Directory of Special Libraries and Information Centers

The Directory of Special Libraries and Information Centers is published in three volumes:

Volume 1—Directory of Special Libraries and Information Centers

Volume 2—Geographic and Personnel Indexes

Volume 3—New Special Libraries (a supplement to Volume 1)

The Subject Directory of Special Libraries and Information Centers, a subject classified edition of material taken from volume 1 of the basic directory, is published in four volumes:

Volume 1—Business and Law Libraries

Volume 2—Social Sciences, Humanities and Education Libraries

Volume 3—Health Sciences Libraries

Volume 4—Science and Engineering Libraries

ISSN 0731-633X

Directory of Special Libraries and Information Centers

12th Edition

A Guide to More Than 18,500 Special Libraries, Research Libraries, Information Centers, Archives, and Data Centers Maintained by Government Agencies, Business, Industry, Newspapers, Educational Institutions, Nonprofit Organizations, and Societies in the Fields of Science and Engineering, Medicine, Law, Art, Religion, the Social Sciences, and Humanities.

1989

BRIGITTE T. DARNAY,
HOLLY M. LEIGHTON
Editors

CAROL SOUTHWARD
Associate Editor

VOLUME 1
PART 2
O-Z
(Entries 10571-18877)
Appendixes and Subject Index

Gale Research Inc. • Book Tower • Detroit, Michigan 48226

Brigitte T. Darnay and Holly M. Leighton, *Editors*

Editorial Staff

Carol Christine Southward, *Associate Editor*
Lori C. Wohlrabe, *Senior Assistant Editor*
Joan M. Hessian and T. James Rapinac, *Assistant Editors*

Research Staff

Lois Lenroot-Ernt and Margaret L. Young, *Contributing Editors*
Henrietta Krohn, *Administrative Services Assistant*

Production Staff

Mary Beth Trimper, *Production Manager*
Darlene K. Maxey, *External Production Associate*

Arthur Chartow, *Art Director*
Cynthia Baldwin, *Graphic Designer*
Linda Davis, *External Production Assistant*

Laura Bryant, *Production Supervisor*
Louise Gagné, *Internal Production Associate*

Library of Congress Catalog Number 84-640165
ISBN 0-8103-2785-6
ISSN 0731-633X

Printed in the United States of America

Contents

Volume 1, Part 1

Volume 1, Part 2

Description of Listings

A simulated listing is shown below. Each numbered item is explained in the descriptive paragraph bearing the same number.

> **(1)** ★562★ **(2) AGRICULTURAL RESEARCH CENTER, INC. - (3) LIBRARY**
> **(4)** (Agri; Biol Sci)
> **(5)** 789 Minnesota Ave. **(6)** Phone: (913)237-8884
> Kansas City, KS 66101 **(7)** Margaret Miller-Holmes, Dir.
> **(8) Founded:** 1972. **(9) Staff:** Prof 6; Other 12. **(10) Subjects:** Agronomy, plant breeding, soil fertility, entomology, dairy science, animal health. **(11) Special Collections:** Biotechnology Research Collection (24 VF drawers of technical reports). **(12) Holdings:** 75,000 books; 150 bound periodical volumes; 85 microfiche; 100 reels of microfilm; 250 AV programs; 6500 internal and technical reports; 4689 government documents. **(13) Subscriptions:** 75 journals and other serials; 12 newspapers. **(14) Services:** Interlibrary loan; copying; SDI; library open to the public for reference use only. **(15) Automated Operations:** Computerized cataloging, acquisitions, serials, and circulation. **(16) Computerized Information Services:** OCLC, DIALOG Information Services; Ag-viser (internal database); Dialcom Inc. (electronic mail service). Performs searches on fee basis. Contact Person: Winston C. Darnay, Online Serv.Libn., 237-8871. **(17) Networks/Consortia:** Member of Bibliographical Center for Research, Rocky Mountain Region, Inc. (BCR). **(18) Publications:** Library Newsletter, quarterly - to selected agricultural libraries; New Acquisitions List, monthly - for internal distribution only. **(19) Special Catalogs:** Catalog of Biotechnology Research Collection (loose-leaf). **(20) Special Indexes:** Indexes to AV programs and internal and technical reports (card). **(21) Remarks:** Maintains a branch library in Lawrence, KS. Telex: **(22) Formerly:** Farming Resources Corporation. **(23) Also Known As:** ARC. **(24) Formed by the Merger of:** Technical Information Center and Corporate Library. **(25) Staff:** Martin Lessner, Chf., Tech.Serv.; Portia F. Leighton, Chf., Pub.Serv.; Kathleen O'Brien, Libn.; Derek Morrison, Libn.

(1) SEQUENTIAL ENTRY NUMBER. The entries in *DSL* are numbered sequentially beginning with the first entry in the U.S. and Canada section and ending with the last entry in the International section. The sequential entry number (rather than the page number) is used in the Subject Index to refer to an entry, and also follows the entry title in Volume 2, Geographic and Personnel Indexes. To facilitate location of an entry, the first entry number on each left-hand page and the last entry number on each right-hand page are provided at the top outer corners of the pages.

(2) NAME OF ORGANIZATION. Name of parent organization, society, or agency which sponsors or is served by the library or information center. Independent libraries and centers and those commonly known by a distinctive name are entered directly under the library's name. Cross-references are included in the body of the work for those entries to which there may be multiple approaches.

(3) NAME OF LIBRARY OR INFORMATION CENTER. Descriptive and memorial names are given as reported. Otherwise the appropriate generic term is used, e.g., library, archives, collection, information center. In many cases the generic term has been supplied by the editors and the inclusion of the term library does not indicate the existence of a formal library.

(4) PRINCIPAL SUBJECT KEYWORD. The major subject or type of material represented by the collection as a whole. When there are two areas of equal importance, both are indicated. When collections have more than

four major subjects or are general in scope no keyword is used. The keywords offer a classification by broad subject category only; each library's more specialized interests are mentioned in the body of each listing. Both the general keywords and specialized interests are used as entry words in the subject index. The following keywords are employed in the 12th edition.

Agri	- agriculture	Info Sci	- information science
Area-Ethnic	- area ethnic	Law	- law
Art	- art	Med	- medicine
Aud-Vis	- audiovisual	Mil	- military
Biol Sci	- biological sciences	Mus	- music
Bus-Fin	- business and finance	Plan	- planning
Comp Sci	- computer science	Publ	- publishing
Educ	- education	Rare Book	- rare book
Energy	- energy	Rec	- recreation
Env-Cons	- environment and conservation	Rel-Phil	- religion and philosophy
Food-Bev	- food and beverages	Sci-Engr	- science and engineering
Geog-Map	- geography and maps	Soc Sci	- social sciences
Hist	- history	Theater	- theater
Hum	- humanities	Trans	- transportation

(5) MAILING ADDRESS. The permanent mailing address of library or center. In some instances this will differ from the headquarters address of the parent organization and the physical location of the library. When there is a separate location address, it is given under "Remarks" (see item 21).

(6) TELEPHONE NUMBER. Area code and telephone number. When more than one telephone number is supplied, alternate ones are listed under "Remarks" (see item 21). Extensions are not provided, since they are subject to frequent change.

(7) HEAD OF LIBRARY OR INFORMATION CENTER. Name and title of the person directly in charge of library or information center. Where no librarian has been identified or where there is no position as such, the name of the administrative officer may be given. When the directorship is shared by two persons the names of both partners are given in the staff names section (see item 25).

(8) FOUNDING DATE. Year when library or information center was established, either formally or informally.

(9) NUMBER OF STAFF. Number of individuals directly engaged in the operation of the library or center on a regular basis. Part-time employees are included but student assistants and other occasional help generally are not. Professional staff includes librarians, bibliographers, subject specialists, information specialists, and other related specialists. Semi-professionals and clerical assistants are grouped in the second category. Distinction between professional and nonprofessional staff is made by the respondents. Where the differentiation is not made, the total number of staff is listed.

(10) SUBJECTS. Terms specifically designating the most important subjects represented in the collection as a whole. This section of the listing, obtained from submitted questionnaires, is ordinarily used as the basis of the subject index.

(11) SPECIAL COLLECTIONS. Separately grouped collections of unusual or notable interest that are identifiable either by subject, form, name of donor, or distinctive name.

(12) HOLDINGS. Quantitative data concerning collections. Numbers of books, bound periodical volumes, pamphlets, and technical reports are given separately when supplied by respondents. When the term "volumes" is used, it generally indicates bound units or collections of bound and unbound items which have been accessioned and cataloged. Unbound material is indicated either by unit count, number of vertical file drawers, linear shelf feet, or cubic storage space. Estimates rather than the exact statistics have frequently been given. Holdings of non book materials are also indicated whenever of significant size and importance.

(13) SUBSCRIPTIONS. Figures generally represent the number of journal and serial titles, not separate copies, received by paid subscription, gift, and exchange. Newspaper subscriptions are given separately when numerically significant.

(14) SERVICES. Most special libraries provide bibliographic or reference services primarily for their own organizations. For these, an appropriate statement of service limitations is given. When the library or center

provides some form of access to outside clientele, it is so indicated. When services offered are of an unusual nature they are noted and indication is given whether such services are for internal or external use. Entries for libraries which honor interlibrary loan requests include the appropriate information, as do those for libraries with copying or reproducing facilities. Normally, copying services to outside users are on a fee basis. Some libraries now charge for interlibrary loans and this information is included when supplied by respondent.

(15) AUTOMATED OPERATIONS. Computerized library management functions such as public access catalog, cataloging, circulation, acquisitions, and serials.

(16) COMPUTERIZED INFORMATION SERVICES. This item indicates a special library's access to online information systems, such as MEDLINE, SDC Information Services, LEXIS, etc. Internally produced databases and electronic mail services are also listed in this section. Also included here are fees for online searches the library may perform for the public, and name and telephone number of contact person.

(17) NETWORKS/CONSORTIA. Here is listed the special library's membership in formal or informal groups involved in cooperative sharing of library resources on the local, regional, or national level. Acronyms are used for networks and consortia which are familiar to the library profession (e.g., CLASS, ILLINET). Appendix A lists geographically the names, acronyms, and addresses of the networks and consortia reported by the special libraries in this directory. An alphabetical index follows.

(18) PUBLICATIONS. Periodical, serial, and other publications issued or prepared by the library or information center are included. Title, frequency, and basis of distribution are indicated when known.

(19) SPECIAL CATALOGS. Unique and unusual catalogs which are locally prepared and maintained, including card, book, computer printout, and other formats.

(20) SPECIAL INDEXES. Unique and unusual indexes which are locally prepared and maintained.

(21) REMARKS. Additional information not adaptable to the standard form of entry, including historical data, explanatory notes, and descriptions of unusual activities. Corporate affiliations are often noted here. Also included is the address of a special library's location when it differs from the mailing address in item 5, and any toll-free phone numbers. For the first time in the 12th edition, telex numbers and telefacsimile numbers are included in this edition.

(22) FORMERLY. Former names and/or locations of a special library or its parent organization when there is a recent change of names under which they were formerly listed. Cross-references are generally supplied from the former names.

(23) ALSO KNOWN AS. Variant names of a special library or its parent organization. Cross-references from these are provided when needed.

(24) FORMED BY THE MERGER OF. When the special library has been created by the merger of two or more units previously listed as separate entries, the names of the components are identified here. Mergers of parent organizations which affect the special library are also noted.

(25) STAFF NAMES. Names and titles of professional and supervisory personnel in the special library or information center. Only principal members of the professional staff are listed for operations with large staffs.

Abbreviations

Acq. —Acquisitions
Act. —Acting
Actv. —Activities, Activity
Adm. —Administration, Administrative, Administrator
Adv. —Advisor
AFB —Air Force Base
Aff. —Affairs
Agri. —Agricultural, Agriculture
AHEC —Area Health Education Center
Amer. —American
ANGB —Air National Guard Base
Anl. —Analysis, Analyst, Analytical
APO —Army Post Office
Arch. —Architect, Architectural, Architecture
Archeo. —Archeological, Archeologist, Archeology
Archv. —Archival, Archives, Archivist
ART —Accredited Record Technician
Assn. —Association
Assoc. —Associate
Asst. —Assistant
Att. —Attorney
Aud. —Audio
AV —Audiovisual
Ave. —Avenue
B.P. —Boite Postale
Bd. —Board
Biblio. —Bibliotechnicien(ne), Bibliothecaire
Bibliog. —Bibliographer, Bibliographic, Bibliographical, Bibliography
Biol. —Biological, Biologist, Biology
Biomed. —Biomedical, Biomedicine
Bk., Bks. —Book, Books
Bldg. —Building
Blvd. —Boulevard
Br. —Branch
Bro. —Brother
Bur. —Bureau
Bus. —Business
C.P. —Caixa Postal, Caja Postale, Case Postale, Casetta Postale
Capt. —Captain
Cart. —Cartographer, Cartographic, Cartography
Cat. —Catalog, Cataloger, Cataloging
CD-ROM —Compact Disk Read-Only Memory
Cedex —Courrier d'Entreprise a Distribution Exceptionnelle
Ch. —Chair, Child, Children, Children's
Chem. —Chemical, Chemist, Chemistry
Chf. —Chief
Chm. —Chairman
Circ. —Circulation
Ck. —Clerk
Class. —Classical, Classification, Classified
Clghse. —Clearinghouse
Clin. —Clinical
Co. —Company
Col. —Colonel
Coll. —Collection(s), College
COM —Computer Output Microfilm/Microfiche
Comm. —Committee
Commn. —Commission
Commnr. —Commissioner
Commun. —Communication(s), Community
Comp. —Computer, Computerized, Computing
Cons. —Conservation, Conservator, Consultant, Consulting
Cont. —Continuing, Control
Coop. —Cooperating, Cooperation, Cooperative
Coord. —Coordinating, Coordination, Coordinator
Corp. —Corporate, Corporation
Coun. —Council
Couns. —Counsel, Counseling, Counselor
Ct. —Court
Ctr. —Center, Centre
Ctrl. —Central
Cur. —Curator, Curatorial
Curric. —Curricular, Curriculum
Cust. —Custodian
Dept., Depts. —Department, Departmental, Departments
Des. —Design, Designer
Dev. —Development, Developmental
Dir. —Director
Dissem. —Dissemination
Dist. —District
Distr. —Distribution, Distributor
Div. —Division, Divisional
Doc., Docs. —Document, Documentalist(e), Documentation, Documents
DOD —U.S. Department of Defense
DOE —U.S. Department of Energy
Dp. —Deputy
Dr. —Doctor, Drive
E. —East
Econ. —Economic(s)
Ed. —Editor, Editorial
Educ. —Education, Educational, Educator
Engr. —Engineer, Engineering
Env. —Environment, Environmental
Exch. —Exchange
Exec. —Executive
Expy. —Expressway
Ext. —Extended, Extension, External
Fac. —Facilitator, Facility, Faculty
Fed. —Federal, Federation
Fin. —Finance, Financial
Fl. —Floor
Fld. —Field
Found. —Foundation
FPO —Fleet Post Office
Fr. —Father
Ft. —Fort
Fwy. —Freeway
G.P.O. —General Post Office
Gen. —General
Geneal. —Genealogical, Genealogist, Genealogy
Geog. —Geographer, Geographic, Geographical, Geography
Geol. —Geological, Geologist, Geology
Govt. —Government, Governmental
Hd. —Head
Hea. —Health
Hist. —Historian, Historic, Historical, History
Hndcp. —Handicap, Handicapped
Hon. —Honorable, Honorary
Hosp. —Hospital
HQ —Headquarters
Hum. —Humanities
Hwy. —Highway
ILL —Interlibrary Loan
Illus. —Illustrated, Illustration, Illustrative, Illustrator
Indiv. —Individual

Indus.	—Industrial, Industry
Info.	—Information, Informational
Inst.	—Institute, Institution, Institutional
Instr.	—Instruction, Instructional, Instructor
Int.	—Internal
Interp.	—Interpretation, Interpreter, Interpretive
Intl.	—International
Jnl.	—Journal
Jr.	—Junior
Kpr.	—Keeper
KWIC	—Keyword in Context
KWOC	—Keyword out of Context
Lab., Labs.	—Laboratory, Laboratories
Lang.	—Language(s)
LATCH	—Literature Attached to the Chart (Medical)
LCDR	—Lieutenant Commander
Ldr.	—Leader
Leg.	—Legal, Legislation, Legislative, Legislator, Legislature
Lib., Libs.	—Library, Libraries
Libn.	—Librarian
Lit.	—Literary, Literature
Ln.	—Lane
LRC	—Learning Resource(s) Center
Lrng.	—Learning
Lt.	—Lieutenant
LTC	—Lieutenant Colonel
Maint.	—Maintenance
Maj.	—Major
Math.	—Mathematical, Mathematics
Med.	—Medical, Medicine
Mfg.	—Manufacturing
Mgr.	—Manager
Mgt.	—Management
Mil.	—Military
Mktg.	—Marketing
Mng.	—Managing
Ms., Mss.	—Manuscript, Manuscripts
Mt.	—Mount
Mtls.	—Materials
Mus.	—Music, Musical
Musm.	—Museum
Myth.	—Mythology
N.	—North
Natl.	—National
NCME	—Network for Continuing Medical Education
No.	—Number, Numero
Nurs.	—Nursing
Off.	—Office, Officer
Oper.	—Operations, Operator
Org.	—Organization, Organizational
P.O.	—Post Office
P.R.	—Public Relations
Per.	—Periodical(s)
Perf.	—Perform, Performing
Pers.	—Personnel
Pharm.	—Pharmaceutical, Pharmacy
Photo.	—Photograph(s), Photographer, Photographic
Photodup.	—Photoduplication
Pict.	—Pictorial, Picture(s)
Pk.	—Park
Pkwy.	—Parkway
Pl.	—Place
Plan.	—Planner, Planning
Pres.	—President
Presrv.	—Preservation
Prin.	—Principal
Proc.	—Process, Processing, Processor
Prod.	—Product, Production
Prof.	—Professional, Professor
Prog.	—Program(s), Programmer, Programming
Proj.	—Project(s)
Prov.	—Province, Provincial
Psych.	—Psychiatric, Psychiatry, Psychological, Psychology
Pub.	—Public
Publ.	—Published, Publisher, Publishing
Pubn., Pubns.	—Publication, Publications
R&D	—Research and Development
Rd.	—Reader(s), Road
Rec.	—Record(s), Recreation
Ref.	—Reference
Reg.	—Region, Regional, Registrar
Rel.	—Relations, Religion, Religious
Rep.	—Representative
Repro.	—Reproduction
Res.	—Research, Researcher
Resp.	—Responsable
Ret.	—Retired, Retrieval
Rev.	—Reverend
Rm., Rms.	—Room, Rooms
Rpt.	—Report(s)
Rsrc., Rsrcs.	—Resource, Resources
Rte.	—Route
S.	—South
S/N	—Sin Numero
Sch.	—School
Sci.	—Science(s), Scientific, Scientist
SDI	—Selective Dissemination of Information
Sec.	—Secretary
Sect.	—Section
Sel.	—Selection
Ser.	—Serial(s)
Serv.	—Service(s)
Sgt.	—Sergeant
SLA	—Special Libraries Association
Soc.	—Social, Society
Spec.	—Special, Specialist, Specialized
Sq.	—Square
Sr.	—Senior, Sister
St.	—Saint, Street
Sta.	—Station
Stat.	—Statistical, Statistics
Ste.	—Sainte, Societe
Sts.	—Saints, Streets
Stud.	—Student(s), Studies, Study
Succ.	—Succursale
Sup.	—Support, Supporting
Supt.	—Superintendent
Supv.	—Supervising, Supervisor, Supervisory
Sys.	—System(s)
Tchg.	—Teaching
TDD	—Telecommunications/Telephone Device for the Deaf
Tech.	—Technical, Technological, Technology
Techn.	—Technician
Theol.	—Theological, Theology
Tpke.	—Turnpike
Trans.	—Transportation
Transl.	—Translation, Translator
Treas.	—Treasurer
Trng.	—Training
TTY	—Teletypewriter
U.N.	—United Nations
U.S.	—United States
UNESCO	—United Nations Educational, Scientific, and Cultural Organization
Univ.	—University
Unpubl.	—Unpublished
V.P.	—Vice President
Vet.	—Veteran(s), Veterinary
VF	—Vertical File(s)
Vis.	—Vision, Visual
Vol., Vols.	—Volume, Volumes
W.	—West

Directory of Special Libraries and Information Centers

Volume 1, Part 2

O-Z

O

★10571★
OAK FOREST HOSPITAL - PROFESSIONAL LIBRARY (Med)
15900 S. Cicero Ave. Phone: (312)928-4200
Oak Forest, IL 60452 Delores I. Quinn, Libn.
Founded: 1973. **Staff:** Prof 1; Other 2. **Subjects:** Medicine, nursing, paramedical sciences. **Holdings:** 2000 books. **Subscriptions:** 250 journals and other serials. **Services:** Library not open to the public.

★10572★
OAK GROVE LUTHERAN CHURCH - MEMORIAL LIBRARY (Rel-Phil)
7045 Lyndale Ave., S. Phone: (612)869-4917
Richfield, MN 55423 Juanita Carpenter, Libn.
Founded: 1959. **Staff:** Prof 1; Other 4. **Subjects:** Bible reference, devotional and inspirational reading, church history, religious education, family life, children's literature, biography, social concerns, world religions. **Holdings:** 3875 books; tape cassettes; religious periodicals; videotapes. **Services:** Library open to the public.

★10573★
OAK HILLS BIBLE COLLEGE - LIBRARY (Rel-Phil)
1600 Oak Hills Rd. Phone: (218)751-8670
Bemidji, MN 56601 John T. Salley, Libn.
Founded: 1946. **Staff:** Prof 1; Other 1. **Subjects:** Biblical, philosophical, and theological studies; religious education. **Holdings:** 15,000 books; 550 bound periodical volumes; 150 files of mission material; 550 AV programs. **Subscriptions:** 90 journals and other serials. **Services:** Interlibrary loan; copying; library open to the public. **Automated Operations:** Computerized cataloging. **Networks/Consortia:** Member of Northern Lights Library Network (NLLN).

★10574★
OAK LAWN PUBLIC LIBRARY - LOCAL HISTORY AREA (Hist)
9427 S. Raymond Ave. Phone: (312)422-4990
Oak Lawn, IL 60453-2434 Gerald R. Anderson, Adult Serv./Local Hist.
Staff: Prof 1. **Subjects:** Local history. **Special Collections:** Southtown Economist newspapers (microfilm); Oral History Collection. **Holdings:** 200 books; 300 photographs; 75 files of clippings; 20 boxes of local government records. **Services:** Interlibrary loan; open to the public. **Automated Operations:** Computerized circulation and indexing. **Computerized Information Services:** LIBS 100 System. **Networks/Consortia:** Member of Suburban Library System (SLS). **Special Indexes:** Index of the South Suburban Region Newspapers (booklet).

★10575★
OAK PARK PUBLIC LIBRARY - LOCAL AUTHOR AND LOCAL HISTORY COLLECTIONS (Hist)
834 Lake St. Phone: (312)383-8200
Oak Park, IL 60301 Barbara Ballinger, Hd.Libn.
Founded: 1903. **Subjects:** Local history, architecture, and authors. **Special Collections:** Local history collection (824 volumes; 8 VF drawers); Ernest Hemingway (309 volumes); Frank Lloyd Wright (351 volumes); Edgar Rice Burroughs (54 volumes); Grant Manson photographs of Wright buildings (350); Gilman Lane photographs of Wright buildings (700). **Holdings:** 1538 books; 5 VF drawers of Oak Park Landmarks Commission files. **Services:** Interlibrary loan; copying; collections open to the public for reference use only. **Automated Operations:** Computerized cataloging and circulation. **Computerized Information Services:** OCLC. **Networks/Consortia:** Member of Suburban Library System (SLS). **Publications:** Frank Lloyd Wright, Prairie School of Architecture (1974; bibliography). **Special Indexes:** Local newspaper index (card). **Staff:** William Jerousek, Libn..

★10576★
OAK RIDGE ASSOCIATED UNIVERSITIES - INSTITUTE FOR ENERGY ANALYSIS - LIBRARY
Box 117
Oak Ridge, TN 37831
Defunct

★10577★
OAK RIDGE ASSOCIATED UNIVERSITIES - MEDICAL LIBRARY (Med)
Box 117 Phone: (615)576-3490
Oak Ridge, TN 37831-0117 Rana Yalcintas, Dir.
Founded: 1974. **Staff:** Prof 1; Other 1. **Subjects:** Biochemistry, occupational medicine, cytogenetics, radiopharmacy, epidemiology, nuclear medicine. **Holdings:** 2300 books; 2849 bound periodical volumes; 9500 reports in microform; 1777 reels of microfilm. **Subscriptions:** 106 journals and other serials. **Services:** Interlibrary loan; copying; SDI; library open to the public for reference use only. **Automated Operations:** Computerized cataloging and ILL. **Computerized Information Services:** DIALOG Information Services, OCLC, Integrated Technical Information System (ITIS), MEDLINE. **Networks/Consortia:** Member of Knoxville Area Health Sciences Library Consortium (KAHSLC). **Remarks:** An alternate telephone number is FTS 626-3490.

★10578★
OAK RIDGE ASSOCIATED UNIVERSITIES - MERT DIVISION - LIBRARY (Info Sci)
Bldg. 2714-F, Rm. E-1
246 Laboratory Rd.
Box 117 Phone: (615)576-3292
Oak Ridge, TN 37831-0117 Harry T. Burn, Libn.
Founded: 1977. **Staff:** Prof 1; Other 1. **Subjects:** Libraries, education, employment, manpower, energy. **Holdings:** 200 volumes; 1000 reports. **Subscriptions:** 55 journals and other serials. **Services:** Interlibrary loan; library open to the public with restrictions. **Computerized Information Services:** OCLC, DIALOG Information Services, DTIC, BRS Information Technologies; MERT Software Systems (internal database). **Remarks:** An alternate telephone number is FTS 626-3292. **Also Known As:** Manpower Education, Research, and Training Division.

★10579★
OAK RIDGE ASSOCIATED UNIVERSITIES - RADIOPHARMACEUTICAL INTERNAL DOSE INFORMATION CENTER (Sci-Engr)
Box 117 Phone: (615)576-3450
Oak Ridge, TN 37831-0117 Evelyn E. Watson, Prog.Mgr.
Founded: 1971. **Staff:** Prof 3; Other 1. **Subjects:** Internal dosimetry, radiation absorbed dose, radionuclide kinetics, nuclear medicine, health and medical physics, radiation protection. **Holdings:** 250 books; 65 bound periodical volumes; Oak Ridge National Laboratory reports; government reports. **Subscriptions:** 15 journals and other serials. **Services:** Center not open to the public. **Computerized Information Services:** RIDIC (internal database). Performs limited searches free of charge. Contact Person: Audrey Schlafke-Stelson, Res.Assoc.. **Publications:** Proceedings of the 4th International Radiopharmaceutical Dosimetry Symposium, 1985 - for sale. **Staff:** Michael G. Stabin, Int. Dosimetry Spec..

OAK RIDGE GASEOUS DIFFUSION PLANT
See: Martin Marietta Energy Systems Inc. - Libraries (8475)

OAK RIDGE NATIONAL LABORATORY
See: Martin Marietta Energy Systems Inc. - Libraries (8475)

★10580★
OAK RIDGE NATIONAL LABORATORY - CARBON DIOXIDE INFORMATION ANALYSIS CENTER (Sci-Engr)
Bldg. 2001/MS 050
Box X Phone: (615)574-0390
Oak Ridge, TN 37831-6050 M.P. Farrell, Dir.
Subjects: Carbon dioxide-climate research, including atmospheric carbon dioxide measurements, fossil fuel use, forest conversion, ocean properties characterization, historical records from ice cores, tree rings. **Holdings:** Figures not available. **Services:** Copying. **Computerized Information Services:** Internal databases. Performs searches free of charge. **Publications:** CDIC Communications (newsletter), semiannual.

★10581★
OAK RIDGE NATIONAL LABORATORY - CENTER FOR ENERGY AND ENVIRONMENTAL INFORMATION - CEEI ENERGY CONSERVATION (Env-Cons, Energy)
Bldg. 4500-N, G-9 Phone: (615)576-1753
Oak Ridge, TN 37831 Rose Weaver, Tech.Anl.
Subjects: Energy planning, nuclear power, environment. **Special Collections:** WMCO (Westinghouse) Feed Materials Power Plant documents and Department of Defense Military Airlift reports. **Holdings:** 2030 documents. **Subscriptions:** 11 journals and other serials. **Services:** Center open to the public with security clearance. **Automated Operations:** Computerized acquisitions. **Computerized Information Services:** DIALOG Information Services; internal database. Performs searches on fee basis. **Publications:** Bibliographies; current awareness newsletter; Energy Conservata.

★10582★
OAK RIDGE NATIONAL LABORATORY - CONTROLLED FUSION ATOMIC DATA CENTER (Sci-Engr)
Bldg. 6003, Box X Phone: (615)574-4707
Oak Ridge, TN 37831-6372 R.A. Phaneuf, Dir.
Staff: Prof 1; Other 1. **Subjects:** Heavy particle collisions, particle interactions with electrons, photons, particle penetration into matter, particle interactions with surfaces. **Services:** Collects, stores, evaluates, recommends, and disseminates atomic and molecular processes information and data. **Computerized Information Services:** Internal database. Performs searches free of charge. **Publications:** Atomic Data for Fusion (compilations of recommended data); Annual Bibliography of Atomic and Molecular Collision Processes (online); topical reports. **Remarks:** The Oak Ridge National Laboratory operates under contract to the U.S. Department of Energy.

★10583★
OAK RIDGE NATIONAL LABORATORY - ENVIRONMENTAL CARCINOGEN INFORMATION CENTER (ECIC) (Med)
Bldg. 9207 MS3
Box Y Phone: (615)574-7871
Oak Ridge, TN 37831 John S. Wassom, Dir.
Subjects: Chemical carcinogenesis. **Holdings:** 5000 records. **Computerized Information Services:** TOXLINE, CHEMLINE, MEDLINE, CANCERLINE, Pergamon ORBIT InfoLine, Inc., DIALOG Information Services; internal database. **Remarks:** Center is a branch of the Environmental Mutagen, Carcinogen, and Teratogen Information Program. ECIC is funded by the Environmental Protection Agency (EPA).

★10584★
OAK RIDGE NATIONAL LABORATORY - ENVIRONMENTAL INFORMATION CENTER - NEVADA APPLIED ECOLOGY INFORMATION CENTER (Env-Cons)
Bldg. 2001
Box X Phone: (616)574-5350
Oak Ridge, TN 37831-0050 Helen Pfuderer, Dir.
Founded: 1968. **Subjects:** Cleanup and treatment of radioactively contaminated land; environmental aspects of the transuranics. **Services:** Interlibrary loan; center open to the public with restrictions. **Computerized Information Services:** DIALOG Information Services; internal databases. Performs searches on fee basis. **Publications:** Bibliographies.

★10585★
OAK RIDGE NATIONAL LABORATORY - ENVIRONMENTAL TERATOLOGY INFORMATION CENTER (ETIC) (Sci-Engr)
Bldg. 9207 MS 003
Box Y Phone: (615)574-7871
Oak Ridge, TN 37831 John S. Wassom, Dir.
Subjects: Evaluation of chemicals, biological agents, and physical agents for teratogenic activity. **Holdings:** 47,000 records. **Computerized Information Services:** TOXLINE, CHEMLINE, MEDLINE, CANCERLINE, Pergamon ORBIT InfoLine, Inc., DIALOG Information Services; internal database. Performs searches free of charge on time-available basis. **Publications:** Bibliographies. **Remarks:** Center is a branch of the Environmental Mutagen, Carcinogen, and Teratogen Information Program. ETIC is supported by the National Toxicology Program/National Institute of Environmental Health Sciences, the Environmental Protection Agency, and the Agency for Toxic Substances and Disease Registry/National Library of Medicine.

★10586★
OAK RIDGE NATIONAL LABORATORY - HEALTH AND SAFETY RESEARCH DIVISION - ENVIRONMENTAL MUTAGEN INFORMATION CENTER (Sci-Engr)
Bldg., 9207 MS 003
Box Y Phone: (615)574-7871
Oak Ridge, TN 37831 John S. Wassom, Dir.
Founded: 1969. **Staff:** Prof 4; Other 1. **Subjects:** Genetic toxicology, chemical mutagenesis. **Holdings:** 66,000 references on the genotoxicity of chemicals. **Services:** Answers information requests on time-available basis. **Computerized Information Services:** TOXLINE. **Remarks:** The Oak Ridge National Laboratory is operated by Martin Marietta Energy Systems, Inc. under contract to the U.S. Department of Energy. **Formerly:** Information Division. **Staff:** E.S. Von Halle; B.L. Whitfield; K. Mavournin.

★10587★
OAK RIDGE NATIONAL LABORATORY - NUCLEAR DATA PROJECT (Sci-Engr)
Box X Phone: (615)574-4699
Oak Ridge, TN 37831 M.J. Martin, Dir.
Founded: 1948. **Staff:** Prof 4; Other 4. **Subjects:** Nuclear physics, nuclear levels, nuclear transitions, nuclear structure, radioactivity, isotopes, nuclear reactions. **Special Collections:** Nuclear data tables (400 compilations of measured or calculated quantities). **Holdings:** 200 books; 180 shelf feet of unbound journals; 9 VF drawers of technical reports. **Subscriptions:** 32 journals and other serials. **Services:** Collection, evaluation, and publication of data on nuclear level structure; answers specific requests for nuclear structure references or data; open to the public with special approval. **Computerized Information Services:** Evaluated Nuclear Structure Data File (ENSDF), Nuclear Structure Reference File. **Remarks:** Maintains computerized bibliographic and keyword files for over 50,000 published references and 30,000 unpublished references in experimental nuclear physics. From these files are produced reference lists for various selectors such as isotope, half-life, specific type of nuclear reaction. The Oak Ridge National Laboratory operates under contract to the U.S. Department of Energy. **Staff:** Y. Ellis-Akovalli, Res.; M.R. Schmorak, Res.; M.R. Lay, Techn..

★10588★
OAK RIDGE NATIONAL LABORATORY - NUCLEAR SAFETY INFORMATION CENTER (Energy)
Bldg. 9201-3, Box Y Phone: (615)574-0391
Oak Ridge, TN 37830 G.T. Mays, Dir.
Founded: 1963. **Staff:** Prof 12; Other 9. **Subjects:** Nuclear facility operation and experience; electrical power systems; general safety considerations; heat transfer and thermal hydraulics; nuclear instrumentation, controls, safety systems; reactor transients, kinetics, stability; risk and reliability. **Special Collections:** Nuclear reactor safety analysis and environmental reports; nuclear facility licensing documents. **Services:** Questions answered; consultation, free to sponsors and their designees, to others on fee basis. **Computerized Information Services:** Sequence Code and Search System (SCSS); internal databases. **Publications:** DOE Nuclear Safety Journal; periodic bibliographies; Licensee Event Report (LER) Monthly Report. **Special Catalogs:** Computer file of LERs from various utilities describing any unusual event occurring at a nuclear plant. **Remarks:** The Oak Ridge National Laboratory is operated by Martin Marietta Energy Systems Inc. under contract to the U.S. Department of Energy.

★10589★
OAK RIDGE NATIONAL LABORATORY - RADIATION SHIELDING INFORMATION CENTER (Sci-Engr)
Box X Phone: (615)574-6176
Oak Ridge, TN 37830 Robert W. Roussin, Dir.
Founded: 1962. **Staff:** Prof 9; Other 5. **Subjects:** Radiation protection, transport, and shielding. **Special Collections:** Digital computer code packages to perform shielding calculations; computer-readable data libraries of nuclear cross sections and data from intranuclear cascade calculations. **Holdings:** 9 VF drawers of reports; 14,000 micronegative cards; 750 computer code packages; 120 nuclear data packages. **Services:** Dissemination of code/data packages; problem-solving; center open to the public. **Automated Operations:** Computerized circulation. **Computerized Information Services:** EasyLink (electronic mail service). Performs searches free of charge. Contact Person: N.A. Hatmaker, Info.Spec.. **Publications:** Bibliographies, irregular; newsletter, monthly; topical reports, irregular; abstracts of code/data packages, annual. **Remarks:** The Oak Ridge National Laboratory is operated by Martin Marietta Energy Systems Inc. under contract to the U.S. Department of Energy. **Staff:** D.K. Trubey, Physicist; B.L. McGill, Mathematician; J.E. White, Mathematician; S.N. Cramer; B.L. Kirk; B.L. McGill; J.L. Bartley.

★10590★
OAK RIDGE NATIONAL LABORATORY - TOXICOLOGY INFORMATION RESPONSE CENTER (Med, Biol Sci)
Bldg. 2001
Box X Phone: (615)576-1743
Oak Ridge, TN 37831-6050 Mary W. Francis, Group Ldr.
Founded: 1971. **Staff:** 1. **Subjects:** Toxicology, pharmacology, veterinary toxicology, heavy metals, pesticides, chemistry, biology, medicine, industrial hygiene. **Holdings:** 7500 search files; 250 microfiche of published bibliographies. **Subscriptions:** 50 journals and other serials. **Services:** SDI; center open to the public with restrictions. **Computerized Information Services:** DIALOG Information Services, MEDLARS, CIS, STN International. **Publications:** State-of-the-art reviews; specialized bibliographies; list of publications for sale - available on request. **Remarks:** Sponsored by the Toxicology Information Program/National Library of Medicine. The Oak Ridge National Laboratory is operated by Martin Marietta Energy Systems Inc. under contract to the U.S. Department of Energy. **Staff:** J.P. Hutson, Tech.Info.Asst..

★10591★
OAKDALE REGIONAL CENTER FOR DEVELOPMENTAL DISABILITIES - STAFF LIBRARY (Med)
2995 W. Genesee St. Phone: (313)664-2951
Lapeer, MI 48446 Rollin Hill, Lib.Coord.
Staff: 1. **Subjects:** Mental retardation, medicine, education, management, nursing, psychiatry. **Holdings:** 2700 books; 1 vertical file collection. **Subscriptions:** 80 journals and other serials. **Services:** Interlibrary loan; copying; library open to the public with restrictions. **Networks/Consortia:** Member of Flint Area Health Science Library Network (FAHSLN). **Remarks:** Maintained by Lapeer County Library System.

★10592★
OAKITE PRODUCTS INC. - CHEMICAL RESEARCH LIBRARY (Sci-Engr)
50 Valley Rd. Phone: (201)464-6900
Berkeley Heights, NJ 07922 Tracy Mason, Libn.
Staff: 1. **Subjects:** Chemistry. **Holdings:** 1000 books; 1250 bound periodical volumes; 90 reports. **Subscriptions:** 80 journals and other serials. **Services:** Interlibrary loan; library open to the public with approval of management.

★10593★
OAKLAND CITY PLANNING DEPARTMENT - LIBRARY (Plan)
City Hall, 6th Fl. Phone: (415)273-3941
Oakland, CA 94612 Christopher Buckley, Libn.
Founded: 1952. **Subjects:** Urban and regional planning. **Holdings:** 1600 books.

★10594★
OAKLAND COUNTY LIBRARY - ADAMS-PRATT LAW LIBRARY DIVISION (Law)
1200 N. Telegraph Rd. Phone: (313)858-0011
Pontiac, MI 48053 Richard L. Beer, Lib.Bd.Adm.
Founded: 1925. **Staff:** Prof 5. **Subjects:** U.S. law, criminal justice, legal medicine. **Special Collections:** Michigan Supreme Court Records and Briefs, 1927-1929 and 1933 to present; House and Senate Bills of Michigan legislature, 1973 to present. **Holdings:** 45,000 volumes; Michigan Attorney General Reports, 1838 to present; Michigan House and Senate Journals, 1929 to present. **Subscriptions:** 1077 journals and other serials; 10 newspapers. **Services:** Interlibrary loan; copying; library open to the public for reference use only. **Automated Operations:** Computerized cataloging. **Computerized Information Services:** WESTLAW, OCLC, LEXIS. **Networks/Consortia:** Member of Michigan Library Consortium (MLC). **Remarks:** Fax: (313)858-1445. **Staff:** Charlotte Liner, Libn..

★10595★
OAKLAND COUNTY LIBRARY FOR THE BLIND & PHYSICALLY HANDICAPPED (Aud-Vis)
32737 W. Twelve Mile Rd. Phone: (313)553-0300
Farmington Hills, MI 48018 Carole Hund, Hd.Libn.
Founded: 1974. **Staff:** Prof 1; Other 3. **Subjects:** General collection of braille, large print, and recorded books. **Holdings:** Figures not available. **Services:** Interlibrary loan; library open to the public with restrictions. **Remarks:** Maintained by Farmington Community Library.

★10596★
OAKLAND COUNTY PIONEER AND HISTORICAL SOCIETY - LIBRARY & ARCHIVES (Hist)
405 Oakland Ave. Phone: (313)338-6732
Pontiac, MI 48058 Beverly Laakko, Exec.Sec.
Founded: 1874. **Staff:** 3. **Subjects:** Local, state, family histories; early Oakland County medical history; genealogy; archeology; architecture. **Special Collections:** Howlett Collection of local history on specific families (20 document boxes; 7000 items); Avery Collection of marriages, births, deaths of Oakland County families (7000 cards). **Holdings:** 2500 books; 1500 bound periodical volumes; 20 volumes of carbons of historical material; 5 VF drawers of photographs; oral histories; clippings; manuscripts; diaries; scrapbooks; maps; newspapers; slides. **Services:** Copying; library open to the public for reference use only by appointment. **Publications:** Oakland Gazette, 4/year - mailed to members, available free at library.

★10597★
OAKLAND COUNTY REFERENCE LIBRARY (Plan)
1200 N. Telegraph Rd. Phone: (313)858-0738
Pontiac, MI 48053 Phyllis Jose, Dir.
Founded: 1972. **Staff:** Prof 1; Other 4. **Subjects:** Planning, solid waste management, transportation, behavioral sciences, census, architecture, municipal government. **Special Collections:** National Research Council publications; Urban Land Institute publications; American Planning Association publications; Southeastern Michigan Council of Government publications; local documents. **Holdings:** 13,900 books. **Subscriptions:** 250 journals and other serials. **Services:** Interlibrary loan; copying; library open to the public. **Automated Operations:** Computerized circulation. **Networks/Consortia:** Member of Wayne/Oakland Library Federation (WOLF), Michigan Library Consortium (MLC). **Publications:** New book list, quarterly; bibliographies. **Special Catalogs:** Oakland County Union List of Serials, biennial.

★10598★
OAKLAND PUBLIC LIBRARY - AMERICAN INDIAN LIBRARY PROJECT (Area-Ethnic)
Dimond Branch Library
3565 Fruitvale Ave. Phone: (415)530-3881
Oakland, CA 94602 Susanna Gilden, Supv.Libn.
Staff: Prof 1; Other 1. **Subjects:** Native Americans - literature, culture, history. **Holdings:** 1500 books. **Subscriptions:** 15 journals and other serials. **Services:** Interlibrary loan; library open to the public. **Automated Operations:** Computerized circulation. **Networks/Consortia:** Member of Bay Area Library and Information System (BALIS).

★10599★
OAKLAND PUBLIC LIBRARY - ART, MUSIC, RECREATION (Art, Mus, Rec)
125 14th St. Phone: (415)273-3178
Oakland, CA 94612 Richard Colvig, Sr.Libn.
Founded: 1961. **Staff:** Prof 3; Other 2. **Subjects:** History of art, architecture, painting, sculpture, decorative and graphic arts, furniture, interior decoration, photography, costume, music, sports and recreation, theater, cinema, dance. **Holdings:** 20,923 books; 2159 bound periodical volumes; 10,000 scores; 30,000 choral music copies; 9000 phonograph records and cassettes. **Services:** Interlibrary loan; copying; open to the public. **Networks/Consortia:** Member of Bay Area Library and Information System (BALIS). **Special Indexes:** Indexes of local events and personalities in music, art, and architecture (on cards). **Staff:** Clinton Arndt, Libn.; David Segall, Libn..

★10600★
OAKLAND PUBLIC LIBRARY - ASIAN BRANCH LIBRARY (Area-Ethnic)
449 9th St. Phone: (415)273-3400
Oakland, CA 94607 Suzanne Lo, Br.Libn.
Founded: 1975. **Staff:** Prof 3. **Subjects:** Asian-American experience; adult and juvenile literature in Asian languages - Chinese, Tagalog, Japanese, Korean, Vietnamese, Thai, Cambodian. **Holdings:** 35,000 books; 8 VF drawers of clippings; 150 historical pictures; 2000 Asian language phonograph records and cassettes; 125 16mm films; 60 sets of filmstrips. **Subscriptions:** 100 journals and other serials; 23 newspapers. **Services:** Interlibrary loan; bilingual staff in all five Asian languages; library tours by bilingual staff; I & R services to Asian Community in East Bay area; library open to the public. **Networks/Consortia:** Member of Bay Area Library and Information System (BALIS). **Staff:** Vera Yip, Ref.Libn..

★10601★
OAKLAND PUBLIC LIBRARY - CITYLINE INFORMATION SERVICE (Soc Sci)
Oakland City Hall, Rm. 108
1 City Hall Plaza Phone: (415)444-2489
Oakland, CA 94612 Mary R. Weinstein, Libn.
Founded: 1977. **Staff:** Prof 1; Other 20. **Subjects:** Local services, community organizations. **Services:** Telephone inquiries answered. **Networks/Consortia:** Member of Bay Area Library and Information System (BALIS). **Special Catalogs:** Cityline Resource File.

★10602★
OAKLAND PUBLIC LIBRARY - HISTORY/LITERATURE DIVISION (Hist, Hum)
125 14th St. Phone: (415)273-3136
Oakland, CA 94612 Richard Ragsdale, Sr.Libn.
Staff: Prof 4; Other 3. **Subjects:** History, travel, biography, English and foreign languages and literature, genealogy, maps. **Special Collections:** Jack London collection (autographed first editions; signed letters; photographs, letters from literary friends; artifacts); logbooks of the cutter BEAR; Ina Coolbrith materials; U.S. Geological Survey Topographical Maps; Schomberg Collection of Black Literature and History (in microform); Negroes of New York, 1939 (Writers Program; in microform); Library of American Civilization (in microform); Sutro Library Family History and Local History Subject Catalogs (in microform); Index to Biographies in State and Local Histories in the Library of Congress (in microform). **Holdings:** 100,663 books; genealogy microfilms. **Subscriptions:** 114 journals and other serials. **Services:** Interlibrary loan; copying; division open to the public. **Networks/Consortia:** Member of Bay Area Library and Information System (BALIS). **Publications:** New Releases. **Special Indexes:** Indexes for Drama, Short Story, Poetry, Literary Criticism (on cards); local newspapers, 1978 to present; Local History. **Staff:** Sherrill Reeves, Libn.; William Sturm, Libn.; Tom Dufour, Libn.; Lois Huish, Libn..

★10603★
OAKLAND PUBLIC LIBRARY - LATIN AMERICAN LIBRARY (Area-Ethnic)
1900 Fruitvale Ave., Suite 1-A Phone: (415)532-7882
Oakland, CA 94601 Roberto Valdez, Libn.
Founded: 1966. **Staff:** Prof 2; Other 4. **Subjects:** Spanish-speaking culture and history, Hispanic literature, Chicano history and culture. **Special Collections:** La Raza/Chicano Reference Collection; juvenile and adult materials in Spanish and English (books; magazines; records; newspapers). **Holdings:** 22,000 books; 115 study print sets; 200 slide sets; 190 tapes; 4 VF drawers of Chicano serials. **Subscriptions:** 70 journals and other serials; 17 newspapers. **Services:** Interlibrary loan; library open to the public. **Networks/Consortia:** Member of Bay Area Library and Information System (BALIS). **Also Known As:** LAL. **Staff:** Patty Wong, Ch.Libn..

★10604★
OAKLAND PUBLIC LIBRARY - SCIENCE/BUSINESS/ SOCIOLOGY DIVISION (Sci-Engr, Soc Sci, Bus-Fin)
125 14th St. Phone: (415)273-3138
Oakland, CA 94612 Marilyn Rowan, Sr.Libn.
Founded: 1953. **Staff:** Prof 6; Other 4. **Subjects:** Business, technology, natural sciences, useful arts, sociology, government, psychology, law, religion. **Special Collections:** Pacific Rim Trade Collection; "Business" Collection; annual reports (hardcopy and microfiche); college catalogs (microfiche); Dun & Bradstreet Market Identifiers (microfiche); Oakland and Alameda County; federal documents (5000). **Holdings:** 65,000 books; 2000 science pamphlets; 384,648 local, state, federal government documents. **Subscriptions:** 625 journals and other serials. **Services:** Interlibrary loan; copying; division open to the public. **Automated Operations:** Computerized cataloging. **Computerized Information Services:** DIALOG Information Services, University of California On-Line Union Catalog (MELVYL); internal databases. Performs searches free of charge. **Networks/Consortia:** Member of Bay Area Library and Information System (BALIS). **Publications:** Urban Scene. **Special Indexes:** City and County Index (cards); Pacific Rim Trade Collection. **Staff:** Patricia Coffey, Docs.Libn.; Joseph Ouyang, Libn.; Barbara Bibel, Libn.; Kevin Roddy, Libn.; Barbara Alessandrini, Libn.; Kathleen DiGiovanni, Libn.; Barbara Humes, Libn..

★10605★
OAKLAND SCHOOLS - EDUCATIONAL RESOURCE CENTER (Educ)
2100 Pontiac Lake Rd. Phone: (313)858-1961
Pontiac, MI 48054 Dr. Robert N. Johnson, Dir.
Founded: 1955. **Staff:** Prof 9; Other 20. **Subjects:** Education. **Holdings:** 40,000 books; complete ERIC microfiche collection; 3000 curriculum guides; 5000 curriculum materials; 7236 films; 1055 kits; 4551 videotapes; 10 VF drawers; 600 journals on microfilm. **Subscriptions:** 500 journals and other serials. **Services:** Interlibrary loan; copying; center open to the public for reference use only. **Computerized Information Services:** DIALOG Information Services. **Remarks:** Center is a state document depository. **Staff:** Judith Brooks, Asst.Libn.; Jennie B. Cross, Asst.Dir.; Robert Kramp, Libn.; Patrick Mardney, Cons., TV Prod.; Linda O'Donnell, Cons., Instr. TV; George Hemingway, Cons., Graphics; Doris Lusk, Mgr., Curric.Sup.Serv.; Larry Shepanek, Cons., Telecommunications.

★10606★
THE (Oakland) TRIBUNE - LIBRARY (Publ)
Box 24424 Phone: (415)645-2745
Oakland, CA 94623 Yae Shinomiya, Libn.
Founded: 1912. **Staff:** Prof 1; Other 4. **Subjects:** Newspaper reference topics. **Holdings:** Figures not available. **Services:** Library not open to the public.

★10607★
OAKLAND UNIVERSITY - LIBRARY - SPECIAL COLLECTIONS AND ARCHIVES (Hist)
Kresge Library Building Phone: (313)370-5355
Rochester, MI 48063 Robert G. Gaylor, Cur. of Archv./Spec.Coll.
Founded: 1959. **Holdings:** James Collection (folklore); Hicks Collection (women in literature, 17th and 18th centuries); Springer Collection (Lincolniana); Underground Press Collection; university archives. **Services:** Interlibrary loan; copying; collections open to the public with restrictions. **Automated Operations:** Computerized cataloging and circulation. **Computerized Information Services:** DIALOG Information Services, BRS Information Technologies, Dow Jones News/Retrieval, Pergamon ORBIT InfoLine, Inc., OCLC, CAB Abstracts. Performs searches on fee basis. **Networks/Consortia:** Member of Michigan Library Consortium (MLC), Wayne/Oakland Library Federation (WOLF), CLASS, Metropolitan Detroit Medical Library Group (MDMLG). **Publications:** Library Guide Series; Instructional Guide Series, both irregular - campus distribution and by request.

★10608★
OAKLAWN PSYCHIATRIC CENTER - PROFESSIONAL LIBRARY (Med)
2600 Oakland Ave. Phone: (219)294-3551
Elkhart, IN 46517 Nancy P. Price, Libn.
Staff: Prof 1. **Subjects:** Psychiatry, mental health, psychology, social work, addictions. **Holdings:** 1805 books; 2065 bound periodical volumes; 20 VF drawers; 450 cassettes. **Subscriptions:** 100 journals and other serials. **Services:** Interlibrary loan; copying; library open to the public with restrictions. **Computerized Information Services:** BRS Information Technologies. **Networks/Consortia:** Member of Area 2 Library Services Authority (ALSA 2).

OAKWOOD FORENSIC CENTER
See: Lima State Hospital (7858)

★10609★
OAKWOOD HOSPITAL - HEALTH SCIENCE LIBRARY (Med)
18101 Oakwood Blvd.
Box 2500 Phone: (313)593-7685
Dearborn, MI 48123-2500 Sharon A. Phillips, Dir.
Staff: Prof 2; Other 3. **Subjects:** Medicine, allied health sciences. **Holdings:** 13,000 volumes; AV programs. **Subscriptions:** 615 journals and other serials; 8 newspapers. **Services:** Interlibrary loan; library not open to the public. **Computerized Information Services:** MEDLINE, DIALOG Information Services, OCLC, BRS Information Technologies. **Networks/Consortia:** Member of Metropolitan Detroit Medical Library Group (MDMLG), Greater Midwest Regional Medical Library Network. **Staff:** Lorraine Obrzut, Asst.Libn..

★10610★
OAO CORPORATION - INFORMATION CENTER (Sci-Engr)
7500 Greenway Center Phone: (301)345-0750
Greenbelt, MD 20770 Rhea Austin, Corp.Libn.
Staff: Prof 1. **Subjects:** Engineering - aerospace, mechanical; data systems, computers. **Holdings:** 400 books; 4000 technical reports. **Subscriptions:** 85 journals and other serials; 15 newspapers. **Services:** Interlibrary loan; center not open to the public. **Computerized Information Services:** DIALOG Information Services, NASA/RECON.

★10611★
OBER, KALER, GRIMES & SHRIVER - LIBRARY (Law)
1600 Maryland National Bank Bldg. Phone: (301)685-1120
Baltimore, MD 21202 Karen C. Hinson, Libn.
Staff: Prof 1; Other 2. **Subjects:** Law - admiralty, hospital/health care, corporate, tax; litigation; estates and trusts. **Holdings:** 10,000 books. **Services:** Library not open to the public. **Computerized Information Services:** DIALOG Information Services, LEXIS, NEXIS, Dow Jones News/Retrieval, WESTLAW.

★10612★
OBERLIN COLLEGE - CLARENCE WARD ART LIBRARY (Art)
Allen Art Bldg. Phone: (216)775-8635
Oberlin, OH 44074 Jeffrey Weidman, Art Libn.
Founded: 1917. **Staff:** 3. **Subjects:** Art, architecture, archeology. **Special Collections:** Artists' books; rare books including duplication of Thomas Jefferson's architectural library. **Holdings:** 45,000 books, exhibition catalogs, bound periodical volumes; 6500 uncataloged exhibition catalogs; 9000 art sales catalogs. **Subscriptions:** 250 journals and other serials. **Services:** Interlibrary loan; copying; library open to the public for reference use only; open to cooperating Great Lakes Colleges Association (GLCA) and NOEMARL libraries with restrictions. **Automated Operations:** Computerized circulation. **Networks/Consortia:** Member of NOEMARL, OHIONET.

★10613★
OBERLIN COLLEGE - CLASS OF 1904 SCIENCE LIBRARY (Sci-Engr, Biol Sci)
Kettering Hall Phone: (216)775-8310
Oberlin, OH 44074 Alison Scott Ricker, Sci.Libn.
Founded: 1961. **Staff:** Prof 1; Other 1. **Subjects:** Biology, chemistry, earth sciences, medicine, technology. **Holdings:** 49,000 volumes; 80 loose-leaf binders of Thermodynamics Research Center Spectral and Thermodynamics Data; 1000 reels of microfilm. **Subscriptions:** 300 journals and other serials. **Services:** Interlibrary loan; copying; library open to the public; open to Great Lakes Colleges Association (GLCA) and NOEMARL libraries with restrictions. **Automated Operations:** Computerized public access catalog, cataloging, acquisitions, serials, and circulation. **Computerized Information Services:** RLIN, WILSONLINE, BRS Information Technologies, DIALOG Information Services. Performs searches on fee basis. **Networks/Consortia:** Member of NOEMARL, OHIONET.

★10614★
OBERLIN COLLEGE - CONSERVATORY OF MUSIC LIBRARY (Mus)
Oberlin, OH 44074 Phone: (216)775-8280
Daniel Zager, Dir.
Staff: Prof 3; Other 7. **Subjects:** Music - chamber, keyboard, vocal, education, history, theory. **Special Collections:** Karl W. Gehrkens Music Education Library; Edmonds Collection of Opera Scores; Rita Benton Collection (reference, research, music librarianship); recital tape archives; Mr. and Mrs. C.W. Best Collection of Autographs. **Holdings:** 91,300 books and scores; 10 VF drawers; 31,000 phonograph records; 800 compact discs; 4100 microcards; 4000 magnetic tapes; 2000 reels of microfilm; 300 microfiche. **Subscriptions:** 433 journals and other serials. **Services:** Interlibrary loan; copying; library open to the public for reference use only; open to cooperating NOEMARL libraries with restrictions. **Automated Operations:** Computerized cataloging, acquisitions, circulation, and ILL. **Computerized Information Services:** OCLC. **Networks/Consortia:** Member of OHIONET, NOEMARL. **Special Catalogs:** Catalog of recital tape archives (computer-generated); Catalog of the Mr. and Mrs. C.W. Best Collection of Autographs; catalog of the George W. Andrews Collection. **Staff:** Carolyn Rabson, Libn., Pub.Serv.; David Knapp, Libn., Tech.Serv..

★10615★
OBERLIN COLLEGE - LIBRARY - ARCHIVES (Hist)
420 Mudd Center Phone: (216)775-8285
Oberlin, OH 44074-1532 Roland M. Baumann, Coll.Archv.
Founded: 1966. **Staff:** Prof 2; Other 8. **Subjects:** Higher education, 19th century reform, temperance, women's history, black education, architecture. **Special Collections:** Missions, the antislavery movement, and temperance in Oberlin; papers of Oberlin College faculty and graduates; Oberlin municipal government records; photographs of Oberlin College and Oberlin. **Holdings:** 2600 linear feet of manuscripts and archival materials. **Services:** Copying; archives open to the public. **Automated Operations:** Computerized public access catalog, cataloging, acquisitions, serials, and circulation. **Computerized Information Services:** DIALOG Information Services, BRS Information Technologies. Performs searches free of charge. Contact Person: Cynthia Comer, Assoc.Hd., Ref.. **Networks/Consortia:** Member of NOEMARL, OHIONET. **Publications:** Library of Congress Rule Interpretation for AACR2; Guide to the Women's History Sources at Oberlin College (1989); Current Scholarship in Women's Studies (1987). **Special Catalogs:** Catalog of the Antislavery Collection.

★10616★
OBERLIN COLLEGE - PHYSICS READING ROOM (Sci-Engr)
Wright Physics Hall Phone: (216)775-8310
Oberlin, OH 44074 Alison Ricker, Sci.Libn.
Founded: 1937. **Subjects:** Physics, astronomy. **Holdings:** 9700 volumes; 200 reels of microfilm of journals. **Subscriptions:** 60 journals and other serials. **Services:** Interlibrary loan; room open to the public with restrictions. **Automated Operations:** Computerized public access catalog, cataloging, acquisitions, and serials. **Networks/Consortia:** Member of NOEMARL, OHIONET.

★10617★
LOUISE OBICI MEMORIAL HOSPITAL - LIBRARY (Med)
1900 N. Main
Box 1100 Phone: (804)539-1511
Suffolk, VA 23434 Patricia D. Herzfeldt, Supv., Med.Rec.
Founded: 1951. **Staff:** Prof 1; Other 1. **Subjects:** Medicine, surgery, obstetrics, pediatrics. **Holdings:** 550 books; 100 Audio-Digest tapes. **Subscriptions:** 25 journals and other serials. **Services:** Interlibrary loan; library not open to the public. **Computerized Information Services:** Online systems.

★10618★
OBLATE FATHERS - BIBLIOTHEQUE DESCHATELETS (Rel-Phil)
175 Main St. Phone: (613)237-0580
Ottawa, ON, Canada K1S 1C3 Leo Laberge, Dir.
Founded: 1885. **Staff:** Prof 1; Other 1. **Subjects:** Theology, spirituality, philosophy, church history, Canadiana, history, literature. **Holdings:** 65,000 books; 15,000 bound periodical volumes. **Subscriptions:** 100 journals and other serials. **Services:** Library not open to the public. **Staff:** Gerard Juneau, Libn..

OBLATE FATHERS - UNIVERSITE ST-PAUL
See: Universite St-Paul (15750)

★10619★
OBLATE SCHOOL OF THEOLOGY - LIBRARY (Rel-Phil)
285 Oblate Dr. Phone: (512)341-1366
San Antonio, TX 78216-6693 James Maney, Dir.
Founded: 1903. **Staff:** Prof 1; Other 1. **Subjects:** Theology. **Special Collections:** Oblate faculty publications. **Holdings:** 24,000 books; 10,000 bound periodical volumes; 390 pamphlets; 220 AV programs. **Subscriptions:** 266 journals and other serials; 8 newspapers. **Services:** Interlibrary loan; copying; library open to the public for reference use only. **Automated Operations:** Computerized cataloging. **Networks/Consortia:** Member of Council of Research & Academic Libraries (CORAL), AMIGOS Bibliographic Council, Inc.. **Publications:** Library Report, monthly - for internal distribution only.

OBLATES OF MARY IMMACULATE - ST. CHARLES SCHOLASTICATE
See: St. Charles Scholasticate (12344)

OBLATES OF MARY IMMACULATE ARCHIVES
See: Oblates Theology Library (10620)

★10620★
OBLATES THEOLOGY LIBRARY (Rel-Phil)
391 Michigan Ave., N.E. Phone: (202)529-5244
Washington, DC 20017 Ward E. Gongoll, Hd.Libn.
Staff: Prof 4. **Subjects:** Theology, sacred scripture. **Special Collections:** Oblates of Mary Immaculate Archives; Oblates of St. Francis De Sales Collection; Special Ministries. **Holdings:** 54,165 volumes. **Subscriptions:** 39 journals and other serials; 9 newspapers. **Services:** Interlibrary loan; copying; library open to the public with restrictions. **Networks/Consortia:** Member of Washington Theological Consortium. **Remarks:** Figures include the holdings of the De Sales Hall School of Theology - Library.

KEVIN F. O'BRIEN HEALTH SCIENCES LIBRARY
See: Marquette General Hospital, Inc. (8450)

O'CALLAHAN SCIENCE LIBRARY
See: College of the Holy Cross (3379)

OLIVER OCASEK REGIONAL MEDICAL INFORMATION CENTER
See: Northeastern Ohio Universities College of Medicine (10404)

★10621★
OCCIDENTAL CHEMICAL CORPORATION - TECHNICAL INFORMATION CENTER (Sci-Engr)
2801 Long Rd. Phone: (716)773-8531
Grand Island, NY 14072 Jane Pattison, Mgr.
Founded: 1916. **Staff:** Prof 4; Other 3. **Subjects:** Chemistry - organic, inorganic, polymer, physical; textiles; business. **Holdings:** 20,000 books; 20,000 bound periodical volumes; 90 VF drawers of technical reports; 10 cabinets of microforms. **Subscriptions:** 500 journals and other serials. **Services:** Interlibrary loan; copying; SDI; center open to the public on request. **Automated Operations:** Computerized cataloging, serials, and circulation. **Computerized Information Services:** DIALOG Information Services, Pergamon ORBIT InfoLine, Inc., NLM, NEXIS, CAS ONLINE. **Networks/Consortia:** Member of Western New York Library Resources Council (WNYLRC). **Special Indexes:** Magnetic disc index of internal reports and patents. **Staff:** Ben Wagner, Assoc.Info.Sci.; Michael Burke, Res.Info.Anl.; Linda Wieland, Res.Info.Anl..

★10622★
OCCIDENTAL COLLEGE - MARY NORTON CLAPP LIBRARY (Hum)
1600 Campus Rd. Phone: (213)259-2852
Los Angeles, CA 90041 Michael C. Sutherland, Spec.Coll.Libn.
Staff: Prof 1. **Subjects:** Western Americana, mystery and detective fiction, romantic literature, railroad history, fine printing, aviation, Lincoln and the Civil War. **Special Collections:** William Jennings Bryan Collection; William Henry Collection; Upton Sinclair Collection; Ward Ritchie Press Collection; Robinson Jeffers Collection; Doheny Foundation papers. **Holdings:** 70,000 volumes. **Services:** Copying; library open to the public. **Automated Operations:** Computerized cataloging. **Computerized Information Services:** OCLC. **Special Indexes:** Index to William Henry Letters; Inventory to Guymon Mystery and Detective Fiction Collection.

★10623★
OCCIDENTAL OIL AND GAS CORPORATION - LIBRARY (Energy)
1200 Discovery Way
Box 12021 Phone: (805)321-6565
Bakersfield, CA 93389-2021 Wendy L. Waldron, Libn.
Founded: 1968. **Staff:** Prof 1; Other 1. **Subjects:** Geology, petroleum, engineering, energy resources, environment, law. **Holdings:** 4000 volumes; 10,000 maps. **Subscriptions:** 400 journals and other serials. **Services:** Interlibrary loan; library not open to the public. **Automated Operations:** Computerized cataloging, serials, and circulation. **Computerized Information Services:** DIALOG Information Services, OCLC, Pergamon ORBIT InfoLine, Inc.; DATALIB (internal database). **Formerly:** Occidental International Exploration & Production Company. **Staff:** Ellen Cantrell, Asst.Libn..

OCCIDENTAL PETROLEUM CORPORATION - CITIES SERVICE OIL & GAS CORPORATION
See: Cities Service Oil & Gas Corporation - Production Library (3228)

★10624★
OCCIDENTAL PETROLEUM CORPORATION - OCCIDENTAL RESEARCH CORPORATION - TECHNICAL INFORMATION CENTER
10889 Wilshire Blvd.
Los Angeles, CA 90024-4201
Defunct

★10625★
OCCIDENTAL SOCIETY OF METEMPIRIC ANALYSIS - LIBRARY AND RESEARCH CENTER (Rel-Phil)
32055 Hwy. 24E
Simla, CO 80835 Robert J. Everhart, Exec.Chm.
Founded: 1977. **Subjects:** Metempirical, occult, and UFO topics. **Special Collections:** Folklore of Americas. **Holdings:** 1500 volumes; biographical archives; research and data tapes. **Services:** Interlibrary loan; answers mail enquiries only.

★10626★
OCEAN CITY HISTORICAL MUSEUM - LIBRARY (Hist)
409 Wesley Ave. Phone: (609)399-1801
Ocean City, NJ 08226 Alberta E. Lamphear, Libn.
Subjects: History of Ocean City. **Holdings:** 200 books; photographs; deeds; documents; periodicals. **Services:** Library open to the public for reference use only.

★10627★
OCEAN AND COASTAL LAW CENTER - LIBRARY (Biol Sci)
School of Law
University of Oregon Phone: (503)686-3845
Eugene, OR 97403-1221 Andrea G. Coffman, Libn.
Founded: 1968. **Staff:** Prof 1; Other 1. **Subjects:** International law of the sea, coastal zone management, ocean management and policy, fisheries, aquaculture, offshore drilling and mining, marine pollution. **Holdings:** 4500 books; 290 bound periodical volumes; 275 reprints; 185 maps; 100 fishery management plans; 7 VF drawers of documents. **Subscriptions:** 139 journals and other serials. **Services:** Interlibrary loan; copying (limited); library open to the public. **Publications:** Recent Acquisitions List, monthly;

Periodical Holdings List, annual; Recent Articles in Marine Legal Affairs, quarterly - all available on request.

★10628★
OCEAN COUNTY LAW LIBRARY (Law)
Justice Complex
120 Hooper Ave. Phone: (201)244-2121
Toms River, NJ 08753 Susan West, Sr.Libn.
Founded: 1930. **Staff:** Prof 1; Other 2. **Subjects:** Law. **Holdings:** 6125 books. **Subscriptions:** 13 journals and other serials. **Services:** Copying; library open to the public. **Computerized Information Services:** WESTLAW. **Remarks:** Maintained by Ocean County Library.

★10629★
OCEANIC INSTITUTE - WORKING LIBRARY (Biol Sci)
Makapuu Point Phone: (808)259-7951
Waimanalo, HI 96795 Ellen Antill, Libn.
Founded: 1964. **Staff:** 1. **Subjects:** Aquaculture, oceanography, general science, marine biology. **Holdings:** Figures not available. **Subscriptions:** 15 journals and other serials. **Services:** Library not open to the public.

★10630★
OCEANROUTES, INC. - TECHNICAL LIBRARY (Sci-Engr)
680 W. Maude Ave., Suite 3 Phone: (408)245-3600
Sunnyvale, CA 94086-3518 Anne Dawson, Libn.
Staff: Prof 1. **Subjects:** Weather, shipping, cargo. **Special Collections:** Historical weather data. **Holdings:** 2500 volumes; 500 technical reports. **Subscriptions:** 78 journals and other serials. **Services:** Interlibrary loan; copying. **Automated Operations:** Computerized cataloging. **Computerized Information Services:** DIALOG Information Services. **Special Catalogs:** Technical paper file.

★10631★
ALTON OCHSNER MEDICAL FOUNDATION - MEDICAL LIBRARY (Med)
1516 Jefferson Hwy. Phone: (504)838-3760
New Orleans, LA 70121 Carol M. Liardon, Hd.Med.Libn.
Founded: 1942. **Staff:** Prof 2; Other 4. **Subjects:** Medicine, nursing, allied health sciences. **Holdings:** 3225 books; 20,120 bound periodical volumes. **Subscriptions:** 600 journals and other serials. **Services:** Interlibrary loan; library not open to the public. **Computerized Information Services:** BRS Information Technologies, DIALOG Information Services, MEDLARS. **Staff:** Mary Claire, Asst.Med.Libn..

★10632★
OCLC, INC. - LIBRARY (Info Sci)
Box 7777 Phone: (614)764-6000
Dublin, OH 43017 Ann T. Dodson, Mgr.
Founded: 1977. **Staff:** Prof 8; Other 6. **Subjects:** Library and information science, computer science and engineering, telecommunications, management and business. **Special Collections:** Library Network Newsletters; state library newsletters. **Holdings:** 10,626 books; 458 bound periodical volumes; 1860 microfiche; 346 cassettes; 1419 slides; 20,754 serial microfiche; 66 maps; 2204 microcomputer software packages; 17,766 OCLC and system manuals. **Subscriptions:** 810 journals and other serials; 6 newspapers. **Services:** Interlibrary loan; copying; SDI; current awareness; library open to the public with restrictions. **Automated Operations:** Computerized public access catalog, cataloging, acquisitions, serials, circulation, and ILL. **Computerized Information Services:** DIALOG Information Services, BRS Information Technologies, Dun & Bradstreet Corporation, CompuServe, Inc., Dow Jones News/Retrieval, Library Control System (LCS), LS/2000. **Networks/Consortia:** Member of CALICO. **Publications:** OCC Libline; accessions lists; bibliographies; list of periodicals (online). **Also Known As:** Online Computer Library Center, Inc. **Staff:** Christine N. Grabenstatter, Mgr., Tech.Serv.Sect.; Mark A. Blanchard, Mgr., Pub.Serv.Sect.; Deborah Tavenner, Ref.Libn.; Christopher Connell, Doc.Libn.; Zelma G. Palestrant, Acq.Libn.; D. Ann Ekstrom, Mgr., Archv./Rec.Mgt.; Lawrence Olszewski, Br.Libn..

CATHERINE B. O'CONNOR LIBRARY
See: Boston College (1729)

★10633★
O'CONNOR, CAVANAGH, ANDERSON, WESTOVER, KILLINGSWORTH & BESHEARS - LAW LIBRARY (Law)
1 E. Camelback Rd., Suite 900 Phone: (602)263-2488
Phoenix, AZ 85012 Philleatra Bridges, Hd. Law Libn.
Staff: Prof 1; Other 3. **Subjects:** Law - medical, insurance, corporate, tax, labor, real estate, bond, employment practice, workers compensation. **Holdings:** 22,000 books. **Services:** Interlibrary loan; copying; library open to attorneys and clients only. **Automated Operations:** Computerized cataloging and acquisitions. **Computerized Information Services:** LEXIS, NEXIS, WESTLAW, VU/TEXT Information Services, DIALOG Information Services, ScanTel Service.

★10634★
LINDSAY A. & OLIVE B. O'CONNOR HOSPITAL - LIBRARY (Med)
Andes Road, Route 28
Box 205A Phone: (607)746-2371
Delhi, NY 13753 Barbara Green, Libn.
Founded: 1968. **Subjects:** Medicine, nursing. **Holdings:** 200 books. **Subscriptions:** 30 journals and other serials. **Services:** Copying; library open to the public on request. **Networks/Consortia:** Member of South Central Research Library Council (SCRLC).

★10635★
OCTAMERON ASSOCIATES, INC. - RESEARCH LIBRARY (Educ)
4805 A Eisenhower Ave. Phone: (703)823-1882
Alexandria, VA 22304-4832 Karen Stokstad, Libn.
Founded: 1975. **Staff:** Prof 1; Other 1. **Subjects:** College admissions and financial aid, career information, higher education. **Holdings:** 2100 books; 500 bound periodical volumes; 20 VF drawers of scholarship information; 20 linear feet of pamphlets. **Subscriptions:** 25 journals and other serials. **Services:** Library not open to the public. **Computerized Information Services:** College financial aid file (internal database). **Publications:** Annual directories of scholarship information - for sale; internal reports. **Special Indexes:** Financial aid data.

HAMILTON ODELL LIBRARY
See: New York State Supreme Court - 3rd Judicial District (10140)

★10636★
ODESSA AMERICAN - EDITORIAL LIBRARY (Publ)
222 E. 4th
Box 2952 Phone: (915)337-4661
Odessa, TX 79760 Johnnie Walker
Founded: 1940. **Staff:** 1. **Subjects:** Newspaper reference topics. **Holdings:** Microfilm; newspaper files. **Subscriptions:** 15 journals and other serials; 35 newspapers. **Services:** Copying; library open to the public for reference use only with supervision. **Remarks:** Published by Freedom Newspapers Chain.

MAYO HAYES O'DONNELL LIBRARY
See: Monterey History & Art Association, Ltd. (9247)

O'DONOGHUE MEDICAL LIBRARY
See: St. Anthony Hospital (12319)

★10637★
ODYSSEY-EASTERN PUMA RESEARCH NETWORK LIBRARY (Biol Sci)
Box 3562 Phone: (301)254-2517
Baltimore, MD 21214 Linda A. Lutz, Sec.
Founded: 1983. **Staff:** Prof 1. **Subjects:** Eastern cougar, mountain lion, panther, and puma - research, study, education, field investigation, nature, characteristics. **Special Collections:** Eastern Puma Network Newsletter (complete). **Holdings:** 150 books; 175 bound periodical volumes; 5000 other cataloged items. **Subscriptions:** 10 journals and other serials. **Services:** Library not open to the public. **Publications:** Eastern Puma Network News, 3/year - by subscription.

OESPER CHEMISTRY-BIOLOGY LIBRARY
See: University of Cincinnati (16057)

OESTERLE LIBRARY
See: North Central College (10339)

★10638★
OFFICE OF BILINGUAL EDUCATION - RESOURCE LIBRARY (Educ)
131 Livingston St., Rm. 204 Phone: (718)935-3905
Brooklyn, NY 11201 Carmen Gloria Burgos, Libn.
Founded: 1973. **Staff:** Prof 1; Other 1. **Subjects:** Bilingual and bicultural education, English as a second language. **Special Collections:** Puerto Rican Heritage Collection. **Holdings:** 53,000 books; 410 curriculum guides; 1500 ERIC microfiche; 220 proposals; 3 VF drawers of reports; 9 VF drawers of clippings and articles; AV programs. **Subscriptions:** 46 journals and other serials. **Services:** Interlibrary loan; library open to the public. **Remarks:**

The language groups served include Spanish, Italian, French, Haitian-Creole, Chinese, Greek, Portuguese, Indochinese, Korean, and Russian.

★10639★
OFFICE OF PERSONNEL MANAGEMENT - LIBRARY (Soc Sci, Bus-Fin)
1900 E St., N.W. Phone: (202)632-4432
Washington, DC 20415 Catherine Tashjean, Supv.Libn.
Founded: 1940. **Staff:** Prof 2; Other 3. **Subjects:** Personnel administration, public administration, civil service, law, legislative reference, social science, political science, management. **Special Collections:** Baruch Collection (personal papers of Ismar Baruch, expert in position classification and salary administration); civil service history. **Holdings:** 95,000 books; 500 bound periodical volumes; 4000 other cataloged items. **Subscriptions:** 500 journals and other serials. **Services:** Interlibrary loan; library open to the public for reference use only. **Computerized Information Services:** DIALOG Information Services, BRS Information Technologies. **Publications:** Personnel Literature, monthly with annual index - for sale through U.S. Government Printing Office. **Staff:** Leon Brody, Ref.Libn.; Laura Vollenweider, Ref.Libn..

★10640★
OGILVIE MILLS LTD. - RESEARCH & DEVELOPMENT LIBRARY (Food-Bev)
Box 6089 Phone: (514)866-7961
Montreal, PQ, Canada H3C 3H1 Muriel E. Henri, Libn.
Founded: 1970. **Staff:** 1. **Subjects:** Cereal chemistry, wheat starch, analytical chemistry. **Holdings:** 2375 books; 1023 bound periodical volumes; 450 patents. **Subscriptions:** 56 journals and other serials. **Services:** Interlibrary loan; copying; library open to the public by appointment. **Computerized Information Services:** DIALOG Information Services, CAN/OLE.

★10641★
OGILVY & MATHER - INFORMATION CENTER (Bus-Fin)
676 St. Clair Phone: (312)988-2766
Chicago, IL 60611 Eileen Pyne, Mgr.
Founded: 1977. **Staff:** Prof 2; Other 1. **Subjects:** Advertising, marketing, business, communications. **Holdings:** 1500 volumes; 150 corporate/industry files; Ogilvy & Mather publications, studies, reports; annual reports of Fortune 500 corporations. **Subscriptions:** 300 journals and other serials; 5 newspapers. **Services:** Interlibrary loan; center not open to the public. **Computerized Information Services:** DIALOG Information Services, NEXIS, Dow Jones News/Retrieval, ProductScan, VU/TEXT Information Services. **Networks/Consortia:** Member of Chicago Library System. **Publications:** New Books, quarterly; Top Resources for Secondary Research, quarterly - for internal distribution only.

★10642★
OGILVY & MATHER - RESEARCH LIBRARY (Bus-Fin)
2 E. 48th St. Phone: (212)907-3502
New York, NY 10017 Joanne Winiarski, Hd.Libn.
Founded: 1955. **Staff:** Prof 5; Other 3. **Subjects:** Advertising, marketing, drugs, cosmetics, food market segments. **Holdings:** 6000 books; 60 periodicals on microfilm; 230 VF drawers of subject files. **Subscriptions:** 400 journals and other serials; 7 newspapers. **Services:** Interlibrary loan; library not open to the public. **Computerized Information Services:** NEXIS, DIALOG Information Services, Dow Jones News/Retrieval, WILSONLINE, TEXTLINE, Marketing Analysis and Information Database (MAID). **Remarks:** An alternate telephone number is 907-3506. **Staff:** Catherine Preston, Sr.Libn.; Margaret Reysen, Libn.; Jerry Foster.

★10643★
OGILVY, RENAULT - LIBRARY (Law)
1981 McGill College Ave., Suite 1100 Phone: (514)286-5424
Montreal, PQ, Canada H3A 3C1 Carole Mehu, Hd.Libn.
Founded: 1879. **Staff:** Prof 1; Other 2. **Subjects:** Law - Quebec, Canada, Great Britain. **Holdings:** 17,000 volumes. **Services:** Library not open to the public. **Automated Operations:** Computerized cataloging. **Computerized Information Services:** BRS Information Technologies.

★10644★
OGLE PETROLEUM INC. - LIBRARY
559 San Ysidro Rd.
Santa Barbara, CA 93108
Defunct

★10645★
OGLEBAY INSTITUTE - MANSION MUSEUM LIBRARY (Hist)
Oglebay Park Phone: (304)242-7272
Wheeling, WV 26003 John A. Artzberger, Dir.
Founded: 1930. **Staff:** Prof 4. **Subjects:** History of local and tri-state area; glass, china, and other decorative arts. **Holdings:** 750 books; 250 archival materials. **Services:** Interlibrary loan; copying; library open to the public for reference use and loan on request. **Staff:** Holly Hoover, Cur. of Educ..

★10646★
OGLESBY HISTORICAL SOCIETY - LIBRARY (Hist)
Oglesby Public Library
128 W. Walnut Phone: (815)883-3619
Oglesby, IL 61348 Albert Moyle, Pres.
Founded: 1919. **Subjects:** Local history. **Holdings:** Figures not available. **Services:** Library open to the public.

★10647★
OGLETHORPE UNIVERSITY - LIBRARY - ARCHIVES (Hist)
4484 Peachtree Rd., N.E. Phone: (404)261-1441
Atlanta, GA 30319 John Ryland, Libn.
Subjects: Oglethorpe University, 1835 to present. **Special Collections:** Records of the "Crypt of Civilization" at Oglethorpe; papers and drawings of the original Oglethorpe University buildings in Atlanta, 1913-1930; minutes of the board of trustees, 1835-1871. **Holdings:** 1 file cabinet and 14 boxes of manuscripts and photographs; the Oglethorpe University "Founder's Book," 1916. **Services:** Copying; archives open to the public for research only. **Networks/Consortia:** Member of University Center in Georgia, Inc..

★10648★
OHEV SHALOM SYNAGOGUE - RAY DOBLITZ MEMORIAL LIBRARY (Rel-Phil)
2 Chester Rd. Phone: (215)874-1465
Wallingford, PA 19086 Evelyn Schott, Libn.
Founded: 1955. **Staff:** Prof 1. **Subjects:** Judaica. **Holdings:** 5500 books; 120 recordings; pamphlets; 80 video cassettes on Jewish subjects. **Subscriptions:** 12 journals and other serials. **Services:** Library open to the public with references.

★10649★
OHIO BELL - CORPORATE INFORMATION RESOURCE CENTER (Bus-Fin)
45 Erieview Plaza, Rm. 820 Phone: (216)822-7285
Cleveland, OH 44114 Jessie L. Martin, Supv.
Founded: 1951. **Staff:** Prof 1; Other 6. **Subjects:** Business, management, telecommunications, personnel, psychology, computers, marketing, Ohio Bell and Bell System history. **Special Collections:** Corporate historical photograph collection (30,000 photographs). **Holdings:** 5000 books; 300 bound periodical volumes. **Subscriptions:** 229 journals and other serials; 10 newspapers. **Services:** Interlibrary loan; copying; library open to public at librarian's discretion. **Automated Operations:** Computerized serials. **Computerized Information Services:** DIALOG Information Services; internal databases. **Publications:** New Book List, monthly - for internal distribution only. **Special Indexes:** Current Awareness File. **Remarks:** Subsidiary of AmeriTech Corp.

★10650★
OHIO COLLEGE OF PODIATRIC MEDICINE - LIBRARY/MEDIA CENTER (Med)
10515 Carnegie Ave. Phone: (216)231-3300
Cleveland, OH 44106 Judy Mehl Cowell, Dir.
Founded: 1916. **Staff:** Prof 1; Other 3. **Subjects:** Podiatric medicine, orthopedics, dermatology, biomechanics, sports medicine. **Special Collections:** Archives; podiatric medicine. **Holdings:** 11,000 books; 2000 bound periodical volumes; 300 AV programs; VF drawers of pamphlet material; 800 reprints; School Papers File; state file. **Subscriptions:** 225 journals and other serials. **Services:** Interlibrary loan; copying; library open to the public with restrictions. **Automated Operations:** Computerized cataloging. **Computerized Information Services:** DIALOG Information Services, MEDLINE. Performs searches on fee basis.

OHIO COOPERATIVE FISH AND WILDLIFE RESEARCH UNIT
See: Ohio State University (10703)

★10651★
OHIO COUNTY COURT - 1ST JUDICIAL DISTRICT - LAW LIBRARY (Law)
County Courthouse
1500 Chapline St. Phone: (304)234-3780
Wheeling, WV 26003 Nancy C. Obecny, Law Libn.
Founded: 1919. **Staff:** Prof 1. **Subjects:** Law. **Holdings:** 37,000 volumes. **Services:** Copying; library open to the public for reference use only. **Remarks:** Maintained by State of West Virginia.

★10652★
OHIO DOMINICAN COLLEGE - SPANGLER LIBRARY (Rel-Phil, Soc Sci)
1216 Sunbury Rd. Phone: (614)253-2741
Columbus, OH 43219 Sr. Rosalie Graham, Dir.
Founded: 1911. **Staff:** Prof 6; Other 3. **Subjects:** Social sciences, theology, philosophy. **Holdings:** 118,000 books; 12,153 bound periodical volumes; 4912 reels of microfilm; 2700 AV programs. **Subscriptions:** 595 journals and other serials; 15 newspapers. **Services:** Interlibrary loan; copying; library open to the public. **Automated Operations:** Computerized cataloging. **Computerized Information Services:** OCLC, DIALOG Information Services. Performs searches on fee basis. **Networks/Consortia:** Member of OHIONET. **Staff:** Gabriella Petrovics, Libn.; P. Miller, Cat.Libn.; Larry Cepek, Dir., Media Ctr..

★10653★
OHIO EDISON COMPANY - CORPORATE LIBRARY (Energy)
76 S. Main St. Phone: (216)384-5367
Akron, OH 44308 Sharon M. Malumphy, Corp.Libn.
Founded: 1981. **Staff:** Prof 2; Other 3. **Subjects:** Engineering, energy, management. **Special Collections:** Electric Power Research Institute reports (4000); Edison Electric Institute reports (525). **Holdings:** 6500 books; 270 bound periodical volumes; 1440 manufacturers' catalogs; 18 shelves of company references and documents; 15 VF drawers of annual reports; 10 VF drawers of newsletters and college catalogs; 950 standards. **Subscriptions:** 268 journals and other serials. **Services:** Interlibrary loan; SDI; library open to the public with permission. **Automated Operations:** Computerized cataloging and acquisitions. **Computerized Information Services:** DIALOG Information Services, LEXIS, NEXIS, Dow Jones News/Retrieval, VU/TEXT Information Services, The Source Information Network. **Networks/Consortia:** Member of Cleveland Area Metropolitan Library System (CAMLS). **Publications:** Library Update, irregular - for internal distribution only. **Special Indexes:** Index to standards. **Staff:** Diane A. Mogren, Asst.Libn..

★10654★
OHIO GENEALOGICAL SOCIETY - LIBRARY (Hist)
419 W. 3rd St.
Box 2625 Phone: (419)522-9077
Mansfield, OH 44906 Florence Main, Libn.
Founded: 1955. **Staff:** Prof 2. **Subjects:** History and genealogy. **Special Collections:** Ancestor file (200,000 cards). **Holdings:** 10,000 books; census for all Ohio counties, 1820-1860, 1880, 1900, on microfilm; 24 file drawers of "First Families of Ohio" applications; 46 drawers of unpublished family history manuscripts. **Services:** Copying; library open to the public. **Publications:** The Report, quarterly; Ohio Records & Pioneer Families, quarterly; OGS Newsletter, monthly. **Special Indexes:** 1812 Ohio tax list (card). **Staff:** Thomas Stephen Neel, Mgr..

★10655★
OHIO GENEALOGICAL SOCIETY - MUSKINGUM COUNTY GENEALOGICAL SOCIETY - LIBRARY (Hist)
Zanesville, OH 43701 Ione B. Supplee, Lib.Comm.Chm.
Founded: 1977. **Staff:** 9. **Subjects:** Genealogy, history. **Holdings:** 2000 books; 400 bound periodical volumes; township, county, and church registers; tombstone inscriptions; Bible records; atlases; genealogical lessons, lectures and guides on tape; directories; court records and local newspapers on microfilm. **Subscriptions:** 12 journals and other serials. **Services:** Copying; library open to the public. **Staff:** Marion Davies, Libn..

★10656★
OHIO HISTORICAL SOCIETY - CAMPUS MARTIUS MUSEUM - LIBRARY (Hist)
601 Second St.
Marietta, OH 45750 John B. Briley, Mgr.
Founded: 1920. **Subjects:** Area history and genealogy prior to 1930, river history. **Holdings:** 1000 books. **Services:** Copying; library open to the public by appointment.

★10657★
OHIO NORTHERN UNIVERSITY - COLLEGE OF LAW - JAY P. TAGGART MEMORIAL LAW LIBRARY (Law)
Ada, OH 45810 Phone: (419)772-2250
James Leonard, Dir./Hd.Libn.
Founded: 1885. **Staff:** Prof 4; Other 5. **Subjects:** Law, international law. **Special Collections:** Papers of Congressman McCullough. **Holdings:** 152,860 volumes; U.S. Government documents (depository library); 20,660 volumes on microfilm. **Subscriptions:** 2450 journals and other serials; 12 newspapers. **Services:** Interlibrary loan; copying; library open to the public. **Automated Operations:** Computerized cataloging. **Computerized Information Services:** LEXIS, NEXIS, WESTLAW. Performs searches on fee basis. Contact Person: Betty Roeske, Ser.Libn., 772-2255. **Networks/Consortia:** Member of OHIONET. **Staff:** Marcia Siebesma, Assoc. Law Libn.; Paul Birch, Circ./Ref.Libn.; Pam Johnson, Acq.; Josephine Ansley, Govt.Doc.; Nancy Biddinger, Circ.; Lora Smith, Tech.Proc..

★10658★
OHIO NORTHERN UNIVERSITY - HETERICK MEMORIAL LIBRARY - SPECIAL COLLECTIONS (Hist)
Ada, OH 45810 Phone: (419)772-2182
Paul M. Logsdon, Dir.
Founded: 1968. **Special Collections:** East Europe and Russia; Theodore Roosevelt; ONU authors; Heterick medals; Taggart paperweights. **Holdings:** 90,906 government documents. **Services:** Interlibrary loan; copying; collections open to the public. **Automated Operations:** Computerized circulation. **Computerized Information Services:** BRS Information Technologies, DIALOG Information Services. Performs searches on fee basis. Contact Person: Charles E. Steele, Jr., Sci.Libn., 772-2188. **Networks/Consortia:** Member of OHIONET, Northwest Ohio Library Consortium. **Publications:** Bibliographies, irregular; government document holdings, annual. **Staff:** Cora Layaou, Ser./Govt.Docs..

★10659★
OHIO POETRY THERAPY CENTER AND LIBRARY (Soc Sci)
Pudding House
60 N. Main St. Phone: (614)279-4188
Johnstown, OH 43031 Jennifer Welch Bosveld, Dir.
Founded: 1981. **Staff:** Prof 2. **Subjects:** Poetry, creative arts in therapy, psychology, self-help and motivation, creative writing, social work, popular culture. **Holdings:** 5000 books; 50 dissertations and reports; 200 cassette tapes. **Subscriptions:** 50 journals and other serials. **Services:** Library open to the public by appointment on fee basis. **Publications:** Pudding Magazine; Association for Applied Poetry Newsletter, quarterly; poetry therapy bibliography (card); printed recommended bibliography, revised annually - for sale; poetry bibliography: recommended reading for the poetry therapist; list of additional publications - available upon request.

★10660★
OHIO POWER COMPANY - LIBRARY (Energy)
Box 400 Phone: (216)438-7235
Canton, OH 44701 James M. Beck, Libn.
Founded: 1956. **Staff:** 1. **Subjects:** Public utility regulations, engineering, law and government, statistics, management development. **Holdings:** 1100 volumes; 8 VF drawers. **Subscriptions:** 150 journals and other serials. **Services:** Library open to the public for reference use only upon request.

★10661★
OHIO (State) AGRICULTURAL RESEARCH AND DEVELOPMENT CENTER - LIBRARY (Agri)
1680 Madison Ave. Phone: (216)263-3773
Wooster, OH 44691-4096 Constance J. Britton, Libn.
Founded: 1892. **Staff:** Prof 1; Other 2. **Subjects:** Agricultural research. **Special Collections:** Virus diseases of corn - Maize Virus Information Service (MAVIS). **Holdings:** 53,200 volumes; microforms. **Subscriptions:** 1200 journals and other serials. **Services:** Interlibrary loan; copying; library open to the public. **Automated Operations:** Computerized cataloging and ILL. **Computerized Information Services:** OCLC, DIALOG Information Services. **Networks/Consortia:** Member of OHIONET. **Publications:** Serials in the Library - to bio-agricultural libraries. **Special Indexes:** Subject indexes to agricultural documents owned by library, monthly; index to publications of this organization. **Remarks:** Maintained by Ohio State University.

★10662★
OHIO STATE ATTORNEY GENERAL'S OFFICE - LAW LIBRARY (Law)
30 E. Broad St., 17th Fl. Phone: (614)466-2465
Columbus, OH 43215 Shelley McLane, Law Libn.
Founded: 1846. **Staff:** Prof 1; Other 1. **Subjects:** Federal and state law. **Holdings:** 23,000 books. **Subscriptions:** 12 journals and other serials; 5 newspapers. **Services:** Copying; SDI; library open to the public by appointment. **Automated Operations:** Computerized acquisitions. **Computerized Information Services:** LEXIS. **Special Indexes:** Tax, securities, newspaper, magazine indexes.

★10663★
OHIO STATE DEPARTMENT OF AGING - RESOURCE CENTER (Soc Sci)
50 W. Broad St. Phone: (614)466-9086
Columbus, OH 43266-0501 Donna L. Burns, Trng.Off.
Founded: 1973. **Staff:** Prof 1; Other 1. **Subjects:** Aging - health care, long-term care, housing, demographics. **Holdings:** 175 AV programs; National Institute on Aging reports; pamphlets; brochures. **Subscriptions:** 37 journals and other serials; 7 newspapers. **Services:** Interlibrary loan; center open to the public for reference use only. **Special Indexes:** Comprehensive cross-reference index of audiovisuals.

★10664★
OHIO STATE DEPARTMENT OF DEVELOPMENT - RESEARCH LIBRARY (Soc Sci)
Box 1001 Phone: (614)466-2115
Columbus, OH 43204 Geraldine Waller, Libn.
Staff: Prof 1; Other 1. **Subjects:** Census, business, statistics, demography, economics. **Special Collections:** Ohio economic data. **Holdings:** 1000 books; 5000 reports; 12 drawers of microfiche. **Subscriptions:** 438 journals and other serials; 12 newspapers. **Services:** Interlibrary loan; copying; library open to the public for reference use only. **Automated Operations:** Computerized cataloging. **Publications:** New Acquisitions List, quarterly; List of Periodicals, annual; Publications Available from ODOD, annual - all for internal distribution and to government, public, and private agencies.

★10665★
OHIO STATE DEPARTMENT OF HEALTH - OFFICE OF PLANNING AND INFORMATION - LIBRARY
Box 118
Columbus, OH 43266-0118
Defunct

★10666★
OHIO STATE DEPARTMENT OF MENTAL HEALTH - BUREAU OF DRUG ABUSE - LIBRARY (Med)
170 N. High St., 3rd Fl.
Columbus, OH 43215 Phone: (614)466-7893
Subjects: Drug abuse. **Holdings:** 1000 books.

★10667★
OHIO STATE DEPARTMENT OF MENTAL HEALTH - EDUCATIONAL MEDIA CENTER (Med)
2401 W. Walnut St. Phone: (614)466-6013
Columbus, OH 43223 Portia McDade, Libn.
Staff: Prof 1; Other 1. **Subjects:** Mental health, prevention of mental illness. **Holdings:** 1000 films. **Services:** Center open to the public. **Special Catalogs:** Media Catalog.

OHIO STATE DEPARTMENT OF MENTAL HEALTH - PORTSMOUTH RECEIVING HOSPITAL
See: Portsmouth Receiving Hospital (11481)

★10668★
OHIO STATE DEPARTMENT OF TAXATION - RESEARCH AND STATISTICS LIBRARY (Bus-Fin)
State Office Tower
Box 530
Columbus, OH 43216 S.L. Shriver, Res.
Founded: 1956. **Subjects:** Taxation, public finance, general statistics. **Holdings:** 1400 books; 120 feet of vertical files. **Services:** Library open to the public.

★10669★
OHIO (State) DEPARTMENT OF TRANSPORTATION - LIBRARY (Trans)
25 S. Front St.
Box 899 Phone: (614)466-7680
Columbus, OH 43216 Ellen Haider, Libn.
Founded: 1976. **Staff:** Prof 1; Other 1. **Subjects:** Road transportation. **Special Collections:** Ohio Department of Transportation publications; Transportation Research Board publications. **Holdings:** 14,000 books and reports; 60 bound periodical volumes. **Subscriptions:** 105 journals and other serials. **Services:** Interlibrary loan; copying; SDI; library open to the public. **Automated Operations:** Computerized cataloging. **Computerized Information Services:** DIALOG Information Services. **Publications:** New Acquisitions, irregular - internal distribution and on request.

★10670★
OHIO (State) DIVISION OF GEOLOGICAL SURVEY - LIBRARY (Sci-Engr)
Fountain Square, Bldg. B Phone: (614)265-6605
Columbus, OH 43224 Merrianne Hackathorn, Geol./Ed.
Staff: 1. **Subjects:** Geology, mineralogy, hydrology, paleontology, petrology, mineral resources. **Holdings:** 3200 books. **Services:** Copying; library open to the public for reference use only.

★10671★
OHIO STATE ENVIRONMENTAL PROTECTION AGENCY - LIBRARY (Env-Cons)
1800 Watermark Dr. Phone: (614)481-7009
Columbus, OH 43215 Ruth Ann Evans, Libn.
Founded: 1976. **Staff:** Prof 1; Other 1. **Subjects:** Pollution control, environmental law, Ohio water quality reports. **Holdings:** 4440 books; 309 microfiche. **Subscriptions:** 118 journals and other serials. **Services:** Interlibrary loan; copying; library open to the public for reference use only. **Automated Operations:** Computerized cataloging. **Computerized Information Services:** DIALOG Information Services, Chemical Information Systems, Inc. (CIS). **Networks/Consortia:** Member of OHIONET. **Formerly:** Environmental Technical Information Center.

★10672★
OHIO STATE INDUSTRIAL COMMISSION - DIVISION OF SAFETY AND HYGIENE - RESOURCE CENTER (Med)
246 N. High St.
Box 16512 Phone: (614)466-7388
Columbus, OH 43215 Rosemary Larkins, Mgr.
Founded: 1974. **Staff:** Prof 1; Other 4. **Subjects:** Occupational safety, industrial hygiene. **Holdings:** 4000 books; 850 standards; 200 microfiche; 2500 16mm films; 20 VF drawers of pamphlets; 650 subject headings; 2 VF drawers of clippings. **Subscriptions:** 125 journals and other serials. **Services:** Interlibrary loan; copying; center open to the public. **Computerized Information Services:** DIALOG Information Services, NLM, Occupational Health Services, Inc. (OHS), Pergamon ORBIT InfoLine, Inc., Telesystemes Questel; Boss-II, Film Library Circulation (internal databases). **Networks/Consortia:** Member of CALICO. **Publications:** Acquisitions, quarterly.

★10673★
OHIO STATE LEGISLATIVE SERVICE COMMISSION - RESEARCH LIBRARY (Soc Sci)
State House Phone: (614)466-7434
Columbus, OH 43215 Barbara J. Laughon, Adm.
Founded: 1953. **Staff:** Prof 2; Other 2. **Subjects:** Public administration, public finance, public education, state government, Ohio history and law. **Special Collections:** Laws of Ohio, 1803 to present; Laws of the Northwest Territory, 1787-1796; Codes for Northwest Territory and State of Ohio; Debates of the Ohio Constitutional Conventions; House and Senate bills and records. **Holdings:** 9000 books; 1000 bound volumes; 50 VF drawers of pamphlets, clippings, unbound and uncataloged documents; 350 reels of microfilm; 120 audiotape cassettes. **Subscriptions:** 262 journals and other serials. **Services:** Copying; library open to the public for reference use only. **Automated Operations:** Computerized cataloging. **Computerized Information Services:** DIALOG Information Services, WILSONLINE, OCLC, LEGISNET. **Networks/Consortia:** Member of CALICO.

★10674★
OHIO STATE SCHOOL FOR THE BLIND - LIBRARY (Educ)
5220 N. High St. Phone: (614)888-8211
Columbus, OH 43214 Beverly Kessler, Libn.
Staff: Prof 1. **Subjects:** Special education with emphasis on blindness. **Holdings:** 9000 books; 1500 AV programs; 150 models. **Subscriptions:** 120 journals and other serials. **Services:** Library not open to the public.

★10675★
OHIO STATE SUPREME COURT LAW LIBRARY (Law)
30 E. Broad St., 4th Fl. Phone: (614)466-2044
Columbus, OH 43266-0419 Paul S. Fu, Law Libn.
Founded: 1858. **Staff:** Prof 6; Other 10. **Subjects:** Law. **Special Collections:** Early laws of Ohio; old legal treatises. **Holdings:** 265,000 volumes. **Subscriptions:** 824 journals and other serials; 23 newspapers. **Services:** Copying; library open to the public. **Publications:** Monthly List of Acquisitions; Law Library Handbook. **Staff:** Niann Lao, Asst.Libn. & Cat.; Edward Weilant, Ref.Libn.; Patsy Duncan, Acq.Libn.; Ellen Siebert, Doc.Libn.; Cathy C. Palombi, Circ.Libn.; Melanie Putnam, Hd., Pub.Serv..

★10676★
OHIO STATE UNIVERSITY - AGRICULTURAL TECHNICAL INSTITUTE - LIBRARY (Agri)
1328 Dover Rd. Phone: (216)264-3911
Wooster, OH 44691 Ella G. Copeland, Dir., Lib. LRC
Founded: 1972. **Staff:** Prof 1; Other 10. **Subjects:** Floriculture, landscape, nursery, turf, crops, food marketing, greenhouse production, agricultural engineering and mechanics, agronomic industries, soil and water management, dairy, horse, livestock, laboratory and research science, wood science, beekeeping. **Special Collections:** Beekeeping journals. **Holdings:** 15,000 books; 1700 bound periodical volumes; 23 VF drawers of pamphlets; journals in microform; 5 VF drawers of Ohio soil surveys; 20,379 microforms. **Subscriptions:** 547 journals and other serials; 12 newspapers. **Services:** Interlibrary loan; library open to the public with restrictions on borrowing. **Automated Operations:** Computerized cataloging.

★10677★
OHIO STATE UNIVERSITY - AGRICULTURE LIBRARY (Agri)
45 Agriculture Bldg.
2120 Fyffe Rd. Phone: (614)292-6125
Columbus, OH 43210 Mary P. Key, Hd.Libn.
Founded: 1956. **Staff:** Prof 1; Other 2. **Subjects:** Animal science, agriculture and allied subjects, food science and nutrition, forestry, dairy science, plant pathology, rural sociology, horticulture, natural resources, poultry science. **Special Collections:** Arnold Library of Agricultural Credit. **Holdings:** 76,000 volumes; 2500 pamphlets; CD-ROM. **Subscriptions:** 1374 journals and other serials. **Services:** Interlibrary loan; copying; library open to the public. **Automated Operations:** Computerized public access catalog, cataloging, acquisitions, serials, and circulation. **Computerized Information Services:** Online systems. **Networks/Consortia:** Member of OHIONET.

★10678★
OHIO STATE UNIVERSITY - ARCHIVES (Hist)
2121 Tuttle Park Place Phone: (614)422-2409
Columbus, OH 43210 Dr. Raimund E. Goerler, Univ.Archv.
Founded: 1963. **Staff:** Prof 2; Other 4. **Subjects:** Ohio State University history. **Special Collections:** Photographic history of OSU (575,000 images). **Holdings:** 6000 cubic feet of records; 625,000 photographs. **Services:** Copying; archives open to the public. **Computerized Information Services:** Internal database. **Special Catalogs:** Inventories of archival collections. **Staff:** Kenneth Grossi, Asst.Archv..

★10679★
OHIO STATE UNIVERSITY - BIOLOGICAL SCIENCES LIBRARY (Biol Sci)
200 B & Z Bldg.
1735 Neil Ave. Phone: (614)292-1744
Columbus, OH 43210 Victoria Welborn, Hd.Libn.
Founded: 1916. **Staff:** Prof 1; Other 3. **Subjects:** Zoology, botany, biology, entomology, microbiology, genetics, biochemistry, biophysics, biotechnology. **Holdings:** 94,000 volumes; CD-ROM. **Subscriptions:** 1037 journals and other serials. **Services:** Interlibrary loan; copying; library open to the public. **Automated Operations:** Computerized public access catalog, cataloging, acquisitions, serials, and circulation. **Computerized Information Services:** Online systems. **Networks/Consortia:** Member of OHIONET. **Publications:** Quarterly lists of acquisitions.

★10680★
OHIO STATE UNIVERSITY - BLACK STUDIES LIBRARY (Area-Ethnic)
1858 Neil Ave. Phone: (614)292-8403
Columbus, OH 43210 Eleanor M. Daniel, Hd.Libn.
Founded: 1971. **Staff:** Prof 1; Other 1. **Subjects:** Black history, African studies. **Special Collections:** Schomburg Collection; Atlanta University Black Culture Collection; Black Newspaper Collection (Bell & Howell); Tuskegee Institute News Clipping File; Martin Luther King, Jr. Assassination File; W.E.B. DuBois papers; Afro-American Rare Book Collection; papers of the National Association for the Advancement of Colored People (NAACP), part 1; papers of the Congress of Racial Equality, 1941-1967. **Holdings:** 23,500 books; 11,000 microforms; 70 major black U.S. newspapers. **Subscriptions:** 173 journals and other serials; 16 newspapers. **Services:** Interlibrary loan; library open to the public. **Automated Operations:** Computerized cataloging, serials, and circulation. **Computerized Information Services:** Online systems. **Publications:** Selected List of Titles Received by the Black Studies Library, monthly.

★10681★
OHIO STATE UNIVERSITY - BUSINESS LIBRARY (Bus-Fin)
110 Page Hall
1810 College Rd. Phone: (614)292-2136
Columbus, OH 43210 Charles Popovich, Hd.Libn.
Founded: 1925. **Staff:** Prof 3; Other 5. **Subjects:** Accounting, business administration, economics, marketing, public administration, geography, finance. **Special Collections:** Annual reports of corporations (84,000 microforms). **Holdings:** 166,000 volumes; 2000 theses and dissertations; 80 loose-leaf services. **Subscriptions:** 2152 journals and other serials; 10 newspapers. **Services:** Interlibrary loan; copying; library open to the public. **Automated Operations:** Computerized public access catalog, cataloging, acquisitions, serials, and circulation. **Computerized Information Services:** Online systems. **Networks/Consortia:** Member of OHIONET. **Staff:** Mel Ankeny, Ref.Libn.; Sue Pease, Ref.Libn..

★10682★
OHIO STATE UNIVERSITY - BYRD POLAR RESEARCH CENTER - GOLDTHWAIT POLAR LIBRARY (Sci-Engr)
125 S. Oval Mall Phone: (614)292-6531
Columbus, OH 43210-1308 Lynn B. Lay, Libn.
Founded: 1960. **Staff:** Prof 1. **Subjects:** Antarctic, Arctic, and Alpine regions - glaciology, geology, climatology, permafrost and soil science, biological sciences; history of polar exploration. **Holdings:** 1350 books; 70 bound periodical volumes; 200 unbound periodical volumes; 19,000 reprints; 75 report series; 1000 maps. **Subscriptions:** 210 journals and other serials. **Services:** Interlibrary loan; copying; library open to qualified researchers. **Publications:** Accessions list, quarterly.

★10683★
OHIO STATE UNIVERSITY - CENTER FOR HUMAN RESOURCE RESEARCH - LIBRARY (Bus-Fin)
650 Ackerman Rd., Suite A
Columbus, OH 43202-1501
Founded: 1965. **Subjects:** Manpower, labor market, education, economics, women, youths, blacks. **Special Collections:** Latin American collection, mostly in Spanish (500 books; reports). **Holdings:** 2500 books; 5 drawers of microforms; 4 VF drawers of seminar and NLS based research papers. **Subscriptions:** 30 journals and other serials. **Services:** Copying; library open to the public with restrictions. **Publications:** NLS (National Longitudinal Surveys) Newsletter, quarterly; NLS Handbook, annual - both available on request.

★10684★
OHIO STATE UNIVERSITY - CENTER FOR LAKE ERIE AREA RESEARCH - LAKE ERIE PROGRAM LIBRARY
1314 Kinnear Rd.
Columbus, OH 43212
Subjects: Great Lakes limnology, Lake Erie science and technology, Great Lakes Wetlands, oceanography, water quality and treatment, coastal engineering, hydrology. **Special Collections:** Great Lakes topographic maps and lake survey charts; early 1900s Lake Erie Survey Charts. **Holdings:** 9000 books; 200 bound periodical volumes; 100 boxes of pamphlets; 150 boxes of reprints; 300 maps; 3000 slides of Lake Erie activities. **Remarks:** Library contains holdings of Ohio State University - Water Resources Library. Presently inactive.

★10685★
OHIO STATE UNIVERSITY - CHEMISTRY LIBRARY (Sci-Engr)
310 McPherson Lab
140 W. 18th Ave. Phone: (614)292-1118
Columbus, OH 43210 Virginia E. Yagello, Hd.Libn.
Founded: 1925. **Staff:** Prof 1; Other 2. **Subjects:** Chemistry, chemical technology and engineering. **Holdings:** 53,000 volumes. **Subscriptions:** 473 journals and other serials. **Services:** Interlibrary loan; copying. **Automated Operations:** Computerized public access catalog, cataloging, acquisitions, serials, and circulation. **Computerized Information Services:** Online systems. **Networks/Consortia:** Member of OHIONET. **Publications:** Classified List of Serial Holdings in Chemistry Library. **Also Known As:** Charles Cutler Sharp Library.

★10686★
OHIO STATE UNIVERSITY - COLE MEMORIAL LIBRARY OF THE PHYSICS AND ASTRONOMY DEPARTMENTS (Sci-Engr)
174 W. 18th Ave. Phone: (614)292-7894
Columbus, OH 43210 Bernard Bayer, Hd.Libn.
Founded: 1930. **Staff:** Prof 1; Other 2. **Subjects:** Physics - solid state, theoretical, mathematical, low temperature, nuclear; astronomy; astrophysics; infrared spectroscopy; condensed matter. **Holdings:** 51,000 books. **Subscriptions:** 341 journals and other serials. **Services:** Interlibrary loan. **Automated Operations:** Computerized public access catalog, cataloging, acquisitions, serials, and circulation. **Computerized Information Services:** Online systems. **Networks/Consortia:** Member of OHIONET.

★10687★
OHIO STATE UNIVERSITY - COUNSELING AND CONSULTATION SERVICE - PACE CENTER (Educ)
Ohio Union, 4th Fl.
1739 N. High St. Phone: (614)292-5766
Columbus, OH 43210 Patricia O. Gapsch, Career Libn.
Staff: Prof 2; Other 8. **Subjects:** Career exploration, job search methods, training opportunities, self-assessment. **Holdings:** 600 books; 35 self-help cassette tapes; 8 VF drawers. **Subscriptions:** 16 journals and other serials. **Services:** Copying; center open to the public for reference use only. **Computerized Information Services:** Sigi, Discover (internal databases). **Remarks:** PACE is an acronym for Personnel and Career Exploration. **Staff:** Dennis Alexander, Chm., Career Comm..

★10688★
OHIO STATE UNIVERSITY - EDGAR DALE EDUCATIONAL MEDIA & INSTRUCTIONAL MATERIALS LABORATORY (Educ)
260 Ramseyer Hall
29 W. Woodruff Ave. Phone: (614)422-1177
Columbus, OH 43210-1177 Dr. Betty P. Cleaver, Dir.
Founded: 1979. **Staff:** Prof 2; Other 16. **Subjects:** Children's literature; K-12 textbooks and curriculum; classroom management and methods; media management. **Special Collections:** Historical collection of children's literature and textbooks (500 volumes). **Holdings:** 19,000 books; 3000 AV kits; 5000 microforms; 2000 textbook series; 165 folders of pamphlets; 4 VF drawers of curriculum guides; 4 VF drawers of transparency originals; 200 microcomputer programs. **Subscriptions:** 11 journals and other serials. **Services:** Copying; media production; laboratory open to the public for reference use only. **Automated Operations:** Computerized cataloging and circulation. **Computerized Information Services:** OCLC, Books in Print Plus; internal database. **Networks/Consortia:** Member of OHIONET. **Special Indexes:** Subject mediagraphy file, K-12. **Staff:** Shirley V. Morrison, Asst.Dir..

★10689★
OHIO STATE UNIVERSITY - EDUCATION/PSYCHOLOGY LIBRARY (Educ)
060 Arps Hall
1945 N. High St. Phone: (614)292-6275
Columbus, OH 43210 Laura Blomquist, Hd.Libn.
Founded: 1926. **Staff:** Prof 4; Other 6. **Subjects:** Education, psychology, physical education and recreation. **Holdings:** 163,000 volumes; 252,000 ERIC microfiche. **Subscriptions:** 1308 journals and other serials. **Services:** Interlibrary loan; copying; library open to the public for reference use only. **Automated Operations:** Computerized public access catalog, cataloging, acquisitions, serials, and circulation. **Computerized Information Services:** Online systems. **Networks/Consortia:** Member of OHIONET. **Special Indexes:** Supplement to Educational Index, 1919-1961 (card). **Staff:** Andrea Gaal, Online Search Coord.; Mary Gouke, Ref.; Martin Jamison, Ref./Circ..

★10690★
OHIO STATE UNIVERSITY - ENGINEERING LIBRARY (Sci-Engr, Plan, Info Sci)
112 Caldwell Lab.
2024 Neil Ave. Phone: (614)292-2852
Columbus, OH 43210 Mary Jo Arnold, Hd.Libn.
Staff: Prof 2; Other 4. **Subjects:** Computer and information science; engineering - industrial, mechanical, aeronautical, civil, electrical; architecture; city and regional planning; welding; landscape architecture. **Holdings:** 148,000 volumes. **Subscriptions:** 1288 journals and other serials. **Services:** Interlibrary loan; copying; library open to the public. **Automated Operations:** Computerized public access catalog, cataloging, acquisitions, serials, and circulation. **Computerized Information Services:** Online systems. **Networks/Consortia:** Member of OHIONET. **Publications:** Book List, biweekly - to campus personnel. **Staff:** Jane McMaster, Ref.Libn..

★10691★
OHIO STATE UNIVERSITY - FINE ARTS LIBRARY (Art)
166 Sullivant Hall
1813 N. High St. Phone: (614)292-6184
Columbus, OH 43210 Susan Wyngaard, Hd.Libn.
Staff: Prof 1; Other 1. **Subjects:** Visual arts (excluding photography); history of art; archeology; art - Western and Eastern European, East Asian, American. **Holdings:** 78,000 books. **Subscriptions:** 421 journals and other serials. **Services:** Interlibrary loan; copying; library open to the public for reference use only. **Automated Operations:** Computerized public access catalog, cataloging, acquisitions, serials, and circulation. **Computerized Information Services:** Online systems. **Networks/Consortia:** Member of OHIONET.

★10692★
OHIO STATE UNIVERSITY - FRANZ THEODORE STONE LABORATORY - LIBRARY (Biol Sci)
Box 119 Phone: (419)285-2341
Put-In-Bay, OH 43456 Victoria Welborn, Hd.
Founded: 1896. **Staff:** Prof 1. **Subjects:** Great Lakes hydrobiology and limnology, field biology, botany, zoology. **Special Collections:** Theses and dissertations (completed at the laboratory or in several departments on the main campus; 80). **Holdings:** 2000 books; 1000 bound periodical volumes; 300 boxes of reprints. **Subscriptions:** 40 journals and other serials. **Services:** Interlibrary loan; copying; library open to the public during the summer only. **Publications:** Contributions from the Franz Theodore Stone Laboratory. **Remarks:** Part of the Biological Sciences Library of The Ohio State University.

★10693★
OHIO STATE UNIVERSITY - HEALTH SCIENCES LIBRARY (Med)
376 W. 10th Ave. Phone: (614)292-9810
Columbus, OH 43210 Elizabeth J. Sawyers, Dir.
Founded: 1849. **Staff:** Prof 9; Other 18. **Subjects:** Clinical medicine, dentistry, nursing, allied health sciences, experimental medicine, optometry. **Holdings:** 168,000 volumes; 2270 government documents. **Subscriptions:** 2040 journals and other serials. **Services:** Interlibrary loan; copying; SDI; library open to the public. **Automated Operations:** Computerized public access catalog, cataloging, acquisitions, serials, and circulation. **Computerized Information Services:** MEDLINE. **Networks/Consortia:** Member of Greater Midwest Regional Medical Library Network, OHIONET. **Publications:** Health Sciences Library Services Bulletin, monthly - to health sciences and library community. **Staff:** Susan Kroll, Asst.Dir.; Barbara Schmidt, Coll.Dev.Coord.; Pamela Bradigan, Hd., Ref.; Carol Mularski, Ref.Libn.; Barbara Van Brimmer, Ref.Libn.; Kathryn McConnell, Ref.Libn.; Deborah Schneider, Outreach Serv.Coord.; Peter LePoer, Automation Coord..

★10694★
OHIO STATE UNIVERSITY - HILANDAR RESEARCH LIBRARY (Area-Ethnic)
227 Main Library
1858 Neil Ave. Phone: (614)292-0634
Columbus, OH 43210 Dr. Predrag Matejic, Cur.
Staff: Prof 1; Other 1. **Subjects:** Medieval Slavic literature, Slavic paleography, history of Slavic languages, Eastern Orthodox Church. **Special Collections:** Microfilm collection of the manuscripts and rare books of the Hilandar Monastery, Mount Athos, Greece; microfilm of Slavic manuscripts obtained through exchanges or field expeditions. **Holdings:** 1500 volumes; 500,000 pages of Slavic Cyrillic Manuscripts in microform; 4 manuscripts. **Services:** Copying (limited); library open to the public with restrictions. **Automated Operations:** Computerized acquisitions, serials, and circulation. **Computerized Information Services:** OCLC. **Publications:** Mateja Matejic, Hilandar Slavic Codices; Predrag Matejic, Watermarks of the Hilandar Slavic Codices, A Descriptive Catalog; Mateja Matejic and Predrag Matejic, Hilandar Slavic Codices, Supplement Number 1. **Remarks:** An alternate telephone number is 292-1327.

★10695★
OHIO STATE UNIVERSITY - HOME ECONOMICS LIBRARY (Soc Sci, Food-Bev)
325 Campbell Hall
1787 Neil Ave. Phone: (614)292-4220
Columbus, OH 43210 Nancy Sanders, Hd.Libn.
Founded: 1962. **Staff:** Prof 1; Other 2. **Subjects:** Family and child development, foods and nutrition, home economics education, home

management and family economics, housing and furnishings, textiles and clothing, institution and hospitality management. **Special Collections:** Costume History. **Holdings:** 21,000 books; 4300 pamphlets. **Subscriptions:** 219 journals and other serials. **Services:** Interlibrary loan; copying; library open to the public for reference use only. **Automated Operations:** Computerized public access catalog, cataloging, acquisitions, serials, and circulation. **Computerized Information Services:** Online systems. **Networks/Consortia:** Member of OHIONET.

★10696★
OHIO STATE UNIVERSITY - JEROME LAWRENCE & ROBERT E. LEE THEATRE RESEARCH INSTITUTE - LIBRARY (Theater)
1410 Lincoln Tower
1800 Cannon Dr. Phone: (614)292-8252
Columbus, OH 43210 Nena Couch, Cur.
Founded: 1951. **Staff:** Prof 2; Other 3. **Subjects:** Theater and theater research. **Special Collections:** McDowell Microfilm Archives (450,000 frames of microfilm of historical theatrical documents); Lawrence & Lee Collection (100 linear feet of manuscripts, books, original cartoons, playbills, photographs); Harmount Uncle Tom's Collection (20 cubic feet of scripts, business records, photographs, scenic drops); Scrapbook Collection (125 scrapbooks); Armbruster Scenic Design Collection (200 renderings); Eileen Heckart Collection (21 linear feet of playscripts, correspondence); Earl Wilson Collection (50 linear feet of manuscripts, photographs, drafts, clippings of Wilson's newspaper column); Robert Breen Collection (200 linear feet of scripts, correspondence, photographs, theater ground plans, posters, clippings, films of 1952-1956 tour of Porgy & Bess and Breen's other activities). **Holdings:** 2500 books; 330 dissertations; 40 VF drawers of playbills; 28 VF drawers of photographs, correspondence, offprints, publicity material; 8450 original documents (posters; scrapbooks; clippings); 3000 photographs. **Subscriptions:** 15 journals and other serials. **Services:** Copying; library open to the public. **Automated Operations:** Computerized public access catalog, cataloging, acquisitions, and serials. **Computerized Information Services:** OCLC; internal database. **Publications:** Theatre Studies, semiannual - by subscription. **Remarks:** An alternate telephone number is 292-6614. **Staff:** Alan Woods, Dir..

★10697★
OHIO STATE UNIVERSITY - JOURNALISM LIBRARY (Info Sci)
100 Journalism Bldg.
242 W. 18th Ave. Phone: (614)292-8747
Columbus, OH 43210 Eleanor Block, Hd.Libn.
Founded: 1967. **Staff:** Prof 1; Other 1. **Subjects:** Journalism - newspaper, magazine, radio, television, advertising, public relations, mass communications, photography and cinema. **Holdings:** 25,000 volumes. **Subscriptions:** 214 journals and other serials; 83 newspapers. **Services:** Interlibrary loan; copying; library open to the public for reference use only. **Automated Operations:** Computerized public access catalog, cataloging, acquisitions, serials, and circulation. **Computerized Information Services:** Online systems. **Networks/Consortia:** Member of OHIONET.

★10698★
OHIO STATE UNIVERSITY - LAW LIBRARY (Law)
College of Law
1659 N. High St. Phone: (614)292-6691
Columbus, OH 43210-1391 S. Alan Holoch, Dir.
Founded: 1885. **Staff:** Prof 8; Other 12. **Subjects:** Anglo-American law. **Special Collections:** Ohio Supreme Court briefs. **Holdings:** 422,601 volumes; 461,890 microforms. **Subscriptions:** 7370 journals and other serials. **Services:** Interlibrary loan; copying; library open to the public for legal research. **Automated Operations:** Computerized cataloging. **Computerized Information Services:** WESTLAW, DIALOG Information Services, NEXIS, Dow Jones News/Retrieval, VU/TEXT Information Services, LEXIS. **Networks/Consortia:** Member of OHIONET. **Staff:** Carole Hinchcliff, Media Ctr.Libn.; Phyllis Post, Hd., Cat.Dept.; Melanie Solon, Hd., Pub.Serv.; George Jackson, Doc.Libn.; Val Bolen, Foreign & Intl. Law Libn.; Deanna Wood, Hd., Acq.Dept.; Thomas G. Spaith, Assoc.Dir..

★10699★
OHIO STATE UNIVERSITY - LIBRARY FOR COMMUNICATION AND GRAPHIC ARTS (Art)
242 W. 18th Ave., Rm. 147 Phone: (614)292-0538
Columbus, OH 43210 Lucy S. Caswell, Cur. & Assoc.Prof.
Staff: Prof 1; Other 1. **Subjects:** Comic strips, editorial cartoons, illustrations, movie posters and stills, photographs, mass media arts. **Special Collections:** Milton Caniff Collection of original comic strips and related materials (500,000 items); Jon Whitcomb Collection of magazine illustrations, photographs, tear sheets, correspondence (44 paintings; 33 boxes); Philip Sills Collection of movie posters and stills (110,000); Richard Teichert Collection of silent film advertising materials (10,000 items); Ray Osrin Collection of original editorial cartoons (1700); Eugene Craig Collection of original comic strips and editorial cartoons (4000); Will Rannells Collection of illustrations (80 paintings; 6 boxes); Katy Keene Collection of comic books (3 boxes); Toni Mendez Collection of business files relating to licensing of comic strip and cartoon feature products (100 boxes); Shel Dorf Collection of historic comic strip materials (30,000 items); Woody Gelman Collection (71 original cartoons and more than 200 newspaper tearsheets by Winsor McCay); Will Eisner Collection (5000 items); comic books and underground comics (14 boxes); Ned White Collection (editorial cartoons by White and 90 other cartoonists including Herblock, Darling, Kirby); Rinhart Collection of historic photographs, 1840-1920 (12,000); papers of Walt Kelly; Noel Sickles Collection (800 items); Ohio News Photographers Association Collection (1000 items); original cartoons of John T. McCutcheon, Jim Larrick, Bill Crawford, Dick Moores, Art Poinier, L.D. Warren, Eugene Payne, Irwin Hasen, Charles Werner, Ed Kuekes, G.T. Maxwell, C.J. Taylor, Louis Dalyrimple, F.B. Opper, M.A. Woolf. **Holdings:** 4000 books on cartoon art; representative holdings of original art from editorial cartoonists and comic strip artists; comic strip clippings; Association of American Editorial Cartoonists and National Cartoonists Society Archives. **Services:** Copying; library open to the public upon registration. **Automated Operations:** Computerized cataloging.

★10700★
OHIO STATE UNIVERSITY - MATERIALS ENGINEERING LIBRARY (Sci-Engr)
197 Watts Hall
2041 N. College Rd. Phone: (614)292-9614
Columbus, OH 43210 Mary Jo Arnold, Hd.Libn.
Staff: Prof 1; Other 1. **Subjects:** Metallurgic and ceramic engineering; materials science. **Holdings:** 18,000 volumes. **Subscriptions:** 209 journals and other serials. **Services:** Interlibrary loan; copying; library open to the public. **Automated Operations:** Computerized public access catalog, cataloging, acquisitions, serials, and circulation. **Computerized Information Services:** Online systems. **Networks/Consortia:** Member of OHIONET.

★10701★
OHIO STATE UNIVERSITY - MATHEMATICS LIBRARY (Sci-Engr)
010 Mathematics Bldg.
231 W. 18th St. Phone: (614)422-2009
Columbus, OH 43210 Heidi Mercado, Hd.Libn.
Founded: 1962. **Staff:** Prof 1; Other 2. **Subjects:** Advanced mathematics, mathematical statistics, geodetic sciences. **Holdings:** 46,000 volumes; 4750 pamphlets. **Subscriptions:** 585 journals and other serials. **Services:** Interlibrary loan; copying; library open to the public for reference use only. **Automated Operations:** Computerized public access catalog, cataloging, acquisitions, serials, and circulation. **Computerized Information Services:** DIALOG Information Services. Performs searches on fee basis. **Networks/Consortia:** Member of OHIONET. **Special Catalogs:** List of Serial Holdings in the Mathematics Library (June, 1965).

★10702★
OHIO STATE UNIVERSITY - MUSIC/DANCE LIBRARY (Mus)
186 Sullivant Hall
1813 N. High St. Phone: (614)292-2319
Columbus, OH 43210 Thomas Heck, Hd.Libn.
Founded: 1946. **Staff:** Prof 2; Other 4. **Subjects:** Music - history, education, theory/composition, performance; dance. **Special Collections:** ABC Radio Collection; Deutsches Musikgeschichtliches Archiv (microfilm collection representing primary source material of German composers published both in Germany and foreign countries and foreign composers living in Germany, 16th and 17th centuries). **Holdings:** 88,000 volumes of music literature and scores; 1224 pamphlets; 1390 microforms; 23,000 phonograph records. **Subscriptions:** 652 journals and other serials. **Services:** Interlibrary loan; library open to the public for reference use only. **Automated Operations:** Computerized public access catalog, cataloging, acquisitions, serials, and circulation. **Computerized Information Services:** Online systems. **Networks/Consortia:** Member of OHIONET. **Staff:** Lois Rowell, Cat. & Ref.Libn..

★10703★
OHIO STATE UNIVERSITY - OHIO COOPERATIVE FISH AND WILDLIFE RESEARCH UNIT - LIBRARY (Biol Sci)
1735 Neil Ave. Phone: (614)292-6112
Columbus, OH 43210 Dr. Theodore A. Bookhout, Unit Leader
Founded: 1936. **Subjects:** Wildlife and fishery research and management, animal ecology, pesticide-wildlife/fishery relationships. **Holdings:** 300 volumes; 160 theses; 300 unit reprints and releases; 30 VF drawers of other reprints; 2500 35mm color transparencies. **Services:** Interlibrary loan; library open to the public with restrictions.

OHIO STATE UNIVERSITY - OHIO (State) AGRICULTURAL RESEARCH AND DEVELOPMENT CENTER
See: Ohio (State) Agricultural Research and Development Center - Library (10661)

★10704★
OHIO STATE UNIVERSITY - ORTON MEMORIAL LIBRARY OF GEOLOGY (Sci-Engr, Geog-Map)
180 Orton Hall
155 S. Oval Dr. Phone: (614)292-2428
Columbus, OH 43210 Regina Brown, Hd.Libn.
Founded: 1917. **Staff:** Prof 1; Other 1. **Subjects:** Geology, mineralogy, paleontology. **Special Collections:** Geologic maps; U.S. Geological Survey topographic maps (85,000 maps). **Holdings:** 62,500 volumes. **Subscriptions:** 650 journals and other serials. **Services:** Interlibrary loan; copying; library open to the public for reference use only. **Automated Operations:** Computerized public access catalog, cataloging, acquisitions, serials, and circulation. **Computerized Information Services:** Online systems. **Networks/Consortia:** Member of OHIONET.

★10705★
OHIO STATE UNIVERSITY - PHARMACY LIBRARY (Med)
Pharmacy Bldg.
500 W. 12th Ave. Phone: (614)292-8026
Columbus, OH 43210 Hazel Benson, Hd.Libn.
Founded: 1930. **Staff:** Prof 1; Other 1. **Subjects:** Pharmacy, pharmaceutical chemistry, pharmacology, pharmacognosy, pharmacy administration. **Holdings:** 33,000 volumes; 2100 pamphlets. **Subscriptions:** 489 journals and other serials. **Services:** Interlibrary loan; library open to the public for reference use only. **Automated Operations:** Computerized public access catalog, cataloging, acquisitions, serials, and circulation. **Computerized Information Services:** Online systems. **Networks/Consortia:** Member of OHIONET. **Also Known As:** Virginia B. Hall Pharmacy Library.

★10706★
OHIO STATE UNIVERSITY - SOCIAL WORK LIBRARY (Soc Sci)
400 Stillman Hall
1947 College Rd. Phone: (614)292-6627
Columbus, OH 43210 Jennifer Kuehn, Hd.Libn.
Founded: 1938. **Staff:** Prof 1; Other 1. **Subjects:** Social work education, criminology, social group work, family, social casework, mental health. **Holdings:** 38,500 volumes; 700 pamphlets. **Subscriptions:** 328 journals and other serials. **Services:** Interlibrary loan; copying; library open to the public. **Automated Operations:** Computerized public access catalog, cataloging, acquisitions, serials, and circulation. **Computerized Information Services:** BRS Information Technologies. **Networks/Consortia:** Member of OHIONET.

★10707★
OHIO STATE UNIVERSITY - TOPAZ MEMORIAL LIBRARY (Med)
College of Optometry
338 W. Tenth Ave. Phone: (614)292-1888
Columbus, OH 43210 Molly A. Phillips, Libn.
Founded: 1965. **Staff:** 1. **Subjects:** Optometry, ophthalmology, optics, vision, reading psychology, visual psychology. **Holdings:** 3058 books; 2270 bound periodical volumes; 112 theses; 5 VF drawers of pamphlets, translations, bibliographies. **Subscriptions:** 67 journals and other serials. **Services:** Interlibrary loan; copying. **Automated Operations:** Computerized public access catalog, cataloging, acquisitions, serials, and circulation. **Computerized Information Services:** Online systems. **Networks/Consortia:** Member of OHIONET.

★10708★
OHIO STATE UNIVERSITY - VETERINARY MEDICINE LIBRARY (Med)
229 Sisson Hall
1900 Coffey Rd.
Columbus, OH 43210 Phone: (614)292-6107
Founded: 1929. **Staff:** Prof 1; Other 1. **Subjects:** Veterinary medicine, medicine, pharmacology, biochemistry, comparative medicine. **Holdings:** 40,000 volumes. **Subscriptions:** 493 journals and other serials. **Services:** Interlibrary loan; copying; library open to the public for reference use only. **Automated Operations:** Computerized public access catalog, cataloging, acquisitions, serials, and circulation. **Computerized Information Services:** Online systems. **Networks/Consortia:** Member of OHIONET.

OHIO STATE UNIVERSITY - WATER RESOURCES LIBRARY
See: Ohio State University - Center for Lake Erie Area Research - Lake Erie Program Library (10684)

★10709★
OHIO STATE UNIVERSITY - WOMEN'S STUDIES LIBRARY (Soc Sci)
220 Main Library
1858 Neil Ave. Mall Phone: (614)292-3035
Columbus, OH 43210 Adrienne Zahniser, Hd.Libn.
Founded: 1977. **Staff:** Prof 1; Other 1. **Subjects:** Women's studies. **Holdings:** 12,000 volumes; 2500 pamphlets and newsletters; 42 microform collections. **Subscriptions:** 100 journals and other serials. **Services:** Interlibrary loan; copying; SDI; library open to the public for reference use only. **Automated Operations:** Computerized cataloging, serials, and circulation. **Computerized Information Services:** Online systems.

★10710★
OHIO UNIVERSITY - DEPARTMENT OF ARCHIVES AND SPECIAL COLLECTIONS - ALDEN LIBRARY (Rare Book, Hist)
Park Place Phone: (614)593-2710
Athens, OH 45701-2978 George W. Bain, Hd.
Founded: 1960. **Staff:** Prof 3; Other 1. **Subjects:** History of Ohio University and Southeastern Ohio; rare books and manuscripts; English literature, 1760-1830 and 1880-1930; 18th century English drama. **Special Collections:** Ohio University Archives (5286 linear feet); Morgan Collection of the History of Chemistry and Science (1600 volumes); Ohioana Collection (1179 volumes); Osteopathic Medicine Collection; Edmund Blunden Collection of Romantic and Georgian Literature (10,000 volumes); author collections including: Arnold Bennett, Thomas Campbell, William Combe, William Cowper, George Crabbe, Charles Dickens, Samuel Foote, John Galsworthy, Lafcadio Hearn, Maurice Hewlett, Thomas Hood, Leigh Hunt, Rudyard Kipling, Arthur Machen, George Moore, Samuel Rogers, John Ruskin, Alfred Tennyson, H.G. Wells; Cornelius Ryan Memorial Collection of World War II Papers (90 cubic feet); United Mine Workers - District 6 (35 cubic feet). **Holdings:** 41,497 volumes; 1116 linear feet of local government records; 1286 linear feet of private papers; 28,749 photographs and slides; 960 maps. **Subscriptions:** 105 journals and other serials. **Services:** Interlibrary loan; copying; archives open to the public. **Automated Operations:** Computerized cataloging and circulation. **Computerized Information Services:** OCLC. **Networks/Consortia:** Member of Ohio Network of American History Research Centers. **Publications:** Guide to Local Government Records at Ohio University Library; brochures. **Special Catalogs:** Manuscript inventories and card catalog; rare book card catalog. **Staff:** Sheppard Black, Spec.Coll.Libn.; William M. Rhinehart, Rec.Mgr..

★10711★
OHIO UNIVERSITY - FINE ARTS COLLECTION (Art)
Alden Library Phone: (614)593-2663
Athens, OH 45701 Anne Braxton, Fine Arts Libn.
Founded: 1962. **Staff:** Prof 1; Other 1. **Subjects:** Art, architecture, photography, film. **Holdings:** 40,000 volumes; 8000 microfiche; 2400 exhibition catalogs; 7000 study plates. **Subscriptions:** 175 journals and other serials. **Services:** Interlibrary loan; copying; collection open to the public. **Automated Operations:** Computerized cataloging. **Computerized Information Services:** OCLC. **Networks/Consortia:** Member of OHIONET.

★10712★
OHIO UNIVERSITY - HEALTH SCIENCES LIBRARY (Med)
Athens, OH 45701 Phone: (614)593-2680
Anne S. Goss, Dir.
Founded: 1977. **Staff:** Prof 3; Other 15. **Subjects:** Medicine, nursing, psychology, basic sciences, allied health fields. **Special Collections:**

Osteopathic medicine (350 books). **Holdings:** 29,480 books; 30,420 bound periodical volumes; 19,471 government documents; 11,687 microfiche. **Subscriptions:** 1478 journals and other serials. **Services:** Interlibrary loan; copying; SDI; library open to the public. **Automated Operations:** Computerized cataloging, circulation, and ILL. **Computerized Information Services:** DIALOG Information Services, MEDLARS, BRS Information Technologies, MEDLINE; internal database. Performs searches on fee basis. Contact Person: Evelyn Constance Powell, Ref.Libn.. **Networks/Consortia:** Member of Greater Midwest Regional Medical Library Network. **Publications:** Shelf Life. **Special Indexes:** Printout of journal holdings. **Staff:** Wayne Evans, Asst.Libn..

★10713★
OHIO UNIVERSITY - MAP COLLECTION (Geog-Map)
Alden Library Phone: (614)593-2659
Athens, OH 45701 Theodore Foster, Map Libn.
Founded: 1960. **Staff:** Prof 1; Other 1. **Subjects:** Maps - U.S. Geological Survey, Defense Mapping Agency, Army Mapping Service, Federal Depository Library Program, Indonesia. **Holdings:** 146,225 maps. **Services:** Interlibrary loan; copying; collection open to the public. **Computerized Information Services:** OCLC, DIALOG Information Services, BRS Information Technologies, WILSONLINE, MEDLARS. Performs searches on fee basis. Contact Person: Nancy Rue, 593-2696. **Networks/Consortia:** Member of OHIONET.

★10714★
OHIO UNIVERSITY - MUSIC/DANCE LIBRARY (Mus)
Music Bldg. Phone: (614)594-5733
Athens, OH 45701 Dr. Holly Oberle, Libn.
Staff: Prof 1; Other 36. **Subjects:** Music, dance. **Holdings:** 30,000 books and scores; 500 bound periodical volumes; 10,000 recordings; 600 college catalogs; microforms; clippings; video cassettes; Catalog of Copyright Entries (Music) and Revision Studies. **Subscriptions:** 130 journals and other serials. **Services:** Interlibrary loan; copying; SDI; listening and microcomputer facilities; library open to residents within 25 mile radius. **Automated Operations:** Computerized cataloging and circulation. **Computerized Information Services:** DIALOG Information Services, BRS Information Technologies, WILSONLINE, OCLC (through main library). Performs searches on fee basis. **Staff:** Shirley Dorman, Asst.Libn..

★10715★
OHIO UNIVERSITY - SOUTHEAST ASIA COLLECTION (Area-Ethnic)
Alden Library Phone: (614)593-2658
Athens, OH 45701 Lian The-Mulliner, Hd.
Founded: 1967. **Staff:** Prof 3; Other 14. **Subjects:** Southeast Asia, with emphasis on Malaysia, Brunei, Singapore, Indonesia, and other members of the Association of Southeast Asian Nations (ASEAN). **Holdings:** 58,500 books; 7300 bound periodical volumes; 8 VF drawers of clippings on Malaysia and Singapore; 6 VF drawers of pamphlets on Southeast Asia; 28,000 titles in microform. **Subscriptions:** 5000 journals and other serials; 20 newspapers. **Services:** Interlibrary loan; copying; collection open to the public. **Automated Operations:** Computerized public access catalog, cataloging, and circulation. **Computerized Information Services:** DIALOG Information Services, BRS Information Technologies, OCLC; internal database. **Networks/Consortia:** Member of OHIONET. **Staff:** David Miller, Asst.Libn.; Swee-Lan Quah, Cat..

★10716★
OHIO VALLEY GENERAL HOSPITAL - PROFESSIONAL LIBRARY (Med)
Heckel Rd. Phone: (412)777-6159
McKee's Rock, PA 15136 Diane Faust, Libn.
Staff: Prof 1. **Subjects:** Nursing, medicine. **Holdings:** 1925 volumes. **Subscriptions:** 101 journals and other serials. **Services:** Interlibrary loan; copying; SDI; library open to the public by appointment. **Networks/Consortia:** Member of Pittsburgh-East Hospital Library Cooperative. **Publications:** Library Bulletin, monthly.

★10717★
OHIO VALLEY HOSPITAL - HEALTH SCIENCES LIBRARY (Med)
One Ross Park Phone: (614)283-7400
Steubenville, OH 43952 Kathryn Pasquarella, Libn.
Staff: Prof 1; Other 5. **Subjects:** Medicine, nursing. **Special Collections:** Pre-1900 Rare medical books. **Holdings:** 1968 books; 2731 bound periodical volumes; 4 theses; 4 VF drawers of pamphlets; 277 filmstrip/tape sets and slide/tape sets; 35 slide sets; 16 overhead transparencies; 276 videotapes; 5 films; 14 charts; 29 audio cassettes; 45 models. **Subscriptions:** 68 journals and other serials. **Services:** Interlibrary loan; copying; library open to the public for reference use only when librarian is present. **Computerized Information Services:** MEDLINE. **Networks/Consortia:** Member of Greater Midwest Regional Medical Library Network, NEOUCOM Council Associated Hospital Librarians. **Publications:** Library Line, quarterly - for internal distribution only. **Special Catalogs:** Resources and Facilities Handbook, annual; Hospital Library Manual.

★10718★
OHIO VALLEY MEDICAL CENTER - HUPP MEDICAL LIBRARY (Med)
2000 Eoff St. Phone: (304)234-8771
Wheeling, WV 26003 Eleanor B. Shonn, Med.Libn.
Staff: Prof 2. **Subjects:** Surgery, internal medicine, obstetrics, gynecology, radiology, hospital administration, pediatrics. **Special Collections:** History of Medicine; Osterman Collection (psychiatry). **Holdings:** 4988 books; 3652 bound periodical volumes; 2073 unbound journals; 630 audio cassettes; 29 video cassettes. **Subscriptions:** 233 journals and other serials. **Services:** Interlibrary loan; copying; library open to the public for reference use only. **Computerized Information Services:** MEDLINE; DOCLINE (electronic mail service). Performs searches on fee basis. **Publications:** Hupp Medical Library Literature. **Special Catalogs:** Audiovisual catalog. **Staff:** Janis Quinlisk, Asst.Libn..

★10719★
OHIOANA LIBRARY ASSOCIATION - OHIOANA LIBRARY AND ARCHIVES (Hum)
1105 Ohio Departments Bldg.
65 S. Front St. Phone: (614)466-3831
Columbus, OH 43266-0334 Kathy B. Gaylor, Libn.
Founded: 1929. **Staff:** Prof 1. **Subjects:** Ohio history, literature and music by or about Ohioans. **Special Collections:** Complete works of William Dean Howells, Sherwood Anderson, Louis Bromfield, and other prominent Ohio authors; "grass roots" poetry; county histories and atlases. **Holdings:** 30,000 books; 200 bound periodical volumes; 5000 musical compositions; 13 VF drawers of clippings about current Ohio subjects; 28 VF drawers of pamphlets; 69 linear feet of scrapbooks containing biographical information about Ohio authors, artists, composers; manuscripts. **Subscriptions:** 30 journals and other serials. **Services:** Copying; reference by mail; library open to the public for reference use only. **Networks/Consortia:** Member of CALICO. **Publications:** Ohioana Quarterly. The autumn issue of the Ohioana Quarterly includes as a supplement an annual bibliography of books and music by or about Ohioans.

★10720★
OHR KODESH CONGREGATION - SISTERHOOD LIBRARY (Area-Ethnic)
8402 Freyman Dr. Phone: (301)589-3880
Chevy Chase, MD 20015-3897 Ethel E. Clemens, Libn.
Founded: 1965. **Staff:** Prof 1; Other 4. **Subjects:** Judaica. **Holdings:** 3700 books. **Services:** Library open to the public for reference use only.

ELIZABETH J. OHRSTROM LIBRARY
See: University of Virginia - Medical Center - Department of Neurology (17039)

★10721★
OIL INFORMATION LIBRARY OF WICHITA FALLS (Sci-Engr)
100 Energy Center
710 Lamar Phone: (817)322-4241
Wichita Falls, TX 76301 Gail Baldon Phillips, Libn.
Founded: 1966. **Staff:** 4. **Subjects:** Oil and gas records, geological information, exploration and development material, well data. **Special Collections:** Original Bess Mason Log File (over 500,000); Independent Operators and Major Oil Companies electric log files (115,000). **Holdings:** 450 books; 81 boxes of microfilm of scout information; 280 miscellaneous county maps; 14 boxes of microfilm of logs; 175 miscellaneous geology maps and plats; 400 VF drawers of miscellaneous oil information. **Services:** Copying; library open to the public with restrictions.

OIL SPILL INFORMATION CENTER ARCHIVES
See: University of California, Santa Barbara - Sciences-Engineering Library (16020)

C.G. O'KELLY LIBRARY
See: Winston-Salem State University (17940)

★10722★
OKLAHOMA ART CENTER - LIBRARY (Art)
3113 Pershing Blvd. Phone: (405)946-4477
Oklahoma City, OK 73107 Jean Gumerson, Interim Dir.
Subjects: Twentieth century American art. **Holdings:** 1300 volumes. **Services:** Library open to the public with restrictions during specified hours.

★10723★
OKLAHOMA CHILDREN'S MEMORIAL HOSPITAL - OCMH LIBRARY (Med)
Oklahoma City, OK 73126 Phone: (405)271-5699
Jean Cavett, Dir.
Founded: 1973. **Staff:** Prof 1; Other 1. **Subjects:** Pediatrics. **Holdings:** 800 books; 1500 bound periodical volumes. **Subscriptions:** 280 journals and other serials. **Services:** Interlibrary loan; SDI. **Computerized Information Services:** MEDLINE; OnTyme Electronic Message Network Service, GTE Telenet Medical Information Network (MINET), DOCLINE (electronic mail services). **Networks/Consortia:** Member of Greater Oklahoma City Area Health Sciences Library Consortium (GOAL), Oklahoma Health Sciences Library Association (OHSLA), BHSL, ALLCeD.

★10724★
OKLAHOMA CITY UNIVERSITY - LAW LIBRARY (Law)
Oklahoma City, OK 73106 Phone: (405)521-5271
Judy Morgan, Law Libn.
Founded: 1956. **Staff:** Prof 4; Other 5. **Subjects:** Law. **Holdings:** 157,000 books. **Subscriptions:** 1700 journals and other serials. **Services:** Interlibrary loan; library open to the public. **Computerized Information Services:** WESTLAW, OCLC. **Networks/Consortia:** Member of AMIGOS Bibliographic Council, Inc.. **Remarks:** Fax: (405)521-5172. **Staff:** Nancy Smith, Hd., Tech.Serv.; Herb Cihak, Asst.Dir./Hd., Pub.Serv..

★10725★
OKLAHOMA COLLEGE OF OSTEOPATHIC MEDICINE & SURGERY - LIBRARY (Med)
1111 W. 17th St. Phone: (918)582-1972
Tulsa, OK 74107 Linda L. Roberts, Coll.Libn.
Founded: 1974. **Staff:** Prof 3; Other 4. **Subjects:** Medicine. **Special Collections:** Osteopathy collection. **Holdings:** 20,249 books; 1185 bound periodical volumes; 2694 AV programs; 22,965 microfiche; 871 reels of microfilm. **Subscriptions:** 547 journals; 181 serials; 4 newspapers. **Services:** Interlibrary loan; copying; library open to the public for reference use only. **Automated Operations:** Computerized cataloging, acquisitions, serials, and circulation. **Computerized Information Services:** MEDLARS, DIALOG Information Services. **Networks/Consortia:** Member of South Central Academic Medical Libraries Consortium (SCAMEL). **Publications:** Library Newsletter, quarterly - to faculty and affiliated hospitals and clinics. **Staff:** Anita Sutrick, Asst.Libn.; David Money, Asst.Libn..

OKLAHOMA CORPORATION COMMISSION - ENERGY CONSERVATION SERVICES DIVISION
See: Oklahoma State Department of Commerce - Energy Conservation Services Division (10737)

★10726★
OKLAHOMA COUNTY LAW LIBRARY (Law)
County Courthouse, Rm. 247 Phone: (405)236-2727
Oklahoma City, OK 73102 Darla J. Schantz, Libn.
Staff: Prof 1; Other 3. **Subjects:** Law. **Holdings:** 28,983 books; 21,682 microfiche. **Subscriptions:** 38 journals and other serials. **Services:** Copying; library open to the public. **Computerized Information Services:** WESTLAW, Dow Jones News/Retrieval, DIALOG Information Services. Performs searches on fee basis. **Networks/Consortia:** Member of Metronet. **Remarks:** An alternate telephone number is 278-4353.

★10727★
OKLAHOMA GAS AND ELECTRIC COMPANY - LIBRARY (Energy, Sci-Engr)
Box 321 Phone: (405)272-3191
Oklahoma City, OK 73102 Ms. Pat Tucker, Libn.
Founded: 1928. **Staff:** 1. **Subjects:** Engineering, electronics, mathematics, management, communication, environment, accident prevention, chemistry, physics, private and public power. **Special Collections:** Oklahoma history; the free enterprise system; world power resources; electrical engineering (185 volumes); American Society of Testing and Materials standards. **Holdings:** 5000 volumes. **Subscriptions:** 124 journals and other serials. **Services:** Interlibrary loan; library open to the public for reference use only. **Automated Operations:** Computerized circulation. **Remarks:** Library located at 321 N. Harvey, Oklahoma City, OK 73101.

★10728★
OKLAHOMA GEOLOGICAL SURVEY - OKLAHOMA GEOPHYSICAL OBSERVATORY LIBRARY (Sci-Engr)
Box 8 Phone: (918)366-4152
Leonard, OK 74043-0008 Charles J. Mankin, Dir.
Founded: 1960. **Staff:** Prof 1; Other 4. **Subjects:** Seismology, geoelectricity, geomagnetism, aeronomy, earth tide gravimetry, meteorology, solar radiation. **Special Collections:** 50 geophysical records are currently recorded on a continuous (24 hour, 7 day) basis (250,000 record days in archives). **Holdings:** 300 books; 1500 other cataloged items. **Subscriptions:** 30 data bulletins. **Services:** Interlibrary loan; library open to the public if advance arrangements are made with the chief geophysicist. **Computerized Information Services:** Oklahoma and regional earthquakes, geomagnetic database (internal databases). Contact Person: J.E. Lawson, Jr., Chf. Geophysicist. **Publications:** P/PKP Arrival Bulletin, biweekly; Phase Amplitude Bulletin, biweekly. **Remarks:** Observatory was previously operated as Leonard Earth Sciences Observatory by the Jersey Production Corporation until 1965, when it was donated to the University of Oklahoma. In 1978 it was transferred to the Oklahoma Geological Survey. **Staff:** Shirley A. Jackson, Libn..

★10729★
OKLAHOMA HISTORICAL SOCIETY - ARCHIVES AND MANUSCRIPT DIVISION (Hist)
Historical Bldg. Phone: (405)521-2491
Oklahoma City, OK 73105 Mary Lee Ervin Boyle, Chf.Archv.
Staff: Prof 5; Other 8. **Subjects:** Oklahoma and Indian territories, Indian tribes of Oklahoma, pioneer life, missionaries, territorial court records, explorers. **Special Collections:** Records from all state Indian agencies, except Osage Agency (3 million document pages; 5000 volumes); Dawes Commission Records (48 cubic feet; 242 bound volumes); Indian-Pioneer History (interviews; 112 volumes); Whipple Collection (8 cubic feet); Joseph Thoburn Collection (20 cubic feet). **Holdings:** 2800 reels of microfilm of Indian and Oklahoma affairs; 20,000 historical photographs; 25,000 reels of microfilm of newspapers; 4200 oral history tapes. **Services:** Copying; archives open to the public. **Publications:** Microfilm of original materials for sale. **Special Indexes:** Inventories of Five Civilized Tribes documents; card index of Indian-Pioneer History. **Special Catalogs:** Catalog listing films for sale. **Staff:** Kay Zahari, Archv.; Robert Nespor, Archv.; William D. Welge, Archv.; Joe L. Todd, Archv./Oral Hist..

★10730★
OKLAHOMA HISTORICAL SOCIETY - CHICKASAW COUNCIL HOUSE LIBRARY (Hist)
Court House Square
Box 717 Phone: (405)371-3351
Tishomingo, OK 73460 Beverly J. Wyatt, Historic Property Mgr.
Founded: 1970. **Staff:** 2. **Subjects:** Chickasaw Indian history, biographies, and statistics. **Special Collections:** Oklahoma Chronicles - Chickasaw Constitution and law books. **Holdings:** 1200 books; 150 maps; county and Chickasaw Nation records; 70 reels of microfilm; pamphlets. **Services:** Library open to the public.

★10731★
OKLAHOMA HISTORICAL SOCIETY - DIVISION OF LIBRARY RESOURCES (Hist)
Wiley Post Historical Bldg. Phone: (405)521-2491
Oklahoma City, OK 73105 Carolyn Grangaard Smith, Lib.Dir.
Founded: 1929. **Staff:** Prof 2; Other 8. **Subjects:** Oklahoma and American Indian history, American west, Oklahoma genealogy. **Holdings:** 55,000 books; 13,100 reels of microfilm of U.S. Census, 1790-1910; 25,000 reels of microfilm of Oklahoma newspapers, 1893 to present. **Subscriptions:** 300 journals and other serials; 280 newspapers. **Services:** Copying; library open to the public for research use only. **Automated Operations:** Computerized cataloging. **Staff:** Edward C. Shoemaker, Tech.Serv.Libn..

★10732★
OKLAHOMA HISTORICAL SOCIETY - MUSEUM OF THE WESTERN PRAIRIE - LIBRARY (Hist)
1100 N. Hightower
Box 574 Phone: (405)482-1044
Altus, OK 73521 Frances Herron, Libn.
Founded: 1982. **Staff:** 1. **Subjects:** History of southwest Oklahoma, pioneer families, Plains Indians, cowboys, early settlers. **Special Collections:** Long Collection (Indians of southwest); Dr. E.E. Dale History Collection; first editions of Oklahoma University Press. **Holdings:** 1500 books; 100 bound periodical volumes; documents; oral history tapes; archival collections; photographs. **Subscriptions:** 18 journals and other serials. **Services:** Copying; SDI; library open to the public for reference use only. **Publications:** Mistletoe Leaves (newsletter), monthly - to the public.

★10733★
OKLAHOMA JUNIOR COLLEGE - LEARNING RESOURCE CENTER (Bus-Fin)
4821 S. 72nd E. Ave. Phone: (918)663-9500
Tulsa, OK 74145 Donna Bishop, Dir. of Lrng.Rsrcs.
Founded: 1916. **Staff:** Prof 2. **Subjects:** Business, accounting, business law, secretarial science, computer science, medical assistance, travel and airlines, electronic technology, fashion merchandising, paralegal professions. **Holdings:** 12,000 books; 6 VF drawers of pamphlets; 150 cassettes; 3 boxes of microfiche. **Subscriptions:** 160 journals and other serials. **Services:** Interlibrary loan; copying; center open to the public with circulation limited to associate members. **Networks/Consortia:** Member of Tulsa Area Library Cooperative (TALC). **Publications:** Subject bibliographies.

★10734★
OKLAHOMA OSTEOPATHIC HOSPITAL - L.C. BAXTER MEDICAL LIBRARY (Med)
744 W. 9th Phone: (918)599-5297
Tulsa, OK 74127 S. Jane Cooper, Lib.Dir.
Founded: 1960. **Staff:** Prof 1; Other 2. **Subjects:** General medicine, internal medicine, surgery, ophthalmology, allied health sciences. **Holdings:** 1500 books; 1900 bound periodical volumes; 1600 AV cassettes; 1900 slides. **Subscriptions:** 200 journals and other serials. **Services:** Interlibrary loan; copying; library open to the public for reference use only. **Networks/Consortia:** Member of TALON.

★10735★
OKLAHOMA REGIONAL LIBRARY FOR THE BLIND AND PHYSICALLY HANDICAPPED (Aud-Vis)
1108 N.E. 36th St. Phone: (405)521-3514
Oklahoma City, OK 73111 Gary R. Minnerath, Lib.Dir.
Founded: 1933. **Staff:** Prof 4; Other 26. **Subjects:** Recreational and informational reading materials in special media collections. **Special Collections:** Locally recorded books on cassette (1400 titles); hand-copied braille books of radio programs (600 titles); braille books (600); LP textbooks (150). **Holdings:** 165,000 books; magnetic tapes; microfiche. **Subscriptions:** 56 journals and other serials. **Services:** Interlibrary loan; LED braille reproduction-machine repair; enlargement of print books; library not open to the public. **Automated Operations:** Computerized circulation. **Networks/Consortia:** Member of National Library Service for the Blind & Physically Handicapped (NLS). **Publications:** Radio Talking Book schedule, monthly - mail distribution; newsletter, monthly. **Special Catalogs:** Catalog for locally produced cassette books (card); braille catalog for braille books other than those produced by the Library of Congress; LP catalog, annual. **Remarks:** Maintained by the Oklahoma State Department of Human Services. **Staff:** Joan Shelton, Libn.; Jerome Simpson, Libn.; Linda Boyd, Libn.; Gerri Beeson, Volunteer Coord.; James Holder, Radio Rd.Serv.; James Gillespie, Comp.Anl..

★10736★
OKLAHOMA SCHOOL FOR THE BLIND - PARKVIEW LIBRARY (Aud-Vis)
3300 Gibson St.
Box 309 Phone: (918)682-6641
Muskogee, OK 74402-0309 Marjorie Moske, Libn.
Founded: 1913. **Staff:** 1. **Subjects:** Books in braille and talking books. **Special Collections:** Education of the blind. **Holdings:** 8440 titles; 2175 talking books. **Subscriptions:** 81 journals and other serials. **Services:** Interlibrary loan; library open to blind, partially-sighted, and multi-handicapped persons. **Remarks:** Maintained by Oklahoma State Department of Human Services.

★10737★
OKLAHOMA STATE DEPARTMENT OF COMMERCE - ENERGY CONSERVATION SERVICES DIVISION - TECHNICAL INFORMATION CENTER (Energy)
301 N.W. 63rd, Suite 130 Phone: (405)521-3941
Oklahoma City, OK 73116-7906 Steven Boggs, Prog.Mgr.
Staff: Prof 1; Other 1. **Subjects:** Energy conservation, renewable energy. **Holdings:** 1000 books. **Services:** Center open to the public with restrictions. **Formerly:** Oklahoma Corporation Commission.

★10738★
OKLAHOMA STATE DEPARTMENT OF CORRECTIONS - PLANNING AND RESEARCH UNIT - LIBRARY (Law)
3400 Martin Luther King Ave. Phone: (405)427-6511
Oklahoma City, OK 73111 Ruthie Steele, Exec.Sec.
Subjects: Criminal justice. **Holdings:** 2000 books. **Services:** Interlibrary loan; copying; library open to the public. **Automated Operations:** Computerized cataloging.

★10739★
OKLAHOMA STATE DEPARTMENT OF HEALTH - INFORMATION & REFERRAL HEALTHLINE (Med)
N.E. 10th & Stonewall
Box 53551 Phone: (405)271-4725
Oklahoma City, OK 73152 Janet Smith, Dir.
Founded: 1938. **Staff:** 1. **Subjects:** Medicine, nursing, psychology, personal health, epidemiology, venereal disease. **Holdings:** 2500 volumes; 90,000 general health pamphlets covering approximately 300 areas. **Subscriptions:** 30 journals and other serials. **Services:** Department open to the public with restrictions.

OKLAHOMA STATE DEPARTMENT OF HUMAN SERVICES - OKLAHOMA SCHOOL FOR THE BLIND
See: Oklahoma School for the Blind (10736)

OKLAHOMA STATE DEPARTMENT OF HUMAN SERVICES - REGIONAL LIBRARY FOR THE BLIND AND PHYSICALLY HANDICAPPED
See: Oklahoma Regional Library for the Blind and Physically Handicapped (10735)

★10740★
OKLAHOMA STATE DEPARTMENT OF LIBRARIES (Hist, Law, Info Sci)
200 N.E. 18th St. Phone: (405)521-2502
Oklahoma City, OK 73105 Robert L. Clark, Jr., Dir.
Founded: 1890. **Staff:** Prof 40; Other 36. **Subjects:** Law; legislative reference materials; Oklahoma government, history, authors; librarianship; juvenile evaluation collection. **Special Collections:** Oklahoma Collection (9000 titles). **Holdings:** 280,295 books; 23,933 cubic feet of state archives and manuscript collections; 13,800 cubic feet of state records; 14,474 linear feet of U.S. Government documents (regional depository); 3870 Oklahoma document titles; 1899 motion picture films; 4484 reels of microfilm; 700,000 microfiche; 150 file drawers of pamphlets and clippings; state government publications. **Subscriptions:** 1972 journals and other serials; 25 newspapers. **Services:** Interlibrary loan; legislative and law reference; archival and state research assistance; department open to the public for reference use only; loans made to state agency personnel only. **Automated Operations:** Computerized cataloging, acquisitions, and circulation. **Computerized Information Services:** OCLC, DIALOG Information Services, LEXIS, The Reference Service (REFSRV), BRS Information Technologies, DataTimes, AgriData Network; legislature's index to statutes (internal database). **Networks/Consortia:** Member of AMIGOS Bibliographic Council, Inc., Western Council of State Libraries. **Publications:** Who Is Who in the Oklahoma Legislature; Annual Report of Oklahoma Libraries; Oklahoma Register (administrative rules and regulations); Annual Directory of Oklahoma Libraries; Biographies of Governors of Oklahoma; ODL Guarantee; ODL Archives, quarterly; Directory of Oklahoma, biennial; Lawdocs, quarterly; GPO: Government Publications for Oklahoma, bimonthly; Oklahoma State Agencies, Boards, Commissions, Courts, Institutions, Legislature and Officers; ODL Source (newsletter), monthly; Oklahoma Government Publications (checklist), quarterly. **Staff:** Sandra Ellison, Pub.Lib.Cons.; Dean Doerr, Cons.; Cathy Cook, Pub.Lib.Cons.; Denny Stephens, Asst.Dir.; Harriet Barbour, Hd., Govt.Serv.; Marilyn Vesely, Pub.Info.Off.; Sue Galloway, Ch.Cons.; Jan Blakely, Pub.Div.; Beverly Jones, Chf.Plan.Off.; Marian Patmon, Hd., Lib.Rsrcs.; Betty Brown, Oklahoma Rm.; Mary Hardin, ILL; Steve Belev, U.S. Govt.Doc.; Susan Gilley, Leg.Ref.; Geraldine Adams, Acq.; Allan Goode, Pub.Lib.Cons.; Howard Lowell, Oklahoma Rsrcs.; Freda Chen, Cat.; Tom Kremm, State Archv.; Donna Skvarla, Adult Serv.Cons.; Chuck Childres, Archv.; Judith McCune, Archv.; Judith Clarke, Law Libn.; Karen Fite, Ref.Libn.; Kitty Pittman, Ref.Libn.; Njambi Kamoche, Docs.Libn.; Lana Cross, AV Cons.; Mike Bruno, Instr.Cons.; Vicki Sullivan, Oklahoma Docs..

★10741★
OKLAHOMA STATE DEPARTMENT OF VOCATIONAL AND TECHNICAL EDUCATION - RESOURCE CENTER (Educ)
1500 W. 7th Ave. Phone: (405)377-2000
Stillwater, OK 74074 Peggy Murphy, Rsrc.Ctr.Mgr.
Founded: 1970. **Staff:** Prof 1; Other 3. **Subjects:** Vocational-technical materials, philosophy of vocational education, curriculum development, career education materials. **Holdings:** 7250 books; 1200 pamphlets. **Subscriptions:** 96 journals and other serials. **Services:** Copying; SDI and ERIC search service (to state staff and Oklahoma vocational teachers); 16mm films and video cassettes circulated free of charge to Oklahoma state vocational teachers on a reservation basis; center open to the public. **Computerized Information Services:** BRS Information Technologies; Adult and Vocational Educational Electronic Mail Network (ADVOCNET; electronic mail service). **Publications:** Bibliographies. **Remarks:** Main purpose is to maintain collection of current materials in subject areas in which vocational instruction or support is offered.

★10742★
OKLAHOMA STATE UNIVERSITY - AUDIO-VISUAL CENTER (Aud-Vis)
Stillwater, OK 74078 Phone: (405)624-7216
Dr. Ron G. Payne, Dir.
Staff: Prof 9; Other 9. **Holdings:** 10,000 books; 5000 16mm films; 300 audiotape masters; 50 video cassettes. **Services:** Copying; SDI; audio recording and duplication; rental and repair; consultations and workshops in various areas of AV communications and operations; films and video cassettes available on rental basis; center open to the public. **Automated Operations:** Computerized cataloging and circulation. **Networks/Consortia:** Member of Consortium of University Film Centers (CUFC). **Special Catalogs:** Film Rental Catalog (regional); Locator III Catalog, both every 3 years; special catalogs by subject and grade level.

★10743★
OKLAHOMA STATE UNIVERSITY - BIOLOGICAL SCIENCES DIVISION (Biol Sci, Agri)
University Library Phone: (405)624-6309
Stillwater, OK 74078 Sheila G. Johnson, Hd.
Founded: 1891. **Staff:** Prof 4; Other 5. **Subjects:** Agriculture, botany, entomology, zoology, bacteriology, anthropology, medicine, home economics. **Holdings:** 87,920 books; 83,436 bound periodical volumes. **Subscriptions:** 2664 journals and other serials. **Services:** Interlibrary loan; copying; division open to the public with borrowing restrictions. **Computerized Information Services:** DIALOG Information Services, BRS Information Technologies, OCLC. **Staff:** M. Kay Gage; William Wiese; Kim Granath.

★10744★
OKLAHOMA STATE UNIVERSITY - CURRICULUM MATERIALS LABORATORY (Educ)
University Library Phone: (405)624-6310
Stillwater, OK 74078 Donna Schwarz, Hd.
Founded: 1957. **Staff:** Prof 1; Other 2. **Subjects:** Materials for preschool-grade 12. **Special Collections:** Preschool-grade 12 fiction and nonfiction; textbooks (5750); curriculum guides (5150); professional materials for teachers and librarians; foreign language books. **Holdings:** 32,500 books; 2300 AV programs. **Subscriptions:** 180 journals and other serials. **Services:** Interlibrary loan; laboratory open to the public with restrictions.

★10745★
OKLAHOMA STATE UNIVERSITY - DOCUMENTS DEPARTMENT (Info Sci)
University Library Phone: (405)624-6546
Stillwater, OK 74078 Vicki W. Phillips, Hd.
Founded: 1907. **Staff:** Prof 6; Other 8. **Special Collections:** U.S. Government Regional Depository; NASA depository; U.S. patent depository; Oklahoma documents depository. **Holdings:** 1.3 million items; 157,237 accessioned volumes; 1.3 million microforms. **Subscriptions:** 4411 journals and other serials. **Services:** Interlibrary loan; copying; department open to the public with restrictions. **Staff:** John Phillips, Asst.Doc.Libn.; Michele McKnelly, Asst.Doc.Libn.; Connie Kirby, Asst.Doc.Libn.; Sharon Egan, Asst.Doc.Libn.; Kevin Harwell, Asst.Doc.Libn..

★10746★
OKLAHOMA STATE UNIVERSITY - HUMANITIES DIVISION (Hum)
University Library
Stillwater, OK 74078 Phone: (405)624-6544
Founded: 1953. **Staff:** Prof 4; Other 4. **Subjects:** Literature, religion, computer science, library science, journalism, language, architecture, film, theater, fine arts, painting, sculpture, interior design, music, sports, recreation. **Holdings:** 133,649 books; 28,463 bound periodical volumes; 83,221 microforms. **Subscriptions:** 1635 journals and other serials. **Services:** Interlibrary loan; copying; division open to the public with restrictions. **Computerized Information Services:** DIALOG Information Services, BRS Information Technologies, OCLC. **Staff:** Janice Bickham, Asst.Hum.Libn.; Terry Basford, Asst.Hum.Libn.; Teresa Fehlig, Arch.Libn..

★10747★
OKLAHOMA STATE UNIVERSITY - MAP COLLECTION (Geog-Map)
University Library Phone: (405)624-6313
Stillwater, OK 74078 Heather M. Lloyd, Hd., Gen.Ref.Dept.
Staff: Prof 2; Other 1. **Subjects:** Agriculture, geology, sociology. **Special Collections:** U.S. Geological Survey maps; Defense Mapping Agency (DMA) maps; aerial photographs of Oklahoma. **Holdings:** 161,633 maps. **Services:** Copying; collection open to the public for reference use only. **Computerized Information Services:** DIALOG Information Services, BRS Information Technologies, OCLC. **Staff:** Rebecca Dinkins, Asst.Ref.Libn..

★10748★
OKLAHOMA STATE UNIVERSITY - OKLAHOMA CITY BRANCH - TECHNICAL BRANCH LIBRARY (Educ)
900 N. Portland Phone: (405)947-4421
Oklahoma City, OK 73107 Annette Duffy, Hd.Libn.
Founded: 1963. **Staff:** Prof 2; Other 2. **Subjects:** Computer science, nursing, electronics, police science, horticulture, fire protection. **Holdings:** 15,000 books. **Subscriptions:** 200 journals and other serials. **Services:** Interlibrary loan; copying; library open to the public with restrictions. **Automated Operations:** Computerized cataloging and circulation. **Computerized Information Services:** OCLC, DIALOG Information Services, WILSONLINE. Performs searches on fee basis. **Networks/Consortia:** Member of AMIGOS Bibliographic Council, Inc.. **Publications:** New Book List, 4/year - for internal distribution only. **Staff:** Donna Denniston, Asst.Libn..

★10749★
OKLAHOMA STATE UNIVERSITY - PHYSICAL SCIENCES AND ENGINEERING DIVISION (Sci-Engr)
University Library Phone: (405)624-6305
Stillwater, OK 74078 Emerson Hilker, Hd.
Founded: 1928. **Staff:** Prof 3; Other 4. **Subjects:** Chemistry; physics; mathematics; geology; engineering - chemical, aeronautical, civil, electrical, mechanical. **Holdings:** 79,806 books; 111,628 bound periodical volumes; 54,700 microforms. **Subscriptions:** 1682 journals and other serials. **Services:** Interlibrary loan; division open to the public with restrictions. **Computerized Information Services:** DIALOG Information Services, OCLC. **Staff:** Sue Ann Johnson, Asst. Physical Sci.Libn.; Linda Zellmer, Asst. Physical Sci.Libn..

★10750★
OKLAHOMA STATE UNIVERSITY - SOCIAL SCIENCE DIVISION (Soc Sci)
University Library
Stillwater, OK 74078 Phone: (405)624-6540
Founded: 1953. **Staff:** Prof 4; Other 3. **Subjects:** Business, economics, history, political science, sociology, management, anthropology, geography, education, psychology, philosophy. **Holdings:** 234,690 books; 64,600 bound periodical volumes; 5 VF drawers of serials; 39 VF drawers of pamphlets; 297,650 microforms. **Subscriptions:** 2080 journals and other serials; 16 newspapers. **Services:** Interlibrary loan; copying; division open to the public with restrictions. **Computerized Information Services:** DIALOG Information Services, BRS Information Technologies, OCLC. **Remarks:** Includes holdings of its Education Division. **Staff:** Jill Holmes, Educ.Libn.; Jeff Levy, Asst.Soc.Sci.Libn.; Brian Wood, Asst.Soc.Sci.Libn..

★10751★
OKLAHOMA STATE UNIVERSITY - SPECIAL COLLECTIONS (Hist)
University Library Phone: (405)624-6311
Stillwater, OK 74078 Heather M. Lloyd, Hd., Gen.Ref.Dept.
Staff: Prof 2; Other 1. **Subjects:** Oklahoma State University; Oklahoma - agriculture, politics, water; journalism. **Holdings:** OSU publications; state agricultural history; papers of Henry Bellmon, Henry S. Johnston, Paul Miller. **Services:** Copying; collections open to the public for reference use only. **Staff:** Kathleen Bledsoe, Asst.Ref.Libn..

★10752★
OKLAHOMA STATE UNIVERSITY - TECHNICAL BRANCH, OKMULGEE - LEARNING RESOURCE CENTER (Sci-Engr)
Fourth & Mission Rd. Phone: (918)756-6211
Okmulgee, OK 74447-0088 Becky Kirkbride, Libn.
Founded: 1946. **Staff:** Prof 2; Other 3. **Subjects:** Automotive engineering, data processing, electrical-electronics technology, diesel trades, machinist trades, drafting, air conditioning and refrigeration, graphic arts, boot making, watch and micro-instrument repair, business education, food trades, commercial art, building trades, computer graphics, numerical control. **Holdings:** 11,000 books; 225 reels of microfilm; 1195 microfiche. **Subscriptions:** 407 journals and other serials; 7 newspapers. **Services:** Interlibrary loan; copying; center open to the public with restrictions. **Networks/Consortia:** Member of AMIGOS Bibliographic Council, Inc.. **Staff:** M.F. Christerson, Coord., LRC.

★10753★
OKLAHOMA STATE UNIVERSITY - VETERINARY MEDICINE LIBRARY (Med)
University Library Phone: (405)624-6655
Stillwater, OK 74078 LaVerne K. Jones, Libn.
Founded: 1948. **Staff:** Prof 1; Other 3. **Subjects:** Veterinary medicine, health sciences, laboratory animal medicine. **Holdings:** 8639 books; 9363 bound periodical volumes; 775 tapes; 694 slides; 30 study guides; 25 films. **Subscriptions:** 307 journals and other serials. **Services:** Interlibrary loan; copying; library open to the public with restrictions. **Computerized Information Services:** DIALOG Information Services, BRS Information Technologies, NLM, OCLC.

★10754★
OKLAHOMA WATER RESOURCES BOARD - LIBRARY (Env-Cons)
1000 N.E. 10th, 12th Fl.
Box 53585 Phone: (405)271-2555
Oklahoma City, OK 73152 Susan E. Lutz, Libn.
Staff: Prof 1. **Subjects:** Water, water quality and planning. **Holdings:** 5500 volumes. **Subscriptions:** 70 journals and other serials. **Services:** Interlibrary loan; copying; library open to the public.

★10755★
OKLAHOMA WELL LOG LIBRARY, INC. (Energy)
1100 Philtower Bldg. Phone: (918)582-6188
Tulsa, OK 74103 Janice R. Jennings, Mgr.
Staff: Prof 1; Other 8. **Subjects:** Geology, oil and gas. **Special Collections:** Electrical logs (450,000); scout tickets (875,000). **Holdings:** 1000 volumes; 560 reels of microfilm. **Services:** Copying; library open to the public with restrictions. **Staff:** Billie R. Weaver, Asst.Mgr..

★10756★
OLANA STATE HISTORIC SITE - LIBRARY (Hist)
R.D. 2 Phone: (518)828-0135
Hudson, NY 12534 James Ryan, Mgr.
Staff: Prof 1; Other 2. **Subjects:** Local history. **Special Collections:** Correspondence and paintings of Frederic Edwin Church (19th century American landscape painter); 19th century photographs. **Holdings:** 3000 books; 34 bound periodical volumes; theses. **Services:** Library open to the public with restrictions. **Publications:** The Crayon, 3/year - to members.

OLCOTT LIBRARY & RESEARCH CENTER
See: Theosophical Society in America (14148)

OLD ACADEMY MUSEUM LIBRARY
See: Wethersfield Historical Society - Old Academy Museum Library (17807)

★10757★
OLD AMERICAN INSURANCE COMPANY - LIBRARY
4900 Oak St.
Kansas City, MO 64112
Subjects: Insurance, law. **Holdings:** 3000 volumes; 4 VF drawers of pamphlets. **Remarks:** Presently inactive.

★10758★
OLD BRUTUS HISTORICAL SOCIETY, INC. - LIBRARY (Hist)
8943 N. Seneca St. Phone: (315)834-6779
Weedsport, NY 13166 Howard J. Finley, Hist.
Staff: 1. **Subjects:** Genealogy, local history. **Special Collections:** Stanley Guppy books on history of Cayuga County (50). **Holdings:** 2000 books; 2000 photographs; 40,000 genealogy sheets; agricultural and household artifacts; products of local manufacturers. **Services:** Library open to the public on limited schedule.

★10759★
OLD CATHEDRAL PARISH CHURCH - BRUTE LIBRARY (Rel-Phil)
205 Church St. Phone: (812)882-7016
Vincennes, IN 47591 Esther Cunningham, Guide/Archv.
Staff: Prof 2. **Subjects:** Rare books, religion. **Special Collections:** Two hand-printed and illuminated documents from the Middle Ages; letter of St. Vincent de Paul dated 1660. **Holdings:** 11,000 books. **Services:** Library open to the public for reference use only.

★10760★
OLD CHARLES TOWN LIBRARY, INC. (Hist)
200 E. Washington St. Phone: (304)725-2208
Charles Town, WV 25414 Anna M. Shewbridge, Libn.
Founded: 1965. **Staff:** Prof 2; Other 7. **Subjects:** Local history, genealogy, West Virginia history. **Special Collections:** Collection of Jefferson County Historical Society; Thorton T. Perry Room (history, genealogy). **Holdings:** 75,000 books; 491 bound periodical volumes. **Subscriptions:** 123 journals and other serials.

★10761★
OLD COLLEGE - HUMANITIES LIBRARY
401 W. Second St.
Reno, NV 89503-5302
Defunct

★10762★
OLD COLONY HISTORICAL SOCIETY - MUSEUM & LIBRARY (Hist)
66 Church Green Phone: (508)822-1622
Taunton, MA 02780 June M. Strojny, Libn.
Founded: 1853. **Staff:** Prof 3; Other 4. **Subjects:** Local and military history, biography, genealogy. **Special Collections:** Books and manuscripts of Francis Baylies. **Holdings:** 6000 books; other cataloged items. **Services:** Copying; museum and library open to the public for reference use only. **Staff:** Lisa A. Compton, Dir..

★10763★
OLD DARTMOUTH HISTORICAL SOCIETY - WHALING MUSEUM LIBRARY (Hist)
18 Johnny Cake Hill Phone: (508)997-0046
New Bedford, MA 02740 Virginia M. Adams, Libn.
Founded: 1903. **Staff:** Prof 4. **Subjects:** History - American whaling, New Bedford area, maritime. **Special Collections:** Ship logbooks (1105); Charles F. Batchelder Collection (whaling); Charles A. Goodwin Collection (maritime history); International Marine Archives (whaling and maritime records on microfilm). **Holdings:** 15,000 books; 500 bound periodical volumes; 750 linear feet of manuscripts; 600 maps and charts; 1800 reels of microfilm. **Subscriptions:** 30 journals and other serials. **Services:** Interlibrary loan (microfilm only); copying; library open to the public. **Publications:** Whaling Logbooks and Journals, 1613-1927: An Inventory of Manuscript Records in Public Collections.

★10764★
OLD DOMINION UNIVERSITY - LIBRARY ARCHIVE (Hist)
Norfolk, VA 23529-0256 Phone: (804)440-4141
Dr. Cynthia B. Duncan, Univ.Libn.
Founded: 1974. **Staff:** Prof 1; Other 2. **Subjects:** Old Dominion University, history of Norfolk and Tidewater cities. **Special Collections:** Papers of Henry E. Howell, Jr., Thomas R. McNamara, Joseph D. Wood, Robert M. Hughes (500 linear feet); records of the Office of the University President. **Holdings:** 403 linear feet of correspondence; legislative and mayoral files; scrapbooks; business papers; political and legal files. **Services:** Interlibrary loan; archive open to the public. **Automated Operations:** Computerized cataloging and circulation. **Special Indexes:** Internal finding aids.

OLD ECONOMY VILLAGE
See: Pennsylvania State Historical & Museum Commission - Old Economy Village (11189)

★10765★
OLD FORT NIAGARA ASSOCIATION - LIBRARY (Hist)
Box 169 Phone: (716)745-7611
Youngstown, NY 14174-0169 Brian Leigh Dunnigan, Exec.Dir.
Staff: Prof 1. **Subjects:** Local and military history. **Special Collections:** Old Fort Niagara Collection (original diaries, orderly books, post records, 1813-1912). **Holdings:** 1500 books; 70 reels of microfilm. **Subscriptions:** 10

journals and other serials. **Services:** Copying; library open to serious researchers by prior arrangement. **Publications:** List of publications - available on request.

OLD FORT WILLIAM
See: Ontario Ministry of Tourism and Recreation (10854)

THE OLD GUARDHOUSE MUSEUM
See: Fort Clark Historical Society (5270)

OLD JAIL MUSEUM LIBRARY
See: Historical Society of Porter County (6351)

★10766★
THE OLD MANSE LIBRARY (Hist)
225 Mary St. Phone: (506)622-0453
Newcastle, NB, Canada E1V 1Z3 Catherine Bryan, Libn.
Founded: 1953. **Staff:** Prof 1; Other 2. **Subjects:** Local history and genealogy. **Special Collections:** Lord Beaverbrook Collection; Miramichi Historical Society Records. **Holdings:** 40,000 books. **Subscriptions:** 10 journals and other serials. **Services:** Interlibrary loan; copying; library open to the public. **Publications:** Newcastle on the Miramichi; The Old Manse Library, Newcastle, N.B.

★10767★
OLD ST. MARY'S CHURCH - PAULIST LIBRARY (Rel-Phil)
614 Grant Ave. Phone: (415)362-0959
San Francisco, CA 94108 Walter Anthony, C.S.P., Dir.
Staff: Prof 1; Other 35. **Subjects:** Catholic religion and history, philosophy, biography, psychology. **Special Collections:** Rare collection of biographical works. **Holdings:** 5000 books; 3500 cassettes. **Subscriptions:** 25 journals and other serials. **Services:** Library open to the public for reference use only. **Special Catalogs:** Cassette catalog.

★10768★
OLD SALEM, INC. - LIBRARY (Hist)
Drawer F, Salem Sta. Phone: (919)723-3688
Winston-Salem, NC 27108 Paula Locklair, Dir., Dept. of Coll.
Staff: Prof 1; Other 1. **Subjects:** Moravians in North Carolina, North Carolina history, traditional American crafts, historic preservation. **Holdings:** 2265 books; 4 VF drawers of Moraviana, preservation, crafts, interpretation clippings; 26 VF drawers of material on life in early Salem, NC and the restoration of Old Salem. **Subscriptions:** 25 journals and other serials. **Services:** Library open to the public with restrictions. **Staff:** Barbara Kendrick, Libn..

★10769★
OLD SALEM, INC. - MUSEUM OF EARLY SOUTHERN DECORATIVE ARTS (MESDA) - LIBRARY (Art)
Box 10310 Phone: (919)722-6148
Winston-Salem, NC 27108 Bradford L. Rauschenberg, Dir. of Res.
Founded: 1965. **Staff:** Prof 1. **Subjects:** Decorative arts of southern United States. **Holdings:** 2500 books; 200 bound periodical volumes; data file of 120,000 cards based on source material; 64 VF drawers of photographs and southern decorative art material; 900 reels of microfilm of newspapers, pre-1821. **Services:** Interlibrary loan; copying; library open to the public upon application.

★10770★
OLD SLAVE MART MUSEUM - LIBRARY
Box 446
Sullivan's Island, SC 29482
Subjects: Slavery, black history, Civil War, Charleston, South Carolina. **Special Collections:** Miriam B. Wilson Collection; Chase/Graves Collection. **Holdings:** 1100 volumes; 1800 photographs; 850 slides; 130 photocopies of documents and 80 original documents; 800 realia; 300 paintings, flatwork, prints; 40 feet of uncataloged record boxes; 35 VF drawers; 10 map case drawers; 500 slides, records, tapes; 65 years of archival records; manuscripts of founder. **Remarks:** Library is the research arm of the Old Slave Mart Museum, 6 Chalmers St., Charleston, SC. Presently inactive.

OLD SONGS LIBRARY
See: Society for the Preservation and Encouragement of Barber Shop Quartet Singing in America (13335)

OLD SPANISH MISSIONS HISTORICAL RESEARCH LIBRARY
See: Our Lady of the Lake University (10956)

★10771★
OLD STURBRIDGE VILLAGE - RESEARCH LIBRARY (Hist)
1 Old Sturbridge Village Rd. Phone: (508)347-3362
Sturbridge, MA 01566-0200 Theresa Rini Percy, Dir.
Founded: 1946. **Staff:** Prof 3; Other 3. **Subjects:** New England rural life, 1790-1840 - state and local history, agriculture, architecture, fine arts, decorative arts (ceramics, furniture, glass, silver), crafts (blacksmithing, cabinet work, pottery), costume and fabrics, politics, economics, education, law, religion; technology and industry. **Special Collections:** Charles W. Eddy Collection of glass plate negatives (turn of the century central Massachusetts townscapes); Powell Collection of printed works on agriculture (1000 volumes); Merino/Dudley Wool Company Records, Dudley, Massachusetts, 1811-1845 (35 linear feet); Bullard Family papers, Holliston, Massachusetts, 1700-1900; Town of Sturbridge, Massachusetts papers, 1738-1915 (13 boxes). **Holdings:** 30,000 volumes; 400 shelf feet of manuscripts; 1184 microforms; 100 daguerreotypes; 50 ambrotypes; 50 tintypes; 150 mounted photographs; 2000 glass plate negatives; 27,000 original negatives; 31,000 black/white prints on paper; 65,000 color slides; archives. **Subscriptions:** 125 journals and other serials. **Services:** Copying (at librarian's discretion); library open to the public for reference use only. **Automated Operations:** Computerized cataloging. **Computerized Information Services:** OCLC. **Publications:** Recent Additions (new book list), occasional. **Staff:** Joan Allen, Asst.Libn.; Kathleen Pratt Frew, Cons.Techn.; Mary Baker-Wood, Vis.Rsrc.Libn..

OLD WEST MUSEUM
See: Sunset Trading Post-Old West Museum (13757)

★10772★
OLD YORK HISTORICAL SOCIETY - LIBRARY (Hist)
George Marshall Store
140 Lindsay Rd.
Box 312 Phone: (207)363-4974
York, ME 03909 Peter Cook, Dir.
Staff: 5. **Subjects:** Local history, decorative arts, genealogy, Maine history, architecture. **Special Collections:** Rare books (600); local manuscripts (3000); local historic photographs (1000); local genealogies (300). **Holdings:** 6000 books; 200 bound periodical volumes; 55 feet of manuscripts and archives; 3000 microfiche; 40 reels of microfilm; 4 VF drawers. **Subscriptions:** 12 journals and other serials. **Services:** Copying; library open to the public for reference use only. **Publications:** York Maine Then and Now; The Old Gaol Museum; Enchanted Ground - for sale; New England Miniature. **Staff:** Debra A. Cunningham, Libn./Geneal..

★10773★
OLD YORK ROAD HISTORICAL SOCIETY - ARCHIVES (Hist)
Jenkintown Library
York and Vista Rds. Phone: (215)884-8058
Jenkintown, PA 19046 Warren Hilton, Libn.
Founded: 1936. **Subjects:** Local history. **Holdings:** Books; newspapers; pamphlets; clippings; photographs; maps; deeds. **Services:** Archives open to the public for reference use on request. **Publications:** Bulletin, annual - to members and libraries.

EARL K. OLDHAM LIBRARY
See: Arlington Baptist College (929)

★10774★
OLDS COLLEGE - LEARNING RESOURCES CENTRE - SPECIAL COLLECTIONS (Agri)
Postal Bag 1 Phone: (403)556-4600
Olds, AB, Canada T0M 1P0 Garry Grisak, Coord.
Holdings: Agricultural Collection; government documents; Agdex (agricultural documents and other pamphlets). **Services:** Interlibrary loan; copying; collections open to the public. **Computerized Information Services:** DIALOG Information Services, Grassroots.

★10775★
OLIN CORPORATION - BUSINESS INFORMATION CENTER (Bus-Fin)
120 Long Ridge Rd. Phone: (203)356-2498
Stamford, CT 06904 L.A. Magistrate, Mgr., Bus.Info.
Staff: Prof 2; Other 1. **Subjects:** Business, law, marketing, chemicals. **Holdings:** 1500 books. **Subscriptions:** 750 journals and other serials. **Services:** Center not open to the public. **Computerized Information Services:** DIALOG Information Services, Pergamon ORBIT InfoLine, Inc., Business International Corporation, Mead Data Central, Trade Information Service, INVESTEXT, Data Resources (DRI), Human Resource Information Network (HRIN), VU/TEXT Information Services.

★10776★
OLIN CORPORATION - CHEMICALS - CHARLESTON TECHNICAL INFORMATION CENTER (Sci-Engr)
Charleston, TN 37310 Phone: (615)336-4347
Connie J. Upton, Coord.
Founded: 1976. **Staff:** Prof 1; Other 1. **Subjects:** Chemistry, chemical engineering, electrochemistry, engineering. **Holdings:** 3000 books; 1000 bound periodical volumes; 5 VF drawers of translated articles and patents; American Chemical Society Journals on microfilm. **Subscriptions:** 100 journals and other serials; 6 newspapers. **Services:** Center not open to the public. **Computerized Information Services:** DIALOG Information Services, Pergamon ORBIT InfoLine, Inc., CAS ONLINE, Chemical Information Systems, Inc. (CIS).

★10777★
OLIN CORPORATION - MARION OPERATIONS - R & D LIBRARY (Sci-Engr)
Box 278 Phone: (618)985-8211
Marion, IL 62959-0278 Martha Rose Rhine, Tech. Writer
Founded: 1958. **Staff:** Prof 1. **Subjects:** Chemistry, chemical engineering, electronics, mechanical engineering, explosives, ammunition, ballistics, computer simulation, solid propellants, munitions testing and evaluation, metals and composites. **Holdings:** 575 books; 500 bound periodical volumes; 100 VF drawers. **Services:** Library not open to the public. **Computerized Information Services:** DIALOG Information Services, DTIC, U.S. National Technical Information Service (NTIS). **Publications:** Progress reports. **Formerly:** Ordnance Products R & D Publications.

★10778★
OLIN CORPORATION - METALS RESEARCH LABORATORIES - METALS INFORMATION CENTER (Sci-Engr)
91 Shelton Ave. Phone: (203)789-5279
New Haven, CT 06511 Marcella C. Tammard, Libn.
Founded: 1961. **Staff:** Prof 1; Other 1. **Subjects:** Metallurgy, corrosion, aluminum, copper and brass. **Holdings:** 1800 books; 700 bound periodical volumes; 5000 internal and external reports; 5000 patents; 3500 translations. **Subscriptions:** 185 journals and other serials. **Services:** Copying; SDI; center open to the public on request. **Computerized Information Services:** DIALOG Information Services, Pergamon ORBIT InfoLine, Inc., Copper Data Center (CDC).

★10779★
OLIN CORPORATION - RESEARCH CENTER - TECHNICAL INFORMATION SERVICES (Sci-Engr)
350 Knotter Dr.
Box 586 Phone: (203)271-4237
Cheshire, CT 06410-0586 Lynn D. Campo, Supv.
Founded: 1941. **Staff:** Prof 3; Other 2. **Subjects:** Chemistry, metallurgy, physics. **Holdings:** 10,000 books; 15,000 bound periodical volumes; 25,000 internal reports; 35 drawers of patents on microfilm; 10 drawers of journals on microfilm. **Subscriptions:** 275 journals and other serials; 10 newspapers. **Services:** Interlibrary loan; services not open to the public. **Automated Operations:** Computerized public access catalog and cataloging. **Computerized Information Services:** DIALOG Information Services, STN International, NewsNet, Inc., Pergamon ORBIT InfoLine, Inc., NLM, BRS Information Technologies. **Publications:** TIS Bulletin - for internal distribution only. **Staff:** J.J. Pitts, Sr.Res.Info.Assoc.; V.C Pitts, Sr.Info.Sci..

JACOB T. OLIPHANT LIBRARY
See: Indiana State Board of Health (6759)

OLIVE VIEW MEDICAL HEALTH CENTER
See: Los Angeles County/Olive View Medical Health Center (7995)

MONSIGNOR JUAN FREMIOT TORRES OLIVER LAW LIBRARY
See: Catholic University of Puerto Rico (2763)

WRENSHALL A. OLIVER PROFESSIONAL LIBRARY
See: Napa State Hospital (9493)

★10780★
OLIVET NAZARENE UNIVERSITY - BENNER LIBRARY AND RESOURCE CENTER (Rel-Phil)
Kankakee, IL 60901 Phone: (815)939-5354
Allan L. Wiens, Dir.
Founded: 1909. **Staff:** Prof 5; Other 5. **Subjects:** Religion, education, literature, business, nursing. **Special Collections:** John Wesley; James Arminius, Archives of Olivet University; geological maps. **Holdings:** 142,000 books; 5183 bound periodical volumes; 3741 reels of microfilm; 29,585 microfiche; 9106 maps; 4460 phonograph records. **Subscriptions:** 906 journals and other serials; 22 newspapers. **Services:** Interlibrary loan; library open to the public with courtesy card. **Automated Operations:** Computerized public access catalog, cataloging, and acquisitions. **Computerized Information Services:** DIALOG Information Services, OCLC. Performs searches on fee basis. Contact Person: Ruth T. Kinnersley, Ref., 939-5355. **Networks/Consortia:** Member of ILLINET. **Staff:** Kathy VanFossan, Hd., Tech.Serv.; Lynette Christensen, Ref./Cat..

★10781★
OLMSTED COUNTY HISTORICAL SOCIETY - LIBRARY AND ARCHIVES (Hist)
Box 6411 Phone: (507)282-9447
Rochester, MN 55903 Beverly Hermes, Libn.
Founded: 1926. **Staff:** Prof 1. **Subjects:** Olmsted County history, Minnesota history, genealogy, 19th century farming. **Holdings:** 5500 books; 400 bound periodical volumes; 540 reels of microfilm of Olmsted County newspapers, 1859 to present; 73 VF drawers of documents, pamphlets, photographs; Minnesota census records through 1910. **Subscriptions:** 21 journals and other serials. **Services:** Copying; library and archives open to the public; fees charged for staff research. **Special Indexes:** Index to newspapers (1859-1912).

FREDERICK LAW OLMSTED NATIONAL HISTORIC SITE
See: U.S. Natl. Park Service (15293)

CHARLES OLSON ARCHIVES
See: University of Connecticut - Homer Babbidge Library - Special Collections (16094)

OTTO OLSON MEMORIAL LIBRARY
See: Lutheran Theological Seminary (8137)

★10782★
OLWINE, CONNELLY, CHASE - LAW LIBRARY (Law)
299 Park Ave. Phone: (212)688-0400
New York, NY 10117 James T. Roscher, Libn.
Staff: Prof 1; Other 1. **Subjects:** Law - corporate, taxation, trust and estates, patents, real estate. **Holdings:** 14,000 books; 550 bound periodical volumes; 150 pamphlets. **Subscriptions:** 75 journals and other serials; 5 newspapers. **Services:** Interlibrary loan; copying; library open to lawyers only. **Computerized Information Services:** LEXIS, WESTLAW.

OLYMPIA FIELDS OSTEOPATHIC MEDICAL CENTER LIBRARY
See: Chicago College of Osteopathic Medicine (3061)

OLYMPIC NATIONAL PARK
See: U.S. Natl. Park Service - Olympic Natl. Park (15334)

★10783★
OMAHA-COUNCIL BLUFFS METROPOLITAN AREA PLANNING AGENCY (MAPA) - LIBRARY (Plan)
2222 Cuming St. Phone: (402)444-6866
Omaha, NE 68102-4328 Pat Jesse, Info.Spec.
Staff: Prof 1. **Subjects:** Planning and community development, transportation, housing, environment, census, employment, local and regional data. **Holdings:** 4000 volumes; 125 periodicals and newsletters; 100 microfiche; 1980 Iowa and Nebraska census tapes; local data; maps; aerial photographs; area newspaper clippings. **Subscriptions:** 90 journals and other serials. **Services:** Copying; library open to the public by appointment.

★10784★
OMAHA PUBLIC LIBRARY - BUSINESS, SCIENCE & TECHNOLOGY DEPARTMENT (Bus-Fin, Sci-Engr, Biol Sci)
215 S. 15th St. Phone: (402)444-4817
Omaha, NE 68102 Janet Davenport, Hd.
Founded: 1952. **Staff:** Prof 3; Other 3. **Subjects:** Economics, insurance, mathematics, physics, investments, chemistry, engineering, agriculture, medicine, health, biology, botany. **Special Collections:** Telephone, city, and trade directories; trade catalogs; Public Document Room Collection of Nuclear Regulatory Commission reports. **Holdings:** 39,212 books; 6358 bound periodical volumes; 75 VF drawers of pamphlets, clippings, house organs, corporate annual reports; 320,583 U.S. Government documents; 56,411 topographic maps; microfilm. **Subscriptions:** 525 journals and other serials. **Services:** Interlibrary loan; copying; department open to the public. **Automated Operations:** Computerized cataloging and acquisitions. **Computerized Information Services:** DIALOG Information Services. **Publications:** Information Bulletin, monthly - to businesses, corporations,

and libraries on request. **Staff:** Barbara Burke, Libn.; Lillian Wunsch, Libn.; Theresa Jehlik, Spec.; Margaret Blackstone, Spec..

★10785★
OMAHA PUBLIC POWER DISTRICT - MANAGEMENT SYSTEMS SERVICES - INFORMATION CENTER-LIBRARY (Comp Sci)
1623 Harney St. Phone: (402)536-4295
Omaha, NE 68102 Suzanne Forbes, Corp.Libn.
Founded: 1982. **Staff:** Prof 1; Other 2. **Subjects:** Data processing, energy, business, nuclear power. **Holdings:** 500 books. **Subscriptions:** 450 journals and other serials. **Services:** Interlibrary loan; library not open to the public. **Computerized Information Services:** DIALOG Information Services.

★10786★
OMAHA WORLD-HERALD - LIBRARY (Publ)
World Herald Square Phone: (402)444-1000
Omaha, NE 68102 Beverly Parisot, Lib.Mgr.
Staff: Prof 1; Other 7. **Subjects:** Newspaper reference topics. **Holdings:** 4.5 million newspaper clippings; 400 drawers of photographs. **Services:** Library not open to the public. **Computerized Information Services:** Omaha World-Herald Data Bank (internal database).

★10787★
O'MELVENY AND MYERS - LIBRARY (Law)
400 S. Hope St. Phone: (213)669-6000
Los Angeles, CA 90071-2899 Maryruth Storer, Law Lib.Mgr.
Founded: 1885. **Staff:** Prof 6; Other 11. **Subjects:** Law - general, labor, tax. **Holdings:** 50,000 volumes; 12,000 research reports and legal memoranda. **Services:** Library not open to the public. **Automated Operations:** Computerized cataloging. **Computerized Information Services:** LEXIS, DIALOG Information Services, WILSONLINE, RLIN, WESTLAW, BRS Information Technologies. **Networks/Consortia:** Member of CLASS. **Special Catalogs:** Book catalog/index of internal research reports. **Staff:** Jill Sidford, Pub.Serv.Libn.; Bill Nazarro, Tech.Serv.Libn.; Catherine Smith, Ref.Libn.; Suzanne Plessinger, Ref.Libn.; Yen-Jane Connie Wang, Cat.Libn..

OMI COLLEGE OF APPLIED SCIENCE
See: University of Cincinnati - OMI College of Applied Science (16058)

★10788★
OMI INTERNATIONAL CORP. - LIBRARY (Sci-Engr)
21441 Hoover Rd. Phone: (313)497-9100
Warren, MI 48089 Lynn M. Pefley, Libn.
Founded: 1955. **Staff:** 1. **Subjects:** Metal finishing and allied sciences. **Holdings:** 1600 books; 200 bound periodical volumes. **Subscriptions:** 70 journals and other serials. **Services:** Interlibrary loan; library not open to the public.

★10789★
OMNIGRAPHICS, INC. - LIBRARY (Bus-Fin)
2500 Penobscot Bldg. Phone: (313)961-1340
Detroit, MI 48226 Annie Brewer, Libn.
Founded: 1987. **Staff:** Prof 1. **Subjects:** Business reference. **Holdings:** 500 volumes. **Subscriptions:** 250 journals and other serials. **Services:** Library not open to the public. **Computerized Information Services:** Access to DIALOG Information Services, WILSONLINE, InfoTrac, CompuServe, Inc., Public Affairs Information Service (PAIS). **Remarks:** Fax: (313)961-1383.

★10790★
OMNIPLEX SCIENCE MUSEUM - LIBRARY (Biol Sci)
2100 N.E. 52nd St. Phone: (405)424-5545
Oklahoma City, OK 73111 Beth Bussey, Educ.Dir.
Founded: 1978. **Subjects:** Life and physical sciences, curriculum aids. **Holdings:** 500 books. **Services:** Copying; library open to the public with restrictions.

★10791★
ON-LINE SOFTWARE INTERNATIONAL - LIBRARY (Comp Sci)
Fort Lee Executive Park
2 Executive Dr. Phone: (201)592-0009
Fort Lee, NJ 07024 Pearl Hutchins, Libn.
Staff: Prof 1. **Subjects:** Software, computers. **Holdings:** 250 books; 200 tapes; periodicals; guides; directories; meetings reports; IBM training manuals. **Subscriptions:** 120 journals and other serials; 30 newspapers. **Services:** Library open to guests of the company. **Automated Operations:** Computerized cataloging. **Publications:** OSI News Bits (newsletter) - for internal distribution only.

★10792★
ONAN CORPORATION - LIBRARY INFORMATION SERVICE (Sci-Engr)
1400 73rd Ave., N.E. Phone: (612)574-5000
Minneapolis, MN 55432 Catherine Glick Nelson, Lib.Mgr.
Founded: 1978. **Staff:** Prof 1; Other 1. **Subjects:** Electric generators, gasoline and diesel engines, automotive engineering, control systems. **Holdings:** 2000 books; 15,000 technical reports; 8000 standards. **Subscriptions:** 200 journals and other serials. **Services:** Interlibrary loan; copying; SDI. **Computerized Information Services:** DIALOG Information Services. **Networks/Consortia:** Member of Metronet.

★10793★
ONE, INC. - BLANCHE M. BAKER MEMORIAL LIBRARY (Soc Sci)
3340 Country Club Dr. Phone: (213)735-5252
Los Angeles, CA 90019 James K. Morrow, Lib.Dir.
Founded: 1953. **Subjects:** Homosexuality, homophile movement, gay liberation movement, gay and lesbian literature, women's and lesbian studies. **Holdings:** 15,000 titles; 60 VF drawers of other cataloged items; archival collections of many organizations; personal papers; foreign language periodicals. **Subscriptions:** 200 journals; 46 newspapers. **Services:** Library open to qualified scholars by appointment only.

ONEIDA COUNTY COMPREHENSIVE PLANNING PROGRAM
See: Herkimer-Oneida Counties Comprehensive Planning Program (6256)

★10794★
ONEIDA COUNTY HISTORICAL SOCIETY - LIBRARY (Hist)
318 Genesee St. Phone: (315)735-3642
Utica, NY 13502 Douglas M. Preston, Dir.
Founded: 1876. **Staff:** Prof 3; Other 8. **Subjects:** History - Oneida County, Utica, Mohawk Valley. **Holdings:** 1500 volumes; 2500 pamphlets; 250,000 manuscript pieces. **Subscriptions:** 10 journals and other serials. **Services:** Copying; library open to the public. **Special Catalogs:** Catalog of manuscripts (book). **Staff:** Betty Carpenter, Libn.; Francis W. Cunningham, Mss.Cat..

★10795★
EUGENE O'NEILL MEMORIAL THEATER CENTER, INC. - MONTE CRISTO COTTAGE LIBRARY (Theater)
325 Pequot Ave. Phone: (203)443-0051
New London, CT 06320 Sally Thomas Pavetti, Cur.
Founded: 1967. **Staff:** Prof 2. **Subjects:** Drama, dramatic literature, costume design, theater memorabilia. **Special Collections:** Johnson Briscoe Drama Collection; Virginia Dean Collection; Harold Friedlander Playbill Collection; Eugene O'Neill letters to Edward R. Keefe and Charles O'Brien Kennedy; O'Neill Theater Center National Playwrights Conference Scripts, 1966-1987; original letters; Pulitzer Prizes and Drama Circle Awards of Tennessee Williams and William Inge; original manuscript material from playwrights Frank Gagliano, Ron Cowen, Paul Foster, Israel Horovitz; Frederick Adler Collection of color movie window cards; Audrey Wood-William Liebling Collection of theater memorabilia. **Holdings:** 5000 books; playbills; theater scrapbooks; photographic stills; manuscripts; letters; set and costume designs; television manuscripts; clipping files; periodicals. **Services:** Copying; library open to the public. **Staff:** Lois E. McDonald, Assoc.Cur..

★10796★
ONGWANADA HOSPITAL - LIBRARY (Med)
117 Park St. Phone: (613)544-9611
Kingston, ON, Canada K7L 1J9 Rhoda McFarlane, Supv., Clin.Rec.
Founded: 1977. **Staff:** Prof 1; Other 1. **Subjects:** Mental retardation. **Holdings:** 750 books; 1 VF drawer of reprints; 95 AV programs; 1 film; 5 pieces of training equipment. **Subscriptions:** 23 journals and other serials. **Services:** Interlibrary loan; copying; library open to the public.

ONLINE COMPUTER LIBRARY CENTER, INC.
See: OCLC, Inc. (10632)

★10797★
ONONDAGA COUNTY PUBLIC LIBRARY - LOCAL HISTORY AND SPECIAL COLLECTIONS (Hist)
Galleries of Syracuse
451 S. Salina St. Phone: (315)473-2701
Syracuse, NY 13202-2417 Patricia F. Finley, Dept.Hd.
Founded: 1852. **Staff:** Prof 4; Other 2. **Subjects:** Genealogy; history - Syracuse, Onondaga County, northeastern U.S. **Holdings:** 37,000 volumes; 40 VF drawers of pamphlets and clippings; 4 VF drawers of genealogical notes; 360 maps; 7500 reels of microfilm. **Subscriptions:** 100 journals and

other serials. **Services:** Copying; collections open to the public. **Automated Operations:** Computerized cataloging, acquisitions, and serials. **Special Indexes:** Onondaga County Pioneer Index (8 catalog drawers).

★10798★
ONONDAGA HISTORICAL ASSOCIATION - LIBRARY (Hist)
311 Montgomery St. Phone: (315)428-1862
Syracuse, NY 13202 Anthony G. King, Exec.Dir.
Founded: 1862. **Staff:** Prof 3. **Subjects:** Local and regional history, New York State canals. **Holdings:** 4000 books; 100,000 photographs; 1000 cubic feet of archival materials. **Services:** Library not open to the public. **Staff:** Suzanne Etherington, Archv.; Edward Lyon, Libn..

ONTARIO AGRICULTURAL MUSEUM
See: Ontario Ministry of Agriculture and Food (10822)

★10799★
THE ONTARIO ARCHAEOLOGICAL SOCIETY - LIBRARY (Soc Sci)
P.O. Box 241, Sta. P
Toronto, ON, Canada M5S 2S8 Charles Garrad, Soc.Adm.
Staff: 1. **Subjects:** Archeology of Ontario, anthropology. **Holdings:** Reports; manuscripts. **Subscriptions:** 10 journals and other serials. **Services:** Copying; library open to the public with restrictions.

★10800★
ONTARIO ARCHIVES OF ONTARIO - LIBRARY (Hist)
Ministry of Culture & Communications
77 Grenville St. Phone: (416)965-4030
Toronto, ON, Canada M7A 2R9 Ethelyn Harlow, Libn.
Founded: 1903. **Staff:** Prof 1; Other 1. **Subjects:** Ontario social, political, military history; archival methodology; government records management. **Special Collections:** County and municipal directories; published minutes of Ontario municipalities; British Army Lists (60 volumes); historical atlases. **Holdings:** 6200 volumes; 13,000 pamphlets; 400 reels of microfilm; 3500 microfiche; 5500 Ontario government publications; 6500 municipal documents. **Subscriptions:** 85 journals and other serials. **Services:** Library open to the public with restrictions. **Special Catalogs:** Separate author, title, and subject card file for pamphlets received prior to 1968. **Staff:** Ian E. Wilson, Archv. of Ontario.

★10801★
ONTARIO BIBLE COLLEGE/ONTARIO THEOLOGICAL SEMINARY - J. WILLIAM HORSEY LIBRARY (Rel-Phil)
25 Ballyconnor Court Phone: (416)226-6380
Willowdale, ON, Canada M2M 4B3 James R. Johnson, Libn.
Staff: Prof 2; Other 7. **Subjects:** Biblical studies, theology, pastoral studies, Christian education, missions. **Holdings:** 39,000 books; 834 volumes in microform; 3900 AV programs. **Subscriptions:** 800 journals and other serials. **Services:** Interlibrary loan; copying; library open to the public with membership fee for borrowing privileges. **Staff:** Miss C. Church, Supv., Tech.Serv.; Mrs. M. Ford, Supv., Pub.Serv.; Mrs. E. Penner, Supv., Acq..

★10802★
ONTARIO CANCER FOUNDATION - HAMILTON REGIONAL CENTRE - LIBRARY (Med)
711 Concession St. Phone: (416)387-9495
Hamilton, ON, Canada L8V 1C3 Anne Devries, Libn.
Staff: Prof 1. **Subjects:** Cancer, medical physics. **Holdings:** 1000 books; 1000 bound periodical volumes. **Subscriptions:** 46 journals and other serials. **Services:** Interlibrary loan; copying. **Computerized Information Services:** MEDLARS. **Networks/Consortia:** Member of Hamilton/Wentworth District Health Library Network.

★10803★
ONTARIO CANCER INSTITUTE - LIBRARY (Med)
500 Sherbourne St. Phone: (416)926-4482
Toronto, ON, Canada M4X 1K9 Carol A. Morrison, Libn.
Founded: 1957. **Staff:** Prof 1; Other 3. **Subjects:** Cancer, cytology, hematology, immunology, radiotherapy, biophysics. **Holdings:** 7000 books; 10,000 bound periodical volumes; pamphlets. **Subscriptions:** 375 journals and other serials. **Services:** Interlibrary loan; library not open to the public. **Computerized Information Services:** MEDLARS, DIALOG Information Services.

★10804★
ONTARIO CHORAL FEDERATION - LIBRARY (Mus)
Maison Chalmers House
20 St. Joseph St. Phone: (416)925-5525
Toronto, ON, Canada M4Y 1J9 Norah Bolton, Exec.Adm.
Staff: 1. **Subjects:** Choral music. **Holdings:** Figures not available. **Services:** Library open to members. **Publications:** Newsletter, quarterly. **Remarks:** An alternate telephone number is 925-5526.

★10805★
ONTARIO COLLEGE OF ART - DOROTHY H. HOOVER LIBRARY (Art)
100 McCaul St. Phone: (416)977-5311
Toronto, ON, Canada M5T 1W1 Ian Carrharris, Dir.
Founded: 1930. **Staff:** Prof 8; Other 4. **Subjects:** Visual arts. **Holdings:** 19,340 books; 200 bound periodical volumes; 51,000 slides; 318 video cassettes; 32,700 items in picture file; 32 VF drawers of information file. **Subscriptions:** 250 journals and other serials. **Services:** Interlibrary loan; copying; AV production; library open to the public with restrictions on borrowing. **Staff:** Richard Milburn, Hd., Pub.Serv.; Diana Myers, Hd., Tech.Serv.; Angelo Rao, Hd., AV Serv..

★10806★
ONTARIO COUNTY HISTORICAL SOCIETY, INC. - ARCHIVES (Hist)
55 N. Main St. Phone: (716)394-4975
Canandaigua, NY 14424 Christopher Clarke-Hazlett, Ph.D., Dir.
Founded: 1902. **Staff:** Prof 4; Other 3. **Subjects:** New York early land dealings, Civil War, history of western New York. **Special Collections:** Oliver Phelps; Oliver L. Phelps; Granger family papers (collection on western New York landholding); Hyland Kirk Collection; Jasper Parrish; Judge Smith papers; John J. Handrahan plans and drawings (landscape architecture, civil engineering). **Holdings:** 3000 books; bound Ontario County newspapers, 1803-1968; 500 maps; 40,000 manuscripts; 250 volumes in Manchester Library Collection; 5000 pieces of ephemera. **Services:** Copying; archives open to the public for use on premises with staff assistance.

★10807★
ONTARIO CRAFTS COUNCIL - CRAFT RESOURCE CENTRE (Art)
346 Dundas St., W. Phone: (416)977-3551
Toronto, ON, Canada M5T 1G5 Ted Rickard, Mgr.
Founded: 1975. **Staff:** Prof 1; Other 1. **Subjects:** All aspects of craft media. **Special Collections:** Archives (provincial, local craft guilds, prominent individuals; vertical file); health hazards in arts and crafts (files; books). **Holdings:** 600 books; 200 bound periodical volumes; 400 portfolios of practicing craftsmen; 250 exhibition catalogs; slide rental/sales programs. **Subscriptions:** 140 journals and other serials. **Services:** Copying; consulting; center open to the public. **Publications:** Annual Craft Fairs in Ontario; Directory of Suppliers of Craft Materials; Ontario Craft; Craft News - to members; list of craft guides and directories for sale. **Special Indexes:** Indexes to publications of the Ontario Crafts Council; card file of Ontario craftspeople. **Staff:** Sandra Dunn, Info.Serv.Off..

★10808★
ONTARIO ENERGY BOARD - LIBRARY (Energy)
14 Carlton St., 8th Fl. Phone: (416)598-4000
Toronto, ON, Canada M5B 1J2 Lina Buccilli, Libn.
Staff: Prof 1. **Subjects:** Energy regulation, natural gas, electricity, gas pipelines, energy rates and pricing, energy economics. **Holdings:** 3000 books; decisions and reports. **Subscriptions:** 165 journals and other serials. **Services:** Interlibrary loan; copying; library open to the public by appointment for reference use only. **Computerized Information Services:** DIALOG Information Services, Info Globe, QL Systems, Infomart, CAN/OLE. **Publications:** Update, irregular.

★10809★
ONTARIO FEDERATION OF LABOUR - RESOURCE CENTRE (Bus-Fin)
15 Gervais Dr., Suite 202 Phone: (416)441-2731
Don Mills, ON, Canada M3C 1Y8 Dr. Jo Surich, Res.Coord.
Founded: 1969. **Staff:** Prof 1. **Subjects:** Labor relations, economic development, labor in politics, labor history. **Special Collections:** OFL Archives. **Holdings:** 800 books; 500 bound periodical volumes. **Subscriptions:** 50 journals and other serials. **Services:** Copying; center open to the public. **Computerized Information Services:** CANSIM. **Publications:** Talking Points: Recent Economic, Social and Political Data, biweekly - for internal distribution only.

★10810★
ONTARIO FILM INSTITUTE - LIBRARY & INFORMATION CENTRE (Theater)
770 Don Mills Rd. Phone: (416)429-4100
Don Mills, ON, Canada M3C 1T3 Sherie Brethour, Libn.
Founded: 1969. **Staff:** Prof 4. **Subjects:** All aspects of the cinema. **Special Collections:** Silent Film Music Selections for Piano (100). **Holdings:** 15,500 books; 900 bound periodical volumes; 100 unpublished screenplays; 4000 soundtracks of motion pictures; 200 BBC recordings on motion pictures; 500,000 files by subject, film title, and biography for all aspects of filmmaking and the industry; 4000 posters and photographs; 1000 video cassettes. **Subscriptions:** 100 journals and other serials; 15 newspapers. **Services:** Copying; library open to the public for reference use only. **Publications:** Film News, quarterly - free upon request. **Remarks:** Maintained by Ontario Science Centre.

★10811★
ONTARIO GENEALOGICAL SOCIETY - LIBRARY (Hist)
c/o Canadiana Collection, North York Public Library

North York Centre, 6th Fl.
5120 Yonge St.
Toronto, ON, Canada M2N 5N9 D. Grant Brown, Libn.
Founded: 1963. **Staff:** 2. **Subjects:** Genealogy and family history, heraldry, local history, biography. **Special Collections:** Cemetery Inscriptions Collection; Family Chart Collection; British County Record Offices Collection. **Holdings:** 2000 books; 45 bound periodical volumes; 1000 family histories. **Subscriptions:** 40 journals and other serials. **Services:** Interlibrary loan (limited); copying; library open to the public for reference use only. **Publications:** OGS Library Holdings (1984) - for sale. **Special Indexes:** Family Chart Collection List (printout); Inventory of Ontario Cemeteries (1987).

ONTARIO GEOLOGICAL SURVEY
See: Ontario Ministry of Northern Development & Mines (10850)

★10812★
ONTARIO HOSPITAL ASSOCIATION - LIBRARY (Bus-Fin)
150 Ferrand Dr. Phone: (416)429-2661
Don Mills, ON, Canada M3C 1H6 John Tagg, Supv.
Staff: Prof 1; Other 1. **Subjects:** Hospital administration, health economics, health insurance, management. **Holdings:** 1500 books. **Subscriptions:** 102 journals and other serials. **Services:** Interlibrary loan; copying; library open to the public for reference use only. **Computerized Information Services:** DIALOG Information Services, MEDLARS. Performs searches on fee basis. **Special Catalogs:** Audiovisuals Catalogue, annual.

★10813★
ONTARIO HYDRO - LIBRARY (Energy, Sci-Engr)
700 University Ave. Phone: (416)592-2719
Toronto, ON, Canada M5G 1X6 M.D. Taylor, Chf.Libn.
Founded: 1916. **Staff:** Prof 15; Other 17. **Subjects:** Electrical engineering, nuclear engineering, electric utilities, management. **Special Collections:** Company reports and documents. **Holdings:** 85,000 volumes; 500,000 reports; microfiche. **Subscriptions:** 1100 journals and other serials. **Services:** Interlibrary loan; copying; SDI; library open to the public in Public Reference Center. **Automated Operations:** Computerized cataloging, acquisitions, and serials routing. **Computerized Information Services:** DIALOG Information Services, Pergamon ORBIT InfoLine, Inc., QL Systems, CAN/OLE, UTLAS, BRS Information Technologies, MEDLARS, WESTLAW, Info Globe, Telesystemes Questel; internal databases; UTLAS, CAN/OLE (electronic mail services). **Publications:** Library bulletin; acquisitions list, monthly; brochure. **Remarks:** Holdings include the Research Division Branch Library, the Atrium Building Branch Library, and the Public Reference Center Consulting Services. **Staff:** Anita Chui, Info.Rsrcs.Supv.; Sylvia Ernesaks, Sr.Libn.; Lorna Bernard, Libn.; Deborah Pazzano, Sr.Libn.; Tran Dam, Info.Rsrcs.Supv.; Kim Cornell, Sr.Libn.; Chris Robinson, Info.Rsrcs.Supv.; Martha Courtright, Libn.; Nancy Fish, Libn.; Richard Toase, Libn.; Carol Elder, Libn.; Jiun Lee, Jr.Libn.; Ingrid Kalnins, Jr.Libn.; Martha Ghent, Libn.; Karen McClymont, Jr.Libn..

★10814★
ONTARIO INSTITUTE FOR STUDIES IN EDUCATION (OISE) - MODERN LANGUAGE CENTRE - LANGUAGE TEACHING LIBRARY (Hum)
252 Bloor St., W. Phone: (416)923-6641
Toronto, ON, Canada M5S 1V6 Alice Weinrib, Res.Assoc./Libn.
Staff: Prof 1; Other 1. **Subjects:** French as a second langauge, English as a second language, theory and methodology of second language teaching, Spanish, German. **Special Collections:** Language curricula resources for the classroom. **Holdings:** 11,000 books; 200 bound periodical volumes; 2750 tapes; 60 language tests; 3500 documents; 110 charts and visuals; 70 filmstrip and slide programs. **Subscriptions:** 50 journals and other serials. **Services:** Copying; library open to the public with restrictions. **Computerized Information Services:** Internal database.

★10815★
ONTARIO INSTITUTE FOR STUDIES IN EDUCATION (OISE) - R.W.B. JACKSON LIBRARY (Educ)
252 Bloor St., W. Phone: (416)923-6641
Toronto, ON, Canada M5S 1V6 Grace F. Bulaong, Chf.Libn.
Staff: Prof 18; Other 26. **Subjects:** Education, psychology, sociology, statistical methodology, linguistics, history, philosophy, computer applications, economics, demography. **Special Collections:** Ontario History of Education Collection (20,000 volumes); Paulo Freire Resource Collection (books and reprints); test collection (3275). **Holdings:** 227,463 books; 23,716 bound periodical volumes; 406,143 microforms; 15,589 films, audio- and videotapes, kits, games, other multimedia resources; 72 linear feet of curriculum guides, curriculum publisher and AV distributor catalogs; 1000 computer disks and tapes. **Subscriptions:** 4436 journals and other serials. **Services:** Interlibrary loan; copying; library open to the public. **Automated Operations:** Computerized cataloging and acquisitions. **Computerized Information Services:** BRS Information Technologies, DIALOG Information Services, ERIC, UTLAS; internal database. Performs searches on fee basis. Contact Person: Don Kinder, 926-4718. **Publications:** Bibliographies. **Special Catalogs:** Catalog of Ontario Textbook Collection (microfiche); Theses Catalog (microfiche). **Special Indexes:** Index to the Paulo Freire Resource Collection (typed list); Index to the Test Collection (card). **Staff:** Ann Neveu, Adm.Off.; Ilze Bregzis, Libn., Tech.Serv.; Jan Schmidt, Libn., Pub.Serv.; Carol Calder, AV Libn.; Mary Campbell, Automation Libn.; Ruth Marks, Curric.Rsrcs.; Valerie Rudkin, Acq.Libn.; Kamlesh Sharma, Supv., Circ..

★10816★
ONTARIO INSTITUTE FOR STUDIES IN EDUCATION (OISE) - WOMEN'S EDUCATIONAL RESOURCES CENTRE (Soc Sci)
252 Bloor St., W., Rm. 6-195 Phone: (416)923-6641
Toronto, ON, Canada M5S 1V6 Frieda Forman, Coord.
Founded: 1976. **Staff:** Prof 2. **Subjects:** Women's studies and issues, children's literature. **Special Collections:** Works of Canadian women authors. **Holdings:** 3200 books; newspaper clipping file; curriculum materials; photographs; AV programs; archival material; vertical files; government reports. **Subscriptions:** 1000 journals and other serials. **Services:** Copying; center open to the public with restrictions. **Special Indexes:** Index of periodical articles. **Staff:** Peggy Bristow, Res.Off..

ONTARIO LABOUR RELATIONS BOARD
See: Ontario Ministry of Labour (10844)

★10817★
ONTARIO LEGISLATIVE ASSEMBLY - LEGISLATIVE LIBRARY (Law, Hist)
Legislative Bldg., Queen's Park Phone: (416)965-4545
Toronto, ON, Canada M7A 1A2 R. Brian Land, Exec.Dir.
Founded: 1867. **Staff:** Prof 43; Other 48. **Subjects:** Political science, especially parliamentary systems; law; public administration and policy; economics; Ontario and Canadian history. **Special Collections:** Full depository for Ontario, Quebec, Canadian government publications; government publications from other provinces, British Parliament, U.S. Congress; U.S. Congressional Information Service, 1970 to present, on microfiche; Microlog and Insider Services on microfiche from Micromedia Limited; Ontario current daily and weekly newspapers; Canadian and British statutes and law reports; Ambler Pricing Service (weekly product prices of five major food chains). **Holdings:** 83,911 books; 6987 bound periodical volumes; 695,966 microfiche; 7556 reels of microfilm; 2687 current data files; 870 videotapes; 75 audio cassettes. **Subscriptions:** 2443 journals and other serials; 298 newspapers. **Services:** Interlibrary loan; copying; library open to the public with restrictions. **Automated Operations:** Computerized cataloging and acquisitions. **Computerized Information Services:** DIALOG Information Services, Pergamon ORBIT InfoLine, Inc., QL Systems, Info Globe, CAN/LAW, Infomart, The

Financial Post Information Service, MEDLINE, Yorkline, CAN/OLE, WESTLAW, BRS Information Technologies, Telichart, LEXIS, NEXIS, VU/TEXT Information Services; internal database. **Networks/Consortia:** Member of Ontario Government Libraries' Council (OGLC). **Publications:** Annual Report of the Executive Director; Features, irregular; Memo to Members, irregular; Periodical Contents, weekly during session; Periodical Selections, monthly; Selected New Titles, monthly; Press Highlights, irregular; Services to the Legislature; Automation Alert, biweekly; Status of Bills Report, weekly during session; Toronto Press Today, daily; Current Issue Papers and Information Kits. **Special Catalogs:** Ontario Government Publications Monthly Checklist (book); Ontario Government Publications Annual Catalogue (book). **Staff:** Wyley L. Powell, Exec.Asst.; Mary E. Dickerson, Dp.Exec.Dir.; Pamela Stoksik, Hd., Tech.Serv. & Sys.; J. Robert Johnson, Mgr., Clipping Serv.; Linda L. Reid, Mgr., Checklist & Cat.Serv.; Cynthia S. Smith, Chf., Leg.Res.Serv.; Thora K. Clarkson, Hd., Coll.Dev..

★10818★
ONTARIO LOTTERY CORPORATION - LIBRARY (Rec)
2 Bloor St., W., 24th Fl. Phone: (416)961-6262
Toronto, ON, Canada M4W 3H8
Suzanne Kemper, Coord.Commun.Rsrcs.
Founded: 1978. **Staff:** Prof 1; Other 1. **Subjects:** Lotteries, casinos, off-track betting, gaming and gambling, public relations, draws, community relations. **Holdings:** 50 books; draw cassettes; gaming reports; casino studies; marketing assessments; rules and regulations for social gaming. **Subscriptions:** 14 journals and other serials. **Services:** Library not open to the public.

★10819★
ONTARIO MEDICAL ASSOCIATION - LIBRARY (Med)
250 Bloor St., E., Suite 600 Phone: (416)963-9383
Toronto, ON, Canada M4W 3P8 Jan Greenwood, Mgr. of Lib.Serv.
Founded: 1972. **Staff:** Prof 1; Other 2. **Subjects:** Canadian medical economics, medico-legal practices and sociomedical affairs, hospital library service. **Special Collections:** Medical office management; reference collection for hospital library consulting service. **Holdings:** 2000 books. **Subscriptions:** 250 journals and other serials. **Services:** Interlibrary loan; copying; library open to the public by appointment. **Automated Operations:** Computerized cataloging and serials. **Computerized Information Services:** MEDLARS; internal database; Envoy 100 (electronic mail service). **Networks/Consortia:** Member of Ontario Hospital Libraries Association (OHLA). **Publications:** Health Sciences Library Manual, 1982; Medical Office Management Bibliography, annual. **Special Indexes:** Ontario Medical Review Index. **Remarks:** Operating under a grant from the PSI Foundation for its collection in Canadian medical economics, the library also provides a consulting service for Ontario hospital libraries.

★10820★
ONTARIO MINISTRY OF AGRICULTURE AND FOOD - HORTICULTURAL RESEARCH INSTITUTE OF ONTARIO - LIBRARY (Agri)
Vineland Station, ON, Canada L0R 2E0 Phone: (416)562-4141
Judith Wanner, Libn.
Staff: Prof 1. **Subjects:** Fruit and vegetable crops, ornamental plants, botany, food science, winemaking, viticulture. **Holdings:** 2000 books; 1500 bound periodical volumes; 2000 pamphlets; annual reports; documents; agricultural statistics. **Subscriptions:** 254 journals and other serials; 6 newspapers. **Services:** Interlibrary loan; copying; library open to the public for reference use only. **Computerized Information Services:** CAN/OLE, DIALOG Information Services. **Publications:** Annual Book Acquisitions List, quarterly - for internal distribution only.

★10821★
ONTARIO MINISTRY OF AGRICULTURE AND FOOD - LIBRARY (Agri)
801 Bay St., 3rd Fl. Phone: (416)965-1816
Toronto, ON, Canada M7A 2B2 Mindy Ginsler, Mgr., Lib.Serv.
Founded: 1969. **Staff:** Prof 3; Other 3. **Subjects:** Agricultural economics, land use, rural agricultural statistics, Ontario and Canadian agriculture, food industry and trade, agriculture and energy, animal husbandry. **Holdings:** 15,000 books; 2500 microfiche. **Subscriptions:** 500 journals and other serials. **Services:** Interlibrary loan; copying; library open to the public for reference use only. **Automated Operations:** Computerized cataloging, acquisitions, serials, and circulation. **Computerized Information Services:** DIALOG Information Services, Info Globe, CAN/OLE, Infomart; SYDNEY (internal database). **Networks/Consortia:** Member of Ontario Government Libraries' Council (OGLC). **Publications:** New Publications, bimonthly - to staff and other interested libraries. **Staff:** Robyn Zuck, Cat.; Donald R. Krueger, Sr.Ref.Libn..

ONTARIO MINISTRY OF AGRICULTURE AND FOOD - NEW LISKEARD COLLEGE OF AGRICULTURAL TECHNOLOGY
See: New Liskeard College of Agricultural Technology (9974)

★10822★
ONTARIO MINISTRY OF AGRICULTURE AND FOOD - ONTARIO AGRICULTURAL MUSEUM - LIBRARY/ ARCHIVES (Agri)
Box 38 Phone: (416)878-8151
Milton, ON, Canada L9T 2X9 Susan Bennett, Res. & Ref.Libn.
Founded: 1974. **Staff:** Prof 4. **Subjects:** Ontario history - agricultural, local, social, political, economic; poultry and animal husbandry; horticulture; botany. **Special Collections:** Agricultural Implement Catalogue Collection (20,000). **Holdings:** 10,000 books; 300 films; 250 reels of microfilm; 25 videotapes; 5000 historical agricultural periodicals; 200 maps and charts; 2000 government publications; 40,000 photographs and negatives; 2000 U.S. patent records; 300 reels of microfilm. **Subscriptions:** 45 journals and other serials. **Services:** Interlibrary loan; copying; library open to the public for reference use only. **Publications:** Occasional Papers, biennial. **Special Indexes:** Subject Index to Government Documents, Monographs, and Periodical Collection; Implement/Manufacturer Index to Agricultural Machinery Collection. **Staff:** Lynn Campbell, Hist.Res..

ONTARIO MINISTRY OF AGRICULTURE AND FOOD - RIDGETOWN COLLEGE OF AGRICULTURAL TECHNOLOGY
See: Ridgetown College of Agricultural Technology (12058)

★10823★
ONTARIO MINISTRY OF AGRICULTURE AND FOOD - VETERINARY SERVICES LABORATORY LIBRARY (Med)
P.O. Box 2005 Phone: (613)258-3804
Kemptville, ON, Canada K0G 1J0 Dr. Peter Lusis, Lab.Hd.
Founded: 1948. **Subjects:** Veterinary medicine, pathology, animal science. **Holdings:** Figures not available. **Subscriptions:** 31 journals and other serials. **Services:** Interlibrary loan; copying; library open to veterinarians only.

★10824★
ONTARIO MINISTRY OF AGRICULTURE AND FOOD - VETERINARY SERVICES LABORATORY LIBRARY (Med)
Box 790 Phone: (705)647-6701
New Liskeard, ON, Canada P0J 1P0 J. Jolette, Lab.Hd.
Founded: 1961. **Subjects:** Veterinary medicine and pathology. **Holdings:** 200 books; 340 bound periodical volumes. **Subscriptions:** 25 journals and other serials; 10 newspapers. **Services:** Library open to veterinarians.

★10825★
ONTARIO MINISTRY OF THE ATTORNEY GENERAL - LIBRARY (Law)
18 King St., E., 12th Fl.
Toronto, ON, Canada M5C 1C5 Phone: (416)965-4714
Staff: Prof 1; Other 2. **Subjects:** Law - criminal, civil, constitutional. **Special Collections:** English reports (178 volumes); Law Reports (including Appeal Cases, Chancery Division, Probate Division, Queen's Bench, King's Bench: 1000 volumes); All England Law Reports (1500 volumes). **Holdings:** 1500 books; 12,000 bound periodical volumes. **Subscriptions:** 100 journals and other serials. **Services:** Interlibrary loan; library not open to the public. **Computerized Information Services:** QL Systems, WESTLAW.

ONTARIO MINISTRY OF CITIZENSHIP AND CULTURE
See: Ontario Ministry of Culture and Communications (10831)

ONTARIO MINISTRY OF COMMUNITY AND SOCIAL SERVICES - HURONIA REGIONAL CENTRE
See: Huronia Regional Centre (6620)

★10826★
ONTARIO MINISTRY OF COMMUNITY AND SOCIAL SERVICES - LIBRARY AND LEARNING RESOURCES (Soc Sci)
880 Bay St., 5th Fl. Phone: (416)965-2300
Toronto, ON, Canada M7A 1E9 Kenneth Sundquist, Mgr., Lib.Serv.
Founded: 1968. **Staff:** Prof 1; Other 4. **Subjects:** Adolescence, adoption, aged, public welfare, developmentally disabled, child abuse, child welfare, physically handicapped, rehabilitation, social problems, social work, juvenile delinquency. **Holdings:** 35,000 books; 1000 bound periodical volumes; 500 reels of microfilm; 16,000 microfiche; 200 audio cassettes; 50 video cassettes; 1500 reprints; 12 VF drawers of journal articles, pamphlets,

computer searches. **Subscriptions:** 450 journals and newsletters. **Services:** Interlibrary loan; copying; library open to the public for reference use only. **Automated Operations:** Computerized cataloging, acquisitions, serials, and circulation. **Computerized Information Services:** DIALOG Information Services, BRS Information Technologies, QL Systems, Info Globe, Infomart, WESTLAW, UTLAS; SYDNEY (internal database); Envoy 100 (electronic mail service). **Networks/Consortia:** Member of Ontario Government Libraries' Council (OGLC). **Publications:** Infocom bulletin (acquisitions list), 3/year; Infocom articles (online), 3/year - both to ministry personnel, affiliated agencies, and government libraries.

ONTARIO MINISTRY OF COMMUNITY AND SOCIAL SERVICES - PRINCE EDWARD HEIGHTS - RESIDENT RECORDS LIBRARY
See: Prince Edward Heights - Resident Records Library (11554)

★10827★
ONTARIO MINISTRY OF COMMUNITY AND SOCIAL SERVICES - RESOURCE LIBRARY (Med)
Highway 59N
P.O. Box 310 Phone: (519)539-1251
Woodstock, ON, Canada N4S 7X9 Rita Thompson, Libn.
Staff: Prof 1. **Subjects:** Mental retardation, epilepsy, tuberculosis. **Holdings:** 1817 books; 403 films, tapes, cassettes. **Subscriptions:** 69 journals and other serials. **Services:** Interlibrary loan; copying; library open to the public with restrictions. **Publications:** Bibliotheca Medica Canadiana, quarterly - to members.

★10828★
ONTARIO MINISTRY OF COMMUNITY AND SOCIAL SERVICES - RIDEAU REGIONAL CENTRE - STAFF LIBRARY & INFORMATION CENTRE (Med)
P.O. Box 2000 Phone: (613)283-5533
Smiths Falls, ON, Canada K7A 4T7 Pat Kiteley, Lib.Techn.
Founded: 1977. **Staff:** Prof 1. **Subjects:** Mental retardation, psychology, social work, medicine. **Holdings:** 4000 books. **Subscriptions:** 127 journals and other serials. **Services:** Interlibrary loan; library open to the public with restrictions. **Publications:** VOX and RefeRenCe (newsletter) - for internal distribution only.

ONTARIO MINISTRY OF COMMUNITY AND SOCIAL SERVICES - THISTLETOWN REGIONAL CENTRE
See: Thistletown Regional Centre (14156)

★10829★
ONTARIO MINISTRY OF CONSUMER AND COMMERCIAL RELATIONS - CONSUMER INFORMATION CENTRE (Bus-Fin)
555 Yonge St., 1st Fl. Phone: (416)963-0200
Toronto, ON, Canada M7A 2H6 Ted Brathwaite, Mgr.
Founded: 1978. **Staff:** 11. **Subjects:** Law; business; securities regulation; consumer information, education, protection; insurance. **Holdings:** 7000 books. **Subscriptions:** 150 journals and other serials. **Services:** Interlibrary loan; public inquiry in person, by phone, and mail; development of educational material; center open to the public for reference use only. **Publications:** New Resources, monthly. **Remarks:** In Ontario, the toll-free number is (800)268-1142; TTY/TTD (416)963-0808.

★10830★
ONTARIO MINISTRY OF CORRECTIONAL SERVICES - LIBRARY SERVICES (Law)
2001 Eglinton Ave., E. Phone: (416)750-3481
Toronto, ON, Canada M1L 4P1 T.J.B. Anderson, Chf.Libn.
Founded: 1958. **Staff:** Prof 2; Other 1. **Subjects:** Penology, criminology. **Holdings:** 3900 books; 50 feet of pamphlets and reports. **Subscriptions:** 150 journals and other serials. **Services:** Interlibrary loan; copying; SDI; library open to bona fide students by appointment. **Automated Operations:** Computerized cataloging and serials. **Computerized Information Services:** DIALOG Information Services. **Networks/Consortia:** Member of Ontario Government Libraries' Council (OGLC). **Publications:** Recent additions list, 3/year - for internal distribution only. **Staff:** Miss H.M. Chan, Libn..

ONTARIO MINISTRY OF CULTURE AND COMMUNICATIONS - ART GALLERY OF ONTARIO
See: Art Gallery of Ontario (957)

★10831★
ONTARIO MINISTRY OF CULTURE AND COMMUNICATIONS - LIBRARIES AND COMMUNITY INFORMATION (Info Sci)
77 Bloor St., W., 3rd Fl. Phone: (416)965-2696
Toronto, ON, Canada M7A 2R9 Wil Vanderelst, Dir.
Staff: 33. **Subjects:** Professional development in librarianship, public library statistics. **Remarks:** Administers Public Libraries Act, promotes public library and community information services, coordinates library services and provides financial aid to public libraries and information centers. Also administers Ontario Library Service. **Formerly:** Ontario Ministry of Citizenship and Culture. **Staff:** Bill Kenny, Mgr., Ontario Lib.Serv.; Brian Beattie, Mgr., Commun.Info.Serv.; Valerie Ridgway, Mgr., Pub.Lib.Serv..

★10832★
ONTARIO MINISTRY OF CULTURE AND COMMUNICATIONS - MAP LIBRARY (Geog-Map)
77 Grenville St. Phone: (416)965-4030
Toronto, ON, Canada M7A 2R9 John W. Fortier, Archv.
Founded: 1903. **Staff:** Prof 2. **Subjects:** Land survey, fire insurance, transportation, land tenure, topography, hydrography, geology. **Special Collections:** David Thompson maps (5 maps; 4 volumes); Simcoe maps (106); Canada Company maps (200 maps; 10 volumes); Talbot maps (3 volumes); fire insurance maps (10,000 sheets); survey records maps (3000). **Holdings:** 200 atlases; 33,000 maps. **Services:** Copying; library open to the public. **Formerly:** Ontario Ministry of Citizenship and Culture.

★10833★
ONTARIO MINISTRY OF CULTURE AND COMMUNICATIONS - MINISTRY OF TOURISM AND RECREATION - LIBRARY/ RESOURCE CENTRE (Rec)
77 Bloor St., W., 9th Fl. Phone: (416)965-6763
Toronto, ON, Canada M7A 2R9 Renata Grodski, Mgr.
Founded: 1975. **Staff:** Prof 1; Other 6. **Subjects:** Recreation and leisure, arts and crafts, sports and fitness, multiculturalism, intercultural communication, literacy, therapeutic recreation, native peoples. **Special Collections:** Drama Collection (1000 plays); English as a Second Language (2500 books); library science collection (1000 books); architectural conservation and preservation reports. **Holdings:** 35,000 books; 1000 unbound periodicals; 4000 pamphlets; 1500 AV programs; 10,000 slides. **Subscriptions:** 450 journals and other serials; 50 newspapers. **Services:** Interlibrary loan; SDI; library open to residents of the Province of Ontario only. **Computerized Information Services:** Online systems. Performs searches on fee basis. **Networks/Consortia:** Member of Ontario Government Libraries' Council (OGLC). **Publications:** New Resources, bimonthly; Resume, monthly - both for internal distribution only. **Special Catalogs:** Audio-Visual Catalogue, by subject (book). **Formerly:** Ontario Ministry of Citizenship and Culture.

★10834★
ONTARIO MINISTRY OF EDUCATION - EDUCATION CENTER LIBRARY (Educ)
199 Larch St., 7th Fl. Phone: (705)675-4427
Sudbury, ON, Canada P3E 5P9 George Whalen, Libn.
Founded: 1967. **Staff:** Prof 1; Other 2. **Subjects:** Education, psychology. **Holdings:** 40,000 books; 5000 unbound periodicals; 2000 microfiche. **Subscriptions:** 200 journals and other serials; 5 newspapers. **Services:** Interlibrary loan; copying.

★10835★
ONTARIO MINISTRY OF EDUCATION - INFORMATION CENTRE (Educ)
Mowat Block, 13th Fl.
Queen's Park Phone: (416)965-1451
Toronto, ON, Canada M7A 1L2 Patricia Grenier, Mgr.
Founded: 1979. **Staff:** Prof 12; Other 5. **Subjects:** Education theory and practice at all levels, apprenticeship training, business/management, systems. **Special Collections:** Multi-year plans for Ontario colleges of applied arts and technology; college and university calendars; briefs of Ontario Education Commissions. **Holdings:** 25,000 books; 22 drawers of microfiche; 45 VF drawers; federal and Ontario sessional papers. **Subscriptions:** 1200 journals and other serials; 7 newspapers. **Services:** Interlibrary loan; copying; SDI; center open to the public for reference use only. **Automated Operations:** Computerized cataloging and serials. **Computerized Information Services:** DIALOG Information Services, BRS Information Technologies, QL Systems, Info Globe, Ontario Education Resources Information System (ONTERIS), CAN/OLE, Telesystemes Questel, UTLAS, WILSONLINE. **Networks/Consortia:** Member of Ontario Government Libraries' Council (OGLC). **Publications:** Contents; InformEd (newsletter), monthly; New Books, monthly; Routing Journals,

irregular; Acronyms List, annual. **Staff:** Martin Ship, Supv., Ref./Res./ILL; Nancy Robinson, Supv., Acq. & Data Description.

★10836★
ONTARIO MINISTRY OF ENERGY - INFORMATION RESOURCE CENTRE (Energy)
56 Wellesley St., W., 12th Fl. Phone: (416)965-9175
Toronto, ON, Canada M7A 2B7 Diane Wenzel, Coord.
Staff: Prof 2; Other 3. **Subjects:** Energy policy, programs, and technologies. **Holdings:** 15,000 books. **Subscriptions:** 500 journals and other serials; 10 newspapers. **Services:** Interlibrary loan; copying; center open to the public by appointment. **Automated Operations:** Computerized cataloging. **Computerized Information Services:** DIALOG Information Services, Pergamon ORBIT InfoLine, Inc., QL Systems, Info Globe, Infomart, The Financial Post Information Service, CAN/OLE, STN International; internal databases. **Networks/Consortia:** Member of Ontario Government Libraries' Council (OGLC). **Publications:** What's New (newsletter), monthly - limited distribution; Quarterly Upcoming Conferences Bulletin.

★10837★
ONTARIO MINISTRY OF THE ENVIRONMENT - LIBRARY (Env-Cons, Sci-Engr)
135 St. Clair Ave., W., 1st Fl. Phone: (416)323-4350
Toronto, ON, Canada M4V 1P5 N.J. McIlroy, Libn.
Founded: 1960. **Staff:** Prof 2; Other 3. **Subjects:** Water pollution, water supply, solid waste, air, noise, engineering, biology, chemistry. **Holdings:** 35,000 books; 2000 bound periodical volumes; 40 VF drawers of reprints, government reports, documents; 60,000 microfiche. **Subscriptions:** 227 journals and other serials. **Services:** Interlibrary loan; library open to the public for reference use only. **Computerized Information Services:** Pergamon ORBIT InfoLine, Inc., QL Systems, CAN/OLE, DIALOG Information Services, MEDLINE. **Publications:** Acquisitions list, monthly. **Remarks:** Includes holdings of the Ministry of the Environment - Laboratory and Research Library.

★10838★
ONTARIO MINISTRY OF GOVERNMENT SERVICES - C.T.S.D. TECHNICAL REFERENCE LIBRARY (Comp Sci)
101 Bloor St., W., 10th Fl. Phone: (416)965-2965
Toronto, ON, Canada M5S 1P8 Joe L. Rees, Coord., Lib.Serv.
Founded: 1975. **Staff:** Prof 1. **Subjects:** Electronic data processing (EDP) technical and product reference. **Holdings:** 250 books; 70 government documents; 25 video reference journals. **Subscriptions:** 65 journals and other serials. **Services:** Library open to government personnel. **Publications:** What's New in the C.T.S.D. Technical Reference Library, monthly - to selected government offices.

★10839★
ONTARIO MINISTRY OF HEALTH - LIBRARY (Med)
15 Overlea Blvd., 7th Fl. Phone: (416)965-7881
Toronto, ON, Canada M4H 1A9 Veronica Brunka, Lib.Supv.
Founded: 1933. **Staff:** Prof 1; Other 5. **Subjects:** Public health, preventive medicine, health care services, hospital administration. **Holdings:** 8500 books; 25 VF drawers; 200 microfiche. **Subscriptions:** 1100 journals and other serials. **Services:** Interlibrary loan; library open to the public with restrictions. **Computerized Information Services:** MEDLARS, DIALOG Information Services, Info Globe. **Networks/Consortia:** Member of Ontario Government Libraries' Council (OGLC). **Publications:** Library Bulletin, bimonthly - to ministry personnel.

ONTARIO MINISTRY OF HEALTH - MENTAL HEALTH DIVISION - HAMILTON PSYCHIATRIC HOSPITAL
See: Hamilton Psychiatric Hospital (5983)

ONTARIO MINISTRY OF HEALTH - MENTAL HEALTH DIVISION - KINGSTON PSYCHIATRIC HOSPITAL
See: Kingston Psychiatric Hospital (7500)

ONTARIO MINISTRY OF HEALTH - MENTAL HEALTH DIVISION - LONDON PSYCHIATRIC HOSPITAL
See: London Psychiatric Hospital (7934)

ONTARIO MINISTRY OF HEALTH - MENTAL HEALTH DIVISION - ST. THOMAS PSYCHIATRIC HOSPITAL
See: St. Thomas Psychiatric Hospital (12679)

★10840★
ONTARIO MINISTRY OF HEALTH - PUBLIC HEALTH LABORATORIES - LIBRARY (Med)
Postal Terminal A, Box 9000 Phone: (416)248-3165
Toronto, ON, Canada M5W 1R5 Doris A. Standing, Libn.
Staff: Prof 1; Other 1. **Subjects:** Medical microbiology, medical laboratory technology. **Holdings:** 3500 volumes; 3 VF drawers of pamphlets. **Subscriptions:** 155 journals and other serials. **Services:** Interlibrary loan (limited); copying; library open to the public by special permission.

★10841★
ONTARIO MINISTRY OF HOUSING - LIBRARY (Plan)
2-777 Bay St. Phone: (416)585-6527
Toronto, ON, Canada M5G 2E5 Frank Szucs, Libn.
Founded: 1965. **Staff:** Prof 2; Other 2. **Subjects:** Housing, community planning, urban renewal, city planning, municipal government and finance. **Holdings:** 20,000 books; 12,500 microfiche. **Subscriptions:** 272 journals and other serials. **Services:** Interlibrary loan; copying; library open to the public for reference use only. **Computerized Information Services:** QL Systems, CAN/OLE, DIALOG Information Services, Info Globe, Canada Systems Group (CSG), DOBIS Canadian Online Library System, Infomart, The Financial Post Information Service. **Publications:** Library Bulletin, irregular - to ministry staff. **Special Indexes:** List of periodical literature. **Staff:** Jennifer Brezina, Asst.Libn..

★10842★
ONTARIO MINISTRY OF INDUSTRY, TRADE AND TECHNOLOGY - INFORMATION CENTRE (Bus-Fin)
Hearst Block
Queen's Park Phone: (416)965-3365
Toronto, ON, Canada M7A 2E1 Dee Phillips, Mgr.
Founded: 1946. **Staff:** Prof 2; Other 2. **Subjects:** Trade, industrial development, small business, technology, management. **Holdings:** 15,000 books. **Subscriptions:** 300 journals and other serials; 7 newspapers. **Services:** Interlibrary loan; copying; center open to the public for reference use only. **Automated Operations:** Computerized cataloging and serials. **Computerized Information Services:** Info Globe, DIALOG Information Services, CAN/OLE, QL Systems, Canadian Financial Database (C.F.D.), SUPPLYLINE, Infomart, Telesystemes Questel, Canada Systems Group (CSG), The Financial Post Information Service. **Publications:** Information Center News, monthly; Current Contents, monthly - limited distribution. **Staff:** Kaili Sermat-Harding, Mgr.; Nazlin Chagpar, Ref./Info.Spec.; Eva Woloszczuk, Cat./Info.Spec..

★10843★
ONTARIO MINISTRY OF LABOUR - LIBRARY AND INFORMATION SERVICES (Bus-Fin)
400 University Ave., 10th Fl. Phone: (416)965-1641
Toronto, ON, Canada M7A 1T7 Sandra A. Walsh, Mgr.
Founded: 1949. **Staff:** Prof 6; Other 10. **Subjects:** Labor relations, occupational health and safety, pay equity, employment, women, manpower. **Special Collections:** International Labor Organization materials. **Holdings:** 73,000 books; 1000 bound periodical volumes; 14,000 pamphlets; 412,500 microforms. **Subscriptions:** 1200 serials. **Services:** Interlibrary loan; copying; SDI; library open to the public. **Automated Operations:** Computerized cataloging, acquisitions, and serials. **Computerized Information Services:** Telesystemes Questel, BRS Information Technologies, Canadian Financial Database (C.F.D.), DIALOG Information Services, Pergamon ORBIT InfoLine, Inc., QL Systems, Infomart, MEDLINE, Info Globe, Occupational Health Services, Inc., CAN/OLE, UTLAS; internal databases; Envoy 100 (electronic mail service). **Networks/Consortia:** Member of Ontario Government Libraries' Council (OGLC). **Publications:** Library bulletins: Occupational Health and Safety; Labour Relations; bibliography series.

★10844★
ONTARIO MINISTRY OF LABOUR - ONTARIO LABOUR RELATIONS BOARD - LIBRARY (Law)
400 University Ave., 4th Fl. Phone: (416)965-0206
Toronto, ON, Canada M7A 1V4 Clare Lyons, Libn.
Founded: 1975. **Staff:** Prof 1; Other 2. **Subjects:** Labor law. **Holdings:** 900 books; 3600 bound periodical volumes; Ontario Labour Relations Board reports, 1944 to present; National Labour Relations Board publications, volume 1 to present. **Subscriptions:** 150 journals and other serials. **Services:** Interlibrary loan; copying; library open to the public. **Automated Operations:** Computerized cataloging. **Computerized Information Services:** QL Systems; internal database. **Special Indexes:** Index to Ontario Labour Relations Board reports (on microfiche).

★10845★
ONTARIO MINISTRY OF LABOUR - RESOURCE CENTRE FOR OCCUPATIONAL HEALTH & SAFETY (Med)
Lakehead University
Oliver Rd. Phone: (807)343-8128
Thunder Bay, ON, Canada P7B 5E1 Shann Brown, Info.Serv.Asst.
Staff: 1. **Subjects:** Hazardous substances, occupational health, toxicology, radiation, noise, health services. **Holdings:** 650 books; 1000 reprints in 4 VF drawers; 25 videotapes; 4 slide programs. **Subscriptions:** 51 journals and other serials. **Services:** Interlibrary loan; copying; center open to the public. **Computerized Information Services:** DIALOG Information Services, CAN/OLE; internal database. Performs searches on fee basis. Contact Person: Sharon Bottomley, Tech.Asst., 343-8001. **Publications:** Northern Ontario Occupational Hygiene Monitor, 3/year - to mailing list.

ONTARIO MINISTRY OF NATURAL RESOURCES - ALGONQUIN PARK MUSEUM
See: Algonquin Park Museum (279)

★10846★
ONTARIO MINISTRY OF NATURAL RESOURCES - GLENORA FISHERIES STATION - LIBRARY (Biol Sci)
Box 50 Phone: (613)476-2400
Maple, ON, Canada L0J 1E0 D.A. Hurley, Libn.
Founded: 1958. **Subjects:** Fisheries and aquatic sciences. **Holdings:** 600 volumes. **Services:** Library not open to the public.

★10847★
ONTARIO MINISTRY OF NATURAL RESOURCES - NATURAL RESOURCES LIBRARY (Rec, Biol Sci)
Whitney Block, Rm. 4540
Queen's Park Phone: (416)965-6319
Toronto, ON, Canada M7A 1W3 Sandra Louet, Mgr.
Founded: 1972. **Staff:** Prof 3; Other 1. **Subjects:** Forestry, ecology, parks and recreation, land use planning, fish and wildlife. **Holdings:** 80,000 books; 500 bound periodical volumes; 60,000 reprints and unpublished papers. **Subscriptions:** 300 journals and other serials. **Services:** Interlibrary loan; library open to the public by appointment for reference use only. **Automated Operations:** Computerized cataloging. **Computerized Information Services:** DIALOG Information Services, BASIS, QL Systems, Info Globe, CAN/OLE, Infomart; Envoy 100 (electronic mail service). **Staff:** Edna Nickie, Libn.; Marusia Borodacz, Libn..

★10848★
ONTARIO MINISTRY OF NATURAL RESOURCES - NATURAL RESOURCES LIBRARY - MAPLE (Biol Sci)
Southern Research Sta. Phone: (416)832-2761
Maple, ON, Canada L0J 1E0 Sandra Louet, Mgr.
Founded: 1942. **Staff:** Prof 1; Other 3. **Subjects:** Forestry, fisheries, wildlife. **Special Collections:** U.S. Forest Service and the U.S. Fish and Wildlife Service publications. **Holdings:** Figures not available. **Subscriptions:** 500 journals and other serials. **Services:** Interlibrary loan; copying; library open to the public with restrictions. **Computerized Information Services:** DIALOG Information Services, Pergamon ORBIT InfoLine, Inc., QL Systems. **Publications:** New Materials List, monthly - for internal distribution only.

★10849★
ONTARIO MINISTRY OF NORTHERN DEVELOPMENT & MINES - LIBRARY, RECORDS AND SERVICES (Area-Ethnic)
10 Wellesley St., E., 8th Fl.
Toronto, ON, Canada M4Y 1G2 Phone: (416)965-1417
Founded: 1978. **Staff:** 2. **Subjects:** Northern Ontario - socioeconomic development, natural resources, community and regional planning, history, culture. **Special Collections:** Ministry Reading Room; Northern Ontario newspapers; college and university calendars for Northern Ontario. **Holdings:** 3000 books and reports; 4 VF drawers of Northern Ontario materials; 4 VF drawers of annual reports. **Subscriptions:** 120 journals and other serials; 55 newspapers. **Services:** Interlibrary loan; library open to the public with restrictions. **Publications:** What's New in the Library (list of periodical contents pages and cataloged material), monthly. **Formerly:** Ontario Ministry of Northern Affairs.

★10850★
ONTARIO MINISTRY OF NORTHERN DEVELOPMENT & MINES - ONTARIO GEOLOGICAL SURVEY - LIBRARY (Sci-Engr)
77 Grenville St., Rm. 812 Phone: (416)965-1352
Toronto, ON, Canada M7A 1W4 Nancy Thurston, Libn.
Founded: 1945. **Staff:** Prof 1; Other 3. **Subjects:** Geology of Ontario, mining, Precambrian geology, metallurgy, mineralogy, environmental geology. **Special Collections:** Geological and aeromagnetic maps (20,000); annual reports of mining companies. **Holdings:** 15,000 texts and reference books; 25,000 government reports. **Subscriptions:** 400 journals and other serials. **Services:** Interlibrary loan; copying; library open to the public for reference use only. **Automated Operations:** Computerized cataloging. **Computerized Information Services:** CAN/OLE, Pergamon ORBIT InfoLine, Inc. **Networks/Consortia:** Member of Ontario Government Libraries' Council (OGLC). **Publications:** Accessions list, monthly - to other libraries on request.

★10851★
ONTARIO MINISTRY OF REVENUE - LIBRARY (Bus-Fin)
33 King St., W.
P.O. Box 627 Phone: (416)433-6135
Oshawa, ON, Canada L1H 8H5 Wendy Craig, Mgr., Lib.Serv.
Founded: 1973. **Staff:** Prof 1; Other 3. **Subjects:** Economics, public finance, taxation, property assessment. **Special Collections:** Technology Collection. **Holdings:** 13,000 books; 390 bound periodical volumes; Statistics Canada, July 1985 to present, on microfiche. **Subscriptions:** 300 journals and other serials. **Services:** Interlibrary loan; copying; library open to the public for reference use only. **Computerized Information Services:** DIALOG Information Services, Info Globe, QL Systems, The Financial Post Information Service. **Publications:** Library Link, irregular; What's New, irregular - both for internal distribution only.

★10852★
ONTARIO MINISTRY OF THE SOLICITOR GENERAL - CENTRE OF FORENSIC SCIENCES - H. WARD SMITH LIBRARY (Law, Sci-Engr)
25 Grosvenor St., 2nd Fl. Phone: (416)965-2561
Toronto, ON, Canada M7A 2G8 Eva Gulbinowicz, Libn.
Founded: 1967. **Staff:** Prof 1; Other 2. **Subjects:** Forensic science, toxicology, biology, chemistry, engineering, firearms, photography, questioned documents. **Special Collections:** Home Office Central Research Establishment (England) reports; Metropolitan Police Forensic Science Laboratory Reports (London, England), 1981 to present. **Holdings:** 10,000 books; 5500 bound periodical volumes; 1000 reports; 11,000 reprints; 2000 government documents and pamphlets; 12,000 slides. **Subscriptions:** 308 journals and other serials. **Services:** Interlibrary loan; copying (limited); library open to criminal justice and medical professionals by telephone appointment. **Automated Operations:** Computerized cataloging, acquisitions, serials, and circulation. **Computerized Information Services:** MEDLARS, BRS Information Technologies, DIALOG Information Services, CAN/OLE, UTLAS; MESSAGES (electronic mail service). **Special Catalogs:** Slide catalog (online).

★10853★
ONTARIO MINISTRY OF THE SOLICITOR GENERAL - OFFICE OF THE FIRE MARSHAL - FIRE SCIENCES LIBRARY (Sci-Engr)
7 Overlea Blvd., 3rd Fl. Phone: (416)965-4855
Toronto, ON, Canada M4H 1A8 Jean Chong, Libn.
Staff: Prof 1; Other 1. **Subjects:** Fire - prevention, protection, science; fire protection engineering; firefighting service. **Special Collections:** National Fire Protection Association Fire Codes; Canadian Standards Association (CSA) and Underwriters Laboratory of Canada (ULC) standards (525). **Holdings:** 5000 books; 200 bound periodical volumes; 200 reports; 2000 catalogs and pamphlets. **Subscriptions:** 145 journals and other serials. **Services:** Interlibrary loan; copying; SDI; library open to the public for reference use only. **Computerized Information Services:** CAN/OLE, DIALOG Information Services. **Networks/Consortia:** Member of Ontario Government Libraries' Council (OGLC). **Publications:** Recent Accessions, monthly; bibliographies of library material, irregular - both free upon request.

ONTARIO MINISTRY OF TOURISM AND RECREATION - HURONIA HISTORICAL PARKS
See: Huronia Historical Parks (6619)

★10854★
ONTARIO MINISTRY OF TOURISM AND RECREATION - OLD FORT WILLIAM - RESOURCE LIBRARY (Hist)
Vicker's Heights Post Office Phone: (807)577-8461
Thunder Bay, ON, Canada P0T 2Z0 Jean Morrison, Supv., Lib./Res.Serv.
Founded: 1975. **Staff:** Prof 2; Other 1. **Subjects:** North American fur trade history and society, North West Company, Ojibway Indians, early 19th century trades and technology, material culture. **Special Collections:** National Heritage Limited (200 transfer cases of primary, secondary, pictorial data); Fort William Archaeological Project (400 files; 20 boxes of subject cards); interpreted buildings (41 kits of specialized data). **Holdings:** 3700 books; 700 documents; 20 VF drawers; 100 reels of microfilm. **Services:** Interlibrary loan; copying; library open to the public by appointment. **Publications:** Acquisitions lists; bibliographies, irregular. **Special Indexes:** Indexes to textiles, voyageurs, tools, material culture, fur trade history, posts, personnel. **Staff:** Helen Hyvarinen, Lib.Techn..

★10855★
ONTARIO MINISTRY OF TRANSPORTATION - LIBRARY AND INFORMATION CENTRE (Trans)
Central Bldg., Rm. 149
1201 Wilson Ave. Phone: (416)235-4546
Downsview, ON, Canada M3M 1J8
Stefanie A. Pavlin, Coord., Lib.Serv.
Founded: 1956. **Staff:** Prof 3; Other 5. **Subjects:** Highway and bridge design, engineering, maintenance; materials testing; transportation economics; photogrammetry; highway safety and accident statistics; personnel management and supervision; traffic engineering; urban and regional studies; energy conservation; laws and regulations. **Special Collections:** Publications and reports of the Transportation Research Board, the Ministry of Transportation, the American Association of State Highway and Transportation Officials. **Holdings:** 81,000 books; 2500 bound periodical volumes; 25,000 microforms. **Subscriptions:** 1000 journals and other serials. **Services:** Interlibrary loan; copying; SDI; library open to qualified users. **Automated Operations:** Computerized cataloging. **Computerized Information Services:** EUROLINE Inc., ESA/IRS, DIALOG Information Services, UTLAS, Infomart, Information Research Services (IRS), CAN/OLE. **Networks/Consortia:** Member of Ontario Government Libraries' Council (OGLC). **Publications:** Library News, monthly; Journal Contents, weekly. **Formerly:** Ontario Ministry of Transportation and Communications. **Staff:** Laila Zvejnieks, Tech.Serv.; Ian Mann, ILL; Noreen Searson, Ref.Serv..

★10856★
ONTARIO MINISTRY OF TREASURY AND ECONOMICS - LIBRARY SERVICES (Bus-Fin, Soc Sci)
Frost Bldg. North, 1st Fl.
Queen's Park Phone: (416)965-2314
Toronto, ON, Canada M7A 1Y8 Barbara Weatherhead, Mgr.
Founded: 1944. **Staff:** Prof 4; Other 7. **Subjects:** Economics, finance, statistics, all levels of government, management, business. **Special Collections:** Budgets, estimates, and public accounts for Canadian federal and all provincial governments. **Holdings:** 186,000 books; 32 VF drawers; 462 linear feet of Statistics Canada reports; 1600 maps of Ontario. **Subscriptions:** 1200 journals and other serials; 12 newspapers. **Services:** Interlibrary loan; library not open to the public. **Automated Operations:** Computerized cataloging, acquisitions, serials, and ILL. **Computerized Information Services:** Pergamon ORBIT InfoLine, Inc., The Reference Service (REFSRV), DIALOG Information Services, BRS Information Technologies, Infomart, QL Systems, Info Globe, CAN/OLE, UTLAS, Publinet Data Base. **Networks/Consortia:** Member of Ontario Government Libraries' Council (OGLC). **Publications:** Current Awareness, weekly; bibliographies; guides; daily book lists; information sheets - all for internal distribution only. **Special Indexes:** Ontario regulations and Ontario debates, both indexed weekly; private acts in Ontario. **Staff:** P. Dunn, Chf.Cat.; Ken Lavin, Ref.Libn..

★10857★
ONTARIO MUNICIPAL BOARD - LIBRARY (Plan)
180 Dundas St., W. Phone: (416)598-2266
Toronto, ON, Canada M5G 1E5 B.C. Alty, Mgr., Adm.
Subjects: Appraisal and assessment, land use and values, planning and zoning. **Holdings:** Figures not available. **Services:** Library not open to the public.

★10858★
ONTARIO NURSES ASSOCIATION - ONA LIBRARY (Med)
85 Grenville St., Suite 600 Phone: (416)964-8833
Toronto, ON, Canada M5S 3A2 Victoria Scott, Libn.
Founded: 1977. **Staff:** Prof 2; Other 1. **Subjects:** Industrial relations, nursing, occupational health and safety, medical and health care. **Holdings:** 3000 books; 200 bound periodical volumes; 4 drawers of ONA archives; 15 VF drawers of nursing and industrial relations materials; 1 drawer of news clippings. **Subscriptions:** 204 journals and other serials. **Services:** Interlibrary loan; copying (limited); library open to the public by appointment for material that is not widely available. **Automated Operations:** Computerized cataloging and acquisitions. **Publications:** ONA Library: Acquisitions, monthly - for internal distribution only. **Special Indexes:** Card index of nursing materials. **Staff:** Jean Buchanan, Lib.Asst..

ONTARIO PAPER COMPANY
See: Quebec and Ontario Paper Company (11757)

★10859★
ONTARIO POLICE COLLEGE - LIBRARY (Law)
Box 1190 Phone: (519)773-5361
Aylmer West, ON, Canada N5H 2T2 Mr. Yen-pin Chao, Libn.
Staff: Prof 1; Other 1. **Subjects:** Police science, criminal law, criminology, sociology. **Holdings:** 10,000 volumes. **Subscriptions:** 330 journals and other serials; 8 newspapers. **Services:** Interlibrary loan; copying (limited); library open to public at librarian's discretion. **Publications:** Acquisitions list.

★10860★
ONTARIO POLICE COMMISSION - LIBRARY (Law)
25 Grosvenor St., 10th Fl. Phone: (416)965-3281
Toronto, ON, Canada M7A 2H3 J. Mark Merryweather, Libn.
Founded: 1981. **Staff:** Prof 1. **Subjects:** Police studies, computer and radio systems, police technology and management, justice. **Holdings:** 6000 books. **Subscriptions:** 69 journals and other serials. **Services:** Interlibrary loan; copying; library open to the public with restrictions. **Automated Operations:** Computerized cataloging. **Computerized Information Services:** DIALOG Information Services. **Networks/Consortia:** Member of Ontario Government Libraries' Council (OGLC).

★10861★
ONTARIO PROVINCIAL POLICE - GENERAL HEADQUARTERS LIBRARY (Law)
90 Harbour St. Phone: (416)965-1372
Toronto, ON, Canada M7A 2S1 Lorna E. Brown, Libn.
Founded: 1979. **Staff:** Prof 1; Other 2. **Subjects:** Criminology, computer science, law enforcement, management, laws and regulations of Ontario and Canada. **Holdings:** 8500 books; 400 bound periodical volumes; 30 AV programs. **Subscriptions:** 200 journals and other serials. **Services:** Interlibrary loan; copying; library open to the public by appointment for reference use only. **Computerized Information Services:** DIALOG Information Services, Infomart, Info Globe, QL Systems, CAN/LAW. **Publications:** List of new acquisitions, bimonthly - for internal distribution only.

★10862★
ONTARIO PUBLIC INTEREST RESEARCH GROUP (OPIRG) - GUELPH LIBRARY (Soc Sci)
University of Guelph
Trent Lane Phone: (519)824-2091
Guelph, ON, Canada N1G 2W1 Carole Milligan, Coord.
Founded: 1973. **Subjects:** Environment, women's issues, nuclear power, energy from waste, other social issues. **Holdings:** 2000 volumes. **Subscriptions:** 50 journals and other serials; 10 newspapers. **Services:** Interlibrary loan; copying; library open to the public.

★10863★
ONTARIO PUBLIC INTEREST RESEARCH GROUP (OPIRG) - PETERBOROUGH LIBRARY (Soc Sci)
Trent University Phone: (705)748-1767
Peterborough, ON, Canada K9J 7B8 Philip White, Coord.
Founded: 1976. **Staff:** Prof 1; Other 10. **Subjects:** Energy, nuclear power, nuclear weapons, environment, civil liberties, Third World development. **Special Collections:** Nuclear Free Press Archives. **Holdings:** 1000 books; 300 vertical files. **Subscriptions:** 40 journals and other serials; 15 newspapers. **Services:** Copying; library open to the public.

★10864★
ONTARIO PUPPETRY ASSOCIATION PUPPET CENTRE - RESOURCE LIBRARY (Theater)
171 Avondale Ave. Phone: (416)222-9029
Willowdale, ON, Canada M2N 2V4 Nancy Kyle, Musm.Dir./Cur.
Founded: 1980. **Staff:** Prof 2. **Subjects:** Puppetry, education and puppetry, museum exhibitions. **Holdings:** 5 VF drawers of research folders. **Services:** Library not open to the public. **Publications:** OPAL, bimonthly.

★10865★
ONTARIO RESEARCH FOUNDATION - LIBRARY (Sci-Engr)
Sheridan Park Phone: (416)822-4111
Mississauga, ON, Canada L5K 1B3 Carl K. Wei, Libn.
Founded: 1928. **Staff:** Prof 1; Other 3. **Subjects:** Chemistry, engineering, metallurgy, textiles, physics, pollution. **Holdings:** 26,000 books; 26,500 bound periodical volumes; 5000 government documents; 50 boxes of annual reports; 5 drawers of microforms. **Subscriptions:** 500 journals and other serials. **Services:** Interlibrary loan; copying; library open to the public. **Computerized Information Services:** CAN/OLE, DIALOG Information Services, ESA/IRS, Pergamon ORBIT InfoLine, Inc., NLM, BRS Information Technologies, QL Systems, CAS ONLINE, Chemical Information Systems, Inc. (CIS), Info Globe, Telesystemes Questel, Mead Data Central, WILSONLINE, VU/TEXT Information Services, Infomart, DIMDI, CompuServe, Inc., JICST On-line Information Service (JOIS), Novatron Information Corporation. **Networks/Consortia:** Member of Ontario Government Libraries' Council (OGLC), Sheridan Park Association - Library and Information Science Committee (LISC). **Publications:** Library Reminder, monthly - for internal distribution only.

★10866★
ONTARIO ST. LAWRENCE PARKS COMMISSION - UPPER CANADA VILLAGE REFERENCE LIBRARY (Hist)
Hwy. 2, Box 740 Phone: (613)253-2911
Morrisburg, ON, Canada K0C 1X0 Jack Schecter, Libn./Archv.
Staff: Prof 1. **Subjects:** Canadian and Eastern Ontario history, local history and genealogy. **Holdings:** 3000 books; 38 bound periodical volumes; 60 boxes of manuscripts, documents, photographs, maps; 242 reels of microfilm; 59 microfiche. **Subscriptions:** 46 journals and other serials. **Services:** Copying; library open to the public for reference use only.

★10867★
ONTARIO SCIENCE CENTRE - LIBRARY (Sci-Engr)
770 Don Mills Rd. Phone: (416)429-4100
Don Mills, ON, Canada M3C 1T3 Jeanne Duperreault, Hd.Libn.
Founded: 1965. **Staff:** Prof 1; Other 2. **Subjects:** Chemistry, physics, biology, astronomy, mathematics, zoology, botany, technology, engineering, graphic arts, museum studies. **Holdings:** 6000 books; 30,000 slides; 30,000 prints and negatives; 500 films; 100 videotapes. **Subscriptions:** 100 journals and other serials. **Services:** Interlibrary loan; copying; library open to the public by appointment. **Computerized Information Services:** DIALOG Information Services, CAN/OLE.

ONTARIO SCIENCE CENTRE - ONTARIO FILM INSTITUTE
See: Ontario Film Institute (10810)

★10868★
ONTARIO SECURITIES COMMISSION - LIBRARY (Law)
20 Queen St., W., 18th Fl. Phone: (416)963-2572
Toronto, ON, Canada M5H 3S8 Sandra Findlay, Libn.
Founded: 1984. **Staff:** Prof 1. **Subjects:** Law, accounting, investment. **Special Collections:** Commission Bulletins and Weekly Summaries, 1949 to present. **Holdings:** 5000 books; 300 bound periodical volumes; 4 drawers of pamphlets. **Subscriptions:** 100 journals and other serials; 6 newspapers. **Services:** Interlibrary loan; library not open to the public. **Computerized Information Services:** QL Systems, Info Globe. **Publications:** Library Insiders' Report, 6/year. **Special Indexes:** Index to Ontario Securites Commission Policies.

★10869★
(Ontario) SUPREME COURT OF ONTARIO - JUDGES' LIBRARY (Law)
Osgoode Hall
130 Queen St., W. Phone: (416)363-4101
Toronto, ON, Canada M5H 2N5 Anne Brown, Mgr.
Staff: Prof 1. **Subjects:** Law. **Holdings:** 20,000 volumes. **Subscriptions:** 20 journals and other serials. **Services:** Interlibrary loan; library not open to the public.

ONTARIO THEOLOGICAL SEMINARY
See: Ontario Bible College/Ontario Theological Seminary (10801)

★10870★
OPPENHEIMER & CO., INC. - INFORMATION CENTER (Bus-Fin)
Oppenheimer Tower
World Financial Center
200 Liberty St. Phone: (212)667-7890
New York, NY 10281 Marilyn H. Adamo, V.P.
Staff: Prof 3; Other 9. **Subjects:** Corporations, investment, government statistics, stock price sources. **Holdings:** 4200 books; 1500 subject files on various industries; 1 million microfiche of U.S. Securities and Exchange Commission documents; corporation files of annual reports, proxy statements, prospectuses. **Subscriptions:** 1200 journals and other serials. **Services:** Interlibrary loan; center not open to the public. **Automated Operations:** Computerized serials and circulation. **Computerized Information Services:** DIALOG Information Services, LEXIS, NEXIS, Dow Jones News/Retrieval, TEXTLINE, Dun & Bradstreet Corporation, Disclosure Information Group, Spectrum Ownership Profiles Online; internal databases. **Staff:** Jeanne Seyffarth, Sr.Ref.Libn..

★10871★
OPPENHEIMER WOLFF & DONNELLY - LIBRARY (Law)
1700 First Bank Bldg. Phone: (612)223-2500
St. Paul, MN 55101 Gretchen Haase, Libn.
Staff: Prof 4; Other 2. **Subjects:** Business law. **Holdings:** 30,000 books; 750 bound periodical volumes. **Subscriptions:** 350 journals and other serials; 11 newspapers. **Services:** Interlibrary loan; library not open to the public. **Automated Operations:** Computerized public access catalog, serials, and routing. **Computerized Information Services:** DIALOG Information Services, WESTLAW, LEXIS; PHINet FedTax Database, Dow Jones News/Retrieval. **Networks/Consortia:** Member of Metronet. **Staff:** Gail McCain, Assoc.Libn.; Trudi Busch, Asst.Libn.; Catherine Magness, Asst.Libn..

★10872★
OPTIKON RESEARCH LABORATORIES - LIBRARY (Sci-Engr)
Box 259 Phone: (203)672-6614
West Cornwall, CT 06796 William Covington, Libn.
Staff: Prof 1; Other 3. **Subjects:** Polymer sciences, optics. **Special Collections:** Dioptric materials. **Holdings:** 9850 books; 700 bound periodical volumes. **Services:** Interlibrary loan; library open to the public by appointment upon written request.

ORAL HISTORY PROJECT IN LABOR HISTORY
See: Roosevelt University (12185)

★10873★
ORANGE COUNTY DEPARTMENT OF EDUCATION - LIBRARY (Educ)
200 Kalmus Dr.
Box 9050 Phone: (714)966-4466
Costa Mesa, CA 92628-9050 Faith M. Herbert, Libn.
Staff: 1. **Subjects:** Educational administration, teaching and teachers, philosophy and psychology of education, school buildings, early childhood education, special education. **Special Collections:** Curriculum guides (300). **Holdings:** 9100 books; 20 VF drawers of pamphlets. **Subscriptions:** 125 journals and other serials. **Services:** Interlibrary loan; copying (limited); library open to the public for reference use only.

★10874★
ORANGE COUNTY ENVIRONMENTAL MANAGEMENT AGENCY - EMA LIBRARY (Env-Cons, Plan)
400 Civic Center Dr., W.
Box 4048 Phone: (714)834-6395
Santa Ana, CA 92702 Janet Hilford, Libn.
Founded: 1963. **Staff:** Prof 1. **Subjects:** Environmental management, water resources, hydrology, flood control, transportation engineering, recreational design, urban planning, land use and zoning, public administration, housing/community development. **Holdings:** 7500 books; 20,000 technical reports. **Subscriptions:** 30 journals and other serials. **Services:** Library not open to the public.

★10875★
ORANGE COUNTY HISTORICAL COMMISSION - MUSEUM LIBRARY (Hist)
812 E. Rollins Ave.
Loch Haven Park
Orlando, FL 32803 Frank Mendola, Libn.
Staff: Prof 1. **Subjects:** Local and state history, Seminole Indians. **Holdings:** 1253 volumes; 614 directories and yearbooks; 225 scrapbooks and ledgers; 54 photograph albums; 4000 pictures; 250 maps; 15 linear feet

of vertical file materials; 5090 postcards; 12 reels of microfilm and 131 sheets of microfiche of newspapers. **Subscriptions:** 11 journals and other serials. **Services:** Copying; library open to the public when librarian is on duty. **Publications:** Orange County Historical Quarterly - to members and visitors.

★10876★
ORANGE COUNTY HISTORICAL SOCIETY - LIBRARY (Hist)
Clove Furnace Historic Site Phone: (914)351-4696
Arden, NY 10910 Michelle P. Figliomeni, Pres.
Founded: 1971. **Subjects:** Local history, iron mining, Harriman family, Peter Parrott family, agricultural records. **Holdings:** Figures not available. **Services:** Copying; library open to the public.

★10877★
ORANGE COUNTY LAW LIBRARY (Law)
515 N. Flower St. Phone: (714)834-3397
Santa Ana, CA 92703 Bethany J. Ochal, Dir.
Founded: 1891. **Staff:** Prof 5; Other 19. **Subjects:** Law. **Special Collections:** Up-to-date codes for the law of all the states, federal government, and U.S. territories as well as case reports and some administrative regulations and rulings; CIS microfiche service. **Holdings:** 132,280 bound volumes; 5416 tapes; 513,597 microfiche; 7860 ultrafiche; depository for California and U.S. Government documents. **Subscriptions:** 1320 journals and other serials; 9 newspapers. **Services:** Interlibrary loan; copying; library open to the public. **Computerized Information Services:** WESTLAW. **Networks/Consortia:** Member of CLASS, RLG. **Staff:** Richard Ayotte, Pub.Serv.Libn.; Michele Finerty, Tech.Serv.Libn.; Kathryn Anne Mettler, Ref.Libn.; Michael Bryant, Ref.Libn..

★10878★
ORANGE COUNTY LAW LIBRARY (Law)
Orlando Public Library
101 E. Central Blvd. Phone: (407)425-4694
Orlando, FL 32801 Judy Mucci, Hd.
Founded: 1980. **Staff:** Prof 4; Other 3. **Subjects:** Law, public policy research. **Special Collections:** Land use planning; local documents. **Holdings:** 33,000 books; 3000 other cataloged items. **Subscriptions:** 150 journals and other serials. **Services:** SDI; library open to the public with referral from another library department or local government staff member. **Automated Operations:** Computerized cataloging and acquisitions. **Computerized Information Services:** OCLC, LOGIN; LOGIN (electronic mail service). **Networks/Consortia:** Member of Florida Library Information Network (FLIN), SOLINET. **Remarks:** Includes holdings of Planning/Local Government Department. **Staff:** Betty Gillard, Sr.Libn.; Chris Testerman, Lib. Aide; Kathy Pratt, Lib. Aide.

★10879★
ORANGE COUNTY LIBRARY SYSTEM - GENEALOGY DEPARTMENT (Hist)
101 E. Central Blvd. Phone: (407)425-4694
Orlando, FL 32801 Eleanor B. Crawford, Dept.Hd.
Staff: Prof 4; Other 2. **Subjects:** Genealogy, family history, heraldry, surnames. **Special Collections:** Barbour Collection of Connecticut Vital Records (97 reels of microfilm); vital records of 190 Massachusetts towns to 1850 (216 volumes); Florida State Society, Daughters of the American Revolution Collection, 1929 to present (5000 volumes); lectures on genealogy (125 cassette tapes). **Holdings:** 10,000 books; 2400 bound periodical volumes; 9000 reels of microfilm; 8 VF drawers of the papers of Beatrice Brown Commander; 14 VF drawers of miscellaneous family papers; 100 exchange periodicals. **Subscriptions:** 65 journals and other serials. **Services:** Interlibrary loan; copying; department open to the public. **Automated Operations:** Computerized cataloging, acquisitions, and circulation. **Computerized Information Services:** OCLC. Performs searches free of charge.

★10880★
ORANGE COUNTY SHERIFF/CORONER - FORENSIC SCIENCE SERVICES LIBRARY (Med)
550 N. Flower St.
Box 449 Phone: (714)834-3073
Santa Ana, CA 92702 Mr. J.L. Ragle, Lab.Dir.
Founded: 1948. **Staff:** Prof 1. **Subjects:** Chemistry, criminalistics, toxicology, forensic medicine, investigation. **Holdings:** 2550 books; 4 VF drawers of catalogs and brochures; 2 VF drawers of lab equipment manuals; 2900 reprints; 3 boxes of microfiche and microfilm. **Subscriptions:** 71 journals and other serials. **Services:** Interlibrary loan; library not open to the public.

★10881★
ORANGE COUNTY TRANSIT DISTRICT - RESOURCE CENTER (Trans)
11800 Woodbury, Annex Bldg. Phone: (714)740-7507
Garden Grove, CA 92642 Terri Sipprelle, Rsrc.Ctr.Asst.
Founded: 1974. **Staff:** 1. **Subjects:** Transportation, employee relations, urban mass transit, light rail, multi-modal transportation, high occupancy vehicles. **Special Collections:** History of transit in Orange County (7 years of documents and pictures). **Holdings:** 7100 books; 500 reports on microfiche; 6515 slides and cassettes. **Subscriptions:** 183 journals and other serials. **Services:** Interlibrary loan; copying; center open to the public. **Automated Operations:** Computerized cataloging, serials, and circulation. **Computerized Information Services:** DIALOG Information Services; RMS (internal database). **Publications:** Technical Reports.

★10882★
ORANGE AND ROCKLAND UTILITIES, INC. - LIBRARY (Energy)
1 Blue Hill Plaza Phone: (914)627-2680
Pearl River, NY 10965 Esther B. Clifford, Libn.
Staff: Prof 1; Other 1. **Subjects:** Electric power, gas industry, energy, environment. **Holdings:** 6000 books; 1200 technical reports and pamphlets; EPRI Collection on microfiche; 25 VF drawers of annual reports; special events clippings, 1970 to present. **Subscriptions:** 200 journals and other serials. **Services:** Interlibrary loan; library not open to the public.

★10883★
ORANGEBURG-CALHOUN TECHNICAL COLLEGE - GRESSETTE LEARNING RESOURCE CENTER (Educ)
3250 Matthews Rd. Phone: (803)536-0311
Orangeburg, SC 29115 Margaret F. Huff, Dean, LRC
Staff: Prof 4; Other 4. **Subjects:** Science and technology, business, allied health sciences. **Special Collections:** Nontraditional power sources. **Holdings:** 29,720 books; 122 bound periodical volumes; 8831 documents; 1405 reels of microfilm; 359 video cassettes; 2803 filmstrips. **Subscriptions:** 412 journals and other serials; 13 newspapers. **Services:** Interlibrary loan; copying; center open to the public. **Automated Operations:** Computerized public access catalog, cataloging, and circulation. **Computerized Information Services:** DIALOG Information Services. Performs searches on fee basis. Contact Person: Mary Anne Braithwaite, Rd.Serv.Libn.. **Publications:** LRC Handbook, irregular - to students; Faculty LRC Handbook, irregular; Multi-Media Handbook, irregular - both to faculty; Monthly Acquisitions List; Special Bibliographies. **Staff:** Christopher Murray, Tech.Serv.Libn.; Henry Hall, Media Rsrcs.Coord..

★10884★
ORATOIRE ST-JOSEPH - CENTRE DE DOCUMENTATION (Rel-Phil)
3800 Queen Mary Rd. Phone: (514)733-8211
Montreal, PQ, Canada H3V 1H6 Mariette Bedard, Libn.
Founded: 1950. **Staff:** Prof 3; Other 3. **Subjects:** Saint Joseph and his cult, patrology, Canadiana, iconography, theology, spirituality, religious history. **Holdings:** 70,000 books; 72 VF drawers of archival materials; 1200 reels of microfilm; 400 titles on microcards. **Subscriptions:** 192 journals and other serials. **Services:** Interlibrary loan; copying; center open to the public for reference use only. **Publications:** Cahiers de Josephologie, semiannual - by subscription. **Also Known As:** St. Joseph's Shrine. **Staff:** Roland Gauthier, Dir..

ORCHESTRA LIBRARY INFORMATION SERVICE (OLIS)
See: American Symphony Orchestra League (699)

ORDER OF FRIARS MINOR (Franciscans) - DUNS SCOTUS LIBRARY
See: Duns Scotus Library (4456)

ORDER OF ST. BENEDICT - ABBEY OF REGINA LAUDIS
See: Abbey of Regina Laudis, Order of St. Benedict (5)

★10885★
ORDER OF SERVANTS OF MARY - EASTERN PROVINCE LIBRARY - MORINI MEMORIAL COLLECTION (Rel-Phil)
3401 S. Home Ave. Phone: (312)484-0063
Berwyn, IL 60402 Rev. Conrad M. Borntrager, O.S.M., Archv.
Staff: 1. **Subjects:** Provincial archives. **Holdings:** 3000 books; 250 bound periodical volumes; 330 linear feet of archival materials; 900 clippings; 60 albums and 4 filing drawers of photographs; 100 blueprints. **Services:** Library open to the public with restrictions. **Also Known As:** Servites.

★10886★
ORDRE DES INFIRMIERES ET DES INFIRMIERS DU QUEBEC - CENTRE DE DOCUMENTATION (Med)
4200 Dorchester, W. Phone: (514)935-2501
Montreal, PQ, Canada H3Z 1V4 Denise Mailhot, Libn.
Staff: 3. **Subjects:** Nursing. **Holdings:** 7500 books; 150 bound periodical volumes; 12 films; 8 slide programs; 25 videotapes. **Subscriptions:** 325 journals and other serials. **Services:** Center open to members only. **Publications:** Nursing Quebec, 6/year.

★10887★
OREGON ART INSTITUTE - NORTHWEST FILM AND VIDEO CENTER - CIRCULATING FILM LIBRARY
1219 S.W. Park Ave.
Portland, OR 97205
Defunct. Holdings absorbed by Portland State University - Continuing Education Film and Video Library.

OREGON ART INSTITUTE - PORTLAND ART MUSEUM
See: Portland Art Museum (11462)

★10888★
OREGON ELECTRIC RAILWAY HISTORICAL SOCIETY, INC. - TROLLEY PARK - LIBRARY (Hist)
HCR 71
Box 1318-A Phone: (503)357-3574
Forest Grove, OR 97116 William Hayes, Hist.
Staff: 1. **Subjects:** Electric railways, tram and trolley history. **Special Collections:** Tram and trolley business records and employment files from street railway companies. **Holdings:** 200 books; 150 unbound periodicals; 2500 photographs, slides, negatives. **Services:** Copying; library open to the public by appointment for reference use only. **Publications:** Trolley Park News, quarterly - to members and by exchange.

★10889★
OREGON GRADUATE CENTER FOR STUDY AND RESEARCH - LIBRARY (Sci-Engr)
19600 N.W. Von Neumann Dr. Phone: (503)690-1060
Beaverton, OR 97006-1999 Maureen G. Sloan, Libn.
Staff: Prof 2; Other 2. **Subjects:** Chemistry, biochemistry, laser physics, solid state and surface physics, computer science and engineering, materials science, welding, environmental science. **Holdings:** 15,000 books; 1500 bound periodical volumes; 600 reels of microfilm; 6000 government reports on microfiche. **Subscriptions:** 500 journals and other serials. **Services:** Interlibrary loan; copying; library open to public by telephone request. **Computerized Information Services:** OCLC, STN International, DIALOG Information Services; OnTyme Electronic Message Network Service (electronic mail service). Performs searches on fee basis. **Networks/Consortia:** Member of Washington County Cooperative Library Services (WCCLS). **Special Catalogs:** OGC Catalog, annual - available on request.

★10890★
OREGON HEALTH SCIENCES UNIVERSITY - DENTAL BRANCH LIBRARY (Med)
611 S.W. Campus Dr. Phone: (503)279-8822
Portland, OR 97201 Dolores Judkins, Dental Libn.
Staff: Prof 1; Other 4. **Subjects:** Dental and oral science. **Special Collections:** History of dentistry (250 books). **Holdings:** 17,650 volumes; 500 AV programs. **Subscriptions:** 350 journals and other serials. **Services:** Interlibrary loan (fee); copying; SDI; library open to the public for reference use only. **Automated Operations:** Computerized cataloging, acquisitions, and serials. **Computerized Information Services:** MEDLINE, OCLC, PHILSOM, BRS Information Technologies, MEDLARS; OnTyme Electronic Message Network Service (electronic mail service). Performs searches on fee basis. **Networks/Consortia:** Member of Pacific Northwest Regional Health Sciences Library Service. **Remarks:** Maintains an Independent Learning Center.

★10891★
OREGON HEALTH SCIENCES UNIVERSITY - LIBRARY (Med)
3181 S.W. Sam Jackson Park Rd.
Box 573 Phone: (503)279-8026
Portland, OR 97207 James E. Morgan, Dir. of Libs.
Staff: Prof 11; Other 25. **Subjects:** Medicine, dentistry, nursing, allied health sciences. **Special Collections:** Pacific Northwest Collection (medical history); History of Medicine Collection. **Holdings:** 172,542 volumes; 2131 AV programs. **Subscriptions:** 2464 journals and other serials. **Services:** Interlibrary loan; copying; SDI; library open to the public for reference use only. **Computerized Information Services:** NLM, BRS Information Technologies, DIALOG Information Services, OCLC, PHILSOM, CAS ONLINE, The Source Information Network, PaperChase, MEDIS. **Networks/Consortia:** Member of Oregon Health Information Network (OHIN), Pacific Northwest Regional Health Sciences Library Service. **Publications:** Accessions list; OHIN News; INFORM (library newsletter). **Remarks:** Figures include holdings of Dental Branch Library. **Staff:** Millard Johnson, Assoc.Dir.; Carol Willman, Cat.Libn.; Dan Kniesner, Asst.Cat.Libn.; Leslie Wykoff, Hd.Ref.Libn.; Patrice O'Donovan, Ser./Acq.Libn.; Heather Rosenwinkel, Coll.Dev.Libn.; Patty Davies, Ref.Libn.; Leslie Cable, Ref.Libn.; Cynthia Cunningham, ILL Libn.; Steve Teich, OHIN Coord.; Linda Simmons, Ref.Libn.; Dolores Judkins, Dental Libn.; Kenneth Harper, Vollum Inst.Libn..

★10892★
OREGON HISTORICAL SOCIETY - LIBRARY (Hist)
1230 S.W. Park Ave. Phone: (503)222-1741
Portland, OR 97205 Louis Flannery, Chf.Libn.
Founded: 1898. **Staff:** Prof 16; Other 7. **Subjects:** History of the Pacific Northwest and the Oregon Country; social, political, and economic growth of the Pacific Northwest; Northwest explorations and voyages; cartography of Northwest. **Special Collections:** Oregon Provisional Government Papers (film); Henry Failing Papers; Oregon Imprints by Belknap; British Collection; Russian-American Studies; Wesley Andrews Collection; M.M. Hazeltine Collection. **Holdings:** 70,000 volumes; 15 million manuscripts in 4500 collections; 16,000 reels of microfilm; 1.5 million photographs; 10,000 maps; 9000 reels of TV film. **Subscriptions:** 600 journals and other serials; 80 newspapers. **Services:** Interlibrary loan; copying; library open to the public. **Automated Operations:** Computerized cataloging. **Computerized Information Services:** OCLC. **Publications:** Guide to Manuscript Collections of the Oregon Historical Society (book with supplements). **Special Catalogs:** Catalog of Microfilm Collections (book); Union Catalog of Photograph Collections in Pacific Northwest. **Staff:** Gordon Manning, Asst.Libn..

OREGON INSTITUTE OF MARINE BIOLOGY
See: University of Oregon (16709)

★10893★
OREGON INSTITUTE OF TECHNOLOGY - LEARNING RESOURCES CENTER (Sci-Engr)
3201 Campus Dr. Phone: (503)882-6321
Klamath Falls, OR 97601-8801 Leonard Freiser, Dir.
Founded: 1950. **Staff:** Prof 8; Other 8. **Subjects:** History of science and technology, engineering, electronics, health sciences, computer science, industrial processes, paramedical sciences, business. **Holdings:** 80,000 books; 18,000 bound periodical volumes; microfilm. **Subscriptions:** 2000 journals and other serials. **Services:** Interlibrary loan; copying; media services; center open to the public. **Automated Operations:** Computerized public access catalog, cataloging, and acquisitions. **Computerized Information Services:** OCLC, DIALOG Information Services. **Networks/Consortia:** Member of CLASS, Southern Oregon Library Federation (SOLF). **Staff:** Charlotte Pierce, Mgt.Asst.; David White, Assoc.Coord.; Gary Gray, Media Coord.; Karen Chase, Tech.Serv.Libn.; Robert Freese, Circ.Libn.; Cecil Chase, Ref.Libn.; Karen L. Peterson, Acq./Ser.Libn.; Judith Chase, Doc.Libn..

★10894★
OREGON INSTITUTE OF TECHNOLOGY - SHAW HISTORICAL LIBRARY (Hist)
Learning Resources Center
3201 Campus Dr. Phone: (503)882-1276
Klamath Falls, OR 97601-8801 Leonard H. Freiser, LRC Dir.
Founded: 1983. **Subjects:** Klamath County and Oregon history, Pacific Northwest, including High Desert Area and Land of the Lakes. **Holdings:** 3000 volumes. **Services:** Interlibrary loan; copying; SDI; library open to the public for reference use only. **Automated Operations:** Computerized acquisitions. **Computerized Information Services:** DIALOG Information Services, OCLC. **Networks/Consortia:** Member of CLASS, Southern Oregon Library Federation (SOLF). **Publications:** The Journal of the Shaw Historical Library, semiannual - for sale.

★10895★
OREGON REGIONAL PRIMATE RESEARCH CENTER - LIBRARY (Biol Sci)
505 N.W. 185th Ave. Phone: (503)645-1141
Beaverton, OR 97006 Isabel McDonald, Libn.
Founded: 1961. **Staff:** Prof 1; Other 1. **Subjects:** Biomedicine, zoology. **Special Collections:** Primatology. **Holdings:** 16,900 volumes; 35 films; 196 reels of microfilm. **Subscriptions:** 175 journals and other serials. **Services:** Interlibrary loan; copying; SDI; library open to visiting scientists and others on request. **Automated Operations:** Computerized cataloging.

Computerized Information Services: MEDLARS, OCLC; OnTyme Electronic Message Network Service (electronic mail service). Performs searches on fee basis. **Networks/Consortia:** Member of Western Library Network (WLN), Washington County Cooperative Library Services (WCCLS), Oregon Health Information Network (OHIN). **Special Catalogs:** Files on center's publications; card files on primate articles, films, and theses.

★10896★
OREGON RESEARCH INSTITUTE - LIBRARY (Soc Sci)
1899 Willamette
Eugene, OR 97401 Linda Rangus, Lib.Mgr.
Founded: 1960. **Staff:** 1. **Subjects:** Psychology, behavioral sciences. **Holdings:** 1000 volumes; 5000 reprints of journal articles. **Services:** Library not open to the public. **Computerized Information Services:** DIALOG Information Services.

★10897★
OREGON SCHOOL OF ARTS AND CRAFTS - LIBRARY (Art)
8245 S.W. Barnes Rd. Phone: (503)297-5544
Portland, OR 97225 Christine Peterson, Libn.
Staff: Prof 1. **Subjects:** Textiles, ceramics, woodworking, drawing and design, metals, calligraphy. **Holdings:** 2000 books; 8000 slides; 4 VF drawers of archival materials. **Subscriptions:** 90 journals and other serials. **Services:** Interlibrary loan; copying; library open to the public for reference use only.

★10898★
OREGON STATE DEPARTMENT OF AGRICULTURE - LIBRARY (Agri)
Agriculture Bldg.
635 Capitol St., N.E. Phone: (503)378-3773
Salem, OR 97310-0110 Dalton Hobbs, Info.Off.
Founded: 1938. **Staff:** Prof 1; Other 1. **Subjects:** Agriculture. **Special Collections:** Oregon Ag in the Classroom Resource Guide Materials (180 items). **Holdings:** 100 books; 5000 slides; U.S.D.A. statistics, data, publications; historic departmental documents; periodicals. **Subscriptions:** 30 journals and other serials; 10 newspapers. **Services:** Library open to the public for reference use only; special collection available for loan. **Publications:** Oregon Agricultural Statistics, annual - available on request; Oregon AgriRecord, quarterly - to mailing list and upon request.

★10899★
OREGON STATE DEPARTMENT OF ECONOMIC DEVELOPMENT - LIBRARY (Bus-Fin)
595 Cottage St., N.E. Phone: (503)373-1200
Salem, OR 97310 Douglas K. Crook, Res.Anl.
Subjects: Economic development and statistics, industrial development, land use. **Holdings:** 5000 books. **Services:** Library not open to the public. **Computerized Information Services:** Produces Directory of Oregon Manufacturers. **Publications:** List of publications - available on request.

★10900★
OREGON STATE DEPARTMENT OF EDUCATION - RESOURCE/DISSEMINATION CENTER (Educ)
700 Pringle Parkway, S.E. Phone: (503)378-8471
Salem, OR 97310 Juanita Maloney, Lib.Asst.
Founded: 1970. **Staff:** Prof 1; Other 1. **Subjects:** General education. **Special Collections:** Career and vocational education; school standards documents; summarized information packets on selected priority topics; collection of files on cost cutting ideas. **Holdings:** 2200 books; 16 VF drawers; 4000 unbound periodicals and newsletters; 260,000 documents on microfiche; complete set of ERIC microfiche. **Subscriptions:** 200 journals and other serials; 6 newspapers. **Services:** Interlibrary loan; copying; SDI; center open to the public with restrictions. **Computerized Information Services:** DIALOG Information Services, BRS Information Technologies, The Source Information Network; SpecialNet, OreNet (electronic mail services). Performs searches free of charge.

★10901★
OREGON STATE DEPARTMENT OF FISH AND WILDLIFE - LIBRARY (Biol Sci)
17330 S.E. Evelyn St.
Clackamas, OR 97015 Mildred Schiewek, Sec./Libn.
Founded: 1957. **Subjects:** Fisheries and fisheries statistics, wildlife. **Holdings:** Figures not available. **Services:** Interlibrary loan; copying; library open to the public for reference use only.

OREGON STATE DEPARTMENT OF FISH & WILDLIFE - NEWPORT LABORATORY LIBRARY
See: Oregon State University - Hatfield Marine Science Center - Library (10916)

★10902★
OREGON STATE DEPARTMENT OF GEOLOGY AND MINERAL INDUSTRIES - LIBRARY (Sci-Engr, Energy)
1400 S.W. 5th Ave. Phone: (503)229-5580
Portland, OR 97201 Klaus Neuendorf, Ed./Libn.
Staff: 1. **Subjects:** Oregon geology, energy. **Special Collections:** Publications of the U.S. Geological Survey, the U.S. Bureau of Mines, other state geological surveys, and some foreign governments. **Holdings:** 23,000 volumes; 20 linear yards of maps; 600 unpublished theses and dissertations on Oregon geology; unpublished open-file reports issued by U.S. Geological Survey. **Subscriptions:** 20 journals and other serials. **Services:** Interlibrary loan (through Oregon State Library); copying (limited); library open to the public with restrictions. **Publications:** Oregon Geology, monthly; Bulletins; Special Papers; Oil and Gas Investigations; Geologic Map Series; open-file reports; bibliography of the geology and mineral resources of Oregon; bibliography of theses and dissertations on the geology of Oregon; bibliography of Oregon paleontology. **Special Indexes:** Index to Ore Bin/Oregon Geology, monthly. **Remarks:** Public access to this collection is more readily obtained through Portland State University Science Library or the Oregon State Library in Salem, OR.

★10903★
OREGON STATE DEPARTMENT OF HUMAN RESOURCES - SENIOR SERVICES DIVISION - LIBRARY (Soc Sci)
313 Public Service Bldg.
Salem, OR 97310 Phone: (503)378-4728
Subjects: Aging and the elderly - abuse and crime, long term care and housing, health; management. **Holdings:** Figures not available.

★10904★
OREGON STATE DEPARTMENT OF LAND CONSERVATION AND DEVELOPMENT - LIBRARY (Plan)
1175 Court St., N.E. Phone: (503)378-2980
Salem, OR 97310 Bonnie Ashford, Libn./Sec.
Staff: Prof 1. **Subjects:** Land use, planning. **Holdings:** 2000 volumes; land use plans. **Subscriptions:** 122 journals and other serials. **Services:** Interlibrary loan; copying; library open to the public. **Publications:** Oregon Lands, quarterly.

★10905★
OREGON STATE DEPARTMENT OF TRANSPORTATION - LIBRARY (Trans)
127 Transportation Bldg. Phone: (503)378-6268
Salem, OR 97310 Marie Y. Elefante, Libn.
Founded: 1938. **Staff:** Prof 1. **Subjects:** Transportation, highway engineering, planning, economics, environment, aeronautics, motor vehicles. **Holdings:** 9000 books. **Subscriptions:** 80 journals and other serials. **Services:** Interlibrary loan; copying; library open to the public with restrictions. **Automated Operations:** Computerized cataloging. **Computerized Information Services:** BRS Information Technologies, DIALOG Information Services, OCLC. **Publications:** ODOT Library News; Acquisitions List.

OREGON STATE DEPARTMENT OF TRANSPORTATION - STATE PARKS AND RECREATION DIVISION - COLLIER STATE PARK LOGGING MUSEUM
See: Collier State Park Logging Museum (3405)

★10906★
OREGON STATE HOSPITAL - MEDICAL LIBRARY
2600 Center St., N.E.
Salem, OR 97310-1319
Founded: 1950. **Subjects:** Psychiatry, medicine, psychology, sociology. **Special Collections:** Complete Psychological Works of Sigmund Freud (24 volumes). **Holdings:** 1500 books. **Remarks:** Presently inactive.

★10907★
OREGON STATE LIBRARY (Info Sci)
State Library Bldg.
Summer and Court Sts. Phone: (503)378-4274
Salem, OR 97310 Wesley A. Doak, State Libn.
Founded: 1848. **Staff:** Prof 17; Other 37. **Subjects:** Oregon history and government, business, librarianship, social sciences, humanities, science and technology. **Special Collections:** Oregoniana; materials for the blind and physically handicapped; history of Oregon library development;

Oregon library statistics; Patent Depository Library; Foundation Center collection. **Holdings:** 282,592 books; 1.2 million government documents and publications; 152,000 microforms; 400 video cassettes; clippings; pamphlets. **Subscriptions:** 1747 journals and other serials; 53 newspapers. **Services:** Interlibrary loan; copying; SDI; library open to the public. **Automated Operations:** Computerized public access catalog, cataloging, and circulation. **Computerized Information Services:** DIALOG Information Services, LEXIS, ISIS, LEGISNET, BRS Information Technologies, NLM, EROS Data Center, Oregon Legislative Information System; ALANET, TYMNET, OCLC, Oregon Public Access Catalog (OPAC) (electronic mail services). **Publications:** Letter to Libraries; Checklist of Official Publications of State of Oregon, quarterly; What's New, monthly; Directory and Statistics of Oregon Libraries, annual - to all Oregon libraries; Reference Satellite, monthly - to all Oregon public libraries. **Special Catalogs:** Oregoniana (card, microfilm, online). **Special Indexes:** Subject and biography index to Salem daily newspaper and other publications. **Staff:** John Webb, Dp. State Libn.; Kathleen McHarg, Asst. State Libn.; Merrialyce Kasner, Adm., Tech.Serv.; Craig Smith, Ref.Supv.; Eva Godwin, Coord., Access Serv..

★10908★
OREGON STATE LIBRARY - TALKING BOOK & BRAILLE SERVICES (Aud-Vis)
State Library Bldg.
Salem, OR 97310-0645 Phone: (503)378-3849
Founded: 1969. **Staff:** Prof 2; Other 8. **Subjects:** General collection. **Special Collections:** Recorded books about Oregon (70 titles); collection of textbooks on cassette (390 titles). **Holdings:** 176,000 volumes, including 10,500 books on records; 2400 braille titles; 14,000 book titles on cassette tapes; 6700 large print titles; CD-ROM. **Subscriptions:** 45 journals and other serials. **Services:** Interlibrary loan; copying; SDI; adaptive computer equipment for blind or visually impaired; services open to legally blind, visually impaired, and physically handicapped Oregonians. **Automated Operations:** Computerized public access catalog and circulation. **Computerized Information Services:** DRANET, BRS Information Technologies; SpecialNet (electronic mail service). Performs searches free of charge. **Networks/Consortia:** Member of National Library Service for the Blind & Physically Handicapped (NLS). **Publications:** Newsletter, quarterly - to registered patrons, other regional libraries, and by request. **Remarks:** An alternate telephone number is 378-3635. The telephone number for Portland residents is 224-0610. Other state residents may call (800)452-0292. **Staff:** Nancy Stewart, Asst.Dir..

★10909★
OREGON STATE SCHOOL FOR THE BLIND - MEDIA CENTER (Aud-Vis)
700 Church St., S.E. Phone: (503)378-8025
Salem, OR 97310 Delphie Schuberg, Media Coord.
Staff: Prof 1. **Subjects:** Visual and hearing impairment. **Holdings:** 3000 books; 500 bound periodical volumes. **Subscriptions:** 12 journals and other serials and newspapers. **Services:** Center not open to the public.

★10910★
OREGON STATE SCHOOL FOR THE DEAF - LIBRARY (Educ, Aud-Vis)
999 Locust St., N.E. Phone: (503)378-6252
Salem, OR 97310 Adoracion A. Alvarez, Curric.Dir.
Staff: Prof 2; Other 1. **Subjects:** Education of deaf children, lipreading, audiology, audio-visual education, vocational education, arts and crafts, science. **Special Collections:** American Annals of the Deaf, 1848 to present; Volta, 1900 to present; Proceedings of Convention of American Instructors of the Deaf, 1870 to present. **Holdings:** 9380 books; 340 bound periodical volumes; 2405 filmstrips. **Subscriptions:** 26 journals and other serials. **Services:** Interlibrary loan; library open to the public with restrictions. **Remarks:** Serves the school's students, teachers and staff members, parents of deaf students, and students in the Education of the Deaf training programs. **Staff:** Robert Bontrager, Media Spec..

★10911★
OREGON (State) SECRETARY OF STATE - STATE ARCHIVES AND RECORDS CENTER (Hist)
1005 Broadway, N.E. Phone: (503)378-4240
Salem, OR 97310 Roy Turnbaugh, State Archv.
Subjects: Oregon state and county agency records. **Special Collections:** Records of the provisional and territorial governments, the Governor's office, the Legislative Assembly, the Supreme Court, the Secretary of State's office, the Justice Department, the Treasurer, the Lands Division, the Labor Bureau, the Military Department, and the Highway Division; files from defunct state agencies, such as the Board of Control, the Capitol Reconstruction Commission, the Defense Council, the Finance and Administration Department, the Planning Board, and the World War I Veterans State Aid Commission. **Holdings:** 72,810 cubic feet of records. **Services:** Copying; center open to the public with restrictions.

★10912★
OREGON STATE SUPREME COURT LIBRARY (Law)
State & 12th Sts. Phone: (503)378-6030
Salem, OR 97310-0260 Roger Andrus, Law Libn.
Staff: Prof 2; Other 1. **Subjects:** Law. **Holdings:** 162,000 volumes. **Subscriptions:** 553 journals and other serials. **Services:** Library open to the public.

★10913★
OREGON STATE TRAFFIC SAFETY COMMISSION - LIBRARY (Trans)
State Library Bldg., 4th Fl.
Salem, OR 97310 Phone: (503)378-3669
Subjects: Traffic safety. **Holdings:** 2000 books.

★10914★
OREGON STATE UNIVERSITY - ARCHIVES (Hist)
Ad.Bldg., BO94 Phone: (503)754-2165
Corvallis, OR 97331 Laurie Filson, Archv.
Founded: 1961. **Staff:** Prof 1; Other 4. **Subjects:** University archives. **Holdings:** 200 record groups; 2300 cubic feet of archival material; 4000 reels of microfilm; 120,000 photographs. **Services:** Copying; archives open to the public during office hours.

★10915★
OREGON STATE UNIVERSITY - DEPARTMENT OF FOREST PRODUCTS - LIBRARY (Sci-Engr)
Corvallis, OR 97331 Phone: (503)754-4258
Mary B. Scroggins, Libn.
Founded: 1947. **Staff:** Prof 1. **Subjects:** Forest products. **Holdings:** 3000 books; 300 bound periodical volumes; 200 dissertations; 3 VF drawers of patents; 60 VF drawers of pamphlets. **Subscriptions:** 80 journals and other serials. **Services:** Copying; library open to the public for reference use only. **Publications:** Research Notes; Research Bulletins; Recent Publications; Special Bulletin; Biennial Report; Research Papers; Special Publications - all available on request. **Formerly:** School of Forestry - FRL Library.

★10916★
OREGON STATE UNIVERSITY - HATFIELD MARINE SCIENCE CENTER - LIBRARY (Biol Sci)
Newport, OR 97365 Phone: (503)867-3011
Marilyn Guin, Libn.
Founded: 1966. **Staff:** Prof 1; Other 2. **Subjects:** Marine biology and fisheries, mariculture, marine pollution. **Holdings:** 7000 books; 9500 bound periodical volumes; 5000 reprints; microforms; ASFA and Life Sciences databases on CD-ROM. **Subscriptions:** 350 journals and other serials. **Services:** Interlibrary loan; copying; library open to the public with restrictions. **Automated Operations:** Computerized cataloging and ILL. **Computerized Information Services:** DIALOG Information Services, OCLC. Performs searches on fee basis. **Remarks:** Contains the holdings of Oregon State Department of Fish and Wildlife - Newport Laboratory Library.

★10917★
OREGON STATE UNIVERSITY - WILLIAM JASPER KERR LIBRARY (Agri, Sci-Engr, Biol Sci)
Corvallis, OR 97331 Phone: (503)754-3411
Melvin R. George, Dir. of Libs.
Founded: 1887. **Staff:** Prof 36; Other 52. **Subjects:** Engineering, agriculture, marine science, forestry. **Special Collections:** Linus Pauling Scientific Collection. **Holdings:** 1.08 million volumes; 174,743 maps; 58,138 photographs, pictures, prints; 315,452 U.N. and U.S. Government documents; 34,573 reels of microfilm; 1.5 million microforms. **Subscriptions:** 7623 journals and other serials; 167 newspapers. **Services:** Interlibrary loan; copying; library open to the public with restrictions. **Automated Operations:** Computerized cataloging, acquisitions, and serials. **Computerized Information Services:** DIALOG Information Services, BRS Information Technologies, Pergamon ORBIT InfoLine, Inc., MEDLARS, STN International, OCLC. Performs searches on fee basis. Contact Person: Karen Starr, Lib.Info.Ret.Coord., 754-2249. **Publications:** Bibliography of forestry theses, annual. **Special Catalogs:** Oregon Union List of Serials. **Special Indexes:** Newspaper index to the Gazette Times. **Staff:** Gloriana St. Clair, Asst.Dir., Tech.Serv.; Robert Lawrence, Sci.-Tech.Ref.Libn.; Patricia Brandt, Soc.Sci./Hum. & Bus.; Michael Kinch, Agri.-Forestry; Doris Tilles, ILL; Craig Wilson, Asst.Dir., Coll.Dev.; Karyle Butcher,

Asst.Dir., Res. & Ref.; John Calhoun, Acq.Libn.; Clifford Mead, Spec.Coll..

★10918★
OREGON STATE WATER RESOURCES DEPARTMENT - LIBRARY & INFORMATION CENTER
3850 Portland Rd., N.E.
Salem, OR 97302
Founded: 1956. **Subjects:** Water, statistics, dams and reservoirs, water rights, ground water. **Holdings:** 6000 books. **Remarks:** Presently inactive.

★10919★
OREGONIAN LIBRARY (Publ)
1320 S.W. Broadway Phone: (503)221-8131
Portland, OR 97201 Doris N. Smith, Hd.Libn.
Staff: Prof 6; Other 3. **Subjects:** Newspaper reference topics. **Holdings:** News photographs; microfilm and microfiche of the Oregonian. **Subscriptions:** 52 journals and other serials. **Services:** Library not open to the public. **Computerized Information Services:** VU/TEXT Information Services. **Remarks:** Published by Oregonian Publishing Co. **Staff:** Sandra Macomber, Asst.Libn..

ORGAN HISTORICAL SOCIETY ARCHIVES
See: Westminster Choir College - Talbott Library (17783)

ORGAN PIPE CACTUS NATIONAL MONUMENT
See: U.S. Natl. Park Service (15335)

★10920★
ORGANIZATION OF AMERICAN STATES - COLUMBUS MEMORIAL LIBRARY (Area-Ethnic)
17th St. & Constitution Ave., N.W. Phone: (202)458-6040
Washington, DC 20006 Thomas L. Welch, Dir.
Founded: 1890. **Staff:** Prof 12; Other 12. **Subjects:** Inter-American system, member states, laws, regional development. **Special Collections:** OAS offical documents and technical and informational publications; publications of the specialized agencies; documents and publications of other international organizations; official gazettes of member states. **Holdings:** 602,000 books; 141,000 bound periodical volumes; 263,000 documents and publications of OAS, its predecessors and specialized agencies; 311,000 microforms. **Subscriptions:** 3618 journals and other serials; 61 newspapers. **Services:** Interlibrary loan; copying; library open to the public for reference use only. **Automated Operations:** Computerized cataloging and ILL. **Computerized Information Services:** DIALOG Information Services; internal database. **Networks/Consortia:** Member of CAPCON. **Publications:** List of Recent Acquisitions; CML Documentation and Information Services; Hipolito Unanue Bibliographic Series. **Special Indexes:** Index to OAS documents; index to Latin American periodical literature. **Also Known As:** OAS. **Staff:** Nora Fernandez, Hd., Cat.; Myriam Figueras, Hd., RD.Serv.; Beverly Wharton-Lake, Archv..

★10921★
ORGANIZATION DEVELOPMENT INSTITUTE - LIBRARY (Soc Sci)
11234 Walnut Ridge Rd.
Chesterland, OH 44026 Phone: (216)461-4333
Subjects: Conflict management, organization development. **Holdings:** 50 volumes.

★10922★
ORGANIZATION FOR ECONOMIC COOPERATION AND DEVELOPMENT - PUBLICATIONS AND INFORMATION CENTER (Soc Sci)
2001 L St., N.W., Suite 700 Phone: (202)785-6323
Washington, DC 20036-4905 Michael W. Moynihan, Hd.
Staff: Prof 3; Other 7. **Subjects:** International economic development, comparative statistics, agriculture, energy, educational research, environment, finance, transportation. **Holdings:** 1000 books; 500 bound periodical volumes. **Subscriptions:** 20 journals and other serials. **Services:** Copying; center open to the public. **Publications:** Recent OECD Publications, 4/year.

★10923★
ORGANIZATION FOR EQUAL EDUCATION OF THE SEXES - LIBRARY (Educ)
438 4th St. Phone: (718)788-3478
Brooklyn, NY 11215-2901 Lucy Simpson, Pres.
Founded: 1978. **Subjects:** Nonsexist curricula, women's history, sexism in education. **Holdings:** 1000 volumes. **Services:** Library not open to the public.

★10924★
ORGANIZATION RESOURCES COUNSELORS, INC. - INFORMATION CENTER (Bus-Fin)
1211 Ave. of the Americas Phone: (212)719-3400
New York, NY 10036 Mary J. DuVal, Libn.
Founded: 1953. **Staff:** Prof 1; Other 1. **Subjects:** Employee relations, collective bargaining, labor law, labor statistics, human relations in industry, labor economics, wages and salaries, management. **Holdings:** 2000 books; 100 VF drawers. **Subscriptions:** 200 journals and other serials. **Services:** Interlibrary loan; center not open to the public. **Computerized Information Services:** DIALOG Information Services, Human Resource Information Network (HRIN).

ORI, INC. - INFORMATION SYSTEMS DIVISION - ERIC PROCESSING AND REFERENCE FACILITY
See: ERIC Processing and Reference Facility (4777)

★10925★
ORLANDO MUNICIPAL REFERENCE SERVICE (Soc Sci)
City Hall
400 S. Orange Ave. Phone: (407)849-2249
Orlando, FL 32801 Nancy Ahlin, Libn.
Founded: 1973. **Staff:** Prof 1; Other 1. **Subjects:** City of Orlando, public administration, other local governments. **Special Collections:** City publications (450 volumes). **Holdings:** 1500 documents; 11 VF drawers; Orlando reports and studies. **Subscriptions:** 63 journals and other serials. **Services:** Interlibrary loan; copying; library open to the public for reference use only. **Computerized Information Services:** LOGIN. Performs searches on fee basis.

★10926★
ORLANDO MUSEUM OF ART - MUSEUM LIBRARY (Art)
2416 N. Mills Ave. Phone: (407)896-4231
Orlando, FL 32803 Jody Feltus, Publicity Coord.
Staff: 2. **Subjects:** Fine arts, American painting and prints, Pre-Columbian and African art. **Holdings:** 1235 books; 425 pamphlets on artists and art; 200 catalogs of museums, collections, exhibitions, galleries. **Services:** Interlibrary loan; copying; library open to museum members. **Automated Operations:** Computerized cataloging. **Formerly:** Orlando Museum of Art at Loch Haven, Inc.

★10927★
ORLANDO REGIONAL MEDICAL CENTER - MEDICAL LIBRARY (Med)
1414 S. Kuhl Ave. Phone: (407)855-8771
Orlando, FL 32806 Mary C. Garmany, Dir.
Staff: Prof 2; Other 1. **Subjects:** Medicine. **Holdings:** 2500 books; 15,000 bound periodical volumes. **Subscriptions:** 225 journals and other serials. **Services:** Interlibrary loan; copying; SDI; library open to the public with permission from Office of Risk Management. **Computerized Information Services:** MEDLARS. **Staff:** Diane Balodis, Assoc.Libn..

★10928★
ORLANDO SENTINEL NEWSPAPER - LIBRARY (Publ)
633 N. Orange Ave., Mail Point 9 Phone: (407)420-5510
Orlando, FL 32801 Judy L. Grimsley, Info.Rsrcs.Mgr.
Staff: Prof 11. **Subjects:** Newspaper reference topics, biography. **Holdings:** 1000 books; 300 bound periodical volumes; 3500 reels of microfilm of newspapers, 1911 to present; 3 million clippings; 750,000 photographs; pamphlets. **Subscriptions:** 30 journals and other serials. **Services:** Library open to journalists by special permission. **Automated Operations:** Computerized acquisitions and serials. **Computerized Information Services:** DataTimes, NEXIS, VU/TEXT Information Services. **Remarks:** Alternative telephone numbers are 420-5535 and 420-5511. **Staff:** Jeannine DeLancett, Res.Libn.; Susan Thompson, News Libn.; Janice Paiano, Info.Sys.Spec.; Jill Simser, Ref.Libn.; Carolyn McClendon, Weekend Supv..

ORLEANS-NIAGARA EDUCATIONAL COMMUNICATIONS CENTER
See: BOCES (1685)

★10929★
OROVILLE HOSPITAL AND MEDICAL CENTER - EDWARD P. GODDARD, M.D., MEMORIAL LIBRARY (Med)
2767 Olive Hwy. Phone: (916)533-8500
Oroville, CA 95966 Gertrude N. Bartley, Libn.
Staff: Prof 1. **Subjects:** Medicine. **Holdings:** 150 books. **Subscriptions:** 29 journals and other serials. **Services:** Interlibrary loan; library not open to

the public. **Computerized Information Services:** MEDLARS. **Networks/ Consortia:** Member of Pacific Southwest Regional Medical Library Service.

★10930★
ORPHAN VOYAGE - KAMMANDALE LIBRARY (Hist)
57 N. Dale Phone: (612)224-5160
St. Paul, MN 55102 Jeanette G. Kamman, Dir.
Founded: 1975. **Staff:** Prof 4. **Subjects:** Local history, genealogy, graphology. **Special Collections:** Local school yearbooks (500); books on books; authors; nationalities (countries); cartoon scrapbooks (450). **Holdings:** 25,000 books; 5000 bound periodical volumes; pamphlets; maps; obituaries; newspaper clippings. **Services:** Copying; library open to the public by appointment. **Staff:** Clark Bradley Hansen, Libn., Bookdealer; Ruth Kudlaty, Libn.; Robert Olson, Geneal..

★10931★
ORPHAN VOYAGE - MUSEUM OF ORPHANHOOD - LIBRARY (Soc Sci)
2141 Road 2300 Phone: (303)856-3937
Cedaredge, CO 81413 Jean Paton, Coord.
Staff: 1. **Subjects:** Orphans as explorers and discoverers, philosophers and religious, fantasy writers, scholars and scientists, painters and poets; fiction by orphans; biographies of orphans in public affairs. **Special Collections:** Americana on orphans; Heritage Press Collection of orphan writers; legislative hearings about adoption. **Holdings:** 850 books; unbound reports; manuscripts; clippings; magnetic tapes; paperbound books. **Subscriptions:** 30 newsletters. **Services:** Copying (limited); library open to the public by appointment for reference use. **Publications:** The Adoption Series.

★10932★
ORRICK, HERRINGTON & SUTCLIFFE - GEORGE HERRINGTON LIBRARY (Law)
600 Montgomery St. Phone: (415)392-1122
San Francisco, CA 94111 Cynthia Papermaster, Libn.
Staff: Prof 2; Other 4. **Subjects:** Law. **Holdings:** 35,000 volumes; 6 drawers of cassettes; microfiche. **Subscriptions:** 260 journals and other serials. **Services:** Interlibrary loan; library open by arrangement to members of the Special Libraries Association and the American Association of Law Libraries. **Automated Operations:** Computerized cataloging. **Computerized Information Services:** LEXIS, DIALOG Information Services, WESTLAW, RLIN, Dow Jones News/Retrieval, VU/TEXT Information Services, DataTimes, Information America, Dun & Bradstreet Corporation; ABA/net (electronic mail service). **Networks/Consortia:** Member of CLASS. **Publications:** OH&S Library News (newsletter) - for internal distribution only. **Special Indexes:** Index to Memoranda of Law (book); index to company prospectuses (online, book). **Staff:** James Mullin, Libn..

★10933★
ORTHO PHARMACEUTICAL (Canada), LTD. - LIBRARY (Med)
19 Green Belt Dr.
Don Mills, ON, Canada M3C 1L9 Phone: (416)449-9444
Founded: 1967. **Staff:** 2. **Subjects:** Contraception, family planning, immunology, business management. **Holdings:** 1565 books; 580 bound periodical volumes; microfiche. **Subscriptions:** 285 journals and other serials. **Services:** Interlibrary loan; library open to the public by appointment. **Automated Operations:** Computerized circulation. **Computerized Information Services:** MEDLINE, TOXLINE, DIALOG Information Services, Infomart, Info Globe, Data-Star, INSIGHT, Pergamon ORBIT InfoLine, Inc., The Financial Post Information Service; internal database. **Publications:** Book List, semiannual; Journal Distribution List, semiannual. **Staff:** Marta Bodnar, Libn.; Irene Meiklejohn, Libn..

★10934★
ORTHO PHARMACEUTICAL CORPORATION - HARTMAN LIBRARY (Med)
Route 202
Box 300 Phone: (201)218-7430
Raritan, NJ 08869-0602 June Bente, Mgr., Lib.Serv.
Founded: 1944. **Staff:** Prof 2; Other 2. **Subjects:** Medicine, pharmacy, endocrinology, biological sciences, chemistry. **Holdings:** 5000 books; 15,000 bound periodical volumes. **Subscriptions:** 700 journals and other serials. **Services:** Interlibrary loan; library open to the public by appointment. **Automated Operations:** Computerized public access catalog, cataloging, acquisitions, serials, and circulation. **Computerized Information Services:** BRS Information Technologies, DIALOG Information Services, Pergamon ORBIT InfoLine, Inc., MEDLINE, U.S. National Technical Information Service (NTIS). **Networks/Consortia:** Member of Medical Resources Consortium of Central New Jersey (MEDCORE). **Staff:** Jean Shepley, Supv., Tech.Serv..

★10935★
ORTHODOX CHURCH IN AMERICA - DEPARTMENT OF HISTORY AND ARCHIVES (Rel-Phil, Hist)
Rte. 25A, Box 675
Syosset, NY 11791 Phone: (516)922-0550
Staff: Prof 1. **Subjects:** Orthodox Church history - American, Carpatho-Russian, Greek; immigration history - Russian, Syrian, Albanian. **Holdings:** 270 linear feet of archival materials; 240 linear feet of periodicals and other print media; parish and individual collections. **Services:** Copying; archives open to the public with restrictions. **Special Catalogs:** Comprehensive guides and catalogs are under preparation.

★10936★
ORTHOPAEDIC AND ARTHRITIC HOSPITAL - HEALTH SCIENCES LIBRARY (Med)
43 Wellesley St., E. Phone: (416)967-8545
Toronto, ON, Canada M4Y 1H1 Sheila M. Lethbridge, Libn.
Staff: Prof 2. **Subjects:** Orthopedics, arthritis, physical and occupational therapy. **Holdings:** 1000 books; 550 bound periodical volumes. **Subscriptions:** 80 journals and other serials. **Services:** Interlibrary loan; library not open to the public.

★10937★
ORTHOPAEDIC HOSPITAL - RUBEL MEMORIAL LIBRARY (Med)
2400 S. Flower St.
Box 60132, Terminal Annex Phone: (213)742-1530
Los Angeles, CA 90060-0132 Veena N. Vyas, Dir., Med.Lib.
Staff: Prof 1; Other 1. **Subjects:** Orthopedics. **Holdings:** 3000 books; 3260 bound periodical volumes. **Subscriptions:** 185 journals and other serials. **Services:** Interlibrary loan; library not open to the public. **Computerized Information Services:** DIALOG Information Services, MEDLINE; DOCLINE (electronic mail service). **Networks/Consortia:** Member of Pacific Southwest Regional Medical Library Service. **Publications:** New Book List; Serials List. **Remarks:** An alternate telephone number is 742-1531.

★10938★
ORTHOPEDIC FOUNDATION FOR ANIMALS - OFA HIP DYSPLASIA REGISTRY (Med)
Middlebush Farm
Hwy. 63 S. Phone: (314)442-0418
Columbia, MO 65211 Dr. E. Al Corley, Proj.Dir.
Staff: 5. **Subjects:** Veterinary medicine. **Holdings:** 120,000 radiographs - Hip Registry X-Ray, evaluated for canine hip dysplasia in purebred dogs. **Remarks:** Sponsored by the Orthopedic Foundation for Animals at the University of Missouri, Columbia - College of Veterinary Medicine.

ORTON MEMORIAL LIBRARY OF GEOLOGY
See: Ohio State University (10704)

★10939★
OSAWATOMIE STATE HOSPITAL - RAPAPORT PROFESSIONAL LIBRARY - MENTAL HEALTH LIBRARY (Med)
Osawatomie, KS 66064 Phone: (913)755-3151
Helen Porter, Dir., Lib.Serv.
Founded: 1949. **Staff:** Prof 2; Other 2. **Subjects:** Psychiatry, psychology, social sciences, medicine, nursing, special education. **Holdings:** 7045 books; 2704 bound periodical volumes; 624 audiotapes; 100 videotapes; 30 VF drawers of dissertations, reprints, pamphlets, documents. **Subscriptions:** 93 journals and other serials. **Services:** Interlibrary loan; copying; library open to public at librarian's discretion. **Networks/Consortia:** Member of Midcontinental Regional Medical Library Program.

★10940★
OSBORN LABORATORIES OF MARINE SCIENCES - NEW YORK AQUARIUM LIBRARY (Biol Sci)
W. Eighth St. & Surf Ave. Phone: (718)266-8500
Brooklyn, NY 11224 G.D. Ruggieri, Ph.D., Dir.
Founded: 1902. **Subjects:** Ichthyology, aquariology, diseases of fish, invertebrates, amphibians and reptiles, marine biochemistry, invertebrate zoology, physiology of fish, marine mammalogy. **Special Collections:** Diseases of aquatic organisms; complete card file of animals of Bay of Naples. **Holdings:** 3000 books; 100 bound periodical volumes; 4000 reprints; 100 theses on aquatic subjects; photographs, films, and slides of aquatic organisms. **Services:** Library open to the public by special

permission. **Also Known As:** New York Zoological Society - New York Aquarium Library.**Staff:** Mildred Montalbano, Libn..

OSBORN LIBRARY OF VERTEBRATE PALEONTOLOGY
See: American Museum of Natural History (610)

STANLEY H. OSBORN MEDICAL LIBRARY
See: Connecticut State Department of Health Services (3654)

OSBORNE COLLECTION OF EARLY CHILDREN'S BOOKS
See: Toronto Public Library (14249)

OSBORNE LIBRARY
See: Connecticut Agricultural Experiment Station (3642)

RICHARD E. OSGOOD, M.D. MEDICAL LIBRARY
See: Los Angeles County/High Desert Hospital (7988)

OSHA
See: U.S. Dept. of Labor - OSHA (15054)

OSHA
See: U.S. Dept. of Labor - OSHA - Billings Area Office Library (15050)

O'SHAUGHNESSY LIBRARY
See: College of St. Thomas (3395)

★10941★
OSHAWA & DISTRICT HISTORICAL SOCIETY - ARCHIVES (Hist)
6 Henry St.
P.O. Box 2303 Phone: (416)436-7624
Oshawa, ON, Canada L1H 7V5 Norah Herd, Archv.
Founded: 1957. **Staff:** Prof 1; Other 5. **Subjects:** Oshawa history, industry. **Special Collections:** Pedlar manuscripts on microfilm. **Holdings:** Family histories; manuscripts; microfilm. **Services:** Copying; archives open to the public for reference use only. **Remarks:** An alternate telephone number is 436-7625.

★10942★
OSHAWA GENERAL HOSPITAL - EDUCATION RESOURCE CENTRE (Med)
24 Alma St. Phone: (416)576-8711
Oshawa, ON, Canada L1G 2B9 Susan Hendricks, Med.Libn.
Founded: 1973. **Staff:** Prof 1; Other 1. **Subjects:** Medicine, nursing, allied health sciences, telemedicine. **Special Collections:** Genetics. **Holdings:** 1000 books; 3000 bound periodical volumes; VF drawers. **Subscriptions:** 155 journals and other serials. **Services:** Interlibrary loan; center not open to the public. **Computerized Information Services:** MEDLARS, MEDLINE, DIALOG Information Services; Envoy 100 (electronic mail service). **Networks/Consortia:** Member of Ontario Hospital Libraries Association (OHLA).

★10943★
OSHKOSH PUBLIC MUSEUM - LIBRARY & ARCHIVES (Hist)
1331 Algoma Blvd. Phone: (414)236-5150
Oshkosh, WI 54901 Kitty A. Hobson, Archv.
Founded: 1924. **Staff:** Prof 1. **Subjects:** Local and state history, anthropology and archeology, arts and crafts, botany and zoology. **Special Collections:** River Steamboat History (3 VF drawers of photographs, clippings, narratives); Lumbering and Logging (3 VF drawers of photographs, clippings, narratives); Inland Lakes Yachting Association minutes, 1899 to present. **Holdings:** 8000 clippings and manuscripts; 200 bound periodical volumes; 68 VF drawers of historical photographs and pamphlets; 400 maps. **Subscriptions:** 25 journals and other serials. **Services:** Interlibrary loan; copying; library open to the public for reference use only.

OSLER LIBRARY
See: Mc Gill University - Osler Library (8210)

★10944★
OSSINING HISTORICAL SOCIETY MUSEUM - LIBRARY (Hist)
196 Croton Ave. Phone: (914)941-0001
Ossining, NY 10562 Roberta Y. Arminio, Info.Dir.
Founded: 1931. **Staff:** Prof 2; Other 3. **Subjects:** Local history and genealogy. **Special Collections:** Goodrich Memorial Law Library. **Holdings:** 1100 books; 122 bound periodical volumes; 390 volumes of newspapers; 10 VF drawers of manuscripts, pamphlets, clippings, documents, reports; 300 maps; 1000 photographs. **Services:** Interlibrary loan; copying; library open to the public.

OTIS ART INSTITUTE
See: Parsons School of Design (11087)

★10945★
OTT WATER ENGINEERS, INC. - LIBRARY (Sci-Engr)
2334 Washington Ave. Phone: (916)244-1920
Redding, CA 96001 Ann S. Wright, Corp.Libn.
Founded: 1978. **Staff:** Prof 1. **Subjects:** Water resources and quality, meteorological data for the western United States, hydropower development. **Holdings:** 3000 books; 1000 other cataloged items. **Subscriptions:** 72 journals and other serials. **Services:** Interlibrary loan; copying; library open to the public. **Automated Operations:** Computerized cataloging. **Computerized Information Services:** DIALOG Information Services; internal databases.

★10946★
(Ottawa) CITIZEN - LIBRARY (Publ)
1101 Baxter Rd.
Box 5020 Phone: (613)596-3746
Ottawa, ON, Canada K2C 3M4 Steven Proulx, Chf.Libn.
Founded: 1970. **Staff:** Prof 5; Other 2. **Subjects:** Biography - local, national, international; newspaper reference topics. **Holdings:** 400 volumes; 20,000 subject clipping files; 15,000 biographical clipping files. **Subscriptions:** 10 journals and other serials; 10 newspapers. **Services:** Library open to the media only. **Computerized Information Services:** Info Globe, QL Systems, DIALOG Information Services, Infomart, NEXIS, Canada Systems Group (CSG); internal database. **Staff:** Ronald P. Tysick, Photo Libn.; Charlene Ruberry, Ref.; James Van Der Mark, Sys.Libn..

★10947★
OTTAWA CIVIC HOSPITAL - DR. GEORGE S. WILLIAMSON HEALTH SCIENCES LIBRARY (Med)
1053 Carling Ave. Phone: (613)725-4450
Ottawa, ON, Canada K1Y 4E9 Mabel C. Brown, Dir., Lib.Serv.
Founded: 1957. **Staff:** Prof 4; Other 5. **Subjects:** Medicine, nursing, allied health sciences. **Holdings:** 3000 books; 5000 bound periodical volumes. **Subscriptions:** 347 journals and other serials. **Services:** Interlibrary loan; copying; SDI; Clinical Librarian Service; Regional Library Service; Current Awareness Service; library open to the public with restrictions. **Computerized Information Services:** Info Globe, CAN/OLE, DIALOG Information Services, MEDLINE; Envoy 100 (electronic mail service). **Networks/Consortia:** Member of O.H.A. Region 9 Hospital Libraries. **Publications:** Acquisition lists, irregular; bibliographies; newsletter. **Staff:** Patricia Johnston, Asst.Libn., Pub.Serv. & Sys.; Kyungja Shin, Asst.Libn., Tech.Serv.; Ursula Riendeau, Reg. & Clin.Libn..

★10948★
OTTAWA GENERAL HOSPITAL - MEDICAL LIBRARY (Med)
501 Smyth Rd. Phone: (613)737-8530
Ottawa, ON, Canada K1H 8L6 Francine Ryan, Supv.
Founded: 1936. **Staff:** Prof 1; Other 1. **Subjects:** Medicine. **Holdings:** 994 books; 3000 bound periodical volumes. **Subscriptions:** 245 journals and other serials. **Services:** Interlibrary loan; library not open to the public. **Also Known As:** Hopital General d'Ottawa.

★10949★
OTTAWA PUBLIC LIBRARY - OTTAWA ROOM (Hist)
120 Metcalfe St., 2nd Fl. Phone: (613)236-0301
Ottawa, ON, Canada K1P 5M2 Thomas Rooney, Libn.
Founded: 1955. **Staff:** Prof 1. **Subjects:** Ottawa - history, municipal affairs, authors, genealogy, imprints; Ottawa Valley. **Holdings:** 9668 books; 108 boxes of archival records, annual reports, periodicals, city and telephone directories; 8 cassettes; 25 microfiche; 302 vertical files; 7 volumes of Ottawa history scrapbooks; 2 volumes of Ottawa schools' scrapbooks; 50 linear feet of municipal documents; 170 rare books; maps. **Subscriptions:** 150 journals and other serials; 35 newspapers. **Services:** Copying; room open to the public for reference use only. **Automated Operations:** Computerized cataloging. **Computerized Information Services:** UTLAS, ULISYS. Performs searches free of charge. **Publications:** Ottawa History Bibliography (in preparation). **Special Indexes:** Ottawa Where-To-Look Index; Ottawa Journal Vital Records Index, 1885-1920.

★10950★
OTTAWA RESEARCH CORPORATION - IRENE HOLM MEMORIAL LIBRARY (Hist)
1465 Osborn Dr. Phone: (614)486-5028
Columbus, OH 43221 Ms. Bobbi Wilson, Libn.
Founded: 1976. **Staff:** Prof 2; Other 1. **Subjects:** Historic recordings, archives of Ottawa Institute, religious music. **Special Collections:** Edwardian music (400 cassette tapes); Arthur Lindner Memorial Collection of Historic Radio Broadcasts (3000 cassette tapes). **Holdings:** 600 books; 6200 audio cassettes; 36 VF drawers of institute archival materials; 100 compact discs; 100 open reel tapes; 1000 discs. **Services:** Interlibrary loan; copying (limited); library open to the public with restrictions. **Publications:** Research reports, irregular - by request. **Staff:** Scott-Eric Lindner, Audio Techn.; Timur Lenk, Audio Engr..

★10951★
OTTER TAIL COUNTY HISTORICAL SOCIETY - LIBRARY (Hist)
1110 Lincoln Ave., W. Phone: (218)736-6038
Fergus Falls, MN 56537 Pamela A. Brunfelt, Archv.
Staff: Prof 1; Other 2. **Subjects:** Local history. **Special Collections:** County newspapers, 1871 to present; War of the Rebellion - Official Records of the Union and Confederate Armies. **Holdings:** 300 books; 100 bound periodical volumes; manuscripts; business records; oral histories; records and newspapers on microfilm; slides; dissertations; maps; photographs. **Subscriptions:** 18 journals and other serials; 7 newspapers. **Services:** Library open to the public with restrictions. **Networks/Consortia:** Member of Northern Lights Library Network (NLLN).

★10952★
OTTER TAIL POWER COMPANY - LIBRARY (Energy)
215 S. Cascade Phone: (218)739-8213
Fergus Falls, MN 56537 Janet Johnson, Lib.Asst.
Staff: 1. **Subjects:** Business management, engineering. **Holdings:** 200 books; 250 Electric Power Research reports; 45 films; 15 videotapes; 11 slide presentations; Federal Registers on microfiche. **Subscriptions:** 145 journals and other serials; 20 newspapers. **Services:** Copying; library open to the public with restrictions. **Publications:** Library Notes, quarterly. **Special Catalogs:** Film catalog, annual.

★10953★
OTTUMWA REGIONAL HEALTH CENTER - ALTA VISTA SITE LIBRARY (Med)
312 E. Alta Vista Phone: (515)684-4651
Ottumwa, IA 52501 Sr. Mary Christine Conaway, Libn.
Founded: 1951. **Staff:** Prof 1; Other 1. **Subjects:** Nursing, medicine, allied health sciences, religion, literature, management. **Special Collections:** Pioneer History of Medicine in Iowa, Mississippi River Valley (5 pieces); archives of St. Joseph School of Nursing, 1914-1970. **Holdings:** 3520 books; 700 bound periodical volumes; 1712 pamphlets; 155 maps; 1542 AV programs; 14 VF drawers of reprints, clippings, diagrams; 4 VF drawers of archival materials; 2 dissertations. **Subscriptions:** 93 journals and other serials. **Services:** Interlibrary loan; copying; library open to the public for reference use only. **Automated Operations:** Computerized public access catalog. **Computerized Information Services:** MEDLINE, BRS Information Technologies. **Networks/Consortia:** Member of Greater Midwest Regional Medical Library Network. **Publications:** Scan (newsheet), quarterly; Scope, quarterly - both for internal distribution only; listing of duplicate journals, semiannual - to members of periodical exchange. **Special Catalogs:** AV catalog file; bibliographic file (card); vertical file subject catalog (card); archival catalog. **Special Indexes:** Archival indexes. **Formerly:** St. Joseph Health and Rehabilitation Center.

★10954★
OUACHITA BAPTIST UNIVERSITY - RILEY-HICKINGBOTHAM LIBRARY (Mus, Hist)
Arkadelphia, AR 71923 Phone: (501)246-4531
Ray Granade, Dir.
Founded: 1886. **Staff:** Prof 3; Other 4. **Subjects:** Liberal arts, music. **Special Collections:** Francis McBeth Collection (original manuscripts of music compositions, primarily for band and orchestra); John L. McClellan Papers, 1942-1978; Baptist history collection; Arkansas history; university archives. **Holdings:** 115,181 books; 16,333 bound periodical volumes; 226,323 microforms including ERIC; 7557 AV programs including 2990 scores, 3161 recordings, 904 tapes; 60,571 documents. **Subscriptions:** 1034 journals and other serials; 8 newspapers. **Services:** Interlibrary loan; copying; library open to the public by request. **Automated Operations:** Computerized cataloging and ILL. **Computerized Information Services:** OCLC. **Networks/Consortia:** Member of AMIGOS Bibliographic Council, Inc.. **Staff:** Schelley Childress, Hd., Tech.Proc.; Jenny Petty, Per.Libn.; Jean Rick, Circ.Libn.; Kim Patterson, AV Supv.; Janice Cockerham, Govt.Docs..

★10955★
OUR LADY OF THE LAKE REGIONAL MEDICAL CENTER - HEALTH SCIENCES LIBRARY (Med)
5000 Hennessy Blvd. Phone: (504)765-6565
Baton Rouge, LA 70809 Diane D. Whited, Libn.
Founded: 1923. **Staff:** Prof 1. **Subjects:** Medicine, nursing. **Holdings:** 5000 volumes. **Subscriptions:** 101 journals and other serials. **Services:** Interlibrary loan; library not open to the public. **Computerized Information Services:** DIALOG Information Services, MEDLARS; DOCLINE (electronic mail service). **Networks/Consortia:** Member of TALON, Baton Rouge Hospital Library Consortium.

★10956★
OUR LADY OF THE LAKE UNIVERSITY - OLD SPANISH MISSIONS HISTORICAL RESEARCH LIBRARY (Hist)
411 S.W. 24th St. Phone: (512)434-6711
San Antonio, TX 78285 Maria Carolina Flores, C.D.P., Archv.
Founded: 1971. **Subjects:** Franciscan missions in Texas, 1682-1834; Spanish shipwrecks off the coast of Texas; Texas Colonial history; Spanish Colonial period in Texas; missions in northern Mexico. **Special Collections:** Archival materials from Mexico, Spain, and other European countries (100 reels of microfilm). **Holdings:** 105 books; 50 maps; 20 photographs; 2000 slides. **Services:** Copying; library open to the public with restrictions. **Computerized Information Services:** DIALOG Information Services. Performs searches on fee basis. Contact Person: Antoinette Garza, Dir. of Lib.Serv., 434-6711, ext. 325. **Publications:** Documentary series, numbers 1-7. **Remarks:** Part of the Learning Resource Center of Our Lady of the Lake University. **Staff:** Margaret Rose Warburton, C.D.P., Cur..

★10957★
OUR LADY OF THE LAKE UNIVERSITY - WORDEN SCHOOL OF SOCIAL SERVICE - LIBRARY (Soc Sci)
411 S.W. 24th St. Phone: (512)434-6711
San Antonio, TX 78285 Sr. Julianna Kozuch, Libn.
Founded: 1942. **Staff:** Prof 1; Other 18. **Subjects:** Social work. **Holdings:** 14,972 books; 2194 bound periodical volumes; 325 case records; 259 theses. **Subscriptions:** 73 journals and other serials. **Services:** Interlibrary loan; copying; library open to the public. **Computerized Information Services:** DIALOG Information Services. Performs searches on fee basis. Contact Person: Judy Larson, Ref.Libn.. **Networks/Consortia:** Member of Council of Research & Academic Libraries (CORAL).

★10958★
OUR LADY OF LIGHT LIBRARY (Rel-Phil)
1500 Chapala Phone: (805)962-9708
Santa Barbara, CA 93101 Sally Dal Pozzo, Pres.
Founded: 1949. **Staff:** Prof 1. **Subjects:** Spiritual reading, biography, fiction, church history, philosophy, psychology. **Holdings:** 5500 books. **Services:** Library open to the public.

★10959★
OUR LADY OF LOURDES MEDICAL CENTER - MEDICAL LIBRARY (Med)
1600 Haddon Ave. Phone: (609)757-3548
Camden, NJ 08103 Fred Kafes, Dir.
Staff: Prof 1. **Subjects:** Medicine, nursing, allied health sciences, hospital administration. **Holdings:** 1160 books; 823 audio cassettes; 45 video cassettes; 10 slide/sound sets. **Subscriptions:** 280 journals and other serials. **Services:** Interlibrary loan; copying; SDI; library open to the public for reference use only. **Automated Operations:** Computerized cataloging and serials. **Computerized Information Services:** BRS Information Technologies. **Networks/Consortia:** Member of Southwest New Jersey Consortium for Health Information Services, New Jersey Health Sciences Library Network (NJHSN), South Jersey Regional Library Cooperative.

★10960★
OUR LADY OF LOURDES REGIONAL MEDICAL CENTER - LEARNING RESOURCE CENTER (Med)
611 St. Landry St.
Box 4027C Phone: (318)231-2141
Lafayette, LA 70502 Annette Tremie, Med.Libn.
Staff: Prof 1; Other 1. **Subjects:** Medicine, nursing, pastoral care. **Holdings:** 2500 books; unbound periodicals. **Subscriptions:** 128 journals and other serials. **Services:** Interlibrary loan; copying; center open to the public with restrictions. **Computerized Information Services:** BRS Information Technologies. **Networks/Consortia:** Member of TALON.

★10961★
OUR LADY OF LOURDES SCHOOL OF NURSING - LIBRARY (Med)
1565 Vesper Blvd. Phone: (609)757-3722
Camden, NJ 08103 Eleanor M. Kelly, Libn.
Founded: 1961. **Staff:** Prof 1. **Subjects:** Medicine, nursing, allied health sciences. **Holdings:** 2580 books; 61 bound periodical volumes; 205 AV programs; 4 VF drawers of clippings, reports, pamphlets. **Subscriptions:** 48 journals and other serials. **Services:** Interlibrary loan; copying; library use restricted to nursing students. **Networks/Consortia:** Member of Southwest New Jersey Consortium for Health Information Services, New Jersey Health Sciences Library Network (NJHSN), BHSL, South Jersey Regional Library Cooperative, Delaware Valley Audiovisual Exchange (DAVE).

★10962★
OUR LADY OF MERCY MEDICAL CENTER - MEDICAL LIBRARY (Med)
600 E. 233rd St., Rm. B-11 Phone: (212)920-9869
Bronx, NY 10466 Sr. Jeanne Atkinson, Chf.Med.Libn.
Staff: Prof 1; Other 2. **Subjects:** Medicine. **Holdings:** 1942 books; 6739 bound periodical volumes; 64 volumes of microforms. **Subscriptions:** 350 journals and other serials. **Services:** Interlibrary loan; copying; library open to health care personnel. **Computerized Information Services:** BRS Information Technologies. **Networks/Consortia:** Member of Medical Library Center of New York (MLCNY), Manhattan-Bronx Health Sciences Library Group.

★10963★
OUR LADY OF PEACE HOSPITAL - MEDICAL LIBRARY (Med)
2020 Newburg Rd. Phone: (502)451-3330
Louisville, KY 40232 Irene Satory, S.C.N., Dir.
Founded: 1951. **Staff:** Prof 1. **Subjects:** Psychiatry, alcoholism and substance abuse, nursing, pediatrics. **Holdings:** 1480 books; 836 bound periodical volumes; 500 cassettes (psychiatric series); 12 VF drawers of pamphlets, clippings, archives. **Subscriptions:** 84 journals and other serials. **Services:** Interlibrary loan; library not open to the public. **Networks/Consortia:** Member of Kentucky Health Sciences Library Consortium.

★10964★
OUR LADY QUEEN OF MARTYRS - ST. LUCIAN LIBRARY (Rel-Phil)
32460 S. Pierce Phone: (313)644-8620
Birmingham, MI 48009 Ruth E. Brady, Lib.Chm.
Founded: 1957. **Staff:** Prof 3; Other 7. **Subjects:** Religion, philosophy, biography, geography, history, travel. **Holdings:** 2500 books. **Services:** Library open to church congregation.

OUR LADY OF THE ROCK
See: Abbey of Regina Laudis, Order of St. Benedict (6)

★10965★
OUR LADY OF SORROWS BASILICA - ARCHIVES (Rel-Phil)
3121 W. Jackson Blvd. Phone: (312)638-5800
Chicago, IL 60612 Rev. Conrad M. Borntrager, O.S.M., Archv.
Staff: 1. **Subjects:** Parish archives. **Holdings:** 66 bound periodical volumes; 78 linear feet of archives; 2 filing drawers of photographs; 56 blueprints. **Services:** Archives open to the public with restrictions.

★10966★
OUR LADY OF VICTORY HOSPITAL - HOSPITAL LIBRARY (Med)
55 Melroy at Ridge Rd. Phone: (716)825-8000
Lackawanna, NY 14218 Ann Hassett, Lib.Ck.
Founded: 1960. **Staff:** 1. **Subjects:** Medicine, surgery, allied health sciences. **Holdings:** 650 books. **Subscriptions:** 48 journals and other serials. **Services:** Interlibrary loan; library not open to the public.

★10967★
OUR LADY OF THE WAY HOSPITAL - MEDICAL LIBRARY (Med)
Box 910 Phone: (606)285-5181
Martin, KY 41649 Naewana Nickles, Act.Libn.
Staff: Prof 1. **Subjects:** Medicine, nursing. **Holdings:** 100 books. **Subscriptions:** 25 journals and other serials. **Services:** Interlibrary loan; library not open to the public. **Automated Operations:** Computerized cataloging. **Networks/Consortia:** Member of Eastern Kentucky Health Science Information Network (EKHSIN).

★10968★
OUR REDEEMERS LUTHERAN CHURCH - LIBRARY (Rel-Phil)
Tenth St., S. & Oakwood Ave. Phone: (612)843-3151
Benson, MN 56215 Marlene Skold, Libn.
Founded: 1958. **Staff:** 1. **Subjects:** Theology, devotional material. **Holdings:** 1500 books; pamphlets; filmstrips. **Services:** Library open to the public with restrictions.

★10969★
OUR SAVIOR'S LUTHERAN CHURCH - LIBRARY (Rel-Phil)
3022 W. Wisconsin Ave. Phone: (414)342-5252
Milwaukee, WI 53208 Karen Roe, Libn.
Founded: 1955. **Subjects:** Religion. **Special Collections:** Cassette tapes recorded by staff members and members of congregation (concerts; sermons; lectures). **Holdings:** 6000 books; 2000 pictures; 400 filmstrips; 200 phonograph records. **Subscriptions:** 35 journals and other serials. **Services:** Library open to the public with restrictions.

★10970★
OUTAGAMIE COUNTY LAW LIBRARY (Law)
410 S. Walnut St., Rm. C304 Phone: (414)735-5149
Appleton, WI 54911 Harriet J. Peppard, Law Ck.
Staff: 1. **Subjects:** Law. **Holdings:** 10,000 volumes. **Services:** Library open to the public.

★10971★
OUTBOARD MARINE CORPORATION - RESEARCH CENTER LIBRARY (Sci-Engr)
4109 N. 27th
Box 663
Milwaukee, WI 53201 Phone: (414)447-5400
Staff: 1. **Subjects:** Mechanical and electrical engineering, mechanics, internal combustion engines, mathematics, metallurgy. **Holdings:** 1900 volumes; 6000 technical reports; 2000 vendors' catalogs; 200 reels of microfilm; 3000 corporation reports; 9000 technical society papers. **Subscriptions:** 60 journals and other serials. **Services:** Interlibrary loan; copying; library open to other technical organizations by special arrangement. **Automated Operations:** Computerized cataloging. **Computerized Information Services:** Internal database. **Networks/Consortia:** Member of Library Council of Metropolitan Milwaukee, Inc. (LCOMM). **Publications:** Library Information Bulletin, monthly.

OUTDOOR EDUCATION RESOURCE LIBRARY
See: National Outdoor Leadership School (9750)

★10972★
W.H. OVER STATE MUSEUM - LIBRARY
University of South Dakota
414 E. Clark Phone: (605)677-5228
Vermillion, SD 57069 Julia R. Vodicka, Musm.Dir.
Staff: Prof 2. **Subjects:** Archeology, anthropology, natural history, history, museology, decorative arts, photography. **Special Collections:** Papers of William H. Over; Morrow Photographic Collection (600). **Holdings:** 1200 books; 36 bound periodical volumes; 22 museum notebooks of clippings; 50 manuscripts. **Subscriptions:** 15 journals and other serials. **Services:** Copying; library open to the public for reference use only. **Special Indexes:** Morrow Photograph Collection. **Remarks:** Maintained by South Dakota State Department of Education and Cultural Affairs. **Staff:** Cleo Kosters, Cur..

★10973★
OVERBROOK SCHOOL FOR THE BLIND - LIBRARY (Aud-Vis)
64th St. & Malvern Ave. Phone: (215)877-0313
Philadelphia, PA 19151 Edith L. Willoughby, Libn.
Founded: 1832. **Staff:** Prof 1. **Subjects:** Standard, large print, and braille books for kindergarten through high school; general library of braille, talking book, tape, and print titles for primary, elementary, and high school; library of print for faculty members. **Special Collections:** Historical material on education of the blind and other aspects of blindness; deafness. **Holdings:** 12,500 braille books; 5000 printed books; 600 large print books; 3000 talking books, tapes, cassettes. **Subscriptions:** 75 journals and other serials in print and braille. **Services:** Library open to the public for reference use only by request.

★10974★
OVERLOOK HOSPITAL - HEALTH SCIENCES LIBRARY (Med)
193 Morris Ave. Phone: (201)522-2119
Summit, NJ 07901 Kathleen A. Moeller, Dir.
Founded: 1946. **Staff:** Prof 1; Other 3. **Subjects:** Medicine, surgery, nursing, radiology, emergency medicine, psychiatry, pediatrics, orthopedics. **Special Collections:** Consumer Health Information Collection (1500 books; 25 journals; free pamphlets). **Holdings:** 6000 books; 12,000 bound periodical volumes; 2000 subject files for LATCH Program; 600 AV programs. **Subscriptions:** 500 journals and other serials. **Services:** Interlibrary loan; copying; library open to the public. **Automated Operations:** Computerized serials and circulation. **Computerized Information Services:** MEDLARS, DIALOG Information Services, BRS Information Technologies. Performs searches on fee basis. **Networks/ Consortia:** Member of Cosmopolitan Biomedical Library Consortium (CBLC), Health Sciences Library Association of New Jersey, Medical Library Center of New York (MLCNY).

★10975★
OVERSEAS DEVELOPMENT COUNCIL - LIBRARY (Soc Sci)
1717 Massachusetts Ave., N.W., Suite 501 Phone: (202)234-8701
Washington, DC 20036 Katherine Bowen, Libn.
Founded: 1970. **Staff:** Prof 1; Other 1. **Subjects:** International trade and industrial policy, international finance and investment, development strategies and development assistance, U.S. foreign policy toward developing countries, U.S.-Mexico relations. **Holdings:** 1300 books. **Subscriptions:** 50 journals and other serials; 6 newspapers. **Services:** Interlibrary loan; copying; library open to the public by appointment.

★10976★
OVERSEAS PRIVATE INVESTMENT CORPORATION - LIBRARY (Bus-Fin)
1615 M St., N.W. Phone: (202)457-7123
Washington, DC 20527 Myra Norton, Libn.
Founded: 1974. **Staff:** Prof 3; Other 2. **Subjects:** Multinational business, foreign investments, international law, economics of developing countries, foreign relations. **Special Collections:** Legislative histories on foreign assistance and international development (300 volumes); country file (54 linear feet). **Holdings:** 6000 books; 8 linear feet of VF drawers. **Subscriptions:** 240 journals and other serials; 10 newspapers. **Services:** Interlibrary loan; copying; SDI; library open to the public by appointment. **Automated Operations:** Computerized cataloging, acquisitions, and circulation. **Computerized Information Services:** DIALOG Information Services, NEXIS, LEXIS, Dow Jones News/Retrieval, LEGI-SLATE, DunSprint, TEXTLINE, OCLC. **Networks/Consortia:** Member of FEDLINK. **Publications:** Information Courier, bimonthly - for internal distribution only; User's Guide to Information Services. **Remarks:** OPIC is an independent U.S. Government agency which provides financing and political risk insurance to U.S. businesses to encourage investment in developing countries.

OVIATT LIBRARY
See: California State University, Northridge (2228)

★10977★
OWATONNA PUBLIC LIBRARY - TOY LIBRARY (Educ)
105 N. Elm
Box 387 Phone: (507)451-4660
Owatonna, MN 55060 Andrea Hoslett, Hd., Ch.Serv.
Staff: Prof 1; Other 2. **Subjects:** Manipulative toys, reading readiness, math and science, parenting. **Holdings:** 300 toys; 50 pamphlets. **Services:** Library open to the public with restrictions. **Automated Operations:** Computerized cataloging, acquisitions, and circulation. **Computerized Information Services:** ATLAS (internal database). **Special Catalogs:** Illustrated toy catalog (loose-leaf).

OWEN SCIENCE AND ENGINEERING LIBRARY
See: Washington State University (17527)

OWENS-CORNING FIBERGLAS CORPORATION - HITCO
See: Hitco (6361)

★10978★
OWENS-CORNING FIBERGLAS CORPORATION - TECHNICAL DATA CENTER (Sci-Engr)
Technical Center
Rte. 16 Phone: (614)587-7265
Granville, OH 43023-0415 Nancy Lemon, Supv., Res.Lib.
Staff: Prof 1; Other 1. **Subjects:** Glass, ceramics, polymers, reinforced plastics, glass textiles, mathematics, chemistry, management, safety engineering, science. **Holdings:** 10,000 books; 20,000 bound periodical volumes; 2500 translations; 500 annual reports. **Subscriptions:** 200 journals and other serials. **Services:** Interlibrary loan; copying; SDI; Current Awareness Service; center open to the public by appointment. **Automated Operations:** Computerized cataloging and acquisitions. **Computerized Information Services:** OCLC, DIALOG Information Services, STN International, BRS Information Technologies, CompuServe, Inc., Pergamon ORBIT InfoLine, Inc. **Networks/Consortia:** Member of OHIONET.

★10979★
OWENS-ILLINOIS - INFORMATION RESEARCH DEPARTMENT
One Seagate
Toledo, OH 43666
Defunct

OWENS LIBRARY
See: Northwest Missouri State University - Owens Library (10474)

★10980★
OWENSBORO AREA MUSEUM - LIBRARY (Sci-Engr)
2829 S. Griffith Ave. Phone: (502)683-0296
Owensboro, KY 42301 Donald M. Boarman, Dir.
Founded: 1966. **Staff:** Prof 8. **Subjects:** Archeology, geology, botany, antiques, astronomy, ornithology. **Holdings:** 300 books; 400 bound periodical volumes; 50 filmstrips; 100 movies; 500 slides; 50 reels of microfilm. **Services:** Library open to the public for reference use only. **Staff:** Kathy Olson, Reg..

★10981★
OWENSBORO-DAVIESS COUNTY PUBLIC LIBRARY - KENTUCKY ROOM (Hist)
450 Griffith Ave. Phone: (502)684-0211
Owensboro, KY 42301 Shelia E. Heflin, Supv.
Staff: 3. **Subjects:** Kentucky history, local history, genealogy. **Special Collections:** Photograph collection; Rotary Club records (4 VF drawers); oral history. **Holdings:** 2500 volumes; 4 VF drawers of family files; 25 VF drawers of clippings and pamphlets; local newspapers and state census on microfilm. **Subscriptions:** 130 journals and other serials. **Services:** Copying; limited research; room open to the public with restrictions. **Special Indexes:** Obituary index to Owensboro Messenger and Inquirer, 1930-1982.

★10982★
OWENSBORO MESSENGER-INQUIRER - LIBRARY (Publ)
1401 Frederica St. Phone: (502)926-0123
Owensboro, KY 42301 Sherri Evans, Libn.
Founded: 1973. **Staff:** Prof 1; Other 2. **Subjects:** Newspaper reference topics. **Holdings:** 2500 books; 50 bound periodical volumes; 127,000 clippings; 30,000 photographs; 1500 pamphlets; Messenger-Inquirer, 1862 to present, on microfilm. **Subscriptions:** 10 journals and other serials; 15 newspapers. **Services:** Library open to the public with restrictions. **Computerized Information Services:** Info-Ky information retrieval system (internal database). **Special Indexes:** Index to microfiche clippings, photographs, books, pamphlets, maps, graphics (online).

★10983★
OWYHEE COUNTY HISTORICAL COMPLEX MUSEUM - LIBRARY (Hist)
Murphy, ID 83650 Phone: (208)495-2319
Linda Morton, Dir.
Staff: 2. **Subjects:** Owyhee County history, agriculture, Indians, mining, ranching. **Holdings:** 1000 books; 10 boxes of reports and manuscripts; 8 VF drawers of clippings and pictures; 20 boxes of archival materials; 1 drawer of microfilm; oral history recordings. **Subscriptions:** 13 journals and other serials. **Services:** Copying; library open to the public with restrictions. **Publications:** Owyhee Outpost, annual.

★10984★
OXFORD MUSEUM - LIBRARY (Hist)
339 Main St. Phone: (508)987-2882
Oxford, MA 01540 Timothy A. Kelley, Hd.Libn.
Founded: 1978. **Staff:** Prof 1. **Subjects:** Local history, genealogy, Huguenots. **Special Collections:** Town records; local newspapers; books by and about Clara Barton and Dr. Elliott P. Joslin. **Holdings:** 1000 volumes. **Services:** Interlibrary loan; copying; library open to the public for reference use only.

★10985★
OXFORD UNITED METHODIST CHURCH - OSCAR G. COOK MEMORIAL LIBRARY (Rel-Phil)
465 Main St.
Oxford, MA 01540 Phone: (508)987-5378
Founded: 1965. **Staff:** 2. **Subjects:** Religion and Bible, family living, theology, history, biography. **Holdings:** 450 books; AV programs. **Services:** Library open to the public. **Staff:** Laura Adams, Co-Libn.; Beth Samuelson, Co-Libn..

★10986★
OXFORD UNIVERSITY PRESS, INC. - LIBRARY (Publ)
200 Madison Ave. Phone: (212)679-7300
New York, NY 10016 Amanda Rust, Libn.
Staff: Prof 1; Other 1. **Subjects:** Humanities; sciences - social, biological, physical. **Holdings:** 8000 books; 42 periodical volumes; publications of the press. **Services:** Library open to the public with restrictions. **Special Catalogs:** Catalog of all titles in print; spring and fall catalog of new publications.

OYER MEMORIAL LIBRARY
See: Washington Bible College/Capital Bible Seminary (17471)

★10987★
OYSTER BAY HISTORICAL SOCIETY - RESEARCH LIBRARY (Hist)
20 Summit St.
Box 297 Phone: (516)922-5032
Oyster Bay, NY 11771-0297 Jane S. Nickerson, Libn.
Founded: 1960. **Staff:** Prof 2. **Subjects:** Long Island - revolutionary, colonial, 18th-19th century history and genealogy; Oyster Bay history. **Special Collections:** Theodore Roosevelt Collection. **Holdings:** 750 books; 20 bound periodical volumes; 20 filing boxes of letters and manuscripts; 200 photographs; 25 maps and atlases; original deeds, letters, documents. **Services:** Copying; library open to the public for reference use only. **Staff:** Julia Clark, Archv..

★10988★
OYSTERPONDS HISTORICAL SOCIETY, INC. - OHS RESEARCH LIBRARY (Hist)
Village Lane
Box 844 Phone: (516)323-2480
Orient, NY 11957 Donald Boerum, Hd.Libn.
Founded: 1944. **Staff:** Prof 1; Other 10. **Subjects:** Genealogy, local history. **Special Collections:** Photographs of Eastern Long Island, 1860-1920 (2000 photographs). **Holdings:** 1350 volumes; 3000 documents and records; 12 VF drawers; 200 glass plates; 19th century diaries and recipe books; whaling logs, 1848-1852; postcards; local wills and papers. **Services:** Copying; library open to the public by appointment.

★10989★
OZARK CHRISTIAN COLLEGE - LIBRARY (Rel-Phil)
1111 N. Main St. Phone: (417)624-2518
Joplin, MO 64801-1188 William F. Abernathy, Lib.Dir.
Founded: 1944. **Staff:** Prof 1; Other 6. **Subjects:** Religion, church history, archeology, Christian education. **Holdings:** 40,568 books; 913 bound periodical volumes; 1074 AV programs; 3000 audio cassettes; 12 VF drawers of missions files; 9 VF drawers of essay files; 7 VF drawers of information about Bible colleges; 715 microfiche. **Subscriptions:** 284 journals and other serials. **Services:** Interlibrary loan; copying; library open to the public. **Networks/Consortia:** Member of Southwest Missouri Library Network. **Special Catalogs:** Audiovisuals Catalog, annual; Audio Cassette Catalog, annual.

★10990★
OZARK FOLK CENTER - LIBRARY (Area-Ethnic)
Mt. View, AR 72560 Phone: (501)269-3851
W.K. McNeil, Folklorist
Staff: Prof 1; Other 1. **Subjects:** Ozark folklore, crafts, and music. **Holdings:** 3000 books; 50 bound periodical volumes; 100 unbound periodicals; 250 pieces of ephemera; sheet music; phonograph records. **Subscriptions:** 40 journals and other serials. **Services:** Interlibrary loan; copying; library open to the public.

★10991★
OZARK-MAHONING COMPANY - RESEARCH LIBRARY (Sci-Engr)
1870 S. Boulder Ave. Phone: (918)585-2661
Tulsa, OK 74119 Judy Tibson, Libn.
Staff: 1. **Subjects:** Chemistry - general, fluorine, inorganic; chemicals for dental application. **Holdings:** 500 books; 300 bound periodical volumes; 50 volumes of unbound journals. **Subscriptions:** 24 journals and other serials. **Services:** Interlibrary loan; copying; library open to the public by appointment. **Remarks:** Library located at 5101 W. 21st St., Tulsa, OK 74107.

P

★10992★
P.T. BOATS, INC. - LIBRARY, ARCHIVES & TECHNICAL INFORMATION CENTER (Mil)
U.S.S. Massachusetts, Battleship Cove Phone: (508)678-1100
Fall River, MA 02721 Frank J. Szczepaniak, P.T. Boat Coord.
Founded: 1975. **Staff:** 1. **Subjects:** Patrol Torpedo (P.T.) boats, naval history. **Special Collections:** Personal photo albums of 43 World War II operating squadrons. **Holdings:** 400 books; 300 bound periodical volumes; 150 manuals; 200 P.T. boat blueprints; 100 designs; 5000 photographs; 15 reels of microfilm; 60 reels of P.T. movies. **Services:** Copying; center open to the public by appointment. **Publications:** Newspaper, semiannual; 3 books on P.T. boats of World War II. **Remarks:** Claims to be the only P.T. Boat Museum and Library in the world. All mail should be sent to the main office of P.T. Boats, Inc., Box 109, Memphis, TN 38101; the telephone number is (901)272-9980.

★10993★
P.T. BOATS, INC. - LIBRARY, ARCHIVES & TECHNICAL INFORMATION CENTER - NATIONAL HEADQUARTERS (Mil)
Box 109 Phone: (901)272-9980
Memphis, TN 38101 Donald Rhoads, Exec. V.P.
Founded: 1946. **Subjects:** Patrol Torpedo (P.T.) boats - World War II operations, squadrons, tenders, bases, training center, P.T. boat builders. **Special Collections:** Photographs (10,000); 78 foot Higgins P.T. Boat; 80 foot Elco P.T. Boat; artifacts, memorabilia, uniforms, weapons. **Holdings:** 500 books; 75 bound periodical volumes; 100 charts; 5000 operation action reports; 5000 clippings; 2000 feet of microfilm; 20,000 feet of World War II film; 20 VF drawers of letters, citations, orders, records of P.T. boaters. **Services:** Interlibrary loan; copying; library open to the public by appointment. **Publications:** The P.T. Boater Newspaper, 2/year; Knights of the Sea - for sale; technical manuals on the history of P.T. Boat squadrons. **Special Catalogs:** Rosters of P.T. Boaters on cards (master, alphabetical, by state, by squadron). **Staff:** Robert Ferrell, Techn..

WILLIAM PACA GARDEN CONSERVATION CENTER
See: Historic Annapolis, Inc. (6318)

★10994★
PACCAR INC. - TECHNICAL CENTER LIBRARY (Sci-Engr)
1261 Hwy. 237 Phone: (206)757-5234
Mount Vernon, WA 98273 Maryanne Ward, Res.Spec.
Founded: 1985. **Staff:** Prof 1; Other 2. **Subjects:** Automotive and mechanical engineering. **Holdings:** 3000 books. **Subscriptions:** 150 journals and other serials; 5 newspapers. **Services:** Interlibrary loan; library not open to the public. **Automated Operations:** Computerized cataloging, serials, and circulation. **Computerized Information Services:** DIALOG Information Services, Pergamon ORBIT InfoLine, Inc.; internal database. **Publications:** PACCAR Technical Center Library Newsletter, biweekly.

PACE CENTER
See: Ohio State University - Counseling and Consultation Service (10687)

JOHN C. PACE LIBRARY
See: University of West Florida (17086)

★10995★
PACE UNIVERSITY - NEW YORK CIVIC CENTER CAMPUS - LIBRARY (Bus-Fin)
Pace Plaza Phone: (212)488-1331
New York, NY 10038 Henry Birnbaum, Univ.Libn.
Staff: Prof 11; Other 20. **Subjects:** Liberal arts and sciences, accounting, finance, management, marketing, real estate, taxation. **Holdings:** 352,500 volumes; domestic and foreign corporation annual reports; 16,000 pamphlets; 26,000 reels of microfilm. **Subscriptions:** 1600 journals and other serials; 6 newspapers. **Services:** Interlibrary loan; library not open to the public. **Automated Operations:** Computerized cataloging. **Computerized Information Services:** BRS Information Technologies, DIALOG Information Services, OCLC. **Networks/Consortia:** Member of New York Metropolitan Reference and Research Library Agency (METRO). **Staff:** Adele Jann, Hd.Cat.; Michelle Fanelli, Rd.Serv.Libn.; Laura Slepetis, ILL Libn..

★10996★
PACE UNIVERSITY - SCHOOL OF LAW LIBRARY (Law)
78 N. Broadway Phone: (914)681-4273
White Plains, NY 10603 Nicholas Triffin, Dir.
Founded: 1976. **Staff:** Prof 7; Other 8. **Subjects:** U.S. and international law, jurisprudence. **Special Collections:** Selective U.S. Government documents depository; environmental law (1000 titles); tax law (800 titles). **Holdings:** 35,904 books; 75,812 bound periodical volumes; 11,809 reels of microfilm; 312,289 microfiche. **Subscriptions:** 2818 journals and other serials. **Services:** Interlibrary loan; copying; library open to the public. **Automated Operations:** Computerized cataloging. **Computerized Information Services:** LEXIS, DIALOG Information Services, WILSONLINE, WESTLAW, OCLC; MCI Mail (electronic mail service). **Networks/Consortia:** Member of New York Metropolitan Reference and Research Library Agency (METRO), SUNY/OCLC Library Network. **Publications:** Acquisitions list, monthly; Informational highlights, bibliographies, and reference aids; government acquisitions list. **Staff:** Martha W. Keister, Hd., Pub.Serv.; Anne Sauter, Ref./Doc.Libn.; Susan Nosseir, Ref./ILL Libn.; Jane Marshall, Hd., Tech.Serv.; Alice Pidgeon, Acq.Libn..

★10997★
PACE UNIVERSITY, PLEASANTVILLE/BRIARCLIFF - EDWARD AND DORIS MORTOLA LIBRARY (Bus-Fin)
861 Bedford Rd. Phone: (914)741-3380
Pleasantville, NY 10570 William J. Murdock, Lib.Dir.
Founded: 1963. **Staff:** Prof 9; Other 6. **Subjects:** Business administration, period histories, accounting, nursing, 19th century English literature, computer science. **Holdings:** 160,000 volumes; 5210 pamphlets; 907 corporation reports; 251 college bulletins; 16,000 reels of microfilm. **Subscriptions:** 1175 journals and other serials. **Services:** Interlibrary loan; copying; library open to the public for reference use only. **Automated Operations:** Computerized cataloging and serials. **Computerized Information Services:** DIALOG Information Services, Dow Jones News/Retrieval, BRS Information Technologies, OCLC. Performs searches on fee basis. Contact Person: P. Chervenie, Rd.Serv.Libn., 993-3504. **Networks/Consortia:** Member of Westchester Library System. **Staff:** R. Yang, Acq.Libn.; Lauren Jackson, Cat.Libn.; R. Loomis, Ref.Libn.; E. Reiman, Ref.Libn.; H. Huang, Ref.Libn.; J. Lee, Ref.Libn.; M. Boyd, Ref.Libn..

★10998★
PACIFIC ASIA MUSEUM - LIBRARY (Area-Ethnic)
46 N. Los Robles Phone: (818)449-2742
Pasadena, CA 91101 Sarah McKay, Libn.
Founded: 1976. **Subjects:** Asia and the Pacific - art, applied art, history, culture. **Special Collections:** Paul Sherbert Collection (India; 1150 volumes). **Holdings:** 1825 volumes. **Services:** Library open to the public by appointment.

★10999★
PACIFIC AND ASIAN AFFAIRS COUNCIL - PACIFIC HOUSE LIBRARY (Area-Ethnic)
2004 University Ave.
Honolulu, HI 96822 Phone: (808)941-5355
Founded: 1925. **Staff:** Prof 3; Other 1. **Subjects:** International affairs, Asia and the Pacific, foreign policy. **Holdings:** 2000 books. **Subscriptions:** 100 journals and other serials; 5 newspapers. **Services:** Interlibrary loan; library open to the public.

PACIFIC/ASIAN AMERICAN MENTAL HEALTH RESEARCH CENTER
See: University of Illinois at Chicago (16268)

★11000★
PACIFIC BELL - CORPORATE INFORMATION CENTER (Info Sci)
2600 Camino Ramon, Rm. 1CS95 Phone: (415)823-8000
San Ramon, CA 94583 Harry Allen, Mgr.
Founded: 1982. **Staff:** Prof 5; Other 3. **Subjects:** Telecommunications, management, business. **Holdings:** 2000 books; 400 bound periodical volumes; Pacific Bell & AT & T annual reports; Bell System publications. **Subscriptions:** 400 journals and other serials; 11 newspapers. **Services:** Interlibrary loan; copying; SDI; center open to the public by appointment. **Automated Operations:** Computerized cataloging, acquisitions, and serials. **Computerized Information Services:** DIALOG Information Services, Pergamon ORBIT InfoLine, Inc., NewsNet, Inc., Dow Jones News/Retrieval, NEXIS, DataTimes, VU/TEXT Information Services, RLIN; internal databases. **Networks/Consortia:** Member of CLASS. **Publications:** CIC Bulletin, quarterly - for internal distribution only. **Staff:** Gina Castro, Info.Res.Anl.; Jensa Woo, Info.Res.Anl.; Martha Ruske, Info.Res.Anl.; Helen Suomela-Tyrrell, Info.Res.Anl..

★11001★
PACIFIC BIO-MARINE LABORATORIES, INC. - RESEARCH LIBRARY (Biol Sci)
124 N. Ash St. Phone: (213)822-5757
Inglewood, CA 90301-1649 Rimmon Fay, Owner
Founded: 1961. **Staff:** 1. **Subjects:** Marine biology, water quality, marine resources. **Special Collections:** Marine resources of southern California. **Holdings:** 2000 books; 500 reports; 2000 reprints. **Subscriptions:** 20 journals and other serials. **Services:** Copying; library open to the public for reference use only.

PACIFIC BIO-MEDICAL RESEARCH CENTER
See: University of Hawaii (16190)

★11002★
PACIFIC CHRISTIAN COLLEGE - HURST MEMORIAL LIBRARY (Rel-Phil)
2500 E. Nutwood Ave. Phone: (714)879-3901
Fullerton, CA 92631 Jeffrey L. Wilson, Lib.Dir.
Founded: 1929. **Staff:** Prof 2; Other 2. **Subjects:** Theology, Christian education, church history, Bible, missions, sociology, psychology, philosophy, world history. **Holdings:** 47,500 books; 300 bound periodical volumes; 1000 other cataloged items; 6 VF drawers Christian Church mission papers; 2200 tapes; 100 reels of microfilm; 1000 microfiche. **Subscriptions:** 320 journals and other serials. **Services:** Interlibrary loan; copying; library open to the public with restrictions. **Automated Operations:** Computerized cataloging and ILL. **Computerized Information Services:** OCLC.

★11003★
PACIFIC COAST BANKING SCHOOL - LIBRARY (Bus-Fin)
2001 Sixth Ave., Suite 1710 Phone: (206)728-2255
Seattle, WA 98121 Debra Rath, Libn.
Founded: 1950. **Staff:** 5. **Subjects:** Bank capital, bank deposits, marketing and personnel operations, economic studies, international banking, regulatory studies, bank investments, loans, trust department studies. **Holdings:** 450 unbound theses. **Services:** Interlibrary loan; library not open to the public.

★11004★
PACIFIC ENERGY & RESOURCES CENTER - LIBRARY (Energy)
Bldg. 1055, Fort Cronkhite
Sausalito, CA 94965 Phone: (415)332-8200
Staff: Prof 1. **Subjects:** Energy, energy management, renewable energy technologies. **Special Collections:** Energy products and services directories and materials; California State Office of Appropriate Technology's Collection (energy issues, technologies, research; 3000 items). **Holdings:** 400 books; 300 bound periodical volumes; 800 other cataloged items. **Services:** Library open to the public by appointment. **Formerly:** Golden Gate Energy Center.

★11005★
PACIFIC GAS AND ELECTRIC COMPANY - CORPORATE LIBRARY (Bus-Fin, Energy)
77 Beale St., Rm. 1220 Phone: (415)972-2573
San Francisco, CA 94106 Michele F. Sullivan, Dir./Corp.Libn.
Staff: Prof 6; Other 2. **Subjects:** Engineering, energy, business, finance. **Special Collections:** Company history. **Holdings:** 6000 volumes; 53 VF drawers. **Subscriptions:** 450 journals and other serials. **Services:** Interlibrary loan; copying; SDI; library open to the public by appointment. **Automated Operations:** Computerized cataloging, acquisitions, serials, circulation, and ILL. **Computerized Information Services:** DIALOG Information Services, Pergamon ORBIT InfoLine, Inc., OCLC; OnTyme Electronic Message Network Service (electronic mail service). **Networks/ Consortia:** Member of CLASS. **Publications:** Library Bulletin, monthly.

★11006★
PACIFIC GAS AND ELECTRIC COMPANY - LAW LIBRARY (Law)
Box 7442 Phone: (415)972-4293
San Francisco, CA 94120 Gary L. Stromme, Law Libn.
Founded: 1906. **Staff:** Prof 2; Other 2. **Subjects:** Law. **Holdings:** 22,000 volumes. **Services:** Library not open to the public. **Staff:** Betty A. Merritt, Asst. Law Libn..

★11007★
PACIFIC GRADUATE SCHOOL OF PSYCHOLOGY - LEARNING RESOURCE CENTER (Med)
431 Burgess Dr. Phone: (415)321-1895
Menlo Park, CA 94025 Jane Riss, Dir.
Founded: 1975. **Staff:** Prof 1; Other 2. **Subjects:** Clinical psychology, psychological assessment, psychopathology, psychotherapy, neuropsychology, developmental psychology, child psychiatry, research methodology and statistics. **Special Collections:** Faculty reprint file. **Holdings:** 4800 books; 2300 bound periodical volumes; 75 psychological tests; 93 dissertations; 250 audio cassettes. **Subscriptions:** 159 journals and other serials. **Services:** Interlibrary loan; copying; center open to graduate students and mental health professionals. **Computerized Information Services:** BRS Information Technologies, NLM; OnTyme Electronic Message Network Service (electronic mail service). **Networks/Consortia:** Member of CLASS, South Bay Cooperative Library System (SBCLS), Northern California Medical Library Group, Pacific Southwest Regional Medical Library Service.

★11008★
PACIFIC GROVE MUSEUM OF NATURAL HISTORY - LIBRARY (Biol Sci)
165 Forest Ave. Phone: (408)372-4212
Pacific Grove, CA 93950 Vernal L. Yadon, Musm.Dir.
Subjects: Natural history of Monterey County. **Holdings:** 2000 books. **Services:** Library open to the public for reference use only.

★11009★
PACIFIC GROVE PUBLIC LIBRARY - ALVIN SEALE SOUTH SEAS COLLECTION (Area-Ethnic)
550 Central Ave. Phone: (408)373-0603
Pacific Grove, CA 93950 Margaret McBride, Lib.Dir.
Subjects: Pacific Islands, voyages. **Holdings:** 1200 volumes. **Services:** Interlibrary loan (limited); copying; collection open to the public with restrictions. **Computerized Information Services:** OnTyme Electronic Message Network Service (electronic mail service). **Networks/Consortia:** Member of Monterey Bay Area Cooperative Library System (MOBAC). **Special Indexes:** Index to Seale Collection.

★11010★
PACIFIC HOSPITAL OF LONG BEACH - MEDICAL STAFF LIBRARY (Med)
2776 Pacific Ave.
Box 1268 Phone: (213)595-1911
Long Beach, CA 90801 Lois E. Harris, Dir., Lib.Serv.
Staff: Prof 1. **Subjects:** General medicine, surgery, osteopathy, nursing, hospital administration. **Holdings:** 5000 volumes. **Subscriptions:** 200 journals and other serials. **Services:** Interlibrary loan; SDI; library open to the public for reference use only when user is sponsored by physician.

★11011★
PACIFIC LIGHTING CORPORATION - LAW LIBRARY (Law)
810 S. Flower St. Phone: (213)689-3352
Los Angeles, CA 90017 Terence Pragnell, Law Libn.
Staff: Prof 2; Other 1. **Subjects:** Law - corporate, utility, oil and gas, energy, environmental. **Holdings:** 23,000 volumes. **Subscriptions:** 350 journals and other serials; 5 newspapers. **Services:** Interlibrary loan; library not open to the public. **Automated Operations:** Computerized cataloging, acquisitions, and circulation. **Computerized Information Services:** LEXIS, NEXIS, DIALOG Information Services; Corporate System (internal database). **Publications:** Law Information Monthly - for internal distribution only; Annotated Bibliography on the California Public Utilities Commission, annual. **Special Indexes:** Index to California PUC General Orders. **Staff:** Kathryn Lee, Lib.Asst..

PACIFIC LIGHTING CORPORATION - SOUTHERN CALIFORNIA GAS COMPANY
See: Southern California Gas Company (13447)

PACIFIC LUTHERAN THEOLOGICAL SEMINARY
See: Graduate Theological Union (5785)

★11012★
PACIFIC MEDICAL CENTER - ELLEN GRIEP MEMORIAL LIBRARY (Med)
1200 12th Ave., S. Phone: (206)326-4085
Seattle, WA 98144 Seungja Song, Mgr., Med.Lib.
Founded: 1969. **Staff:** Prof 1; Other 1. **Subjects:** Ambulatory care medicine, medicine, dentistry, hospital administration. **Holdings:** 1300 books; 5000 bound periodical volumes. **Subscriptions:** 190 journals and

other serials. **Services:** Interlibrary loan; library not open to the public. **Automated Operations:** Computerized ILL. **Computerized Information Services:** WLN, MEDLARS, BRS Information Technologies, DIALOG Information Services. **Networks/Consortia:** Member of Seattle Area Hospital Library Consortium (SAHLC). **Publications:** Library News, 3/month.

PACIFIC NORTHWEST AGRICULTURAL HISTORY ARCHIVES
See: Washington State University - Manuscripts, Archives, & Special Collections (17526)

PACIFIC NORTHWEST ANTHROPOLOGICAL ARCHIVES
See: University of Idaho (16221)

PACIFIC NORTHWEST NATIONAL PARKS ASSOCIATION - FORT VANCOUVER NATIONAL HISTORIC SITE
See: U.S. Natl. Park Service - Fort Vancouver Natl. Historic Site - Library (15292)

PACIFIC NORTHWEST PUBLISHERS' ARCHIVES
See: Washington State University - Manuscripts, Archives, & Special Collections (17526)

★11013★
PACIFIC POWER AND LIGHT COMPANY - LIBRARY (Energy)
920 S.W. Sixth Ave. Phone: (503)243-4095
Portland, OR 97204 Susan Jackson, Libn.
Founded: 1960. **Staff:** Prof 1. **Subjects:** Electric engineering, electric utility management, energy resources, environment. **Holdings:** 10,000 volumes; 15,000 U.S. Government documents; 5000 state documents; 10,000 pamphlets, 7500 annual reports, 1000 standards in 150 VF drawers; 1000 reels of microfilm; 5000 microfiche; 200 aperture cards. **Subscriptions:** 560 journals and other serials. **Services:** Interlibrary loan; copying; library open to the public for reference use only. **Computerized Information Services:** DIALOG Information Services, Dow Jones News/Retrieval, DunSprint. **Networks/Consortia:** Member of CLASS.

★11014★
PACIFIC PRESBYTERIAN MEDICAL CENTER/UNIVERSITY OF THE PACIFIC - HEALTH SCIENCES LIBRARY (Med)
2395 Sacramento St.
Box 7999 Phone: (415)923-3240
San Francisco, CA 94120 Harold R. Gibson, Libn.
Staff: Prof 2; Other 2. **Subjects:** Medicine, dentistry, anesthesiology. **Holdings:** 10,313 books; 61,312 bound periodical volumes. **Subscriptions:** 894 journals and other serials. **Services:** Interlibrary loan; library not open to the public. **Computerized Information Services:** MEDLARS, DIALOG Information Services. Performs searches on fee basis.

★11015★
PACIFIC PRESS, LTD. - PRESS LIBRARY (Publ)
2250 Granville St. Phone: (604)732-2519
Vancouver, BC, Canada V6H 3G2 Shirley E. Mooney, Mgr.
Staff: Prof 3; Other 17. **Subjects:** Newspaper reference topics. **Holdings:** 1000 volumes; 260 VF drawers of newspaper clipping files; 325,000 microjackets of clipping files; 200 VF drawers of pictures; 250 VF drawers of biographical files; 360 boxes of pamphlets. **Subscriptions:** 37 journals and other serials. **Services:** Copying; library open to the public with restrictions. **Computerized Information Services:** Infomart. Performs searches on fee basis. Contact Person: Debra Millward, Jr.Libn., 732-2605. **Staff:** Janice Butler, Asst.Libn..

PACIFIC REGIONAL ORAL HISTORY PROGRAM
See: University of Hawaii - Department of History (16187)

PACIFIC RIM BUSINESS INFORMATION SERVICE
See: Library Association of Portland (7802)

★11016★
PACIFIC SALMON COMMISSION - LIBRARY (Biol Sci)
1155 Robson St., Suite 600 Phone: (604)684-8081
Vancouver, BC, Canada V6E 1B9 Glenna J. Westwood, Libn.
Founded: 1947. **Staff:** Prof 1. **Subjects:** Fisheries management, salmon research and biology. **Special Collections:** Commission field notes and data records; history of fisheries in British Columbia. **Holdings:** 600 books; 600 bound periodical volumes; 6000 reports; 75 meters of archival material; 800 reprints; 1 box of microfiche; 50 dissertations; 17 file drawers of data sheets; 375 maps. **Subscriptions:** 32 journals and other serials. **Services:** Interlibrary loan; copying; library open to the public for reference use only. **Automated Operations:** Computerized cataloging. **Computerized Information Services:** Internal database. **Publications:** Annual Report; Technical Report.

PACIFIC SCHOOL OF RELIGION
See: Graduate Theological Union (5785)

★11017★
PACIFIC SCIENCE CENTER FOUNDATION - LIBRARY
200 Second Ave., N.
Seattle, WA 98109
Founded: 1978. **Subjects:** Science, science and museum education. **Holdings:** 3000 books. **Remarks:** Presently inactive.

PACIFIC-SIERRA RESEARCH CORPORATION
See: Eaton Corporation (4576)

★11018★
PACIFIC STUDIES CENTER - LIBRARY (Bus-Fin)
222B View St. Phone: (415)969-1545
Mountain View, CA 94041 Leonard M. Siegel, Dir.
Founded: 1969. **Staff:** Prof 2. **Subjects:** Multinational corporations, high technology industry, defense industry, Southeast Asia, U.S. military and foreign policy. **Holdings:** 7000 books; 165 drawers of working research files arranged by geographical area, country, industry, corporation. **Subscriptions:** 150 periodicals. **Services:** Copying; library open to the public. **Publications:** Global Electronics (newsletter), monthly - by subscription.

★11019★
PACIFIC-UNION CLUB - LIBRARY (Hist)
1000 California St. Phone: (415)775-1234
San Francisco, CA 94108 Barbara Borden, Libn.
Staff: Prof 1. **Special Collections:** Californiana. **Holdings:** 32,700 books. **Services:** Library open to members only.

★11020★
PACIFIC UNION COLLEGE - PITCAIRN ISLANDS STUDY CENTER - LIBRARY (Area-Ethnic)
Angwin, CA 94508-9705 Phone: (707)965-6675
Gary Shearer, Cur.
Founded: 1977. **Staff:** Prof 1; Other 1. **Subjects:** Pitcairn Islands. **Holdings:** 90 books; 700 indexed articles; 300 other indexed materials; pamphlets; articles; clippings; stamp collection, including first day covers; films; slides; photographs; cassettes; island artifacts and curios; correspondence of Pitcairn Islanders; complete file of Pitcairn Miscellany; partial file of Pitcairn Pilhi; obituary file. **Services:** Copying; library open to the public for reference use only.

★11021★
PACIFIC UNIVERSITY - HARVEY SCOTT MEMORIAL LIBRARY - MUSIC LIBRARY (Mus)
College Way Phone: (503)357-6151
Forest Grove, OR 97116 Nancy Kenney, Mus.Libn.
Staff: Prof 1; Other 2. **Subjects:** Music. **Holdings:** 8845 books and scores; 4640 phonograph records and tapes. **Services:** Interlibrary loan; library open to the public with restrictions. **Computerized Information Services:** OCLC.

★11022★
PACIFICA FOUNDATION - PACIFICA RADIO NETWORK - PACIFICA RADIO ARCHIVE (Aud-Vis)
5316 Venice Blvd. Phone: (213)931-1625
Los Angeles, CA 90019 Roger Bowerman, Archv.
Founded: 1968. **Staff:** Prof 2; Other 3. **Subjects:** Civil rights, public affairs, politics, Third World, psychology, women's studies, literature, music. **Holdings:** 22,000 sound recordings. **Services:** Copying; archive open to the public by appointment. **Automated Operations:** Computerized cataloging.

★11023★
PACKAGING CORPORATION OF AMERICA - INFORMATION SERVICES DEPARTMENT (Sci-Engr)
5401 Old Orchard Rd. Phone: (312)470-0080
Skokie, IL 60077 Jacqueline J. True, Info.Spec.
Staff: Prof 1. **Subjects:** Paper chemistry; packaging; manufacture of paper, pulpboard, plastics. **Holdings:** 1000 books; 2500 bound periodical volumes; 150 VF drawers of Institute of Paper Chemistry, Technical Association of Pulp & Paper Industry, and Boxboard Research & Development Association publications. **Subscriptions:** 184 journals and other serials. **Services:** Interlibrary loan; copying; department open to the public with restrictions. **Computerized Information Services:** DIALOG Information

Services, STN International, Pergamon ORBIT InfoLine, Inc., Dow Jones News/Retrieval. **Networks/Consortia:** Member of ILLINET, North Suburban Library System (NSLS).

★11024★
PACKAGING INSTITUTE INTERNATIONAL - LIBRARY AND RESOURCE CENTER
20 Summer St.
Stamford, CT 06901-2304
Subjects: Packaging and allied fields. **Holdings:** 500 books; 10 VF drawers; international packaging periodicals, reports, manuscripts. **Remarks:** Presently inactive.

★11025★
PACKANACK COMMUNITY CHURCH OF WAYNE - LIBRARY (Rel-Phil)
120 Lake Dr., E. Phone: (201)694-0608
Wayne, NJ 07470 Marjorie Q. Vaiden, Libn.
Staff: Prof 1. **Subjects:** Religion, Bible study, counseling. **Holdings:** 2250 books; church history notebooks; church newsletters; AV programs. **Services:** Library open to the public with restrictions.

PACKARD LIBRARY
See: Columbus College of Art and Design (3499)

PACKARD READING ROOM
See: Pennsylvania Hospital - Department for Sick and Injured - Medical Library (11165)

★11026★
PACKARD TRUCK ORGANIZATION - LIBRARY (Trans)
1196 Mountain Rd. Phone: (717)528-4920
York Springs, PA 17372 David B. Lockard, Founder
Founded: 1981. **Subjects:** Packard trucks. **Holdings:** Truck manuals; advertisements; general information. **Services:** Copying; written inquiries only.

PADDOCK MUSIC LIBRARY
See: Dartmouth College (4047)

INMAN E. PAGE LIBRARY
See: Lincoln University of Missouri (7876)

★11027★
PAIER COLLEGE OF ART, INC. - LIBRARY (Art)
44 Circular Ave. Phone: (203)287-1585
Hamden, CT 06514 Gail J. Nachin, Lib.Dir.
Staff: Prof 2; Other 8. **Subjects:** Art, graphic design, interior design, photography. **Holdings:** 9000 books; 200 bound periodical volumes; 40,000 pictures; 2500 slides. **Subscriptions:** 80 journals and other serials. **Services:** Interlibrary loan; copying; library open to the public for research only. **Networks/Consortia:** Member of Southern Connecticut Library Council (SCLC).

DR. HARRY PAIKIN LIBRARY
See: Hamilton Board of Education (5978)

★11028★
PAINE ART CENTER AND ARBORETUM - GEORGE P. NEVITT LIBRARY (Art)
1410 Algoma Blvd. Phone: (414)235-4530
Oshkosh, WI 54901 Corinne H. Spoo, Libn.
Staff: Prof 2; Other 3. **Subjects:** Art, interior decoration, English houses, gardening. **Holdings:** 2683 volumes. **Subscriptions:** 10 journals and other serials. **Services:** Interlibrary loan; library open to the public for reference use only. **Special Catalogs:** Exhibition catalogs, irregular - available on request. **Staff:** Genevieve Kusche, Slide Libn..

THOMAS PAINE HISTORICAL ASSOCIATION OF NEW ROCHELLE
See: Huguenot-Thomas Paine Historical Association of New Rochelle (6585)

★11029★
PAINE WEBBER INC. - LIBRARY (Bus-Fin)
1285 Ave. of the Americas Phone: (212)713-3669
New York, NY 10019 Barbara A. Fody, Asst. V.P.
Staff: Prof 6; Other 15. **Subjects:** Finance, investments, money and banking, economic and business conditions. **Special Collections:** Corporation records. **Holdings:** 3000 books; 700 industry subject files; 500 shelves of corporation records; 300 reels of microfilm; microfiche. **Subscriptions:** 700 journals and other serials; 15 newspapers. **Services:** Interlibrary loan; library open to members of Special Libraries Association. **Computerized Information Services:** DIALOG Information Services, Dow Jones News/Retrieval, TEXTLINE, BRS Information Technologies, NEXIS, DunSprint, Vickers Institutional Stock System, LEXIS, VU/TEXT Information Services, DataTimes, Investment Dealers Digest. **Publications:** Paine Webber Library Bulletin, monthly - for internal distribution only. **Staff:** Penny Cagan, Asst.Mgr.; Molly Russell, Ref.Libn.; Cindy Furlinger, Asst.Ref.Libn.; Andrea Crone, Corp.Docs.Supv.; Frederick Nesta, Tech.Serv.Libn..

★11030★
PAJARO VALLEY HISTORICAL ASSOCIATION - WILLIAM H. VOLCK MUSEUM - ARCHIVES (Hist)
261 E. Beach St. Phone: (408)722-0305
Watsonville, CA 95076 Alzora Snyder, Archv.
Staff: 1. **Subjects:** History of the Pajaro Valley, 1865 to present. **Holdings:** 102 linear feet of letters, literary manuscripts, genealogical source materials, account books, business and financial records, noncurrent records of schools, city and county government agencies, community groups and associations, architectural drawings, aerial photographs, oral history tapes and transcripts, photographs. **Services:** Copying; archives open to the public.

★11031★
PALEONTOLOGICAL RESEARCH INSTITUTION - LIBRARY (Biol Sci)
1259 Trumansburg Rd. Phone: (607)273-6623
Ithaca, NY 14850 Peter R. Hoover, Dir.
Staff: Prof 1. **Subjects:** Paleontology, geology, conchology, fossils, mollusca. **Holdings:** 50,000 volumes; 48 VF cabinets; 6000 reprints and papers; microfilm; maps; photographs. **Subscriptions:** 400 journals and other serials. **Services:** Interlibrary loan (fee); library open to specialists by appointment. **Publications:** Library Serials List, 1979.

★11032★
PALINET/ULC (Info Sci)
3401 Market St., Suite 262 Phone: (215)382-7031
Philadelphia, PA 19104 Dr. James G. Schoenung, Exec.Dir.
Founded: 1935. **Staff:** Prof 12; Other 4. **Publications:** PALINET News (newsletter), 6/year - to members and for sale; PALINET Annual Report. **Remarks:** Headquarters of PALINET & Union Library Catalogue of Pennsylvania (library network). Card file closed in 1975; microfilm available since 1976. Provides full OCLC and microcomputer support services for 290 member libraries in Pennsylvania, New Jersey, Delaware, Maryland, and Washington, D.C. Brokers CD-ROM products and reference database services and provides archive tape management services. **Staff:** Rian Miller-McIrvine, Mgr., OCLC Serv.Div.; Meryl Cinnamon, Mgr., Microcomputer Serv.Div.; Donna Wright, Mgr., Adm.Serv.Div..

★11033★
PALL CORPORATION - LIBRARY (Sci-Engr)
30 Sea Cliff Ave. Phone: (516)671-4000
Glen Cove, NY 11724 Lucy Bara Lettis, Mgr., Lib.Serv.
Staff: Prof 1; Other 1. **Subjects:** Filtration, chemistry, technology, medicine. **Holdings:** 3000 books; 350 periodical titles; industrial market directories. **Subscriptions:** 400 journals and other serials. **Services:** Interlibrary loan; library not open to the public. **Computerized Information Services:** DIALOG Information Services, Pergamon ORBIT InfoLine, Inc., DunSprint. **Networks/Consortia:** Member of Long Island Library Resources Council, Inc. (LILRC). **Publications:** Acquisitions Report.

★11034★
PALLOTTINE PROVINCIALATE LIBRARY (Rel-Phil)
5424 W. Blue Mound Rd. Phone: (414)258-0653
Milwaukee, WI 53208 Rev. Jerome Kuskowski, S.A.C., Libn.
Founded: 1923. **Staff:** Prof 1. **Subjects:** Theology, philosophy, hagiography. **Special Collections:** St. Vincent Pallotti Collection (29 items). **Holdings:** 3273 books. **Subscriptions:** 20 journals and other serials; 7 newspapers. **Services:** Interlibrary loan; copying; library open to the public. **Remarks:** Maintained by the Society of the Catholic Apostolate.

★11035★
PALM BEACH COUNTY LAW LIBRARY (Law)
County Courthouse, Rm. 339
300 N. Dixie Hwy. Phone: (407)820-2928
West Palm Beach, FL 33401 Cheryl L. Rovinelli, Law Libn.
Staff: Prof 1; Other 3. **Subjects:** Law. **Holdings:** 19,600 volumes; 1930 microfiche. **Services:** Interlibrary loan; copying; library open to the public for reference use only.

ROLAND PALMEDO NATIONAL SKI LIBRARY
See: National Ski Hall of Fame and Museum (9786)

★11036★
PALMER COLLEGE OF CHIROPRACTIC - DAVID D. PALMER HEALTH SCIENCES LIBRARY (Med)
1000 Brady St. Phone: (319)326-9641
Davenport, IA 52803 Dennis Peterson, Interim Dir.
Founded: 1895. **Staff:** Prof 7; Other 15. **Subjects:** Chiropractic, health sciences. **Special Collections:** B.J. Palmer papers; chiropractic history and research; conservative health care; Lyndon Lee papers; Kenneth Cronk papers. **Holdings:** 25,978 books; 13,839 bound periodical volumes; 9145 microfiche; 1226 reels of microfilm; 1350 audiotapes; 991 videotapes; 19,800 slides; 910 biological specimens and models; 1434 x-ray sets. **Subscriptions:** 900 journals and other serials; 14 newspapers. **Services:** Interlibrary loan; copying; SDI; library open to the public with restrictions. **Automated Operations:** Computerized cataloging and serials. **Computerized Information Services:** MEDLARS, DIALOG Information Services; internal database; DIALMAIL (electronic mail service). Performs searches on fee basis. Contact Person: Robert Stout, Pub.Serv.Libn., 326-9890. **Networks/Consortia:** Member of Greater Midwest Regional Medical Library Network, River Bend Library System (RBLS), Chiropractic Library Consortium (CLIBCON). **Publications:** NEXUS, biweekly - campus distribution and by subscription; Chiropractic Contents, biweekly - campus distribution. **Special Indexes:** Chiropractic Literature Index, 1970-1979 (online). **Staff:** Glenda Wiese, Tech.Serv.Libn.; Susan Barns, Tech.Serv.Libn.; Ruth Hall, Pub.Serv.Libn.; Richard Parkinson, Instr. Media Supv..

★11037★
PALMER COLLEGE OF CHIROPRACTIC - WEST - LIBRARY (Med)
1095 Dunford Way Phone: (408)244-8907
Sunnyvale, CA 94087 Phyllis Hazekamp, Dir.
Staff: Prof 2; Other 1. **Subjects:** Chiropractic, health sciences, medicine, basic sciences, education. **Special Collections:** Chiropractic history (300 volumes). **Holdings:** 5308 books; 1954 bound periodical volumes; 86 skeletal parts; 1548 x-rays; 120 audiotapes; 29 carousels of slides; 2 films; 320 videotapes; periodicals. **Subscriptions:** 177 journals and other serials. **Services:** Interlibrary loan (fee); library open to the public for reference use only. **Automated Operations:** Computerized serials. **Computerized Information Services:** Internal database. **Networks/Consortia:** Member of Pacific Southwest Regional Medical Library Service, Northern California and Nevada Medical Library Group (NCNMLG), Chiropractic Library Consortium (CLIBCON). **Publications:** New in the Library, bimonthly - for internal distribution only. **Special Indexes:** Historical books (online); index to articles. **Staff:** Jaxon Matthews, Asst.Libn..

DAVID D. PALMER HEALTH SCIENCES LIBRARY
See: Palmer College of Chiropractic (11036)

GEORGE B. PALMER MEMORIAL LIBRARY
See: The Hunt Hospital (6597)

★11038★
PALMER, O'CONNELL, LEGER, RODERICK, GLENNIE - LAW LIBRARY (Law)
One Brunswick Square, Suite 1600
P.O. Box 1324
Saint John, NB, Canada E2L 4H8 Phone: (506)632-8900
Staff: Prof 1; Other 1. **Subjects:** Law. **Special Collections:** Canadian and English common law. **Holdings:** 2000 books; 5000 bound periodical volumes. **Subscriptions:** 20 journals and other serials; 10 newspapers. **Services:** Library open to the public with restrictions.

SOPHIA F. PALMER LIBRARY
See: American Journal of Nursing Company (577)

★11039★
PALO ALTO MEDICAL FOUNDATION - BARNETT-HALL LIBRARY (Med)
860 Bryant St. Phone: (415)321-4121
Palo Alto, CA 94301 Eileen E. Cassidy, Hd.Libn.
Founded: 1950. **Staff:** Prof 3. **Subjects:** Medicine, medical research, basic sciences, nursing, pharmacology. **Holdings:** 12,555 volumes; 13 VF drawers of pamphlets. **Subscriptions:** 321 journals and other serials. **Services:** Interlibrary loan; copying; library open to physicians and technological researchers of the county. **Computerized Information Services:** MEDLINE. **Networks/Consortia:** Member of Pacific Southwest Regional Medical Library Service, Northern California and Nevada Medical Library Group (NCNMLG). **Publications:** Annual Report. **Special Indexes:** Periodical holdings visible file index. **Staff:** Natalie Hazen, Ser.Libn.; Judith Cummings, Ref.Libn..

★11040★
PALO ALTO UNIFIED SCHOOL DISTRICT - INSTRUCTIONAL MATERIALS CENTER (Educ)
Cubberley School
4000 Middlefield Rd. Phone: (415)856-0678
Palo Alto, CA 94306 Jack Gibbany, Prog.Coord.
Founded: 1950. **Staff:** Prof 13; Other 7. **Subjects:** Curriculum materials, children's fiction. **Holdings:** 200,000 books. **Subscriptions:** 15 journals and other serials; 8 newspapers. **Services:** Interlibrary loan; copying; center open to the public for reference use only. **Automated Operations:** Computerized cataloging. **Computerized Information Services:** Picodyne (internal database).

★11041★
PALOMAR COMMUNITY COLLEGE - LIBRARY - SPECIAL COLLECTIONS (Hum)
1140 Mission Rd. Phone: (619)744-1150
San Marcos, CA 92069 Judy J. Carter, Lib.Dir.
Holdings: Fine arts (15,200 volumes); American Indian (3200 volumes); Iceland (200 volumes); World War I poster collection. **Services:** Interlibrary loan; copying; collections open to the public with restrictions. **Automated Operations:** Computerized cataloging and serials. **Computerized Information Services:** BRS Information Technologies, DIALOG Information Services, OCLC. **Networks/Consortia:** Member of Learning Resources Cooperative, CLASS.

★11042★
PALOMINO HORSE BREEDERS OF AMERICA - LIBRARY (Rec)
15253 E. Skelly Dr. Phone: (918)438-1234
Tulsa, OK 74116-2620 Cindy Chilton, Gen.Mgr.
Subjects: Horses and equine-related activities, the Palomino horse. **Special Collections:** Palomino Horse Breeders of America Stud Book Listings. **Holdings:** Figures not available.

★11043★
PALOS COMMUNITY HOSPITAL - MEDICAL LIBRARY (Med)
123rd & 80th Aves. Phone: (312)361-4500
Palos Heights, IL 60463 Gail Waldoch, Libn.
Staff: Prof 1. **Subjects:** Medicine, allied health sciences. **Holdings:** 600 books. **Subscriptions:** 83 journals and other serials. **Services:** Interlibrary loan; library not open to the public. **Computerized Information Services:** DIALOG Information Services. **Networks/Consortia:** Member of Chicago and South Consortium.

PAN-AMERICAN ASSOCIATION OF FORENSIC SCIENCES - SECRETARIAT
See: International Reference Organization in Forensic Medicine & Sciences - Library and Reference Center (7062)

★11044★
PAN AMERICAN HEALTH ORGANIZATION - DOCUMENTATION AND HEALTH INFORMATION CENTER (Med)
525 23rd St., N.W.
Mail Code HBD Phone: (202)861-3300
Washington, DC 20037 Dr. Carlos A. Gamboa, Chf.
Staff: Prof 3; Other 2. **Subjects:** Health sciences. **Special Collections:** Documents of the World Health Organization, Pan American Health Organization, and Latin American Ministries of Health. **Holdings:** 15,000 books; 5000 bound periodical volumes; 25 file drawers of microfilm. **Subscriptions:** 130 journals and other serials. **Services:** Interlibrary loan; copying; SDI; extramural educational programs; center open to the public. **Automated Operations:** Computerized cataloging, acquisitions, and serials.

Computerized Information Services: MEDLINE, DIALOG Information Services; PAHOLINE (internal database); ECONET (electronic mail service). Performs searches on fee basis. **Publications:** Acquisitions Bulletin; PAHODOC, quarterly; PAHOSTC, quarterly. **Remarks:** A regional office of the World Health Organization. **Staff:** Olga Rojo, Indexer; Olinda Glorioso, Acq.Libn.; Evelyn Elena, Asst.Acq.Libn..

★11045★
PAN AMERICAN SOCIETY OF NEW ENGLAND - SHATTUCK MEMORIAL LIBRARY
Box 1906
Brookline, MA 02146-0016
Defunct. Holdings absorbed by Boston University Libraries.

★11046★
PAN AMERICAN WORLD AIRWAYS - CORPORATE LIBRARY (Trans)
200 Park Ave., Rm. 904 Phone: (212)880-1917
New York, NY 10166 Liwa Chiu, Libn.
Founded: 1943. **Staff:** Prof 1. **Subjects:** Air transportation worldwide, business, economics, U.S. and foreign travel. **Holdings:** 2000 books; 300 bound periodical volumes; 70 VF drawers of clippings and pamphlets; 1200 microforms; 3000 microfiche; Official Airline Guide, 1928 to present. **Subscriptions:** 86 journals and other serials. **Services:** Interlibrary loan; copying; library open to the public by appointment. **Automated Operations:** Computerized circulation. **Publications:** Monthly Acquisition Bulletin. **Special Indexes:** Index of inauguration of services.

★11047★
PANAMA CANAL COMMISSION - LIBRARY (Area-Ethnic)
APO Miami, FL 34011 Beverly C. Williams, Libn.
Founded: 1914. **Staff:** Prof 5; Other 14. **Subjects:** Panama Canal, shipping, engineering, Isthmus of Panama. **Special Collections:** Panama Collection (36,088 items, including 5 VF drawers of newspaper clippings; 5459 photographs; manuscripts). **Holdings:** 209,423 books; 1045 bound periodical volumes; 122 manuscripts; 841 maps and prints; 4657 reels of microfilm; 3403 microfiche. **Subscriptions:** 305 journals and other serials; 8 newspapers. **Services:** Copying; library open to researchers and university students referred by other libraries. **Automated Operations:** Computerized cataloging, acquisitions, and serials. **Publications:** A History of the Panama Canal (1984); bibliographies, irregular; Library Resources Up-date, monthly; - all for internal distribution only. **Remarks:** The telephone number for the library is 011-507-52-7761. **Staff:** Naomi A. Wolf, Rsrcs.Libn.; Nan S. Chong, Libn., Panama Canal Coll.; Mary Ann Nita, Ref.Libn.; Consuelo B. Baker, Cat..

★11048★
PANCANADIAN PETROLEUM LTD. - CORPORATE LIBRARY (Energy)
P.O. Box 2850 Phone: (403)290-2386
Calgary, AB, Canada T2P 2S5 Marcia G. Kennedy, Corp.Libn.
Founded: 1981. **Staff:** Prof 2; Other 5. **Subjects:** Petroleum, natural gas, geology. **Holdings:** 20,000 books. **Subscriptions:** 425 journals and other serials; 10 newspapers. **Services:** Interlibrary loan; library not open to the public. **Automated Operations:** Computerized cataloging, acquisitions, serials, and circulation. **Computerized Information Services:** Online systems. **Publications:** Current Awareness, monthly - for internal distribution only. **Staff:** J. Nixon, Cat.Libn..

★11049★
PANEL DISPLAYS, INC. - TECHNICAL LIBRARY (Sci-Engr)
211 S. Hindry Ave. Phone: (213)641-6661
Inglewood, CA 90301 K.O. Fugate, Pres. & Libn.
Staff: Prof 1. **Subjects:** Electronics, electro-acoustics and electro-optics, radar, solid state physics, computers, mathematics, oceanography, ultrasonics. **Holdings:** 2100 books; 5200 bound periodical volumes; 1000 product catalogs; 3000 special subject technical papers. **Subscriptions:** 102 journals and other serials. **Services:** Interlibrary loan; library open to the public by appointment.

★11050★
PANHANDLE EASTERN PIPE LINE COMPANY - TECHNICAL INFORMATION CENTER (Sci-Engr)
3444 Broadway
Box 1348 Phone: (816)753-5600
Kansas City, MO 64141 Vernie Hedger, Libn.
Founded: 1967. **Staff:** Prof 1. **Subjects:** Engineering, management, natural gas industry, geology, mathematics, finance. **Special Collections:** Conference Board Reports; Stanford Research Institute Reports; SRI Energy Supply and Demand to 1980; Institute of Gas Technology (IGT) and American Gas Association (AGA) Reports. **Holdings:** 2000 volumes; standards for American National Standards Institute (ANSI), National Fluid Power Association (NFPA), American Society of Mechanical Engineers (ASME), American Petroleum Institute (API). **Subscriptions:** 70 journals and other serials; 6 newspapers. **Services:** Interlibrary loan; copying; answers brief inquiries and makes referrals; center open to the public for reference use only on request. **Publications:** Newsletter - for internal distribution only. **Remarks:** An alternate telephone number is 753-2849.

★11051★
PANHANDLE-PLAINS HISTORICAL MUSEUM - RESEARCH CENTER (Hist)
Wt. Sta., Box 967 Phone: (806)655-7191
Canyon, TX 79016 Claire R. Kuehn, Archv./Libn.
Founded: 1932. **Staff:** Prof 2; Other 2. **Subjects:** Texas and Southwest history; ranching; Indians of the Great Plains; archeology of Texas Panhandle; ethnology; clothing and textiles; fine arts; antiques; museum science. **Special Collections:** Interviews with early settlers collected over a period of 60 years; Bob Wills Memorial Archive of Popular Music, 1915 to present (5000 phonograph records). **Holdings:** 14,000 books; 12,000 cubic feet of manuscripts; 20 VF drawers of pamphlets; 800 maps; 1600 reels of microfilm; 45 cubic feet of manufacturers' trade literature; 31,000 historic photographs. **Subscriptions:** 250 journals and other serials; 12 newspapers. **Services:** Copying; center open to the public. **Special Indexes:** Index to the Panhandle-Plains Historical Review (card); Index to the Canyon (Texas) News. **Remarks:** Center is the Regional Historical Resource Depository for noncurrent county documents for 24 Texas Panhandle counties (a Texas State Library program). **Staff:** Dorothy Johnson, Asst.Archv./Libn..

★11052★
PANHANDLE STATE UNIVERSITY - NO MAN'S LAND HISTORICAL MUSEUM - LIBRARY (Hist)
Sewel St.
Box 278 Phone: (405)349-2670
Goodwell, OK 73939 Dr. Harold S. Kachel, Cur.
Subjects: Western history, No Man's Land, Dust Bowl, genealogy. **Holdings:** 3000 books; 2000 bound periodical volumes; 2000 other cataloged items. **Services:** Copying; library open to the public with restrictions.

★11053★
PANNELL KERR FORSTER - LIBRARY (Bus-Fin)
420 Lexington Ave. Phone: (212)867-8000
New York, NY 10170 Lorraine Hodges Williams, Libn.
Founded: 1945. **Staff:** Prof 1; Other 1. **Subjects:** Management advisory services, general business. **Special Collections:** Management - hotel, real estate, restaurant, health care; accounting and auditing. **Holdings:** 1000 volumes; pamphlets; clippings; government documents. **Subscriptions:** 300 journals and other serials. **Services:** Interlibrary loan; library not open to the public. **Computerized Information Services:** DIALOG Information Services, LEXIS, NEXIS, Dun & Bradstreet Corporation, Dow Jones News/Retrieval.

★11054★
PANNELL KERR FORSTER - LIBRARY (Bus-Fin)
5847 San Felipe, Rm. 2300 Phone: (713)780-8007
Houston, TX 77057-3010 Cheryl Jones, Off.Serv.Mgr.
Staff: 2. **Subjects:** Hotel operations, travel, tourism. **Holdings:** 5015 volumes; 5000 manuscripts and studies. **Subscriptions:** 25 journals and other serials; 10 newspapers. **Services:** Library not open to the public. **Computerized Information Services:** DIALOG Information Services; INFOSTAR, DATASTAR (internal databases). **Publications:** Texas Annual Trends - free upon request; Monthly Trends in the Hotel Industry (for Texas, Houston, Dallas/Fort Worth, San Antonio, Austin).

★11055★
PANNELL KERR FORSTER - MANAGEMENT ADVISORY SERVICES - LIBRARY (Bus-Fin)
150 N. Michigan Ave., Suite 3700 Phone: (312)427-7955
Chicago, IL 60601 Mary Beth Fanto, Market Res.
Staff: Prof 1. **Subjects:** Hotels and motels, food service and restaurants, travel and tourism, economics and demographics, commercial real estate. **Holdings:** 100 books; 15 hotel/motel and foodservice operation manuals; statistics and trends of the hotel industry. **Subscriptions:** 34 journals and other serials; 12 newspapers. **Services:** Library not open to the public. **Publications:** Newsletter - for internal distribution only. **Special Indexes:** Index of market demand and economic feasibility studies for hotels, motels, condominiums; food and beverage operation studies; economic valuations and data processing studies.

PANZNER MEMORIAL LIBRARY
See: Providence Hospital (11642)

★11056★
PAOLI MEMORIAL HOSPITAL - ROBERT M. WHITE MEMORIAL LIBRARY (Med)
Lancaster Pike — Phone: (215)648-1218
Paoli, PA 19301 — Virginia M. Dick, Med.Libn.
Staff: Prof 1. **Subjects:** Clinical and pre-clinical medicine. **Holdings:** 800 books; 110 publications of medical staff members; 4 VF drawers of pamphlets. **Subscriptions:** 159 journals and other serials. **Services:** Interlibrary loan; copying; library open to the public for reference use only. **Computerized Information Services:** BRS Information Technologies, MEDLARS. **Networks/Consortia:** Member of Consortium for Health Information & Library Services (CHI).

★11057★
PAPANICOLAOU COMPREHENSIVE CANCER CENTER - THE CANCER INFORMATION SERVICE (Med)
1475 N.W. 12th Ave. — Phone: (305)548-4821
Miami, FL 33136 — Jo Beth Speyer, Dir.
Founded: 1976. **Staff:** Prof 5; Other 1. **Subjects:** Cancer, nutrition. **Holdings:** Figures not available. **Services:** Interlibrary loan; open to the public. **Computerized Information Services:** Physician Data Query (PDQ). Performs searches free of charge. Contact Person: Gepsie Mary.

★11058★
PAPANICOLAOU COMPREHENSIVE CANCER CENTER - RESEARCH LIBRARY (Med)
1155 N.W. 14th St.
Box 016188
Miami, FL 33101 — Lari Wenzel, Dir.
Founded: 1968. **Subjects:** Biochemistry, enzymology, protein chemistry, molecular biology, immunology, cancer research, biophysics, pathology, genetics, microbiology, virology, professional and patient cancer education materials. **Special Collections:** Russian technical publications (150). **Holdings:** 2300 books; 2000 bound periodical volumes; 1500 unbound journals; 5 boxes of staff publications. **Services:** Library open to the public with restrictions. **Networks/Consortia:** Member of Consortium of Health Sciences Libraries of the Eastern Shore. **Publications:** Spanish/English Cancer Educational/Informational Fact Sheets.

★11059★
PAPETERIE REED LTD. - DEVELOPMENT LIBRARY (Sci-Engr)
Box 1487 — Phone: (418)525-2886
Quebec, PQ, Canada G1K 7H9 — Paule Gagnon, Libn.
Founded: 1965. **Staff:** 2. **Subjects:** Pulp and paper, science and engineering. **Holdings:** 3000 books; 700 bound periodical volumes. **Subscriptions:** 120 journals and other serials. **Services:** Interlibrary loan (limited); library open to the public by appointment.

PAPPAS LAW LIBRARY
See: Boston University (1763)

★11060★
PARADE PUBLICATIONS, INC. - LIBRARY (Publ)
750 Third Ave., 6th Fl. — Phone: (212)573-7189
New York, NY 10017 — Roberta J. Gardner, Lib.Dir.
Staff: Prof 5. **Subjects:** Editorial research materials. **Special Collections:** Parade Magazine, 1941 to present (bound and on microfiche). **Holdings:** 1200 volumes; internal research material; pamphlets; clippings. **Subscriptions:** 125 journals and other serials; 6 newspapers. **Services:** Library not open to the public. **Computerized Information Services:** NEXIS. **Publications:** Parade Magazine; Sunday News Magazine. **Staff:** Anita B. Goss, Sr.Res.Libn.; David Hegeman, Ed.Res.Asst.; Linda Mohler, Sr.Libn.; Teressa Platt, Sr.Res.Libn..

★11061★
PARADISE VALLEY HOSPITAL - MEDICAL LIBRARY (Med)
2400 E. Fourth St. — Phone: (714)470-6311
National City, CA 92050 — Vicky A. Kaili, Libn.
Founded: 1974. **Subjects:** Medicine, nursing. **Holdings:** 800 books; 166 bound periodical volumes; 50 other cataloged items. **Subscriptions:** 60 journals and other serials. **Services:** Library not open to the public.

★11062★
PARAPSYCHOLOGY FOUNDATION INC. - EILEEN J. GARRETT LIBRARY (Rel-Phil)
228 E. 71st St. — Phone: (212)628-1550
New York, NY 10021-5136 — Wayne Norman, Libn.
Founded: 1951. **Staff:** 1. **Subjects:** Experimental parapsychology and allied sciences, altered states of consciousness, hypnosis, psi in anthropology, paranormal healing, studies of survival after death. **Special Collections:** Rare books dealing with the paranormal and occult. **Holdings:** 9400 books; 991 bound periodical volumes; 11 VF drawers of pamphlets, clippings, reprints. **Subscriptions:** 100 journals and other serials. **Services:** Copying (limited); library open to the public for reference use only. **Publications:** Guide to Sources of Information on Parapsychology, annual - for sale. **Special Indexes:** Index to periodical literature in parapsychology, 1966 to present (card).

★11063★
PARAPSYCHOLOGY SOURCES OF INFORMATION CENTER (Rel-Phil)
2 Plane Tree Lane — Phone: (516)271-1243
Dix Hills, NY 11746 — Rhea A. White, Dir.
Staff: Prof 1; Other 3. **Subjects:** Experimental parapsychology, psychical research, consciousness studies, mysticism, transpersonal psychology, analytical psychology/Jung. **Special Collections:** Sports and mysticism (4000 items); parapsychology from a nonparapsychological viewpoint (12,000 articles); parapsychology and transpersonal psychology organizations (files on 100 organizations); biographies of parapsychologists (350 files). **Holdings:** 4400 books; 40 bound periodical volumes; 65 manuscripts; 20 dissertations; 70 cassette tapes. **Subscriptions:** 111 journals and other serials. **Services:** Interlibrary loan; copying; SDI; center open to the public by appointment. **Computerized Information Services:** The Source Information Network; PsiLine Database System (internal database). Performs searches on fee basis. **Publications:** PSI Center bibliographies; Higher degrees granted for work in parapsychology: An international list; Parapsychology in Print: Subject List to the Best Books in English, AN; Parapsychology in Print: Author List to the Best Books in English, annual - all for sale; Parapsychology Abstracts International, semiannual. **Special Indexes:** Index to reviews of parapsychology books; parapsychology index; index to biographical information on parapsychologists; index to sports and mysticism collection (all on cards).

S.C. PARDEE MEDICAL LIBRARY
See: Adventist Health Systems Sunbelt - Walker Memorial Hospital (68)

WILLIAM J. PARISH MEMORIAL LIBRARY
See: University of New Mexico (16606)

★11064★
PARK AVENUE SYNAGOGUE - ROTHSCHILD LIBRARY (Rel-Phil)
50 E. 87th St. — Phone: (212)369-2600
New York, NY 10128 — Susan Vogelstein, Libn.
Founded: 1956. **Staff:** Prof 2; Other 1. **Subjects:** Judaica. **Special Collections:** Holocaust; Jewish biographies; early childhood Judaica; Jewish history; Bible; Jewish art and music. **Holdings:** 8000 books. **Subscriptions:** 20 journals and other serials. **Services:** Library open to the public with special permission. **Staff:** Rose Rudich, Sunday Libn.; Irma Adler, Asst.Libn..

★11065★
PARK CITY HOSPITAL - CARLSON FOUNDATION MEMORIAL LIBRARY (Med)
695 Park Ave.
Bridgeport, CT 06604 — Phone: (203)579-5097
Staff: Prof 1. **Subjects:** Medicine, nursing, dentistry, allied health sciences. **Holdings:** 1813 books; 2770 bound periodical volumes; 253 videotapes; 2 VF drawers. **Subscriptions:** 185 journals and other serials. **Services:** Interlibrary loan; copying; library open to the public for reference use only. **Computerized Information Services:** BRS Information Technologies, MEDLINE. Performs searches on fee basis. **Networks/Consortia:** Member of Southwestern Connecticut Library Council (SWLC), Connecticut Association of Health Science Libraries (CAHSL), North Atlantic Health Science Libraries (NAHSL). **Special Catalogs:** Catalog of the Videotape Collection, updated periodically - for internal distribution only.

★11066★
PARK COUNTY BAR ASSOCIATION - LAW LIBRARY (Law)
Court House
1002 Sheridan Ave. Phone: (307)587-2204
Cody, WY 82414 Jerry Hoag, Libn.
Staff: 2. **Subjects:** Law. **Holdings:** 10,600 volumes. **Services:** Library open to the public with restrictions. **Computerized Information Services:** WESTLAW. Performs searches on fee basis.

★11067★
PARK COUNTY MUSEUM ASSOCIATION - MUSEUM LIBRARY (Hist)
118 W. Chinook Phone: (406)222-3506
Livingston, MT 59047 Sherral K. Jerde, Caretaker
Founded: 1976. **Staff:** 5. **Subjects:** State and local history, railroads. **Holdings:** 1400 books; 1000 bound periodical volumes; 32,000 newspapers; 140 cassettes; 1120 family history reports; association scrapbooks and minutes. **Services:** Library open to the public with restrictions.

★11068★
PARK FOREST PUBLIC LIBRARY - ORAL HISTORY OF PARK FOREST COLLECTION (Hist)
400 Lakewood Blvd. Phone: (312)748-3731
Park Forest, IL 60466 Neal Ney, Adm.Libn.
Subjects: Park Forest history, especially 1948-1960. **Holdings:** 99 audiotapes; 69 transcripts of audiotapes; 7 tapes; 14 video cassette titles; 231 mounted photographs; 1200 photographs; 200 slides; 3 scrapbooks; 5 VF drawers of local government documents; 2 VF drawers of local history materials; newspapers, 1949 to present, hardcopy and microfilm. **Services:** Interlibrary loan (limited); copying; collection open to the public. **Publications:** Booklet.

★11069★
PARK-NICOLLET MEDICAL FOUNDATION - ARNESON LIBRARY (Med)
5000 W. 39th St. Phone: (612)927-3097
Minneapolis, MN 55416 Barbara K. Latta, Dir.
Staff: Prof 2; Other 1. **Subjects:** Medicine, nursing, allied health sciences. **Holdings:** 1150 books; 3840 bound periodical volumes; 5 boxes of pamphlets and reprints. **Subscriptions:** 148 journals and other serials. **Services:** Interlibrary loan (limited); library not open to the public. **Computerized Information Services:** DIALOG Information Services, BRS Information Technologies, MEDLARS. Performs searches on fee basis. **Networks/Consortia:** Member of Twin Cities Biomedical Consortium (TCBC). **Publications:** Bulletin, quarterly.

PHILIP M. PARK MEMORIAL LIBRARY
See: Jesse Besser Museum (1538)

★11070★
PARK PLACE CHURCH OF GOD - CARL KARDATZKE MEMORIAL LIBRARY (Rel-Phil)
501 College Dr.
Anderson, IN 46012 Trish B. Janutolo, Chm., Lib.Comm.
Subjects: Bibles, religion, Christian education, doctrinal theology, family ethics, biography, missions, children's books. **Holdings:** 2000 books.

★11071★
PARK RIDGE HOSPITAL - NATHANIEL J. HURST LIBRARY (Med)
1555 Long Pond Rd. Phone: (716)723-7755
Rochester, NY 14626 Eileen P. Shirley, Libn.
Founded: 1975. **Staff:** Prof 1. **Subjects:** Medicine, nursing, surgery, hospital administration, alcoholism and drug abuse. **Holdings:** 1760 books; 1984 bound periodical volumes; 817 audio cassettes; 228 videotapes. **Subscriptions:** 117 journals and other serials. **Services:** Interlibrary loan; copying; library open to the public upon request. **Automated Operations:** Computerized ILL. **Computerized Information Services:** MEDLARS, OCLC; DOCLINE (electronic mail service). **Networks/Consortia:** Member of Rochester Regional Library Council (RRLC). **Publications:** Highlights of Health, bimonthly - for internal distribution only.

★11072★
PARK SYNAGOGUE LIBRARY - KRAVITZ MEMORIAL LIBRARY (Rel-Phil)
3300 Mayfield Rd. Phone: (216)371-2244
Cleveland Heights, OH 44118 Tikvah Krieger, Libn.
Staff: Prof 1. **Subjects:** Judaica, Jewish history. **Holdings:** 15,000 books; 100 bound periodical volumes. **Subscriptions:** 70 journals and other serials; 10 newspapers. **Services:** Interlibrary loan; library open to the public for reference use only.

WILLIAM HALLOCK PARK MEMORIAL LIBRARY
See: New York City Public Health Laboratories (10018)

PARKE-DAVIS
See: Warner-Lambert/Parke-Davis (17451)

★11073★
PARKER, CHAPIN, FLATTAU AND KLIMPL - LIBRARY (Law)
1211 Ave. of the Americas Phone: (212)704-6000
New York, NY 10036 Lucy Maret, Libn.
Founded: 1940. **Staff:** Prof 2; Other 3. **Subjects:** Law - litigation, antitrust, tax, labor, trusts and estates, corporations, banking, securities, real estate. **Holdings:** 15,500 books; 150 bound periodical volumes; 600 pamphlets. **Subscriptions:** 200 journals and other serials. **Services:** Interlibrary loan; library not open to the public. **Computerized Information Services:** LEXIS, DIALOG Information Services. **Publications:** PCF & K Library Memo, monthly. **Special Catalogs:** Catalog of memoranda and briefs (card); corporate forms catalog (card). **Staff:** Mitchell Feir, Asst.Libn..

★11074★
PARKER MEMORIAL BAPTIST CHURCH - LIBRARY (Rel-Phil)
1205 Quintard Ave.
Box 2104 Phone: (205)236-5628
Anniston, AL 36201 Mrs. Gale Main, Libn.
Founded: 1932. **Staff:** Prof 1; Other 6. **Subjects:** Religion, fiction, biography, history, geography. **Holdings:** 3500 books; 1 VF drawer of pamphlets. **Services:** Library open to the public.

★11075★
PARKLAND COLLEGE - LEARNING RESOURCE CENTER (Educ)
2400 W. Bradley Ave. Phone: (217)351-2241
Champaign, IL 61820 David L. Johnson, Dir.
Founded: 1967. **Staff:** Prof 7; Other 20. **Subjects:** Education. **Holdings:** 90,500 books; 15,000 other cataloged items. **Subscriptions:** 815 journals and other serials; 38 newspapers. **Services:** Interlibrary loan; copying; center open to the public with restrictions. **Automated Operations:** Computerized cataloging and acquisitions. **Computerized Information Services:** DIALOG Information Services, OCLC. **Networks/Consortia:** Member of Metropolitan Consortium of Chicago, ILLINET. **Staff:** William C. Gaines, Pub.Serv.Libn.; Ann Neely, Ref.Libn.; Ken Strickler, Tech.Serv.Libn.; Raymond Bial, Acq.Libn.; Larry Johnson, Media Spec..

PARKLAWN HEALTH LIBRARY
See: U.S. Public Health Service (15491)

TIMOTHY PARKMAN MEMORIAL LIBRARY
See: Newman Catholic Student Center (10216)

★11076★
PARKRIDGE CENTRE - STAFF LIBRARY (Med)
110 Gropper Crescent Phone: (306)978-2333
Saskatoon, SK, Canada S7M 5N9 Kristine Wisser, Dir. of Hea.Rec.
Founded: 1987. **Staff:** Prof 1. **Subjects:** Medical guidelines, nursing, gerontology, psychosocial and rehabilitation therapies. **Holdings:** 345 volumes. **Subscriptions:** 21 journals and other serials. **Services:** Copying; library open to the public with restrictions. **Computerized Information Services:** Internal database. **Formerly:** Frank Eliason Centre - Health Sciences Library.

PARKS COLLEGE
See: St. Louis University (12548)

★11077★
PARKVIEW EPISCOPAL MEDICAL CENTER - MEDICAL LIBRARY (Med)
400 W. 16th St. Phone: (719)584-4582
Pueblo, CO 81003 Alma Williams, Lib.Coord.
Founded: 1959. **Staff:** Prof 1. **Subjects:** Medicine, nursing, surgery, hospital administration, allied health sciences. **Holdings:** 2119 books; 1648 bound periodical volumes; pamphlet file. **Subscriptions:** 120 journals and other serials. **Services:** Interlibrary loan; copying; SDI; library open to the public for reference use only. **Computerized Information Services:** MEDLARS, BRS Information Technologies; Mile High Mail (electronic mail service). Performs searches on fee basis. **Networks/Consortia:** Member of Colorado Council of Medical Librarians, Peaks and Valleys (Medical) Library Consortium.

PARKVIEW LIBRARY
See: Oklahoma School for the Blind (10736)

★11078★
PARKVIEW MEMORIAL HOSPITAL - HEALTH SCIENCE LIBRARY (Med)
2200 Randallia Dr. Phone: (219)484-6636
Fort Wayne, IN 46805 Dorothy Gitlin, Lib.Mgr.
Staff: Prof 2; Other 1. **Subjects:** Medicine, nursing, and allied health sciences. **Holdings:** 3000 books. **Subscriptions:** 180 journals and other serials. **Services:** Interlibrary loan (fee); copying; library open to staff and health science students. **Automated Operations:** Computerized cataloging and circulation. **Computerized Information Services:** MEDLINE, BRS Information Technologies. **Networks/Consortia:** Member of Northeast Indiana Health Sciences Libraries, Tri-ALSA, Greater Midwest Regional Medical Library Network. **Staff:** Phyllis Eckman, Asst.Libn..

★11079★
PARKVIEW OSTEOPATHIC HOSPITAL - LIBRARY (Med)
1920 Parkwood Ave. Phone: (419)242-8471
Toledo, OH 43624 Mary Bracey, Libn.
Staff: 1. **Subjects:** Osteopathy, orthopedics, radiology, surgery, anesthesiology, pediatrics, clinical and family medicine. **Special Collections:** Osteopathic Collection (including rare books by the founder of the osteopathic medical profession). **Holdings:** 1050 books; 1450 bound periodical volumes; Audio-Digest tapes. **Subscriptions:** 74 journals and other serials. **Services:** Interlibrary loan; library not open to the public. **Computerized Information Services:** MEDLINE.

★11080★
PARLEE, MC LAWS BARRISTERS & SOLICITORS - LIBRARY (Law)
10405 Jasper Ave., No. 1800 Phone: (403)423-8594
Edmonton, AB, Canada T5J 3N4
Priscilla Kennedy, Dir. of Legal Res.
Subjects: Law, government. **Holdings:** 10,000 books. **Services:** Copying; library open to the public with permission. **Automated Operations:** Computerized cataloging. **Computerized Information Services:** QL Systems, WESTLAW, LEXIS. Performs searches on fee basis. **Remarks:** A branch library is maintained at 300 Fifth Ave., S.W., 21st Fl., Calgary, AB T2P 3C4; telephone: (403)294-7000. **Staff:** Phyllis Thornton, Libn..

A.F. PARLOW LIBRARY OF THE HEALTH SCIENCES
See: Los Angeles County/Harbor-UCLA Medical Center (7987)

PARMA TECHNICAL CENTER
See: Union Carbide Corporation (14465)

★11081★
PARMLY BILLINGS LIBRARY - MONTANA ROOM (Hist)
510 N. Broadway Phone: (406)657-8290
Billings, MT 59101 Linda Weirather
Staff: Prof 1. **Subjects:** Montana history, Battle of Little Bighorn, Crow Indians. **Special Collections:** Local histories (100); city archives (75 archival materials). **Holdings:** 6000 books; 100 bound periodical volumes; 120 filing drawers. **Subscriptions:** 12 journals and other serials; 6 newspapers.

PARRAL ARCHIVES
See: Amerind Foundation, Inc. - Fulton-Hayden Memorial Library (718)

★11082★
PARRISH ART MUSEUM - LIBRARY
25 Job's Lane
Southampton, NY 11968
Founded: 1954. **Subjects:** American and European art, architecture, crafts. **Special Collections:** William Merritt Chase Archives; Aline B. Saarinen Library; Moses and Ida Soyer Library; Samuel Parrish Library. **Holdings:** 4300 books; 3000 catalogs. **Remarks:** Presently inactive.

JUNE AUSTIN PARRISH MEMORIAL LIBRARY
See: Employers Reinsurance Corporation (4693)

SAMUEL PARRISH LIBRARY
See: Parrish Art Museum - Library (11082)

PARROT HEALTH SCIENCES LIBRARY
See: Eastern Maine Medical Center (4533)

DR. VICTOR PARSONNET MEMORIAL LIBRARY
See: Newark Beth Israel Medical Center (10190)

★11083★
PARSONS, BRINCKERHOFF, QUADE & DOUGLAS, INC. - LIBRARY (Sci-Engr)
One Penn Plaza
250 W. 34th St. Phone: (212)613-5290
New York, NY 10119 Laura A. Marino, Libn.
Founded: 1976. **Staff:** Prof 1; Other 1. **Subjects:** Transportation, civil and structural engineering, urban and environmental planning. **Holdings:** 5500 books; 4500 technical reports. **Subscriptions:** 250 journals and other serials. **Services:** Interlibrary loan; copying; library open to the public by appointment. **Automated Operations:** Computerized periodicals routing. **Computerized Information Services:** BRS Information Technologies, DIALOG Information Services, Pergamon ORBIT InfoLine, Inc., American Society of Civil Engineers (ASCE).

PARSONS CORPORATION - CHAS. T. MAIN, INC.
See: Chas. T. Main, Inc. (8313)

★11084★
ELBERT H. PARSONS PUBLIC LAW LIBRARY (Law)
205 East Side Square Phone: (205)532-3740
Huntsville, AL 35801 Cleo S. Cason, Libn.
Staff: Prof 1. **Subjects:** Law. **Holdings:** 14,000 books; 1000 bound periodical volumes. **Subscriptions:** 54 journals and other serials. **Services:** Copying; library open to the public. **Remarks:** Maintained by Madison County.

★11085★
RALPH M. PARSONS COMPANY - CENTRAL LIBRARY (Sci-Engr)
100 W. Walnut St. Phone: (818)440-3999
Pasadena, CA 91124 Jennifer Stein, Libn.
Staff: Prof 1; Other 1. **Subjects:** Engineering, mining, nuclear engineering, power. **Holdings:** 6000 books; 1000 bound periodical volumes; 7000 reports; 3500 vendor equipment catalogs. **Subscriptions:** 200 journals and other serials; 5 newspapers. **Services:** Interlibrary loan.

RALPH M. PARSONS LABORATORY
See: Massachusetts Institute of Technology - Civil Engineering Department (8531)

★11086★
PARSONS SCHOOL OF DESIGN - ADAM AND SOPHIE GIMBEL DESIGN LIBRARY (Art)
2 W. 13th St., 2nd Fl. Phone: (212)741-8914
New York, NY 10011 Sharon Chickanzeff, Lib.Dir.
Founded: 1896. **Staff:** Prof 2; Other 5. **Subjects:** Art, architecture, costume, crafts, design, environmental design, fashion, graphic arts, photography, typography. **Special Collections:** Sketchbooks by American fashion designer Claire McCardell (125 volumes). **Holdings:** 32,000 books; 40,000 mounted picture plates. **Subscriptions:** 230 journals and other serials. **Services:** Interlibrary loan; library open to the public by appointment. **Automated Operations:** Computerized cataloging and circulation. **Computerized Information Services:** RLIN. **Networks/Consortia:** Member of New York Metropolitan Reference and Research Library Agency (METRO). **Remarks:** Affiliated with New School for Social Research. **Staff:** Claire Petrie, Ref./Tech.Serv.Libn..

★11087★
PARSONS SCHOOL OF DESIGN - OTIS ART INSTITUTE - LIBRARY (Art)
2401 Wilshire Blvd. Phone: (213)251-0560
Los Angeles, CA 90057 Tom Goff, Dir.
Founded: 1947. **Staff:** Prof 3; Other 1. **Subjects:** Fine arts, communication design, architecture, fashion, design, photography. **Special Collections:** Artists' books (750 titles); fine prints and artists' realia (54 titles). **Holdings:** 50,000 books; 3000 bound periodical volumes; 60,000 slides; 54 VF drawers of artists' ephemera files; 16 VF drawers of clipping files; 9 VF drawers of art reproduction files; 267 audio cassettes; 123 films; 87 videotapes and cassettes. **Subscriptions:** 207 journals and other serials. **Services:** Copying; library open to the public by appointment only. **Automated Operations:** Computerized cataloging. **Staff:** Brian Mains, Cat.Libn.; Russ Cangealosi, Slide/Media Cur..

★11088★
PARSONS SCHOOL OF DESIGN - SLIDE DEPARTMENT - LIBRARY (Art)
66 Fifth Ave.
New York, NY 10011 Christina Kane, Cur.
Subjects: Art history, architecture, interior design, industrial design, costume history and fashion, illustration, graphic design. **Holdings:** 70,000 slides. **Staff:** Susan Miller, Asst.Cur..

★11089★
PARSONS STATE HOSPITAL AND TRAINING CENTER - MEDICAL LIBRARY (Med)
2601 Gabriel
Box 738 Phone: (316)421-6550
Parsons, KS 67357-0738 Linda Lee Stahlman, Med.Libn.
Founded: 1953. **Staff:** Prof 1. **Subjects:** Mental retardation, psychiatry, psychology, psychiatric nursing, social service, speech pathology, audiology, behavioral science, operant conditioning. **Holdings:** 5200 books; 4 VF drawers of pamphlets; 282 working papers. **Subscriptions:** 75 journals and other serials. **Services:** Interlibrary loan; copying; library open to the public. **Computerized Information Services:** Online systems. Performs searches on fee basis. **Special Indexes:** Index to Parsons Sun articles concerning the hospital (in preparation). **Remarks:** Maintained by the Kansas State Department of Social & Rehabilitation Services. Center maintains an active library for mentally retarded and emotionally disturbed children and young people, aged 6 to adult.

★11090★
PASADENA COLLEGE OF CHIROPRACTIC - LIBRARY (Med)
8420 Beverly Rd. Phone: (213)692-0331
Pico Rivera, CA 90660 Mary Beth Hayes, Lib.Dir.
Staff: Prof 1; Other 1. **Subjects:** Chiropractic. **Holdings:** 8000 books; 900 bound periodical volumes; 5000 unbound periodicals. **Subscriptions:** 80 journals and other serials. **Services:** Interlibrary loan; copying; library open to the public for reference use only. **Networks/Consortia:** Member of Chiropractic Library Consortium (CLIBCON).

★11091★
PASADENA HISTORICAL SOCIETY - LIBRARY & ARCHIVES (Hist)
470 W. Walnut St. Phone: (818)795-3002
Pasadena, CA 91103 Carol H. Buge, Archv./Libn.
Founded: 1924. **Staff:** Prof 1; Other 12. **Subjects:** History of the Pasadena area. **Special Collections:** Photographs and slides of early Pasadena (500,000). **Holdings:** 1500 books; pamphlets; clippings; albums; diaries; maps; documents; magazines. **Services:** Copying; library and archives open to the public for research only.

★11092★
PASADENA PRESBYTERIAN CHURCH - LIBRARY (Rel-Phil)
100 Pasadena Ave., N. Phone: (813)345-0148
St. Petersburg, FL 33710-8315 Elizabeth Howe, Libn.
Founded: 1960. **Staff:** Prof 2; Other 2. **Subjects:** Religion, religious education. **Holdings:** 5000 books; 75 filmstrips; 24 videotapes; Presbyterian curriculum materials. **Subscriptions:** 10 journals and other serials. **Services:** Copying; library open to the public for reference use only. **Staff:** Maxine Perry, Cat.Libn.; Richard Howe, AV Libn..

★11093★
PASADENA PUBLIC LIBRARY - ALICE COLEMAN BATCHELDER MUSIC LIBRARY (Mus)
285 E. Walnut St. Phone: (818)577-4052
Pasadena, CA 91101 Anne Cain, Prin.Libn.
Founded: 1955. **Staff:** Prof 4; Other 3. **Subjects:** Music history, theory, biography; dance; musical instruments; cinema. **Special Collections:** Popular sheet music, 1858-1956 (1500 pieces). **Holdings:** 4850 books; 296 bound periodical volumes; 5342 scores; 6 VF drawers of clippings and pamphlets; 19 boxes of opera librettos; 33 boxes of miniature scores; 13,056 phonograph records; 22 scrapbooks; 600 cassettes. **Subscriptions:** 29 journals and other serials. **Services:** Interlibrary loan; copying; library open to the public. **Automated Operations:** Computerized circulation. **Networks/Consortia:** Member of Metropolitan Cooperative Library System (MCLS), South State Cooperative Library System. **Special Indexes:** Card index to song collections; card index to piano, organ, and violin music in collections. **Staff:** Laurie Whitcomb; Ruth Quirk.

★11094★
PASADENA PUBLIC LIBRARY - BUSINESS-TECHNOLOGY DIVISION (Bus-Fin, Sci-Engr)
285 E. Walnut St. Phone: (818)577-4052
Pasadena, CA 91101 Anne Cain, Prin.Libn.
Founded: 1970. **Staff:** Prof 5; Other 1. **Subjects:** Investments, finance, business management, real estate, taxation, industrial technology, engineering. **Special Collections:** Pasadena industries; state industrial directories; tax and investment services. **Holdings:** 20,485 books; 705 trade and professional directories; 350 company catalogs; 1670 corporate annual reports; 20 VF drawers of clippings and pamphlets; 1450 microfiche; 144 cassettes. **Subscriptions:** 178 journals and other serials; 16 newspapers. **Services:** Interlibrary loan; division open to the public. **Automated Operations:** Computerized cataloging, acquisitions, and circulation. **Computerized Information Services:** OCLC, DIALOG Information Services, VU/TEXT Information Services, RLIN, Mead Data Central, WILSONLINE, BRS Information Technologies. Performs searches on fee basis. Contact Person: Daniel Hanne, 405-4052. **Networks/Consortia:** Member of Metropolitan Cooperative Library System (MCLS), South State Cooperative Library System. **Special Indexes:** Subject index to trade directories; subject index to company catalogs.

★11095★
PASADENA PUBLIC LIBRARY - FINE ARTS DIVISION (Art)
285 E. Walnut St. Phone: (818)577-4049
Pasadena, CA 91101 Anne Cain, Prin.Libn.
Founded: 1927. **Staff:** Prof 4; Other 3. **Subjects:** Art history and theory, architecture, antiques, crafts, painting, printmaking, photography, costume, art biographies. **Holdings:** 15,126 books; 1550 bound periodical volumes; 377 16mm film titles; 12 VF drawers of clippings and pamphlets; 132,568 pictures; 92 scrapbooks. **Subscriptions:** 94 journals and other serials. **Services:** Interlibrary loan; copying; division open to the public. **Automated Operations:** Computerized circulation. **Networks/Consortia:** Member of Metropolitan Cooperative Library System (MCLS), South State Cooperative Library System. **Special Indexes:** Index to Architectural Digest from 1920-1950 for Southern California Architecture; Picture File Index. **Staff:** Laurie Whitcomb; Ruth Quirk.

★11096★
PASADENA PUBLIC LIBRARY - REFERENCE DIVISION (Hist)
285 E. Walnut St. Phone: (818)577-4054
Pasadena, CA 91101 Anne Cain, Prin.Libn.
Staff: Prof 5; Other 2. **Special Collections:** California and Pasadena local history, Pasadena Playhouse, genealogy. **Holdings:** 28,057 books; 425 bound periodical volumes; 1752 Pasadena photographs; 210 Pasadena scrapbooks; 47 pamphlet boxes of local city reports; 90,603 U.S. Government documents; 14,043 California government documents; 44 VF drawers; 5047 maps; 8958 reels of microfilm; 8399 pamphlets; 1395 photographs; 109 negatives; 861 telephone directories; 9239 microfiche; 723 college catalogs; 1272 reels of microfilm of Pasadena newspapers. **Subscriptions:** 395 journals and other serials; 30 newspapers. **Services:** Interlibrary loan; copying; division open to the public. **Automated Operations:** Computerized cataloging and acquisitions. **Computerized Information Services:** OCLC, DIALOG Information Services, VU/TEXT Information Services, RLIN, Mead Data Central, WILSONLINE, BRS Information Technologies. Performs searches on fee basis. Contact Person: Elaine Zorbas, 405-4052. **Networks/Consortia:** Member of Metropolitan Cooperative Library System (MCLS), South State Cooperative Library System. **Staff:** Dorothy Potter.

★11097★
PASCACK VALLEY HOSPITAL - DAVID GOLDBERG MEMORIAL MEDICAL LIBRARY (Med)
Old Hook Rd. Phone: (201)358-3240
Westwood, NJ 07675 Debbie Michaels, Dir.
Founded: 1968. **Staff:** Prof 1; Other 1. **Subjects:** Medicine, surgery, nursing, allied health sciences, management. **Special Collections:** Sports medicine. **Holdings:** 1200 books; 25 bound periodical volumes; 4 indexes; 7 audiotape subscriptions; 50 videotapes; pamphlets. **Subscriptions:** 186 journals and other serials. **Services:** Interlibrary loan; copying; SDI; library open to the public with restrictions. **Computerized Information Services:** NLM, DIALOG Information Services, BRS Information Technologies; MESSAGES (electronic mail service). Performs searches on fee basis. **Networks/Consortia:** Member of Bergen-Passaic Health Sciences Library Consortium, Health Sciences Library Association of New Jersey, New Jersey Multitype Library Network.

★11098★
PASQUA HOSPITAL - HEALTH SCIENCES LIBRARY (Med)
4101 Dewdney Ave. Phone: (306)527-9641
Regina, SK, Canada S4T 1A5 Leona Lang, Dir.
Founded: 1953. **Staff:** 1. **Subjects:** Medicine, nursing, administration. **Holdings:** 1200 books; 2800 bound periodical volumes; Audio-Digest tapes; videotapes. **Subscriptions:** 72 journals and other serials. **Services:** Library not open to the public.

MALCA PASS LIBRARY
See: Agudath Israel Congregation (100)

★11099★
PASSAIC COUNTY HISTORICAL SOCIETY - LOCAL HISTORY AND GENEALOGY LIBRARY (Hist)
Lambert Castle
Valley Rd. Phone: (201)881-2761
Paterson, NJ 07503 Susan Pumilia, Dir.
Founded: 1926. **Subjects:** Genealogy, local history. **Special Collections:** Society for the Establishment of Useful Manufactures papers; Abraham Hewitt papers (iron industry); Family Group Sheets Collection (3 filing cabinets). **Holdings:** 2000 books. **Services:** Copying; library open to the public by appointment. **Publications:** A Guide to the Collections - for sale. **Special Catalogs:** Researchers Card File.

★11100★
PASSAIC RIVER COALITION - ENVIRONMENTAL LIBRARY (Env-Cons)
246 Madisonville Rd. Phone: (201)766-7550
Basking Ridge, NJ 07920 Alfred J. Porro, Jr., Chm.
Founded: 1971. **Subjects:** Environmental quality in the Passaic River Watershed, urban river systems, water pollution, water quality and supply, flood control, sewage and garbage disposal, urban decay, land use, wildlife and vegetation, historic preservation, solid waste energy, environmental education. **Holdings:** 8000 volumes; special interest collections. **Subscriptions:** 15 journals and other serials; 5 newspapers. **Services:** Copying; library open to the public. **Publications:** Vibes from the Libe, bimonthly.

★11101★
PASSAVANT AREA HOSPITAL - SIBERT LIBRARY (Med)
1600 W. Walnut St. Phone: (217)245-9541
Jacksonville, IL 62650 Dorothy H. Knight, Libn.
Founded: 1902. **Staff:** Prof 1. **Subjects:** Nursing, medicine. **Holdings:** 2227 books; 140 bound periodical volumes; AV programs. **Subscriptions:** 315 journals and other serials. **Services:** Interlibrary loan; copying; library open to the public. **Networks/Consortia:** Member of Greater Midwest Regional Medical Library Network, Capital Area Consortium, Great River Library System (GRLS). **Remarks:** Maintains Community Health Information Center. Fax: (217)245-9331.

★11102★
PASSIONIST MONASTIC SEMINARY - LIBRARY (Rel-Phil)
86-45 178th St. Phone: (718)739-6502
Jamaica, NY 11432 Br. James G. Johnson, C.P., Libn.
Founded: 1934. **Staff:** Prof 1. **Subjects:** Theology, spirituality, preaching, philosophy, Passion of Christ, adult education. **Holdings:** 53,648 books; 142 bound periodical volumes. **Subscriptions:** 125 journals and other serials. **Services:** Copying; library open to the public by appointment.

★11103★
PASSIVE SOLAR INSTITUTE - LIBRARY (Energy)
Box 722 Phone: (419)937-2225
Bascom, OH 44809 Joseph Deahl, Pres.
Founded: 1973. **Subjects:** Passive solar energy and building designs. **Holdings:** 10,000 volumes.

SHERMAN PASTOR MEMORIAL LIBRARY
See: Congregation Shalom (3633)

PASTORE LIBRARY
See: Philadelphia College of Textiles and Science (11272)

★11104★
PATENT, TRADEMARK AND COPYRIGHT RESEARCH FOUNDATION - LIBRARY (Law)
Franklin Pierce Law Center
2 White St.
Concord, NH 03301 Phone: (603)228-1541
Staff: Prof 3. **Subjects:** Patents, trademarks, copyright. **Holdings:** 1000 items. **Publications:** IDEA; Journal of Law and Technology, quarterly.

PATERNO LIBRARY
See: Columbia University (3490)

CHANCELLOR PATERSON LIBRARY
See: Lakehead University (7619)

★11105★
(Paterson) HERALD & NEWS - LIBRARY/NEWSPAPER MORGUE (Publ)
988 Main Ave. Phone: (201)684-3000
Paterson, NJ 07055 Sheldon Matson, Libn.
Founded: 1890. **Staff:** 1. **Subjects:** Newspaper reference topics. **Special Collections:** New Jersey Legislative Directory, 1879 to present; Passaic County Freeholders Reports, 1975 to present; Paterson Morning Call and News, 1889 to present (microfilm). **Holdings:** Photographs; reference books; local sports material. **Subscriptions:** 16 journals and other serials. **Services:** Library open to the public by appointment. **Formerly:** Paterson News.

NORMAN PATERSON SCHOOL OF INTERNATIONAL AFFAIRS
See: Carleton University (2661)

★11106★
WILLIAM PATERSON COLLEGE OF NEW JERSEY - SARAH BYRD ASKEW LIBRARY - SPECIAL COLLECTIONS (Hist)
300 Pompton Rd. Phone: (201)595-2116
Wayne, NJ 07470 Michelle Ruhlin, Docs./Spec.Coll.Libn.
Founded: 1924. **Special Collections:** New Jerseyana (1500 volumes); first and limited editions of American and English authors (525); professional papers of William Paterson (senator, governor, Supreme Court Justice). **Services:** Interlibrary loan; copying; collections open to the public for reference use only. **Automated Operations:** Computerized cataloging, acquisitions, and circulation. **Computerized Information Services:** WILSONLINE, BRS Information Technologies, DIALOG Information Services, OCLC. **Networks/Consortia:** Member of PALINET, New Jersey Academic Library Network. **Publications:** New Books List, monthly.

PATHFINDERS MEMORIAL RESOURCE LIBRARY
See: Chapelwood United Methodist Church (2977)

★11107★
PATIENT CARE - LIBRARY (Publ)
690 Kinderkamack Rd. Phone: (201)599-8029
Oradell, NJ 07649-1506 Christine T. O'Connor, Libn.
Staff: Prof 1; Other 1. **Subjects:** Medicine, family practice, medical marketing. **Special Collections:** Patient Care magazine archives. **Holdings:** 600 books; 100 audio cassettes; 30 VF drawers. **Subscriptions:** 152 journals and other serials. **Services:** Interlibrary loan; copying; SDI; library open to the public by appointment. **Computerized Information Services:** BRS Information Technologies. **Networks/Consortia:** Member of Southwestern Connecticut Library Council (SWLC), Connecticut Association of Health Science Libraries (CAHSL), Bergen-Passaic Health Sciences Library Consortium. **Publications:** Library acquisitions, 6/year - for internal distribution only. **Special Indexes:** Subject file of patient education aids. **Formerly:** Patient Care Communications, Inc.

PATMOS MEMORIAL LIBRARY
See: Emma L. Bixby Hospital (1631)

★11108★
JAMES PATON MEMORIAL HOSPITAL - STAFF LIBRARY (Med)
Trans Canada Hwy. Phone: (709)256-5527
Gander, NF, Canada A1V 1P7 Cherry Candow, Libn.
Staff: Prof 1. **Subjects:** Medicine, orthopedics, ophthalmology, pediatrics, obstetrics, gynecology, allied health sciences. **Holdings:** 700 books. **Subscriptions:** 130 journals and other serials. **Services:** Interlibrary loan; copying; library open to the public. **Automated Operations:** Computerized cataloging, acquisitions, serials, and circulation.

★11109★
ALAN PATRICOF ASSOCIATES - INFORMATION CENTER (Bus-Fin)
545 Madison Ave. Phone: (212)753-6300
New York, NY 10022 Myra Rubin, Info.Mgr.
Founded: 1984. **Staff:** Prof 1; Other 1. **Subjects:** Venture capital. **Holdings:** 100 books. **Subscriptions:** 80 journals and other serials; 5 newspapers. **Services:** Interlibrary loan; copying; SDI; center open to SLA members. **Automated Operations:** Computerized cataloging, acquisitions, and serials. **Computerized Information Services:** DIALOG Information Services, Dow Jones News/Retrieval, VU/TEXT Information Services, TEXTLINE, CompuServe, Inc., NewsNet, Inc.; internal database; Dialcom Inc. (electronic mail service). **Special Indexes:** Index to conference material (online).

★11110★
PATRIOT NEWS COMPANY - LIBRARY (Publ)
812 King Blvd.
Box 2265 Phone: (717)255-8402
Harrisburg, PA 17105 Deanna Mills, Libn.
Staff: Prof 2; Other 2. **Subjects:** Newspaper reference topics. **Holdings:** 200 books; newspapers clipping files on microfiche; photographs; local paper, 1911 to present, on microfilm. **Services:** Library not open to the public. **Computerized Information Services:** DataTimes. **Special Indexes:** Clippings index; graphics index; photo index.

A.B. PATTERSON PROFESSIONAL LIBRARY
See: Scarborough Board of Education (12943)

★11111★
PATTERSON, BELKNAP, WEBB & TYLER - LIBRARY (Law)
30 Rockefeller Plaza Phone: (212)698-2500
New York, NY 10112 Penny Tarpley, Chf.Libn.
Staff: Prof 2; Other 7. **Subjects:** Law - litigation, corporate, tax, patent/copyright, media/communication. **Holdings:** 25,000 volumes; 6000 current annual reports; 15 VF drawers; 150 audio cassettes. **Subscriptions:** 360 journals and other serials; 12 newspapers. **Services:** Interlibrary loan; library not open to the public. **Computerized Information Services:** WESTLAW, The Reference Service (REFSRV), DIALOG Information Services, Dow Jones News/Retrieval, NewsNet, Inc., Mead Data Central. **Publications:** Res Communes (newsletter), monthly - for internal distribution only. **Special Catalogs:** Cataloging Manual (online, printout). **Special Indexes:** Tax Club Memoranda Index; List of On-Line Databases; Annual Reports List; Periodicals List (all online and printout). **Staff:** Christina Senezak, Asst.Libn.; Carol Mahoney, Asst.Libn..

PATTERSON REFERENCE LIBRARY AND ECONOMICS REFERENCE CENTER
See: Midwest Research Institute (8973)

JAMES R. PATTILLO LIBRARY OF BANKING AND FINANCE
See: University of California, Los Angeles - John E. Anderson Graduate School of Management - Library (15975)

★11112★
PATTON BOGGS AND BLOW - LAW LIBRARY (Law)
2550 M St., N.W. Phone: (202)457-6000
Washington, DC 20036 Kevin McCall, Libn.
Staff: Prof 1. **Subjects:** Law. **Holdings:** 7000 books. **Subscriptions:** 36 journals and other serials. **Services:** Interlibrary loan. **Computerized Information Services:** WESTLAW, DIALOG Information Services, LEXIS.

★11113★
GEORGE S. PATTON, JR. HISTORICAL SOCIETY - LIBRARY (Hist)
3116 Thorn St. Phone: (619)271-6517
San Diego, CA 92104-4618 Charles M. Province, Pres.
Founded: 1970. **Staff:** Prof 1; Other 1. **Subjects:** George S. Patton, Jr., Third U.S. Army, military science and history. **Holdings:** 200 books; 300 bound periodical volumes; videotapes; films. **Services:** Copying; library open to the public. **Automated Operations:** Computerized cataloging, acquisitions, and serials.

PATTON MUSEUM OF CAVALRY & ARMOR
See: U.S. Army - TRADOC - Patton Museum of Cavalry & Armor (14804)

★11114★
PATTON STATE HOSPITAL - STAFF LIBRARY (Med)
3102 E. Highland Ave. Phone: (714)862-8121
Patton, CA 92369 Mary Sue Stumberg, Staff Libn.
Founded: 1947. **Staff:** Prof 1. **Subjects:** Psychiatry, psychology, neurology, psychiatric nursing. **Holdings:** 3600 books; 2025 bound periodical volumes; 1100 unbound periodical volumes; 2 VF drawers of unbound reports; 2 VF drawers of documents. **Subscriptions:** 101 journals and other serials. **Services:** Interlibrary loan; copying; library open to mental health professionals. **Networks/Consortia:** Member of Pacific Southwest Regional Medical Library Service, San Bernardino, Inyo, Riverside Counties United Library Services (SIRCULS), Medical Library Group of Southern California and Arizona (MLGSCA). **Remarks:** Maintained by California State Department of Mental Health.

PATUXENT WILDLIFE RESEARCH CENTER
See: U.S. Fish & Wildlife Service (15087)

★11115★
PAUL, HASTINGS, JANOFSKY AND WALKER - LAW LIBRARY (Law)
555 S. Flower, 22nd Floor Phone: (213)489-4000
Los Angeles, CA 90071 Karen Rogers, Adm.Libn.
Founded: 1972. **Staff:** Prof 2; Other 3. **Subjects:** Federal and state law. **Holdings:** 15,000 volumes. **Subscriptions:** 185 journals and other serials. **Services:** Interlibrary loan; library open to the public on request. **Automated Operations:** Computerized cataloging. **Computerized Information Services:** DIALOG Information Services, LEXIS, WESTLAW, Dow Jones News/Retrieval, I.P. Sharp Associates Limited, VU/TEXT Information Services; MCI Mail, OnTyme Electronic Message Network Service (electronic mail services). **Networks/Consortia:** Member of CLASS. **Special Indexes:** Computerized index to research memos.

★11116★
PAUL SMITH'S COLLEGE OF ARTS AND SCIENCES - FRANK L. CUBLEY LIBRARY (Educ)
Paul Smiths, NY 12970 Phone: (518)327-6313
Theodore D. Mack, Libn.
Staff: Prof 2; Other 4. **Subjects:** Hotel and restaurant management, chef training, cookery, forestry, urban tree management, environmental science, forest recreation, surveying. **Holdings:** 43,775 books; 26,200 forestry pamphlets; 6342 forestry and surveying slides. **Subscriptions:** 424 journals and other serials; 8 newspapers. **Services:** Interlibrary loan; copying; library open to the public with restrictions. **Automated Operations:** Computerized cataloging. **Computerized Information Services:** OCLC. **Networks/Consortia:** Member of North Country Reference and Research Resources Council (NCRRRC). **Staff:** Neil Surprenant, Asst.Libn..

★11117★
PAUL, WEISS, RIFKIND, WHARTON AND GARRISON - LIBRARY (Law)
1285 Ave. of the Americas Phone: (212)373-2401
New York, NY 10019 Deborah S. Panella, Chf.Libn.
Founded: 1927. **Staff:** Prof 10; Other 31. **Subjects:** Law. **Holdings:** 75,000 books; 1000 bound periodical volumes; 7500 reels of microfilm. **Subscriptions:** 600 journals and other serials; 25 newspapers. **Services:** Interlibrary loan; library not open to the public. **Automated Operations:** Computerized cataloging, acquisitions, and serials. **Computerized Information Services:** LEXIS, WESTLAW, DIALOG Information Services, Pergamon ORBIT InfoLine, Inc., RLIN, BRS Information Technologies, I.P. Sharp Associates Limited, VU/TEXT Information Services, Dow Jones News/Retrieval, LEGI-SLATE, ELSS (Electronic Legislative Search System). **Staff:** Marsha Stein, Asst.Libn.; Diane Rosenberg, Corp.Libn.; Christine Fisher, Hd., Ref.; Paula Berger, Ref.Libn.; Kathleen McCartin, Ref.Libn.; B. Susan McGlamery, Ref.Libn.; Joanne Scala, Ref.Libn.; Theresa A. O'Leary, Tax Libn.; John Davey, ILL Libn.; Fanny L. Tibay, Cat.Libn..

PAULIST LIBRARY
See: Old St. Mary's Church (10767)

PAVEMENTS & SOIL TRAFFICABILITY INFORMATION ANALYSIS CENTER
See: U.S. Army - Engineer Waterways Experiment Station (14750)

PAVILLON ALBERT-PREVOST
See: Hopital du Sacre Coeur (6464)

★11118★
PAWTUCKET MEMORIAL HOSPITAL - HEALTH SCIENCES LIBRARY (Med)
Prospect & Pond Sts. Phone: (401)722-6000
Pawtucket, RI 02860 Joyce Brothers, Med.Lib.Coord.
Founded: 1959. **Staff:** Prof 2. **Subjects:** Medicine, family medicine. **Special Collections:** Videocassette Resource Center (Network for Continuing Medical Education - American Medical Association Category Credit Programs). **Holdings:** 660 books; 6904 bound periodical volumes. **Subscriptions:** 150 journals and other serials. **Services:** Interlibrary loan; copying; library open to the public upon special request. **Computerized Information Services:** MEDLINE; DOCLINE (electronic mail service). **Networks/Consortia:** Member of Consortium of Rhode Island Academic and Research Libraries, Inc. (CRIARL), Association of Rhode Island Health Sciences Librarians (ARIHSL). **Publications:** Newsletter. **Staff:** Carol-Ann Rausch, Ref.Libn..

★11119★
PAYETTE ASSOCIATES - LIBRARY (Plan)
40 Isabella St. Phone: (617)423-0070
Boston, MA 02116 Ellen W. Brackett, Corp.Libn.
Founded: 1979. **Staff:** Prof 1; Other 1. **Subjects:** Architecture, design and construction of health care facilities. **Holdings:** 1000 books; 2000 catalogs; 500 samples; 10 VF drawers of reports and clippings; 15 drawers of prints and plans; 17,000 slides. **Subscriptions:** 80 journals and other serials. **Services:** Interlibrary loan; library open to the public upon request to librarian.

BISHOP PAYNE LIBRARY
See: Virginia Theological Seminary (17388)

★11120★
PAYNE THEOLOGICAL SEMINARY - R.C. RANSOM MEMORIAL LIBRARY (Rel-Phil, Area-Ethnic)
Box 474 Phone: (513)376-2946
Wilberforce, OH 45384 J. Dale Balsbaugh, Hd.Libn.
Founded: 1844. **Staff:** Prof 1; Other 1. **Subjects:** Philosophy, Biblical studies, pastoral theology, doctrinal theology, black studies, African Methodist Episcopal Church history. **Special Collections:** Arno Press Black Studies Program - The American Negro, His History and Literature (150 volumes). **Holdings:** 20,000 books; 500 archival materials. **Services:** Interlibrary loan; copying; library open to the public. **Special Catalogs:** Union Serials List of Seminaries, every 4 years.

★11121★
PAYNE WHITNEY PSYCHIATRIC CLINIC LIBRARY (Med)
New York Hospital-Cornell University Medical College
525 E. 68th St. Phone: (212)472-6442
New York, NY 10021 Patricia Tomasulo, Dept.Libn.
Staff: Prof 1; Other 2. **Subjects:** Psychiatry, psychology, behavioral sciences. **Special Collections:** History of psychiatry; Archives of Psychiatry. **Holdings:** 20,500 volumes; 125 video cassettes; 50 audio cassettes. **Subscriptions:** 175 journals and other serials. **Services:** Interlibrary loan; library open to qualified researchers. **Automated Operations:** Computerized public access catalog, cataloging, acquisitions, and serials. **Computerized Information Services:** miniMEDLINE. **Networks/Consortia:** Member of Medical Library Center of New York (MLCNY). **Publications:** Acquisitions List, quarterly. **Special Catalogs:** Media Catalog.

DANIEL CARROLL PAYSON MEDICAL LIBRARY
See: North Shore University Hospital (10371)

★11122★
PCL-BRAUN-SIMONS LTD. - PBS LIBRARY
1202 Centre St., S.E.
Calgary, AB, Canada T2G 5A5
Subjects: Engineering, project management, construction, procurement. **Special Collections:** Engineering standards (2000). **Holdings:** 500 books; 200 periodical volumes. **Remarks:** Presently inactive.

PEA RIDGE NATIONAL MILITARY PARK
See: U.S. Natl. Park Service (15336)

PEABODY CONSERVATORY OF MUSIC
See: Johns Hopkins University (7241)

GEORGE PEABODY COLLECTION
See: Johns Hopkins University - Milton S. Eisenhower Library (7238)

★11123★
GEORGE PEABODY COLLEGE FOR TEACHERS OF VANDERBILT UNIVERSITY - KENNEDY CENTER - MATERIALS CENTER (Educ)
Box 62 Phone: (615)322-8184
Nashville, TN 37203 Mrs. Jamesie Rodney, Mgr.
Founded: 1968. **Staff:** Prof 1; Other 1. **Subjects:** Mental retardation, special education, psychology, remedial reading, educational and psychological tests. **Holdings:** 4000 volumes; 23 VF drawers and 50 shelves containing 475 tests; AV equipment. **Subscriptions:** 11 journals and other serials. **Services:** Copying; center is open to students and faculty only. **Also Known As:** John F. Kennedy Center for Research of Education and Human Development.

★11124★
PEABODY INSTITUTE LIBRARY - DANVERS ARCHIVAL CENTER (Hist)
15 Sylvan St. Phone: (617)774-0554
Danvers, MA 01923 Richard B. Trask, Town Archv.
Staff: Prof 1; Other 1. **Subjects:** History and development of Danvers and Salem Village, Salem Village witchcraft. **Special Collections:** Ellerton J. Brehaut Witchcraft Collection (1000 items); Parker Pillsbury Anti-Slavery Collection (179 volumes). **Holdings:** 4000 books; 200,000 manuscript materials; 300 reels of microfilm; 600 maps; 50 magnetic tapes. **Subscriptions:** 10 journals and other serials. **Services:** Copying; center open to the public. **Special Catalogs:** Catalogs of witchcraft, manuscripts, history.

★11125★
PEABODY MUSEUM OF SALEM - PHILLIPS LIBRARY (Hist)
East India Square Phone: (617)745-1876
Salem, MA 01970-1682 Gregor Trinkaus-Randall, Libn./Archv.
Founded: 1799. **Staff:** Prof 2; Other 20. **Subjects:** Maritime history, ethnology of non-European peoples, natural history, Asian Export Art. **Holdings:** 110,000 volumes; 1100 linear feet of logbooks; account books; shipping papers. **Subscriptions:** 200 journals and other serials. **Services:** Interlibrary loan; copying; library open to the public. **Computerized Information Services:** Internal database.

★11126★
ROBERT S. PEABODY FOUNDATION FOR ARCHEOLOGY - LIBRARY (Soc Sci)
Phillips Academy Phone: (617)475-0248
Andover, MA 01810 Dr. Donald W. McNemar, Act.Dir.
Staff: Prof 1; Other 1. **Subjects:** North American archeology and ethnography, especially Eastern North America; general anthropology. **Holdings:** 4400 books; 100 bound periodical volumes; 5000 reprints and pamphlets. **Services:** Library open to the public. **Publications:** Papers of the Robert S. Peabody Foundation for Archeology, irregular; first annual report of the Coxcatlan Project; Prehistory of the Ayacucho Basin, Peru series; First Annual Report of the Belize Archaic Archaeological Reconnaissance.

★11127★
PEACE CORPS - INFORMATION SERVICES DIVISION (Soc Sci, Sci-Engr)
806 Connecticut Ave., N.W., Rm. M-407 Phone: (202)254-3307
Washington, DC 20526 Victoria Reich, Dir.
Founded: 1966. **Staff:** Prof 2; Other 1. **Subjects:** Developing countries in Asia, Africa, Latin America, the South Pacific Islands, Caribbean; economic development; cross-cultural studies; community development; appropriate technology; women in development. **Special Collections:** Peace Corps; foreign language learning materials. **Holdings:** 27,000 books; 54 shelves of folder materials. **Subscriptions:** 265 journals and other serials. **Services:** Interlibrary loan; division open to the public with restrictions. **Computerized Information Services:** DIALOG Information Services, OCLC. **Networks/Consortia:** Member of FEDLINK, Metropolitan Washington Library Council. **Publications:** List of Acquisitions, monthly; country and specialized bibliographies and resource lists. **Staff:** Marian P. Francois, Libn..

★11128★
PEACE RIVER CENTENNIAL MUSEUM - ARCHIVES (Hist)
Box 747 Phone: (403)624-4261
Peace River, AB, Canada T0H 2X0 Kirstin Clausen, Dir./Cur.
Founded: 1967. **Staff:** Prof 1; Other 2. **Subjects:** Pioneers, fur trade, river and rail transportation, petroleum industry, native culture. **Special Collections:** Local area histories (25); local photograph negatives (300); pre-1930 fictional monographs. **Holdings:** 200 books; 20 bound periodical volumes; 8 VF drawers of manuscripts and documents; 42 reels of

microfilm; 500 photograph negatives; 3 reels of 16mm film; 52 audio cassettes; 1476 slides. **Subscriptions:** 10 journals and other serials. **Services:** Copying; archives open to the public with restrictions. **Publications:** Programme calendar, monthly - to special mailing list. **Special Catalogs:** Artifacts catalog. **Remarks:** Maintained by the Town of Peace River and Sir Alexander Mackenzie Historical Society.

PEALE MUSEUM
See: Baltimore City Life Museums (1266)

★11129★
PEARL HARBOR SURVIVORS ASSOCIATION - ARCHIVES (Hist)
1106 Maplewood Ave. Phone: (603)436-5835
Portsmouth, NH 03801 Mr. W.M. Cleveland, Hist.
Subjects: Japanese attack on Pearl Harbor. **Special Collections:** Nameplates from plane shot down December 7, 1941. **Holdings:** Books; oral history tapes; 5 cubic feet of combat records, reports, artifacts; 10 photograph albums; administrative and historical records, 1962-1986. **Services:** Copying; archives open to the public with restrictions. **Publications:** Bibliography of Pearl Harbor Attack; Pearl Harbor Gram, quarterly.

A.S. PEARSE MEMORIAL LIBRARY
See: Duke University - Marine Laboratory (4439)

★11130★
LESTER B. PEARSON COLLEGE OF THE PACIFIC - NORMAN MC KEE LANG LIBRARY (Hist)
RR 1 Phone: (604)478-5591
Victoria, BC, Canada V8X 3W9 Margaret McAvity, Libn.
Founded: 1974. **Staff:** Prof 1; Other 1. **Special Collections:** Personal library of the late Lester B. Pearson (history and international affairs; 1000 titles); videotape collection of lectures by Dr. Giovanni Costigan, professor emeritus at University of Washington (history and international relations; 50 videotapes). **Holdings:** 13,000 books; 500 phonograph records; 50 cassettes; 900 slides; 2500 microfiche; 150 video cassettes. **Subscriptions:** 100 journals and other serials; 10 newspapers. **Services:** Interlibrary loan; copying; SDI; library open to the public by appointment. **Remarks:** Affiliated with the United World Colleges.

PEARSON LIBRARY
See: California Lutheran University (2154)

PEAT, MARWICK, MAIN & CO.
See: KPMG Peat Marwick Main & Co. (7553)

PEAT, MARWICK, MITCHELL & CO.
See: KPMG Peat Marwick Main & Co. (7550)

★11131★
PECHNER, DORFMAN, WOLFFE, ROUNICK & CABOT - LIBRARY (Law)
3 Benjamin Franklin Parkway Phone: (215)561-7100
Philadelphia, PA 19102 Eugenie Tyburski, Law Libn.
Staff: Prof 1; Other 1. **Subjects:** Law - U.S., Pennsylvania, New Jersey, tax, labor, corporate; personal injury litigation. **Holdings:** 12,000 books; pamphlet files. **Subscriptions:** 350 journals and other serials; 10 newspapers. **Services:** Interlibrary loan; copying; library open to public at librarian's discretion. **Computerized Information Services:** LEXIS, NEXIS, DIALOG Information Services. **Publications:** Pechner, Dorfman, Wolffe, Rounick & Cabot Library News, monthly - for internal distribution only.

★11132★
PEE DEE AREA HEALTH EDUCATION CENTER LIBRARY (Med)
McLeod Regional Medical Center
555 E. Cheves St. Phone: (803)667-2275
Florence, SC 29501 Lillian Fisher, Reg.Libn.
Founded: 1975. **Staff:** Prof 3; Other 1. **Subjects:** Clinical medicine, nursing, allied health sciences, competency-based nursing orientation, management. **Holdings:** 1565 books; 2087 bound periodical volumes; 1181 AV programs. **Subscriptions:** 317 journals and other serials. **Services:** Interlibrary loan; copying; SDI; library open to professional health personnel, students, and community members. **Automated Operations:** Computerized cataloging. **Computerized Information Services:** MEDLARS, BRS Information Technologies; SCHIN (internal database); DOCLINE (electronic mail service). Performs searches on fee basis. **Networks/Consortia:** Member of South Carolina Health Information Network (SCHIN). **Publications:** Serials List; Media Holdings. **Special Indexes:** Subject index to periodicals.

BRUCE PEEL SPECIAL COLLECTIONS LIBRARY
See: University of Alberta - Bruce Peel Special Collections Library (15791)

★11133★
PEEL COUNTY BOARD OF EDUCATION - J.A. TURNER PROFESSIONAL LIBRARY (Educ)
5650 Hurontario St. Phone: (416)890-1099
Mississauga, ON, Canada L5R 1C6 Catherine Roy, Prof.Libn.
Founded: 1969. **Staff:** Prof 1; Other 3. **Subjects:** Education, child psychology, sociology, educational research, educational administration. **Special Collections:** Peel curriculum collection; Ontario Ministry of Education documents. **Holdings:** 2000 books; 1000 other cataloged items. **Subscriptions:** 300 journals and other serials; 5 newspapers. **Services:** Interlibrary loan; library open to the public for reference use only. **Automated Operations:** Computerized public access catalog, cataloging, serials, and circulation. **Computerized Information Services:** BRS Information Technologies, DIALOG Information Services, CAN/OLE, Infomart, The Financial Post Information Service, WILSONLINE, Info Globe, UTLAS. **Networks/Consortia:** Member of Education Libraries Sharing of Resources Network (ELSOR). **Publications:** Research Bulletin, monthly - for internal distribution only. **Remarks:** Fax: (416)890-6747.

★11134★
PEEL REGIONAL POLICE FORCE - LIBRARY (Law)
7750 Hurontario St. Phone: (416)453-3311
Brampton, ON, Canada L6V 3W6 Lorna Mays, Lib.Techn.
Founded: 1974. **Staff:** Prof 1. **Subjects:** Police science, law, behavioral sciences, management. **Holdings:** 2000 books; 280 bound periodical volumes. **Subscriptions:** 80 journals and other serials. **Services:** Interlibrary loan; copying; library open to law enforcement personnel.

PEER ASSISTANCE NETWORK IN EXPERIENTIAL LEARNING
See: National Society for Internships and Experiential Education - PANEL Technical Assistance Services Library (9793)

★11135★
PEI ASSOCIATES, INC. - TECHNICAL LIBRARY (Env-Cons)
11499 Chester Rd. Phone: (513)782-4700
Cincinnati, OH 45246 Judith E. Le Blanc, Tech.Libn.
Founded: 1973. **Staff:** Prof 1; Other 1. **Subjects:** Environment; engineering - environmental, civil, mechanical; industrial hygiene; chemistry; air and water pollution; water treatment and hazardous waste. **Holdings:** 1500 books; 900 EPA reports and 25,000 government/contractor reports on microfiche; 1500 U.S. Government reports. **Subscriptions:** 125 journals and other serials. **Services:** Interlibrary loan; library open to the public by appointment. **Computerized Information Services:** Integrated Technical Information System (ITIS). **Publications:** Recent Acquisitions, weekly.

★11136★
PEIRCE JUNIOR COLLEGE - LIBRARY - SPECIAL COLLECTIONS (Bus-Fin)
1420 Pine St. Phone: (215)545-6400
Philadelphia, PA 19102 Debra S. Schrammel, Dir.
Founded: 1963. **Holdings:** Pre-1900 business textbooks; legal collection (3400 volumes). **Services:** Interlibrary loan; copying; collections open to local college students.

PEIRCE MEMORIAL LIBRARY
See: First Presbyterian Church of Flint (5093)

PELL MARINE SCIENCE LIBRARY
See: University of Rhode Island, Narragansett Bay (16812)

PAUL PELTASON LIBRARY
See: Temple Israel (13967)

★11137★
PEMAQUID HISTORICAL ASSOCIATION - HARRINGTON MEETING HOUSE - MUSEUM (Hist)
Old Harrington Rd. Phone: (207)677-2193
Pemaquid, ME 04558 Margo W. Hope, Pres.
Founded: 1965. **Subjects:** Local history, religion. **Holdings:** 100 volumes; genealogical records; pamphlets; local records and maps; hymnals; ledgers; early school books; newspapers; historical documents. **Services:** Museum open to the public by appointment.

PEMBROKE CENTER FOR TEACHING AND RESEARCH ON WOMEN
See: Brown University (1978)

★11138★
PEN AND BRUSH INC. - LIBRARY (Hum)
16 E. Tenth St. Phone: (212)475-3669
New York, NY 10003 Mercy Dobell Wolfe, Pres.
Founded: 1893. **Staff:** 2. **Subjects:** Literature, art. **Holdings:** 1200 books.

★11139★
PENDLE HILL - LIBRARY (Rel-Phil)
Wallingford, PA 19086 Phone: (215)566-4507
Yuki T. Brinton, Libn.
Founded: 1930. **Staff:** Prof 1. **Subjects:** Religion, Quakers. **Special Collections:** Quaker Collection. **Holdings:** 14,000 volumes. **Subscriptions:** 35 journals and other serials. **Services:** Interlibrary loan; library open to the public.

★11140★
PENDLETON DISTRICT HISTORICAL AND RECREATIONAL COMMISSION - REFERENCE LIBRARY (Hist)
125 E. Queen St.
Box 565 Phone: (803)646-3782
Pendleton, SC 29670 Hurley Badders, Commn.Dir.
Founded: 1974. **Staff:** Prof 2; Other 1. **Subjects:** History - Pendleton district, South Carolina, U.S.; genealogy; church history; travel, tourism, and recreation; antiques and historic preservation; archeology. **Special Collections:** Anderson Cotton Mill Records (71 ledgers, 1890-1950s); Speaking of History (interviews with citizens of Anderson, Oconee, and Pickens counties; 35 oral history tapes). **Holdings:** 800 books; 200 boxes of clippings, unbound reports, other cataloged items; 90 books and documents on microfilm; 10 drawers of photographs; 1 drawer of family histories; 75 maps; 90 ledgers. **Subscriptions:** 19 journals and other serials. **Services:** Copying; library open to the public for reference use only. **Special Indexes:** Index to names mentioned in library materials (card). **Staff:** Donna Roper, Asst.Dir..

PENFIELD LIBRARY
See: SUNY - College at Oswego (13773)

★11141★
PENICK CORPORATION - PPT LIBRARY
158 Mt. Olivet Ave.
Newark, NJ 07114
Founded: 1920. **Subjects:** Organic chemistry, chemistry of natural products, botany, medicinal drugs, entomology, fish diseases, agricultural chemicals. **Holdings:** 1500 books; 5000 bound periodical volumes; 4000 patents; 700 reprints; 6 VF drawers of literature searches; Chemical Abstracts, 1907 to present, on microfilm. **Remarks:** Presently inactive.

★11142★
PENINSULA COMMUNITY FOUNDATION - COMMUNITY RESOURCE LIBRARY (Bus-Fin)
1204 Burlingame Ave.
Box 627 Phone: (415)342-2505
Burlingame, CA 94011-0627 Martha Simpson, Libn.
Staff: Prof 1. **Subjects:** Funding sources and management assistance for nonprofit organizations; fundraising activities; proposal writing. **Holdings:** 600 books; 460 foundation annual reports. **Subscriptions:** 50 journals and other serials; 10 newspapers. **Services:** Library open to the public. **Computerized Information Services:** DIALOG Information Services. Performs searches on fee basis. **Publications:** Community Resource Library News, quarterly - to organizations upon request.

★11143★
PENINSULA CONSERVATION FOUNDATION - LIBRARY OF THE ENVIRONMENT (Env-Cons)
2253 Park Blvd. Phone: (415)328-5313
Palo Alto, CA 94306 Connie S. Sutton, Libn.
Founded: 1971. **Staff:** Prof 1. **Subjects:** Conservation, ecology, energy, wildlife and endangered species, backpacking and trails, pollution control. **Special Collections:** Environmental Volunteers Collection; Audubon Collection (250); Conservation Collection (2000); Trails Collection (300 books; 4 VF drawers). **Holdings:** 5000 books; 636 bound periodical volumes; 43 VF drawers; 2000 maps. **Subscriptions:** 23 journals and other serials; 5 newspapers. **Services:** Interlibrary loan; copying; library open to the public. **Networks/Consortia:** Member of Energy Librarians of the Bay Area, South Bay Cooperative Library System (SBCLS). **Publications:** The Center View, quarterly - to members or on exchange. **Special Indexes:** The Harbinger File.

★11144★
PENINSULA HOSPITAL CENTER - MEDICAL LIBRARY (Med)
51-15 Beach Channel Dr. Phone: (718)945-7100
Far Rockaway, NY 11691 Edith Rubinstein, Dir.
Founded: 1970. **Staff:** Prof 1; Other 1. **Subjects:** Medicine, surgery, nursing, dentistry, podiatry, orthopedics. **Holdings:** 1182 books; 2150 bound periodical volumes; 75 video cassettes; 228 audio cassettes. **Subscriptions:** 105 journals and other serials. **Services:** Interlibrary loan; copying; library open to the public for reference use only. **Computerized Information Services:** MEDLARS; DOCLINE (electronic mail service). **Networks/Consortia:** Member of Brooklyn-Queens-Staten Island Health Sciences Librarians (BQSI), Medical & Scientific Libraries of Long Island (MEDLI), BHSL.

★11145★
PENINSULA LIBRARY AND HISTORICAL SOCIETY (Hist)
6105 Riverview Rd. Phone: (216)657-2291
Peninsula, OH 44264 Edith M. Minns, Libn.
Founded: 1943. **Staff:** Prof 3; Other 6. **Subjects:** History, biography, literature, arts. **Special Collections:** Local history (2000 volumes; manuscripts; clippings; maps; pictures; cemetery records). **Holdings:** 35,000 books; 162 bound periodical volumes; 1050 AV programs; depository for U.S. Army Corps of Engineer reports; 24 VF drawers of pamphlets and clippings; 150 maps. **Subscriptions:** 103 journals and other serials; 5 newspapers. **Services:** Interlibrary loan; copying; library open to the public. **Publications:** Newsletter, monthly - local distribution. **Special Indexes:** Index to Local History (card). **Staff:** Randolph Bergdorf, Archv..

★11146★
PENINSULA TEMPLE BETH EL - LIBRARY (Rel-Phil)
1700 Alameda de Las Pulgas Phone: (415)341-7701
San Mateo, CA 94403 Ann Levin, Libn.
Founded: 1961. **Staff:** Prof 2; Other 7. **Subjects:** Philosophy of Judaism; history of Judaism and the Jewish religion; fiction of Jewish content or by Jewish authors; Israel - description and travel; history of the Jews in the U.S. **Special Collections:** Biographies of Jewish leaders. **Holdings:** 3200 books; periodicals; cassettes; records. **Services:** Library open to the public.

★11147★
ANNIE PENN MEMORIAL HOSPITAL - MEDICAL LIBRARY (Med)
618 S. Main St. Phone: (919)349-8461
Reidsville, NC 27320 Sandra King, Libn.
Staff: Prof 1. **Subjects:** Medicine, nursing, allied health sciences. **Holdings:** 500 books. **Subscriptions:** 43 journals and other serials. **Services:** Interlibrary loan; library not open to the public.

★11148★
PENN MUTUAL LIFE INSURANCE COMPANY - LAW LIBRARY (Law, Bus-Fin)
Independence Square Phone: (215)625-5020
Philadelphia, PA 19172 Doris Nardin, Asst.Libn.
Founded: 1940. **Staff:** 1. **Subjects:** Insurance, law. **Holdings:** 15,000 books; 30 bound periodical volumes. **Subscriptions:** 38 journals and other serials; 7 newspapers. **Services:** Library not open to the public. **Publications:** List of periodical holdings, annual; New Books List, irregular.

★11149★
PENN MUTUAL LIFE INSURANCE COMPANY - SHARED RESOURCE CENTER (Comp Sci)
Penn Mutual Independence Place
600 Dresher Rd. Phone: (215)956-8178
Horsham, PA 19044 Sheri C. Reinhart, Supv./Libn.
Founded: 1984. **Staff:** Prof 1; Other 1. **Subjects:** Microcomputers, mainframes, management training and development, insurance, business. **Holdings:** 300 books; 350 manuals; 75 computer programs; 120 video cassettes; 100 telephone books. **Subscriptions:** 45 journals and other serials. **Services:** Center not open to the public. **Automated Operations:** Computerized cataloging and circulation. **Computerized Information Services:** Internal database; Ethernet (electronic mail service). **Publications:** SRC News (newsletter), monthly; Micro News (newsletter), monthly.

★11150★
PENN VIRGINIA CORPORATION - LIBRARY
2500 Fidelity Bldg.
Philadelphia, PA 19109
Subjects: Energy, coal, oil, gas, business, environment, mining equipment, industrial minerals. **Holdings:** 300 books; 500 government documents. **Remarks:** Presently inactive.

★11151★
WILLIAM PENN COLLEGE - WILCOX LIBRARY - SPECIAL COLLECTIONS (Rel-Phil)
Oskaloosa, IA 52577 Phone: (515)673-8311
Edward Goedeken, Libn.
Staff: Prof 2; Other 2. **Subjects:** Quakers - history, biography, genealogy. **Holdings:** 2010 books; 350 bound periodical volumes; cemetery records on microfilm; clippings; scrapbooks; pictures. **Subscriptions:** 22 journals and other serials. **Services:** Interlibrary loan; copying; collections open to the public. **Computerized Information Services:** OCLC. **Networks/Consortia:** Member of Bibliographical Center for Research, Rocky Mountain Region, Inc. (BCR). **Publications:** William Penn College: A Product and a Producer, 1973.

GEORGE PENNAL LIBRARY
See: St. Joseph's Health Centre (12482)

★11152★
J.C. PENNEY COMPANY, INC. - LAW LIBRARY (Law, Bus-Fin)
Box 659000 Phone: (214)591-1284
Dallas, TX 75265-9000 Kaethryn Luetkemeyer, Law Libn.
Staff: Prof 1; Other 2. **Subjects:** Law, business. **Holdings:** 20,000 books; 400 bound periodical volumes; 2800 volumes of West's reporters on ultrafiche. **Subscriptions:** 200 journals and other serials; 16 newspapers. **Services:** Interlibrary loan; library not open to the public. **Computerized Information Services:** WESTLAW, LEXIS, DIALOG Information Services. **Formerly:** Located in New York, NY.

★11153★
PENNIE & EDMONDS - LAW LIBRARY (Law)
1155 Ave. of the Americas Phone: (212)790-0909
New York, NY 10036 Mary Gilligan, Libn.
Founded: 1884. **Staff:** Prof 2; Other 1. **Subjects:** Law - patent, copyright, trademark; biotechnology; chemistry; electronics. **Special Collections:** Foreign Collection (intellectual property). **Holdings:** 20,000 books; 100 bound periodical volumes; videotapes. **Subscriptions:** 125 serials; 10 newspapers. **Services:** Interlibrary loan (limited); library not open to the public. **Computerized Information Services:** DIALOG Information Services, WESTLAW, LEXIS, Pergamon ORBIT InfoLine, Inc., VU/TEXT Information Services, Telesystemes Questel. **Publications:** Library Acquisitions Bulletin, quarterly - for internal distribution only. **Staff:** Lynne Burkey, Asst.Libn..

REV. DR. GEORGE PENNIMAN GENEALOGICAL LIBRARY
See: Braintree Historical Society, Inc. - Library (1805)

★11154★
PENNOCK HOSPITAL - MEDICAL LIBRARY (Med)
1009 W. Green St. Phone: (616)945-3451
Hastings, MI 49058 Mary Diane Hawkins, Med.Libn.
Staff: Prof 1; Other 1. **Subjects:** Medicine, nursing, pharmacy, allied health sciences. **Holdings:** 750 books. **Subscriptions:** 125 journals and other serials. **Services:** Interlibrary loan; copying; library open to the public by appointment. **Computerized Information Services:** MEDLARS, DIALOG Information Services. Performs searches on fee basis. **Networks/Consortia:** Member of Capitol Area Library Network (CALNET), Michigan Library Consortium (MLC), Michigan Health Sciences Libraries Association (MHSLA).

★11155★
PENNSYLVANIA ACADEMY OF THE FINE ARTS - LIBRARY (Art)
Broad & Cherry Sts. Phone: (215)972-7611
Philadelphia, PA 19102 Marietta P. Bushnell, Libn.
Founded: 1805. **Staff:** Prof 1. **Subjects:** Art history, painting, sculpture, graphics, with concentration on American art. **Holdings:** 10,000 books; 56 VF drawers of artists clippings; 16 VF drawers of subject-idea clippings. **Subscriptions:** 58 journals and other serials. **Services:** Interlibrary loan; copying; library open to the public.

★11156★
PENNSYLVANIA COLLEGE OF OPTOMETRY - ALBERT FITCH MEMORIAL LIBRARY (Med)
1200 W. Godfrey Ave. Phone: (215)276-6270
Philadelphia, PA 19141 Marita J. Krivda, Lib.Dir.
Staff: Prof 1; Other 3. **Subjects:** Optometry, ophthalmology, optics theory, ophthalmic optics, contact lenses, low vision rehabilitation, clinical medicine, public health. **Special Collections:** Visual Science Rare Book Collection, 17th-19th centuries (250 books); eye spectacles, turn of the century ophthalmic instruments, and ophthalmoscopes. **Holdings:** 4500 books; 7000 bound periodical volumes; 3 VF drawers of government documents; 2 VF drawers of old instruments pamphlets; 50 video cassettes; 800 audio cassettes; 6640 slides. **Subscriptions:** 290 journals and other serials. **Services:** Interlibrary loan; copying; library open to the public with restrictions. **Computerized Information Services:** MEDLARS, OCLC, BRS Information Technologies. Performs searches on fee basis. **Networks/Consortia:** Member of Greater Northeastern Regional Medical Library Program, PALINET, Association of Visual Science Librarians (AVSL). **Publications:** Acquisitions list, monthly; annual report. **Special Indexes:** Ophthalmic Literature.

★11157★
PENNSYLVANIA COLLEGE OF PODIATRIC MEDICINE - CENTER FOR THE HISTORY OF FOOT CARE AND FOOT WEAR (Med)
Charles E. Krausz Library
Eighth St. at Race Phone: (215)629-0300
Philadelphia, PA 19107 Lisabeth M. Holloway, Dir.
Staff: Prof 2. **Subjects:** Podiatric medicine, anatomy and diseases of the foot, podiatry/chiropody as a profession, ethnic footwear. **Holdings:** 1800 books; 200 bound periodical volumes; 130 linear feet of archival materials; 700 other cataloged items. **Services:** Copying; center open to the public for reference use only. **Publications:** The ClioPedic Items (newsletter), irregular - to members; A Fast Pace Forward: Chronicles of American Podiatry (1987). **Special Indexes:** Index of graduates of chiropody/podiatry colleges in the U.S.; index of foreign practitioners.

★11158★
PENNSYLVANIA COLLEGE OF PODIATRIC MEDICINE - CHARLES E. KRAUSZ LIBRARY (Med)
Eighth St. at Race Phone: (215)629-0300
Philadelphia, PA 19107 Linda C. Stanley, Coll.Libn.
Founded: 1962. **Staff:** Prof 4; Other 2. **Subjects:** Podiatry, the foot, general medicine. **Special Collections:** **Holdings:** 10,203 books; 9025 bound periodical volumes; reprint file of faculty publications; 16 VF drawers of reprints of articles pertaining to the foot; 2500 pamphlets on medical subjects; 325 reels of microfilm; 900 video cassettes; 101 films; 625 audio cassettes; 13,000 slides. **Subscriptions:** 278 journals and other serials; 5 newspapers. **Services:** Interlibrary loan; copying; SDI; library open to the public for reference use only. **Computerized Information Services:** BRS Information Technologies. Performs searches on fee basis. **Networks/Consortia:** Member of Greater Northeastern Regional Medical Library Program, Delaware Valley Information Consortium (DEVIC). **Publications:** Foot Notes (newsletter); list of new acquisitions, bimonthly; periodical holdings list.

★11159★
PENNSYLVANIA DUTCH FOLK CULTURE SOCIETY, INC. - BAVER MEMORIAL LIBRARY (Hist)
Lenhartsville, PA 19534 Phone: (215)562-4803
Florence Baver, Pres.
Founded: 1978. **Staff:** Prof 1. **Subjects:** Genealogy, folklore, local history. **Holdings:** 1000 books; 200 bound periodical volumes; pamphlets; photographs; diaries; tape recordings; clippings; postcards; church records. **Services:** Copying; library open to the public. **Publications:** Pennsylvania Dutch News & Views, semiannual.

★11160★
PENNSYLVANIA ECONOMY LEAGUE - EASTERN DIVISION - LIBRARY (Soc Sci, Bus-Fin)
1211 Chestnut St., Suite 600 Phone: (215)864-9562
Philadelphia, PA 19107-4116 Ellen Brennan, Libn.
Founded: 1932. **Staff:** Prof 1. **Subjects:** Public administration, charters and constitutions, city government, municipal finance. **Holdings:** 16,000 volumes. **Services:** Interlibrary loan; copying; library open to the public with restrictions.

★11161★
PENNSYLVANIA ECONOMY LEAGUE - WESTERN DIVISION - LIBRARY (Soc Sci)
Two Gateway Center Phone: (412)471-1477
Pittsburgh, PA 15222 Judith A. Eves, Libn.
Founded: 1932. **Staff:** Prof 2. **Subjects:** State and local government, finance, taxation, public personnel. **Holdings:** 1025 volumes; 2500 pamphlets; 24 VF drawers of financial reports and news clippings. **Subscriptions:** 160 journals and other serials; 10 newspapers. **Services:** Copying; library open to the public with restrictions. **Computerized Information Services:** Internal database. **Staff:** Martha E. Mantilla, Asst.Libn..

★11162★
PENNSYLVANIA ELECTRIC COMPANY - TECHNICAL LIBRARIES (Energy)
1001 Broad St. Phone: (814)533-8633
Johnstown, PA 15907 Jean C. Johnson, Libn.
Founded: 1962. **Staff:** Prof 1; Other 2. **Subjects:** Fossil fuel generation, electric transmission and distribution, environmental affairs, utility-based engineering, electric utility business. **Holdings:** 1760 books; Electric Power Research Institute (EPRI) microfiche. **Subscriptions:** 87 journals and other serials. **Services:** Copying; libraries open to public utility companies only. **Computerized Information Services:** CARIRS (internal database). **Publications:** Newsletter - for internal distribution only.

PENNSYLVANIA FARM MUSEUM OF LANDIS VALLEY
See: Landis Valley Museum (7647)

★11163★
PENNSYLVANIA HORTICULTURAL SOCIETY - LIBRARY (Biol Sci, Agri)
325 Walnut St. Phone: (215)625-8268
Philadelphia, PA 19106 Janet Evans, Libn.
Founded: 1827. **Staff:** Prof 2; Other 3. **Subjects:** Ornamental horticulture, botany, landscape design, garden history. **Special Collections:** Rare herbals and gardening books; 19th century horticulture; Pennsylvania horticulture. **Holdings:** 14,000 books; 4000 bound periodical volumes; 16 VF drawers of horticultural information; 1000 slides. **Subscriptions:** 200 journals and other serials. **Services:** Interlibrary loan; copying; slide sets available for rent; library open to the public for reference use only. **Special Catalogs:** Early and contemporary seed and nursery catalogs (card).

★11164★
PENNSYLVANIA HOSPITAL - DEPARTMENT FOR SICK AND INJURED - HISTORICAL LIBRARY (Med)
Eighth & Spruce Sts. Phone: (215)829-3998
Philadelphia, PA 19107 Caroline Morris, Dir. of Libs.
Founded: 1761. **Staff:** 1. **Subjects:** Pre-1800 chemistry, physics, botany, zoology, natural history, materia medica; medicine and surgery prior to 1940. **Special Collections:** Hospital archives and case reports; early M.D. dissertations. **Holdings:** 8500 books; 4464 bound periodical volumes. **Services:** Library open to the public by appointment requested in writing.

★11165★
PENNSYLVANIA HOSPITAL - DEPARTMENT FOR SICK AND INJURED - MEDICAL LIBRARY (Med)
Eighth & Spruce Sts. Phone: (215)829-3998
Philadelphia, PA 19107 Caroline Morris, Dir. of Libs.
Founded: 1940. **Staff:** Prof 1; Other 2. **Subjects:** Medicine, nursing, allied health sciences. **Holdings:** 2122 books; 9500 bound periodical volumes; 3700 other cataloged items; 2 VF drawers. **Subscriptions:** 540 journals and other serials. **Services:** Interlibrary loan; copying (limited); library open to the public by appointment. **Remarks:** Includes holdings of School of Nursing - Lydia Jane Clark Library. **Also Known As:** Packard Reading Room.

PENNSYLVANIA INDUSTRIAL ARTS ASSOCIATION ARCHIVES
See: Millersville University of Pennsylvania - Helen A. Ganser Library - Special Collections (8990)

★11166★
PENNSYLVANIA INSTITUTE OF TECHNOLOGY - LIBRARY (Sci-Engr)
800 Manchester Ave. Phone: (215)565-7900
Media, PA 19063 Rita Burgess, Libn.
Staff: Prof 1; Other 1. **Subjects:** Electronics, computers, architecture, civil and mechanical engineering. **Holdings:** 9835 books; 10 boxes of pamphlets. **Subscriptions:** 190 journals and other serials. **Services:** Interlibrary loan; copying; library open to the public for reference use only. **Publications:** List of Recently Processed Books, quarterly - to faculty, staff, and students.

★11167★
PENNSYLVANIA INTERGOVERNMENTAL COUNCIL - LIBRARY (Soc Sci)
Box 11880
Harrisburg, PA 17108 Phone: (717)783-3700
Subjects: Municipal fiscal distress; intergovernmental informational problems, needs, and services. **Holdings:** Figures not available. **Computerized Information Services:** Internal database.

PENNSYLVANIA LUMBER MUSEUM
See: Pennsylvania State Historical & Museum Commission (11190)

★11168★
PENNSYLVANIA PUBLIC UTILITY COMMISSION - LIBRARY (Energy)
Box 3265 Phone: (717)787-4466
Harrisburg, PA 17120 Thais Gardy, Libn.
Staff: Prof 1; Other 1. **Subjects:** Public utility law, energy conservation, economics, transportation, coal, oil, gas technology. **Holdings:** 6200 books; 204 bound periodical volumes; 3100 unbound reports; 46 maps; 4 VF drawers; 16 sets of loose-leaf reporters. **Subscriptions:** 118 journals and other serials. **Services:** Interlibrary loan; copying; library open to the public for reference use only. **Computerized Information Services:** LEXIS, DIALOG Information Services.

★11169★
PENNSYLVANIA RESOURCES AND INFORMATION CENTER FOR SPECIAL EDUCATION (Educ)
200 Anderson Rd. Phone: (215)265-7321
King of Prussia, PA 19406 Dr. Marianne Price, Dir.
Staff: Prof 7; Other 2. **Subjects:** Education of exceptional students. **Special Collections:** Publishers and supply catalogs (12 VF drawers). **Holdings:** 7000 books; tests; curriculum guides; special education dissertations on microfiche; ERIC indexes and microfiche. **Subscriptions:** 425 journals and other serials; 200 newsletters. **Services:** Center open to the public for reference use only. **Computerized Information Services:** DIALOG Information Services, BRS Information Technologies. **Publications:** PRISE, 6/year. **Remarks:** Holdings are shared with Regional Resources Center of Eastern Pennsylvania for Special Education. **Staff:** Mary D'Ippolits, Asst.Dir.; Philip Juska, Asst.Dir./Adm..

★11170★
PENNSYLVANIA SCHOOL FOR THE DEAF - LIBRARY (Educ)
100 W. School House Lane Phone: (215)951-4743
Philadelphia, PA 19144 Barbara Jo Bartels, Libn.
Staff: Prof 1; Other 2. **Subjects:** Deafness, children's literature. **Holdings:** 13,000 books; 205 bound periodical volumes. **Subscriptions:** 50 journals and other serials; 5 newspapers. **Services:** Interlibrary loan; library open to the public for reference use only. **Automated Operations:** Computerized cataloging.

PENNSYLVANIA SOCIOLOGICAL ASSOCIATION ARCHIVES
See: Millersville University of Pennsylvania - Helen A. Ganser Library - Special Collections (8990)

★11171★
PENNSYLVANIA STATE DEPARTMENT OF EDUCATION - STATE LIBRARY OF PENNSYLVANIA (Info Sci)
Box 1601 Phone: (717)787-2646
Harrisburg, PA 17105 David R. Hoffman, Act. State Libn.
Founded: 1745. **Staff:** Prof 36; Other 61. **Subjects:** Government, law, education, public welfare and administration, Pennsylvania history and biography, Central Pennsylvania genealogy, social and behavioral science, economics, library science. **Special Collections:** Americana; Pennsylvania Imprints; Colonial Assembly Collection. **Holdings:** 972,221 books; federal and Pennsylvania government publications; Congressional Information Service and American Statistics Index microfiche series; Newsbank, 1977 to present; ERIC microfiche. **Subscriptions:** 4311 journals and other serials; 177 newspapers. **Services:** Interlibrary loan; copying; library open to the public. **Automated Operations:** Computerized cataloging, acquisitions, and circulation. **Computerized Information Services:** DIALOG Information Services, BRS Information Technologies, LEXIS, NLM, VU/TEXT Information Services, Datext, Inc., WILSONLINE. Performs searches on fee basis. Contact Person: Joan Schrader, Online Ref.Libn., 787-4440. **Networks/Consortia:** Member of PALINET, Interlibrary Delivery Service of Pennsylvania (IDS), Association of College Libraries of Central Pennsylvania (ACLCP). **Publications:** Directory-

Pennsylvania Libraries, annual; Pennsylvania Public Library Statistics, annual. **Special Catalogs:** Pennsylvania Imprints, 1689-1789; Union List of Current Periodical Holdings of the Capitol Hill Libraries and State Library of Pennsylvania; Catalog of Pennsylvania Newspapers and Selected Out-of-State Newspapers. **Staff:** Judith M. Foust, Dir., Lib.Dev.Div.; Ruth B. Coble, Coord., Tech.Serv.; Donald R. Brown, Coord., Coll.Mgt.; Alice L. Lubrecht, Ref./Info.Serv.; Thomas R. Beddoes, Hd., Ref.Sect.; Doris M. Epler, Dir., Sch.Lib. Media Serv.Div.; Sally T. Felix, Coord., Advisory Serv.; Barbara Cole, Adm., Subsidies & Grants; Blaze J. Gusic, Coord., ITV; Gary Neights, Coord., Instr.Mtls.Serv.; Charles R. Peguese, Coord., Networking & Acad.Libs.; Richard Cassel, Coord., Sch.Lib. Network.

★11172★
PENNSYLVANIA STATE DEPARTMENT OF ENVIRONMENTAL RESOURCES - BUREAU OF TOPOGRAPHIC & GEOLOGIC SURVEY LIBRARY (Geog-Map)
916 Executive House Apts.
Second & Chestnut Sts. Phone: (717)783-8077
Harrisburg, PA 17120 Sandra Blust, Libn.
Founded: 1854. **Staff:** Prof 1; Other 1. **Subjects:** Geology, geography. **Special Collections:** Maps Collection; aerial photographs of Pennsylvania. **Holdings:** 5500 books; 7800 bound periodical volumes; 5000 government publications; 150 unpublished manuscripts; 200 dissertations on Pennsylvania geology, hardcopy and microfilm. **Subscriptions:** 83 journals and other serials. **Services:** Interlibrary loan; copying; library open to the public for reference use only. **Computerized Information Services:** GeoRef (Geological Reference File), DIALOG Information Services.

★11173★
PENNSYLVANIA STATE DEPARTMENT OF ENVIRONMENTAL RESOURCES - ENVIRONMENTAL PROTECTION TECHNICAL REFERENCE LIBRARY (Env-Cons)
Fulton Bldg., 17th Fl.
Box 2063 Phone: (717)787-9647
Harrisburg, PA 17120 Julie K. Weaver, Lib.Techn.
Founded: 1965. **Staff:** 1. **Subjects:** Water quality, sewerage, industrial waste, mining and reclamation, air quality, surface mines, solid waste, radiation protection, community environmental control. **Special Collections:** Water Pollution Control Federation Research Series on Clean Water (480 volumes); Pennsylvania State University Special Research Report on Coal (90 volumes); U.S. and Pennsylvania Geological Surveys (700 items). **Holdings:** 2400 books; 215 bound periodical volumes; 10,000 microfiche of EPA Technology Series to 1974; 200 linear feet of technical material concerning water pollution; 500 river basin and stream file reports. **Subscriptions:** 170 journals and other serials; 10 newsletters. **Services:** Interlibrary loan; copying; library open to the public for reference use only. **Publications:** User's Guide to the Technical Reference Library.

★11174★
PENNSYLVANIA STATE DEPARTMENT OF HEALTH - BUREAU OF LABORATORIES - HERBERT FOX MEMORIAL LIBRARY (Biol Sci)
Pickering Way & Welsh Pool Rd. Phone: (215)363-8500
Lionville, PA 19353 Leonard Sideman, Libn.
Staff: Prof 1; Other 2. **Subjects:** Clinical chemistry, microbiology and virology, toxicology, hematology, laboratory legislation. **Holdings:** 500 books. **Subscriptions:** 50 journals and other serials. **Services:** Interlibrary loan; copying; library open to the public by appointment.

PENNSYLVANIA STATE DEPARTMENT OF PUBLIC WELFARE - HAMBURG CENTER FOR THE MENTALLY RETARDED
See: Hamburg Center for the Mentally Retarded (5975)

PENNSYLVANIA STATE DEPARTMENT OF PUBLIC WELFARE - HAVERFORD STATE HOSPITAL
See: Haverford State Hospital (6140)

★11175★
PENNSYLVANIA STATE DEPARTMENT OF PUBLIC WELFARE - MAYVIEW STATE HOSPITAL - MENTAL HEALTH AND MEDICAL LIBRARY (Med)
1601 Mayview Rd. Phone: (412)429-6496
Bridgeville, PA 15017-1599 William A. Suvak, Jr., Libn.Supv. I
Founded: 1966. **Staff:** Prof 1. **Subjects:** Psychiatry, psychoanalysis, psychiatric nursing, psychology, hospital administration, psychiatric social work, psychopharmacology. **Holdings:** 4000 books; 1200 bound periodical volumes. **Subscriptions:** 75 journals and other serials. **Services:** Interlibrary loan; copying; library open to community mental health professionals. **Networks/Consortia:** Member of Greater Northeastern Regional Medical Library Program. **Publications:** Newsletter,

★11176★
PENNSYLVANIA STATE DEPARTMENT OF PUBLIC WELFARE - NORRISTOWN STATE HOSPITAL - PROFESSIONAL/STAFF LIBRARY (Med)
Bldg. 11 Phone: (215)270-1369
Norristown, PA 19401 Frieda Liem, Libn.
Staff: Prof 1; Other 1. **Subjects:** Psychiatry and neurology; clinical psychology; psychiatric nursing; psychiatric and clinical social work; activities therapy - recreational, music, occupational, vocational; aging; geriatrics; gerontology. **Holdings:** 8450 books; 800 AV programs; 2 VF drawers; pamphlets. **Subscriptions:** 200 journals and other serials. **Services:** Interlibrary loan; library open to the public with restrictions. **Automated Operations:** Computerized cataloging. **Computerized Information Services:** OCLC. **Networks/Consortia:** Member of Confederation of State & State Related Institutions. **Remarks:** An alternate telephone number is 270-1370.

★11177★
PENNSYLVANIA STATE DEPARTMENT OF PUBLIC WELFARE - OFFICE OF CHILDREN, YOUTH & FAMILIES - RESEARCH AND INFORMATION CENTER (Soc Sci)
Harrisburg State Hospital
Lanco Lodge Bldg.
Box 2675 Phone: (717)257-7291
Harrisburg, PA 17105-2675 Richard Fiene, Ph.D, Res.Dir.
Founded: 1979. **Staff:** Prof 6; Other 4. **Subjects:** Day care, program evaluation, child care research, child welfare, child abuse, youth services. **Holdings:** 5000 books; 500 bound periodical volumes; 2000 other cataloged items. **Subscriptions:** 10 journals and other serials. **Services:** Interlibrary loan; copying; SDI; center open to the public. **Automated Operations:** Computerized public access catalog. **Staff:** Lawrence Woods, Info.Chf.; Vickie Harle, Trng.Coord..

★11178★
PENNSYLVANIA STATE DEPARTMENT OF PUBLIC WELFARE - PHILADELPHIA STATE HOSPITAL - STAFF LIBRARY (Med)
W3 Bldg.
14000 Roosevelt Blvd. Phone: (215)671-4145
Philadelphia, PA 19114 Greta Clark, Libn.
Staff: Prof 1; Other 4. **Subjects:** Psychiatry, psychology, psychiatric nursing, social services, family therapy. **Special Collections:** Robert S. Smith Behavioral Science Library. **Holdings:** 4000 volumes; 40 dissertations; 4 VF drawers. **Subscriptions:** 185 journals and other serials. **Services:** Interlibrary loan; copying; library open to the public at the discretion of librarian. **Publications:** Library information booklet; periodicals list; bibliographies, all irregular.

★11179★
PENNSYLVANIA STATE DEPARTMENT OF PUBLIC WELFARE - PHILIPSBURG STATE GENERAL HOSPITAL - LIBRARY (Med)
Loch Lomond Rd. Phone: (814)342-3320
Philipsburg, PA 16866 Elaine G. Filsinger, Libn.
Staff: Prof 1; Other 1. **Subjects:** Medicine, hospital administration, patient education. **Holdings:** 2430 books; 92 bound periodical volumes; 88 videotapes; 39 film loops; 2 drawers of audio cassettes; 2 shelves of patient education materials. **Subscriptions:** 89 journals and other serials. **Services:** Interlibrary loan; copying; library open to the public for reference use only. **Networks/Consortia:** Member of Central Pennsylvania Health Sciences Library Association (CPHSLA).

★11180★
PENNSYLVANIA STATE DEPARTMENT OF PUBLIC WELFARE - SOMERSET STATE HOSPITAL - LIBRARY (Med)
Box 631 Phone: (814)445-6501
Somerset, PA 15501 Eve Kline, Dir., Lib.Serv.
Staff: Prof 2; Other 1. **Subjects:** Psychiatry, psychology, mental retardation. **Holdings:** 7000 books; 500 filmstrips; 500 cassettes. **Subscriptions:** 150 journals and other serials; 7 newspapers. **Services:** Interlibrary loan. **Computerized Information Services:** OCLC, DIALOG Information Services, VU/TEXT Information Services, BRS Information Technologies. Performs searches on fee basis. **Networks/Consortia:** Member of Health Information Resources Consortium (HIRESCU), State System of Higher Education Libraries Council (SSHELCO), Greater

Northeastern Regional Medical Library Program. **Publications:** Newsletter, weekly. **Staff:** Kathy Plaso, Libn..

★11181★
PENNSYLVANIA STATE DEPARTMENT OF PUBLIC WELFARE - WESTERN CENTER - LIBRARY SERVICES (Med)
333 Curry Hill Rd. Phone: (412)873-3200
Canonsburg, PA 15317 Nicholas L. Liguori, Libn.
Founded: 1962. **Staff:** Prof 1. **Subjects:** Medicine, psychology, special education. **Holdings:** 1080 volumes. **Subscriptions:** 41 journals and other serials. **Services:** Interlibrary loan; copying; library open to the public with restrictions.

★11182★
PENNSYLVANIA (State) DEPARTMENT OF TRANSPORTATION - HIGHWAY ADMINISTRATION - BUREAU OF CONSTRUCTION AND MATERIALS - LIBRARY
Transportation & Safety Bldg., Rm. 1212
Commonwealth & Foster St.
Harrisburg, PA 17123
Defunct. Holdings absorbed by Pennsylvania (State) Department of Transportation - Technical Reference Center.

★11183★
PENNSYLVANIA (State) DEPARTMENT OF TRANSPORTATION - TECHNICAL REFERENCE CENTER (Trans)
903 Transportation & Safety Bldg. Phone: (717)787-6527
Harrisburg, PA 17120 Judy H. Gutshall, Libn.
Founded: 1979. **Staff:** Prof 1; Other 2. **Subjects:** Transportation and allied subjects, management, engineering. **Special Collections:** TRB Publications; U.S. and Pennsylvania Department of Transportation documents; audiovisual collection (600 programs). **Holdings:** 14,000 publications. **Subscriptions:** 300 journals and other serials. **Services:** Interlibrary loan; copying; center open to the public for research purposes. **Automated Operations:** Computerized public access catalog, serials, and circulation. **Computerized Information Services:** DIALOG Information Services, VU/TEXT Information Services, LOGIN, DataTimes; DIALMAIL (electronic mail service). **Publications:** Technical Reference Center News/Notes and Acquisitions. **Special Catalogs:** Audio/Visual Catalog; Internal Reports Catalog (in preparation). **Remarks:** Contains the holdings of the former Highway Administration - Bureau of Construction and Materials - Library.

★11184★
PENNSYLVANIA STATE FISH COMMISSION LIBRARY - BENNER SPRING FISH RESEARCH STATION (Biol Sci)
1225 Shiloh Rd. Phone: (814)355-4837
State College, PA 16801-8495 Thomas R. Bender, Jr., Biol.
Staff: 1. **Subjects:** Freshwater fisheries, fish culture, fish disease. **Holdings:** 450 books; 3500 reprints of manuscripts. **Subscriptions:** 50 journals and other serials. **Services:** Library not open to the public.

★11185★
PENNSYLVANIA (State) HISTORICAL & MUSEUM COMMISSION - DIVISION OF ARCHIVES AND MANUSCRIPTS (Hist)
William Penn Memorial Museum & Archives Bldg.
Box 1026 Phone: (717)787-3023
Harrisburg, PA 17108-1026 Harry E. Whipkey, State Archv.
Founded: 1903. **Staff:** Prof 11; Other 5. **Subjects:** Archives of Pennsylvania and historical manuscripts. **Special Collections:** Record groups of the holdings of state agencies and political subdivisions (57); manuscript collections (409). **Holdings:** 17,500 books; 24,000 cubic feet of archival materials; 14,200 cubic feet of personal papers; 12,000 reels of microfilm; 4025 maps. **Subscriptions:** 180 journals and other serials. **Services:** Interlibrary loan (limited); division not open to the public. **Automated Operations:** Computerized cataloging. **Computerized Information Services:** OCLC, RLIN; internal databases. **Networks/Consortia:** Member of RLG. **Publications:** List of publications - available on request; Finding Aids. **Staff:** Carol Tallman, Libn., Bur. of Archv. & Hist..

★11186★
PENNSYLVANIA STATE HISTORICAL & MUSEUM COMMISSION - DRAKE WELL MUSEUM - LIBRARY (Hist)
R.D. 3 Phone: (814)827-2797
Titusville, PA 16354 Lois Jackson, Lib.Asst.
Founded: 1934. **Staff:** 1. **Subjects:** Petroleum industry, local area history, geological surveys. **Special Collections:** Brewer Papers (50 letters and papers of Dr. Francis B. Brewer); Mather Photographic Collection, 1860-1890 (2500 prints, 2761 identified negatives, 1061 unidentified negatives of the oil region). **Holdings:** 1500 books; 900 bound periodical volumes; 1500 other cataloged items; 115 cubic feet of Roberts Torpedo Company papers, 1865-1881; 8 cubic feet of John H. Scheide Papers, 1860-1890; 5 cubic feet of Ida M. Tarbell Papers; early maps, atlas, ledgers, scrapbooks. **Subscriptions:** 1300 oil company periodicals and early newspapers of the region. **Services:** Interlibrary loan; copying; library open to the public by appointment.

★11187★
PENNSYLVANIA STATE HISTORICAL & MUSEUM COMMISSION - EPHRATA CLOISTER - LIBRARY (Hist)
632 W. Main St. Phone: (717)733-6600
Ephrata, PA 17522 Nadine A. Steinmetz, Dir.
Subjects: History of Ephrata Cloister, Pennsylvania German culture. **Special Collections:** Eighteenth and nineteenth century imprints printed at Ephrata Cloister. **Holdings:** 250 books. **Services:** Copying; library open to the public by appointment.

★11188★
PENNSYLVANIA STATE HISTORICAL & MUSEUM COMMISSION - FORT PITT MUSEUM - LIBRARY (Hist)
Point State Park Phone: (412)281-9284
Pittsburgh, PA 15222 Robert J. Trombetta, Dir.
Founded: 1967. **Staff:** 5. **Subjects:** French and Indian War, Western Pennsylvania to 1800, 18th century forts and artillery, regimental histories. **Holdings:** 450 volumes; unbound periodicals; 10 French and Indian War letters and documents.

★11189★
PENNSYLVANIA STATE HISTORICAL & MUSEUM COMMISSION - OLD ECONOMY VILLAGE - HARMONY SOCIETY LIBRARY (Hist)
14th & Church Sts. Phone: (412)266-4500
Ambridge, PA 15003 Raymond V. Shepherd, Jr., Dir.
Founded: 1919. **Staff:** Prof 2; Other 10. **Subjects:** History of Harmony Society, communitarian and social experiments in U.S., industrial and economic history, religion, German language, natural science. **Special Collections:** Music of Harmony Society (5000 manuscripts). **Holdings:** 5000 original books; 325,000 pages of manuscripts on microfilm. **Services:** Library open to the public by appointment. **Remarks:** Historic correspondence, pamphlets, and documents have been transferred to the Pennsylvania State Historical & Museum Commission - Division of Archives and Manuscripts, Harrisburg, PA. Site contains 17 historic buildings, 1824-1830.

★11190★
PENNSYLVANIA STATE HISTORICAL & MUSEUM COMMISSION - PENNSYLVANIA LUMBER MUSEUM - LIBRARY (Hist)
Box K Phone: (814)435-2652
Galeton, PA 16922 Dolores M. Buchsen, Adm.
Staff: 1. **Subjects:** History of logging, antique tools, logging railroads. **Special Collections:** Disston Crucible (113 copies on milling, 1912-1926). **Holdings:** 1200 books; 500 bound periodical volumes. **Services:** Interlibrary loan; copying (limited); library open to the public for reference use only.

★11191★
PENNSYLVANIA (State) HISTORICAL & MUSEUM COMMISSION - REFERENCE LIBRARY (Hist)
William Penn Memorial Museum & Archives Bldg.
Third & N Sts.
Box 1026 Phone: (717)783-9898
Harrisburg, PA 17108-1026 Carol W. Tallman, Libn.
Founded: 1947. **Staff:** Prof 1. **Subjects:** Pennsylvania history, museum technology. **Holdings:** 17,500 volumes; 15 VF drawers of pamphlets and clippings. **Subscriptions:** 180 journals and other serials. **Services:** Interlibrary loan (limited); library open to the public by appointment. **Automated Operations:** Computerized cataloging. **Computerized Information Services:** OCLC; internal databases. **Publications:** Finding aids.

★11192★
PENNSYLVANIA STATE JOINT STATE GOVERNMENT COMMISSION - LIBRARY (Soc Sci)
108 Finance Bldg. Phone: (717)787-6803
Harrisburg, PA 17120 Carol A. Himmelright, Libn.
Staff: Prof 1. **Subjects:** Education, state legislation, finance, taxes, medical statistics. **Holdings:** 3000 books; 500 bound periodical volumes; 5000 reports and pamphlets; 12 VF drawers of federal and state releases. **Subscriptions:** 30 journals and other serials; 10 newspapers. **Services:**

Research on Pennsylvania laws for other states' agencies; library open to members of legislature and authorized visitors. **Publications:** Studies prepared by the staff - limited distribution.

★11193★
PENNSYLVANIA STATE LEGISLATIVE REFERENCE BUREAU LIBRARY (Law)
Box 1127 Phone: (717)787-4816
Harrisburg, PA 17120 Susan K. Zavacky, Libn.
Founded: 1909. **Staff:** Prof 1. **Subjects:** State legislation, law, bill drafting, state court cases, federal case and statutory law. **Special Collections:** Laws of Pennsylvania; Senate and House journals, 1906 to present; Senate and House histories; Senate and House bills, 1826 to present. **Holdings:** 8000 volumes; 75 pamphlet files of state documents; 16 VF cases of pamphlets and newspaper clippings; 4 drawers of microfilm; 4 boxes of microfiche. **Subscriptions:** 55 journals and other serials. **Services:** Copying (limited); library open to the public for reference use only. **Computerized Information Services:** Internal databases.

PENNSYLVANIA STATE MODERN LANGUAGE ASSOCIATION ARCHIVES
See: Millersville University of Pennsylvania - Helen A. Ganser Library - Special Collections (8990)

★11194★
PENNSYLVANIA STATE OFFICE OF ATTORNEY GENERAL - LAW LIBRARY (Law)
1525 Strawberry Square Phone: (717)787-3176
Harrisburg, PA 17120 Ellen R. Chack, Chf., Law Lib.Sect.
Founded: 1873. **Staff:** Prof 1; Other 2. **Subjects:** Law. **Holdings:** 30,000 books; 500 bound periodical volumes. **Subscriptions:** 50 journals and other serials; 10 newspapers. **Services:** Library not open to the public. **Computerized Information Services:** LEXIS, NEXIS. **Special Indexes:** Pennsylvania Official Opinions of the Attorney General (card).

★11195★
PENNSYLVANIA STATE SUPERIOR COURT - APPELLATE COURTS LIBRARY (Law)
2061 Robert N.C. Nix, Sr. Federal Bldg. Phone: (215)560-5840
Philadelphia, PA 19107 Nancy R. McGowan, Libn.
Staff: Prof 1; Other 1. **Subjects:** Law, court administration. **Holdings:** 12,200 volumes; 2500 microfiche. **Subscriptions:** 120 journals and other serials; 8 newspapers. **Services:** Interlibrary loan; library not open to the public. **Automated Operations:** Computerized cataloging. **Computerized Information Services:** LEXIS, NEXIS, OCLC. Performs searches free of charge. **Networks/Consortia:** Member of PALINET. **Publications:** Library Bulletin, monthly - for internal distribution only; quarterly and annual reports.

★11196★
PENNSYLVANIA STATE UNIVERSITY - APPLIED RESEARCH LABORATORY - LIBRARY (Sci-Engr)
Box 30 Phone: (814)865-6621
State College, PA 16804 Charles G. Murphy, Sr.Asst.Libn.
Founded: 1945. **Staff:** Prof 1; Other 1. **Subjects:** Electronics, engineering, acoustics, physics, applied mathematics, hydrodynamics, oceanography, materials engineering, manufacturing technology. **Holdings:** 3500 books; 1300 bound periodical volumes; 5000 technical reports. **Subscriptions:** 250 journals and other serials. **Services:** Library not open to the public. **Automated Operations:** Computerized cataloging, acquisitions, serials, and circulation. **Computerized Information Services:** DIALOG Information Services, DTIC; Library Information Access System (LIAS), INMAGIC (internal databases). **Publications:** Accessions Listing, monthly - to ARL personnel.

★11197★
PENNSYLVANIA STATE UNIVERSITY - ARCHITECTURE READING ROOM (Plan)
207 Engineering Unit C Phone: (814)863-0511
University Park, PA 16802 Jean Smith, Arts & Arch.Libn.
Staff: Prof 1; Other 2. **Subjects:** Architecture, history of architecture, building construction, architectural engineering. **Holdings:** 16,342 volumes. **Subscriptions:** 125 journals. **Services:** Interlibrary loan; copying; room open to the public. **Automated Operations:** Computerized cataloging, serials, and circulation. **Computerized Information Services:** DIALOG Information Services.

★11198★
PENNSYLVANIA STATE UNIVERSITY - ARTS LIBRARY (Art, Mus)
University Library, Rm. E405 Phone: (814)865-6481
University Park, PA 16802 Jean Smith, Arts & Arch.Libn.
Founded: 1964. **Staff:** Prof 2; Other 4. **Subjects:** History of art and architecture, painting, sculpture, drawing, graphic arts, decorative arts, music. **Special Collections:** Warren Mack Memorial Collection (535 original prints); Charles Wakefield Cadman Collection. **Holdings:** 86,634 books, including 18,374 scores; 1027 spoken word phonograph records; 23,074 phonograph records and cassette tapes. **Subscriptions:** 610 journals and other serials. **Services:** Interlibrary loan; copying; library open to the public. **Automated Operations:** Computerized cataloging, serials, and circulation. **Computerized Information Services:** DIALOG Information Services, BRS Information Technologies.

★11199★
PENNSYLVANIA STATE UNIVERSITY - AUDIOVISUAL SERVICES (Aud-Vis)
Special Services Bldg. Phone: (814)863-3100
University Park, PA 16802 Robert L. Allen, Dir.
Founded: 1942. **Subjects:** Anthropology, psychology, life sciences, sociology, arts, humanities. **Special Collections:** Psychological Cinema Register (350 film titles); American Archive of Encyclopaedia Cinematographica (2000 film titles). **Holdings:** 21,000 motion picture films and videotapes. **Services:** Film and video rental and sales; materials available to public with some restrictions. **Computerized Information Services:** Internal database. **Publications:** 11 catalogs in series organized along lines of recognized interest areas; alphabetical listing by title only of 16mm films and video cassettes; reference publication.

★11200★
PENNSYLVANIA STATE UNIVERSITY - COLLEGE OF BUSINESS ADMINISTRATION - CENTER FOR RESEARCH - RESEARCH SUPPORT CENTER (Bus-Fin)
104 Beam Business Adm. Bldg. Phone: (814)863-0598
University Park, PA 16802 Margaret E. Smith, Libn.
Staff: Prof 1; Other 7. **Subjects:** Accounting and management information systems, business logistics, finance, international business and business law, insurance and real estate, marketing, management science and operations management, organizational behavior. **Holdings:** Doctoral dissertations, masters theses, MBA professional papers; Pennsylvania State University publications; Association for University Business and Economic Research publications; trade association and accounting firm publications; Financial Accounting Standards Board publications; Bureau of National Affairs Tax Management Portfolios; Pennsylvania state and federal government documents. **Subscriptions:** 650 journals and other serials. **Services:** SDI; center open to the public with special permission. **Automated Operations:** Computerized acquisitions and serials. **Computerized Information Services:** DIALOG Information Services. **Special Catalogs:** Journal Holdings List (printout).

★11201★
PENNSYLVANIA STATE UNIVERSITY - COLLEGE OF MEDICINE - GEORGE T. HARRELL LIBRARY (Med)
Milton S. Hershey Medical Center Phone: (717)534-8629
Hershey, PA 17033 Lois J. Lehman, Libn.
Founded: 1965. **Staff:** Prof 6; Other 8. **Subjects:** Medicine. **Special Collections:** Rare medical books (372 volumes). **Holdings:** 18,513 books; 77,559 bound periodical volumes; 200 motion pictures, videotapes, video discs, cassettes; 950 phonograph records, audiotapes, audio cassettes; 80 slide programs; 6 filmstrips. **Subscriptions:** 1734 journals and other serials. **Services:** Interlibrary loan; copying; SDI; library open to the public for reference use only. **Computerized Information Services:** Online systems. **Networks/Consortia:** Member of Greater Northeastern Regional Medical Library Program, Health Sciences Library Consortium. **Publications:** Library Bulletin, irregular - to state medical school libraries and Hershey Medical Center. **Special Catalogs:** Library Serials Title Catalog. **Staff:** M. Sandra Wood, Libn./Hd., Ref.; Barbara E. Nwoke, Sr.Asst.Libn./Hd.Cat.; Virginia A. Lingle, Asst.Libn./Ref.; Loretta D. Ulincy, Asst.Libn./Ref.; Irmgard Boker, Lib.Asst./Hd., Circ.; Dorthy Malcom, Asst.Libn./Ref..

★11202★
PENNSYLVANIA STATE UNIVERSITY - DEPARTMENT OF PUBLIC ADMINISTRATION - LIBRARY (Bus-Fin)
215 Burrowes Bldg. Phone: (814)865-2536
University Park, PA 16802 Robert D. Lee, Jr.
Staff: Prof 1; Other 2. **Subjects:** Public administration, budgeting systems, personnel systems, information systems. **Holdings:** 4059 books; 2043 bound periodical volumes; 1300 masters' degree papers. **Subscriptions:** 45 journals

and other serials. **Services:** Library open to the public. **Formerly:** Institute of Public Administration.

★11203★
PENNSYLVANIA STATE UNIVERSITY - DOCUMENTS/MAPS SECTION (Geog-Map)
Pattee Library Phone: (814)863-0094
University Park, PA 16802 Diane H. Smith, Hd., Docs. & Maps
Staff: Prof 1; Other 5. **Subjects:** Topography, city planning, place names, map reading and interpretation. **Special Collections:** Sanborn Fire Insurance maps and atlases of Pennsylvania towns and cities (24,000 sheets); Pennsylvania County boundary maps, 1790-1876; Pennsylvania Land Ownership Maps (microfiche); Pennsylvania Warrentee Maps. **Holdings:** 1200 books; 78 bound periodical volumes; 300,000 maps; 200 raised relief maps; 1740 aerial photographs; 107 reels of microfilm; 464 microfiche; 2700 atlases; 8 globes; 5 VF drawers of map interpretation files; 36 VF drawers of travel files. **Subscriptions:** 29 journals and other serials. **Services:** Interlibrary loan; library open to the public. **Publications:** Map Collection: New Acquisitions/Cartographic Notes, quarterly. **Special Indexes:** Atlas Index File (card).

★11204★
PENNSYLVANIA STATE UNIVERSITY - EARTH AND MINERAL SCIENCES LIBRARY (Sci-Engr, Energy)
105 Deike Bldg. Phone: (814)865-9517
University Park, PA 16802 Emilie T. McWilliams, Hd.
Founded: 1931. **Staff:** Prof 1; Other 4. **Subjects:** Geosciences, materials science, meteorology, mineral economics and mineral engineering. **Special Collections:** Coal mining and processing as a fuel (1300 items). **Holdings:** 80,000 books; 21,905 geologic and topographic maps; 9750 microfiche. **Subscriptions:** 1300 journals and other serials. **Services:** Interlibrary loan; copying; library open to the public. **Automated Operations:** Computerized circulation. **Computerized Information Services:** DIALOG Information Services, Pergamon ORBIT InfoLine, Inc., BRS Information Technologies, OCLC. Performs searches on fee basis. **Networks/Consortia:** Member of RLG.

★11205★
PENNSYLVANIA STATE UNIVERSITY - ENGINEERING LIBRARY (Sci-Engr)
325 Hammond Bldg. Phone: (814)865-3451
University Park, PA 16802 Thomas W. Conkling, Hd.
Founded: 1950. **Staff:** Prof 2; Other 5. **Subjects:** Engineering. **Special Collections:** Schweitzer, diesel engines and diesel research. **Holdings:** 75,000 volumes; 275,000 technical reports and papers from NASA, DOE, DOD, American Institute of Aeronautics and Astronautics, Society of Automotive Engineers, Society of Manufacturing Engineers, American Society of Mechanical Engineers. **Subscriptions:** 1000 journals and other serials. **Services:** Interlibrary loan; copying; library open to the public. **Automated Operations:** Computerized public access catalog, cataloging, and circulation. **Computerized Information Services:** DIALOG Information Services, BRS Information Technologies, Integrated Technical Information System (ITIS), WILSONLINE, Pergamon ORBIT InfoLine, Inc. **Staff:** Linda Gruber, Libn..

★11206★
PENNSYLVANIA STATE UNIVERSITY - ENVIRONMENTAL RESOURCES RESEARCH INSTITUTE - CENTER FOR AIR ENVIRONMENT STUDIES - CAES INFORMATION SERVICES (Env-Cons)
225 Fenske Laboratory Phone: (814)865-1415
University Park, PA 16802 Elizabeth J. Carroll, Hd.
Founded: 1963. **Staff:** 2. **Subjects:** Air pollution monitoring, control, effects on health; atmospheric environment research; fossil fuel emissions and acid rain research. **Holdings:** 600 volumes; 44,000 microfiche and reprints. **Subscriptions:** 35 journals and other serials. **Services:** Interlibrary loan; services open to the public. **Automated Operations:** Computerized serials. **Computerized Information Services:** DIALOG Information Services; Library Information Access System (LIAS; internal database). **Publications:** Air Pollution Titles, bimonthly - by subscription; ERRI reports and publications.

★11207★
PENNSYLVANIA STATE UNIVERSITY - ENVIRONMENTAL RESOURCES RESEARCH INSTITUTE - LIBRARY (Env-Cons)
Land & Water Research Bldg. Phone: (814)863-0140
University Park, PA 16802 Eunice Roe, Info.Anl.
Founded: 1963. **Staff:** Prof 1. **Subjects:** Acid precipitation, hazardous waste, land economics, water quality and conservation, land reclamation, acid mine drainage. **Special Collections:** Water Center Reports listed by state; institute publications. **Holdings:** 1000 books; 12,000 technical reports; pamphlets; 2500 microfiche; maps. **Subscriptions:** 35 journals and other serials; 75 newsletters. **Computerized Information Services:** DIALOG Information Services. **Publications:** Acquisition list - monthly.

★11208★
PENNSYLVANIA STATE UNIVERSITY - FROST ENTOMOLOGICAL MUSEUM - TAXONOMIC RESEARCH LIBRARY (Biol Sci)
106 Patterson Bldg. Phone: (814)865-1895
University Park, PA 16802 Ke Chung Kim, Cur.
Founded: 1972. **Staff:** Prof 2; Other 2. **Subjects:** Taxonomy, entomology, insect identification and information, Anoplura information. **Holdings:** 1000 books; bound volumes; taxonomic references and reprints. **Services:** Library open for research use by appointment.

★11209★
PENNSYLVANIA STATE UNIVERSITY - GERONTOLOGY CENTER - HUMAN DEVELOPMENT COLLECTION (Soc Sci)
S109 Henderson Human Development Bldg. Phone: (814)863-0776
University Park, PA 16802 Faye Wohlwill, Coll.Dir.
Staff: Prof 1; Other 2. **Subjects:** Gerontology, adolescent and child psychology. **Holdings:** 3500 volumes. **Subscriptions:** 25 journals and other serials. **Services:** Copying; collection open to the public.

★11210★
PENNSYLVANIA STATE UNIVERSITY - INSTITUTE FOR POLICY RESEARCH AND EVALUATION - LIBRARY (Soc Sci)
N253 Burrowes Phone: (814)865-5541
University Park, PA 16802 Mary Jane Johnson, Sec.
Founded: 1964. **Subjects:** Human resources, education, manpower, corrections, environment, science policy, welfare, medical care, technology, population. **Holdings:** Vertical file materials. **Services:** Library open to the public on limited basis. **Publications:** List of publications - available on request. **Staff:** Irwin Feller, Dir..

PENNSYLVANIA STATE UNIVERSITY - KING OF PRUSSIA CENTER
See: Pennsylvania State University, Great Valley (11217)

★11211★
PENNSYLVANIA STATE UNIVERSITY - LIFE SCIENCES LIBRARY (Biol Sci, Med, Agri)
E205 Pattee Library Phone: (814)865-7056
University Park, PA 16802 Keith Roe, Hd.
Founded: 1888. **Staff:** Prof 5; Other 3. **Subjects:** Agriculture, biology, forestry, microbiology, biophysics, biochemistry, veterinary science, health planning and administration, nursing, food science, nutrition. **Special Collections:** Mycology and mushrooms; early American agricultural journals; Lumbering in Pennsylvania Collection (manuscripts; films; slides). **Holdings:** 185,000 books. **Subscriptions:** 3800 journals and other serials. **Services:** Interlibrary loan; library open to the public. **Automated Operations:** Computerized cataloging and circulation. **Computerized Information Services:** Pergamon ORBIT InfoLine, Inc., RLIN, DIALOG Information Services, BRS Information Technologies, The Faxon Company, OCLC; Library Information Access System (LIAS; internal database). **Publications:** Acquisitions List, monthly. **Special Indexes:** Ready-Reference Index to U.S.D.A. Statistical Series. **Staff:** Robert Seeds, Hea.Sci.Libn.; Frederick Sepp, Sr.Asst.Libn.; Amy Paster, Asst.Libn.; Helen Smith, Asst.Libn..

★11212★
PENNSYLVANIA STATE UNIVERSITY - MATHEMATICS LIBRARY (Sci-Engr, Comp Sci)
109 McAllister Bldg. Phone: (814)865-6822
University Park, PA 16802 Miriam D. Pierce, Hd.
Founded: 1966. **Staff:** Prof 1; Other 1. **Subjects:** Mathematics, statistics, computer science. **Special Collections:** PSU mathematics dissertations; artificial intelligence technical reports (microfiche). **Holdings:** 38,912 volumes. **Subscriptions:** 470 journals and other serials. **Services:** Interlibrary loan; copying; library open to the public. **Automated Operations:** Computerized public access catalog, cataloging, acquisitions, serials, and circulation. **Computerized Information Services:** BRS Information Technologies, DIALOG Information Services, Pergamon ORBIT InfoLine, Inc., WILSONLINE, OCLC, RLIN; Library Information Access System (LIAS; internal database); BITNET (electronic mail service). Performs searches on fee basis. **Networks/Consortia:** Member of RLG, Pittsburgh Regional Library Center (PRLC).

★11213★
PENNSYLVANIA STATE UNIVERSITY - PHYSICAL SCIENCES LIBRARY (Sci-Engr)
230 Davey Laboratory Phone: (814)865-7617
University Park, PA 16802 C.J. McKown, Hd.
Staff: Prof 1; Other 4. **Subjects:** Chemistry, physics, chemical engineering, astronomy, biophysics, biochemistry. **Special Collections:** PSU dissertations in chemistry, physics, and chemical engineering. **Holdings:** 91,200 volumes. **Subscriptions:** 1192 journals and other serials. **Services:** Interlibrary loan; copying. **Automated Operations:** Computerized cataloging, acquisitions, serials, and circulation. **Computerized Information Services:** DIALOG Information Services, STN International, CAS ONLINE, BRS Information Technologies; Library Information Access System (LIAS; internal database). Performs searches on fee basis. **Networks/Consortia:** Member of RLG. **Publications:** New Books Received, weekly - to faculty. **Staff:** J.F. Ferrainolo, Physical Sci.Libn..

★11214★
PENNSYLVANIA STATE UNIVERSITY - SLAVIC AND SOVIET LANGUAGE AND AREA CENTER - LIBRARY (Area-Ethnic)
306 Burrowes Bldg. Phone: (814)865-0436
University Park, PA 16802 Linda Verbeck, Libn.
Founded: 1965. **Subjects:** Eastern Europe - history, politics, foreign policy, society, economics, geography, language, literature. **Holdings:** 1050 books. **Subscriptions:** 62 journals and other serials; 16 newspapers.

★11215★
PENNSYLVANIA STATE UNIVERSITY - TRANSPORTATION INSTITUTE WORKING COLLECTION (Trans)
Research Bldg. B Phone: (814)863-3953
University Park, PA 16802 Del Sweeney, Res.Assoc.
Founded: 1968. **Staff:** Prof 1; Other 1. **Subjects:** Transportation engineering and materials, automotive research, public transportation, transportation planning, policy analysis. **Special Collections:** Tire-Pavement Interaction Collection (2600 items); Bureau of Highway Traffic theses. **Holdings:** 3100 books; 700 bound periodical volumes; 8500 reports. **Subscriptions:** 150 journals and other serials. **Services:** Interlibrary loan; copying; collection open to the public. **Computerized Information Services:** DIALOG Information Services.

★11216★
PENNSYLVANIA STATE UNIVERSITY, BERKS CAMPUS - MEMORIAL LIBRARY (Sci-Engr)
Tulpehocken Rd.
Box 7009 Phone: (215)375-4211
Reading, PA 19610-6009 Sally S. Small, Hd.Libn.
Founded: 1958. **Staff:** Prof 2; Other 5. **Subjects:** Engineering, business, liberal arts, food service, science. **Holdings:** 33,000 books; 3100 bound periodical volumes; 42 VF drawers of pamphlets; 1900 microforms; 700 phonograph records; 70 maps; 287 film loops; 34 art reproductions; 17 videotapes; 17 media kits. **Subscriptions:** 400 journals and other serials; 6 newspapers. **Services:** Interlibrary loan; copying; library open to the public with restrictions. **Computerized Information Services:** Library Information Access System (LIAS; internal database). **Publications:** Library Notes for Students. **Staff:** Deena H. Morganti, Hd., Pub.Serv..

★11217★
PENNSYLVANIA STATE UNIVERSITY, GREAT VALLEY - LIBRARY (Sci-Engr, Educ)
30 E. Swedesford Rd.
Malvern, PA 19355
Founded: 1964. **Staff:** Prof 1; Other 1. **Subjects:** Engineering, public administration, mathematics, elementary and special education. **Holdings:** 18,000 books; 2200 bound periodical volumes. **Subscriptions:** 260 journals and other serials. **Services:** Interlibrary loan; copying; library open to the public. **Automated Operations:** Computerized cataloging, acquisitions, and circulation. **Computerized Information Services:** BRS Information Technologies, DIALOG Information Services, OCLC; internal database. Performs searches on fee basis. **Formerly:** King of Prussia Center.

★11218★
PENNWALT CORPORATION - INFORMATION SERVICES DEPARTMENT (Sci-Engr)
900 First Ave. Phone: (215)337-6776
King of Prussia, PA 19406 Kathryn M. Donovan, Mgr.
Founded: 1944. **Staff:** Prof 4; Other 4. **Subjects:** Chemistry. **Holdings:** 10,000 books; 20,000 bound periodical volumes. **Subscriptions:** 400 journals and other serials. **Staff:** Susan Hunsicker; Leah Yocum; Kathryn L. Waterston.

★11219★
PENNWALT CORPORATION - LUCIDOL DIVISION - RESEARCH LIBRARY (Sci-Engr)
1740 Military Rd. Phone: (716)877-1740
Buffalo, NY 14240 Susan E. Jones, Tech.Libn.
Founded: 1932. **Staff:** Prof 1; Other 1. **Subjects:** Peroxides, organic chemistry, free radicals, chemical safety, polymerization, toxicology. **Holdings:** 6000 monographs; 2500 bound periodical volumes; 15 VF drawers of peroxide literature. **Subscriptions:** 180 journals and other serials. **Services:** Interlibrary loan (fee); copying; library open to the public with restrictions. **Computerized Information Services:** DIALOG Information Services, STN International, BRS Information Technologies, Technical Database Services, Inc. **Networks/Consortia:** Member of Western New York Library Resources Council (WNYLRC). **Special Catalogs:** Peroxides, polymerization, azo compounds catalog (card).

★11220★
PENNWALT CORPORATION - PENNWALT PHARMACEUTICAL DIVISION - RESEARCH LIBRARY (Med)
755 Jefferson Rd.
Box 1710 Phone: (716)475-9000
Rochester, NY 14603 Angela M. Scarfia, Libn.
Staff: Prof 1; Other 2. **Subjects:** Pharmacology, pharmacy, chemistry, bioscience, medicine. **Holdings:** 3000 books; 4750 bound periodical volumes. **Subscriptions:** 475 journals and other serials. **Services:** Interlibrary loan; copying; library open to the public by appointment. **Automated Operations:** Computerized ILL. **Computerized Information Services:** MEDLARS, DIALOG Information Services, Pergamon ORBIT InfoLine, Inc., BRS Information Technologies, CAS ONLINE, Telesystemes Questel, Data-Star. **Networks/Consortia:** Member of Rochester Regional Library Council (RRLC).

★11221★
PENNZOIL EXPLORATION AND PRODUCTION COMPANY - TECHNICAL INFORMATION SERVICES (Sci-Engr)
700 Milam
Box 2967 Phone: (713)546-6481
Houston, TX 77252-2967 Joan K. Baldwin, Libn.
Founded: 1981. **Staff:** Prof 1. **Subjects:** Geology, geophysics, reservoir engineering, enhanced recovery. **Holdings:** 7000 books; 2000 bound periodical volumes; 1500 technical reports; 2000 maps. **Subscriptions:** 125 journals and other serials. **Services:** Interlibrary loan; copying; services open to the public by appointment. **Automated Operations:** Computerized cataloging and circulation. **Computerized Information Services:** DIALOG Information Services, Pergamon ORBIT InfoLine, Inc., BRS Information Technologies, WILSONLINE, NEXIS, Dow Jones News/Retrieval, OCLC. **Networks/Consortia:** Member of AMIGOS Bibliographic Council, Inc.. **Publications:** Journals Received, weekly; Books Cataloged, monthly - both for internal distribution only.

★11222★
PENOBSCOT COUNTY LAW LIBRARY (Law)
Penobscot County Court House
97 Hammond St.
Bangor, ME 04401 Lynda Ryder, Libn.
Subjects: Law. **Holdings:** 14,000 volumes. **Services:** Library open to the public.

★11223★
PENOBSCOT MARINE MUSEUM - STEPHEN PHILLIPS MEMORIAL LIBRARY (Hist)
Church St.
Box 498 Phone: (207)548-2529
Searsport, ME 04974 William A. Bayreuther, Cur.
Founded: 1936. **Staff:** Prof 4; Other 7. **Subjects:** Maritime history, biography of mariners. **Special Collections:** Local history and genealogy (83 linear feet); ships registers; logbooks and journals. **Holdings:** 6000 volumes; archival materials; clippings; 1900 navigational charts; manuscripts; vital records and census data of Knox, Waldo, Hancock counties on microfilm. **Subscriptions:** 10 journals and other serials. **Services:** Interlibrary loan; copying; library open to the public.

★11224★
PENROSE HOSPITAL - WEBB MEMORIAL LIBRARY (Med)
2215 N. Cascade Ave.
Box 7021 Phone: (719)630-5288
Colorado Springs, CO 80933 Nina Janes, Dir.
Founded: 1959. **Staff:** Prof 2. **Subjects:** Medicine, hospital administration. **Special Collections:** Penrose Cancer Hospital Collection; partial depository

for government documents on cancer; history of medicine/historical medical texts (100 volumes); rare medical books. **Holdings:** 1000 books; 12,000 bound periodical volumes. **Subscriptions:** 300 journals and other serials. **Services:** Interlibrary loan; copying; SDI; library open to persons employed in medical fields and students of local colleges. **Automated Operations:** Computerized acquisitions, serials, and circulation. **Computerized Information Services:** DIALOG Information Services, MEDLARS, MEDLINE; ABACUS (electronic mail service). **Networks/Consortia:** Member of Colorado Council of Medical Librarians, Peaks and Valleys (Medical) Library Consortium. **Staff:** W. Robin Waters, Med.Libn..

PENROSE LIBRARY
See: University of Denver (16122)

★11225★
PENSACOLA HISTORICAL SOCIETY - LELIA ABERCROMBIE HISTORICAL LIBRARY (Hist)
405 S. Adams St. Phone: (904)433-1559
Pensacola, FL 32501 Gordon N. Simons, Cur.
Founded: 1960. **Staff:** Prof 3. **Subjects:** Pensacola, Escambia County, and West Florida history. **Special Collections:** Stephen R. Mallory letters, 1861-1870; Brosnaham Collection (land transfers, 1821; letters, deeds, documents, ledgers, 1782-1935); manuscripts (80 Hollinger manuscript boxes). **Holdings:** 2500 books; 700 maps, charts, architectural drawings; 30 hours of oral history recordings by local citizens; 3600 genealogical family data sheets; VF drawers; 140 reels of microfilm; 25,000 photographs; 20,000 glass negatives. **Services:** Copying; library open to the public. **Staff:** Claire N. LeMacher, Asst.Cur.; Sandra Johnson, Asst.Cur..

★11226★
PENSACOLA MUSEUM OF ART - HARRY THORNTON MEMORIAL LIBRARY (Art)
407 S. Jefferson St. Phone: (904)432-6247
Pensacola, FL 32501 M.H. Takach, Dir.
Founded: 1964. **Subjects:** Fine arts. **Holdings:** 1500 books; catalogs; AV programs.

★11227★
PENSION BENEFIT GUARANTY CORPORATION - OFFICE OF THE GENERAL COUNSEL - LIBRARY (Law)
2020 K St., N.W., Suite 7200 Phone: (202)778-8821
Washington, DC 20006-1806 Pat Martinez, Libn.
Founded: 1976. **Staff:** Prof 1. **Subjects:** Pension law, pensions. **Holdings:** 10,000 volumes. **Subscriptions:** 200 journals and other serials. **Services:** Interlibrary loan. **Computerized Information Services:** LEXIS. **Networks/Consortia:** Member of FEDLINK. **Special Indexes:** Indexes to PBGC regulations and notices in the Federal Register; PBGC congressional testimony. **Remarks:** Pension Benefit Guaranty Corporation is a government corporation that insures private pension plans.

★11228★
PENTON PUBLISHING - MARKETING INFORMATION CENTER (Publ)
1100 Superior Ave. Phone: (216)696-7000
Cleveland, OH 44114 Kenneth Long, Mgr.
Founded: 1960. **Staff:** Prof 4; Other 2. **Subjects:** Industrial and consumer markets, advertising, marketing. **Special Collections:** Penton market studies. **Holdings:** 3400 books; 3100 government documents; 190 VF drawers of market data, articles, annual reports, company catalogs, government reports. **Subscriptions:** 220 journals and other serials. **Services:** Interlibrary loan; copying; SDI; center open to advertisers and potential advertisers by staff referral. **Computerized Information Services:** DIALOG Information Services, NEXIS. **Publications:** Marketing Information Center News, quarterly - to Penton editors and marketing executives; Market Profiles (computation of product sales to consuming industries), annual; industry analyses for Penton magazines. **Remarks:** Center is part of Marketing Research & Economic Analysis Department. **Staff:** Michael Keating, Sr. Market Anl.; Barbara Pierce, Market Anl.; Mark Fosselman, Market Anl..

★11229★
PEOPLES GAS LIGHT AND COKE COMPANY - LIBRARY (Energy)
122 S. Michigan Ave., Rm. 727 Phone: (312)431-4677
Chicago, IL 60603 Anne C. Roess, Chf.Libn.
Founded: 1911. **Staff:** Prof 1; Other 2. **Subjects:** Gas industry for manufactured and natural gas; public utilities; accounting; engineering; energy; management; federal statistics. **Special Collections:** Federal Power Commission Reports; American Gas Association Proceedings. **Holdings:** 6314 books; 1200 reports. **Subscriptions:** 373 journals; 10 newspapers. **Services:** Interlibrary loan; library not open to the public. **Automated Operations:** Computerized cataloging. **Computerized Information Services:** DIALOG Information Services, Pergamon ORBIT InfoLine, Inc., WILSONLINE, VU/TEXT Information Services, A.G.A. GasNet, OCLC, Integrated Technical Information System (ITIS), NEXIS; A.G.A. GasNet (electronic mail service). **Networks/Consortia:** Member of ILLINET, Chicago Library System. **Publications:** Newsclips, daily; Infoline, monthly.

PEOPLE'S MUSIC WEEKEND ARCHIVE
See: New Song Library (10001)

★11230★
PEOPLES NATURAL GAS COMPANY - LAW LIBRARY (Law, Energy)
625 Liberty Ave. Phone: (412)471-5100
Pittsburgh, PA 15222 Horace P. Payne, Jr., Att.
Staff: 1. **Subjects:** Law - general, oil and gas, public utilities. **Holdings:** 7500 books; 185 bound periodical volumes. **Subscriptions:** 10 journals and other serials. **Services:** Library not open to the public.

PEORIA BAHAI ASSEMBLY - BAHA'I FAITH LIBRARY & ARCHIVES
See: Baha'i Faith Library & Archives (1227)

★11231★
PEORIA COUNTY LAW LIBRARY (Law)
Peoria County Court House, Rm. 209 Phone: (309)672-6084
Peoria, IL 61602 Mary Louise Jacquin, Libn.
Subjects: Law. **Holdings:** 12,000 volumes. **Subscriptions:** 17 journals and other serials. **Services:** Copying; library open to the public. **Networks/Consortia:** Member of Illinois Valley Library System.

★11232★
PEORIA HISTORICAL SOCIETY - LIBRARY (Hist)
Bradley University Library Phone: (309)677-2822
Peoria, IL 61625 Charles Frey, Spec.Coll.Libn.
Founded: 1962. **Staff:** Prof 1; Other 2. **Subjects:** Peoria - pictures, biographies, churches, schools, business and industry, authors. **Special Collections:** Ernest E. East Collection; A. Wilson Oakford Collection of Peoria history and pictures (34 loose-leaf binders); Journal of Illinois State Historical Society, complete with index, 1909 to present; Peoria and Peoria County Atlas; historical encyclopedias; Works Progress Administration (WPA) file. **Holdings:** 1600 books; 32 VF drawers; 12,000 photographic images. **Services:** Interlibrary loan (limited); copying; library open to the public. **Automated Operations:** Computerized cataloging, acquisitions, serials, and circulation. **Computerized Information Services:** DIALOG Information Services, BRS Information Technologies, OCLC. **Networks/Consortia:** Member of Illinois Valley Library System, Resource Sharing Alliance of West Central Illinois, Inc., ILLINET.

ANTHONY PEPE MEMORIAL LAW LIBRARY
See: Hamilton Law Association (5982)

★11233★
PEPPER, HAMILTON AND SCHEETZ - LAW LIBRARY (Law)
123 S. Broad St. Phone: (215)893-3080
Philadelphia, PA 19109 Robyn L. Beyer, Dir., Lib.Serv.
Staff: Prof 2; Other 4. **Subjects:** Law. **Holdings:** 26,000 volumes. **Subscriptions:** 150 journals and other serials; 5 newspapers. **Services:** Interlibrary loan; SDI; library open to other law libraries and those connected with the firm. **Computerized Information Services:** LEXIS, NEXIS, DIALOG Information Services, VU/TEXT Information Services. **Remarks:** An alternate telephone number is 893-3000. **Staff:** Anne W. Levy, Asst.Libn..

★11234★
PEPPERDINE UNIVERSITY - LAW LIBRARY (Law)
24255 Pacific Coast Hwy. Phone: (213)456-4647
Malibu, CA 90265 Nancy J. Kitchen, Dir.
Founded: 1969. **Staff:** Prof 5; Other 4. **Subjects:** Law. **Holdings:** 99,575 volumes; 85,015 other cataloged items. **Subscriptions:** 2786 journals and other serials; 20 newspapers. **Services:** Interlibrary loan; copying; library open to the public for reference use only. **Automated Operations:** Computerized public access catalog, cataloging, and circulation. **Computerized Information Services:** LEXIS, WESTLAW, OCLC. **Staff:** Joleen Heather, Acq.; Paula Popma, Cat.; Ramona Stahl, Circ.; Carole Levitt, Ref..

★11235★
PEPPERDINE UNIVERSITY - LIBRARY - SPECIAL COLLECTIONS (Hum, Hist)
24255 Pacific Coast Hwy. Phone: (213)456-4263
Malibu, CA 90265 Virginia Randolph, Spec.Coll.Libn.
Subjects: California history, early children's literature. **Holdings:** Archives of Churches of Christ, West Coast. **Services:** Interlibrary loan; copying; collections open to the public. **Automated Operations:** Computerized cataloging and serials. **Computerized Information Services:** DIALOG Information Services, OCLC.

★11236★
PEPPERDINE UNIVERSITY - NATIONAL SCHOOL SAFETY CENTER - LIBRARY (Educ)
16830 Ventura Blvd., Suite 200 Phone: (213)306-5693
Encino, CA 91436-1704 Beverly Gandy Beatty, Libn.
Subjects: School safety, discipline, and social climate. **Holdings:** 500 volumes; 100,000 clippings.

★11237★
PEPSICO - TECHNICAL INFORMATION CENTER (Food-Bev)
100 Stevens Ave. Phone: (914)742-4882
Valhalla, NY 10595 Myron E. Menewitch, Mgr.
Founded: 1950. **Staff:** Prof 2; Other 3. **Subjects:** Carbonated and other beverages, sweeteners, chemistry, microbiology, food technology, toxicology, nutrition. **Holdings:** 3000 books. **Subscriptions:** 250 journals and other serials. **Services:** Interlibrary loan; center not open to the public. **Computerized Information Services:** DIALOG Information Services, Food Regulation Enquiries (FOREGE), PIERS (Port Import/Export Reporting Services), MEDLARS, Dow Jones News/Retrieval, NewsNet, Inc.; DIALMAIL (electronic mail service). **Publications:** Technical Information Center News, 10/year - for internal distribution only.

★11238★
PERELMAN ANTIQUE TOY MUSEUM - LIBRARY (Rec)
270 S. 2nd St. Phone: (215)922-1070
Philadelphia, PA 19106 Michael Tritz, Cur.
Founded: 1969. **Staff:** Prof 1. **Subjects:** Toys, antiques, banks, dolls, historic guidebooks, catalogs. **Special Collections:** Patent papers on antique toy mechanical banks. **Holdings:** 226 books; 100 bound periodical volumes; 100 newsletters; 1 VF drawer of clippings; 2 VF drawers of early toy catalogs. **Services:** Interlibrary loan; library open to the public with restrictions. **Special Catalogs:** Perelman Antique Toy Museum.

PERES OBLAT
See: Oblate Fathers - Bibliotheque Deschatelets (10618)

★11239★
PERGAMON PRESS, INC. - LIBRARY (Publ)
Maxwell House Phone: (914)592-7700
Elmsford, NY 10523 Maureen Madden, Libn.
Founded: 1957. **Staff:** Prof 1; Other 3. **Subjects:** Science, social sciences, technology, humanities and medicine. **Special Collections:** Vergilliana on microfiche; History of Economics (business and annual reports). **Holdings:** 4000 books; 2000 bound periodical volumes; microforms; VF drawers. **Subscriptions:** 250 journals and other serials. **Services:** Library not open to the public. **Publications:** Microforms Annual; Librarian's Guide to International Periodicals; Collection Development Guide.

PERHAM FOUNDATION - FOOTHILL ELECTRONICS MUSEUM - DE FOREST MEMORIAL ARCHIVES
See: Electronics Museum - De Forest Memorial Archive (4651)

★11240★
PERIODICALS INSTITUTE - LIBRARY (Publ)
Box 899 Phone: (201)882-1130
West Caldwell, NJ 07007 John E. Fitzmaurice, Jr., Pres.
Founded: 1979. **Subjects:** Marketing for the publishing industry. **Holdings:** 2000 volumes.

★11241★
PERKIN-ELMER CORPORATION - APPLIED SCIENCE DIVISION - LIBRARY
2771 N. Garey Ave.
Pomona, CA 91767
Founded: 1981. **Subjects:** Mass spectrometry, electronics, atmospheric and respiratory monitors, analytical instrumentation, medicine, surgery, optics. **Holdings:** 659 books; 374 government documents, reports, patents. **Remarks:** Presently inactive.

★11242★
PERKIN-ELMER CORPORATION - CORPORATE LIBRARY & INFORMATION SERVICE (Sci-Engr)
761 Main Ave. Phone: (203)834-4798
Norwalk, CT 06859-0249 Debra Kaufman, Mgr.
Founded: 1958. **Staff:** Prof 3; Other 6. **Subjects:** Instrumentation, optics, electronics, semiconductors. **Holdings:** 25,000 books; 1500 bound periodical volumes; 20,000 documents; 40 VF drawers of reprints. **Subscriptions:** 700 journals and other serials. **Services:** Interlibrary loan; copying; library open to the public by appointment. **Automated Operations:** Computerized acquisitions, serials, and circulation. **Computerized Information Services:** DIALOG Information Services, BRS Information Technologies, NEXIS, Pergamon ORBIT InfoLine, Inc., Dow Jones News/Retrieval, NASA/RECON, DTIC; STAIRS (internal database). **Networks/Consortia:** Member of Southwestern Connecticut Library Council (SWLC). **Publications:** List of papers presented by company personnel, annual - for internal distribution only. **Special Catalogs:** Catalog of internal and external engineering reports (book). **Staff:** Judy M. Irete, Supv., Br.Oper./Tech.Serv.; Rosemary Augliera, Ref.Libn..

PERKIN-ELMER CORPORATION - METCO INC.
See: Metco Inc. - Engineering Library (8791)

★11243★
PERKIN-ELMER DATA SYSTEMS GROUP - CONCURRENT COMPUTER CORPORATION - LIBRARY (Comp Sci)
2 Crescent Place Phone: (201)870-4500
Oceanport, NJ 07757 Nancy B. Lynott, Libn.
Founded: 1977. **Staff:** Prof 1; Other 1. **Subjects:** Computer science, electrical engineering, math, management. **Holdings:** 2000 books. **Subscriptions:** 150 journals and other serials. **Services:** Interlibrary loan; copying; SDI; library open to the public by appointment. **Computerized Information Services:** DIALOG Information Services. **Remarks:** A branch library is maintained at 106 Apple St., Tinton Falls, NJ 07724.

RICHARD S. PERKIN LIBRARY
See: American Museum of Natural History - Hayden Planetarium (609)

★11244★
PERKINS COIE - LIBRARY (Law)
1900 Washington Bldg. Phone: (206)682-8770
Seattle, WA 98101 Jane Stewart, Libn.
Staff: Prof 4; Other 5. **Subjects:** Law. **Holdings:** 40,000 volumes. **Subscriptions:** 1000 journals and other serials. **Services:** Interlibrary loan; library not open to the public. **Staff:** Susan Schulkin, Assoc.Libn.; Carol Warner, Assoc.Libn.; Mark W. Munson, Assoc.Libn..

RALPH PERKINS MEMORIAL LIBRARY
See: John D. Archbold Memorial Hospital (844)

★11245★
PERKINS SCHOOL FOR THE BLIND - SAMUEL P. HAYES RESEARCH LIBRARY (Educ)
175 N. Beacon St. Phone: (617)924-3434
Watertown, MA 02172 Kenneth A. Stuckey, Res.Libn.
Founded: 1880. **Staff:** Prof 1; Other 1. **Subjects:** Nonmedical aspects of blindness and deaf-blindness, including education, rehabilitation, welfare. **Special Collections:** Historical collection of embossed books printed for the blind; pictures of blind people; books by blind and deaf-blind; postage stamps which honor and aid the blind. **Holdings:** 18,000 volumes; bound newspaper clippings; Helen Keller material. **Subscriptions:** 125 journals and other serials. **Services:** Interlibrary loan; copying (articles and pamphlets only); library open to the public for reference use only. **Publications:** Accessions List, biennial - free upon request. **Remarks:** Collection includes a museum showing the history of education of the blind and aids and appliances for the blind.

PERKINS SCHOOL OF THEOLOGY
See: Southern Methodist University - Perkins School of Theology - The Bridwell Library (13484)

★11246★
PERKINS AND WILL ARCHITECTS, INC. - RESOURCE CENTER (Plan)
2 N. LaSalle Phone: (312)977-1100
Chicago, IL 60602 Diane Johnson, Libn.
Staff: 1. **Subjects:** Building technology and products, architecture, art, design, planning, interior decorating, engineering. **Holdings:** 2500 books; 300 bound periodical volumes; 12 drawers and 450 linear feet of product

literature; 9 drawers of code files. **Subscriptions:** 75 journals and other serials. **Services:** Interlibrary loan; center not open to the public.

★11247★
PERMIAN BASIN PETROLEUM MUSEUM, LIBRARY AND HALL OF FAME - ARCHIVES CENTER (Energy)
1500 Interstate 20 W. Phone: (915)683-4403
Midland, TX 79701 Betty Orbeck, Archv.
Staff: Prof 1; Other 1. **Subjects:** Petroleum industry and company history; biographies and autobiographies of oil personnel; oil well exploration, drilling, production, refining, marketing, transportation, service, supply; Permian Basin of West Texas and Southeastern New Mexico. **Holdings:** 1000 books; 600 bound periodical volumes; 500 taped oral history interviews with typed transcripts; 6000 photographic prints and negatives; equipment and tool catalogs, 1884, 1891-1982; oil company internal journals, 1918-1936; motion picture films, 1926-1951 and 1985; newspapers, 1911-1963; maps. **Subscriptions:** 20 journals and other serials. **Services:** Interlibrary loan; copying; center open to the public. **Publications:** Museum Memo, bimonthly.

★11248★
PERRY MEMORIAL HOSPITAL - DR. KENNETH O. NELSON LIBRARY OF THE HEALTH SCIENCES (Med)
530 Park Ave., E. Phone: (815)875-2811
Princeton, IL 61356 Mary Ann Butler, Lib.Coord.
Staff: Prof 1. **Subjects:** Medicine. **Holdings:** 318 books. **Subscriptions:** 67 journals and other serials. **Services:** Interlibrary loan; copying; library open to the public with restrictions. **Automated Operations:** Computerized cataloging, acquisitions, serials, and circulation. **Networks/Consortia:** Member of Greater Midwest Regional Medical Library Network, Heart of Illinois Library Consortium (HILC), ILLINET, Starved Rock Library System.

MERLE G. PERRY ARCHIVES
See: Alfred P. Sloan, Jr. Museum (13228)

PERRY'S VICTORY & INTERNATIONAL PEACE MEMORIAL
See: U.S. Natl. Park Service (15337)

★11249★
PERSONAL PRODUCTS COMPANY - RESEARCH & DEVELOPMENT LIBRARY (Sci-Engr)
Van Liew Ave. Phone: (201)524-7544
Milltown, NJ 08850 Kathryn Hummer, Res.Libn.
Founded: 1954. **Staff:** Prof 1; Other 1. **Subjects:** Chemistry, paper, textiles, medicine, microbiology, cosmetics. **Holdings:** 3150 books; 2550 bound periodical volumes; 2 VF drawers and 21 reels of microfilm of patents; 35 VF drawers and 700 microfiche of company reports; 5 VF drawers of pamphlets. **Subscriptions:** 154 journals and other serials. **Services:** Interlibrary loan; library not open to the public. **Automated Operations:** Computerized patent files, circulation, and indexing of research reports. **Computerized Information Services:** Online systems. **Remarks:** A subsidiary of Johnson and Johnson.

PERTH AMBOY GENERAL HOSPITAL
See: Raritan Bay Medical Center (11883)

W.T. PERYAM LIBRARY
See: Grand Encampment Museum, Inc. - Library (5792)

★11250★
PET INCORPORATED - CORPORATE INFORMATION CENTER (Food-Bev)
400 S. 4th St. Phone: (314)622-6134
St. Louis, MO 63102 Laurence R. Walton, Mgr.
Founded: 1960. **Staff:** Prof 2; Other 1. **Subjects:** Food science and technology, nutrition, microbiology, dairy science, food business, food economics, marketing. **Special Collections:** Cookbook Collection (2500 volumes; 400 pre-1900 volumes. **Holdings:** 24,000 books; 2000 bound periodical volumes; microfiche; government research reports on food. **Subscriptions:** 550 journals and other serials; 12 newspapers. **Services:** Interlibrary loan; copying; center open to the public by appointment. **Automated Operations:** Computerized cataloging and serials. **Computerized Information Services:** DIALOG Information Services, Dow Jones News/Retrieval, Pergamon ORBIT InfoLine, Inc., NEXIS. **Networks/Consortia:** Member of St. Louis Regional Library Network. **Publications:** PET News Notes, weekly. **Staff:** Roseann Huddleston, Asst.Libn..

PETAWAWA NATIONAL FORESTRY INSTITUTE
See: Canada - Canadian Forestry Service (2335)

PETER MEMORIAL LIBRARY
See: Moravian Music Foundation, Inc. (9297)

★11251★
PETERBOROUGH HISTORICAL SOCIETY - LIBRARY (Hist)
Grove St.
Box 58 Phone: (603)924-3235
Peterborough, NH 03458 Ellen Derby, Exec.Dir.
Founded: 1902. **Staff:** Prof 1; Other 2. **Subjects:** History of Peterborough and New Hampshire, antiques. **Special Collections:** 19th century photographs of local people and scenes; early school books; antiques (books; pamphlets). **Holdings:** 1000 books; tax records; clippings; early mill account books; maps; letters; early deeds; scrapbooks. **Services:** Library open to the public.

PETERS HEALTH SCIENCES LIBRARY
See: Rhode Island Hospital (12017)

★11252★
PETERSBURG GENERAL HOSPITAL - MEDICAL LIBRARY MEDIA SERVICES (Med)
801 S. Adams St. Phone: (804)732-7220
Petersburg, VA 23803 Joan B. Pollard, Med.Lib./Media Serv.Dir.
Founded: 1956. **Staff:** Prof 1; Other 4. **Subjects:** Medicine, nursing. **Special Collections:** Old medical books. **Holdings:** 1002 books; 5230 bound periodical volumes; 4 VF drawers of reprints; 120 video cassettes; 1260 Audio-Digest tapes. **Subscriptions:** 125 journals and other serials. **Services:** Interlibrary loan; library not open to the public. **Networks/Consortia:** Member of Southeastern/Atlantic Regional Medical Library Services. **Publications:** Monthly News-Acquisitions.

PETERSBURG NATIONAL BATTLEFIELD
See: U.S. Natl. Park Service (15338)

★11253★
PETERSHAM HISTORICAL SOCIETY, INC. - LIBRARY (Hist)
Main St. Phone: (508)724-3380
Petersham, MA 01366 Delight Gale Haines, Libn./Cur.
Founded: 1930. **Staff:** Prof 1. **Subjects:** Petersham history and genealogy. **Special Collections:** Shays' Rebellion. **Holdings:** 800 books; 600 pamphlets and reports; 15 VF drawers of documents, diaries, pictures; 8 VF drawers of clippings and manuscripts; 20 maps. **Services:** Library open to the public with restrictions.

C. LLOYD PETERSON MEMORIAL LIBRARY
See: Rocky Mountain Hospital (12157)

★11254★
SYMON PETLURA INSTITUTE - ARCHIVES (Area-Ethnic)
620 Spadina Ave. Phone: (416)536-5083
Toronto, ON, Canada M5S 2H4 Dr. Oleh S. Pidhainy, Pres./Archv.Dir.
Founded: 1977. **Staff:** Prof 1. **Subjects:** Ukraine. **Special Collections:** Ukrainian and East European scholarship in North America and the world; The Great Artificial Famine in Ukraine, 1932-1933; Christianization of the Ukraine, 988 A.D.; Symon Petlura, 1869-1926; 20th century Ukraine. **Holdings:** Figures not available.

PETRIFIED FOREST NATIONAL PARK
See: U.S. Natl. Park Service (15339)

★11255★
PETRO-CANADA - LAW LIBRARY (Law)
150 6th Ave., S.W.
P.O. Box 2844 Phone: (403)296-8592
Calgary, AB, Canada T2P 3E3 Susan Beugin, Law Libn.
Founded: 1984. **Staff:** Prof 1. **Subjects:** Law. **Holdings:** 7500 volumes. **Subscriptions:** 171 journals and other serials. **Services:** Interlibrary loan; library not open to the public. **Automated Operations:** Computerized cataloging, acquisitions, and serials. **Computerized Information Services:** QL Systems, Canada Systems Group (CSG), DIALOG Information Services, Info Globe.

★11256★
PETRO-CANADA - LIBRARY SERVICES (Energy)
150 6th Ave., S.W.
P.O. Box 2844 Phone: (403)296-8959
Calgary, AB, Canada T2P 3E3 Janet Ferro, Hd.Libn.
Staff: Prof 3; Other 5. **Subjects:** Petroleum geology and engineering, environment, energy economics, marketing. **Holdings:** 15,000 books; 600 company reports. **Subscriptions:** 500 journals and other serials; 10 newspapers. **Services:** Interlibrary loan; library not open to the public. **Automated Operations:** Computerized cataloging, acquisitions, serials, circulation, and ILL. **Computerized Information Services:** Online systems.

★11257★
PETRO-CANADA PRODUCTS INC. - TECHNICAL LIBRARY (Energy)
2489 N. Sheridan Way Phone: (416)822-6770
Mississauga, ON, Canada L5K 1A8 Roy E. Metcalfe, Supv.
Founded: 1965. **Staff:** Prof 3. **Subjects:** Petroleum chemistry and technology. **Special Collections:** Society of Automotive Engineers Transactions, 1965 to present; Canadian Patents, 1977-1985; U.S. Chemical Patents, 1952 to present. **Holdings:** 9000 books; 1600 bound periodical volumes. **Subscriptions:** 275 journals and other serials; 5 newspapers. **Services:** Interlibrary loan; copying; SDI; library open to the public by appointment. **Automated Operations:** Computerized cataloging and serials. **Computerized Information Services:** CAN/OLE, DIALOG Information Services, Info Globe, STN International, Pergamon ORBIT InfoLine, Inc., BRS Information Technologies. **Networks/Consortia:** Member of Sheridan Park Association - Library and Information Science Committee (LISC). **Formerly:** Research & Development Library. **Staff:** A. Neilson, Libn.; W. Davis, Libn..

PETROLEUM HISTORY AND RESEARCH CENTER LIBRARY
See: University of Wyoming (17190)

PETROLEUM RECOVERY INSTITUTE - I.N. MC KINNON MEMORIAL LIBRARY
See: I.N. Mc Kinnon Memorial Library (8235)

★11258★
PETROLITE CORPORATION - INFORMATION CENTER (Sci-Engr)
369 Marshall Ave. Phone: (314)968-6008
St. Louis, MO 63119 Pauline C. Beinbrech, Mgr.
Founded: 1959. **Staff:** Prof 2; Other 2. **Subjects:** Chemistry - organic, petroleum, corrosion; water treatment; wax. **Holdings:** 7200 books; 8500 bound periodical volumes; 94,000 patents; 33,000 microfiche; 10 VF drawers of trade literature. **Subscriptions:** 250 journals and other serials. **Services:** Interlibrary loan; copying; center open to the public by appointment. **Automated Operations:** Computerized circulation and periodical routing. **Computerized Information Services:** DIALOG Information Services, Pergamon ORBIT InfoLine, Inc., Chemical Information Systems, Inc. (CIS), STN International, Oil & Gas Journal Energy Database, NLM, CHEMEST, OCLC; internal database. **Networks/Consortia:** Member of St. Louis Regional Library Network, Missouri Library Network (MLNC). **Publications:** Procedures Manual, irregular; Recent Acquisitions, quarterly. **Staff:** Joyce Hanebrink, Info.Spec..

★11259★
PETTAQUAMSCUTT HISTORICAL SOCIETY - LIBRARY (Hist)
2636 Kingstown Rd. Phone: (401)783-1328
Kingston, RI 02881 Elizabeth R. Albro, Cur.
Founded: 1958. **Subjects:** Local history and genealogy, Rhode Island history. **Holdings:** 1000 books; manuscripts; 10 boxes of local government papers. **Services:** Library open to the public by appointment. **Publications:** Pettaquamscutt Reporter, 5/year - to members.

★11260★
PETTIT & MARTIN - LIBRARY (Law)
101 California, 35th Fl. Phone: (415)434-4000
San Francisco, CA 94111 Lynn Brazil, Hd.Libn.
Staff: Prof 2; Other 2. **Subjects:** Law. **Holdings:** 28,000 books; 1100 bound periodical volumes. **Subscriptions:** 400 journals and other serials. **Services:** Interlibrary loan; copying; library open to the public by permission only. **Computerized Information Services:** LEXIS, NEXIS, DIALOG Information Services, Dow Jones News/Retrieval, RLIN, DataTimes, Information America. **Networks/Consortia:** Member of CLASS. **Staff:** Molly Young, Asst.Libn..

ALMEDA MAY CASTLE PETZINGER LIBRARY
See: The Haggin Museum - Almeda May Castle Petzinger Library (5950)

JOHN G. PEW MEMORIAL LIBRARY
See: Delaware County Historical Society (4148)

JOSEPH N. PEW, JR. MEDICAL LIBRARY
See: Bryn Mawr Hospital - Joseph N. Pew, Jr. Medical Library (2002)

★11261★
THE PFAUDLER COMPANY - TECHNICAL LIBRARY (Sci-Engr)
1000 West Ave.
Box 1600 Phone: (716)235-1000
Rochester, NY 14692 Candice M. Johnson, Libn.
Founded: 1960. **Staff:** 1. **Subjects:** Metallurgy - steel and refractory metal fabrication; protective coatings - ceramic, metallic, plastic; chemical engineering. **Holdings:** 1900 books; 1065 bound periodical volumes; 6 VF drawers of government reports; 4 VF drawers of patents; 3 VF drawers of microforms; 8 VF drawers of internal reports. **Subscriptions:** 250 journals and other serials. **Services:** Interlibrary loan; copying; translations; library open to the public by appointment. **Automated Operations:** Computerized serials. **Computerized Information Services:** DIALOG Information Services. **Networks/Consortia:** Member of Rochester Regional Library Council (RRLC). **Special Catalogs:** Journal catalog. **Special Indexes:** Patent and internal reports indexes.

ANNIE MERNER PFEIFFER LIBRARY
See: West Virginia Wesleyan College (17685)

PFEIFFER PHYSICS LIBRARY
See: Washington University (17544)

RICHARD C. PFEIFFER LIBRARY
See: Tiffin University (14193)

★11262★
PFIZER CANADA INC. - MEDICAL LIBRARY (Med)
P.O. Box 800 Phone: (514)695-0500
Pointe Claire-Dorval, PQ, Canada H9R 4V2
Miriam Hayward, Sci.Info.Off.
Staff: Prof 1. **Subjects:** Pharmacology, drug therapy, rheumatology, cardiovasology, psychotherapy, microbiology, allergies, dermatology. **Holdings:** 650 books; 480 bound periodical volumes; 50 audio cassettes; 6500 reprints; 125 meeting and symposia proceedings; 90 pieces of product information; 80 other cataloged items. **Subscriptions:** 122 journals and other serials. **Services:** SDI; library open to health professionals, sales representatives, and students. **Computerized Information Services:** MEDLARS, DIALOG Information Services, Lithium Library; MEDNET (internal database); Envoy 100 (electronic mail service). **Publications:** Bibliographies; Current Awareness - both for internal distribution only.

★11263★
PFIZER, INC. - CENTRAL RESEARCH - RESEARCH LIBRARY (Med, Sci-Engr)
Eastern Point Rd. Phone: (203)441-3688
Groton, CT 06340 Dr. Jay S. Buckley, Jr., Dir.
Founded: 1960. **Staff:** Prof 6; Other 6. **Subjects:** Organic and pharmaceutical chemistry, pharmacology, clinical medicine, antibiotics, fermentation. **Holdings:** 7000 books; 30,000 bound periodical volumes; 2500 reels of microfilm of patent specifications. **Subscriptions:** 1000 journals and other serials. **Services:** Library open to students and researchers. **Automated Operations:** Computerized cataloging, acquisitions, and serials. **Computerized Information Services:** DIALOG Information Services, Pergamon ORBIT InfoLine, Inc., NLM, CAS ONLINE. **Networks/Consortia:** Member of Southeastern Connecticut Library Association (SECLA). **Publications:** Periodical Holdings List, semiannual; Infosource, quarterly. **Special Indexes:** Central Patents Index - Sections A, B, D, and E; Unlisted Drugs (card). **Staff:** John B. Hare, Info.Sci.; Roberta Lewis Morton, Libn.; Dr. Roger P. Nelson, Mgr.; E. Shoop, Info.Sci..

★11264★
PFIZER, INC. - N.Y.O. LIBRARY (Med)
235 E. 42nd St. Phone: (212)573-2966
New York, NY 10017 Veronica Plucinski, Chf.Libn.
Staff: Prof 3; Other 1. **Subjects:** Pharmaceuticals, pharmacology, clinical medicine. **Holdings:** 15,000 volumes; 1270 reels of microfilm. **Subscriptions:** 630 journals and other serials. **Services:** Interlibrary loan; SDI; library open to students and researchers by appointment. **Automated Operations:** Computerized serials. **Computerized Information Services:**

DIALOG Information Services, Pergamon ORBIT InfoLine, Inc., BRS Information Technologies, Data-Star, MEDLARS. **Networks/Consortia:** Member of Medical Library Center of New York (MLCNY). **Publications:** Periodical Subscription List, annual; Periodical Subject List, annual - free upon request. **Staff:** Karen Erani, Assoc.Libn.; Clara Henson, Lib.Asst..

ANTHONY C. PFOHL HEALTH SCIENCE LIBRARY
See: Mercy Health Center (8738)

CARL & LILY PFORZHEIMER FOUNDATION, INC. - CARL H. PFORZHEIMER LIBRARY
See: New York Public Library - Carl H. Pforzheimer Shelley and His Circle Collection (10051)

PFORZHEIMER LIBRARY OF ENGLISH LITERATURE
See: University of Texas, Austin - Harry Ransom Humanities Research Center (16931)

★11265★
PHARMACIA P-L BIOCHEMICALS, INC. - RESEARCH LIBRARY (Biol Sci)
2202 N. Bartlett Ave. Phone: (414)225-2601
Milwaukee, WI 53202 Symie Menitove, Res.Libn.
Founded: 1944. **Staff:** Prof 1. **Subjects:** Microbiology, biochemistry, chemistry. **Holdings:** 2786 books; 1482 bound periodical volumes. **Subscriptions:** 90 journals and other serials. **Services:** Interlibrary loan; SDI; library open to the public by appointment. **Computerized Information Services:** DIALOG Information Services, BRS Information Technologies, NLM, Pergamon ORBIT InfoLine, Inc., STN International. **Networks/Consortia:** Member of Library Council of Metropolitan Milwaukee, Inc. (LCOMM), Southeastern Wisconsin Health Science Library Consortium (SWHSL). **Publications:** P-L Library News - for internal distribution only.

PHASE DIAGRAMS FOR CERAMISTS
See: U.S. Natl. Bureau of Standards - Phase Diagrams for Ceramists (15201)

GERALD B. PHELAN ARCHIVES
See: University of Toronto - Pontifical Institute of Mediaeval Studies - Library (16996)

★11266★
PHILADELPHIA ASSOCIATION FOR PSYCHOANALYSIS - LOUIS KAPLAN MEMORIAL LIBRARY (Med)
15 St. Asaph's Rd.
Bala Cynwyd, PA 19004 June M. Strickland, Libn.
Founded: 1950. **Staff:** Prof 1. **Subjects:** Psychoanalysis. **Holdings:** 2500 books; 2400 bound periodical volumes. **Subscriptions:** 10 journals and other serials. **Services:** Library not open to the public.

★11267★
PHILADELPHIA CITY ARCHIVES (Hist)
Dept. of Records
City Hall Annex, Rm. 523 Phone: (215)686-2276
Philadelphia, PA 19107 Ward J. Childs, City Archv.
Founded: 1952. **Staff:** Prof 4; Other 9. **Subjects:** Archives of the City and County of Philadelphia, 1683 to present. **Special Collections:** Official records of the 1876 Centennial Exhibition, 1926 Sesquicentennial Exposition, and 1976 Bicentennial celebration of the city of Philadelphia. **Holdings:** 20,000 cubic feet of archives; 98,000 cubic feet of Records Center holdings. **Services:** Copying; archives open to the public with restrictions. **Publications:** City Archives Newsletter; list of other publications - available on request. **Special Catalogs:** Descriptive Inventory of the Archives of the City and County of Philadelphia (book). **Special Indexes:** Subject Index to the Photograph Collection of the Philadelphia City Archives (book); Warrants and Surveys of the Province of Pennsylvania including the Three Lower Counties, 1759. **Staff:** Lee Stanley, Archv. II; Alfonso Harrell, Supv., Rec. Storage Ctr.; Jefferson M. Moak, Archv. II.

★11268★
PHILADELPHIA CITY PLANNING COMMISSION - LIBRARY
1515 Market St., 17th Fl.
Philadelphia, PA 19103
Founded: 1944. **Subjects:** City and regional planning, housing, transportation, government, architecture, engineering, business and industry, sociology, statistics. **Special Collections:** Archives of the commission (2 VF drawers); Philadelphia renewal areas (4000 35mm slides). **Holdings:** 22,000 books and pamphlets; 1000 bound periodical volumes. **Remarks:** Presently inactive.

★11269★
PHILADELPHIA COLLEGE OF BIBLE - LIBRARY (Rel-Phil)
Langhorne Manor
Manor Ave. Phone: (215)752-5800
Langhorne, PA 19047 Julius C. Bosco, Dir.
Founded: 1913. **Staff:** Prof 2; Other 1. **Subjects:** Theology and Bible study, music, Christian education, elementary education, social work, missions. **Special Collections:** Hymnals; C.I. Scofield Library of Biblical Studies. **Holdings:** 56,042 books, bound periodical volumes, scores; 3600 slides; 1112 reels of microfilm; 17,009 microfiche; 3500 phonograph records; 316 filmstrips; 36 films; 903 cassettes; 2544 curriculum materials. **Subscriptions:** 509 journals and other serials; 8 newspapers. **Services:** Copying; library open to the public for reference use only. **Automated Operations:** Computerized cataloging. **Computerized Information Services:** OCLC. **Publications:** Music Reference Sources. **Staff:** Dorothy M. Black, Asst.Libn..

★11270★
PHILADELPHIA COLLEGE OF OSTEOPATHIC MEDICINE - O.J. SNYDER MEMORIAL MEDICAL LIBRARY (Med)
4150 City Ave. Phone: (215)581-6526
Philadelphia, PA 19131 Dr. Shanker H. Vyas, Prof./Dir. of Libs.
Founded: 1898. **Staff:** Prof 3; Other 7. **Subjects:** Osteopathy, medicine, surgery. **Special Collections:** First editions of works on osteopathy, many autographed; archives of osteopathy. **Holdings:** 57,943 volumes; 4467 audiotapes; 1396 videotapes; 112 reels of 35mm microfilm; 6009 slides; 323 view master reels; 946 filmstrips. **Subscriptions:** 676 journals; 109 osteopathic serials. **Services:** Interlibrary loan; copying; microfilming; library open to the public for reference use only with permission. **Computerized Information Services:** MEDLINE. **Networks/Consortia:** Member of Greater Northeastern Regional Medical Library Program, Health Sciences Consortium. **Publications:** List of publications - available upon request. **Special Indexes:** Union List of Osteopathic Literature. **Staff:** Prof. Hansa S. Vyas, Search Anl./Ref.Libn.; Kathryn Picardo, Asst.Prof./Cat.Libn..

★11271★
PHILADELPHIA COLLEGE OF PHARMACY AND SCIENCE - JOSEPH W. ENGLAND LIBRARY (Med)
42nd St. & Woodland Ave. Phone: (215)596-8960
Philadelphia, PA 19104 Mignon Adams, Dir., Lib.Serv.
Founded: 1822. **Staff:** Prof 7; Other 8. **Subjects:** Pharmacy, pharmacology, biological sciences, chemistry, pharmacognosy, toxicology. **Special Collections:** History of pharmacy. **Holdings:** 55,000 volumes; 4900 reels of microfilm; 20,000 microfiche; 150 audio cassettes; 24 VF drawers of pamphlets; AV programs. **Subscriptions:** 900 journals and other serials. **Services:** Interlibrary loan; copying; library open to the public for reference use only by appointment. **Automated Operations:** Computerized cataloging, serials, and ILL. **Computerized Information Services:** DIALOG Information Services, BRS Information Technologies, NLM, Chemical Information Systems, Inc. (CIS), OCLC, STN International, WILSONLINE, VU/TEXT Information Services, EasyNet. Performs searches on fee basis. Contact Person: Sue Brizuela, Coord., ILL, 596-8964. **Networks/Consortia:** Member of Greater Northeastern Regional Medical Library Program, PALINET, Interlibrary Delivery Service of Pennsylvania (IDS), Philadelphia Area Reference Librarians Information Exchange (PARLIE), Tri-State College Library Cooperative (TCLC). **Publications:** J.W. England Newsletter & Booklist, monthly. **Remarks:** Fax: (215)222-5060. **Staff:** Joyce Zogott, Hd., AV Dept.; Leslie Bowman, Hd., Tech.Serv./Cat.; Judith Hesp, Coord., Bibliog.Instr.; Marjorie Smink, Ref./Ser..

★11272★
PHILADELPHIA COLLEGE OF TEXTILES AND SCIENCE - PASTORE LIBRARY (Sci-Engr)
School House Lane & Henry Ave. Phone: (215)951-2840
Philadelphia, PA 19144 Evelyn Minick, Dir. of Lib.Serv.
Founded: 1949. **Staff:** Prof 5; Other 3. **Subjects:** Textiles, business. **Special Collections:** Textile history. **Holdings:** 75,000 books; 12,000 bound periodical volumes; 6000 reels of microfilm. **Subscriptions:** 1542 journals and other serials; 12 newspapers. **Services:** Interlibrary loan; copying; library open to the public for reference use only. **Automated Operations:** Computerized cataloging, acquisitions, and serials. **Computerized Information Services:** DIALOG Information Services, Pergamon ORBIT InfoLine, Inc. **Networks/Consortia:** Member of Tri-State College Library Cooperative (TCLC), PALINET. **Staff:** J. Thomas Vogel, Coll.Dev.; Barbara Lowry, Hd., Pub.Serv.; Mary Phalan, Hd., Tech.Serv.; Wilfred Frisby, Ref.Libn.; Barry Cohen, Audiovisual Serv..

PHILADELPHIA COLLEGES OF THE ARTS
See: University of the Arts - Libraries (15844)

★11273★
PHILADELPHIA COMMON PLEAS & MUNICIPAL COURT - LAW LIBRARY (Law)
City Hall, Rm. 600 Phone: (215)686-3799
Philadelphia, PA 19107 James M. Clark, Law Libn.
Staff: Prof 1; Other 4. **Subjects:** U.S. and Pennsylvania law. **Special Collections:** Philadelphia Judges Memorial Collection. **Holdings:** 30,000 books; 200 bound periodical volumes; 3 VF drawers of Pennsylvania House and Senate bills; 3 VF drawers of Pennsylvania Appellate Court Slip opinions; 40 audio cassettes. **Subscriptions:** 125 journals and other serials; 10 newspapers. **Services:** Interlibrary loan; library not open to the public. **Computerized Information Services:** LEXIS. **Special Indexes:** Subject index to Pennsylvania Appellate Court Slip opinions. **Formerly:** Philadelphia Court of Common Pleas.

★11274★
PHILADELPHIA COMMUNITY LEGAL SERVICES, INC. - LAW LIBRARY (Law)
Sylvania House
1324 Locust at Juniper St. Phone: (215)893-5368
Philadelphia, PA 19107 John O'Connor, Libn.
Founded: 1968. **Staff:** Prof 1; Other 3. **Subjects:** Civil and poverty law. **Holdings:** 30,000 books; 200 unbound periodicals; 100 internal publications. **Subscriptions:** 50 journals and other serials; 5 newspapers. **Services:** Interlibrary loan; library open to the public by appointment. **Computerized Information Services:** LEXIS, DIALOG Information Services; LSC Brief Bank (internal database). **Publications:** Newsletter, 6/year - for internal distribution only. **Remarks:** Maintained by Legal Services Corporation.

★11275★
PHILADELPHIA CORPORATION FOR AGING - LIBRARY (Soc Sci)
111 N. Broad St. Phone: (215)496-0520
Philadelphia, PA 19107 Maureen Neville, Ref.Libn.
Founded: 1978. **Staff:** Prof 1; Other 1. **Subjects:** Gerontology, gerontological literature, programs for the aging. **Special Collections:** Service Center for Aging Information Microfiche Repository Collection (SCAN; 3000 gerontology-related research documents on microfiche). **Holdings:** 1500 books; 102 periodical volumes on microfiche; 400 government publications; 6525 documents; 16 VF drawers of pamphlets and reports. **Subscriptions:** 70 journals and other serials; 7 newspapers. **Services:** Interlibrary loan; copying; library open to the public for reference use only by appointment. **Computerized Information Services:** BRS Information Technologies. **Networks/Consortia:** Member of Greater Northeastern Regional Medical Library Program. **Remarks:** Corporation is an Area Agency on Aging.

★11276★
PHILADELPHIA ELECTRIC COMPANY - LIBRARY (Energy)
2301 Market St. Phone: (215)841-4358
Philadelphia, PA 19101 Sabina D. Tannenbaum, Libn.
Founded: 1909. **Staff:** Prof 3; Other 3. **Subjects:** Engineering - civil, electrical, mechanical, chemical; generating stations - hydro, nuclear, steam; nuclear energy; public utilities. **Special Collections:** Electric Power Research Institute reports. **Holdings:** 7000 volumes; 10,000 pamphlets and reports. **Subscriptions:** 250 journals and other serials. **Services:** Interlibrary loan; library open to the public by appointment. **Computerized Information Services:** DIALOG Information Services, Pergamon ORBIT InfoLine, Inc., VU/TEXT Information Services, Dow Jones News/Retrieval, Unicom News, A.G.A. GasNet, WESTLAW. **Publications:** Current Topics (abstracts of current articles and books) - for internal distribution only.

PHILADELPHIA EVENING BULLETIN LIBRARY
See: Temple University - Central Library System - Urban Archives (13996)

★11277★
PHILADELPHIA GERIATRIC CENTER - LIBRARY (Soc Sci, Med)
5301 Old York Rd. Phone: (215)456-2971
Philadelphia, PA 19141 Joyce A. Post, Libn.
Staff: Prof 1; Other 1. **Subjects:** Gerontology, geriatrics, psychology, sociology, housing, medicine, long-term care administration. **Holdings:** 10,000 books; 1000 bound periodical volumes. **Subscriptions:** 200 journals and other serials. **Services:** Interlibrary loan; copying; library open to the public by appointment. **Computerized Information Services:** MEDLINE, BRS Information Technologies. Performs searches on fee basis. **Networks/Consortia:** Member of Delaware Valley Information Consortium (DEVIC). **Publications:** Acquisitions list, 10/year.

★11278★
PHILADELPHIA HISTORICAL COMMISSION - LIBRARY (Hist)
1313 City Hall Annex Phone: (215)686-4543
Philadelphia, PA 19107 Dr. Richard Tyler, Hist.
Founded: 1955. **Staff:** Prof 8. **Subjects:** Philadelphia - architectural history, architecture, history. **Holdings:** 1500 books; 25 cabinets of manuscript records including insurance surveys, briefs of titles, photostats of old prints, photographs of buildings in Philadelphia. **Subscriptions:** 10 journals and other serials. **Services:** Library open to the public.

★11279★
PHILADELPHIA JEWISH ARCHIVES CENTER (Area-Ethnic)
Balch Institute
18 S. 7th St. Phone: (215)923-8090
Philadelphia, PA 19106 Lily G. Schwartz, Archv.
Staff: Prof 2. **Subjects:** Jewish community of Philadelphia - social welfare agencies, synagogues, fraternal organizations. **Holdings:** 1500 books; 1800 cubic feet of archival materials; 270 reels of microfilm. **Services:** Interlibrary loan; copying; center open to the public for reference use only. **Publications:** PJAC News, biennial; Guide to the Holdings of the Philadelphia Jewish Archives Center (1977). **Remarks:** Maintained by Federation of Jewish Agencies of Greater Philadelphia.

★11280★
PHILADELPHIA MARITIME MUSEUM - LIBRARY (Hist)
321 Chestnut St. Phone: (215)925-5439
Philadelphia, PA 19106 Dorothy Mueller Schneider, Libn.
Founded: 1974. **Staff:** 2. **Subjects:** Philadelphia port and general maritime history. **Special Collections:** Vessel registers (1500 volumes); Port Records, 1798 to present; Boat Plans (9000). **Holdings:** 10,000 books; 12 VF drawers of photographs; manuscripts; oral history tapes; microfilm; pamphlets; charts; maps. **Subscriptions:** 160 journals and other serials. **Services:** Copying; library open to the public by appointment. **Automated Operations:** Computerized cataloging. **Computerized Information Services:** OCLC. **Networks/Consortia:** Member of PALINET. **Staff:** Anna Smyth, Asst.Libn..

★11281★
PHILADELPHIA MUSEUM OF ART - LIBRARY (Art)
Box 7646 Phone: (215)763-8100
Philadelphia, PA 19101 Barbara Sevy, Libn.
Founded: 1876. **Staff:** Prof 4; Other 2. **Subjects:** Fine arts. **Special Collections:** Kienbusch Library of Arms and Armour (2500 volumes); museum archives. **Holdings:** 130,000 books, periodicals, pamphlets. **Subscriptions:** 450 journals and other serials. **Services:** Copying; library open to the public for reference use only on limited schedule. **Automated Operations:** Computerized cataloging and acquisitions. **Computerized Information Services:** RLIN. **Networks/Consortia:** Member of RLG, PALINET. **Special Indexes:** Index to Philadelphia Museum of Art Bulletin (card). **Staff:** Gina Erdreich, Res. & Ref.Libn.; Alice Lefton, Archv.; Thomas Donio, Slide Libn..

★11282★
PHILADELPHIA MUSEUM OF ART - SLIDE LIBRARY (Aud-Vis, Art)
Parkway at 26th St.
Box 7646 Phone: (215)763-8100
Philadelphia, PA 19101 Thomas S. Donio, Slide Libn.
Founded: 1939. **Staff:** 1. **Subjects:** History of art and architecture. **Holdings:** 112,225 slides (noncirculating). **Services:** Department not open to the public. **Remarks:** Figures include slides of works in the Rodin Museum and John G. Johnson Collection. Sales requests should be referred to Rosenthal Art Slides, 5456 S. Ridgewood Court, Chicago, IL 60615.

★11283★
PHILADELPHIA NEWSPAPERS, INC. - INQUIRER AND DAILY NEWS LIBRARY (Publ)
400 N. Broad St. Phone: (215)854-4665
Philadelphia, PA 19101 Mary Jo Crowley, Mgr.
Founded: 1925. **Staff:** 15. **Subjects:** Newspaper reference topics. **Holdings:** 6000 volumes; 600 pamphlets; clippings and photographs from Inquirer, Daily News, and selected New York papers and periodicals; Philadelphia Inquirer, 1926 to present, Daily News, 1960 to present, and New York Times, 1958 to present, on microfilm. **Subscriptions:** 32 journals and other serials; 50 newspapers. **Services:** Library not open to the public.

Computerized Information Services: NEXIS, DIALOG Information Services, VU/TEXT Information Services, DataTimes, Dow Jones News/Retrieval; electronic retrieval system for Daily News and Inquirer (internal database). **Special Indexes:** Philadelphia Inquirer index, 1926-1954 (card); selective index, 1955-1979.

★11284★
PHILADELPHIA ORCHESTRA ASSOCIATION - LIBRARY (Mus)
Academy of Music
Broad and Locust Sts. Phone: (215)893-1929
Philadelphia, PA 19102 Clinton F. Nieweg, Prin.Libn.
Founded: 1900. **Staff:** Prof 3. **Subjects:** Symphony orchestra music. **Holdings:** 4200 orchestrations with complete scores and parts; 15,200 choral parts (150 titles); 1500 scores. **Services:** Library open for research on premises only. **Remarks:** Alternate telephone numbers are 893-1954 and 893-1960. **Staff:** Robert M. Grossman, Libn.; Nancy M. Bradburd, Asst.Libn..

★11285★
PHILADELPHIA PSYCHIATRIC CENTER - PROFESSIONAL LIBRARY (Med)
Ford Rd. & Monument Ave. Phone: (215)877-2000
Philadelphia, PA 19131 Ann Vosburgh, Libn.
Staff: Prof 1. **Subjects:** Psychiatry, psychology, psychoanalysis, family therapy. **Holdings:** 7500 volumes. **Subscriptions:** 90 journals and other serials. **Services:** Interlibrary loan; copying (limited); library open to the public with restrictions. **Networks/Consortia:** Member of Greater Northeastern Regional Medical Library Program, PALINET.

PHILADELPHIA STATE HOSPITAL
See: Pennsylvania State Department of Public Welfare - Philadelphia State Hospital - Staff Library (11178)

★11286★
PHILATELIC FOUNDATION - ARCHIVES AND LIBRARY (Rec)
270 Madison Ave. Phone: (212)889-6483
New York, NY 10016 John F. Dunn, Dir. of Educ.
Staff: 3. **Subjects:** Philately. **Special Collections:** Luff Reference Collection; Ashbrook Correspondence and Special Service. **Holdings:** 1500 books; 200 bound periodical volumes; 5000 documents and archival materials. **Subscriptions:** 25 journals and other serials; 10 newspapers. **Services:** Copying; library open to members.

PHILBRICK LIBRARY OF DRAMATIC LITERATURE AND THEATER HISTORY
See: The Claremont Colleges - Libraries (3247)

★11287★
PHILBROOK MUSEUM OF ART - LIBRARY (Art)
Box 52510 Phone: (918)749-7941
Tulsa, OK 74152 Thomas E. Young, Libn.
Founded: 1939. **Staff:** Prof 1. **Subjects:** Art. **Special Collections:** Roberta Campbell Lawson Indian Library (1105 volumes). **Holdings:** 8000 books; 7000 bound periodical volumes; 81 VF drawers; 150 boxes of archival materials. **Subscriptions:** 143 journals and other serials. **Services:** Interlibrary loan; copying; library open to the public by appointment. **Remarks:** Located at 2727 South Rockford Road, Tulsa, OK 74114. **Formerly:** Philbrook Art Center.

★11288★
PHILIP MORRIS, U.S.A. - RESEARCH CENTER LIBRARY (Biol Sci)
Box 26583 Phone: (804)274-2877
Richmond, VA 23261 Marian Z. DeBardeleben, Assoc.Sr.Sci.
Founded: 1959. **Staff:** Prof 3; Other 3. **Subjects:** Tobacco, chemistry, biochemistry, botany, physics, plant physiology. **Holdings:** 30,000 books; 10,000 bound periodical volumes; 250 AV programs; 5000 microfiche; 21 VF drawers of clippings; 6500 reels of microfilm of periodicals. **Subscriptions:** 750 journals and other serials; 6 newspapers. **Services:** Interlibrary loan; library open to the public by appointment. **Automated Operations:** Computerized cataloging, acquisitions, serials, and circulation. **Computerized Information Services:** DIALOG Information Services, Pergamon ORBIT InfoLine, Inc., NLM, Mead Data Central, RLIN, CAS ONLINE, Dow Jones News/Retrieval, International Patent Documentation Center (INPADOC); Philip Morris Information Network (internal database). **Publications:** TIF Patent Update, monthly - for internal distribution only; Dictionary of Tobacco Terminology (book). **Special Catalogs:** Published Papers and Journal Holdings, annual (both printouts). **Staff:** Charity McDonald, Assoc.Libn.; Lucy Cook, Asst.Libn..

ISIDORE PHILIPP ARCHIVE AND MEMORIAL LIBRARY
See: University of Louisville - Dwight Anderson Memorial Music Library (16331)

★11289★
PHILIPPINE RESOURCE CENTER - LIBRARY (Area-Ethnic)
2288 Fulton St., No. 103
Box 40090 Phone: (415)548-2546
Berkeley, CA 94704 Victoria Flores, Adm.Off.
Founded: 1984. **Staff:** 4. **Subjects:** Philippines - economy, politics, society, culture, history. **Holdings:** 80 books; 75 bound periodical volumes; 400 other cataloged items. **Subscriptions:** 10 journals and other serials; 8 newspapers. **Services:** Library open to the public. **Publications:** Philippine Report (newsletter), monthly - to the public.

PHILIPS AUTOGRAPH LIBRARY
See: West Chester University - Francis Harvey Green Library - Special Collections (17645)

PHILIPS LABORATORIES RESEARCH LIBRARY
See: North American Philips Corporation (10293)

PHILIPSBURG STATE GENERAL HOSPITAL
See: Pennsylvania State Department of Public Welfare (11179)

★11290★
PHILLIPS 66 NATURAL GAS COMPANY - LIBRARY (Energy)
910 Plaza Office Bldg. Phone: (918)661-5803
Bartlesville, OK 74004 E. Jane Nichols, Supv., Rec.Mgt. & Lib.
Founded: 1951. **Staff:** 7. **Subjects:** Natural gas industry, natural gas liquids, energy industries. **Holdings:** 215 books; 262 paperback books. **Subscriptions:** 17 journals and other serials. **Services:** Library not open to the public.

★11291★
PHILLIPS ACADEMY - OLIVER WENDELL HOLMES LIBRARY - SPECIAL COLLECTIONS (Hum)
Andover, MA 01810 Phone: (617)475-3400
Linda Demmers, Dir.
Founded: 1796. **Staff:** Prof 5; Other 6. **Special Collections:** Charles H. Forbes Collection of Vergiliana and Bancroft Collection of Vergil Translations (1000 volumes and 450 pamphlets). **Services:** Interlibrary loan; copying; collections open to the public for reference use only on request. **Special Catalogs:** Catalog of the Charles H. Forbes Collection of Vergiliana in the Oliver Wendell Holmes Library.

★11292★
THE PHILLIPS COLLECTION - LIBRARY (Art)
1600 21st St., N.W. Phone: (202)387-2151
Washington, DC 20009 Karen Schneider, Libn.
Staff: 1. **Subjects:** 19th and 20th century European and American painting and sculpture. **Special Collections:** Phillips Collection exhibition catalogs; monographs on artists represented in the Phillips Collection. **Holdings:** 4000 books; 65 reels of microfilm of the Phillips Collection correspondence, 1920-1960; 20 VF drawers of exhibition catalogs, clippings, articles. **Subscriptions:** 30 journals and other serials. **Services:** Copying; library open to researchers by appointment.

★11293★
FRANK PHILLIPS FOUNDATION, INC. - WOOLAROC MUSEUM - LIBRARY (Area-Ethnic)
Rte. 3 Phone: (918)336-0307
Bartlesville, OK 74003 Linda Stone Laws, Cur. of Art
Subjects: Native American culture, art, early Americana, weaponry, natural history, history. **Holdings:** 800 books. **Subscriptions:** 15 journals and other serials. **Services:** Library open to the public with director's permission.

JAMES DUNCAN PHILLIPS LIBRARY
See: Essex Institute (4804)

PHILLIPS LIBRARY
See: Peabody Museum of Salem (11125)

★11294★
PHILLIPS, LYTLE, HITCHCOCK, BLAINE AND HUBER - LIBRARY (Law)
3400 Maine Midland Center Phone: (716)847-8400
Buffalo, NY 14203 Jeanne M. Kern, Libn.
Staff: Prof 2; Other 3. **Subjects:** New York law, federal law, taxation. **Holdings:** 24,000 books; 500 bound periodical volumes; 50 cassettes. **Subscriptions:** 430 journals and other serials; 7 newspapers. **Services:** Interlibrary loan; library not open to the public. **Computerized Information Services:** LEXIS, DIALOG Information Services, WESTLAW, Legislative Retrieval System (LRS). **Publications:** Library Newsletter; bibliographies, irregular - both for internal distribution only. **Special Catalogs:** Internal catalogs. **Staff:** Mary Ellen O'Hara, Asst.Libn..

PHILLIPS MEMORIAL LIBRARY
See: Providence College (11638)

★11295★
PHILLIPS PETROLEUM COMPANY - R&D LIBRARY (Energy, Sci-Engr)
102 PLB Phone: (918)661-3433
Bartlesville, OK 74004 Annabeth Robin, Lib.Supv.
Founded: 1945. **Staff:** Prof 2; Other 4. **Subjects:** Chemistry, petroleum science and technology, polymer science and technology, biotechnology, geosciences, plastics, physics. **Holdings:** 30,000 books; 25,000 bound periodical volumes; 2 million U.S. and foreign patents; 5500 microfilm cartridges; 20,000 U.S. Government reports on microfiche. **Subscriptions:** 1213 journals and other serials. **Services:** Library not open to the public. **Automated Operations:** Computerized public access catalog, cataloging, acquisitions, serials, and circulation. **Computerized Information Services:** Pergamon ORBIT InfoLine, Inc., DIALOG Information Services, NEXIS, OCLC; internal database. **Networks/Consortia:** Member of AMIGOS Bibliographic Council, Inc.. **Publications:** Selected Patent Listings; Library Bulletin - both for internal distribution only. **Staff:** Myrtle Ingerson, Cat.; Tanya Corle, ILL Libn.; Delpha Murphy, Acq.Libn.; Janet Elias, Ser.Libn..

SEYMOUR J. PHILLIPS HEALTH SCIENCES LIBRARY
See: Beth Israel Medical Center Hospital for Joint Diseases Orthopaedic Institute (1548)

STEPHEN PHILLIPS MEMORIAL LIBRARY
See: Penobscot Marine Museum (11223)

★11296★
PHILLIPS UNIVERSITY - GRADUATE SEMINARY LIBRARY (Rel-Phil)
University Sta., Box 2218 Phone: (405)237-4433
Enid, OK 73701 John L. Sayre, Dir.
Founded: 1907. **Staff:** Prof 5. **Subjects:** Religion. **Special Collections:** Discipliana. **Holdings:** 85,053 books; 11,319 bound periodical volumes; 22 VF drawers of pamphlets. **Subscriptions:** 413 journals and other serials. **Services:** Interlibrary loan; copying; library open to the public. **Automated Operations:** Computerized cataloging. **Computerized Information Services:** OCLC. **Networks/Consortia:** Member of AMIGOS Bibliographic Council, Inc.. **Staff:** Roberta Hamburger, Seminary Libn.; Linda Matthews, Acq.Libn.; Marilee Pralle, Pub.Serv.Libn.; Mary Louise Pendleton, Circ.Libn..

★11297★
PHILOSOPHICAL HERITAGE INSTITUTE - LIBRARY OF ESOTERIC STUDIES
Box 929
Fairbanks, AK 99707
Founded: 1971. **Subjects:** Esoterics, metaphysics, comparative religions, Tibetan studies, cosmology, New Age interests. **Holdings:** 2900 books; 3 VF drawers of unbound periodicals; 200 magnetic tapes; 1 drawer of past life regression research. **Remarks:** Presently inactive.

★11298★
PHILOSOPHICAL RESEARCH SOCIETY, INC. - PRS LIBRARY (Rel-Phil)
3910 Los Feliz Blvd. Phone: (213)663-2167
Los Angeles, CA 90027 Pearl M. Thomas, Libn.
Founded: 1934. **Staff:** Prof 1; Other 8. **Subjects:** Alchemy; astrology; Baconiana; ancient and modern philosophy; metaphysics; theosophy; rosicrucianism; orientalia - philosophy, culture, customs; freemasonry. **Special Collections:** Reiser; Parker; Manly P. Hall (founder and president); Le Plongeon (Yucatan; books; slides). **Holdings:** 50,000 books. **Services:** Interlibrary loan; copying; library open to the public. **Automated Operations:** Computerized public access catalog. **Publications:** Library Bulletin, irregular; Art Bulletin, quarterly; bibliography of alchemy and rosicrucian holdings. **Special Indexes:** Quarterly journal index; titles of holdings, special collections, and lecture notes by Manly P. Hall, founder and president (all on cards).

★11299★
FORD PHILPOT EVANGELISTIC ASSOCIATION - LIBRARY (Rel-Phil)
Box 3000 Phone: (606)276-1479
Lexington, KY 40533 Dr. Ford Philpot, Pres.
Subjects: Christianity. **Holdings:** 500 volumes. **Remarks:** Library located at 1815 Nicholasville Rd., Lexington, KY 40503.

★11300★
PHOENIX ART MUSEUM - LIBRARY (Art)
1625 N. Central Ave. Phone: (602)257-1222
Phoenix, AZ 85004 Clayton C. Kirking, Libn.
Founded: 1959. **Staff:** Prof 1; Other 1. **Subjects:** Painters and sculptors, history of painting and art, Egyptology, prints, museums and galleries (collections and exhibitions); 19th and 20th century American painting; 20th century Mexican art. **Special Collections:** Ambrose Lansing Collection of Egyptology (208 volumes); exhibition catalogs for one-man shows (9000); international auction records; museum bulletins (100 boxes); Orme Lewis Collection of Rembrandt Etching Catalogs; Art Libraries Societies Archives of Arizona Artists; Arizona Costume Institute Library (1000 volumes); P.A.M. Slide Collection (39,000 images). **Holdings:** 25,000 books; 520 bound periodical volumes; 152 file drawers of gallery catalogs, museum publications, artistic biographies, archives. **Subscriptions:** 109 journals and other serials. **Services:** Interlibrary loan; copying; library open to the public for reference use only. **Special Indexes:** Index of artists and subjects in exhibition and museum catalogs (card).

★11301★
PHOENIX DAY SCHOOL FOR THE DEAF - LIBRARY/MEDIA CENTER (Educ)
1935 W. Hayward Ave. Phone: (602)255-3448
Phoenix, AZ 85021 Donna L. Farman, Libn.
Staff: Prof 2. **Subjects:** Juvenile fiction, signed English. **Holdings:** 7000 books. **Subscriptions:** 18 journals and other serials. **Services:** Library not open to the public. **Staff:** Lois O. Carlson, Media Coord..

★11302★
PHOENIX ELEMENTARY SCHOOL DISTRICT NO. 1 - CURRICULUM LIBRARY (Educ)
125 E. Lincoln St. Phone: (602)257-3774
Phoenix, AZ 85004 Tom Lind, Media Supv.
Founded: 1956. **Staff:** Prof 2; Other 8. **Subjects:** Elementary education, Arizona history. **Special Collections:** Juvenile Trade Book Examination Center; 16mm film library (2500 films); Arizona Collection (800 volumes). **Holdings:** 12,000 books; 750 bound periodical volumes; 140 cassettes. **Subscriptions:** 60 journals and other serials. **Services:** Library not open to the public. **Automated Operations:** Computerized cataloging and circulation. **Publications:** Media News, monthly. **Staff:** Mary Brewer, Lib.Cat..

PHOENIX GAZETTE
See: Phoenix Newspapers, Inc. (11306)

★11303★
PHOENIX GENERAL HOSPITAL - MEDICAL LIBRARY (Med)
1950 W. Indian School Rd.
Box 21331 Phone: (602)279-4411
Phoenix, AZ 85015 Myrtle Idland, Libn.
Founded: 1958. **Staff:** Prof 1. **Subjects:** Internal medicine, surgery, pediatrics, orthopedics, obstetrics/gynecology. **Holdings:** 1294 books; 1784 bound periodical volumes. **Subscriptions:** 90 journals and other serials. **Services:** Interlibrary loan; copying; library open to the public for reference use only.

★11304★
PHOENIX INDIAN MEDICAL CENTER - LIBRARY (Med)
4212 N. 16th St. Phone: (602)263-1200
Phoenix, AZ 85016 Thomas Mead, Adm.Libn.
Founded: 1965. **Staff:** Prof 1; Other 1. **Subjects:** Medicine, nursing, dentistry. **Special Collections:** Indian history; Indian health. **Holdings:** 1800 books; 2000 bound periodical volumes; 524 medical tapes; 3000 unbound journals; 5 VF drawers of pamphlets and reprints. **Subscriptions:** 180 journals and other serials. **Services:** Interlibrary loan; copying (both limited); SDI; library open to the public for reference use only. **Automated**

Operations: Computerized cataloging, serials, and ILL. **Computerized Information Services:** MEDLINE, BRS Information Technologies; Indian Health (internal database); OnTyme Electronic Message Network Service (electronic mail service). **Publications:** List of acquisitions - for internal distribution only.

★11305★
PHOENIX MUTUAL LIFE INSURANCE COMPANY - LIBRARY (Bus-Fin)
One American Row Phone: (203)278-1212
Hartford, CT 06115 Margaret Colton, Libn.
Founded: 1915. **Staff:** 2. **Subjects:** Insurance, business, salesmanship, management, data processing. **Holdings:** 17,500 volumes. **Subscriptions:** 200 journals and other serials; 5 newspapers. **Services:** Interlibrary loan; copying; library open to the public by referral.

★11306★
PHOENIX NEWSPAPERS, INC. - LIBRARY (Publ)
Box 1950 Phone: (602)271-8115
Phoenix, AZ 85001 Paula Stevens, Lib.Dir.
Founded: 1948. **Staff:** Prof 6; Other 15. **Subjects:** Newspaper reference topics. **Special Collections:** Subject file of Arizona Republic and Phoenix Gazette clippings, 1948-1986 (7 million). **Holdings:** 2000 books; Arizona Republic and Phoenix Gazette, 1880 to present, on microfilm; 100,000 photographs; pamphlets; maps. **Subscriptions:** 120 journals and other serials; 30 newspapers. **Services:** Library not open to the public. **Automated Operations:** Computerized cataloging. **Computerized Information Services:** DIALOG Information Services, NEXIS, VU/TEXT Information Services, DataTimes, Dow Jones News/Retrieval, Washington Alert Service. **Publications:** Inside Information (newsletter), monthly - for internal distribution only. **Remarks:** Publishes the Arizona Republic, Phoenix Gazette, and Arizona Business Gazette. **Staff:** DeDe Leshy, Ref.Libn.; Philip Curdy, Ref.Libn.; Jennie Miller, Ref.Libn.; Heather Goebel, Ref.Libn.; Donna Colletta, Ref.Libn..

★11307★
PHOENIX PLANNING DEPARTMENT - LIBRARY (Plan)
Plaza Municipal Bldg.
125 E. Washington St.
Phoenix, AZ 85004-2342 Phone: (602)262-6881
Staff: 1. **Subjects:** General urban development, land use, economics, population, community facilities, public utilities, urban renewal, central business district, transportation. **Holdings:** 3200 books; 70 bound periodical volumes. **Subscriptions:** 65 journals and other serials. **Services:** Library open to the public.

★11308★
PHOENIX PUBLIC LIBRARY - ARIZONA ROOM (Area-Ethnic)
12 E. McDowell Rd. Phone: (602)262-6538
Phoenix, AZ 85004 Don Ellinghausen, Jr., Libn.
Staff: Prof 1; Other 1. **Subjects:** Phoenix and Arizona history, Southwestern Indians, Southwestern water and land use, Mexican Americans, Southwestern art. **Special Collections:** James Harvey McClintock papers, 1864-1934. **Holdings:** 17,500 books; 225 bound periodical volumes; Phoenix municipal records; Arizona Republic clipping file, 1977 to present. **Subscriptions:** 45 journals and other serials. **Services:** Copying; room open to the public.

★11309★
PHOENIX PUBLIC LIBRARY - ART OF THE BOOK ROOM (Rare Book)
12 E. McDowell Rd. Phone: (602)262-6110
Phoenix, AZ 85004 Edwin J. Saeger, Rare Bk.Libn.
Staff: Prof 1. **Subjects:** Shakespeare, Napoleon, book arts, rare books, fine editions, small presses. **Special Collections:** Alfred Knight Collection (Shakespeare, Napoleon, first editions, incunabula, Bibles; 2900 volumes). **Holdings:** 4000 volumes; incunabula; cuneiform tablets; scrolls; manuscripts. **Services:** Copying; room open to the public with restrictions. **Automated Operations:** Computerized cataloging, acquisitions, serials, and circulation. **Computerized Information Services:** OCLC, LIBRIS; internal database. Performs searches on fee basis. Contact Person: Tim Wherry, 262-4795. **Networks/Consortia:** Member of AMIGOS Bibliographic Council, Inc.. **Publications:** Newsletter - for internal distribution only.

★11310★
PHOENIX PUBLIC LIBRARY - ARTS & HUMANITIES UNIT (Hum)
12 E. McDowell Rd. Phone: (602)262-4602
Phoenix, AZ 85004 Clarence Dial, Libn.
Staff: Prof 8; Other 11. **Subjects:** History, Arizona history, literature, art, biography, music, religion. **Holdings:** 200,000 books. **Subscriptions:** 400 journals and other serials. **Services:** Interlibrary loan; copying; open to the public. **Automated Operations:** Computerized circulation. **Computerized Information Services:** Internal database. **Staff:** Elizabeth Belot, Libn.; Maria Eldringhoff, Libn.; Brenda Tevis, Libn..

★11311★
PHOENIX PUBLIC LIBRARY - BUSINESS & SCIENCES DEPARTMENT (Bus-Fin, Sci-Engr)
12 E. McDowell Rd. Phone: (602)262-6451
Phoenix, AZ 85004 Shera Farnham, Hd.
Staff: Prof 12; Other 6. **Subjects:** Business and economics, technology, social sciences, sciences, medicine, psychology. **Special Collections:** Arizona business; Arizona law; Career Center. **Holdings:** 200,000 books; government documents. **Subscriptions:** 900 journals and other serials. **Services:** Interlibrary loan; department open to the public. **Automated Operations:** Computerized cataloging, acquisitions, and serials. **Computerized Information Services:** DIALOG Information Services, VU/TEXT Information Services, OCLC. Contact Person: Tim Wherry, Comp.Serv.Ref.Coord., 261-8667. **Networks/Consortia:** Member of AMIGOS Bibliographic Council, Inc.. **Special Indexes:** Arizona business index (card). **Staff:** Stefanie Moritz, Libn.; Elizabeth Laurent, Bus.Spec.; Fern Eckhardt, Govt.Docs..

★11312★
PHOENIX PUBLIC LIBRARY - CRAFTS GALLERY (Art, Rec)
12 E. McDowell Rd. Phone: (602)262-4768
Phoenix, AZ 85004 Sandra Liberman, Libn.
Staff: Prof 1. **Subjects:** Ceramics, drawing, sewing, painting, needle arts, photography. **Holdings:** 15,300 books. **Subscriptions:** 58 journals and other serials. **Services:** Interlibrary loan; copying; gallery open to the public. **Special Indexes:** Handicrafts project index (card).

★11313★
PHOENIX PUBLIC LIBRARY - FOREIGN LANGUAGES - LIBRARY (Hum)
12 E. McDowell Rd. Phone: (602)262-4608
Phoenix, AZ 85004 Yvonne Murphy, Libn.
Staff: Prof 1. **Subjects:** Foreign language books in 29 languages - fiction, nonfiction, biography, literature, poetry, history, children's literature. **Holdings:** 10,000 books. **Subscriptions:** 20 journals and other serials; 7 newspapers. **Services:** Interlibrary loan; copying; open to the public. **Computerized Information Services:** DIALOG Information Services. Performs searches on fee basis. **Special Indexes:** Spanish collection index (vertical file).

★11314★
PHOENIX PUBLIC LIBRARY - MOTOR AND APPLIANCE REPAIR COLLECTION (Sci-Engr)
12 E. McDowell Rd. Phone: (602)262-6534
Phoenix, AZ 85004 Marjorie Sykes, Engr.Spec.
Staff: Prof 1. **Subjects:** Vehicle and motor repair; electronic data and schematics for computers, appliances, transistor and ham radios, and guns. **Holdings:** 3050 books; 10,000 schematics and 20 volumes of SAMS publications. **Subscriptions:** 17 journals and other serials. **Services:** Interlibrary loan; collection open to the public. **Computerized Information Services:** DIALOG Information Services.

★11315★
PHOENIX PUBLIC LIBRARY - SPECIAL NEEDS CENTER (Aud-Vis)
12 E. McDowell Rd. Phone: (602)261-8690
Phoenix, AZ 85004 Mary Roatch, Supv.
Staff: Prof 3; Other 4. **Subjects:** General collection. **Special Collections:** Learning disabilities (200 volumes); Technology for People with Disabilities (200 volumes); manual communication (150 volumes); basic adult collection (700 volumes). **Holdings:** 5800 books; 4000 large type books; 65 videotapes; 200 toys in toybrary. **Subscriptions:** 180 journals and other serials. **Services:** Center open to the public. **Publications:** Technology and the Handicapped (bibliography), annual; Manual Communications (bibliography), annual. **Special Catalogs:** Toybrary Catalog (large type).

★11316★
PHOTO RESEARCHERS, INC. - LIBRARY (Aud-Vis)
60 E. 56th St. Phone: (212)758-3420
New York, NY 10022 Robert L. Zentmaier, Pres.
Founded: 1956. **Staff:** 24. **Subjects:** Color and black/white photographic prints in the fields of natural history, travel, social studies, industry, technology, anthropology, biology, botany, medicine, education. **Special Collections:** Edited files of 1200 photographers; Science Library; National Audubon Society Collection. **Holdings:** 1 million original color transparencies and custom black/white prints. **Subscriptions:** 27 journals and other serials. **Services:** Photographs available for reproduction; library open to the public on fee basis. **Staff:** Terry Cordasci, Gen. Color Lib.; Cindy Popkin, Black/White Lib.; Bug Sutton, Sci.Libn.; John Kaprielian, Nat.Hist.Libn..

★11317★
PHOTO TRENDS - LIBRARY (Aud-Vis)
Box 650 Phone: (516)379-1440
Freeport, NY 11520 R. Eugene Keesee, Owner
Founded: 1968. **Staff:** Prof 1; Other 2. **Subjects:** Events of the last 60 years; children, education, nature, recent youth trends; science subjects, notably psychology, sociology and medicine, world figures, performers, artists, intellectuals. **Holdings:** 500,000 photographs. **Services:** Library not open to the public; sells photographs for reproduction in qualified publications; represents the library of Syndication International (London Daily Mirror), Camera Press (London, England), and Shooting Star (Hollywood, CA).

PHOTON AND CHARGED PARTICLE DATA CENTER
See: U.S. Natl. Bureau of Standards (15202)

★11318★
PHOTOPHILE - LIBRARY (Aud-Vis)
2311 Kettner Blvd. Phone: (619)234-4431
San Diego, CA 92101 Donna Wall, Dir.
Founded: 1968. **Staff:** Prof 1. **Subjects:** Industry, business, scenic photography, Southern California, recreation. **Holdings:** 150,000 color transparencies. **Services:** Copying; library open to the public. **Remarks:** Photophile is a stock photograph agency. Usage is for publications and advertising only.

★11319★
PHYSICS INTERNATIONAL COMPANY - LIBRARY (Sci-Engr)
2700 Merced St. Phone: (415)577-7278
San Leandro, CA 94577 M. Misegades, Libn.
Staff: Prof 1. **Subjects:** Physics, nuclear physics, electronics, mechanical engineering, computer software. **Holdings:** 3000 books; 8000 technical reports; 150 reels of microfilm of military and commercial standards and specifications. **Subscriptions:** 292 journals and other serials. **Services:** Interlibrary loan; library not open to the public. **Automated Operations:** Computerized cataloging, acquisitions, serials, and circulation. **Computerized Information Services:** DIALOG Information Services, Information Handling Services (IHS); PILIB (internal database). **Networks/Consortia:** Member of Bay Area Library and Information System (BALIS).

★11320★
JEAN PIAGET SOCIETY - LIBRARY (Soc Sci)
College of Education
University of Delaware Phone: (302)451-2311
Newark, DE 19716 Robert Wozniak, Pres.
Founded: 1971. **Staff:** Prof 1; Other 1. **Subjects:** Psychology, child development, education, language development, cognition. **Special Collections:** Catalog of the archives of Jean Piaget. **Holdings:** 400 books; 150 cataloged articles; 10 shelves of dissertations; journal articles; original manuscripts; speeches; films; cassette tapes. **Services:** Copying; library open to the public for reference use only. **Publications:** Journal, quarterly; Proceedings,

PICATINNY ARSENAL ARCHIVE
See: U.S. Army - Armament, Munitions & Chemical Command - Armament Research, Development & Engineering Center - Scientific & Tech.Info. Branch - Information Center (14705)

ALBERT PICK MUSIC LIBRARY
See: University of Miami - School of Music - Albert Pick Music Library (16409)

LAWRENCE MERCER PICK MEMORIAL LIBRARY
See: LaRabida Children's Hospital and Research Center (7662)

★11321★
PICKAWAY COUNTY LAW LIBRARY (Law)
Courthouse
Box 727 Phone: (614)474-6026
Circleville, OH 43113 William Ammer, Treas.
Subjects: Law. **Holdings:** 19,000 volumes.

COLONEL TIMOTHY PICKERING LIBRARY
See: Wenham Historical Association and Museum (17624)

PICKETT LIBRARY MEDIA CENTER
See: Alderson-Broaddus College (265)

RALPH E. PICKETT MEDICAL LIBRARY
See: Licking Memorial Hospital (7846)

PICKLER MEMORIAL LIBRARY
See: Northeast Missouri State University (10392)

★11322★
PICTORIAL PARADE INC. - LIBRARY (Aud-Vis)
130 W. 42nd St. Phone: (212)840-2026
New York, NY 10036 Baer M. Frimer, Pres.
Staff: Prof 6. **Subjects:** Current and historical events, foreign and domestic personalities, picture stories, Hollywood and TV stars. **Holdings:** Black/white photographs and prints; color transparencies. **Services:** Library open to bona fide researchers in the publishing and communications fields only.

★11323★
PIEDMONT BIBLE COLLEGE - GEORGE M. MANUEL MEMORIAL LIBRARY (Rel-Phil)
716 Franklin St. Phone: (919)725-8344
Winston-Salem, NC 27107 William P. Thompson, Hd.Libn.
Founded: 1947. **Staff:** Prof 2; Other 2. **Subjects:** Theology, religious education, education, philosophy, history, music. **Holdings:** 46,566 books; 1218 bound periodical volumes; 3600 other cataloged items. **Subscriptions:** 243 journals and other serials. **Services:** Interlibrary loan; copying; library open to the public. **Automated Operations:** Computerized cataloging. **Computerized Information Services:** Bibliofile (internal database). **Staff:** Cathie L. Chatmon, Asst.Libn./Ref..

★11324★
PIEDMONT HOSPITAL - SAULS MEMORIAL LIBRARY (Med)
1968 Peachtree Rd., N.W. Phone: (404)350-2222
Atlanta, GA 30309 Alice DeVierno, Med.Libn.
Staff: Prof 2; Other 1. **Subjects:** Clinical medicine, nursing. **Special Collections:** Patient education (1000 items). **Holdings:** 2500 books; 3500 bound periodical volumes; 200 video cassettes. **Subscriptions:** 200 journals and other serials. **Services:** Interlibrary loan; library not open to the public. **Computerized Information Services:** MEDLARS. **Networks/Consortia:** Member of Atlanta Health Science Libraries Consortium.

PIEDMONT PUBLISHING COMPANY - WINSTON-SALEM JOURNAL
See: Winston-Salem Journal (17939)

★11325★
PIEDMONT TECHNICAL COLLEGE - LIBRARY (Educ)
Emerald Rd.
P.O. Drawer 1467 Phone: (803)223-8357
Greenwood, SC 29648 Dan Koenig, Dean, Gen.Educ. & Lrng.Rscs.
Staff: Prof 2; Other 2. **Subjects:** Economics, technology, allied health, small business. **Holdings:** 24,000 books; 1700 AV programs. **Subscriptions:** 350 journals and other serials; 12 newspapers. **Services:** Interlibrary loan; copying; library open to the public. **Automated Operations:** Computerized public access catalog, cataloging, and circulation. **Computerized Information Services:** DIALOG Information Services, OCLC. **Networks/Consortia:** Member of SOLINET. **Staff:** Ruth Nicholson, Lib.Coord..

★11326★
PIERCE COUNTY LAW LIBRARY (Law)
930 Tacoma Ave., S. Phone: (206)591-7494
Tacoma, WA 98402 Janet Gildenhar, Law Libn.
Founded: 1933. **Staff:** Prof 2; Other 1. **Subjects:** Primary and secondary law. **Holdings:** 25,000 books. **Subscriptions:** 21 journals and other serials. **Services:** Copying; library open to the public for reference use only. **Automated Operations:** Computerized public access catalog and cataloging. **Computerized Information Services:** WESTLAW; internal database. Performs searches on fee basis. **Staff:** Tina Aure, Asst. Law Libn..

★11327★
PIERCE COUNTY MEDICAL LIBRARY (Med)
315 South K St.
Box 5299 Phone: (206)572-5340
Tacoma, WA 98405-0986 Ms. Marion Von Bruck, Coord., Lib.Serv.
Staff: 3. **Subjects:** Medicine. **Holdings:** 1553 books; 1222 bound periodical volumes; 10 VF drawers. **Subscriptions:** 165 biomedical and administrative journals. **Services:** Interlibrary loan; copying; translations; library open to members of the Medical Society of Pierce County, hospital employees of participating hospitals, and by private membership to other professionals. **Computerized Information Services:** NLM, MEDLARS, Knowledge Index. **Networks/Consortia:** Member of Western Library Network (WLN). **Publications:** Pierce County Medical Library Bulletin, monthly. **Special Catalogs:** Union Catalog of consortium's holdings. **Remarks:** Central resource facility of Pierce County Medical Library Consortium, a consortium that includes the satellite libraries of eight hospitals; holdings of the consortium total 2932 books and 264 journal subscriptions.

★11328★
FRANKLIN PIERCE LAW CENTER - LIBRARY (Law)
2 White St. Phone: (603)228-1541
Concord, NH 03301 Judith A. Gire, Law Libn./Asst.Prof.
Staff: Prof 5; Other 3. **Subjects:** Law. **Holdings:** 107,429 volumes; 194,906 microfiche. **Subscriptions:** 1894 journals and other serials. **Services:** Interlibrary loan; copying; SDI; library open to the public. **Computerized Information Services:** WESTLAW, DIALOG Information Services. Performs searches on fee basis. Contact Person: Sherry Gratton, Tech.Serv.Libn.. **Networks/Consortia:** Member of New England Law Library Consortium (NELLCO). **Staff:** Cynthia Landau, Asst. Law Libn.; Joyce Galvin, Ser.Supv..

★11329★
PIERCE/GOODWIN/ALEXANDER - LIBRARY/RESOURCE CENTER (Plan)
800 Bering Dr.
Box 13319 Phone: (713)977-5777
Houston, TX 77219 Peggy Kelley, Libn.
Founded: 1980. **Staff:** Prof 1. **Subjects:** Architecture, interiors. **Holdings:** 690 books; 79 bound periodical volumes; 1600 vendor catalogs; vendor samples; 100 maps. **Subscriptions:** 72 journals and other serials. **Services:** Library not open to the public. **Special Indexes:** Index to product literature (card).

LAWRENCE J. PIERCE RHODODENDRON LIBRARY
See: Rhododendron Species Foundation (12033)

DEAN PIEROSE MEMORIAL HEALTH SCIENCES LIBRARY
See: Moritz Community Hospital (9314)

★11330★
PIERSON, BALL & DOWD - LAW LIBRARY (Law)
1200 18th St., N.W. Phone: (202)429-3830
Washington, DC 20036 Sandra Peterson, Libn.
Staff: Prof 2; Other 3. **Subjects:** Law - communications, labor, taxation, health care; government contracts. **Holdings:** 12,000 books; 300 bound periodical volumes. **Subscriptions:** 150 journals and other serials; 10 newspapers. **Services:** Interlibrary loan; copying; library open to the public with restrictions. **Automated Operations:** Computerized cataloging and serials. **Computerized Information Services:** LEXIS, NEXIS, DIALOG Information Services, Dun & Bradstreet Corporation, LEGI-SLATE, NewsNet, Inc., Dow Jones News/Retrieval, VU/TEXT Information Services; ABA/net (electronic mail service). **Staff:** Margaret Allin, Asst.Libn..

WILLIAM PIERSON MEDICAL LIBRARY
See: Hospital Center at Orange (6481)

★11331★
PIGEON DISTRICT LIBRARY - SPECIAL COLLECTIONS (Hist)
7236 Nitz St. Phone: (517)453-2341
Pigeon, MI 48755 Naomi R. Jantzi, Dir.
Founded: 1913. **Special Collections:** Michigan Collection; toys (300). **Services:** Interlibrary loan; copying; SDI; collections open to the public. **Automated Operations:** Computerized cataloging, serials, and circulation. **Computerized Information Services:** OCLC. Performs searches free of charge.

★11332★
PIKES PEAK LIBRARY DISTRICT - LOCAL HISTORY COLLECTION (Hist, Aud-Vis)
20 N. Cascade
Box 1579 Phone: (719)473-2080
Colorado Springs, CO 80901 Ree Mobley, Local Hist.Libn.
Staff: Prof 4; Other 4. **Subjects:** History - Pikes Peak, Colorado High Plains, local gold mining towns. **Special Collections:** Myron Wood photograph collection (5000 photographs documenting the Southwest); Mathews Collection (100 glass negatives, circa 1890); Payne Collection (52,000 negatives from Colorado Springs Gazette, 1950-1975); Stewart Collection (3000 photographs and negatives of Colorado Springs/Pikes Peak area, 1896-1970). **Holdings:** 23,000 books; 2000 bound periodical volumes; 5000 pamphlets; 1000 maps; 27,000 clippings; 100 cubic feet of manuscript material from League of Women Voters of Pikes Peak Region; 30 cubic feet of manuscript material from Mental Health Association; 30 cubic feet of Chase Stone papers; 50 cubic feet of Cliff House papers; 50 Gordon Sweet blueprints; 30 cubic feet of Ghost Town papers; 2 reels of microfilm of Pike National Forest History file. **Subscriptions:** 110 journals and other serials; 16 newspapers. **Services:** Interlibrary loan; copying; collection open to the public. **Automated Operations:** Computerized cataloging, acquisitions, and circulation. **Computerized Information Services:** LOGIN; Local Authors, Local Documents Data Base (internal databases). **Publications:** TIP Sheet, monthly - for internal distribution and to mailing list. **Special Indexes:** Indexes to Gazette Telegraph (book), Free Press (card), Colorado City Iris (book), and Pike National Forest (book). **Staff:** Nancy Thaler, Asst.Libn.; Orlando Archibeque, Local Docs.Libn..

★11333★
PILGRIM CONGREGATIONAL CHURCH - LIBRARY (Rel-Phil)
2310 E. 4th St. Phone: (218)724-8503
Duluth, MN 55812 Judy Casserberg, Libn.
Staff: 4. **Subjects:** Bible, liberal theology, church and social action, United Church of Christ and Congregational history, social issues, meditation and prayer. **Holdings:** 1670 books. **Services:** Library open to the public. **Automated Operations:** Computerized cataloging. **Publications:** Newsletter - for internal distribution only.

★11334★
PILGRIM PSYCHIATRIC CENTER - HEALTH SCIENCES LIBRARY (Med)
Bldg. 23
Box A Phone: (516)231-8000
West Brentwood, NY 11717 Aime Atlas, Sr.Libn.
Founded: 1932. **Staff:** Prof 2; Other 2. **Subjects:** Psychiatry, social sciences, psychology, medicine, nursing. **Holdings:** 6000 books; 120 bound periodical volumes; 8 VF drawers of pamphlets and clippings; 3 VF drawers of reports and manuscripts; 1 VF drawer of documents; 145 reels of microfilm; 260 cassette tapes. **Subscriptions:** 120 journals and other serials; 7 newspapers. **Services:** Interlibrary loan; copying; library open to the public. **Staff:** Irving Tredwell, Jr., Asst.Libn..

★11335★
PILGRIM SOCIETY - PILGRIM HALL LIBRARY (Hist)
75 Court St. Phone: (617)746-1620
Plymouth, MA 02360-3891 Laurence R. Pizer, Dir.
Founded: 1820. **Staff:** Prof 4; Other 1. **Subjects:** Pilgrim history, Plymouth, Massachusetts and Plymouth Colony, 1620-1692. **Special Collections:** William Brewster imprints; books that belonged to the Pilgrims; rare book collection (300 volumes). **Holdings:** 10,000 books; 1000 bound periodical volumes; 4000 photographs; 12,000 manuscripts, maps, prints, charts, ephemera. **Services:** Copying; library open to researchers by appointment. **Publications:** The Pilgrim Journal; A Brief Guide to the Pilgrim Society Library Collections. **Special Catalogs:** Catalog of artifacts. **Special Indexes:** Index to manuscripts, Rare Book Inventory. **Staff:** Elizabeth L. Balcom, Cur., Mss. & Bks..

★11336★
PILLSBURY COMPANY - BUSINESS REFERENCE LIBRARY (Bus-Fin)
Pillsbury Center, 27th Fl.
Mail Station 2754 Phone: (612)330-4047
Minneapolis, MN 55402 Rachel Berry, Dir.
Founded: 1959. **Staff:** Prof 6; Other 2. **Subjects:** Consumer products marketing, marketing research, food industry, foodservice industry, supermarket industry, advertising research, management training. **Special Collections:** Pillsbury primary market research projects (15,000 documents). **Holdings:** 700 books; 790 reference titles; 3500 subject documents; 5000 microfiche. **Subscriptions:** 260 journals and other serials. **Services:** Library not open to the public. **Computerized Information**

Services: Online systems. **Publications:** Extracts from Current Periodicals, weekly; New Products Bulletin, weekly; Consumerism Issues Status, monthly; Acquisitions Listing, monthly - all for internal distribution only. **Special Indexes:** New Products Index, classed by company; Company Index; internally generated subject index; internal materials indexed via library-developed thesaurus. **Remarks:** Maintains a Consumer Service Library specializing in cookbooks and recipe development materials. **Staff:** Barbara Rostad, Res.Libn.; Sandra Date, Sr.Libn.; Peter Sidney, Sr.Libn..

★11337★
PILLSBURY COMPANY - TECHNICAL INFORMATION CENTER (Food-Bev)
311 Second St., S.E. Phone: (612)330-4750
Minneapolis, MN 55414 James B. Tchobanoff, Mgr.
Founded: 1941. **Staff:** Prof 3; Other 3. **Subjects:** Food science and technology, cereal chemistry, microbiology, mathematics, statistics, agriculture, plant science. **Holdings:** 6200 books; 8500 bound periodical volumes; 40,000 patents; 35,000 internal reports. **Subscriptions:** 425 journals and other serials. **Services:** Interlibrary loan; SDI; center open to the public by appointment on limited schedule. **Automated Operations:** Computerized cataloging and circulation of journals. **Computerized Information Services:** DIALOG Information Services, MEDLINE, CAS ONLINE, Pergamon ORBIT InfoLine, Inc., OCLC; internal database; OnTyme Electronic Message Network Service, DIALMAIL (electronic mail services). **Networks/Consortia:** Member of Metronet. **Publications:** Food Patent Digest, monthly; Current Literature, monthly - all for internal distribution only. **Special Indexes:** KWIC index to research notebooks and internal reports. **Staff:** Patricia Schumacher, Tech.Serv.Libn.; Dennis Pedersen, Sr.Tech.Info.Sci..

★11338★
PILLSBURY, MADISON AND SUTRO - LIBRARY (Law)
Box 7880 Phone: (415)983-1130
San Francisco, CA 94120 Lynn A. Green, Dir., Lib. & Info.Serv.
Staff: Prof 5; Other 17. **Subjects:** Law. **Holdings:** Figures not available. **Services:** Interlibrary loan; library not open to the public. **Remarks:** Library located at 225 Bush St., San Francisco, CA 94104.

★11339★
PILOTS INTERNATIONAL ASSOCIATION - LIBRARY (Sci-Engr)
Box 907 Phone: (612)588-5175
Minneapolis, MN 55440 Sharon Neuenfeldt, Libn.
Staff: Prof 1; Other 1. **Subjects:** Aviation. **Holdings:** 75 books; 2 VF drawers of aviation clippings; 3 VF drawers of information on aviation organizations. **Subscriptions:** 15 journals and other serials. **Services:** Interlibrary loan; copying; library open to the public with restrictions.

PILSUDSKI ARCHIVES
See: Yale University - Slavic & East European Collections (18148)

★11340★
JOZEF PILSUDSKI INSTITUTE OF AMERICA - LIBRARY AND ARCHIVES (Hist, Area-Ethnic)
381 Park Ave., S., Suite 701 Phone: (212)683-4342
New York, NY 10016 Mr. Jan Weiss, Dir.
Founded: 1943. **Staff:** Prof 2. **Subjects:** Polish history and politics, 1863 to present; United States history. **Special Collections:** Diplomatic and military documents of Polish Chief of State Jozef Pilsudski's Military Chancellery (45,000). **Holdings:** 13,000 books; 220 linear feet of bound periodical volumes; 399 linear feet of archival documents; 30,000 clippings; 1900 titles of cataloged pamphlets; 15,000 pictures; 500 maps; 498 reels of microfilm. **Subscriptions:** 21 journals and other serials; 19 newspapers. **Services:** Interlibrary loan; copying; SDI; library open to the public. **Publications:** Niepodleglusi (in Polish with English summaries). **Staff:** Zofia Doliwa, Libn..

★11341★
PIMA COUNCIL ON AGING - LIBRARY (Soc Sci)
2955 E. Broadway Phone: (602)795-5800
Tucson, AZ 85716-5311 Mary C. Guilbert, Libn.
Staff: Prof 1; Other 1. **Subjects:** Aging programs and services, gerontology, longterm care. **Holdings:** 100 books; 24 VF drawers; 4000 other cataloged items. **Subscriptions:** 30 journals and other serials; 200 newsletters; 6 newspapers. **Services:** Interlibrary loan; copying; SDI; library open to the public by appointment. **Automated Operations:** Computerized cataloging and acquisitions.

★11342★
PIMA COUNTY JUVENILE COURT CENTER - LIBRARY (Law)
2225 E. Ajo Way Phone: (602)882-2082
Tucson, AZ 85713 Gwen Reid, Ct.Libn.
Founded: 1978. **Staff:** Prof 1. **Subjects:** Juvenile crime, penal institutions, adolescent problems, drug addiction, status offenses, sexual and child abuse. **Holdings:** 800 books. **Subscriptions:** 30 journals and other serials. **Services:** Copying; library open to the public with restrictions.

★11343★
PIMA COUNTY LAW LIBRARY (Law)
New Courts Bldg.
110 W. Congress
Tucson, AZ 85701-1317 Phone: (602)792-8456
Founded: 1915. **Staff:** Prof 1; Other 3. **Subjects:** Law, taxation. **Special Collections:** Conciliation Court - Family, Marriage, and Woman (605 periodicals); Court Clinic Social Pathology and Criminology (100 periodicals). **Holdings:** 42,700 volumes. **Subscriptions:** 80 journals and other serials. **Services:** Copying; library open to judges, attorneys, and authorized legal personnel. **Special Catalogs:** State Supreme Court & Court of Appeals current slip opinions. **Remarks:** Maintained by Pima County Superior Courts.

★11344★
PIMA COUNTY PLANNING AND DEVELOPMENT SERVICES DEPARTMENT - LIBRARY (Plan)
130 W. Congress St. Phone: (602)792-8361
Tucson, AZ 85701-1317 Paul Matty, Libn.
Founded: 1975. **Staff:** Prof 1. **Subjects:** Land use planning, demography, natural features. **Holdings:** 4000 books; 300 maps. **Subscriptions:** 50 journals and other serials. **Services:** Interlibrary loan; copying; SDI; library open to the public by appointment.

★11345★
PIMERIA ALTA HISTORICAL SOCIETY - MUSEUM/ ARCHIVES (Hist)
223 Grand Ave.
Box 2281
Nogales, AZ 85628-2281 Phone: (602)287-5402
Subjects: Prehistory and history of Southern Arizona and Northern Sonora, 1000 to present; border history; mining; ranching; archeology. **Special Collections:** City of Nogales archives; oral history tapes of local history, business activities, ranching, women's history. **Holdings:** 2000 books; 5 periodicals. **Services:** Copying; museum and archives open to the public for reference use only.

★11346★
PINAL COUNTY HISTORICAL SOCIETY, INC. - LIBRARY (Hist)
715 S. Main St.
Box 851 Phone: (602)868-4382
Florence, AZ 85232 Mary A. Faul, Libn.
Staff: Prof 1. **Subjects:** Arizona and Southwest history, Pinal County. **Holdings:** 460 books; 75 bound periodical volumes; clippings and pictures of local history. **Services:** Library open to researchers with restrictions.

★11347★
PINE REST CHRISTIAN HOSPITAL - VAN NOORD HEALTH SCIENCES LIBRARY (Med)
300 68th St., S.E. Phone: (616)455-5000
Grand Rapids, MI 49508-6999 Thomas Van Dam, Libn.
Founded: 1962. **Staff:** Prof 1; Other 1. **Subjects:** Psychiatry, psychiatric nursing, psychiatric social work, clinical psychology. **Holdings:** 3000 books; 75 other cataloged items; 4 VF drawers of pamphlets. **Subscriptions:** 110 journals and other serials. **Services:** Interlibrary loan (fee); copying; library open to mental health professionals.

★11348★
PINE RIDGE HOSPITAL - LIBRARY (Med)
150 Wyoming St. Phone: (307)332-5700
Lander, WY 82520 Jane Heuer, Libn.
Founded: 1986. **Staff:** 1. **Subjects:** Alcohol and drug abuse, psychiatry, anorexia and bulemia. **Holdings:** 100 books. **Subscriptions:** 19 journals and other serials. **Services:** Interlibrary loan; copying; library open to public at librarian's discretion. **Computerized Information Services:** MEDLARS. Performs searches on fee basis. **Networks/Consortia:** Member of Wind River Health Science Library Consortium.

★11349★
PINELAND CENTER - LIBRARY AND MEDIA CENTER (Med)
Box E Phone: (207)688-4811
Pownal, ME 04069-0902 Sally Ward, Dir., Staff Dev.
Founded: 1958. **Staff:** 3. **Subjects:** Developmental disabilities, mental retardation, epilepsy, autism, cerebral palsy, medicine. **Holdings:** 400 books; 20 videotapes; 5 films. **Subscriptions:** 20 journals and other serials. **Services:** Interlibrary loan; copying; library open to the public. **Computerized Information Services:** BRS Information Technologies, MEDLINE. **Networks/Consortia:** Member of Health Science Library and Information Cooperative of Maine (HSLIC).

★11350★
PINELLAS COUNTY JUVENILE WELFARE BOARD - MAILANDE W. HOLLAND LIBRARY (Soc Sci)
4140 49th St., N. Phone: (813)521-1853
St. Petersburg, FL 33709 Alison R. Birmingham, Libn.
Founded: 1976. **Staff:** Prof 1; Other 1. **Subjects:** Child welfare, marriage and family therapy, juvenile delinquency, substance abuse, child abuse and neglect, day care and early childhood education, primary prevention, adolescent health, mental health, advocacy for economically disadvantaged, legislation, administration, funding and grant writing, community planning and development, community education. **Special Collections:** Funding collection (20 volumes). **Holdings:** 800 books; 300 government documents; 150 AV programs. **Subscriptions:** 82 journals and other serials. **Services:** Interlibrary loan; library open to Pinellas County residents and child-serving professionals. **Networks/Consortia:** Member of Tampa Bay Library Consortium, Inc.. **Publications:** Bulletin, quarterly.

★11351★
PINELLAS COUNTY LAW LIBRARY - CLEARWATER BRANCH (Law)
315 Court St.
Clearwater, FL 34616-5165 Phone: (813)462-3411
Staff: 2. **Subjects:** Law, taxes. **Holdings:** 20,100 volumes. **Subscriptions:** 43 journals and other serials. **Services:** Copying; library open to the public for reference use only. **Staff:** Patricia E. Spaulding, Libn.; Margaret Shewell, Libn..

★11352★
PINELLAS COUNTY LAW LIBRARY - ST. PETERSBURG BRANCH - ALLEN C. ANDERSON MEMORIAL LAW LIBRARY (Law)
Judicial Bldg., Rm. 500
545 1st Ave., N. Phone: (813)825-1875
St. Petersburg, FL 33701 Martha F. Otting, Libn.
Founded: 1949. **Staff:** 2. **Subjects:** Law. **Holdings:** 30,000 volumes. **Subscriptions:** 100 journals and other serials. **Services:** Copying; library open to the public for reference use only. **Staff:** Alice J. Snyder, Asst.Libn..

★11353★
PINELLAS COUNTY SCHOOL BOARD - MIRROR LAKE/ TOMLINSON ADULT VOCATIONAL CENTER - LIBRARY/ MEDIA CENTER (Educ)
709 Mirror Lake Dr. Phone: (813)821-4593
St. Petersburg, FL 33701 Helen G. Campbell, Media Spec.
Founded: 1969. **Staff:** Prof 2; Other 3. **Subjects:** Adult education - Adult Basic Education (ABE), high school, General Equivalency Diploma (GED); art; painting; English for foreign born; commercial art and advertising; office skills training; cosmetology; industrial sewing; jewelry design, manufacturing, repair; watch repair; arts and crafts; foreign languages; music; reupholstery; sewing; creative writing; woodworking and wood carving; lip reading; sign language; private investigation. **Holdings:** 9900 books; 1451 filmstrips; 431 phonograph records; 8765 slides; 5 16mm films; 1685 tape recordings; 20 microfiche; 39 videotapes; charts; models. **Subscriptions:** 160 journals and other serials. **Services:** Interlibrary loan; copying; center open to the public.

★11354★
PIONEER HI-BRED INTERNATIONAL, INC. - CORPORATE LIBRARY (Agri)
400 Locust, Suite 700 Phone: (515)245-3518
Des Moines, IA 50309 Gala J. Rolofson, Corp.Libn.
Founded: 1983. **Staff:** Prof 1; Other 1. **Subjects:** Agriculture, agribusiness, law, taxation, business. **Holdings:** 1500 books. **Subscriptions:** 399 journals and other serials. **Services:** Interlibrary loan; library not open to the public. **Automated Operations:** Computerized cataloging, serials, and circulation. **Computerized Information Services:** DIALOG Information Services, Pergamon ORBIT InfoLine, Inc., BRS Information Technologies, LEXIS, NEXIS, OCLC, On-Line Research, Inc., I/S Datacentralen, Dow Jones News/Retrieval, Occupational Health Services, Inc.; BASIS (internal database). Performs searches on fee basis.

★11355★
PIONEER HI-BRED INTERNATIONAL, INC. - PLANT BREEDING RESEARCH LIBRARY (Agri)
7301 N.W. 62nd Ave. Phone: (515)270-3147
Johnston, IA 50131 Helen Hoeven, Res.Libn.
Founded: 1982. **Staff:** Prof 1. **Subjects:** Plant breeding, crop science, plant genetics, agriculture. **Holdings:** 1521 books; 250 bound periodical volumes. **Subscriptions:** 220 journals and other serials. **Services:** Interlibrary loan; copying; SDI; library open to the public with restrictions. **Automated Operations:** Computerized cataloging, acquisitions, and serials. **Computerized Information Services:** DIALOG Information Services, Pergamon ORBIT InfoLine, Inc., BRS Information Technologies, AGNET, National Pesticide Information Retrieval System (NPIRS), AgriData Network, Telenet Communications Corporation, TYMNET, Germplasm Resources Information Network (GRIN); internal database. **Networks/Consortia:** Member of Bibliographical Center for Research, Rocky Mountain Region, Inc. (BCR). **Publications:** Newsletter - for internal distribution only.

PIONEER MEMORIAL MUSEUM
See: U.S. Natl. Park Service - Olympic Natl. Park (15334)

PIONEER MUSEUM, ARIZONA HISTORICAL SOCIETY ARCHIVES
See: Northern Arizona University - Cline Library - Special Collections (10414)

PIONEER VALLEY RESOURCE CENTER
See: Greenfield Community College (5870)

PIONEERS' MUSEUM
See: Colorado Springs Pioneers' Museum (3418)

★11356★
PIPER & MARBURY - LAW LIBRARY (Law)
36 S. Charles St., Suite 1100 Phone: (301)576-1617
Baltimore, MD 21201 Katherine E. Hobner, Libn.
Staff: 4. **Subjects:** Law. **Holdings:** 35,000 volumes. **Subscriptions:** 70 journals and other serials; 16 newspapers. **Services:** Interlibrary loan; library not open to the public. **Automated Operations:** Computerized cataloging. **Computerized Information Services:** LEXIS, DIALOG Information Services, WESTLAW.

★11357★
PIPESTONE COUNTY HISTORICAL SOCIETY - RESEARCH LIBRARY (Hist)
113 S. Hiawatha Phone: (507)825-2563
Pipestone, MN 56164 David Rambow, Asst.Musm.Dir.
Subjects: Local, county, and state history. **Special Collections:** Rose biographies (unpublished). **Holdings:** 500 books; 150 bound periodical volumes; 212 reels of microfilm; oral history transcripts; county newspapers. **Services:** Copying; library open to the public with restrictions. **Special Indexes:** Obituary index (card); biography index (card).

PIPESTONE NATIONAL MONUMENT
See: U.S. Natl. Park Service (15340)

CHESLEY A. PIPPY, JR. MEDICAL LIBRARY
See: Grace General Hospital (5770)

PIRATE HOUSE LIBRARY
See: Cumberland County Historical Society (3924)

★11358★
MALCOLM PIRNIE, INC. - TECHNICAL LIBRARY (Env-Cons, Sci-Engr)
2 Corporate Park Dr.
Box 751
White Plains, NY 10602 Phone: (914)694-2100
Staff: Prof 1; Other 1. **Subjects:** Environmental engineering, water supply and treatment, pollution control. **Holdings:** 15,000 volumes; 1000 U.S. Environmental Protection Agency reports. **Subscriptions:** 150 journals and other serials. **Services:** Copying; requests for library access individually evaluated. **Computerized Information Services:** DIALOG Information Services. **Publications:** Current Awareness, weekly - for internal distribution only.

GEORGE W. PIRTLE GEOLOGICAL SCIENCES LIBRARY
See: University of Kentucky (16316)

★11359★
PISCATAQUIS COUNTY LAW LIBRARY (Law)
Court House Annex Phone: (207)564-2181
Dover-Foxcroft, ME 04426 Elaine H. Roberts, Libn.
Staff: 1. **Subjects:** Law. **Holdings:** 5500 volumes. **Services:** Library not open to the public.

PITCAIRN ISLANDS STUDY CENTER
See: Pacific Union College (11020)

★11360★
PITMAN-MOORE, INC. - RESEARCH & DEVELOPMENT LIBRARY (Sci-Engr)
1331 S. First St.
Box 207 Phone: (812)232-0121
Terre Haute, IN 47808 Lori E. Wahl, Lib.Supv.
Founded: 1927. **Staff:** Prof 2; Other 5. **Subjects:** Chemistry, microbiology, animal health and nutrition, mining, agriculture. **Holdings:** 10,000 books; 30,000 bound periodical volumes; 40,000 internal reports; chemical patents in microform; microfilm. **Subscriptions:** 450 journals and other serials. **Services:** Interlibrary loan; SDI; library open to the public by appointment. **Automated Operations:** Computerized public access catalog, cataloging, serials, and circulation. **Computerized Information Services:** DIALOG Information Services, Pergamon ORBIT InfoLine, Inc., OCLC, NLM, Mead Data Central, Dow Jones News/Retrieval, Dun & Bradstreet Corporation, NewsNet, Inc., INVESTEXT; internal database. **Networks/Consortia:** Member of INCOLSA. **Formerly:** International Minerals & Chemicals Corporation. **Staff:** Kurt O. Baumgartner, Sr.Assoc.Info.Sci..

★11361★
PITNEY BOWES - TECHNICAL INFORMATION CENTER (Info Sci)
World Headquarters
Location 26-00 Phone: (203)854-7569
Stamford, CT 06926-0786 Teresa Wilkins, Mgr.
Founded: 1953. **Staff:** Prof 1; Other 2. **Subjects:** Telecommunications, electronics, optics, chemistry, printing technology, physics, electrophotography, computers. **Holdings:** 3500 books; 75 reels of microfilm. **Subscriptions:** 350 journals and other serials. **Services:** Interlibrary loan; center not open to the public. **Automated Operations:** Computerized cataloging, serials, and circulation. **Computerized Information Services:** DIALOG Information Services, BRS Information Technologies, OCLC; internal database. **Networks/Consortia:** Member of Southwestern Connecticut Library Council (SWLC). **Publications:** New Acquisitions, monthly; orientation sheet. **Special Catalogs:** Technical report file; laboratory notebook.

★11362★
PITNEY, HARDIN, KIPP & SZUCH - LAW LIBRARY (Law)
163 Madison Ave.
CN 1945 Phone: (201)267-3333
Morristown, NJ 07960 Julie L. Von Schrader, Libn.
Staff: Prof 1; Other 3. **Subjects:** Law. **Special Collections:** New Jersey Statutes, 1680 to present (200 publications). **Holdings:** 27,000 books; 1000 bound periodical volumes; 100 video cassettes. **Subscriptions:** 70 journals and other serials; 7 newspapers. **Services:** Interlibrary loan; copying; library open to attorneys for reference use only on request. **Computerized Information Services:** LEXIS, DIALOG Information Services, WESTLAW, CIS, Dow Jones News/Retrieval.

★11363★
PITT-DES MOINES, INC. - ENGINEERING LIBRARY (Sci-Engr)
3400 Grand Ave. Phone: (412)331-3000
Pittsburgh, PA 15225-1508 Louise Franz, Libn.
Staff: Prof 1. **Subjects:** Engineering. **Holdings:** 800 books; 200 bound periodical volumes; 16 VF drawers of technical reports; 700 binders of clippings. **Subscriptions:** 50 journals and other serials. **Services:** Interlibrary loan; library not open to the public.

AMELIA WHITE PITTS MEMORIAL LIBRARY
See: Baptist Medical Center (1320)

PITTS THEOLOGY LIBRARY
See: Emory University - Pitts Theology Library (4684)

★11364★
PITTSBURG STATE UNIVERSITY - LEONARD H. AXE LIBRARY - SPECIAL COLLECTIONS (Hist)
S. Joplin Phone: (316)231-7000
Pittsburg, KS 66762 Eugene H. DeGruson, Spec.Coll.Libn.
Founded: 1903. **Special Collections:** Haldeman-Julius Collection (45,000 items); Southeast Kansas Collection (110,500 items); Kansas and U.S. documents (161,000); college and community archives (21,300 archival materials). **Services:** Interlibrary loan; copying; collections open to the public. **Automated Operations:** Computerized cataloging, serials, circulation, and ILL. **Computerized Information Services:** DIALOG Information Services, Pergamon ORBIT InfoLine, Inc., BRS Information Technologies, MEDLARS. **Networks/Consortia:** Member of Southeast Kansas Library System, Bibliographical Center for Research, Rocky Mountain Region, Inc. (BCR).

★11365★
PITTSBURGH BOARD OF EDUCATION - PROFESSIONAL LIBRARY (Educ)
635 Ridge Ave. Phone: (412)323-4146
Pittsburgh, PA 15212 Dorothy Hopkins, Libn.
Founded: 1928. **Staff:** Prof 1. **Subjects:** Education, early childhood through high school. **Special Collections:** Depository for Pittsburgh Public School textbooks; courses of study and Board of Education minutes. **Holdings:** 15,000 books; 20 drawers of pamphlets, clippings, reports, articles; 12 VF drawers of archival material. **Subscriptions:** 230 journals, newsletters, and other serials; 5 newspapers. **Services:** Interlibrary loan; copying; library open to the public for research only. **Computerized Information Services:** BRS Information Technologies, OCLC. **Networks/Consortia:** Member of Pittsburgh Regional Library Center (PRLC). **Staff:** Judy G. Mizik, Dir., Lib.Serv..

★11366★
PITTSBURGH CORNING CORPORATION - TECHNICAL LIBRARY (Sci-Engr)
800 Presque Isle Dr. Phone: (412)327-6100
Pittsburgh, PA 15239 Lorraine Wellosencuk, Libn.
Founded: 1962. **Subjects:** Glass, ceramics, chemistry, physics, materials engineering. **Holdings:** 2000 books; 2600 bound periodical volumes; 3500 patents.

★11367★
PITTSBURGH HISTORY & LANDMARKS FOUNDATION - JAMES D. VAN TRUMP LIBRARY (Hist)
450 Landmarks Bldg.
Station Square Phone: (412)471-5808
Pittsburgh, PA 15219 Walter C. Kidney, Archv.
Staff: Prof 2. **Subjects:** History of Pittsburgh and Western Pennsylvania, architecture, architectural history, historic preservation, landscaping, transportation. **Special Collections:** Architectural drawings, maps, sketches, prints; speeches of James D. Van Trump (manuscripts; recordings; notes); engineering drawings by Samuel Diescher. **Holdings:** 3000 books; 20 bound periodical volumes; 20 VF drawers of Pittsburgh clippings and brochures; 40 drawers of slides; 50 audiotapes; 30 drawers of architectural and engineering drawings and maps; 32 shelves of plat books; 50 loose-leaf manuscripts; 20 unbound periodical titles. **Subscriptions:** 12 journals and other serials. **Services:** Library open to the public with restrictions.

PITTSBURGH PLATE GLASS COMPANY
See: PPG Industries, Inc. (11499)

★11368★
PITTSBURGH POST-GAZETTE PUBLISHING COMPANY - LIBRARY (Publ)
50 Blvd. of the Allies Phone: (412)263-1397
Pittsburgh, PA 15222 Angelika R. Kane, Libn.
Staff: Prof 4. **Subjects:** Newspaper reference topics. **Special Collections:** Movie stills. **Holdings:** 500 books; 30 bound periodical volumes; 400 VF drawers of clippings; 6 VF drawers of subject files; 150,000 picture files; 15 drawers of microfilm. **Subscriptions:** 32 journals and other serials; 24 newspapers. **Services:** Copying (limited); library open to the public. **Automated Operations:** Computerized circulation. **Computerized Information Services:** NEXIS. **Special Catalogs:** Photograph catalog (card). **Special Indexes:** Index to newspaper clippings files (notebooks).

★11369★
PITTSBURGH PRESS - LIBRARY (Publ)
Boulevard of the Allies Phone: (412)263-1480
Pittsburgh, PA 15230 Eileen E. Finster, Hd.Libn.
Founded: 1884. **Staff:** Prof 1; Other 5. **Subjects:** Newspaper reference topics. **Holdings:** 250 books; clippings; photographs; Pittsburgh Press, 1884 to present, on microfilm. **Services:** Library not open to the public.

★11370★
PITTSBURGH THEOLOGICAL SEMINARY - CLIFFORD E. BARBOUR LIBRARY (Rel-Phil)
616 N. Highland Ave. Phone: (412)362-5610
Pittsburgh, PA 15206 Stephen D. Crocco, Libn.
Founded: 1794. **Staff:** Prof 2; Other 4. **Subjects:** Theology, philosophy. **Special Collections:** Newburgh Collection (17th and 18th century theological works); James Warrington Collection of hymnology. **Holdings:** 211,389 volumes; 5285 microforms; 616 phonograph records; 896 theses; 1131 tapes; 6050 archival materials. **Subscriptions:** 886 journals and other serials. **Services:** Interlibrary loan; library open to undergraduate students with special permission from their institutions. **Automated Operations:** Computerized cataloging and serials. **Computerized Information Services:** Online systems. **Networks/Consortia:** Member of Pittsburgh Regional Library Center (PRLC). **Publications:** Bibliographia Tripotamopolitana, irregular.

★11371★
PITTSBURGH TOY LENDING LIBRARY, INC. (Educ)
5410 Baum Blvd.
Pittsburgh, PA 15232 Phone: (412)682-4430
Founded: 1974. **Staff:** 21. **Subjects:** Toys - imaginative play, cognitive development, infant; parenting; children's books. **Holdings:** 1000 books; 5000 toys. **Services:** Interlibrary loan; library open to members. **Networks/Consortia:** Member of U.S.A. Toy Library Association.

PLACE NAME SURVEY OF THE UNITED STATES
See: American Name Society (614)

★11372★
PLACER COUNTY LAW LIBRARY (Law)
350 Nevada St. Phone: (916)823-4391
Auburn, CA 95603 Tanemi Klahn, Law Libn.
Staff: Prof 1. **Subjects:** Law. **Holdings:** 5030 volumes; 26 cassettes. **Services:** Interlibrary loan; library open to the public.

★11373★
PLACER DOME INC. - LIBRARY (Sci-Engr)
Bentall Postal Sta., P.O. Box 49330 Phone: (604)682-7082
Vancouver, BC, Canada V7X 1P1 Julie Bolden
Staff: 1. **Subjects:** Geology, mining, metallurgy, business and economics. **Holdings:** 10,000 books. **Subscriptions:** 280 journals and other serials; 20 newspapers. **Services:** Interlibrary loan; library not open to the public. **Automated Operations:** Computerized serials and acquisitions. **Computerized Information Services:** DIALOG Information Services, QL Systems; Envoy 100 (electronic mail service). **Formerly:** Placer Development, Ltd.

★11374★
PLAIN DEALER PUBLISHING COMPANY - LIBRARY (Publ)
1801 Superior Ave. Phone: (216)344-4195
Cleveland, OH 44114 Patti A. Graziano, Lib.Dir.
Founded: 1956. **Staff:** Prof 4; Other 7. **Subjects:** Newspaper reference topics. **Special Collections:** Great Lakes; Ohio and Cleveland history. **Holdings:** 3970 books; 500,000 pictures; 4.8 million clippings; 4811 reels of microfilm; 38 VF drawers of pamphlets. **Subscriptions:** 200 journals and other serials; 65 newspapers. **Services:** Interlibrary loan; library not open to the public. **Special Catalogs:** Subject Authority File (printout).

★11375★
PLAINFIELD PUBLIC LIBRARY - GUILFORD TOWNSHIP HISTORICAL COLLECTION (Hist)
1120 Stafford Rd. Phone: (317)839-6602
Plainfield, IN 46168 Susan Miller Carter, Hist.Libn.
Staff: Prof 1; Other 2. **Subjects:** History and genealogy - Plainfield, Hendricks, Morgan, Montgomery, Putnam, and Boone counties; Society of Friends Western Yearly Meeting; local authors. **Holdings:** 4769 books; 120 bound periodical volumes; 24 oral history tapes and transcripts; 2 file drawers of photographs; 14 file drawers of clippings and pamphlets; 84 boxes of manuscripts; obituary file; 360 reels of microfilm of local newspapers; 23 reels of microfilm of census data; 100 reels of microfilm of local history materials. **Subscriptions:** 22 journals and other serials; 7 newspapers. **Services:** Copying; collection open to the public by appointment. **Special Indexes:** Indexes for Hendricks County authors, biographies, 50th wedding anniversaries, place-names, obituaries, local newspapers, Maple Hill cemetery (cards); name indexes for books of local interest (book).

★11376★
PLAINS ART MUSEUM - LIBRARY (Art)
106 5th St., S. Phone: (218)236-7171
Moorhead, MN 56560 Susan Talbot-Stanaway, Cur., Educ.
Staff: 1. **Subjects:** Art history, museology. **Holdings:** 40 books; 200 unbound periodicals; 30 videotapes; 30 cassette tapes. **Services:** Library not open to the public.

★11377★
PLAINS HEALTH CENTRE - DR. W.A. RIDDELL HEALTH SCIENCES LIBRARY (Med)
4500 Wascana Pkwy. Phone: (306)584-6426
Regina, SK, Canada S4S 5W9 Beth Silzer, Dir.
Staff: Prof 1; Other 3. **Subjects:** Medicine, nursing, pharmacy, physiotherapy. **Holdings:** 4764 books; 4500 bound periodical volumes; 800 AV programs. **Subscriptions:** 294 journals and other serials. **Services:** Interlibrary loan; SDI; library open to health sciences personnel. **Automated Operations:** Computerized cataloging. **Computerized Information Services:** DIALOG Information Services; Envoy 100 (electronic mail service).

★11378★
PLANETARY ASSOCIATION FOR CLEAN ENERGY, INC. (PACE) - CLEAN ENERGY CENTRE (Energy)
191 Promenade du Portage, No. 600 Phone: (819)777-9696
Hull, PQ, Canada J8X 2K6 Monique Michaud, Hd.
Founded: 1984. **Staff:** Prof 4; Other 3. **Subjects:** Biological effects of electromagnetic radiation, clean energy systems, emerging energy sciences, food irradiation; biomass energy; problems associated with video display systems. **Special Collections:** Nikola Tesla Collection; T. Henry Moray Collection. **Holdings:** 10,000 books; 500 bound periodical volumes; emerging energy science and technology manuscripts. **Subscriptions:** 160 journals and other serials. **Services:** Interlibrary loan; copying; center open to the public. **Computerized Information Services:** Emerging Energy Science (internal database). Performs searches on fee basis. Contact Person: Dr. Andrew Michrowski.

PLANETARY IMAGE CENTER
See: Lunar and Planetary Institute (8107)

★11379★
PLANETREE - HEALTH RESOURCE CENTER (Med)
2040 Webster St. Phone: (415)923-3680
San Francisco, CA 94115 Tracey Cosgrove, Med.Libn.
Staff: Prof 1; Other 5. **Subjects:** Consumer health information, preventive medicine, self-care, holistic health, body systems and diseases, nutrition, fitness, pharmaceutical drugs. **Holdings:** 2000 books; 19 VF drawers of clippings; 2000 entries in Information and Reference System. **Subscriptions:** 55 journals and other serials; 5 newspapers. **Services:** Copying; center open to the public. **Computerized Information Services:** DIALOG Information Services, DataTimes, NLM. **Networks/Consortia:** Member of San Francisco Biomedical Library Group. **Publications:** Planetalk Newsletter, 2/year. **Formerly:** Program Planetree.

★11380★
PLANNED PARENTHOOD ASSOCIATION OF ST. LOUIS - FAMILY PLANNING LIBRARY (Med)
2202 S. Hanley Rd. Phone: (314)781-3800
St. Louis, MO 63144 Cindy Mohrhard, Info. & Ref.Asst.
Founded: 1972. **Staff:** Prof 2. **Subjects:** Family planning, human reproduction, sexually transmitted diseases, pregnancy, homosexuality, human sexuality, abortion, parenting. **Special Collections:** Birth Control Review, 1922-1927 (complete); Social Welfare Forum, 1948-1965. **Holdings:** 500 books; 20 bound periodical volumes; clippings and articles. **Subscriptions:** 11 journals and other serials. **Services:** Copying; library open to the public by appointment for reference use.

★11381★
PLANNED PARENTHOOD CENTER OF SAN ANTONIO - LIBRARY (Med)
104 Babcock Rd. Phone: (512)736-2244
San Antonio, TX 78201 Susan Cox, Exec.Dir.
Founded: 1939. **Staff:** Prof 2. **Subjects:** Birth control, population, human sexuality, sex education, family planning, ecology, environment, women's

health, teenage pregnancy. **Holdings:** 1500 books; 500 periodicals; pamphlets; vertical files; 100 films, filmstrips, slide sets. **Subscriptions:** 35 journals and other serials. **Services:** Interlibrary loan; copying; library open to the public with restrictions. **Networks/Consortia:** Member of Planned Parenthood Federation of America, Inc.. **Publications:** Pamphlets on V.D and birth control. **Special Catalogs:** Interregional Library Loan Catalog; PPCSA Media Catalog. **Staff:** Diane Trujillo, Commun.Educ.Coord..

★11382★
PLANNED PARENTHOOD OF CENTRAL INDIANA - RESOURCE CENTER (Med)
3209 N. Meridian St. Phone: (317)925-6686
Indianapolis, IN 46208 Katy Smith, Libn.
Founded: 1980. **Staff:** 1. **Subjects:** Birth control, human sexuality, teen pregnancy, human reproduction, abortion, sex education, women's health. **Holdings:** 1000 books; 110 films and videotapes; vertical files; poster collection. **Subscriptions:** 66 journals and other serials. **Services:** Copying; center open to the public. **Networks/Consortia:** Member of Central Indiana Area Library Services Authority (CIALSA).

★11383★
PLANNED PARENTHOOD OF CLEVELAND, INC. - LIBRARY (Med)
1501 Euclid Ave., Suite 300 Phone: (216)781-0410
Cleveland, OH 44115 Betsey C. Kaufman, Exec.Dir.
Founded: 1928. **Staff:** 1. **Subjects:** Birth control and contraceptives, family planning, population, sexuality, family life education. **Special Collections:** Historical information on the birth control movement. **Holdings:** 600 books; 12 films. **Subscriptions:** 10 journals and other serials. **Services:** Copying; library open to health, social, and medical professionals and parents.

★11384★
PLANNED PARENTHOOD FEDERATION OF AMERICA, INC. - KATHARINE DEXTER MC CORMICK LIBRARY (Med)
810 Seventh Ave. Phone: (212)541-7800
New York, NY 10019 Gloria A. Roberts, Hd.Libn.
Staff: Prof 2; Other 1. **Subjects:** Family planning in the U.S., contraceptives, abortion and sterilization, history of birth control, population, sex, sex education. **Holdings:** 4000 books; 35 VF drawers of journal articles, reprints, unpublished mimeographs. **Subscriptions:** 150 journals and other serials. **Services:** Interlibrary loan (articles only); copying; library open to the public for reference use only. **Computerized Information Services:** DIALOG Information Services; LINK (Library and Information Network; internal database). Performs searches on fee basis. **Networks/Consortia:** Member of APLIC International Census Network, New York Metropolitan Reference and Research Library Agency (METRO), Manhattan-Bronx Health Sciences Library Group. **Publications:** A Family Planning Library Manual; A Small Library in Family Planning; Current Literature in Family Planning (review of books and journal articles in the field, annotated and classified), monthly; Directory of Population Research and Family Planning Training Centers in the U.S.A., 1980-1981. **Remarks:** An alternate phone number is 603-4637. **Staff:** Zeau D. Modig, Assoc.Libn..

★11385★
PLANNED PARENTHOOD OF HOUSTON & SOUTHEAST TEXAS, INC. - MARY ELIZABETH HUDSON LIBRARY (Med)
3601 Fannin St. Phone: (713)522-6363
Houston, TX 77004 Natalie H. Thrall, Volunteer Libn.
Founded: 1970. **Staff:** 3. **Subjects:** Sexuality education, family planning, parenting, reproductive health, reproductive rights, population, women's issues. **Holdings:** 2500 books; 100 bound periodical volumes; 400 file folders of reprints and newspaper clippings. **Subscriptions:** 23 journals and other serials. **Services:** Copying; library open to the public with restrictions.

★11386★
PLANNED PARENTHOOD OF MINNESOTA - PHYLLIS COOKSEY RESOURCE CENTER (Med)
1965 Ford Pkwy. Phone: (612)698-2401
St. Paul, MN 55116 Catherine J. McMahon, Rsrc.Ctr.Coord.
Founded: 1972. **Staff:** Prof 2. **Subjects:** Family planning, population growth, human sexuality, abortion, sex education. **Special Collections:** Works of Margaret Sanger (8 volumes). **Holdings:** 1500 books; 12 VF drawers of pamphlets and ephemera; 100 films, filmstrips, video and audio cassettes. **Subscriptions:** 90 journals and other serials. **Services:** Copying; center open to the public. **Publications:** Acquisitions lists, newsnotes, semiannual - free upon request; list of other publications - available upon request. **Staff:** Sandi Milburn, Rsrc.Libn..

PLANNED PARENTHOOD NEW YORK CITY
See: Margaret Sanger Center-Planned Parenthood New York City (12856)

★11387★
PLANNED PARENTHOOD OF NORTHERN NEW ENGLAND - PPNNE RESOURCE CENTER (Med)
23 Mansfield Ave. Phone: (802)862-9637
Burlington, VT 05401 Jan Hughes Fuller, Educ.Rsrc.Coord.
Founded: 1967. **Staff:** Prof 1. **Subjects:** Family life education, sexual development, parenting and child care, women's health, infertility. **Special Collections:** Agency history; sex education. **Holdings:** 2300 books; 4 VF drawers of articles. **Subscriptions:** 30 journals and other serials; 30 newsletters. **Services:** Interlibrary loan; copying; center open to the public. **Computerized Information Services:** Internal database. **Publications:** Edsource, 3/year - to area educators; K-12 Family Life Curriculum - for sale.

★11388★
PLANNED PARENTHOOD OF SOUTHEASTERN PENNSYLVANIA - RESOURCE CENTER (Med)
1220 Sansom St. Phone: (215)592-4108
Philadelphia, PA 19107 Martha Fuller, Rsrc.Ctr.Adm.
Founded: 1975. **Staff:** Prof 1. **Subjects:** Family planning, reproductive health, venereal diseases, childbearing and pregnancy options, sex education. **Holdings:** 2500 books; 40 bound periodical volumes; 10 VF drawers; 70 slides, videotapes, films, filmstrips. **Subscriptions:** 61 journals and other serials. **Services:** Copying; SDI; center open to the public for reference use only. **Networks/Consortia:** Member of Greater Northeastern Regional Medical Library Program. **Publications:** List of publications - available on request.

★11389★
PLANNED PARENTHOOD OF SOUTHWESTERN INDIANA, INC. - RESOURCE CENTER (Med)
Hebron Plaza
971 Kenmore Dr. Phone: (812)473-8800
Evansville, IN 47715-7503 Donna Reed, Dir. of Educ.
Subjects: Contraceptives, sexuality, family life education curriculum, women's health, infertility, population. **Holdings:** 300 books; 5 VF drawers. **Services:** Interlibrary loan; copying; center open to the public by appointment for reference use. **Networks/Consortia:** Member of Evansville Area Health Sciences Libraries Consortium, Planned Parenthood Federation of America, Inc..

★11390★
PLANNED PARENTHOOD OF WISCONSIN - MAURICE RITZ RESOURCE LIBRARY AND BOOKSTORE (Med)
1046 N. 12th St. Phone: (414)271-6033
Milwaukee, WI 53233 Ann H. McIntyre, Libn.
Founded: 1972. **Staff:** Prof 1; Other 1. **Subjects:** Birth control, nursing education, human sexuality, sex education, population. **Holdings:** 3000 books; 12 VF drawers of clippings and reports; 100 pamphlets, booklets, reprints; 80 films, slides, tapes, filmstrip kits, videotapes. **Subscriptions:** 31 journals and other serials. **Services:** Interlibrary loan; copying; library open to the public. **Networks/Consortia:** Member of Library Council of Metropolitan Milwaukee, Inc. (LCOMM). **Publications:** Audiovisual list; pamphlets list; material available for rent or purchase; subject bibliographies.

★11391★
PLANNING COUNCIL FOR HEALTH AND HUMAN SERVICES - RESOURCE INFORMATION CENTER (Med)
1442 N. Farwell, No. 300 Phone: (414)224-0404
Milwaukee, WI 53202-2913 Nancy Fletcher, Coord.
Founded: 1976. **Staff:** Prof 1. **Subjects:** Health and health facility planning, health care cost containment, health promotion/wellness, hospitals, worksite wellness, business and health. **Holdings:** 2000 books and unbound reports. **Subscriptions:** 20 journals and other serials. **Services:** Copying; center open to the public with restrictions on circulation. **Networks/Consortia:** Member of Library Council of Metropolitan Milwaukee, Inc. (LCOMM), Southeastern Wisconsin Health Science Library Consortium (SWHSL). **Formerly:** Southeastern Wisconsin Health Systems Agency.

★11392★
PLANNING FORUM - LIBRARY (Bus-Fin)
5500 College Corner Pike Phone: (513)523-4185
Oxford, OH 45056 Ron Lerman, Pres.
Founded: 1985. **Subjects:** Corporate planning. **Holdings:** 700 volumes. **Services:** Library open to members only.

★11393★
PLANNING RESEARCH CORPORATION - TECHNICAL LIBRARY (Comp Sci, Info Sci)
1500 Planning Research Dr. Phone: (703)556-1131
McLean, VA 22102 Marion C. Kersey, Lib.Mgr.
Founded: 1961. **Staff:** Prof 5. **Subjects:** Computer software, engineering, information science. **Holdings:** 10,000 books; 100 bound periodical volumes; 5000 company reports; 3000 documents. **Subscriptions:** 350 journals and other serials; 10 newspapers. **Services:** Interlibrary loan; library not open to the public. **Automated Operations:** Computerized cataloging, acquisitions, serials, and circulation. **Computerized Information Services:** DIALOG Information Services, Pergamon ORBIT InfoLine, Inc., DTIC, NEXIS, Procurement Automated Source System (PASS), Dow Jones News/Retrieval, Dun & Bradstreet Corporation, Aerospace Online, InfoMaster, LS/2000; OCLC; EasyLink (electronic mail service). **Networks/Consortia:** Member of Metropolitan Washington Library Council, Interlibrary Users Association (IUA), CAPCON. **Publications:** Journal Holdings list; library brochure. **Staff:** Jo E. Mueller, Ref./Info.Serv.Libn.; LeAnn Vliet, ILL; Patricia Wolf, Acq./Cat.; Patricia Gorman, Ref./Info.Serv.Libn..

★11394★
MORTON F. PLANT HOSPITAL - MEDICAL LIBRARY (Med)
323 Jeffords St.
Box 210 Phone: (813)462-7889
Clearwater, FL 34617 Cynthia Schmid, Med.Libn.
Founded: 1955. **Staff:** Prof 1. **Subjects:** Medicine, nursing, hospital administration. **Holdings:** 1050 books; 900 bound periodical volumes; 400 volumes on microfiche. **Subscriptions:** 143 journals and other serials. **Services:** Interlibrary loan; copying; SDI; library open to the public by appointment. **Automated Operations:** Computerized serials. **Computerized Information Services:** MEDLARS, DIALOG Information Services; OnTyme Electronic Message Network Service, DOCLINE (electronic mail services). Performs searches on fee basis. **Networks/Consortia:** Member of Tampa Bay Medical Library Network.

★11395★
PLANTING FIELDS ARBORETUM - HORTICULTURAL LIBRARY (Biol Sci)
Planting Fields Rd. Phone: (516)922-9024
Oyster Bay, NY 11771 Elizabeth K. Reilley, Dir.
Founded: 1975. **Staff:** Prof 2; Other 1. **Subjects:** Horticulture, botany. **Holdings:** 5000 books. **Subscriptions:** 50 journals and other serials. **Services:** Copying; library open to the public for reference use only. **Staff:** Helen S. Moskowitz, Asst. to Dir..

★11396★
PLASTICS INSTITUTE OF AMERICA - LIBRARY (Sci-Engr)
Stevens Institute of Technology
Castle Point Sta. Phone: (201)420-5552
Hoboken, NJ 07030 Mary Ann Sherger, Educ.Coord.
Staff: 1. **Subjects:** Polymer science and engineering. **Holdings:** Figures not available. **Services:** Copying; library open to the public with restrictions. **Publications:** Polymer Science and Engineering Programs, biennial; Foodplas Proceedings; Recyclingplas Proceedings; Secondary Reclamation of Plastics Waste - all for sale. **Remarks:** An alternate telephone number is 420-5553.

★11397★
PLATT SACO LOWELL CORPORATION - ENGINEERING LIBRARY (Sci-Engr)
Drawer 2327 Phone: (803)859-3211
Greenville, SC 29602 Alice K. Dill, Patent Techn.
Founded: 1850. **Staff:** Prof 1. **Subjects:** Engineering, textile machinery and manufacture, patent and trademark law. **Special Collections:** U.S. and British patents on textile machinery. **Holdings:** 3000 books; 1500 bound periodical volumes; 300,000 patent copies; 1500 microfiche cards of abstracts and patents; 2000 paper copies of abstracts and patents. **Subscriptions:** 85 journals and other serials. **Services:** Library not open to the public except with prior permission.

★11398★
PLATTE RIVER POWER AUTHORITY - LIBRARY (Energy)
Timberline & Horsetooth Rds. Phone: (303)226-4000
Fort Collins, CO 80525 Rosalie Feldman, Libn.
Staff: Prof 1; Other 1. **Subjects:** Electric energy. **Holdings:** 2000 books; 300 reports; clippings. **Subscriptions:** 240 journals and other serials; 25 newspapers. **Services:** Interlibrary loan; copying; library open to the public with restrictions. **Automated Operations:** Computerized cataloging, serials, and routing. **Computerized Information Services:** DIALOG Information Services. **Networks/Consortia:** Member of High Plains Regional Library Service System. **Publications:** Additions to the Library, quarterly.

★11399★
PLAYBOY ENTERPRISES, INC. - PHOTO LIBRARY (Aud-Vis)
919 N. Michigan Ave. Phone: (312)751-8000
Chicago, IL 60611 Clydia Jones, Pict.Libn.
Staff: 3. **Holdings:** 10 million pictures. **Services:** Library not open to the public.

PLAYWRIGHTS UNION OF CANADA
See: Manitoba Association of Playwrights - Library/Archive (8354)

MARIAM J. PLEAK MEMORIAL LIBRARY AND ARCHIVE
See: Hobart Historical Society, Inc. (6367)

PLENUM PUBLISHING CORPORATION - IFI/PLENUM DATA COMPANY
See: IFI/Plenum Data Company (6677)

★11400★
PLESSEY/STROMBERG-CARLSON - ENGINEERING LIBRARY (Info Sci)
400 Rinehart Rd. Phone: (407)244-1438
Lake Mary, FL 32746 Harriet Watkins, Libn.
Staff: Prof 1. **Subjects:** Telephony, engineering, computer science and language, mathematics, science. **Holdings:** 1000 books; 100 bound periodical volumes; 200 archival materials; 100 reels of microfilm; reports. **Subscriptions:** 100 journals and other serials; 5 newspapers. **Services:** Interlibrary loan; library not open to the public.

★11401★
PLIMOTH PLANTATION, INC. - LIBRARY (Hist)
Warren Ave.
Box 1620 Phone: (617)746-1622
Plymouth, MA 02360 James W. Baker, Hd. of Res.
Founded: 1949. **Staff:** Prof 2; Other 2. **Subjects:** New England history, 16th and 17th century social history, early travel and exploration, crafts, antiques, colonial archeology. **Holdings:** 3000 books; 3000 pamphlets; 4 volumes of Plymouth Colony wills (photocopies). **Subscriptions:** 80 journals and other serials. **Services:** Library open to the public for reference use only. **Staff:** Carolyn Freeman Travers, Res.Libn..

PLIMPTON LIBRARY
See: Columbia University - Rare Book and Manuscript Library (3493)

OSCAR PLOTKIN LIBRARY
See: North Shore Congregation Israel - Romanek Cultural Center (10368)

★11402★
PLOUGH, INC. - RESEARCH LIBRARY (Med)
3030 Jackson Ave.
Box 377 Phone: (901)320-2702
Memphis, TN 38151 Martha Hurst, Libn.
Staff: Prof 1. **Subjects:** Pharmacology, cosmetics, medicine, chemistry. **Holdings:** 1600 books; 1800 bound periodical volumes; 3000 reprints. **Subscriptions:** 113 journals and other serials. **Services:** Interlibrary loan; library open to the public by permission only. **Computerized Information Services:** DIALOG Information Services, NLM. **Networks/Consortia:** Member of Association of Memphis Area Health Sciences Libraries (AMAHSL).

★11403★
PLUMAS COUNTY LAW LIBRARY (Law)
Court House
Box 686
Quincy, CA 95971 Phone: (916)283-1840
Staff: Prof 1. **Subjects:** State and federal law. **Holdings:** 8000 volumes. **Services:** Interlibrary loan; copying; library open to the public for reference use only.

★11404★
PLUMBING AND HEATING WHOLESALERS OF NEW ENGLAND, INC. - LIBRARY (Sci-Engr)
262 Main St.
Box 638 Phone: (508)478-8621
Milford, MA 01757 Maurice A. Desmarais, Exec. V.P.
Subjects: Plumbing and heating. **Holdings:** 300 surveys and reports, training manuals, management and sales texts.

★11405★
PLUMMER MEMORIAL PUBLIC HOSPITAL - LIBRARY (Med)
969 Queen St., E. Phone: (705)759-3434
Sault Ste. Marie, ON, Canada P6A 2C4 Kathy You, Dir., Lib.Serv.
Founded: 1979. **Staff:** Prof 1. **Subjects:** Medicine, nursing, allied health sciences, management, psychiatry, social work. **Holdings:** 1000 books. **Subscriptions:** 100 journals and other serials. **Services:** Interlibrary loan; copying; SDI; library open to the public for reference use only. **Computerized Information Services:** MEDLARS. Performs searches on fee basis.

★11406★
PLUNKETT & COONEY - LAW LIBRARY (Law)
900 Marquette Bldg. Phone: (313)965-3900
Detroit, MI 48226 Ann Kondak, Hd.Libn.
Founded: 1913. **Staff:** Prof 2; Other 2. **Subjects:** Statutes and court decisions in Michigan and the U.S.; products liability; insurance and tax law; bankruptcy. **Holdings:** 11,000 books; 500 bound periodical volumes; 2000 monographs and reports; microfiche. **Services:** Interlibrary loan; copying; library open to the public with restrictions. **Computerized Information Services:** WESTLAW, DIALOG Information Services, Dow Jones News/Retrieval, VU/TEXT Information Services, WILSONLINE, ABA/net, NLM; INTERACT (electronic mail service). **Networks/ Consortia:** Member of Michigan Library Consortium (MLC). **Staff:** Jill Davidson, Asst.Libn..

★11407★
PLYMOUTH CONGREGATIONAL CHURCH - LIBRARY (Rel-Phil)
1900 Nicollet Ave., S. Phone: (612)871-7400
Minneapolis, MN 55403 Joanne Lee, Libn.
Staff: Prof 1. **Subjects:** Religion and theology, global concerns, social and women's issues, art, children's literature. **Special Collections:** Free to Be collection (women's issues; 40 books); Global Concerns collection (60 books and pamphlets); art lending library (35 framed pictures). **Holdings:** 2000 books; 100 tapes. **Subscriptions:** 12 journals and other serials. **Services:** Library open to the public.

★11408★
PLYMOUTH CONGREGATIONAL CHURCH - VIDA B. VAREY LIBRARY (Rel-Phil)
1217 6th Ave.
Seattle, WA 98101 Anna F. Chiong, Libn.
Subjects: Religion. **Holdings:** 3000 books. **Services:** Interlibrary loan; library open to the public.

★11409★
PLYMOUTH STATE COLLEGE - GEOGRAPHERS ON FILM COLLECTION (Geog-Map)
Ellen Reed House, Off. 4 Phone: (603)536-1550
Plymouth, NH 03264 Prof. Maynard Weston Dow, Dir.
Staff: Prof 1; Other 1. **Subjects:** Geographers, geography, oral history. **Holdings:** 205 films and television tapes of special conferences, paper sessions, longer interviews. **Services:** Library open to the public for film rental by request. **Publications:** Geographers on Film (brochure; 1987) - available on request.

★11410★
PLYMOUTH STATE COLLEGE - HERBERT H. LAMSON LIBRARY - ROBERT FROST COLLECTION (Hum)
Plymouth, NH 03264 Phone: (603)536-5000
Philip C. Wei, Dir.
Subjects: Robert Frost. **Special Collections:** George H. Browne Collection (150 titles and 1 drawer of Robert Frost material). **Holdings:** 200 books; 25 films and recordings; 30 letters from Frost, 1915-1922; 10 typescripts of poems, 1915-1922; 15 photographs, 1915-1920; 200 clippings, memorabilia, pamphlets, lecture notes. **Services:** Copying; collection open to the public. **Publications:** Finding aid - available on request.

★11411★
PLYMOUTH STATE COLLEGE - HERBERT H. LAMSON LIBRARY - SPECIAL COLLECTIONS (Educ, Hist)
Plymouth, NH 03264 Phone: (603)536-5000
Philip C. Wei, Dir.
Founded: 1871. **Subjects:** Education, African affairs, New Hampshire and Plymouth (town) history. **Special Collections:** Ernest L. Silver Collection of Early Textbooks; Educational Materials Center. **Holdings:** 4200 archival materials; 274,000 microforms, including ERIC; 500 maps. **Services:** Interlibrary loan; copying; collections open to the public. **Automated Operations:** Computerized cataloging. **Computerized Information Services:** DIALOG Information Services, BRS Information Technologies, OCLC. **Networks/Consortia:** Member of NELINET, New Hampshire College & University Council Library Policy Committee (NHCUC). **Publications:** Handbook; Newsletter, semimonthly; bibliography of holdings in African affairs. **Staff:** Gary A. McCool, Educ.Ctr.Libn.; Lissa A. Pearson.

★11412★
POCONO HOSPITAL - MARSHALL R. METZGAR MEDICAL LIBRARY (Med)
206 E. Brown St. Phone: (717)421-4000
East Stroudsburg, PA 18301 Ellen P. Woodhead, Lib.Dir.
Staff: Prof 1. **Subjects:** Medicine, nursing. **Holdings:** 780 books; 1100 bound periodical volumes; 16 VF drawers and 1270 pamphlets of patient education materials and AV programs. **Subscriptions:** 128 journals and other serials. **Services:** Interlibrary loan; copying; SDI; library open to the public by appointment. **Computerized Information Services:** BRS Information Technologies, NLM. **Networks/Consortia:** Member of Delaware Valley Information Consortium (DEVIC), Health Information Library Network of Northeastern Pennsylvania (HILNNEP). **Publications:** QUEST (library newsletter) - for internal distribution only.

POCUMTUCK VALLEY MEMORIAL ASSOCIATION
See: Historic Deerfield, Inc. - Henry N. Flynt Library (6322)

★11413★
POETRY SOCIETY OF AMERICA - VAN VOORHIS LIBRARY (Hum)
15 Gramercy Park Phone: (212)254-9628
New York, NY 10003 Kristine Chalifoux, Asst.Dir.
Founded: 1910. **Staff:** Prof 1; Other 1. **Subjects:** American poetry and poetics, biography. **Special Collections:** Turn of the century and contemporary American poetry. **Holdings:** 8000 books. **Services:** Library open to researchers by appointment. **Remarks:** Large holograph collection and memorabilia of the Poetry Society of America are included in the Rare Book Division of the New York Public Library.

★11414★
POINT LOMA NAZARENE COLLEGE - RYAN LIBRARY (Rel-Phil)
3900 Lomaland Dr. Phone: (619)221-2355
San Diego, CA 92106 James D. Newburg, Dir.
Staff: Prof 6; Other 8. **Subjects:** Religion. **Special Collections:** Arminianism and Wesleyana Collection; 19th and 20th century Christian Holiness movement; Pasadena and Point Loma College authors; college archives (170 linear feet). **Holdings:** 181,111 books; 23,790 bound periodical volumes; 4929 microforms. **Subscriptions:** 665 journals and other serials; 6 newspapers. **Services:** Interlibrary loan; copying; library open to the public. **Automated Operations:** Computerized cataloging. **Computerized Information Services:** DIALOG Information Services, OCLC. Performs searches on fee basis. **Networks/Consortia:** Member of Learning Resources Cooperative, CLASS. **Staff:** Vernell Posey, Cat.Libn.; Sharon Bull, Instr.Serv.Libn.; Clem Guthro, Instr.Serv.Libn.; Virgil Vail, Media Spec.; Ann Ruppert, Instr.Serv.Libn..

★11415★
POINT PELEE NATIONAL PARK - LIBRARY (Biol Sci)
R.R. 1 Phone: (519)322-2365
Leamington, ON, Canada N8H 3V4 Rob A. Watt, Chf.Pk.Interp.
Founded: 1968. **Staff:** 5. **Subjects:** Ornithology, botany, biology, natural history, history, geology. **Special Collections:** Herbarium (1000 specimens); live mounts; study skins; insects (300 specimens). **Holdings:** 2000 books; 20,000 35mm slides; 1500 reprints and manuscripts; 1500 black/white prints; 30 16mm film titles. **Subscriptions:** 10 journals and other serials. **Services:** Library not open to the public. **Remarks:** Maintained by Environment Canada, Parks.

★11416★
POINT OF PURCHASE ADVERTISING INSTITUTE - INFORMATION CENTER (Bus-Fin)
66 N. Van Brunt St.
Englewood, NJ 07631-2707 John Kawula
Subjects: Point of purchase information, slide and videotape presentation. **Holdings:** 162 volumes; 15 VF drawers; reports; surveys. **Subscriptions:** 90 journals and other serials; 10 newspapers. **Services:** Interlibrary loan; copying; center open to those involved with point of purchase. **Also Known As:** POPAI Information Center.

POINT REYES NATIONAL SEASHORE
See: U.S. Natl. Park Service (15341)

★11417★
POLAROID CORPORATION - RESEARCH LIBRARY (Sci-Engr)
730 Main St. Phone: (617)577-3368
Cambridge, MA 02139 Jean M. Vnenchak, Dept.Mgr.
Staff: Prof 3; Other 3. **Subjects:** Photography, chemistry, physics, engineering, mathematics, social sciences, general business. **Special Collections:** Photography and polarized light; Polaroid issued patents; photographs. **Holdings:** 30,000 books; 8000 bound periodical volumes; 60 drawers of annual reports, standards, government documents, translations, scientific papers, technical reports. **Subscriptions:** 1100 journals and other serials; 10 newspapers. **Services:** Interlibrary loan; copying; library open to the public for reference use only with approval of the department manager or the library administrator. **Automated Operations:** Computerized cataloging, acquisitions, serials, and circulation. **Computerized Information Services:** DIALOG Information Services, STN International, Pergamon ORBIT InfoLine, Inc., BRS Information Technologies, Image Technology Patent Information System (ITPAIS). **Publications:** Library Bulletin, monthly; Journal and Periodical Listings, semiannual - both for internal distribution only. **Staff:** Dorothy M. Davis, Assoc.Tech.Libn.; Richard Gurner, Lib.Adm.; Rebecca Kenney, Assoc.Tech.Libn..

SHAD POLIER MEMORIAL LIBRARY
See: American Jewish Congress - Commission on Law and Social Action (573)

★11418★
POLISH AMERICAN CONGRESS - SOUTHERN CALIFORNIA-ARIZONA DIVISION - POLAND'S MILLENIUM LIBRARY
(Area-Ethnic)
3424 W. Adams Blvd. Phone: (213)664-0662
Los Angeles, CA 90018 Dr. Frances Tuszynski, Libn.
Founded: 1966. **Staff:** Prof 1; Other 6. **Subjects:** Polish history, literature, sociology, geography, 1918 to present. **Holdings:** 8000 books; 12 magazines. **Services:** Library not open to the public.

★11419★
POLISH INSTITUTE OF ARTS AND SCIENCES OF AMERICA, INC. - ALFRED JURZYKAWSKI MEMORIAL LIBRARY
(Area-Ethnic)
208 E. 30th St. Phone: (212)686-4164
New York, NY 10016 Krystyna Baron, Chf.Libn.
Founded: 1959. **Staff:** Prof 2; Other 1. **Subjects:** Poland - humanities, social sciences, ethnicity. **Special Collections:** Polish art collection; Polish history, 1918-1945 (pamphlets). **Holdings:** 20,000 books; 300 bound periodical volumes; newspapers on microfilm; maps. **Subscriptions:** 400 journals and other serials. **Services:** Library open to the public. **Publications:** Guide to the archives. **Staff:** Krystyna Swierbutowicz, Asst.Libn..

★11420★
POLISH INSTITUTE OF ARTS AND SCIENCES IN CANADA - POLISH LIBRARY (Area-Ethnic)
McGill University
3479 Peel St. Phone: (514)398-6978
Montreal, PQ, Canada H3A 1W7
Dr. Anna Poray-Wybranowski, Chf.Libn.
Staff: Prof 3; Other 2. **Subjects:** Polish literature, history, social science, political science, art, folklore; East European problems. **Special Collections:** Wartime publications in English and Polish. **Holdings:** 35,000 books; 5000 periodicals; reports; videotapes; manuscripts; clippings; documents; files; 200 engravings; 30 paintings; 700 slides; 15 atlases; 40 maps; 300 photographs. **Subscriptions:** 85 journals and other serials; 15 newspapers. **Services:** Interlibrary loan; copying; library open to the public. **Publications:** Biuletyn Informacyjny P.I.N.u (bulletin), annual. **Special Indexes:** Index to "Tygodnik Powszechny"; "Kultura," Paris; "Polish Review," New York; "News," London; Abstracts of articles in library periodical holdings in English, French, and Polish (4000 cards). **Staff:** Wanda Stachiewicz, Hon.Cur.; Stefan Wladysuik, Libn.; Sophie Bogdanski, Cat.Libn..

★11421★
POLISH MUSEUM OF AMERICA - ARCHIVES & LIBRARY
(Area-Ethnic)
984 Milwaukee Ave. Phone: (312)384-3352
Chicago, IL 60622 Jacek M. Nowakowski, Cur.
Founded: 1935. **Staff:** Prof 3; Other 3. **Subjects:** Polonica. **Special Collections:** 16th and 17th century original Polish works; 16th-18th century royal Polish manuscripts; original manuscripts of Kosciuszko, Pulaski, Tyssowski, Paderewski, and others; Polish American newspapers and magazines. **Holdings:** 38,000 books; 6000 periodical titles and reels of microfilm; 400 art pieces, reports, clippings, booklets, museum and archival materials. **Subscriptions:** 25 journals and other serials; 7 newspapers. **Services:** Interlibrary loan; copying; library open to the public. **Remarks:** Maintained by the Polish Roman Catholic Union of America. **Staff:** Krzysztof Kamyszew, Archv..

★11422★
POLISH NOBILITY ASSOCIATION - VILLA ANNESLIE ARCHIVES (Area-Ethnic)
529 Dunkirk Rd. Phone: (301)752-1087
Anneslie, MD 21212 Leonard Suligowski, Dir. of Heraldry
Staff: Prof 2. **Subjects:** Polish history, heraldry, nobility. **Special Collections:** Heraldry of Eastern Europe; nobility-family archives. **Holdings:** 500 books; 100 other cataloged items. **Subscriptions:** 10 journals and other serials. **Services:** Archives not open to the public. **Staff:** Thomas Hollowak, Res. Herald.

★11423★
POLISH SINGERS ALLIANCE OF AMERICA - LIBRARY (Mus)
Seven Norwood Court Phone: (212)720-6089
Staten Island, NY 10304 Walter Witkowicki, Libn.
Subjects: Choral and orchestral music. **Holdings:** 200,000 sheets of music for male, female, mixed choruses, and orchestra.

★11424★
POLK COUNTY DEPARTMENT OF SOCIAL SERVICES - CHILD CARE RESOURCE CENTER (Educ)
Box 756 Phone: (515)286-3536
Des Moines, IA 50303-0756 Emilie Duimstra, Trng.Coord.
Staff: Prof 1; Other 1. **Subjects:** Child development. **Holdings:** 500 books; 1500 toys and equipment; musical instruments; children's books; craft items. **Subscriptions:** 10 journals and other serials. **Services:** Center not open to the public. **Publications:** Local newsletter - to childcare givers, parents, trainers, and patrons.

★11425★
POLK COUNTY HISTORICAL AND GENEALOGICAL LIBRARY (Hist)
100 E. Main St., Rm. 101 Phone: (813)533-1161
Bartow, FL 33830 LaCona Raines Padgett, Hd.Libn.
Founded: 1937. **Staff:** Prof 2. **Subjects:** History - Polk County, Florida, Southeastern United States; genealogies of Southeastern United States families. **Special Collections:** Florida history. **Holdings:** 12,000 books; 610 bound periodical volumes; 800 family histories; 4000 reels of microfilm of census reports; 600 reels of microfilm of early newspapers, court records, church records. **Subscriptions:** 80 journals and other serials; 8 newspapers. **Services:** Copying; library open to the public. **Publications:** Polk County Historical Quarterly and Historical Calendar. **Remarks:** Maintained by Polk County Historical Commission (Board of County Commissioners). **Staff:** Kathleen M. Greer, Asst.Libn..

★11426★
POLK COUNTY LAW LIBRARY (Law)
Courthouse, Rm. 3076
255 N. Broadway Phone: (813)534-4013
Bartow, FL 33830 Nancy H. Tabler, Libn.
Founded: 1955. **Staff:** Prof 1; Other 1. **Subjects:** Law. **Holdings:** 16,000 volumes. **Subscriptions:** 75 journals and other serials. **Services:** Copying; library open to the public for reference use only. **Automated Operations:** Computerized circulation. **Computerized Information Services:** WESTLAW, WILSONLINE. Performs searches on fee basis. **Remarks:** Maintained by Polk County Board of County Commissioners.

★11427★
JAMES K. POLK ANCESTRAL HOME - LIBRARY (Hist)
Box 741 Phone: (615)388-2354
Columbia, TN 38402 John C. Holtzapple, Coord.
Founded: 1929. **Staff:** 2. **Subjects:** James K. Polk. **Holdings:** 100 books; 2000 artifacts. **Services:** Library open to the public by written permission. **Remarks:** Maintained by James K. Polk Memorial Association. Personal letters and memorabilia are on deposit at the Tennessee State Archives.

★11428★
POLK MUSEUM OF ART - MEMORIAL LIBRARY (Hum)
800 E. Palmetto Phone: (813)688-7743
Lakeland, FL 33801 Ken Rollins, Dir.
Staff: Prof 1; Other 2. **Subjects:** Art, antiques, history, music, natural history, literature. **Holdings:** 400 books; 20 bound periodical volumes; 150 clippings. **Services:** Library open to the public for reference use only. **Staff:** Marjorie Gilvin, Libn..

POLLACK LIBRARY
See: Maimonides Hospital Geriatric Centre (8311)

POLLACK LIBRARY
See: Yeshiva University - Pollack Library (18172)

CALVIN E. POLLINS MEMORIAL LIBRARY
See: Westmoreland County Historical Society (17791)

CHANNING POLLOCK THEATRE COLLECTION
See: Howard University (6536)

★11429★
POLLUTION PROBE FOUNDATION - ECOLOGY HOUSE LIBRARY (Env-Cons)
12 Madison Ave. Phone: (416)926-1907
Toronto, ON, Canada M5R 2S1 Vanessa Alexander, Pubn.Coord.
Founded: 1980. **Subjects:** Environment, pollution, energy alternatives and conservation. **Holdings:** 1500 books; reports. **Services:** Copying; library open to the public for reference use only.

BRIAN POLSLEY MEMORIAL AUDIO/VIDEO LIBRARY
See: ALS and Neuromuscular Research Foundation (336)

★11430★
POLYCHROME CORPORATION - RESEARCH & DEVELOPMENT LIBRARY (Art)
137 Alexander St. Phone: (914)965-8800
Yonkers, NY 10702 Peg Otis, Libn.
Staff: Prof 1. **Subjects:** Graphic arts, chemistry, business management. **Holdings:** 1500 books; 100 unbound periodicals; 4 drawers of U.S. patents; 1 drawer of foreign patents. **Subscriptions:** 100 journals and other serials. **Services:** Copying; library open to the public for reference use only on request.

★11431★
POLYCLINIC MEDICAL CENTER - MEDICAL LIBRARY (Med)
2601 N. 3rd St. Phone: (717)782-4292
Harrisburg, PA 17110 Suzanne M. Shultz, Libn.
Founded: 1925. **Staff:** 1. **Subjects:** Medicine, medical specialities. **Holdings:** 1500 books; 5000 bound periodical volumes. **Subscriptions:** 189 journals and other serials. **Services:** Interlibrary loan; copying; library open to students and medical professionals. **Computerized Information Services:** MEDLARS. **Networks/Consortia:** Member of Central Pennsylvania Health Sciences Library Association (CPHSLA).

★11432★
POLYMER CORPORATION - LIBRARY
501 Crescent Ave.
Reading, PA 19603
Founded: 1966. **Subjects:** Polymer science, polymer technology, engineering, chemistry, physics, management, mathematics. **Holdings:** 2500 volumes; 1275 laboratory notebooks. **Remarks:** Presently inactive.

★11433★
POLYSAR, LTD. - INFORMATION CENTRE (Sci-Engr)
Vidal St., S. Phone: (519)337-8251
Sarnia, ON, Canada N7T 7M2 Rosemary O'Donnell, Gp.Ldr.
Founded: 1944. **Staff:** Prof 5; Other 7. **Subjects:** Rubber, latexes, plastics, chemicals, polymer science, organic chemistry. **Holdings:** 12,000 books; 5000 bound periodical volumes; 1800 reels of microfilm; 10,000 microfiche; 34,000 internal reports. **Subscriptions:** 700 journals and other serials; 30 newspapers. **Services:** Interlibrary loan; copying; SDI; center open to the public by advance request. **Automated Operations:** Computerized public access catalog, cataloging, serials, and circulation. **Computerized Information Services:** DIALOG Information Services, Pergamon ORBIT InfoLine, Inc., Info Globe, Mead Data Central, Dun & Bradstreet Corporation; internal databases. **Publications:** Polysar Information Bulletin. **Special Indexes:** Index to internal reports (book). **Staff:** Sharon Freeman, Info.Spec.-Bus.; Tina DeMars, Info.Spec.-Tech.; Mary Mahoney, Info.Spec.-Tech.; Carol Anne O'Brien, Info.Spec.-Bus..

★11434★
POLYSCIENCES INCORPORATED - LIBRARY (Sci-Engr)
Paul Valley Industrial Park
Warrington, PA 18976 Phone: (215)343-6484
Founded: 1961. **Subjects:** Plastics, polymers in dentistry and medicine. **Holdings:** Figures not available.

★11435★
POLYTECHNIC UNIVERSITY - LIBRARY (Sci-Engr)
333 Jay St. Phone: (718)260-3109
Brooklyn, NY 11201 Richard T. Sweeney, Dean of Libs.
Staff: Prof 7; Other 8. **Subjects:** Aerospace technology; engineering - civil, industrial, electrical; electrophysics; chemistry; industrial management; mathematics; physics. **Special Collections:** Joseph Mattiello Collection of works of interest to the paint, varnish, and lacquer industries; history of science and technology collection. **Holdings:** 219,673 volumes; 31,966 microtexts. **Subscriptions:** 1233 journals and other serials. **Services:** Interlibrary loan; copying; library open to the public with letter from parent organization. **Automated Operations:** Computerized cataloging, acquisitions, serials, and interlibrary loans. **Computerized Information Services:** DIALOG Information Services, OCLC. Performs searches on fee basis. Contact Person: Irene Frye, Hd., Infodash Div.. **Publications:** Serials 1988, irregular. **Staff:** James Jarman, Asst. Dean of Libs..

★11436★
POLYTECHNIC UNIVERSITY - LONG ISLAND CAMPUS LIBRARY (Sci-Engr)
Route 110 Phone: (516)454-5020
Farmingdale, NY 11735 Lorraine Schein, Lib.Mgr.
Founded: 1960. **Staff:** Prof 3; Other 2. **Subjects:** Electrical engineering, electrophysics, aeronautics, fluid mechanics, physics, mathematics. **Holdings:** 25,000 books; 10,000 bound periodical volumes; NASA depository library; 20 VF drawers of pamphlets; 1 file drawer of cassettes. **Subscriptions:** 250 journals and other serials. **Services:** Interlibrary loan; copying; library open to the public with restrictions. **Networks/Consortia:** Member of Long Island Library Resources Council, Inc. (LILRC).

★11437★
POMONA PUBLIC LIBRARY - SPECIAL COLLECTIONS DEPARTMENT (Hist)
625 S. Garey Ave.
Box 2271 Phone: (714)620-2033
Pomona, CA 91766 David Streeter, Supv.
Founded: 1887. **Special Collections:** Californiana (3000 items); philately (1200 items); genealogy (3000 items); Citrus Company Records (28 companies); citrus box labels (4200); water company records (16 companies); Frasher photographs (60,000); Cooper photographs (4000); historical photographs (10,000); Tatum photographs (150); post card collection (35,000); glass plate negatives and prints (2500); California Wine Labels (10,000); non-California wine labels (1500); Laura Ingalls Wilder Collection (Little House on the Prairie holograph manuscripts; letters; photographs); Clara Webber Collection of Historic Children's Books; Padua Theater Collection (Mexican Players; 15 linear feet of uncataloged manuscripts and photographs). **Services:** Interlibrary loan; copying; department open to the public. **Automated Operations:** Computerized cataloging, acquisitions, and circulation. **Computerized Information Services:** OCLC. **Networks/Consortia:** Member of Metropolitan Cooperative Library System (MCLS), Southern California Answering Network (SCAN). **Special Indexes:** Pomona Progress Bulletin Index (card); CULP; CATALIST.

★11438★
POMONA VALLEY COMMUNITY HOSPITAL - MEDICAL LIBRARY (Med)
1798 N. Garey Ave. Phone: (714)865-9878
Pomona, CA 91767 Deborah Klein, Libn.
Staff: Prof 1. **Subjects:** Clinical medicine, nursing, bioethics. **Holdings:** 1400 books; 5000 bound periodical volumes; 600 audiotapes. **Subscriptions:** 180 journals and other serials; 10 audiotape subscriptions. **Services:** Interlibrary loan; library open to the public for reference use only. **Computerized Information Services:** DIALOG Information Services, MEDLARS. **Networks/Consortia:** Member of Medical Library Group of Southern California and Arizona (MLGSCA).

★11439★
PONCA CITY CULTURAL CENTER & MUSEUMS - LIBRARY (Area-Ethnic)
1000 E. Grand Ave. Phone: (405)762-6123
Ponca City, OK 74601 LaWanda French, Supv.
Founded: 1938. **Staff:** 1. **Subjects:** American Indian, anthropology, archeology, American cowboy, museology. **Special Collections:** Personal letters and photographs of Bryant Baker, sculptor of the Pioneer Woman; Ponca Indian music (tape recordings). **Holdings:** 200 books; 15 bound periodical volumes; VF drawers of unbound reports, clippings, pamphlets, dissertations, documents. **Subscriptions:** 15 journals and other serials. **Services:** Copying (limited); library open to the public. **Publications:** Museum Brochure; Museum Educational Leaflet Series. **Special Catalogs:**

Classification, Source, Tribe, Location, and Documents Catalogs (card file).

★11440★
PONCE SCHOOL OF MEDICINE FOUNDATION - MEDICAL LIBRARY (Med)
University Ave. No. 1
Box 7004 Phone: (809)844-3865
Ponce, PR 00731 Nestor M. Jeremias, Hd.Libn.
Founded: 1977. **Staff:** Prof 2; Other 5. **Subjects:** Clinical and basic sciences, anatomy, microbiology. **Special Collections:** Puerto Rican medical authors; hispanic medical journals. **Holdings:** 6200 books; 6250 bound periodical volumes. **Subscriptions:** 300 journals and other serials; 7 newspapers. **Services:** Interlibrary loan; copying; library open to the public. **Computerized Information Services:** BRS Information Technologies, MEDLINE, internal database. Performs searches on fee basis. Contact Person: Victoria Panelli, Res.Techn.. **Publications:** Library guide; acquisitions list, monthly; library procedures. **Special Indexes:** Index to the Journal: Asociacion Medica de Puerto Rico Boletin. **Staff:** Carmen G. Malavet, Assoc.Libn..

★11441★
PONTIAC GENERAL HOSPITAL - LIBRARY (Med)
Seminole & W. Huron Phone: (313)857-7412
Pontiac, MI 48053 Naim K. Sahyoun, Dir. of Libs.
Staff: Prof 2; Other 2. **Subjects:** Medicine, health care administration, nursing. **Holdings:** 3000 books; 10,000 bound periodical volumes; Audio-Digest tapes. **Subscriptions:** 400 journals and other serials. **Services:** Interlibrary loan; copying; SDI; library open to nursing and allied health students and physicians. **Computerized Information Services:** NLM, DIALOG Information Services. Performs searches on fee basis. **Publications:** Media News.

★11442★
PONTIAC OSTEOPATHIC HOSPITAL - MEDICAL LIBRARY (Med)
50 N. Perry St. Phone: (313)338-5000
Pontiac, MI 48058 Janis M. Fox-Heroux, Libn.
Founded: 1963. **Staff:** 2. **Subjects:** Medicine. **Holdings:** 2586 books; 3100 bound periodical volumes; 125 AV programs; 7 drawers of Audio-Digest tapes; 90 slide/tape sets. **Subscriptions:** 149 journals and other serials. **Services:** Interlibrary loan; library not open to the public.

★11443★
PONTIFICAL COLLEGE JOSEPHINUM - A.T. WEHRLE MEMORIAL LIBRARY (Rel-Phil)
7625 N. High St. Phone: (614)885-5585
Columbus, OH 43085 Peter G. Veracka, Dir.
Founded: 1889. **Staff:** Prof 2; Other 3. **Subjects:** Patristics, scholastic philosophy, Catholic theology. **Special Collections:** Dissertations on the work and thought of Bernard Lonergan (53). **Holdings:** 88,350 books; 11,845 bound periodical volumes; 68 reels of microfilm; 468 microfiche. **Subscriptions:** 432 journals and other serials; 51 newspapers. **Services:** Interlibrary loan; copying; library open to the public on request. **Automated Operations:** Computerized cataloging. **Computerized Information Services:** OCLC. **Networks/Consortia:** Member of OHIONET. **Staff:** Eleanor Byerly, Ref. & Bibliog.Instr.Libn..

PONTIFICAL INSTITUTE OF MEDIAEVAL STUDIES
See: University of Toronto - Pontifical Institute of Mediaeval Studies - Library (16996)

POPAI INFORMATION CENTER
See: Point of Purchase Advertising Institute - Information Center (11416)

★11444★
POPE, BALLARD, SHEPARD AND FOWLE - LIBRARY (Law)
69 W. Washington St. Phone: (312)630-4283
Chicago, IL 60602 Ronald E. Feret
Staff: Prof 1; Other 1. **Subjects:** Law. **Holdings:** 25,950 books; 200 bound periodical volumes. **Subscriptions:** 18 journals and other serials. **Services:** Library not open to the public.

★11445★
POPE COUNTY HISTORICAL SOCIETY & MUSEUM - LIBRARY (Hist)
Hwy. 104 Phone: (612)634-3293
Glenwood, MN 56334 Merlin Berglin, Cur.
Founded: 1932. **Staff:** Prof 2. **Subjects:** History - local, business, personal. **Special Collections:** Bound newspapers, 1891 to present. **Holdings:** 1343 volumes. **Services:** Copying; library open to the public for reference use only.

★11446★
POPE JOHN XXIII NATIONAL SEMINARY - LIBRARY (Rel-Phil)
558 South Ave. Phone: (617)899-5500
Weston, MA 02193 Rev. James L. Fahey, Libn.
Founded: 1964. **Staff:** Prof 2; Other 12. **Subjects:** Theology, philosophy, scripture, humanities, social sciences. **Holdings:** 44,680 books; 4287 bound periodical volumes; 2 vertical files. **Subscriptions:** 298 journals and other serials. **Services:** Interlibrary loan; copying; library open to the public for reference use only. **Remarks:** Maintained by the Archdiocese of Boston. **Staff:** Ann Kidney, Asst.Libn..

★11447★
POPULATION COUNCIL - LIBRARY (Soc Sci)
1 Dag Hammarskjold Plaza Phone: (212)644-1620
New York, NY 10017 H. Neil Zimmerman, Libn.
Staff: Prof 1; Other 1. **Subjects:** Population; demography; family planning; contraception; statistics; public health; development - economic, social, agricultural. **Holdings:** 20,000 books; 6,000 pamphlets, mimeographs, reprints, other cataloged items. **Subscriptions:** 350 journals and other serials. **Services:** Interlibrary loan; library open to researchers by appointment. **Automated Operations:** Computerized serials. **Networks/Consortia:** Member of Consortium of Foundation Libraries, APLIC International Census Network, New York Metropolitan Reference and Research Library Agency (METRO). **Publications:** Acquisitions List, irregular.

★11448★
POPULATION CRISIS COMMITTEE/DRAPER FUND - LIBRARY (Soc Sci)
1120 19th St., N.W., Suite 550 Phone: (202)659-1833
Washington, DC 20036 Anne Marie B. Amantia, Sr.Libn./Info.Mgr.
Staff: Prof 1; Other 1. **Subjects:** Family planning, demography, contraceptive technology, status of women, food, environment. **Special Collections:** Female circumcision; history of population legislation. **Holdings:** 5000 books; 65 VF drawers. **Subscriptions:** 500 journals and other serials. **Services:** Interlibrary loan; copying; SDI; library open to the public by appointment only. **Networks/Consortia:** Member of APLIC International Census Network. **Publications:** Library acquisitions list, monthly - free upon request.

★11449★
POPULATION DYNAMICS, INC. - INFORMATION CENTER
2442 N.W. Market St., Rm. 42
Seattle, WA 98107-4177
Founded: 1967. **Subjects:** Population growth, family planning, contraception, environmental quality. **Holdings:** Films; 8 rental films. **Remarks:** Presently inactive.

★11450★
POPULATION REFERENCE BUREAU, INC. - LIBRARY/INFORMATION SERVICE (Soc Sci)
777 14th St., N.W., Suite 800 Phone: (202)785-4664
Washington, DC 20005 Denise Molajo, Hd.Libn.
Founded: 1929. **Staff:** Prof 2; Other 1. **Subjects:** Demography, U.S. census, family planning, migration, energy/resources. **Holdings:** 12,000 books; 2500 reprints and papers; 15 VF drawers of pamphlets, clippings, reprints; historical U.S. census collection, including complete set of 1930-1980 census volumes. **Subscriptions:** 450 journals and other serials. **Services:** Interlibrary loan; copying; library open to the public. **Computerized Information Services:** MEDLARS, DIALOG Information Services.

★11451★
PORT AUTHORITY OF ALLEGHENY COUNTY - TRANSIT RESEARCH LIBRARY (Trans)
Beaver & Island Aves. Phone: (412)237-7334
Pittsburgh, PA 15233 Sandra L. Demas, Res.Asst.
Founded: 1974. **Staff:** Prof 1. **Subjects:** Rapid transit, paratransit, urban mass transit. **Holdings:** 3500 books; 200 reels of microfilm; Federal Register. **Subscriptions:** 81 journals and other serials. **Services:** Interlibrary loan; copying; library open to the public.

★11452★
PORT AUTHORITY OF NEW YORK AND NEW JERSEY - LIBRARY (Trans, Bus-Fin)
55 N., One World Trade Center Phone: (212)466-4062
New York, NY 10048 Jane M. Janiak, Chf.Libn.
Founded: 1946. **Staff:** Prof 7; Other 6. **Subjects:** Transportation, public administration, international trade, business, management, engineering, aviation. **Holdings:** 25,000 books; 25,000 documents; 150 titles on microfilm; Urban Mass Transportation Administration Depository. **Subscriptions:** 1200 journals; 500 serials. **Services:** Interlibrary loan; SDI; library open to students and librarians by appointment. **Automated Operations:** Computerized cataloging. **Computerized Information Services:** NEXIS, DIALOG Information Services, Pergamon ORBIT InfoLine, Inc., VU/TEXT Information Services, Washington Alert Service, WILSONLINE, TEXTLINE, RLIN, OCLC, LEGI-SLATE; THESAURUS (internal database). **Networks/Consortia:** Member of SUNY/OCLC Library Network. **Publications:** Library Bulletin; Port Authority Bibliography. **Staff:** Rhonda Marker, Asst.Chf.Libn., Cat.; Diane Sciattara, Ref.Libn.; Patricia Cose, Asst.Chf.Libn., Ref. ; James J. Ryan, Ref.Libn.; Armilda Laats, Sr.Cat.; Barbara Lafave, Cat..

★11453★
PORT HURON TIMES HERALD - LIBRARY (Publ)
911 Military St. Phone: (313)985-7171
Port Huron, MI 48060 Joann M. Maxwell, Lib.Ck.
Staff: 1. **Subjects:** Newspaper reference topics. **Holdings:** 10,000 files of clippings and photographs; 670 reels of microfilm. **Services:** Library open to the public with permission.

★11454★
PORT MOODY STATION MUSEUM - LIBRARY AND ARCHIVES (Hist)
2734 Murray St. Phone: (604)939-1648
Port Moody, BC, Canada V3H 1X2 Diane Rogers, Cur.
Staff: Prof 1. **Subjects:** Museum training materials, Canadian Pacific Railway history, local history, Salish art and culture. **Special Collections:** Archives (100 linear feet of archival materials, including Port Moody City records, newspapers, and local business records, Canadian Pacific Railway papers, film and cassette recordings). **Holdings:** 500 books. **Subscriptions:** 35 journals and other serials. **Services:** Copying; library open to the public with restrictions. **Publications:** Original Inhabitants... (1983); History of Port Moody 1880's; museum notes series; Heritage Express (newsletter), monthly - for internal distribution and upon request. **Remarks:** Maintained by Port Moody Heritage Society.

★11455★
PORT OF PORTLAND - LIBRARY (Bus-Fin, Trans)
700 N.E. Multnomah Phone: (503)231-5000
Portland, OR 97232 Katie Hill, Lib.Info.Spec.
Staff: Prof 1; Other 1. **Subjects:** Maritime and waterborne commerce, aviation. **Special Collections:** Port of Portland studies (Port-run airports, ship repair yard, marine terminals); archives. **Holdings:** 10,000 books. **Subscriptions:** 350 journals and other serials; 20 newspapers. **Services:** Interlibrary loan; library open to the public. **Automated Operations:** Computerized cataloging.

★11456★
PORTAGE COUNTY HISTORICAL SOCIETY - LIBRARY AND MUSEUM (Hist)
6549-51 N. Chestnut St. Phone: (216)296-3523
Ravenna, OH 44266 Thomas E. Cadwallader, Pres.
Founded: 1951. **Subjects:** County history - families, industries, organizations, genealogy. **Special Collections:** Frederick J. Loudin Collection; Alford photograph collection. **Holdings:** 500 books; 40 family histories; early tax records; county records, documents, atlas; cemetery records. **Services:** Copying; library open to the public for reference use only. **Staff:** Bonita S. Lock, Libn..

PORTAGE COUNTY HISTORICAL SOCIETY COLLECTION
See: University of Wisconsin, Stevens Point - University Archives & Portage County Historical Society (17181)

DANA PORTER LIBRARY
See: University of Waterloo - Dana Porter Library (17081)

KATHERINE ANNE PORTER ROOM
See: University of Maryland, College Park Libraries - Mc Keldin Library (16381)

★11457★
LANGLEY PORTER PSYCHIATRIC INSTITUTE - PROFESSIONAL LIBRARY (Med)
University of California
401 Parnassus Ave.
Box 13-B/C Phone: (415)476-7380
San Francisco, CA 94143-0984 Lisa M. Dunkel, Libn.
Founded: 1943. **Staff:** Prof 1; Other 2. **Subjects:** Psychiatry, psychoanalysis, clinical psychology, allied mental health sciences. **Holdings:** 6575 books; 4145 bound periodical volumes; pamphlets. **Subscriptions:** 187 journals and other serials. **Services:** Interlibrary loan; library not open to the public. **Computerized Information Services:** MEDLARS, DIALOG Information Services, BRS Information Technologies. Performs searches on fee basis. **Remarks:** An alternate telephone number is 476-7203.

★11458★
PORTER MEDICAL CENTER - MEDICAL LIBRARY & INFORMATION SERVICE (Med)
South St. Phone: (802)388-7901
Middlebury, VT 05753 Lori Munson, Libn.
Founded: 1974. **Staff:** Prof 1; Other 1. **Subjects:** Medicine, nursing. **Holdings:** 500 books. **Subscriptions:** 20 journals and other serials. **Services:** Interlibrary loan; library not open to the public. **Networks/Consortia:** Member of Vermont/New Hampshire Health Science Libraries.

★11459★
PORTER MEMORIAL HOSPITAL - HARLEY E. RICE MEMORIAL LIBRARY (Med)
2525 S. Downing St. Phone: (303)778-5656
Denver, CO 80210 Karla Britain, Dir.
Staff: Prof 2. **Subjects:** Medicine. **Holdings:** 2250 books; 6500 bound periodical volumes; 125 audiotapes; 4 VF drawers. **Subscriptions:** 395 journals and other serials. **Services:** Interlibrary loan; copying; SDI; library open to the public for reference use only. **Automated Operations:** Computerized cataloging. **Computerized Information Services:** BRS Information Technologies, MEDLARS; ABACUS (electronic mail service). Performs searches on fee basis. **Networks/Consortia:** Member of Denver Area Health Sciences Library Consortium, Bibliographical Center for Research, Rocky Mountain Region, Inc. (BCR). **Staff:** Roseanne Vercio, Asst.Libn..

SISTER ESTHER PORTER MEDICAL-NURSING LIBRARY
See: Bethesda Lutheran Hospital - Library (1564)

★11460★
PORTER, WRIGHT, MORRIS & ARTHUR - LIBRARY (Law)
41 S. High St. Phone: (614)227-2090
Columbus, OH 43215 Susan M. Schaefgen, Hd.Libn.
Founded: 1852. **Staff:** Prof 2; Other 3. **Subjects:** Law, Ohio law. **Holdings:** 25,000 books; 1000 bound periodical volumes. **Subscriptions:** 250 journals and other serials; 10 newspapers. **Services:** Library not open to the public. **Automated Operations:** Computerized cataloging. **Computerized Information Services:** LEXIS, NEXIS, WESTLAW, DIALOG Information Services, VU/TEXT Information Services, Dow Jones News/Retrieval; ZyIndex (internal database). **Networks/Consortia:** Member of OHIONET. **Special Indexes:** Memo, prospectus, expert witness, and lawyer referral files. **Staff:** Edward Hosey, Asst.Libn..

★11461★
PORTERVILLE DEVELOPMENTAL CENTER - PROFESSIONAL LIBRARY (Med)
Box 2000 Phone: (209)782-2609
Porterville, CA 93258 Mary Jane Berry, Libn.
Staff: Prof 1. **Subjects:** Mental retardation - psychology, medical aspects, education, social welfare. **Holdings:** 6000 books; 3800 bound periodical volumes. **Subscriptions:** 125 journals and other serials. **Services:** Interlibrary loan; copying; library open to the public for reference use only on request.

★11462★
PORTLAND ART MUSEUM - LIBRARY (Art)
1219 S.W. Park Phone: (503)226-2811
Portland, OR 97205 Emily Evans Elsner, Libn.
Founded: 1892. **Staff:** Prof 1. **Subjects:** Art. **Special Collections:** Art of Indian tribes of the Pacific Northwest; Oriental art, especially Japanese prints; English silver books. **Holdings:** 21,430 books; 1026 bound periodical volumes; 365 pamphlet cases of catalogs relating to artists, movements, and exhibitions; 175 pamphlet cases of museum reports and bulletins; 71,500 slides. **Subscriptions:** 84 journals and other serials. **Services:** Interlibrary

loan; library open to the public for reference use only. **Remarks:** Maintained by the Oregon Art Institute. **Staff:** Dan Lucas, Slide Libn..

PORTLAND CEMENT ASSOCIATION - CONSTRUCTION TECHNOLOGY LABORATORIES INC.
See: Construction Technology Laboratories Inc. (3698)

★11463★
PORTLAND CITY BUREAU OF PLANNING - LIBRARY (Plan)
1120 S.W. 5th Ave., 10th Fl. Phone: (503)796-7717
Portland, OR 97204-1966 Neal Van Horn, Libn.
Founded: 1975. **Staff:** Prof 1. **Subjects:** City planning, historic and urban design, housing and land use policy, development and administration. **Special Collections:** Planning Commission minutes. **Holdings:** 8000 books, reports, bound periodical volumes. **Subscriptions:** 20 journals and other serials. **Services:** Library open to the public for reference use only. **Automated Operations:** Computerized cataloging. **Computerized Information Services:** Internal database. **Special Indexes:** Keyword index to book titles.

★11464★
PORTLAND GENERAL ELECTRIC - CORPORATE AND TECHNICAL LIBRARIES (Sci-Engr, Energy)
121 S.W. Salmon St. Phone: (503)226-8695
Portland, OR 97204 Donna B. Shaver, Supv., Lib.Rsrcs.
Founded: 1914. **Staff:** Prof 3; Other 4. **Subjects:** Electrical and nuclear engineering, management, alternative energy sources, environmental sciences. **Holdings:** 16,000 books; 48,000 technical reports, hardcopy and microfiche; 1500 standards. **Subscriptions:** 1300 journals and other serials; 25 newspapers. **Services:** Interlibrary loan; copying (limited); library open to the public with restrictions. **Automated Operations:** Computerized cataloging, acquisitions, serials, and ILL. **Computerized Information Services:** DIALOG Information Services, BRS Information Technologies, Utility Data Institute, Dow Jones News/Retrieval, OCLC; LINX Courier (electronic mail service). **Special Indexes:** Keyword index of technical reports (microfiche). **Staff:** Bob Weber, Tech.Libn.; Barb Buckley, Tech.Serv.Libn..

★11465★
PORTLAND GENERAL ELECTRIC - ENERGY RESOURCE CENTER - TECHNICAL LIBRARY (Energy)
7895 S.W. Mohawk St. Phone: (503)692-9417
Tualatin, OR 97062 Bette L. Stewart, Info.Spec.
Founded: 1986. **Staff:** Prof 1; Other 1. **Subjects:** Heating, ventilation, and air conditioning; electrical applications; commercial food facilities; lighting; industrial processes; construction. **Holdings:** 600 books; 100 technical reports; standards. **Subscriptions:** 65 journals and other serials. **Services:** Library open to the public with restrictions. **Automated Operations:** Computerized cataloging and acquisitions. **Computerized Information Services:** DIALOG Information Services; Inmagic (internal database).

★11466★
PORTLAND PUBLIC LIBRARY - ART DEPARTMENT (Art, Mus)
5 Monument Square Phone: (207)773-4761
Portland, ME 04101-4072 Judith Wentzell, Art Libn.
Founded: 1867. **Staff:** Prof 1; Other 3. **Subjects:** Visual and performing arts, music, costume. **Special Collections:** Picture file (18 drawers); Maine composers, artists, musicians; choral music; art school catalogs. **Holdings:** 16,815 books; 19 drawers of sheet music. **Subscriptions:** 96 journals and other serials. **Services:** Interlibrary loan; copying; SDI; department open to the public. **Automated Operations:** Computerized cataloging, acquisitions, and circulation. **Computerized Information Services:** DIALOG Information Services. Performs searches on fee basis. Contact Person: Suzanne Thompson, Ref.Libn., 773-4761.

★11467★
PORTLAND PUBLIC SCHOOLS - PROFESSIONAL LIBRARY (Educ)
501 N. Dixon St.
Box 3107 Phone: (503)249-2000
Portland, OR 97208 Connie Stanton, Libn.
Staff: Prof 1; Other 2. **Subjects:** Education. **Holdings:** 15,000 books. **Subscriptions:** 170 journals and other serials; 7 newspapers. **Services:** Interlibrary loan; copying; SDI; library open to the public with restrictions. **Computerized Information Services:** DIALOG Information Services, OCLC, ED-LINE, WILSONLINE.

★11468★
PORTLAND PUBLIC SCHOOLS DISTRICT NO. 1 - RECORDS MANAGEMENT OFFICE (Educ)
531 S.E. 14th Ave. Phone: (503)280-6477
Portland, OR 97214 Christine Blackburn, Rec.Mgr.
Founded: 1979. **Staff:** Prof 2; Other 2. **Subjects:** School district history, 1858 to present. **Holdings:** 4000 cubic feet of inactive district records; 150 cubic feet of Portland Public Schools archival materials; 3 cubic feet of microfilm of permanent records, including minutes, class lists, annual reports, censuses. **Services:** Copying; office open to the public with restrictions. **Computerized Information Services:** Internal databases. **Staff:** D. Evans, Archv..

★11469★
PORTLAND SCHOOL OF ART - LIBRARY (Art)
619 Congress St. Phone: (207)761-1772
Portland, ME 04101 Joanne Waxman, Libn.
Founded: 1973. **Staff:** Prof 3; Other 12. **Subjects:** Art and art history, biographies of artists, local architecture and arts, liberal arts, photography, crafts. **Holdings:** 17,000 books; 38,000 slides. **Subscriptions:** 80 journals and other serials. **Services:** Interlibrary loan; copying; library open to the public with restrictions. **Staff:** Jeffory Clough, Asst.Libn.; Catherine Nugent, Ck..

★11470★
PORTLAND STATE UNIVERSITY - AUDIO-VISUAL SERVICES (Aud-Vis)
Box 1151 Phone: (503)464-4514
Portland, OR 97207 Frank F. Kuo, Dir.
Founded: 1953. **Staff:** Prof 2; Other 9. **Subjects:** General AV collection to support university curriculum. **Holdings:** 610 guides and indexes to media materials; media catalogs; 370 media kits; 70 videotapes; 1700 16mm films; 400 8mm films; 3268 35mm filmstrips; 46,000 35mm slides; 11,900 phonograph records; 7500 audiotapes; 4100 scores; 2470 cassettes; 90 compact discs; 6 laser discs; 50 microcomputer programs. **Services:** Copying (limited); production of AV materials; services open to the public for campus use only. **Networks/Consortia:** Member of Western Library Network (WLN). **Special Catalogs:** Film catalog; Media Kits Catalog; Foreign Languages (26) Audiotape Catalog - all for internal distribution only. **Special Indexes:** Slide index; cassette tape index - both for internal distribution only. **Staff:** Stan Nuffer, Asst.Dir., Lrng./Comp.Labs..

★11471★
PORTLAND STATE UNIVERSITY - CONTINUING EDUCATION FILM AND VIDEO LIBRARY (Aud-Vis)
1633 S.W. Park Ave.
Box 1383 Phone: (503)464-4890
Portland, OR 97207 Anthony J. Midson, Dir.
Founded: 1932. **Staff:** Prof 1; Other 5. **Subjects:** General subjects. **Holdings:** 8000 16mm films; 1000 videotapes. **Services:** Rental collection available to public. **Remarks:** Contains the holdings of the former Oregon Art Institute - Northwest Film and Video Center - Circulating Film Library.

★11472★
PORTLAND STATE UNIVERSITY - MIDDLE EAST STUDIES CENTER
Box 751
Portland, OR 97207
Subjects: Arabic, Hebrew, Persian, and Turkish languages. **Holdings:** 33,000 volumes in vernacular languages; additional volumes in Western languages to supplement area studies. **Remarks:** Presently inactive.

★11473★
JOHN PORTMAN & ASSOCIATES - LIBRARY (Plan)
231 Peachtree St., N.E., Suite 200 Phone: (404)522-8811
Atlanta, GA 30303 Alice S. Butler, Rsrc.Coord.
Staff: Prof 2. **Subjects:** Architecture, civil engineering, construction industry, real estate, art. **Special Collections:** Archives of John Portman. **Holdings:** 2750 books; 259 bound periodical volumes; 6 VF drawers of reports and clippings; 7650 sheets of microfilm; 5700 photographs and slides; drawings. **Subscriptions:** 114 journals and other serials; 7 newspapers. **Services:** Interlibrary loan; library not open to the public. **Special Catalogs:** File of manufacturers' catalogs (card); microfilm catalog (book).

★11474★
PORTSMOUTH ATHENAEUM - LIBRARY AND MUSEUM (Hist)
9 Market Square
Box 848 Phone: (603)431-2538
Portsmouth, NH 03801-0848 Richard M. Candee, Pres.
Founded: 1817. **Subjects:** Local history, genealogy, 19th century travel and description, biography. **Special Collections:** Local and New England Maritime/Naval History; New Hampshire Fire & Marine Insurance Company records, 1801-1812; local history, politics, and military affairs, 1700-1900 (450 manuscripts); Green's Drug Store records (83 volumes; 7 boxes); Portsmouth Fire Societies and Companies (5 volumes); Arthur D. Hill Collection (17 boxes); Peirce and Haven family manuscripts (3 boxes); 18th and 19th century English and American magazines. **Holdings:** 30,000 books; 350 bound volumes of New Hampshire newspapers; charts; maps; photographs. **Subscriptions:** 25 journals and other serials. **Services:** Library open to the public on a limited schedule or by appointment. **Staff:** Jane M. Porter, Kpr.; F. Jeanette Mitchell, Libn..

★11475★
PORTSMOUTH BAR AND LAW LIBRARY (Law)
Scioto County Court House, 3rd Fl. Phone: (614)353-5111
Portsmouth, OH 45662 Otha Sanderlin, Libn.
Staff: 1. **Subjects:** Law. **Holdings:** 25,000 volumes. **Services:** Library not open to the public.

★11476★
PORTSMOUTH GENERAL HOSPITAL - MEDICAL LIBRARY (Med)
850 Crawford Pkwy. Phone: (804)398-4217
Portsmouth, VA 23704 Sallie B. Dellinger, Libn.
Staff: Prof 1. **Subjects:** Medicine, allied health sciences. **Special Collections:** Continuing Medical Education Video Cassette Tapes. **Holdings:** 707 books; 1105 bound periodical volumes; 60 other cataloged items. **Subscriptions:** 30 journals and other serials. **Services:** Interlibrary loan; library not open to the public.

★11477★
PORTSMOUTH MILITARY MUSEUM AND LIBRARY - MILITARY AVIATION ARCHIVES AND LIBRARY (Mil)
1106 Maplewood Ave.
Portsmouth, NH 03801 Mr. W.M. Cleveland, Hist.
Founded: 1973. **Staff:** Prof 1. **Subjects:** World War II; air war in the Pacific, Korea, Vietnam; U.S. military aviation history and military history. **Holdings:** 1250 books; 11 cubic feet of reports and archival materials; 200 reels of microfilm; 6 VF drawers; 20 boxes; 20 shelves. **Subscriptions:** 11 journals and other serials. **Services:** Copying; library open to the public by appointment.

★11478★
PORTSMOUTH NAVAL SHIPYARD MUSEUM - MARSHALL W. BUTT LIBRARY (Mil)
2 High St.
Box 248 Phone: (804)393-8591
Portsmouth, VA 23705 Alice C. Hanes, Cur.
Founded: 1962. **Staff:** 3. **Subjects:** Naval history and ordnance, local history, Norfolk naval shipyard. **Special Collections:** Early naval ordnance books and engineer journals. **Holdings:** 4000 books. **Subscriptions:** 10 journals and other serials. **Services:** Copying; library open to the public by appointment.

★11479★
PORTSMOUTH PSYCHIATRIC CENTER - MEDICAL LIBRARY (Med)
301 Fort Lane Phone: (804)393-0061
Portsmouth, VA 23704 Virginia M. Kerstetter, Med.Libn.
Staff: Prof 1. **Subjects:** Psychiatry, psychology, clinical social work, adjunct therapies, nursing, alcoholism. **Holdings:** 1400 books; 700 bound periodical volumes; 277 audio cassettes. **Subscriptions:** 80 journals and other serials. **Services:** Interlibrary loan; copying; library open to the public with administrative approval. **Computerized Information Services:** MEDLARS, DIALOG Information Services.

★11480★
PORTSMOUTH PUBLIC LIBRARY - LOCAL HISTORY ROOM (Hist)
601 Court St. Phone: (804)393-8501
Portsmouth, VA 23704 Mrs. Brook Maupin, Lib.Asst.
Staff: 1. **Subjects:** Local history, lighthouses and lightships, genealogy. **Special Collections:** Judge White Collection. **Holdings:** 2800 books; 200 bound periodical volumes; 55 maps; 280 documents; 21,400 photographs. **Services:** Interlibrary loan; copying; room open to the public. **Automated Operations:** Computerized public access catalog, cataloging, and circulation. **Computerized Information Services:** CAVALIR. Performs searches on fee basis. Contact Person: Susan H. Burton, Hd. of Ref.. **Special Indexes:** Portsmouth and Norfolk County Documents; Emmerson Papers (abstracts of local newspapers, 1700-1880); Butt papers (17th century land holdings in Norfolk county; all on cards).

★11481★
PORTSMOUTH RECEIVING HOSPITAL - MEDICAL LIBRARY (Med)
25th St. & Elmwood Dr.
Box 561 Phone: (614)354-2804
Portsmouth, OH 45662 Jack W. Haffner, Educ.Coord.
Founded: 1966. **Staff:** Prof 1. **Subjects:** Psychiatry, psychology, allied health sciences. **Holdings:** 1509 books; 26 bound periodical volumes. **Subscriptions:** 24 journals and other serials. **Services:** Interlibrary loan; library open to college students for reference use only. **Networks/Consortia:** Member of Ohio Valley Area Libraries (OVAL). **Remarks:** Maintained by Ohio State Department of Mental Health.

★11482★
PORTUGUESE CONTINENTAL UNION OF THE U.S.A. - LIBRARY (Area-Ethnic)
899 Boylston St. Phone: (617)536-2916
Boston, MA 02115 Jose S. Fernandes, Supreme Sec.
Founded: 1955. **Staff:** 2. **Subjects:** Portugal and overseas provinces - history, geography, statistics, literature. **Holdings:** 2200 volumes. **Services:** Library open to members for reference and research work on request.

★11483★
POS PILOT PLANT CORPORATION - LIBRARY (Food-Bev)
118 Veterinary Rd. Phone: (306)665-7791
Saskatoon, SK, Canada S7N 2R4 Betty Vankoughnett, Libn.
Founded: 1977. **Staff:** Prof 1; Other 1. **Subjects:** Oilseeds, chemistry, food science and technology. **Special Collections:** Corporate archives; slide and photograph collection (3000). **Holdings:** 750 books; 230 bound periodical volumes; 1 VF drawer of patents; 1 VF drawer of reports; 5000 reprints. **Subscriptions:** 150 journals and other serials; 5 newspapers. **Services:** Interlibrary loan; copying; library open to the public for reference use only. **Computerized Information Services:** DIALOG Information Services, CAN/OLE, Info Globe; internal database. Performs searches on fee basis.

C.W. POST CAMPUS
See: Long Island University (7958)

★11484★
POST-TRIBUNE - LIBRARY (Publ)
1065 Broadway Phone: (219)881-3134
Gary, IN 46402 Louise K. Tucker, Chf.Libn.
Founded: 1936. **Staff:** Prof 1; Other 2. **Subjects:** Newspaper reference topics. **Special Collections:** Gary history; anniversary and special editions. **Holdings:** 300 books; 55 VF drawers of biographical clippings; 67 VF drawers of subject clipping files; 30 VF drawers of local and national photographs; microfilm, 1906 to present. **Services:** Library open to the public on fee basis with written request. **Computerized Information Services:** VU/TEXT Information Services; internal database. Performs searches on fee basis.

★11485★
WINFRED L. AND ELIZABETH C. POST FOUNDATION - POST MEMORIAL ART REFERENCE LIBRARY (Art)
300 Main St. Phone: (417)782-5419
Joplin, MO 64801-2384 Leslie Simpson, Libn./Dir.
Founded: 1981. **Staff:** Prof 1; Other 1. **Subjects:** Visual arts, antiques, architecture, photography, historic preservation, heraldry. **Special Collections:** Picture file (reproductions of works of art; 4000 pictures); 16th and 17th century furniture; sculpture and paintings, 13th century to present; Joplin's historic buildings and homes (slides; photographs). **Holdings:** 2000 books; 228 bound periodical volumes; 16 VF drawers of pictures, articles, pamphlets. **Subscriptions:** 31 journals and other serials. **Services:** Copying; library open to the public.

★11486★
RUBIN POSTAER AND ASSOCIATES - MARKETING INFORMATION CENTER (Bus-Fin)
11601 Wilshire Blvd. Phone: (213)208-5000
Los Angeles, CA 90025 Maria Hinds, Mgr., Info.Serv.
Founded: 1981. **Staff:** Prof 1; Other 1. **Subjects:** Advertising, marketing. **Holdings:** 300 books; 350 subject and company files. **Subscriptions:** 195 journals and other serials; 5 newspapers. **Services:** Center not open to the public. **Computerized Information Services:** DIALOG Information Services, NEXIS.

POSTAL HISTORY SOCIETY LIBRARY
See: American Philatelic Research Library (633)

★11487★
POSTGRADUATE CENTER FOR MENTAL HEALTH - EMIL A. GUTHEIL MEMORIAL LIBRARY (Med)
124 E. 28th St. Phone: (212)689-7700
New York, NY 10016 Leona Mackler, Dir.
Founded: 1947. **Staff:** Prof 2; Other 2. **Subjects:** Psychiatry, psychology, community mental health, psychoanalysis. **Holdings:** 10,000 books; 150 bound periodical volumes; 7000 unbound journals; 2 VF cabinets of pamphlets. **Subscriptions:** 100 journals and other serials. **Services:** Interlibrary loan; copying; SDI; library open to nonaffiliated professionals on fee basis. **Computerized Information Services:** BRS Information Technologies, DIALOG Information Services, MEDLINE. Performs searches on fee basis. **Networks/Consortia:** Member of Greater Northeastern Regional Medical Library Program, Manhattan-Bronx Health Sciences Library Group, New York Metropolitan Reference and Research Library Agency (METRO). **Publications:** Acquisitions list, quarterly - to staff and fellows.

★11488★
POTASH CORPORATION OF SASKATCHEWAN - LIBRARY SERVICES (Agri)
122 1st Ave., S., Suite 500 Phone: (306)933-8501
Saskatoon, SK, Canada S7K 7G3 Marybelle Peet, Lib.Techn.
Founded: 1979. **Staff:** Prof 1. **Subjects:** Fertilizers, agriculture, engineering, chemicals, computers, business. **Holdings:** 3500 books. **Subscriptions:** 350 journals and other serials; 20 newspapers. **Services:** Library open to students with restrictions. **Automated Operations:** Computerized cataloging. **Computerized Information Services:** DIALOG Information Services, MINISIS.

★11489★
POTOMAC ELECTRIC POWER COMPANY - CORPORATE LIBRARY - 601 (Sci-Engr)
1900 Pennsylvania Ave., N.W. Phone: (202)872-2361
Washington, DC 20068 Helen C. Jessup, Libn.
Founded: 1932. **Staff:** 1. **Subjects:** Electrical and mechanical engineering, energy, finance, accounting, personnel management, computers, data processing, Washingtoniana. **Holdings:** 9000 volumes; Electric Power Research Institute (EPRI) research reports on microfilm. **Subscriptions:** 200 journals and other serials; 6 newspapers. **Services:** Interlibrary loan; library not open to the public. **Automated Operations:** Computerized acquisitions and circulation. **Computerized Information Services:** DIALOG Information Services, Dow Jones News/Retrieval. **Publications:** Accessions list of new books.

WILLIAM POTOROKA MEMORIAL LIBRARY
See: Alcoholism Foundation of Manitoba (257)

★11490★
POTTER COUNTY LAW LIBRARY (Law)
601 S. Fillmore, Suite 201B Phone: (806)379-2347
Amarillo, TX 79101 Charlotte Hill, Libn.
Founded: 1911. **Staff:** Prof 1; Other 1. **Subjects:** Law. **Special Collections:** State reporters, 1800-1900. **Holdings:** 17,000 books; 3000 bound periodical volumes. **Subscriptions:** 14 journals and other serials. **Services:** Copying; library open to the public. **Remarks:** Also serves the Amarillo Bar Association.

★11491★
POTTSTOWN MEMORIAL MEDICAL CENTER - MEDICAL STAFF LIBRARY (Med)
1600 E. High St. Phone: (215)327-7468
Pottstown, PA 19464 Marilyn D. Chapis, Med. Staff Libn.
Staff: 1. **Subjects:** Medical and surgical specialties. **Holdings:** 250 books; 850 bound periodical volumes. **Subscriptions:** 50 journals and other serials. **Services:** Interlibrary loan; library not open to the public. **Computerized Information Services:** BRS Information Technologies. **Networks/Consortia:** Member of Delaware Valley Information Consortium (DEVIC).

★11492★
POTTSVILLE HOSPITAL AND WARNE CLINIC - MEDICAL LIBRARY (Med)
420 S. Jackson St. Phone: (717)622-6120
Pottsville, PA 17901 Diane Leinheiser, Libn.
Founded: 1955. **Staff:** Prof 1. **Subjects:** Medicine, surgery. **Holdings:** 530 books; 1668 bound periodical volumes; audiotapes of surgery, internal medicine, family practice, pediatrics. **Subscriptions:** 46 journals and other serials. **Services:** Interlibrary loan; copying; will answer brief inquiries and make referrals. **Networks/Consortia:** Member of Central Pennsylvania Health Sciences Library Association (CPHSLA), Greater Northeastern Regional Medical Library Program.

★11493★
POUDRE VALLEY HOSPITAL - MEDICAL LIBRARY (Med)
1024 Lemay Ave. Phone: (303)482-4111
Fort Collins, CO 80524 Mary McVicar, Med.Libn.
Founded: 1969. **Staff:** Prof 1. **Subjects:** Medicine, nursing. **Special Collections:** Ethics; management. **Holdings:** 3000 books; 3500 bound periodical volumes. **Subscriptions:** 225 journals and other serials. **Services:** Interlibrary loan; copying; library open to the public for reference use only. **Computerized Information Services:** MEDLINE; internal database. Performs searches on fee basis. **Networks/Consortia:** Member of Colorado Council of Medical Librarians, Midcontinental Regional Medical Library Program, High Plains Regional Library Service System. **Formerly:** Media Resources Library.

EZRA POUND INSTITUTE OF CIVILIZATION
See: Bankers Research Institute (1305)

★11494★
ROSCOE POUND FOUNDATION - LIBRARY (Law)
1050 31st St., N.W. Phone: (202)965-3500
Washington, DC 20007 Marcia Feldman, Exec.Dir.
Founded: 1956. **Staff:** Prof 1. **Subjects:** Jurisprudence, philosophy, social sciences, history, literature, botany. **Special Collections:** Personal library of Dean Roscoe Pound. **Holdings:** 8700 volumes. **Services:** Interlibrary loan; copying; library open to scholars and students with appropriate credentials. **Special Catalogs:** Catalog of publications listed by author (card). **Formerly:** Association of Trial Lawyers of America.

★11495★
POWELL, GOLDSTEIN, FRAZER & MURPHY - LIBRARY (Law)
1100 C & S National Bank Bldg. Phone: (404)572-6600
Atlanta, GA 30335 Barbara Geier, Dir.
Staff: Prof 4; Other 4. **Subjects:** Law - corporation, banking, securities, tax, labor, real estate. **Holdings:** 23,000 books; 417 bound periodical volumes. **Subscriptions:** 92 journals and other serials. **Services:** Interlibrary loan; library not open to the public. **Automated Operations:** Computerized cataloging and acquisitions. **Computerized Information Services:** Dun & Bradstreet Corporation, LEGI-SLATE, LEXIS, DIALOG Information Services, PHINet FedTax Database, WESTLAW, NewsNet, Inc., Washington Alert Service, Information America, VU/TEXT Information Services, Dow Jones News/Retrieval; internal databases; ABA/net, MCI Mail (electronic mail services). **Staff:** Ruth Fuller, Oper.Libn.; Linda Jackson, Ref./Info.Spec.; Julie Schein, Cat..

★11496★
JOHN WESLEY POWELL MEMORIAL MUSEUM - LIBRARY (Hist)
6 N. Lake Powell Blvd.
Box 547
Page, AZ 86040 Phone: (602)645-9496
Subjects: John Wesley Powell (1834-1902) and his explorations of the Colorado Plateau areas of Utah and Arizona; Dominguez-Escalante expedition of 1776; Lake Powell Country and the Colorado River, 1776-1909; history of the City of Page. **Holdings:** 8 file drawers of manuscripts and photographs. **Services:** Library open to the public with restrictions from February to November.

ROBERT L. POWELL MEMORIAL LIBRARY
See: The Master's College and Seminary - Robert L. Powell Memorial Library (8576)

F.B. POWER PHARMACEUTICAL LIBRARY
See: University of Wisconsin, Madison (17132)

HOWARD ANDERSON POWER MEMORIAL LIBRARY
See: Magee-Womens Hospital (8304)

PATRICK POWER LIBRARY
See: St. Mary's University (12621)

★11497★
POYNTER INSTITUTE FOR MEDIA STUDIES - LIBRARY (Info Sci)
801 3rd St., S. Phone: (813)821-9494
St. Petersburg, FL 33701 Jo A. Cates, Chf.Libn.
Founded: 1985. **Staff:** Prof 1; Other 3. **Subjects:** Journalism, mass communications, newspaper design and graphics, journalistic ethics, media management, writing and composition. **Special Collections:** Newsleaders videotape series. **Holdings:** 6000 books; 400 videotapes; vertical files; microfiche. **Subscriptions:** 225 journals and other serials; 30 newspapers. **Services:** Interlibrary loan; library not open to the public. **Computerized Information Services:** DIALOG Information Services, VU/TEXT Information Services, WILSONLINE, DataTimes. Performs searches on fee basis. **Publications:** Bibliographies on newspaper design, media management, ethics, writing coaching (printout).

DR. JOSEPH POZSONYI MEMORIAL LIBRARY
See: University of Western Ontario - Dr. Joseph Pozsonyi Memorial Library (17093)

★11498★
PPG INDUSTRIES, INC. - BARBERTON TECHNICAL CENTER - TECHNICAL INFORMATION CENTER (Sci-Engr)
Wooster Rd. & 16th St.
Box 31 Phone: (216)848-4161
Barberton, OH 44203 Deborah K. Oberlander, Libn.
Founded: 1940. **Staff:** Prof 3; Other 3. **Subjects:** Agricultural and analytical chemistry, ophthalmic materials, industrial and specialty chemicals, pigments, toxicology. **Holdings:** 12,000 books; 5000 bound periodical volumes; 30,000 internal research reports on microfilm; 5 VF drawers of translations; Chemical Abstracts; U.S. Chemical Patents in microform. **Subscriptions:** 300 journals and other serials. **Services:** Interlibrary loan; SDI; center open to the public with restrictions. **Automated Operations:** Computerized cataloging, acquisitions, serials, and circulation. **Computerized Information Services:** DIALOG Information Services, Pergamon ORBIT InfoLine, Inc., NLM, OCLC, WILSONLINE, STN International; internal database. **Networks/Consortia:** Member of Pittsburgh Regional Library Center (PRLC). **Publications:** Contents of periodicals, weekly; Barberton Technical Center Newsletter, monthly - for internal distribution only. **Formerly:** Chemical Division Library. **Staff:** Yvonne Pringle, Info.Spec.; Krystal Kassay, Info.Spec..

★11499★
PPG INDUSTRIES, INC. - C & R GROUP - TECHNICAL INFORMATION CENTER (Sci-Engr)
Rosanna Dr.
Box 1009 Phone: (412)492-5268
Allison Park, PA 15101 Helen Lamrey, Supv., Info.Serv.
Founded: 1924. **Staff:** Prof 2; Other 4. **Subjects:** Chemistry - paint, polymer, organic; plastics; resins. **Holdings:** 5000 books; 6000 bound periodical volumes; 150 linear feet of patents; 105 linear feet of trade literature; 142 linear feet of pamphlets, government documents. **Subscriptions:** 500 journals and other serials. **Services:** Interlibrary loan; copying; center open to the public with restrictions. **Automated Operations:** Computerized serials routing. **Computerized Information Services:** CAS ONLINE, OCLC, DIALOG Information Services, Pergamon ORBIT InfoLine, Inc. **Networks/Consortia:** Member of Pittsburgh Regional Library Center (PRLC). **Publications:** Research Review, monthly - for internal distribution only. **Also Known As:** Pittsburgh Plate Glass Company.

★11500★
PPG INDUSTRIES, INC. - CHEMICAL DIVISION - NATRIUM RESEARCH AND DEVELOPMENT LIBRARY
Box 191
New Martinsville, WV 26155
Defunct

★11501★
PPG INDUSTRIES, INC. - FIBER GLASS RESEARCH CENTER - LIBRARY (Sci-Engr)
Box 2844 Phone: (412)782-5130
Pittsburgh, PA 15230 Beverly Malak, Lib.Asst.
Staff: 1. **Subjects:** Fiber glass, glass, plastics, rubber, polymer science. **Special Collections:** Foreign and domestic patents on fiber glass science and technology; Visual Search Microfilm File American Society of Testing and Materials standards/collection. **Holdings:** 1500 books; 310 technical reports; 100 translations; 50 college catalogs; internal documents control. **Subscriptions:** 220 journals and other serials. **Services:** Interlibrary loan; copying; SDI; library open to the public with permission. **Automated Operations:** Computerized cataloging. **Computerized Information Services:** DIALOG Information Services, Pergamon ORBIT InfoLine, Inc. **Networks/Consortia:** Member of Pittsburgh Regional Library Center (PRLC). **Publications:** Patent Bulletin, semimonthly; Current Contents, biweekly. **Special Indexes:** Index of internal documents (card).

★11502★
PPG INDUSTRIES, INC. - GLASS RESEARCH CENTER - INFORMATION SERVICES (Sci-Engr)
Box 11472 Phone: (412)665-8566
Pittsburgh, PA 15238 Patricia C. Edge, Supv.
Founded: 1912. **Staff:** Prof 2; Other 1. **Subjects:** Glass technology, physics, mathematics, chemistry, engineering, industrial management. **Special Collections:** U.S. patents on microfilm. **Holdings:** 25,000 books; 18,000 translations and technical reports; 1000 16mm cartridges of microfilm of journals; 2000 microfiche of technical reports. **Subscriptions:** 400 journals and other serials. **Services:** Interlibrary loan; services not open to the public. **Automated Operations:** Computerized cataloging, serials, and circulation. **Computerized Information Services:** DIALOG Information Services, BRS Information Technologies, OCLC, Pergamon ORBIT InfoLine, Inc. **Networks/Consortia:** Member of Pittsburgh Regional Library Center (PRLC). **Publications:** Technical Information Bulletin, monthly - for internal distribution only. **Special Catalogs:** Catalog of internal research reports (card). **Staff:** Hazel Green, Tech.Serv.Libn..

★11503★
PPG INDUSTRIES, INC. - SPECIALTY PRODUCTS UNIT - LIBRARY
12555 W. Higgins Rd.
Box 66251
Chicago, IL 60666
Defunct

★11504★
PQ CORPORATION - BUSINESS LIBRARY (Bus-Fin)
Box 840 Phone: (215)293-7255
Valley Forge, PA 19482 Barbara S. Mattscheck, Bus.Libn.
Staff: Prof 1; Other 1. **Subjects:** Business, marketing, chemistry, engineering. **Holdings:** 1500 books. **Subscriptions:** 150 journals and other serials. **Services:** Interlibrary loan; SDI; library open by personal invitation. **Automated Operations:** Computerized cataloging, acquisitions, serials, and circulation. **Computerized Information Services:** DIALOG Information Services, Pergamon ORBIT InfoLine, Inc., Dun & Bradstreet Corporation, Piers (Port Import/Export Reporting Service). **Publications:** Business Page, bimonthly - for internal distribution only.

★11505★
PQ CORPORATION - RESEARCH LIBRARY (Sci-Engr)
Box 258 Phone: (215)825-5000
Lafayette Hill, PA 19444-0258 Dolores A. Whitehurst, Libn.
Founded: 1927. **Staff:** Prof 1. **Subjects:** Inorganic chemistry, specializing in soluble silicates and silica. **Holdings:** 2450 books; 550 bound periodical volumes; 42 VF drawers of reports and patents. **Subscriptions:** 159 journals and other serials. **Services:** Interlibrary loan; copying; library open to the public with approval. **Automated Operations:** Computerized cataloging. **Computerized Information Services:** DIALOG Information Services, Pergamon ORBIT InfoLine, Inc., U.S. Patents Files, STN International, OCLC.

★11506★
PRACTISING LAW INSTITUTE - LIBRARY (Law)
810 Seventh Ave. Phone: (212)765-5700
New York, NY 10019 Henry W. Enberg, Sr. Legal Ed.
Founded: 1933. **Staff:** Prof 1. **Subjects:** Law. **Holdings:** 3000 books. **Subscriptions:** 50 journals and other serials. **Services:** Library not open to the public.

★11507★
PRAIRIE AGRICULTURAL MACHINERY INSTITUTE - LIBRARY (Agri)
Box 1900 Phone: (306)682-2555
Humboldt, SK, Canada S0K 2A0 Sharon Doepker, Libn.
Staff: Prof 1. **Subjects:** Agriculture, farm machinery testing, electronics, business management, photography. **Holdings:** 2283 books; 80 bound periodical volumes; 11,350 technical papers. **Subscriptions:** 100 journals and other serials; 5 newspapers. **Services:** Interlibrary loan; copying; SDI; library open to the public. **Automated Operations:** Computerized cataloging. **Publications:** Evaluation reports - by subscription; master bibliography and updates to technical papers.

★11508★
PRAIRIE BIBLE INSTITUTE - LIBRARY (Rel-Phil)
Box 4020 Phone: (403)443-5511
Three Hills, AB, Canada T0M 2A0 Ron Jordahl, Lib.Dir.
Staff: 4. **Subjects:** Biblical studies, Christian missions, Christian biography, Christian education. **Holdings:** 41,000 books; 715 bound periodical volumes; 40 VF drawers of clippings; 240 reels of microfilm; 13,400 microfiche; 3700 cassettes. **Subscriptions:** 400 journals and other serials. **Services:** Interlibrary loan; copying; library open to the public. **Automated Operations:** Computerized cataloging and acquisitions. **Staff:** Dr. Fred Youngs, Pub.Serv.Libn.; Jacob Geddert, Tech.Serv.Libn.; Colleen Charter, Acq.Libn..

PRAIRIE FARM REHABILITATION ADMINISTRATION
See: Canada - Prairie Farm Rehabilitation Administration (2470)

PRAIRIE MIGRATORY BIRD RESEARCH CENTRE
See: Canada - Environment Canada, Conservation & Protection - Canadian Wildlife Service (2370)

★11509★
PRAIRIE VIEW A & M UNIVERSITY - W.R. BANKS LIBRARY - SPECIAL COLLECTIONS (Hum, Area-Ethnic)
Third St. Phone: (409)857-3119
Prairie View, TX 77446
Ruth Wachter-Nelson, Archv. & Spec.Coll.Libn.
Founded: 1912. **Special Collections:** Afro-American Collection (by and about Negroes); Black Heritage of the West Collection; children's literature; university archives; photograph collection (1300 photographs); rare books collection. **Services:** Interlibrary loan; copying; collections open to the public. **Automated Operations:** Computerized cataloging. **Computerized Information Services:** DIALOG Information Services, OCLC; internal databases. Performs searches on fee basis. Contact Person: Mrs. Jimmizine Taylor, Hd., Ref., 857-2612. **Networks/Consortia:** Member of Houston Area Research Library Consortium (HARLIC), AMIGOS Bibliographic Council, Inc.. **Staff:** Frank Francis, Jr., Coll.Mgr..

MARGARET PRALL MUSIC LIBRARY
See: Mills College - Margaret Prall Music Library (8997)

PRANG-MARK SOCIETY
See: American Life Foundation (587)

★11510★
ENOCH PRATT FREE LIBRARY - AUDIO-VISUAL DEPARTMENT (Aud-Vis)
400 Cathedral St. Phone: (301)396-4616
Baltimore, MD 21201 Helen W. Cyr, Hd.
Founded: 1949. **Staff:** Prof 4; Other 10. **Subjects:** History of film, experimental film, music, art, social sciences, other arts and crafts, religion, black history/culture, children's films. **Special Collections:** Maryland and Baltimore history. **Holdings:** 5194 16mm films; 161 super and standard 8mm films; 486 filmstrips; 36,805 slides; 926 videotapes; 120 videodiscs; 412 audiotape cassettes. **Subscriptions:** 14 journals and other serials. **Services:** Interlibrary loan (within Maryland only); department open to the public. **Staff:** Marc Sober, AV Spec.; Barry Stahl, Ref.Libn..

★11511★
ENOCH PRATT FREE LIBRARY - BUSINESS, SCIENCE AND TECHNOLOGY DEPARTMENT (Bus-Fin, Sci-Engr)
400 Cathedral St. Phone: (301)396-5316
Baltimore, MD 21201 Sherry Ledbetter, Dept.Hd.
Founded: 1916. **Staff:** Prof 12; Other 3. **Subjects:** Science, business, economics, technology, census material, medicine, consumerism. **Special Collections:** Directories (14 shelves); auto repair (40 VF drawers). **Holdings:** 122,769 books; 3750 bound periodical volumes; 128 VF drawers of pamphlets; 2176 shelves of U.S. documents; 360 periodical titles on microfiche; 34 drawers of U.S. documents on microfiche. **Subscriptions:** 1002 journals and other serials. **Services:** Interlibrary loan; copying; department open to the public. **Computerized Information Services:** The Reference Service (REFSRV). **Networks/Consortia:** Member of Maryland Interlibrary Organization (MILO). **Staff:** Richard Bonnell, Asst.Hd..

★11512★
ENOCH PRATT FREE LIBRARY - FINE ARTS AND RECREATION DEPARTMENT (Art, Mus)
400 Cathedral St. Phone: (301)396-5491
Baltimore, MD 21201 Joan Stahl, Dept.Hd.
Staff: Prof 5; Other 3. **Subjects:** Art, music, architecture, sports and recreation, antiques, dance, prints. **Special Collections:** Holme Collection (a chronological record of illustrated books). **Holdings:** 41,000 volumes; 18,865 musical recordings; 64 VF drawers; 196 VF drawers of pictures; 35,000 libretti; 11,800 pieces of sheet music. **Subscriptions:** 172 journals and other serials. **Services:** Interlibrary loan; copying; department open to the public. **Computerized Information Services:** The Reference Service (REFSRV). **Networks/Consortia:** Member of Maryland Interlibrary Organization (MILO). **Special Indexes:** Song index; analytical index; popular sheet music index; dance index; games index (all on cards). **Staff:** Elaine Bradtke, Prof.Asst.; Judith Goodyear, Prof.Asst.; Ruth Sundermeyer, Prof.Asst.; Ellen Luchinsky, Asst.Hd..

★11513★
ENOCH PRATT FREE LIBRARY - JOB AND CAREER INFORMATION CENTER (Soc Sci)
400 Cathedral St.
Baltimore, MD 21201 Patricia Dougherty, Libn./Couns.
Founded: 1981. **Subjects:** Vocational guidance, job/person matching, trades. **Holdings:** 270 reference titles; 16 VF drawers. **Subscriptions:** 22 journals and other serials. **Services:** Center open to the public. **Remarks:** Center located in Business, Science and Technology Department.

★11514★
ENOCH PRATT FREE LIBRARY - MARYLAND DEPARTMENT (Hist)
400 Cathedral St. Phone: (301)396-5468
Baltimore, MD 21201 Wesley Wilson, Dept.Hd.
Founded: 1934. **Staff:** Prof 4; Other 2. **Subjects:** State of Maryland - persons, places, subjects. **Holdings:** 40,000 volumes; 7000 uncataloged documents; 2100 maps; 24,000 photographs; 1272 fine prints; 4000 postcards; clippings; pamphlets. **Subscriptions:** 40 journals and other serials. **Services:** Interlibrary loan; copying; department open to the public. **Special Indexes:** Biography file, query file, documents file (all card). **Staff:** Eva Slezak, Spec.; Jeffrey Korman, Asst.Hd..

★11515★
ENOCH PRATT FREE LIBRARY - SOCIAL SCIENCE AND HISTORY DEPARTMENT (Soc Sci, Hist)
400 Cathedral St. Phone: (301)396-5430
Baltimore, MD 21201 Marva Belt, Hd.
Staff: Prof 9; Other 2. **Subjects:** Sociology, biography, travel, anthropology, political science, law, history, education. **Special Collections:** Foundation Center Collection; college catalogs (4225). **Holdings:** 250,000 volumes; 161 VF drawers; 250 recordings; depository library for government documents. **Subscriptions:** 625 journals and other serials. **Services:** Interlibrary loan; copying; department open to the public. **Computerized Information Services:** The Reference Service (REFSRV). **Networks/Consortia:** Member of Maryland Interlibrary Organization (MILO). **Staff:** Harriet Jenkins, Asst.Hd..

★11516★
PRATT INSTITUTE - LIBRARY (Art, Sci-Engr)
200 Willoughby Ave. Phone: (718)636-3545
Brooklyn, NY 11205 George Lowy, Dean of Libs.
Founded: 1887. **Staff:** Prof 9; Other 13. **Subjects:** Fine arts, architecture, library science, science and technology. **Special Collections:** History of printing (2000 volumes). **Holdings:** 189,000 books; 29,200 bound periodical volumes; 153,000 government documents; 160,000 prints; 51,000 art slides; 16,000 microforms. **Subscriptions:** 644 journals. **Services:** Interlibrary loan; copying; library open to the public with restrictions. **Automated Operations:** Computerized public access catalog, cataloging, acquisitions, serials, and circulation. **Computerized Information Services:** DIALOG Information Services, OCLC. **Networks/Consortia:** Member of New York Metropolitan Reference and Research Library Agency (METRO). **Special Catalogs:** Periodicals in the Library. **Staff:** Tad G. Kumatz, Asst.Dir., Pub.Serv.; Josephine McSweeney, Ref.Libn.; Margot Karp, Ref.Libn.; Sydney Keaveney, Art & Arch.Libn.; Beverly Robertson, Art &

Arch.Libn.; Christine Stenstrom, Sci.Libn.; Roger Cartwill, Tech.Serv.Libn.; Christopher Thornton, Cat..

★11517★
PRATT INSTITUTE - PRATT MANHATTAN LIBRARY (Art)
295 Lafayette St. Phone: (212)925-8481
New York, NY 10012 George Lowy, Dean of Libs.
Founded: 1974. **Staff:** Prof 1. **Subjects:** Decoration and ornament; interiors; furnishings; fashion illustration; portrait, figure, still life, landscape painting; advertising design and illustration; magazine and book illustration; photography and film; furniture design; airbrush technique. **Holdings:** 500 books; 8 VF drawers; 7500 pictures; photograph file. **Subscriptions:** 20 journals and other serials. **Services:** Library not open to the public. **Networks/Consortia:** Member of New York Metropolitan Reference and Research Library Agency (METRO). **Remarks:** A branch of the Pratt Institute Library, Brooklyn, NY 11205.

★11518★
PRATT AND WHITNEY CANADA INC. - LIBRARY (Sci-Engr)
P.O. Box 10 Phone: (514)677-9411
Longueuil, PQ, Canada J4K 4X9 Joyce Whiting, Chf.Libn.
Founded: 1958. **Staff:** Prof 4; Other 5. **Subjects:** Aeronautics, mechanical and materials engineering, gas turbine engines, industrial management. **Holdings:** 10,000 books; 2500 periodical volumes; 40,000 reports, patents, standards; 13,000 reports on microfiche. **Subscriptions:** 875 journals and other serials. **Services:** Interlibrary loan; library not open to the public. **Automated Operations:** Computerized cataloging and serials routing. **Computerized Information Services:** CAN/OLE, WILSONLINE, DIALOG Information Services, Information/Documentation (INFO/DOC); internal database. **Publications:** Periodical Articles bulletin, biweekly - for internal distribution only; Periodicals in the Library, annual; Library Bulletin, Technical Reports Bulletin, both bimonthly - for internal distribution only. **Remarks:** A subsidiary of United Technologies Corporation. **Staff:** Elizabeth Reader, Ref.Libn.; Suzanne Carlaw, Ref.Libn.; Linda Kuchta, Cat.Libn..

PRATT & WHITNEY INFORMATION SERVICES
See: United Technologies Corporation (15682)

PRC CONSOER, TOWNSEND, INC.
See: Consoer Townsend & Associates (3686)

PRC ENGINEERING, INC.
See: Fredric R. Harris, Inc. (6037)

★11519★
PRECISION CASTPARTS CORPORATION - TECHNICAL INFORMATION CENTER (Sci-Engr)
4600 S.E. Harney Dr. Phone: (503)777-3881
Portland, OR 97206 Patrick Spurlock, Mgr.
Staff: Prof 2; Other 1. **Subjects:** Materials, metals, ceramics, physical sciences, robotics and automation, statistics, process control. **Holdings:** 500 books; 12 bound periodical volumes; 500 unbound reports; 900 patents; 1000 government reports; 800 reprints. **Subscriptions:** 125 journals and other serials. **Services:** Interlibrary loan; copying; SDI; center open to the public by appointment. **Automated Operations:** Computerized cataloging and serials. **Computerized Information Services:** BRS Information Technologies, DIALOG Information Services, OCLC, Pergamon ORBIT InfoLine, Inc.; OnTyme Electronic Message Network Service (electronic mail service). **Publications:** Current Awareness Bulletins. **Special Indexes:** Topical index to Current Awareness Bulletins.

★11520★
PREDICASTS, INC. - LIBRARY (Publ)
11001 Cedar Ave. Phone: (216)795-3000
Cleveland, OH 44106 Diane Oberbeck, Mgr.
Founded: 1960. **Staff:** Prof 2; Other 7. **Subjects:** Business, industries, economics, statistics. **Holdings:** 250 books. **Subscriptions:** 1200 journals and other serials; 100 newspapers. **Services:** Library not open to the public. **Automated Operations:** Computerized serials. **Staff:** Cary McCullough, Thesauri Ed./Cat..

★11521★
PREFORMED LINE PRODUCTS - RESEARCH & ENGINEERING LIBRARY (Sci-Engr)
Box 91129 Phone: (216)461-5200
Cleveland, OH 44101 Edwina T. Barron, Libn.
Founded: 1956. **Staff:** Prof 1. **Subjects:** Vibration, fatigue, strains and stresses, pole line hardware, underground distribution, electric power lines. **Special Collections:** CIGRE (International Conference on Large Electric Systems); American Institute of Electrical Engineers. **Holdings:** 6550 books; 300 bound periodical volumes; 60 VF drawers of technical papers (indexed); internal reports on microfiche (indexed); 125 16mm films; 35 videotapes. **Subscriptions:** 130 journals and other serials. **Services:** Interlibrary loan; copying; library open by permission. **Remarks:** Library located at 660 Beta Dr., Cleveland, OH 44143.

★11522★
PREGNANCY AND INFANT LOSS CENTER - LENDING LIBRARY (Med)
1415 E. Wayzata Blvd., Suite 22 Phone: (612)473-9372
Wayzata, MN 55391 Susan Erling, Exec.Dir.
Founded: 1983. **Staff:** Prof 2. **Subjects:** Perinatal bereavement, coping with grief, children and death. **Holdings:** 100 books. **Subscriptions:** 25 newspapers.

★11523★
PREMARK INTERNATIONAL - BUSINESS INFORMATION CENTER (Bus-Fin)
1717 Deerfield Rd. Phone: (312)498-8569
Deerfield, IL 60015 Mary E. Tyner, Info.Spec.
Founded: 1981. **Staff:** Prof 2. **Subjects:** Business, finance. **Holdings:** 600 books; 50 unbound reports; 3 drawers of microfiche. **Subscriptions:** 240 journals and other serials; 5 newspapers. **Services:** Interlibrary loan; copying; library open to the public with special permission. **Automated Operations:** Computerized cataloging and serials. **Computerized Information Services:** DIALOG Information Services, BRS Information Technologies, Pergamon ORBIT InfoLine, Inc., Dow Jones News/Retrieval, Dun & Bradstreet Corporation, DataTimes, Inc., Data-Star, TEXTLINE, Info Globe, VU/TEXT Information Services, WILSONLINE. **Networks/Consortia:** Member of North Suburban Library System (NSLS). **Staff:** Yvonne Hoff, Bus.Info.Coord..

PRENTIS MEMORIAL LIBRARY
See: Temple Beth El (13938)

★11524★
PRESBYTERIAN CHURCH OF THE ATONEMENT - LIBRARY (Rel-Phil)
10613 Georgia Ave. Phone: (301)649-4131
Silver Spring, MD 20902 Vicky Hess, Libn.
Staff: 1. **Subjects:** Christian doctrine, life and character, missions, biography, education; Bible. **Holdings:** 6500 books; pictures; 500 AV programs; 490 phonograph records; 80 filmstrips; 735 cassette tapes; 135 music tapes; 50 videotapes; 28 maps. **Subscriptions:** 25 journals and other serials. **Services:** Library open to the public.

PRESBYTERIAN CHURCH (U.S.A.) - GHOST RANCH CONFERENCE CENTER
See: Ghost Ranch Conference Center (5653)

★11525★
PRESBYTERIAN CHURCH (U.S.A.) - PRESBYTERIAN HISTORICAL SOCIETY - LIBRARY (Hist, Rel-Phil)
425 Lombard St. Phone: (215)627-1852
Philadelphia, PA 19147 William B. Miller, Dir.
Founded: 1852. **Staff:** Prof 5; Other 6. **Subjects:** Presbyterian Church history, history of Protestantism, hymnology, slavery. **Special Collections:** Sheldon Jackson Collection (Alaska, circa 1870-1905); Westminster Assembly of Divines Collection (300 17th century pamphlets dealing with British church history); Westminster Press Depository Collection (2800 volumes). **Holdings:** 200,000 books; 500,000 manuscripts and primary source materials; 1875 reels of microfilm; 9000 pictures of churches and ministers; 5000 communion tokens; 18 million arranged archival materials. **Subscriptions:** 407 journals and other serials. **Services:** Copying; library open to the public. **Publications:** Journal of Presbyterian History, quarterly - to members and by subscription. **Staff:** Gerald W. Gillette, Mgr., Res. & Lib.Serv.; Barbara Roy, Cat.Libn.; Frederick J. Heuser, Archv..

★11526★
PRESBYTERIAN COLLEGE - LIBRARY (Rel-Phil)
3495 University St. Phone: (514)288-5257
Montreal, PQ, Canada H3A 2A8 Rev. Daniel Shute, Libn.
Founded: 1867. **Staff:** Prof 1; Other 2. **Subjects:** Reformed theology and history, philosophy. **Special Collections:** Patrologia Graeco-Latina (Migne; 382 volumes). **Holdings:** 22,200 volumes. **Subscriptions:** 50 journals and other serials. **Services:** Interlibrary loan; library open to the public during academic year.

★11527★
PRESBYTERIAN DENVER HOSPITAL - BRADFORD MEMORIAL LIBRARY (Med)
1719 E. 19th Ave. Phone: (303)839-6440
Denver, CO 80218 Darcy Burdick, Libn.
Founded: 1950. **Staff:** Prof 1. **Subjects:** Medicine, nursing, hospital administration, hospital chaplaincy. **Holdings:** 2500 books; 1200 bound periodical volumes; 4 drawers of LATCH bibliographies and articles on specific subjects. **Subscriptions:** 55 journals and other serials. **Services:** Interlibrary loan; library not open to the public. **Computerized Information Services:** MEDLINE, DIALOG Information Services, Octanet. **Networks/Consortia:** Member of Denver Area Health Sciences Library Consortium, Colorado Council of Medical Librarians.

★11528★
PRESBYTERIAN HOSPITAL - HEALTH SERVICES LIBRARY (Med)
Box 26666 Phone: (505)841-1516
Albuquerque, NM 87125-6666 Helen Saylor, Med.Libn.
Founded: 1962. **Staff:** Prof 2; Other 3. **Subjects:** Medicine. **Holdings:** 1200 books; 1544 bound periodical volumes; 11,808 unbound materials. **Services:** Interlibrary loan; copying; library open to the public by permission. **Networks/Consortia:** Member of New Mexico Consortium of Biomedical and Hospital Libraries, TALON. **Remarks:** Library located at 1100 Central Ave., S.E., Albuquerque, NM 87102. **Staff:** Mary Beth Jordan, Lib. Media Asst..

★11529★
PRESBYTERIAN HOSPITAL - LEARNING RESOURCE CENTER (Med)
Box 33549 Phone: (704)371-4258
Charlotte, NC 28233-3549 Mary Wallace Berry, Libn.
Staff: Prof 2; Other 2. **Subjects:** Nursing, medicine, allied health education. **Holdings:** 6000 books; 3 VF drawers; AV programs. **Subscriptions:** 200 journals and other serials. **Services:** Interlibrary loan; center not open to the public. **Computerized Information Services:** MEDLINE. **Networks/Consortia:** Member of North Carolina Area Health Education Centers Program Library and Information Services Network.

★11530★
PRESBYTERIAN HOSPITAL - MEDICAL LIBRARY (Med)
N.E. 13th and Lincoln Blvd. Phone: (405)271-4266
Oklahoma City, OK 73104 Dorothy Williams, Lib.Dir.
Founded: 1919. **Staff:** Prof 1; Other 1. **Subjects:** Medicine, nursing, surgery, cardiology. **Holdings:** 4000 books; 6000 bound periodical volumes; 24 boxes of pamphlets; 175 file boxes of unbound periodicals; 2 VF drawers; 800 cassettes. **Subscriptions:** 257 journals and other serials. **Services:** Interlibrary loan; library open to medical and health personnel for reference use only. **Computerized Information Services:** MEDLINE. **Networks/Consortia:** Member of Greater Oklahoma City Area Health Sciences Library Consortium (GOAL), Metronet.

PRESBYTERIAN-UNIVERSITY HOSPITAL
See: University of Pittsburgh (16776)

★11531★
PRESBYTERIAN-UNIVERSITY OF PENNSYLVANIA MEDICAL CENTER - MARY ELLEN BROWN MEDICAL CENTER LIBRARY (Med)
51 N. 39th St. Phone: (215)662-9181
Philadelphia, PA 19104 Kathleen M. Ahrens, Libn.
Staff: Prof 1; Other 4. **Subjects:** Clinical medicine and nursing. **Holdings:** 2200 books; 3500 bound periodical volumes; 300 archival materials; 70 AV programs; 3 VF drawers. **Subscriptions:** 246 journals and other serials. **Services:** Interlibrary loan; copying; library open to the public with restrictions. **Computerized Information Services:** MEDLARS. **Networks/Consortia:** Member of Delaware Valley Information Consortium (DEVIC), Greater Northeastern Regional Medical Library Program.

★11532★
PRESBYTERY OF LONG ISLAND - RESOURCE CENTER (Rel-Phil)
50 Hauppauge Rd. Phone: (516)499-7171
Commack, NY 11725 Rev. Anita E. Hendrix, Assoc.Exec.
Founded: 1983. **Staff:** Prof 1; Other 1. **Subjects:** Christian education, worship, social issues, women's studies. **Holdings:** 1500 books. **Subscriptions:** 35 journals and other serials; 12 newspapers. **Services:** Interlibrary loan; copying; center open to the public. **Automated Operations:** Computerized cataloging, acquisitions, and circulation. **Computerized Information Services:** Internal database.

PRESCOTT HISTORICAL SOCIETY
See: Sharlot Hall/Prescott Historical Societies (13105)

★11533★
PRESENTATION COLLEGE - LIBRARY (Med, Rel-Phil)
1500 North Main Phone: (605)229-8468
Aberdeen, SD 57401 Arvyce Burns, Lib.Dir.
Founded: 1950. **Staff:** Prof 1; Other 2. **Subjects:** Nursing, theology. **Holdings:** 33,782 books; 2245 bound periodical volumes; 2256 recordings, filmstrips, reels of microfilm, cassettes; 8 VF drawers of pamphlets. **Subscriptions:** 192 journals and other serials; 9 newspapers. **Services:** Interlibrary loan; copying; library open to the public with restrictions. **Automated Operations:** Computerized cataloging. **Computerized Information Services:** OCLC. **Networks/Consortia:** Member of MINITEX, Bibliographical Center for Research, Rocky Mountain Region, Inc. (BCR).

PRESIDENT'S COMMITTEE ON EMPLOYMENT OF THE HANDICAPPED ARCHIVES
See: Marquette University - Department of Special Collections and University Archives (8451)

PRESIDENTS HEALTH SCIENCES LIBRARY
See: St. Anne's Hospital (12315)

★11534★
PRESS CLUB OF SAN FRANCISCO - WILL AUBREY MEMORIAL LIBRARY (Hum)
555 Post St.
San Francisco, CA 94102 Phone: (415)775-7800
Founded: 1888. **Subjects:** Biography, Californiana, fiction, history. **Holdings:** 5000 volumes. **Services:** Library not open to the public.

PRESS HERALD-EVENING EXPRESS-MAINE SUNDAY TELEGRAM
See: Guy Gannett Publishing Company (5463)

PRESTON LIBRARY
See: Virginia Military Institute (17361)

PRESTON MEDICAL LIBRARY
See: University of Tennessee - Medical Center, Knoxville (16904)

★11535★
PRESTON, THORGRIMSON, ELLIS & HOLMAN - LIBRARY (Law)
1735 New York Ave., N.W., Suite 500 Phone: (202)628-1700
Washington, DC 20006 Gretchen W. Asmuth, Libn.
Founded: 1982. **Staff:** Prof 1; Other 1. **Subjects:** Law - federal, maritime, insurance; lobbying; U.S. Congress and politics; federal administrative practice. **Special Collections:** Washington state legal materials. **Holdings:** 6000 books. **Subscriptions:** 135 journals and other serials; 15 newspapers. **Services:** Interlibrary loan; copying; library open to the public by appointment. **Computerized Information Services:** LEXIS, NEXIS, LEGI-SLATE, Washington On-Line, DIALOG Information Services, Aviation Online; internal database. Performs searches on fee basis.

★11536★
PRESTON, THORGRIMSON, ELLIS & HOLMAN - LIBRARY (Law)
5400 Columbia Center Phone: (206)623-7580
Seattle, WA 98104 Peggy Roebuck-Jarrett, Hd.Libn.
Staff: Prof 2; Other 1. **Subjects:** Law. **Holdings:** 25,000 books. **Subscriptions:** 200 journals and other serials; 9 newspapers. **Services:** Interlibrary loan; copying; SDI; library open to the public with permission. **Computerized Information Services:** LEXIS, WESTLAW, DIALOG Information Services, DataTimes, VU/TEXT Information Services. **Publications:** New Acquisitions List, irregular. **Staff:** Lee Jackson, Asst.Libn..

PREUS LIBRARY
See: Luther College (8109)

★11537★
PREVENTION RESEARCH CENTER - LIBRARY (Med)
2532 Durant Ave. Phone: (415)486-1111
Berkeley, CA 94704 Elva Yanez, Libn.
Founded: 1984. **Staff:** Prof 2; Other 1. **Subjects:** Alcohol and drug abuse prevention research. **Holdings:** 700 books; 2500 reprints. **Subscriptions:** 85 journals and other serials. **Services:** Interlibrary loan; library not open to

the public. **Automated Operations:** Computerized cataloging. **Computerized Information Services:** DIALOG Information Services; INFOMAR (internal database); DIALMAIL (electronic mail service). **Networks/Consortia:** Member of Substance Abuse Librarians and Information Specialists (SALIS). **Staff:** Leslie Fisher, Asst.Libn..

ISSER AND RAE PRICE LIBRARY OF JUDAICA
See: University of Florida (16151)

★11538★
PRICE-POTTENGER NUTRITION FOUNDATION - LIBRARY
5871 El Cajon Blvd.
San Diego, CA 92115
Founded: 1975. **Subjects:** Nutrition, health, agrobiology, gardening, pesticides, poisoning, medicine. **Special Collections:** Complete works of Dr. Weston A. Price and Dr. Francis M. Pottenger; pesticide research of Dr. G.F. Knight; papers of Dr. William A. Albrecht; scientific studies. **Holdings:** Scientific reprints; tapes; film. **Remarks:** Presently inactive.

★11539★
PRICE WATERHOUSE - INFORMATION CENTER (Bus-Fin)
400 S. Hope St. Phone: (213)236-3515
Los Angeles, CA 90071-2889 Mignon Veasley, Hd.Libn.
Staff: Prof 1; Other 2. **Subjects:** Accounting, business, management, investment, auditing, taxation. **Holdings:** Figures not available. **Subscriptions:** 400 journals and other serials. **Services:** Interlibrary loan; center not open to the public. **Computerized Information Services:** LEXIS, NEXIS, DIALOG Information Services, DataTimes, WILSONLINE, VU/TEXT Information Services, INVESTEXT, Dow Jones News/Retrieval, UMI Article Clearinghouse (UMAC), Interactive Data Services. **Publications:** Periodical list.

★11540★
PRICE WATERHOUSE - INFORMATION CENTER (Bus-Fin)
200 S. Biscayne Blvd., Suite 3000 Phone: (305)358-3682
Miami, FL 33131 Lynne Becton, Info.Spec.
Staff: Prof 1; Other 1. **Subjects:** Accounting and auditing, taxation, business. **Holdings:** 1500 books; 600 annual reports; Price Waterhouse external publications; 55 loose-leaf services. **Subscriptions:** 80 journals and other serials; 6 newspapers. **Services:** Interlibrary loan; center open to the public by appointment. **Computerized Information Services:** DIALOG Information Services, LEXIS, NEXIS.

★11541★
PRICE WATERHOUSE - INFORMATION CENTER (Bus-Fin)
160 Federal St. Phone: (617)439-7412
Boston, MA 02110 Jean M. Scanlan, Mgr.
Founded: 1976. **Staff:** Prof 2. **Subjects:** Accounting, taxation, management, finance. **Holdings:** 2500 books; 60 reels of microfilm; microfiche. **Subscriptions:** 250 journals and other serials. **Services:** Interlibrary loan; copying; SDI; center open to the public by appointment. **Automated Operations:** Computerized cataloging. **Computerized Information Services:** DunSprint, DIALOG Information Services, Pergamon ORBIT InfoLine, Inc., LEXIS, NewsNet, Inc.; DIALMAIL (electronic mail service). Performs searches on fee basis. **Publications:** What's New in the Price Waterhouse Information Center, monthly - for internal distribution only. **Staff:** James N. Cooper, Asst to Dir..

★11542★
PRICE WATERHOUSE - INFORMATION CENTER (Bus-Fin)
200 Renaissance Center, Suite 3900 Phone: (313)259-0500
Detroit, MI 48243 Jerrie Calloway, Info.Spec.
Founded: 1976. **Staff:** Prof 1. **Subjects:** Accounting, taxation. **Holdings:** 5000 books; 6 boxes of microfiche; 1 drawer of microfilm; Price Waterhouse publications. **Subscriptions:** 132 journals and other serials; 13 newspapers. **Services:** Center not open to the public. **Automated Operations:** Computerized cataloging. **Computerized Information Services:** DIALOG Information Services, VU/TEXT Information Services, LEXIS, NEXIS.

★11543★
PRICE WATERHOUSE - INFORMATION CENTER (Bus-Fin)
1001 Fourth Avenue Plaza, Suite 4200 Phone: (206)622-1505
Seattle, WA 98154 Roxanna Frost, Info.Spec.
Founded: 1972. **Staff:** Prof 1; Other 1. **Subjects:** Accounting, taxation, auditing, management, data processing. **Holdings:** 3000 books; loose-leaf tax services. **Subscriptions:** 340 journals and other serials; 10 newspapers. **Services:** Center not open to the public. **Automated Operations:** Computerized cataloging. **Computerized Information Services:** DIALOG Information Services, Dun & Bradstreet Corporation, Dow Jones News/Retrieval, LEXIS, NEXIS, National Automated Accounting Research System (NAARS), DataTimes; internal databases. Performs searches on fee basis. **Publications:** Acquisitions list, monthly - for internal distribution only.

★11544★
PRICE WATERHOUSE - LIBRARY (Bus-Fin)
200 E. Randolph Dr., Suite 6200 Phone: (312)565-1500
Chicago, IL 60601 E. Ann Raup, Libn.
Founded: 1970. **Staff:** 2. **Subjects:** Accounting, auditing, management. **Holdings:** 1000 books; 120 bound periodical volumes; 49 VF drawers of corporate annual reports. **Subscriptions:** 133 journals and other serials. **Services:** Interlibrary loan (local only); library open to the public by appointment.

★11545★
PRICE WATERHOUSE - LIBRARY (Bus-Fin)
101 S.W. Main, Suite 1700 Phone: (503)224-9040
Portland, OR 97204 Betty Woerner, Libn.
Founded: 1979. **Staff:** Prof 1. **Subjects:** Tax law, accounting, auditing, management consulting. **Holdings:** Figures not available. **Subscriptions:** 80 journals and other serials; 7 newspapers. **Services:** Interlibrary loan; copying; SDI; library open to the public by appointment. **Publications:** New books list, bimonthly. **Special Catalogs:** Management proposals and reports; brochures (both online).

★11546★
PRICE WATERHOUSE - LIBRARY (Bus-Fin)
601 W. Hastings St. Phone: (604)682-4711
Vancouver, BC, Canada V6B 5A5
Janet A. Parkinson, Supv., Lib. and Res.
Staff: Prof 1. **Subjects:** Accounting, auditing, taxation. **Holdings:** 2000 volumes; newspaper clipping file and financial pages; Price Waterhouse external publications; corporate annual reports for 500 Canadian companies. **Subscriptions:** 30 journals and other serials; 7 newspapers. **Services:** Interlibrary loan; library not open to the public.

★11547★
PRICE WATERHOUSE - LIBRARY (Bus-Fin)
1100, blvd. Dorchester, W. Phone: (514)879-5600
Montreal, PQ, Canada H3B 2G4 Martha Nugent
Founded: 1945. **Staff:** Prof 1. **Subjects:** Accounting, auditing, management, consulting, taxation. **Holdings:** 1800 books; 100 bound periodical volumes. **Subscriptions:** 80 journals and other serials. **Services:** Interlibrary loan; library not open to the public.

★11548★
PRICE WATERHOUSE - NATIONAL INFORMATION CENTER (Bus-Fin)
1251 Ave. of the Americas Phone: (212)489-8900
New York, NY 10020 Masha Zipper, Dir.
Staff: Prof 9; Other 10. **Subjects:** Accounting, auditing, business, United States and international taxation. **Holdings:** 15,000 books; 70 VF drawers; 1000 reels of microfilm; 10 million microfiche. **Subscriptions:** 500 journals and other serials. **Services:** Interlibrary loan (to clients and SLA members); center open to clients. **Automated Operations:** Computerized cataloging and routing system. **Computerized Information Services:** DIALOG Information Services, Dow Jones News/Retrieval, LEXIS, NEXIS, National Automated Accounting Research System (NAARS), Pergamon ORBIT InfoLine, Inc., CompuServe, Inc., TEXTLINE, WILSONLINE, VU/TEXT Information Services. **Publications:** National Information Center Acquisitions. **Special Indexes:** Price Waterhouse Review Twenty-Five Year Index, 1955-1980. **Staff:** Ann Alexanian, Asst. to Mgr.; Terry Bennett, Info.Spec.; Nancy Trott, Info.Spec.; Deborah Yaffe, Info.Spec.; Jane Axelrod, U.S. Tax Spec.; Rita Van Buren, Intl. Tax Spec.; Dennis Dilno, Hd.Cat.; Chung Lee, Asst.Cat..

★11549★
PRICE WATERHOUSE - NATIONAL/TORONTO OFFICE LIBRARY (Bus-Fin)
Toronto Dominion Centre
P.O. Box 51 Phone: (416)863-1133
Toronto, ON, Canada M5K 1G1
Dorothy L. Sedgwick, Mgr., Info. and Lib.Serv.
Staff: Prof 2; Other 2. **Subjects:** Accounting, auditing, business, finance, management. **Holdings:** 5000 volumes; annual reports for 1200 Canadian, U.S., and other corporations; Conference Board publications; annual reports for Canadian federally incorporated companies on microfiche. **Subscriptions:** 150 journals and other serials; 6 newspapers. **Services:** Interlibrary loan; library not open to the public. **Automated Operations:**

Computerized cataloging. **Computerized Information Services:** Pergamon ORBIT InfoLine, Inc., Info Globe, QL Systems, DIALOG Information Services, Dun & Bradstreet Corporation; internal database. **Publications:** Professional Reading, bimonthly. **Staff:** Nancy Wells, Asst.Libn..

★11550★
PRICE WATERHOUSE - NEW YORK OFFICE INFORMATION CENTER (Bus-Fin)
153 E. 53rd St. Phone: (212)371-2000
New York, NY 10022 Patricia R. Pauth, Mgr.
Founded: 1972. **Staff:** Prof 4; Other 4. **Subjects:** Accounting, auditing, business, finance. **Holdings:** 5000 books; 90 bound periodical volumes; corporation reports for 3000 companies; securities prices in microform. **Subscriptions:** 350 journals and other serials. **Services:** Interlibrary loan; center open to the public by appointment. **Automated Operations:** Computerized cataloging. **Computerized Information Services:** DIALOG Information Services, Dow Jones News/Retrieval, LEXIS, NEXIS, Dun & Bradstreet Corporation; internal database. **Staff:** Elizabeth Croft, Asst.; Maura Sostack, Info.Spec..

★11551★
PRICE WATERHOUSE - TAX LIBRARY (Law)
153 E. 53rd St. Phone: (212)371-2000
New York, NY 10022 Ann Hayes, Tax Libn.
Staff: Prof 1. **Subjects:** Taxation law, international tax law. **Holdings:** 3300 books; 324 bound periodical volumes; 150 vertical files on taxation. **Subscriptions:** 22 journals and other serials. **Services:** Interlibrary loan; library open to clients and SLA members. **Computerized Information Services:** LEXIS.

CLEVELAND PRICHARD MEMORIAL LIBRARY
See: Bienville Historical Society (1592)

PRIMATE INFORMATION CENTER
See: University of Washington - Regional Primate Research Center (17077)

★11552★
PRIME COMPUTER, INC. - INFORMATION CENTER (Comp Sci)
500 Old Connecticut Path Phone: (617)879-2960
Framingham, MA 01701 Susan Keith, Mgr.
Founded: 1978. **Staff:** Prof 2; Other 1. **Subjects:** Computer science, business, management, library science. **Holdings:** 2500 books; 6000 technical reports, patents, dissertations; 80 journal titles on microfiche. **Subscriptions:** 250 journals and other serials; 10 newspapers. **Services:** Interlibrary loan; library not open to the public. **Automated Operations:** Computerized cataloging, serials, and circulation. **Computerized Information Services:** OCLC, DIALOG Information Services; internal database. **Networks/Consortia:** Member of NELINET. **Publications:** Newsletter, monthly - for internal distribution only. **Special Indexes:** KWIC index to technical reports.

PRIMERICA CORP.
See: American National Can Co. (615)

PRIMERICA CORP. - AMERICAN CAPITAL ASSET MANAGEMENT, INC.
See: American Capital Asset Management, Inc. (434)

★11553★
PRINCE COUNTY HOSPITAL - MEDICAL LIBRARY (Med)
259 Beattie Ave. Phone: (902)436-9131
Summerside, PE, Canada C1N 2A9 Dr. J.P. Schaefer, Dir.
Subjects: Medicine. **Holdings:** 2000 books; 200 bound periodical volumes. **Subscriptions:** 20 journals and other serials. **Services:** Interlibrary loan; library open to the public with restrictions.

★11554★
PRINCE EDWARD HEIGHTS - RESIDENT RECORDS LIBRARY (Med)
Box 440 Phone: (613)476-2104
Picton, ON, Canada K0K 2T0 Sharon Morch, Libn.
Staff: 1. **Subjects:** Mental retardation, psychology, medicine, pharmacy, social work, management. **Holdings:** 730 volumes; 93 files of reference material; 2 educational kits. **Subscriptions:** 34 journals and other serials. **Services:** Interlibrary loan; copying; library open to the public. **Remarks:** Maintained by Ontario Ministry of Community and Social Services.

★11555★
PRINCE EDWARD ISLAND DEPARTMENT OF EDUCATION - MEDIA CENTRE (Aud-Vis)
202 Richmond St. Phone: (902)368-4639
Charlottetown, PE, Canada C1A 1J2
Bill Ledwell, Chf. of Educ. Media
Founded: 1974. **Staff:** Prof 1; Other 5. **Subjects:** General collection. **Holdings:** 3500 16mm films; 3200 videotapes; 200 multimedia kits. **Subscriptions:** 10 journals and other serials. **Services:** Center open to the public. **Remarks:** Media centre serves as distribution outlet for National Film Board of Canada in Prince Edward Island.

★11556★
PRINCE EDWARD ISLAND GOVERNMENT SERVICES LIBRARY (Plan)
Box 2000 Phone: (902)368-4653
Charlottetown, PE, Canada C1A 7N8 Nichola Cleaveland, Libn.
Founded: 1968. **Staff:** Prof 1. **Subjects:** Planning and development, economics, education, social services, recreation and tourism, health services administration. **Holdings:** 8000 books; 1080 linear feet of Canadian federal government publications (depository); 150 linear feet of provincial government publications. **Subscriptions:** 200 journals and other serials. **Services:** Interlibrary loan; copying; library open to the public.

★11557★
PRINCE EDWARD ISLAND MUSEUM AND HERITAGE FOUNDATION - GENEALOGICAL COLLECTION (Hist)
2 Kent St. Phone: (902)892-9127
Charlottetown, PE, Canada C1A 1M6 Miss Orlo Jones, Geneal.Coord.
Staff: Prof 2. **Subjects:** Genealogy. **Holdings:** 215 books; 140 bound periodical volumes; 11 drawers of manuscript genealogies; 125 bound genealogies; 2 VF drawers of manuscript transcriptions of local cemetery records. **Subscriptions:** 50 journals and other serials. **Services:** Copying (limited); collection open to the public. **Special Indexes:** Index to persons having lived on Prince Edward Island (650,000 cards); baptismal records (130,000 cards); burial records (14,000 cards).

★11558★
PRINCE EDWARD ISLAND PUBLIC ARCHIVES (Hist)
P.O. Box 1000 Phone: (902)368-4290
Charlottetown, PE, Canada C1A 7M4 N.J. De Jong, Prov.Archv.
Founded: 1964. **Staff:** Prof 2; Other 1. **Subjects:** History and government of Prince Edward Island. **Holdings:** 600 books; 40 linear meters of bound periodical volumes; 3000 linear meters of archival materials; microfilm. **Subscriptions:** 10 journals and other serials. **Services:** Copying; archives open to the public.

★11559★
PRINCE GEORGE CITIZEN - NEWSPAPER LIBRARY (Publ)
150 Brunswick St.
P.O. Box 5700 Phone: (604)562-2441
Prince George, BC, Canada V2L 5K9 Sharon L. Moffat, Libn.
Staff: Prof 1. **Subjects:** Newspaper reference topics. **Holdings:** 100 books; 2000 files of clippings; 420 files of photographs; 365 reels of microfilm; 200 documents and pamphlets. **Subscriptions:** 16 journals and other serials. **Services:** Library open to the public with restrictions. **Special Indexes:** Editorial index (card).

★11560★
PRINCE GEORGE CITY PLANNING DEPARTMENT - PLANNING LIBRARY (Plan)
1100 Patricia Blvd. Phone: (604)564-5151
Prince George, BC, Canada V2L 3V9 Kent Sedgwick, Libn.
Subjects: Planning, policy, environmental studies, economic development, design, housing, zoning bylaws. **Holdings:** 1300 books; 50 bound periodical volumes. **Subscriptions:** 25 journals and other serials. **Services:** Library open to the public with prior permission of librarian. **Computerized Information Services:** Internal database.

★11561★
PRINCE GEORGE'S COUNTY CIRCUIT COURT - LAW LIBRARY (Law)
Courthouse
Box 580 Phone: (301)952-3438
Upper Marlboro, MD 20772-0580 Pamela J. Gregory, Law Libn.
Staff: Prof 1; Other 2. **Subjects:** Law, Maryland law and history. **Special Collections:** Maryland State documents depository. **Holdings:** 34,000 books; 500 bound periodical volumes; 3 VF drawers of state agency regulations and materials; 15 years of county local legislation. **Subscriptions:** 300 journals and other serials. **Services:** Interlibrary loan;

copying; library open to the public. **Computerized Information Services:** WESTLAW, LEXIS, DIALOG Information Services. **Publications:** Selected List of Acquisitions. **Special Indexes:** Index to County Charter; Index to Prince George's County Legislation.

★11562★
PRINCE GEORGE'S COUNTY HEALTH DEPARTMENT - PUBLIC HEALTH RESOURCE CENTER (Med)
Cheverly, MD 20785 Peggy H. Roeder, Mgr.
Staff: Prof 1; Other 1. **Subjects:** Public health, health education, nursing, mental health, administration, geriatrics. **Holdings:** 1500 books; educational pamphlets. **Subscriptions:** 100 journals and other serials. **Services:** Interlibrary loan; copying; center open to the public. **Publications:** Resource Center Register, quarterly - for internal distribution only.

★11563★
PRINCE GEORGE'S COUNTY MEMORIAL LIBRARY SYSTEM - PARENT CHILD ROOM (Soc Sci)
6530 Adelphi Rd. Phone: (301)779-9330
Hyattsville, MD 20782-2098 Peggy Ransom, Ch.Libn.
Founded: 1984. **Staff:** Prof 1. **Subjects:** Parenting. **Holdings:** 1200 books. **Services:** Interlibrary loan; copying; room open to the public.

★11564★
PRINCE GEORGE'S COUNTY MEMORIAL LIBRARY SYSTEM - PUBLIC DOCUMENTS REFERENCE LIBRARY (Plan)
County Adm. Bldg., Rm. 2198 Phone: (301)952-3904
Upper Marlboro, MD 20772 Ellen Lodwick, Docs.Libn.
Founded: 1977. **Staff:** Prof 1; Other 1. **Subjects:** County government, regional planning, zoning. **Special Collections:** Published county documents; documents from bi-county and regional agencies, municipalities (3000). **Holdings:** 800 books; 3000 documents; 250 microfilm cartridges; 63 feet of bill files; 192 feet of zoning files. **Subscriptions:** 50 journals and other serials; 8 newspapers. **Services:** Copying; library open to the public for reference use only. **Computerized Information Services:** LOGIN (electronic mail service). **Publications:** Newsletter, bimonthly - to county departments and selected libraries. **Special Catalogs:** Catalog of county publications. **Special Indexes:** Subject index to county council bills and resolutions (card).

★11565★
PRINCE GEORGE'S COUNTY MEMORIAL LIBRARY SYSTEM - SOJOURNER TRUTH ROOM (Area-Ethnic)
6200 Oxon Hill Rd. Phone: (301)839-2400
Oxon Hill, MD 20745 Teresa M. Stakem, Libn. II
Staff: Prof 1; Other 1. **Subjects:** Blacks - women, family, slavery, civil rights; literature; military. **Special Collections:** Slave narratives (30). **Holdings:** 3600 books; 130 bound periodical volumes; 12 VF drawers of clippings, pamphlets, government documents; 100 reels of microfilm and 35 microfiche of periodicals. **Subscriptions:** 20 journals and other serials. **Services:** Copying; room open to the public with restrictions. **Automated Operations:** Computerized circulation. **Computerized Information Services:** CLSI (internal database).

★11566★
PRINCE GEORGE'S COUNTY PUBLIC SCHOOLS - PROFESSIONAL LIBRARY (Educ)
8437 Landover Rd. Phone: (301)773-9790
Landover, MD 20785 Dr. Edward W. Barth, Coord.Supv.
Founded: 1960. **Staff:** Prof 3; Other 2. **Subjects:** Education. **Special Collections:** Maryland Collection; Prince George's County Collection (150 books). **Holdings:** 11,500 books; 200 AV programs; 300 public school curriculum guides; 295 journals in microform. **Subscriptions:** 349 journals and other serials. **Services:** Interlibrary loan; copying; library open to the public for reference use only. **Automated Operations:** Computerized cataloging, acquisitions, serials, and circulation. **Computerized Information Services:** Online systems. **Networks/Consortia:** Member of Maryland Interlibrary Organization (MILO), Metropolitan Washington Library Council. **Publications:** Bits and Pieces (newsletter), 4/academic year - for internal distribution only. **Staff:** Joyce E. Meucci, Lib.Assoc.; Mary Ellen Lentz, Libn..

★11567★
PRINCE GEORGE'S HOSPITAL CENTER - SAUL SCHWARTZBACH MEMORIAL LIBRARY (Med)
Cheverly, MD 20785 Phone: (301)341-2440
Eleanor Kleman, Med.Libn.
Staff: Prof 1. **Subjects:** Medicine. **Holdings:** 1000 books; 2500 bound periodical volumes; 2350 AV programs. **Subscriptions:** 180 journals and other serials. **Services:** Interlibrary loan; copying; library open to the public for reference use only. **Computerized Information Services:** MEDLARS. **Networks/Consortia:** Member of Maryland and D.C. Consortium of Resource Sharing (MADCORS).

★11568★
PRINCE OF PEACE LUTHERAN CHURCH - LIBRARY (Rel-Phil)
4419 S. Howell Ave. Phone: (414)483-3828
Milwaukee, WI 53207 Mrs. Robert Heinritz, Hd.Libn.
Founded: 1963. **Staff:** 6. **Subjects:** Religion, missions, children's literature. **Special Collections:** Works of Martin Luther. **Holdings:** 3085 books; archival materials; VF drawers; cassette tapes; maps. **Services:** Library not open to the public.

★11569★
PRINCE OF WALES NORTHERN HERITAGE CENTRE - NORTHWEST TERRITORIES ARCHIVES - LIBRARY (Hist)
Yellowknife, NT, Canada X1A 2L9 Phone: (403)873-7177
Carolynn Kobelka, Libn.
Founded: 1982. **Staff:** Prof 1; Other 1. **Subjects:** History of the Northwest Territories, archeology, Arctic exploration, heritage resource management. **Special Collections:** Admiral Sir Leopold M'Clintock and Rear Admiral Noel Wright Collections (600 19th century imprints of Arctic exploration). **Holdings:** 7000 books; federal and provincial government publications; microfilm; microfiche; reprints. **Subscriptions:** 150 journals and other serials; 15 newspapers. **Services:** Copying; library open to the public for reference use only. **Publications:** Acquisitions list, monthly.

★11570★
PRINCE WILLIAM COUNTY SCHOOLS - STAFF LIBRARY (Educ)
Box 389 Phone: (703)791-7334
Manassas, VA 22110 Chris Burton, Libn.
Founded: 1962. **Staff:** Prof 1; Other 2. **Subjects:** Education, psychology, management, library science. **Holdings:** 6066 books; 2399 pamphlets, monographs, special reports; commercial catalog and educational material files; unbound periodicals; newsletters. **Subscriptions:** 163 journals and other serials. **Services:** SDI; library open to the public.

★11571★
PRINCETON ANTIQUES BOOKFINDERS - ART MARKETING REFERENCE LIBRARY (Art, Sci-Engr)
2915-17-31 Atlantic Ave. Phone: (609)344-1943
Atlantic City, NJ 08401 Robert Eugene, Cur.
Founded: 1974. **Staff:** Prof 1. **Subjects:** Science and technology, living arts, fiction, collectibles. **Special Collections:** Postcard Photo Library (250,000). **Holdings:** 175,000 books. **Subscriptions:** 25 journals and other serials. **Services:** Library open to the public by appointment.

★11572★
PRINCETON LIBRARY IN NEW YORK (Hist)
15 W. 43rd St., Fifth Fl. Phone: (212)840-6400
New York, NY 10036 Constance Clark, Libn.
Founded: 1962. **Subjects:** Princetoniana. **Holdings:** 9000 books. **Subscriptions:** 90 journals and other serials. **Services:** Library open to Princeton Club members, alumni, visiting scholars, and accredited members of historical, literary, or comparable organizations.

★11573★
PRINCETON POLYMER LABORATORIES, INC. - LIBRARY (Sci-Engr)
501 Plainsboro Rd. Phone: (609)799-2060
Plainsboro, NJ 08536 Carol Troy, Libn.
Founded: 1972. **Staff:** Prof 1. **Subjects:** Polymer technology; chemistry - organic, inorganic, physical. **Holdings:** 1000 books; 3 VF drawers of U.S. and foreign patents. **Subscriptions:** 23 journals and other serials. **Services:** Interlibrary loan; copying; library open to the public with permission of president.

★11574★
PRINCETON THEOLOGICAL SEMINARY - SPEER LIBRARY (Rel-Phil)
Mercer St. & Library Place
Box 111 Phone: (609)921-8300
Princeton, NJ 08540 James Armstrong, Libn.
Founded: 1812. **Staff:** Prof 6; Other 9. **Subjects:** Theology, Presbyterianism, Semitic philology, Biblical studies, church history. **Special Collections:** Benson Collection of Hymnology; collection of Puritan and English theological literature; Agnew Collection on the Baptism

Controversy; Sprague Collection of Early American Pamphlets. **Holdings:** 321,741 volumes; 58,388 bound pamphlets; 100,000 manuscripts; 2911 reels of microfilm; 3000 cuneiform tablets. **Subscriptions:** 2000 journals and other serials. **Services:** Interlibrary loan; copying; library open to the public. **Automated Operations:** Computerized cataloging, acquisitions, and serials. **Computerized Information Services:** DIALOG Information Services, RLIN, OCLC, BRS Information Technologies. **Networks/Consortia:** Member of RLG. **Staff:** Sandra Boyd, Ref.Libn.; Dr. James S. Irvine, Assoc.Libn., Tech.Serv.; Tom Ray, Cat.Libn.; Julie Dawson, Ser.Libn.; Sharon Taylor, Coll.Dev.Libn.; Donald Vorp, Archv..

PRINCETON UNIVERSITY - AMERICAN CIVIL LIBERTIES UNION - ARCHIVES
See: American Civil Liberties Union - Library/Archives (445)

★11575★
PRINCETON UNIVERSITY - ASTRONOMY LIBRARY (Sci-Engr)
Peyton Hall — Phone: (609)452-3820
Princeton, NJ 08544 — Ludmilla Wightman
Subjects: Astronomy, astrophysics. **Special Collections:** European Southern Observatory (ESO) Atlas of the Southern Sky; Mount Palomar Sky Atlas. **Holdings:** 17,000 volumes. **Subscriptions:** 350 journals and other serials. **Services:** Interlibrary loan; copying; library open to the public for reference use only. **Computerized Information Services:** RLIN.

★11576★
PRINCETON UNIVERSITY - BIOLOGY LIBRARY (Biol Sci)
Guyot Hall — Phone: (609)452-3235
Princeton, NJ 08544 — Helen Y. Zimmerberg, Libn.
Staff: Prof 1; Other 3. **Subjects:** Biology, biochemistry, microbiology, zoology, botany, molecular biology, genetics, ecology, population biology. **Holdings:** 18,500 books; 21,500 bound periodical volumes. **Subscriptions:** 1000 journals and other serials. **Services:** Interlibrary loan; copying; library open to the public. **Automated Operations:** Computerized public access catalog. **Computerized Information Services:** DIALOG Information Services, BRS Information Technologies. Performs searches on fee basis. **Publications:** Acquisitions List.

★11577★
PRINCETON UNIVERSITY - CHEMISTRY LIBRARY (Sci-Engr, Biol Sci)
Frick Chemical Laboratory — Phone: (609)452-3238
Princeton, NJ 08544 — Dr. David Goodman, Libn.
Staff: Prof 1; Other 2. **Subjects:** Chemistry - general, physical, organic, inorganic, biochemistry, molecular biology. **Holdings:** 20,000 books; 24,000 bound periodical volumes; 1200 departmental dissertations. **Subscriptions:** 600 journals and other serials. **Services:** Interlibrary loan (through main library); copying; library open to the public for reference use only. **Computerized Information Services:** DIALOG Information Services, CAS ONLINE, BRS Information Technologies. **Networks/Consortia:** Member of RLG. **Publications:** New Books and News.

★11578★
PRINCETON UNIVERSITY - DEPARTMENT OF ART & ARCHAEOLOGY - INDEX OF CHRISTIAN ART (Art)
McCormick Hall — Phone: (609)452-3773
Princeton, NJ 08544 — Elizabeth Sears, Act.Dir.
Founded: 1917. **Staff:** Prof 4; Other 2. **Subjects:** Christian art before 1400. **Holdings:** Iconographic index of 700,000 cards; 200,000 photographs. **Services:** Reference for visiting scholars, mainly in history of art. **Staff:** A.L. Bennett Hagens; R. Melzak; L. Drewer.

★11579★
PRINCETON UNIVERSITY - ENGINEERING LIBRARY (Sci-Engr)
Engineering Quadrangle — Phone: (609)452-3200
Princeton, NJ 08544 — Dolores M. Hoelle, Libn.
Staff: Prof 4; Other 6. **Subjects:** Engineering - chemical, civil, electrical, mechanical, nuclear, aeronautical; solid state physics; polymers; computers; transportation; environmental studies; water resources. **Special Collections:** DOE and NASA reports (microfilm); SAE and Aerospace Industries Association of America (AIAA) conference papers (microfiche). **Holdings:** 60,000 books; 60,000 bound periodical volumes; 400,000 technical reports and government documents, including 52 file cabinets of microfiche. **Subscriptions:** 1500 journals and other serials. **Services:** Interlibrary loan; copying; library open to the public for reference use only. **Automated Operations:** Computerized public access catalog, cataloging, acquisitions, and circulation. **Computerized Information Services:** DIALOG Information Services, WILSONLINE, BRS Information Technologies, STN International, NASA/RECON, Geac Library Information System, DTIC. Performs searches on fee basis. **Networks/Consortia:** Member of RLG. **Staff:** Lois M. Nase, Asst.Libn.; Ann C. Doyle, Asst.Libn..

★11580★
PRINCETON UNIVERSITY - GEOLOGY LIBRARY (Sci-Engr)
Guyot Hall — Phone: (609)452-3267
Princeton, NJ 08544 — David C. Stager, Geol.Libn.
Staff: Prof 2; Other 5. **Subjects:** Geology - crystallography, geochemistry, geomorphology, geophysics, mineralogy, oceanography, paleontology, petrology, sedimentation, stratigraphy, structural geology. **Holdings:** 60,000 volumes; 900 theses; 276,000 maps; 450 technical reports. **Subscriptions:** 1200 journals and other serials. **Services:** Interlibrary loan; copying; library open to the public. **Computerized Information Services:** DIALOG Information Services, RLIN; GEOMAP (internal database). Performs searches on fee basis. Contact Person: Patricia Gaspari Bridges, Asst.Libn./Map Libn., 452-3247.

★11581★
PRINCETON UNIVERSITY - GEST ORIENTAL LIBRARY AND EAST ASIAN COLLECTIONS (Area-Ethnic)
317 Palmer Hall — Phone: (609)452-3182
Princeton, NJ 08544 — Diane Perushek, Cur.
Founded: 1926. **Staff:** Prof 7; Other 14. **Subjects:** China, Japan, Korea. **Special Collections:** Buddhist sutras, Sung and Yuan editions (2864 volumes); Ming editions (24,000 volumes); Hishi copies, Ming works reproduced in Japan (2100 volumes); Chinese medicine and materia medica (1700 volumes); "Go" collection (500 volumes); rare books including Mongolian, Tibetan, and Manchurian titles (1300). **Holdings:** 396,900 books; 3000 manuscripts; 17,400 microforms. **Subscriptions:** 1900 journals and other serials; 23 newspapers. **Services:** Interlibrary loan; copying; information service for outside inquirers on questions relating to China, Japan, and Korea. **Automated Operations:** Computerized cataloging. **Computerized Information Services:** RLIN catalog (internal database); BITNET (electronic mail service). Contact Person: Charmian Cheng, Hd., Pub.Serv.Sect., 452-5336. **Networks/Consortia:** Member of RLG. **Special Catalogs:** A Catalogue of the Chinese Rare Books in the Gest Collection of the Princeton University Library (book); Union List of Current Japanese Periodicals in the East Asian Libraries of Columbia, Harvard, Princeton, and Yale, 1985. **Special Indexes:** List of Periodicals in Japanese in the Gest Oriental Library and East Asian Collections, 1980. **Staff:** Iping K. Wei, Hd., Tech.Serv.Sect.; Soowon Y. Kim, Japanese/Korean Bibliog.; Mariko Shimomura, Asst.Hd., Tech.Serv.; Shu-Sheng Wang, Chinese/Japanese Cat.; Ch'iu-Kuei Wang, Chinese/Western Lang.Bibliog..

★11582★
PRINCETON UNIVERSITY - INDUSTRIAL RELATIONS LIBRARY (Bus-Fin)
Princeton, NJ 08544 — Phone: (609)452-4936
Kevin P. Barry, Libn.
Founded: 1922. **Staff:** Prof 1; Other 2. **Subjects:** Industrial relations, labor legislation, labor unions, human resource planning, labor economics, social insurance, benefit plans, personnel administration. **Holdings:** 8000 volumes; 105 VF drawers; 100,000 pamphlets, company personnel documents, labor union publications; International Labor Organization (ILO) documents. **Subscriptions:** 650 journals and other serials. **Services:** Library open to the public with restrictions. **Computerized Information Services:** DIALOG Information Services, LEXIS, BRS Information Technologies, WILSONLINE. **Networks/Consortia:** Member of RLG. **Publications:** Selected References, 5/year - by subscription.

★11583★
PRINCETON UNIVERSITY - MARQUAND LIBRARY (Art)
McCormick Hall — Phone: (609)452-3783
Princeton, NJ 08544 — Mary M. Schmidt, Libn.
Founded: 1908. **Staff:** Prof 3; Other 6. **Subjects:** History of art, history of architecture, archeology. **Special Collections:** Barr Ferree Collection (architecture); Friend Collection (early Christian and manuscript illumination); sales catalogs; exhibition catalogs. **Holdings:** 150,000 volumes. **Subscriptions:** 900 journals and other serials. **Services:** Library not open to the public. **Networks/Consortia:** Member of RLG.

★11584★
PRINCETON UNIVERSITY - MATHEMATICS, PHYSICS AND STATISTICS LIBRARY (Sci-Engr)
Princeton, NJ 08544 — Phone: (609)452-3188
Peter Cziffra, Libn.
Staff: Prof 1; Other 4. **Subjects:** Mathematics, physics, statistics - history, development, philosophy. **Holdings:** 44,000 books; 35,000 bound periodical volumes; 5000 pamphlets; 10 VF drawers of Princeton theses; 250 VF drawers of uncataloged pamphlets; 16 VF drawers of undergraduate theses.

Subscriptions: 805 journals and other serials. **Services:** Interlibrary loan; copying; library open to qualified readers for reference use only. **Automated Operations:** Computerized public access catalog, cataloging, acquisitions, and circulation. **Computerized Information Services:** DIALOG Information Services, RLIN. Performs searches on fee basis.

★11585★
PRINCETON UNIVERSITY - MUSIC COLLECTION (Mus)
Firestone Library Phone: (609)452-3230
Princeton, NJ 08544 Paula Morgan, Mus.Libn.
Staff: Prof 1; Other 1. **Subjects:** Music. **Holdings:** 18,000 books; 3000 bound periodical volumes; 19,000 volumes of music; 2500 microforms. **Subscriptions:** 150 journals and other serials. **Services:** Interlibrary loan; copying; collection open to the public for reference use only.

★11586★
PRINCETON UNIVERSITY - NEAR EAST COLLECTIONS (Area-Ethnic)
Firestone Library Phone: (609)452-3279
Princeton, NJ 08544 James Weinberger, Cur.
Staff: Prof 4; Other 3. **Subjects:** Arabic, Persian, Turkish, and Hebrew languages and literature. **Special Collections:** Garrett Collection of Near Eastern Manuscripts. **Holdings:** 130,000 volumes; 12,000 volumes of manuscripts. **Services:** Interlibrary loan; copying; collections open to the public on fee basis. **Networks/Consortia:** Member of RLG, Center for Research Libraries (CRL) Consortia. **Staff:** Joan Biella, Ldr., Cat. Team; Mr. Kambiz Eslami; David Hirsch; Kathy Van der Vate.

★11587★
PRINCETON UNIVERSITY - OFFICE OF POPULATION RESEARCH - LIBRARY (Soc Sci)
21 Prospect Ave. Phone: (609)452-4874
Princeton, NJ 08544 Thomas Holzmann, Libn.
Founded: 1936. **Staff:** Prof 2; Other 1. **Subjects:** Population studies, demography (emphasis on methodology), fertility, mortality, census, vital statistics. **Holdings:** 26,000 volumes; 5500 reprints; 10,000 manuscripts and pamphlets; 1100 reels of microfilm. **Subscriptions:** 400 journals and other serials. **Services:** Interlibrary loan; copying; library open to the public for reference use only. **Publications:** Acquisitions list - for local distribution. **Special Indexes:** Population Index (quarterly index of the demographic field). **Staff:** Olga Boemeke, Asst.Libn..

★11588★
PRINCETON UNIVERSITY - PHONOGRAPH RECORD LIBRARY (Mus)
Woolworth Center of Musical Studies Phone: (609)452-4251
Princeton, NJ 08544 Marjorie Hassen, Recordings Libn.
Staff: Prof 1; Other 1. **Subjects:** Music - western classical, nonwestern, jazz. **Holdings:** 1200 score titles in multiple copies; 25,000 phonograph records; 2000 tapes. **Subscriptions:** 30 journals and other serials. **Services:** Library not open to the public.

★11589★
PRINCETON UNIVERSITY - PLASMA PHYSICS LIBRARY (Sci-Engr)
Box 451 Phone: (609)683-3567
Princeton, NJ 08544 Jane Holmquist, Libn.
Staff: Prof 2; Other 3. **Subjects:** Fusion reactor technology, plasma physics. **Holdings:** 5000 books; 6000 bound periodical volumes; 3000 project reports; 18,000 technical reports and reprints; 33,000 microfiche. **Subscriptions:** 130 journals and other serials. **Services:** Interlibrary loan; library open to the public for reference use only. **Computerized Information Services:** DIALOG Information Services, STN International. **Publications:** Monthly Bulletin and Acquisitions List - for internal distribution only. **Staff:** Rhoda Stasiak, Asst.Libn..

★11590★
PRINCETON UNIVERSITY - PLINY FISK LIBRARY OF ECONOMICS AND FINANCE (Bus-Fin)
Firestone Library Phone: (609)452-3211
Princeton, NJ 08544 Louise Tompkins, Libn.
Founded: 1915. **Staff:** Prof 1; Other 2. **Subjects:** Economics, finance, international economics. **Special Collections:** Pliny Fisk Collection of Railroad and Corporation Finance (annual reports and other financial documents, 1830-1900). **Holdings:** 5575 books; current annual reports of 800 corporations; 21 VF drawers of pamphlets; selected economics working papers. **Subscriptions:** 942 journals and other serials. **Services:** Interlibrary loan; library open to the public with restrictions.

★11591★
PRINCETON UNIVERSITY - PSYCHOLOGY LIBRARY (Soc Sci)
Green Hall Phone: (609)452-3239
Princeton, NJ 08544 Mary C. Chaikin, Psych.Libn.
Staff: Prof 1; Other 2. **Subjects:** Psychology - cognitive, developmental, social, experimental, health, physiological; neuropsychology; perception; personality; psychotherapy; psycholinguistics. **Holdings:** 16,070 books; 12,448 bound periodical volumes; 4664 microfiche. **Subscriptions:** 402 journals and other serials. **Services:** Interlibrary loan; copying; library open to the public for reference use only. **Automated Operations:** Computerized cataloging and circulation. **Computerized Information Services:** DIALOG Information Services, RLIN. **Networks/Consortia:** Member of RLG. **Publications:** Acquisition list and bibliographies - local distribution.

★11592★
PRINCETON UNIVERSITY - PUBLIC ADMINISTRATION COLLECTION (Soc Sci)
Firestone Library Phone: (609)452-3209
Princeton, NJ 08544 Rosemary Allen Little, Libn.
Founded: 1930. **Staff:** Prof 1; Other 4. **Subjects:** Public administration; government on the national, state, county, and municipal levels; law; politics; planning. **Special Collections:** Recent U.S. censuses in housing and population; depository for New Jersey state government documents; official depository for United Nations publications. **Holdings:** 5000 books; 2000 bound periodical volumes; 18,000 pamphlets; 28 VF drawers of clippings. **Subscriptions:** 1600 journals and other serials. **Services:** Interlibrary loan; collection open to the public. **Networks/Consortia:** Member of RLG.

★11593★
PRINCETON UNIVERSITY - RARE BOOKS AND SPECIAL COLLECTIONS (Rare Book)
Firestone Library Phone: (609)452-3184
Princeton, NJ 08544 William L. Joyce, Assoc.Libn.
Subjects: Papyri; Babylonian clay tablets; Medieval, Renaissance, Ethiopian, Batak manuscripts; early printing; English and American literature and history of the 18th to 20th centuries; theater history; dramatic literature; New Jerseyana; emblem books; Western Americana; American Indians; Mormons; history and examples of bookmaking, printmaking, fine printing, binding, photography; motion picture history; private press books. **Special Collections:** Sylvia Beach Collection; Carton Hunting Collection; Grover Cleveland Library; Cook Chess Collection; College of One Collection of Sheilah Graham; Meirs Collection of George Cruikshank; de Coppet Collection of American Historical Manuscripts; Derrydale Press Collection and The Sporting Books of Eugene V. Connett; general rare books collection; Jonathan Edwards Library; J. Harlin O'Connell Collection of English Literature of the 1890's; Kenneth McKenzie Fable Collection; Sinclair Hamilton Collection of American Illustrated Books; incunabula; Otto von Kienbusch Angling Collection; Charles Scribner Collection of Charles Lamb; James McCosh Library; Robert F. Metzdorf Collection of Victorian Bookbindings; Harry B. Vandeventer Poetry Collection; Orlando F. Weber Collection of Economic History; Goertz Collection; Gryphius Imprints Collection; Laurence Hutton Collection; Miriam Y. Holden Collection on the History of Women (Rare Books Section); Grenville Kane Collection of Americana; Stanley Lieberman Memorial Collection of Hero Fiction; Cyrus McCormick Collection of Americana; William Nelson Collection of New Jerseyana; New Jersey Imprints; Morris L. Parrish Collection of Victorian Novelists; Princeton Borough Collection; Princeton Borough Agricultural Association Records; Pitney Collection on International Law and Diplomacy (Rare Books Section); Robert Patterson Collection of Horace; Kenneth H. Rockey Angling Collection (Rare Books Section); Richard Sheridan Collection; Robert H. Taylor Library; Junius Spencer Morgan Collection of Virgil; John Shaw Pierson Civil War Collection; John Witherspoon Library; Woodrow Wilson Collection; Scribner papers; papers of: F. Scott Fitzgerald, Ernest Hemingway, Allen Tate, Caroline Gordon, John Day (publisher), Henry Holt (publisher), Luigi Pirandello (playwright), John Foster Dulles, American Civil Liberties Union (ACLU), other 20th century literary and historical papers. **Holdings:** 250,000 books; 1000 manuscript collections; 210,000 maps and charts; 25,000 prints and drawings. **Staff:** Stephen Ferguson, Cur. of Rare Bks.; Jean F. Preston, Cur. of Mss.; Alfred L. Bush, Cur., W. Americana/Historic Maps; Brooks Levy, Cur. of Numismatics; Nancy Bressler, Cur., Pub.Aff./Papers; Dale Roylance, Cur., Graphic Arts; Alexander D. Wainwright, Cur., Parrish Coll.; Mary Ann Jensen, Cur. of Theatre Coll.; Ann Hanson, Cur. of Papyrology; Mark R. Farrell, Cur. of Taylor Lib..

★11594★
PRINCETON UNIVERSITY - SCHOOL OF ARCHITECTURE LIBRARY (Plan)
Princeton, NJ 08544 Phone: (609)452-3256
Frances Chen, Libn.
Founded: 1967. **Staff:** Prof 1; Other 3. **Subjects:** Current architectural practice, urban affairs, physical planning, transportation, sociology. **Special Collections:** Library of the former Bureau of Urban Research. **Holdings:** 25,000 books; 5000 pamphlets. **Subscriptions:** 450 journals and other serials. **Services:** Interlibrary loan; copying; library open to the public for reference use only. **Networks/Consortia:** Member of RLG.

★11595★
PRINCETON UNIVERSITY - WILLIAM SEYMOUR THEATRE COLLECTION (Theater)
Firestone Library Phone: (609)452-3223
Princeton, NJ 08544 Mary Ann Jensen, Cur.
Founded: 1936. **Staff:** Prof 1; Other 5. **Subjects:** Performing arts - theater, musical theater, popular music, dance, circus, film. **Special Collections:** Papers of: William Seymour, Fanny Davenport, Mathews family, Otto Kahn, E.L. Davenport, George Crouse Tyler, Alan S. Downer, Sarah Enright, Woody Allen; collections of: Ashton Sly, Lulu Glaser, Max Gordon, Joseph McCaddon, Bretaigne Windust, Clinton Wilder, Sam H. Harris; archives of: Warner Bros. Inc., Tams-Witmark, Theatre Intime, Triangle Club, McCarter Theatre; A.M. Friend Collection of 18th century theatre drawings. **Holdings:** 13,000 books; 3300 VF drawers of programs, pictures, pamphlets; 50 map drawers of posters; 500 scrapbooks; 1250 paperbound playbooks. **Subscriptions:** 150 journals and other serials. **Services:** Copying (limited); collection open to qualified scholars. **Automated Operations:** Computerized public access catalog and circulation. **Networks/Consortia:** Member of RLG.

★11596★
PRINCETON UNIVERSITY - WOODROW WILSON SCHOOL OF PUBLIC AND INTERNATIONAL AFFAIRS - LIBRARY (Soc Sci)
Princeton, NJ 08544 Phone: (609)452-5455
Linda Oppenheim, Libn.
Founded: 1964. **Staff:** Prof 1; Other 4. **Subjects:** Political science, economics, international affairs. **Holdings:** 18,000 books; 1361 bound periodical volumes. **Subscriptions:** 284 journals and other serials; 7 newspapers. **Services:** Interlibrary loan; library open to the public for reference use only. **Automated Operations:** Computerized circulation and reserves. **Computerized Information Services:** DIALOG Information Services, BRS Information Technologies, LEXIS, VU/TEXT Information Services, NEXIS, RLIN; internal database; BITNET (electronic mail service). Performs searches on fee basis.

PRINGLE HERBARIUM
See: University of Vermont (17018)

★11597★
PRINTING BROKERAGE ASSOCIATION - LIBRARY (Art)
Wyncote House 7A
Wyncote, PA 19095 Glenna T. McWilliams, Exec.Dir.
Founded: 1985. **Subjects:** Management in graphic arts industries. **Holdings:** 1500 volumes. **Formerly:** Located in Arlington, VA.

WALTER F. PRIOR MEDICAL LIBRARY
See: Frederick Memorial Hospital (5366)

★11598★
PRISON FELLOWSHIP MINISTRIES - INFORMATION CENTER (Soc Sci)
Justice Fellowship Information Center
Box 17500 Phone: (703)478-0100
Washington, DC 20041 Elizabeth A. Leahy, Coord.
Staff: Prof 1; Other 2. **Subjects:** Criminal justice and criminal justice reform, corrections, Christian theology and life. **Holdings:** 2500 books; 1000 technical reports; 1100 cassettes; 1500 audio and video cassettes 7 VF drawers of clippings; 2 VF drawers of archival materials; 20 VF drawers. **Subscriptions:** 103 journals and other serials. **Services:** Interlibrary loan; copying; center open to the public with prior approval of librarian. **Computerized Information Services:** DIALOG Information Services.

H. WAYNE PRITCHARD LIBRARY
See: Soil and Water Conservation Society (13346)

PRITZKER INSTITUTE OF MEDICAL ENGINEERING
See: Illinois Institute of Technology (6690)

★11599★
PRO FOOTBALL HALL OF FAME - LIBRARY/RESEARCH CENTER (Rec)
2121 George Halas Dr., N.W. Phone: (216)456-8207
Canton, OH 44708 Sandi Lang, Libn.
Founded: 1963. **Staff:** Prof 2; Other 1. **Subjects:** Professional football. **Special Collections:** Spalding football guides, 1892-1940; Scrapbooks of Commissioner Bert Bell; 98 players' personal scrapbooks; pre-NFL rare documents (player contracts). **Holdings:** 3400 volumes; 2800 bound periodical volumes; 6100 game programs; 20,000 photographs of players, teams, officials, coaches; 700 slides of player and game action; 50 audiotapes; 1100 16mm films; 1020 team media guides; 7200 microforms; 80 VF drawers of present, defunct league, and semi-pro team files. **Subscriptions:** 18 journals and other serials; 5 newspapers. **Services:** Interlibrary loan; copying; library open to researchers and writers by appointment. **Also Known As:** National Football Museum.

PRO-LIFE LIBRARY
See: Diocese of Allentown (4275)

★11600★
PROCTER & GAMBLE COMPANY - BUCKEYE CELLULOSE CORPORATION - CELLULOSE & SPECIALTIES DIVISION TECHNICAL INFORMATION SERVICES (Sci-Engr)
949 Tillman Ave.
Memphis, TN 38108 Phone: (901)320-8311
Founded: 1953. **Staff:** Prof 1; Other 1. **Subjects:** Chemistry - cellulose, physical, organic, analytical; polymer sciences; colloid science; textiles. **Holdings:** 5000 books; 5000 bound periodical volumes; 10,000 technical reports; 8 VF drawers of government documents; 10,000 U.S. and foreign patents; 500 reels of microfilm. **Subscriptions:** 354 journals and other serials. **Services:** Interlibrary loan. **Computerized Information Services:** Pergamon ORBIT InfoLine, Inc., NLM, DIALOG Information Services.

★11601★
PROCTER & GAMBLE COMPANY - IVORYDALE TECHNICAL CENTER - LIBRARY (Sci-Engr)
Cincinnati, OH 45217 Joyce Wheeler, Libn.
Holdings: Figures not available. **Services:** Library not open to the public. **Remarks:** Library is one of several units comprising the Procter & Gamble Company Information Management Group.

★11602★
PROCTER & GAMBLE COMPANY - LIBRARY (Bus-Fin)
Box 599
Cincinnati, OH 45201 Shirley Caldwell, Libn.
Subjects: Detergents, advertising, business. **Holdings:** Figures not available. **Services:** Library not open to the public.

★11603★
PROCTER & GAMBLE COMPANY - MIAMI VALLEY LABORATORIES - TECHNICAL LIBRARY (Sci-Engr)
Box 39175
Cincinnati, OH 45247 Emelyn L. Hiland, Lib.Mgr.
Staff: Prof 1; Other 4. **Subjects:** Chemistry, surface and colloid sciences, life sciences. **Holdings:** 8000 books; 12,000 bound periodical volumes. **Subscriptions:** 600 journals and other serials. **Services:** Library not open to the public. **Computerized Information Services:** DIALOG Information Services, Pergamon ORBIT InfoLine, Inc., OCLC, BRS Information Technologies, CAS ONLINE, Chemical Information Systems, Inc. (CIS); internal database.

PROCTER & GAMBLE COMPANY - NORWICH EATON PHARMACEUTICALS, INC.
See: Norwich Eaton Pharmaceuticals, Inc. (10522)

★11604★
PROCTER & GAMBLE COMPANY - SHARON WOODS TECHNICAL CENTER - HB LIBRARY (Sci-Engr)
11511 Reed Hartman Hwy.
Cincinnati, OH 45241 Eleanor Scott, Lib.Mgr.
Founded: 1982. **Holdings:** Figures not available. **Subscriptions:** 100 journals and other serials. **Services:** Library not open to the public. **Remarks:** Library is one of several units comprising the Procter & Gamble Company Information Management Group.

★11605★
PROCTER & GAMBLE COMPANY - VICKS RESEARCH CENTER - LIBRARY (Biol Sci, Med)
One Far Mill Crossing Phone: (203)929-2500
Shelton, CT 06484 Susanne Silverman, Libn.
Founded: 1942. **Staff:** Prof 1; Other 1. **Subjects:** Drugs and pharmaceuticals, medicine, cosmetics and cosmetic science, analytical and physical chemistry, microbiology, biochemistry, biology, nutrition. **Holdings:** 6500 books; 7000 bound periodical volumes. **Subscriptions:** 275 journals and other serials. **Services:** Interlibrary loan; library not open to the public. **Automated Operations:** Computerized serials. **Networks/Consortia:** Member of Southwestern Connecticut Library Council (SWLC), Connecticut Association of Health Science Libraries (CAHSL), BHSL. **Formerly:** Richardson-Vicks, Inc. - Vicks Research Center.

★11606★
PROCTER & GAMBLE COMPANY - WINTON HILL TECHNICAL CENTER - LIBRARY (Sci-Engr)
Administration Bldg.
6090 Center Hill Rd. Phone: (513)983-4240
Cincinnati, OH 45224 Irene L. Myers, Sect.Hd.
Holdings: Figures not available. **Services:** Library not open to the public. **Remarks:** Library is one of five units comprising the Procter & Gamble Company Technical Information Service with combined holdings of 35,000 volumes.

★11607★
PROCTOR COMMUNITY HOSPITAL - MEDICAL LIBRARY (Med)
5409 N. Knoxville Ave. Phone: (309)691-4702
Peoria, IL 61614 Nancy Camacho, Libn.
Founded: 1972. **Staff:** Prof 1. **Subjects:** Medicine, nursing, allied health sciences. **Holdings:** 500 books; 210 bound periodical volumes; 550 unbound journal volumes. **Subscriptions:** 120 journals and other serials. **Services:** Interlibrary loan; copying; SDI; library open to qualified patrons. **Computerized Information Services:** MEDLINE. **Networks/Consortia:** Member of Heart of Illinois Library Consortium (HILC), Illinois Valley Library System, Greater Midwest Regional Medical Library Network, ILLINET. **Publications:** Internal pamphlets.

★11608★
PROCTOR & REDFERN, CONSULTING ENGINEERS - LIBRARY (Sci-Engr, Plan)
45 Green Belt Dr. Phone: (416)445-3600
Don Mills, ON, Canada M3C 3K3 Catherine Spark, Hd.Libn.
Staff: Prof 1; Other 1. **Subjects:** Civil and environmental engineering, urban and regional planning, hydrology, transportation, waste management. **Holdings:** 18,000 books; 600 bound periodical volumes. **Subscriptions:** 125 journals and other serials; 20 newspapers. **Services:** Interlibrary loan; copying; library open to the public with restrictions. **Automated Operations:** Computerized cataloging. **Computerized Information Services:** DIALOG Information Services, Pergamon ORBIT InfoLine, Inc., QL Systems. **Publications:** Information Centre News, monthly - for internal distribution only.

★11609★
PROCUREMENT ASSOCIATES - LIBRARY (Bus-Fin)
733 N. Dodsworth Ave. Phone: (818)966-4576
Covina, CA 91724 Marie Sirney, Libn.
Staff: Prof 1; Other 2. **Subjects:** Government contracts, business administration. **Holdings:** 4000 books; 6500 government and industry reports; government courses in the field of government contracts. **Subscriptions:** 91 journals and other serials. **Services:** Interlibrary loan; copying; library open to the public.

★11610★
PRODUCE MARKETING ASSOCIATION - PMA INFORMATION CENTER (Food-Bev)
1500 Casho Mill Rd.
Box 6036 Phone: (302)738-7100
Newark, DE 19714-6036 Bryan Silbermann, Staff V.P.
Founded: 1949. **Staff:** 4. **Subjects:** Fresh fruit and vegetables, floral products, packaging, marketing. **Special Collections:** Microfilm Library (75,000 pages). **Holdings:** 22,000 volumes. **Subscriptions:** 40 journals and other serials; 15 newspapers. **Computerized Information Services:** Internal database. Performs searches on fee basis for nonmembers. **Staff:** Julie E. Stewart, Info.Spec..

PROESCHER PATHOLOGY LIBRARY
See: Santa Clara Valley Medical Center - Milton J. Chatton Medical Library (12871)

PROFESSIONAL CORPORATION OF PHYSICIANS OF QUEBEC
See: Corporation Professionnelle des Medecins du Quebec (3802)

★11611★
PROFESSIONAL GOLFERS' ASSOCIATION OF AMERICA - LIBRARY
100 Ave. of the Champions
Box 109601
Palm Beach Gardens, FL 33410
Subjects: Golf and the golf profession. **Holdings:** 3000 books; 2000 bound periodical volumes; 100 VF drawers. **Remarks:** Presently inactive.

★11612★
PROFESSIONAL INSURANCE AGENTS - LIBRARY (Bus-Fin)
400 N. Washington St. Phone: (703)836-9340
Alexandria, VA 22314 Donald K. Gardiner, Exec. V.P.
Subjects: Insurance. **Holdings:** 1000 volumes.

★11613★
PROFESSIONAL PSYCHICS UNITED - LIBRARY (Rel-Phil)
1839 S. Elmwood Phone: (312)484-3252
Berwyn, IL 60402 Phyllis Allen Spies, Contact
Founded: 1977. **Subjects:** Extrasensory perception. **Holdings:** 203 volumes; biographical archives.

★11614★
PROFESSIONAL SCHOOL OF PSYCHOLOGY - LIBRARY (Med)
1714 Lombard St. Phone: (415)563-2277
San Francisco, CA 94123 Sandra J. Duzak, Libn.
Founded: 1978. **Staff:** Prof 1; Other 1. **Subjects:** Psychology - general, clinical, organizational. **Holdings:** 2800 books; dissertations. **Subscriptions:** 23 journals and other serials. **Services:** Interlibrary loan; copying; library open to the public with restrictions. **Automated Operations:** Computerized cataloging. **Computerized Information Services:** BRS Information Technologies. Performs searches on fee basis.

PROGRAM PLANETREE
See: Planetree (11379)

★11615★
PROGRAM PLANNERS, INC. - LIBRARY/INFORMATION CENTER (Bus-Fin)
230 W. 41st St. Phone: (212)840-2600
New York, NY 10036 Doreen Lilore, Info.Off.
Founded: 1970. **Staff:** Prof 1; Other 2. **Subjects:** Collective bargaining, education, public employee pensions/retirement systems, local government, urban affairs, health care, insurance, sanitation. **Special Collections:** Annual budgets and financial reports for major U.S. cities and school districts; fire, police, sanitation, and transportation departments annual reports; retirement system annual reports; reports of the New York City Special Deputy Comptroller and the New York Financial Control Board, 1976 to present. **Holdings:** 10,000 books and reports; 26 VF drawers of clippings. **Subscriptions:** 110 journals and other serials. **Services:** Interlibrary loan; library open to the public by appointment only. **Computerized Information Services:** Internal databases. **Publications:** Monthly New York City Economic Report.

★11616★
PROGRESSIVE FOUNDATION - NUKEWATCH INFORMATION CENTER (Soc Sci)
315 W. Gorham St. Phone: (608)256-4146
Madison, WI 53703 Samuel H. Day, Jr., Dir.
Founded: 1981. **Staff:** 3. **Subjects:** Nuclear industry, weapons, power, and waste. **Holdings:** 70 books; films; slides. **Services:** Center open to the public. **Publications:** Time Bomb; A Consumers Guide to the Military; Maps of Missile Fields of U.S.; Nukewatch (newsletter), quarterly - available on request.

★11617★
PROJECT FOR PUBLIC SPACES - LIBRARY (Plan)
153 Waverly Place Phone: (212)620-5660
New York, NY 10014 Steven Davies, Proj.Dir.
Subjects: Pedestrian circulation, urban studies, transportation planning, playground and recreation area research, social behavior in public spaces,

landscape architecture. **Holdings:** 40 books; 175 research reports and articles. **Subscriptions:** 15 journals and other serials. **Services:** Library open to the public. **Computerized Information Services:** MCI Mail (electronic mail service). **Publications:** List of publications - available on request.

PROJECT SHARE
See: Berul Associates, Ltd. - Project SHARE (1536)

★11618★
PROJECT STARLIGHT INTERNATIONAL - LIBRARY (Sci-Engr)
Box 599
College Park, MD 20740 Ray Stanford, Dir.
Founded: 1964. **Subjects:** UFOs - physical effects, optical images, locations. **Holdings:** 470 volumes; films emphasizing physics of UFOs and UFO events.

PROJECT TALENT DATA BANK
See: American Institutes for Research (564)

PROMOTION AUSTRALIA
See: Australian Overseas Information Service (1183)

★11619★
THE PROPRIETARY ASSOCIATION - LIBRARY (Med)
1150 Connecticut Ave., N.W. Phone: (202)429-9260
Washington, DC 20036 Phyllis M. Taylor, Libn.
Founded: 1977. **Staff:** 2. **Subjects:** Medicines - nonprescription, limited prescription, allied-type groups; regulations affecting over-the-counter medicine. **Holdings:** 1000 volumes; U.S. Food and Drug Administration monographs and reports; AV programs. **Subscriptions:** 78 journals and other serials. **Services:** Interlibrary loan; copying; library open to the public with restrictions.

★11620★
PROSKAUER, ROSE, GOETZ & MENDELSOHN - LIBRARY (Law)
300 Park Ave. Phone: (212)906-8794
New York, NY 10022 Marsha Pront, Hd.Libn.
Staff: Prof 5; Other 7. **Subjects:** Law. **Holdings:** 25,000 books; 1000 bound periodical volumes. **Subscriptions:** 250 journals and other serials; 10 newspapers. **Services:** Interlibrary loan; copying; library open to the public with permission. **Computerized Information Services:** LEXIS, NEXIS, WESTLAW, Dun & Bradstreet Corporation, BRS Information Technologies, Dow Jones News/Retrieval, NewsNet, Inc., RLIN. **Networks/Consortia:** Member of Library Consortium of Health Institutions in Buffalo (LCHIB). **Publications:** Library News (newsletter), monthly - internal distribution and to selected libraries. **Staff:** Karen Frankel, Labor Libn.; Nathan Rosen, Asst.Libn.; Ann Rauch, Ref.Libn.; Sadako Oracca, Tech.Serv.Libn.; David Johnson, Tax Libn..

★11621★
PROSPEROS - INNER SPACE CENTER (Rel-Phil)
Box 27189
Los Angeles, CA 90027 Phone: (213)663-8747
Founded: 1956. **Subjects:** Metaphysics, psychology, philosophy, sociology, astrology, religion. **Special Collections:** Thane of Hawaii; C.G. Jung; Emma Curtis Hopkins; Lillian DeWaters. **Holdings:** 4500 volumes. **Services:** Center open to the public for reference use only. **Remarks:** Located at 2449 Hyperion, No. 106, Los Angeles, CA 90027.

★11622★
PROTESTANT EPISCOPAL CHURCH - ARCHIVES (Rel-Phil)
Box 2247 Phone: (512)472-6816
Austin, TX 78768 Dr. Virginia Nelle Bellamy, Archv.
Staff: Prof 3; Other 1. **Subjects:** History of the Protestant Episcopal Church in America. **Special Collections:** Correspondence of the Domestic and Foreign Missionary Society; archives of the General Convention. **Holdings:** 10,000 volumes; manuscripts; documents. **Services:** Copying; archives open to the public.

★11623★
PROTESTANT EPISCOPAL CHURCH - DIOCESE OF INDIANAPOLIS, INDIANA - ARCHIVES (Rel-Phil)
Indiana State Library
140 N. Senate Ave. Phone: (317)926-5454
Indianapolis, IN 46208 Dr. Wendell Calkins, Historiographer
Subjects: Church history. **Special Collections:** Diocesan manuscripts, 1833 to present (85 file boxes). **Holdings:** 40 books; bishop's correspondence; church records; personnel jackets. **Services:** Interlibrary loan; copying; archives open to the public with restrictions. **Special Catalogs:** Archive inventory; catalog of bishop's correspondence (card). **Remarks:** Correspondence and requests for permission to work in the archives should go to Bishop Edward W. Jones, Episcopal Diocesan Headquarters, 1100 W. 42nd St., Indianapolis, IN, 46208.

★11624★
PROTESTANT EPISCOPAL CHURCH - DIOCESE OF PENNSYLVANIA - INFORMATION CENTER (Rel-Phil)
IVB Bldg., Suite 2616
1700 Market St.
Philadelphia, PA 19103 Phone: (215)567-6650
Staff: 1. **Subjects:** Episcopal Church, Diocese of Pennsylvania, Anglicanism. **Holdings:** 300 books; parish records; diocesan journals; confirmation records; archives. **Services:** Center open to public.

★11625★
PROTESTANT EPISCOPAL CHURCH - EPISCOPAL DIOCESE OF CONNECTICUT - DIOCESAN LIBRARY AND ARCHIVES (Rel-Phil)
1335 Asylum Ave. Phone: (203)233-4481
Hartford, CT 06105 Rev. Dr. Robert G. Carroon, Archv.
Founded: 1850. **Staff:** Prof 1; Other 2. **Subjects:** History of the Episcopal Church in Connecticut. **Special Collections:** Papers of the Bishops of Connecticut, 1784-1955 (6000 pieces); letters and historical documents of the Episcopal Church in Connecticut, 1786-1885 (6000 pieces); early sermons (Colonial period); cathedral and parochial historical materials; parish registers and records of diocesan organizations, 1790 to present; papers of the Standing Committee, 1796 to present; papers of the Society for the Increase of the Ministry (12,000 pieces); films of reports of the missionaries under the Society for the Propagation of the Gospel in Foreign Parts, 1700-1776; records of the Episcopal Academy of Connecticut at Cheshire. **Holdings:** 100,000 manuscripts and films; 400 reference books; 3000 bound pamphlets. **Services:** Interlibrary loan; copying; library open to the public by appointment. **Publications:** Historiographer of the Episcopal Diocese of Connecticut, annual - by subscription.

★11626★
PROTESTANT EPISCOPAL CHURCH - EPISCOPAL DIOCESE OF EASTERN OREGON - ARCHIVES (Rel-Phil)
7799 S.W. Scholls Ferry Rd., Suite 151 Phone: (503)646-8464
Beaverton, OR 97005-6584 Rev. Louis L. Perkins
Staff: Prof 1. **Subjects:** Diocese history. **Holdings:** 100 books; 50 bound periodical volumes; manuscripts; correspondence; archival materials; microfilm; pictures; statistics. **Services:** Interlibrary loan; archives open to the public.

★11627★
PROTESTANT EPISCOPAL CHURCH - EPISCOPAL DIOCESE OF MASSACHUSETTS - DIOCESAN LIBRARY AND ARCHIVES (Rel-Phil)
1 Joy St. Phone: (617)742-4720
Boston, MA 02108 Mary Eleanor Murphy, Archv.
Staff: 2. **Subjects:** History of churches in the diocese and published work of the clergy. **Special Collections:** Americana (Colonial sermons); published records of the Society for the Propagation for the Gospel, 1701-1892. **Holdings:** Offical papers of the diocese, its bishops and affiliated agencies; historical manuscripts and pre-1905 vital records of its parishes; 50 linear feet of 19th and 20th century pamphlets. **Services:** Copying; archives open to the public for reference use only. **Publications:** Guide for Parish Historians (1961); brochures on history of the Diocese of Massachusetts; Littera Scripta Manet (newsletter); Guide to the Parochial Archives of the Episcopal Church in Boston (1981). **Remarks:** A description of the manuscript collection was published by Works Progress Administration, Boston, 1939. **Staff:** Katherine A. Powers, Asst.Archv.; Ruth S. Leonard, Lib.Cons..

★11628★
PROTESTANT EPISCOPAL CHURCH - EPISCOPAL DIOCESE OF SOUTH DAKOTA - ARCHIVES (Rel-Phil)
Center for Western Studies
Augustana College
Box 727 Phone: (605)336-4007
Sioux Falls, SD 57197 Harry F. Thompson, Cur.
Staff: Prof 1; Other 2. **Subjects:** History - Episcopal church, South Dakota, Great Plains, United States; missionary work; Indian culture. **Special Collections:** Bishop William H. Hare papers (10 cubic feet); Rev. Joseph W. Cook journals (28 volumes); Bishop Hugh L. Burleson papers (4 cubic feet); Bishop W. Blair Roberts papers (25 cubic feet); Bishop Conrad H.

Gesner papers (25 cubic feet). **Holdings:** 40 volumes of church registers. **Services:** Copying; archives open to the public with restrictions.

★11629★
PROTESTANT EPISCOPAL CHURCH - EPISCOPAL DIOCESE OF SPRINGFIELD, ILLINOIS - DIOCESAN CENTER LIBRARY (Hist)
821 S. 2nd St. Phone: (217)525-1876
Springfield, IL 62704 Philip L. Shutt, Reg./Historiographer
Staff: Prof 1. **Subjects:** Diocesan archives. **Special Collections:** Journals of Diocese of Illinois, 1835-1877; journals of Diocese of Springfield, 1878 to present; journals of the General Convention of the Episcopal Church, 1823 to present. **Holdings:** 187 volumes; manuscripts; reports; diocesan records; defunct parish records; maps; photographs. **Services:** Interlibrary loan; library open to the public.

★11630★
PROTESTANT EPISCOPAL CHURCH - EPISCOPAL DIOCESE OF UTAH - ARCHIVES (Rel-Phil)
231 East 100 South
Salt Lake City, UT 84111 Phone: (801)322-3400
Subjects: History of the Episcopal Diocese of Utah, 1867 to present. **Holdings:** 65 cubic feet of diocesan records, journals of annual conventions, confirmation records, financial records, parish statistical reports, diaries and registers of the clergy. **Services:** Archives open to the public by appointment.

★11631★
PROTESTANT EPISCOPAL CHURCH - EPISCOPAL DIOCESE OF WEST TEXAS - CATHEDRAL HOUSE ARCHIVES (Rel-Phil)
111 Torcido Dr.
Box 6885 Phone: (512)824-5387
San Antonio, TX 78209 Zethyl T. LeStourgeon, Dir.
Subjects: Religion, history, education. **Special Collections:** History of the Episcopal Diocese of West Texas and its institutions, including St. Philip's College, St. Mary's Hall, and Texas Military Institute, 1874 to present. **Holdings:** 5000 books; 50 linear feet of letters, minutes, diaries, records, scrapbooks, manuscripts. **Services:** Copying; archives open to other churches. **Automated Operations:** Computerized cataloging and acquisitions.

★11632★
PROTESTANT EPISCOPAL CHURCH - EPISCOPAL DIOCESE OF WESTERN NORTH CAROLINA - LIBRARY & ARCHIVES (Rel-Phil)
Box 368 Phone: (704)669-2921
Black Mountain, NC 28711 Elizabeth W. Thomson, Archv.
Founded: 1975. **Staff:** Prof 2; Other 2. **Subjects:** Theology, religion, Christian education, church history, handicrafts, music, drama, biography. **Special Collections:** Diocese and congregational papers, 1800 to present. **Holdings:** 4200 books; AV programs; hymn and prayer books; handicrafts; archival material. **Subjects:** 11 journals and other serials. **Services:** Interlibrary loan; copying; library open to the public with restrictions. **Also Known As:** Episcopal Church in the U.S.A. **Staff:** Carolyn Hughes, Libn..

★11633★
PROTESTANT EPISCOPAL CHURCH - MISSOURI DIOCESE - DIOCESAN ARCHIVES (Rel-Phil)
1210 Locust St. Phone: (314)231-1220
St. Louis, MO 63103 Charles F. Rehkopf, Archv./Reg.
Staff: Prof 1; Other 2. **Subjects:** History - diocesan, parish, Anglican Church, Missouri, St. Louis. **Special Collections:** Journals of the General Convention, 1784 to present (69 volumes); Journals of the Diocese of Missouri, 1841 to present (147 volumes); The Spirit of Missions and Forth, 1835 to present (125 volumes); Historical Magazine of the Episcopal Church, 1932 to present; Episcopal Church Almanacs and Annuals, 1830 to present (102 volumes); Episcopal Clerical Directories, 1785 to present (24 volumes). **Holdings:** 572 books; 223 bound periodical volumes; 83.5 linear feet of diocesan archives; 18 linear feet of parish files. **Subscriptions:** 13 journals and other serials. **Services:** Interlibrary loan; copying; archives open to the public by appointment. **Special Indexes:** Index of diocesan publications and official records (card); finding aids for diocesan historical collections.

★11634★
PROTESTANT EPISCOPAL CHURCH OF WESTERN WASHINGTON - DIOCESE OF OLYMPIA - ARCHIVES (Rel-Phil)
1551 Tenth Ave., E.
Box 12126 Phone: (206)325-4200
Seattle, WA 98102 Peggy Ann Hansen, Archv.
Staff: Prof 1. **Subjects:** Diocesan archives. **Special Collections:** Bishop Stephen Fielding Bayne, Jr. Collection; Bishop Simeon Arthur Huston Collection. **Holdings:** 100 books; bishop's office and diocesan records; journals; newspapers; pictures; tapes. **Services:** Copying; archives open to the public with restrictions.

★11635★
PROTESTANT EPISCOPAL CHURCH OF WESTERN WASHINGTON - DIOCESE OF OLYMPIA - DIOCESAN RESOURCE CENTER (Rel-Phil)
1551 Tenth Ave., E.
Box 12126 Phone: (206)325-4200
Seattle, WA 98102 Janice Matsumoto, Libn.
Founded: 1965. **Staff:** Prof 1; Other 1. **Subjects:** Religion, theology, religious education, leadership training. **Holdings:** 4000 volumes; 46 films; 30 filmstrips; 140 video cassettes; 50 cassette tapes. **Subscriptions:** 18 journals and other serials. **Services:** Interlibrary loan; copying; center open to the public. **Special Catalogs:** Audio-visual catalog. **Formerly:** Education Resource Center.

★11636★
PROTESTANT SCHOOL BOARD OF GREATER MONTREAL - SARAH MAXWELL LIBRARY (Educ)
6000 Fielding Ave. Phone: (514)483-7269
Montreal, PQ, Canada H3X 1T4 M.E. Montague, Lib.Techn.
Founded: 1963. **Subjects:** Education, child psychology, school administration, curriculum, special education. **Holdings:** 8000 books; 452 bound periodical volumes; unbound materials. **Subscriptions:** 100 journals and other serials. **Services:** Interlibrary loan; copying; library open to the public for reference use only. **Publications:** Copycat, semiannual.

PROUTY-CHEW MUSEUM AND LIBRARY
See: Geneva Historical Society - James D. Luckett Memorial Archives (5581)

★11637★
PROVIDENCE ATHENAEUM - LIBRARY (Hum)
251 Benefit St. Phone: (401)421-6970
Providence, RI 02903 Sally Duplaix, Dir./Libn.
Founded: 1753. **Staff:** Prof 8; Other 7. **Subjects:** History, literature, biography, art, voyage and travel, natural history. **Special Collections:** Audubon Collection; Bowen Collection; Burns Collection; collections in 19th century fiction and juvenile literature; rare books. **Holdings:** 159,499 books; 304 bound periodical titles. **Subscriptions:** 155 journals and other serials. **Services:** Interlibrary loan; copying; research facilities; library open to the public. **Networks/Consortia:** Member of Rhode Island Interrelated Library Network. **Publications:** Providence Athenaeum Bulletin; Annual Report. **Special Catalogs:** Travel and Exploration: Catalogue of the Providence Athenaeum Collection, 1988. **Staff:** Juliet T. Saunders, Asst.Dir.; Risa Gilpin, Hd. of Pub.Serv.; Dolly Borts, Hd., Tech.Serv.; Judy Aaron, Ch.Libn.; Carleigh Hoff, Ch.Libn.; Candis Dixon, Cons.Mgr.; Carol Cook, Bibliog..

★11638★
PROVIDENCE COLLEGE - PHILLIPS MEMORIAL LIBRARY (Rel-Phil, Soc Sci)
River Ave. at Eaton St. Phone: (401)865-2242
Providence, RI 02918 Joseph H. Doherty, Dir.
Founded: 1919. **Staff:** Prof 7; Other 22. **Subjects:** Works of St. Thomas Aquinas, Thomistic philosophy and theology, Dominican Order. **Special Collections:** John E. Fogarty Papers (500,000 pieces); Dennis J. Roberts Papers (3000 pieces); William Henry Chamberlin Papers (120 pieces and 40 diaries on microfilm); Louis Francis Budenz Papers (9500 pamphlets and periodicals); Rhode Island Constitutional Convention Collection, 1964-1968 (1000 pieces); Cornelius Moore Papers (250 pieces); J. Lyons Moore Collection (3000 pieces); Robert E. Quinn Papers and Oral History Project; Rhode Island Urban League Papers (200,000 items); Nazi Bund Collection (300 pieces); John J. Fawcett Collection (3000 drawings); Limited Constitutional Convention, 1973 (500 pieces); Quonset Point Collection (9000 pieces); Blackfriars' Guild Collection (2500 pieces); Joseph A. Doorley, Jr. Collection (60,000 pieces); Black Regiment Collection (600 pieces); Bonniwell Liturgical Collection (2100 pieces); Coutu Genealogy; Aime J. Forand Collection (4500 pieces); Irish Literature Collection (50

pieces); John O. Pastore Collection (100,000 pieces); Rhode Island Library Association Collection (5000 pieces); Social Justice Collection, 1936-1942 (325 pieces); Walsh Civil War Diary (30 pages); Black Newspapers, 1932-1957 (8 reels of microfilm); Confederation Period in Rhode Island Newspapers Collection (47 pieces); Reunification of Ireland Clippings (7 pieces); National Association for the Advancement of Colored People Collection (pending); English and Colonial 18th Century Trade Statistics Collection (500,000 I.B.M. cards); Alice Lafond Altieri Collection (925 pieces); Rhode Island Court Records Collection, 1657-1905 (1 million pieces); J. Howard McGrath Collection (62,000 pieces); Thomas Matthew McGlynn, O.P. Collection (5000 pieces and art objects); Edward J. Higgins Collection; Edward P. Beard Collection. **Holdings:** 275,000 books; 44,450 bound periodical volumes; 91,850 government documents; 24,597 microforms; 1143 AV programs. **Subscriptions:** 1892 journals and other serials; 27 newspapers. **Services:** Interlibrary loan (books only); copying; library open to the public for reference use only. **Automated Operations:** Computerized cataloging and ILL. **Computerized Information Services:** OCLC. **Networks/Consortia:** Member of Consortium of Rhode Island Academic and Research Libraries, Inc. (CRIARL), NELINET. **Staff:** Edgar C. Bailey, Jr., Ref.Libn.; Elaine Shanley, Hd.Cat.; Norman Desmarais, Acq.Libn.; Malinda Carpenter, Ref.Libn..

★11639★
PROVIDENCE HOSPITAL - HEALTH SCIENCE LIBRARY (Med)
Box 850724 Phone: (205)633-1373
Mobile, AL 36685 Mary Ann Donnell, Libn.
Staff: Prof 1. **Subjects:** Nursing, medicine, hospital administration, allied health sciences. **Holdings:** 1800 books; bound periodical volumes. **Subscriptions:** 111 journals and other serials. **Services:** Interlibrary loan; copying; library open to public at librarian's discretion. **Computerized Information Services:** MEDLARS, BRS Information Technologies. Performs searches on fee basis. **Networks/Consortia:** Member of National Library of Medicine (NLM), Alabama Health Libraries Association (ALHELA). **Remarks:** Library located at 6801 Airport Blvd., Mobile, AL 36609.

★11640★
PROVIDENCE HOSPITAL - HEALTH SCIENCES LIBRARY (Med)
1150 Varnum St., N.E. Phone: (202)269-7144
Washington, DC 20017 RoseMarie G. Leone, Dir.
Staff: Prof 1; Other 3. **Subjects:** Medicine, nursing, hospital administration, allied health sciences. **Holdings:** 3200 books; 3500 bound periodical volumes. **Subscriptions:** 155 journals and other serials. **Services:** Interlibrary loan; library not open to the public. **Computerized Information Services:** MEDLARS, DIALOG Information Services. **Networks/Consortia:** Member of Southeastern/Atlantic Regional Medical Library Services.

★11641★
PROVIDENCE HOSPITAL - MEDICAL LIBRARY (Med)
2446 Kipling Ave. Phone: (513)853-5806
Cincinnati, OH 45239 Nirupama Emani, Libn.
Founded: 1978. **Staff:** Prof 1. **Subjects:** Medicine, nursing, and allied health sciences. **Holdings:** 300 books; 4000 bound periodical volumes. **Subscriptions:** 179 journals and other serials. **Services:** Interlibrary loan; library not open to the public. **Computerized Information Services:** BRS Information Technologies; DOCLINE (electronic mail service). **Networks/Consortia:** Member of Greater Midwest Regional Medical Library Network.

★11642★
PROVIDENCE HOSPITAL - PANZNER MEMORIAL LIBRARY (Med)
16001 W. Nine Mile Rd.
Box 2043 Phone: (313)424-3294
Southfield, MI 48037 Carole M. Gilbert, Dir., Lib.Serv.
Founded: 1965. **Staff:** Prof 2; Other 1. **Subjects:** Medicine, nursing, allied health sciences, hospitals. **Holdings:** 3000 books; 8500 bound periodical volumes; 700 Audio-Digest tapes; 125 teaching slides. **Subscriptions:** 300 journals and other serials. **Services:** Interlibrary loan; library not open to the public. **Automated Operations:** Computerized cataloging, acquisitions, serials, and circulation. **Computerized Information Services:** DIALOG Information Services, BRS Information Technologies, MEDLARS, WILSONLINE, VU/TEXT Information Services. **Networks/Consortia:** Member of Metropolitan Detroit Medical Library Group (MDMLG), Wayne Oakland Region of Interlibrary Cooperation. **Staff:** Diane Dustin, Libn..

★11643★
PROVIDENCE HOSPITAL - SCHOOL OF NURSING LIBRARY (Med)
1912 Hayes Ave. Phone: (419)625-8450
Sandusky, OH 44870 Marion McGurk, Libn.
Founded: 1905. **Staff:** Prof 1; Other 1. **Subjects:** Nursing, medicine, allied health sciences. **Holdings:** 5000 volumes; 20 VF drawers of pamphlets, leaflets, pictures, articles. **Subscriptions:** 73 journals and other serials. **Services:** Interlibrary loan; copying; library open to the public with restrictions. **Automated Operations:** Computerized cataloging. **Computerized Information Services:** BRS Information Technologies.

PROVIDENCE HOSPITAL, EVERETT - HEALTH INFORMATION NETWORK SERVICES
See: Health Information Network Services (6198)

★11644★
PROVIDENCE JOURNAL COMPANY - NEWS LIBRARY (Publ)
75 Fountain St. Phone: (401)277-7390
Providence, RI 02902 Joseph O. Mehr, Libn.
Founded: 1920. **Staff:** Prof 2; Other 6. **Subjects:** Newspaper reference topics. **Special Collections:** Journal Bulletin Almanacs, 1892 to present. **Holdings:** 2500 books; clippings; picture collection; microforms; pamphlets. **Subscriptions:** 35 journals and other serials; 13 newspapers. **Services:** Copying; library open to the public by appointment. **Computerized Information Services:** DIALOG Information Services, Dow Jones News/Retrieval, VU/TEXT Information Services; J/TEXT (internal database). **Publications:** Journal Bulletin Almanac. **Special Indexes:** Index to Rhode Island State General Assembly materials. **Staff:** Linda Henderson, Asst.Libn..

★11645★
PROVIDENCE MEDICAL CENTER - HORTON HEALTH SCIENCES LIBRARY (Med)
500 17th Ave., C-34008 Phone: (206)326-5621
Seattle, WA 98124 Kathleen Murray, Dir., Lib.Serv.
Staff: 4. **Subjects:** Clinical medicine, surgery, cardiology, nursing, psychiatry. **Holdings:** 6000 volumes; 12 VF drawers. **Subscriptions:** 500 journals and other serials. **Services:** Interlibrary loan; copying; SDI; library open to patients with approval of physician. **Automated Operations:** Computerized cataloging, serials, and circulation. **Computerized Information Services:** Western Library Network (WLN), MEDLINE, BRS Information Technologies, DIALOG Information Services; OnTyme Electronic Message Network Service (electronic mail service). Performs searches on fee basis. **Networks/Consortia:** Member of Seattle Area Hospital Library Consortium (SAHLC).

★11646★
PROVIDENCE MEDICAL CENTER - MEDICAL LIBRARY (Med)
4805 N.E. Glisan Phone: (503)230-6075
Portland, OR 97213 Peggy R. Burrell, Med.Lib.Dir.
Staff: Prof 1. **Subjects:** Nursing, medicine. **Holdings:** 600 books. **Subscriptions:** 202 journals and other serials. **Services:** Interlibrary loan; copying; library open to the public with restrictions. **Computerized Information Services:** MEDLARS, DIALOG Information Services, MEDIS; OnTyme Electronic Message Network Service (electronic mail service). **Networks/Consortia:** Member of Oregon Health Information Network (OHIN).

★11647★
PROVIDENCE PRESBYTERIAN CHURCH - LIBRARY (Rel-Phil)
Box 64033
Virginia Beach, VA 23464 Phone: (804)420-6159
Founded: 1985. **Staff:** Prof 1; Other 6. **Staff:** Presbyterian Church, Bible. **Holdings:** 350 books. **Services:** Library open to the public for reference use only.

★11648★
PROVIDENCE PUBLIC LIBRARY - BUSINESS-INDUSTRY-SCIENCE DEPARTMENT (Bus-Fin, Sci-Engr)
150 Empire St. Phone: (401)521-7722
Providence, RI 02903 Shirley Long, Hd., Adult Serv.
Founded: 1923. **Staff:** Prof 3; Other 1. **Subjects:** Pure and applied sciences, technology, business. **Special Collections:** Historical textiles collection. **Holdings:** 20,000 books; 18,500 bound periodical volumes; 20 VF drawers of federal and military specifications; 3400 annual reports; U.S. patents, 1790 to present, on microfilm; indexes to U.S. patents, 1790 to present; official gazettes, 1872 to present, on microfilm; pamphlets. **Subscriptions:** 306 journals and other serials. **Services:** Interlibrary loan; copying;

department open to the public. **Automated Operations:** Computerized acquisitions and circulation. **Computerized Information Services:** DIALOG Information Services, OCLC. Performs searches on fee basis. **Networks/Consortia:** Member of Consortium of Rhode Island Academic and Research Libraries, Inc. (CRIARL), Rhode Island Interrelated Library Network, Cooperating Libraries Automated Network (CLAN). **Special Indexes:** Index to Rhode Island Inventors and Inventions. **Staff:** Cheryl R. Hunt, Ref./Patent Libn.; Peter Holscher, Ref.Libn.; Dawn Oliveri, Ref.Libn..

★11649★
PROVIDENCE-ST. MARGARET HEALTH CENTER - LIBRARY (Med)
8929 Parallel Pkwy. Phone: (913)596-4795
Kansas City, KS 66112 Mary Hollingshead, Med.Libn.
Staff: Prof 1; Other 1. **Subjects:** Medicine, surgery, nursing, health sciences. **Holdings:** 1000 books; 773 bound periodical volumes; AV programs; video cassettes; cassette tapes; 6 VF drawers. **Subscriptions:** 130 journals and other serials. **Services:** Interlibrary loan; copying; library open to hospital staff and students. **Computerized Information Services:** MEDLINE, DIALOG Information Services. **Networks/Consortia:** Member of Kansas City Library Network, Inc. (KCLN).

★11650★
PROVIDENT HOSPITAL - HEALTH SCIENCES LIBRARY
2600 Liberty Heights Ave.
Baltimore, MD 21215
Defunct

PROVINCE OF ST. JOSEPH OF THE CAPUCHIN ORDER - ST. LAWRENCE SEMINARY
See: St. Lawrence Seminary (12514)

PROVINCIAL ARCHIVES OF ALBERTA
See: Alberta Culture and Multiculturalism (201)

PROVINCIAL ARCHIVES OF NEW BRUNSWICK
See: (New Brunswick) Provincial Archives of New Brunswick (9908)

★11651★
PROWERS COUNTY HISTORICAL SOCIETY - BIG TIMBERS MUSEUM - LIBRARY (Hist)
North Santa Fe Trail
Box 362 Phone: (719)336-2472
Lamar, CO 81052 Edith Birchler, Cur.
Subjects: Local history. **Holdings:** 200 books; Prowers County newspapers. **Services:** Library open to the public for reference use only.

★11652★
PRUDENTIAL INSURANCE COMPANY OF AMERICA - BUSINESS LIBRARY (Bus-Fin)
24 Greenway Plaza, Suite 1900 Phone: (713)993-3526
Houston, TX 77046 Fred Suza, Sr. Group Cons.
Founded: 1952. **Subjects:** Group life insurance, group accident and health insurance, sales promotion, business and business methods, statistics, economics. **Holdings:** 150 volumes. **Subscriptions:** 15 journals and other serials. **Services:** Library not open to the public.

★11653★
PRUDENTIAL INSURANCE COMPANY OF AMERICA - CAPITAL MARKETS GROUP - FINANCIAL RESEARCH CENTER (Bus-Fin)
2 Gateway Three, 2nd Fl. Phone: (201)877-9268
Newark, NJ 07102 Marilyn Lukas, Mgr.
Staff: Prof 2; Other 2. **Subjects:** Finance, business, industry. **Holdings:** 1000 books. **Subscriptions:** 350 journals and other serials; 25 newspapers. **Services:** Center not open to the public. **Automated Operations:** Computerized cataloging, acquisitions, serials, and circulation. **Computerized Information Services:** BRS Information Technologies, Dow Jones News/Retrieval, TEXTLINE, DIALOG Information Services, Inmagic Inc.; READMORE (internal database). **Publications:** Acquisitions list, bimonthly. **Staff:** Rochelle Yates, Asst.Fin.Res.Cons.; Lynn Reiff, Asst.Fin.Res.Cons..

★11654★
PRUDENTIAL INSURANCE COMPANY OF AMERICA - DRYDEN BUSINESS LIBRARY (Bus-Fin)
213 Washington St., 2nd Fl. Phone: (201)877-7583
Newark, NJ 07101 Barbara Ciccone, Mktg.Res.Cons.
Founded: 1941. **Staff:** Prof 3; Other 4. **Subjects:** Insurance, personnel management, office management, census statistics. **Special Collections:** Actuarial proceedings. **Holdings:** 5600 books; 95 VF drawers. **Subscriptions:** 150 journals and other serials. **Services:** Interlibrary loan; library not open to the public. **Computerized Information Services:** DIALOG Information Services, BRS Information Technologies, NEXIS, The Source Information Network, Washington Alert Service, Public Affairs Information Service (PAIS); internal database. **Publications:** Competitive Intelligence Report, monthly; Capsules, weekly - both for internal distribution only.

★11655★
PRUDENTIAL INSURANCE COMPANY OF AMERICA - EMPLOYEES' BUSINESS & RECREATIONAL LIBRARY
Prudential Dr.
Jacksonville, FL 32207
Founded: 1953. **Subjects:** Business, recreation, research. **Holdings:** 4000 books; 750 other cataloged items. **Remarks:** Presently inactive.

★11656★
PRUDENTIAL INSURANCE COMPANY OF AMERICA - LAW LIBRARY (Law, Bus-Fin)
22 Prudential Plaza Phone: (201)877-6804
Newark, NJ 07101 Diane Narr, Assoc.Mgr.
Staff: Prof 1; Other 4. **Subjects:** Law, insurance. **Holdings:** 36,000 volumes. **Subscriptions:** 138 journals and other serials. **Services:** Interlibrary loan; copying; library open to the public on limited schedule. **Computerized Information Services:** DIALOG Information Services, ELSS (Electronic Legislative Search System), LEXIS.

★11657★
PRYOR, CARNEY AND JOHNSON - LIBRARY (Law)
6200 S. Syracuse, Suite 400 Phone: (303)771-6200
Englewood, CO 80111 Michele Bickford, Lib.Asst.
Staff: Prof 1. **Subjects:** Law. **Holdings:** 5000 books. **Subscriptions:** 225 journals and other serials. **Services:** Library not open to the public. **Computerized Information Services:** DIALOG Information Services, WESTLAW; internal database. **Special Indexes:** Document file (online, card).

★11658★
PSI RESEARCH - LIBRARY (Rel-Phil)
484 B Washington St., Suite 317 Phone: (408)646-0661
Monterey, CA 93940-3090 Larissa Vilenskaya, Dir.
Founded: 1982. **Subjects:** Parapsychological studies in the USSR, Eastern Europe, and China. **Holdings:** 250 books; 4 filing drawers and 20 boxes of unbound periodicals, manuscripts, archival materials. **Subscriptions:** 16 journals and other serials. **Services:** Copying; library open to the public by appointment.

★11659★
PSYCHIC SCIENCE INTERNATIONAL SPECIAL INTEREST GROUP - LIBRARY (Rel-Phil)
7514 Belleplain Dr. Phone: (513)236-0361
Dayton, OH 45424 Richard Allen Strong, Pres.
Founded: 1976. **Subjects:** Psychic studies, allied research and education. **Holdings:** 200 volumes; biographical archives. **Computerized Information Services:** Internal database.

★11660★
PSYCHICAL RESEARCH FOUNDATION - DAVID WAYNE HOOKS MEMORIAL LIBRARY (Rel-Phil)
Psychology Department
West Georgia College
Carrollton, GA 30118 William George Roll, Res.Dir.
Founded: 1961. **Subjects:** Parapsychology, death, meditation and religion, mediumship, hauntings and poltergeists, states of consciousness, physics and biophysics, psychology, anthropology. **Special Collections:** Journals and Proceedings of the British Society for Psychical Research, 1882 to present; American Society for Psychical Research Journal, 1941 to present; Journal of Parapsychology, 1937 to present; Proceedings of Parapsychology Association (complete series); Proceedings of American Society for Psychical Research, 1886 to present. **Holdings:** 1500 books; 300 bound periodical volumes; 200 journals; 4 VF drawers of manuscripts, reprints, articles. **Subscriptions:** 35 journals and other serials. **Services:**

Library open to students and faculty. **Publications:** THETA, quarterly - international distribution.

PSYCHO-MOTOR SKILL DESIGN ARCHIVE
See: Justice System Training Association (7303)

PSYCHOANALYTIC FOUNDATION OF MINNESOTA LIBRARY
See: Ramsey County Medical Society - Boeckmann Library (11873)

★11661★
PSYCHOANALYTIC SOCIETY OF SEATTLE - EDITH BUXBAUM LIBRARY (Med)
4027 E. Madison St. Phone: (206)728-1188
Seattle, WA 98112 James O. Raney, M.D., Chm., Lib.Comm.
Staff: Prof 1; Other 3. **Subjects:** Psychoanalysis, allied health sciences. **Holdings:** 1750 volumes; 24 pamphlet boxes of journal reprints; 811 unbound journals; videotapes. **Subscriptions:** 20 journals and other serials. **Services:** Library open to Seattle Institute for Psychoanalysis members.

★11662★
PSYCHOLOGICAL SERVICE OF PITTSBURGH - LIBRARY (Soc Sci)
429 Forbes Ave. Phone: (412)261-1333
Pittsburgh, PA 15219 Dina J. Fulmer, Libn.
Staff: Prof 1. **Subjects:** Industrial psychology; counseling - educational, career, personal; mental health; organization development; psychological testing; work attitudes and motivation; personnel selection; research techniques and statistical methods. **Holdings:** 1000 volumes; 16 VF drawers of reports, pamphlets, reprints, clippings. **Subscriptions:** 40 journals and other serials. **Services:** Interlibrary loan; copying; SDI; library open to qualified persons by appointment.

PSYCHOLOGY TODAY LIBRARY
See: American Psychological Association (644)

★11663★
PSYNETICS FOUNDATION - LIBRARY (Rel-Phil)
1212 E. Lincoln Ave. Phone: (714)533-2311
Anaheim, CA 92805 Marilyn Livingston, Off.Mgr.
Staff: 3. **Subjects:** Metaphysics, occultism, philosophy. **Holdings:** Figures not available. **Services:** Library not open to the public.

★11664★
PUBLIC AFFAIRS RESEARCH COUNCIL OF LOUISIANA - RESEARCH LIBRARY (Soc Sci)
Box 3118 Phone: (504)343-9204
Baton Rouge, LA 70821 Jan Carlock, Res.Libn.
Founded: 1951. **Staff:** Prof 1. **Subjects:** State and local government and finance; education; statistics; public administration; elections and voting; Louisiana law. **Holdings:** 4000 books; 20 pamphlet boxes of state agency reports. **Subscriptions:** 44 journals and other serials. **Services:** Copying; library open to the public for reference use only. **Publications:** PAR List of Publications: Selective Subject Index to PAR Research, annual - to members, press, libraries; PAR Analysis, irregular; Legislative Bulletin, weekly during Louisiana legislative session. **Remarks:** Library located at 300 Louisiana Ave., Baton Rouge, LA 70802.

PUBLIC ARCHIVES OF NOVA SCOTIA
See: (Nova Scotia) Public Archives of Nova Scotia (10549)

★11665★
PUBLIC BROADCASTING SERVICE - PTV ARCHIVES (Info Sci)
1320 Braddock Place Phone: (703)739-5014
Alexandria, VA 22314-1698 Glenn Clatworthy, Prog. Data Anl.
Staff: Prof 3. **Subjects:** Fine arts, public affairs, science, history, natural history. **Special Collections:** National Educational Television (NET) Film and Videotape Collection; Public Broadcasting Service (PBS) Videotape Collection; NET and PBS program files. **Holdings:** 38,000 tapes; 18,000 video cassettes. **Services:** Archives open to the public by appointment. **Special Catalogs:** Biographical Catalog, 1953-1973 (printout). **Remarks:** An alternate telephone number is 739-5230.

★11666★
PUBLIC CITIZEN - CONGRESS WATCH LIBRARY (Law, Soc Sci)
215 Pennsylvania Ave., S.E. Phone: (202)546-4996
Washington, DC 20003 Michael McCauley, Libn./Res.Asst.
Founded: 1973. **Staff:** Prof 1. **Subjects:** Congressional, consumer, and environmental issues. **Special Collections:** Complete collection of Public Citizen reports, studies, voting indices; publications of other Ralph Nader groups (books; reports; articles). **Holdings:** 3000 books; 200 bound periodical volumes; congressional hearings and reports. **Subscriptions:** 10 journals and other serials; 6 newspapers. **Services:** Interlibrary loan; copying; library open to the public by appointment.

★11667★
PUBLIC CITIZEN - CRITICAL MASS ENERGY PROJECT - LIBRARY (Energy)
215 Pennsylvania Ave., S.E. Phone: (202)546-4996
Washington, DC 20003 Ken Bossong, Dir.
Founded: 1974. **Staff:** Prof 4. **Subjects:** Nuclear power, least-cost energy planning, energy conservation, solar energy. **Special Collections:** Collection of antinuclear materials (250 books). **Holdings:** 800 books. **Subscriptions:** 153 journals and other serials. **Services:** Library open to the public by appointment. **Computerized Information Services:** Internal database.

★11668★
PUBLIC EDUCATION ASSOCIATION - LIBRARY AND ARCHIVES (Educ)
39 W. 32nd St., 15th Fl. Phone: (212)868-1640
New York, NY 10018 Judith Baum, Dir., Info.Serv.
Staff: Prof 2. **Subjects:** Education, New York City. **Special Collections:** Integration; decentralization; P.E.A. Archives; collective bargaining; special education (handicapped); alternative education; school finance reform. **Holdings:** 5060 volumes and documents; 28 VF drawers; 40 drawers of archival materials. **Subscriptions:** 31 journals and other serials. **Services:** Interlibrary loan; copying; library open to the public by appointment. **Computerized Information Services:** Internal database. **Publications:** Public Education Alert, 6/year; internal subject bibliography.

★11669★
PUBLIC LAW EDUCATION INSTITUTE - LIBRARY (Law)
1601 Connecticut Ave., N.W., Suite 450 Phone: (202)232-1400
Washington, DC 20009 William J. Straub, Circ.Mgr.
Staff: 5. **Subjects:** Military, civil, criminal law; allied federal law; selective service law and administration; veterans law. **Special Collections:** Principal U.S. archive of selective service court opinions, 1968-1987; Defense Department regulations on manpower/military justice. **Holdings:** 1100 volumes; 35 VF drawers of federal court opinions. **Subscriptions:** 50 journals and other serials. **Services:** Interlibrary loan; copying; facsimile service and selective service document locator; library open to the public. **Publications:** Military Law Reporter, 1973-1988 (16 volumes). **Special Catalogs:** Catalog of Selected Litigation - Selective Service, 1980-1983.

★11670★
PUBLIC LIBRARY OF CINCINNATI AND HAMILTON COUNTY - ART AND MUSIC DEPARTMENT (Art, Mus)
800 Vine St. Phone: (513)369-7954
Cincinnati, OH 45202 R. Jayne Craven, Hd.
Founded: 1872. **Staff:** Prof 7; Other 2. **Subjects:** Art, music, architecture, theater arts, photography, crafts, dance, cinema, costume. **Special Collections:** Choral Music (208,752 copies of 1840 titles); Delta Omicron Music Composers Library (1221 items); Valentines, 1835-1920s (225). **Holdings:** 134,712 books and cataloged scores; 18,385 bound periodical volumes; 30,986 pieces of sheet music; 726,371 clippings; 16,625 theater, dance, music programs; 6064 exhibition catalogs; 2432 librettos; 1035 Strobridge circus posters; 944 reels of microfilm; 6548 microfiche. **Subscriptions:** 617 journals and other serials. **Services:** Interlibrary loan; copying; department open to the public. **Computerized Information Services:** OCLC. **Networks/Consortia:** Member of Art Research Libraries of Ohio (ARLO). **Special Indexes:** 26 Symphony Orchestra program notes; Cincinnati Summer Opera Index by season, opera, artist, character; Index to Langstroth Reference Lithographs Collection; Matinee Musicale Recital Series; Analytic Index of Published Songs and Music Collections; Cincinnati Composers Manuscript Collection. **Staff:** Charles E. Ishee, First Asst..

★11671★
PUBLIC LIBRARY OF CINCINNATI AND HAMILTON COUNTY - CHILDREN'S DEPARTMENT (Educ)
800 Vine St. Phone: (513)369-6900
Cincinnati, OH 45202 Consuelo W. Harris, Hd.
Staff: Prof 4; Other 3. **Subjects:** Children's literature, children's literature reference materials. **Special Collections:** Jean Alva Goldsmith Memorial Collection (juvenile titles - fiction, easy, nonfiction, foreign language, toy books; 5000); Historical Collection (examples of late 19th and early 20th century children's books; 1000). **Holdings:** 54,142 books; 230 bound periodical volumes; 3 file drawers; 20 notebooks on authors and

illustrators; 4 bibliography notebooks; 2000 other uncataloged items. **Subscriptions:** 86 journals and other serials. **Services:** Interlibrary loan; copying; department open to the public. **Staff:** Rebecca Shea, First Asst..

★11672★
PUBLIC LIBRARY OF CINCINNATI AND HAMILTON COUNTY - DEPARTMENT OF RARE BOOKS & SPECIAL COLLECTIONS (Rare Book, Hum)
800 Vine St. Phone: (513)369-6957
Cincinnati, OH 45202 Alfred Kleine-Kreutzmann, Cur.
Founded: 1955. **Staff:** Prof 2; Other 1. **Subjects:** Discovery and exploration of America; Ohio Valley; Cincinnatiana; Bibles; author collections: Lafcadio Hearn, Mark Twain, William Faulkner, Ernest Hemingway, John Steinbeck, W. Somerset Maugham, Charles Dickens, Sir Winston Churchill, Sinclair Lewis, Pearl Buck, Eugene O'Neill, Edgar Rice Burroughs, A. Edward Newton, Saul Bellow, Isaac B. Singer, Hugh Walpole; English language dictionaries; books about books and fine printing; George Cruikshank; Milestone Books; Mormons and Shakers. **Special Collections:** Inland Rivers Library (books, manuscripts, photographs on commercial transportation on the Ohio and Mississippi Rivers and their navigable tributaries). **Holdings:** 36,000 books; 1400 bound periodical volumes; 22,000 photographs of steamboats; 40 VF drawers of pamphlets; 157 boxes; 5 drawers of manuscripts; 15 map case drawers of maps, blueprints, broadsides, prints of steamboats. **Subscriptions:** 36 journals and other serials. **Services:** Copying; department open to the public. **Publications:** Occasional checklists and brochures describing holdings. **Special Catalogs:** Printed catalog of Inland Rivers Library; Catalog of Kahn English Language Dictionary Collection - both for sale. **Staff:** Claire Pancero, First Asst. & Cat..

★11673★
PUBLIC LIBRARY OF CINCINNATI AND HAMILTON COUNTY - EDUCATION AND RELIGION DEPARTMENT (Educ, Rel-Phil)
800 Vine St. Phone: (513)369-6940
Cincinnati, OH 45202 Susan F. Hettinger, Hd.
Founded: 1952. **Staff:** Prof 7; Other 1. **Subjects:** Education, library science, religion, grantsmanship, sports and recreation, philosophy, psychology, sociology. **Special Collections:** Theological and Religious Collection (church history and 19th-20th century Protestant theological writings); Foundation Center Regional Collection. **Holdings:** 153,000 books; 19,750 bound periodical volumes; 20,000 microfiche of Internal Revenue Service (IRS) 990 forms for foundations in Kentucky, Indiana, Ohio; 65 VF drawers of pamphlets and vocational literature; 25 VF drawers of government documents; college catalogs of 2400 institutions on microfiche; ERIC microfiche, 1976 to present. **Subscriptions:** 600 journals and other serials. **Services:** Interlibrary loan; copying. **Computerized Information Services:** BRS Information Technologies, DIALOG Information Services, NEXIS, VU/TEXT Information Services. **Staff:** Joan Hamilton, First Asst..

★11674★
PUBLIC LIBRARY OF CINCINNATI AND HAMILTON COUNTY - EXCEPTIONAL CHILDREN'S DIVISION (Educ)
800 Vine St. Phone: (513)369-6065
Cincinnati, OH 45202 Coy Kate Hunsucker, Hd.
Founded: 1966. **Staff:** Prof 2; Other 3. **Subjects:** Programs and materials for deaf, mentally handicapped, learning disabled, physically handicapped, socially maladjusted, emotionally disturbed, and gifted and talented children and young adults from pre-school through high school ages. **Special Collections:** Deposit collections in 7 hospitals and institutions (2500 books). **Holdings:** 16,000 volumes. **Subscriptions:** 16 journals and other serials. **Services:** Story hours; book talks and puppet shows for children; talks for parent groups, teachers, and workers with special needs children; special summer programs for gifted and talented children. **Publications:** Feelings and Emotions for Younger Children; Books for Developmentally Handicapped Children; Books for Severe and Profoundly Handicapped Children. **Staff:** Mark A. Kelso, First Asst..

★11675★
PUBLIC LIBRARY OF CINCINNATI AND HAMILTON COUNTY - FILMS AND RECORDINGS CENTER (Aud-Vis)
800 Vine St. Phone: (513)369-6924
Cincinnati, OH 45202 Robert Hudzik, Hd.
Founded: 1947. **Staff:** Prof 5; Other 8. **Subjects:** Audiovisual advisory service in all subjects. **Special Collections:** Slides on the history of Cincinnati (1750); The Fountain Speaks (26 radio programs of local history on 78rpm records); Reference Collection of Cincinnati Symphony recordings (40). **Holdings:** 3460 reels of sound film (2590 titles); 435 8mm films; 1600 35mm filmstrips; 31,600 slides; 42,000 sound recordings; 13,500 tape cassettes; 1200 video cassettes; 2875 compact discs. **Services:** 16mm films and video cassettes loaned to individuals, organizations, schools in Hamilton County and surrounding counties for a fee; circulation of other holdings free to card holders; center open to the public. **Special Catalogs:** 16mm Film Catalog; 35mm Filmstrip Catalog; Slide Catalog; Tape Cassette Catalog; Video Cassette Catalog. **Staff:** Kent Newlon, First Asst..

★11676★
PUBLIC LIBRARY OF CINCINNATI AND HAMILTON COUNTY - GOVERNMENT AND BUSINESS DEPARTMENT (Bus-Fin, Soc Sci)
800 Vine St. Phone: (513)369-6932
Cincinnati, OH 45202 Carl G. Marquette, Jr., Hd.
Founded: 1952. **Staff:** Prof 9; Other 7. **Subjects:** Economics, business, labor, accounting, statistics, finance, government, law, insurance, international relations, military science. **Special Collections:** Telephone directories (1025; Phonefiche); Murray Seasongood Collection of Government, Law and Public Administration (5000 items); Lenke Insurance Library (1000 items). **Holdings:** 134,000 books; 36,200 bound periodical volumes; complete U.S. Government depository, 1884 to present; 40 VF drawers of pamphlets; 80 VF drawers of documents; 130 drawers of microfilm. **Subscriptions:** 1080 journals and other serials. **Services:** Interlibrary loan; copying. **Computerized Information Services:** BRS Information Technologies, DIALOG Information Services, NEXIS, Dow Jones News/Retrieval, WILSONLINE, VU/TEXT Information Services. Performs searches on fee basis after first 10 minutes of searching. **Staff:** Martha Heitkamp, First Asst..

★11677★
PUBLIC LIBRARY OF CINCINNATI AND HAMILTON COUNTY - HISTORY DEPARTMENT (Hist, Geog-Map)
800 Vine St. Phone: (513)369-6905
Cincinnati, OH 45202 J. Richard Abell, Hd.
Staff: Prof 7; Other 4. **Subjects:** History, genealogy, maps, bibliography, geography, travel. **Special Collections:** Travel files (U.S. and foreign); genealogy and family history collection (U.S. census population schedules, 1790-1910, on microfilm; state census indexes); town, county, and state histories (U.S. and foreign); military unit histories rosters, indexes; local history collection (local history index; local newspaper index). **Holdings:** 163,000 books; 26,100 bound periodical volumes; 9640 bound newspaper volumes; 31,000 reels of microfilm; 100,000 microfiche. **Subscriptions:** 1200 journals and other serials; 50 newspapers. **Services:** Interlibrary loan; copying. **Staff:** Susan J. Kober, First Asst..

★11678★
PUBLIC LIBRARY OF CINCINNATI AND HAMILTON COUNTY - HISTORY DEPARTMENT - MAP UNIT (Geog-Map)
800 Vine St. Phone: (513)369-6909
Cincinnati, OH 45202 Douglas S. Magee, Map Libn.
Founded: 1955. **Staff:** Prof 1; Other 1. **Subjects:** Maps, atlases, cartography, place name studies, gazetteers. **Special Collections:** Ohio county cadastral atlases; maps of Cincinnati; U.S. county cadastral atlases (1550); current street maps of U.S. cities with population of 20,000 and over. **Holdings:** 147,139 maps; 1605 atlases; 423 gazetteers; 225 carto-bibliographies; 87 reels of microfilm; 4500 microfiche; 12 globes; 1051 bound periodical volumes. **Subscriptions:** 38 journals and other serials. **Services:** Copying; unit open to the public.

★11679★
PUBLIC LIBRARY OF CINCINNATI AND HAMILTON COUNTY - INSTITUTIONS/BOOKS BY MAIL/BOOKMOBILE (Info Sci)
Library Square
800 Vine St. Phone: (513)369-6070
Cincinnati, OH 45202 Keith C. Kuhn, Hd.
Founded: 1969. **Staff:** Prof 3; Other 12. **Subjects:** Fiction and nonfiction. **Special Collections:** Large-print materials (20,884 books). **Holdings:** 40,000 volumes; 897 sound recordings; 214 cassettes. **Subscriptions:** 46 journals and other serials. **Services:** Interlibrary loan; books-by-mail for the homebound; specialized services for the institutionalized; deposit collections for hospitals, senior centers, schools, correctional facilities; Special Services Area in main library. **Special Catalogs:** Large-print catalog of holdings, annual; Books-by-Mail catalog, annual. **Staff:** Tonia H. Moorman, First Asst..

★11680★
PUBLIC LIBRARY OF CINCINNATI AND HAMILTON COUNTY - LIBRARY FOR THE BLIND AND PHYSICALLY HANDICAPPED (Aud-Vis)
Library Square
800 Vine St. Phone: (513)369-6075
Cincinnati, OH 45202 Carol Heideman, Reg.Libn.
Founded: 1901. **Staff:** Prof 1; Other 12. **Subjects:** Books for the blind and physically handicapped in braille, on discs (talking books) and cassettes. **Holdings:** 15,744 volumes in braille; 61,490 recorded disc containers; 94,171 cassette containers. **Subscriptions:** 44 on talking books; 34 in braille; 25 on cassettes. **Services:** Interlibrary loan; library open to residents of 33 Ohio counties who are certified as eligible for services. **Automated Operations:** Computerized circulation; automatic subject selection by reader interest categories. **Publications:** Newsletter, monthly. **Remarks:** A toll-free telephone number for Ohio residents is (800)582-0335.

★11681★
PUBLIC LIBRARY OF CINCINNATI AND HAMILTON COUNTY - LITERATURE DEPARTMENT (Hum)
800 Vine St. Phone: (513)369-6991
Cincinnati, OH 45202 Donna S. Monnig, Hd.
Founded: 1983. **Staff:** Prof 6; Other 2. **Subjects:** Literature, foreign fiction, folklore, journalism, linguistics. **Special Collections:** Ohio author bibliographies. **Holdings:** 197,000 books; 12,800 bound periodical volumes; 12,720 reels of microfilm; dictionaries. **Subscriptions:** 400 journals and other serials. **Services:** Interlibrary loan; copying; department open to the public. **Special Indexes:** Ohioana Hamilton County Authors Bibliography (pamphlet), annual. **Staff:** Georganne F. Bradford, First Asst..

★11682★
PUBLIC LIBRARY OF CINCINNATI AND HAMILTON COUNTY - MUNICIPAL REFERENCE LIBRARY (Soc Sci)
801 Plum St. Phone: (513)369-6076
Cincinnati, OH 45202 Barbara J. Perkins, Libn.
Staff: Prof 1. **Subjects:** Municipal administration, business and economics, criminology and law enforcement, waste collection and management, public health and safety, transportation. **Holdings:** 8000 books; 42,000 other cataloged items. **Subscriptions:** 65 journals and other serials. **Services:** Library open to the public.

★11683★
PUBLIC LIBRARY OF CINCINNATI AND HAMILTON COUNTY - SCIENCE AND TECHNOLOGY DEPARTMENT (Sci-Engr)
800 Vine St. Phone: (513)369-6936
Cincinnati, OH 45202 Rosemary Dahmann, Hd.
Founded: 1902. **Staff:** Prof 7; Other 4. **Subjects:** Pure and applied science, especially chemistry. **Special Collections:** U.S. Depository Library, including U.S. patents, 1790 to present, and Official Gazette, 1872 to present; U.S. military and federal, ASTM, and ANSI standards and specifications; trade directories; Rand Corporation documents. **Holdings:** 197,000 books; 62,300 bound periodical volumes; 54,000 pamphlets; 261,000 microforms. **Subscriptions:** 1200 journals and other serials. **Services:** Interlibrary loan; copying. **Computerized Information Services:** DIALOG Information Services, WILSONLINE, BRS Information Technologies, NEXIS, U.S. Patent Classification System. Performs U.S. Patent searches free of charge; other searches on fee basis. **Staff:** John E. Johns, First Asst..

PUBLIC LIBRARY OF THE HIGH SEAS
See: United Seaman's Service - American Merchant Marine Library Association (14573)

★11684★
PUBLIC LIBRARY OF NASHVILLE AND DAVIDSON COUNTY - BUSINESS INFORMATION DIVISION (Bus-Fin)
8th and Union Phone: (615)244-4700
Nashville, TN 37203 Alyne R. Gundlach, Chf.
Founded: 1931. **Staff:** Prof 2; Other 2. **Subjects:** Management, finance, investments, advertising, technology. **Holdings:** 8500 books; 4500 bound periodical volumes; 17,500 government documents. **Subscriptions:** 454 journals and other serials. **Services:** Interlibrary loan; copying; division open to the public. **Automated Operations:** Computerized cataloging. **Publications:** Newsletter Quarterly: Information For Profit. **Staff:** Ron Perry, Bus.Libn..

★11685★
PUBLIC LIBRARY OF NASHVILLE AND DAVIDSON COUNTY - THE NASHVILLE ROOM (Hist)
8th Ave., N. & Union Phone: (615)244-4700
Nashville, TN 37203-3585 Mary Glenn Hearne, Dir.
Staff: Prof 2; Other 3. **Subjects:** History and genealogy of Nashville and its residents, 1779 to present. **Special Collections:** Jeter-Smith Dance Collection; Naff Collection of performing artists; Weil Ornithological Collection; Stahlman Collection of Southern Books. **Holdings:** 10,000 books; scrapbooks; school diaries of the 1890s; 5 file drawers of census microfilm; manuscripts of local authors; interviews with local authors; Nashville obituaries (online); Nashville movies; photographs; slides; oral history tapes. **Services:** Copying; room open to the public. **Special Indexes:** Index to photographs (cards); index to Naff Collection; index to scrapbooks and maps (cards); index to Jeter-Smith Collection (cards). **Staff:** Dorothy Dale, Libn..

★11686★
PUBLIC LIBRARY OF YOUNGSTOWN AND MAHONING COUNTY - SCIENCE AND INDUSTRY COLLECTION (Bus-Fin, Sci-Engr)
305 Wick Ave. Phone: (216)744-8636
Youngstown, OH 44503 Janet K. Moy, Hd.
Staff: Prof 5; Other 4. **Subjects:** Science and technology, business and finance. **Holdings:** 50,000 books; 6300 bound periodical volumes; 55 VF drawers of pamphlets, documents, house organs, clippings; 1500 reels of microfilm. **Subscriptions:** 270 journals and other serials. **Services:** Interlibrary loan; copying; collection open to the public. **Networks/Consortia:** Member of NOLA Regional Library System.

★11687★
PUBLIC POLICY FORUM - LIBRARY (Soc Sci)
633 W. Wisconsin Ave., Suite 406 Phone: (414)276-8240
Milwaukee, WI 53203-1918 Jean B. Tyler, Exec.Dir.
Founded: 1913. **Subjects:** Local government, urban concerns of state government, municipal administration, local school districts. **Special Collections:** Data about local governments and school districts in 5-county Milwaukee metropolitan area. **Holdings:** 3000 books; clippings files; unbound reports, manuscripts, archives, documents. **Subscriptions:** 50 journals and other serials; 25 newspapers. **Services:** Interlibrary loan; copying (both limited); library open to the public with permission. **Publications:** Bulletin, 10-20/year - to mailing list of public officials and other opinion leaders, citizen activists, civic organizations across the U.S. **Formerly:** Citizens' Governmental Research Bureau, Inc.

★11688★
PUBLIC/PRIVATE VENTURES - RESOURCE CENTER (Bus-Fin)
399 Market St. Phone: (215)592-9099
Philadelphia, PA 19106 Donna R. Thomas, Info.Mgr.
Staff: Prof 1; Other 1. **Subjects:** Employment, youth unemployment, labor market information, training programs, economic development, supported work, vocational and remedial education, foundations, disadvantaged populations. **Holdings:** 1750 books; 16 VF drawers of brochures, clippings, annual reports. **Subscriptions:** 47 journals and other serials. **Services:** Copying; SDI; center open to the public by appointment. **Publications:** List of publications - available on request.

★11689★
PUBLIC RELATIONS SOCIETY OF AMERICA - PRSA INFORMATION CENTER (Bus-Fin)
33 Irving Place, 3rd Fl. Phone: (212)995-0148
New York, NY 10003 Tesse Santoro, Mgr.
Founded: 1955. **Staff:** Prof 3. **Subjects:** Public relations. **Special Collections:** Public relations plans and proposals; examples of employee communications. **Holdings:** 1000 books; 90 VF drawers. **Subscriptions:** 52 journals and other serials. **Services:** Interlibrary loan; center open to the public on fee basis. **Automated Operations:** Computerized public access catalog. **Publications:** Bibliography of PR Materials, annual - for sale.

★11690★
PUBLIC SERVICE COMPANY OF COLORADO - LIBRARY (Energy)
550 15th St.
Box 840 Phone: (303)571-7084
Denver, CO 80201 Mary Ann Hamm, Libn.
Staff: 1. **Subjects:** Business management, public utilities, economics, electrical engineering. **Special Collections:** Electric Power Research Institute reports; Conference Board publications. **Holdings:** 3500 books; 500 government documents. **Subscriptions:** 175 journals and other serials; 6 newspapers. **Services:** Interlibrary loan; copying; library open to the

public through other librarians and for specific research in utility field. **Computerized Information Services:** DIALOG Information Services, Utility Data Institute, A.G.A. GasNet. **Publications:** Library bulletin, monthly - for internal distribution only; bibliographies - available on request.

★11691★
PUBLIC SERVICE CO. OF OKLAHOMA - CORPORATE REFERENCE CENTER (Energy)
212 E. 6th St.
Box 201 Phone: (918)599-2367
Tulsa, OK 74119 Carol A. Bartley, Res.Anl.
Founded: 1967. **Staff:** Prof 1. **Subjects:** Electric utilities, electrical engineering, business. **Holdings:** 10,000 volumes; 6200 technical and conference papers. **Subscriptions:** 451 journals and other serials. **Services:** Interlibrary loan; center not open to the public. **Automated Operations:** Computerized serials. **Computerized Information Services:** DIALOG Information Services. **Networks/Consortia:** Member of Tulsa Area Library Cooperative (TALC). **Special Indexes:** KWIC/KWOC index of technical papers.

★11692★
PUBLIC SERVICE ELECTRIC AND GAS COMPANY - CORPORATE LIBRARY (Energy, Sci-Engr)
80 Park Plaza, P3C
Box 570 Phone: (201)430-7333
Newark, NJ 07101 Harriet Mayer, Corp.Libn.
Founded: 1911. **Staff:** Prof 3; Other 5. **Subjects:** Public utilities, electric industry, electrical engineering, gas industry, mechanical engineering, business, management, nuclear power. **Holdings:** 18,400 books; 6000 bound periodical volumes; 800 directories; 165 VF drawers of pamphlets, reports, separates; 60 shelves of government documents; 5 shelves of annual reports and prospectuses of public utility companies; 100,000 microfiche of U.S. Government energy-related reports. **Subscriptions:** 765 journals and other serials. **Services:** Interlibrary loan; copying; limited service to public by appointment only. **Automated Operations:** Computerized cataloging and serials. **Computerized Information Services:** DIALOG Information Services, OCLC, Pergamon ORBIT InfoLine, Inc., LEXIS, NEXIS, Dun & Bradstreet Corporation, NLM, TOXNET, Dow Jones News/Retrieval, BRS Information Technologies, WILSONLINE, VU/TEXT Information Services; Corporate Information System (internal database); SourceMail (electronic mail service). **Networks/Consortia:** Member of PALINET, Essex-Hudson Regional Library Cooperative. **Publications:** Library Guide, irregular. **Special Indexes:** Index to selected periodical articles on public utilities (card). **Staff:** Sheila E. Cassels, Assoc.Libn., Ref.; Patrice M. Otani, Asst.Libn., Ref..

★11693★
PUBLIC SERVICE ELECTRIC AND GAS COMPANY - NUCLEAR LIBRARY (Energy)
Box 236, MC N02 Phone: (609)339-4135
Hancocks Bridge, NJ 08308 Virginia L. Swichel, Libn.
Founded: 1983. **Staff:** Prof 1; Other 2. **Subjects:** Nuclear power and engineering. **Holdings:** 2000 books; 1100 unbound reports; 70,000 vendor catalogs on microfilm; 218 reels of microfilm of current and Retrospective Industry Standards; 600 reels of microfilm of Military Standards; 944 hardcopy Industry Standards; 7 drawers of microfiche; 2345 reels of microfilm; 2 VF drawers of pamphlets; 3 VF drawers of clippings. **Subscriptions:** 171 journals and other serials; 7 newspapers. **Services:** Interlibrary loan; library not open to the public. **Automated Operations:** Computerized cataloging, acquisitions, and serials. **Computerized Information Services:** DIALOG Information Services, BRS Information Technologies, Pergamon ORBIT InfoLine, Inc., VU/TEXT Information Services, LEXIS, NEXIS, WILSONLINE; Corporate Information System (internal database); SourceMail (electronic mail service). **Networks/ Consortia:** Member of South Jersey Regional Library Cooperative. **Publications:** Nuclear Library Newsletter, 6/year - for internal distribution only.

★11694★
PUBLIC SERVICE ELECTRIC AND GAS COMPANY - NUCLEAR TRAINING CENTER LIBRARY (Energy)
244 Chestnut St. Phone: (609)339-3773
Salem, NJ 08079 Richard E. Bater, Info.Coord.
Founded: 1983. **Staff:** Prof 1; Other 2. **Subjects:** Nuclear reactor operations - training, engineering, management. **Holdings:** 6000 books; plant documents. **Subscriptions:** 44 journals and other serials. **Services:** Copying; SDI; library open to the public with restrictions. **Automated Operations:** Computerized cataloging. **Computerized Information Services:** DIALOG Information Services, Dow Jones News/Retrieval, CDC, Institute of Nuclear Power Operations (INPO); internal database. **Publications:** Acquisition list, monthly; holdings list, semiannual.

PUBLIC TECHNOLOGY INC. - INFORMATION CENTER
See: National League of Cities - Municipal Reference Service (9722)

★11695★
PUBLIC UTILITIES COMMISSION OF OHIO (PUCO) - PUCO RESEARCH LIBRARY (Law, Energy)
180 E. Broad St. Phone: (614)466-5082
Columbus, OH 43215 Ms. Riek A. Oldenquist, Libn.
Founded: 1975. **Staff:** Prof 3. **Subjects:** Law, public utilities, economics, forecasting, accounting, engineering, management, transportation. **Special Collections:** PUCO annual reports, 1867 to present; official copies of session and administrative orders, 1913 to present; National Association of Regulatory Utility Commissioners (NARUC) publications, 1922 to present; Public Utilities Fortnightly, 1945 to present; long-term forecasts of the Ohio Utility companies, 1976 to present. **Holdings:** 16,780 books; 2727 government documents; 504 staff reports of investigations; 100 technical reports. **Subscriptions:** 194 journals and other serials; 15 newspapers. **Services:** Interlibrary loan; copying; library open to the public with restrictions. **Computerized Information Services:** LEXIS, WESTLAW, LEGI-SLATE; internal database. **Publications:** PUCO Code of Rules and Regulations, volumes 1 and 2, second edition and revisions; Gas Pipeline Safety Code; A Portion of the Laws of Ohio Applying to Railroads. **Special Catalogs:** PUCO Recent Acquisitions, quarterly. **Staff:** Ina Walker, Asst.Libn.; Edna Newkirk, Acq.Libn..

★11696★
PUBLIC UTILITY COMMISSION OF TEXAS - LIBRARY (Energy, Law)
7800 Shoal Creek Blvd. Phone: (512)458-0299
Austin, TX 78757 Suzi Williams, Libn.
Founded: 1976. **Staff:** Prof 1. **Subjects:** Public utilities, law, telecommunications, electric utilities, economics, energy. **Holdings:** 10,000 books; 700 unbound periodical volumes; 12 VF drawers; 2000 microfiche; 100 videotapes. **Subscriptions:** 352 journals and other serials; 9 newspapers. **Services:** Interlibrary loan; SDI; library open to the public by appointment. **Computerized Information Services:** LEXIS; internal database. **Publications:** PUC Library Bulletin, monthly - for internal distribution only. **Special Indexes:** Citation index to PUC Bulletin.

PUBLIC WORKS CANADA
See: Canada - Public Works Canada (2474)

NEWBELL NILES PUCKETT MEMORIAL ARCHIVES
See: Cleveland Public Library - Fine Arts and Special Collections Department - Special Collections Section - John G. White Collection and Rare Books (3318)

★11697★
PUEBLO CHIEFTAIN - LIBRARY (Publ)
825 W. 6th St. Phone: (719)544-3520
Pueblo, CO 81003 Betty M. Carnes, Libn.
Staff: Prof 1; Other 1. **Subjects:** Newspaper reference topics. **Special Collections:** Bound volumes of the Pueblo Daily Chieftain, 1868-1947, microfilm volumes, 1947 to present; bound volumes of the Pueblo Star-Journal, 1901 to present, microfilm volumes, 1947 to present. **Holdings:** 300 books; 6000 filing envelopes of clippings; 10,000 personal files; 1000 historical files. **Services:** Copying; library open to the public.

★11698★
PUEBLO CITY INFORMATION DEPARTMENT - MUNICIPAL REFERENCE LIBRARY (Soc Sci)
Box 1427 Phone: (719)545-0561
Pueblo, CO 81002 Donald R. Vest, Libn.
Founded: 1960. **Staff:** 1. **Subjects:** Municipal government, urban and regional planning, environmental quality, census documents, human services planning, zoning. **Special Collections:** Municipal reports. **Holdings:** 2400 volumes; 8 VF drawers; 1000 maps; planning reports. **Subscriptions:** 36 journals and other serials; 6 newspapers. **Services:** Copying; library open to the public with restrictions. **Computerized Information Services:** LOGIN; Colorado County Profiles (internal database); LINUS (electronic mail service). **Publications:** Municipal Reports, 6-10/year; Pueblo Economic Statistics Retrieval System (economic report), quarterly; City of Pueblo Data Book, annual. **Remarks:** Library located at One City Hall Place, Pueblo, CO 81003.

★11699★
PUEBLO GRANDE MUSEUM - RESEARCH LIBRARY (Soc Sci)
4619 E. Washington St. Phone: (602)275-3452
Phoenix, AZ 85034 Chad T. Phinney, Musm.Asst.
Founded: 1926. **Staff:** Prof 1. **Subjects:** Archeology, anthropology. **Holdings:** Figures not available. **Services:** Library open to public for reference use on request.

JOHN G. PUENTE LIBRARY
See: Capitol College (2645)

★11700★
PUERTO RICAN CONGRESS OF MUSIC & ART - LIBRARY (Area-Ethnic)
2315 W. North Ave. Phone: (312)772-4223
Chicago, IL 60647 Nilda Ruiz-Pauley, Exec.Dir.
Founded: 1948. **Staff:** Prof 4. **Subjects:** Music composition, Latin American music, Puerto Rican arts and crafts. **Special Collections:** Postcards of Puerto Rican towns and municipalities; History of the Puerto Ricans in Chicago and Illinois; articles written by local Puerto Rican writers. **Holdings:** 153 books; 500 Latin magazines; Estrellita's Gossip; Latin and Puerto Rican artist information. **Services:** Interlibrary loan; copying; SDI; library open to the public by appointment. **Automated Operations:** Computerized circulation.

★11701★
PUERTO RICAN CULTURE INSTITUTE - LUIS MUNOZ RIVERA LIBRARY AND MUSEUM (Area-Ethnic)
Calle Padre Berrios
Barranquitas, PR 00618 Maria L. Valencia, Libn.
Founded: 1916. **Staff:** Prof 1; Other 1. **Subjects:** History, literature, language, art, folklore. **Special Collections:** Puerto Rican authors; information about Luis Munoz Rivera and Barranquitas. **Holdings:** 2500 books; 500 pamphlets and journals; 3 VF drawers of clippings and documents. **Services:** Interlibrary loan; library open to the public for reference use only. **Publications:** Boletin Cultural, monthly - to high school students. **Remarks:** Library affiliated with the General Library of Puerto Rico.

★11702★
PUERTO RICO CENTRAL OFFICE OF PERSONNEL ADMINISTRATION - INSTITUTE OF PERSONNEL DEVELOPMENT - LIBRARY (Bus-Fin)
Ponce de Leon Ave., Stop 22
Fernandez Juncos Sta., Box 8476 Phone: (809)721-4300
Santurce, PR 00910 Jacqueline Rivera, Libn.
Founded: 1979. **Staff:** Prof 1. **Subjects:** Public and personnel administration, Puerto Rico history. **Holdings:** 2008 volumes; 576 pamphlets; 203 reports; 56 scrapbooks of clippings. **Subscriptions:** 14 journals and other serials. **Services:** Interlibrary loan; library open to the public. **Automated Operations:** Computerized cataloging and circulation. **Publications:** Boletin Informativo, quarterly. **Special Indexes:** Public Administration (card). **Also Known As:** Puerto Rico Oficina Central Administracion Personal - Biblioteca Instituto Desarrollo Personal.

★11703★
PUERTO RICO DEPARTMENT OF HEALTH - MEDICAL LIBRARY (Med)
Ant. Hospital de Psiquiatria - Bo. Monacillos
Call Box 70184 Phone: (809)767-6060
San Juan, PR 00936 Esther Rosario Hernandez, Libn.
Founded: 1952. **Staff:** Prof 1; Other 2. **Subjects:** Public health, emergency and ambulatory services, mental health services, planning and evaluation of hospital development, health services administration, continuing medical education, allied health professions. **Holdings:** 3500 books; 180 bound periodical volumes; 1110 monographs and pamphlets; 600 bound reports and documents; 260 state reports; 558 unbound periodical volumes; 14 VF drawers of leaflets. **Subscriptions:** 563 journals and other serials. **Services:** Interlibrary loan; copying; library open to the public for reference use only. **Publications:** Lista de revistas y series recibidas en la biblioteca, annual; bibliographies of publications edited by department, irregular. **Special Catalogs:** Catalog of Puerto Rican agencies publications.

★11704★
PUERTO RICO DEPARTMENT OF HEALTH - MENTAL HEALTH LIBRARY (Med)
Asst. Secretariat for Mental Health
Box G.P.O. 61 Phone: (809)781-5660
San Juan, PR 00936 Consuelo Serrano Romero, Libn.
Founded: 1957. **Staff:** Prof 1; Other 1. **Subjects:** Psychiatry, drugs, neurology, psychotherapy, alcoholism, psychology, psychoanalysis, hypnosis, T-groups. **Special Collections:** Collection of Dr. Luis Morales in psychiatry and psychoanalysis (2000 items); Dr. Jose Rafael Mayme Collection (200 items). **Holdings:** 5665 books; 300 bound periodical volumes; 100 special theme materials; 200 annual reports of the Mental Health Program; 50 publications of the Division of Human Resources. **Services:** Interlibrary loan; copying; library open to the public for reference use only. **Automated Operations:** Computerized cataloging. **Special Indexes:** Index to magazine articles (card).

★11705★
PUERTO RICO DEPARTMENT OF HEALTH - RAMON EMETERIO BETANCES MEDICAL CENTER LIBRARY (Med)
Bo. Sabalos Ave., Carr. no. 2
Box 1868 Phone: (809)834-8686
Mayaguez, PR 00708 Myrna Y. Ramirez, Libn.
Founded: 1970. **Staff:** Prof 2. **Subjects:** Medicine, pediatrics, surgery, laboratory medicine, obstetrics and gynecology, dentistry, family medicine. **Special Collections:** CIBA Collection. **Holdings:** 2173 books; 1040 bound periodical volumes; 13 reports. **Subscriptions:** 74 journals and other serials. **Services:** Interlibrary loan; copying; library open to the public with restrictions on circulation. **Computerized Information Services:** MEDLINE. Performs searches on fee basis. **Networks/Consortia:** Member of Consorcio Educativo Del Oeste - Recinto Ciencias Medicas. **Staff:** Awilda Mercado, Awxiliar de Biblioteca.

★11706★
PUERTO RICO DEPARTMENT OF JUSTICE - LIBRARY (Law)
Box 192 Phone: (809)721-2900
San Juan, PR 00902 Antonio Nadal, Dir.
Founded: 1936. **Staff:** Prof 2; Other 3. **Subjects:** Common and civil law. **Special Collections:** Puerto Rican law. **Holdings:** 85,000 volumes; 25 VF drawers. **Subscriptions:** 315 journals and other serials; 30 newspapers. **Services:** Interlibrary loan; library open to the public with restrictions. **Publications:** Opiniones del Secretario Justicia, annual; Informe anual del Secretario de Justicia, Anuario Estadistico. **Remarks:** An alternate telephone number is 724-6869.

★11707★
PUERTO RICO DEPARTMENT OF NATURAL RESOURCES - LIBRARY (Env-Cons)
Munoz Rivera Ave., Stop 3
Box 5887 Phone: (809)724-8774
San Juan, PR 00906 Carmen Anna Abrahamson, Libn.
Subjects: Natural resources. **Holdings:** 5000 books.

★11708★
PUERTO RICO DEPARTMENT OF SOCIAL SERVICES - LIBRARY (Soc Sci)
Box 11398, Fernandez Juncos Sta. Phone: (809)721-4624
San Juan, PR 00910 Nereida Pardo-de-Grant, Libn.
Subjects: Social services to families, child welfare, social rehabilitation, child abuse and delinquency. **Holdings:** 2119 books; 8669 pamphlets.

★11709★
PUERTO RICO ECONOMIC DEVELOPMENT ADMINISTRATION - PUERTO RICO INDUSTRIAL DEVELOPMENT COMPANY - BIBLIOTECA DE FOMENTO (Bus-Fin)
G.P.O. Box 2350 Phone: (809)758-4747
San Juan, PR 00936 Isabel Lopez, Libn.
Founded: 1946. **Staff:** Prof 2. **Subjects:** Economy, industry, statistics, economic planning, finance. **Special Collections:** Unpublished studies of the economic and industrial development of Puerto Rico. **Holdings:** 15,200 books. **Subscriptions:** 90 journals and other serials; 7 newspapers. **Services:** Interlibrary loan; library open to the public. **Publications:** Bibliografia del desarrollo economico e industrial de Puerto Rico - suplementos, irregular. **Remarks:** Library located at Fomento Bldg., 355 Franklin D. Roosevelt Ave. & Lamar Guerra St., Hato Rey, PR 00918. **Formerly:** Office of Economic Research. **Staff:** Nimia Tosca, Ref.Libn..

★11710★
PUERTO RICO GENERAL COURT OF JUSTICE - OFFICE OF COURT ADMINISTRATION - LIBRARY SERVICE DIVISION (Law)
Call Box 22-A, Hato Rey Sta. Phone: (809)751-8670
Hato Rey, PR 00919 Manuela O. Martinez, Dir.
Staff: Prof 3; Other 12. **Subjects:** Law - civil, criminal, labor; management; judicial administration. **Special Collections:** Spain's civil law. **Holdings:** 150,000 books; 3300 bound periodical volumes; 1100 pamphlets; 2000 reports; 100 dissertations; 500 Judicial & Criminal Statistics. **Subscriptions:** 350 journals and other serials; 7 newspapers. **Services:** Interlibrary loan; copying; division open to the public. **Computerized Information Services:** LEXIS. **Publications:** List of Recent Acquisitions. **Special Catalogs:** Puerto Rico Court Libraries Collective Catalogue (title, subject, author). **Remarks:** Library service division organizes and supervises the Superior Court libraries. **Staff:** German Nogueras, Tech.Serv.Supv.; Miriam L. Del Valle, S.J. Judicial Ctr.Lib..

★11711★
(Puerto Rico) INSTITUTE OF PUERTO RICAN CULTURE - ARCHIVO GENERAL DE PUERTO RICO (Hist)
Ponce de Leon 500, Apartado 4184 Phone: (809)722-2113
San Juan, PR 00905 Miguel Angel Nieves, Dir.
Staff: Prof 8; Other 16. **Subjects:** Public works, municipal records, legislation, notarial protocols, treasury, court records, health. **Holdings:** 40,000 cubic feet of documents; 5000 pieces of music; 600 cubic feet of private collections. **Subscriptions:** 15 journals and other serials. **Services:** Copying; archives open to the public. **Publications:** Guia Al Archivo General De Puerto Rico; Loa Archivos Historicos De Puerto Rico. **Staff:** Eduardo Leon, Archv.Supv.; Carmen Alicia Davila, Archv.; Luis De La Rosa, Archv.; Jose Flores, Archv.; Milagros Pepin, Archv.; Hilda Chicon, Archv..

★11712★
(Puerto Rico) INSTITUTE OF PUERTO RICAN CULTURE - LA CASA DEL LIBRO (Publ)
Calle Del Cristo 225
Box S-2265 Phone: (809)723-0354
San Juan, PR 00903 David Jackson McWilliams, Dir.
Founded: 1955. **Staff:** 2. **Subjects:** Typography, history and art of the book, early printed books especially Spanish, fine editions of modern press books. **Holdings:** Figures not available. **Services:** Open to public.

★11713★
PUERTO RICO MUNICIPAL SERVICES ADMINISTRATION - LIBRARY (Law)
Box 70167 Phone: (809)754-1600
San Juan, PR 00936 Duncan Renaldo Maldonado, Dir., Commun.Off.
Subjects: Municipal law, state legislation. **Holdings:** Figures not available. **Remarks:** Library located at 306 Barbosa Ave., Hato Rey, PR 00917.

★11714★
PUERTO RICO OFFICE OF BUDGET & MANAGEMENT - LIBRARY (Bus-Fin)
254 Tetuan & Cruz Sts.
Box 4515 Phone: (809)725-9420
San Juan, PR 00904 Gladys Santiago, Hd.Libn.
Founded: 1942. **Staff:** Prof 1; Other 2. **Subjects:** Public administration, budget management, economics, auditing, computers. **Special Collections:** Puerto Rico and U.S. Law; budget documents of the states and the federal government. **Holdings:** 5000 books; 500 bound periodical volumes; 18,000 clippings; 5100 pamphlets; 10,000 public documents. **Subscriptions:** 156 journals and other serials. **Services:** Interlibrary loan; library open to the public for reference use only. **Publications:** New acquisitions, quarterly. **Special Indexes:** Index of professional magazines (card); Indice tematico de la Revista Presupuesto y Gerencia 1952-1983.

★11715★
PUERTO RICO STATE DEPARTMENT OF CONSUMER AFFAIRS - LIBRARY (Law)
Minillas Govt. Center
North Tower, 3rd Fl.
Minillas Sta., Box 41059
Santurce, PR 00940 Phone: (809)722-7555
Staff: Prof 1. **Subjects:** Law, economics. **Holdings:** 1717 books; 200 bound periodical volumes. **Subscriptions:** 11 journals and other serials. **Services:** Interlibrary loan; library open to the public with restrictions.

★11716★
PUERTO RICO SUPREME COURT - LAW LIBRARY (Law)
Box 2392 Phone: (809)723-3863
San Juan, PR 00903 Roberto Segarra-Olivencia, Lib.Dir.
Founded: 1842. **Staff:** Prof 5; Other 10. **Subjects:** Law. **Special Collections:** Puerto Rican and Spanish civil law collections. **Holdings:** 80,100 volumes; 24 VF drawers; 53 drawers of microforms. **Subscriptions:** 494 journals and other serials; 7 newspapers. **Services:** Interlibrary loan; copying; library open to the public with restrictions. **Computerized Information Services:** LEXIS. **Publications:** Nuevas Adquisiciones, monthly. **Special Indexes:** Index to articles in Spanish and to South American legal periodicals received in the library; list of magazines and law reviews received (organized by title, country, subject). **Remarks:** An alternate telephone number is 723-9894. **Staff:** Maria E. Montijo, Tech.Serv.Libn.; Mirta Colon, Cat.Libn.; Ivette Torres, Cat.Libn.; Jose Marin, Ref.Libn..

★11717★
PUGET SOUND COUNCIL OF GOVERNMENTS - INFORMATION CENTER (Plan)
216 First Ave., S. Phone: (206)464-7090
Seattle, WA 98104 Howard Feltmann, Libn.
Founded: 1967. **Staff:** Prof 1. **Subjects:** Regional planning, transportation, housing, population, land use. **Special Collections:** Small area regional forecasts including population, households, employment; 1980 census tape files. **Holdings:** 3000 books. **Subscriptions:** 85 journals and other serials; 10 newspapers. **Services:** Center open to the public by appointment. **Networks/Consortia:** Member of Western Library Network (WLN).

PUGET SOUND MARITIME HISTORICAL SOCIETY
See: Historical Society of Seattle & King County - Sophie Frye Bass Library of Northwest Americana (6356)

★11718★
PUGET SOUND POWER AND LIGHT COMPANY LIBRARY (Bus-Fin, Energy)
Box 97034 Phone: (206)454-6363
Bellevue, WA 98009-9734 Susan Campbell Ball, Libn.
Founded: 1968. **Staff:** Prof 2; Other 2. **Subjects:** Electric utility operations, economics, management, energy conservation. **Holdings:** 3000 books; 10,000 documents and technical reports; 300 videotapes; 200 audio cassettes. **Subscriptions:** 600 journals and other serials. **Services:** Interlibrary loan; copying; SDI; library open to the public by appointment. **Automated Operations:** Computerized public access catalog routing. **Computerized Information Services:** DIALOG Information Services, DataTimes, LEXIS; OnTyme Electronic Message Network Service (electronic mail service). **Networks/Consortia:** Member of Western Library Network (WLN).

DELIA BIDDLE PUGH LIBRARY
See: Burlington County Historical Society (2044)

PULASKI COUNTY LAW LIBRARY
See: University of Arkansas, Little Rock (15837)

PULLING LAW LIBRARY
See: Villanova University - School of Law (17342)

★11719★
PULP AND PAPER RESEARCH INSTITUTE OF CANADA - LIBRARY (Sci-Engr)
570 St. John's Blvd. Phone: (514)630-4100
Pointe Claire, PQ, Canada H9R 3J9 Hella Stahl, Mgr.
Founded: 1929. **Staff:** Prof 4; Other 2. **Subjects:** Paper, pulp, forestry, mechanical engineering, chemistry, chemical engineering, environmental biology, physics, metallurgy, economics, mathematics. **Holdings:** 8000 books; 10,000 bound periodical volumes; pamphlets; reports; translations; technical papers; patents. **Subscriptions:** 400 journals and other serials. **Services:** Interlibrary loan. **Automated Operations:** Computerized public access catalog and cataloging. **Computerized Information Services:** DIALOG Information Services, Pergamon ORBIT InfoLine, Inc., CISTI, CAS ONLINE, Info Globe, QL Systems; PAPRICAN (internal database). **Also Known As:** Institut Canadien de Recherches sur les Pates et Papiers. **Staff:** Sylvia McVicar, Supv.Libn.; Margot Dube, Libn., Info.Ret.Serv..

★11720★
PURDUE FREDERICK COMPANY - CORPORATE LIBRARY (Med)
100 Connecticut Ave. Phone: (203)853-0123
Norwalk, CT 06856 Kathryn Walsh, Mgr., Lib.Serv.
Founded: 1970. **Staff:** Prof 2; Other 1. **Subjects:** Pharmacology, chemistry, medicine, business. **Holdings:** 2300 books; 7000 bound periodical volumes; patent file. **Subscriptions:** 450 journals and other serials. **Services:** Interlibrary loan; library open to the public by appointment. **Computerized Information Services:** DIALOG Information Services, BRS Information Technologies, NLM, LEXIS, Dow Jones News/Retrieval, Data-Star; internal database.

★11721★
PURDUE UNIVERSITY - AVIATION TECHNOLOGY LIBRARY (Sci-Engr)
Purdue University Airport Phone: (317)494-7640
West Lafayette, IN 47907 Greg Youngen, Libn.
Founded: 1960. **Staff:** 2. **Subjects:** Aviation technology, flight, aerospace education. **Special Collections:** General Aviation Manufacturers Association designated Aviation Education Resource Center (over 500 educators materials). **Holdings:** 3996 volumes. **Subscriptions:** 75 journals and other serials. **Services:** Interlibrary loan; copying; library open to the public.

★11722★
PURDUE UNIVERSITY - BIOCHEMISTRY LIBRARY (Sci-Engr)
Biochemistry Bldg. Phone: (317)494-1621
West Lafayette, IN 47907 Martha J. Bailey, Life Sci.Libn.
Founded: 1952. **Staff:** Prof 1; Other 1. **Subjects:** Biochemistry, carbohydrate chemistry. **Holdings:** 11,403 volumes. **Subscriptions:** 117 journals and other serials. **Services:** Interlibrary loan; copying; library open to the public. **Publications:** Acquisitions list, quarterly.

★11723★
PURDUE UNIVERSITY - CHEMISTRY LIBRARY (Sci-Engr)
Chemistry Bldg. Phone: (317)494-2862
West Lafayette, IN 47907 John Pinzelik, Chem.Libn.
Founded: 1874. **Staff:** Prof 1; Other 3. **Subjects:** Chemistry - inorganic, organic, biological, analytical. **Special Collections:** Archives of Herbert C. Brown, 1979 Nobel Laureate in chemistry. **Holdings:** 41,457 volumes; 7700 microforms; patents. **Subscriptions:** 493 journals and other serials. **Services:** Interlibrary loan; copying; library open to the public. **Computerized Information Services:** DIALOG Information Services, CAS ONLINE, Pergamon ORBIT InfoLine, Inc. **Publications:** Biweekly Acquisitions List. **Also Known As:** M.G. Mellon Library of Chemistry.

★11724★
PURDUE UNIVERSITY - CINDAS - ELECTRONIC PROPERTIES INFORMATION CENTER (Sci-Engr)
2595 Yeager Rd. Phone: (317)494-6300
West Lafayette, IN 47906 C.Y. Ho, Dir.
Founded: 1960. **Subjects:** Absorption coefficient; dielectric constant; dielectric strength; effective mass; electrical hysteresis; electrical resistivity; energy bands; energy gaps; energy levels; hall coefficient; magnetic hysteresis; magnetic susceptibility; mobility; refractive index; work function; electron emission; luminescence; magnetoelectric, magnetomechanical, photoelectronic, piezoelectric, thermoelectric properties. **Holdings:** 95,000 indexed abstracts; 90,000 complete papers on microfiche and microfilm. **Services:** Research and special searches; reproductions; center open to the public by appointment. **Publications:** Electronic Properties Research Literature - Retrieval Guide, Basic Edition (4 volumes; 1979); McGraw-Hill/CINDAS Data Series on Material Properties, 2-4 handbooks/year; Special Studies - list available on request. **Remarks:** CINDAS is the acronym for Center for Information and Numerical Data Analysis and Synthesis.

★11725★
PURDUE UNIVERSITY - CINDAS - THERMOPHYSICAL PROPERTIES RESEARCH CENTER - LIBRARY (Sci-Engr)
2595 Yeager Rd. Phone: (317)494-6300
West Lafayette, IN 47906 C.Y. Ho, Dir.
Founded: 1957. **Subjects:** Thermophysical properties of matter - theoretical, experimental, numerical data; thermal conductivity; accommodation coefficient; thermal contact conductance; thermal diffusivity; specific heat; viscosity; emittance; reflectance; absorptance; transmittance; solar radiation to emittance ratio; Prandtl number; thermal linear expansion coefficient; thermal volumetric expansion coefficient. **Holdings:** 98,000 indexed abstracts; 97,000 complete papers on microfiche. **Services:** Reproductions; research; special searches; center may be visited by appointment. **Publications:** Thermophysical Properties Research Literature - Retrieval Guide, Basic Edition (7 volumes; 1981); Masters Theses in the Pure and Applied Sciences, volumes 1-26, annual; Thermophysical Properties of Matter, 14 volumes; McGraw-Hill/CINDAS Data Series on Material Properties, 2-4 handbooks/year.

★11726★
PURDUE UNIVERSITY - CINDAS - UNDERGROUND EXCAVATION AND ROCK PROPERTIES INFORMATION CENTER
2595 Yeager Rd.
West Lafayette, IN 47906
Founded: 1972. **Subjects:** Mechanical, thermophysical, electrical, and magnetic properties of selected rocks and minerals; codification of the literature on tunnels and other underground excavations. **Holdings:** 3500 indexed abstracts and complete papers on microfiche. **Remarks:** Presently inactive.

★11727★
PURDUE UNIVERSITY - CONSUMER AND FAMILY SCIENCES LIBRARY (Bus-Fin, Soc Sci)
Stone Hall Phone: (317)494-2914
West Lafayette, IN 47907 Judith Nixon, Libn.
Founded: 1957. **Staff:** Prof 1; Other 2. **Subjects:** Retail management; apparel technology; textile science; consumer affairs; consumer financial advising; early childhood education; child development and family life; environmental design; nutrition science; dietetics; food science; food and nutrition business; restaurant, hotel, and institutional management. **Holdings:** 20,124 volumes and theses; 7 file drawers of pamphlets and clippings. **Subscriptions:** 375 journals and other serials. **Services:** Interlibrary loan; copying; library open to the public. **Computerized Information Services:** DIALOG Information Services, NEXIS, WILSONLINE. Performs searches on fee basis. **Special Indexes:** Restaurant, Hotel & Institution Management (computer produced journal index).

★11728★
PURDUE UNIVERSITY - EARTH & ATMOSPHERIC SCIENCES LIBRARY (Sci-Engr, Biol Sci)
Geosciences Bldg. Phone: (317)494-3264
West Lafayette, IN 47907 D.S. Brandt, Libn.
Founded: 1970. **Staff:** Prof 1; Other 1. **Subjects:** Geology, oceanography, earth science, engineering, remote sensing, stratigraphy, meteorology, paleontology, tectonophysics, astronomy, climatology, mineralogy, sedimentology, geochemistry, biogeography, petrology, geoastrophysical geomorphology, geophysical geography. **Holdings:** 17,926 volumes and theses. **Subscriptions:** 354 journals and other serials. **Services:** Interlibrary loan; copying; library open to the public. **Computerized Information Services:** DIALOG Information Services.

★11729★
PURDUE UNIVERSITY - ENGINEERING LIBRARY (Sci-Engr)
Potter Bldg. Phone: (317)494-2867
West Lafayette, IN 47907 Edwin D. Posey, Engr.Libn.
Founded: 1977. **Staff:** Prof 3; Other 11. **Subjects:** Engineering - aeronautical, chemical, civil, electrical, industrial, materials, mechanical, nuclear. **Special Collections:** Goss History of Engineering Library, with focus on railways and transportation. **Holdings:** 266,382 volumes, technical reports, theses; 714,000 microforms; 1300 maps. **Subscriptions:** 2059 journals and other serials. **Services:** Interlibrary loan; copying; library open to the public. **Automated Operations:** Computerized cataloging and serials. **Computerized Information Services:** Online systems. **Special Catalogs:** New books (online). **Staff:** Charlotte Erdmann, Asst.Engr.Libn.; Greg Youngen, Asst.Engr.Libn..

★11730★
PURDUE UNIVERSITY - FILM LIBRARY (Aud-Vis)
Stewart Center Phone: (317)494-6742
West Lafayette, IN 47907 Carl E. Snow, Film Libn.
Founded: 1948. **Staff:** Prof 2; Other 4. **Subjects:** Agriculture, electrical engineering, aviation technology, home economics, horticulture, psychology. **Special Collections:** Medieval Archives (10,000 35mm slides of Medieval illuminations in 500 sets). **Holdings:** 2570 films; 500 filmstrip sets; 5000 tape recordings; 150 media kits; 1000 videotapes; 2200 slide sets. **Services:** Interlibrary loan; library open to organized groups. **Special Catalogs:** Film Catalog - to library users; special subject catalogs (printout). **Staff:** R.J. Kovac, Media Ref.Libn..

★11731★
PURDUE UNIVERSITY - HUMANITIES, SOCIAL SCIENCE AND EDUCATION LIBRARY (Educ, Soc Sci, Hum)
West Lafayette, IN 47907 Phone: (317)494-2828
Laszlo L. Kovacs, Hum.Libn.
Staff: Prof 9; Other 34. **Subjects:** English and American literature, U.S. history, education, audiology and speech science, political science, sociology. **Holdings:** 674,743 volumes; 405,920 government documents; 725,000 microforms; United Nations documents; ERIC documents. **Subscriptions:** 3918 journals and other serials. **Services:** Interlibrary loan; copying; SDI; library open to state residents. **Automated Operations:** Computerized cataloging. **Computerized Information Services:** OCLC. **Networks/Consortia:** Member of INCOLSA. **Staff:** Barbara Pinzelik, Assoc.Hum.Libn.; Mark Tucker, Sr.Ref.Libn.; Stewart Saunders, Ref.Coll.Dev.; Kathleen McCullough, Hum.Bibliog.; James Bracken, Bibliog.; Pam Baxter, Ref.Libn., Psych./Soc.Sci.; Mary E. Collins, Ref.; J.P. Herubel, Ref.; L. Murdock, Govt.Docs.; C. Polit, Bibliog..

★11732★
PURDUE UNIVERSITY - LIBRARY - SPECIAL COLLECTIONS UNIT (Hist)
West Lafayette, IN 47907 Phone: (317)494-2906
Helen Q. Schroyer, Libn.
Subjects: History of Purdue University, 1873 to present. **Special Collections:** Papers of George Ade, John T. McCutcheon, Bruce Rogers, Charles Major, John Purdue, Amelia Earhart; records of the Midwest Program on Airborne Television Instruction; New Harmony, Indiana collection; university archives (student theses; faculty papers; administrative records; alumni papers; oral histories). **Holdings:** 55,262 volumes, theses, technical reports; 60 journals; 257 cubic feet and 2480 linear feet of archival material. **Services:** Copying; unit open to the public during business hours. **Formerly:** Documents and Special Collections Unit.

★11733★
PURDUE UNIVERSITY - LIFE SCIENCE LIBRARY (Agri, Biol Sci)
Lilly Hall of Life Sciences Phone: (317)494-2910
West Lafayette, IN 47907 Martha J. Bailey, Life Sci.Libn.
Founded: 1959. **Staff:** Prof 3; Other 6. **Subjects:** Biological sciences, entomology, forestry, horticulture, agronomy, botany, animal science, plant pathology, soil science. **Holdings:** 71,965 volumes; 1600 dissertations; 7000 microforms. **Subscriptions:** 1526 journals and other serials. **Services:** Interlibrary loan; copying; SDI; library open to the public. **Computerized Information Services:** DIALOG Information Services, Pergamon ORBIT InfoLine, Inc., MEDLARS. **Publications:** Acquisitions list, monthly. **Staff:** Sarah A. Kelly, Asst. Life Sci.Libn.; Nancy S. Hewison, Asst. Life Sci.Libn..

★11734★
PURDUE UNIVERSITY - MANAGEMENT AND ECONOMICS LIBRARY (Bus-Fin)
Krannert Graduate School of Management Phone: (317)494-2922
West Lafayette, IN 47907 Gordon Law, Libn.
Founded: 1959. **Staff:** Prof 3; Other 8. **Subjects:** Business organization and management; economics - applied, history, principles, theory, systems; industrial relations; agricultural economics; statistics and mathematics; marketing; taxation; real estate; finance; accounting. **Special Collections:** Estey Collection (business cycles); rare books in economics and business history, 16th-19th century (7500 volumes). **Holdings:** 153,194 volumes and theses; 4000 bound annual reports; 1482 reels of microfilm; 10,032 microforms; newspaper clippings. **Subscriptions:** 1163 journals and other serials. **Services:** Interlibrary loan; copying; library open to the public. **Automated Operations:** Computerized serials. **Computerized Information Services:** DIALOG Information Services, Pergamon ORBIT InfoLine, Inc., BRS Information Technologies, OCLC, Dow Jones News/Retrieval, NEXIS, I.P. Sharp Associates Limited, Human Resource Information Network (HRIN). **Networks/Consortia:** Member of INCOLSA. **Publications:** Monthly Acquisitions List; occasional publications - available on request. **Special Catalogs:** Catalog of rare books (book). **Staff:** Priscilla C. Geahigan, Asst.Libn.; Kay Smith, Asst.Libn..

★11735★
PURDUE UNIVERSITY - MATHEMATICAL SCIENCES LIBRARY (Sci-Engr, Comp Sci)
Mathematical Sciences Phone: (317)494-2855
West Lafayette, IN 47907 Richard L. Funkhouser, Sci.Libn.
Founded: 1910. **Staff:** Prof 2; Other 2. **Subjects:** Mathematics, statistics, computer sciences. **Holdings:** 48,508 volumes and theses; 493 reels of microfilm; 3800 technical reports. **Subscriptions:** 607 journals and other serials. **Services:** Interlibrary loan; copying; library open to the public. **Staff:** Kevin Hilton.

★11736★
PURDUE UNIVERSITY - PHARMACY, NURSING AND HEALTH SCIENCES LIBRARY (Med)
Pharmacy Bldg. Phone: (317)494-1416
West Lafayette, IN 47907 Theodora Andrews, Libn.
Founded: 1982. **Staff:** Prof 2; Other 4. **Subjects:** Pharmaceutical sciences, pharmacy, clinical medicine, nursing, bionucleonics, environmental sciences. **Special Collections:** Drug abuse collection (1275 volumes); herbal medicine (350 volumes). **Holdings:** 38,547 volumes; 24 VF drawers of pamphlets; 150 audio cassettes; 93,700 microforms. **Subscriptions:** 630 journals and other serials. **Services:** Interlibrary loan; copying; SDI; library open to the public. **Automated Operations:** Computerized cataloging and serials (through General Library). **Computerized Information Services:** Online systems. **Networks/Consortia:** Member of Greater Midwest Regional Medical Library Network. **Publications:** Purdue University Pharmacy, Nursing and Health Sciences Library Notes, quarterly - to faculty, graduate students, pharmacy libraries, and mailing list. **Staff:** Sharon Martino, Prof.Asst..

★11737★
PURDUE UNIVERSITY - PHYSICS LIBRARY (Sci-Engr)
Physics Bldg. Phone: (317)494-2858
West Lafayette, IN 47907 D.S. Brandt, Libn.
Founded: 1905. **Staff:** Prof 1; Other 3. **Subjects:** Physics - classical, mathematical, modern, solid state, nuclear; pure and applied mathematics; astronomy. **Holdings:** 44,210 volumes and theses. **Subscriptions:** 349 journals and other serials. **Services:** Interlibrary loan; copying; library open to the public. **Computerized Information Services:** DIALOG Information Services. **Publications:** New Acquisitions List, monthly; Library Handbook - both available on request.

★11738★
PURDUE UNIVERSITY - PSYCHOLOGICAL SCIENCES LIBRARY (Soc Sci)
Peirce Hall Phone: (317)494-2969
West Lafayette, IN 47907 Pam Baxter, Psych.Libn.
Founded: 1966. **Staff:** Prof 1; Other 2. **Subjects:** Psychology. **Holdings:** 24,855 volumes and theses. **Subscriptions:** 339 journals and other serials. **Services:** Interlibrary loan; copying; library open to the public. **Computerized Information Services:** DIALOG Information Services, BRS Information Technologies, WILSONLINE.

★11739★
PURDUE UNIVERSITY - VETERINARY MEDICAL LIBRARY (Med)
C.V. Lynn Hall, Rm. 108 Phone: (317)494-2852
West Lafayette, IN 47907 Gretchen Stephens, Libn.
Founded: 1960. **Staff:** Prof 2; Other 2. **Subjects:** Comparative and veterinary medicine, animal behavior, comparative anatomy, neuroanatomy, pathology, laboratory animal medicine. **Holdings:** 31,191 volumes. **Subscriptions:** 776 journals and other serials. **Services:** Interlibrary loan; copying; SDI; library open to the public. **Automated Operations:** Computerized cataloging. **Computerized Information Services:** OCLC, MEDLINE, DIALOG Information Services, BRS Information Technologies. **Networks/Consortia:** Member of INCOLSA. **Publications:** New & Notable (acquisitions list), quarterly - by request. **Remarks:** An alternate telephone number is 494-2853. **Staff:** Lynn Ogles, Prof.Asst..

★11740★
PURDUE UNIVERSITY, CALUMET - LIBRARY (Sci-Engr, Hum, Soc Sci)
Hammond, IN 46323-2094 Phone: (219)989-2224
Bernard H. Holicky, Dir., Lib./AV Serv.
Founded: 1947. **Staff:** Prof 5; Other 13. **Subjects:** Science and technology, humanities, social science. **Holdings:** 189,769 volumes; 7702 reels of microfilm; 425,155 microforms. **Subscriptions:** 1409 journals and other serials. **Services:** Interlibrary loan; copying; library open to the public with limited circulation. **Automated Operations:** Computerized cataloging, acquisitions, and ILL. **Computerized Information Services:** BRS Information Technologies, DIALOG Information Services, MEDLARS, Pergamon ORBIT InfoLine, Inc., OCLC. **Networks/Consortia:** Member of INCOLSA, Northwest Indiana Area Library Services Authority (NIALSA). **Staff:** Peter P. Chojenski, Ref.Libn.; Karen M. Corey, Rd.Serv.Libn.; Sheila A. Rezak, Teacher Educ.Rsrcs.; Rebecca R. House, Tech.Serv.Libn..

PURDUE UNIVERSITY AT FORT WAYNE
See: Indiana University/Purdue University at Fort Wayne (6811)

PURDY/KRESGE LIBRARY
See: Wayne State University (17592)

PURDY MEMORIAL LIBRARY
See: Canton Art Institute (2631)

ROSS COFFIN PURDY MUSEUM OF CERAMICS
See: American Ceramic Society - Library (439)

★11741★
PURE CARBON CO., INC. - ENGINEERING LIBRARY (Sci-Engr)
441 Hall Ave. Phone: (814)781-1573
St. Marys, PA 15857 Betty J. Clark, Libn.
Founded: 1966. **Staff:** 1. **Subjects:** Carbon. **Holdings:** 1272 books; 3003 technical brochures; 2020 U.S. and foreign patents. **Services:** Library not open to the public.

PURVIS LIBRARY
See: Kemptville College of Agricultural Technology (7397)

★11742★
PUTNAM COMPANIES - INVESTMENT RESEARCH LIBRARY (Bus-Fin)
One Post Office Square Phone: (617)292-1335
Boston, MA 02109 Jill M. Hayes, Mgr., Lib.Serv./Asst. V.P.
Founded: 1968. **Staff:** Prof 3; Other 5. **Subjects:** Mutual funds, financial and economic data. **Holdings:** 400 books; 3000 files on major American and foreign companies including annual, quarterly, 10K, brokerage reports. **Subscriptions:** 350 journals and other serials; 20 newspapers. **Services:** Interlibrary loan; library not open to the public. **Computerized Information Services:** DIALOG Information Services, LEXIS, NEXIS; internal database. **Remarks:** A subsidiary of Marsh and McLennan, Inc. **Staff:** Ellen Callahan, Libn.; Marian Schwaller, Libn..

★11743★
PUTNAM COUNTY HISTORICAL SOCIETY - ARCHIVES (Hist)
Roy O. West Library
DePauw University Phone: (317)658-4500
Greencastle, IN 46135 Wesley W. Wilson, Archv.
Staff: Prof 1; Other 3. **Subjects:** County history and genealogy. **Holdings:** 50 books; 86 linear feet including of clippings, letters, diaries, scrapbooks; microfilm; tape recordings; movies. **Services:** Copying; genealogical research on fee basis; archives open to the public. **Remarks:** Maintains collection of 500 photographs, 1850-1980, at Putnam County Public Library.

★11744★
PUTNAM COUNTY HISTORICAL SOCIETY - FOUNDRY SCHOOL MUSEUM - REFERENCE LIBRARY (Hist)
63 Chestnut St. Phone: (914)265-4010
Cold Spring, NY 10516 Abby Hartman, Libn.
Founded: 1962. **Staff:** 1. **Subjects:** Genealogy; Putnam, Westchester, and Dutchess County history; West Point; American Revolution; Hudson River; West Point Foundry. **Special Collections:** Works of Susan and Anna Warner (24 volumes). **Holdings:** 1200 volumes; 2 VF drawers of clippings and newspapers; 30 boxes of archival materials and letters; 2 VF drawers of maps; manuscripts. **Services:** Library open to the public by appointment.

HENRY W. PUTNAM MEMORIAL HOSPITAL
See: Southwestern Vermont Medical Center (13531)

★11745★
PUTNAM MUSEUM - LIBRARY (Hist)
1717 W. 12th St. Phone: (319)324-1933
Davenport, IA 52804 Michael J. Smith, Dir.
Founded: 1867. **Staff:** 14. **Subjects:** Local and regional history, natural history, anthropology, geology, steamboat history. **Special Collections:** Upper Mississippi River steamboat history; photographs; Civil War; early settlers; newspapers. **Holdings:** 45,000 volumes; 50 VF drawers of documents, pamphlets, maps, broadsides, handbills; 12 VF drawers of Black Store papers. **Subscriptions:** 15 journals and other serials. **Services:** Library open to the public by appointment. **Staff:** Carol Hunt, Cur., Hist.Coll..

★11746★
PUTNEY, TWOMBLY, HALL & HIRSON - LAW LIBRARY (Law)
36 W. 44th St., 6th Fl. Phone: (212)704-0300
New York, NY 10036-8102 Lois Liss, Libn.
Staff: Prof 1. **Subjects:** Law - labor, corporate, trust, estate, tax. **Holdings:** 8000 books. **Subscriptions:** 12 journals and other serials. **Services:** Library not open to the public.

PU'UHONUA O HONAUNAU NATIONAL HISTORICAL PARK
See: U.S. Natl. Park Service (15342)

HOWARD PYLE LIBRARY
See: Delaware Art Museum - Helen Farr Sloan Library (4147)

PYMATUNING LABORATORY OF ECOLOGY
See: University of Pittsburgh - Pymatuning Laboratory of Ecology (16777)

Q

★11747★
Q.I.T. - FER ET TITANE INC. - BIBLIOTHEQUE (Sci-Engr)
B.P. 560 Phone: (514)742-6671
Sorel, PQ, Canada J3P 5P6 C. Stroemgren, Libn.
Founded: 1950. **Subjects:** Chemistry, engineering, business. **Holdings:** Figures not available. **Services:** Interlibrary loan; copying; library open to the public by appointment. **Also Known As:** Fer et Titane du Quebec, Inc.; Quebec Iron and Titanium Corporation.

★11748★
QUACO HISTORICAL SOCIETY - LIBRARY (Hist)
St. Martins, NB, Canada E0G 2Z0 Phone: (506)833-4740
Elizabeth Thibodeau, Libn.
Subjects: Atlantic maritime history, wooden shipbuilding, local history. **Holdings:** 5000 books. **Services:** Copying; library open to the public.

★11749★
QUAIN AND RAMSTAD CLINIC - MEDICAL LIBRARY (Med)
622 Ave. A East Phone: (701)222-5390
Bismarck, ND 58501 Leeila Bina, Med.Libn.
Founded: 1920. **Staff:** Prof 1; Other 2. **Subjects:** Clinical medicine. **Special Collections:** Pediatric peptic ulcer. **Holdings:** 6000 books; 9000 bound periodical volumes; 4 VF drawers of pamphlets and reprints. **Subscriptions:** 232 journals and other serials. **Services:** Interlibrary loan; copying; SDI; library open to the public with permission. **Computerized Information Services:** MEDLINE; EasyLink, DOCLINE (electronic mail services). **Networks/Consortia:** Member of Greater Midwest Regional Medical Library Network. **Publications:** Childhood Gastroenterology Registry.

★11750★
QUAKER CHEMICAL CORPORATION - INFORMATION RESOURCES CENTER (Sci-Engr)
Conshohocken, PA 19428-0873 Phone: (215)828-4250
Ellen B. Morrow, Mgr.
Founded: 1952. **Staff:** Prof 1; Other 5. **Subjects:** Chemical technology for the metals and paper specialty fields. **Holdings:** 5500 volumes; 5500 pamphlets; 18 VF drawers of vendor literature; 85 VF drawers of documents and miscellanea; chemical patents, 1966 to present, on microfilm; 425 reels of microfilm of journals; 365 reels of microfilm of documents; 4 VF drawers of government reports on microfiche; 45 audio cassettes. **Subscriptions:** 257 journals and other serials. **Services:** Interlibrary loan; copying; SDI; center open to the public by appointment. **Automated Operations:** Computerized circulation. **Computerized Information Services:** DIALOG Information Services, Pergamon ORBIT InfoLine, Inc., U.S. Patents Files; internal databases. **Publications:** Current awareness lists; Current Contents Alert. **Staff:** Jane L. Williams, Info.Rsrcs.Coord..

★11751★
QUAKER OATS COMPANY - JOHN STUART RESEARCH LABORATORIES - RESEARCH LIBRARY (Food-Bev, Sci-Engr)
617 W. Main St. Phone: (312)381-1980
Barrington, IL 60010 Geraldine R. Horton, Mgr., Lib.
Staff: Prof 3; Other 2. **Subjects:** Food, biochemistry, nutrition, chemical engineering, organic chemistry. **Holdings:** 10,000 books; 4000 bound periodical volumes; 50 VF drawers of reprints and pamphlets; internal reports. **Subscriptions:** 500 journals and other serials. **Services:** Interlibrary loan; copying (limited); library open to the public with permission. **Automated Operations:** Computerized cataloging. **Computerized Information Services:** DIALOG Information Services, Pergamon ORBIT InfoLine, Inc. **Staff:** Jeanne M. Head, Acq.Libn.; Adrienne Jasnich, Sr.Info.Sci..

★11752★
QUAKERTOWN COMMUNITY HOSPITAL - HEALTH SCIENCES LIBRARY (Med)
11th St. & Park Ave. Phone: (215)538-4563
Quakertown, PA 18951 Elaine P. O'Connor, Lib.Dir.
Staff: Prof 1; Other 1. **Subjects:** Internal medicine, geriatrics, psychiatry. **Holdings:** 300 books; 175 bound periodical volumes. **Subscriptions:** 111 journals and other serials. **Services:** Interlibrary loan; copying; SDI; library open to the public. **Computerized Information Services:** BRS Information Technologies, MEDLINE. Performs searches on fee basis.

QUANTUM CHEMICAL CORPORATION - USI CHEMICALS COMPANY
See: USI Chemicals Company - CRL Library (17222)

★11753★
QUANTUM CHEMICAL CORPORATION - USI DIVISION - LIBRARY (Sci-Engr)
3100 Golf Rd. Phone: (312)437-7800
Rolling Meadows, IL 60008 Frieda R. Oetting, Hd.Libn.
Founded: 1967. **Staff:** Prof 1; Other 1. **Subjects:** Polymer chemistry, polymer physics, general business, chemical engineering. **Holdings:** 5000 books; 460 technical abstracts (card); 650 annual reports and house organs; 390 pamphlets. **Subscriptions:** 230 journals and other serials. **Services:** Interlibrary loan; library open to the public for reference use only by request. **Automated Operations:** Computerized public access catalog and circulation. **Computerized Information Services:** DIALOG Information Services, Pergamon ORBIT InfoLine, Inc.

★11754★
QUANTUM CHEMICAL CORPORATION - USI DIVISION - TECHNICAL CENTER - LIBRARY
8935 N. Tabler Rd. Phone: (815)942-7558
Morris, IL 60450-9988 Ingrid M. Voss, Info.Spec.
Founded: 1970. **Staff:** Prof 1; Other 2. **Subjects:** Plastics, chemistry, physics, chemical engineering, packaging. **Holdings:** 2500 books; 1875 bound periodical volumes; 8 VF drawers of company archives; 4 shelves of conference material; 3 drawers of competitor notes; 3 drawers of AV programs and microfilm; 5 VF drawers; 4 drawers of specifications; 8 drawers of central files; patents on microfilm. **Subscriptions:** 157 journals and other serials. **Services:** Interlibrary loan; copying; SDI; library open to the public for reference use only. **Automated Operations:** Computerized cataloging, acquisitions, and circulation. **Computerized Information Services:** CAS ONLINE, NERAC, Inc., Pergamon ORBIT InfoLine, Inc.; internal database. **Networks/Consortia:** Member of ILLINET, Bur Oak Library System. **Formerly:** USI Chemicals Co. - ENRON Chemical Company.

★11755★
QUARLES & BRADY - LIBRARY (Law)
411 E. Wisconsin Ave. Phone: (414)277-5000
Milwaukee, WI 53202-4497 Susan H. Jankowski, Libn.
Staff: Prof 3; Other 3. **Subjects:** Law - litigation, labor, tax, patent, securities, pension, banking. **Special Collections:** Wisconsin Statutes, 1898 to present; Federal Register, 1970 to present. **Holdings:** 42,000 volumes; microfiche. **Subscriptions:** 110 journals and other serials; 15 newspapers. **Services:** Library not open to the public. **Computerized Information Services:** LEXIS, DIALOG Information Services; internal database. **Networks/Consortia:** Member of Library Council of Metropolitan Milwaukee, Inc. (LCOMM), Private Downtown Law Librarians. **Special Catalogs:** Hospital brief, memo, and litigation file. **Staff:** Linda Marifke, Sr.Asst.Libn.; Kay Christiansen, Asst.Libn..

★11756★
THE QUATREFOIL LIBRARY (Soc Sci)
1619 Dayton Ave., Suite 325 Phone: (612)522-7185
St. Paul, MN 55104-6208 David D. Irwin, Exec.Dir.
Founded: 1983. **Staff:** Prof 4; Other 24. **Subjects:** Gay and lesbian materials. **Holdings:** 3200 books; 20 bound periodical volumes; unbound newspapers and magazines, 1953 to present; 24 videotapes; 80 audiotapes; 28 sound recordings; 4 file cabinets of clippings; button collection; clothing; art work; Out and About Theater archives; posters. **Subscriptions:** 25 journals and other serials. **Services:** Copying; library open to the public. **Publications:** Newsletter,

QUAYLE RARE BIBLE COLLECTION
See: Baker University (1244)

QUEBEC ASSOCIATION FOR HEARING-IMPAIRED CHILDREN - INFORMATION CENTER FOR DEAFNESS
See: Association Quebecoise pour Enfants avec Problemes Auditifs - Centre de Documentation en Deficience Auditive (1032)

QUEBEC CEREBRAL PALSY ASSOCIATION
See: Association de Paralysie Cerebrale du Quebec, Inc. (1029)

QUEBEC IRON AND TITANIUM CORPORATION
See: Q.I.T. - Fer et Titane Inc. (11747)

★11757★
QUEBEC AND ONTARIO PAPER COMPANY - LIBRARY (Sci-Engr)
Allanburg Rd. Phone: (416)227-1121
Thorold, ON, Canada L2V 3Z5 Isabelle Ridgway, Libn.
Founded: 1949. **Staff:** 1. **Subjects:** Pulp and paper (newsprint); forestry and logging; chemical byproducts of paper manufacture; chemical engineering; business. **Special Collections:** Patents concerning all phases of pulp and paper manufacture (6000 patents). **Holdings:** 2400 books; 2250 bound periodical volumes; 1900 pamphlets; 1750 unbound company reports; 125 filing boxes of other reports. **Subscriptions:** 300 journals and other serials; 6 newspapers. **Services:** Interlibrary loan; copying; library open to the public for reference use only on request. **Automated Operations:** Computerized cataloging and circulation. **Computerized Information Services:** Info Globe, DIALOG Information Services. **Publications:** Monthly Accession List; Newsclips, monthly - both for internal distribution only. **Formerly:** Ontario Paper Company.

QUEBEC PENSION BOARD
See: Quebec Province Regie des Rentes (11796)

★11758★
(Quebec Province) **ARCHIVES NATIONALES DU QUEBEC - BIBLIOTHEQUE** (Hist)
C.P. 10450 Phone: (418)643-8904
Ste. Foy, PQ, Canada G1V 4N1 Gilles Heon, Archv.
Founded: 1920. **Staff:** Prof 1; Other 2. **Subjects:** History of Quebec, Canada, French Canada; biography; numismatics; genealogy; church history; sociology. **Holdings:** 40,000 books; 6000 bound periodical volumes; 7000 other cataloged items; 800,000 photographs; 20,000 maps; 260 reels of microfilm of journals. **Subscriptions:** 120 journals and other serials. **Services:** Interlibrary loan; copying; library open to the public with permission. **Publications:** Rapport des Archives Nationales du Quebec. **Remarks:** Maintained by the Ministere des Affaires Culturelles.

★11759★
QUEBEC PROVINCE BIBLIOTHEQUE DE L'ASSEMBLEE NATIONALE (Law, Soc Sci)
Edifice Pamphile-Le May
Bureau 5 Phone: (418)643-2896
Quebec, PQ, Canada G1A 1A5 Jacques Premont, Dir.
Founded: 1802. **Staff:** Prof 27; Other 45. **Subjects:** Law - Canadian, French, English, American; political science; economics; legislation; Canadiana. **Special Collections:** British Parliamentary Papers. **Holdings:** 525,620 books; 59,200 bound periodical volumes; 26,000 Canadian pamphlets and other cataloged items; 22,100 reels of microfilm of journals and newspapers; 210,000 microfiche of government publications. **Subscriptions:** 975 journals and other serials. **Services:** Interlibrary loan; copying. **Automated Operations:** Computerized cataloging. **Computerized Information Services:** DIALOG Information Services, Pergamon ORBIT InfoLine, Inc., IST-Informatheque, Inc., UTLAS. **Publications:** Bulletin de la Bibliotheque de la Legislature; Bibliographie et Documentation (series). **Special Indexes:** Index to the laws of the Province of Quebec (card).

★11760★
(Quebec Province) **BIBLIOTHEQUE NATIONALE DU QUEBEC** (Info Sci)
1700, rue St-Denis Phone: (514)873-4553
Montreal, PQ, Canada H2X 3K6 M. Georges Cartier, Dir.
Founded: 1967. **Staff:** Prof 46; Other 75. **Subjects:** Quebec. **Special Collections:** Books printed before 1821. **Holdings:** 325,769 volumes; 28,457 reels of microfilm; 5982 monographic map titles; 34,753 serial maps; 1383 linear meters of manuscripts; 75,000 pieces of sheet music. **Subscriptions:** 15,465 journals and other serials; 642 newspapers. **Services:** Interlibrary loan; copying; library open to the public. **Automated Operations:** Computerized cataloging. **Computerized Information Services:** UTLAS, Telesystemes Questel, DOBIS Canadian Online Library System, REFCATTS; Envoy 100 (electronic mail service). Performs searches free of charge. Contact Person: Milada Vlach, 873-2156. **Publications:** Bibliographies; list of additional publications - available on request. **Staff:** Marcel Fontaine, Dir., Pub.Serv./Cons.; Pierre Deslauriers, Dir., Bibliog.Serv. & Coll.Dev..

★11761★
(Quebec Province) **BIBLIOTHEQUE NATIONALE DU QUEBEC - SECTEUR DES COLLECTIONS SPECIALES - SECTION DES CARTES ET PLANS** (Geog-Map)
125, rue Sherbrooke Ouest Phone: (514)873-4408
Montreal, PQ, Canada H2X 1X4 Pierre Lepine, Map Libn.
Founded: 1968. **Staff:** Prof 1. **Subjects:** Quebec maps. **Holdings:** 5982 map titles; 34,753 sheets in maps series. **Services:** Copying; section open to the public. **Automated Operations:** Computerized cataloging. **Computerized Information Services:** UTLAS, REFCATSS; Envoy 100 (electronic mail service). Performs searches free of charge. **Special Catalogs:** Documents cartographiques depuis la decouverte de l'Amerique jusqu'a 1820: inventaire sommaire, 1985 - for sale.

★11762★
(Quebec Province) **BIBLIOTHEQUE NATIONALE DU QUEBEC - SECTEUR DES COLLECTIONS SPECIALES - SECTION DES MANUSCRITS** (Hum)
1700, rue Saint-Denis Phone: (514)873-7593
Montreal, PQ, Canada H2X 3K6 Michel Biron, Mss.Libn.
Staff: Prof 1; Other 2. **Subjects:** Literary manuscripts of Quebec. **Holdings:** 1350 linear meters of manuscripts. **Services:** Copying; section open to the public.

★11763★
(Quebec Province) **BIBLIOTHEQUE NATIONALE DU QUEBEC - SECTEUR DES COLLECTIONS SPECIALES - SECTION DE LA MUSIQUE** (Mus)
1700, rue St-Denis Phone: (514)873-4512
Montreal, PQ, Canada H2X 3K6 Denis Rivest, Hd.
Staff: Prof 1. **Subjects:** Music from Quebec, Canada, and other countries. **Holdings:** 75,000 pieces of sheet music; 400 boxes of clippings; 20,000 phonograph records. **Services:** Copying; section open to the public for reference use only. **Remarks:** Books and periodicals relating to music are included in the general collection of the library.

★11764★
(Quebec Province) **BIBLIOTHEQUE NATIONALE DU QUEBEC - SECTEUR DES COLLECTIONS SPECIALES - SECTION DE LA RESERVE** (Hist)
1700, rue Saint-Denis Phone: (514)873-1928
Montreal, PQ, Canada H2X 3K6 Joseph Blonde, Rare Bks.Libn.
Staff: Prof 1. **Subjects:** Quebec history and society, voyages and exploration, European history and philosophy, artists. **Holdings:** 10,000 books; 200 reels of microfilm; Quebec imprints, 1764-1820; Quebec artists' books; incunabula. **Services:** Interlibrary loan; copying; section open to the public. **Special Catalogs:** Laurentiana Parus Avant 1821 (book); Catalogue Collectif des Impressions Quebecoises, 1764-1820 (book); Repertoire des Livres d'Artistes au Quebec, 1900-1980 (book).

★11765★
QUEBEC PROVINCE COMMISSION DE LA CONSTRUCTION DU QUEBEC - RESSOURCES DOCUMENTAIRES (Plan)
3530, rue Jean-Talon W. Phone: (514)341-7740
Montreal, PQ, Canada H3R 2G3 Nicole Cote, Chf.
Founded: 1979. **Staff:** Prof 3. **Subjects:** Construction industry, collective agreements, fringe benefits. **Holdings:** 3800 books; 500 judgments; 120 subject files. **Subscriptions:** 240 journals and other serials; 8 newspapers. **Services:** Interlibrary loan; copying; open to the public. **Computerized Information Services:** Quebec Society for Legal Information, Terminology Bank of Quebec, DIALOG Information Services. **Publications:** Liste des acquisitions, bimonthly; Repertoire des periodiques, annual. **Staff:** Ghislaine Jette, Lib.Techn.; Rachel Gauthier, Lib.Techn..

★11766★
QUEBEC PROVINCE COMMISSION DES DROITS DE LA PERSONNE - LIBRARY (Law, Soc Sci)
360, rue Saint-Jacques, W. Phone: (514)873-5146
Montreal, PQ, Canada H2Y 1P5 Madeleine Beaudoin, Libn.
Founded: 1976. **Staff:** Prof 1; Other 2. **Subjects:** Human rights, law, sociology, economics, criminology, social sciences. **Special Collections:** Decisions of the Human Rights Commission. **Holdings:** 8191 books; 14,297 bound periodical volumes; 415 reports and files. **Subscriptions:** 377 journals and other serials. **Services:** Interlibrary loan; copying; library open to the public for reference use only. **Automated Operations:** Computerized cataloging. **Computerized Information Services:** UTLAS. **Networks/Consortia:** Member of Nova Scotia On-Line Consortium. **Publications:** New Books List; Periodicals, monthly. **Special Catalogs:** Catalogue Collectif, 3/year (on microfiche).

★11767★
QUEBEC PROVINCE COMMISSION DES NORMES DU TRAVAIL - CENTRE DE DOCUMENTATION (Bus-Fin)
400 Boul. Jean-Lesage Phone: (418)643-1420
Quebec, PQ, Canada G1K 8W1 Sylvia Dupuis, Biblio.
Founded: 1978. **Staff:** 1. **Subjects:** Labor standards. **Holdings:** 1675 books. **Subscriptions:** 100 journals and other serials; 10 newspapers. **Services:** Interlibrary loan; copying; center open to the public. **Publications:** Liste des nouveautes, quarterly.

★11768★
QUEBEC PROVINCE COMMISSION DE LA SANTE ET DE LA SECURITE DU TRAVAIL - CENTRE DE DOCUMENTATION (Med, Sci-Engr)
1199 de Bleury, 4th Fl.
C.P. 6067, Succ. A Phone: (514)873-3160
Montreal, PQ, Canada H3C 4E2 Renee Morin, Chef de Serv.
Staff: Prof 7; Other 14. **Subjects:** Occupational health and safety. **Holdings:** 28,800 books; 50 bound periodical volumes; 350 AV programs; 20,000 other cataloged items. **Subscriptions:** 500 journals and other serials; 5 newspapers. **Services:** Interlibrary loan; copying; center open to the public. **Automated Operations:** Computerized cataloging, acquisitions and ILL. **Computerized Information Services:** DIALOG Information Services, Pergamon ORBIT InfoLine, Inc., MEDLARS, IST-Informatheque Inc.; internal databases. **Publications:** Sommaire des Periodiques, 25/year; liste des nouvelles acquisitions, 12/year. **Staff:** Rosedany Enea; Ginette Laurin; Marc Fournier; Pierre Vincent; Stephane Aumont; Germain Roy.

★11769★
QUEBEC PROVINCE CONSEIL SUPERIEUR DE L'EDUCATION - CENTRE DE DOCUMENTATION (Educ)
2050 St-Cyrille Blvd., W. Phone: (418)643-3850
Ste. Foy, PQ, Canada G1V 2K8 Bernard Audet, Resp.
Founded: 1975. **Staff:** Prof 1; Other 1. **Subjects:** Education. **Special Collections:** Ministere de l'Education publications. **Holdings:** 5000 books; 40 bound periodical volumes. **Subscriptions:** 90 journals and other serials; 5 newspapers. **Services:** Interlibrary loan; copying; center open to the public.

QUEBEC PROVINCE ELECTRICITY AND GAS BOARD
See: Quebec Province Regie de l'Electricite et du Gaz (11795)

★11770★
QUEBEC PROVINCE L'INSPECTEUR GENERAL DES INSTITUTIONS FINANCIERES - BIBLIOTHEQUE (Bus-Fin)
800, place d'Youville, 7th Fl. Phone: (418)643-5236
Quebec, PQ, Canada G1R 4Y5 Sylvie Nadeau, Biblio.
Founded: 1969. **Staff:** Prof 1; Other 1. **Subjects:** Financial institutions, finance, insurance, law. **Holdings:** 9000 books; 175 bound periodical volumes; 200 annual reports. **Subscriptions:** 350 journals and other serials; 20 newspapers. **Services:** Interlibrary loan; copying; library open to the public with restrictions. **Publications:** Bibliotheque Documentation, monthly.

QUEBEC PROVINCE MINISTERE DES AFFAIRES CULTURELLES - ARCHIVES NATIONALES DU QUEBEC
See: (Quebec Province) Archives Nationales du Quebec (11758)

★11771★
QUEBEC PROVINCE MINISTERE DES AFFAIRES CULTURELLES - CENTRE DE DOCUMENTATION
225, Grande-Allee Est
Quebec, PQ, Canada G1R 5G5
Subjects: Politics, humanities, museology, cultural heritage, archeology, architecture, music, theater. **Holdings:** 20,000 books; microcards; microfilm; slides; maps. **Remarks:** Presently inactive.

★11772★
QUEBEC PROVINCE MINISTERE DES AFFAIRES CULTURELLES - CONSERVATOIRE D'ART DRAMATIQUE - BIBLIOTHEQUE (Theater)
100 Notre-Dame St., E. Phone: (514)873-3002
Montreal, PQ, Canada H2Y 1C1 Louise Rousseau, Doc.Techn.
Founded: 1967. **Staff:** 2. **Subjects:** Theater, film, literature, biography. **Holdings:** 9050 books; slides; reel-to-reel tapes; video and audio cassettes; phonograph records. **Subscriptions:** 44 journals and other serials. **Services:** Interlibrary loan; library open to the public.

QUEBEC PROVINCE MINISTERE DES AFFAIRES CULTURELLES - MUSEE DU QUEBEC
See: Musee du Quebec (9432)

★11773★
QUEBEC PROVINCE MINISTERE DES AFFAIRES MUNICIPALES - CENTRE DE DOCUMENTATION (Plan)
20, rue Chauveau
Secteur B, 2nd Fl. Phone: (418)691-2018
Quebec, PQ, Canada G1R 4J3 Ernest Bertrand Roy, Resp.
Founded: 1976. **Staff:** Prof 1; Other 2. **Subjects:** Municipal administration, urban affairs, planning, urbanization, real estate. **Holdings:** 9000 books; 130 bound periodical volumes; maps. **Subscriptions:** 120 journals and other serials. **Services:** Interlibrary loan; copying (limited); center open to the public with restrictions. **Automated Operations:** Computerized cataloging and acquisitions. **Computerized Information Services:** UTLAS. **Publications:** Monthly Bulletin for Acquisitions. **Special Indexes:** Index of authors, titles, subjects, regions (online).

★11774★
QUEBEC PROVINCE MINISTERE DE L'AGRICULTURE, DES PECHERIES ET DE L'ALIMENTATION - CENTRE DE DOCUMENTATION (Agri)
200-A, chemin Ste-Foy, 1st Fl. Phone: (418)643-2428
Quebec, PQ, Canada G1R 4X6 Sylvie Belanger, Chf.Libn.
Founded: 1942. **Staff:** Prof 1; Other 6. **Subjects:** Agriculture, food, fisheries, veterinary medicine. **Special Collections:** Ministry publications. **Holdings:** 12,000 books; 1200 bound periodical volumes; 55 AV programs. **Subscriptions:** 274 journals and other serials. **Services:** Interlibrary loan; center not open to the public. **Computerized Information Services:** DIALOG Information Services, CAN/OLE, IST-Informatheque Inc., Banque de Terminologie du Quebec. **Publications:** Sommaire des periodiques.

★11775★
QUEBEC PROVINCE MINISTERE DES COMMUNAUTES CULTURELLES ET DE L'IMMIGRATION - CENTRE DE DOCUMENTATION (Soc Sci)
355, rue McGill Phone: (514)873-3255
Montreal, PQ, Canada H2Y 2E8 Denis Robichaud, Chf.
Founded: 1968. **Staff:** Prof 1; Other 4. **Subjects:** Immigration, demography, population, ethnicity, refugees. **Holdings:** 5000 books; 100 bound periodical volumes; 25,000 newspaper clippings on immigration; 7000 documents. **Subscriptions:** 200 journals and other serials; 30 newspapers. **Services:** Interlibrary loan; copying; center open to the public. **Computerized Information Services:** CAN/SDI. **Publications:** Revue de Presse Hebdomadaire; En Revue, weekly; A La Fiche, monthly.

★11776★
QUEBEC PROVINCE MINISTERE DES COMMUNICATIONS - BIBLIOTHEQUE ADMINISTRATIVE (Bus-Fin, Soc Sci)
1056, rue Conroy, rez-de-chaussee Phone: (418)643-1515
Quebec, PQ, Canada G1R 5E6 Luc Dufour, Dir.
Founded: 1972. **Staff:** Prof 9; Other 23. **Subjects:** Public administration, management, education, communications, labor and manpower, law. **Holdings:** 110,000 volumes; 200,000 microforms. **Subscriptions:** 750 journals and other serials. **Services:** Interlibrary loan; copying; SDI; library open to the public for reference use only. **Automated Operations:** Computerized cataloging. **Computerized Information Services:** DIALOG Information Services, Pergamon ORBIT InfoLine, Inc., CAN/OLE, QL Systems, UTLAS, Telesystemes Questel, Info Globe, IST-Informatheque Inc. **Publications:** Nouveautes de la Bibliotheque Administrative; Administration & Gestion, Communications, Relations de Travail, Sciences de l'Education; Apercu de la Documentation Courante; Economie et Politique. **Special Catalogs:** Union catalog of periodicals in Quebec government libraries; CDM union catalog. **Remarks:** The Bibliotheque Administrative includes two libraries which jointly serve sixteen Quebec government departments. **Staff:** Lise Villeneuve, Network; Claude Lamarre, Coll.Dev.; Jean-Marc Labrie, Online Serv.; Edward Collister, Ref.; Veronique Pare, Ref., Edifice H.

★11777★
QUEBEC PROVINCE MINISTERE DE L'ENERGIE ET DES RESSOURCES - BUREAU DES ECONOMIES D'ENERGIE - CENTRE DE DOCUMENTATION (Energy)
425 Viger Ave., W., 6th Fl. Phone: (514)873-5463
Montreal, PQ, Canada H2Z 1W9 Louise Marcil, Libn.
Founded: 1980. **Staff:** Prof 1; Other 1. **Subjects:** Energy conservation in industry, commerce, housing, urban planning, transportation. **Special Collections:** Provincial and federal publications on energy conservation.

Holdings: 5000 books; slide sets; video cassettes. **Subscriptions:** 33 journals and other serials. **Services:** Interlibrary loan; copying; SDI; center open to the public for reference use only. **Computerized Information Services:** CAN/OLE, DIALOG Information Services.

★11778★
QUEBEC PROVINCE MINISTERE DE L'ENERGIE ET DES RESSOURCES - CENTRE DE DOCUMENTATION (Sci-Engr, Agri)
200, chemin Ste-Foy, 7th Fl. Phone: (418)643-6004
Quebec, PQ, Canada G1R 4X7 Jacques Fournier, Chef de Serv.
Founded: 1979. **Staff:** Prof 4; Other 16. **Subjects:** Forests and forestry, forest economics, mines and mining, geology, mineral chemistry, energy, surveying, geodesy, pollution, metallurgy, law, conservation, entomology. **Special Collections:** U.S. Bureau of Mines (microfiche); departmental records (microfiche). **Holdings:** 70,000 books; 30,000 bound periodical volumes; 350 patents; 1600 reels of microfilm; 1250 microfiche. **Subscriptions:** 1700 journals and other serials; 75 newspapers. **Services:** Interlibrary loan (fee); copying; SDI; center open to the public with restrictions. **Automated Operations:** Computerized cataloging and serials. **Computerized Information Services:** DIALOG Information Services, QL Systems, Pergamon ORBIT InfoLine, Inc., CAN/OLE, CAN/SDI, IST-Informatheque Inc., Telesystemes Questel. **Publications:** List of Periodicals; Info-Mer-Mines, monthly; Info-Mer-Terres et Forets, monthly; Info-Mer-Energie, monthly - all free upon request. **Special Indexes:** Index of Northern Miner. **Staff:** Reine Tremblay, Mines/Hd., Automated Sys.; Johanne Belanger, Forest; Irenee Gourde, Energy.

QUEBEC PROVINCE MINISTERE DE L'ENERGIE ET DES RESSOURCES - REGIE DE L'ELECTRICITE ET DU GAZ
See: Quebec Province Regie de l'Electricite et du Gaz (11795)

★11779★
QUEBEC PROVINCE MINISTERE DE L'ENERGIE ET DES RESSOURCES - SECTEUR FORETS - DIRECTION DE LA RECHERCHE ET DU DEVELOPPEMENT - BIBLIOTHEQUE (Agri)
2700, rue Einstein Phone: (418)643-7994
Ste. Foy, PQ, Canada G1P 3W8 Lucie Jobin, Lib.Techn.
Founded: 1967. **Staff:** Prof 1. **Subjects:** Forestry, soils, research. **Holdings:** 2800 volumes. **Services:** Library not open to the public. **Computerized Information Services:** Internal database.

★11780★
QUEBEC PROVINCE MINISTERE DE L'ENSEIGNEMENT SUPERIEUR ET DE LA SCIENCE - CENTRE DE DOCUMENTATION (Educ)
1033, rue de la Chevrotiere, 20th Fl. Phone: (418)643-1572
Quebec, PQ, Canada G1R 5K9 Claudine Tremblay, Techn.
Founded: 1981. **Staff:** 1. **Subjects:** Higher education, research, university finances, teacher education. **Special Collections:** Commission d'etude sur les universites archives; university publications concerning continuing education for French teachers. **Holdings:** 8000 books. **Subscriptions:** 60 journals and other serials; 10 newspapers. **Services:** Interlibrary loan; copying; center open to the public with restrictions. **Automated Operations:** Computerized cataloging. **Computerized Information Services:** EDiBASE; UNIV (internal database). Performs searches free of charge. **Publications:** Guide du Centre de documentation; Bulletin de nouveautes, monthly; Revue de presse universitaire, weekly - all for internal distribution only.

★11781★
QUEBEC PROVINCE MINISTERE DE L'ENVIRONNEMENT - LIBRARY (Env-Cons)
3900, rue Marly Phone: (418)643-5363
Ste-Foy, PQ, Canada G1X 4E4 Gerard Nobrega, Chf.Libn.
Founded: 1980. **Staff:** Prof 6; Other 7. **Subjects:** Pollution control, acid rain, Quebec environmental issues. **Holdings:** 20,000 books; 10,000 bound periodical volumes; 10,000 maps; 6000 government documents. **Subscriptions:** 200 journals and other serials. **Services:** Interlibrary loan; library open to the public. **Automated Operations:** Computerized cataloging. **Computerized Information Services:** IST-Informatheque Inc., DIALOG Information Services, CAN/OLE, QL Systems, MEDLARS. **Publications:** List of acquisitions, monthly - for internal distribution only. **Special Indexes:** Indexes to materials on acid precipitation and Quebec environment (online). **Staff:** Alain Aubin, Ref.; Carole Bergeron, Cat.; Johanne Lauzon; Lucie Gobeil.

★11782★
QUEBEC PROVINCE MINISTERE DE L'INDUSTRIE ET DU COMMERCE - BIBLIOTHEQUE MINISTERIELLE (Bus-Fin)
710, place d'Youville, local 203 Phone: (418)643-5081
Quebec, PQ, Canada G1R 4Y4 Mario Day, Resp.
Founded: 1957. **Staff:** Prof 2; Other 5. **Subjects:** Economics, industrial development, commerce, statistics, finance, cooperative societies. **Special Collections:** Statistics Canada (32,000 documents); Financial Post Corporation Service Cards (complete set); Stanford Research Institute publications (500). **Holdings:** 14,000 books; 100 bound periodical volumes; 36,000 unbound periodicals. **Subscriptions:** 600 journals and other serials; 25 newspapers. **Services:** Interlibrary loan (limited); copying; library open to the public with restrictions. **Automated Operations:** Computerized cataloging. **Computerized Information Services:** DIALOG Information Services, IST-Informatheque Inc., Info Globe. **Publications:** Bulletin mensuel de la documentation courante, monthly - for internal distribution only; revue de presse quotidienne du MIC, daily - for internal distribution only. **Staff:** Edith Healy, Ref.Libn..

★11783★
QUEBEC PROVINCE MINISTERE DE LA JUSTICE - BIBLIOTHEQUE (Law)
1200, route de l'Eglise
Edifice Delta, 4th Fl. Phone: (418)643-8409
Ste. Foy, PQ, Canada G1V 4M1 Michel Ricard, Responsable
Founded: 1965. **Staff:** Prof 1; Other 2. **Subjects:** Law. **Special Collections:** Statutes. **Holdings:** 13,000 books; 225 bound periodical volumes; 250 reports and government documents; 450 unbound periodicals; 14,000 microfiche. **Subscriptions:** 170 journals and other serials. **Services:** Copying; SDI; library open to the public. **Computerized Information Services:** QL Systems, CAN/LAW, WESTLAW. **Publications:** New acquisitions list. **Staff:** Solange Tardif, Biblio..

★11784★
QUEBEC PROVINCE MINISTERE DU LOISIR, DE LA CHASSE ET DE LA PECHE - BIBLIOTHEQUE (Env-Cons, Biol Sci)
150 est, blvd. St-Cyrille, 4th Fl.
Quebec, PQ, Canada G1R 4Y1 Madeleine Savard, Hd.Libn.
Founded: 1967. **Subjects:** Wildlife management, conservation, ecology, zoology, ornithology, fish culture, game, hunting, sport fishing, recreation. **Holdings:** 20,000 books; 1500 bound periodical volumes; 44 VF drawers of reprints and pamphlets; 6000 research reports and manuscripts.

★11785★
QUEBEC PROVINCE MINISTERE DU LOISIR, DE LA CHASSE ET DE LA PECHE - BIBLIOTHEQUE DE LA FAUNE (Env-Cons, Biol Sci)
6255 13th Ave. Phone: (514)374-5840
Montreal, PQ, Canada H1X 3E6 Richard Mathieu, Chf.Libn.
Founded: 1945. **Staff:** Prof 1; Other 2. **Subjects:** Aquatic fauna, limnology, mammology, ecology, North American birds, environmental pollution. **Special Collections:** 16th-18th century natural history; 17th-19th century works of French, American, English naturalists. **Holdings:** 8500 books; 160,000 periodical volumes; 3000 reprints. **Subscriptions:** 185 journals and other serials. **Services:** Interlibrary loan; copying; library open to qualified users only. **Publications:** Monthly recent books list.

★11786★
QUEBEC PROVINCE MINISTERE DU REVENU - BIBLIOTHEQUE (Bus-Fin)
3800, rue Marly Phone: (418)652-6835
Ste. Foy, PQ, Canada G1X 4A5 Pierre-Paul Blais, Dir.
Staff: 2. **Subjects:** Tax law and administration, management. **Holdings:** 8000 books; 450 bound periodical volumes. **Subscriptions:** 50 journals and other serials; 10 newspapers. **Services:** Interlibrary loan; library open to government employees.

★11787★
QUEBEC PROVINCE MINISTERE DE LA SANTE ET DES SERVICES SOCIAUX - SERVICE DE LA DOCUMENTATION (Soc Sci, Med)
1005, chemin Ste-Foy, R.C. Phone: (418)643-6392
Quebec, PQ, Canada G1S 4N4 Yvon Papillon, Hd.Libn.
Staff: Prof 6; Other 13. **Subjects:** Health and social services, medical economics, aging, occupational and environmental health, family. **Special Collections:** World Health Organization publications. **Holdings:** 35,000 books. **Subscriptions:** 325 journals and other serials. **Services:** Interlibrary loan; service not open to the public. **Automated Operations:** Computerized cataloging. **Computerized Information Services:** DIALOG Information

Services, IST-Informatheque Inc. **Publications:** Informations Documentaires, 10/year. **Remarks:** An alternate telephone number is 643-5572. **Staff:** Francois Allard, Ref. & Coll.Dev.Libn.; Jacqueline Vallee, Ref.Techn.; Michel Dupuis, Cat. & Rec.Mgr.Libn.; Gerard Darlington, Br.Libn.; Lise Lefrancois, Cat.Techn.; Carol Murphy, Rec.Mgt.Mgr..

★11788★
QUEBEC PROVINCE MINISTERE DES TRANSPORTS - CENTRE DE DOCUMENTATION (Trans)
1410 Stanley St., 8th Fl. Phone: (514)873-5467
Montreal, PQ, Canada H3A 1P8 Mr. Vy-Khanh Nguyen, Libn.
Founded: 1979. **Staff:** Prof 1; Other 2. **Subjects:** Transportation - urban, school, design and construction; local transit; subways; transportation of the physically handicapped. **Special Collections:** Ministry working papers and studies (600); annual reports and studies from Canadian Transit Commissions; studies and reports from other transportation agencies. **Holdings:** 12,000 books; 1000 newspaper reviews; 240 subject and organization files; 35 microfiche; 12 videotapes. **Subscriptions:** 156 journals and other serials. **Services:** Interlibrary loan; copying; center open to the public. **Automated Operations:** Computerized cataloging and circulation. **Computerized Information Services:** DIALOG Information Services, CAN/OLE, Telesystemes Questel, Banque de Terminologie du Quebec, DOBIS Canadian Online Library System, ESA/IRS, QL Systems; internal database; CAN/OLE (electronic mail service). Performs searches free of charge. **Publications:** Acquisitions Recentes, bimonthly; Sommaire des Periodiques, bimonthly - to ministry services and concerned libraries and organizations.

★11789★
QUEBEC PROVINCE MINISTERE DES TRANSPORTS - CENTRE DE DOCUMENTATION (Trans)
700, blvd. St. Cyrille E., 24th Fl. Phone: (418)643-3578
Quebec, PQ, Canada G1R 5H1 Donald Blais, Dir.
Staff: Prof 3; Other 10. **Subjects:** Transportation - air, road, maritime, railroad, urban. **Special Collections:** Annual reports of the ministry, 1907 to present; Transportation Research Board publications; Transport and Road Research Laboratory publications. **Holdings:** 5000 books; 28,000 reports. **Subscriptions:** 700 journals and other serials; 15 newspapers. **Services:** Interlibrary loan; copying; SDI; center open to the public. **Computerized Information Services:** DIALOG Information Services, IST-Informatheque Inc., DOBIS Canadian Online Library System, CAN/OLE, ESA/IRS. **Publications:** Sommaire des Periodiques, bimonthly; Acquisitions Recentes, bimonthly - both free upon request. **Staff:** Marya Bradicich, Ref.Libn.; Vy-Khanh Nguyen, Ref.Libn..

★11790★
QUEBEC PROVINCE MINISTERE DU TRAVAIL - CENTRE DE DOCUMENTATION (Bus-Fin)
425 St-Amable, 2nd Fl. Phone: (418)643-7587
Quebec, PQ, Canada G1R 4Z1 Lise Laprise, Biblio.
Founded: 1962. **Staff:** 2. **Subjects:** Labor, industrial relations, employment, statistics, industry, finances. **Holdings:** 10,000 books. **Subscriptions:** 175 journals and other serials. **Services:** Interlibrary loan; copying; center open to the public with restrictions.

★11791★
QUEBEC PROVINCE OFFICE DES COMMUNICATIONS SOCIALES - BIBLIOTHEQUE ET CENTRE DE DOCUMENTATION (Info Sci)
4005, rue de Bellechasse Phone: (514)729-6391
Montreal, PQ, Canada H1X 1J6 Lucien Labelle, Gen.Dir.
Founded: 1957. **Staff:** Prof 1; Other 3. **Subjects:** Cinema, radio, television, cablevision, videotex, the press. **Holdings:** 6000 books; 400 bound periodical volumes; microfilm; unbound documents. **Subscriptions:** 60 journals and other serials; 10 newspapers. **Services:** Copying; library open to the public with restrictions. **Computerized Information Services:** Computerized information and evaluation on 22,000 feature films. **Publications:** List of publications for sale - available on request. **Special Indexes:** Index to film documentation. **Remarks:** Provides facilities for Centre de Documentation Cinematographique.

★11792★
QUEBEC PROVINCE OFFICE DE LA LANGUE FRANCAISE - BIBLIOTHEQUE (Hum, Sci-Engr)
800, place Victoria, 15th Fl. Phone: (514)873-2997
Montreal, PQ, Canada H4Z 1G8 Chantal Robinson, Chf., Lib./Pub.Serv.
Founded: 1970. **Staff:** Prof 2; Other 5. **Subjects:** Terminology, technology, French language. **Special Collections:** Association Francaise de Normalisation (AFNOR) standards; Bibliotheque Nationale du Quebec (BNQ) standards; Techniques de Ingenieur. **Holdings:** 17,000 books; internal publications. **Subscriptions:** 175 journals and other serials; 5 newspapers. **Services:** Interlibrary loan; copying; library open to the public. **Automated Operations:** Computerized cataloging. **Computerized Information Services:** DIALOG Information Services, CAN/OLE, Telesystemes Questel, Banque de Terminologie du Quebec (BTQ). **Publications:** Parutions Recentes, monthly; selective bibliographies. **Staff:** Mireille Cliche, Chf., Tech.Serv..

★11793★
QUEBEC PROVINCE OFFICE DES PERSONNES HANDICAPEES DU QUEBEC - CENTRE DE DOCUMENTATION (Soc Sci)
C.P. 820 Phone: (819)477-7100
Drummondville, PQ, Canada J2B 6X1 Sophie Janik, Doc.
Founded: 1979. **Staff:** Prof 1; Other 2. **Subjects:** Handicapped persons - social and vocational integration, adaptation and rehabilitation, deinstitutionalization, general and psychological impairment. **Holdings:** 5000 books; bound periodical volumes; 500 audio cassettes; ministry reports; AV programs. **Subscriptions:** 75 journals and other serials. **Services:** Interlibrary loan; copying; center open to the public. **Computerized Information Services:** Fichier informatise (internal database); Arctel (electronic mail service). **Networks/Consortia:** Member of Reseau d'acces a la documentation pour les personnes handicapees. **Publications:** Liste d'acquisition, quarterly; Thesaurus: Personne handicapee; Bibliographies thematiques; Bibliographie quebecoise. **Special Indexes:** Repertoires audiovisuels. **Staff:** Francois Malouin, Biblio..

★11794★
QUEBEC PROVINCE OFFICE DE LA PROTECTION DU CONSOMMATEUR - CENTRE DE DOCUMENTATION (Bus-Fin)
400, boul. Jean-Lesage
Bureau 450 Phone: (418)643-1484
Quebec, PQ, Canada G1K 8W4 Denise Martineau, Doc.Techn.
Founded: 1975. **Staff:** 2. **Subjects:** Consumers, credit, law, housing, advertising, food supply. **Holdings:** 5000 books; 300 bound periodical volumes; annual reports; government publications. **Subscriptions:** 300 journals and other serials. **Services:** Interlibrary loan; copying; SDI; center open to the public with restrictions. **Publications:** Nouvelles Acquisitions Recues au Centre de Documentation de Quebec et au Bureau Administratif de Montreal, monthly; Sommaire des Periodiques Recus au Centre de Documentation, monthly - both for internal distribution only. **Special Indexes:** Index des Tests (looseleaf).

★11795★
QUEBEC PROVINCE REGIE DE L'ELECTRICITE ET DU GAZ - BIBLIOTHEQUE (Energy)
2100, rue Drummond Phone: (514)873-2452
Montreal, PQ, Canada H3G 1X1 Marielle Bernard, Lib.Techn.
Founded: 1973. **Staff:** Prof 1. **Subjects:** Public utilities, energy, oil and gas, accounting, law, economics. **Holdings:** 525 books; 110 bound periodical volumes; 100 other cataloged items; annual reports; conference proceedings; regulations. **Subscriptions:** 33 journals and other serials. **Services:** Interlibrary loan; copying; library open to the public by appointment. **Remarks:** Maintained by Ministere de l'Energie et des Ressources. **Also Known As:** Electricity and Gas Board.

★11796★
QUEBEC PROVINCE REGIE DES RENTES - CENTRE DE DOCUMENTATION (Bus-Fin)
C.P. 5200 Phone: (418)643-8250
Quebec, PQ, Canada G1K 7S9 Nicole Paquin, Asst.Libn.
Founded: 1965. **Staff:** Prof 1; Other 3. **Subjects:** Social security, private pension plans. **Holdings:** 15,000 volumes; 5500 microfiche; 430 pamphlets and reprints. **Subscriptions:** 299 journals and other serials. **Services:** Interlibrary loan; copying; SDI; center open to the public with permission. **Automated Operations:** Computerized cataloging. **Computerized Information Services:** DIALOG Information Services, IST-Informatheque Inc., QL Systems, Banque de Terminologie du Quebec. Performs searches on fee basis. **Publications:** Nouvelles acquisitions, bimonthly - for exchange; Periodiques recus, annual with supplements - for internal distribution only; Repertoire des periodiques, 1986 - limited distribution. **Also Known As:** Quebec Pension Board.

(Quebec Province) SOCIETE DE RADIO-TELEVISION DU QUEBEC - RADIO QUEBEC
See: Radio Quebec (11859)

★11797★
QUEBEC SAFETY LEAGUE - INFORMATION CENTER (Sci-Engr)
6785, rue St-Jacques, W. Phone: (514)482-9110
Montreal, PQ, Canada H4B 1V3 Jacques Bisson, Lib.Techn.
Founded: 1986. **Staff:** Prof 1. **Subjects:** Road and work safety, safety at home, safety in sports and leisure. **Holdings:** 2000 books. **Subscriptions:** 31 journals and other serials. **Services:** Copying; center open to the public. **Automated Operations:** Computerized cataloging. **Also Known As:** Ligue de Securite du Quebec.

★11798★
QUEBEC YOUNG FARMERS PROVINCIAL FEDERATION - LIBRARY (Agri)
Box 80 Phone: (514)457-2010
Ste. Anne de Bellevue, PQ, Canada H9X 3L4
Shannon Keenan, Prov.Coord.
Staff: 8. **Subjects:** Rural youth, agriculture. **Holdings:** Figures not available. **Services:** Library not open to the public.

QUEBEC ZOOLOGICAL GARDEN
See: Jardin Zoologique du Quebec (7165)

★11799★
QUEEN ANNE'S COUNTY LAW LIBRARY (Law)
Court House Phone: (301)758-0216
Centreville, MD 21617 Mary F. Engle, Libn.
Staff: 1. **Subjects:** U.S. and Maryland law. **Holdings:** 2800 books; 52 bound periodical volumes. **Services:** Library open to the public.

★11800★
QUEEN ELIZABETH HOSPITAL - LIBRARY (Med)
P.O. Box 6600 Phone: (902)566-6371
Charlottetown, PE, Canada C1A 8T5 Marion J. Kielly, Libn.
Founded: 1982. **Staff:** Prof 1; Other 1. **Subjects:** Medicine, nursing, allied health sciences, hospital administration. **Holdings:** 500 books; 500 bound periodical volumes. **Subscriptions:** 119 journals and other serials. **Services:** Interlibrary loan; copying; library open to health science workers. **Computerized Information Services:** MEDLARS; Envoy 100 (electronic mail service).

★11801★
QUEEN ELIZABETH II HOSPITAL - STAFF LIBRARY (Med)
10409 98th St.
Postal Bag 2600 Phone: (403)538-7186
Grande Prairie, AB, Canada T8V 2E8 Phyllis Brazeau, Lib.Techn.
Founded: 1984. **Staff:** 1. **Subjects:** Medicine. **Holdings:** 2000 books; 220 bound periodical volumes; 300 videotapes. **Subscriptions:** 251 journals and other serials. **Services:** Interlibrary loan; copying; library open to the public for reference use only.

QUEEN ELIZABETH II LIBRARY
See: Memorial University of Newfoundland - Queen Elizabeth II Library (8665)

★11802★
QUEEN STREET MENTAL HEALTH CENTRE - HEALTH SCIENCES LIBRARY (Med)
1001 Queen St., W. Phone: (416)535-8501
Toronto, ON, Canada M6J 1H4 Mary Ann Georges, Staff Libn.
Founded: 1965. **Staff:** Prof 1. **Subjects:** Psychiatry, psychology, nursing, psychopharmacology, sociology, administration, rehabilitation. **Special Collections:** Hospital History File (history of Queen Street Mental Health Centre); Griffin-Greenland History of Canadian Psychiatry Collection. **Holdings:** 3000 books; 3000 bound periodical volumes; 50 theses; 150 AV cassettes; 4 VF drawers. **Subscriptions:** 185 journals and other serials. **Services:** Interlibrary loan; copying; library open to the public for reference use only. **Publications:** Acquisitions list, 2/year; journals list, annual.

★11803★
QUEEN'S BENCH - COURT OF APPEAL JUDGES' LIBRARY (Law)
Law Courts Bldg.
1A Churchill Square
Edmonton, AB, Canada T5J 0R2Shih-Sheng Hu, Chf.Prov. Law Libn.
Subjects: Law. **Holdings:** 6300 volumes. **Services:** Library not open to the public. **Remarks:** Housed with Law Society of Alberta - Edmonton Library.

★11804★
QUEENS BOROUGH PUBLIC LIBRARY - ART AND MUSIC DIVISION (Art, Mus)
89-11 Merrick Blvd. Phone: (718)990-0755
Jamaica, NY 11432 Dorothea Wu, Hd.
Founded: 1933. **Staff:** Prof 6; Other 3. **Subjects:** Art, music, theater, dance, games, sports. **Special Collections:** Picture collection (1 million reproductions, photographs, postcards, clippings). **Holdings:** 111,050 books; 5645 bound periodical volumes; 18,380 phonograph records; 7060 cassettes; 600 compact discs; 2248 reels of microfilm; 46 VF drawers of pamphlets; 490 libretto titles;178 framed pictures. **Subscriptions:** 285 periodical titles. **Services:** Interlibrary loan; copying; division open to the public. **Automated Operations:** Computerized cataloging and circulation. **Computerized Information Services:** ALANET (electronic mail service). **Special Indexes:** Subject Index to Picture Collection; Song Index; Symphonic Program Note Index. **Staff:** Claire Kach, Asst.Div.Hd.; Shirley Evans, Ref.Libn.; Wendy Wiederhorn, Ref.Libn.; Heidi Gottman, Ref.Libn.; Sharon Kugler, Ref.Libn..

★11805★
QUEENS BOROUGH PUBLIC LIBRARY - HISTORY, TRAVEL & BIOGRAPHY DIVISION (Hist, Geog-Map)
89-11 Merrick Blvd. Phone: (718)990-0762
Jamaica, NY 11432 Deborah Hammer, Hd.
Founded: 1930. **Staff:** Prof 6; Other 3. **Subjects:** History, Indians of North America, biography, geography, travel, exploration. **Special Collections:** Carter G. Woodson Collection of Afro-American Culture and Life; Schomburg microfilm collection; U.S. Geographic Survey topographic maps (4800); physical/thematic maps of countries of the world (126); nautical charts (813); jet/ocean/world navigation charts (520); national forest maps (75); Latin American topographic maps (97); New York State planimetric maps (968); New York state, county, road maps (78); railroad transportation zone maps (82); historic/city maps (442). **Holdings:** 135,000 books; 3500 bound periodical volumes; 6100 microforms; 36 VF drawers of pamphlets; New York Daily News, 1950 to present; Christian Science Monitor, 1966 to present; Los Angeles Times, 1980 to present; Washington Post, 1981 to present, all newspapers on microfilm. **Subscriptions:** 87 journals and other serials; 31 newspapers. **Services:** Interlibrary loan; copying; division open to the public. **Automated Operations:** Computerized cataloging and circulation. **Computerized Information Services:** ALANET (electronic mail service). **Special Indexes:** Collective biography analytics (card). **Staff:** John Moran, Asst.Div.Hd.; Arthur Sherman, Ref.Libn.; Bernice Sims, Ref.Libn.; Roy Berg, Ref.Libn.; Emanuele Zoberman, Ref.Libn..

★11806★
QUEENS BOROUGH PUBLIC LIBRARY - INFORMATION/ TELEPHONE REFERENCE DIVISION (Info Sci)
89-11 Merrick Blvd. Phone: (718)990-0714
Jamaica, NY 11432 Dr. Rosemarie Riechel, Div.Hd.
Staff: Prof 8; Other 1. **Subjects:** Reference, online information retrieval, information and referral. **Holdings:** 6000 books. **Subscriptions:** 14 journals and other serials; 5 newspapers. **Services:** Interlibrary loan; copying; SDI; division open to the public. **Automated Operations:** Computerized cataloging and circulation. **Computerized Information Services:** NEXIS, DIALOG Information Services, BRS Information Technologies, OCLC; Community Information Resource File (internal database); ALANET (electronic mail service). Performs searches free of charge. **Special Indexes:** Index to newspaper clippings (card); index to Community Information Resource File (computer printout); file of obscure questions (card). **Remarks:** An alternate telephone number is 990-0778. **Staff:** Malcolm Spensley, Asst.Hd.; Edward Weiss, Ref.Libn.; Maria Berde, Ref.Libn.; David Alperstein, Ref.Libn.; Ms. Ilham Al-Basri, Ref.Libn.; Susan James, Ref.Libn.; Steven Sachar, Ref.Libn..

★11807★
QUEENS BOROUGH PUBLIC LIBRARY - LANGUAGE & LITERATURE DIVISION (Hum)
89-11 Merrick Blvd. Phone: (718)990-0763
Jamaica, NY 11432 Inge M. Judd, Div.Hd.
Founded: 1928. **Staff:** Prof 7; Other 4. **Subjects:** Literature, linguistics, fiction and nonfiction in 75 languages (not including English). **Special Collections:** Foreign language books. **Holdings:** 226,593 books; 10,361 bound periodical volumes; 583 sets of phonograph records; 550 language cassettes; 36 VF drawers of pamphlets; 215 microfiche; 3142 reels of microfilm. **Subscriptions:** 303 journals and other serials. **Services:** Interlibrary loan; copying; division open to the public. **Automated Operations:** Computerized cataloging and circulation. **Computerized Information Services:** ALANET (electronic mail service). **Special Indexes:** Play Index (card). **Staff:** Esther Pollock, Asst.Div.Hd.; Daniel Gutoff,

Ref.Libn.; Anca Costea, Foreign Lang.Libn.; Dana Aylor, Foreign Lang.Libn.; Casper Morsello, Foreign Lang.Libn.; Desiree Lee, Foreign Lang.Libn..

★11808★
QUEENS BOROUGH PUBLIC LIBRARY - LIBRARY ACTION COMMITTEE OF CORONA-EAST ELMHURST, INC. - LANGSTON HUGHES COMMUNITY LIBRARY AND CULTURAL CENTER (Soc Sci)
102-09 Northern Blvd. Phone: (718)651-1100
Corona, NY 11368 Andrew P. Jackson, Exec.Dir.
Founded: 1969. **Staff:** Prof 14; Other 34. **Subjects:** Third World, children's literature, law. **Special Collections:** Langston Hughes Collection (books by and about the author); Black Heritage Reference Collection. **Holdings:** 110,000 books; 150 documents, manuscripts, reels of microfilm. **Subscriptions:** 105 journals and other serials; 15 newspapers. **Services:** Copying; library open to the public. **Publications:** Library Center Brochure. **Staff:** Marsha Stewart, Supv.; Rodney Lee, Cur., Black Heritage Ctr.; Ruby Sprott, Dir., Homework Assist.Prog..

★11809★
QUEENS BOROUGH PUBLIC LIBRARY - LONG ISLAND DIVISION (Hist)
89-11 Merrick Blvd. Phone: (718)990-0770
Jamaica, NY 11432 C.F.J. Young, Div.Hd.
Founded: 1912. **Staff:** Prof 3; Other 2. **Subjects:** Long Island local history and genealogy. **Special Collections:** Books published at Marion Press (private press in Jamaica, NY); publications of Christopher Morley. **Holdings:** 24,000 books; 2100 bound periodical volumes; 90 VF drawers of clippings; 5300 maps; 40,000 manuscripts; 8200 reels of microfilm; 50,000 pictures, prints, photographs, postcards, glass plate negatives. **Subscriptions:** 187 journals and other serials; 31 newspapers. **Services:** Interlibrary loan; copying; division open to the public. **Automated Operations:** Computerized cataloging and circulation. **Computerized Information Services:** ALANET (electronic mail service). **Staff:** William Asadorian, Archv.; Robert Friedrich, Ref.Libn..

★11810★
QUEENS BOROUGH PUBLIC LIBRARY - SCIENCE & TECHNOLOGY DIVISION (Sci-Engr, Bus-Fin)
89-11 Merrick Blvd. Phone: (718)990-0760
Jamaica, NY 11432 John D. Brady, Jr., Div.Hd.
Founded: 1930. **Staff:** Prof 7; Other 4. **Subjects:** Mathematics, engineering, accounting, chemistry, biological sciences, advertising, nursing, physics, business administration, aeronautics, patents. **Special Collections:** Telephone directories for all major U.S. and foreign cities; automobile and household repair manuals; Sams Photofacts and Computerfacts. **Holdings:** 217,373 books; 29,612 bound periodical volumes; 12,374 reels of microfilm of back issue periodicals; 50 VF drawers. **Subscriptions:** 1196 journals and other serials. **Services:** Interlibrary loan; copying; division open to the public. **Automated Operations:** Computerized cataloging and circulation. **Computerized Information Services:** ALANET (electronic mail service). **Staff:** Linda Scavetti, Asst.Div.Hd.; Joseph R. Morris, Ref.Libn.; Norman Malwitz, Ref.Libn.; Dana Gordon, Ref.Libn.; Mr. Artis Klavins, Ref.Libn..

★11811★
QUEENS BOROUGH PUBLIC LIBRARY - SOCIAL SCIENCES DIVISION (Soc Sci, Bus-Fin, Rel-Phil)
89-11 Merrick Blvd. Phone: (718)990-0761
Jamaica, NY 11432 Nathan Shoengold, Div.Hd.
Founded: 1930. **Staff:** Prof 7; Other 5. **Subjects:** Philosophy, psychology, religion, sociology, economics and investments, political science, government, law, education, costumes, folklore. **Special Collections:** Investment, law, and tax services; college catalogs; civil service study guides; corporate reports; curriculum-related pamphlets; Hiler Costume Collection. **Holdings:** 261,436 books; 20,508 bound periodical volumes; 116 VF drawers; 325 drawers of microfiche; 10,850 reels of microfilm; 154 microcards; 721,626 ERIC microfiche. **Subscriptions:** 1261 journals and other serials; 30 newspapers. **Services:** Interlibrary loan; copying; division open to the public. **Automated Operations:** Computerized cataloging and circulation. **Computerized Information Services:** ALANET (electronic mail service). **Staff:** Renee Kaplan, Asst.Div.Hd.; Lucille Vener, Ref.Libn.; Muriel Marcus, Ref.Libn.; Martin Sedacca, Ref.Libn.; Delia Wong, Ref.Libn.; Anne Murphy, Ref.Libn..

★11812★
QUEENS CHILDREN'S PSYCHIATRIC CENTER - LAURETTA BENDER STAFF LIBRARY (Med)
74-03 Commonwealth Blvd. Phone: (718)464-2900
Bellerose, NY 11426 Annie Sarwee, Libn.
Staff: Prof 1. **Subjects:** Psychiatry, psychology, social work. **Special Collections:** Collection of reprints from psychiatric journals (300); Lauretta Bender series (books on Bender-gestalt; reprints and limited works of Dr. Paul Ferdinand Schilder). **Holdings:** 5000 books; 300 bound periodical volumes; 650 reprints and pamphlets; 300 reels of tape; Audio-Digest tapes on psychiatry. **Subscriptions:** 80 journals and other serials. **Services:** Library open to other health facilities.

★11813★
QUEENS COLLEGE OF THE CITY UNIVERSITY OF NEW YORK - BENJAMIN S. ROSENTHAL LIBRARY - ART LIBRARY (Art)
65-30 Kissena Blvd. Phone: (718)520-7243
Flushing, NY 11367-0904 Suzanne Simor, Hd.
Founded: 1937. **Staff:** Prof 2; Other 5. **Subjects:** Art, architecture, archeology, design, photography. **Holdings:** 40,000 books; 4000 bound periodical volumes; 18,000 pamphlets; 12,000 exhibition catalogs; 35,000 mounted reproductions; 2000 microfiche; 10,000 slides. **Subscriptions:** 200 journals and other serials. **Services:** Interlibrary loan; copying; library open to the public for reference use only. **Automated Operations:** Computerized public access catalog, cataloging, serials, and circulation. **Computerized Information Services:** DIALOG Information Services, RLIN, OCLC. Performs searches on fee basis. **Networks/Consortia:** Member of SUNY/OCLC Library Network. **Publications:** New Books, quarterly; List of Periodicals Available, semiannual - both for internal distribution only; Collection Development Policy (2nd edition; 1985) - internal distribution and available upon request. **Formerly:** Paul Klapper Library. **Staff:** Deborah Barlow, Art Libn..

★11814★
QUEENS COLLEGE OF THE CITY UNIVERSITY OF NEW YORK - BENJAMIN S. ROSENTHAL LIBRARY - HISTORICAL DOCUMENTS COLLECTION (Hist)
65-30 Kissena Blvd.
Flushing, NY 11367-0904
Subjects: State and local history, 1660-1860. **Holdings:** 18,000 cubic feet of legal records, wills, inventories, administrative papers, assessment lists, criminal court records. **Services:** Copying; collection open to the public. **Formerly:** Paul Klapper Library.

★11815★
QUEENS COLLEGE OF THE CITY UNIVERSITY OF NEW YORK - CENTER FOR BYZANTINE & MODERN GREEK STUDIES - LIBRARY (Hum)
Jefferson Hall, Rm. 303 Phone: (718)520-7035
Flushing, NY 11367 E. Lekas, Libn.
Staff: Prof 1; Other 2. **Subjects:** Modern Greek language, literature, history; Greek American community; Cyprus. **Holdings:** 2000 books; 100 other cataloged items. **Subscriptions:** 10 journals and other serials.

★11816★
QUEENS COLLEGE OF THE CITY UNIVERSITY OF NEW YORK - ETHNIC MATERIALS INFORMATION CENTER (Area-Ethnic)
Graduate School of Lib. & Info. Studies
NSF 300
65-30 Kissena Blvd. Phone: (718)520-7194
Flushing, NY 11367 David Cohen, Prog.Dir.
Staff: Prof 1; Other 1. **Subjects:** Ethnic studies resources, minority groups in America. **Holdings:** 2000 volumes; 40 filmstrips; 10 tapes; 250 pamphlets; curriculum materials. **Services:** Center open to the public. **Remarks:** An alternate telephone number is 520-7139.

★11817★
QUEENS COLLEGE OF THE CITY UNIVERSITY OF NEW YORK - SCIENCE LIBRARY (Sci-Engr, Med)
65-30 Kissena Blvd. Phone: (718)520-7254
Flushing, NY 11367 Jackson B. Cohen, Hd., Sci.Lib.
Staff: Prof 2; Other 2. **Subjects:** Biology, psychology, chemistry, mathematics, physics, geology, computer science, home economics, speech pathology, audiology, sports physiology and medicine. **Holdings:** 67,500 books; 33,000 bound periodical volumes; microfilm. **Subscriptions:** 1850 journals and other serials. **Services:** Interlibrary loan; copying; library open to the public for reference use only. **Automated Operations:** Computerized cataloging, serials, and circulation. **Computerized Information Services:**

DIALOG Information Services, BRS Information Technologies, STN International. **Networks/Consortia:** Member of New York Metropolitan Reference and Research Library Agency (METRO). **Publications:** Science Library Reference Guide series, irregular - to library users; Science Fair Research in a College Library - for sale. **Staff:** Gail Ronnermann, Sci.Libn..

QUEENS HOSPITAL CENTER
See: Long Island Jewish Medical Center (7954)

★11818★
QUEEN'S UNIVERSITY AT KINGSTON - ART LIBRARY (Art)
Ontario Hall Phone: (613)545-2841
Kingston, ON, Canada K7L 5C4 Vivien Taylor, Mus./Art Libn.
Founded: 1957. **Staff:** Prof 1; Other 2. **Subjects:** Art history, art education, art conservation. **Holdings:** 25,000 volumes; 600 microfiche; 300 reels of microfilm; 8500 exhibition catalogs; 100,000 35mm slides; 50,000 photographs. **Subscriptions:** 110 journals and other serials. **Services:** Interlibrary loan; library open to the public with restrictions. **Remarks:** Slides and photographs are owned and administered by the Department of Art. They are inaccessible to the public.

★11819★
QUEEN'S UNIVERSITY AT KINGSTON - BIOLOGY LIBRARY (Biol Sci)
Earl Hall
Barrie St. Phone: (613)545-2834
Kingston, ON, Canada K7L 5C4 Denise Hodge, Lib.Asst.
Staff: 2. **Subjects:** Biology. **Holdings:** 23,000 volumes. **Subscriptions:** 358 journals and other serials. **Services:** Interlibrary loan; copying; SDI; library open to teachers and technical staff of local institutions. **Computerized Information Services:** CAN/OLE, QL Systems, BRS Information Technologies, DIALOG Information Services.

★11820★
QUEEN'S UNIVERSITY AT KINGSTON - BRACKEN LIBRARY (Med)
Kingston, ON, Canada K7L 3N6 Phone: (613)545-2510
Mrs. V. Ludwin, Libn.
Staff: Prof 4; Other 9. **Subjects:** Medicine, nursing, rehabilitation. **Holdings:** 92,675 volumes. **Subscriptions:** 1293 journals and other serials. **Services:** Interlibrary loan; copying; library open to health sciences personnel. **Automated Operations:** Computerized cataloging and circulation. **Computerized Information Services:** MEDLINE, BRS Information Technologies, DIALOG Information Services. **Publications:** Subscription List, annual. **Staff:** Monica Webster, Pub.Serv.Libn.; Jane Law, Pub.Serv.Libn.; Mrs. J. Eikelboom, Tech.Serv. & Ser.Libn.; Suzanne Maranda, Pub.Serv.Libn..

★11821★
QUEEN'S UNIVERSITY AT KINGSTON - CHEMISTRY LIBRARY (Sci-Engr)
Frost Wing, Gordon Hall Phone: (613)545-2610
Kingston, ON, Canada K7L 5C4 Janet Innis, Lib.Asst.
Staff: 2. **Subjects:** Chemistry. **Holdings:** 10,996 books; 11,920 bound periodical volumes. **Subscriptions:** 315 journals and other serials. **Services:** Interlibrary loan; copying; SDI; library open to teachers and technical staff of local industries. **Computerized Information Services:** CAN/OLE, QL Systems, BRS Information Technologies.

★11822★
QUEEN'S UNIVERSITY AT KINGSTON - CIVIL ENGINEERING LIBRARY (Sci-Engr)
Ellis Hall Phone: (613)545-2835
Kingston, ON, Canada K7L 5C4 Jane Walker, Lib.Techn.
Staff: 1. **Subjects:** Civil engineering. **Holdings:** 16,197 volumes. **Subscriptions:** 266 journals and other serials. **Services:** Interlibrary loan; SDI; library open to the public with restrictions. **Automated Operations:** Computerized circulation. **Computerized Information Services:** DIALOG Information Services, CAN/OLE, BRS Information Technologies, QL Systems. Performs searches on fee basis.

★11823★
QUEEN'S UNIVERSITY AT KINGSTON - DOCUMENTS LIBRARY (Info Sci)
Mackintosh-Corry Hall Phone: (613)545-6313
Kingston, ON, Canada K7L 3N6 Peter Girard, Hd., Doc.Lib.
Founded: 1960. **Staff:** Prof 4; Other 14. **Subjects:** Economics and business, sociology, political science, urban affairs, planning, history, geography, public administration, ecology. **Special Collections:** Royal Commissions of Canada (3600 volumes); 17th century British documents; pre-Confederation official publications (1500 volumes); federal and provincial Parliamentary publications for Canada; United Nations, EEC and OECD, IMF, ILO documents. **Holdings:** 500,000 volumes; 313,030 microfiche; 324,160 microcards; 5567 reels of microfilm; 85,000 maps; complete set of Statistics Canada publications; census documents. **Services:** Interlibrary loan; copying; library open to the public with restrictions. **Automated Operations:** Computerized coding. **Special Indexes:** KWOC index of document holdings. **Remarks:** An alternate telephone number is 547-5767. **Staff:** John Offenbeck, Pub.Serv.Libn.; Carmen Konigsreuther Socknat, Tech.Serv.Libn.; Jeffrey Moon, Ref.Libn..

★11824★
QUEEN'S UNIVERSITY AT KINGSTON - DUPUIS HALL LIBRARY (Sci-Engr)
Division & Clergy Sts. Phone: (613)545-2833
Kingston, ON, Canada K7L 5C4 Ms. M.L. Ranger, Lib.Asst.
Staff: 2. **Subjects:** Engineering - chemical, mining, metallurgical. **Holdings:** 22,000 volumes. **Subscriptions:** 360 journals and other serials. **Services:** Interlibrary loan; SDI; library open to teachers and technical staff of local industries. **Computerized Information Services:** QL Systems, BRS Information Technologies, CAN/OLE.

★11825★
QUEEN'S UNIVERSITY AT KINGSTON - EDUCATION LIBRARY (Educ)
Duncan McArthur Hall Phone: (613)545-2191
Kingston, ON, Canada K7L 3N6 Sandra Casey, Educ.Libn.
Founded: 1966. **Staff:** Prof 2; Other 7. **Subjects:** Education, psychology. **Holdings:** 90,000 volumes; 400,000 microfiche titles; 4000 filmstrips and film loops; 3500 35mm slides; 1800 phonograph records, cassettes, audiotapes; 2000 transparencies. **Subscriptions:** 878 journals and other serials. **Services:** Interlibrary loan; copying; library open to teachers. **Computerized Information Services:** BRS Information Technologies, Ontario Education Resources Information System (ONTERIS). **Publications:** Periodicals List, annual. **Staff:** Judith Fraser, Asst.Libn..

★11826★
QUEEN'S UNIVERSITY AT KINGSTON - ELECTRICAL ENGINEERING LIBRARY (Sci-Engr)
Technology Centre Phone: (613)545-2836
Kingston, ON, Canada K7L 5C4 Angela Madden, Lib.Techn.
Founded: 1930. **Staff:** 1. **Subjects:** Electrical engineering. **Holdings:** 8048 volumes. **Subscriptions:** 204 journals and other serials. **Services:** Interlibrary loan; SDI; library open to technical staff of local industries and institutions. **Computerized Information Services:** CAN/OLE, BRS Information Technologies, QL Systems.

★11827★
QUEEN'S UNIVERSITY AT KINGSTON - GEOLOGICAL SCIENCES LIBRARY (Sci-Engr)
Miller Hall, Bruce Wing Phone: (613)545-2840
Kingston, ON, Canada K7L 5C4 Mary Mayson, Sr.Lib.Techn.
Founded: 1932. **Staff:** 2. **Subjects:** Geological sciences. **Holdings:** 55,000 volumes; 1020 theses; 35,000 maps; microfiche; microfilm. **Subscriptions:** 450 journals and other serials. **Services:** Interlibrary loan; SDI; library open to the public. **Automated Operations:** Computerized circulation. **Computerized Information Services:** CAN/OLE, BRS Information Technologies, QL Systems. **Special Indexes:** Index to maps.

★11828★
QUEEN'S UNIVERSITY AT KINGSTON - INDUSTRIAL RELATIONS CENTRE - LIBRARY (Bus-Fin)
Kingston, ON, Canada K7L 3N6 Phone: (613)547-6917
Carol Williams, Lib.Coord.
Founded: 1937. **Staff:** Prof 2; Other 2. **Subjects:** Industrial relations, labor economics, personnel administration. **Special Collections:** Canadian Government documents (20,000); United States Government documents (5000); International Labor Organization documents (5000). **Holdings:** 5000 books; 2000 bound periodical volumes; 200 VF drawers of pamphlets, reports, dissertations; 616 reels of microfilm. **Subscriptions:** 500 journals and other serials. **Services:** Library open to the public for reference use only, by request. **Publications:** Bibliographies. **Special Indexes:** Index of Industrial Relations Literature (book), annual. **Staff:** Wendy Gower, Libn..

★11829★
QUEEN'S UNIVERSITY AT KINGSTON - LAW LIBRARY (Law)
Sir John A. Macdonald Hall Phone: (613)545-2842
Kingston, ON, Canada K7L 3N6 Irene Bessette, Libn.
Founded: 1957. **Staff:** Prof 4; Other 9. **Subjects:** Law. **Special Collections:** Law - international, Quebec, French, labour, criminal, public. **Holdings:** 140,500 volumes. **Subscriptions:** 3850 journals and other serials. **Services:** Interlibrary loan; copying; library open to the public. **Computerized Information Services:** QL Systems. **Staff:** Mrs. Mai Chen, Coord., Tech.Serv.; Jeffrey Johnson, Supv., Pub.Serv.; Elizabeth Fox, Cat.Libn.; Elizabeth Read, RECON Libn..

★11830★
QUEEN'S UNIVERSITY AT KINGSTON - MAP AND AIR PHOTO LIBRARY (Geog-Map)
Mackintosh-Corry Hall Phone: (613)545-6314
Kingston, ON, Canada K7L 5C4 Kathy Harding, Sr.Lib.Asst.
Staff: 2. **Subjects:** Cartography, aerial photography, photogrammetry. **Special Collections:** Historical cartography collection. **Holdings:** 1100 books; 850 atlases; 68,000 maps; 27,000 aerial photographs; theses; soil surveys; working papers. **Subscriptions:** 50 journals and other serials. **Services:** Interlibrary loan; library open to the public with restrictions.

★11831★
QUEEN'S UNIVERSITY AT KINGSTON - MATHEMATICS AND STATISTICS LIBRARY (Sci-Engr)
Jeffery Hall Phone: (613)545-2838
Kingston, ON, Canada K7L 5C4 Janet Burgess, Lib.Asst.
Staff: 2. **Subjects:** Mathematics, statistics. **Holdings:** 26,000 volumes. **Subscriptions:** 372 journals and other serials.

★11832★
QUEEN'S UNIVERSITY AT KINGSTON - MECHANICAL ENGINEERING LIBRARY (Sci-Engr)
McLaughlin Hall
Stuart St. Phone: (613)545-2584
Kingston, ON, Canada K7L 3N6 Hilary Richardson, Lib.Asst.
Staff: 1. **Subjects:** Mechanical engineering. **Holdings:** 8200 volumes. **Subscriptions:** 150 journals and other serials. **Services:** Interlibrary loan; copying; SDI; library open to technical staff of local firms. **Computerized Information Services:** CAN/OLE, QL Systems, BRS Information Technologies, DIALOG Information Services.

★11833★
QUEEN'S UNIVERSITY AT KINGSTON - MUSIC LIBRARY (Mus)
Harrison-LeCaine Hall Phone: (613)545-2839
Kingston, ON, Canada K7L 5C4 Vivien Taylor, Mus./Art Libn.
Staff: Prof 1; Other 2. **Subjects:** Musicology, music education, ethnomusicology. **Holdings:** 10,000 volumes; 10,500 scores; 50 cassettes; 540 open reel tapes; 230 reels of microfilm; 6000 sound recordings. **Subscriptions:** 120 journals and other serials. **Services:** Interlibrary loan; library open to the public with restrictions. **Remarks:** Maintains a Performance Library of choral, band, orchestral, and chamber music.

★11834★
QUEEN'S UNIVERSITY AT KINGSTON - PHYSICS LIBRARY (Sci-Engr)
Stirling Hall
Queen's Crescent Phone: (613)545-2722
Kingston, ON, Canada K7L 5C4 Diane Nuttall, Lib.Asst.
Staff: 2. **Subjects:** Physics, astronomy. **Holdings:** 20,000 volumes. **Subscriptions:** 265 journals and other serials. **Services:** Interlibrary loan; SDI; library open to teachers and technical staff of local industries. **Automated Operations:** Computerized circulation. **Computerized Information Services:** CAN/OLE, BRS Information Technologies, QL Systems.

★11835★
QUEEN'S UNIVERSITY AT KINGSTON - PSYCHOLOGY LIBRARY (Soc Sci)
Humphrey Hall Phone: (613)545-2837
Kingston, ON, Canada K7L 5C4 Bonnie Bowes, Lib.Techn.
Staff: 2. **Subjects:** Psychology. **Holdings:** 13,428 volumes. **Subscriptions:** 218 journals and other serials. **Services:** Interlibrary loan. **Computerized Information Services:** CAN/OLE, QL Systems, BRS Information Technologies.

★11836★
QUEEN'S UNIVERSITY AT KINGSTON - SPECIAL COLLECTIONS (Hum)
Douglas Library Phone: (613)545-2528
Kingston, ON, Canada K7L 5C4 Barbara Teatero, Cur., Spec.Coll.
Founded: 1965. **Staff:** Prof 1; Other 3. **Subjects:** Canadiana, British history, Anglo-Irish literature. **Special Collections:** Edith and Lorne Pierce Collection of Canadiana (43,700 items); John Buchan Collection (Scotland; 5200 volumes); 18th century British pamphlets (3000); McNicol Collection on Telegraphy, Telephony, and Radio (1200 volumes); Riche-Covington Collection (astrophysics; 1000 volumes); Victor Hugo (150 volumes); dated, rare books, published prior to 1700 (1100 volumes); Bible collection (1200 volumes); Non-Canadian Children's Book Collection (2000 volumes); Gothic Fantasy collection (1000 volumes); F.R. Scott Collection (little magazines; 900); Dickens British and American first editions (350 volumes); Galsworthy (230 volumes); Masefield (240 volumes); Disraeli (1350 volumes); sample Canadian journals (1500). **Holdings:** 119,408 books, bound periodical volumes, Canadian pamphlets; 1000 non-Canadian pamphlets; 650 volumes in Canadian School Text collection; 200 atlases; 500 items in Canadian Centennial Collection; 65,200 microforms; 10 boxes of artifacts; 3 drawers of information materials; 7000 Canadian programmes; 1000 pieces of Canadian sheet music; 600 maps and plans; 2000 broadsides and posters; 3000 postcards; 500 greeting cards; 2400 ephemera; 1000 bookplates; 27,762 items in papers collections. **Services:** Interlibrary loan; copying; collections open to the public. **Automated Operations:** Computerized cataloging. **Publications:** Douglas Library Occasional Papers, irregular - to Canadian libraries and others on request. **Special Indexes:** Card indexes - publisher, printer, date, provenance, Canadian imprints in English and French, 18th century British political pamphlets, maps, private presses, broadsides, sheet music, sample journals. Book indexes - Galsworthy, Masefield, sheet music, F.R. Scott, Gothic Fantasy, McNicol, Bible, Dickens, Riche-Covington, Victor Hugo, Canadian School Text, 18th Century British Pamphlets, Bishop Macdonell, Cartwright Kingston, and Children's Collections.

QUEENSBURY HISTORICAL ASSOCIATION, INC.
See: Glens Falls-Queensbury Historical Association, Inc. - Chapman Historical Museum (5688)

★11837★
QUEENSWOOD HOUSE - LIBRARY (Rel-Phil)
2494 Arbutus Rd. Phone: (604)477-3822
Victoria, BC, Canada V8N 1V8 Patricia Dickinson, SSA, Libn.
Founded: 1963. **Staff:** 2. **Subjects:** Spirituality, dogma, theology, liturgy, church history, English literature, history, geography, psychology, art, music. **Holdings:** 6000 books; 2000 audiotapes. **Subscriptions:** 10 journals and other serials. **Services:** Library open to the public on fee basis. **Remarks:** Maintained by The Sisters of Saint Ann.

★11838★
QUEST RESEARCH CORPORATION - LIBRARY (Sci-Engr)
6858 Old Dominion Dr. Phone: (703)893-6401
McLean, VA 22101 Christine T. Rudolf, Libn.
Founded: 1975. **Staff:** Prof 1. **Subjects:** Electrical engineering, optics, radar, microwaves, military-related subjects. **Holdings:** 2500 books; 50 bound periodical volumes; 1200 NTIS/DDC documents; 250 documents on microfiche; 14 volumes of data descriptions; 35 volumes of military regulations, standards, specifications. **Subscriptions:** 50 journals and other serials. **Services:** Interlibrary loan; library not open to the public. **Computerized Information Services:** DIALOG Information Services, DTIC; DIRS (internal database).

★11839★
QUESTAR CORPORATION - CORPORATE LIBRARY (Energy)
Box 11150 Phone: (801)530-2113
Salt Lake City, UT 84147 Scott Dean, Bus.Info.Anl.
Founded: 1980. **Staff:** Prof 1; Other 1. **Subjects:** Energy, oil and gas, business and industry, utilities, telecommunications, data processing. **Holdings:** 500 books; 2500 other cataloged items. **Subscriptions:** 20 journals and other serials; 5 newspapers. **Services:** Library not open to the public. **Automated Operations:** Computerized cataloging, acquisitions, serials, and circulation. **Computerized Information Services:** DIALOG Information Services, Dow Jones News/Retrieval, Dun & Bradstreet Corporation, A.G.A. GasNet; internal database; DIALMAIL, A.G.A. GasNet (electronic mail services). **Networks/Consortia:** Member of American Gas Association - Library Services (AGA-LSC).

HAROLD SCOTT QUIGLEY LIBRARY
See: University of Minnesota - Institute of International Studies (16474)

MAY G. QUIGLEY COLLECTION
See: Grand Rapids Public Library (5809)

QUIGLEY PHOTOGRAPHIC ARCHIVE
See: Georgetown University - Special Collections Division - Lauinger Memorial Library (5597)

ELLEN SCHULTZ QUILLIN MEMORIAL LIBRARY
See: San Antonio Museum Association (12742)

★11840★
QUINCY HISTORICAL SOCIETY - WIRTANEN LIBRARY (Hist)
Adams Academy Bldg.
8 Adams St. Phone: (617)773-1144
Quincy, MA 02169 Dr. Elliott W. Hoffman, Dir.
Founded: 1893. **Staff:** Prof 2; Other 4. **Subjects:** Quincy area history and genealogy. **Holdings:** 3000 books; 1000 pamphlets; 1000 photographs; manuscripts. **Services:** Copying; library open to the public with restrictions.

★11841★
QUINCY MUSEUM OF NATURAL HISTORY AND ART - LIBRARY (Biol Sci)
1601 Maine St. Phone: (217)224-7669
Quincy, IL 62301 Dr. John L. Snow, Dir.
Staff: Prof 1; Other 1. **Subjects:** Anthropology, ornithology, paleobotany, paleozoology, American Indian, fossils, mollusks, shells, minerals. **Holdings:** 350 books; 600 bound periodical volumes. **Services:** Library not open to the public.

★11842★
QUINCY RESEARCH CENTER - INFORMATION SERVICES* (Med)
5100 E. 24th St.
Kansas City, MO 64127
Founded: 1984. **Staff:** Prof 1; Other 1. **Subjects:** Pharmaceutical research, pharmacology, medicine. **Holdings:** 500 books; 100 bound periodical volumes. **Subscriptions:** 87 journals and other serials. **Services:** Interlibrary loan; services not open to the public. **Computerized Information Services:** MEDLARS, DIALOG Information Services, BRS Information Technologies; MEDFILES (internal database). **Networks/Consortia:** Member of CLASS.

★11843★
QUODDY TIDES FOUNDATION - MARINE LIBRARY (Biol Sci)
123 Water St. Phone: (207)853-4806
Eastport, ME 04631 Susan Esposito, Libn.
Founded: 1974. **Staff:** 1. **Subjects:** Marine sciences, local literature. **Special Collections:** Tidal power studies of Cobscook and Passamaquoddy Bays; environmental impact studies of proposed Pittston Company Project; government reports on commercial fishing in U.S. and Canadian waters. **Holdings:** 784 books; 650 bound periodical volumes; reports; manuscripts. **Services:** Copying; library open to the public with restrictions.

R

★11844★
R & D ASSOCIATES - TECHNICAL INFORMATION CENTER (Sci-Engr)
4640 Admiralty Way
Box 9695 Phone: (213)822-1715
Marina del Rey, CA 90295 Shirley L. Lee, Mgr.
Staff: Prof 4; Other 7. **Subjects:** Defense systems, nuclear physics, electronics, energy systems, systems engineering, weapon systems, computer science, national security. **Holdings:** 16,000 books; 100,000 reports. **Subscriptions:** 400 journals and other serials. **Services:** Interlibrary loan; center not open to the public. **Automated Operations:** Computerized cataloging and circulation. **Computerized Information Services:** DIALOG Information Services, BRS Information Technologies, VU/TEXT Information Services, NASA/RECON, RLIN, Aerospace Online; OnTyme Electronic Message Network Service (electronic mail service). **Networks/Consortia:** Member of CLASS. **Staff:** Christine L. Lincoln, Hd., Ref.; Janet Katz, Cat.Libn.; Christine Anderson, Classified Doc.Supv..

R & D ENGINEERING ASSOCIATES, INC. - ATL TESTING LABORATORIES
See: ATL Testing Laboratories (1101)

★11845★
RACAL-MILGO, INC. - INFORMATION RESOURCES (Info Sci)
Box 407044 Phone: (305)592-8600
Fort Lauderdale, FL 33340 Jan Stern, Mgr.
Founded: 1963. **Staff:** Prof 2; Other 3. **Subjects:** Telecommunications, computer science, electronics. **Holdings:** Figures not available. **Services:** Interlibrary loan; resources open to the public by appointment. **Computerized Information Services:** Online systems; internal database.

RACHMANINOFF ARCHIVES
See: Library of Congress - Music Division (7831)

★11846★
RACINE COUNTY HISTORICAL SOCIETY AND MUSEUM, INC. - LOCAL HISTORY AND GENEALOGICAL REFERENCE LIBRARY (Hist)
701 Main St. Phone: (414)637-8585
Racine, WI 53403 Jeffrey R. Schultz, Dir.
Founded: 1969. **Subjects:** Local history, Racine County, military history. **Special Collections:** Local history photographs. **Holdings:** 500 books; 48 VF drawers of clippings and pamphlets; ephemera; lineage society materials. **Services:** Copying; library open to the public on a limited schedule. **Special Catalogs:** Surname file for early marriages, histories, cemetery inscriptions, 1858 landowners, Declaration of Intent or Naturalization, and censuses for Racine County for years 1840, 1850, 1860, and 1880.

★11847★
RACINE COUNTY LAW LIBRARY (Law)
730 Wisconsin Ave. Phone: (414)636-3862
Racine, WI 53403 Lawrence E. Flynn, Ck. of Courts
Founded: 1850. **Subjects:** Law. **Holdings:** 16,500 books; Wisconsin Briefs on microfiche. **Services:** Copying; library open to the public.

★11848★
RACINE JOURNAL TIMES - LIBRARY (Publ)
212 4th St. Phone: (414)634-3322
Racine, WI 53403 Jill Makovsky, Libn.
Founded: 1958. **Staff:** 1. **Subjects:** Newspaper reference topics. **Holdings:** 300 books; 930 reels of microfilm of the Journal Times, through 1888; miscellaneous pamphlets; 10,900 obituaries; 10,000 biographical files. **Subscriptions:** 18 journals and other serials. **Services:** Library not open to the public. **Special Indexes:** Clippings, mostly of local stories; biographical files, editorials; business and industry activities (card).

★11849★
RACQUET AND TENNIS CLUB - LIBRARY (Rec)
370 Park Ave. Phone: (212)753-9700
New York, NY 10022 Gerard J. Belliveau, Jr., Libn.
Founded: 1916. **Staff:** Prof 2. **Subjects:** Sports, court and lawn tennis, early American sport. **Holdings:** 18,000 books. **Subscriptions:** 45 journals and other serials. **Services:** Mail queries answered; copying; library open to researchers by appointment. **Publications:** Annual Report - to members. **Special Catalogs:** A Dictionary Catalog of the Library of Sports in the Racquet and Tennis Club (1970). **Staff:** Todd M. Thompson, Asst.Libn..

PAL RACZ MEMORIAL LIBRARY
See: Institute for East-West Security Studies (6904)

★11850★
RADCLIFFE COLLEGE - ARTHUR AND ELIZABETH SCHLESINGER LIBRARY ON THE HISTORY OF WOMEN IN AMERICA (Soc Sci, Hist)
10 Garden St. Phone: (617)495-8647
Cambridge, MA 02138 Dr. Patricia M. King, Dir.
Founded: 1943. **Staff:** Prof 9; Other 4. **Subjects:** Women - suffrage, medicine, education, law, social service, labor, family, organizations; history of American women in all phases of public and private life. **Special Collections:** Beecher-Stowe; Woman's Rights; Blackwell Family; Charlotte Perkins Gilman; Emma Goldman; Somerville-Howorth; Dr. Martha May Eliot; Jeannette Rankin; National Organization for Women; Black Women Oral History Project; cookbooks; etiquette books; picture collection (55,000). **Holdings:** 29,500 volumes; 850 major collections of papers on individual American women, families, women's organizations; 9500 reels of microfilm; 2250 magnetic tapes; 52 VF drawers. **Subscriptions:** 425 journals and other serials. **Services:** Interlibrary loan; copying; library open to the public. **Automated Operations:** Computerized cataloging and serials. **Publications:** Occasional Reports, sent on request. **Special Catalogs:** Manuscript Inventories; Catalogs of the Manuscripts, Books and Periodicals, 1984 (10 volumes). **Staff:** Eva Moseley, Cur., Mss.; Barbara Haber, Cur., Printed Bks.; Ruth E. Hill, AV Coord.; Jane S. Knowles, Archv..

★11851★
RADCLIFFE COLLEGE - HENRY A. MURRAY RESEARCH CENTER (Soc Sci)
10 Garden St. Phone: (617)495-8140
Cambridge, MA 02138 Anne Colby, Dir.
Founded: 1976. **Staff:** Prof 5; Other 6. **Subjects:** Human development and social change; women - work, careers, education, mental health, political participation, family life, widowhood, aging. **Special Collections:** Archival materials dealing with data sets of raw and computer-accessible social science research studies. **Holdings:** 150 data sets; 50 books; 350 boxes of raw data; 35 dissertations; 150 unpublished reports; 75 computer magnetic tapes. **Services:** Center open to the public. **Automated Operations:** Computerized acquisitions. **Publications:** Murray Center News, semiannual - free upon request. **Special Indexes:** Guide to the Data Resources of the Henry A. Murray Research Center. **Staff:** Erin Phelps, Res.Assoc.; Sally Powers, Res.Assoc..

RADCLIFFE COLLEGE - MORSE MUSIC LIBRARY
See: Harvard University - Radcliffe College - Morse Music Library (6115)

★11852★
RADER COMPANIES, INC. - INFORMATION CENTER
6005 N.E. 82nd Ave.
Portland, OR 97220
Founded: 1970. **Subjects:** Engineering, materials handling, pulp and paper, forest products. **Holdings:** 1045 books; 2700 technical reports; 2200 vendor files. **Remarks:** Presently inactive.

★11853★
RADFORD UNIVERSITY - DEPARTMENT OF GEOGRAPHY - MAP COLLECTION (Geog-Map)
Box 5811 Phone: (703)831-5558
Radford, VA 24142 Dr. Bernd H. Kuennecke, Cur.
Founded: 1977. **Staff:** 2. **Subjects:** Maps - Virginia, topographic, land use. **Holdings:** 20,000 maps. **Services:** Copying; collection open to the public with restrictions.

★11854★
RADFORD UNIVERSITY - LIBRARY - VIRGINIA ROOM AND SPECIAL COLLECTIONS (Hist)
Radford, VA 24142 Phone: (703)831-5471
Subjects: Southwestern Virginia - institutions, people, culture; Civil War; Christiansburg Institute (originally a black Freedmen's Bureau school); folklore. **Holdings:** 7000 manuscripts, photographs, slides, tapes; unpublished literary manuscripts. **Services:** Copying; collection open to the public. **Automated Operations:** Computerized public access catalog, cataloging, and circulation. **Staff:** Robert L. Turner, Jr., Asst.Dir., Pub.Serv.

★11855★
RADIAN CORPORATION - LIBRARY (Env-Cons)
10395 Old Placerville Rd. Phone: (916)362-5332
Sacramento, CA 95824 Susan Scheibel, Libn.
Founded: 1986. **Staff:** Prof 1; Other 1. **Subjects:** Environment, air quality, hazardous waste. **Holdings:** 3000 books; technical and government reports; government agency rules and regulations. **Subscriptions:** 62 journals and other serials. **Services:** Interlibrary loan; library not open to the public. **Computerized Information Services:** DIALOG Information Services, NLM, National Ground Water Information Center Data Base, Legi-Tech, Dialcom Inc.

★11856★
RADIAN CORPORATION - LIBRARY (Energy)
8501 MoPac Blvd.
Box 201088 Phone: (512)454-4797
Austin, TX 78720 Barbara J. Maxey, Mgr., Lib.Serv.
Staff: Prof 2; Other 4. **Subjects:** Coal conversion processes, air and water pollution control, petroleum refining emissions, ambient air monitoring, artificial intelligence. **Special Collections:** Gasification and liquefaction (20,000 items); sulphur dioxide control (3250 items). **Holdings:** 1950 volumes; 2500 microforms; 21,000 articles, patents, maps; 21,000 technical reports. **Subscriptions:** 380 journals and other serials. **Services:** Interlibrary loan; copying; library open to the public by appointment. **Automated Operations:** Computerized cataloging and circulation. **Computerized Information Services:** Online systems. **Publications:** Library Briefs, irregular; Biweekly List of Books and Reports - both for internal distribution only. **Staff:** Jane E. McDowell, Tech.Libn..

RADIATION RESEARCH ARCHIVES
See: University of Tennessee - Special Collections (16907)

★11857★
RADIO ADVERTISING BUREAU - MARKETING INFORMATION CENTER (Bus-Fin)
304 Park Ave., S., 7th Fl. Phone: (212)254-4800
New York, NY 10010-4302 Susan Raehse, Dir.
Founded: 1951. **Staff:** Prof 2; Other 1. **Subjects:** Radio, advertising and marketing, consumer markets, demographics, competitive media, leading advertisers, retailing. **Special Collections:** Tape Library (30,000 commercials; separate department); company and radio industry archives; Broadcasting Yearbook, 1935 to present. **Holdings:** 600 volumes; 70 VF drawers of clippings. **Subscriptions:** 152 journals and other serials. **Services:** Interlibrary loan (limited); copying; center open to the public by special permission. **Staff:** Peggy Jordan, Asst..

★11858★
RADIO FREE EUROPE/RADIO LIBERTY INC. - REFERENCE LIBRARY (Area-Ethnic)
1775 Broadway Phone: (212)397-5343
New York, NY 10019 Irene V. Dutikow, Ref.Libn.
Founded: 1958. **Staff:** Prof 1; Other 2. **Subjects:** Soviet Union and Eastern European cultural, economic, and political life. **Special Collections:** Soviet magazines and newspapers (184); biographical file on Soviet personalities; Samizdat materials depository (underground documents; 8 drawers and bound volumes); RFE research papers, 1973 to present; RL Research Bulletin, 1964 to present. **Holdings:** 19,000 books; 126 VF drawers; 3300 reels of microfilm. **Subscriptions:** 260 journals and other serials; 70 newspapers. **Services:** Interlibrary loan; copying; library open to the public by appointment. **Automated Operations:** Computerized public access catalog, cataloging, acquisitions, serials, and circulation. **Computerized Information Services:** Internal database. Performs searches free of charge.

★11859★
RADIO QUEBEC - CENTRE DES RESSOURCES DOCUMENTAIRES (Info Sci)
800, rue Fullum Phone: (514)521-2424
Montreal, PQ, Canada H2K 3L7 Nicole Charest, Dir.
Founded: 1969. **Staff:** Prof 8; Other 20. **Subjects:** Canadian and Quebec history, communications, television, graphic arts. **Special Collections:** Collection of Radio-Quebec production and administrative documents, 1968 to present (800 documents in French). **Holdings:** 18,000 books; 20,000 phonograph records; 23,000 slides; 6000 photographs; 4000 television programs on videotape; 3 million feet of film; 100 archival materials; 2000 clipping files; 1000 biographical files. **Subscriptions:** 360 journals and other serials; 30 newspapers. **Services:** Interlibrary loan; center not open to the public. **Automated Operations:** Computerized cataloging. **Publications:** List of serials, semiannual; New Books, bimonthly; New Records, bimonthly; list of consultants in various fields related to public affairs and news, semiannual. **Remarks:** Maintained by (Quebec Province) Societe de Radio-Television du Quebec. **Staff:** Michel Boisvert, Hd. of Ref.Serv.; Micheline Godbout-Mercure, Hd. of Tech.Serv.; Marie Leclaire, Hd. of Film Lib..

RADIO WRITERS GUILD ARCHIVES
See: New York Public Library - Performing Arts Research Center - Billy Rose Theatre Collection (10079)

★11860★
RADIOLOGICAL SOCIETY OF NORTH AMERICA, INC. - LIBRARY (Med)
Oak Brook Regency Towers, Tower B
1415 W. 22nd St.
Oak Brook, IL 60521 Phone: (312)920-2670
Subjects: Clinical radiology, allied health sciences. **Holdings:** 800 volumes; records of manuscripts received annually. **Subscriptions:** 120 journals and other serials. **Services:** Library not open to the public. **Publications:** Radiology, monthly; Radio Graphics, bimonthly. **Special Indexes:** Indexes of selected radiological journals.

RADIOPHARMACEUTICAL INTERNAL DOSE INFORMATION CENTER
See: Oak Ridge Associated Universities (10579)

★11861★
RADNOR HISTORICAL SOCIETY - RESEARCH LIBRARY AND MUSEUM (Hist)
Finley House
113 W. Beech Tree Lane Phone: (215)688-2668
Wayne, PA 19087 George W. Smith, Pres.
Founded: 1948. **Subjects:** Local and Pennsylvania history. **Holdings:** 300 volumes; 4 boxes of genealogical papers; 4 drawers of maps; 4 boxes of photographs, 1880 to present. **Services:** Library open to the public. **Publications:** Bulletin of the Radnor Historical Society, annual - to members and for sale. **Special Indexes:** Index to articles on local history (card).

MORRIS P. RADOV LIBRARY
See: Congregation Brith Shalom - Jewish Center (3622)

RAE COLLECTION ON ARCHITECTURE
See: Monterey Public Library (9250)

BERNARD B. RAGINSKY RESEARCH LIBRARY
See: Institute for Research in Hypnosis (6932)

★11862★
RAHR-WEST ART MUSEUM - LIBRARY (Art)
Park St. at N. 8th
Manitowoc, WI 54220 Richard C. Quick, Dir.
Subjects: Art, county and state history. **Holdings:** 1000 volumes.

RAILROAD COMMISSION OF TEXAS
See: (Texas State) Railroad Commission of Texas (14119)

★11863★
RAILROAD AND PIONEER MUSEUM - LIBRARY (Hist)
710 Jack Baskin St.
Box 5126 Phone: (817)778-6873
Temple, TX 76505 Mary L. Irving, Libn. & Dir.
Founded: 1977. **Staff:** Prof 1. **Subjects:** Railroads, local and pioneer history. **Special Collections:** Original manuscripts. **Holdings:** 400 books. **Subscriptions:** 19 journals and other serials. **Services:** Interlibrary loan; copying; library open to the public for reference use only. **Remarks:** Maintained by the City of Temple, Texas.

★11864★
RAILROAD RETIREMENT BOARD - LIBRARY (Soc Sci, Law)
844 Rush St. Phone: (312)751-4928
Chicago, IL 60611 Kay G. Collins, Hd.Libn.
Founded: 1940. **Staff:** Prof 2. **Subjects:** Law, legislation, social sciences. **Holdings:** 80,000 volumes; 83 VF drawers of legislative materials; 28 VF drawers of miscellaneous unbound materials. **Subscriptions:** 179 journals and other serials. **Services:** Interlibrary loan; library open to the public by appointment. **Networks/Consortia:** Member of FEDLINK, Chicago Library System. **Staff:** Katherine M. Tsang, Asst.Libn..

★11865★
RAILWAY MAIL SERVICE - LIBRARY (Hist)
18 E. Rosemont Ave. Phone: (703)549-4095
Alexandria, VA 22301-2325 Dr. Frank R. Scheer, Cur.
Founded: 1950. **Staff:** Prof 1. Post office transportation, postal markings and labor unions. **Special Collections:** E.B. Bergman Schedule of Mail Routes Collection (2000 postal schedules); H.E. Rankin General Scheme Collection (1500 post office distribution schemes). **Holdings:** 900 books; 65 bound periodical volumes; 380,000 documents; 650 copies of rare publications; 400 unbound periodicals; 80 oral history audio cassettes; 5 video cassettes; 4 16mm films. **Subscriptions:** 14 journals and other serials. **Services:** Interlibrary loan; copying; library open to the public.

★11866★
RAILWAYS TO YESTERDAY, INC. - LEHIGH VALLEY TRANSPORTATION RESEARCH CENTER (Trans)
12th and Cumberland Sts.
General Office, 2nd Fl. Phone: (215)797-3242
Allentown, PA 18103 Douglas E. Peters, Hist./Libn.
Staff: 1. **Subjects:** Electric and steam railways. **Special Collections:** Company records of the Lehigh Valley Transit Company; Howard Sell Collection (photographs and negatives of Lehigh Valley area railways and trolley lines); trolley artifacts; James MacDonald Collection (railway photographs and negatives); Tom Ruddell Collection (railway negatives). **Holdings:** 150 volumes; 10 VF cabinets and 15 boxes of railway material, including railway maps and timetables; newspaper clippings. **Subscriptions:** 10 journals and other serials. **Services:** Center open to the public by appointment. **Publications:** Trolley Museum Reporter, 6/year.

★11867★
RAINBOW CHILD CARE COUNCIL - RAINBOW RESOURCE & TOY LIBRARY (Educ)
1801 Oak St. Phone: (707)253-0366
Napa, CA 94559 Jill Treseder, Rsrc.Libn.
Founded: 1979. **Staff:** Prof 1; Other 2. **Subjects:** Toys - infant, toddler, puzzles, large and small motor skill development, puppets, dramatic play, educational. **Holdings:** 515 books; 900 toys; puzzles; puppets; cassettes; phonograph records; musical instruments. **Subscriptions:** 13 journals and other serials. **Services:** Copying; library open to the public. **Networks/Consortia:** Member of U.S.A. Toy Library Association. **Publications:** Rainbow Newsletter, monthly - to members and available by request. **Special Indexes:** Toy inventory; picture index.

★11868★
RAINBOW FLEET, INC. - LIBRARY (Educ)
3016 Paseo Phone: (405)521-1426
Oklahoma City, OK 73103 Susan Moore Myers, Exec.Dir.
Staff: Prof 5. **Subjects:** Child development; infant stimulation; preschool enhancement, including language and sensorial development, pre-math skills, and practical life skills. **Special Collections:** Toys for handicapped children. **Holdings:** 2500 books; 3000 toys and games. **Services:** Library open to licensed daycare centers and homes, preschools, other programs providing group care for children, and parents.

★11869★
RAINIER NATIONAL BANK - INFORMATION CENTER (Bus-Fin)
Box 3966
Seattle, WA 98124 Vivienne C. Burke, Asst. V.P./Mgr.
Founded: 1968. **Staff:** Prof 3; Other 1. **Subjects:** Banking and finance. **Holdings:** 3200 books; 600 annual reports. **Subscriptions:** 600 journals and other serials; 32 newspapers. **Services:** Interlibrary loan; copying; center open to the public for reference use only with permission. **Automated Operations:** Computerized cataloging and serials. **Computerized Information Services:** DIALOG Information Services, DataTimes, OCLC. **Staff:** Vivian Chun, Res.Anl.; Krishna Sharma, Res.Anl..

RAINIER SCHOOL BRANCH LIBRARY
See: Washington State Library (17519)

WILLIAM M. RAINS LIBRARY
See: Loyola Law School (8086)

THE LEONARD S. AND JULIETTE K. RAKOW LIBRARY
See: Corning Museum of Glass (3799)

★11870★
RALSTON PURINA COMPANY - INFORMATION CENTER (Food-Bev, Med)
Checkerboard Square, 2RS Phone: (314)982-2056
St. Louis, MO 63164 Linda S. Lincks, Mgr.
Founded: 1929. **Staff:** Prof 3; Other 1. **Subjects:** Animal and human nutrition, veterinary medicine, food processing, food sanitation. **Special Collections:** Food and Agricultural Organization of the United Nations (FAO) Publications (20 VF drawers). **Holdings:** 13,000 volumes; 20 VF drawers of proceedings; 69 VF drawers of government reports. **Subscriptions:** 392 journals and other serials. **Services:** Interlibrary loan; copying; SDI; center open to the public by appointment. **Automated Operations:** Computerized cataloging, acquisitions, and ILL. **Computerized Information Services:** DIALOG Information Services, Pergamon ORBIT InfoLine, Inc., BRS Information Technologies, NLM, Dow Jones News/Retrieval, Mead Data Central, OCLC, I.P. Sharp Associates Limited, CAS ONLINE. **Networks/Consortia:** Member of St. Louis Regional Library Network. **Staff:** Beverly Sanders, Libn.; Peggy Zabel, Supv., Search Serv..

WILLO RALSTON MEMORIAL LIBRARY FOR HISTORICAL RESEARCH
See: Mondak Heritage Center (9188)

RALPH K. RAMSAYER, M.D. LIBRARY
See: Stark County Historical Society (13631)

★11871★
RAMSEY COUNTY HISTORICAL SOCIETY - JOSEPH E. KARTH RESEARCH CENTER - LIBRARY (Hist)
75 W. Fifth St., Rm. 323 Phone: (612)222-0701
St. Paul, MN 55102 Virginia B. Kunz, Exec.Dir.
Staff: Prof 5. **Subjects:** Local history. **Special Collections:** Heman Gibbs papers. **Holdings:** 300 books; maps; pamphlets; documents; pictures. **Services:** Library open to the public for reference use only.

★11872★
RAMSEY COUNTY LAW LIBRARY (Law)
1815 Court House Phone: (612)298-5208
St. Paul, MN 55102 Carol C. Florin, Lib.Dir.
Founded: 1935. **Staff:** Prof 1; Other 1. **Subjects:** Law - Minnesota, tax, real property, criminal, corporate; practice. **Special Collections:** Minnesota Supreme Court Briefs and Paperbooks, 1950 to present (1400 volumes). **Holdings:** 20,000 books; 300 bound periodical volumes. **Subscriptions:** 15 journals and other serials. **Services:** Interlibrary loan; copying; library open to the public with restrictions. **Networks/Consortia:** Member of Metronet.

★11873★
RAMSEY COUNTY MEDICAL SOCIETY - BOECKMANN LIBRARY (Med)
345 N. Smith Ave. Phone: (612)291-1209
St. Paul, MN 55102 Mary Sandra Tarman, Libn.
Founded: 1897. **Staff:** Prof 2; Other 3. **Subjects:** Medicine, nursing, hospital administration. **Special Collections:** Psychoanalytic Foundation of Minnesota Library (300 books; 7 periodicals). **Holdings:** 15,000 books; 28,500 bound periodical volumes; 6500 unbound periodical volumes; 18 VF drawers of pamphlets and clippings; 800 medical instruments and memorabilia. **Subscriptions:** 550 journals and other serials; 8 newspapers. **Services:** Interlibrary loan; copying; library open to the public with restrictions. **Computerized Information Services:** DIALOG Information Services, MEDLINE. **Networks/Consortia:** Member of Twin Cities Biomedical Consortium (TCBC), Greater Midwest Regional Medical Library Network.

RAMSEY LIBRARY
See: U.S. Army - TRADOC - Military Police School - Ramsey Library (14801)

★11874★
RANCHO LOS AMIGOS MEDICAL CENTER - HEALTH SCIENCES LIBRARY (Med)
7601 E. Imperial Hwy.
Downey, CA 90242-3456
Staff: Prof 1; Other 3. **Subjects:** Rehabilitation medicine, orthopedics, nursing, diabetes, pulmonary disease, rheumatology. **Holdings:** 6500 books; 15,000 bound periodical volumes; 250 Rancho resident papers; 650 audio cassettes. **Subscriptions:** 634 journals and other serials. **Services:** Interlibrary loan; copying; SDI; library open to the public. **Computerized Information Services:** MEDLINE, Pergamon ORBIT InfoLine, Inc. **Networks/Consortia:** Member of Los Angeles County Health Sciences

Library Consortium, Medical Library Group of Southern California and Arizona (MLGSCA), Pacific Southwest Regional Medical Library Service. **Publications:** New Book List, quarterly.

RANCHO LOS CERRITOS HISTORIC SITE
See: Long Beach Public Library (7945)

★11875★
RANCHO SANTA ANA BOTANIC GARDEN - LIBRARY (Biol Sci)
1500 N. College Ave. Phone: (714)625-8767
Claremont, CA 91711 Beatrice M. Beck, Libn.
Founded: 1927. **Staff:** Prof 1; Other 2. **Subjects:** Botany, horticulture, drought tolerant plants, ethnobotany of California Indians, evolutionary biology. **Special Collections:** Floras of the world. **Holdings:** 33,000 items; reprint collection; nursery catalogs. **Subscriptions:** 500 journals and other serials. **Services:** Interlibrary loan (limited); copying; library open to qualified users. **Automated Operations:** Computerized cataloging. **Computerized Information Services:** OCLC.

ANNE RAND RESEARCH LIBRARY
See: International Longshoremen's and Warehousemen's Union (7039)

★11876★
RAND CORPORATION - LIBRARY (Soc Sci)
1700 Main St.
Box 2138 Phone: (213)393-0411
Santa Monica, CA 90406-2138 Elizabeth D. Gill, Lib.Dir.
Founded: 1948. **Staff:** Prof 10; Other 26. **Subjects:** Policy analysis, decision-making, military strategy, international affairs, urban development, education, economics of medical care services, criminal and civil justice, regulatory policy, labor, population. **Special Collections:** Russian language collection in economics, political science, and military science (5000 monographs; 300 periodical titles). **Holdings:** 74,000 books; 21,000 bound periodical volumes; 213,000 documents and reports; 5000 maps. **Subscriptions:** 3400 journals and other serials; 52 newspapers. **Services:** Interlibrary loan; library not open to the public. **Automated Operations:** Computerized cataloging and serials. **Computerized Information Services:** Aerospace Online, BRS Information Technologies, Groupement de la Caisse des Depots Automatisation pour le Management (G.CAM), Data Resources (DRI), DataTimes, DIALOG Information Services, DTIC, Inter-university Consortium for Political and Social Research (ICPSR), Survey Methodology Information System (SMIS), LEXIS, MEDLARS, University of California On-Line Union Catalog (MELVYL), NASA/RECON, NewsNet, Inc., NEXIS, ORION, Pergamon ORBIT InfoLine, Inc., RLIN, RLIN, Roper Center for Public Opinion Research, I.P. Sharp Associates Limited, The Source Information Network, VU/TEXT Information Services, Washington Alert Service, WESTLAW, WILSONLINE. **Networks/Consortia:** Member of CLASS. **Publications:** Accessions List, monthly; Interest List, irregular; periodicals listing, monthly. **Special Catalogs:** Microfiche catalog, monthly. **Staff:** Jill Brophy, Assoc.Dir.; Andrea Burkenroad, Hd., Per.Serv.; Doris Helfer, Hd., Tech.Serv.; Roberta Shanman, Hd., Ref.Serv.; Joan Schlimgen, Hd., User Serv.; Marge Behrens, Slavic/Oriental Libn.; Walter Nelson, Hd., Class.Info.Serv.; Barbara Neff, Hd., ILL.

★11877★
RAND CORPORATION - LIBRARY (Soc Sci, Mil)
2100 M St., N.W. Phone: (202)296-5000
Washington, DC 20037-1270 Casey Kane, Libn.
Staff: 2. **Subjects:** Social studies, military studies, housing and urban affairs, education. **Holdings:** 10,000 books; 2000 Congressional hearings. **Subscriptions:** 250 journals and other serials; 6 newspapers. **Services:** Interlibrary loan; library not open to the public. **Automated Operations:** Computerized serials. **Networks/Consortia:** Member of Interlibrary Users Association (IUA).

★11878★
RAND MC NALLY AND COMPANY - LIBRARY (Geog-Map, Publ)
8255 Central Park Ave. Phone: (312)673-9100
Skokie, IL 60076 Philip L. Forstall, Libn.
Founded: 1949. **Staff:** Prof 1. **Subjects:** U.S. history, geography, cartography, graphic arts, place names, railroads, business. **Special Collections:** Toponymy (place names); historical/archival collection of company publications. **Holdings:** 17,000 volumes; 800 atlases; 30,000 sheet maps (in cartographic department); 400 pamphlets. **Subscriptions:** 120 journals and other serials. **Services:** Interlibrary loan (to libraries and specialized research institutions); geographical reference service to librarians; library open to graduate researchers for reference use. **Publications:** Accessions lists; subject bibliographies.

OLLIE A. RANDALL LIBRARY
See: The National Council on the Aging, Inc. (9640)

WILLIAM MADISON RANDALL LIBRARY
See: University of North Carolina, Wilmington - William Madison Randall Library (16648)

★11879★
RANDOLPH CIRCUIT COURT - LAW LIBRARY (Law)
Courthouse, Rm. 307 Phone: (317)584-7070
Winchester, IN 47394 Joan Benson, Libn.
Subjects: Law. **Holdings:** 15,000 volumes. **Services:** Library open to the public with restrictions.

★11880★
RANDOLPH COUNTY GENEALOGICAL SOCIETY - LIBRARY (Hist)
Asheboro Public Library
201 Worth St.
Asheboro, NC 27203 Phone: (919)629-3329
Subjects: Genealogy. **Holdings:** 2000 books; 82 reels of microfilm; photographs; VF drawers of memorabilia; historical maps. **Services:** Copying; library open to the public with restrictions.

LYDIA RANKIN TECHNICAL LIBRARY
See: Boeing Helicopter Company (1693)

HARRY RANSOM HUMANITIES RESEARCH CENTER
See: University of Texas, Austin - Harry Ransom Humanities Research Center (16931)

R.C. RANSOM MEMORIAL LIBRARY
See: Payne Theological Seminary (11120)

RAPAPORT PROFESSIONAL LIBRARY
See: Osawatomie State Hospital (10939)

★11881★
RAPID CITY REGIONAL HOSPITAL - HEALTH SCIENCES LIBRARY (Med)
353 Fairmont Blvd. Phone: (605)341-7101
Rapid City, SD 57700-6000 Patricia J. Hamilton, Dept.Mgr./Lib.Serv.
Founded: 1927. **Staff:** Prof 2; Other 1. **Subjects:** Medicine, nursing, natural and social sciences. **Holdings:** 6673 books; 4735 unbound periodicals; 2300 government documents. **Subscriptions:** 426 journals and other serials. **Services:** Interlibrary loan; copying; library open to the public with restrictions. **Computerized Information Services:** OCLC, MEDLARS, BRS Information Technologies; EasyLink, DOCLINE (electronic mail services). **Networks/Consortia:** Member of Greater Midwest Regional Medical Library Network. **Formerly:** Rushmore National Health System. **Staff:** Carol Davis, Ref.Libn..

★11882★
RAPIDES GENERAL HOSPITAL - MEDICAL LIBRARY (Med)
Box 30101 Phone: (318)473-3563
Alexandria, LA 71301 Janet Dawkins, Libn.
Founded: 1963. **Staff:** Prof 1. **Subjects:** Medicine. **Holdings:** 1800 books; 1112 bound periodical volumes. **Subscriptions:** 65 journals and other serials. **Services:** Interlibrary loan; library open to public at librarian's discretion.

★11883★
RARITAN BAY MEDICAL CENTER - HEALTH SCIENCE LIBRARY (Med)
530 New Brunswick Ave. Phone: (201)442-3700
Perth Amboy, NJ 08861 Catherine A. Hilman, Hea.Sci.Libn.
Staff: Prof 1; Other 1. **Subjects:** Medicine, nursing, allied health sciences. **Special Collections:** Administrative collection (200 volumes). **Holdings:** 1800 books; 770 bound periodical volumes. **Subscriptions:** 140 journals and other serials. **Services:** Library not open to the public. **Formerly:** Perth Amboy General Hospital.

RASCHE MEMORIAL LIBRARY
See: Milwaukee Area Technical College (9003)

RASPET FLIGHT RESEARCH LABORATORY
See: Mississippi State University (9115)

ERICH RATH MUSIC LIBRARY & LISTENING CENTER
See: Hollins College - Music Department (6394)

★11884★
JACK G. RAUB COMPANY - LIBRARY (Sci-Engr)
24741 Chrisanta Dr. Phone: (714)859-4948
Mission Viejo, CA 92691 Lorraine B. Boies, Libn.
Staff: Prof 1; Other 1. **Subjects:** Soil engineering, civil engineering, water resources, public works, transportation, laws and codes. **Special Collections:** Environmental Impact Reports; Advance and Community Planning; geotechnical documents. **Holdings:** 7000 books; 5000 periodical volumes; 5000 engineering drawings; 8 VF drawers of newspaper clippings; 5 trays of microfiche; 6000 plans; 2000 photographs and slides. **Subscriptions:** 253 journals and other serials. **Services:** Library not open to the public. **Automated Operations:** Computerized cataloging, acquisitions, serials, and circulation. **Staff:** Norma L. Chakrabarty, Assoc.Libn..

RAUH MEMORIAL LIBRARY
See: Children's Museum of Indianapolis (3121)

★11885★
RAVENSWOOD HOSPITAL MEDICAL CENTER - MEDICAL-NURSING LIBRARY (Med)
4550 N. Winchester at Wilson Phone: (312)878-4300
Chicago, IL 60640 Mr. Zia Solomon Gilliana, Med.Libn.
Founded: 1908. **Staff:** Prof 1; Other 2. **Subjects:** Medicine, nursing. **Special Collections:** History of medicine; history of nursing. **Holdings:** 3747 books; 4415 bound periodical volumes. **Subscriptions:** 201 journals and other serials. **Services:** Interlibrary loan; copying; SDI; library open to the public with restrictions. **Publications:** Guide to the Library.

MARGUERITE RAWALT RESOURCE CENTER
See: Business and Professional Women's Foundation (2073)

★11886★
RAWLE AND HENDERSON - LAW LIBRARY (Law)
211 S. Broad St. Phone: (215)875-4000
Philadelphia, PA 19107 Christine Harvan, Libn.
Founded: 1783. **Staff:** Prof 1; Other 2. **Subjects:** Law - ships and shipping, medical malpractice, tax, securities, general practice. **Holdings:** 10,000 books; 505 Paper Books. **Subscriptions:** 203 journals and other serials. **Services:** Interlibrary loan; library not open to the public. **Computerized Information Services:** LEXIS, DIALOG Information Services, WESTLAW. **Publications:** Paper Books (firm's important cases). **Remarks:** This is said to be the oldest established law firm and law library in Philadelphia.

ALEXANDER RAXLEN MEMORIAL LIBRARY
See: Doctors Hospital (4326)

ISAAC RAY MEDICAL LIBRARY
See: Butler Hospital (2079)

★11887★
RAY-O-VAC CORP. - TECHNOLOGY CENTER LIBRARY (Sci-Engr)
630 Forward Dr. Phone: (608)275-3340
Madison, WI 53711 C. Saxe, Sr.Tech.Adv.
Founded: 1967. **Staff:** Prof 1. **Subjects:** Electrochemistry, primary batteries, chemical engineering, plastics, management. **Special Collections:** U.S. Government and internal reports. **Holdings:** 2200 books; 1100 bound periodical volumes; 3000 patents; 9600 technical reports. **Subscriptions:** 100 journals and other serials. **Services:** Interlibrary loan; copying; library open to the public by appointment. **Networks/Consortia:** Member of Multitype Advisory Library Committee (MALC). **Publications:** Acquisition List, monthly; Current Awareness Bulletin - both for internal distribution only. **Special Indexes:** Uniterm Index to documents collection.

OTTO ERNEST RAYBURN LIBRARY OF FOLKLORE
See: University of Arkansas, Fayetteville - Special Collections Division (15835)

★11888★
SAM RAYBURN FOUNDATION - SAM RAYBURN LIBRARY (Hist)
Bonham, TX 75418 Phone: (214)583-2455
H.G. Dulaney, Lib.Dir.
Founded: 1957. **Staff:** Prof 4; Other 2. **Subjects:** History of Congress and its leaders; history of political parties; Texas history, especially in 4th Congressional District. **Special Collections:** Congressional documents from the First Continental Congress to present. **Holdings:** 15,000 books; 100 bound periodical volumes; 30 VF drawers of personal papers and correspondence (microfilm) of Honorable Sam Rayburn, Speaker; Presidential letters to the Speaker; original letters from his mother to the Speaker; tape recordings of his speeches. **Services:** Library open to the public with restrictions. **Special Indexes:** Guide to contents of Speaker's papers. **Remarks:** Library is also a museum concerning the career of Speaker Rayburn.

SAM RAYBURN MEMORIAL VETERANS CENTER
See: U.S. Veterans Administration (TX-Bonham) (15651)

★11889★
RAYCHEM CORPORATION - CORPORATE LIBRARY (Sci-Engr)
300 Constitution Dr. Phone: (415)361-3282
Menlo Park, CA 94025 Phyllis Oda, Mgr.
Staff: Prof 3; Other 4. **Subjects:** Chemistry, polymer science, electronics. **Holdings:** 6000 books; 8000 bound periodical volumes. **Subscriptions:** 450 journals and other serials. **Services:** Interlibrary loan; library not open to the public. **Computerized Information Services:** Pergamon ORBIT InfoLine, Inc., DIALOG Information Services, BRS Information Technologies; BASIS (internal database).

★11890★
RAYMOND, CHABOT, MARTIN, PARE - LIBRARY/BIBLIOTHEQUE (Bus-Fin)
600, de la Gauchetiere, W., No. 1900 Phone: (514)878-2691
Montreal, PQ, Canada H3B 4L8 Huguette Thibault, Libn.
Founded: 1979. **Staff:** Prof 1. **Subjects:** Accounting, management, business, computer science. **Holdings:** 4500 books; 125 bound periodical volumes. **Services:** Interlibrary loan; library open to the public. **Automated Operations:** Computerized cataloging. **Computerized Information Services:** Dun & Bradstreet Corporation, DIALOG Information Services.

JOHN RAYMOND MEMORIAL LIBRARY
See: Waukegan Historical Society (17573)

★11891★
RAYTHEON COMPANY - BADGER ENGINEERS, INC. - LIBRARY (Sci-Engr)
One Broadway Phone: (617)494-7565
Cambridge, MA 02142 Jacqueline Bassett, Libn.
Staff: Prof 1; Other 1. **Subjects:** Chemical engineering, energy, petroleum refining, environmental engineering. **Holdings:** 4500 books; 1500 bound periodical volumes; 8 VF drawers of patents; 16 VF drawers of codes and specifications; 20 VF drawers of process data files; 41 VF drawers of pamphlets, reprints, special services. **Subscriptions:** 100 journals and other serials. **Services:** Interlibrary loan; library not open to the public. **Computerized Information Services:** DIALOG Information Services.

★11892★
RAYTHEON COMPANY - BUSINESS INFORMATION CENTER (Bus-Fin)
141 Spring St. Phone: (617)860-2579
Lexington, MA 02173 Jerry O'Connor, Mgr.
Founded: 1960. **Staff:** Prof 1; Other 1. **Subjects:** General business, marketing, economics, census, finance. **Special Collections:** Annual reports; Arthur D. Little reports; SRI Long Range Planning reports; Conference Board reports. **Holdings:** 1200 books; 10,000 archival materials and back copies of journals; 80 VF drawers; 2 cabinets of microfilm. **Subscriptions:** 350 journals and other serials; 15 newspapers. **Services:** Interlibrary loan; center not open to the public. **Computerized Information Services:** DIALOG Information Services, LEXIS, NEXIS, Dow Jones News/Retrieval, Dun & Bradstreet Corporation. **Publications:** Periodical holdings, annual.

★11893★
RAYTHEON COMPANY - ELECTROMAGNETIC SYSTEMS DIVISION - ENGINEERING LIBRARY (Sci-Engr)
6380 Hollister Ave. Phone: (805)967-5511
Goleta, CA 93117 Sheila Anderson, Libn.
Founded: 1957. **Staff:** Prof 1. **Subjects:** Electrical and electronic engineering; communications; electrochemical machining; navigation and guidance systems and equipment; materials science. **Holdings:** 3000 volumes; 2 drawers of microfiche of government documents; 2400 microfilm cartridges of specifications, standards, military documents, vendor information; 88 VF drawers of hardcopy specifications and standards. **Subscriptions:** 126 journals and other serials.

★11894★
RAYTHEON COMPANY - EQUIPMENT DIVISION - TECHNICAL INFORMATION CENTER (Sci-Engr)
528 Boston Post Rd. Phone: (617)443-9521
Sudbury, MA 01776 Robert Seidel, Libn.
Founded: 1963. **Staff:** Prof 2; Other 2. **Subjects:** Electronics, computers, communications. **Holdings:** 5000 books; 30 bound periodical volumes; 300 other cataloged items; 330,000 microfiche of NASA reports; 350 tape cassettes; 2 files of reports on microfiche. **Subscriptions:** 160 journals and other serials. **Services:** Interlibrary loan; center not open to the public. **Computerized Information Services:** DIALOG Information Services, DTIC, OCLC. **Networks/Consortia:** Member of NELINET. **Publications:** Technical Information Center Bulletin, monthly - for internal distribution only. **Special Catalogs:** Raytheon Libraries Union List of Books; Raytheon Libraries Union List of Serials.

★11895★
RAYTHEON COMPANY - EQUIPMENT DIVISION - TECHNICAL INFORMATION CENTER (Sci-Engr)
Boston Post Rd. Phone: (617)440-8065
Wayland, MA 01778 Joanne Portsch-Snow, Libn.
Founded: 1955. **Staff:** Prof 1; Other 3. **Subjects:** Electronics, electrical engineering, physics, radar, mathematics. **Holdings:** 6000 books; 555 bound periodical volumes; 2 files of reports on microfiche; 350 tape cassettes. **Subscriptions:** 350 journals and other serials. **Services:** Interlibrary loan; center not open to the public. **Automated Operations:** Computerized cataloging. **Computerized Information Services:** DIALOG Information Services, OCLC. **Publications:** TIC Bulletin, monthly - for internal distribution only. **Special Catalogs:** Raytheon Libraries Union List of Serials, monthly (printout); Raytheon Libraries Union List of Books, quarterly (printout). **Special Indexes:** Technical Information Center Index to internal memos and reports, annual (printout).

★11896★
RAYTHEON COMPANY - LAW LIBRARY (Law)
Office of the General Counsel
141 Spring St. Phone: (617)860-4829
Lexington, MA 02173 Joan Cook, Libn.
Founded: 1930. **Subjects:** Law. **Holdings:** 2600 volumes. **Subscriptions:** 10 journals and other serials. **Services:** Library not open to the public.

★11897★
RAYTHEON COMPANY - MISSILE SYSTEMS DIVISION - BEDFORD LABORATORIES - TECHNICAL INFORMATION CENTER (Sci-Engr)
Hartwell Rd. Phone: (617)274-2231
Bedford, MA 01730 Lorraine Bick-Gregoire, Mgr.
Staff: Prof 3; Other 2. **Subjects:** Guided missiles, electronics, aerodynamics, physics, mathematics, management techniques. **Holdings:** 25,000 books; 50,000 research reports; 40,000 microfiche. **Subscriptions:** 175 journals and other serials. **Services:** Interlibrary loan; center not open to the public. **Computerized Information Services:** DIALOG Information Services, DTIC, NASA/RECON. **Publications:** Technical Abstract Bulletin, monthly - for internal distribution only; Library Scanner. **Staff:** Patricia Healey, Ref.Libn.; Michael Hedrich, Archv..

★11898★
RAYTHEON COMPANY - RESEARCH DIVISION - LIBRARY (Sci-Engr)
131 Spring St. Phone: (617)860-3190
Lexington, MA 02173 Vicary Maxant, Hd.Libn.
Founded: 1952. **Staff:** Prof 3. **Subjects:** Applied physics, advanced materials, semiconductor physics, physical chemistry. **Holdings:** 6000 books; 5000 bound periodical volumes; 15,000 technical reports; 9000 archival materials. **Subscriptions:** 350 journals and other serials. **Services:** Interlibrary loan; library open to the public with approval of security officer. **Automated Operations:** Computerized cataloging, serials, circulation, and ILL. **Computerized Information Services:** DIALOG Information Services, OCLC, DTIC, CAS ONLINE. **Networks/Consortia:** Member of NELINET. **Publications:** Accessions Bulletin, monthly; special bibliographies; Update, monthly. **Staff:** Irene Buono, Ser. & ILL Libn.; Johanna Grenda, Tech.Info.Spec..

★11899★
RAYTHEON COMPANY - SUBMARINE SIGNAL DIVISION - TECHNICAL INFORMATION CENTER (Sci-Engr)
1847 W. Main Rd.
Box 360 Phone: (401)847-8000
Portsmouth, RI 02871 Mark F. Baldwin, Mgr.
Founded: 1960. **Staff:** Prof 3; Other 2. **Subjects:** Electronics, acoustics, oceanography, antisubmarine warfare, environmental science. **Holdings:** 12,000 books; 1200 bound periodical volumes; 30,000 reports and documents. **Subscriptions:** 220 journals and other serials; 5 newspapers. **Services:** Interlibrary loan; center not open to the public. **Automated Operations:** Computerized cataloging, acquisitions, and circulation. **Computerized Information Services:** DIALOG Information Services, DTIC, OCLC, NEXIS, Data Resources (DRI); internal database. **Publications:** Accession Bulletin, monthly; News & Views, biweekly; TIC Bulletin, monthly. **Staff:** Bea Digovanni, Class.Docs.; Stephanie Mutty, Cat. & Res..

★11900★
RAYTHEON COMPANY - TECHNICAL INFORMATION CENTER (Info Sci)
400 Nickerson Rd. Phone: (617)460-8347
Marlborough, MA 01752 Dayle Reilly, Sr.Libn.
Staff: Prof 1. **Subjects:** Communications. **Holdings:** 1400 books. **Subscriptions:** 71 journals and other serials. **Services:** Interlibrary loan; center not open to the public. **Automated Operations:** Computerized cataloging and circulation. **Computerized Information Services:** DIALOG Information Services. **Networks/Consortia:** Member of NELINET.

RAYTHEON COMPANY - UNITED ENGINEERS & CONSTRUCTORS INC.
See: United Engineers & Constructors Inc. (14532)

★11901★
RAYTHEON SERVICE COMPANY - INFORMATION CENTER (Bus-Fin)
Spencer Laboratory
2 Wayside Rd. Phone: (617)272-9300
Burlington, MA 01803 Jean Cameron, Info.Spec.
Founded: 1970. **Staff:** Prof 1; Other 1. **Subjects:** Business, marketing. **Holdings:** 2000 books; 3000 reports. **Subscriptions:** 100 journals and other serials. **Services:** Interlibrary loan; copying; center open to the public by arrangement. **Computerized Information Services:** DIALOG Information Services, Dun & Bradstreet Corporation, OCLC. **Publications:** Accessions bulletin, bimonthly; Current Contents, monthly - both for internal distribution only.

RAZA UNIDA PARTY ARCHIVE
See: University of Texas, Austin - Benson Latin American Collection (16917)

★11902★
RCA CORPORATION - AEROSPACE & DEFENSE/ AUTOMATED SYSTEMS DIVISION - ENGINEERING LIBRARY (Sci-Engr)
Box 588 Phone: (617)229-3322
Burlington, MA 01803 Veronica Hsu, Tech.Libn.
Founded: 1955. **Staff:** Prof 1; Other 1. **Subjects:** Electronics, electrical engineering, optics, mathematics, computer technology, management. **Holdings:** 6000 books; 2500 bound periodical volumes; 2000 technical reports. **Subscriptions:** 200 journals and other serials. **Services:** Interlibrary loan; library not open to the public. **Computerized Information Services:** DIALOG Information Services, BRS Information Technologies, OCLC, DTIC. **Remarks:** An alternate telephone number is 229-5000.

RCA CORPORATION - DAVID SARNOFF LIBRARY
See: David Sarnoff Library (12887)

RCA CORPORATION - ENGINEERING LIBRARY
See: GE Aerospace - RCA Electronic Systems Department - Engineering Library (5486)

★11903★
RCA CORPORATION - GCS-GOVERNMENT COMMUNICATIONS SYSTEMS DIVISION - LIBRARY (Sci-Engr)
Delaware Ave. & Cooper St., Bldg. 10-6-5 Phone: (609)338-4046
Camden, NJ 08102 Nina R. Arrowood, Mgr., Lib.Rsrcs.
Founded: 1927. **Staff:** Prof 1; Other 2. **Subjects:** Electronics, mathematics, physics, computers, telecommunications. **Holdings:** 14,000 books; 3500

bound periodical volumes; 375 VF drawers of reports, reprints, conference proceedings. **Subscriptions:** 300 journals and other serials. **Services:** Interlibrary loan; library open to the public by appointment. **Automated Operations:** Computerized serials. **Computerized Information Services:** DIALOG Information Services, BRS Information Technologies. **Publications:** Library News. **Special Catalogs:** Catalog of reports (card).

RCA CORPORATION - LIBRARY
See: Burle Industries - Library (2043)

RCA CORPORATION - PICTURE TUBE DIVISION
See: Thomson Consumer Electronics, Inc. - Picture Tube Division (14168)

RCA CORPORATION - RCA AEROSPACE AND DEFENSE - ASTRO-SPACE DIVISION - LIBRARY
See: General Electric Company - Astro-Space Division (5525)

RCA CORPORATION - RCA CONSUMER ELECTRONICS
See: Thomson Consumer Electronics, Inc. (14167)

RCA CORPORATION - SOLID STATE DIVISION
See: General Electric Company - Solid State Division (5536)

★11904★
RCM CAPITAL MANAGEMENT - RESEARCH LIBRARY (Bus-Fin)
Four Embarcadero Center, Suite 2900 Phone: (415)954-5474
San Francisco, CA 94111 Maggie O'Brien, Res.Libn.
Founded: 1976. **Staff:** Prof 2; Other 2. **Subjects:** Investment. **Holdings:** 50 books; 6000 company reports; 5000 broker reports; 20,000 company reports on microfiche. **Subscriptions:** 350 journals and other serials; 10 newspapers. **Services:** Interlibrary loan; library not open to the public. **Computerized Information Services:** DIALOG Information Services, Dow Jones News/Retrieval, NewsNet, Inc., VU/TEXT Information Services. **Formerly:** Rosenberg Capital Management.

SIR HERBERT READ ARCHIVES
See: University of Victoria - Mc Pherson Library - Special Collections (17024)

★11905★
READER'S DIGEST - ADVERTISING AND MARKETING LIBRARY (Publ)
200 Park Ave. Phone: (212)907-6898
New York, NY 10166 Helen Fledderus, Libn.
Staff: 2. **Subjects:** Advertising, marketing, media research. **Holdings:** 800 volumes; 125 VF drawers of commodity and industry data; 6 VF drawers of media information. **Subscriptions:** 150 journals and other serials. **Services:** Interlibrary loan. **Computerized Information Services:** NEXIS, DIALOG Information Services, The Source Information Network.

★11906★
READER'S DIGEST - INDEX (Publ)
Pleasantville, NY 10570 Phone: (914)241-5194
Adrienne Bova Velardi, Ed.
Founded: 1922. **Staff:** 6. **Holdings:** Articles and book condensations; anecdotes in the magazine, 1950 to present. **Services:** Index area not open to the public; staff will answer inquiries. **Computerized Information Services:** STAIRS, RAMIS (internal databases).

★11907★
READER'S DIGEST ASSOCIATION - GENERAL BOOKS LIBRARY (Publ)
260 Madison Ave., 6th Fl. Phone: (212)850-7044
New York, NY 10016 Jo Manning, Libn./Hd.
Founded: 1975. **Staff:** Prof 2; Other 1. **Subjects:** Bible, arts and crafts, American history, nature. **Special Collections:** Reader's Digest, 1922 to present; Reader's Digest international books (microfiche). **Holdings:** 30,000 books; New York Times, 1851 to present, on microfilm. **Subscriptions:** 150 journals and other serials. **Services:** Interlibrary loan; library not open to the public. **Computerized Information Services:** DIALOG Information Services, NEXIS. **Publications:** Books! (acquisition list), monthly. **Staff:** Nettie Seaberry, Assoc.Libn..

★11908★
READER'S DIGEST MAGAZINES LIMITED - EDITORIAL LIBRARY (Publ)
215 Redfern Ave. Phone: (514)934-0751
Montreal, PQ, Canada H3Z 2V9 Colette Nishizaki, Libn.
Founded: 1973. **Staff:** Prof 1; Other 1. **Subjects:** Canadiana. **Holdings:** 6000 books; 22 VF drawers of newspaper clippings. **Subscriptions:** 200 journals and other serials; 10 newspapers. **Services:** Interlibrary loan; library not open to the public. **Automated Operations:** Computerized cataloging. **Computerized Information Services:** Info Globe, Infomart; internal database. **Special Indexes:** Index to Canadian Reader's Digest.

★11909★
READING HOSPITAL & MEDICAL CENTER - MEDICAL LIBRARY (Med)
Sixth & Spruce Sts. Phone: (215)378-6418
Reading, PA 19603 Melinda Robinson Paquette, Med.Libn.
Founded: 1940. **Staff:** Prof 1. **Subjects:** Medicine, medical specialties, medical ethics, consumer health education. **Holdings:** 4000 books; 18,000 bound periodical volumes; 4 VF drawers; 300 audiotapes. **Subscriptions:** 200 journals and other serials. **Services:** Interlibrary loan; copying; SDI; library open to the public by appointment for research and reference. **Computerized Information Services:** BRS Information Technologies. **Networks/Consortia:** Member of Greater Northeastern Regional Medical Library Program, Central Pennsylvania Health Sciences Library Association (CPHSLA), Berks County Library Association (BCLA). **Publications:** Newsletter - for internal distribution only.

★11910★
READING HOSPITAL & MEDICAL CENTER - READING HOSPITAL SCHOOL OF NURSING LIBRARY (Med)
Reading, PA 19603 Phone: (215)378-6359
Catherine R. Boyer, Libn.
Founded: 1935. **Staff:** Prof 1; Other 1. **Subjects:** Nursing, psychiatry, psychology. **Special Collections:** History of nursing. **Holdings:** 8590 volumes. **Subscriptions:** 63 journals and other serials. **Services:** Interlibrary loan; copying; SDI; library open to the public by appointment. **Networks/Consortia:** Member of Berks County Library Association (BCLA), Central Pennsylvania Health Sciences Library Association (CPHSLA). **Publications:** RHSN Library News, irregular.

★11911★
READING PUBLIC MUSEUM AND ART GALLERY - REFERENCE LIBRARY (Art, Sci-Engr)
500 Museum Rd. Phone: (215)371-5850
Reading, PA 19611-1425 Bruce L. Dietrich, Dir.
Staff: Prof 1; Other 1. **Subjects:** Art, natural science, anthropology. **Special Collections:** Unger Geology Collection; American Bureau of Ethnology Collection. **Holdings:** 3000 books; 2000 bound periodical volumes; 4 VF drawers of museum catalogs; 4 VF drawers of artist catalogs; 4 VF drawers of art catalogs; 3000 unbound periodicals. **Subscriptions:** 30 journals and other serials. **Services:** Interlibrary loan; library open to the public for reference use only with advance written permission. **Publications:** List of publications - available upon request.

★11912★
READING REHABILITATION HOSPITAL - MEDICAL LIBRARY (Med)
Rte. 1, Box 250 Phone: (215)777-7615
Reading, PA 19607 Margaret Hsieh, Libn.
Founded: 1977. **Staff:** Prof 1. **Subjects:** Rehabilitation, physical medicine, neurology, diabetes, spinal cord and head injuries, communication disorders. **Holdings:** 1000 books; 1000 bound periodical volumes; 217 videotapes; 114 audio cassettes; 82 filmstrips; 56 slide programs. **Subscriptions:** 102 journals and other serials. **Services:** Interlibrary loan; copying; library open to the public by appointment. **Automated Operations:** Computerized serials. **Computerized Information Services:** BRS Information Technologies. Performs searches on fee basis. **Networks/Consortia:** Member of Central Pennsylvania Health Sciences Library Association (CPHSLA), Cooperative Hospital Libraries, Berks County Library Association (BCLA). **Publications:** Rehab. Scanner, quarterly - for internal distribution only.

★11913★
READING SCHOOL DISTRICT PLANETARIUM - LIBRARY (Sci-Engr)
1211 Parkside Dr., S. Phone: (215)371-5854
Reading, PA 19611-1441 Bruce L. Dietrich, Dir. of Planetarium
Founded: 1969. **Staff:** 1. **Subjects:** Astronomy. **Holdings:** 900 books; 100 bound periodical volumes; 7000 35mm slides; 1 VF drawer of manuscripts;

500 magnetic tapes; 2 VF drawers of clippings and pamphlets; 25 film loops; 15 movies. **Services:** Library open to the public with written permission.

WILLIAM READY DIVISION OF ARCHIVES AND RESEARCH COLLECTIONS
See: Mc Master University - The William Ready Division of Archives and Research Collections (8256)

LINDLEY B. REAGAN HEALTH SCIENCES LIBRARY
See: Memorial Hospital of Burlington County (8647)

★11914★
REAL ESTATE RESEARCH CORPORATION - LIBRARY (Bus-Fin)
72 W. Adams St. Phone: (312)346-5885
Chicago, IL 60603 Mary Oleksy, Libn.
Staff: Prof 2; Other 2. **Subjects:** Real estate management, urban planning, appraisal, land use, housing. **Holdings:** 1100 books; 100 bound periodical volumes; 20,000 internal reports on microfiche; 40 VF drawers. **Subscriptions:** 300 journals and other serials; 6 newspapers. **Services:** Interlibrary loan; library open to the public with permission of librarian.

REAL ESTATE, SHOPPING CENTER & URBAN DEVELOPMENT INFORMATION CENTER
See: The Vineyard (17346)

LAUREN TAYLOR REARDON FAMILY LIBRARY
See: Children's Medical Center of Dallas (3117)

GEORGE REAVIS LIBRARY
See: Boulder Valley Public Schools, Region 2 - Professional Library (1775)

★11915★
REAVIS & MC GRATH - LAW LIBRARY (Law)
345 Park Ave. Phone: (212)486-9500
New York, NY 10154 Steven A. Lastres, Hd.Libn.
Staff: Prof 3; Other 3. **Subjects:** Law, securities, corporate law. **Holdings:** 20,000 books; 1000 bound periodical volumes; 4 drawers of microfiche; 36 reels of microfilm. **Subscriptions:** 80 journals and other serials; 10 newspapers. **Services:** Interlibrary loan; copying; library open to SLA members by appointment. **Computerized Information Services:** DIALOG Information Services, LEXIS, NEXIS, WESTLAW, Dow Jones News/ Retrieval, Dun & Bradstreet Corporation, ABA/net, VU/TEXT Information Services, PHINet FedTax Database. Performs searches on fee basis. **Special Indexes:** Prospectus and tender offer file (card). **Staff:** Priscilla Toribio, Cat.; Stuart C. Hancock, Asst.Libn.; Damian Calderon, ILL Coord..

★11916★
REBOUND, INC. - CORPORATE LIBRARY (Med)
103 Hazel Path Phone: (615)822-9010
Hendersonville, TN 37075 Virginia Collier, Libn.
Founded: 1987. **Staff:** Prof 1; Other 1. **Subjects:** Head injuries, rehabilitation, medical management, administration. **Special Collections:** Brain injury (periodicals). **Holdings:** 150 books; 85 audiotapes; 100 videotapes. **Subscriptions:** 40 journals and other serials. **Services:** Interlibrary loan; copying; library open to the public for reference use only. **Automated Operations:** Computerized cataloging. **Computerized Information Services:** DIALOG Information Services.

RECON/OPTICAL, INC. - CAI
See: CAI (2109)

★11917★
RECONSTRUCTIONIST RABBINICAL COLLEGE - MORDECAI M. KAPLAN LIBRARY (Rel-Phil)
Church Rd. & Greenwood Ave. Phone: (215)576-0800
Wyncote, PA 19095 Susan Frank, Libn.
Founded: 1968. **Staff:** Prof 1; Other 2. **Subjects:** Judaica, Hebraica, Rabbinics, Bible, Jewish history and sociology, religion, philosophy. **Special Collections:** Mordecai M. Kaplan Collection; President's Library. **Holdings:** 30,000 books; 1500 bound periodical volumes. **Subscriptions:** 150 journals and other serials; 20 newspapers. **Services:** Interlibrary loan; copying; library open to the public. **Networks/Consortia:** Member of Southeastern Pennsylvania Theological Library Association (SEPTLA).

★11918★
RECORDING FOR THE BLIND, INC. - LIBRARY SERVICES DEPARTMENT (Aud-Vis)
20 Roszel Rd. Phone: (609)452-0606
Princeton, NJ 08540 John Kelly, Mgr., Lib.Serv.
Founded: 1948. **Staff:** Prof 4; Other 1. **Subjects:** Collection consists of recorded educational materials. **Holdings:** 70,000 titles on master tapes. **Services:** Library and recording service available to qualified print-handicapped students who are registered with RFB. **Automated Operations:** Computerized cataloging and circulation. **Computerized Information Services:** BRS Information Technologies, OCLC; MINISIS (internal database); SpecialNet (electronic mail service). Performs searches free of charge to registered borrowers. **Networks/Consortia:** Member of FEDLINK, National Library Service for the Blind & Physically Handicapped (NLS). **Special Catalogs:** Catalog of recorded books.

★11919★
RECORDING INDUSTRY ASSOCIATION OF AMERICA - REFERENCE LIBRARY (Bus-Fin)
1020 Nineteenth St., N.W., Suite 200 Phone: (202)775-0101
Washington, DC 20036 James Fishel, Exec.Dir.
Subjects: Audio and video recording industry. **Holdings:** Books; magazines; clippings; other cataloged materials. **Formerly:** Located in New York, NY.

★11920★
RED CROSS OF CONSTANTINE - UNITED GRAND IMPERIAL COUNCIL - EDWARD A. GLAD MEMORIAL LIBRARY (Rec)
14 E. Jackson Blvd., Suite 1700 Phone: (312)427-5670
Chicago, IL 60604 G. Wilbur Bell, Grand Recorder
Founded: 1974. **Staff:** 2. **Subjects:** Freemasonry, American history. **Holdings:** 1700 books; 50 periodical volumes; 200 tapes. **Subscriptions:** 20 journals and other serials; 5 newspapers. **Services:** Library open to Masonic researchers.

★11921★
RED DEER ADVOCATE - NEWSPAPER LIBRARY (Publ)
2950 Bremner Ave. Phone: (403)343-2400
Red Deer, AB, Canada T4N 5G3 Patricia J. Goulet, Libn.
Staff: Prof 1. **Subjects:** Newspaper reference topics. **Special Collections:** Biography files (240). **Holdings:** 100 books; 300 bound periodical volumes; 100 VF drawers of newspaper clippings; 312 reels of microfilm; 15,000 photographs. **Subscriptions:** 10 journals and other serials; 10 newspapers. **Services:** Copying; library open to the public.

★11922★
RED DEER REGIONAL HOSPITAL CENTRE - LEARNING RESOURCE CENTRE (Med)
3942 50A Ave. Phone: (403)343-4557
Red Deer, AB, Canada T4N 4E7 Elizabeth Kavanagh, Libn.
Founded: 1981. **Staff:** Prof 1. **Subjects:** Medicine, nursing, allied health sciences, hospital administration. **Holdings:** 850 books; 520 bound periodical volumes; 200 videotapes; 500 audiotapes; 120 filmstrips. **Subscriptions:** 115 journals and other serials. **Services:** Interlibrary loan; copying; center open to the public for reference use only.

★11923★
REDDY COMMUNICATIONS, INC. - INFORMATION/ RESEARCH SERVICES (Energy)
4300 San Mateo, N.E. Phone: (505)884-7500
Albuquerque, NM 87110 Ann M. Klos, Mgr.
Staff: Prof 1; Other 1. **Subjects:** Public utilities, energy, communication techniques, public relations. **Holdings:** 800 books; 50 VF drawers of clippings, publications, reports, speeches. **Subscriptions:** 75 journals and other serials. **Services:** Services not open to the public. **Computerized Information Services:** DIALOG Information Services; internal database.

★11924★
REDEEMER COLLEGE - LIBRARY (Rel-Phil, Hum)
777 Hwy. 53, E.
P.O. Box 7349 Phone: (416)648-2131
Ancaster, ON, Canada L9G 3N6 Daniel A. Savage, Chf.Libn.
Founded: 1982. **Staff:** Prof 1; Other 7. **Subjects:** English, history, theology, philosophy, business, biology. **Special Collections:** Dutch Reformed theology and literature (in Dutch; 3000 volumes). **Holdings:** 75,000 books; 7386 bound periodical volumes. **Subscriptions:** 386 journals and other serials. **Services:** Interlibrary loan; copying; SDI; library open to the public. **Publications:** Monthly Acquisitions List; Annual Report; Library Handbook - available upon request.

★11925★
REDFIELD STATE HOSPITAL AND SCHOOL - MEDIA CENTER (Med)
Box 410 Phone: (605)472-2400
Redfield, SD 57469-0410 Lynn Loveland, Libn.
Founded: 1970. **Staff:** Prof 1. **Subjects:** Mental retardation, developmentally disabled, special education. **Holdings:** 3259 books; 838 filmstrips; 33 films; 932 phonograph records; 214 cassettes; 1200 games and manipulative toys; 19 videotapes; 6 computer programs; 25 microfiche. **Services:** Interlibrary loan; center open to Redfield and surrounding area residents. **Special Indexes:** Professional holdings purchased by other areas of this institution (online, card).

REDINGTON MUSEUM
See: Waterville Historical Society - Library and Archives (17568)

JULES REDISH MEMORIAL MEDICAL LIBRARY
See: South Nassau Communities Hospital (13409)

★11926★
J.W. REDMOND COMPANY - LIBRARY (Bus-Fin)
1750 Pennsylvania Ave., N.W.
Washington, DC 20006 June Johnson, Libn.
Staff: 1. **Subjects:** Stock market. **Holdings:** 3000 corporate files. **Services:** Interlibrary loan; copying; library open to the public by appointment.

★11927★
REDWOOD COMMUNITY ACTION AGENCY - ENERGY DEMONSTRATION CENTER - APPROPRIATE TECHNOLOGY LIBRARY
539 T St.
Eureka, CA 95501
Subjects: Passive solar energy, energy conservation, weatherization, solar retrofits, wind energy, wood stoves. **Holdings:** 1000 books; 18 bound periodical volumes; 2 shelves of energy policy and planning documents; 2 shelves of California Energy Commission reports; 1 shelf of energy curriculum; 3 VF drawers of general information files; 1 VF drawer of organization and agency files. **Remarks:** Presently inactive.

★11928★
REDWOOD EMPIRE ASSOCIATION - INFORMATION CENTER (Aud-Vis)
One Market Plaza
Spear St. Tower, Suite 1001 Phone: (415)543-8334
San Francisco, CA 94105 Stuart Nixon, Gen.Mgr.
Founded: 1925. **Staff:** Prof 3. **Subjects:** Scenic, recreational, and travel photos of nine counties in Northwestern California and Southwestern Oregon. **Holdings:** 100 reference books; news releases and fact sheets; 5000 black/white photographic negatives; 500 color transparencies and slides. **Services:** Interlibrary loan; copying; photographs and news releases available without charge; special stories on this area prepared to order; center open to the public by appointment. **Publications:** Visitors Guide to the Redwood Empire, Wine Country, irregular.

★11929★
REEBIE ASSOCIATES - LIBRARY (Trans)
200 Railroad Ave.
Box 1436 Phone: (203)661-8661
Greenwich, CT 06836 J.R. Thomson, Res.Assoc.
Founded: 1968. **Staff:** Prof 1. **Subjects:** Freight transportation. **Holdings:** 3500 books and reports; 450 subject and statistics files; annual reports; maps. **Subscriptions:** 54 journals and other serials. **Services:** Library not open to the public.

★11930★
REED COLLEGE - ERIC V. HAUSER MEMORIAL LIBRARY - SPECIAL COLLECTIONS (Hist)
Portland, OR 97202-8199 Phone: (503)771-1112
Victoria Hanawalt, Coll.Libn.
Subjects: College and Oregon history. **Special Collections:** Simeon Gannett Reed papers (19th century Oregon business); papers of Indian scout Edouard Chambreau, Thomas Lamb Eliot, poet Philip Whalen. **Holdings:** 81.5 linear feet of archival material. **Services:** Interlibrary loan; copying; collections open to the public with restrictions. **Automated Operations:** Computerized public access catalog, cataloging, and acquisitions. **Computerized Information Services:** DIALOG Information Services, BRS Information Technologies, MEDLARS, CAS ONLINE, WILSONLINE.

★11931★
REED INC. - TECHNICAL INFORMATION CENTRE (Sci-Engr)
207 Queen's Quay, W. Phone: (416)862-5006
Toronto, ON, Canada M5J 1A7 Jim Drake, Info.Spec.
Staff: Prof 1; Other 1. **Subjects:** Pulp and paper. **Holdings:** 2000 books; 30 bound periodical volumes. **Subscriptions:** 70 journals and other serials; 10 newspapers. **Services:** Interlibrary loan; copying; center open to the public by appointment. **Automated Operations:** Computerized cataloging, serials, and circulation. **Computerized Information Services:** DIALOG Information Services. **Publications:** Acquisitions list.

★11932★
REED LIGNIN INC. - LIGNIN CHEMICAL RESEARCH LIBRARY (Sci-Engr)
100 Hwy. 51, S. Phone: (715)359-6544
Rothschild, WI 54474-1198 Julie M. Stephany, Rec.Ck./Libn.
Founded: 1949. **Subjects:** Lignins. **Holdings:** 2100 volumes; 850 bound periodical volumes. **Subscriptions:** 70 journals and other serials. **Services:** Library open to the public with permission.

★11933★
REED, SMITH, SHAW AND MC CLAY - LAW LIBRARY (Law)
435 Sixth Ave. Phone: (412)288-3377
Pittsburgh, PA 15219 Barbara Rose Stewart, Hd.Libn.
Staff: Prof 2; Other 3. **Subjects:** Law. **Holdings:** 32,000 volumes. **Subscriptions:** 130 journals and other serials. **Services:** Library not open to the public. **Computerized Information Services:** DIALOG Information Services, LEXIS, Compu-Mark U.S., Dow Jones News/Retrieval.

★11934★
REED STENHOUSE, LTD. - RESEARCH DEPARTMENT LIBRARY (Bus-Fin)
20 Bay St., 18th Fl. Phone: (416)868-5520
Toronto, ON, Canada M5J 2N9
G.R.E. Bromwich, V.P., Res. & Info.Dept.
Founded: 1957. **Staff:** 3. **Subjects:** Insurance. **Holdings:** 300 volumes; clippings. **Subscriptions:** 80 journals and other serials. **Services:** Library not open to the public.

WALTER REED ARCHIVES
See: University of Virginia - Medical Center - Claude Moore Health Sciences Library (17038)

WALTER REED ARMY INSTITUTE OF RESEARCH
See: U.S. Army - Medical Research & Development Command - Walter Reed Army Institute of Research (14770)

WALTER REED ARMY MEDICAL CENTER
See: U.S. Army Hospitals - Walter Reed Army Medical Center - Medical Library (14839)

LLOYD REEDS MAP LIBRARY/URBAN DOCUMENTATION CENTRE
See: Mc Master University (8254)

WILLIAM MARION REEDY LIBRARY
See: St. Louis Public Library - Rare Book & Special Collections Department (12538)

MINA REES LIBRARY
See: CUNY - Graduate School and University Center (3941)

★11935★
MICHAEL REESE HOSPITAL & MEDICAL CENTER - DEPARTMENT OF LIBRARY & MEDIA RESOURCES (Med)
2908 S. Ellis Ave. Phone: (312)791-2474
Chicago, IL 60616 Dr. George Mozes, Dir.
Founded: 1935. **Staff:** Prof 2; Other 2. **Subjects:** Medicine, dentistry, nursing. **Holdings:** 12,000 books; 18,000 bound periodical volumes; 500 audio- and videotapes. **Subscriptions:** 435 journals and other serials. **Services:** Interlibrary loan; computer assisted instruction; library open to the public for reference use only. **Automated Operations:** Computerized cataloging. **Computerized Information Services:** NLM, Pergamon ORBIT InfoLine, Inc.

DAVID L. REEVES MEDICAL LIBRARY
See: Cottage Hospital (3813)

REEVES LIBRARY
See: Moravian College and Theological Seminary (9296)

REEVES MEMORIAL LIBRARY
See: Bridgeport Hospital (1840)

★11936★
REFLECTONE, INC. - ENGINEERING LIBRARY (Sci-Engr)
5125 Tampa West Blvd. Phone: (813)885-7481
Tampa, FL 33634 Betsy King, Libn.
Staff: Prof 1. **Subjects:** Aerodynamics of aircraft and helicopters; electronics; engineering. **Special Collections:** Flight simulation; military standards; aircraft manuals. **Holdings:** 350 books. **Subscriptions:** 80 journals and other serials. **Services:** Interlibrary loan; copying; SDI; library open to the public with prior permission. **Computerized Information Services:** DIALOG Information Services.

★11937★
REFORM CONGREGATION KENESETH ISRAEL - MEYERS LIBRARY (Rel-Phil)
York Rd. & Township Line Phone: (215)887-8700
Elkins Park, PA 19117 Sidney August, Libn.
Founded: 1870. **Staff:** Prof 1; Other 1. **Subjects:** Judaica. **Holdings:** 10,200 books; 200 bound periodical volumes. **Subscriptions:** 30 journals and other serials. **Services:** Interlibrary loan; library open to the public with permission.

★11938★
REFORMED BIBLE COLLEGE - LIBRARY (Rel-Phil)
1869 Robinson Rd., S.E. Phone: (616)458-0404
Grand Rapids, MI 49506 Dianne Zandbergen, Libn.
Staff: Prof 1; Other 10. **Subjects:** Reformed theology, religious education, missions, Bible study, cults. **Holdings:** 43,060 books; 20 VF drawers; 2793 tapes; 1005 volumes in microform; 706 filmstrips. **Subscriptions:** 289 journals and other serials. **Services:** Interlibrary loan; copying; library open to the public. **Automated Operations:** Computerized cataloging and acquisitions. **Networks/Consortia:** Member of Lakeland Area Library Network (LAKENET). **Publications:** Library handbook.

★11939★
REFORMED EPISCOPAL CHURCH - THEOLOGICAL SEMINARY - KUEHNER MEMORIAL LIBRARY (Rel-Phil)
4225 Chestnut St. Phone: (215)222-5158
Philadelphia, PA 19104-2998 Walter G. Truesdell, Libn.
Founded: 1886. **Subjects:** Theology, church history, Oxford Movement, English Reformation. **Holdings:** 25,000 volumes. **Subscriptions:** 85 journals and other serials. **Services:** Interlibrary loan; library open to the public for reference use only.

★11940★
REFORMED PRESBYTERIAN THEOLOGICAL SEMINARY - LIBRARY (Rel-Phil)
7418 Penn Ave. Phone: (412)731-8690
Pittsburgh, PA 15208 Rachel George, Libn.
Staff: Prof 1; Other 2. **Subjects:** Biblical studies, systematic and pastoral theology, church history, devotional works, sermons. **Special Collections:** Covenanter history and testimony; Psalms and psalmody. **Holdings:** 26,000 books; 3000 bound periodical volumes; 131 boxes of pamphlets; 1099 tapes; 57 reels of microfilm; 1256 microfiche. **Subscriptions:** 181 journals and other serials. **Services:** Interlibrary loan; copying; library open to the public by appointment with fee for borrowing. **Automated Operations:** Computerized cataloging and ILL. **Computerized Information Services:** DIALOG Information Services, BRS Information Technologies, OCLC; OCLC Link (electronic mail service). **Networks/Consortia:** Member of Pittsburgh Regional Library Center (PRLC).

★11941★
REFORMED THEOLOGICAL SEMINARY - LIBRARY (Rel-Phil)
5422 Clinton Blvd. Phone: (601)922-4988
Jackson, MS 39209 Thomas G. Reid, Jr., Dir.
Founded: 1966. **Staff:** Prof 3; Other 4. **Subjects:** Theology, religion, Biblical studies, Southern Presbyterianism, Christian education, marriage and family therapy. **Special Collections:** George C. Blackburn Memorial Library (Southern Presbyterian history and theology; 1100 volumes; pamphlets; periodicals; manuscripts); Southern Presbyterian Collection. **Holdings:** 70,000 books; 5000 bound periodical volumes; 5000 tapes; 32,000 microfiche; 2200 reels of microfilm. **Subscriptions:** 675 journals and other serials. **Services:** Interlibrary loan; copying; library open to the public. **Automated Operations:** Computerized cataloging. **Computerized Information Services:** BRS Information Technologies. **Networks/Consortia:** Member of SOLINET. **Staff:** William Yount, Pub.Serv.Libn.; John Delivuk, Tech.Serv.Libn..

★11942★
THE REFRIGERATION RESEARCH FOUNDATION - LIBRARY (Sci-Engr)
7315 Wisconsin Ave., Suite 1200N Phone: (301)652-5674
Bethesda, MD 20814 J. William Hudson, Exec.Dir.
Founded: 1944. **Subjects:** Handling of perishable commodities. **Holdings:** 500 volumes. **Subscriptions:** 50 journals and other serials. **Services:** Library open to the public.

★11943★
REFRIGERATION SERVICE ENGINEERS SOCIETY - LIBRARY (Sci-Engr)
1666 Rand Rd. Phone: (312)297-6464
Des Plaines, IL 60016-3552 Mr. Nari Sethna, Exec. V.P.
Subjects: Refrigeration and air conditioning. **Holdings:** Figures not available.

REGINA CLERI RESOURCE LIBRARY
See: Diocese of Tucson (4285)

REGINA COELI SEMINARY - AMERICAN CATHOLIC UNION - LIBRARY
See: American Catholic Union - Library (438)

★11944★
REGINA GENERAL HOSPITAL - HEALTH SCIENCES LIBRARY (Med)
1440 14th Ave. Phone: (306)359-4314
Regina, SK, Canada S4P 0W5
Ms. Terry Bouchard-DeVenney, Hea.Sci.Libn.
Founded: 1942. **Staff:** Prof 1; Other 2. **Subjects:** Pediatrics, obstetrics/gynecology, surgery, medicine, family practice, radiology, psychiatry, nursing, allied health sciences. **Holdings:** 8000 books; bound periodical volumes; VF drawers; AV programs. **Subscriptions:** 350 journals and other serials; 5 newspapers. **Services:** Interlibrary loan; copying; library open to the public by appointment. **Computerized Information Services:** BRS Information Technologies; Envoy 100 (electronic mail service). **Networks/Consortia:** Member of Health Sciences Library Council.

REGINA LIBRARY
See: Rivier College (12086)

★11945★
REGINA URBAN PLANNING DEPARTMENT - LIBRARY (Plan)
P.O. Box 1790 Phone: (306)569-7533
Regina, SK, Canada S4P 3C8 Eva Lukomski, Lib.Serv.Ck.
Founded: 1976. **Staff:** Prof 1. **Subjects:** Urban planning, zoning, housing, heritage conservation, land use and controls. **Holdings:** 5000 books. **Subscriptions:** 51 journals and other serials. **Services:** Interlibrary loan; copying; library open to the public for reference use only. **Publications:** Planning Department Publication Guide, annual. **Formerly:** Regina City Planning Department.

★11946★
REGIONAL MEMORIAL HOSPITAL - HEALTH SCIENCES LIBRARY (Med)
58 Baribeau Dr. Phone: (207)729-0181
Brunswick, ME 04011 Sylvia K. Norton, Libn.
Founded: 1972. **Staff:** Prof 1. **Subjects:** Internal medicine, orthopedics, surgery, pediatrics, psychiatry, nursing. **Holdings:** 800 books; 2000 bound periodical volumes; 100 audio cassettes; 50 videotapes. **Subscriptions:** 146 journals and other serials. **Services:** Interlibrary loan; copying; SDI; library open to the public with restrictions. **Computerized Information Services:** DIALOG Information Services, MEDLINE. Performs searches on fee basis. **Networks/Consortia:** Member of Health Science Library and Information Cooperative of Maine (HSLIC).

★11947★
REGIONAL MUNICIPALITY OF OTTAWA-CARLETON - TRANSPORTATION-WORKS LIBRARY (Trans)
222 Queen St., 10th Fl. Phone: (613)560-2064
Ottawa, ON, Canada K1P 5Z3 Calvin Skuce, Tech.Lib.Cust.
Founded: 1973. **Staff:** Prof 1. **Subjects:** Urban transportation, road and bridge construction, pollution and water quality control, sewer systems. **Special Collections:** RMOC reports and studies. **Holdings:** 12,154 volumes. **Services:** Interlibrary loan.

★11948★
REGIONAL PLAN ASSOCIATION, INC. - LIBRARY (Plan)
1040 Ave. of the Americas Phone: (212)398-1140
New York, NY 10018 Peter Haskel, Libn.
Founded: 1929. **Staff:** Prof 1; Other 1. **Subjects:** Urban and regional planning, housing, transportation, land use, public administration, environment. **Special Collections:** Municipal and county planning reports. **Holdings:** 2000 books; 8000 research and technical reports; 8 file drawers of newspaper clippings; 8 VF drawers. **Subscriptions:** 302 journals and other serials. **Services:** Interlibrary loan; copying; library open to members. **Publications:** Accessions list, biennial - to members.

★11949★
REGIONAL PLANNING COUNCIL - LIBRARY (Plan)
2225 N. Charles St. Phone: (301)554-5614
Baltimore, MD 21218 Mary Logan, Libn.
Staff: Prof 1; Other 1. **Subjects:** Planning, economic development, urban affairs, environment, transportation, demography. **Special Collections:** Maryland and Baltimore region government publications; Regional Planning Council publications. **Holdings:** 10,000 books; 60 bound periodical volumes; 500 technical reports on microfiche. **Subscriptions:** 320 journals and other serials; 15 newspapers. **Services:** Interlibrary loan; copying; library open to the public for reference use only. **Networks/Consortia:** Member of Maryland Interlibrary Organization (MILO). **Publications:** Acquisitions list, quarterly; List of Current Publications of the Regional Planning Council, annual - both free upon request.

REGIONAL RESOURCES CENTER OF EASTERN PENNSYLVANIA FOR SPECIAL EDUCATION
See: Pennsylvania Resources and Information Center for Special Education (11169)

★11950★
REGIONAL TRANSPORTATION DISTRICT (Metropolitan Denver Area) - RESEARCH & RECORDS SERVICES (Trans)
1600 Blake St. Phone: (303)573-2120
Denver, CO 80202 Ms. Yem Fong, Supv., Res. & Rec.
Founded: 1975. **Staff:** Prof 1; Other 2. **Subjects:** Public transportation, land use, urban planning, civil engineering. **Holdings:** 6275 books; 5000 reports; 2394 microfiche; 4 films; 38 videotapes; 8000 slides. **Subscriptions:** 250 journals and other serials; 11 newspapers. **Services:** Interlibrary loan; services open to the public by appointment. **Automated Operations:** Computerized cataloging and serials. **Computerized Information Services:** DIALOG Information Services; SYDNEY (internal database); DIALMAIL (electronic mail service). **Networks/Consortia:** Member of Central Colorado Library System (CCLS), Bibliographical Center for Research, Rocky Mountain Region, Inc. (BCR).

★11951★
REGIS COLLEGE - LIBRARY (Rel-Phil)
15 St. Mary St. Phone: (416)922-0536
Toronto, ON, Canada M4Y 2R5
Rev. Vincent MacKenzie, S.J., Chf.Libn.
Founded: 1931. **Staff:** Prof 1; Other 4. **Subjects:** Theology, religion, allied subjects. **Special Collections:** Lonergan Centre (manuscripts; books; tapes; off-prints). **Holdings:** 95,321 books; 20,000 bound periodical volumes. **Subscriptions:** 445 journals and other serials; 5 newspapers. **Services:** Interlibrary loan (fee); copying; library open to University of Toronto and Toronto School of Theology students, and outside readers with approval of chief librarian. **Automated Operations:** Computerized cataloging, acquisitions, serials, and circulation.

★11952★
REGISTER-GUARD - LIBRARY (Publ)
975 High St.
Box 10188 Phone: (503)485-1234
Eugene, OR 97440 Suzanne Boyd, Lib.Mgr.
Founded: 1950. **Staff:** Prof 1; Other 1. **Subjects:** Newspaper reference topics. **Holdings:** 1500 books; newspaper clippings. **Subscriptions:** 25 journals and other serials; 10 newspapers. **Services:** Library open to the public with restrictions.

★11953★
REGISTERED NURSES' ASSOCIATION OF BRITISH COLUMBIA - LIBRARY (Med)
2855 Arbutus St. Phone: (604)736-7331
Vancouver, BC, Canada V6J 3Y8 Joan I. Aufiero, Libn.
Staff: Prof 1; Other 2. **Subjects:** Nursing. **Holdings:** 2500 books; 450 bound periodical volumes; 30 shelves of pamphlets; 400 audiotapes; 25 videotapes. **Subscriptions:** 75 journals and other serials. **Services:** Interlibrary loan; copying; library open to RNABC members and holders of temporary library cards.

★11954★
REGISTERED NURSES' ASSOCIATION OF ONTARIO - LIBRARY (Med)
33 Price St. Phone: (416)923-3523
Toronto, ON, Canada M4W 1Z2 Mary Boite, Libn.
Staff: Prof 1; Other 1. **Subjects:** Nursing, health. **Special Collections:** RNAO Archives. **Holdings:** 4000 books; 258 bound periodical volumes; 8 VF drawers of reports; 20 VF drawers of clippings. **Subscriptions:** 120 journals and other serials. **Services:** Interlibrary loan; copying; library open to the public by appointment for reference use only. **Publications:** RNAO library acquisitions, bimonthly; bibliographies on different aspects of nursing - to members.

REGNER HEALTH SCIENCES LIBRARY
See: St. Michael's Hospital (12629)

★11955★
REHABILITATION INSTITUTE OF CHICAGO - LEARNING RESOURCES CENTER (Med)
345 E. Superior, Rms. 1671 and 1679 Phone: (312)908-2859
Chicago, IL 60611 Karen Kaluzsa, Med.Libn.
Staff: Prof 1. **Subjects:** Physical rehabilitation, spinal cord injury, stroke, vocational rehabilitation, brain trauma. **Holdings:** 800 books; 20 bound periodical volumes; 300 films and videotapes; 50 slide/sound sets and filmstrips; 400 research reports; 7 VF drawers. **Subscriptions:** 136 journals and other serials. **Services:** Interlibrary loan; copying; center open to the public by appointment. **Computerized Information Services:** BRS Information Technologies, DIALOG Information Services, NLM, OCLC; DOCLINE (electronic mail service). **Networks/Consortia:** Member of Greater Midwest Regional Medical Library Network, Chicago Library System, ILLINET, Metropolitan Consortium of Chicago. **Publications:** Recent Acquisitions, irregular - to staff. **Remarks:** Affiliated with Northwestern University.

★11956★
REHABILITATION INSTITUTE, INC. - LEARNING RESOURCES CENTER (Med)
261 Mack Blvd. Phone: (313)745-9860
Detroit, MI 48201 Daria Shackelford, Med.Libn./Dir.
Founded: 1958. **Staff:** Prof 1; Other 2. **Subjects:** Physical medicine, rehabilitation, general medicine, physical therapy, occupational therapy, social service, patient education. **Holdings:** 1800 books; 3200 bound periodical volumes; 6 VF drawers of pamphlets; 5 boxes of reports; 1 VF drawer of reprints; 15 16mm films; 1000 35mm slides; 30 videotapes. **Subscriptions:** 125 journals and other serials. **Services:** Interlibrary loan; copying; center open to the public with permission. **Computerized Information Services:** BRS Information Technologies, NLM. **Networks/Consortia:** Member of Greater Midwest Regional Medical Library Network.

REHABILITATION INTERNATIONAL
See: International Society for Rehabilitation of the Disabled/ Rehabilitation International (7070)

REHN GALLERY ARCHIVE
See: SUNY - College at Buffalo - Burchfield Art Center - Research Library (13763)

★11957★
REICHHOLD CHEMICALS, INC. - INFORMATION RESOURCES CENTER (Sci-Engr)
407 S. Pace Blvd.
Box 1433 Phone: (904)433-7621
Pensacola, FL 32596 Terry Burrill, Info.Spec.
Founded: 1950. **Staff:** Prof 1. **Subjects:** Chemistry - coatings, inks, adhesives; paper and rubber chemicals. **Holdings:** 1000 books; 1500 bound periodical volumes; 4 VF drawers of laboratory reports; 6 VF drawers of U.S. and foreign patents. **Subscriptions:** 58 journals and other serials. **Services:** Interlibrary loan; copying; center open to qualified persons with permission. **Computerized Information Services:** DIALOG Information Services.

★11958★
REID & PRIEST - LAW LIBRARY (Law)
40 W. 57th St. Phone: (212)603-2265
New York, NY 10019 Ruth Ulferts, Dir., Lib.Serv.
Founded: 1935. **Staff:** Prof 2; Other 3. **Subjects:** Law - securities, public utilities, international, tax. **Special Collections:** Securities and Exchange Commission (SEC) releases; state tax. **Holdings:** 20,000 books. **Services:** Interlibrary loan; library not open to the public. **Computerized Information Services:** DIALOG Information Services, VU/TEXT Information Services, DataTimes, Pergamon ORBIT InfoLine, Inc., NewsNet, Inc., Finsbury Data Services, Ltd., WESTLAW, LEXIS, QL Systems, DunSprint, Dow Jones News/Retrieval.

REIGNER MEDICAL LIBRARY
See: Liberty Medical Center, Inc. (7790)

★11959★
REILLY TRANSLATIONS - LIBRARY
Box 1702
Glendale, CA 91209-1702
Founded: 1967. **Subjects:** Linguistics, science and technology. **Holdings:** 2000 books; 750 foreign patents; 30 magnetic tapes; 150 videotapes. **Remarks:** Presently inactive.

WILLIAM F. REILLY LIBRARY
See: Katharine Gibbs School (5656)

REIMER LIBRARY
See: Winnipeg Bible College (17929)

FRITZ REINER LIBRARY
See: Northwestern University - Music Library (10502)

REINERT/ALUMNI MEMORIAL LIBRARY
See: Creighton University (3882)

MAX REINHARDT ARCHIVE AND LIBRARY
See: SUNY at Binghamton - Special Collections (13789)

★11960★
REINHART, BOERNER, VAN DEUREN, NORRIS & RIESELBACH - LIBRARY (Law)
1800 Marine Plaza Phone: (414)271-1190
Milwaukee, WI 53202 Carol Bannen, Libn.
Founded: 1975. **Staff:** Prof 2; Other 2. **Subjects:** Law - taxation, real estate, labor, employee benefits, banking, corporate, securities. **Holdings:** 9000 books; 110 cassette tapes; 20 reels of microfilm; 6 boxes of microfiche; 30 video cassettes. **Subscriptions:** 250 journals and other serials. **Services:** Interlibrary loan; copying; SDI; library open to the public with restrictions. **Computerized Information Services:** DIALOG Information Services, WESTLAW, LEXIS. **Networks/Consortia:** Member of Library Council of Metropolitan Milwaukee, Inc. (LCOMM), Private Downtown Law Librarians. **Publications:** New Book List, monthly; Current Education Opportunities in Law, monthly - for internal distribution only. **Special Indexes:** Information Retrieval Index (online).

REIS LAW LIBRARY
See: Western State University - College of Law (17755)

★11961★
JOY REISINGER RESEARCH LIBRARY (Hist)
1020 Central Ave. Phone: (608)269-6361
Sparta, WI 54656 Joy Reisinger, Owner
Founded: 1975. **Subjects:** Genealogy, Canadian history, Quebec and Ontario history. **Special Collections:** Rapports de l'Archiviste du Quebec (complete collection); inventories of notaries; published marriage repertoires of Quebec (complete collection); Ontario county and local histories; Repertoire des Actes de Bapteme, Mariage, Sepulture et des Recensements du Quebec Ancien (30 volumes); Wisconsin Historical Collections (complete collection). **Holdings:** Figures not available. **Subscriptions:** 80 journals and other serials. **Services:** Copying; library open to subscribers by appointment. **Publications:** Lost in Canada Canadian-American Genealogical Journal.

★11962★
REISS-DAVIS CHILD STUDY CENTER - RESEARCH LIBRARY (Soc Sci)
3200 Motor Ave. Phone: (213)204-1666
Los Angeles, CA 90034 Leonore W. Freehling, Libn.
Founded: 1950. **Staff:** Prof 1. **Subjects:** Child psychology, child psychiatry, child development, psychiatric social work, educational psychology, child analysis. **Special Collections:** Freud Collection. **Holdings:** 12,500 books; 3500 bound periodical volumes; 10 VF drawers of information files; 25 films; 500 audiotapes. **Subscriptions:** 125 journals and other serials. **Services:** Interlibrary loan; copying; SDI; library open to the public on payment of membership fee. **Networks/Consortia:** Member of Pacific Southwest Regional Medical Library Service. **Automated Operations:** Computerized acquisitions. **Computerized Information Services:** MEDLINE. Performs searches on fee basis. **Publications:** Acquisitions list, quarterly. **Special Indexes:** Index to contributions by authors in collections.

★11963★
REL INCORPORATED - CORPORATE LIBRARY (Sci-Engr)
3800 S. Congress Ave. Phone: (407)732-0300
Boynton Beach, FL 33435 Karen Anderson, Libn.
Staff: Prof 1. **Subjects:** Radar, electronic warfare, tropospheric scatter, radio communications, electronics. **Holdings:** 1500 books; 40 bound periodical volumes; 800 Air Force technical orders; 70 VF drawers and 500 microfilm cartridges of vendor catalogs; 60 VF drawers and 824 microfilm cartridges of military specifications and standards. **Subscriptions:** 131 journals and other serials. **Services:** Interlibrary loan; copying; library open to the public with restrictions. **Publications:** New Titles in the Library, irregular - for internal distribution only.

CLICK RELANDER COLLECTION
See: Yakima Valley Regional Library - Reference Department (18112)

★11964★
RELIABILITY ENGINEERING & MANAGEMENT INSTITUTE - TECHNICAL INFORMATION CENTER (Sci-Engr)
7340 N. La Oesta Ave. Phone: (602)297-2679
Tucson, AZ 85704 Dr. Dimitri Kececioglu, Cons.
Founded: 1963. **Staff:** Prof 3; Other 2. **Subjects:** Reliability; maintainability; availability; testing - life, accelerated, Bayesian. **Special Collections:** Mechanical reliability. **Holdings:** 3350 books; reports. **Subscriptions:** 18 journals and other serials. **Special Collections:** Copying; center open to the public by appointment.

★11965★
RELIANCE GROUP HOLDINGS, INC. - CORPORATE LIBRARY (Bus-Fin)
Park Ave. Plaza
New York, NY 10055 Ellen Rubin-Berk, Corp.Libn.
Founded: 1980. **Staff:** Prof 1; Other 1. **Subjects:** Investment, business, management. **Special Collections:** Investment and Insurance Reference Collection. **Holdings:** 400 books; 150 unbound periodicals; 20 drawers of microfiche. **Subscriptions:** 200 journals and other serials; 10 newspapers. **Services:** Interlibrary loan; library not open to the public. **Automated Operations:** Computerized cataloging, acquisitions, and serials. **Computerized Information Services:** DIALOG Information Services, Pergamon ORBIT InfoLine, Inc., Dun & Bradstreet Corporation, Info Globe, COMPUSTAT Services, Inc. (C/S), Dow Jones News/Retrieval, LEXIS, NEXIS, INVESTEXT, VU/TEXT Information Services, Spectrum Ownership Profiles Online, Vickers Stock Research Corporation, ADP Network Services, TEXTLINE, NewsNet, Inc., DataTimes, A.M. Best Company.

★11966★
RELIGIOUS NEWS SERVICE - LIBRARY AND MORGUE (Publ)
Radio City Sta., Box 1015 Phone: (212)315-0870
New York, NY 10101 Gary O'Guinn, Off.Mgr.
Founded: 1933. **Staff:** 1. **Subjects:** News stories of the world's religions. **Holdings:** Figures not available. **Services:** Library open on limited basis for research by authorized personnel. **Computerized Information Services:** NewsNet, Inc. **Remarks:** Library carries stories from the past 3-4 years only. Older files are available through the United Presbyterian Church in the U.S.A. - Presbyterian Historical Society in Philadelphia, PA.

★11967★
RELIGIOUS NEWS SERVICE - PHOTOGRAPH LIBRARY (Aud-Vis)
Radio City Sta., Box 1015 Phone: (212)315-0870
New York, NY 10101 Sean B. Murray, Photo Ed.
Founded: 1945. **Staff:** Prof 1. **Subjects:** Religion, current events, social concerns. **Holdings:** 200,000 black/white photographs. **Services:** Library not open to the public.

REMBERT-STOKES LEARNING CENTER
See: Wilberforce University (17871)

★11968★
REMINGTON ARMS COMPANY, INC. - RESEARCH LIBRARY
939 Barnum Ave.
Bridgeport, CT 06602
Defunct

★11969★
RENEWABLE ENERGY INFORMATION CENTER (Energy)
Box 251 Phone: (805)482-3068
Tarzana, CA 91356 Alan A. Tratner, Dir.
Founded: 1978. **Staff:** Prof 3. **Subjects:** Renewable energy and geothermal energy research and development. **Special Collections:** Geothermal World Directory, 1972-1986. **Holdings:** 500 volumes; Geothermal Energy Monthly Journal, 1973-1986, on microfiche; maps; slides. **Subscriptions:** 10 journals and other serials. **Services:** Copying; accepts mail requests for information. **Special Indexes:** Geothermal Energy, cumulative index; Geothermal World Directory index. **Formerly:** Geothermal World Corporation - Information Center, located in Camarillo, CA.

FREDERIC G. RENNER MEMORIAL LIBRARY
See: Charles M. Russell Museum (12246)

★11970★
RENSSELAER COUNTY HISTORICAL SOCIETY - LIBRARY (Hist)
59 Second St. Phone: (518)272-7232
Troy, NY 12180 Mrs. Frederick R. Walsh, Dir.
Staff: Prof 1; Other 2. **Subjects:** Rensselaer County history. **Special Collections:** City directories; collection of photographs of Troy and Rensselaer County; Tibbitts Collection. **Holdings:** 2500 books; letters; local business daybooks; pamphlets. **Services:** Copying; library open to the public.

★11971★
RENSSELAER POLYTECHNIC INSTITUTE - ARCHITECTURE LIBRARY (Art, Plan)
Troy, NY 12181 Phone: (518)276-6465
Virginia S. Bailey, Arch.Libn.
Founded: 1930. **Staff:** Prof 2; Other 2. **Subjects:** Architecture, art, city and regional planning, landscaping. **Special Collections:** Vance Architecture Bibliography Series; Historic American Building Survey (microfiche); Armenian Architecture (a documented photo-archival collection on microfiche). **Holdings:** 26,100 books; 4600 bound periodical volumes; 8 VF drawers of manufacturers' literature; 63,600 slides; 1900 maps. **Subscriptions:** 241 journals and other serials. **Services:** Interlibrary loan; copying; library open to the public. **Automated Operations:** Computerized cataloging, acquisitions, serials, and circulation. **Staff:** Jeanne Keefe-Watkinson, Graphics Cur..

★11972★
RENSSELAER POLYTECHNIC INSTITUTE - CENTER FOR MANUFACTURING PRODUCTIVITY AND TECHNOLOGY TRANSFER - LIBRARY (Comp Sci)
110 Eighth St. Phone: (518)266-6724
Troy, NY 12180 Laurie Rattner, Prog.Mgr.
Founded: 1979. **Subjects:** Robotics, sensor technologies, computer-aided design and manufacturing, artificial intelligence, advanced powder processing. **Holdings:** 250 books; technical reports; theses; dissertations. **Services:** Library open to the public with restrictions on circulation.

★11973★
RENSSELAER POLYTECHNIC INSTITUTE - RPI LIBRARIES (Sci-Engr, Soc Sci)
Troy, NY 12181 Phone: (518)276-8300
Barbara A. Lockett, Dir. of Lib.
Founded: 1824. **Staff:** Prof 14; Other 29. **Subjects:** Science, engineering, management, social sciences, architecture, humanities. **Special Collections:** History of Science and Technology; technical reports; Geological Survey Quadrangle Maps. **Holdings:** 364,300 books; 129,300 bound periodical volumes; 750,968 microforms; 2000 recordings; 63,700 slides; 801,300 reports, documents, maps; government documents. **Subscriptions:** 4600 journals and other serials; 34 newspapers. **Services:** Interlibrary loan; copying; libraries open to the public. **Automated Operations:** Computerized cataloging, acquisitions, and serials. **Computerized Information Services:** MicroLinx, BRS Information Technologies, DIALOG Information Services, Dow Jones News/Retrieval, New York State Union Education and Research Network (NYSERNet). **Networks/Consortia:** Member of Capital District Library Council for Reference & Research Resources (CDLC), SUNY/OCLC Library Network. **Publications:** Library Guide; library use manuals; Guide to the Roebling Collections. **Formerly:** Folsom Library. **Staff:** Pat Molholt, Assoc.Dir.; Irving E. Stephens, Hd., Bldg.Serv.; Richard Kaplan, Hd., Ref.; Liz Lane, Hd., Tech.Serv.; Alice R. Browne, Sci.Libn.; Colette O'Connell, Engr.Libn.; Polly-Alida Farrington, Docs. & Maps/Software Libn.; Clare Merrill, Ser.Libn.; Kathleen Rose, Cat.Libn.; Kristina MacCormick, Cat.Libn.; John Dojka, Archv.; Jonathan Penn, ILL Libn.; Susan Zappen, Acq.Libn.; Virginia Bailey, Arch.Libn..

★11974★
REORGANIZED CHURCH OF JESUS CHRIST OF LATTER DAY SAINTS - LIBRARY & ARCHIVES (Rel-Phil)
RLDS Auditorium
Box 1059 Phone: (816)833-1000
Independence, MO 64051 Sara Hallier, Libn.
Staff: Prof 2; Other 1. **Subjects:** Mormon history, Reorganized Latter Day Saint thought and doctrine, religion and theology. **Special Collections:** Herald House publications; state histories related to Latter Day Saint movement; Latter Day Saints pamphlets; archival collection (320 linear feet of unpublished records, journals, manuscripts, photographs). **Holdings:** 15,000 books; 2700 bound periodical volumes; 900 reels of microfilm; 250 cassettes. **Subscriptions:** 100 journals and other serials. **Services:** Interlibrary loan; copying; library open to the public. **Networks/Consortia:** Member of Kansas City Metropolitan Library Network (KCMLN). **Special Indexes:** Index to current periodical publications of the Reorganized Church of Jesus Christ of Latter Day Saints. **Staff:** Madelon Brunson, Archv..

★11975★
REORGANIZED CHURCH OF JESUS CHRIST OF LATTER DAY SAINTS - SERVICES TO THE BLIND (Rel-Phil, Aud-Vis)
1001 Walnut
Box 1059
Independence, MO 64051 Phone: (816)833-1000
Staff: 2. **Subjects:** Religion. **Holdings:** 200 books on cassette; 1200 volumes in braille; 30 large print pamphlets; brochures; instruction manuals; braille calendars. **Services:** Braille transcription instruction and service; thermoform and computer duplication of braille materials; services open to the public.

★11976★
REPERTOIRE INTERNATIONAL D'ICONOGRAPHIE MUSICALE - RESEARCH CENTER FOR MUSICAL ICONOGRAPHY - LIBRARY (Mus)
Dept. of Music
CUNY - Graduate Center
33 W. 42nd St. Phone: (212)642-2336
New York, NY 10036 Dr. Barry S. Brook, Dir.
Staff: Prof 3. **Subjects:** Musical iconography, portraits of musicians, paintings with musical subjects. **Special Collections:** Martin Bernstein Slide Collection; Viennese Classical Period Collection (Haydn, Mozart, Beethoven, Schubert iconography - slides and transparencies); Vienna Gesellschaft der Musikfreunde Portrait Collection (transparencies). **Holdings:** 800 volumes; 1500 documents and pictures with accompanying catalog card; 2000 slides; 8000 pictures. **Services:** Copying; library open to the public. **Publications:** RIDIM/RCMI Newsletter, semiannual; RICIM/RCMI Inventories of Music Iconography, irregular. **Special Catalogs:** The Musical Ensemble, circa 1730-1830 (exhibition catalog; 1978); Autour de la viole de gambe (exhibition catalog; 1979); catalogs and indexes of artwork with musical subject matter in individual museums (card). **Special Indexes:** Index to pictures housed in the center. **Staff:** Terence Ford, Assoc.Dir..

★11977★
REPTILE BREEDING FOUNDATION - LIBRARY (Biol Sci)
R.R. 3, Box 1450 Phone: (613)476-3351
Picton, ON, Canada K0K 2T0 Thomas A. Huff, Dir.
Founded: 1976. **Staff:** 5. **Subjects:** Herpetology, reptiles, amphibians, wildlife conservation, zoology, zoos. **Holdings:** 2200 books; 250 bound periodical volumes; 4000 reprints; 50 microfiche; 4 VF drawers of

clippings, reports, regional surveys. **Subscriptions:** 145 journals and other serials. **Services:** Copying; library open to the public by appointment. **Publications:** The Herpetoculturist, quarterly; Scales & Tales, quarterly. **Special Catalogs:** Taxonomic catalog dealing with captive husbandry and propagation of reptiles and amphibians.

★11978★
REPUBLICAN ASSOCIATES OF LOS ANGELES COUNTY - RESEARCH LIBRARY (Soc Sci)
1153 N. Brand Blvd. Phone: (818)240-9100
Glendale, CA 91202 June Boehle, Libn.
Founded: 1951. **Staff:** Prof 2; Other 3. **Subjects:** Current issues; state and federal administrations; political officeholders; assembly, senate, and congressional districts. **Special Collections:** Richard Nixon Collection (120 items); campaign materials (100 items); Governor Jerry Brown clipping file; Governor George Deukmejian clipping file; President Reagan and Reagan Administration clipping file. **Holdings:** 170 VF drawers of newspaper clippings; Governor Ronald Reagan Press releases, 1966-1974 (complete and inclusive); Congressional Quarterly Weekly Reports, 1956 to present. **Subscriptions:** 29 journals and other serials; 11 newspapers. **Services:** Copying; library open to the public with restrictions (no Democratic candidates or office holders). **Networks/Consortia:** Member of Southern California Answering Network (SCAN). **Publications:** Newsletter, monthly - to members and Republican office holders; campaign material - on request. **Special Catalogs:** Catalog of judicial appointments. **Special Indexes:** List of speeches by Governor Reagan, 1966-1974; list of appointments by Governor Reagan, 1966-1974; index of past and present political figures; index of current federal and California issues. **Staff:** Gene Wiberg, Exec.Dir.; William Graham, Res.Dir..

★11979★
REPUBLICAN NATIONAL COMMITTEE - LIBRARY (Soc Sci)
310 First St., S.E. Phone: (202)863-8626
Washington, DC 20003 Linda Smith, Lib.Dir.
Founded: 1936. **Staff:** Prof 1; Other 1. **Subjects:** Government, legislation, politics, election results, demographic material, voting statistics, political history, presidential documents. **Special Collections:** Collection of Republican National Committee Proceedings of Nominating Conventions, 1856 to present. **Holdings:** 5000 books; microfilm. **Subscriptions:** 180 journals and other serials; 12 newspapers. **Services:** Library open to the public by special arrangement. **Computerized Information Services:** The Reference Service (REFSRV), NEXIS.

★11980★
REPUBLICBANK CORPORATION - ECONOMIC RESEARCH LIBRARY (Bus-Fin)
Box 660020 Phone: (214)653-5807
Dallas, TX 75266-0020 Sandra Pearman, Econ.Libn.
Staff: Prof 1; Other 2. **Subjects:** Economics, banking, finance, political science, energy. **Holdings:** 2500 books; 400 bound periodical volumes. **Subscriptions:** 400 journals and other serials; 8 newspapers. **Services:** Interlibrary loan; copying; library open to the public by appointment. **Automated Operations:** Computerized serials. **Computerized Information Services:** DIALOG Information Services, NEXIS, Data Resources (DRI), Dow Jones News/Retrieval, I.P. Sharp Associates Limited; internal database.

★11981★
RESEARCH FOR BETTER SCHOOLS, INC. - RESOURCE CENTER (Educ)
444 N. Third St. Phone: (215)574-9300
Philadelphia, PA 19123 Ellen I. Newcombe, Dir., Info.Serv.
Founded: 1978. **Staff:** Prof 1; Other 1. **Subjects:** Elementary and secondary education. **Special Collections:** Basic Skills (1200 documents); Competency-based education (600 documents); educational technology (500 items); Research for Better Schools (900 documents); school improvement (1000 documents); training materials (150 documents). **Holdings:** 1500 books; complete ERIC microfiche collection. **Subscriptions:** 92 journals and other serials. **Services:** SDI; center open to the public by appointment for reference use only. **Computerized Information Services:** DIALOG Information Services, BRS Information Technologies. **Publications:** Tracings, monthly - to all professional staff. **Special Indexes:** Indexes to special collections (card).

RESEARCH CENTRE FOR MANAGEMENT OF NEW TECHNOLOGY
See: Wilfrid Laurier University (7685)

RESEARCH CENTER FOR MUSICAL ICONOGRAPHY
See: Repertoire International d'Iconographie Musicale (11976)

★11982★
RESEARCH CENTER FOR RELIGION & HUMAN RIGHTS IN CLOSED SOCIETIES - INFORMATION CENTER (Rel-Phil)
475 Riverside Dr., Suite 448 Phone: (212)870-2481
New York, NY 10115 Rev. B.S. Hruby, Exec.Dir.
Staff: 4. **Subjects:** Religion and human rights in Communist countries; religious and atheistic literature published in Communist countries. **Holdings:** Periodicals; clippings; reports; occasional papers; underground publications from Communist countries. **Subscriptions:** 100 journals and other serials. **Services:** Center open to members and scholars by special arrangement only. **Publications:** RCDA - Religion in Communist Dominated Areas, quarterly. **Special Indexes:** Index to RCDA, annual.

★11983★
RESEARCH AND DEVELOPMENT ASSOCIATES FOR MILITARY FOOD & PACKAGING SYSTEMS - LIBRARY (Food-Bev)
103 Biltmore Dr., Suite 106 Phone: (512)344-5773
San Antonio, TX 78213 Merton Singer, Exec.Dir.
Subjects: Food and container developments. **Holdings:** 600 volumes.

★11984★
RESEARCH & EDUCATION ASSOCIATION - LIBRARY (Sci-Engr)
505 Eighth Ave. Phone: (212)695-9487
New York, NY 10018 Carl Fuchs, Libn.
Staff: Prof 2. **Subjects:** Science and technology, mathematics, physics, chemistry. **Holdings:** 2000 books. **Services:** Library not open to the public. **Staff:** P. Weston.

★11985★
RESEARCH FOUNDATION FOR JEWISH IMMIGRATION, INC. - ARCHIVES (Area-Ethnic)
570 7th Ave., 16th Fl. Phone: (212)921-3871
New York, NY 10018 Dennis E. Rohrbaugh, Archv.
Subjects: Biography, bibliography, oral history. **Special Collections:** International Biographical Archive of Central European Emigres, 1933-1945 (data on 25,000 emigres from German-speaking Central Europe). **Holdings:** 300 transcriptions of oral history interviews with German-Jewish emigres in the United States. **Services:** Archives open to the public by appointment; telephone and written inquiries accepted. **Publications:** Jewish Immigrants of the Nazi Period in the U.S.A. (series); International Biographical Dictionary of Central European Emigres 1933-1945. **Remarks:** Affiliated with the American Federation of Jews from Central Europe, Inc. **Staff:** Dr. Herbert A. Strauss, Sec. & Coord. of Res..

★11986★
RESEARCH & INFORMATION SERVICES FOR EDUCATION - MONTGOMERY COUNTY INTERMEDIATE UNIT LIBRARY (Educ)
725 Caley Rd. Phone: (215)265-6056
King of Prussia, PA 19406 Richard R. Brickley, Dir.
Founded: 1966. **Staff:** Prof 1. **Subjects:** Education, curriculum design, educational research, administration, methodology and evaluation, program dissemination. **Holdings:** 8000 volumes; 310 literature searches; 4 vertical files of newsletters; ERIC microfiche collection. **Subscriptions:** 100 journals and other serials; 150 newspapers. **Services:** Copying; library open to the public. **Computerized Information Services:** BRS Information Technologies, DIALOG Information Services, The Source Information Network; internal database. Performs searches on fee basis. Contact Person: Emma Peterson, Info.Spec.. **Publications:** RISE Newsletter, 4/year. **Special Catalogs:** Search catalog (book).

★11987★
RESEARCH INSTITUTE ON ALCOHOLISM - LIBRARY (Med)
1021 Main St. Phone: (716)887-2511
Buffalo, NY 14203 Diane Augustino, Res.Sci. I
Staff: Prof 1; Other 1. **Subjects:** Alcoholism and alcohol abuse - physiological, psychological, sociological, biochemical, pharmacological aspects; drug abuse. **Holdings:** 3850 books; 700 bound periodical volumes; 10 VF drawers. **Subscriptions:** 100 journals and other serials; 5 newspapers. **Services:** Copying; library open to the public for reference use only. **Computerized Information Services:** BRS Information Technologies. **Networks/Consortia:** Member of Western New York Library Resources Council (WNYLRC), Library Consortium of Health Institutions in Buffalo (LCHIB). **Publications:** RIA Publications List, annual; List of Serials, annual; Library Acquisitions List, monthly.

RESEARCH INSTITUTE FOR INNER ASIAN STUDIES
See: Indiana University (6799)

★11988★
RESEARCH INSTITUTE FOR THE STUDY OF MAN - LIBRARY (Area-Ethnic)
162 E. 78th St. Phone: (212)535-8448
New York, NY 10021 Judith Selakoff, Libn.
Founded: 1955. **Staff:** Prof 2; Other 1. **Subjects:** Social sciences of the Caribbean and non-Hispanic West Indies. **Special Collections:** Caribbeana (pamphlets; dissertations; manuscripts; government publications). **Holdings:** 16,000 books. **Subscriptions:** 120 journals and other serials. **Services:** Interlibrary loan (limited); copying; library open to the public for reference use only. **Special Indexes:** Index to West Indian Periodical Literature at RISM; periodical holdings; Listing of RISM Associated Publications (punched card). **Staff:** Sheila Bourne, Libn..

★11989★
RESEARCH MEDICAL CENTER - CARL R. FERRIS, M.D. MEDICAL LIBRARY (Med)
2316 E. Meyer Blvd. Phone: (816)276-4310
Kansas City, MO 64132-1199 Gerald R. Kruse, Lib.Dir.
Founded: 1963. **Staff:** Prof 1; Other 4. **Subjects:** Medicine, nursing. **Holdings:** 8500 books; 8500 bound periodical volumes; 350 reels of microfilm; 900 tapes; 150 filmstrips. **Subscriptions:** 330 journals and other serials. **Services:** Interlibrary loan; copying; SDI; library open to the public for reference use only. **Computerized Information Services:** MEDLARS, DIALOG Information Services.

RESEARCH AND REVIEW SERVICE OF AMERICA
See: Longman Financial Services Publishing (7959)

★11990★
RESEARCH SERVICES CORPORATION - THE O.A. BATTISTA RESEARCH INSTITUTE - LIBRARY (Sci-Engr)
3863 Southwest Loop - 820, Suite 100 Phone: (817)292-4272
Fort Worth, TX 76133-2076 Naomi L. Matous, Libn.
Founded: 1971. **Staff:** Prof 2; Other 3. **Subjects:** Polymer science and technology, chemistry, medicine. **Holdings:** 3000 books. **Subscriptions:** 102 journals and other serials. **Automated Operations:** Computerized cataloging, acquisitions, serials, and circulation. **Publications:** Knowledge Magazine. **Staff:** S. Scott Lee, Inst.Mgr..

★11991★
RESEARCH TRIANGLE INSTITUTE - TECHNICAL LIBRARY (Sci-Engr, Biol Sci)
Box 12194 Phone: (919)541-6455
Research Triangle Park, NC 27709 Lois Melton, Libn.
Founded: 1960. **Staff:** Prof 4; Other 1. **Subjects:** Organic and inorganic chemistry, life sciences, health research, engineering, social sciences, environmental sciences, statistics. **Holdings:** 40,000 books. **Subscriptions:** 900 journals and other serials. **Services:** Library not open to the public. **Automated Operations:** Computerized serials. **Computerized Information Services:** DIALOG Information Services, Pergamon ORBIT InfoLine, Inc., BRS Information Technologies, CAS ONLINE, MEDLARS.

★11992★
RESOURCE CENTER FOR NONVIOLENCE - ROY C. KEPLER LIBRARY OF PEACE (Soc Sci)
Box 2324 Phone: (408)423-1626
Santa Cruz, CA 95063 Doug Rand, Off.Coord.
Staff: 1. **Subjects:** Theory and practice of nonviolence, peace education, draft resistance. **Special Collections:** Gandhi (300 volumes); Garland Library of War and Peace (300 volumes). **Holdings:** 4000 books. **Subscriptions:** 20 journals and other serials. **Services:** Library open to the public.

RESOURCE ENGINEERING, INC. - ERT, INC.
See: ERT, Inc. - Information Center (4792)

★11993★
RESOURCE POLICY INSTITUTE - TECHNICAL INFORMATION PROJECT (Env-Cons)
Box 39185 Phone: (202)363-1133
Washington, DC 20016 D. Ross
Founded: 1975. **Staff:** Prof 1. **Subjects:** Hazardous waste, toxic substances, environmental issues, energy and energy conservation, nuclear power, waste/recycling. **Holdings:** 200 books; 500 bound periodical volumes. **Services:** Project not open to the public. **Publications:** Periodic reports.

★11994★
RESOURCE & RESEARCH CENTER FOR BEAVER COUNTY & LOCAL HISTORY (Hist)
Carnegie Free Library
1301 7th Ave. Phone: (412)846-4340
Beaver Falls, PA 15010 Vivian C. McLaughlin, Dir.
Founded: 1974. **Staff:** Prof 2. **Subjects:** Local history, genealogy. **Special Collections:** Beaver County newspapers, 1830 to present, on microfilm. **Holdings:** 3000 books; marriage and death notices; cemetery listings; census microfilm; Pennsylvania archives; Daughters of the American Revolution lineage materials. **Services:** Interlibrary loan; copying; center open to the public for reference use only. **Publications:** Gleanings (genealogical journal), quarterly; Milestones (historical journal), quarterly - by subscription; cemetery listings - for sale. **Special Indexes:** Index to census; index to deeds and articles.

★11995★
RESOURCES FOR CHILD CARING INC. - LIBRARY
Fairview Community Center
County Rd. B & Fairview
Roseville, MN 55113
Defunct. Merged with Roseville Early Childhood Education Programs-Play 'n' Learn Library to form Roseville Early Childhood Education Program - Toy Library.

★11996★
RESPONSE ANALYSIS CORPORATION - LIBRARY (Soc Sci)
377 Wall St.
Box 158 Phone: (609)921-3333
Princeton, NJ 08542 Anne R. Frihart, Libn.
Staff: Prof 1. **Subjects:** Survey research methodology, energy consumption and conservation, marketing and market research, advertising and advertising research, communications and media, employee relations. **Holdings:** 1000 books; 1 VF drawer of clippings; 56 reels of microfilm; 1000 internal company reports; 700 corporate annual reports. **Subscriptions:** 50 journals and other serials. **Services:** Interlibrary loan; copying; library open to the public with restrictions. **Automated Operations:** Computerized public access catalog and serials. **Computerized Information Services:** DIALOG Information Services, Dow Jones News/Retrieval; internal databases. Performs searches on fee basis for clients only. **Publications:** BookRAC, monthly - for internal distribution only. **Special Catalogs:** Catalog of master records for company reports (book).

★11997★
RESURRECTION HOSPITAL - MEDICAL LIBRARY (Med)
7435 W. Talcott Rd. Phone: (312)774-8000
Chicago, IL 60631 Laura M. Wimmer, Med.Libn.
Founded: 1953. **Staff:** Prof 1; Other 2. **Subjects:** Medicine, allied health sciences. **Holdings:** 1307 books; 3671 bound periodical volumes; 624 cassettes. **Subscriptions:** 109 journals and other serials. **Services:** Interlibrary loan; library not open to the public. **Automated Operations:** Computerized cataloging and ILL. **Computerized Information Services:** MEDLINE; DOCLINE (electronic mail service). Performs searches on fee basis. **Networks/Consortia:** Member of Greater Midwest Regional Medical Library Network, Metropolitan Consortium of Chicago, Chicago Library System.

RETINA FOUNDATION
See: Eye Research Institute of Retina Foundation (4870)

REU MEMORIAL LIBRARY
See: Schools of Theology in Dubuque - Libraries (12976)

★11998★
REVEILLE UNITED METHODIST CHURCH - REVEILLE MEMORIAL LIBRARY (Rel-Phil)
4200 Cary Street Rd. Phone: (804)359-6041
Richmond, VA 23221 Janet P. Sigman, Adult Libn.
Staff: Prof 5; Other 6. **Subjects:** Bible studies, devotions, travel, art, philosophy, psychology, fiction. **Holdings:** 11,062 books; 10 bound periodical volumes; tapes; pictures; slides; films; 4 VF drawers. **Subscriptions:** 18 journals and other serials. **Services:** Interlibrary loan; library open to the public. **Publications:** In-church book reviews, monthly; reading lists for United Methodist Women's Circles, annual. **Staff:** Mrs. William Guthrie, Cat.; Martha Kurtz, AV Rm. 33.

REVENUE CANADA
See: Canada - Revenue Canada (2478)

★11999★
REVIEW & HERALD PUBLISHING ASSOCIATION - LIBRARY (Rel-Phil, Publ)
55 W. Oak Ridge Dr. Phone: (301)791-7000
Hagerstown, MD 21740 Betty F. Ullrich, Libn.
Staff: Prof 1; Other 1. **Subjects:** Seventh-Day Adventism, church history. **Special Collections:** Early Seventh-Day Adventist publications; William Miller Collection. **Holdings:** 40,000 books; 3000 bound periodical volumes; 2500 pamphlets; 18 VF drawers; Review & Herald, 1850-1971, on microcard. **Subscriptions:** 143 journals and other serials. **Services:** Copying (limited); library open for research on written request to chairman of library committee. **Special Indexes:** Index and catalogs to church periodicals (Adventist Review; Insight).

★12000★
REVLON, INC. - REVLON RESEARCH CENTER LIBRARY (Sci-Engr)
2121 Rte. 27 Phone: (201)287-7649
Edison, NJ 08817 Lee J. Tanen, Mgr., Lib./Info.Serv.
Founded: 1955. **Staff:** Prof 2; Other 1. **Subjects:** Cosmetics, soaps, chemistry, perfumery, dermatology, pharmacology, microbiology, aerosols. **Holdings:** 11,000 books; 4000 bound periodical volumes; 650 boxes of reports, pamphlets, reprints, documents; research notebooks. **Subscriptions:** 300 journals and other serials. **Services:** Interlibrary loan; copying; library open to the public by appointment. **Automated Operations:** Computerized acquisitions, serials, and circulation. **Computerized Information Services:** DIALOG Information Services, STN International, NLM; internal database. **Publications:** RRC Abstracts, biweekly; Cosmetics Patents Abstracts, monthly - both for internal distribution only. **Special Indexes:** Index to research notebooks. **Staff:** Susan Joseph, Asst.Libn..

★12001★
REX HOSPITAL - LIBRARY (Med)
4420 Lake Boone Trail Phone: (919)783-3100
Raleigh, NC 27607 Dorothy T. McCallum, Libn.
Founded: 1937. **Staff:** Prof 1; Other 1. **Subjects:** Medicine, nursing. **Holdings:** 1650 books; 2000 bound periodical volumes; 4 VF drawers of pamphlets, brochures, clippings. **Subscriptions:** 100 journals and other serials. **Services:** Interlibrary loan; library not open to the public.

★12002★
REXHAM CORPORATION - PACKAGING TECHNICAL LIBRARY
Church St. Extension
Box 111
Flemington, NJ 08822
Defunct

★12003★
REYNOLDA HOUSE, INC. - LIBRARY (Art)
Reynolda Rd.
Box 11765 Phone: (919)725-5325
Winston-Salem, NC 27106 Ruth Mullen, Libn.
Staff: Prof 1; Other 2. **Subjects:** American art and literature, art appreciation for children and adults. **Holdings:** 1700 books; 370 museum, gallery, special art collection catalogs; clippings and other items about American artists and American life; 3000 slides; musical recordings. **Subscriptions:** 23 journals and other serials. **Services:** Copying; library open to the public with restrictions.

REYNOLDS AUDIO-VISUAL DEPARTMENT
See: Rochester Public Library (12124)

★12004★
REYNOLDS ELECTRICAL AND ENGINEERING COMPANY, INC. - COORDINATION AND INFORMATION CENTER (Sci-Engr, Energy)
3084 S. Highland Phone: (702)295-0731
Las Vegas, NV 89109 Bernardo Maza, Supv.
Founded: 1979. **Staff:** Prof 9; Other 10. **Subjects:** Radioactive fallout, radiation monitoring, nuclear weapons testing, biological effects of radiation. **Special Collections:** U.S. Public Health Service Archive (effects of nuclear weapons testing on health; 76 reels of microfilm; 12,000 documents); U.S. Environmental Protection Agency's Las Vegas files 1955-1972 (23,000 documents); U.S. Department of Energy Historian Archives Office (14,000 documents); Los Alamos National Laboratory (8000 documents). **Holdings:** 661 books; 21,678 reports; 63,756 letters and memos; 6523 data documents; 1256 Atomic Energy Commission staff papers; 2257 articles; 1302 listings; 1812 meeting minutes; 2842 clippings; 12,207 press releases; 2148 field and monitoring logs; 14,691 other cataloged items. **Services:** Copying; center open to the public. **Automated Operations:** Computerized cataloging. **Special Indexes:** KWIC author and document indexes (microfiche). **Remarks:** Operates under contract to the U.S. Department of Energy. **Staff:** Thomas C. Mehas, Proj.Mgr.; Martha E. DeMarre, Hea. Physicist III.

★12005★
REYNOLDS ELECTRICAL AND ENGINEERING COMPANY, INC. - TECHNICAL LIBRARY
2501 Wyandotte St.
Box 14400, M/S 613
Las Vegas, NV 89114
Defunct

FRED J. REYNOLDS HISTORICAL GENEALOGY COLLECTION
See: Allen County Public Library (299)

★12006★
REYNOLDS METALS COMPANY - ALUMINA DIVISION TECHNOLOGY - TECHNICAL INFORMATION CENTER (Sci-Engr)
Box 9911 Phone: (512)643-6531
Corpus Christi, TX 78469 Dolores J. Mancias Phegan, Tech.Info.Spec.
Founded: 1979. **Staff:** 1. **Subjects:** Aluminum industry, engineering. **Holdings:** 755 volumes; 30 file cabinets of internal documents; 2 VF drawers of patents; 6 VF drawers of journal articles; drawings. **Subscriptions:** 61 journals and other serials; 7 newspapers. **Services:** Interlibrary loan; copying; center open to the public with restrictions. **Automated Operations:** Computerized cataloging and acquisitions. **Computerized Information Services:** DIALOG Information Services, BRS Information Technologies; INQUIRE (internal database). Performs searches on fee basis.

★12007★
REYNOLDS METALS COMPANY - BUSINESS AND TECHNICAL INFORMATION CENTER (Sci-Engr)
6603 W. Broad St.
Richmond, VA 23261 Phone: (804)281-2804
Founded: 1958. **Staff:** Prof 1. **Subjects:** Aluminum industry, business and marketing, international trade, engineering. **Holdings:** 200 books; 5 drawers of journals on microfiche. **Subscriptions:** 10 journals and other serials. **Services:** Interlibrary loan. **Computerized Information Services:** DIALOG Information Services.

★12008★
REYNOLDS METALS COMPANY - FLEXIBLE PACKAGING DIVISION - TECHNOLOGY CENTER LIBRARY (Sci-Engr)
2101 Reymet Rd. Phone: (804)743-6649
Richmond, VA 23237 Lorna K. Joyner, Adm.
Staff: 1. **Subjects:** Adhesives, inks and coatings, chemistry, foods and food packaging. **Holdings:** 1200 books; 190 bound periodical volumes; 12 VF drawers of company, project, subject files. **Subscriptions:** 75 journals and other serials. **Services:** Interlibrary loan; copying; library open to the public by appointment.

★12009★
REYNOLDS METALS COMPANY - MANUFACTURING TECHNOLOGY LABORATORY LIBRARY (Sci-Engr)
E. Second St.
Box 1200 Phone: (205)386-9536
Sheffield, AL 35660 Beth B. Stanford, Libn.
Founded: 1956. **Staff:** Prof 1. **Subjects:** Engineering, electrochemistry, aluminum production, material science, extraction metallurgy of aluminum physics, physical chemistry. **Holdings:** 1800 books; 700 bound periodical volumes; 11 VF drawers of patents. **Subscriptions:** 125 journals and other serials. **Services:** Interlibrary loan; library not open to the public. **Automated Operations:** Computerized cataloging and acquisitions. **Computerized Information Services:** DIALOG Information Services; INQUIRE (internal database).

★12010★
REYNOLDS METALS COMPANY - TECHNICAL INFORMATION SERVICES LIBRARY (Sci-Engr)
Fourth & Canal Sts.
Box 27003 Phone: (804)788-7409
Richmond, VA 23261 L. Pace Phillips, Lib.Spec.
Founded: 1965. **Staff:** Prof 1. **Subjects:** Metallurgy, materials science, applied sciences, engineering, chemistry, physics. **Holdings:** 15,000 books;

4600 bound periodical volumes; 6200 microfiche; 300 microfilm cartridges; 2200 internal technical reports. **Subscriptions:** 200 journals and other serials. **Services:** Interlibrary loan; copying; SDI; library open to the public by appointment. **Computerized Information Services:** DIALOG Information Services.

★12011★
REYNOLDS MUSEUM - LIBRARY (Hist)
4118 57th St. Phone: (403)352-5201
Wetaskiwin, AB, Canada T9A 2B6 Stanley G. Reynolds, Cur.
Founded: 1956. **Staff:** 1. **Subjects:** Antique automobiles, aircraft, gas tractors, and steam engines. **Holdings:** 3000 books and catalogs; 100 VF drawers of photographs, photocopies, illustrations. **Subscriptions:** 10 journals and other serials. **Services:** Library not open to the public.

★12012★
R.J. REYNOLDS TOBACCO COMPANY - ENGINEERING - TECHNICAL INFORMATION/RECORDS SECTION (Sci-Engr)
RJR Plaza, 11th Fl.
401 N. Main Phone: (919)777-4130
Winston-Salem, NC 27102 Pansy D. Broughton, Ref.Libn.
Staff: 1. **Subjects:** Mechanical engineering, environmental data, standards and codes. **Holdings:** 3200 books. **Subscriptions:** 140 journals and other serials. **Services:** Interlibrary loan; copying (limited); section open to the public with restrictions.

★12013★
R.J. REYNOLDS TOBACCO COMPANY - R&D SCIENTIFIC INFORMATION SERVICES LIBRARY (Sci-Engr, Agri)
Bowman Gray Technical Ctr., 611-12, 205C Phone: (919)741-4360
Winston-Salem, NC 27102 Randy D. Ralph, Master R&D Lit.Sci.
Founded: 1951. **Staff:** Prof 5; Other 8. **Subjects:** Tobacco, chemistry, biochemistry, agriculture, chemical engineering. **Holdings:** 25,528 books; 25,346 bound periodical volumes; 1405 unbound periodicals; 6500 internal reports; 1.5 million patents on microfilm. **Subscriptions:** 976 journals and other serials; 17 newspapers. **Services:** Interlibrary loan; copying; SDI; library open to the public with permission. **Automated Operations:** Computerized cataloging, acquisitions, serials, and circulation. **Publications:** Current awareness bulletin. **Staff:** Hana Rozsypal, Sr. R&D Lit.Sci.; Helen Chung, Sr. R&D Lit.Sci.; Nellie W. Sizemore, R&D Lit.Sci.; Richard W. Williams, R&D Lit.Sci..

REYNOLDS RESEARCH CENTER
See: Hall County Museum - Stuhr Museum (5967)

★12014★
RUSSELL REYNOLDS ASSOCIATES, INC. - LIBRARY (Bus-Fin)
200 S. Wacker Dr., Suite 3600 Phone: (312)993-9696
Chicago, IL 60606-4958 Gerri Hilt, Dir. of Res.
Staff: Prof 5; Other 3. **Subjects:** Business, financial services, banking. **Holdings:** 1000 books; company annual reports; subject files. **Subscriptions:** 50 journals and other serials. **Services:** Interlibrary loan; copying; library open to the public by appointment. **Automated Operations:** Computerized cataloging. **Computerized Information Services:** DIALOG Information Services, Dow Jones News/Retrieval, Dun & Bradstreet Corporation, NEXIS, VU/TEXT Information Services; Compulog (internal database). **Staff:** Barbara Dolmon, Res.Assoc.; Patricia Mortensen, Sr.Res.Assoc.; Kim Agriesti, Anl.; Kathy Kelly, Res.Assoc..

★12015★
REYNOLDS, SMITH & HILLS - LIBRARY (Sci-Engr, Plan)
6737 Southpoint Dr., S.
Box 4850 Phone: (904)396-2011
Jacksonville, FL 32201 Andrea Pennington
Founded: 1973. **Staff:** 1. **Subjects:** Architecture, engineering, planning. **Holdings:** 17,600 books; 600 bound periodical volumes; 8 VF drawers of pamphlets; 9000 government documents; microforms; maps. **Subscriptions:** 250 journals and other serials; 8 newspapers. **Services:** Interlibrary loan; copying; library open to the public by appointment. **Automated Operations:** Computerized cataloging, acquisitions, and circulation. **Computerized Information Services:** DIALOG Information Services, BRS Information Technologies; internal database. Performs searches on fee basis.

J.B. AND L.E. RHINE ARCHIVES
See: Foundation for Research on the Nature of Man - Library/Archives (5322)

★12016★
RHODE ISLAND HISTORICAL SOCIETY - LIBRARY (Hist)
121 Hope St. Phone: (401)331-8575
Providence, RI 02906 Paul R. Campbell, Lib.Dir.
Founded: 1822. **Staff:** Prof 5; Other 2. **Subjects:** Rhode Island history, New England genealogy, local history. **Special Collections:** Film Archives (feature films, newsreels, TV footage on Rhode Island); Rhode Island newspapers; Rhode Island imprints; business history. **Holdings:** 150,000 volumes; 1500 linear feet of manuscripts; 12,000 reels of microfilm of newspapers. **Subscriptions:** 1000 journals and other serials; 600 newspapers. **Services:** Interlibrary loan; copying; library open to the public. **Automated Operations:** Computerized cataloging. **Networks/Consortia:** Member of Consortium of Rhode Island Academic and Research Libraries, Inc. (CRIARL), Rhode Island Interrelated Library Network. **Publications:** Rhode Island History, quarterly - to members, by subscription to institutions. **Special Indexes:** Indexes to the Rhode Island Census for 1850, 1860 and 1865 (card). **Staff:** Suckey Lutman, Ref.Libn.; Harold E. Kemble, Mss.Cur.; Denise Bastien, Graphics Cur.; Madeleine Telfeyan, Tech.Serv.Libn..

★12017★
RHODE ISLAND HOSPITAL - PETERS HEALTH SCIENCES LIBRARY (Med)
593 Eddy St. Phone: (401)277-4671
Providence, RI 02902 Irene Lathrop, Dir. of Lib.Serv.
Founded: 1931. **Staff:** Prof 5; Other 7. **Subjects:** Medicine, medical specialities, nursing, hospital administration. **Special Collections:** Pratt Collection in Hospital Administration. **Holdings:** 9000 books; 11,000 bound periodical volumes. **Subscriptions:** 602 journals and other serials. **Services:** Interlibrary loan; copying; AV facilities; library open to the public with restrictions. **Automated Operations:** Computerized cataloging. **Computerized Information Services:** MEDLINE, OCLC. **Networks/Consortia:** Member of Consortium of Rhode Island Academic and Research Libraries, Inc. (CRIARL), NELINET. **Publications:** Library Access (newsletter); Peters Library Guides.

★12018★
RHODE ISLAND JEWISH HISTORICAL ASSOCIATION - LIBRARY (Area-Ethnic)
130 Sessions St. Phone: (401)331-1360
Providence, RI 02906 Eleanor F. Horvitz, Libn./Archv.
Founded: 1951. **Staff:** Prof 1; Other 1. **Subjects:** History of Rhode Island Jews, Jews in the United States. **Special Collections:** Family papers; papers and pictures of organizations and institutions; oral history tapes. **Holdings:** Figures not available. **Subscriptions:** 13 journals and other serials. **Services:** Library open to the public in presence of librarian. **Publications:** Rhode Island Jewish Historical Notes, annual - to members and by subscription; newsletter.

★12019★
RHODE ISLAND MEDICAL SOCIETY - LIBRARY
106 Francis St.
Providence, RI 02903
Defunct. Holdings absorbed by Brown University - Sciences Library.

RHODE ISLAND ORAL HISTORY PROJECT
See: University of Rhode Island (16810)

★12020★
RHODE ISLAND PUBLIC EXPENDITURE COUNCIL - LIBRARY (Soc Sci)
222 Richmond St. Phone: (401)521-6320
Providence, RI 02903-4214 Gary S. Sasse, Exec.Dir.
Founded: 1932. **Staff:** Prof 3; Other 2. **Subjects:** State and local government administration and finance. **Holdings:** 200 books; 500 research reports and government documents. **Subscriptions:** 100 journals and other serials. **Services:** Copying; library open to the public for reference use only on request. **Publications:** RIPEC Comments on Your Government, irregular - both to members and government officials.

★12021★
RHODE ISLAND SCHOOL OF DESIGN - LIBRARY (Art)
2 College St. Phone: (401)331-3511
Providence, RI 02903 Carol S. Terry, Dir.
Founded: 1878. **Staff:** Prof 4; Other 10. **Subjects:** Fine arts, architecture, applied arts. **Special Collections:** Lowthorpe Collection of Landscape Architecture (1200 volumes); artists' books (500 volumes). **Holdings:** 67,000 books; 7440 bound periodical volumes; 94,000 slides; 301,000 clippings; 30,000 mounted photographs; 1500 posters and color reproductions; 780 phonograph records. **Subscriptions:** 350 journals and

other serials. **Services:** Interlibrary loan; copying; library open to the public for reference use only. **Networks/Consortia:** Member of Consortium of Rhode Island Academic and Research Libraries, Inc. (CRIARL), RLG. **Staff:** Elinor Nacheman, Hd., Cat.Dept.; Annette Cooke-Tracey, Coord., Media Coll.; Laurie Averill, Rd.Serv.Libn..

★12022★
RHODE ISLAND STATE ARCHIVES (Hist)
State House, Rm. 43, Smith St. Phone: (401)277-2353
Providence, RI 02903 Phyllis C. Silva, Archv.
Staff: 1. **Subjects:** Rhode Island history. **Special Collections:** Private letters of Ellery and Huntington. **Holdings:** Acts and resolves of the General Assembly; colony records; Revolutionary War records; petitions and reports to the General Assembly; military and maritime charters. **Services:** Copying; archives open to the public with restrictions.

★12023★
RHODE ISLAND STATE DEPARTMENT OF ADMINISTRATION AFFAIRS - REFERENCE LIBRARY (Soc Sci)
275 Westminster Mall
Providence, RI 02903-3415 Phone: (401)277-2869
Founded: 1969. **Staff:** Prof 1. **Subjects:** Planning, government administration, legislation, health, census, land use. **Holdings:** 8422 volumes. **Subscriptions:** 14 journals and other serials; 6 newspapers. **Services:** Interlibrary loan.

★12024★
RHODE ISLAND STATE DEPARTMENT OF ECONOMIC DEVELOPMENT - RESEARCH DIVISION LIBRARY (Bus-Fin)
7 Jackson Walkway Phone: (401)277-2601
Providence, RI 02903 John A. Iemma, Res.Dir.
Subjects: Economic statistics. **Holdings:** Figures not available. **Remarks:** Telex: WUI 6814132.

★12025★
RHODE ISLAND STATE DEPARTMENT OF ELDERLY AFFAIRS - LIBRARY (Soc Sci)
79 Washington St. Phone: (401)277-2858
Providence, RI 02903 Eve M. Goldberg, Libn.
Founded: 1958. **Staff:** Prof 1. **Subjects:** Gerontology, geriatrics, retirement. **Special Collections:** Legislation and programs relating to aging. **Holdings:** 600 volumes; 50 state studies on aging; 100 pamphlets; 20 films; 10 video cassettes. **Subscriptions:** 20 journals and other serials. **Services:** Interlibrary loan; library open to the public.

★12026★
RHODE ISLAND STATE DEPARTMENT OF HEALTH - GERTRUDE E. STURGES MEMORIAL LIBRARY (Med)
75 Davis St., Rm. 407 Phone: (401)277-2506
Providence, RI 02908 A. William Pett, Libn.
Founded: 1939. **Staff:** Prof 1; Other 1. **Subjects:** Public health, preventive medicine, nursing. **Holdings:** 9400 books and pamphlets; 1200 bound periodical volumes; 4 drawers of newsletters; 2 cabinets of vertical files. **Subscriptions:** 275 journals and other serials; 5 newspapers. **Services:** Interlibrary loan; copying; library open to the public. **Computerized Information Services:** MEDLARS. **Networks/Consortia:** Member of Consortium of Rhode Island Academic and Research Libraries, Inc. (CRIARL).

★12027★
RHODE ISLAND STATE DEPARTMENT OF SOCIAL AND REHABILITATIVE SERVICES - STAFF DEVELOPMENT LIBRARY (Soc Sci)
600 New London Ave.
Cranston, RI 02920 Phone: (401)464-3111
Staff: 1. **Subjects:** Social work, psychology, social welfare policy. **Holdings:** 1000 books. **Subscriptions:** 14 journals and other serials. **Services:** Copying; library open to the public with restrictions. **Automated Operations:** Computerized cataloging.

★12028★
RHODE ISLAND (State) DEPARTMENT OF STATE LIBRARY SERVICES (Info Sci)
95 Davis St. Phone: (401)277-2726
Providence, RI 02908 Bruce E. Daniels, Dir.
Staff: Prof 20; Other 11. **Special Collections:** Professional Library Science Collection (3300 volumes); books on handicaps (350 volumes). **Holdings:** 50,000 books; 410 bound periodical volumes; pamphlet files. **Subscriptions:** 180 journals and other serials. **Services:** Interlibrary loan; copying; bookmobile services; library open to librarians, library school students, trustees, and the blind and handicapped. **Automated Operations:** Computerized cataloging and circulation. **Computerized Information Services:** DIALOG Information Services, OCLC; electronic mail service. **Networks/Consortia:** Member of NELINET, Rhode Island Interrelated Library Network. **Publications:** Newsletter, bimonthly - to libraries. **Special Catalogs:** Books about Handicaps (book); Non-print Media: Accession List (book). **Remarks:** Administers grants-in-aid to public libraries, serves as the Regional Library for the Blind and Handicapped, and gives professional leadership and consultant services for the development of improved library service. **Staff:** Barbara Wilson, Chf., Reg.Lib. for Blind; Sheila Carlson, Act.Chf., Lib.Plan.; Dorothy Frechette, Act.Dp.Dir..

★12029★
RHODE ISLAND STATE DEPARTMENT OF TRANSPORTATION - PLANNING DIVISION - LIBRARY (Trans)
State Office Bldg.
Smith St. Phone: (401)277-2694
Providence, RI 02903 Mark D. Joseph, Sr.Plan.
Staff: Prof 1. **Subjects:** Transportation. **Holdings:** 7500 volumes. **Services:** Library open to the public by appointment. **Staff:** Everett Carvalho, Engr.Techn.

★12030★
RHODE ISLAND STATE GOVERNOR'S OFFICE OF ENERGY ASSISTANCE - LIBRARY (Energy)
275 Westminster Mall
Providence, RI 02903-3393 Phone: (401)277-3370
Subjects: Energy conservation, oil, gas. **Holdings:** 2000 books.

★12031★
RHODE ISLAND STATE LAW LIBRARY (Law)
Providence County Court House
250 Benefit St. Phone: (401)277-3275
Providence, RI 02903 Kendall F. Svengalis, State Law Libn.
Founded: 1827. **Staff:** Prof 4; Other 4. **Subjects:** Law. **Special Collections:** Rare law books. **Holdings:** 101,000 volumes. **Subscriptions:** 268 journals and other serials; 7 newspapers. **Services:** Interlibrary loan; copying; library open to the public. **Networks/Consortia:** Member of New England Law Library Consortium (NELLCO). **Automated Operations:** Computerized cataloging. **Remarks:** Maintained by Rhode Island State Supreme Court. **Staff:** Sondra L. Giles, Asst.Libn.; Marcia LaKomski, Ref.Libn..

★12032★
RHODE ISLAND STATE LIBRARY (Info Sci, Law)
State House Phone: (401)277-2473
Providence, RI 02903 Beth I. Perry, State Libn.
Founded: 1851. **Staff:** Prof 4; Other 5. **Subjects:** Legislative law; reference and research. **Special Collections:** Rhode Island history and law. **Holdings:** 150,000 books; 250,000 U.S. Government documents. **Subscriptions:** 100 journals and other serials; 50 newspapers. **Services:** Interlibrary loan; copying; library open to the public with restrictions. **Automated Operations:** Computerized cataloging. **Computerized Information Services:** DIALOG Information Services, J-text. **Networks/Consortia:** Member of NELINET. **Publications:** List of documents received, quarterly. **Special Catalogs:** Reports filed for all state agencies with special emphasis on governor's office and legislative materials. **Staff:** Karen Quinn, Leg.Ref.; Robert Chase, Hd., Doc.Distr.Ctr.; Gretchen Pfeffer, Asst.Leg.Ref.Libn..

RHODE ISLAND STATE SUPREME COURT - RHODE ISLAND STATE LAW LIBRARY
See: Rhode Island State Law Library (12031)

★12033★
RHODODENDRON SPECIES FOUNDATION - LAWRENCE J. PIERCE RHODODENDRON LIBRARY (Biol Sci)
2525 S. 336th St.
Box 3798 Phone: (206)927-6960
Federal Way, WA 98063-3798 Frances P. Harrison, Chm., Lib.Comm.
Staff: Prof 2; Other 3. **Subjects:** Rhododendrons, azaleas, companion plants, trees and shrubs, general horticulture, plant explorers. **Special Collections:** Collections of field notes, photographs, and personal memorabilia of recent plant collectors. **Holdings:** 1000 books; 60 bound periodical volumes; 1500 files of other cataloged items. **Subscriptions:** 20 journals and other serials; 28 newsletters. **Services:** Copying; library open to the public. **Automated Operations:** Computerized cataloging. **Computerized Information Services:** Internal database. Performs searches

on fee basis. **Networks/Consortia:** Member of Council on Botanical Horticultural Libraries. **Publications:** Selected Rhododendron Bibliography.

★12034★
RHONE-POULENC AG COMPANY - LIBRARY (Sci-Engr, Agri)
2 T.W. Alexander Dr.
Box 12014 Phone: (919)549-2649
Research Triangle Park, NC 27709 Valerie Eslyn Wolford, Mgr.
Founded: 1981. **Staff:** Prof 1; Other 3. **Subjects:** Biochemistry, biotechnology, agricultural marketing, plant growth regulators, weed identification and control, insect identification and control, organic chemistry. **Holdings:** 11,600 books; 5000 bound periodical volumes; 650 volumes of Agriculture Marketing Reports; 100 VF drawers of statistics, product information; crop reports; 1700 reels of microfilm; 13,400 microfiche. **Subscriptions:** 700 journals and other serials. **Services:** Interlibrary loan; library open to the public by appointment for reference use only. **Computerized Information Services:** DIALOG Information Services, Pergamon ORBIT InfoLine, Inc., CAS ONLINE, National Pesticide Information Retrieval System (NPIRS), OCLC, INVESTEXT. **Formerly:** Union Carbide Agricultural Products Company, Inc. **Staff:** Deborah K. Doerr, Cat..

★12035★
RICE COUNTY HISTORICAL SOCIETY - ARCHIVES (Hist)
1814 Second Ave., N.W.
Box 5 Phone: (507)332-2121
Faribault, MN 55021 Susan McKenna, Dir.-Cur.
Founded: 1926. **Staff:** Prof 1. **Subjects:** Rice County, Minnesota. **Special Collections:** Rice County directories, 1895 to present. **Holdings:** 800 books; 500 manuscripts; 250 magazines and scrapbooks. **Services:** Copying; research; archives open to the public with restrictions.

HARLEY E. RICE MEMORIAL LIBRARY
See: Porter Memorial Hospital (11459)

JAMES E. RICE POULTRY LIBRARY
See: Cornell University - Albert R. Mann Library (3763)

RICE LIBRARY
See: U.S. Natl. Marine Fisheries Service - Southeast Fisheries Center (15223)

★12036★
RICE MEMORIAL HOSPITAL - HEALTH SCIENCE LIBRARY (Med)
301 Becker Ave., S.W. Phone: (612)235-4543
Willmar, MN 56201 Carol Conradi, Libn.
Staff: Prof 1. **Subjects:** Clinical medicine. **Holdings:** 1100 books; 900 bound periodical volumes. **Subscriptions:** 120 journals and other serials. **Services:** Interlibrary loan; copying; library open to the public with restrictions. **Computerized Information Services:** DIALOG Information Services.

RICE MILLERS ASSOCIATION ARCHIVES
See: University of Southwestern Louisiana - Jefferson Caffery Louisiana Room - Southwestern Archives and Manuscripts Collection (16895)

★12037★
RICE UNIVERSITY - ALICE PRATT BROWN LIBRARY (Art, Mus)
Fondren Library
Box 1892
Houston, TX 77251-1892 Phone: (713)527-4832
Founded: 1986. **Staff:** Prof 2. **Subjects:** Art history, architecture, music performance, music composition and theory, conducting. **Special Collections:** American music imprints, 1850-1950 (5100 titles); Halford Collection (Renaissance and Baroque keyboard; 200 titles); Richard Lert Library (conductor and student of Strauss; 250 books; 260 scores); Sylvester Collection (607 titles of stone lithographed music; 400 acoustical recordings). **Holdings:** 63,314 books and bound periodical volumes; 16,957 sound recordings; 16,405 scores; art exhibition catalogs. **Subscriptions:** 450 journals and other serials. **Services:** Interlibrary loan; copying; SDI; library open to the public. **Automated Operations:** Computerized cataloging and circulation. **Computerized Information Services:** DIALOG Information Services, Pergamon ORBIT InfoLine, Inc., BRS Information Technologies, Knowledge Index, RLIN, VU/TEXT Information Services, DataTimes; LIBRIS (internal database). Performs searches on fee basis. **Networks/Consortia:** Member of AMIGOS Bibliographic Council, Inc., Houston Area Research Library Consortium (HARLIC), Houston Music Librarians' Consort (HMLC). **Publications:** Rice Notes (newsletter), irregular. **Staff:** Jet Prendeville, Art & Arch.Libn.; Sandy Wenner, Mus.Libn..

★12038★
RICE UNIVERSITY - DIVISION OF GOVERNMENT PUBLICATIONS & SPECIAL RESOURCES (Info Sci)
Fondren Library
Box 1892 Phone: (713)527-8101
Houston, TX 77251-1892 Barbara Kile, Dir.
Staff: Prof 2; Other 3. **Holdings:** 230,000 government documents; 500,000 technical reports; 1.5 million microforms; U.S. patents: utility, 1960 to present; design, 1842 to present; reissues, 1838 to present; plant, 1978 to present. **Services:** Interlibrary loan; copying; department open to the public. **Computerized Information Services:** U.S. Patent Classification System, LEGI-SLATE. Performs searches free of charge. **Publications:** Guides to the collections, irregular - free upon request.

★12039★
RICE UNIVERSITY - JONES GRADUATE SCHOOL OF ADMINISTRATION - BUSINESS INFORMATION CENTER (Bus-Fin)
Herring Hall Phone: (713)527-8108
Houston, TX 77251 Peggy Shaw, Bus.Libn.
Staff: Prof 1; Other 1. **Subjects:** Accounting, finance, public administration, management, marketing. **Holdings:** 15,000 books; New York Stock Exchange companies' annual reports, 1980 to present, on microfiche. **Subscriptions:** 175 journals and other serials. **Services:** Interlibrary loan; copying; center open to the public. **Automated Operations:** Computerized cataloging. **Computerized Information Services:** DIALOG Information Services, BRS Information Technologies, Pergamon ORBIT InfoLine, Inc. Performs searches on fee basis.

★12040★
RICE UNIVERSITY - WOODSON RESEARCH CENTER (Hist, Hum)
Fondren Library Phone: (713)527-8101
Houston, TX 77251-1892 Nancy L. Boothe, Dir.
Staff: Prof 2; Other 2. **Subjects:** Texas history and entrepreneurship, Civil War, Rice University history, history of U.S. spaceflight, 20th century American literature, history of aeronautics and science. **Special Collections:** Masterson Texana (1200 volumes); Julian S. Huxley (90 linear feet of papers; 1000 volumes); Johnson Space Center History Archive (445 cubic feet); James A. Baker III Political Archive (75 linear feet); Anderson History of Aeronautics (3800 volumes); Axson 18th Century British Drama (5500 volumes); Confederate imprints (2500); Carlota and Maximilian manuscript collection (3 linear feet). **Holdings:** 20,000 books and bound periodical volumes; 1500 linear feet of university archives; 2000 linear feet of literary, historical, political, scientific, business, and artistic manuscript collections; 232 linear feet of faculty papers. **Services:** Copying (limited); center open to the public. **Publications:** Bibliography of cataloged archival publications in the Fondren Library (book). **Special Catalogs:** Manuscript collection guides: Julian Sorell Huxley papers; Johnson Space Center History Archive, 1952-1980; William Ward Watkin papers; Walter Benona and Estelle Sharp Collection, 1868-1978; Thomas Moore letters; Walter Gardner Hall papers; James Lockhart Autry papers; Masterson Texana Collection catalog.

★12041★
RICERCA INFORMATION SERVICES (Bus-Fin, Sci-Engr)
7528 Auburn Rd.
Box 1000 Phone: (216)357-3475
Painesville, OH 44077 Carol Duane, Mgr.Info.Serv.
Founded: 1980. **Staff:** Prof 3; Other 4. **Subjects:** Chemistry, agriculture, business, biotechnology, engineering, management, marketing research, finance. **Holdings:** 10,000 books; 4500 bound periodical volumes; 8800 reels of microfilm; 300,000 patents; 550 dissertations. **Subscriptions:** 253 journals and other serials. **Services:** Interlibrary loan; copying; SDI; consulting; fee-based information services; services open to companies and persons under contract. **Automated Operations:** Computerized acquisitions and circulation. **Computerized Information Services:** DIALOG Information Services, Pergamon ORBIT InfoLine, Inc., BRS Information Technologies, WILSONLINE, STN International, NewsNet, Inc., Telesystemes Questel, DataStar, Finsbury Data Services Ltd., NLM, Dow Jones News/Retrieval; MACCS (chemical registry database), Central Files Index database (internal databases). Performs searches on fee basis. **Networks/Consortia:** Member of Cleveland Area Metropolitan Library System (CAMLS). **Publications:** Quarterly newsletter. **Remarks:** An alternate telephone number is 357-3471. **Staff:** Elizabeth Wainio, Supv. of Rec., Tech.Info.Serv.; Susan Branchick, Supv., Corp.Lib., Chem.Info.Sys..

★12042★
BUDDY RICH FAN CLUB - LIBRARY (Mus)
Box 2014
Warminster, PA 18974 Charles Braun, Pres.
Founded: 1984. **Staff:** 5. **Subjects:** Buddy Rich. **Holdings:** Recordings; videotapes; paper memorabilia; photographs; access to 2000 hours of taped concerts. **Services:** Library not open to the public.

★12043★
RICHARDS, LAYTON & FINGER - LAW LIBRARY (Law)
One Rodney Square, 10th Fl.
Box 551 Phone: (302)658-6541
Wilmington, DE 19899 Jean D. Winstead, Law Libn.
Staff: 2. **Subjects:** Law - corporate, commercial, labor, tax, real estate. **Holdings:** 8400 books; 100 bound periodical volumes; 9 VF drawers of unreported Chancery, Supreme, and District Court opinions; 7 VF drawers of current and past Delaware legislation. **Subscriptions:** 115 journals and other serials. **Services:** Interlibrary loan; copying; library open to the public by referral only. **Computerized Information Services:** LEXIS. **Special Indexes:** Indexes to unreported Chancery Court opinions, reference file, and state legislation.

RICHARDSON ARCHIVES
See: University of South Dakota - I.D. Weeks Library (16859)

★12044★
RICHARDSON GREENSHIELDS OF CANADA, LTD. - RESEARCH LIBRARY (Bus-Fin)
130 Adelaide St., W., Suite 1400 Phone: (416)860-3432
Toronto, ON, Canada M5H 1T8 Vickie Cantelon, Libn.
Founded: 1921. **Staff:** Prof 1; Other 3. **Subjects:** Securities industry, economics, business, finance. **Holdings:** 1200 books and bound periodical volumes; 4800 classified files. **Subscriptions:** 140 journals and other serials. **Services:** Library open to university students and associate firms. **Publications:** Research publications. **Formerly:** Located in Winnipeg, MB.

RICHARDSON MEMORIAL LIBRARY
See: St. Louis Art Museum (12516)

★12045★
RICHARDSON-VICKS, INC. - MARKETING INFORMATION CENTER (Bus-Fin)
10 Westport Rd. Phone: (203)834-5000
Wilton, CT 06897 Mary Lou Wells, Mgr.
Staff: Prof 1; Other 1. **Subjects:** Market research, marketing, drugs. **Holdings:** 500 books; 70 VF drawers of reports, pamphlets, clippings. **Subscriptions:** 150 journals and other serials. **Services:** Interlibrary loan; center open to the public by permission.

RICHARDSON-VICKS, INC. - VICKS RESEARCH CENTER
See: Procter & Gamble Company - Vicks Research Center (11605)

WILLIAM S. RICHARDSON SCHOOL OF LAW
See: University of Hawaii (16201)

★12046★
RICHLAND COLLEGE - ADULT RESOURCE CENTER (Educ)
12800 Abrams Rd. Phone: (214)238-6034
Dallas, TX 75243-2199 Elaine Sullivan, Dir.
Staff: 6. **Subjects:** Personal growth, career development, women's issues. **Holdings:** 105 volumes. **Services:** Center open to clients and community.

★12047★
RICHLAND COUNTY LAW LIBRARY (Law)
Court House
50 Park Ave., E. Phone: (419)524-9944
Mansfield, OH 44902 Arthur W. Negin, Pres.
Founded: 1896. **Staff:** Prof 2. **Subjects:** Law and allied subjects. **Holdings:** 20,000 books. **Services:** Library open to students on introduction.

★12048★
RICHLAND MEMORIAL HOSPITAL - JOSEY MEMORIAL HEALTH SCIENCES LIBRARY (Med)
5 Richland Medical Park Phone: (803)765-6312
Columbia, SC 29203 Kay F. Harwood, Dir.
Founded: 1940. **Staff:** Prof 1; Other 2. **Subjects:** Medicine, medical specialities, nursing, hospital administration. **Holdings:** 2600 books; 4000 bound periodical volumes; 300 videotapes; 950 audiotapes; 2800 slides. **Subscriptions:** 420 journals and other serials. **Services:** Interlibrary loan; copying; SDI; library open to the public. **Computerized Information Services:** MEDLARS, DIALOG Information Services. Performs searches on fee basis. **Networks/Consortia:** Member of Columbia Area Medical Librarians' Association (CAMLA), South Carolina Health Information Network (SCHIN).

★12049★
RICHLAND MEMORIAL HOSPITAL - STAFF LIBRARY (Med)
800 East Locust Phone: (618)395-2131
Olney, IL 62450 Carolyn K. Wells, Dir., Med.Rec.
Staff: 1. **Subjects:** Internal medicine, surgery, oncology, hematology, orthopedics, obstetrics-gynecology. **Holdings:** 448 books. **Subscriptions:** 12 journals and other serials. **Services:** Library not open to the public.

RICHMOND AREA DEVELOPMENT ARCHIVES
See: Virginia Commonwealth University - James Branch Cabell Library - Special Collections and Archives (17356)

MARY RICHMOND ARCHIVES
See: Columbia University - Whitney M. Young, Jr. Memorial Library of Social Work (3496)

★12050★
RICHMOND MEMORIAL HOSPITAL - MEDICAL AND NURSING SCHOOL LIBRARIES (Med)
1300 Westwood Ave. Phone: (804)254-6008
Richmond, VA 23227 Merle L. Colglazier, Libn.
Founded: 1960. **Staff:** Prof 1; Other 1. **Subjects:** Medicine, nursing, health sciences. **Holdings:** 8000 books and bound periodical volumes; nursing AV programs. **Subscriptions:** 149 journals and other serials. **Services:** Interlibrary loan; copying; libraries open to qualified users for reference use only. **Networks/Consortia:** Member of Richmond Health Information Group.

RICHMOND NATIONAL BATTLEFIELD PARK
See: U.S. Natl. Park Service (15343)

★12051★
RICHMOND NEWSPAPERS, INC. - LIBRARY (Publ)
Box C-32333 Phone: (804)649-6000
Richmond, VA 23293 Charles D. Saunders, Libn.
Staff: 8. **Subjects:** Newspaper reference topics. **Holdings:** 2000 books; 56 file cases of clippings; 59 file cases of pictures; newspapers on microfilm. **Services:** Copying; library open to the public.

★12052★
RICHMOND PUBLIC LIBRARY - ART AND MUSIC DEPARTMENT (Art, Mus)
101 E. Franklin St. Phone: (804)780-4740
Richmond, VA 23219 Helen M. Ogden, Sr.Libn.
Staff: Prof 4; Other 1. **Subjects:** Fine arts, crafts, decoration, antiques, music, dance. **Special Collections:** Scott Fund Orchestral Scores (280). **Holdings:** 23,500 books; 2132 bound periodical volumes; 12,400 scores; 271 large print reproductions; 13 VF drawers of art and music clippings; 15 VF drawers of pamphlets; 31 VF drawers of sheet music; 10,900 recordings; 32 VF drawers of pictures. **Subscriptions:** 74 journals and other serials. **Services:** Interlibrary loan; copying (limited); department open to the public. **Staff:** Judy Fiscus, Libn.; Margaret Harter, Libn.Asst.; Theresa Wagenknecht, Libn..

★12053★
RICHMOND PUBLIC LIBRARY - BUSINESS, SCIENCE & TECHNOLOGY DEPARTMENT (Bus-Fin, Sci-Engr)
101 E. Franklin St. Phone: (804)780-8223
Richmond, VA 23219 Alice L. DeCamps, Hd.
Founded: 1972. **Staff:** Prof 4; Other 2. **Subjects:** Social sciences, business, pure sciences, applied sciences. **Holdings:** Books; Foundation Center Regional Collection; 1100 annual reports of business corporations; government publications; city documents. **Subscriptions:** 415 journals and other serials; 8 newspapers. **Services:** Interlibrary loan; copying (limited); department open to the public. **Publications:** Miscellaneous book lists. **Staff:** F. Rebecca Walker, Libn.; Elizabeth H. Holmes, Libn.; Carol Callahan, Libn..

★12054★
RICHMOND PUBLIC LIBRARY - SPECIAL COLLECTIONS (Educ)
325 Civic Center Plaza Phone: (415)620-6561
Richmond, CA 94804 Marie Contreras, City Libn.
Founded: 1905. **Special Collections:** Local history; job information center; AV collection (film; video cassettes); motor manuals; art prints; Afro-

American history; LEAP (literacy program). **Services:** Interlibrary loan; copying; collections open to the public. **Automated Operations:** Computerized cataloging and circulation. **Computerized Information Services:** DIALOG Information Services, WILSONLINE; CLSI (internal database); OnTyme Electronic Message Network Service (electronic mail service). Performs searches on fee basis. Contact Person: Douglas Holtzman. **Networks/Consortia:** Member of Bay Area Library and Information Network (BALIN), Bay Area Library and Information System (BALIS).

★12055★
RICHMOND PUBLIC SCHOOLS - CURRICULUM MATERIALS CENTER (Educ)
301 N. Ninth St. Phone: (804)780-5370
Richmond, VA 23219 Dr. Delores Z. Pretlow, Supv., Media Serv.
Founded: 1964. **Staff:** Prof 1; Other 3. **Subjects:** Education. **Holdings:** 11,500 books; 800 pamphlets; multimedia kits for grades K-12. **Subscriptions:** 150 journals and other serials. **Services:** Center open to school and city employees. **Automated Operations:** Computerized cataloging, acquisitions, and circulation. **Computerized Information Services:** DIALOG Information Services.

RICHTER LIBRARY
See: Desert Botanical Garden (4207)

OTTO G. RICHTER LIBRARY
See: University of Miami (16405)

RICKER LIBRARY OF ARCHITECTURE AND ART
See: University of Illinois (16258)

HELEN RICKSON LIBRARY
See: Taylor Business Institute (13895)

DR. W.A. RIDDELL HEALTH SCIENCES LIBRARY
See: Plains Health Centre (11377)

RIDEAU REGIONAL CENTRE
See: Ontario Ministry of Community and Social Services (10828)

★12056★
RIDER, BENNETT, EGAN & ARUNDEL - LIBRARY (Law)
2500 First Bank Place W.
Minneapolis, MN 55402 Phone: (612)340-7960
Staff: Prof 2. **Subjects:** Law. **Holdings:** 5500 books. **Subscriptions:** 50 journals and other serials. **Services:** Library not open to the public. **Computerized Information Services:** LEXIS, WESTLAW. **Staff:** Marillyn Soulen, Libn.; Kathy McGuire, Libn..

★12057★
RIDER COLLEGE - FRANKLIN F. MOORE LIBRARY (Bus-Fin)
2083 Lawrenceville Rd. Phone: (609)896-5111
Lawrenceville, NJ 08648-0399 Ross Stephen, Dir., Lib.Serv.
Founded: 1934. **Staff:** Prof 13; Other 13. **Subjects:** Business. **Special Collections:** Kendric C. Hill Shorthand Collection; Riderana. **Holdings:** 325,000 books; 40,000 bound periodical volumes; Delaware Valley newspapers. **Subscriptions:** 1800 journals and other serials. **Services:** Interlibrary loan; copying; library open to the public. **Automated Operations:** Computerized cataloging, acquisitions, and circulation. **Computerized Information Services:** DIALOG Information Services, Dow Jones News/Retrieval, OCLC. **Networks/Consortia:** Member of PALINET, New Jersey Library Network.

★12058★
RIDGETOWN COLLEGE OF AGRICULTURAL TECHNOLOGY - LIBRARY (Agri)
Ridgetown, ON, Canada N0P 2C0 Phone: (519)674-5456
Mrs. I.R. Roadhouse, Libn.
Founded: 1951. **Staff:** Prof 2; Other 3. **Subjects:** Agriculture, soils, crops, horticulture, biology, agricultural engineering and chemistry, livestock, farm economics, English and communication. **Holdings:** 10,000 books and bound periodical volumes; 2000 pamphlets and clippings. **Subscriptions:** 140 journals and other serials; 15 newspapers. **Services:** Interlibrary loan; copying; library open to the public. **Computerized Information Services:** Online systems. **Publications:** Bibliographies. **Remarks:** College is a branch of the Ontario Ministry of Agriculture and Food.

RIECKER MEMORIAL LIBRARY
See: Catherine Mc Auley Health Center (8160)

RIEMENSCHNEIDER BACH INSTITUTE
See: Baldwin-Wallace College - Riemenschneider Bach Institute (1250)

★12059★
RIFKIND CENTER FOR GERMAN EXPRESSIONIST STUDIES - ART LIBRARY AND GRAPHICS COLLECTION (Art)
Los Angeles County Museum of Art
5905 Wilshire Blvd. Phone: (213)278-0970
Los Angeles, CA 90036 Susan Trauger, Art Libn.
Founded: 1979. **Staff:** Prof 3. **Subjects:** German Expressionist art. **Special Collections:** German Expressionist art exhibition catalogs, monographs, illustrated books, and portfolios; Expressionist periodicals; German Expressionist graphics collection. **Holdings:** 5000 volumes. **Services:** Library open to qualified art professionals by appointment only. **Publications:** List of publications - available upon request.

★12060★
AUSTEN RIGGS CENTER, INC. - AUSTEN FOX RIGGS LIBRARY (Med)
Main St. Phone: (413)298-5511
Stockbridge, MA 01262 Helen Linton, Libn.
Founded: 1919. **Staff:** Prof 1. **Subjects:** Psychoanalysis, psychiatry, psychology. **Holdings:** 8543 books; 2013 bound periodical volumes; 54 cassettes. **Subscriptions:** 121 journals and other serials. **Services:** Interlibrary loan; library open to the public upon recommendation of staff member or librarian. **Computerized Information Services:** DIALOG Information Services. Performs searches free of charge.

★12061★
RIGHT TO LIFE LEAGUE OF SOUTHERN CALIFORNIA - LIBRARY (Soc Sci)
1616 W. 9th St., Suite 220 Phone: (213)380-8750
Los Angeles, CA 90015 David Wilkinson, Dir. of Educ.
Founded: 1969. **Staff:** Prof 5; Other 6. **Subjects:** Abortion, pre-natal development, euthanasia, genetic engineering, infanticide, human experimentation, population control. **Special Collections:** The Human Life Review, 1975-1986. **Holdings:** Books; periodicals; clippings; pamphlets; cassettes. **Services:** Copying; library open to the public with restrictions. **Publications:** Living (newsletter), quarterly - free upon request. **Special Catalogs:** Catalog of pro-life materials; catalog of audiovisual aids.

ERLING RIIS RESEARCH LABORATORY
See: International Paper Company (7054)

★12062★
RILEY COUNTY GENEALOGICAL SOCIETY - LIBRARY (Hist)
2005 Claflin Rd. Phone: (913)537-2205
Manhattan, KS 66502 Evelyn Brown, Pres.
Founded: 1963. **Staff:** Prof 2; Other 2. **Subjects:** Genealogy, state and local history. **Holdings:** 3600 books; 600 bound periodical volumes; 3 VF drawers of original biographies; 1 VF drawer and 15 card file drawers of genealogical charts of society members' ancestors; 50 reels of microfilm of census materials; 6 card drawers of microfiche of genealogical and land records. **Subscriptions:** 125 journals and other serials. **Services:** Copying; SDI; library open to the public. **Publications:** Kansas Kin, quarterly - by subscription or exchange. **Special Indexes:** Indexes to censuses of Riley County and 1880 census of surrounding counties; index to cemetery records. **Staff:** Mildred Loeffler, Res.; Helen R. Long, Cat./Acq.Libn..

★12063★
RILEY COUNTY HISTORICAL SOCIETY - SEATON MEMORIAL LIBRARY (Hist)
2309 Claflin Rd. Phone: (913)537-2210
Manhattan, KS 66502 D. Cheryl Collins, Archv./Libn.
Founded: 1914. **Staff:** Prof 2; Other 2. **Subjects:** History of Manhattan City and Riley County, Kansas, Kansas State University. **Holdings:** 4000 books; 100 bound periodical volumes; 100 scrapbooks; 425 cubic feet of archival materials; 4100 local photographs; 2 architect's filing cabinets of maps, documents, newspaper tear sheets and special issues; 350 cubic feet of manuscripts; 20 oral history tapes. **Services:** Copying; library open to the public. **Staff:** Jeanne Mithen, Asst.Libn..

RILEY-HICKINGBOTHAM LIBRARY
See: Ouachita Baptist University (10954)

★12064★
RILEY STOKER CORPORATION - LIBRARY (Sci-Engr, Energy)
5 Neponset St.
Box 2040 Phone: (508)852-7100
Worcester, MA 01613 Jane M. Milligan, Info.Spec.
Staff: Prof 1. **Subjects:** Steam generation, fuel burning equipment, power generation, boilers and pressure vessels, petroleum chemicals, coal gasification. **Special Collections:** American Society of Mechanical Engineers (ASME) Boiler and Pressure Vessel Codes; Environmental Protection Agency, U.S. Dept. of Energy, and Electric Power Research Institute reports. **Holdings:** 1400 books; 18 VF drawers of reports and papers; 500 patents. **Subscriptions:** 130 journals and other serials; 5 newspapers. **Services:** Interlibrary loan; copying; SDI; library open to the public by appointment. **Automated Operations:** Computerized cataloging. **Computerized Information Services:** DIALOG Information Services; VAX (internal database). Performs searches on fee basis. **Networks/Consortia:** Member of Worcester Area Cooperating Libraries (WACL). **Publications:** Monthly Bulletin.

★12065★
JOHN AND MABLE RINGLING MUSEUM OF ART - ART RESEARCH LIBRARY (Art, Rare Book)
Box 1838 Phone: (813)355-5101
Sarasota, FL 33578 Lynell A. Morr, Art Libn.
Founded: 1930. **Staff:** Prof 1; Other 1. **Subjects:** Baroque art; 16th, 17th, and 18th century European art; contemporary art; Rubens. **Special Collections:** Rare books (16th, 17th, and 18th century art history sources); Emblem books; Iconography; Gluck (Gustav) collection of offprints of materials on early Flemish and Dutch painters. **Holdings:** 15,500 books; 1815 bound periodical volumes; 36,000 art catalogs; 100 VF drawers of art auction sale catalogs; 4 VF drawers of clippings; 16 VF drawers of Phototeca files. **Subscriptions:** 100 journals and other serials. **Services:** Interlibrary loan; copying; library open to the public. **Computerized Information Services:** OCLC. **Networks/Consortia:** Member of SOLINET. **Special Catalogs:** Exhibition Catalogs: Rare Books of the 16th, 17th, and 18th centuries from the Library of the Ringling Museum of Art, Sarasota, FL, November 3-23, 1969.

★12066★
RINGLING SCHOOL OF ART AND DESIGN - LIBRARY (Art)
1111 27th St. Phone: (813)351-4614
Sarasota, FL 33580 Yvonne Morse, Lib.Dir.
Founded: 1928. **Staff:** Prof 2; Other 3. **Subjects:** Art history, interior design, advertising design, architecture, graphics, painting. **Special Collections:** Print Collection of Japanese Art (Robert M. Jackson Collection; 800 items); European prints of 17th and 18th century (500 items). **Holdings:** 11,000 books; 800 bound periodical volumes; 800 museum catalogs; 24,000 art slides; 34 16mm films. **Subscriptions:** 212 journals and other serials. **Services:** Interlibrary loan; copying; library open to artists and researchers. **Networks/Consortia:** Member of Florida Library Information Network (FLIN), West Coast Library Consortium (WELCO). **Staff:** Allen R. Novak, AV Libn..

★12067★
RIO ALGOM, LTD. - INFORMATION CENTRE (Sci-Engr)
120 Adelaide St., W. Phone: (416)365-6800
Toronto, ON, Canada M5H 1W5 Penny Lipman, Libn.
Founded: 1966. **Staff:** Prof 1. **Subjects:** Mining, uranium, copper, tin, potash, coal. **Holdings:** 3000 books; 1000 bound periodical volumes; annual reports for 1000 companies; Canadian and U.S. federal and provincial geological reports. **Subscriptions:** 150 journals and other serials; 12 newspapers. **Services:** Interlibrary loan; copying; library open to librarians. **Computerized Information Services:** DIALOG Information Services, Info Globe, QL Systems, Dow Jones News/Retrieval, TEXTLINE, Dunserve II, WILSONLINE, Infomart, CAN/LAW. **Remarks:** Fax: (416)365-6870.

MAURICE RITZ RESOURCE LIBRARY AND BOOKSTORE
See: Planned Parenthood of Wisconsin (11390)

LUIS MUNOZ RIVERA LIBRARY AND MUSEUM
See: Puerto Rican Culture Institute (11701)

★12068★
RIVERSIDE COMMUNITY MEMORIAL HOSPITAL - HEALTH SCIENCE LIBRARY (Med)
800 Riverside Dr. Phone: (715)258-1063
Waupaca, WI 54981 Andrea Crane, Libn.
Founded: 1978. **Staff:** Prof 2. **Subjects:** Medicine, nursing, health care administration, pathology. **Holdings:** 630 books. **Subscriptions:** 90 journals and other serials. **Services:** Interlibrary loan; library not open to the public. **Automated Operations:** Computerized cataloging, acquisitions, serials, and circulation. **Networks/Consortia:** Member of Fox River Valley Area Library Consortium.

RIVERSIDE COUNTY ART & CULTURE CENTER - EDWARD-DEAN MUSEUM OF DECORATIVE ARTS
See: Edward-Dean Museum Art Reference Library (4621)

★12069★
RIVERSIDE COUNTY HISTORICAL COMMISSION - LIBRARY (Hist)
4600 Crestmore Rd.
Box 3507 Phone: (714)787-2551
Rubidoux, CA 92509 Diana Seider, Dir.
Founded: 1974. **Staff:** Prof 3. **Subjects:** Local and California history, Indian history. **Special Collections:** History of Riverside County. **Holdings:** 500 volumes; manuscripts and ephemera relating to Riverside County history; 90 oral history tapes. **Services:** Copying; library open to the public for reference use only. **Publications:** Historical Commission Press, annual. **Staff:** Don Kleinhesselink, Cur. of Hist..

★12070★
RIVERSIDE COUNTY LAW LIBRARY (Law)
3535 Tenth St., Suite 100 Phone: (714)787-2460
Riverside, CA 92501 Gayle Webb, Law Libn.
Staff: Prof 2; Other 5. **Subjects:** Law. **Holdings:** 43,001 books and bound periodical volumes; 3808 microforms; 128 cassettes; county ordinances and codes; state and federal statutes; treatises. **Subscriptions:** 62 journals and other serials. **Services:** Copying; SDI; library open to the public. **Computerized Information Services:** WESTLAW, OCLC.

★12071★
RIVERSIDE COUNTY LAW LIBRARY - INDIO LAW LIBRARY (Law)
46-209 Oasis St. Phone: (619)342-8316
Indio, CA 92201 Peggy Snyder, Lib.Asst.
Staff: 3. **Subjects:** Law. **Holdings:** 15,000 volumes. **Services:** Copying; library open to the public. **Computerized Information Services:** WESTLAW.

★12072★
RIVERSIDE GENERAL HOSPITAL - MEDICAL LIBRARY (Med)
9851 Magnolia Ave. Phone: (714)351-7066
Riverside, CA 92503 Rosalie Reed, Med.Lib.Asst.
Staff: Prof 1; Other 1. **Subjects:** Medicine, surgery, nursing, allied health sciences. **Holdings:** 1015 books; 5337 bound periodical volumes. **Subscriptions:** 216 journals and other serials. **Services:** Interlibrary loan; copying; SDI; library open to the public with permission from administration. **Computerized Information Services:** NLM. **Networks/Consortia:** Member of Inland Empire Medical Library Cooperative, Medical Library Group of Southern California and Arizona (MLGSCA).

★12073★
RIVERSIDE HOSPITAL - HEALTH SCIENCES LIBRARY (Med)
J. Clyde Morris Blvd.
Newport News, VA 23601 Phone: (804)599-2175
Staff: Prof 2; Other 5. **Subjects:** Family practice, medicine, pediatrics, obstetrics-gynecology, nursing, allied health sciences. **Holdings:** 4038 books; 6742 bound periodical volumes. **Subscriptions:** 203 journals and other serials. **Services:** Interlibrary loan; copying; library open to the public for reference use only. **Computerized Information Services:** MEDLINE. **Remarks:** An alternate telephone number is 599-2682. **Staff:** Joan Taylor, Nurs.Libn.; Peggy Rogers, Med.Libn..

★12074★
RIVERSIDE HOSPITAL - MEDICAL LIBRARY (Med)
700 Lea Blvd. Phone: (302)764-6120
Wilmington, DE 19802 Gail P. Gill, Dir.
Founded: 1967. **Staff:** Prof 1; Other 1. **Subjects:** Osteopathic medicine, internal medicine, nursing. **Holdings:** 300 books and bound periodical volumes; 400 cassettes; 3 VF drawers of pamphlets. **Subscriptions:** 52 journals and other serials. **Services:** Interlibrary loan; library not open to the public. **Networks/Consortia:** Member of Wilmington Area Biomedical Library Consortium (WABLC), Libraries in the New Castle County System (LINCS).

★12075★
RIVERSIDE HOSPITAL - SARAH AND JULIUS STEINBERG MEMORIAL LIBRARY (Med)
1600 N. Superior St. Phone: (419)729-6198
Toledo, OH 43604 Kathryn Maluchnik, Libn.
Staff: Prof 1; Other 1. **Subjects:** Medicine, nursing, podiatry, sports medicine, health promotion, hospital management. **Holdings:** 1000 books; 850 bound periodical volumes. **Subscriptions:** 240 journals and other serials. **Services:** Interlibrary loan; copying; SDI; library open to qualified users by request. **Computerized Information Services:** MEDLINE, BRS Information Technologies. **Networks/Consortia:** Member of Greater Midwest Regional Medical Library Network.

★12076★
RIVERSIDE HOSPITAL - SCOBIE MEMORIAL LIBRARY (Med)
1967 Riverside Dr. Phone: (613)738-8230
Ottawa, ON, Canada K1H 7W9 Jean E. White, Libn.
Founded: 1968. **Staff:** Prof 1; Other 5. **Subjects:** Medicine, nursing, hospital administration. **Holdings:** 1000 books; 500 bound periodical volumes; 200 videotapes and cassettes. **Subscriptions:** 175 journals and other serials. **Services:** Interlibrary loan; copying; library open to the public.

★12077★
RIVERSIDE MEDICAL CENTER - HEALTH SCIENCES LIBRARY (Med)
Riverside at 25th Ave., S. Phone: (612)371-6545
Minneapolis, MN 55454 Linda McIntosh, Dir.
Founded: 1971. **Staff:** Prof 1; Other 4. **Subjects:** Medicine, orthopedics, nursing. **Holdings:** 3067 books; 4500 bound periodical volumes; 233 audiotapes. **Subscriptions:** 300 journals and other serials. **Services:** Library not open to the public. **Computerized Information Services:** BRS Information Technologies, MEDLINE. **Networks/Consortia:** Member of Twin Cities Biomedical Consortium (TCBC).

★12078★
RIVERSIDE MEDICAL CENTER - MEDICAL LIBRARY (Med)
350 N. Wall St. Phone: (815)933-1671
Kankakee, IL 60901 Brenda Brower, Libn.
Founded: 1977. **Staff:** Prof 1; Other 6. **Subjects:** Medicine, nursing, hospital administration, mental health, substance abuse. **Holdings:** 300 books; 200 bound periodical volumes; 110 cassettes; 120 slide/cassette sets. **Subscriptions:** 230 journals and other serials; 10 newspapers. **Services:** Interlibrary loan; library open to the public with physician referral. **Automated Operations:** Computerized acquisitions. **Computerized Information Services:** MEDLINE. **Networks/Consortia:** Member of Chicago and South Consortium, Bur Oak Library System, Greater Midwest Regional Medical Library Network.

★12079★
RIVERSIDE METHODIST HOSPITAL - D.J. VINCENT MEDICAL LIBRARY (Med)
3535 Olentangy River Rd. Phone: (614)261-5230
Columbus, OH 43214 Josephine W. Yeoh, Dir.
Staff: Prof 2; Other 6. **Subjects:** Clinical medicine, nursing, hospital administration, microcomputers, management, patient education, fiction. **Special Collections:** Complete collection of American Journal of Nursing, 1901 to present; historical medical books. **Holdings:** 21,000 books; 10,000 bound periodical volumes; 4 Audio-Digest tapes; NCME video cassettes; pamphlet files for patient education; professional reprints file; 500 archives of papers published by professionals connected with the hospital. **Subscriptions:** 500 journals and other serials. **Services:** Interlibrary loan; copying; SDI; library open to the public for reference use only. **Automated Operations:** Computerized cataloging and circulation. **Computerized Information Services:** MEDLINE, DIALOG Information Services, OCLC, BRS Information Technologies. Performs searches on fee basis. **Networks/Consortia:** Member of OHIONET, CALICO, Central Ohio Hospital Library Consortium. **Publications:** Newsletter, bimonthly - for internal distribution only; bibliographies - by request. **Staff:** Lynn Cooper, Med.Libn..

★12080★
RIVERSIDE MUNICIPAL MUSEUM - LIBRARY (Hist)
3720 Orange St. Phone: (714)782-5273
Riverside, CA 92501 William G. Dougall, Dir.
Subjects: History, anthropology, decorative arts, geology and paleontology, botany, zoology. **Holdings:** 1600 books; 400 bound periodical volumes; 250 feet of archival material; 2200 unbound periodicals. **Subscriptions:** 15 journals and other serials. **Services:** Library open to the public with restrictions. **Staff:** Bryn Barabas, Reg..

★12081★
RIVERSIDE OSTEOPATHIC HOSPITAL - MEDICAL LIBRARY (Med)
150 Truax St. Phone: (313)676-4200
Trenton, MI 48183 Susan E. Skoglund, Dir. of Lib.Serv.
Staff: Prof 1; Other 1. **Subjects:** Medicine, nursing. **Holdings:** 1231 books; 1158 bound periodical volumes; 3 VF drawers of pamphlets; 576 Audio-Digest tapes; University of Michigan Media Library slide-cassette programs. **Subscriptions:** 125 journals and other serials. **Services:** Interlibrary loan; library open to the public with restrictions. **Computerized Information Services:** MEDLINE, DIALOG Information Services, BRS Information Technologies, WILSONLINE.

★12082★
RIVERSIDE PRESBYTERIAN CHURCH - JEAN MILLER LIBRARY (Rel-Phil)
849 Park St. Phone: (904)355-4585
Jacksonville, FL 32204 Evelyn Parker, Libn.
Staff: Prof 2. **Subjects:** Religion, general subjects. **Holdings:** 1500 books.

★12083★
RIVERSIDE PRESS-ENTERPRISE COMPANY - EDITORIAL LIBRARY (Publ)
3512 14th St. Phone: (714)684-1200
Riverside, CA 92501 Joan K. Douglas, Lib.Dir.
Founded: 1968. **Staff:** Prof 1; Other 5. **Subjects:** Newspaper reference topics. **Holdings:** 350 books; clippings; microfilm. **Subscriptions:** 10 journals and other serials. **Services:** Copying; library open to the public on a limited schedule. **Computerized Information Services:** NEXIS. **Special Indexes:** Index of newspapers (notebooks and microfiche).

★12084★
RIVERVIEW HOSPITAL - LIBRARY SERVICES (Med)
500 Lougheed Hwy. Phone: (604)524-7018
Port Coquitlam, BC, Canada V3C 4J2 Min-Ja Laubental, Libn.
Founded: 1949. **Staff:** Prof 1; Other 2. **Subjects:** Psychiatry, psychology, psychiatric nursing, social sciences, medicine, hospital administration, forensic psychiatry. **Special Collections:** Audiovisual collection (125 tapes; 100 filmstrips). **Holdings:** 4450 books; 1510 bound periodical volumes; 160 staff publications; 50 annual reports; 580 pamphlets; 250 bibliographies. **Subscriptions:** 250 journals and other serials. **Services:** Interlibrary loan; copying; library open to the public for reference use only on request. **Automated Operations:** Computerized cataloging. **Computerized Information Services:** MEDLINE. **Publications:** In the Journals, monthly; acquisitions list, bimonthly - both for internal distribution only. **Remarks:** Maintains a Patients' Library of 5000 volumes. Also maintains the British Columbia Ministry of Health - Mental Health Programs - Staff Reference Library.

★12085★
RIVERVIEW MEDICAL CENTER - CLINICAL LIBRARY (Med)
1 Riverview Plaza Phone: (201)530-2275
Red Bank, NJ 07701 Cheryl Newman, Med.Libn.
Staff: Prof 1; Other 1. **Subjects:** Clinical medicine. **Holdings:** 2500 books; 900 audio cassettes; microfilm. **Subscriptions:** 250 journals and other serials. **Services:** Interlibrary loan; copying; library open to health professionals only. **Computerized Information Services:** MEDLARS, BRS Information Technologies; MESSAGES (electronic mail service). Performs searches on fee basis. **Networks/Consortia:** Member of Monmouth-Ocean Biomedical Information Consortium (MOBIC).

★12086★
RIVIER COLLEGE - REGINA LIBRARY (Area-Ethnic, Hum)
429 Main St. Phone: (603)888-1311
Nashua, NH 03060 Sr. Arlene Callahan, Lib.Dir.
Founded: 1933. **Staff:** Prof 5; Other 5. **Subjects:** French-Canadians, education, business, law. **Holdings:** 113,500 volumes; 39,306 nonprint items. **Subscriptions:** 550 journals and other serials; 15 newspapers. **Services:** Interlibrary loan; copying; library open to the public for reference use only. **Automated Operations:** Computerized cataloging. **Networks/Consortia:** Member of New Hampshire College & University Council Library Policy Committee (NHCUC), New Hampshire Automated Information System (NHAIS). **Publications:** Now and New (acquisitions list), biweekly - for internal distribution only. **Special Catalogs:** Regina Library Union List of Serials (printout). **Staff:** Sr. Albina-Marie, Hd., Tech.Serv.; Elaine Bean, Hd., Info.Serv..

★12087★
RJR NABISCO - NABISCO BRANDS, INC. - TECHNOLOGY CENTER LIBRARY (Food-Bev)
100 River Rd.
Box 1942 Phone: (201)503-3467
East Hanover, NJ 07936-1942 Sonia D. Meurer, Supv., Lib.
Founded: 1922. **Staff:** Prof 2; Other 2. **Subjects:** Food science. **Holdings:** 12,000 books; 3000 bound periodical volumes. **Subscriptions:** 800 journals and other serials. **Services:** Interlibrary loan; SDI; library open to the public. **Automated Operations:** Computerized cataloging, circulation, and serials. **Computerized Information Services:** DIALOG Information Services, Pergamon ORBIT InfoLine, Inc., LEXIS, NEXIS, Dun & Bradstreet Corporation, Dow Jones News/Retrieval, PRODUCTSCAN, BRS Information Technologies, CAS ONLINE. **Publications:** Guide to Current Literature, weekly; Library Bulletin, monthly; Technical Meetings List, annual. **Staff:** Carol Butler, Libn..

RKO PICTURES ARCHIVE
See: University of California, Los Angeles - Theater Arts Library (15987)

★12088★
RMS - VS PROGRAM LIBRARY (Mil)
5 Eves Dr. Phone: (609)596-5775
Marlton, NJ 08053 Robert Kudless, Tech.Libn.
Staff: Prof 1; Other 1. **Subjects:** Military specifications, aircraft, weapons. **Special Collections:** Information on the S-3 aircraft used by the U.S. Navy. **Holdings:** 9000 books; 470 tapes; 200 reels of microfilm; 100 microfiche. **Services:** Library not open to the public. **Automated Operations:** Computerized cataloging and circulation. **Computerized Information Services:** Internal database.

★12089★
RMT, INC. - LIBRARY (Sci-Engr)
1406 E. Washington Ave., Suite 124 Phone: (608)255-2134
Madison, WI 53703 Mary Jane Kayes, Libn.
Staff: Prof 2; Other 1. **Subjects:** Solid and hazardous waste management, environmental engineering, industrial hygiene, regulatory compliance, hydrogeology, consulting engineering. **Holdings:** Figures not available. **Subscriptions:** 300 journals and other serials. **Services:** Interlibrary loan; copying; SDI; library open to the public for reference use only and by appointment. **Computerized Information Services:** The Source Information Network, DIALOG Information Services, Chemical Information Systems, Inc. (CIS), Environmental Technical Information System (ETIS). Performs searches on fee basis. **Networks/Consortia:** Member of Multitype Advisory Library Committee (MALC). **Staff:** Sarah K. Castello, Assoc.Libn..

★12090★
ROADS AND TRANSPORTATION ASSOCIATION OF CANADA - TECHNICAL INFORMATION SERVICE (Trans)
1765 St. Laurent Blvd. Phone: (613)521-4052
Ottawa, ON, Canada K1G 3V4 Chris Hedges, Libn.
Founded: 1956. **Staff:** Prof 1. **Subjects:** Road construction, surface transportation, urban transit, transportation planning. **Holdings:** 16,000 books. **Subscriptions:** 200 journals and other serials. **Services:** Interlibrary loan; copying; service open to the public. **Automated Operations:** Computerized cataloging, circulation, and ILL. **Computerized Information Services:** DIALOG Information Services, ESA-QUEST, CAN/OLE. Performs searches on fee basis. **Publications:** Surface Transportation R & D in Canada, annual - by subscription; RTAC News, bimonthly - to members; Transportation Forum, quarterly - by subscription.

★12091★
ROANOKE LAW LIBRARY (Law)
315 Church Ave., S.W. Phone: (703)981-2268
Roanoke, VA 24016 Clayne Calhoun, Libn.
Staff: Prof 1. **Subjects:** State and federal law, federal taxation. **Holdings:** 15,000 volumes; 20,000 microfiche. **Subscriptions:** 120 journals and other serials. **Services:** Interlibrary loan; copying; library open to the public.

★12092★
ROANOKE MEMORIAL HOSPITALS - MEDICAL LIBRARY (Med)
Belleview at Jefferson St.
Box 13367 Phone: (703)981-7371
Roanoke, VA 24033 Lucy D. Glenn, Chf.Med.Libn.
Founded: 1959. **Staff:** Prof 2; Other 3. **Subjects:** Medicine, nursing, allied health sciences. **Holdings:** 5230 books; 4896 bound periodical volumes; 66 slide sets. **Subscriptions:** 254 journals and other serials. **Services:** Interlibrary loan; copying; SDI; library open to medical and health agencies staff. **Computerized Information Services:** BRS Information Technologies, MEDLINE; OnTyme Electronic Message Network Service (electronic mail service). Performs searches free of charge. **Networks/Consortia:** Member of Southwestern Virginia Health Information Librarians. **Publications:** Newsletter, quarterly - for internal distribution only; notices of new books, journals, and services. **Remarks:** Hospitals maintained by Carilion Health Systems.

ROANOKE TIMES & WORLD-NEWS
See: Times-World Corporation (14202)

★12093★
ROANOKE VALLEY HISTORICAL SOCIETY - LIBRARY (Hist)
1 Market Square, Center in The Square Phone: (703)342-5770
Roanoke, VA 24011 Clare White, Hd.Libn.
Founded: 1957. **Staff:** 4. **Subjects:** Roanoke and Southwest Virginia history. **Special Collections:** James Breckinridge and William Preston family letters and papers (1030 items). **Holdings:** 500 books. **Services:** Library open to researchers by appointment.

★12094★
ROARING FORK ENERGY CENTER - LIBRARY (Energy)
242 Main St.
Carbondale, CO 81623 Phone: (303)963-0311
Subjects: Solar energy, alternative energy, solar greenhouses, energy planning and conservation, renewable resources, wind and water power. **Holdings:** 1200 books; films; videotapes; slides; computer software programs. **Subscriptions:** 12 journals and other serials.

★12095★
ROATH & BREGA, P.C. - LAW LIBRARY (Law)
1873 S. Bellaire, Suite 1700
Box 5560, Terminal Annex Phone: (303)691-5400
Denver, CO 80217 Dorothy Norbie, Law Libn.
Staff: Prof 1; Other 2. **Subjects:** Law. **Holdings:** 10,000 books; 5000 volumes on microfiche. **Subscriptions:** 60 journals and other serials; 5 newspapers. **Services:** Interlibrary loan (to local libraries). **Automated Operations:** Computerized cataloging. **Computerized Information Services:** DIALOG Information Services, WESTLAW, LEXIS.

JEROME ROBBINS ARCHIVE
See: New York Public Library - Performing Arts Research Center - Dance Collection (10080)

JOHN E. ROBBINS LIBRARY
See: Brandon University (1817)

ROBBINS LIBRARY
See: Harvard University (6116)

ROBBINS MUSEUM
See: Massachusetts Archaeological Society - Robbins Museum (8518)

WARREN M. ROBBINS NATIONAL MUSEUM OF AFRICAN ART
See: Smithsonian Institution Libraries (13289)

ROBERSON CENTER FOR THE ARTS AND SCIENCES - BROOME COUNTY HISTORICAL SOCIETY
See: Broome County Historical Society - Josiah T. Newcomb Library (1954)

A. WEBB ROBERTS LIBRARY
See: Southwestern Baptist Theological Seminary (13522)

★12096★
H. ARMSTRONG ROBERTS, INC. - STOCK PHOTOGRAPHY LIBRARY (Aud-Vis)
4203 Locust St. Phone: (215)386-6300
Philadelphia, PA 19104 H. Armstrong Roberts, III, Pres.
Founded: 1920. **Subjects:** Photography of H. Armstrong Roberts and select contributing photographers. **Special Collections:** Charles Phelps Cushing Collection of historical engravings and photographs. **Holdings:** 1 million black/white original contemporary photographs and color transparencies. **Remarks:** Also maintains offices or representatives in New York City, Chicago, Los Angeles, and Toronto, Canada.

★12097★
ORAL ROBERTS UNIVERSITY - GRADUATE THEOLOGY LIBRARY - JOHN MESSICK LEARNING RESOURCE CENTER (Rel-Phil)
7777 S. Lewis Phone: (918)495-6894
Tulsa, OK 74171 Oon-Chor Khoo, Libn.
Founded: 1962. **Staff:** Prof 2; Other 8. **Subjects:** Biblical literature, historical and theological studies, Christianity and culture, practices of ministry. **Holdings:** 77,106 books and bound periodical volumes; 9045 microforms; 7524 AV programs; 45 VF drawers of pamphlets; 141 tracts. **Subscriptions:** 1208 journals and other serials. **Services:** Interlibrary loan; center open to the public with special permission. **Automated Operations:** Computerized cataloging, acquisitions, circulation, and reference. **Computerized Information Services:** DIALOG Information Services, BRS Information Technologies, OCLC; ALIS (internal database). Performs searches on fee basis. **Networks/Consortia:** Member of AMIGOS Bibliographic Council, Inc..

★12098★
ORAL ROBERTS UNIVERSITY - HEALTH SCIENCES LIBRARY (Med)
7777 S. Lewis
Box 2187 Phone: (918)493-6975
Tulsa, OK 74171 Timothy C. Judkins, Asst.Dir.
Founded: 1976. **Staff:** Prof 3; Other 4. **Subjects:** Medicine, dentistry, nursing. **Holdings:** 20,193 books; 36,088 bound periodical volumes; 700 AV programs. **Subscriptions:** 1334 journals and other serials. **Services:** Interlibrary loan; copying; library open to the public with restrictions. **Automated Operations:** Computerized cataloging, acquisitions, and circulation. **Computerized Information Services:** DIALOG Information Services, MEDLINE, BRS Information Technologies, OCLC. **Networks/Consortia:** Member of AMIGOS Bibliographic Council, Inc., South Central Academic Medical Libraries Consortium (SCAMEL). **Publications:** New acquisitions list, quarterly.

★12099★
ORAL ROBERTS UNIVERSITY - LIBRARY - HOLY SPIRIT RESEARCH CENTER (Rel-Phil)
Box 2187 Phone: (918)495-6899
Tulsa, OK 74171 Karen Jermyn, Libn.
Founded: 1962. **Staff:** Prof 1; Other 1. **Subjects:** History of Pentecostalism, history of Pentecostal/Charismatic denominations and organizations, gifts or manifestations of the Holy Spirit, divine healing, baptism of the Holy Spirit, Neo-Pentecostalism (Charismatic Movement), Catholic Pentecostalism, glossolalia, eschatology. **Special Collections:** Bishop Dan T. Muse (8 boxes of manuscripts; 27 photograph albums); J.G. Lake Photograph Collection (1 box); William Braham Photograph Collection (1 box). **Holdings:** 10,000 books; 1800 bound periodical volumes; 1000 tapes and cassettes; 40 VF drawers of pamphlets; 27 reels of microfilm; 35 theses and dissertations; 30 records; AV programs. **Subscriptions:** 500 journals and other serials. **Services:** Center open to the public for reference use only. **Automated Operations:** Computerized cataloging and acquisitions. **Publications:** Bibliographies on Pentecostal and charismatic materials, the Holy Spirit and divine healing; Microfilm Holdings in HSRC; Annotated Bibliography of Catholic Charismatic Materials in HSRC; General Works on the Baptism in the Holy Spirit as Taught by Pentecostals - for sale; Oral Roberts books.

★12100★
ROBERTS WESLEYAN COLLEGE - KENNETH B. KEATING LIBRARY - ARCHIVES (Hist, Rel-Phil)
2301 Westside Dr. Phone: (716)594-9471
Rochester, NY 14624 Charles H. Canon, III, Archv.
Staff: Prof 1. **Subjects:** History of the college and the Free Methodist Church. **Special Collections:** Papers of Benjamin Titus Roberts, founder of the college (manuscripts; photographs; diaries; ephemera). **Holdings:** 3946 archival items. **Services:** Copying; archives open to the public by appointment. **Computerized Information Services:** DIALOG Information Services. Performs searches on fee basis. Contact Person: Carolyn Bowman, Dir., Pub.Serv.. **Networks/Consortia:** Member of Rochester Regional Library Council (RRLC).

J.C. ROBERTSON MEMORIAL LIBRARY
See: Indian River Memorial Hospital (6749)

ROBERTSON LIBRARY
See: University of Prince Edward Island (16786)

PAUL ROBESON LIBRARY
See: SUNY - Syracuse Educational Opportunity Center - Paul Robeson Library (13784)

E. CLAIBORNE ROBINS SCHOOL OF BUSINESS
See: University of Richmond (16813)

ARTHUR H. ROBINSON MAP LIBRARY
See: University of Wisconsin, Madison (17116)

★12101★
ROBINSON & COLE - LIBRARY (Law)
One Commercial Plaza Phone: (203)275-8200
Hartford, CT 06103-3597 David S. Matthewson, Law Libn.
Staff: Prof 1; Other 2. **Holdings:** Law, business. **Holdings:** 15,000 books; 350 bound periodical volumes. **Subscriptions:** 65 journals and other serials; 10 newspapers. **Services:** Interlibrary loan; library not open to the public. **Computerized Information Services:** DIALOG Information Services, Dow Jones News/Retrieval, ABA/net, WESTLAW, LEXIS, NEXIS.

ELWYN B. ROBINSON DEPARTMENT OF SPECIAL COLLECTIONS
See: University of North Dakota (16650)

ROBINSON-LEHANE LIBRARY
See: Dorchester Historical Society (4354)

ROBINSON LIBRARY
See: Hartford Hospital - Health Science Libraries (6053)

MARY & LOUIS ROBINSON LIBRARY
See: Jewish Board of Family & Children Services (7194)

★12102★
ROBINSON, SHEPPARD, BORENSTEIN, SHAPIRO - LAW LIBRARY (Law)
800 Place Victoria, Suite 4700
Box 322, Succ. Tour de la Bourse Phone: (514)878-2631
Montreal, PQ, Canada H4Z 1H6 Angela Belle Tietolman, Law Libn.
Staff: Prof 1. **Subjects:** Law - civil, insurance, corporate, commercial, family and divorce, taxation, labor, criminal. **Holdings:** Figures not available. **Services:** Interlibrary loan; library not open to the public. **Computerized Information Services:** QL Systems, WESTLAW, SOQUIJ.

★12103★
ROBINSON, SILVERMAN, PEARCE, ARONSOHN, & BERMAN - LIBRARY & INFORMATION CENTER (Law)
230 Park Ave. Phone: (212)687-0400
New York, NY 10169 Janice E. Henderson, Law Libn.
Staff: Prof 1; Other 1. **Subjects:** Law. **Holdings:** 12,000 books; New York Law Journal, 1979 to present, on microfiche. **Subscriptions:** 80 journals and other serials; 8 newspapers. **Services:** Interlibrary loan; library not open to the public. **Automated Operations:** Computerized cataloging, acquisitions, and serials. **Computerized Information Services:** LEXIS, DIALOG Information Services, Dow Jones News/Retrieval, Information America, WESTLAW; internal databases. **Publications:** Robinson, Silverman, et al Library Bulletin, monthly.

ROBOTICS INTERNATIONAL OF THE SOCIETY OF MANUFACTURING ENGINEERS COLLECTION
See: Society of Manufacturing Engineers - SME Library (13331)

★12104★
ROCHESTER ACADEMY OF MEDICINE - LIBRARY (Med)
1441 East Ave.
Rochester, NY 14610 Phone: (716)271-1313
Founded: 1900. **Staff:** 1. **Subjects:** Medicine and allied health sciences. **Holdings:** 31,300 volumes. **Subscriptions:** 90 journals. **Services:** Interlibrary loan; copying; library open to the public. **Networks/Consortia:** Member of Rochester Area Libraries in Healthcare.

★12105★
ROCHESTER BUSINESS INSTITUTE - BETTY CRONK MEMORIAL LIBRARY (Bus-Fin)
107 Clinton Ave., N. Phone: (716)325-7290
Rochester, NY 14604 Paula Henry, Libn.
Founded: 1970. **Staff:** Prof 1. **Subjects:** Business and allied subjects. **Holdings:** 2000 volumes. **Subscriptions:** 31 journals and other serials. **Services:** Interlibrary loan; copying; library open to the public by appointment for research.

ROCHESTER DEMOCRAT & CHRONICLE
See: Rochester Times-Union and Rochester Democrat & Chronicle (12126)

★12106★
ROCHESTER GAS AND ELECTRIC CORPORATION - TECHNICAL INFORMATION CENTER (Sci-Engr, Energy)
89 East Ave. Phone: (716)546-2700
Rochester, NY 14649 Linda L. Phillips, Supv., Off.Serv./Doc.Ctr.
Staff: Prof 2; Other 1. **Subjects:** Electrical power generation, nuclear power, energy, engineering, environment, management. **Special Collections:** Electric Power Research Institute (EPRI) reports (3000). **Holdings:** 2500 books and reports; 3000 items on nuclear power, including codes, standards, and regulations; 1500 power plant documents; 500 internal reports; 8 drawers of pamphlets and company historical information. **Subscriptions:** 125 journals and other serials. **Services:** Interlibrary loan; copying; center open to the public by appointment and with escort. **Automated Operations:** Computerized cataloging, circulation, and indexing. **Computerized Information Services:** DIALOG Information Services, Pergamon ORBIT InfoLine, Inc., Integrated Technical Information System (ITIS). **Networks/Consortia:** Member of Rochester Regional Library Council (RRLC). **Publications:** RG & E News, bimonthly; book review columns and acquisitions lists. **Special Indexes:** Industry codes & standards; technical manuals for power plant systems & components; technical reports (all online). **Staff:** Sharon M. Paprocki, Tech.Info.Coord..

★12107★
ROCHESTER GENERAL HOSPITAL - LILLIE B. WERNER HEALTH SCIENCES LIBRARY (Med)
1425 Portland Ave. Phone: (716)338-4743
Rochester, NY 14621 Bernie Todd Smith, Lib.Dir.
Founded: 1883. **Staff:** Prof 4; Other 5. **Subjects:** Medicine, psychiatry, nursing. **Special Collections:** History of Medicine Collection (200 books). **Holdings:** 6000 books; 6000 bound periodical volumes; 1500 AV programs. **Subscriptions:** 400 journals and other serials. **Services:** Interlibrary loan; library not open to the public. **Computerized Information Services:** MEDLINE, DIALOG Information Services, BRS Information Technologies. **Networks/Consortia:** Member of Rochester Regional Library Council (RRLC). **Publications:** Information Alert, quarterly; Library Guide; Circuit Librarian Program brochure; New Arrivals (acquisitions list), biennial. **Special Catalogs:** Catalog of AV materials, quarterly (computer-generated book). **Staff:** Edward Lewek, Asst.Lib.Dir.; Tami Hartzell, Circuit Libn.; Lana Rudy, Circuit Libn..

★12108★
ROCHESTER HISTORICAL SOCIETY - LIBRARY (Hist)
485 East Ave. Phone: (716)271-2705
Rochester, NY 14607 Mary Widger, Libn.
Staff: Prof 1. **Subjects:** Local history. **Holdings:** 3000 books; manuscript and archival material; photographs; maps; genealogical material; complete file of Rochester directories, 1827 to present. **Services:** Library open to the public with restrictions.

★12109★
ROCHESTER INSTITUTE OF TECHNOLOGY - CHEMISTRY GRADUATE RESEARCH LIBRARY (Sci-Engr)
One Lomb Memorial Dr. Phone: (716)475-2520
Rochester, NY 14623 Christine DeGolyer, Sci.Libn.
Founded: 1968. **Staff:** Prof 1; Other 2. **Subjects:** Advanced chemistry. **Holdings:** 4885 books; 4640 bound periodical volumes; 70 masters' theses; 110 pamphlets; 800 microfiche; 84 reels of microfilm. **Subscriptions:** 153 journals and other serials. **Services:** Interlibrary loan; copying; library open to the public. **Automated Operations:** Computerized cataloging and circulation. **Computerized Information Services:** DIALOG Information Services, BRS Information Technologies, STN International. Performs searches on fee basis. **Networks/Consortia:** Member of Rochester Regional Library Council (RRLC).

★12110★
ROCHESTER INSTITUTE OF TECHNOLOGY - MELBERT B. CARY, JR. GRAPHIC ARTS COLLECTION (Art, Publ)
School of Printing Management and Sciences Phone: (716)475-2408
Rochester, NY 14623 David Pankow, Cur.
Founded: 1969. **Staff:** Prof 2. **Subjects:** Printing history, typography, book arts, press books, calligraphy, papermaking, graphic arts. **Special Collections:** Rudolf Koch; Fritz Kredel; Officina Bodoni; Grabhorn Press; Spiral Press; W.A. Dwiggins; T.M. Cleland; Press of the Woolly Whale; Laboratory Press; Bruce Rogers; Frederic W. Goudy; Type Specimen books; broadsides and posters; fore edge paintings. **Holdings:** 12,000 books; 16 VF drawers of clippings; ephemera; pamphlets; 12 boxes of posters, broadsides, drawings. **Subscriptions:** 18 journals and other serials. **Services:** Copying (limited); collection open to the public.

★12111★
ROCHESTER INSTITUTE OF TECHNOLOGY - NATIONAL TECHNICAL INSTITUTE FOR THE DEAF - STAFF RESOURCE CENTER (Med)
Lyndon Baines Johnson Bldg., Rm. 2490
1 Lomb Memorial Dr. Phone: (716)475-6823
Rochester, NY 14623 Gail Wilson, Res.Spec.
Founded: 1978. **Staff:** Prof 1; Other 1. **Subjects:** Deafness. **Special Collections:** National Center on Employment of the Deaf information collection (4 VF drawers). **Holdings:** 800 books; 200 bound periodical volumes; 1100 videotapes; 300 AV programs; 1500 pamphlets. **Subscriptions:** 31 journals and other serials. **Services:** Interlibrary loan; copying; center open to the public by appointment. **Networks/Consortia:** Member of Rochester Regional Library Council (RRLC). **Publications:** A Deafness Collection: Selected and Annotated, ASCLA/ALA, 1985.

★12112★
ROCHESTER INSTITUTE OF TECHNOLOGY - TECHNICAL & EDUCATION CENTER INFORMATION SERVICES (Sci-Engr)
One Lomb Memorial Dr. Phone: (716)475-2791
Rochester, NY 14623 Helga Birth, Mgr. of Info.Serv.
Founded: 1952. **Staff:** Prof 1; Other 2. **Subjects:** Printing technology and management, photographic science, imaging science and technology. **Holdings:** 1000 books; 300 unbound periodical titles; 25,000 articles on microfilm; 12 VF drawers of pamphlets; 4 VF drawers of research reports; printing and photoscience masters' theses. **Subscriptions:** 275 journals and other serials. **Services:** Interlibrary loan; copying; services open to the public. **Computerized Information Services:** Image Technology Patent Information System (I.T.P.A.I.S.; internal database). Performs searches on fee basis. **Publications:** Graphic Arts Literature Abstracts, monthly - by subscription; Photographiconservation, quarterly - by subscription; T & E Center Newsletter - free upon request; bibliographies on printing and imaging science topics. **Special Indexes:** Annual Cumulative Author/Keyword Index to Graphic Arts Literature Abstracts.

★12113★
ROCHESTER INSTITUTE OF TECHNOLOGY - WALLACE MEMORIAL LIBRARY (Art, Sci-Engr, Soc Sci, Comp Sci)
One Lomb Memorial Dr. Phone: (716)475-2565
Rochester, NY 14623 Patricia A. Pitkin, Dir.
Staff: Prof 23; Other 15. **Subjects:** Art, business, criminal justice, printing, micro-optics, computer science, imaging science, photography, social work, engineering, science. **Special Collections:** The deaf and deafness. **Holdings:** 285,000 books and bound periodical volumes; 1542 theses; 140 VF drawers of archives; 70,000 slides; 400 films; 15,778 reels of microfilm; 234,730 microfiche. **Subscriptions:** 5462 journals and other serials; 35 newspapers. **Services:** Interlibrary loan; library open to the public. **Automated Operations:** Computerized cataloging, acquisitions, and circulation. **Computerized Information Services:** OCLC; internal databases. Performs searches on fee basis. **Networks/Consortia:** Member of Rochester Regional Library Council (RRLC). **Publications:** Faculty Writings and Achievements, 1951 to present; Yet Another Newsletter; bibliographies. **Staff:** Lois A. Goodman, Asst.Dir., Info.Serv.; Virginia Church, Asst.Dir., Tech.Serv.; Joan Green, Dir., Instr. Media Serv.; Gladys Taylor, Archv.; Chandra Mckenzie, Asst.Dir., Circ.Serv.; Loretta Caren, Hd., Ref.; Margaret Fallon, Hd., Ser..

★12114★
ROCHESTER METHODIST HOSPITAL - METHODIST KAHLER LIBRARY (Med)
Rochester, MN 55902 Phone: (507)286-7425
Jean M. Brose, Hd.Libn.
Staff: Prof 2; Other 2. **Subjects:** Nursing services and education, hospital administration and management. **Special Collections:** History of Nursing. **Holdings:** 11,500 books; 500 bound periodical volumes; 1000 AV programs; 12 VF drawers of newspaper clippings and pamphlets. **Subscriptions:** 350 journals and other serials. **Services:** Interlibrary loan; copying; library open to the public with limited outside circulation. **Computerized Information Services:** DIALOG Information Services. Performs searches on fee basis. **Networks/Consortia:** Member of Greater Midwest Regional Medical Library Network. **Staff:** Karen Larsen, Asst.Libn..

★12115★
ROCHESTER MUSEUM AND SCIENCE CENTER - LIBRARY (Hist, Sci-Engr, Soc Sci)
657 East Ave.
Box 1480 Phone: (716)271-4320
Rochester, NY 14603 Leatrice M. Kemp, Libn.
Founded: 1914. **Staff:** Prof 2; Other 1. **Subjects:** Natural sciences, anthropology, local history, American Indians, antiques, archeology, costume, technology, museology. **Special Collections:** Albert Stone Collection of local photographs, 1904-1934 (15,000); slide library. **Holdings:** 26,000 volumes; museum bulletins; archival material and ephemera. **Subscriptions:** 60 journals and other serials. **Services:** Copying; library open to the public. **Automated Operations:** Computerized cataloging. **Networks/Consortia:** Member of Rochester Regional Library Council (RRLC).

★12116★
ROCHESTER MUSEUM AND SCIENCE CENTER - STRASENBURGH PLANETARIUM - TODD LIBRARY (Sci-Engr)
657 East Ave. Phone: (716)244-6060
Rochester, NY 14607 Grace Matthews, Libn.
Staff: Prof 1. **Subjects:** Astronomy, space science. **Holdings:** 1500 books; 500 bound periodical volumes. **Subscriptions:** 21 journals and other serials. **Services:** Library open to the public for reference use only.

★12117★
ROCHESTER POST-BULLETIN - LIBRARY (Publ)
18 First Ave., S.E. Phone: (507)285-7737
Rochester, MN 55903 Marit D. Bang, Libn.
Staff: Prof 1; Other 1. **Subjects:** Newspaper reference topics, Mayo Clinic, IBM. **Holdings:** 260 books; 2 drawers of microfilm of Rochester Post-Bulletin, 1977 to present; Agri News, 1976 to present, on microfilm. **Subscriptions:** 19 journals and other serials; 17 newspapers. **Services:** Interlibrary loan; library not open to the public. **Computerized Information Services:** DIALOG Information Services. **Networks/Consortia:** Member of Southeastern Libraries Cooperating (SELCO).

ROCHESTER PSYCHIATRIC CENTER
See: New York State Office of Mental Health (10129)

★12118★
ROCHESTER PUBLIC LIBRARY - ART DIVISION (Art, Mus)
115 South Ave. Phone: (716)428-7332
Rochester, NY 14604 Mary Lee Miller, Hd.
Staff: Prof 4; Other 7. **Subjects:** Fine arts, music, photography, film history, antiques, ornamental gardening, architecture, urban planning, crafts. **Special Collections:** Picture file (84 VF drawers). **Holdings:** 39,000 books; 12,000 slides; 20,000 sound recordings; choir music; framed prints. **Subscriptions:** 157 journals and other serials. **Services:** Interlibrary loan; copying. **Networks/Consortia:** Member of Rochester Regional Library Council (RRLC).

★12119★
ROCHESTER PUBLIC LIBRARY - BUSINESS, ECONOMICS AND LAW DIVISION (Bus-Fin, Soc Sci, Law)
115 South Ave. Phone: (716)428-7328
Rochester, NY 14604 Carolyn Johnson, Hd.
Staff: Prof 6; Other 3. **Subjects:** Business, economics, labor, employment, political science, law. **Special Collections:** Industrial directories; financial services; corporation annual reports; Foundation Center Collection. **Holdings:** 69,000 books; 15 VF drawers of pamphlets and clippings; federal, state, and local documents; microfilm; recordings. **Subscriptions:** 700 journals and other serials. **Services:** Interlibrary loan; copying. **Networks/Consortia:** Member of Rochester Regional Library Council (RRLC).

★12120★
ROCHESTER PUBLIC LIBRARY - EDUCATION, SOCIOLOGY AND RELIGION DIVISION (Educ, Rel-Phil, Soc Sci)
115 South Ave. Phone: (716)428-7330
Rochester, NY 14604 Judith Prevratil, Hd.
Staff: Prof 3; Other 4. **Subjects:** Education, religion, philosophy, psychology, psychiatry, ethics, sociology, folklore, etiquette. **Special Collections:** College catalog collection (paperback and microfiche); Education/Job Information Center. **Holdings:** 47,000 books; 300 pamphlets. **Subscriptions:** 170 journals and other serials. **Services:** Interlibrary loan; copying; Regents External Degree Advisory Service. **Computerized Information Services:** The Guidance Information System (GIS). **Networks/Consortia:** Member of Rochester Regional Library Council (RRLC). **Publications:** New Books for Teachers - distributed to city and county school districts for duplication and distribution to teachers.

★12121★
ROCHESTER PUBLIC LIBRARY - HISTORY, GOVERNMENT AND TRAVEL DIVISION (Hist, Soc Sci)
115 South Ave. Phone: (716)428-7323
Rochester, NY 14604 Winn McCray, Hd.
Staff: Prof 3; Other 2. **Subjects:** History, government, travel, international law and relations, archeology, the military. **Special Collections:** Map collection including topographic maps for New York State. **Holdings:** 53,000 volumes; 26 VF drawers of pamphlets and travel brochures; slides; recordings. **Subscriptions:** 150 journals and other serials. **Services:** Interlibrary loan; copying. **Networks/Consortia:** Member of Rochester Regional Library Council (RRLC). **Publications:** Booklists, irregular.

★12122★
ROCHESTER PUBLIC LIBRARY - LITERATURE, BIOGRAPHY AND SPORTS DIVISION (Hum, Rec)
115 South Ave. Phone: (716)428-7315
Rochester, NY 14604 William J. Cuseo, Hd.
Staff: Prof 5; Other 4. **Subjects:** Literature, fiction, biography, language, speech, journalism, sports and games. **Special Collections:** Talking books; books in French, Spanish, German, Italian, Hungarian. **Holdings:** 140,000 books; 3000 large print books; 12 VF drawers of pamphlets and clippings; 3000 phonograph records; 3500 cassettes. **Subscriptions:** 160 journals and other serials. **Services:** Interlibrary loan; copying. **Networks/Consortia:** Member of Rochester Regional Library Council (RRLC).

★12123★
ROCHESTER PUBLIC LIBRARY - LOCAL HISTORY AND GENEALOGY DIVISION (Hist)
115 South Ave. Phone: (716)428-7338
Rochester, NY 14604 Wayne Arnold, Hd.
Staff: Prof 4; Other 1. **Subjects:** History of Rochester and Genesee area, genealogy (primarily New York and New England). **Special Collections:** Local newspapers. **Holdings:** 25,000 books; 15 cases and 400 volumes of manuscripts; 1800 maps; 500 scrapbooks; 145 VF drawers of newspaper clippings; 80 VF drawers of pamphlets and ephemera; 20 VF drawers of pictures; 12 drawers of postcards; 638 reels of microfilm; 120 films. **Subscriptions:** 200 journals and other serials; 78 newspapers. **Services:** Copying (limited). **Networks/Consortia:** Member of Rochester Regional Library Council (RRLC). **Remarks:** The majority of the holdings of the Rochester Historical Society are on permanent loan to the Local History Division.

★12124★
ROCHESTER PUBLIC LIBRARY - REYNOLDS AUDIO-VISUAL DEPARTMENT (Aud-Vis)
115 South Ave. Phone: (716)428-7335
Rochester, NY 14604 Robert Barnes, Hd.
Staff: Prof 2; Other 7. **Holdings:** 265 books; 5500 16mm films; 937 filmstrips; 2300 video cassettes. **Subscriptions:** 50 journals and other serials. **Services:** Interlibrary loan; media preview facilities; equipment loans. **Networks/Consortia:** Member of Rochester Regional Library Council (RRLC). **Special Catalogs:** Catalogs of 16mm films and video cassette tapes.

★12125★
ROCHESTER PUBLIC LIBRARY - SCIENCE AND TECHNOLOGY DIVISION (Sci-Engr, Biol Sci)
115 South Ave. Phone: (716)428-7327
Rochester, NY 14604 Jeffrey Levine, Hd.
Staff: Prof 5; Other 3. **Subjects:** Physical and natural sciences, applied science and technology, health sciences, environmental sciences, agriculture, home economics. **Special Collections:** Trade catalogs of national firms; automobile shop manuals; Sam's Photofacts Service; Official Gazette of U.S. Patent Office, 1846 to present. **Holdings:** 54,000 books; 15 VF drawers of pamphlets; 130 slide sets; 100 phonograph records; 70 cassettes. **Subscriptions:** 425 journals and other serials. **Services:** Interlibrary loan; copying. **Networks/Consortia:** Member of Rochester Regional Library Council (RRLC). **Publications:** Booklists, irregular.

★12126★
ROCHESTER TIMES-UNION AND ROCHESTER DEMOCRAT & CHRONICLE - LIBRARY (Publ)
55 Exchange St. Phone: (716)232-7100
Rochester, NY 14614 Peter Ford, Lib.Mgr.
Founded: 1929. **Staff:** Prof 3; Other 3. **Subjects:** Newspaper reference topics. **Holdings:** 1500 books; clippings; photographs; microfilm. **Services:** Library not open to the public.

★12127★
ROCK COUNTY HEALTH CARE CENTER - STAFF LIBRARY (Med)
Box 351
Janesville, WI 53547 Phone: (608)755-2590
Founded: 1971. **Staff:** Prof 1. **Subjects:** Psychiatry, psychiatric social work, geriatrics, nursing. **Holdings:** 1052 books; 29 bound periodical volumes; AV programs. **Subscriptions:** 63 journals and other serials. **Services:** Interlibrary loan; copying; library open to the public. **Networks/Consortia:** Member of South Central Wisconsin Health Planning Area Cooperative.

★12128★
ROCK COUNTY HISTORICAL SOCIETY - ARCHIVES OF ROCK COUNTY HISTORY (Hist)
10 S. High
Box 896 Phone: (608)756-4509
Janesville, WI 53545 Maurice J. Montgomery, Archv.
Founded: 1948. **Staff:** Prof 1. **Subjects:** Rock County local history; land speculation. **Special Collections:** Tallman Family papers (3000 items dealing with land speculation, railroad matters, building construction, 1830-1880). **Holdings:** 1500 books; 40 VF drawers of manuscripts and photocopies of clippings; 500 volumes of school records, business records, diaries; 4 boxes and 15 cubic feet of maps; 50 drawers of cataloged photographs and other miscellaneous items; 4000 abstracts of title of Rock County Lands; 9000 probate records, 1839-1900. **Subscriptions:** 15 journals and other serials; 5 newspapers. **Services:** Copying; archives open to the public on a limited schedule. **Publications:** Recorder, bimonthly. **Special Catalogs:** Iconographic catalog; artifact catalog (both card). **Special Indexes:** Biographical index to Rock County (card); cemetery records (card); index to published and nonpublished materials (book).

ROCK CREEK NATURE CENTER LIBRARY
See: U.S. Natl. Park Service - National Capital Region (15332)

★12129★
LARRY ROCK AUTOMATION ASSOCIATES
1760 Dewberry Ln.
Cherry Hill, NJ 08003-3357
Defunct

ROCKBRIDGE HISTORICAL SOCIETY COLLECTION
See: Washington & Lee University - Special Collections Department (17492)

ROCKDALE TEMPLE
See: K.K. Bene Israel/Rockdale Temple (7304)

ABBY ALDRICH ROCKEFELLER FOLK ART CENTER
See: Colonial Williamsburg Foundation (3408)

★12130★
ROCKEFELLER FOUNDATION - LIBRARY (Soc Sci, Bus-Fin)
1133 Ave. of the Americas Phone: (212)869-8500
New York, NY 10036 Meredith S. Averill, Libn.
Staff: Prof 2; Other 1. **Subjects:** Philanthropy, social sciences, biography. **Special Collections:** College catalogs; annual reports of philanthropic institutions; Rockefeller Foundation reports and publications. **Holdings:** 5000 volumes. **Subscriptions:** 500 journals and other serials. **Services:** Interlibrary loan; copying; current awareness; library serves members of staff only. **Automated Operations:** Computerized cataloging and serials. **Computerized Information Services:** DIALOG, OCLC, NEXIS, VU/TEXT Information Services, MEDLINE, WILSONLINE. **Networks/Consortia:** Member of Consortium of Foundation Libraries, New York Metropolitan Reference and Research Library Agency (METRO), Medical Library Center of New York (MLCNY). **Staff:** Erroll J. Cantlin, III, Asst.Libn..

★12131★
ROCKEFELLER UNIVERSITY - LIBRARY (Biol Sci, Med, Sci-Engr)
1230 York Ave.
RU Box 263 Phone: (212)570-8901
New York, NY 10021-6399 Sonya Wohl Mirsky, Univ.Libn.
Founded: 1906. **Staff:** Prof 3; Other 24. **Subjects:** Biological sciences, medicine, chemistry, physics, mathematics. **Holdings:** 229,800 volumes. **Subscriptions:** 2470 journals and other serials. **Services:** Interlibrary loan; library not open to the public. **Automated Operations:** Computerized cataloging, acquisitions, serials, and circulation. **Computerized Information Services:** DIALOG Information Services, BRS Information Technologies, NLM, WILSONLINE, NEXIS. **Networks/Consortia:** Member of Medical Library Center of New York (MLCNY), Greater Northeastern Regional Medical Library Program.

★12132★
ROCKEFELLER UNIVERSITY - ROCKEFELLER ARCHIVE CENTER (Hist, Soc Sci)
Hillcrest, Pocantico Hills Phone: (914)631-4505
North Tarrytown, NY 10591 Dr. Darwin H. Stapleton, Dir.
Founded: 1975. **Staff:** Prof 10; Other 6. **Subjects:** American philanthropy; Rockefeller family; education; medicine; physical, natural, and social sciences; public health; arts; humanities. **Special Collections:** Rockefeller Foundation (3300 cubic feet); General Education Board (350 cubic feet); Laura Spelman Rockefeller Memorial (58 cubic feet); Bureau of Social Hygiene (32 cubic feet); John D. Rockefeller (550 cubic feet); Office of the Messrs. Rockefeller (580 cubic feet); International Education Board (22 cubic feet); Spelman Fund of New York (42 cubic feet); Rockefeller University (2400 cubic feet); The Commonwealth Fund (400 cubic feet); International Basic Economy Corporation (94 cubic feet; microforms); Russell Sage Foundation (43 cubic feet); Products of Asia (27 cubic feet); China Medical Board (122 cubic feet); Rockefeller Brothers Fund (255 cubic feet); Agricultural Development Council (88 cubic feet); American International Association for Economic and Social Development (33 cubic feet); Population Council (51 cubic feet); Arts, Education and Americans Panel (21 cubic feet); Davison Fund, Inc. (16 cubic feet); John D. Rockefeller, III Fund (143 cubic feet); Memorial Sloan-Kettering Cancer Center (50 cubic feet); Rockefeller Sanitary Commission for the Eradication of Hookworm Disease (6.5 cubic feet); Union Tank Car Company (6 cubic feet); Lawrence B. Dunham (2 cubic feet); Frederick T. Gates (2 cubic feet); Lewis W. Hackett (20 cubic feet); J. George Harrar (15 cubic feet); John H. Knowles (23 cubic feet); William Rockefeller (12 cubic feet). **Holdings:** 20,000 cubic feet of archival and manuscript collections; 250,000 photographs; 4000 microfiche. **Services:** Copying; center open to scholars by appointment. **Computerized Information Services:** RLIN. **Networks/Consortia:** Member of RLG. **Publications:** Newsletter, annual; occasional papers. **Special Catalogs:** Archives and Manuscripts in the Rockefeller Archive Center, 1984 (pamphlet); Photograph Collections in the Rockefeller Archive Center, 1986. **Staff:** Claire Collier, Archv.; Barbara Gilson, Archv.; Lee Hiltzik, Archv.; Erwin Levold, Archv.; Thomas Rosenbaum, Archv.; Emily Oakhill, Archv.; Harold Oakhill, Archv.; Kenneth W. Rose, Asst. to the Dir.; Melissa Smith, Archv..

★12133★
ROCKFORD MEMORIAL HOSPITAL - HEALTH SCIENCE LIBRARY (Med)
2400 N. Rockton Ave. Phone: (815)968-6861
Rockford, IL 61101 Phyllis Nathan, Coord., Lib.Serv.
Staff: Prof 2; Other 1. **Subjects:** Clinical medicine, nursing, health care administration. **Special Collections:** Hunter Memorial Pediatric Library (300 volumes); School of Nursing (3000 volumes). **Holdings:** 2000 books; 2000 bound periodical volumes; 2 VF drawers; 100 nonprint items. **Subscriptions:** 240 journals and other serials. **Services:** Interlibrary loan; copying; library open to the public by arrangement. **Computerized Information Services:** DIALOG Information Services, MEDLARS. **Networks/Consortia:** Member of Greater Midwest Regional Medical Library Network, Northern Illinois Library System (NILS), Upstate Illinois Consortium.

★12134★
ROCKINGHAM MEMORIAL HOSPITAL - HEALTH SCIENCES LIBRARY (Med)
235 Cantrell Ave. Phone: (703)433-4166
Harrisonburg, VA 22801-3293 Ilene N. Smith, Med.Libn.
Founded: 1912. **Staff:** Prof 1. **Subjects:** Clinical medicine, nursing, allied health subjects. **Holdings:** 6000 books and bound periodical volumes; 337 AV programs. **Subscriptions:** 280 journals and other serials. **Services:** Interlibrary loan; SDI; library open to the public with restrictions.

Computerized Information Services: BRS Information Technologies, MEDLINE, ASTD, ICOA; DOCLINE (electronic mail service). **Networks/Consortia:** Member of Southwestern Virginia Health Information Librarians. **Publications:** Library newsletter, quarterly - for internal distribution only.

★12135★
ROCKLAND COUNTY CAREER INFORMATION CENTER (Educ)
83 Main St. Phone: (914)358-9390
Nyack, NY 10960 Henrietta Hendrick, Career Info.Asst.
Founded: 1966. **Staff:** Prof 1; Other 3. **Subjects:** Career information, employment, education, financial aid. **Holdings:** 500 books; 16 VF drawers of pamphlets; college catalogs for New York, New Jersey, and Connecticut; 400 audiotapes; 6 videotapes. **Subscriptions:** 12 journals and other serials. **Services:** Copying; center open to the public. **Automated Operations:** Computerized public access catalog. **Publications:** Newsletter, semiannual.

★12136★
ROCKVILLE GENERAL HOSPITAL - MEDICAL LIBRARY/ RESOURCE ROOM (Med)
31 Union St. Phone: (203)872-0501
Rockville, CT 06066 Dorothea M. Zabilansky, Med.Libn.
Founded: 1960. **Staff:** Prof 1. **Subjects:** Medicine. **Holdings:** 600 books; 300 bound periodical volumes; Audio-Digest tapes, 1960 to present. **Subscriptions:** 102 journals and other serials. **Services:** Interlibrary loan; copying; library open to the public by appointment. **Networks/Consortia:** Member of Connecticut Association of Health Science Libraries (CAHSL).

ROCKWELL CHEMISTRY LIBRARY
See: Tufts University (14380)

★12137★
ROCKWELL INTERNATIONAL - ATOMICS INTERNATIONAL DIVISION - ROCKY FLATS PLANT - TECHNICAL LIBRARY (Sci-Engr, Energy)
Box 938 Phone: (303)966-2863
Golden, CO 80402 Mary Ann Paliani, Lib.Mgr.
Founded: 1952. **Staff:** Prof 2; Other 4. **Subjects:** Atomic energy, chemistry, metallurgy, physics. **Holdings:** 15,000 volumes; 10,000 technical reports; 50,000 reports on microcards and microfiche. **Subscriptions:** 797 journals and other serials. **Services:** Interlibrary loan; library not open to the public. **Automated Operations:** Computerized cataloging, acquisitions, and internal reports. **Computerized Information Services:** DIALOG Information Services, RLIN, Pergamon ORBIT InfoLine, Inc., The Reference Service (REFSRV), Integrated Technical Information System (ITIS). **Publications:** Library and Technical Information Office Bulletin, monthly - for internal distribution only; Journals Currently Received by the Rocky Flats Library. **Special Indexes:** Indexes to classified and unclassified IRF reports (book). **Formerly:** Rockwell International - Energy Systems Group.

★12138★
ROCKWELL INTERNATIONAL - AUTOMOTIVE BUSINESSES - REFERENCE CENTER (Sci-Engr)
2135 W. Maple Rd. Phone: (313)435-1668
Troy, MI 48084 Cheryl Varga, Libn.
Founded: 1960. **Staff:** Prof 1; Other 1. **Subjects:** Automotive engineering, marketing, technical sciences. **Special Collections:** Society of Automotive Engineers technical papers; American Society for Testing and Materials (ASTM) standards. **Holdings:** 2600 books; 33 bound periodical volumes; 750 annual reports; 300 laboratory reports. **Subscriptions:** 732 journals and other serials; 5 newspapers. **Services:** Interlibrary loan; center not open to the public. **Computerized Information Services:** DIALOG Information Services, Pergamon ORBIT InfoLine, Inc., Dow Jones News/Retrieval, NEXIS, Dun & Bradstreet Corporation; internal database; OnTyme Electronic Message Network Service (electronic mail service). **Publications:** Reference Center Notes, monthly - for internal distribution only. **Formerly:** Heavy Vehicles Components Operation.

★12139★
ROCKWELL INTERNATIONAL - BUSINESS RESEARCH CENTER (Bus-Fin)
600 Grant St. Phone: (412)565-5880
Pittsburgh, PA 15219 Ruth T. Gunning, Mgr., Bus.Info.Serv.
Founded: 1967. **Staff:** Prof 2. **Subjects:** Business, economic, and financial information for the aerospace, automotive, electronic, general industries, and industrial automation businesses. **Holdings:** 1000 books; 1300 pamphlets and reports; 5000 Securities and Exchange Commission reports. **Subscriptions:** 410 journals and other serials; 7 newspapers. **Services:** Interlibrary loan; center not open to the public. **Computerized Information Services:** DIALOG Information Services, Dow Jones News/Retrieval, Dun & Bradstreet Corporation, NEXIS, NewsNet, Inc., VU/TEXT Information Services, WILSONLINE; OnTyme Electronic Message Network Service (electronic mail service). **Publications:** Annotated Checklist of Acquisitions, monthly - for internal distribution only; annual list of periodicals and services; Companies of Interest, annual.

★12140★
ROCKWELL INTERNATIONAL - COLLINS CANADA DIVISION - TIC LIBRARY (Sci-Engr)
150 Bartley Dr. Phone: (416)757-1101
Toronto, ON, Canada M4A 1C7 Joan Ann Hall, Libn.
Founded: 1960. **Staff:** Prof 1. **Subjects:** Electronics and communications. **Holdings:** Books; bound periodical volumes; pamphlets; reports; government documents. **Services:** Interlibrary loan; library open to the public.

★12141★
ROCKWELL INTERNATIONAL - COLLINS DIVISIONS - INFORMATION CENTER (Sci-Engr)
400 Collins Rd., N.E. Phone: (319)395-3070
Cedar Rapids, IA 52498 Judith A. Leavitt, Supv.
Founded: 1942. **Staff:** Prof 1; Other 5. **Subjects:** Electronics, management, space, navigation, mathematics, aeronautics, communication equipment, computers, physics. **Holdings:** 6000 books and bound periodical volumes; military, federal, and industrial specifications. **Subscriptions:** 400 journals and other serials. **Services:** Center not open to the public. **Automated Operations:** Computerized public access catalog, cataloging, acquisitions, serials, and circulation. **Computerized Information Services:** DIALOG Information Services, NewsNet, Inc., VU/TEXT Information Services, Pergamon ORBIT InfoLine, Inc., WILSONLINE, DTIC, BRS Information Technologies, Dow Jones News/Retrieval, Dun & Bradstreet Corporation, NASA/RECON, NEXIS, DMS/ONLINE, DataTimes, LEXIS; Rockwell Technical Information System (RTIS; internal database); OnTyme Electronic Message Network Service (electronic mail service). **Networks/Consortia:** Member of Linn County Library Consortium (LCLC). **Publications:** Acquisition list, biweekly; Communique (newsletter), bimonthly - both for internal distribution only.

★12142★
ROCKWELL INTERNATIONAL - ELECTRONICS OPERATIONS - DALLAS INFORMATION CENTER (Sci-Engr)
Dallas Information Center 407-120
Box 10462 Phone: (214)996-6022
Dallas, TX 75207 Wanda J. Fox, Supv.
Founded: 1960. **Staff:** Prof 6; Other 4. **Subjects:** Electronics, communications. **Special Collections:** International Business Collection (500 volumes); military, commercial, and international specifications and standards. **Holdings:** 9000 books; 2500 bound periodical volumes; 55,000 internal reports and working papers; 1500 financial and marketing files. **Subscriptions:** 500 journals and other serials. **Services:** Interlibrary loan; center not open to the public. **Computerized Information Services:** DIALOG Information Services, Data Resources (DRI), NEXIS, Dow Jones News/Retrieval, Dun & Bradstreet Corporation, DataTimes, WILSONLINE. **Publications:** Working Paper Bulletin; Current Awareness Bulletin; Daily News Briefs; Business Information Update. **Special Indexes:** Working Paper Index. **Staff:** David L. Clifton, Mgr., Info.Serv.; Joyce Deegan, Libn.; Stacy Cotter, Sr.Res.Libn..

ROCKWELL INTERNATIONAL - ENERGY SYSTEMS GROUP
See: Rockwell International - Atomics International Division (12137)

★12143★
ROCKWELL INTERNATIONAL - FLOW CONTROL DIVISION - TECHNICAL INFORMATION CENTER (Sci-Engr)
400 N. Lexington Ave. Phone: (412)247-3095
Pittsburgh, PA 15208 Kathleen M. Witkowski, Lib.Coord.
Founded: 1950. **Staff:** Prof 1. **Subjects:** Engineering - mechanical, hydraulic, electrical, metallurgy, instrumentation, technology. **Holdings:** 5800 books; 200 bound periodical volumes; 2500 government research and development reports; 7 VF drawers of clippings and pamphlets; 250 cartridges of microfilm; 2200 microfiche. **Subscriptions:** 140 journals and other serials; 10 newspapers. **Services:** Interlibrary loan; center not open to the public. **Automated Operations:** Computerized serials. **Computerized Information Services:** DIALOG Information Services, Pergamon ORBIT InfoLine, Inc., BRS Information Technologies; OnTyme Electronic Message Network Service (electronic mail service). **Publications:** Information Bulletin, bimonthly; List of Standards and Specifications, annual; List of Annual Reports, annual; List of Periodicals, semiannual -

all for internal distribution only. **Special Catalogs:** Catalog of NTIS Reports (card).

★12144★
ROCKWELL INTERNATIONAL - GRAPHIC SYSTEMS - TECHNICAL INFORMATION CENTER (Sci-Engr)
3100 S. Central Ave.
Chicago, IL 60650 Marlene J. Slifka, Adm.
Founded: 1965. **Staff:** Prof 1. **Subjects:** Engineering, graphic arts, electronics. **Holdings:** 3000 books. **Subscriptions:** 100 journals and other serials. **Services:** Interlibrary loan; center not open to the public. **Computerized Information Services:** DIALOG Information Services, STN International.

ROCKWELL INTERNATIONAL - HEAVY VEHICLES COMPONENTS OPERATION
See: Rockwell International - Automotive Businesses (12138)

★12145★
ROCKWELL INTERNATIONAL - NEWPORT BEACH INFORMATION CENTER (Sci-Engr, Comp Sci)
4311 Jamboree Blvd., 501-345 Phone: (714)833-4389
Newport Beach, CA 92660-9969 K.H. Preston, Mgr.
Staff: Prof 1. **Subjects:** Electronics; communications; data systems/materials; automatic navigation; sensing, monitoring, and reporting; computers; manufacturing research and development. **Special Collections:** Transactions and proceedings of electronics and communications conferences and societies. **Holdings:** 8200 books; 550 bound periodical volumes; 20 VF drawers of working papers (last 5 years, earlier ones on microfilm); 10 VF drawers of engineers' notebooks; 5 VF drawers of procedures. **Subscriptions:** 300 journals and other serials. **Services:** Interlibrary loan; center not open to the public. **Computerized Information Services:** DIALOG Information Services, DTIC.

★12146★
ROCKWELL INTERNATIONAL - NORTH AMERICAN AIRCRAFT OPERATIONS - TECHNICAL INFORMATION CENTER (Sci-Engr)
Box 92098 Phone: (213)647-2961
Los Angeles, CA 90009 Robert Panek, Libn.
Founded: 1940. **Staff:** Prof 2; Other 8. **Subjects:** Aeronautics, materials, mathematics and computer sciences, electronics and electrical engineering. **Holdings:** 11,500 books; 5400 bound periodical volumes; 282,000 technical reports; microfiche. **Subscriptions:** 230 journals and other serials. **Services:** Interlibrary loan; center not open to the public. **Automated Operations:** Computerized cataloging. **Computerized Information Services:** DTIC, NASA/RECON, DIALOG Information Services, Pergamon ORBIT InfoLine, Inc., BRS Information Technologies, ESA-QUEST; Rockwell Technical Information System (RTIS; internal database); OnTyme Electronic Message Network Service (electronic mail service). **Remarks:** Center located at 201 N. Douglas St., El Segundo, CA 90245.

★12147★
ROCKWELL INTERNATIONAL - ROCKETDYNE DIVISION - TECHNICAL INFORMATION CENTER (Sci-Engr)
6633 Canoga Ave. Phone: (818)710-2575
Canoga Park, CA 91303 Julia Keim, Mgr.
Founded: 1955. **Staff:** Prof 5; Other 3. **Subjects:** Engineering, chemistry, physics, nuclear engineering, directed energy, materials science. **Holdings:** 38,000 books; 8709 bound periodical volumes; 6000 reels of microfilm of periodicals; 145,000 technical reports. **Subscriptions:** 635 journals and other serials. **Services:** Interlibrary loan; center not open to the public. **Automated Operations:** Computerized public access catalog, cataloging, acquisitions, and circulation. **Computerized Information Services:** DIALOG Information Services, BRS Information Technologies, Integrated Technical Information System (ITIS), NASA/RECON, DTIC, LEXIS, NEXIS; Rockwell Technical Information System (RTIS; internal database); OnTyme Electronic Message Network Service (electronic mail service). **Networks/Consortia:** Member of CLASS. **Publications:** Current Technical Information; demand bibliographies. **Special Catalogs:** Catalog of microcomputer software programs. **Staff:** Haroldeane Snell, Br.Supv.; Marie Sigari, Cat.; Scott Peters, Lit. Search; Nancy Brown, Acq..

ROCKWELL INTERNATIONAL - ROCKWELL HANFORD OPERATIONS
See: Westinghouse Hanford Company (17777)

★12148★
ROCKWELL INTERNATIONAL - ROCKWELL HANFORD OPERATIONS - BASALT WASTE ISOLATION PROJECT - LIBRARY
H9-16/300 Area
Richland, WA 99352
Defunct

ROCKWELL INTERNATIONAL - ROCKWELL HANFORD OPERATIONS - LEGAL LIBRARY
See: Battelle-Northwest - Legal Library (1383)

★12149★
ROCKWELL INTERNATIONAL - SCIENCE CENTER LIBRARY (Sci-Engr)
1049 Camino Dos Rios
Box 1085 Phone: (805)373-4722
Thousand Oaks, CA 91360 Yolanda O. Fackler, Supv.
Founded: 1962. **Staff:** Prof 1; Other 2. **Subjects:** Electronics, physics and chemistry, fracture and metal physics, structural materials, semiconductor devices, fluid mechanics, physical metallurgy, computer science, artificial intelligence, robotics. **Holdings:** 13,500 books; 6500 bound periodical volumes; 5500 technical reports; 6000 microfiche. **Subscriptions:** 300 journals and other serials. **Services:** Interlibrary loan; copying; SDI; library open to the public by appointment. **Automated Operations:** Computerized cataloging and circulation. **Computerized Information Services:** DIALOG Information Services, NASA/RECON, DTIC, BRS Information Technologies, Dow Jones News/Retrieval, Pergamon ORBIT InfoLine, Inc.; Rockwell Technical Information System (RTIS; internal database). **Networks/Consortia:** Member of Total Interlibrary Exchange (TIE). **Publications:** Library Announcements - for internal distribution only. **Special Catalogs:** Catalog of technical report holdings of Rockwell International libraries (machine produced microfiche). **Staff:** Florina Carvalho, ILL.

★12150★
ROCKWELL INTERNATIONAL - SPACE TRANSPORTATION SYSTEMS DIVISION (STSD) - TECHNICAL INFORMATION CENTER (Sci-Engr, Comp Sci)
12214 Lakewood Blvd. Phone: (213)922-4648
Downey, CA 90241 Nan H. Paik, Supv.
Founded: 1947. **Staff:** Prof 5; Other 5. **Subjects:** Aerospace technology, information systems, electronics, astronautics, mathematics, engineering, computer sciences. **Holdings:** 48,000 books; 7000 bound periodical volumes; 75,000 technical reports; 500,000 microfiche. **Subscriptions:** 600 journals and other serials. **Services:** Interlibrary loan; copying; SDI and retrospective search; center open to the public by appointment for reference use only. **Automated Operations:** Computerized cataloging, serials, and circulation. **Computerized Information Services:** DIALOG Information Services, BRS Information Technologies, NASA/RECON, DTIC; Rockwell Technical Information System (RTIS; internal database). **Publications:** Custom bibliographies. **Staff:** Theodore Cranford, Lib.Res.Anl.; Alberta Donlan, Lib.Res.Anl.; Charlotte Baughman, Lib.Res.Anl.; Margaret Russell, Mktg..

★12151★
ROCKWELL INTERNATIONAL - SWITCHING SYSTEMS DIVISION - TECHNICAL LIBRARY (Comp Sci)
1431 Opus Place Phone: (312)960-8019
Downers Grove, IL 60515 Carol Brade, Tech.Libn.
Founded: 1984. **Staff:** Prof 1. **Subjects:** Telecommunications, switching systems, electronics, computers. **Holdings:** 1934 books; 73 NTIS and government reports; 3935 marketing and business reports; 3149 standards and recommendations. **Subscriptions:** 165 journals and other serials. **Services:** Interlibrary loan; library not open to the public. **Computerized Information Services:** DIALOG Information Services, Dun & Bradstreet Corporation, Dow Jones News/Retrieval; OnTyme Electronic Message Network Service, ALANET (electronic mail services). **Networks/Consortia:** Member of Suburban Library System (SLS). **Publications:** Current Literature Accession List, semimonthly - for internal distribution only.

★12152★
ROCKWELL INTERNATIONAL - TECHNICAL INFORMATION CENTER (Sci-Engr)
3370 Miraloma Ave. Phone: (714)762-2089
Anaheim, CA 92803 Carol Pryor, Mgr.
Founded: 1955. **Staff:** Prof 3; Other 9. **Subjects:** Electronics, chemistry, physics, solid state electronics, microelectronics, inertial navigation, computers, radar, lasers. **Special Collections:** Management Development.

Holdings: 68,000 books; 5500 bound periodical volumes; 130,000 technical reports; 80,000 technical reports on microfiche. **Subscriptions:** 519 journals and other serials. **Services:** Interlibrary loan; center not open to the public. **Computerized Information Services:** DIALOG Information Services. **Publications:** Weekly Accession Bulletin.

★12153★
ROCKWELL INTERNATIONAL - TECHNICAL INFORMATION CENTER (Sci-Engr)
2000 N. Memorial Dr.
Box 582808 Phone: (918)835-3111
Tulsa, OK 74158 Mary B. Sewell, Adm.
Founded: 1962. **Staff:** Prof 2. **Subjects:** Aerospace, aircraft, manufacturing and industrial engineering, management. **Holdings:** 1500 books; 6000 military and federal specifications on microfilm; 3000 NASA and DOD reports; 5600 industry technical reports. **Services:** Interlibrary loan (limited); copying; center open to the public with restrictions. **Computerized Information Services:** NASA/RECON, DTIC; Rockwell Technical Information System (RTIS; internal database). **Publications:** Technical Documents - Rockwell Briefings & Reports. **Special Indexes:** Indexes of Engineering Specifications.

★12154★
NORMAN ROCKWELL MUSEUM AT STOCKBRIDGE - REFERENCE DEPARTMENT (Art)
Main St. Phone: (413)298-3869
Stockbridge, MA 01262 Laurie Norton Moffatt, Dir.
Staff: Prof 4. **Subjects:** Norman Rockwell. **Holdings:** 4000 photographic images of Rockwell art work; 10,000 negatives of artist's models and sketches; archive of 4000 original publications; 100 books with Rockwell images; 20 drawers of information on artist's works; clippings file; business and fan letters. **Services:** Department not open to the public. **Staff:** Linda Russell, Cur.Asst..

SOLOMON ROCKWELL HOUSE
See: Winchester Historical Society (17916)

ROCKY FLATS PLANT
See: Rockwell International - Atomics International Division (12137)

★12155★
ROCKY HILL HISTORICAL SOCIETY - ACADEMY HALL MUSEUM - LIBRARY (Hist)
785 Old Main St.
Box 185 Phone: (203)563-8710
Rocky Hill, CT 06067 Ethel M. Cooke, Libn.
Staff: 1. **Subjects:** Local history. **Special Collections:** 19th century general reading matter; antiques; costumes; accessories; farm implements; tools; handmade quilts; local Indian artifacts; Treat & Davis Melodeon; Ruth Wilcox Collection (antique salts; 500 items). **Holdings:** 1000 books; 3 boxes of letters and documents; 20 magnetic tapes (some oral history); local news scrapbooks; 18th and 19th century school texts; local Indian artifacts. **Services:** Library open to the public by appointment.

★12156★
ROCKY MOUNT HISTORICAL ASSOCIATION - LIBRARY (Hist)
Route 2, Box 70
Piney Flats, TN 37686 Phone: (615)538-7396
Founded: 1961. **Staff:** Prof 1. **Subjects:** Local history, Southwest Territory history, genealogy, technology, biography. **Holdings:** 1000 books; 1000 bound periodical volumes; 7 VF drawers of clippings; 2 VF drawers and 2 boxes of manuscripts; photographs. **Subscriptions:** 10 journals and other serials. **Services:** Copying; library open to the public for reference use only.

ROCKY MOUNTAIN ENERGY
See: Union Pacific Resources Company (14481)

★12157★
ROCKY MOUNTAIN HOSPITAL - C. LLOYD PETERSON MEMORIAL LIBRARY (Med)
4701 E. Ninth Ave. Phone: (303)393-5784
Denver, CO 80220 Kathy K. Mueller, Libn.
Staff: 1. **Subjects:** Medicine. **Special Collections:** Osteopathic texts (20). **Holdings:** 600 books; 250 bound periodical volumes; 500 cassette tapes; 200 serials. **Subscriptions:** 101 journals and other serials. **Services:** Interlibrary loan; copying; library open to the public with restrictions. **Networks/Consortia:** Member of Colorado Council of Medical Librarians, Midcontinental Regional Medical Library Program, Denver Area Health Sciences Library Consortium.

★12158★
ROCKY MOUNTAIN JEWISH HISTORICAL SOCIETY - IRA M. BECK MEMORIAL LIBRARY (Rel-Phil)
Center for Judaic Studies
University of Denver Phone: (303)753-3178
Denver, CO 80208 Jeanne Abrams, Archv.
Staff: Prof 1. **Subjects:** Judaica. **Holdings:** Figures not available. **Services:** Copying; library open to the public. **Publications:** Rocky Mountain Notes, quarterly; Rocky Mountain Chai newsletter, quarterly.

ROCKY MOUNTAIN NATIONAL PARK
See: U.S. Natl. Park Service (15344)

★12159★
ROCKY MOUNTAIN NEWS - LIBRARY (Publ)
400 W. Colfax Ave. Phone: (303)892-5000
Denver, CO 80204 Susan Schwellenbach, Libn.
Founded: 1859. **Staff:** Prof 2; Other 6. **Subjects:** Newspaper reference topics. **Special Collections:** Index to historic houses of Denver. **Holdings:** 500 books; 5 million newspaper clippings; 6000 filing inches of photographs. **Services:** Library not open to the public.

ROD LIBRARY
See: University of Northern Iowa (16663)

★12160★
RODDEY, CARPENTER, AND WHITE, P.A. - GUARDIAN BUILDING LAW LIBRARY (Law)
P.O. Drawer 560 Phone: (803)324-4500
Rock Hill, SC 29731 Julie B. Luppino, Libn.
Founded: 1984. **Staff:** Prof 1. **Subjects:** Law. **Holdings:** 4500 books. **Subscriptions:** 200 journals and other serials; 8 newspapers. **Services:** Copying; library open to area attorneys. **Computerized Information Services:** WESTLAW, ABA/net, PHINet FedTax Database, DIALOG Information Services; ABA/net (electronic mail service). **Remarks:** Library located at One Law Place, Suite 600, Rock Hill, SC 29730.

BILLIE DAVIS RODENBERG MEMORIAL LIBRARY
See: Temple Beth El (13935)

★12161★
RODEY, DICKASON, SLOAN, AKIN & ROBB, P.A. - LIBRARY (Law)
20 First Plaza, Suite 700
Box 1888 Phone: (505)765-5900
Albuquerque, NM 87102 Shirley A. Meridith, Libn.
Staff: Prof 2; Other 1. **Subjects:** Law - antitrust, labor, tax. **Holdings:** 15,000 books. **Subscriptions:** 250 journals and other serials; 5 newspapers. **Services:** Interlibrary loan; library not open to the public. **Computerized Information Services:** LEXIS, WESTLAW, DIALOG Information Services; internal database. Performs searches on fee basis. **Staff:** Sarah Knox Morley, Asst.Libn..

RODGERS & HAMMERSTEIN ARCHIVES OF RECORDED SOUND
See: New York Public Library - Performing Arts Research Center - Rodgers & Hammerstein Archives of Recorded Sound (10082)

★12162★
RODMAN HALL ARTS CENTRE/NATIONAL EXHIBITION CENTRE - OFFICE REFERENCE LIBRARY (Art)
109 St. Paul Crescent Phone: (416)684-2925
St. Catharines, ON, Canada L2R 7B3
Debra Attenborough, Cur. of Ed.
Founded: 1960. **Staff:** Prof 1. **Subjects:** Canadian art history, 15th-19th century European masters, contemporary international artists. **Holdings:** 500 books; 1000 bound periodical volumes; 2500 other cataloged items. **Services:** Copying; library open to the public for reference use only. **Automated Operations:** Computerized public access catalog.

★12163★
G. ALLAN ROEHER INSTITUTE - NATIONAL INFORMATION EXCHANGE NETWORK (Med)
Kinsmen Bldg., York University
4700 Keele St. Phone: (416)661-9611
Downsview, ON, Canada M3J 1P3 Mary Ann Hutton, Libn.
Founded: 1964. **Staff:** Prof 3; Other 1. **Subjects:** Mental retardation, developmental disabilities, rehabilitation, special education, community organization. **Holdings:** 12,000 books; 12 VF drawers of pamphlets and reprints; 75 films. **Subscriptions:** 100 journals and other serials. **Services:**

Interlibrary loan; copying; network open to the public. **Automated Operations:** Computerized cataloging. **Publications:** Specialized bibliographies. **Special Catalogs:** Film and videotape catalog. **Remarks:** Network is sponsored by the Canadian Association for Community Living.

WINONA ROEHL LIBRARY
See: First Christian Church (Disciples of Christ) (5058)

FERDINAND ROEMER GEOLOGICAL LIBRARY
See: Baylor University - Department of Geology (1417)

ROESCH LIBRARY
See: University of Dayton (16106)

★12164★
ROGERS CORPORATION - ELECTRONICS LIBRARY (Sci-Engr)
2001 W. Chandler Blvd. Phone: (602)963-4584
Chandler, AZ 85224 Tracey Alsid, Libn.
Founded: 1984. **Staff:** Prof 1. **Subjects:** Electronics. **Holdings:** 700 books. **Subscriptions:** 60 journals and other serials. **Services:** Interlibrary loan; copying; library open to the public with restrictions. **Automated Operations:** Computerized cataloging, acquisitions, serials, and circulation. **Computerized Information Services:** OCLC, DIALOG Information Services; Bibliotech - Comstow Inc. (internal database).

EDITH NOURSE ROGERS MEMORIAL VETERANS HOSPITAL
See: U.S. Veterans Administration (MA-Bedford) (15575)

★12165★
LAUREN ROGERS MUSEUM OF ART - LIBRARY (Art, Hist)
Box 1108 Phone: (601)649-6374
Laurel, MS 39441 Jerry Scott Goodwin, Libn.
Founded: 1922. **Staff:** Prof 1; Other 2. **Subjects:** Fine arts, genealogy, Mississippiana. **Holdings:** 19,300 books; 1185 bound periodical volumes. **Subscriptions:** 110 journals and other serials. **Services:** Interlibrary loan; copying; library open to the public. **Remarks:** Maintained by the Eastman Memorial Foundation. Library located at 5th Ave. at 7th St., Laurel, MS 39440.

★12166★
MILLICENT ROGERS MUSEUM - LIBRARY (Area-Ethnic)
Box A Phone: (505)758-2462
Taos, NM 87571 Linda Geroy, Libn.
Staff: 1. **Subjects:** Indians of North America, local history, fine arts, museology, anthropology. **Special Collections:** Registry of Hispanic artists in New Mexico (109 artists). **Holdings:** 904 books; 81 subject classification files. **Subscriptions:** 36 journals and other serials. **Services:** Interlibrary loan; library open to the public by appointment for reference use only.

★12167★
ROGERS & WELLS - LIBRARY (Law)
201 N. Figueroa St., 15th Fl. Phone: (213)580-1000
Los Angeles, CA 90012-2638 Susan C. Trauger, Libn.
Staff: Prof 1; Other 1. **Subjects:** Taxation, real property, securities, corporations, litigation, finance. **Holdings:** 8000 books. **Services:** Library not open to the public. **Automated Operations:** Computerized cataloging. **Computerized Information Services:** LEXIS, NEXIS, DIALOG Information Services, WESTLAW, Information America.

★12168★
ROGERS & WELLS - LIBRARY (Law)
1737 H St., N.W. Phone: (202)331-7760
Washington, DC 20006 Julian Reckert, Libn.
Staff: Prof 1. **Subjects:** Law. **Holdings:** 5700 volumes; 4.5 shelves of U.S. International Trade Commission publications; U.S. Bureau of the Census statistics and Custom Service decisions and rulings on microfiche. **Subscriptions:** 41 journals and other serials. **Services:** Interlibrary loan; library open to the public by appointment. **Computerized Information Services:** LEXIS, NEXIS, WESTLAW.

★12169★
ROGERS & WELLS - LIBRARY (Law)
200 Park Ave., 52nd Fl. Phone: (212)878-8210
New York, NY 10166 Daniel J. Pelletier, Libn.
Staff: Prof 2; Other 3. **Subjects:** Law - tax, antitrust, securities, labor, trusts and estates. **Holdings:** 20,000 volumes; 10 drawers of microfiche; 8 drawers of microfilm. **Subscriptions:** 125 journals and other serials; 10 newspapers. **Services:** Interlibrary loan; library not open to the public. **Computerized Information Services:** DIALOG Information Services, Dow Jones News/Retrieval, VU/TEXT Information Services, NewsNet, Inc., LEXIS, WESTLAW. **Publications:** Information Bulletin, monthly - for internal distribution only. **Staff:** Margaret W. Nicol, Asst.Libn..

★12170★
WILL ROGERS LIBRARY (Hist)
121 N. Weenonah Phone: (918)341-1564
Claremore, OK 74017 Margaret L. Guffey, Libn.
Founded: 1936. **Staff:** Prof 2; Other 1. **Subjects:** Will Rogers, American Indians, Oklahoma and regional history. **Holdings:** 40,320 books; 225 bound periodical volumes; 1 VF drawer of clippings and pamphlets. **Subscriptions:** 65 journals and other serials; 10 newspapers. **Services:** Interlibrary loan; copying; library open to the public. **Automated Operations:** Computerized circulation. **Remarks:** Maintained by the City of Claremore. **Staff:** Vera Baker, Asst.Libn..

★12171★
ROHM & HAAS COMPANY - HOME OFFICE LIBRARY (Bus-Fin, Law)
Independence Mall, W. Phone: (215)592-3631
Philadelphia, PA 19105 Sandra F. Hostetter, Libn.
Founded: 1965. **Staff:** Prof 1; Other 1. **Subjects:** Law, management, finance, marketing, employee relations. **Holdings:** 5500 books and bound periodical volumes; 500 pamphlets; microfiche; annual reports. **Subscriptions:** 250 journals and other serials. **Services:** Interlibrary loan; library open to the public by appointment. **Automated Operations:** Computerized serials and circulation. **Computerized Information Services:** DIALOG Information Services, Pergamon ORBIT InfoLine, Inc., Dow Jones News/Retrieval, NewsNet, Inc., BRS Information Technologies, VU/TEXT Information Services, PIERS (Port Import/Export Reporting Services), OCLC, LEXIS, NEXIS. **Networks/Consortia:** Member of PALINET. **Publications:** Library Bulletin, bimonthly - for internal distribution only.

★12172★
ROHM & HAAS COMPANY - RESEARCH DIVISION - INFORMATION SERVICES DEPARTMENT (Sci-Engr)
727 Norristown Rd. Phone: (215)641-7816
Spring House, PA 19477 Dr. Frederick H. Owens, Mgr., Info.Serv.
Founded: 1936. **Staff:** Prof 9; Other 11. **Subjects:** Agricultural chemistry, coatings, plastics, textiles and fibers, petroleum chemicals. **Holdings:** 53,000 volumes; 8500 reels of microfilm; 5000 microfiche; 200 VF drawers of pamphlets, government reports, patents, trade literature. **Subscriptions:** 1000 journals and other serials. **Services:** Interlibrary loan; copying; library open to the public by appointment. **Automated Operations:** Computerized cataloging, serials, and circulation. **Computerized Information Services:** DIALOG Information Services, Chemical Information Systems, Inc. (CIS), WILSONLINE, NewsNet, Inc., The Source Information Network, CAS ONLINE, OCLC, LEXIS, VU/TEXT Information Services, DARC Pluridata System (DPDS) Data Base, Pergamon ORBIT InfoLine, Inc., BRS Information Technologies, NLM. Performs searches on fee basis. **Networks/Consortia:** Member of PALINET. **Publications:** Monthly library bulletin - for internal distribution only. **Staff:** Ellen C. Dotterrer, Acq.; Joanne L. Witiak, Info.Sci.; Margot B. Licitis, Transl.; Dominic R. Falgiatore, Info.Sci.; Helen M. Curran, Libn.; Virginia Piccolini, Info.Sci.; Helen M. Welsh, Info.Sci.; Barbara G. Wood, Libn..

★12173★
ROHM & HAAS COMPANY - RESEARCH DIVISION - INFORMATION SERVICES DEPARTMENT - LIBRARY (Sci-Engr)
Box 718 Phone: (215)785-8055
Bristol, PA 19007 Barbara G. Wood, Res.Lib.Mgr.
Staff: Prof 2; Other 5. **Subjects:** Polymer chemistry, chemical engineering, chemistry. **Holdings:** 23,000 volumes; government reports. **Subscriptions:** 1000 journals and other serials. **Services:** Interlibrary loan; copying; SDI; library open to the public by appointment. **Automated Operations:** Computerized serials, circulation, and ILL. **Computerized Information Services:** DIALOG Information Services, Pergamon ORBIT InfoLine, Inc., NLM, BRS Information Technologies, STN International, OCLC. **Networks/Consortia:** Member of PALINET, Greater Northeastern Regional Medical Library Program. **Staff:** Helen Welsh, Info.Chem..

★12174★
ROHR INDUSTRIES, INC. - CORPORATE LIBRARY (Trans)
Box 1516 Phone: (619)691-3010
Chula Vista, CA 92012 Richard J. Tommey, Tech.Libn.Sr.
Staff: Prof 1; Other 2. **Subjects:** Aerospace, materials, metallurgy, manufacturing. **Special Collections:** Advanced composites. **Holdings:** 5000 books; 24,000 reports. **Subscriptions:** 152 journals and other serials. **Services:** Interlibrary loan; library not open to the public. **Computerized**

Information Services: DIALOG Information Services, NASA/RECON, DTIC. **Publications:** Library Bulletin, quarterly.

ROHRBACH LIBRARY
See: Kutztown University (7574)

ROLFING MEMORIAL LIBRARY
See: Trinity Evangelical Divinity School (14335)

★12175★
ROLLINS COLLEGE - BEAL-MALTBIE SHELL MUSEUM - LIBRARY* (Biol Sci)
Box 2753
Winter Park, FL 32789 Linda L. Mojer, Cur.
Subjects: Shells. **Holdings:** Figures not available.

★12176★
C.A. ROLLOFF TRI-COUNTY LAW LIBRARY (Law)
Chippewa County Courthouse
11th St. & Hwy. 7 Phone: (612)269-7733
Montevideo, MN 56265 C.A. Rolloff, Sec.
Staff: 1. **Subjects:** Law. **Holdings:** 5000 volumes; Briefs from the Minnesota Supreme Court, 1943-1980. **Services:** Interlibrary loan; library open to the public.

★12177★
ROLLS-ROYCE INC. - INFORMATION CENTER (Sci-Engr)
1895 Phoenix Blvd. Phone: (404)996-8400
Atlanta, GA 30349 Karen L. Bell, Info.Mgr.
Staff: Prof 1; Other 1. **Subjects:** Jet engine technology, thermodynamics, metallurgy, aeronautics, contract management. **Holdings:** 2000 books; 4000 government documents. **Subscriptions:** 150 journals and other serials. **Services:** Center not open to the public. **Computerized Information Services:** DIALOG Information Services, DMS/ONLINE, Aerospace Online; INMAGIC (internal database); DIALMAIL (electronic mail service). **Networks/Consortia:** Member of Georgia Library Information Network (GLIN).

ROMANEK CULTURAL CENTER
See: North Shore Congregation Israel - Romanek Cultural Center (10368)

★12178★
ROMANIAN LIBRARY (Area-Ethnic)
200 E. 38th St.
New York, NY 10016 Phone: (212)687-0180
Founded: 1971. **Staff:** 2. **Subjects:** Romania - literature, history, arts, science, economy. **Special Collections:** Constantin Brancusi (30 volumes); minorities in Romania (50 volumes); Romania's present day domestic policy; Romania's foreign policy (50 volumes). **Holdings:** 15,000 books; 500 bound periodical volumes; 500 phonograph records; 1000 slides; 500 photographs; films. **Subscriptions:** 100 journals and other serials; 10 newspapers. **Services:** Interlibrary loan; annual Romanian language courses; library open to the public. **Publications:** Romanian Library monthly program - free upon request; bibliographies on Romanian topics. **Remarks:** Maintained by the Ministry of Foreign Affairs, Central State Library at Bucharest.

★12179★
ROME HISTORICAL SOCIETY - WILLIAM E. SCRIPTURE MEMORIAL LIBRARY (Hist)
200 Church St. Phone: (315)336-5870
Rome, NY 13440 Thomas J. Kernan, Res.Libn.
Founded: 1936. **Staff:** Prof 1; Other 3. **Subjects:** Central New York and local history, genealogy, Civil War, American Revolution, social history. **Holdings:** 3500 books; 350 bound periodical volumes; 7000 archival documents; La Vita (Italian language newspaper), 1918-1945, on microfilm; historical documents on microfilm. **Subscriptions:** 11 journals and other serials. **Services:** Copying; library open to the public.

MILES ROMNEY MEMORIAL LIBRARY
See: Bitter Root Valley Historical Society - Miles Romney Memorial Library (1630)

★12180★
ROOKS, PITTS, FULLAGAR & POUST - LIBRARY (Law)
55 W. Monroe, Suite 1500 Phone: (312)372-5600
Chicago, IL 60603 Nancy J. Henry, Hd.Libn.
Staff: Prof 1; Other 2. **Subjects:** Law. **Holdings:** 16,000 volumes. **Subscriptions:** 644 journals and other serials. **Services:** Interlibrary loan; copying; library open to the public with restrictions. **Computerized Information Services:** LEXIS, WESTLAW, DIALOG Information Services. **Networks/Consortia:** Member of Chicago Library System, ILLINET.

FRANKLIN D. ROOSEVELT LIBRARY
See: U.S. Presidential Libraries (15482)

★12181★
ROOSEVELT HOSPITAL - HEALTH SCIENCE LIBRARY (Med)
Box 151 Phone: (201)321-6800
Metuchen, NJ 08840 Karen Rubin, Libn.
Staff: 1. **Subjects:** Medicine, nursing. **Holdings:** 800 books. **Subscriptions:** 60 journals and other serials. **Services:** Library open to the public for reference use only.

★12182★
ROOSEVELT HOSPITAL - MEDICAL LIBRARY (Med)
428 W. 59th St. Phone: (212)554-6872
New York, NY 10019 Paul E. Barth, Libn.
Founded: 1955. **Staff:** Prof 1; Other 1. **Subjects:** Medicine, surgery, gerontology, geriatrics, hospital administration, pediatrics, anesthesia. **Holdings:** 25,000 books and bound periodical volumes. **Subscriptions:** 530 journals and other serials. **Services:** Interlibrary loan; copying; library open to the public for reference use only by appointment. **Computerized Information Services:** NLM, BRS Information Technologies. **Networks/Consortia:** Member of Medical Library Center of New York (MLCNY), New York Metropolitan Reference and Research Library Agency (METRO).

THEODORE ROOSEVELT HUNTING LIBRARY
See: Library of Congress - Rare Book & Special Collections Division (7836)

THEODORE ROOSEVELT NATIONAL PARK
See: U.S. Natl. Park Service (15356)

★12183★
ROOSEVELT UNIVERSITY - ARCHIVES (Hist)
430 S. Michigan Ave. Phone: (312)341-3643
Chicago, IL 60605 Calvin S. Byre, Hd.Ref.Libn.
Staff: Prof 1. **Subjects:** University and Chicago history. **Special Collections:** Auditorium Theater records and broadsides (30 boxes; 30 volumes; 80 broadsides). **Holdings:** 30 books; 100 boxes of university records. **Services:** Copying; archives open to the public.

★12184★
ROOSEVELT UNIVERSITY - MUSIC LIBRARY (Mus)
430 S. Michigan Ave. Phone: (312)341-3651
Chicago, IL 60605 Donald Draganski, Libn.
Founded: 1945. **Staff:** Prof 1; Other 3. **Subjects:** Music, music education. **Holdings:** 35,000 volumes; 10,000 phonograph records; 100 reels of microfilm; 200 dissertations; 400 magnetic tapes. **Subscriptions:** 105 journals and other serials. **Services:** Interlibrary loan; copying; library open to the public for reference use only. **Computerized Information Services:** OCLC. **Networks/Consortia:** Member of ILLINET.

★12185★
ROOSEVELT UNIVERSITY - ORAL HISTORY PROJECT IN LABOR HISTORY (Hist)
430 S. Michigan Ave. Phone: (219)931-9791
Chicago, IL 60605 Elizabeth Balanoff, Prof. of Hist.
Subjects: Oral histories in labor history. **Holdings:** 193 hours of taped interviews. **Services:** Copying. **Remarks:** The oral history transcripts are held in the Roosevelt University library where they may be read but not checked out. People who wish to read a transcript for scholarly research but are unable to come to Roosevelt University may order the transcript they need through their own university library. Orders should be sent to Director of Oral History Project.

ROOSEVELT-VANDERBILT NATIONAL HISTORIC SITES
See: U.S. Natl. Park Service (15345)

ROPER CENTER ARCHIVES
See: Yale University - Social Science Library (18149)

ROPER CENTER FOR PUBLIC OPINION RESEARCH
See: University of Connecticut (16102)

★12186★
ROPES & GRAY - CENTRAL LIBRARY (Law)
225 Franklin St. Phone: (617)423-6100
Boston, MA 02110 Cornelia Trubey, Dir., Lib.Serv.
Staff: Prof 2; Other 3. **Subjects:** Law. **Holdings:** 25,000 books; 1000 bound periodical volumes. **Subscriptions:** 600 journals and other serials; 10 newspapers. **Services:** Interlibrary loan; library not open to the public. **Computerized Information Services:** LEXIS, NEXIS, DIALOG Information Services, WESTLAW, Dow Jones News/Retrieval, VU/TEXT Information Services, CDA Investment Technologies, Inc., Dialcom Inc.

★12187★
RORER GROUP, INC. - ARMOUR PHARMACEUTICAL COMPANY - LIBRARY (Med)
Box 511 Phone: (815)932-6771
Kankakee, IL 60901 Mary Blunk, Libn.
Staff: 1. **Subjects:** Chemistry, biology, medicine, pharmacy. **Holdings:** 1000 books; 2000 bound periodical volumes. **Subscriptions:** 200 journals and other serials. **Services:** Interlibrary loan; library not open to the public.

★12188★
RORER GROUP, INC. - RESEARCH LIBRARY
500 Virginia Dr.
Fort Washington, PA 19034
Defunct. Holdings absorbed by Rorer Pharmaceutical Corporation, Inc. - Research Library.

★12189★
RORER PHARMACEUTICAL CORPORATION, INC. - RESEARCH LIBRARY (Med)
640 Allendale Rd. Phone: (215)962-3937
King of Prussia, PA 19406 George H. Bell, Supv.
Staff: Prof 2; Other 3. **Subjects:** Organic chemistry, biochemistry, pharmacology, medicine, pharmacy. **Holdings:** 13,000 books; 45,000 bound periodical volumes; 1000 reels of microfilm. **Subscriptions:** 650 journals and other serials. **Services:** Interlibrary loan; library not open to the public. **Computerized Information Services:** DIALOG Information Services, Pergamon ORBIT InfoLine, Inc., STN International, NLM, Telesystemes Questel, BRS Information Technologies, Data-Star, IMSBASE. **Formed by the merger of:** Rorer Central Research - Research Library and Rorer Group, Inc. - Research Library. **Staff:** Catherine Heslin, Info.Spec.; Mary Kay Ludovicy, Coord., Tech.Serv..

BILLY ROSE THEATRE COLLECTION
See: New York Public Library - Performing Arts Research Center - Billy Rose Theatre Collection (10079)

DAVID J. ROSE LIBRARY
See: Massachusetts Institute of Technology - Plasma Fusion Center (8545)

★12190★
ROSE-HULMAN INSTITUTE OF TECHNOLOGY - JOHN A. LOGAN LIBRARY (Sci-Engr)
5500 E. Wabash Ave. Phone: (812)877-1511
Terre Haute, IN 47803-3999 John M. Robson, Dir.
Founded: 1874. **Staff:** Prof 1; Other 2. **Subjects:** Engineering and science. **Holdings:** 41,000 books; 18,000 bound periodical volumes; 1200 records; 6000 documents; 675 reels of microfilm; 800 archival volumes. **Subscriptions:** 500 journals and other serials; 10 newspapers. **Services:** Interlibrary loan; copying; library open to the public. **Automated Operations:** Computerized public access catalog and cataloging. **Computerized Information Services:** OCLC. **Networks/Consortia:** Member of INCOLSA.

★12191★
ROSE MEDICAL CENTER - LIBRARY (Med)
4567 E. 9th Ave. Phone: (303)320-2160
Denver, CO 80220 Nancy Simon, Med.Libn.
Founded: 1949. **Staff:** Prof 1. **Subjects:** Medicine. **Holdings:** 1000 books; 2989 bound periodical volumes; 257 Audio-Digest tapes. **Subscriptions:** 197 journals and other serials. **Services:** Interlibrary loan; library not open to the public. **Computerized Information Services:** MEDLARS, DIALOG Information Services. **Networks/Consortia:** Member of Colorado Council of Medical Librarians. **Publications:** Annual Report; procedure manual.

ROSE MEMORIAL LIBRARY
See: Biola University - Rose Memorial Library (1601)

SIDNEY G. ROSE MEMORIAL LIBRARY
See: K.K. Bene Israel/Rockdale Temple (7304)

★12192★
ROSELAND COMMUNITY HOSPITAL - HEALTH SCIENCE LIBRARY (Med)
45 W. 111th St. Phone: (312)995-3191
Chicago, IL 60628 Mary T. Hanlon, Libn.
Staff: Prof 1. **Subjects:** Medicine and nursing. **Holdings:** 850 books; 2 VF drawers of pamphlets. **Subscriptions:** 37 journals and other serials. **Services:** Interlibrary loan; copying. **Networks/Consortia:** Member of Greater Midwest Regional Medical Library Network, ILLINET, Chicago and South Consortium.

ROSEMEAD GRADUATE SCHOOL OF PROFESSIONAL PSYCHOLOGY - LIBRARY
See: Biola University - Rose Memorial Library (1601)

★12193★
ROSEMONT COLLEGE - GERTRUDE KISTLER MEMORIAL LIBRARY - SPECIAL COLLECTIONS (Educ)
Rosemont, PA 19010 Phone: (215)527-0200
Sr. Mary Dennis Lynch, S.H.C.J., Dir., Lib.Serv.
Founded: 1922. **Staff:** Prof 6; Other 8. **Special Collections:** Early Pennsylvania history; Education Resource Center. **Services:** Interlibrary loan; copying; SDI; library open to persons with academic credentials. **Automated Operations:** Computerized cataloging and ILL. **Computerized Information Services:** DIALOG Information Services, Pergamon ORBIT InfoLine, Inc., OCLC, BRS Information Technologies. Performs searches on fee basis. Contact Person: Barbara J. Williams, Rd.Serv.Libn.. **Networks/Consortia:** Member of Tri-State College Library Cooperative (TCLC), PALINET, Interlibrary Delivery Service of Pennsylvania (IDS). **Publications:** Your Path to Success (bibliographic instruction text) - for sale; Guide - to regular users. **Staff:** April Nelson, Tech.Proc.Serv.Libn.; Sr. Annette Dawson, S.H.C.J., Coord., ILL; Diana M. Cowling, Coord., Per. & Circ..

★12194★
ROSEN, WACHTELL & GILBERT - LAW LIBRARY & INFORMATION CENTER (Law)
1888 Century Park E., Suite 2100 Phone: (213)553-2900
Los Angeles, CA 90067-1725 Cookie Lewis, Dir.
Staff: Prof 2. **Subjects:** Banking and commercial law, financial institutions, municipal finance. **Holdings:** 4000 books; 50 bound periodical volumes; 10K and annual reports; research files. **Subscriptions:** 400 loose-leaf services and newsletters; 8 newspapers. **Services:** Interlibrary loan; library open to clients and legal professionals. **Computerized Information Services:** LEXIS, DataTimes, WESTLAW, NEXIS, Dow Jones News/Retrieval, DIALOG Information Services; internal database. **Staff:** Judith Gross, Asst. Law Libn..

★12195★
ROSENBACH MUSEUM & LIBRARY (Hist, Hum)
2010 DeLancey Pl. Phone: (215)732-1600
Philadelphia, PA 19103 Ellen S. Dunlap, Dir.
Founded: 1954. **Staff:** Prof 6; Other 8. **Subjects:** Americana, English literature, incunabula, Judaica, book illustration. **Special Collections:** Marianne Moore Archive; Maurice Sendak original drawings; Latin-American historical manuscripts. **Holdings:** 30,000 books; 270,000 manuscripts. **Subscriptions:** 35 journals and other serials. **Services:** Interlibrary loan; copying; museum open for tours and exhibitions; library open to scholars by appointment. **Automated Operations:** Computerized cataloging. **Networks/Consortia:** Member of RLG. **Publications:** Recent Acquisitions, irregular; fine press and facsimile editions of important rare books and manuscripts; collection guides; Rosenbach Newsletter. **Special Catalogs:** Exhibition catalogs on aspects of collection. **Staff:** Leslie A. Morris, Cur., Bks. & Mss.; Kimerly Rorschach, Cur., Art.

ROSENBERG CAPITAL MANAGEMENT
See: RCM Capital Management (11904)

JOSEPH H. ROSENBERG AMERICAN JEWISH ARCHIVES
See: Hebrew Union College - Jewish Institute of Religion - Frances-Henry Library (6215)

★12196★
ROSENBERG LIBRARY - SPECIAL COLLECTIONS (Hist)
2310 Sealy Ave. Phone: (409)763-8854
Galveston, TX 77550 Jane A. Kenamore, Hd.
Founded: 1904. **Staff:** Prof 2; Other 1. **Subjects:** State and local history, Civil War, historic preservation. **Holdings:** 8000 books; 1000 bound periodical volumes; 1600 linear feet of manuscripts; 15,000 photographs; 800 maps; microfilm; architectural drawings; newspapers; vertical files. **Subscriptions:** 75 journals and other serials. **Services:** Copying; collections open to the public. **Computerized Information Services:** Marcon (internal database). **Networks/Consortia:** Member of Houston Area Library System (HALS). **Publications:** Manuscript Sources in the Rosenberg Library: A Selective Guide. **Special Catalogs:** Book and manuscript catalogs. **Special Indexes:** News article index; biographical index; map index; photograph subject index; lists of newspaper holdings; architectural and engineering drawings and films. **Staff:** Casey Greene, Asst.Archv.; Jane A. Kenamore, Archv./Hd., Spec.Coll.; Lise Darat, Cur..

★12197★
PAUL ROSENBERG ASSOCIATES - LIBRARY (Sci-Engr)
Box 729 Phone: (914)834-3939
Larchmont, NY 10538 Miss M. Hill, Libn.
Founded: 1945. **Staff:** Prof 1; Other 1. **Subjects:** Applied physics, engineering, aerospace, photogrammetry, remote sensing, energy, navigation, lasers, electro-optics, ultrasonics, radon. **Holdings:** 1000 books; 800 bound periodical volumes; 2000 reports and reprints. **Subscriptions:** 40 journals and other serials. **Services:** Library not open to the public.

★12198★
M. ROSENBLATT & SON, INC. - TECHNICAL EXCHANGE (Sci-Engr)
350 Broadway Phone: (212)431-6900
New York, NY 10013 Hon H. Lee, Libn.
Founded: 1947. **Staff:** Prof 1; Other 4. **Subjects:** Naval architecture; engineering - marine, ocean, civil; naval science; offshore structures. **Special Collections:** Mandell Rosenblatt Collection of sports vessels and yachts, 1910-1959. **Holdings:** 2400 books; 1650 bound periodical volumes; 2400 reports; 3000 reels of microfilm; 2000 microfiche; 9000 ships plans. **Subscriptions:** 25 journals and other serials; 10 newspapers. **Services:** Interlibrary loan; not open to the public. **Computerized Information Services:** DIALOG Information Services, MCAUTO (McDonnell Douglas Automation Company); INFO MFD 2: Ships Maneuvering, Vibration, Stability Programs (internal database). **Publications:** Library List (newsletter), irregular - for internal distribution only.

SOL ROSENBLOOM LIBRARY
See: Hebrew Institute of Pittsburgh (6211)

BLANCHE AND IRA ROSENBLUM MEMORIAL LIBRARY
See: Beth Shalom Congregation (1550)

★12199★
ROSENMAN & COLIN - LAW LIBRARY (Law)
575 Madison Ave. Phone: (212)940-8598
New York, NY 10022 Eleanor A. Sabo, Hd.Libn.
Staff: Prof 4; Other 6. **Subjects:** Law. **Holdings:** 35,000 books and bound periodical volumes; New York Law Journal, 1964 to present, on microfilm. **Subscriptions:** 300 journals and other serials; 8 newspapers. **Services:** Interlibrary loan; library open to clients and library community by appointment. **Computerized Information Services:** LEXIS, NEXIS, WESTLAW, DIALOG Information Services.

★12200★
ROSENN, JENKINS & GREENWALD, ATTORNEYS AT LAW - LIBRARY (Law)
15 S. Franklin St. Phone: (717)826-5663
Wilkes-Barre, PA 18711 Sarah P. Carr, Libn.
Staff: Prof 1. **Subjects:** State and federal law. **Holdings:** 8000 books; 200 bound periodical volumes. **Subscriptions:** 350 journals and other serials. **Services:** Interlibrary loan; library not open to the public. **Computerized Information Services:** LEXIS.

DOROTHY & LEWIS ROSENSTIEL SCHOOL OF MARINE & ATMOSPHERIC SCIENCES
See: University of Miami (16401)

BENJAMIN S. ROSENTHAL LIBRARY
See: Queens College of the City University of New York (11814)

BENJAMIN S. ROSENTHAL LIBRARY
See: Queens College of the City University of New York - Benjamin S. Rosenthal Library (11813)

SAMUEL ROSENTHAL MEMORIAL LIBRARY
See: St. Joseph's Hospital (12494)

EDWARD ROSENTHALL MATHEMATICS AND STATISTICS LIBRARY
See: Mc Gill University - Edward Rosenthall Mathematics and Statistics Library (8194)

ROSENZWEIG HEALTH SCIENCES LIBRARY
See: St. Luke's Medical Center (12570)

★12201★
ROSEVILLE COMMUNITY HOSPITAL - MEDICAL LIBRARY (Med)
333 Sunrise Ave. Phone: (916)781-1580
Roseville, CA 95661 Helen R. Asher, Libn.
Founded: 1976. **Staff:** Prof 1. **Subjects:** Medicine, nursing, surgery. **Holdings:** 1560 books; 55 bound periodical volumes; 8 VF drawers of pamphlets. **Subscriptions:** 174 journals and other serials. **Services:** Interlibrary loan; copying; library open to the public for reference use only. **Computerized Information Services:** NLM. Performs searches on fee basis. **Networks/Consortia:** Member of Northern California and Nevada Medical Library Group (NCNMLG), Mountain Valley Library System, Sacramento Area Health Sciences Librarians Group (SAHSL).

★12202★
ROSEVILLE EARLY CHILDHOOD FAMILY EDUCATION PROGRAM - TOY LIBRARY (Educ)
Parkview Center
701 W. County Rd. B Phone: (612)633-8150
Roseville, MN 55113 Linda L. Merte, Libn.
Staff: Prof 1; Other 3. **Subjects:** Educational toys, children's literature, and activity kits for children up to 5 years of age; parenting. **Holdings:** 1000 books; 4000 toys; 150 folders of clippings and documents. **Services:** Library open to the public on fee basis. **Formed by the merger of:** Play 'n' Learn Library and Resources for Child Caring Inc. - Library.

★12203★
ROSEWOOD CENTER - MIRIAM LODGE PROFESSIONAL LIBRARY (Med, Educ)
Owings Mills, MD 21117 Phone: (301)363-0300
Thelma W. Newton, Supv., Lib. & Files
Founded: 1955. **Staff:** Prof 1. **Subjects:** Mental retardation, special education, social work, learning disorders, pediatrics, psychology. **Holdings:** 3000 books; 1000 bound periodical volumes; 6 VF drawers of pamphlets; 7 VF drawers of staff papers; 30 manuscripts. **Subscriptions:** 69 journals and other serials. **Services:** Interlibrary loan; copying; library open to the public. **Networks/Consortia:** Member of Maryland Association of Health Science Librarians. **Staff:** Yvette Dixon, Lib.Coord..

★12204★
ROSICRUCIAN FELLOWSHIP - LIBRARY (Rel-Phil)
2222 Mission Ave.
Box 713 Phone: (619)757-6600
Oceanside, CA 92054 Helen Schroeder, Libn.
Staff: Prof 1. **Subjects:** Christian mysticism, Bible study, spiritual astrology, health and healing. **Holdings:** 1500 books. **Services:** Library open to members for reference use only.

★12205★
ROSICRUCIAN FRATERNITY - LIBRARY (Rel-Phil)
Beverly Hall
Box 220 Phone: (215)536-5168
Quakertown, PA 18951 Gerald E. Poesnecker, Pres.
Subjects: Religion, philosophy. **Holdings:** Figures not available. **Services:** Library not open to the public. **Remarks:** Library serves as the archive for the fraternity and as study reference center for students enrolled in the fraternity.

★12206★
ROSICRUCIAN ORDER, AMORC - ROSICRUCIAN RESEARCH LIBRARY (Rel-Phil)
Rosicrucian Park
Park & Naglee Aves. Phone: (408)287-9176
San Jose, CA 95191 Clara Campbell, Libn.
Founded: 1939. **Staff:** Prof 1; Other 1. **Subjects:** Egyptology, Rosicrucianism, parapsychology, mysticism, Baconiana. **Holdings:** 14,000 books; 260 bound periodical volumes; 6 VF drawers of pamphlets and manuscripts. **Subscriptions:** 25 journals and other serials. **Services:** Library not open to the public. **Publications:** Rosicrucian Digest, monthly - to members and by subscription. **Special Indexes:** Rosicrucian Digest index; Rosicrucian Forum index (card); Index to Rosicrucian books (book); Rosicrucian Lessons (book).

★12207★
ROSS COUNTY LAW LIBRARY (Law)
67 N. Paint St. Phone: (614)773-1075
Chillicothe, OH 45601 Rita Fuchsman, Libn.
Staff: 1. **Subjects:** Law. **Holdings:** 17,700 books; 337 bound periodical volumes; 4300 microfiche. **Subscriptions:** 60 journals and other serials. **Services:** Copying; library open to the public with restrictions. **Computerized Information Services:** WESTLAW. Performs searches on fee basis. **Remarks:** Maintained by Ross County Law Library Association.

★12208★
ROSS & HARDIES - LIBRARY (Law)
150 N. Michigan Ave., 24th Fl. Phone: (312)558-1000
Chicago, IL 60601 Carol Furnish, Libn.
Founded: 1902. **Staff:** Prof 1; Other 2. **Subjects:** Law, health. **Holdings:** 26,196 volumes. **Subscriptions:** 52 journals and other serials. **Services:** Interlibrary loan; library open to the public. **Computerized Information Services:** DIALOG Information Services, Dow Jones News/Retrieval, LEXIS, WESTLAW, OCLC.

HOWARD ROSS LIBRARY OF MANAGEMENT
See: Mc Gill University (8196)

★12209★
ROSS LABORATORIES - LIBRARY (Food-Bev)
625 Cleveland Ave. Phone: (614)227-3503
Columbus, OH 43216 Linda Mitro Hopkins, Mgr.
Staff: Prof 2; Other 2. **Subjects:** Nutrition, food technology, business, analytical chemistry. **Holdings:** 3500 books; 6000 bound periodical volumes. **Subscriptions:** 550 journals and other serials. **Services:** Interlibrary loan; copying; SDI; library open to the public with restrictions. **Automated Operations:** Computerized cataloging, serials, and circulation. **Computerized Information Services:** DIALOG Information Services, OCLC, MEDLINE, Pergamon ORBIT InfoLine, Inc., The Source Information Network, BRS Information Technologies; internal databases. **Networks/Consortia:** Member of OHIONET. **Publications:** Internal newsletter and journal holdings list.

ROSS LIBRARY
See: U.S. Dept. of Energy - Bonneville Power Administration (15002)

★12210★
ROSS ROY, INC. - LIBRARY (Bus-Fin)
100 Bloomfield Pkwy. Phone: (313)568-6000
Bloomfield Hills, MI 48013-3100 April Vossberg, Libn.
Founded: 1920. **Staff:** Prof 1; Other 1. **Subjects:** Marketing, sales promotion, automobile data, advertising. **Holdings:** 700 books. **Subscriptions:** 600 journals and other serials; 10 newspapers. **Services:** Library open to public at librarian's discretion. **Automated Operations:** Computerized cataloging and budget. **Computerized Information Services:** DIALOG Information Services, VU/TEXT Information Services, NEXIS, Dun & Bradstreet Corporation. **Special Indexes:** Periodicals list.

★12211★
ROSSLAND HISTORICAL MUSEUM ASSOCIATION - ARCHIVES (Hist)
Box 26 Phone: (604)362-7722
Rossland, BC, Canada V0G 1Y0 Joyce Tadevic, Archv.
Founded: 1955. **Staff:** 1. **Subjects:** Rossland history including mining, biography, business, entertainment, sports. **Holdings:** 400 books; 50 bound periodical volumes; 50 items of city records; 48 drawers of indexed documents, clippings, reports, letters; 2700 photographs of Rossland area. **Services:** Copying (limited); archives open to the public for reference use only.

ROSTAD LIBRARY
See: Evangelical School of Theology (4835)

★12212★
ROSWELL MUSEUM AND ART CENTER - RESEARCH LIBRARY (Art)
100 W. 11th St. Phone: (505)624-6744
Roswell, NM 88201 William Ebie, Dir.
Founded: 1950. **Subjects:** Art - contemporary, Native American, Spanish Colonial, Western United States; rocketry; archeology. **Holdings:** 2500 books; 3600 bound periodical volumes; 3500 color slides. **Subscriptions:** 75 journals and other serials. **Services:** Copying; library open to scholars.

★12213★
ROSWELL PARK MEMORIAL INSTITUTE - LIBRARY AND INFORMATION MANAGEMENT SERVICES (Med)
666 Elm St. Phone: (716)845-5966
Buffalo, NY 14263 Ann P. Hutchinson, Lib.Dir.
Founded: 1898. **Staff:** Prof 4; Other 6. **Subjects:** Cancer and allied diseases. **Holdings:** 65,000 books and bound periodical volumes; 400 AV programs. **Subscriptions:** 1200 journals and other serials. **Services:** Interlibrary loan; copying; SDI; library open to the public. **Automated Operations:** Computerized cataloging, acquisitions, and serials. **Computerized Information Services:** DIALOG Information Services, BRS Information Technologies, OCLC, MEDLINE; OnTyme Electronic Message Network Service, DOCLINE (electronic mail services). **Networks/Consortia:** Member of Western New York Library Resources Council (WNYLRC), Medical Library Center of New York (MLCNY). **Publications:** Library Bulletin, quarterly. **Remarks:** Maintained by New York State Department of Health. **Staff:** Gail Franke, Pub.Serv.; Suzanne Zajac, Tech.Serv.; Gayle Ablove, Ref.Serv..

ROTCH LIBRARY OF ARCHITECTURE AND PLANNING
See: Massachusetts Institute of Technology (8550)

ROTHSCHILD LIBRARY
See: Park Avenue Synagogue (11064)

ROTHSCHILD MEDICAL LIBRARY
See: Jewish Hospital at Washington University Medical Center (7216)

★12214★
ROUNCE AND COFFIN CLUB, LOS ANGELES - LIBRARY (Hum)
Occidental College Library
1600 Campus Rd. Phone: (213)259-2852
Los Angeles, CA 90041 Tyrus G. Harmsen, Book Arts Prog.
Staff: Prof 1. **Subjects:** Western printing, 1938 to present. **Holdings:** 1400 books. **Special Catalogs:** Western Books Catalog, annual.

PERE ROUQUETTE LIBRARY
See: St. Joseph Seminary College (12478)

★12215★
ROWAN PUBLIC LIBRARY - EDITH M. CLARK HISTORY ROOM (Hist)
201 W. Fisher St.
Box 4039 Phone: (704)633-5578
Salisbury, NC 28144 Shirley Hoffman, Local Hist., Geneal.Spec.
Staff: Prof 1; Other 1. **Subjects:** Local and regional history and genealogy. **Special Collections:** McCubbins Collection (Rowan County families; 150,000 abstracts of court records, wills, deeds, Bible records); Smith Collection (families who migrated to Kentucky and westward; correspondence; family charts); Archibald Henderson Collection (historical materials of North Carolina); James Brawley Collection (local history; family histories; maps; original newspapers of the 1800s). **Holdings:** 5500 books; 226 bound periodical volumes; 920 reels of microfilm; 100 microfiche; 25 VF drawers of personal papers; 100 maps. **Subscriptions:** 45 journals and other serials. **Services:** Copying; room open to the public.

ROWE MEMORIAL LIBRARY
See: Southeastern Bible College (13422)

DR. HUGH GRANT ROWELL CIRCUS LIBRARY COLLECTION
See: Somers Historical Society (13358)

NELLIE LANGFORD ROWELL LIBRARY
See: York University (18203)

ROWND HISTORICAL LIBRARY
See: Cedar Falls Historical Society (2781)

GRADIE R. ROWNTREE MEDICAL LIBRARY
See: Humana Hospital University (6594)

★12216★
ROXBOROUGH MEMORIAL HOSPITAL - SCHOOL OF NURSING AND MEDICAL STAFF LIBRARIES (Med)
5800 Ridge Ave. Phone: (215)487-4345
Philadelphia, PA 19128 Barbara D. Bernoff, Libn.
Staff: Prof 1. **Subjects:** Nursing, medicine, psychology, sociology, science. **Holdings:** 3500 books; 1550 bound periodical volumes; 6 VF drawers of pamphlets; 3 VF drawers of National League for Nursing pamphlets; 300 AV programs; 20 computer programs. **Subscriptions:** 168 journals and other serials. **Services:** Interlibrary loan; copying; library open to the public for reference use only. **Automated Operations:** Computerized cataloging and serials. **Computerized Information Services:** BRS Information Technologies. Performs searches on fee basis. **Networks/Consortia:** Member of Greater Northeastern Regional Medical Library Program, Delaware Valley Information Consortium (DEVIC). **Special Indexes:** Classified list of new acquisitions, bimonthly - for internal distribution only.

★12217★
ROYAL ALEXANDRA HOSPITAL - LIBRARY SERVICES (Med)
10240 Kingsway Ave. Phone: (403)477-4135
Edmonton, AB, Canada T5H 3V9 Donna Dryden, Supv.
Founded: 1963. **Staff:** Prof 1; Other 1. **Subjects:** Medicine, allied health sciences. **Holdings:** 1600 books. **Subscriptions:** 180 journals and other serials. **Services:** Interlibrary loan; copying; SDI; services open to hospital personnel. **Computerized Information Services:** MEDLINE, DIALOG Information Services.

★12218★
ROYAL ALEXANDRA HOSPITAL - SCHOOL OF NURSING LIBRARY (Med)
10415 111th Ave. Phone: (403)477-4939
Edmonton, AB, Canada T5G 0B8 Juliana Zia, Libn.
Founded: 1960. **Staff:** Prof 1; Other 1. **Subjects:** Nursing, medicine, social and behavioral sciences. **Holdings:** 13,073 books; 13 drawers of clippings, reports, pamphlets. **Subscriptions:** 76 journals and other serials. **Services:** Interlibrary loan; copying; library open to nursing students, faculty, and hospital personnel.

★12219★
ROYAL ASTRONOMICAL SOCIETY OF CANADA - NATIONAL LIBRARY (Sci-Engr)
136 Dupont St. Phone: (416)924-7973
Toronto, ON, Canada M5R 1V2 Brian Beattie, Libn.
Subjects: Astronomy and allied sciences. **Holdings:** 2000 volumes; 600 35mm slides; 11 16mm films. **Subscriptions:** 50 journals and other serials. **Services:** Library open to the public.

★12220★
ROYAL BANK OF CANADA - INFORMATION RESOURCES (Bus-Fin)
Royal Bank Plaza, 4th Fl. Phone: (416)974-2780
Toronto, ON, Canada M5J 2J5 Jane Dysart, Mgr.
Founded: 1972. **Staff:** Prof 4; Other 4. **Subjects:** Banking, finance, Canadian industry, business, world economic conditions, economics, management. **Holdings:** 9500 books; 250 subject files; 200 association files; 200 country files; 200 industry files; 4 drawers of microfiche of financial statements of Canadian companies. **Subscriptions:** 1200 journals and other serials; 50 newspapers. **Services:** Interlibrary loan; not open to the public. **Automated Operations:** Computerized cataloging, acquisitions, serials, and circulation. **Computerized Information Services:** DIALOG Information Services, TEXTLINE, Info Globe, BRS Information Technologies, Pergamon ORBIT InfoLine, Inc., Dow Jones News/Retrieval, I.P. Sharp Associates Limited, Canada Systems Group (CSG), Telesystemes Questel, QL Systems, NewsNet, Inc.; Envoy 100 (electronic mail service). **Publications:** On the Shelf (current awareness bulletin), monthly - for internal distribution only. **Staff:** Deirdre Grimes, Asst.Mgr.; Barbara Dance, Asst.Mgr.; Lesley Tiringer, Libn..

★12221★
ROYAL BANK OF CANADA - INFORMATION RESOURCES (Bus-Fin)
P.O. Box 6001 Phone: (514)874-2452
Montreal, PQ, Canada H3C 3A9 Anthea Downing, Mgr.
Founded: 1913. **Staff:** Prof 3; Other 3. **Subjects:** Banks and banking; finance and international finance; economics and business; Canadian and world economic conditions; management. **Holdings:** 55,000 volumes; pamphlets; speeches; archives. **Subscriptions:** 1200 journals and other serials; 35 newspapers. **Services:** Interlibrary loan; copying; open to the public. **Automated Operations:** Computerized cataloging, acquisitions, and serials. **Computerized Information Services:** Pergamon ORBIT InfoLine, Inc., DIALOG Information Services, Info Globe, Dow Jones News/Retrieval, QL Systems, IST-Informatheque Inc., LEXIS, NEXIS, TEXTLINE; ROBIN (internal database). **Publications:** On the Shelf, monthly; Notes of the Week. **Staff:** Adelaide Richter, Asst.Mgr., Info.Serv.; John O'Shaughnessy, Asst.Mgr., Tech.Sys.

★12222★
ROYAL BANK OF CANADA - LIBRARY
335 8th Ave., S.W.
P.O. Box 2534
Calgary, AB, Canada T2P 2N5
Defunct

★12223★
ROYAL BANK OF CANADA - TAXATION LIBRARY/ INTERNATIONAL
Royal Bank Plaza
Toronto, ON, Canada M5J 2J5
Defunct

★12224★
ROYAL BOTANICAL GARDENS - LIBRARY (Biol Sci)
Box 399 Phone: (416)527-1158
Hamilton, ON, Canada L8N 3H8 Ina Vrugtman, Libn./Cur.
Founded: 1947. **Staff:** Prof 1; Other 2. **Subjects:** Botany, ornamental horticulture, natural history and conservation, ornithology. **Special Collections:** Centre for Canadian Historical Horticulture Studies (CCHHS). **Holdings:** 8000 books; 1500 bound periodical volumes; 2500 pamphlets and reprints; 10,000 nursery and seed trade catalogs. **Subscriptions:** 400 journals and other serials. **Services:** Interlibrary loan; copying; library open to the public for reference use only. **Special Indexes:** Gray Herbarium card index.

★12225★
ROYAL CANADIAN ARTILLERY MUSEUM - LIBRARY (Mil)
Canadian Forces Base Phone: (204)765-2282
Shilo, MB, Canada R0K 2A0 Mr. W.M. Lunan, Cur.
Founded: 1956. **Staff:** Prof 1. **Subjects:** Military history; artillery - ordnance, carriages, ammunition, technical data, small arms. **Special Collections:** War diaries of the Canadian Artillery from World War II and the Korean Conflict (640 boxes). **Holdings:** 10,567 books; 10,567 bound periodical volumes; 404 maps; 71 boxes of documents; 65 videotapes; pamphlets. **Subscriptions:** 14 journals and other serials; 5 newspapers. **Services:** Copying; library open to the public by appointment for research. **Remarks:** Library is maintained by Royal Regiment of Canadian Artillery. **Also Known As:** RCA Museum.

★12226★
ROYAL CANADIAN MILITARY INSTITUTE - LIBRARY (Mil)
426 University Ave. Phone: (416)597-0286
Toronto, ON, Canada M5G 1S9 Ann Melvin, Libn.
Founded: 1890. **Staff:** Prof 1; Other 1. **Subjects:** Military science; military, naval, and air force history; army, navy, and air force technical topics; Canadiana. **Special Collections:** Denison Collection (500 volumes); Frost Collection (200 volumes); War of the Rebellion: compilation of official records of Union and Confederate Armies. **Holdings:** 25,000 books; 2000 bound periodical volumes; 1000 antique volumes; 2500 photographs (World Wars I and II). **Subscriptions:** 40 journals and other serials. **Services:** Interlibrary loan; library open to the public for reference use only.

★12227★
ROYAL CANADIAN MOUNTED POLICE - CENTENNIAL MUSEUM RESEARCH ROOM (Mil, Hist)
P.O. Box 6500 Phone: (306)780-5838
Regina, SK, Canada S4P 3J7 Malcolm J.H. Wake, Musm.Dir.
Founded: 1933. **Staff:** 4. **Subjects:** Royal Canadian Mounted Police, military, Saskatchewan and Canadian history. **Special Collections:** History of the Royal Canadian Mounted Police (500 volumes). **Holdings:** 800

books; 200 bound periodical volumes; historical photographs; 8 VF drawers of R.C.M.P. archives. **Subscriptions:** 10 journals and other serials. **Services:** Copying; room open to the public by appointment.

★12228★
ROYAL CANADIAN MOUNTED POLICE - RCMP LAW ENFORCEMENT REFERENCE CENTRE (LERC) (Law)
N Division
St. Laurent Blvd., N. & Sandridge Rd.
Box 8900 Phone: (613)993-3225
Ottawa, ON, Canada K1G 3J2 Helen T. Booth, Mgr.
Founded: 1936. **Staff:** Prof 3; Other 15. **Subjects:** Police science, criminal justice, management, criminology, sociology, physical fitness. **Holdings:** 40,000 books; 40,000 microforms; 950 motion pictures; 40 VF drawers. **Subscriptions:** 1926 journals and other serials; 7 newspapers. **Services:** Interlibrary loan; center open to the public with permission of RCMP Commissioner. **Automated Operations:** Computerized public access catalog, cataloging, acquisitions, and serials. **Computerized Information Services:** QL Systems, CAN/LAW, CAN/OLE, Info Globe, DOBIS; Library Automated System (LAS; internal database); Envoy 100 (electronic mail service). **Publications:** Bibliographies, irregular; Acquisitions List, monthly - available to libraries upon request. **Special Catalogs:** Subject listing of AV material. **Also Known As:** Gendarmerie Royale du Canada, Centre de Documentation Policiere (CDP). **Staff:** Atsuko Cooke, Hd., Tech.Serv.; Joan Beavis, Ref.Spec.; Shawn Aitken, Ref.Libn..

★12229★
ROYAL CANADIAN ORDNANCE CORPS MUSEUM - LIBRARY (Mil)
6560 Hochelaga St.
P.O. Box 4000, Succursale K Phone: (514)252-2241
Montreal, PQ, Canada H1N 3R9 Maurice Brown, Cur.
Founded: 1962. **Staff:** 1. **Subjects:** Military history and equipment, weapons, ammunition and explosives. **Holdings:** 2000 volumes. **Services:** Library open to the public by appointment. **Remarks:** Maintained by Canada - National Defence.

★12230★
ROYAL COLUMBIAN HOSPITAL - LIBRARY (Med)
330 E. Columbia St. Phone: (604)520-4255
New Westminster, BC, Canada V3L 3W7 Ms. S. Abzinger, Libn.
Founded: 1978. **Staff:** 2. **Subjects:** Medicine, allied health sciences. **Holdings:** 2100 books; 2200 bound periodical volumes. **Subscriptions:** 160 journals and other serials. **Services:** Interlibrary loan; library not open to the public. **Computerized Information Services:** MEDLARS.

★12231★
ROYAL MILITARY COLLEGE OF CANADA - MASSEY LIBRARY & SCIENCE/ENGINEERING LIBRARY (Mil)
Kingston, ON, Canada K7K 5L0 Phone: (613)541-6330
Keith Crouch, Chf.Libn.
Staff: Prof 5. **Subjects:** Engineering; military history, arts, and science. **Special Collections:** Military Studies (28,485 volumes). **Holdings:** 196,098 volumes; 43,953 documents; 16,674 technical reports; 10,169 microforms; 2353 artifacts, manuscripts, prints, photographs. **Subscriptions:** 993 journals; 12 newspapers. **Services:** Interlibrary loan; copying; library open to the public by permission. **Automated Operations:** Computerized public access catalog and cataloging. **Computerized Information Services:** DIALOG Information Services, CAN/OLE. **Networks/Consortia:** Member of Ontario Council of University Libraries (OCUL). **Remarks:** Maintained by Canada - National Defence. **Staff:** Mr. D. Kissoore, Hd., Sys. & Proc.; Mrs. N. Turkington, Hd., Sci./Engr.Div.; Mr. B. Cameron, Act.Hd., Massey Lib.Div..

★12232★
ROYAL ONTARIO MUSEUM - CANADIANA GALLERY LIBRARY (Art, Hist)
14 Queen's Park Crescent, W. Phone: (416)586-5524
Toronto, ON, Canada M5S 2C6 Janet Holmes, Curatorial Fellow
Staff: Prof 1; Other 1. **Subjects:** North American decorative arts, Canadian history, 16th and 17th century geographical works. **Holdings:** 7000 books. **Subscriptions:** 20 journals and other serials. **Services:** Interlibrary loan; copying; library open to the public by appointment for reference use only. **Automated Operations:** Computerized cataloging.

★12233★
ROYAL ONTARIO MUSEUM - FAR EASTERN LIBRARY (Area-Ethnic, Art)
100 Queen's Park Phone: (416)586-5718
Toronto, ON, Canada M5S 2C6 Jack Howard, Assoc.Libn.
Founded: 1933. **Staff:** Prof 2. **Subjects:** Art and archeology of the Far East including China, Japan, India, and Southeast Asia. **Special Collections:** Stone inscriptions and carvings from monuments in China; Chinese and Japanese rare books. **Holdings:** 20,000 books and bound periodical volumes; 8 VF drawers. **Subscriptions:** 300 journals and other serials. **Services:** Interlibrary loan; copying; library open to the public with restrictions. **Automated Operations:** Computerized cataloging. **Computerized Information Services:** UTLAS. **Staff:** Shyh-Charng Lo, Lib.Techn..

★12234★
ROYAL ONTARIO MUSEUM - MAIN LIBRARY (Art, Sci-Engr, Biol Sci)
100 Queen's Park Phone: (416)586-5595
Toronto, ON, Canada M5S 2C6 Julia Matthews, Hd.Libn.
Founded: 1961. **Staff:** Prof 4; Other 6. **Subjects:** Anthropology, archeology, astronomy, botany, geology, mineralogy, museology, paleontology, zoology, decorative arts, ethnology. **Holdings:** 100,000 books and bound periodical volumes. **Subscriptions:** 800 journals and other serials. **Services:** Interlibrary loan; copying; library open to the public for reference use only. **Automated Operations:** Computerized cataloging, acquisitions, and serials. **Computerized Information Services:** UTLAS, DIALOG Information Services, Telesystemes Questel; Envoy 100 (electronic mail service). **Publications:** Accessions list, monthly - internal distribution and by request; Current Contents, monthly; newsletter, irregular - both for internal distribution only. **Special Indexes:** Index to Rotunda (disk file and printout). **Staff:** Isabella Guthrie-McNaughton, Libn.; Mrs. Pat Trunks, ILL; Sharon Hick, Libn.; Anne Federer, Asst.Libn..

★12235★
ROYAL ROADS MILITARY COLLEGE - CORONEL MEMORIAL LIBRARY (Mil, Hist)
Victoria, BC, Canada V0S 1B0 Phone: (604)388-1483
Susan E. Day, Chf.Libn.
Founded: 1952. **Staff:** Prof 3; Other 3. **Subjects:** Academic topics, military science and history, Pacific Northwest history. **Holdings:** 75,000 books; 20,000 bound periodical volumes. **Subscriptions:** 550 journals and other serials; 25 newspapers. **Services:** Interlibrary loan; copying; library open to the public by permission only. **Automated Operations:** Computerized cataloging. **Computerized Information Services:** CAN/OLE, DIALOG Information Services, BRS Information Technologies; Envoy 100 (electronic mail service). **Special Catalogs:** Periodical list (printout). **Remarks:** Maintained by Canada - National Defence. **Staff:** J.C. Inkster, User Serv.; L.B. Jensen, Tech.Serv..

★12236★
ROYAL SOCIETY OF CANADA - LIBRARY (Sci-Engr, Hum, Biol Sci)
344 Wellington St. Phone: (613)992-3468
Ottawa, ON, Canada K1A 0N4 Michael R. Dence, Exec.Dir.
Founded: 1882. **Staff:** 4. **Subjects:** Humanities, social sciences, mathematics, chemistry, physics, earth sciences, animal and plant biology, microbiology and biochemistry, applied science, medical science. **Special Collections:** Proceedings and Transactions, annually, 1882 to present. **Holdings:** Proceedings of symposiums. **Services:** Copying (limited); library open to the public. **Publications:** List of publications - available on request. **Remarks:** Society's collections are stored in the Canada Institute for Scientific and Technical Information and the National Library of Canada. **Also Known As:** Societe Royale du Canada.

★12237★
ROYAL TRUST CORPORATION OF CANADA - CORPORATE INFORMATION CENTRE (Bus-Fin)
P.O. Box 7500, Sta. A Phone: (416)864-6170
Toronto, ON, Canada M5W 1P9 Alison Verwijk-O'Sullivan, Mgr.
Founded: 1978. **Staff:** Prof 3; Other 4. **Subjects:** Banking, trust industry, business, investment, finance, security analysis, Canadian and U.S. corporations and industries. **Holdings:** 1000 books; corporation annual reports. **Subscriptions:** 120 journals and other serials. **Services:** Interlibrary loan; center not open to the public. **Computerized Information Services:** Info Globe, DIALOG Information Services, Dow Jones News/Retrieval, Canada Systems Group (CSG), Infomart, LEXIS, NEXIS, The Financial Post Information Service.

★12238★
ROYAL TRUST CORPORATION OF CANADA - CORPORATE INFORMATION CENTRE - INFORMATION SYSTEMS (Comp Sci)
P.O. Box 7500, Sta. A
Toronto, ON, Canada M5W 1P9 Phone: (416)864-6171
Subjects: Computers, programming, automation support, telecommunications, computer networks, personal computers. **Holdings:** 1800 IBM program manuals. **Subscriptions:** 60 journals and other serials.

★12239★
ROYAL VICTORIA HOSPITAL - ALLAN MEMORIAL INSTITUTE OF PSYCHIATRY - LIBRARY (Med)
1025 Pine Ave., W. Phone: (514)842-1251
Montreal, PQ, Canada H3A 1A1 Robert MacKay-Melrose, Libn.
Founded: 1946. **Staff:** Prof 1. **Subjects:** Psychiatry, psychology, psychopharmacology, biochemistry, social work. **Holdings:** 2000 books; 1100 bound periodical volumes; 120 unbound journals; 850 pamphlets. **Subscriptions:** 27 journals and other serials. **Services:** Interlibrary loan; copying; library open to hospital staff and McGill University medical students.

★12240★
ROYAL VICTORIA HOSPITAL - MEDICAL LIBRARY (Med)
687 Pine Ave., W., Rm. H4.01 Phone: (514)842-1231
Montreal, PQ, Canada H3A 1A1 Sandra R. Duchow, Chf.Med.Libn.
Founded: 1935. **Staff:** Prof 2; Other 2. **Subjects:** Medicine, surgery, anesthesia, nursing. **Holdings:** 2000 books; 10,000 bound periodical volumes. **Subscriptions:** 225 journals and other serials. **Services:** Interlibrary loan; library not open to the public. **Computerized Information Services:** MEDLINE. **Networks/Consortia:** Member of McGill Medical and Health Libraries Association (MMHLA). **Staff:** Ada M. Ducas, Asst.Med.Libn..

★12241★
ROYAL VICTORIA HOSPITAL - WOMEN'S PAVILION LIBRARY (Med)
687 Pine Ave., W. Phone: (514)842-1231
Montreal, PQ, Canada H3A 1A1 Lynda Dickson, Libn.
Founded: 1957. **Staff:** Prof 1. **Subjects:** Gynecology, obstetrics, newborn physiology, neuroendocrinology. **Holdings:** 700 books; 600 bound periodical volumes; 4 drawers of reprints. **Subscriptions:** 30 journals and other serials. **Services:** Interlibrary loan; audiovisual lectures (cassette tapes, slides, and prints) on obstetrics and gynecology available to medical students and other interested personnel for use on the premises only; telephone reference service; library open to members of medical and paramedical professions. **Computerized Information Services:** MEDLINE. **Publications:** Placenta and Fetus Abstracts; Uterine Physiology Abstracts; Gynaecological Cancer Abstracts, all irregular - to research personnel.

★12242★
RPPW, INC. - LIBRARY (Plan)
555 White Plains Rd. Phone: (914)631-9003
Tarrytown, NY 10591 Lesley Vanderpot, Libn.
Staff: Prof 1. **Subjects:** Land and park planning, environmental studies, traffic and transportation, urban design, zoning and comprehensive planning, economic and market analyses. **Holdings:** 550 books; 175 bound periodical volumes; 12,990 documents; 10 VF drawers of pamphlets. **Subscriptions:** 100 journals and other serials. **Services:** Interlibrary loan; library open to the public with restrictions. **Publications:** Current contents, monthly; acquisitions lists, monthly - both for internal distribution only.

RUBEL MEMORIAL LIBRARY
See: Orthopaedic Hospital (10937)

RUBEN LIBRARY
See: Temple Adath Israel (13933)

BERNARD RUBINSTEIN LIBRARY
See: Congregation Agudas Achim (3613)

RUDNYC'KI ARCHIVES
See: Concordia University - Loyola Campus - Georges P. Vanier Library (3587)

IDA AND MATTHEW RUDOFKER LIBRARY
See: Har Zion Temple (6015)

RICHARD C. RUDOLPH ORIENTAL LIBRARY
See: University of California, Los Angeles (15986)

GEORGE C. RUHLE LIBRARY
See: U.S. Natl. Park Service - Glacier Natl. Park (15298)

RUPPEL MEMORIAL LIBRARY
See: Vandercook College of Music (17288)

RURAL ADVANCEMENT FUND
See: National Sharecroppers Fund/Rural Advancement Fund (9784)

CHARLES ANDREW RUSH LEARNING CENTER/LIBRARY
See: Birmingham-Southern College (1620)

★12243★
RUSH-PRESBYTERIAN-ST. LUKE'S MEDICAL CENTER - LIBRARY OF RUSH UNIVERSITY (Med)
600 S. Paulina St. Phone: (312)942-5950
Chicago, IL 60612 Trudy Gardner, Dir.
Founded: 1898. **Staff:** Prof 9; Other 14. **Subjects:** Biomedical sciences, hospital administration, health care delivery, nursing, allied health fields. **Special Collections:** Rare medical books (3500). **Holdings:** 53,523 books; 51,133 bound periodical volumes; 482 microforms; 4961 AV programs. **Subscriptions:** 2310 journals and other serials; 6 newspapers. **Services:** Interlibrary loan; copying; SDI; library open to the public. **Automated Operations:** Computerized cataloging, acquisitions, serials, and circulation. **Computerized Information Services:** MEDLINE, DIALOG Information Services, BRS Information Technologies, OCLC, LOGIN (Local Government Information Network) Data Base; internal databases. Performs searches on fee basis. Contact Person: Joanne Sparks, Hd., Ref.Libn., 942-5952. **Networks/Consortia:** Member of Rush Affiliates Information Network (RAIN), Greater Midwest Regional Medical Library Network, ILLINET. **Special Catalogs:** Serials list; AV catalog. **Staff:** Christine Frank, Assoc.Dir., Info.Serv; Lucyna Szymanski, Tech.Serv.Coord.; Paul DiMauro, Coll.Dev.Libn.; Marianne Doherty, Ref.Libn.; Gerald Perry, Ref.Libn.; Eleanor Hill, ILL Libn.; Maggie Marshall, Circ.Libn.; Virginia Kimsey, LRC Libn..

★12244★
RUSH UNIVERSITY - CENTER FOR HEALTH MANAGEMENT STUDIES - LIBRARY (Med)
202 Academic Facility
1753 W. Harrison St. Phone: (312)942-5402
Chicago, IL 60612 Dr. Michael Counte, Assoc.Dir.
Founded: 1982. **Subjects:** Health care organizations and management. **Holdings:** 1000 books and professional journals. **Services:** Library not open to the public.

RUSHMORE NATIONAL HEALTH SYSTEM
See: Rapid City Regional Hospital (11881)

★12245★
BERTRAND RUSSELL SOCIETY, INC. - LIBRARY (Hum)
29 Gillette St.
Box 434
Wilder, VT 05088 Thomas Stanley, Libn.
Founded: 1975. **Staff:** 1. **Subjects:** Bertrand Russell. **Holdings:** 100 books; 8 films; 6 video cassettes; 25 audio cassettes; archives of the Bertrand Russell Society. **Services:** Library open to the public with restrictions.

RUSSELL CAVE NATIONAL MONUMENT
See: U.S. Natl. Park Service (15346)

★12246★
CHARLES M. RUSSELL MUSEUM - FREDERIC G. RENNER MEMORIAL LIBRARY (Art)
400 13th St., N. Phone: (406)727-8787
Great Falls, MT 59401 Janet W. Postler, Reg./Libn.
Founded: 1952. **Staff:** Prof 1; Other 4. **Subjects:** Artist Charles M. Russell, Western art and artists. **Holdings:** 1200 books; 1000 bound periodical volumes; 300 manuscripts and letters. **Services:** Interlibrary loan; copying; library open to the public by appointment for reference use only. **Automated Operations:** Computerized cataloging and acquisitions.

★12247★
RUSSELL AND DUMOULIN - LIBRARY (Law)
MacMillan Bloedel Bldg., 17th Fl.
1075 W. Georgia St. Phone: (604)688-3411
Vancouver, BC, Canada V6E 3G2 Diana E. Inselberg, Libn.
Staff: Prof 1; Other 3. **Subjects:** Law, labor law. **Holdings:** 17,000 volumes. **Services:** Library not open to the public. **Automated Operations:** Computerized cataloging, acquisitions, and serials. **Computerized**

Information Services: QL Systems, WESTLAW, Info Globe, Infomart, CAN/LAW, The Financial Post Information Service, DIALOG Information Services; Labour Index (internal database); QL Mail (electronic mail service). **Networks/Consortia:** Member of Central Vancouver Library Group.

HELEN CROCKER RUSSELL LIBRARY OF HORTICULTURE
See: Strybing Arboretum Society - Helen Crocker Russell Library of Horticulture (13718)

INA DILLARD RUSSELL LIBRARY
See: Georgia College (5600)

RICHARD B. RUSSELL AGRICULTURAL RESEARCH CENTER LIBRARY
See: U.S.D.A. - Agricultural Research Service - South Atlantic Area (14975)

RICHARD B. RUSSELL MEMORIAL LIBRARY
See: University of Georgia (16175)

SUSAN V. RUSSELL TAPE LIBRARY
See: Wittenberg University - Thomas Library (17983)

RUSSELL VERMONTIANA COLLECTION
See: Canfield Memorial Library (2628)

RUSSIAN ORTHODOX DIOCESE OF ALASKA - ARCHIVES
See: St. Herman's Theological Seminary - St. Innocent Veniaminov Research Institute - Library (12409)

★12248★
RUST INTERNATIONAL CORPORATION - LIBRARY (Sci-Engr)
Meadow Brook Corporate Park
100 Corporate Pkwy.
Box 101 Phone: (205)930-1400
Birmingham, AL 35201 Calberta O. Atkinson, Libn.
Founded: 1957. **Staff:** Prof 1; Other 1. **Subjects:** Engineering - environmental, civil, chemical, electrical, mechanical; pulp and paper. **Holdings:** 6452 books; 330 bound periodical volumes; 5030 technical reports; 77 microfiche. **Subscriptions:** 180 journals and other serials. **Services:** Interlibrary loan; copying; library open to the public for reference use only. **Computerized Information Services:** DIALOG Information Services, WILSONLINE, Dow Jones News/Retrieval. **Remarks:** Corporation is a subsidiary of Wheelabrator Technologies, Inc.

★12249★
RUST-OLEUM CORPORATION - R & D LIBRARY (Sci-Engr)
2301 Oakton St.
Evanston, IL 60204 Phone: (312)864-8200
Founded: 1972. **Staff:** Prof 1; Other 1. **Subjects:** Coatings, resins, corrosion, environment. **Holdings:** 430 books; 100 bound periodical volumes; 100 patents; 100 suppliers' catalogs. **Subscriptions:** 122 journals and other serials. **Services:** Library not open to the public. **Publications:** Technical Newsletter, quarterly; Book List, Periodical List - annual.

★12250★
RUTAN AND TUCKER - LIBRARY (Law)
611 Anton, Suite 1400 Phone: (714)641-3460
Costa Mesa, CA 92626 Louise Whitaker, Libn.
Subjects: Law. **Holdings:** 33,000 volumes. **Services:** Library not open to the public.

RUTGERS CENTER OF ALCOHOL STUDIES
See: Rutgers University, the State University of New Jersey (12266)

★12251★
RUTGERS UNIVERSITY, THE STATE UNIVERSITY OF NEW JERSEY - ART LIBRARY (Art)
Voorhees Hall Phone: (201)932-7739
New Brunswick, NJ 08903 Halina Rusak, Hd.
Staff: Prof 2; Other 1. **Subjects:** Art, architecture. **Special Collections:** Louis E. Stern Collection of Modern Art; Bartlett Cowdrey Collection of American Art; Howard Hibbard Collection of Italian Renaissance and Baroque Art. **Holdings:** 45,000 books; 6077 bound periodical volumes; 10,000 items in microform; 24 VF drawers of exhibition catalogs, museum guides, reports, ephemeral materials. **Subscriptions:** 118 journals and other serials. **Services:** Copying; library open to the public. **Automated Operations:** Computerized cataloging and acquisitions. **Computerized Information Services:** DIALOG Information Services, BRS Information Technologies, WILSONLINE; internal database. Performs searches on fee basis. **Networks/Consortia:** Member of RLG. **Staff:** Beryl Smith, Asst.Libn..

★12252★
RUTGERS UNIVERSITY, THE STATE UNIVERSITY OF NEW JERSEY - BLANCHE AND IRVING LAURIE MUSIC LIBRARY (Mus)
Chapel Dr. Phone: (201)932-9783
New Brunswick, NJ 08903 Jan R. Cody, Mus.Libn.
Founded: 1982. **Staff:** Prof 3; Other 6. **Subjects:** Music. **Holdings:** 36,125 books; 2882 bound periodical volumes; 19,812 sound recordings. **Subscriptions:** 422 journals and other serials. **Services:** Interlibrary loan; library open to the public for reference use only. **Automated Operations:** Computerized cataloging, acquisitions, and circulation. **Computerized Information Services:** DIALOG Information Services, BRS Information Technologies, OCLC, RLIN; internal database. Performs searches on fee basis. Contact Person: Lil Maman, 932-9407. **Networks/Consortia:** Member of RLG. **Staff:** Roger Tarman, Chf.Bibliog.; Janet Aaronson, Mus.Cat.Libn.; Rich AmRhein, Media Supv.; John Bewley, Rec.Cat..

★12253★
RUTGERS UNIVERSITY, THE STATE UNIVERSITY OF NEW JERSEY - CENTER FOR COMPUTER AND INFORMATION SERVICES (Comp Sci)
Computer Reference Ctr.
Busch Campus
Box 879 Hill Center Phone: (201)932-2296
Piscataway, NJ 08854 Christopher P. Jarocha-Ernst, Coord.
Founded: 1964. **Staff:** Prof 2; Other 2. **Subjects:** Computers, data archives, U.S. Census, electronics. **Special Collections:** University newsletters (200 serials); IBM manuals (1000 volumes); Digital Equipment Corporation (DEC) manuals (200 volumes); U.S. Census tapes and documents; Inter-University Consortium for Political and Social Research (ICPSR) archives. **Holdings:** 1500 books; 500 vendor manuals. **Subscriptions:** 350 journals and other serials. **Services:** Center open to the public for reference use only. **Automated Operations:** Computerized cataloging, acquisitions, and serials. **Computerized Information Services:** Internal database. **Publications:** CCIS Newsletter, bimonthly; CCIS Education Series, monthly - by subscription. **Special Catalogs:** CCIS Technical Documents catalog; Data Archives catalog; ICPSR and Census Material catalog; CCIS AS/9000-2 Software Catalog (all online).

★12254★
RUTGERS UNIVERSITY, THE STATE UNIVERSITY OF NEW JERSEY - CENTER FOR PLASTICS RECYCLING RESEARCH (Sci-Engr)
Busch Campus, Bldg. 3529 Phone: (201)932-4402
Piscataway, NJ 08855 John C. Adams, Mgr., Info.Serv.
Staff: Prof 3; Other 2. **Subjects:** Plastics recycling. **Holdings:** Periodicals; monographs; pamphlets; government publications. **Subscriptions:** 200 journals and other serials. **Services:** Copying; center open to the public. **Publications:** Plastics Recycling Report, bimonthly - to qualified recipients.

★12255★
RUTGERS UNIVERSITY, THE STATE UNIVERSITY OF NEW JERSEY - CENTER FOR URBAN POLICY RESEARCH LIBRARY (Soc Sci, Plan)
Bldg. 4051, Kilmer Campus Phone: (201)932-3136
New Brunswick, NJ 08903 Edward E. Duensing, Jr., Dir.
Founded: 1962. **Staff:** Prof 2; Other 1. **Subjects:** Urban/regional planning, environmental planning, municipal finance, intergovernmental relations, housing. **Holdings:** 3584 books; 5320 other cataloged items; 119 VF drawers of research papers, manuscripts, government documents. **Subscriptions:** 179 journals and other serials. **Services:** Interlibrary loan; library open to the public. **Automated Operations:** Computerized cataloging and acquisitions. **Networks/Consortia:** Member of RLG.

★12256★
RUTGERS UNIVERSITY, THE STATE UNIVERSITY OF NEW JERSEY - CHEMISTRY LIBRARY (Sci-Engr)
Busch Campus
Wright-Riemann Laboratories Phone: (201)932-2625
Piscataway, NJ 08854 Dr. Howard M. Dess, Physical Sci.Rsrc.Libn.
Staff: Prof 1; Other 2. **Subjects:** Chemistry. **Holdings:** 9600 books; 14,285 bound periodical volumes. **Subscriptions:** 320 journals and other serials. **Services:** Interlibrary loan; copying; library open to the public. **Computerized Information Services:** DIALOG Information Services, BRS Information Technologies, CAS ONLINE, NLM. Performs searches on fee

basis. **Networks/Consortia:** Member of RLG. **Publications:** Additions to the Chemistry Library, monthly. **Staff:** Barbara Cavallo, Supv..

★12257★
RUTGERS UNIVERSITY, THE STATE UNIVERSITY OF NEW JERSEY - CRIMINAL JUSTICE/NCCD COLLECTION (Law)
John Cotton Dana Library
185 University Ave. Phone: (201)648-5522
Newark, NJ 07102 Phyllis A. Schultze, Libn.
Founded: 1921. **Staff:** Prof 1. **Subjects:** Crime and juvenile delinquency - prevention, control, and treatment; criminology and correction. **Holdings:** 9000 books; 650 bound periodical volumes; 10,000 documents on microfiche; 50,000 unpublished and published reports, studies, monographs, letters, clippings, pictures. **Subscriptions:** 200 journals and other serials. **Services:** Interlibrary loan (to organizations only); copying; telephone information service; collection open to the public. **Computerized Information Services:** Criminal Justice Abstracts (internal database).

★12258★
RUTGERS UNIVERSITY, THE STATE UNIVERSITY OF NEW JERSEY - EAST ASIAN LIBRARY (Area-Ethnic)
College Ave. Phone: (201)932-7161
New Brunswick, NJ 08903 Dr. Nelson Ling-Sun Chou, Libn.
Founded: 1970. **Staff:** Prof 1; Other 1. **Subjects:** China - language, literature, history, philosophy, religion, children's literature, arts and sciences; Japanese history, language, literature; Korean history. **Special Collections:** Complete microfilm collection of the rare books in the National Central Library, Taiwan (up to Series 7); Pamphlet Collection of Tiao-yu-t'ai Problems. **Holdings:** 100,000 volumes; 4000 reels of microfilm; 5000 pamphlets. **Subscriptions:** 360 journals and other serials; 12 newspapers. **Services:** Interlibrary loan; SDI (limited); library open to the public. **Automated Operations:** Computerized cataloging and acquisitions. **Networks/Consortia:** Member of RLG. **Publications:** Serial Holding List, irregular - available on request.

★12259★
RUTGERS UNIVERSITY, THE STATE UNIVERSITY OF NEW JERSEY - GOTTSCHO PACKAGING INFORMATION CENTER (Sci-Engr)
Busch Campus, Bldg. 3529 Phone: (201)932-3044
Piscataway, NJ 08855 John C. Adams, Mgr., Info.Serv.
Staff: Prof 3; Other 2. **Subjects:** Packaging. **Holdings:** Periodicals; monographs; pamphlets; government publications. **Subscriptions:** 200 journals and other serials. **Services:** Copying; center open to the public. **Publications:** Current Packaging Abstracts, semimonthly - by subscription.

★12260★
RUTGERS UNIVERSITY, THE STATE UNIVERSITY OF NEW JERSEY - INSTITUTE OF JAZZ STUDIES (Mus)
135 Bradley Hall
Warren St. and Martin Luther King Blvd. Phone: (201)648-5595
Newark, NJ 07102 Dan Morgenstern, Dir.
Founded: 1952. **Staff:** Prof 4; Other 1. **Subjects:** Jazz, blues, popular music. **Special Collections:** National Endowment for the Arts (NEA) Jazz Oral History Project Repository (120 taped interviews and transcriptions). **Holdings:** 6000 books; 650 bound periodical volumes; 75,000 records and transcriptions; 2000 audiotapes; cylinders; 30 VF drawers of clippings; manuscripts; piano rolls; jazz periodicals; sheet music; instruments; dissertations; works of art; photographs; memorabilia. **Subscriptions:** 152 journals and other serials. **Services:** Copying; institute open to the public by appointment. **Automated Operations:** Computerized cataloging. **Computerized Information Services:** RLIN; IJS Jazz Register (register of recorded jazz performances; internal database). Performs searches free of charge. Contact Person: Vincent Pelote, Libn.. **Networks/Consortia:** Member of RLG. **Publications:** Annual Review of Jazz Studies - by subscription; Studies in Jazz (monograph series): Benny Carter, 1982; Art Tatum, 1982; Erroll Garner, 1984; James P. Johnson, 1986. **Special Indexes:** Index to IJS Jazz Register (microfiche). **Staff:** Edward Berger, Cur..

★12261★
RUTGERS UNIVERSITY, THE STATE UNIVERSITY OF NEW JERSEY - INSTITUTE OF MANAGEMENT/LABOR RELATIONS LIBRARY (Soc Sci)
New Brunswick, NJ 08903 Phone: (201)932-9513
Marjorie Watson, Act.Libn.
Founded: 1947. **Staff:** Prof 1; Other 5. **Subjects:** Industrial relations, labor education, human resources, collective bargaining, labor-management cooperation. **Holdings:** 3400 books; 820 bound periodical volumes; 78 VF drawers of pamphlets; state and federal documents; 38 VF drawers of union and company reports. **Subscriptions:** 673 journals and other serials. **Services:** Interlibrary loan; copying; library open to the public. **Automated Operations:** Computerized public access catalog. **Computerized Information Services:** DIALOG Information Services. Performs searches on fee basis. **Networks/Consortia:** Member of RLG, New Jersey Library Network. **Publications:** Selected Acquisitions List, irregular. **Remarks:** An alternate telephone number is 932-9608.

★12262★
RUTGERS UNIVERSITY, THE STATE UNIVERSITY OF NEW JERSEY - JUSTICE HENRY ACKERSON LAW LIBRARY (Law)
Samuel I. Newhouse Ctr. for Law & Justice
15 Washington St. Phone: (201)648-5675
Newark, NJ 07102-3192 Charlie Harvey, Law Libn.
Founded: 1946. **Staff:** Prof 9; Other 14. **Subjects:** Law, criminology. **Special Collections:** Justice Bradley Law Library (1000 volumes). **Holdings:** 281,000 books and bound periodical volumes; 4372 linear feet of New Jersey and other state records and briefs; 4583 linear feet of U.S. Government documents; 118,000 volumes in microform. **Subscriptions:** 3180 journals and other serials; 6 newspapers. **Services:** Interlibrary loan; copying; library open to the public. **Automated Operations:** Computerized cataloging. **Computerized Information Services:** LEXIS, WESTLAW. **Networks/Consortia:** Member of RLG. **Publications:** Selected New Acquisitions, monthly - by exchange. **Special Catalogs:** Shelf lists of Federal and New Jersey documents. **Staff:** Ermina Hahn, Hd., Tech.Serv.; Barbara Sanders-Harris, Hd., User Serv.; Ernest Nardone, Ref.; Paul Axel-Lute, Coll.Dev.; Brenda Adams, Doc.Libn.; Virginia Lemmon, Ref.; Robert Schriek, Ref.; Betsy Reidinger, Cat.; Marjorie Crawford, ILL/Circ..

★12263★
RUTGERS UNIVERSITY, THE STATE UNIVERSITY OF NEW JERSEY - LIBRARY OF SCIENCE & MEDICINE (Med, Sci-Engr, Biol Sci)
Box 1029 Phone: (201)932-3850
Piscataway, NJ 08854 Shirley W. Bolles, Dir.
Founded: 1963. **Staff:** Prof 14; Other 29. **Subjects:** Medicine, agriculture, biology and biochemistry, engineering, geology, pharmacy, pharmacology, psychology. **Holdings:** 165,000 books; 155,000 bound periodical volumes; 430,000 government documents. **Subscriptions:** 3500 periodicals. **Services:** Interlibrary loan; copying; library open to the public. **Automated Operations:** Computerized circulation. **Computerized Information Services:** DIALOG Information Services, BRS Information Technologies, STN International, Pergamon ORBIT InfoLine, Inc. **Networks/Consortia:** Member of RLG.

★12264★
RUTGERS UNIVERSITY, THE STATE UNIVERSITY OF NEW JERSEY - MATHEMATICAL SCIENCES LIBRARY (Comp Sci, Sci-Engr)
Piscataway, NJ 08854 Phone: (201)932-3735
Sylvia Walsh, Libn.
Founded: 1971. **Staff:** Prof 1; Other 2. **Subjects:** Pure and applied mathematics, computer science, statistics, artificial intelligence, operations research. **Holdings:** 22,000 books; 14,500 bound periodical volumes; 283 reels of microfilm; 4500 technical reports. **Subscriptions:** 625 journals and other serials. **Services:** Copying; library open to the public. **Automated Operations:** Computerized circulation. **Computerized Information Services:** BRS Information Technologies, RLIN, Geac Library Information System. **Networks/Consortia:** Member of RLG. **Publications:** Daily Acquisitions List (hardcopy and online). **Special Indexes:** Index to technical reports.

★12265★
RUTGERS UNIVERSITY, THE STATE UNIVERSITY OF NEW JERSEY - PHYSICS LIBRARY (Sci-Engr)
Busch Campus
Serin Physics Laboratory Phone: (201)932-2500
Piscataway, NJ 08854 Dr. Howard M. Dess, Physical Sci.Rsrc.Libn.
Staff: Prof 1; Other 2. **Subjects:** Physics, astronomy. **Holdings:** 10,000 books; 8400 bound periodical volumes; 4000 preprints; 200 dissertations. **Subscriptions:** 260 journals and other serials. **Services:** Interlibrary loan; copying; library open to the public. **Computerized Information Services:** DIALOG Information Services, CAS ONLINE, NLM, BRS Information Technologies. Performs searches on fee basis. **Networks/Consortia:** Member of RLG. **Staff:** Barbara Cavallo, Supv..

★12266★
RUTGERS UNIVERSITY, THE STATE UNIVERSITY OF NEW JERSEY - RUTGERS CENTER OF ALCOHOL STUDIES - LIBRARY (Soc Sci)
Busch Campus
Smithers Hall Phone: (201)932-4442
Piscataway, NJ 08854 Penny B. Page, Libn.
Founded: 1940. **Staff:** Prof 2; Other 3. **Subjects:** Alcohol, drinking, alcoholism. **Special Collections:** McCarthy Memorial Collection (40,000 documents). **Holdings:** 7775 books; 134 boxes of archival materials; 20,000 abstracts on 6x7 edge notched cards (Classified Abstract Archive of the Alcohol Literature); 1600 doctoral dissertations on microfilm; 500 alcohol-related bibliographies; 500 questionnaires, interview schedules, survey forms. **Subscriptions:** 200 journals and other serials. **Services:** Interlibrary loan; copying; reference service for researchers and students; library open to the public. **Networks/Consortia:** Member of Substance Abuse Librarians and Information Specialists (SALIS). **Publications:** Bibliographies.

★12267★
RUTGERS UNIVERSITY, THE STATE UNIVERSITY OF NEW JERSEY - SCHOOL OF LAW LIBRARY (Law)
Fifth & Penn Sts. Phone: (609)757-6173
Camden, NJ 08102 Arno Liivak, Law Libn.
Founded: 1926. **Staff:** Prof 7; Other 13. **Subjects:** Law. **Special Collections:** George Ginsburg's Collection of Soviet Legal Materials, 1945 to present (20,000 volumes). **Holdings:** 273,782 volumes; 137,379 government documents; 3686 reels of microfilm; 360,160 microfiche. **Subscriptions:** 2100 journals and other serials. **Services:** Interlibrary loan; copying; library open to the public with restrictions. **Automated Operations:** Computerized cataloging, acquisitions, and serials. **Computerized Information Services:** LEXIS, WESTLAW, RLIN, INNOVACQ Automated Library System; RLG (electronic mail service). **Networks/Consortia:** Member of RLG, Center for Research Libraries (CRL) Consortia. **Staff:** Anne Dalesandro, Ref.Libn.; Jessie Matthews, Night Ref.Libn.; Gloria Chao, Tech.Serv.Libn.; Lucy Cox; Vicky Kristian; Pat LaPierre.

★12268★
RUTGERS UNIVERSITY, THE STATE UNIVERSITY OF NEW JERSEY - SPECIAL COLLECTIONS AND ARCHIVES (Hist, Hum)
Alexander Library
College Ave. & Huntington St. Phone: (201)932-7006
New Brunswick, NJ 08903 Ruth J. Simmons, Dir./Univ.Archv.
Founded: 1946. **Staff:** Prof 9; Other 4. **Subjects:** History of education, social policy and social welfare, exploration and travel, Puritanism, genealogy, Latin America, history of science and technology. **Special Collections:** New Jersey Collections; Rutgers University Archives (6500 cubic feet of archival material); Women's Archives (including the records of SIGNS and the Womens Caucus for Art); literary collection (including Philip Freneau, William Cobbett, and the J. Alexander Symington Collection of 19th and early 20th century British authors); political papers collection (including the papers of Robert Morris, William Paterson, Clifford Case, Harrison Williams, Millicent Fenwick); westerners in the Orient collections (including the William Elliot Griffis Collection); consumer movement collections; Roebling Family Collections; social policy collections (records of the American Council of Voluntary Agencies for Foreign Services, World Policy Institute, World Hunger Year); Edward J. Bloustein Dictionary Collection; early American newspapers. **Holdings:** 152,000 volumes; 1000 newspaper titles; 2000 manuscript collections; 200,000 pictures; 5500 almanacs; 4400 maps; 12,500 broadsides; 500 reels of microfilm; genealogical materials; ephemera; museum objects. **Subscriptions:** 842 journals and other serials. **Services:** Interlibrary loan; copying; collections open to the public. **Automated Operations:** Computerized cataloging. **Computerized Information Services:** IRIS (internal database); RLG (electronic mail service). **Networks/Consortia:** Member of RLG, Center for Research Libraries (CRL) Consortia. **Publications:** Acquisitions reports; User guides. **Special Catalogs:** Checklist of New Jersey Periodicals in Special Collections, Rutgers University Libraries, 1982 (book); Guide to the Manuscript Collections, 1964; Guide to Manuscript Diaries and Journals, 1980. **Staff:** Clark L. Beck, Jr., Mss.Libn.; Ronald Becker, Mss.Cur.; Anne Brugh, NJ Bibliog.; Bonita Grant, Ref.Serv.Libn.; Albert King, Mss.Libn./Archv.; Janice Kraus, Rare Books Cur.; Maxine Lurie, Asst.Univ.Archv.; Janet Riemer, Presrv..

★12269★
RUTGERS UNIVERSITY, THE STATE UNIVERSITY OF NEW JERSEY - WAKSMAN INSTITUTE OF MICROBIOLOGY LIBRARY (Biol Sci)
Box 759 Phone: (201)932-2906
Piscataway, NJ 08855 Helen Hoffman, Libn.
Founded: 1954. **Staff:** Prof 1; Other 1. **Subjects:** Microbiology. **Holdings:** 8010 volumes. **Subscriptions:** 80 journals and other serials. **Services:** Interlibrary loan; copying; library open to the public for reference use only. **Automated Operations:** Computerized cataloging and acquisitions. **Computerized Information Services:** DIALOG Information Services, BRS Information Technologies, NLM. **Networks/Consortia:** Member of RLG. **Staff:** Mary Jane Werner, Supv..

★12270★
RUTLAND REGIONAL MEDICAL CENTER - HEALTH SCIENCE LIBRARY (Med)
Allen St. Phone: (802)775-7111
Rutland, VT 05701 Cherie L. Goderwis, R.N., Dir.
Founded: 1970. **Staff:** Prof 1. **Subjects:** Medicine, nursing, allied health professions, management. **Holdings:** 3000 books; 35 bound periodical volumes; unbound reports, clippings; journal reprints. **Subscriptions:** 102 journals and other serials. **Services:** Interlibrary loan; copying; literature searches. **Networks/Consortia:** Member of Vermont/New Hampshire Health Science Libraries.

★12271★
RYAN-BIGGS ASSOCIATES, P.C. - LIBRARY (Plan)
291 River St. Phone: (518)272-6266
Troy, NY 12180 Susan Benjamin, Libn.
Founded: 1977. **Staff:** Prof 1; Other 1. **Subjects:** Building codes and specifications; construction - concrete, steel, masonry, wood; structural engineering. **Holdings:** 800 books; 130 bound periodical volumes; 160 technical reports. **Subscriptions:** 42 journals and other serials. **Services:** SDI; library open to local companies.

THE C. RYAN LIBRARY
See: San Diego Aero-Space Museum - N. Paul Whittier Historical Aviation Library (12758)

CALVIN T. RYAN LIBRARY
See: Kearney State College (7384)

RYAN LIBRARY
See: Point Loma Nazarene College (11414)

RYAN MEMORIAL LIBRARY
See: St. Charles Borromeo Seminary (12342)

RYERSON LIBRARY
See: Art Institute of Chicago - Ryerson and Burnham Libraries (961)

RYERSON NATURE LIBRARY
See: Lake County Forest Preserve District (7602)

★12272★
RYERSON POLYTECHNICAL INSTITUTE - LEARNING RESOURCES CENTRE (Sci-Engr, Bus-Fin, Soc Sci)
350 Victoria St. Phone: (416)979-5031
Toronto, ON, Canada M5B 2K3 John North, Dir.
Founded: 1948. **Staff:** Prof 12; Other 69. **Subjects:** Business, nursing, engineering, mathematics, technology, architecture, urban planning, interior design, physics, photography, nutrition, family studies. **Special Collections:** Rare books (830); Urban Planning Collection (4500 volumes). **Holdings:** 271,800 books; 22,700 bound periodical volumes; 30,515 AV programs; 5130 reels of microfilm; 44,840 microfiche; 13,966 maps. **Subscriptions:** 2481 journals and other serials; 35 newspapers. **Services:** Interlibrary loan (fee); copying; center open to the public. **Automated Operations:** Computerized public access catalog, cataloging, acquisitions, and circulation. **Computerized Information Services:** DIALOG Information Services, Info Globe, International Development Research Centre (IDRC), DOBIS Canadian Online Library System; Envoy 100 (electronic mail service). **Networks/Consortia:** Member of Bibliocentre. **Publications:** Periodicals holdings list, annual. **Special Catalogs:** Reserve list; urban planning keyword index; map index (all printout). **Staff:** Diane Granfield, Info.Ctr.Libn.; Lucia Martin, Supv., Circ.; Sue Giles, Coord., Lib.Serv.; Eva Friesen, Tech.Serv.Libn.; Joan Parsons, Hum.Libn.; Olive King, Bus.Mgt.Libn.; Elizabeth Bishop, Arts & Lit.Libn.; Robert Jackson, Soc.Serv.Libn.; Sandra Kendall, Sci. & Tech.Libn.; Zita Murphy, Soc. &

Political Sci.Libn.; Ophelia Kam, Econ. & Adm.Stud.Libn.; Daniel Phelan, Media Libn..

★12273★
RYERSON POLYTECHNICAL INSTITUTE - THIRD WORLD RESOURCE CENTRE (Sci-Engr, Soc Sci)
350 Victoria St., 7th Fl. Phone: (416)979-5000
Toronto, ON, Canada M5B 2K3 Olive King, Bus.Mgt.Libn.
Founded: 1977. **Subjects:** Economic development, technology transfer, development education, communications, microelectronics and development, women and development, developing regions and countries. **Holdings:** 1000 volumes; 16 VF drawers of uncataloged documents. **Subscriptions:** 110 journals and other serials. **Services:** Copying; library open to the public for reference use only. **Automated Operations:** Computerized cataloging and acquisitions. **Computerized Information Services:** DIALOG Information Services, MINISIS; ECONET (electronic mail service). **Publications:** List of Acquisitions, 3/year - by exchange and to other institutions.

S

★12274★
S-CUBED - TECHNICAL LIBRARY (Sci-Engr)
Box 1620 Phone: (619)453-0060
La Jolla, CA 92038-1620 LaDonna L. Rowe, Libn.
Staff: Prof 1; Other 1. **Subjects:** Physics, geophysics, seismology, energy technology, nuclear technology, chemistry. **Holdings:** 2500 books; 1000 bound periodical volumes. **Subscriptions:** 150 journals and other serials. **Services:** Library open to the public by appointment. **Computerized Information Services:** DIALOG Information Services. **Networks/Consortia:** Member of Learning Resources Cooperative. **Remarks:** S-Cubed is a division of Maxwell Laboratories, Inc.

ALINE B. SAARINEN LIBRARY
See: Parrish Art Museum - Library (11082)

★12275★
SAATCHI & SAATCHI COMPTON HAYHURST LTD. - MEDIA RESEARCH LIBRARY (Bus-Fin)
55 Eglinton Ave., E. Phone: (416)487-4371
Toronto, ON, Canada M4P 1G9 J. Marcotte, Media Supv.
Founded: 1959. **Staff:** Prof 1. **Subjects:** Advertising, media, marketing. **Holdings:** 230 books; 2600 magazines and periodicals; 16 drawers of clippings; 12 drawers of Statistics Canada material. **Subscriptions:** 20 journals and other serials. **Services:** Library not open to the public. **Publications:** Media Research Bulletin, monthly - to company personnel and agency clients.

★12276★
SAATCHI & SAATCHI DFS COMPTON ADVERTISING - RESEARCH LIBRARY (Bus-Fin)
405 Lexington Ave. Phone: (212)878-1819
New York, NY 10174 Shirley Damon, Hd.Libn.
Staff: Prof 2. **Subjects:** Advertising, marketing. **Holdings:** 6500 books. **Subscriptions:** 170 journals and other serials; 6 newspapers. **Services:** Interlibrary loan; library not open to the public. **Computerized Information Services:** DIALOG Information Services. **Publications:** Bulletin, irregular. **Formerly:** Compton Advertising Inc. **Staff:** Joyce Melito, Ref.Libn..

C.B. SACHER LIBRARY
See: St. Paul Hospital (12639)

ARTHUR M. SACKLER GALLERY LIBRARY
See: Smithsonian Institution - Freer Gallery of Art (13264)

★12277★
SACRAMENTO AREA COUNCIL OF GOVERNMENTS - LIBRARY (Plan)
Box 808 Phone: (916)441-5930
Sacramento, CA 95804 Rhonda R. Egan, Libn.
Founded: 1974. **Staff:** Prof 1; Other 1. **Subjects:** Planning, census. **Special Collections:** 1975 special census for SACOG region and Placer and Nevada counties. **Holdings:** 5000 cataloged items; 1 drawer of microfiche. **Subscriptions:** 24 journals and other serials. **Services:** Interlibrary loan; copying; library open to the public for reference use only. **Automated Operations:** Computerized public access catalog and cataloging. **Remarks:** Library located at 106 K St., Suite 200, Sacramento, CA 95814.

★12278★
SACRAMENTO BEE - REFERENCE LIBRARY (Publ)
Box 15779
Sacramento, CA 95852 Anna M. Michael, Libn.
Staff: 8. **Subjects:** Newspaper reference topics. **Special Collections:** Sacramento city history. **Holdings:** 500 books; 45 file cabinets of clippings, photographs, and pamphlets. **Services:** Library not open to the public. **Remarks:** Library located at 21st & Q Sts., Sacramento, CA 95814.

★12279★
SACRAMENTO CITY AND COUNTY ARCHIVES (Hist)
1930 J St. Phone: (916)449-2072
Sacramento, CA 95816 James E. Henley, Mgr.
Founded: 1953. **Staff:** Prof 5; Other 2. **Subjects:** Regional history, printing, theater, ethnic history, photography. **Special Collections:** McClatchy Collection (Gold Rush, printing, California theater; 500 linear feet); Natomas Collection (water, gold mining; 300 linear feet); California Almond Growers Association Collection (business records). **Holdings:** 5000 books; 1.5 million photographs; 3000 linear feet of government records; 150 VF drawers of regional maps; lithographs; 9 million feet of local NBC-TV affiliate news film, 1955-1973; 4000 linear feet of personal and business records; 19th century newspapers. **Subscriptions:** 15 journals and other serials. **Services:** Copying; archives open to the public by appointment. **Computerized Information Services:** Internal database. **Special Indexes:** Finding aids to the collection. **Formerly:** Sacramento Museum and History Division - Archives. **Staff:** Sherry A. Hatch, Registrar; Charlene Gilbert, Archv..

★12280★
SACRAMENTO COUNCIL FOR DELAYED PRESCHOOLERS - DAISY TOY LENDING LIBRARY (Educ)
890 Morse Ave. Phone: (916)485-7494
Sacramento, CA 95825 Joan Melamed, Libn.
Staff: Prof 2. **Subjects:** Infant stimulation - language, creative play, fine and gross motor skills, auditory and tactile skills. **Holdings:** 8000 toys. **Subscriptions:** 12 journals and other serials. **Services:** Library open to families, professionals, and paraprofessionals working with developmentally delayed children. **Publications:** Homemade Toy Book. **Staff:** Alicia Condon, Asst.Libn..

★12281★
SACRAMENTO COUNTY LAW LIBRARY (Law)
Sacramento County Courthouse
720 9th St. Phone: (916)440-6011
Sacramento, CA 95814 Shirley H. David, Dir.
Founded: 1903. **Staff:** Prof 2; Other 2. **Subjects:** Law, taxes, California and federal documents. **Holdings:** 33,866 volumes; 4493 bound periodical volumes; 3118 audiotapes; 612 volumes on microfiche. **Subscriptions:** 245 journals and other serials; 11 newspapers. **Services:** Interlibrary loan; copying; library open to the public. **Automated Operations:** Computerized cataloging, acquisitions, and serials. **Computerized Information Services:** LEXIS. Performs searches on fee basis. **Networks/Consortia:** Member of CLASS. **Remarks:** An alternate telephone number is 440-6013. **Staff:** Tana S. Smith, Asst.Libn..

★12282★
SACRAMENTO-EL DORADO MEDICAL SOCIETY - PAUL H. GUTTMAN LIBRARY (Med)
5380 Elvas Ave. Phone: (916)456-2687
Sacramento, CA 95819 Julia G. Barry, Libn.
Founded: 1949. **Staff:** Prof 2. **Subjects:** Clinical medicine. **Holdings:** 1500 books; 1200 bound periodical volumes. **Subscriptions:** 110 journals and other serials. **Services:** Interlibrary loan; copying; library open to the public for reference use only. **Computerized Information Services:** MEDLARS, DIALOG Information Services. Performs searches on fee basis. **Staff:** Mary Curtis, Asst.Libn..

★12283★
SACRAMENTO UNION - EDITORIAL LIBRARY (Publ)
301 Capitol Mall Phone: (916)442-7811
Sacramento, CA 95812 Tracey Miller, Act.Libn.
Staff: Prof 1; Other 1. **Subjects:** Newspaper reference topics. **Special Collections:** Sacramento Union, 1846 to present (bound volumes). **Holdings:** 300 books; 180,000 newspaper clipping files. **Subscriptions:** 5 newspapers. **Services:** Interlibrary loan; copying; library open to the public by appointment. **Special Indexes:** Index to Sacramento Union, 1977 to present.

★12284★
SACRED HEART GENERAL HOSPITAL AND MEDICAL CENTER - LIBRARY SERVICES (Med)
1255 Hilyard
Box 10905 Phone: (503)686-6837
Eugene, OR 97440 Deborah L. Graham, Dir., Lib.Serv.
Founded: 1971. **Staff:** Prof 4; Other 3. **Subjects:** Medicine, nursing, paramedicine, hospital administration, patient education. **Special Collections:** School of Nursing archives, 1942-1970 (2 boxes). **Holdings:** 3000 books; 7000 bound periodical volumes. **Subscriptions:** 450 journals and other serials. **Services:** Interlibrary loan (fee); copying; SDI; library open to the public with physician referral. **Automated Operations:** Computerized cataloging. **Computerized Information Services:** MEDLARS, DIALOG Information Services, Western Library Network (WLN); OnTyme Electronic Message Network Service (electronic mail service). Performs searches on fee basis. **Networks/Consortia:** Member of Marine-Valley Health Information Network (MarVHIN). **Staff:** Beverly Bowers, Ref.Libn.; Anne Fraser, Ref.Libn.; Kim Tyler, Ref.Libn..

★12285★
SACRED HEART HOSPITAL - HEALTH SCIENCE LIBRARY (Med)
900 Seton Dr. Phone: (301)759-5229
Cumberland, MD 21502 Sr. Martha, Libn.
Founded: 1967. **Staff:** Prof 1; Other 1. **Subjects:** Medicine, nursing, allied health sciences. **Holdings:** 1900 books; 50 bound periodical volumes. **Subscriptions:** 63 journals and other serials. **Services:** Interlibrary loan; copying; library open to the public with restrictions. **Computerized Information Services:** MEDLINE.

★12286★
SACRED HEART HOSPITAL - MEDICAL LIBRARY (Med)
5151 N. 9th Ave. Phone: (904)476-7851
Pensacola, FL 32504 Florence V. Ruby, Hosp.Libn.
Founded: 1959. **Staff:** 2. **Subjects:** Medicine, pediatrics, nursing, management. **Special Collections:** Pediatrics library. **Holdings:** 854 books; 3312 bound periodical volumes. **Subscriptions:** 136 journals and other serials. **Services:** Interlibrary loan; copying; library open to the public by appointment. **Computerized Information Services:** MEDLARS.

★12287★
SACRED HEART HOSPITAL - MEDICAL LIBRARY (Med)
501 Summit Phone: (605)665-9371
Yankton, SD 57078 Roxie Olson, Med.Libn.
Founded: 1975. **Staff:** Prof 1. **Subjects:** Life and health sciences, nursing, hospital administration. **Holdings:** 2700 volumes; 300 AV programs; 5 VF drawers. **Subscriptions:** 200 journals and other serials. **Services:** Interlibrary loan; copying; library open to the public with restrictions. **Computerized Information Services:** MEDLARS, NLM; EasyLink (electronic mail service). Performs searches on fee basis. **Networks/Consortia:** Member of Midcontinental Regional Medical Library Program.

★12288★
SACRED HEART HOSPITAL - MEDICAL LIBRARY (Med)
900 W. Clairemont Ave. Phone: (715)839-4330
Eau Claire, WI 54701 Bruno Warner, Libn.
Founded: 1964. **Staff:** Prof 1. **Subjects:** Medicine, nursing, dentistry, hospital administration, patient teaching. **Special Collections:** Neurology. **Holdings:** 5000 books; 1000 bound periodical volumes; 2000 unbound periodicals; 4 VF drawers of pamphlets. **Subscriptions:** 286 journals and other serials. **Services:** Interlibrary loan; copying; library open to the public. **Networks/Consortia:** Member of Greater Midwest Regional Medical Library Network.

★12289★
SACRED HEART HOSPITAL - WILLIAM A. HAUSMAN MEDICAL LIBRARY (Med)
4th & Chew Sts. Phone: (215)776-4747
Allentown, PA 18102 Diane M. Horvath, Libn.
Founded: 1928. **Staff:** Prof 1. **Subjects:** Nursing, medicine. **Holdings:** 1438 books; 5290 bound periodical volumes; 804 Audio-Digest tapes; clippings of Sacred Heart Hospital and School of Nursing history. **Subscriptions:** 77 journals and other serials. **Services:** Interlibrary loan; copying; library open to medical, nursing, and allied health personnel and students for reference use. **Computerized Information Services:** MEDLARS.

SACRED HEART JESUIT CENTER - JESUIT CENTER LIBRARY
See: California Province of the Society of Jesus - Jesuit Center Library (2161)

★12290★
SACRED HEART MEDICAL CENTER - HEALTH SCIENCES LIBRARY (Med)
W. 101 8th Ave.
TAF-C9 Phone: (509)455-3094
Spokane, WA 99220-4045 Elizabeth J. Guilfoil, Dir.
Staff: Prof 3; Other 1. **Subjects:** Medicine and surgery, nursing, dietetics, psychology, administration and personnel, clinical laboratory. **Holdings:** 5000 books; 3000 bound periodical volumes; 8 VF drawers of clippings, pamphlets, pictures; slides; cassettes; filmstrips. **Subscriptions:** 210 journals and other serials. **Services:** Interlibrary loan; copying; library open to the public for reference use only. **Staff:** Agnes Wright, Lib.Techn.; Sandy Keno, Lib.Techn..

★12291★
SACRED HEART MONASTERY - LEO DEHON LIBRARY (Rel-Phil)
7335 S. Lovers Lane Rd.
Box 429 Phone: (414)425-8300
Hales Corners, WI 53130-0429 Sr. Agnese Jasko, P.H.J.C., Libn.
Founded: 1932. **Staff:** Prof 2; Other 2. **Subjects:** Dogmatic theology, ascetical theology, canon law, church history, scripture, liturgy, moral theology, comparative religion, philosophy. **Special Collections:** Sacred Heart Collection (500 titles). **Holdings:** 65,637 books; 5499 bound periodical volumes; 1000 pamphlets; 316 reels of microfilm; 38 volumes on microfiche; 1120 cassette tapes; 10,784 phonograph records. **Subscriptions:** 366 journals and other serials. **Services:** Library open to the public. **Staff:** Rev. Charles Yost, S.C.J., Cons..

★12292★
SACRED HEART SEMINARY - WARD MEMORIAL LIBRARY (Rel-Phil)
2701 W. Chicago Blvd. Phone: (313)868-2700
Detroit, MI 48206 Arnold M. Rzepecki, Libn.
Founded: 1919. **Staff:** Prof 1; Other 1. **Subjects:** Catholic theology, scholastic philosophy, modern philosophy, church history. **Special Collections:** Cardinal Mooney Collection (church and social problems); Michigan Historical Collection (church history in Michigan). **Holdings:** 65,000 books; 15,000 bound periodical volumes; 500 reels of microfilm. **Subscriptions:** 250 journals and other serials; 25 newspapers. **Services:** Interlibrary loan; copying; library open to public at librarian's discretion.

★12293★
SACRED HEART UNIVERSITY - LIBRARY (Rel-Phil)
5229 Park Ave. Phone: (203)371-7700
Bridgeport, CT 06606 Dorothy Kijanka, Dir.
Founded: 1963. **Staff:** Prof 7; Other 9. **Subjects:** Religious studies, business administration. **Special Collections:** International Children's Literature Collection; Heywood Hale Broun Collection; Msgr. Ronald Knox Collection. **Holdings:** 146,000 books; 58,000 AV programs. **Subscriptions:** 731 journals and other serials. **Services:** Interlibrary loan; copying; library open to the public. **Automated Operations:** Computerized cataloging and ILL. **Computerized Information Services:** OCLC, DIALOG Information Services, BIBLIOMATION CAM. **Networks/Consortia:** Member of Southwestern Connecticut Library Council (SWLC), NELINET. **Publications:** Acquisitions List, monthly - for internal distribution only; newsletter, semiannual; handbook; study guides; bibliographies, irregular. **Staff:** Mary Rogers, Hd., Pub.Serv.; Josephine Smith, Tech.Serv.Libn.; Ronald Fontaine, Evening Ref.Libn..

★12294★
SADTLER RESEARCH LABORATORIES - LIBRARY (Sci-Engr)
3316 Spring Garden St. Phone: (215)382-7800
Philadelphia, PA 19104 Bernadette Steiner, Libn.
Founded: 1966. **Staff:** 1. **Subjects:** Spectroscopy - infrared, ultraviolet, nuclear magnetic resonance; gas chromatography; analytical chemistry. **Special Collections:** Spectra consisting of infrared, ultraviolet, nuclear magnetic resonance, attenuated total reflectance, and differential thermal analysis for 100,000 compounds. **Holdings:** 3500 books; 2500 bound periodical volumes. **Subscriptions:** 50 journals and other serials. **Services:** Interlibrary loan; copying; library open to the public for reference use only with appointment. **Remarks:** Sadtler Research Laboratories is a division of Bio-Rad Laboratories, Inc.

★12295★
SAFECO INSURANCE COMPANY - LIBRARY (Bus-Fin)
Safeco Plaza Phone: (206)545-5505
Seattle, WA 98185 Esther J. Delaney, Libn.
Founded: 1958. **Staff:** 2. **Subjects:** Insurance, finance, management, business. **Holdings:** 9500 books; 1 VF drawer of unbound materials; 360 AV programs; 15 phonograph records; 150 16mm films; 20 shelves of archives; 2 VF drawers of pamphlets, brochures; 150 video cassettes. **Subscriptions:** 210 journals and other serials; 15 newspapers. **Services:** Interlibrary loan; copying; library open to the public with restrictions. **Automated Operations:** Computerized serials and circulation.

★12296★
SAFEWAY STORES, INC. - LIBRARY (Food-Bev, Bus-Fin)
201 Fourth St. Phone: (415)891-3236
Oakland, CA 94660 Catherine Ghent, Lib.Mgr.
Founded: 1938. **Staff:** Prof 1; Other 1. **Subjects:** Food, retail food chains, business. **Holdings:** 23,500 books; clippings; corporate reports. **Subscriptions:** 160 journals and other serials. **Services:** Interlibrary loan; library not open to the public. **Automated Operations:** Computerized

serials. **Computerized Information Services:** DIALOG Information Services, DataTimes.

★12297★
SAG HARBOR WHALING AND HISTORICAL MUSEUM - LIBRARY (Hist)
Main St. Phone: (516)725-0770
Sag Harbor, NY 11963 George A. Finckenor, Sr., Cur.
Staff: Prof 1; Other 3. **Subjects:** Whaling, fishing, antiques, shipping, Indians. **Special Collections:** Log books of whaling ships; scrimshaw (on sperm whale teeth, walrus tusks, and narwhal tusks). **Holdings:** 300 books; memorabilia. **Services:** Library open to the public for reference use only on application.

★12298★
SAGADAHOC COUNTY LAW LIBRARY (Law)
County Court House
752 High St.
Box 246
Bath, ME 04530 Phone: (207)443-9734
Subjects: Law. **Holdings:** 5500 books.

ELLIOT L. AND ANNETTE Y. SAGALL LIBRARY
See: American Society of Law & Medicine (673)

★12299★
SAGAMORE HILLS CHILDREN'S PSYCHIATRIC HOSPITAL - STAFF MEDICAL LIBRARY (Med)
11910 Dunham Rd.
Northfield, OH 44067 Phone: (614)467-7955
Subjects: Child psychology, institutional care, nursing, activity and educational therapy, psychiatry. **Holdings:** 950 books; tapes. **Subscriptions:** 15 journals and other serials. **Services:** Library not open to the public.

GARDNER A. SAGE LIBRARY
See: New Brunswick Theological Seminary (9910)

★12300★
RUSSELL SAGE FOUNDATION - LIBRARY (Soc Sci)
112 E. 64th St. Phone: (212)750-6008
New York, NY 10021 Pauline M. Rothstein, Dir. of Info.Serv.
Staff: Prof 1; Other 1. **Subjects:** Social science. **Special Collections:** Foundation publications. **Holdings:** 1500 books. **Subscriptions:** 100 journals and other serials; 5 newspapers. **Services:** Interlibrary loan; copying; library open to the public by appointment. **Computerized Information Services:** DIALOG Information Services, OCLC. **Networks/Consortia:** Member of Consortium of Foundation Libraries, New York Metropolitan Reference and Research Library Agency (METRO). **Publications:** Reporting from the Russell Sage Foundation, irregular - free upon request. **Remarks:** Foundation archives are held at Rockefeller Archive Center, Pocantico Hills, North Tarrytown, NY 10591-1598.

★12301★
SAGINAW COUNTY LAW LIBRARY (Law)
Courthouse, Rm. 215
111 S. Michigan Ave. Phone: (517)790-5490
Saginaw, MI 48602 Jannis Corley, Law Libn.
Founded: 1945. **Staff:** Prof 4. **Subjects:** Law. **Holdings:** 20,000 volumes. **Services:** Copying; library open to the public with restrictions.

★12302★
SAGINAW HEALTH SCIENCES LIBRARY (Med)
1000 Houghton St., Suite 2000 Phone: (517)771-6846
Saginaw, MI 48602 Stephanie John, Dir.
Founded: 1978. **Staff:** Prof 3; Other 7. **Subjects:** Medicine, nursing, allied health sciences, dentistry, health care administration. **Holdings:** 10,500 books; 14,750 bound periodical volumes; 1448 AV programs; 6 VF drawers of pamphlets. **Subscriptions:** 494 journals and other serials. **Services:** Interlibrary loan; copying; SDI; library open to the public for reference use only. **Automated Operations:** Computerized cataloging. **Computerized Information Services:** OCLC, CompuServe, Inc., NewsNet, Inc., PaperChase, NLM, BRS Information Technologies, NurseSearch, MEDLINE, DIALOG Information Services. Performs searches on fee basis. Contact Person: Nancy Nicholson, Assoc.Dir., 771-6950. **Networks/Consortia:** Member of Michigan Library Consortium (MLC). **Remarks:** Library maintained by Saginaw Cooperative Hospitals, Inc. which serves 4 area hospitals. Library functions as Learning Resources Center for a 32 county federal AHEC. **Staff:** June Cronenberger, Extramural Libn., NMAHEC; Nancy Nicholson, Assoc.Dir..

★12303★
SAGINAW NEWS - LIBRARY (Publ)
203 S. Washington Ave. Phone: (517)776-9672
Saginaw, MI 48605 Leland R. Watrous, Hd.Libn.
Founded: 1946. **Staff:** Prof 1; Other 1. **Subjects:** Newspaper reference topics. **Holdings:** 1000 books; 5.5 million clippings; area newspapers, 1840 to present, on microfilm. **Subscriptions:** 12 journals and other serials; 12 newspapers. **Services:** Library open to the public with restrictions.

★12304★
SAGINAW OSTEOPATHIC HOSPITAL - LIBRARY
Box 420
East Detroit, MI 48021-0420
Defunct

SAGUENAY REGION HISTORICAL SOCIETY
See: Societe Historique du Saguenay (13305)

SAHEL DOCUMENTATION CENTER
See: Michigan State University - Africana Library (8902)

★12305★
SAIC INFORMATION SERVICES CENTER (Sci-Engr)
1710 Goodridge Dr.
Mail Stop T-14-4 Phone: (703)749-8701
McLean, VA 22102-3799 Madeleine Hahn, Libn.
Staff: Prof 3; Other 7. **Subjects:** Engineering. **Holdings:** Military and federal specifications and standards on microfiche. **Services:** Interlibrary loan; center not open to the public. **Automated Operations:** Computerized acquisitions. **Computerized Information Services:** DIALOG Information Services, DTIC. Performs searches on fee basis. Contact Person: Jane Amesse, Asst.Dir., 749-8704. **Publications:** SAIC Crier (newsletter), semiannual. **Networks/Consortia:** Member of Interlibrary Users Association (IUA). **Staff:** M. Kamaluddin, ILL Spec..

★12306★
ST. AGNES HOSPITAL - GAVIN MEMORIAL HEALTH SCIENCE LIBRARY (Med)
430 E. Division St. Phone: (414)929-1695
Fond du Lac, WI 54935-0385 Sr. Sharon McEnery, C.S.A., Dir.
Founded: 1918. **Staff:** Prof 1; Other 1. **Subjects:** Medical science, nursing education, health care science, administration. **Holdings:** 1780 books; 2605 bound periodical volumes. **Subscriptions:** 96 journals and other serials. **Services:** Interlibrary loan; library not open to the public. **Automated Operations:** Computerized serials. **Computerized Information Services:** BRS Information Technologies, MEDLINE. **Networks/Consortia:** Member of Fox River Valley Area Library Consortium, Greater Midwest Regional Medical Library Network.

★12307★
ST. AGNES HOSPITAL - L.P. GUNDRY HEALTH SCIENCES LIBRARY (Med)
900 S. Caton Ave. Phone: (301)368-7565
Baltimore, MD 21229 Joanne Sullivan, Dir.
Founded: 1959. **Staff:** Prof 1; Other 4. **Subjects:** Medicine, surgery, pediatrics, obstetrics, gynecology, pathology, nursing, psychiatry. **Holdings:** 2000 books; 5000 bound periodical volumes. **Subscriptions:** 250 journals and other serials. **Services:** Interlibrary loan; copying; library open to the public with restrictions. **Automated Operations:** Computerized cataloging. **Computerized Information Services:** BRS Information Technologies, MEDLARS.

★12308★
ST. AGNES MEDICAL CENTER - HEALTH SCIENCE LIBRARY (Med)
1900 S. Broad St. Phone: (215)339-4448
Philadelphia, PA 19145 Marian Schaner, Dir.
Founded: 1975. **Staff:** Prof 2; Other 1. **Subjects:** Medicine, nursing, and allied health sciences. **Holdings:** 4000 books; 2000 bound periodical volumes; 8 VF drawers. **Subscriptions:** 200 journals and other serials. **Services:** Interlibrary loan; library not open to the public. **Networks/Consortia:** Member of Delaware Valley Information Consortium (DEVIC). **Computerized Information Services:** BRS Information Technologies.

★12309★
ST. ALEXIS HOSPITAL - HEALTH SCIENCES LIBRARY (Med)
5163 Broadway Ave. Phone: (216)429-8245
Cleveland, OH 44127 Jean Stanley, Lib.Cons.
Staff: Prof 1; Other 1. **Subjects:** Medicine, allied health sciences, hospitals, nursing. **Holdings:** 2000 books; 1500 bound periodical volumes; 400 AV

programs; pamphlets; reprints. **Subscriptions:** 175 journals and other serials. **Services:** Interlibrary loan; library not open to the public. **Automated Operations:** Computerized cataloging. **Computerized Information Services:** MEDLINE, DIALOG Information Services.

★12310★
ST. ALPHONSUS REGIONAL MEDICAL CENTER - HEALTH SCIENCES LIBRARY (Med)
1055 N. Curtis Rd. Phone: (208)378-2271
Boise, ID 83706 Martha R. Stolz, Libn.
Founded: 1970. **Staff:** Prof 1; Other 1. **Subjects:** Medicine, nursing, and allied health sciences. **Holdings:** 1000 books; 2 VF drawers of pamphlets (uncataloged). **Subscriptions:** 224 journals and other serials. **Services:** Interlibrary loan; copying; library open to the medical community for reference use only. **Computerized Information Services:** MEDLINE; OnTyme Electronic Message Network Service (electronic mail service). **Networks/Consortia:** Member of Boise Valley Health Sciences Library Consortium, Idaho Health Information Association (IHIA).

★12311★
ST. AMANT CENTRE INC. - MEDICAL LIBRARY (Med)
440 River Rd.
Winnipeg, MB, Canada R2M 3Z9 Pauline Dufresne, Techn.
Staff: Prof 1. **Subjects:** Mental retardation, genetics. **Holdings:** 600 books. **Subscriptions:** 20 journals and other serials. **Services:** Copying; library open to the public with restrictions.

★12312★
ST. ANDREW'S COLLEGE - LIBRARY (Rel-Phil)
1121 College Dr. Phone: (306)966-8983
Saskatoon, SK, Canada S7N 0W3 Anne Craggs, Libn.
Founded: 1912. **Staff:** Prof 1; Other 2. **Subjects:** Religion and theology. **Holdings:** 26,000 books; 1005 bound periodical volumes; 400 microfiche; 200 cassettes; 25 reels of microfilm; dissertations. **Subscriptions:** 137 journals and other serials. **Services:** Interlibrary loan; copying; library open to the public. **Automated Operations:** Computerized cataloging. **Remarks:** College is an autonomous affiliate of the University of Saskatchewan.

★12313★
ST. ANDREWS HOSPITAL - MEDICAL LIBRARY (Med)
3 St. Andrews Ln. Phone: (207)633-2121
Boothbay Harbor, ME 04538 Margaret Pinkham, R.N., Educ.Dir.
Staff: 1. **Subjects:** Medicine, surgery, orthopedics, obstetrics/gynecology, pediatrics, urology, ophthalmology. **Holdings:** 100 books. **Services:** Interlibrary loan; library open for general hospital use.

★12314★
ST. ANDREWS PRESBYTERIAN COLLEGE - MUSIC LIBRARY (Mus)
Vardell Bldg.
Laurinburg, NC 28352 Phone: (919)276-3652
Founded: 1961. **Subjects:** Music. **Holdings:** 18,000 scores; 4 VF drawers of unbound scores; 2000 phonograph records. **Services:** Library open to students.

★12315★
ST. ANNE'S HOSPITAL - PRESIDENTS HEALTH SCIENCES LIBRARY (Med)
4950 W. Thomas St.
Chicago, IL 60651 Phone: (312)378-7100
Staff: Prof 1. **Subjects:** Medicine, nursing, and allied health sciences. **Holdings:** 1000 books. **Subscriptions:** 110 journals and other serials. **Services:** Interlibrary loan; library not open to the public. **Automated Operations:** Computerized acquisitions, serials, and accounting. **Computerized Information Services:** BRS Information Technologies. Performs searches on fee basis. **Networks/Consortia:** Member of Metropolitan Consortium of Chicago. **Publications:** Newsletter, bimonthly - for internal distribution only.

★12316★
ST. ANNE'S HOSPITAL - SULLIVAN MEDICAL LIBRARY† (Med)
795 Middle St. Phone: (508)674-5741
Fall River, MA 02721 Elaine M. Crites, Med.Libn.
Founded: 1956. **Staff:** Prof 1. **Subjects:** Oncology, medicine, surgery, allied health sciences. **Holdings:** 100 books; 4000 bound periodical volumes. **Subscriptions:** 80 journals and other serials. **Services:** Interlibrary loan; copying; library open to the public with restrictions. **Networks/Consortia:** Member of Southeastern Massachusetts Consortium of Health Science Libraries (SEMCO). **Publications:** Hospital Newsletter - local distribution.

★12317★
ST. ANSELM COLLEGE - GEISEL LIBRARY (Rel-Phil)
Manchester, NH 03102 Phone: (603)669-1030
James R. Kennedy, Libn.
Founded: 1929. **Staff:** Prof 6; Other 14. **Subjects:** Church history, theology, medieval history, sociology, nursing. **Special Collections:** New England Collection (3000 volumes). **Holdings:** 156,000 books; 17,000 bound periodical volumes; 16,000 reels of microfilm; 36,000 microfiche; 6500 phonograph records and tapes. **Subscriptions:** 1650 journals and other serials; 50 newspapers. **Services:** Interlibrary loan; copying; library open to the public for reference use only. **Automated Operations:** Computerized cataloging, acquisitions, circulation, and ILL. **Computerized Information Services:** DIALOG Information Services, BRS Information Technologies, OCLC. Performs searches on fee basis. **Networks/Consortia:** Member of NELINET, New Hampshire College & University Council Library Policy Committee (NHCUC). **Publications:** Accession list, monthly; subject bibliographies. **Staff:** Eunice Wang, Tech.Serv.; Jeanne Welch, ILL; Florence Cimon, Per.; Nancy S. Urtz, Asst.Libn., Circ.; Karen Metz, Ref..

★12318★
ST. ANSGAR HOSPITAL - HEALTH SCIENCE LIBRARY (Med)
715 N. 11th St. Phone: (218)299-2252
Moorhead, MN 56560-2088 Char Myhre, Libn.
Staff: Prof 1. **Subjects:** Medicine, nursing, hospital administration. **Holdings:** 1200 books; 2 VF drawers of documents and reports; 4 VF drawers of other cataloged items. **Subscriptions:** 150 journals and other serials. **Services:** Interlibrary loan; copying; SDI; library open to public at librarian's discretion. **Computerized Information Services:** Access to BRS Information Technologies, MEDLARS. **Networks/Consortia:** Member of Valley Medical Network (VMN), Northern Lights Library Network (NLLN), Greater Midwest Regional Medical Library Network, Tri-College University Library Consortium.

ST. ANTHONY FALLS HYDRAULIC LABORATORY
See: University of Minnesota - St. Anthony Falls Hydraulic Laboratory (16489)

★12319★
ST. ANTHONY HOSPITAL - O'DONOGHUE MEDICAL LIBRARY (Med)
1000 N. Lee St.
Box 205 Phone: (405)272-6284
Oklahoma City, OK 73102 Mary Huffman, Dir.
Founded: 1950. **Staff:** Prof 1; Other 3. **Subjects:** Cardiovascular medicine, neurosurgery and neurology, general medicine, nursing, community health, allied health sciences. **Holdings:** 4000 books; 3800 bound periodical volumes; 13 VF drawers of pamphlets, reports, clippings, illustrations, and reprints. **Subscriptions:** 185 journals and other serials. **Services:** Interlibrary loan; copying; library open to the public. **Computerized Information Services:** MEDLINE, TOXLINE. **Networks/Consortia:** Member of Greater Oklahoma City Area Health Sciences Library Consortium (GOAL).

★12320★
ST. ANTHONY HOSPITAL - PHILIP B. HARDYMON LIBRARY (Med)
1492 E. Broad St. Phone: (614)251-3248
Columbus, OH 43205 Pamela L. Caruzzi, Chf.Med.Libn.
Founded: 1956. **Staff:** Prof 1; Other 1. **Subjects:** Medicine, medical specialties. **Special Collections:** Reprint file of articles published by staff physicians (26). **Holdings:** 2800 books; 3500 bound periodical volumes; 92 pamphlets; 392 audio cassettes; holdings in various hospital departments. **Subscriptions:** 200 journals and other serials. **Services:** Interlibrary loan; copying; SDI; library open to the public by appointment. **Automated Operations:** Computerized cataloging and ILL. **Computerized Information Services:** DIALOG Information Services, NLM. **Networks/Consortia:** Member of Greater Midwest Regional Medical Library Network, Central Ohio Hospital Library Consortium. **Publications:** Bibliographies - to doctors, nursing personnel, and administration. **Special Indexes:** Index to reprint file of articles published by staff physicians.

★12321★
ST. ANTHONY HOSPITAL - SISTER M. FRANCIS MEDICAL LIBRARY (Med)
1313 St. Anthony Pl. Phone: (502)587-1161
Louisville, KY 40204 Alma Hall Fielden, Libn.
Subjects: Medicine. **Holdings:** 500 books; 100 bound periodical volumes. **Subscriptions:** 25 journals and other serials. **Services:** Interlibrary loan; library not open to the public.

★12322★
ST. ANTHONY HOSPITAL - SPRAFKA MEMORIAL HEALTH SCIENCE LIBRARY (Med)
2875 W. 19th St. Phone: (312)521-1710
Chicago, IL 60623 Karen Ambrose, Lib.Cons.
Founded: 1945. **Staff:** 2. **Subjects:** Medicine, nursing, administration. **Holdings:** 600 books; 100 bound periodical volumes; 1000 pamphlets. **Subscriptions:** 88 journals and other serials. **Services:** Interlibrary loan; library open to the public with restrictions. **Networks/Consortia:** Member of Greater Midwest Regional Medical Library Network, Chicago and South Consortium, Chicago Library System. **Publications:** Bibliographies.

★12323★
ST. ANTHONY HOSPITAL MEDICAL CENTER - SCHOOL OF NURSING - BISHOP LANE LIBRARY (Med)
5666 E. State St. Phone: (815)226-2000
Rockford, IL 61108 Mary Patricia Pryor, Libn.
Staff: Prof 1. **Subjects:** Nursing. **Holdings:** 4500 books; 742 bound periodical volumes. **Subscriptions:** 40 journals and other serials. **Services:** Interlibrary loan; library not open to the public. **Networks/Consortia:** Member of Upstate Consortium of Medical and Allied Libraries in Northern Illinois. **Special Indexes:** Cumulative index to nursing and allied health literature.

★12324★
ST. ANTHONY HOSPITAL SYSTEMS - MEMORIAL MEDICAL LIBRARY (Med)
4231 W. 16th Ave. Phone: (303)629-3790
Denver, CO 80204 Christine Yolanda Crespin, Supv.Libn.
Founded: 1948. **Staff:** Prof 1; Other 1. **Subjects:** Emergency medicine, trauma, critical care, allied health sciences. **Holdings:** 900 books; 3500 bound periodical volumes; 50 pamphlets. **Subscriptions:** 254 journals and other serials. **Services:** Interlibrary loan; library not open to the public. **Automated Operations:** Computerized cataloging and serials. **Computerized Information Services:** DIALOG Information Services. **Networks/Consortia:** Member of Denver Area Health Sciences Library Consortium. **Publications:** Current Awareness Service, monthly.

★12325★
ST. ANTHONY MEDICAL CENTER - LIBRARY (Med)
5666 E. State St. Phone: (815)226-2000
Rockford, IL 61108 Nancy Dale, Med.Libn.
Staff: Prof 1. **Subjects:** Clinical medicine. **Holdings:** 300 books; 1400 bound periodical volumes. **Subscriptions:** 100 journals and other serials. **Services:** Interlibrary loan; copying; SDI; library open to the public by prior arrangement. **Computerized Information Services:** MEDLARS, DIALOG Information Services. **Networks/Consortia:** Member of Greater Midwest Regional Medical Library Network, Northern Illinois Library System (NILS), Upstate Consortium of Medical and Allied Libraries in Northern Illinois.

★12326★
ST. ANTHONY-ON-HUDSON THEOLOGICAL LIBRARY (Rel-Phil)
St. Anthony-on-Hudson Phone: (518)463-2261
Rensselaer, NY 12144 Bro. James J. Doyle, Libn.
Founded: 1912. **Staff:** Prof 1. **Subjects:** Theology. **Special Collections:** Franciscana (4000 volumes); Newmaniana (300 volumes); patristic-monastic-medieval theology (10,000 items). **Holdings:** 110,000 books; 15,000 bound periodical volumes; 60 incunabula and post-incunabula; 3 medieval codices; 60 manuscripts; 400 pamphlets; 260 volumes on microfilm; 75 boxes of archival material; 1000 phonograph records. **Subscriptions:** 300 journals and other serials. **Services:** Copying; library open to scholars by appointment.

★12327★
ST. ANTHONY'S HOSPITAL - MEDICAL LIBRARY (Med)
Saint Anthony's Way Phone: (618)465-2571
Alton, IL 62002 Darla Ann Reif, Libn.Asst.
Staff: Prof 1. **Subjects:** Medicine, nursing. **Holdings:** 500 books. **Subscriptions:** 90 journals and other serials. **Services:** Interlibrary loan; library not open to the public. **Networks/Consortia:** Member of Areawide Hospital Library Consortium of Southwestern Illinois (AHLC).

★12328★
ST. ANTHONY'S HOSPITAL, INC. - MEDICAL LIBRARY (Med)
601 12th St., N.
Box 12588
St. Petersburg, FL 33705 Phone: (813)825-1100
Founded: 1958. **Subjects:** Medicine. **Holdings:** 1000 books; 2500 bound periodical volumes. **Subscriptions:** 77 journals and other serials. **Services:** Interlibrary loan; library not open to the public.

★12329★
ST. ANTHONY'S MEMORIAL HOSPITAL - HEALTH SCIENCE LIBRARY (Med)
503 N. Maple St. Phone: (217)342-2121
Effingham, IL 62401 Sr. M. Angelus Gardiner, Libn.
Staff: 2. **Subjects:** Health, illness. **Holdings:** 1268 books; 455 tapes; 15 video cassettes; archives; 12 VF drawers of other cataloged items. **Subscriptions:** 197 journals and other serials. **Services:** Interlibrary loan; copying; library open to the public with restrictions. **Networks/Consortia:** Member of ILLINET, Rolling Prairie Library System (RPLS).

★12330★
ST. AUGUSTINE HISTORICAL SOCIETY - LIBRARY (Hist)
271 Charlotte St. Phone: (904)824-2872
St. Augustine, FL 32084 Jacqueline K. Fretwell, Lib.Dir.
Founded: 1883. **Staff:** 7. **Subjects:** History of St. Augustine and environs and related subjects. **Special Collections:** Cathedral Parish records, St. Augustine, 1594-1763 and 1784-1882 (marriages, baptisms, burials); archives (manuscripts; city papers; St. Johns County court records). **Holdings:** 8000 books; photocopies; manuscripts; documents; microfilm; photographs; maps; pictures; card calendar of Spanish documents, 1512-1764; card index of St. Augustine people, 1821 to present. **Subscriptions:** 12 journals and other serials. **Services:** Interlibrary loan; copying; library open to the public for reference use only. **Publications:** El Escribano, annual - by subscription; East Florida Gazette, quarterly.

ST. AUGUSTINE RETREAT CENTER - LIBRARY
See: Divine Word Seminary of St. Augustine - Library (4317)

★12331★
ST. AUGUSTINE'S SEMINARY - LIBRARY (Rel-Phil)
2661 Kingston Rd. Phone: (416)261-7207
Scarborough, ON, Canada M1M 1M3 Sr. Jean Harris, Libn.
Founded: 1913. **Staff:** Prof 1; Other 2. **Subjects:** Theology, scripture, canon law, church history. **Holdings:** 39,000 books; 3750 bound periodical volumes. **Subscriptions:** 190 journals and other serials; 9 newspapers. **Services:** Interlibrary loan; copying; library open to Toronto School of Theology students, St. Augustine's alumni, and to religious education students with permission.

★12332★
ST. BARNABAS MEDICAL CENTER - MEDICAL LIBRARY (Med)
Old Short Hills Rd. Phone: (201)533-5050
Livingston, NJ 07039 A. Christine Connor, Lib.Dir.
Staff: Prof 1; Other 3. **Subjects:** Medicine, nursing. **Special Collections:** Plastic surgery (225 books). **Holdings:** 4500 books; 6800 bound periodical volumes. **Subscriptions:** 325 journals and other serials. **Services:** Interlibrary loan (fee); copying; library open to qualified researchers and members of the community with restrictions. **Computerized Information Services:** MEDLINE. **Networks/Consortia:** Member of Medical Library Center of New York (MLCNY), Cosmopolitan Biomedical Library Consortium (CBLC), Health Sciences Library Association of New Jersey.

★12333★
ST. BENEDICT'S ABBEY - BENET LIBRARY (Rel-Phil)
Benet Lake, WI 53102 Phone: (414)396-4311
Bro. Vincent Wedig, O.S.B., Libn.
Founded: 1945. **Staff:** Prof 2. **Subjects:** Theology, scripture, psychosocial sciences, history, literature. **Holdings:** 17,000 books; 1000 bound periodical volumes; 200 unbound periodicals. **Subscriptions:** 35 journals and other serials; 10 newspapers. **Services:** Interlibrary loan; copying; library open to the public for reference use only. **Staff:** Sr. Mary Benedict, O.S.B., Asst.Libn..

★12334★
ST. BENEDICT'S FAMILY MEDICAL CENTER - LIBRARY (Med)
709 N. Lincoln Phone: (208)324-4301
Jerome, ID 83338 Priscilla Malone, Libn.
Staff: Prof 1. **Subjects:** Medicine, nursing. **Holdings:** 250 books. **Subscriptions:** 25 journals and other serials. **Services:** Interlibrary loan; copying; library open to the public with restrictions. **Networks/Consortia:** Member of Southeast Idaho Health Information Consortium. **Publications:** Bene Bugle (newsletter), monthly - for internal distribution only.

★12335★
ST. BENEDICT'S HOSPITAL - HEALTH SCIENCES LIBRARY (Med)
5475 S. 500 East Phone: (801)479-2055
Ogden, UT 84405-6978 Sandy Eckersley, Info.Spec.
Founded: 1947. **Staff:** Prof 1. **Subjects:** Medicine, nursing, and allied health sciences. **Special Collections:** Dr. J.G. Olson Cardiovascular Collection (200 volumes). **Holdings:** 2000 books; 150 bound periodical volumes; 125 videotapes; 30 audio cassettes. **Subscriptions:** 202 journals and other serials. **Services:** Interlibrary loan; copying; library open to the public. **Computerized Information Services:** MEDLARS, MEDLINE. **Networks/Consortia:** Member of Midcontinental Regional Medical Library Program.

★12336★
ST. BERNARDINE MEDICAL CENTER - NORMAN F. FELDHEYM LIBRARY (Med)
2101 N. Waterman Ave. Phone: (714)883-8711
San Bernardino, CA 92399 Kathy Crumpacker, Lib.Asst.
Founded: 1981. **Staff:** 1. **Subjects:** Medicine, paramedical fields, nursing, surgery. **Holdings:** 800 books. **Subscriptions:** 125 journals and other serials. **Services:** Interlibrary loan; copying; library open to the public. **Computerized Information Services:** MEDLINE. **Networks/Consortia:** Member of Medical Library Group of Southern California and Arizona (MLGSCA), Inland Empire Medical Library Cooperative, San Bernardino, Inyo, Riverside Counties United Library Services (SIRCULS).

ST. BERNARD'S INSTITUTE - AMBROSE SWASEY LIBRARY
See: Ambrose Swasey Library (13830)

★12337★
ST. BERNARD'S PARISH - HAZARDVILLE CATHOLIC LIBRARY (Rel-Phil)
426 Hazard Ave. Phone: (203)749-9490
Enfield, CT 06082 Rose Hartman, Libn.
Founded: 1957. **Staff:** 20. **Subjects:** Encyclicals, theology, retreats, religion, Mariology, children's literature. **Holdings:** 8000 volumes; 2000 other cataloged items. **Services:** Library open to the public.

★12338★
ST. CATHARINES GENERAL HOSPITAL - HEALTH SCIENCES LIBRARY (Med)
142 Queenston St. Phone: (416)684-7271
St. Catharines, ON, Canada L2R 7C6 Susan P. Armbrust, Libn.
Founded: 1978. **Staff:** Prof 1; Other 2. **Subjects:** Medicine, nursing, laboratory and business administration. **Holdings:** 1000 books; 100 bound periodical volumes; audiotapes; vertical files. **Subscriptions:** 152 journals and other serials. **Services:** Interlibrary loan; copying; SDI; library open to the public. **Computerized Information Services:** MEDLINE, CAN/OLE. Performs searches on fee basis. **Networks/Consortia:** Member of Niagara Peninsula Hospital Libraries.

★12339★
ST. CATHARINES HISTORICAL MUSEUM - LIBRARY (Hist)
343 Merritt St. Phone: (416)227-2962
St. Catharines, ON, Canada L2T 1K7 Mr. Arden Phair, Dir.
Staff: 4. **Subjects:** History - St. Catharines, Niagara region, Welland Canal. **Special Collections:** St. Lawrence Seaway Authority Collection (121 maps); Norris Papers (mid-19th century shipping business; 60.95 centimeters); Ingersoll Papers (19th century business and household accounts; 25.4 centimeters); Niagara Grape and Wine Festival Archives; DeCew Falls Waterworks Collection; James Kidd Marine Photographs Collection. **Holdings:** 1600 books; 2000 maps and plans; 350 pamphlets and leaflets; 210 unbound periodicals; 187 reels of microfilm; 79 street directories; 5 drawers of documents; 3400 historical photographs. **Subscriptions:** 11 journals and other serials. **Services:** Copying; library open to the public. **Publications:** A Guide to the Grand River Canal (1982); Recollections of St. Catharines, 1837-1902 (1982); Glimpses Into Our Past, Volumes 1 and 2 (1984), Volume 3 (1986); A Canadian Enterprise - The Welland Canals (1984). **Special Catalogs:** Port of St. Catharines Shipping Register (card); Catalog of the Niagara Heritage Collection. **Special Indexes:** Index the ship names appearing in the St. Catharines Standard Newspaper column "Ships That Ply the Lakes" (booklet). **Remarks:** Library includes the St. Catharines and Lincoln Historical Society Collection.

★12340★
ST. CATHERINE HOSPITAL - REGIONAL EDUCATIONAL SERVICES - MC GUIRE MEMORIAL LIBRARY (Med)
4321 Fir St. Phone: (219)392-7230
East Chicago, IN 46312 Madeline E. Downen, Coord., Lib.Serv.
Founded: 1935. **Subjects:** Medicine and allied health sciences. **Holdings:** 7600 volumes. **Subscriptions:** 300 journals and other serials. **Services:** Interlibrary loan; copying; library open to public at librarian's discretion. **Computerized Information Services:** BRS Information Technologies, MEDLARS. **Networks/Consortia:** Member of Northwest Indiana Health Science Library Consortium. **Publications:** AV Software, annual update - free upon request.

★12341★
ST. CATHERINE'S HOSPITAL - MEDICAL LIBRARY (Med)
3556 Seventh Ave. Phone: (414)656-3230
Kenosha, WI 53140 Mary Sipsma, Med.Libn.
Founded: 1962. **Staff:** 1. **Subjects:** Medicine, family practice. **Holdings:** 1500 volumes; 300 video cassettes. **Subscriptions:** 150 journals and other serials. **Services:** Interlibrary loan; copying; library open to the public with restrictions. **Computerized Information Services:** MEDLINE. **Networks/Consortia:** Member of Southeastern Wisconsin Health Science Library Consortium (SWHSL), Greater Midwest Regional Medical Library Network.

★12342★
ST. CHARLES BORROMEO SEMINARY - RYAN MEMORIAL LIBRARY (Rel-Phil)
Overbrook Phone: (215)839-3760
Philadelphia, PA 19151 Lorena A. Boylan, Dir. of Libs.
Founded: 1832. **Staff:** Prof 5; Other 5. **Subjects:** Theology, philosophy, patristics, scripture, church history. **Special Collections:** Ryan Library Archives; historical collections of American Catholic Historical Society of Philadelphia; Pre-1850 Book Collection (incunabula, 16th and 17th century books in sacred sciences; 23,000 volumes). **Holdings:** 118,411 books; 20,971 bound periodical volumes; 6715 AV programs and microforms; 400,000 manuscripts; 600 museum pieces; 4000 prints and photographs; 195 paintings. **Subscriptions:** 588 journals and other serials; 19 newspapers. **Services:** Interlibrary loan; copying; library open to the public with registration. **Automated Operations:** Computerized cataloging, acquisitions, and ILL. **Computerized Information Services:** OCLC. **Networks/Consortia:** Member of PALINET, Tri-State College Library Cooperative (TCLC), Southeastern Pennsylvania Theological Library Association (SEPTLA). **Publications:** Acquisitions bibliography, monthly. **Special Catalogs:** Holdings of periodicals and newspapers (card); art collections (book). **Staff:** Eileen Kearney, Rd.Serv.Libn.; Francis X. Ounan, Per.; Rita A. DeStefano, Tech.Serv.Libn.; Joseph J. Casino, Archv.; Sr. Rose Lorena, S.S.J., Circ.Libn..

★12343★
ST. CHARLES COUNTY HISTORICAL SOCIETY - ARCHIVES (Hist)
101 S. Main St.
St. Charles, MO 63301 Carol Wilkins, Archv.
Staff: Prof 1; Other 6. **Subjects:** St. Charles County and Missouri history; genealogy. **Special Collections:** Mrs. Edna McElhiney Olson's Collection (genealogy and local history; 24 VF drawers); St. Charles Banner-News collection of newspapers, 1870-1978 (140 reels of microfilm). **Holdings:** Figures not available for books; 12 VF drawers of court records; 7 VF drawers of miscellanea; 4 VF drawers of photographs; 161 reels of microfilm; deeds; cemetery records; school records. **Services:** Copying; archives open to the public on fee basis. **Special Indexes:** Index of cemetery, church, and land records for St. Charles County; card indexes to Mrs. Olson's Collection, court records, and genealogy.

★12344★
ST. CHARLES SCHOLASTICATE - LIBRARY (Rel-Phil)
Box 99 Phone: (306)937-2355
Battleford, SK, Canada S0M 0E0 Ron Zimmer, Libn.
Founded: 1932. **Staff:** Prof 1; Other 2. **Subjects:** Theology, scripture, philosophy, social sciences, history. **Holdings:** 30,560 books; 2120 bound periodical volumes. **Subscriptions:** 40 journals and other serials. **Services:** Library open to the public. **Remarks:** Maintained by the Oblates of Mary Immaculate.

★12345★
ST. CHARLES SEMINARY - LIBRARY (Rel-Phil)
Carthagena, OH 45822 Phone: (419)925-4516
Bro. Jude Brown, Libn./Treas.
Founded: 1861. **Staff:** 1. **Subjects:** Scholastic philosophy, Catholic theology, hagiography. **Holdings:** 28,000 books; 6000 bound periodical volumes.

★12346★
ST. CHRISTOPHER'S EPISCOPAL CHURCH - LIBRARY (Rel-Phil)
93 N. Kainalu Dr.
Box 456
Kailua, HI 96734 Phone: (808)262-8176
Staff: 3. **Subjects:** Religion. **Holdings:** 700 books; tapes; filmstrips. **Subscriptions:** 20 journals and other serials. **Services:** Library open to the public.

★12347★
ST. CHRISTOPHER'S HOSPITAL FOR CHILDREN - MARGERY H. NELSON MEDICAL LIBRARY (Med)
2600 N. Lawrence St. Phone: (215)427-5374
Philadelphia, PA 19133 Frances B. Pinnel, Med.Libn.
Staff: Prof 1; Other 1. **Subjects:** Pediatrics. **Holdings:** 3790 books; 2284 bound periodical volumes. **Subscriptions:** 150 journals and other serials. **Services:** Interlibrary loan; library open to parents and guardians of patients. **Networks/Consortia:** Member of Delaware Valley Information Consortium (DEVIC), BHSL. **Publications:** Literature List, monthly; Periodical List, annual. **Remarks:** Fax: (215)427-5598.

★12348★
ST. CLAIRE MEDICAL CENTER - MEDICAL LIBRARY (Med)
222 Medical Circle
Morehead, KY 40351 Phone: (606)784-6661
Staff: Prof 1. **Subjects:** Medicine, nursing, pharmacy, allied health sciences. **Holdings:** 2115 books; 910 bound periodical volumes; pamphlets. **Subscriptions:** 95 journals and other serials; 10 newspapers. **Services:** Interlibrary loan; copying; library open to the public. **Networks/Consortia:** Member of Eastern Kentucky Health Science Information Network (EKHSIN), Kentucky Library Network, Inc. (KLN).

★12349★
ST. CLARE'S HOSPITAL & HEALTH CENTER - MEDICAL LIBRARY (Med)
415 W. 51st St. Phone: (212)586-1500
New York, NY 10019 Mitchell A. Bogen, Med.Libn.
Founded: 1934. **Staff:** Prof 1; Other 1. **Subjects:** Medicine, surgery. **Special Collections:** Surgical Reprints (8 VF drawers). **Holdings:** 1500 books; 8000 bound periodical volumes; tapes. **Subscriptions:** 45 journals and other serials. **Services:** Interlibrary loan; library not open to the public. **Networks/Consortia:** Member of Manhattan-Bronx Health Sciences Library Group, New York Metropolitan Reference and Research Library Agency (METRO).

★12350★
ST. CLARE'S MERCY HOSPITAL - EDUCATION RESOURCE CENTRE (Med)
St. Clare Ave. Phone: (709)778-3414
St. John's, NF, Canada A1C 5B8 Valerie Benson, Libn.
Founded: 1974. **Staff:** 1. **Subjects:** Medicine, nursing, hospital administration, allied health sciences. **Holdings:** 300 books; 100 AV tapes. **Subscriptions:** 70 journals and other serials. **Services:** Interlibrary loan; copying; center open to visiting doctors for reference use.

★12351★
ST. CLARE'S MERCY HOSPITAL - SCHOOL OF NURSING LIBRARY (Med)
Lemarchant Rd. Phone: (709)778-3577
St. John's, NF, Canada A1C 5B8
Dora M. Braffet, Instr.Mtls.Spec.Libn.
Founded: 1958. **Staff:** Prof 1; Other 4. **Subjects:** Nursing. **Holdings:** 3000 books; 26 bound periodical volumes; AV programs. **Subscriptions:** 31 journals and other serials. **Services:** Interlibrary loan; copying; library open to the public with restrictions. **Automated Operations:** Computerized cataloging and acquisitions. **Special Catalogs:** AV Catalog.

★12352★
ST. CLARES-RIVERSIDE MEDICAL CENTER - HEALTH SCIENCES LIBRARY (Med)
Pocono Rd. Phone: (201)625-6547
Denville, NJ 07834 Jan Hyde, Libn.
Staff: 1. **Subjects:** Medicine, surgery, dentistry, mental health, allied health sciences. **Holdings:** 300 books; 300 bound periodical volumes; unbound periodicals; microfiche. **Subscriptions:** 81 journals and other serials. **Services:** Interlibrary loan; library not open to the public. **Computerized Information Services:** Access to MEDLINE, TOXLINE. **Networks/Consortia:** Member of Cosmopolitan Biomedical Library Consortium (CBLC).

★12353★
ST. CLARES-RIVERSIDE MEDICAL CENTER - SELF-HELP CLEARINGHOUSE (Soc Sci)
Pocono Rd. Phone: (201)625-7101
Denville, NJ 07834 Edward J. Madara, Dir.
Founded: 1981. **Staff:** Prof 6; Other 5. **Subjects:** Self-help organizations. **Special Collections:** Collection of how-to materials for starting and maintaining self-help groups. **Holdings:** Self-help literature; directories of state and national self-help groups; conference proceedings. **Computerized Information Services:** MASHnet (internal database); CompuServe, Inc. (electronic mail service). **Publications:** The Self-Help Sourcebook; The Self-Help Group Directory, both annual. **Remarks:** A toll-free telephone number in New Jersey is (800)367-6274. **Staff:** Margaret Duthie, Educ. & Outreach Coord.; Andrew D. Bernstein, Prog.Coord.; Abigail Meese, Info. & Referral Coord..

★12354★
ST. CLOUD HOSPITAL - HEALTH SCIENCES LIBRARY (Med)
1406 Sixth Ave., N. Phone: (612)251-2700
St. Cloud, MN 56301 Judith Heeter, Libn.
Staff: Prof 1. **Subjects:** Medicine, nursing, hospital management. **Holdings:** 1000 books; 800 bound periodical volumes; 120 videotapes; 25 16mm films; 50 audio cassettes; 20 AV programs. **Subscriptions:** 100 journals and other serials. **Services:** Interlibrary loan; library not open to the public. **Computerized Information Services:** MEDLARS. Performs searches on fee basis.

ST. CLOUD STATE UNIVERSITY - CENTRAL MINNESOTA HISTORICAL CENTER
See: Central Minnesota Historical Center (2910)

ST. CROIX VALLEY ROOM
See: Stillwater Public Library (13683)

★12355★
ST. CYRIL AND METHODIUS BYZANTINE CATHOLIC SEMINARY - LIBRARY (Rel-Phil)
3605 Perrysville Ave. Phone: (412)321-8383
Pittsburgh, PA 15214 Msgr. Raymond Balta, Rector
Founded: 1950. **Staff:** Prof 1; Other 2. **Subjects:** Theology, philosophy, Byzantine studies, Ruthenian studies, Slavic studies, Byzantine art. **Special Collections:** Byzantine and Ruthenian theological studies; Slavonic rare books. **Holdings:** 16,603 books; 3155 bound periodical volumes; 2 VF drawers of pamphlets. **Subscriptions:** 60 journals and other serials. **Services:** Library open to the public with permission of rector of the seminary. **Special Catalogs:** Language file; rare book file. **Staff:** Jody John Baran, Hd.Libn..

★12356★
ST. DAVID'S UNITED CHURCH - LIBRARY (Rel-Phil)
3303 Capitol Hill Crescent, N.W.
Calgary, AB, Canada T2M 2R2 Phone: (403)284-2276
Founded: 1968. **Subjects:** Religion, theology, Bible. **Holdings:** 480 books; 210 filmstrips and slides; 30 transparencies; 5 tapes. **Services:** Copying; library open to the public with restrictions.

★12357★
ST. DOMINIC-JACKSON MEMORIAL HOSPITAL - LUTHER MANSHIP MEDICAL LIBRARY (Med)
969 Lakeland Drive Phone: (601)982-0121
Jackson, MS 39216 Nyla Stevens, Libn.
Founded: 1973. **Staff:** Prof 1. **Subjects:** Medicine, nursing, mental health. **Holdings:** 1911 books; 439 bound periodical volumes. **Subscriptions:** 127 journals and other serials. **Services:** Interlibrary loan; library not open to the public. **Computerized Information Services:** MEDLARS. **Networks/**

Consortia: Member of Central Mississippi Library Council, Central Mississippi Council of Medical Libraries.

★12358★
ST. ELIAS ORTHODOX CHURCH - LIBRARY (Rel-Phil)
Box 1446 Phone: (512)476-2314
Austin, TX 78767 Rev. James D. Kenna
Staff: 1. **Subjects:** Orthodox theology, church history, liturgics. **Holdings:** 600 books; 500 unbound periodicals. **Services:** Copying; library open to the public.

★12359★
ST. ELIZABETH COMMUNITY HEALTH CENTER - MEDICAL LIBRARY (Med)
555 South 70th St.
Lincoln, NE 68510 Phone: (402)489-7181
Staff: Prof 1; Other 1. **Subjects:** Medicine, nursing. **Holdings:** 2783 books; 1643 bound periodical volumes; 38 AV programs; 2524 unbound journals; 16 files. **Subscriptions:** 116 journals and other serials. **Services:** Interlibrary loan; copying; library open to the public. **Networks/Consortia:** Member of Lincoln Health Science Library Group, Midcontinental Regional Medical Library Program. **Special Catalogs:** Lincoln Health Science Library Group Union List of Serials.

★12360★
ST. ELIZABETH HOSPITAL - HEALTH SCIENCE LIBRARY (Med)
1506 S. Oneida St. Phone: (414)738-2324
Appleton, WI 54915 Mary M. Bayorgeon, Dir., Lib.Serv.
Founded: 1973. **Staff:** Prof 1; Other 1. **Subjects:** Medicine, nursing, hospital administration. **Holdings:** 2754 books; 3101 bound periodical volumes; 1113 audiotapes; 304 videotapes. **Subscriptions:** 280 journals and other serials. **Services:** Interlibrary loan; copying; library open to the public with restrictions. **Computerized Information Services:** DIALOG Information Services, MEDLINE. **Networks/Consortia:** Member of Greater Midwest Regional Medical Library Network, Fox Valley Library Council, Fox River Valley Area Library Consortium.

★12361★
ST. ELIZABETH HOSPITAL - HEALTH SCIENCES LIBRARY (Med)
225 Williamson St. Phone: (201)527-5371
Elizabeth, NJ 07207 Sally Holdorf, Libn.
Staff: Prof 1; Other 3. **Subjects:** Medicine, nursing, and allied health fields. **Holdings:** 1000 books; 1200 bound periodical volumes. **Subscriptions:** 117 journals and other serials. **Services:** Interlibrary loan; copying. **Computerized Information Services:** DIALOG Information Services, NLM. **Networks/Consortia:** Member of Cosmopolitan Biomedical Library Consortium (CBLC), Health Sciences Library Association of New Jersey. **Publications:** Health Sciences Library Newsletter, quarterly.

★12362★
ST. ELIZABETH HOSPITAL - HEALTH SCIENCES LIBRARY (Med)
2830 Calder Ave.
Box 5405 Phone: (409)892-7171
Beaumont, TX 77702 Sue Martin, Libn.
Founded: 1958. **Staff:** Prof 1; Other 2. **Subjects:** Medicine, dentistry, allied health sciences. **Holdings:** 900 books; 5400 bound periodical volumes; AV programs. **Subscriptions:** 120 journals and other serials. **Services:** Interlibrary loan; copying; SDI; library open to the public. **Computerized Information Services:** NLM, DIALOG Information Services, BRS Information Technologies.

★12363★
ST. ELIZABETH HOSPITAL - MEDICAL LIBRARY (Med)
600 Sager Ave. Phone: (217)442-6300
Danville, IL 61832 Evelyn J. Vail, Med.Libn.
Staff: Prof 1. **Subjects:** Medicine, nursing. **Holdings:** 537 books. **Subscriptions:** 85 journals. **Services:** Interlibrary loan; library not open to the public. **Networks/Consortia:** Member of Champaign-Urbana Consortium.

★12364★
ST. ELIZABETH HOSPITAL MEDICAL CENTER - BANNON HEALTH SCIENCE LIBRARY (Med)
1501 Hartford St.
Box 7501 Phone: (317)423-6143
Lafayette, IN 47903 Ruth Pestalozzi Pape, Dir., Prof.Lib.Serv.
Founded: 1919. **Staff:** 1. **Subjects:** Medicine, health care management, allied subjects. **Holdings:** 1000 books; 3500 bound periodical volumes; 1102 other books in departmental libraries; 500 audio cassette tapes; periodicals on microfiche; video cassette tapes. **Subscriptions:** 275 journals and other serials. **Services:** Interlibrary loan; copying; library open to medical staff, hospital personnel, and health care students. **Computerized Information Services:** BRS Information Technologies, MEDLINE. **Networks/Consortia:** Member of Greater Midwest Regional Medical Library Network.

★12365★
ST. ELIZABETH HOSPITAL MEDICAL CENTER - MEDICAL LIBRARY (Med)
1044 Belmont Ave. Phone: (216)746-7231
Youngstown, OH 44501 Barbara G. Rosenthal, Med.Libn.
Founded: 1929. **Staff:** 3. **Subjects:** Medicine and related subjects. **Holdings:** 2500 books; 7000 bound periodical volumes; 720 reels of microfilm. **Subscriptions:** 289 journals and other serials. **Services:** Interlibrary loan; copying; library open to public at librarian's discretion. **Computerized Information Services:** MEDLINE, DIALOG Information Services; Freedom Network (electronic mail service). **Publications:** Bibliographies.

★12366★
ST. ELIZABETH HOSPITAL MEDICAL CENTER - SCHOOL OF NURSING - LIBRARY (Med)
1044 Belmont Ave. Phone: (216)746-7211
Youngstown, OH 44501 Doris L. Crawford, Libn.
Founded: 1911. **Staff:** Prof 1; Other 2. **Subjects:** Nursing, health education, medicine, allied health fields. **Special Collections:** Historical Collection (nursing). **Holdings:** 7876 books; 1954 bound periodical volumes; 20 lateral file drawers of pamphlets; 10 drawers of microfiche; 762 AV programs. **Subscriptions:** 304 journals and other serials. **Services:** Interlibrary loan; copying; SDI; library open to the public for reference use only. **Automated Operations:** Computerized cataloging. **Computerized Information Services:** DIALOG Information Services, MEDLINE. **Networks/Consortia:** Member of NEOUCOM Council Associated Hospital Librarians. **Publications:** Library News, bimonthly - to faculty, students, and hospital departments; Library Information: Guide Series - to faculty, students, and library users; bibliographies - to library users. **Special Catalogs:** Audiovisual Catalog (card and book). **Special Indexes:** Subject Index to New Acquisitions (book); Serials List (book); TIC/TOC Service.

★12367★
ST. ELIZABETH MEDICAL CENTER - ALLNUTT HEALTH SCIENCES LIBRARY (Med)
One Medical Village Dr. Phone: (606)344-2248
Edgewood, KY 41017 Donald R. Smith, Libn.
Founded: 1978. **Staff:** Prof 1; Other 1. **Subjects:** Health sciences. **Holdings:** 2450 books; 4000 bound periodical volumes. **Subscriptions:** 200 journals and other serials; 5 newspapers. **Services:** Interlibrary loan; copying; library open to health professionals. **Computerized Information Services:** BRS Information Technologies. **Publications:** Interface, bimonthly.

★12368★
ST. ELIZABETH MEDICAL CENTER - HEALTH SCIENCES LIBRARY (Med)
601 Edwin Moses Blvd., W. Phone: (513)229-6061
Dayton, OH 45408 Ann L. Lewis, Med.Libn.
Staff: 4. **Subjects:** Medicine, sports medicine, rehabilitation, physical medicine, family practice, gastroenterology. **Special Collections:** Archives of St. Elizabeth Medical Center. **Holdings:** 7239 books; 6752 bound periodical volumes; AV programs. **Subscriptions:** 450 journals and other serials. **Services:** Interlibrary loan; copying; SDI; library open to the public for reference use only. **Computerized Information Services:** MEDLINE, OCLC, BRS Information Technologies.

★12369★
ST. ELIZABETH MEDICAL CENTER - HEALTH SCIENCES LIBRARY (Med)
110 S. 9th Ave. Phone: (509)575-5073
Yakima, WA 98902 Sr. Irene Charron, S.P., Med.Libn.
Founded: 1969. **Staff:** Prof 1; Other 1. **Subjects:** Medicine, nursing, health sciences, hospital administration. **Holdings:** 3080 books; 494 bound periodical volumes; 4 VF drawers of health sciences material; 124 Audio-

Digest tapes; archives (20 books; 222 bound periodical volumes). **Subscriptions:** 254 journals and other serials. **Services:** Interlibrary loan; copying; library open to the public. **Computerized Information Services:** MEDLARS. Performs searches on fee basis. **Networks/Consortia:** Member of Pacific Northwest Regional Health Sciences Library Service. **Publications:** Health Sciences Newsletter, quarterly. **Special Indexes:** Vertical File Index (notebook); Index to National Library of Medicine Bibliographies.

★12370★
ST. ELIZABETH MEDICAL CENTER - ST. ELIZABETH HOSPITAL SCHOOL OF NURSING - LIBRARY (Med)
1508 Tippecanoe St. Phone: (317)423-6125
Lafayette, IN 47904 Lorraine Rund, Libn.
Staff: Prof 1. **Subjects:** Nursing, medicine, psychiatry. **Holdings:** 4000 books; 302 filmstrips; 6 16mm films; 50 charts; 300 videotapes. **Subscriptions:** 160 journals and other serials; 10 newspapers. **Services:** Interlibrary loan; copying; library open to the public. **Publications:** Annual report; bibliographies of various fields in nursing.

★12371★
ST. ELIZABETH'S HOSPITAL - HEALTH SCIENCE LIBRARY (Med)
211 S. Third St. Phone: (618)234-2120
Belleville, IL 62221 Michael A. Campese, Lib.Dir.
Staff: Prof 1; Other 2. **Subjects:** Medicine, nursing, hospital administration. **Special Collections:** Medical books, 1879-1890. **Holdings:** 2000 books; 1200 bound periodical volumes. **Subscriptions:** 323 journals and other serials. **Services:** Interlibrary loan; copying; library open to the public on a limited schedule. **Computerized Information Services:** MEDLARS. **Networks/Consortia:** Member of Greater Midwest Regional Medical Library Network, Kaskaskia Library System, Areawide Hospital Library Consortium of Southwestern Illinois (AHLC).

★12372★
ST. ELIZABETHS HOSPITAL - HEALTH SCIENCES LIBRARY (Med)
Administration Bldg.
2700 Martin Luther King Jr. Ave., S.E. Phone: (202)373-7274
Washington, DC 20032 Toby G. Port, Adm.Libn.
Staff: Prof 2; Other 4. **Subjects:** Psychiatry, occupational therapy, general medicine, Protestant and Catholic chaplaincy, neurology, dance therapy, dentistry, therapeutic recreation, clinical psychology, social work, speech pathology and audiology, psychiatric nursing, psychoanalysis, psychodrama. **Special Collections:** William Alanson White Library. **Holdings:** 20,000 books; 18,000 bound periodical volumes. **Subscriptions:** 300 journals and other serials. **Services:** Interlibrary loan; copying; library open to the public for reference use only with librarian's permission. **Automated Operations:** Computerized cataloging. **Computerized Information Services:** MEDLINE. **Networks/Consortia:** Member of District of Columbia Health Sciences Information Network (DOCHSIN). **Publications:** Accessions lists, monthly - for internal distribution only. **Staff:** Marcella Fludd, ILL; Stephen O. Newton, Cat..

★12373★
ST. ELIZABETH'S HOSPITAL - LUKEN HEALTH SCIENCES LIBRARY (Med)
1431 N. Claremont Ave.
Chicago, IL 60622 Phone: (312)278-2000
Founded: 1955. **Staff:** Prof 1; Other 1. **Subjects:** Medicine, nursing and allied health sciences. **Holdings:** 1500 books; 722 bound periodical volumes; 309 volumes of unbound medical journals; 160 cassette tapes; 81 filmstrips. **Subscriptions:** 101 journals and other serials. **Services:** Interlibrary loan; library not open to the public. **Networks/Consortia:** Member of Metropolitan Consortium of Chicago.

★12374★
ST. ELIZABETH'S HOSPITAL - NURSING SCHOOL LIBRARY (Med)
2215 Genesee St. Phone: (315)798-5209
Utica, NY 13501 Ann M. Kelly, Libn.
Staff: Prof 1; Other 2. **Subjects:** Nursing, medicine, sociology, psychology. **Holdings:** 5592 books; 671 bound periodical volumes; 9 VF drawers; 220 phonograph records; 157 videotapes; 326 AV programs. **Subscriptions:** 100 journals and other serials. **Services:** Interlibrary loan; copying; library open to the public for reference use only with permission from librarian.

★12375★
ST. ELIZABETH'S HOSPITAL - SCHOOL OF NURSING - LIBRARY (Med)
159 Washington St. Phone: (617)789-2304
Brighton, MA 02135 Robert L. Loud, Libn.
Staff: 1. **Subjects:** Nursing, medicine. **Holdings:** 2235 books; 953 bound periodical volumes. **Subscriptions:** 80 journals and other serials. **Services:** Interlibrary loan; library not open to the public. **Networks/Consortia:** Member of Libraries and Information for Nursing Consortium (LINC).

★12376★
ST. ELIZABETH'S HOSPITAL - STOHLMAN LIBRARY (Med)
736 Cambridge St. Phone: (617)789-2177
Brighton, MA 02135 Robin E. Braun, Dir.
Staff: Prof 1; Other 1. **Subjects:** Medicine. **Holdings:** 1500 books; 5135 bound periodical volumes. **Subscriptions:** 172 journals and other serials. **Services:** Interlibrary loan; copying; library open to the public with restrictions. **Computerized Information Services:** MEDLARS, BRS Information Technologies; MEDLINK (electronic mail service). **Networks/Consortia:** Member of Boston Biomedical Library Consortium, Massachusetts Health Sciences Library Network (MAHSLIN).

★12377★
ST. FRANCES CABRINI HOSPITAL - MEDICAL LIBRARY (Med)
3330 Masonic Dr. Phone: (318)487-1122
Alexandria, LA 71301 Denise Dupont, Act.Libn.
Founded: 1957. **Staff:** Prof 1; Other 1. **Subjects:** Medicine, nursing, and allied health sciences. **Holdings:** 3471 books and bound periodical volumes; 276 tapes and phonograph records; 157 unbound journals. **Subscriptions:** 59 journals and other serials. **Services:** Interlibrary loan; copying; SDI; library open to the public with restrictions.

ST. FRANCIS CHAPEL INFORMATION CENTER & FREE-LENDING LIBRARY
See: St. Francis Monastery and Chapel (12400)

★12378★
ST. FRANCIS COLLEGE - JAMES A. KELLY INSTITUTE FOR LOCAL HISTORICAL STUDIES - LIBRARY (Hist)
180 Remsen St. Phone: (718)522-2300
Brooklyn, NY 11201 Arthur J. Konop, Dir.-Archv.
Founded: 1956. **Staff:** 2. **Subjects:** Local history of Brooklyn. **Holdings:** 10,000 books; 2 million folios of archival material. **Services:** Library open to the public for reference use only. **Special Catalogs:** Guide to Materials in the John Rooney Collection (book).

★12379★
ST. FRANCIS DE SALES ARCHDIOCESAN PASTORAL CENTER - ECUMENICAL LIBRARY
Box 32180
Oklahoma City, OK 73123
Founded: 1967. **Subjects:** Ecumenism, theology, church history, biblical studies. **Holdings:** 36,500 books and bound periodical volumes. **Remarks:** Presently inactive.

★12380★
ST. FRANCIS HOSPITAL - BIOETHICS INSTITUTE - LIBRARY (Med)
250 W. 63rd St. Phone: (305)868-5000
Miami Beach, FL 33141 Wilma S. Grover, Libn.
Founded: 1985. **Staff:** Prof 1. **Subjects:** Judeo-Christian medical ethics, withholding treatment, living wills, allocation of health care resources, ethics committees, nursing ethics. **Holdings:** Figures not available. **Subscriptions:** 25 journals and other serials. **Services:** Copying; library open to members. **Computerized Information Services:** BIOETHICSLINE, MEDLINE. Performs searches free of charge for members. **Networks/Consortia:** Member of Southeastern/Atlantic Regional Medical Library Services, Miami Health Sciences Library Consortium (MHSLC). **Publications:** Bibliographies.

★12381★
ST. FRANCIS HOSPITAL - HEALTH SCIENCE LEARNING CENTER (Med)
3237 S. 16th St. Phone: (414)647-5156
Milwaukee, WI 53215 Joy Shong, Dir.
Founded: 1974. **Staff:** Prof 2; Other 1. **Subjects:** Medicine, nursing, paramedicine. **Special Collections:** Materials relating to and serving patient education. **Holdings:** 2000 books; 3200 bound periodical volumes; 896 AV programs. **Subscriptions:** 245 journals and other serials. **Services:**

Interlibrary loan; copying; SDI; center open to the public. **Automated Operations:** Computerized serials. **Computerized Information Services:** MEDLINE, BRS Information Technologies. **Networks/Consortia:** Member of Southeastern Wisconsin Health Science Library Consortium (SWHSL), Library Council of Metropolitan Milwaukee, Inc. (LCOMM). **Staff:** Mary Jo Baertschy, Libn..

★12382★
ST. FRANCIS HOSPITAL - HEALTH SCIENCE LIBRARY (Med)
North Rd. Phone: (914)431-8132
Poughkeepsie, NY 12601 Linda Lee Paquin, Med.Libn.
Staff: Prof 1. **Subjects:** Internal medicine, surgery, dentistry, pediatrics, health care administration. **Holdings:** 1200 books; 120 unbound journals. **Subscriptions:** 120 journals and other serials. **Services:** Interlibrary loan; copying; library open to public at librarian's discretion. **Computerized Information Services:** BRS Information Technologies. Performs searches on fee basis. **Networks/Consortia:** Member of Southeastern New York Library Resources Council (SENYLRC), Health Information Libraries of Westchester (HILOW).

★12383★
ST. FRANCIS HOSPITAL - HEALTH SCIENCES LIBRARY (Med)
6161 S. Yale Ave. Phone: (918)494-1210
Tulsa, OK 74316 Darryl Logan, Med.Libn.
Staff: Prof 1; Other 2. **Subjects:** Health sciences, nursing, hospital management. **Holdings:** 2002 books; 4904 bound periodical volumes; 278 government documents. **Subscriptions:** 250 journals and other serials. **Services:** Interlibrary loan; library not open to the public.

★12384★
ST. FRANCIS HOSPITAL - MEDICAL LIBRARY (Med)
601 E. Micheltorena Phone: (805)962-7661
Santa Barbara, CA 93103 Marilyn Shearer, Dir.
Staff: 2. **Subjects:** Medicine and medical specialties. **Holdings:** 1020 books; 469 bound periodical volumes; videotapes; cassettes. **Subscriptions:** 38 journals and other serials. **Services:** Library not open to the public.

★12385★
ST. FRANCIS HOSPITAL - MEDICAL LIBRARY (Med)
E. Pikes Peak Ave. & Prospect Phone: (719)636-8256
Colorado Springs, CO 80903 Sr. Mary Louis Wenzl, Lib.Ck.
Staff: 1. **Subjects:** Medicine, surgery, pediatrics, obstetrics, psychiatry, orthopedics. **Holdings:** 144 books; 182 bound periodical volumes; 1 volume of tape cassettes. **Subscriptions:** 14 journals and other serials. **Services:** Interlibrary loan; copying; library open to the public with restrictions.

★12386★
ST. FRANCIS HOSPITAL - MEDICAL LIBRARY (Med)
250 W. 63rd St. Phone: (305)868-5000
Miami Beach, FL 33141 Wilma S. Grover, Libn.
Founded: 1927. **Staff:** Prof 1. **Subjects:** Medicine and allied health sciences. **Holdings:** 700 books; 2750 bound periodical volumes; 856 audiotapes; 12 phonograph records; 576 slides; videotapes. **Subscriptions:** 100 journals and other serials. **Services:** Interlibrary loan; library not open to the public; bioethics collection and services open to Bioethics Institute members. **Computerized Information Services:** BRS Information Technologies. **Networks/Consortia:** Member of Southeastern/Atlantic Regional Medical Library Services, Miami Health Sciences Library Consortium (MHSLC).

★12387★
ST. FRANCIS HOSPITAL - MEDICAL LIBRARY (Med)
2230 Liliha St. Phone: (808)547-6481
Honolulu, HI 96817 Julie J. Sirois, Libn.
Founded: 1955. **Staff:** Prof 1; Other 2. **Subjects:** Nursing, medicine, hospital administration, sociology, psychology, pre-clinical sciences. **Holdings:** 5000 books; 1600 bound periodical volumes; 500 slides and tapes; 6 VF drawers of pamphlets. **Subscriptions:** 387 journals and other serials. **Services:** Interlibrary loan; copying; SDI; library open to the public. **Computerized Information Services:** MEDLARS. Performs searches on fee basis. **Networks/Consortia:** Member of Pacific Southwest Regional Medical Library Service. **Publications:** Brochure, annual - to library users; Library Acquisition List, monthly - for internal distribution only.

★12388★
ST. FRANCIS HOSPITAL - MEDICAL LIBRARY (Med)
100 Port Washington Blvd. Phone: (516)627-6200
Roslyn, NY 11576 Judith Weinstein, Med.Libn.
Staff: Prof 1; Other 1. **Subjects:** Cardiology, pulmonary diseases, biomedical sciences, hospitals, management. **Special Collections:** Thoracic and cardiovascular surgery. **Holdings:** 2000 books; 1000 bound periodical volumes; 200 audio cassettes; pamphlets. **Subscriptions:** 70 journals and other serials. **Services:** Interlibrary loan; library not open to the public. **Computerized Information Services:** MEDLINE. **Networks/Consortia:** Member of Long Island Library Resources Council, Inc. (LILRC), BHSL.

★12389★
ST. FRANCIS HOSPITAL - SCHOOL OF NURSING LIBRARY (Med)
319 Ridge Ave. Phone: (312)492-6268
Evanston, IL 60202 Patricia Gibson, Libn.
Staff: Prof 1; Other 1. **Subjects:** Medicine, nursing, allied health sciences. **Holdings:** 3000 books; 420 bound periodical volumes; 6 VF drawers of clippings and pamphlets; 234 filmstrip programs; 160 film loops; 60 audio cassettes; 150 video cassettes; 6 16mm films. **Subscriptions:** 60 journals and other serials. **Services:** Interlibrary loan; copying; library open to medical and nursing personnel. **Networks/Consortia:** Member of Metropolitan Consortium of Chicago, North Suburban Library System (NSLS).

★12390★
ST. FRANCIS HOSPITAL, INC. - MEDICAL LIBRARY (Med)
7th & Clayton Sts. Phone: (302)421-4834
Wilmington, DE 19805 Sr. Joan Ignatius McCleary, O.S.F., Libn.
Founded: 1936. **Staff:** Prof 2; Other 1. **Subjects:** Medicine, nursing, surgery, psychiatry, continuing education for acute care. **Holdings:** 3227 books; 123 bound periodical volumes; 12 VF drawers of reprints, original articles, ephemera; 114 audiotapes. **Subscriptions:** 150 journals and other serials. **Services:** Interlibrary loan; copying; library open to the public with restrictions. **Networks/Consortia:** Member of Wilmington Area Biomedical Library Consortium (WABLC). **Publications:** Library News, bimonthly - to staff and consortium members. **Special Indexes:** Vertical file subject index (card). **Remarks:** An alternate telephone number is 421-4835. **Staff:** Helen E. Gravell, Asst.Libn..

★12391★
ST. FRANCIS HOSPITAL AND MEDICAL CENTER - SCHOOL OF NURSING LIBRARY (Med)
338 Asylum St. Phone: (203)247-4411
Hartford, CT 06103 Ruth Carroll, Dir. of Libs.
Founded: 1942. **Staff:** Prof 2; Other 1. **Subjects:** Nursing, psychiatry, psychology, pre-clinical medicine. **Holdings:** 6000 books; 400 bound periodical volumes; 15 VF drawers. **Subscriptions:** 150 journals and other serials. **Services:** Interlibrary loan; copying; library open to the public. **Computerized Information Services:** MEDLARS. **Staff:** Gloria Harrison, Libn..

★12392★
ST. FRANCIS HOSPITAL AND MEDICAL CENTER - WILSON C. JAINSEN LIBRARY (Med)
114 Woodland St. Phone: (203)548-4746
Hartford, CT 06105 Ruth Carroll, Dir. of Libs.
Staff: Prof 6; Other 7. **Subjects:** Medicine, nursing, management, psychiatry, psychology. **Holdings:** 13,000 books; 450 periodical titles on microfilm. **Subscriptions:** 850 journals and other serials. **Services:** Interlibrary loan; copying; SDI; library open to the public. **Computerized Information Services:** BRS Information Technologies, NLM, DIALOG Information Services. **Publications:** Library Notes. **Staff:** Carolyn Walcox, Asst.Dir.; Ted Friedmann, Clin. Libn.; Nancy Bianchi, Clin.Libn.; Mark Gentry, Clin.Libn.; Florence Hidalgo, Clin.Libn..

★12393★
ST. FRANCIS MEDICAL CENTER - CAPE COUNTY MEMORIAL MEDICAL LIBRARY, INC. (Med)
211 St. Francis Dr. Phone: (314)335-1251
Cape Girardeau, MO 63701 June Johnston, Med.Rec.Dir.
Founded: 1950. **Staff:** Prof 2; Other 2. **Subjects:** Medicine, nursing, hospital administration, mental health. **Holdings:** 1300 books; 135 bound periodical volumes; 2 shelves of tapes and cassettes. **Subscriptions:** 139 journals and other serials. **Services:** Interlibrary loan; copying; library open with permission of medical and hospital administrative staff. **Networks/ Consortia:** Member of Midcontinental Regional Medical Library Program. **Publications:** Cape County Journal, monthly - to members. **Staff:** Mrs. Kilja Israel, Libn..

★12394★
ST. FRANCIS MEDICAL CENTER - COMMUNITY HEALTH SCIENCE LIBRARY (Med)
415 Oak St.
Breckenridge, MN 56520 Karen Engstrom, Dir., Lib.Serv.
Founded: 1975. **Staff:** Prof 1; Other 1. **Subjects:** Medicine, nursing, and allied health sciences. **Holdings:** 416 books; 4 VF drawers of pamphlets; 23 AV programs. **Subscriptions:** 168 journals and other serials. **Services:** Interlibrary loan; SDI; library open to health care professionals. **Networks/Consortia:** Member of Valley Medical Network (VMN), Greater Midwest Regional Medical Library Network, Prairie Library Network. **Remarks:** Library contains holdings of the School of Nursing library.

★12395★
ST. FRANCIS MEDICAL CENTER - HEALTH SCIENCES LIBRARY (Med)
601 Hamilton Ave. Phone: (609)599-5068
Trenton, NJ 08629 Donna Barlow, Dir.
Founded: 1930. **Staff:** Prof 2; Other 1. **Subjects:** Medicine, nursing, allied health sciences. **Holdings:** 5000 books. **Subscriptions:** 300 journals and other serials. **Services:** Interlibrary loan; SDI; library open to the public. **Computerized Information Services:** BRS Information Technologies, NLM; MESSAGES (electronic mail service). Performs searches on fee basis. **Networks/Consortia:** Member of Central Jersey Health Science Libraries Association, Health Sciences Library Association of New Jersey. **Publications:** Library Bulletin, quarterly. **Staff:** Eileen Monroe, Tech.Info.Spec..

★12396★
ST. FRANCIS MEDICAL CENTER - HEALTH SCIENCES LIBRARY (Med)
615 S. 10th St. Phone: (608)785-0940
La Crosse, WI 54601 Sr. Louise Therese Lotze, Lib.Supv.
Staff: Prof 2. **Subjects:** Medicine, dentistry, nursing, allied health sciences. **Special Collections:** History of medicine. **Holdings:** 3200 books; 4500 bound periodical volumes; 12 VF drawers of clippings and articles. **Subscriptions:** 360 journals and other serials. **Services:** Interlibrary loan; library open to the public. **Networks/Consortia:** Member of Western Wisconsin Health Sciences Library Consortium. **Publications:** Library Bulletin, quarterly - for internal distribution only.

★12397★
ST. FRANCIS MEDICAL CENTER - MEDICAL LIBRARY (Med)
530 N.E. Glen Oak Ave. Phone: (309)672-2210
Peoria, IL 61637 Mary Anne Parr, Med.Libn.
Founded: 1942. **Staff:** Prof 1; Other 4. **Subjects:** Surgery, internal medicine, orthopedics, family practice, pediatrics. **Holdings:** 3500 books; 6600 bound periodical volumes; 300 slide sets; 550 video cassettes; 1000 audio cassettes. **Subscriptions:** 325 journals and other serials. **Services:** Interlibrary loan; copying; library open to the public. **Computerized Information Services:** MEDLINE. **Networks/Consortia:** Member of Heart of Illinois Library Consortium (HILC), Greater Midwest Regional Medical Library Network. **Publications:** Newsletter, monthly; acquisitions list, monthly.

★12398★
ST. FRANCIS MEDICAL CENTER - MOTHER MACARIA HEALTH SCIENCE LIBRARY (Med)
3630 E. Imperial Hwy. Phone: (213)603-6045
Lynwood, CA 90262 Eva Kratz, Dir. of Lib.Serv.
Founded: 1971. **Staff:** Prof 1; Other 2. **Subjects:** Medicine, nursing, hospital administration, paramedical sciences. **Holdings:** 3000 books; 4000 bound periodical volumes; 120 other cataloged items; 800 audiotapes; 90 boxes of peripheral material; 175 archival materials; 48 videotapes. **Subscriptions:** 300 journals and other serials. **Services:** Interlibrary loan; copying; SDI; library open to health professionals. **Computerized Information Services:** Online systems. **Publications:** Annual report; Monthly Acquisitions List.

★12399★
ST. FRANCIS MEMORIAL HOSPITAL - WALTER F. SCHALLER MEMORIAL LIBRARY (Med)
Box 7726 Phone: (415)775-4321
San Francisco, CA 94120 Maryann Zaremska, Dir., Lib.Serv.
Staff: Prof 1; Other 1. **Subjects:** Medicine, nursing. **Special Collections:** Plastic and reconstructive surgery; burns. **Holdings:** 6300 volumes; 650 audiotapes. **Subscriptions:** 145 journals and other serials and newspapers. **Services:** Interlibrary loan; SDI; library open to affiliated personnel only. **Computerized Information Services:** MEDLARS, BRS Information Technologies, DIALOG Information Services; OnTyme Electronic Message Network Service (electronic mail service). **Networks/Consortia:** Member of San Francisco Biomedical Library Group, Pacific Southwest Regional Medical Library Service.

★12400★
ST. FRANCIS MONASTERY AND CHAPEL - ST. FRANCIS CHAPEL INFORMATION CENTER & FREE-LENDING LIBRARY (Rel-Phil)
20 Page St. Phone: (401)331-6510
Providence, RI 02903 Fr. John Bosco Valente, O.F.M., Libn.
Staff: Prof 2; Other 25. **Subjects:** Religion. **Special Collections:** Franciscana. **Holdings:** 12,000 books; pamphlets; picture files. **Subscriptions:** 20 journals and other serials. **Services:** Interlibrary loan; copying; library open to the public.

★12401★
ST. FRANCIS REGIONAL MEDICAL CENTER - PROFESSIONAL LIBRARY (Med)
929 N. St. Francis Phone: (316)268-5979
Wichita, KS 67214 Betty B. Wood, Libn.
Founded: 1945. **Staff:** Prof 2; Other 3. **Subjects:** Medicine, nursing, surgery, orthopedics, management. **Holdings:** 6000 books; 10,000 bound periodical volumes. **Subscriptions:** 550 journals and other serials. **Services:** Interlibrary loan; copying. **Computerized Information Services:** MEDLINE. **Publications:** Journal Holdings, annual - to hospital staff and local special libraries.

★12402★
ST. FRANCIS-ST. GEORGE HOSPITAL - HEALTH SCIENCES LIBRARY (Med)
3131 Queen City Ave. Phone: (513)389-5118
Cincinnati, OH 45238 Carol Mayor, Libn.
Staff: Prof 1. **Subjects:** Medicine, nursing, hospital administration. **Holdings:** 830 books; 365 periodicals. **Subscriptions:** 143 journals and other serials. **Services:** Interlibrary loan; copying; library open to the public with special permission. **Computerized Information Services:** Online systems.

★12403★
ST. FRANCIS SEMINARY - SALZMANN LIBRARY (Rel-Phil)
3257 South Lake Dr. Phone: (414)747-6477
Milwaukee, WI 53207 Rev. Lawrence K. Miech, Lib.Dir.
Founded: 1908. **Staff:** Prof 3. **Subjects:** Scripture, theology, church history, social science, behavioral science, canon law. **Special Collections:** Wisconsin Catholic Church History; Catholic Americana. **Holdings:** 75,000 books; 14,000 bound periodical volumes; 1350 dissertations; 10 VF drawers of pamphlets, documents; 250 reels of microfilm; 2500 AV programs. **Subscriptions:** 325 journals and other serials; 20 newspapers. **Services:** Interlibrary loan; copying; library open to the public for reference use only. **Staff:** Sr. Colette Zirbes, Asst.Libn.; Rev. Thomas Fait, Archv..

★12404★
ST. FRANCIS OF THE WOODS - CIMARRON HEIGHTS LIBRARY (Rel-Phil)
Rt. 1 Phone: (405)466-3774
Coyle, OK 73027 Kay E. Adair, Lib.Mgr.
Founded: 1983. **Staff:** 2. **Subjects:** Eastern Orthodox theology, patristics, Biblical theology, liturgics, Byzantine music, philosophy, psychology, homiletics, Roman Catholic theology, Anglican theology. **Special Collections:** Monumentae Musicae Byzantinae (11th-17th century Byzantine music manuscripts on microfilm; 100); Carl G. Jung; sustainable agriculture; St. Francis of Asissi (books; journals). **Holdings:** 18,000 books; 5000 bound periodical volumes; 300 reels of microfilm; 3000 unbound periodicals; 1000 leaflets, pamphlets; 500 phonograph recordings. **Subscriptions:** 12 journals and other serials. **Services:** Library open to the public with restrictions. **Staff:** Diane Lamecker, Libn.; David Green, Asst.Libn..

★12405★
ST. FRANCIS XAVIER UNIVERSITY - ANGUS L. MAC DONALD LIBRARY - SPECIAL COLLECTIONS (Area-Ethnic)
Antigonish, NS, Canada B2G 1C0 Phone: (902)867-2267
Maureen Williams, Cur.
Staff: Prof 1. **Subjects:** Celtic studies. **Holdings:** Celtic Collection (includes writings in Gaelic); 6150 books; pamphlets; family trees; private correspondence; Scottish works. **Subscriptions:** 25 journals and other serials. **Services:** Copying; collections open to the public for reference use only. **Automated Operations:** Computerized cataloging. **Computerized Information Services:** DIALOG Information Services.

★12406★
ST. FRANCIS XAVIER UNIVERSITY - COADY INTERNATIONAL INSTITUTE - MARIE MICHAEL LIBRARY (Bus-Fin, Educ)
Antigonish, NS, Canada B2G 1C0 Phone: (902)867-3964
Sr. Berthold Mackey, Chf.Libn.
Founded: 1974. **Staff:** Prof 1. **Subjects:** Cooperatives, community development, adult education, health education, labor economics, technology. **Holdings:** 4000 volumes; seminar reports. **Subscriptions:** 80 journals and other serials; 11 newspapers. **Services:** Interlibrary loan; copying; library open to the public.

★12407★
ST. GABRIEL'S HOSPITAL - LIBRARY (Med)
815 S.E. 2nd St. Phone: (612)632-5441
Little Falls, MN 56345 Peggy Martin, Dir. of Educ.
Founded: 1942. **Staff:** Prof 1. **Subjects:** Nursing, medicine, science. **Holdings:** Figures not available. **Services:** Interlibrary loan; copying; library open to the public.

ST. GEORGE HOSPITAL
See: St. Francis-St. George Hospital (12402)

★12408★
ST. GEORGE'S EPISCOPAL MISSION - LIBRARY (Rel-Phil)
First & Arizona Sts.
Box V Phone: (602)524-2361
Holbrook, AZ 86025 Allen P. Rothlisberg, Libn.
Founded: 1975. **Staff:** Prof 1. **Subjects:** Theology. **Special Collections:** Clyde Smallwood Theology Collection. **Holdings:** 1000 books. **Services:** Interlibrary loan; copying; library open to the public. **Networks/Consortia:** Member of Channelled Arizona Information Network (CHAIN).

ST. HELENA PUBLIC LIBRARY - NAPA VALLEY WINE LIBRARY ASSOCIATION
See: Napa Valley Wine Library Association (9495)

★12409★
ST. HERMAN'S THEOLOGICAL SEMINARY - ST. INNOCENT VENIAMINOV RESEARCH INSTITUTE - LIBRARY (Rel-Phil, Area-Ethnic)
414 Mission Rd.
Box 728 Phone: (907)486-3524
Kodiak, AK 99615 Oleg Kobtzeff, Dir.
Staff: Prof 3. **Subjects:** Alaskan history, theology, Native American culture, Russian and Siberian studies. **Special Collections:** Archives of the Russian Orthodox Diocese of Alaska, 1823-1940 (10 cubic meters); Ilvani File (tapes of interviews with Kodiak senior citizens). **Holdings:** 6000 books; 35 bound periodical volumes; 100 cassette tapes; 10,000 ethnographic photographs. **Subscriptions:** 40 journals and other serials; 13 newspapers. **Services:** Interlibrary loan; copying; institute open to the public. **Automated Operations:** Computerized cataloging. **Publications:** Occasional papers.

ST. INNOCENT VENIAMINOV RESEARCH INSTITUTE
See: St. Herman's Theological Seminary - St. Innocent Veniaminov Research Institute - Library (12409)

★12410★
ST. JAMES COMMUNITY HOSPITAL - HEALTH SCIENCES LIBRARY (Med)
400 S. Clark Phone: (406)782-8361
Butte, MT 59702 Deni Donich Corrigan, Med.Libn.
Staff: Prof 1; Other 1. **Subjects:** Oncology, nursing, medicine, ethics, pediatrics, obstetrics, gynecology. **Holdings:** 450 books; 600 bound periodical volumes; 400 video cassettes. **Subscriptions:** 432 journals and other serials. **Services:** Interlibrary loan; copying; library open to the public. **Computerized Information Services:** MEDLINE; OnTyme Electronic Message Network Service (electronic mail service). **Publications:** Monthly Report - for internal distribution only. **Special Catalogs:** Audiovisual Catalog. **Special Indexes:** Health Sciences Serial List.

★12411★
ST. JAMES HOSPITAL - MEDICAL LIBRARY (Med)
610 E. Water St. Phone: (815)842-2828
Pontiac, IL 61764 Karen Harty
Staff: 1. **Subjects:** Medicine and allied health sciences. **Holdings:** 103 volumes; 13 video cassettes. **Subscriptions:** 17 journals and other serials. **Services:** Interlibrary loan; copying; library open to the public for reference use only. **Networks/Consortia:** Member of Greater Midwest Regional Medical Library Network, Heart of Illinois Library Consortium (HILC). **Remarks:** Fax: (815)842-3485.

★12412★
ST. JAMES HOSPITAL MEDICAL CENTER - HUGO LONG LIBRARY (Med)
1423 Chicago Rd. Phone: (312)756-1000
Chicago Heights, IL 60411 Margaret A. Lindstrand, Libn.
Founded: 1956. **Staff:** 1. **Subjects:** Medicine and related subjects. **Holdings:** 800 books; 800 bound periodical volumes. **Subscriptions:** 75 journals and other serials. **Services:** Interlibrary loan; library open to the public with restrictions. **Networks/Consortia:** Member of Chicago and South Consortium.

★12413★
ST. JAMES MERCY HOSPITAL - MEDICAL & SCHOOL OF NURSING LIBRARY (Med)
440 Monroe Ave. Phone: (607)324-0841
Hornell, NY 14843 Brian Smith, Libn.
Staff: Prof 1. **Subjects:** Nursing. **Holdings:** 3500 books; 475 bound periodical volumes; 300 AV programs. **Subscriptions:** 43 journals and other serials. **Services:** Interlibrary loan; copying; SDI; library open to the public. **Automated Operations:** Computerized acquisitions and serials. **Computerized Information Services:** MEDLARS, OCLC. Performs searches on fee basis. **Networks/Consortia:** Member of South Central Research Library Council (SCRLC).

★12414★
ST. JOHN HOSPITAL - MEDICAL LIBRARY (Med)
22101 Moross Rd. Phone: (313)343-3733
Detroit, MI 48236 Ellen E. O'Donnell, Dir.
Founded: 1952. **Staff:** Prof 2; Other 3. **Subjects:** Medicine, nursing, allied health sciences, health care administration and management. **Holdings:** 5000 books; 5900 bound periodical volumes; 600 AV programs; 10 VF drawers of pamphlets, documents; 7 series of medical audiotapes; 245 journal titles on microfiche. **Subscriptions:** 525 journals and other serials. **Services:** Interlibrary loan; copying; SDI; library open to the public with permission of the director. **Automated Operations:** Computerized serials and circulation. **Computerized Information Services:** MEDLINE, DIALOG Information Services, BRS Information Technologies. **Staff:** Sheryl Summers, Ref.Libn..

★12415★
ST. JOHN MEDICAL CENTER - HEALTH SCIENCES LIBRARY (Med)
1923 S. Utica Phone: (918)744-2970
Tulsa, OK 74104 James M. Donovan, Libn.
Founded: 1946. **Staff:** 1. **Subjects:** Medicine, nursing, allied health sciences, management. **Special Collections:** Training and development; history of medicine; Catholic bioethics. **Holdings:** 3041 books; 7050 bound periodical volumes; Audio-Digest tapes. **Subscriptions:** 148 journals and other serials. **Services:** Interlibrary loan; copying; library open to the public by appointment. **Computerized Information Services:** MEDLINE. **Networks/Consortia:** Member of TALON, Tulsa Area Library Cooperative (TALC).

ST. JOHN DEL REY MINING COMPANY ARCHIVES
See: University of Texas, Austin - Benson Latin American Collection (16917)

★12416★
ST. JOHN UNITED CHURCH OF CHRIST - LIBRARY (Rel-Phil)
307 W. Clay St. Phone: (618)344-2526
Collinsville, IL 62234 Jean Nuernberger, Libn.
Founded: 1959. **Staff:** Prof 1; Other 7. **Subjects:** Bible, life and teachings of Jesus, prayer and devotions, faith and theology, religions, worship and music. **Holdings:** 5708 books; 35 phonograph records; 35 cassettes; 6 videotapes.

★12417★
ST. JOHN VIANNEY COLLEGE SEMINARY - MARY LOUISE MAYTAG MEMORIAL LIBRARY (Rel-Phil)
2900 S.W. 87th Ave. Phone: (305)223-4561
Miami, FL 33165 Diane Maguire, Dir.
Founded: 1960. **Staff:** Prof 1; Other 2. **Subjects:** Religion, philosophy. **Special Collections:** Paintings by Jehan Georges Vibert. **Holdings:** 45,680 books. **Subscriptions:** 227 journals and other serials. **Services:** Library not open to the public. **Publications:** Library handbook. **Special Catalogs:** Periodical directory (booklet); AV catalog.

★12418★
ST. JOHN AND WEST SHORE HOSPITAL - MEDIA CENTER (Med)
29000 Center Ridge Rd. Phone: (216)835-6000
Westlake, OH 44145 Jennifer Gallant, Dir.
Founded: 1981. **Staff:** Prof 1. **Subjects:** Medicine, nursing, allied health sciences. **Special Collections:** Osteopathic historical collections (35 items). **Holdings:** 2300 books; 2 drawers of pamphlets. **Subscriptions:** 130 journals and other serials. **Services:** Interlibrary loan; copying; center open to the public with restrictions. **Computerized Information Services:** MEDLARS, DIALOG Information Services, BRS Information Technologies.

★12419★
ST. JOHN'S ABBEY AND UNIVERSITY - HILL MONASTIC MANUSCRIPT LIBRARY - BUSH CENTER (Rel-Phil, Hist)
Collegeville, MN 56321 Phone: (612)363-3514
Dr. Julian G. Plante, Exec.Dir.
Founded: 1965. **Staff:** Prof 9; Other 1. **Subjects:** Medieval theology, science, literature, philosophy, medicine, church history, codicology, papyrology, monasticism, paleography, calligraphy, art, liturgy. **Special Collections:** Pre-1600 manuscripts of 76 Austrian libraries; manuscripts from Spain, Ethiopia, Malta, England, Germany, Portugal, Italy, and Hungary (68,000 total manuscript books); 100,000 papyri totalling 22 million pages of documentation (microfilm). **Services:** Copying; research assistance; center open to the public. **Publications:** Progress Reports; Festschrift. **Special Catalogs:** Checklists of manuscripts, occasional; Descriptive Inventories of Manuscripts, occasional. **Staff:** Dr. Getatchew Haile, Mss.Cat.; Richard Oliver, O.S.B., Field Dir.; Dr. Thomas Amos, Mss.Cat.; Dr. Jonathan G. Black, Mss.Cat.; Gregory Sebastian, O.S.B., Mss.Cat..

ST. JOHN'S COLLEGE
See: University of Manitoba (16357)

ST. JOHN'S EASTSIDE HOSPITAL - FREDERICK J. PLONDKE MEDICAL LIBRARY
See: St. John's Northeast Hospital - Memorial Medical Library (12427)

ST. JOHN'S EPISCOPAL HOSPITAL
See: Interfaith Medical Center (6968)

★12420★
ST. JOHN'S HOSPITAL - HEALTH SCIENCE LIBRARY (Med)
800 E. Carpenter Phone: (217)544-6464
Springfield, IL 62769 Kathryn Wrigley, Dir.
Staff: Prof 1; Other 2. **Subjects:** Cardiovascular system, surgery, pediatrics, emergency medicine, nursing, pathology, psychiatry. **Holdings:** 3611 books; 196 AV programs; pamphlets. **Subscriptions:** 335 journals and other serials. **Services:** Interlibrary loan; copying; SDI; library open to the public for reference use only on request. **Computerized Information Services:** NLM, DIALOG Information Services, OCLC. **Networks/Consortia:** Member of Capital Area Consortium, ILLINET, Greater Midwest Regional Medical Library Network. **Publications:** Libri (acquisitions list). **Special Catalogs:** Periodical holdings; media holdings.

★12421★
ST. JOHN'S HOSPITAL - HEALTH SCIENCE LIBRARY (Med)
Box 30 Phone: (508)458-1411
Lowell, MA 01853 Gale Cogan, Dir.
Founded: 1970. **Staff:** Prof 1; Other 1. **Subjects:** Medicine and allied health sciences, hospital administration. **Holdings:** 1500 books. **Subscriptions:** 450 journals and other serials. **Services:** Interlibrary loan; copying; library open to the public. **Computerized Information Services:** MEDLARS, BRS Information Technologies. **Networks/Consortia:** Member of Northeastern Consortium for Health Information (NECHI), Massachusetts Health Sciences Library Network (MAHSLIN), Boston Biomedical Library Consortium.

★12422★
ST. JOHN'S HOSPITAL AND HEALTH CENTER - HOSPITAL LIBRARY (Med)
1328 22nd St. Phone: (213)829-8494
Santa Monica, CA 90404 Cathey L. Pinckney, Libn.
Founded: 1952. **Staff:** Prof 1; Other 1. **Subjects:** Medicine, nursing, and hospital administration. **Holdings:** 5878 books; 2706 bound periodical volumes; 3142 unbound journal volumes. **Subscriptions:** 321 journals and other serials. **Services:** Interlibrary loan; copying; library open to qualified users.

★12423★
ST. JOHN'S LUTHERAN CHURCH - LIBRARY (Rel-Phil)
5th and Wilhelm Phone: (316)564-2044
Ellinwood, KS 67526 Paula Knop, Libn.
Founded: 1980. **Staff:** Prof 1. **Subjects:** Children's literature, Biblical fiction, Christian biographies, Christian life, bibliotherapy, reference. **Special Collections:** Christian phonograph records (140); Dr. James Dobson Collection (90 cassettes). **Holdings:** 2350 books. **Services:** Interlibrary loan; copying; library open to the public.

★12424★
ST. JOHN'S MEDICAL CENTER - HEALTH SCIENCES LIBRARY (Med)
2015 Jackson St. Phone: (317)646-8264
Anderson, IN 46014 Scott S. Loman, Hea.Sci.Libn.
Staff: Prof 1. **Subjects:** Medicine, nursing, allied health sciences, health administration, marketing. **Holdings:** 2000 books; 4000 bound periodical volumes; 150 audio cassettes; 400 video cassettes. **Subscriptions:** 200 journals and other serials; 7 newspapers. **Services:** Interlibrary loan; copying; SDI; library open to public at librarian's discretion. **Computerized Information Services:** NLM, BRS Information Technologies. Performs searches on fee basis. **Networks/Consortia:** Member of Greater Midwest Regional Medical Library Network, East Central Indiana Health Sciences Library Consortium. **Publications:** Library Update (newsletter), monthly. **Remarks:** An alternate telephone number is 646-8262.

★12425★
ST. JOHN'S MERCY MEDICAL CENTER - JOHN YOUNG BROWN MEMORIAL LIBRARY (Med)
621 S. New Ballas Rd. Phone: (314)569-6340
St. Louis, MO 63141-8221 Saundra H. Brenner, Dir.
Founded: 1912. **Staff:** Prof 2; Other 3. **Subjects:** Medicine. **Holdings:** 1391 books; 8000 bound periodical volumes. **Subscriptions:** 550 journals and other serials. **Services:** Interlibrary loan; copying; SDI; current awareness; library open to the public for reference use only with physician's permission. **Automated Operations:** Computerized public access catalog, cataloging, acquisitions, serials, circulation, and ILL. **Computerized Information Services:** MEDLARS, OCLC, BRS Information Technologies, DIALOG Information Services; DOCLINE, Philnet (electronic mail services). Performs searches free of charge. **Networks/Consortia:** Member of St. Louis Regional Library Network. **Staff:** Bridget Kowalczyk, Asst.Dir..

★12426★
ST. JOHN'S MUSEUM OF ART, INC. - LIBRARY (Art)
114 Orange St. Phone: (919)763-0281
Wilmington, NC 28401 C. Reynolds Brown, Dir.
Subjects: Art. **Holdings:** 600 books and periodicals. **Services:** Library open to the public by appointment.

★12427★
ST. JOHN'S NORTHEAST HOSPITAL - MEMORIAL MEDICAL LIBRARY (Med)
1575 Beam Ave. Phone: (612)779-4276
Maplewood, MN 55109 Terri Cover, Lib.Serv.Dir.
Staff: Prof 1. **Subjects:** Medicine, nursing, allied health sciences. **Holdings:** 1200 books; 40 bound periodical volumes; 150 AV programs. **Subscriptions:** 170 journals and other serials. **Services:** Interlibrary loan; copying; library open to students and health professionals by appointment only. **Computerized Information Services:** BRS Information Technologies. **Networks/Consortia:** Member of Twin Cities Biomedical Consortium (TCBC), MINITEX, Greater Midwest Regional Medical Library Network, Metronet. **Publications:** Library newsletter, 9/year - for internal distribution only. **Remarks:** Maintained by HealthEast. **Formerly:** St. John's Eastside Hospital - Frederick J. Plondke Medical Library.

★12428★
ST. JOHN'S PROVINCIAL SEMINARY - LIBRARY (Rel-Phil)
44011 Five Mile Rd. Phone: (313)453-6200
Plymouth, MI 48170 Jean McGarty, Lib.Dir.
Founded: 1949. **Staff:** Prof 2; Other 2. **Subjects:** Theology and scripture. **Special Collections:** Gabriel Richard Collection. **Holdings:** 50,000 books; 11,000 bound periodical volumes; 1700 cassettes; 2200 microforms. **Subscriptions:** 400 journals and other serials; 19 newspapers. **Services:** Interlibrary loan; copying; library open to the public for reference use only. **Publications:** About Books, quarterly. **Staff:** Estelle De Bear, Tech.Serv.Libn..

★12429★
ST. JOHN'S REGIONAL HEALTH CENTER - MEDICAL LIBRARY (Med)
1235 E. Cherokee Phone: (417)885-2795
Springfield, MO 65804-2263 Anna Beth Crabtree, Dir., Med.Lib.Serv.
Founded: 1904. **Staff:** Prof 1; Other 1. **Subjects:** Medicine, nursing, and allied health sciences. **Holdings:** 750 books; 4200 bound periodical volumes; 65 videotapes; 200 audiotapes. **Subscriptions:** 310 journals and other serials; 25 newspapers. **Services:** Interlibrary loan; copying; SDI; library open to health care professionals. **Automated Operations:** Computerized cataloging, serials, and ILL. **Computerized Information Services:** MEDLARS, WILSONLINE, OCLC, BRS Information Technologies; Octanet, DOCLINE, Philnet (electronic mail services). **Publications:** Medical Library Express, quarterly - for internal distribution and to physicians in Southwest Missouri.

★12430★
ST. JOHN'S REGIONAL HEALTH CENTER - SCHOOL OF NURSING LIBRARY (Med)
1930 S. National Ave. Phone: (417)885-2104
Springfield, MO 65804 Sandy J. Anderson, Libn.
Founded: 1909. **Staff:** Prof 1; Other 4. **Subjects:** Nursing, medicine, and allied health sciences. **Holdings:** 8000 books; 155 reels of microfilm; 7 VF drawers of pamphlets; slides; recordings; charts; models; pictures; cassette tapes. **Subscriptions:** 70 journals and other serials. **Services:** Library open to the public for reference use only. **Publications:** Book Acquisitions List, monthly.

★12431★
ST. JOHN'S REGIONAL MEDICAL CENTER - HEALTH SCIENCE LIBRARY (Med)
333 N. F St. Phone: (805)988-2820
Oxnard, CA 93030 Joanne Kennedy, Libn.
Founded: 1973. **Staff:** Prof 1. **Subjects:** Clinical medicine, nursing, health management. **Holdings:** 3200 volumes. **Subscriptions:** 180 journals and other serials. **Services:** Interlibrary loan; copying; library open to the public with restrictions. **Computerized Information Services:** MEDLINE, BRS Information Technologies; OnTyme Electronic Message Network Service (electronic mail service). Performs searches on fee basis.

★12432★
ST. JOHNS RIVER WATER MANAGEMENT DISTRICT - LIBRARY (Sci-Engr, Env-Cons)
Hwy. 100, W.
Box 1429 Phone: (904)328-8321
Palatka, FL 32078-1429 Judith G. Hunter, Libn.
Founded: 1975. **Staff:** Prof 1; Other 1. **Subjects:** Hydrology, water management, engineering, ecology, botany, agriculture. **Holdings:** 7000 books. **Subscriptions:** 195 journals and other serials. **Services:** Interlibrary loan; copying; library open to the public for reference use only. **Publications:** Monthly Bibliography of recent acquisitions - for internal distribution only.

★12433★
ST. JOHN'S RIVERSIDE HOSPITAL - MEDICAL LIBRARY (Med)
967 N. Broadway
Yonkers, NY 10701 Phone: (914)964-4344
Subjects: Medicine. **Holdings:** 430 books. **Subscriptions:** 31 journals and other serials. **Services:** Library not open to the public.

★12434★
ST. JOHN'S SEMINARY - EDWARD LAURENCE DOHENY MEMORIAL LIBRARY (Rel-Phil)
5012 E. Seminary Rd. Phone: (805)482-2755
Camarillo, CA 93010 Mark Lager, Dir.
Founded: 1940. **Staff:** Prof 2; Other 3. **Subjects:** Theology, philosophy, history. **Holdings:** 50,000 books; 10,000 bound periodical volumes. **Subscriptions:** 280 journals and other serials; 10 newspapers. **Services:** Interlibrary loan copying; library open to the public. **Automated Operations:** Computerized cataloging. **Computerized Information Services:** DIALOG Information Services, OCLC. Performs searches free of charge.

★12435★
ST. JOHN'S SEMINARY - LIBRARY (Rel-Phil)
99 Lake St. Phone: (617)254-2610
Brighton, MA 02135 Rev. L.W. McGrath, Hd.
Staff: Prof 2; Other 3. **Subjects:** Ecclesiastical sciences. **Holdings:** 120,000 books; 7600 bound periodical volumes. **Subscriptions:** 325 journals and other serials. **Services:** Interlibrary loan; copying; library open to accredited scholars. **Automated Operations:** Computerized cataloging. **Computerized Information Services:** OCLC. **Networks/Consortia:** Member of NELINET, Boston Theological Institute Libraries.

★12436★
ST. JOHN'S UNIVERSITY - ARCHIVES (Hist)
Grand Central & Utopia Pkwys. Phone: (718)990-6161
Jamaica, NY 11439 Rev. John E. Young, C.M., Archv.
Staff: Prof 1. **Special Collections:** James L. Buckley Senatorial Papers; Paul O'Dwyer and Cormac O'Malley Collections (Irish-American affairs); James J. Needham Papers (Wall Street business affairs); American League for an Undivided Ireland Collection, 1947-1963; American Friends of Irish Neutrality Collection; Meehan Collection (ecclesiastical and civic historical clippings); Vincentian Papers (Archives of the Eastern Province of the Congregation of the Mission); university archives; autograph collection. **Holdings:** 1510 books and bound periodical volumes. **Services:** Copying; archives open to the public by appointment.

★12437★
ST. JOHN'S UNIVERSITY - ASIAN COLLECTION - LIBRARY (Area-Ethnic)
Grand Central & Utopia Pkwys. Phone: (718)990-6161
Jamaica, NY 11439 Mr. Hou Ran Ferng, Hd.Libn.
Founded: 1966. **Staff:** Prof 1; Other 3. **Subjects:** Chinese and Japanese literature, religions, history, arts, philosophy, social sciences. **Special Collections:** Taoism (7000 volumes); Buddhism (9000 volumes); Oriental Art Books Collection (1200 volumes); Serial Collections (22,500 volumes). **Holdings:** 62,000 books; 745 bound periodical volumes; survey of China mainland press, 1958-1978; selections from China mainland magazines, 1960-1978; Mainichi Daily News (Japanese daily newspaper), 1960 to present, on microfilm; current background, 1958-1978; The Asian Wall Street Journal, 1982 to present. **Subscriptions:** 167 journals and other serials; 14 newspapers. **Services:** Interlibrary loan; copying; library open to the public with restrictions.

★12438★
ST. JOHN'S UNIVERSITY - COLLEGE OF PHARMACY & ALLIED HEALTH PROFESSIONS - HEALTH EDUCATION RESOURCE CENTER (Med)
Grand Central & Utopia Pkwys. Phone: (718)990-6162
Jamaica, NY 11439 Mary A. Grant, Dir.
Staff: Prof 3; Other 1. **Subjects:** Clinical pharmacy, pharmacology, pharmacy administration, toxicology, pharmacokinetics, industrial pharmacy. **Holdings:** 1575 books; 20 newsletters; 632 video cassettes and audio slide programs; 16 drawers of article and pamphlet files; 280 transparencies; 41 Computer Assisted Learning programs. **Subscriptions:** 90 journals and other serials. **Services:** Center open to health care professionals with a special need. **Computerized Information Services:** MEDLARS. **Staff:** Richard Goldberg, Media Spec.; Ann Hurt, Asst. to Dir..

★12439★
ST. JOHN'S UNIVERSITY - GOVERNMENT DOCUMENTS DEPARTMENT (Soc Sci)
Grand Central & Utopia Pkwys. Phone: (718)990-6071
Jamaica, NY 11439 Shu-fang Lin, Govt.Docs.Libn.
Staff: Prof 1; Other 3. **Subjects:** Politics and government, education, business and economics. **Special Collections:** Congressional Record, 1st Congress to present; Congressional Serial Set; Joint Publications Research Service and Foreign Broadcast Information Service publications on microfiche. **Holdings:** 78,592 books; 2290 bound periodical volumes; 3978 reels of microfilm; 91,296 microfiche. **Subscriptions:** 171 journals and other serials. **Services:** Interlibrary loan; copying; SDI; department open to the public for reference use only. **Automated Operations:** Computerized cataloging. **Computerized Information Services:** DIALOG Information Services, BRS Information Technologies.

★12440★
ST. JOHN'S UNIVERSITY - HUGH L. CAREY COLLECTION (Hist)
Grand Central & Utopia Parkways Phone: (718)990-6201
Jamaica, NY 11439 Szilvia E. Szmuk, Spec.Coll.Libn.
Founded: 1984. **Staff:** Prof 1. **Subjects:** American government and legislation, 1960s-1970s; education; handicapped; New York state public policy; naval shipyards; urban planning in Park Slope, New York. **Special Collections:** Hugh L. Carey Collection, including Congressional Papers, 1960-1974, and Gubernatorial Papers, 1975-1983. **Holdings:** Elementary and Secondary Education Act (ESEA) papers; American government, campaign, and convention files. **Services:** Interlibrary loan (limited); copying; collection open to the public by appointment. **Computerized**

Information Services: DIALOG Information Services, BRS Information Technologies, WILSONLINE; internal database. **Networks/Consortia:** Member of New York Metropolitan Reference and Research Library Agency (METRO). **Publications:** Brochure on Hugh L. Carey and collection; guide to the collection.

★12441★
ST. JOHN'S UNIVERSITY - INSTRUCTIONAL MATERIALS CENTER (Educ, Aud-Vis)
Grand Central & Utopia Pkwys. Phone: (718)990-6161
Jamaica, NY 11439 Sharon Krauss, Libn./Assoc.Prof.
Staff: Prof 1; Other 3. **Subjects:** Education. **Special Collections:** Drug and alcohol education books and films; educational and psychological tests; educational software. **Holdings:** 10,000 books; 2000 curriculum guides; 1700 filmstrips; 1300 study prints; 1400 cassettes; 1650 slides. **Services:** Copying; center open to the public for reference use only. **Networks/Consortia:** Member of New York Metropolitan Reference and Research Library Agency (METRO). **Special Catalogs:** Film catalog (book).

★12442★
ST. JOHN'S UNIVERSITY - LAW LIBRARY (Law)
Fromkes Hall
Grand Central & Utopia Pkwys. Phone: (718)990-6651
Jamaica, NY 11439 Julius Marke, Dir.
Founded: 1925. **Staff:** Prof 7; Other 10. **Subjects:** Law - Anglo-American, international, ecclesiastical, foreign, comparative, Roman; jurisprudence. **Special Collections:** Collected works of St. Thomas More (original editions and works about); canon law. **Holdings:** 200,516 books; 8654 bound periodical volumes; 3909 reels of microfilm; 47,155 microcards; 745,188 microfiche. **Subscriptions:** 5138 journals and other serials; 10 newspapers. **Services:** Interlibrary loan; copying; library open to the public with restrictions. **Automated Operations:** Computerized cataloging and serials. **Computerized Information Services:** LEXIS, WESTLAW, NEXIS, DIALOG Information Services, OCLC; ABA/net (electronic mail service). **Staff:** Robert Nagy, Cat.; Karl Christensen, Circ./Ref.; Paul Shore, Ref.Libn.; Irene Shapiro, Ref.Libn.; Catherine Pennington, Assoc.Dir.; Ruth Rosner, Comp.Serv./Ref.; William Manz, Media/Ref..

★12443★
ST. JOHN'S UNIVERSITY - LIBRARY AND INFORMATION SCIENCE LIBRARY (Info Sci)
Grand Central & Utopia Pkwys. Phone: (718)990-6161
Jamaica, NY 11439 Drew K. Selvar, LIS Libn.
Staff: Prof 1; Other 1. **Subjects:** Library and information science, children's/young adult literature. **Holdings:** 21,500 books; 1250 bound periodical volumes; 605 reels of microfilm. 3 cabinets of vertical files and annual reports. **Subscriptions:** 400 journals and other serials; 185 newsletters. **Services:** Interlibrary loan; copying; library open to the public with identification. **Automated Operations:** Computerized cataloging. **Computerized Information Services:** OCLC.

★12444★
ST. JOHN'S UNIVERSITY - LORETTO MEMORIAL LIBRARY (Bus-Fin)
300 Howard Ave. Phone: (718)390-4545
Staten Island, NY 10301 Sr. Monica Wood, S.C., Asst.Dir.
Staff: Prof 7; Other 16. **Subjects:** Education, business administration. **Special Collections:** Myer Collection (accounting). **Holdings:** 110,000 books; 35,620 bound periodical volumes; 14,023 reels of microfilm; 20 VF drawers. **Subscriptions:** 976 journals and other serials. **Services:** Interlibrary loan; copying; SDI; library open to the public with restrictions. **Computerized Information Services:** BRS Information Technologies, DIALOG Information Services, Pergamon ORBIT InfoLine, Inc., OCLC, WILSONLINE; MULTICS (internal database). Performs searches on fee basis. Contact Person: Francine Russo. **Publications:** Library handbook. **Staff:** Lois Cherepon; Sandra Math; Eugene Hunt; Mark Padnos; Francine Russo; Kathleen Delaney.

★12445★
ST. JOHN'S UNIVERSITY - SPECIAL COLLECTIONS (Bus-Fin, Hum)
Grand Central & Utopia Pkwys. Phone: (718)990-6201
Jamaica, NY 11439 Szilvia E. Szmuk, Spec.Coll.Libn.
Founded: 1870. **Staff:** Prof 1; Other 1. **Subjects:** Lawn tennis, accounting, American literature. **Special Collections:** Art exhibition catalogs; William M. Fischer Tennis Collection (2500 volumes); Myer Collection (accounting; 170 volumes); Baxter Collection (American literature; 350 volumes); Heller Collection. **Holdings:** 6000 books; 40 papal letters. **Services:** Collections open to the public by appointment. **Automated Operations:** Computerized cataloging. **Computerized Information Services:** DIALOG Information Services, Pergamon ORBIT InfoLine, Inc. **Networks/Consortia:** Member of New York Metropolitan Reference and Research Library Agency (METRO), SUNY/OCLC Library Network.

★12446★
ST. JOSEPH ABBEY - LIBRARY (Rel-Phil)
St. Benedict, LA 70457 Phone: (504)892-1800
Fr. Timothy J. Burnett, O.S.B., Dir.
Founded: 1910. **Staff:** Prof 1; Other 2. **Subjects:** Theology, scripture, patristics, monastica, church history. **Holdings:** 16,000 books; 1850 bound periodical volumes. **Subscriptions:** 65 journals and other serials. **Services:** Interlibrary loan; library not open to the public.

ST. JOSEPH COLLEGE OF ORANGE
See: Loyola Marymount University - Orange Campus Library (8087)

★12447★
ST. JOSEPH COMMUNITY HOSPITAL - LIBRARY (Med)
600 N.E. 92nd Ave.
Box 1600 Phone: (206)256-2045
Vancouver, WA 98668 Sylvia E. MacWilliams, Lib.Coord.
Staff: Prof 1. **Subjects:** Medicine, nursing. **Holdings:** 1054 books. **Subscriptions:** 354 journals and other serials. **Services:** Interlibrary loan; library not open to the public. **Computerized Information Services:** MEDLARS. **Remarks:** Maintained by Southwest Washington Hospitals.

★12448★
ST. JOSEPH COUNTY LAW LIBRARY (Law)
Court House Phone: (219)284-9657
South Bend, IN 46601 Jan E. Quigley, Libn.
Staff: 1. **Subjects:** Law. **Holdings:** 17,716 volumes. **Services:** Library open to the public for reference use only.

★12449★
ST. JOSEPH HEALTH CENTER - HEALTH SCIENCE LIBRARY (Med)
300 First Capitol Dr. Phone: (314)724-2810
St. Charles, MO 63301 Lucille Dykas, Lib.Mgr.
Staff: Prof 1. **Subjects:** Medicine. **Holdings:** 500 books; 320 bound periodical volumes. **Subscriptions:** 80 journals and other serials. **Services:** Interlibrary loan; library not open to the public.

ST. JOSEPH HEALTH AND REHABILITATION CENTER
See: Ottumwa Regional Health Center (10953)

★12450★
ST. JOSEPH HOSPITAL - BURLEW MEDICAL LIBRARY (Med)
1100 Stewart Dr. Phone: (714)771-8291
Orange, CA 92668 Julie Smith, Lib.Mgr.
Founded: 1929. **Staff:** Prof 2; Other 3. **Subjects:** Medicine, nursing, hospital administration. **Holdings:** 10,000 books; 4798 bound periodical volumes; 7800 AV programs. **Subscriptions:** 713 journals and other serials. **Services:** Interlibrary loan (fee); copying; library open to the public. **Automated Operations:** Computerized cataloging, serials, and circulation. **Computerized Information Services:** MEDLINE, DIALOG Information Services, BRS Information Technologies; OnTyme Electronic Message Network Service (electronic mail service). Performs searches on fee basis. **Networks/Consortia:** Member of Pacific Southwest Regional Medical Library Service, Nursing Information Consortium of Orange County (NICOC), Medical Library Group of Southern California and Arizona (MLGSCA).

ST. JOSEPH HOSPITAL - CARLSON MEMORIAL MEDICAL LIBRARY
See: St. Joseph Hospital and Health Center - Medical Library (12468)

★12451★
ST. JOSEPH HOSPITAL - EDUCATIONAL RESOURCES LIBRARY (Med)
915 E. 5th St. Phone: (618)463-5284
Alton, IL 62002 Betty Byrd, Libn.
Staff: Prof 1. **Subjects:** Medicine, hospital administration, nursing. **Holdings:** 2800 volumes; 12 legal files of pamphlets. **Subscriptions:** 200 journals and other serials. **Services:** Interlibrary loan; copying; library open to health personnel. **Computerized Information Services:** MEDLINE. **Networks/Consortia:** Member of Areawide Hospital Library Consortium of Southwestern Illinois (AHLC), ILLINET, Greater Midwest Regional Medical Library Network. **Publications:** Current Journal Contents, weekly - to department heads and doctors; bibliographies.

★12452★
ST. JOSEPH HOSPITAL - HEALTH REACH PATIENT & COMMUNITY LIBRARY (Med)
1835 Franklin St. Phone: (303)837-7188
Denver, CO 80218 Margaret Bandy, Libn.
Founded: 1985. **Staff:** Prof 1; Other 6. **Subjects:** Consumer health. **Holdings:** 450 books. **Subscriptions:** 10 journals and other serials. **Services:** Interlibrary loan; library open to the public.

★12453★
ST. JOSEPH HOSPITAL - HEALTH SCIENCE LIBRARY (Med)
1000 Carondelet Dr. Phone: (816)942-4400
Kansas City, MO 64114 Janice Foster, Libn.
Founded: 1929. **Staff:** Prof 1; Other 1. **Subjects:** Medicine, nursing, and allied health sciences. **Holdings:** 1000 books; 1200 bound periodical volumes. **Subscriptions:** 156 journals and other serials. **Services:** Interlibrary loan; copying. **Computerized Information Services:** MEDLARS, BRS Information Technologies, DIALOG Information Services. **Networks/Consortia:** Member of Kansas City Library Network, Inc. (KCLN), Midcontinental Regional Medical Library Program.

★12454★
ST. JOSEPH HOSPITAL - HEALTH SCIENCE LIBRARY (Med)
200 High Service Ave. Phone: (401)456-3036
North Providence, RI 02904 Sylvia Raymond, Lib.Asst.
Founded: 1977. **Staff:** 1. **Subjects:** Medicine, surgery, nursing, allied health sciences. **Holdings:** 3969 books; 2302 bound periodical volumes; 4 VF drawers; 12 files of pamphlets. **Subscriptions:** 132 journals and other serials. **Services:** Interlibrary loan; copying; library open to the public by appointment.

★12455★
ST. JOSEPH HOSPITAL - HEALTH SCIENCE LIBRARY (Med)
220 Overton
Box 178 Phone: (901)577-2828
Memphis, TN 38101-0178 Patricia Irby, Libn.
Founded: 1935. **Staff:** 2. **Subjects:** Medicine, nursing, management. **Holdings:** 2735 books; 2834 bound periodical volumes. **Subscriptions:** 172 journals and other serials. **Services:** Interlibrary loan; copying; SDI; library open to the public for reference use only on request. **Computerized Information Services:** NLM, MEDLINE. Performs searches on fee basis. **Networks/Consortia:** Member of Association of Memphis Area Health Sciences Libraries (AMAHSL).

★12456★
ST. JOSEPH HOSPITAL - HEALTH SCIENCE LIBRARY (Med)
1919 LaBranch Phone: (713)757-1000
Houston, TX 77002 Shelley G. Mao, Dir.
Founded: 1940. **Staff:** Prof 1; Other 1. **Subjects:** Medicine, sciences, management. **Holdings:** 3518 books; 4620 bound periodical volumes; 127 volumes in microform; 72 volumes of Audio-Digest tapes. **Subscriptions:** 200 journals and other serials. **Services:** Interlibrary loan; copying; library open to professionals by appointment. **Computerized Information Services:** NLM; internal database.

★12457★
ST. JOSEPH HOSPITAL - HEALTH SCIENCES LIBRARY (Med)
1835 Franklin St. Phone: (303)837-7188
Denver, CO 80218 Margaret Bandy, Libn.
Staff: Prof 1; Other 1. **Subjects:** Medicine, nursing, hospital management. **Holdings:** 2102 books; pamphlets. **Subscriptions:** 208 journals and other serials. **Services:** Interlibrary loan; copying; library open to the public. **Automated Operations:** Computerized public access catalog, cataloging, circulation, and ILL. **Computerized Information Services:** MEDLINE, DIALOG Information Services, OCLC, BRS Information Technologies. **Networks/Consortia:** Member of Denver Area Health Sciences Library Consortium, Midcontinental Regional Medical Library Program.

★12458★
ST. JOSEPH HOSPITAL - HEALTH SCIENCES LIBRARY (Med)
302 Kensington Ave. Phone: (313)762-8519
Flint, MI 48502 Ria Brown Lukes, Med.Libn.
Staff: Prof 1; Other 3. **Subjects:** Medicine, nursing. **Holdings:** 2313 books; 5271 bound periodical volumes; 1227 audio cassettes; 108 video cassettes. **Subscriptions:** 220 journals and other serials. **Services:** Interlibrary loan; copying; library open to the public for reference use only. **Automated Operations:** Computerized acquisitions and serials. **Computerized Information Services:** MEDLINE, DIALOG Information Services; INTERACT (electronic mail service). **Networks/Consortia:** Member of Flint Area Health Science Library Network (FAHSLN), Michigan Health Sciences Libraries Association (MHSLA). **Publications:** New book lists.

★12459★
ST. JOSEPH HOSPITAL - HEALTH SCIENCES LIBRARY (Med)
12th & Walnut Sts. Phone: (215)378-2389
Reading, PA 19603 Kathleen A. Izzo, Libn.
Founded: 1973. **Staff:** Prof 2; Other 2. **Subjects:** Medicine, nursing, patient education, allied health professions, hospital administration, public health. **Holdings:** 2982 books; 4526 bound periodical volumes; 4 VF drawers of pamphlets. **Subscriptions:** 214 journals and other serials. **Services:** Interlibrary loan; copying; SDI; library open to the public. **Automated Operations:** Computerized cataloging. **Computerized Information Services:** DIALOG Information Services, NLM, BRS Information Technologies. Performs searches on fee basis. **Networks/Consortia:** Member of Greater Northeastern Regional Medical Library Program, Berks County Library Association (BCLA), Central Pennsylvania Health Sciences Library Association (CPHSLA). **Publications:** Library Ledger, monthly - for internal distribution only. **Special Catalogs:** AV Catalog (notebook). **Staff:** Carol M. Morey, Asst.Libn..

★12460★
ST. JOSEPH HOSPITAL - HOSPITAL LIBRARY (Med)
250 College Ave.
Box 3509 Phone: (717)291-8119
Lancaster, PA 17604 Eileen B. Doudna, Dir., Lib.Rsrcs.
Founded: 1940. **Staff:** Prof 1; Other 1. **Subjects:** Medicine, nursing, and allied health sciences. **Holdings:** 3000 books; 500 AV programs. **Subscriptions:** 250 journals and other serials. **Services:** Interlibrary loan; copying; library open to the public. **Computerized Information Services:** MEDLARS, BRS Information Technologies. Performs searches on fee basis. **Networks/Consortia:** Member of Central Pennsylvania Health Sciences Library Association (CPHSLA).

★12461★
ST. JOSEPH HOSPITAL - MEDICAL LIBRARY (Med)
One St. Joseph Dr. Phone: (606)278-3436
Lexington, KY 40504 Jerri Trimble, Libn.
Founded: 1968. **Staff:** 1. **Subjects:** Medicine, nursing, and allied health sciences. **Holdings:** 1115 books; 2935 bound periodical volumes; 10 directories; 818 audiotapes; 55 AV programs. **Subscriptions:** 177 journals and other serials. **Services:** Interlibrary loan; library not open to the public. **Networks/Consortia:** Member of Kentucky Health Sciences Library Consortium.

★12462★
ST. JOSEPH HOSPITAL - MEDICAL LIBRARY (Med)
400 Walter Ave., N.E. Phone: (505)848-8291
Albuquerque, NM 87102 Melba Clark, Med.Libn.
Founded: 1959. **Staff:** 1. **Subjects:** Medicine, nursing, hospital administration, social work, public health. **Holdings:** 700 books; 800 bound periodical volumes. **Subscriptions:** 90 journals and other serials. **Services:** Interlibrary loan; copying; library open to students and workers in health professions. **Remarks:** Maintained by the Sisters of Charity.

★12463★
ST. JOSEPH HOSPITAL - OTTO C. BRANTIGAN, M.D. MEDICAL LIBRARY (Med)
7620 York Rd. Phone: (301)337-1210
Towson, MD 21204 Marianne Prenger, Med.Libn.
Founded: 1940. **Staff:** Prof 2; Other 2. **Subjects:** Medicine, surgery, obstetrics, gynecology, pediatrics. **Holdings:** 1445 books; 404 bound periodical volumes; Audio-Digest tapes; audio and video cassette tapes. **Subscriptions:** 151 journals and other serials. **Services:** Interlibrary loan; copying; library open to students. **Computerized Information Services:** MEDLINE, MEDLARS; DOCLINE, MedSig (electronic mail services). **Networks/Consortia:** Member of Maryland Association of Health Science Librarians.

★12464★
ST. JOSEPH HOSPITAL - OUR LADY OF PROVIDENCE UNIT - HEALTH SCIENCE LIBRARY (Med)
21 Peace St. Phone: (401)456-4035
Providence, RI 02907 Marcia A. Sessions, Dir., Lib.Serv.
Founded: 1940. **Staff:** Prof 1; Other 2. **Subjects:** Medicine, nursing, and allied health sciences. **Holdings:** 3016 books; 3972 bound periodical volumes; 8 VF drawers of pamphlets, reports. **Subscriptions:** 141 journals and other serials. **Services:** Interlibrary loan; copying; library open to the public by appointment with referral from another library. **Computerized Information Services:** MEDLARS. **Networks/Consortia:** Member of Consortium of Rhode Island Academic and Research Libraries, Inc. (CRIARL), Association of Rhode Island Health Sciences Librarians (ARIHSL).

★12465★
ST. JOSEPH HOSPITAL - SISTER MARY ALVINA NURSING LIBRARY (Med)
7620 York Rd. Phone: (301)337-1641
Towson, MD 21204 Marcella Siemienski, Libn.
Founded: 1949. **Staff:** Prof 1. **Subjects:** Nursing. **Holdings:** 2281 books; 162 bound periodical volumes; 12 VF drawers of pamphlets and clippings; 939 AV programs. **Subscriptions:** 52 journals and other serials. **Services:** Interlibrary loan; copying; library open to the public for reference use only. **Networks/Consortia:** Member of Maryland Association of Health Science Librarians.

★12466★
ST. JOSEPH HOSPITAL AND HEALTH CARE CENTER - HOSPITAL LIBRARY (Med)
1718 South I St.
Box 2197 Phone: (206)627-4101
Tacoma, WA 98401 Cheryl M. Goodwin, Libn.
Staff: Prof 1. **Subjects:** Medicine, nursing, health sciences, autism, anorexia nervosa. **Holdings:** 2000 books; 150 bound periodical volumes. **Subscriptions:** 100 journals and other serials. **Services:** Interlibrary loan; copying; library open to the public for reference use only. **Computerized Information Services:** DIALOG Information Services, MEDLINE. **Networks/Consortia:** Member of Pierce County Medical Library Consortium, Pacific Northwest Regional Health Sciences Library Service, Western Library Network (WLN).

★12467★
ST. JOSEPH HOSPITAL AND HEALTH CARE CENTER - LIBRARY (Med)
2900 N. Lake Shore Phone: (312)975-3038
Chicago, IL 60657 Katherine Wimmer, Libn.
Staff: Prof 1. **Subjects:** Medicine, nursing. **Special Collections:** Hospital archives. **Holdings:** 5500 books; 8000 bound periodical volumes; 2500 audiotapes; 48 sets of slides and filmstrips; 10 VF drawers; 200 videotapes; 50 8mm films. **Subscriptions:** 260 journals and other serials; 10 newspapers. **Services:** Interlibrary loan; copying; LATCH; current awareness; library open to the public with director's authorization. **Computerized Information Services:** NLM. **Networks/Consortia:** Member of ILLINET, Metropolitan Consortium of Chicago, Greater Midwest Regional Medical Library Network. **Publications:** Quarterly Accession List.

★12468★
ST. JOSEPH HOSPITAL AND HEALTH CENTER - MEDICAL LIBRARY (Med)
205 W. 20th St. Phone: (216)245-6851
Lorain, OH 44052 Susan M. Blaskevica, Libn.
Staff: Prof 1; Other 1. **Subjects:** Medicine, nursing. **Holdings:** 1597 books; 1650 bound periodical volumes; 386 video cassettes. **Subscriptions:** 183 journals and other serials. **Services:** Interlibrary loan; copying; SDI; library open to the public. **Computerized Information Services:** DIALOG Information Services, MEDLINE. Performs searches on fee basis. **Networks/Consortia:** Member of Lake Erie Medical Librarians Association, Cleveland Area Metropolitan Library System (CAMLS). **Formerly:** St. Joseph Hospital - Carlson Memorial Medical Library.

★12469★
ST. JOSEPH INTERCOMMUNITY HOSPITAL - LIBRARY (Med)
2605 Harlem Rd.
Cheektowaga, NY 14225 Phone: (716)896-6300
Staff: Prof 1; Other 1. **Subjects:** Medicine. **Holdings:** 725 books; 57 bound periodical volumes; 657 cassettes; 374 slides. **Subscriptions:** 25 journals and other serials. **Services:** Interlibrary loan; library not open to the public. **Networks/Consortia:** Member of Western New York Library Resources Council (WNYLRC). **Publications:** Library Handbook; Cataloging Handbook.

★12470★
ST. JOSEPH MEDICAL CENTER - HEALTH SCIENCE LIBRARY (Med)
Buena Vista & Alameda Sts. Phone: (818)843-5111
Burbank, CA 91505 Sr. Naomi Hurd, S.P., Libn.
Founded: 1953. **Staff:** Prof 2; Other 2. **Subjects:** Medicine, nursing, hospital administration. **Special Collections:** History of Medicine; rare book collection. **Holdings:** 17,500 books; 5000 bound periodical volumes; 1438 audio cassettes; 238 video cassettes; 101 16mm films; 90 filmstrips; 65 slide programs; 4 transparency programs; 50 microfiche; 36 items of miscellanea. **Subscriptions:** 623 journals and other serials. **Services:** Interlibrary loan; copying; library open to the public for reference use only. **Automated Operations:** Computerized cataloging and serials. **Computerized Information Services:** MEDLINE; DOCLINE (electronic mail service). Performs searches on fee basis. **Networks/Consortia:** Member of Pacific Southwest Regional Medical Library Service. **Publications:** Journal list, annual. **Staff:** Ann Miller, Asst.Libn./AV Coord..

★12471★
ST. JOSEPH MEDICAL CENTER - HEALTH SCIENCE LIBRARY (Med)
333 N. Madison St. Phone: (815)725-7133
Joliet, IL 60435 Catherine Siron, Coord., Lib.Serv.
Founded: 1976. **Staff:** Prof 2; Other 1. **Subjects:** Clinical medicine and nursing. **Special Collections:** Nursing library (4000 volumes). **Holdings:** 2000 books; 2500 bound periodical volumes. **Subscriptions:** 300 journals and other serials. **Services:** Interlibrary loan; copying; library open to the public for reference use only. **Computerized Information Services:** NLM, DIALOG Information Services. Performs searches on fee basis. **Networks/Consortia:** Member of Chicago and South Consortium, Greater Midwest Regional Medical Library Network, Bur Oak Library System. **Staff:** Virginia Gale, Asst.Libn..

★12472★
ST. JOSEPH MEDICAL CENTER - HEALTH SCIENCES LIBRARY (Med)
128 Strawberry Hill Ave.
Box 1222 Phone: (203)353-2095
Stamford, CT 06904-1222 Lucille Lieberman, Dir.
Staff: Prof 1; Other 1. **Subjects:** Medicine, nursing, and allied health sciences. **Holdings:** 1412 books; 160 bound periodical volumes; 106 video cassettes. **Subscriptions:** 160 journals and other serials. **Services:** Interlibrary loan; copying; SDI; library open to the public by arrangement. **Computerized Information Services:** Online systems. **Networks/Consortia:** Member of Connecticut Association of Health Science Libraries (CAHSL), North Atlantic Health Science Libraries (NAHSL). **Publications:** A Guide to Use of the Health Sciences Library, updated annually - to new employees and the medical community.

★12473★
ST. JOSEPH MEMORIAL HOSPITAL - HEALTH SCIENCE LIBRARY (Med)
1907 W. Sycamore St. Phone: (317)452-5611
Kokomo, IN 46901 Jean Romack, Personnel Asst.
Staff: 1. **Subjects:** Medicine, nursing, hospital administration and management. **Holdings:** 1609 books; 736 bound periodical volumes; 348 AV programs; 4 VF drawers. **Subscriptions:** 129 journals and other serials. **Services:** Interlibrary loan; copying; library open to the public with limited circulation. **Networks/Consortia:** Member of Greater Midwest Regional Medical Library Network.

★12474★
ST. JOSEPH MERCY HOSPITAL - LIBRARY (Med)
900 Woodward Phone: (313)858-3495
Pontiac, MI 48053 Mollie S. Lynch, Lib.Mgr.
Staff: Prof 2; Other 2. **Subjects:** Medicine, nursing, health care administration, allied health sciences. **Special Collections:** Consumer health information. **Holdings:** 5000 books; 8000 bound periodical volumes; 300 media programs. **Subscriptions:** 600 journals and other serials. **Services:** Interlibrary loan; copying; SDI; LATCH; library open to students of the health sciences. **Automated Operations:** Computerized acquisitions, serials, and ILL. **Computerized Information Services:** MEDLARS, BRS Information Technologies, OCLC, WILSONLINE, DIALOG Information Services. Performs searches on fee basis. **Networks/Consortia:** Member of Metropolitan Detroit Medical Library Group

(MDMLG), Health Instructional Resources Associated (HIRA), Michigan Health Sciences Libraries Association (MHSLA), SMHC Library Group. **Publications:** Acquisitions List, monthly; Info-Pack, semiannual - both for internal distribution only. **Staff:** Elaine Kissel, Libn..

★12475★
ST. JOSEPH MERCY HOSPITAL - MEDICAL LIBRARY (Med)
84 Beaumont Dr. Phone: (515)424-7699
Mason City, IA 50401 Judy I. Madson, Dir.
Staff: Prof 1; Other 1. **Subjects:** Medicine, nursing, hospital administration. **Holdings:** 5300 volumes. **Subscriptions:** 250 journals and other serials. **Services:** Interlibrary loan; copying; SDI; library open to the public with restrictions. **Automated Operations:** Computerized cataloging, serials, and ILL. **Computerized Information Services:** MEDLARS, BRS Information Technologies. Performs searches on fee basis. **Networks/ Consortia:** Member of Greater Midwest Regional Medical Library Network.

★12476★
ST. JOSEPH MUSEUM - LIBRARY (Hist)
Eleventh at Charles Phone: (816)232-8471
St. Joseph, MO 64501 Richard A. Nolf, Dir.
Staff: Prof 8; Other 5. **Subjects:** Natural history, North American Indians, Pony Express, history of Western expansion, local and area history. **Special Collections:** American Indian Collection; Civil War period local history collection; Pony Express; bird, mammal, and fish exhibits. **Holdings:** 5600 volumes. **Subscriptions:** 45 journals and other serials. **Services:** Copying; library open to the public for reference use only. **Publications:** Newsletter, bimonthly. **Staff:** Bonnie Harlow, Cur., Coll.; Jackie Lewin, Cur., Hist.; Marilyn Taylor, Cur., Ethnology; June Swift, Exec.Sec.; David Mead, Cur., Natural Hist..

★12477★
ST. JOSEPH NEWS-PRESS & GAZETTE - LIBRARY (Publ)
9th & Edmond Sts. Phone: (816)279-5671
St. Joseph, MO 64502 Don E. Thornton, Dir.
Staff: 1. **Subjects:** Newspaper reference topics. **Holdings:** 55,000 clippings; microfilm. **Subscriptions:** 18 newspapers. **Services:** Library open to the public with director's consent.

★12478★
ST. JOSEPH SEMINARY COLLEGE - PERE ROUQUETTE LIBRARY (Hum, Rel-Phil)
St. Benedict, LA 70457 Phone: (504)892-9895
Rev. Timothy J. Burnett, O.S.B., Dir. of Lib.
Staff: Prof 1; Other 9. **Subjects:** Literature, religion, history, social sciences, psychology, philosophy, sciences, languages, fine arts. **Holdings:** 75,000 books; 6000 bound periodical volumes. **Subscriptions:** 200 journals and other serials. **Services:** Interlibrary loan; copying; SDI; library open to the public for reference use only on request.

★12479★
ST. JOSEPH STATE HOSPITAL - PROFESSIONAL LIBRARY (Med)
3400 Frederick Ave.
Box 263 Phone: (816)232-8431
St. Joseph, MO 64502 Cynthia McAdam, Lib.Dir.
Founded: 1966. **Staff:** Prof 1; Other 1. **Subjects:** Psychiatry, psychology, social service, nursing, education, alcoholism, chaplaincy, therapy, dietetics, pharmacy. **Special Collections:** Complete works of Sigmund Freud. **Holdings:** 1000 books; 600 bound periodical volumes; 700 Audio-Digest tapes; 35 films; AV kits; 8 boxes of slides; 53 cassettes; 100 video cassettes. **Subscriptions:** 62 journals and other serials. **Services:** Interlibrary loan; copying; SDI; library open to the public with restrictions. **Networks/Consortia:** Member of Midcontinental Regional Medical Library Program, Northwest Missouri Library Network. **Publications:** Alcohol and other drugs, quarterly - by mail. **Special Catalogs:** AV holdings.

★12480★
ST. JOSEPH'S ABBEY - LIBRARY (Rel-Phil)
Rte. 31, N. Spencer Rd. Phone: (508)885-3901
Spencer, MA 01562 Fr. Basil Byrne, Libn.
Founded: 1951. **Staff:** Prof 1. **Subjects:** Theology; Biblical studies; philosophy; patristics; history - church, ancient, medieval, modern; psychology; sociology. **Holdings:** 40,000 books. **Subscriptions:** 65 journals and other serials; 5 newspapers. **Services:** Interlibrary loan; library open to the public with restrictions.

★12481★
ST. JOSEPH'S GENERAL HOSPITAL - MEDICAL LIBRARY (Med)
P.O. Box 3251 Phone: (807)343-2431
Thunder Bay, ON, Canada P7B 5G7 Karen Houseman, Libn.
Founded: 1961. **Staff:** Prof 1. **Subjects:** Medicine, nursing, management, rehabilitation, ethics. **Holdings:** 800 books; 460 bound periodical volumes. **Subscriptions:** 42 journals and other serials. **Services:** Interlibrary loan; copying; library open to college and university students with permission. **Networks/Consortia:** Member of Northwestern Ontario Medical Programme Library Network (NOMP).

★12482★
ST. JOSEPH'S HEALTH CENTRE - GEORGE PENNAL LIBRARY (Med)
30 The Queensway Phone: (416)530-6726
Toronto, ON, Canada M6R 1B5 Barbara Iwasiuk, Med.Libn.
Founded: 1963. **Staff:** Prof 1; Other 1. **Subjects:** Medicine, nursing, hospital administration, pastoral care. **Holdings:** 3500 books; 3000 bound periodical volumes. **Subscriptions:** 172 journals and other serials. **Services:** Interlibrary loan; library not open to the public. **Automated Operations:** Computerized cataloging, acquisitions, serials, and circulation. **Computerized Information Services:** MEDLARS. **Publications:** Health Administration Update, quarterly.

★12483★
ST. JOSEPH'S HEALTH CENTRE OF LONDON - LIBRARY SERVICES (Med)
268 Grosvenor St. Phone: (519)439-3271
London, ON, Canada N6A 4V2 Louise Lin, Mgr., Lib.Serv.
Founded: 1966. **Staff:** Prof 1; Other 2. **Subjects:** Clinical medicine, nursing, allied health sciences. **Special Collections:** World Health Organization International Histological Classification of Tumors (books and slides). **Holdings:** 3000 books; 5422 bound periodical volumes; 2000 physical diagnosis teaching slides; 2000 hematology teaching slides. **Subscriptions:** 342 journals and other serials. **Services:** Interlibrary loan; copying; services open to the public for reference use only. **Computerized Information Services:** MEDLINE. Performs searches on fee basis.

★12484★
ST. JOSEPH'S HOSPITAL - DRUG INFORMATION CENTRE (Med)
50 Charlton Ave., E. Phone: (416)522-4941
Hamilton, ON, Canada L8N 4A6
Mrs. D. Thompson, Dir., Pharm.Serv.
Staff: 1. **Subjects:** Drugs, pharmacology, disease, clinical pharmacy services, pharmaceutical techniques. **Holdings:** 175 volumes; 75 cassette tapes; 25 videotapes; archives and teaching files. **Subscriptions:** 17 journals and other serials. **Services:** Interlibrary loan; center open to public with approval.

★12485★
ST. JOSEPH'S HOSPITAL - HEALTH SCIENCE LIBRARY (Med)
220 Pawtucket St. Phone: (508)453-1761
Lowell, MA 01854 Anne C. Dick, Lib.Dir.
Founded: 1971. **Staff:** Prof 1; Other 1. **Subjects:** Medicine and nursing. **Holdings:** 3050 volumes. **Subscriptions:** 200 journals and other serials. **Services:** Interlibrary loan; copying; library open to the public for reference use only. **Networks/Consortia:** Member of Northeastern Consortium for Health Information (NECHI).

★12486★
ST. JOSEPH'S HOSPITAL - HEALTH SCIENCES LIBRARY (Med)
350 W. Thomas Rd.
Box 2071 Phone: (605)285-3299
Phoenix, AZ 85001 Kay E. Wellik, Mgr., Lib.Serv.
Founded: 1942. **Staff:** Prof 1; Other 3. **Subjects:** Medicine. **Special Collections:** Library of neurological sciences. **Holdings:** 4500 books; 8500 bound periodical volumes. **Subscriptions:** 380 journals and other serials. **Services:** Interlibrary loan; library not open to the public. **Computerized Information Services:** MEDLARS, BRS Information Technologies, DIALOG Information Services; OnTyme Electronic Message Network Service (electronic mail service).

★12487★
ST. JOSEPH'S HOSPITAL - HELENE FULD LEARNING RESOURCE CENTER (Med)
555 E. Market St. Phone: (607)733-6541
Elmira, NY 14902 Arlene C. Pien, Libn.
Founded: 1975. **Staff:** Prof 1; Other 1. **Subjects:** Medicine, nursing. **Holdings:** 5000 books; 4000 bound periodical volumes; 1500 AV programs; 10 drawers of pamphlets. **Subscriptions:** 165 journals and other serials. **Services:** Interlibrary loan; copying. **Computerized Information Services:** Online systems. Performs searches on fee basis.

★12488★
ST. JOSEPH'S HOSPITAL - HOSPITAL LIBRARY (Med)
50 Charlton Ave., E. Phone: (416)522-4941
Hamilton, ON, Canada L8N 1Y4 Mrs. S.L. Rogers, Hosp.Libn.
Founded: 1964. **Staff:** 2. **Subjects:** Medicine, hospital administration. **Special Collections:** Sir William Osler Collection. **Holdings:** 1600 books; 7000 bound periodical volumes. **Subscriptions:** 150 journals and other serials. **Services:** Library not open to the public.

★12489★
ST. JOSEPH'S HOSPITAL - JEROME MEDICAL LIBRARY (Med)
69 W. Exchange St. Phone: (612)291-3193
St. Paul, MN 55102 Karen Brudvig, Med.Libn.
Founded: 1949. **Staff:** Prof 1. **Subjects:** Medicine, hospital administration, nursing. **Holdings:** 2500 books; 2900 bound periodical volumes. **Subscriptions:** 153 journals and other serials. **Services:** Interlibrary loan; copying; library open to the public for reference use only. **Computerized Information Services:** BRS Information Technologies. **Networks/Consortia:** Member of Twin Cities Biomedical Consortium (TCBC).

★12490★
ST. JOSEPH'S HOSPITAL - LEARNING RESOURCE CENTER (Med)
611 St. Joseph Ave. Phone: (715)387-7374
Marshfield, WI 54449 Margaret A. Allen, Libn.
Founded: 1914. **Staff:** Prof 1; Other 2. **Subjects:** Nursing. **Holdings:** 7800 books; 881 bound periodical volumes; 10 VF drawers of pamphlets; school archives; 1054 AV programs. **Subscriptions:** 120 journals and other serials. **Services:** Interlibrary loan; copying; center open to the public with restrictions. **Networks/Consortia:** Member of Northern Wisconsin Health Science Libraries Cooperative. **Publications:** Current Awareness Service, biweekly. **Special Catalogs:** Audiovisual catalog. **Remarks:** Includes a 2800 volume patient library.

★12491★
ST. JOSEPH'S HOSPITAL - MEDICAL LIBRARY (Med)
3000 W. Buffalo Ave.
Box 4227 Phone: (813)870-4658
Tampa, FL 33677 Adelia P. Seglin, Dir., Med.Lib.
Staff: Prof 2; Other 1. **Subjects:** Medicine, nursing, cancer, pharmacology, management, cardiology. **Holdings:** 1500 books; 5800 bound periodical volumes. **Subscriptions:** 257 journals and other serials. **Services:** Interlibrary loan; library not open to the public. **Computerized Information Services:** MEDLARS, DIALOG Information Services, BRS Information Technologies, WILSONLINE. Performs searches on fee basis. **Networks/Consortia:** Member of Tampa Bay Medical Library Network. **Staff:** Mrs. Gita Halder, Med.Libn..

★12492★
ST. JOSEPH'S HOSPITAL - MEDICAL LIBRARY (Med)
11705 Mercy Blvd. Phone: (912)925-4100
Savannah, GA 31419 Judy G. Henry, Libn.
Staff: Prof 1. **Subjects:** Medicine, surgery, nursing, allied health sciences. **Holdings:** 750 books; 150 bound periodical volumes; 100 pamphlets; 80 filmstrips with records; 4 VF drawers. **Subscriptions:** 104 journals and other serials. **Services:** Interlibrary loan; copying; library open to the public with restrictions. **Computerized Information Services:** Online systems.

★12493★
ST. JOSEPH'S HOSPITAL - RUSSELL BELLMAN MEDICAL LIBRARY (Med)
5665 Peachtree Dunwoody Rd., N.E. Phone: (404)851-7040
Atlanta, GA 30342 Gail Waverchak, Hea.Sci.Libn.
Founded: 1965. **Staff:** Prof 1; Other 1. **Subjects:** Medicine, nursing, hospital administration, allied health sciences. **Special Collections:** Medical Ethics. **Holdings:** 4000 books; 4113 bound periodical volumes. **Subscriptions:** 210 journals and other serials. **Services:** Interlibrary loan. **Automated Operations:** Computerized cataloging and ILL. **Computerized Information Services:** NLM, OCLC. Performs searches on fee basis. **Networks/Consortia:** Member of Atlanta Health Science Libraries Consortium, Georgia Library Information Network (GLIN), Georgia Health Sciences Library Association (GHSLA), SOLINET.

★12494★
ST. JOSEPH'S HOSPITAL - SAMUEL ROSENTHAL MEMORIAL LIBRARY (Med)
5000 W. Chambers St. Phone: (414)447-2194
Milwaukee, WI 53210 Sunja Shaikh, Med.Libn.
Founded: 1967. **Staff:** Prof 1. **Subjects:** Medicine. **Holdings:** 3000 books; 8000 bound periodical volumes; 150 Audio-Digest tapes. **Subscriptions:** 150 journals and other serials. **Services:** Interlibrary loan; copying; SDI; library open to the public for reference use only. **Computerized Information Services:** BRS Information Technologies, MEDLINE; DOCLINE (electronic mail service). Performs searches on fee basis. **Networks/Consortia:** Member of Southeastern Wisconsin Health Science Library Consortium (SWHSL). **Publications:** Library Newsletter, bimonthly. **Special Indexes:** Library Journal Holdings List (online).

★12495★
ST. JOSEPH'S HOSPITAL - SCHOOL OF NURSING LIBRARY
700 Broadway
Fort Wayne, IN 46802
Defunct

★12496★
ST. JOSEPH'S HOSPITAL CENTERS - MEDICAL LIBRARY (East Site) (Med)
215 North Ave. Phone: (313)466-9485
Mt. Clemens, MI 48043 Sandra A. Studebaker, Dir.
Staff: Prof 2. **Subjects:** Medicine, nursing, allied health sciences, consumer health, management. **Holdings:** 3650 titles; 3500 bound periodical volumes. **Subscriptions:** 485 journals and other serials. **Services:** Interlibrary loan; copying; current awareness; library open to the public for reference use only. **Computerized Information Services:** NLM, BRS Information Technologies. **Networks/Consortia:** Member of Metropolitan Detroit Medical Library Group (MDMLG). **Publications:** Library Acquisitions List, monthly - for internal distribution only. **Remarks:** The west site library is located at 15855 19 Mile Rd., Mt. Clemens, MI 48044; the telephone number is 263-2485. **Staff:** Mary Lou Hubbard, Med.Libn..

★12497★
ST. JOSEPH'S HOSPITAL & HEALTH CENTER - BRUCE M. COLE MEMORIAL LIBRARY (Med)
350 N. Wilmot Phone: (602)296-3211
Tucson, AZ 85711 Marcia Church, Libn.
Staff: Prof 1; Other 5. **Subjects:** Surgery, internal medicine, infection control, ophthalmology, nursing. **Special Collections:** Alcoholism (45 books; 25 AV programs; 6 journal subscriptions). **Holdings:** 1000 books; 1100 bound periodical volumes; 50 other cataloged items. **Subscriptions:** 154 journals and other serials. **Services:** Interlibrary loan; copying; SDI; library open to the public with doctor's approval. **Computerized Information Services:** MEDLARS, BRS Information Technologies; OnTyme Electronic Message Network Service (electronic mail service). **Networks/Consortia:** Member of Pacific Southwest Regional Medical Library Service.

★12498★
ST. JOSEPH'S HOSPITAL AND HEALTH CENTER - MEDICAL LIBRARY (Med)
30 W. 7th St. Phone: (701)225-7267
Dickinson, ND 58601 Sr. Salome Tlusty, Lib.Ck.
Founded: 1951. **Staff:** 1. **Subjects:** Medicine. **Holdings:** 1328 books. **Subscriptions:** 206 journals and other serials. **Services:** Interlibrary loan; library not open to the public. **Automated Operations:** Computerized cataloging and circulation. **Networks/Consortia:** Member of Greater Midwest Regional Medical Library Network.

★12499★
ST. JOSEPH'S HOSPITAL HEALTH CENTER - MEDICAL AND SCHOOL OF NURSING LIBRARIES (Med)
301 Prospect Ave. Phone: (315)424-5053
Syracuse, NY 13203 Mr. V. Juchimek, Hd.Libn.
Founded: 1940. **Staff:** Prof 2; Other 2. **Subjects:** Nursing, medicine, psychology, social sciences, religion. **Holdings:** 10,000 books; 2000 bound periodical volumes; 30 VF drawers of pamphlets; 200 cassette programs; models; slides; filmstrips; recordings. **Subscriptions:** 195 journals and other serials. **Services:** Interlibrary loan (limited); libraries open to the public for reference use only. **Publications:** Accessions List, monthly; Exchange List.

★12500★
ST. JOSEPH'S HOSPITAL AND MEDICAL CENTER - HEALTH SCIENCES LIBRARY (Med)
703 Main St. Phone: (201)977-2104
Paterson, NJ 07503 Patricia May, Lib.Serv.
Staff: Prof 4; Other 1. **Subjects:** Medicine, biological sciences, dentistry, psychology, nursing. **Holdings:** 4500 books; 4800 bound periodical volumes. **Subscriptions:** 275 journals and other serials. **Services:** Interlibrary loan; copying; library open to the public for reference use only. **Computerized Information Services:** MEDLARS, DIALOG Information Services. **Networks/Consortia:** Member of Bergen-Passaic Health Sciences Library Consortium. **Staff:** Hannah Berkley, Libn.; Eleanor Cohen, Asst.Med.Libn.; Mary Ann Obremski, Asst.Med.Libn.; Vicky Spitalniak, Asst.Med.Libn..

★12501★
ST. JOSEPH'S MEDICAL CENTER - LIBRARY (Med)
1800 N. California St. Phone: (209)467-6332
Stockton, CA 95204 Doreen Brown, Lib.Coord.
Staff: Prof 1. **Subjects:** Medicine, nursing, hospital administration, human relations. **Holdings:** 400 books; 840 bound periodical volumes; 50 video cassettes. **Subscriptions:** 106 journals and other serials. **Services:** Interlibrary loan; library not open to the public. **Formerly:** St. Joseph's Hospital - Hospital Library.

★12502★
ST. JOSEPH'S MEDICAL CENTER - LIBRARY (Med)
700 Broadway Phone: (219)423-3094
Fort Wayne, IN 46802 Michael T. Sheets, Dir., Med.Lib.
Founded: 1945. **Staff:** Prof 3; Other 1. **Subjects:** Medicine, hospital administration. **Holdings:** 1500 books; 3000 bound periodical volumes; 350 reels of microfilm; 105,000 microfiche. **Subscriptions:** 391 journals and other serials. **Services:** Interlibrary loan; library not open to the public. **Computerized Information Services:** NLM, BRS Information Technologies. **Networks/Consortia:** Member of Northeastern Indiana Health Science Library Consortium. **Staff:** Marla Baden, Med.Libn..

★12503★
ST. JOSEPH'S MEDICAL CENTER - MEDICAL LIBRARY (Med)
811 E. Madison St.
Box 1935 Phone: (219)237-7228
South Bend, IN 46634-1935 Donna J. Bayless, Libn.
Founded: 1981. **Staff:** Prof 1; Other 1. **Subjects:** Medicine, nursing, pharmacy, health administration, pastoral care, social work. **Holdings:** 2955 books; 13,170 unbound periodicals; 580 documents, pamphlets, brochures, and clippings; 50 video cassettes; 13 drawers of microfiche. **Subscriptions:** 280 journals and other serials. **Services:** Interlibrary loan; copying; library open to the public. **Computerized Information Services:** BRS Information Technologies, MEDLARS. Performs searches free of charge. **Networks/Consortia:** Member of Area 2 Library Services Authority (ALSA 2), INCOLSA, Greater Midwest Regional Medical Library Network, National Library of Medicine (NLM).

★12504★
ST. JOSEPH'S MEDICAL CENTER - MEDICAL LIBRARY (Med)
127 S. Broadway Phone: (914)965-6700
Yonkers, NY 10701 Anita H. Weatherup, Lib.Mgr.
Staff: Prof 1; Other 1. **Subjects:** Medicine. **Holdings:** 2218 volumes. **Subscriptions:** 110 journals and other serials. **Services:** Interlibrary loan; library open to the public by appointment.

★12505★
ST. JOSEPH'S SEMINARY - ARCHBISHOP CORRIGAN MEMORIAL LIBRARY (Rel-Phil)
201 Seminary Ave. Phone: (914)968-6200
Yonkers, NY 10704 Sr. Ellen E. Gaffney, RDC, Lib.Dir.
Founded: 1953. **Staff:** Prof 3; Other 3. **Subjects:** Sacred scripture, moral and dogmatic theology, liturgy, canon law, patristics. **Special Collections:** Archdiocesan Archives. **Holdings:** 95,000 books; 10,600 bound periodical volumes. **Subscriptions:** 400 journals and other serials; 7 newspapers. **Services:** Interlibrary loan; copying; library open to the public for reference use only. **Automated Operations:** Computerized cataloging. **Computerized Information Services:** OCLC. **Networks/Consortia:** Member of SUNY/OCLC Library Network. **Publications:** Recent Acquisitions, monthly - to faculty and students. **Staff:** Barbara Carey, Asst.Libn.; Sr. Kathleen McCann, Per.Libn..

★12506★
ST. JOSEPH'S SEMINARY - LIBRARY (Rel-Phil, Area-Ethnic)
1200 Varnum St., N.E. Phone: (202)526-4231
Washington, DC 20017 Laurence A. Schmitt, Libn.
Founded: 1930. **Staff:** Prof 1; Other 1. **Subjects:** Philosophy and theology, black studies. **Holdings:** 24,000 volumes. **Subscriptions:** 75 journals and other serials. **Services:** Interlibrary loan (limited); library open to the public by appointment.

ST. JOSEPH'S SHRINE
See: Oratoire St-Joseph (10884)

★12507★
ST. JOSEPH'S UNIVERSITY - ACADEMY OF FOOD MARKETING - CAMPBELL LIBRARY (Food-Bev)
54th & City Line Ave. Phone: (215)879-7489
Philadelphia, PA 19131 Anna Mae Penrose, Libn.
Founded: 1965. **Staff:** Prof 1; Other 2. **Subjects:** Food marketing, retailing, consumerism, agricultural products. **Special Collections:** Bound food trade journals; U.S. Department of Agriculture Yearbooks, 1865 to present. **Holdings:** 3905 books; 1350 bound periodical volumes; 1710 items in corporation files; 160 reels of microfilm; journals and doctoral dissertations; 4372 subject information files. **Subscriptions:** 233 journals and other serials. **Services:** Interlibrary loan; copying; library open to the public for reference use only, reciprocal privileges extended to food industry libraries and organizations. **Computerized Information Services:** DIALOG Information Services. **Publications:** Serials Holdings, annual; Selected Acquisitions; internal bibliographies.

★12508★
ST. JUDE CHILDREN'S RESEARCH HOSPITAL - RESEARCH LIBRARY (Med)
332 N. Lauderdale
Box 318 Phone: (901)525-0388
Memphis, TN 38101 Mary Edith Walker, Med.Libn.
Founded: 1962. **Staff:** Prof 1; Other 2. **Subjects:** Medicine, biological sciences, chemistry. **Holdings:** 2100 books; 10,000 bound periodical volumes; 15 dissertations; 300 audio cassettes; 80 AV programs. **Subscriptions:** 255 journals and other serials. **Services:** Interlibrary loan; copying; SDI; library open to medical professionals only for reference use. **Computerized Information Services:** DIALOG Information Services, PaperChase, MEDLINE; DOCLINE, OnTyme Electronic Message Network Service (electronic mail services). **Networks/Consortia:** Member of Association of Memphis Area Health Sciences Libraries (AMAHSL). **Publications:** Library Notes - for internal distribution only.

★12509★
ST. JUDE HOSPITAL & REHABILITATION CENTER - MEDICAL LIBRARY (Med)
101 E. Valencia Mesa Dr. Phone: (714)992-2000
Fullerton, CA 92635 Barbara Garside, Med.Libn.
Founded: 1974. **Staff:** Prof 1. **Subjects:** Medicine, nursing. **Holdings:** 500 books; 20 sound-slide sets; 100 video cassettes. **Subscriptions:** 105 journals and other serials. **Services:** Interlibrary loan; copying; SDI; library open to consortia members and local librarians. **Networks/Consortia:** Member of Nursing Information Consortium of Orange County (NICOC), Medical Library Group of Southern California and Arizona (MLGSCA).

★12510★
ST. LAWRENCE COLLEGE SAINT-LAURENT - LEARNING RESOURCE CENTRE (Educ)
Windmill Point Phone: (613)933-6080
Cornwall, ON, Canada K6H 4Z1 Shirley E. McGlynn, Libn.
Founded: 1967. **Staff:** 6. **Subjects:** Education, psychology, social sciences, literature, art, technology. **Special Collections:** St. Lawrence College Saint-Laurent (Cornwall) Archives. **Holdings:** 50,000 volumes. **Subscriptions:** 210 journals and other serials; 7 newspapers. **Services:** Interlibrary loan; copying; center open to the public. **Remarks:** Maintains a toy lending library.

★12511★
ST. LAWRENCE COLLEGE SAINT-LAURENT - LEARNING RESOURCE CENTRE (Hum, Sci-Engr)
King & Portsmouth
Box 6000 Phone: (613)544-5400
Kingston, ON, Canada K7L 5A6 Sherwin Raichman, Hd.
Founded: 1967. **Staff:** Prof 2; Other 9. **Subjects:** Humanities, technologies, nursing, arts, business. **Holdings:** 73,000 books; 1725 bound periodical volumes; 4100 government documents; 9700 nonprint items. **Subscriptions:** 590 journals and other serials; 18 newspapers. **Services:** Interlibrary loan;

copying; center open to the public. **Automated Operations:** Computerized cataloging. **Computerized Information Services:** QL Systems, Info Globe, DIALOG Information Services, Infomart, CAN/OLE. **Special Catalogs:** Union list of campus libraries in Brockville and Cornwall, Ontario; union list of medical serials in Kingston and area institutions. **Staff:** Barbara Carr, Ref.Libn.; Barbara Love, Ref.Libn..

★12512★
ST. LAWRENCE COUNTY HISTORICAL ASSOCIATION - ARCHIVES (Hist)
3 E. Main St.
Box 8
Canton, NY 13617 Phone: (315)386-8133
Founded: 1947. **Staff:** Prof 2; Other 6. **Subjects:** St. Lawrence County history. **Special Collections:** Silas Wright Papers (250 items); local genealogy (1000 items). **Holdings:** 1500 books; 150 bound periodical volumes; 4000 maps, clippings, pamphlets, documents. **Services:** Copying; archives open to the public. **Staff:** Marcia Thompson Archv. Aide.

★12513★
ST. LAWRENCE HOSPITAL - MEDICAL LIBRARY (Med)
1210 W. Saginaw Phone: (515)377-0354
Lansing, MI 48915 Jane B. Claytor, Mgr.
Staff: Prof 2. **Subjects:** Medicine, nursing, mental health, hospital management. **Holdings:** 2560 books; 4900 bound periodical volumes. **Subscriptions:** 325 journals and other serials. **Services:** Interlibrary loan; copying; library open to health care professionals. **Computerized Information Services:** MEDLARS, BRS Information Technologies, WILSONLINE, DIALOG Information Services. Performs searches free of charge. **Networks/Consortia:** Member of Capitol Area Library Network (CALNET), Michigan Library Consortium (MLC), Michigan Health Sciences Libraries Association (MHSLA). **Staff:** CiSi Dillberger, Med.Lib.Asst..

ST. LAWRENCE PSYCHIATRIC CENTER
See: New York State Office of Mental Health (10130)

★12514★
ST. LAWRENCE SEMINARY - LIBRARY (Rel-Phil)
301 Church St. Phone: (414)753-3911
Mount Calvary, WI 53057 Sr. Elaine Basche, Libn.
Staff: Prof 1; Other 1. **Subjects:** Religion, English literature, classical studies. **Holdings:** 15,465 books; 2 VF drawers of pamphlets; 288 reels of microfilm of periodicals; 400 video cassettes; 325 sound filmstrip titles. **Subscriptions:** 100 journals and other serials; 10 newspapers. **Services:** Library not open to the public. **Remarks:** Maintained by the Province of St. Joseph of the Capuchin Order.

★12515★
ST. LAWRENCE UNIVERSITY - SPECIAL COLLECTIONS (Hist)
Owen D. Young Library Phone: (315)379-5476
Canton, NY 13617 Lynn Ekfelt, Cur.
Subjects: 19th century farm, village, and family life in the northern counties of New York; political, cultural, and industrial history of the area. **Special Collections:** Papers of Irving Bacheller, Frederic Remington, David Parish, Nathaniel Hawthorne, Redington, and Robert McEwen. **Holdings:** 1500 linear feet of manuscripts, documents, and other materials. **Services:** Interlibrary loan (limited); copying; collections open to the public. **Automated Operations:** Computerized cataloging and acquisitions. **Computerized Information Services:** DIALOG Information Services, OCLC, BRS Information Technologies. **Networks/Consortia:** Member of New York State Interlibrary Loan Network (NYSILL), Associated Colleges of the St. Lawrence Valley, Inc. (ACSLV).

★12516★
ST. LOUIS ART MUSEUM - RICHARDSON MEMORIAL LIBRARY (Art)
Forest Park Phone: (314)721-0067
St. Louis, MO 63110 Stephanie C. Sigala, Hd.Libn.
Founded: 1915. **Staff:** Prof 3; Other 4. **Subjects:** Art history, painting, sculpture, decorative arts, American art, graphic arts. **Special Collections:** Museum archives. **Holdings:** 40,000 books and bound periodical volumes; 35,000 pamphlets; 20,000 mounted photographs; 25,000 slides; 15,000 art auction catalogs. **Subscriptions:** 300 journals and other serials. **Services:** Interlibrary loan; copying (both limited); library open to adult public. **Automated Operations:** Computerized cataloging. **Networks/Consortia:** Member of St. Louis Regional Library Network, RLG. **Special Indexes:** Bulletin of St. Louis Art Museum; St. Louis Artist Files. **Staff:** Norma Sindelar, Archv.; Dana L. Beth, Asst.Libn..

★12517★
ST. LOUIS CHILDREN'S HOSPITAL - CHILDREN'S HOSPITAL LIBRARY (Med)
400 S. Kingshighway Blvd.
Box 14871 Phone: (314)454-6000
St. Louis, MO 63178 Ileen R. Kendall, Libn.
Founded: 1968. **Staff:** Prof 1. **Subjects:** Medicine, pediatrics, nursing. **Holdings:** 1800 books; 1239 bound periodical volumes; 187 audio cassettes; 27 volumes of staff publications, 1920-1983; annuals. **Subscriptions:** 117 journals and other serials. **Services:** Interlibrary loan; copying; SDI; library open to the public for reference use only. **Computerized Information Services:** BACS Data Base; internal database.

★12518★
ST. LOUIS CHRISTIAN COLLEGE - LIBRARY (Rel-Phil)
1360 Grandview Dr. Phone: (314)837-6777
Florissant, MO 63033 Jerry D. Kennedy, Libn.
Founded: 1956. **Staff:** Prof 1; Other 2. **Subjects:** Restoration, Christian Church, Bible, church history, religions. **Holdings:** 44,000 books; 60 bound periodical volumes; 14,000 volumes on microfiche; 1500 reels of microfilm of Restoration-Christian Church history and Bible commentaries. **Subscriptions:** 138 journals and other serials. **Services:** Interlibrary loan; copying; library open to the public. **Special Catalogs:** Booklet of new additions.

★12519★
ST. LOUIS COLLEGE OF PHARMACY - O.J. CLOUGHLY ALUMNI LIBRARY (Med)
4588 Parkview Place Phone: (314)367-8700
St. Louis, MO 63110 Helen F. Silverman, Lib.Dir.
Staff: Prof 2; Other 2. **Subjects:** Pharmacy, pharmacology, medicine, drug information. **Holdings:** 28,000 books; 5000 bound periodical volumes; 500 audiotapes and microforms. **Subscriptions:** 410 journals and other serials; 8 newspapers. **Services:** Interlibrary loan; copying; library open to the public for reference use only. **Automated Operations:** Computerized cataloging. **Computerized Information Services:** BRS Information Technologies, DIALOG Information Services. **Networks/Consortia:** Member of Missouri Library Network (MLNC), St. Louis Regional Library Network. **Publications:** New Accession List, bimonthly. **Staff:** Beth Carlin, Asst.Libn..

★12520★
ST. LOUIS COMPTROLLERS OFFICE - MICROFILM DEPARTMENT (Hist)
1200 Market St. Phone: (314)622-4274
St. Louis, MO 63103 Edward J. Machowski, Mgr.
Founded: 1960. **Staff:** Prof 3; Other 9. **Subjects:** St. Louis, Missouri; genealogy. **Special Collections:** French, English, and Spanish documents to 1901; French and Spanish land grants; birth records, 1863-1909; death records, 1850-1909; cancelled voter affidavits, 1896-1983; building information, 1876-1977; plans, 1940 to present. **Holdings:** 50,000 reels of microfilm of fiscal records, vital statistics, building and tax records. **Services:** Copying; department open to the public with restrictions. **Staff:** Ruth Brown, Asst.Mgr.; Mary Kelso, Adm.Asst..

★12521★
ST. LOUIS CONSERVATORY AND SCHOOLS FOR THE ARTS (CASA) - MAE M. WHITAKER LIBRARY (Mus)
560 Trinity Ave. Phone: (314)863-3033
St. Louis, MO 63130 Marion Sherman, Libn.
Founded: 1974. **Staff:** Prof 1; Other 4. **Subjects:** Music. **Special Collections:** Performance and listening libraries; Thomas B. Sherman Collection; Robert Orchard Opera Collection; Max Risch Wind Ensemble and Bassoon Music Collection. **Holdings:** 12,336 books and scores; 198 bound periodical volumes; 9114 phonograph records and tapes; 2 VF drawers of music publishers' catalogs; 1915 microfiche. **Subscriptions:** 40 journals and other serials. **Services:** Interlibrary loan; library open to the public for reference use only. **Networks/Consortia:** Member of St. Louis Regional Library Network. **Special Catalogs:** Catalog of music for performance.

ST. LOUIS COUNTY HISTORICAL SOCIETY - NORTHEAST MINNESOTA HISTORICAL CENTER
See: Northeast Minnesota Historical Center (10391)

★12522★
ST. LOUIS COUNTY LAW LIBRARY (Law)
100 N. Fifth Ave., W., Rm. 515 Phone: (218)726-2611
Duluth, MN 55802 Michele Des Rosier, Law Libn.
Founded: 1889. **Staff:** Prof 1. **Subjects:** Law. **Holdings:** 20,000 books. **Services:** Copying; library open to the public for reference use only.

★12523★
ST. LOUIS COUNTY LAW LIBRARY (Law)
Courts Bldg.
7900 Carondelet Ave., Suite 536 Phone: (314)889-2726
Clayton, MO 63105 Mary C. Dahm, Libn.
Staff: Prof 1; Other 2. **Subjects:** Law. **Holdings:** 18,600 volumes. **Subscriptions:** 17 journals and other serials. **Services:** Copying; library open to the public.

★12524★
ST. LOUIS GENEALOGICAL SOCIETY - LIBRARY (Hist)
University City Public Library
1695 S. Brentwood Blvd., Rm. 210 Phone: (314)968-2763
St. Louis, MO 63144 Lorraine Cates, Libn.
Subjects: Genealogy. **Special Collections:** Daughters of the American Revolution collection (lineage books and indexes; bound volumes of DAR Magazine, 1896 to present). **Holdings:** 18,000 books; microfilm; microfiche; cassette tapes. **Services:** Copying; library open to the public. **Special Indexes:** Index to 1860 St. Louis City & County Census (book).

★12525★
ST. LOUIS HEARING AND SPEECH CENTER - LIBRARY (Med)
9526 Manchester Phone: (314)968-4710
St. Louis, MO 63119 Peggy Thompson, Exec.Dir.
Staff: 18. **Subjects:** Audiology, speech pathology, sign language, industrial hearing conservation, noise pollution, stutterers, preschool language. **Holdings:** 600 volumes. **Services:** Interlibrary loan; library open to the public. **Publications:** Health Information.

★12526★
ST. LOUIS MERCANTILE LIBRARY ASSOCIATION - LIBRARY (Hum)
510 Locust St.
Box 633 Phone: (314)621-0670
St. Louis, MO 63188 Charles F. Bryan, Jr., Exec.Dir.
Founded: 1846. **Staff:** Prof 4; Other 10. **Subjects:** History, biography, social sciences, science, fine arts, fiction, literature. **Special Collections:** Alchemy, dating to 1420; early Western Americana; early French and German literature; early state papers; Colonial Dames of America (155 items; pamphlets); Herman T. Pott National Inland Waterways Collection (10,000 volumes; pamphlets; documents); John W. Barriger, III Railroad Collection (11,000 volumes; 40,000 photographs; papers and files); St. Louis Globe-Democrat morgue (10 million clippings; 125,000 photographs). **Holdings:** 255,000 books; manuscripts; broadsides. **Subscriptions:** 241 journals and other serials. **Services:** Interlibrary loan; copying; library open to the public with restrictions. **Automated Operations:** Computerized cataloging. **Computerized Information Services:** OCLC. **Networks/Consortia:** Member of St. Louis Regional Library Network. **Publications:** New Books Bulletin, monthly; annual reports. **Staff:** John N. Hoover, Asst. & Spec.Coll.Libn.; Mark Cedeck, Barriger Lib.Cur.; David Cassens, Pott Lib.Cur..

★12527★
ST. LOUIS METROPOLITAN MEDICAL SOCIETY - ST. LOUIS SOCIETY FOR MEDICAL AND SCIENTIFIC EDUCATION - LIBRARY (Med)
3839 Lindell Blvd. Phone: (314)371-5225
St. Louis, MO 63108 Audrey L. Berkley, Libn.
Founded: 1899. **Staff:** Prof 2; Other 1. **Subjects:** Clinical application of medicine. **Special Collections:** Paracelsus Collection (400 items); St. Louis history of medicine (500 items). **Holdings:** 25,000 books; 44,000 bound periodical volumes; 10 file cabinets of archives. **Subscriptions:** 400 journals and other serials; 8 newspapers. **Services:** Interlibrary loan (fee); copying; library open to the public for reference use only. **Computerized Information Services:** BRS Information Technologies, Octanet, MEDLINE, AMA/NET. Performs searches on fee basis. **Networks/Consortia:** Member of Missouri Library Network (MLNC). **Staff:** Kala Sirdesmuth, Asst.Libn..

★12528★
ST. LOUIS METROPOLITAN POLICE DEPARTMENT - LIBRARY (Soc Sci, Law)
315 S. Tucker Phone: (314)444-5581
St. Louis, MO 63102 Barbara L. Miksicek, Libn.
Founded: 1947. **Staff:** Prof 1. **Subjects:** Police science, criminology, corrections, juvenile delinquency, criminal law, narcotics. **Special Collections:** Annual Reports, 1861 to present. **Holdings:** 21,000 books; 1002 bound periodical volumes; 515 titles on microfiche; 20 VF drawers of reports, pamphlets, clippings, manuscripts; 466 pictures. **Subscriptions:** 153 journals and other serials. **Services:** Interlibrary loan; copying; library open to the public for reference use only. **Networks/Consortia:** Member of St. Louis Regional Library Network, Criminal Justice Information Exchange Group. **Publications:** Bibliographies; Directory of Law Enforcement Agencies in Metropolitan St. Louis. **Special Indexes:** Index of articles in eight police journals (card); index of St. Louis Police Journal, 1912 to present (card).

★12529★
ST. LOUIS POST-DISPATCH - REFERENCE LIBRARY (Publ)
900 N. Tucker Blvd. Phone: (314)622-7535
St. Louis, MO 63101 Gerald D. Brown, Lib.Dir.
Staff: Prof 2; Other 13. **Subjects:** Newspaper reference topics. **Holdings:** 800 books; 2500 reports and pamphlets; 10 million clippings; 2.5 million photographs. **Subscriptions:** 15 journals and other serials. **Services:** Copying; library open to the public by appointment on fee basis. **Computerized Information Services:** VU/TEXT Information Services; UNIDAS 1100/72 (internal database). Performs searches on fee basis by mail only. **Staff:** Michael A. Marler, Asst.Lib.Dir..

★12530★
ST. LOUIS PSYCHOANALYTIC INSTITUTE - BETTY GOLDE SMITH MEMORIAL LIBRARY (Med)
4524 Forest Park Blvd. Phone: (314)361-7075
St. Louis, MO 63108 Rheba Symeonoglou, Libn.
Founded: 1956. **Staff:** Prof 1; Other 1. **Subjects:** Psychoanalysis and related subjects. **Holdings:** 6000 volumes. **Subscriptions:** 33 journals and other serials. **Services:** Interlibrary loan; copying; literature searching; library open to the public. **Publications:** Newsletter, 3/year - to mailing list.

★12531★
ST. LOUIS PUBLIC LIBRARY - APPLIED SCIENCE DEPARTMENT (Sci-Engr)
Central Library
1301 Olive St. Phone: (314)241-2288
St. Louis, MO 63103-2389 Stephanie Dohner, Dept.Hd.
Founded: 1912. **Staff:** Prof 2; Other 1. **Subjects:** Engineering; electricity and electronics; materials science; manufacturing processes; home remodeling; radio, TV, and automobile repair. **Holdings:** 20,000 books; 45,000 bound periodical volumes; complete collection of U.S. patents; complete collection of British standards; 34 VF drawers of Sams Photofacts; 2000 VF envelopes; 24 VF drawers and 2 boxes of microfiche of industrial standards; 2000 automobile repair manuals. **Subscriptions:** 1000 journals and other serials. **Services:** Interlibrary loan; copying; department open to the public. **Computerized Information Services:** U.S. Patent Classification System, BRS Information Technologies. **Staff:** Carol A. Giles, Libn..

★12532★
ST. LOUIS PUBLIC LIBRARY - ART DEPARTMENT (Art)
Central Library
1301 Olive St.
St. Louis, MO 63103-2389 Phone: (314)241-2288
Founded: 1912. **Staff:** Prof 2. **Subjects:** Art and related fields - painting, sculpture, costume, architecture, photography, graphics. **Special Collections:** Steedman Architectural Collection; Bill Collection of Mississippi Riverboat pictures; Boehl photographs of early St. Louis; pictures of St. Louis architecture, past and present. **Holdings:** 50,000 books; 135 VF drawers; 14,500 slides; 131,150 postcards; framed and unframed prints. **Subscriptions:** 105 journals and other serials. **Services:** Interlibrary loan; copying; department open to the public. **Special Catalogs:** Steedman Architectural Library Catalog. **Staff:** Shannon Paul, Libn..

★12533★
ST. LOUIS PUBLIC LIBRARY - CHILDREN'S LITERATURE ROOM (Hum)
Central Library
1301 Olive St. Phone: (314)241-2288
St. Louis, MO 63103-2389 Julanne M. Good, Coord., Ch.Serv.
Staff: Prof 1; Other 1. **Subjects:** Children's literature, emphasizing fairy tales, folklore; history and criticism of children's literature. **Special Collections:** Award-winning American children's books; Jacob Abbott (50 titles); William Taylor Adams (38 titles); Horatio Alger (60 titles); Beatrix Potter; Charles Austin Fordick (32 titles); early children's literature (2000 books); history of children's literature (500 books); folklore (2000 titles); Mother Goose (50 editions, 1878 to present); St. Nicholas (complete run); story telling; representative collection of early fantasy illustrators including Arthur Rackham, Kay Nielsen, Maxfield Parrish and others. **Holdings:** 28,500 volumes. **Subscriptions:** 20 journals and other serials. **Services:** Interlibrary loan; copying; room open to the public.

★12534★
ST. LOUIS PUBLIC LIBRARY - FILM LIBRARY SERVICE (Aud-Vis)
1624 Locust St. Phone: (314)241-2288
St. Louis, MO 63103-2389 Diane Freiermuth, Supv.
Founded: 1948. **Staff:** Prof 1; Other 4. **Holdings:** 3000 16mm sound educational films; 600 video cassettes. **Services:** Service open to the public within the City of St. Louis and St. Louis County Library Districts. **Publications:** New additions list, annual. **Special Catalogs:** Catalog of 16mm sound films and educational video cassettes, semiannual.

★12535★
ST. LOUIS PUBLIC LIBRARY - HISTORY AND GENEALOGY DEPARTMENT (Hist)
Central Library
1301 Olive St. Phone: (314)241-2288
St. Louis, MO 63103-2389 Noel C. Holobeck, Chf.
Founded: 1973. **Staff:** Prof 3. **Subjects:** U.S. history; local history; genealogy of Missouri, Illinois, and most states east of the Mississippi River; heraldry; maps. **Special Collections:** Complete set of St. Louis city directories; early printed records of Eastern States; British learned societies publications; American Colonial and State Papers: passenger lists of the 19th century (microfilm); St. Louis newspapers; Boston Evening Transcript: Genealogical Queries (microfiche); U.S. state and county histories and genealogical materials; Missouri Union and Confederate service records (microfilm); federal population censuses (microfilm) and indexes; territorial papers of U.S.; family histories (3800). **Holdings:** 118,000 volumes; 1150 genealogy files; 10,000 local history files; 8288 reels of microfilm; U.S. Geological Survey map depository for topographic maps; U.S. Army maps of foreign countries; U.S. and foreign gazetteers. **Subscriptions:** 521 journals and other serials. **Services:** Interlibrary loan; copying; department open to the public. **Publications:** Genealogical Materials and Local Histories in the St. Louis Public Library (bibliography of holdings), 1965, 1st supplement, 1971. **Special Indexes:** Heraldry Index of the St. Louis Public Library, 1980 (4 volumes); Genealogy index (card); local history index (card); heraldry index supplement (card); map index; surname and locations file. **Staff:** Cynthia Millar.

★12536★
ST. LOUIS PUBLIC LIBRARY - HUMANITIES AND SOCIAL SCIENCES DEPARTMENT (Hum, Bus-Fin)
Central Library
1301 Olive St. Phone: (314)241-2288
St. Louis, MO 63103-2389 Edna J. Reinhold, Dept.Hd.
Founded: 1973. **Staff:** Prof 3; Other 4. **Subjects:** Business, religion and philosophy, social sciences, English and American literature, languages, education, performing arts, recreation. **Holdings:** Books; pamphlets; journals; clippings; 2000 domestic and foreign telephone directories; COLT microfiche library of state industrial directories; vertical file on St. Louis area urban affairs; investment newsletters and indexes; annual shareholders' reports on microfiche. **Subscriptions:** 200 journals. **Services:** Interlibrary loan; copying; department open to the public. **Special Indexes:** Ready reference file (card); local association index (card). **Staff:** Nicolette Ehernberger; Celia Bouchard.

★12537★
ST. LOUIS PUBLIC LIBRARY - POPULAR LIBRARY - MUSIC SECTION (Mus)
Central Library
1301 Olive St. Phone: (314)241-2288
St. Louis, MO 63103-2389 Margaret Ganyard, Dept.Hd.
Founded: 1956. **Staff:** Prof 2; Other 1. **Subjects:** Music. **Holdings:** 5500 books; 119 bound periodical volumes; 24,000 scores; 25,000 phonograph records; 16 drawers of clippings; 1800 cassette tapes. **Subscriptions:** 65 journals and other serials. **Services:** Interlibrary loan; copying; section open to the public. **Special Indexes:** Catalog and indices for songs in songbooks and on phonograph records. **Staff:** Mary Lou Allen; Michael Lohmar.

★12538★
ST. LOUIS PUBLIC LIBRARY - RARE BOOK & SPECIAL COLLECTIONS DEPARTMENT (Rare Book)
Central Library
1301 Olive St. Phone: (314)241-2288
St. Louis, MO 63103-2389 Erik Bradford Stocker, Rare Bk.Libn.
Founded: 1965. **Staff:** Prof 1. **Subjects:** St. Louis authors and imprints, history of the book and printing, natural history. **Special Collections:** Reedy's Mirror, volumes 4-29, 1894-1920; Blake Collection of Bewick materials; William K. Bixby Collection; N.J. Werner Typographic Collection; Benjamin Franklin Shumard Library; William Marion Reedy Library; Grolier Society Collection (history of writing and the book). **Holdings:** 10,000 books; archives of St. Louis Public Library; manuscripts. **Subscriptions:** 25 journals and other serials. **Services:** Department open to the public with restrictions. **Special Indexes:** Reedy's Mirror Index, 1894-1914 (card).

★12539★
ST. LOUIS PUBLIC LIBRARY - READERS SERVICES/ DOCUMENTS DEPARTMENT (Info Sci, Geog-Map)
Central Library
1301 Olive St. Phone: (314)241-2288
St. Louis, MO 63103-2389 Anne Watts, Supv.
Founded: 1865. **Staff:** Prof 3; Other 9. **Special Collections:** Defense Mapping Agency map and chart depository; U.S. Geological Survey map depository; Missouri state document depository, 1976 to present; U.S. Government document depository, 1866 to present. **Holdings:** Missouri documents; St. Louis city documents. **Services:** Interlibrary loan; copying; department open to the public. **Staff:** Lori Smith, Libn..

★12540★
ST. LOUIS PUBLIC SCHOOLS - LIBRARY SERVICES CENTER (Educ)
1100 Farrar St. Phone: (314)865-4550
St. Louis, MO 63107 Robert G. Nador, Dir.
Staff: Prof 5; Other 15. **Subjects:** Education. **Holdings:** Figures not available for books; ERIC microfiche, 1968 to present. **Services:** Interlibrary loan; copying; center open to the public by appointment. **Automated Operations:** Computerized cataloging and acquisitions. **Networks/Consortia:** Member of St. Louis Regional Library Network. **Staff:** Howard Thomas, Coord., Fac.; Reola Boyd, Coord., Instr.; Helen Grauel, Coord., Acq.; Nancy McCullough, Coord., Ref. & Sel.; Robert Levitt, Cat..

★12541★
ST. LOUIS REGIONAL MEDICAL CENTER - MEDICAL LIBRARY (Med)
5535 Delmar Blvd. Phone: (314)361-1212
St. Louis, MO 63112 Mrs. Bernie Ferrell, Med.Libn.
Founded: 1985. **Staff:** Prof 1. **Subjects:** Medicine, surgery, pediatrics, orthopedics, obstetrics and gynecology, neurology. **Holdings:** 1000 books; 10,000 bound periodical volumes. **Subscriptions:** 100 journals and other serials. **Services:** Interlibrary loan; library not open to the public.
See: Kenrick Seminary (7424).

★12542★
ST. LOUIS SCIENCE CENTER - LIBRARY (Sci-Engr)
5050 Oakland Ave. Phone: (314)289-4400
St. Louis, MO 63110 Virginia Warakomski, Libn.
Founded: 1984. **Staff:** 1. **Subjects:** General science, natural history, astronomy, aeronautics, technology. **Holdings:** 3200 books; 18 bound periodical volumes. **Subscriptions:** 25 journals and other serials. **Services:** Library not open to the public.

ST. LOUIS SOCIETY FOR MEDICAL AND SCIENTIFIC EDUCATION
See: St. Louis Metropolitan Medical Society (12527)

★12543★
ST. LOUIS UNIVERSITY - CENTER FOR URBAN PROGRAMS - LIBRARY* (Plan)
221 N. Grand Blvd. Phone: (314)658-3934
St. Louis, MO 63103 Donna MacBridge-Braun, Adm.Asst.
Subjects: Urban affairs, urban planning. **Holdings:** 7500 volumes.

★12544★
ST. LOUIS UNIVERSITY - DIVINITY LIBRARY (Rel-Phil)
Pius XII Memorial Library
3650 Lindell Blvd. Phone: (314)658-3082
St. Louis, MO 63108 Rev. W. Charles Heiser, S.J., Libn.
Founded: 1848. **Staff:** Prof 1; Other 4. **Subjects:** Catholic church, monasticism and religious orders, mysticism, patrology, Bible, canon law. **Holdings:** 125,971 books; 16,218 bound periodical volumes; 157 reels of microfilm; 517 microfiche. **Subscriptions:** 1274 journals and other serials. **Services:** Interlibrary loan; copying; library open to the public for reference use only.

★12545★
ST. LOUIS UNIVERSITY - KNIGHTS OF COLUMBUS VATICAN FILM LIBRARY (Hum)
Pius XII Memorial Library
3650 Lindell Blvd.
St. Louis, MO 63108 Charles J. Ermatinger, Vatican Film Libn.
Founded: 1953. **Staff:** Prof 2; Other 1. **Subjects:** Greek, Latin, Arabic, Ethiopic, and Hebrew manuscripts from Vatican Library; Jesuitica and Hispanic Americana from European and Latin American collections; rare and out-of-print books. **Holdings:** 27,522 reels of microfilm (including 40,000 volumes of manuscript material); 52,003 slides of illuminated manuscripts. **Services:** Interlibrary loan; copying (both limited); library open to the public with restrictions. **Publications:** Manuscripta, 3/year - by subscription and exchange. **Special Catalogs:** Published and unpublished catalogs of manuscripts. **Staff:** Thomas Tolle, Assoc.Libn..

★12546★
ST. LOUIS UNIVERSITY - LAW LIBRARY (Law)
3700 Lindell Blvd. Phone: (314)658-2755
St. Louis, MO 63108 Eileen H. Searls, Law Libn.
Staff: Prof 6; Other 7. **Subjects:** American law, urban legal problems, jurisprudence, taxation, health and business law. **Special Collections:** U.S. Government documents, 1967 to present; Missouri government documents, 1977 to present; Congressman Leonor Sullivan papers, 1952-1976; Father Leo Brown papers; Smurfit Irish Law Center. **Holdings:** 222,480 books; 19,000 bound periodical volumes; 3046 reels of microfilm; 32,259 microcards; 233,064 microfiche; 565 cassettes and videotapes. **Subscriptions:** 4091 journals and other serials; 13 newspapers. **Services:** Interlibrary loan; copying; library open to the public for reference use only. **Automated Operations:** Computerized cataloging. **Computerized Information Services:** LEXIS, WESTLAW, DIALOG Information Services, OCLC, VERALEX, Electronic Legislative Search System (ELSS). **Networks/Consortia:** Member of Mid-America Law School Library Consortium, Missouri Library Network (MLNC), St. Louis Regional Library Network. **Publications:** Faculty Bibliography, irregular; Recent Acquisitions, monthly. **Special Catalogs:** Smurfit Irish Law Center Bibliographic Guide. **Staff:** Richard Amelung, Hd., Tech.Serv.; Kristy Elam, Law Libn.; Betsy McKinzie, Hd., Pub.Serv.; Carol Moody, Hd., Govt.Docs..

★12547★
ST. LOUIS UNIVERSITY - MEDICAL CENTER LIBRARY (Med)
1402 S. Grand Blvd. Phone: (314)577-8605
St. Louis, MO 63104 Judith Messerle, Dir.
Founded: 1890. **Staff:** Prof 9; Other 22. **Subjects:** Medicine, nursing, orthodontics, allied health sciences. **Special Collections:** Patrick Henry Griffin Surgical Library. **Holdings:** 48,000 books; 70,000 bound periodical volumes; 15 VF drawers of pamphlets; 400 pictures; 500 historical volumes; 3000 microfiche; 26,000 slides; 700 video cassettes; instrument collection. **Subscriptions:** 1500 journals and other serials. **Services:** Interlibrary loan; copying; SDI; library open to the public with restrictions. **Automated Operations:** Computerized cataloging and serials. **Computerized Information Services:** MEDLINE, BRS Information Technologies, DIALOG Information Services, OCLC, PHILSOM. Performs searches on fee basis. **Networks/Consortia:** Member of Center for Research Libraries (CRL) Consortia, Midcontinental Regional Medical Library Program, St. Louis Regional Library Network. **Staff:** Carolyn L. Taylor, Asst.Dir., Spec.Proj.; Suzanne Conway, Asst.Dir., Info.Serv.; Christine Sullivan, Ref.Libn.; Scott Pluchak, Assoc.Dir.; Linda Hulbert, Asst.Dir., Tech.Serv.; Kathy Gallagher, Ref.Libn.; Beth Carlin, Hd., Cat..

★12548★
ST. LOUIS UNIVERSITY - PARKS COLLEGE - LIBRARY (Sci-Engr)
Cahokia, IL 62206 Phone: (618)337-7500
Paul L. Anthony, Dir., Instr.Rsrcs.
Founded: 1927. **Staff:** Prof 1; Other 7. **Subjects:** Aeronautics, aerospace, science and technology. **Special Collections:** Federal Aviation Administration, Civil Aeronautics Board, International Civil Aviation Organization, and NASA Documents Depository. **Holdings:** 23,855 books; 8824 bound periodical volumes; 1741 reels of microfilm; 18,154 unbound government documents; 14,182 microfiche. **Subscriptions:** 299 journals and other serials; 11 newspapers. **Services:** Interlibrary loan; copying; library open to the public for reference use only. **Automated Operations:** Computerized cataloging and ILL. **Computerized Information Services:** OCLC, DIALOG Information Services. Performs searches on fee basis. **Networks/Consortia:** Member of Kaskaskia Library System, St. Louis Regional Library Network, ILLINET.

★12549★
ST. LOUIS ZOOLOGICAL PARK - LIBRARY (Biol Sci)
Forest Park
St. Louis, MO 63110 Charles Hoessle, Dir.
Subjects: Zoos, zoology, mammals, birds, reptiles, animal behavior. **Holdings:** 400 publications; 200 annual reports. **Services:** Library open to the public for reference use only by request.

ST. LUC HOSPITAL
See: Hopital St-Luc (6468)

ST. LUCIAN LIBRARY
See: Our Lady Queen of Martyrs (10964)

★12550★
ST. LUCIE COUNTY HISTORICAL MUSEUM - LIBRARY (Hist)
414 Seaway Dr. Phone: (407)464-6635
Fort Pierce, FL 34949 Scott W. Loehr, Musm.Div.Supt.
Founded: 1968. **Staff:** Prof 3; Other 3. **Subjects:** History of Indian River area; national, state, and local history; genealogy and archives of early families. **Holdings:** 235 volumes. **Services:** Library open to the public for reference use only.

★12551★
ST. LUCIE COUNTY LAW LIBRARY (Law)
County Courthouse, 3rd Fl. Phone: (407)461-2549
Fort Pierce, FL 34950 Audrey A. Robinson, Libn.
Subjects: Law. **Holdings:** 14,000 volumes. **Services:** Library open to the public by appointment.

★12552★
ST. LUKE THE EVANGELIST, CATHOLIC COMMUNITY - RESOURCE LIBRARY (Rel-Phil)
11011 Hall Rd. Phone: (713)481-2137
Houston, TX 77089 Rita M. Hubbard, Libn.
Founded: 1985. **Staff:** Prof 1; Other 17. **Subjects:** Religion, parenting and family life, self-help, biography, children's literature. **Special Collections:** Local authors (3 collections); St. Luke (4 collections). **Holdings:** 1400 books. **Services:** Library not open to the public.

★12553★
ST. LUKE MEDICAL CENTER - WILLIAM P. LONG MEDICAL LIBRARY (Med)
2632 E. Washington Blvd., Bin 7021 Phone: (818)797-1141
Pasadena, CA 91109-7021 Christine De Cicco, Cons.Libn.
Founded: 1948. **Staff:** Prof 1. **Subjects:** Clinical medicine, surgery, nursing. **Holdings:** 625 books; 110 bound periodical volumes; 200 cassettes. **Subscriptions:** 97 journals and other serials. **Services:** Interlibrary loan; copying; SDI; library open to the public for reference use only. **Networks/Consortia:** Member of Medical Library Group of Southern California and Arizona (MLGSCA).

★12554★
ST. LUKE'S EPISCOPAL & TEXAS CHILDREN'S HOSPITALS - MEDICAL LIBRARY (Med)
6621 Fannin St. Phone: (715)791-3054
Houston, TX 77030 Robert C. Park, Dir. of Lib.Serv.
Founded: 1954. **Staff:** Prof 1; Other 1. **Subjects:** Medicine and related fields. **Holdings:** 15,000 books. **Subscriptions:** 154 journals and other serials. **Services:** Interlibrary loan; copying; library open to physicians only.

★12555★
ST. LUKES HOSPITAL - DR. PAUL G. BUNKER MEMORIAL MEDICAL LIBRARY (Med)
305 S. State St. Phone: (605)229-3355
Aberdeen, SD 57401 Jay Tobin, Med.Libn.
Founded: 1972. **Staff:** Prof 1. **Subjects:** Medicine, nursing. **Holdings:** 1200 books. **Subscriptions:** 220 journals and other serials; 7 newspapers. **Services:** Interlibrary loan; copying; library open to the public with restrictions. **Computerized Information Services:** MEDLARS, DIALOG Information Services; DOCLINE (electronic mail service). Performs searches on fee basis. **Networks/Consortia:** Member of Greater Midwest Regional Medical Library Network.

★12556★
ST. LUKE'S HOSPITAL - HEALTH SCIENCE LIBRARY (Med)
1026 A Ave., N.E. Phone: (319)369-7864
Cedar Rapids, IA 52402 Donald Pohnl, Dir.
Staff: Prof 1; Other 2. **Subjects:** Medicine, nursing, allied health sciences, health administration. **Holdings:** 7000 books; 9000 bound periodical volumes; 2000 AV programs. **Subscriptions:** 500 journals and other serials. **Services:** Interlibrary loan; copying; library open to the public with restrictions. **Automated Operations:** Computerized cataloging. **Computerized Information Services:** DIALOG Information Services, MEDLARS, AMA/NET, BRS Information Technologies; internal database. **Networks/Consortia:** Member of Linn County Library Consortium (LCLC), Greater Midwest Regional Medical Library Network. **Special Catalogs:** Book Catalog; Area Serials List.

★12557★
ST. LUKE'S HOSPITAL - HEALTH SCIENCES LIBRARY (Med)
601 E. 19th Ave. Phone: (303)869-2395
Denver, CO 80203 Karen Guth, Dir.
Founded: 1954. **Staff:** Prof 1. **Subjects:** Medicine, nursing, oncology, geriatrics, womens' health, cardiology. **Holdings:** 2599 books; 5815 bound periodical volumes. **Subscriptions:** 247 journals and other serials. **Services:** Interlibrary loan; library not open to the public. **Computerized Information Services:** DIALOG Information Services, MEDLINE; ABACUS (electronic mail service). **Networks/Consortia:** Member of Denver Area Health Sciences Library Consortium, Colorado Council of Medical Librarians. **Remarks:** Maintained by American Medical International.

★12558★
ST. LUKE'S HOSPITAL - HILDING MEDICAL LIBRARY (Med)
915 E. First St. Phone: (218)726-5320
Duluth, MN 55805 Doreen Roberts, Libn.
Founded: 1944. **Staff:** Prof 1; Other 1. **Subjects:** Clinical medicine, nursing. **Holdings:** 1100 books; 8000 bound periodical volumes; 300 videotapes. **Subscriptions:** 270 journals and other serials. **Services:** Interlibrary loan; library not open to the public. **Computerized Information Services:** MEDLINE, BRS Information Technologies. **Networks/Consortia:** Member of Arrowhead Professional Libraries Association (APLA).

★12559★
ST. LUKE'S HOSPITAL - LIBRARY (Med)
720 4th St., N. Phone: (701)280-5571
Fargo, ND 58122 Margaret Wagner, Lib.Supv.
Founded: 1925. **Staff:** 4. **Subjects:** Medicine, paramedicine, nursing, hospital administration. **Holdings:** 3407 books; 3842 bound periodical volumes; 402 volumes on microfiche; 83 volumes on microfilm; 984 AV programs; 280 other cataloged items. **Subscriptions:** 379 journals and other serials. **Services:** Interlibrary loan; copying; SDI; library open to the public for reference use only. **Computerized Information Services:** MEDLINE, BRS Information Technologies; EasyLink, DOCLINE (electronic mail services). Performs searches on fee basis. Contact Person: Eileen Chamberlain, 280-5572. **Networks/Consortia:** Member of Valley Medical Network (VMN). **Publications:** Recent Additions, monthly - distributed internally and to members of Valley Medical Network.

★12560★
ST. LUKE'S HOSPITAL - MEDICAL LIBRARY (Med)
3555 Army St. Phone: (415)647-8600
San Francisco, CA 94110 Corazon O'S. Ismarin, Libn.
Founded: 1959. **Staff:** Prof 1. **Subjects:** Medicine and nursing. **Holdings:** 6651 books; 4319 bound periodical volumes. **Subscriptions:** 106 journals and other serials. **Services:** Interlibrary loan; library not open to the public. **Computerized Information Services:** MEDLINE. **Networks/Consortia:** Member of San Francisco Biomedical Library Group.

★12561★
ST. LUKE'S HOSPITAL - MEDICAL LIBRARY (Med)
11311 Shaker Blvd. Phone: (216)368-7691
Cleveland, OH 44104 Pam Billick, Dir.
Founded: 1936. **Staff:** Prof 2; Other 1. **Subjects:** Medicine, nursing, management. **Holdings:** 2500 books; 6300 bound periodical volumes. **Subscriptions:** 350 journals and other serials. **Services:** Interlibrary loan; copying; SDI; library open to the public. **Automated Operations:** Computerized cataloging and circulation. **Computerized Information Services:** MEDLINE, BRS Information Technologies, DIALOG Information Services; internal database; DOCLINE (electronic mail service). Performs searches on fee basis. **Networks/Consortia:** Member of Cleveland Area Metropolitan Library System (CAMLS). **Publications:** Library Link (newsletter), bimonthly. **Staff:** Pat Bresien, Clin.Libn..

★12562★
ST. LUKE'S HOSPITAL ASSOCIATION - MEDICAL, NURSING AND ALLIED HELP LIBRARY (Med)
4201 Belfort Rd. Phone: (904)739-3735
Jacksonville, FL 32216 Margarette Wally, Libn.
Staff: Prof 1; Other 1. **Subjects:** Medicine, nursing. **Holdings:** 1155 books; 2128 bound periodical volumes. **Subscriptions:** 77 journals and other serials. **Services:** Interlibrary loan; library not open to the public. **Computerized Information Services:** Online systems.

★12563★
ST. LUKE'S HOSPITAL OF BETHLEHEM, PENNSYLVANIA - AUDIOVISUAL LIBRARY (Aud-Vis, Med)
801 Ostrum St. Phone: (215)691-4341
Bethlehem, PA 18015 Robert R. Fields, AV Coord.
Staff: 1. **Subjects:** Medicine, nursing, allied health sciences, patient education. **Holdings:** 700 AV programs. **Services:** Interlibrary loan; library open to the public with permission of librarian.

★12564★
ST. LUKE'S HOSPITAL OF BETHLEHEM, PENNSYLVANIA - SCHOOL OF NURSING - TREXLER NURSES' LIBRARY (Med)
Bishopthorpe & Ostrum Sts. Phone: (215)691-4355
Bethlehem, PA 18015 Diane Frantz, Libn.
Staff: Prof 1; Other 2. **Subjects:** Nursing and allied health sciences. **Special Collections:** Historical Nursing Collection. **Holdings:** 4600 volumes; 15 VF drawers. **Subscriptions:** 63 journals and other serials. **Services:** Interlibrary loan; copying; library open to the public for reference use only. **Computerized Information Services:** MEDLINE, DIALOG Information Services.

★12565★
ST. LUKE'S HOSPITAL OF BETHLEHEM, PENNSYLVANIA - W.L. ESTES, JR. MEMORIAL LIBRARY (Med)
801 Ostrum St. Phone: (215)691-4227
Bethlehem, PA 18015 Maria D. Collette, Libn.
Founded: 1947. **Staff:** Prof 1; Other 1. **Subjects:** Medicine, medical specialities, allied health sciences. **Special Collections:** Historical collection (251 books). **Holdings:** 2150 books; 5250 bound periodical volumes; 164 folders of ephemeral file articles. **Subscriptions:** 425 journals and other serials; 5 newspapers. **Services:** Interlibrary loan; copying; library open to the public for reference use only. **Automated Operations:** Computerized serials. **Computerized Information Services:** DIALOG Information Services, MEDLARS, BRS Information Technologies. Performs searches on fee basis. **Networks/Consortia:** Member of Greater Northeastern Regional Medical Library Program.

★12566★
ST. LUKE'S HOSPITAL CENTER - RICHARD WALKER BOLLING MEMORIAL MEDICAL LIBRARY (Med)
Amsterdam Ave. & 114th St. Phone: (212)870-1861
New York, NY 10025 Nancy Mary Panella, Libn.
Founded: 1884. **Staff:** Prof 3; Other 2. **Subjects:** Medicine, surgery, psychiatry, child psychiatry, health care administration. **Special**

Collections: History of medicine; old and/or rare medical books; historical collections of St. Luke's Hospital, Women's Hospital, and School of Nursing. **Holdings:** 10,000 books; 32,000 bound periodical volumes; 4 VF drawers; staff reprints. **Subscriptions:** 450 journals and other serials. **Services:** Interlibrary loan; copying; library open to the public by appointment. **Automated Operations:** Computerized cataloging. **Computerized Information Services:** MEDLINE, OCLC. Performs searches on fee basis. **Networks/Consortia:** Member of Medical Library Center of New York (MLCNY). **Staff:** Elizabeth Skerritt, Asst.Libn.; Joan Carvajed, Archv.; C.H. Otis, Ser.; R.J. Garrett, ILL.

★12567★
ST. LUKE'S HOSPITAL OF KANSAS CITY - MEDICAL LIBRARY (Med)
Spencer Center for Education
44th & Wornall Rd. Phone: (816)932-2333
Kansas City, MO 64111 Karen Wiederaenders, Dir. of Lib.Serv.
Founded: 1948. **Staff:** Prof 3; Other 6. **Subjects:** Cardiology, nursing, sports medicine, medicine. **Holdings:** 5000 books; 10,000 bound periodical volumes; 1000 other cataloged items. **Subscriptions:** 624 journals and other serials. **Services:** Interlibrary loan; copying; library open to the public for reference use only. **Automated Operations:** Computerized cataloging. **Computerized Information Services:** NLM, DIALOG Information Services, OCLC, BRS Information Technologies. **Networks/Consortia:** Member of Kansas City Library Network, Inc. (KCLN), Kansas City Metropolitan Library Network (KCMLN). **Publications:** News and Notes, monthly - for internal distribution only. **Staff:** Richard Dalton, Asst.Libn.; Mary Webb, Ser.Libn..

★12568★
ST. LUKE'S HOSPITAL OF MIDDLEBOROUGH - MEDICAL STAFF LIBRARY (Med)
52 Oak St. Phone: (617)947-6000
Middleboro, MA 02346 Gail Twomey, Med.Libn.
Staff: Prof 1. **Subjects:** Medicine and allied health sciences. **Holdings:** 112 volumes; 2000 unbound periodicals. **Subscriptions:** 45 journals and other serials. **Services:** Interlibrary loan; copying; library open to the public with permission. **Networks/Consortia:** Member of Massachusetts Health Sciences Library Network (MAHSLIN), Southeastern Massachusetts Consortium of Health Science Libraries (SEMCO).

★12569★
ST. LUKE'S MEDICAL CENTER - MEDICAL LIBRARY (Med)
2900 W. Oklahoma Ave. Phone: (414)649-7357
Milwaukee, WI 53215 Midge Wos, Mgr.
Founded: 1967. **Staff:** Prof 1; Other 3. **Subjects:** Medicine, nursing, paramedicine. **Holdings:** 20,760 books; 7646 bound periodical volumes; 13,958 filmstrips, records, transparencies, slides, film reels; 3500 cassettes; 1176 video cassettes; 1174 volumes on microfilm. **Subscriptions:** 1268 journals and other serials; 35 newspapers. **Services:** Interlibrary loan; copying; SDI; library open to professional staff and employees only. **Automated Operations:** Computerized acquisitions, serials, circulation, and ILL. **Computerized Information Services:** MEDLINE, BRS Information Technologies, DIALOG Information Services; DOCLINE (electronic mail service). **Networks/Consortia:** Member of Southeastern Wisconsin Health Science Library Consortium (SWHSL). **Publications:** New Book List and Audiovisual List, both monthly - for internal distribution only.

★12570★
ST. LUKE'S MEDICAL CENTER - ROSENZWEIG HEALTH SCIENCES LIBRARY (Med)
1800 E. Van Buren St. Phone: (602)251-8100
Phoenix, AZ 85006 Barbara Hasan
Founded: 1983. **Staff:** Prof 1. **Subjects:** Cardiology, nursing, behavioral health. **Holdings:** 1005 books; 2050 bound periodical volumes. **Subscriptions:** 225 journals and other serials. **Services:** Interlibrary loan; library not open to the public. **Computerized Information Services:** DIALOG Information Services, MEDLARS; OnTyme Electronic Message Network Service (electronic mail service). Performs searches free of charge. **Networks/Consortia:** Member of Maricopa Biomedical Librarians (MABL).

★12571★
ST. LUKE'S MEMORIAL HOSPITAL - MEDICAL LIBRARY (Med)
711 S. Cowley St. Phone: (509)838-4771
Spokane, WA 99210 Delores Brewer, Libn.
Staff: 1. **Subjects:** Orthopedics, nursing, medicine, surgery, pathology, neurology. **Holdings:** 400 books; 21 bound periodical volumes; 39 titles of Medcom slides; Audio-Digest tapes. **Subscriptions:** 35 journals and other serials. **Services:** Interlibrary loan; library not open to the public.

★12572★
ST. LUKE'S REGIONAL MEDICAL CENTER - LIBRARY-MEDIA CENTER (Med)
2720 Stone Park Blvd. Phone: (712)279-3156
Sioux City, IA 51104 Barbara Knight, Tech.Serv.Mgr.
Staff: Prof 2. **Subjects:** Medicine, nursing. **Holdings:** 1500 books; 200 filmstrips; 600 video cassettes. **Subscriptions:** 90 journals and other serials. **Services:** Interlibrary loan; copying; library open to the public. **Computerized Information Services:** MEDLINE.

★12573★
ST. LUKE'S REGIONAL MEDICAL CENTER - MEDICAL LIBRARY (Med)
190 E. Bannock Phone: (208)386-2277
Boise, ID 83712 Pamela S. Spickelmier, Dir.
Staff: Prof 1; Other 2. **Subjects:** Medicine, nursing, administration. **Holdings:** 1200 volumes. **Subscriptions:** 200 journals and other serials. **Services:** Interlibrary loan; copying; SDI; library open to the public with restrictions. **Automated Operations:** Computerized cataloging and circulation. **Computerized Information Services:** MEDLARS, BRS Information Technologies. **Remarks:** Library also houses the Idaho Health Information Retrieval Center.

ST. MARGARET HEALTH CENTER
See: Providence-St. Margaret Health Center (11649)

★12574★
ST. MARGARET HOSPITAL - SALLIE M. TYRRELL, M.D. MEMORIAL LIBRARY (Med)
5454 Hohman Ave. Phone: (219)932-2300
Hammond, IN 46320 Laurie Broadus, Lib.Coord.
Staff: Prof 1; Other 1. **Subjects:** Medicine, nursing. **Holdings:** 2000 books; 1500 bound periodical volumes; Audio-Digest tapes. **Subscriptions:** 150 journals and other serials. **Services:** Interlibrary loan; library not open to the public. **Networks/Consortia:** Member of Greater Midwest Regional Medical Library Network, Northwest Indiana Health Science Library Consortium.

★12575★
ST. MARGARET MEMORIAL HOSPITAL - PAUL TITUS MEMORIAL LIBRARY AND SCHOOL OF NURSING LIBRARY (Med)
4631 Davison St. Phone: (412)622-7075
Pittsburgh, PA 15201 Dorothy Schiff, Libn.
Staff: Prof 2; Other 2. **Subjects:** Medicine, nursing, allied health sciences. **Holdings:** 3500 books; 1500 bound periodical volumes; 8 VF drawers of pamphlets; 3 shelves of archives; audiotapes; filmstrips; slides; AV programs. **Subscriptions:** 281 journals and other serials. **Services:** Interlibrary loan; library not open to the public. **Computerized Information Services:** MEDLINE. **Networks/Consortia:** Member of Pittsburgh-East Hospital Library Cooperative. **Remarks:** The Paul Titus Memorial Library is located at 815 Freeport Rd., Pittsburgh, PA 15215. An alternate telephone number is 784-4239. **Staff:** Sandra Arjona, Med.Libn..

★12576★
ST. MARIA GORETTI CHURCH LIBRARY† (Rel-Phil)
5405 Flad Ave.
Madison, WI 53711 Phone: (608)271-8244
Founded: 1962. **Subjects:** Religion and allied subjects. **Holdings:** 3000 books. **Subscriptions:** 15 journals and other serials. **Services:** Library open to the public on a limited schedule.

★12577★
ST. MARK'S EPISCOPAL CHURCH - BISHOP JONES LIBRARY (Rel-Phil)
315 E. Pecan St. Phone: (512)226-2426
San Antonio, TX 78205 Dorothy B. Brown, Parish Libn.
Staff: Prof 1; Other 5. **Subjects:** Religion, children's literature. **Special Collections:** Jack Kent Collection (children's author; 56 books). **Holdings:** 3870 books; 500 AV programs. **Subscriptions:** 10 journals and other serials. **Services:** Copying; library open to the public with restrictions.

★12578★
ST. MARK'S EPISCOPAL CHURCH - PARISH LIBRARY (Rel-Phil)
680 Calder Phone: (409)832-3405
Beaumont, TX 77701 Mrs. W.E. Krueger, Libn.
Staff: Prof 1. **Subjects:** Religion, social sciences, history, arts, philosophy, literature. **Holdings:** Figures not available. **Subscriptions:** 16 journals and other serials. **Services:** Library not open to the public.

★12579★
ST. MARK'S HOSPITAL - LIBRARY AND MEDIA SERVICES (Med)
1200 East 3900 South St. Phone: (801)268-7004
Salt Lake City, UT 84124 Kerry F. Skidmore, Libn.
Staff: Prof 1; Other 1. **Subjects:** Medicine and allied health sciences. **Holdings:** 2250 books; 454 bound periodical volumes; unbound periodicals; microfiche; 100 pamphlets; 1000 AV programs. **Subscriptions:** 425 journals and other serials. **Services:** Interlibrary loan (fee); copying; SDI; patient education instruction; library open to the public with restrictions. **Automated Operations:** Computerized cataloging, acquisitions, serials, circulation, and indexing. **Computerized Information Services:** MEDLINE, INFONET, Octanet; DOCLINE (electronic mail service). Performs searches on fee basis. **Networks/Consortia:** Member of Utah Health Sciences Library Consortium. **Special Indexes:** AV index (pamphlet). **Remarks:** Maintained by Hospital Corporation of America.

ST. MARK'S LIBRARY
See: General Theological Seminary (5575)

★12580★
ST. MARK'S PRESBYTERIAN CHURCH - LIBRARY (Rel-Phil)
3809 E. 3rd St. Phone: (602)325-1519
Tucson, AZ 85716 Janet M. Tower, Lib.Adm.
Founded: 1965. **Staff:** 6. **Subjects:** Theology, Bible and Bible study, devotions, church history, social problems. **Holdings:** 3000 books. **Services:** Library open to church members.

★12581★
ST. MARTHA'S HOSPITAL - SCHOOL OF NURSING LIBRARY (Med)
25 Bay St. Phone: (902)863-2830
Antigonish, NS, Canada B2G 2G5 Sr. Mary Chisholm, Libn.
Staff: Prof 1. **Subjects:** Nursing. **Holdings:** 4152 books; 158 bound periodical volumes; 20 videotapes; AV programs. **Subscriptions:** 70 journals and other serials. **Services:** Library open to the public.

★12582★
SAINT MARY COLLEGE - DE PAUL LIBRARY - SPECIAL COLLECTIONS CENTER (Hum, Hist)
Leavenworth, KS 66048 Phone: (913)682-5151
Sr. S. Therese Deplazes, Spec.Coll.Libn.
Founded: 1972. **Staff:** Prof 1; Other 1. **Holdings:** Sir John and Mary Craig Scripture-Theology Collection (2000 titles in 100 languages: Bibles; scriptural texts and exegesis; leaves; manuscripts; scrolls; codices; incunabula; facsimiles; transcriptions; printed books, 15th century to present; memorabilia); Bernard H. Hall Abraham Lincoln Collection (1500 books; 700 pamphlets; 300 postcards; 150 framed and unframed portraits and prints; sheet music and song sheets; documents; memorabilia); Americana (Holographs of American personalities; manuscripts documenting United States and Kansas history: slave papers, ships papers, property deeds, contracts, territorial textbooks); Shakespeariana (785 volumes; scrapbooks of theater programs and photographs; memorabilia); Charles Dickens (60 rare volumes; 3 titles in original monthly paper wrappings; first editions; facsimiles; rare print collections; journals; memorabilia); Maurice C. Fields, 1915-1938 (108 items: letters from his mother, teachers, friends; poems about him; masters' thesis on his life and work; published works). **Services:** Copying; center open to the public for viewing and research. **Networks/Consortia:** Member of Kansas City Regional Council for Higher Education (KCRCHE). **Special Catalogs:** Descriptive bibliographic lists for Americana, rare Dickensania, and special subjects; catalogs for Scripture-Theology and Abraham Lincoln collections (card).

★12583★
ST. MARY-CORWIN HOSPITAL - FINNEY MEMORIAL LIBRARY (Med)
1008 Minnequa Ave. Phone: (719)560-5598
Pueblo, CO 81004-9988 Shirley Chun-Harper, Med.Libn.
Founded: 1958. **Staff:** Prof 1. **Subjects:** Internal medicine, surgery, pediatrics, pathology, allied health sciences. **Holdings:** 2568 volumes; 66 video cassettes; 1154 Audio-Digest tapes. **Subscriptions:** 125 journals and other serials. **Services:** Interlibrary loan; copying; library open to the public for reference use only. **Automated Operations:** Computerized cataloging. **Computerized Information Services:** MEDLINE, OCLC.

★12584★
ST. MARY HOSPITAL - HEALTH SCIENCE LIBRARY (Med)
3600 Gates Blvd.
Box 3696
Port Arthur, TX 77643-3696 Phone: (409)985-7431
Founded: 1930. **Staff:** Prof 2. **Subjects:** Allergic diseases, dermatology, radiology, pathology, genitourinary medicine, physicians and surgeons, family practice, hemodialysis, thoracic and cardiovascular surgery, internal medicine, obstetrics/gynecology, child specialists, dentistry, infection. **Special Collections:** Industrial medicine (340 items). **Holdings:** 3590 books; 690 bound periodical volumes; 400 unbound reports; 168 Audio-Digest tapes; 32 video cassettes. **Subscriptions:** 135 journals and other serials. **Services:** Interlibrary loan; library open to the public with approval of administrator. **Automated Operations:** Computerized cataloging, circulation, and ILL. **Computerized Information Services:** NLM. **Special Indexes:** Cumulated Index Medicus, annual; Index Medicus, monthly. **Staff:** Ethel M. Granger, Libn..

★12585★
ST. MARY HOSPITAL - MEDICAL LIBRARY (Med)
36475 Five Mile Rd. Phone: (313)464-4800
Livonia, MI 48154 Shirley Welch, Asst.Libn.
Founded: 1959. **Staff:** Prof 1; Other 2. **Subjects:** Medicine, surgery, radiology, nursing, obstetrics and gynecology, pediatrics, mental health. **Holdings:** 2143 books; 1230 bound periodical volumes; 800 tapes; 7 16mm films; 8 35mm filmstrips; Audio-Digest tapes; filmstrip/tape sets. **Subscriptions:** 40 journals and other serials. **Services:** Interlibrary loan; library not open to the public. **Networks/Consortia:** Member of Metropolitan Detroit Medical Library Group (MDMLG), Wayne/Oakland Library Federation (WOLF). **Remarks:** Maintained by the Felician Sisters.

★12586★
ST. MARY MEDICAL CENTER - BELLIS MEDICAL LIBRARY (Med)
1050 Linden Ave.
Box 887 Phone: (213)491-9295
Long Beach, CA 90801-0887 Lorraine B. Attarian, Mgr.
Founded: 1955. **Staff:** Prof 2; Other 1. **Subjects:** Medicine, nursing. **Holdings:** 30,000 volumes; pamphlet files; historical collection. **Subscriptions:** 500 journals and other serials. **Services:** Interlibrary loan; copying; SDI; library open to the public with restrictions. **Computerized Information Services:** Pergamon ORBIT InfoLine, Inc., MEDLARS, DIALOG Information Services. Performs searches on fee basis. **Staff:** Vicki Michaels, Med.Libn..

★12587★
ST. MARY OF NAZARETH HOSPITAL CENTER - SISTER STELLA LOUISE HEALTH SCIENCE LIBRARY (Med)
2233 W. Division St. Phone: (312)770-2219
Chicago, IL 60622 Terri Windle, Med.Libn.
Founded: 1949. **Staff:** Prof 1; Other 2. **Subjects:** Medicine, surgery. **Special Collections:** Hospital Satellite Videotape Network. **Holdings:** 1400 books; 2200 bound periodical volumes; 300 pamphlets and reprints; 1000 Audio-Digest tapes; 65 slide sets; 200 video cassettes. **Subscriptions:** 153 journals and other serials. **Services:** Interlibrary loan; SDI; library open to the public by appointment. **Automated Operations:** Computerized cataloging and serials. **Computerized Information Services:** DIALOG Information Services, MEDLINE. **Networks/Consortia:** Member of Greater Midwest Regional Medical Library Network, Metropolitan Consortium of Chicago. **Publications:** Monthly Acquisitions Lists; Hospital Satellite Network Newsletter. **Special Catalogs:** Audiovisual Catalog.

★12588★
ST. MARY SEMINARY - JOSEPH M. BRUENING LIBRARY (Rel-Phil)
1227 Ansel Rd. Phone: (216)721-2100
Cleveland, OH 44108 Alan Rome, Libn.
Founded: 1848. **Staff:** Prof 1; Other 1. **Subjects:** Liturgy, dogmatic and moral theology, history of the Catholic Church, patristic writings, sacred scripture, ecumenism, canon law, religious education, pastoral care. **Special Collections:** Bishop Horstmann Collection (1600 books). **Holdings:** 40,000 books; 9000 bound periodical volumes; 250 drafts and reports of Vatican Council II; 5 boxes of U.S. Catholic Conference pamphlets; 759 cassettes; 293 filmstrips; 367 microfiche; 253 reels of microfilm; 281 theses.

Subscriptions: 358 journals and other serials; 5 newspapers. **Services:** Interlibrary loan; copying; library open to the public by appointment. **Networks/Consortia:** Member of Cleveland Area Metropolitan Library System (CAMLS), Ohio Theological Librarians.

★12589★
SAINT MARY'S COLLEGE - CUSHWA-LEIGHTON LIBRARY - SPECIAL COLLECTIONS (Hum)
Notre Dame, IN 46556 Phone: (219)284-5280
Sr. Bernice Hollenhorts, C.S.C., Lib.Dir.
Holdings: Books by and about Dante Alighieri (600 titles). **Services:** Interlibrary loan; copying; collections open to the public with restrictions. **Computerized Information Services:** BRS Information Technologies, OCLC. **Networks/Consortia:** Member of INCOLSA, Area 2 Library Services Authority (ALSA 2).

★12590★
ST. MARY'S COLLEGE - MUSIC SEMINAR ROOM (Mus)
Moreau Hall, Rm. 322 Phone: (219)284-4638
Notre Dame, IN 46556 Sr. Rita Claire, C.S.C., Dir.
Founded: 1957. **Staff:** Prof 2; Other 7. **Subjects:** Music. **Holdings:** 719 books; 3276 scores; 3351 phonograph records; 181 tapes and cassettes. **Subscriptions:** 10 journals and other serials. **Services:** Interlibrary loan; copying; room open to professors and students. **Automated Operations:** Computerized cataloging. **Staff:** Robert Hohl, Cat..

★12591★
ST. MARY'S COLLEGE OF CALIFORNIA - LIBRARY - SPECIAL COLLECTIONS (Rel-Phil)
St. Mary's Rd.
Box N Phone: (415)376-4411
Moraga, CA 94575 Andrew Simon, Spec.Coll.Libn.
Staff: Prof 1. **Subjects:** Cardinal John Henry Newman, Saint Jean Baptiste de la Salle, Brothers of the Christian Schools, 17th and 18th century French Catholic spirituality. **Special Collections:** John Henry Newman and His Times (5000 items); Library for Lasallian Studies (5000 volumes). **Services:** Collections open to the public for reference use only by appointment. **Networks/Consortia:** Member of CLASS, Bay Area Library and Information Network (BALIN). **Special Catalogs:** Catalog of the Library for Lasallian Studies. **Remarks:** The Library for Lasallian Studies is owned by De La Salle Institute of Moraga, CA.

★12592★
ST. MARY'S GENERAL HOSPITAL - HEALTH SCIENCES LIBRARY (Med)
45 Golder St. Phone: (207)786-2901
Lewiston, ME 04240 Evelyn A. Greenlaw, Dir.
Founded: 1908. **Staff:** Prof 1. **Subjects:** Medicine, nursing, hospital administration. **Special Collections:** Crisis intervention. **Holdings:** 840 books; 510 bound periodical volumes. **Subscriptions:** 145 journals and other serials. **Services:** Interlibrary loan; copying; SDI; library open to the public. **Computerized Information Services:** MEDLARS, DIALOG Information Services, BRS Information Technologies, WILSONLINE; DIALMAIL, DOCLINE (electronic mail services). Performs searches on fee basis. **Networks/Consortia:** Member of Health Science Library and Information Cooperative of Maine (HSLIC).

★12593★
ST. MARY'S HEALTH CENTER - HEALTH SCIENCES LIBRARY (Med)
6420 Clayton Rd. Phone: (314)768-8112
St. Louis, MO 63117 Candace W. Thayer, Libn.
Founded: 1933. **Staff:** Prof 1; Other 3. **Subjects:** Clinical medicine, nursing, allied health sciences. **Holdings:** 1000 books; 12,000 bound periodical volumes. **Subscriptions:** 200 journals and other serials. **Services:** Interlibrary loan; library not open to the public. **Computerized Information Services:** MEDLARS. **Networks/Consortia:** Member of Sisters of St. Mary - System Wide Library Consortium, St. Louis Regional Library Network.

ST. MARY'S HOSPITAL
See: Catholic Medical Center of Brooklyn & Queens, Inc. (2746)

★12594★
ST. MARY'S HOSPITAL - FAMILY PRACTICE & NATIONAL PATIENT EDUCATION LIBRARY (Med)
2900 Baltimore
Kansas City, MO 64108 Phone: (816)753-5700
Founded: 1982. **Staff:** Prof 1. **Subjects:** Family practice, medical business management, bioethics. **Special Collections:** Patient education. **Holdings:** 2000 books. **Subscriptions:** 50 journals and other serials; 10 newspapers. **Services:** Interlibrary loan; copying; library open to the public with restrictions. **Computerized Information Services:** MEDLINE, DIALOG Information Services. **Networks/Consortia:** Member of Kansas City Library Network, Inc. (KCLN).

★12595★
ST. MARY'S HOSPITAL - FINKELSTEIN LIBRARY (Med)
56 Franklin St. Phone: (203)574-6408
Waterbury, CT 06702 Jean Fuller, Libn.
Founded: 1970. **Staff:** Prof 1; Other 2. **Subjects:** Medicine and nursing. **Holdings:** 1200 books; 2584 bound periodical volumes. **Subscriptions:** 237 journals and other serials. **Services:** Interlibrary loan; copying; SDI; library open to the public for reference use only.

★12596★
ST. MARY'S HOSPITAL - HEALTH SCIENCE LIBRARY (Med)
1800 E. Lake Shore Dr. Phone: (217)429-2966
Decatur, IL 62525 Laura L. Brosamer, Libn.
Staff: Prof 1; Other 1. **Subjects:** Medicine, nursing, hospital administration. **Holdings:** 2000 books; 1700 bound periodical volumes; 184 slide/tape programs; 9 linear feet of vertical files; 200 video cassettes. **Subscriptions:** 300 journals and other serials. **Services:** Interlibrary loan; copying; SDI; library open to the public with librarian's permission. **Computerized Information Services:** MEDLARS, DIALOG Information Services. **Networks/Consortia:** Member of Rolling Prairie Library System (RPLS), Greater Midwest Regional Medical Library Network, Capitol Area Consortium of Health Science Libraries. **Publications:** The Appendix (new book list), quarterly.

★12597★
ST. MARY'S HOSPITAL - HEALTH SCIENCES LIBRARY (Med)
901 45th St. Phone: (407)844-6300
West Palm Beach, FL 33407 Jacqueline Taylor, Libn.
Founded: 1946. **Staff:** Prof 1. **Subjects:** Medicine, nursing, allied health sciences. **Special Collections:** Historical Collection in Medicine. **Holdings:** 1000 books; 6200 bound periodical volumes; 200 rare books. **Subscriptions:** 185 journals and other serials. **Services:** Interlibrary loan; copying; library open to the public with restrictions. **Computerized Information Services:** DIALOG Information Services, MEDLARS. **Networks/Consortia:** Member of Palm Beach County Health Sciences Library Consortium, Miami Health Sciences Library Consortium (MHSLC).

★12598★
ST. MARY'S HOSPITAL - HEALTH SCIENCES LIBRARY (Med)
5801 Bremo Rd. Phone: (804)281-8247
Richmond, VA 23226 Sandra H. Parham, Libn.
Founded: 1966. **Staff:** Prof 2. **Subjects:** Medicine, hospital administration, nursing. **Holdings:** 600 books; 1000 bound periodical volumes. **Subscriptions:** 115 journals and other serials. **Services:** Interlibrary loan; copying; library open to the public with permission. **Computerized Information Services:** BRS Information Technologies. Performs searches on fee basis. Contact Person: Damon Persiani, Search Anl..

★12599★
ST. MARY'S HOSPITAL - HEALTH SCIENCES LIBRARY (Med)
2323 N. Lake Dr.
Box 503 Phone: (414)289-7000
Milwaukee, WI 53201 Sharon A. Wochos, Libn.
Founded: 1959. **Staff:** Prof 1. **Subjects:** Nursing, medicine, management. **Holdings:** 2000 books; 2000 bound periodical volumes. **Subscriptions:** 225 journals and other serials. **Services:** Interlibrary loan; copying; SDI; library open to the public for reference use only. **Computerized Information Services:** DIALOG Information Services, MEDLINE, BRS Information Technologies; DOCLINE (electronic mail service). Performs searches on fee basis. **Networks/Consortia:** Member of Southeastern Wisconsin Health Science Library Consortium (SWHSL). **Remarks:** An alternate telephone number is 225-8149.

★12600★
ST. MARY'S HOSPITAL - LIBRARY (Med)
200 Jefferson, S.E. Phone: (616)774-6243
Grand Rapids, MI 49503 Mary A. Hanson, Med.Libn.
Founded: 1927. **Staff:** Prof 2; Other 1. **Subjects:** Medicine, nursing. **Special Collections:** Historical medical collections from Kent County Medical Society, St. Mary's Hospital, and Mercy Central School of Nursing. **Holdings:** 3500 books; 7500 bound periodical volumes; 12 VF drawers. **Subscriptions:** 230 journals and other serials. **Services:** Interlibrary loan; copying; library open to the public with restrictions. **Computerized Information Services:** MEDLINE, DIALOG Information Services. Performs searches on fee basis. **Networks/Consortia:** Member of Lakeland

Area Library Network (LAKENET), Sisters of Mercy Health Corporation. **Staff:** Yvonne Mathis, Asst.Libn..

★12601★
ST. MARY'S HOSPITAL - LIBRARY (Med)
1216 2nd St., S.W. Phone: (507)285-5647
Rochester, MN 55902 Mona Stevermer, Libn.
Founded: 1913. **Staff:** Prof 2; Other 6. **Subjects:** Nursing, allied health sciences, nutrition, hospital administration. **Holdings:** 4500 books. **Subscriptions:** 250 journals and other serials. **Services:** Interlibrary loan; current awareness; library open to the public for reference use only. **Computerized Information Services:** DIALOG Information Services. **Publications:** New Books List, monthly; Library News Column, monthly. **Staff:** Janet Behrens, Asst.Libn..

★12602★
ST. MARY'S HOSPITAL - MEDICAL ALLIED HEALTH LIBRARY (Med)
211 Pennington Ave. Phone: (201)470-3055
Passaic, NJ 07055 Sr. Gertrude Doremus, S.C., Dir.
Staff: Prof 1. **Subjects:** Medicine, surgery, orthopedics, vascular surgery, psychiatry, urology, gastrointestinal diseases, cardiovascular systems, hematology, gynecology and obstetrics. **Holdings:** 450 books; 1900 bound periodical volumes. **Subscriptions:** 120 journals and other serials. **Services:** Interlibrary loan; copying; library open to the public with identification. **Automated Operations:** Computerized cataloging and circulation. **Networks/Consortia:** Member of New Mexico Consortium of Biomedical and Hospital Libraries, Bergen-Passaic Health Sciences Library Consortium.

★12603★
ST. MARY'S HOSPITAL - MEDICAL LIBRARY (Med)
2800 Main St. Phone: (816)753-5700
Kansas City, MO 64108 Kitty Serling, Lib.Mgr.
Founded: 1936. **Staff:** Prof 1. **Subjects:** Medicine, nursing, allied health sciences. **Holdings:** 1600 books; 600 bound periodical volumes; 100 journal titles on microfilm. **Subscriptions:** 151 journals and other serials. **Services:** Interlibrary loan; copying; SDI; library open to the public with restrictions. **Computerized Information Services:** DIALOG Information Services, MEDLARS, BRS Information Technologies, WILSONLINE. Performs searches on fee basis. **Networks/Consortia:** Member of Kansas City Library Network, Inc. (KCLN), Sisters of St. Mary - System Wide Library Consortium, Kansas City Metropolitan Library Network (KCMLN).

★12604★
ST. MARY'S HOSPITAL - MEDICAL LIBRARY (Med)
305 S. Fifth St.
Box 232 Phone: (405)233-6100
Enid, OK 73701 Jean McDaniel, Med.Libn.
Staff: Prof 1. **Subjects:** Medicine, nursing, hospital administration. **Holdings:** 2405 books; 2292 bound periodical volumes; 250 videotapes. **Subscriptions:** 160 journals and other serials. **Services:** Interlibrary loan; copying; library open to medical and paramedical professionals.

★12605★
ST. MARY'S HOSPITAL - MEDICAL LIBRARY (Med)
803 E. Dakota Ave. Phone: (605)224-3178
Pierre, SD 57501 DeAnn DeKay Hilmoe, Med.Libn.
Staff: Prof 1. **Subjects:** Medicine, nursing, allied health sciences. **Holdings:** 2100 books; 25 bound periodical volumes. **Subscriptions:** 195 journals and other serials. **Services:** Interlibrary loan; copying; SDI; library open to the public with restrictions. **Automated Operations:** Computerized cataloging. **Computerized Information Services:** BRS Information Technologies, MEDLARS; EasyLink, DOCLINE (electronic mail services). Performs searches on fee basis. **Networks/Consortia:** Member of Central South Dakota Health Science Library Consortium. **Publications:** CSDHSLC Newsletter, monthly - to members and interested professionals in the region.

★12606★
ST. MARY'S HOSPITAL - MEDICAL LIBRARY (Med)
911B Queen's Blvd. Phone: (519)744-3311
Kitchener, ON, Canada N2M 1B2 Elaine Baldwin, Libn.
Founded: 1963. **Staff:** Prof 1. **Subjects:** Medicine, nursing, hospital administration. **Holdings:** 1000 books; 900 bound periodical volumes. **Subscriptions:** 100 journals and other serials. **Services:** Library not open to the public.

★12607★
ST. MARY'S HOSPITAL - MEDICAL LIBRARY (Med)
3830 Lacombe Phone: (514)344-3317
Montreal, PQ, Canada H3T 1M5 Lucile Lavigueur, Libn.
Founded: 1952. **Staff:** Prof 1; Other 1. **Subjects:** Medicine, nursing, obstetrics, gynecology, psychiatry, surgery. **Holdings:** 2600 books; 5600 bound periodical volumes; 1300 audio cassettes; 20 video cassettes; 5065 slides; 60 slide/tape sets. **Subscriptions:** 230 journals and other serials. **Services:** Interlibrary loan; library not open to the public.

★12608★
ST. MARY'S HOSPITAL - MEDICAL LIBRARY (6-East) (Med)
Huntington, WV 25702-1271 Phone: (304)526-1314
Kay Gibson, Med.Libn.
Founded: 1929. **Staff:** Prof 1; Other 1. **Subjects:** Medicine, surgery, allied health sciences. **Holdings:** 757 books; 1526 bound periodical volumes; 731 unbound periodicals; 89 pamphlets. **Subscriptions:** 152 journals and other serials; 5 newspapers. **Services:** Interlibrary loan; copying; SDI; library open to the public. **Computerized Information Services:** Access to MEDLARS, MEDLINE. **Networks/Consortia:** Member of Huntington Health Science Library Consortium. **Publications:** Bibliographies - to physicians. **Special Catalogs:** Huntington Health Science Library Consortium Serial Holdings; St. Mary's Hospital serial holdings by title and subject; book holdings by author and subject.

★12609★
ST. MARY'S HOSPITAL - MEDICAL STAFF LIBRARY (Med)
1300 Massachusetts Ave. Phone: (518)272-5000
Troy, NY 12180 Audna T. Clum, Libn.
Founded: 1960. **Staff:** Prof 1. **Subjects:** Medicine. **Holdings:** 450 books; 1300 bound periodical volumes; 719 other cataloged items. **Subscriptions:** 78 journals and other serials. **Services:** Interlibrary loan; library open to the public. **Networks/Consortia:** Member of Capital District Library Council for Reference & Research Resources (CDLC).

★12610★
ST. MARY'S HOSPITAL & HEALTH CENTER - RALPH FULLER MEDICAL LIBRARY (Med)
1601 W. St. Mary's Rd.
Box 5386 Phone: (602)622-5833
Tucson, AZ 85703 Jeffrey W. St. Clair, Libn.
Founded: 1939. **Staff:** Prof 1; Other 3. **Subjects:** Medicine, nursing, hospital administration, allied health sciences. **Holdings:** 900 books; 3000 bound periodical volumes; 166 videotapes; 4 VF drawers of pamphlets and reprints. **Subscriptions:** 133 journals and other serials. **Services:** Interlibrary loan; library not open to the public. **Automated Operations:** Computerized cataloging and acquisitions. **Computerized Information Services:** MEDLINE, DIALOG Information Services; OnTyme Electronic Message Network Service (electronic mail service). Performs searches on fee basis. **Networks/Consortia:** Member of Pacific Southwest Regional Medical Library Service, Southeast Arizona Medical Library Consortium. **Publications:** Serials Holdings List, annual - free upon request; Audiovisual Holdings List, annual. **Remarks:** Maintained by Carondelet Health Services, Inc.

★12611★
ST. MARY'S HOSPITAL AND MEDICAL CENTER - MEDICAL LIBRARY (Med)
450 Stanyan St. Phone: (415)750-5784
San Francisco, CA 94117 Rochelle Perrine Schmalz, Dir., Lib.Serv.
Staff: Prof 2; Other 1. **Subjects:** Medicine, surgery, psychiatry, nursing. **Holdings:** 5250 books; 7800 bound periodical volumes; medical, surgical, and psychiatry tape cassettes. **Subscriptions:** 275 journals and other serials. **Services:** Interlibrary loan; copying; library open to the public by appointment. **Computerized Information Services:** DIALOG Information Services, BRS Information Technologies, MEDLINE. **Networks/Consortia:** Member of Pacific Southwest Regional Medical Library Service, San Francisco Biomedical Library Group.

★12612★
ST. MARY'S HOSPITAL MEDICAL EDUCATION FOUNDATION - MEDICAL LITERATURE INFORMATION CENTER (Med)
101 Memorial Dr. Phone: (816)753-5700
Kansas City, MO 64108 Dr. George X. Trimble, Dir.
Founded: 1947. **Staff:** Prof 1; Other 2. **Subjects:** Clinical medicine, medical education, medical staff organization, toxicology, history of medicine. **Special Collections:** Medical literature reprint technology. **Holdings:** 500 volumes; 900 monographs; 485,000 medical literature reprints. **Subscriptions:** 150 journals and other serials. **Services:** Copying; will

answer brief inquiries and make referrals; center open for medical or academic use by appointment. **Publications:** Reports and critical reviews, irregular; medical literature critiques, irregular. **Special Indexes:** Index and cross-index to medical literature reprints; index to therapeutic drugs in generic and proprietary terms; index of eponyms.

★12613★

ST. MARY'S OF THE LAKE HOSPITAL - GIBSON MEDICAL LIBRARY (Med)
340 Union St., W.
Box 3600 Phone: (613)544-5220
Kingston, ON, Canada K7L 5A2 Penny G. Levi, Dir., Lib.Serv.
Founded: 1978. **Staff:** Prof 1; Other 1. **Subjects:** Geriatrics and chronic care, rehabilitation, allied health sciences. **Special Collections:** Hospital archives, 1946-1987. **Holdings:** 2500 books; 500 bound periodical volumes. **Subscriptions:** 120 journals and other serials. **Services:** Interlibrary loan; copying; library open to the public with restrictions. **Computerized Information Services:** MEDLARS; Envoy 100 (electronic mail service). Performs searches on fee basis. **Publications:** New Book List, monthly - local distribution on request; Patient/Family Resource Guide: Arthritis (pamphlet).

★12614★

ST. MARY'S MEDICAL CENTER - HERMAN M. BAKER, M.D. MEMORIAL LIBRARY (Med)
3700 Washington Ave. Phone: (812)479-4151
Evansville, IN 47750 E. Jane Saltzman, Mgr.
Staff: Prof 1; Other 5. **Subjects:** Medicine, nursing, health administration. **Holdings:** 1200 volumes; 300 AV programs. **Subscriptions:** 120 journals and other serials; 10 newspapers. **Services:** Interlibrary loan; copying; library open to the public with restrictions. **Computerized Information Services:** MEDLARS. **Networks/Consortia:** Member of Greater Midwest Regional Medical Library Network, Evansville Area Health Sciences Libraries Consortium.

★12615★

ST. MARY'S MEDICAL CENTER, INC. - MEDICAL LIBRARY (Med)
Oak Hill Ave. Phone: (615)971-7916
Knoxville, TN 37917 Glenda Clark, Libn.
Staff: Prof 1. **Subjects:** Medicine, nursing, hospital administration. **Holdings:** 1500 books; 425 bound periodical volumes; 300 pamphlets. **Subscriptions:** 122 journals and other serials. **Services:** Interlibrary loan; copying; library open to the public for reference use only. **Computerized Information Services:** MEDLARS. Performs searches on fee basis. **Networks/Consortia:** Member of Knoxville Area Health Sciences Library Consortium (KAHSLC).

★12616★

ST. MARY'S MEDICAL CENTER, INC. - SCHOOL OF NURSING LIBRARY (Med)
900 Emerald Ave. Phone: (615)971-7839
Knoxville, TN 37917 Beth Barret, Libn.
Founded: 1944. **Staff:** Prof 1. **Subjects:** Medicine, nursing. **Holdings:** 3018 volumes; 6 drawers of clippings and pamphlets. **Subscriptions:** 75 journals and other serials. **Services:** Interlibrary loan; copying; library open to the public for reference use only. **Networks/Consortia:** Member of Knoxville Area Health Sciences Library Consortium (KAHSLC).

★12617★

ST. MARY'S REGIONAL MEDICAL CENTER - MAX C. FLEISCHMANN MEDICAL LIBRARY (Med)
235 W. Sixth St. Phone: (702)789-3108
Reno, NV 89520-0108 Kathleen L. Pratt, Libn.
Founded: 1958. **Staff:** Prof 1. **Subjects:** Medicine, nursing, management. **Holdings:** 1446 books; 1244 bound periodical volumes. **Subscriptions:** 152 journals and other serials. **Services:** Interlibrary loan; copying; library open to the public for reference use only. **Networks/Consortia:** Member of Pacific Southwest Regional Medical Library Service, Northern California and Nevada Medical Library Group (NCNMLG), Nevada Medical Libraries Group (NMLG). **Formerly:** St. Mary's Hospital.

★12618★

ST. MARY'S SCHOOL FOR THE DEAF - INFORMATION CENTER (Educ)
2253 Main St. Phone: (716)834-7200
Buffalo, NY 14214 Collette Sangster, Dir.
Staff: Prof 2; Other 1. **Subjects:** Deafness, audiology, speech, special education. **Holdings:** 10,951 books; 652 bound periodical volumes; 436 microfiche. **Subscriptions:** 57 journals and other serials. **Services:** Interlibrary loan; copying; center open to the public with restrictions. **Automated Operations:** Computerized cataloging. **Staff:** Jean Odien, Libn..

★12619★

ST. MARY'S SEMINARY - CARDINAL BERAN LIBRARY (Rel-Phil)
9845 Memorial Dr. Phone: (713)681-5544
Houston, TX 77024 Constance Walker, Libn.
Staff: Prof 1; Other 2. **Subjects:** Philosophy, theology, canon law, church history. **Holdings:** 39,500 books; 4118 bound periodical volumes; 1816 cassette tapes; 1400 microforms; 436 phonograph records. **Subscriptions:** 325 journals and other serials; 13 newspapers. **Services:** Interlibrary loan; library open to the public for reference use only. **Computerized Information Services:** Access to OCLC.

★12620★

ST. MARY'S UNIVERSITY - GEOGRAPHY DEPARTMENT - MAP LIBRARY (Geog-Map)
Robie St. Phone: (902)420-5742
Halifax, NS, Canada B3M 3M7 Benoit Ouellette, Cart./Map Libn.
Founded: 1975. **Staff:** 1. **Subjects:** Maps - North America, Western Europe, Asia. **Special Collections:** Atlantic region; urban and regional development; marine and coastal studies. **Holdings:** 1000 books, pamphlets, journals, atlases; 25,000 maps. **Services:** Library open to the public for reference use only. **Remarks:** Library is depository for Canadian topographical maps from Canada Map Office.

★12621★

ST. MARY'S UNIVERSITY - PATRICK POWER LIBRARY (Rel-Phil, Bus-Fin)
Halifax, NS, Canada B3H 3C3 Phone: (902)429-9780
Ronald A. Lewis, Univ.Libn.
Staff: Prof 7; Other 36. **Subjects:** Religious studies, Canadiana, business administration. **Special Collections:** Eric Gill Collection (30 volumes); Santamariana Collection (575 volumes). **Holdings:** 250,000 volumes; ERIC microfiche, 1969 to present; 200 titles of Canadian labor newspapers on microfilm; corporate reports for 1400 companies. **Subscriptions:** 1802 journals and other serials; 33 newspapers. **Services:** Interlibrary loan; copying; library open to the public with restrictions. **Automated Operations:** Computerized cataloging, acquisitions, and serials. **Computerized Information Services:** CAN/OLE, DIALOG Information Services, Pergamon ORBIT InfoLine, Inc., QL Systems, The Reference Service (REFSRV), Info Globe, International Development Research Centre (IDRC), UTLAS. Performs searches on fee basis. Contact Person: Douglas Vaisey. **Networks/Consortia:** Member of Nova Scotia On-Line Consortium. **Publications:** The Perfect Term Paper: A Do-It-Yourself Guide; Guide to the Patrick Power Library, irregular; statistics collected by the Federal Government of Canada, irregular; The Census of Canada, irregular; statistics published by provincial governments in Canada, irregular; pamphlets on corporate reports and group study rooms - all free upon request. **Staff:** Cynthia Tanner, Coll.Dev./User Educ.; Rashid Tayyeb, Hd., Tech.Serv.; Margot Schenk, Hd., Pub.Serv.; Paul Rooney, Media Serv.; Arthur Smith, Cat.; Ken Clare, Circ.; David Manning, Acq.; Bob Cook, Bibliog. Searching Unit.

★12622★

ST. MARY'S UNIVERSITY - SARITA KENNEDY EAST LAW LIBRARY (Law)
One Camino Santa Maria Phone: (512)436-3435
San Antonio, TX 78284-0440 Robert L. Summers, Jr., Dir.
Founded: 1937. **Staff:** Prof 6; Other 30. **Subjects:** Law. **Special Collections:** Early Spanish law; land titles (Spanish and American). **Holdings:** 78,865 books; 11,079 bound periodical volumes. **Subscriptions:** 1488 journals and other serials. **Services:** Interlibrary loan; copying (limited); library open to the public for reference use only. **Automated Operations:** Computerized cataloging. **Computerized Information Services:** WESTLAW, LEXIS. **Staff:** Douglas Ferrier, Hd., Tech.Serv.; Duane Henricks, Govt.Doc.Libn.; Lee Unterborn, Acq./Ref.Libn.; Caroline Byrd, Hd., Pub.Serv.; James Bass, Cat..

★12623★

ST. MATTHEW'S & ST. TIMOTHY'S NEIGHBORHOOD CENTER, INC. - TUTORIAL PROGRAM LIBRARY (Educ)
26 W. 84th St. Phone: (212)362-6750
New York, NY 10024 Delfa Castillo, Dir., Reading Ctr.
Staff: Prof 2. **Subjects:** Remedial reading and mathematics. **Special Collections:** Remedial reading and mathematics materials and professional literature; children's literature (600 volumes). **Holdings:** 11,000 books. **Services:** Library open to Neighborhood Center participants. **Staff:** Jennifer Anderson, Asst.Dir., Tutoring Prog..

★12624★
ST. MEINRAD ARCHABBEY - COLLEGE & SCHOOL OF THEOLOGY - LIBRARY (Rel-Phil)
St. Meinrad, IN 47577 Phone: (812)357-6401
Rev. Simeon Daly, O.S.B., Libn.
Staff: Prof 2; Other 7. **Subjects:** Religion, Catholic theology. **Holdings:** 126,000 books; 15,000 bound periodical volumes. **Subscriptions:** 567 journals and other serials. **Services:** Interlibrary loan; copying; library open to the public for reference use only. **Automated Operations:** Computerized cataloging and ILL. **Computerized Information Services:** BRS Information Technologies. Performs searches on fee basis. **Networks/Consortia:** Member of INCOLSA, Four Rivers Area Library Services Authority. **Staff:** Rev. Justin DuVall, O.S.B., Asst.Libn..

★12625★
ST. MICHAEL MEDICAL CENTER - AQUINAS MEDICAL LIBRARY (Med)
268 Dr. Martin Luther King Jr. Blvd. Phone: (201)877-5471
Newark, NJ 07102 Betty L. Garrison, Dir., Med.Lib.
Staff: Prof 1; Other 1. **Subjects:** Medicine, pediatrics, obstetrics and gynecology, surgery, infectious diseases. **Special Collections:** Podiatry; hematology. **Holdings:** 2000 books; 4500 bound periodical volumes; 1 VF drawer of clippings. **Subscriptions:** 95 journals and other serials. **Services:** Interlibrary loan; library not open to the public. **Computerized Information Services:** NLM, BRS Information Technologies. Performs searches on fee basis. **Networks/Consortia:** Member of Cosmopolitan Biomedical Library Consortium (CBLC), Health Sciences Library Association of New Jersey, BHSL.

ST. MICHAEL'S COLLEGE
See: University of Toronto - St. Michael's College - John M. Kelly Library (16997)

★12626★
ST. MICHAEL'S IN THE HILLS EPISCOPAL CHURCH - PARISH LIBRARY (Rel-Phil)
4718 Brittany Rd. Phone: (419)531-1616
Toledo, OH 43615-2312 Claudia Hannaford, Libn.
Staff: 3. **Subjects:** Religion, devotion, interpersonal relations, Christian social concerns. **Special Collections:** Summa Theologicae (St. Thomas Aquinas; 60 volumes). **Holdings:** 1850 books; 13 audio cassettes; 20 phonograph records; 21 games; 3 VF drawers of pictures; 12 video cassettes. **Subscriptions:** 12 journals and other serials. **Services:** Library open to the public with restrictions.

★12627★
ST. MICHAEL'S HOSPITAL - HEALTH SCIENCE LIBRARY (Med)
30 Bond St. Phone: (416)864-5059
Toronto, ON, Canada M5B 1W8 Anita Wong, Dir.
Founded: 1956. **Staff:** Prof 1; Other 4. **Subjects:** Medicine and surgery. **Holdings:** 7000 books; 9000 bound periodical volumes; reprints of staff publications. **Subscriptions:** 500 journals and other serials. **Services:** Interlibrary loan; library not open to the public. **Computerized Information Services:** MEDLARS, CAN/OLE, DIALOG Information Services. **Publications:** Monthly Library Bulletin; library journal holdings by title and by subject, annual.

★12628★
ST. MICHAEL'S HOSPITAL - HEALTH SCIENCES LIBRARY (Med)
900 Illinois Ave. Phone: (715)344-4400
Stevens Point, WI 54481 Barbara DeWeerd, Libn.
Founded: 1967. **Staff:** Prof 1; Other 1. **Subjects:** Medicine, nursing. **Holdings:** 900 books. **Subscriptions:** 95 journals and other serials. **Services:** Interlibrary loan; copying; library open to the public for reference use only. **Computerized Information Services:** MEDLINE. **Networks/Consortia:** Member of Greater Midwest Regional Medical Library Network, Northern Wisconsin Health Science Libraries Cooperative.

★12629★
ST. MICHAEL'S HOSPITAL - REGNER HEALTH SCIENCES LIBRARY (Med)
2400 W. Villard Ave. Phone: (414)527-8477
Milwaukee, WI 53209 Vicki Schluge, Dir., Lib.Serv.
Staff: Prof 1; Other 4. **Subjects:** Medicine, nursing, allied health sciences, management. **Holdings:** 2000 books; 4600 periodicals (bound and on microfilm); 80 video cassettes. **Subscriptions:** 270 journals and other serials. **Services:** Interlibrary loan; copying; library open to the public for reference use only. **Automated Operations:** Computerized cataloging. **Computerized Information Services:** DIALOG Information Services, BRS Information Technologies, NLM; DOCLINE (electronic mail service). Performs searches on fee basis. **Networks/Consortia:** Member of Southeastern Wisconsin Health Science Library Consortium (SWHSL), Greater Midwest Regional Medical Library Network.

★12630★
ST. MONICA'S CHURCH - LIBRARY (Rel-Phil)
31 Mather St.
Hartford, CT 06112 Ilene Tahey, Libn.
Founded: 1985. **Subjects:** Religion. **Holdings:** 100 books. **Services:** Copying; library open to the public.

★12631★
ST. NICHOLAS HOSPITAL - HEALTH SCIENCES LIBRARY (Med)
1601 N. Taylor Dr. Phone: (414)459-4713
Sheboygan, WI 53081 Kathleen Blaser, Coord., Lib.Serv.
Staff: Prof 1. **Subjects:** Medicine, nursing, management, philosophy. **Holdings:** 850 books. **Subscriptions:** 125 journals and other serials. **Services:** Interlibrary loan; copying; literature searches; library open to persons in health fields. **Computerized Information Services:** DOCLINE (electronic mail service). **Networks/Consortia:** Member of Fox River Valley Area Library Consortium, Greater Midwest Regional Medical Library Network.

★12632★
ST. NORBERT ABBEY - AUGUSTINE LIBRARY (Rel-Phil)
1016 N. Broadway Phone: (414)336-1321
De Pere, WI 54115 Rev. Aaron Walschinski, Libn./Archv.
Staff: Prof 1. **Subjects:** Theology, philosophy. **Special Collections:** Abbey Archives (1200 rare books); Premonstratensian Order history (1300 books); manuscripts and letters (90,000 items). **Holdings:** 12,000 books; 350 bound periodical volumes. **Subscriptions:** 40 journals and other serials. **Services:** Interlibrary loan; copying; library open to the public by appointment.

★12633★
ST. OLAF COLLEGE - HOWARD AND EDNA HONG KIERKEGAARD LIBRARY (Rel-Phil, Hum)
Northfield, MN 55057 Phone: (612)663-3846
Dr. C. Stephen Evans, Cur.
Founded: 1976. **Staff:** Prof 3. **Subjects:** Translation, philosophy, theology, religion, history. **Special Collections:** Kierkegaard's writings (complete set of first editions and later editions); replication of Kierkegaard's personal library; Kierkegaard's manuscripts (microfilm); critical secondary sources and background materials published after 1855. **Holdings:** 9000 volumes; doctoral dissertations; microfilm; cassette tapes. **Services:** Library open to the public with restrictions. **Staff:** Howard V. Hong, Assoc.Cur.; Cynthia Lund, Asst.Cur..

★12634★
ST. OLAF LUTHERAN CHURCH - CARLSEN MEMORIAL LIBRARY (Rel-Phil)
29th & Emerson Ave., N. Phone: (612)529-7726
Minneapolis, MN 55411 Donna Weflen, Libn.
Founded: 1962. **Staff:** 2. **Subjects:** Religion and related topics. **Special Collections:** Books in Norwegian. **Holdings:** 1457 books. **Services:** Library not open to the public.

★12635★
ST. PATRICK HOSPITAL - LIBRARY (Med)
500 W. Broadway
Box 4587 Phone: (406)543-7271
Missoula, MT 59806 Cara Lou Mackay, Libn.
Staff: Prof 1; Other 1. **Subjects:** Nursing, medicine, hospital administration, patient education. **Holdings:** 1500 books; 20 VF drawers of pamphlets; 800 video cassettes. **Subscriptions:** 250 journals and other serials. **Services:** Interlibrary loan; copying; literature searches; library open to the public. **Computerized Information Services:** MEDLARS; DOCLINE, EMSCL (electronic mail services). Performs searches free of charge. **Networks/Consortia:** Member of Pacific Northwest Regional Health Sciences Library Service.

★12636★
ST. PATRICK'S SEMINARY - MC KEON MEMORIAL LIBRARY (Rel-Phil)
320 Middlefield Rd. Phone: (415)321-5655
Menlo Park, CA 94025 John F. Mattingly, Dir.
Founded: 1898. **Staff:** Prof 2. **Subjects:** Theology, philosophy, scripture, patrology. **Special Collections:** Bibliotheca Sancti Francisci Archdioceseos.

Holdings: 68,000 books; 4500 bound periodical volumes; 950 tapes. **Subscriptions:** 270 journals and other serials; 11 newspapers. **Services:** Interlibrary loan; copying; library open to the public for reference use only. **Staff:** Pamela Nurse, Asst.Libn..

★12637★
ST. PAUL CITY COUNCIL - RESEARCH LIBRARY (Plan)
502 City Hall
15 W. Kellogg Blvd. Phone: (612)298-4163
St. Paul, MN 55102 Rosanne D'Agostino
Founded: 1973. **Staff:** 1. **Subjects:** St. Paul, urban affairs. **Special Collections:** St. Paul city documents. **Holdings:** 3200 books; 150 bound periodical volumes; 29 VF drawers; 8 drawers of microfilm; newsletters. **Subscriptions:** 150 journals and other serials. **Services:** Interlibrary loan; copying; library open to the public with restrictions. **Special Indexes:** Document index (book).

★12638★
ST. PAUL FIRE & MARINE INSURANCE COMPANY - LIBRARY (Bus-Fin)
385 Washington St. Phone: (612)221-8226
St. Paul, MN 55102 Eleanor Hamilton, Lib.Supv.
Founded: 1953. **Staff:** Prof 1; Other 3. **Subjects:** Insurance, management, data processing. **Holdings:** 12,000 volumes. **Subscriptions:** 350 journals and other serials. **Services:** Interlibrary loan; copying; library open to the public.

★12639★
ST. PAUL HOSPITAL - C.B. SACHER LIBRARY (Med)
5909 Harry Hines Blvd. Phone: (214)879-2390
Dallas, TX 75235 Sheila Ross Carter, Dir.
Founded: 1900. **Staff:** Prof 1; Other 2. **Subjects:** Nursing, medicine, and allied health sciences. **Holdings:** 3500 books; 1100 bound periodical volumes; 750 audio cassettes. **Subscriptions:** 150 journals and other serials. **Services:** Interlibrary loan; copying; library open to the public with restrictions. **Automated Operations:** Computerized cataloging. **Computerized Information Services:** DIALOG Information Services, BRS Information Technologies, NLM, Compact Cambridge; DOCLINE (electronic mail service). Performs searches on fee basis. **Networks/Consortia:** Member of Dallas-Tarrant County Consortium of Health Science Libraries, Northeast Texas Library System (NETLS). **Remarks:** An alternate telephone number is 879-3790.

★12640★
ST. PAUL LUTHERAN CHURCH AND SCHOOL - PARISH LIBRARY (Rel-Phil)
5201 Galitz
Skokie, IL 60077 Phone: (312)673-5030
Founded: 1960. **Staff:** 8. **Subjects:** Religion. **Holdings:** 9000 books; 40 bound periodical volumes; 9 VF drawers of pamphlets; AV programs; pictures; posters; phonograph records; filmstrips. **Subscriptions:** 25 journals and other serials. **Services:** Interlibrary loan; copying; library open to the public on request. **Automated Operations:** Computerized cataloging. **Publications:** Book lists, irregular - to parishioners.

★12641★
ST. PAUL PIONEER PRESS AND DISPATCH - LIBRARY (Publ)
345 Cedar St. Phone: (612)228-5557
St. Paul, MN 55101 Linda James, Hd.Libn.
Founded: 1906. **Staff:** Prof 1; Other 7. **Subjects:** Newspaper reference topics. **Holdings:** 500 books; 500,000 clippings; 1 million pictures. **Services:** Library not open to the public.

★12642★
ST. PAUL PUBLIC LIBRARY - ART AND MUSIC (Art, Mus)
90 W. Fourth St. Phone: (612)292-6186
St. Paul, MN 55102 Delores Sundbye, Supv.
Staff: Prof 4; Other 1. **Subjects:** Fine and applied arts, music. **Holdings:** 33,500 books; 3528 bound periodical volumes; 24,000 mounted pictures; 52,000 unmounted pictures; 1080 exhibit catalogs; 311 framed pictures; 39 sculptures; 1941 art slides; 5295 phonograph records; 364 music and language cassettes; 19,240 scores; 141 compact discs. **Subscriptions:** 150 journals and other serials. **Services:** Interlibrary loan; copying; library open to the public. **Networks/Consortia:** Member of Metronet, Metropolitan Library Service Agency (MELSA), Cooperating Libraries in Consortium (CLIC). **Special Indexes:** Song Index; Art and Music Biography/Criticism Indexes; Piano/Organ Index; Arts Ephemera Index. **Staff:** Carole Brysky, Prof.Asst..

★12643★
ST. PAUL PUBLIC LIBRARY - BUSINESS & SCIENCE ROOM (Bus-Fin, Sci-Engr)
90 W. Fourth St. Phone: (612)292-6176
St. Paul, MN 55102 Virginia B. Stavn, Supv.
Staff: Prof 4; Other 4. **Subjects:** Economics, business, labor, finance, science, technology, popular medicine. **Holdings:** 65,000 books; 7300 bound periodical volumes; 65 VF drawers. **Subscriptions:** 485 journals and other serials. **Services:** Interlibrary loan; copying; room open to the public. **Networks/Consortia:** Member of Metropolitan Library Service Agency (MELSA), Cooperating Libraries in Consortium (CLIC), Metronet. **Special Indexes:** Indexes for handicraft materials and consumer information (card). **Staff:** Karen Kolb, Prof.Asst.; Doris Wahl, Libn.; Joan Gens, Libn..

★12644★
ST. PAUL PUBLIC LIBRARY - FILM & VIDEO CENTER (Aud-Vis)
90 W. Fourth St. Phone: (612)292-6336
St. Paul, MN 55102 Marti Lybeck, Supv.
Staff: Prof 1; Other 3. **Subjects:** Film, video, computer software. **Holdings:** 50 books; 50 catalogs of video software; 1300 videotapes and cassettes; 650 16mm films. **Subscriptions:** 12 journals and other serials. **Services:** Interlibrary loan (for print material); center open to the public with restrictions. **Networks/Consortia:** Member of Metropolitan Library Service Agency (MELSA), MINITEX, Metronet. **Publications:** Occasional booklists, bibliographies, tapelists, filmlists. **Special Catalogs:** Catalog of films - for sale.

★12645★
ST. PAUL PUBLIC LIBRARY - GOVERNMENT PUBLICATIONS OFFICE (Info Sci)
90 W. 4th St. Phone: (612)292-6178
St. Paul, MN 55102 Rosamond T. Jacob, Libn.
Staff: Prof 1; Other 1. **Subjects:** Federal and state depository publications. **Holdings:** 250,000 documents. **Services:** Interlibrary loan; copying; office open to the public. **Computerized Information Services:** DIALOG Information Services, DATANET. Performs searches free of charge. **Networks/Consortia:** Member of Metropolitan Library Service Agency (MELSA), Cooperating Libraries in Consortium (CLIC), Metronet. **Publications:** Documents/Classified, monthly.

★12646★
ST. PAUL PUBLIC LIBRARY - HIGHLAND PARK BRANCH - PERRIE JONES MEMORIAL ROOM (Rare Book)
1974 Ford Pkwy. Phone: (612)292-6622
St. Paul, MN 55116 Kathleen Tregilgas, Supv.
Special Collections: Sumerian Clay Tablets (41); Horn Collection: classics published in the 16th, 17th, and 18th centuries (154); Cruikshank Collection: books illustrated and/or written by George Cruikshank and his brother (26); Fitzgerald Collection: books by or about F. Scott Fitzgerald and his times (38); Johnston Collection: rare books, 16th century to present (1430); Local Collection: miscellaneous books on Twin Cities and Minnesota (43); Perrie Jones Collection: books and other material by or related to Perrie Jones (50). **Holdings:** 1800 books; letters; manuscripts; photographs; autographs. **Services:** Copying; room open to the public by appointment for reference use only.

★12647★
ST. PAUL PUBLIC LIBRARY - SOCIAL SCIENCES & LITERATURE (Soc Sci, Hum)
90 W. Fourth St. Phone: (612)292-6206
St. Paul, MN 55102 Elaine Wagner, Supv.
Staff: Prof 5; Other 8. **Subjects:** Literature, fiction, history and travel, philosophy and religion, biography, political and social sciences, dance, sports and games. **Special Collections:** Large print books (2000); costume (50 books); foreign languages (5104 titles in 15 languages); spoken word cassettes (275). **Holdings:** 220,000 volumes. **Services:** Interlibrary loan; copying; library open to the public. **Networks/Consortia:** Member of Metronet, Metropolitan Library Service Agency (MELSA), Cooperating Libraries in Consortium (CLIC). **Special Indexes:** Card indexes to biography and literary criticism file; short story file; drama file; ballet story index; dance index; games and sports index. **Staff:** Richard Hemming, Prof.Asst..

★12648★
ST. PAUL PUBLIC LIBRARY - SOCIAL SCIENCES & LITERATURE REFERENCE ROOM (Hum, Soc Sci)
90 W. Fourth St. Phone: (612)292-6307
St. Paul, MN 55102 Elizabeth McMonigal, Supv.
Staff: Prof 5; Other 6. **Subjects:** Literature, philosophy, religion, history, biography, sports, geography, travel, education, politics, government. **Special Collections:** St. Paul Collection (city documents; newspapers; clippings); selected Minnesota documents; telephone directories (35,000 U.S. cities). **Holdings:** 20,000 volumes. **Subscriptions:** 231 journals; 257 serials; 9 newspapers. **Services:** Interlibrary loan; room open to the public. **Computerized Information Services:** DIALOG Information Services, DataTimes, DATANET, WILSONLINE. **Networks/Consortia:** Member of Metropolitan Library Service Agency (MELSA), Metronet. **Special Indexes:** St. Paul Pioneer Press and St. Paul Dispatch Index, 1967 to present; local clubs and organization file; St. Paul Pioneer Press and Dispatch Morgue File, 1910-1945. **Staff:** Carol Martinson, Asst. to Supv..

★12649★
ST. PAUL PUBLIC SCHOOLS INDEPENDENT SCHOOL DISTRICT 625 - DISTRICT PROFESSIONAL LIBRARY (Educ)
1930 Como Ave. Phone: (612)293-8990
St. Paul, MN 55108 Walter M. Ostrem, Libn.
Staff: Prof 1. **Subjects:** Education, psychology, child development. **Special Collections:** Archives of St. Paul School District (1000 items). **Holdings:** 7000 books; 22,000 unbound periodicals; 500 reels of microfilm of periodicals; 1500 textbooks; 900 documents; 3000 clippings. **Subscriptions:** 184 journals and other serials. **Services:** Interlibrary loan; copying; library open to the public. **Networks/Consortia:** Member of MINITEX, Cooperating Libraries in Consortium (CLIC).

★12650★
ST. PAUL RAMSEY MEDICAL CENTER - MEDICAL LIBRARY (Med)
640 Jackson St. Phone: (612)221-3607
St. Paul, MN 55101 Mary Dwyer, Hd.Libn.
Founded: 1961. **Staff:** Prof 2; Other 2. **Subjects:** Medicine and nursing. **Holdings:** 4000 books; 6000 bound periodical volumes. **Subscriptions:** 390 journals and other serials. **Services:** Interlibrary loan; library open to professionals only. **Computerized Information Services:** MEDLARS. **Networks/Consortia:** Member of Twin Cities Biomedical Consortium (TCBC). **Staff:** Audrey Woodke, Asst.Libn..

★12651★
ST. PAUL SCHOOL OF THEOLOGY - DANA DAWSON LIBRARY (Rel-Phil)
5123 Truman Rd. Phone: (816)483-9600
Kansas City, MO 64127-2499 Dr. William S. Sparks, Libn.
Founded: 1958. **Staff:** Prof 1; Other 4. **Subjects:** Theology. **Holdings:** 64,000 volumes. **Subscriptions:** 350 journals and other serials. **Services:** Interlibrary loan; copying; library open to the public with restrictions. **Computerized Information Services:** BRS Information Technologies, DIALOG Information Services.

★12652★
ST. PAUL TECHNICAL VOCATIONAL INSTITUTE - LIBRARY (Sci-Engr)
235 Marshall Ave. Phone: (612)221-1410
St. Paul, MN 55102 S. Haugen, Libn.
Founded: 1967. **Staff:** Prof 1; Other 1. **Subjects:** Trades and technical occupations, business subjects. **Holdings:** 7000 books. **Subscriptions:** 185 journals and other serials. **Services:** Copying; library open to the public for reference use only.

★12653★
ST. PAUL'S CHURCH - ARCHIVES (Rel-Phil)
605 Reynolds St.
Augusta, GA 30901 Phone: (404)724-2485
Subjects: St. Paul's Church history, 1750 to present. **Holdings:** 4000 church records, meetings minutes, correspondence of church officers, church registers, and marriage, baptism, and communicant records. **Services:** Archives open to the public.

ST. PAUL'S COLLEGE
See: University of Manitoba (16358)

★12654★
ST. PAUL'S COLLEGE - LIBRARY† (Rel-Phil)
3015 Fourth St., N.E. Phone: (202)832-6262
Washington, DC 20017 Lawrence E. Boadt, C.S.P., Libn.
Founded: 1889. **Staff:** Prof 1; Other 3. **Subjects:** Philosophy, scripture, church history, liturgy, theology, American history, canon law. **Special Collections:** Paulist Fathers Archival Materials (4 filing cases). **Holdings:** 45,000 books; 5000 bound periodical volumes; 2500 pamphlets; 1000 recordings; 100 reels of microfilm. **Subscriptions:** 137 journals and other serials. **Services:** Copying; library open to the public with permission of librarian. **Networks/Consortia:** Member of Washington Theological Consortium.

★12655★
ST. PAUL'S EPISCOPAL CHURCH - LIBRARY (Rel-Phil)
1066 Washington Rd.
Pittsburgh, PA 15228 Sandra W. Ludman, Libn.
Staff: Prof 3; Other 2. **Subjects:** Church and local history. **Holdings:** 2000 books; tapes. **Services:** Copying; library open to the public.

★12656★
ST. PAUL'S EPISCOPAL CHURCH - LIBRARY (Rel-Phil)
815 E. Grace St. Phone: (804)643-3589
Richmond, VA 23219 Leigh S. Hulcher, Lib.Cons.
Staff: 1. **Subjects:** Bible, theology, Christian art, worship, meditation, Christian education, church history, children's books. **Holdings:** 3500 books. **Subscriptions:** 12 journals and other serials. **Services:** Copying; library open to the public.

★12657★
ST. PAUL'S HOSPITAL (Grey Nuns') OF SASKATOON - MEDICAL LIBRARY (Med)
1702 20th St., W. Phone: (306)664-1438
Saskatoon, SK, Canada S7M 0Z9 Sandra Boucher, Lib.Techn.
Founded: 1962. **Staff:** Prof 1. **Subjects:** Medicine, nursing. **Holdings:** 880 books. **Subscriptions:** 64 journals and other serials. **Services:** Interlibrary loan; library not open to the public.

ST. PAUL'S HOSPITAL HEALTH SCIENCES LIBRARY
See: University of British Columbia (15873)

ST. PAUL'S HOSPITAL MUSEUM AND ARCHIVES
See: University of British Columbia (15873)

★12658★
ST. PAUL'S UNITED METHODIST CHURCH - JOHNSON MEMORIAL LIBRARY (Rel-Phil)
225 W. Griggs Phone: (505)526-6689
Las Cruces, NM 88005 Iona McMahon, Libn.
Staff: Prof 3. **Subjects:** Bible, philosophy, prayer, missions, psychology, history, biography, Byzantine and Medieval art, church histories. **Holdings:** 5512 books; tapes. **Services:** Interlibrary loan; copying; library open to the public. **Automated Operations:** Computerized cataloging, acquisitions, and circulation.

★12659★
ST. PAUL'S UNITED METHODIST CHURCH - LIBRARY (Rel-Phil)
3334 Breton Rd., S.E. Phone: (616)949-0880
Kentwood, MI 49508 Loni Soderfelt, Libn.
Staff: Prof 2; Other 4. **Subjects:** Religion. **Holdings:** Figures not available. **Services:** Library open to the public.

★12660★
ST. PAUL'S UNITED METHODIST CHURCH - LIBRARY (Rel-Phil)
9500 Constitution Ave., N.E. Phone: (505)298-5596
Albuquerque, NM 87112 Nancy Smith, Libn.
Founded: 1957. **Staff:** Prof 1; Other 1. **Subjects:** Religion, children's literature, teacher training and aids, contemporary living. **Holdings:** 3000 books; 150 reels of microfilm; 25 tapes; 50 phonograph records. **Services:** Library not open to the public.

★12661★
ST. PETER HOSPITAL - LIBRARY SERVICES (Med)
413 N. Lilly Rd. Phone: (206)456-7222
Olympia, WA 98506 Edean Berglund, Dir.
Staff: Prof 2. **Subjects:** Health care. **Holdings:** Figures not available. **Subscriptions:** 300 journals and other serials. **Services:** Interlibrary loan; copying; library open to the public with restrictions. **Computerized**

Information Services: NLM, MEDLINE, BRS Information Technologies, WILSONLINE, DIALOG Information Services; DOCLINE, OnTyme Electronic Message Network Service (electronic mail services). Performs searches on fee basis. **Remarks:** Fax: (206)456-7924.

★12662★
ST. PETER REGIONAL TREATMENT CENTER - BURTON P. GRIMES STAFF LIBRARY (Med)
100 Freeman Dr. Phone: (507)931-7720
St. Peter, MN 56082 James Twait, Libn.
Founded: 1869. **Staff:** Prof 1; Other 4. **Subjects:** Medicine, nursing, drug addiction, mental retardation, and allied health sciences. **Holdings:** 1300 books; 650 bound periodical volumes; 3 VF drawers; 400 audiotapes; 200 microfiche; clippings. **Subscriptions:** 30 journals and other serials; 10 newspapers. **Services:** Interlibrary loan; copying; library open to the public but must register first. **Computerized Information Services:** Access to DIALOG Information Services. **Networks/Consortia:** Member of Minnesota Department of Human Services Library Consortium.

★12663★
ST. PETER'S ABBEY & COLLEGE - LIBRARY (Rel-Phil)
Box 10 Phone: (306)682-5431
Muenster, SK, Canada S0K 2Y0 Andrew M. Britz, Libn.
Founded: 1892. **Staff:** Prof 1; Other 2. **Subjects:** Arts and science, Roman Catholic theology, monasticism. **Holdings:** 35,000 volumes. **Subscriptions:** 100 journals and other serials. **Services:** Interlibrary loan; copying; library open to the public.

★12664★
ST. PETER'S HOSPITAL - HEALTH SCIENCES LIBRARY (Med)
315 S. Manning Blvd. Phone: (518)454-1670
Albany, NY 12208 Phyllis Miyauchi, Dir.
Founded: 1950. **Staff:** Prof 1; Other 1. **Subjects:** Medicine, surgery, nursing. **Holdings:** 1200 books; 4800 bound periodical volumes; 400 audiotapes. **Subscriptions:** 191 journals and other serials. **Services:** Interlibrary loan; copying; library open to the public for reference use only. **Computerized Information Services:** BRS Information Technologies, NLM. **Networks/Consortia:** Member of Capital District Library Council for Reference & Research Resources (CDLC). **Formerly:** Medical Staff Library.

★12665★
ST. PETER'S HOSPITAL - PROFESSIONAL LIBRARY (Med)
88 Maplewood Ave.
Hamilton, ON, Canada L8M 1W9 Peggy Ross, Libn.
Founded: 1971. **Staff:** 1. **Subjects:** Geriatrics, nursing. **Holdings:** 1100 books. **Subscriptions:** 45 journals and other serials. **Services:** Interlibrary loan; library not open to the public.

★12666★
ST. PETER'S MEDICAL CENTER - LIBRARY (Med)
254 Easton Ave. Phone: (201)745-8545
New Brunswick, NJ 08903 Linda De Muro, Mgr., Lib.Serv.
Founded: 1907. **Staff:** Prof 2; Other 6. **Subjects:** Medicine, nursing. **Special Collections:** History of medicine. **Holdings:** 10,000 books; 20,000 bound periodical volumes; 3600 AV programs. **Subscriptions:** 550 journals and other serials. **Services:** Interlibrary loan; copying; library open to the public for reference use only. **Computerized Information Services:** MEDLINE, DIALOG Information Services, BRS Information Technologies, Physician Data Query (PDQ); DOCLINE (electronic mail service). Performs searches on fee basis. **Networks/Consortia:** Member of Medical Resources Consortium of Central New Jersey (MEDCORE), Health Sciences Library Association of New Jersey. **Publications:** Up-Dates, monthly. **Staff:** Elisabeth Jacobsen, Asst.Lib.Mgr..

★12667★
ST. PETER'S SEMINARY - A.P. MAHONEY LIBRARY (Rel-Phil)
1040 Waterloo St., N. Phone: (519)432-1824
London, ON, Canada N6A 3Y1 Lois Cote, Libn.
Founded: 1926. **Staff:** Prof 1; Other 3. **Subjects:** Theology, philosophy. **Holdings:** 43,000 books and bound periodical volumes. **Subscriptions:** 400 journals and other serials. **Services:** Interlibrary loan; copying; library open to the public with restrictions.

★12668★
ST. PETERSBURG HISTORICAL SOCIETY, INC. - LIBRARY AND ARCHIVES (Hist)
335 Second Ave., N.E. Phone: (813)894-1052
St. Petersburg, FL 33701 Mary Wyatt Allen, Pres.
Staff: 7. **Subjects:** St. Petersburg history. **Special Collections:** Newman Collection (autographs and holographs of American historical figures); books by local authors; local photograph collection. **Holdings:** 500 books; manuscripts; documents; records. **Services:** Copying; library open to members. **Staff:** Ellen Babb, Cur.; Lisa Budreau White, Asst.Cur.; Julia Robinson, Reg..

★12669★
ST. RITA HOSPITAL - HEALTH SCIENCES LIBRARY (Med)
409 King's Rd. Phone: (902)562-2322
Sydney, NS, Canada B1S 1B4 Patricia Keough, Libn.
Founded: 1963. **Staff:** Prof 1. **Subjects:** Health sciences, medicine, nursing, obstetrics, gynecology, pediatrics, anatomy, physiology, nutrition, psychiatry. **Holdings:** 2466 books; 15 bound periodical volumes. **Subscriptions:** 84 journals and other serials. **Services:** Interlibrary loan; copying; library open to public at librarian's discretion. **Automated Operations:** Computerized cataloging, acquisitions, serials, and circulation.

★12670★
ST. RITA'S MEDICAL CENTER - MEDICAL LIBRARY (Med)
730 W. Market St. Phone: (419)227-3361
Lima, OH 45801 Sharon A. Bilopavlovich, Libn.
Staff: 1. **Subjects:** Medicine. **Holdings:** 1484 volumes. **Subscriptions:** 57 journals and other serials. **Services:** Library open to physicians, medical staff, and paramedical personnel. **Networks/Consortia:** Member of Greater Midwest Regional Medical Library Network.

★12671★
ST. STEPHEN UNITED CHURCH OF CHRIST - CENTENNIAL LIBRARY (Rel-Phil)
905 E. Perkins Ave. Phone: (419)626-1612
Sandusky, OH 44870 Linda Richards, Libn.
Founded: 1982. **Staff:** 7. **Subjects:** Religion, church history, Bible. **Special Collections:** Historical Bibles (many in German; 40). **Holdings:** 1957 books. **Services:** Copying; library open to the public. **Automated Operations:** Computerized cataloging, acquisitions, and serials.

★12672★
ST. STEPHEN'S COLLEGE - LIBRARY (Rel-Phil)
University of Alberta Phone: (403)439-7311
Edmonton, AB, Canada T6G 2J6 Sharon Costall, Libn.
Founded: 1909. **Staff:** 1. **Subjects:** Religion and theology. **Special Collections:** Liberation theology; feminist theology. **Holdings:** 10,000 books; United Church and World Council of Churches regular publications. **Subscriptions:** 46 journals and other serials. **Services:** Interlibrary loan; library open to the public with librarian's approval. **Remarks:** Maintained by the United Church of Canada, the college serves as a Centre for Continuing Education for the professional ministry and laity.

★12673★
ST. STEPHEN'S UNITED METHODIST CHURCH - LIBRARY (Rel-Phil)
4601 Juan Tabo, N.E. Phone: (505)293-9673
Albuquerque, NM 87111 Eleanor McDonald, Libn.
Founded: 1980. **Staff:** 3. **Subjects:** Christianity. **Holdings:** 1500 books. **Services:** Library open to the public.

★12674★
ST. THOMAS CATHOLIC CHURCH - BARR MEMORIAL LIBRARY (Rel-Phil)
2210 Lincoln Way Phone: (515)292-3810
Ames, IA 50010 Anne Recker, Libn.
Subjects: Bible, Catholic doctrine, family/ethics, saints/biography, meditations, children's literature. **Special Collections:** Concilium; John Henry Cardinal Newman; western spirituality; Fathers of the Church. **Holdings:** 5000 books. **Subscriptions:** 50 journals and other serials; 9 newspapers. **Services:** Library open to the public.

★12675★
ST. THOMAS EPISCOPAL CHURCH - GARDNER MEMORIAL LIBRARY (Rel-Phil)
231 Sunset Ave. Phone: (408)736-4155
Sunnyvale, CA 94086 Carol Campbell, Parish Libn.
Founded: 1979. **Staff:** 5. **Subjects:** Christian life, prayer, parenting, psychology. **Special Collections:** Summa Theologicae (St. Thomas Aquinas). **Holdings:** 2300 books; 500 cassette tapes; 50 phonograph records; 2 VF drawers; 20 filmstrips; 50 video recordings; 150 slides. **Services:** Interlibrary loan; library open to the public with restrictions.

★12676★
ST. THOMAS INSTITUTE - LIBRARY (Sci-Engr, Med)
1842 Madison Rd. Phone: (513)861-3460
Cincinnati, OH 45206 Sr. M. Virgil Ghering, O.P., Libn.
Founded: 1935. **Staff:** Prof 1. **Subjects:** Biology, experimental medicine, physics, biophysics, chemistry, biochemistry. **Special Collections:** Ph.D. dissertations; original laboratory notes; Classical Studies (1100 volumes). **Holdings:** 8200 books; 21,400 bound periodical volumes; 45 boxes and 4 VF drawers of reprints; 10 volumes of press clippings; 14 boxes of dissertation summaries. **Subscriptions:** 173 journals and other serials. **Services:** Interlibrary loan; copying; library open to the public with restrictions. **Networks/Consortia:** Member of Greater Cincinnati Library Consortium (GCLC), Greater Midwest Regional Medical Library Network.

★12677★
ST. THOMAS MEDICAL CENTER - MEDICAL LIBRARY (Med)
444 N. Main St. Phone: (216)379-1111
Akron, OH 44310 Linda E. Bunyan, Med.Libn.
Founded: 1929. **Staff:** Prof 1; Other 2. **Subjects:** Medicine, nursing, and allied health sciences. **Holdings:** 1758 books; 3381 bound periodical volumes; 400 cassette tapes; 600 slides; 1 file case of clippings and pamphlets; AV programs; computer software. **Subscriptions:** 170 journals and other serials. **Services:** Interlibrary loan; library not open to the public. **Computerized Information Services:** NLM. **Networks/Consortia:** Member of NEOUCOM Council Associated Hospital Librarians.

★12678★
ST. THOMAS MORE COLLEGE - SHANNON LIBRARY (Rel-Phil, Soc Sci)
1437 College Dr. Phone: (306)966-8962
Saskatoon, SK, Canada S7N 0W6 Dr. Margot King, Libn.
Staff: Prof 1; Other 2. **Subjects:** Theology, women in monasticism, church history, Christian sociology, history, English, philosophy, psychology, sociology, economics, political science, Biblical literature. **Special Collections:** St. Thomas More (all books and all editions); complete holdings of Chesterton, Belloc, Wells, and Christopher Dawson. **Holdings:** 50,000 volumes. **Subscriptions:** 175 journals and other serials. **Services:** Interlibrary loan; library open to the public. **Remarks:** College is an autonomous affiliate of the University of Saskatchewan. **Staff:** Jane Morris, Assoc.Libn..

★12679★
ST. THOMAS PSYCHIATRIC HOSPITAL - LIBRARY SERVICES† (Med)
Box 2004 Phone: (519)631-8510
St. Thomas, ON, Canada N5P 3V9 Jean Heriot, Libn.
Founded: 1973. **Staff:** Prof 1; Other 1. **Subjects:** Psychiatry, psychology, medicine, nursing, allied health professions. **Holdings:** 2000 books; 1500 bound periodical volumes; 250 videotapes. **Subscriptions:** 175 journals and other serials; 10 newspapers. **Services:** Interlibrary loan; copying; SDI; library open to the public with restrictions. **Publications:** Current Awareness, monthly - for internal distribution only. **Remarks:** Maintained by Ontario Ministry of Health - Mental Health Division.

★12680★
ST. THOMAS SEMINARY - LIBRARY (Rel-Phil)
1300 S. Steele Phone: (303)722-4687
Denver, CO 80210 Joyce L. White, Dir.
Founded: 1906. **Staff:** Prof 3; Other 1. **Subjects:** Theology, Bible, social problems. **Special Collections:** Catholic theology; Anglican theology; social problems; Minorities Collection, with emphasis on the Chicano; De Andreis Seminary Collection. **Holdings:** 145,000 volumes. **Subscriptions:** 400 journals and other serials. **Services:** Interlibrary loan; copying; library open to those with an identification card. **Staff:** Dig Chinn, Assoc.Libn.; Sharon Figlino, Circ.; Patricia Regal, Per.; Frank Germovnik, C.M., Retrospective Cat..

★12681★
ST. THOMAS SEMINARY - LIBRARY - ALUMNI COLLECTION (Rel-Phil, Rare Book)
467 Bloomfield Ave. Phone: (201)242-5573
Bloomfield, CT 06002 Lucille S. Halfpenny, Libn.
Founded: 1950. **Staff:** Prof 1. **Subjects:** Catholic Americana, 1790-1860; Catholic theology. **Special Collections:** Incunabula; Bibles, 1522 to present. **Holdings:** 13,700 books; 1500 bound periodical volumes; 600 pamphlets; 220 cassette tapes; 34 video cassettes. **Subscriptions:** 98 journals and other serials; 10 newspapers. **Services:** Interlibrary loan; copying; collection open to the public for reference use only. **Publications:** Reading Guide for Religious Studies; What Do You Think of the Priest, a bibliographic commentary on the priesthood.

★12682★
ST. TIKHON'S SEMINARY - LIBRARY (Rel-Phil)
South Canaan, PA 18459 Phone: (717)937-4411
Staff: Prof 1; Other 2. **Subjects:** Theology. **Holdings:** 20,000 books; 500 bound periodical volumes. **Subscriptions:** 40 journals and other serials; 10 newspapers. **Services:** Interlibrary loan; library open to the public with restrictions.

ST. TIMOTHY'S NEIGHBORHOOD CENTER
See: St. Matthew's & St. Timothy's Neighborhood Center, Inc. (12623)

★12683★
ST. VINCENT CHARITY HOSPITAL - LIBRARY (Med)
2351 E. 22nd St. Phone: (216)861-6200
Cleveland, OH 44115 Joanne Billiar, Hd.Libn.
Founded: 1937. **Staff:** Prof 2. **Subjects:** Medicine, nursing, administration, allied health sciences. **Special Collections:** Historical ophthalmology. **Holdings:** 2500 titles; 3 audio cassette series. **Subscriptions:** 180 journals and other serials. **Services:** Interlibrary loan; copying; library open to the public for reference use only. **Computerized Information Services:** NLM. Performs searches on fee basis. **Staff:** Suzanne R. Arnold, Asst.Libn..

★12684★
ST. VINCENT COLLEGE AND ARCHABBEY - LIBRARIES (Rel-Phil, Hist)
Latrobe, PA 15650-2690 Phone: (412)539-9761
Rev. Chrysostom V. Schlimm, O.S.B., Dir., Libs.
Founded: 1846. **Staff:** Prof 5; Other 8. **Subjects:** Liberal arts, Benedictina, patrology, Catholic Church history, medieval studies, Pennsylvaniana, ecclesiastical history. **Special Collections:** Incunabula, Austria-Hungary, England, France, Germany, Switzerland (87 volumes; 15 leaves). **Holdings:** 200,475 books; 34,924 bound periodical volumes; 88,704 microcards; 879 microfiche; 8197 reels of microfilm; 449 cassettes. **Subscriptions:** 791 journals and other serials; 27 newspapers. **Services:** Interlibrary loan; copying; library open to the public. **Automated Operations:** Computerized cataloging. **Computerized Information Services:** OCLC. **Networks/Consortia:** Member of Pittsburgh Regional Library Center (PRLC). **Special Catalogs:** A Descriptive Catalogue of the Incunabula in the St. Vincent College and Archabbey Library (book). **Staff:** Rev. Fintan R. Shoniker, O.S.B., Spec.Coll.; Dr. John F. Macey, Hd.Cat.; John C. Benyo, Asst.Libn.; Rev. Lawrence H. Hill, O.S.B., Ref. & Per.Libn..

★12685★
ST. VINCENT COLLEGE AND ARCHABBEY - MUSIC LIBRARY
Latrobe, PA 15650
Subjects: Music. **Special Collections:** Wimmer Music Collection, 1750-1900 (2500 items). **Holdings:** 1100 music scores. **Remarks:** Presently inactive.

★12686★
ST. VINCENT COLLEGE AND ARCHABBEY - PHYSICS DEPARTMENTAL LIBRARY
Latrobe, PA 15650
Subjects: Physics, astronomy, mathematics. **Holdings:** 1000 books; 200 bound periodical volumes; 600 unbound periodicals. **Remarks:** Presently inactive.

★12687★
ST. VINCENT DE PAUL REGIONAL SEMINARY - LIBRARY (Rel-Phil)
10701 S. Military Trail Phone: (407)732-4424
Boynton Beach, FL 33436-4811
Bro. Frank J. Mazsick, C.F.X., Lib.Dir.
Founded: 1962. **Staff:** Prof 1; Other 1. **Subjects:** Theology, philosophy, Latin American studies, philosophical and theological classics in Spanish

and English. **Holdings:** 52,564 books; 7219 bound periodical volumes; 682 tapes and cassettes; 4101 microforms. **Subscriptions:** 490 journals and other serials; 18 newspapers. **Services:** Interlibrary loan; library open to the public for reference use only.

★12688★
ST. VINCENT HEALTH CENTER - HEALTH SCIENCE LIBRARY (Med)
232 W. 25th St. Phone: (814)452-5740
Erie, PA 16512 Joni M. Alex, Med.Libn.
Founded: 1894. **Staff:** Prof 1; Other 3. **Subjects:** Clinical medicine, nursing, dentistry. **Holdings:** 3500 books; 5000 bound periodical volumes; 8 filing drawers of pamphlets; 200 cassettes and slides. **Subscriptions:** 227 journals and other serials. **Services:** Interlibrary loan; copying; library open to the public for reference use only. **Computerized Information Services:** DIALOG Information Services. Performs searches on fee basis. **Networks/Consortia:** Member of Greater Northeastern Regional Medical Library Program, Erie Area Health Information Library Cooperative (EAHILC).

★12689★
ST. VINCENT HOSPITAL - HEALTH SCIENCE LIBRARY (Med)
835 S. VanBuren St.
Box 13508
Green Bay, WI 54305 Phone: (414)433-8171
Founded: 1982. **Staff:** Prof 2; Other 3. **Subjects:** Medicine, allied health sciences. **Holdings:** 3100 books; 450 bound periodical volumes. **Subscriptions:** 140 journals and other serials. **Services:** Interlibrary loan; copying; SDI; library open to the public with restrictions. **Computerized Information Services:** DIALOG Information Services, MEDLINE; NEWIL (electronic mail service). Performs searches on fee basis. Contact Person: Polly Snider, Libn.. **Networks/Consortia:** Member of Northeast Wisconsin Intertype Libraries (NEWIL), Fox River Valley Area Library Consortium. **Staff:** Betty Gorsegner, Libn..

★12690★
ST. VINCENT HOSPITAL - JOHN J. DUMPHY MEMORIAL LIBRARY (Med)
25 Winthrop St. Phone: (508)798-6117
Worcester, MA 01604 Theresa B. Davitt, Libn.
Staff: Prof 1; Other 2. **Subjects:** Medicine, allied health sciences. **Holdings:** 950 books; 5500 bound periodical volumes. **Subscriptions:** 162 journals and other serials. **Services:** Interlibrary loan; copying; library open to the public by appointment. **Computerized Information Services:** MEDLARS; MEDLINK (electronic mail service). Performs searches on fee basis. **Networks/Consortia:** Member of Central Massachusetts Consortium of Health Related Libraries (CMCHRL).

★12691★
ST. VINCENT HOSPITAL - MEDICAL LIBRARY/AV DEPARTMENT (Med)
60 Cambridge St. Phone: (613)782-2751
Ottawa, ON, Canada K1R 7A5 Anita Beausoleil, Hd.
Staff: Prof 2; Other 1. **Subjects:** Gerontology, physiotherapy, occupational therapy, speech and hearing therapy, long term psychotherapy, rehabilitation. **Holdings:** 4500 books; 50 unbound documents; 4 VF drawers; 118 video cassettes; 26 slide kits; 21 filmstrip kits; 95 audio cassettes; government documents, catalogs, and theses on microfiche. **Subscriptions:** 271 journals and other serials. **Services:** Interlibrary loan; copying; library open to interns and field practice students. **Networks/Consortia:** Member of Disability Research Library Network. **Publications:** Acquisitions lists (book), monthly. **Special Catalogs:** AV Catalog (book), annual. **Staff:** Mireille Ethier-Danis, Lib.Techn..

★12692★
ST. VINCENT HOSPITAL AND MEDICAL CENTER - HEALTH SCIENCES LIBRARY (Med)
9205 S.W. Barnes Rd.
Portland, OR 97225 Edith H. Throckmorton, Dir.
Staff: Prof 1; Other 2. **Subjects:** Medicine, nursing, hospital administration. **Special Collections:** Patient education (400 books, pamphlets, AV programs). **Holdings:** 3800 books; 6000 bound periodical volumes. **Subscriptions:** 425 journals and other serials. **Services:** Interlibrary loan; library not open to the public. **Automated Operations:** Computerized cataloging. **Computerized Information Services:** MEDLINE. **Networks/Consortia:** Member of Oregon Health Information Network (OHIN), Washington County Cooperative Library Services (WCCLS).

★12693★
ST. VINCENT INFIRMARY - MEDICAL LIBRARY (Med)
2 St. Vincent Circle Phone: (501)661-3991
Little Rock, AR 72205 Sr. Jean B. Roberts, S.C.N., Med.Libn.
Founded: 1900. **Staff:** Prof 1; Other 1. **Subjects:** Medicine, medical specialties. **Special Collections:** Hospital Archives (35 volumes). **Holdings:** 4935 books; 3500 bound periodical volumes. **Subscriptions:** 200 journals and other serials. **Services:** Interlibrary loan; copying; library open to students and interns of University of Arkansas Medical Center; open to the public with restrictions. **Networks/Consortia:** Member of TALON.

★12694★
ST. VINCENT MEDICAL CENTER - HEALTH SCIENCE LIBRARY (Med)
2213 Cherry St.
Toledo, OH 43608 Phone: (419)321-4324
Founded: 1970. **Staff:** Prof 2; Other 3. **Subjects:** Clinical medicine and surgery, nursing, hospital administration. **Holdings:** 9661 books; 7228 bound periodical volumes. **Subscriptions:** 608 journals and other serials. **Services:** Interlibrary loan; library not open to the public. **Automated Operations:** Computerized cataloging and circulation. **Computerized Information Services:** MEDLARS, OCLC, BRS Information Technologies. Performs searches on fee basis. **Networks/Consortia:** Member of Health Science Librarians of Northwest Ohio (HSLNO). **Staff:** Claudia Grainger, Co-Dir.; Susan Schafer, Co-Dir..

★12695★
ST. VINCENT MEDICAL CENTER - HEALTH SCIENCES LIBRARY (Med)
2131 W. Third St. Phone: (213)484-5530
Los Angeles, CA 90057 Marsha Gelman-Kmec, Dir., Lib.Serv.
Founded: 1938. **Staff:** Prof 1; Other 1. **Subjects:** Medicine, nursing, nursing education, cardiology, kidney transplantation. **Holdings:** 1200 books; 400 bound periodical volumes. **Subscriptions:** 202 journals and other serials. **Services:** Interlibrary loan; copying; SDI; library open to the public with restrictions. **Automated Operations:** Computerized acquisitions. **Computerized Information Services:** MEDLINE, BRS Information Technologies. Performs searches on fee basis. **Networks/Consortia:** Member of Medical Library Group of Southern California and Arizona (MLGSCA). **Publications:** Monthly newsletter - for internal distribution only.

★12696★
ST. VINCENT'S HOSPITAL - CUNNINGHAM WILSON LIBRARY (Med)
Box 12407 Phone: (205)320-7830
Birmingham, AL 35202-2407 Joyce Sims, Libn.
Staff: Prof 1; Other 2. **Subjects:** Medicine, nursing, hospital administration. **Special Collections:** Historical Nursing Collection. **Holdings:** 2537 books; 1316 bound periodical volumes; 335 vertical files; 20 videotapes; 240 audiotapes. **Subscriptions:** 170 journals and other serials. **Services:** Interlibrary loan; copying; SDI; library open to the public with restrictions. **Computerized Information Services:** MEDLINE. Performs searches free of charge for physicians; on fee basis to others. **Networks/Consortia:** Member of Jefferson County Hospital Librarians' Association, Alabama Health Libraries Association (ALHELA).

★12697★
ST. VINCENT'S HOSPITAL - GARCEAU LIBRARY (Med)
2001 W. 86th St. Phone: (317)871-2095
Indianapolis, IN 46260 Virginia Durkin, Mgr., Lib.Serv.
Founded: 1927. **Staff:** Prof 2. **Subjects:** Medicine, paramedical sciences, nursing, hospital administration. **Special Collections:** Hospital archives. **Holdings:** 6980 volumes; 420 audiotapes; 4 VF drawers of pamphlets; 400 AV programs; microfiche. **Subscriptions:** 200 journals and other serials. **Services:** Interlibrary loan; copying; SDI; library open with approval of librarian. **Computerized Information Services:** BRS Information Technologies, MEDLINE, OCLC. **Networks/Consortia:** Member of Central Indiana Health Science Library Consortium, Greater Midwest Regional Medical Library Network, INCOLSA. **Publications:** Acquisitions list, biannual; library handbook. **Staff:** Louise Hass, Libn..

★12698★
ST. VINCENT'S HOSPITAL - SCHOOL OF NURSING LIBRARY (Med)
27 Christopher St. Phone: (212)790-8486
New York, NY 10014 Clare E. Higgins, Libn.
Founded: 1892. **Staff:** Prof 1. **Subjects:** Nursing and allied professional sciences, social sciences, medicine, religion, humanities. **Holdings:** 3000 books; 225 bound periodical volumes; 8 VF drawers of pamphlets; 825 AV

programs. **Subscriptions:** 65 journals and other serials. **Services:** Copying; library open to faculty, students, hospital personnel.

★12699★
ST. VINCENT'S HOSPITAL AND MEDICAL CENTER OF NEW YORK - MEDICAL LIBRARY (Med)
153 W. Eleventh St. Phone: (212)790-7811
New York, NY 10011 Agnes T. Frank, Dept.Hd.
Founded: 1934. **Staff:** Prof 2; Other 2. **Subjects:** Health sciences, psychology. **Holdings:** 8805 volumes. **Subscriptions:** 276 journals and other serials. **Services:** Interlibrary loan; library not open to the public. **Computerized Information Services:** MEDLINE, BRS Information Technologies. Performs searches on fee basis. **Networks/Consortia:** Member of Medical Library Center of New York (MLCNY). **Staff:** Nina Hollander, Asst.Dept.Hd..

★12700★
ST. VINCENT'S HOSPITAL AND MEDICAL CENTER OF NEW YORK, WESTCHESTER BRANCH - MEDICAL LIBRARY (Med)
240 North St. Phone: (914)967-6500
Harrison, NY 10528 Ethel Eisenberg, Med.Libn.
Staff: Prof 1. **Subjects:** Psychiatry, psychology, alcoholism, drug abuse. **Holdings:** 3000 books; 2000 bound periodical volumes; cassettes. **Subscriptions:** 60 journals and other serials. **Services:** Interlibrary loan; library not open to the public. **Networks/Consortia:** Member of Greater Northeastern Regional Medical Library Program.

★12701★
ST. VINCENT'S MEDICAL CENTER - DANIEL T. BANKS HEALTH SCIENCE LIBRARY (Med)
2800 Main St. Phone: (203)576-5336
Bridgeport, CT 06606 Janet Goerig, Dir., Lib.Serv.
Founded: 1903. **Staff:** Prof 1; Other 5. **Subjects:** Medicine, nursing, and allied health sciences. **Holdings:** 4059 books; 4035 bound periodical volumes; 40 VF drawers of reprints and pamphlets; 5904 AV programs. **Subscriptions:** 310 journals and other serials. **Services:** Interlibrary loan; library not open to the public.

★12702★
ST. VINCENT'S MEDICAL CENTER OF RICHMOND - MEDICAL LIBRARY (Med)
355 Bard Ave. Phone: (718)390-1327
Staten Island, NY 10310 Lucy DiMatteo, Dir.
Founded: 1925. **Staff:** Prof 1; Other 1. **Subjects:** Medicine, nursing, health administration. **Holdings:** 5000 books; 3000 bound periodical volumes. **Subscriptions:** 180 journals and other serials. **Services:** Interlibrary loan; copying; library open to students. **Automated Operations:** Computerized circulation. **Computerized Information Services:** MEDLARS; DOCLINE (electronic mail service). **Networks/Consortia:** Member of Brooklyn-Queens-Staten Island Health Sciences Librarians (BQSI), BHSL, New York Metropolitan Reference and Research Library Agency (METRO).

★12703★
ST. VLADIMIR INSTITUTE - ST. VLADIMIR INSTITUTE LIBRARY: A RESOURCE CENTER FOR UKRAINIAN STUDIES (Area-Ethnic)
620 Spadina Ave. Phone: (416)923-8266
Toronto, ON, Canada M5S 2H4 Donna A. Wilk, Libn.
Founded: 1969. **Staff:** Prof 1; Other 1. **Subjects:** Ukrainian Canadiana; Ukrainian folk and fine arts, history, geography, archeology, politics, literature, language, and music; Ukrainian Orthodox Church. **Special Collections:** Photograph archives (2 boxes); Ukrainians in Canada 1979 Collection (clippings). **Holdings:** 20,000 books; 15 VF drawers of clippings and pamphlets; 50 AV programs; 500 phonograph records; 1000 posters; 500 cassette tapes; 3 boxes of printed archival material. **Subscriptions:** 100 journals and other serials; 17 newspapers. **Services:** Copying; library open to the public.

★12704★
ST. VLADIMIR'S ORTHODOX THEOLOGICAL SEMINARY - FR. GEORGES FLOROVSKY LIBRARY (Rel-Phil)
575 Scarsdale Rd. Phone: (914)961-8313
Yonkers, NY 10707 Rev. Paul N. Tarzi, Act.Libn.
Founded: 1938. **Staff:** Prof 1; Other 1. **Subjects:** Russian Orthodox church history and theology, Byzantine and Balkan church history and theology, Russian church music, iconography, Orthodox Church in America church history. **Special Collections:** 19th century theological periodicals. **Holdings:** 55,000 books; 400 volumes of dissertations; 600 sound recordings; 1290 titles in microform. **Subscriptions:** 330 journals and other serials. **Services:** Interlibrary loan; copying; library open to the public for reference use only. **Automated Operations:** Computerized public access catalog, cataloging, serials, and circulation. **Computerized Information Services:** Unix (internal database). Performs searches free of charge. Contact Person: Eleana Silk, Asst. to Libn. for Circ..

★12705★
ST. VLADIMIR'S UKRAINIAN ORTHODOX CHURCH - CULTURAL CENTRE LIBRARY AND ARCHIVES (Area-Ethnic)
404 Meredith Rd., N.E. Phone: (403)264-3437
Calgary, AB, Canada T2E 5A6 Mykola Woron, Libn.
Founded: 1959. **Staff:** 3. **Subjects:** Ukraine. **Special Collections:** Programs of Ukrainian events (1 VF drawer). **Holdings:** 6684 books; 73 bound periodical volumes; 570 unbound periodicals; 15 video cassettes; 799 cards; 19 maps; 956 clippings; 161 photographs; 118 items from XXI Olympic Games in Montreal. **Subscriptions:** 24 journals and other serials; 6 newspapers. **Services:** Interlibrary loan; library open to public at librarian's discretion. **Staff:** Bill Swiityk, Asst.Libn.; Al Boykiw, Asst.Libn..

★12706★
ST. WALBURG MONASTERY OF BENEDICTINE SISTERS OF COVINGTON, KENTUCKY - ARCHIVES (Rel-Phil)
2500 Amsterdam Rd. Phone: (606)331-6771
Covington, KY 41017 Sr. Teresa Wolking, O.S.B., Archv.
Staff: Prof 1; Other 3. **Subjects:** History and records of the Benedictine Sisters of Covington. **Holdings:** 150 square feet of archival material, focusing on religious women. **Subscriptions:** 12 newspapers. **Services:** Copying; archives open to the public with restrictions by appointment.

★12707★
STS. MARY AND ELIZABETH HOSPITAL - HEALTH SCIENCES LIBRARY (Med)
4400 Churchman Ave. Phone: (502)361-6428
Louisville, KY 40215 Anne Wagner, Libn.
Founded: 1897. **Staff:** Prof 1; Other 1. **Subjects:** Medicine and nursing. **Holdings:** 1800 books; 1600 bound periodical volumes; 2 VF drawers of clippings and pamphlets. **Subscriptions:** 200 journals and other serials. **Services:** Interlibrary loan; copying; library open to hospital staff and students from surrounding area only. **Computerized Information Services:** MEDLINE. **Networks/Consortia:** Member of Kern Health Science Libraries Consortium. **Publications:** Bibliographies; Library Handbook, semiannual.

★12708★
SALEM COUNTY HISTORICAL SOCIETY - LIBRARY (Hist)
79-83 Market St. Phone: (609)935-5004
Salem, NJ 08079 Alice G. Boggs, Sec.
Founded: 1884. **Staff:** Prof 2. **Subjects:** Genealogy and history of Salem County. **Holdings:** Scrapbooks; photographs; architectural drawings; microfilm; oral histories; documents. **Subscriptions:** 10 journals and other serials. **Services:** Copying; library open to the public for reference use only during restricted hours for a fee.

★12709★
SALEM COUNTY LAW LIBRARY (Law)
Salem County Court House
92 Market St. Phone: (609)935-7510
Salem, NJ 08079 Fred B. Gross, Law Ck./Libn.
Staff: Prof 2. **Subjects:** Law. **Holdings:** 3500 books; 200 bound periodical volumes. **Services:** Interlibrary loan; library open to the public with permission of librarian. **Staff:** Marion Moriarty.

★12710★
SALEM FREE PUBLIC LIBRARY - SPECIAL COLLECTIONS (Hist)
112 W. Broadway Phone: (609)935-0526
Salem, NJ 08079 Elizabeth C. Fogg, Dir.
Staff: Prof 1; Other 1. **Subjects:** South Jersiana, especially Salem County history. **Special Collections:** Granville S. Thomas South Jersey Collection (700 items); U.S. Nuclear Regulatory Commission/Public Service Electric & Gas Company Salem I & II Nuclear Power Station document collection (316 linear feet of reports and documents). **Holdings:** 700 books; 6 reels of microfilm of Salem County census information; 200 audio cassettes; 7 cases of pamphlets, reports, newspaper clippings. **Services:** Interlibrary loan (limited); copying; collections open to the public with restrictions. **Networks/Consortia:** Member of South Jersey Regional Library Cooperative.

★12711★
SALEM HOSPITAL - HEALTH SCIENCES LIBRARY (Med)
81 Highland Ave. Phone: (617)741-1200
Salem, MA 01970 Nancy Fazzone, Dir., Lib.Serv.
Founded: 1928. **Staff:** Prof 1; Other 2. **Subjects:** Medicine, nursing, and allied health sciences. **Holdings:** 3500 books; 6000 bound periodical volumes. **Subscriptions:** 265 journals and other serials. **Services:** Interlibrary loan; library open to the public. **Computerized Information Services:** NLM, PaperChase, BRS Information Technologies; internal database. **Networks/Consortia:** Member of Northeastern Consortium for Health Information (NECHI).

★12712★
SALEM HOSPITAL - HEALTH SCIENCES LIBRARY (Med)
665 Winter St., S.E.
Box 14001 Phone: (503)370-5377
Salem, OR 97309-5014 Carol Jones, Dir., Lib.Serv.
Staff: Prof 1; Other 2. **Subjects:** Clinical medicine, allied health sciences. **Special Collections:** Veterinary medicine. **Holdings:** 2300 monographs. **Subscriptions:** 420 journals and other serials. **Services:** Interlibrary loan (fee); library open to the public with restrictions. **Automated Operations:** Computerized cataloging, acquisitions, and serials. **Computerized Information Services:** MEDLARS, DIALOG Information Services, BRS Information Technologies, OCLC; internal database; OnTyme Electronic Message Network Service (electronic mail service). **Networks/Consortia:** Member of Marine-Valley Health Information Network (MarVHIN). **Special Indexes:** Citation Index; clinical and medical indexes. **Remarks:** An alternate telephone number is 370-5559.

SALEM MARITIME NATIONAL HISTORIC SITE
See: U.S. Natl. Park Service (15347)

★12713★
SALEM STATE COLLEGE - LIBRARY - SPECIAL COLLECTIONS (Soc Sci)
352 Lafayette St. Phone: (617)745-0556
Salem, MA 01970 Neil B. Olson, Dir. of Libs.
Special Collections: Congressmen George and William Bates Archives (140 boxes of papers and books); Congressman Michael Harrington papers (200 boxes); 19th century school materials (800 items); U.S. Geological Survey maps (71,000). **Services:** Interlibrary loan; copying; SDI; microform reproduction; collections open to the public for reference use only. **Automated Operations:** Computerized cataloging and ILL. **Computerized Information Services:** DIALOG Information Services, OCLC; internal database. **Networks/Consortia:** Member of Massachusetts Conference of Chief Librarians in Public Higher Educational Institutions, Essex County Cooperating Libraries (ECCL), Northeast Consortium of Colleges and Universities in Massachusetts (NECCUM), Northeastern Consortium for Health Information (NECHI). **Publications:** Library Handbook. **Staff:** Marie Malone, Archv.; Camilla M. Glynn, Asst.Dir..

★12714★
SALEM STATE COLLEGE - LIBRARY OF SOCIAL ALTERNATIVES (Soc Sci)
Salem, MA 01970 Phone: (617)745-0556
Margaret Andrews, Coord.
Staff: Prof 1. **Subjects:** Alternative lifestyles, Third World, social change, ecology, gays/lesbians, health care, women, hobbies, radical left. **Special Collections:** Community Resource Referral File. **Holdings:** 3000 books; magazine archives. **Subscriptions:** 20 journals and other serials. **Services:** Library open to the public. **Publications:** Community Resource File.

★12715★
SALEM STATE COLLEGE - PROFESSIONAL STUDIES RESOURCES CENTER (Educ)
Library, 352 Lafayette St. Phone: (617)745-0556
Salem, MA 01970 Gertrude L. Fox, Libn.
Founded: 1964. **Staff:** Prof 1. **Subjects:** Nursing; business; marine science; education - materials, textbooks and trade books (K-12), nonprint materials, standardized tests. **Special Collections:** Resource Center for Marine Science (elementary and secondary). **Holdings:** 14,463 books; 126 bound periodical volumes; ERIC microfiche, 1968 to present; 5 filing cabinets of curriculum guides; 2 file drawers of pamphlets; 1 file drawer of pictures and maps; 5000 curriculum guides on microfiche. **Services:** Interlibrary loan; copying; center open to the public. **Automated Operations:** Computerized serials.

★12716★
SALES AND MARKETING MANAGEMENT - LIBRARY (Bus-Fin, Publ)
633 Third Ave.
New York, NY 10017 Phone: (212)986-4800
Founded: 1940. **Staff:** Prof 1. **Subjects:** Marketing, sales management, salesmanship, advertising, general management. **Special Collections:** Complete bound sets of Sales and Marketing Management Magazine, 1918 to present, and Survey of Buying Power, 1928 to present. **Holdings:** 500 books; 50 VF drawers. **Subscriptions:** 90 journals and other serials. **Services:** Interlibrary loan (limited); library open to the public by appointment. **Special Indexes:** Index to Sales and Marketing Management Magazine.

★12717★
SALINAS PUBLIC LIBRARY - JOHN STEINBECK LIBRARY (Hum)
110 W. San Luis St. Phone: (408)758-7311
Salinas, CA 93901 Mary Gamble, Steinbeck Libn.
Staff: 1. **Holdings:** John Steinbeck Collection (first and foreign language editions of Steinbeck's works); 100 oral interview recordings; 2000 photographs; letters; movie posters; manuscripts; galley proofs. **Services:** Interlibrary loan; copying; library open to the public by appointment. **Networks/Consortia:** Member of Monterey Bay Area Cooperative Library System (MOBAC). **Publications:** John Steinbeck: A Guide to the Collection of the Salinas Public Library, 1979; Guide to Steinbeck Country, 1984.

★12718★
SALISBURY HISTORICAL SOCIETY - ARCHIVES (Hist)
Box 91, R.D. 1 Phone: (603)648-2436
Andover, NH 03216 Janet H. Ball, Cur.
Founded: 1968. **Staff:** 2. **Subjects:** Local history, genealogy. **Holdings:** 50 books; manuscripts and original documents pertaining to Salisbury. **Services:** Interlibrary loan; genealogical research; archives open to the public by appointment. **Publications:** News Letter, monthly - to members and friends.

★12719★
SALISBURY STATE COLLEGE - BLACKWELL LIBRARY - SPECIAL COLLECTIONS (Hist)
Salisbury, MD 21801 Phone: (301)543-6130
Charletta House, Spec.Coll.
Founded: 1925. **Special Collections:** Maryland Room (3200 volumes; 12 VF drawers of clippings); Education Resources Center; U.S. Government documents depository (selected); Leisure Studies; juvenile literature; Les Callette Memorial Civil War Collection; Maryland State documents depository. **Services:** Interlibrary loan; copying; collections open to the public. **Automated Operations:** Computerized cataloging and circulation. **Computerized Information Services:** DIALOG Information Services, WILSONLINE, OCLC, BRS Information Technologies. Performs searches on fee basis. Contact Person: Dorothy Newcomb, Asst.Dir.. **Networks/Consortia:** Member of PALINET.

★12720★
SALK INSTITUTE FOR BIOLOGICAL STUDIES - LIBRARY (Biol Sci, Sci-Engr)
Box 85800 Phone: (619)453-4100
San Diego, CA 92138 June A. Gittings, Libn.
Founded: 1962. **Staff:** 4. **Subjects:** Biochemistry, molecular biology, plant biology, chemistry, genetics, virology, neurobiology, philosophy of science. **Holdings:** 14,355 books and serials. **Subscriptions:** 211 journals; 5 newspapers. **Services:** Interlibrary loan; copying; library open to the public for reference use only by permission. **Computerized Information Services:** MEDLINE.

★12721★
SALMAGUNDI CLUB - LIBRARY (Art)
47 Fifth Ave. Phone: (212)255-7740
New York, NY 10003 Joseph Levenson, Libn.
Founded: 1899. **Subjects:** Art. **Holdings:** 8000 books. **Services:** Library open to qualified persons submitting written applications and references.

★12722★
SALMON BROOK HISTORICAL SOCIETY - REFERENCE AND EDUCATIONAL CENTER (Hist)
208 Salmon Brook St. Phone: (203)653-3965
Granby, CT 06035 Carol Laun, Cur.
Founded: 1959. **Staff:** 1. **Subjects:** Local and area history, genealogy, religion, agriculture and industry, military history. **Special Collections:**

James L. Loomis Collection (Loomis Store, 1862-1931, and Connecticut Home Guard, 1917-1918; 600 items); Richard E. Holcomb Papers (Panama Canal and Civil War; 250 items). **Holdings:** 1500 books; 50 bound periodical volumes; 250 other cataloged items; 9 VF drawers of original documents; 10 VF drawers of research information and clippings; 20 boxes of pamphlets, booklets, newspapers; 300 deeds; 150 account books. **Services:** Center open to the public by appointment. **Publications:** Collections I, II, and III - to members and for sale; Granby Town Records 1786-1853 - for sale.

SALOMON BROTHERS CENTER FOR THE STUDY OF FINANCIAL INSTITUTIONS
See: New York University (10179)

★12723★
SALOMON BROTHERS INC. - CORPORATE FINANCE LIBRARY (Bus-Fin)
One New York Plaza, 46th Fl. Phone: (212)747-7933
New York, NY 10004 Gloria D. McDonald, Lib.Mgr.
Founded: 1976. **Staff:** Prof 6; Other 31. **Subjects:** Investment banking, corporate and international finance, securities industry. **Special Collections:** Eurobond prospectuses (7100); underwriting indentures on microfiche (7500). **Holdings:** 8300 books; 420 subject files of clippings, pamphlets, documents, reports; 3000 international files of annual reports and prospectuses; 5000 corporate files; transaction files; 900,000 microforms. **Subscriptions:** 700 journals and other serials; 25 newspapers. **Services:** Interlibrary loan; library not open to the public. **Automated Operations:** Computerized cataloging and acquisitions. **Computerized Information Services:** DIALOG Information Services, Dun & Bradstreet Corporation, ADP Network Services, Data Resources (DRI), Dow Jones News/Retrieval, Info Globe, NEXIS, BRS Information Technologies, Spectrum Ownership Profiles Online, Securities Data Company, Inc., NewsNet, Inc., OCLC. **Publications:** Business Publications, quarterly; Financial News Checklist, weekly; Precedent Document Submissions, monthly; Periodicals in the Library, quarterly - all for internal distribution only. **Staff:** Elizabeth Bryant, Hd., Domestic Res.; Louise Klusek, Hd., Intl.Res.; Arthur Di Meglio, Res.Assoc.; Brian Gallagher, Res.Assoc.; Cecelia B. Scotti, Tech.Serv.Assoc.; Susan Capozzoli, Doc.Supv..

SOPHIE AND IVAN SALOMON LIBRARY COLLECTION
See: Congregation Shearith Israel - Sophie and Ivan Salomon Library Collection (3634)

NATHAN SALON RESOURCE CENTER
See: Indiana (State) Department of Human Services (6766)

★12724★
SALT LAKE CITY SCHOOLS - DISTRICT MEDIA CENTER (Educ, Aud-Vis)
1575 S. State St. Phone: (801)328-7279
Salt Lake City, UT 84115 Marian Karpisek, Supv., Lib. Media Serv.
Founded: 1965. **Staff:** Prof 1; Other 18. **Subjects:** School curriculum. **Holdings:** 100 audio cassettes; 2492 16mm films; 7085 videotapes; 1335 sound filmstrips; 1140 kits; 148 filmstrips; 66 slides; 73 models; 1165 pictures; 436 transparencies; 624 ditto masters; 101 Alcohol & Drug kits. **Subscriptions:** 11 journals and other serials. **Services:** Center open to district related organizations. **Automated Operations:** Computerized cataloging, acquisitions, and circulation. **Computerized Information Services:** WILSONLINE; Email (electronic mail service). **Special Catalogs:** District holdings.

★12725★
SALT LAKE COUNTY LAW LIBRARY (Law)
240 E. 400 South, Rm. 219A Phone: (801)535-7518
Salt Lake City, UT 84111 Nancy Cheng, Law Libn.
Founded: 1900. **Staff:** Prof 1. **Subjects:** Law. **Holdings:** 13,000 volumes. **Services:** Copying; library open to the public with restrictions. **Remarks:** Maintained by Third Judicial District Court.

★12726★
SALT LAKE TRIBUNE - LIBRARY (Publ)
143 S. Main St. Phone: (801)237-2001
Salt Lake City, UT 84117 Laurene A. Sowby, Hd.Libn.
Staff: 7. **Subjects:** Newspaper reference topics. **Holdings:** 2500 books; photographs; microfilm; clipping files. **Services:** Interlibrary loan (fee); copying; library open to the public with restrictions. **Special Indexes:** Annual Index.

★12727★
SALT RIVER PROJECT - LIBRARY (Energy, Bus-Fin)
Box 52025 Phone: (602)236-3405
Phoenix, AZ 85072-2025 Bonnie M. Klassen, Supv.
Staff: Prof 2; Other 2. **Subjects:** Business, management, finance, utilities, energy, water, engineering, computer science, environment, law, government, Arizona history, professional development. **Holdings:** 8000 books and reports. **Subscriptions:** 210 journals and other serials; 13 newspapers. **Services:** Interlibrary loan; copying; SDI; library open to the public by appointment. **Automated Operations:** Computerized cataloging, acquisitions, serials, circulation, and ILL. **Computerized Information Services:** DIALOG Information Services, VU/TEXT Information Services, NLM, RLIN, BRS Information Technologies; internal databases; MCI Mail (electronic mail service). **Publications:** New Publications List. **Remarks:** Library located at 1521 Project Dr., Tempe, AZ 85281.

★12728★
SALVATION ARMY - ARCHIVES AND RESEARCH CENTER (Hist, Rel-Phil)
145 W. 15th St. Phone: (212)337-7427
New York, NY 10011 Thomas Wilsted, Archv./Adm.
Founded: 1975. **Staff:** Prof 4; Other 3. **Subjects:** Salvation Army history and records, social service, churches, religion. **Holdings:** 2300 books; 800 bound periodical volumes; 1000 cubic feet of archives; 31 cubic feet of manuscript collections; 23,000 photographs; 1340 reels of microfilm; 750 microfiche; 35 VF drawers; 300 sound recordings; 280 audiotapes; 250 slides; 500 films. **Subscriptions:** 15 journals and other serials. **Services:** Interlibrary loan; copying; library open to the public. **Automated Operations:** Computerized cataloging, acquisitions, and serials. **Computerized Information Services:** DIALOG Information Services, BRS Information Technologies. Performs searches on fee basis. Contact Person: Susan Miller, Asst.Archv., 337-7433. **Publications:** Historical Newsview, quarterly - available upon request. **Special Indexes:** Inventories of processed archives and manuscript collections; Index to Salvation Army Social Service Periodicals (card); Index to The War Cry (card). **Staff:** Judith Johnson, Archv..

SALVATION ARMY - BOOTH MEMORIAL MEDICAL CENTER
See: Booth Memorial Medical Center (1709)

SALVATION ARMY - CATHERINE BOOTH BIBLE COLLEGE
See: Catherine Booth Bible College (1708)

★12729★
SALVATION ARMY - EDUCATION DEPARTMENT LIBRARY (Hist)
120 W. 14th St., 6th Fl. Phone: (212)337-7349
New York, NY 10011 Mrs. C.W. Kinnet
Staff: Prof 1. **Subjects:** Salvation Army - biography, history, activities. **Holdings:** 2400 books; clippings; manuscripts; pamphlets; documents. **Services:** Library open to the public by appointment.

SALVATION ARMY - GRACE GENERAL HOSPITAL
See: Grace General Hospital (5770)

★12730★
SALVATION ARMY GRACE GENERAL HOSPITAL - LIBRARY (Med)
300 Booth Dr. Phone: (204)837-0127
Winnipeg, MB, Canada R3J 3M7 M. Dyck, Staff Educ.Dir.
Founded: 1974. **Staff:** Prof 1; Other 3. **Subjects:** Medicine, nursing, and allied health sciences. **Holdings:** 9821 books; 803 AV programs; 18 linear feet of pamphlets. **Subscriptions:** 192 journals and other serials. **Services:** Interlibrary loan; copying; library open to the public with restrictions.

★12731★
SALVATION ARMY GRACE HOSPITAL - LIBRARY (Med)
339 Crawford Ave. Phone: (519)255-2245
Windsor, ON, Canada N9A 5C6 Anna Henshaw, Libn.
Staff: Prof 1; Other 1. **Subjects:** Medicine, nursing. **Holdings:** 2000 books; 880 bound periodical volumes. **Subscriptions:** 112 journals and other serials. **Services:** Interlibrary loan; library not open to the public.

★12732★
SALVATION ARMY GRACE HOSPITAL - MEDICAL STAFF LIBRARY (Med)
1402 8th Ave., N.W. Phone: (403)284-1141
Calgary, AB, Canada T2N 1B9 Dr. A. Rothwell, Chm., Lib.Comm.
Founded: 1967. **Subjects:** Medicine, paramedicine, history and poetry of medicine. **Holdings:** 2000 books; 50 bound periodical volumes; 40 tapes.

Subscriptions: 30 journals and other serials. Services: Library not open to the public.

★12733★
SALVATION ARMY SCHOOL FOR OFFICERS TRAINING - ELFTMAN MEMORIAL LIBRARY (Rel-Phil, Soc Sci)
30840 Hawthorne Blvd. Phone: (213)377-0481
Rancho Palos Verdes, CA 90274 Lavonne D. Robertson, Hd.Libn.
Staff: 3. **Subjects:** Salvation Army history and services, Bible and theology, social welfare. **Holdings:** 30,000 books; AV programs. **Subscriptions:** 206 journals and other serials. **Services:** Library open to the public by appointment.

SALZMANN LIBRARY
See: St. Francis Seminary (12403)

★12734★
SAMARITAN HOSPITAL - MEDICAL LIBRARY (Med)
2215 Burdett Ave. Phone: (518)271-3200
Troy, NY 12180 Annie J. Smith, Med.Libn.
Staff: Prof 1. **Subjects:** Medicine, allied health sciences. **Special Collections:** Spafford Collection (health-related books for laymen; 450 books). **Holdings:** 290 books; 1500 bound periodical volumes. **Subscriptions:** 64 journals and other serials. **Services:** Interlibrary loan; library not open to the public. **Networks/Consortia:** Member of Capital District Library Council for Reference & Research Resources (CDLC). **Publications:** Bookbag.

★12735★
SAMBORN, STEKETEE, OTIS & EVANS, INC. - RESOURCE & INFORMATION CENTER (Sci-Engr)
1001 Madison Ave. Phone: (419)255-3830
Toledo, OH 43624 Mary Jo Coates
Founded: 1972. **Staff:** 1. **Subjects:** Architecture, engineering, planning, building codes. **Special Collections:** Solid waste. **Holdings:** 6712 books; 4 VF drawers of technical papers; 16,000 engineering drawings on microfilm; 10 loose-leaf volumes of newspaper clippings; 437 loose-leaf volumes and 12 VF drawers of product catalogs; 42 file drawers of blueprints. **Subscriptions:** 98 journals and other serials. **Services:** Center open to the public with restrictions.

★12736★
SAMFORD UNIVERSITY - BAPTIST HISTORICAL COLLECTION (Rel-Phil)
Harwell Goodwin Davis Library
800 Lakeshore Dr. Phone: (205)870-2749
Birmingham, AL 35229 Dr. William Nelson, Cur.
Founded: 1958. **Staff:** Prof 1; Other 1. **Subjects:** Alabama Baptist history and biography. **Holdings:** 2500 books; 2200 bound periodical volumes; 10,000 Baptist Association Annuals; Baptist Church minutes and records; oral history tapes and transcripts. **Subscriptions:** 55 journals and other serials. **Services:** Interlibrary loan; copying; collection open to the public. **Computerized Information Services:** DIALOG Information Services. **Publications:** Alabama Baptist Historian. **Special Indexes:** Index to Alabama Baptist newspaper (card and computerized book form); Annuals, Alabama Baptist State Convention; Analytical Information Index. **Remarks:** Library is the official depository of the archives of the Alabama Baptist State Convention.

SAMFORD UNIVERSITY - BAPTIST MEDICAL CENTERS
See: Baptist Medical Centers-Samford University - Ida V. Moffett School of Nursing (1326)

★12737★
SAMFORD UNIVERSITY - CUMBERLAND SCHOOL OF LAW - CORDELL HULL LAW LIBRARY (Law)
800 Lakeshore Dr. Phone: (205)870-2714
Birmingham, AL 35229 Laurel R. Clapp, Law Libn.
Founded: 1847. **Staff:** Prof 4; Other 7. **Subjects:** American law, common law. **Holdings:** 196,553 books; documents; microfilm. **Subscriptions:** 3323 journals and other serials. **Services:** Interlibrary loan; copying; library open to the public. **Automated Operations:** Computerized cataloging. **Computerized Information Services:** WESTLAW, LEXIS. **Publications:** Selected List of Recent Acquisitions, monthly - to faculty. **Staff:** Linda Jones, Acq.Libn.; Rebecca Hutto, Cat.Libn..

★12738★
SAMFORD UNIVERSITY - HARWELL GOODWIN DAVIS LIBRARY - SPECIAL COLLECTIONS (Hist)
800 Lakeshore Dr. Phone: (205)870-2749
Birmingham, AL 35229 Elizabeth C. Wells, Spec.Coll.Libn.
Founded: 1957. **Staff:** Prof 1; Other 3. **Subjects:** Alabama history, literature, and imprints; Early Southeast - Indians, travel, law; genealogical source records; Southern Reconstruction; Irish history and genealogy. **Special Collections:** William H. Brantley Collection (books; 19th and 20th century manuscripts; 18th and 19th century maps); Albert E. Casey Collection (books; manuscripts; periodicals; maps of Ireland); Douglas C. McMurtrie Collection; John Ruskin Collection; John Masefield Collection; Alfred Tennyson Collection; Lafcadio Hearn Collection. **Holdings:** 25,653 books; 2562 bound periodical volumes; 806 microcards; 349 phonograph records; 2725 maps; 218,167 manuscripts; 7414 reels of microfilm; 7828 prints and photographs; 2910 microfiche; 150 oral histories; 37 atlases; 1 globe; 60 relief models. **Subscriptions:** 330 journals and other serials. **Services:** Interlibrary loan; copying; collections open to the public. **Computerized Information Services:** DIALOG Information Services. **Special Catalogs:** Map Catalog; Catalog of the Casey Collection of Irish History and Genealogy. **Special Indexes:** Analytical Information Index; index to The Alabama Baptist (newspaper).

BERNARD SAMUELS LIBRARY
See: New York Eye and Ear Infirmary (10026)

SAN ANGELO STANDARD-TIMES
See: Harte-Hanks Communications, Inc. (6051)

★12739★
SAN ANTONIO COLLEGE - LEARNING RESOURCES CENTER - SPECIAL COLLECTIONS (Hist)
1001 Howard St. Phone: (512)733-2480
San Antonio, TX 78284 Oscar F. Metzger, Dir., Lrng.Rsrcs.
Founded: 1925. **Subjects:** Texana. **Special Collections:** Morrison Collection of 18th century British imprints (6100 volumes); McAllister Collection of Texas and Western America (7250 volumes). **Services:** Interlibrary loan; copying; collections open to the public for reference use only. **Automated Operations:** Computerized cataloging, acquisitions, and circulation. **Computerized Information Services:** DIALOG Information Services, BRS Information Technologies, OCLC, WILSONLINE; Computer Augmented Resources System (internal database). **Networks/Consortia:** Member of AMIGOS Bibliographic Council, Inc., Council of Research & Academic Libraries (CORAL), Health Oriented Libraries of San Antonio (HOLSA).

★12740★
SAN ANTONIO COMMUNITY HOSPITAL - WEBER MEMORIAL LIBRARY (Med)
999 San Bernardino Rd. Phone: (714)985-2811
Upland, CA 91786 Francena Johnston, Med.Libn.
Founded: 1956. **Staff:** Prof 1; Other 1. **Subjects:** Medicine, health services management, allied health sciences. **Holdings:** 4500 books; 2720 bound periodical volumes; 1715 other cataloged items; 720 audio cassettes; 550 Audio-Digest tapes; 284 videotapes; 120 filmstrip/cassette sets; 15 films. **Subscriptions:** 550 journals and other serials; 17 newspapers. **Services:** Interlibrary loan; library not open to the public. **Automated Operations:** Computerized cataloging, acquisitions, and serials. **Computerized Information Services:** DIALOG Information Services, MEDLINE; internal databases; QMODEN, OnTyme Electronic Message Network Service (electronic mail services). Performs searches on fee basis. **Networks/Consortia:** Member of Medical Library Group of Southern California and Arizona (MLGSCA), Inland Empire Medical Library Cooperative. **Staff:** Marilyn Hope, Asst.Libn..

★12741★
SAN ANTONIO CONSERVATION SOCIETY - LIBRARY & ARCHIVES (Hist)
107 King William St. Phone: (512)224-6163
San Antonio, TX 78204 Marianna C. Jones, Libn.
Founded: 1971. **Staff:** Prof 4. **Subjects:** History of San Antonio; historic preservation; architectural history. **Special Collections:** Ernst Raba Photograph Collection (250 glass negatives); Texas Heritage Resource Center (300 publications); Dorothy Matthis Postcard Collection (early San Antonio, Galveston, Houston; 767 items); John M. Sr. & Eleanor Freeborn Bennett Collection (Texana); Historic American Buildings Survey: Texas (microfiche). **Holdings:** 1500 books; archives; documents; maps; blueprints; pictures; AV programs; clippings. **Subscriptions:** 20 journals and other serials. **Services:** Interlibrary loan; copying; library open to the public on a limited schedule.

SAN ANTONIO MUSEUM OF ART
See: San Antonio Museum Association (12742)

★12742★
SAN ANTONIO MUSEUM ASSOCIATION - ELLEN SCHULTZ QUILLIN MEMORIAL LIBRARY (Art)
3801 Broadway
Box 2601 Phone: (512)226-5544
San Antonio, TX 78299-2601 George Anne Cormier, Libn.
Founded: 1926. **Staff:** Prof 1; **Subjects:** Texana; art - American, Indian, folk, decorative; natural history; transportation. **Holdings:** 13,500 books; 4000 bound periodical volumes; 20 drawers of documents, maps, pictures; 12 VF drawers; 25 boxes of archival materials; 17,000 slides. **Subscriptions:** 78 journals and other serials. **Services:** Interlibrary loan; copying; library open to the public for reference use only by appointment. **Remarks:** The association maintains libraries at the Witte Memorial Museum, located at 3801 Broadway; the San Antonio Museum of Art, located at 200 West Jones.

★12743★
SAN ANTONIO PUBLIC LIBRARY AND INFORMATION CENTER - ART, MUSIC AND FILMS DEPARTMENT (Art, Mus, Rec)
203 S. St. Mary's St. Phone: (512)299-7795
San Antonio, TX 78205 Mary A. Wright, Hd.
Founded: 1959. **Staff:** Prof 4; Other 7. **Subjects:** Art history and criticism; painting, sculpture, and crafts; architecture - history, criticism, design; interior decoration; antiques; glass; graphics; photography; music; theater; performing arts; sports; stamp and coin collecting. **Holdings:** 105,306 books; picture file; local artists' biographical file; pamphlet file; 4100 phonograph records; 5350 scores; 500 libretti; 2540 films; 3000 video cassettes; 300 audio cassettes; compact discs; books on tape. **Subscriptions:** 170 journals and other serials. **Publications:** News releases on art gallery exhibits and special display case gallery. **Special Catalogs:** Catalog of recordings and books (microfiche); catalog of films and video cassettes (book). **Special Indexes:** Indexes to sheet music and theater archives.

★12744★
SAN ANTONIO PUBLIC LIBRARY AND INFORMATION CENTER - BUSINESS, SCIENCE AND TECHNOLOGY DEPARTMENT (Bus-Fin, Sci-Engr)
203 S. St. Mary's St. Phone: (512)299-7800
San Antonio, TX 78205 James Sosa, Hd.
Founded: 1959. **Staff:** Prof 4; Other 2. **Subjects:** Business, science, technology, economics, statistics, population demographics, useful arts, commerce, business and realty law. **Special Collections:** Trade directories; corporate annual reports; Texas business. **Holdings:** 23,399 bound periodical volumes; 17,024 hardbound U.S. Government documents; 80 VF drawers of pamphlets, clippings, and reports; 468,419 government pamphlets; 25,179 AEC reports; 65,700 AEC microcards; 273,991 U.S. Government documents on microfiche; 22,088 Texas State documents.

★12745★
SAN ANTONIO PUBLIC LIBRARY AND INFORMATION CENTER - HARRY HERTZBERG CIRCUS COLLECTION (Hist)
210 W. Market St.
San Antonio, TX 78205 Phone: (512)299-7810
Founded: 1942. **Staff:** Prof 1; Other 1. **Subjects:** Circus and circus history. **Special Collections:** Jenny Lind; P.T. Barnum; Charles S. Stratton (Tom Thumb); Townsend Walsh Scrapbook Collection; rare books. **Holdings:** 8849 volumes; 1521 lithographs; 200 circus route books; 43 19th century clown songsters; photographs; circus necrological file; archives; memorabilia; letters; documents. **Services:** Copying; collection open to historians, graduate students, publishers, and authors.

★12746★
SAN ANTONIO PUBLIC LIBRARY AND INFORMATION CENTER - HISTORY, SOCIAL SCIENCE & GENERAL REFERENCE DEPARTMENT (Soc Sci, Hist)
203 S. St. Mary's St. Phone: (512)299-7813
San Antonio, TX 78205 Marie Berry, Hd.
Founded: 1959. **Staff:** Prof 4; Other 5. **Subjects:** History, travel, biography, social science, Texana, genealogy, education, general reference. **Special Collections:** Texana Collection; genealogy. **Holdings:** 107,680 books; 3897 bound periodical volumes; 14,402 reels of microfilm; 58,819 microfiche; 2397 ultrafiche; San Antonio and Texas vertical file. **Subscriptions:** 418 journals and other serials. **Services:** Interlibrary loan. **Special Indexes:** Index to San Antonio and Texas vertical file.

★12747★
SAN ANTONIO PUBLIC LIBRARY AND INFORMATION CENTER - LITERATURE, PHILOSOPHY AND RELIGION DEPARTMENT (Hum)
203 S. St. Mary's St. Phone: (512)299-7817
San Antonio, TX 78205 Eugene R. Sanders, Hd.
Founded: 1959. **Staff:** Prof 4; Other 5. **Subjects:** Library science, psychology, languages, literature, philosophy, religion. **Special Collections:** Reading Development Collection; Spanish Collection. **Holdings:** 77,138 books; 5489 bound periodical volumes; 6102 reels of microfilm; 200 ultrafiche; 3000 large print books; talking and braille books. **Subscriptions:** 226 journals and other serials; 40 newspapers. **Services:** Interlibrary loan; department open to the public.

★12748★
SAN ANTONIO STATE CHEST HOSPITAL - HEALTH SCIENCE LIBRARY (Med)
Highland Hills Sta., Box 23340 Phone: (512)534-8857
San Antonio, TX 78223 Patricia Beaman, Libn.
Staff: Prof 1. **Subjects:** Medicine, chest diseases, nursing. **Holdings:** 1800 books; 1500 bound periodical volumes; 450 AV programs. **Subscriptions:** 120 journals and other serials. **Services:** Interlibrary loan; copying; library open to the public for reference use only. **Automated Operations:** Computerized serials. **Computerized Information Services:** MEDLINE. **Networks/Consortia:** Member of Health Oriented Libraries of San Antonio (HOLSA). **Publications:** Newsletter (includes recent acquisitions), bimonthly.

★12749★
SAN ANTONIO STATE HOSPITAL - STAFF LIBRARY (Med)
Highland Hills Sta., Box 23310
San Antonio, TX 78223 Phone: (512)532-8811
Staff: Prof 1; Other 1. **Subjects:** Medical sciences, psychology, psychiatric medicine, theology, mental health, mental hospitals. **Holdings:** 4000 books and bound periodical volumes; 12 VF drawers of reports, pamphlets, and documents; cassette tapes. **Subscriptions:** 130 journals and other serials. **Services:** Interlibrary loan; copying; library open to the public; outside users may check out materials only through ILL. **Networks/Consortia:** Member of Health Oriented Libraries of San Antonio (HOLSA), TALON. **Publications:** Current Awareness, monthly - for internal distribution only. **Remarks:** Maintained by Texas State Department of Mental Health & Mental Retardation.

★12750★
SAN ANTONIO SYMPHONY ORCHESTRA - SYMPHONY LIBRARY (Mus)
109 Lexington Ave., Suite 207 Phone: (512)222-8573
San Antonio, TX 78205 Gregory Vaught, Libn.
Staff: Prof 2. **Subjects:** Orchestral and choral music, opera. **Holdings:** 1800 orchestrations with operas, full scores, and miniature scores. **Services:** Library open to the public for reference use only. **Publications:** Report of all performances and timings by the San Antonio Symphony, annual. **Staff:** William Moore, Asst.Libn..

★12751★
SAN BERNARDINO COMMUNITY HOSPITAL - MEDICAL LIBRARY (Med)
1500 W. 17th St. Phone: (714)887-6333
San Bernardino, CA 92411 Marlene Nourok, Med.Libn.
Staff: Prof 1. **Subjects:** Medicine. **Holdings:** 1500 books; 5000 bound periodical volumes. **Subscriptions:** 139 journals and other serials. **Services:** Interlibrary loan; library not open to the public. **Computerized Information Services:** DIALOG Information Services, MEDLINE; OnTyme Electronic Message Network Service (electronic mail service). **Networks/Consortia:** Member of Inland Empire Medical Library Cooperative, Medical Library Group of Southern California and Arizona (MLGSCA). **Publications:** Library Notes, bimonthly.

★12752★
SAN BERNARDINO COUNTY ENVIRONMENTAL PUBLIC WORKS AGENCY - RESOURCE CENTER
385 N. Arrowhead Ave.
San Bernardino, CA 92415
Defunct

★12753★
SAN BERNARDINO COUNTY HISTORICAL ARCHIVES (Hist)
104 W. Fourth St. Phone: (714)383-3374
San Bernardino, CA 92415 Jeanette Bernthaler, Act.Archv.
Founded: 1979. **Staff:** Prof 2. **Subjects:** County government records. **Special Collections:** Sullivan Collection (emphasis on San Bernardino history, 1923-1974, and southern California highway system; 25 volumes); W. Jacob Schaefer Collection (Chino, California agricultural history, 1898-1959; journals and ledgers); transcripts of Mormon diaries, journals, and life sketches (microfilm). **Holdings:** 12,000 books; county maps; early newspapers; government documents; resident journals; scrapbooks. **Services:** Interlibrary loan; copying; archives open to the public by appointment. **Remarks:** Archives located at 741 S. Lugo, Suite E, San Bernardino, CA 92408.

★12754★
SAN BERNARDINO COUNTY MEDICAL CENTER - MEDICAL LIBRARY (Med)
780 E. Gilbert St. Phone: (714)383-3367
San Bernardino, CA 92404 Jacqueline M. Wakefield, Med.Libn.
Staff: Prof 1. **Subjects:** Medicine. **Holdings:** 1700 volumes; 1020 Audio-Digest tapes; 4 VF drawers of pamphlets. **Subscriptions:** 207 journals and other serials. **Services:** Interlibrary loan; copying; library open to the public for reference use only. **Automated Operations:** Computerized cataloging. **Computerized Information Services:** MEDLINE, DIALOG Information Services. **Networks/Consortia:** Member of Pacific Southwest Regional Medical Library Service, Medical Library Group of Southern California and Arizona (MLGSCA), Inland Empire Medical Library Cooperative, San Bernardino, Inyo, Riverside Counties United Library Services (SIRCULS).

★12755★
SAN BERNARDINO COUNTY MUSEUM - WILSON C. HANNA LIBRARY/RESEARCH LIBRARY (Hist, Biol Sci)
2022 Orange Tree Lane
Box 2258 Phone: (714)793-9684
Redlands, CA 92373 Dr. Allan D. Griesemer, Dir.
Founded: 1963. **Subjects:** Local history, anthropology, archeology, natural history. **Special Collections:** Ornithology. **Holdings:** 6000 books; 2000 bound periodical volumes. **Subscriptions:** 20 journals and other serials. **Services:** Library not open to the public. **Publications:** Technical Series; occasional papers.

★12756★
SAN BERNARDINO SUN - EDITORIAL LIBRARY (Publ)
399 North D St. Phone: (714)889-9666
San Bernardino, CA 92401 Anita Kaschube, Hd.Libn.
Founded: 1950. **Staff:** Prof 2; Other 1. **Subjects:** Newspaper reference topics. **Holdings:** 900 books; San Bernardino Sun, 1894 to present; 150 archival materials; 4 file cabinets; 1084 films; clippings; microfilm; photographs. **Subscriptions:** 20 journals and other serials. **Services:** Library not open to the public. **Staff:** Peggy Hardy, Asst.Libn..

★12757★
SAN CLEMENTE PRESBYTERIAN CHURCH - LIBRARY (Rel-Phil)
119 Estrella Ave. Phone: (714)492-4068
San Clemente, CA 92672 Margaret Helm, Libn.
Staff: 3. **Subjects:** Religion, christian living, Presbyterian Church, church policy. **Holdings:** 1200 books; 100 cassettes. **Services:** Library open to the public.

★12758★
SAN DIEGO AERO-SPACE MUSEUM - N. PAUL WHITTIER HISTORICAL AVIATION LIBRARY (Mil, Hist)
2001 Pan America Plaza, Balboa Park Phone: (619)234-8291
San Diego, CA 92101 Ray Wagner, Archv.
Founded: 1980. **Staff:** Prof 2; Other 3. **Subjects:** History of World Wars I and II including military aircraft, civil aircraft, personnel, early aircraft history, Lighter than Air aircraft, rotary wing, gliding engines. **Special Collections:** L.N. Forden Collection (photographs); L.R. Hackney Collection (Air Cargo Library); T.P. Hall; W.F. Schult; E. Cooper Air Mail Pioneers; Wally Wiberg; Lou E. Gordon; Willard F. Schmitt Air Mail History (3 VF drawers); Early Birds of Aviation (3 file cabinets); U.S. Navy Helicopter Association; George E.A. Hallett; Warren S. Eaton; Frank T. Courtney; Errold G. Bahl; T.C. MacAulay; Hugh M. Rockwell; John Sloan; Admiral Mitscher; American Aviators in China; The C. Ryan Library. **Holdings:** 8600 books; 2800 bound and unbound periodicals; 850,000 microfiche; 1176 airline insignia; 3400 aircraft drawings; 2500 aircraft and engine manuals; 42,000 photographs; 2000 negatives; 4000 slides; 85 scrapbooks; 300 aircraft brochures; 80 cassette tapes. **Subscriptions:** 15 journals and other serials. **Services:** Interlibrary loan; copying; library open to the public by appointment. **Staff:** Marion L. Buckner, Libn..

★12759★
SAN DIEGO COUNTY DEPARTMENT OF PLANNING AND LAND USE - LIBRARY (Plan)
5201 Ruffin Rd., Suite B-2 Phone: (619)565-3043
San Diego, CA 92123 Sonya Heiserman, Libn.
Staff: Prof 1; Other 1. **Subjects:** Urban planning, zoning, hydrology. **Holdings:** 1000 books; 1500 other cataloged items. **Subscriptions:** 35 journals and other serials; 10 newspapers. **Services:** Library open to the public for reference use only.

★12760★
SAN DIEGO COUNTY LAW LIBRARY (Law)
1105 Front St. Phone: (619)531-3900
San Diego, CA 92101-3999 Charles R. Dyer, Dir.
Founded: 1891. **Staff:** Prof 11; Other 15. **Subjects:** Law. **Special Collections:** California Appellate Court Briefs, 1950 to present; legal history of San Diego County. **Holdings:** 206,156 books and bound periodical volumes; 830 volumes of microcards; 28,478 volumes of microfiche; 950 volumes of ultrafiche; 2007 audio cassettes; 945 reels of microfilm; 94 videotapes. **Subscriptions:** 900 journals and other serials; 10 newspapers. **Services:** Interlibrary loan; copying; library open to the public; borrowing restricted to those with deposit accounts. **Computerized Information Services:** WESTLAW, OCLC, DIALOG Information Services, Pergamon ORBIT InfoLine, Inc., PHINet FedTax Database, CIM Data Base, WILSONLINE. **Networks/Consortia:** Member of CLASS. **Publications:** Recent Acquisitions, monthly - to mailing list; Guide to San Diego County Law Library, irregular - to patrons and other interested persons. **Special Indexes:** Index of Current Mexican Legal Materials; Index of Opinions of Appellate Division, Superior Court, San Diego. **Staff:** Sandra Utz, Circ.Libn.; Thomas Johnsrud, Asst.Libn.; Colleen Buskirk, Acq.Libn.; Elaine Peabody, Asst.Libn.; Florence Ewing, Ref.Libn.; Mewail Mebrahtu, Ref.Libn.; Saw Ch'ng, Ref.Libn.; Michael Kaye, Ref.Libn..

★12761★
SAN DIEGO COUNTY LAW LIBRARY - EAST COUNTY BRANCH (Law)
250 E. Main Phone: (619)441-4451
El Cajon, CA 92020-3941 Charles R. Dyer, Dir.
Founded: 1983. **Staff:** Prof 1. **Subjects:** Law. **Holdings:** 7351 books and bound periodical volumes; 22 audio cassettes; 1744 volumes of microfiche. **Subscriptions:** 49 journals and other serials. **Services:** Copying; library open to the public for reference use only. **Staff:** Carolyn Dulude, Br.Lib.Assoc..

★12762★
SAN DIEGO COUNTY LAW LIBRARY - SOUTH BAY BRANCH (Law)
500 Third Ave. Phone: (619)691-4929
Chula Vista, CA 92010-5617 Charles R. Dyer, Dir.
Founded: 1982. **Staff:** 1. **Subjects:** Law. **Holdings:** 13,191 books; 32 audio cassettes; 590 volumes of microfiche. **Subscriptions:** 49 journals and other serials. **Services:** Copying; library open to the public for reference use only. **Staff:** Edna Thiel, Br.Lib.Assoc..

★12763★
SAN DIEGO COUNTY LAW LIBRARY - VISTA BRANCH (Law)
325 S. Melrose Phone: (619)940-4386
Vista, CA 92083-6627 Charles R. Dyer, Dir.
Founded: 1973. **Staff:** 2. **Subjects:** Law. **Holdings:** 15,130 books and bound periodical volumes; 111 audio cassettes; 237 volumes of microfiche. **Subscriptions:** 50 journals and other serials. **Services:** Copying; library open to the public for reference use only. **Staff:** Ellis Swadley, Br.Lib.Assoc..

★12764★
SAN DIEGO COUNTY LIBRARY - GOVERNMENTAL REFERENCE LIBRARY (Soc Sci, Plan, Bus-Fin)
602 County Administration Center
1600 Pacific Hwy. Phone: (619)531-5787
San Diego, CA 92101 Ann Terrell, Govt.Ref.Libn.
Founded: 1946. **Staff:** Prof 1; Other 2. **Subjects:** Local government, public administration, public finance, health and welfare, public works, transportation, parks and recreation, crime and delinquency, personnel management. **Special Collections:** City and county documents (15,000);

surveys and studies by consultants. **Holdings:** 11,000 books; 8527 bound periodical volumes; 28,000 pamphlets, surveys, reports. **Subscriptions:** 250 journals and other serials; 7 newspapers. **Services:** Interlibrary loan; copying; library open to the public for reference use only. **Computerized Information Services:** DIALOG Information Services, DataTimes, WILSONLINE. **Networks/Consortia:** Member of Serra Cooperative Library System. **Publications:** Timely Topics, irregular.

★12765★
SAN DIEGO COUNTY OFFICE OF EDUCATION - RESEARCH AND REFERENCE CENTER (Educ)
6401 Linda Vista Rd. Phone: (619)292-3608
San Diego, CA 92111 P. Marvin Barbula, Dir.
Staff: Prof 2; Other 3. **Subjects:** Education and related subjects. **Special Collections:** Administrator's Corner; grant research materials. **Holdings:** 20,000 books and bound periodical volumes; 270,562 ERIC microfiche; 25,000 pamphlets, courses of study; state adopted textbooks for grades K-8; secondary textbook collection; instructional materials. **Subscriptions:** 230 journals and other serials. **Services:** Interlibrary loan; center open to public school personnel within San Diego County. **Computerized Information Services:** DIALOG Information Services. **Publications:** Curriculum Currents; bibliographies - on request. **Remarks:** Alternate telephone numbers are 292-3556 and 292-3669. **Staff:** Dorothy Smith Collins, Coord..

★12766★
SAN DIEGO ECOLOGY CENTRE - LIBRARY (Env-Cons)
2270 5th Ave. Phone: (619)238-1984
San Diego, CA 92101-2104 Chandler Deming, Lib.Coord.
Staff: 1. **Subjects:** Environmental quality, energy, land use, solid waste management, recycling, resource recovery, bio-degradable packaging, water quality and supply, air quality, wildlife, population, noise, gardening. **Holdings:** 605 books; 2000 handbooks, pamphlets; 44 VF drawers of reports, guidebooks, teaching materials; 12 AV programs. **Subscriptions:** 21 journals and other serials. **Services:** Library open to the public. **Publications:** Environmental Reporter (newsletter), bimonthly - limited distribution; Eco-Logic (newsletter), quarterly - to members and elected officials.

★12767★
SAN DIEGO GAS AND ELECTRIC COMPANY - LIBRARY (Energy)
Box 1831 Phone: (619)696-2188
San Diego, CA 92112 Marie A. Peelman, Hd.Libn.
Founded: 1921. **Staff:** Prof 1. **Subjects:** Electrical and gas engineering, steam power, environment, business, economics, Californiana, science and technology, nuclear science. **Special Collections:** Public Utilities Reports and Digest. **Holdings:** 1000 books; 10 boxes of microfilm of Electric Power Research Institute (EPRI) reports. **Subscriptions:** 400 journals and other serials; 75 newspapers. **Services:** Interlibrary loan; library not open to the public. **Automated Operations:** Computerized cataloging, acquisitions, and circulation. **Computerized Information Services:** Internal database. **Publications:** Acquisitions, monthly - for internal distribution only.

★12768★
SAN DIEGO HALL OF SCIENCE - BERNICE HARDING LIBRARY† (Sci-Engr)
Box 33303 Phone: (619)238-1233
San Diego, CA 92103 Lynne Kennedy, Educ.Coord.
Founded: 1976. **Staff:** 1. **Subjects:** Astronomy, photography, scientific research. **Holdings:** 1000 books; 200 bound periodical volumes. **Subscriptions:** 14 journals and other serials. **Services:** Interlibrary loan; library open to members. **Publications:** Space Reflections, bimonthly - to members.

★12769★
SAN DIEGO HISTORICAL SOCIETY - RESEARCH ARCHIVES (Hist)
Box 81825 Phone: (619)232-6203
San Diego, CA 92138 Sylvia Arden, Hd., Lib. and Mss.Coll.
Founded: 1929. **Staff:** Prof 2. **Subjects:** History - San Diego County, California, Baja California. **Special Collections:** San Diego Biography (374 notebooks); oral history (550 transcripts); Kerr Collection (California ranchos; 19 notebooks). **Holdings:** 9500 volumes; 4500 bound periodical volumes; 500 photostats of documents in the Archivo General, Cuidad de Mejico Collection, 1769-1840; 1200 feet of local public records; business ledgers and reports; census reports; maps; architectural records; newspapers on microfilm. **Subscriptions:** 15 journals and other serials. **Services:** Copying; clipping service; archives open to the public with restrictions. **Remarks:** Library located at Balboa Park, Casa de Balboa, 1649 El Prado, San Diego, CA 92101. **Staff:** Richard Crawford, Archv..

★12770★
SAN DIEGO HISTORICAL SOCIETY - RESEARCH ARCHIVES - PHOTOGRAPH COLLECTION (Aud-Vis)
Box 81825 Phone: (619)232-6203
San Diego, CA 92138 Larry Booth, Cur., Photo.
Subjects: San Diego city and county, 1867-1986. **Holdings:** 1.25 million large format professional negatives, vintage prints, and reference prints; slides; films. **Services:** Collection open to the public on a limited schedule; photographs available for research, display, publication, and advertising on fee basis. **Remarks:** Collection is located at Balboa Park, Casa de Balboa, 1649 El Prado, San Diego, CA 92101. An alternate telephone number is 297-3258.

★12771★
SAN DIEGO MUSEUM OF ART - REFERENCE LIBRARY (Art)
Balboa Park
Box 2107 Phone: (619)232-7931
San Diego, CA 92112 Nancy J. Andrews, Libn.
Founded: 1926. **Staff:** Prof 1; Other 1. **Subjects:** Art, especially Spanish Baroque, Oriental, and Italian Renaissance. **Holdings:** 10,000 books; 1100 bound periodical volumes; 80,000 art exhibition catalogs; 25 cabinets of artists files; 18,000 slides. **Subscriptions:** 35 journals and other serials. **Services:** Copying; library open to the public for reference use only. **Special Catalogs:** Bibliographical card file to artists in art exhibition catalogs.

★12772★
SAN DIEGO MUSEUM OF MAN - SCIENTIFIC LIBRARY (Hist)
Balboa Park
1350 El Prado Phone: (619)239-2001
San Diego, CA 92101 Jane Bentley, Libn.
Founded: 1916. **Staff:** Prof 2. **Subjects:** Anthropology, pre-Columbian art, Indians of the Americas, archeology, ethnology, physical anthropology. **Special Collections:** North American Indians. **Holdings:** 5500 books; 2000 bound periodical volumes; 51 archival manuscripts. **Subscriptions:** 325 journals and other serials. **Services:** Interlibrary loan; copying (both limited); library open to the public by appointment. **Publications:** Ethnic Technology Notes, irregular; San Diego Museum Papers, irregular - both for sale or exchange.

★12773★
SAN DIEGO PUBLIC LIBRARY - ART, MUSIC & RECREATION SECTION (Art, Mus, Rec)
820 E St. Phone: (619)236-5810
San Diego, CA 92101 Kathleen M. Griffin, Supv.
Staff: Prof 4; Other 2. **Subjects:** Art and music history, architecture, sculpture, antiques, interior decoration, crafts, music theory and techniques, painting, drawing, printmaking, photography, sports, games, theater, cinema, dance. **Special Collections:** Language instruction recordings; pop songs, 1900-1970. **Holdings:** 89,500 books; 510,000 pictures; 25,000 picture postcards; 10,000 choral music pieces; 25,000 phonograph records; 14,000 scores; 4000 audio cassettes; libretti, miniature scores. **Subscriptions:** 339 journals and other serials. **Services:** Chamber music series; monthly art exhibitions. **Automated Operations:** Computerized cataloging and circulation. **Computerized Information Services:** DIALOG Information Services. Performs searches free of charge. **Networks/Consortia:** Member of Serra Cooperative Library System, CLASS. **Special Catalogs:** Phono-Record Catalog. **Special Indexes:** Song Title Index; Choral Music Index; Film Review File. **Staff:** Barbara Carroll, Libn.; Evelyn Kooperman, Libn.; Christina Clifford, Libn..

★12774★
SAN DIEGO PUBLIC LIBRARY - CALIFORNIA ROOM (Hist)
820 E St. Phone: (619)236-5834
San Diego, CA 92101 Mary Allely, Supv.
Staff: Prof 2. **Subjects:** History of California counties, especially San Diego and Imperial Counties; history and description of Baja California. **Special Collections:** Records of the Little Landers Colony, San Ysidro, California; Kelly Papers (records of a pioneer family); Hatfield (rainmaker) papers; San Diego Park Department records, including exposition material; official repository of San Diego 200th Anniversary Committee papers; San Diego Great Registers, 1866-1909; Horton House registers. **Holdings:** 18,000 books; 300 maps; 52 VF drawers of pamphlets and clippings; 800,000 index cards covering San Diego Herald, 1851-1860, San Diego Union, 1868-1903 and 1930 to present. **Services:** Copying; room open to the public for reference use only. **Staff:** Eileen Boyle, Libn..

★12775★
SAN DIEGO PUBLIC LIBRARY - GENEALOGY ROOM (Hist)
820 E St.
San Diego, CA 92101 Mary Allely, Supv.
Founded: 1940. **Subjects:** General genealogy. **Special Collections:** California census, 1850-1900, on microfilm. **Holdings:** 3600 books. **Services:** Copying; room open to the public for reference use only.

★12776★
SAN DIEGO PUBLIC LIBRARY - HISTORY & WORLD AFFAIRS SECTION (Hist)
820 E St. Phone: (619)236-5820
San Diego, CA 92101 Jean Hughes, Supv.
Staff: Prof 4; Other 2. **Subjects:** World history, travel, biography, archeology, atlases and maps. **Special Collections:** World Wars I and II personal narratives. **Holdings:** 92,000 books; 2400 maps; 40 VF drawers of pamphlets and clippings; Facts on File, 1944-1983; Editorials on File. **Subscriptions:** 260 journals and other serials. **Services:** Interlibrary loan; copying; section open to the public. **Automated Operations:** Computerized cataloging and circulation. **Computerized Information Services:** DIALOG Information Services. Performs searches free of charge. **Networks/Consortia:** Member of Serra Cooperative Library System, CLASS. **Staff:** Don Silva, Libn.; Kathleen Burns, Libn.; Brinn Vaniman, Libn..

★12777★
SAN DIEGO PUBLIC LIBRARY - INFORMATION/DIRECTORY SERVICE SECTION (Info Sci)
820 E St. Phone: (619)236-5800
San Diego, CA 92101 Jean Hughes, Supv.
Staff: Prof 1; Other 6. **Holdings:** 1400 telephone directories; 845 trade directories; 88 city directories; U.S. telephone directories on microfiche. **Services:** Copying; section open to the public. **Automated Operations:** Computerized cataloging and circulation. **Computerized Information Services:** DIALOG Information Services. Performs searches free of charge. **Networks/Consortia:** Member of Serra Cooperative Library System, CLASS. **Special Indexes:** Index to directories (card).

★12778★
SAN DIEGO PUBLIC LIBRARY - LITERATURE & LANGUAGES SECTION (Rel-Phil, Hum)
820 E St. Phone: (619)236-5816
San Diego, CA 92101 Ellen Sneberger, Supv.
Staff: Prof 4; Other 2. **Subjects:** Literature, psychology, languages, philosophy, religion, information science. **Special Collections:** Occult sciences; Bacon-Shakespeare controversy; theosophy. **Holdings:** 164,000 books; 4 VF drawers of pamphlets; large print books; 10,000 foreign language books (especially Spanish). **Subscriptions:** 500 journals and other serials. **Services:** Home delivery for shut-ins; section open to the public. **Automated Operations:** Computerized cataloging and circulation. **Computerized Information Services:** DIALOG Information Services. Performs searches free of charge. **Networks/Consortia:** Member of Serra Cooperative Library System, CLASS. **Publications:** Booklists, irregular. **Staff:** Linda Griffin, Libn.; John Vanderby, Libn.; Susanna Engelsman, Libn..

★12779★
SAN DIEGO PUBLIC LIBRARY - SCIENCE & INDUSTRY SECTION (Sci-Engr, Bus-Fin)
820 E St. Phone: (619)236-5813
San Diego, CA 92101 Joanne Anderson, Supv.
Staff: Prof 3; Other 4. **Subjects:** Business, industry, science, cookery, automobile repair. **Special Collections:** Space and aeronautics historical collection; depository for U.S., California, and San Diego city and county government publications (over 1.3 million); American National Standards Institute (ANSI) and American Society for Testing and Materials (ASTM) standards on microfiche; U.S. Utility Patents, 1955 to present; U.S. Design Patents, 1951 to present. **Holdings:** 61,600 books; 23,000 maps; 265,000 microforms; Sams Photofacts (complete collection); Atomic Energy Commission (AEC) and NASA depository collections. **Subscriptions:** 500 journals and other serials. **Services:** Interlibrary loan; copying. **Automated Operations:** Computerized cataloging and circulation. **Computerized Information Services:** DIALOG Information Services, U.S. Patent Classification System. Performs searches free of charge. **Networks/Consortia:** Member of Serra Cooperative Library System, CLASS. **Special Indexes:** Subject index to government documents (card); California Mines Index (card). **Staff:** Robert Taylor, Libn.; Thomas Karras, Libn..

★12780★
SAN DIEGO PUBLIC LIBRARY - SOCIAL SCIENCES SECTION (Soc Sci)
820 E St. Phone: (619)236-5564
San Diego, CA 92101 Matt J. Katka, Supv.
Staff: Prof 4; Other 2. **Subjects:** Sociology, education, political science, law, economics, finance, conservation, transportation, military service, folklore. **Holdings:** 71,154 books; 7 VF drawers of corporation annual reports; 6 VF drawers of vocational pamphlets; 31 VF drawers of miscellaneous pamphlets; 5000 college catalogs on microfiche; corporation annual reports, 1978 to present, on microfiche; talking books and cassette tapes for the visually handicapped. **Subscriptions:** 511 journals and other serials. **Automated Operations:** Computerized cataloging and circulation. **Computerized Information Services:** DIALOG Information Services. Performs searches free of charge. **Networks/Consortia:** Member of Serra Cooperative Library System, CLASS. **Publications:** Booklists, irregular. **Special Indexes:** Black American Firsts File (card); Women Firsts File (card). **Staff:** Marian Avila, Libn.; James Castro, Libn.; Frances Bookheim, Libn..

★12781★
SAN DIEGO PUBLIC LIBRARY - WANGENHEIM ROOM (Rare Book)
820 E St. Phone: (619)236-5807
San Diego, CA 92101 Eileen Boyle, Libn.
Founded: 1954. **Staff:** Prof 1. **Subjects:** History of printing and the development of the book with specimens ranging from Babylonian tablets to cassettes; famous presses and modern private presses; incunabula; fine book bindings. **Special Collections:** Dime novels (769 items); bookplates (8000); fore-edge paintings (185 volumes); works of John Ruskin (250 volumes); Curtis' North American Indians (20 volumes and 20 portfolios of photographs); Monumenta Scenica (12 portfolios). **Holdings:** 8800 books; selected antiquarian book dealers' catalogs; periodicals; manuscripts; autographs; artifacts. **Services:** Room open to the public by appointment. **Special Catalogs:** Chronological card catalog arranged by date and place of publication.

★12782★
SAN DIEGO SOCIETY OF NATURAL HISTORY - NATURAL HISTORY MUSEUM LIBRARY (Biol Sci)
Box 1390 Phone: (619)232-3821
San Diego, CA 92112 Carol B. Barsi, Libn.
Founded: 1874. **Staff:** Prof 1; Other 1. **Subjects:** Birds and mammals, botany, geology, paleontology, mineralogy, entomology, marine invertebrates, herpetology, biology. **Special Collections:** A.W. Vodges Library of Geology and Paleontology (20,000 volumes); L. Klauber Herpetological Library (1462 volumes; 19,000 pamphlets and reprints). **Holdings:** 80,000 volumes; maps; photograph archives; Valentein wildflower originals. **Subscriptions:** 850 journals and other serials. **Services:** Interlibrary loan; copying; library open to the public by appointment for reference use only.

★12783★
SAN DIEGO STATE UNIVERSITY - BUREAU OF BUSINESS & ECONOMIC RESEARCH LIBRARY (Bus-Fin)
College of Business Administration Phone: (619)265-6838
San Diego, CA 92182 Oliver Galbraith, Dir.
Founded: 1958. **Staff:** Prof 1; Other 2. **Subjects:** Accounting, auditing, business, business education, economics, finance, management, marketing, labor. **Special Collections:** Research studies of Bureau members; Arthur Young Tax Research Library; regional data on San Diego and southern California; national data by states. **Holdings:** Figures not available. **Subscriptions:** 27 serials. **Services:** Interlibrary loan; library open to the public. **Publications:** Monographs; Business Case Studies; Faculty Working Papers.

★12784★
SAN DIEGO STATE UNIVERSITY - CENTER FOR ENERGY STUDIES - LIBRARY (Energy)
Dept. of Physics Phone: (619)265-5847
San Diego, CA 92182 Kati Harkanyi, Libn.
Founded: 1980. **Subjects:** Energy systems and allied topics. **Special Collections:** U.S. Department of Energy publications. **Holdings:** 7000 volumes. **Services:** Library open to the public. **Remarks:** An alternate telephone number is 265-6240.

★12785★
SAN DIEGO STATE UNIVERSITY - CENTER FOR PUBLIC ECONOMICS LIBRARY (Plan, Bus-Fin)
ACE 124-126 Phone: (619)265-6707
San Diego, CA 92182-0511 Dr. George Babilot, Dir.
Staff: Prof 9; Other 5. **Subjects:** Economics, health and welfare, land use and taxation, natural resources and environment, population and demography, poverty, public finance, urban regional studies. **Special Collections:** Fiscal studies from all 50 states; San Diego County documents. **Holdings:** 4000 books. **Subscriptions:** 80 journals and other serials. **Services:** Interlibrary loan; library open to the public with restrictions. **Automated Operations:** Computerized cataloging. **Computerized Information Services:** DIALOG Information Services; Macroeconomic Data, San Diego Regional Economic (internal databases). **Publications:** Working papers in public economics. **Staff:** Joseph Drew, Coord..

★12786★
SAN DIEGO STATE UNIVERSITY - EUROPEAN STUDIES CENTER - LIBRARY (Area-Ethnic)
San Diego, CA 92182-0511 Phone: (619)265-5928
Dr. Leon Rosenstein, Dir.
Staff: Prof 12; Other 1. **Subjects:** European studies. **Holdings:** 1500 books; 200 bound periodical volumes; 18,000 slides; 1000 records and tapes. **Services:** Library not open to the public.

★12787★
SAN DIEGO STATE UNIVERSITY - GOVERNMENT PUBLICATIONS DIVISION (Info Sci)
San Diego, CA 92182-0511 Phone: (619)265-5832
Charles V. Dintrone, Div.Hd.
Staff: Prof 4; Other 3. **Holdings:** 481,030 U.S., United Nations, and California documents; 1.5 million microforms. **Services:** Interlibrary loan; copying; division open to the public. **Computerized Information Services:** DIALOG Information Services. **Special Catalogs:** U.S., California, United Nations card catalogs. **Staff:** Patricia Moore-Crisley, Ref.Libn.; Joann Goodwin, Ref.Libn.; Walter Posner, Ref.Libn..

★12788★
SAN DIEGO STATE UNIVERSITY - INSTITUTE FOR PUBLIC AND COMMUNITY HISTORY (Hist)
College of Arts and Letters Phone: (619)265-5751
San Diego, CA 92182-0400 M.M. Gerlach, Archv.
Founded: 1976. **Staff:** Prof 2. **Subjects:** 20th century San Diego history. **Special Collections:** Archival collections of American Tunaboat Association, Hotel Del Coronado, San Diego Convention and Visitors Bureau, National Conference of Christians and Jews, La Jolla Museum of Contemporary Art, San Diego County Medical Society, San Diego Symphony, U.S. Congressman Robert Carlton Wilson, San Diego Chamber of Commerce, San Diego Center for Children, United Way of San Diego County, San Diego County National Organization for Women (NOW), and 108 additional archival collections (total holdings: 2500 linear feet). **Holdings:** 1200 books; 400 oral history tapes; 85 reels of microfilm; 700 photographs; 7000 cores of newsfilm. **Subscriptions:** 20 journals and other serials; 5 newspapers. **Services:** Copying; institute open to the public. **Publications:** A Guide to the Collections of the San Diego History Research Center, 1978; San Diego History Research Center News, irregular - both available upon request. **Special Catalogs:** Inventories of archival collections; catalog of published works and archival collections (card). **Formerly:** Center for Regional History.

★12789★
SAN DIEGO STATE UNIVERSITY - MALCOLM A. LOVE LIBRARY - SPECIAL COLLECTIONS (Hum, Sci-Engr)
San Diego, CA 92182-0511 Phone: (619)265-6014
Don L. Bosseau, Univ.Libn.
Founded: 1897. **Services:** Lord Chesterfield Collection (150 volumes); Norland Collection on the History of Biology (3500 volumes; 1000 other cataloged items); Davis Orchid Collection (2000 volumes); Chater Collection in Science Fiction; Archive of Popular American Music; H.L. Mencken Collection of Autographed First Editions. **Services:** Interlibrary loan; copying; collections open to the public for reference use only. **Automated Operations:** Computerized cataloging, serials, and circulation. **Computerized Information Services:** DIALOG Information Services, BRS Information Technologies, WILSONLINE, NLM. **Networks/Consortia:** Member of Serra Cooperative Library System. **Staff:** Ruth Leerhoff, Spec.Coll.Libn.; William Pease, Coll.Dev.Libn.; Christina Woo, Ref.Dept.; Carol Lea Goyne, Cat.Dept..

★12790★
SAN DIEGO STATE UNIVERSITY - MEDIA & CURRICULUM CENTER (Educ, Aud-Vis)
University Library Phone: (619)265-6757
San Diego, CA 92182-0511
Stephen D. Fitt, Ph.D., Hd., Spec.Rsrcs.Div.
Founded: 1951. **Staff:** 4. **Subjects:** Textbooks and curriculum materials for K-12, children's literature, nonprint media for all levels. **Holdings:** 14,000 K-12 textbooks; 10,000 K-12 curriculum guides, teachers' resource books, pamphlets; 15,000 children's books; 10 VF drawers of publishers' and AV producers' catalogs; 18,000 nonbook media. **Services:** Facilities for previewing and listening. **Staff:** Judith Arbogast, Media Supv..

★12791★
SAN DIEGO STATE UNIVERSITY - PUBLIC ADMINISTRATION CENTER LIBRARY (Soc Sci)
PSFA 100 Phone: (619)286-6084
San Diego, CA 92182-0367 Elaine Wonsowicz, Mgr.
Founded: 1950. **Staff:** Prof 1; Other 3. **Subjects:** American and comparative public administration; urban affairs; public policy and planning; resource utilization; city planning; criminal justice. **Special Collections:** San Diego Region Collection. **Holdings:** 3000 books; 70,000 other cataloged items; depository of public institutional reports. **Subscriptions:** 300 journals and other serials. **Services:** Copying; library open to the public for reference use only. **Publications:** Selected monographs; reports.

★12792★
SAN DIEGO STATE UNIVERSITY - SCIENCE DIVISION (Sci-Engr, Biol Sci)
University Library Phone: (619)265-6715
San Diego, CA 92182-0511 Lillian Chan, Sci.Libn.
Staff: Prof 5; Other 3. **Subjects:** Biology, chemistry, mathematics, geology, physics, engineering, industrial arts, astronomy, military science, history of sciences, nursing, public health. **Special Collections:** Natural history and sciences collection (4500 volumes); Ernst Zinner Collection on the History of Astronomy and Science (1500 volumes; 4200 other cataloged items); W.M. Pearce Spider Collection (300 items). **Holdings:** 192,400 books; 126,700 bound periodical volumes; 12,030 hardcopy science reports; 145,000 microfiche of science reports; 1300 reels of microfilm and filmstrips; 245,000 microfiche; 46,668 microcards. **Subscriptions:** 3308 journals and other serials. **Services:** Interlibrary loan; copying; division open to the public with fee for borrowing. **Automated Operations:** Computerized cataloging and serials. **Computerized Information Services:** DIALOG Information Services, Pergamon ORBIT InfoLine, Inc., MEDLINE. **Publications:** Union List of Standards in the San Diego County Area; serials printout, quarterly - limited number free upon request; Literature of Time in the Ernst Zinner Collection, a checklist; Copernicus; Johann Kepler, a bibliography; Tycho Brahe, a bibliography; Geology of Baja California, a bibliography; Botany of San Diego County, guide to research materials; Guide to the Botanical Literature of Baja California in the Collections of the San Diego State University Library; Sunbeams and Solar Energy; Science and Engineering Resource Series; Guide to Special Information in Scientific and Engineering Journals. **Staff:** Robert Carande, Sr.Asst.Libn.; Katalin Harkanyi, Assoc.Sci.Libn.; Mary E. Harris, Assoc.Sci.Libn.; Anne Turhollow, Assoc.Sci.Libn.; Eric Lamb, Div.Supv..

★12793★
SAN DIEGO UNIFIED SCHOOL DISTRICT - PROFESSIONAL LIBRARY
2441 Cardinal Ln.
San Diego, CA 92123
Defunct

★12794★
SAN DIEGO UNION-TRIBUNE PUBLISHING COMPANY - LIBRARY (Publ)
350 Camino De La Reina Phone: (619)299-3131
San Diego, CA 92108 Sharon Stewart Reeves, Lib.Dir.
Staff: Prof 3; Other 22. **Subjects:** Newspaper reference topics. **Holdings:** 2000 books; 240 drawers of newspaper clippings; 4000 reels of microfilm. **Subscriptions:** 50 journals and other serials; 8 newspapers. **Services:** Library not open to the public. **Automated Operations:** Computerized cataloging. **Computerized Information Services:** DIALOG Information Services, NEXIS, VU/TEXT Information Services, DataTimes, Dow Jones News/Retrieval; internal databases. **Special Indexes:** Index of negatives of photographs taken by staff photographers (online). **Staff:** Linda F. Ritter, Asst.Libn.; Richard D. Harrington, Asst.Libn..

★12795★
SAN FRANCISCO ACADEMY OF COMIC ART - LIBRARY (Art, Hum)
2850 Ulloa Phone: (415)681-1737
San Francisco, CA 94116 Bill Blackbeard, Dir.
Founded: 1968. **Staff:** 5. **Subjects:** Science fiction, crime fiction, popular literature, comic strip art in all aspects, dime novels, pulp and other popular magazines, motion picture data, critical literature. **Special Collections:** Dickensiana; Sherlockiana; Oz books; foreign popular literature; 19th century fiction and art; children's books; nationally representative bound newspaper runs, including many rare Hearst papers. **Holdings:** 59,000 books; one million comic strips; 25,000 unbound periodicals; manuscripts, original comic strips, and other graphic work; movie stills and pressbooks; newspaper and magazine ads and art; science fiction fanzines and fanzines of other areas of interest; segregated editorial pages, columns, film and auto sections, comic strips. **Subscriptions:** 100 journals and other serials; 100 newspapers. **Services:** Interlibrary loan; copying; library open to the public by appointment. **Staff:** William Loughman, Dir.; Chris Berglas, Dir.; William Murr, Dir.; Gale Paulson, Dir.; Barbara Tyger, Dir.; Rick Marschall, Dir..

SAN FRANCISCO ART INSTITUTE
See: College of the San Francisco Art Institute (3397)

★12796★
SAN FRANCISCO CHRONICLE - LIBRARY (Publ)
901 Mission St. Phone: (415)777-1111
San Francisco, CA 94119 Richard Geiger, Lib.Dir.
Founded: 1879. **Staff:** Prof 16. **Subjects:** Newspaper reference topics. **Holdings:** 1500 books; 100 pamphlets; 7.5 million clippings; 3 million news photographs; San Francisco Chronicle Database, 1985 to present. **Services:** Copying; library open to the public by telephone during limited hours. **Computerized Information Services:** DataTimes, NEXIS, DIALOG Information Services, VU/TEXT Information Services, Dow Jones News/Retrieval. **Staff:** June Dellapa, Asst.Hd.Libn..

★12797★
SAN FRANCISCO CITY ATTORNEY'S OFFICE - LIBRARY (Law)
206 City Hall Phone: (415)554-4247
San Francisco, CA 94102 Ruth B. Stevenson, Law Libn.
Staff: Prof 1; Other 3. **Subjects:** San Francisco municipal law and codes; city attorney opinions. **Holdings:** 25,000 volumes. **Subscriptions:** 75 journals and other serials. **Services:** Library not open to the public. **Remarks:** Maintains a branch library at 214 Van Ness Ave., San Francisco, CA 94102.

★12798★
SAN FRANCISCO COLLEGE OF MORTUARY SCIENCE - LIBRARY (Sci-Engr)
1363 Divisadero St. Phone: (415)567-0674
San Francisco, CA 94115-3912 Michael C. Hawkins, Pres.
Subjects: Embalming, restorative art, anatomy, pathology, bacteriology, chemistry, funeral directing and management. **Special Collections:** Burial customs of foreign countries (16mm color films); death and dying (20 filmstrips). **Holdings:** 512 books and bound periodical volumes. **Subscriptions:** 12 journals and other serials. **Services:** Library open to the public with permission.

★12799★
SAN FRANCISCO CONSERVATORY OF MUSIC - LIBRARY (Mus)
1201 Ortega St. Phone: (415)564-8086
San Francisco, CA 94122 Lucretia Wolfe, Libn.
Founded: 1967. **Staff:** Prof 2; Other 3. **Subjects:** Music. **Special Collections:** Performance materials. **Holdings:** 17,000 books; 200 bound periodical volumes; 450 tapes; 450 slides; 6000 phonograph records; 40 holographic scores and manuscripts of 20th century music. **Subscriptions:** 57 journals and other serials. **Services:** Interlibrary loan; library open to the public for reference use only.

★12800★
SAN FRANCISCO EXAMINER - LIBRARY (Publ)
110 Fifth St. Phone: (415)777-7845
San Francisco, CA 94103 Judy Gerritts Canter, Chf.Libn.
Founded: 1865. **Staff:** Prof 1; Other 13. **Subjects:** Newspaper reference topics, state and local history. **Special Collections:** San Francisco Examiner, 1865 to present (microfilm); historical photographs and clippings of San Francisco and California. **Holdings:** 5000 books and pamphlets; 12 million newspaper clippings on microjackets; negatives; photographs. **Subscriptions:** 24 journals and other serials; 10 newspapers. **Services:** Interlibrary loan; library not open to the public. **Computerized Information Services:** NEXIS, DataTimes, DIALOG Information Services, VU/TEXT Information Sevices. **Remarks:** Published by Hearst Corporation.

★12801★
SAN FRANCISCO GENERAL HOSPITAL MEDICAL CENTER - BARNETT-BRIGGS LIBRARY (Med)
1001 Potrero Ave. Phone: (415)821-3113
San Francisco, CA 94110 [illegible]
Founded: 1950. **Staff:** Prof 1; Other 5. **Subjects:** Medicine. **Holdings:** 13,359 books; 17,947 bound periodical volumes. **Subscriptions:** 428 journals and other serials. **Services:** Interlibrary loan; copying; library open to the public. **Computerized Information Services:** NLM, BRS Information Technologies, DIALOG Information Services. Performs searches on fee basis. **Networks/Consortia:** Member of Pacific Southwest Regional Medical Library Service, San Francisco Biomedical Library Group, CLASS.

★12802★
SAN FRANCISCO LAW LIBRARY (Law)
436 City Hall
400 Van Ness Ave. Phone: (415)558-4627
San Francisco, CA 94102-4672 John H. Hauff, Libn.
Founded: 1870. **Staff:** Prof 5; Other 8. **Subjects:** Law. **Holdings:** 271,689 volumes. **Subscriptions:** 436 journals and other serials. **Services:** Library open to the public for reference use only. **Remarks:** Maintains branch library at 685 Market St., Rm. 420. **Staff:** Coral Henning, Chf.Asst.Libn.; John M. Moore, Br.Libn..

★12803★
SAN FRANCISCO MUNICIPAL RAILWAY - LIBRARY (Trans)
949 Presidio Ave., Rm. 204 Phone: (415)923-6100
San Francisco, CA 94115 Dr. Marc Hofstadter, Libn.
Staff: Prof 1. **Subjects:** Transportation planning, public transit, Bay Area transportation history. **Holdings:** 3500 books; 250 Bay Area Environmental Impact Reports; 500 San Francisco transit maps. **Subscriptions:** 50 journals and other serials. **Services:** Interlibrary loan; library open to the public by appointment for reference use only. **Computerized Information Services:** DIALOG Information Services. **Networks/Consortia:** Member of Metropolitan Transit & Planning (MTP).

★12804★
SAN FRANCISCO MUSEUM OF MODERN ART - LOUISE S. ACKERMAN FINE ARTS LIBRARY (Art)
401 Van Ness Ave. Phone: (415)863-8800
San Francisco, CA 94102 Eugenie Candau, Libn.
Founded: 1935. **Staff:** Prof 1; Other 5. **Subjects:** Modern and contemporary visual arts, history of photography. **Special Collections:** Margery Mann Collection of the Literature of Photography. **Holdings:** 10,000 books; 40,000 art exhibition catalogs; 100 VF drawers of biographical clippings; 18 files of archives. **Services:** Copying; library open to the public for reference use only. **Networks/Consortia:** Member of Bay Area Reference Center (BARC).

★12805★
SAN FRANCISCO PSYCHOANALYTIC INSTITUTE - ERIK H. ERIKSON LIBRARY (Med)
2420 Sutter St. Phone: (415)563-4477
San Francisco, CA 94115 Anne L. Regner-Hyatt, Libn.
Founded: 1954. **Staff:** Prof 1; Other 1. **Subjects:** Psychoanalysis. **Special Collections:** Siegfried Bernfield Collection (300 books); Bernice S. Engle Memorial Collection (80 books). **Holdings:** 4500 books; 1500 bound periodical volumes; 2 VF drawers of pamphlets; 3000 reprints and manuscripts; 5 boxes of audiotapes; 150 audio cassette tapes; 3 VF drawers of archives. **Subscriptions:** 90 journals and other serials. **Services:** Interlibrary loan; copying; SDI; library open to institute members, candidates, and to the public upon payment of membership fee. **Networks/Consortia:** Member of Pacific Southwest Regional Medical Library Service, San Francisco Biomedical Library Group, Northern California and Nevada Medical Library Group (NCNMLG). **Publications:** Journal holdings list - available on request.

★12806★
SAN FRANCISCO PUBLIC LIBRARY - BAY AREA REFERENCE CENTER (BARC) (Info Sci)
Civic Ctr. Phone: (415)558-2941
San Francisco, CA 94102 Fauneil McInnis, Dir.
Staff: Prof 8; Other 3. **Holdings:** Figures not available. **Computerized Information Services:** DIALOG Information Services, Pergamon ORBIT InfoLine, Inc., BRS Information Technologies, NEXIS, VU/TEXT Information Services, RLIN; OnTyme Electronic Message Network Service (electronic mail service). **Publications:** BARC Notes, monthly.

★12807★
SAN FRANCISCO PUBLIC LIBRARY - BUSINESS LIBRARY (Bus-Fin)
530 Kearny St. Phone: (415)558-3946
San Francisco, CA 94108 John Fetros, Prin.Libn.
Staff: Prof 4; Other 3. **Subjects:** Accounting, advertising, economics, finance, banking, business planning, insurance, management, investments, retail, real estate. **Special Collections:** Trade directories; corporation annual reports (1500); bank publications (125); historical insurance collection. **Holdings:** 13,000 books; 434 bound periodical volumes; 200 local, state, and federal publications; 40 business newspapers; 173 business services; 800 VF drawers; newspaper clipping file. **Services:** Copying.

★12808★
SAN FRANCISCO PUBLIC LIBRARY - SAN FRANCISCO ROOM AND ARCHIVES (Hist)
Civic Ctr. Phone: (415)558-3949
San Francisco, CA 94102 Gladys Hansen, City Archv.
Founded: 1963. **Staff:** Prof 1; Other 1. **Subjects:** History of San Francisco and California. **Holdings:** 2.5 million morgue clips from the San Francisco Examiner, 1906 to present; News-Call-Bulletin morgue photographs, 1925-1965; 125,000 historical San Francisco and California photographs; 299 VF drawers of pamphlets; 6000 postcards; periodicals; newspapers. **Services:** Copying.

★12809★
SAN FRANCISCO PUBLIC LIBRARY - SPECIAL COLLECTIONS DEPARTMENT (Rare Book)
Civic Ctr. Phone: (415)558-3940
San Francisco, CA 94102 Johanna Goldschmid, Spec.Coll.Libn.
Founded: 1963. **Staff:** Prof 1; Other 1. **Special Collections:** Robert Grabhorn Collection on the history of printing and the development of the book; Max John Kuhl Collection of printing; Richard Harrison Collection of calligraphy and lettering; James D. Phelan Collection of California authors; Schmulowitz Collection of wit and humor; George M. Fox Collection of early children's books; Scowrers Sherlockiana Collection; Robert Frost Collection; Panama Canal Collection. **Holdings:** 25,000 books; 100 VF drawers of pamphlets and other ephemera. **Subscriptions:** 40 journals and other serials. **Services:** Copying; collections open to serious researchers and advanced students.

★12810★
SAN FRANCISCO STATE UNIVERSITY - FRANK V. DE BELLIS COLLECTION (Area-Ethnic)
1630 Holloway Ave. Phone: (415)338-1649
San Francisco, CA 94132 Serena De Bellis, Cur.
Founded: 1963. **Staff:** Prof 1; Other 4. **Subjects:** Italian and Roman civilization, including history, literature, fine arts, music. **Holdings:** 12,500 books; 10,000 music scores; 700 manuscripts; 25,000 sound recordings; 500 reels of microfilm; 450 prints; 356 artifacts; 400 coins. **Subscriptions:** 53 journals. **Services:** Interlibrary loan; copying; collection open to the public. **Publications:** The Frank V. de Bellis Collection (revised edition, 1967). **Special Catalogs:** Published catalog of artifacts: Etruscan, Greek and Roman Artifacts in the Frank V. de Bellis Collection (revised edition, 1975).

★12811★
SAN FRANCISCO STATE UNIVERSITY - J. PAUL LEONARD LIBRARY - SPECIAL COLLECTIONS/ARCHIVES (Hist, Aud-Vis)
1630 Holloway Ave. Phone: (415)338-1856
San Francisco, CA 94132 Helene Whitson, Coord.
Staff: Prof 1; Other 1. **Subjects:** San Francisco Bay Area. **Special Collections:** KQED Film Archive, including Bay Area news and events, 1967-1980 (student protests; gay rights and activities; interviews with local political, social, and cultural figures; 1.8 million feet of 16mm newsfilm); university archives (newspapers; catalogs; yearbooks; publications; photographs; microfiche; President's records; materials on San Francisco State College strike, 1968-1969). **Holdings:** 70 linear feet of printed books and records; 68 cubic feet of records; 2500 special collections of books and records. **Services:** KQED Film Archives open to the public for research and educational purposes; other collections open to the public.

SAN FRANCISCO THEOLOGICAL SEMINARY
See: Graduate Theological Union (5785)

★12812★
SAN FRANCISCO THEOSOPHICAL SOCIETY - LIBRARY (Rel-Phil)
809 Mason St. Phone: (415)771-8777
San Francisco, CA 94108 Richard Power, Libn.
Founded: 1892. **Staff:** 2. **Subjects:** Theosophy, religion, metaphysics, psychic research, anthropology, healing. **Special Collections:** Popular American metaphysics, circa 1880-1950. **Holdings:** 5000 books; 200 bound periodical volumes; 6 file drawers of pamphlets and clippings; 3 cases of manuscripts. **Services:** Library open to the public.

★12813★
SAN FRANCISCO UNIFIED SCHOOL DISTRICT - TEACHERS PROFESSIONAL LIBRARY (Educ)
135 Van Ness Ave. Phone: (415)565-9272
San Francisco, CA 94102 Helen M. Boutin, Lib.Techn.
Staff: 1. **Subjects:** Educational philosophy and psychology, guidance and personnel, human relations, social work, curriculum development, educational administration, educational practices. **Special Collections:** Californiana and San Franciscana (archives files of the school district). **Holdings:** 38,375 books; 2300 bound periodical volumes; 388 reels of microfilm of periodicals; 2251 microfiche; 9 drawers of pamphlets; 135 feet of documents and curriculum guides. **Subscriptions:** 104 journals and other serials. **Services:** Interlibrary loan; copying; library open to the public for reference use only. **Publications:** Bibliographies of special collections and recent acquisitions (mimeographed) - to district personnel only.

★12814★
SAN GORGONIO PASS MEMORIAL HOSPITAL - MEDICAL LIBRARY (Med)
600 N. Highland Springs Ave.
Banning, CA 92220 Phone: (714)845-1121
Subjects: Medicine. **Holdings:** 783 volumes; 18 boxes of clippings and pamphlets. **Services:** Library not open to the public.

★12815★
SAN JACINTO MUSEUM OF HISTORY ASSOCIATION - LIBRARY (Hist)
3800 Park Rd. 1836 Phone: (713)479-2421
La Porte, TX 77571 Winston Atkins, Libn.
Founded: 1939. **Staff:** Prof 1. **Subjects:** Texas and regional history, church and commerce in New Spain, anglo colonization and republic of Texas. **Special Collections:** Espinosa Hacienda Papers, 1740-1840; Duncan Papers, 1820s-1860s; Austin-Bryan-Perry Families, 1820s-1900. **Holdings:** 10,000 books; 250 linear feet of manuscripts and documents; historic maps; photographs. **Services:** Copying; library open to qualified scholars by appointment. **Publications:** The Advance, quarterly; occasional monographs.

★12816★
SAN JOAQUIN COLLEGE OF LAW - LIBRARY (Law)
3385 E. Shields Ave. Phone: (209)225-4953
Fresno, CA 93726 Diane Johnson, Libn.
Staff: Prof 1; Other 5. **Subjects:** Law. **Holdings:** 18,000 books; 2100 bound periodical volumes; 200 audiotapes. **Subscriptions:** 45 journals and other serials. **Services:** Library not open to the public. **Computerized Information Services:** LEXIS.

★12817★
SAN JOAQUIN COUNTY HISTORICAL MUSEUM - LIBRARY (Hist)
Micke Grove Park
Box 21 Phone: (209)368-9154
Lodi, CA 95241 Michael W. Bennett, Musm.Dir.
Founded: 1966. **Staff:** 6. **Subjects:** Local and agricultural history. **Holdings:** 2000 books; 1000 bound periodical volumes; clippings; depository for county archives; county maps, plats, survey reports, records; bound newspapers. **Subscriptions:** 11 journals and other serials. **Services:** Library open to the public for reference use only with supervision.

★12818★
SAN JOAQUIN COUNTY LAW LIBRARY (Law)
County Court House, Rm. 300 Phone: (209)944-2207
Stockton, CA 95202 Gertrudes J. Ladion, Law Libn.
Founded: 1984. **Staff:** 1. **Subjects:** Law. **Holdings:** 26,005 volumes. **Subscriptions:** 33 journals and other serials. **Services:** Copying; library open to the public.

★12819★
SAN JOSE BIBLE COLLEGE - MEMORIAL LIBRARY (Rel-Phil)
790 S. 12th St.
Box 1090 Phone: (408)295-9058
San Jose, CA 95108-1090 Kay Llovio, Libn.
Staff: Prof 1; Other 3. **Subjects:** Bible, church history, psychology, Greek, Hebrew. **Special Collections:** History of Christian Church. **Holdings:** 32,515 books; 129 bound periodical volumes; 2190 other cataloged items; 2554 unbound periodicals; 644 microfiche; 51 missionary papers. **Subscriptions:** 94 journals and other serials. **Services:** Interlibrary loan; copying; library open to the public.

★12820★
SAN JOSE HISTORICAL MUSEUM - ARCHIVES (Hist)
635 Phelan Ave. Phone: (408)287-2290
San Jose, CA 95112 Leslie Masunaga, Archv.
Founded: 1971. **Staff:** Prof 1; Other 1. **Subjects:** Santa Clara Valley and San Jose history, Victorian materials. **Special Collections:** New Almaden Mines Collection; pueblos and ranchos (original papers). **Holdings:** 200 cubic feet of books, ledgers, pamphlets; 374 linear feet of manuscripts and public records. **Services:** Copying (limited); archives open to the public with limited access to materials.

★12821★
SAN JOSE HOSPITAL - HEALTH SCIENCES LIBRARY (Med)
675 E. Santa Clara St. Phone: (408)998-3212
San Jose, CA 95114 Deloris Osby, Dir.
Founded: 1934. **Staff:** Prof 1; Other 2. **Subjects:** Medicine, nursing, health care administration, family practice, allied health sciences, wellness. **Special Collections:** Family practice; Health Care Management/ Administration. **Holdings:** 20,100 books; 8726 bound periodical volumes; 12 VF drawers of pamphlets and clippings; 150 AV programs; 80 filmstrips; 19 films; 200 archival items. **Subscriptions:** 450 journals and other serials; 6 newspapers. **Services:** Interlibrary loan; copying; SDI; library open to the public by appointment. **Automated Operations:** Computerized cataloging, acquisitions, and serials. **Computerized Information Services:** MEDLINE, BRS Information Technologies, WILSONLINE, DIALOG Information Services; OnTyme Electronic Message Network Service (electronic mail service). Performs searches on fee basis. **Networks/Consortia:** Member of Medical Library Consortium of Santa Clara Valley, Northern California and Nevada Medical Library Group (NCNMLG). **Remarks:** Maintained by Health Dimensions Inc.

★12822★
SAN JOSE MERCURY NEWS - LIBRARY (Publ)
750 Ridder Park Dr. Phone: (408)920-5345
San Jose, CA 95190 Gary L. Lance, Lib.Mgr.
Staff: Prof 8; Other 1. **Subjects:** Newspaper reference topics, local history. **Holdings:** 2000 volumes; 3.5 million clippings; 400,000 photographs; 7000 reels of microfilm of newspapers. **Subscriptions:** 60 journals and other serials; 30 newspapers. **Services:** Interlibrary loan; library not open to the public. **Computerized Information Services:** DIALOG Information Services, NEXIS, VU/TEXT Information Services, Dow Jones News/ Retrieval.

★12823★
SAN JOSE MUSEUM OF ART - LIBRARY (Art)
110 S. Market St. Phone: (408)294-2787
San Jose, CA 95113 Mildred Vick Chatton, Libn.
Founded: 1978. **Staff:** Prof 2; Other 1. **Subjects:** Art. **Special Collections:** Children's art books. **Holdings:** 1500 books; 1700 exhibition catalogs; 4 VF drawers of art information files; 1800 slides. **Services:** Library open to the public with permission of curator. **Staff:** Jean F. Wheeler, Libn..

★12824★
SAN JOSE PUBLIC LIBRARY - SILICON VALLEY INFORMATION CENTER (Hist)
180 W. San Carlos St. Phone: (408)277-5754
San Jose, CA 95113 Mike Ferrero, Proj.Dir.
Founded: 1985. **Staff:** Prof 8; Other 4. **Subjects:** Santa Clara County, California - high technology industries, history, environmental issues, social and cultural impact, personalities. **Special Collections:** Corporate document archives (400 companies represented). **Holdings:** 1020 books; 30 bound periodical volumes; 7000 clippings; 470 annual reports; 317 photographs; 50 videotapes. **Subscriptions:** 50 journals and other serials; 5 newspapers. **Services:** Copying; center open to the public. **Automated Operations:** Computerized cataloging. **Computerized Information Services:** DIALOG Information Services; internal database. Performs searches on fee basis. **Publications:** Tomorrow, 2/year - to the public. **Remarks:** Center is the "first centralized public facility to document the birth, development, and impact of the high technology industries in Santa Clara Valley, California."

★12825★
SAN JOSE STATE UNIVERSITY - IRA F. BRILLIANT CENTER FOR BEETHOVEN STUDIES (Mus)
1 Washington Square Phone: (408)924-4590
San Jose, CA 95192-0171 Dr. William Meredith, Dir.
Founded: 1983. **Staff:** Prof 2; Other 1. **Subjects:** Beethoven. **Special Collections:** First and early editions of Beethoven's music; William S. Newman Beethoven Collection. **Holdings:** 1200 books; 115 bound periodical volumes; 700 scores; 400 recordings; 2 Beethoven manuscripts; 50 reels of microfilm; 40 slides; 2 videotapes. **Subscriptions:** 10 journals and other serials. **Services:** Interlibrary loan; copying; center open to the public. **Automated Operations:** Computerized cataloging. **Publications:** Bibliography of Beethoven materials (card and online); The Beethoven Newsletter, 3/year - by subscription. **Staff:** Patricia Elliott, Cur..

★12826★
SAN JOSE STATE UNIVERSITY - STEINBECK RESEARCH CENTER (Hum)
Wahlquist Library
One Washington Square Phone: (408)277-3377
San Jose, CA 95192-0028 Susan Shillinglaw, Dir.
Staff: Prof 1; Other 1. **Subjects:** John Steinbeck. **Holdings:** 5000 manuscripts, typescripts, pieces of correspondence, first editions, photographs, and memorabilia. **Services:** Center open to the public with restrictions. **Publications:** List of publications - available upon request.

★12827★
SAN JOSE STATE UNIVERSITY - WAHLQUIST LIBRARY - CHICANO LIBRARY RESOURCE CENTER (Area-Ethnic)
1 Washington Sq. Phone: (408)924-2707
San Jose, CA 95192 Jeff Paul, Coord.
Staff: Prof 1; Other 2. **Subjects:** Chicano studies. **Special Collections:** Hispanic Link (newspaper articles and editorials on the role of the Hispanic in the United States); National Hispanic Feminist Conference Papers, 1980; United Farm Workers Resources (pictures; songs; poems; accounts of Cesar Chavez; a history of the UFW; announcements of boycotts, 1973-1975). **Holdings:** 1400 books; 700 unbound periodicals; 400 reels of microfilm; 1200 clippings and pamphlets; 50 posters. **Subscriptions:** 15 journals and other serials. **Services:** Interlibrary loan; center open to the public. **Publications:** CLRC Bibliography. **Special Indexes:** Index to Chicano Serials (microfilm).

★12828★
SAN JUAN COUNTY ARCHAEOLOGICAL RESEARCH CENTER & LIBRARY (Soc Sci)
975 Hwy. 64 Phone: (505)632-2013
Farmington, NM 87401 Barbara Jenkins, Libn.
Staff: Prof 1; Other 2. **Subjects:** Archeology, history, anthropology, botany. **Special Collections:** Slide/tape programs; historical records of San Juan Basin (3 VF drawers); Four Corners area rock art (1700 slides and photographs); archival records of excavation of Salmon Ruin Site (224 feet); Navaho Mythology Collection. **Holdings:** 900 books; 3000 reports, pamphlets, dissertations; 1 VF drawer of clippings; 1 VF drawer of photographs; 36 oral history tapes and transcriptions; 2 reels of microfilm; 3 VF drawers of botany specimens; 5 drawers of historic maps. **Subscriptions:** 56 journals and other serials. **Services:** Copying; library open to the public for reference use only. **Publications:** Contributions to Anthropology Series, irregular; cemeteries in San Juan County, biennial. **Special Indexes:** Computer index to pioneer families in the area. **Remarks:** Library located at the upper level of the Research Center. Maintained by the San Juan County Museum Association.

★12829★
SAN JUAN COUNTY HISTORICAL SOCIETY - ARCHIVE (Hist)
1111 Reese St. Phone: (303)387-5770
Silverton, CO 81433 Allen Nossaman, Dir.
Staff: 1. **Subjects:** San Juan County and Colorado history. **Holdings:** 40 books; 700 photographs; 36 reels of microfilm; 100 oral history tapes; 50 cubic feet of maps, slides, correspondence, records. **Services:** Copying;

archive open to the public. **Publications:** Hillside Cemetery-Silverton - for sale. **Special Catalogs:** Oral history catalog. **Special Indexes:** San Juan County Newspaper Index, 1879-1883 and 1884-1887.

★12830★
SAN LUIS OBISPO COUNTY LAW LIBRARY (Law)
Government Center, Rm. 125 Phone: (805)549-5855
San Luis Obispo, CA 93408 Jean Borraccino, Law Libn.
Founded: 1896. **Staff:** Prof 1; Other 3. **Subjects:** Law. **Holdings:** 22,043 volumes; 1000 pamphlets; 209 tapes; 3100 microforms. **Subscriptions:** 50 journals and other serials. **Services:** Interlibrary loan; copying; library open to the public with restrictions. **Networks/Consortia:** Member of Total Interlibrary Exchange (TIE).

★12831★
SAN LUIS OBISPO COUNTY PLANNING DEPARTMENT - TECHNICAL INFORMATION LIBRARY (Env-Cons)
County Government Center Phone: (805)549-5600
San Luis Obispo, CA 93408 Vivian Lassanske, Libn.
Founded: 1969. **Subjects:** Conservation and natural resources, recreation, circulation, land data, social and economic analysis, public utilities and services, aesthetic and historical data, administration data, housing and building research. **Holdings:** 600 books; 1000 pamphlets and documents; 5000 maps. **Subscriptions:** 30 journals and other serials; 7 newspapers. **Services:** Interlibrary loan; library open to the public for reference use only on request.

★12832★
SAN MARTIN SOCIETY OF WASHINGTON, DC - INFORMATION CENTER (Hist)
Box 33 Phone: (703)883-0950
McLean, VA 22101-0033 Dr. Christian Garcia-Godoy, Pres.
Subjects: General Jose de San Martin; the emancipation of Argentina, Chile, and Peru. **Holdings:** 1300 volumes; microfilm; dissertations; speeches; pamphlets; documents. **Services:** Copying; center open to the public by written request.

★12833★
SAN MATEO COUNTY DEPARTMENT OF HEALTH SERVICES - LIBRARY (Soc Sci)
225 37th Ave. Phone: (415)573-2520
San Mateo, CA 94403 Mark Quinn Constantz, Med.Libn.
Founded: 1967. **Staff:** Prof 1. **Subjects:** Clinical medicine, emergency medicine, psychiatry, public health, mental health, rehabilitation. **Holdings:** 4000 books; 6000 bound periodical volumes. **Subscriptions:** 120 journals and other serials. **Services:** Interlibrary loan; copying; library open to the public for reference use only. **Automated Operations:** Computerized cataloging. **Computerized Information Services:** DIALOG Information Services, BRS Information Technologies, TYMNET, MEDLARS; Health Services Bibliographic Source (internal database). **Networks/Consortia:** Member of Pacific Southwest Regional Medical Library Service, Northern California and Nevada Medical Library Group (NCNMLG), San Mateo County Hospital Library Consortium, CLASS. **Publications:** San Mateo County Hospital Library Consortia Newsletter.

SAN MATEO COUNTY EDUCATIONAL RESOURCES CENTER
See: San Mateo County Office of Education - The SMERC Library (12836)

★12834★
SAN MATEO COUNTY HISTORICAL ASSOCIATION - LIBRARY (Hist)
College of San Mateo Campus
1700 W. Hillsdale Blvd. Phone: (415)574-6441
San Mateo, CA 94402 Marion C. Holmes, Archv.
Founded: 1935. **Staff:** Prof 1. **Subjects:** San Mateo County history. **Holdings:** 1018 books; 2973 pamphlets; 25,000 photographs; 337 manuscripts; 390 student monographs; 535 documents, including assessment books, diaries, municipal and county records. **Services:** Copying; library open to the public. **Publications:** La Peninsula (journal), annual - to members. **Special Indexes:** La Peninsula index; alphabetical list of 1860 and 1870 censuses; alphabetical list of Richard N. Schellens Collection.

★12835★
SAN MATEO COUNTY LAW LIBRARY (Law)
710 Hamilton St. Phone: (415)363-4160
Redwood City, CA 94063 Robert D. Harrington, Dir.
Staff: 4. **Subjects:** Law. **Holdings:** 40,000 volumes. **Services:** Library open to the public.

★12836★
SAN MATEO COUNTY OFFICE OF EDUCATION - THE SMERC LIBRARY (Educ, Comp Sci)
333 Main St. Phone: (415)363-5470
Redwood City, CA 94063 Mrs. Karol Thomas, Dir.
Founded: 1967. **Staff:** Prof 3; Other 8. **Subjects:** Education, microcomputers. **Holdings:** 22,000 books; 2000 textbooks; 350,000 microfiche. **Subscriptions:** 500 education journals. **Services:** Interlibrary loan; copying; library open to the public with restrictions. **Computerized Information Services:** DIALOG Information Services, ERIC. **Networks/Consortia:** Member of South Bay Cooperative Library System (SBCLS). **Publications:** Newsnotes; SMERC Alert - both 6/year. **Formerly:** San Mateo County Educational Resources Center. **Staff:** Anna Joe, Ref.Coord.; Linda Bolash, Lib.Serv.Supv..

★12837★
SAN MATEO PUBLIC LIBRARY - BUSINESS SECTION (Bus-Fin)
55 W. Third Ave. Phone: (415)377-4680
San Mateo, CA 94402 Thos. S. Fowler, Bus.Ref.Libn.
Staff: Prof 1; Other 2. **Subjects:** Small business, investment. **Holdings:** 8000 books. **Subscriptions:** 75 journals and other serials; 10 newspapers. **Services:** Interlibrary loan; section open to the public. **Automated Operations:** Computerized cataloging and circulation. **Computerized Information Services:** DIALOG Information Services; OnTyme Electronic Message Network Service (electronic mail service). **Networks/Consortia:** Member of Peninsula Library System (PLS). **Publications:** Business Collection Bibliography (book).

★12838★
SAN PEDRO PENINSULA HOSPITAL - JOHN T. BURCH, M.D. MEMORIAL LIBRARY (Med)
1300 W. 7th St. Phone: (213)832-3311
San Pedro, CA 90732-3593 James H. Harlan, Libn.
Founded: 1940. **Staff:** Prof 1; Other 3. **Subjects:** Clinical medicine, nursing. **Holdings:** 650 books; 1850 bound periodical volumes; 250 Audio-Digest tapes; 22 videotapes; 8 reels of microfilm. **Subscriptions:** 180 journals and other serials. **Services:** Interlibrary loan; copying; SDI; library open to the public by special permission. **Computerized Information Services:** MEDLINE, DIALOG Information Services; OnTyme Electronic Message Network Service (electronic mail service). Performs searches on fee basis.

SANBORN HOUSE ENGLISH LIBRARY
See: Dartmouth College (4048)

CARL SANDBURG HOME NATIONAL HISTORIC SITE
See: U.S. Natl. Park Service (15263)

★12839★
SANDERS ASSOCIATES - LIBRARY SERVICES (Mil, Comp Sci)
95 Canal St., NCA 1-1342 Phone: (603)885-4144
Nashua, NH 03061-2004 Art Berlin, Mgr., Lib.Serv.
Founded: 1955. **Staff:** Prof 4; Other 5. **Subjects:** Defense electronics, computer graphics. **Holdings:** 10,000 books; 2000 bound periodical volumes; 20,000 microfiche. **Subscriptions:** 700 journals and other serials; 7 newspapers. **Services:** Interlibrary loan; library open to industrial community by appointment only. **Computerized Information Services:** DIALOG Information Services, Pergamon ORBIT InfoLine, Inc., Integrated Technical Information System (ITIS), DTIC. **Staff:** Cynthia Davis, Supv.; David Morrison, Supv..

★12840★
SANDERS & THOMAS, INC. - LIBRARY (Sci-Engr)
11 Robinson St. Phone: (215)326-4600
Pottstown, PA 19464 Carol S. Leh, Tech.Libn.
Founded: 1962. **Staff:** Prof 1. **Subjects:** Engineering, architecture, planning. **Special Collections:** Solid Waste/Energy Collection (708 titles). **Holdings:** 769 books; catalogs for 1731 companies; 5 information file boxes; 3 films; 591 specifications; 148 transportation reports. **Subscriptions:** 64 journals and other serials. **Services:** Library not open to the public.

LEONARD M. SANDHAUS MEMORIAL LIBRARY
See: Temple Israel (13961)

★12841★
SANDIA BAPTIST CHURCH - MEDIA CENTER (Rel-Phil)
9429 Constitution, N.E. Phone: (505)292-2713
Albuquerque, NM 87112 Margaret Haynes Mills, Media Serv.Dir.
Staff: 4. **Subjects:** Bible study, Christian life, family living, children's books. **Holdings:** 2500 books; 150 filmstrips; 15 AV programs; 25

audiotapes. **Subscriptions:** 10 journals and other serials. **Services:** Center open to the public.

★12842★
SANDIA NATIONAL LABORATORIES - TECHNICAL LIBRARY (Sci-Engr)
Box 969 Phone: (415)422-2525
Livermore, CA 94550 Saundra Lormand, Group Ldr.
Founded: 1957. **Staff:** Prof 2; Other 6. **Subjects:** Engineering materials, electrical and mechanical engineering, physics, chemistry, electronics, defense. **Holdings:** 8000 books; 8632 bound periodical volumes; 900 reels of microfilm of periodicals; 45,000 technical reports. **Subscriptions:** 387 journals and other serials. **Services:** Interlibrary loan; library not open to the public. **Automated Operations:** Computerized cataloging, acquisitions, serials, and circulation. **Computerized Information Services:** DIALOG Information Services, BRS Information Technologies, Pergamon ORBIT InfoLine, Inc., NEXIS, CAS ONLINE, WILSONLINE, DTIC. **Remarks:** The Sandia National Laboratories operate under contract to the U.S. Department of Energy. **Staff:** Hugh Keleher, Tech.Info.Spec..

★12843★
SANDIA NATIONAL LABORATORIES - TECHNICAL LIBRARY (Sci-Engr, Energy)
Dept. 3140
Box 5800 Phone: (505)844-2869
Albuquerque, NM 87185 D.E. Robertson, Mgr.
Founded: 1948. **Staff:** Prof 20; Other 32. **Subjects:** Nuclear weapons, nuclear waste management, nuclear safety and security, electronics, explosives, materials, aerodynamics, solid state physics, ordnance, energy research. **Special Collections:** Videotapes on Sandia's weekly colloquia, 1976 to present. **Holdings:** 50,000 volumes; 22,000 bound periodical volumes; 20,000 periodical volumes on microfilm; 100,000 hardcopy technical reports; 876,000 technical reports on microfiche; 69,000 internal reports. **Subscriptions:** 1700 journals and other serials. **Services:** Interlibrary loan; library not open to the public. **Automated Operations:** Computerized cataloging, acquisitions, serials, and circulation. **Computerized Information Services:** DIALOG Information Services, Integrated Technical Information System (ITIS), BRS Information Technologies, DTIC, NEXIS, NASA/RECON, RLIN, STN International, WILSONLINE, NLM, United States Naval Institute (USNI), Pergamon ORBIT InfoLine, Inc.; internal database. **Publications:** SCAN (Sandia Laboratories Accession News), monthly. **Remarks:** The Sandia National Laboratories operate under contract to the U.S. Department of Energy. **Staff:** Sally Landenberger, Supv., Tech.Proc.; George R. Dalphin, Ref.Supv.; Dennis Rowley, Sys.Supv.; Cathy E. Pasterczyk, Subject Spec.; Joyce Van Berkel, Subject Spec.; Gloria Zamora, Subject Spec.; Marge Meyer, Subject Spec.; Sue Sozanski, Subject Spec.; Walter R. Roose, Subject Spec.; Gladys E. Rowe, Subject Spec.; Willie M. Servis, Subject Spec.; Ferne Allan, Subject Spec.; Linda Erickson, Subject Spec.; Patricia Newman, Transl.; Kim Denton-Hill, Info.Sys.Anl.; Paul Kirby, Info.Sys.Anl.; Joe Maloney, Info.Sys.Anl.; Chris Morgan, Info.Sys.Anl.; Nancy Pruett, Lib.Sys.Anl.; Cathy Pasterczyk, Subject Spec.; Lynn Llull-Kaczor, Subject Spec..

★12844★
SANDOZ CANADA INC. - INFORMATION SERVICES (Med)
385 Bouchard Blvd. Phone: (514)631-6775
Dorval, PQ, Canada H9R 4P5 Diane Boisvert, Supv.
Founded: 1950. **Staff:** Prof 2; Other 1. **Subjects:** Medicine, pharmaceuticals, cardiology, immunology, endocrinology, neurology. **Holdings:** 4000 books; 500 bound periodical volumes; 30,000 microfiche; company publications. **Subscriptions:** 300 journals and other serials; 5 newspapers. **Services:** Interlibrary loan; services not open to the public. **Automated Operations:** Computerized cataloging. **Computerized Information Services:** MEDLARS, DIALOG Information Services, Data-Star, CAN/OLE; internal database; Envoy 100 (electronic mail service). Performs limited searches free of charge. **Staff:** Laura King-Morgan, Asst. to Supv..

★12845★
SANDOZ CHEMICALS CORPORATION - LIBRARY (Sci-Engr)
Box 669246 Phone: (704)827-9651
Charlotte, NC 28266 Jacqueline N. Kirkman, Corp.Libn.
Founded: 1963. **Staff:** Prof 1; Other 1. **Subjects:** Dyestuffs, organic chemistry. **Holdings:** 2200 books; 2320 bound periodical volumes; 11,000 patents; 300 unbound reports; 102 reels of microfilm; 4000 microfiche. **Subscriptions:** 164 journals and other serials. **Services:** Interlibrary loan; library open to the public with restrictions. **Computerized Information Services:** DIALOG Information Services, CAS ONLINE, Occupational Health Services, Inc., Pergamon ORBIT InfoLine, Inc., NLM.

★12846★
SANDOZ CROP PROTECTION CORPORATION - CORPORATE TECHNICAL SERVICES/LIBRARY (Agri, Biol Sci)
1300 E. Touhy Ave. Phone: (312)390-3859
Des Plaines, IL 60018 Candy J. Ortman, Libn.
Founded: 1940. **Staff:** Prof 1; Other 1. **Subjects:** Pesticides, herbicides, organic chemistry, entomology, botany, agribusiness. **Special Collections:** Proceedings and reports of various weed society conferences from 1945 to present. **Holdings:** 5000 books; 5000 bound periodical volumes; 5000 reels of microfilm. **Subscriptions:** 201 journals and other serials. **Services:** Interlibrary loan; copying; library open to the public by appointment. **Computerized Information Services:** DIALOG Information Services, Pergamon ORBIT InfoLine, Inc., Chemical Information Systems, Inc. (CIS), National Pesticide Information Retrieval System (NPIRS), NLM, Occupational Health Services, Inc. **Networks/Consortia:** Member of ILLINET, North Suburban Library System (NSLS).

★12847★
SANDOZ CROP PROTECTION CORPORATION - ZOECON RESEARCH INSTITUTE - LIBRARY (Biol Sci, Sci-Engr)
975 California Ave.
Box 10975 Phone: (415)354-3475
Palo Alto, CA 94303 Martha L. Manion, Mgr., Lib.
Staff: Prof 2; Other 1. **Subjects:** Organic chemistry, invertebrate biochemistry, molecular biology, plant genetics, entomology, pest control. **Holdings:** 6500 books; 3500 bound periodical volumes; 17,000 reprints; 900 cartridges of microfilm; 4000 microfiche. **Subscriptions:** 350 journals and other serials. **Services:** Interlibrary loan; copying; library open to the public by request. **Computerized Information Services:** DIALOG Information Services, Pergamon ORBIT InfoLine, Inc., BRS Information Technologies, STN International, National Pesticide Information Retrieval System (NPIRS), OCLC, NLM. **Networks/Consortia:** Member of CLASS. **Staff:** Julie Beer, Info.Spec..

★12848★
SANDOZ, INC. - LIBRARY (Biol Sci, Med)
Route 10 Phone: (201)503-8306
East Hanover, NJ 07936 Carol Bekar, Mgr., Lib./Info.Serv.
Staff: Prof 7; Other 5. **Subjects:** Medicine, chemistry, pharmacology, toxicology, biochemistry. **Holdings:** 7500 books; 24,850 bound periodical volumes; 16 drawers of microfilm; 2 drawers of annual reports; 2 drawers of company publications. **Subscriptions:** 647 journals and other serials; 5 newspapers. **Services:** Interlibrary loan; copying; SDI; library open to the public by appointment. **Automated Operations:** Computerized cataloging. **Computerized Information Services:** DIALOG Information Services, Pergamon ORBIT InfoLine, Inc., MEDLINE, BRS Information Technologies, CAS ONLINE. **Networks/Consortia:** Member of PALINET. **Publications:** LIBLINE, quarterly - available on request. **Staff:** Veong Kwon, Supv., Tech.Serv.; Sue Mellen, Supv., Clin./Bus.Info.; Sigfried Wahrman, Supv., Preclinical Info..

★12849★
SANDOZ PHARMACEUTICALS - MEDICAL COMMUNICATIONS AND INFORMATION SERVICES (Med, Bus-Fin)
Route 10 Phone: (201)503-8105
East Hanover, NJ 07936 Joyce G. Koelle, Asst.Dir.
Founded: 1939. **Staff:** Prof 10; Other 6. **Subjects:** Corporation products, biomedicine, business. **Holdings:** Figures not available. **Computerized Information Services:** DIALOG Information Services, Pergamon ORBIT InfoLine, Inc., INVESTEXT, IMSBASE, Data-Star, NLM; Sandoz Product Information System (internal database). **Publications:** Current Awareness Bulletin, biweekly - for internal distribution only.

★12850★
SANDUSKY COUNTY LAW LIBRARY (Law)
Courthouse, 100 N. Park Ave. Phone: (419)334-6165
Fremont, OH 43420 Ann Rooks, Supv.
Staff: Prof 1. **Subjects:** Law. **Special Collections:** Historical law books (especially early Ohio legal history). **Holdings:** 11,000 books; 1100 bound periodical volumes; 600 other cataloged items. **Subscriptions:** 200 journals and other serials. **Services:** Library open to the public for reference use only on request. **Staff:** Shirley Schiets, Asst. Law Libn..

★12851★
SANDY BAY HISTORICAL SOCIETY AND MUSEUM - LIBRARY (Hist)
Box 63
Rockport, MA 01966-0063 Dr. Marshall W.S. Swan, Pres.
Founded: 1925. **Staff:** Prof 1. **Subjects:** History of Rockport (Sandy Bay), Cape Ann, Essex County; Rockport families. **Holdings:** 300 books; 7500 manuscripts. **Services:** Interlibrary loan; copying; library open to qualified researchers.

★12852★
SANDY CORPORATION - LIBRARY (Bus-Fin)
1500 W. Big Beaver Rd. Phone: (313)649-0800
Troy, MI 48084 Judith Wilson, Libn.
Founded: 1971. **Staff:** Prof 1; Other 2. **Subjects:** Consulting, training, communication. **Holdings:** 3000 books; 2000 pamphlets; 32 VF drawers of automotive product information; 36 VF drawers of business and management literature; 3000 square feet of periodicals, videodiscs, cartridges, slides, filmstrips, motion pictures, scripts. **Subscriptions:** 150 journals and other serials. **Services:** Interlibrary loan; library not open to the public. **Computerized Information Services:** DIALOG Information Services, VU/TEXT Information Services. **Networks/Consortia:** Member of Library Cooperative of Macomb (LCM). **Publications:** Library Bulletin, biweekly; Acquisitions Bulletin, 5/year - both for internal distribution only.

★12853★
SANFORD MUSEUM & PLANETARIUM - LIBRARY (Sci-Engr)
117 E. Willow St. Phone: (712)225-3922
Cherokee, IA 51012 J. Terry Walker, Dir.
Founded: 1951. **Staff:** 4. **Subjects:** Archeology, astronomy, geology, history, paleontology, museology. **Holdings:** 5000 volumes. **Services:** Interlibrary loan; library open to the public.

★12854★
SANGAMON STATE UNIVERSITY - EAST CENTRAL NETWORK FOR CURRICULUM COORDINATION - LIBRARY (Educ)
F-2 Phone: (217)786-6375
Springfield, IL 62708 Susie Shackleton, Libn.
Staff: Prof 6; Other 7. **Subjects:** Education - vocational, career, adult. **Holdings:** 27,340 books; 926 AV programs; 8 VF drawers of publishers files. **Subscriptions:** 100 journals and other serials. **Services:** Interlibrary loan; copying; library open to the public. **Automated Operations:** Computerized public access catalog, cataloging, and circulation. **Computerized Information Services:** BRS Information Technologies; Task Listing File (internal database). Performs searches free of charge. Contact Person: Jeff Lake, Microcomp.Cons.. **Networks/Consortia:** Member of Rolling Prairie Library System (RPLS). **Publications:** Center Critiques, semiannual; Monthly Memo; occasional papers; subject bibliographies. **Remarks:** The network is funded by the U.S. Department of Education. **Staff:** Rebecca Douglass, Dir.; Ruth Patton, Coord..

★12855★
SANGAMON STATE UNIVERSITY - ORAL HISTORY OFFICE - LIBRARY (Hist)
Brookens Library, Rm. 377 Phone: (217)786-6521
Springfield, IL 62794-9243 Cullom Davis, Dir.
Founded: 1972. **Staff:** Prof 2; Other 5. **Subjects:** History - 20th century American, Illinois, ethnic and minority, coal mining, labor, agricultural; state and local politics. **Holdings:** 750 oral history memoirs (2500 hours of taped interviews and 75,000 pages of transcripts). **Services:** Interlibrary loan; copying; library open to the public for reference use only. **Publications:** History with a Tape Recorder: an Oral History Handbook; Oral History: From Tape to Type. **Special Catalogs:** Subject descriptions and inventories for Coal Mining and Union Activities, The Jewish Experience, Agricultural History, Women's History, and Sangamon County History. **Also Known As:** Illinois Oral History Clearinghouse.

★12856★
MARGARET SANGER CENTER-PLANNED PARENTHOOD NEW YORK CITY - ABRAHAM STONE LIBRARY (Soc Sci)
380 Second Ave. Phone: (212)677-6474
New York, NY 10010 Jeanne Swinton, Libn.
Subjects: Abortion, adolescent sexuality, infertility, sex, family living, demography, population, sexuality of the handicapped. **Holdings:** 6000 books; 3000 bound periodical volumes; 60 VF drawers of reprints and newspaper clippings. **Subscriptions:** 85 journals and other serials. **Services:** Interlibrary loan; copying; library open by appointment to graduate students and agencies.

★12857★
SANTA BARBARA BOTANIC GARDEN - LIBRARY (Biol Sci)
1212 Mission Canyon Rd. Phone: (805)682-4726
Santa Barbara, CA 93105 Nancy Hawver, Libn.
Founded: 1942. **Staff:** Prof 1; Other 1. **Subjects:** Botany; floras of Western North America and Mediterranean climates; California horticulture; California offshore islands; cactus and succulents. **Special Collections:** Oral history collection (60 taped interviews). **Holdings:** 6500 books; 2000 bound periodical volumes; 1200 reprints; 1000 nursery and seed catalogs; 42 boxes of pamphlets and reports; maps (indexed); 1 file cabinet of exchange newsletters from other gardens. **Subscriptions:** 95 journals and other serials. **Services:** Copying; library open to the public with permission. **Automated Operations:** Computerized indexing. **Computerized Information Services:** OCLC. **Networks/Consortia:** Member of Total Interlibrary Exchange (TIE).

★12858★
SANTA BARBARA COUNTY GENEALOGICAL SOCIETY - LIBRARY (Hist)
Box 1303
Santa Barbara, CA 93116-1303 Ruth B. Scollin, Libn.
Founded: 1974. **Staff:** Prof 1; Other 8. **Subjects:** Genealogy. **Holdings:** 1000 books; 1100 bound periodical volumes; 12 boxes of Earl Hazard Family History Papers; family histories; ancestral charts. **Subscriptions:** 110 journals and other serials. **Services:** Library open to the public. **Publications:** Ancestors West, quarterly - to members, by subscription or exchange. **Remarks:** Library located at 5679 Hollister, Goleta, CA 93116.

★12859★
SANTA BARBARA COUNTY LAW LIBRARY (Law)
County Courthouse Phone: (805)568-2296
Santa Barbara, CA 93101 Raymond W. MacGregor, Law Libn.
Founded: 1891. **Staff:** Prof 3; Other 2. **Subjects:** Law. **Special Collections:** Historical Treatises: Collection of California Codes, 1885 to present. **Holdings:** 40,211 volumes; 3247 microfiche; 495 cassettes. **Services:** Interlibrary loan; copying; library open to the public for reference use only. **Automated Operations:** Computerized cataloging and acquisitions. **Computerized Information Services:** Internal database. **Networks/Consortia:** Member of Total Interlibrary Exchange (TIE). **Remarks:** Figures include holdings of a branch library located in Santa Maria, CA. **Staff:** Steven Zaharias, Asst. Libn.; Phyllis Cooper, Asst.Libn..

★12860★
SANTA BARBARA HISTORICAL SOCIETY - GLEDHILL LIBRARY (Hist)
136 E. De La Guerra St.
Box 578 Phone: (805)966-1601
Santa Barbara, CA 93102 Michael Redmon, Hd.Libn.
Founded: 1967. **Staff:** Prof 1; Other 4. **Subjects:** Local history and genealogy. **Holdings:** 5000 books; 17,000 photographs; 200 oral history tapes. **Subscriptions:** 20 journals and other serials. **Services:** Copying; photograph reproduction; library open to the public.

★12861★
SANTA BARBARA MISSION ARCHIVE-LIBRARY (Hist, Rel-Phil)
Old Mission, Upper Laguna St. Phone: (805)682-4713
Santa Barbara, CA 93105 Fr. Virgilio Biasiol, O.F.M., Dir.
Founded: 1786. **Staff:** Prof 1. **Subjects:** Early missions and missionaries in the Santa Barbara area, Californiana and Mexicana, Spain and Hispanic America. **Special Collections:** De la Guerra Collection (12,000 pages of documents on California); Wilson Collection (rare books; globes; works of art); Alexander Taylor Collection (copies of 2300 documents from the Archdiocesan Archives in San Francisco); photographs of the late mission period in California, Spain, and Mexico (4000); original mission music (1000 brochures); original mission documents (3500). **Holdings:** 14,000 books; 100 scrapbooks, newspaper clippings; 1000 pamphlets. **Services:** Library open to the public. **Publications:** Newsletter, irregular - to Friends of Archive-Library; list of other publications - available on request. **Special Catalogs:** Catalog of documents and old books. **Remarks:** Maintained by the Franciscan Fathers of California. **Staff:** Rev. Francis F. Guest, O.F.M., Archv.-Hist..

★12862★
SANTA BARBARA MUSEUM OF ART - MUSEUM LIBRARY AND ARCHIVES (Art)
1130 State St. Phone: (805)963-4364
Santa Barbara, CA 93101 Ron Crozier, Libn.
Founded: 1941. **Staff:** Prof 1; Other 2. **Subjects:** Art, artists. **Special Collections:** Exhibition catalogs (20,000); Single Artist File. **Holdings:** 3000

books; 500 linear feet of archives; pamphlet library consisting of museum calendars and artists' exhibition notices; museum and gallery bulletins; annual reports; newspaper clipping file; sale catalogs; slides. **Subscriptions:** 45 journals and other serials. **Services:** Interlibrary loan; copying; library open to the public with restrictions.

★12863★
SANTA BARBARA MUSEUM OF NATURAL HISTORY - LIBRARY (Biol Sci)
2559 Puesta del Sol Rd. Phone: (805)682-4711
Santa Barbara, CA 93105 Susan G. Dixon, Libn.
Founded: 1929. **Staff:** Prof 1. **Subjects:** Natural history - anthropology, botany, geology, zoology, astronomy. **Special Collections:** Chumash Indians; Harrington California Indian Archives; Stillman Berry Malacology Collection; Channel Islands Archive; Dick Smith Archives; Pacific Voyages Collection; antique nature illustrations. **Holdings:** 30,000 volumes; 200 feet of reprints. **Subscriptions:** 200 journals and other serials. **Services:** Interlibrary loan (limited); copying; library open to the public for reference use only. **Automated Operations:** Computerized cataloging. **Computerized Information Services:** OCLC. **Publications:** Occasional papers on natural history - by gift and exchange.

★12864★
SANTA BARBARA NEWS PRESS - LIBRARY (Publ)
72 De La Guerra Plaza
Drawer NN Phone: (805)966-3911
Santa Barbara, CA 93102 Susan V. DeLapa, Libn.
Staff: Prof 1; Other 1. **Subjects:** Newspaper reference topics. **Holdings:** 1490 books; microfilm; pictures; negatives; 512 linear feet of clippings; 80 pamphlets; 100 maps. **Services:** Library open to the public on a limited schedule.

★12865★
SANTA CLARA COUNTY DEPARTMENT OF LAND USE AND DEVELOPMENT - LIBRARY (Plan)
County Government Center, East Wing
70 W. Hedding St. Phone: (408)299-2521
San Jose, CA 95110 Cheriel Jensen, Libn./Assoc.Plan.
Founded: 1955. **Subjects:** Urban planning, housing, census, economics, water, air quality, noise, geology, transportation, energy, environmental assessment. **Special Collections:** General local plans; energy ordinances from local communities. **Holdings:** 6500 volumes; 350 environmental impact statements; 1300 maps; 9 file drawers of microfiche; 2 VF cabinets of pamphlets. **Subscriptions:** 40 journals and other serials. **Services:** Library open to the public with restrictions. **Publications:** Acquisitions Lists, irregular - for internal distribution only; Santa Clara County general and specific plans and studies related to planning.

★12866★
SANTA CLARA COUNTY HEALTH DEPARTMENT - LIBRARY (Med)
2220 Moorpark Ave. Phone: (408)299-6021
San Jose, CA 95128 Felicia Angeles, Lib.Supv.
Staff: 3. **Subjects:** Public health, psychology, nutrition, environmental health, medicine, alcoholism and drug abuse. **Holdings:** 7000 books; 1200 bound periodical volumes; pamphlets; reprints; hearing reports; clippings. **Subscriptions:** 300 journals and other serials. **Services:** Copying; library open to the public for reference use only. **Networks/Consortia:** Member of Medical Library Consortium of Santa Clara Valley, Northern California and Nevada Medical Library Group (NCNMLG).

★12867★
SANTA CLARA COUNTY LAW LIBRARY (Law)
360 N. First St. Phone: (408)299-3567
San Jose, CA 95113 Susan B. Kuklin, Dir.
Founded: 1874. **Staff:** Prof 3; Other 7. **Subjects:** Law. **Holdings:** 62,000 bound volumes. **Subscriptions:** 315 journals and other serials. **Services:** Interlibrary loan; copying.

★12868★
SANTA CLARA COUNTY OFFICE OF EDUCATION - EMC/ PROFESSIONAL LIBRARY (Educ)
100 Skyport Dr., Mail Code 232 Phone: (408)947-6808
San Jose, CA 95115 Susan Choi, Lib.Serv.Supv.
Staff: Prof 1; Other 5. **Subjects:** Education, administration, technology. **Special Collections:** Curriculum Resource Center (500 government-funded curriculum programs); Technology Demonstration Center (2000 software programs); Indochinese Collection (300 volumes); MEPIC Resource Center (30 migrant education programs). **Holdings:** 13,000 books; 18 VF drawers of newspaper clippings; 12 VF drawers of publisher and vendor catalogs. **Subscriptions:** 341 journals and other serials. **Services:** Interlibrary loanL; copying; library open to residents of Santa Clara County. **Automated Operations:** Computerized circulation. **Computerized Information Services:** DIALOG Information Services. Performs limited searches free of charge. Contact Person: Donna Wheelehan, Lib.Tech.Asst., 947-6808. **Networks/Consortia:** Member of SOUTHNET.

★12869★
SANTA CLARA UNIVERSITY - ARCHIVES (Hist, Rel-Phil)
Santa Clara, CA 95053 Phone: (408)554-4117
Julia O'Keefe, Univ.Archv.
Staff: Prof 1; Other 3. **Subjects:** Mission Santa Clara, Santa Clara University, Jesuits, higher education. **Special Collections:** John J. Montgomery Aviation Collection; Bernard J. Reid Papers; Bernard R. Hubbard, S.J., Collection; Mission Santa Clara sacramental registers, 1777-1903. **Holdings:** 1000 books and bound periodical volumes; university archives; all Santa Clara University publications and newspapers. **Services:** Copying; archives open to the public by appointment.

★12870★
SANTA CLARA UNIVERSITY - HEAFEY LAW LIBRARY (Law)
Santa Clara University Law School Phone: (408)554-4072
Santa Clara, CA 95053 Mary B. Emery, Dir.
Founded: 1963. **Staff:** Prof 6; Other 5. **Subjects:** Law. **Special Collections:** Collection on the development of water and power legislation in the U.S. and California (joint collection with the city of Santa Clara). **Holdings:** 104,114 volumes; 473 AV programs; 2650 volumes on ultrafiche; 47,346 volumes on microfiche. **Subscriptions:** 7498 journals and other serials; 17 newspapers. **Services:** Interlibrary loan; library not open to the public. **Automated Operations:** Computerized cataloging and acquisitions. **Computerized Information Services:** LEXIS, WESTLAW, RLIN. **Networks/Consortia:** Member of CLASS, South Bay Cooperative Library System (SBCLS). **Publications:** Acquisitions List, irregular. **Staff:** Regina T. Wallen, Hd., Tech.Serv.; Mary D. Hood, Hd., Pub.Serv.; Marilyn Earhart, Acq.; Barbara Friedrich, Ref.Libn.; Fe Snider, Cat..

★12871★
SANTA CLARA VALLEY MEDICAL CENTER - MILTON J. CHATTON MEDICAL LIBRARY (Med)
751 S. Bascom Ave. Phone: (408)299-5650
San Jose, CA 95128 Barbara A. Wilson, Med.Libn.
Staff: Prof 2; Other 3. **Subjects:** Clinical medicine, nursing, pathology, physical medicine. **Special Collections:** Tumor Library; Proescher Pathology Library. **Holdings:** 4000 books; 25,000 bound periodical volumes. **Subscriptions:** 650 journals and other serials. **Services:** Interlibrary loan; copying; SDI; library open to students or professionals in the health care field. **Computerized Information Services:** MEDLINE, DIALOG Information Services. Performs searches on fee basis. **Networks/Consortia:** Member of Medical Library Consortium of Santa Clara Valley.

★12872★
SANTA CRUZ APIARIES - AMERICAN APICULTURAL LENDING LIBRARY (Agri)
350 San Miguel Canyon Phone: (408)724-8201
Watsonville, CA 95076 James Meyer, Dir.
Founded: 1985. **Staff:** 1. **Subjects:** Beekeeping, honey, bees, social insects, beeswax, pollen, propolis. **Holdings:** 400 books. **Services:** Library open to the public by mail.

★12873★
SANTA CRUZ COUNTY HISTORICAL TRUST - ARCHIVES (Hist)
118 Cooper St. Phone: (408)425-2540
Santa Cruz, CA 95060 John Lisher, Musm.Dir.
Founded: 1954. **Staff:** Prof 3; Other 1. **Subjects:** Santa Cruz County history, lumbering, tourism, local historical preservation issues. **Special Collections:** Paul D. Johnston Photo Collection (mid-county history; 700 photographs); letters from the Gold Rush era; history of the town band; photographs, 1865 to present; special event programs and memorabilia; history of the Santa Cruz Mission Adobe. **Holdings:** Figures not available. **Services:** Archives open to the public by appointment for specific research requests. **Publications:** Newsletter, monthly - to members and by subscription. **Remarks:** Additional archival materials are located at Octagon Historical Museum, 118 Cooper St., Santa Cruz, CA 95060. **Staff:** Carolyn Franks, Coll.Mgr..

★12874★
SANTA CRUZ COUNTY LAW LIBRARY (Law)
Courts Bldg.
701 Ocean St. Phone: (408)425-2211
Santa Cruz, CA 95060 Patricia J. Pfremmer, Law Libn.
Founded: 1896. **Staff:** Prof 1; Other 1. **Subjects:** Law. **Holdings:** 20,000 books; 1000 bound periodical volumes. **Services:** Interlibrary loan; copying; library open to the public. **Computerized Information Services:** WESTLAW. Performs searches on fee basis. **Networks/Consortia:** Member of South Bay Cooperative Library System (SBCLS). **Remarks:** Maintains branch library of 3600 volumes in Watsonville, CA.

★12875★
SANTA FE BRAUN INC. - REFERENCE LIBRARY (Sci-Engr, Energy)
1000 S. Fremont Ave.
Box 4000 Phone: (818)300-2234
Alhambra, CA 91802-3900 Beverly Muller, Lib.Mgr.
Founded: 1935. **Staff:** Prof 2; Other 2. **Subjects:** Petrochemicals; petroleum; energy; engineering - civil, chemical, electrical, mechanical, hydraulic, ocean; naval architecture; offshore oil well drilling; pipelines; biotechnology; business and management. **Holdings:** 33,800 books; 4000 bound periodical volumes; 6000 microfiche; language tapes; standards and codes; maps and nautical charts; reports. **Subscriptions:** 500 journals and other serials. **Services:** Interlibrary loan; copying. **Computerized Information Services:** DIALOG Information Services, NEXIS, Pergamon ORBIT InfoLine, Inc., Dun & Bradstreet Corporation, Petroleum Abstracts Information Services (PAIS). **Publications:** Periodicals list; New Acquisitions List - for internal distribution only. **Staff:** Helen A. Kramer, Libn..

SANTA FE TRAIL CENTER LIBRARY
See: Fort Larned Historical Society, Inc. (5277)

★12876★
SANTA MONICA HOSPITAL MEDICAL CENTER - LIBRARY (Med)
1225 15th St. Phone: (213)319-4000
Santa Monica, CA 90404 Lenore F. Orfirer, Libn.
Staff: Prof 2. **Subjects:** Medicine. **Holdings:** 1500 books; 900 bound periodical volumes; 1900 unbound periodical volumes; 500 video cassettes. **Subscriptions:** 200 journals and other serials. **Services:** Interlibrary loan; library not open to the public. **Computerized Information Services:** MEDLARS. **Staff:** Linda Moore, Asst.Libn..

★12877★
SANTA MONICA PUBLIC LIBRARY · CALIFORNIA SPECIAL COLLECTION (Hist)
1343 Sixth St. Phone: (213)451-5751
Santa Monica, CA 90401 Carol Aronoff, City Libn.
Staff: Prof 12. **Subjects:** Local history. **Special Collections:** Photographs of the Santa Monica Bay area, 1875 to present (1383). **Holdings:** 2600 books; 300 bound periodical volumes; Santa Monica Evening Outlook, 1875 to present, on microfilm. **Subscriptions:** 10 journals and other serials. **Services:** Interlibrary loan (limited); copying; collection open to the public with restrictions. **Networks/Consortia:** Member of Metropolitan Cooperative Library System (MCLS). **Special Indexes:** Selective indexing of Santa Monica Evening Outlook.

★12878★
SANTA ROSA MEDICAL CENTER - HEALTH SCIENCE LIBRARY (Med)
519 W. Houston St.
Sta. A, Box 7330 Phone: (512)228-2284
San Antonio, TX 78285 Marjorie McFarland, Dir.
Founded: 1939. **Staff:** Prof 1. **Subjects:** Pediatrics, orthopedics, medicine, nursing, hospital administration. **Special Collections:** Terminal Care (30 books). **Holdings:** 1744 books; 4680 bound periodical volumes; 155 audio cassette tapes; 4 file drawers of pamphlets. **Subscriptions:** 191 journals and other serials. **Services:** Interlibrary loan (limited); copying; library open to the public with restrictions. **Computerized Information Services:** NLM. **Networks/Consortia:** Member of Health Oriented Libraries of San Antonio (HOLSA).

★12879★
SANTA ROSA PRESS DEMOCRAT - EDITORIAL LIBRARY (Publ)
427 Mendocino Ave.
Box 569 Phone: (707)526-8585
Santa Rosa, CA 95402 Elaine Cant, Lib.Dir.
Staff: Prof 1; Other 3. **Subjects:** Newspaper reference topics. **Holdings:** Books; bound periodical volumes; 1.5 million clippings; 75 drawers of photographs; newspapers, 1857 to present, on microfilm. **Services:** Copying; SDI; telephone and mail requests only. **Special Indexes:** Criminal file index; biographical file index (both on cards). **Remarks:** Published by New York Times Group.

★12880★
SANTA YNEZ VALLEY HISTORICAL SOCIETY - ELLEN GLEASON LIBRARY (Hist)
Box 181 Phone: (805)688-7889
Santa Ynez, CA 93460 Phil Lockwood, Cur.
Founded: 1961. **Subjects:** History of Santa Ynez Valley, Santa Barbara County, early California. **Special Collections:** Early land deeds. **Holdings:** 1000 books. **Services:** Copying; library open to the public for reference use only.

SANTE ET BIEN-ETRE SOCIAL CANADA
See: Canada - Health and Welfare Canada (2396)

★12881★
SARASOTA MEMORIAL HOSPITAL - MEDICAL LIBRARY (Med)
1700 S. Tamiami Trail Phone: (813)953-1730
Sarasota, FL 34239-3555 Doris Marose, Dir.
Staff: Prof 1. **Subjects:** Medicine, nursing. **Holdings:** 3000 books; 6000 bound periodical volumes; 1400 audio- and videotapes. **Subscriptions:** 175 journals. **Services:** Interlibrary loan; copying; library open to the public. **Computerized Information Services:** NLM. **Networks/Consortia:** Member of West Coast Library Consortium (WELCO).

★12882★
SARATOGA COMMUNITY HOSPITAL - HEALTH SCIENCE LIBRARY (Med)
15000 Gratiot Ave. Phone: (313)245-1200
Detroit, MI 48205 Viju Karnik, Med.Libn.
Staff: Prof 1. **Subjects:** Medicine, nursing, hospital administration. **Holdings:** 1100 books; 300 bound periodical volumes. **Subscriptions:** 137 journals and other serials. **Services:** Interlibrary loan; library not open to the public. **Computerized Information Services:** BRS Information Technologies, MEDLINE.

★12883★
SARATOGA COUNTY HISTORICAL SOCIETY - LIBRARY (Hist)
Brookside
Ballston Spa, NY 12020 Phone: (518)885-4000
Subjects: Saratoga County, New York. **Holdings:** 901 volumes; manuscripts; photographs. **Services:** Library open to the public by appointment. **Publications:** Grist Mill, quarterly; Brookside Columns, monthly. **Special Catalogs:** Catalogue of the Manuscript Collection (1979); Genealogical Guide to Saratoga County, NY (1980).

★12884★
SARATOGA HOSPITAL - MEDICAL STAFF LIBRARY (Med)
211 Church St. Phone: (518)584-6000
Saratoga Springs, NY 12866 Julie Van Dussen
Staff: 4. **Subjects:** Medicine, nursing, surgery. **Holdings:** 340 books; 85 bound periodical volumes. **Subscriptions:** 32 journals and other serials. **Services:** Interlibrary loan; copying; library open to the public for reference use only. **Networks/Consortia:** Member of Capital District Library Council for Reference & Research Resources (CDLC).

SARATOGA NATIONAL HISTORICAL PARK
See: U.S. Natl. Park Service (15348)

SARGEANT MEMORIAL ROOM
See: Norfolk Public Library (10279)

★12885★
SARGENT & LUNDY ENGINEERS - COMPUTER INFORMATION CENTER (Comp Sci)
55 E. Monroe Phone: (312)269-3656
Chicago, IL 60603 William J. Kakish, Supv., Info.Rsrc.Mgmt.
Staff: Prof 1; Other 8. **Subjects:** Computer applications. **Holdings:** 250 books; 723 computer program manuals; 70 VF drawers of computer program documentation; microfiche. **Subscriptions:** 27 journals and other serials. **Services:** Copying; library open to the public by appointment. **Automated Operations:** Computerized circulation. **Computerized Information Services:** DIALOG Information Services, Telenet Telecommunications Corporation; DIALMAIL (electronic mail service). **Networks/Consortia:** Member of ILLINET.

★12886★
SARGENT & LUNDY ENGINEERS - TECHNICAL LIBRARY (Sci-Engr)
55 E. Monroe St., Rm. 26V63 Phone: (312)269-3526
Chicago, IL 60603 Helen P. Heisler, Libn.
Founded: 1969. **Staff:** Prof 1; Other 1. **Subjects:** Engineering - civil, mechanical, electrical; nuclear science; public utilities; air and water pollution. **Holdings:** 1000 books; 85 bound periodical volumes; 20 drawers of standards and specifications; 20 VF drawers. **Subscriptions:** 315 journals and other serials. **Services:** Interlibrary loan; copying; library open to the public by appointment.

★12887★
DAVID SARNOFF LIBRARY (Info Sci)
CN 5300 Phone: (609)734-2608
Princeton, NJ 08543-5300 Wendy Chu, Mgr., Lib.Serv.
Special Collections: David Sarnoff Collection (history of communications). **Holdings:** 1000 books. **Services:** Copying; library open to the public. **Formerly:** RCA Corporation - David Sarnoff Library.

DAVID SARNOFF RESEARCH CENTER
See: SRI International (13589)

★12888★
SASAKI ASSOCIATES, INC. - LIBRARY (Plan)
64 Pleasant St. Phone: (617)926-3300
Watertown, MA 02172 Carole E. Twombly, Libn.
Founded: 1966. **Staff:** Prof 1; Other 1. **Subjects:** Landscape architecture, architecture, planning, environment, engineering. **Holdings:** 2000 books; 55 bound periodical volumes; 300 office publications. **Subscriptions:** 100 journals and other serials. **Services:** Library not open to the public. **Computerized Information Services:** DIALOG Information Services. **Publications:** DIALOGUE, biweekly - for internal distribution only.

★12889★
SASKATCHEWAN ALCOHOL & DRUG ABUSE COMMISSION - LIBRARY (Med)
3475 Albert St. Phone: (306)787-4656
Regina, SK, Canada S4S 6X6 Karen P. King, Libn.
Staff: Prof 1. **Subjects:** Alcohol and alcoholism, drugs and other dependencies, health care. **Holdings:** 3000 books; 400 bound periodical volumes; 100 archival items; reports; pamphlets; government publications. **Subscriptions:** 90 journals and other serials. **Services:** Interlibrary loan; copying; library open to the public. **Automated Operations:** Computerized cataloging, acquisitions, and circulation. **Computerized Information Services:** BRS Information Technologies, DIALOG Information Services. Performs searches free of charge.

★12890★
SASKATCHEWAN ARCHIVES BOARD (Hist)
University of Regina Phone: (306)787-4068
Regina, SK, Canada S4S 0A2 Trevor J.D. Powell, Act.Prov.Archv.
Founded: 1945. **Staff:** Prof 11; Other 15. **Subjects:** Saskatchewan history. **Holdings:** 600 books; 2000 bound periodical volumes; 30,000 feet of archives; 240,000 historical photographs; 8000 reels of microfilm; 8000 hours of sound recordings. **Services:** Copying; archives open to the public. **Publications:** Saskatchewan History, 3/year; Saskatchewan Archives Reference Series; irregular reports. **Special Indexes:** Index to Saskatchewan History (volumes 1-30). **Remarks:** Maintains additional office at Murray Bldg., University of Saskatchewan, Saskatoon, SK S7N 0W0. **Staff:** Mr. E.C. Morgan, Staff Archv.; Mr. D. Herperger, Act.Dir., Rec. & Tech.Serv.; Mr. D. Hande, Act.Dir., Saskatoon Off.; Mr. K.M. Gebhard, Hd., Sound Archv.; Margaret Hutchison, Staff Archv.; Don Richan, City of Regina Archv.; Wayne Crockett, Staff Archv.; Marie-Louise Perron, Francophone Archv.; Glennda Leslie, City of Saskatoon Archv.; Maureen Fox, Staff Archv.

★12891★
SASKATCHEWAN ARTS BOARD - LIBRARY (Art)
2550 Broad St. Phone: (306)787-4056
Regina, SK, Canada S4P 3V7 Nik L. Burton, Literary Prog.Off.
Staff: 10. **Subjects:** Literary, visual, and performing arts. **Holdings:** 500 books. **Subscriptions:** 12 journals and other serials; 10 newspapers.

★12892★
SASKATCHEWAN CANCER FOUNDATION - ALLAN BLAIR MEMORIAL CLINIC - LIBRARY (Med)
4101 Dewdney Ave. Phone: (306)359-2203
Regina, SK, Canada S4T 7T1 Barbara Karchewski, Libn.
Founded: 1948. **Staff:** 1. **Subjects:** Cancer, medical and radiation oncology, physics. **Holdings:** 900 books; 500 bound periodical volumes; 1500 reprint articles on cancer. **Subscriptions:** 100 journals and other serials. **Services:** Interlibrary loan; copying; library open to medical professionals and some research personnel.

★12893★
SASKATCHEWAN DEPARTMENT OF ADVANCED EDUCATION AND MANPOWER - WOMEN'S SECRETARIAT - WOMEN'S RESOURCE CENTRE
1855 Victoria Ave.
Regina, SK, Canada S4P 3V5
Defunct. Absorbed by Saskatchewan Department of Human Resources, Labour and Employment - Library.

★12894★
SASKATCHEWAN DEPARTMENT OF AGRICULTURE - LIBRARY (Agri, Bus-Fin)
Walter Scott Bldg.
3085 Albert St. Phone: (306)787-5151
Regina, SK, Canada S4S 0B1 Helene Stewart, Libn.
Founded: 1974. **Staff:** Prof 1; Other 3. **Subjects:** Agricultural economics, marketing, and statistics; extension; current Canadian agriculture. **Holdings:** 1100 books; 360 bound periodical volumes; 6000 pamphlets and technical reports; 1450 Canadian, U.S., international government annuals; 10,000 fact sheets; 8 VF drawers. **Subscriptions:** 650 journals and other serials; 10 newspapers. **Services:** Interlibrary loan; copying; library open to the public for reference use only. **Computerized Information Services:** BRS Information Technologies, DIALOG Information Services, CAN/OLE, Grassroots, AgriData Network, Sydney Library Systems; Envoy 100 (electronic mail service). **Publications:** Information Notes, 6/year; periodical list, annual.

★12895★
SASKATCHEWAN DEPARTMENT OF THE ATTORNEY GENERAL - COURT OF APPEAL LIBRARY (Law)
Court House, 2425 Victoria Ave. Phone: (306)787-7399
Regina, SK, Canada S4P 3V7 Shirley A. Hurnard, Libn.
Staff: Prof 1. **Subjects:** Law - Canadian, American, English. **Holdings:** 8000 volumes. **Subscriptions:** 30 journals and other serials. **Services:** Library not open to the public.

★12896★
SASKATCHEWAN DEPARTMENT OF CO-OPERATION AND CO-OPERATIVE - RESOURCE CENTRE
2055 Albert St., 5th Fl.
Regina, SK, Canada S4P 3V7
Defunct. Absorbed by Saskatchewan Department of Tourism, Small Business and Co-operatives - Business Library.

★12897★
SASKATCHEWAN DEPARTMENT OF CONSUMER AND COMMERCIAL AFFAIRS - CONSUMER INFORMATION CENTRE (Bus-Fin)
1871 Smith St. Phone: (306)787-5578
Regina, SK, Canada S4P 3V7 Kari Norman, Lib.Techn.
Founded: 1973. **Staff:** 4. **Subjects:** Consumer education and information, insurance, credit, advertising and marketing, money management. **Special Collections:** Marketplace/consumer issues and information files; consumer education resources (AV programs). **Holdings:** 3000 books; 400 AV programs; 15 VF drawers, including Statistics Canada material. **Subscriptions:** 150 journals and other serials; 10 newspapers. **Services:** Interlibrary loan; copying; center open to the public with restrictions. **Publications:** Acquisition List, irregular; special bibliographies.

SASKATCHEWAN DEPARTMENT OF CULTURE AND RECREATION
See: Saskatchewan Department of Parks, Recreation and Culture (12905)

★12898★
SASKATCHEWAN DEPARTMENT OF EDUCATION - RESOURCE CENTRE (Educ)
2220 College Ave. Phone: (306)787-5977
Regina, SK, Canada S4P 3V7 Jane Naisbitt, Libn.
Founded: 1976. **Staff:** Prof 2; Other 2. **Subjects:** Education. **Holdings:** 10,000 books; ERIC microfiche; vertical files; test collections; large print books; audiotapes; braille books. **Subscriptions:** 200 journals and other serials. **Services:** Interlibrary loan; copying; center open to the public for reference use only. **Computerized Information Services:** DIALOG Information Services; internal database. **Publications:** Bibliographies - for internal distribution only. **Remarks:** An alternate telephone number is 787-5998. **Staff:** Wilma Olmsted, Lib.Techn.; Rebecca Landau, Spec.Mtls.Libn..

★12899★
SASKATCHEWAN DEPARTMENT OF ENVIRONMENT AND PUBLIC SAFETY - LIBRARY (Env-Cons)
Walter Scott Bldg.
3085 Albert St. Phone: (306)787-6114
Regina, SK, Canada S4S 0B1 Janice Szuch, Lib.Supv.
Founded: 1974. **Staff:** 2. **Subjects:** Water pollution, air pollution, environmental protection and policy, impact assessments, chemicals. **Holdings:** 1000 books; 25 bound periodical volumes; 4000 reports; 8 VF drawers of pamphlets; 32 shelves of unbound periodicals. **Subscriptions:** 100 journals and other serials. **Services:** Interlibrary loan; library open to the public. **Publications:** Acquisitions list, irregular. **Formerly:** Saskatchewan Department of the Environment.

★12900★
SASKATCHEWAN DEPARTMENT OF HIGHWAYS AND TRANSPORTATION - PLANNING SUPPORT LIBRARY (Trans, Plan)
1855 Victoria Ave. Phone: (306)787-4778
Regina, SK, Canada S4P 3V5 Ellen Basler, Libn.
Founded: 1957. **Staff:** Prof 1. **Subjects:** Highway and traffic engineering, transportation planning, urban and regional studies, management. **Holdings:** 10,000 books; 70 bound periodical volumes. **Subscriptions:** 150 journals and other serials. **Services:** Interlibrary loan; copying; SDI; library open to employees from other Saskatchewan government departments. **Computerized Information Services:** DIALOG Information Services. **Publications:** Library acquisitions, quarterly.

★12901★
SASKATCHEWAN DEPARTMENT OF HUMAN RESOURCES, LABOUR AND EMPLOYMENT - LIBRARY (Bus-Fin, Soc Sci)
1870 Albert St. Phone: (306)787-2422
Regina, SK, Canada S4P 3V7 Fraser Russell, Libn.
Founded: 1957. **Staff:** Prof 1; Other 2. **Subjects:** Labor law and legislation, occupational health, women in the work force, sexism in society, changing roles of women, economic conditions of Canada, industrial relations, income security, trade unions, employment programs. **Special Collections:** Saskatchewan collective labor agreements (500). **Holdings:** 4500 books; 500 bound periodical volumes; 860 linear feet of Canada and Saskatchewan government publications and other documents. **Subscriptions:** 530 journals and other periodicals; 5 newspapers. **Services:** Interlibrary loan; copying; library open to the public. **Computerized Information Services:** DIALOG Information Services, QL Systems, CAN/OLE, WILSONLINE, CCINFO. **Publications:** Labour Bibliographies, irregular. **Formed by the merger of:** Saskatchewan Department of Labour - Library and Saskatchewan Department of Advanced Education and Manpower - Women's Secretariat - Women's Resource Centre.

★12902★
SASKATCHEWAN DEPARTMENT OF JUSTICE - CIVIL LAW LIBRARY (Law)
1874 Scarth St., 9th Fl. Phone: (306)787-7281
Regina, SK, Canada S4P 3V7 Dawn Snedker, Lib.Techn.
Staff: 1. **Subjects:** Law. **Holdings:** Figures not available. **Subscriptions:** 78 journals and other serials. **Services:** Library not open to the public.

SASKATCHEWAN DEPARTMENT OF LABOUR
See: Saskatchewan Department of Human Resources, Labour and Employment (12901)

★12903★
SASKATCHEWAN DEPARTMENT OF PARKS, RECREATION AND CULTURE - FISHERIES MANAGEMENT LIBRARY (Biol Sci)
Box 3003 Phone: (306)953-2891
Prince Albert, SK, Canada S6V 6G1
Brian Christensen, Fisheries Ecologist
Staff: 1. **Subjects:** Fisheries management, fisheries and aquatic biology, fish enhancement, aquaculture, aquatic habitat protection, commercial and sport fishing. **Holdings:** Books; pamphlets; reports; bulletins; periodical volumes. **Subscriptions:** 11 journals and other serials. **Services:** Library open to the public. **Formerly:** Saskatchewan Department of Parks and Renewable Resources - Fish Enhancement Division Library.

★12904★
SASKATCHEWAN DEPARTMENT OF PARKS, RECREATION AND CULTURE - FORESTRY BRANCH LIBRARY (Agri, Biol Sci)
P.O. Box 3003 Phone: (306)952-2333
Prince Albert, SK, Canada S6V 6G1 Felix Casavant
Founded: 1946. **Staff:** Prof 1. **Subjects:** Forestry, forest inventory and products, plant ecology, soil science, silviculture, forest injuries, mensuration, wildlife. **Special Collections:** Soil surveys. **Holdings:** 10,000 books; 2000 other cataloged items. **Subscriptions:** 36 journals and other serials. **Services:** Interlibrary loan; copying; library open to the public with restrictions on some publications. **Publications:** Technical bulletins, annual.

★12905★
SASKATCHEWAN DEPARTMENT OF PARKS, RECREATION AND CULTURE - RESOURCE CENTRE (Rec, Env-Cons)
1942 Hamilton St. Phone: (306)787-5715
Regina, SK, Canada S4P 3V7 Debby Smith, Libn.
Founded: 1987. **Staff:** Prof 2; Other 3. **Subjects:** Heritage archeology, architectural conservation, Saskatchewan history, Canadian arts and multiculturalism, recreation, sports and sports administration, parks management, fisheries, wildlife, forestry, lands management, historic parks. **Special Collections:** Saskatchewan local histories. **Holdings:** 7000 books; 200 bound periodical volumes; 500 other cataloged items. **Subscriptions:** 200 journals and other serials; 20 newspapers. **Services:** Interlibrary loan; center not open to the public. **Automated Operations:** Computerized public access catalog, cataloging, serials, and circulation. **Computerized Information Services:** Envoy 100 (electronic mail service). **Special Indexes:** Saskatchewan Local History Geographical Index. **Formed by the merger of:** Saskatchewan Department of Culture and Recreation and Saskatchewan Department of Parks and Renewable Resources. **Staff:** Robyn Froese, Libn..

SASKATCHEWAN DEPARTMENT OF PARKS AND RENEWABLE RESOURCES
See: Saskatchewan Department of Parks, Recreation and Culture (12904)

★12906★
SASKATCHEWAN DEPARTMENT OF SOCIAL SERVICES - RESOURCE CENTRE (Soc Sci)
1920 Broad St. Phone: (306)787-3680
Regina, SK, Canada S4P 3V6 Muriel Griffiths, Lib.Techn.
Staff: 1. **Subjects:** Social work, child welfare, social policy and welfare, management, juvenile delinquency and corrections, social sciences. **Holdings:** 4600 books; 200 bound periodical volumes. **Subscriptions:** 120 journals and other serials. **Services:** Interlibrary loan; copying; center open to the public.

★12907★
SASKATCHEWAN DEPARTMENT OF TOURISM, SMALL BUSINESS AND CO-OPERATIVES - BUSINESS LIBRARY (Bus-Fin)
Bank of Montreal Bldg., 4th Fl.
2103 11th Ave. Phone: (306)787-2254
Regina, SK, Canada S4P 3V7 Rochelle Smith, Coord.
Founded: 1984. **Staff:** Prof 2; Other 2. **Subjects:** Tourism, small business, economic development, trade, co-operatives, economics, marketing. **Holdings:** 1000 books; 2000 reports; trade directories; government documents; files. **Subscriptions:** 300 journals and other serials; 6 newspapers. **Services:** Interlibrary loan; copying; library open to the public. **Automated Operations:** Computerized cataloging. **Computerized Information Services:** DIALOG Information Services, Info Globe, Canada Systems Group (CSG), Dunserve II, CAN/OLE. **Staff:** Jane Mihalyko, Res.Off..

★12908★
SASKATCHEWAN GENEALOGICAL SOCIETY - LIBRARY (Hist)
1870 Lorne St. Phone: (206)359-9707
Regina, SK, Canada S4P 2L7 Laura M. Hanowski, Libn.
Founded: 1969. **Staff:** Prof 2. **Subjects:** Genealogy, local and family history. **Special Collections:** I.G.I. Ontario Land Records Index; 1891 census information for Northwest Territories, Manitoba, and Ontario; Index to St. Catherines House, 1863-1866; Saskatchewan Cemetery Record; Loiselle Index. **Holdings:** 5000 books; 35 bound periodical volumes; 3000 microfiche; 200 reels of microfilm; 3 videotapes. **Subscriptions:** 250 journals and other serials. **Services:** Interlibrary loan; copying; library open to the public for reference use only. **Special Indexes:** Periodical Index; Obituary Index; Cemetery Index. **Staff:** Marge Thomas, Asst.Libn..

★12909★
SASKATCHEWAN HEALTH - LIBRARY (Med)
3475 Albert St.
Regina, SK, Canada S4S 6X6 Phone: (306)565-3090
Staff: 5. **Subjects:** Public health, nutrition, public health nursing, medicine. **Holdings:** 10,000 books; 8000 bound periodical volumes; 7000 pamphlets; 2000 technical reports. **Subscriptions:** 358 journals and other serials. **Services:** Interlibrary loan; copying (limited); library open to health professionals. **Computerized Information Services:** DIALOG Information Services, CAN/OLE, iNet 2000. **Publications:** Library Acquisitions, monthly.

★12910★
SASKATCHEWAN HOSPITAL - DEPARTMENT OF PSYCHIATRIC SERVICES - STAFF LIBRARY (Med)
P.O. Box 39 Phone: (306)445-9411
North Battleford, SK, Canada S9A 2X8 Doris Allan, Libn.
Staff: 1. **Subjects:** Psychiatry, medicine, psychology, nursing, hospital administration. **Holdings:** 1500 books; 700 bound periodical volumes. **Subscriptions:** 35 journals and other serials; 5 newspapers. **Services:** Interlibrary loan; copying; library open to the public with special permission.

★12911★
SASKATCHEWAN INDIAN FEDERATED COLLEGE - LIBRARY (Area-Ethnic)
University of Regina
127 College W. Phone: (306)584-8333
Regina, SK, Canada S4S 0A2 Phyllis G. Lerat, Libn.
Founded: 1977. **Staff:** Prof 1; Other 2. **Subjects:** Indian studies, art, band administration; health careers. **Special Collections:** Eeniwuk collection. **Holdings:** 10,700 books; 120 bound periodical volumes; 20 VF drawers; 32 VF drawers of clippings, pamphlets, reports. **Subscriptions:** 80 journals and other serials; 12 newspapers. **Services:** Interlibrary loan; copying; library open to the public with restrictions. **Publications:** Acquisitions list, monthly.

★12912★
SASKATCHEWAN LEGISLATIVE LIBRARY (Hist, Law, Soc Sci)
234 Legislative Bldg. Phone: (306)787-2276
Regina, SK, Canada S4S 0B3 Marian Powell, Leg.Libn.
Founded: 1905. **Staff:** Prof 5; Other 9. **Subjects:** Political and social sciences with emphasis on Canada; history, especially Canadian and Western Canadian; law. **Special Collections:** Saskatchewan, Canadian, and Ontario Government documents (165,360 volumes). **Holdings:** 34,900 books; 152,840 microforms, including 140,018 government publications. **Subscriptions:** 518 journals and other serials; 146 newspapers. **Services:** Interlibrary loan; copying; library open to the public with restrictions on borrowing. **Computerized Information Services:** CODOC (Cooperative Documents Network Project), DIALOG Information Services, CAN/OLE, QL Systems, LEXIS, NEXIS, Info Globe, I.P. Sharp Associates Limited; Envoy 100 (electronic mail service). **Publications:** Selected List of Accessions, bimonthly; Checklist of Saskatchewan Government Publications, monthly; Annual Report. **Special Catalogs:** Publications of the governments of the North-West Territories, 1876-1905, and the Province of Saskatchewan, 1905-1952; **Special Indexes:** Saskatchewan Newspaper Index, 1978-1981. **Staff:** Laura Pogue, Ref.Libn.; Judy Brennan, Govt.Pubn.Libn.; Pat Kolesar, Tech.Serv.Libn..

★12913★
SASKATCHEWAN MUSEUM OF NATURAL HISTORY - LIBRARY (Biol Sci)
Dept. of Culture and Recreation
Wascana Park Phone: (306)787-2815
Regina, SK, Canada S4P 3V7 Ruby Apperley, Supv., Musm.Serv.
Staff: Prof 3. **Subjects:** Archeology, anthropology and ethnology, paleontology and earth sciences, botany and other life sciences, conservation and wildlife, taxidermy. **Special Collections:** Whooping Crane Archival Library. **Holdings:** 1937 books; 225 bound periodical volumes; 200 unbound items. **Subscriptions:** 50 journals and other serials. **Services:** Library open to researchers and students by appointment only. **Staff:** Donna Susa, Curatorial Libn.; M. Hanna, Archeo.Libn.; T. Tokaryk, Earth Sci.Libn..

★12914★
SASKATCHEWAN PIPING INDUSTRY - JOINT TRAINING BOARD - LIBRARY (Sci-Engr)
1366 Cornwall St. Phone: (306)522-4237
Regina, SK, Canada S4R 2H5 Darlene Pellerin
Founded: 1971. **Staff:** 1. **Subjects:** Plumbing, pipefitting, welding. **Holdings:** 500 volumes; 28 visual aids; training manuals. **Services:** Library not open to the public.

★12915★
SASKATCHEWAN POWER CORPORATION - LIBRARY (Energy)
2025 Victoria Ave. Phone: (306)566-2697
Regina, SK, Canada S4P 0S1 K. Watts, Lib.Ck.
Founded: 1959. **Staff:** 1. **Subjects:** Electric power engineering, gas engineering, economics, statistics, management. **Holdings:** 10,000 books; 300 unbound periodical volumes; 6000 reports. **Subscriptions:** 250 journals and other serials. **Services:** Interlibrary loan; library not open to the public.

★12916★
SASKATCHEWAN PROPERTY MANAGEMENT CORPORATION - PHOTOGRAPHIC SERVICES AGENCY - LIBRARY (Aud-Vis)
Walter Scott Bldg., Rm. 307
3085 Albert St.
Regina, SK, Canada S4S 0B1 Phone: (306)787-6298
Staff: Prof 1. **Subjects:** Saskatchewaniana. **Holdings:** 40,000 black/white negatives; 100,000 color negatives; 10,000 slides. **Services:** Library open to the public with restrictions. **Formerly:** Saskatchewan Supply & Services - Photographic Services Agency.

★12917★
SASKATCHEWAN PROVINCIAL LIBRARY (Info Sci)
1352 Winnipeg St. Phone: (306)787-2976
Regina, SK, Canada S4P 3V7 Karen Adams, Prov.Libn.
Founded: 1953. **Staff:** Prof 15; Other 26. **Subjects:** Library science, Canada and Saskatchewan documents, general reference. **Special Collections:** Multicultural Collection (26 languages; 66,600 titles); Native Collection (4000 titles); large print and talking books (8400 titles). **Holdings:** 200,000 volumes; 5900 cassettes and tapes; 5000 phonograph records. **Subscriptions:** 870 journals and other serials. **Services:** Interlibrary loan; coordinates public library services throughout the province; direct services to individuals remote from public libraries; centralized cataloging service to public libraries; library not open to the public. **Automated Operations:** Computerized cataloging. **Computerized Information Services:** DIALOG Information Services, Pergamon ORBIT InfoLine, Inc., BRS Information Technologies, CAN/OLE, Info Globe, QL Systems, MEDLARS, DOBIS Canadian Online Library System, REFCATSS; Envoy 100 (electronic mail service). Performs searches on fee basis. Contact Person: Marie Sakon, Hd., Ref. & Res.Serv., 787-2984. **Publications:** Focus, bimonthly; Directory of Saskatchewan Libraries; Saskatchewan Bibliography. **Special Catalogs:** Saskatchewan Union Catalog; Saskatchewan Union List of Serials. **Staff:** Gloria Materi, Dir., Tech.Serv.; Joylene Campbell, Dir., Prof.Serv.; Ved Arora, Hd., Bibliog.Serv.; Jim Oxman, Info.Serv..

★12918★
SASKATCHEWAN REGISTERED NURSES ASSOCIATION - NURSES MEMORIAL RESOURCE CENTRE (Med)
2066 Retallack St. Phone: (306)757-4643
Regina, SK, Canada S4T 2K2 Alice Lalonde, Lib.Techn.
Founded: 1979. **Staff:** Prof 1. **Subjects:** Nursing. **Holdings:** 2000 books; 140 bound periodical volumes. **Subscriptions:** 100 journals and other serials. **Services:** Interlibrary loan; copying; center open to the public for reference use only.

★12919★
SASKATCHEWAN RESEARCH COUNCIL - INFORMATION CENTRE (Sci-Engr)
15 Innovation Place Phone: (306)933-5454
Saskatoon, SK, Canada S7N 2X8 Margaret Samms, Mgr.
Staff: Prof 1; Other 5. **Subjects:** Geology and engineering resources; analytical chemistry; environmental studies - land, water, air; small business assistance and technology transfer. **Holdings:** 10,000 books; 40,000 government publications and technical reports. **Subscriptions:** 430 journals and other serials. **Services:** Interlibrary loan; copying; center open to the public with restrictions. **Automated Operations:** Computerized cataloging. **Computerized Information Services:** DIALOG Information Services, Info Globe, QL Systems, CAN/OLE. Performs searches on fee basis.

★12920★
SASKATCHEWAN RESEARCH COUNCIL - PETROLEUM DIVISION TECHNICAL LIBRARY (Sci-Engr)
515 Henderson Dr. Phone: (306)787-9327
Regina, SK, Canada S4N 5X1 Doreen Sinclair, Tech.Info.Off.
Founded: 1981. **Staff:** 2. **Subjects:** Engineering - petroleum, chemical, reservoir; enhanced recovery; analytical chemistry. **Holdings:** 1100 books; 1200 technical reports; 850 patents; 14,200 reports, papers, articles on microfiche. **Subscriptions:** 85 journals and other serials. **Services:** Interlibrary loan; copying; library open to the public.

SASKATCHEWAN SUPPLY & SERVICES - PHOTOGRAPHIC SERVICES AGENCY
See: Saskatchewan Property Management Corporation - Photographic Services Agency (12916)

★12921★
SASKATCHEWAN SUPPLY & SERVICES - SYSTEMS DIVISION - INFORMATICS RESOURCE CENTER
3rd Fl., T.C. Douglas Bldg.
3475 Albert St.
Regina, SK, Canada S4S 6X6
Founded: 1985. **Subjects:** Information processing technology, office automation, data processing, communications technologies, networking, management education. **Holdings:** 520 books; 65 technical manuals; 3 VF drawers of clippings and pamphlets. **Remarks:** Presently inactive.

★12922★
SASKATCHEWAN TEACHERS' FEDERATION - STEWART RESOURCES CENTRE (Educ)
2317 Arlington Ave.
Box 1108
Saskatoon, SK, Canada S7K 3N3 Phone: (306)373-1660
Founded: 1958. **Staff:** Prof 2; Other 2. **Subjects:** Education, educational psychology, psychology, economic and social conditions. **Special Collections:** Current elementary and secondary school textbooks; Mary Ellen Burgess Drama Library (12,000 play titles). **Holdings:** 20,000 volumes; 4000 pamphlets. **Subscriptions:** 680 journals and other serials; 15 newspapers. **Services:** Interlibrary loan; copying; center open to the public with restrictions. **Publications:** Acquisition list - limited distribution; booklists in subject areas.

★12923★
SASKATCHEWAN TELECOMMUNICATIONS - CORPORATE LIBRARY (Sci-Engr)
2121 Saskatchewan Dr., 2nd Fl. Phone: (306)347-2229
Regina, SK, Canada S4P 3Y2
Basil G. Pogue, Mgr., Corp. Practices & Libs.
Founded: 1980. **Staff:** Prof 2; Other 3. **Subjects:** Electronics, management, data processing, planning, telecommunications, engineering. **Holdings:** 4000 books; 50 bound periodical volumes; 2000 government documents; 4 drawers of microfiche. **Subscriptions:** 550 journals and other serials; 25 newspapers. **Services:** Interlibrary loan; library not open to the public. **Automated Operations:** Computerized cataloging, acquisitions, serials, and circulation. **Computerized Information Services:** DIALOG Information Services, Dun & Bradstreet Corporation, The Financial Post Information Service, Info Globe, CAN/OLE, QL Systems; Envoy 100 (electronic mail service). **Publications:** Library Bulletin, 11/year - for internal distribution only. **Staff:** Tanya Evancio, Corp.Libn..

★12924★
SASKATCHEWAN WESTERN DEVELOPMENT MUSEUMS - GEORGE SHEPHERD LIBRARY (Agri, Trans)
2935 Melville St.
P.O. Box 1910 Phone: (306)934-1400
Saskatoon, SK, Canada S7K 3S5 Warren A. Clubb, Res.Coord.
Founded: 1972. **Subjects:** Technology - general, agricultural, transportation; Western Canadian history; advertising. **Special Collections:** Agricultural implement catalogs, 1880 to present (120 feet). **Holdings:** 10,000 books; 1500 catalogs and other items; 9 drawers of photographs; 1000 glass slides. **Subscriptions:** 30 journals and other serials; 5 newspapers. **Services:** Copying; library open to serious researchers by appointment. **Special Indexes:** Index to Agricultural Implement Catalog collection; Index to Automotive Catalog collection; pamphlet subject indexes.

★12925★
SASKATCHEWAN WHEAT POOL - REFERENCE LIBRARY (Agri)
2625 Victoria Ave. Phone: (306)569-4480
Regina, SK, Canada S4T 7T9 Diane Grodzinski, Libn.
Founded: 1925. **Staff:** 1. **Subjects:** Agriculture, economics, cooperation. **Special Collections:** Saskatchewan Wheat Pool history; history of co-operatives. **Holdings:** 5000 books; documents and special reports from Statistics Canada, Royal Commissions, and others. **Subscriptions:** 150 journals and other serials; 15 newspapers. **Services:** Interlibrary loan; copying; library open to the public for reference use only. **Computerized Information Services:** BRS Information Technologies, Agricultural Computer Network (AGNET); Envoy 100 (electronic mail service).

★12926★
SASKATOON CANCER CLINIC - LIBRARY (Med)
University Hospital
Saskatoon, SK, Canada S7N 0X0 Phone: (306)966-2684
Subjects: Treatment and diagnosis of cancer, radiation therapy, physics, nuclear medicine. **Holdings:** 1000 books; 3500 bound periodical volumes; 25 tapes. **Subscriptions:** 50 journals and other serials. **Services:** Library open to staff members.

★12927★
SASKATOON CITY HOSPITAL - MEDICAL LIBRARY (Med)
701 Queen St. Phone: (306)934-0228
Saskatoon, SK, Canada S7K 0M7 Shirley Blanchette, Lib.Techn.
Founded: 1967. **Staff:** Prof 1. **Subjects:** Medicine. **Holdings:** 300 books; 257 bound periodical volumes. **Subscriptions:** 62 journals and other serials. **Services:** Interlibrary loan; copying; library open to hospital personnel. **Computerized Information Services:** BRS Information Technologies.

★12928★
SASKATOON GALLERY AND CONSERVATORY CORPORATION - MENDEL ART GALLERY - LIBRARY (Art)
950 Spadina Crescent E.
P.O. Box 569 Phone: (306)664-9610
Saskatoon, SK, Canada S7K 3L6 Joan Steel, Libn.
Staff: Prof 1. **Subjects:** Art, museology. **Holdings:** 8500 books; 416 bound periodical volumes; 11,507 slides; 41 VF drawers of clippings and exhibition announcements; 1000 photographs. **Subscriptions:** 44 journals and other serials. **Services:** Interlibrary loan; copying; library open to the public for reference use only.

★12929★
SASKATOON PUBLIC LIBRARY - FINE AND PERFORMING ARTS DEPARTMENT (Art, Mus)
311 23rd St., E. Phone: (306)975-7579
Saskatoon, SK, Canada S7K 0J6 Frances Bergles, Dept.Hd.
Staff: Prof 2; Other 9. **Subjects:** Art, music, theater, crafts, cinema. **Holdings:** 25,000 books; 1500 16mm films; 25,000 sound recordings; 2000 cassettes; 500 videotapes. **Subscriptions:** 350 journals and other serials. **Services:** Interlibrary loan; copying; department open to the public. **Automated Operations:** Computerized cataloging and circulation. **Computerized Information Services:** Envoy 100 (electronic mail service).

★12930★
SASKATOON STAR-PHOENIX - LIBRARY (Publ)
204 5th Ave., N. Phone: (306)652-9200
Saskatoon, SK, Canada S7K 2P1 Miriam Clemence, Libn.
Staff: 1. **Subjects:** Newspaper reference topics, local and provincial news. **Holdings:** 520 books; 105 drawers of photographs and cuts; 30 VF drawers of clippings; 1080 reels of microfilm. **Subscriptions:** 80 journals and other

serials; 21 newspapers. **Services:** Copying; library open to the public for reference use only.

★12931★
SASQUATCH INVESTIGATIONS OF MID-AMERICA - LIBRARY (Sci-Engr)
Box 441 Phone: (405)947-1332
Edmond, OK 73083 Hayden C. Hewes, Dir. of Res.
Founded: 1976. **Subjects:** Bigfoot. **Holdings:** 300 books and magazines.

★12932★
SATELLITE VIDEO EXCHANGE SOCIETY - VIDEO IN LIBRARY (Info Sci, Aud-Vis)
1160 Hamilton St. Phone: (604)688-4336
Vancouver, BC, Canada V6B 2S2 Karen Knights, Libn.
Founded: 1973. **Staff:** Prof 15. **Subjects:** Media arts, arts, national and international politics, community service. **Special Collections:** International videotapes (2000). **Holdings:** 6000 volumes; 6 VF drawers; clippings. **Subscriptions:** 3000 journals and other serials; 300 newspapers. **Services:** Interlibrary loan; copying; library open to the public for reference use only. **Automated Operations:** Computerized cataloging and circulation. **Computerized Information Services:** Online systems. Performs searches on fee basis. **Publications:** Video Guide, 5/year - by subscription. **Special Catalogs:** Video Out (catalog for distribution of independently produced videotapes).

★12933★
SATURDAY EVENING POST SOCIETY - ARCHIVES (Publ, Bus-Fin)
1100 Waterway Blvd. Phone: (317)634-1100
Indianapolis, IN 46202 Steven Cornelius Pettinga, Archv.
Staff: Prof 1; Other 1. **Subjects:** Advertising, marketing, general fiction. **Special Collections:** Correspondence of Cyrus H.K. Curtis, 1900-1930 (15 VF drawers); complete files of Saturday Evening Post, Jack and Jill, Country Gentleman. **Holdings:** 4500 volumes; 4 VF drawers of manuscripts; clippings; pamphlets. **Subscriptions:** 100 journals and other serials. **Services:** Archives not open to the public. **Computerized Information Services:** DIALOG Information Services. **Special Indexes:** Author, title, and subject card index of the Saturday Evening Post, 1900 to present; Saturday Evening Post cartoonists, 1971 to present, and artists, 1920 to present.

SAUGUS IRON WORKS NATIONAL HISTORIC SITE
See: U.S. Natl. Park Service (15349)

★12934★
SAUK COUNTY HISTORICAL SOCIETY, INC. - HISTORICAL MUSEUM LIBRARY (Hist)
531 Fourth Ave. Phone: (608)356-6549
Baraboo, WI 53913 Nijole Etzwiler, Cur.
Founded: 1905. **Staff:** 1. **Subjects:** State and local history, Indian ethnology, religion. **Special Collections:** William H. Canfield writings; H.E. Cole notes and negatives. **Holdings:** 2000 books; 2000 newspaper clippings. **Services:** Library open to the public for reference use only by appointment. **Publications:** Old Sauk Trails.

★12935★
SAUL, EWING, REMICK & SAUL - LAW LIBRARY (Law)
3800 Centre Square W. Phone: (215)972-7873
Philadelphia, PA 19102 Judith W. Abriss, Libn.
Staff: 2. **Subjects:** Law. **Holdings:** 21,000 books; 680 bound periodical volumes. **Subscriptions:** 160 journals and other serials; 5 newspapers. **Services:** Interlibrary loan; library not open to the public. **Computerized Information Services:** LEXIS, NEXIS, DIALOG Information Services, Dun & Bradstreet Corporation, Dow Jones News/Retrieval, VU/TEXT Information Services, WESTLAW. **Staff:** Christine M. Amadio, Asst.Libn..

SAULS MEMORIAL LIBRARY
See: Piedmont Hospital (11324)

★12936★
SAULT STE. MARIE GENERAL HOSPITAL - HEALTH SCIENCES LIBRARY (Med)
941 Queen St., E. Phone: (705)759-3333
Sault Ste. Marie, ON, Canada P6A 2B8 Kathy You, Dir., Lib.Serv.
Founded: 1978. **Staff:** Prof 1; Other 1. **Subjects:** Medicine, nursing, hospital administration. **Holdings:** 900 books; unbound journals kept for 10 years. **Subscriptions:** 100 journals and other serials. **Services:** Interlibrary loan; copying; library open to the public for reference use only. **Computerized Information Services:** MEDLARS. Performs searches on fee basis.

★12937★
SAVANNAH (City) POLICE DEPARTMENT - LIBRARY (Law)
323 Oglethorpe Ave.
Box 1027 Phone: (912)233-9321
Savannah, GA 31402 Glenda E. Anderson, Res.Libn.
Staff: 1. **Subjects:** Police management and organization, criminal justice. **Holdings:** 906 volumes. **Subscriptions:** 21 journals and other serials. **Services:** Interlibrary loan; library not open to the public. **Networks/Consortia:** Member of Georgia Library Information Network (GLIN), Criminal Justice Information Exchange Group.

★12938★
SAVANNAH MORNING NEWS-SAVANNAH EVENING PRESS - LIBRARY (Publ)
111 W. Bay St.
Box 1088 Phone: (912)236-9511
Savannah, GA 31402 Julia C. Muller, Chf.Libn.
Staff: Prof 2. **Subjects:** Newspaper reference topics. **Holdings:** Newspaper clippings; local and wire pictures; microfilm. **Subscriptions:** 10 newspapers. **Services:** Library not open to the public. **Staff:** Sara Wright, Asst.Libn..

★12939★
SAVANNAH MUNICIPAL RESEARCH LIBRARY (Soc Sci)
City Hall, Rm. 402
Box 1027 Phone: (912)235-4094
Savannah, GA 31402 Glenda E. Anderson, Res.Libn.
Founded: 1974. **Staff:** Prof 2. **Subjects:** Urban administration, municipal management, public services, community development, municipal finance/budgeting, urban public works. **Special Collections:** Savannah Area Local Documents Collection (1486 items). **Holdings:** 4294 volumes; 933 periodical volumes; 1552 microfiche. **Subscriptions:** 150 journals and other serials. **Services:** Interlibrary loan; copying; SDI; library open to the public for reference use only. **Computerized Information Services:** LOGIN; LINUS, PTI-NET (electronic mail services). **Networks/Consortia:** Member of Georgia Library Information Network (GLIN). **Publications:** Savannah Area Local Documents, 1960-1979 (bibliography and indexes). **Staff:** Judith C. Wood, Cat.Libn..

★12940★
SAVANNAH RIVER LABORATORY - TECHNICAL LIBRARY (Energy, Sci-Engr)
E.I. Du Pont de Nemours & Company
Bldg. 773A Phone: (803)725-2940
Aiken, SC 29808 C. Tom Sutherland, Supv., Tech.Serv.
Founded: 1952. **Staff:** Prof 2; Other 6. **Subjects:** Nuclear science, chemistry, physics, metallurgy, engineering, mathematics. **Holdings:** 35,000 books; 45,000 bound periodical volumes; 51,000 technical reports. **Subscriptions:** 1500 journals and other serials. **Services:** Interlibrary loan; library not open to the public. **Automated Operations:** Computerized cataloging, serials, and circulation. **Computerized Information Services:** DIALOG Information Services, Pergamon ORBIT InfoLine, Inc., Integrated Technical Information System (ITIS). **Remarks:** The Savannah River Laboratory operates under contract to the U.S. Department of Energy. **Staff:** Ermina U. Kauer, Ref.Libn..

★12941★
SAVANNAH SCIENCE MUSEUM - ENERGY LIBRARY (Energy)
4405 Paulsen St. Phone: (912)355-6705
Savannah, GA 31405 Robert Graham, Cur.
Founded: 1981. **Staff:** Prof 1. **Subjects:** Energy - solar, wind, alternative, conservation; appropriate technology. **Holdings:** 400 books; 200 pamphlets; 150 Department of Energy publications. **Services:** Library not open to the public.

★12942★
SAVE THE CHILDREN FEDERATION - LIBRARY (Soc Sci)
54 Wilton Rd. Phone: (203)226-7271
Westport, CT 06880 Nancy N. Faesy, Libn.
Staff: Prof 1; Other 1. **Subjects:** Community development - planning and evaluation; health and nutrition; technical foreign aid; appropriate technology; North American Indians. **Holdings:** 3200 books; 6 VF drawers of pamphlets; 6 VF drawers of information on organizations; 2 VF drawers of United Nations information. **Subscriptions:** 300 journals and other serials; 20 newspapers. **Services:** Interlibrary loan; copying; library open to the public with restrictions. **Networks/Consortia:** Member of Information Network for Materials Effecting Development (INFORMED),

Southwestern Connecticut Library Council (SWLC). **Publications:** New materials list, bimonthly; Core Bibliographies.

SAVITT MEDICAL LIBRARY
See: University of Nevada, Reno (16583)

SAVITZ LIBRARY
See: Glassboro State College - Savitz Library (5676)

MILDRED F. SAWYER LIBRARY
See: Suffolk University (13733)

RUTH SAWYER COLLECTION
See: College of St. Catherine - Library (3392)

SAYERS MEMORIAL LIBRARY
See: U.S. Army Post - Fort Benning (14844)

★12943★
SCARBOROUGH BOARD OF EDUCATION - A.B. PATTERSON PROFESSIONAL LIBRARY (Educ)
140 Borough Dr., Level 2 Phone: (416)396-7515
Scarborough, ON, Canada M1P 4N6 Rowan Amott, Supv.
Founded: 1956. **Staff:** Prof 2; Other 4. **Subjects:** Education, child study, sociology. **Holdings:** 30,000 books; 600 reels of microfilm; 86,000 microfiche; 15 VF drawers; ONTERIS microfiche. **Subscriptions:** 378 journals and other serials. **Services:** Interlibrary loan; copying; library open to the public by appointment. **Automated Operations:** Computerized cataloging and acquisitions. **Computerized Information Services:** DIALOG Information Services, Pergamon ORBIT InfoLine, Inc., Infomart, BRS Information Technologies, UTLAS, CAN/OLE. **Networks/Consortia:** Member of Education Libraries Sharing of Resources Network (ELSOR). **Special Catalogs:** Book Catalogue; journal listing, both annual - for internal distribution only. **Staff:** Martha Murphy, Asst.Libn..

★12944★
SCARBOROUGH CITY HEALTH DEPARTMENT - HEALTH RESOURCE CENTRE - JEAN CREW DEEKS MEMORIAL LIBRARY (Med)
160 Borough Dr. Phone: (416)396-7453
Scarborough, ON, Canada M1P 4N8 Dianne Beal, Libn.
Founded: 1967. **Staff:** Prof 1. **Subjects:** Nursing; prenatal, maternal, and child care; psychology; geriatrics; nutrition. **Special Collections:** Nutrition; sexually transmitted disease; family planning; health inspection; dentistry. **Holdings:** 1200 books; 400 studies and reports; 100 posters; 700 pamphlet titles; 100 audio cassettes; 15 videotapes; 20 resource kits. **Subscriptions:** 82 journals and other serials. **Services:** Center not open to the public. **Publications:** Library Bulletin, biweekly - for internal distribution only. **Special Catalogs:** Studies and reports; resource kits and audio- and videotapes (both on cards).

★12945★
SCARBOROUGH GENERAL HOSPITAL - HEALTH SCIENCES LIBRARY (Med)
3050 Lawrence Ave., E. Phone: (416)431-8114
Scarborough, ON, Canada M1P 2V5 Helvi Thomas, Libn.
Founded: 1958. **Staff:** Prof 1. **Subjects:** Health sciences. **Holdings:** 1200 books; 85 bound periodical volumes. **Subscriptions:** 200 journals and other serials. **Services:** Interlibrary loan; library not open to the public. **Computerized Information Services:** MEDLARS.

SCARBOROUGH MEMORIAL LIBRARY
See: College of the Southwest (3398)

★12946★
SCARBOROUGH RESOURCE CENTRE (Plan)
Scarborough Civic Centre
150 Borough Dr. Phone: (416)296-7215
Scarborough, ON, Canada M1P 4N7 Dave Hawkins, Mgr.
Founded: 1973. **Staff:** Prof 1; Other 2. **Subjects:** Urban affairs with emphasis on Scarborough and metropolitan Toronto. **Holdings:** 2000 books; 16 VF drawers of documents. **Subscriptions:** 400 journals and other serials; 10 newspapers. **Services:** Interlibrary loan; copying; center open to the public. **Publications:** Recent Additions, bimonthly - to city staff and interested individuals.

★12947★
SCARRITT GRADUATE SCHOOL - VIRGINIA DAVIS LASKEY LIBRARY (Rel-Phil)
1104 19th Ave., S. Phone: (615)340-7479
Nashville, TN 37203 Dale E. Bilbrey, Libn.
Founded: 1892. **Staff:** Prof 2; Other 1. **Subjects:** Christian education, church music. **Special Collections:** Bibles (297). **Holdings:** 49,850 books; 5200 bound periodical and curriculum volumes; 40 reels of microfilm; 420 recordings; 250 tapes and AV kits. **Subscriptions:** 115 journals and other serials. **Services:** Interlibrary loan; copying; library open to the public with restrictions on borrowing. **Remarks:** Library has mutual borrowing privileges with Vanderbilt University Library System.

★12948★
SCENIC GENERAL HOSPITAL - STANISLAUS COUNTY MEDICAL LIBRARY (Med)
830 Scenic Dr. Phone: (209)526-6926
Modesto, CA 95350 Margie A. Felt, Med.Lib.Asst.
Founded: 1956. **Staff:** Prof 1; Other 1. **Subjects:** General and family practice, orthopedics, surgery, pediatrics, radiology, nursing, psychiatry. **Holdings:** 3563 books; 4330 bound periodical volumes; 931 other cataloged items; 97 slides; Audio-Digest tapes. **Subscriptions:** 162 journals and other serials. **Services:** Interlibrary loan; copying; library open to the public with doctor's referral.

DR. OTTO SCHAEFER HEALTH LIBRARY AND RESOURCE CENTRE
See: Northwest Territories Ministry of Health and Social Services (10482)

PHILIP SCHAFF LIBRARY
See: Lancaster Theological Seminary of the United Church of Christ (7641)

SCHAFFER LAW LIBRARY
See: Union University - Albany Law School (14486)

SCHAFFER LIBRARY
See: Union College - Schaffer Library - Special Collections (14469)

SCHAFFER LIBRARY OF THE HEALTH SCIENCES
See: Albany Medical College (177)

WALTER F. SCHALLER MEMORIAL LIBRARY
See: St. Francis Memorial Hospital (12399)

SCHEIDEMANTEL HOUSE
See: Aurora Historical Society, Inc. - ScheideMantel House (1169)

★12949★
SCHEIE EYE INSTITUTE - LIBRARY
Myrin Circle
51 N. 39th St.
Philadelphia, PA 19104
Defunct

SCHENDEL MEMORIAL LIBRARY
See: First Lutheran Church of the Lutheran Church in America (5073)

SCHENECTADY ARCHIVES OF SCIENCE AND TECHNOLOGY
See: Union College - Schaffer Library - Special Collections (14469)

★12950★
SCHENECTADY CHEMICALS, INC. - W. HOWARD WRIGHT RESEARCH CENTER - LIBRARY (Sci-Engr)
2750 Balltown Rd. Phone: (518)370-4200
Schenectady, NY 12309 Dorothy M. Kraus, Mgr., Tech.Info.Serv.
Staff: Prof 1; Other 1. **Subjects:** Polymer and organic chemistry. **Holdings:** 1100 books; 1200 bound periodical volumes. **Subscriptions:** 70 journals and other serials. **Services:** Interlibrary loan; copying; SDI; library open to the public with restrictions. **Computerized Information Services:** DIALOG Information Services, STN International, Pergamon ORBIT InfoLine, Inc. **Networks/Consortia:** Member of Capital District Library Council for Reference & Research Resources (CDLC).

★12951★
SCHENECTADY COUNTY HISTORICAL SOCIETY - LIBRARY AND ARCHIVES (Hist)
32 Washington Ave. Phone: (518)374-0263
Schenectady, NY 12305 Mrs. C.A. Church, Archv.
Founded: 1905. **Staff:** 2. **Subjects:** Schenectady County and New York State history, genealogy. **Special Collections:** Local church and cemetery records; Revolutionary War documents; family record file; 1850 census of New York State counties (microfilm); federal census of Schenectady County, 1790-1900; state census of Schenectady County, 1835, 1855; 1900 federal census of New York State counties. **Holdings:** 1500 volumes; clippings; manuscripts; pamphlets; documents; slides; pictures; maps. **Services:** Copying; family research (fee); library open to the public on fee basis.

★12952★
SCHENECTADY GAZETTE - LIBRARY (Publ)
332 State St. Phone: (518)374-4141
Schenectady, NY 12301 Colleen J. Daze, Libn.
Staff: 2. **Subjects:** Newspaper reference topics. **Holdings:** 250 books; 250,000 newspaper clippings; newspaper on microfilm, 1899 to present. **Subscriptions:** 15 journals and newspapers. **Services:** Copying; library open to the public by appointment. **Special Indexes:** Index to Schenectady Gazette, 1979 to present.

★12953★
SCHENECTADY MUSEUM AND PLANETARIUM - LIBRARY (Art, Sci-Engr)
Nott Terrace Heights Phone: (518)382-7890
Schenectady, NY 12308 Mary Dagan, Reg.
Founded: 1934. **Subjects:** Art, history, science, industry, technology, natural history. **Special Collections:** Early electricity; Charles P. Steinmetz Collection. **Holdings:** 1000 books. **Services:** Interlibrary loan; library open to the public with restrictions.

HEINRICH SCHENKER ARCHIVE
See: University of California, Riverside - Music Library (16001)

FRANK H. SCHEPLER, JR. MEMORIAL LIBRARY
See: Chatsworth Historical Society (2998)

★12954★
R.P. SCHERER CORPORATION - LIBRARY (Med)
2075 W. Big Beaver Rd. Phone: (313)649-0900
Troy, MI 48094 Sandra Abrams, Libn.
Staff: 1. **Subjects:** Chemistry, pharmacy. **Holdings:** 3000 books; 1000 bound periodical volumes. **Subscriptions:** 50 journals and other serials. **Services:** Library not open to the public.

SCHERING FOUNDATION LIBRARY OF HEALTH CARE
See: Harvard University - School of Medicine (6119)

★12955★
SCHERING-PLOUGH CORPORATION - LIBRARY INFORMATION CENTER (Bus-Fin)
Galloping Hill Rd. Phone: (201)558-5121
Kenilworth, NJ 07033 Esther M. Jankovics, Supv.
Staff: Prof 3; Other 1. **Subjects:** Management, pharmaceutical marketing, business. **Holdings:** 2500 books and bound periodical volumes; 2 drawers of annual reports; 7 card catalog drawers of In the News; 5 VF drawers. **Subscriptions:** 303 journals and other serials; 5 newspapers. **Services:** Interlibrary loan; copying; SDI; center open to the public with restrictions. **Computerized Information Services:** Online systems. **Publications:** In the News, 2/week. **Staff:** Amy Ipp, Libn.; Virginia Hughes, Ed., In The News.

★12956★
SCHERING-PLOUGH CORPORATION - PHARMACEUTICAL RESEARCH DIVISION - LIBRARY INFORMATION CENTER (Biol Sci, Med)
60 Orange St. Phone: (201)429-3737
Bloomfield, NJ 07003 Sidney L. Blumenthal, Mgr.
Founded: 1940. **Staff:** Prof 10; Other 9. **Subjects:** Pharmacy, biomedicine, microbiology, organic chemistry. **Holdings:** 30,000 volumes. **Subscriptions:** 1400 journals and other serials. **Services:** Interlibrary loan; copying; SDI; center open to qualified users by appointment only. **Automated Operations:** Computerized public access catalog, cataloging, acquisitions, serials, and circulation. **Computerized Information Services:** DIALOG Information Services, WILSONLINE, Telesystemes Questel, CAS ONLINE; ICON, SCHOLAR/Inquire (internal databases). **Staff:** Jean R. Hudson, Supv., Tech.Serv.; Jean Nocka, Supv., Lit. Dissemination.

SCHERING-PLOUGH LIBRARY
See: Massachusetts Institute of Technology (8552)

HARRY SCHERMAN LIBRARY
See: Mannes College of Music (8385)

GALKA E. SCHEYER ARCHIVES
See: Norton Simon Museum of Art at Pasadena - Library and Archives (13190)

★12957★
SCHICK SHADEL HOSPITAL - MEDICAL LIBRARY (Med)
Box 48149 Phone: (206)244-8100
Seattle, WA 98148 Pamela W. Miles, Med.Libn.
Staff: Prof 1. **Subjects:** Medicine, smoking, alcoholism and substance abuse, behavior modification. **Holdings:** 800 books; 80 unbound periodical volumes; 15 VF drawers of reports, reprints, clippings. **Subscriptions:** 80 journals and other serials. **Services:** Interlibrary loan; copying. **Computerized Information Services:** MEDLARS, BRS Information Technologies; OnTyme Electronic Message Network Service (electronic mail service). **Networks/Consortia:** Member of Seattle Area Hospital Library Consortium (SAHLC).

★12958★
SCHIELE MUSEUM OF NATURAL HISTORY AND PLANETARIUM - LIBRARY (Biol Sci)
1500 E. Garrison Blvd.
Box 953 Phone: (704)864-3962
Gastonia, NC 28053-0953 M. Turney, Reg./Libn.
Staff: Prof 1; Other 17. **Subjects:** Ecology, natural history, marine biology, archeology, anthropology, land use, zoology, botany, local history. **Holdings:** 6000 books; 141 films; 15,000 slides; 89 planetarium program tapes; 5000 wildflower transparencies; 400 items in research egg collection; serial publications of the Natural History Museum of Los Angeles County; biweekly bulletins of Wildlife Management Institute, 1972 to present. **Subscriptions:** 37 journals and other serials. **Services:** Interlibrary loan; copying; library open to the public with restrictions. **Publications:** Newsletter, quarterly; annual report. **Remarks:** Library serves as an Environmental Reference Center for the State of North Carolina and also as a Regional Reference Center for the Library of Congress.

RABBI SCHIFF LIBRARY
See: Telshe Yeshiva - Rabbi A.N. Schwartz Library (13932)

ARTHUR AND ELIZABETH SCHLESINGER LIBRARY ON THE HISTORY OF WOMEN IN AMERICA
See: Radcliffe College (11850)

CHARLES H. SCHLICHTER, M.D. HEALTH SCIENCE LIBRARY
See: Elizabeth General Medical Center (4655)

★12959★
SCHLUMBERGER-DOLL RESEARCH LIBRARY (Sci-Engr, Energy)
Old Quarry Rd. Phone: (203)431-5600
Ridgefield, CT 06877-4108 Mary Ellen Banks, Supv., SDR Lib.
Staff: Prof 3. **Subjects:** Oil well logging, physics, nuclear science, mathematics, computer science, chemistry, geology, geoscience, artificial intelligence, petroleum exploration. **Holdings:** 12,000 books; 2500 bound periodical volumes; microforms; 10,000 articles and reports; 3000 government reports. **Subscriptions:** 400 journals and other serials. **Services:** Interlibrary loan; copying (limited); library open to the public by appointment. **Automated Operations:** Computerized cataloging, acquisitions, and circulation. **Computerized Information Services:** Pergamon ORBIT InfoLine, Inc., STN International, DIALOG Information Services, BRS Information Technologies, Sci-Mate, OCLC, DATALIB; LINX Courier (electronic mail service). **Networks/Consortia:** Member of NELINET, Southwestern Connecticut Library Council (SWLC). **Remarks:** An alternate telephone number is 431-5604. **Staff:** Maureen Jones, Bk./ILL Libn..

★12960★
SCHLUMBERGER, LTD. - EMR PHOTOELECTRIC CENTER - INFORMATION CENTER (Sci-Engr)
Box 44 Phone: (609)799-1000
Princeton, NJ 08542 Nora L. Kugler, Lib.Adm.
Founded: 1954. **Staff:** Prof 1; Other 1. **Subjects:** Photomultiplier tubes, thin films, optical physics, electro-optics, vacuum technology. **Holdings:** 1000 books; 1500 bound periodical volumes; 15 VF drawers of company

technical reports; 2 VF drawers of patents. **Subscriptions:** 65 journals and other serials. **Services:** Interlibrary loan; center not open to the public. **Automated Operations:** Computerized cataloging. **Computerized Information Services:** DIALOG Information Services; internal database. **Publications:** Monthly Library Acquisitions Bulletin; Current Interest Profiles, monthly.

SCHLUMBERGER, LTD. - FAIRCHILD-WESTON SYSTEMS INC.
See: Fairchild-Weston Systems Inc. (4881)

SCHLUMBERGER PALO ALTO RESEARCH
See: Lucid Information Services (8101)

★12961★
SCHLUMBERGER WELL SERVICES - HDS LIBRARY (Sci-Engr)
5000 Gulf Fwy.
Box 2175 Phone: (713)928-4411
Houston, TX 77252-2175 Margaret Kuo, Libn.
Founded: 1953. **Staff:** Prof 1. **Subjects:** Engineering, electronics, geology. **Holdings:** 4480 books; 100 bound periodical volumes; 30 drawers of company reports. **Subscriptions:** 114 journals and other serials. **Services:** Interlibrary loan; library not open to the public. **Automated Operations:** Computerized cataloging and circulation. **Computerized Information Services:** Pergamon ORBIT InfoLine, Inc., DIALOG Information Services; internal database. **Publications:** Monthly New Acquisitions Online.

GRACE SCHMIDT ROOM OF LOCAL HISTORY
See: Waterloo Historical Society - Grace Schmidt Room of Local History (17563)

SCHMIDT HERPETOLOGY LIBRARY
See: Field Museum of Natural History - Library (5005)

SCHMIDT LIBRARY
See: York College of Pennsylvania (18179)

SCHMIDT MEDICAL LIBRARY
See: California College of Podiatric Medicine (2133)

DIETRICH SCHMITZ MEMORIAL LIBRARY
See: Washington Mutual Savings Bank - Information Center & Dietrich Schmitz Memorial Library (17498)

★12962★
SCHNADER, HARRISON, SEGAL & LEWIS - LIBRARY (Law)
1600 Market St., Suite 3600 Phone: (215)751-2111
Philadelphia, PA 19103 Paul B. Gloeckner, Dir.
Staff: Prof 4; Other 3. **Subjects:** Law. **Holdings:** 30,000 volumes. **Subscriptions:** 100 journals and other serials; 10 newspapers. **Services:** Interlibrary loan; copying; library open to the public with restrictions. **Computerized Information Services:** DIALOG Information Services, LEXIS, VU/TEXT Information Services, WILSONLINE, Dow Jones News/Retrieval, Dun & Bradstreet Corporation, NewsNet, Inc., WESTLAW.

SCHNEIDER SERVICES INTERNATIONAL - ARNOLD ENGINEERING DEVELOPMENT CENTER
See: Arnold Engineering Development Center (946)

KENNETH H. SCHNEPP MEDICAL LIBRARY
See: Memorial Medical Center (8654)

ARTHUR SCHNITZLER ARCHIVES
See: SUNY at Binghamton - Special Collections (13789)

★12963★
ARNOLD SCHOENBERG INSTITUTE - ARCHIVES (Mus)
University of Southern California
University Park - MC 1101 Phone: (213)743-5393
Los Angeles, CA 90089-1101 R. Wayne Shoaf, Archv.
Founded: 1975. **Staff:** Prof 2; Other 1. **Subjects:** Arnold Schoenberg, 20th century music, Los Angeles war emigres. **Holdings:** 2400 books; 6000 pages of manuscripts; 230 audiotapes; 730 phonograph records; 200 microfiche; 60 reels of microfilm; 15 boxes of concert programs, news clippings; 2500 photographs; 120 theses and dissertations; 1000 scores; 5 maps; 18 films; 500 AV programs. **Subscriptions:** 10 journals and other serials. **Services:** Copying; archives open to the public by appointment. **Automated Operations:** Computerized cataloging. **Computerized Information Services:** RLIN; RLIN (electronic mail service). **Remarks:** Institute is jointly maintained and supported by the University of Southern California and California Institute of the Arts.

★12964★
SCHOHARIE COUNTY HISTORICAL SOCIETY - REFERENCE LIBRARY (Hist)
Old Stone Fort Museum
N. Main St.
R.D. 2, Box 30A Phone: (518)295-7192
Schoharie, NY 12157 Helene S. Farrell, Dir.
Founded: 1888. **Subjects:** Schoharie County history and genealogy, regional and New York State history. **Special Collections:** Early Schoharie County land patents. **Holdings:** 1500 books; 200 bound periodical volumes; 500 pamphlets; scrapbooks; maps; pictures. **Services:** Copying; library open to the public for reference use only on a fee basis. **Publications:** Schoharie County Historical Review, semiannual - to members.

★12965★
SCHOLASTIC MAGAZINES & BOOK SERVICES - GENERAL LIBRARY (Publ)
730 Broadway Phone: (212)505-3000
New York, NY 10003 Lucy Evankow, Chf.Libn.
Founded: 1931. **Staff:** Prof 2; Other 3. **Subjects:** Current affairs, biography, sports, education of youth, juvenile and teenage literature, political cartoons, arts. **Holdings:** 205 VF drawers of biographical and pamphlet material; periodical volumes; syllabi; photographs. **Subscriptions:** 300 journals and other serials. **Services:** Interlibrary loan; library not open to the public.

SAMUEL R. SCHOLES LIBRARY OF CERAMICS
See: New York State College of Ceramics at Alfred University (10096)

★12966★
DR. WILLIAM M. SCHOLL COLLEGE OF PODIATRIC MEDICINE - LIBRARY (Med)
1001 N. Dearborn St. Phone: (312)280-2891
Chicago, IL 60610 Richard S. Klein, Dir., Lib.Serv.
Staff: Prof 2; Other 2. **Subjects:** Podiatric medicine, orthopedics, dermatology, anatomy, neurology, sports medicine, biomechanics. **Special Collections:** Historical shoes; historical podiatric books. **Holdings:** 16,000 books and bound periodical volumes; AV programs. **Subscriptions:** 330 journals and other serials. **Services:** Interlibrary loan; copying; SDI; library open to the public for reference use only. **Automated Operations:** Computerized cataloging. **Computerized Information Services:** OCLC, DIALOG Information Services, Pergamon ORBIT InfoLine, Inc., MEDLINE; OnTyme Electronic Message Network Service, DOCLINE (electronic mail services). Performs searches on fee basis. Contact Person: Donald Nagolski, Assoc.Dir., 280-2493. **Networks/Consortia:** Member of Greater Midwest Regional Medical Library Network, Metropolitan Consortium of Chicago, Chicago Library System. **Publications:** Acquisitions List, quarterly; Library User's Manual, annual; Library Report, annual; Periodicals Holdings List, annual; MEDLINE Fact Sheet.

SCHOMBURG CENTER FOR RESEARCH IN BLACK CULTURE
See: New York Public Library (10086)

★12967★
SCHOOL OF AMERICAN RESEARCH - LIBRARY (Sci-Engr, Area-Ethnic)
Box 2188 Phone: (505)982-3583
Santa Fe, NM 87504-2188 Jane P. Gillentine, Libn.
Staff: Prof 1. **Subjects:** Anthropology, archeology, ethnology, Southwest Indian arts. **Holdings:** 6000 books; 300 bound periodical volumes. **Subscriptions:** 25 journals and other serials. **Services:** Interlibrary loan; library not open to the public. **Publications:** Exploration, annual; monographs, irregular; advanced seminar publications, annual; Indian Arts Series books; Archaeology of the Grand Canyon series; Arroyo Hondo Archaeological series.

SCHOOL OF THE ART INSTITUTE OF CHICAGO
See: Art Institute of Chicago (962)

★12968★
SCHOOL DISTRICT OF PHILADELPHIA - PEDAGOGICAL LIBRARY (Educ)
Adm. Bldg., Rm. 301
21st St. & Parkway Phone: (215)299-7783
Philadelphia, PA 19103 Helen E. Howe, Hd.Libn.
Founded: 1883. **Staff:** Prof 2; Other 2. **Subjects:** Elementary and secondary education, psychology and testing, intercultural human relations, special education, reading. **Holdings:** 48,000 books and bound periodical volumes; ERIC microfiche; VF drawers of Philadelphia courses of study, pictures, teaching units, bibliographies, pamphlets; 300,000 documents on microfiche. **Subscriptions:** 425 journals and other serials; 6 newspapers. **Services:** Interlibrary loan; copying; library open to the public for reference use only. **Automated Operations:** Computerized cataloging. **Computerized Information Services:** BRS Information Technologies, OCLC. **Publications:** New book lists and flyers, monthly; current list of periodicals, annual. **Staff:** Dorothy L. Williams, Dir.; Patricia Buck, Asst.Libn..

★12969★
SCHOOL OF FINE ARTS - LIBRARY (Mus, Theater)
38660 Mentor Ave. Phone: (216)951-7500
Willoughby, OH 44094 Edith Reed, Act.Libn.
Founded: 1978. **Staff:** 2. **Subjects:** Music, theater, art, dance. **Special Collections:** Opera collection. **Holdings:** 3600 books; 700 phonograph records. **Services:** Library not open to the public.

★12970★
SCHOOL OF LIVING - RALPH BORSODI MEMORIAL LIBRARY AND ARCHIVES (Soc Sci)
R.D. 1
Box 1508AA Phone: (717)225-3745
Spring Grove, PA 17362 True Ritchie, Libn.
Staff: Prof 1; Other 1. **Subjects:** Philosophy, spiritual man, human nature, historiography, nature of truth, values and purposes, esthetics, economics, mental and physical health, occupations, possessions, organization, production, distribution, politics, civic government, institutions, education. **Special Collections:** Complete collection of Green Revolution; antique books (100); books written by Ralph Borsodi and Mildred Loomis. **Holdings:** 1500 books; 2 VF drawers of articles; microfilm. **Subscriptions:** 200 journals and other serials. **Services:** Interlibrary loan; library open to the public. **Publications:** Green Revolution, quarterly - by subscription.

★12971★
SCHOOL MANAGEMENT STUDY GROUP - LIBRARY (Educ)
860 18th Ave. Phone: (801)532-5340
Salt Lake City, UT 84103 Dr. Donald Thomas, Exec.Dir.
Founded: 1969. **Staff:** Prof 2; Other 1. **Subjects:** Educational administration and management. **Special Collections:** Incentive Pay; Character Education. **Holdings:** 100 books; 200 bound periodical volumes; manuscripts. **Services:** Interlibrary loan; copying; library open to the public.

★12972★
SCHOOL OF THE OZARKS - RALPH FOSTER MUSEUM - LOIS BROWNELL RESEARCH LIBRARY (Hist)
Point Lookout, MO 65726 Phone: (417)334-6411
Robert S. Esworthy, Dir.
Staff: Prof 1; Other 1. **Subjects:** Firearms, archeology, Ozarks regional history, antiques, fine art, natural history, early man. **Special Collections:** Congressman Dewey Short's papers. **Holdings:** 1500 books; 300 bound periodical volumes; 5 VF drawers of archives. **Subscriptions:** 25 journals and other serials; 7 newspapers. **Services:** Copying; library open to the public with permission of director.

SCHOOL OF THEOLOGY AT CLAREMONT - CENTER FOR PROCESS STUDIES
See: Center for Process Studies (2859)

★12973★
SCHOOL OF THEOLOGY AT CLAREMONT - THEOLOGY LIBRARY (Rel-Phil)
1325 N. College Ave. Phone: (714)626-3521
Claremont, CA 91711 Michael P. Boddy, Dir.
Founded: 1968. **Staff:** Prof 4; Other 2. **Subjects:** Bible, Ancient Near East, church history, theology, ethics, pastoral care, homiletics. **Special Collections:** Methodistica; Kirby Page Manuscripts (8 VF drawers); Bishop James C. Baker Manuscripts; archives for the California Pacific Conference and the Desert Southwest Conference of the United Methodist Church. **Holdings:** 143,681 books; 18,259 bound periodical volumes; 2635 microforms; 48 audio cassettes; dissertations; manuscripts. **Subscriptions:** 635 journals and other serials. **Services:** Interlibrary loan; copying; library open to the public with proper identification. **Automated Operations:** Computerized cataloging. **Computerized Information Services:** OCLC. **Staff:** Jean Cobb, Ref.Libn.; Elsie Freudenberger, Cat.Libn.; Elaine Walker, Circ.Libn..

★12974★
SCHOOL OF VISUAL ARTS - LIBRARY (Art)
209 E. 23rd St. Phone: (212)679-7350
New York, NY 10010 Zuki Landau, Chf.Libn.
Founded: 1961. **Staff:** Prof 4; Other 2. **Subjects:** Fine arts, graphic arts, advertising, photography, film, humanities. **Holdings:** 55,000 books and bound periodical volumes; 900 pamphlets; 47 VF drawers of pictures; 400 mounted reproductions; 82,000 slides. **Subscriptions:** 200 journals and other serials. **Services:** Copying; library open to staff, faculty, students, and alumni. **Networks/Consortia:** Member of New York Metropolitan Reference and Research Library Agency (METRO). **Publications:** Accessions lists, monthly - to staff and students. **Staff:** William Buckley, Slide Cur.; Robert Lobe, Asst.Libn..

★12975★
SCHOOLCRAFT COLLEGE - WOMEN'S RESOURCE CENTER (Soc Sci)
18600 Haggerty Rd. Phone: (313)591-6400
Livonia, MI 48152 Virginia Wilhelm, Dir.
Founded: 1975. **Staff:** Prof 3; Other 2. **Subjects:** Women and single parents - career information, education, employment, counseling, health. **Holdings:** 500 books; 1000 newsletters, pamphlets, government publications, research reports, reprints; 6 VF drawers. **Subscriptions:** 18 journals and other serials. **Services:** Copying; center open to the public for reference use only. **Publications:** Reprints, irregular; Newsletter, quarterly - free upon request.

★12976★
SCHOOLS OF THEOLOGY IN DUBUQUE - LIBRARIES (Rel-Phil)
2000 University Phone: (319)589-3215
Dubuque, IA 52001 Duncan Brockway, Dir. of Libs.
Staff: Prof 6; Other 4. **Subjects:** Theology, missions, ecumenical studies. **Special Collections:** Hymnals; Lutheran irenics and polemics. **Holdings:** 222,256 volumes. **Subscriptions:** 800 journals and other serials; 10 newspapers. **Services:** Interlibrary loan; copying; library open to the public. **Automated Operations:** Computerized cataloging, serials, and circulation. **Computerized Information Services:** OCLC, DIALOG Information Services, BRS Information Technologies. Performs searches free of charge. **Publications:** STD Library Bulletin, monthly - for internal distribution only. **Remarks:** Includes the holdings of the Couchman Memorial Library located at 2050 University Ave. and the Reu Memorial Library located at 333 Wartburg Place. An alternate telephone number is 589-0265. **Staff:** Vera L. Robinson, Cat.; Mary Anne Knefel, Ref.Libn.; Debbie Fliegel, Ref.Libn.; Carolynne Lathrop, Ref.Libn..

★12977★
SCHREIBER FOODS, INC. - LIBRARY (Food-Bev)
Box 19010
Green Bay, WI 54307-9010 Phone: (414)437-7601
Founded: 1977. **Staff:** Prof 1. **Subjects:** Cheese, food industry. **Holdings:** 1200 books; 200 bound periodical volumes; government documents. **Subscriptions:** 315 journals and other serials. **Services:** Library not open to the public. **Computerized Information Services:** DIALOG Information Services.

★12978★
IBJ SCHRODER BANK & TRUST COMPANY - LIBRARY (Bus-Fin)
One State St., 8th Fl. Phone: (212)269-6500
New York, NY 10004 Mary Montalto, Libn.
Founded: 1930. **Staff:** 2. **Subjects:** Banking, investments, international finance, economic and business conditions, international trade, corporate records. **Special Collections:** Foreign bank letters. **Holdings:** 200 books. **Subscriptions:** 450 journals and other serials. **Services:** Interlibrary loan; library not open to the public.

WALTER SCHROEDER LIBRARY
See: Milwaukee School of Engineering (9019)

SCHUBERT HALL LIBRARY
See: California Historical Society - Schubert Hall Library (2137)

ANDREW S. SCHULER EDUCATIONAL RESOURCES CENTER
See: Clarkson University (3274)

★12979★
SCHUMANN MEMORIAL FOUNDATION, INC. - LIBRARY
2904 E. Lake Rd.
Livonia, NY 14487
Subjects: Music marked for performance by outstanding performers of past years; musicology; music therapy. **Special Collections:** Dickinson collection of Schumann memorabilia. **Holdings:** 3000 books; 7000 items of sheet music and opera scores; music manuscripts. **Remarks:** Presently inactive.

★12980★
SCHUMPERT MEDICAL CENTER - MEDICAL LIBRARY (Med)
915 Margaret Place
Box 21976 Phone: (318)227-4501
Shreveport, LA 71120-1976 Marilyn Willis, Med.Libn.
Staff: Prof 1. **Subjects:** Medicine, surgery, and allied health sciences. **Holdings:** 1200 books; 3400 bound periodical volumes. **Subscriptions:** 205 journals and other serials. **Services:** Interlibrary loan; library not open to the public. **Computerized Information Services:** MEDLINE. **Remarks:** Hospital network also includes Pathology, Radiology, and Anesthesiology Libraries.

★12981★
SCHUYLER COUNTY HISTORICAL SOCIETY - RESEARCH LIBRARY (Hist)
108 N. Catharine St.
Box 651 Phone: (607)535-9741
Montour Falls, NY 14891 Belva Dickinson, Musm.Dir.
Founded: 1960. **Staff:** 1. **Subjects:** Schuyler County history and genealogy. **Special Collections:** Larroka and Seneca Indian artifacts (300 times); period toys and clothing (700 items); paintings by Talitha Botsford (22). **Holdings:** 5000 books; 220 bound periodical volumes; 3000 cemetery records; 5000 clippings; 100 manuscripts; 20 maps. **Services:** Copying; library open to the public with restrictions. **Special Catalogs:** Newspaper, scrapbook, and photograph catalogs. **Special Indexes:** Index to Schuyler County Historical Society Journal. **Staff:** Barbara H. Bell, Hist..

★12982★
SCHUYLER TECHNICAL LIBRARY (Sci-Engr)
615 Brandywine Dr. Phone: (804)877-5860
Newport News, VA 23602 Gilbert S. Bahn, Hd.
Founded: 1952. **Subjects:** Chemical thermodynamics, combustion processes, chemical kinetics, analysis of digital imagery. **Special Collections:** Private technical papers of Gilbert S. Bahn. **Holdings:** Figures not available. **Services:** Library not open to the public. **Remarks:** Most of the library's holdings are now located at the University of Virginia, on permanent loan.

★12983★
SCHUYLKILL COUNTY LAW LIBRARY (Law)
Court House Phone: (717)622-5570
Pottsville, PA 17901 Patricia G. Kellet, Law Libn.
Staff: Prof 1. **Subjects:** Law. **Holdings:** 24,000 volumes; 1500 ultrafiche. **Subscriptions:** 25 journals and other serials. **Services:** Copying; library open to the public for reference use only.

★12984★
SCHUYLKILL VALLEY NATURE CENTER - LIBRARY (Biol Sci, Env-Cons)
8480 Hagy's Mill Rd. Phone: (215)482-7300
Philadelphia, PA 19128 Karin James, Libn.
Founded: 1965. **Staff:** 1. **Subjects:** Natural history, zoology, ornithology, botany, ecology, geology/mineralogy, environmental concerns, astronomy, weather, gardening. **Special Collections:** Rare books on the natural sciences (100 volumes); environmental science teaching resource center (2700 books). **Holdings:** 6000 books; 8 VF drawers of clippings and leaflets; 3 VF drawers of nature center brochures; 3 VF drawers of descriptive material of environmental organizations and newsletters. **Subscriptions:** 42 journals and other serials. **Services:** Library open to the public for reference use only. **Publications:** The Spider's Web (calendar of events), annual - to members and for sale; The Quill (newsletter), 4/year; brochures of courses and workshops - both sent to members and others on request.

ARNOLD & MARIE SCHWARTZ COLLEGE OF PHARMACY & HEALTH SCIENCES
See: Long Island University (7956)

ARNOLD & MARIE SCHWARTZ LIBRARY
See: Temple Beth-El of Great Neck (13941)

CHARLES AND BERTIE G. SCHWARTZ JUDAICA READING ROOM & LIBRARY
See: American Jewish Congress (572)

★12985★
J. & H. SCHWARTZ TECHNICAL INFORMATION CENTER - LIBRARY (Sci-Engr)
161 Rosenhayn Ave.
Upper Deerfield Township
Bridgeton, NJ 08302-1241 Phone: (609)455-4393
Founded: 1964. **Staff:** Prof 2. **Subjects:** Space technology, chemistry, physics, biochemistry, drafting, German and Dutch languages, astronomy, astrophysics, pesticides, medicine, biology. **Special Collections:** Books by Carl Sagan and Isaac Asimov (complete sets); chemical collection; Abrams Planetarium sky calendar. **Holdings:** 250 books; 200 bound periodical volumes; 250 U.S. patents. **Services:** Copying; translation; library open to the public with restrictions on fee basis. **Staff:** Dr. Herbert Schwartz, Libn., Res.Coord; Johanna Schwartz, Libn., Res.Coord..

JOSEPH & ELIZABETH SCHWARTZ LIBRARY
See: Beth Sholom Congregation (1551)

★12986★
SCHWARTZ, KELM, WARREN & RUBENSTEIN - LAW LIBRARY (Law)
41 S. High St., Suite 2300 Phone: (614)224-3168
Columbus, OH 43215 Mary Grace Hune, Coord. of Info.Serv.
Staff: 2. **Subjects:** Securities, taxation, general litigation. **Holdings:** 8500 books; 7 drawers of microfiche. **Subscriptions:** 70 journals and other serials; 7 newspapers. **Services:** Library not open to the public. **Computerized Information Services:** LEXIS, NEXIS, DIALOG Information Services, Dow Jones News/Retrieval, VU/TEXT Information Services, WESTLAW.

MARIE SMITH SCHWARTZ MEDICAL LIBRARY
See: Brookdale Hospital Medical Center (1920)

RABBI A.N. SCHWARTZ LIBRARY
See: Telshe Yeshiva - Rabbi A.N. Schwartz Library (13932)

SAUL SCHWARTZBACH MEMORIAL LIBRARY
See: Prince George's Hospital Center (11567)

ERNST SCHWARZ LIBRARY
See: Zoological Society of San Diego - Ernst Schwarz Library (18252)

★12987★
SCHWENKFELDER LIBRARY (Rel-Phil)
Pennsburg, PA 18073 Phone: (215)679-3103
Dennis K. Moyer, Dir.
Founded: 1946. **Staff:** Prof 1; Other 2. **Subjects:** Schwenkfelder Church history, history of Perkiomen Valley, history of Protestant Reformation in Silesia. **Special Collections:** Writings of Caspar von Schwenkfeld. **Holdings:** 30,000 volumes. **Subscriptions:** 10 journals and other serials. **Services:** Interlibrary loan; copying; library open to the public.

SIMON SCHWOB MEDICAL LIBRARY
See: Medical Center (8605)

★12988★
SCIENCE APPLICATIONS INTERNATIONAL CORPORATION - FOREIGN SYSTEMS RESEARCH CENTER - LIBRARY (Mil, Soc Sci)
6021 S. Syracuse Way, Suite 300 Phone: (303)773-6900
Greenwood Village, CO 80111 Jennifer Doran, Mgr.
Founded: 1979. **Staff:** Prof 2; Other 4. **Subjects:** Military science, international relations, political science, economics. **Special Collections:** Translations and Soviet Union source materials (8000 books; 14,000 journals). **Holdings:** 13,000 books; 23,000 journal issues. **Subscriptions:** 125 journals and other serials; 6 newspapers. **Services:** Library open to government and scholastic researchers with approval. **Computerized Information Services:** FILMS (internal database). **Publications:** Monthly newsletter.

★12989★
SCIENCE APPLICATIONS INTERNATIONAL CORPORATION - SAIC/REQUIREMENTS ANALYSIS DIVISION LIBRARY
803 W. Broad St., Suite 100
Falls Church, VA 22046-3199
Founded: 1986. 2. **Subjects:** Military science, systems acquisition and management, remote sensing, image processing, data processing, telecommunications. **Holdings:** 700 books; 32 bound periodical volumes; 12 videotapes; 85 computer programs; 325 microfiche; 450 unbound technical reports; 300 graphs; 200 items of graphic artwork; 400 navigation charts; 50 computer printouts. **Remarks:** Presently inactive.

★12990★
SCIENCE ASSOCIATES/INTERNATIONAL, INC. - LIBRARY (Publ, Info Sci)
1841 Broadway Phone: (212)265-4995
New York, NY 10023 Roxy Bauer, Libn.
Staff: Prof 4; Other 1. **Subjects:** Information science, library science, documentation, publishing, computer science. **Holdings:** 2500 books; 1000 library and information science reports; 200 newsletters. **Subscriptions:** 200 journals and other serials. **Services:** Library not open to the public.

SCIENCE COUNCIL OF CANADA
See: Canada - Science Council of Canada (2481)

★12991★
SCIENCE MUSEUM OF MINNESOTA - LOUIS S. HEADLEY MEMORIAL LIBRARY (Biol Sci, Sci-Engr)
30 E. 10th St. Phone: (612)221-9488
St. Paul, MN 55101 Mary S. Finlayson, Libn.
Founded: 1907. **Staff:** Prof 1. **Subjects:** Geology, anthropology, biology, archeology, paleontology, botany, technology. **Holdings:** 20,000 books; 439 bound periodical volumes; 2437 U.S. Geological Survey publications; International Catalog, 1903-1919; Zoological Record, 1915 to present; 9 VF drawers of pamphlets; 208 file boxes of museum publications. **Subscriptions:** 150 journals and other serials. **Services:** Interlibrary loan; copying; library open to the public by special request.

★12992★
THE SCIENCE PLACE - LIBRARY (Sci-Engr)
Fair Park, Box 11158
Dallas, TX 75223 Phone: (214)428-7200
Founded: 1961. **Subjects:** Health, astronomy, medicine, earth sciences, astronautics, sex education, natural science. **Holdings:** 1600 books and bound periodical volumes. **Remarks:** The official name is the Southwest Museum of Science and Technology. The Science Place is supported in part by funds from the Dallas Park and Recreation Department - Division of Cultural Affairs.

★12993★
SCIENCE SERVICE, INC. - LIBRARY (Sci-Engr, Med)
1719 N St., N.W. Phone: (202)785-2255
Washington, DC 20036 Jane M. Livermore, Libn.
Staff: Prof 1. **Subjects:** Science, medicine, technology. **Holdings:** 3600 books; 1500 unbound periodicals. **Subscriptions:** 246 journals and other serials. **Services:** Interlibrary loan; copying; library open to the public with restrictions.

★12994★
SCIENCE TRENDS - LIBRARY (Sci-Engr)
National Press Bldg., Suite 1079 Phone: (202)393-0031
Washington, DC 20045 Arthur Kranish, Hd.
Founded: 1958. **Subjects:** Government sponsored research and development, science, energy, environment. **Holdings:** Figures not available. **Services:** Maintains information and documents relating to government sponsorship of research and development; subscription includes inquiry service without additional charge. **Publications:** Science Trends, weekly, monthly in July and August - by subscription; Energy Today, monthly; Environment Report, semimonthly; Scientific Information Notes, quarterly. **Also Known As:** Trends Publishing, Inc.

★12995★
SCIENTIFIC-ATLANTA, INC. - LIBRARY (Sci-Engr)
3845 Pleasantdale Rd. Phone: (404)449-2000
Atlanta, GA 30340 Jaki Cone, Libn.
Founded: 1965. **Staff:** Prof 1. **Subjects:** Antennas, electronic engineering, mechanical engineering, telecommunications. **Holdings:** 4000 books; 450 bound periodical volumes; 2700 documents and technical reports; manufacturers' catalogs on microfilm; 450 microfiche of technical reports. **Subscriptions:** 230 journals and other serials. **Services:** Interlibrary loan; library not open to the public. **Publications:** Acquisitions Bulletin, every 3 weeks - for internal distribution only.

★12996★
SCITUATE HISTORICAL SOCIETY - LIBRARY (Hist)
43 Cudworth Rd.
Scituate, MA 02066 Dorothy B. Wood, Libn.
Staff: Prof 1. **Subjects:** Local history, genealogy. **Holdings:** 600 books. **Services:** Library open to the public. **Publications:** Bulletin, semiannual - to members.

★12997★
SCM CHEMICALS - LIBRARY (Sci-Engr)
3901 Glidden Rd. Phone: (301)355-3600
Baltimore, MD 21226 Nancy Freeman, Libn.
Founded: 1944. **Staff:** Prof 1; Other 1. **Subjects:** Chemistry - inorganic, physical, analytical; ceramics; inorganic pigments; paint; paper; colors; rubbers; plastics; enamels. **Holdings:** 4000 books and bound periodical volumes; U.S. and foreign patents; reprints; clippings; pamphlets; reports. **Subscriptions:** 135 journals and other serials; 10 newspapers. **Services:** Interlibrary loan; copying; library open to the public with prior approval. **Computerized Information Services:** Pergamon ORBIT InfoLine, Inc., DIALOG Information Services, STN International. **Publications:** Resource Update, bimonthly - for internal distribution only. **Remarks:** SCM Chemicals is a division of Hanson Industries. **Formerly:** SCM Corporation - Pigments Division.

SCM CORPORATION - ORGANIC CHEMICALS DIVISION
See: SCM Glidco Organics (12998)

SCM CORPORATION - PIGMENTS DIVISION
See: SCM Chemicals (12997)

★12998★
SCM GLIDCO ORGANICS - TECHNICAL LIBRARY
Box 389
Jacksonville, FL 32201
Founded: 1958. **Subjects:** Organic and analytical chemistry, chemical engineering, flavor and fragrance chemicals, polymers, marketing. **Special Collections:** Catalysis; terpene chemicals; fatty acids. **Holdings:** 5730 books; 5000 bound periodical volumes; 5500 patents; 2050 technical reports; 201,000 abstracts on cards; chemical abstracts on microfilm. **Remarks:** Presently inactive. **Formerly:** SCM Corporation - Organic Chemicals Division.

SCOBIE MEMORIAL LIBRARY
See: Riverside Hospital (12076)

C.I. SCOFIELD LIBRARY OF BIBLICAL STUDIES
See: Philadelphia College of Bible - Library (11269)

SCOTCH-IRISH FOUNDATION LIBRARY AND ARCHIVES
See: Balch Institute for Ethnic Studies (1248)

★12999★
SCOTT COUNTY BAR ASSOCIATION - GRANT LAW LIBRARY (Law)
416 W. 4th St. Phone: (319)326-8741
Davenport, IA 52801 Ginger F. Wolfe, Libn.
Staff: 1. **Subjects:** Law. **Special Collections:** Iowa Supreme Court records and briefs. **Holdings:** 10,000 volumes. **Services:** Library open to lawyers and judges; open to the public on a limited schedule. **Computerized Information Services:** WESTLAW.

★13000★
SCOTT, FORESMAN & COMPANY, INC. - EDITORIAL LIBRARY (Publ, Educ)
1900 E. Lake Ave. Phone: (312)729-3000
Glenview, IL 60025 S. Donald Robertson, Hd.Libn.
Staff: Prof 2; Other 1. **Subjects:** Education, children's literature, study and teaching of reading. **Special Collections:** Company publications. **Holdings:** 40,000 books; 3500 bound periodical volumes; 200 phonograph records; 2500 reels of microfilm of periodicals; 8 VF drawers of publishers' catalogs. **Subscriptions:** 400 journals and other serials; 5 newspapers. **Services:** Interlibrary loan; copying; library open to the public for reference use only. **Networks/Consortia:** Member of North Suburban Library System (NSLS). **Publications:** List of Recent Additions, bimonthly. **Staff:** Jane F. Harris, Asst.Libn..

HARVEY SCOTT MEMORIAL LIBRARY
See: Pacific University (11021)

★13001★
SCOTT, HULSE, MARSHALL, FEUILLE, FINGER & THURMOND - LIBRARY (Law)
Texas Commerce Bank Bldg., 11th Fl. Phone: (512)533-2493
El Paso, TX 79901 Brenda D. McDonald, Libn.
Staff: Prof 1; Other 1. **Subjects:** Law. **Special Collections:** Firm correspondence and docket books, 1897-1946. **Holdings:** 15,000 books; 500 bound periodical volumes. **Subscriptions:** 403 journals and other serials. **Services:** Interlibrary loan (limited); copying; SDI; library open to the public by appointment. **Automated Operations:** Computerized cataloging. **Computerized Information Services:** DIALOG Information Services, Information America, LEXIS. Performs searches on fee basis. **Publications:** Acquisitions list, monthly - for internal distribution only. **Special Catalogs:** Expert witness deposition file (online); brief and memorandum file (card).

JOHN W. SCOTT HEALTH SCIENCES LIBRARY
See: University of Alberta (15803)

SCOTT MEMORIAL LIBRARY
See: Thomas Jefferson University (7181)

★13002★
O.M. SCOTT AND SONS - INFORMATION SERVICES (Biol Sci, Sci-Engr)
Dwight G. Scott Research Center Phone: (513)644-0011
Marysville, OH 43041 Betty Seitz, Supv., Info.Serv.
Staff: 1. **Subjects:** Horticulture, botany, chemistry, business. **Special Collections:** Lawn Care magazine (15 volumes). **Holdings:** 5100 books; 275 bound periodical volumes; 15 VF drawers of research reports. **Subscriptions:** 150 journals and other serials. **Services:** Services open to the public with prior arrangement. **Computerized Information Services:** Online systems.

★13003★
SCOTT PAPER COMPANY - INFORMATION RESOURCE CENTER (Bus-Fin)
Scott Plaza Phone: (215)522-6262
Philadelphia, PA 19113 Eva K. Butler, Mgr.
Founded: 1960. **Staff:** Prof 1; Other 1. **Subjects:** Paper industry, statistics, marketing, marketing research, management. **Holdings:** 2350 books; 97 bound periodical volumes; 45 VF drawers of pamphlets; 8 drawers of microfiche; 30 VF drawers of internal research reports. **Subscriptions:** 123 journals and other serials. **Services:** Interlibrary loan; center open to the public for reference use only on request. **Computerized Information Services:** DIALOG Information Services. **Publications:** Magazine article highlights, monthly; acquisitions bulletin, monthly - both for internal distribution only.

★13004★
SCOTT PAPER COMPANY - S.D. WARREN COMPANY - RESEARCH LIBRARY (Sci-Engr)
Research Laboratory Phone: (207)856-6911
Westbrook, ME 04092 Deborah G. Chandler, Info.Spec.
Staff: Prof 1; Other 2. **Subjects:** Papermaking, printing, chemistry, physics, engineering. **Holdings:** 3500 books; 1000 bound periodical volumes; 20 VF drawers of U.S. and foreign patents. **Subscriptions:** 150 journals and other serials. **Services:** Copying (limited); library open to the public with prior permission. **Computerized Information Services:** DIALOG Information Services, STN International.

★13005★
SCOTT PAPER COMPANY - TECHNOLOGY LIBRARY & TECHNICAL INFORMATION SERVICE (Sci-Engr)
Scott Plaza 3
Philadelphia, PA 19113 George Burna, Mgr.
Founded: 1958. **Staff:** Prof 2; Other 2. **Subjects:** Pulp and paper, chemistry, engineering, physics, textiles, management. **Holdings:** 10,000 volumes; 150,000 patents; internal research reports; microfilm; dissertations. **Subscriptions:** 300 journals and other serials. **Services:** Interlibrary loan; copying; library open to the public for reference use only on request. **Computerized Information Services:** DIALOG Information Services, CAS ONLINE, Pergamon ORBIT InfoLine, Inc. **Publications:** Biweekly bulletin listing recent acquisitions - for internal distribution only. **Staff:** Cheryl R. Stickle, Libn..

★13006★
SCOTT & WHITE MEMORIAL HOSPITAL - RICHARD D. HAINES MEDICAL LIBRARY (Med)
2401 S. 31st St. Phone: (817)774-2228
Temple, TX 76508 Penny Worley, Dir.
Founded: 1897. **Staff:** Prof 3; Other 8. **Subjects:** Clinical medicine, nursing care and education, allied health sciences. **Holdings:** 8600 books; 22,600 bound periodical volumes. **Subscriptions:** 875 journals and other serials. **Services:** Interlibrary loan; copying; library open to medical, nursing, and allied health personnel. **Automated Operations:** Computerized cataloging and serials. **Computerized Information Services:** DIALOG Information Services, MEDLARS, BRS Information Technologies; internal database. Performs searches on fee basis. Contact Person: Leta Dannelley, Pub.Serv.Libn., 774-2230. **Networks/Consortia:** Member of TALON, TAMU Consortium of Medical Libraries, AMIGOS Bibliographic Council, Inc.. **Publications:** List of Acquisitions.

WILLIAM A. SCOTT BUSINESS LIBRARY
See: University of Wisconsin, Madison (17160)

SCOTTISH RESEARCH LIBRARY
See: American-Scottish Foundation, Inc. (656)

★13007★
SCOTTISH RITE BODIES, SAN DIEGO - SCOTTISH RITE MASONIC LIBRARY (Rec)
1895 Camino Del Rio Phone: (714)297-0395
San Diego, CA 92108 Alfred D. Sawyer, Chm., Lib.Comm.
Founded: 1974. **Staff:** 15. **Subjects:** Masonic literature and history. **Special Collections:** New Age Magazine, 1904 to present; Quatuor Coronati Research Lodge, London, England, 1880 to present. **Holdings:** 4000 books; 200 bound periodical volumes; video and audio cassette tapes. **Subscriptions:** 20 journals and other serials. **Services:** Interlibrary loan (limited); copying; library open to the public with restrictions on borrowing. **Publications:** Library Newsletter, monthly - for internal distribution only.

★13008★
SCOTTISH RITE SUPREME COUNCIL - LIBRARY (Hist, Rec)
1733 Sixteenth St., N.W. Phone: (202)232-3579
Washington, DC 20009 Inge Baum, Libn.
Founded: 1888. **Staff:** Prof 1. **Subjects:** Freemasonry and all its aspects, American history, biography, philosophy, religion. **Special Collections:** Claudy Collection (Goethe); Louis D. Carman Collection (Lincolniana); William R. Smith Collection (Burnsiana); Albert Pike Collection; Maurice H. Thatcher Collection (Panama Canal). **Holdings:** 175,000 books and bound periodical volumes; 50 cases of Masonic patents, documents, clippings; manuscripts; prints; photographs; microfilm. **Subscriptions:** 175 journals and other serials. **Services:** Interlibrary loan; copying; library open to the public. **Publications:** Dynamic Freedoms Series; The New Age Magazine, monthly.

SCOTTS BLUFF NATIONAL MONUMENT
See: U.S. Natl. Park Service (15350)

★13009★
SCOTTSDALE MEMORIAL HOSPITAL - DR. ROBERT C. FOREMAN HEALTH SCIENCES LIBRARY (Med)
7400 E. Osborn Rd. Phone: (602)481-4870
Scottsdale, AZ 85251 Marihelen O'Connor, Med.Libn.
Founded: 1968. **Staff:** Prof 1; Other 4. **Subjects:** Family practice, medicine, surgery, pediatrics, cardiology, orthopedics, radiology, nursing. **Holdings:** 2000 books; 5000 bound periodical volumes; 40 VF items; videotapes. **Subscriptions:** 200 journals and other serials. **Services:** Interlibrary loan; library not open to the public. **Computerized Information Services:** DIALOG Information Services, BRS Information Technologies, WILSONLINE, MEDLINE; OnTyme Electronic Message Network Service (electronic mail service).

★13010★
SCRANTONIAN TRIBUNE - LIBRARY (Publ)
338 N. Washington Ave. Phone: (717)344-7221
Scranton, PA 18503 Hal Lewis, Exec.Ed.
Staff: Prof 1. **Subjects:** Newspaper reference topics. **Holdings:** 500 books. **Services:** Copying; library open to the public with restrictions. **Formerly:** Scranton Tribune and Scrantonian.

★13011★
SCRIPPS CLINIC & RESEARCH FOUNDATION - KRESGE MEDICAL LIBRARY (Med)
10666 N. Torrey Pines Rd. Phone: (714)455-8705
La Jolla, CA 92037 Jesse G. Neely, Med.Libn.
Staff: 3. **Subjects:** Immunology, medicine, molecular and cellular biology, biochemistry, psychiatry. **Holdings:** 4369 books; 33,895 bound periodical volumes. **Subscriptions:** 545 journals and other serials. **Services:** Interlibrary loan; copying; library open to the public for reference use only on request. **Computerized Information Services:** MEDLINE, DIALOG Information Services.

E.W. SCRIPPS CO. - CINCINNATI POST
See: Cincinnati Post (3210)

SCRIPPS HOWARD PUBLISHING COMPANY - THE COMMERCIAL APPEAL
See: The Commercial Appeal (3522)

SCRIPPS INSTITUTION OF OCEANOGRAPHY LIBRARY
See: University of California, San Diego (16008)

WILLIAM E. SCRIPTURE MEMORIAL LIBRARY
See: Rome Historical Society (12179)

★13012★
SCUDDER, STEVENS & CLARK - LIBRARY (Bus-Fin)
175 Federal St. Phone: (617)482-3990
Boston, MA 02110 Helen Doikos, Libn.
Staff: Prof 1. **Subjects:** Investments. **Holdings:** 1750 volumes; 135 drawers of 10K reports, clippings, and pamphlets; microfilm. **Subscriptions:** 200 journals and other serials. **Services:** Interlibrary loan; library not open to the public. **Computerized Information Services:** COMPUSTAT Services, Inc. (C/S), Interactive Data Services, Inc., Data Resources (DRI), FactSet Data Systems, Inc., Wharton Econometric Forecasting Associates, Inc.

★13013★
SCUDDER, STEVENS & CLARK - LIBRARY (Sci-Engr)
345 Park Ave. Phone: (212)326-6200
New York, NY 10154 Linda Osborne
Founded: 1926. **Staff:** Prof 2. **Subjects:** Cosmetics, pharmaceuticals, health supplies and services, nonferrous metals, chemicals, general economics, petroleum, gas utilities, construction, paper, forest products, automobiles, steel, railroads, home and leisure. **Holdings:** 2000 books; 300 VF drawers. **Services:** Interlibrary loan; copying; library open to clients and other financial librarians.

SEA LAMPREY CONTROL CENTRE
See: Canada - Fisheries & Oceans - Central & Arctic Region (2381)

★13014★
SEA VIEW HOSPITAL AND HOME - MEDICAL LIBRARY (Med)
460 Brielle Ave. Phone: (718)390-8689
Staten Island, NY 10314 Selma Amtzis, Dept.Sr.Libn.
Founded: 1932. **Staff:** Prof 1; Other 1. **Subjects:** Medicine, nursing, geriatrics, hospital administration. **Holdings:** 3000 books; 4160 bound periodical volumes. **Subscriptions:** 150 journals and other serials. **Services:** Interlibrary loan; copying; library open to the public for reference use only. **Computerized Information Services:** NLM. Performs searches on fee basis. **Networks/Consortia:** Member of Brooklyn-Queens-Staten Island Health Sciences Librarians (BQSI).

★13015★
SEA WORLD, INC. - EDUCATION DEPARTMENT LIBRARY (Biol Sci)
1720 S. Shores Rd. Phone: (619)222-6363
San Diego, CA 92109 Sandra De La Garza, Dir., Educ.Dept.
Founded: 1973. **Staff:** Prof 10. **Subjects:** Marine biology. **Holdings:** 2000 books; 1000 periodicals, scientific and government reports. **Subscriptions:** 15 journals and other serials. **Services:** Library open to the public for reference use only. **Publications:** Information sheets on marine mammals and curriculum guides on marine life for teachers. **Remarks:** Maintained by Harcourt Brace Jovanovich, Inc. **Staff:** Ruth A. Musgrave, Libn..

★13016★
SEA WORLD RESEARCH INSTITUTE - HUBBS MARINE RESEARCH CENTER (Biol Sci)
1700 S. Shores Rd. Phone: (619)226-3870
San Diego, CA 92109 Suzanne I. Bond, Res.Asst.
Founded: 1978. **Staff:** 1. **Subjects:** Marine mammals, acoustics, aquatic animal behavior, population biology, mariculture. **Holdings:** 500 books; 50 bound periodical volumes. **Subscriptions:** 30 journals and other serials. **Services:** Copying; center open to the public for reference use only. **Publications:** Currents, 4/year - free upon request.

★13017★
SEABOARD COAST LINE RAILROAD COMPANY - LAW LIBRARY (Law)
500 Water St., Rm. 1523
Jacksonville, FL 32202 Phone: (904)353-2011
Subjects: Law. **Holdings:** 10,000 volumes.

SEABURN AND ROBERTSON, INC.
See: Law Environmental, Inc. (7691)

SEABURY MC COY LIBRARY
See: Los Angeles College of Chiropractic (7983)

SEABURY-WESTERN THEOLOGICAL SEMINARY
See: United Library of Garrett-Evangelical and Seabury-Western Theological Seminaries (14545)

★13018★
JOSEPH E. SEAGRAM & SONS, INC. - CORPORATE LIBRARY (Food-Bev)
800 Third Ave. Phone: (212)572-7873
New York, NY 10022 Alice Gross, Mgr., Lib.Serv.
Founded: 1973. **Staff:** Prof 3; Other 3. **Subjects:** Distilled spirits and wine, corporate finance, statistics. **Holdings:** 500 books; 200 newsletters; microfiche. **Subscriptions:** 300 journals and other serials; 75 newspapers. **Services:** Interlibrary loan; library not open to the public. **Automated Operations:** Computerized serials. **Computerized Information Services:** DIALOG Information Services, NEXIS. Performs searches on fee basis. **Special Catalogs:** Library union catalog.

★13019★
SEAGRAM MUSEUM LIBRARY (Food-Bev)
57 Erb St., W. Phone: (519)885-1857
Waterloo, ON, Canada N2L 6C2 Sandra Lowman, Archv./Libn.
Founded: 1970. **Staff:** Prof 2. **Subjects:** Beverage alcohol industry; wine, beer, and spirits; alcoholism; prohibition; cooperage; copper-smithing; cork production; glassmaking; decorative arts. **Special Collections:** Label and Advertising Collections, 1880 to present (100,000 labels; 6000 advertisements); Photograph, Slide and Film Library (industry and company activities; 25,000 items); Packaging and Bottle Library (5000 items, 1880s to present); Alfred Fromm Rare Wine Books Library; fine art collection (drawings and engravings related to the history of beverage alcohol). **Holdings:** 6000 books (in 7 languages); 100 bound periodical volumes; 1200 company reports and industry booklets. **Subscriptions:** 50 journals. **Services:** Interlibrary loan; copying; library open to the public by appointment. **Automated Operations:** Computerized cataloging. **Staff:** Don Spencer, Coll.Mgr..

ALVIN SEALE SOUTH SEAS COLLECTION
See: Pacific Grove Public Library (11009)

A.E. SEAMAN MINERALOGICAL MUSEUM
See: Michigan Technological University (8931)

★13020★
SEAMEN'S CHURCH INSTITUTE OF NEW YORK - CENTER FOR SEAFARERS' RIGHTS (Law)
50 Broadway Phone: (212)269-2710
New York, NY 10004 Paul Chapman, Dir.
Subjects: Seafarers' rights, laws protecting seafarers, legal and human rights. **Holdings:** Figures not available. **Services:** Center open to the public by appointment for research.

★13021★
SEAMEN'S CHURCH INSTITUTE OF NEW YORK - JOSEPH CONRAD LIBRARY
50 Broadway
New York, NY 10004
Founded: 1834. **Subjects:** Marine engineering, ship registers, maritime history, navigation, shipping, maritime law, seamanship, voyages, naval architecture. **Special Collections:** Ship pictures and photographs; SCI Archives; Untermeyer Collection of Maritime History and Fiction (300 volumes). **Holdings:** 16,000 books; 125 bound periodical volumes; 21 VF cabinets of photographs, pictures of ships and related material; Merchant Marine study guides. **Remarks:** Presently inactive.

★13022★
SEAR-BROWN ASSOCIATES, P.C. - INFORMATION CENTER (Sci-Engr)
85 Metro Park — Phone: (716)475-1440
Rochester, NY 14623 — Ulrich Bobitz, Info.Ctr.Coord.
Staff: Prof 1. **Subjects:** Civil and structural engineering, architecture, surveying, water and waste treatment, hydraulics. **Holdings:** 2800 books; 10 VF drawers of product information; 1300 manufacturers' catalogs; 4 VF drawers of planning information on local municipalities; 31 VF drawers, 27 shelves, 3 drawing files, and 210 reels of microfilm of Sear-Brown project files and drawings; 10 reels of microfilm of Rand Data for Monroe and Ontario counties. **Subscriptions:** 130 journals and other serials; 5 newspapers. **Services:** Interlibrary loan; center open to the public by appointment. **Automated Operations:** Computerized records management. **Computerized Information Services:** DIALOG Information Services; internal databases. **Networks/Consortia:** Member of Rochester Regional Library Council (RRLC). **Publications:** New From the Information Center (list of new books), bimonthly - for internal distribution only.

★13023★
SEARCH GROUP, INC. - LIBRARY (Law)
925 Secret River Dr. — Phone: (916)392-2550
Sacramento, CA 95831 — Judith Anne Ryder, Mgr., Corp.Commun.
Staff: Prof 1; Other 1. **Subjects:** Law enforcement, corrections, courts, identification, statistics. **Holdings:** 250 books; 300 technical reports; 85 unbound periodicals; state statutes on criminal history record information and victim/witness legislation. **Subscriptions:** 24 journals and other serials. **Services:** Library not open to the public. **Computerized Information Services:** Internal database. Performs searches on fee basis. Contact Person: Cheryl Moore, Res.Anl..

★13024★
G.D. SEARLE & COMPANY - RESEARCH LIBRARY (Med)
4901 Searle Pkwy. — Phone: (312)982-8285
Skokie, IL 60077 — Anthony Petrone, Mgr.
Founded: 1952. **Staff:** Prof 2; Other 2. **Subjects:** Chemistry, biology, gastroenterology, gynecology and contraception, hypertension, pharmacology. **Holdings:** 4500 books. **Subscriptions:** 1000 journals and other serials; 35 newsletters. **Services:** Interlibrary loan; SDI; library open to the public by appointment on a limited basis. **Automated Operations:** Computerized cataloging, acquisitions, serials, and circulation. **Computerized Information Services:** DIALOG Information Services, Pergamon ORBIT InfoLine, Inc., BRS Information Technologies. **Networks/Consortia:** Member of North Suburban Library System (NSLS), Center for Research Libraries (CRL) Consortia. **Publications:** Acquisitions List, monthly; Science Scan, daily - both for internal distribution only. **Staff:** M. Louise Lasworth, Ser.Supv..

★13025★
G.D. SEARLE & COMPANY OF CANADA, LIMITED - MEDICAL LIBRARY (Med)
400 Iroquois Shore Rd.
Oakville, ON, Canada L6H 1M5 — Phone: (416)844-1040
Subjects: Pharmacy and pharmacology, cardiology, gastroenterology, obstetrics and gynecology, therapeutics. **Holdings:** 900 books; 300 bound periodical volumes; 4 drawers of microfiche; 120 boxes. **Subscriptions:** 50 journals and other serials. **Services:** Interlibrary loan; library not open to the public. **Computerized Information Services:** Internal database.

SEARLS HISTORICAL LIBRARY
See: Nevada County Historical Society (9878)

CHARLES B. SEARS LAW LIBRARY
See: SUNY at Buffalo (13791)

SEARS LIBRARY
See: Case Western Reserve University (2728)

★13026★
SEARS, ROEBUCK AND CO. - ARCHIVES, BUSINESS HISTORY AND INFORMATION CENTER (Bus-Fin, Hist)
Sears Tower, Dept. 703 — Phone: (312)875-8321
Chicago, IL 60684 — Lenore Swoiskin, Archv.
Founded: 1955. **Staff:** Prof 3; Other 1. **Subjects:** Company history, retailing. **Special Collections:** Historical material covering company development, 1886 to present; biographical collection of papers of officers, directors, key personalities, Americana; catalog collection of Sears, Roebuck and Co., 1888 to present (7500 volumes). **Holdings:** 150 VF drawers of pamphlets; 36,500 photographs; 350 reels of microfilm. **Services:** Copying; research services available; center open to researchers only with approval. **Staff:** Manny Banayo, Dir. of Info.Ctr..

★13027★
SEARS, ROEBUCK AND CO. - MERCHANDISE DEVELOPMENT AND TESTING LABORATORY - LIBRARY, DEPARTMENT 817 (Sci-Engr)
Sears Tower, 23rd Fl.
Chicago, IL 60684 — Phone: (312)875-5991
Founded: 1928. **Staff:** Prof 1; Other 1. **Subjects:** Textiles, electrical and electronics engineering, design. **Holdings:** 8000 books; 60 VF drawers of government and state publications, specifications and standards of standards organizations. **Subscriptions:** 377 journals and other serials. **Services:** Interlibrary loan; library open to the public with restrictions. **Automated Operations:** Computerized serials. **Computerized Information Services:** DIALOG Information Services.

MURRAY SEASONGOOD LIBRARY
See: National Civic League, Inc. - Murray Seasongood Library (9623)

SEATON MEMORIAL LIBRARY
See: Riley County Historical Society (12063)

★13028★
SEATTLE AQUARIUM - STAFF LIBRARY (Biol Sci)
Pier 59
Waterfront Park — Phone: (206)625-4359
Seattle, WA 98101 — Richard Hocking, Aquarium Biol.
Founded: 1977. **Subjects:** Marine biology, marine animal husbandry. **Holdings:** 665 books; 101 bound periodical volumes. **Subscriptions:** 14 journals and other serials. **Services:** Library open to the public by appointment.

★13029★
SEATTLE ART MUSEUM - LIBRARY (Art)
Volunteer Park
14th E. & E. Prospect — Phone: (206)447-4686
Seattle, WA 98112 — Elizabeth De Fato, Libn.
Founded: 1933. **Staff:** Prof 1; Other 1. **Subjects:** Art, history of art, archeology. **Holdings:** 12,000 books; 4000 exhibition catalogs; 5 drawers of Northwest artists clipping files. **Subscriptions:** 50 journals and other serials. **Services:** Copying; library open to the public.

★13030★
SEATTLE-FIRST NATIONAL BANK - LIBRARY (Bus-Fin)
Box 3586 — Phone: (206)358-3292
Seattle, WA 98124 — Jeannette M. Privat, A.V.P. & Mgr.
Founded: 1968. **Staff:** Prof 2; Other 5. **Subjects:** Finance and financial institutions; investments and public corporations; economies of Washington state, United States, and other countries; small business operations. **Holdings:** 8700 books; 100 bound periodical volumes; 356 VF drawers of pamphlets; 4000 microfiche; 15,000 financial reports; 150 videotapes. **Subscriptions:** 2200 journals and other serials; 30 newspapers. **Services:** Interlibrary loan; copying; library open to the public with permission of librarian. **Automated Operations:** Computerized cataloging, acquisitions, and serials. **Computerized Information Services:** DIALOG Information Services, Pergamon ORBIT InfoLine, Inc., Dow Jones News/Retrieval, TEXTLINE, OCLC, VU/TEXT Information Services, SEC Online, DataTimes; LINX Courier (electronic mail service). **Staff:** James G. Gong, Ref.Libn..

★13031★
SEATTLE GENEALOGICAL SOCIETY - GENEALOGICAL LIBRARY (Hist)
Box 549 — Phone: (206)682-1410
Seattle, WA 98111 — Sarah T. Little, Pres.
Founded: 1967. **Subjects:** Genealogy, family history, Washington state history. **Holdings:** 3000 books; microfilm. **Subscriptions:** 200 journals and other serials. **Services:** Copying; library open to the public on fee basis.

★13032★
(Seattle) METRO LIBRARY (Trans, Env-Cons)
821 Second Ave. Phone: (206)684-1129
Seattle, WA 98104 Anne McBride, Libn.
Staff: Prof 2; Other 2. **Subjects:** Urban transportation, wastewater treatment, water quality, toxicants. **Holdings:** 7000 books and documents. **Subscriptions:** 245 journals and other serials; 20 newspapers. **Services:** Interlibrary loan; copying; library open to the public for reference use only. **Computerized Information Services:** DIALOG Information Services, OCLC, DataTimes, VU/TEXT Information Services; ALICE (internal database). **Networks/Consortia:** Member of Western Library Network (WLN). **Formerly:** Municipality of Metropolitan Seattle - Metro Library. **Staff:** Jeannette Squire, Asst.Libn..

★13033★
SEATTLE POST-INTELLIGENCER - NEWSPAPER LIBRARY (Publ)
101 Elliott West Phone: (206)448-8000
Seattle, WA 98119 Lytton Smith, Chf.Libn.
Founded: 1890. **Staff:** Prof 1; Other 3. **Subjects:** Newspaper reference topics. **Holdings:** 700 books; news photographs; index files; pamphlets; Post-Intelligencer, 1876 to present, on microfilm. **Services:** Library not open to the public. **Computerized Information Services:** VU/TEXT Information Services; internal database.

★13034★
SEATTLE PUBLIC LIBRARY - ART AND MUSIC DEPARTMENT (Art, Mus)
1000 Fourth Ave. Phone: (206)386-4636
Seattle, WA 98104 Charles P. Coldwell, Mng.Libn.
Staff: Prof 9; Other 9. **Subjects:** Art, music literature, architecture, music scores, flower and ornamental gardening, dance. **Special Collections:** Scrapbooks containing information on Northwest artists (30,723 items); photographs of Seattle and the Northwest (29,484). **Holdings:** 107,108 books; 10,000 bound periodical volumes; 26,071 pictures; 33,738 pieces of sheet music; 35,854 phonograph records; 681,722 clippings. **Subscriptions:** 570 journals and other serials. **Services:** Interlibrary loan; copying; department open to the public. **Computerized Information Services:** DIALOG Information Services, Pergamon ORBIT InfoLine, Inc. **Networks/Consortia:** Member of Western Library Network (WLN). **Special Indexes:** Song Titles Index; premieres index; program notes index (all on cards).

★13035★
SEATTLE PUBLIC LIBRARY - BUSINESS AND SCIENCE DEPARTMENT (Sci-Engr, Bus-Fin)
1000 Fourth Ave. Phone: (206)386-4645
Seattle, WA 98104 Jean Coberly, Mng.Libn.
Founded: 1978. **Staff:** Prof 13; Other 9. **Subjects:** Local marketing and employment, motor vehicle repair, investments, skilled trades, domestic science, history of aviation. **Special Collections:** Aeronautics collection (12,000 books; 76 periodicals); Washington Companies File (268 drawers of cards; 2500 microfiche of clippings); Pacific Northwest historical telephone and city directory collection (1450 volumes); Ornithology Collection (500 volumes); Clock and Watch Repair Collection (107 volumes); Automotive Repair Collection (30,000 volumes). **Holdings:** 250,000 books; 80 VF drawers of pamphlets, directories, clippings, annual reports; 28 VF drawers of standards and specifications; federal document depository (state, local, and foreign document holdings). **Subscriptions:** 2300 journals and other serials. **Services:** Interlibrary loan; copying; department open to the public. **Automated Operations:** Computerized cataloging. **Computerized Information Services:** DIALOG Information Services, NEXIS, VU/TEXT Information Services, NewsNet, Inc., DataTimes. **Networks/Consortia:** Member of Western Library Network (WLN). **Special Indexes:** Boat and Ship file; Washington science and business subject index.

★13036★
SEATTLE PUBLIC LIBRARY - DOUGLASS-TRUTH BRANCH LIBRARY (Area-Ethnic)
23rd Ave. & E. Yesler Way Phone: (206)684-4704
Seattle, WA 98122 Marcia Myers, South Reg.Libn.
Founded: 1965. **Staff:** Prof 3; Other 4. **Subjects:** Afro-American history and literature - the black experience in the Pacific Northwest, the portrayal of blacks in children's literature. **Special Collections:** Afro-Americana Collection; Children's Literature Reference Collection. **Holdings:** 6020 books; 346 bound periodical volumes; 5 VF drawers of pictures and pamphlets; 95 sound recordings; 3 boxes of microfiche. **Subscriptions:** 17 journals and other serials; 6 newspapers. **Services:** Interlibrary loan (fee); copying; library open to the public. **Automated Operations:** Computerized circulation. **Networks/Consortia:** Member of Western Library Network (WLN). **Special Indexes:** Afro-American History Index (card). **Staff:** Nancy Foley, Coord., Adult Serv.; Barbara McKeon, Pub.Serv.Libn..

★13037★
SEATTLE PUBLIC LIBRARY - EDUCATION, PSYCHOLOGY, SOCIOLOGY, SPORTS DEPARTMENT (Soc Sci)
1000 Fourth Ave. Phone: (206)625-2665
Seattle, WA 98104 Jean Coberly, Mng.Libn.
Staff: Prof 6; Other 7. **Subjects:** Education, psychology, sociology, human relations, recreation, sports and games, vocations, occult, etiquette, childbirth, child care, criminology, sex, marriage and family. **Special Collections:** Adult reading and enrichment collection (adult literacy); Career Information Center Collection; Regional Foundation Center Collection. **Holdings:** 70,300 books; microforms; college catalogs. **Services:** Interlibrary loan; department open to the public. **Computerized Information Services:** DIALOG Information Services, NEXIS. **Special Catalogs:** Local club file; Seattle-King County social agencies file.

★13038★
SEATTLE PUBLIC LIBRARY - GOVERNMENTAL RESEARCH ASSISTANCE LIBRARY (Soc Sci)
Municipal Bldg.
600 Fourth Ave. Phone: (206)625-2665
Seattle, WA 98104 Barbara Guptill, Mng.Libn.
Founded: 1931. **Staff:** Prof 3; Other 4. **Subjects:** Public administration, local government, police science, fire fighting, city planning, public personnel administration, municipal finance. **Special Collections:** City and county documents. **Holdings:** 18,000 volumes; 68 VF drawers. **Subscriptions:** 175 journals and other serials. **Services:** Interlibrary loan; Municipal Reference Exchange Program; library open to the public for reference use only. **Computerized Information Services:** DIALOG Information Services, NEXIS, LOGIN. **Publications:** Recent Additions, biweekly - to city and county personnel, civic organizations, and other municipal reference libraries. **Staff:** Jeannette Voiland, Libn.; Rose Bias, Lib.Asst..

★13039★
SEATTLE PUBLIC LIBRARY - HISTORY, GOVERNMENT AND BIOGRAPHY DEPARTMENT (Hist)
1000 Fourth Ave. Phone: (206)386-4636
Seattle, WA 98104 Paula Green, Sr.Asst.Mng.Libn.
Staff: Prof 8; Other 7. **Subjects:** Northwest history and politics, biography, genealogy, travel. **Special Collections:** Northwest history; Sayre-Carkeek Theater Program Collection; Balch Autograph Collection. **Holdings:** General periodicals; microrecords; newspapers; maps. **Services:** Interlibrary loan; copying; department open to the public. **Automated Operations:** Computerized cataloging and circulation. **Computerized Information Services:** DIALOG Information Services, Pergamon ORBIT InfoLine, Inc., DataTimes, The Reference Service (REFSRV). Performs searches on fee basis. **Special Indexes:** Northwest history index; Seattle newspaper index.

★13040★
SEATTLE PUBLIC LIBRARY - LITERATURE, LANGUAGES, PHILOSOPHY & RELIGION DEPARTMENT (Hum)
1000 Fourth Ave. Phone: (206)386-4636
Seattle, WA 98104 James B. Taylor, Mgr.
Staff: Prof 8; Other 14. **Subjects:** Literature, languages, philosophy, religion, drama, poetry, fiction, general bibliography. **Special Collections:** Multilingual collection (52 languages; 40,000 volumes); young adult collection (6000 volumes); popular library (25,000 volumes). **Holdings:** 200,000 books and bound periodical volumes; 28 VF drawers of unbound plays and scripts; 31 volumes of Seattle Theatre scrapbooks. **Subscriptions:** 800 journals and other serials. **Services:** Interlibrary loan; copying; department open to the public. **Automated Operations:** Computerized cataloging, acquisitions, and circulation. **Computerized Information Services:** DIALOG Information Services, WILSONLINE, DataTimes, VU/TEXT Information Services. Performs searches free of charge. Contact Person: Yvonne Onen, 386-4678. **Networks/Consortia:** Member of Western Library Network (WLN). **Staff:** Norma Arnold, Sr.Asst.Mng.Libn..

★13041★
SEATTLE PUBLIC LIBRARY - MEDIA & PROGRAM SERVICES (Aud-Vis)
1000 Fourth Ave. Phone: (206)386-4666
Seattle, WA 98104 Raymond Serebrin, Mng.Libn.
Staff: Prof 4; Other 10. **Subjects:** Adult education, child development, general collection. **Special Collections:** 16mm film collection (1700 prints, all subjects). **Holdings:** 117 books; 52 bound periodical volumes; 165 slide

sets; 18 filmstrip sets; 2500 video cassettes. **Subscriptions:** 18 journals and other serials. **Services:** Services open to the public, books and periodicals for reference use only. **Special Catalogs:** 16mm Film Catalog (book); AV Catalog (video and 16mm film; microfiche). **Staff:** Glennie Ruth Webb, Media Libn.; Sharon Simes, Media Libn.; Elizabeth Yee, Prog.Libn..

SEATTLE PUBLIC LIBRARY - WASHINGTON LIBRARY FOR THE BLIND AND PHYSICALLY HANDICAPPED
See: Washington Library for the Blind and Physically Handicapped (17493)

★13042★
SEATTLE TIMES - LIBRARY (Publ)
Fairview, N. & John Sts. Phone: (206)464-2307
Seattle, WA 98109 Theresa Redderson, Lib.Mgr.
Founded: 1900. **Staff:** Prof 3; Other 14. **Subjects:** Newspaper reference topics. **Holdings:** 4000 books; 13 bound periodical volumes; 8000 pamphlets and maps; 1 million photographs; 10 million news clippings; 30 drawers of microfilm. **Subscriptions:** 75 journals and other serials; 5 newspapers. **Services:** Library not open to the public. **Computerized Information Services:** DIALOG Information Services, NEXIS, DataTimes, VU/TEXT Information Services; internal database; DataTimes (electronic mail service). **Staff:** Ann Carver, Asst.Libn.; Sandra Freeman, Asst.Libn..

SEATTLE TRUST & SAVINGS BANK
See: Key Bank of Puget Sound (7473)

SEAVER CENTER FOR WESTERN HISTORY RESEARCH
See: Natural History Museum of Los Angeles County (9829)

★13043★
SEBASTIAN COUNTY LAW LIBRARY (Law)
Stephens Bldg., Suite 418 Phone: (501)783-4730
Fort Smith, AR 72901 Rachel L. Piercy, Libn.
Founded: 1972. **Staff:** Prof 1. **Subjects:** Law. **Holdings:** 14,000 volumes. **Services:** Copying; library open to the public.

SEBRING MEMORIAL LIBRARY
See: Chevy Chase Baptist Church (3050)

★13044★
SECOND BAPTIST CHURCH - LIBRARY (Rel-Phil)
2800 Silverside Rd. Phone: (302)478-5921
Wilmington, DE 19810 Nancy P. Minnich, Libn.
Staff: Prof 1; Other 4. **Subjects:** Religion, philosophy. **Holdings:** 3000 books. **Services:** Interlibrary loan; library not open to the public. **Networks/Consortia:** Member of Libraries in the New Castle County System (LINCS).

★13045★
SECOND PRESBYTERIAN CHURCH - CAPEN MEMORIAL LIBRARY (Rel-Phil)
313 N. East St.
Bloomington, IL 61701 Phone: (309)828-6297
Founded: 1939. **Subjects:** Religion, religious education, missions. **Special Collections:** Local church history. **Holdings:** 3200 books; 150 pamphlets; 3 VF drawers. **Services:** Library open to the public upon request to church office.

★13046★
SECURITIES AND EXCHANGE COMMISSION - LIBRARY (Bus-Fin)
450 5th St., N.W. Phone: (202)272-2618
Washington, DC 20549 Charlene C. Derge, Libn.
Founded: 1934. **Staff:** Prof 4; Other 4. **Subjects:** Accounting, corporations, economics, finance, government, investments, law, public utilities, securities, statistics, stock exchanges. **Special Collections:** Legislative histories of statutes administered by agency. **Holdings:** 60,000 books; 5000 bound periodical volumes. **Subscriptions:** 400 journals and other serials. **Services:** Interlibrary loan (to other government agencies only); copying; library open to the public by appointment. **Computerized Information Services:** LEXIS, OCLC. **Publications:** Library Bulletin, biweekly. **Also Known As:** SEC. **Staff:** Raymond J. Kramer, Asst.Libn..

★13047★
SECURITIES AND EXCHANGE COMMISSION - PUBLIC REFERENCE LIBRARY (Bus-Fin)
219 S. Dearborn, Rm. 1242 Phone: (312)353-7433
Chicago, IL 60604 Donald J. Evers, Chf.Ref.Libn.
Founded: 1940. **Staff:** Prof 1; Other 3. **Subjects:** Securities laws, SEC releases and special studies. **Holdings:** 500 bound periodical volumes; financial statements; corporate annual reports; 20,000 files of reports by publicly owned companies on microfiche; registration statements, applications, and financial data for regional broker/dealers and investment advisors; annual reports for registered investment companies. **Services:** Copying; library open to the public. **Remarks:** Other repositories of this same information are located in SEC headquarters in Washington, DC and a regional office in New York City. Requests for copies of documents should be sent to Securities and Exchange Commission, Washington, DC 20549. **Also Known As:** SEC.

★13048★
SECURITY BENEFIT LIFE INSURANCE COMPANY - LIBRARY (Bus-Fin)
700 Harrison St. Phone: (913)295-3000
Topeka, KS 66636 Elizabeth Liebig, Lib.Serv./Educ.Coord.
Subjects: Insurance, law, securities, marketing, Life Office Management Association. **Holdings:** 3000 books; company records and annual reports; case histories. **Subscriptions:** 25 journals and other serials. **Services:** Library not open to the public.

★13049★
SECURITY PACIFIC NATIONAL BANK - ECONOMICS AND BUSINESS LIBRARY (Bus-Fin)
333 S. Hope St. Phone: (213)345-5388
Los Angeles, CA 90071 Ann W. Shea, Res.Off.
Founded: 1920. **Staff:** Prof 1; Other 2. **Subjects:** Banking and finance, real estate, general business, agriculture. **Special Collections:** California history collection (2500 volumes). **Holdings:** 5000 books; 450 bound periodical volumes; 370 theses; 15,000 VF materials; 370 masters' theses on banking; 50 serials on microfiche. **Subscriptions:** 475 journals and other serials; 30 newspapers. **Services:** Interlibrary loan; copying; library open to the public by appointment. **Automated Operations:** Computerized serials. **Computerized Information Services:** NEXIS. **Publications:** Monthly Acquisitions List. **Special Catalogs:** Union Catalog.

★13050★
SED SYSTEMS, INC. - LIBRARY (Sci-Engr)
Box 1464 Phone: (306)933-1672
Saskatoon, SK, Canada S7K 3P7 Lynn Kennedy, Lib.Tech.
Founded: 1968. **Staff:** Prof 1. **Subjects:** Space and communications systems. **Holdings:** 500 books; 300 reports, standards, manuals; 3500 project documents. **Subscriptions:** 73 journals and other serials. **Services:** Interlibrary loan; copying; library open to the public. **Automated Operations:** Computerized cataloging. **Computerized Information Services:** DIALOG Information Services, CAN/OLE; internal databases.

★13051★
SEDGWICK COUNTY LAW LIBRARY (Law)
255 N. Market, Suite 210 Phone: (316)263-2251
Wichita, KS 67202 Sara I. Hill, Law Libn.
Founded: 1915. **Staff:** Prof 1; Other 1. **Subjects:** Law. **Holdings:** 25,700 books; 4000 bound periodical volumes. **Subscriptions:** 5 newspapers. **Services:** Interlibrary loan; library open to the public.

★13052★
SEDGWICK, DETERT, MORAN & ARNOLD - LIBRARY AND INFORMATION CENTER (Law)
One Embarcadero Ctr., 16th Fl. Phone: (415)781-7900
San Francisco, CA 94111 Ann Borkin, Libn.
Staff: Prof 1; Other 1. **Subjects:** Law. **Holdings:** 7500 books. **Services:** Interlibrary loan; library not open to the public. **Computerized Information Services:** LEXIS, WESTLAW, DIALOG Information Services, RLIN. **Networks/Consortia:** Member of CLASS.

★13053★
SEDGWICK TOMENSON INC. - NATIONAL RESOURCE CENTRE (Bus-Fin)
Toronto-Dominion Center
P.O. Box 439 Phone: (416)361-6830
Toronto, ON, Canada M5K 1M3 Kabita Choudhuri, Mgr.
Staff: 4. **Subjects:** Insurance, employee benefits, risk management, pensions, insurance law, actuarial science. **Special Collections:** Client reports and presentations. **Holdings:** 3000 monographs; 10 VF drawers of

annual reports; 6 VF drawers of internal reports; 3000 subject files. **Subscriptions:** 104 journals and other serials; 6 newspapers. **Services:** Interlibrary loan; copying; center open to the public by appointment. **Automated Operations:** Computerized cataloging. **Computerized Information Services:** Info Globe, The Financial Post Information Service, QL Systems. **Publications:** National Information Bulletin; Information Update (newsletter), bimonthly - to clients; Adviser (newsletter) - to clients.

LINDON SEED LIBRARY
See: Grant Hospital of Chicago (5823)

★13054★
SEEK INFORMATION SERVICE (Info Sci)
416 N. Glendale Ave., Suite M Phone: (818)242-2793
Glendale, CA 91206-3309 M.T. Grenier, Pres.
Founded: 1976. **Staff:** Prof 3; Other 2. **Services:** SDI; service accepts telephone requests for database searches. **Computerized Information Services:** DIALOG Information Services, BRS Information Technologies, VU/TEXT Information Services, WILSONLINE, TEXTLINE, ESA/IRS, Dow Jones News/Retrieval. **Remarks:** SEEK is an online information retrieval service. A toll-free telephone number in Southern California is (800)722-SEEK. **Staff:** L.M. Ecklund, V.P..

★13055★
SEINGALT SOCIETY - LIBRARY (Hum)
41 Birch Place Phone: (203)846-6800
Stratford, CT 06497 Tom Vitelli, Pres.
Subjects: Giacomo Casanova de Seingalt. **Holdings:** 1000 volumes. **Special Indexes:** Index to manuscripts. **Remarks:** An alternate telephone number is 378-2298.

★13056★
SELF WINDING CLOCK ASSOCIATION - SWC LIBRARY (Rec)
3736 Atlantic Ave., No. 4
Box 7704 Phone: (213)427-8001
Long Beach, CA 90807 B.E. Honning, Ph.D., Dir.
Founded: 1979. **Staff:** Prof 1; Other 2. **Subjects:** Horology; machine tool; U.S. history, 1850-1971. **Special Collections:** Horology manuscripts (50). **Holdings:** 325 books; 600 bound periodical volumes; 65 reels of microfilm. **Subscriptions:** 14 journals and other serials. **Services:** Library open to members

★13057★
J. & W. SELIGMAN & CO. INCORPORATED - RESEARCH LIBRARY (Bus-Fin)
One Bankers Trust Place Phone: (212)488-0456
New York, NY 10006 Paula A. Gray, Libn.
Founded: 1931. **Staff:** Prof 1; Other 3. **Subjects:** Corporations, finance, investment companies, general business statistics, economics. **Holdings:** 1000 books; 450 bound periodical volumes; 3500 corporate and industry files; 2 drawers of maps; telephone directories; 186 reels of microfilm; 1200 microfiche. **Subscriptions:** 300 journals and other serials; 25 newspapers. **Services:** Interlibrary loan; library not open to the public. **Publications:** Serials List, semiannual - for internal distribution only. **Special Catalogs:** Catalog of Company History.

SELIGMAN LIBRARY
See: Columbia University - Rare Book and Manuscript Library (3493)

★13058★
SELKIRK MENTAL HEALTH CENTRE - CENTRAL LIBRARY (Med)
Box 9600 Phone: (204)482-3810
Selkirk, MB, Canada R1A 2B5 B. Scarsbrook, Chm., Lib.Comm.
Founded: 1976. **Staff:** Prof 1. **Subjects:** Psychiatry, psychiatric nursing, psychology, social service, nursing, allied health sciences. **Holdings:** 4000 books; 1000 bound periodical volumes; AV programs. **Subscriptions:** 110 journals and other serials. **Services:** Interlibrary loan; library not open to the public. **Staff:** Lorna Weiss, Lib.Techn..

SELLES SOLA MEMORIAL COLLECTION
See: University of Puerto Rico - College of Education (16789)

DAVID O. SELZNICK FILM ARCHIVES
See: University of Texas, Austin - Harry Ransom Humanities Research Center (16931)

★13059★
SEMANTODONTICS, INC. - LIBRARY (Med)
Box 15668 Phone: (602)955-5662
Phoenix, AZ 85060 Jim Rhode, Pres.
Staff: 1. **Subjects:** Dentistry, patient care, dental staff training, psychology, communications, transactional analysis, motivation. **Holdings:** 400 books; 50 bound periodical volumes; 200 magnetic tapes; 100 patient education pamphlets. **Subscriptions:** 43 journals and other serials; 8 newspapers. **Services:** Copying; library open to the public by appointment. **Publications:** Practice Smart (newsletter), 11/year - to the public. **Remarks:** Semantodontics means Semantics in Dentistry.

★13060★
SEMICONDUCTOR EQUIPMENT AND MATERIALS INTERNATIONAL (SEMI) - LIBRARY (Sci-Engr)
805 E. Middlefield Rd. Phone: (415)940-6924
Mountain View, CA 94043 Roger Sherman, Libn.
Founded: 1984. **Staff:** Prof 1. **Subjects:** Semiconductor and electronics industries. **Special Collections:** Semiconductor industry standards; annual reports of member companies. **Holdings:** 500 books. **Subscriptions:** 110 journals and other serials; 10 newspapers. **Services:** Copying; library open to the public on fee basis. **Computerized Information Services:** DIALOG Information Services. **Networks/Consortia:** Member of CLASS.

★13061★
SEMINAIRE DE CHICOUTIMI - BIBLIOTHEQUE (Rel-Phil, Hum)
679, rue Chabanel Phone: (418)549-0190
Chicoutimi, PQ, Canada G7H 1Z7 Clement-Jacques Simard, Dir.
Founded: 1873. **Staff:** Prof 2. **Subjects:** Religion, theology, science, philosophy, philology, art, history, literature. **Special Collections:** Canadian literature; Latin and ancient Greek literature. **Holdings:** 80,000 books; 20,000 archival materials. **Subscriptions:** 100 journals and other serials. **Services:** Interlibrary loan; copying; library open to the public with restrictions. **Staff:** Lucien Fortin, Lib.Techn./Asst..

★13062★
SEMINAIRE DE QUEBEC - ARCHIVES (Hist)
9, rue de l'Universite
Box 460 Phone: (418)692-2843
Quebec, PQ, Canada G1R 4R7 Rev. Laurent Tailleur, Dir.
Founded: 1941. **Staff:** Prof 1; Other 2. **Subjects:** History - local, Canadian, American, economic, religious. **Special Collections:** Canadian public documents, 1763-1867 (250 volumes). **Holdings:** 2000 books; 250 bound periodical volumes; 1500 boxes of manuscripts; 160 feet of bound documents; 250 reels of microfilm. **Services:** Copying; archives open to the public with restrictions.

★13063★
SEMINAIRE ST-ALPHONSE - BIBLIOTHEQUE (Hum)
10026, rue Royale Phone: (418)827-3744
Ste. Anne de Beaupre, PQ, Canada G0A 3C0 Robert Boucher, Dir.
Staff: 3. **Subjects:** Literature, Canadian history, education, art. **Holdings:** 32,000 volumes; 10,000 slides; 2000 phonograph records. **Subscriptions:** 80 journals and other serials. **Services:** Copying; library open to the public with restrictions.

SEMINAIRE ST-JOSEPH - ARCHIVES DU SEMINAIRE DE TROIS-RIVIERES
See: Corporation du Seminaire St-Joseph de Trois-Rivieres - Archives du Seminaire de Trois-Rivieres (3803)

★13064★
SEMINAIRE ST-JOSEPH - BIBLIOTHEQUE (Rel-Phil, Hum)
858, rue Laviolette
C.P. 548 Phone: (819)378-5167
Trois-Rivieres, PQ, Canada G9A 5J1 Jean Perigny, Dir.
Founded: 1860. **Staff:** Prof 1; Other 2. **Subjects:** Religion, French literature, history, foreign literature, sciences. **Special Collections:** Canadiana. **Holdings:** 85,000 books; 15,000 bound periodical volumes; 225 films; 18,000 slides; 125 magnetic tapes; 4500 phonograph records. **Subscriptions:** 162 journals and other serials; 12 newspapers. **Services:** Library not open to the public.

SEMINARIO EVANGELICO DE PUERTO RICO
See: Evangelical Seminary of Puerto Rico (4836)

★13065★
SEMINARY OF THE IMMACULATE CONCEPTION - LIBRARY (Rel-Phil)
440 West Neck Rd. Phone: (516)423-0483
Huntington, NY 11743 Jiri (George) Lipa, Ph.D., Libn.
Founded: 1930. **Staff:** Prof 1; Other 3. **Subjects:** Theology, scripture, church history, patrology, canon law, liturgy, catechetics. **Holdings:** 49,000 books; 6800 bound periodical volumes. **Subscriptions:** 320 journals and other serials. **Services:** Interlibrary loan; copying; library open to the public by appointment. **Networks/Consortia:** Member of Long Island Library Resources Council, Inc. (LILRC).

SEMINEX LIBRARY
See: Christ Seminary (3142)

★13066★
SEMIOTIC SOCIETY OF AMERICA - LIBRARY (Hum)
Applied Behavioral Science
University of California Phone: (916)752-6437
Davis, CA 98616 Dean MacConnell, Act.Exec.Dir.
Founded: 1975. **Subjects:** Semiotics. **Holdings:** 200 volumes; offprint files. **Formerly:** Located in Bloomington, IN.

★13067★
SEMMES, BOWEN & SEMMES - LAW LIBRARY (Law)
250 W. Pratt St., 14th Fl. Phone: (301)539-5040
Baltimore, MD 21201 Helen Y. Harris, Libn.
Staff: Prof 2; Other 4. **Subjects:** Law. **Special Collections:** Admiralty and maritime law. **Holdings:** 19,500 books; 330 bound periodical volumes; 225 volumes and 16 pamphlet boxes of memos and briefs. **Subscriptions:** 70 journals and other serials. **Services:** Library open to the public by appointment. **Automated Operations:** Computerized acquisitions. **Computerized Information Services:** DIALOG Information Services, LEXIS, WESTLAW, PHINet FedTax Database; internal database. **Publications:** Semmes Library Information Publication (SLIP), monthly - for internal distribution only. **Special Indexes:** Index to firm memoranda and briefs (computerized). **Staff:** Delia S. Stark, Cat..

★13068★
SEMMES-MURPHEY CLINIC - LIBRARY (Med)
920 Madison Ave., Suite 201 Phone: (901)522-7700
Memphis, TN 38103 Charles M. Prest, Libn.
Staff: Prof 1. **Subjects:** Neurosurgery, neurology. **Holdings:** 1327 books; 819 bound periodical volumes. **Subscriptions:** 38 journals and other serials. **Services:** Library not open to the public. **Networks/Consortia:** Member of Association of Memphis Area Health Sciences Libraries (AMAHSL).

SENATE HOUSE STATE HISTORIC SITE
See: New York State Office of Parks, Recreation and Historic Preservation (10134)

★13069★
SENECA COLLEGE OF APPLIED ARTS AND TECHNOLOGY - LESLIE CAMPUS LIBRARY/RESOURCE CENTRE (Med)
1255 Sheppard Ave., E. Phone: (416)491-5050
North York, ON, Canada M2K 1E2 Vinh P. Le, Ref.Libn.
Staff: Prof 1; Other 4. **Subjects:** Nursing, dentistry. **Special Collections:** International health (500 volumes). **Holdings:** 14,723 books; 169 filmstrips; 250 AV programs; 250 audiotapes; 550 videotapes; 81 films; 176 slide sets; 150 dental models. **Subscriptions:** 111 journals and other serials. **Services:** Interlibrary loan; copying; center open to the public on fee basis. **Automated Operations:** Computerized cataloging, acquisitions, and circulation. **Computerized Information Services:** DIALOG Information Services, DOBIS; internal databases; DOBIS (electronic mail service). Performs searches on fee basis. **Networks/Consortia:** Member of Bibliocentre. **Publications:** Health Sciences Programs Required Reading Lists; Seneca Union List of Periodicals, both annual - both for internal distribution only; bibliographies.

★13070★
SENECA FALLS HISTORICAL SOCIETY - JESSIE BEACH WATKINS MEMORIAL LIBRARY (Hist)
55 Cayuga St. Phone: (315)568-8412
Seneca Falls, NY 13148 Ed Polk Douglas, Exec.Dir.
Subjects: Local and state history, Victoriana. **Special Collections:** Women's Rights Collection (documents, 1848 to present). **Holdings:** 1300 books; 300 bound periodical volumes; 17 VF drawers; local newspaper, 1839 to present, on microfilm. **Services:** Copying; library open to the public. **Staff:** George Covert, Archv.; Jane Wood, Res..

★13071★
SENECA ZOOLOGICAL SOCIETY - LIBRARY (Biol Sci)
2222 St. Paul St. Phone: (716)338-2308
Rochester, NY 14621 Mary Coykendall, Libn.
Founded: 1978. **Staff:** Prof 1. **Subjects:** Zoos, zoo animals, veterinary medicine, ecology, zoology, herpetology. **Holdings:** 2100 books; 7800 slides; 1900 photographs; 30 zoo guidebooks. **Subscriptions:** 55 journals and other serials. **Services:** Copying; library open to the public.

★13072★
SENTRY INSURANCE COMPANY - LIBRARY (Bus-Fin)
1800 N. Point Dr.
Stevens Point, WI 54481 Phone: (715)346-6787
Founded: 1930. **Staff:** 3. **Subjects:** Insurance - property/casualty and life; pensions; law; business management. **Holdings:** 21,000 books; 6000 bound periodical volumes; 125 VF drawers of monographs, booklets, clippings, pamphlets, reports, pictures, and archives. **Subscriptions:** 475 journals and other serials; 17 newspapers. **Services:** Interlibrary loan; copying; library open to the public by permission. **Publications:** Acquisition List - for internal distribution only. **Staff:** Annette Whelihan, Asst.Libn..

★13073★
SEQUA CORPORATION - KOLLSMAN DIVISION - KIC LIBRARY (Sci-Engr)
220 Daniel Webster Hwy. Phone: (603)886-2083
Merrimack, NH 03054 Gerald W. Rice, Libn.
Staff: Prof 1. **Subjects:** Aeronautics, optics, electronics, engineering, mathematics, management, marketing, accounting. **Holdings:** 4241 volumes; 5 volumes of patents. **Subscriptions:** 80 journals and other serials. **Services:** Interlibrary loan; library not open to the public. **Computerized Information Services:** DIALOG Information Services, NERAC, Inc. **Publications:** Library Newsletter, bimonthly. **Formerly:** Kollsman Company.

★13074★
SERGENT, HAUSKINS & BECKWITH, CONSULTING GEOTECHNICAL ENGINEERS - LIBRARY (Sci-Engr)
3232 W. Virginia Ave. Phone: (602)272-6848
Phoenix, AZ 85009 Susanne M. Jerome, Libn.
Staff: Prof 2. **Subjects:** Engineering - geology, geotechnical, earthquake, mining, environmental; hydrology; dam safety. **Special Collections:** Geotechnical engineering problems in arid regions (1500 volumes). **Holdings:** 7050 books and bound periodical volumes; 13,000 other cataloged items; 2 VF drawers; 70 boxes of unbound periodicals; 2 drawers of microfiche. **Subscriptions:** 94 journals and other serials. **Services:** Copying; library open to the public with permission. **Automated Operations:** Computerized cataloging and acquisitions. **Computerized Information Services:** Pergamon ORBIT InfoLine, Inc., DIALOG Information Services. **Staff:** Tom Zupin, Res.Asst..

★13075★
SERVANTS OF THE IMMACULATE HEART OF MARY - ARCHIVES (Rel-Phil)
Villa Maria House of Studies Phone: (215)647-2160
Immaculata, PA 19345 Sr. Genevieve Mary, Archv.
Subjects: Congregation history, 1840 to present. **Holdings:** 160 cubic feet of correspondence, journals, financial records, architectural drawings, and photographs. **Services:** Copying; archives open to the public on a limited schedule.

★13076★
SERVIO LOGIC CORPORATION - CORPORATE INFORMATION CENTER (Comp Sci)
15025 S.W. Koll Pkwy. 1-A Phone: (503)644-4242
Beaverton, OR 97006 Susan F. Sudduth, Mgr.
Founded: 1983. **Staff:** Prof 1. **Subjects:** Computer science, programming, software management, electronics industry. **Special Collections:** Institute of Electrical and Electronics Engineers (IEEE) and Association for Computing Machinery (ACM) journals, 1983 to present; electronics industry market research reports. **Holdings:** 2000 books; 400 IBM PC software packages; 100 linear feet of vertical files; company and product literature. **Subscriptions:** 163 journals and other serials. **Services:** Interlibrary loan; copying; SDI; center open to public at librarian's discretion. **Automated Operations:** Computerized cataloging and ILL. **Computerized Information Services:** DIALOG Information Services, DunSprint, NewsNet, Inc., OCLC; Inmagic (internal database). Performs searches on fee basis.

SERVITES
See: Order of Servants of Mary - Eastern Province Library (10885)

★13077★
SESSIONS, FISHMAN, ROSENSON, BOISFONTAINE, NATHAN & WINN - LAW LIBRARY (Law)
201 St. Charles Ave., Suite 3500 Phone: (504)582-1563
New Orleans, LA 70170 Cynthia Harper, Libn.
Staff: Prof 1; Other 1. **Subjects:** Law. **Holdings:** 10,000 books; 600 bound periodical volumes. **Subscriptions:** 100 journals and other serials; 6 newspapers. **Services:** Interlibrary loan; copying; library open to the public with restrictions. **Computerized Information Services:** WESTLAW, LEXIS, DIALOG Information Services. **Publications:** Now Hear This (newsletter) - for internal distribution only.

★13078★
SETON HALL UNIVERSITY - IMMACULATE CONCEPTION SEMINARY - LIBRARY (Rel-Phil)
400 S. Orange Ave. Phone: (201)761-9198
South Orange, NJ 07079 Fr. James C. Turro, Lib.Dir.
Staff: Prof 2; Other 1. **Subjects:** Theology, philosophy, Bible studies, ethics, liturgy, pastoral ministries. **Special Collections:** Sacred books (rare). **Holdings:** 71,000 books; 3000 bound periodical volumes; 478 dissertations; 585 reels of microfilm; 344 tapes and cassettes; 507 microforms. **Subscriptions:** 712 journals and other serials; 30 newspapers. **Services:** Interlibrary loan; copying; library open to the public with restrictions. **Automated Operations:** Computerized cataloging. **Publications:** Bibliography of new titles in library, bimonthly. **Staff:** Sr. Concetta Russo, Libn..

★13079★
SETON HALL UNIVERSITY - MC LAUGHLIN LIBRARY - SPECIAL COLLECTIONS (Hist, Hum)
400 South Orange Ave. Phone: (201)761-9000
South Orange, NJ 07079 Dr. Robert A. Jones, Univ.Libn.
Holdings: Gerald Murphy Civil War Collection (1000 volumes); Oriental Collection (10,000 volumes). **Services:** Interlibrary loan; copying; collections open to the public on fee basis. **Automated Operations:** Computerized cataloging and ILL. **Computerized Information Services:** DIALOG Information Services, BRS Information Technologies, OCLC. **Networks/Consortia:** Member of County of Essex Cooperating Libraries (CECLS), Essex-Hudson Regional Library Cooperative.

★13080★
SETON HALL UNIVERSITY - MAC MANUS COLLECTION (Area-Ethnic)
McLaughlin Library
400 South Orange Ave. Phone: (201)761-9000
South Orange, NJ 07079 Rev. William Noe Field, Cur., Spec.Coll.
Founded: 1958. **Subjects:** Irish literature, history, and politics, particularly the home rule question. **Special Collections:** Complete works of Liam O'Flaherty (300 autographed 1st editions; periodicals and news clippings). **Holdings:** 4000 volumes; autographs; clippings; letters. **Services:** Copying; collection open to the public with letter of introduction. **Automated Operations:** Computerized cataloging. **Computerized Information Services:** DIALOG Information Services, OCLC. Performs searches on fee basis. **Networks/Consortia:** Member of County of Essex Cooperating Libraries (CECLS).

★13081★
SETON HALL UNIVERSITY - SCHOOL OF LAW - LAW LIBRARY (Law)
1111 Raymond Blvd. Phone: (201)642-8766
Newark, NJ 07102 Deborah D. Herrera, Dir.
Founded: 1950. **Staff:** Prof 6; Other 12. **Subjects:** Law. **Holdings:** 210,000 books, bound periodical volumes, and volumes in microform; 300 audiovisual programs. **Subscriptions:** 4200 journals and other serials. **Services:** Interlibrary loan; library open to the public with restrictions. **Automated Operations:** Computerized cataloging and serials. **Computerized Information Services:** OCLC, LEXIS, WESTLAW. **Networks/Consortia:** Member of PALINET, Essex-Hudson Regional Library Cooperative. **Staff:** Eileen Denner, Hd., Rd.Serv./Ref.Libn.; Kathleen McCarthy, Ref.Libn.; Maja Basioli, Ref./Circ.Libn.; Constance Nourse, Ref.Libn., Weekends; Barbara J. Meade, Hd., Tech.Serv./Cat.Libn.; Diane West, Asst.Cat..

★13082★
SETON HALL UNIVERSITY - SCHOOL OF THEOLOGY - LIBRARY (Rel-Phil)
400 South Orange Ave. Phone: (201)761-9198
South Orange, NJ 07079 Rev. James C. Turro, Dir.
Staff: Prof 2; Other 2. **Subjects:** Theology, philosophy, Catholic church history. **Special Collections:** Rare sacred books. **Holdings:** 70,000 books; 4000 bound periodical volumes; 300 microforms; 300 tapes. **Subscriptions:** 430 journals and other serials; 16 newspapers. **Services:** Interlibrary loan; copying; library open to the public with special permission. **Automated Operations:** Computerized cataloging. **Computerized Information Services:** OCLC. **Networks/Consortia:** Member of County of Essex Cooperating Libraries (CECLS). **Publications:** Bibliography of new titles. **Staff:** Sr. Concetta Russo, Asst.Libn..

★13083★
SETON HALL UNIVERSITY - UNIVERSITY ARCHIVES (Hist, Rel-Phil)
Duffy Hall
400 South Orange Ave. Phone: (201)761-9476
South Orange, NJ 07079 Barbara Geller, Univ.Archv.
Founded: 1978. **Staff:** Prof 2; Other 1. **Subjects:** New Jersey Catholicism and Catholic history. **Special Collections:** Archives of the Archdiocese of Newark (300 linear feet); Seton Hall University Archives (250 linear feet); Bernard Shanley papers (25 linear feet); archives of the Seton family, Leonard Dreyfuss, Chief Justice Richard Hughes; archival and manuscript collections (40 linear feet). **Services:** Copying; archives open to the public. **Publications:** New Jersey Catholic Records Newsletter, 3/year - for sale. **Special Catalogs:** Catholic Parish and Institutional Histories in the State of New Jersey; Guide to Northern New Jersey Catholic Parish and Institutional Records.

★13084★
SETON, JOHNSON & ODELL, INC. - ENGINEERING LIBRARY (Sci-Engr)
133 S.W. 2nd Ave.
Portland, OR 97204 Phone: (503)226-3921
Founded: 1978. **Staff:** Prof 1; Other 1. **Subjects:** Engineering - mechanical, structural, civil, electrical, air/noise. **Special Collections:** Environmental Protection Agency materials on air/noise pollution control. **Holdings:** 810 volumes; 50 reports; 8 VF drawers of vendors' brochures. **Subscriptions:** 79 journals and other serials. **Services:** Interlibrary loan; copying; SDI; library open to the public with restrictions. **Computerized Information Services:** Online systems.

★13085★
SETON MEDICAL CENTER - LIBRARY (Med)
1900 Sullivan Ave. Phone: (415)991-6700
Daly City, CA 94015 Marie Grace Abbruzzese, Libn.
Staff: Prof 1. **Subjects:** Medicine, nursing, hospital administration. **Holdings:** 2000 books; 2000 bound periodical volumes; 8 shelves of audio cassettes and tapes. **Subscriptions:** 125 journals and other serials. **Services:** Interlibrary loan; copying; library open to professionals and by referral. **Publications:** Acquisitions List, irregular - for internal distribution only.

★13086★
SETON MEMORIAL LIBRARY
Philmont Scout Ranch
Cimarron, NM 87714
Founded: 1967. **Subjects:** Books written by Ernest T. Seton, Boy Scouts, Southwest, natural history, Indian Art, Bureau of American Ethnology. **Special Collections:** Ernest T. Seton Collection (200 volumes; 7 VF drawers of manuscripts and correspondence). **Holdings:** 6000 books; 250 bound periodical volumes; 2000 photographs; 46 boxes of pamphlets; 90 maps; local archeology reports (2 VF drawers). **Remarks:** Maintained by Boy Scouts of America-Philmont Scout Ranch. Presently inactive.

★13087★
SETTLEMENT MUSIC SCHOOL - BLANCHE WOLF KOHN LIBRARY (Mus)
416 Queen St.
Box 25120
Philadelphia, PA 19147 Phone: (215)336-0400
Staff: Prof 2; Other 2. **Subjects:** Music. **Special Collections:** J. Gershon Cohen Chamber Music; William M. Kincaid Flute Music; Mischa Schneider Cello Music; Herman Busch Violin Music; woodwind music. **Holdings:** 1200 books; 10,000 scores; 100,000 pieces of classical sheet music. **Subscriptions:** 20 journals and other serials. **Services:** Copying; library open to alumni and noted musicians. **Special Catalogs:** Catalogs of special collections and woodwind music (both card).

SEUFERT MEMORIAL LIBRARY
See: Norwegian-American Hospital, Inc. (10519)

ERIC SEVAREID JOURNALISM LIBRARY
See: University of Minnesota - Eric Sevareid Journalism Library (16466)

★13088★
SEVENTH-DAY ADVENTISTS GENERAL CONFERENCE - ARCHIVES (Rel-Phil)
6840 Eastern Ave., N.W. Phone: (202)722-6374
Washington, DC 20012 F. Donald Yost, Dir.
Founded: 1973 **Staff:** Prof 3; Other 1. **Subjects:** Seventh-day Adventism - history, theology, missions, institutions. **Special Collections:** Personal collections of prominent SDA leaders. **Holdings:** 50 books; 2000 bound periodical volumes; pamphlets; administrative records. **Services:** Copying; archives open to the public. **Publications:** Guide to Holdings of Archives. **Staff:** Bert Haloviak, Asst.Dir..

★13089★
SEVENTH DAY BAPTIST HISTORICAL SOCIETY - LIBRARY (Rel-Phil, Hist)
3120 Kennedy Rd.
Box 1678 Phone: (608)752-5055
Janesville, WI 53547 Don A. Sanford, Hist.
Founded: 1916. **Staff:** Prof 2. **Subjects:** Seventh Day Baptist history; Sabbatarian literature, church history, religion; New England history; genealogy. **Special Collections:** Julius F. Sachse Ephrata Collection; Nyasaland-Malawi Collection, 1895-1915. **Holdings:** 2500 books; 500 bound and indexed periodical volumes; 250 society record books; tracts; reports; church records; letters; manuscripts. **Services:** Interlibrary loan; copying; library open to the public. **Publications:** Annual Report; occasional bulletins. **Staff:** Janet Thorngate, Libn..

SEVERSON NATIONAL INFORMATION CENTER
See: Family Service America (4913)

SEWARD HOUSE
See: Foundation Historical Association (5318)

★13090★
SEWARD & KISSEL - LIBRARY (Law)
Wall Street Plaza Phone: (212)412-4270
New York, NY 10005 Robert J. Davis, Libn.
Staff: Prof 1; Other 2. **Subjects:** Law. **Holdings:** 18,000 volumes; 17 VF drawers of pamphlets. **Subscriptions:** 185 journals and other serials. **Services:** Interlibrary loan; library not open to the public. **Computerized Information Services:** LEXIS, DIALOG Information Services, Dow Jones News/Retrieval, NEXIS, WESTLAW.

★13091★
SEX INFORMATION & EDUCATION COUNCIL OF THE U.S. (SIECUS) - MARY S. CALDERONE LIBRARY (Soc Sci)
New York University
32 Washington Place
New York, NY 10003 Phone: (212)673-3850
Founded: 1979. **Staff:** Prof 1; Other 3. **Subjects:** Sex education, behavior, and research; human sexuality; family life education. **Holdings:** 3500 books; 200 curriculum items; 10 VF drawers; 500 pamphlets and booklets. **Subscriptions:** 70 journals and other serials. **Services:** Copying; library open to the public on fee basis. **Networks/Consortia:** Member of APLIC International Census Network. **Computerized Information Services:** Internal databases. Performs searches on fee basis. **Publications:** List of bibliographies and other publications available on request.

★13092★
SEYFARTH, SHAW, FAIRWEATHER & GERALDSON - LIBRARY (Law)
2029 Century Park East, Suite 3300 Phone: (213)277-7200
Los Angeles, CA 90067 Beth Bernstein, Libn.
Staff: Prof 1. **Subjects:** Labor and agricultural labor law. **Special Collections:** California Agricultural Labor Relations Board decisions, 1975 to present. **Holdings:** 12,000 books. **Services:** Interlibrary loan; library open to area law firms. **Automated Operations:** Computerized cataloging. **Computerized Information Services:** LEXIS, DIALOG Information Services. **Special Indexes:** Index to Agricultural Labor Relations Board decisions.

★13093★
SEYFARTH, SHAW, FAIRWEATHER & GERALDSON - LIBRARY (Law)
55 E. Monroe St. Phone: (312)346-8000
Chicago, IL 60603 Deborah Reeber, Libn.
Staff: Prof 3; Other 3. **Subjects:** Labor law, industrial relations, taxation, corporate law. **Holdings:** 2500 books; 96 VF drawers of pamphlets, decisions, briefs, agreements. **Subscriptions:** 354 journals and other serials. **Services:** Interlibrary loan; library not open to the public. **Automated Operations:** Computerized cataloging and circulation. **Computerized Information Services:** DataTimes, DIALOG Information Services, VU/TEXT Information Systems, WESTLAW, Information America, BRS Information Technologies, LEXIS, Legislative Information System (LIS), Labor Relations Press (LRP); internal database. **Networks/Consortia:** Member of ILLINET. **Staff:** Deborah Abram, Ref..

★13094★
SEYFARTH, SHAW, FAIRWEATHER & GERALDSON - LIBRARY (Law)
757 Third Ave., 12th Fl. Phone: (212)715-9635
New York, NY 10017 Catherine Inglis, Libn.
Staff: Prof 1; Other 1. **Subjects:** Law - labor, securities, corporate, tax, real estate. **Holdings:** 10,000 books; 100 bound periodical volumes. **Subscriptions:** 53 journals and other serials; 8 newspapers. **Services:** Interlibrary loan; library not open to the public. **Automated Operations:** Computerized cataloging and serials. **Computerized Information Services:** DIALOG Information Services, LEXIS, WESTLAW.

WILLIAM SEYMOUR THEATRE COLLECTION
See: Princeton University - William Seymour Theatre Collection (11595)

SHADEK-FACKENTHAL LIBRARY
See: Franklin and Marshall College (5355)

SHADELANDS RANCH HISTORICAL MUSEUM
See: Walnut Creek Historical Society (17436)

★13095★
SHADYSIDE HOSPITAL - JAMES FRAZER HILLMAN HEALTH SCIENCES LIBRARY (Med)
5230 Centre Ave. Phone: (412)622-2415
Pittsburgh, PA 15232 Malinda Fetkovich, Dir.
Staff: Prof 2; Other 7. **Subjects:** Thoracic medicine, cardiology, internal medicine, nursing. **Holdings:** 3000 books; 7000 bound periodical volumes. **Subscriptions:** 250 journals and other serials. **Services:** Interlibrary loan; copying; library open to the public with restrictions. **Computerized Information Services:** MEDLARS, DIALOG Information Services, BRS Information Technologies. Performs searches on fee basis. **Networks/Consortia:** Member of Pittsburgh-East Hospital Library Cooperative. **Remarks:** An alternate telephone number is 622-2441.

CHARLES E. SHAIN LIBRARY
See: Connecticut College - Charles E. Shain Library (3644)

★13096★
SHAKER COMMUNITY, INC. - LIBRARY
Box 898
Pittsfield, MA 01202
Defunct. Holdings absorbed by Hancock Shaker Village, Inc. - Library.

THE SHAKER LIBRARY
See: United Society of Believers (14575)

SHAKER LIBRARY
See: Warren County Historical Society - Museum and Library (17456)

★13097★
SHAKER MUSEUM FOUNDATION - EMMA B. KING LIBRARY (Rel-Phil)
Old Chatham, NY 12136 Phone: (518)794-9100
Jerry V. Grant, Asst.Dir. for Coll. & Res.
Founded: 1950. **Staff:** Prof 1; Other 1. **Subjects:** Shakers and Shakerism - industry, economy, history, music, theology, religious practices, material culture. **Holdings:** 2000 books; 50 bound periodical volumes: 550 pamphlets; 2500 other cataloged items; 2500 slides; 120 reels of microfilm; AV programs; 2500 manuscripts; 3500 photographs; 40 maps; diaries; account books; drawings. **Subscriptions:** 20 journals and other serials. **Services:** Copying; library open to the public on fee basis. **Publications:** List of publications - available on request. **Remarks:** Library is a repository of Shaker Society manuscripts and records.

★13098★
THE SHAKESPEARE DATA BANK, INC. - LIBRARY (Hum)
1217 Ashland Ave. Phone: (312)475-7550
Evanston, IL 60202 Louis Marder
Founded: 1984. **Subjects:** William Shakespeare - life, times, theater, plays, authorship controversy, criticism; English Renaissance literature. **Holdings:** 7800 books. **Services:** Library open to professors, teachers, students, theater personnel, Shakespeare Club members, and press service.

Computerized Information Services: Shakespeare Data Bank, Inc. (SDB). **Publications:** Shakespeare Newsletter, quarterly. **Remarks:** Maintains Shakespeare Hall of Fame, said to be the world's largest collection of Shakespeare memorabilia.

SHAKESPEARE RESEARCH COLLECTION
See: University of Wisconsin, Milwaukee - Golda Meir Library (17169)

★13099★
SHAKESPEARE SOCIETY OF AMERICA - NEW PLACE RARE BOOK LIBRARY (Hum)
1107 N. Kings Rd. Phone: (213)654-5623
West Hollywood, CA 90069 R. Thad Taylor, Pres.
Founded: 1967. **Staff:** Prof 3; Other 2. **Subjects:** Shakespeare - all aspects of his works. **Special Collections:** Renaissance literature; early science; antique furniture; Shakespeare Stamp Collection; Shakespeare coins and medals. **Holdings:** 3000 books; 1500 bound periodical volumes; 1000 catalogs; 500 magazines and pamphlets; 450 clippings and articles; 2000 photographs and slides; 100 tapes and phonograph records. **Subscriptions:** 50 journals and other serials; 5 newspapers. **Services:** Interlibrary loan; library open to the public with written request. **Publications:** Shakespeare's Proclamation - to members, for sale to nonmembers. **Remarks:** The library is adjacent to a one-half scale replica of Shakespeare's Globe Theatre.

★13100★
SHAND, MORAHAN & COMPANY, INC. - LIBRARY (Bus-Fin)
Shand Morahan Plaza Phone: (312)866-2800
Evanston, IL 60201 Constance N. Field, Libn.
Staff: Prof 1; Other 1. **Subjects:** Property and casualty insurance, reinsurance, professional liability, management. **Holdings:** 1500 books; 150 bound periodical volumes; pamphlets and clippings. **Subscriptions:** 240 journals and other serials. **Services:** Interlibrary loan; copying; SDI; library open to the public by appointment. **Computerized Information Services:** DIALOG Information Services, WESTLAW, VU/TEXT Information Services; internal database. **Networks/Consortia:** Member of ILLINET. **Publications:** Library Bulletin, bimonthly - for internal distribution only.

WILLIAM SHAND, JR. MEMORIAL LIBRARY
See: Franklin and Marshall College - Chemistry Department (5353)

SHANK MEMORIAL LIBRARY
See: Good Samaritan Hospital (5733)

★13101★
SHANLEY & FISHER - LAW LIBRARY (Law)
131 Madison Ave. Phone: (201)285-1000
Morristown, NJ 07960-1979 Margaret M. Wang, Libn.
Staff: Prof 2; Other 2. **Subjects:** Law. **Holdings:** 20,000 volumes. **Computerized Information Services:** LEXIS, WESTLAW.

SHANNON LIBRARY
See: St. Thomas More College (12678)

★13102★
SHANNON & WILSON, INC. - TECHNICAL LIBRARY (Sci-Engr)
1105 N. 38th St.
Box C-30313 Phone: (206)632-8020
Seattle, WA 98103-8067 Jean Boucher, Info.Rsrcs.Spec.
Staff: Prof 1; Other 1. **Subjects:** Geotechnical engineering, rock mechanics, applied geophysics, earthquake effects on soils. **Holdings:** 4000 volumes; 6000 reports, documents, and clippings; 1400 maps. **Subscriptions:** 90 journals and other serials. **Services:** Interlibrary loan; copying; library open to the public with permission of librarian. **Computerized Information Services:** Pergamon ORBIT InfoLine, Inc. **Networks/Consortia:** Member of Western Library Network (WLN). **Publications:** Recent acquisitions, monthly.

SHAPIRO LIBRARY
See: New Hampshire College (9937)

MAX SHAPIRO LIBRARY
See: Beth El Synagogue (1542)

★13103★
SAMUEL H. SHAPIRO DEVELOPMENTAL CENTER - PROFESSIONAL LIBRARY (Med)
100 E. Jeffery St. Phone: (815)939-8419
Kankakee, IL 60901 Juanita Licht, Br.Libn.
Founded: 1877. **Staff:** 1. **Subjects:** Developmental disabilities, mental retardation. **Holdings:** 2200 volumes; videotapes; educational games. **Subscriptions:** 62 journals and other serials. **Services:** Interlibrary loan; library open to the public by appointment. **Remarks:** Maintained by the Corn Belt Library System.

★13104★
SHARED MEDICAL SYSTEMS (SMS) - RESOURCE LIBRARY & INFORMATION CENTER (Comp Sci)
51 Valley Stream Pkwy. Phone: (215)296-6300
Malvern, PA 19355 Dorothy E. Young, Lib.Info.Spec.
Founded: 1981. **Staff:** Prof 2; Other 1. **Subjects:** Computers, health care administration. **Holdings:** 500 books. **Subscriptions:** 225 journals and other serials; 10 newspapers. **Services:** Interlibrary loan; library not open to the public. **Automated Operations:** Computerized serials. **Computerized Information Services:** DIALOG Information Services, BRS Information Technologies. **Networks/Consortia:** Member of Consortium for Health Information & Library Services (CHI).

★13105★
SHARLOT HALL/PRESCOTT HISTORICAL SOCIETIES - LIBRARY/ARCHIVES (Hist)
415 W. Gurley St. Phone: (602)445-3122
Prescott, AZ 86301 Sue Abbey, Archv.
Founded: 1929. **Staff:** Prof 1; Other 1. **Subjects:** Anglo and Indian history of the Southwest, especially Arizona; Arizona history and mining. **Special Collections:** Sharlot Hall Collection (7 cubic feet); cowboy folklore and music collection (100 cassette tapes). **Holdings:** 9000 volumes; 200 linear feet of uncataloged items; 200 oral history/folklore tapes; photographs; manuscripts; diaries; artifacts; letters. **Subscriptions:** 13 journals and other serials. **Services:** Interlibrary loan; copying; library/archives open to the public. **Publications:** Quarterly newsletter.

★13106★
SHARON GENERAL HOSPITAL - MEDICAL STAFF LIBRARY (Med)
740 E. State St. Phone: (412)981-1700
Sharon, PA 16146 Eugenia Christenson, Libn.
Staff: 1. **Subjects:** Medicine and allied health sciences. **Holdings:** 283 books; 679 bound periodical volumes; 2422 unbound journals; 2 VF drawers of clip sheets and pamphlets. **Subscriptions:** 33 journals and other serials. **Services:** Interlibrary loan; copying; library open to community residents.

★13107★
SHARON GENERAL HOSPITAL - SCHOOL OF NURSING - LIBRARY (Med)
740 E. State St. Phone: (412)981-1700
Sharon, PA 16146 Eugenia Christenson, Libn.
Staff: 1. **Subjects:** Nursing, medicine, nutrition, and allied health sciences. **Holdings:** 1500 books; 200 bound periodical volumes; 50 volumes of unbound journals; 4 VF drawers of clipsheets and pamphlets; 117 videotapes; 261 filmstrips and records; 14 slide cassette programs; 23 audio cassettes. **Subscriptions:** 25 journals and other serials. **Services:** Interlibrary loan; copying; library open to community residents.

★13108★
SHARON HOSPITAL - HEALTH SCIENCES LIBRARY (Med)
W. Main St. Phone: (203)364-4095
Sharon, CT 06069 Jackie Rorke, Libn.
Subjects: Medicine. **Holdings:** 400 books; 1440 bound periodical volumes. **Subscriptions:** 107 journals and other serials. **Services:** Interlibrary loan; copying; library open to the public for reference use only. **Networks/Consortia:** Member of Northwestern Connecticut Health Science Library Consortium.

SHARON WOODS TECHNICAL CENTER
See: Procter & Gamble Company (11604)

CHARLES CUTLER SHARP LIBRARY
See: Ohio State University - Chemistry Library (10685)

★13109★
ELLA SHARP MUSEUM - RESEARCH LIBRARY (Hist)
3225 Fourth St. Phone: (517)787-2320
Jackson, MI 49203 Ruthellen M. Sharp, Libn./Archv.
Founded: 1965. **Staff:** Prof 1; Other 4. **Subjects:** Local history, Victorian culture, art, museum techniques, space science and history. **Special Collections:** Merriman-Sharp Collection (family papers, 1835-1912); Anna Berger-Lynch Papers; Withington Papers; Hurst Collection (16th to 18th century European prints); rare books. **Holdings:** 4000 books; 20 bound periodical volumes; 100 boxes of Victorian era periodicals; 40 boxes of archival materials; club programs; photographs. **Subscriptions:** 25 journals and other serials. **Services:** Interlibrary loan; copying; library open to the public for reference use only.

★13110★
SHARP MEMORIAL HOSPITAL - HEALTH SCIENCES LIBRARY (Med)
7901 Frost St. Phone: (619)541-3242
San Diego, CA 92123 A. Peri Worthington, Dir. of Lib.Serv.
Founded: 1970. **Staff:** Prof 1; Other 2. **Subjects:** Clinical medicine, nursing. **Holdings:** 1416 books; 2380 bound periodical volumes. **Subscriptions:** 180 journals and other serials; 5 newspapers. **Services:** Interlibrary loan; copying; SDI; library open to the public by appointment. **Automated Operations:** Computerized cataloging, serials, and circulation. **Computerized Information Services:** MEDLARS, DIALOG Information Services; DOCLINE, OnTyme Electronic Message Network Service (electronic mail services). Performs searches on fee basis. **Networks/Consortia:** Member of Medical Library Group of Southern California and Arizona (MLGSCA), Pacific Southwest Regional Medical Library Service. **Publications:** Newsletter, quarterly - for internal distribution only. **Special Catalogs:** Journal holdings list.

REUBEN L. SHARP HEALTH SCIENCE LIBRARY
See: Cooper Hospital/University Medical Center (3735)

★13111★
SHASTA COUNTY LAW LIBRARY (Law)
Court House, Rm. 301
1500 Court St. Phone: (916)225-5645
Redding, CA 96001 Carol Tracy, Law Libn.
Founded: 1851. **Subjects:** Law. **Holdings:** 13,500 books and bound periodical volumes. **Subscriptions:** 12 journals and other serials. **Services:** Interlibrary loan; copying; library open to the public.

★13112★
LEMUEL SHATTUCK HOSPITAL - MEDICAL LIBRARY (Med)
170 Morton St. Phone: (617)522-8110
Jamaica Plain, MA 02130 Ann Collins, Libn.
Founded: 1954. **Staff:** Prof 1; Other 1. **Subjects:** Medicine and allied health sciences. **Holdings:** 940 books; 4360 bound periodical volumes; 320 audio cassettes. **Subscriptions:** 185 journals and other serials. **Services:** Interlibrary loan; library not open to the public. **Computerized Information Services:** NLM, BRS Information Technologies; MEDLINK, DOCLINE (electronic mail services). **Networks/Consortia:** Member of Boston Biomedical Library Consortium.

SHATTUCK MEMORIAL LIBRARY
See: Bisbee Mining and Historical Museum (1622)

★13113★
SHAVER HOSPITAL - HEALTH SCIENCES LIBRARY (Med)
541 Glenridge Ave. Phone: (416)685-1381
St. Catharines, ON, Canada L2R 6S5 Ruth Servos, Dir., Med.Rec.
Staff: 1. **Subjects:** Medicine, nursing, and allied health sciences. **Special Collections:** Canadian Tuberculosis Association, 1927 to present; Tuberculosis in Industry, 1941 to present; Financial & Medical Statistics of Sanitoria of Ontario, 1930 to present. **Holdings:** 3000 books; 300 bound periodical volumes; manuscripts; reports and clippings. **Subscriptions:** 31 journals and other serials. **Services:** Interlibrary loan; copying; library open to medical personnel.

ROBERT E. SHAVER LIBRARY OF ENGINEERING
See: University of Kentucky (16325)

ALFRED SHAW AND EDWARD DURELL STONE LIBRARY
See: Boston Architectural Center - Alfred Shaw and Edward Durell Stone Library (1725)

CHARLES E. SHAW HERPETOLOGICAL LIBRARY
See: Zoological Society of San Diego - Ernst Schwarz Library (18252)

EDWIN SHAW ARCHIVES
See: Akron Art Museum - Library (122)

SHAW HISTORICAL LIBRARY
See: Oregon Institute of Technology (10894)

J. PORTER SHAW LIBRARY
See: National Maritime Museum (9742)

★13114★
THE LLOYD SHAW FOUNDATION - ARCHIVES (Rec)
1620 Los Alamos Ave., S.W. Phone: (515)247-3921
Albuquerque, NM 87104 Dr. William M. Litchman, Dir.
Founded: 1977. **Staff:** Prof 1. **Subjects:** Dancing - square, round, contra, social, folk. **Special Collections:** Dance Away Library (5000 items); Charlie Thomas Collection (square dance; 2000 items); Bob Osgood Collection (square dance recordings). **Holdings:** 3000 books; 1000 unbound periodicals; letters; sheet music; phonograph records; audio- and videotapes; wire recordings; photographs; Square Dancing Hall of Fame portraits; clothing. **Subscriptions:** 50 journals and other serials. **Services:** Copying; archives open to the public. **Automated Operations:** Computerized cataloging. **Computerized Information Services:** Internal databases. **Publications:** Bibliography of Square Dance History; Bibliography of American Square Dance; Bibliography of American Round Dance; Bibliography of American Contra Dance. **Special Catalogs:** Catalog of Dance Videos; Catalog of Videotapes (printout); Catalog of the Dance Away Library (printout). **Remarks:** An alternate telephone number is 255-2661. Library is located at 5506 Coal Ave., S.E., Albuquerque, NM 87108.

★13115★
SHAW, PITTMAN, POTTS & TROWBRIDGE - LIBRARY (Law)
2300 N St., N.W. Phone: (202)663-8500
Washington, DC 20037 Carolyn P. Ahearn, Libn.
Staff: Prof 3; Other 5. **Subjects:** Law. **Holdings:** 24,000 books; 550 bound periodical volumes; 1000 congressional hearings; 8 VF drawers of pamphlets. **Subscriptions:** 200 journals and other serials. **Services:** Interlibrary loan; copying; library open to the public with restrictions. **Computerized Information Services:** LEXIS, DIALOG Information Services, WESTLAW, Dow Jones News/Retrieval.

SHAWINIGAN CONSULTANTS INC.
See: Lavalin Inc. (7688)

★13116★
SHAWMUT BANK, N.A. - LIBRARY (Bus-Fin)
1 Federal St., 8th Fl. Phone: (617)292-2550
Boston, MA 02211 Leslie C. Knapp, Libn.
Founded: 1981. **Staff:** Prof 1; Other 1. **Subjects:** Banking, finance, business. **Special Collections:** D.T. Trigg Collection on Lending and Credit Practices (120 items). **Holdings:** 2500 books; 120 bound periodical volumes; 220 other cataloged items; 10 VF drawers of subject files. **Subscriptions:** 100 journals and other serials; 20 newspapers. **Services:** Interlibrary loan; library not open to the public. **Computerized Information Services:** DIALOG Information Services, Dow Jones News/Retrieval. **Publications:** Library Morning News Service; Monthly Bulletin; Library Review; FOCUS; Article Alert - all for internal distribution only.

★13117★
SHAWNEE MISSION MEDICAL CENTER - MEDICAL LIBRARY (Med)
9100 W. 74th
Box 2923 Phone: (913)676-2101
Shawnee Mission, KS 66201 Clifford L. Nestell, Lib.Dir.
Staff: Prof 1; Other 4. **Subjects:** Medicine. **Holdings:** 6831 books; 6904 bound periodical volumes; 2350 audiotapes; 435 videotapes. **Subscriptions:** 619 journals and other serials. **Services:** Interlibrary loan; copying; SDI; library open to the public with restrictions. **Automated Operations:** Computerized cataloging, acquisitions, serials, circulation, and ILL. **Computerized Information Services:** DIALOG Information Services, NLM, OCLC, AMA/NET. **Networks/Consortia:** Member of Kansas City Library Network, Inc. (KCLN), Kansas City Metropolitan Library Network (KCMLN).

★13118★
SH&E, INC. - LIBRARY (Trans)
708 Third Ave., 17th Fl. Phone: (212)682-8455
New York, NY 10017 Beth L. Geltman, Libn.
Founded: 1963. **Staff:** Prof 1. **Subjects:** Transportation, aircraft, airport planning, tourism, travel, economics, finance, marketing. **Holdings:** 10,000

books; 100 bound periodical volumes; 500 statistical volumes. **Subscriptions:** 100 journals and other serials. **Services:** Interlibrary loan; copying; library open to the public with restrictions.

★13119★
SHEA & GARDNER - LIBRARY (Law)
1800 Massachusetts Ave., N.W. Phone: (202)828-2019
Washington, DC 20036 Sharon Kissel, Libn.
Founded: 1950. **Staff:** Prof 1; Other 3. **Subjects:** Law - labor, transportation, environment. **Special Collections:** Legislative histories (500 volumes). **Holdings:** 28,000 books; 600 bound periodical volumes; 1500 other cataloged items. **Subscriptions:** 1000 journals and other serials. **Services:** Interlibrary loan; library not open to the public. **Computerized Information Services:** LEXIS, NEXIS, DIALOG Information Services, WESTLAW, VU/TEXT Information Services, NewsNet,

★13120★
SHEA & GOULD - LIBRARY (Law)
1251 Avenue of the Americas Phone: (212)827-3489
New York, NY 10020 Jean P. O'Grady, Law Libn.
Founded: 1964. **Staff:** Prof 4; Other 8. **Subjects:** Law - real estate, corporate, tax, trusts and estates, administrative, public utilities, bankruptcy, labor; litigation. **Holdings:** 20,000 books. **Subscriptions:** 100 journals and other serials; 10 newspapers. **Services:** Interlibrary loan; library not open to the public. **Automated Operations:** Computerized public access catalog and cataloging. **Computerized Information Services:** Information America, LEGI-SLATE, LEXIS, NEXIS, DIALOG Information Services, WESTLAW, DataTimes, Dow Jones News/Retrieval, Dun & Bradstreet Corporation, VU/TEXT Information Services, OCLC, Legislative Information System (LIS); KILS-Keyword in Context Litigation System (internal database); ABA/net (electronic mail service). **Publications:** Library News (newsletter), monthly - for internal distribution only. **Staff:** Lynn R. Stram, Sys.Libn.; C. Shireen Kumar, Asst.Libn.; Patricia Barbone, Corp.Info.Spec.; Estelita Cuna, Acq..

JAMES J. SHEA MEMORIAL LIBRARY
See: American International College (567)

★13121★
SHEARMAN & STERLING - LIBRARY (Law)
153 E. 53rd St., Rm. 3205 Phone: (212)484-4624
New York, NY 10022 Jack S. Ellenberger, Dir. of Libs.
Staff: Prof 5. **Subjects:** Law. **Holdings:** 65,000 volumes. **Services:** Interlibrary loan; library not open to the public. **Automated Operations:** Computerized cataloging. **Computerized Information Services:** Dow Jones News/Retrieval, LEXIS, WESTLAW, DIALOG Information Services. **Remarks:** An alternate telephone number is 484-4626. **Staff:** Joseph Florio, Ref.Libn.; John Lai, Cat. & Sys.; Katharine Wolpe, Ref.Coord. & Bibliog..

★13122★
SHEARSON LEHMAN BROTHERS INC. - RESEARCH LIBRARY
14 Wall St.
New York, NY 10005
Defunct

★13123★
SHEARSON LEHMAN HUTTON - CORPORATE LIBRARY (Bus-Fin)
American Express Tower
200 Vesey St. Phone: (212)298-2783
New York, NY 10285-1590 Ronald F. Dow, V.P., Corp.Lib.Serv.
Founded: 1930. **Staff:** Prof 12; Other 47. **Subjects:** Finance. **Special Collections:** Annual reports; Securities and Exchange Commission (SEC) filings and pricings. **Holdings:** 1000 volumes; 900 VF drawers of pamphlets. **Subscriptions:** 800 journals and other serials; 20 newspapers. **Services:** Interlibrary loan; library not open to the public. **Automated Operations:** Computerized cataloging, acquisitions, and serials. **Computerized Information Services:** DIALOG Information Services, NEXIS, Dow Jones News/Retrieval, International Data Corporation (IDC), I.P. Sharp Associates Limited, Spectrum Ownership Profiles Online, Vickers Stock Research Corporation, Dun & Bradstreet Corporation, Disclosure Information Group, Bechtel Information Services (BIS), INVESTEXT, Finsbury Data Services Ltd. **Remarks:** Contains the holdings of American Express Company - Card Information Center and American Express Company - CFS Technical Information Center. **Formerly:** Shearson Lehman Brothers Inc. **Staff:** Louise Gent-Sandford, Libn.; Harriet Wisner, Libn.; Andrea Goodman, Libn.; Sizeekumar Menon, Libn.; Cheryl Wacher, Libn.; Robert Alfonso, Libn.; Sarika Mahant, Libn.; Sarah Gross, Libn.; Elizabeth Boutinon, Libn.; Joe Dottavio, Tech.Serv.; Deonna Taylor, Libn..

PAUL B. SHEATSLEY LIBRARY
See: University of Chicago - National Opinion Research Center (16034)

★13124★
SHEBOYGAN COUNTY HISTORICAL RESEARCH CENTER (Hist)
518 Water St. Phone: (414)467-4667
Sheboygan Falls, WI 53085 Janice Hildebrand, Libn.
Founded: 1983. **Staff:** Prof 1; Other 1. **Subjects:** County history and genealogy. **Special Collections:** Civil War; World War I. **Holdings:** 5000 books; historic photographs; county land records. **Services:** Copying; center open to the public for reference use only. **Remarks:** Jointly maintained by Sheboygan County Genealogy Society, Sheboygan County Historical Society, and Sheboygan County Landmarks, Ltd.

★13125★
SHEBOYGAN PRESS LIBRARY (Publ)
632 Center Ave. Phone: (414)457-7711
Sheboygan, WI 53081 Janice Hildebrand, Libn.
Staff: Prof 1. **Subjects:** Newspaper reference topics. **Special Collections:** Wisconsin Blue Books; city directories; local and state histories. **Holdings:** 200 books; 600 bound periodical volumes; newspapers, 1907 to present, on microfilm. **Subscriptions:** 10 journals and other serials; 30 newspapers. **Services:** Copying; library open to the public. **Special Catalogs:** Local obituaries, 1966 to present.

★13126★
JOHN G. SHEDD AQUARIUM - LIBRARY (Biol Sci)
1200 S. Lake Shore Dr. Phone: (312)939-2426
Chicago, IL 60605 Janet E. Powers, Libn.
Founded: 1975. **Staff:** Prof 1; Other 2. **Subjects:** Marine and freshwater biology, fishes, water pollution, fisheries, Lake Michigan, aquatic education. **Holdings:** 7500 books; 300 file folders of clippings, reprints, pamphlets. **Subscriptions:** 250 journals and other serials. **Services:** Interlibrary loan (limited); copying; library open to the public by appointment. **Automated Operations:** Computerized cataloging. **Networks/Consortia:** Member of Chicago Library System.

SHEELY-LEE LAW LIBRARY
See: Dickinson School of Law (4258)

FULTON J. SHEEN ARCHIVES
See: Ambrose Swasey Library (13830)

★13127★
SHELBURNE MUSEUM, INC. - RESEARCH LIBRARY (Hist, Art)
Shelburne, VT 05482 Phone: (802)985-3346
Founded: 1947. **Subjects:** Antiques, art, Vermontiana, furniture, architecture, textiles, transportation. **Holdings:** 7000 books; 600 bound periodical volumes; 1400 pamphlets; 164 magazines on antiques; 260 manuscripts; 600 volumes of records of museum holdings. **Subscriptions:** 55 journals and other serials. **Services:** Copying; library open to the public by appointment.

★13128★
SHELBY COUNTY LAW LIBRARY (Law)
Courthouse Phone: (513)498-4541
Sidney, OH 45365 Rita Miller, Libn.
Staff: 2. **Subjects:** Law. **Holdings:** 18,000 books; microfiche. **Subscriptions:** 75 journals and other serials. **Services:** Copying; library open to the public for reference use only.

★13129★
SHELDON MUSEUM - LIBRARY (Hist)
1 Park St. Phone: (802)388-2117
Middlebury, VT 05753 Polly C. Darnell, Libn.
Founded: 1882. **Staff:** Prof 2. **Subjects:** Addison County and Vermont history. **Special Collections:** Newspapers published in Middlebury, 1801 to present (bound); letters (filed by date; 30,000). **Holdings:** 4000 books; pamphlets; 200 scrapbooks compiled by Henry L. Sheldon; 350 linear feet of manuscripts, account books, diaries; 1000 photographs of local scenes and people; 117 maps; 57 audiotapes; 3 videotapes. **Services:** Library open to the public for reference use only. **Publications:** Annual report; newsletter - to members; Addison County Heritage: Historical Studies from the Library of the Sheldon Museum, irregular - for sale. **Special Indexes:** Index

of letters (author and subject; card). **Staff:** Phyllis B. Cunningham, Asst.Libn..

SHELDON MUSEUM & CULTURAL CENTER
See: Chilkat Valley Historical Society (3125)

★13130★
SHELL CANADA LIMITED - LIBRARY (Energy)
400 4th Ave., S.W.
Sta. M, P.O. Box 100 Phone: (403)232-4070
Calgary, AB, Canada T2P 2H5 Mila E. Carozzi, Hd.Libn.
Founded: 1958. **Staff:** Prof 3; Other 4. **Subjects:** Geology, earth sciences, petroleum and chemical engineering, minerals, business and economics. **Special Collections:** Geological Survey of Canada publications. **Holdings:** 6500 books; 120 bound periodical volumes; 9000 government documents; 160 microfiche; 200 reels of microfilm; 575 theses. **Subscriptions:** 1200 journals and other serials; 12 newspapers. **Services:** Interlibrary loan (limited); library open to the public for reference use only. **Automated Operations:** Computerized cataloging, serials, and circulation. **Computerized Information Services:** DIALOG Information Services, NEXIS, Pergamon ORBIT InfoLine, Inc., CANSIM, Compusearch Market and Social Research Ltd., CAN/OLE, Info Globe; SCROLL (internal database). **Publications:** Current Awareness Bulletin, monthly - for internal distribution only. **Remarks:** An alternate telephone number is 232-3249. **Staff:** Dorothy Gilbert, Libn..

★13131★
SHELL CANADA LIMITED - OAKVILLE RESEARCH CENTRE - SHELL RESEARCH CENTRE LIBRARY (Energy)
P.O. Box 2100 Phone: (416)827-1141
Oakville, ON, Canada L6J 5C7 Mr. Lan C. Sun, Libn.
Founded: 1970. **Staff:** Prof 1; Other 4. **Subjects:** Petroleum technology products and processes. **Holdings:** 5000 volumes; 40,000 proprietary research and technical reports; 6000 pamphlets, journal articles, patents. **Subscriptions:** 110 journals and other serials; 5 newspapers. **Services:** Interlibrary loan; copying; library open to the public with restrictions on proprietary materials. **Automated Operations:** Computerized cataloging, acquisitions, serials, circulation, and ILL. **Computerized Information Services:** CAN/OLE, DIALOG Information Services, NLM, Pergamon ORBIT InfoLine, Inc., Canadian Center for Occupational Health and Safety; INFO/ORC (internal database); Envoy 100, DIALMAIL, Shell PROFS System (electronic mail services). **Networks/Consortia:** Member of Shell Canada Technical Information System. **Publications:** Monthly Accession List of Final Reports and Monographs; Monthly Subject List of Shell Periodical Report Articles. **Special Indexes:** Eight separate indexes (corporate author, title, personal author, series, project, subject, KWIC index, and shelf list or master file), produced cumulatively every month on COM microfiche from computer tape and merged annually with previous years.

★13132★
SHELL DEVELOPMENT COMPANY - BELLAIRE RESEARCH CENTER LIBRARY (Energy)
Box 481 Phone: (713)663-2293
Houston, TX 77001 Aphrodite Mamoulides, Lib.Supv.
Founded: 1946. **Staff:** Prof 2; Other 1. **Subjects:** Geology, geophysics, petroleum-reservoir engineering, drilling and production, computer science. **Holdings:** 14,000 books; 6000 bound periodical volumes; 3000 pamphlets; 20,000 government reports; 3000 dissertations. **Subscriptions:** 600 journals and other serials. **Services:** Interlibrary loan; copying; library open to the public. **Automated Operations:** Computerized public access catalog, cataloging, acquisitions, and serials. **Computerized Information Services:** Pergamon ORBIT InfoLine, Inc. **Publications:** Weekly Acquisitions List; Weekly Library Bulletin. **Staff:** F.B. Melde, Libn..

★13133★
SHELL DEVELOPMENT COMPANY - WESTHOLLOW RESEARCH CENTER LIBRARY (Sci-Engr, Energy)
3333 Hwy. 6, S.
Box 1378 Phone: (713)493-7530
Houston, TX 77001 Linda Jeff Pharis, Supv.
Founded: 1975. **Subjects:** Corrosion, petrochemicals, petroleum refining, toxicology. **Holdings:** 14,000 volumes. **Subscriptions:** 1430 journals and other serials. **Computerized Information Services:** DIALOG Information Services, Pergamon ORBIT InfoLine, Inc.

JOHN N. SHELL LIBRARY
See: Nassau County Medical Society - Nassau Academy of Medicine (9527)

★13134★
SHELL OIL COMPANY - INFORMATION & LIBRARY SERVICES (Energy, Bus-Fin)
Box 587 Phone: (713)241-5433
Houston, TX 77001 Jane C. Rodgers, Lib.Supv.
Founded: 1971. **Staff:** Prof 7; Other 9. **Subjects:** Petroleum, business, chemistry, management. **Holdings:** 16,000 volumes. **Subscriptions:** 900 journals and other serials. **Services:** Interlibrary loan; SDI; services open to the public. **Automated Operations:** Computerized cataloging, acquisitions, serials, and circulation. **Computerized Information Services:** DIALOG Information Services, Pergamon ORBIT InfoLine, Inc., Dow Jones News/Retrieval, NEXIS, RLIN, PIERS (Port Import/Export Reporting Service), STN International, VU/TEXT Information Services, Data Resources (DRI), DataTimes, Oil & Gas Journal Energy Database; OnTyme Electronic Message Network Service, DIALMAIL (electronic mail services). **Staff:** Patricia A. Kanter, Sect.Supv.; M. Caldwell, Info.Anl.; M. Pappas, Sr.Info.Anl.; K. Johnson, Info.Anl.; D. Baier, Anl.; C. Wehmeyer, Anl..

★13135★
SHELL OIL COMPANY - PUBLIC AFFAIRS RESEARCH SERVICE (Energy)
Box 2463 Phone: (713)241-4231
Houston, TX 77001 Anita W. Dorsett, Pub.Aff.Rep.
Founded: 1980. **Staff:** Prof 1; Other 3. **Subjects:** Oil and chemical industries, government affairs, news media. **Holdings:** 400 books; 10,000 photographs and slides; Shell Oil Company publications. **Subscriptions:** 25 journals and other serials; 8 newspapers. **Services:** Copying; SDI; service open to the public with restrictions. **Computerized Information Services:** DIALOG Information Services, BRS Information Technologies, Pergamon ORBIT InfoLine, Inc., NEXIS, LEGI-SLATE, The Source Information Network, CompuServe, Inc., NewsNet, Inc.; internal database; DIALMAIL (electronic mail service). **Remarks:** Library located at 900 Louisiana, Rm. 1579, Houston, TX 77002.

★13136★
SHELL OIL COMPANY - SHELL WESTERN E & P INC. - WOODCREEK LIBRARY (Sci-Engr)
Box 4423 Phone: (713)870-4025
Houston, TX 77210-4423 Frances K. Brown, Sr.Info.Anl.
Founded: 1981. **Staff:** Prof 3; Other 10. **Subjects:** Geology, production technology, energy, mining, minerals. **Holdings:** 32,000 books; 5200 bound periodical volumes; 50,000 Shell proprietary reports. **Subscriptions:** 432 journals and other serials. **Services:** Interlibrary loan; copying; SDI; library open to the public by appointment. **Automated Operations:** Computerized cataloging, acquisitions, serials, circulation, and journal routing. **Computerized Information Services:** DIALOG Information Services, Pergamon ORBIT InfoLine, Inc., RLIN, NEXIS, VU/TEXT Information Services, WILSONLINE, Dow Jones News/Retrieval; internal databases; DIALMAIL (electronic mail service). **Publications:** Awareness Bulletin (for proprietary reports), monthly - for internal distribution only. **Staff:** Anne H. Krum, Anl.; Michael B. Schuldt, Info.Anl..

SHELL WESTERN E & P INC.
See: Shell Oil Company (13136)

★13137★
SHELTER ISLAND HISTORICAL SOCIETY - HAVENS HOUSE MUSEUM - ARCHIVES (Hist)
16 S. Ferry Rd. Phone: (516)749-0025
Shelter Island, NY 11964 Margaret Joyce, Chm.
Staff: 9. **Subjects:** Local history. **Special Collections:** Worthington journals and notebooks (ornithology); Shelter Island historic house research and photographic records. **Holdings:** 200 books; 25 bound periodical volumes; 200 postcards; 400 literary documents; 100 financial documents; 30 maps; 1600 clippings; 425 photographs; genealogical material. **Services:** Copying; archives open to the public for reference use only.

HERBERT SHELTON LIBRARY
See: American Natural Hygiene Society, Inc. (617)

★13138★
SHENANDOAH COLLEGE & CONSERVATORY - HOWE LIBRARY - SPECIAL COLLECTIONS (Rel-Phil)
Winchester, VA 22601 Phone: (703)665-4553
Subjects: History of Evangelical United Brethren Church. **Holdings:** Figures not available. **Services:** Interlibrary loan; copying; collection open to the public, registration required. **Computerized Information Services:** DIALOG Information Services. Performs searches on fee basis.

★13139★
SHENANGO VALLEY MEDICAL CENTER - MEDICAL LIBRARY (Med)
2200 Memorial Dr. Extended Phone: (412)981-3500
Farrell, PA 16121 Ethelnel Baron, Staff Sec.
Staff: 1. **Subjects:** Medicine. **Holdings:** 500 books; 200 video cassettes; 200 Audio-Digest tapes. **Subscriptions:** 40 journals and other serials. **Services:** Interlibrary loan; library not open to the public. **Networks/Consortia:** Member of Greater Northeastern Regional Medical Library Program.

DRS. BEN AND A. JESS SHENSON LIBRARY
See: Triton Museum of Art (14352)

CARL F. SHEPARD MEMORIAL LIBRARY
See: Illinois College of Optometry (6687)

EDWARD M. SHEPARD MEMORIAL ROOM
See: Springfield-Greene County Public Libraries (13574)

★13140★
SHEPARD'S/MC GRAW-HILL - LIBRARY (Law)
420 N. Cascade Ave.
Box 1235 Phone: (719)475-7230
Colorado Springs, CO 80901 Gregory P. Harris, Libn.
Founded: 1873. **Staff:** Prof 3. **Subjects:** Law. **Holdings:** 60,000 books; 30,000 reports; 20,000 statutes, digests. **Subscriptions:** 500 journals and other serials. **Services:** Library not open to the public. **Computerized Information Services:** WESTLAW, LEXIS.

GEORGE SHEPHERD LIBRARY
See: Saskatchewan Western Development Museums (12924)

SHEPPARD LIBRARY
See: Massachusetts College of Pharmacy and Allied Health Sciences (8522)

★13141★
SHEPPARD, MULLIN, RICHTER & HAMPTON - LAW LIBRARY (Law)
333 S. Hope St., 48th Fl. Phone: (213)620-1780
Los Angeles, CA 90071 James S. Hauger, Libn.
Staff: Prof 1; Other 3. **Subjects:** Law. **Holdings:** 30,000 books. **Subscriptions:** 75 journals and other serials. **Services:** Interlibrary loan; library not open to the public. **Automated Operations:** Computerized cataloging, acquisitions, and circulation. **Computerized Information Services:** LEXIS, DIALOG Information Services, WESTLAW, Dow Jones News/Retrieval, VU/TEXT Information Services, PHINet FedTax Database, DataTimes, LEGI-SLATE, Information America.

SHEPPARD PROFESSIONAL LIBRARY
See: Baptist Medical System - Sheppard Professional Library (1327)

★13142★
SHERIDAN COLLEGE - GRIFFITH MEMORIAL LIBRARY - SPECIAL COLLECTIONS (Rare Book, Hist)
Box 1500 Phone: (307)674-6446
Sheridan, WY 82801 Deborah Iverson, Lib.Dir.
Staff: Prof 1; Other 5. **Special Collections:** Reynolds Memorial Collection of Western Americana; Sheridan College history; Thorne-Rider memorabilia; Griffith artifact collection; rare book collection. **Subscriptions:** 325 journals and other serials. **Services:** Interlibrary loan; copying; collections open to the public. **Automated Operations:** Computerized cataloging. **Computerized Information Services:** BRS Information Technologies, MEDLARS; DOCLINE (electronic mail service). Performs searches on fee basis. **Networks/Consortia:** Member of Bibliographical Center for Research, Rocky Mountain Region, Inc. (BCR), Northeastern Wyoming Medical Library Consortium.

★13143★
SHERIDAN COLLEGE OF APPLIED ARTS AND TECHNOLOGY - SCHOOL OF DESIGN - LIBRARY
1460 S. Sheridan Way
Mississauga, ON, Canada L5H 1Z7
Defunct. Holding absorbed by Sheridan College of Applied Arts and Technology, Oakville Campus - Arts and Crafts Library.

★13144★
SHERIDAN COUNTY HISTORICAL SOCIETY, INC. - AGNES & CLARENCE BENSCHOTER MEMORIAL LIBRARY (Hist)
Box 274 Phone: (308)327-2961
Rushville, NE 69360 Robert W. Buchan, Cur.
Founded: 1958. **Staff:** Prof 1; Other 1. **Subjects:** Western and Nebraska history; military; genealogy. **Special Collections:** Camp Sheridan, Nebraska archives, 1874-1881. **Holdings:** 700 books; 100 bound periodical volumes; clippings; manuscripts; albums. **Services:** Copying; library open to the public by appointment. **Publications:** Recollections of Sheridan County.

SHERMAN ART LIBRARY
See: Dartmouth College (4049)

★13145★
SHERMAN COLLEGE OF STRAIGHT CHIROPRACTIC - TOM AND MAE BAHAN LIBRARY (Med)
Box 1452 Phone: (803)578-8770
Spartanburg, SC 29304 David M. Bowles, Lib.Dir.
Staff: Prof 1; Other 6. **Subjects:** Chiropractic, clinical and basic sciences. **Special Collections:** B.J. Palmer Collection. **Holdings:** 9100 books; 1137 bound periodical volumes; 243 audiotapes; 81 videotapes; 2471 slides; 3 16mm films; 8 phonograph records; 4 VF drawers. **Subscriptions:** 104 journals and other serials; 10 newspapers. **Services:** Interlibrary loan; copying; library open to chiropractic doctors. **Automated Operations:** Computerized cataloging and ILL. **Computerized Information Services:** OCLC, MEDLINE; internal database. Performs searches on fee basis.

★13146★
SHERMAN RESEARCH LIBRARY (Hist)
614 Dahlia Ave. Phone: (714)673-1880
Corona Del Mar, CA 92625 Dr. William O. Hendricks, Dir.
Founded: 1966. **Staff:** Prof 2. **Subjects:** Pacific Southwest history, 1870 to present - economic development, land and water, transportation, immigration. **Special Collections:** Sherman papers; Brant papers; Colorado River Land Company documents. **Holdings:** 15,000 books; 400 bound periodical volumes; 2500 pamphlets; 375 document boxes of business papers; 1475 reels of microfilm of newspapers; 200 theses and dissertations on microfilm; 2000 maps. **Subscriptions:** 30 journals and other serials. **Services:** Interlibrary loan; library open to the public. **Special Catalogs:** Inventory catalogs to the papers. **Staff:** Reva McFarlane, Res.Asst..

HENRY KNOX SHERRILL RESOURCE CENTER
See: Episcopal Church Executive Council (4751)

★13147★
SHERRITT GORDON MINES, LTD. - RESEARCH CENTRE LIBRARY (Sci-Engr)
Fort Saskatchewan, AB, Canada T8L 2P2 Phone: (403)998-6419
Anne Poulton, Libn.
Founded: 1953. **Staff:** 1. **Subjects:** Hydrometallurgy, inorganic chemistry, physical chemistry, fertilizers. **Holdings:** 7000 books and bound periodical volumes; 1500 slides; 1000 laboratory reports, pilot plant reports, Sherritt-published papers. **Subscriptions:** 250 journals and other serials. **Services:** Interlibrary loan; library not open to the public. **Computerized Information Services:** EBSCONET; internal database. **Publications:** Acquisitions report, monthly - for internal distribution only.

★13148★
SHERWIN-WILLIAMS COMPANY - INFORMATION CENTER (Comp Sci)
13 Midland Bldg.
101 Prospect Ave., N.W. Phone: (216)234-6444
Cleveland, OH 44115 Gary Weske, Info.Ctr.Dir.
Founded: 1982. **Staff:** Prof 5. **Subjects:** Data processing, business. **Holdings:** 300 books; 1500 computer listings; 300 technical manuals; 3 VF drawers of hardware/software product brochures. **Subscriptions:** 100 journals and other serials; 5 newspapers. **Services:** Center not open to the public. **Automated Operations:** Computerized cataloging, serials, circulation, and routing. **Computerized Information Services:** DIALOG Information Services, The Source Information Network; internal database. **Publications:** Education Newsletter, monthly; Information Center Bulletin, bimonthly - both for internal distribution only. **Staff:** Pamela J. Kuzma, Anl./Libn.; Ron Kubalski, Anl.; Robert Holland, Anl.; Ken Schlosser, Anl..

K.K. SHERWOOD LIBRARY
See: University of Washington - Health Sciences Library and Information Center (17065)

★13149★
SHEVCHENKO SCIENTIFIC SOCIETY, INC. - LIBRARY AND ARCHIVES (Area-Ethnic)
63 4th Ave. Phone: (212)254-5130
New York, NY 10003 Svitlana Andrushkiw, Dir.
Founded: 1873. **Staff:** Prof 1; Other 2. **Subjects:** Ukrainian and Slavic languages, Ukrainians in the U.S. and in foreign countries, literature, history, arts, music, geography, ethnography, sciences. **Special Collections:** World Wars I and II; Displaced Person Camps archives. **Holdings:** 50,000 books; 5000 periodicals; 3000 manuscripts, archives, pamphlets; rare books. **Subscriptions:** 21 journals and other serials. **Services:** Copying; library open to serious researchers only. **Publications:** Publications catalog; pamphlets. **Staff:** G. Navrosky, Cat.; Wasyl Lev, Acq..

★13150★
SHIBLEY, RIGHTON & MC CUTCHEON - LIBRARY AND INFORMATION SERVICES (Law)
401 Bay St.
Box 32 Phone: (416)363-9381
Toronto, ON, Canada M5H 2Z1 Vivienne Denton, Libn.
Staff: Prof 1; Other 1. **Subjects:** Law - corporate, commercial, labor; Ontario litigation. **Holdings:** 2000 books; law reports. **Subscriptions:** 22 journals and other serials. **Services:** Interlibrary loan; copying; SDI; library open to Toronto law librarians. **Computerized Information Services:** QL Systems, WESTLAW, Info Globe. **Publications:** Library Bulletin, weekly - for internal distribution only. **Special Indexes:** Index to internal memoranda of law.

VERA PARSHALL SHIFFMAN MEDICAL LIBRARY
See: Wayne State University - School of Medicine (17593)

SHIKAR/SAFARI CLUB LIBRARY
See: Museum of York County - Library (9466)

★13151★
SHILOH MILITARY TRAIL, INC. - LIBRARY (Hist)
Box 17386 Phone: (901)454-5600
Memphis, TN 38187-0386 Edward F. Williams, III, Res.Hist.
Founded: 1961. **Staff:** 1. **Subjects:** Civil War history and American history. **Special Collections:** Civil War manuscripts and material related to the Battle of Shiloh and Confederate General Nathan Bedford Forrest (4 VF drawers). **Holdings:** 1000 books; 20 bound periodical volumes. **Subscriptions:** 10 journals and other serials. **Services:** Library open to the public by appointment. **Remarks:** Located in Memphis Pink Palace Museum Library, 232 Tilton, Memphis, TN 38111.

SHILOH NATIONAL MILITARY PARK
See: U.S. Natl. Park Service (15351)

★13152★
SHIPPENSBURG HISTORICAL SOCIETY - ARCHIVES (Hist)
52 W. King St.
Shippensburg, PA 17257 Phone: (717)532-4508
Subjects: History and genealogy of Shippensburg area. **Holdings:** Figures not available. **Services:** Archives open to the public by appointment.

★13153★
SHIPPENSBURG UNIVERSITY OF PENNSYLVANIA - EZRA LEHMAN MEMORIAL LIBRARY (Bus-Fin, Soc Sci)
Shippensburg, PA 17257 Phone: (717)532-1463
Virginia M. Crowe, Ph.D., Dir.
Founded: 1871. **Staff:** Prof 9; Other 18. **Subjects:** Business, education, arts and sciences, criminal justice, public administration. **Special Collections:** Media/Curricular Center; Pennsylvaniana; rare books; university archives (560 linear feet). **Holdings:** 398,500 books; 20,389 bound periodical volumes; 50,278 reels of microfilm; 1.2 million microfiche; 10,970 microprints; 7000 microcards; U.S. and Pennsylvania government documents. **Subscriptions:** 1788 journals and other serials; 33 newspapers. **Services:** Interlibrary loan; library open to the public for serious research. **Automated Operations:** Computerized cataloging and acquisitions. **Computerized Information Services:** DIALOG Information Services. Performs searches on fee basis. Contact Person: Madelyn Valunas, Sys. & Automation, 532-1479. **Networks/Consortia:** Member of PALINET, State System of Higher Education Libraries Council (SSHELCO). **Staff:** Judith Culbertson, Spec.Coll.; Linda Gatchel, Tech.Serv.; Signe Kelker, Ref./ILL; Berkley Laite, Dir. of Media/Curric.Ctr.; Hugh O'Brien, Coll.Mgt.; Fred Smith, Ref. and Lib./Bibliog.Instr.; Katherine Warkentin, Govt.Docs.; Robert Gimmi, Ser. & Circ..

★13154★
SHIPPENSBURG UNIVERSITY OF PENNSYLVANIA - SMALL BUSINESS INSTITUTE - LIBRARY
Shippen Hall
Shippensburg, PA 17257
Defunct. Holdings absorbed by Ezra Lehman Memorial Library.

★13155★
SHIPS OF THE SEA MARITIME MUSEUM - LIBRARY (Hist)
503 East River St.
Savannah, GA 31401 Phone: (912)232-1511
Founded: 1966. **Subjects:** Maritime history. **Holdings:** Figures not available. **Services:** Library open to the public for reference use only.

SHOALS MARINE LABORATORY
See: Cornell University (3794)

★13156★
SHODAIR CHILDREN'S HOSPITAL - MEDICAL INFORMATION & LIBRARY SERVICES (Med)
Box 5539 Phone: (406)442-1980
Helena, MT 59604 Suzy Holt, Info.Spec.
Founded: 1979. **Staff:** Prof 1; Other 1. **Subjects:** Genetics - human medical, disorders, counseling; cytogenetics; prenatal diagnosis; pediatrics. **Special Collections:** Lay Library for parents/patients with genetic disorders (250 booklets and brochures; fact sheets on 100 disorders). **Holdings:** 2000 books; 1000 bound periodical volumes; 15,000 reprints. **Subscriptions:** 65 journals and other serials. **Services:** Interlibrary loan; copying; SDI; services open to the public by prior arrangement. **Computerized Information Services:** DIALOG Information Services, WLN, MEDLARS; OnTyme Electronic Message Network Service (electronic mail service). Performs searches on fee basis. **Networks/Consortia:** Member of Helena Area Health Sciences Library Consortium (HAHSLC). **Remarks:** Fax: (406)443-0320.

MOSES SHOENBERG MEMORIAL LIBRARY
See: Jewish Hospital at Washington University Medical Center - School of Nursing (7217)

★13157★
SHOOK, HARDY & BACON - LIBRARY (Law)
Mercantile Bank Tower, 20th Fl.
1101 Walnut Phone: (816)474-6550
Kansas City, MO 64106 Lori Hunt, Dir., Lib. & Info.Serv.
Staff: Prof 4; Other 2. **Subjects:** Law - federal and state, products liability, antitrust, corporate, tax, labor. **Holdings:** 27,000 books; legal memoranda; 3000 ultrafiche. **Subscriptions:** 300 journals and other serials. **Services:** Interlibrary loan; library not open to the public. **Computerized Information Services:** NEXIS, VU/TEXT Information Services, Dow Jones News/Retrieval, LEXIS, WESTLAW, DIALOG Information Services; ABA/net, MCI Mail (electronic mail services). **Networks/Consortia:** Member of Kansas City Library Network, Inc. (KCLN). **Publications:** Law Review and Legal Periodical Current Awareness Services, monthly. **Special Indexes:** Index to Expert Witness File; index to Legal Memoranda File; index to Local Counsel File (all online). **Staff:** Janet Peters, Ref.Libn.; Michael McReynolds, Ref.Libn..

★13158★
SHORTER COLLEGE - MEMORABILIA ROOM (Hist)
Rome, GA 30161 Phone: (404)291-2121
Robert Gardner, Coll.Hist./Archv.
Subjects: History of Shorter College. **Holdings:** 350 books; 25 VF drawers of archives, manuscripts, documents, unbound reports, clippings; 300 artifacts. **Services:** Copying; room open to the public by appointment.

SHORTT LIBRARY OF CANADIANA
See: University of Saskatchewan - Special Collections (16841)

★13159★
SHOSTAL ASSOCIATES, INC. (Aud-Vis)
10 W. 20th St. Phone: (212)633-0101
New York, NY 10011 J.D. Barnell, Pres.
Founded: 1940. **Subjects:** Complete, up-to-date file of stock color transparencies of subjects of general interest with worldwide geographical coverage; special emphasis on educational projects and advertising. **Special Collections:** Large format original color transparencies representing hundreds of photographers from around the world. **Holdings:** Figures not available.

KENNETH J. SHOULDICE LIBRARY
See: Lake Superior State College (7616)

★13160★
SHOW BUSINESS ASSOCIATION - LIBRARY (Theater, Law)
1501 Broadway Phone: (212)354-7600
New York, NY 10036 Leo Shull, Pres.
Subjects: Entertainment industry, legislation pertinent to the arts. **Holdings:** 14,000 volumes.

G.H.P. SHOWALTER LIBRARY
See: Institute for Christian Studies - Library (6894)

★13161★
THE (Shreveport) TIMES - LIBRARY (Publ)
222 Lake St. Phone: (318)459-3283
Shreveport, LA 71130 Johnny L. King, Libn.
Founded: 1951. **Staff:** Prof 1; Other 3. **Subjects:** Newspaper reference topics. **Special Collections:** Shreveport Times, bound and on microfilm, 1871 to present; bound issues of the Sunday Magazine with index. **Holdings:** 2300 books; 20 bound periodical volumes; 50,000 newspaper clippings; 113 reels of microfilm; 15 VF drawers of photographs; caricatures; files of art work; 300 VF drawers. **Subscriptions:** 20 journals and other serials; 20 newspapers. **Services:** Library not open to the public. **Special Indexes:** Index to Sunday Magazine; index of daily clippings; index to Shreveport Magazine. **Remarks:** Published by Gannett Newspapers.

★13162★
SHREWSBURY DAILY-SUNDAY REGISTER - LIBRARY (Publ)
One Register Plaza Phone: (201)542-4000
Shrewsbury, NJ 07702 Carol Fenwick, Hd.Libn.
Staff: Prof 1; Other 1. **Subjects:** Newspaper reference topics. **Holdings:** 400 books; 75 bound periodical volumes; newspapers, 1878 to present, on microfilm; pamphlets; photographs; clippings. **Services:** Interlibrary loan; library not open to the public.

★13163★
SHRINE TO MUSIC MUSEUM - LIBRARY (Mus)
University of South Dakota
414 E. Clark St. Phone: (605)677-5306
Vermillion, SD 57069-2390 Andre P. Larson, Dir.
Founded: 1966. **Staff:** Prof 4; Other 1. **Subjects:** Musical instruments, musical history including American music, sheet and wind music. **Holdings:** 2100 books; 4000 musical instruments; 15,000 musical items; 8500 photographs; 10,000 sound recordings. **Services:** Copying; library open to the public with permission of director. **Publications:** Newsletter, quarterly - free upon request. **Remarks:** Maintained by Center for Study of the History of Musical Instruments of the University of South Dakota. **Staff:** Arne B. Larson, Res.Cons.; Margaret D. Banks, Cur.; Gary Stewart, Consrv..

★13164★
SHRINERS HOSPITAL FOR CRIPPLED CHILDREN - ORTHOPEDIC LIBRARY (Med)
1402 Outerbelt Dr. Phone: (713)797-1616
Houston, TX 77030 Jean Rasmussen, Med. Staff Coord.
Staff: Prof 2. **Subjects:** Orthopedics. **Holdings:** 200 books; 668 bound periodical volumes. **Subscriptions:** 20 journals and other serials. **Services:** Library not open to the public. **Automated Operations:** Computerized cataloging. **Computerized Information Services:** NLM, BRS Information Technologies. **Publications:** Newsletter - for internal distribution only.

★13165★
EUNICE KENNEDY SHRIVER CENTER FOR MENTAL RETARDATION, INC. - BIOCHEMISTRY LIBRARY (Med)
200 Trapelo Rd.
Waltham, MA 02254
Founded: 1970. **Staff:** Prof 1. **Subjects:** Biochemistry, chemistry, neurochemistry, neuroscience, genetics, cell biology. **Holdings:** 200 books; 400 bound periodical volumes; 50 pamphlets. **Subscriptions:** 30 journals and other serials. **Services:** Library not open to the public. **Computerized Information Services:** DIALOG Information Services.

MAX SHULMAN ZIONIST LIBRARY
See: Hebrew Theological College - Saul Silber Memorial Library (6212)

★13166★
SHUMAKER, LOOP & KENDRICK - LIBRARY (Law)
1000 Jackson Phone: (419)241-9000
Toledo, OH 43624-1573 Martha Esbin, Libn.
Staff: Prof 1. **Subjects:** Law. **Holdings:** 17,000 books; 550 bound periodical volumes; 600 research memoranda; 800 employee benefit materials. **Subscriptions:** 150 journals and other serials. **Services:** Interlibrary loan; library not open to the public. **Computerized Information Services:** LEXIS. **Publications:** S,L&K Library Letter (newsletter) - for internal distribution only. **Special Indexes:** Index to research and employee benefits files.

BENJAMIN FRANKLIN SHUMARD LIBRARY
See: St. Louis Public Library - Rare Book & Special Collections Department (12538)

★13167★
HERBERT V. SHUSTER, INC. - TECHNICAL LIBRARY (Food-Bev, Sci-Engr)
5 Hayward St. Phone: (617)328-7600
Quincy, MA 02171 Dr. George W. Bierman, Pres.
Subjects: Foods, pharmaceuticals, chemistry, microbiology, engineering, smoked fish processing. **Holdings:** 4200 volumes; regulatory, scientific, and industrial publications. **Services:** Library not open to the public.

SIBERT LIBRARY
See: Passavant Area Hospital (11101)

CLYDE L. SIBLEY MEDICAL LIBRARY
See: Baptist Medical Center (1321)

★13168★
SIBLEY MEMORIAL HOSPITAL - MEDICAL LIBRARY (Med)
5255 Loughboro Rd., N.W. Phone: (202)537-4110
Washington, DC 20016 Annie B. Footman, Libn.
Founded: 1903. **Staff:** Prof 1. **Subjects:** Medicine. **Holdings:** 3240 books; 1913 bound periodical volumes; 8 VF drawers of clippings, reports, and documents. **Subscriptions:** 152 journals and other serials. **Services:** Interlibrary loan; library not open to the public. **Computerized Information Services:** NLM. **Networks/Consortia:** Member of Southeastern/Atlantic Regional Medical Library Services, Maryland and D.C. Consortium of Resource Sharing (MADCORS).

SIBLEY MUSIC LIBRARY
See: University of Rochester - Eastman School of Music (16821)

★13169★
SIDLEY AND AUSTIN - LIBRARY (Law)
1722 Eye St., N.W. Phone: (202)429-4295
Washington, DC 20006 Sabrina I. Pacifici, Libn.
Staff: Prof 1; Other 4. **Subjects:** Law. **Holdings:** 25,000 books; 1000 bound periodical volumes; 800 reels of microfilm; 8 boxes of microfiche; legislative histories. **Subscriptions:** 150 journals and other serials; 7 newspapers. **Services:** Interlibrary loan; library open to the public by appointment. **Automated Operations:** Computerized cataloging and acquisitions. **Computerized Information Services:** LEXIS, NEXIS, WESTLAW, DIALOG Information Services, Dow Jones News/Retrieval, DataTimes, LEGI-SLATE, OCLC. **Networks/Consortia:** Member of RLG.

★13170★
SIDLEY AND AUSTIN - LIBRARY (Law)
One First National Plaza, Suite 4800 Phone: (312)853-7475
Chicago, IL 60603 Allyson D. Withers, Hd. Law Libn.
Staff: Prof 1; Other 7. **Subjects:** Law. **Holdings:** 45,000 volumes. **Services:** Interlibrary loan; library open to the public for reference use only. **Automated Operations:** Computerized cataloging. **Computerized Information Services:** LEXIS, DIALOG Information Services, Information America, VU/TEXT Information Services, NEXIS, Dow Jones News/Retrieval, DataTimes, WESTLAW; MCI Mail (electronic mail service). **Networks/Consortia:** Member of ILLINET.

★13171★
SIECOR CORPORATION - LIBRARY/INFORMATION SERVICES (Sci-Engr)
489 Siecor Park
800 17th St., N.W. Phone: (704)328-2171
Hickory, NC 28603-0489 Nola V. Callahan, Supv.
Staff: Prof 1; Other 2. **Subjects:** Telephone and cable industries, telecommunications, fiber optics. **Holdings:** 1000 books; 500 bound periodical volumes; 6000 reports and documents. **Subscriptions:** 130 journals and other serials. **Services:** Interlibrary loan; library not open to

the public. **Automated Operations:** Computerized cataloging. **Computerized Information Services:** DIALOG Information Services, VU/TEXT Information Services, WILSONLINE, NewsNet, Inc., BRS Information Technologies.

★13172★
ELI SIEGEL COLLECTION (Hum, Rel-Phil)
498 Broome St. Phone: (212)966-9787
New York, NY 10013 Richita Anderson, Libn.
Founded: 1982. **Staff:** Prof 3; Other 3. **Subjects:** Poetry, world literature, philosophy, art and literary criticism, history, labor and economics, approaches to mind, the sciences. **Special Collections:** Original manuscripts of the poetry and prose of Eli Siegel, founder of Aesthetic Realism; poems by Eli Seigel in holograph on pages of many of the books in this collection; French, German, and Spanish literature; early American history; 19th century periodical literature; British and American poetry. **Holdings:** 30,000 books; 500 bound periodical volumes; 1000 tapes of Aesthetic Realism lessons and lectures by Eli Siegel. **Services:** Collection is open by appointment to persons seriously studying Aesthetic Realism of Eli Siegel. **Publications:** The Right of Aesthetic Realism to be Known, weekly international periodical, edited by Ellen Reiss, published by the Aesthetic Realism Foundation, Inc. **Special Catalogs:** Cataloging of manuscripts within books is in process. **Remarks:** The books in this collection, with original manuscripts, poetry, and annotations by Eli Siegel, were used by him to develop and teach the philosophy of Aesthetic Realism. **Staff:** Leila Rosen, Libn.; Meryl Simon, Libn..

★13173★
SIEMENS GAMMASONICS, INC. - NUCLEAR MEDICAL DIVISION - RESEARCH LIBRARY (Sci-Engr)
2000 Nuclear Dr. Phone: (312)390-1989
Des Plaines, IL 60018 Jan Graham, Libn.
Founded: 1957. **Staff:** Prof 1. **Subjects:** Nuclear instrumentation, computers, engineering, electronics, gamma camera imaging, nuclear medicine, nuclear cardiology, mathematics, software, computed tomography. **Holdings:** 4000 books; 1000 bound periodical volumes; 200 reports. **Subscriptions:** 84 journals and other serials. **Services:** Interlibrary loan (limited); library open to the public by appointment. **Computerized Information Services:** DIALOG Information Services. **Networks/Consortia:** Member of North Suburban Library System (NSLS), Metropolitan Consortium of Chicago.

★13174★
SIERRA CLUB - WILLIAM E. COLBY MEMORIAL LIBRARY (Env-Cons)
730 Polk St. Phone: (415)776-2211
San Francisco, CA 94109 Richard Presby, Libn.
Founded: 1892. **Staff:** Prof 2. **Subjects:** Environmental policy, conservation, energy policy, mountaineering, natural history, Sierra Nevada. **Special Collections:** Foreign mountaineering journals (800 bound volumes); selected Sierra Club archives and memorabilia (500 items). **Holdings:** 7000 books; 1300 bound periodical volumes; 10,000 indexed documents and reports; 10 VF drawers of maps; 5000 slides; 5 file boxes of photographs. **Subscriptions:** 300 journals and other serials; 10 newspapers. **Services:** Interlibrary loan; copying; library open to the public for reference use only. **Automated Operations:** Computerized cataloging and serials. **Computerized Information Services:** OCLC. **Networks/Consortia:** Member of Bay Area Reference Center (BARC), Bay Area Library and Information System (BALIS). **Publications:** New Environmental Literature, annual; Sierra Club Periodicals Holdings List, 1982; Selected Acquisitions List, 3/year. **Special Indexes:** Subject index to documents holdings. **Staff:** Helmi S. Nock, Cat./Asst.Libn..

★13175★
SIERRA COUNTY LAW LIBRARY (Law)
Courthouse
Downieville, CA 95936 Phone: (916)289-3269
Founded: 1920. **Staff:** 2. **Subjects:** Law. **Holdings:** 4000 volumes. **Services:** Library open to the public with restrictions.

★13176★
SIERRA VIEW DISTRICT HOSPITAL - MEDICAL LIBRARY (Med)
465 W. Putnam Ave. Phone: (209)784-1110
Porterville, CA 93257 Marilyn R. Pankey, Dir., Med.Rec.
Staff: 1. **Subjects:** Anatomy, physiology, medicine, surgery. **Holdings:** 150 books. **Subscriptions:** 22 journals and other serials. **Services:** Library not open to the public. **Networks/Consortia:** Member of Areawide Library Network (AWLNET).

★13177★
SIGMA ALPHA EPSILON FOUNDATION - LEVERE MEMORIAL TEMPLE LIBRARY (Rec)
Box 1856 Phone: (312)475-1856
Evanston, IL 60204 Kenneth D. Tracey, Exec.Dir.
Founded: 1930. **Staff:** Prof 1. **Subjects:** Fraternities and sororities. **Special Collections:** Complete collection of all fraternity and sorority journals; Sigma Alpha Epsilon books, authors, and papers. **Holdings:** 225 books; 4000 bound periodical volumes; 407 chapter scrapbooks. **Services:** Library open to the public for reference use only. **Remarks:** Library located at 1856 Sheridan Rd., Evanston, IL 60201.

★13178★
SIGNETICS CORPORATION - PHILIPS RESEARCH LABORATORIES SUNNYVALE - TECHNICAL LIBRARY (Sci-Engr)
811 E. Arques Ave., MS 64 Phone: (408)991-5061
Sunnyvale, CA 94086 Sally Turk, Libn.
Founded: 1970. **Staff:** Prof 1. **Subjects:** Electronics, semiconductors, spectroscopy, materials science. **Holdings:** 2000 books; 2000 bound periodical volumes; 30 VF drawers of internal reports. **Subscriptions:** 150 journals and other serials. **Services:** Interlibrary loan; library not open to the public. **Automated Operations:** Computerized cataloging, acquisitions, serials, and circulation. **Computerized Information Services:** DIALOG Information Services, BRS Information Technologies, STN International, ESA/IRS; internal database; OnTyme Electronic Message Network Service (electronic mail service). **Networks/Consortia:** Member of CLASS, SOUTHNET. **Remarks:** Signetics Corporation is a subsidiary of N.V. Phillips Corporation.

SIKORSKY AIRCRAFT
See: United Technologies Corporation (15683)

SAUL SILBER MEMORIAL LIBRARY
See: Hebrew Theological College - Saul Silber Memorial Library (6212)

SILCOX MEMORIAL LIBRARY
See: Huron College (6616)

SILICON VALLEY INFORMATION CENTER
See: San Jose Public Library (12824)

O.P. SILLIMAN MEMORIAL LIBRARY
See: Hartnell Community College - Library (6064)

LUIGI SILVA COLLECTION
See: University of North Carolina, Greensboro (16639)

ABBA HILLEL SILVER ARCHIVES
See: Temple Library (13972)

★13179★
SILVER BURDETT & GINN - EDITORIAL LIBRARY (Publ)
250 James St. Phone: (201)285-7961
Morristown, NJ 07960 Theresa W. Barasch, Hd.Libn.
Staff: Prof 1. **Subjects:** General education, business, market research. **Special Collections:** Silver Burdett publications. **Holdings:** 10,000 books. **Subscriptions:** 100 journals and other serials. **Services:** Library not open to the public. **Networks/Consortia:** Member of New Jersey Library Network. **Publications:** Guidelines for Developing Bias-Free Instructional Materials.

★13180★
SILVER BURDETT & GINN - LIBRARY (Educ, Publ)
160 Gould St. Phone: (617)455-1200
Needham Heights, MA 02194-2310 Michele Sullivan, Libn.
Founded: 1867. **Staff:** Prof 1; Other 1. **Subjects:** English, reading, mathematics, science, social science, education, home economics, testing. **Special Collections:** Complete first editions of every title published by Ginn and Company in all subject areas. **Holdings:** 40,000 books; 9 filing cabinets of pamphlets and dissertations; 1000 microfiche. **Subscriptions:** 200 journals and other serials. **Services:** Library not open to the public.

★13181★
SILVER CROSS HOSPITAL - LLOYD W. JESSEN HEALTH SCIENCE LIBRARY (Med)
1200 Maple Rd. Phone: (815)740-1100
Joliet, IL 60432 Mary Ingmire, Libn.
Founded: 1956. **Staff:** Prof 1. **Subjects:** Medicine, nursing, hospital administration, social science. **Holdings:** 750 books; 1500 bound periodical volumes; 8 VF drawers of articles and pamphlets. **Subscriptions:** 102

journals and other serials. **Services:** Interlibrary loan; copying; library open to the public with referrals. **Computerized Information Services:** DIALOG Information Services. Performs searches on fee basis. **Networks/Consortia:** Member of Chicago and South Consortium.

★13182★
SILVER INSTITUTE - LIBRARY (Sci-Engr)
1026 16th St., N.W., Suite 101 Phone: (202)783-0500
Washington, DC 20036 John H. Lutley, Exec.Dir.
Staff: Prof 4; Other 6. **Subjects:** Silver. **Holdings:** 100 volumes; newsletters. **Subscriptions:** 15 journals and other serials. **Services:** Library open to the public. **Special Catalogs:** Catalog of abstracts on silver (11,000 items).

★13183★
SILVERADO MUSEUM (Hum)
1490 Library Lane
Box 409 Phone: (707)963-3757
St. Helena, CA 94574 Ellen Shaffer, Cur.
Staff: Prof 1. **Subjects:** Life and works of Robert Louis Stevenson. **Holdings:** 3500 books; 1200 original letters; 110 manuscripts; 1000 photographs; 120 paintings, prints, drawings; 8 sculptures; 7900 pieces of memorabilia. **Services:** Copying; museum open to the public.

SAUL A. SILVERMAN LIBRARY
See: C.M. Hincks Treatment Centre (6310)

★13184★
SILVERMINE SCHOOL OF ART - LIBRARY (Art)
1037 Silvermine Rd. Phone: (203)966-6668
New Canaan, CT 06840 Michael Costello, Dir.
Founded: 1959. **Subjects:** Art and allied subjects. **Holdings:** 3000 books. **Remarks:** Maintained by Silvermine Guild of Artists, Inc.

★13185★
SIMCOE COUNTY ARCHIVES (Hist)
R.R. 2 Phone: (705)726-9331
Minesing, ON, Canada L0L 1Y0 Peter P. Moran, Archv.
Founded: 1966. **Staff:** Prof 3. **Subjects:** Simcoe County history, business, and genealogy; cartography; lumbering history. **Special Collections:** Jacques and Hay Papers, 1854 to 1872 (the operation of New Lowell, Ontario; 2000 items, mainly letters); A.F. Hunter Papers (personal notes of local historian); Clarke Collection (500 books; 200 maps; 20,000 photographs, slides, negatives; correspondence); Sports Heritage Collection; C. Beck Manufacturing Company records (250 cubic feet); Cavana family records, 1860-1970 (land surveying; 20 cubic feet). **Holdings:** 1500 books; 500 bound periodical volumes; 50 Women's Institute histories; 130 county assessment rolls; 800 feet of municipal records; 150 magnetic tapes; 50 feet of Georgian Bay Lumber Company papers; 400 maps; 2000 photographs; census records on microfilm. **Subscriptions:** 29 journals and other serials. **Services:** Copying; archives open to the public. **Special Indexes:** Index of newspaper Barrie Northern Advance, 1847-1940; index of photographs; index of maps (all on cards). **Staff:** Bruce Beacock, Archv.Techn.; Su Murdoch, Asst.Archv..

★13186★
SIMCOE COUNTY LAW ASSOCIATION - LAW LIBRARY (Law)
Court House
30 Poyntz St. Phone: (705)728-1221
Barrie, ON, Canada L4M 1M1 Patricia Henry, Libn.
Staff: 1. **Subjects:** Law - criminal, civil, family, income tax, corporate. **Special Collections:** Ontario Municipal Board Decisions; Ontario Government Bills and Statutes (revisions). **Holdings:** 7000 books and bound periodical volumes. **Services:** Library not open to the public.

★13187★
SIMI VALLEY HISTORICAL SOCIETY - ARCHIVES (Hist)
R.P. Strathearn Historical Park Simi Valley, CA 93065
137 Strathearn Place
Box 351
Phone: (805)526-6453
Subjects: Simi Valley history, 1874-1960. **Holdings:** 500 letters and archival materials. **Services:** Archives open to the public by appointment.

SIMMEL-FENICHEL LIBRARY
See: Los Angeles Psychoanalytic Society and Institute (8012)

★13188★
SIMMONS COLLEGE - GRADUATE SCHOOL OF LIBRARY AND INFORMATION SCIENCE - LIBRARY (Info Sci)
300 The Fenway Phone: (617)738-2226
Boston, MA 02115 Linda H. Watkins, Libn.
Founded: 1902. **Staff:** Prof 1; Other 12. **Subjects:** Library and information science, publishing, media resources and study, library management. **Special Collections:** Annual reports of New England libraries; History of Publishing. **Holdings:** 22,827 books; 7340 bound periodical volumes; 4935 microfiche; 873 reels of microfilm; 34 VF drawers; 13 videotapes; 20 cassettes; School of Library Science doctoral field studies; information files on 100 library-related subjects; doctoral dissertations on microfilm. **Subscriptions:** 500 journals and other serials; 153 newsletters. **Services:** Interlibrary loan; copying; library open to the public for reference use only. **Automated Operations:** Computerized reserve holdings and union periodicals list. **Computerized Information Services:** OCLC, DIALOG Information Services, BRS Information Technologies. **Networks/Consortia:** Member of NELINET, Fenway Library Consortium (FLC).

★13189★
SIMMONS COLLEGE - SCHOOL OF SOCIAL WORK LIBRARY (Soc Sci)
51 Commonwealth Ave. Phone: (617)266-8435
Boston, MA 02116 Marilyn Smith Bregoli, Libn.
Founded: 1904. **Staff:** Prof 1; Other 3. **Subjects:** Social work, public welfare, psychiatry. **Holdings:** 21,000 books; 2600 bound periodical volumes; 1200 theses. **Subscriptions:** 185 journals and other serials. **Services:** Interlibrary loan; library not open to the public. **Automated Operations:** Computerized cataloging. **Computerized Information Services:** DIALOG Information Services, BRS Information Technologies.

SIMON-LOWENSTEIN COLLECTION
See: The American Institute of Wine and Food (561)

★13190★
NORTON SIMON MUSEUM OF ART AT PASADENA - LIBRARY AND ARCHIVES (Art)
411 W. Colorado Blvd.
Pasadena, CA 91105 Phone: (818)449-6840
Subjects: Art history. **Special Collections:** The Knoedler Library (auction and exhibition catalogs on microfiche, 18th century to 1970); The Galka E. Scheyer Archives (materials pertaining to the life and collections of Galka E. Scheyer and "The Blue Four" - Paul Klee, Wassily Kandinsky, Lyonel Feininger, and Alexei Jawlensky). **Holdings:** 150 books; 200 brochures and catalogs; letters of "The Blue Four"; photographs of artists and collections. **Services:** Use of archives limited to scholars.

★13191★
H.A. SIMONS LTD. - CORPORATE LIBRARY (Sci-Engr)
425 Carrall St. Phone: (604)664-4311
Vancouver, BC, Canada V6B 2J6 David Pepper, Corp.Libn.
Staff: Prof 2; Other 1. **Subjects:** Pulp/paper, automation. **Holdings:** 5000 books; annual reports; standards. **Subscriptions:** 250 journals and other serials; 10 newspapers. **Services:** Interlibrary loan; copying; SDI; library open to the public. **Automated Operations:** Computerized cataloging, acquisitions, serials, and circulation. **Computerized Information Services:** DIALOG Information Services, Pergamon ORBIT InfoLine, Inc., Dow Jones News/Retrieval, QL Systems, TEXTLINE, Info Globe, CAN/OLE; Envoy 100, Dialcom, Inc., Immedia Telematics, Inc. (electronic mail services). Performs searches on fee basis. **Networks/Consortia:** Member of Central Vancouver Library Group. **Publications:** TREND Report; Economic Indicators, bimonthly; Daily Newsflash - all for internal distribution only. **Remarks:** An alternate telephone number is 664-4305. **Staff:** Kit Tam, Asst.Corp.Libn..

HARRY SIMONS LIBRARY
See: Beth David Congregation (1540)

LEONARD N. SIMONS RESEARCH LIBRARY
See: Michigan Cancer Foundation (8881)

MENNO SIMONS HISTORICAL LIBRARY AND ARCHIVES
See: Eastern Mennonite College (4535)

ALBERT B. SIMPSON HISTORICAL LIBRARY & ARCHIVES
See: Christian and Missionary Alliance (3147)

SIMPSON GEOGRAPHIC RESEARCH CENTER
See: University of Wisconsin, Eau Claire (17105)

SIMPSON LIBRARY OF PALEONTOLOGY
See: University of Florida - Florida State Museum (16148)

★13192★
SIMPSON, THACHER & BARTLETT - LIBRARY (Law)
1 Battery Park Plaza Phone: (212)483-9000
New York, NY 10004 John S. Marsh, Libn.
Founded: 1884. **Staff:** Prof 2; Other 7. **Subjects:** Law - antitrust, corporate, labor, banking, trade regulations, public utilities, taxation, securities. **Holdings:** 40,000 volumes. **Services:** Interlibrary loan; library not open to the public. **Computerized Information Services:** LEXIS, NEXIS, WESTLAW, DIALOG Information Services, Dow Jones News/Retrieval. **Remarks:** Branch library located at 270 Park Ave., New York, NY 10017. **Staff:** Bobby Smith, 1st Asst.Libn.; Michael Bronson, Ref.Libn..

L.A. SIMS MEMORIAL LIBRARY
See: Southeastern Louisiana University (13425)

★13193★
SIMSBURY HISTORICAL SOCIETY - BLANCHE C. SKOGLUND MEMORIAL LIBRARY (Hist)
800 Hopmeadow St.
Box 2 Phone: (203)658-2500
Simsbury, CT 06070 Mary L. Nason, Dir.
Founded: 1975. **Subjects:** Simsbury area history and genealogy. **Holdings:** 2000 books, pamphlets, serials; 30 boxes of manuscripts; photographs; slides; maps. **Services:** Library open to the public by request. **Remarks:** Established as a bicentennial project, the library includes materials that had been in storage since 1911.

★13194★
SINAI HOSPITAL OF BALTIMORE, INC. - EISENBERG MEDICAL STAFF LIBRARY (Med)
Belvedere & Greenspring Phone: (301)578-5015
Baltimore, MD 21215 Rita Matcher, Dir., Lib.Serv.
Staff: Prof 1; Other 2. **Subjects:** Medicine, nursing, Jewish medicine, management. **Holdings:** 5000 books; 10,000 bound periodical volumes. **Subscriptions:** 279 journals and other serials. **Services:** Interlibrary loan; library not open to the public. **Computerized Information Services:** MEDLINE, DIALOG Information Services. Performs searches on fee basis. **Networks/Consortia:** Member of Maryland Association of Health Science Librarians.

★13195★
SINAI HOSPITAL OF DETROIT - SAMUEL FRANK MEDICAL LIBRARY (Med)
6767 W. Outer Dr. Phone: (313)493-5140
Detroit, MI 48235 Barbara L. Finn, Dir. of Med.Lib.
Founded: 1953. **Staff:** Prof 3; Other 5. **Subjects:** Medicine, nursing, and allied health sciences. **Special Collections:** History of Medicine (emphasis on Jewish contributions). **Holdings:** 9600 books; 15,135 bound periodical volumes; 9 VF drawers of reprints and pamphlets; cassettes; Audio-Digest tapes. **Subscriptions:** 571 journals and other serials. **Services:** Interlibrary loan; copying; SDI; library open to medical and paramedical personnel. **Computerized Information Services:** Online systems. **Publications:** Accession list of new books, monthly - for internal distribution only. **Staff:** Cathy Palmer, Lib.Supv.; Laura Grab, Asst.Dir..

SINGER COMPANY - DALMO VICTOR
See: Dalmo Victor (4013)

★13196★
SINGER COMPANY - KEARFOTT DIVISION - TECHNICAL INFORMATION CENTER (Sci-Engr)
150 Totowa Rd. Phone: (201)785-6462
Wayne, NJ 07470 B.R. Meade, Mgr.
Founded: 1956. **Staff:** Prof 3; Other 1. **Subjects:** Aerospace sciences, metallurgy, mathematics, electrical and electronic engineering. **Holdings:** 25,000 books; 1800 bound serials; 20,000 reports, pamphlets, reprints; 4500 microforms. **Subscriptions:** 215 journals and other serials. **Services:** Interlibrary loan; center not open to the public. **Computerized Information Services:** DIALOG Information Services, DTIC, NASA/RECON.

★13197★
SINGER COMPANY - LIBRASCOPE DIVISION - TECHNICAL INFORMATION CENTER (Sci-Engr, Comp Sci)
833 Sonora Ave. Phone: (818)244-6541
Glendale, CA 91201 Linda K. Zoeckler, Hd.Libn.
Founded: 1954. **Staff:** Prof 1; Other 1. **Subjects:** Computers; engineering - systems, electronic, mechanical, electrical; data processing; military electronics; electro-optics; instruments; mathematics; management. **Holdings:** 20,000 books; 1000 bound periodical volumes; 20,000 reports; VSMF microfilm files; 25,000 microfiche; 12 VF drawers of pamphlets. **Subscriptions:** 250 journals and other serials. **Services:** Interlibrary loan; copying; project data bank management; center open to the public by appointment. **Automated Operations:** Computerized cataloging and circulation. **Computerized Information Services:** Internal database. **Publications:** Accessions List, quarterly; computer-generated data bank lists.

★13198★
SINGER COMPANY - LINK DIVISION - TECHNICAL LIBRARY (Comp Sci)
1077 E. Arques Ave. Phone: (408)720-5719
Sunnyvale, CA 94088-3484 Shu-nan T. Chiang, Tech.Libn.
Staff: Prof 1. **Subjects:** Computer science, electrical engineering, computer graphics, simulation, Link trainers, flight simulation, flight trainers, radar, electronics. **Holdings:** 1500 volumes; 500 technical reports. **Subscriptions:** 90 journals and other serials. **Services:** Interlibrary loan; library not open to the public. **Publications:** Information from the Technical Library, monthly - for internal distribution only.

★13199★
SINGER COMPANY - LINK FLIGHT SIMULATION DIVISION - INFORMATION CENTER (Sci-Engr)
Colesville Rd., MS659
Binghamton, NY 13902 Eileen M. Hamlin, Mgr.
Founded: 1951. **Staff:** Prof 3; Other 1. **Subjects:** Electrical and electronic engineering; aeronautics; economics; mathematics; computers. **Holdings:** 6000 books; internal and technical reports; manuals; reprints; handbooks; microforms. **Subscriptions:** 400 journals and other serials. **Services:** Interlibrary loan; copying; center open to the public by appointment. **Computerized Information Services:** DIALOG Information Services, BRS Information Technologies, DTIC, OCLC, NASA/RECON, NEXIS. **Networks/Consortia:** Member of South Central Research Library Council (SCRLC). **Staff:** Robin Petrus, Info.Couns..

★13200★
H. DOUGLAS SINGER MENTAL HEALTH CENTER - LIBRARY (Med)
4402 N. Main St. Phone: (815)987-7092
Rockford, IL 61105 Pat Ellison, Lib.Assoc.
Founded: 1966. **Staff:** Prof 1. **Subjects:** Mental health, psychology, psychiatry, psychotherapy, sociology, religion, medicine. **Holdings:** 2000 books. **Subscriptions:** 100 journals and other serials. **Services:** Interlibrary loan; library open to the public with restrictions. **Networks/Consortia:** Member of Northern Illinois Library System (NILS), Upstate Consortium of Medical and Allied Libraries in Northern Illinois. **Remarks:** Maintained by Illinois State Department of Mental Health and Developmental Disabilities.

SINGEWALD READING ROOM
See: Johns Hopkins University - Department of Earth and Planetary Sciences (7235)

★13201★
SINGING RIVER HOSPITAL - MEDICAL LIBRARY (Med)
2809 Denny Ave. Phone: (601)938-5040
Pascagoula, MS 39567 Mary Evelyn Dowell, Dir., Med.Lib.
Staff: Prof 1; Other 1. **Subjects:** Medicine, nursing, allied health sciences, hospital administration. **Holdings:** 2000 books; 8000 bound periodical volumes. **Subscriptions:** 250 journals and other serials. **Services:** Interlibrary loan; copying; SDI; library open to Jackson County allied health students and hospital system employees and physicians. **Automated Operations:** Computerized cataloging. **Computerized Information Services:** MEDLARS, DIALOG Information Services; OnTyme Electronic Message Network Service (electronic mail service). **Networks/Consortia:** Member of Mississippi Biomedical Library Consortium. **Publications:** Library Lifeline - for internal distribution only. **Remarks:** Maintains Community Health Information Library.

★13202★
SINGLE DAD'S LIFESTYLE MAGAZINE - LIBRARY (Publ)
4723 N. 44th St.
Phoenix, AZ 85018 Robert A. Hirschfeld, Ed./Publ.
Founded: 1978. **Staff:** 1. **Subjects:** Father's rights, divorce law, psychology of divorce, paternal custody, visitation and child support, child rearing by single parents. **Special Collections:** Father's Rights/Divorce Reform Organization newsletters (400); case law collection of paternal custody, visitation, child support materials (50 items). **Holdings:** 210 volumes; 15

videotapes. **Subscriptions:** 13 journals and other serials. **Services:** Library not open to the public. **Special Indexes:** Annual blue list of Father's Rights/Divorce Reform organizations.

SINO-SOVIET INFORMATION CENTER
See: George Washington University - Melvin Gelman Library (17486)

★13203★
SIOUX CITY ART CENTER ASSOCIATION - LIBRARY (Art)
513 Nebraska St. Phone: (712)279-6272
Sioux City, IA 51101 Sheila Webb, Educ.Cur.
Subjects: Art and art history. **Holdings:** 800 books; exhibition catalogs; reproduction slides. **Subscriptions:** 15 journals and other serials. **Services:** Library open to the public for reference use only. **Publications:** Artifact, quarterly. **Special Catalogs:** Exhibition catalogs.

★13204★
SIOUX FALLS ARGUS LEADER - LIBRARY (Publ)
Box 5034 Phone: (605)331-2300
Sioux Falls, SD 57117-5034 Monique Potratz, Libn.
Staff: Prof 1. **Subjects:** Newspaper reference topics. **Holdings:** Figures not available. **Services:** Library not open to the public. **Remarks:** Library located at 200 S. Minnesota, Sioux Falls, SD 57102.

★13205★
SIOUX VALLEY HOSPITAL - MEDICAL LIBRARY (Med)
1100 S. Euclid Ave.
Box 5039 Phone: (605)333-6330
Sioux Falls, SD 57117 Anna Gieschen, Libn.
Founded: 1954. **Staff:** 3. **Subjects:** Medicine, nursing, allied health sciences. **Holdings:** 4195 books; 3925 bound periodical volumes; 4 VF drawers of pamphlets, reprints, articles, clippings. **Subscriptions:** 153 journals and other serials. **Services:** Interlibrary loan; copying; library open to the public for reference use only. **Computerized Information Services:** MEDLINE.

★13206★
SIOUXLAND HERITAGE MUSEUMS - LIBRARY (Hist)
131 N. Duluth Ave. Phone: (605)339-7097
Sioux Falls, SD 57104 John E. Rycktarik, Cur. of Coll.
Founded: 1926. **Staff:** Prof 1. **Subjects:** South Dakota history; U.S. history - silver question; 19th century works on ethnology and natural science; Indians. **Special Collections:** Arthur C. Phillips Collection; Northern League Baseball records (4 linear feet); library and private papers of U.S. Senator R.F. Pettigrew (1000 volumes); South Dakota history (1500 items). **Holdings:** 9000 books; 200 bound periodical volumes; 100 maps; 50 linear feet of manuscripts; 3000 photographs. **Subscriptions:** 10 journals and other serials. **Services:** Copying; library open to the public. **Publications:** Community Report, bimonthly - free upon request. **Remarks:** An alternate telephone number is 335-4210.

★13207★
SIPPICAN, INC. - LIBRARY (Sci-Engr)
7 Barnabas Rd. Phone: (508)748-1160
Marion, MA 02738 Kendra J. St. Aubin, Tech.Libn.
Founded: 1984. **Staff:** Prof 1. **Subjects:** Engineering, underwater acoustics, physical oceanography, electronic and antisubmarine warfare, computer science. **Holdings:** 810 books; 35 bound periodical volumes; 1020 technical reports; 16 microfiche titles on 1200 microfiche; 1225 internal reports; 298 patents; 1376 specifications and standards; 28 video cassettes; 17 audio cassettes. **Subscriptions:** 107 journals and other serials. **Services:** Interlibrary loan; library not open to the public. **Automated Operations:** Computerized public access catalog, cataloging, and acquisitions. **Computerized Information Services:** DIALOG Information Services, WILSONLINE, DTIC; internal databases; DIALMAIL (electronic mail service). **Publications:** Sippican Library Online, monthly - for internal distribution only.

★13208★
SIROTE, PERMUTT, MC DERMOTT, SLEPIAN, FRIEND, FRIEDMAN, HELD & APOLINSKY - LAW LIBRARY (Law)
2222 Arlington Ave., S. Phone: (205)933-7111
Birmingham, AL 35205 Patricia M. Levine, Libn.
Staff: Prof 1; Other 1. **Subjects:** Law - taxation, litigation, business, collection. **Holdings:** 15,000 volumes; 100 cassettes; 82 binders of legal briefs and memos; 50 speech outlines. **Subscriptions:** 79 journals and other serials. **Services:** Interlibrary loan; copying; library open to the public with permission of member of the firm. **Computerized Information Services:** WESTLAW. **Special Indexes:** Legal Brief/Memo index (card and online); holdings list of tax materials (card).

★13209★
SISKIYOU COUNTY HISTORICAL SOCIETY - LIBRARY (Hist)
910 S. Main St. Phone: (916)842-3836
Yreka, CA 96097 Michael Hendryx, Musm.Dir.
Founded: 1950. **Staff:** Prof 1; Other 1. **Subjects:** History of Siskiyou County. **Holdings:** 1000 books; 21 bound periodical volumes; 250 ledgers and account books; 1500 documents; 10,000 photographs; 248 bound volumes of county newspapers, 1917-1952. **Services:** Library open to the public by appointment. **Publications:** Siskiyou Pioneer, annual; occasional papers. **Special Indexes:** Index to Siskiyou Pioneer.

★13210★
SISKIYOU COUNTY LAW LIBRARY (Law)
311 Fourth St., Courthouse Phone: (916)842-3531
Yreka, CA 96097 Janet L. Whitaker, Libn.
Founded: 1939. **Staff:** 1. **Subjects:** Law. **Holdings:** 13,506 volumes; 12 bound periodical volumes; 3350 volumes on ultrafiche. **Services:** Copying; library open to the public for reference use only. **Remarks:** Maintained by Siskiyou County Law Library Association.

SISTER FORMATION CONFERENCE/RELIGIOUS FORMATION CONFERENCE ARCHIVES
See: Marquette University - Department of Special Collections and University Archives (8451)

SISTERS OF CHARITY - ST. JOSEPH HOSPITAL
See: St. Joseph Hospital (12462)

★13211★
SISTERS OF CHARITY HOSPITAL - MEDICAL STAFF LIBRARY (Med)
2157 Main St. Phone: (716)862-2846
Buffalo, NY 14214 Anne Cohen, Med.Libn.
Founded: 1948. **Staff:** Prof 1. **Subjects:** Medicine, surgery, obstetrics and gynecology, pediatrics. **Holdings:** 5974 books and bound periodical volumes. **Subscriptions:** 99 journals and other serials. **Services:** Interlibrary loan; copying; library open to medical staff only.

★13212★
SISTERS OF THE HOLY FAMILY OF NAZARETH - PROVINCIAL ARCHIVES (Rel-Phil, Hist)
Grant & Torresdale Aves. Phone: (215)637-6464
Philadelphia, PA 19114 Sr. Mary Frances, Info.Dir.
Founded: 1973. **Staff:** Prof 2. **Subjects:** History of the Sisters of the Holy Family of Nazareth and the Immaculate Conception Province. **Special Collections:** Autobiography and biographies of the Foundress of the Sisters of the Holy Family of Nazareth; Constitutions of the Congregation, 1887-1983; Proceedings of the General Chapters, 1895-1983; Books of Customs, 1894-1966; Reports of Provincial Superiors; Educational Conference Proceedings, 1941-1979; circular letters of the General and Provincial Superiors; Album of Fine Arts of the Sisters of the Holy Family of Nazareth (CSFN); information on various programs held in the province; Inter-Province News Letters; blueprints of all institutions of the province. **Holdings:** 1180 books; 41 bound periodical volumes; 120 doctoral and masters' dissertations; active files of convents and members; chronicles and annals of homes; necrologies of deceased sisters. **Services:** Archives not open to the public. **Publications:** Guide to Nazareth Literature 1873-1973 (1st edition).

★13213★
SISTERS OF NOTRE DAME DE NAMUR - OHIO PROVINCE - ARCHIVES (Rel-Phil)
Provincial House
701 E. Columbia Ave.
Cincinnati, OH 45215 Phone: (513)821-7448
Subjects: Houses, institutions, and works of the Ohio Province of the Sisters of Notre Dame de Namur, 1840 to present; work of St. Julie Billiart. **Special Collections:** Manuscripts (original and copied letters of church officials and sisters of the convent); biographies and memoirs of sisters, Catholic women, and clergy. **Holdings:** 650 cubic feet of church records, conference proceedings, catechisms, educational writings, academic theses, institutional histories, cemetery records, necrologies, church rules, prayers; photographs; slides. **Services:** Copying; archives open to public with permission.

★13214★
SISTERS OF PROVIDENCE - SACRED HEART PROVINCE - ARCHIVES (Rel-Phil)
4800 37th Ave., S.W. Phone: (206)937-4600
Seattle, WA 98126 Sr. Rita Bergamini, S.P., Archv.
Founded: 1856. **Staff:** Prof 2. **Subjects:** Sisters of Providence; history of health care, education, missions, social welfare institutions, Catholic church. **Special Collections:** Mother Joseph, a Sister of Providence (1823-1902); medical history of the Sisters of Providence hospitals and health care institutions in Alaska, Washington, Oregon, and California, 1856 to present; educational history of the Sisters of Providence schools in Alaska, Washington, Oregon, and California, 1856 to present. **Holdings:** 3000 books; 2800 linear feet of archival materials; 50 file drawers of photographs, film, slides. **Services:** Copying; archives open to the public by appointment. **Staff:** Loretta Zwolak Greene, Asst.Archv..

★13215★
SISTERS OF PROVIDENCE HEALTHCARE CORPORATION - CORPORATE LIBRARY (Med)
Box C11038 Phone: (206)464-3028
Seattle, WA 98111 Kathy Cushman, Lib.Coord.
Founded: 1985. **Staff:** 1. **Subjects:** Health care - administration, planning, law, financing. **Holdings:** 800 books. **Subscriptions:** 473 journals and other serials; 10 newspapers. **Services:** Interlibrary loan; library not open to the public. **Computerized Information Services:** DIALOG Information Services; internal database.

SISTERS OF SAINT ANN - QUEENSWOOD HOUSE
See: Queenswood House (11837)

SISTERS OF ST. FRANCIS - LOURDES COLLEGE
See: Lourdes College (8072)

★13216★
SISTERS OF ST. JOSEPH OF CARONDELET - ST. PAUL PROVINCE - ARCHIVES (Rel-Phil)
1884 Randolph Ave. Phone: (612)690-7000
St. Paul, MN 55105 Mary E. Kraft, C.S.J., Archv.
Staff: Prof 1; Other 1. **Subjects:** Religious life, education, health care, social justice, women. **Holdings:** Archival collections. **Services:** Copying; archives open to the public with restrictions.

★13217★
SISTERS OF ST. MARY OF NAMUR - MOUNT ST. MARY RESEARCH CENTER (Rel-Phil, Hist)
3756 Delaware Ave. Phone: (716)875-4705
Kenmore, NY 14217 Sr. M. Xavier, Archv./Libn.
Founded: 1975. **Staff:** Prof 2. **Subjects:** History of Sisters of St. Mary, Bible, biography, church history. **Special Collections:** Slides of Dante. **Holdings:** 5025 books and bound periodical volumes; 8 boxes of slides; 300 cassettes. **Subscriptions:** 25 journals and other serials. **Services:** Interlibrary loan; copying; center open to the public. **Staff:** Sr. Martin Joseph, Cat..

SITKA NATIONAL HISTORICAL PARK
See: U.S. Natl. Park Service (15352)

★13218★
SKADDEN, ARPS, SLATE, MEAGHER & FLOM - LIBRARY (Law)
919 3rd Ave. Phone: (212)735-3000
New York, NY 10022 Carrie Hirtz, Libn.
Staff: Prof 7; Other 22. **Subjects:** Law. **Holdings:** 60,000 books; 500 bound periodical volumes; 150 VF drawers. **Subscriptions:** 500 journals and other serials; 6 newspapers. **Services:** Interlibrary loan; library not open to the public. **Automated Operations:** Computerized circulation. **Computerized Information Services:** DIALOG Information Services, WESTLAW, Dow Jones News/Retrieval, Pergamon ORBIT InfoLine, Inc., LEXIS, VU/TEXT Information Services, TEXTLINE, DataTimes, Newsnet, Inc.

★13219★
SKAGIT COUNTY HISTORICAL MUSEUM - HISTORICAL REFERENCE LIBRARY (Hist)
Box 818 Phone: (206)466-3365
La Conner, WA 98257 David J. Van Meer, Cur.
Founded: 1968. **Staff:** Prof 4; Other 2. **Subjects:** Skagit County history, pioneer family genealogies, local Indian histories, late 19th century novels and periodicals. **Special Collections:** Diaries of Grant Sisson, W.J. Cornelius, Arthur Champenois, and others, 1844-1964; Darius Kinsey Photographs; personal and legal papers of Key Pittman, U.S. Senator from Nevada, 1913-1940. **Holdings:** 1500 books; 308 bound periodical volumes; 6000 photographs; 599 newspapers; 658 business documents; 109 old letters; 106 old district school accounts/records; 81 maps; 626 clippings and clipping scrapbooks; 183 old programs/announcements; 64 pioneer diaries; 220 oral history tapes with transcripts; old American popular music, 1866-1954; local newspapers, 1900 to present. **Subscriptions:** 14 journals and other serials. **Services:** Copying; library open to the public by appointment. **Staff:** Eunice Darvill, Dir.; Pat Dovan, Reg.; Janet Saunders, Archv.Asst..

★13220★
SKAGIT COUNTY LAW LIBRARY (Law)
County Court House Phone: (206)336-9313
Mount Vernon, WA 98273 A.J. (Rusty) Kuntze, Libn.
Subjects: Law, decisions of appellate courts. **Holdings:** 6500 volumes. **Services:** Library open to the public for reference use only.

SKIDAWAY INSTITUTE OF OCEANOGRAPHY
See: University of Georgia (16178)

LOUIS SKIDMORE ROOM
See: Massachusetts Institute of Technology - Rotch Library of Architecture and Planning - Visual Collections (8551)

★13221★
SKIDMORE, OWINGS & MERRILL - INFORMATION SERVICES DEPARTMENT (Plan, Art)
220 E. 42nd St. Phone: (212)309-9500
New York, NY 10017 Frances C. Gretes, Dir., Info.Serv.
Staff: Prof 1. **Subjects:** Architecture, art, engineering, interior design, New York history, planning. **Special Collections:** Archives. **Holdings:** 3000 books; 170 bound periodical volumes; 200 master plans; 10,000 drawings; specifications; 300 reels of microfilm; 5000 project clippings; 5000 photographs; 1000 unbound periodicals. **Subscriptions:** 160 journals and other serials. **Services:** Interlibrary loan (limited); copying; SDI; department open to other librarians and students for reference use only. **Computerized Information Services:** Pergamon ORBIT InfoLine, Inc., NewsNet, Inc., Avery Index to Architectural Periodicals, Civil Engineering Database, DIALOG Information Services, RLIN. **Publications:** Monthly list of new publications; bibliography on the work of the firm (published articles).

★13222★
SKIDMORE, OWINGS & MERRILL - LIBRARY (Plan, Art)
1201 Pennsylvania Ave., N.W. Phone: (202)393-1400
Washington, DC 20004 Susan Wilcox, Dir., Commun.
Founded: 1976. **Staff:** Prof 1. **Subjects:** Architecture, interior design, urban planning and transportation, landscape architecture. **Holdings:** 2000 books; 100 bound periodical volumes; 1000 SOM reports; 500 SOM proposals; slides; maps; photographs; clippings. **Services:** Interlibrary loan; copying; library open to the public by appointment.

★13223★
SKIDMORE, OWINGS & MERRILL - LIBRARY (Plan)
33 W. Monroe St. Phone: (312)641-5959
Chicago, IL 60603 Ann Dutt, Libn.
Founded: 1973. **Staff:** Prof 1. **Subjects:** Engineering and architecture design and technology. **Holdings:** 7000 books; 50 bound periodical volumes; 20 VF drawers of photographs and pamphlets. **Subscriptions:** 50 journals and other serials. **Services:** Interlibrary loan; library not open to the public. **Networks/Consortia:** Member of Chicago Library System.

FREDERICK W. SKILLIN HEALTH SCIENCES LIBRARY
See: Northern Cumberland Memorial Hospital (10416)

BLANCHE C. SKOGLUND MEMORIAL LIBRARY
See: Simsbury Historical Society (13193)

★13224★
SKYNET - LIBRARY (Sci-Engr)
257 Sycamore Glen Phone: (213)256-8655
Pasadena, CA 91105 Ann Druffel, Proj.Coord.
Founded: 1965. **Subjects:** UFO research, parapsychology, geomancy. **Holdings:** 500 books; 700 periodicals; 5 cases of magnetic tapes; 800 other cataloged items. **Services:** Accepts mail inquiries. **Computerized Information Services:** Internal database.

SLA
See: Special Libraries Association (13546)

SLAC HIGH ENERGY PREPRINT LIBRARY
See: University of California, Los Angeles - Physics Library (15984)

FRANK J. SLADEN LIBRARY
See: Henry Ford Hospital (5242)

★13225★
SLATER MILL HISTORIC SITE - RESEARCH LIBRARY (Hist)
Roosevelt Ave.
Box 727 Phone: (401)725-8638
Pawtucket, RI 02862 Ruth Macaulay, Cur.
Founded: 1955. **Staff:** 1. **Subjects:** Handicraft and factory textile production, machine tools, local industrial and social history. **Holdings:** 500 volumes. **Services:** Library open to the public by appointment. **Publications:** The Newsletter, quarterly.

★13226★
SLAVIA LIBRARY (Area-Ethnic)
418 W. Nittany Ave. Phone: (814)238-5215
State College, PA 16801 Dr. W.O. Luciw, Dir.
Staff: Prof 1; Other 2. **Subjects:** Ukrainian history, literature, language, social studies, art, science. **Special Collections:** Ukrainian and Slavic archives. **Holdings:** 45,000 books; 5000 unbound periodical volumes; 17,000 other cataloged items; 40,000 items in microform; Slavic book plates; American and Slavic historical documents. **Subscriptions:** 60 journals and other serials. **Services:** Copying; SDI; library open to the public by appointment for reference use only. **Publications:** Life and School, 5/year; Free World. **Special Catalogs:** Book publications catalog.

★13227★
SLAVONIC BENEVOLENT ORDER OF THE STATE OF TEXAS - LIBRARY, ARCHIVES, MUSEUM (Area-Ethnic)
520 N. Main St. Phone: (817)773-1575
Temple, TX 76501 Thelma Bartosh, Libn./Cur.
Staff: 1. **Subjects:** Education, medicine, religion, history, music. **Holdings:** 28,000 volumes (mostly in Czech language); over 500 Czech plays. **Services:** Interlibrary loan; copying; library open to the public.

SLEEPY HOLLOW RESTORATIONS, INC.
See: Historic Hudson Valley (6323)

THOMAS BAKER SLICK MEMORIAL LIBRARY
See: Southwest Research Institute (13518)

★13228★
ALFRED P. SLOAN, JR. MUSEUM - MERLE G. PERRY ARCHIVES (Trans)
1221 E. Kearsley St. Phone: (313)762-1170
Flint, MI 48503 Phillip C. Kwiatkowski, Dir.
Subjects: Automotive history, carriage industry, local history. **Special Collections:** Automotive catalogs (300). **Holdings:** 750 volumes. **Subscriptions:** 24 journals and other serials. **Services:** Copying; archives open to the public for reference use only. **Staff:** Carol DeKalands, Archv..

HELEN FARR SLOAN LIBRARY
See: Delaware Art Museum - Helen Farr Sloan Library (4147)

JOHN SLOAN MEMORIAL LIBRARY
See: Delaware Art Museum - Helen Farr Sloan Library (4147)

★13229★
SLOAN-KETTERING INSTITUTE FOR CANCER RESEARCH - DONALD S. WALKER LABORATORY - C.P. RHOADS MEMORIAL LIBRARY (Med)
145 Boston Post Rd.
Rye, NY 10580
Defunct. Holdings absorbed by Memorial Sloan-Kettering Cancer Center - Medical Library.

SLOANE ART LIBRARY
See: University of North Carolina, Chapel Hill (16631)

DR. BARNEY A. SLOTKIN MEMORIAL LIBRARY
See: Kennedy Memorial Hospitals - Cherry Hill Division (7417)

★13230★
SLOVAK CATHOLIC CHARITABLE ORGANIZATION - SLOVAK CULTURAL CENTER - LIBRARY (Area-Ethnic)
5900 W. 147th St. Phone: (312)687-2877
Oak Forest, IL 60452 Sr. M. Methodia Machalica, Dir.
Staff: Prof 1. **Subjects:** Slovakia. **Holdings:** 2030 books and bound periodical volumes; Slovak encyclopedias, periodicals, stamps; manuscripts; clippings; archival materials; documents; magnetic tapes. **Services:** Library open to the public with restrictions.

★13231★
SLOVAK WRITERS AND ARTISTS ASSOCIATION - SLOVAK INSTITUTE - LIBRARY (Area-Ethnic)
St. Andrew's Abbey
2900 Martin Luther King Dr.
Cleveland, OH 44104
Staff: Prof 2. **Subjects:** Slovak history, Slovak art, Slovak literature, cultural achievements of Americans of Slovak ancestry. **Holdings:** 5000 books. **Services:** Library open to the public for reference use only by special arrangement.

★13232★
SMALL BUSINESS ADMINISTRATION - REFERENCE LIBRARY (Bus-Fin)
1441 L St., N.W. Phone: (202)653-6914
Washington, DC 20416 Margaret Hickey, Libn.
Founded: 1958. **Staff:** Prof 1; Other 1. **Subjects:** Business, finance, management. **Holdings:** 8000 volumes; 80 VF drawers of reports, pamphlets, documents. **Subscriptions:** 203 journals and other serials. **Services:** Interlibrary loan; library open to the public for reference use only.

★13233★
SMALL BUSINESS COMPUTER SYSTEMS, INC. - AGRI-SOURCE SOFTWARE LIBRARY (Agri, Comp Sci)
3815 Adams St. Phone: (402)467-3591
Lincoln, NE 68504 Diane Walkowiak, Ed.
Founded: 1983. **Staff:** Prof 3. **Subjects:** Agriculture. **Special Collections:** Public domain agricultural software. **Holdings:** 15 books; spreadsheet templates and programs. **Subscriptions:** 15 journals and other serials; 6 newspapers. **Services:** Library open to the public.

★13234★
SMALL, CRAIG & WERKENTHIN - LIBRARY (Law)
100 Congress Ave., Suite 1100 Phone: (512)472-8355
Austin, TX 78701-4099 Donna Doby, Libn.
Staff: Prof 1; Other 1. **Subjects:** Law. **Holdings:** 10,700 books; 50 bound periodical volumes; 600 volumes on microfiche; 2 boxes of microfiche. **Subscriptions:** 50 journals and other serials. **Services:** Interlibrary loan; copying; library open to the public by appointment. **Computerized Information Services:** DIALOG Information Services, WESTLAW, LEXIS, NEXIS; Research Retrieval (internal database).

SMALL NEWSPAPER GROUP, INC. - (Moline) DAILY DISPATCH
See: (Moline) Daily Dispatch (9181)

ROBERT SCOTT SMALL LIBRARY
See: College of Charleston - Robert Scott Small Library - Special Collections (3372)

WALTER M. SMALL GEOLOGY LIBRARY
See: Allegheny College (285)

SMATHERS & THOMPSON
See: Kelly, Drye & Warren (7393)

A.K. SMILEY PUBLIC LIBRARY - LINCOLN MEMORIAL SHRINE
See: Lincoln Memorial Shrine (7869)

MARY MILLER SMISER HERITAGE LIBRARY
See: Johnson County Historical Society (7255)

★13235★
SMITH, ANDERSON, BLOUNT, DORSETT, MITCHELL & JERNIGAN - LIBRARY (Law)
1300 St. Mary's St.
Box 12807 Phone: (919)821-1220
Raleigh, NC 27605 Constance M. Matzen, Libn.
Staff: Prof 1. **Subjects:** Law. **Holdings:** 2000 volumes. **Services:** Library not open to the public. **Computerized Information Services:** LEXIS, DIALOG Information Services, WESTLAW. Performs searches on fee basis. **Publications:** Library News (newsletter), monthly - for internal distribution only.

ANDRE SMITH COLLECTION
See: Maitland Public Library (8331)

★13236★
SMITH BARNEY, HARRIS UPHAM & COMPANY, INC. - LIBRARY (Bus-Fin)
1345 Ave. of the Americas Phone: (212)698-6294
New York, NY 10105 James J. Fichter, Libn.
Founded: 1922. **Staff:** Prof 4; Other 5. **Subjects:** Investments and securities. **Special Collections:** Corporation records. **Holdings:** 1000 books and bound periodical volumes; 500 VF drawers. **Subscriptions:** 450 journals and other serials. **Services:** Interlibrary loan; library open to clients only.

BERTHA SMITH LIBRARY
See: Luther Rice Seminary (8112)

BETTY GOLDE SMITH MEMORIAL LIBRARY
See: St. Louis Psychoanalytic Institute (12530)

★13237★
SMITH COLLEGE - ARCHIVES (Hist)
Northampton, MA 01063 Phone: (413)584-2700
Susan Grigg, Dir.
Founded: 1922. **Staff:** Prof 2; Other 1. **Subjects:** Smith College - administration, faculty, students, alumnae organizations. **Special Collections:** Records of central administrative offices and academic departments; official publications; papers of faculty members; records of student organizations; letters, diaries, and memorabilia of students; records of alumnae organizations. **Holdings:** 2700 linear feet. **Services:** Copying (limited); archives open to the public with restrictions. **Staff:** Margery N. Sly, Coll.Archv..

★13238★
SMITH COLLEGE - CLARK SCIENCE LIBRARY (Sci-Engr, Biol Sci)
Northampton, MA 01063 Phone: (413)584-2700
Founded: 1966. **Staff:** Prof 1; Other 3. **Subjects:** Astronomy, biological sciences, chemistry, geology, mathematics, physics, psychology, computer science. **Holdings:** 112,211 volumes; 30,000 government documents and pamphlets; 11,938 microforms; 84 audiotapes. **Subscriptions:** 750 journals and other serials. **Services:** Interlibrary loan; copying; library open to the public for reference use only. **Automated Operations:** Computerized cataloging. **Computerized Information Services:** BRS Information Technologies, DIALOG Information Services.

★13239★
SMITH COLLEGE - HILLYER ART LIBRARY (Art)
Fine Arts Ctr. Phone: (413)584-2700
Northampton, MA 01063 Karen J. Harvey, Libn.
Staff: Prof 1; Other 4. **Subjects:** History of art, painting, design, architecture, sculpture, graphic arts, landscape architecture. **Holdings:** 51,000 books and bound periodical volumes; 72,000 study photographs; color reproductions; 11,000 microfiche. **Subscriptions:** 202 journals and other serials. **Services:** Interlibrary loan; copying; library open to the public for reference use only by special permission.

★13240★
SMITH COLLEGE - NONPRINT RESOURCES CENTER (Aud-Vis)
Library Phone: (413)584-2700
Northampton, MA 01063 David Vikre, Dir.
Founded: 1985. **Staff:** Prof 1; Other 4. **Subjects:** Film studies, science. **Holdings:** 350 videotapes; 280 audiotapes; 30 16mm films. **Services:** Center open to the public with restrictions. **Automated Operations:** Computerized cataloging.

★13241★
SMITH COLLEGE - RARE BOOK ROOM (Rare Book)
Northampton, MA 01063 Phone: (413)584-2700
Ruth Mortimer, Cur.
Staff: Prof 2. **Subjects:** 18th century English literature, early science, history of printing, economics, 19th century English lithography. **Special Collections:** English and American children's books, 17th-20th centuries (525 titles); Rudyard Kipling (275 items); William Faulkner (100 items); George Bernard Shaw (264 items); Ernest Hemingway (250 items); Sylvia Plath (700 items, including 4000 pages of manuscripts); Virginia Woolf (450 items, including manuscripts); E. Thornton Botanical Books (89 titles). **Holdings:** 20,000 books. **Services:** Copying; room open to the public by appointment. **Special Indexes:** Chronological index (card). **Staff:** Alison Scott, Asst.Cur..

★13242★
SMITH COLLEGE - SOPHIA SMITH COLLECTION - WOMEN'S HISTORY ARCHIVE (Hist, Soc Sci)
Northampton, MA 01063 Phone: (413)584-2700
Susan Grigg, Dir.
Founded: 1942. **Staff:** Prof 3; Other 1. **Subjects:** U.S. women's history, 1820 to present, especially birth control, social welfare, professions, women's suffrage and rights, international affairs; 19th century families. **Special Collections:** 200 major collections of personal papers and organizational records, including: Margaret Sanger; Planned Parenthood of America and Massachusetts; Hale, Ames, Garrison, and Bodman families; Ellen Gates Starr; Mary van Kleeck. **Holdings:** 3000 linear feet of manuscripts, archives, periodicals, printed ephemera, books. **Subscriptions:** 75 journals and other serials. **Services:** Copying (limited); archive open to the public with restrictions. **Special Catalogs:** Catalog of the Sophia Smith Collection; Picture Catalog of the Sophia Smith Collection - both for sale. **Staff:** Susan L. Boone, Cur..

★13243★
SMITH COLLEGE - WERNER JOSTEN LIBRARY OF THE PERFORMING ARTS (Mus, Theater)
Mendenhall Center Phone: (413)584-2700
Northampton, MA 01063 Marlene M. Wong, Libn.
Staff: Prof 2; Other 4. **Subjects:** Music, theater, dance. **Special Collections:** Einstein Collection (music of the 16th and 17th centuries copied in score by Alfred Einstein); music and correspondence of Werner Josten. **Holdings:** 30,526 books and bound periodical volumes; 38,000 scores; 45,596 sound recordings; 547 reels of microfilm. **Subscriptions:** 269 journals and other serials. **Services:** Interlibrary loan (books and periodicals only); library open to the public for reference use only. **Automated Operations:** Computerized cataloging. **Computerized Information Services:** OCLC. **Networks/Consortia:** Member of NELINET. **Special Indexes:** Index to articles in periodicals published prior to 1949; index to American sheet music collection; index to selected song collections; index to microfilm collection of musical and dramatic criticism by Philip Hale and others. **Staff:** Kathryn E. Burnett, Assoc.Libn..

★13244★
SMITH, CURRIE & HANCOCK - LAW LIBRARY (Law)
233 Peachtree St., N.E., Suite 2600 Phone: (404)521-3800
Atlanta, GA 30043-6601 Susan C. Lisi, Law Libn.
Founded: 1972. **Staff:** Prof 2. **Subjects:** Law - building and construction, government contract, labor. **Holdings:** 10,000 volumes; 1500 other cataloged items; 1300 internal materials. **Subscriptions:** 80 journals and other serials. **Services:** Interlibrary loan; library open to members of the Atlanta Law Libraries Association. **Computerized Information Services:** DIALOG Information Services, LEXIS, VU/TEXT Information Services, Information America, WESTLAW. **Publications:** Library Newsletter, monthly - for internal distribution only; Construction Law; Labor Law (both annotated bibliographies).

DAVID EUGENE SMITH MATHEMATICAL LIBRARY
See: Columbia University - Rare Book and Manuscript Library (3493)

★13245★
DEAF SMITH GENERAL HOSPITAL - LIBRARY (Med)
801 E. 3rd St. Phone: (806)364-2141
Hereford, TX 79045 Debbie Foerster, Dir., Med.Rec.
Staff: Prof 1; Other 2. **Subjects:** Medicine and allied health sciences. **Holdings:** 175 volumes. **Services:** Library not open to the public.

DICK SMITH ARCHIVES
See: Santa Barbara Museum of Natural History - Library (12863)

DR. C.W. SMITH TECHNICAL INFORMATION CENTER
See: General Electric Company - Aircraft Engine Business Group (5520)

EDGAR FAHS SMITH MEMORIAL COLLECTION IN THE HISTORY OF CHEMISTRY
See: University of Pennsylvania (16732)

★13246★
FREDERICK C. SMITH CLINIC - MEDICAL LIBRARY (Med)
1040 Delaware Ave. Phone: (614)383-8098
Marion, OH 43302 Doris P. Hurn, Libn.
Staff: Prof 1. **Subjects:** Medicine. **Holdings:** 750 books; 2000 bound periodical volumes. **Subscriptions:** 135 journals and other serials. **Services:** Interlibrary loan; copying; library open to the public by appointment. **Networks/Consortia:** Member of Central Ohio Hospital Library Consortium.

FREDERICK MADISON SMITH LIBRARY
See: Graceland College (5782)

FURMAN SMITH LIBRARY
See: Mercer University - Law School (8720)

GEORGE F. SMITH LIBRARY
See: University of Medicine and Dentistry of New Jersey (16397)

★13247★
GEORGE WALTER VINCENT SMITH ART MUSEUM - LIBRARY (Art)
222 State St.
Springfield, MA 01103 Phone: (413)733-4214
Founded: 1898. **Subjects:** Chinese and Japanese decorative arts, American art, arms and armor. **Holdings:** 2500 volumes. **Subscriptions:** 10 journals and other serials. **Services:** Library not open to the public. **Special Catalogs:** Exhibition catalogs. **Remarks:** Maintained by Springfield Library and Museums Association. **Staff:** Janet Gelman, Act.Co-Dir.; Steven Kern, Act.Co-Dir..

H. WARD SMITH LIBRARY
See: Ontario Ministry of the Solicitor General - Centre of Forensic Sciences (10852)

★13248★
SMITH HELMS MULLISS & MOORE - JULIUS C. SMITH LAW LIBRARY & EQUIPMENT, INC. (Law)
101 W. Friendly Ave. Phone: (919)378-1450
Greensboro, NC 27420 Anne Washburn, Libn.
Staff: Prof 1; Other 1. **Subjects:** Law. **Holdings:** 16,000 books. **Subscriptions:** 153 journals and other serials. **Services:** Copying; library open to the public with restrictions. **Computerized Information Services:** DIALOG Information Services, WESTLAW. **Remarks:** Branch libraries are maintained in Charlotte and Raleigh.

★13249★
HERMAN SMITH ASSOCIATES - LIBRARY† (Plan)
120 E. Ogden Ave. Phone: (312)323-3510
Hinsdale, IL 60521 Gail M. Langer, Libn.
Staff: Prof 1; Other 1. **Subjects:** Hospital planning, design and construction, administration, regional health planning. **Holdings:** 1500 books; 7000 documents and reports; 55 VF drawers. **Subscriptions:** 200 journals and other serials. **Services:** Interlibrary loan; copying; library open to the public with librarian's permission and by appointment. **Networks/Consortia:** Member of Suburban Library System (SLS). **Publications:** Library Bulletin, bimonthly.

HERVEY GARRETT SMITH RESEARCH LIBRARY
See: Suffolk Marine Museum (13731)

J.D. SMITH MEMORIAL LIBRARY
See: Akron General Medical Center (127)

★13250★
JOHN PETER SMITH HOSPITAL - MARIETTA MEMORIAL MEDICAL LIBRARY (Med)
1500 S. Main Phone: (817)921-3431
Fort Worth, TX 76104 M. June Bowman, Med.Libn.
Founded: 1963. **Staff:** Prof 1; Other 3. **Subjects:** Medicine, nursing, and allied health sciences. **Holdings:** 4200 books; 12,000 bound periodical volumes; 800 audiotapes. **Subscriptions:** 325 journals and other serials. **Services:** Interlibrary loan (limited); copying; complete services to the personnel of the Tarrant County Hospital District and the Tarrant County Medical Society; library open to the public but services available to health professionals only. **Computerized Information Services:** NLM, MEDLINE. **Networks/Consortia:** Member of Dallas-Tarrant County Consortium of Health Science Libraries. **Publications:** Acquisitions List, monthly; current awareness. **Special Catalogs:** Union List of Serials, biennial - to members.

JOSEPH F. SMITH LIBRARY AND MEDIA CENTER
See: Brigham Young University, Hawaii Campus (18224)

JULIUS C. SMITH LAW LIBRARY & EQUIPMENT, INC.
See: Smith Helms Mulliss & Moore (13248)

KENT H. SMITH LIBRARY
See: Foundation Center - Cleveland (5310)

★13251★
SMITH-KETTLEWELL EYE RESEARCH FOUNDATION - IN-HOUSE LIBRARY (Med)
2232 Webster St. Phone: (415)561-1620
San Francisco, CA 94115 Dr. Alex Cogan
Founded: 1959. **Subjects:** Vision research and rehabilitation engineering. **Holdings:** 2000 volumes. **Services:** Library not open to the public.

★13252★
SMITH KLINE BECKMAN - SMITH KLINE CONSUMER PRODUCTS - INFORMATION CENTER
1 Franklin Plaza
Box 8082
Philadelphia, PA 19101
Founded: 1983. **Subjects:** Medicine, chemistry, polymers. **Holdings:** 1200 books; U.S. chemistry patents. **Remarks:** Presently inactive. **Formerly:** Smith, Kline & French Laboratories.

★13253★
SMITH KLINE BIO-SCIENCE LABORATORIES - LIBRARY (Med, Biol Sci)
7600 Tyrone Ave. Phone: (818)376-6270
Van Nuys, CA 91405 Lois M. Mackey, Info.Spec.
Founded: 1948. **Staff:** Prof 1. **Subjects:** Clinical chemistry, microbiology, endocrinology and immunology, business management. **Holdings:** 2000 books; 5000 bound periodical volumes; 200 doctors' papers written at laboratories. **Subscriptions:** 125 journals and other serials. **Services:** Interlibrary loan; copying; library open to cooperating libraries. **Computerized Information Services:** MEDLARS, BRS Information Technologies, DIALOG Information Services. **Publications:** Reprints of doctors' papers - free upon request.

★13254★
SMITH, KLINE & FRENCH CANADA, LTD. - MEDICAL/ MARKETING LIBRARY (Med)
1940 Argentia Rd. Phone: (416)821-2200
Mississauga, ON, Canada L5N 2V7 Janet B. Hillis, Lib.Techn.
Founded: 1960. **Staff:** 1. **Subjects:** Medicine, pharmacy, pharmacology, biochemistry, microbiology, marketing. **Holdings:** 1000 books; 650 bound periodical volumes; 600 volumes of reprints; 170 reels of microfilm. **Subscriptions:** 160 journals and other serials. **Services:** Library not open to the public. **Computerized Information Services:** DIALOG Information Services; PRODOL (internal database).

★13255★
SMITH, KLINE & FRENCH LABORATORIES - MARKETING RESEARCH DEPARTMENT - LIBRARY (Bus-Fin)
1500 Spring Garden St. Phone: (215)751-5576
Philadelphia, PA 19101 Doris P. Shalley, Mktg.Libn.
Founded: 1945. **Staff:** 2. **Subjects:** Business and marketing aspects of the healthcare and pharmaceutical industries; drug therapy; disease information; general business. **Holdings:** 1000 books and bound periodical volumes; 10,000 internal reports; 15 shelves of clip files; 1000 government reports. **Subscriptions:** 180 journals and other serials. **Services:** Library not open to the public. **Computerized Information Services:** DIALOG Information Services, INVESTEXT, Dun & Bradstreet Corporation, Pharmaprojects, NEXIS, Dow Jones News/Retrieval, IMSBASE; BASIS (internal database). **Publications:** Marketing Research Reports, monthly; MarkAlert, 4/year; CAB Bulletin - all for internal distribution only.

★13256★
SMITH, KLINE & FRENCH LABORATORIES - RESEARCH AND DEVELOPMENT LIBRARY (L322) (Med)
709 Swedeland Rd.
Box 1539 Phone: (215)270-6400
King of Prussia, PA 19406-1539 Penny Young, R&D Libn.
Founded: 1947. **Staff:** Prof 7; Other 4. **Subjects:** Medicine, chemistry, pharmacology, pharmacy, biological sciences. **Holdings:** 11,000 books 12,000 bound periodical volumes; 2500 reels of microfilm. **Subscriptions:** 1100 journals and other serials. **Services:** Interlibrary loan; library not open to the public. **Automated Operations:** Computerized public access catalog, cataloging, acquisitions, serials, and circulation. **Computerized Information Services:** DIALOG Information Services, Pergamon ORBIT InfoLine, Inc., BRS Information Technologies, NLM, AMA/NET, Mead Data Central; LION, PRODOL (internal databases). **Networks/Consortia:** Member of PALINET. **Publications:** List of Acquisitions, monthly - for internal distribution only. **Staff:** Alice Dempsey, Hd., Pub.Serv.; Arlene Smith, Hd., Tech.Serv.; Daniel Law, Coll.Dev.Coord..

LILLIAN H. SMITH COLLECTION OF CHILDREN'S BOOKS
See: Toronto Public Library (14247)

★13257★
SMITH, LYONS, TORRANCE, STEVENSON & MAYER - LIBRARY (Law)
2 First Canadian Place, Suite 3400
P.O. Box 420 Phone: (416)369-7285
Toronto, ON, Canada M5X 1J3 Martha L. Foote, Libn.
Staff: Prof 1; Other 2. **Subjects:** Canadian law. **Holdings:** 3400 books; 3900 bound periodical volumes. **Subscriptions:** 200 journals and other serials; 6 newspapers. **Services:** Interlibrary loan; library open to the public by appointment. **Computerized Information Services:** QL Systems, Info Globe, CAN/LAW, The Financial Post Information Service, WESTLAW, Infomart, LEXIS, Dow Jones News/Retrieval, Canada Systems Group (CSG). **Publications:** Library Bulletin, weekly - for internal distribution only. **Special Indexes:** Index to Legal Memoranda (computer printout).

★13258★
MARGARET CHASE SMITH LIBRARY CENTER (Hist)
Norridgewock Avenue
Box 366 Phone: (207)474-8844
Skowhegan, ME 04976 Russell W. Fridley, Dir.
Founded: 1982. **Staff:** Prof 3; Other 5. **Subjects:** Senator Margaret Chase Smith's personal and professional records, American political history and biography. **Holdings:** Figures not available. **Services:** Copying; library open to qualified scholars. **Remarks:** Maintained by Northwood Institute, Midland, Michigan.

MARJORIE SMITH LIBRARY
See: University of British Columbia (15870)

★13259★
SMITH MEMORIAL LIBRARY - HISTORICAL COLLECTION (Hum)
Clark & Miller Ave. Phone: (716)357-5844
Chautauqua, NY 14722 Barbara Haug, Cur.
Founded: 1906. **Subjects:** Chautauqua. **Holdings:** Books and history of the Chautauqua Institution, 1874 to present. **Services:** Interlibrary loan; copying; collection open to the public. **Networks/Consortia:** Member of Chautauqua-Cattaraugus Library System. **Remarks:** Maintained by Chautauqua Institution. **Staff:** T. Isaac, Libn..

★13260★
SMITH PETERSON BECKMAN WILLSON LAW FIRM - SMITH PETERSON LAW LIBRARY (Law)
370 Midlands Mall
Box 249 Phone: (712)328-1833
Council Bluffs, IA 51501 Beverly Hobbs, Libn.
Staff: Prof 1. **Subjects:** Law. **Holdings:** 6824 books; expert witness files. **Subscriptions:** 51 journals and other serials. **Services:** Library not open to the public. **Computerized Information Services:** WESTLAW.

RALPH SMITH MEMORIAL LIBRARY
See: American Collectors Association, Inc. (449)

RICHARD ROOT SMITH LIBRARY
See: Blodgett Memorial Medical Center (1653)

ROBERT S. SMITH BEHAVIORAL SCIENCE LIBRARY
See: Pennsylvania State Department of Public Welfare - Philadelphia State Hospital - Staff Library (11178)

★13261★
SMITH & SCHNACKE - LAW LIBRARY (Law)
2000 Courthouse Plaza, N.E. Phone: (513)226-6623
Dayton, OH 45401 Greta K. Southard, Libn.
Staff: Prof 1; Other 3. **Subjects:** Law. **Holdings:** 25,000 books; 550 volumes on microfiche. **Subscriptions:** 450 journals and other serials; 7 newspapers. **Services:** Interlibrary loan; library not open to the public. **Computerized Information Services:** DIALOG Information Services, LEXIS.

SOPHIA SMITH COLLECTION
See: Smith College (13242)

★13262★
WILBUR SMITH ASSOCIATES - LIBRARY (Plan)
1301 Gervais St.
Box 92 Phone: (803)738-0580
Columbia, SC 29202 Jasper Salmond, Info.Dir.
Founded: 1952. **Staff:** Prof 2. **Subjects:** Transportation, planning, architecture, civil engineering, economics, energy. **Holdings:** 18,000 books and technical reports; speeches; vertical file. **Subscriptions:** 50 journals and other serials. **Services:** Interlibrary loan; library open to the public with restrictions. **Publications:** Acquisitions list; Federal Register Report, both monthly - both for internal distribution only.

WILLIAM HENRY SMITH MEMORIAL LIBRARY
See: Indiana Historical Society (6753)

SMITHKLINE BECKMAN, INC. - BECKMAN INSTRUMENTS, INC.
See: Beckman Instruments, Inc. (1456)

★13263★
SMITHSONIAN INSTITUTION - ARCHIVES (Hist)
Arts and Industries Bldg., Rm. 2135
900 Jefferson Dr., S.W. Phone: (202)357-1420
Washington, DC 20560 William W. Moss, Archv.
Founded: 1967. **Staff:** Prof 9; Other 11. **Subjects:** Smithsonian Institution history, history of 19th century natural science. **Special Collections:** Papers of Joseph Henry, Spencer F. Baird, Samuel P. Langley, Charles D. Walcott, Charles G. Abbot, and Alexander Wetmore (Smithsonian Secretaries). **Holdings:** 12,000 cubic feet of records, manuscripts, private papers, and collections relating to the Smithsonian, its staff members, and other scientists. **Services:** Copying; archives open to the public. **Publications:** Guide to the Smithsonian Archives, 1983; Guides to Collections, irregular.

SMITHSONIAN INSTITUTION - ARCHIVES OF AMERICAN ART
See: Archives of American Art/Smithsonian Institution (859)

★13264★
SMITHSONIAN INSTITUTION - FREER GALLERY OF ART - ARTHUR M. SACKLER GALLERY LIBRARY (Art)
1050 Independence Ave. Phone: (202)357-2091
Washington, DC 20560 Lily Kecskes, Hd.Libn.
Founded: 1923. **Staff:** Prof 2; Other 2. **Subjects:** Art and cultures of the Far East, Near East, and South Asia; history and civilization; art and art history; archeology; pottery; painting. **Special Collections:** Washington Biblical manuscript facsimiles; C.L. Freer Letter Books (30 volumes); letters of Whistler, Tryon, Dewing, Thayer, Freer acquaintances, dealers, and business associates (2500-3000). **Holdings:** 45,000 books and bound periodical volumes (both Western and Oriental languages); 102 reels of microfilm; 49 microfiche; 4 VF drawers of maps; 12 VF drawers of study photographs; 30,000 slides. **Subscriptions:** 260 journals. **Services:** Library reading room open to the public; slides loaned to public. **Automated Operations:** Computerized cataloging. **Computerized Information Services:** RLIN. **Networks/Consortia:** Member of RLG. **Special Indexes:** Index to KOKKA; index to sales catalogs; index to Chinese calligraphers.

★13265★
SMITHSONIAN INSTITUTION - HIRSHHORN MUSEUM AND SCULPTURE GARDEN - LIBRARY (Art)
Independence Ave. & 8th St., S.W. Phone: (202)357-3223
Washington, DC 20560 Anna Brooke, Libn.
Founded: 1966. **Staff:** Prof 1; Other 3. **Subjects:** Fine arts, European and American 20th century painting and sculpture, American 19th century

painting. **Special Collections:** Samuel Murray scrapbooks; Thomas Eakins memorabilia. **Holdings:** 35,000 books; exhibition catalogs; 31 VF drawers of artist files. **Subscriptions:** 50 journals and other serials. **Services:** Copying; library open to scholars by appointment. **Computerized Information Services:** RLIN, DIALOG Information Services, WILSONLINE, Geac Library Information System. Performs searches on fee basis. **Remarks:** An alternate telephone number is 357-3222.

★13266★
SMITHSONIAN INSTITUTION - NATIONAL ANTHROPOLOGICAL ARCHIVES (Soc Sci)
National Museum of Natural History Bldg., MRC 152
10th & Constitution Ave., N.W. Phone: (202)357-1976
Washington, DC 20560 James R. Glenn, Act.Dir.
Founded: 1879. **Staff:** Prof 3; Other 5. **Subjects:** Anthropology, linguistics, archeology, history of anthropology, history of American Indians, history of geography. **Special Collections:** Bureau of American Ethnology manuscript collection (5000); photographs of American Indians (60,000); Center for the Study of Man; Department of Anthropology records; Institute for Social Anthropology records; River Basin Surveys; professional papers of anthropologists; records of anthropological organizations. **Holdings:** 4000 cubic feet of archives and private papers; 350,000 photographs; 500 recordings; 100 reels of microfilm. **Services:** Copying; archives open to the public. **Computerized Information Services:** Smithsonian Institution - SIBIS System (internal database). **Special Catalogs:** Guide; manuscripts catalog (card, book); catalog of photographs (card); inventory and registers (booklets). **Staff:** Paula J. Fleming, Photo.Archv.; Kathleen T. Baxter, Ref.Archv..

★13267★
SMITHSONIAN INSTITUTION - NATIONAL MUSEUM OF AMERICAN ART - INVENTORY OF AMERICAN PAINTINGS EXECUTED BEFORE 1914 (Art)
8th and G Sts., N.W. Phone: (202)357-2941
Washington, DC 20560 Eleanor Fink, Dir.
Founded: 1971. **Staff:** Prof 2; Other 1. **Subjects:** American painting. **Holdings:** Photographic study collection of over 85,000 images of American paintings. **Services:** Copying; open to the public with restrictions. **Automated Operations:** Computerized cataloging. **Publications:** Directory to the Bicentennial Inventory of American Paintings Executed Before 1914, 1976. **Special Indexes:** Listings of approximately 250,000 American paintings indexed by artist, subject matter, owner/location, and title. **Staff:** Christine Hennessey, Coord..

★13268★
SMITHSONIAN INSTITUTION - NATIONAL MUSEUM OF AMERICAN ART - OFFICE OF RESEARCH SUPPORT - SLIDE AND PHOTOGRAPH ARCHIVES (Art)
Washington, DC 20560 Phone: (202)357-2283
Eleanor E. Fink, Chf.
Founded: 1973. **Staff:** Prof 2; Other 1. **Subjects:** American art, painting, sculpture, and decorative arts; graphics. **Special Collections:** Slide Library (90,000); photographic negatives for the New York photographic firm of Peter Juley and Son (127,000); the collection documents 80 years of American artists and their works of art. **Services:** Archives open to the public with restrictions. **Automated Operations:** Computerized cataloging. **Special Indexes:** Indexes by artist, subject, source, and location (computerized). **Staff:** Rachel M. Allen, Asst.Chf.; Margaret Harman, Photo Archv.; Nancy Yeide, Slide Libn..

★13269★
SMITHSONIAN INSTITUTION - NATIONAL MUSEUM OF AMERICAN ART/NATIONAL PORTRAIT GALLERY - LIBRARY (Art)
8th & F Sts., N.W. Phone: (202)357-1886
Washington, DC 20560 Cecilia Chin, Chf.Libn.
Founded: 1930. **Staff:** Prof 3; Other 5. **Subjects:** American painting, sculpture, graphic arts, biography, history, photography; portraiture; contemporary art. **Special Collections:** Ferdinand Perret Collection (scrapbooks on California and West Coast art). **Holdings:** 60,000 books and bound periodical volumes; 400 VF drawers of clippings, pamphlets, correspondence, photographs. **Subscriptions:** 1000 journals and other serials. **Services:** Interlibrary loan; copying; library open to adult researchers and graduate students. **Automated Operations:** Computerized cataloging and acquisitions. **Computerized Information Services:** DIALOG Information Services, WILSONLINE, OCLC, RLIN. **Staff:** Pat Lynagh, Asst.Libn./Ref.Libn.; Charles H. King, Jr., Cat..

★13270★
SMITHSONIAN INSTITUTION - NATIONAL MUSEUM OF AMERICAN HISTORY - ARCHIVES CENTER (Hist)
NMAH C340
14th St. & Constitution Ave., N.W. Phone: (202)357-3270
Washington, DC 20560 John A. Fleckner, Archv.
Staff: Prof 6. **Subjects:** History of advertising and technology, American history. **Special Collections:** Warshaw Collection of Business Americana (800 cubic feet); Clark Radioana Collection (early history of radio; 300 cubic feet). **Holdings:** 4000 cubic feet of manuscripts and other items. **Services:** Copying; center open to the public. **Computerized Information Services:** Smithsonian Institution Bibliographic Information System (internal database). **Publications:** Registers of collections, irregular.

★13271★
SMITHSONIAN INSTITUTION - OFFICE OF FOLKLIFE PROGRAMS - ARCHIVES (Mus)
955 L'Enfant Plaza, S.W., Suite 2600 Phone: (202)287-3424
Washington, DC 20560 Jeff Place, Archv.Coord.
Subjects: American and international music. **Holdings:** 12,000 hours of recordings.

SMITHSONIAN INSTITUTION - WOODROW WILSON INTERNATIONAL CENTER FOR SCHOLARS
See: Woodrow Wilson International Center for Scholars (17914)

★13272★
SMITHSONIAN INSTITUTION LIBRARIES (Sci-Engr, Hist, Art)
National Museum of Natural History
10th & Constitution Ave., N.W. Phone: (202)357-2240
Washington, DC 20560 Vija Karklins, Act.Dir.
Founded: 1846. **Staff:** Prof 47; Other 76. **Subjects:** Natural history and ethnology; ecology; history of science, technology, and flight; American history and culture; decorative and graphic arts; American and contemporary art. **Holdings:** 1 million volumes; 35,000 archival materials; manuscripts; pictures; photographs; clippings. **Subscriptions:** 15,941 journals and other serials. **Services:** Interlibrary loan; copying; open to qualified scholars. **Automated Operations:** Computerized public access catalog, cataloging and acquisitions. **Computerized Information Services:** DIALOG Information Services, BRS Information Technologies, Mead Data Central, RLIN, STN International. **Networks/Consortia:** Member of FEDLINK. **Remarks:** Figures given above represent combined holdings and staff for all branches. The Smithsonian Tropical Research Institute's address is P.O. Box 2072, Balboa, Republic de Panama. **Staff:** Margaret Child, Asst.Dir.; Nancy E. Gwinn, Asst.Dir.; Mary Augusta Rosenfeld, Adm.Libn.; Victoria Avera, Chf., Auto.Bibliog.Cont.; Brooke Henley, Chf., Cat.Rec.; Sylvia Churgin, Chf., STRI Lib..

★13273★
SMITHSONIAN INSTITUTION LIBRARIES - ASTROPHYSICAL OBSERVATORY - LIBRARY (Sci-Engr)
60 Garden St. Phone: (617)495-7264
Cambridge, MA 02138 Joyce Rey, Libn.
Founded: 1959. **Staff:** Prof 1. **Subjects:** Astrophysics, astronomy, physics, mathematics, satellite and earth geophysics. **Holdings:** 12,000 books; 3500 bound periodical volumes; 12,000 unbound reports; 20,000 microfiche. **Subscriptions:** 400 journals and other serials. **Services:** Interlibrary loan; copying; library open to the public by arrangement.

★13274★
SMITHSONIAN INSTITUTION LIBRARIES - CENTER FOR EARTH AND PLANETARY STUDIES - REGIONAL PLANETARY IMAGE FACILITY (Sci-Engr)
National Air and Space Museum, Rm. 3101 Phone: (202)357-1457
Washington, DC 20560 Ted A. Maxwell, Dir.
Staff: Prof 2. **Subjects:** Planetary sciences. **Special Collections:** Planetary images and cartographic products; spacecraft-image documentation; selected earth images. **Holdings:** 300,000 planetary images taken by manned and unmanned space probes. **Services:** Facility open to the public by appointment. **Computerized Information Services:** Telenet Communications Corporation (electronic mail service).

★13275★
SMITHSONIAN INSTITUTION LIBRARIES - CENTRAL REFERENCE AND LOAN SERVICE (Info Sci)
Museum of Natural History
10th & Constitution Ave., N.W. Phone: (202)357-2139
Washington, DC 20560 Maureen Canick, Chf.Libn.
Staff: Prof 3; Other 4. **Subjects:** General reference, bibliography, library and information sciences, management/administration, social sciences.

Special Collections: Smithsoniana (publications by and about the Smithsonian Institution); national bibliographies. **Holdings:** 28,000 volumes. **Services:** Copying; service open to the public for reference use only. **Automated Operations:** Computerized public access catalog, cataloging, and acquisitions. **Computerized Information Services:** DIALOG Information Services, Mead Data Central, OCLC, RLIN; Email (electronic mail service).

★13276★
SMITHSONIAN INSTITUTION LIBRARIES - COOPER-HEWITT MUSEUM OF DESIGN - DORIS & HENRY DREYFUSS MEMORIAL STUDY CENTER (Art)
2 E. 91st St. Phone: (212)860-6887
New York, NY 10128 Rhoda S. Ratner, Act.Chf.
Staff: Prof 1; Other 4. **Subjects:** Decorative arts, design, textiles, architecture. **Special Collections:** Rare books (4000); American and foreign auction catalogs; George W. Kubler Collection (18th and 19th century line engravings); Color Archive; Henry Dreyfuss Archive; Donald Deskey Archive; Ladislav Sutnar Archive; Therese Bonney photographs; trade catalogs. **Holdings:** 35,000 books; 3500 bound periodical volumes; 16 VF drawers; picture collection of over 350,000 items arranged by subject for designers. **Subscriptions:** 275 journals and other serials. **Services:** Interlibrary loan; copying; center open to the public. **Automated Operations:** Computerized cataloging, acquisitions, serials, and circulation. **Computerized Information Services:** OCLC.

★13277★
SMITHSONIAN INSTITUTION LIBRARIES - MUSEUM REFERENCE CENTER (Hum, Bus-Fin)
Arts & Industries Bldg., Rm. 2235
900 Jefferson Dr., S.W. Phone: (202)357-3101
Washington, DC 20560 Catherine D. Scott, Libn.
Founded: 1974. **Staff:** Prof 1; Other 2. **Subjects:** Museology, museum programs, nonprofit organization management, fundraising and membership development, voluntarism. **Special Collections:** American Law Institute-American Bar Association annual conference proceedings, 1978 to present (legal problems of museum administration); American Association of Museums annual meeting proceedings, 1984 to present (audio cassettes). **Holdings:** 3000 books; 9000 files of documentary materials. **Subscriptions:** 1200 journals and other serials. **Services:** Interlibrary loan; copying; center open to the public by appointment. **Automated Operations:** Computerized cataloging and acquisitions. **Computerized Information Services:** DIALOG Information Services; OnTyme Electronic Message Network Service (electronic mail service). **Networks/Consortia:** Member of FEDLINK. **Publications:** List of publications - available on request. **Remarks:** The Museum Reference Center contains resources on all aspects of museum operations. It is the only central source of museological information in the United States that makes such materials available to researchers and all members of the museum community.

★13278★
SMITHSONIAN INSTITUTION LIBRARIES - MUSEUM SUPPORT CENTER BRANCH (Biol Sci, Sci-Engr)
Washington, DC 20560 Phone: (202)287-3666
Karen Preslock, Chf.Libn.
Founded: 1964. **Staff:** Prof 2; Other 1. **Subjects:** Conservation of materials and museum objects; conservation science, including archeometry, study of museum environments, and analysis of materials by such means as x-ray diffraction and gas chromatography; occupational health hazards; medical entomology; taxonomic aspects of marine and estuarine fauna. **Holdings:** 10,000 books; 1800 bound periodical volumes; 30,000 reprints; 200 reels of microfilm; 800 microfiche. **Subscriptions:** 120 journals and other serials. **Services:** Interlibrary loan; copying; SDI; branch open to the public by appointment only. **Automated Operations:** Computerized cataloging and acquisitions. **Computerized Information Services:** DIALOG Information Services, OCLC, STN International, BRS Information Technologies.

★13279★
SMITHSONIAN INSTITUTION LIBRARIES - NATIONAL AIR AND SPACE MUSEUM - LIBRARY (Sci-Engr, Trans)
National Air & Space Museum, Rm. 3100
Independence Ave. & Seventh St., S.W. Phone: (202)357-3133
Washington, DC 20560 Martin A. Smith, Libn.
Founded: 1972. **Staff:** Prof 4; Other 2. **Subjects:** Aeronautics, astronautics, astronomy, earth and planetary sciences. **Special Collections:** Sherman Fairchild Photographic Collection; William A.M. Burden Collection (early ballooning works and aeronautica); Bella Landauer Aeronautical Sheet Music Collection (1500 pieces); Jerome Hunsaker papers; Samuel P. Langley aerodrome manuscripts; Harold E. Morehouse biographical files on early aircraft pioneers; Juan Trippe correspondence and papers. **Holdings:** 40,000 books; 7000 bound periodical volumes; 95 reels of microfilm of periodicals. **Subscriptions:** 452 journals and other serials. **Services:** Interlibrary loan; copying; library open to the public by appointment. **Automated Operations:** Computerized cataloging and acquisitions. **Computerized Information Services:** DIALOG Information Services, NEXIS, OCLC. **Networks/Consortia:** Member of FEDLINK. **Publications:** NASM Library Brochure. **Special Indexes:** Aeronautical periodical index (computerized). **Staff:** Mary Clare Gray, Ref.Libn.; Amy Levin, Ref.Libn.; Philip Edwards, Info.Spec..

★13280★
SMITHSONIAN INSTITUTION LIBRARIES - NATIONAL MUSEUM OF AMERICAN HISTORY - LIBRARY (Sci-Engr, Hist)
Museum of American History Phone: (202)357-2414
Washington, DC 20560 Rhoda S. Ratner, Chf.Libn.
Staff: Prof 3; Other 4. **Subjects:** American history, history of science and technology, applied science, decorative arts, domestic and community life. **Special Collections:** Exhibitions and expositions (1500 items); trade catalogs (275,000). **Holdings:** 165,000 volumes. **Services:** Interlibrary loan; copying; library open to the public with restrictions.

★13281★
SMITHSONIAN INSTITUTION LIBRARIES - NATIONAL MUSEUM OF NATURAL HISTORY - ANTHROPOLOGY DIVISION LIBRARY (Soc Sci)
Natural History Bldg., Rm. 330/331 Phone: (202)357-1819
Washington, DC 20560 Mary Kay Davies, Libn.
Staff: Prof 1; Other 1. **Subjects:** Ethnology, physical anthropology, archeology. **Special Collections:** Bureau of American Ethnology Library Collection. **Holdings:** 63,000 books and bound periodicals. **Subscriptions:** 1300 journals and other serials. **Services:** Interlibrary loan; copying; library open to the public by appointment. **Automated Operations:** Computerized acquisitions. **Computerized Information Services:** Smithsonian Institution Bibliographic Information System (internal database). **Publications:** Monthly acquisitions list.

★13282★
SMITHSONIAN INSTITUTION LIBRARIES - NATIONAL MUSEUM OF NATURAL HISTORY - BOTANY LIBRARY (Biol Sci)
Natural History Bldg.
10th & Constitution Ave. Phone: (202)357-2715
Washington, DC 20560 Ruth F. Schallert, Libn.
Subjects: Taxonomic botany, history of botany. **Special Collections:** Hitchcock-Chase Collection (grasses; 1500 books and reprints); Dawson Collection (algae; 1000 books and reprints). **Holdings:** 32,000 volumes; 14 shelves of collectors' field notebooks; 325 boxes of reprints; 21 herbaria on microfiche. **Subscriptions:** 400 journals and other serials. **Services:** Interlibrary loan; copying; library open to the public by appointment.

★13283★
SMITHSONIAN INSTITUTION LIBRARIES - NATIONAL MUSEUM OF NATURAL HISTORY - BRANCH LIBRARY (Biol Sci)
Natural History Bldg., Rm. 51
10th & Constitution Ave. Phone: (202)357-4696
Washington, DC 20560 Ann Juneau, Natural Hist.Libn.
Staff: Prof 5; Other 7. **Subjects:** Paleobiology, systematic botany, geology, oceanography, ecology, entomology, vertebrate and invertebrate zoology and paleontology, mineralogy, limnology, anthropology, North and South American Indians. **Special Collections:** J.D. Smith Collection (botany); Cushman Collection (Foraminifera); Springer Collection (crinoids); Wilson Collection (copepoda); Remington-Kellogg Collection of Marine Mammalogy. **Holdings:** 329,000 books and bound periodical volumes. **Services:** Interlibrary loan; copying. **Automated Operations:** Computerized cataloging and acquisitions. **Computerized Information Services:** DIALOG Information Services, RLIN, NEXIS, OCLC, Geac Library Information System; SIBIS (internal database). **Networks/Consortia:** Member of FEDLINK. **Staff:** David Steere, Ref.Libn.; Robert Skarr, Ref.Libn.; Carolyn Hahn, ILL Coord.; Ronald Lindsey, Sr.Techn..

★13284★
SMITHSONIAN INSTITUTION LIBRARIES - NATIONAL MUSEUM OF NATURAL HISTORY - ENTOMOLOGY LIBRARY (Biol Sci)
Natural History Bldg., Rm. W629C Phone: (202)357-2354
Washington, DC 20560 Robert J. Skarr, Libn.
Staff: 1. **Subjects:** Taxonomic and medical entomology. **Special Collections:** Casey Collection (Coleoptera). **Holdings:** 23,000 volumes. **Subscriptions:** 280 journals and other serials. **Services:** Interlibrary loan; copying; library open to the public by appointment. **Automated Operations:** Computerized public access catalog.

★13285★
SMITHSONIAN INSTITUTION LIBRARIES - NATIONAL ZOOLOGICAL PARK - LIBRARY (Biol Sci)
3000 Block of Connecticut Ave., N.W. Phone: (202)673-4771
Washington, DC 20008 Kay A. Kenyon, Chf.Libn.
Staff: Prof 1. **Subjects:** Animal behavior, animal husbandry, wildlife conservation, animal nutrition, veterinary medicine, horticulture. **Special Collections:** Zoo publications. **Holdings:** 4000 volumes. **Subscriptions:** 320 journals and other serials. **Services:** Interlibrary loan; copying; library open to the public by appointment. **Automated Operations:** Computerized public access catalog, cataloging and acquisitions. **Computerized Information Services:** DIALOG Information Services, OCLC; Email (electronic mail service). **Publications:** Library News for Zoos and Aquariums, 3/year - to zoos and aquariums.

★13286★
SMITHSONIAN INSTITUTION LIBRARIES - OFFICE OF HORTICULTURE - BRANCH LIBRARY (Biol Sci)
Arts & Industries Bldg., Rm. 2401 Phone: (202)357-1544
Washington, DC 20560 Susan R. Gurney, Chf.Libn.
Founded: 1984. **Staff:** Prof 1. **Subjects:** History of American horticulture and landscape design. **Special Collections:** W. Atlee Burpee Seed and Nursery Catalog Collection (15,000 catalogs, 19th and 20th centuries). **Holdings:** 3000 books; 1600 bound periodical volumes; clipping files. **Subscriptions:** 80 journals and other serials. **Services:** Interlibrary loan; copying; library open to the public by appointment. **Automated Operations:** Computerized cataloging and acquisitions. **Computerized Information Services:** DIALOG Information Services.

★13287★
SMITHSONIAN INSTITUTION LIBRARIES - SMITHSONIAN ENVIRONMENTAL RESEARCH CENTER LIBRARY-EDGEWATER (Env-Cons)
Box 28 Phone: (301)261-4190
Edgewater, MD 21037 Angela N. Haggins, Chf.Libn.
Founded: 1972. **Staff:** 1. **Subjects:** Environment, ecology, estuarine research, marine ecology, aquatic microbiology. **Holdings:** 1160 books; 995 bound periodical volumes; 1000 technical reports. **Subscriptions:** 82 journals and other serials. **Services:** Interlibrary loan; copying; library open to the public by appointment. **Automated Operations:** Computerized cataloging and acquisitions. **Computerized Information Services:** DIALOG Information Services. **Special Indexes:** List of technical reports.

★13288★
SMITHSONIAN INSTITUTION LIBRARIES - SPECIAL COLLECTIONS BRANCH (Biol Sci, Sci-Engr)
MAH 5016 Phone: (202)357-1568
Washington, DC 20560 Ellen B. Wells, Chf.
Staff: Prof 1; Other 1. **Subjects:** Physical sciences, natural history, technology, applied arts. **Special Collections:** Smithson Collection (200 books and offprints); Wetmore Ornithology Collection (400 books); Dibner Library (Americana and science and technology; 10,000 books); Comegys Library (19th century Philadelphia family library; 900 volumes). **Holdings:** 25,000 books and bound periodical volumes; 350 bound manuscripts; 1500 engraved portraits; 200 science medals. **Services:** Copying; library open to the public by appointment for reference use only. **Publications:** Operations of the Geometric and Military Compass 1606, 1978; Heralds of Science, 1980; Manuscripts of the Dibner Collection, 1985.

★13289★
SMITHSONIAN INSTITUTION LIBRARIES - WARREN M. ROBBINS NATIONAL MUSEUM OF AFRICAN ART - BRANCH LIBRARY (Art, Area-Ethnic)
950 Independence Ave., S.W. Phone: (202)357-4875
Washington, DC 20560 Janet L. Stanley, Chf.Libn.
Founded: 1971. **Staff:** Prof 1; Other 1. **Subjects:** Africa - art, material culture, anthropology, folklore history. **Holdings:** 15,000 books; 500 vertical files. **Subscriptions:** 200 journals and other serials. **Services:** Interlibrary loan; copying; SDI; library open to the public by appointment. **Publications:** National Museum of African Art Library Acquisitions List, monthly.

★13290★
SMITHSONIAN INSTITUTION LIBRARIES - WARREN M. ROBBINS NATIONAL MUSEUM OF AFRICAN ART - ELIOT ELISOFON ARCHIVES (Art)
950 Independence Ave., S.W. Phone: (202)347-4600
Washington, DC 20560 Judith Luskey, Archv./Cur. of Photo.Colls.
Staff: Prof 2. **Subjects:** Africa, African art. **Holdings:** 150,000 color slides; 70,000 black/white negatives; 50 feature films; 100,000 feet of unedited outtakes, 1860 to present. **Services:** Archives open to the public by appointment.

SMITHSONIAN TROPICAL RESEARCH INSTITUTE
See: Smithsonian Institution Libraries (13272)

★13291★
SMITHTOWN HISTORICAL SOCIETY - LIBRARY (Hist)
Box 69 Phone: (516)265-6768
Smithtown, NY 11787 Louise P. Hall, Dir.
Founded: 1955. **Staff:** 2. **Subjects:** Local history and genealogy. **Holdings:** 1000 books; 300 bound periodical volumes; 5000 deeds, ledgers, documents, letters, surveys. **Services:** Copying; library open to the public by appointment for research use only.

★13292★
SMITHTOWN LIBRARY - SPECIAL COLLECTIONS (Hist)
1 North Country Rd. Phone: (516)265-2072
Smithtown, NY 11787 Vera Toman, L.I. Coll.Libn.
Founded: 1907. **Special Collections:** Long Island Collection (23,075 items). **Services:** Interlibrary loan; copying; collections open to the public. **Automated Operations:** Computerized acquisitions and circulation. **Networks/Consortia:** Member of Suffolk Cooperative Library System, Long Island Library Resources Council, Inc. (LILRC). **Publications:** Pamphlets on Long Island History, irregular.

SMURFIT IRISH LAW CENTER
See: St. Louis University - Law Library (12546)

★13293★
R.M. SMYTHE AND COMPANY - OBSOLETE AND INACTIVE SECURITIES LIBRARY (Bus-Fin)
26 Broadway, Suite 271 Phone: (212)668-1880
New York, NY 10004 Diana E. Herzog, Pres.
Staff: Prof 7; Other 6. **Subjects:** Obsolete securities, inactive U.S. securities, foreign securities, active securities, collector's certificate reference. **Holdings:** 5000 books and bound periodical volumes; 35 VF drawers of correspondence; 20 boxes of pamphlets; 250,000 cards of company records; 50,000 cards of company reports; lost stockholder tracing reference material; reference material for antique certificate collectors. **Services:** Copying; library open to the public with restrictions.

★13294★
SNC INC. - LIBRARY (Sci-Engr, Bus-Fin)
1 Complexe Desjardins
C.P. 10 Phone: (514)282-9551
Montreal, PQ, Canada H5B 1C8 Martine Bousquet, Chf.Libn.
Founded: 1911. **Staff:** Prof 1; Other 1. **Subjects:** Engineering, construction, business, international affairs. **Holdings:** 10,000 books; 3000 standards; 100 microfiche. **Subscriptions:** 300 journals and other serials; 10 newspapers. **Services:** Interlibrary loan; library not open to the public. **Automated Operations:** Computerized circulation. **Computerized Information Services:** DIALOG Information Services, Telesystemes Questel, CAN/OLE, QL Systems; Envoy 100 (electronic mail service).

★13295★
SNELL & WILMER - LAW LIBRARY (Law)
3100 Valley Bank Center Phone: (602)257-7316
Phoenix, AZ 85073 Mary Grace Oakes, Law Libn.
Staff: Prof 2; Other 8. **Subjects:** Law - tax, utilities, real estate, water, corporate, securities. **Special Collections:** Arizona archival law materials. **Holdings:** 45,310 books; 417 bound periodical volumes; 700 other cataloged items. **Subscriptions:** 700 journals and other serials; 11 newspapers. **Services:** Interlibrary loan; library not open to the public. **Computerized Information Services:** LEXIS, DIALOG Information Services, WESTLAW, VU/TEXT Information Services, OCLC. **Networks/Consortia:** Member of AMIGOS Bibliographic Council, Inc.. **Publications:** Monthly Book List of New Titles. **Special Indexes:** Medical indexes of

articles used in cases; memorandum index. **Staff:** Barbara Miller, Ref.Libn..

SNITE MUSEUM OF ART
See: University of Notre Dame (16675)

★13296★
SNOHOMISH COUNTY LAW LIBRARY (Law)
County Court House Phone: (206)259-5326
Everett, WA 98201 Betty Z. Scott, Libn.
Staff: Prof 1; Other 1. **Subjects:** Law - federal, state, local. **Holdings:** 18,000 volumes. **Subscriptions:** 17 journals and other serials. **Services:** Interlibrary loan; copying; library open to the public with restrictions on circulation.

SNYDER COLLECTION OF AMERICANA
See: University of Missouri, Kansas City (16540)

★13297★
SNYDER COUNTY HISTORICAL SOCIETY, INC. - LIBRARY (Hist)
30 E. Market St.
Box 276 Phone: (717)837-6191
Middleburg, PA 17842 Kathryn Gift, Libn.
Staff: Prof 1. **Subjects:** Local history, Pennsylvania history, Pennsylvania military history, genealogy. **Special Collections:** Civil War letters; Dr. Charles A. Fisher Collection. **Holdings:** 3000 volumes; 1000 historical bulletins, early land grants, warrants, deeds. **Services:** Copying; library open to the public with permission. **Publications:** Snyder County Annual Bulletin.

★13298★
H.L. SNYDER MEMORIAL RESEARCH FOUNDATION - LIBRARY (Med)
1407 Wheat Rd. Phone: (316)221-4080
Winfield, KS 67156 Barbara Smith, Libn.
Founded: 1947. **Staff:** Prof 1. **Subjects:** Biochemistry, medicine, clinical chemistry. **Holdings:** 2000 books; 1000 bound periodical volumes. **Subscriptions:** 30 journals and other serials. **Services:** Interlibrary loan; copying; library open to the public. **Networks/Consortia:** Member of Midcontinental Regional Medical Library Program. **Remarks:** Includes holdings of the Snyder Clinic Library.

O.J. SNYDER MEMORIAL MEDICAL LIBRARY
See: Philadelphia College of Osteopathic Medicine (11270)

★13299★
SOAP AND DETERGENT ASSOCIATION - LIBRARY (Sci-Engr)
475 Park Ave., S. Phone: (212)725-1262
New York, NY 10016 Rose D. Api, Off.Mgr.
Staff: 1. **Subjects:** Detergents. **Holdings:** 1000 books; 200 bound periodical volumes. **Subscriptions:** 205 journals and other serials. **Services:** Copying; library open to the public by appointment.

★13300★
SOCIAL LAW LIBRARY (Law)
1200 Court House Phone: (617)523-0018
Boston, MA 02108 Edgar J. Bellefontaine, Libn.
Founded: 1804. **Staff:** Prof 28; Other 25. **Subjects:** Anglo-American law. **Special Collections:** Papers of the Inferior Court of Common Pleas for Suffolk County, 1692-1830; Supreme Judicial Court Records and Briefs; Papers of Lemuel Shaw. **Holdings:** 220,000 volumes; 360,000 microfiche; 2160 audio cassettes; 240 videotapes. **Subscriptions:** 3436 journals and other serials; 20 newspapers. **Services:** Interlibrary loan (limited); copying; library open to members and other authorized persons. **Computerized Information Services:** DIALOG Information Services, LEXIS, VU/TEXT Information Services, PHINet FedTax Database, WESTLAW. **Networks/Consortia:** Member of New England Law Library Consortium (NELLCO). **Publications:** Newsletter, quarterly - to members; Legal Video Review, quarterly - by subscription.

SOCIAL SECURITY ADMINISTRATION
See: U.S. Social Security Administration (15494)

★13301★
SOCIETE D'ARCHEOLOGIE ET DE NUMISMATIQUE DE MONTREAL - BIBLIOTHEQUE (Hist)
280 est, rue Notre-Dame
Montreal, PQ, Canada H2Y 1C5 Phone: (514)861-3708
Founded: 1895. **Staff:** 1. **Subjects:** Canadian history, numismatics. **Holdings:** 10,000 books; manuscripts; archives; documents. **Services:** Library not open to the public, but the society will consider appropriate requests by researchers. **Remarks:** Library is in process of reorganization after being inactive for over twenty years. **Also Known As:** Antiquarian and Numismatic Society of Montreal.

SOCIETE CANADIENNE D'HYPOTHEQUES ET DE LOGEMENT
See: Canada - Mortgage and Housing Corporation (2414)

SOCIETE CANADIENNE DE PSYCHANALYSE
See: Canadian Psychoanalytic Society (2600)

★13302★
SOCIETE CULINAIRE PHILANTHROPIQUE DE NEW YORK, INC. - LIBRARY (Food-Bev)
250 W. 57th St., Rm. 1532 Phone: (212)246-6754
New York, NY 10019 Andre Rene, Pres.
Subjects: Professional cooking. **Holdings:** Cookbooks. **Services:** Library open to members only.

★13303★
SOCIETE DE GENEALOGIE DE QUEBEC - LIBRARY (Hist)
C.P. 9066 Phone: (418)651-9127
Ste. Foy, PQ, Canada G1V 4A8 Rene Doucet, Libn.
Staff: 15. **Subjects:** Genealogy. **Holdings:** 3000 books; microfiche. **Subscriptions:** 20 journals and other serials. **Services:** Copying; library open to the public. **Publications:** L'Ancetre (newsletter), 10/year.

★13304★
SOCIETE D'HISTOIRE DES CANTONS DE L'EST - BIBLIOTHEQUE (Hist)
1304 Portland Blvd. Phone: (819)562-0616
Sherbrooke, PQ, Canada J1J 1S3 Andree Desilets, Pres.
Founded: 1927. **Staff:** Prof 2. **Subjects:** Local and regional history of the Eastern Townships. **Holdings:** 5000 volumes; 3000 photographs; 400 maps; archives. **Also Known As:** Eastern Townships Historical Society. **Staff:** Christine Beaudoin, Coord..

SOCIETE HISTORIQUE-DE-LA-COTE-DU-SUD
See: College de Ste-Anne-de-la-Pocatiere (3400)

★13305★
SOCIETE HISTORIQUE DU SAGUENAY - BIBLIOTHEQUE (Hist)
C.P. 456
Chicoutimi, PQ, Canada G7H 5C8 Roland Belanger, Archv.
Founded: 1934. **Staff:** Prof 1. **Subjects:** Regional history and geography, genealogy, oral history, folklore. **Special Collections:** Newspaper clippings, 1859 to present, concerning the Saguenay region. **Holdings:** 12,000 books; 200 bound periodical volumes; 200,000 photographs; 65,000 negatives; 1500 maps. **Subscriptions:** 50 journals and other serials; 30 newspapers. **Services:** Copying; library open to the public for reference use only. **Automated Operations:** Computerized cataloging. **Publications:** Saguenayensia, quarterly. **Also Known As:** Saguenay Region Historical Society.

SOCIETE DES MISSIONS-ETRANGERES
See: Foreign Missions Society of Quebec (5252)

★13306★
SOCIETE NATIONALE DE DIFFUSION EDUCATIVE ET CULTURELLE - SERVICE D'INFORMATION SONDEC
8770, Blvd. Langelier, Suite 230
St. Leonard, PQ, Canada H1P 3E8
Defunct

SOCIETE RADIO-CANADA
See: Canadian Broadcasting Corporation (2529)

SOCIETE ROYALE DU CANADA
See: Royal Society of Canada (12236)

SOCIETE DE TRANSPORT DE LA COMMUNAUTE URBAINE DE MONTREAL
See: Montreal Urban Community Transit Corporation (9279)

★13307★
SOCIETY FOR ACADEMIC ACHIEVEMENT - LIBRARY (Educ)
220 WCU Bldg.
510 Maine St. Phone: (217)224-0570
Quincy, IL 62301 C. Richard Heitholt, Exec.Dir./Libn.
Staff: 2. **Subjects:** Academic excellence, communication skills. **Holdings:** 1075 volumes. **Subscriptions:** 15 journals and other serials. **Services:** Library not open to the public.

★13308★
SOCIETY OF ACTUARIES - LIBRARY (Bus-Fin)
500 Park Blvd. Phone: (312)773-3010
Itasca, IL 60143 Donna Richardson, Res.Libn.
Founded: 1949. **Subjects:** Application of mathematical probabilities to the design of insurance, pension, and employee benefit programs. **Holdings:** 2500 volumes.

★13309★
SOCIETY OF AMERICAN FORESTERS - INFORMATION CENTER
5400 Grosvenor Ln.
Bethesda, MD 20814
Subjects: Forestry education, forest economics, silviculture, forest fires, forest land use, history of professional forestry. **Holdings:** Figures not available. **Remarks:** Presently inactive.

SOCIETY OF AMERICAN FORESTERS ARCHIVES
See: Forest History Society, Inc. - Library and Archives (5256)

★13310★
SOCIETY FOR THE APPLICATION OF FREE ENERGY - LIBRARY (Energy)
1315 Apple Ave. Phone: (301)587-8686
Silver Spring, MD 20910 William C. Moore, Sec.
Founded: 1973. **Subjects:** Research and application of natural forms of energy, including solar, wind, metaphysical (energy of the mind), and biocybernetic (energy of living things). **Holdings:** 2000 volumes.

SOCIETY OF ARTS AND CRAFTS, BOSTON ARCHIVES
See: Boston Public Library - Fine Arts Department (1742)

★13311★
SOCIETY OF AUTOMOTIVE ENGINEERS, INC. - SAE LIBRARY (Sci-Engr)
400 Commonwealth Dr. Phone: (412)776-4841
Warrendale, PA 15096-0001 Janet M. Jedlicka, Libn./Res.Ck.
Founded: 1905. **Staff:** Prof 1; Other 1. **Subjects:** Automotive and aerospace engineering, including trucks, buses, and farm machinery; design and development; fuels and lubricants; fuel economy. **Special Collections:** SAE publications, 1905 to present. **Holdings:** 1700 books; 160 bound periodical volumes; 25,000 technical papers; 5000 aerospace material specifications; 1700 automotive standards; mechanical engineering publications. **Subscriptions:** 203 journals and other serials. **Services:** Copying; library open to the public by appointment. **Computerized Information Services:** Pergamon ORBIT InfoLine, Inc. Performs searches on fee basis. Contact Person: Amy Haugh, Info.Spec..

★13312★
SOCIETY OF CALIFORNIA PIONEERS - JOSEPH A. MOORE LIBRARY (Hist)
456 McAllister St. Phone: (415)861-5278
San Francisco, CA 94102 Grace E. Baker, Libn.
Founded: 1850. **Staff:** Prof 1. **Subjects:** California - primarily pre-1870 with emphasis on the activities of 1849ers. **Special Collections:** Correspondence of Thomas Starr King, Unitarian Minister, 1861-1864; letters of Jessie Benton Fremont, writer; Jacob Rink Snyder Collection (California Battalion documents; 295 items); handwritten diaries of forty-niners and other pioneers (200); reminiscences of pioneers (8 volumes); photographs of the San Francisco Bay Area and California (25,000); political scrapbooks, 1863-1910 (18 linear feet); scrapbooks on early San Francisco history and prominent figures (9 linear feet); Cooper-Molera Papers, 1828-1910 (10 linear feet of ship logs, account books, business papers, legal documents, taxation and assessment papers for Monterey County, Mexican mining deeds, household papers of Monterey adobe); Patterson Ranch Papers, 1849-1965 (ranch history; 81 linear feet); Sherman Music Collection, 1852-1923 (early theatrical posters and biographical sketches of California musicians; rare sheet music; playbills; musical manuscripts); mining company stock certificates and business records, 1850 to present. **Holdings:** Diaries and county histories on microfilm. **Services:** Copying; photographs made of paintings and duplicate prints made of photos; library open to the public. **Publications:** The Pioneer - to members and by mailing list. **Special Catalogs:** Catalog of pioneers (card).

★13313★
SOCIETY FOR CALLIGRAPHY - LIBRARY (Art)
Box 64174 Phone: (213)457-2968
Los Angeles, CA 90064 Andree Weinman
Founded: 1974. **Subjects:** Calligraphy. **Holdings:** 450 volumes; slides; movies.

SOCIETY OF THE CATHOLIC APOSTOLATE - PALLOTTINE PROVINCIALATE LIBRARY
See: Pallottine Provincialate Library (11034)

★13314★
SOCIETY OF THE CINCINNATI LIBRARY - ANDERSON HOUSE MUSEUM (Hist)
2118 Massachusetts Ave., N.W. Phone: (202)785-2040
Washington, DC 20008 John D. Kilbourne, Dir.
Founded: 1783. **Staff:** Prof 1; Other 1. **Subjects:** U.S. history, American Revolution. **Holdings:** 15,000 books; 25,500 items in manuscript archives and collections of the society. **Subscriptions:** 52 journals and other serials. **Services:** Interlibrary loan; copying; library and museum open to the public. **Publications:** Annual Report of the Library and Museum; Cincinnati 14 (newsletter), semiannual; George Rogers Clark Lectures on the American Revolution.

SOCIETY OF CIVIL WAR SURGEONS LIBRARY
See: Lincoln Memorial University - Abraham Lincoln Library and Museum (7870)

SOCIETY OF COLLECTORS, INC. - DUNHAM TAVERN MUSEUM
See: Dunham Tavern Museum (4451)

★13315★
SOCIETY FOR COMPUTER APPLICATIONS IN ENGINEERING, PLANNING, AND ARCHITECTURE, INC. (CEPA) - LIBRARY OF PROGRAM ABSTRACTS (Comp Sci, Plan)
15713 Crabbs Branch Way Phone: (301)926-7070
Rockville, MD 20855 Patricia C. Johnson, Exec.Dir.
Subjects: Engineering, architecture, computers, computer software and hardware. **Holdings:** Figures not available. **Services:** Library not open to the public. **Publications:** Conference Proceedings, semiannual - for sale; Newsletter, quarterly - by subscription. **Special Catalogs:** Software title list; keyword index.

★13316★
SOCIETY OF COSMETIC CHEMISTS - LIBRARY (Sci-Engr)
1995 Broadway, 17th Fl. Phone: (212)874-0600
New York, NY 10023 Jo Rathgeber, Chm., Lib.Comm.
Subjects: Chemistry, pharmacy, cosmetic sciences. **Holdings:** 550 volumes. **Subscriptions:** 25 journals and other serials. **Services:** Interlibrary loan; library open to the public. **Computerized Information Services:** DIALOG Information Services.

★13317★
SOCIETY OF DIE CASTING ENGINEERS, INC. - H.L. "RED" HARVILL MEMORIAL LIBRARY (Sci-Engr)
Triton College Campus
2000 N. Fifth Ave. Phone: (312)452-0700
River Grove, IL 60171-1992 Larry G. Hayes, Found.Sec.
Founded: 1986. **Subjects:** Die casting and allied aspects of metal casting, mechanics, engineering, and other arts and sciences. **Holdings:** 5600 volumes. **Services:** Library open to the public. **Computerized Information Services:** The Harvill Information System (internal database).

★13318★
SOCIETY OF THE FOUNDERS OF NORWICH, CONNECTICUT - LEFFINGWELL INN LIBRARY (Hist)
348 Washington St. Phone: (203)889-5990
Norwich, CT 06360 Linda Kate Edgerton, Libn.
Staff: Prof 1; Other 1. **Subjects:** Local history and genealogy. **Holdings:** 400 books; 32 bound periodical volumes; 15 linear feet of documents and

letters. **Services:** Interlibrary loan (limited); copying; library open to the public by appointment.

★13319★
SOCIETY OF THE FOUR ARTS - LIBRARY (Art)
Four Arts Plaza Phone: (407)655-2766
Palm Beach, FL 33480 Joanne Rendon, Libn.
Founded: 1936. **Staff:** Prof 1; Other 4. **Subjects:** Painting, decorative arts, architecture, photography. **Special Collections:** Addison Mizner Collection. **Holdings:** 32,000 books and bound periodical volumes. **Subscriptions:** 35 journals and other serials; 10 newspapers. **Services:** Interlibrary loan; copying; library open to the public. **Remarks:** An alternate telephone number is 655-2776.

★13320★
SOCIETY OF FRIENDS - FRIENDS HOUSE LIBRARY (Rel-Phil)
60 Lowther Ave. Phone: (416)921-0368
Toronto, ON, Canada M5R 1C7 Jane Sweet, Lib.Coord.
Founded: 1890. **Staff:** 1. **Subjects:** History of Quakerism, peace and nonviolence, native concerns. **Holdings:** 5200 books; 102 bound periodical volumes; 12 boxes of pamphlets and reports. **Subscriptions:** 25 journals and other serials. **Services:** Interlibrary loan; library open to the public.

★13321★
SOCIETY OF FRIENDS - FRIENDS MEETING OF WASHINGTON - LIBRARY (Rel-Phil)
2111 Florida Ave., N.W. Phone: (202)483-3310
Washington, DC 20008 Katharine Durand, Libn.
Founded: 1932. **Staff:** 1. **Subjects:** Quaker history and beliefs. **Holdings:** 5500 books; 55 audiotapes; 5 videotapes; 50 other cataloged items. **Subscriptions:** 32 journals and other serials. **Services:** Interlibrary loan; library open to the public. **Publications:** Bibliographies.

★13322★
SOCIETY OF FRIENDS - NEW ENGLAND YEARLY MEETING OF FRIENDS - ARCHIVES (Rel-Phil)
121 Hope St. Phone: (401)331-8575
Providence, RI 02906 Rosalind Wiggins, Cur.
Founded: 1661. **Staff:** 1. **Subjects:** Archives and records of Society of Friends in New England; Quaker historical material. **Special Collections:** Moses and Obadiah Brown Libraries (512 volumes); Moses Brown Papers and Pamphlets, 1774-1836 (29 file boxes). **Holdings:** 1570 books; 155 bound periodical volumes; 635 volumes of archives; 158 file boxes of pamphlets and papers; 47 boxes of unbound periodicals; 173 reels of microfilm of archives; 1 box of newspaper clippings; 7 dissertations; 40 magnetic tapes. **Services:** Copying; archives open to the public upon written request to curator.

★13323★
SOCIETY OF FRIENDS - NEW YORK YEARLY MEETING - RECORDS COMMITTEE - HAVILAND RECORDS ROOM (Rel-Phil)
15 Rutherford Pl. Phone: (212)673-6866
New York, NY 10003 Elizabeth Haas Moger, Kpr. of the Rec.
Founded: 1900. **Staff:** 1. **Subjects:** Quaker genealogy and history in New York and surrounding states. **Special Collections:** New York Quaker imprints - Samuel Wood, Mahlon Day, Isaac T. Hopper (70 volumes); papers relating to Friends and New York State Indians in the 19th century. **Holdings:** 2500 books; 2000 manuscript records. **Services:** Room open to the public by appointment. **Special Catalogs:** Catalog of manuscript records (card). **Remarks:** Official depository for New York Yearly Meeting and its subordinate meetings in New York State, western Vermont, Connecticut, and northern New Jersey.

★13324★
SOCIETY OF FRIENDS - OHIO YEARLY MEETING - WESTGATE FRIENDS LIBRARY (Rel-Phil)
3750 Sullivant Ave. Phone: (614)274-5131
Columbus, OH 43228 William T. Peters, Libn.
Founded: 1968. **Staff:** Prof 1; Other 3. **Subjects:** Quaker history and theology. **Holdings:** 2000 books and pamphlets; 10 VF drawers. **Subscriptions:** 65 journals and other serials. **Services:** Interlibrary loan; library open to the public with restrictions. **Remarks:** Maintained by Evangelical Friends Church, Eastern Region.

★13325★
SOCIETY OF FRIENDS - PHILADELPHIA YEARLY MEETING - LIBRARY (Rel-Phil, Soc Sci)
1515 Cherry St. Phone: (215)241-7220
Philadelphia, PA 19102 Mary V. Davidson, Libn.
Founded: 1960. **Staff:** Prof 1; Other 1. **Subjects:** Quakerism; education; religious education; social concerns - religion, native Americans, criminal justice, race, service, sex, family relations, hunger, poverty, nuclear energy, peace education, nuclear weapons and disarmament. **Special Collections:** Dora Wilson Collection (religion and psychology); E. Vesta Haines Collection of Christmas Literature; Jean C. Hollingshead Poetry Corner; Peace Education Resource Center; Frances Ferris Collection (books for and about children). **Holdings:** 18,000 books. **Subscriptions:** 104 journals and other serials. **Services:** Interlibrary loan; copying; library open to the public on fee basis. **Publications:** Subject reading lists.

★13326★
SOCIETY FOR INFORMATION DISPLAY - LIBRARY (Comp Sci)
8055 W. Manchester Ave., Suite 615 Phone: (213)305-1502
Playa Del Rey, CA 90293 Bettye B. Burdett, Off.Mgr.
Founded: 1962. **Subjects:** Information display and allied arts, sciences, and effects on the human senses. **Holdings:** 4800 volumes. **Services:** Copying; library open to the public. **Publications:** List of publications - available on request. **Remarks:** Affiliated with American Federation of Information Processing Societies.

★13327★
SOCIETY FOR THE INVESTIGATION OF THE UNEXPLAINED (SITU) - LIBRARY (Sci-Engr)
Box 265 Phone: (201)842-5229
Little Silver, NJ 07739 Nancy Warth, Sec.
Founded: 1965. **Staff:** Prof 2; Other 3. **Subjects:** Forteana (works on tangible objects or events not yet accepted by orthodox science, e.g., sea monsters, abominable snowmen, poltergeists, UFOs); geology and geography; natural history; biology (all phases); cultural anthropology; astronomy; physics; chemistry; mathematics. **Special Collections:** Personal papers, original manuscripts and drawings of society's former director, the late Ivan T. Sanderson. **Holdings:** 2000 books; 105 bound periodical volumes; 95 shelf feet of unbound periodicals; 22 boxes of pamphlets; 260 ring binders of clippings, original reports, tear sheets; 300 maps; 2 map case drawers and 1 VF drawer of charts, diagrams, original drawings; 6 VF drawers of photographs, clippings, slides; 25 magnetic tapes. **Subscriptions:** 59 journals and other serials. **Services:** Library not open to the public. **Publications:** Pursuit Quarterly Journal - to members.

★13328★
SOCIETY OF JESUS - OREGON PROVINCE ARCHIVES (Rel-Phil, Hist)
Crosby Library, Gonzaga University
E. 502 Boone Ave. Phone: (509)328-4220
Spokane, WA 92588 Rev. Neill R. Meany, S.J., Archv.
Founded: 1931. **Staff:** Prof 1; Other 2. **Subjects:** History - Northwest Church, Alaska Church and missions, Doukhobor, local; Alaskan and Indian languages. **Special Collections:** Joset Papers; Cataldo Papers; Crimont Papers; Neil Byrne Papers; Monaghan Papers; Cowley Papers; Prando Papers; Jesuit Mission Papers. **Holdings:** 3600 books; 800 bound periodical volumes; 123,000 manuscripts; 25,000 photographs. **Subscriptions:** 35 journals and other serials; 18 newspapers. **Services:** Copying; library open to those with scholarly credentials. **Automated Operations:** Computerized cataloging. **Publications:** Guides to Microfilm Editions of the Oregon Province Archives of the Society of Jesus Indian Language Collection: (1) The Alaska Native Languages; (2) The Pacific Northwest Tribes; The Alaska Mission Papers; Guide to Microfilm Editions of Papers on Pacific Northwest Jesuit Missions & Missionaries. **Staff:** Bro. Ed Jennings, S.J., Asst.Archv..

SOCIETY OF JESUS, MARYLAND PROVINCE - ARCHIVES
See: Georgetown University - Special Collections Division - Lauinger Memorial Library (5597)

SOCIETY OF JESUS, MARYLAND PROVINCE - WOODSTOCK THEOLOGICAL CENTER
See: Woodstock Theological Center - Library (18017)

★13329★
SOCIETY OF MANAGEMENT ACCOUNTANTS OF CANADA - RESOURCE CENTRE (Bus-Fin)
154 Main St., E.
Box 176 Phone: (416)525-4100
Hamilton, ON, Canada L8N 3C3 Helen Hill, Libn.
Founded: 1920. **Staff:** Prof 1. **Subjects:** Accounting, management, systems, communication, economics, marketing, mathematics, production, taxation. **Holdings:** 8000 books. **Subscriptions:** 125 journals and other serials. **Services:** Interlibrary loan; copying (limited); center open to the public for reference use only.

★13330★
SOCIETY FOR MANITOBANS WITH DISABILITIES INC. - STEPHEN SPARLING LIBRARY (Med)
825 Sherbrook St. Phone: (204)786-5601
Winnipeg, MB, Canada R3A 1M5 Cheryl Manness, Lib.Techn.
Founded: 1957. **Staff:** 1. **Subjects:** Rehabilitation, social work, learning disorders, physical disabilities, therapy, psychology, psychiatry. **Holdings:** 1340 books and bound periodical volumes; 1000 monographs, reprints, and pamphlets. **Subscriptions:** 50 journals and other serials. **Services:** Interlibrary loan; copying; library open to the public. **Publications:** Monthly Library Additions.

★13331★
SOCIETY OF MANUFACTURING ENGINEERS - SME LIBRARY (Comp Sci, Sci-Engr)
One SME Dr.
Box 930 Phone: (313)271-1500
Dearborn, MI 48121 Paulette Groen, Libn.
Founded: 1932. **Staff:** 1. **Subjects:** Business, manufacturing engineering and materials, metallurgical processing, robotics, computerized automation in manufacturing. **Special Collections:** SME annual reports, minutes, papers, and other publications; Computerized Automation and Robotics Information Center (CARIC; books; documents; related resource materials). **Holdings:** 2500 books; 11,000 technical reports, 1951 to present. **Subscriptions:** 420 journals and other serials. **Services:** Copying; library open to the public by appointment. **Automated Operations:** Computerized serials. **Computerized Information Services:** DIALOG Information Services; INTIME (internal database). Performs searches on fee basis. **Remarks:** Library contains Robotics International of the Society of Manufacturing Engineers Collection.

★13332★
SOCIETY OF MARY - CINCINNATI PROVINCE - ARCHIVES (Rel-Phil)
Roesch Library, Rm. 313
University of Dayton
Box 445 Phone: (513)229-2724
Dayton, OH 45469 Bro. Bernard Laurinaitis, S.M., Archv.
Founded: 1938. **Staff:** Prof 1. **Subjects:** Church history, theology, and philosophy. **Special Collections:** Archives of the Society of Mary (Marianists) from its origin in U.S. in 1850 to the present. **Holdings:** 3200 storage boxes of archival material; 15 oral history tapes of the University of Dayton; collection of slides and photographs about various schools conducted by Marianists. **Services:** Copying; archives open to the public by appointment. **Special Indexes:** Indexes of Serial Publications of Marianists (card).

★13333★
SOCIETY OF NAVAL ARCHITECTS AND MARINE ENGINEERS - LIBRARY (Sci-Engr)
601 Pavonia Ave. Phone: (201)798-4800
Jersey City, NJ 07306 Robert G. Mende, Sec./Exec.Dir.
Founded: 1893. **Subjects:** Naval architecture, shipbuilding, marine engineering, and allied fields. **Holdings:** 1000 volumes. **Formerly:** Located in New York, NY.

★13334★
SOCIETY OF PHILATICIANS - LIBRARY (Rec)
154 Laguna Ct.
St. Augustine, FL 32086-7031 Gustav Detjen, Jr., Ed.
Founded: 1972. **Staff:** Prof 1. **Subjects:** Philately, Rooseveltiana. **Holdings:** 800 books. **Subscriptions:** 15 journals and other serials; 5 newspapers. **Services:** Interlibrary loan; copying. **Publications:** The Philatelic Journalist; Philatelic Directory; Handbook for Philatelic Writers.

★13335★
SOCIETY FOR THE PRESERVATION AND ENCOURAGEMENT OF BARBER SHOP QUARTET SINGING IN AMERICA - OLD SONGS LIBRARY (Mus)
6315 Third Ave. Phone: (414)654-9111
Kenosha, WI 53140-5199 Ruth Marks, Harmony Found.Adm.
Staff: 1. **Subjects:** Piano-vocal sheet music, 1880s to present. **Special Collections:** Walter F. Wade Collection; Ken Grant Collection. **Holdings:** 65,000 pieces. **Services:** Library open to the public with restrictions. **Also Known As:** Harmony Foundation.

★13336★
SOCIETY FOR THE PRESERVATION OF NEW ENGLAND ANTIQUITIES - ARCHIVES (Hist)
141 Cambridge St. Phone: (617)227-3956
Boston, MA 02114 Elinor Reichlin, Dir. of Archv.
Founded: 1910. **Staff:** Prof 2; Other 1. **Subjects:** New England architecture and decorative arts, local history, transportation, history of photography. **Special Collections:** Photographic collections: N.L. Stebbins, Henry Peabody, Baldwin Coolidge, Soule Art Photo Company, Halliday Historic Photograph Company, New England News Company, George Noyes, Arthur Haskell, Wilfred French, Mary Northend, Emma Coleman, Fred Quimby, Boston and Albany Railroad, Wallace Nutting, and other regional photographers; Manuscript collections: Codman Family papers (100 linear feet); Rundlet-May papers (5 linear feet); Sayward Family papers (2 linear feet); Casey Family papers (40 linear feet); Harrison Gray Otis business records (1 linear foot); architectural drawings, originals, and blueprints including works of Asher Benjamin, Luther Briggs, Ogden Codman, Jr., Frank Chouteau Brown, Arthur Little, Herbert Brown, George Clough, and Arland Dirlham (10,000 items); rare architectural pattern books (18th and 19th centuries; 500); Boston Transit Commission Archives, 1894-1940s (12,000 glass negatives). **Holdings:** 400,000 photographic prints, including 10,000 stereopticion views, 10,000 postcards, 175 albums, 2500 cartes de visite portraits, 100,000 standard size prints, 800 daguerreotypes and ambrotypes; 70,000 negatives including 40,000 glass plates; 2500 lithographs, wood engravings, and drawings primarily of New England architecture and landscape. **Services:** Copying; photography; archives open to the public, appointment preferred. **Publications:** Guide and Checklist to Library Collections. **Special Catalogs:** Printed catalog to N.L. Stebbins marine photographs. **Special Indexes:** Typed inventories to photograph albums, prints and drawings, account books, maps, Soule Art Company photographs, and trade catalogs and manuscripts; card index to rare architectural pattern books; card index to landscape architecture and design; inventories to all manuscript collections; card index to all architectural drawings (by architect, location, and building types). **Staff:** Lorna Condon, Asst.Dir..

★13337★
SOCIETY FOR PROMOTING AND ENCOURAGING ARTS & KNOWLEDGE OF THE CHURCH - HOWARD LANE FOLAND LIBRARY
Hillspeak
Eureka Springs, AR 72632-9705
Founded: 1980. **Subjects:** Bible, eschatology, theology, pastoral relations, liturgies. **Holdings:** 7500 books. **Remarks:** Presently inactive.

★13338★
SOCIETY OF REAL ESTATE APPRAISERS - LIBRARY (Plan)
225 N. Michigan Ave., Suite 724 Phone: (312)819-2400
Chicago, IL 60601 Jan Seefeldt, Libn.
Founded: 1957. **Subjects:** Real estate appraisal, land use, urban planning, investment analysis, real estate. **Holdings:** 500 books; 37 bound periodical volumes; 408 pamphlets. **Services:** Library not open to the public.

★13339★
SOCIETY OF ST. VINCENT DE PAUL - LIBRARY (Rel-Phil)
4140 Lindell Blvd. Phone: (314)371-4980
St. Louis, MO 63108 Rita W. Porter, Exec.Sec.
Subjects: History and work of the Society of St. Vincent de Paul. **Holdings:** Figures not available.

SOCIETY FOR SOUTHEASTERN FLORA AND FAUNA - BROOKGREEN GARDENS
See: Brookgreen Gardens - Library (1921)

★13340★
SOCIETY FOR THE STUDY OF MALE PSYCHOLOGY & PHYSIOLOGY - LIBRARY (Med)
321 Iuka
Montpellier, OH 43543 Jerry Bergman, Ph.D., Dir.
Staff: 1. **Subjects:** Male psychology. **Holdings:** 1475 books; 450 bound periodical volumes. **Special Collections:** Interlibrary loan; copying; SDI; library open to the public by appointment. **Automated Operations:** Computerized cataloging, acquisitions, and serials.

★13341★
SOCIETY OF WIRELESS PIONEERS, INC. - BRENIMAN NAUTICAL-WIRELESS LIBRARY & MUSEUM OF COMMUNICATIONS (Sci-Engr)
Box 530 Phone: (707)542-0898
Santa Rosa, CA 95402 Elmer Burgman, Dir.
Staff: Prof 2; Other 5. **Subjects:** Wireless telegraphy, communication, radio and television broadcasting, ships and shipping. **Special Collections:** Dickow Wireless Collection; Brown Lighthouses of the World. **Holdings:** 2755 books; 1500 bound periodical volumes; 4500 maps and other cataloged items; 2300 historical papers and monographs. **Subscriptions:** 23 journals and other serials. **Services:** Copying; library open to the public with restrictions.

★13342★
SOCIETY OF WOMEN ENGINEERS - INFORMATION CENTER (Sci-Engr)
345 E. 47th St., Rm. 305 Phone: (212)705-7855
New York, NY 10017 B.J. Harrod, Act.Exec.Dir.
Subjects: Women in engineering. **Holdings:** Figures not available. **Services:** Center open to the public. **Publications:** Career guidance brochures; article reprints; Survey of Women Engineers; U.S. Woman Engineer (magazine) - bimonthly. **Remarks:** This is an information center on women in engineering with emphasis on career guidance for the younger girl and advancement of women in the engineering profession.

★13343★
SOD TOWN PIONEER HOMESTEAD MUSEUM - LIBRARY (Hist)
Rte. 1, Box 225 Phone: (913)462-6787
Colby, KS 67701 Ronald E. Thiel, Dir.
Founded: 1955. **Staff:** 2. **Subjects:** Sod houses, dugouts, adobe buildings, pioneer homestead history. **Special Collections:** Old photographs of sod buildings in North America (500). **Holdings:** 20,000 personal letters and family history reports from persons with sod house heritage. **Services:** Library open to the public for reference use only. **Publications:** Sod Houses and Dugouts in North America - for sale. **Remarks:** Maintained by Sons and Daughters of the Soddies.

SODARCAN, LTD. - DALE-PARIZEAU
See: Dale-Parizeau (3975)

★13344★
SOFTWARE ACCESS INTERNATIONAL, INC. - MARKET ACCESS DIVISION - INFORMATION CENTER
1260 L Avenida St.
Mountain View, CA 94043-1426
Defunct

SOHN MEMORIAL HEALTH SERVICES LIBRARY
See: Fort Hamilton-Hughes Memorial Hospital Center (5274)

★13345★
SOHO CENTER FOR VISUAL ARTISTS - LIBRARY (Art)
110 Prince St.
New York, NY 10012 Rhonda Wall, Libn.
Founded: 1974. **Staff:** Prof 1; Other 1. **Subjects:** Twentieth century painting, sculpture, photography, and film; architecture; crafts. **Holdings:** 2000 volumes; exhibition catalogs; unbound reference materials; 10 VF drawers of limited edition print portfolios and reproductions of art work. **Subscriptions:** 50 journals and other serials. **Services:** Library open to visual artists. **Remarks:** Includes the library of the Aldrich Museum of Contemporary Art, Ridgefield, CT. The Soho Center consists of the library and an Exhibition Gallery at 114 Prince St.

SOIL MECHANICS INFORMATION ANALYSIS CENTER
See: U.S. Army - Engineer Waterways Experiment Station (14751)

SOIL SCIENCE SOCIETY OF AMERICA - AMERICAN SOCIETY OF AGRONOMY
See: American Society of Agronomy (662)

★13346★
SOIL AND WATER CONSERVATION SOCIETY - H. WAYNE PRITCHARD LIBRARY (Env-Cons)
7515 N.E. Ankeny Rd. Phone: (515)289-2331
Ankeny, IA 50021-9764 James L. Sanders, Mng.Ed.
Subjects: Soil and water conservation, land use planning, natural resources management. **Special Collections:** Papers of leaders in soil and water conservation. **Holdings:** 2500 books. **Services:** Copying; library open to the public for reference use only.

ALBERT SOILAND MEMORIAL LIBRARY
See: California Medical Center Los Angeles (2157)

★13347★
SOLANO COUNTY LAW LIBRARY (Law)
Hall of Justice
600 Union Ave. Phone: (707)429-6655
Fairfield, CA 94533 Susanne Pierce Dyer, Law Libn.
Staff: Prof 1. **Subjects:** California and Federal law. **Special Collections:** Solano County Ordinance Code; codes of Solano County municipalities. **Holdings:** 15,000 books. **Subscriptions:** 16 journals and other serials. **Services:** Copying; library open to the public.

★13348★
SOLANO COUNTY LIBRARY - SPECIAL COLLECTIONS (Rare Book)
1150 Kentucky St. Phone: (707)429-6601
Fairfield, CA 94533 Anne Marie Gold, Dir., Lib.Serv.
Founded: 1914. **Holdings:** Donovan J. McCune Collection (printing history, rare books; 1500 volumes); U.S. and state government documents depository (5000 volumes); local history (500 volumes). **Services:** Interlibrary loan; copying; collections open to the public. **Automated Operations:** Computerized cataloging, acquisitions, and circulation. **Computerized Information Services:** DIALOG Information Services; OnTyme Electronic Message Network Service (electronic mail service). Performs searches free of charge. **Networks/Consortia:** Member of North Bay Cooperative Library System (NBCLS).

★13349★
SOLAR ENERGY INSTITUTE OF NORTH AMERICA (SEINAM) - LIBRARY
3404 Connecticut Ave., N.W.
Washington, DC 20008
Defunct

★13350★
SOLAR ENERGY RESEARCH INSTITUTE - SERI TECHNICAL LIBRARY (Energy)
1617 Cole Blvd. Phone: (303)231-1415
Golden, CO 80401 Jerome T. Maddock, Br.Chf.
Founded: 1977. **Staff:** Prof 5; Other 4. **Subjects:** Energy - solar, wind, ocean, biomass; photovoltaics; biotechnology; solid state physics. **Holdings:** 13,000 books; 3500 bound periodical volumes; 20,500 technical reports; 8000 patents; 46,000 reports on microfiche. **Subscriptions:** 600 journals and other serials; 5 newspapers. **Services:** Interlibrary loan; copying; SDI; library open to the public by appointment. **Automated Operations:** Computerized cataloging and serials. **Computerized Information Services:** DIALOG Information Services, Pergamon ORBIT InfoLine, Inc., Integrated Technical Information System (ITIS), RLIN, OCLC, BRS Information Technologies, CAS ONLINE, CIS; internal database. **Networks/Consortia:** Member of FEDLINK. **Publications:** Serials Holdings List; New Acquisitions Lists, both irregular. **Remarks:** The Solar Energy Research Institute operates under contract to the U.S. Department of Energy. **Staff:** Nancy Greer, Sect.Mgr.; Joe Chervenak, Acq.; Soon Duck Kim, Cat.; Al Berger, Ref..

SOLAR LOBBY - CENTER FOR RENEWABLE RESOURCES
See: Center for Renewable Resources (2867)

★13351★
SOLAR TURBINES INCORPORATED - LIBRARY (Sci-Engr)
Box 80966 Phone: (714)238-5992
San Diego, CA 92138 George Hall, Libn.
Founded: 1959. **Staff:** Prof 1. **Subjects:** Gas turbines, ceramics, high temperature metals. **Holdings:** 2700 books; 700 bound periodical volumes; 5000 technical reports and society papers. **Subscriptions:** 30 journals and

other serials; 10 newspapers. **Services:** Interlibrary loan; library not open to the public. **Computerized Information Services:** DIALOG Information Services. **Publications:** New Material Bulletin, monthly. **Remarks:** Solar Turbines Incorporated is a subsidiary of Caterpillar Tractor Company.

★13352★
SOLARTHERM - LIBRARY (Energy)
1315 Apple Ave. Phone: (301)587-8686
Silver Spring, MD 20910 Dr. Carl Schleicher, Pres.
Founded: 1977. **Subjects:** Solar energy; alternative energy systems - high-temperature solar, conservation, solid waste, tidal and methane systems. **Holdings:** 8000 volumes.

★13353★
SOLDIERS AND SAILORS MEMORIAL HOSPITAL - HEALTH SCIENCE LIBRARY (Med)
Central Ave. Phone: (717)724-1631
Wellsboro, PA 16901 Charlean Patterson, Libn.
Staff: 1. **Subjects:** Clinical medicine, nursing, hospital administration, allied health sciences, patient education. **Holdings:** 900 books; 300 bound periodical volumes; 200 NCME videotapes. **Subscriptions:** 115 journals and other serials. **Services:** Interlibrary loan; copying; SDI; library open to the public. **Networks/Consortia:** Member of Susquehanna Library Cooperative, Central Pennsylvania Health Sciences Library Association (CPHSLA), Greater Northeastern Regional Medical Library Program.

★13354★
SOLEIL LIMITEE - CENTRE DE DOCUMENTATION (Publ)
390 E. St. Vallier Phone: (418)647-3394
Quebec, PQ, Canada G1K 7J6 Berthold Landry, Adm.Asst.
Founded: 1967. **Staff:** Prof 4; Other 5. **Subjects:** Newspaper reference topics. **Holdings:** 1500 books; 50 bound periodical volumes; 700,000 black/white photographs; 1000 color photographs; 1 million clippings; 20,000 reels of microfilm; 150 VF drawers. **Subscriptions:** 120 journals and other serials; 30 newspapers. **Services:** Copying; center open to the public by appointment. **Staff:** Claudine Gagnon, Coord..

PAOLO SOLERI ARCHIVES
See: Arizona State University - Howe Architecture and Environmental Design Library (907)

★13355★
SOLUTION MINING RESEARCH INSTITUTE - LIBRARY (Sci-Engr)
812 Muriel St. Phone: (815)338-8579
Woodstock, IL 60098 Howard W. Fiedelman, Exec.Dir.
Subjects: Solution mining industry, environmental issues pertinent to industry. **Holdings:** 112 research reports; 250 papers published by others; 136 meeting papers. **Services:** Copying.

★13356★
SOMBRA TOWNSHIP MUSEUM - REFERENCE ROOM (Hist)
146 St. Clair St.
Sombra, ON, Canada N0P 2H0 Maude Dalgety, Cur.
Subjects: Local history. **Holdings:** Biographies; diaries; family histories. **Services:** Room open to the public for reference use only.

★13357★
SOMERS HISTORICAL SOCIETY - ARCHIVES (Hist)
574 Main St. Phone: (203)749-7273
Somers, CT 06071 Jeanne K. DeBell, Cur.
Staff: 3. **Subjects:** Local and state history, genealogy. **Special Collections:** Civil War Letters; Sermons, 1750-1865; Public School Readers, 1830-1890. **Holdings:** 200 books; 1 VF drawer of local history material; 1 box of early deeds and letters, 1730-1865. **Services:** Archives open to the public with restrictions. **Publications:** Somers, History of a Connecticut Town, 1973; Somers, Connecticut Through the Camera's Eye, 1978 - both for sale. **Special Indexes:** Genealogical File of Somers Families.

★13358★
SOMERS HISTORICAL SOCIETY - DR. HUGH GRANT ROWELL CIRCUS LIBRARY COLLECTION (Hist)
Elephant Hotel
Box 336 Phone: (914)277-4977
Somers, NY 10589 Elizabeth Macaulay, Pres.
Subjects: Circus, genealogy. **Holdings:** 600 books; 4 VF drawers of uncataloged pamphlets and manuscripts; 10 maps; 1000 circus-related materials. **Services:** Collection open to the public for reference use only on a limited schedule.

★13359★
SOMERSET COUNTY LAW LIBRARY (Law)
Court House
Box 3000 Phone: (201)231-7612
Somerville, NJ 08876 Robert G. Gennett, Law Libn.
Staff: 1. **Subjects:** Law. **Holdings:** 20,000 volumes. **Services:** Copying; library open to the public for reference use only. **Computerized Information Services:** WESTLAW.

★13360★
SOMERSET COUNTY LAW LIBRARY (Law)
Court House Phone: (814)443-9770
Somerset, PA 15501 David E. Rickabaugh, Libn.
Subjects: Law. **Holdings:** 20,500 volumes. **Services:** Library not open to the public.

SOMERSET STATE HOSPITAL
See: Pennsylvania State Department of Public Welfare (11180)

★13361★
SOMERVILLE HOSPITAL - CARR HEALTH SCIENCES LIBRARY (Med)
230 Highland Ave. Phone: (617)666-4400
Somerville, MA 02143 Celeste F. Kozlowski, Med.Libn.
Staff: Prof 2; Other 2. **Subjects:** Medicine, nursing. **Holdings:** 2709 books; 118 bound periodical volumes; pamphlets. **Subscriptions:** 130 journals and other serials. **Services:** Interlibrary loan; copying; library open to the public with permission. **Computerized Information Services:** MEDLARS, MEDLINE; DOCLINE (electronic mail service). Performs searches on fee basis. **Networks/Consortia:** Member of Libraries and Information for Nursing Consortium (LINC). **Staff:** Anne Hughes, Libn..

SONAHEND FAMILY LIBRARY
See: Temple Emanu-El - Sonahend Family Library (13954)

★13362★
SONAT INC. - CORPORATE LIBRARY (Bus-Fin, Energy)
1900 5th Ave., N.
Birmingham, AL 35203 Phone: (205)325-7409
Staff: Prof 1; Other 1. **Subjects:** Energy, natural gas industry, alternative fuels, oil industry, business, corporate law. **Special Collections:** Financial data on major natural gas pipeline companies (53 VF drawers). **Holdings:** 8200 books; 8 VF drawers of clippings; 6 VF drawers of speeches. **Subscriptions:** 400 journals and other serials; 10 newspapers. **Services:** Copying; SDI; library open to the public for reference use only. **Computerized Information Services:** NEXIS, LEXIS, A.G.A. GasNet; A.G.A. GasNet (electronic mail service).

★13363★
SONAT OFFSHORE DRILLING, INC. - CORPORATE LIBRARY
5599 San Felipe
Box 2765
Houston, TX 77252-2765
Founded: 1978. **Subjects:** Engineering, naval engineering, geology, social sciences. **Holdings:** 2200 books; 100 bound periodical volumes; 250 brochures. **Remarks:** Presently inactive.

★13364★
SONNENSCHEIN CARLIN NATH & ROSENTHAL - LIBRARY (Law)
8000 Sears Tower
233 S. Wacker Dr. Phone: (312)876-7906
Chicago, IL 60606 Colleen L. McCarroll, Libn.
Staff: Prof 3; Other 3. **Subjects:** Law. **Special Collections:** Insurance statutes and regulations for all states. **Holdings:** 30,000 books; 240 bound periodical volumes; 500 microfiche; 1200 internal research reports. **Services:** Interlibrary loan; copying; SDI; library open to public at librarian's discretion. **Automated Operations:** Computerized cataloging and serials. **Computerized Information Services:** DIALOG Information Services, OCLC, LEXIS, WESTLAW, Pergamon ORBIT InfoLine, Inc., Dow Jones News/Retrieval, ELSS (Electronic Legislative Search System). **Networks/Consortia:** Member of Chicago Library System. **Special Indexes:** Internal research index (book and magnetic disk); corporate precedents file (card). **Staff:** Carolyn L. Hayes, Ref.Libn.; Carol J. Dawe, Tech.Serv.Libn..

SONNTAG LIBRARY
See: Manhattan College (8350)

★13365★
SONOMA COUNTY LAW LIBRARY (Law)
Hall of Justice, Rm. 213-J
600 Administration Dr. Phone: (707)527-2668
Santa Rosa, CA 95403-2879 Charlotte S. Von Gunten, Law Libn.
Founded: 1891. **Staff:** Prof 2; Other 1. **Subjects:** Law. **Holdings:** 22,500 volumes; 514 tapes. **Services:** Library open to the public.

★13366★
SONOMA COUNTY PLANNING DEPARTMENT - LIBRARY (Plan)
575 Administration Dr., Rm. 105A Phone: (707)527-2412
Santa Rosa, CA 95401 Ruth Lund, Supv.Ck.
Founded: 1961. **Staff:** Prof 1. **Subjects:** Planning, transportation, land use, housing, zoning and environmental impact information related to Sonoma County and surrounding areas. **Holdings:** Books; reports; special studies. **Services:** Copying; library open to the public with restrictions.

★13367★
SONOMA DEVELOPMENTAL CENTER - STAFF LIBRARY (Med)
Box 1493 Phone: (707)938-6244
Eldridge, CA 95431 Eric M. Mosier, Sr.Libn.
Founded: 1951. **Staff:** Prof 1. **Subjects:** Mental retardation, psychology, nursing, social work, rehabilitation therapy, medicine. **Special Collections:** History of the hospital. **Holdings:** 9000 books; 8417 bound periodical volumes; 70 AV programs. **Subscriptions:** 91 journals and other serials. **Services:** Interlibrary loan; copying; library open to the public. **Computerized Information Services:** MEDLARS. **Networks/Consortia:** Member of North Bay Health Sciences Library Group, Northern California and Nevada Medical Library Group (NCNMLG).

★13368★
SONOMA STATE UNIVERSITY - NORTHWEST INFORMATION CENTER - CALIFORNIA ARCHAEOLOGICAL INVENTORY (Hist)
Rohnert Park, CA 94928 Phone: (707)664-2494
Founded: 1975. **Subjects:** Archeology, anthropology, history, cultural resource management. **Holdings:** 20,000 reports, records, and maps. **Services:** Copying; open to the public with restrictions. **Computerized Information Services:** Internal database. Performs searches on fee basis. **Publications:** Bibliography of holdings.

SONORA DESERT MUSEUM
See: Arizona-Sonora Desert Museum (887)

SONS OF THE AMERICAN REVOLUTION
See: National Society of the Sons of the American Revolution (9796)

SONS AND DAUGHTERS OF THE SODDIES - SOD TOWN PIONEER HOMESTEAD MUSEUM
See: Sod Town Pioneer Homestead Museum (13343)

★13369★
SONS OF NORWAY INTERNATIONAL - NORTH STAR LIBRARY (Area-Ethnic)
1455 W. Lake St. Phone: (612)827-3611
Minneapolis, MN 55408 Liv Lyons, Mgr.
Staff: Prof 1. **Subjects:** Literature, World War II, travel, art, history, insurance, social studies. **Special Collections:** Norwegian Pictorial Review (55); Norwegian-American Studies (20); Norwegian-American Emigration Lists (15); 19th century Norwegian literary classics; Norwegian immigration to the U.S. **Holdings:** 2500 books (half in Norwegian, half in English); insurance reports; census and legal reference materials; photographs. **Services:** Library open to the public for reference use only.

★13370★
SONS OF THE REVOLUTION IN THE STATE OF CALIFORNIA - LIBRARY (Hist)
600 S. Central Ave. Phone: (818)240-1775
Glendale, CA 91204 Anne Coe, Libn.
Founded: 1893. **Staff:** Prof 1. **Subjects:** Genealogy, history. **Holdings:** 35,000 volumes; 2000 bound periodical volumes; 2500 family genealogies. **Subscriptions:** 20 journals and other serials. **Services:** Copying; genealogical research; library open to the public with donation.

★13371★
SONS OF THE REVOLUTION IN THE STATE OF NEW YORK - LIBRARY (Hist)
Fraunces Tavern Museum
Broad & 54 Pearl Sts. Phone: (212)425-1776
New York, NY 10004 Patricia Kesling, Exec.Dir.
Subjects: Colonial and Revolutionary War period. **Holdings:** Figures not available. **Services:** Library not open to the public.

P.A. SOROKIN LIBRARY
See: University of Saskatchewan - Special Collections (16841)

★13372★
SOTHEBY'S LIBRARY (Art)
1334 York Ave. Phone: (212)606-7000
New York, NY 10021 Rosalyn Narbutas, Libn.
Staff: Prof 1. **Subjects:** Fine arts, decorative arts. **Special Collections:** Auction catalogs; company archives. **Holdings:** Figures not available. **Subscriptions:** 200 journals and other serials; newspapers. **Services:** Library not open to the public. **Special Indexes:** Index to archive files.

★13373★
SOURIS VALLEY REGIONAL CARE CENTER - MEDICAL & HEALTH SCIENCES LIBRARY (Med)
Box 2001 Phone: (306)842-7481
Weyburn, SK, Canada S4H 2L7 Melva Cooke, Libn.
Founded: 1971. **Staff:** 1. **Subjects:** Gerontology, psychiatry, nursing, nutrition, physical and occupational therapy. **Holdings:** 800 books; 90 bound periodical volumes; 300 articles; 3 VF drawers of clippings. **Subscriptions:** 75 journals and other serials; 7 newspapers. **Services:** Interlibrary loan; copying; library open to the public with restrictions.

JOHN PHILIP SOUSA MUSIC LIBRARY
See: U.S. Marine Corps - Marine Band Library (15187)

★13374★
SOUTH AFRICA AS THE FIFTY-FIRST STATE LIBRARY (Area-Ethnic)
4845 S. Raymond Phone: (206)725-7417
Seattle, WA 98118 William H. Davis, Libn.
Founded: 1986. **Staff:** Prof 1. **Subjects:** Events which will cause the "White Tribe" to favor union; cultural conditions to which blacks from South Africa would have to adjust; winter resort possibilities. **Holdings:** 25 books; 648 issues of National Geographic, 1933-1987; 18 scrapbooks. **Services:** Interlibrary loan; copying; library open to the public. **Computerized Information Services:** Performs searches on fee basis. **Publications:** Leaflets, bimonthly - available on request.

★13375★
SOUTH AMERICAN EXPLORERS CLUB - LIBRARY (Sci-Engr)
1510 York St. Phone: (303)320-0388
Denver, CO 80206 Ethel L. Greene, Mgr.
Founded: 1977. **Subjects:** Scientific field exploration research, recreation, and travel in South America; environmental and ecological concerns; history of South America. **Holdings:** 1000 volumes.

★13376★
SOUTH BALTIMORE GENERAL HOSPITAL - MEDICAL LIBRARY (Med)
3001 S. Hanover St. Phone: (301)347-3419
Baltimore, MD 21230 Shirley Lay, Libn.
Staff: Prof 1; Other 1. **Subjects:** Internal medicine, nursing. **Special Collections:** Ciba Collection of Medical Illustrations. **Holdings:** 1485 books; 3465 bound periodical volumes; 250 Network for Continuing Medical Education programs; 554 other AV programs. **Subscriptions:** 149 journals and other serials. **Services:** Interlibrary loan; library not open to the public. **Automated Operations:** Computerized cataloging. **Computerized Information Services:** MEDLARS, DIALOG Information Services; internal database. **Networks/Consortia:** Member of Maryland Association of Health Science Librarians. **Publications:** Library Newsletter.

★13377★
SOUTH CAROLINA CONFEDERATE RELIC ROOM & MUSEUM - LIBRARY (Hist)
World War Memorial Bldg.
920 Sumter St.
Columbia, SC 29201
Founded: 1896. **Staff:** 5. **Subjects:** South Carolina history, Southern Confederacy, Revolutionary history. **Special Collections:** Civil War era

histories (225 volumes); War of the Rebellion (150 volumes). **Holdings:** 450 books; 50 bound periodical volumes; scrapbooks; diaries; Muster Rolls; 100 pamphlets; 50 newspapers. **Subscriptions:** 10 journals and other serials. **Services:** Research on request; library open to the public for reference use only.

★13378★
SOUTH CAROLINA ELECTRIC AND GAS COMPANY - CORPORATE LIBRARY (Energy, Bus-Fin)
Palmetto Center
1426 Main St. Phone: (803)748-3942
Columbia, SC 29218 Patsy G. Moss, Libn.
Founded: 1984. **Staff:** Prof 1. **Subjects:** Public utilities, business, engineering. **Holdings:** 2220 books; 150 unbound periodicals; Electric Power Research Institute reports. **Services:** Interlibrary loan; copying; library open to the public with restrictions. **Computerized Information Services:** DIALOG Information Services.

★13379★
SOUTH CAROLINA HISTORICAL SOCIETY - LIBRARY (Hist)
Fireproof Bldg.
Meeting & Chalmers Sts. Phone: (803)723-3225
Charleston, SC 29401 David Moltke-Hansen, Dir.
Staff: Prof 7; Other 3. **Subjects:** South Carolina history, architecture, economy, genealogy. **Holdings:** 30,000 books and bound periodical volumes; 9000 pamphlets; 1500 linear feet of manuscripts; microfiche; 10,000 architectural drawings; 10,000 photographs; ephemera. **Subscriptions:** 50 journals and other serials. **Services:** Copying; library open to the public on fee basis. **Publications:** Carologue, 4/year. **Staff:** Harlan Greene, Asst.Dir.; Stephen Hoffius, Dir. of Pubns..

★13380★
SOUTH CAROLINA STATE ATTORNEY GENERAL'S OFFICE - DANIEL R. MC LEOD LAW LIBRARY (Law)
1000 Assembly St., Suite 701
Box 11549 Phone: (803)734-3769
Columbia, SC 29211 Susan Husman, Libn.
Staff: Prof 1; Other 1. **Subjects:** Law. **Special Collections:** South Carolina Attorney Generals' opinions (published and unpublished). **Holdings:** 15,000 books; 53 bound periodical volumes. **Subscriptions:** 15 journals and other serials. **Services:** Interlibrary loan; copying; library open to the public for reference use only. **Automated Operations:** Computerized cataloging and opinion index. **Computerized Information Services:** LEXIS. **Publications:** Annual Report of the Attorney General of South Carolina. **Special Indexes:** Index of published and unpublished opinions.

★13381★
SOUTH CAROLINA STATE COLLEGE - SOUTH CAROLINA STATE COLLEGE HISTORICAL COLLECTION (Hist)
Miller F. Whittaker Library
College Ave.
Box 1991
Orangeburg, SC 29117 Phone: (803)536-7045
Subjects: College history, 1897 to present. **Holdings:** College records; presidential papers; photographs; blueprints; college publications; yearbooks; newspapers; oral history recordings; documents concerning the development of South Carolina State College. **Services:** Copying; collection open to the public.

★13382★
SOUTH CAROLINA (State) COMMISSION ON ALCOHOL AND DRUG ABUSE - THE DRUGSTORE INFORMATION CLEARINGHOUSE (Med)
3700 Forest Dr. Phone: (803)734-9559
Columbia, SC 29204 Elizabeth G. Peters, Adm.
Staff: Prof 1; Other 1. **Subjects:** Alcohol and drug abuse - education, prevention, intervention, treatment. **Special Collections:** South Carolina State Commission on Alcohol and Drug Abuse publications (complete set). **Holdings:** 1500 books; 150 bound periodical volumes; 16 VF drawers; 50 pamphlet titles; 200 16mm films. **Subscriptions:** 44 journals and other serials. **Services:** Interlibrary loan; copying; clearinghouse open to the public with restrictions. **Computerized Information Services:** SCHIN. **Networks/Consortia:** Member of Columbia Area Medical Librarians' Association (CAMLA). **Special Catalogs:** AV catalog (book). **Remarks:** An alternate telephone number is 734-9559.

★13383★
SOUTH CAROLINA STATE DEPARTMENT OF ARCHIVES & HISTORY - ARCHIVES SEARCH ROOM (Hist)
Capitol Sta., Box 11669 Phone: (803)734-8577
Columbia, SC 29211 George L. Vogt, Dir.
Founded: 1905. **Staff:** 120. **Subjects:** History of South Carolina - political, constitutional, legal, economic, social, religious. **Special Collections:** Noncurrent public records of South Carolina, including: land records of the colony and state; Revolutionary War accounts; confederate service records; executive, legislative, and judicial records of the colony and state; probate records of the colony; county records (13,000 cubic feet of records; 15,000 reels of microfilm). **Holdings:** 2000 books; 250 bound periodical volumes. **Subscriptions:** 200 journals and other serials. **Services:** Copying; search room open to the public for reference use only. **Publications:** Colonial Records of South Carolina, 16 volumes; State Records of South Carolina, 10 volumes; South Carolina Archives Microcopies, 15 series; New South Carolina State Gazette (newsletter), quarterly; other documentary publications. **Special Catalogs:** Catalog of reference library (card). **Special Indexes:** Published Summary Guide to Archives; consolidated computer output microfilm index to documents; bound volume indexes to land plats and grants, marriage settlements and other records; map catalog (card); Revolutionary and Confederate War service records (card). **Remarks:** Library is located at 1430 Senate St., Columbia, SC 29201. **Staff:** William L. McDowell, Jr., Dp.Dir.; Charles H. Lesser, Asst.Dir., Archv. & Pubns..

★13384★
SOUTH CAROLINA STATE DEPARTMENT OF HEALTH & ENVIRONMENTAL CONTROL - EDUCATIONAL RESOURCE CENTER (Med)
2600 Bull St. Phone: (803)734-4769
Columbia, SC 29201 Michael Kronenfeld, Dir.
Founded: 1981. **Staff:** Prof 1; Other 8. **Subjects:** Public health, medicine, nursing, epidemiology, environmental sciences, nutrition, health education. **Holdings:** 3000 books; 3000 bound periodical volumes; 1500 films; 300 pamphlet and poster titles. **Subscriptions:** 232 journals and other serials. **Services:** Interlibrary loan; copying; SDI; center open to the public with restrictions. **Automated Operations:** Computerized cataloging. **Computerized Information Services:** DIALOG Information Services, MEDLARS, OCLC, SCHIN, BRS Information Technologies, LEXIS, NEXIS; South Carolina Health Promotion Clearinghouse (internal database); EPAMAIL (electronic mail service). **Networks/Consortia:** Member of Columbia Area Medical Librarians' Association (CAMLA), SOLINET.

★13385★
SOUTH CAROLINA STATE DEPARTMENT OF MENTAL HEALTH - EARLE E. MORRIS, JR. ALCOHOL & DRUG ADDICTION TREATMENT CENTER - LIBRARY (Med)
610 Faison Dr. Phone: (803)737-7791
Columbia, SC 29203 Jane K. Olsgaard, Libn.
Founded: 1975. **Staff:** Prof 1. **Subjects:** Alcoholism, drug addiction, group and family therapy. **Holdings:** 3704 books. **Subscriptions:** 39 journals and other serials. **Services:** Interlibrary loan; library not open to the public. **Networks/Consortia:** Member of Columbia Area Medical Librarians' Association (CAMLA).

SOUTH CAROLINA STATE DEPARTMENT OF MENTAL HEALTH - GREENVILLE MENTAL HEALTH CENTER
See: Greenville Mental Health Center (5885)

★13386★
SOUTH CAROLINA STATE DEPARTMENT OF MENTAL RETARDATION - MIDLANDS CENTER LIBRARY (Educ, Med)
8301 Farrow Rd. Phone: (803)737-7548
Columbia, SC 29203 Mrs. Clannie H. Washington, Libn.
Staff: Prof 1; Other 1. **Subjects:** Mental retardation, special education. **Holdings:** 2500 books; 33 video cassettes; 10 16mm films; 295 slides. **Subscriptions:** 28 journals and other serials. **Services:** Interlibrary loan; copying; library open to state employees and local school districts.

★13387★
SOUTH CAROLINA STATE DEPARTMENT OF MENTAL RETARDATION - WHITTEN CENTER LIBRARY & MEDIA RESOURCE SERVICES (Educ, Med)
Columbia Hwy.
Box 239 Phone: (803)833-2736
Clinton, SC 29325 Mr. Hsiu-Yun Keng, Dir.
Founded: 1965. **Staff:** Prof 1; Other 1. **Subjects:** Mental retardation, social services for mentally retarded, special education, special media for mentally

retarded, psychology. **Special Collections:** Mental retardation; low reading level/high interest books for mentally retarded; special education. **Holdings:** 20,000 books; 170 bound periodical volumes; 18 volumes of South Carolina laws; 250 microfiche; 18,500 AV programs. **Subscriptions:** 30 journals and other serials. **Services:** Interlibrary loan; copying; library open to residents and employees of state institutions for the mentally retarded. **Publications:** Bibliography of Professional Materials on Mental Retardation, 2nd edition and annual supplements. **Special Catalogs:** Simplified card catalog for mentally retarded people; Audiovisual Materials in Teaching Mentally Retarded; Subject Headings and Classification Index in Mental Retardation, 1983.

★13388★
SOUTH CAROLINA STATE LIBRARY (Info Sci)
1500 Senate St.
Box 11469 Phone: (803)734-8666
Columbia, SC 29211 Betty E. Callaham, Dir.
Founded: 1943. **Staff:** Prof 20; Other 28. **Subjects:** Reference, government, business, political science, education, history, fine arts, South Caroliniana. **Special Collections:** Foundation Center Regional Depository. **Holdings:** 188,869 books; 1823 bound periodical volumes; 29,434 South Carolina state documents; 12,823 reels of microfilm of periodicals; 340,216 ERIC microfiche; 176,352 government documents; 348 filmstrips; 1813 slides; 2654 films; 8041 large print books. **Subscriptions:** 2213 journals and other serials; 27 newspapers. **Services:** Interlibrary loan; copying; library open to the public. **Automated Operations:** Computerized cataloging, circulation, periodicals list, and ILL. **Computerized Information Services:** DIALOG Information Services, OCLC, BRS Information Technologies; ALANET (electronic mail service). Performs searches on fee basis. Contact Person: Deborah Hotchkiss, Ref.Libn.. **Networks/Consortia:** Member of SOLINET. **Publications:** News for South Carolina Libraries, monthly - to public, school, and academic libraries and trustees; New Resources for State Government and Agencies - to state government agencies; Checklist of State Documents, quarterly; News about library services for the blind and physically handicapped, quarterly - to handicapped readers; News about the AV scene, quarterly - to public; South Carolina Foundation Directory, irregular - for sale. **Staff:** James B. Johnson, Jr., Dp.Dir. for Lib.Dev.; Margie E. Herron, Dir., Fld.Serv.; Frances Case, Dir., Dept. of Blind & Phys.Hndcp.; John H. Landrum, Dp.Dir., Lib.Serv.; Marjorie Mazur, Dir., Tech.Serv.; Mark Dumphrey, Inst.Cons.; Mary Bostick, Doc.Libn.; Wesley Sparks, Cat.Libn.; Libby Law, Fld.Serv.Libn.; Larry Freeman, Fld.Serv.Libn.; Alice I. Nolte, Fld.Serv.Libn.; Anne M. Schneider, Dir., Rd.Serv.; Jane McGregor, Fld.Serv.Libn./Ch.; Lea Walsh, ILL Libn.; Ron Anderson, Fld.Serv.Libn./AV; Ora Dickens, Hndcp.Serv.; Mary Morgan, Asst.Ref.Libn.; Guynell Williams, Ref.Libn.; Edna White, Asst.Ref.Libn.; William Ellett, Coord., Automated Serv..

★13389★
SOUTH CAROLINA STATE SUPREME COURT - LIBRARY (Law)
Box 11330 Phone: (803)758-3741
Columbia, SC 29211 Angela D. Bardin, Libn.
Staff: Prof 1; Other 1. **Subjects:** Law. **Holdings:** 51,440 books; 1005 bound periodical volumes. **Subscriptions:** 75 journals and other serials. **Services:** Copying; library open to the public.

★13390★
SOUTH CAROLINA STATE WILDLIFE AND MARINE RESOURCES DEPARTMENT - LIBRARY (Biol Sci)
Box 12559 Phone: (803)795-6350
Charleston, SC 29412 Ann Horan
Founded: 1972. **Staff:** Prof 1; Other 2. **Subjects:** Marine biology and ecology; fisheries; aquaculture; marine resources management. **Holdings:** 16,500 books; 6700 bound periodical volumes; 22,000 reprints; 10 reels of microfilm; 749 microfiche. **Subscriptions:** 350 journals and other serials. **Services:** Interlibrary loan; copying; library open to the public with restrictions. **Automated Operations:** Computerized cataloging. **Networks/Consortia:** Member of Charleston Higher Education Consortium (CHEC).

★13391★
SOUTH CENTRAL BELL TELEPHONE COMPANY - RESOURCE CENTER (Info Sci)
600 N. 19th St., 12th Fl.
Box 771 Phone: (205)321-2064
Birmingham, AL 35201 Bonnie B. Browning, Asst. Staff Supv.
Subjects: Telecommunications. **Holdings:** 500 books. **Subscriptions:** 62 journals and other serials. **Services:** Interlibrary loan; copying; center open to the public on a limited basis. **Computerized Information Services:** NEXIS.

SOUTH CENTRAL MONTANA REGIONAL MENTAL HEALTH CENTER
See: Mental Health Center (8705)

★13392★
SOUTH CHICAGO COMMUNITY HOSPITAL - DEPARTMENT OF LIBRARY SERVICES (Med)
2320 E. 93rd St. Phone: (312)978-2000
Chicago, IL 60617 Ronald Rayman, Dir.
Staff: Prof 1; Other 3. **Subjects:** Clinical medicine, nursing, chemical dependency. **Holdings:** 4500 books; 3000 bound periodical volumes. **Subscriptions:** 275 journals and other serials. **Services:** Interlibrary loan; copying; library open to the public with restrictions. **Automated Operations:** Computerized cataloging and serials. **Computerized Information Services:** DIALOG Information Services, BRS Information Technologies, WILSONLINE, NLM. Performs searches on fee basis. **Networks/Consortia:** Member of Chicago and South Consortium, Greater Midwest Regional Medical Library Network.

★13393★
SOUTH CONGREGATIONAL CHURCH - ETHEL L. AUSTIN LIBRARY† (Rel-Phil)
242 Salmon Brook St.
Box 779 Phone: (203)653-7289
Granby, CT 06035 Joan Griswold, Libn.
Staff: 1. **Subjects:** Christian living, devotions, Bible study, biography. **Holdings:** 1650 books. **Services:** Library open to the public.

★13394★
SOUTH DAKOTA HUMAN SERVICES CENTER - MEDICAL LIBRARY (Med)
Box 76 Phone: (605)665-3671
Yankton, SD 57078 Mary Lou Kostel, Libn.
Staff: 1. **Subjects:** Psychiatry, psychology, psychiatric nursing, gerontology, social work, medicine. **Special Collections:** Hospital history. **Holdings:** 2603 books; 140 bound periodical volumes; 466 audiotapes; VF drawers of pamphlets; manuscripts; historical clippings. **Subscriptions:** 62 journals and other serials. **Services:** Interlibrary loan; copying; library open to staff, students, and professionals. **Automated Operations:** Computerized serials. **Computerized Information Services:** EasyLink, DOCLINE (electronic mail services).

★13395★
SOUTH DAKOTA SCHOOL OF MINES & TECHNOLOGY - DEVEREAUX LIBRARY (Sci-Engr)
501 E. St. Joseph St. Phone: (605)394-2418
Rapid City, SD 57701 Dr. Bernice C. McKibben, Lib.Dir.
Founded: 1886. **Staff:** Prof 4; Other 10. **Subjects:** Engineering, computer science, chemistry, chemical engineering, physics, mathematics, mining geology. **Special Collections:** Black Hills and Western South Dakota History; Mining Histories of South Dakota and Adjacent Areas. **Holdings:** 82,656 volumes; 20,332 bound periodical volumes; 1502 theses and dissertations; 10,961 maps; 4356 South Dakota documents; 933 VF items; 18,000 archival items; 194,614 microfiche. **Subscriptions:** 1317 journals and other serials; 10 newspapers. **Services:** Interlibrary loan; copying; library open to the public. **Automated Operations:** Computerized public access catalog, cataloging, and circulation. **Computerized Information Services:** DIALOG Information Services, Pergamon ORBIT InfoLine, Inc., WILSONLINE; EasyLink (electronic mail service). Performs searches on fee basis. Contact Person: Janet Taylor, Act.Ref.Libn., 394-1255. **Networks/Consortia:** Member of Bibliographical Center for Research, Rocky Mountain Region, Inc. (BCR), MINITEX. **Publications:** Acquisitions List; Guide Series. **Special Catalogs:** Thesis/Dissertation listing; periodical holdings (book); Catalog of Reference Collection Materials; Catalog of Black Hills Mines (in preparation). **Special Indexes:** Indexes to State Geological Materials (in preparation). **Staff:** Margaret Sandine, Cat.Libn.; Donna Neal, ILL Supv.; Jo Ann Meyer, Circ.Supv.; Patty Anderson, Hd., Info./Pub.Serv.; Cindy Davies, Cat.; Barbara Hansen, Gov.Doc.; Mary Mickelson, Acq..

SOUTH DAKOTA STATE ARCHIVES
See: South Dakota State Historical Society - Office of History (13397)

SOUTH DAKOTA STATE DEPARTMENT OF EDUCATION AND CULTURAL AFFAIRS - W.H. OVER STATE MUSEUM
See: W.H. Over State Museum (10972)

★13396★
SOUTH DAKOTA STATE DEPARTMENT OF TRANSPORTATION - RESEARCH LIBRARY (Trans)
700 Broadway Ave., E. Phone: (605)773-3292
Pierre, SD 57501 David L. Huft, Res.Engr.
Staff: Prof 1; Other 1. **Subjects:** Transportation, highway engineering. **Special Collections:** South Dakota Research Reports. **Holdings:** 17,000 volumes. **Services:** Interlibrary loan; copying; library open to the public.

★13397★
SOUTH DAKOTA STATE HISTORICAL SOCIETY - OFFICE OF HISTORY - SOUTH DAKOTA STATE ARCHIVES (Hist)
800 Governors Dr. Phone: (605)773-3804
Pierre, SD 57501 Linda M. Sommer, State Archv.
Founded: 1986. **Staff:** Prof 4; Other 5. **Subjects:** South Dakota history, culture and government; Great Plains; government administration. **Holdings:** 26,000 volumes; 6000 cubic feet of records; 70 cubic feet of photographs; 4000 maps. **Subscriptions:** 140 newspapers. **Services:** Interlibrary loan; copying; office open to the public. **Automated Operations:** Computerized cataloging. **Publications:** Guide to holdings; Where Are They Now: Guide to Noncurrent South Dakota School Records. **Staff:** Ann Jenks, Libn..

★13398★
SOUTH DAKOTA STATE LIBRARY (Info Sci)
800 Governors Dr. Phone: (605)773-3131
Pierre, SD 57501-2294 Jane Kolbe, State Libn.
Founded: 1913. **Staff:** Prof 10; Other 34. **Subjects:** General collection. **Special Collections:** South Dakota; large print books; South Dakota documents. **Holdings:** 140,796 volumes; 174,541 documents; 6147 pictures; 581 maps; 8117 films, filmstrips, videotapes, and other media; 27,000 talking book titles; 358,568 microfiche; 8051 reels of microfilm. **Subscriptions:** 1197 journals and other serials. **Services:** Interlibrary loan; copying; library open to South Dakota residents. **Automated Operations:** Computerized cataloging and ILL. **Computerized Information Services:** DIALOG Information Services, Pergamon ORBIT InfoLine, Inc., BRS Information Technologies, TYMNET, ALANET, OCLC, RLIN, Western Library Network (WLN). **Networks/Consortia:** Member of CLASS, MINITEX, Western Council of State Libraries. **Publications:** South Dakota State Library Newsletter. **Special Catalogs:** South Dakota Union Card Catalog (microfiche). **Staff:** Dorothy Liegl, Dp. State Libn.; Rebecca Bell, Tech.Serv.Libn.; Ann Eichinger, Ref.Libn.; Margaret Bezpaletz, Doc.Supv.; Daniel Boyd, Dir., Hndcp.Serv.; Donna Gilliland, Sch.Lib.Cons.; Jerome Wagner, Inst.Lib.Cons.; Beth Marie Quanbeck.

★13399★
SOUTH DAKOTA STATE SUPREME COURT - LIBRARY (Law)
State Capitol
500 E. Capitol Ave.
Pierre, SD 57501 Phone: (605)773-4898
Staff: Prof 1; Other 1. **Subjects:** Law. **Holdings:** 27,802 volumes. **Subscriptions:** 60 journals and other serials. **Services:** Library open to the public.

★13400★
SOUTH DAKOTA STATE UNIVERSITY - HILTON M. BRIGGS LIBRARY (Biol Sci, Agri, Sci-Engr, Med)
Box 2115 Phone: (605)688-5106
Brookings, SD 57007-1098 Dr. Leon Raney, Dean of Lib.
Founded: 1886. **Staff:** Prof 12; Other 15. **Subjects:** Agriculture; pharmacy; engineering - civil, mechanical, electrical; chemistry; entomology; plant pathology; biological sciences; nursing; home economics. **Holdings:** 395,005 books and bound periodical volumes; 341,944 documents; 228,540 microforms. **Subscriptions:** 3501 journals and other serials; 87 newspapers. **Services:** Interlibrary loan; library open to the public. **Automated Operations:** Computerized cataloging and acquisitions. **Computerized Information Services:** OCLC, DIALOG Information Services, BRS Information Technologies. Performs searches on fee basis. Contact Person: Clark Hallman, Hd., Ref.Dept.. **Publications:** South Dakota Union List of Serials, 1979. **Special Indexes:** Sioux Falls Argus Leader Index, 1979 to present; Index to SDSU Agricultural Experiment Station and Extension Service Publications, 1975 (tape; book); South Dakota Farm and Home Research, KWIC Index, 1976 (tape; book). **Staff:** B.J. Kim, Hd., Cat.Dept.; Mark Bronson, Hd., Circ.Dept.; Philip Brown, Hd., Doc.; Gary Hudson, Hd., Acq.Dept.; Susan Richards, Hd., Ser.Dept..

★13401★
SOUTH DAKOTA STATE UNIVERSITY - WEST RIVER AGRICULTURAL RESEARCH AND EXTENSION CENTER - LIBRARY (Agri)
801 San Francisco St. Phone: (605)394-2236
Rapid City, SD 57701 F.R. Gartner, Dir.
Founded: 1969. **Staff:** Range, animal, plant, crop, and soil sciences. **Holdings:** 2000 volumes.

★13402★
SOUTH FLORIDA REGIONAL PLANNING COUNCIL - LIBRARY* (Plan)
3440 Hollywood Blvd., Suite 140 Phone: (305)961-2999
Hollywood, FL 33021 M. Keegan, Info.Spec.
Founded: 1971. **Staff:** Prof 1. **Subjects:** Planning - regional, transportation, housing, land use, coastal zone, energy. **Holdings:** 8000 books. **Subscriptions:** 150 journals and other serials. **Services:** Interlibrary loan; copying; library open to the public. **Automated Operations:** Computerized cataloging.

★13403★
SOUTH FLORIDA STATE HOSPITAL - MEDICAL LIBRARY (Med)
1000 S.W. 84th Ave. Phone: (305)983-4321
Hollywood, FL 33025 Mabel E. Randall, Med.Libn.
Staff: 1. **Subjects:** Psychiatry, neurology, psychology, nursing, social work. **Holdings:** 2650 books; 230 bound periodical volumes; cassettes; 3 masters' theses; tape cassettes. **Subscriptions:** 63 journals and other serials. **Services:** Interlibrary loan; copying; library open to the public with restrictions.

★13404★
SOUTH GEORGIA MEDICAL CENTER - MEDICAL LIBRARY (Med)
Box 1727 Phone: (912)333-1160
Valdosta, GA 31603-1727 Susan T. Statom, Med.Libn.
Staff: Prof 1. **Subjects:** Medicine, nursing, and allied health sciences. **Holdings:** 200 books; 300 bound periodical volumes. **Subscriptions:** 70 journals and other serials. **Services:** Interlibrary loan; copying; SDI; current awareness; library open to the public with restrictions. **Computerized Information Services:** NLM, BRS Information Technologies. Performs searches on fee basis. **Networks/Consortia:** Member of South Georgia Associated Libraries, Southwest Georgia Health Sciences Library Consortium (SWGHSLC), Georgia Interactive Network for Medical Information (GAIN).

★13405★
SOUTH HIGHLANDS HOSPITAL - MEDICAL LIBRARY (Med)
1127 S. 12th St. Phone: (205)930-7703
Birmingham, AL 35205 Dena Metts, Libn.
Founded: 1910. **Staff:** 1. **Subjects:** Medicine, nursing, and allied health sciences. **Holdings:** 500 books; 450 bound periodical volumes. **Subscriptions:** 125 journals and other serials. **Services:** Interlibrary loan; library not open to the public.

★13406★
SOUTH HILLS HEALTH SYSTEM - BEHAN HEALTH SCIENCE LIBRARY (Med)
Coal Valley Rd.
Box 18119 Phone: (412)664-5786
Pittsburgh, PA 15236 Barbara Palso, Libn.
Founded: 1975. **Staff:** Prof 1. **Subjects:** Medicine, nursing, and allied health sciences. **Special Collections:** Dr. Richard J. Behan Memorial Collection (cancer, trauma, legal aspects of medicine, pain, medical monographs). **Holdings:** 2000 books; 150 video cassettes. **Subscriptions:** 96 journals and other serials. **Services:** Interlibrary loan; library not open to the public. **Networks/Consortia:** Member of Greater Northeastern Regional Medical Library Program.

★13407★
SOUTH JERSEY REGIONAL FILM LIBRARY (Aud-Vis)
Echelon Urban Center
Laurel Rd. Phone: (609)772-1642
Voorhees, NJ 08043 Katherine Schalk-Greene, Dir.
Founded: 1970. **Staff:** Prof 1; Other 4. **Subjects:** Films - entertainment, social documentaries, film art, health and safety, classic features, cartoons. **Special Collections:** State Department films; National Gallery of Art. **Holdings:** 1900 16mm films; 500 videotapes. **Services:** Interlibrary loan; library open to the public with restrictions. **Automated Operations:** Computerized cataloging. **Networks/Consortia:** Member of New Jersey

State Library Regional Film Centers, South Jersey Regional Library Cooperative. **Special Catalogs:** Catalogs, annual.

★13408★
SOUTH MOUNTAIN LABORATORIES, INC. - LIBRARY (Med)
380 Lackawanna Place Phone: (201)762-0045
South Orange, NJ 07079 C.N. Mangieri, Dir.
Staff: 30. **Subjects:** Biology, chemistry, medicine, pharmaceutics. **Holdings:** 1000 books; 500 bound periodical volumes. **Subscriptions:** 14 journals and other serials. **Services:** Library not open to the public.

★13409★
SOUTH NASSAU COMMUNITIES HOSPITAL - JULES REDISH MEMORIAL MEDICAL LIBRARY (Med)
Oceanside Rd. Phone: (516)536-1600
Oceanside, NY 11572 Claire Strelzoff, Med.Libn.
Subjects: Medicine, surgery, nursing. **Holdings:** 1000 books; 6000 bound periodical volumes. **Subscriptions:** 111 journals and other serials. **Services:** Interlibrary loan; copying; library open to the public for reference use only.

★13410★
SOUTH STREET SEAPORT MUSEUM - LIBRARY (Hist)
207 Front St. Phone: (212)669-9438
New York, NY 10038 Norman J. Brouwer, Hist. & Cur.
Founded: 1967. **Staff:** Prof 1; Other 1. **Subjects:** Maritime history, technology, New York City. **Holdings:** 7000 books; 400 bound periodical volumes; 15,000 plans of ships and marine engines; 7 drawers of New York Harbor photographs and negatives; 38 drawers of archives; 21 drawers of shipping photographs and negatives. **Services:** Copying; library open to the public. **Staff:** Gerard Boardman, Libn..

★13411★
SOUTH SUBURBAN GENEALOGICAL & HISTORICAL SOCIETY - LIBRARY (Hist)
Box 96 Phone: (312)333-9474
South Holland, IL 60473 Alice DeBoer, Hd.Libn.
Staff: Prof 1; Other 10. **Subjects:** Genealogy, local history. **Special Collections:** Eddy Collection; Bishop Collection. **Holdings:** 4000 books; 450 bound periodical volumes; 115 reels of microfilm; federal census; land indexed wills; Bible records; obituaries; family work sheet files. **Subscriptions:** 110 journals and other serials. **Services:** Copying; library open to the public. **Networks/Consortia:** Member of Suburban Library System (SLS). **Publications:** Where the Trails Cross, quarterly; newsletter, monthly. **Special Indexes:** Family sheets of members, wills, Bibles, and obituary notices; surname indexes.

★13412★
SOUTH TEXAS COLLEGE OF LAW - LIBRARY (Law)
1303 San Jacinto Phone: (713)659-8040
Houston, TX 77002 Ann Puckett, Dir., Law Lib.
Founded: 1923. **Staff:** Prof 8; Other 4. **Subjects:** Law. **Holdings:** 250,000 volumes. **Services:** Interlibrary loan; copying; library open to alumni and law students; government documents section open to the public. **Automated Operations:** Computerized cataloging. **Computerized Information Services:** WESTLAW, DIALOG Information Services, VU/TEXT Information Services, LEXIS, InfoTrac. Performs searches on fee basis. Contact Person: Susan Spillman.

★13413★
SOUTHAM COMMUNICATIONS LTD. - LIBRARY (Publ)
1450 Don Mills Rd. Phone: (416)445-6641
Don Mills, ON, Canada M3B 2X7 Eileen M. Wise, Libn.
Founded: 1957. **Staff:** Prof 1; Other 2. **Subjects:** Industrial advertising, business journalism, magazine design, business periodical publishing. **Special Collections:** Southam publications. **Holdings:** 1500 books; 500 bound periodical volumes. **Subscriptions:** 60 journals and other serials. **Services:** Copying (limited); library open to advertising and library professionals. **Computerized Information Services:** DIALOG Information Services, The Financial Post Information Service, Infomart, Info Globe; DIALMAIL, Envoy 100 (electronic mail services).

★13414★
SOUTHEAST ALABAMA MEDICAL CENTER - MEDICAL LIBRARY (Med)
Drawer 6987 Phone: (205)793-8102
Dothan, AL 36302 Ruth R. Baxter, Libn.
Founded: 1963. **Staff:** Prof 1. **Subjects:** General medicine, nursing, hospital administration. **Holdings:** 700 books; 2400 bound periodical volumes; 150 unbound journals and other serials. **Subscriptions:** 102 journals and other serials. **Services:** Interlibrary loan; copying; library open to the public for reference use only. **Computerized Information Services:** MEDLARS. Performs searches on fee basis.

★13415★
SOUTHEAST ASIA RESCUE FOUNDATION, INC. - REFERENCE COLLECTION (Soc Sci)
Box 5060 Phone: (904)471-8424
St. Augustine, FL 32085 Theodore G. Schweitzer, III, Founder
Founded: 1982. **Staff:** Prof 1; Other 2. **Subjects:** Vietnamese boat refugees, refugee experiences vis-a-vis pirates. **Special Collections:** Firsthand accounts, manuscripts, scripts, and photographs of actual pirates and victims. **Holdings:** 1000 books; 100 bound periodical volumes; 2000 photographs. **Subscriptions:** 12 journals and other serials. **Services:** Library open to public at librarian's discretion. **Remarks:** Located at 1-1 LP Ocean Gallery, St. Augustine Beach, FL 32084. **Formerly:** Located in Lewistown, MO.

★13416★
SOUTHEAST HUMAN SERVICES CENTER - LIBRARY (Med)
700 1st Ave., S. Phone: (701)239-1620
Fargo, ND 58103 Diane Nordeng, Libn.
Staff: Prof 1. **Subjects:** Mental health, child growth and development, counseling. **Holdings:** 210 books; 4 VF drawers. **Services:** Interlibrary loan; copying; library open to the public with restrictions.

★13417★
SOUTHEAST INSTITUTE FOR GROUP AND FAMILY THERAPY - LIBRARY (Soc Sci)
103 Edwards Ridge Phone: (919)929-1171
Chapel Hill, NC 27514 Vann Joines, Pres.
Founded: 1969. **Staff:** 5. **Subjects:** Transactional analysis, psychotherapy, family therapy, race relations, Gestalt therapy. **Special Collections:** Audio- and videotapes on racism (not available to public). **Holdings:** 2500 volumes. **Services:** Library open only to institute students.

★13418★
SOUTHEAST LOUISIANA HOSPITAL - PROFESSIONAL LIBRARY (Med)
Box 3850 Phone: (504)626-8161
Mandeville, LA 70448 Carol C. Adams, Libn.
Staff: Prof 1; Other 1. **Subjects:** Psychiatry, psychology, sociology, psychiatric nursing, human physiology, biochemistry, philosophy. **Holdings:** 3000 books; 2800 bound periodical volumes; 70 other cataloged items; 3 VF drawers of doctoral dissertations, pamphlets, state vital statistics reports; 10 newsletters; 216 cassette tapes. **Subscriptions:** 112 journals and other serials. **Services:** Interlibrary loan; copying; SDI; library open to the public with restrictions. **Publications:** Brochure of Professional Library Services - for internal distribution only.

★13419★
SOUTHEAST METROPOLITAN BOARD OF COOPERATIVE SERVICES - PROFESSIONAL INFORMATION CENTER (Educ)
3301 S. Monaco Phone: (303)757-6201
Denver, CO 80222 Jim Foyle, Mgr.
Founded: 1968. **Staff:** Prof 2; Other 4. **Subjects:** Education - elementary, secondary, early childhood, special. **Holdings:** 3000 books; microcomputer software; textbooks. **Subscriptions:** 300 journals and other serials. **Services:** Interlibrary loan; copying; center open to educators in member districts. **Automated Operations:** Computerized cataloging. **Computerized Information Services:** DIALOG Information Services, WILSONLINE, BRS Information Technologies; EasyLink (electronic mail service). Performs searches on fee basis. **Networks/Consortia:** Member of Bibliographical Center for Research, Rocky Mountain Region, Inc. (BCR). **Staff:** Mary Asper, Info.Spec..

★13420★
SOUTHEAST MICHIGAN COUNCIL OF GOVERNMENTS - SEMCOG LIBRARY (Plan, Trans)
1900 Edison Plaza
660 Plaza Dr. Phone: (313)961-4266
Detroit, MI 48226 Pamela L. Lazar, Libn.
Staff: Prof 2. **Subjects:** Economic development, transportation, environmental issues, intergovernmental cooperation, regional planning, public safety. **Special Collections:** Detroit Metropolitan Area Regional Planning Commission (3 VF drawers of publications); Detroit Regional Transportation and Land Use Study (TALUS; 110 volumes). **Holdings:** 10,975 books and reports; 42 VF drawers of publications; 10 VF drawers of SEMCOG archives; 5 VF drawers of zoning ordinances; 3080 reports on microfiche. **Subscriptions:** 280 journals and other serials; 13 newspapers.

Services: Interlibrary loan; copying; SDI; library open to the public for reference use only. **Computerized Information Services:** CDC. Performs searches free of charge for members. **Networks/Consortia:** Member of Detroit Associated Libraries Region of Cooperation. **Publications:** Bibliographic accession list, monthly; periodical master list, annual - both for internal distribution only. **Staff:** Katherine Smith, Lib.Techn..

★13421★
SOUTHEAST MICHIGAN REGIONAL FILM LIBRARY (Aud-Vis)
c/o Monroe County Library System
3700 S. Custer Rd. Phone: (313)241-5277
Monroe, MI 48161 Bernard A. Margolis, Dir.
Founded: 1975. **Staff:** Prof 1; Other 4. **Special Collections:** 16mm feature films. **Holdings:** 800 reels of film. **Services:** Library not open to the public. **Special Catalogs:** Film catalog, annual.

★13422★
SOUTHEASTERN BIBLE COLLEGE - ROWE MEMORIAL LIBRARY (Rel-Phil)
2901 Pawnee Ave., S. Phone: (205)251-2311
Birmingham, AL 35256 Edith Taff, Libn.
Staff: Prof 1. **Subjects:** Theology, Church education, missions, church music. **Holdings:** 30,000 books and bound periodical volumes. **Subscriptions:** 159 journals and other serials; 5 newspapers. **Services:** Interlibrary loan; copying; library open to the public with restrictions.

★13423★
SOUTHEASTERN COLLEGE OF OSTEOPATHIC MEDICINE - MEDICAL LIBRARY (Med)
1750 N.E. 168th St. Phone: (305)947-6130
North Miami Beach, FL 33162 Naomi F. Elia, Lib.Dir.
Founded: 1981. **Staff:** Prof 1; Other 4. **Subjects:** Clinical medicine, basic sciences, osteopathy, pharmacy. **Special Collections:** Osteopathic medicine. **Holdings:** 8062 books; 5453 bound periodical volumes; 118 state osteopathic journals and newsletters. **Subscriptions:** 446 journals and other serials. **Services:** Interlibrary loan; copying; library open to the public for reference use only. **Computerized Information Services:** BRS Information Technologies, NLM; DOCLINE (electronic mail service). **Networks/Consortia:** Member of Miami Health Sciences Library Consortium (MHSLC). **Staff:** Marsha R. Mudrey, Lib.Assoc..

★13424★
SOUTHEASTERN GENERAL HOSPITAL, INC. - LIBRARY (Med)
300 W. 27th St.
Box 1408 Phone: (919)738-6441
Lumberton, NC 28358 Ann Stephens, Libn.
Staff: Prof 1; Other 1. **Subjects:** Medicine, surgery, nursing. **Holdings:** 500 books. **Subscriptions:** 120 journals and other serials. **Services:** Interlibrary loan; copying; SDI; library open to the public for reference use only. **Computerized Information Services:** MEDLINE. **Networks/Consortia:** Member of Cape Fear Health Sciences Information Consortium.

SOUTHEASTERN LESBIAN ARCHIVES
See: Atlanta Lesbian Feminist Alliance (1109)

★13425★
SOUTHEASTERN LOUISIANA UNIVERSITY - L.A. SIMS MEMORIAL LIBRARY (Educ)
Drawer 896, Univ. Sta. Phone: (504)549-2234
Hammond, LA 70402 F. Landon Greaves, Jr., Lib.Dir.
Founded: 1925. **Staff:** Prof 8; Other 16. **Subjects:** Education, mathematics, music, American history. **Special Collections:** Papers of Congressman James H. Morrison. **Holdings:** 265,000 books; 55,000 bound periodical volumes; 91,266 AV programs. **Subscriptions:** 1900 journals and other serials; 23 newspapers. **Services:** Interlibrary loan; copying; library open to the public for reference use only. **Computerized Information Services:** DIALOG Information Services, BRS Information Technologies, WILSONLINE, OCLC. **Networks/Consortia:** Member of SOLINET.

★13426★
SOUTHEASTERN MASSACHUSETTS UNIVERSITY - LIBRARY COMMUNICATIONS CENTER - ROBERT F. KENNEDY ASSASSINATION ARCHIVE (Hist)
North Dartmouth, MA 02747 Phone: (508)999-8686
Helen Koss, Univ.Archv.
Founded: 1985. **Staff:** Prof 1; Other 1. **Subjects:** Robert F. Kennedy assassination, U.S. assassinations, political violence. **Special Collections:** Nelson-Castellano Collection; Robert Blair Kaiser Collection; Lowenstein-Stone Collection. **Holdings:** 100 books; 30 boxes of manuscripts; 175 audiotapes; 40 photographs. **Services:** Copying; archive open to the public with restrictions. **Automated Operations:** Computerized cataloging. **Computerized Information Services:** DIALOG Information Services, BRS Information Technologies. Performs searches on fee basis. Contact Person: Barbara Donnelly. **Networks/Consortia:** Member of NELINET, Southeastern Massachusetts Cooperating Libraries (SMCL).

SOUTHEASTERN NEWSPAPERS CORPORATION - AUGUSTA CHRONICLE-HERALD NEWS
See: Augusta Chronicle-Herald News (1160)

★13427★
SOUTHEASTERN OKLAHOMA STATE UNIVERSITY - CENTRAL INDUSTRIAL APPLICATIONS CENTER (Sci-Engr)
Durant, OK 74701 Phone: (405)924-6822
Dr. Dickie Deel, Dir.
Founded: 1964. **Staff:** Prof 6; Other 3. **Subjects:** Aviation, astronautics, science, electronics, instrumentation, photography, mathematics, physics, computer science, space sciences. **Special Collections:** NASA-sponsored research documents. **Holdings:** 15,000 books; 1500 bound periodical volumes; 275,000 microfiche of reports. **Subscriptions:** 32 journals and other serials. **Services:** Interlibrary loan; copying; center open to the public with restrictions. **Computerized Information Services:** NASA/RECON, DIALOG Information Services, Pergamon ORBIT InfoLine, Inc. **Publications:** Quarterly and annual reports; General Aviation Technical News Letter. **Remarks:** CIAC is a NASA Industrial Applications Center serving the states of Oklahoma, Texas, Kansas, Nebraska, North Dakota, and South Dakota. **Formerly:** Kerr Industrial Applications Center. **Staff:** Chris Dill, Tech. Applications Anl.; A. Chambers-Craig, Bus.Anl./Adm.Asst.; Susy Davis, Comp.Sys.Mgr..

★13428★
SOUTHEASTERN PENNSYLVANIA TRANSPORTATION AUTHORITY - SEPTA LIBRARY (Trans)
841 Chestnut St., 11th Fl. Phone: (215)574-7387
Philadelphia, PA 19107 Rena E. Hawes, Libn.
Founded: 1966. **Staff:** Prof 1. **Subjects:** Public transportation, commuter railroads, urban planning. **Special Collections:** Urban Traffic and Transportation Board Collection (history and early planning of public transportation in Philadelphia; 300 items). **Holdings:** 6000 books and technical reports; 8 VF drawers of pamphlets; 4 VF drawers of annual reports of other agencies; 8 VF drawers of clippings. **Subscriptions:** 61 journals and other serials; 5 newspapers. **Services:** Interlibrary loan; copying; library open to the public by appointment. **Computerized Information Services:** DIALOG Information Services. **Networks/Consortia:** Member of PALINET. **Publications:** Annual Reports of Agency, 1964 to present; News Highlight - Transit, USA; Acquisitions List, both bimonthly - both for internal distribution only.

★13429★
SOUTHEASTERN UNIVERSITIES RESEARCH ASSOCIATION - CONTINUOUS ELECTRON BEAM ACCELERATOR FACILITY LIBRARY (Sci-Engr)
12070 Jefferson Ave. Phone: (804)875-7800
Newport News, VA 23606 Elois A. Morgan, Libn.
Staff: Prof 1; Other 1. **Subjects:** Physics, engineering, nuclear physics. **Holdings:** 7000 books; 10,000 bound periodical volumes; 3500 government documents; 15,000 microfiche. **Subscriptions:** 135 journals and other serials; 5 newspapers. **Services:** Interlibrary loan; copying; library open to the public. **Automated Operations:** Computerized public access catalog and cataloging. **Computerized Information Services:** Integrated Technical Information System (ITIS), SPIRES, DIALOG Information Services; SCIMATE (internal database). **Publications:** Using the CEBAF Library, annual; Serials in the CEBAF Library; New Books in the CEBAF Library; Library Handbook; Preprints Received in the CEBAF Library, monthly.

SOUTHEASTERN WISCONSIN HEALTH SYSTEMS AGENCY
See: Planning Council for Health and Human Services (11391)

★13430★
SOUTHEASTERN WISCONSIN REGIONAL PLANNING COMMISSION - LIBRARY (Plan)
916 N. East Ave.
Box 1607 Phone: (414)547-6721
Waukesha, WI 53187-1607 Arno M. Klausmeier, Libn.
Founded: 1960. **Staff:** Prof 1. **Subjects:** Regional planning, land use, transportation, population, housing, sewerage, drainage and flood control, environmental quality, parks and open space. **Special Collections:** Publications of Transportation Research Board, Southeastern Wisconsin

Regional Planning Commission, Urban Land Institute, American Society of Planning Officials, and American Society of Civil Engineers. **Holdings:** 6500 books; census data; weather maps; climatological data. **Subscriptions:** 100 journals and other serials. **Services:** Interlibrary loan; copying; library open to students and researchers only. **Networks/Consortia:** Member of Library Council of Metropolitan Milwaukee, Inc. (LCOMM).

★13431★
SOUTHERN ALBERTA ART GALLERY - LIBRARY (Art)
601 3rd Ave., S. Phone: (403)327-8770
Lethbridge, AB, Canada T1J 0H4 Clark Wilson, Reg./Libn.
Founded: 1976. **Staff:** Prof 1. **Subjects:** Art history, art techniques, artists. **Holdings:** 500 books; 6000 artists' catalogs; 600 unbound periodicals. **Subscriptions:** 11 journals and other serials. **Services:** Copying; library open to the public with restrictions.

★13432★
SOUTHERN ALBERTA INSTITUTE OF TECHNOLOGY - EDUCATIONAL RESOURCES - LIBRARY (Comp Sci, Sci-Engr)
1301 16th Ave., N.W. Phone: (403)284-8616
Calgary, AB, Canada T2M 0L4 R.C. Thornborough, Hd., Educ.Rsrcs.
Founded: 1920. **Staff:** Prof 5; Other 23. **Subjects:** Electronics, computer technology, business, chemical technology, engineering technologies, automotives, cookery, medical science, communication arts, drafting. **Holdings:** 72,000 books; 194 bound periodical volumes; 2000 film titles; 3000 videotapes; 1500 audiotapes; 86,700 microfiche; 6850 reels of microfilm; 500 film loop and filmstrip titles; 180 machine readable data files; 50 VF drawers of pamphlets. **Subscriptions:** 1001 journals and newspapers. **Services:** Interlibrary loan; copying; center open to the public. **Automated Operations:** Computerized cataloging, acquisitions, and circulation. **Computerized Information Services:** DIALOG Information Services, Pergamon ORBIT InfoLine, Inc., CAN/OLE, Info Globe; Envoy 100 (electronic mail service). **Publications:** Periodicals List, annual; Pathfinders. **Staff:** Robert Wilson, Info. Access Serv.; Thomas Skinner, Tech. & Sys.Serv.; May Chan, Sys.Coord..

SOUTHERN APPALACHIAN ARCHIVES
See: Berea College - Hutchins Library - Special Collections (1514)

★13433★
SOUTHERN BAPTIST CONVENTION - FOREIGN MISSION BOARD - ARCHIVES CENTER (Rel-Phil)
3806 Monument Ave.
Box 6767
Richmond, VA 23230 Phone: (804)353-0151
Staff: Prof 1. **Subjects:** Missions, missionaries, Southern Baptist Convention. **Holdings:** Board minutes; minutes of missions; administrative correspondence; correspondence with missionaries in the field. **Services:** Copying; center open to qualified users upon request.

★13434★
SOUTHERN BAPTIST CONVENTION - FOREIGN MISSION BOARD - JENKINS RESEARCH LIBRARY (Rel-Phil)
3806 Monument Ave.
Box 6767 Phone: (804)353-0151
Richmond, VA 23230 Kathryn K. Purks, Rsrc.Mgr.
Founded: 1960. **Staff:** Prof 4; Other 4. **Subjects:** Missions, mission history, management theory and practice, history, anthropology, area studies, travel. **Holdings:** 10,000 books. **Subscriptions:** 550 journals and other serials; 6 newspapers. **Services:** Interlibrary loan; library open to the public by written request and appointment scheduled in advance. **Automated Operations:** Computerized cataloging, acquisitions, and serials. **Computerized Information Services:** DIALOG Information Services, NEXIS; The Commission (internal database). **Networks/Consortia:** Member of SOLINET. **Staff:** Judith F. Bernicchi, Tech.Serv.Libn.; Terry L. Hanks, Ref.Libn.; Wayne Casey, Cat..

★13435★
SOUTHERN BAPTIST CONVENTION - HISTORICAL COMMISSION - SOUTHERN BAPTIST HISTORICAL LIBRARY & ARCHIVES (Rel-Phil, Hist)
901 Commerce St., Suite 400
Nashville, TN 37203-3620 Phone: (615)244-0344
Founded: 1938. **Staff:** Prof 2; Other 1. **Subjects:** Baptist history. **Holdings:** 22,000 books; 1500 linear feet of archival material; 15,000 reels of microfilm. **Subscriptions:** 150 journals and other serials; 100 newspapers. **Services:** Copying; library open to the public. **Automated Operations:** Computerized cataloging. **Computerized Information Services:** OCLC. **Networks/Consortia:** Member of SOLINET. **Publications:** Baptist History and Heritage, quarterly - by subscription; Baptist Heritage Update, quarterly - to members. **Special Catalogs:** Microfilm catalog. **Staff:** Pat Brown, Libn.; Bill Sumners, Archv..

SOUTHERN BAPTIST CONVENTION - SUNDAY SCHOOL BOARD - E.C. DARGAN RESEARCH LIBRARY
See: E.C. Dargan Research Library (4039)

★13436★
SOUTHERN BAPTIST HOSPITAL - LEARNING RESOURCE CENTER (Med)
2700 Napoleon Ave. Phone: (504)899-9311
New Orleans, LA 70115 Pauline Fulda, Dir.
Staff: Prof 2; Other 1. **Subjects:** Medicine, nursing, allied health sciences, pastoral care and counseling. **Special Collections:** Harriet L. Mather Archives. **Holdings:** 3333 books; 461 bound periodical volumes; 1509 AV programs. **Subscriptions:** 175 journals and other serials; 9 newspapers. **Services:** Interlibrary loan; center not open to the public. **Publications:** Library Users' Handbook. **Staff:** Marylynn Rooney, Lib.Asst..

★13437★
SOUTHERN BAPTIST THEOLOGICAL SEMINARY - AUDIOVISUAL CENTER (Aud-Vis)
2825 Lexington Rd. Phone: (502)897-4508
Louisville, KY 40280 Andrew B. Rawls, AV Libn.
Staff: Prof 1; Other 6. **Subjects:** Sermons, religious education, theology, church history, Christian missions, pastoral counseling. **Holdings:** 1935 filmstrips; 14,014 audiotapes; 1829 videotapes; 421 16mm films; 72,326 slides; 1387 phonograph records. **Services:** Center open to the public for reference use only.

★13438★
SOUTHERN BAPTIST THEOLOGICAL SEMINARY - BILLY GRAHAM ROOM (Rel-Phil)
2825 Lexington Rd. Phone: (502)897-4807
Louisville, KY 40280 Dr. Ronald F. Deering, Libn.
Founded: 1960. **Subjects:** Ministry of Billy Graham. **Holdings:** Books; sermons; movies and records of revivals throughout the world. **Services:** Copying; room open to the public.

★13439★
SOUTHERN BAPTIST THEOLOGICAL SEMINARY - CHURCH MUSIC LIBRARY (Mus, Rel-Phil)
2825 Lexington Rd. Phone: (502)897-4712
Louisville, KY 40280 Martha C. Powell, Church Music Libn.
Founded: 1944. **Staff:** Prof 1; Other 3. **Subjects:** Hymnody; music - history, education, instruments, choral, folk; musicians; voice; worship. **Special Collections:** Converse Hymnal Collection; Ingersoll Evangelistic Music Collection (3000 titles); Everett B. Helm Score Collection. **Holdings:** 18,583 books; 1879 bound periodical volumes; 8935 phonograph records; 5151 audiotapes; 491 compact discs; 147,825 scores; 275 titles on microfilm. **Subscriptions:** 112 journals and other serials. **Services:** Interlibrary loan; copying; library open to the public.

★13440★
SOUTHERN BAPTIST THEOLOGICAL SEMINARY - JAMES P. BOYCE CENTENNIAL LIBRARY (Rel-Phil)
2825 Lexington Rd. Phone: (502)897-4807
Louisville, KY 40280 Dr. Ronald F. Deering, Dir.
Founded: 1859. **Staff:** Prof 7; Other 27. **Subjects:** Bible, theology, philosophy, psychology, religious education, church history and music, comparative religions, sociology. **Special Collections:** Baptist Historical Collection. **Holdings:** 320,432 volumes; 102,498 pamphlets; 32,420 microforms. **Subscriptions:** 1492 journals and other serials. **Services:** Interlibrary loan; copying; library open to the public. **Staff:** Nancy Robinson, Cat.; Elsa A. Miller, Circ.Libn.; Paul M. Debusman, Ref./Ser.Libn.; Melody Mazuk, Tech.Serv.Libn..

★13441★
SOUTHERN BELL TELEPHONE AND TELEGRAPH COMPANY - LAW LIBRARY (Law)
4300 Southern Bell Center
675 W. Peachtree St., N.E. Phone: (404)529-7937
Atlanta, GA 30375 Linda Gray, Libn.
Staff: Prof 1. **Subjects:** Law. **Holdings:** 14,000 volumes. **Services:** Library not open to the public.

SOUTHERN CALIFORNIA ACADEMY OF SCIENCE LIBRARY
See: Natural History Museum of Los Angeles County - Research Library (9828)

★13442★
SOUTHERN CALIFORNIA ASSOCIATION OF GOVERNMENTS - INFORMATION RESOURCE CENTER
600 S. Commonwealth Ave., Suite 1000
Los Angeles, CA 90005
Defunct

SOUTHERN CALIFORNIA CENTER FOR EDUCATIONAL IMPROVEMENT
See: Los Angeles County Office of Education (7994)

★13443★
SOUTHERN CALIFORNIA COLLEGE OF OPTOMETRY - M.B. KETCHUM MEMORIAL LIBRARY (Med)
2565 Yorba Linda Blvd. Phone: (714)870-7226
Fullerton, CA 92631-1699 Mrs. Pat Carlson, Hd.Libn.
Founded: 1948. **Staff:** Prof 1; Other 2. **Subjects:** Optometry, optics, ophthalmology. **Holdings:** 8000 books; 5000 bound periodical volumes; 380 theses; 325 AV programs. **Subscriptions:** 330 serials. **Services:** Interlibrary loan; copying; SDI; library open to the public with restrictions. **Computerized Information Services:** DIALOG Information Services, MEDLINE, LION. **Publications:** Recent Publications Received, bimonthly - by request.

★13444★
SOUTHERN CALIFORNIA EDISON COMPANY - LIBRARY (Sci-Engr)
2244 Walnut Grove Ave.
Box 800 Phone: (818)302-8971
Rosemead, CA 91770 N.P. Morton, Corp.Libn.
Founded: 1905. **Staff:** Prof 4; Other 4. **Subjects:** Electrical engineering and allied fields, nuclear engineering, management. **Holdings:** 12,332 books; 1253 bound periodical volumes; 33 VF drawers; 67 shelves of government documents; 14 shelves of reports; 1600 reels of microfilm of periodicals. **Subscriptions:** 570 journals and other serials. **Services:** Interlibrary loan; copying (limited); library open to the public by appointment only. **Automated Operations:** Computerized public access catalog, cataloging, acquisitions, serials, and circulation. **Computerized Information Services:** DIALOG Information Services, Pergamon ORBIT InfoLine, Inc., BRS Information Technologies, Electric Power Database (EPD); internal database. **Publications:** Library Bulletin, monthly. **Staff:** Barbara L. Netzley, Assoc.Doc.Anl.; Terry Taylor, Asst.Libn.; Michael Culbertson, Asst.Libn..

★13445★
SOUTHERN CALIFORNIA EDISON COMPANY - NUCLEAR TRAINING DIVISION RESOURCE CENTER
San Onofre Nuclear Generating Station, E-50B MESA
Box 700
San Clemente, CA 92672
Founded: 1983. **Subjects:** Nuclear power, radiation, education, and training. **Special Collections:** Electric Power Research Institute - Nuclear Power collection; Institute of Nuclear Power Operations (INPO) collection. **Holdings:** 1200 books; 75 unbound volumes; 120,000 aperture cards; 60,000 microfiche; 592 standards (392 binders); 6000 vendor manuals; 150 telephone directories; 10,000 procedures; 2000 documents; 1500 NUREGS (NRC). **Remarks:** Presently inactive.

★13446★
SOUTHERN CALIFORNIA GAS COMPANY - ENGINEERING INFORMATION CENTER (Energy)
Box 3249, Terminal Annex, ML730D Phone: (818)307-2872
Los Angeles, CA 90051 Gordon L. Sandviken, Info.Ctr.Spec.
Founded: 1975. **Staff:** Prof 1; Other 2. **Subjects:** Engineering - civil, mechanical, structural; natural gas; energy. **Special Collections:** Project Collection (20 project holdings). **Holdings:** 3000 books; 1000 codes. **Subscriptions:** 252 journals and other serials. **Services:** Interlibrary loan; copying; center open to the public. **Automated Operations:** Computerized cataloging, acquisitions, serials, and circulation. **Computerized Information Services:** DIALOG Information Services, Pergamon ORBIT InfoLine, Inc. **Publications:** Acquisitions list, monthly.

★13447★
SOUTHERN CALIFORNIA GAS COMPANY - GAS SUPPLY INFORMATION CENTER (Energy)
720 W. 8th St. - ML 10MW
Box 3249, Terminal Annex Phone: (213)689-3930
Los Angeles, CA 90051 Janice Young, Res. & Info.Ctr.Supv.
Staff: Prof 3. **Subjects:** Energy, natural gas, gas supply. **Special Collections:** Federal Energy Regulatory Commission (FERC) forms. **Holdings:** 250 books. **Subscriptions:** 200 journals and other serials. **Services:** Interlibrary loan; center open to the public with restrictions. **Automated Operations:** Computerized cataloging, acquisitions, and circulation. **Computerized Information Services:** DIALOG Information Services, Pergamon ORBIT InfoLine, Inc., BRS Information Technologies, InfoMaster, NEXIS, The Source Information Network, Integrated Technical Information System (ITIS), LEXIS; internal databases; A.G.A. GasNet, EasyLink (electronic mail services). **Publications:** Acquisitions List, monthly. **Remarks:** Southern California Gas Company is a subsidiary of Pacific Lighting Corporation.

★13448★
SOUTHERN CALIFORNIA GAS COMPANY - PUBLIC AFFAIRS LIBRARY (Hist, Energy)
810 S. Flower St. Phone: (213)689-2179
Los Angeles, CA 90017 Stephanie L. Thompson, Supv.
Staff: Prof 1; Other 1. **Subjects:** Southern California Gas Company history, early 1800s to present. **Holdings:** 15,000 books, directories, pamphlets, reports; photographs; slides; documents. **Services:** Interlibrary loan. **Automated Operations:** Computerized cataloging, acquisitions, serials, and circulation. **Computerized Information Services:** LEXIS, NEXIS, A.G.A. GasNet, DIALOG Information Services, BRS Information Technologies; A.G.A. GasNet (electronic mail service). **Publications:** Quarterly current awareness bulletin.

★13449★
SOUTHERN CALIFORNIA GENEALOGICAL SOCIETY, INC. - LIBRARY (Hist)
122 S. San Fernando Blvd.
Box 4377 Phone: (818)843-7247
Burbank, CA 91503 Jan Jennings, Pres.
Founded: 1965. **Staff:** 50. **Subjects:** State and local history, family history. **Special Collections:** Alabama county records; Massachusetts town records; Brossman genealogical columns (16 years); Pennsylvania area keys; Texas Robertson Colony records; North Carolina Moravian records; New England History and Genealogy Register; Joseph Brown Turner Collection (microfiche). **Holdings:** 6000 books; 2000 bound periodical volumes; 3 file drawers of maps; 36 drawers of manuscripts. **Subscriptions:** 200 journals and other serials. **Services:** Copying; library open to the public. **Publications:** The Searcher, monthly - to members. **Special Indexes:** Index in process to family histories, periodicals and manuscripts (card).

★13450★
SOUTHERN CALIFORNIA INSTITUTE OF ARCHITECTURE (SCI-ARC) - ARCHITECTURE LIBRARY (Plan)
1800 Berkeley St. Phone: (213)829-3482
Santa Monica, CA 90404 Kevin McMahon, Lib.Mgr.
Founded: 1974. **Staff:** Prof 1; Other 1. **Subjects:** Architectural history and theory, planning, art. **Holdings:** 7000 books; 700 bound periodical volumes. **Subscriptions:** 30 journals and other serials. **Services:** Copying; library open to the public for reference use only. **Publications:** Modern Architecture: Mexico.

★13451★
SOUTHERN CALIFORNIA LIBRARY FOR SOCIAL STUDIES AND RESEARCH (Soc Sci)
6120 S. Vermont Ave. Phone: (213)759-6063
Los Angeles, CA 90044 Sarah Cooper, Dir.
Founded: 1963. **Staff:** Prof 3; Other 8. **Subjects:** Labor; Communism; Marxism; liberalism; black, Chicano, and women's movements; southern California grassroots organizations. **Special Collections:** Civil Rights Congress (Los Angeles area) archival records; Harry Bridges papers on deportation trials; Los Angeles Committee for the Protection of the Foreign Born records; personal manuscript collections from Charlotta A. Bass, Richard Gladstein, Robert W. Kenny, and Earl Robinson. **Holdings:** 35,000 books; 30,000 pamphlets; 3500 tapes; 500,000 news clippings; 600 VF drawers of periodicals and files from labor, peace, and civil rights organizations, 1930s to present; 50 documentary films, 1930s-1970s. **Services:** Copying; library open to the public. **Publications:** Heritage (newsletter), quarterly.

★13452★
SOUTHERN CALIFORNIA PERMANENTE MEDICAL CENTER - HEALTH SCIENCES LIBRARY/MEDIA CENTER (Med)
9400 E. Rosecrans Ave. Phone: (213)920-4938
Bellflower, CA 90706 Geraldine N. Graves, Dir., Lib.Serv.
Founded: 1965. **Staff:** Prof 2; Other 4. **Subjects:** Medicine and medical specialties, nursing. **Holdings:** 5495 books; 3890 bound periodical volumes; 1200 Audio-Digest tapes; 2 VF drawers of pamphlets; 1035 AV programs; videotapes. **Subscriptions:** 319 journals and other serials. **Services:**

Interlibrary loan; copying; SDI; library open to the public by appointment. **Automated Operations:** Computerized cataloging, acquisitions, serials, circulation, and ordering. **Computerized Information Services:** MEDLINE, DIALOG Information Services; internal database; OnTyme Electronic Message Network Service (electronic mail service). Performs searches on fee basis. Contact Person: Mary White, Asst.Libn., 920-4247. **Networks/Consortia:** Member of Pacific Southwest Regional Medical Library Service. **Publications:** Library Newsletter - for internal distribution only. **Special Catalogs:** Computerized union book catalog of all Kaiser libraries in southern region.

★13453★
SOUTHERN CALIFORNIA PSYCHOANALYTIC INSTITUTE - FRANZ ALEXANDER LIBRARY (Med)
9024 Olympic Blvd. Phone: (213)276-2455
Beverly Hills, CA 90211 Lena Pincus, Libn.
Founded: 1950. **Staff:** Prof 1. **Subjects:** Psychoanalysis, psychiatry, psychology. **Holdings:** 4000 volumes; 2200 reprints. **Subscriptions:** 45 journals and other serials. **Services:** Interlibrary loan; copying; library open to the public with restrictions.

★13454★
SOUTHERN CALIFORNIA RAPID TRANSIT DISTRICT - INFORMATION CENTER/LIBRARY (Trans)
425 S. Main St., 5th Fl.,
Los Angeles, CA 90013 Phone: (213)972-6467
Founded: 1971. **Staff:** Prof 2. **Subjects:** Urban transportation, local transit, urban planning, parent organization history. **Special Collections:** Public domain software (600 diskettes). **Holdings:** 20,000 books and bound periodical volumes; 2000 reports on microfiche; 50 maps. **Subscriptions:** 150 journals and other serials. **Services:** Interlibrary loan; copying; library open to the public with restrictions. **Automated Operations:** Computerized cataloging, acquisitions, and serials. **Computerized Information Services:** DIALOG Information Services, LEXIS, NEXIS, OCLC. **Publications:** Infocus (acquisitions list), quarterly - for internal distribution only. **Staff:** Robert Bremer, Asst.Libn..

★13455★
SOUTHERN CALIFORNIA SOCIETY FOR PSYCHICAL RESEARCH, INC. - LIBRARY (Rel-Phil)
Box 3901 Phone: (213)936-0904
Thousand Oaks, CA 91359 Andrew T. Shields, Lib.Coord.
Founded: 1968. **Subjects:** Parapsychology. **Special Collections:** Journal of Parapsychology (50); Journal of the American Society for Psychic Research (300); rare books by early psychical researchers (100); UFOs (15 books). **Holdings:** 1000 books; 18 bound periodical volumes. **Services:** Library open to members for reference use only by appointment. **Publications:** Southern California Society for Psychical Research Monthly Bulletin.

SOUTHERN CENTER FOR STUDIES IN PUBLIC POLICY
See: Clark College (3255)

★13456★
SOUTHERN COLLEGE - LIBRARY (Sci-Engr)
5600 Lake Underhill Rd. Phone: (407)273-1000
Orlando, FL 32807 Mary Love Hammond, Libn.
Staff: Prof 1; Other 1. **Subjects:** Interior design, dentistry, computers, data processing, electronics, business and general education, computer repair. **Holdings:** 7000 books; 1500 unbound periodicals; 1747 slides; 16 film cassettes; 8 filmstrips. **Subscriptions:** 134 journals and other serials; 6 newspapers. **Services:** Library not open to the public. **Computerized Information Services:** Internal database. **Publications:** Handbook.

★13457★
SOUTHERN COLLEGE OF OPTOMETRY - LIBRARY (Med)
1245 Madison Ave. Phone: (901)722-3237
Memphis, TN 38104 Nancy Gatlin, Dir.
Founded: 1938. **Staff:** Prof 2; Other 1. **Subjects:** Optometry, optics, ophthalmology, psychology, exceptional education. **Holdings:** 14,516 books; 3749 bound periodical volumes; 12,302 slides; 376 microfiche; 153 reels of microfilm; 230 video cassettes. **Subscriptions:** 191 journals and other serials. **Services:** Interlibrary loan; copying; SDI; library open to the public for reference use only. **Automated Operations:** Computerized cataloging, acquisitions, and serials. **Computerized Information Services:** DIALOG Information Services; LION (internal database); Mail Call (electronic mail service). Performs searches on fee basis. **Networks/Consortia:** Member of Association of Memphis Area Health Sciences Libraries (AMAHSL), Association of Visual Science Librarians (AVSL). **Special Indexes:** Vision Science Index (online); ocular pathology slide index. **Staff:** Deborah Lawless, Asst.Dir..

SOUTHERN COLLEGE OF PHARMACY
See: Mercer University - Southern College of Pharmacy (8722)

★13458★
SOUTHERN COLLEGE OF SEVENTH-DAY ADVENTISTS - MC KEE LIBRARY - SPECIAL COLLECTIONS (Rel-Phil, Hist)
Box 629 Phone: (615)238-2788
Collegedale, TN 37315 Peg Bennett, Dir. of Libs.
Founded: 1892. **Staff:** Prof 3; Other 5. **Special Collections:** Dr. Vernon Thomas Memorial Civil War Collection (1400 books; 2000 letters; manuscripts; newspapers; pamphlets; pictures; maps); Dr. Vernon Thomas Memorial Abraham Lincoln Collection (2000 books, letters, manuscripts, newspapers, pamphlets, pictures, paintings, maps, artifacts); Seventh-Day Adventist Church publications (10,000 books, current periodicals, bound periodicals, microforms, archives). **Services:** Interlibrary loan; copying; SDI; collections open to the public with restrictions. **Automated Operations:** Computerized cataloging, acquisitions, serials, and circulation. **Computerized Information Services:** OCLC. **Networks/Consortia:** Member of SOLINET.

★13459★
SOUTHERN COLLEGE OF TECHNOLOGY - LIBRARY (Sci-Engr)
1112 Clay St. Phone: (404)424-7275
Marietta, GA 30060 John W. Pattillo, Dir.
Founded: 1948. **Staff:** Prof 5; Other 3. **Subjects:** Engineering and technology - apparel, architectural, civil, computer, electrical, industrial, mechanical, textile. **Holdings:** 68,000 books; 16,000 bound periodical volumes; 9000 serials; 11,000 AV programs; 2000 company reports. **Subscriptions:** 1400 journals and other serials. **Services:** Interlibrary loan; copying; library open to the public with restrictions. **Automated Operations:** Computerized cataloging and serials. **Computerized Information Services:** OCLC. **Networks/Consortia:** Member of SOLINET. **Staff:** Nancy S. Shofner, Asst.Dir.; Dorothy Ingram, Ref.Libn.; Eddie McLoed, Ser.Libn.; Mary Day, Acq.Libn..

★13460★
SOUTHERN CONNECTICUT NEWSPAPERS INC. - ADVOCATE & GREENWICH TIME LIBRARY (Publ)
75 Tresser Blvd. Phone: (203)964-2297
Stamford, CT 06904-9307 Leigh Baker Michels, Hd.Libn.
Founded: 1829. **Staff:** Prof 2; Other 2. **Subjects:** Newspaper reference topics. **Special Collections:** Antique newspapers, photographs, and posters. **Holdings:** Clippings; local and state documents; microfilm; photographs. **Subscriptions:** 10 journals and other serials; 12 newspapers. **Services:** Library not open to the public. **Special Catalogs:** Catalogs of clipping file and photograph file. **Staff:** Pamela Malley, Asst.Libn..

★13461★
SOUTHERN CONNECTICUT STATE UNIVERSITY - H.C. BULEY LIBRARY - SPECIAL COLLECTIONS (Hist, Hum)
501 Crescent St. Phone: (203)397-4505
New Haven, CT 06515 Kenneth G. Walter, Dir.
Founded: 1893. **Special Collections:** Connecticut Room (5865 volumes; 28 VF drawers); Contemporary Juvenile Collection (15,276 volumes); Carolyn Sherwin Bailey Historical Collection of Children's Books (2302 volumes); government documents (157,772 items); archives (40 VF drawers); Hartford Times newspaper morgue (300 VF drawers). **Services:** Interlibrary loan; copying; collections open to the public with restrictions. **Automated Operations:** Computerized cataloging. **Computerized Information Services:** DIALOG Information Services, BRS Information Technologies, WILSONLINE. **Special Catalogs:** Catalog of Carolyn Sherwin Bailey Children's Collection (printed). **Special Indexes:** Magazine Index (online). **Staff:** Shirley Bickoff, Docs.; Claire Bennett, CT Rm. & Assoc.Ref.Libn..

SOUTHERN ENERGY/ENVIRONMENTAL INFORMATION CENTER (SEEIC)
See: Southern States Energy Board (SSEB) (13498)

★13462★
SOUTHERN ENGINEERING - LIBRARY (Sci-Engr)
1800 Peachtree St., N.W.
Atlanta, GA 30367 Phone: (404)352-9200
Founded: 1945. **Subjects:** Electric utilities, engineering. **Holdings:** Figures not available.

★13463★
SOUTHERN FOREST PRODUCTS ASSOCIATION - LIBRARY (Bus-Fin)
Box 52468 Phone: (504)443-4464
New Orleans, LA 70152 Ivy Riley, Libn.
Staff: Prof 1. **Subjects:** Lumber industry economics. **Special Collections:** History of Southern Pine Association/Southern Forest Products Association. **Holdings:** Figures not available. **Subscriptions:** 80 journals and other serials. **Services:** Interlibrary loan; library not open to the public. **Publications:** List of association publications and films available for sale - free upon request.

★13464★
SOUTHERN HIGHLAND HANDICRAFT GUILD - FOLK ART CENTER LIBRARY (Art)
Box 9545 Phone: (704)298-7928
Asheville, NC 28815 Rosemary Maxwell, Volunteer Libn.
Staff: Prof 1; Other 6. **Subjects:** History, traditional and contemporary crafts of the southern highlands. **Special Collections:** Goodrich Collection; textiles study collection; craft objects (750). **Holdings:** 2500 books; historical materials. **Subscriptions:** 36 journals and other serials. **Services:** Library open to the public for reference and research use only. **Publications:** Bibliographies. **Remarks:** Library located at Blue Ridge Parkway and Riceville Road, Asheville, NC 28805.

SOUTHERN HIGHLANDS RESEARCH CENTER
See: University of North Carolina, Asheville (16610)

★13465★
SOUTHERN ILLINOIS UNIVERSITY - SCHOOL OF MEDICINE - MEDICAL LIBRARY (Med)
801 N. Rutledge
Box 3926 Phone: (217)782-2658
Springfield, IL 62708 Robert Berk, Ph.D., Dir.
Founded: 1970. **Staff:** Prof 7; Other 19. **Subjects:** Medical sciences. **Special Collections:** History of medicine (4000 volumes). **Holdings:** 50,175 books; 52,813 bound periodical volumes; 1600 reels of microfilm; 3803 AV programs. **Subscriptions:** 1752 journals and other serials. **Services:** Interlibrary loan; copying; library open to the public. **Automated Operations:** Computerized cataloging, serials, and circulation. **Computerized Information Services:** MEDLINE, DIALOG Information Services, OCLC, BRS Information Technologies, Statewide Library Computer System (LCS). Performs searches free of charge for primary users; on fee basis for others. **Networks/Consortia:** Member of Greater Midwest Regional Medical Library Network, ILLINET, Sangamon Valley Academic Library Consortium (SVALC), Capital Area Consortium. **Special Catalogs:** Subject and title listings of current subscriptions; subject guide to AV collection. **Staff:** Gail Hitchcock, Cat.Libn.; Joyce Horney, Hd.Info. Access Serv.Libn.; Richard Dilley, Hd., Tech.Serv.; Martha Ann Klestinski, Spec.Coll.Libn.; Janice Prior, Ref. & Educ.Serv.Libn.; Rhona Kelley, Hd.Ref. & Educ.Serv.Libn..

★13466★
SOUTHERN ILLINOIS UNIVERSITY, CARBONDALE - EDUCATION AND PSYCHOLOGY DIVISION LIBRARY (Educ, Info Sci)
Morris Library Phone: (618)453-2274
Carbondale, IL 62901 Dr. Ruth E. Bauner, Educ. & Psych.Libn.
Founded: 1950. **Staff:** Prof 4; Other 1. **Subjects:** Education, psychology, library science, recreation, sports, guidance. **Special Collections:** John Dewey Collection; historical children's book collection. **Holdings:** 128,500 books; 33,170 bound periodical volumes; 33,000 curriculum guides, children's books, textbooks in instructional materials center. **Subscriptions:** 1624 journals and other serials. **Services:** Interlibrary loan; copying; library open to the public for reference use only. **Automated Operations:** Computerized cataloging and circulation. **Computerized Information Services:** DIALOG Information Services, Pergamon ORBIT InfoLine, Inc., OCLC, BRS Information Technologies, Statewide Library Computer System (LCS). **Networks/Consortia:** Member of ILLINET, Center for Research Libraries (CRL) Consortia. **Staff:** Dr. Kathy Cook, Asst.Libn.; Mary Isbell, Asst.Libn.; Lorene Pixley, Asst.Libn..

★13467★
SOUTHERN ILLINOIS UNIVERSITY, CARBONDALE - HUMANITIES DIVISION LIBRARY (Hum)
Morris Library Phone: (618)536-3391
Carbondale, IL 62901 Alan M. Cohn, Hum.Libn.
Founded: 1956. **Staff:** Prof 3; Other 2. **Subjects:** Literature, linguistics, music, art, philosophy, religion, speech, theater, journalism. **Holdings:** 525,000 books; 86,000 bound periodical volumes; 87,000 microtexts; 16,500 phonograph records; 25,000 prints. **Subscriptions:** 3600 journals and other serials. **Services:** Interlibrary loan; copying; library open to the public for reference use only. **Automated Operations:** Computerized cataloging and circulation. **Computerized Information Services:** OCLC, DIALOG Information Services, Pergamon ORBIT InfoLine, Inc., Statewide Library Computer System (LCS). **Networks/Consortia:** Member of ILLINET, Center for Research Libraries (CRL) Consortia. **Staff:** Angela Rubin, Asst.Libn.; Blake Landor, Asst.Libn.; Carole L. Palmer, Asst.Libn..

★13468★
SOUTHERN ILLINOIS UNIVERSITY, CARBONDALE - SCHOOL OF LAW LIBRARY (Law)
Carbondale, IL 62901 Phone: (618)536-7711
Frank G. Houdek, Law Lib.Dir.
Founded: 1973. **Staff:** Prof 6; Other 12. **Subjects:** Law. **Special Collections:** Mining law; water law (208 water quality plans); federal and state government documents depository. **Holdings:** 251,194 volumes. **Subscriptions:** 6537 journals and other serials. **Services:** Interlibrary loan; copying; library open to the public. **Automated Operations:** Computerized cataloging and ILL. **Computerized Information Services:** WESTLAW, LEXIS, OCLC, DIALOG Information Services, ELSS (Electronic Legislative Search System); ABA/net (electronic mail service). **Networks/Consortia:** Member of ILLINET, Mid-America Law School Library Consortium. **Publications:** Recent Acquisitions and Developments, irregular - to campus and other libraries; Law Library Publication Series. **Special Catalogs:** Rare Book Collection catalog; Loose-leaf Service Holdings (both book). **Staff:** Laurel A. Wendt, Assoc. Law Lib.Dir.; R. Kathy Garner, Ref./Instr.Serv.Libn.; Elizabeth W. Matthews, Cat.Libn.; Kay L. Andrus, Rd.Serv.Libn.; Heija B. Ryoo, Acq./Ser.Libn..

★13469★
SOUTHERN ILLINOIS UNIVERSITY, CARBONDALE - SCIENCE DIVISION LIBRARY (Sci-Engr, Agri, Med)
Morris Library Phone: (618)453-2700
Carbondale, IL 62901 George W. Black, Sci.Libn.
Founded: 1956. **Staff:** Prof 4; Other 1. **Subjects:** Agriculture, science, medicine, engineering. **Holdings:** 200,000 books; 170,000 bound periodical volumes; 2200 theses; 225,000 maps and aerial photographs; 9600 serial reports on microfilm; 1500 books on microfilm. **Subscriptions:** 5200 journals and other serials. **Services:** Interlibrary loan; copying; library open to the public for reference use only. **Automated Operations:** Computerized cataloging and circulation. **Computerized Information Services:** DIALOG Information Services, Pergamon ORBIT InfoLine, Inc., MEDLARS, BRS Information Technologies, OCLC, WILSONLINE, Statewide Library Computer System (LCS). **Networks/Consortia:** Member of ILLINET. **Staff:** Kathy Fahey, Asst.Sci.Libn. & ILL Libn.; Harry O. Davis, Asst.Sci.Libn./Map Libn.; Andrew Tax, Med.Libn..

★13470★
SOUTHERN ILLINOIS UNIVERSITY, CARBONDALE - SOCIAL STUDIES DIVISION LIBRARY (Soc Sci)
Morris Library Phone: (618)453-2708
Carbondale, IL 62901 James Fox, Soc.Stud.Libn.
Founded: 1956. **Staff:** Prof 4; Other 2. **Subjects:** Anthropology, business, economics, geography, history, political science, sociology, Latin American studies. **Holdings:** 314,000 books; 101,200 bound periodical volumes; 337,000 U.S. Government documents in hardcopy; 388,000 government documents on microfiche; 57 cabinets of Human Relations Area Files; one file of Classified Abstract Archive of Alcohol Literature; microprints of U.S. Government documents (1953-1976 ND, 1956-1976 D), British Sessional Papers, 1731 to present, and American Antiquarian Society's early American newspapers and imprints; 55,000 reels of microfilm of newspapers, journals, National Archives material. **Subscriptions:** 3514 journals and other serials; 86 newspapers. **Services:** Interlibrary loan; copying; library open to the public for reference use only. **Automated Operations:** Computerized cataloging and circulation. **Computerized Information Services:** DIALOG Information Services, Pergamon ORBIT InfoLine, Inc., Statewide Library Computer System (LCS). **Networks/Consortia:** Member of ILLINET, Center for Research Libraries (CRL) Consortia. **Staff:** Charles Holliday, Asst.Soc.Stud.Libn.; Catherine Martinsek, Asst.Soc.Stud.Libn.; Walter Stubbs, Asst.Soc.Stud.Libn..

★13471★
SOUTHERN ILLINOIS UNIVERSITY, CARBONDALE - SPECIAL COLLECTIONS (Hum)
Morris Library Phone: (618)453-2516
Carbondale, IL 62901 David V. Koch, Cur./Archv.
Founded: 1956. **Staff:** Prof 3; Other 3. **Special Collections:** Irish Literary Renaissance; 20th century British and American literature, theater, and philosophy; private press books (Black Sun, Trovillion, Nash, Cuala);

Southern Illinois history; Ulysses S. Grant; John Dewey; Paul Weiss; James K. Feibleman; Open Court Press; Christian Century Magazine; Library of Living Philosophers; Henry Nelson Wieman; Robert Graves; James Joyce; D.H. Lawrence; Richard Aldington; Lawrence Durrell; Erwin Piscator; Henry Miller; Kay Boyle; John Howard Lawson; First Amendment freedoms; university archives. **Holdings:** 55,000 books; 650,000 manuscripts and letters. **Services:** Copying; collection open to qualified scholars. **Automated Operations:** Computerized cataloging and circulation. **Computerized Information Services:** OCLC, Statewide Library Computer System (LCS). **Networks/Consortia:** Member of ILLINET. **Publications:** Bibliographic Contributions; ICarbS (journal), semiannual. **Special Catalogs:** Catalogs of special exhibits. **Staff:** Shelley Cox, Rare Bks.Libn.; Sheila Ryan, Cur., Mss..

★13472★
SOUTHERN ILLINOIS UNIVERSITY, CARBONDALE - UNDERGRADUATE LIBRARY (Hum)
Morris Library Phone: (618)453-2818
Carbondale, IL 62901 Dr. Judith Ann Harwood, Libn.
Founded: 1971. **Staff:** Prof 4; Other 3. **Subjects:** Automotive technology, thanatology, cinema and photography, women's studies, radio and television, general studies. **Holdings:** 104,720 books; 9533 bound periodical volumes; 2437 reels of microfilm. **Subscriptions:** 450 journals and other serials. **Services:** Interlibrary loan; copying; library open to the public for reference use only. **Automated Operations:** Computerized cataloging and circulation. **Computerized Information Services:** DIALOG Information Services, BRS Information Technologies, OCLC, Statewide Library Computer System (LCS). **Networks/Consortia:** Member of ILLINET. **Staff:** Wilma Lampman, Asst.Libn.; Roland Person, Asst.Libn.; Willie Scott, Asst.Libn..

★13473★
SOUTHERN ILLINOIS UNIVERSITY, EDWARDSVILLE - DOCUMENTS COLLECTION (Info Sci)
Lovejoy Library Phone: (618)692-2606
Edwardsville, IL 62026 Robert J. Fortado, Doc.Libn.
Staff: Prof 1; Other 1. **Holdings:** 500,000 U.S. Government documents. **Services:** Interlibrary loan; copying; collection open to the public. **Automated Operations:** Computerized cataloging and circulation. **Computerized Information Services:** OCLC, DIALOG Information Services; internal database.

★13474★
SOUTHERN ILLINOIS UNIVERSITY, EDWARDSVILLE - RESEARCH & PROJECTS OFFICE LIBRARY (Bus-Fin)
Graduate School
Box 1046 Phone: (618)692-3162
Edwardsville, IL 62026-1046 Sheila Lischwe, Rsrcs.Anl.
Founded: 1970. **Staff:** Prof 1. **Subjects:** Federal, state, and private grant support; federal legislation. **Holdings:** 15 VF drawers of federal and state program guidelines and applications; education directories; foundation annual reports; directories of federal and private grant support. **Subscriptions:** 20 newsletters. **Services:** Library open to the public for reference use only. **Computerized Information Services:** IRIS (Illinois Researcher Information System; internal database). Performs searches on fee basis. **Networks/Consortia:** Member of Illinois Resource Network. **Publications:** Research Highlights, monthly - to faculty and staff.

★13475★
SOUTHERN MAINE MEDICAL CENTER - HEALTH SCIENCES LIBRARY (Med)
1 Mountain Rd.
Box 626 Phone: (207)283-3663
Biddeford, ME 04005 Patricia Goodwin, Libn.
Staff: Prof 1. **Subjects:** Medicine and allied health sciences. **Holdings:** 500 books; 30 bound periodical volumes. **Subscriptions:** 90 journals and other serials. **Services:** Interlibrary loan; copying; SDI; library open to the public by appointment. **Computerized Information Services:** BRS Information Technologies, NLM. Performs searches on fee basis. **Networks/Consortia:** Member of Health Science Library and Information Cooperative of Maine (HSLIC).

★13476★
SOUTHERN MAINE VOCATIONAL TECHNICAL INSTITUTE - LIBRARY (Educ)
Fort Rd. Phone: (207)799-7303
South Portland, ME 04106 Donald A. Bertsch, Jr., Libn.
Staff: Prof 2; Other 1. **Subjects:** Electronics, marine science, building technology, culinary arts, plant and soil sciences, nursing and allied health sciences. **Holdings:** 15,000 books. **Subscriptions:** 350 journals and other serials; 10 newspapers. **Services:** Interlibrary loan; copying; SDI; library open to the public. **Computerized Information Services:** DIALOG Information Services. Performs searches on fee basis. **Networks/Consortia:** Member of Health Science Library and Information Cooperative of Maine (HSLIC).

★13477★
SOUTHERN METHODIST UNIVERSITY - BRIDWELL THEOLOGY LIBRARY - CENTER FOR METHODIST STUDIES
Dallas, TX 75275
Defunct. Holdings absorbed by Southern Methodist University - Perkins School of Theology - The Bridwell Library.

★13478★
SOUTHERN METHODIST UNIVERSITY - DE GOLYER LIBRARY - FIKES HALL OF SPECIAL COLLECTIONS (Hist, Trans)
Central University Libraries, SMU Sta. Phone: (214)692-3231
Dallas, TX 75275 David Farmer, Dir.
Founded: 1956. **Staff:** Prof 4; Other 5. **Subjects:** Western United States history, history of the Spanish borderlands, history of the American railroad, history and technology of transportation. **Special Collections:** E.L. DeGolyer, Sr. papers; Baldwin Locomotive Works papers; S.M. Vauclain papers; John Insley Blair papers; Texas and Pacific Railway papers; Muskogee Corporation papers. **Holdings:** 85,000 monographs; 5000 periodical volumes; 300,000 railroad photographs; 1500 cubic feet of manuscript and archival collections; 3000 reels of microfilm. **Subscriptions:** 400 journals and other serials. **Services:** Copying; collections open to the public. **Automated Operations:** Computerized cataloging, acquisitions, indexing, and processing of manuscripts and photographs. **Computerized Information Services:** OCLC; internal database. **Networks/Consortia:** Member of AMIGOS Bibliographic Council, Inc.. **Publications:** DeGolyer Library Publication Series, irregular; De Golyer Library Keepsake Series; occasional publications, irregular. **Special Catalogs:** Finding aids to processed manuscript, serial, photograph, and archival collections available; chronological file to all printed holdings. **Staff:** Michael Vinson, Ref.Libn.; Dawn Letson, Mss.Cur.; Jeanne Byron, Cat.Libn..

★13479★
SOUTHERN METHODIST UNIVERSITY - FINE ARTS LIBRARY (Art)
Owens Art Center Phone: (214)692-2796
Dallas, TX 75275 Kay Krochman Marks, Asst.Mus./Fine Arts Libn.
Staff: Prof 1. **Subjects:** Art history. **Special Collections:** Spanish art. **Holdings:** 16,953 books. **Services:** Interlibrary loan (limited); copying; library open to the public for reference use only.

★13480★
SOUTHERN METHODIST UNIVERSITY - FORT BURGWIN RESEARCH CENTER - LIBRARY & HERBARIUM
Box 300
Ranchos de Taos, NM 87557
Founded: 1957. **Subjects:** Anthropology, biology, ecology, geology, linguistics. **Special Collections:** Herbarium of flora of Carson National Forest; Pollen Reference Collection for modern and paleoenvironments; Taos and Llano Estacado. **Holdings:** 2500 books; 800 bound periodical volumes. **Remarks:** Presently inactive.

★13481★
SOUTHERN METHODIST UNIVERSITY - INSTITUTE FOR THE STUDY OF EARTH AND MAN (ISEM) - LIBRARY (Sci-Engr, Soc Sci)
Heroy Bldg. Phone: (214)692-2430
Dallas, TX 75275 John Phinney
Staff: 1. **Subjects:** Anthropology, geology, Texas archeology. **Special Collections:** Reprint files in archeology, anthropology, paleobotany. **Holdings:** 5000 books; 5000 bound periodical volumes; reels of microfilm. **Subscriptions:** 145 journals and other serials. **Services:** Interlibrary loan; copying (limited); library open to the public with restrictions.

★13482★
SOUTHERN METHODIST UNIVERSITY - MC CORD THEATER COLLECTION (Theater)
Fondren Library Phone: (214)692-2400
Dallas, TX 75275 Edyth Renshaw, Cur.
Staff: 1. **Subjects:** Theater, opera, vaudeville, cinema, dance, radio, television. **Special Collections:** Texas Theater; Dallas Little Theater; Arden Club Collection; Corsicana Opera House Collections (records and artifacts); Harriet Bacon McDonald Collection of photographs. **Holdings:**

Archival material, photographs, and clippings; theater and cinema realia. **Services:** Copying; collection open to the public by appointment. **Publications:** McCord Theater Collection (pamphlet).

★13483★
SOUTHERN METHODIST UNIVERSITY - MUSIC LIBRARY (Mus)
Owen Arts Center Phone: (214)692-2894
Dallas, TX 75275 Robert Skinner, Mus./Fine Arts Libn.
Founded: 1965. **Staff:** Prof 1; Other 1. **Subjects:** Music, music history. **Special Collections:** Van Katwijk Collection (3000 books, scores, manuscripts); Charles Wakefield Cadman correspondence (100 items); Ferde Grofe Library (2000 scores, manuscripts). **Holdings:** 30,000 books, scores, and bound periodical volumes; 15,000 audiotapes and phonograph records. **Subscriptions:** 125 journals and other serials. **Services:** Interlibrary loan; copying; library open to the public. **Computerized Information Services:** Internal database. **Networks/Consortia:** Member of AMIGOS Bibliographic Council, Inc.. **Publications:** Musicalia Nova (newsletter), irregular - available upon request.

★13484★
SOUTHERN METHODIST UNIVERSITY - PERKINS SCHOOL OF THEOLOGY - THE BRIDWELL LIBRARY (Rel-Phil)
Dallas, TX 75275 Phone: (214)692-3483
Dr. Robert Maloy, Libn.
Founded: 1915. **Staff:** Prof 5; Other 10. **Subjects:** Theology; Methodist Church in Texas, the United States and England; Methodist hymnology; Wesleyana; 18th century theological literature; Judaica; biblical archeology; early and fine printing. **Special Collections:** New Thought Archive; Levi Olan Collection of Fine Books; Robert and Lessie Curl Collection of New Testament Literature; Joseph Walker Elston III Collection of David Hume; Violet Hayden Joyce Collection; George Leinwall James Joyce Collection; Corey Collection; Thomas J. Harrison Bible Collection; Ferguson Collection of Texana and Americana; Laura and Carl Brannin Collection of Religion in Social Action; Selecman Savonarola Collection; Margaret Bridwell Bowdle Collection of Fifteenth Century Printing; Bridwell-DeBellis Collection of Fifteenth Century Printing; Steindorff Collection of Egyptology; William Perry Bentley Collection (psychical research, parapsychology, and cognate subjects); Archives of the Perkins School of Theology (60 boxes); Methodist manuscripts collection (640 boxes). **Holdings:** 188,045 books; 29,045 bound periodical volumes; 3472 reels of microfilm; 79,139 microfiche. **Subscriptions:** 832 journals and other serials. **Services:** Interlibrary loan; copying; library use restricted to registered users. **Automated Operations:** Computerized public access catalog, cataloging, acquisitions, and ILL. **Computerized Information Services:** OCLC. **Networks/Consortia:** Member of AMIGOS Bibliographic Council, Inc.. **Staff:** Roger L. Loyd, Assoc.Libn.; Page A. Thomas, Cat.; Laura H. Randall, Ref.; Ellen L Frost, Acq.; Lillie R. Jenkins-Carter, ILL.

★13485★
SOUTHERN METHODIST UNIVERSITY - SCIENCE/ ENGINEERING LIBRARY (Biol Sci, Sci-Engr)
Dallas, TX 75275 Phone: (214)692-2276
Devertt D. Bickston, Libn.
Founded: 1961. **Staff:** Prof 5; Other 7. **Subjects:** Biology, botany, chemistry, engineering, geology, mathematics, physics, statistics. **Special Collections:** E. DeGolyer Collection (petroleum, history of geology, guide books); Edwin Foscue Map Library; SMU Herbarium with Lloyd Shinners Collection of Taxonomic Botany. **Holdings:** 187,451 books; 78,696 bound periodical volumes; 250,519 government documents; 190,763 maps. **Subscriptions:** 1648 journals and other serials. **Services:** Interlibrary loan; copying; library open to the public. **Computerized Information Services:** DIALOG Information Services, Pergamon ORBIT InfoLine, Inc., BRS Information Technologies. Performs searches on fee basis. **Networks/ Consortia:** Member of Association for Higher Education of North Texas (AHE). **Remarks:** Business and industrial special libraries should contact Industrial Information Services at 692-2271 for service. **Staff:** Jim Stephens, Ref.Libn.; Sandra Setnick, Ref.Libn.; Mary Ellen Batchelor, Ref.Libn.; Linda Samuels, Ref.Libn..

★13486★
SOUTHERN METHODIST UNIVERSITY - UNDERWOOD LAW LIBRARY (Law)
Dallas, TX 75275-0354 Phone: (214)692-3258
Earl C. Borgeson, Dir.
Staff: Prof 10; Other 13. **Subjects:** International law and business, commercial transactions, corporations, securities, taxation, jurisprudence, oil and gas. **Holdings:** 350,000 volumes. **Subscriptions:** 5027 journals and other serials. **Services:** Interlibrary loan; copying. **Automated Operations:** Computerized cataloging. **Computerized Information Services:** LEXIS, WESTLAW, DIALOG Information Services, NEXIS, VU/TEXT Information Services, PHINet FedTax Database. **Networks/Consortia:** Member of AMIGOS Bibliographic Council, Inc.. **Staff:** Ora E. Addis, Assoc.Dir.; L. Kurt Adamson, Assoc.Dir., Coll.Dev.; Dolores Stewart, Acq.Mgr.; Joan Englander, Sr.Cat.; Sue Wright, Cat.; Bruce Muck, Sr.Ref.Libn.; Kenneth Chadwick, Sr.Ref.Libn.; Kimberly Tolman, Sr.Ref.Libn.; Winston Tubb, Coll.Mgr..

★13487★
SOUTHERN MINNESOTA HISTORICAL CENTER - LIBRARY (Hist)
Mankato State University Phone: (507)389-1029
Mankato, MN 56001 Dr. William E. Lass, Dir.
Founded: 1969. **Staff:** 1. **Subjects:** Mankato civic affairs, Minnesota politics and government, business, education in Southern Minnesota. **Special Collections:** Mankato State University archives; necrology file; H.H. King Flour Mills Company records; Mankato YWCA records. **Holdings:** 1500 linear feet of local history materials and university archives; oral history cassettes; microfilm. **Services:** Copying; library open to the public. **Remarks:** Maintained by Mankato State University.

★13488★
SOUTHERN NEW ENGLAND TELEPHONE COMPANY - BUSINESS RESEARCH LIBRARY
227 Church St., 7th Fl.
New Haven, CT 06506
Defunct

★13489★
SOUTHERN NEW ENGLAND TELEPHONE COMPANY - NETWORK TECHNOLOGY LIBRARY (Comp Sci)
555 Long Wharf Dr., 3rd Fl. Phone: (203)553-6238
New Haven, CT 06511 Monica Denman, Libn.
Founded: 1984. **Staff:** Prof 1; Other 3. **Subjects:** Electronics, computer science, telecommunications, management, fiber optics, engineering. **Special Collections:** Telecommunications documents. **Holdings:** 2400 books; 200 bound periodical volumes; 3000 unbound materials; 40,000 microcards; 2000 microfiche; 5 videotapes. **Subscriptions:** 100 journals and other serials; 5 newspapers. **Services:** Interlibrary loan; library not open to the public. **Automated Operations:** Computerized cataloging and circulation. **Computerized Information Services:** DIALOG Information Services, NewsNet, Inc.; FOCUS (internal database). **Networks/Consortia:** Member of Southern Connecticut Library Council (SCLC). **Special Catalogs:** Book, document, and periodical lists. **Special Indexes:** Documents Index. **Formerly:** ITT Advanced Technology Center - Library.

★13490★
SOUTHERN OHIO COLLEGE, NORTHEAST CAMPUS - LIBRARY (Educ)
2791 Mogadore Rd. Phone: (216)733-8766
Akron, OH 44312 Kathryn M. Paine, Libn.
Staff: 1. **Subjects:** Business administration, economics, accounting, business law, medicine, computers, secretarial science, travel, real estate. **Holdings:** 2970 books; 1984-1985 Official Airline Guide publications. **Subscriptions:** 61 journals and other serials. **Services:** Library open to the public for reference use only. **Networks/Consortia:** Member of North Central Library Cooperative (NCLC).

★13491★
SOUTHERN OHIO GENEALOGICAL SOCIETY - REFERENCE LIBRARY (Hist)
Southern State Community College Learning Center
100 Hobart Dr.
Box 414
Hillsboro, OH 45133
Founded: 1978. **Staff:** Prof 1; Other 10. **Subjects:** Genealogy, local history. **Special Collections:** Jewish genealogical records; International Genealogical Index on microfiche (65 million names and accompanying information). **Holdings:** 1200 books; 250 bound periodical volumes; 100 family files; 250 reels of microfilm of Highland County records from Probate Court, Clerk of Courts, and Recorder's Office, 1805 to present; 85 family history files; 3700 burial records of veterans buried in Highland County, OH; 83 volumes of published family histories; 75 family history manuscripts; census maps; passenger and immigration records. **Services:** Copying; library open to the public with restrictions. **Publications:** Roots & Shoots, quarterly. **Special Indexes:** Surname/Locality Index, annual; Surname Index (card); Family File Index (card). **Remarks:** The society acts as a clearinghouse for local and out-of-state patrons in finding and establishing their genealogical lines.

★13492★
SOUTHERN OREGON HISTORICAL SOCIETY - RESEARCH LIBRARY (Hist)
206 N. 5th St.
Box 480 Phone: (503)899-1847
Jacksonville, OR 97530 Paul A. Richardson, Libn./Archv.
Staff: Prof 1; Other 2. **Subjects:** Jackson County and southern Oregon history, historic preservation, museum techniques. **Special Collections:** Peter Britt photographic collection and work of other photographers (30,000 photographs dealing with southern Oregon subjects). **Holdings:** 3100 books; 100 bound periodical volumes; 460 manuscript collections; 240 oral histories. **Subscriptions:** 55 journals and other serials; 8 newspapers. **Services:** Interlibrary loan (limited); copying; library open to the public. **Special Catalogs:** Preliminary Guide to Local History Materials, 1978 (booklet).

★13493★
SOUTHERN OREGON STATE COLLEGE - LIBRARY (Educ)
1250 Siskiyou Blvd. Phone: (503)482-6445
Ashland, OR 97520 Sue A. Burkholder, Lib.Dir.
Founded: 1926. **Staff:** Prof 10; Other 15. **Subjects:** Liberal arts, education, business. **Special Collections:** Margery Bailey Renaissance Collection (6000 volumes); Southern Oregon History (1120 volumes). **Holdings:** 230,000 books and bound periodical volumes; 25,000 maps; 2800 photographs and pamphlets; 195,000 state and federal government documents; 523,000 microforms. **Subscriptions:** 1850 journals and other serials; 30 newspapers. **Services:** Interlibrary loan; copying; library open to the public. **Automated Operations:** Computerized cataloging. **Computerized Information Services:** OCLC, DIALOG Information Services, WILSONLINE, BRS Information Technologies; OnTyme Electronic Message Network Service (electronic mail service). Performs searches on fee basis. Contact Person: Ruth Monical, 482-6441. **Networks/Consortia:** Member of Southern Oregon Library Federation (SOLF). **Publications:** Bibliography series, irregular; list of serials, annual. **Special Indexes:** Index to Ashland Daily Tidings, 1958 to present. **Staff:** Deborah Hollens; Harold Otness; David Russell; Richard Moore; Timothy Shove; James Rible; Ruth Monical.

★13494★
SOUTHERN POVERTY LAW CENTER - KLANWATCH - LIBRARY (Soc Sci)
Box 2087 Phone: (205)264-0286
Montgomery, AL 36102 Patricia Clark, Dir.
Founded: 1980. **Staff:** 5. **Subjects:** Ku Klux Klan, neo-Nazi organizations, other right-wing extremists, anti-KKK information. **Holdings:** 50 books; 100 legal documents; 10,000 news clippings; 50 audio- and videotapes; 1000 letters. **Subscriptions:** 30 journals and other serials. **Services:** Copying; library open to the public with restrictions. **Publications:** Klanwatch Intelligence Report, bimonthly - for internal distribution only; Klanwatch Law Report; The Ku Klux Klan: A History of Racism and Violence.

SOUTHERN RAILWAY PREDECESSORS ARCHIVE
See: Virginia Polytechnic Institute and State University - Carol M. Newman Library (17365)

★13495★
SOUTHERN REGIONAL COUNCIL, INC. - REFERENCE LIBRARY (Soc Sci)
60 Walton St., N.W., 2nd Fl. Phone: (404)522-8764
Atlanta, GA 30303-2199 Stephen T. Suitts, Exec.Dir.
Subjects: Civil rights, civil liberties, politics, suffrage. **Holdings:** 1200 books; civil rights movement newspaper collection on microfilm; newsclip collection, 1946-1975; special studies. **Services:** Copying; library open to the public with restrictions. **Publications:** Southern Changes, bimonthly - by subscription; Special Reports and Studies.

★13496★
SOUTHERN REGIONAL EDUCATION BOARD - LIBRARY (Educ)
592 10th St., N.W. Phone: (404)875-9211
Atlanta, GA 30318-5790 Leon Benham, Res.Asst./Libn.
Founded: 1949. **Staff:** Prof 1. **Subjects:** Higher education in the South, southern education, mental health, computer science, nursing, medical education. **Holdings:** 10,000 books; 4 VF drawers of pamphlets; 15 linear feet of college catalogs; 22 drawers of documents on microfiche. **Subscriptions:** 50 journals and other serials.

★13497★
SOUTHERN RESEARCH INSTITUTE - THOMAS W. MARTIN MEMORIAL LIBRARY (Sci-Engr, Energy, Biol Sci)
2000 Ninth Ave., S.
Box 55305 Phone: (205)323-6592
Birmingham, AL 35255-5305 Mary L. Pullen, Lib.Mgr.
Founded: 1945. **Staff:** Prof 2; Other 3. **Subjects:** Chemistry, biology, biomaterials, genetics, virology, microbiology, engineering, energy, pollution, metallurgy, physics. **Holdings:** 13,000 books; 33,000 bound periodical volumes. **Subscriptions:** 800 journals and other serials. **Services:** Interlibrary loan; copying; library open to qualified users. **Staff:** Mary W. White, Doc.Libn.; Richard Remy, Info.Sci..

★13498★
SOUTHERN STATES ENERGY BOARD (SSEB) - SOUTHERN ENERGY/ENVIRONMENTAL INFORMATION CENTER (SEEIC) (Energy)
3091 Governors Lakes Dr., Suite 400 Phone: (404)242-7712
Norcross, GA 30071-1113 Nancy E. Kaiser, Mgr., Info.Serv.
Staff: Prof 1; Other 2. **Subjects:** Energy, environment, energy policy and development. **Holdings:** 110 books; 2000 technical reports; 200 state publications; 20 VF drawers. **Subscriptions:** 199 journals and other serials. **Services:** Interlibrary loan; copying (limited); center open to the public by appointment. **Computerized Information Services:** DIALOG Information Services, Integrated Technical Information System (ITIS). **Publications:** Southern Sources, monthly - to state officials, legislators, association members, and by subscription.

★13499★
SOUTHERN UNION COMPANY - LAW LIBRARY (Law)
Renaissance Tower, Suite 1800 Phone: (214)748-8511
Dallas, TX 75270 Bruce Henderson, Asst.Gen.Couns.
Staff: Prof 2; Other 3. **Subjects:** Law. **Holdings:** 5920 books. **Subscriptions:** 10 journals and other serials. **Services:** Interlibrary loan; library not open to the public.

★13500★
SOUTHERN UNIVERSITY - LAW CENTER - LIBRARY (Law)
Southern Branch Post Office Phone: (504)771-4900
Baton Rouge, LA 70813 Melbarose H. Manuel, Law Libn.
Founded: 1947. **Staff:** Prof 5; Other 6. **Subjects:** Law, political science, public policy, civil rights, criminal procedure, international law. **Special Collections:** U.S. Government and state of Louisiana documents depository; civil rights; civil liberties; computer-aided legal research; international law. **Holdings:** 226,352 volumes; 20,500 bound periodical volumes; 76,699 volumes of microfilm; 12 VF drawers. **Subscriptions:** 500 journals and other serials; 11 newspapers. **Services:** Interlibrary loan; copying; library open to the public with special permission from the library director. **Automated Operations:** Computerized cataloging. **Computerized Information Services:** OCLC, WESTLAW; internal database. **Networks/Consortia:** Member of SOLINET. **Publications:** Periodical list; acquisitions list, bimonthly; subject bibliography. **Staff:** Roberta S. Cummings, Asst.Libn.; Harold Isadore, Assoc.Libn.; Clarence T. Nalls, Asst.Libn.; Alvin Roche, Assoc.Libn..

★13501★
SOUTHERN UTAH STATE COLLEGE - LIBRARY - SPECIAL COLLECTIONS DEPARTMENT (Hist, Hum)
300 W. Center St. Phone: (801)586-7945
Cedar City, UT 84720 Blanche C. Clegg, Spec.Coll.Coord.
Founded: 1962. **Staff:** Prof 1; Other 2. **Subjects:** Southern Paiute Indians history, local history, college history, Shakespeare. **Special Collections:** William Rees Palmer Western History Collection; Gladys McConnell Collection; Rhoda M. Wood Collection; E.D. Woolley Collection; Amasa Redd Collection; Alva and Zella Matheson Collection; Belle Armstrong Collection; John Laurence Seymour Collection (music, theater, humanities). **Holdings:** 7000 volumes; 925 oral history tapes; 457 phonograph records; 1445 linear feet of manuscript collections; 11,200 photographs and negatives; 3068 pamphlets; 804 linear feet of archives; 3250 microforms. **Subscriptions:** 13 journals and other serials. **Services:** Interlibrary loan; copying; department open to the public for reference use only. **Automated Operations:** Computerized cataloging. **Computerized Information Services:** DIALOG Information Services; internal database. **Networks/Consortia:** Member of Utah College Library Council. **Special Indexes:** Index of library's holdings on women; index of library's holdings of Latter-Day Saints periodicals; index to Palmer Western History Collection.

★13502★
SOUTHERN WISCONSIN CENTER FOR THE DEVELOPMENTALLY DISABLED - MEDICAL STAFF LIBRARY (Med)
21425 Spring St. Phone: (414)878-2411
Union Grove, WI 53182-9708 Margaret A. Basley, Med.Sec.
Founded: 1965. **Staff:** 1. **Subjects:** Medicine, mental retardation, medical specialties, current therapy, syndromes, malformations. **Holdings:** 124 books; 260 Audio-Digest tapes; statistical reports. **Subscriptions:** 15 journals and other serials. **Services:** Library not open to the public.

★13503★
SOUTHERN WISCONSIN CENTER FOR THE DEVELOPMENTALLY DISABLED - NURSING EDUCATION LIBRARY† (Med)
21425 Spring St.
Union Grove, WI 53182-9708 Phone: (414)878-2411
Subjects: Nursing, pharmacology, nutrition, mental retardation. **Holdings:** Figures not available for books; AV programs. **Services:** Interlibrary loan (limited); library not open to the public.

SOUTHERN WOMEN'S ARCHIVES
See: Birmingham Public and Jefferson County Free Library - Linn-Henley Library for Southern Historical Research - Department of Archives and Manuscripts (1613)

★13504★
SOUTHFIELD PUBLIC LIBRARY - SPECIAL COLLECTIONS (Bus-Fin, Hum)
26000 Evergreen Rd.
Box 2055 Phone: (313)354-9100
Southfield, MI 48037-2055 Douglas A. Zyskowski, City Libn.
Founded: 1960. **Special Collections:** Business Collection; Census Affiliate Collection; Shakespeare Collection. **Services:** Interlibrary loan; copying; collections open to the public. **Automated Operations:** Computerized circulation. **Computerized Information Services:** DIALOG Information Services, Dow Jones News/Retrieval, WESTLAW, VU/TEXT Information Services, National Planning Data Corporation (NPDC), Information Access Company (IAC), Huttonline; L.G.F.S. (internal database). Performs searches on fee basis. Contact Person: June Hund, Coord., Sup.Serv.. **Networks/Consortia:** Member of Wayne/Oakland Library Federation (WOLF). **Staff:** Paul Deane, Coord., Adult Pub.Serv.; Carol Mueller, Dp. City Libn.; Irene Smeyers, Coord., Ch.Serv..

★13505★
SOUTHLAND CORPORATION - CORPORATE BUSINESS RESEARCH CENTER
2828 N. Haskell
Dallas, TX 75204
Defunct

★13506★
SOUTHOLD HISTORICAL SOCIETY MUSEUM - LIBRARY (Hist)
Main Rd. & Maple Ln. Phone: (516)765-5500
Southold, NY 11971 George D. Wagoner, Dir.
Founded: 1960. **Subjects:** Local and state history, local fishing and farming, early textbooks, decorative arts, local cabinet makers. **Special Collections:** Early and local music; doll collection; unique doll house from 1903. **Holdings:** 3000 books; diaries. **Services:** Library open to the public by appointment. **Publications:** Newsletter, annual.

★13507★
SOUTHSIDE HOSPITAL - MEDICAL LIBRARY (Med)
Montauk Hwy. Phone: (516)968-3026
Bay Shore, NY 11706 Jane Travers, Med.Libn.
Founded: 1955. **Staff:** Prof 1. **Subjects:** Family practice, internal medicine, surgery, nursing, dentistry, psychiatry. **Special Collections:** Family practice collections; dental collections. **Holdings:** 700 books; 100 bound periodical volumes; 5 VF drawers of pamphlets; 150 audio cassette programs. **Subscriptions:** 150 journals and other serials; 10 newspapers. **Services:** Interlibrary loan; library not open to the public. **Automated Operations:** Computerized cataloging. **Computerized Information Services:** MEDLINE. Performs searches on fee basis. **Networks/Consortia:** Member of Greater Northeastern Regional Medical Library Program, Medical & Scientific Libraries of Long Island (MEDLI), Brooklyn-Queens-Staten Island Health Sciences Librarians (BQSI), Long Island Library Resources Council, Inc. (LILRC).

★13508★
SOUTHWEST ARKANSAS REGIONAL ARCHIVES (SARA) (Hist)
Box 134 Phone: (501)983-2633
Washington, AR 71862 Mary Medearis, Dir.
Founded: 1978. **Staff:** Prof 1. **Subjects:** History of Southwest Arkansas, Caddo Indians. **Special Collections:** Rare books collection on Southwest Arkansas and Texas; Dawson Collection (research on Nicholas Trammel and Trammel's Trace); Claud Garner Collection (first editions and manuscripts); census and court records for twelve southwest Arkansas counties; newspapers of southwest Arkansas; index and service records for Civil War soldiers who served in Arkansas units. **Holdings:** 1500 books; 3000 reels of microfilm; original court records of Hempstead County, 1819-1910; pictures; manuscripts; family histories; theses; sheet music; newspapers; maps; pamphlets; journals; genealogical records. **Services:** Copying; archives open to the public. **Publications:** SARA Newsletter, quarterly.

★13509★
SOUTHWEST FLORIDA WATER MANAGEMENT DISTRICT - LIBRARY (Env-Cons, Plan)
2379 Broad St. Phone: (904)796-7211
Brooksville, FL 34609 Charles Tornabene, Jr., Libn.
Founded: 1961. **Staff:** Prof 1; Other 1. **Subjects:** Water resources, urban planning, ecology, engineering. **Holdings:** 10,000 books. **Subscriptions:** 50 journals and other serials. **Services:** Copying; library open to the public for reference use only. **Automated Operations:** Computerized cataloging. **Computerized Information Services:** DIALOG Information Services. **Publications:** Basin Literature Assessments, annual. **Formerly:** Florida State Southwest Florida Management District.

★13510★
SOUTHWEST FOUNDATION FOR BIOMEDICAL RESEARCH - PRESTON G. NORTHROP MEMORIAL LIBRARY (Biol Sci, Med)
Box 28147 Phone: (512)674-1410
San Antonio, TX 78284 Maureen D. Funnell, Libn.
Founded: 1959. **Staff:** Prof 3; Other 1. **Subjects:** Biomedicine. **Special Collections:** Primatology. **Holdings:** 8600 books; 38,000 bound periodical volumes. **Subscriptions:** 772 journals and other serials. **Services:** Interlibrary loan; copying; library open to the public. **Automated Operations:** Computerized cataloging, acquisitions, serials, and circulation. **Computerized Information Services:** DIALOG Information Services, Pergamon ORBIT InfoLine, Inc., MEDLARS, CAS ONLINE. **Networks/Consortia:** Member of AMIGOS Bibliographic Council, Inc., Council of Research & Academic Libraries (CORAL), Health Oriented Libraries of San Antonio (HOLSA). **Staff:** Ruth H. Brooks, Asst.Libn.; Mary Ann Smith, ILL.

★13511★
SOUTHWEST MINNESOTA HISTORICAL CENTER - LIBRARY (Hist)
Southwest State University Phone: (507)537-7373
Marshall, MN 56258 Joseph Amato, Dir.
Founded: 1972. **Staff:** Prof 1; Other 4. **Subjects:** Local history, church histories, Iceland, agricultural history, genealogy. **Special Collections:** Minnesota Farm Holiday Association (tapes); Globe Land and Loan Company records; Verzlunarfelag Islendinga records; regional newspapers. **Holdings:** 150 books; records; 200 oral history interviews. **Services:** Interlibrary loan; copying; library open to the public on a varying schedule. **Remarks:** Maintained by Southwest State University.

★13512★
SOUTHWEST MISSOURI STATE UNIVERSITY - MAP COLLECTION (Geog-Map)
Duane G. Meyer Library
Box 175 Phone: (417)836-4534
Springfield, MO 65804-0095 James A. Coombs, Map Libn.
Founded: 1980. **Staff:** Prof 1; Other 2. **Subjects:** Cartography, outdoor recreation. **Special Collections:** Tourist information (5000 items); pre-1920 U.S. Geological Survey topographic quadrangles; U.S. Geological Survey Geologic Atlas of the United States (221 volumes). **Holdings:** 180 books; 114,000 maps; 52,399 aerial photographs; 1102 atlases; 6 globes; 9 raised relief maps; 265 microforms; 46 gazetteers. **Subscriptions:** 18 journals and other serials. **Services:** Interlibrary loan; copying; collection open to the public. **Automated Operations:** Computerized public access catalog and cataloging. **Special Indexes:** Indexes to U.S. Geological Survey geologic atlases and to small- and medium-scale geologic maps in U.S.

★13513★
SOUTHWEST MUSEUM - BRAUN RESEARCH LIBRARY (Hist)
Box 128 Phone: (213)221-2164
Los Angeles, CA 90042 Daniela Moneta, Hd.Libn.
Founded: 1907. **Staff:** Prof 4; Other 4. **Subjects:** Anthropology, Native American studies, western history. **Special Collections:** Munk Library of Arizoniana; Hector Alliott Memorial Library of Archaeology; Charles F. Lummis Collection; George Wharton James Collection; papers of Frank Hamilton Cushing, John Charles Fremont, George Bird Grinnell, Frederick Webb Hodge, Charles F. Lummis; rare Western American imprints; children's books; fine printing. **Holdings:** 50,000 volumes; 100,000 pamphlets and ephemera; 150,000 photographs; 700 linear feet of manuscripts; sound archives; government publications; VF drawers. **Subscriptions:** 300 journals and other serials; 15 newspapers. **Services:** Library open to the public. **Automated Operations:** Computerized public access catalog and cataloging. **Computerized Information Services:** OCLC; ARGUS (internal database). Performs searches free of charge. Contact Person: Richard Buchen, Ref.Libn.. **Remarks:** Library located at 234 Museum Dr., Los Angeles, CA 90065. **Staff:** Kenneth Bicknell, Cat.; Craig Klyver, Photo Archv..

SOUTHWEST MUSEUM OF SCIENCE AND TECHNOLOGY
See: The Science Place (12992)

★13514★
SOUTHWEST RAILROAD HISTORICAL SOCIETY - AGE OF STEAM MUSEUM - LIBRARY (Hist)
Box 26369 Phone: (214)421-8754
Dallas, TX 75226 Steven C. Longley, Exec.Dir
Founded: 1963. **Subjects:** Railroad history. **Holdings:** 200 books; 200 bound periodical volumes. **Services:** Library open to the public with restrictions. **Publications:** Clearance Card (newsletter), bimonthly - available on request. **Remarks:** Library located at Washington & Parry Ave., Dallas, TX 75226.

★13515★
SOUTHWEST REGIONAL LABORATORY FOR EDUCATIONAL RESEARCH AND DEVELOPMENT - LIBRARY
4665 Lampson Ave.
Los Alamitos, CA 90720
Subjects: Education, psychology, linguistics, computer sciences, music, art. **Holdings:** 5500 books; 819 bound periodical volumes; 1675 other cataloged items; 2 million archives; 70,000 ERIC microfiche; 1800 items in Curriculum Library; 250 items in Juvenile Library; 93 VF drawers of pamphlets and miscellaneous information. **Remarks:** Presently inactive. **Also Known As:** SWRL.

★13516★
SOUTHWEST RESEARCH & INFORMATION CENTER (Soc Sci, Env-Cons)
Box 4524 Phone: (505)262-1862
Albuquerque, NM 87106 Don Hancock, Info.Coord.
Founded: 1971. **Staff:** Prof 2; Other 1. **Subjects:** Environmental, consumer, and social issues. **Special Collections:** Uranium publications and clippings (3000 items); nuclear waste management publications and clippings. **Holdings:** 3000 books; 7 cabinets of clippings in 1000 categories; 100 sourcebooks. **Subscriptions:** 350 journals and other serials; 15 newspapers. **Services:** Copying; center open to the public for reference use only. **Publications:** The Workbook, quarterly; Nuclear Waste News (newsletter), bimonthly.

★13517★
SOUTHWEST RESEARCH INSTITUTE - NONDESTRUCTIVE TESTING INFORMATION ANALYSIS CENTER (Sci-Engr)
Drawer 28510 Phone: (512)522-2737
San Antonio, TX 78284 Dr. George A. Matzkanin, Dir.
Founded: 1974. **Staff:** Prof 2; Other 2. **Subjects:** Nondestructive testing, inspection, and evaluation; quality control; inspection using liquid penetrants; radiography; electricity and magnetism; ultrasonics; heat; optical-visual devices; audible-sonic devices. **Special Collections:** Series of abstracts devoted to nondestructive evaluation. **Holdings:** 37,000 reports and journals. **Services:** Rapid response literature searching; consultation; SDI; center open to U.S. citizens. **Computerized Information Services:** DIALOG Information Services, DTIC, Pergamon ORBIT InfoLine, Inc.; NTIAC (internal database). Performs searches on fee basis. Contact Person: Frances P. Hicks, Info.Anl., 522-2362. **Publications:** Quarterly newsletter; list of additional publications - available on request. **Remarks:** Center is an official DOD Information Analysis Center. Operated by SWRI for the U.S. Department of Defense under technical cognizance of the Under Secretary of Defense for Research and Engineering. Sponsors a biennial symposium on nondestructive evaluation.

★13518★
SOUTHWEST RESEARCH INSTITUTE - THOMAS BAKER SLICK MEMORIAL LIBRARY (Sci-Engr)
Drawer 28510 Phone: (512)684-5111
San Antonio, TX 78284 Robert D. Armor, Libn.
Founded: 1948. **Staff:** Prof 3; Other 5. **Subjects:** Engineering - chemical, electrical, mechanical, aeronautical; chemistry; geology; physics; mathematics. **Holdings:** 41,840 books; 14,356 bound periodical volumes; 26,480 unbound periodicals; 85,000 reports on microfiche. **Subscriptions:** 1441 journals and other serials. **Services:** Interlibrary loan; copying; library open to the public for reference use only. **Computerized Information Services:** DIALOG Information Services, Pergamon ORBIT InfoLine, Inc. **Networks/Consortia:** Member of Council of Research & Academic Libraries (CORAL), Health Oriented Libraries of San Antonio (HOLSA). **Staff:** Oralia R. Ruiz, Assoc.Libn.; Anita Lang, Asst.Libn..

SOUTHWEST STATE UNIVERSITY - SOUTHWEST MINNESOTA HISTORICAL CENTER
See: Southwest Minnesota Historical Center (13511)

★13519★
SOUTHWEST TEXAS METHODIST HOSPITAL - LIBRARY (Med)
7700 Floyd Curl Dr. Phone: (512)692-4583
San Antonio, TX 78229 Christy Floerke, Libn.
Staff: Prof 1. **Subjects:** Medicine, nursing. **Holdings:** 1275 books; 195 bound periodical volumes. **Subscriptions:** 91 journals and other serials. **Services:** Interlibrary loan; copying; library open to the public with restrictions. **Computerized Information Services:** MEDLINE. **Networks/Consortia:** Member of Health Oriented Libraries of San Antonio (HOLSA).

SOUTHWEST WASHINGTON HOSPITALS - ST. JOSEPH COMMUNITY HOSPITAL
See: St. Joseph Community Hospital (12447)

SOUTHWEST WASHINGTON HOSPITALS - VANCOUVER MEMORIAL HOSPITAL
See: Vancouver Memorial Hospital (17264)

★13520★
SOUTHWEST WISCONSIN VOCATIONAL-TECHNICAL INSTITUTE - LEARNING RESOURCES CENTER (Bus-Fin, Sci-Engr)
Bronson Blvd.
Rte. 1, Box 500 Phone: (608)822-3262
Fennimore, WI 53809 Patricia Payson, Libn.
Founded: 1971. **Staff:** Prof 1; Other 3. **Subjects:** Business education, agriculture, automotive mechanics, home economics, health occupations, technical and industrial occupations. **Holdings:** 28,000 books; 2500 AV programs; 18 drawers of pamphlets; 1147 microforms. **Subscriptions:** 250 journals and other serials. **Services:** Interlibrary loan; copying; center open to the public.

★13521★
SOUTHWESTERN ASSEMBLIES OF GOD COLLEGE - P.C. NELSON MEMORIAL LIBRARY (Rel-Phil)
1200 Sycamore Phone: (214)937-4010
Waxahachie, TX 75165 Mr. Murl M. Winters, Dir.
Founded: 1927. **Staff:** Prof 2; Other 2. **Subjects:** Bible, liberal arts, education. **Special Collections:** Pentecostal Materials Collection (1794 volumes); William Burton McCafferty Pentecostal Periodical Collection (4 cabinets; 20 cubic feet). **Holdings:** 74,090 books; 6091 bound periodical volumes; 9804 pamphlets; 615 flannelgraphs; 924 tapes; 1466 slides; 132 maps; 1360 phonograph records; 790 filmstrips; 873 reels of microfilm; 19,129 microfiche; 1511 directories and catalogs; 235 documents; 1649 ultrafiche; 56 puppets. **Subscriptions:** 617 journals and other serials. **Services:** Interlibrary loan; copying; library open to the public on fee basis. **Special Indexes:** Index to Pentecostal Evangel, 1920, 1924, 1926, 1927, 1930-1961 (card); index to Pentecost Magazine (card); index to Church of God Evangel (card; in preparation); index to Christ's Ambassadors Herald (card; in preparation); index to Missionary Challenge (card; in preparation); index to Pentecostal Holiness Advocate (card; in preparation). **Staff:** Pearl Ellis, Asst.Dir..

★13522★
SOUTHWESTERN BAPTIST THEOLOGICAL SEMINARY - A. WEBB ROBERTS LIBRARY (Rel-Phil)
Box 22000-2E Phone: (817)923-1921
Fort Worth, TX 76122 Dr. Carl R. Wrotenbery, Dir. of Libs.
Founded: 1909. **Staff:** Prof 9; Other 42. **Subjects:** Religion and theology, Bible, music and hymnology, Baptist history, religious education. **Special Collections:** Personal items and correspondence of B.H. Carroll, L.R. Scarborough, George W. Truett, M.E. Dodd, James M. Carroll (Baptist leaders); Texas Baptist Historical Collection (63,737 items). **Holdings:** 258,251 books; 27,149 bound periodical volumes; 49,844 convention and association annuals; 153,337 pieces of printed music; 23,088 tapes and discs; 3313 films and filmstrips; 1906 videotapes; 234 VF drawers of manuscripts; church minutes and histories. **Subscriptions:** 2002 journals and other serials. **Services:** Interlibrary loan; copying; SDI; library open to the public. **Automated Operations:** Computerized cataloging, acquisitions and circulation. **Computerized Information Services:** OCLC, BRS Information Technologies, WILSONLINE. Performs searches on fee basis. Contact Person: Robert Phillips, Asst.Dir./Pub.Serv., 294-7142. **Networks/Consortia:** Member of AMIGOS Bibliographic Council, Inc.. **Publications:** New Titles Added, monthly. **Special Indexes:** Baptist biography index (card). **Staff:** Phil Sims, Music Libn.; Carol Bastien, Acq.Libn.; Lori Robertson, Circ.Libn.; Bob Trimble, AV Libn.; Steve Story, Media Coord.; Barbara Russell, Cat.Libn.; Ben Rogers, Archv.; Myrta Garrett, Asst.Dir./Tech.Serv.; Kellie Glass, Ser.Libn..

★13523★
SOUTHWESTERN BAPTIST THEOLOGICAL SEMINARY - HISPANIC BAPTIST THEOLOGICAL SEMINARY - LIBRARY (Rel-Phil)
8019 S. Pan Am Expy. Phone: (512)924-4338
San Antonio, TX 78224-1397 James O. Wallace, Dir.
Founded: 1956. **Staff:** Prof 1; Other 2. **Subjects:** Theology, Baptist history. **Holdings:** 15,632 books; 1425 bound periodical volumes. **Subscriptions:** 202 journals and other serials. **Services:** Interlibrary loan; copying; library open to seminary students. **Automated Operations:** Computerized cataloging.

★13524★
SOUTHWESTERN CONSERVATIVE BAPTIST BIBLE COLLEGE - DR. R.S. BEAL, SR. LIBRARY (Rel-Phil)
2625 E. Cactus Rd. Phone: (602)992-6101
Phoenix, AZ 85032 Alice Eickmeyer, Libn.
Founded: 1960. **Staff:** Prof 1; Other 1. **Subjects:** Bible, theology, missions, Christian education, elementary education. **Holdings:** 23,307 books; 1365 bound periodical volumes; 19,432 microforms; 1260 AV programs; 39 scores; 415 teaching aids. **Subscriptions:** 113 journals and other serials. **Services:** Interlibrary loan; copying; library open to the public with restrictions on circulation.

★13525★
SOUTHWESTERN ILLINOIS METROPOLITAN AND REGIONAL PLANNING COMMISSION - TECHNICAL LIBRARY (Plan)
203 W. Main St. Phone: (618)344-4250
Collinsville, IL 62234 Bonnie C. Moore, Info.Mgr.
Founded: 1965. **Staff:** Prof 1. **Subjects:** Urban and regional planning, census data, legislation, codes and ordinances, transportation, recreation, water and sewage. **Holdings:** 4000 volumes. **Subscriptions:** 65 journals and other serials. **Services:** Interlibrary loan; copying; library open to the public.

SOUTHWESTERN INDIAN POLYTECHNIC INSTITUTE
See: U.S. Bureau of Indian Affairs (14883)

★13526★
SOUTHWESTERN INDIANA MENTAL HEALTH CENTER, INC. - LIBRARY (Med)
415 Mulberry St. Phone: (812)423-7791
Evansville, IN 47713 Ina Freeman, Libn.
Staff: Prof 1. **Subjects:** Psychology, psychiatry, social work, child development, sexuality, therapeutic recreation, drug abuse. **Holdings:** 1000 books; 700 pamphlets; 125 AV programs. **Subscriptions:** 80 journals and other serials. **Services:** Interlibrary loan; copying; library open to the public for reference use only. **Networks/Consortia:** Member of Evansville Area Health Sciences Libraries Consortium, Four Rivers Area Library Services Authority.

★13527★
SOUTHWESTERN OKLAHOMA STATE UNIVERSITY - AL HARRIS LIBRARY (Educ, Med, Bus-Fin)
Weatherford, OK 73096 Phone: (405)772-6611
Sheila Wilder Hoke, Lib.Dir.
Founded: 1902. **Staff:** Prof 6; Other 9. **Subjects:** Pharmacy, education, psychology, business administration. **Holdings:** 228,638 books and bound periodical volumes; 15,862 reels of microfilm; 312,124 microfiche; 90,250 microcards; 26,950 government documents. **Subscriptions:** 1496 journals and other serials. **Services:** Interlibrary loan; library open to the public. **Staff:** James Wilkerson, Ser.Libn.; Daniel Nutter, Acq.Libn.; George Alsbach, Cat.; Caroline Armold Torrence, Ref./ILL/Govt.Docs.; Vicki Buettner, Circ..

★13528★
SOUTHWESTERN PUBLIC SERVICE COMPANY - LIBRARY (Bus-Fin, Energy)
6th at Tyler
Box 1261 Phone: (806)378-2741
Amarillo, TX 79170 Beth Perry, Libn.
Founded: 1971. **Staff:** Prof 1. **Subjects:** Engineering, power transmission and distribution, business administration, finance, economics, agriculture, data processing, law. **Special Collections:** Electric Power Research Institute Reports; Texas Water Development Board Reports; ASTM standards. **Holdings:** 3000 books; 250 bound periodical volumes; 100 audio cassettes; 3 drawers of microfilm; 3 drawers of microfiche; 63 films; 2 VF drawers of standards; 3 VF drawers of annual reports. **Subscriptions:** 400 journals and other serials; 6 newspapers. **Services:** Interlibrary loan; library not open to the public. **Automated Operations:** Computerized cataloging and serials. **Computerized Information Services:** DIALOG Information Services. **Special Catalogs:** Film catalog - on request.

★13529★
SOUTHWESTERN STATE HOSPITAL - PROFESSIONAL LIBRARY (Med)
E. Main St.
Box 670 Phone: (703)783-3171
Marion, VA 24354 Kathleen G. Overbay, Dir., Lib.Serv.
Founded: 1941. **Staff:** Prof 1. **Subjects:** Psychiatry. **Holdings:** 804 volumes; 479 AV programs. **Subscriptions:** 23 journals and other serials. **Services:** Interlibrary loan; copying; library open to the public.

★13530★
SOUTHWESTERN UNIVERSITY - SCHOOL OF LAW LIBRARY (Law)
675 S. Westmoreland Ave. Phone: (213)738-6725
Los Angeles, CA 90005 Linda Whisman, Dir.
Founded: 1913. **Staff:** Prof 8; Other 12. **Subjects:** Law. **Holdings:** 175,529 books; 1046 audiotapes; 445,590 microforms. **Subscriptions:** 3913 journals and other serials; 25 newspapers. **Services:** Interlibrary loan; library not open to the public. **Automated Operations:** Computerized cataloging. **Computerized Information Services:** LEXIS, RLIN, WESTLAW. **Networks/Consortia:** Member of CLASS. **Staff:** S. Streiker, Ref./Media; D. Johnson-Champ, Ref.; C. Weiner, Circ.; P. Lambert, Cat.; D. McFadden, Ref.; T. Tsui, Cat..

★13531★
SOUTHWESTERN VERMONT MEDICAL CENTER - HENRY W. PUTNAM MEMORIAL HOSPITAL - MEDICAL LIBRARY (Med)
100 Hospital Dr. Phone: (802)442-6361
Bennington, VT 05201 Jack Hall, Med.Libn.
Staff: Prof 1. **Subjects:** Medicine, surgery. **Holdings:** 1200 books; Audio-Digest tapes. **Subscriptions:** 123 journals and other serials. **Services:** Interlibrary loan; copying; library open to the public with restrictions. **Networks/Consortia:** Member of Greater Northeastern Regional Medical Library Program.

★13532★
SOUTHWIRE COMPANY - R & D TECHNICAL LIBRARY (Sci-Engr)
Fertilla St.
Carrollton, GA 30117 Phone: (404)832-5099
Founded: 1964. **Staff:** 1. **Subjects:** Aluminum, copper, rod, wire and cable, metallurgy, environment, management. **Holdings:** 1000 books; 500 bound periodical volumes; 4000 information files. **Subscriptions:** 62 journals and other serials. **Services:** Library open to company employees only.

★13533★
SOUTHWOOD COMMUNITY HOSPITAL - MEDICAL LIBRARY (Med)
111 Dedham St. Phone: (617)668-0385
Norfolk, MA 02056 Edna Sacco, Med.Libn.
Founded: 1927. **Staff:** 1. **Subjects:** Oncology, medicine, surgery, nursing, radiology. **Special Collections:** CIBA Collection, Volumes 1-7. **Holdings:** 1896 books and bound periodical volumes. **Subscriptions:** 94 journals and other serials. **Services:** Interlibrary loan; copying; library open to the public with restrictions. **Automated Operations:** Computerized acquisitions, serials, and circulation. **Computerized Information Services:** DOCLINE (electronic mail service). **Networks/Consortia:** Member of Southeastern Massachusetts Consortium of Health Science Libraries (SEMCO), Consortium for Information Resources (CIR).

CHARLES L. SOUVAY MEMORIAL LIBRARY
See: Kenrick Seminary (7424)

★13534★
SOVEREIGN HOSPITALLER ORDER OF ST. JOHN - VILLA ANNESLIE - ARCHIVES (Rel-Phil)
529 Dunkirk Rd. Phone: (301)752-1087
Anneslie, MD 21212 Rev. F. James, H.O.S.J.
Staff: Prof 1. **Subjects:** History of the Order of St. John. **Holdings:** 1000 books and documents. **Subscriptions:** 34 journals and other serials. **Services:** Archives open to the public by appointment.

★13535★
SOVRAN FINANCIAL CORPORATION - CORPORATE LIBRARY (Bus-Fin)
Two Commercial Place
Box 600 Phone: (804)441-4419
Norfolk, VA 23510 Lois Reeves, Libn.
Founded: 1968. **Staff:** Prof 1; Other 1. **Subjects:** Banking, finance, management, personnel administration, law, accounting. **Holdings:** 2510 volumes; 15 VF drawers; 337 cassettes; 16 directories; 45 theses; microfilm. **Subscriptions:** 200 journals and other serials. **Services:** Interlibrary loan; copying; library open to the public for reference use only. **Computerized Information Services:** TRAINET, DIALOG Information Services. **Publications:** Recent Acquisitions, monthly; Periodical Holdings List, quarterly; Audio Cassette List, quarterly - all for internal distribution only; Guide to the Corporate Library, irregular. **Remarks:** An alternate telephone number is 441-4489.

MOSES AND IDA SOYER LIBRARY
See: Parrish Art Museum - Library (11082)

★13536★
SOYFOODS CENTER LIBRARY AND INFORMATION CENTER (Food-Bev)
Box 234 Phone: (415)283-2991
Lafayette, CA 94549 William R. Shurtleff, Dir.
Staff: Prof 2; Other 1. **Subjects:** Soyfoods and the soybean industry - history, food technology, nutrition, industrial statistics, marketing information. **Special Collections:** Traditional, low technology soyfoods; East Asian soyfoods; European soyfoods; historical collection. **Holdings:** 925 books; 30,000 article reprints, interviews, and letters; color slides. **Subscriptions:** 15 journals and other serials. **Services:** Copying; library open to the public by appointment. **Automated Operations:** Computerized cataloging. **Computerized Information Services:** SoyaScan Publications, SoyaScan Products, SoyaScan Directory (internal databases). Performs searches on fee basis. **Publications:** International Bibliography of Soyfoods and the Soybean Industry, biennial; Soyfoods Industry and Market: Directory and Databook, annual; list of other publications - available on request. **Remarks:** Center located at 1021 Dolores Dr., Lafayette, CA 94549. **Staff:** Akiko Aoyagi, Asst.Dir..

★13537★
SPACE TELESCOPE SCIENCE INSTITUTE - LIBRARY (Sci-Engr)
3700 San Martin Dr. Phone: (301)338-4961
Baltimore, MD 21218 Sarah Stevens-Rayburn, Libn.
Founded: 1983. **Staff:** Prof 2. **Subjects:** Astrophysics, astronomy, space sciences, computers. **Special Collections:** Palomar, European Southern Observatory, and Space Research Council photographic sky surveys. **Holdings:** 3000 books; 2000 bound periodical volumes; 210 linear feet of observatory publications. **Subscriptions:** 436 journals and other serials. **Services:** Interlibrary loan; copying; SDI; library open to qualified users by appointment. **Automated Operations:** Computerized cataloging, serials, and circulation. **Computerized Information Services:** DIALOG Information Services, NASA/RECON, STN International; internal database; SPAN, ARPAnet, UUCP (electronic mail services). **Networks/Consortia:** Member of FEDLINK. **Publications:** STEPsheet (preprint listing), biweekly; acquisitions list, monthly; duplicates list, quarterly.

SPACED OUT LIBRARY
See: Toronto Public Library (14250)

SPANGLER LIBRARY
See: Ohio Dominican College (10652)

★13538★
SPAR AEROSPACE LTD. - SATELLITE & AEROSPACE SYSTEMS DIVISION - LIBRARY (Sci-Engr)
21025 Trans Canada Hwy. Phone: (514)457-2150
Ste. Anne de Bellevue, PQ, Canada H9X 3R2
Margaret B. Gross, Libn.
Staff: Prof 1; Other 1. **Subjects:** Electronics, satellite communications, radar, mechanical engineering, space research, materials science. **Holdings:** 4000 books; 10,000 reports; 5000 microfiche. **Subscriptions:** 160 journals and other serials. **Services:** Interlibrary loan; library not open to the public. **Computerized Information Services:** DIALOG Information Services, BRS Information Technologies, CAN/OLE, Pergamon ORBIT InfoLine, Inc., WILSONLINE, Infomart; internal databases; Envoy 100, GLOBETEX (electronic mail services). **Publications:** Library Bulletin, 9/year; Current Contents, semimonthly.

★13539★
SPARBER, SHEVIN, SHAPO & HEILBRONNER, P.A. - LIBRARY (Law)
One S.E. 3rd Ave. Phone: (305)347-4891
Miami, FL 33131 Jeannette Neuschaefer, Libn.
Staff: Prof 1; Other 1. **Subjects:** Litigation; law - tax, real estate, banking, corporate, securities. **Holdings:** Figures not available. **Services:** Library not open to the public. **Computerized Information Services:** LEXIS. **Publications:** Financial Institutions Newsletter, quarterly; Real Estate Newsletter, quarterly; Health Law News, quarterly.

★13540★
SPARKS REGIONAL MEDICAL CENTER - REGIONAL HEALTH SCIENCES LIBRARY (Med)
1311 S. Eye St. Phone: (501)441-4000
Fort Smith, AR 72901 Grace Anderson, Dir.
Founded: 1951. **Staff:** Prof 1; Other 1. **Subjects:** Medicine and biological sciences. **Holdings:** 2000 books; 3000 bound periodical volumes. **Subscriptions:** 237 journals and other serials. **Services:** Interlibrary loan (fee); copying; library open to students and researchers. **Automated Operations:** Computerized cataloging. **Computerized Information Services:** MEDLINE, BRS Information Technologies; OnTyme Electronic Message Network Service, DOCLINE (electronic mail services). Performs searches on fee basis. **Remarks:** Designated as an Area Health Education Center Library.

STEPHEN SPARLING LIBRARY
See: Society for Manitobans with Disabilities Inc. (13330)

★13541★
EDWARD W. SPARROW HOSPITAL - MEDICAL LIBRARY (Med)
1215 E. Michigan Ave.
Box 30480 Phone: (517)483-2274
Lansing, MI 48909 Doris H. Asher, Med.Libn.
Founded: 1950. **Staff:** 1. **Subjects:** Medicine, nursing. **Holdings:** 3300 books. **Subscriptions:** 310 journals and other serials. **Services:** Interlibrary loan; copying; library open to health care professionals.

★13542★
SPARTANBURG REGIONAL MEDICAL CENTER - HEALTH SCIENCES LIBRARY (Med)
101 E. Wood St. Phone: (803)573-6220
Spartanburg, SC 29303 Mary Ann Camp, Dir., Lib.Serv.
Staff: Prof 1; Other 1. **Subjects:** Medicine, nursing, allied health sciences, hospital administration. **Holdings:** 4000 books; 3200 bound periodical volumes; 200 AV programs. **Subscriptions:** 225 journals and other serials. **Services:** Interlibrary loan; copying; library open to the public for reference use only. **Computerized Information Services:** NLM, SCHIN; DOCLINE (electronic mail service). Performs searches on fee basis. **Networks/Consortia:** Member of Health Communications Network (HCN), South Carolina Health Information Network (SCHIN).

HARRIET M. SPAULDING LIBRARY
See: New England Conservatory of Music (9922)

MARTIN SPEARE MEMORIAL LIBRARY
See: New Mexico Institute of Mining and Technology (9976)

★13543★
SPEARS, LUBERSKY, CAMPBELL, BLEDSOE, ANDERSON & YOUNG - LIBRARY (Law)
800 Pacific Bldg.
520 S.W. Yamhill St. Phone: (503)226-6151
Portland, OR 97204 Joe K. Stephens, Law Libn.
Staff: Prof 1; Other 1. **Subjects:** Law. **Holdings:** 20,000 volumes; 2000 internal legal memoranda. **Subscriptions:** 400 journals and other serials. **Services:** Interlibrary loan; library not open to the public. **Computerized Information Services:** WESTLAW, LEXIS. **Special Indexes:** Index to legal memoranda (punch cards).

★13544★
SPECIAL EDUCATION RESOURCE CENTER (Educ)
25 Industrial Park Rd. Phone: (203)632-1485
Middletown, CT 06457-1520 Arnold Fassler, Dir.
Founded: 1968. **Staff:** Prof 3; Other 4. **Subjects:** Special education, education and training of handicapped people (birth to 21 years). **Special Collections:** ERIC indexes (complete) and microfiche, 1982 to present. **Holdings:** 3200 books; 16 VF drawers of material; 329 tests; 200 inservice training materials; 41 newsletters; 3250 instructional materials; 278 literature searches; 70 computer search reprints; 188 computer software packages. **Subscriptions:** 139 journals and other serials. **Services:** Copying; center open to the public with restrictions. **Computerized Information Services:** DIALOG Information Services, WILSONLINE; SpecialNet (electronic mail service). Performs searches free of charge for special education administrators. **Publications:** How to Do Research in Special Education; Computer Software at SERC; bibliographies of research and instructional materials. **Special Catalogs:** Books and test catalog (card); instructional materials and inservice training catalog. **Staff:** Stephen Krasner, Coord., Lib.Rsrcs. & Exhibits.

★13545★
SPECIAL ELITE FORCES SOCIETY - DOCUMENT CONTROL CENTER (Mil)
Box 174
Bryson, TX 76027 Ley Lovett-DeLouvetier, Adm.
Founded: 1978. **Staff:** Prof 3. **Subjects:** Special, overt, and covert field operations; anti-terrorist and anti-guerrilla operations. **Holdings:** 500 books. **Services:** Center not open to the public. **Computerized Information Services:** Online systems. **Publications:** Debrief, monthly - for internal distribution only. **Formerly:** Located in Kansas City, MO.

★13546★
SPECIAL LIBRARIES ASSOCIATION - INFORMATION RESOURCES CENTER (Info Sci)
1700 18th St., N.W. Phone: (202)234-4700
Washington, DC 20009 Tobi A. Brimsek, Mgr., Info.Rsrcs.
Staff: Prof 1. **Subjects:** Special libraries, librarianship, information science, library management. **Special Collections:** Association's Archives; History of Special Library Movement. **Holdings:** 3000 volumes. **Subscriptions:** 140 journals and other serials. **Services:** Interlibrary loan; center open to the public by appointment. **Automated Operations:** Computerized cataloging and serials. **Also Known As:** SLA.

★13547★
SPECIAL METALS CORPORATION - TECHNICAL LIBRARY/ INFORMATION CENTER (Sci-Engr)
Middle Settlement Rd. Phone: (315)798-2936
New Hartford, NY 13413 Elizabeth A. Lazore, Libn.
Founded: 1957. **Staff:** Prof 1. **Subjects:** Metallurgy, business management, ceramics, vacuum melting, industrial maintenance. **Holdings:** 2500 books and bound periodical volumes; 5000 technical documents; 900 technical reports; company records. **Subscriptions:** 126 journals and other serials. **Services:** Interlibrary loan; library open to the public upon request. **Computerized Information Services:** DIALOG Information Services. **Networks/Consortia:** Member of Central New York Library Resources Council (CENTRO).

JOHN SPECK MEMORIAL LIBRARY
See: Mountaineering Foundation of Chicago, Inc. (9398)

★13548★
J.B. SPEED ART MUSEUM - LIBRARY (Art)
2035 S. Third St. Phone: (502)636-2893
Louisville, KY 40208 Mary Jane Benedict, Libn.
Staff: Prof 1. **Subjects:** Art, decorative arts, architecture, archeology, film, photography. **Special Collections:** J.B. Speed's Lincoln Collection; Weygold Indian collection. **Holdings:** 12,900 books and bound periodical volumes; 48 VF drawers. **Subscriptions:** 73 journals and other serials. **Services:** Copying; library open to the public for reference use only. **Special Indexes:** Speed Bulletin Index; Speed Scrapbook Index; Kennedy Quarterly Index; Index of Contemporary Artists file; Index of Reproduction file; Index to Gallery Catalogs (all on cards).

SPEER LIBRARY
See: Princeton Theological Seminary (11574)

SPEIZMAN JEWISH LIBRARY AT SHALOM PARK
See: The Foundation of the Charlotte Jewish Community (5314)

★13549★
CARDINAL SPELLMAN PHILATELIC MUSEUM, INC. - LIBRARY (Rec)
235 Wellesley St. Phone: (617)894-6735
Weston, MA 02193 Ruth Koved, Libn.
Founded: 1960. **Staff:** Prof 1; Other 2. **Subjects:** Philately, postal service. **Holdings:** 9500 books; 2300 bound periodical volumes; 2100 pamphlets; 4000 volumes of auction catalogs; 6500 unbound periodical volumes; 2 VF drawers of pamphlets, clippings, and documents. **Subscriptions:** 83 journals and other serials. **Services:** Interlibrary loan; copying; library open to the public.

DAVID SPENCE LIBRARY
See: University of Southern California - Science & Engineering Library (16885)

SPENCER ART REFERENCE LIBRARY
See: Nelson-Atkins Museum of Art - Spencer Art Reference Library (9867)

SPENCER COLLECTION
See: New York Public Library (10089)

SPENCER ENTOMOLOGICAL MUSEUM
See: University of British Columbia (15877)

SPENCER KELLOGG PRODUCTS
See: NL Industries, Inc. (10259)

ALBERT F. SPERRY LIBRARY
See: Instrument Society of America (6943)

SPERRY FLIGHT SYSTEMS
See: Honeywell, Inc. - Sperry Aerospace Group (6442)

★13550★
SPERRY MARINE INC. - ENGINEERING LIBRARY (Sci-Engr, Comp Sci)
Rte. 29 North Phone: (804)974-2441
Charlottesville, VA 22906 Grace McKenzie, Libn.
Staff: 1. **Subjects:** Engineering - electrical, mechanical; computer technology. **Holdings:** 4000 books; 300 bound periodical volumes; 20,000 technical reports; 175 volumes of standards; 1500 patents; 1000 reels of microfilm. **Subscriptions:** 200 journals and other serials. **Services:** Library not open to the public. **Automated Operations:** Computerized cataloging. **Computerized Information Services:** DIALOG Information Services. **Publications:** Acquisitions Bulletin, bimonthly - for internal distribution only. **Remarks:** Sperry Marine Inc. is a subsidiary of Tenneco, Inc. - Newport News Shipbuilding.

★13551★
SPERTUS COLLEGE OF JUDAICA - NORMAN AND HELEN ASHER LIBRARY (Area-Ethnic, Rel-Phil)
618 S. Michigan Ave.
Chicago, IL 60605 Phone: (312)922-9012
Founded: 1925. **Staff:** Prof 5; Other 2. **Subjects:** Judaica, Hebraica, Rabbinics, Yiddish language and literature, Zionism, Israel, Jewish current events. **Special Collections:** Badona Spertus Art Collection; Chicago Jewish Archives; Levine Microform Collection. **Holdings:** 72,000 books; 5800 bound periodical volumes; 1382 reels of microfilm. **Subscriptions:** 340 journals and other serials; 9 newspapers. **Services:** Interlibrary loan;

copying; library open to the public. **Networks/Consortia:** Member of Chicago Library System, Judaica Library Network of Chicago. **Staff:** Dan Sharon, Libn.; Robbin Saltzman, Libn.; Kathleen Ladien, Adm.Libn.; Isaac Kornfeld, Cur., Rare Bks..

★13552★
SPIE - THE INTERNATIONAL SOCIETY FOR OPTICAL ENGINEERING - LIBRARY (Sci-Engr)
Box 10 Phone: (206)676-3290
Bellingham, WA 98227-0010 Joseph Yaver, Exec.Dir.
Subjects: Optical and electro-optical technology - electro-optics, laser, infrared, photographic. **Holdings:** 736 books. **Services:** Library open to the public. **Publications:** S.P.I.E. Proceedings of approximately 100 conferences per year; Optical Engineering Reports (newspaper), monthly; Optical Engineering journal, monthly. **Remarks:** Library located at 1022 19th St., Bellingham, WA 98225.

★13553★
SPILL CONTROL ASSOCIATION OF AMERICA - LIBRARY (Env-Cons)
400 Renaissance Center, 10th Fl. Phone: (313)552-0500
Detroit, MI 48243-1895 Marc K. Shaye, General Counsel
Founded: 1972. **Staff:** 4. **Subjects:** Federal and state water laws, current proposed legislation, equipment and contractor listings, government agencies, oil and hazardous substances spill statistics, industry history. **Special Collections:** Current abstracts of technical documents relating to oil and hazardous substances spill control and containment research and techniques employed in the United States, Canada, and around the world. **Holdings:** Figures not available for books; SCAA Newsletters. **Services:** Interlibrary loan; copying; library open to the public upon request. **Remarks:** Library includes the most current information regarding laws and regulations relating to oil and hazardous materials spill control, cleanup, transport, and disposal.

★13554★
SPIRITUAL FRONTIERS FELLOWSHIP - LIBRARY (Rel-Phil)
10819 Winner Rd. Phone: (816)254-8585
Independence, MO 64052 Ruth Rickner, Off.Mgr.
Founded: 1956. **Staff:** 1. **Subjects:** Psychic research and experiences, spiritual healing and development, prayer, mysticism, meditation. **Special Collections:** Gertrude Tubby Collection (papers and books from the former secretary of the American Society for Psychical Research). **Holdings:** 12,000 books. **Subscriptions:** 25 journals and other serials. **Services:** Library open to members only. **Publications:** Progressive Reading List. **Special Catalogs:** Lending Library Catalog.

RENE A. SPITZ PSYCHIATRIC LIBRARY
See: University of Colorado Health Sciences Center (16087)

★13555★
SPOHN HOSPITAL - MEDICAL LIBRARY (Med)
600 Elizabeth St. Phone: (512)881-3261
Corpus Christi, TX 78404 Sr. Julia Delaney, Libn.
Staff: Prof 1; Other 2. **Subjects:** Medicine, nursing, medical technology, management, x-ray. **Holdings:** 3500 books; 1200 bound periodical volumes; 8 VF drawers of pamphlets; AV programs. **Subscriptions:** 50 journals and other serials. **Services:** Interlibrary loan; library open to the public for reference use only. **Networks/Consortia:** Member of Coastal Bend Health Sciences Library Consortium.

★13556★
SPOKANE COUNTY LAW LIBRARY (Law)
1020 Paulsen Bldg. Phone: (509)456-3680
Spokane, WA 99201-0402 Emily E. Wadden, Law Libn.
Founded: 1909. **Staff:** Prof 1. **Subjects:** Law. **Holdings:** 22,000 volumes. **Services:** Interlibrary loan; copying; library open to the public.

★13557★
SPOKANE MEDICAL LIBRARY (Med)
705 W. 1st Phone: (509)458-6251
Spokane, WA 99204-0409 Jay W. Rea, Libn.
Founded: 1929. **Staff:** Prof 1; Other 2. **Subjects:** Clinical medicine. **Holdings:** 3000 books; 30,000 bound periodical volumes. **Subscriptions:** 250 journals and other serials. **Services:** Interlibrary loan; copying; library open to the public. **Automated Operations:** Computerized cataloging. **Computerized Information Services:** DIALOG Information Services, MEDLINE; OnTyme Electronic Message Network Service (electronic mail service). Performs searches on fee basis. **Remarks:** Jointly maintained by the Spokane County Medical Society and Eastern Washington University.

★13558★
(Spokane) SPOKESMAN-REVIEW AND SPOKANE CHRONICLE - NEWSPAPER REFERENCE LIBRARY (Publ)
Box 2160
Spokane, WA 99210 Phone: (509)459-5468
Staff: 8. **Subjects:** Newspaper reference topics. **Holdings:** 3000 books; newspapers, 1881 to present, on microfilm; newspaper clipping files; pictures. **Services:** Library not open to the public. **Remarks:** Both newspapers are published by the Cowles Publishing Company. Library located at 479 Review Tower, Spokane, WA 99210.

★13559★
SPORT INFORMATION RESOURCE CENTRE (Rec)
333 River Rd. Phone: (613)748-5658
Ottawa, ON, Canada K1L 8H9 Gilles Chiasson, Pres.
Founded: 1973. **Staff:** Prof 8; Other 5. **Subjects:** Sports, physical education, coaching, the handicapped and sports, exercise physiology, sports history, recreation, physical fitness, sports medicine. **Holdings:** 25,000 books; 3000 bound periodical volumes; 6500 microfiche. **Subscriptions:** 1400 journals and other serials. **Services:** Interlibrary loan; copying; SDI; center open to the public. **Automated Operations:** Computerized cataloging and acquisitions. **Computerized Information Services:** DIALOG Information Services, German Institute for Medical Documentation and Information (DIMDI), BRS Information Technologies, Info Globe, CAN/OLE. Performs searches on fee basis. Contact Person: Linda Wheeler, Hd., Ref.Serv.. **Publications:** Sport Thesaurus, 1987; Sport Database User Aid; Sport and Recreation for the Disabled; Sport Bibliography, 1981-1982 and updates; SportSearch (current awareness), monthly - by subscription. **Remarks:** The Resource Centre creates SPORT, an online database containing 210,000 documents. **Staff:** Richard Stark, V.P., Oper.; Christine Lalande, Hd., Tech.Serv..

★13560★
SPORTS RESEARCH INSTITUTE - LIBRARY
109 Sports Research Bldg.
Pennsylvania State University
University Park, PA 16802
Founded: 1969. **Subjects:** Sports - research, safety, injuries; biomechanics of sport. **Holdings:** 150 books; 250 bound periodical volumes; 2 VF drawers of reprints; 15 theses. **Remarks:** Presently inactive.

★13561★
SPOTSYLVANIA HISTORICAL ASSOCIATION, INC. - FRANCES L.N. WALLER RESEARCH MUSEUM AND LIBRARY (Hist)
Court House, Box 64 Phone: (703)582-7167
Spotsylvania, VA 22553 Frances L.N. Waller, Dir.
Founded: 1962. **Staff:** Prof 4; Other 2. **Subjects:** Spotsylvania County history, Civil War battlefields, colonial settlers and forts since 1671, genealogy statistics, Lafayette's campaign through Spotsylvania County 1781. **Special Collections:** Early medicine; Civil War arms; Indian artifacts; colonial farm implements; family histories and collection of old home and church histories in the county. **Holdings:** 2500 books; 100 bound periodical volumes; 800 booklets; 1 bookcase of Ohio and Virginia historical reports; 4 VF drawers of local manuscripts; maps; tapes; photostats; slides; film; reprints. **Subscriptions:** 10 journals and other serials. **Services:** Copying; library open to the public for reference use only. **Publications:** Association reports; Revolutionary Times in Spotsylvania County, 1976; Spotsylvania County Historical Map, 1978; Spotsylvania County Patriots, 1774-1786. **Staff:** Merle Strickler; John E. Pruitt, Jr.; A.N. Waller; Sonya Harvison, Asst.Dir..

SPRAFKA MEMORIAL HEALTH SCIENCE LIBRARY
See: St. Anthony Hospital (12322)

★13562★
SPRAGUE ELECTRIC COMPANY - RESEARCH LIBRARY (Sci-Engr)
96 Marshall St. Phone: (413)664-4524
North Adams, MA 01247 Jill Coghlan, Res.Libn.
Founded: 1944. **Staff:** Prof 1. **Subjects:** Electronics, chemistry, physics, materials sciences, mathematics, engineering. **Holdings:** 5800 books; 1100 bound periodical volumes; 10 VF drawers of internal reports; government documents on microfiche. **Subscriptions:** 240 journals and other serials. **Services:** Interlibrary loan; copying; library open to the public for reference use only with permission. **Computerized Information Services:** DIALOG Information Services, STN International.

HARRY A. SPRAGUE LIBRARY
See: Montclair State College (9237)

NORMAN F. SPRAGUE MEMORIAL LIBRARY
See: The Claremont Colleges (3248)

WILLIAM MERCER SPRIGG MEMORIAL LIBRARY
See: Capitol Hill Hospital (2646)

★13563★
SPRING GARDEN COLLEGE - LIBRARY (Sci-Engr)
7500 Germantown Ave. Phone: (215)248-7900
Chestnut Hill, PA 19119 Mildred Glushakow, Dir.
Staff: Prof 2. **Subjects:** Engineering - electrical, electronic, civil, mechanical, computer; building construction; architecture; medical technology; business management. **Holdings:** 21,900 volumes; 8 VF drawers of catalogs and pamphlets. **Subscriptions:** 454 journals and other serials. **Services:** Interlibrary loan; copying; library open to the public. **Automated Operations:** Computerized cataloging. **Networks/Consortia:** Member of Tri-State College Library Cooperative (TCLC). **Publications:** Library Handbook; Library Research Quiz; Alphabetical and Subject Lists of Periodicals - to students and faculty. **Staff:** Ella Strattis, Asst.Libn..

★13564★
SPRING GROVE HOSPITAL CENTER - SULZBACHER MEMORIAL LIBRARY (Med)
Isidore Tuerk Bldg.
Wade Ave. Phone: (301)455-7824
Baltimore, MD 21228 Charles H. Johnson, Supv., Lib. & Files
Founded: 1938. **Staff:** 1. **Subjects:** Psychiatry, psychology, psychotherapy, pharmacology, sociology, social work, neurology, pastoral care, nursing education, therapy. **Special Collections:** History of Spring Grove Hospital Center; Rare Book Collection. **Holdings:** 2835 books; 1000 bound periodical volumes; 954 cassettes; 10 films; 15 phonograph records; 2045 pamphlets; 13 AV programs; 20 archives; 30 dissertations; 25 reels of microfilm. **Subscriptions:** 297 journals and other serials; 10 newspapers. **Services:** Interlibrary loan; copying; library open to the public for reference use only. **Computerized Information Services:** MEDLINE, DIALOG Information Services, BRS Information Technologies. **Networks/ Consortia:** Member of Maryland Association of Health Science Librarians. **Publications:** Bibliographies; SML Acquisitions (newsletter). **Remarks:** Maintained by Maryland State Department of Health & Mental Hygiene.

★13565★
SPRINGFIELD ACADEMY OF MEDICINE - HEALTH SCIENCE LIBRARY (Med)
1400 State St. Phone: (413)734-5445
Springfield, MA 01109 Linda Rodger, Lib.Dir.
Founded: 1907. **Staff:** Prof 1; Other 1. **Subjects:** Medicine, nursing, dentistry. **Special Collections:** Medical history. **Holdings:** 10,000 books; 18,000 bound periodical volumes. **Subscriptions:** 44 journals and other serials. **Services:** Interlibrary loan; copying; library open to the public. **Automated Operations:** Computerized ILL. **Computerized Information Services:** MEDLINE; MEDLINK, DOCLINE (electronic mail services). Performs searches on fee basis. **Networks/Consortia:** Member of Western Massachusetts Health Information Consortium, Massachusetts Health Sciences Library Network (MAHSLIN). **Remarks:** Affiliated with the Hampden District Medical Society.

SPRINGFIELD ARMORY NATIONAL HISTORIC SITE
See: U.S. Natl. Park Service (15353)

★13566★
SPRINGFIELD ART ASSOCIATION - MICHAEL VICTOR II ART LIBRARY (Art)
700 N. Fourth St. Phone: (217)523-2631
Springfield, IL 62702 Annadean Bull, Libn.
Staff: Prof 1; Other 4. **Subjects:** Visual and related arts. **Holdings:** 3000 books; prints; booklets; exhibition catalogs. **Subscriptions:** 12 journals and other serials. **Services:** Library open to the public for reference use only.

★13567★
SPRINGFIELD ART CENTER - LIBRARY (Art)
107 Cliff Park Rd. Phone: (513)325-4673
Springfield, OH 45501 Mary McG. Miller, Chm. of Lib.Comm.
Subjects: Art, art history, photography. **Special Collections:** Axel Bahnson Collection (historical photographic books and periodicals). **Holdings:** 2500 books. **Subscriptions:** 15 journals and other serials. **Services:** Library open to the public with restrictions. **Publications:** Newsletter - to members.

★13568★
SPRINGFIELD ART MUSEUM - ART REFERENCE LIBRARY (Art)
1111 E. Brookside Dr. Phone: (417)866-2716
Springfield, MO 65807 Patricia Leembruggen, Libn.
Staff: Prof 1. **Subjects:** Art history, painting, sculpture, graphics, decorative arts, photography. **Holdings:** 3500 books; 1000 bound periodical volumes; 1000 slides; 5000 clippings; 3000 unbound magazines; 2500 exhibition catalogs. **Subscriptions:** 56 journals and other serials. **Services:** Interlibrary loan; copying; library open to the public.

★13569★
SPRINGFIELD CITY LIBRARY - ARCHIVES
Local History and Genealogy Department
220 State St.
Springfield, MA 01103
Defunct. Absorbed by Genealogy and Local History Department.

★13570★
SPRINGFIELD CITY LIBRARY - FINE ARTS DEPARTMENT (Art, Mus)
220 State St. Phone: (413)739-3871
Springfield, MA 01103 Karen A. Dorval, Supv./Art Libn.
Founded: 1857. **Staff:** Prof 4; Other 3. **Subjects:** Art, crafts, needlework, music, photography, coins. **Special Collections:** Aston Collection of wood-engravings (2250 prints). **Holdings:** 33,250 books; 3200 bound periodical volumes; 18,000 recordings; 2000 compact discs; 3000 audio cassettes; 125,000 pictures; 8000 pamphlets. **Subscriptions:** 112 journals and other serials. **Services:** Interlibrary loan; copying; department open to the public, card required to borrow books. **Automated Operations:** Computerized circulation. **Staff:** Sylvia St. Amand, Mus.Libn..

★13571★
SPRINGFIELD CITY LIBRARY - GENEALOGY COLLECTION
220 State St.
Springfield, MA 01103
Defunct. Absorbed by Genealogy and Local History Department.

★13572★
SPRINGFIELD CITY LIBRARY - GENEALOGY AND LOCAL HISTORY DEPARTMENT (Hist)
220 State St. Phone: (413)739-3871
Springfield, MA 01103 Joseph Carvalho, III, Supv.
Staff: Prof 4. **Subjects:** Springfield history and genealogy, 1636 to present; historic architecture. **Special Collections:** Donald Macaulay papers; John Cotton Dana papers, 1898-1902; 17th-20th century manuscripts; Springfield First Church Records, 1636-1900; Ames Sword Co. Collection; Massachusetts Mutual Life Insurance Records; Springfield Fire and Marine Insurance Co. Collection; World Wars I and II Propaganda Collection; Farr Alpaca Co. Records; Civil War Collection; Roger L. Putnam Collection. **Holdings:** 20,000 volumes; 2000 linear feet of archival documents; 25,000 photographs and printed illustrations; 300 feet of vertical files; International Genealogical Index microfiche; atlases and maps; ephemera. **Services:** Copying; department open to the public. **Automated Operations:** Computerized cataloging, acquisitions, and circulation. **Publications:** Pathfinders for Italian, Jewish, Irish, Polish, and Afro-American genealogy - free on request; French Canadian genealogy booklet, 6th edition - for sale. **Formed by the merger of:** Genealogy Collection, Springfield History Collection, and Archives. **Staff:** Guy McLain, Archv. & Local Hist.Libn.; Edmond Lonergan, Local Hist. & Geneal.Libn.; Margaret Humberston, Libn.; Valerie McQuillan, Libn..

★13573★
SPRINGFIELD COLLEGE - BABSON LIBRARY - SPECIAL COLLECTIONS (Educ, Rec)
263 Alden St. Phone: (413)788-3307
Springfield, MA 01109 Gerald F. Davis, Lib.Dir.
Founded: 1885. **Special Collections:** Physical education; recreation. **Holdings:** Figures not available. **Services:** Interlibrary loan; copying; collections open to the public with permission. **Computerized Information Services:** DIALOG Information Services, WILSONLINE, BRS Information Technologies; DIALMAIL (electronic mail service). Performs searches on fee basis for college community. Contact Person: Andrea Taupier, Sr.Ref.Libn., 788-3315. **Networks/Consortia:** Member of Cooperating Libraries of Greater Springfield, A CCGS Agency (CLGS), C/W MARS, Inc.. **Staff:** Raymond Lin, Cat.; MaryJane Sobinski-Smith, Ref.; Dr. Charles Weckwerth, Archv..

★13574★
SPRINGFIELD-GREENE COUNTY PUBLIC LIBRARIES - EDWARD M. SHEPARD MEMORIAL ROOM (Hist)
397 E. Central Phone: (417)869-4621
Springfield, MO 65801 Michael D. Glenn, Ref.Libn.
Founded: 1961. **Staff:** Prof 1; Other 3. **Subjects:** Missouri, Greene County, Springfield, and the Ozarks - history, biography, genealogy, literature, Missouri authors, archeology, geology, religion, language. **Special Collections:** Edward M. Shepard Collection of Rare Missouri and Ozark books; Collection of Historical Photographs; Max Hunter Collection of Ozark Folksong (1000 songs on cassette tapes). **Holdings:** 7000 books; Federal Census, Missouri, 1830-1880, 1900, 1910, on microfilm; 1200 reels of microfilm of Springfield newspapers, 1870 to present; 54 reels of microfilm of miscellaneous genealogical material; 16 VF drawers of pictures and clippings. **Subscriptions:** 75 journals and other serials. **Services:** Copying; room open to the public. **Automated Operations:** Computerized circulation. **Computerized Information Services:** CLSI (internal database). **Networks/Consortia:** Member of Southwest Missouri Library Network. **Special Indexes:** Card index to Springfield newspapers (articles pertaining primarily to Springfield and Greene County, also includes Missouri and the Ozarks).

★13575★
SPRINGFIELD HISTORICAL SOCIETY - LIBRARY (Hist)
126 Morris Ave.
Box 124 Phone: (201)376-7737
Springfield, NJ 07081 Janice P. Bongiovanni, Pres.
Founded: 1953. **Subjects:** Local history, genealogy, New Jersey history. **Holdings:** 1000 books. **Services:** Library open to the public by appointment for reference use only. **Staff:** Howard Wiseman, Cur..

★13576★
SPRINGFIELD HOSPITAL - INFORMATION CENTER/ LIBRARY† (Med)
25 Ridgewood Rd. Phone: (802)885-2151
Springfield, VT 05156 Hania L. McAuliffe, Med.Libn.
Staff: Prof 1. **Subjects:** Medicine, surgery, nursing. **Holdings:** 304 volumes. **Subscriptions:** 41 journals and other serials. **Services:** Interlibrary loan; copying; center open to the public with restrictions. **Computerized Information Services:** BRS Information Technologies. **Networks/ Consortia:** Member of Vermont/New Hampshire Health Science Libraries, COOP Group II of Southern Vermont/New Hampshire Librarians, North Atlantic Health Science Libraries (NAHSL).

★13577★
SPRINGFIELD HOSPITAL CENTER - MEDICAL LIBRARY (Med)
Sykesville, MD 21784 Phone: (301)795-2100
Elizabeth D. Mercer, Libn.
Founded: 1954. **Staff:** 1. **Subjects:** Psychiatry, neurology, clinical psychology, psychotherapy, psychiatric nursing, psychiatric social work, medicine, practical nursing. **Holdings:** 2000 books; 1000 bound periodical volumes. **Subscriptions:** 84 journals and other serials. **Services:** Interlibrary loan; library open to the public for reference use only on request. **Publications:** Acquisition lists, quarterly.

★13578★
SPRINGFIELD, ILLINOIS STATE JOURNAL & REGISTER - EDITORIAL LIBRARY (Publ)
1 Copley Plaza Phone: (217)788-1300
Springfield, IL 62705 Sandra Vance, Libn.
Staff: 2. **Subjects:** Newspaper reference topics. **Holdings:** 460 books; 90 bound periodical volumes; 2.9 million newspaper clippings on microfiche; newspapers on microfilm; photo negative file; photos of subjects and people. **Services:** Library open to the public. **Computerized Information Services:** Battelle Software Products Center. Performs searches on fee basis. **Remarks:** An alternate telephone number is 788-1504.

SPRINGFIELD LIBRARY AND MUSEUMS ASSOCIATION - GEORGE WALTER VINCENT SMITH ART MUSEUM
See: George Walter Vincent Smith Art Museum (13247)

★13579★
SPRINGFIELD NEWSPAPERS - LIBRARY (Publ)
1860 Main St. Phone: (413)788-1018
Springfield, MA 01102 Diane A. Blais, Supv.
Staff: Prof 1; Other 5. **Subjects:** Newspaper reference topics. **Special Collections:** Springfield city directories, 1852 to present; Springfield Union Index, 1912-1941. **Holdings:** 80,000 subject headings of clippings and microfiche. **Services:** Library not open to the public.

★13580★
SPRINGHOUSE CORPORATION - CORPORATE LIBRARY (Med, Publ)
1111 Bethlehem Pike Phone: (215)646-8700
Spring House, PA 19477 Nancy H. Lange, Libn.
Staff: Prof 1; Other 1. **Subjects:** Nursing, health care, education. **Holdings:** 6000 books; company archives. **Subscriptions:** 360 journals and other serials. **Services:** Interlibrary loan; library not open to the public. **Automated Operations:** Computerized cataloging and serials. **Computerized Information Services:** BRS Information Technologies. Performs searches free of charge for consortium members. **Networks/ Consortia:** Member of Delaware Valley Information Consortium (DEVIC), Tri-State College Library Cooperative (TCLC).

SPRUANCE LIBRARY
See: Bucks County Historical Society (2009)

★13581★
SPS TECHNOLOGIES, INC. - RESEARCH AND DEVELOPMENT LABORATORIES - CORPORATE TECHNICAL LIBRARY (Sci-Engr)
Highland Ave. Phone: (215)572-3564
Jenkintown, PA 19046 Stephanie Woodlock, Corp.Tech.Libn.
Staff: Prof 1. **Subjects:** Fastener engineering and technology, mechanical engineering, metallurgy, management. **Holdings:** 1500 books; 10,000 internal technical reports; 250 technical reports; specifications; industry standards; annual reports. **Subscriptions:** 53 journals and other serials. **Services:** Interlibrary loan; copying; SDI; library open to the public by appointment. **Computerized Information Services:** DIALOG Information Services, BRS Information Technologies; internal database. Performs searches on fee basis. **Publications:** Acquisitions List, monthly; Technical Reports Issued by the Corporation, monthly - both for internal distribution only. **Special Indexes:** Chronological, author, and subject indexes to SPS technical reports and lab notes (book), annual.

★13582★
SQUARE D COMPANY - LIBRARY (Sci-Engr)
4041 N. Richards St. Phone: (414)332-2000
Milwaukee, WI 53212 Susan Paul, Corp.Libn.
Founded: 1960. **Staff:** 1. **Subjects:** Electrical engineering. **Holdings:** 3000 books. **Subscriptions:** 150 journals and other serials. **Services:** Interlibrary loan; library not open to the public. **Computerized Information Services:** DIALOG Information Services.

★13583★
SQUIBB CANADA INC. - MEDICAL LIBRARY (Med)
2365 Cote de Liesse Rd. Phone: (514)331-7423
Montreal, PQ, Canada H4N 2M7 Donna Gibson, Med.Libn.
Staff: 1. **Subjects:** Medicine, pharmacology. **Holdings:** 2000 unbound periodical volumes; 300 monographs. **Subscriptions:** 65 journals; 5 newspapers. **Services:** Interlibrary loan; copying; library open to the public by appointment. **Computerized Information Services:** MEDLARS.

★13584★
E.R. SQUIBB AND SONS, INC. - NEW BRUNSWICK LIBRARY (Med, Sci-Engr)
Rte. 1 & College Farm Rd., Bldg. 100 Phone: (201)519-2269
New Brunswick, NJ 08903 Dorothy McLaughlin, Supv., Lib.Oper.
Staff: Prof 1; Other 2. **Subjects:** Analytical chemistry, pharmaceutics, pharmacology, microbiology, biochemistry. **Holdings:** 4000 books; 6600 bound periodical volumes. **Subscriptions:** 300 journals and other serials. **Services:** Interlibrary loan; copying; SDI; library open to other librarians and researchers with authorization. **Automated Operations:** Computerized routing. **Computerized Information Services:** DIALOG Information Services, Pergamon ORBIT InfoLine, Inc., STN International, OCLC. **Networks/Consortia:** Member of Medical Resources Consortium of Central New Jersey (MEDCORE).

★13585★
E.R. SQUIBB AND SONS, INC. - SQUIBB INSTITUTE FOR MEDICAL RESEARCH - SCIENCE INFORMATION DEPARTMENT (Sci-Engr, Med)
Box 4000 Phone: (609)921-4844
Princeton, NJ 08540 Dr. Frank L. Weisenborn, Dir.
Founded: 1925. **Staff:** Prof 9; Other 10. **Subjects:** Pharmacology, chemistry, medicine, pharmacy. **Holdings:** 17,300 books; 40,000 bound periodical volumes; 7000 volumes on microfilm; 100 VF drawers. **Subscriptions:** 1000 journals and other serials. **Services:** Interlibrary loan; copying; department open to the public by appointment. **Automated Operations:** Computerized cataloging and serials. **Computerized**

Information Services: DIALOG Information Services, Pergamon ORBIT InfoLine, Inc., OCLC, MEDLINE, U.S. Patents Files. **Networks/Consortia:** Member of Medical Resources Consortium of Central New Jersey (MEDCORE). **Publications:** Index Squibbicus, bimonthly - for internal distribution only; Monthly Acquisitions Bulletin. **Staff:** Dr. Nick Semenuk, Sec.Hd., Lit. Search; Helen Kosowski, Mgr., Lib.Oper..

ELEANOR SQUIRE LIBRARY
See: Garden Center of Greater Cleveland (5465)

★13586★
SRI INTERNATIONAL - BUSINESS INTELLIGENCE CENTER - INFORMATION CENTER (Bus-Fin)
333 Ravenswood Ave. Phone: (415)859-2400
Menlo Park, CA 94025 Edward F. Christie, Dir., Client Serv.
Founded: 1958. **Staff:** 25. **Subjects:** Trends - business and industrial, technological, government, sociological; business planning. **Holdings:** 650 books; 150,000 clippings, pamphlets, and reports indexed by subject. **Subscriptions:** 500 journals and other serials. **Services:** Center use restricted to SRI staff and subscribers to Business Intelligence Program Service. **Computerized Information Services:** DIALOG Information Services, NEXIS. **Special Indexes:** Index to BIP publications (computerized), quarterly - to subscribers.

★13587★
SRI INTERNATIONAL - CHEMICAL MARKETING RESEARCH CENTER/PROCESS INDUSTRIES - DIVISION RESEARCH LIBRARY (Sci-Engr)
333 Ravenswood Ave. Phone: (415)859-5041
Menlo Park, CA 94025 Lani Ritchey, Supv., Lit.Serv.
Founded: 1950. **Staff:** Prof 1; Other 2. **Subjects:** Chemicals - commodity, agricultural, inorganic, specialty; minerals; metals; agriculture. **Holdings:** Figures not available. **Subscriptions:** 425 journals and other serials; 6 newspapers. **Services:** Interlibrary loan; library not open to the public.

★13588★
SRI INTERNATIONAL - COMPUTER SCIENCE LITERATURE CENTER (Comp Sci)
333 Ravenswood Ave. Phone: (415)859-6187
Menlo Park, CA 94025 Elizabeth Redfield, Mgr., Lib.Serv.
Founded: 1975. **Staff:** Prof 1; Other 1. **Subjects:** Computer science, engineering, artificial intelligence, network telecommunications. **Holdings:** 5000 books; 300 bound periodical volumes. **Subscriptions:** 88 journals and other serials. **Services:** Center not open to the public. **Computerized Information Services:** DIALOG Information Services; BIBLIO (internal database); Telenet Communication Corporation, ARPANET Network (electronic mail services). **Publications:** CSLC Journals List, semiannual; DDN Protocol Handbook; TCP/IP Vendors Guide, quarterly. **Special Indexes:** Index to protocol literature (online).

★13589★
SRI INTERNATIONAL - DAVID SARNOFF RESEARCH CENTER - LIBRARY (Sci-Engr)
Princeton, NJ 08540 Phone: (609)734-2608
Wendy Chu, Mgr.
Founded: 1941. **Staff:** Prof 2; Other 3. **Subjects:** Radio, electronics, television, physics, chemistry, mathematics, metallurgy, acoustics, computers, semiconducting materials, space technology. **Holdings:** 32,000 books; 12,000 bound periodical volumes; 1000 reels of microfilm; 110 VF drawers of company reports; 100 VF drawers of pamphlets. **Subscriptions:** 450 journals and other serials. **Services:** Interlibrary loan; copying; library open to the public. **Automated Operations:** Computerized cataloging, acquisitions, serials, and circulation. **Computerized Information Services:** DIALOG Information Services, BRS Information Technologies, Electronic Markets and Information Systems, Inc. (EMIS). **Publications:** Weekly Bulletin - for internal distribution only. **Staff:** Larry Eubank, Coord., Info.Serv..

★13590★
SRI INTERNATIONAL - RESEARCH INFORMATION SERVICES DEPARTMENT (Sci-Engr, Bus-Fin)
333 Ravenswood Ave. Phone: (415)326-6200
Menlo Park, CA 94025 Marjorie Wilson, Dir.
Founded: 1946. **Staff:** Prof 8; Other 16. **Subjects:** Engineering, physical sciences, life sciences, management sciences, research and development, economics. **Holdings:** 60,000 books; 8500 bound periodical volumes; 65,500 technical reports; 29,412 corporate annual reports; 6384 pamphlets; 135,000 government documents. **Subscriptions:** 1730 journals and other serials. **Services:** Interlibrary loan; copying; SDI; information systems design; department open to the public for reference use only by prior arrangement. **Automated Operations:** Computerized cataloging, acquisitions, and serials. **Computerized Information Services:** STN International, DunSprint, ESA/IRS, VU/TEXT Information Services, WILSONLINE, Faxon, BRS Information Technologies, DIALOG Information Services, DTIC, Finsbury Data Services Ltd., Dow Jones News/Retrieval, MEDLARS, Pergamon ORBIT InfoLine, Inc., Telesystemes Questel, RLIN; LIBRI (internal database); OnTyme Electronic Message Network Service (electronic mail service). Performs searches on fee basis. Contact Person: Donna Kleiner, Sr.Info.Spec., 859-5983. **Networks/Consortia:** Member of SOUTHNET, CLASS. **Publications:** Library Notes, 6/year; Serials List, 2/year - both for internal distribution only. **Staff:** Helen Rolen, Supv., Tech.Serv.; Lucille Steelman, Rsrcs.Coord.; Josh Duberman, Info.Spec.; Nancy Myers, Hd., Ref.; Geraldine Wong, Rec.Ctr.Mgr..

★13591★
SRI INTERNATIONAL - STRATEGIC STUDIES CENTER (SSC) LIBRARY
1611 N. Kent St.
Arlington, VA 22209
Defunct

JOAN STAATS LIBRARY
See: Jackson Laboratory (7145)

SAMUEL J. STABINS, M.D. MEDICAL LIBRARY
See: Genesee Hospital (5578)

★13592★
STACK'S RARE COIN COMPANY OF NEW YORK - TECHNICAL INFORMATION CENTER (Rec)
123 W. 57th St. Phone: (212)582-2580
New York, NY 10019 James C. Risk, Mgr., Tech.Oper.
Staff: Prof 2. **Subjects:** Rare coins - U.S., ancient, foreign; medals and decorations. **Special Collections:** Historical busts of famous world personalities. **Holdings:** 15,000 books; 5000 bound periodical volumes. **Services:** Center open to the public with permission and by appointment.

★13593★
STAGECOACH LIBRARY FOR GENEALOGICAL RESEARCH (Hist)
1840 S. Wolcott Ct. Phone: (303)922-8856
Denver, CO 80219 Donna J. Porter, Owner
Staff: Prof 2; Other 1. **Subjects:** Genealogy, local history. **Holdings:** 4500 books; 400 other cataloged items. **Subscriptions:** 10 journals and other serials. **Services:** Copying; library open to the public by mail only. **Publications:** Catalog of holdings - for sale. **Remarks:** An alternate telephone number is 936-0118.

HELEN STAHLER LIBRARY
See: Christ United Methodist Church - Helen Stahler Library (3143)

RALPH C. STAIGER LIBRARY
See: International Reading Association (7060)

★13594★
A.E. STALEY MANUFACTURING COMPANY - TECHNICAL INFORMATION CENTER (Food-Bev)
2200 E. Eldorado St. Phone: (217)421-2543
Decatur, IL 62525 Richard E. Wallace, Mgr.
Founded: 1920. **Staff:** Prof 2; Other 2. **Subjects:** Carbohydrates, sweeteners, fats-oils, polymers, starch, corn products. **Holdings:** 10,000 books; 10,000 bound and microfilm periodical volumes; 3000 reprints, translations, pamphlets; 15,000 patents; 16 VF drawers. **Subscriptions:** 500 journals and other serials. **Services:** Interlibrary loan; copying; center open to the public with restrictions. **Automated Operations:** Computerized cataloging, serials, and circulation. **Computerized Information Services:** DIALOG Information Services, Pergamon ORBIT InfoLine, Inc., STN International, MEDLARS, OCLC, BRS Information Technologies, Dow Jones News/Retrieval; Famulus (internal database). **Networks/Consortia:** Member of Rolling Prairie Library System (RPLS). **Publications:** Abstracts, weekly; New Additions to the Library, bimonthly.

STALEY LIBRARY
See: Millikin University (8992)

J. KENNETH STALLMAN MEMORIAL LIBRARY
See: Atlantic Salmon Federation (1128)

HERBERT S. STAMATS ART LIBRARY
See: Cedar Rapids Museum of Art - Herbert S. Stamats Art Library (2782)

★13595★
STAMFORD CATHOLIC LIBRARY, INC. (Rel-Phil)
14 Peveril Rd. Phone: (203)348-4422
Stamford, CT 06902-3019 Mary C. Cash, Libn.
Founded: 1948. **Staff:** Prof 1. **Subjects:** Religion, theology, American literature, history, biography, psychology. **Holdings:** 3000 books; 25 documentary series; 200 pre-Vatican II pamphlets; 20 encyclicals; 12 scripture studies; 100 papal and episcopal documents; 24 tapes. **Services:** Interlibrary loan; library open to the public on a fee basis. **Publications:** Annual Report.

★13596★
STAMFORD HISTORICAL SOCIETY - LIBRARY (Hist)
1508 High Ridge Rd. Phone: (203)329-1183
Stamford, CT 06903-4107 Ronald Marcus, Libn.
Founded: 1901. **Staff:** 2. **Subjects:** History - Stamford, Fairfield County, State of Connecticut. **Special Collections:** Catherine Aiken School Collection, 1855-1913; Charles Kurz Photographic Collection on Stamford, 1868-1941; Eaton, Yale and Towne Collection on Yale and Towne Manufacturing Company of Stamford, 1868-1949; F. Stewart Andrews Collection on Stamford Foundry Company, 1850-1950; Anson Dickinson Collection, 1779-1852. **Holdings:** 2800 books and pamphlets; 50 Stamford tax lists manuscripts, 1712-1876; 136 Stamford Revolutionary War damage claims manuscripts, 1776-1783; 300 Stamford newspapers, 1829-1925; 2000 Stamford pictures, 1870-1940; 1000 Stamford slides, 1870-1920; 25 Stamford maps, 1800-1961; 65 Stamford account books manuscripts, 1787-1941; 12 Stamford diaries, 1850-1929; 12 VF drawers of documents and clippings. **Services:** Copying; library open to the public. **Publications:** Stamford Revolutionary War Damage Claims; Stamford - Pictures from the Past; Stamford - Journey through Time; Fort Stamford; Stamford in the Gilded Age - The Political Life of a Connecticut Town 1868-1893; Stamford from Puritan to Patriot 1641-1774; list of other publications - available on request.

★13597★
STAMFORD HOSPITAL - HEALTH SCIENCES LIBRARY (Med)
Shelburne Rd.
Box 9317 Phone: (203)325-7522
Stamford, CT 06904-9317 Joanna Faraday, Dir.
Staff: Prof 1; Other 1. **Subjects:** Clinical medicine, nursing. **Holdings:** 2376 books; 5174 bound periodical volumes; 6454 microfiche; 1177 tapes; 3607 slides. **Subscriptions:** 353 journals and other serials. **Services:** Interlibrary loan; copying; library open to the public by appointment only. **Computerized Information Services:** BRS Information Technologies, NLM. **Networks/Consortia:** Member of Connecticut Association of Health Science Libraries (CAHSL), Health Information Libraries of Westchester (HILOW), Southwestern Connecticut Library Council (SWLC). **Publications:** Newsletter, quarterly - to hospital staff and Connecticut medical libraries.

★13598★
STANDARD ALASKA PRODUCTION COMPANY - INFORMATION RESOURCE CENTER (Energy, Sci-Engr)
900 E. Benson Blvd.
Box 196612 Phone: (907)564-4594
Anchorage, AK 99519-6612
Jacqueline Lauren Barker, Supv., Info.Serv.
Staff: Prof 2; Other 3. **Subjects:** Geology, environmental aspects of petroleum development, management, engineering, maintenance, petroleum production. **Holdings:** 6000 books; 1500 reports; 1500 reels of microfilm of industry standards and vendor catalogs; 500 reels of microfilm of journals. **Subscriptions:** 100 journals and other serials. **Services:** Interlibrary loan; copying; SDI (limited); center open to the public by appointment. **Automated Operations:** Computerized cataloging. **Computerized Information Services:** DIALOG Information Services, Pergamon ORBIT InfoLine, Inc. **Networks/Consortia:** Member of Alaska Library Network (ALN). **Publications:** Acquisitions List, quarterly - for internal distribution only; subscription list, annual; special bibliographies and handouts, irregular.

★13599★
STANDARD EDUCATIONAL CORPORATION - EDITORIAL LIBRARY (Publ)
200 W. Monroe St. Phone: (312)346-7440
Chicago, IL 60606 David E. King, Libn.
Staff: 2. **Subjects:** General reference. **Holdings:** 10,000 books; 400 microforms; 88 VF drawers. **Subscriptions:** 161 journals and other serials. **Services:** Interlibrary loan; copying; library open to the public by appointment. **Networks/Consortia:** Member of ILLINET. **Publications:** New Books List, monthly; Serials List, annual.

STANDARD OIL COMPANY
See: BP America, Inc. (1791)

★13600★
STANDARD & POOR'S COMPUSTAT SERVICES, INC. - DATA RESOURCE CENTER (Bus-Fin)
7400 S. Alton Court Phone: (303)771-6510
Engelwood, CO 80112 Alice Dewey, Libn.
Founded: 1968. **Staff:** Prof 1; Other 7. **Subjects:** Financial reports. **Special Collections:** Daily Stock Price Record Books; Moody publications. **Holdings:** 50 books; 7 filing cabinets of Federal Reserve publications; 400,000 microfiche of financial reports; financial reports from over 10,000 companies; Standard & Poor's publications; Canadian Stock Exchange listings. **Subscriptions:** 30 journals and other serials; 5 newspapers. **Services:** Center open to the public by appointment. **Automated Operations:** Computerized cataloging. **Computerized Information Services:** Compustat (internal database). **Publications:** Compustat; Financial Dynamics, both weekly.

★13601★
STANDARD & POOR'S CORPORATION - RESEARCH LIBRARY (Bus-Fin)
25 Broadway Phone: (212)208-8514
New York, NY 10004 Dennis F. Jensen, Lib.Mgr.
Founded: 1917. **Staff:** Prof 5; Other 17. **Subjects:** Corporations and industries, securities and investments, finance and banking, public utilities. **Special Collections:** Annual and quarterly reports, prospectuses, documents describing corporations and their activities (500 VF drawers); Standard & Poor's publications, 1860 to present; disclosure reports to Securities and Exchange Commission (SEC), 1968 to present, on microfiche (2 million pieces). **Holdings:** 22,000 volumes; 600 reels of microfilm; 50 VF drawers of pamphlets and newsletters. **Subscriptions:** 2000 journals and other serials; 40 newspapers. **Services:** Copying (limited); library open to the public with restrictions. **Automated Operations:** Computerized acquisitions. **Computerized Information Services:** DIALOG Information Services, Dow Jones News/Retrieval, Data Resources (DRI), Progressive Grocer Company, Stock Pak; Corporate Files Information Systems (internal database). Performs searches on fee basis. Contact Person: Douglas Green, Ctrl. Inquiry Supv., 208-1199 or Sawn Shulka, Ref.Serv., 208-8520. **Publications:** Acquisitions list/newsletter, monthly; Library Notes, monthly - both for internal distribution and to others on request. **Remarks:** Fax: (212)514-7016. **Staff:** Richard Zain Eldeen, Tech.Serv.Supv.; Cynthia A. Gagen, Corp. Files Mgr..

★13602★
STANDARD REGISTER COMPANY - CORPORATE LIBRARY (Sci-Engr)
Box 1167 Phone: (513)443-1000
Dayton, OH 45401 Dorothea P. Adkinson, Libn.
Staff: Prof 1. **Subjects:** Chemistry; printing; paper; physics; business; engineering - chemical, mechanical, electronic. **Holdings:** 5500 books; 104 bound periodical volumes; 3000 company catalogs. **Subscriptions:** 250 journals and other serials. **Services:** Interlibrary loan; library not open to the public.

STANDARDBRED CANADA LIBRARY
See: Canadian Trotting Association (2614)

★13603★
STANDARDS COUNCIL OF CANADA - INFORMATION DIVISION (Sci-Engr)
350 Sparks St., Suite 1200 Phone: (613)238-3222
Ottawa, ON, Canada K1P 6N7 D. Thompson, Mgr.
Founded: 1977. **Staff:** Prof 6; Other 2. **Subjects:** Standards, specifications, codes and related documents, technical regulations. **Holdings:** 400,000 documents. **Subscriptions:** 90 journals and other serials. **Services:** Copying; division open to the public. **Computerized Information Services:** CAN/OLE, iNET 2000, Standards Information Service (SIS). **Special Catalogs:**

National Standards of Canada (book). **Special Indexes:** KWIC Directory and Index of Standards and Specifications. **Remarks:** The toll-free telephone number in Canada is (800)267-8220. **Also Known As:** Conseil Canadien des Normes. **Staff:** Z. Ignatowicz, Comp.Anl..

STANFORD ARCHIVE OF RECORDED SOUND
See: Stanford University - Music Library (13619)

★13604★
STANFORD LINEAR ACCELERATOR CENTER - LIBRARY (Sci-Engr)
Box 4349 Phone: (415)854-3300
Stanford, CA 94305 Robert C. Gex, Chf.Libn.
Staff: Prof 5; Other 4. **Subjects:** High energy physics, particle accelerators. **Holdings:** 12,000 books; 6000 bound periodical volumes; 98,000 technical reports and preprints; 20,000 reports on microfiche. **Subscriptions:** 1214 journals and other serials. **Services:** Interlibrary loan; copying; library open to the public. **Automated Operations:** Computerized cataloging, acquisitions, and serials. **Computerized Information Services:** DIALOG Information Services, Chemical Information Systems, Inc. (CIS). Contact Person: Louise Addis, Assoc.Hd.Libn.. **Publications:** Preprints in Particles and Fields, weekly - by subscription; Anti-Preprint Cumulation, annual - for sale. **Remarks:** The Stanford Linear Acceleralor Center operates under contract to the U.S. Department of Energy. Located at 2575 Sand Hill Rd., Menlo Park, CA 94305. **Staff:** Arsella Raman, Ser.Libn.; Rita Taylor, Libn.; Shirley Livengood, Tech. Data Libn..

★13605★
STANFORD UNIVERSITY - ART AND ARCHITECTURE LIBRARY (Art)
Nathan Cummings Art Bldg. Phone: (415)723-3408
Stanford, CA 94305-2018 Alexander D. Ross, Hd.Libn.
Staff: Prof 2; Other 5. **Subjects:** Art - 19th and 20th century, Medieval, Renaissance, Baroque, Far Eastern, ancient; classical archeology; architectural history. **Special Collections:** Thomas Rowlandson Collection; Paris Salon Catalogues, 1673-1952; J.D. Chen Collection (Chinese art and archeology). **Holdings:** 125,000 volumes. **Subscriptions:** 480 journals and other serials. **Services:** Copying; library use limited to library card holders. **Computerized Information Services:** DIALOG Information Services, BRS Information Technologies; Socrates (internal database). **Networks/Consortia:** Member of CLASS, South Bay Cooperative Library System (SBCLS), RLG.

★13606★
STANFORD UNIVERSITY - BRANNER EARTH SCIENCES LIBRARY (Sci-Engr)
School of Earth Sciences Phone: (415)723-2300
Stanford, CA 94305 Charlotte R.M. Derksen, Libn./Bibliog.
Founded: 1915. **Staff:** Prof 1; Other 4. **Subjects:** Geology, applied earth sciences, geophysics, petroleum engineering, micropaleontology, geochemistry. **Special Collections:** Hayden, King, and Wheeler surveys; state geological survey open-file reports; geothermal, technical reports. **Holdings:** 100,000 books and bound periodical volumes; 107,000 maps; 960 Stanford dissertations; 500 Stanford student reports; 50,000 microfiche. **Subscriptions:** 2450 journals and other serials. **Services:** Interlibrary loan; copying; library open to the public for reference use only. **Automated Operations:** Computerized cataloging. **Computerized Information Services:** DIALOG Information Services, Pergamon ORBIT InfoLine, Inc., STN International, BRS Information Technologies, Telesystemes Questel, RLIN; BITNET (electronic mail service). **Networks/Consortia:** Member of CLASS, RLG. **Special Indexes:** Technical reports/open-file reports file (online); map series index (card); thesis series index (online).

★13607★
STANFORD UNIVERSITY - CENTER FOR AERONAUTICS AND SPACE INFORMATION SCIENCES (CASIS) - LIBRARY (Comp Sci)
STAR Lab
Stanford, CA 94305 Phone: (415)497-2848
Subjects: Computer science, systems, and applications in the space sciences. **Holdings:** Figures not available.

★13608★
STANFORD UNIVERSITY - CENTRAL MAP COLLECTION (Geog-Map)
Cecil H. Green Library Phone: (415)497-1811
Stanford, CA 94305 Karyl Tonge, Map Libn.
Founded: 1948. **Staff:** 1. **Holdings:** 78,000 maps. **Services:** Copying; circulation to authorized Stanford borrowers; library open to the public with restrictions. **Networks/Consortia:** Member of CLASS, South Bay Cooperative Library System (SBCLS), RLG. **Publications:** Selected Additions to the Central Map Collection, irregular; Map Collections (guides).

★13609★
STANFORD UNIVERSITY - CUBBERLEY EDUCATION LIBRARY (Educ)
Stanford, CA 94305 Phone: (415)723-2121
Barbara Celone, Hd.Libn.
Founded: 1938. **Staff:** Prof 2; Other 7. **Subjects:** Education, allied social sciences. **Special Collections:** 19th century textbooks (2000); college catalogs (78,000). **Holdings:** 134,489 volumes; 15,000 volumes of historical curriculum materials; 12,000 domestic and foreign government documents; 12,000 historical textbooks; 270,600 ERIC microfiche. **Subscriptions:** 1252 journals and other serials. **Services:** Interlibrary loan; copying; library open to the public; borrowing limited to library card holders. **Automated Operations:** Computerized cataloging and acquisitions. **Computerized Information Services:** DIALOG Information Services, BRS Information Technologies; Socrates (internal database). **Networks/Consortia:** Member of CLASS, South Bay Cooperative Library System (SBCLS), RLG. **Publications:** Selected Acquisitions, monthly - to faculty and interested individuals; Contemporary Cuban Education: An Annotated Bibliography, 1980; Education in Bolivia: A Bibliography, 1980; Education in Tanzania: A Working Bibliography, 1981 - available for sale. **Staff:** Juanita McKinley, Asst.Hd.Libn..

★13610★
STANFORD UNIVERSITY - ENGINEERING LIBRARY (Sci-Engr)
Terman Engineering Center Phone: (415)723-1013
Stanford, CA 94305 Eleanor Goodchild, Hd.
Founded: 1942. **Staff:** Prof 3; Other 5. **Subjects:** Engineering - civil, electrical, industrial, mechanical; engineering-economic systems; aeronautics and astronautics; materials science. **Special Collections:** Timoshenko Collection (applied mechanics; 1800 volumes). **Holdings:** 30,000 books; 36,000 bound periodical volumes; 350,000 microfiche; 60,000 technical reports. **Subscriptions:** 1851 journals and other serials; 13 newspapers. **Services:** Interlibrary loan; copying; library open to the public. **Automated Operations:** Computerized cataloging and acquisitions. **Computerized Information Services:** DIALOG Information Services, Pergamon ORBIT InfoLine, Inc., BRS Information Technologies, STN International, RLIN; Socrates (internal database); OnTyme Electronic Message Network Service (electronic mail service). **Networks/Consortia:** Member of CLASS, South Bay Cooperative Library System (SBCLS), RLG. **Staff:** John Broadwin, Ref., Bibliog.Instr.; Lois Sher, Oper.Mgr.; Steven Gass, Asst.Hd. & Bibliog..

★13611★
STANFORD UNIVERSITY - FALCONER BIOLOGY LIBRARY (Biol Sci)
Stanford, CA 94305 Phone: (415)723-1528
Joseph G. Wible, Hd.Libn.
Founded: 1926. **Staff:** Prof 1; Other 4. **Subjects:** Biochemistry, molecular biology, population genetics and ecology, organismal biology. **Holdings:** 79,000 volumes. **Subscriptions:** 1300 journals and other serials. **Services:** Interlibrary loan; copying; library open to the public for reference use only. **Automated Operations:** Computerized public access catalog. **Computerized Information Services:** DIALOG Information Services, Pergamon ORBIT InfoLine, Inc., BRS Information Technologies, NLM; Socrates (internal database); BITNET, DIALMAIL (electronic mail services). **Networks/Consortia:** Member of CLASS, South Bay Cooperative Library System (SBCLS), RLG.

★13612★
STANFORD UNIVERSITY - FOOD RESEARCH INSTITUTE - LIBRARY (Agri, Food-Bev)
Stanford, CA 94305 Phone: (415)723-3943
Charles C. Milford, Hd.Libn.
Founded: 1921. **Staff:** Prof 1; Other 2. **Subjects:** Economic aspects of agriculture, food supply, population, underdeveloped areas. **Special Collections:** Documents of foreign governments and international organizations. **Holdings:** 76,500 books; 25,000 pamphlets. **Subscriptions:** 2000 journals and other serials. **Services:** Interlibrary loan; copying; library open to the public for reference use only. **Computerized Information Services:** RLIN. **Networks/Consortia:** Member of RLG.

★13613★
STANFORD UNIVERSITY - HOOVER INSTITUTION ON WAR, REVOLUTION AND PEACE - LIBRARY (Soc Sci)
Stanford, CA 94305 Phone: (415)723-2058
Neil J. McElroy, Hd., Rd.Serv.
Founded: 1919. **Staff:** Prof 30; Other 45. **Subjects:** 20th century economic, political, and social problems with special emphasis on World Wars I and II and the following geographical areas: Africa, China, Eastern Europe, U.S.S.R., Japan, North and Latin America, Middle East, United States, Central and Western Europe. **Special Collections:** American Relief Administration records; military journals; international organizations; communist party materials; Paris Peace Conference records; propaganda and psychological warfare; underground movements. **Holdings:** 1.6 million volumes; 55,000 reels of microfilm; 43,000 microfiche; 3700 archival collections of national and international organizations, military government, political personnel; 774 videotapes; 164,491 photographs; 2933 slides; 68,324 posters; pamphlets; government documents; newspaper and periodical file in Slavic, Western, and East Asian languages (38,000 titles). **Subscriptions:** 3572 journals and other serials; 370 newspapers. **Services:** Interlibrary loan; copying; library open to the public. **Automated Operations:** Computerized cataloging. **Computerized Information Services:** DIALOG Information Services, RLIN; Socrates (internal database). **Networks/Consortia:** Member of RLG. **Publications:** List of publications - available on request. **Special Catalogs:** Middle East languages catalog; survey of area collection holdings. **Staff:** Charles Palm, Assoc.Dir.; Joseph Kladko, Hd., Tech.Serv.; Robert Conquest, Cur., Russia & Eastern Europe; Peter Duignan, Cur., Africa Mid East; Ramon H. Myers, Cur., E. Asia Coll.; William Ratliff, Cur., Latin & N. Amer.Coll.; Agnes Peterson, Cur., Central & Western Europe Coll..

★13614★
STANFORD UNIVERSITY - HOPKINS MARINE STATION - LIBRARY (Biol Sci)
Cabrillo Point Phone: (408)373-0460
Pacific Grove, CA 93950 Alan Baldridge, Hd.Libn.
Founded: 1920. **Staff:** Prof 1; Other 1. **Subjects:** Marine zoology and phycology, physiology and neurobiology, cell and developmental biology, biochemistry, immunology, ecology and population biology, oceanography. **Special Collections:** MacFarland Opisthobranchiate Molluscan Collection (800 items); G.M. Smith Algae Reprint Collection (300 volumes). **Holdings:** 24,000 volumes; 132 maps; 1400 other cataloged items. **Subscriptions:** 450 journals and other serials. **Services:** Interlibrary loan; copying; library open to the public by appointment. **Automated Operations:** Computerized cataloging and acquisitions. **Computerized Information Services:** DIALOG Information Services. **Networks/Consortia:** Member of RLG, CLASS. **Publications:** List of faculty and student publications, annual; bibliographies of common local marine invertebrates.

★13615★
STANFORD UNIVERSITY - J. HUGH JACKSON LIBRARY (Bus-Fin)
Graduate School of Business Phone: (415)723-2161
Stanford, CA 94305-5016 Bela Gallo, Dir.
Founded: 1932. **Staff:** Prof 11; Other 24. **Subjects:** Accounting, business economics, finance, international business, investment, management, marketing, quantitative analysis. **Special Collections:** Favre Collection (Pacific Northwest economics); Jackson Collection (accounting information files of former Dean of School). **Holdings:** 354,928 books and other cataloged items; government documents; pamphlets; 350,000 corporate reports; 3756 reels of microfilm; 921,536 microfiche. **Subscriptions:** 2256 periodicals; 102 newspapers. **Services:** Interlibrary loan (limited to faculty and graduate students); library not open to the public. **Automated Operations:** Computerized serials. **Computerized Information Services:** RLIN. **Publications:** Selected Additions to the J. Hugh Jackson Library, 6/year. **Special Catalogs:** Jackson Library Periodicals, annual (book); Jackson Library Annuals on Standing Order, annual (book). **Staff:** Evelyn Hu, Cat.Libn.; Janna Leffingwell, Cat.Libn.; Karen Wilson, Hd.Pub.Serv.Libn.; Robert Mayer, Asst.Dir./Hd., Tech.Serv.; Esther Pike, Acq.Libn.; Peter Latusek, Ser.Libn.; Henry Wang, Doc.Libn.; Hanna Slocum, Hd.Ref.Serv.Libn.; Luisa T. Claeys, Asst.Ref.Libn..

★13616★
STANFORD UNIVERSITY - LANE MEDICAL LIBRARY (Med)
Stanford University Medical Center Phone: (415)723-6831
Stanford, CA 94305 Peter Stangl, Dir.
Founded: 1906. **Staff:** Prof 14; Other 25. **Subjects:** Clinical medicine and its specialties, preclinical and basic sciences, public health, nursing and allied fields. **Special Collections:** History of Medicine; Barkan Ophthalmology Collection. **Holdings:** 295,466 volumes; 28,648 pamphlets and theses; 485 audio recordings; 545 videotapes and cassettes; 95 computer materials. **Subscriptions:** 3244 journals and other serials; 6 newspapers. **Services:** Interlibrary loan; copying; SDI; library open to the public for reference use; borrowing limited to library card holders. **Automated Operations:** Computerized public access catalog, cataloging, acquisitions, and circulation. **Computerized Information Services:** MEDLARS, DIALOG Information Services, Pergamon ORBIT InfoLine, Inc., UTLAS, BRS Information Technologies, CAS ONLINE; OnTyme Electronic Message Network Service, RLG (electronic mail services). Performs searches on fee basis. Contact Person: **Networks/Consortia:** Member of Pacific Southwest Regional Medical Library Service, CLASS, RLG. **Special Catalogs:** Serials list, annual. **Special Indexes:** Reference index. **Staff:** Valerie Su, Dp.Dir./Hd., Pub.Serv.; Dick Miller, Sys.Libn./Hd., Tech.Serv.; Anne Brewer, Hd., LRC; Marcia Epelbaum, Hd., Circ. & Stacks Maint.; Marsha Mielke, Info.Cons.; Michael Newman, Info.Cons.; Marilyn Tinsley, Info.Cons.; Betty Vadeboncoeur, Info.Cons.; Susan Anderes, Tech.Serv.Libn.; Herman Pai, Tech.Serv.Libn.; Bruce Flath, Asst.Sys./Info.Cons..

★13617★
STANFORD UNIVERSITY - LAW LIBRARY (Law)
Stanford, CA 94305 Phone: (415)497-2721
Lance E. Dickson, Law Libn.
Founded: 1894. **Staff:** Prof 8; Other 18. **Subjects:** Law, with particular emphasis on Anglo-American legislative and administrative materials. **Special Collections:** Maritime law; air law; French law; German law. **Holdings:** 315,000 volumes. **Subscriptions:** 5111 journals and other serials. **Services:** Interlibrary loan; library not open to the public. **Automated Operations:** Computerized cataloging. **Networks/Consortia:** Member of CLASS, RLG. **Staff:** Rosalee Long, Assoc. Law Libn.; J. Paul Lomio, Pub.Serv.Libn.; Eliska Ryznar, Hd.Cat.Libn.; Iris J. Wildman, Sr.Ref. & Spec.Proj.Libn..

★13618★
STANFORD UNIVERSITY - MATHEMATICAL AND COMPUTER SCIENCES LIBRARY (Sci-Engr, Comp Sci)
Bldg. 380, Sloan Mathematics Center Phone: (415)723-4672
Stanford, CA 94305 Rebecca Lasher, Hd.Libn.
Founded: 1964. **Staff:** Prof 1; Other 5. **Subjects:** Mathematics, statistics, operations research, computer science. **Holdings:** 54,847 volumes; 35,000 technical reports. **Subscriptions:** 1127 journals and other serials. **Services:** Interlibrary loan; copying; library open to the public for reference use only. **Automated Operations:** Computerized public access catalog, cataloging, and acquisitions. **Computerized Information Services:** DIALOG Information Services, Pergamon ORBIT InfoLine, Inc., BRS Information Technologies, RLIN, STN International; Socrates (internal database); ARPANET, BITNET (electronic mail services). **Networks/Consortia:** Member of CLASS, RLG, South Bay Cooperative Library System (SBCLS). **Publications:** New Technical Reports List, semimonthly.

★13619★
STANFORD UNIVERSITY - MUSIC LIBRARY (Mus)
Braun Music Center Phone: (415)723-1211
Stanford, CA 94305 Karen N. Nagy, Hd.Libn.
Founded: 1948. **Staff:** Prof 4; Other 6. **Subjects:** Music. **Special Collections:** Stanford Archive of Recorded Sound (134,000 sound recordings). **Holdings:** 70,000 books and scores; 2400 reels of microfilm; 1700 microcards and microfiche; 26,000 phonograph records. **Subscriptions:** 500 journals and other serials. **Services:** Interlibrary loan; copying; listening facilities for phonograph records and reel-to-reel tapes; library use limited to library card holders. **Automated Operations:** Computerized cataloging and acquisitions. **Computerized Information Services:** DIALOG Information Services, Pergamon ORBIT InfoLine, Inc., BRS Information Technologies; Socrates (internal database). **Networks/Consortia:** Member of CLASS, RLG, South Bay Cooperative Library System (SBCLS). **Publications:** List of publications - available on request. **Staff:** Barbara Sawka, Archv.; Mimi Tashiro, Asst.Mus.Libn..

★13620★
STANFORD UNIVERSITY - PHYSICS LIBRARY (Sci-Engr)
Stanford, CA 94305 Phone: (415)723-4342
Henry Lowood, Hd.Libn.
Staff: Prof 1; Other 3. **Subjects:** Physics, astronomy, astrophysics, meteorology. **Special Collections:** Microwave and high-energy physics. **Holdings:** 45,000 books and bound periodical volumes; technical reports; sky atlas photographs. **Subscriptions:** 630 journals and other serials. **Services:** Interlibrary loan; copying; library use limited to library card holders. **Automated Operations:** Computerized cataloging and acquisitions (through Green Library). **Computerized Information Services:** DIALOG Information Services, Pergamon ORBIT InfoLine, Inc., BRS Information Technologies, STN International, Integrated Technical Information

System (ITIS); Socrates (internal database). **Networks/Consortia:** Member of CLASS, RLG, South Bay Cooperative Library System (SBCLS).

★13621★
STANFORD UNIVERSITY - SPECIAL COLLECTIONS AND UNIVERSITY ARCHIVES (Hum, Hist)
Cecil H. Green Library Phone: (415)723-4054
Stanford, CA 94305 Michael T. Ryan, Chf.
Staff: Prof 5; Other 11. **Subjects:** British and American literature of the 19th and 20th centuries, book arts and the history of the book, 16th-18th century continental books, history of science, music, theater, the Mexican-American experience, California history and politics, Stanford University history, higher education, science and technology. **Special Collections:** Charlotte Ashley Felton Memorial Library (British and American literature); Morgan A. and Aline D. Gunst Memorial Library of the Book Arts; Samuel I. and Cecile M. Barchas Collection on the History of Science and Ideas; Frederick E. Brasch Collection on Sir Isaac Newton and the History of Scientific Thought; Memorial Library of Music; Elmer E. Robinson Collection in American History; Antoine Borel Collection (manuscripts pertaining to California history and politics); James A. Healy Collection of Irish Literature; John Steinbeck Collection; Ernest Hemingway Collection; Mary L. Schofield Collection of Children's Literature; Taube-Baron Collection of Jewish History and Culture; Fanino Collection of Dante. **Holdings:** 120,000 books; 15.8 million manuscripts; 2700 maps; 197,000 photographs and prints; administrative records of the university; personal papers of faculty, trustees, staff, students; Stanford family papers; oral histories; 300 3-dimensional objects; 530 reels of microfilm; 56,000 maps; 1100 sound recordings and films; prints; posters; ephemera. **Subscriptions:** 330 journals and other serials. **Services:** Copying; archives not open to the public. **Automated Operations:** Computerized cataloging, acquisitions, and serials. **Computerized Information Services:** RLIN; Socrates (internal database). **Publications:** List of publications - available on request. **Special Catalogs:** Exhibition catalogs; descriptive guide to manuscript/archival collections; special card catalogs for maps, photographs, posters, 3-dimensional objects, theses, and dissertations. **Staff:** Roxanne-Louise Nilan, Asst.Chf.; Mark Dimunation, Rare Bk.Libn.; Margaret Kimball, Mss. & Archv.Libn..

★13622★
STANFORD UNIVERSITY - SWAIN LIBRARY OF CHEMISTRY AND CHEMICAL ENGINEERING (Sci-Engr)
Stanford, CA 94305 Phone: (415)723-9237
Joseph G. Wible, Act.Hd.Libn.
Founded: 1901. **Staff:** Prof 1; Other 3. **Subjects:** Chemistry, chemical engineering. **Holdings:** 40,700 volumes; 2400 microfiche; 375 reels of microfilm; 600 dissertations. **Subscriptions:** 690 journals and other serials. **Services:** Interlibrary loan; copying; library open to the public for reference use only. **Automated Operations:** Computerized public access catalog. **Computerized Information Services:** DIALOG Information Services, RLIN, Pergamon ORBIT InfoLine, Inc., BRS Information Technologies, CAS ONLINE; Socrates (internal database); BITNET (electronic mail service). **Networks/Consortia:** Member of CLASS, RLG, South Bay Cooperative Library System (SBCLS).

★13623★
STANFORD UNIVERSITY - TANNER MEMORIAL PHILOSOPHY LIBRARY (Rel-Phil)
Department of Philosophy Phone: (415)723-1539
Stanford, CA 94305 Zita Zukowsky, Libn.
Founded: 1960. **Staff:** Prof 1; Other 4. **Subjects:** Symbolic logic; philosophical logic; philosophy of mathematics, language, and science; metaphysics and epistemology; ethics and philosophy of action; history of philosophy; aesthetics. **Special Collections:** Clarence Irving Lewis Memorial Collection (235 volumes). **Holdings:** 5500 books; 850 bound periodical volumes; 200 dissertations; 925 reprints and typescripts. **Subscriptions:** 75 journals and other serials. **Services:** Interlibrary loan; library open to the public with approval of Stanford University Libraries. **Automated Operations:** Computerized cataloging and acquisitions. **Computerized Information Services:** Online systems. Performs searches on fee basis.

★13624★
STANISLAUS COUNTY LAW LIBRARY (Law)
Rm. 223, Courthouse
1100 I St. Phone: (209)571-6967
Modesto, CA 95354 Janice K. Milliken, Law Libn.
Founded: 1893. **Staff:** Prof 1. **Subjects:** Law. **Holdings:** 18,000 volumes. **Services:** Interlibrary loan (limited); copying; library open to the public for reference use only.

STANISLAUS COUNTY MEDICAL LIBRARY
See: Scenic General Hospital (12948)

★13625★
STANISLAUS COUNTY SCHOOLS - TEACHERS' PROFESSIONAL LIBRARY (Educ)
801 County Center No. 3 Ct. Phone: (209)571-6593
Modesto, CA 95355 V. Ruth Smith, Hd.
Staff: Prof 1; Other 1. **Subjects:** Education. **Holdings:** 9000 books. **Subscriptions:** 35 journals and other serials. **Services:** Library open to teachers only.

★13626★
STANLEY ASSOCIATES ENGINEERING, LTD. - LIBRARY (Env-Cons, Plan)
10160 112th St. Phone: (403)423-4777
Edmonton, AB, Canada T5P 2L6 Louise Ball, Libn.
Staff: Prof 1; Other 1. **Subjects:** Pollution control, transportation, environmental and municipal engineering, land development, water supply and distribution, urban and regional planning, structural engineering. **Holdings:** 10,000 books; 300 bound periodical volumes; 12,000 internal reports and proposals; 30,000 engineering drawings on microfilm; 6000 original drawings; 1000 topographic maps. **Subscriptions:** 200 journals and other serials; 20 newspapers. **Services:** Interlibrary loan; copying; library open to the public by request. **Computerized Information Services:** DIALOG Information Services, QL Systems, CAN/OLE, National Ground Water Information Center Data Base, Info Globe.

★13627★
STANLEY CONSULTANTS - TECHNICAL LIBRARY (Sci-Engr, Plan)
Stanley Bldg. Phone: (319)264-6234
Muscatine, IA 52761 Terri M. Goos, Libn.
Staff: 1. **Subjects:** Engineering, architecture, urban and regional planning. **Holdings:** 12,500 books; 1000 bound periodical volumes; 15,000 vendor catalogs on microfilm; 115 videotapes of internal seminars; 24 cassettes. **Subscriptions:** 222 journals and other serials. **Services:** Interlibrary loan; copying; library open to the public with restrictions. **Computerized Information Services:** DIALOG Information Services, Institute of Electrical and Electronics Engineers, Inc. (IEEE).

EDMUND STANLEY LIBRARY
See: Friends University - Edmund Stanley Library - Special Collections (5417)

PATRICK J. STAPLETON, JR. LIBRARY
See: Indiana University of Pennsylvania (6810)

★13628★
STAR MAGAZINE - LIBRARY (Publ)
660 White Plains Rd. Phone: (914)332-5000
Tarrytown, NY 10591 Christopher E. Bowen, Lib.Dir.
Staff: Prof 1; Other 4. **Subjects:** People, entertainment, news events. **Holdings:** 350,000 clippings; 230,000 photographs; 22,500 color slides and transparencies. **Subscriptions:** 26 journals and other serials; 40 newspapers. **Services:** Library not open to the public.

★13629★
STAR OF THE REPUBLIC MUSEUM - LIBRARY (Hist)
Box 317 Phone: (409)878-2461
Washington, TX 77880 Houston McGaugh, Dir.
Subjects: Texas history, museums and museology, artifact identification. **Special Collections:** Showers-Brown Collection (Texana). **Holdings:** 3000 books; 100 bound periodical volumes; 2000 manuscripts, documents; 300 maps; 100 newspapers, census documents, dissertations on microfilm. **Subscriptions:** 40 journals and other serials. **Services:** Copying; library open to the public. **Special Indexes:** Special Formats Index (booklet).

★13630★
STAR TREK: THE OFFICIAL FAN CLUB - LIBRARY (Rec)
Box 111000 Phone: (303)366-8550
Aurora, CO 80011 John S. Davis, V.P./Assoc.Ed.
Founded: 1980. **Subjects:** Star Trek (television show and movies). **Holdings:** Figures not available.

★13631★
STARK COUNTY HISTORICAL SOCIETY - RALPH K. RAMSAYER, M.D. LIBRARY (Hist)
Box 483 Phone: (216)455-7043
Canton, OH 44701 Sally Donze, Libn.
Staff: Prof 1; Other 5. **Subjects:** President William McKinley and family, Stark County history and industry, local genealogy. **Special Collections:** McKinleyana Collection (records of William McKinley, 25th President of the United States; 9 VF drawers); letters and reports of Captain W.F. Raynolds; Civil War letters; Stark County Clipping files (19 VF drawers). **Holdings:** 3200 books; 200 bound periodical volumes; 1000 other cataloged items; 83 reels of microfilm of McKinley papers and McKinleyana. **Subscriptions:** 53 journals and other serials; 7 newspapers. **Services:** Library open to the public for research only by permission. **Automated Operations:** Computerized public access catalog. **Remarks:** Located at 800 McKinley Monument Dr., N.W., Canton, OH 44708. **Formerly:** Mc Kinley Museum of History, Science and Industry.

★13632★
STARK COUNTY LAW LIBRARY ASSOCIATION - ALLIANCE BRANCH LAW LIBRARY† (Law)
City Hall
470 E. Market
Alliance, OH 44601 Phone: (216)823-6181
Founded: 1930. **Subjects:** U.S. law. **Holdings:** 3500 volumes.

★13633★
STARK COUNTY LAW LIBRARY ASSOCIATION - LAW LIBRARY (Law)
Court House, 4th Fl. Phone: (216)456-2330
Canton, OH 44702 Martha M. Cox, Dir.
Founded: 1890. **Staff:** Prof 1; Other 2. **Subjects:** U.S. and Ohio law. **Holdings:** 43,307 volumes; 37,678 microfiche; 210 reels of microfilm. **Subscriptions:** 70 journals. **Services:** Copying; library open to the public for reference use only. **Computerized Information Services:** WESTLAW, DIALOG Information Services, LEXIS, PHINet FedTax Database.

★13634★
STARK COUNTY LAW LIBRARY ASSOCIATION - MASSILLON BRANCH LAW LIBRARY (Law)
Massillon Municipal Court
Law and Safety Bldg.
102 City Hall, S.E. Phone: (216)830-1725
Massillon, OH 44646 Ida Pedrotty, Libn.
Founded: 1940. **Subjects:** Ohio law. **Holdings:** 2500 volumes.

MIRIAM LUTCHER STARK LIBRARY
See: University of Texas, Austin - Harry Ransom Humanities Research Center (16931)

C.V. STARR EAST ASIAN LIBRARY
See: Columbia University (3475)

DOROTHY C.S. STARR CIVIL WAR RESEARCH LIBRARY
See: Fort Ward Museum (5290)

STARR KING SCHOOL FOR THE MINISTRY
See: Graduate Theological Union (5785)

STARSMORE RESEARCH CENTER
See: Colorado Springs Pioneers' Museum (3418)

★13635★
STATE BAR OF MICHIGAN - LIBRARY (Law)
306 Townsend St. Phone: (517)372-9030
Lansing, MI 48933 Douglas L. Sweet, Dir., R. & D.
Staff: 1. **Subjects:** Law. **Holdings:** 3000 books; 700 bound periodical volumes. **Subscriptions:** 10 journals and other serials; 5 newspapers. **Services:** Library open to lawyers only.

★13636★
STATE CAPITAL HISTORICAL ASSOCIATION - LIBRARY AND PHOTO ARCHIVES (Hist)
211 W. 21st Ave. Phone: (206)753-2580
Olympia, WA 98501 Derek R. Valley, Dir.
Founded: 1941. **Staff:** Prof 7. **Subjects:** Washington history, Victoriana, museology, art. **Special Collections:** Collection of Washington photographs, including early photos of pioneers, towns, industries, Indians, and state governments; archives of Northwest Indian art. **Holdings:** 3000 historical photographs. **Services:** Copying; archives open to the public by arrangement.

★13637★
STATE FARM MUTUAL AUTOMOBILE INSURANCE COMPANY - LAW LIBRARY (Law)
One State Farm Plaza Phone: (309)766-5224
Bloomington, IL 61710 Laura Garrett, Corp.Libn.
Founded: 1962. **Staff:** Prof 3; Other 3. **Subjects:** Law, insurance, commerce, management. **Holdings:** 30,000 books; 30 bound periodical volumes. **Subscriptions:** 400 journals and other serials; 8 newspapers. **Services:** Interlibrary loan; library open to the public for reference use only. **Computerized Information Services:** DIALOG Information Services, Pergamon ORBIT InfoLine, Inc., LEXIS, NEXIS, WESTLAW; Executive Communications Network (internal database). **Networks/Consortia:** Member of Corn Belt Library System. **Publications:** New Acquisitions, monthly; Resource, bimonthly - for internal distribution only. **Staff:** Sylvia Justice, Asst.Corp.Libn.; Mary Crumley, Lib.Res.Asst..

★13638★
STATE HISTORICAL SOCIETY OF IOWA - LIBRARY (Hist)
Historical Bldg.
600 E. Locust Phone: (515)281-5472
Des Moines, IA 50319 Lowell R. Wilbur, Libn.
Staff: Prof 2; Other 2. **Subjects:** History - Iowa, Midwest, American; genealogy. **Special Collections:** Manuscript collections - Grenville Dodge, Charles Mason, Albert Cummins, William Boyd Allison, John A. Kasson, and others; Aldrich Autograph Collection. **Holdings:** 62,000 volumes. **Subscriptions:** 160 journals and other serials. **Services:** Library open to the public. **Staff:** Soudabeh Janssens, Mss.Div..

★13639★
STATE HISTORICAL SOCIETY OF IOWA - LIBRARY (Hist)
402 Iowa Ave. Phone: (319)338-5471
Iowa City, IA 52240 Nancy Kraft, Hd.Libn.
Founded: 1857. **Staff:** Prof 6; Other 8. **Subjects:** History - Iowa, the frontier, agriculture, railroad, Indians of the region; genealogy. **Special Collections:** Robert Lucas papers; Jonathan P. Dolliver papers; Gilbert Haugen papers; Cyrus Carpenter papers; Iowa industry house organs; historical Iowa photographs (100,000). **Holdings:** 100,000 books; 10,000 bound periodical volumes; 15,000 pamphlets; 14,000 reels of microfilm; 10,000 bound newspapers; 25 VF drawers of newspaper clippings; 1400 oral history interviews; 2500 linear feet of manuscripts. **Subscriptions:** 575 journals and other serials; 65 newspapers. **Services:** Interlibrary loan; copying; library open to the public. **Automated Operations:** Computerized cataloging. **Computerized Information Services:** OCLC. Performs searches on fee basis. Contact Person: Linda Brown-Link, Cat.Libn.. **Networks/Consortia:** Member of Bibliographical Center for Research, Rocky Mountain Region, Inc. (BCR). **Publications:** Bibliography of Iowa newspapers, 1831-1976 (book and online); bibliographies on immigrant groups, women in Iowa, and historic Iowa homes. **Special Catalogs:** Newspaper Collection of the State Historical Society of Iowa, compiled by L.O. Cheever, 1969; manuscript catalog; Fire Insurance Maps of Iowa Cities and Towns. **Special Indexes:** Indexes to selected history and genealogy serials. **Staff:** Mary Bennett, Spec.Coll.Libn.; Karen Laughlin, Ref.Libn.; Susan Rogers, Acq.Libn.; Linda Brown-Link, Cat..

★13640★
STATE HISTORICAL SOCIETY OF MISSOURI - LIBRARY (Hist)
1020 Lowry St. Phone: (314)882-7083
Columbia, MO 65201 James W. Goodrich, Dir.
Founded: 1898. **Staff:** Prof 17; Other 5. **Subjects:** Missouri and midwestern history, works by and about Missourians. **Special Collections:** J. Christian Bay Rare Book Collection (5200 books and documents); special collection of the writings of Mark Twain and Eugene Field; Bishop William Fletcher McMurray Collection; Francis A. Sampson Collection; Alice Irene Fitzgerald Collection of Missouri's Literary Heritage for Children and Youth (1000 volumes). **Holdings:** 435,000 volumes; 1900 bound volumes of newspapers; 700 reels of microfilm of manuscripts; 325,000 pages of original manuscripts; 1600 maps; 36,700 reels of microfilm of Missouri newspapers; 100,000 photographs; 6216 reels of microfilm of genealogical records. **Subscriptions:** 520 journals and other serials; 293 newspapers. **Services:** Interlibrary loan; copying; library open to the public. **Special Catalogs:** Catalog of Missouri Newspapers on Microfilm, irregular - for sale.

STATE HISTORICAL SOCIETY OF MISSOURI - MANUSCRIPTS COLLECTION
See: Western Historical Manuscript Collection/State Historical Society of Missouri Manuscripts Joint Collection (17708)

★13641★
STATE HISTORICAL SOCIETY OF NORTH DAKOTA - STATE ARCHIVES AND HISTORICAL RESEARCH LIBRARY (Hist)
Heritage Center Phone: (701)224-2668
Bismarck, ND 58505 Gerald Newborg, State Archv./Div.Dir
Founded: 1905. **Staff:** Prof 8; Other 3. **Subjects:** North Dakota; social, cultural, economic, and political history; early exploration and travel; fur trade; plains military history; Northern Plains region - archeology, prehistory, ethnology, ethnohistory; historic preservation; genealogy. **Holdings:** 87,000 volumes; 2000 cubic feet of manuscripts; 7000 cubic feet of state and county archives; 58,237 photographs; 7800 reels of microfilm of newspapers; 800 titles of North Dakota newspapers; 2100 titles of periodicals; 1200 oral history interviews; sound recordings; maps; videotapes; motion pictures. **Subscriptions:** 300 journals and other serials; 103 newspapers. **Services:** Interlibrary loan (limited); copying; library open to the public for reference use only. **Automated Operations:** Computerized cataloging. **Computerized Information Services:** OCLC. **Networks/Consortia:** Member of MINITEX. **Publications:** North Dakota History: Journal of the Northern Plains, quarterly; Plains Talk (newsletter), quarterly; Guide to the North Dakota State Archives, 1985; Guide to Manuscripts, 1985. **Staff:** Dolores Vyzralek, Chf.Libn.; David Gray, Dp. State Archv.; Todd Strand, Photo.Archv..

★13642★
STATE HISTORICAL SOCIETY OF WISCONSIN - ARCHIVES DIVISION (Hist)
816 State St. Phone: (608)262-3338
Madison, WI 53706 F. Gerald Ham, State Archv.
Staff: Prof 17; Other 9. **Subjects:** Wisconsin history; American frontier, 1750-1815; labor and industrial relations; socialism; mass communications; theater; agricultural history; civil rights; contemporary social action movements. **Special Collections:** Sigrid Schultz Collection (66 boxes of Nazi documents, personal papers, World War II memorabilia); Draper Collection (frontier); McCormick Collection (agriculture and agricultural manufacturing); manuscript collections of American Institute of the History of Pharmacy, Mass Communications History Center, Wisconsin Center for Film and Theatre Research, and Wisconsin Jewish Archives. **Holdings:** 45,037 cubic feet of Wisconsin state and local public records; 37,776 cubic feet of nongovernmental archives and manuscripts; 15,000 unbound maps; 2000 atlases; 500 titles on 3100 audiotapes; 110 titles on 3500 phonograph records; 1.5 million iconographic items; 50 machine-readable data files of state government records. **Services:** Interlibrary loan; copying; photo and film reproduction and dubbing of recordings for television. **Automated Operations:** Computerized cataloging. **Publications:** Accession reports in Wisconsin Magazine of History, quarterly; guides and inventories. **Remarks:** Administers the Wisconsin Area Research Center Network. **Staff:** Michael E. Stevens, Pub.Rec.; Harry Miller, Ref.Archv.; George A. Talbot, Sound & Vis.Archv.; Barbara J. Kaiser, Coll.Dev..

STATE HISTORICAL SOCIETY OF WISCONSIN - CIRCUS WORLD MUSEUM
See: Circus World Museum (3218)

★13643★
STATE HISTORICAL SOCIETY OF WISCONSIN - LIBRARY (Hist)
816 State St.
Madison, WI 53706-1482 Phone: (608)262-3421
Founded: 1846. **Staff:** Prof 18; Other 12. **Subjects:** History - American, Canadian, state, local, labor, U.S. church; radical/reform movements and groups in the U.S. and Canada; ethnic and minority groups in North America; genealogy; women's history. **Holdings:** 2 million items. **Subscriptions:** 7000 periodicals; 320 newspapers. **Services:** Interlibrary loan; copying; library open to the public. **Automated Operations:** Computerized cataloging. **Computerized Information Services:** OCLC. **Networks/Consortia:** Member of Wisconsin Interlibrary Services (WILS), Center for Research Libraries (CRL) Consortia. **Publications:** Wisconsin Public Documents (checklist of state government documents) - free upon request; bibliographies; guides. **Special Indexes:** Index to names in Wisconsin federal census, 1820-1870 and 1905 state census; Wisconsin necrology index; index of names in Wisconsin county histories. **Remarks:** This library is a U.S. Federal Government regional depository, a Wisconsin State official depository, and a Canadian Federal Government selective depository for government publications. **Staff:** Gerald R. Eggleston, Acq.Libn.; Jonathan D. Cooper, Cat.Libn.; Michael J. Edmonds, Pub.Serv.Libn.; John A. Peters, Govt.Pubns.Libn..

★13644★
STATE LAW LIBRARY OF MONTANA (Law)
Justice Bldg.
215 N. Sanders Phone: (406)444-3660
Helena, MT 59620-3004 Judith Meadows, State Law Libn.
Founded: 1873. **Staff:** Prof 4; Other 5. **Subjects:** Law. **Holdings:** 65,000 books; 4000 bound periodical volumes; 82,000 microfiche. **Subscriptions:** 400 journals and other serials. **Services:** Interlibrary loan; copying; SDI; library open to the public. **Automated Operations:** Computerized cataloging. **Computerized Information Services:** WESTLAW, DIALOG Information Services, LEXIS, NEXIS, VU/TEXT Information Services, Washington Alert Service; MCI Mail (electronic mail service). Performs searches on fee basis. **Networks/Consortia:** Member of Bibliographical Center for Research, Rocky Mountain Region, Inc. (BCR), Northwest Consortium of Law Libraries. **Publications:** Handbook on Dispute Resolution; Library Guidebook; Historical Sketch of State Law Library of Montana. **Remarks:** Fax: (406)444-3603. **Staff:** Brenda Grasmick, Tech.Serv.Libn.; Edith Roos, Circ.Coord..

★13645★
STATE LIBRARY OF FLORIDA (Info Sci)
R.A. Gray Bldg. Phone: (904)487-2651
Tallahassee, FL 32399-0250 Barratt Wilkins, State Libn.
Founded: 1845. **Staff:** Prof 31; Other 37. **Subjects:** Florida, history, social sciences, library science. **Special Collections:** Floridana (19,638 items). **Holdings:** 247,095 books; 7350 bound periodical volumes; 101,634 Florida public documents; 159,464 U.S. documents; 15,337 reels of microfilm; 188,454 microfiche; 4010 films. **Subscriptions:** 1283 journals and other serials; 12 newspapers. **Services:** Interlibrary loan; copying; SDI; library open to the public. **Automated Operations:** Computerized cataloging, serials, circulation, and film booking. **Computerized Information Services:** OCLC. **Networks/Consortia:** Member of SOLINET, Florida Library Information Network (FLIN). **Publications:** Orange Seed (technical bulletin) - to libraries; Intercom (technical bulletin) - to trustees and friends; Keystone (technical bulletin) - to institutions; New Books, monthly - to state agency personnel; Florida Library Directory with Statistics, annual - free to libraries; Florida Public Documents, monthly. **Special Indexes:** KWIC Index to Florida Public Documents, quarterly. **Remarks:** Maintained by Florida State Department of State - Division of Library and Information Services. **Staff:** Lorraine D. Summers, Asst. State Libn.; Virginia C. Grigg, Chf., Bur.Lib.Dev.; Loretta Flowers, Fed.Proj.Cons.; Kathleen Mayo, Inst.Cons.; Betty Miller, Youth Serv.Cons.; Elizabeth Curry, Lib.Cons.; Laura Hodges, Lib.Cons.; Betty Ann Scott, Lib.Cons.; Ethel Hughes, Lib.Cons.; Glenn Tripplett, Lib.Cons.; Freddie Ann Mellichamp, Chf., ILL Coop.; Marvin Mounce, ILL Coop.Cons.; Bob Gorin, ILL Coop.Cons.; William E. Paplinski, Chf., Bur.Lib.Serv.; Patty Paul, Lib.Serv.Mgr.; Debra Sears, Ref.Libn.; Evelyn Turkington, Doc.Libn.; Beverly Byrd, Florida Libn.; Helen Morgan Moeller, Lib.Serv.Mgr.; Sheila Rider, AV Libn.; Darnell Pratt, Acq.Libn.; Ann Lo, Cat.Libn..

★13646★
STATE LIBRARY OF IOWA (Info Sci)
E. 12th & Grand Phone: (515)281-4118
Des Moines, IA 50319 Shirley George, State Libn.
Staff: Prof 15; Other 25. **Subjects:** State government, law, medicine, library science. **Special Collections:** Iowa Collection; State Documents Archival Collection; Federal Documents Depository; Iowa Census Information Depository. **Holdings:** 262,460 books; 10 cabinets of vertical files about Iowa; 14,423 reels of microfilm; 525,136 microfiche. **Subscriptions:** 1610 journals and other serials. **Services:** Interlibrary loan; copying; SDI; library open to the public. **Computerized Information Services:** DIALOG Information Services, Pergamon ORBIT InfoLine, Inc., BRS Information Technologies. **Networks/Consortia:** Member of Bibliographical Center for Research, Rocky Mountain Region, Inc. (BCR), Iowa Computer Assisted Network (ICAN). **Publications:** Footnotes, monthly; Public Library Statistics, annual; Regional Library Statistics, annual; In Service to Iowa: Public Library Measures of Quality; Iowa Certification Manual for Public Libraries; 1988 LSCA Handbook; Iowa Library Quarterly; Iowa Library Laws; Iowa Library Directory, both annual; Summer Reading Program - Manual, annual - to public and regional libraries of Iowa. **Special Catalogs:** Periodical Holdings List (book); Iowa Documents Catalog (book). **Remarks:** Maintained by the Iowa State Department of Cultural Affairs. Includes the holdings of the Iowa State Law Library and the Iowa State Medical Library. **Staff:** Linda Robertson, Dir., Off. of Lib.Dev..

★13647★
STATE LIBRARY OF OHIO (Info Sci)
65 S. Front St. Phone: (614)462-7061
Columbus, OH 43266-0334 Richard M. Cheski, State Libn.
Founded: 1817. **Staff:** Prof 37; Other 95. **Subjects:** Management, social sciences, education, public administration, Ohio history. **Special Collections:** Genealogy (7200 items); Ohio and federal documents (1.1 million). **Holdings:** 555,833 books; 29,986 bound periodical volumes; 363,216 microforms. **Subscriptions:** 467 journals and other serials; 16 newspapers. **Services:** Interlibrary loan; copying; library open to the public. **Automated Operations:** Computerized cataloging, acquisitions, serials, and circulation. **Computerized Information Services:** DIALOG Information Services, SilverPlatter Information, Ltd., OCLC, LIBRIS, ALANET, WILSONLINE, Library Control System (LCS), OHIONET; ALANET, SourceMail (electronic mail services). Performs searches on fee basis. Contact Person: Michael Lucas, Hd., Ref., 462-6960. **Networks/Consortia:** Member of Greater Midwest Regional Medical Library Network, OHIONET, CALICO. **Publications:** Directory of Ohio Libraries, annual; Ohio Documents, quarterly; Statistics of Ohio Libraries, annual; Recent Acquisitions, irregular; News from the State Library, monthly; Library Opportunities, monthly; Annual Report. **Staff:** Susan Thomas, Dp. State Libn.; Catherine Mead, Hd., Ref. & Info.Serv.; John Philip, Hd., Field Oper.; Floyd Dickman, Prog.Dev.Supv.; William A. Crowley, Jr., Dp. State Libn.; Richard Palmer, Dp. State Libn..

STATE LIBRARY OF PENNSYLVANIA
See: Pennsylvania State Department of Education (11171)

★13648★
STATE MUTUAL LIFE ASSURANCE COMPANY OF AMERICA - LIBRARY (Bus-Fin)
440 Lincoln St. Phone: (508)852-1000
Worcester, MA 01605 Mary F. Duffy, Assoc.Libn.
Founded: 1957. **Staff:** 2. **Subjects:** Insurance, actuarial science, business, law. **Holdings:** 25,000 books; 650 bound periodical volumes; 35 VF drawers of pamphlets and reports. **Subscriptions:** 750 journals and other serials. **Services:** Library open to the public by request.

★13649★
STATE STREET CONSULTANTS, INC. - INFORMATION CENTER (Bus-Fin)
84 State St., Suite 905 Phone: (617)720-2020
Boston, MA 02109 Denise Cloutier, Info.Mgr.
Staff: Prof 1; Other 1. **Subjects:** Management, marketing, financial marketing, industry collections. **Holdings:** 1600 books; 100 VF drawers; 100 unbound reports; 150 cases of periodicals. **Subscriptions:** 95 journals and other serials. **Services:** SDI; center open to the public with restrictions. **Staff:** Ilene McLaughlin, Asst.Info.Mgr..

★13650★
STATE TECHNICAL INSTITUTE AT MEMPHIS - GEORGE E. FREEMAN LIBRARY (Sci-Engr)
5983 Macon Cove Phone: (901)377-4106
Memphis, TN 38134 Rosa S. Burnett, Dir.
Founded: 1968. **Staff:** Prof 3; Other 4. **Subjects:** Engineering - electrical, electronics, instrumentation, civil, architectural, mechanical, environmental, biomedical; chemical technology; data processing technologies. **Holdings:** 35,162 books; 5000 bound periodical volumes; 36 VF drawers; 15,088 microforms. **Subscriptions:** 349 journals and other serials; 19 newspapers. **Services:** Interlibrary loan; copying; library open to the public for reference use only. **Publications:** Library Handbook. **Staff:** Bettie W. Boyd, Assoc.Libn.; Virginia Ann Howard, Asst.Libn..

STATE UNIVERSITY OF NEW YORK
See: SUNY (13758)

STATE UNIVERSITY OF NORTH DAKOTA
See: Minot State University (9086)

★13651★
STATEN ISLAND COOPERATIVE CONTINUUM - EDUCATIONAL RESOURCE CENTER (Educ)
130 Stuyvesant Place, Rm. 704 Phone: (718)390-7985
Staten Island, NY 10301 John Gino, Prog.Dir.
Founded: 1973. **Staff:** Prof 1; Other 3. **Subjects:** Education, curriculum (K-12). **Holdings:** 9000 books; 50 bound periodical volumes; 1200 curriculum guides; 200 multimedia kits; 200 testing materials; 9 microcomputers. **Services:** Interlibrary loan; copying; videotaping and editing for students and the educational community; center open to the public. **Publications:** A/V Guide to ERC, irregular; ERC Newsletter, semiannual.

★13652★
STATEN ISLAND HISTORICAL SOCIETY - LIBRARY (Hist)
Court & Center Sts. Phone: (718)351-1611
Staten Island, NY 10306 Stephen C. Barto, Archv.
Staff: Prof 1; Other 3. **Subjects:** History of Staten Island and neighboring communities, U.S. history. **Special Collections:** Rare books. **Holdings:** 5000 books; 350 bound periodical volumes; 30 VF drawers of Staten Island history; 8 VF drawers of Staten Island genealogies; 110 reels of microfilm; 545 cubic feet of manuscripts; 9000 uncataloged items; 75 audiotapes; 30 videotapes; 320 bound volumes of newspapers. **Subscriptions:** 25 journals and other serials. **Services:** Copying; library open to the public by appointment only. **Publications:** Staten Island Historian, quarterly - to members.

★13653★
STATEN ISLAND HOSPITAL - MEDICAL STAFF LIBRARY (Med)
475 Seaview Ave. Phone: (718)390-9545
Staten Island, NY 10305 Song Ja Oh, Dir.
Founded: 1952. **Staff:** Prof 2; Other 2. **Subjects:** Internal medicine, surgery, pediatrics, obstetrics, gynecology. **Holdings:** 5000 books; 9000 bound periodical volumes; 920 Audio-Digest tapes. **Subscriptions:** 300 journals and other serials. **Services:** Interlibrary loan; copying; library open to the public with restrictions. **Computerized Information Services:** MEDLINE.

★13654★
STATEN ISLAND INSTITUTE OF ARTS AND SCIENCES - ARCHIVES AND LIBRARY (Sci-Engr, Hist)
75 Stuyvesant Place Phone: (718)727-1135
Staten Island, NY 10301 Kristine K. Hogan, Archv.
Founded: 1881. **Staff:** Prof 2; Other 1. **Subjects:** Natural history, Staten Island history, archeology, black history, women's history, urban planning. **Special Collections:** Architecture; N.L. Britton; G.W. Curtis; J.P. Chapin; W.T. Davis (total of 1000 cubic feet); photographs and prints of old Staten Island; local black history; repository for U.S. Geological Survey publications; complete list of special collections available on request. **Holdings:** 12,000 books; 22,000 bound periodical volumes; 3000 maps; 1200 prints; 50,000 photographs; 1500 art museum and gallery catalogs; 1500 cubic feet of manuscripts, letters, and documents; 80 reels of microfilm of Staten Island newspapers. **Subscriptions:** 200 journals and other serials. **Services:** Interlibrary loan; copying; library open to the public by appointment. **Publications:** Proceedings, 2/year - by subscription and exchange; Guide to Special Collections, 16 volumes. **Special Indexes:** Guide to Institute Archives, 2 volumes; indexes to newspapers, iconography of Staten Island, special collections (all on cards). **Remarks:** Basic library has been divided into two sections, a Science Library and a History Library.

★13655★
STATEN ISLAND INSTITUTE OF ARTS AND SCIENCES - HIGH ROCK PARK CONSERVATION CENTER - LIBRARY (Env-Cons, Biol Sci)
200 Nevada Ave. Phone: (718)987-6233
Staten Island, NY 10306 Evelyn Hare, Libn.
Founded: 1964. **Staff:** Prof 1. **Subjects:** Environmental education, mammalogy, salt and fresh water ecology, ornithology, botany, dendrology, geology, ichthyology, zoology, astronomy, energy, photography. **Holdings:** 2748 books; 4 boxes of Cornell Science leaflets; 2 boxes of Department of Agriculture leaflets; 2 boxes of Botanic Gardens pamphlets; 12 phonograph records of bird songs; filmstrips; AV programs; Outdoor Biology Instructional Strategies (OBIS) materials. **Subscriptions:** 15 journals and other serials. **Services:** Videotape facilities; library

★13656★
STATEN ISLAND ZOOLOGICAL SOCIETY - LIBRARY (Biol Sci)
614 Broadway Phone: (718)442-3101
Staten Island, NY 10310 Kathy Quinn, Adm.Asst.
Founded: 1936. **Staff:** 1. **Subjects:** Herpetology, environmental education, mammals, invertebrates, fish, birds. **Holdings:** 750 books; 180 bound periodical volumes. **Subscriptions:** 10 journals and other serials. **Services:** Copying; library open to the public by appointment.

STATES INFORMATION CENTER
See: Council of State Governments (3827)

STATISTICS CANADA
See: Canada - Statistics Canada (2485)

ALICE STATLER LIBRARY
See: City College of San Francisco - Hotel and Restaurant Department (3235)

STATUE OF LIBERTY NATIONAL MONUMENT
See: U.S. Natl. Park Service (15354)

STAUFFER CHEMICAL COMPANY - DE GUIGNE TECHNICAL CENTER
See: ICI Americas Inc. - De Guigne Technical Center (6662)

STAUFFER CHEMICAL COMPANY - EASTERN RESEARCH CENTER
See: AKZO Chemicals Inc. (132)

STAUFFER CHEMICAL COMPANY - SWS SILICONES
See: Wacker Silicones Corporation - SWS Silicones (17410)

★13657★
STAUFFER CHEMICAL COMPANY - TECHNICAL INFORMATION CENTER (Biol Sci, Med)
400 Farmington Ave. Phone: (203)674-6312
Farmington, CT 06032 Joanna W. Eickenhorst, Supv., Info.Serv.
Staff: Prof 2. **Subjects:** Toxicology, environmental health, mutagenicity, genetics, inhalation toxicology, biochemistry, metabolism, pharmacokinetics. **Holdings:** 4000 books. **Subscriptions:** 140 journals and other serials. **Services:** Interlibrary loan; SDI. **Computerized Information Services:** NLM, Pergamon ORBIT InfoLine, Inc., DIALOG Information Services, OCLC, Occupational Health Services, Inc. **Networks/Consortia:** Member of Capitol Region Library Council (CRLC). **Publications:** Acquisitions list, monthly; Journal Holdings List; style manual. **Special Indexes:** Technical Reports Index; Reprints Collection Index.

STAUFFER HEALTH SCIENCES LIBRARY
See: Stormont-Vail Regional Medical Center (13699)

STEACIE SCIENCE LIBRARY
See: York University (18205)

★13658★
STEAMSHIP HISTORICAL SOCIETY OF AMERICA COLLECTION (Hist, Trans)
414 Pelton Ave. Phone: (718)727-9583
Staten Island, NY 10310 Alice S. Wilson, Sec./Libn.
Founded: 1940. **Staff:** Prof 3; Other 1. **Subjects:** Marine transportation, steamship and steamboat history, naval history. **Special Collections:** Tracey Brooks Collection; T.H. Franklin's collection of 19th century steamboats; B.M. Boyles' collection of Maine material; Hudson River Day Line Collection; R. Loren Graham marine photographs; Everett Viez ocean liner photographs. **Holdings:** 5000 books; 800 pamphlets; 30,000 ship photograph negatives; 60,000 pictures of ships; 1000 steamship company folders; 200 deck and cabin plans; 25,000 colored postcards. **Subscriptions:** 100 journals and other serials. **Services:** Copying; collection open to the public. **Automated Operations:** Computerized cataloging. **Computerized Information Services:** OCLC. **Publications:** Steamboat Bill, quarterly; list of other publications - available on request. **Remarks:** Located at University of Baltimore Library, 1420 Maryland Ave., Baltimore, MD 21201.

★13659★
STEARNS COUNTY HISTORICAL SOCIETY - RESEARCH CENTER & ARCHIVES (Hist)
Box 702 Phone: (612)253-8424
St. Cloud, MN 56302-0702 John W. Decker, Archv.
Founded: 1975. **Staff:** Prof 2. **Subjects:** Genealogy, county history, architecture. **Special Collections:** Glanville W. Smith papers (14 boxes); Stearns County aerial sectional photographs, 1938 (474); Byron E. Barr (Gig Young) papers (2 boxes); Frank W. Jackson Architectural Firm records (12 Hollinger boxes; 100 plans); Cold Spring Granite Company photographs (250); State Senator Ed Schrom papers (10 boxes); Russell T. Wing papers (12 boxes); maps of Stearns County and Central Minnesota, 1855 to present (150); Stearns County census reports, 1850-1910; John Clark Granite Company photographs (200). **Holdings:** 1500 books; 500 bound periodical volumes; 14 VF drawers of biographical and family files (10,000 names); 1800 oral history tapes; 900 reels of microfilm of Stearns County newspapers; 14,000 photographs and slides; 22 reels of microfilm of Stearns County naturalization records, 1852-1954; 7 reels of microfilm of Stearns County Land Office tract index records, 1853-1910; St. Cloud city directories, 1888-1986; Stearns County birth and death records, 1946-1982, and marriage records, 1916-1982. **Subscriptions:** 16 journals and other serials. **Services:** Copying; center open to the public. **Networks/Consortia:** Member of Central Minnesota Libraries Exchange (CMLE). **Publications:** Crossings (newsletter), bimonthly - to the public. **Special Indexes:** Gravestone surname index for Stearns, Benton, and Sherburne Counties; St. Cloud Daily Times News index, 1928 to present. **Staff:** Robert Lommel, Res..

★13660★
STEELE COUNTY HISTORICAL SOCIETY - ARCHIVES (Hist)
Box 144 Phone: (701)945-2394
Hope, ND 58046 Helen Parkman, Cur.
Staff: 1. **Subjects:** Local history. **Holdings:** 400 books; 158 bound periodical volumes; 31 oral history tapes; old catalogs and magazines; photograph collection; town and school records. **Services:** Copying; archives open to the public with restrictions.

STEEN LIBRARY
See: Stephen F. Austin State University (1180)

STEENBOCK MEMORIAL LIBRARY
See: University of Wisconsin, Madison (17153)

STEIN MEMORIAL LIBRARY
See: Agudas Achim Congregation (98)

★13661★
STEIN ROE AND FARNHAM - LIBRARY (Bus-Fin)
One S. Wacker Dr. Phone: (312)368-7777
Chicago, IL 60606 Nancy Marano, Libn.
Founded: 1932. **Staff:** Prof 2; Other 2. **Subjects:** Business, finance. **Holdings:** 4200 books; 110 bound periodical volumes; 111,000 microfiche. **Subscriptions:** 400 journals and other serials; 30 newspapers. **Services:** Interlibrary loan; copying; library open to the public for reference use only on request. **Computerized Information Services:** DIALOG Information Services, WILSONLINE, Dun & Bradstreet Corporation, INVESTEXT, DataTimes, VU/TEXT Information Services, Dow Jones News/Retrieval. **Staff:** Celeste Jannusch, Asst.Libn..

★13662★
STEINBACH BIBLE COLLEGE - LIBRARY (Rel-Phil)
Box 1420 Phone: (204)326-6451
Steinbach, MB, Canada R0A 2A0 Myrna Friesen, Libn.
Founded: 1936. **Staff:** Prof 1; Other 1. **Subjects:** Bible, theology, Mennonite history, music. **Holdings:** 14,300 books; 354 bound periodical volumes. **Subscriptions:** 80 journals and other serials. **Services:** Interlibrary loan; copying; library open to the public. **Publications:** The Servant (newsletter), 5/year.

RABBI A. ALAN STEINBACH MEMORIAL LIBRARY
See: Temple Ahavath Sholom (13934)

JOHN STEINBECK LIBRARY
See: Salinas Public Library (12717)

STEINBECK RESEARCH CENTER
See: San Jose State University (12826)

HEDI STEINBERG LIBRARY
See: Yeshiva University (18169)

STEINBERG INFORMATION CENTER
See: Ciba Corning Diagnostics Corporation (3191)

SARAH AND JULIUS STEINBERG MEMORIAL LIBRARY
See: Riverside Hospital (12075)

RUDOLPH STEINER LIBRARY
See: Anthroposophical Society of Canada (805)

WALTER STEINER MEMORIAL LIBRARY
See: Hartford Medical Society (6057)

STEINHEIMER COLLECTION OF SOUTHWESTERN CHILDREN'S LITERATURE
See: Tucson Public Library (14372)

KATE TRAUMAN STEINITZ ARCHIVES
See: University of California, Los Angeles - Art Library - Elmer Belt Library of Vinciana (15959)

★13663★
STELCO INC. - TECHNICAL INFORMATION CENTER (Sci-Engr)
P.O. Box 2030 Phone: (416)528-2511
Hamilton, ON, Canada L8N 3T1 David W. Rosenplot, Info.Spec.
Staff: Prof 2. **Subjects:** Ferrous metallurgy, engineering, pollution control. **Holdings:** 2200 books; 300 bound periodical volumes; microforms; patents; internal reports. **Subscriptions:** 250 journals and other serials. **Services:** Interlibrary loan; center not open to the public. **Automated Operations:** Computerized cataloging and circulation. **Computerized Information Services:** DIALOG Information Services, CAN/OLE; internal database. **Networks/Consortia:** Member of Ontario Library Service - Escarpment. **Publications:** Current Awareness Bulletin, weekly. **Special Indexes:** Index of project and report files (computer printout).

SISTER STELLA LOUISE HEALTH SCIENCE LIBRARY
See: St. Mary of Nazareth Hospital Center (12587)

★13664★
STEP FAMILY FOUNDATION, INC. - LIBRARY (Soc Sci)
333 West End Ave. Phone: (212)877-3244
New York, NY 10023 Jeannette Lofas, Exec.Dir.
Staff: Prof 1; Other 2. **Subjects:** Self-awareness, the family, the stepfamily. **Holdings:** 1100 books; 100 audiotapes. **Services:** Library not open to the public. **Publications:** Newsletter, quarterly.

★13665★
STEPAN COMPANY - TECHNICAL INFORMATION CENTER (Sci-Engr)
22 W. Frontage Rd. Phone: (312)501-2277
Northfield, IL 60093 Patricia L. Brown, Mgr.
Staff: Prof 2; Other 2. **Subjects:** Chemistry. **Holdings:** 3000 books; 6000 bound periodical volumes; internal R&D documents; 5000 technical reports; 1200 microfilm cartridges of patents. **Subscriptions:** 185 journals and other serials. **Services:** Interlibrary loan; center open to the public by appointment. **Computerized Information Services:** Pergamon ORBIT InfoLine, Inc., BRS Information Technologies, Telesystemes Questel, Chemical Economics Handbook (CEH) Program, DIALOG Information Services, NLM, CAS ONLINE, CompuServe, Inc; internal databases. **Publications:** Current Literature. **Staff:** Lois A. Bey. Tech.Info.Sci..

STEPHENS BROS. BOAT WORKS ARCHIVES
See: The Haggin Museum - Almeda May Castle Petzinger Library (5950)

★13666★
STEPTOE AND JOHNSON - LIBRARY (Law)
1330 Connecticut Ave., N.W. Phone: (202)429-3000
Washington, DC 20036 Thomas B. Fleming, Libn.
Staff: Prof 7; Other 6. **Subjects:** Law. **Holdings:** 44,000 volumes. **Services:** Library not open to the public.

★13667★
STEREO CLUB OF SOUTHERN CALIFORNIA - LIBRARY (Aud-Vis, Rec)
Box 2368 Phone: (213)837-2368
Culver City, CA 90231 David Starkman, Tech.Dir.
Founded: 1977. **Staff:** 3. **Subjects:** Stereoscopy; 3-D photography, movies, television; View-Master products and history. **Holdings:** 50 books; 6 VF drawers of articles, instructional manuals, pamphlets. **Services:** Copying (limited); library open to the public with restrictions. **Publications:** 3-D News, monthly - by subscription.

STERLING CHEMISTRY LIBRARY
See: Yale University (18151)

STERLING DRUG, INC. - LEHN & FINK PRODUCTS GROUP
See: Lehn & Fink Products Group (7756)

★13668★
STERLING DRUG, INC. - STERLING-WINTHROP RESEARCH INSTITUTE - LIBRARY (Med, Biol Sci)
81 Columbia Turnpike Phone: (518)445-8262
Rensselaer, NY 12144-3493 Patsy L. Schulenberg, Sr.Adm., Lib.Serv.
Staff: Prof 3; Other 5. **Subjects:** Biomedicine, chemistry, pharmacology, biology. **Holdings:** 20,000 books; 30,000 bound periodical volumes; 2600 reels of microfilm; 8300 microfiche. **Subscriptions:** 780 journals and other serials. **Services:** Interlibrary loan; copying; SDI; library open to the public by appointment. **Automated Operations:** Computerized cataloging, serials, and ILL. **Computerized Information Services:** Pergamon ORBIT InfoLine, Inc., DIALOG Information Services, BRS Information Technologies, Data-Star, OCLC, CAS ONLINE, MEDLINE; internal database. **Networks/Consortia:** Member of SUNY/OCLC Library Network, Capital District Library Council for Reference & Research Resources (CDLC). **Publications:** Library Bulletin, quarterly - to mailing list. **Staff:** Ann Marie Weis, Supv., Lib.Serv.; D. Lynn Siegelman, Info.Spec., Lib.Serv.; Patricia Carroll, ILL Libn..

★13669★
STERLING DRUG, INC. - WINTHROP LABORATORIES - MEDICAL LIBRARY (Med)
90 Park Ave. Phone: (212)907-2504
New York, NY 10016 Irene Frisch, Lib.Mgr.
Founded: 1927. **Staff:** Prof 7; Other 2. **Subjects:** Drugs, pharmaceuticals, clinical medicine. **Special Collections:** Articles on drugs (abstracted and indexed); company history. **Holdings:** 6400 books and bound periodical volumes; 115 VF drawers of articles; 2 drawers of microfiche; manuscripts; clippings; pamphlets. **Subscriptions:** 260 journals and other serials. **Services:** Interlibrary loan; copying; SDI; library open to the public by appointment. **Computerized Information Services:** MEDLINE, DIALOG Information Services; Inquire (internal database). **Networks/Consortia:** Member of Greater Northeastern Regional Medical Library Program. **Publications:** Current References, semimonthly.

★13670★
STERLING DRUG, INC. - ZIMPRO INC. - REFERENCE AND RESOURCE CENTER (Sci-Engr)
Military Rd.
Rothschild, WI 54474 Phone: (715)359-7211
Subjects: Environmental control systems, sewage treatment. **Holdings:** 2000 books; 200 bound periodical volumes; 500 technical reports; 400 standards; 12 VF drawers of patents; 4 VF drawers of clippings. **Subscriptions:** 155 journals and other serials. **Services:** Interlibrary loan; library not open to the public. **Networks/Consortia:** Member of Wisconsin Valley Library Service (WVLS).

STERLING FEDERAL SYSTEMS - FISH AND WILDLIFE REFERENCE SERVICE
See: Fish and Wildlife Reference Service (5113)

STERLING SOFTWARE, INC. - INFORMATION SERVICES DIVISION
See: ATLIS Federal Services, Inc. - Library Services Division (1135)

STERLING-WINTHROP RESEARCH INSTITUTE
See: Sterling Drug, Inc. (13668)

STERNBERG MEMORIAL MUSEUM
See: Fort Hays State University (5276)

★13671★
STETSON UNIVERSITY - ARCHIVES (Hist)
Box 1418 Phone: (904)734-4121
De Land, FL 32720 Dorothy C. Minor, Archv.
Subjects: Stetson University, 1883 to present. **Special Collections:** Stetson correspondence; catalogs and annuals. **Holdings:** 150 linear feet (5 file cabinets) of correspondence and letters from early De Land settlers; campus photographs (including faculty, students, and athletics); biographies of all presidents and faculty members. **Services:** Interlibrary loan; copying; archives open to the public.

★13672★
STETSON UNIVERSITY - CHEMISTRY LIBRARY (Sci-Engr)
N. Woodland Blvd.
Box 1271 Phone: (904)734-4121
De Land, FL 32720 Theodore W. Beiler, Chm.
Staff: 1. **Subjects:** Chemistry. **Holdings:** 2200 books; 4400 bound periodical volumes; 10 drawers of microfiche. **Subscriptions:** 28 journals and other serials. **Services:** Interlibrary loan; copying; library open to the public.

★13673★
STETSON UNIVERSITY - COLLEGE OF LAW - CHARLES A. DANA LAW LIBRARY (Law)
1401 61st St., S. Phone: (813)345-1335
St. Petersburg, FL 33707 J. Lamar Woodard, Libn./Prof. of Law
Founded: 1900. **Staff:** Prof 5; Other 6. **Subjects:** Law. **Holdings:** 245,000 volumes. **Subscriptions:** 700 journals and other serials. **Services:** Interlibrary loan; copying; library open to qualified persons. **Automated Operations:** Computerized cataloging. **Computerized Information Services:** WESTLAW, LEXIS, OCLC. **Networks/Consortia:** Member of SOLINET, Tampa Bay Library Consortium, Inc.. **Staff:** Roman Yoder, Asst.Libn.,

Tech.Serv.; Earlene Hurst, Ser.Libn.; Sally Ginsberg, Ref.Libn.; Pamela Burdett, Asst.Libn., Pub.Serv..

★13674★
STETSON UNIVERSITY - DU PONT-BALL LIBRARY - GARWOOD BAPTIST HISTORICAL COLLECTION (Hist, Rel-Phil)
Box 8247 Phone: (904)734-4121
De Land, FL 32720 Dr. E. Earl Joiner, Cur.
Staff: Prof 2. **Subjects:** History of Baptist, Southern Baptist, and Florida Baptist Churches. **Holdings:** 1300 books; 825 bound periodical volumes; 260 reels of microfilm; 155 boxes of Baptist Association records; 4 cabinets of manuscripts and papers; vertical files. **Subscriptions:** 37 journals and other serials. **Services:** Interlibrary loan; copying; collection open to the public by appointment with restrictions on circulation. **Automated Operations:** Computerized cataloging and acquisitions. **Computerized Information Services:** Internal database. **Networks/Consortia:** Member of SOLINET. **Special Indexes:** Florida Baptist Historical Collection Index; Stetson Baptist Archives Index; Index to Florida Baptist Witness (online).

★13675★
STETSON UNIVERSITY - SCHOOL OF MUSIC LIBRARY (Mus)
Woodland Blvd. Phone: (904)734-4121
De Land, FL 32720 Janice Jenkins, Music Libn.
Founded: 1936. **Staff:** Prof 1; Other 15. **Subjects:** Music. **Special Collections:** Organ music recordings (370). **Holdings:** 6117 books; 1040 bound periodical volumes; 9187 scores; 7779 phonograph records; 740 pieces of old, popular sheet music; 55 cassettes; 45 compact discs; ensemble music for brass choir, band, orchestra, and choir; collected editions and monuments. **Subscriptions:** 33 journals. **Services:** Interlibrary loan; copying; library open to the public for reference use only. **Automated Operations:** Computerized cataloging. **Computerized Information Services:** DIALOG Information Services. Performs searches on fee basis. **Networks/Consortia:** Member of SOLINET.

IVAN M. STETTENHEIM LIBRARY
See: Congregation Emanu-El (3623)

★13676★
CHARLES E. STEVENS AMERICAN ATHEIST LIBRARY AND ARCHIVES INC. (Rel-Phil, Soc Sci)
Box 14505 Phone: (512)458-1244
Austin, TX 78761 R. Murray-O'Hair, Dir.
Founded: 1971. **Staff:** Prof 2; Other 4. **Subjects:** Atheism, agnosticism, free thought, humanism, objectivism, rationalism, iconoclasm, ethical culturism, separation of state and church. **Special Collections:** Atheist and Freethought magazines, pre-Civil War to present. **Holdings:** 40,000 books; 2000 bound periodical volumes; 600,000 pamphlets, booklets, throw-aways, manuscripts, documents, clippings, leaflets; 500 radio tapes; 500 videotapes. **Subscriptions:** 50 journals and other serials; 10 newspapers. **Services:** Copying; library open to scholars only by appointment. **Remarks:** Library located at 7215 Cameron Rd., Suite B, Austin, TX 78756.

★13677★
STEVENS CLINIC HOSPITAL - LIBRARY (Med)
U.S. 52, East Phone: (304)436-3161
Welch, WV 24801 Karen Peery, Libn.
Staff: 2. **Subjects:** Medicine, surgery, allied health sciences. **Holdings:** 800 volumes. **Services:** Copying; library open to the public with restrictions.

★13678★
STEVENS INSTITUTE OF TECHNOLOGY - SAMUEL C. WILLIAMS LIBRARY (Sci-Engr)
Castle Point Sta. Phone: (201)420-5198
Hoboken, NJ 07030 Richard P. Widdicombe, Dir.
Founded: 1890. **Staff:** Prof 5; Other 7. **Subjects:** Engineering, science, mathematics, scientific management. **Special Collections:** Lieb Library of Leonardo Da Vinci; F.W. Taylor Collection (scientific management). **Holdings:** 100,000 books and bound periodical volumes; 2500 reels of microfilm; 8 VF drawers. **Subscriptions:** 1000 journals and other serials. **Services:** Interlibrary loan; copying; library open to the public. **Automated Operations:** Computerized serials, circulation, and accounting. **Computerized Information Services:** DIALOG Information Services, Pergamon ORBIT InfoLine, Inc., Dow Jones News/Retrieval, WILSONLINE, BRS Information Technologies, VU/TEXT Information Services, NEXIS, OCLC, Civil Engineering Database, RLIN, NewsNet, Inc. Performs searches on fee basis. Contact Person: Robin Merrill, Info.Serv.Libn., 420-5410. **Staff:** Joy Johnsen, Asst.Dir.; Ourida Oubraham, Info.Serv.Libn.; Robert Freeman, Tech.Serv.Libn..

★13679★
J.P. STEVENS AND CO., INC. - TECHNICAL LIBRARY (Sci-Engr)
400 E. Stone Ave.
Box 2850 Phone: (803)239-4211
Greenville, SC 29602-2850 Ann Sims, Dir.
Founded: 1948. **Staff:** Prof 1. **Subjects:** Textiles, chemistry. **Holdings:** 4000 books; 1700 bound periodical volumes; 8 VF drawers of U.S. Government reports; 8 VF drawers of pamphlets and clippings; 100 microfiche. **Subscriptions:** 153 journals and other serials. **Services:** Copying; library open to the public with permission. **Computerized Information Services:** DIALOG Information Services, Pergamon ORBIT InfoLine, Inc., BRS Information Technologies, Telesystemes Questel.

GEORGE B. STEVENSON LIBRARY
See: Lock Haven University (7912)

MARION STEVENSON LIBRARY
See: Christian Board of Publication (3145)

★13680★
DAVID M. STEWART MUSEUM - DAVID M. STEWART LIBRARY (Mil, Hist)
Sta. A, P.O. Box 1024 Phone: (514)861-6701
Montreal, PQ, Canada H3C 2W9 Elizabeth F. Hale, Libn.Cons.
Staff: Prof 1; Other 1. **Subjects:** Canadian history to 1763, including military and social history; American Revolution; War of 1812; Rebellion of 1837-1838. **Special Collections:** Macdonald Stewart Collection (rare books, documents, engravings, and 19th century Montreal history); pre-1764 rare books (1000). **Holdings:** 8000 books; 30 bound periodical volumes. **Subscriptions:** 30 journals and other serials. **Services:** Copying; consultation; library open to qualified researchers by appointment only. **Publications:** 4 M's Bulletins, irregular (both French and English editions) - to members; Discovery of the World: Maps of the Earth and the Cosmos (1985).

STEWART RESOURCES CENTRE
See: Saskatchewan Teachers' Federation - Stewart Resources Centre (12922)

STEWART ROOM
See: Glassboro State College - Savitz Library (5676)

★13681★
STIEFEL LABORATORIES, INC. - RESEARCH INSTITUTE LIBRARY (Med)
Oak Hill, NY 12460 Phone: (518)239-6901
Loretta Lounsbury, Act.Libn.
Founded: 1967. **Staff:** 2. **Subjects:** Dermatology. **Holdings:** 300 books; 10 bound periodical volumes. **Subscriptions:** 40 journals and other serials. **Services:** Library not open to the public.

A.T. STILL MEMORIAL LIBRARY
See: Kirksville College of Osteopathic Medicine (7510)

A.T. STILL OSTEOPATHIC LIBRARY AND RESEARCH CENTER
See: American Osteopathic Association (628)

★13682★
STILL WATERS FOUNDATION, INC. - STILL WATERS CENTRE LIBRARY (Rel-Phil)
615 Stafford Ln.
Pensacola, FL 32506 Dana Faye Cobb
Staff: Prof 1; Other 3. **Subjects:** Metaphysics, parapsychology, comparative religions, earth science, space program, planetary discoveries, unexplained UFOs, astronomy, animal rights, anti-vivisection issues, animal care, preventive medicine, holistic health care theory, herbal medicine. **Special Collections:** Blavatsky; M.P. Hall; Edgar Cayce. **Holdings:** 5000 books; 2000 bound periodical volumes; 84 other cataloged items. **Subscriptions:** 23 journals and other serials. **Services:** Copying; library open to the public on a limited basis for reference use only.

STILLMAN LIBRARY
See: Tobey Hospital (14216)

STILLWATER DISTRICT 834 - EARLY CHILDHOOD FAMILY EDUCATION - TOY LENDING LIBRARY
See: Early Childhood Family Education - Toy Lending Library (4489)

★13683★
STILLWATER PUBLIC LIBRARY - ST. CROIX VALLEY ROOM (Hist)
223 N. 4th St. Phone: (612)439-1675
Stillwater, MN 55082 Sue Collins, Hist.
Founded: 1859. **Staff:** Prof 1. **Subjects:** Local history, with emphasis on Washington County. **Special Collections:** John Runk pictures (700). **Holdings:** 800 books; newspaper clippings; manuscripts; scrapbooks; city directories, 1876 to present. **Services:** Interlibrary loan; copying; room open to the public for reference use only. **Special Indexes:** Index to scrapbooks by subject.

STIMSON LIBRARY
See: U.S. Army - Health Services Command - Academy of Health Sciences (14755)

RUSSELL L. STIMSON OPHTHALMIC REFERENCE LIBRARY
See: Canada College (2514)

STINE LABORATORY LIBRARY
See: E.I. Du Pont de Nemours & Company, Inc. (4421)

STIRTON-KELSON LIBRARY
See: Idaho State University - Idaho Museum of Natural History (6672)

EDWARD RHODES STITT LIBRARY
See: U.S. Navy - Naval Hospital (MD-Bethesda) (15416)

STITT LIBRARY
See: Austin Presbyterian Theological Seminary (1177)

EDITH L. STOCK MEMORIAL LIBRARY
See: Trinity United Church of Christ (14345)

★13684★
STOCKBRIDGE LIBRARY ASSOCIATION - HISTORICAL ROOM (Hist)
Main & Elm Sts. Phone: (413)298-5501
Stockbridge, MA 01262 Pauline D. Pierce, Cur.
Founded: 1938. **Subjects:** Local and area history, genealogy, books by and about Stockbridge authors, Stockbridge imprints, Stockbridge Indians. **Special Collections:** Anson Clark, Jonathan Edwards, Field family, Daniel Chester French, and Sedgwick Collections. **Holdings:** 1700 books and pamphlets; vital records and cemetery inscriptions; memorabilia and manuscripts; account books. **Services:** Interlibrary loan; copying; room open to the public. **Special Catalogs:** Stockbridge Library Historical Room: An Inventory to the Collection. **Staff:** Rosemary Schneyer, Hd.Libn..

★13685★
STOCKMEN'S MEMORIAL FOUNDATION - LIBRARY (Agri, Hist)
2116 27th Ave., N.E., No. 126 Phone: (403)250-7529
Calgary, AB, Canada T2E 7A6 Helgi Leesment, Cons.Libn.
Founded: 1982. **Staff:** Prof 2; Other 2. **Subjects:** Alberta ranching history, beef cattle industry, Western art, ranching fiction. **Special Collections:** Local community histories (100); Alberta Brand Books, 1900 to present (complete set); interviews of pioneer families and historically significant ranchers (90 videotapes). **Holdings:** 1900 books; 50 bound periodical volumes; 25 pamphlet boxes of cattle breed organizations materials. **Subscriptions:** 35 journals and other serials; 5 newspapers. **Services:** Copying; library open to the public with restrictions. **Staff:** JoAnn Hooper, Libn..

★13686★
STOCKPHOTOS, INC. - LIBRARY (Aud-Vis)
373 Park Ave., S., 6th Fl. Phone: (212)686-1196
New York, NY 10016 Robert E. Carol, Photo.Ed.
Founded: 1967. **Staff:** Prof 6; Other 2. **Subjects:** Contemporary human interest photography, industrial photography, European and religious art. **Holdings:** 1 million photographs; catalogs of representative photographs. **Services:** Library open to the public. **Automated Operations:** Computerized cataloging. **Formerly:** The Image Bank. **Staff:** Daniel Conway; Seema Bajaj; Thomas Creavin; Joseph S. Lada, Dir..

★13687★
STOCKTON DEVELOPMENTAL CENTER - STAFF LIBRARY (Med)
510 E. Magnolia St. Phone: (209)948-7181
Stockton, CA 95202 Walter Greening, Sr.Libn.
Staff: Prof 1. **Subjects:** Mentally handicapped, mentally ill, behavior therapy, child psychiatry, community mental health, psychiatric nursing. **Holdings:** 6700 books; 1200 bound periodical volumes; 158 reels of microfilm of periodicals; 300 audiotapes. **Subscriptions:** 100 journals and other serials. **Services:** Interlibrary loan; copying; library open to the public. **Networks/Consortia:** Member of Pacific Southwest Regional Medical Library Service, Northern California and Nevada Medical Library Group (NCNMLG), North San Joaquin Health Sciences Library Consortium. **Remarks:** Maintained by California State Department of Developmental Services.

★13688★
STOCKTON NEWSPAPERS INC. - STOCKTON RECORD LIBRARY (Publ)
530 Market St. Phone: (209)943-6397
Stockton, CA 95201 Kenneth A. Mimms, Libn.
Founded: 1952. **Staff:** Prof 2; Other 1. **Subjects:** Newspaper reference topics, local history. **Holdings:** 300 books; 468 VF drawers of newspaper clippings; 42 drawers of large pictures; 875 reels of microfilm. **Subscriptions:** 15 journals and other serials; 15 newspapers. **Services:** Library open to accredited journalists. **Staff:** Dorothy Frankhouse, Asst.Libn..

★13689★
STOCKTON-SAN JOAQUIN COUNTY PUBLIC LIBRARY - LOCAL HISTORY ROOM (Hist)
603 N. El Dorado Phone: (209)944-8415
Stockton, CA 95202 Isabel Benson, Ref.Libn.
Subjects: History of Stockton, San Joaquin County, and gold mining regions of California, 1850 to present. **Special Collections:** Writings of local pioneers concerning library development, theater, and government; early public documents and periodicals. **Holdings:** 3000 items. **Automated Operations:** Computerized cataloging.

STOECKEL ARCHIVES
See: Ball State University - Bracken Library - Special Collections (1256)

★13690★
STOEL, RIVES, BOLEY, ET AL - LIBRARY (Law)
900 S.W. Fifth Ave. Phone: (503)294-9576
Portland, OR 97204 Larry W. Piper, Libn.
Staff: Prof 3; Other 3. **Subjects:** Law. **Holdings:** 33,000 books; 1200 bound periodical volumes. **Subscriptions:** 450 journals and other serials; 10 newspapers. **Services:** Interlibrary loan (limited); copying; library open to the public with restrictions. **Computerized Information Services:** LEXIS, WESTLAW, DIALOG Information Services, Oregon Legislative Information System, BRS Information Technologies, ABA/net. **Staff:** Ann W. Van Hassel; Nancy Hoover.

STOHLMAN LIBRARY
See: St. Elizabeth's Hospital (12376)

★13691★
LEOPOLD STOKOWSKI SOCIETY OF AMERICA - STOKOWSKI ARCHIVE (Mus)
870 N. Meadows Court, No. E Phone: (614)846-8659
Columbus, OH 43229 Robert M. Stumpf, II, Pres.
Founded: 1983. **Staff:** Prof 1. **Subjects:** Leopold Stokowski, classical music. **Holdings:** 500 recordings by Stokowski, 1917-1977. **Services:** Interlibrary loan; copying; archive open to the public with restrictions. **Publications:** Maestrino, semiannual - to mailing list.

STOLL MEMORIAL LIBRARY
See: Lancaster Bible College (7635)

ABRAHAM STONE LIBRARY
See: Margaret Sanger Center-Planned Parenthood New York City (12856)

EDWARD DURELL STONE LIBRARY
See: Boston Architectural Center - Alfred Shaw and Edward Durell Stone Library (1725)

FRANZ THEODORE STONE LABORATORY
See: Ohio State University (10692)

GEORGE G. STONE CENTER FOR CHILDREN'S BOOKS
See: The Claremont Graduate School (3251)

★13692★
STONE, MARRACCINI & PATTERSON - RESEARCH & DEVELOPMENT LIBRARY (Plan, Med)
455 Beach St. Phone: (415)775-7300
San Francisco, CA 94133 Mary E. Brackeen, Libn.
Founded: 1965. **Staff:** 1. **Subjects:** Health planning, health care facilities design, medical facility planning, architecture, population statistics, urban planning. **Holdings:** 7280 books; 24 VF drawers of articles, clippings, pamphlets, reports, and maps. **Subscriptions:** 140 journals and other serials. **Services:** Library not open to the public.

OLIVE CLIFFORD STONE LIBRARY
See: Butler County Historical Society (2076)

★13693★
STONE AND WEBSTER ENGINEERING CORPORATION - STONE AND WEBSTER MANAGEMENT CONSULTANTS, INC. - INFORMATION CENTER (Bus-Fin, Energy)
One Penn Plaza, 30th Fl. Phone: (212)290-7041
New York, NY 10119 Marcel Robichaud, Libn.
Staff: Prof 1. **Subjects:** Finance, accounting, public utilities, power, oil, gas, management. **Holdings:** 1000 books; corporation records; microfiche of New York and American Stock Exchanges and selected over-the-counter stocks. **Subscriptions:** 100 journals and other serials; 10 newspapers. **Services:** Interlibrary loan; center open to special libraries. **Computerized Information Services:** DIALOG Information Services, WESTLAW. **Publications:** SWMCI Library Bulletin - for internal distribution only.

★13694★
STONE AND WEBSTER ENGINEERING CORPORATION - TECHNICAL INFORMATION CENTER (Sci-Engr, Energy)
Box 5406 Phone: (303)741-7486
Denver, CO 80217 Nancy E. Pearson, Libn.
Founded: 1975. **Staff:** Prof 1. **Subjects:** Engineering, energy resources, power plants. **Holdings:** 5000 books; 200 reports on microfiche; plant engineering service on microfilm; 800 computer program manuals. **Subscriptions:** 100 journals and other serials. **Services:** Interlibrary loan; center not open to the public. **Automated Operations:** Computerized cataloging. **Computerized Information Services:** DIALOG Information Services. **Publications:** Acquisition list, monthly - for internal distribution only.

★13695★
STONE AND WEBSTER ENGINEERING CORPORATION - TECHNICAL INFORMATION CENTER (Sci-Engr, Energy)
245 Summer St. Phone: (617)589-8891
Boston, MA 02110 Nancy M. Pellini, Mgr.
Staff: Prof 1; Other 4. **Subjects:** Engineering - chemical, civil, nuclear, electrical, environmental, mechanical, structural; petroleum and petroleum processing; electric power transmission and generation; geology and soil mechanics; gas processing and transmission; pulp and paper processing and manufacture; water desalination; synfuels. **Special Collections:** Visual Search microfilm file of vendors, commercial standards, and International Organization for Standardization and IEC standards. **Holdings:** 14,000 books and bound periodical volumes; 25,000 reports. **Subscriptions:** 1000 journals and other serials; 20 newspapers. **Services:** Interlibrary loan; copying; library open to the public by appointment. **Computerized Information Services:** WESTLAW, DIALOG Information Services, Pergamon ORBIT InfoLine, Inc., Integrated Technical Information System (ITIS), Institute of Nuclear Power Operations (INPO), TECH DATA, Occupational Health Services, Inc. (OHS); CRS (internal database); LINX Courier (electronic mail service). **Publications:** Guide to the Technical Information Center. **Special Catalogs:** List of Stone and Webster Serial and Journal Holdings.

★13696★
STONEHENGE STUDY GROUP - STONEHENGE VIEWPOINT LIBRARY (Hist)
2821 De La Vina St. Phone: (805)687-9350
Santa Barbara, CA 93105 Joan L. Cyr, Libn.
Staff: Prof 2; Other 2. **Subjects:** Archeoastronomy, astroarcheology, canopy theory, Hidden Halo hypothesis, Vailian canopy research, halo motifs, pre-Columbian Ogam epigraphy sites in America. **Special Collections:** Unpublished manuscripts and published works of Isaac N. Vail, 1840-1912 (7000 pages). **Holdings:** 3400 books; 5000 pages on microfilm. **Subscriptions:** 32 journals and other serials. **Services:** Copying; library open to the public by appointment. **Publications:** Stonehenge Viewpoint, 4/year. **Staff:** Donald L. Cyr, Ed..

★13697★
STONEHILL COLLEGE - ARNOLD B. TOFIAS INDUSTRIAL ARCHIVES (Bus-Fin)
Washington St. Phone: (617)238-1081
North Easton, MA 02357 Louise M. Kenneally, Archv.
Founded: 1973. **Staff:** Prof 1. **Subjects:** Business archives. **Special Collections:** O. Ames & Co. shovel papers; Union Pacific Railroad. **Holdings:** 1500 linear feet of manuscripts. **Services:** Archives open to the public by appointment.

STONES RIVER NATIONAL BATTLEFIELD
See: U.S. Natl. Park Service (15355)

★13698★
STONINGTON HISTORICAL SOCIETY - WHITEHALL LIBRARY (Hist)
Box 103
Stonington, CT 06378 Norman F. Boas, Libn.
Staff: Prof 1; Other 1. **Subjects:** Genealogy, local history, biography. **Holdings:** 700 books; manuscripts; photographs; ships' logs; biographies; maps; newspaper clippings; memorabilia. **Publications:** Historical Footnotes, quarterly.

EMERY STOOPS AND JOYCE KING-STOOPS EDUCATION LIBRARY
See: University of Southern California (16870)

EFFIE M. STOREY LEARNING CENTER
See: Northwest Hospital (10470)

★13699★
STORMONT-VAIL REGIONAL MEDICAL CENTER - STAUFFER HEALTH SCIENCES LIBRARY (Med)
1500 S.W. 10th St. Phone: (913)354-5800
Topeka, KS 66604-1353 Shirley Borglund, Dir.
Founded: 1889. **Staff:** Prof 3; Other 6. **Subjects:** Medicine, nursing. **Holdings:** 8500 books; 15,000 unbound periodicals. **Subscriptions:** 400 journals and other serials. **Services:** Interlibrary loan; copying; research; library open to the public upon referral by a physician. **Computerized Information Services:** MEDLARS; Octanet (electronic mail service). Performs searches on fee basis. **Networks/Consortia:** Member of Midcontinental Regional Medical Library Program. **Publications:** Journal holdings list; acquisitions list - both available on request. **Staff:** Carol Wadley, Asst.Dir..

STOTT EXPLORERS LIBRARY
See: Martin and Osa Johnson Safari Museum (7264)

★13700★
STOVE KING - LIBRARY
1116 Capistrano Dr.
Salt Lake City, UT 84116
Defunct

★13701★
STOWE-DAY FOUNDATION - LIBRARY (Hist, Art)
77 Forest St. Phone: (203)728-5507
Hartford, CT 06105 Joseph S. Van Why, Dir.
Founded: 1964. **Staff:** Prof 3. **Subjects:** Art, architecture, decorative arts, history, literature, slavery, women's suffrage. **Special Collections:** William H. Gillette papers, plays, and photographs, 1853-1937; suffrage papers of Isabella Beecher Hooker; Katharine S. Day Collection; Saturday Morning Club Collection; literary manuscripts of Mark Twain and Harriet Beecher Stowe; 19th century wallpaper samples. **Holdings:** 15,000 books; 1500 bound periodical volumes; 150,000 manuscripts, especially Beecher family; 1500 pamphlets, 1850-1900; 3500 miscellaneous 19th century pamphlets; photographs. **Subscriptions:** 10 journals and other serials. **Services:** Interlibrary loan; copying; library open to the public for reference use only. **Networks/Consortia:** Member of Capitol Region Library Council (CRLC). **Special Catalogs:** Catalog of Nineteenth Century Chairs; American Artist Jared Flagg; William H. Gillette; microfiche of suffrage papers of Isabella Beecher Hooker. **Remarks:** The books, manuscripts, and photographs of the Mark Twain Memorial, Hartford, Connecticut, are also cataloged and housed in the Stowe-Day Library. The Stowe-Day Foundation maintains an active publishing program, consisting of original and reprint works, which reflects the interests of the library. **Staff:** Diana Royce, Libn..

LYMAN MAYNARD STOWE LIBRARY
See: University of Connecticut - Health Center (16093)

STOXEN LIBRARY
See: Dickinson State University (4259)

★13702★
STRADLEY, RONON, STEVENS & YOUNG - LAW LIBRARY (Law)
1100 One Franklin Plaza — Phone: (215)564-8190
Philadelphia, PA 19102 — Linda-Jean Smith, Libn.
Founded: 1972. **Staff:** Prof 1; Other 2. **Subjects:** Law - corporate, Pennsylvania, tax, labor; securities. **Special Collections:** Pennsylvania Pamphlet Laws since the 1700s (200 volumes). **Holdings:** 8500 books; 200 bound periodical volumes; 4 VF drawers of annual reports. **Subscriptions:** 200 journals and other serials. **Services:** Interlibrary loan; copying; library open to the public by appointment. **Computerized Information Services:** LEXIS. **Publications:** Information Items, monthly - for internal distribution only.

STRASENBURGH PLANETARIUM
See: Rochester Museum and Science Center - Strasenburgh Planetarium (12116)

★13703★
THE STRATEGIC CORPORATION - ISSUES NEWS SERVICE (Soc Sci)
2188 S.W. Park Place. — Phone: (503)222-9028
Portland, OR 97205-1125 — Susan Dole, Exec.Ed.
Founded: 1982. **Staff:** Prof 2; Other 3. **Subjects:** Social, economic, technological, political, governmental, natural resources, work, demographic, and global issues. **Holdings:** 59 environmental files; 10,000 other cataloged items. **Subscriptions:** 165 journals and other serials; 10 newspapers. **Services:** Service open to the public with restrictions. **Automated Operations:** Computerized cataloging and serials. **Computerized Information Services:** Mikado (internal database). Performs searches on fee basis. **Publications:** Strategic Moves, monthly - by subscription.

★13704★
STRATFORD HALL PLANTATION - JESSIE BALL DU PONT MEMORIAL LIBRARY (Hist)
Stratford Post Office — Phone: (804)493-8572
Stratford, VA 22558 — C. Vaughan Stanley, Libn./Hist.
Founded: 1980. **Staff:** Prof 5; Other 1. **Subjects:** Lee family history; 18th century Virginia history; Robert E. Lee. **Special Collections:** Lee Family manuscripts (1200 items); Thomas Lee Shippen 1790 Inventory and Collection (600 volumes); Ditchley Collection of 16th, 17th, and 18th century books (2400 volumes). **Holdings:** 7500 books; 200 bound periodical volumes; 332 cubic feet of Stratford Hall archives; 125 reels of microfilm. **Services:** Copying; library open to researchers by appointment. **Staff:** Donna J. Smith, Asst.Libn.; E. Pearl Cantrell, Archv.; Jeanne A. Calhoun, Res.; Grace Rhinesmith, Seminar Fellow.

★13705★
STRATFORD HISTORICAL SOCIETY - LIBRARY (Hist)
967 Academy Hill
Box 382 — Phone: (203)378-0630
Stratford, CT 06497 — Mrs. Einar M. Larson, Libn.
Founded: 1926. **Staff:** 2. **Subjects:** Stratford history and genealogy, Connecticut history. **Holdings:** 800 volumes; genealogical records and documents. **Services:** Library open to the public by appointment only.

★13706★
STRATFORD SHAKESPEAREAN FESTIVAL FOUNDATION OF CANADA - STRATFORD FESTIVAL ARCHIVES (Theater)
Box 520 — Phone: (519)271-4040
Stratford, ON, Canada N5A 6V2 — Daniel W. Ladell, Archv.
Staff: Prof 1. **Subjects:** The Stratford Festival. **Holdings:** 1500 linear feet of production, publicity, and administration records; 1500 AV programs; 130,000 photographs and transparencies; 350,000 press clippings; 1500 costumes and property pieces; 4000 plans and design renderings. **Services:** Archives not open to the public.

★13707★
STRATHY, ARCHIBALD & SEAGRAM - LAW LIBRARY (Law)
3801 Commerce Court, W.
Box 438 — Phone: (416)863-7525
Toronto, ON, Canada M5L 1J3 — Alison J. Colvin, Libn.
Staff: Prof 1. **Subjects:** Law. **Holdings:** 5500 volumes. **Services:** Interlibrary loan (limited); library not open to the public. **Computerized Information Services:** DIALOG Information Services, Info Globe, QL Systems, WESTLAW. Performs searches on fee basis. **Publications:** Library bulletin, biweekly -

LESLIE M. STRATTON NURSING LIBRARY
See: Methodist Hospitals of Memphis - Educational Resources Department (8800)

★13708★
STRAUB CLINIC & HOSPITAL, INC. - ARNOLD LIBRARY (Med)
888 S. King St. — Phone: (808)544-0317
Honolulu, HI 96813 — Frances P. Smith, Hd.Libn.
Founded: 1921. **Staff:** Prof 2. **Subjects:** Medicine - internal, nuclear, pediatric, adolescent, dermatology, surgery. **Special Collections:** Straub Clinic Proceedings; reprints of articles written and published by staff members. **Holdings:** 2500 books; 100 bound periodical volumes. **Subscriptions:** 280 journals and other serials. **Services:** Interlibrary loan; copying; SDI; library open to the public for reference use only. **Computerized Information Services:** MEDLINE, DIALOG Information Services, BRS Information Technologies. Performs searches on fee basis. **Networks/Consortia:** Member of Medical Library Group of Hawaii. **Publications:** Straub Clinic Proceedings, quarterly - free upon request; ALS News, quarterly. **Special Indexes:** Reprint index, 1929 to present (card). **Staff:** Patty Mazzola, Asst.Libn.

LORENZ G. STRAUB MEMORIAL LIBRARY
See: University of Minnesota - St. Anthony Falls Hydraulic Laboratory (16489)

NATHAN STRAUS YOUNG ADULT LIBRARY
See: New York Public Library - Donnell Library Center (10057)

ANNA LORD STRAUSS LIBRARY
See: Foundation for Citizen Education (5315)

★13709★
LEVI STRAUSS & COMPANY - BUSINESS ENVIRONMENT RESEARCH - LIBRARY (Bus-Fin)
1155 Battery St.
Box 7215
San Francisco, CA 94120-6935 — Michelle H. Ridgway, Mgr.
Founded: 1978. **Staff:** Prof 2; Other 1. **Subjects:** Apparel industry, marketing, retailing, advertising, demographics. **Holdings:** Books; reports; periodicals; subject files. **Services:** Interlibrary loan; center not open to the public. **Computerized Information Services:** DIALOG Information Services, NEXIS, Data Resources (DRI). **Formerly:** Corporate Information Center.

★13710★
LEVI STRAUSS & COMPANY - CORPORATE LAW LIBRARY (Law)
1155 Battery St. — Phone: (415)544-7676
San Francisco, CA 94106 — Yvonne B. Marty, Mgr., Law Lib.
Staff: 2. **Subjects:** Antitrust law, trademarks, copyrights. **Holdings:** 3500 books; 2000 bound periodical volumes; 25 cassettes; 45 loose-leaf services; worldwide listing of trademarks and copyrights. **Subscriptions:** 15 journals and other serials; 14 newspapers. **Services:** Interlibrary loan; copying; library open to members of private law libraries and state, city, and local federal libraries. **Computerized Information Services:** DIALOG Information Services, WESTLAW.

★13711★
STRAWBERY BANKE, INC. - THAYER CUMINGS HISTORICAL REFERENCE LIBRARY (Hist, Art)
454 Court St. — Phone: (603)436-8010
Portsmouth, NH 03801 — Janet R. Nourse Clark, Libn.
Staff: Prof 1. **Subjects:** Portsmouth history, decorative arts, architecture, archeology, horticulture. **Special Collections:** Business and family papers of Governor Ichabod and Sarah Parker Rice Goodwin, 1790s-1890s (8 cubic feet); Lowell Boat Shop Collection, 1881-1914 (5 boxes); papers of William and Charles Neil, Capt. John Hill, and Stephen Chase. **Holdings:** 2800 books; 30 bound periodical volumes; 25 reports; 24 cubic feet of

manuscripts; 45 reels of microfilm. **Subscriptions:** 58 journals and other serials. **Services:** Copying; library open to the public for reference use only.

★13712★
STRAYER COLLEGE - LEARNING RESOURCES CENTER (Bus-Fin)
3045 Columbia Pike Phone: (703)861-5241
Arlington, VA 22204 Marilyn Mackhrandilal, LRC Mgr.
Staff: 4. **Subjects:** Data processing, business, office administration, court and conference reporting, accounting, electronics. **Holdings:** 4000 books; 4 VF drawers of pamphlets; 160 dictation cassettes. **Subscriptions:** 40 journals and other serials. **Services:** Interlibrary loan; copying; center open to the public by appointment. **Publications:** Library Handbook.

★13713★
STRAYER COLLEGE - WILKES LIBRARY (Bus-Fin)
1015 14th St., N.W. Phone: (202)467-6966
Washington, DC 20005 David A. Moulton, Dir. of Libs.
Staff: Prof 1; Other 3. **Subjects:** Business administration, data processing, accounting, court and conference reporting, office administration. **Holdings:** 15,000 books; 12 drawers of pamphlets. **Subscriptions:** 120 journals and other serials; 15 newspapers. **Services:** Interlibrary loan; copying; library open to the public. **Computerized Information Services:** DIALOG Information Services. **Publications:** Library Handbook, annual.

STRECKER MUSEUM LIBRARY
See: Baylor University (1420)

★13714★
STREICH, LANG, WEEKS & CARDON - LIBRARY (Law)
100 W. Washington, Suite 2100 Phone: (602)257-0999
Phoenix, AZ 85008 Winifred Edwards, Libn.
Staff: Prof 1; Other 2. **Subjects:** Law - corporate, tax, real estate, banking. **Holdings:** 15,000 volumes. **Subscriptions:** 217 journals and other serials; 5 newspapers. **Services:** Library not open to the public. **Automated Operations:** Computerized cataloging. **Computerized Information Services:** LEXIS, WESTLAW.

★13715★
STROH BREWERY COMPANY - STROH TECHNICAL LIBRARY (Food-Bev)
100 River Place Phone: (313)446-2635
Detroit, MI 48207 Patricia D. Pindzia, Libn.
Founded: 1982. **Staff:** 1. **Subjects:** Brewing, chemistry, biosciences. **Holdings:** Figures not available. **Services:** Library not open to the public. **Computerized Information Services:** DIALOG Information Services.

STROKE INFORMATION AND RESOURCE CLEARINGHOUSE
See: National Stroke Association (9808)

JOSEPH G. STROMBERG LIBRARY OF THE HEALTH SCIENCES
See: Swedish Covenant Hospital (13836)

★13716★
G.F. STRONG REHABILITATION CENTRE - STAFF MEDICAL LIBRARY (Med)
4255 Laurel St. Phone: (604)734-1313
Vancouver, BC, Canada V5Z 2G9 Robert Trowsdale, Chf.Libn.
Founded: 1978. **Staff:** Prof 1. **Subjects:** Rehabilitation, physical medicine. **Holdings:** 7600 books; 100 cassette tapes. **Subscriptions:** 70 journals and other serials. **Services:** Interlibrary loan; library not open to the public. **Automated Operations:** Computerized cataloging. **Computerized Information Services:** DIALOG Information Services, MEDLARS, CAN/OLE; internal databases; Envoy 100 (electronic mail service). Performs searches on fee basis. **Publications:** Library Bulletin - for internal distribution only.

KATE STRONG HISTORICAL LIBRARY
See: Museums at Stony Brook (9468)

★13717★
MARGARET WOODBURY STRONG MUSEUM - LIBRARY (Art, Hist)
One Manhattan Square Phone: (716)263-2700
Rochester, NY 14607 Elaine M. Challacombe, Libn.
Founded: 1972. **Staff:** Prof 3; Other 1. **Subjects:** U.S. social history, 19th century decorative arts in the U.S., 19th century woman in the home. **Special Collections:** Children's literature from late 19th and early 20th centuries (400 titles); Victorian publishers' bindings (600); miniature books (680); fore-edge paintings (74); Winslow Homer's library (20 volumes). **Holdings:** 25,000 books; 600 Parke-Bernet auction catalogs, 1938-1957; 4000 trade catalogs. **Subscriptions:** 130 journals and other serials. **Services:** Interlibrary loan; copying; library open to the public. **Automated Operations:** Computerized cataloging. **Networks/Consortia:** Member of Rochester Regional Library Council (RRLC), SUNY/OCLC Library Network. **Publications:** New Acquisitions list, monthly - for internal distribution only. **Staff:** Anna K. Wang, Asst.Libn./Cat.; Carol Sandler, Asst.Libn./Ref./Archv..

STROSACKER LIBRARY
See: Northwood Institute (10506)

STRUGHOLD AEROMEDICAL LIBRARY
See: U.S. Air Force - Air Force Systems Command - Human Systems Division - School of Aerospace Medicine (14589)

★13718★
STRYBING ARBORETUM SOCIETY - HELEN CROCKER RUSSELL LIBRARY OF HORTICULTURE (Biol Sci)
Golden Gate Park
9th Ave. & Lincoln Way Phone: (415)661-1514
San Francisco, CA 94122 Jane Potter Gates, Hd.Libn.
Founded: 1972. **Staff:** Prof 2. **Subjects:** Horticulture, plant propagation, landscape gardening, flora of Mediterranean climates, plant hunting, history of gardening. **Holdings:** 11,500 books, including 300 rare volumes; 700 bound periodical volumes; 1 shelf of William Hammond Hall Archives; 4250 slide transparencies of plants; 12 VF drawers of brochures and pamphlets; old and current nursery catalogs. **Subscriptions:** 220 journals and other serials. **Services:** Copying; library open to the public. **Networks/Consortia:** Member of Council on Botanical Horticultural Libraries. **Special Catalogs:** Catalog of slide collection (card); catalog of old and current nursery catalog collections. **Remarks:** "The basic purpose of the library is to assist the home gardener and to provide information about the 5000 plants in the Strybing Arboretum." **Staff:** Barbara M. Pitschel, Asst.Libn..

★13719★
STS CONSULTANTS LTD. - LIBRARY (Sci-Engr)
111 Pfingsten Rd. Phone: (312)272-6520
Northbrook, IL 60062 William J. Burns, Libn.
Staff: Prof 1. **Subjects:** Engineering - civil, environmental, materials; engineering geology; hydrology; geohydrology. **Holdings:** 1400 books. **Subscriptions:** 40 journals and other serials. **Services:** Interlibrary loan; copying; library open to the public by appointment. **Automated Operations:** Computerized cataloging. **Computerized Information Services:** DIALOG Information Services, BRS Information Technologies, Pergamon ORBIT InfoLine, Inc., American Society of Civil Engineers (ASCE). **Networks/Consortia:** Member of North Suburban Library System (NSLS).

JOHN STUART RESEARCH LABORATORIES
See: Quaker Oats Company (11751)

STUART LIBRARY OF WESTERN AMERICANA
See: University of the Pacific - Holt-Atherton Center for Western Studies (16723)

LYLE STUART LIBRARY OF SEXUAL SCIENCE
See: Institute for Advanced Study of Human Sexuality - Research Library (6879)

STUART MEMORIAL LIBRARY
See: Alta Bates-Herrick Hospitals (338)

STUCK MEDICAL LIBRARY
See: Mount Clemens General Hospital (9367)

★13720★
STUDEBAKER NATIONAL MUSEUM INC. - RESEARCH LIBRARY (Hist)
120 S. St. Joseph St. Phone: (219)284-9714
South Bend, IN 46601 Thomas Brubaker, Dir.
Staff: Prof 1. **Subjects:** Studebaker corporation and vehicles, South Bend industries, automotive history. **Special Collections:** Studebaker Archives (3000 linear feet); Oliver Photographic Collection (10,000 negatives, circa 1900-1950, from Oliver Corporation, manufacturers of farm equipment). **Holdings:** 300 books; 60 reels of microfilm; 15 VF drawers of trade catalogs and advertising; 12 VF drawers of photographs. **Subscriptions:** 27 journals and other serials. **Services:** Interlibrary loan; copying; library open to the public for reference use only. **Formerly:** Discovery Hall Museum.

STUDENT VOLUNTEER MOVEMENT - ARCHIVES
See: Yale University - Divinity School Library (18126)

★13721★
STUDENTS' MUSEUM, INC. - LIBRARY (Sci-Engr)
Box 6204 Phone: (615)637-1121
Knoxville, TN 37914 David R. Sincerbox, Dir.
Founded: 1976. **Staff:** Prof 5; Other 6. **Subjects:** Science, history, nature, arts and crafts. **Special Collections:** Old tools (400); dolls (300); costumes (25); fossils (300); rocks and minerals (5000); Indian artifacts (1000); man-made artifacts (20,000); shells (5000); stuffed animals (300); charts (300). **Holdings:** 2500 books; 200 manuscripts; 15,000 slides; 300 pamphlets; 2500 postcards. **Subscriptions:** 30 journals and other serials. **Services:** Library not open to the public. **Automated Operations:** Computerized cataloging and acquisitions. **Computerized Information Services:** Internal database. **Staff:** Sylvia Gloeckner, Cur. of Educ..

STUDENTS STRUGGLE FOR SOVIET JEWRY
See: Center for Russian & East European Jewry (2869)

STUHR MUSEUM
See: Hall County Museum - Stuhr Museum (5967)

RICHARD J. STULL MEMORIAL LEARNING RESOURCES CENTER
See: American College of Healthcare Executives (454)

★13722★
STURDY MEMORIAL HOSPITAL - HEALTH SCIENCES LIBRARY (Med)
211 Park St. Phone: (508)222-5200
Attleboro, MA 02703 Juliet I. Mansfield, Libn.
Staff: Prof 1; Other 2. **Subjects:** Medicine, nursing. **Special Collections:** Rare editions of medical and surgical books (82 volumes). **Holdings:** 866 books; 584 bound periodical volumes; 8 VF drawers of articles, clippings, pamphlets. **Subscriptions:** 132 journals and other serials. **Services:** Interlibrary loan; copying; library open to the public for reference use only. **Networks/Consortia:** Member of Southeastern Massachusetts Consortium of Health Science Libraries (SEMCO), Massachusetts Health Sciences Library Network (MAHSLIN), Association of Rhode Island Health Sciences Librarians (ARIHSL).

STURGEON MUSIC LIBRARY
See: Mount Union College (9387)

GERTRUDE E. STURGES MEMORIAL LIBRARY
See: Rhode Island State Department of Health (12026)

GERTRUDE STURGES MEMORIAL LIBRARY
See: Group Health Association of America, Inc. (5903)

★13723★
STURGIS LIBRARY (Hist)
Main St.
Box 606 Phone: (508)362-6636
Barnstable, MA 02630 Susan R. Klein, Chf.Libn.
Founded: 1867. **Staff:** Prof 2; Other 2. **Subjects:** Genealogy, Barnstable County history, maritime history, 19th century English and American literature. **Special Collections:** Stanley W. Smith Collection (original Cape Cod documents and land deeds); Kittredge Collection (marine history). **Holdings:** 43,960 books; 200 bound periodical volumes; 250 sound recordings, tapes, and cassettes; 125 reels of microfilm; 60 flat pictures; 1500 land deeds; 25 maps and charts. **Subscriptions:** 105 journals and other serials. **Services:** Interlibrary loan; copying; service to homebound and institutionalized; library open to the public on fee basis. **Publications:** Sturgis Library Newsletter, quarterly; A Short History of the Sturgis Library; 19th Century Literary Gentlemen. **Remarks:** This library has been declared the oldest library building in the U.S.; its original structure was built in 1644. **Staff:** Diane Nielsen, Ref.Libn..

★13724★
MARY RILEY STYLES PUBLIC LIBRARY - LOCAL HISTORY COLLECTION (Hist)
120 N. Virginia Ave. Phone: (703)241-5030
Falls Church, VA 22046 Anna W. Rups, Libn.
Staff: Prof 1; Other 3. **Subjects:** Falls Church history. **Holdings:** 821 books; 56 bound periodical volumes; 336 public records; 145 manuscripts; 5000 photographs; 20,000 negatives; 258 maps; 130 oral history tapes; 41 reels of microfilm; 24 VF drawers of archival materials; 5 scrapbooks; 800 slides; 8 videotapes. **Subscriptions:** 22 journals and other serials. **Services:** Copying; collection open to the public by appointment for reference use. **Remarks:** Maintained by the city of Falls Church.

SUBBAROW MEMORIAL LIBRARY
See: American Cyanamid Company - Lederle Laboratories Division (480)

★13725★
SUBURBAN HENNEPIN REGIONAL PARK DISTRICT - LOWRY NATURE CENTER - LIBRARY (Biol Sci)
Carver Park Reserve
7025 Victoria Dr. Phone: (612)472-4911
Excelsior, MN 55331 Dale Rock, Naturalist
Founded: 1970. **Staff:** Prof 4. **Subjects:** Natural history, ornithology, mammalogy, ichthyology, herpetology, botany and forestry, wildlife management, ecology, entomology. **Holdings:** 650 books; 4 VF drawers of natural history material, organizational material, maps, pamphlets. **Services:** Library open to the public for reference use only.

★13726★
SUBURBAN TEMPLE - GRIES LIBRARY (Rel-Phil)
22401 Chagrin Blvd. Phone: (216)991-0700
Beachwood, OH 44122 Tamara M. Katz, Libn.
Staff: Prof 1. **Subjects:** Judaica. **Holdings:** 6000 books; 100 phonograph records; 4 VF drawers. **Subscriptions:** 10 journals and other serials. **Services:** Interlibrary loan; copying; library open to the public by appointment. **Publications:** New acquisitions list, semiannual - for internal distribution only.

★13727★
SUDBURY GENERAL HOSPITAL - HOSPITAL LIBRARY (Med)
700 Paris St., Station B Phone: (705)674-3181
Sudbury, ON, Canada P3E 3B5 D.M. Hawryliuk, Libn.
Founded: 1950. **Staff:** Prof 1. **Subjects:** Clinical medicine. **Special Collections:** Archival history of hospital (8 volumes of newspaper clippings). **Holdings:** 1200 books; 1120 bound periodical volumes. **Subscriptions:** 130 journals and other serials. **Services:** Interlibrary loan; copying; SDI; library open to the public with restrictions. **Publications:** Health Science Serials,

★13728★
SUFFOLK ACADEMY OF MEDICINE - LIBRARY (Med)
850 Veterans Memorial Hwy. Phone: (516)724-7970
Hauppauge, NY 11788 Isabel V. Hathorn, Dir.
Founded: 1966. **Staff:** Prof 1; Other 1. **Subjects:** Medicine, dentistry, nursing. **Holdings:** 2950 books; 2600 periodicals; 90 bulletin collections; 24 shelves of pamphlets. **Subscriptions:** 390 journals and other serials. **Services:** Interlibrary loan; copying; library open to the public for reference use only. **Automated Operations:** Computerized cataloging. **Computerized Information Services:** BRS Information Technologies, DIALOG Information Services, MEDLARS. Performs searches on fee basis. **Networks/Consortia:** Member of Long Island Library Resources Council, Inc. (LILRC), Greater Northeastern Regional Medical Library Program.

★13729★
SUFFOLK COOPERATIVE LIBRARY SYSTEM - AUDIOVISUAL DEPARTMENT (Aud-Vis)
627 N. Sunrise Service Rd. Phone: (516)286-1600
Bellport, NY 11713 Philip Levering, AV Cons.
Staff: Prof 1; Other 4. **Subjects:** Films - children's, documentaries, nature study, feature length, old-time comedy classics; film as art. **Holdings:** 2600 16mm films; 900 VHS video cassettes. **Services:** Interlibrary loan; copying; department open to members of the library system. **Special Catalogs:** Film catalog, biennial - for sale; video catalog, biennial - free upon request.

★13730★
SUFFOLK COUNTY HISTORICAL SOCIETY - LIBRARY (Hist)
300 W. Main St. Phone: (516)727-2881
Riverhead, NY 11901 Joanne J. Brooks, Libn.
Founded: 1886. **Staff:** 12. **Subjects:** Suffolk County and Long Island history and genealogy. **Special Collections:** Revolutionary War documents of Colonel Josiah Smith; Modern Times (Brentwood); Fullerton negatives, circa 1900; E.T. Talmage weaving collection; Professional Resources (Museum) Collection. **Holdings:** 15,000 volumes; microfilm; manuscripts; clippings; records; documents; photographs; fiber swatch-books. **Subscriptions:** 12 journals and other serials. **Services:** Copying; library open to the public with restrictions. **Publications:** Register. **Special Indexes:** Index to scrapbooks, glass negatives (card); vital statistics (card); index to documents (card); abstracts of documents (book). **Staff:** Eileen Earl, Res.Asst..

★13731★
SUFFOLK MARINE MUSEUM - HERVEY GARRETT SMITH RESEARCH LIBRARY (Hist)
Montauk Hwy.
Box 144 Phone: (516)567-1733
West Sayville, NY 11796 Ruth Dougherty, Res.Libn.
Founded: 1966. **Staff:** Prof 1. **Subjects:** Boat building, yachting, racing, shipwrecks, U.S. Life Saving Service, shellfishing, history of the America's Cup Race, the Merchant Marine, U.S. Navy, and U.S. Coast Guard. **Special Collections:** Ships' logs (4); vessel construction plans; U.S. Life Saving Service records; historical photograph collection. **Holdings:** 1700 books; 50 bound periodical volumes; 2 slide programs; 40 navigational charts; glass plate negatives. **Subscriptions:** 11 journals and other serials. **Services:** Copying; library open to the public for reference use only.

★13732★
SUFFOLK UNIVERSITY - LAW LIBRARY (Law)
41 Temple St. Phone: (617)723-4700
Boston, MA 02114 Edward Bander, Law Libn.
Founded: 1906. **Staff:** Prof 7; Other 9. **Subjects:** Law. **Holdings:** 210,000 books and bound periodical volumes; 45,000 volumes on microfiche; U.S. Government documents depository. **Subscriptions:** 900 journals and other serials; 20 newspapers. **Services:** Interlibrary loan; copying; library open to the public for use of government documents. **Automated Operations:** Computerized cataloging, acquisitions, and serials. **Computerized Information Services:** LEXIS, WESTLAW, OCLC, ABA/net, PHINet FedTax Database, DIALOG Information Services. **Networks/Consortia:** Member of NELINET. **Staff:** Susan Sweetgall, Sr.Ref.Libn.; Patricia I. Brown, Assoc. Law Libn.; Susan Silver, Govt.Docs.Libn..

★13733★
SUFFOLK UNIVERSITY - MILDRED F. SAWYER LIBRARY - COLLECTION OF AFRO-AMERICAN LITERATURE (Area-Ethnic)
8 Ashburton Place Phone: (617)723-4700
Boston, MA 02108 E.G. Hamann, Dir.
Staff: Prof 6; Other 6. **Subjects:** Afro-Americans - literature, bibliography, history, biography, literary criticism. **Holdings:** 4000 books; 150 bound periodical volumes. **Services:** Interlibrary loan; copying; collection open to the public for reference use only. **Automated Operations:** Computerized cataloging. **Computerized Information Services:** InfoTrac. Performs searches free of charge. **Networks/Consortia:** Member of NELINET, Fenway Library Consortium (FLC). **Publications:** Black Writers in New England, a Bibliography, 1985 - for sale; Acquisitions List, annual - free upon request. **Staff:** James R. Coleman, Ref.Libn.; Joseph Middleton, Ref.Libn.; Kathleen Maio, Ref.Libn.; Elisa McKnight, Ref.Libn..

★13734★
THE SUGAR ASSOCIATION, INC. - LIBRARY (Food-Bev)
1101 15th St., N.W., No. 600 Phone: (202)785-1122
Washington, DC 20005 Nancy M. Cassel, Libn.
Founded: 1943. **Staff:** Prof 1. **Subjects:** Sugar, nutrition and health, food technology. **Holdings:** 1500 books; 1000 bound periodical volumes; 50 VF drawers of pamphlets, clippings, patents, miscellaneous documents. **Subscriptions:** 100 journals and other serials; 7 newspapers. **Services:** Interlibrary loan; copying; library open to the public.

SUGARLANDS VISITOR CENTER
See: U.S. Natl. Park Service - Great Smoky Mountains Natl. Park (15303)

SUICIDE INFORMATION AND EDUCATION CENTRE
See: Canadian Mental Health Association (2581)

★13735★
SULLIVAN AND CROMWELL - LIBRARY (Law)
125 Broad St. Phone: (212)558-4000
New York, NY 10004 Helene A. Weatherill, Libn.
Subjects: Law. **Holdings:** 29,500 volumes. **Services:** Library not open to the public. **Staff:** Barbara A. Clyne, Asst.Libn.; Stephanie Heacox, Asst.Libn..

★13736★
SULLIVAN AND CROMWELL - WASHINGTON D.C. LIBRARY (Law)
1775 Pennsylvania Ave., N.W. Phone: (202)956-7538
Washington, DC 20006 Denise Noller, Libn.
Founded: 1977. **Staff:** Prof 1; Other 2. **Subjects:** Law - antitrust, securities, tax; trade regulation. **Holdings:** 9000 books; 1000 bound periodical volumes; documents; microforms. **Subscriptions:** 150 journals and other serials; 8 newspapers. **Services:** Interlibrary loan; SDI; library open to the public with permission. **Computerized Information Services:** LEXIS, NEXIS, DIALOG Information Services.

SULLIVAN MEDICAL LIBRARY
See: St. Anne's Hospital (12316)

★13737★
SULPHUR INSTITUTE - LIBRARY (Sci-Engr)
1725 K St., N.W. Phone: (202)331-9660
Washington, DC 20006 Robin Smith, Libn.
Subjects: Sulphur in industry and agriculture. **Holdings:** 500 books; 200 bound periodical volumes; 20 VF drawers. **Services:** Interlibrary loan; library open to the public by appointment.

SULZBACHER MEMORIAL LIBRARY
See: Spring Grove Hospital Center (13564)

SULZBERGER JOURNALISM LIBRARY
See: Columbia University (3494)

★13738★
SUMMER INSTITUTE OF LINGUISTICS - DALLAS/NORMAN LIBRARY (Hum, Soc Sci)
7500 W. Camp Wisdom Rd.
Dallas, TX 75236 Phone: (214)298-3331
Staff: Prof 3; Other 2. **Subjects:** Linguistics, anthropology. **Special Collections:** Summer Institute of Linguistics archives (9000 items on microfiche). **Holdings:** 13,500 books; 1000 bound periodical volumes; 5000 vertical files. **Subscriptions:** 151 journals and other serials. **Services:** Interlibrary loan; copying; library open to the public for reference use only. **Computerized Information Services:** DIALOG Information Services. **Publications:** Acquisitions list, irregular. **Staff:** Dorothy L. White, Cat..

W.W. SUMMERVILLE MEDICAL LIBRARY
See: Bethany Medical Center (1556)

SUMMIT COUNTY PUBLIC LIBRARY
See: Akron-Summit County Public Library (129)

★13739★
SUMTER AREA TECHNICAL COLLEGE - LIBRARY (Bus-Fin, Sci-Engr)
506 N. Guignard Dr. Phone: (803)778-1961
Sumter, SC 29150 Chris Bruggman, Coord.
Founded: 1963. **Staff:** Prof 2; Other 2. **Subjects:** Business, civil engineering, secretarial science, marketing, machine shop technology, automotive mechanics, criminal justice, accounting, electricity, natural resources management, nursing, welding, climate control, electronics, paralegal science, fashion merchandising, environmental quality control technology, drafting, tool and dye technology, industrial maintenance. **Holdings:** 18,592 books; 618 bound periodical volumes; 74 journal titles on microfiche; 250 VF drawers; 967 AV programs. **Subscriptions:** 225 journals and other serials; 16 newspapers. **Services:** Interlibrary loan; copying; library open to the public for reference use only. **Publications:** Workstudy Handbook; Library Handbook; Policies and Procedures Manual. **Special Catalogs:** Catalog to AV programs.

★13740★
SUN CHEMICAL CORPORATION - RESEARCH LIBRARY (Sci-Engr)
631 Central Ave. Phone: (201)933-4500
Carlstadt, NJ 07072 Kendal Funk, Tech.Info.Spec.
Founded: 1938. **Staff:** Prof 1; Other 1. **Subjects:** Graphic arts, polymer chemistry, photochemistry, organic chemistry. **Holdings:** 2500 books; 3000 bound periodical volumes; 48 shelf feet of unbound official gazettes; 200 boxes of unbound periodicals; 7 VF drawers of reports. **Subscriptions:** 150 journals and other serials; 6 newspapers. **Services:** Library not open to the public. **Computerized Information Services:** DIALOG Information Services, Pergamon ORBIT InfoLine, Inc. **Publications:** Library Bulletin, weekly - for internal distribution only.

★13741★
SUN EXPLORATION & PRODUCTION COMPANY - TECHNOLOGY CENTER LIBRARY (Energy)
Box 830936 Phone: (214)470-1168
Richardson, TX 75083-0936 Irene Darrow, Libn.
Founded: 1966. **Staff:** Prof 1; Other 2. **Subjects:** Geology and geophysics, petroleum engineering, chemistry. **Holdings:** 20,000 volumes; 6000 dissertations, guidebooks, and government documents; 6500 reports on microfiche. **Subscriptions:** 272 journals and other serials. **Services:**

Interlibrary loan; copying; library open to the public with restrictions. **Computerized Information Services:** DIALOG Information Services, Pergamon ORBIT InfoLine, Inc., Petroleum Data System (PDS). **Formerly:** Information Resources Center.

★13742★
SUN FINANCIAL GROUP - REFERENCE LIBRARY (Bus-Fin)
One Sun Life Executive Park Phone: (617)237-6030
Wellesley Hills, MA 02181 Pamela A. Mahaney, Libn.
Founded: 1973. **Staff:** Prof 2. **Subjects:** Insurance, management, data processing, law, labor, taxation. **Holdings:** 12,000 books; 29 VF drawers. **Subscriptions:** 667 journals and other serials; 14 newspapers. **Services:** Interlibrary loan; copying; library open to the public with restrictions. **Publications:** Selected Articles of Interest, weekly; Book News, monthly; LIMRA Accessions, bimonthly. **Staff:** Merrill H. Walsh, Asst.Libn..

★13743★
SUN LIBRARY AND INFORMATION CENTER (Energy)
Box 1135 Phone: (215)485-1121
Marcus Hook, PA 19061 Norman D. Morphet, Sect.Chf.
Staff: Prof 3; Other 6. **Subjects:** Petroleum, physics, chemistry, mathematics, chemical marketing, engineering, business, management. **Holdings:** 14,000 books; 14,000 bound periodical volumes; 65 VF drawers of pamphlets; 40 VF drawers of patents; 40 VF drawers of pamphlets (uncataloged); API project reports; 14,000 government documents; microfilm; microcards. **Subscriptions:** 800 journals and other serials; 19 newspapers. **Services:** Interlibrary loan; copying; library open to scholars for research by application. **Automated Operations:** Computerized serials. **Computerized Information Services:** Online systems. **Publications:** Book Accession List, monthly; Pamphlet Accession List, weekly - both for internal distribution only. **Special Indexes:** National Petroleum Refiners Association Question and Answer Sessions Index. **Staff:** Phoebe Cassidy, Res.Libn.; Dale Rodenhaver, Bus.Libn..

★13744★
SUN LIFE OF CANADA - BUSINESS LIBRARY (Bus-Fin)
200 University Ave. Phone: (416)595-7894
Toronto, ON, Canada M5H 3C7 Elizabeth Gibson, Mgr.
Founded: 1980. **Staff:** Prof 2; Other 5. **Subjects:** Life insurance, management, financial services, pensions, investments, data processing. **Holdings:** 10,000 books; annual reports. **Subscriptions:** 700 journals and other serials; 20 newspapers. **Services:** Interlibrary loan; copying; library open to the public by appointment. **Automated Operations:** Computerized cataloging. **Computerized Information Services:** DIALOG Information Services, Info Globe, BRS Information Technologies, TEXTLINE, Dow Jones News/Retrieval, The Financial Post Information Service, Canada Systems Group (CSG), Infomart, UTLAS, WILSONLINE, Canadian Financial Database (C.F.D.), Report on Business Corporate Database; Envoy 100 (electronic mail service). Performs searches on fee basis. **Publications:** List of new books, bimonthly - distributed internally and to selected libraries; List of Periodicals, annual. **Staff:** Sarah Carvalho, Libn..

★13745★
SUN LIFE OF CANADA - REFERENCE LIBRARY (Bus-Fin)
Box 6075, Sta. A Phone: (514)866-6411
Montreal, PQ, Canada H3C 3G5 Claire De Grandpre, Libn.
Staff: Prof 1. **Subjects:** Life insurance, finance, management, economics. **Holdings:** 700 books. **Subscriptions:** 150 journals and other serials; 10 newspapers. **Services:** Interlibrary loan; copying; SDI; library open to the public with restrictions. **Computerized Information Services:** DIALOG Information Services, UTLAS.

★13746★
SUNBURY SHORES ARTS AND NATURE CENTRE, INC. - SUNBURY SHORES LIBRARY (Art, Env-Cons)
139 Water St.
P.O. Box 100 Phone: (506)529-3386
St. Andrews, NB, Canada E0G 2X0 Nancy Aiken
Staff: 2. **Subjects:** Art history, crafts, natural science, ecology, photography. **Special Collections:** Kroenberger Memorial Collection (fine art); Vaughan Collection (fine art and natural science). **Holdings:** 800 books; 10 drawers of pictures; 15 sleeves of slides. **Subscriptions:** 10 journals and other serials. **Services:** Interlibrary loan; copying; library open to members and area schools.

★13747★
SUNCOR INC. - LIBRARY (Sci-Engr, Energy)
500 4th Ave., S.W.
P.O. Box 38 Phone: (403)269-8128
Calgary, AB, Canada T2P 2V5 Pat Strong, Libn.
Founded: 1959. **Staff:** 2. **Subjects:** Petroleum industry, geology, geophysics, engineering, economics, office management, statistics. **Holdings:** 500 books; 700 government publications; 1000 pamphlets, reprints, and clippings; 600 annual reports of other companies. **Subscriptions:** 72 journals and other serials. **Services:** Interlibrary loan; copying; library open to the public for reference use only. **Publications:** Library Newsletter, monthly - for internal distribution only.

★13748★
SUNDSTRAND AVIATION - INFORMATION RESOURCE CENTER (Sci-Engr)
4747 Harrison Ave.
Box 7002 Phone: (815)226-6753
Rockford, IL 61125 D'Ann Hamilton, Info.Spec.
Staff: Prof 1. **Subjects:** Aviation design, research, and manufacturing. **Holdings:** 3500 books; government and corporate reports; specifications and standards. **Subscriptions:** 110 journals and other serials. **Services:** Interlibrary loan; library not open to the public. **Automated Operations:** Computerized cataloging. **Computerized Information Services:** NERAC, Inc., DIALOG Information Services. **Networks/Consortia:** Member of Northern Illinois Library System (NILS). **Formerly:** Engineering Library. **Staff:** Danita Duncan, Libn..

★13749★
SUNDSTRAND DATA CONTROL - ENGINEERING LIBRARY (Sci-Engr)
15001 N.E. 36th St., MS 1
Box 97001 Phone: (206)885-8420
Redmond, WA 98073-9701 Doris M. Smart, Engr.Res.Libn.
Founded: 1957. **Staff:** Prof 1. **Subjects:** Aerospace, electronics, avionics systems, instruments, passenger entertainment systems, industrial components. **Holdings:** 1200 books; military specifications and standards on microfilm; vendor catalogs on microfilm. **Subscriptions:** 100 journals and other serials. **Services:** Interlibrary loan; library not open to the public. **Automated Operations:** Computerized cataloging. **Computerized Information Services:** DIALOG Information Services, OCLC, TECH DATA; internal database; High Security (electronic mail service). **Networks/Consortia:** Member of Western Library Network (WLN).

★13750★
SUNHEALTH, INC. - SUNHEALTH RESOURCE CENTER (Med)
Box 668800 Phone: (704)529-3324
Charlotte, NC 28266-8800 Carroll H. Backman, Mgr., Res.Ctr.
Founded: 1978. **Staff:** Prof 1; Other 1. **Subjects:** Hospitals, health care, safety, marketing. **Holdings:** 3100 books; 180 bound periodical volumes; 3000 confidential reports; 20 magazine volumes on microfiche; 10 sound slide sets; 100 audio cassettes; 20 video cassettes. **Subscriptions:** 125 journals and other serials. **Services:** Interlibrary loan; copying; library open to the public with prior arrangement. **Computerized Information Services:** BRS Information Technologies; internal databases. **Publications:** Library Newsletter, bimonthly - for internal distribution only.

★13751★
SUNKIST GROWERS, INC. - CORPORATE LIBRARY (Bus-Fin, Food-Bev)
14130 Riverside Dr. Phone: (818)986-4800
Sherman Oaks, CA 91423 Leo R. Bald, Corp.Libn.
Founded: 1975. **Staff:** Prof 1; Other 1. **Subjects:** Business, management, marketing, citrus industry, agricultural economics, international trade. **Special Collections:** Archives (3000 citrus crate labels, early advertisements, historical photographs). **Holdings:** 2000 books; 10,000 government documents; 30 VF drawers; 25,000 microfiche. **Subscriptions:** 350 journals and other serials; 15 newspapers. **Services:** Interlibrary loan; copying; library open to the public by appointment only. **Computerized Information Services:** RLIN, DIALOG Information Services. **Publications:** Corporate Contents, irregular - for internal distribution only. **Special Indexes:** Index to citrus crate labels by brand name (card).

★13752★
SUNKIST GROWERS, INC. - RESEARCH LIBRARY
760 E. Sunkist St.
Ontario, CA 91761
Founded: 1939. **Subjects:** Citrus and citrus products technology; chemistry - organic, analytical, food. **Holdings:** 1100 books; 1230 bound periodical volumes; 2000 reprints. **Remarks:** Presently inactive.

★13753★
SUNLAND CENTER AT GAINESVILLE - LIBRARY (Med)
Box 1150 Phone: (904)395-1650
Gainesville, FL 32602 Susan L. Stephan, Libn. II
Founded: 1954. **Staff:** Prof 1; Other 1. **Subjects:** Mental retardation, exceptional child education. **Holdings:** 6800 volumes; 3500 AV programs; high interest-low vocabulary picture books; professional materials. **Subscriptions:** 25 journals and other serials. **Services:** Interlibrary loan; library open to the public with restrictions.

★13754★
SUNNYBROOK MEDICAL CENTRE - HEALTH SCIENCES LIBRARY (Med)
2075 Bayview Ave. Phone: (416)486-4562
Toronto, ON, Canada M4N 3M5 Linda McFarlane, Hea.Sci.Libn.
Staff: Prof 2; Other 10. **Subjects:** Medicine and nursing, hospital administration. **Holdings:** 8000 books; 18,000 bound periodical volumes; 2500 audiotapes; 260 videotapes; 15 drawers of pamphlets. **Subscriptions:** 535 journals and other serials. **Services:** Interlibrary loan; copying; SDI; library open to area medical practitioners. **Computerized Information Services:** MEDLINE, DIALOG Information Services, BRS Information Technologies.

★13755★
SUNNYVALE PATENT INFORMATION CLEARINGHOUSE (Law)
1500 Partridge Ave., Bldg. 7 Phone: (408)730-7290
Sunnyvale, CA 94087 Beverley J. Simmons, Dir. of Libs.
Founded: 1965. **Staff:** Prof 2; Other 2. **Subjects:** U.S. patents, 1836 to present; patent, trademark, and copyright registration information. **Holdings:** 7800 volumes; 4 million patents; Federal Trademark Register; Report of the Commissioner of Patents, 1790-1835; Official Gazette, 1836 to present; list of patentees, 1870 to present; English language abstracts of Japanese patents (physical field, 1980 to present; electrical field, 1979 to present); European Patent Bulletin, 1979 to present; PCT Gazette, 1981 to present. **Subscriptions:** 12 journals and other serials. **Services:** Copying; mail service for patent copies; clearinghouse open to the public. **Computerized Information Services:** DIALOG Information Services, U.S. Patent Classification System. Performs searches on fee basis. Contact Person: Mary-Jo Di Muccio, Adm.Libn.. **Networks/Consortia:** Member of South Bay Cooperative Library System (SBCLS). **Publications:** Information brochures; guides for conducting a patent search and trademark search. **Remarks:** Maintained by Sunnyvale Public Library. This clearinghouse is a self-search center which is said to have the only subject-classified patent collection in the United States outside of Arlington, VA.

SUNNYVALE PUBLIC LIBRARY - FRIENDS OF THE WESTERN PHILATELIC LIBRARY
See: Friends of the Western Philatelic Library (5418)

★13756★
SUNRISE MUSEUMS, INC. - LIBRARY (Art, Sci-Engr)
746 Myrtle Rd.
Charleston, WV 25314 Phone: (304)344-8035
Founded: 1961. **Staff:** 1. **Subjects:** Fine arts, natural sciences, anthropology. **Holdings:** 3000 volumes. **Subscriptions:** 40 journals and other serials. **Services:** Library open to the public for reference use only.

★13757★
SUNSET TRADING POST-OLD WEST MUSEUM - LIBRARY (Hist)
Rte. 1 Phone: (817)872-2027
Sunset, TX 76270 Jack Glover, Owner
Subjects: Barbed wire, frontier, American Indian, cowboys and cattlemen, Civil War, Western painting, county history, guns and knives. **Special Collections:** Barbed Wire. **Holdings:** 2500 books; 200 pamphlets; clippings; drawings; Indian artifacts; Bronzes of the West by Jack Glover; unpublished stories; pictures; negatives. **Subscriptions:** 25 journals and other serials. **Services:** Library open to the public with restrictions. **Publications:** Barbed Wire Bible VII - for sale.

SUNY - AGRICULTURAL AND TECHNICAL COLLEGE AT ALFRED
See: SUNY - College of Technology at Alfred (13777)

★13758★
SUNY - AGRICULTURAL AND TECHNICAL COLLEGE AT COBLESKILL - JARED VAN WAGENEN, JR. LEARNING RESOURCE CENTER (Agri)
Cobleskill, NY 12043 Phone: (518)234-5841
Eleanor M. Carter, Dean
Founded: 1920. **Staff:** Prof 5; Other 9. **Subjects:** Agriculture, business, education of young children, food service, applied biology, reference. **Special Collections:** Career and adult basic skills collection (1000 items); Schoharie County history. **Holdings:** 81,139 books; 5511 bound periodical volumes; 5137 juvenile books; 64 VF drawers of pamphlets and documents; 5247 reels of microfilm; 20,192 AV programs. **Subscriptions:** 541 journals and other serials; 19 newspapers. **Services:** Interlibrary loan; copying; media production; instructional design; center open to the public. **Automated Operations:** Computerized cataloging, acquisitions, circulation, and ILL. **Computerized Information Services:** BRS Information Technologies. Performs searches on fee basis. Contact Person: Winifred Nelson, Hd., Access Serv.. **Networks/Consortia:** Member of Capital District Library Council for Reference & Research Resources (CDLC), SUNY/OCLC Library Network. **Special Indexes:** Index to Times Journal (local newspaper; book format); slide-tape programs on library use. **Staff:** Patricia Hults, Ser.Libn.; Loraine Funk, Supv.Ck. Staff; Nancy Galasso, Hd., Tech.Serv.; Nancy Niles, Bibliog.Instr.; Gerald B. Kirsch, ILL Libn..

SUNY - AGRICULTURAL AND TECHNICAL COLLEGE AT DELHI
See: SUNY - College of Technology at Delhi (13778)

★13759★
SUNY - AGRICULTURAL AND TECHNICAL COLLEGE AT FARMINGDALE - THOMAS D. GREENLEY LIBRARY (Agri, Sci-Engr)
Melville Rd. Phone: (516)420-2040
Farmingdale, NY 11735 Michael G. Knauth, Hd.Libn.
Founded: 1912. **Staff:** Prof 14; Other 16. **Subjects:** Technology, engineering, business, horticulture, dental hygiene, nursing, liberal arts. **Holdings:** 125,000 books and bound periodical volumes; 22,000 pamphlets; 100,000 government documents; 11,000 reels of microfilm; 22,500 AV programs; 14,500 microfiche. **Subscriptions:** 1510 journals and other serials. **Services:** Interlibrary loan; copying (limited); library open to the public for reference use only. **Automated Operations:** Computerized cataloging, acquisitions, and serials. **Computerized Information Services:** OCLC, DIALOG Information Services, WILSONLINE, InfoTrac. Performs searches on fee basis. Contact Person: Irene Keogh, Hd., Ref., 420-2184. **Networks/Consortia:** Member of Long Island Library Resources Council, Inc. (LILRC). **Publications:** Newsletter, irregular; bibliographic guides. **Staff:** Judi Bird, Hd., Acq.; Charlotte Schart, Hd., Ser.; Carol Greenholz, Hd., Tech.Serv./Cat.; Sue Schapiro, Govt.Docs.; George LoPresti, Sys.Libn.; Marian Gromet, Cat./Acq.; Helene Cerky, Ref.; Jeri McCarthy, Ser./Ref.; Ann Meronet, Hd., Circ./ILL/AV.

★13760★
SUNY - AGRICULTURAL AND TECHNICAL COLLEGE AT MORRISVILLE - LIBRARY (Agri, Sci-Engr)
Morrisville, NY 13408 Phone: (315)684-6055
Colleen Stella, Dir.
Founded: 1910. **Staff:** Prof 5; Other 5. **Subjects:** Food processing, food service, agriculture, wood and automotive technology, natural resources conservation, nursing, horse husbandry, journalism. **Special Collections:** New York State Historical Collection. **Holdings:** 91,920 books; 5600 bound periodical volumes; 9957 microforms; 403 audio cassettes; 250 video cassettes. **Subscriptions:** 563 journals and other serials; 23 newspapers. **Services:** Interlibrary loan; copying; library open to the public. **Automated Operations:** Computerized cataloging and ILL. **Computerized Information Services:** OCLC. **Networks/Consortia:** Member of Central New York Library Resources Council (CENTRO). **Publications:** Periodicals Received Currently; Library Guide; Basics, Bits and Books (library newsletter). **Staff:** Wilfred E. Drew, Ref./ILL Libn.; Michael Gieryic, Ref./ILL Libn.; Charles Skewis, Acq.Libn.; Phyllis Petersen, Hd. of Tech.Serv..

★13761★
SUNY - CENTRAL ADMINISTRATION RESEARCH LIBRARY (Educ)
State University Plaza, Rm. S540 Phone: (518)443-5635
Albany, NY 12246 M. Joan Tauber, Dir.
Founded: 1967. **Staff:** Prof 1; Other 1. **Subjects:** Education - higher, professional, international; management; finance; statistics. **Special Collections:** SUNY archival collection (300 items). **Holdings:** 25,000 books; 150 bound periodical volumes; 1500 VF items; 2000 government documents; 1000 microforms; 200 dissertations; 3000 ERIC research

reports. **Subscriptions:** 250 journals and other serials. **Services:** Interlibrary loan; copying; SDI; library open to the public with restrictions. **Computerized Information Services:** OCLC. **Publications:** Tables of Contents of Significant Journals; Acquisitions List, both bimonthly; annotated lists of selected books; listing of new microforms, both

★13762★
SUNY - COLLEGE AT BROCKPORT - DRAKE MEMORIAL LIBRARY (Educ)
Brockport, NY 14420 Phone: (716)395-2141
Ms. Raj Madan, Dir. of Lib.Serv.
Founded: 1860. **Staff:** Prof 16; Other 21. **Subjects:** Nursing, physical and general education, U.S. history, criminal justice. **Special Collections:** Early American Imprints, 1639-1800 (Readex); Early English Books, 1475-1700 (Readex). **Holdings:** 373,093 books; 79,188 bound periodical volumes; 20,425 reels of microfilm; 363,672 microfiche; 952,867 micro-opaque cards. **Subscriptions:** 2900 journals and other serials; 50 newspapers. **Services:** Interlibrary loan; copying; library open to the public. **Automated Operations:** Computerized cataloging, acquisitions, and circulation. **Computerized Information Services:** OCLC. **Networks/Consortia:** Member of Rochester Regional Library Council (RRLC). **Publications:** Drake Library Review, quarterly; subject bibliographies. **Special Indexes:** Indexes to New York State Museum Bulletins (numerical, author, subject); Index to U.S. Government Serials, 1953-1970. **Staff:** Steven F. Buckley, Assoc.Dir..

★13763★
SUNY - COLLEGE AT BUFFALO - BURCHFIELD ART CENTER - RESEARCH LIBRARY (Art)
Rockwell Hall
1300 Elmwood Ave. Phone: (716)878-6011
Buffalo, NY 14222 Nancy M. Weekly, Cur./Archv.
Staff: Prof 2; Other 5. **Subjects:** American art, art education. **Special Collections:** Charles E. Burchfield Archive; Rehn Gallery Archive; George William Eggers Archive; Charles Cary Rumsey Archive; Western New York State Artists; Buffalo Society of Artists records; Patteran Society records. **Holdings:** 2500 books; 1 drawer of microfiche; 10,000 exhibition catalogs, slides, photographs, artist files, clippings, letters, manuscripts, original materials, AV programs. **Services:** Copying; library open to the public by appointment. **Automated Operations:** Computerized public access catalog. **Formerly:** Burchfield Center - Western New York Forum for American Art. **Staff:** Michele Ryan, Reg./Asst.Archv..

★13764★
SUNY - COLLEGE AT BUFFALO - EDWARD H. BUTLER LIBRARY (Hum)
1300 Elmwood Ave. Phone: (716)878-6302
Buffalo, NY 14222 Dr. George C. Newman, Dir.
Founded: 1871. **Staff:** Prof 25; Other 29. **Subjects:** Education, sciences and humanities, fine and applied arts. **Special Collections:** Curriculum Laboratory Collection (26,000 volumes); Hertha Ganey Historical Children's Book Collection (310 volumes); Root-Kempke Historical Textbook Collection (676 volumes); Lois Lenski Collection (241 autographed first edition titles; 310 original illustrations, notes, research, and dummies); Creative Studies Library (2750 volumes; 1870 dissertations on microfilm); Independent Learning Center (8500 AV programs, nonprint items, educational games); Francis E. Fronczak Collection (18 linear feet); college archives (1560 linear feet); Paul G. Reilly Seneca Indian Land Claims Collection (27 linear feet). **Holdings:** 428,378 books; 87,344 bound periodical volumes; 5491 reels of microfilm; 565,928 microtexts; 499 maps. **Subscriptions:** 4393 journals and other serials; 42 newspapers. **Services:** Interlibrary loan; copying; library open to the public for reference use only. **Automated Operations:** Computerized cataloging. **Computerized Information Services:** DIALOG Information Services, BRS Information Technologies, WILSONLINE. Contact Person: Susan Stievater, Coord., Search Serv.. **Networks/Consortia:** Member of SUNY/OCLC Library Network, Western New York Library Resources Council (WNYLRC). **Publications:** Lois Lenski Children's Collection (booklet); Frances E. Fronczak Collection Inventory (booklet). **Staff:** Maryruth Glogowski, Assoc.Dir.; Mary Karen Delmont, Asst. to Dir.; Paul Zadner, Hd., Circ./Per.; Carol Richards, Hd., Ref.; Shirley Posner, Hd., Acq.; Sr. Martin Joseph Jones, Hd., Archv./Spec.Coll.; Gail Ellmann, Lrng.Sys.; Mary Lee Xanco, Hd., Coll.Dev.; Marjorie Lord, ILL; Amy DiBartolo, Microforms; Carol Richard, Hd., Info.Serv..

★13765★
SUNY - COLLEGE AT CORTLAND - MEMORIAL LIBRARY (Educ)
Prospect Terrace
Box 2000 Phone: (607)753-2221
Cortland, NY 13045 Selby U. Gration, Dir. of Libs.
Founded: 1869. **Staff:** Prof 14; Other 17. **Subjects:** Education, recreation, physical education, health education. **Special Collections:** Teaching Materials (21,672 books; 20,882 teaching materials); Cortland College Archives (8100 items); Knowlton Collection of Social Studies Textbooks (875 items); rare book collection (800). **Holdings:** 266,924 books; 39,398 bound periodical volumes; 454,420 microforms; 13,412 AV programs; 271 VF drawers; 15,529 pictures; 10 files of pamphlets; 19,848 government documents. **Subscriptions:** 1650 journals and other serials; 8 newspapers. **Services:** Interlibrary loan; copying; SDI; library open to the public with restrictions. **Automated Operations:** Computerized cataloging, serials, and ILL. **Computerized Information Services:** DIALOG Information Services, OCLC, BRS Information Technologies. Performs searches on fee basis. Contact Person: Leonard Cohen, Hd., Rd.Serv., 753-2525. **Networks/Consortia:** Member of SUNY/OCLC Library Network, South Central Research Library Council (SCRLC). **Publications:** Facets; subject bibliographies; Setting the Book Straight on the Library; occasional publications - campus distribution. **Special Indexes:** Serials and periodicals list; lists of abstracts/indexes by subject. **Staff:** Mary Beilby, Coll.Dev.Libn.; James Chapman, Electronic Media Ctr.Supv.; Catherine Hanchett, Hd., Bibliog.Serv.; Gretchen Herrmann, Soc.Sci.Ref.-Bibliog.; Eileen Schroeder, Tchg.Mtls.Ctr.Libn.; Ellen Paterson, Sci.Ref.-Bibliog.; Johanna Bowen, Ser./Per.Libn.; Suzanne Peterson, Pub.Serv.Libn.; David Ritchie, Cat.Libn.; Stephen Hearn, Cat.Libn.; Lauren Stiles, Hum.Ref.-Bibliog.; David Kreh, Educ.Ref.-Bibliog.; Thomas Bonn, Pol.Sci./Phys.Educ.Ref.-Bibliog..

★13766★
SUNY - COLLEGE OF ENVIRONMENTAL SCIENCE & FORESTRY - F. FRANKLIN MOON LIBRARY (Env-Cons, Sci-Engr, Biol Sci)
Syracuse, NY 13210 Phone: (315)470-6716
Donald F. Webster, Libn.
Founded: 1919. **Staff:** Prof 8; Other 6. **Subjects:** Forests and forestry, environment, botany, zoology, polymer and cellulose chemistry, paper science, wildlife management, entomology, wood products engineering, soil science. **Holdings:** 93,507 books; 28,994 bound periodical volumes; 4152 bound theses; 91,929 microforms. **Subscriptions:** 2938 journals and other serials. **Services:** Interlibrary loan; copying; library open to the public for reference use only. **Automated Operations:** Computerized cataloging. **Computerized Information Services:** BRS Information Technologies, OCLC; SULIRS (internal database). **Publications:** New Accessions List; user guides. **Staff:** Elizabeth A. Elkins, Coord., Pub.Serv; Salvacion S. De La Paz, Coord., Bibliog.Oper.; Dianne Juchimek, Coord., Coll.Dev..

★13767★
SUNY - COLLEGE OF ENVIRONMENTAL SCIENCE & FORESTRY - HUNTINGTON WILDLIFE FOREST LIBRARY (Env-Cons)
Newcomb, NY 12852 Phone: (518)582-4551
Donald Webster, Dir. of Libs.
Staff: 1. **Subjects:** Wildlife, wildlife management and research, forestry, ecology. **Special Collections:** Collection of birds, mammals, insects, and plants indigenous to the area; local history (notes; photographs; maps). **Holdings:** 370 books; 290 bound periodical volumes; 200 other cataloged items. **Subscriptions:** 18 journals and other serials. **Services:** Copying; library open to the public with restrictions.

★13768★
SUNY - COLLEGE AT FREDONIA - MUSIC COLLECTION (Mus)
Daniel A. Reed Library Phone: (716)673-3183
Fredonia, NY 14063 Joseph Chouinard, Mus.Libn.
Founded: 1940. **Staff:** Prof 1. **Subjects:** Music - education, performance and study, history, biography, criticism; monumenta. **Holdings:** 29,753 scores; 13,907 music recordings; 2054 music titles in microform; 11,595 music books; 1307 cassettes; 2000 dance band arrangements; 2000 pieces of popular sheet music, 1900-1950. **Subscriptions:** 119 journals and other serials. **Services:** Interlibrary loan; copying; library open to the public. **Automated Operations:** Computerized cataloging. **Computerized Information Services:** OCLC, DIALOG Information Services, BRS Information Technologies. **Networks/Consortia:** Member of SUNY/OCLC Library Network, Western New York Library Resources Council (WNYLRC). **Staff:** Susan P. Besemer, Dir., Lib.Serv..

★13769★
SUNY - COLLEGE AT GENESEO - COLLEGE LIBRARIES (Educ)
Milne Library & Fraser Library Phone: (716)245-5591
Geneseo, NY 14454 Richard C. Quick, Dir. of Libs.
Founded: 1871. **Staff:** Prof 15; Other 16. **Subjects:** English and American literature, natural and physical sciences, music, computer science, education and special education, business management and accounting. **Special Collections:** Aldous Huxley (600 items); Genesee Valley Historical Collection (7500 items); Carl F. Schmidt Collection in American Architecture (5000 items); Wadsworth Family Papers, 1790-1952 (50,000 items); College Archives. **Holdings:** 340,797 books; 50,100 bound periodical volumes; 690,000 microforms, including 282,000 ERIC microfiche; 240,000 U.S. Government documents. **Subscriptions:** 2330 journals and other serials; 19 newspapers. **Services:** Interlibrary loan; copying; library open to the public with restrictions. **Automated Operations:** Computerized cataloging, acquisitions, and serials. **Computerized Information Services:** BRS Information Technologies. **Networks/Consortia:** Member of SUNY/OCLC Library Network, Rochester Regional Library Council (RRLC). **Publications:** Serials Holdings List (computer printout). **Remarks:** Figures reflect the holdings of Milne Library and Fraser Library. **Staff:** Janet A. Neese, Assoc. for Admin.; Paula M. Henry, Acq.Libn.; Adelaide L. LaVerdi, Hd.Cat.; Barbara Clarke, Libn., CRC; David W. Parish, Govt.Docs.Libn.; Diane Johnson, Ser.Libn.; Mary McGrath, Circ.Mgr.; Harriet Sleggs, ILL Libn.; Paul MacLean, Mng.Libn., Fraser Lib..

★13770★
SUNY - COLLEGE AT NEW PALTZ - SOJOURNER TRUTH LIBRARY - SPECIAL COLLECTIONS (Area-Ethnic, Hist)
New Paltz, NY 12561 Phone: (914)257-2204
William E. Connors, Dir.
Founded: 1833. **Holdings:** Africa and Asia collections; New Paltz collection; college archives; U.S. Government documents (selective); Early American Imprints (Readex); Early English Books (Readex microprint). **Services:** Interlibrary loan; copying; collections open to the public. **Automated Operations:** Computerized cataloging and ILL. **Computerized Information Services:** DIALOG Information Services, BRS Information Technologies. Performs searches on fee basis. Contact Person: Gerlinde Barley, 257-2212. **Networks/Consortia:** Member of SUNY/OCLC Library Network, Southeastern New York Library Resources Council (SENYLRC). **Staff:** James R. Goodrich, Coord. of Rd.Serv..

★13771★
SUNY - COLLEGE AT ONEONTA - JAMES M. MILNE LIBRARY - SPECIAL COLLECTIONS (Hist)
Oneonta, NY 13820 Phone: (607)431-3702
Diane A. Clark, Spec.Coll.Libn.
Founded: 1889. **Staff:** Prof 1; Other 1. **Special Collections:** New York State Historical Collection; 19th and Early 20th Century Popular Fiction; New York State Verse Collection; Early Textbooks and Early Educational Theory. **Holdings:** 6635 volumes; 300 masters' theses; 463 linear feet of archival material; 30 tapes. **Services:** Interlibrary loan; collections open to the public with restrictions. **Automated Operations:** Computerized cataloging, serials, and ILL. **Computerized Information Services:** OCLC, DIALOG Information Services, BRS Information Technologies, WILSONLINE. Performs searches on fee basis. Contact Person: Debora Rougeux, 431-3454. **Networks/Consortia:** Member of South Central Research Library Council (SCRLC). **Publications:** Grist.

★13772★
SUNY - COLLEGE OF OPTOMETRY - HAROLD KOHN MEMORIAL VISUAL SCIENCE LIBRARY (Med, Sci-Engr)
100 E. 24th St. Phone: (212)477-7965
New York, NY 10010-3677 Margaret Lewis, Libn.
Founded: 1956. **Staff:** Prof 2; Other 2. **Subjects:** Physiological optics, perception, developmental psychology, theory of optometry, public health, learning disabilities, ocular pathology, orthoptics. **Holdings:** 27,000 books; 7000 bound periodical volumes; 1800 tapes; 90 phonograph records; 25,500 slides; 400 reels of microfilm; 7000 pamphlets; 1200 indexed reprints on optics. **Subscriptions:** 540 journals and other serials. **Services:** Interlibrary loan; copying; library open to the public for reference use only. **Automated Operations:** Computerized cataloging. **Computerized Information Services:** MEDLARS, OCLC, DIALOG Information Services. **Networks/Consortia:** Member of New York Metropolitan Reference and Research Library Agency (METRO). **Special Indexes:** Visual science articles, 1900-1947 (card). **Staff:** Jeffery Garverick, Sr.Asst.Libn..

★13773★
SUNY - COLLEGE AT OSWEGO - PENFIELD LIBRARY - SPECIAL COLLECTIONS (Hist)
Oswego, NY 13126 Phone: (315)341-3110
Founded: 1861. **Special Collections:** College archives; Oswego County history; rare books; President Millard Fillmore papers. **Holdings:** 6398 books; 560 linear feet of other cataloged items; 602 reels of microfilm; 15 microfiche; 511 audio cassettes; 4535 vertical files. **Services:** Interlibrary loan; copying; library open to the public by appointment. **Computerized Information Services:** OCLC. **Networks/Consortia:** Member of North Country Reference and Research Resources Council (NCRRRC). **Staff:** Nancy Osborne, Coord.; Judith Wellman, Coord.; Lois Stolp, Libn./Cat.; Alexander Beattie, Libn..

★13774★
SUNY - COLLEGE AT PLATTSBURGH - BENJAMIN F. FEINBERG LIBRARY - SPECIAL COLLECTIONS (Hist)
Plattsburgh, NY 12901 Phone: (518)564-5206
Joseph G. Swinyer, Spec.Coll.Libn.
Founded: 1961. **Staff:** Prof 1; Other 2. **Subjects:** History of Upstate New York and northwestern Vermont; Canadiana; folklore of Adirondacks and Champlain Valley; recent environmental, industrial, and demographic studies of the region; Rockwell Kent; university archives. **Special Collections:** History of Northern New York (4470 monographs; 15,000 ephemera and manuscripts); Marjorie Lansing Porter Folklore Collection (original discs and tapes); Kent-Delord papers; William Bailey papers; Truesdell Print Collection; Signor/Langlois Collection of architectural drawings and maps; Rockwell Kent Collection (1500 items); Feinberg Collection; 1980 Lake Placid Olympics. **Holdings:** 4700 volumes; 65,000 manuscripts; 4000 maps and atlases; 3500 photographs; 1900 reels of microfilm; 400 recordings; 3500 pamphlets; 7200 clippings. **Subscriptions:** 36 journals and other serials. **Services:** Interlibrary loan; copying; collections open to the public. **Special Catalogs:** Manuscripts for Research: Report of the Director, 1961-1974.

★13775★
SUNY - COLLEGE AT POTSDAM - CRANE MUSIC LIBRARY (Mus)
Potsdam, NY 13676 Sally Skyrm, Mus.Libn.
Staff: Prof 1; Other 2. **Subjects:** Music - education, performance, study, history, biography, criticism, monuments. **Special Collections:** Julia E. Crane School of Music Archives; Helen M. Hosmer Papers. **Holdings:** 12,000 books; 2100 bound periodical volumes; 22,500 scores; 14,575 phonograph records. **Subscriptions:** 140 journals and other serials. **Services:** Interlibrary loan; library open to the public. **Networks/Consortia:** Member of Associated Colleges of the St. Lawrence Valley, Inc. (ACSLV), North Country Reference and Research Resources Council (NCRRRC). **Staff:** David Ossenkop, Assoc.Libn..

★13776★
SUNY - COLLEGE AT POTSDAM - FREDERICK W. CRUMB MEMORIAL LIBRARY (Hum)
Pierrepont Ave. Phone: (315)267-2481
Potsdam, NY 13676 Germaine C. Linkins, Dir. of Libs.
Founded: 1880. **Staff:** Prof 13; Other 10. **Subjects:** Education and curriculum materials, art, 19th and 20th century German history, urban sociology, northern New York State history, Anglo-Irish literature. **Special Collections:** Bertrand A. Snell Collection (public and private papers); college archives. **Holdings:** 243,578 books; 54,218 bound periodical volumes; 7903 public school textbooks; 1041 phonograph records; 465,738 microforms; 5672 government documents; 243 linear feet of archives; 4667 maps and charts. **Subscriptions:** 1736 journals and other serials; 27 newspapers. **Services:** Interlibrary loan; copying; library open to the public. **Automated Operations:** Computerized cataloging, acquisitions, and serials. **Computerized Information Services:** BRS Information Technologies, DIALOG Information Services, OCLC. Performs searches on fee basis. Contact Person: David Trithart, Ref., 267-2486. **Networks/Consortia:** Member of Associated Colleges of the St. Lawrence Valley, Inc. (ACSLV), North Country Reference and Research Resources Council (NCRRRC). **Publications:** Subject bibliographies and library guides, irregular. **Staff:** Keith Compeau, Asst. to Dir./Circ.; Selma V. Foster, OCLC Coord.; Holly Chambers, Ref.; Nancy Edblom, Doc./ILL; Kay Brown, Cat.Libn.; Frances Finch, Ref.; Jane Subramanian, Ser.; Mary P. Kaduck, Acq.Libn.; Nancy Alzo, Cat.Libn.; Margaret Weitzmann, Arch./Ref.Libn.; Susan Omohundro, Cat..

★13777★
SUNY - COLLEGE OF TECHNOLOGY AT ALFRED - WALTER C. HINKLE MEMORIAL LIBRARY (Agri, Sci-Engr)
Alfred, NY 14802 Phone: (607)587-4313
Barry Lash, Dir.
Founded: 1911. **Staff:** Prof 6; Other 6. **Subjects:** Agriculture, business, health and engineering technologies. **Special Collections:** Western New York History. **Holdings:** 55,000 books; 7300 bound periodical volumes; 77,000 pamphlets; 4800 reels of microfilm; 12,000 microfiche; 1100 AV programs; 2800 corporation reports. **Subscriptions:** 1400 journals and other serials; 12 newspapers. **Services:** Interlibrary loan; copying; library open to the public. **Automated Operations:** Computerized cataloging and serials. **Computerized Information Services:** BRS Information Technologies, WILSONLINE, OCLC. Performs searches free of charge. Contact Person: Ellen H. Ehrig, Assoc.Libn.. **Networks/Consortia:** Member of South Central Research Library Council (SCRLC). **Publications:** Salmagundi (newsletter), 1/semester; Alfred Tech Periodicals - both for local distribution only. **Special Indexes:** Index to Alfred Sun newspaper, 1883 to present. **Formerly:** Agricultural and Technical College at Alfred. **Staff:** Diana Hovorka, Asst.Ref.Libn.; Suzanne Wood, Tech.Serv.Libn.; Barbara Greil, Ser./Ref.Libn.; Kenneth Maracek, Asst.Ref.Libn.; David Haggstrom, AV Libn..

★13778★
SUNY - COLLEGE OF TECHNOLOGY AT DELHI - LIBRARY (Agri, Sci-Engr)
Delhi, NY 13753 Phone: (607)746-4107
Herbert J. Sorgen, Libn.
Founded: 1913. **Staff:** Prof 4; Other 4. **Subjects:** Agriculture and life sciences, engineering technologies, management, vocational education, nontraditional studies, liberal arts. **Holdings:** 49,196 books; 700 bound periodical volumes. **Subscriptions:** 867 journals and other serials. **Services:** Interlibrary loan; library open to the public. **Automated Operations:** Computerized cataloging. **Computerized Information Services:** BRS Information Technologies. Performs searches on fee basis. **Networks/Consortia:** Member of SUNY/OCLC Library Network, South Central Research Library Council (SCRLC). **Publications:** Booklist, bimonthly; Pathfinders. **Formerly:** Agricultural and Technical College at Delhi. **Staff:** Donald Young, Assoc.Libn.; Anna Zilles, Asst.Libn.; Ronald Rosenblum, Asst.Libn..

★13779★
SUNY - DOWNSTATE MEDICAL CENTER - DEPARTMENT OF PSYCHIATRY LIBRARY (Med)
451 Clarkson Ave.
Brooklyn, NY 11203 Phone: (718)735-3131
Founded: 1947. **Staff:** Prof 1. **Subjects:** Psychiatry, psychoanalysis, child psychiatry, psychology. **Holdings:** 2038 books; 1150 bound periodical volumes; 5 VF drawers of pamphlets and reprints. **Subscriptions:** 50 journals and other serials. **Services:** Interlibrary loan; library not open to the public. **Also Known As:** Kings County Hospital - Psychiatry Library.

★13780★
SUNY - HEALTH SCIENCE CENTER AT BROOKLYN - LIBRARY (Med)
450 Clarkson Ave.
Box 14 Phone: (718)270-1041
Brooklyn, NY 11203 Kenneth E. Moody, Dir.
Staff: Prof 14; Other 22. **Subjects:** Medicine, nursing, and allied health sciences. **Holdings:** 64,700 books; 175,300 bound periodical volumes; archives and memorabilia of various Brooklyn hospitals and medical societies. **Subscriptions:** 1600 journals and other serials. **Services:** Interlibrary loan; copying; SDI; library open to qualified scientists who need access to the collection. **Automated Operations:** Computerized cataloging, acquisitions, and serials. **Computerized Information Services:** BRS Information Technologies, MEDLINE. **Networks/Consortia:** Member of Greater Northeastern Regional Medical Library Program, SUNY/OCLC Library Network, Medical Library Center of New York (MLCNY). **Staff:** Julie Semkow, Hd., AV; Sonia Sields-Obalanlege, Hd., Circ.; Rolfe DePuy, Hd., Tech.Serv..

★13781★
SUNY - HEALTH SCIENCE CENTER AT SYRACUSE - LIBRARY (Med)
766 Irving Ave. Phone: (315)473-4582
Syracuse, NY 13210 Suzanne H. Murray, Dir.
Founded: 1834. **Staff:** Prof 7; Other 12. **Subjects:** Medicine, nursing, and allied health sciences. **Special Collections:** Medical Americana (350 volumes); Geneva Medical College Library (300 volumes); Rare Books (1500 volumes); Medical School Archives and History of Medicine in Syracuse (3 VF cabinets). **Holdings:** 49,000 books; 101,000 bound periodical volumes; 1444 AV program titles. **Subscriptions:** 1541 journals and other serials. **Services:** Interlibrary loan; copying; SDI; library open to the public. **Automated Operations:** Computerized cataloging and serials. **Computerized Information Services:** DIALOG Information Services, MEDLARS, OCLC, MEDLINE, BRS Information Technologies; EasyLink (electronic mail service). Performs searches on fee basis. Contact Person: Peter Uva, Assoc.Libn./Hd., Pub.Serv., 473-4580. **Networks/Consortia:** Member of SUNY/OCLC Library Network, Central New York Library Resources Council (CENTRO), Health Resources Council of Central New York (HRCCNY). **Publications:** Library Bulletin, quarterly; Library Guide, biennial; Annual Report; Subject List of AV Titles, semiannual; Alphabetical and Subject List of Currently Received Serials, annual - all available on request. **Staff:** James Capodagli, Sr.Asst.Ref.Libn.; Shakeh Mardikian, Sr.Asst.Ref.Libn.; Patricia Onsi, Assoc.Dir./Hd., Tech.Serv.; Christine Kucharski, Asst.Libn., Media.

★13782★
SUNY - MARITIME COLLEGE - STEPHEN B. LUCE LIBRARY (Sci-Engr, Trans)
Fort Schuyler Phone: (212)409-7231
Bronx, NY 10465 Richard H. Corson, Libn.
Founded: 1946. **Staff:** Prof 6; Other 6. **Subjects:** Marine transportation, maritime history, marine engineering, naval architecture, merchant marine. **Holdings:** 87,500 books, bound periodical volumes, and government documents; 13,000 microfiche; 6143 reels of microfilm; 236 motion picture titles. **Subscriptions:** 540 journals; 305 serials; 8 newspapers. **Services:** Interlibrary loan; copying; library open to the public with identification. **Automated Operations:** Computerized cataloging, acquisitions, and ILL. **Computerized Information Services:** OCLC, DIALOG Information Services, WILSONLINE. **Networks/Consortia:** Member of SUNY/OCLC Library Network. **Publications:** Maritima, 2/year - to faculty and students; Stephen B. Luce Library Accessions, quarterly; bibliographic series, irregular. **Staff:** Filomena Magavero, Libn., Rd.Serv.; Alvina Kalsch, Assoc.Libn., Tech.Serv.; John Lee, Assoc.Libn., Ref.; Tereze Rancans, Sr.Asst.Libn., Cat.; Anita Zutis, Asst.Libn., Docs..

★13783★
SUNY - SCHOOL OF PHARMACY - DRUG INFORMATION SERVICE - LIBRARY (Med)
Erie County Medical Center
462 Grider St. Phone: (716)898-3927
Buffalo, NY 14215 Dr. Susan L. Rozek, Dir.
Founded: 1966. **Staff:** Prof 1. **Subjects:** Medicinals, pharmacology, therapeutics. **Holdings:** 70 books; 5 bound periodical volumes; microfilm. **Subscriptions:** 25 journals and other serials. **Services:** Library not open to the public. **Publications:** Therapeutic Perspectives, bimonthly - to medical staff and other drug information centers.

★13784★
SUNY - SYRACUSE EDUCATIONAL OPPORTUNITY CENTER - PAUL ROBESON LIBRARY (Area-Ethnic)
100 New St. Phone: (315)472-0130
Syracuse, NY 13202 Florence Beer, Libn.
Staff: Prof 1; Other 1. **Subjects:** Afro-Americans, job preparation, women, African fiction, business skills, minorities. **Special Collections:** Frazier Library of Afro-American Books (500 volumes); National Archives Collection of Afro-American Artists (23 trays of slides). **Holdings:** 11,000 books and bound periodical volumes; 40 VF drawers. **Subscriptions:** 139 journals and other serials; 20 newspapers. **Services:** Interlibrary loan; copying; library open to the public. **Networks/Consortia:** Member of Central New York Library Resources Council (CENTRO). **Publications:** Periodical Holdings, annual - for internal distribution only; New Acquisitions Listings, semiannual. **Special Catalogs:** Catalog to audiovisual collection.

★13785★
SUNY AT ALBANY - FILM & TELEVISION DOCUMENTATION CENTER (Aud-Vis)
Richardson 390
1400 Washington Ave.
Albany, NY 12222 Phone: (518)442-5745
Founded: 1981. **Staff:** Prof 3. **Subjects:** Film and television. **Special Collections:** Film and television journals from 28 countries, 1973 to present (160 items). **Holdings:** 2000 unbound periodical volumes. **Subscriptions:** 201 journals and other serials. **Services:** Interlibrary loan; copying; center open to the public. **Computerized Information Services:** Film literature index, 1976 to present (internal database). Performs searches on fee basis. **Staff:** Vincent J. Aceto, Co-Dir.; Fred Silva, Co-Dir.; Kevin Hagopian, Ed..

★13786★
SUNY AT ALBANY - GRADUATE LIBRARY FOR PUBLIC AFFAIRS AND POLICY (Soc Sci, Law)
Hawley Library
1400 Washington Ave. Phone: (518)442-3690
Albany, NY 12222 Jacquelyn A. Gavryck, Act.Hd.
Founded: 1981. **Staff:** Prof 5; Other 6. **Subjects:** Public policy, criminal justice, social welfare, library and information science, law. **Special Collections:** Children's historical collection (9000 volumes); public policy archives. **Holdings:** 100,000 books; microfiche; periodicals. **Services:** Interlibrary loan; library open to the public. **Automated Operations:** Computerized cataloging and circulation. **Computerized Information Services:** BRS Information Technologies, DIALOG Information Services, VU/TEXT Information Services, WILSONLINE, WESTLAW, RLIN, OCLC. **Networks/Consortia:** Member of Capital District Library Council for Reference & Research Resources (CDLC), Criminal Justice Information Exchange Group. **Staff:** Barbara Via, Ref./Bibliog.; Richard Irving, Bibliog.; H. Mendelsohn, Bibliog.; Mary Jane Brustman, Ref./Bibliog..

★13787★
SUNY AT BINGHAMTON - CENTER FOR MEDIEVAL AND EARLY RENAISSANCE STUDIES (Hum)
Binghamton, NY 13901 Phone: (607)777-2730
Robin S. Oggins, Dir.
Founded: 1966. **Subjects:** Latin and Arabic paleography and codicology, Medieval England. **Remarks:** Supporting materials housed in Main Library include Vaticana Arabic manuscripts (1678 manuscripts on 425 reels of microfilm); Rare Books Collection; Manuscripta series (microfilm); Italian Archives, 13th-19th century (1000 pieces in Latin and Italian); English Public Records (microfilm; includes Household and Wardrobe records to 1307); Slide Archive (20,000 slides including Bodleian and Morgan Library slides and slides of selected British library manuscripts).

★13788★
SUNY AT BINGHAMTON - SCIENCE LIBRARY (Biol Sci, Sci-Engr)
Binghamton, NY 13901 Phone: (607)777-2166
Ina C. Brownridge, Hd., Sci.Lib.
Staff: Prof 6; Other 9. **Subjects:** Biological sciences, chemistry, geological sciences, health sciences, engineering, physics, psychology, nursing, general science, technology. **Holdings:** 110,000 books; 101,443 maps; microforms. **Subscriptions:** 2050 journals. **Services:** Interlibrary loan; copying; library open to the public with courtesy card. **Computerized Information Services:** BRS Information Technologies, DIALOG Information Services, STN International. **Networks/Consortia:** Member of South Central Research Library Council (SCRLC), RLG.

★13789★
SUNY AT BINGHAMTON - SPECIAL COLLECTIONS (Rare Book, Hist)
Glenn G. Bartle Library
Vestal Pkwy., E. Phone: (607)777-4844
Binghamton, NY 13901
Marion Hanscom, Asst.Dir. for Fine Arts & Spec
Staff: Prof 3. **Subjects:** History of books and printing; literary and historical collections. **Special Collections:** Padraic and Mary Colum papers (750 items); Max Reinhardt Library (theater); Max Reinhardt Archive (250,000 papers, letters, documents, and original prompt books); photograph and negative collection (14,000 items); scene design materials; Loften Mitchell Papers; Tillie Losch Papers; Charles Monroe Dickinson Family Papers (2000 items relating to journalist and diplomat C.M. Dickinson, 1842-1924); Edwin Link (1904-1981) papers; Broome County Medical Society Collection; Arthur Schnitzler Archives (microfilm); Frances R. Conole Archive of Sound Recordings (54,320 phonograph records with a concentration of vocal/operatic recordings); Mary Lavin papers (250 items); Associated Colleges of Upper New York Archives (5000 items). **Holdings:** 20,500 volumes; 11,000 local and regional archives; 6000 publications, photographs, and reports in university archives; 385 linear feet of archives and manuscripts; 124 films. **Services:** Interlibrary loan; copying; collections open to the public during limited hours by appointment. **Publications:** Lamont Montgomery Bowers Papers (pamphlet). **Special Catalogs:** Edwin Link Papers (pamphlet); Catalogue of the Colum Collection (pamphlet); Catalogue of the Lavin Collection (pamphlet); Catalog of Reinhardt Library (card); manuscript catalog (card); supplementary rare book catalogs (card).

★13790★
SUNY AT BUFFALO - ARCHITECTURE & ENVIRONMENTAL DESIGN LIBRARY (Plan)
Hayes Hall
Main Street Campus
Buffalo, NY 14214 Phone: (716)831-3505
Staff: Prof 2; Other 1. **Subjects:** Architecture, environmental design. **Special Collections:** Slide collection (20,000). **Holdings:** 13,000 volumes; product catalogs; VF drawers of pamphlets. **Subscriptions:** 160 journals and other serials. **Services:** Interlibrary loan; copying; library open to the public with restrictions. **Automated Operations:** Computerized cataloging and circulation. **Networks/Consortia:** Member of RLG. **Publications:** AED Library Acquisitions List, quarterly - to faculty and upon request.

★13791★
SUNY AT BUFFALO - CHARLES B. SEARS LAW LIBRARY (Law)
O'Brian Hall, Amherst Campus Phone: (716)636-2048
Buffalo, NY 14260 Ellen M. Gibson, Dir.
Founded: 1887. **Staff:** Prof 9; Other 11. **Subjects:** Law. **Special Collections:** John Lord O'Brian Papers; Morris L. Cohen Rare Book Collection. **Holdings:** 304,697 volumes. **Subscriptions:** 2516 journals and other serials. **Services:** Interlibrary loan; library open to the public for reference use only. **Automated Operations:** Computerized cataloging and circulation. **Computerized Information Services:** LEXIS, NEXIS, WESTLAW. **Networks/Consortia:** Member of RLG. **Staff:** Marcia Zubrow, Hd.Ref.Libn.; Susan Dow, Docs.Libn.; Mary Miller, Ser./Acq.Libn.; Terry McCormack, AV Libn.; Karen Spencer, Ref.Libn.; Nina Cascio, Intl. Law Libn.; Renee Chapman, Hd., Tech.Serv.Libn..

★13792★
SUNY AT BUFFALO - CURRICULUM CENTER (Educ)
Faculty of Educational Studies
17 Baldy Hall Phone: (716)636-2488
Amherst, NY 14260 Dr. William Eller, Dir.
Founded: 1954. **Staff:** Prof 1; Other 3. **Subjects:** Education, textbooks and teacher guides (K-12), courses of study, curriculum guides. **Special Collections:** Gray Collection of Research in Reading. **Holdings:** 10,000 volumes; 5 VF drawers of publishers' catalogs; 5 VF drawers of Teaching Ideas; 15 VF drawers of resource files; 5000 retrospective and historical textbooks; 350 tests; 200 supplementary instructional materials. **Subscriptions:** 60 newsletters. **Services:** Copying; center open to the public. **Publications:** In the Center, 3/year - free upon request. **Staff:** Norma Shatz, Lib.Coord..

★13793★
SUNY AT BUFFALO - DEPARTMENT OF GEOLOGICAL SCIENCES - ICE CORE LABORATORY - LIBRARY (Sci-Engr)
4240 Ridge Lea Rd. Phone: (716)831-3054
Amherst, NY 14226 Chester C. Langway, Jr., Proj.Dir.
Subjects: Glaciology, ice research. **Holdings:** 1000 volumes. **Remarks:** Laboratory is active in ice core studies and interacts on a national basis as well as with universities in Japan, Switzerland, Denmark, the USSR, France, West Germany, and Austria.

★13794★
SUNY AT BUFFALO - HEALTH-CARE INSTRUMENTS AND DEVICES INSTITUTE (HIDI) - LIBRARY (Med)
105 Parker Hall Phone: (716)831-2446
Buffalo, NY 14214 Eileen L. Hassett, Res.Adm.
Founded: 1984. **Subjects:** Medical technology. **Holdings:** 500 volumes. **Services:** Library not open to the public.

★13795★
SUNY AT BUFFALO - HEALTH SCIENCES LIBRARY (Med)
Main St. Campus Phone: (716)831-3337
Buffalo, NY 14214 Mr. C.K. Huang, Dir.
Founded: 1846. **Staff:** Prof 18; Other 28. **Subjects:** Medicine, nursing, dentistry, pharmacy, allied health sciences, basic sciences. **Special Collections:** History of Medicine Collection (12,000 volumes). **Holdings:** 118,084 books; 143,552 bound periodical volumes; 1857 AV programs; 3000 pamphlets. **Subscriptions:** 2594 journals and other serials. **Services:** Interlibrary loan; copying; SDI; library open to the public. **Automated Operations:** Computerized cataloging, acquisitions, serials, and circulation. **Computerized Information Services:** MEDLINE, BRS Information Technologies. Performs searches on fee basis. **Networks/Consortia:** Member of Library Consortium of Health Institutions in Buffalo (LCHIB), Greater Northeastern Regional Medical Library Program, Western New York Library Resources Council (WNYLRC). **Publications:** Progress Report, annual - for exchange. **Special Catalogs:** Pre-Nineteenth Century

Catalog of the Robert L. Brown History of Medicine Collection. **Staff:** Nancy Fabrizio, Assoc.Dir.; Remedios Silva, Hd.Cat.; Sharon Keller, Hd., Info.Serv.; Amy Lyons, Asst.Dir. for Circ.; Luella Allen, Hd., Media Rsrc.Ctr.; Cindy Bertuca, Hd., Info. Dissemination Serv.; Linda Lohr, Asst. to Dir.; Wilson Prout, Asst. to Dir.; Cythia Hepfer, Hd., Ser.; Bradley Chase, Tech.Asst.; Lilli Sentz, Hist. of Med.Libn.; Karen Miller Allen, Info.Serv./Libn.; Martha Manning, Info.Serv./Libn.; Theresa Dombrowski, Asst.Libn., Cat.; Pam Rose, Acq.; Carol Lelonek, Comp.Prog..

★13796★
SUNY AT BUFFALO - MUSIC LIBRARY (Mus)
Baird Hall Phone: (716)636-2923
Buffalo, NY 14260 James Coover, Dir.
Staff: Prof 5; Other 2. **Subjects:** Music - history, theory, performance; jazz history; music education. **Special Collections:** Archives of the Center of the Creative and Performing Arts (10 linear meters); History of Music Librarianship in the U.S. (9 linear meters); Arnold Cornelissen and Ferdinand Praeger Manuscript Collections (6 linear meters); Buffalo Musicians Collection (8 linear meters). **Holdings:** 23,000 books; 11,800 bound periodical volumes; 52,000 scores and parts; 24,000 sound recordings; 5500 microforms; 2100 slides and photographs. **Subscriptions:** 1370 journals and other serials. **Services:** Interlibrary loan; copying; library open to the public. **Automated Operations:** Computerized cataloging and acquisitions. **Computerized Information Services:** RLIN. **Publications:** Current Acquisitions List, irregular; Newsletter, irregular. **Special Catalogs:** Evenings for New Music: A Catalogue, 1964-1977; Supplement, 1977-1980. **Staff:** Dr. Carol June Bradley, Assoc.Dir.; Nancy Nuzzo, Record Cat.; Gudrun Kilburn, Lit.Cat./Ref.Libn.; Andrea Adema, Score Cat./Ref.Libn..

★13797★
SUNY AT BUFFALO - POETRY/RARE BOOKS COLLECTION (Hum, Rare Book)
University Libraries
420 Capen Hall Phone: (716)636-2918
Buffalo, NY 14260 Robert J. Bertholf, Cur.
Founded: 1935. **Staff:** Prof 1; Other 2. **Subjects:** Twentieth-century poetry in English and in translation; rare books. **Special Collections:** Robert Graves; James Joyce; Wyndham Lewis; Dylan Thomas; William Carlos Williams. **Holdings:** 86,000 books and ephemera; 3600 periodical titles; 911 phonograph records; 1200 tapes; photographs; paintings; sculpture; 105,000 manuscripts; 95,000 letters; microfilm. **Services:** Interlibrary loan; copying; collection open to the public. **Automated Operations:** Computerized serials. **Computerized Information Services:** RLIN. **Publications:** Lockwood Memorial Library Christmas Broadsides, annual. **Special Catalogs:** James Joyce's Manuscripts and Letters at the University of Buffalo, 1962; The Personal Library of James Joyce; The Manuscripts and Letters of William Carlos Williams in the Poetry Collection, SUNYAB; A Descriptive Catalog of the Private Library of Thomas B. Lockwood.

★13798★
SUNY AT BUFFALO - SCIENCE AND ENGINEERING LIBRARY (Sci-Engr, Biol Sci, Comp Sci)
Capen Hall Phone: (716)636-2946
Buffalo, NY 14260 Ken Hood, Act.Dir.
Founded: 1949. **Staff:** Prof 7; Other 4. **Subjects:** Engineering, chemistry, physics, mathematics, geology, statistics, computer science, biology. **Special Collections:** Rare books in chemistry and metallurgy. **Holdings:** 375,000 books; 125,000 bound periodical volumes; 130,000 technical reports; 160,000 maps; 1.4 million microforms; 34 video cassettes; 1100 audio cassettes. **Subscriptions:** 2500 journals and other serials. **Services:** Interlibrary loan; copying; library open to the public. **Automated Operations:** Computerized cataloging and circulation. **Computerized Information Services:** DIALOG Information Services, BRS Information Technologies, RLIN. Performs searches on fee basis. Contact Person: Carol A. Kizis, ILL. **Networks/Consortia:** Member of RLG, Western New York Library Resources Council (WNYLRC). **Publications:** SEL NEWS, monthly; subject bibliographies, occasional; New Books, monthly; Current Awareness Lists, occasional; audiovisual material list, occasional. **Remarks:** Includes the holdings of the Chemistry, Mathematics, and Geology Libraries and the Earthquake Engineering Information Center. **Staff:** P.J. Koshy, Hd., AV Ctr./Microcomp.Libn.; E.L. Woodson, Map Libn.; J.K. Webster, Engr.Libn..

★13799★
SUNY AT BUFFALO - UNIVERSITY ARCHIVES (Hist)
420 Capen Hall Phone: (716)636-2916
Buffalo, NY 14260 Shonnie Finnegan, Univ.Archv.
Subjects: Archives of the State University of New York at Buffalo and its predecessor, University of Buffalo, 1846 to present. **Special Collections:** Documents pertaining to the Darwin D. Martin House and other Buffalo buildings designed by Frank Lloyd Wright; records of social action and women's organizations; history of Buffalo area in the 20th century; Fran Striker Collection (early radio scripts, including The Lone Ranger, 1932-1937). **Holdings:** 7000 linear feet of manuscripts, papers, and other archival materials. **Services:** Copying; archives open to the public.

★13800★
SUNY AT STONY BROOK - BIOLOGICAL SCIENCES LIBRARY (Biol Sci)
Stony Brook, NY 11794-5260 Phone: (516)632-7152
Doris Williams, Libn.
Founded: 1975. **Staff:** Prof 1; Other 3. **Subjects:** Zoology, botany, general biology, biochemistry, microbiology, physiology, agriculture. **Special Collections:** Raymond Pearle Reprint Collection (625 volumes). **Holdings:** 35,514 books; 35,099 bound periodical volumes. **Subscriptions:** 785 journals. **Services:** Interlibrary loan; copying; library open to the public for reference use only. **Computerized Information Services:** Online systems.

★13801★
SUNY AT STONY BROOK - CHEMISTRY LIBRARY (Sci-Engr)
Stony Brook, NY 11794-3425 Phone: (516)632-7150
Janet Steins, Libn.
Founded: 1965. **Staff:** Prof 1; Other 2. **Subjects:** Chemistry, biochemistry. **Holdings:** 21,565 books; 23,269 bound periodical volumes. **Subscriptions:** 350 journals and other serials. **Services:** Interlibrary loan; copying; library open to the public for reference use only.

★13802★
SUNY AT STONY BROOK - COMPUTER SCIENCE LIBRARY (Comp Sci)
Lab Office Building Phone: (516)632-7628
Stony Brook, NY 11794-4400 Donna M. Albertus, Hd.
Founded: 1987. **Staff:** Prof 1; Other 3. **Subjects:** Computer science, logic programming, artificial intelligence. **Holdings:** 1400 books; 1520 bound periodical volumes; 2170 reports. **Subscriptions:** 114 journals and other serials. **Services:** Interlibrary loan; copying; SDI; library open to the public. **Computerized Information Services:** DIALOG Information Services, BRS Information Technologies; electronic mail systems. **Publications:** Computer Science Library Acquisitions Update, monthly - distributed via electronic mail.

★13803★
SUNY AT STONY BROOK - DEPARTMENT OF SPECIAL COLLECTIONS AND UNIVERSITY ARCHIVES (Hist, Hum)
Stony Brook, NY 11794-3323 Phone: (516)632-7119
Evert Volkersz, Hd.
Founded: 1969. **Staff:** Prof 2; Other 3. **Subjects:** Contemporary letters and literature, children's literature, Ibero-Americana, Long Island, 20th century political and social movements, printing and publishing, SUNY at Stony Brook. **Special Collections:** Conrad Potter Aiken (102 volumes; 44 periodicals); Jorge Carrera Andrade (85 volumes; manuscripts); children's literature, 1820 to present (2500 volumes); Chilean Theater Pamphlets (57 bound volumes; 570 pamphlets); Robert Creeley (130 volumes, manuscripts); Fortune Press, London (110 volumes); Oakley Calvin Johnson Papers (10 volumes; 31 linear feet of manuscripts); Latin American Pamphlets (1215 items); Pablo Neruda (175 volumes and manuscripts); Robert Payne (200 volumes and manuscripts); Perishable Press, Ltd. (100 volumes; 20 linear feet of manuscripts); Juan and Eva Peron Pamphlets (380 items); Printing and Publishing Collection (750 volumes); Spanish-American Colonial Trade (103 16th century unbound pamphlets); The Typophiles, New York (120 volumes); early 19th century Chilean newspapers and journals (41 titles); Irish political pamphlets, 1789-1829 (503 pamphlets bound in 78 volumes); Environmental Defense Fund, 1967-1975 (600 linear feet); Performing Arts Foundation Collection (80 linear feet); Jacob K. Javits Collection (1200 linear feet); Fielding Dawson (45 volumes and manuscripts); Robert E. Duncan (75 volumes and manuscripts); Emery Long Island Railroad Collection (40 volumes; 5000 photographs; 262 timetables); William Everson (45 volumes and manuscripts); Allen Ginsburg (60 volumes and manuscripts); League for Industrial Democracy (150 pamphlets); Denise Levertov (35 volumes and manuscripts); Long Island manuscript collections; Long Island fiction (250 volumes); Michael McClure (45 volumes and manuscripts); Charles Olson (65 volumes and manuscripts); Ezra Pound (125 volumes); William Butler

Yeats Microfilm Manuscripts Collection (80,000 frames). **Holdings:** 25,000 volumes; 4000 linear feet of manuscripts; 10,000 pieces of ephemera and clippings; 48 linear feet of pamphlets. **Services:** Copying (limited); department open to the public for reference use only. **Publications:** Information leaflets. **Special Catalogs:** Chronological imprints catalog (card).

★13804★
SUNY AT STONY BROOK - EARTH AND SPACE SCIENCES LIBRARY (Sci-Engr)
Stony Brook, NY 11794-2199 Phone: (516)632-7146
Rosalind Walcott, ESS Libn.
Founded: 1968. **Staff:** Prof 1; Other 2. **Subjects:** Geology, astronomy, oceanography, paleontology, meteorology, geomorphology. **Holdings:** 35,600 books; 14,650 bound periodical volumes; 7000 sheets of geological maps; 2500 Palomar Sky Survey and Southern Sky Survey photographic prints; film copies of seismograms from 20 stations of the National Geophysical Data Center, 1964 to present. **Subscriptions:** 735 journals and other serials. **Services:** Interlibrary loan; copying; library open to the public for reference use only. **Computerized Information Services:** Online systems.

★13805★
SUNY AT STONY BROOK - ENGINEERING LIBRARY (Sci-Engr)
Stony Brook, NY 11794-2225 Phone: (516)632-7148
Founded: 1964. **Staff:** Prof 1; Other 2. **Subjects:** Engineering, electrical sciences, mechanics and mechanical engineering, materials sciences, technology, medical technology, mathematics and applied mathematics, chemical technology, applied physics, aerospace sciences. **Holdings:** 27,000 books; 24,000 bound periodical volumes. **Subscriptions:** 685 journals and other serials. **Services:** Interlibrary loan; copying; library open to the public for reference use only.

★13806★
SUNY AT STONY BROOK - ENVIRONMENTAL INFORMATION SERVICE (Env-Cons)
Stony Brook, NY 11794-3331 Phone: (516)632-7161
Sandra Neal, Sr.Asst.Libn.
Founded: 1970. **Staff:** Prof 1; Other 1. **Subjects:** Environment of Long Island; general environmental problems and energy issues. **Holdings:** 6350 books and pamphlets; 1500 research and technical report titles; 1655 federal, state, and local document titles; 25 drawers of newspaper clippings. **Services:** Interlibrary loan; copying; service open to the public for reference use only. **Computerized Information Services:** Online systems.

★13807★
SUNY AT STONY BROOK - HEALTH SCIENCES LIBRARY (Med)
Box 66 Phone: (516)444-2512
East Setauket, NY 11733-0066 Ruth Marcolina, Dir.
Founded: 1969. **Staff:** Prof 10; Other 18. **Subjects:** Medicine, dentistry, nursing, health and basic medical sciences, pharmacology, social welfare. **Special Collections:** History of medicine and dentistry. **Holdings:** 230,387 books and bound periodical volumes; microfilm. **Subscriptions:** 4424 journals and other serials; 7 newspapers. **Services:** Interlibrary loan; copying; SDI; library open to those involved in Nassau and Suffolk County health care. **Automated Operations:** Computerized cataloging and serials. **Computerized Information Services:** NLM, DIALOG Information Services, BRS Information Technologies. **Networks/Consortia:** Member of SUNY/OCLC Library Network, Long Island Library Resources Council, Inc. (LILRC), Greater Northeastern Regional Medical Library Program. **Publications:** Guide to Health Sciences Library, annual - to patrons. **Staff:** Antonija Prelec, Assoc. Dir./Coll.Dev.; Arlee May, Asst.Dir./Pub.Serv.; Laura Blohm, Cat.Libn.; Esther Wei, Hd., Ref.; Julitta Jo, Ser.Libn.; Robert Williams, Circ.Libn.; Betty Emilio, Sr.Asst.Libn.; Colleen Kenefick, Ref.Libn.; Godfrey Belleh, Ref.Libn..

★13808★
SUNY AT STONY BROOK - MAP LIBRARY (Geog-Map)
Stony Brook, NY 11794-3331 Phone: (516)632-7110
David Y. Allen, Libn.
Founded: 1974. **Staff:** Prof 1. **Subjects:** U.S. topography, nautical information, Long Island, U.S. soil maps. **Holdings:** 1300 volumes; 54,000 U.S. Geological Survey topographic maps; 2000 Defense Mapping Agency depository items, 1975 to present; 3000 National Ocean Survey depository items; 9000 U.S. sheet maps; 19,000 maps of areas other than the United States. **Services:** Interlibrary loan; library

★13809★
SUNY AT STONY BROOK - MATHEMATICS-PHYSICS LIBRARY (Sci-Engr)
Physics Bldg., C Fl. Phone: (516)632-7145
Stony Brook, NY 11794-3855 Sherry Chang, Libn.
Founded: 1964. **Staff:** Prof 1; Other 3. **Subjects:** Mathematics, physics, applied mathematics. **Holdings:** 37,700 books; 26,100 bound periodical volumes; 500 unbound lecture notes of academic organizations; 300 reels of microfilm of journals; 2100 unbound documents; 1000 dissertations; 650 microfiche. **Subscriptions:** 700 journals and other serials. **Services:** Interlibrary loan; copying; library open to the public for reference use only. **Computerized Information Services:** Online systems.

★13810★
SUNY AT STONY BROOK - MUSIC LIBRARY (Mus)
Stony Brook, NY 11794-3333 Phone: (516)632-7097
Daniel W. Kinney, Act.Hd.
Founded: 1974. **Staff:** Prof 2; Other 4. **Subjects:** Music. **Holdings:** 50,000 books, scores, and periodical volumes; 18,200 sound recordings; 6700 microforms. **Subscriptions:** 360 journals and other serials. **Services:** Interlibrary loan; copying; library open to the public. **Automated Operations:** Computerized cataloging. **Staff:** Ruben E. Weltsch, Mus.Cat..

★13811★
SUOMI COLLEGE - FINNISH-AMERICAN HISTORICAL ARCHIVES (Hist, Area-Ethnic)
Hancock, MI 49930 Phone: (906)482-5300
Dr. Marsha E. Penti, Dir.
Founded: 1932. **Staff:** Prof 1; Other 1. **Subjects:** Suomi Synod and Finnish-American church history; Finnish Americans, especially in the Upper Midwest; temperance; mutual benefit societies. **Holdings:** 7000 books, periodicals, and pamphlets; 600 cassette tapes and transcripts; 12 linear feet of photographs; 400 linear feet of manuscript collections; college records; organizational and personal papers. **Subscriptions:** 29 journals and other serials; 6 newspapers. **Services:** Copying; archives open to the public by appointment.

★13812★
SUPER VALU STORES, INC. - RESOURCE CENTER (Comp Sci)
Box 990 Phone: (612)828-4372
Minneapolis, MN 55440 Linda Canfield, Info.Anl.
Founded: 1984. **Staff:** Prof 1; Other 1. **Subjects:** Data processing, personal computers, business. **Holdings:** 250 books; 100 internal reports; 500 technical manuals. **Subscriptions:** 60 journals and other serials. **Services:** SDI; center open to the public with restrictions. **Automated Operations:** Computerized cataloging, acquisitions, and serials. **Computerized Information Services:** DIALOG Information Services, American Society for Information Science (ASIS). **Publications:** Guide to the Resource Center, annual. **Special Catalogs:** Personal computer catalog, 2/year.

★13813★
SUPPLEE MEMORIAL PRESBYTERIAN CHURCH - LIBRARY (Rel-Phil)
855 Welsh Rd. Phone: (215)646-4123
Maple Glen, PA 19002 Suzanne P. Stahler, Libn.
Founded: 1982. **Staff:** 3. **Subjects:** Religion, social concerns, children's books. **Holdings:** 1717 books; tapes; college and seminary catalogs; periodicals. **Subscriptions:** 13 journals and other serials. **Services:** Library open to the public. **Staff:** Sylvia Eagano, Dir. of Christian Educ..

SUPREME COURT OF CANADA
See: Canada - Supreme Court of Canada (2495)

SUPREME COURT OF THE UNITED STATES
See: U.S. Supreme Court (15502)

★13814★
SURFACE MINING RESEARCH LIBRARY (Energy)
Box 5024 Phone: (304)346-3408
Charleston, WV 25361 Norman Kilpatrick, Dir.
Founded: 1971. **Staff:** Prof 1. **Subjects:** Surface coal mining, deep coal mining, coal prices, international coal competition, deep coal, utility reform, energy policy. **Holdings:** 300 volumes; 160 8x10 photos, 500 3x5 photos, and 900 slides of surface coal mining. **Services:** Copying; consulting. **Publications:** Technical Information Kit - free upon request; slide show on modern surface mining methods - for sale.

★13815★
SURGIKOS - TECHNICAL INFORMATION CENTER (Biol Sci, Sci-Engr)
2500 Arbrook Blvd.
Box 130 Phone: (817)465-3141
Arlington, TX 76010 W.B. Scroggs, Tech.Info.Coord.
Founded: 1970. **Staff:** Prof 1; Other 1. **Subjects:** Chemical and biological sciences. **Special Collections:** Antimicrobial chemistry (5000 reprints). **Holdings:** 2400 books; 4500 bound periodical volumes. **Subscriptions:** 352 journals and other serials. **Services:** Interlibrary loan; copying; center open to the public by appointment. **Automated Operations:** Computerized cataloging. **Computerized Information Services:** DIALOG Information Services. **Networks/Consortia:** Member of Dallas-Tarrant County Consortium of Health Science Libraries. **Publications:** Library information bulletin - for internal distribution only. **Remarks:** Surgikos is a subsidiary of Johnson and Johnson.

★13816★
SURREY CENTENNIAL MUSEUM - ARCHIVES (Hist)
Box 1006, Sta. A
Cloverdale Phone: (604)574-5744
Surrey, BC, Canada V3S 4P5 Linda Johnston, Prog.Mgr.
Founded: 1958. **Staff:** Prof 1; Other 4. **Subjects:** Local history. **Holdings:** 1000 books; school registers; municipal records; maps; photographs. **Services:** Copying; archives open to the public for reference use only on a limited schedule and by appointment. **Remarks:** Archives located at 17679 60th Ave., Surrey, BC V3S 1V3.

★13817★
SURVEYORS HISTORICAL SOCIETY - LIBRARY (Geog-Map)
31457 Hugh Way Phone: (415)581-2345
Hayward, CA 94554 Myron A. Lewis, Sec.
Founded: 1977. **Subjects:** Surveying. **Holdings:** 100 books, manuals, catalogs; archives. **Computerized Information Services:** Internal database. **Special Catalogs:** Artifact collection catalog (online).

★13818★
SURVIVAL RESEARCH FOUNDATION - LIBRARY (Rel-Phil)
Box 8565 Phone: (305)435-2730
Pembroke Pines, FL 33084 Arthur S. Berger, Pres.
Founded: 1971. **Subjects:** Life after death, immortality, hauntings, apparitions, poltergeists, reincarnation, out-of-body experiences. **Holdings:** 200 volumes.

★13819★
SUSQUEHANNA COUNTY HISTORICAL SOCIETY AND FREE LIBRARY ASSOCIATION (Hist)
Monument Square Phone: (717)278-1881
Montrose, PA 18801 Mary O. Garm, Dir.
Founded: 1907. **Staff:** Prof 2; Other 11. **Subjects:** Genealogy, natural science, art, music, humanities, religion. **Holdings:** 71,641 volumes; 475 genealogical items. **Subscriptions:** 75 journals and other serials; 7 newspapers. **Services:** Interlibrary loan; copying; library open to the public with restrictions. **Staff:** Elizabeth Smith, Cur., Hist.Dept.; Susan Stone, Asst.Libn.; David Colwell, Ref.Libn..

★13820★
SUSSEX COUNTY HISTORICAL SOCIETY - LIBRARY (Hist)
82 Main St.
Box 913 Phone: (201)383-6010
Newton, NJ 07860 Barbara Lewis Waskowich, Cur./Sec.
Founded: 1904. **Staff:** Prof 2. **Subjects:** New Jersey and Sussex County history, archeology, genealogy, antiques. **Special Collections:** Roy Papers. **Holdings:** 2000 books; 10 bound periodical volumes; 600 genealogical files; newspapers. **Services:** Library open to the public on a limited schedule.

★13821★
SUSSEX COUNTY LAW LIBRARY† (Law)
Court House
3 High St. Phone: (201)383-4590
Newton, NJ 07860 Barbara J. Smith, Ck. to Jury Comm.
Subjects: Law. **Holdings:** 45,000 books; 5000 bound periodical volumes. **Services:** Copying; library open to the public.

★13822★
SUTHERLAND, ASBILL & BRENNAN - LIBRARY (Law)
1275 Pennsylvania Ave., N.W. Phone: (202)383-0450
Washington, DC 20004 Robert S. Stivers, Mgr., Lib.Serv.
Staff: Prof 3; Other 4. **Subjects:** Law - tax, energy, insurance, securities. **Special Collections:** History of tax legislation, 1921 to present. **Holdings:** 30,000 books. **Subscriptions:** 200 journals and other serials. **Services:** Interlibrary loan; copying; library open to the public with librarian's permission. **Computerized Information Services:** DIALOG Information Services, OCLC, WESTLAW, Dow Jones News/Retrieval, LEXIS. **Staff:** Ronald Pramberger, Leg.Libn.; Monica Parry, Ref. & Res.Libn.; Kim Walton, Pub.Serv.Libn..

LADISLAV SUTNAR ARCHIVE
See: Smithsonian Institution Libraries - Cooper-Hewitt Museum of Design - Doris & Henry Dreyfuss Memorial Study Center (13276)

ADOLPH SUTRO ARCHIVE
See: University of San Francisco - Special Collections Department/ Donohue Rare Book Room (16834)

SUTRO LIBRARY
See: California State Library (2206)

★13823★
SUTTER COUNTY LAW LIBRARY (Law)
Court House Phone: (916)741-7360
Yuba City, CA 95991 Pamela J. Mastelotto, Interim Law Libn.
Staff: 1. **Subjects:** Law. **Holdings:** 7699 volumes. **Services:** Library open to the public.

WILLIAM M. SUTTLE MEDICAL LIBRARY
See: Hinds General Hospital (6311)

★13824★
SVERDRUP CORPORATION - TECHNICAL LIBRARY (Sci-Engr)
801 N. 11th Blvd. Phone: (314)436-7600
St. Louis, MO 63101 R.A. Bodapati, Libn.
Founded: 1966. **Staff:** Prof 1. **Subjects:** Engineering - civil, structural, electrical, mechanical, environmental; architecture; urban and regional planning. **Holdings:** 8000 books. **Subscriptions:** 80 journals and other serials. **Services:** Interlibrary loan (limited); library not open to the public.

GEORGE SVERDRUP LIBRARY AND MEDIA CENTER
See: Augsburg College (1159)

SWAIN HALL LIBRARY
See: Indiana University (6802)

SWAIN LIBRARY OF CHEMISTRY AND CHEMICAL ENGINEERING
See: Stanford University (13622)

ROBERT S. SWAIN NATURAL HISTORY LIBRARY
See: Thornton W. Burgess Society, Inc. - Museum and Nature Center (2041)

★13825★
SWAIN SCHOOL OF DESIGN - MELVILLE LIBRARY (Art)
1213 Purchase St., 2nd Fl. Phone: (617)997-7831
New Bedford, MA 02740-6688 Martine Hargreaves, Libn.
Founded: 1882. **Staff:** Prof 1. **Subjects:** Fine arts, liberal arts, graphic and decorative arts. **Special Collections:** Rare books on fine arts; local artists (pamphlets and clippings); slide collection (30,000 slides). **Holdings:** 18,000 volumes. **Subscriptions:** 57 journals and other serials. **Services:** Interlibrary loan; copying; library open to the public with restrictions on borrowing. **Networks/Consortia:** Member of Southeastern Association for Cooperation in Higher Education in Massachusetts (SACHEM).

JAMES SWANN ARCHIVES
See: Cedar Rapids Museum of Art - Herbert S. Stamats Art Library (2782)

SWANSON READING ROOM
See: Kansas State University - Grain Science and Industry (7361)

★13826★
SWARTHMORE COLLEGE - CORNELL LIBRARY OF SCIENCE AND ENGINEERING (Sci-Engr)
Swarthmore, PA 19081 Phone: (215)328-8261
Emi K. Horikawa, Sci.Libn.
Founded: 1982. **Staff:** Prof 1; Other 2. **Subjects:** Mathematics, physics, chemistry, engineering, biology, astronomy, computer science. **Holdings:** 35,800 books; 26,200 bound periodical volumes and periodicals on microfilm; 2100 government documents. **Subscriptions:** 802 journals and other serials. **Services:** Interlibrary loan; copying; library open to the public

with courtesy card. **Computerized Information Services:** DIALOG Information Services, BRS Information Technologies, OCLC, CAS ONLINE. Performs searches on fee basis. **Networks/Consortia:** Member of PALINET. **Publications:** Current Periodicals List.

★13827★
SWARTHMORE COLLEGE - DANIEL UNDERHILL MUSIC LIBRARY (Mus)
Swarthmore, PA 19081 Phone: (215)328-8231
George K. Huber, Mus.Libn.
Founded: 1973. **Staff:** Prof 1. **Subjects:** Music, dance. **Holdings:** 4700 books; 1100 bound periodical volumes; 9000 scores; 14,000 phonograph records. **Subscriptions:** 40 journals and other serials. **Services:** Interlibrary loan; library open to the public with a fee charged in some cases. **Computerized Information Services:** OCLC. **Networks/Consortia:** Member of PALINET. **Special Catalogs:** Catalog for chamber music (card).

★13828★
SWARTHMORE COLLEGE - FRIENDS HISTORICAL LIBRARY (Hist, Rel-Phil)
Swarthmore, PA 19081 Phone: (215)328-8496
J. William Frost, Dir..
Founded: 1871. **Staff:** Prof 2; Other 5. **Subjects:** Quaker faith, history, and genealogy; Quaker social concerns - abolition of slavery, race relations, women's rights, peace, education, prison reform, mental health, Indian rights, temperance. **Special Collections:** Friends Meeting records (2000 volumes of manuscripts); Whittier (1700 books, 900 manuscripts); Quaker manuscripts (250 collections); Lucretia Mott manuscripts (7 boxes); Samuel Janney manuscripts (7 boxes); Elias Hicks manuscripts (12 boxes); journals of Quaker ministers (18 boxes); Charles F. Jenkins Autograph Collection (6 boxes). **Holdings:** 36,434 books; 1772 bound periodical volumes; 100 boxes of pictures; 81 chart case drawers of pictures, maps, broadsides, deeds, genealogical charts, marriage certificates; 2357 reels of microfilm. **Subscriptions:** 201 journals and other serials. **Services:** Interlibrary loan; copying; library open to the public. **Computerized Information Services:** OCLC. **Networks/Consortia:** Member of PALINET. **Publications:** Descriptive leaflet; Guide to the Manuscript Collections of Friends Historical Library of Swarthmore College, 1982. **Special Indexes:** Quaker picture index (card); William Wade Hinshaw Index to Quaker Meeting Records (card); checklists for Quaker manuscript collections (loose-leaf); index to Whittier Collection (card). **Staff:** Albert W. Fowler, Assoc.Dir..

★13829★
SWARTHMORE COLLEGE - PEACE COLLECTION (Soc Sci)
McCabe Library Phone: (215)328-8557
Swarthmore, PA 19081 Eleanor M. Barr, Cur.
Founded: 1930. **Staff:** Prof 4; Other 1. **Subjects:** History of peace movement, nonviolence, pacifism, conscientious objection and conscription, disarmament, women and peace and justice. **Special Collections:** Jane Addams (350 books; 13,000 manuscripts; 170 document boxes of clippings and pictures); A.J. Muste (23 feet of manuscripts, correspondence, writings); Emily Greene Balch (36 feet of manuscripts, correspondence, writings); Fellowship of Reconciliation; Friends Committee on National Legislation; Clergy and Laity Concerned; Women's International League for Peace and Freedom; War Resisters League; SANE; National Interreligious Service Board for Conscientious Objectors; Women Strike for Peace; CCCO/An Agency for Military and Draft Counseling; World Conference on Religion and Peace; World Peace Foundation. **Holdings:** 9200 books; 475 bound periodical volumes; 3500 peace posters and broadsides; 1100 reels of microfilm; 147 document groups. **Subscriptions:** 300 journals and other serials. **Services:** Interlibrary loan; copying; library open to the public with restrictions on some collections. **Automated Operations:** Computerized cataloging and serials. **Computerized Information Services:** OCLC. **Networks/Consortia:** Member of PALINET. **Publications:** Guide to Swarthmore College Peace Collection. **Special Catalogs:** Checklists for major collections (loose-leaf). **Special Indexes:** Index for Jane Addams correspondence (card); index for archival collections (card). **Staff:** Barbara Addison, Cat.; Mary Ellen Clark, Asst. to Cur.; Martha P. Shane, Archv..

MINOR SWARTHOUT MEMORIAL LIBRARY
See: Glenn H. Curtiss Museum of Local History (3952)

★13830★
AMBROSE SWASEY LIBRARY (Rel-Phil)
1100 S. Goodman St. Phone: (716)271-1320
Rochester, NY 14620 Norman J. Kansfield, Dir. of Lib.Serv.
Founded: 1819. **Staff:** Prof 4; Other 5. **Subjects:** World religions, Christian history, theology, worship and liturgy, marriage and family, Bible. **Special Collections:** McQuaid Papers; Fulton J. Sheen Archives. **Holdings:** 263,000 books and bound periodical volumes; 3610 microforms; 2626 audio recordings; 566 theses. **Subscriptions:** 874 journals and other serials. **Services:** Interlibrary loan; copying; library open to the public for reference use only. **Automated Operations:** Computerized cataloging and acquisitions. **Computerized Information Services:** OCLC. **Networks/Consortia:** Member of Rochester Regional Library Council (RRLC). **Publications:** Book Lists, monthly; Guide to Ambrose Swasey Library. **Remarks:** Maintained by Colgate Rochester Divinity School/Bexley Hall/Crozer Theological Seminary and St. Bernard's Institute. **Staff:** Christopher Brennan, Asst. for Tech.Serv.; Bonnie Van Delinder, Asst. for Pub.Serv.; Lily Shung, Cat.; Gail McClain, Cat..

★13831★
SWEDENBORG FOUNDATION - LIBRARY (Rel-Phil)
139 E. 23rd St. Phone: (212)673-7310
New York, NY 10010 John R. Seekamp, Pres.
Staff: 6. **Subjects:** Works by and about Emanuel Swedenborg. **Special Collections:** Rare editions; image archive (slides; photographs; drawings). **Holdings:** 3000 books; 100 bound periodical volumes; engravings and prints; 10 paintings and drawings; 5 films. **Services:** Library open to the public with restrictions. **Publications:** LOGOS newsletter.

SWEDENBORG LIBRARY
See: Academy of the New Church (23)

★13832★
SWEDENBORG LIBRARY AND BOOKSTORE (Rel-Phil)
79 Newbury St. Phone: (617)262-5918
Boston, MA 02116 Rafael Guiu, Mgr.
Founded: 1865. **Staff:** Prof 3. **Subjects:** Swedenborg theological works, American and English Swedenborgian Church, collateral works of Swedenborgian writers. **Special Collections:** First editions of Swedenborg's writings; photolithographic and photostatic copies of Swedenborg's manuscripts. **Holdings:** 2100 books; 210 bound periodical volumes; 1000 pamphlets. **Services:** Copying; library open to the public. **Special Catalogs:** Books for Sale Catalogue - free upon request. **Remarks:** Maintained by the Massachusetts New Church Union. **Staff:** Michelle Joan, Cat./Asst.Libn..

SWEDENBORG MEMORIAL LIBRARY
See: Urbana University (17215)

★13833★
SWEDENBORG SCHOOL OF RELIGION - LIBRARY (Rel-Phil)
48 Sargent St. Phone: (617)244-0504
Newton, MA 02158 Patricia Lyons Basu, Dir.
Founded: 1866. **Staff:** 2. **Subjects:** Writings of Emanuel Swedenborg, theology. **Special Collections:** History and literature of the Swedenborgian Church (also known as the New Church or the Church of the New Jerusalem). **Holdings:** 33,000 books and bound periodical volumes; Swedenborgian Church archive materials including letters, manuscripts, committee reports, sermons. **Subscriptions:** 67 journals and other serials. **Services:** Interlibrary loan; copying; library open to the public by appointment. **Remarks:** Incorporated as the New Church Theological School in 1881. **Staff:** Louise Woofenden, Archv..

SWEDISH-AMERICAN ARCHIVES OF GREATER CHICAGO
See: Swedish Pioneer Historical Society (13840)

★13834★
SWEDISH AMERICAN HOSPITAL - HEALTH CARE LIBRARY† (Med)
1400 Charles St. Phone: (815)968-4400
Rockford, IL 61108 Peggy Fuller, Med.Libn.
Staff: Prof 1; Other 1. **Subjects:** Clinical medicine, hospital administration. **Holdings:** 1200 books; 300 video cassettes; 8 year backlog of periodicals. **Subscriptions:** 200 journals and other serials. **Services:** Interlibrary loan; copying; library open to the public. **Computerized Information Services:** MEDLARS. **Networks/Consortia:** Member of Upstate Consortium of Medical and Allied Libraries in Northern Illinois, Northern Illinois Library System (NILS).

★13835★
SWEDISH CONSULATE GENERAL - SWEDISH INFORMATION SERVICE (Area-Ethnic)
825 Third Ave. Phone: (212)751-5900
New York, NY 10022 Elisabeth Halvarsson-Stapen, Lib.Asst.
Founded: 1921. **Staff:** 2. **Subjects:** Contemporary Sweden. **Holdings:** 7000 books; 50 VF drawers of pamphlets and clippings. **Subscriptions:** 89 journals and other serials. **Services:** Copying; service open to the public for reference use only. **Publications:** New accessions, semiannual - to users. **Staff:** Marna Feldt, Info.Off..

★13836★
SWEDISH COVENANT HOSPITAL - JOSEPH G. STROMBERG LIBRARY OF THE HEALTH SCIENCES (Med)
5145 N. California Ave. Phone: (312)878-8200
Chicago, IL 60625 Cynthia Sanchez, Hea.Sci.Lib.Techn.
Staff: 1. **Subjects:** Family practice, medicine, nursing. **Holdings:** 2000 books; 3100 bound periodical volumes; AV programs. **Subscriptions:** 103 journals. **Services:** Interlibrary loan; library not open to the public. **Computerized Information Services:** BRS Information Technologies, MEDLINE. **Networks/Consortia:** Member of Greater Midwest Regional Medical Library Network, Metropolitan Consortium of Chicago. **Publications:** Acquisitions List, quarterly - to staff and other medical libraries in area.

★13837★
SWEDISH EMBASSY - LIBRARY-INFORMATION CENTER (Area-Ethnic)
Watergate 600, Suite 1200
600 New Hampshire Ave., N.W. Phone: (202)944-5600
Washington, DC 20037 Larilyn Congdon, Libn.
Staff: 1. **Subjects:** Sweden - social policy, ethnology, government, history, education, literature. **Holdings:** 4000 books and bound periodical volumes; yearly publications by the Swedish government including the Yearbook of Nordic Statistics. **Services:** Library not open to the public.

★13838★
SWEDISH HOSPITAL MEDICAL CENTER - REFERENCE LIBRARY (Med)
747 Summit Ave. Phone: (206)386-2484
Seattle, WA 98104 Jean C. Anderson, Chf.Libn.
Staff: Prof 2; Other 2. **Subjects:** Surgery, medicine, nursing, hospital administration. **Special Collections:** Nursing Baccalaureate Collection (420 volumes; 12 videotapes); CIBA slides. **Holdings:** 2900 volumes; 40 videotapes; 6100 slides. **Subscriptions:** 367 journals and other serials. **Services:** Interlibrary loan; library not open to the public. **Automated Operations:** Computerized acquisitions and serials. **Computerized Information Services:** MEDLARS, DIALOG Information Services, BRS Information Technologies, DataTimes; OnTyme Electronic Message Network Service (electronic mail service). **Networks/Consortia:** Member of Seattle Area Hospital Library Consortium (SAHLC), Western Library Network (WLN). **Special Catalogs:** Catalog of serials holding (print). **Staff:** Barbara A. Ivester, Asst.Libn..

★13839★
SWEDISH MEDICAL CENTER - LIBRARY (Med)
501 E. Hampden Ave., Dept. 8640
Box 2901 Phone: (303)788-6616
Englewood, CO 80110-0101 Sandra Parker, Dir., Lib.Serv.
Founded: 1967. **Staff:** Prof 2; Other 1. **Subjects:** Neurosciences, medicine, nursing, health administration, rehabilitation, spinal cord/head injuries. **Holdings:** 1500 books; 2500 bound periodical volumes; 1110 unbound periodicals. **Subscriptions:** 350 journals and other serials. **Services:** Interlibrary loan; copying; library open to the public by appointment. **Automated Operations:** Computerized cataloging. **Computerized Information Services:** NLM, DIALOG Information Services, BRS Information Technologies, Pergamon ORBIT InfoLine, Inc. Performs searches on fee basis. **Networks/Consortia:** Member of Denver Area Health Sciences Library Consortium. **Staff:** Alice B. Smith, Asst.Libn..

★13840★
SWEDISH PIONEER HISTORICAL SOCIETY - SWEDISH-AMERICAN ARCHIVES OF GREATER CHICAGO (Area-Ethnic)
5125 N. Spaulding Ave. Phone: (312)583-5722
Chicago, IL 60625 Timothy Johnson, Archv.
Founded: 1965. **Staff:** Prof 1; Other 2. **Subjects:** Swedish settlement in the U.S., Swedish culture, Swedish-American organizations, Swedish contributions to development of the U.S., outstanding Swedish-Americans. **Special Collections:** Contributions of Swedes to American life and culture; Swedish music; records of Swedish organizations in the U.S.; documents and papers of outstanding Swedish Americans; Henry Bengston; Carl Hjalmar Lundquist; Selma Jacobson; Swedish Royalty and Chicago; Sweden, the Land of Our Forefathers. **Holdings:** 5000 books (largely in Swedish); 400 archive boxes of records; Swedish newspapers printed in Chicago, 1871-1981. **Subscriptions:** 100 journals and other serials; 5 newspapers. **Services:** Copying; translations; archives open to the public by appointment. **Automated Operations:** Computerized cataloging. **Publications:** Items in Swedish Pioneer Historical Society Quarterly. **Staff:** C. Hobart Edgren, Exec.Dir..

★13841★
SWEDLOW, INC. - TECHNICAL LIBRARY (Sci-Engr)
12122 Western Ave. Phone: (714)893-7531
Garden Grove, CA 92645 Marjorie M. Ford, Info.Spec.
Staff: Prof 1; Other 1. **Subjects:** Polymers, engineering, plastics. **Holdings:** 500 books; 250 bound periodical volumes; 2000 patents; 175 VF drawers; 31 cartridges of microfilm of company files **Subscriptions:** 30 journals and other serials. **Services:** Interlibrary loan; library not open to the public. **Automated Operations:** Computerized cataloging, serials, and circulation. **Computerized Information Services:** DIALOG Information Services. **Publications:** What's New in the Library, biweekly - for internal distribution only.

BEATRICE S. SWEENEY ARCHIVE
See: Historical Society of Saratoga Springs (6355)

★13842★
SWEETWATER COUNTY HISTORICAL MUSEUM - INFORMATION CENTER (Sci-Engr)
Courthouse
80 W. Flaming Gorge Way Phone: (307)875-2611
Green River, WY 82935 Henry F. Chadey, Dir.
Founded: 1967. **Staff:** Prof 2; Other 1. **Subjects:** Coal mining. **Special Collections:** Pictures of coal mining in southwestern Wyoming (4000 items); pictures of Chinese employed in coal mining industry. **Holdings:** 300 books; 25 bound periodical volumes; 8 VF drawers of clippings and reports; 4 cubic feet of archival mining materials including payroll, maps, and contracts; 200 other publications; 20,000 photographs. **Services:** Copying; center open to the public for research.

EARL GREGG SWEM LIBRARY
See: College of William and Mary (3402)

★13843★
SWENSON SWEDISH IMMIGRATION RESEARCH CENTER (Area-Ethnic)
Augustana College
Box 175 Phone: (309)794-7204
Rock Island, IL 61201 Dag Blanck, Dir.
Staff: Prof 2; Other 1. **Subjects:** Swedish immigration to the U.S., Swedish-American life and culture, biography of Swedes in the U.S. **Special Collections:** G.N. Swan Book Collection (6000 volumes); Oliver A. Linder Book Collection (600 volumes); Scandinaviana Book Collection (750 volumes); Swedish Topographical Map Collection (5 flat case drawers); Immigration Book Collection (2000 volumes). **Holdings:** 9000 books; 1000 bound periodical volumes; 200 uncataloged periodicals; 5.5 linear feet of Scandinavian-American Picture Collection; 120 linear feet of manuscripts; 8 linear feet of Oliver A. Linder clipping files; 1560 reels of microfilm of Swedish-American newspapers; 2000 reels of microfilm of Swedish-American church records; 412 reels of microfilm of records and papers of Swedish-American benevolent, fraternal, and cultural organizations and their institutions; 59 reels of microfilm of personal and professional papers of immigrants; 89 reels of microfilm and 6 loose-leaf volumes of name indexes to Swedish port of embarkation records: Gothenburg, 1869-1930 and Malmo, 1874-1895; other Swedish emigrant lists, 1850-1861. **Subscriptions:** 30 journals and other serials. **Services:** Copying; center open to the public. **Automated Operations:** Computerized cataloging and acquisitions (through Augustana College Library). **Computerized Information Services:** OCLC (through Augustana College Library). **Publications:** Swenson Center News - free upon request; Swedish-American Newspapers: A Guide to the Microfilms held by SSIRC at Augustana College, Rock Island, Illinois, compiled by Lilly Setterdahl, 1981; Guide to Resources and Holdings. **Special Indexes:** Index to O.A. Linder clipping file; index to George M. Stephenson photostat collection; index to Scandinavian-American Picture Collection; index to personal data on first generation immigrants; index of studio names and addresses of photographers represented in general photograph collection; index to subject files (all on cards). **Staff:** Kermit B. Westerberg, Archv./Libn.; Vicky Oliver, Res..

MORRIS SWETT TECHNICAL LIBRARY
See: U.S. Army - TRADOC - Field Artillery School (14794)

SHERMAN SWIFT REFERENCE LIBRARY
See: Canadian National Institute for the Blind - National Library Services (2588)

★13844★
SWIGART MUSEUM - LIBRARY (Hist, Trans)
Museum Park, Box 214 Phone: (814)643-3000
Huntingdon, PA 16652 William E. Swigart, Jr., Exec.Dir.
Founded: 1927. **Staff:** Prof 1; Other 3. **Subjects:** Automotive history, transportation, automobiliana. **Special Collections:** Early transportation evolving into the automobile. **Holdings:** 1000 books; 612 bound periodical volumes; automobile literature; extensive uncataloged material. **Subscriptions:** 12 journals and other serials. **Services:** Copying; library open to the public with restrictions. **Remarks:** Said to have world's largest collection of license plates, emblems, and nameplates.

★13845★
SYMES BUILDING LAW LIBRARY
820 16th St., Suite 800 Phone: (303)370-9490
Denver, CO 80202 Frank Thompson
Subjects: Law. **Holdings:** 20,000 volumes. **Remarks:** Sherman Agency, Inc. is agent for owner.

★13846★
SYMMERS, FISH AND WARNER - RESEARCH LIBRARY (Law)
111 E. 50th St. Phone: (212)751-6400
New York, NY 10022 Barbara Kochan, Libn.
Founded: 1956. **Staff:** Prof 1. **Subjects:** Law - insurance, marine, aviation. **Special Collections:** Admiralty and English Law Reports. **Holdings:** 12,500 volumes; pamphlets; maps. **Subscriptions:** 97 journals and other serials. **Services:** Interlibrary loan.

SYNAGOGUE ARCHITECTURAL AND ART LIBRARY
See: Union of American Hebrew Congregations (14452)

★13847★
SYNCRUDE CANADA, LTD. - OPERATIONS LIBRARY (Sci-Engr, Energy)
P.O. Bag 4009, Mail Drop 1140 Phone: (403)790-8317
Fort McMurray, AB, Canada T9H 3L1 Stephen Sloan, Lib./Info.Spec.
Founded: 1977. **Staff:** Prof 1; Other 2. **Subjects:** Oil sands, petroleum technology, engineering. **Holdings:** 5000 books; 100 bound periodical volumes; 13 lateral files of technical information; 800 microfiche; 150 videotapes; 100 16mm films; 50 AV programs. **Subscriptions:** 150 journals and other serials; 6 newspapers. **Services:** Interlibrary loan; library not open to the public. **Automated Operations:** Computerized cataloging. **Computerized Information Services:** DIALOG Information Services, CAN/OLE, Info Globe, Dow Jones News/Retrieval.

★13848★
SYNCRUDE CANADA, LTD. - RESEARCH AND DEVELOPMENT LIBRARY (Sci-Engr, Energy)
10120 17th St.
P.O. Box 5790, Sta. L Phone: (403)464-8400
Edmonton, AB, Canada T6C 4G3 Peter J. Bates, Info.Spec.
Founded: 1960. **Staff:** Prof 1; Other 1. **Subjects:** Tar sands, chemistry, chemical engineering, petroleum, environment, mining. **Holdings:** 8000 books; 750 bound periodical volumes; 4000 patents; 2000 company reports; 1000 microfiche; reprints. **Subscriptions:** 170 journals and other serials; 5 newspapers. **Services:** Interlibrary loan; library not open to the public. **Automated Operations:** Computerized public access catalog and indexing. **Computerized Information Services:** Online systems. **Publications:** Current awareness bulletin, monthly - for internal distribution only.

★13849★
SYNERGY POWER INSTITUTE - LIBRARY (Soc Sci)
64 Via La Cambre Phone: (415)461-7854
Greenbrae, CA 94904 James H. Craig, Dir.
Founded: 1968. **Staff:** Prof 1; Other 1. **Subjects:** Psychology, power, political science, sociology, U.S. history. **Holdings:** 6000 books. **Subscriptions:** 25 journals and other serials. **Services:** Library not open to the public. **Publications:** Synergic Power: Beyond Domination and Permissiveness, 2nd edition, 1979; occasional papers. **Remarks:** Institute founded to research and disseminate information about power and ways it can be used humanely and responsibly to change society.

SYNOD OF EVANGELICAL LUTHERAN CHURCH ARCHIVES
See: Concordia Historical Institute - Department of Archives and History (3581)

★13850★
SYNTEX, U.S.A. - CORPORATE LIBRARY/INFORMATION SERVICES (Med, Biol Sci)
3401 Hillview Ave. Phone: (415)855-5431
Palo Alto, CA 94304 Faye M. Chartoff, Mgr.
Founded: 1961. **Staff:** Prof 7; Other 6. **Subjects:** Organic chemistry, biochemistry, pharmacology, clinical medicine, veterinary medicine, physiology. **Special Collections:** Career/Management (300 items). **Holdings:** 7000 books; 16,000 bound periodical volumes; 1400 microfilm cartridges; 22 volumes of bound reprints of papers authored by Syntex personnel. **Subscriptions:** 500 journals and other serials. **Services:** Interlibrary loan; copying; SDI; library open to the public by application to librarian. **Automated Operations:** Computerized cataloging, acquisitions, serials, and circulation. **Computerized Information Services:** DIALOG Information Services, NLM, Pergamon ORBIT InfoLine, Inc., BRS Information Technologies, CAS ONLINE, Pergamon ORBIT InfoLine, Inc., TEXTLINE, OCLC; SPIF (internal database). **Networks/Consortia:** Member of Pacific Southwest Regional Medical Library Service. **Publications:** Booklist, monthly; bibliographies; Periodicals List - all for internal distribution only. **Staff:** Caren Cavanaugh, Supv., Info.Serv. Unit; Vicki Garlow, Info.Spec.; Ann Nishimoto, Info.Spec.; Kathy Trimble, Sr.Info.Spec.; Catherine Sanborn, Sr.Info.Spec..

★13851★
SYRACUSE RESEARCH CORPORATION - LIBRARY (Sci-Engr, Energy)
Merrill Lane Phone: (315)425-5200
Syracuse, NY 13210 Bonnie B. Armstrong, Dir.
Founded: 1957. **Staff:** Prof 1. **Subjects:** Environmental sciences, policy analysis and evaluation, electrical and electronics engineering. **Holdings:** 2000 books; 1500 archival items. **Subscriptions:** 100 journals and other serials. **Services:** Interlibrary loan; library not open to the public. **Computerized Information Services:** DIALOG Information Services, BRS Information Technologies, STN International, Chemical Information Systems, Inc. (CIS), MEDLARS, TOXNET, Pergamon ORBIT InfoLine, Inc.; internal databases. **Networks/Consortia:** Member of Central New York Library Resources Council (CENTRO), SUNY/OCLC Library Network.

★13852★
SYRACUSE UNIVERSITY - E.S. BIRD LIBRARY - AREA STUDIES DEPARTMENT
Syracuse, NY 13244-2010
Defunct. Holdings absorbed by general library.

★13853★
SYRACUSE UNIVERSITY - E.S. BIRD LIBRARY - FINE ARTS DEPARTMENT (Art, Mus)
Syracuse, NY 13244-2010 Phone: (315)423-2440
Barbara Opar, Act.Dept.Hd./Arch.Libn.
Staff: Prof 4; Other 8. **Subjects:** Art, architecture, music, photography. **Special Collections:** Italian libretto collection (19th century Italian opera libretti; 1350); Liechtenstein Music Archive (microfilm collection of 17th century music preserved in Czechoslovakia); papers of Marcel Breuer and Pietro Belluschi; papers of William Lescaze; working drawings of a number of contemporary buildings; papers of American artists and critics including John Canaday, Richard Florsheim, John Singer Sargent, Eastman Johnson, Elihu Vedder, Jacob Lawrence, Edwin Dickinson, George Cruikshank, and photographer Margaret Bourke White. **Holdings:** 110,000 volumes; 16,484 recordings; 21,700 scores; 969 tapes; 240,000 slides; 10,550 mounted photographs; 27,000 pictures; 12,000 exhibition catalogs; 3685 pamphlets; 1421 microcards; 1323 microfiche. **Subscriptions:** 437 journals and other serials. **Services:** Interlibrary loan; copying; department open to the public with restrictions on circulation. **Automated Operations:** Computerized cataloging, acquisitions, and circulation. **Computerized Information Services:** OCLC. **Networks/Consortia:** Member of SUNY/OCLC Library Network. **Special Catalogs:** Catalog of art exhibition catalogs (card). **Staff:** Randall Bond, Art Libn.; Johanna Prins, Slide Cur.; Donald Seibert, Music Libn..

★13854★
SYRACUSE UNIVERSITY - E.S. BIRD LIBRARY - HUMANITIES DEPARTMENT
Syracuse, NY 13244-2010
Defunct. Holdings absorbed by general library.

★13855★
SYRACUSE UNIVERSITY - E.S. BIRD LIBRARY - MEDIA SERVICES DEPARTMENT (Aud-Vis)
B101 Bird Library Phone: (315)423-2438
Syracuse, NY 13244-2010 George Abbott, Hd.
Staff: Prof 2; Other 10. **Subjects:** Audiovisual materials. **Special Collections:** Film Study Center (500 films); Broadcast Foundation of America audio recordings (5000 reels). **Holdings:** 100,000 items, including AV programs and microforms. **Subscriptions:** 75 newspapers. **Services:** Copying; department open to the public. **Computerized Information Services:** Email, ALANET, BITNET (electronic mail services). **Staff:** Diana Reinstein, Online/Media Serv.Libn..

★13856★
SYRACUSE UNIVERSITY - E.S. BIRD LIBRARY - SOCIAL SCIENCES DEPARTMENT
Syracuse, NY 13244-2010
Defunct. Holdings absorbed by general library.

★13857★
SYRACUSE UNIVERSITY - GEOLOGY LIBRARY (Sci-Engr)
300 Heroy Geology Lab Phone: (315)423-3337
Syracuse, NY 13244-1070 Eileen Snyder, Libn.
Subjects: Geology, economic geology, geomorphology, geophysics, geochemistry. **Holdings:** 27,343 volumes. **Subscriptions:** 195 journals. **Services:** Interlibrary loan; copying; library open to the public with restrictions. **Automated Operations:** Computerized cataloging, acquisitions, and circulation. **Computerized Information Services:** OCLC; SULIRS (internal database). **Networks/Consortia:** Member of SUNY/OCLC Library Network.

★13858★
SYRACUSE UNIVERSITY - GEORGE ARENTS RESEARCH LIBRARY FOR SPECIAL COLLECTIONS (Rare Book)
E.S. Bird Library Phone: (315)423-2585
Syracuse, NY 13244-2010 Amy S. Doherty, Act.Hd./Univ.Archv.
Staff: Prof 7; Other 14. **Subjects:** Rare books, manuscripts, audio archives, university archives. **Holdings:** RARE BOOKS (120,000 volumes) - general collection of 15th-18th century imprints; early American imprints; finely printed and privately printed books; finely illustrated books; fine bindings; 19th and 20th century literature collections arranged by author; Spire Collection on Loyalists in the American Revolution; Novotny Library of Economic History; Stephen Crane Collection; William Hobart-Royce Balzac Collection; Mayfield Library; Leopold von Ranke Library. MANUSCRIPTS (30,000 linear feet) - Art (papers of artists, cartoonists, industrial designers, photographers, sculptors, architects); Business History (corporate records of various types of companies including forest industries, public utilities, publishing, printing, transportation, banking, voluntary associations, manufacturing); Government and Public Administration (papers of federal administrators, diplomats and military officers, federal and state judicial officers, state governors, department heads and administrators, federal legislators, and statesmen); American Literature (papers of nonfiction authors, novelists, poets, playwrights, dramatists, historians, literary critics); Science Fiction (papers of science fiction writers, anthologists, and publishers as well as documents related to societies, international meetings, science fiction art, radio and television programs, and fantasy literature); Mass Communications (news photography, periodical and newspaper administration, editing and reporting, news commentators and columnists, foreign correspondents, personalities in music, entertainment, radio, and television); Religion and Theology (papers of philosophers, missionaries, theologians, Christian church administrators, and clergy); Social Science (documents relating to American military and naval history, local history, law, education, families, philanthropy, economics, explorations); Adult Education (papers of prominent adult educators and researchers and corporate records of international adult educational organizations). AUDIO ARCHIVES (250,000 recordings) - first eighty years of commercial sound recordings from the earliest of the Thomas Edison cylinder recordings to the most modern audiotapes; sound recordings of political leaders, poets, actresses, singers; transcriptions of audio broadcastings, musical and theatrical performances, folk music, and contemporary compositions of the 20th century. UNIVERSITY ARCHIVES (10,500 linear feet) - history and development of Syracuse University; all relevant books, pamphlets, photographs, manuscripts; records of university faculty and staff; semiofficial papers of university life such as student publications, records of students clubs and organizations, files relating to student classes and activities, papers of faculty members; administrative records of university schools, colleges, offices, and other units; records of university governing boards including Board of Trustees, University Senate, Board of Graduate Studies, and records of students groups. **Services:** Copying; library open to the public with restrictions. **Automated Operations:** Computerized cataloging. **Computerized Information Services:** RLIN, OCLC. **Networks/Consortia:** Member of SUNY/OCLC Library Network, RLG. **Staff:** Mark F. Weimer, Rare Bk.Libn.; Carolyn A. Davis, Mss.Libn.; Terrance Keenan, Adult Educ.Mss.Libn.; Lydia Wasylenko, Cat.Libn.; William Storm, Dir., Audio Archv.; Walter L. Welch, Audio Archv.Cur..

★13859★
SYRACUSE UNIVERSITY - H. DOUGLAS BARCLAY LAW LIBRARY (Law)
College of Law Phone: (315)423-2527
Syracuse, NY 13244-1030 David L. Naylor, Act.Dir.
Founded: 1899. **Staff:** Prof 5; Other 9. **Subjects:** Law - Anglo-American, tax, criminal, New York State. **Special Collections:** Depository for U.S. Government documents. **Holdings:** 147,000 volumes; 50,000 microforms. **Subscriptions:** 1150 journals and other serials; 15 newspapers. **Services:** Interlibrary loan; copying; library open to the public. **Automated Operations:** Computerized cataloging and circulation. **Computerized Information Services:** LEXIS, WESTLAW, OCLC, NEXIS; SULIRS (internal database). **Networks/Consortia:** Member of SUNY/OCLC Library Network. **Staff:** Brenda B. Adams, Assoc.Libn./Cat.; M. Louise Lantzy, Assoc.Libn./Coll.Dev.; Janet Fleckenstein, Sr.Asst.Libn./Circ..

★13860★
SYRACUSE UNIVERSITY - MATHEMATICS LIBRARY (Sci-Engr)
308 Carnegie Bldg. Phone: (315)423-2092
Syracuse, NY 13244-2010 Mary DeCarlo, Libn.
Staff: Prof 1; Other 1. **Subjects:** Mathematics, history of mathematics, mathematical statistics, logic, algebra, numerical analysis, combinatorics, topology. **Special Collections:** Russian journals (translated). **Holdings:** 20,493 books; 15,895 bound periodical volumes; 1400 reports. **Subscriptions:** 341 journals. **Services:** Interlibrary loan; library open to the public with restrictions. **Automated Operations:** Computerized cataloging, acquisitions, and circulation. **Computerized Information Services:** OCLC; SULIRS (internal database) **Networks/Consortia:** Member of SUNY/OCLC Library Network.

★13861★
SYRACUSE UNIVERSITY - PHYSICS LIBRARY (Sci-Engr)
208 Physics Bldg. Phone: (315)423-2692
Syracuse, NY 13244-1070 Eileen Snyder, Libn.
Staff: Prof 1; Other 1. **Subjects:** Physics, astronomy. **Holdings:** 23,804 volumes. **Subscriptions:** 234 journals. **Services:** Interlibrary loan; copying; library open to the public. **Automated Operations:** Computerized cataloging, acquisitions and circulation. **Computerized Information Services:** OCLC. **Networks/Consortia:** Member of SUNY/OCLC Library Network.

★13862★
SYRACUSE UNIVERSITY - SCHOOL OF EDUCATION - EDUCATIONAL RESOURCE CENTER (Educ)
150 Marshall St. Phone: (315)423-3800
Syracuse, NY 13210 Dr. Tom Rusk Vickery, Dir.
Staff: Prof 5; Other 10. **Subjects:** Education. **Special Collections:** Diagnostic tests for school psychologists; collection of public school textbooks; children's books. **Holdings:** 19,000 books; multimedia material; curriculum material on microfiche; AV and production equipment; complete ERIC microfiche collection. **Services:** Center open to students and faculty.

★13863★
SYRACUSE UNIVERSITY - SCIENCE AND TECHNOLOGY LIBRARY (Biol Sci, Sci-Engr, Med)
105 Carnegie Phone: (315)423-2160
Syracuse, NY 13244-2010 Lee M. Murray, Act.Hd., Sci. & Tech.Dept.
Staff: Prof 4; Other 6. **Subjects:** Engineering - chemical, civil, electrical, industrial, mechanical; computers and data processing; biology; botany; zoology; microbiology; biochemistry; chemistry; immunology; genetics; ecology; public health; general medicine; medicine and society; nursing; neuroscience; psychiatry; general science and technology; history and philosophy of science; nutrition; mining and metallurgy; physical geography. **Special Collections:** Reports on microform from Atomic Energy Commission (AEC), Energy Research and Development Administration (ERDA), DOE, NASA, and Society of Automotive Engineers (SAE). **Holdings:** 190,000 books and bound periodical volumes; 700,000 microforms. **Subscriptions:** 2100 journals and other serials. **Services:** Interlibrary loan; copying; library open to the public. **Automated Operations:** Computerized cataloging, acquisitions, serials, and circulation. **Computerized Information Services:** DIALOG Information Services, BRS

Information Technologies, WILSONLINE, OCLC; SULIRS (internal database). **Networks/Consortia:** Member of SUNY/OCLC Library Network. **Staff:** Lockhart Russell, Engr.Libn.; Nancy Herrington, Ref.Libn.; H. Thomas Keays, Chem.Libn..

★13864★
SYSTEM PLANNING CORPORATION - TECHNICAL LIBRARY (Mil, Comp Sci)
1500 Wilson Blvd.
Arlington, VA 22209 — Phyllis W. Moon, Mgr.
Staff: Prof 2; Other 2. **Subjects:** Military science, international relations, computer science, radar. **Holdings:** 30,000 books. **Subscriptions:** 225 journals and other serials. **Services:** Interlibrary loan; library not open to the public. **Automated Operations:** Computerized cataloging. **Computerized Information Services:** DTIC, DIALOG Information Services, DMS/ONLINE. **Staff:** Barbara A. Mack, ILL Libn.; Helena Pitsvada, Libn..

★13865★
SYSTEMATICS GENERAL CORPORATION - LIBRARY
1606 Old Ox Rd.
Box 28
Sterling, VA 22170
Defunct

★13866★
SYSTEMS APPLICATIONS, INC. - LIBRARY (Sci-Engr)
101 Lucas Valley Rd. — Phone: (415)472-4011
San Rafael, CA 94903 — Janet McDonald, Libn./Info.Spec.
Founded: 1975. **Staff:** Prof 1. **Subjects:** Air quality, meteorology, computer modeling. **Holdings:** 2000 books; 8000 technical reports. **Subscriptions:** 150 journals and other serials. **Services:** Interlibrary loan; copying; SDI; library open to the public by appointment. **Automated Operations:** Computerized cataloging. **Computerized Information Services:** DIALOG Information Services, NLM; internal database. Performs searches on fee basis. **Publications:** Acquisition list, irregular - for internal distribution only.

★13867★
SYSTEMS CONTROL INC. - TECHNICAL LIBRARY (Comp Sci)
1801 Page Mill Rd.
Box 10025 — Phone: (408)494-1165
Palo Alto, CA 94303 — Martha Liles, Libn.
Staff: Prof 1. **Subjects:** Computer software. **Holdings:** Figures not available. **Services:** Interlibrary loan; library open to the public with approval of librarian. **Computerized Information Services:** DIALOG Information Services.

★13868★
SYVA COMPANY - LIBRARY/INFORMATION CENTER (Biol Sci, Med)
900 Arastradero Rd.
Box 10058 — Phone: (415)493-2200
Palo Alto, CA 94303 — Louise Lohr, Mgr.
Founded: 1966. **Staff:** Prof 4; Other 4. **Subjects:** Organic chemistry, biochemistry, microbiology, medicine. **Holdings:** 6000 books. **Subscriptions:** 300 journals and other serials. **Services:** Interlibrary loan; library not open to the public. **Computerized Information Services:** DIALOG Information Services, Pergamon ORBIT InfoLine, Inc., BRS Information Technologies, Telesystemes Questel, OCLC, CAS ONLINE. **Networks/Consortia:** Member of CLASS. **Staff:** Paul S. Hanson, Tech.Info.Spec.; Kim Kubik, Tech.Info.Spec.; Meaghan Wheeler, Supv., Tech.Serv..

T

★13869★
TABOR OPERA HOUSE - LIBRARY
815 Harrison Ave.
Leadville, CO 80461
Founded: 1955. **Subjects:** History of Leadville, Colorado, Tabor Opera House history, Colorado history, paintings. **Remarks:** Presently inactive.

★13870★
TACKAPAUSHA MUSEUM - LIBRARY (Biol Sci)
Washington Ave. Phone: (516)785-2802
Seaford, NY 11783 Richard D. Ryder, Cur.
Staff: 2. **Subjects:** Natural history, zoology, botany, ornithology, mammalogy, herpetology. **Holdings:** 1100 books. **Subscriptions:** 10 journals and other serials. **Services:** Library open for reference use by appointment. **Remarks:** Maintained by Nassau County Department of Recreation and Parks.

★13871★
TACOMA ART MUSEUM - LIBRARY (Art)
12th & Pacific Ave. Phone: (206)272-4258
Tacoma, WA 98402 Sally Norris, Libn.
Staff: 2. **Subjects:** Art. **Special Collections:** The Constance Lyon Collection of Japanese prints. **Holdings:** 1780 books; 5 vertical files. **Subscriptions:** 38 journals and other serials. **Services:** Copying; library open to the public for reference use only.

★13872★
(Tacoma) MORNING NEWS TRIBUNE - LIBRARY (Publ)
Box 11000 Phone: (206)597-8626
Tacoma, WA 98411 Pilaivan H. Britton, Libn.
Founded: 1955. **Staff:** Prof 1; Other 2. **Subjects:** Newspaper reference topics. **Holdings:** 500 books; newspaper clippings; 5 VF drawers of pamphlets; 250 maps; News Tribune, 1909 to present, on microfilm. **Subscriptions:** 80 journals and other serials; 40 newspapers. **Services:** Library not open to the public. **Automated Operations:** Computerized acquisitions and serials. **Computerized Information Services:** DataTimes. **Special Indexes:** Roll Microfilm Index (book, online); Index to News Tribune (book, online); index to negatives (book); subject thesauri to files (book, online).

★13873★
TACOMA PUBLIC LIBRARY - SPECIAL COLLECTIONS (Hist)
1102 Tacoma Ave., S. Phone: (206)591-5622
Tacoma, WA 98402 Kevin Hegarty, Dir.
Staff: Prof 2; Other 1. **Subjects:** Pacific Northwest and Washington state history. **Special Collections:** Genealogy and local history; John B. Kaiser Collection (World War I posters and propaganda; 2000 volumes); Civil War and Abraham Lincoln (3000 volumes). **Holdings:** 25,000 books; 2000 bound periodical volumes; 20,000 photographs and photographic negatives; 900 linear feet of manuscripts; 750 linear feet of local government archives; 15,000 slides; 35,000 maps; 80 VF drawers of clippings. **Subscriptions:** 40 journals and other serials. **Services:** Interlibrary loan; copying; collections open to the public. **Automated Operations:** Computerized cataloging, acquisitions, and circulation. **Computerized Information Services:** DIALOG Information Services, DataTimes, OCLC. **Special Indexes:** Northwest Note File (200,000 cards); Northwest Biography File (75,000 cards); Calendars of Manuscripts. **Staff:** Gary Fuller Reese, Mng.Libn..

LORADO TAFT ARCHIVES
See: Northern Illinois University - Taft Field Campus - Instructional Materials Center (10424)

★13874★
TAFT MUSEUM - LIBRARY (Art)
316 Pike St. Phone: (513)241-0343
Cincinnati, OH 45202 David T. Johnson, Reg.
Founded: 1932. **Staff:** 1. **Subjects:** Art, historical buildings, museology. **Holdings:** 1200 books; 900 bound periodical volumes; 800 slides of permanent art collections. **Subscriptions:** 10 journals and other serials. **Services:** Copying; library open to the public by appointment for reference use only. **Special Catalogs:** Taft Art Collection handbook; special exhibition catalogs. **Remarks:** Maintained by Cincinnati Institute of Fine Arts.

★13875★
TAFT, STETTINIUS & HOLLISTER - LAW LIBRARY (Law)
First National Bank Center Phone: (513)381-2838
Cincinnati, OH 45202 Barbara Flanagan, Libn.
Staff: Prof 1; Other 3. **Subjects:** Law. **Holdings:** 25,000 volumes. **Services:** Library not open to the public. **Computerized Information Services:** LEXIS, WESTLAW, DIALOG Information Services. **Publications:** Newsletter - for internal distribution only.

WILLIAM HOWARD TAFT NATIONAL HISTORIC SITE
See: U.S. Natl. Park Service (15362)

JAY P. TAGGART MEMORIAL LAW LIBRARY
See: Ohio Northern University - College of Law (10657)

★13876★
TALBOT ASSOCIATES, INC. - LIBRARY (Sci-Engr)
11 Cleveland Place Phone: (201)376-9570
Springfield, NJ 07081 Duncan A. Talbot, Jr., Pres.
Founded: 1954. **Subjects:** Metal casting, alloys. **Holdings:** References files; cross references; specifications.

★13877★
TALBOT COUNTY FREE LIBRARY - MARYLAND ROOM (Hum, Hist)
100 W. Dover St. Phone: (301)822-1626
Easton, MD 21601 Miss Scotti Oliver, Cur.
Subjects: History - local and state, with emphasis on Talbot County and other locations on the eastern shore; genealogy. **Special Collections:** H.L. Mencken (80 volumes); manuscripts and notes for James Michener's Chesapeake (25 boxes); manuscript of Dickson Preston's Young Frederick Douglass (1 box); manuscripts and notes for L.G. Shreve's Tench Tilghman, the Life and Times of Washington's Aide-de-Camp (3 boxes); history of the Society of Friends, 1773 to present (50 volumes); Lloyd Family papers (41 reels of microfilm); Maryland Colonial Society papers (31 reels of microfilm); Charles Carroll papers (3 reels of microfilm); Talbot County Register of Deaths, 1930-1969 (13 reels of microfilm). **Holdings:** 4000 books; unbound periodicals; 16 VF drawers; 63 boxes of manuscripts and ephemera; 84 boxes and bound volumes of newspapers; 96 reels of microfilm of newspapers; 32 reels of microfilm of census data; 30 reels of microfilm of church records; 6 reels of microfilm of tax lists; 2 reels of microfilm of dissertations. **Subscriptions:** 37 journals and other serials. **Services:** Copying; room open to the public for reference use only. **Special Catalogs:** Catalog of subject headings (card); catalog to manuscript and ephemera collection (card); catalog of microfilm, newspapers, and maps.

TALBOT RESEARCH LIBRARY
See: Institute for Cancer Research - Talbot Research Library (6887)

TALBOTT LIBRARY
See: Westminster Choir College - Talbott Library (17783)

★13878★
TALL TIMBERS RESEARCH STATION - LIBRARY (Biol Sci, Env-Cons)
Rte. 1, Box 678 Phone: (904)893-4153
Tallahassee, FL 32312 Sharri Moroshok, Libn.
Staff: Prof 1. **Subjects:** Fire ecology, wildlife management, ornithology, earthworms, plant and general ecology, forestry. **Special Collections:** Dr. Gordon E. Gates collection (earthworms; 5000 reprints); E.V. Komarek Fire File (fire ecology; 20,000 reprints and monographs). **Holdings:** 2300 books; 2900 bound periodical volumes; 7000 reprints; 10,000 state, federal, and international documents; 5 VF drawers of scientific research data; 150 maps. **Subscriptions:** 240 journals and other serials. **Services:** Interlibrary loan (limited); copying; library open to the public by appointment. **Automated Operations:** Computerized cataloging. **Computerized Information Services:** Internal database. Performs searches on fee basis.

★13879★
TALLADEGA COLLEGE - HISTORICAL COLLECTIONS (Area-Ethnic, Hist)
627 W. Battle St.
Talladega, AL 35160 Phone: (205)362-0206
Subjects: American blacks; missions in Angola, Mozambique, Zaire, and South Africa; the black church; civil rights; education. **Special Collections:** College archives (includes the activities of Talladega alumni); Historical Collections (the black church, African missions, southern Africa, civil rights, education). **Holdings:** 120 linear feet of archival items. **Services:** Copying; collections open to serious researchers and noncampus undergraduates with letter from supervising faculty. **Publications:** A Guide

to the Archives of Talladega College, 1981; A Guide to the Collections, 1981.

★13880★
TALLADEGA COUNTY LAW LIBRARY (Law)
Judicial Bldg.
Northeast St. Phone: (205)362-2050
Talladega, AL 35160 Franklin Self, Law Libn.
Founded: 1951. **Staff:** Prof 1; Other 2. **Subjects:** Law. **Holdings:** 20,000 books; 3000 bound periodical volumes; 2000 pamphlets and documents. **Subscriptions:** 100 journals and other serials. **Services:** Copying; library open to the public for research only.

★13881★
TALLMADGE HISTORICAL SOCIETY - LIBRARY & ARCHIVES (Hist)
One Tallmadge Circle
Box 25 Phone: (216)633-2217
Tallmadge, OH 44278 Richard L. Smith, Pres.
Founded: 1858. **Staff:** 1. **Subjects:** History - Tallmadge, Summit County, Ohio. **Holdings:** Figures not available. **Services:** Library open to the public by appointment.

TAMBURITZANS CULTURAL CENTER
See: Duquesne University - Institute of Folk Arts (4458)

TAMIMENT LIBRARY
See: New York University - Tamiment Library (10182)

LT. DAVID TAMIR LIBRARY AND READING ROOM
See: Consulate General of Israel (3701)

★13882★
TAMPA BAY REGIONAL INFORMATION CENTER (Plan)
9455 Koger Blvd., Suite 206 Phone: (813)577-5151
St. Petersburg, FL 33702 Claudia R. Ward, Libn.
Founded: 1962. **Staff:** Prof 1; Other 2. **Subjects:** Urban and regional planning, land use, energy, housing, human resources, transportation, environment. **Special Collections:** Local and regional comprehensive plans; environmental impact statements; development of regional impacts; U.S. Census data; aging. **Holdings:** 6000 books and technical documents; 400 maps. **Subscriptions:** 107 journals and other serials. **Services:** Library open to the public. **Networks/Consortia:** Member of Tampa Bay Library Consortium, Inc.. **Publications:** Bay Bulletin, monthly; Regional Review; technical plans.

★13883★
TAMPA ELECTRIC COMPANY - TECHNICAL REFERENCE CENTER (Energy)
702 N. Franklin St. Phone: (813)228-1205
Tampa, FL 33602 Patricia W. Boody, Supv., Lib.Serv.
Founded: 1982. **Staff:** Prof 1; Other 2. **Subjects:** Electric power generation, energy, environment, business and economics, management, data processing. **Holdings:** 1500 books; unbound periodicals; 2000 documents; 2500 microfiche; 680 computer manuals. **Subscriptions:** 450 journals and other serials; 15 newspapers. **Services:** Interlibrary loan; copying; SDI; center open to the public. **Automated Operations:** Computerized cataloging, serials, and circulation. **Computerized Information Services:** DIALOG Information Services, The Source Information Network, Dun & Bradstreet Corporation, LEXIS, NEXIS, VU/TEXT Information Services; SourceMail (electronic mail service). **Networks/Consortia:** Member of Tampa Bay Library Consortium, Inc..

★13884★
TAMPA GENERAL HOSPITAL - MEDICAL LIBRARY (Med)
Davis Islands
Box 1289 Phone: (813)251-7328
Tampa, FL 33601 Loretta Holliday, Dir.
Founded: 1961. **Staff:** Prof 3. **Subjects:** Medicine, otorhinolaryngology, pediatrics, obstetrics, gynecology, surgery, clinical medicine. **Special Collections:** Audio-Digest tapes on surgery, pediatrics, internal medicine, anesthesia, otolaryngology (750 tapes); Network for Continuing Medical Education tapes. **Holdings:** 3100 books; 3600 bound periodical volumes; 12 drawers of microfiche. **Subscriptions:** 273 journals and other serials. **Services:** Interlibrary loan; copying; SDI; library open to the public with authorization from administration. **Computerized Information Services:** MEDLINE, DIALOG Information Services; OnTyme Electronic Message Network Service (electronic mail service). Performs searches on fee basis. **Networks/Consortia:** Member of Tampa Bay Medical Library Network. **Publications:** TGH Medical Library Newsletter, quarterly - to medical staff. **Staff:** Kathleen Everall, Libn.; George Benettini, Lib.Techn..

★13885★
TAMPA TRIBUNE & TAMPA TIMES - LIBRARY (Publ)
202 S. Parker St. Phone: (813)272-7665
Tampa, FL 33601 Louise N. LeGette, Chf.Libn.
Founded: 1895. **Staff:** Prof 12; Other 5. **Subjects:** Newspaper reference topics. **Holdings:** 2500 volumes; clippings; pamphlets; pictures; microfilm; reference books. **Services:** Library open to newspaper personnel only. **Staff:** Thomas Banks, Asst.Libn..

★13886★
TAMS ENGINEERS, ARCHITECTS & PLANNERS - LIBRARY
655 Third Ave.
New York, NY 10017
Founded: 1950. **Subjects:** Civil engineering, soil mechanics, water resources, traffic engineering, architecture, environmental planning, socioeconomics. **Holdings:** 6500 books; 300 bound periodical volumes; 3000 company reports; 3 VF drawers of pamphlets. **Remarks:** Presently inactive.

TAMS-WITMARK ARCHIVES
See: Princeton University - William Seymour Theatre Collection (11595)

★13887★
TANDEM COMPUTERS, INC. - CORPORATE INFORMATION CENTER (Comp Sci)
19333 Vallco Pkwy., 3-07 Phone: (408)725-6000
Cupertino, CA 95014 Selma Zinker, Corp.Libn.
Staff: Prof 3; Other 3. **Subjects:** Computer science, data processing, computer programming, communications, marketing, business. **Holdings:** 7000 books; 3000 research reports; 2000 microfiche; 600 technical reports. **Subscriptions:** 325 journals and other serials; 13 newspapers. **Services:** Interlibrary loan; center not open to the public. **Automated Operations:** Computerized cataloging. **Computerized Information Services:** DIALOG Information Services, RLIN, The Source Information Network, VU/TEXT Information Services, Dow Jones News/Retrieval, OCLC, NEXIS, NewsNet, Inc. **Networks/Consortia:** Member of CLASS. **Staff:** Jane Differding, Ref.Libn.; Barbara Nepple, Asst.Libn..

Z.T. TANG MEDICAL LIBRARY
See: Westerly Hospital (17692)

TANGENT GROUP - HOMOSEXUAL INFORMATION CENTER
See: Homosexual Information Center - Tangent Group (6425)

TANNER MEMORIAL PHILOSOPHY LIBRARY
See: Stanford University (13623)

★13888★
TAPPI INFORMATION RESOURCE CENTER (Sci-Engr)
Box 105113
Atlanta, GA 30348 Phone: (404)446-1400
Founded: 1915. **Staff:** Prof 2; Other 2. **Subjects:** Pulp, paper, packaging, and allied subjects. **Holdings:** 2400 books; 1500 bound periodical volumes. **Subscriptions:** 170 journals and other serials. **Services:** Copying; technical inquiries; center open to the public. **Automated Operations:** Computerized cataloging and serials. **Computerized Information Services:** DIALOG Information Services, Pergamon ORBIT InfoLine, Inc.; internal database; ALANET (electronic mail service). Performs searches on fee basis. **Staff:** D. Gail Stahl, Info.Rsrcs.Coord..

TARLTON LAW LIBRARY
See: University of Texas, Austin - School of Law (16942)

★13889★
TARRANT COUNTY LAW LIBRARY (Law)
420 Courthouse Phone: (817)334-1481
Fort Worth, TX 76196 Frances Perry, Law Libn.
Founded: 1945. **Staff:** Prof 3; Other 2. **Subjects:** Law. **Holdings:** 27,000 books; 1050 bound periodical volumes; 580 cassette tapes. **Subscriptions:** 200 journals and other serials. **Services:** Interlibrary loan; copying (limited); library open to the public for reference use only. **Special Indexes:** Index of Texas Law Review Articles.

★13890★
BEN TAUB GENERAL HOSPITAL - DOCTOR'S MEDICAL LIBRARY (Med)
1502 Taub Loop Phone: (713)791-7441
Houston, TX 77030 Angie Ortiz, Lib.Ck.
Founded: 1958. **Staff:** 1. **Subjects:** Medicine. **Holdings:** 1100 books; 110 bound periodical volumes; 12 VF drawers. **Subscriptions:** 110 journals and other serials; 8 newspapers. **Services:** Library not open to the public. **Automated Operations:** Computerized cataloging and acquisitions.

ALFRED TAUBMAN MEDICAL LIBRARY
See: University of Michigan (16411)

★13891★
TAUNTON STATE HOSPITAL - MEDICAL LIBRARY (Med)
60 Hodges Ave.
Box 151
Taunton, MA 02780 Phone: (508)824-7551
Staff: 1. **Subjects:** Psychiatry, psychology, medicine, social science. **Holdings:** 909 books; 1516 bound periodical volumes. **Subscriptions:** 81 journals and other serials; 10 newspapers. **Services:** Interlibrary loan; copying; library open to the public for reference and overnight loan. **Networks/Consortia:** Member of Southeastern Massachusetts Consortium of Health Science Libraries (SEMCO).

TAX COURT OF CANADA
See: Canada - Tax Court of Canada (2496)

★13892★
TAX EXECUTIVES INSTITUTE, INC. - LIBRARY (Bus-Fin)
1001 Pennsylvania Ave., N.W., Suite 320
Washington, DC 20004-2505 Thomas P. Kerester, Exec.Dir.
Founded: 1944. **Staff:** Prof 4; Other 5. **Subjects:** Taxation; tax - legislation, administration, management. **Holdings:** 1000 books; 500 professional memoranda. **Subscriptions:** 20 journals and other serials. **Services:** Library open to TEI members upon written request.

★13893★
TAX FOUNDATION - LIBRARY (Bus-Fin)
One Thomas Circle, N.W., Suite 500 Phone: (202)822-9050
Washington, DC 20005 Marion B. Marshall, Res.Libn.
Founded: 1937. **Staff:** Prof 1; Other 1. **Subjects:** Taxation, public finance, economics. **Special Collections:** Annual reports of the Secretary of the Treasury, 1852-1980; proceedings of the National Tax Association, 1907 to present; state tax studies. **Holdings:** 16,500 books; 85 VF drawers of clippings, documents, and pamphlets. **Subscriptions:** 200 journals and other serials. **Services:** Interlibrary loan; copying; library open to the public. **Publications:** Library Bulletin, quarterly.

ABBOT VINCENT TAYLOR LIBRARY
See: Belmont Abbey College (1495)

★13894★
BAYARD TAYLOR MEMORIAL LIBRARY (Art, Rare Book)
216 E. State St. Phone: (215)444-2702
Kennett Square, PA 19348 Joseph A. Lordi, Dir.
Founded: 1895. **Staff:** Prof 1; Other 5. **Subjects:** Antiques, arts, social sciences, history, gardening. **Special Collections:** Harlan R. Cole Memorial Collection (reference collection on antiques); Bayard Taylor Collection (pre-1900 rare books); Pennsylvania Collection (local history); Rare Books of the Union Library Company of Kennett Square (pre-1896); Botanica Collection of Trees, Shrubs and Wildflowers. **Holdings:** 45,000 books; 4 VF drawers of pamphlets, clippings, local history materials, maps. **Subscriptions:** 150 journals and other serials; 8 newspapers. **Services:** Interlibrary loan; copying; library open to the public.

★13895★
TAYLOR BUSINESS INSTITUTE - HELEN RICKSON LIBRARY (Bus-Fin)
One Penn Plaza Phone: (212)947-6677
New York, NY 101019 Mary E. Cardwell, Libn.
Founded: 1973. **Staff:** Prof 1. **Subjects:** Business, secretarial studies, accounting, travel and tourism, electronics. **Holdings:** 3478 books; 13 VF drawers; 48 video cassettes. **Subscriptions:** 88 journals and other serials. **Services:** Library not open to the public. **Publications:** New Books in the Library -

★13896★
DAVID TAYLOR RESEARCH CENTER - TECHNICAL INFORMATION CENTER (Sci-Engr)
Code 5220 Phone: (202)227-1309
Bethesda, MD 20084-5000 Dr. Michael Dankewych, Libn.
Subjects: Naval architecture; hydromechanics; structural mechanics; acoustics and vibration; mathematics; underwater ballistics; pure and applied physics; engineering - marine, electrical, mechanical, civil; environmental protection and safety; fabrication technology; energy; aerodynamics. **Special Collections:** DTNSRDC reports. **Holdings:** 35,000 books; 18,000 bound periodical volumes; 100,000 technical reports; 23,000 classified documents; 280,000 microfiche. **Subscriptions:** 900 journals and other serials. **Services:** Interlibrary loan (to other government agencies); copying; SDI; center is open for staff use only and for other government employees by special arrangement. **Automated Operations:** Computerized cataloging, serials, and circulation. **Computerized Information Services:** DIALOG Information Services, Institute for Scientific Information (ISI), Integrated Technical Information System (ITIS), DTIC, NASA/RECON, BRS Information Technologies, Pergamon ORBIT InfoLine, Inc. **Publications:** Accession Bulletin, biweekly - for internal distribution only. **Special Indexes:** DTNSRDC Report index. **Formerly:** U.S. Navy - David W. Taylor Naval Ship Research and Development Center. **Staff:** Alvetta D. Smythe, Hd., Annapolis TIC; Margaret Holland, Ref.Libn..

EDWARD P. TAYLOR AUDIO-VISUAL CENTRE
See: Art Gallery of Ontario (957)

EDWARD P. TAYLOR REFERENCE LIBRARY
See: Art Gallery of Ontario (958)

ELIZABETH PREWITT TAYLOR MEMORIAL LIBRARY
See: Arkansas Arts Center (914)

FREDERICK W. TAYLOR ARCHIVES
See: Hive Publishing Company - John Franklin Mee Memorial Library (6362)

IRA J. TAYLOR LIBRARY
See: Iliff School of Theology (6683)

★13897★
MOSES TAYLOR HOSPITAL - LIBRARY (Med)
745 Quincy Ave. Phone: (717)963-2145
Scranton, PA 18510 Jo-Ann M. Babish, Dir., Lib.Serv.
Staff: Prof 1; Other 1. **Subjects:** Medicine, health administration, nursing. **Holdings:** 1200 books; journals on microfilm. **Subscriptions:** 250 journals and other serials. **Services:** Interlibrary loan; copying; SDI; library open to the public with restrictions. **Computerized Information Services:** DIALOG Information Services, MEDLARS. **Networks/Consortia:** Member of Health Information Library Network of Northeastern Pennsylvania (HILNNEP).

TAYLOR MUSEUM LIBRARY
See: Colorado Springs Fine Arts Center - Reference Library and Taylor Museum Library (3416)

ROBERT H. TAYLOR LIBRARY
See: Princeton University - Rare Books and Special Collections (11593)

STANLEY TAYLOR SOCIOLOGY READING ROOM
See: University of Alberta (15807)

★13898★
TAYLOR UNIVERSITY - ZONDERVAN LIBRARY - ARCHIVES/SPECIAL COLLECTIONS (Rel-Phil)
Upland, IN 46989 Phone: (317)998-5520
Staff: Prof 1. **Subjects:** Protestant theology. **Special Collections:** Hillis congressional papers; Wesley materials; African, Oriental, and rare book collections; rare historical documents. **Holdings:** 1000 books. **Services:** Copying; collections open to the public. **Automated Operations:** Computerized cataloging. **Computerized Information Services:** DIALOG Information Services. Performs searches on fee basis. Contact Person: Roger Phillips. **Networks/Consortia:** Member of INCOLSA.

★13899★
TDS HEALTHCARE SYSTEMS CORPORATION - TECHNICAL LIBRARY (Med, Comp Sci)
3255-1 Scott Blvd. Phone: (408)727-9400
Santa Clara, CA 95051 Margaret Yesso Watson, Libn.
Founded: 1982. **Staff:** Prof 1; Other 1. **Subjects:** Hospital information systems, physicians and computers. **Special Collections:** Federal Information Processing Standards (FIPS) publications (complete set). **Holdings:** 1300 books; 74 bound periodical volumes; 50 other cataloged items. **Subscriptions:** 78 journals and other serials. **Services:** Interlibrary loan; copying; SDI; library open to the public by appointment. **Computerized Information Services:** DIALOG Information Services, VU/TEXT Information Services. **Networks/Consortia:** Member of CLASS, South Bay Cooperative Library System (SBCLS). **Formerly:** Technicon Data Systems.

★13900★
TEACHERS COLLEGE - MILBANK MEMORIAL LIBRARY (Educ)
Columbia University
DB, Box 307 Phone: (212)678-3494
New York, NY 10027 Jane P. Franck, Dir.
Founded: 1887. **Staff:** Prof 30; Other 16. **Subjects:** Education, psychology, speech pathology and audiology, nursing education, communications, computers and learning technology, nutrition and allied subjects. **Special Collections:** Darton Collection (early English children's books); Annie E. Moore Collection (illustrated children's literature); chapbook collection; U.S. and foreign elementary and secondary school textbooks; rare books on education, 15th-19th centuries; Adelaide Nutting Collection (history of nursing); Teachers College Archives (administrative records, papers of faculty members, and related materials); Archives of the Board of Education of the City of New York (printed records; manuscripts; photographs); records of the National Kindergarten Association; National Council for the Social Studies; New York Juvenile Asylum. **Holdings:** 424,369 volumes; 343,812 microforms; 5961 AV programs and nonprint materials; 3715 cubic feet of manuscript material; 75,000 photographs; 68,612 titles in microform; 1170 software programs. **Subscriptions:** 2180 journals and other serials. **Services:** Interlibrary loan; library open to the public with special permits. **Computerized Information Services:** DIALOG Information Services, BRS Information Technologies, OCLC, RLIN, ERIC. **Networks/Consortia:** Member of RLG, New York State Interlibrary Loan Network (NYSILL). **Publications:** Circulation and Borrowing Information; ILL Guide; Online Search Services; Special Collections; Photocopy Services; Resource Center; New Titles. **Staff:** Donna Barkman, Asst.Dir./Chf., Coll.Dev.Serv.; Maureen Horgan, Plan.Coord.; David Ment, Hd., Spec.Coll.; Kathleen Murphy, Hd., Access; Allen Foresta, Hd., Ref.Serv.; B. Woodburn McRae, Ser.Cat.; Sergio Gaitan; Patrick Casey, Hd., Microcomputer Rsrc.Ctr.; Cecile Hastie, Ref.Libn.; Yodit Kebede, Hd., Bibliog.Acq.; Anita Lauer, Hd., Bibliog. Control; Jennifer Whitten, Res.Libn.; Amy Farber, Hd., Cat.Maint.; Nora Ligorano, Cons.; Virginia Buchan, Cons.; Bette Weneck, Mss.Cur.; Daniel P. Walsh, Res.Libn.; Minoo Gharai, Bibliog.; Richard Gibboney, Ref. Intern; Rohinie Munzel, Asst.Archv.; VaNee Van Vleck, Acq. Intern; Lily Wu, Non-Print Cat.; Frank Webster, Hd., Bibliog.Tech..

★13901★
TEACHERS OF ENGLISH TO SPEAKERS OF OTHER LANGUAGES - TESOL LENDING LIBRARY
1118 22nd St., N.W., Suite 205
Washington, DC 20037
Defunct

★13902★
TEACHERS INSURANCE AND ANNUITY ASSOCIATION OF AMERICA - BUSINESS LIBRARY (Bus-Fin)
730 Third Ave. Phone: (212)490-9000
New York, NY 10017 Kathleen Kelleher, Libn.
Founded: 1959. **Staff:** Prof 2; Other 3. **Subjects:** Insurance, pensions and annuities, law, investment, higher education, old age. **Special Collections:** Carnegie Foundation reports. **Holdings:** 8000 books; 382 reels of microfilm; 45 VF drawers. **Subscriptions:** 420 journals and other serials; 12 newspapers. **Services:** Interlibrary loan; library open to SLA members by appointment only. **Automated Operations:** Computerized serials. **Computerized Information Services:** DIALOG Information Services. **Staff:** Mary-Lynne Bancone, Asst.Libn..

TEACHOUT-PRICE MEMORIAL LIBRARY
See: Hiram College (6313)

EDWIN WAY TEALE ARCHIVES
See: University of Connecticut - Homer Babbidge Library - Special Collections (16094)

★13903★
TEAM FOUR INC. - LIBRARY (Plan)
14 N. Newstead Ave. Phone: (314)533-2200
St. Louis, MO 63108 Rita M. Probst, Lib.Dir.
Staff: Prof 1. **Subjects:** Architecture, urban planning, master plans, planning, landscape architecture. **Holdings:** 3300 books; 30 bound periodical volumes; 100 reports. **Subscriptions:** 30 journals and other serials; 5 newspapers. **Services:** Interlibrary loan; copying; library open to the public by appointment.

★13904★
TEANECK PUBLIC LIBRARY - ORAL AND LOCAL HISTORY PROJECT (Hist)
840 Teaneck Rd. Phone: (201)837-4171
Teaneck, NJ 07666 Michael McCue, Dir.
Staff: Prof 13; Other 15. **Subjects:** Local history, early families, Jewish community, black community. **Holdings:** 100 cassettes; 4 notebooks; 1000 index cards; photographs; transcriptions; documentary film; historical exhibits; slide/tape show. **Services:** Copying; project open to the public by appointment.

CHARLTON W. TEBEAU LIBRARY OF FLORIDA HISTORY
See: Historical Association of Southern Florida (6332)

★13905★
TECHNIC INC. - LIBRARY (Sci-Engr)
1 Spectacle St. Phone: (401)781-6100
Providence, RI 02910 Alfred M. Weisberg, V.P.
Staff: Prof 1. **Subjects:** Electrochemistry, surface finishing and electroplating, metallurgy, electronics, manufacturing, jewelry. **Special Collections:** Precious metals. **Holdings:** 250 shelves of books and bound periodical volumes. **Subscriptions:** 75 journals and other serials; 5 newspapers. **Services:** Copying; library open to the public with restrictions. **Publications:** TechnicNews (newsletter).

TECHNICAL COLLEGE OF ALAMANCE
See: Alamance Community College (147)

TECHNICAL LIBRARY FOR TROPICAL AND HURRICANE METEOROLOGY
See: U.S. Natl. Oceanic & Atmospheric Administration - National Hurricane Center - Library (15238)

★13906★
TECHNICAL UNIVERSITY OF NOVA SCOTIA - LIBRARY (Sci-Engr)
Barrington & Bishop St.
P.O. Box 1000 Phone: (902)429-8300
Halifax, NS, Canada B3J 2X4 Mohammad Riaz Hussain, Libn.
Founded: 1949. **Staff:** Prof 4; Other 11. **Subjects:** Engineering - civil, chemical, mechanical, mineral, electrical, industrial; geology; mathematics; architecture. **Special Collections:** Fletcher Memorial Collection (geology and mining); Foulis Collection (environmental sciences). **Holdings:** 90,000 volumes; 70,000 microfiche; 12,000 slides; 100 video cassettes. **Subscriptions:** 1250 journals and other serials. **Services:** Interlibrary loan; copying; SDI; microfilming; library open to the public. **Automated Operations:** Computerized cataloging. **Computerized Information Services:** DIALOG Information Services, CAN/OLE; UTLAS (electronic mail service). **Networks/Consortia:** Member of Association of Atlantic Universities Librarians Council. **Publications:** Library Holdings of Serial Publications, annual. **Staff:** Tahira Hussain, Sr.Libn.; Sandra Scott, Pub.Serv.; Helen Powell, Tech.Serv..

TECHNICON DATA SYSTEMS
See: TDS Healthcare Systems Corporation (13899)

★13907★
TECHNICON INSTRUMENTS CORPORATION - LIBRARY (Med, Sci-Engr, Comp Sci)
511 Benedict Ave. Phone: (914)333-6338
Tarrytown, NY 10591 Gitta Benglas, Libn.
Founded: 1962. **Staff:** Prof 1; Other 1. **Subjects:** Medicine, chemistry, computer science. **Holdings:** 15,000 books; laboratory notebooks; dissertations; reports; microfilm; microfiche; 30 VF drawers; 200 audiotapes. **Subscriptions:** 320 journals and other serials. **Services:** Interlibrary loan; library not open to the public. **Automated Operations:**

Computerized acquisitions and serials. **Computerized Information Services:** DIALOG Information Services.

★13908★
TECHNOLOGY APPLICATIONS, INC. - TECHNICAL LIBRARY (Sci-Engr)
6101 Stevenson Ave. Phone: (703)461-2000
Alexandria, VA 22304 Frances M. Oliver, Tech.Libn.
Founded: 1984. **Staff:** Prof 2. **Subjects:** Engineering - naval, industrial, civil, aerospace; automated information systems; facilities management. **Holdings:** 1336 books, bound reports, proposals. **Subscriptions:** 252 journals and other serials. **Services:** Interlibrary loan; library not open to the public. **Computerized Information Services:** DMS/ONLINE, DIALOG Information Services, Dun & Bradstreet Corporation; internal database. **Staff:** Suzanne Baxter, Tech.Libn..

★13909★
TECHNOLOGY TRANSFER SOCIETY - LIBRARY (Sci-Engr)
611 N. Capitol Ave. Phone: (317)262-5022
Indianapolis, IN 46204 Barbara Ostermeier, Off.Mgr.
Founded: 1975. **Staff:** 1. **Subjects:** Technology transfer. **Special Collections:** Proceedings of the Technology Transfer Society. **Holdings:** 200 volumes. **Services:** Copying; library open to the public. **Formerly:** Located in Los Angeles, CA.

★13910★
TECHNOMIC, INC. - INFORMATION SERVICES (Food-Bev)
300 S. Riverside Plaza, Suite 1940 S. Phone: (312)876-0004
Chicago, IL 60606 Mollie R. Brumbaugh, Mgr., Info.Rsrcs.
Founded: 1976. **Staff:** Prof 1; Other 1. **Subjects:** Management, food/food service, packaging. **Special Collections:** Food Service Resource Center (500 books; 100 periodicals; 60 VF drawers). **Holdings:** 606 books; 60 VF drawers of clippings. **Subscriptions:** 150 journals and other serials; 5 newspapers. **Services:** Interlibrary loan; copying; services open to the public with approval. **Computerized Information Services:** DIALOG Information Services, Dow Jones News/Retrieval, Dun & Bradstreet Corporation; Restaurant Concepts, Acquisition Database (internal databases). Performs searches on fee basis. **Networks/Consortia:** Member of Chicago Library System. **Publications:** TRA Foodservice Abstracts, monthly - by subscription; Restaurant Information Service (updates), monthly; Dynamics of the Chain Restaurant Market, annual.

★13911★
TECHNOMIC PUBLISHING CO., INC. (TPC) - BUSINESS LIBRARY (Sci-Engr, Publ)
851 New Holland Ave.
Box 3535
Lancaster, PA 17604 Richard Dunn, Lib.Dir.
Staff: Prof 1. **Subjects:** Plastics, resins, composites, materials engineering, sanitary engineering, environmental science, biotechnology. **Holdings:** 750 books; 40 bound periodical volumes. **Subscriptions:** 18 journals and other serials. **Services:** Library not open to the public.

★13912★
TECK MINING GROUP LTD. - LIBRARY (Sci-Engr)
1199 W. Hastings St. Phone: (604)687-1117
Vancouver, BC, Canada V6E 2K5 Elizabeth J. Watson, Libn.
Staff: Prof 1; Other 1. **Subjects:** Mining, geology. **Holdings:** 3000 books; 500 bound periodical volumes; 500 maps; 300 newspaper clippings. **Subscriptions:** 220 journals and other serials; 50 newspapers. **Services:** Library not open to the public.

★13913★
TECSULT, INC. - LIBRARY DEPARTMENT (Sci-Engr)
85 W. Ste. Catherine Phone: (514)287-8546
Montreal, PQ, Canada H2X 3P4 Louise Rickerd, Libn.
Founded: 1975. **Staff:** Prof 1. **Subjects:** Engineering, construction, economy, developing countries, environment. **Holdings:** 6100 books; 1500 bound periodical volumes; 100 annual reports; 4300 standards and Canadian Government specifications. **Subscriptions:** 244 journals and other serials. **Services:** Interlibrary loan; library open to the public. **Automated Operations:** Computerized public access catalog, cataloging, serials, and circulation. **Computerized Information Services:** DIALOG Information Services, CAN/OLE, QL Systems, Telesystemes Questel; Envoy 100 (electronic mail service). **Publications:** Liste des nouveautes, monthly; liste des periodiques, biennial - for internal distribution only.

CESARE GEORGE TEDESCHI LIBRARY
See: Framingham Union Hospital (5331)

★13914★
TEHAMA COUNTY LAW LIBRARY (Law)
Court House, Rm. 35
Red Bluff, CA 96080 Jill Miller, Lib.Ck.
Staff: 1. **Subjects:** Law. **Holdings:** 8925 books; 200 bound periodical volumes; annotated codes; reports and reporters; decennials; digests; U.S. Supreme Court reports. **Subscriptions:** 11 journals and other serials. **Services:** Library open to the public.

★13915★
TEKTRONIX, INC. - CORPORATE LIBRARY (Sci-Engr, Comp Sci)
Box 500, MS 50-210 Phone: (503)627-5388
Beaverton, OR 97077 Julianne Williams, Lib.Mgr.
Founded: 1958. **Staff:** Prof 1; Other 3. **Subjects:** Electronics, solid state physics, analytical chemistry, management, information display, computers, instrumentation, electron optics, materials science. **Holdings:** 10,000 books. **Subscriptions:** 600 journals and other serials. **Services:** Interlibrary loan; copying; SDI; library open to the public by appointment only. **Computerized Information Services:** DIALOG Information Services, Pergamon ORBIT InfoLine, Inc., NEXIS. **Networks/Consortia:** Member of Washington County Cooperative Library Services (WCCLS).

★13916★
TEKTRONIX, INC. - WALKER ROAD TECHNICAL INFORMATION CENTER (Comp Sci)
MS 94-501
Box 4600 Phone: (503)629-1062
Beaverton, OR 97075 Yan Y. Soucie, Libn.
Founded: 1980. **Staff:** Prof 1. **Subjects:** Automated test equipment, computer-aided engineering, software engineering. **Holdings:** 3000 books. **Subscriptions:** 139 journals and other serials. **Services:** Interlibrary loan; library not open to the public. **Automated Operations:** Computerized cataloging. **Computerized Information Services:** DIALOG Information Services. **Networks/Consortia:** Member of Washington County Cooperative Library Services (WCCLS). **Publications:** Newsletter, quarterly - for internal distribution only.

★13917★
TEKTRONIX, INC. - WILSONVILLE LIBRARY (Comp Sci)
Box 1000, M/S 63-531 Phone: (503)685-3986
Wilsonville, OR 97070 Linda K. Appel, Libn.
Staff: Prof 1; Other 1. **Subjects:** Computer graphics and programming, electronics, business and management. **Holdings:** 2000 books. **Subscriptions:** 175 journals and other serials; 7 newspapers. **Services:** Interlibrary loan; copying; SDI; library open to the public by appointment. **Computerized Information Services:** DIALOG Information Services. **Networks/Consortia:** Member of CLASS, Western Library Network (WLN), Washington County Cooperative Library Services (WCCLS). **Publications:** Wilsonville Library Bulletin, biweekly - for internal distribution only.

TEL-MED HEALTH INFORMATION SERVICE
See: Fairview Southdale Hospital (4900)

★13918★
TELE-UNIVERSITE - SERVICE DE LA DOCUMENTATION (Educ)
214, ave. St-Sacrement Phone: (418)657-2262
Quebec, PQ, Canada G1N 4M6 Lise Roberge, Resp.
Founded: 1978. **Staff:** Prof 3; Other 4. **Subjects:** Education by correspondence, educational technology, adult education, lifelong learning, didactics, communication. **Special Collections:** Education by correspondence (1000 items). **Holdings:** 9000 volumes; 122 reels of microfilm; 800 microfiche; 185 films; 328 videotapes; 269 audiotapes; 21 records; 1105 transparencies; 25 dioramas; 75 educational games. **Subscriptions:** 235 journals and other serials; 5 newspapers. **Services:** Interlibrary loan; copying; service open to the public with restrictions. **Automated Operations:** Computerized cataloging. **Computerized Information Services:** DIALOG Information Services, BADADUQ, DOBIS Canadian Online Library System, Telesystemes Questel; Envoy 100 (electronic mail service). **Publications:** Les Nouveautes (a list of new acquisitions and abstracts of periodicals), weekly. **Staff:** Reine Belanger, Doc.; Claude Tousignant, Libn..

★13919★
TELECOM CANADA - INFORMATION RESOURCE CENTRE (Bus-Fin)
410 Laurier Ave., W. Phone: (613)560-3953
Ottawa, ON, Canada K1P 6H5 Susan Grohn, Mgr.
Founded: 1978. **Staff:** Prof 1; Other 2. **Subjects:** Telecommunications, telephone industry, business, marketing. **Holdings:** 1000 books. **Subscriptions:** 250 journals and other serials. **Services:** Interlibrary loan; center not open to the public. **Automated Operations:** Computerized acquisitions and circulation. **Computerized Information Services:** Pergamon ORBIT InfoLine, Inc., DIALOG Information Services, QL Systems, CAN/OLE, BRS Information Technologies, Info Globe; internal databases. **Publications:** Acquisition lists, quarterly - for internal distribution only; Periodicals, annual (both annotated).

★13920★
TELEDYNE BROWN ENGINEERING - TECHNICAL LIBRARY (Sci-Engr)
Cummings Research Park
300 Sparkman Dr., N.W. Phone: (205)532-1433
Huntsville, AL 35807 Mark Sutherland, Chf.Libn.
Founded: 1962. **Staff:** Prof 1; Other 2. **Subjects:** Research and development. **Holdings:** 200 bound periodical volumes; 50,000 documents; 3000 microfiche; military specifications and standards. **Subscriptions:** 200 journals and other serials. **Services:** Interlibrary loan; library not open to the public. **Automated Operations:** Computerized circulation.

★13921★
TELEDYNE CAE CORPORATION - ENGINEERING LIBRARY (Sci-Engr)
1330 Laskey Rd. Phone: (419)470-3027
Toledo, OH 43612 Marlene S. Dowdell, Libn.
Founded: 1970. **Staff:** Prof 1. **Subjects:** Aeronautical engineering, aircraft gas turbine engines, jet engines, aerospace, metallurgy. **Special Collections:** National Advisory Committee for Aeronautics (NACA) Technical Memoranda and Technical Notes, 1920 to present. **Holdings:** 2900 books; 57 VF cabinets of reports; 2500 microfiche. **Subscriptions:** 100 journals and other serials. **Services:** Interlibrary loan; library not open to the public. **Automated Operations:** Computerized cataloging, acquisitions, and circulation. **Computerized Information Services:** DIALOG Information Services, Aerospace Online, NASA/RECON, DTIC. **Publications:** Acquisitions Bulletin, bimonthly - for internal distribution only.

★13922★
TELEDYNE ENERGY SYSTEMS - LIBRARY (Energy)
110 W. Timonium Rd. Phone: (301)252-8220
Timonium, MD 21093 Cathy Layne, Libn.
Founded: 1976. **Staff:** Prof 1. **Subjects:** Energy conversion, aerospace engineering. **Holdings:** 2400 books; 101,000 technical reports. **Subscriptions:** 80 journals and other serials. **Services:** Interlibrary loan; copying; SDI; library open to the public with restrictions. **Computerized Information Services:** DTIC.

★13923★
TELEDYNE ENGINEERING SERVICES - INFORMATION CENTER (Sci-Engr)
130 Second Ave. Phone: (617)890-3350
Waltham, MA 02254 Susan Fingerman, Mgr., Info.Serv.
Staff: Prof 1. **Subjects:** Mechanical and civil engineering, materials, stress analysis. **Holdings:** 1500 books; 2000 other cataloged items. **Subscriptions:** 80 journals and other serials. **Services:** Copying; SDI; center open to the public with approval of manager. **Automated Operations:** Computerized cataloging. **Computerized Information Services:** BRS Information Technologies, OCLC, DIALOG Information Services, Pergamon ORBIT InfoLine, Inc.; internal database; DIALMAIL (electronic mail service). **Networks/Consortia:** Member of NELINET, Route 128 Librarians Group. **Publications:** Recent Acquisitions, bimonthly; Reports Received, irregular; Periodical Holdings, annual.

★13924★
TELEDYNE GEOTECH - ALEXANDRIA LABORATORIES - LIBRARY (Sci-Engr)
314 Montgomery St. Phone: (703)836-3882
Alexandria, VA 22314 Carolyn Lewis, Libn.
Subjects: Seismology, geophysics. **Holdings:** Figures not available for research materials. **Services:** Library open to the public.

★13925★
TELEDYNE ISOTOPES - BUSINESS LIBRARY (Sci-Engr)
50 Vanburen Ave. Phone: (201)664-7070
Westwood, NJ 07675 Helen Principe, Res.Libn./Adm.Asst.
Founded: 1957. **Staff:** 2. **Subjects:** Oil recovery/TeleTrace, radiochemistry, health physics, waste disposal, thermoluminescent dosimetry, carbon, nuclear instruments, geochemistry, geology. **Holdings:** Figures not available. **Subscriptions:** 55 journals and other serials. **Services:** Interlibrary loan; library open to the public by appointment. **Automated Operations:** Computerized circulation.

★13926★
TELEDYNE RYAN AERONAUTICAL - TECHNICAL LIBRARY (Sci-Engr)
2701 N. Harbor Dr. Phone: (619)260-4458
San Diego, CA 92101 William E. Ebner, Chf.
Founded: 1943. **Staff:** Prof 1. **Subjects:** Aerodynamics, avionics, materials. **Holdings:** 4000 books; 200 bound periodical volumes; 2400 other cataloged items; 100,000 Defense Documentation Center Technical Reports; 60,000 NASA Documentation items. **Subscriptions:** 150 journals and other serials. **Services:** Interlibrary loan; copying; SDI; services open to the public for reference use only by appointment. **Computerized Information Services:** DIALOG Information Services, NASA/RECON. **Publications:** Library Acquisitions List, irregular - for internal distribution only.

★13927★
TELEDYNE SYSTEMS COMPANY - TECHNICAL LIBRARY (Comp Sci)
19601 Nordhoff St. Phone: (818)886-2211
Northridge, CA 91324 Linda Zazueta, Tech.Libn.
Staff: 1. **Subjects:** Communication systems, computers, microprocessors, digital signal processing. **Holdings:** 2000 books; 300 bound periodical volumes; 700 technical reports. **Subscriptions:** 63 journals and other serials. **Services:** Interlibrary loan; copying; library open to the public with government clearance. **Special Catalogs:** Technical reports catalog; journal catalog (card).

★13928★
TELEMEDIA, INC. - INFORMATION CENTER (Educ)
310 S. Michigan Ave.
Chicago, IL 60604 Phone: (312)987-4000
Staff: Prof 2. **Subjects:** Education-training, language instruction, English as a second language, petroleum industry, aviation, geography. **Holdings:** 1700 books; 500 military documents; 1000 internal publications; 14 VF drawers of corporate annual reports; 11 VF drawers serials; 2100 unbound periodicals. **Subscriptions:** 72 journals and other serials; 5 newspapers. **Services:** Center not open to the public. **Automated Operations:** Computerized cataloging. **Computerized Information Services:** DIALOG Information Services.

★13929★
TELENET COMMUNICATIONS CORPORATION - CHRISTOPHER B. NEWPORT INFORMATION RESOURCE CENTER (Info Sci)
12490 Sunrise Valley Dr. Phone: (703)689-6000
Reston, VA 22096 Judith A. Adams, Mgr.
Founded: 1981. **Staff:** Prof 5; Other 2. **Subjects:** Data communications, telecommunications, computer science. **Holdings:** 1350 books; 1370 technical and marketing reports; 185 company tariffs; 190 computer manuals; 40 VF drawers of subject/competitive files; 24 drawers of microforms of journals, standards, Securities and Exchange Commission filings; 455 government and industry standards. **Subscriptions:** 360 journals and other serials; 6 newspapers. **Services:** Interlibrary loan; SDI; center open to the public by appointment only. **Automated Operations:** Computerized cataloging, acquisitions, and serials. **Computerized Information Services:** DIALOG Information Services, Mead Data Central, NewsNet, Inc., CompuServe, Inc., The Source Information Network, LS/2000, OCLC, Dun & Bradstreet Corporation; Infocomm, Infolib (internal databases). **Networks/Consortia:** Member of GTE LIBNET. **Staff:** Victoria Harriston, Info.Spec.; Deborah McClain, Acq.Spec.; Charlaine Cook, Cat.Spec.; Patricia Huff, Rec.Spec..

TELESAT CANADA
See: Canada - Telesat Canada (2497)

★13930★
TELEVISION INFORMATION OFFICE OF THE NATIONAL ASSOCIATION OF BROADCASTERS - RESEARCH SERVICES (Info Sci)
745 Fifth Ave., 17th Fl. Phone: (212)759-6800
New York, NY 10151 James Poteat, Mgr., Res.Serv.
Founded: 1959. **Staff:** Prof 2; Other 3. **Subjects:** Television (except technical aspects). **Holdings:** 4500 books; 650 bound periodical volumes; 155 vertical files. **Subscriptions:** 265 journals and other serials; 10 newspapers. **Services:** Interlibrary loan; copying; services open to the public by appointment only. **Publications:** Bibliography series. **Staff:** Leslie Slocum.

★13931★
TELFAIR ACADEMY OF ARTS AND SCIENCES, INC. - LIBRARY (Art)
121 Barnard St. Phone: (912)232-1177
Savannah, GA 31412 Wilma M. Wierwill, Libn.
Founded: 1885. **Staff:** Prof 1. **Subjects:** American art and artists; writings and art of Kahlil Gibran. **Holdings:** 3000 books; auction catalogs; 20 VF drawers of material on artists, associations, and museums. **Subscriptions:** 130 journals and other serials. **Services:** Copying. **Automated Operations:** Computerized cataloging and acquisitions. **Publications:** Exhibition catalogs.

★13932★
TELSHE YESHIVA - RABBI A.N. SCHWARTZ LIBRARY (Rel-Phil)
28400 Euclid Ave. Phone: (216)289-1605
Wickliffe, OH 44092 Rabbi Reuven Gerson, Hd.Libn.
Founded: 1945. **Staff:** Prof 7; Other 2. **Subjects:** Talmud, Pentateuch, Jewish ethics and philosophy, Jewish law, Jewish history, Kabala, homiletics, Midrash. **Special Collections:** Hagaon Reb Eliezer Silver Collection; rare Sepharadic commentaries and Responsa; early printed volumes of Biblical commentaries (1500); Rabbi Elazari Collection; Rabbi Abramowitz Collection; Rabbi Schiff Library; Rabbi Arnst Collection; Rabbi Levitan Collection. **Holdings:** 20,000 books; 1200 separate periodicals; 500 dissertations; 50 school publications; 25 manuscripts. **Subscriptions:** 10 journals and other serials. **Services:** Interlibrary loan; copying; library open to the public but a security deposit is required. **Publications:** Kol Hayeshiva, quarterly; Pe'er Mordechai, annual; Pri Etz Chaim, annual. **Remarks:** A section of this library has been named the Rabbi Neuhaus Library.

★13933★
TEMPLE ADATH ISRAEL - RUBEN LIBRARY (Rel-Phil)
Old Lancaster Rd. & Highland Ave. Phone: (215)664-5150
Merion, PA 19066 Fred Kazan, Rabbi
Founded: 1955. **Staff:** Prof 1. **Subjects:** Judaica. **Holdings:** 5000 books; 8 drawers of clippings; 100 filmstrips. **Services:** Interlibrary loan; library open to area college students or by member sponsorship.

★13934★
TEMPLE AHAVATH SHOLOM - RABBI A. ALAN STEINBACH LIBRARY (Rel-Phil)
1906 Ave. V Phone: (718)769-5350
Brooklyn, NY 11229-4506 Gloria Weinrich, Libn.
Founded: 1938. **Staff:** Prof 1. **Subjects:** Jewish ethics, history, music; comparative religion; biography. **Holdings:** 4500 books; Rabbi Steinbach's manuscripts; Jewish antiquities. **Services:** Library open to the public with restrictions.

★13935★
TEMPLE BETH EL - BILLIE DAVIS RODENBERG MEMORIAL LIBRARY (Rel-Phil)
1351 S. 14th Ave. Phone: (305)920-8225
Hollywood, FL 33020 Roslyn Kurland, Libn.
Staff: Prof 1; Other 4. **Subjects:** Judaica. **Holdings:** 7000 volumes. **Subscriptions:** 25 journals and other serials; 6 newspapers. **Services:** Interlibrary loan; copying; library open to the public for reference use only.

★13936★
TEMPLE BETH EL - LIBRARY (Rel-Phil)
225 E. 7th St. Phone: (201)756-2333
Plainfield, NJ 07060 Fran Dorio, Libn.
Founded: 1966. **Staff:** 3. **Subjects:** Judaica and Hebraica - juvenile and adult. **Holdings:** 3500 books. **Services:** Copying; library open to the public.

★13937★
TEMPLE BETH EL - LIBRARY (Rel-Phil)
139 Winton Rd., S. Phone: (716)473-1770
Rochester, NY 14610 Anne Kirshenbaum, Libn.
Founded: 1946. **Staff:** Prof 1; Other 1. **Subjects:** Judaica - religion, philosophy, social science, history, art, literature, language, fiction, biography for adults and juveniles. **Holdings:** 6592 books; 7 file drawers of pamphlets and clippings. **Subscriptions:** 31 journals and other serials. **Services:** Interlibrary loan; library open to the public with special permission.

★13938★
TEMPLE BETH EL - PRENTIS MEMORIAL LIBRARY (Rel-Phil)
7400 Telegraph Rd. Phone: (313)851-1100
Birmingham, MI 48010 Marilyn R. Brenner, Libn.
Founded: 1878. **Staff:** Prof 1. **Subjects:** Judaica, Christianity, philosophy, the arts, sociology, archeology, Bible, Jewish history, Jewish Americana. **Special Collections:** Leonard N. Simons Collection of Rare Judaica; Irving I. Katz Collection of Jewish Americana. **Holdings:** 15,000 books; AV programs; recordings; pamphlets; large print books; talking books. **Subscriptions:** 65 journals and other serials. **Services:** Copying; library open to the public with restrictions.

★13939★
TEMPLE BETH-EL - WILLIAM G. BRAUDE LIBRARY (Rel-Phil)
70 Orchard Ave. Phone: (401)331-6070
Providence, RI 02906 Reini Silverman, Libn.
Founded: 1894. **Staff:** Prof 1. **Subjects:** Judaica, Hebraica, Yiddish, Biblical studies, Holocaust, philosophy, folklore, music, rabbinics, antisemitism, Latin American Jewry. **Special Collections:** Englander Collection. **Holdings:** 25,000 books; 258 bound periodical volumes; 432 pamphlets; clippings; programs of interest to Rhode Island Jews; Yiddish and Hebrew books. **Subscriptions:** 73 journals and other serials; 10 newspapers. **Services:** Interlibrary loan; library open to the public. **Automated Operations:** Computerized cataloging.

★13940★
TEMPLE BETH-EL - ZISKIND MEMORIAL LIBRARY (Rel-Phil)
385 High St. Phone: (508)674-3529
Fall River, MA 02720 Ida C. Pollock, Libn.
Staff: 1. **Subjects:** English Judaica. **Holdings:** 6000 volumes; 200 phonograph records; 300 pamphlets and clippings. **Subscriptions:** 35 journals and other serials. **Services:** Library open to the public.

★13941★
TEMPLE BETH-EL OF GREAT NECK - ARNOLD & MARIE SCHWARTZ LIBRARY (Rel-Phil)
5 Old Mill Rd. Phone: (516)487-0900
Great Neck, NY 11023 Linda Zimbalist, Libn.
Founded: 1950. **Staff:** Prof 1. **Subjects:** Judaica - history, Holocaust, literature, biography; Israel. **Special Collections:** Children's collection. **Holdings:** 8000 books; records; reference books. **Subscriptions:** 25 journals and other serials. **Services:** Interlibrary loan; library open to students enrolled in adult education at the temple and all congregants.

★13942★
TEMPLE BETH EL OF GREATER BUFFALO - LIBRARY (Rel-Phil)
2368 Eggert Rd. Phone: (716)836-3762
Tonawanda, NY 14150 Sandra Freed Gralnick, Libn.
Founded: 1920. **Staff:** Prof 1; Other 4. **Subjects:** Judaica. **Special Collections:** Samuel S. Luskin Memorial Music Reference Library; Cantor Gerald De Bruin Music, Tapes and Record Library; Edward Weiss Reading Center for the Visually Impaired; reference collection on Jewish art; large print books; children's collection; Holocaust collection; Janet S. Adler Special Israeli Collection. **Holdings:** 5000 books; phonograph records; tapes. **Services:** Library open to the public. **Publications:** Lists of Recent Acquisitions, annual.

★13943★
TEMPLE BETH ISRAEL - LIBRARY (Rel-Phil)
3310 N. 10th Ave. Phone: (602)264-4428
Phoenix, AZ 85013 Mrs. Elliot Tempkin, Libn.
Staff: Prof 1. **Subjects:** Jewish history, Bible, literature, rabbinics, biography, art, music. **Special Collections:** Judaica Music Library (245 phonograph records, tapes, and cassettes). **Holdings:** 17,541 books; 26 VF drawers of pamphlets, clippings, and maps; 6 boxes of temple archives.

Subscriptions: 72 journals and other serials. **Services:** Interlibrary loan; copying; library open to the public.

★13944★
TEMPLE BETH JOSEPH - ROSE BASLOE LIBRARY (Rel-Phil)
North Prospect St.
Herkimer, NY 13350 Phone: (315)866-4270
Founded: 1957. **Staff:** 2. **Subjects:** Judaica. **Holdings:** 3500 books. **Services:** Library open to the public.

★13945★
TEMPLE BETH SHOLOM - HERBERT GOLDBERG MEMORIAL LIBRARY (Rel-Phil)
Green St. & White Horse Pike Phone: (609)547-6113
Haddon Heights, NJ 08035 Doris Corman, Libn.
Staff: Prof 1. **Subjects:** Judaica. **Holdings:** 3000 books. **Subscriptions:** 12 journals and other serials.

★13946★
TEMPLE BETH SHOLOM - LIBRARY (Rel-Phil)
4144 Chase Ave. Phone: (305)538-7231
Miami Beach, FL 33140 Celia R. Huber, Libn.
Staff: Prof 1; Other 4. **Subjects:** Judaica (adult and juvenile), rabbinics. **Holdings:** 5000 books. **Subscriptions:** 60 journals and other serials. **Services:** Interlibrary loan; copying; library open to the public with restrictions.

★13947★
TEMPLE BETH ZION - LIBRARY (Rel-Phil)
805 Delaware Ave. Phone: (716)886-7151
Buffalo, NY 14209 Linda Herman, Libn.
Founded: 1915. **Staff:** Prof 1. **Subjects:** Jewish religion, history, literature, art. **Special Collections:** Reform Judaism; Jewish beliefs and practices; American Jewish history. **Holdings:** 12,100 books; 250 filmstrips and slides; 180 records and cassettes; video cassettes. **Subscriptions:** 38 journals and other serials. **Services:** Interlibrary loan; library open to the public. **Publications:** Lest We Forget: A Selected Annotated List of Books on the Holocaust; American Jewish Odyssey (annotated bibliography of the Jewish experience in America, as reflected in the library holdings); Jewish Children's Literature (annotated bibliography of books on Judaism and Jewish history for children up to age 14); Books on the Holocaust (list of library's holdings); Basic List for a Jewish Home Library.

★13948★
TEMPLE B'NAI ISRAEL - LASKER MEMORIAL LIBRARY (Rel-Phil)
3006 Ave. O Phone: (409)765-5796
Galveston, TX 77550 Sophie Nussenblatt
Founded: 1956. **Staff:** 3. **Subjects:** Judaism, Jewish history, biblical history, Bible commentaries. **Holdings:** 2000 books. **Subscriptions:** 15 journals and other serials. **Services:** Library open to the public.

★13949★
TEMPLE B'RITH KODESH - LIBRARY (Rel-Phil)
2131 Elmwood Ave. Phone: (716)244-7060
Rochester, NY 14618 Annette Sheiman, Libn.
Staff: Prof 1; Other 1. **Subjects:** Judaica. **Holdings:** 8000 books. **Subscriptions:** 25 journals and other serials. **Services:** Library open to members of local congregations and students of local colleges and universities.

★13950★
TEMPLE EMANU-EL - ALEX F. WEISBERG LIBRARY (Rel-Phil)
8500 Hillcrest Rd. Phone: (214)368-3613
Dallas, TX 75225 Maureen Reister, Libn.
Founded: 1957. **Staff:** Prof 1. **Subjects:** Judaica and related topics. **Holdings:** 6000 books. **Subscriptions:** 30 journals and other serials; 7 newspapers. **Services:** Interlibrary loan; copying; programs for interfaith and senior citizens groups; library open to the public with annual fee.

★13951★
TEMPLE EMANU-EL - CONGREGATIONAL LIBRARY (Rel-Phil)
99 Taft Ave. Phone: (401)331-1616
Providence, RI 02906 Lillian Schwartz, Libn.
Founded: 1953. **Staff:** Prof 1. **Subjects:** Judaica, comparative religion. **Holdings:** 7000 books. **Subscriptions:** 20 journals and other serials. **Services:** Interlibrary loan; copying; library open to the public with deposit. **Publications:** Booklists, occasional - for school use.

★13952★
TEMPLE EMANU-EL - DAVIS LIBRARY (Rel-Phil)
225 N. Country Club Rd. Phone: (602)327-4501
Tucson, AZ 85716 Beverly H. Morgen, Libn.
Founded: 1947. **Staff:** Prof 1. **Subjects:** Judaica. **Holdings:** 8000 books; 150 phonograph records; 50 filmstrips; 50 videotapes; 20 audiotapes. **Subscriptions:** 12 journals and other serials. **Services:** Copying; library open to the public for reference use only.

★13953★
TEMPLE EMANU-EL - LIBRARY (Rel-Phil)
1701 Washington Ave. Phone: (305)538-2503
Miami Beach, FL 33139 Ruth M. Abelow, Libn.
Staff: Prof 1; Other 1. **Subjects:** Judaica including religion, Bible, Israel, biography, literature, history, sociology, and education. **Special Collections:** Samuel Friedland Collection of Rare Books (600 volumes, mainly printed in Europe). **Holdings:** 8000 books; 55 cataloged periodicals; 270 pamphlets; 40 pamphlet boxes of uncataloged pamphlets on Israel and religion; 8 books of clippings. **Subscriptions:** 48 journals and other serials; 6 newspapers. **Services:** Library open to the public with refundable deposit.

★13954★
TEMPLE EMANU-EL - SONAHEND FAMILY LIBRARY (Rel-Phil)
455 Neptune Blvd. Phone: (516)431-4060
Long Beach, NY 11561 Beth Moscowitz, Libn.
Founded: 1954. **Staff:** Prof 1. **Subjects:** Jewish religion and literature; Bible; Hebraica; current events in Israel. **Holdings:** 2975 books; 30 bound periodical volumes; 10 VF drawers; 35 videotapes; audiotapes; filmstrips; sound recordings. **Subscriptions:** 15 newspapers. **Services:** Library open to members. **Automated Operations:** Computerized cataloging and circulation.

★13955★
TEMPLE EMANU-EL - WILLIAM P. BUDNER RELIGIOUS SCHOOL - LIBRARY (Rel-Phil)
8500 Hillcrest Rd. Phone: (214)368-3613
Dallas, TX 75225 Maureen Reister, Libn.
Founded: 1980. **Staff:** Prof 1. **Subjects:** Juvenile Judaica. **Holdings:** 1300 books. **Services:** Library not open to the public. **Remarks:** Library is maintained by the Alex F. Weisberg Library and operated by a volunteer staff.

★13956★
TEMPLE EMANU-EL - WILLIAM P. ENGEL LIBRARY (Rel-Phil)
2100 Highland Ave. Phone: (205)933-8037
Birmingham, AL 35255 Adele Cohn, Libn.
Staff: Prof 2; Other 1. **Subjects:** Judaica, religion. **Holdings:** 3500 books. **Services:** Interlibrary loan; copying; library open to the public. **Staff:** Florence Goldstein, Asst..

★13957★
TEMPLE EMANU-EL OF YONKERS - LEVITAS LIBRARY (Rel-Phil)
306 Rumsey Rd. Phone: (914)963-0575
Yonkers, NY 10705 Irving Levitas, Libn.
Staff: Prof 1; Other 5. **Subjects:** Judaica, history, comparative religions, American literature, Asian studies. **Holdings:** 5000 volumes. **Subscriptions:** 12 journals and other serials. **Services:** Interlibrary loan; library open to students.

★13958★
TEMPLE EMANUEL - LIBRARY (Rel-Phil)
150 Derby Ave.
Box 897 Phone: (203)397-3000
Orange, CT 06477 Michael S. Chosak, Chm., Lib.Comm.
Subjects: Judaica. **Holdings:** 1000 books; 25 phonograph records. **Services:** Library open to the public with permission.

★13959★
TEMPLE EMANUEL - LIBRARY (Rel-Phil)
Cooper River Pkwy. at Donahue Phone: (609)665-0669
Cherry Hill, NJ 08002 Rene Batterman, Libn.
Staff: Prof 1. **Subjects:** Judaism. **Special Collections:** Holocaust. **Holdings:** 5000 books; records; tapes. **Subscriptions:** 12 journals and other serials. **Services:** Copying; library open to the public with restrictions.

★13960★
TEMPLE DE HIRSCH SINAI - LIBRARY (Rel-Phil)
1511 E. Pike
Seattle, WA 98122-4199 Kathryn K. Crane, Libn.
Staff: Prof 1. **Subjects:** Judaism, Jewish history, literature, biography, Holocaust, children's literature. **Holdings:** 4500 books. **Subscriptions:** 24 journals and other serials. **Services:** Interlibrary loan; copying (limited); library open to the public with restrictions.

★13961★
TEMPLE ISRAEL - LEONARD M. SANDHAUS MEMORIAL LIBRARY† (Rel-Phil)
125 Pond St.
Sharon, MA 02067 Phone: (617)784-3986
Founded: 1953. **Staff:** Prof 1; Other 4. **Subjects:** Jewish religion, philosophy, history; American Jewish life; Israel and Zionism. **Special Collections:** Jewish literature. **Holdings:** 5200 books; 200 pamphlets; 50 tapes. **Subscriptions:** 14 journals and other serials. **Services:** Interlibrary loan; library open to the public with restrictions.

★13962★
TEMPLE ISRAEL - LIBRARY (Rel-Phil)
1901 N. Flagler Dr. Phone: (407)833-8421
West Palm Beach, FL 33407 Elsie Leviton, Chm., Lib.Comm.
Founded: 1958. **Staff:** Prof 1; Other 5. **Subjects:** Judaica - history, literature, sociology, arts. **Special Collections:** Americana Judaica; Holocaust. **Holdings:** 7000 books; 12 bound periodical volumes; 1000 pamphlets, bibliographies, archives, clippings; 8 VF drawers; phonograph records; filmstrips. **Subscriptions:** 16 journals and other serials; 7 newspapers. **Services:** Library open to residents of Palm Beach County. **Staff:** Adele Sayles, Libn..

★13963★
TEMPLE ISRAEL - LIBRARY (Rel-Phil)
Longwood Ave. & Plymouth St. Phone: (617)566-3960
Boston, MA 02215 Ann Carol Abrams, Libn.
Staff: Prof 1; Other 1. **Subjects:** Judaica. **Special Collections:** Jewish Peace Collection (20 books). **Holdings:** 9000 books. **Subscriptions:** 30 journals and other serials. **Services:** Library open to congregation and religious school.

★13964★
TEMPLE ISRAEL - LIBRARY (Rel-Phil)
2324 Emerson Ave., S. Phone: (612)377-8680
Minneapolis, MN 55405 Georgia Kalman, Libn.
Founded: 1928. **Staff:** Prof 1. **Subjects:** Judaica, Jewish religion, philosophy. **Holdings:** 6000 books. **Subscriptions:** 20 journals and other serials; 6 newspapers. **Services:** Library open to the public.

★13965★
TEMPLE ISRAEL - LIBRARY (Rel-Phil)
140 Central Ave. Phone: (516)239-1140
Lawrence, NY 11559 Donna Z. Lifland, Libn.
Founded: 1949. **Staff:** Prof 1; Other 6. **Subjects:** Judaica and allied subjects. **Holdings:** 5100 books; 20 bound periodical volumes; 225 filmstrips; 10 cassettes. **Subscriptions:** 19 journals and other serials. **Services:** Library open to the public with permission.

★13966★
TEMPLE ISRAEL - MAX AND EDITH WEINBERG LIBRARY (Rel-Phil)
5725 Walnut Lake Rd. Phone: (313)661-5700
West Bloomfield, MI 48033 Bertha Wember, Libn.
Founded: 1962. **Staff:** Prof 1; Other 1. **Subjects:** Judaism - history, biography, literature, arts; Holocaust; Bible study; Israel. **Holdings:** 9000 books; 8 VF drawers of clippings and pamphlets. **Subscriptions:** 35 journals and other serials. **Services:** Library open to the public.

★13967★
TEMPLE ISRAEL - PAUL PELTASON LIBRARY (Rel-Phil)
10675 Ladue Rd. Phone: (314)432-8050
Creve Coeur, MO 63141 Mrs. Barry Katz
Founded: 1930. **Staff:** 1. **Subjects:** Judaica. **Holdings:** 4000 books. **Services:** Library open to the public with restrictions.

★13968★
TEMPLE ISRAEL - RABBI LOUIS WITT MEMORIAL LIBRARY (Rel-Phil)
1821 Emerson Ave. Phone: (513)278-9621
Dayton, OH 45406 Janie Fletcher, Libn.
Founded: 1925. **Subjects:** Judaica. **Holdings:** Figures not available. **Services:** Library not open to the public.

★13969★
TEMPLE ISRAEL OF GREATER MIAMI - LIBRARY (Rel-Phil)
137 N.E. 19th St. Phone: (305)573-5900
Miami, FL 33132 Beatrice T. Muskat, Libn.
Founded: 1944. **Staff:** Prof 1; Other 1. **Subjects:** Judaica. **Special Collections:** Biblical and juvenile collections; Haggadahs. **Holdings:** 10,000 books; pamphlets; American Jewish Archives; Near East reports; records; tapes; slides. **Subscriptions:** 30 journals and other serials. **Services:** Library open to the public for reference use only. **Remarks:** Maintains a small branch library at 9990 N. Kendall Dr., Miami, FL 33176.

★13970★
TEMPLE JUDEA - MEL HARRISON MEMORIAL LIBRARY (Rel-Phil)
5500 Granada Blvd.
Coral Gables, FL 33146 Zelda Harrison, Chf.Libn.
Founded: 1967. **Staff:** 5. **Subjects:** Judaica. **Holdings:** 4500 books. **Services:** Library not open to the public.

★13971★
TEMPLE JUDEA MIZPAH - LIBRARY (Rel-Phil)
8610 Niles Center Rd. Phone: (312)676-1566
Skokie, IL 60077 Claire Alport, Lib.Chm.
Staff: Prof 3; Other 14. **Subjects:** Judaica. **Holdings:** 3900 books; 20 bound periodical volumes. **Services:** Copying; library open to the public with restrictions. **Networks/Consortia:** Member of Judaica Library Network of Chicago. **Staff:** Beatrice Silver, Co-Chm..

★13972★
TEMPLE LIBRARY (Rel-Phil)
University Circle & Silver Park Phone: (216)791-7755
Cleveland, OH 44106 Claudia Z. Fechter, Libn.
Founded: 1896. **Staff:** Prof 1; Other 2. **Subjects:** Judaica. **Special Collections:** Abba Hillel Silver Archives. **Holdings:** 40,000 books; pamphlets; maps; filmstrips; slides. **Subscriptions:** 50 journals and other serials; 10 newspapers. **Services:** Interlibrary loan; copying; library open to the public. **Special Indexes:** Jewish Union List (JUL) periodic list of holdings of institutions in the Greater Cleveland area. **Remarks:** Branch library, located at 26000 Shaker Blvd., contains a children's collection, adult fiction, and holocaust material.

★13973★
TEMPLE OHABAI SHALOM - LIBRARY (Rel-Phil)
5015 Harding Rd. Phone: (615)352-7620
Nashville, TN 37205 Annette Levy Ratkin, Libn.
Staff: Prof 1; Other 1. **Subjects:** Bible commentary, Jewish history, children's literature. **Holdings:** 5000 books. **Subscriptions:** 10 journals and other serials. **Services:** Interlibrary loan; copying; library open to the public.

★13974★
TEMPLE OHABEI SHALOM - SISTERHOOD LIBRARY (Rel-Phil)
1187 Beacon St. Phone: (617)277-6610
Brookline, MA 02146 Mary R. Rosen, Libn.
Founded: 1938. **Staff:** 1. **Subjects:** Bible, Judaism, biography, history, Israel, religion, theology. **Holdings:** 3500 books. **Subscriptions:** 14 journals and other serials. **Services:** Library open to the public with restrictions. **Remarks:** An alternate telephone number is 734-9109.

★13975★
TEMPLE SHAAREY ZEDEK - RABBI ISAAC KLEIN LIBRARY (Rel-Phil)
621 Getzville Rd. Phone: (716)838-3232
Amherst, NY 14226 Ferne E. Mittleman, Libn.
Founded: 1959. **Staff:** Prof 1; Other 4. **Subjects:** Judaica. **Holdings:** 3300 volumes. **Subscriptions:** 13 journals and other serials. **Services:** Library open to the public.

★13976★
TEMPLE SHAREY TEFILO-ISRAEL - EDWARD EHRENKRANTZ/ELCHANAN ECHIKSON MEMORIAL LIBRARY (Rel-Phil)
432 Scotland Rd. Phone: (201)763-4116
South Orange, NJ 07079 Ann R. Zeve, Libn.
Staff: Prof 1. **Subjects:** Bible; Jewish religion, history, customs, ceremonies, holidays, practices, theology, philosophy, social sciences; fiction. **Holdings:** 4755 volumes. **Services:** Library not open to the public.

★13977★
TEMPLE SINAI - DR. ALEX MORRISON LIBRARY (Rel-Phil)
50 Alberta Dr. Phone: (716)834-0708
Buffalo, NY 14226 Vivien G. Krieger, Hd.Libn.
Founded: 1972. **Staff:** Prof 1; Other 2. **Subjects:** Judaica, Holocaust. **Holdings:** 3008 volumes. **Services:** Library open to the public.

★13978★
TEMPLE SINAI - JACK BALABAN MEMORIAL LIBRARY (Rel-Phil)
New Albany Rd. Phone: (609)829-0658
Cinnaminson, NJ 08077 Joseph Alterescu, Libn.
Staff: 1. **Subjects:** Holocaust; Jewish history, religion, holidays, authors. **Special Collections:** Encyclopaedia Judaica. **Holdings:** 1000 books. **Services:** Interlibrary loan; library open to the public with restrictions.

★13979★
TEMPLE SINAI - LIBRARY (Rel-Phil)
3100 Military Rd., N.W. Phone: (202)363-6394
Washington, DC 20015 Margaret Chachkin, Libn.
Founded: 1960. **Staff:** Prof 1; Other 2. **Subjects:** Judaism - philosophy, history; Bible; theology; Jews in the United States; Jewish rituals, traditions, folklore, art, literature, and music; Israeli history; Holocaust. **Special Collections:** Celia B. Friedman Collection of Hebrew Material (60 books); Selis Memorial Collection (comparative religion; 55 volumes); Bianka Zwick Memorial Collection (American-Jewish immigrant experience). **Holdings:** 4000 volumes; 2 VF drawers of clippings. **Subscriptions:** 37 journals and other serials. **Services:** Copying; library open to the public. **Publications:** Bibliographies; guides.

★13980★
TEMPLE SINAI - LIBRARY (Rel-Phil)
50 Sewall Ave. Phone: (617)277-5888
Brookline, MA 02146 Jane Taubenfield Cohen, Prin., Rel.Sch.
Staff: Prof 1. **Subjects:** Judaica, religion, Bible, Talmud. **Holdings:** 2200 books. **Services:** Library not open to the public.

★13981★
TEMPLE UNIVERSITY - CENTER FOR THE STUDY OF FEDERALISM - LIBRARY (Soc Sci)
Gladfelter Hall, 10th Fl., 025-25 Phone: (215)787-1483
Philadelphia, PA 19122 Rasheeda Didi, Res.Asst.
Staff: Prof 1; Other 1. **Subjects:** American federalism, comparative federal systems, federal theory, political culture, state and local governments, environmental problems, covenants. **Holdings:** 1500 books; 1200 bound periodical volumes; 1000 uncataloged items; 5 VF drawers. **Subscriptions:** 102 journals and other serials. **Services:** Copying; library open to the public with director's supervision. **Publications:** CSF Notebook; Publius: The Journal of Federalism, quarterly; special reports and books on key subject areas. **Remarks:** "The center is dedicated to the study of federal principles, institutions, and processes as a practical means of organizing political power in a free society. By initiating, sponsoring, and conducting research projects and educational programs related to them, the center seeks to increase and disseminate knowledge of federalism in general and to develop specialists in the growing field of intergovernmental relations."

★13982★
TEMPLE UNIVERSITY - CENTRAL LIBRARY SYSTEM - AMBLER CAMPUS LIBRARY (Biol Sci, Educ)
Meetinghouse Rd. Phone: (215)283-1383
Ambler, PA 19002 Linda Cotilla, Hd.Libn.
Founded: 1958. **Staff:** Prof 3; Other 6. **Subjects:** Horticulture, education, literature, history, landscape design, science, botany, sociology, business. **Special Collections:** Horticulture and landscape design (3000 volumes); Pennsylvania Affiliate Data Center (census materials). **Holdings:** 62,000 books; 5250 bound periodical volumes; 3545 recordings; 8600 pamphlets; 3500 reels of microfilm. **Subscriptions:** 600 journals and other serials; 20 newspapers. **Services:** Interlibrary loan; copying; library open to the public for reference use only. **Computerized Information Services:** RLIN, DIALOG Information Services, BRS Information Technologies, Association of Research Libraries (ARL). **Networks/Consortia:** Member of RLG, Center for Research Libraries (CRL) Consortia, PALINET. **Staff:** Steven V. Baumeister, Asst.Libn./Serv.; Sandra Thompson, Asst.Libn./Rsrcs..

★13983★
TEMPLE UNIVERSITY - CENTRAL LIBRARY SYSTEM - AUDIO UNIT (Mus)
Broad & Montgomery Phone: (215)787-8205
Philadelphia, PA 19122 Steve Landstreet, Hd. of Coll.
Subjects: Music - classical, jazz, popular, folk; musical comedy; spoken word recordings. **Special Collections:** Paley Presents Lecture Series (257 tape recordings). **Holdings:** 15,109 phonograph records; 292 reel-to-reel tapes; 65 compact discs; 70 cassettes. **Special Catalogs:** Partial Individual Song Catalog for phonograph records in the popular collection (card; in preparation).

★13984★
TEMPLE UNIVERSITY - CENTRAL LIBRARY SYSTEM - BIOLOGY LIBRARY (Biol Sci)
248 Life Science Bldg. Phone: (215)787-8878
Philadelphia, PA 19122 Raelaine Ballou, Hd., Eng. & Sci.Libs.
Staff: 1. **Subjects:** Biology - cell, molecular, developmental; biochemistry; genetics; physiology. **Holdings:** 1400 books; 12,000 bound periodical volumes; 11 VF drawers of reprints; 50 volumes of dissertations and theses. **Services:** Interlibrary loan; copying; library open to qualified users. **Automated Operations:** Computerized public access catalog and circulation. **Computerized Information Services:** Association of Research Libraries (ARL). **Networks/Consortia:** Member of Center for Research Libraries (CRL) Consortia, PALINET, RLG.

★13985★
TEMPLE UNIVERSITY - CENTRAL LIBRARY SYSTEM - CHARLES L. BLOCKSON AFRO-AMERICAN HISTORICAL COLLECTION (Hist, Area-Ethnic)
Sullivan Hall, 1st Fl. Phone: (215)787-6632
Philadelphia, PA 19122 Charles L. Blockson, Cur.
Founded: 1983. **Staff:** Prof 3; Other 2. **Subjects:** Afro-American history, literature, and religion; African history; blacks in sports; Caribbean; sociology; education. **Special Collections:** History of blacks in Pennsylvania; underground railroad; John Mosley Photo Collection; Paul Robeson Collection; Bishop R.R. Wright, Jr. Collection. **Holdings:** 13,642 books; 169 bound periodical volumes; 15,000 other cataloged items. **Subscriptions:** 19 journals and other serials. **Services:** Copying; collection open to the public for reference use only. **Automated Operations:** Computerized cataloging and circulation. **Computerized Information Services:** RLIN, Geac Library Information System. **Networks/Consortia:** Member of , , , . **Publications:** Afro-Americana: An Exhibition of Selected Books, Manuscripts & Prints, 1984. **Staff:** James Gordon, Asst.Cur.; Margaret Jarrette, Libn..
Founded: 1968. **Staff:** 1. **Subjects:** Chemistry - organic, inorganic, physical, analytical, theoretical; biochemistry. **Special Collections:** Guy F. Allen Memorial Collection in Chemical Education (100 volumes). **Holdings:** 5596 books; 12,223 bound periodical volumes; 2 VF of reprints; 135 volumes of theses and dissertations. **Subscriptions:** 253 journals and other serials. **Services:** Interlibrary loan; copying; library open to qualified users. **Automated Operations:** Computerized circulation. **Computerized Information Services:** Association of Research Libraries (ARL). **Networks/Consortia:** Member of RLG, Center for Research Libraries (CRL) Consortia, PALINET.

★13986★
TEMPLE UNIVERSITY - CENTRAL LIBRARY SYSTEM - CHEMISTRY LIBRARY (Sci-Engr)
Beury Hall, 1st Fl. Phone: (215)787-7120
Philadelphia, PA 19122 Dolores Michalak, Bibliog.Asst.
Founded: 1968. **Staff:** 1. **Subjects:** Chemistry - organic, inorganic, physical, analytical, theoretical; biochemistry. **Special Collections:** Guy F. Allen Memorial Collection in Chemical Education (100 volumes). **Holdings:** 5596 books; 12,223 bound periodical volumes; 2 VF of reprints; 135 volumes of theses and dissertations. **Subscriptions:** 253 journals and other serials. **Services:** Interlibrary loan; copying; library open to qualified users. **Automated Operations:** Computerized circulation. **Computerized Information Services:** Association of Research Libraries (ARL). **Networks/Consortia:** Member of RLG, Center for Research Libraries (CRL) Consortia, PALINET.

★13987★
TEMPLE UNIVERSITY - CENTRAL LIBRARY SYSTEM - COLLEGE OF ENGINEERING, COMPUTER SCIENCES, AND ARCHITECTURE - LIBRARY (Plan, Sci-Engr)
12th & Norris Sts. Phone: (215)787-7828
Philadelphia, PA 19122 Betsy Tabas, Libn.
Founded: 1921. **Staff:** Prof 1; Other 4. **Subjects:** Engineering - biomedical, civil, electrical, environmental, mechanical; architecture. **Holdings:** 18,000 books; 2000 bound periodical volumes. **Subscriptions:** 350 journals and other serials. **Services:** Interlibrary loan; copying; library open to the public. **Automated Operations:** Computerized public access catalog and circulation. **Computerized Information Services:** DIALOG Information Services, Association of Research Libraries (ARL). Performs searches on fee basis. **Networks/Consortia:** Member of RLG, Center for Research Libraries (CRL) Consortia, PALINET.

★13988★
TEMPLE UNIVERSITY - CENTRAL LIBRARY SYSTEM - CONTEMPORARY CULTURE COLLECTION (Soc Sci)
13th & Berks Sts. Phone: (215)787-8667
Philadelphia, PA 19122 Elaine Cox Clever, Cur.
Founded: 1969. **Staff:** 1. **Subjects:** Social change, peace and disarmament, small press poetry, fringe politics, alternative life styles, animal rights, feminism, gays. **Special Collections:** Counter culture and peace movement newspapers from the Vietnam era; early second wave feminist publications and literary chapbooks; Liberation News Service Archive (160 linear feet); Youth Liberation Archive (40 linear feet); Committee of Small Press Editors and Publishers Archive (32 linear feet); small presses archives (83 linear feet); personal papers of poet Lyn Lifshin (36 linear feet). **Holdings:** 7500 books and pamphlets; 3500 periodical, newspaper, and newsletter titles; 700 reels of microfilm; 70 linear feet of ephemera. **Subscriptions:** 290 journals and other serials; 90 newspapers. **Services:** Copying; collection open to the public for reference use only. **Automated Operations:** Computerized cataloging. **Computerized Information Services:** Association of Research Libraries (ARL). **Networks/Consortia:** Member of RLG, Center for Research Libraries (CRL) Consortia, PALINET. **Publications:** Periodical holdings lists, 1972, 1976; Alternative Press Periodicals: A Listing of Periodicals Microfilmed at The Collection, 1976; Exhibits with related bibliographies.

★13989★
TEMPLE UNIVERSITY - CENTRAL LIBRARY SYSTEM - CONWELLANA-TEMPLANA COLLECTION (Hist)
13th & Berks Sts. Phone: (215)787-8240
Philadelphia, PA 19122 Carol Harris, Bibliog.Asst.
Founded: 1946. **Staff:** Prof 1; Other 2. **Subjects:** University archives; life and activities of Russell Conwell. **Special Collections:** Faculty and alumni publications (3900 volumes); sermons, manuscripts, and publications of Russell Conwell (38 linear feet); personal library of Russell Conwell (1800 volumes); personal papers of faculty and alumni (156 linear feet); Barrows Dunham-Fred Zimring Collection (128 tapes and 66 transcriptions of oral history interviews and research materials related to dismissal of faculty members and academic freedom issues; 7 linear feet); Frank Ankenbrand papers, manuscript notebooks, and publications (3 linear feet); Frank Brookhouser papers, correspondence, manuscripts, and published columns (5 linear feet); Negley K. Teeters personal papers, correspondence, manuscripts, and related files (5 linear feet); personal papers of Melville S. Green, 1950-1979 (statistical physicist; 14 linear feet); personal papers of Daniel Swern, 1961-1982 (chemist and pioneer in plastics; 35 linear feet); personal papers of Henry Dexter Learned, 1893-1978 (linguistic scholar; 7 linear feet); Weiss-Karlen Collection (papers of novelist David Weiss and poet-playwright Stymean Karlen, 1940-1982; 20 linear feet); papers of William W. Tomlinson, 1950-1980 (including diaries of his travels; 50 linear feet); papers of Miriam Allen De Ford, 1903-1975 (mystery and historical writer; 2 linear feet). **Holdings:** 6561 books; 2770 bound periodical volumes; 1506 catalogs and reports; 9632 theses and dissertations; 738 linear feet of archives and manuscripts; 18 drawers of clippings, pictures, pamphlets; 620 reels of microfilm; 630 tape recordings; 2580 slides, posters, phonograph records, and memorabilia. **Subscriptions:** 121 journals and other serials. **Services:** Interlibrary loan; copying; collection open to the public for reference use only. **Computerized Information Services:** Association of Research Libraries (ARL). **Networks/Consortia:** Member of RLG, Center for Research Libraries (CRL) Consortia, PALINET. **Publications:** General Guide to Archives and Manuscripts; Russell Herman Conwell: The Individual and His Influence, compiled by M.I. Crawford, 1977; Walk 100 Years in a Hundred Feet: The Temple Centennial, An Illustrated Guide to the History of Temple University; A Descriptive Guide to the University Archives of Temple University, 1986. **Special Catalogs:** Inventories of manuscripts and archives collections; Inventories of certain Record Groups and Personal Papers (in sheet form).

★13990★
TEMPLE UNIVERSITY - CENTRAL LIBRARY SYSTEM - FILM LIBRARY (Aud-Vis)
Samuel Paley Library
13th & Berks Mall Phone: (215)787-8571
Philadelphia, PA 19122 Lawrence W. Marble, Hd.
Staff: Prof 1; Other 1. **Subjects:** History, anthropology, film as art, filmmaking, psychology, political science, feature films. **Special Collections:** Science fiction. **Holdings:** 800 films. **Services:** Library not open to the public. **Publications:** Film catalog, every other year - for internal distribution only.

★13991★
TEMPLE UNIVERSITY - CENTRAL LIBRARY SYSTEM - MATHEMATICAL SCIENCES LIBRARY (Sci-Engr, Comp Sci)
407 Computer Sciences Bldg. Phone: (215)787-8434
Philadelphia, PA 19122 Kimberly Jones, Bibliog.Asst.
Founded: 1968. **Staff:** 1. **Subjects:** Pure and applied mathematics, statistics, computer and information sciences. **Holdings:** 2682 books; 10,396 bound periodical volumes; 9 linear feet of technical reports. **Subscriptions:** 350 journals and other serials. **Services:** Interlibrary loan; copying; library open to qualified users. **Automated Operations:** Computerized public access catalog and circulation. **Computerized Information Services:** Association of Research Libraries (ARL). **Networks/Consortia:** Member of RLG, Center for Research Libraries (CRL) Consortia, PALINET.

★13992★
TEMPLE UNIVERSITY - CENTRAL LIBRARY SYSTEM - PHYSICS LIBRARY (Sci-Engr)
209A Barton Hall Phone: (215)787-7649
Philadelphia, PA 19122 Rhea Mihalisin, Bibliog.Asst.
Founded: 1968. **Staff:** 1. **Subjects:** Physics, astronomy. **Holdings:** 3200 books; 10,000 bound periodical volumes; 1 VF drawer of reprints; 50 volumes of theses and dissertations; 1 VF drawer of preprints; 1 VF drawer of society newsletters. **Subscriptions:** 190 journals and other serials. **Services:** Interlibrary loan; copying; library open to qualified users. **Automated Operations:** Computerized circulation. **Computerized Information Services:** Association of Research Libraries (ARL). **Networks/Consortia:** Member of RLG, Center for Research Libraries (CRL) Consortia, PALINET.

★13993★
TEMPLE UNIVERSITY - CENTRAL LIBRARY SYSTEM - RARE BOOK & MANUSCRIPT COLLECTION (Rare Book)
13th & Berks St. Phone: (215)787-8230
Philadelphia, PA 19122 Thomas M. Whitehead, Hd., Spec.Coll.Dept.
Staff: Prof 2; Other 2. **Subjects:** English, French, American, and Symbolist literature; business history; science fiction; horticulture; lithography; printing, publishing, and bookselling history. **Special Collections:** Charles Morice papers; Constable & Company correspondence collection; Cochran History of Business Collection (500 volumes); Bush-Brown Horticulture Collection (500 volumes); Nordell 17th Century England Collection (150 volumes); Richard Ellis Library and Archive; Albert Caplan Limited Editions Club Collection; Sir Richard Owen correspondence collection; Walter de la Mare Collection; Paskow/Knuf Science Fiction and Fantasy Collection. **Holdings:** 40,000 books; 2500 bound periodical volumes; 3000 war posters; 2000 linear feet of manuscripts. **Subscriptions:** 15 journals and other serials. **Services:** Copying; collection open to the public with restrictions. **Computerized Information Services:** OCLC, DIALOG Information Services, BRS Information Technologies, Pergamon ORBIT InfoLine, Inc., Association of Research Libraries (ARL). **Networks/Consortia:** Member of PALINET, Center for Research Libraries (CRL) Consortia, RLG. **Special Catalogs:** Andre Girard, 1970; Lithography, 1973; Richard Aldington, 1973; 30 issued registers to manuscript collection. **Remarks:** Includes the holdings of Temple University - Central Library System - Science Fiction Collection. **Staff:** Sharon Fitzpatrick, Bibliog.Asst..

★13994★
TEMPLE UNIVERSITY - CENTRAL LIBRARY SYSTEM - REFERENCE & INFORMATION SERVICES DEPARTMENT MAP UNIT (Geog-Map)
Paley Library
13th & Berks Sts. Phone: (215)787-8213
Philadelphia, PA 19122 Ida G. Ginsburgs, Map Libn.
Staff: Prof 1. **Subjects:** Topography, geography, geology, hydrology. **Holdings:** 83,000 maps; 1300 atlases and gazetteers. **Services:** Interlibrary

loan; copying; collection open to the public on a limited schedule. **Computerized Information Services:** BRS Information Technologies, Pergamon ORBIT InfoLine, Inc., DIALOG Information Services, Telesystemes Questel, VU/TEXT Information Services, WILSONLINE. Performs searches on fee basis. Contact Person: David Dillard.

★13995★
TEMPLE UNIVERSITY - CENTRAL LIBRARY SYSTEM - TYLER SCHOOL OF FINE ARTS - LIBRARY (Art)
Beech & Penrose Aves. Phone: (215)782-2849
Philadelphia, PA 19126 Mary Ivy Bayard, Libn.
Founded: 1935. **Staff:** 3. **Subjects:** Fine and applied arts. **Holdings:** 27,000 volumes; 6 VF drawers of pictures; 5 periodical titles on microfilm. **Subscriptions:** 118 journals and other serials. **Services:** Interlibrary loan; copying. **Computerized Information Services:** Association of Research Libraries (ARL). **Networks/Consortia:** Member of RLG, Center for Research Libraries (CRL) Consortia, PALINET.

★13996★
TEMPLE UNIVERSITY - CENTRAL LIBRARY SYSTEM - URBAN ARCHIVES (Soc Sci)
13th & Berks Sts. Phone: (215)787-8257
Philadelphia, PA 19122 Dr. Fredric Miller, Cur.
Founded: 1967. **Staff:** Prof 3; Other 4. **Subjects:** Philadelphia area - history, housing, planning, social welfare, urban renewal, civil rights, politics, settlement houses, education, labor, criminal justice, business, photojournalism, news photography. **Special Collections:** WPVI-TV News Film, 1947-1983; Philadelphia Inquirer Newspaper Photographic Archival Collection, 1937-1979; Philadelphia Evening Bulletin Library, 1847-1982. **Holdings:** 3000 books; 20,000 pamphlets; 200 manuscript collections; 750 maps; 5000 photographs; 10,000 canisters of news film; 240 filing cabinets of clippings; 550 filing cabinets of photographic prints and negatives. **Subscriptions:** 10 journals and other serials. **Services:** Copying; archives open to the public. **Computerized Information Services:** RLIN, Association of Research Libraries (ARL). **Networks/Consortia:** Member of RLG, Center for Research Libraries (CRL) Consortia, PALINET. **Publications:** Urban Archives Notes, biennial; Guides to Housing and Social Services Collections. **Special Catalogs:** Folder lists of manuscripts; catalog of pamphlets and photographs (card). **Staff:** George D. Brightbill, Photojournalism Cur.; David Weinberg, Asst.Cur..

TEMPLE UNIVERSITY - CENTRAL LIBRARY SYSTEM - URBAN ARCHIVES - HOUSING ASSOCIATION OF DELAWARE VALLEY
See: Housing Association of Delaware Valley (6507)

★13997★
TEMPLE UNIVERSITY - CENTRAL LIBRARY SYSTEM - ZAHN INSTRUCTIONAL MATERIALS CENTER/SCHOOL OF SOCIAL ADMINISTRATION - LIBRARY (Educ, Soc Sci)
Ritter Annex 139
13th & Columbia Ave. Phone: (215)787-8481
Philadelphia, PA 19122 Lawrence W. Marble, Hd.Libn.
Staff: Prof 2; Other 3. **Subjects:** Instructional materials, education, social administration, welfare. **Holdings:** 34,605 books; 697 bound periodical volumes; 542 volumes of masters' projects and theses; 2489 nonprint curricular materials. **Subscriptions:** 156 journals and other serials. **Services:** Interlibrary loan; copying; library open to the public. **Computerized Information Services:** Association of Research Libraries (ARL). **Networks/Consortia:** Member of RLG, Center for Research Libraries (CRL) Consortia, PALINET.

★13998★
TEMPLE UNIVERSITY - DEPARTMENT OF JOURNALISM - BLITMAN READING ROOM (Info Sci)
303 Annenberg Hall
13th & Diamond Sts. Phone: (215)787-7350
Philadelphia, PA 19122 Robert G. Roberts, Libn.
Staff: Prof 1; Other 1. **Subjects:** Reporting, newspaper industry, media law, radio and television broadcasting, telecommunications. **Holdings:** 10,200 books. **Subscriptions:** 80 journals and other serials; 25 newspapers. **Services:** Copying; library open to the public.

★13999★
TEMPLE UNIVERSITY - ESTHER BOYER COLLEGE OF MUSIC - NEW SCHOOL INSTITUTE - ALICE TULLY LIBRARY (Mus)
301 S. 21st St. Phone: (215)732-3966
Philadelphia, PA 19103 Susan L. Koenig, Libn.
Staff: Prof 1; Other 6. **Subjects:** Music, music literature. **Holdings:** 2000 books; 6500 scores; 2300 phonograph records; 300 tapes. **Subscriptions:** 25 journals and other serials. **Services:** Library not open to the public.

★14000★
TEMPLE UNIVERSITY - EXPERIMENTAL PARTICLE PHYSICS PROGRAM - LIBRARY
Physics Dept., 009-00
Philadelphia, PA 19122
Defunct

★14001★
TEMPLE UNIVERSITY - HEALTH SCIENCES CENTER - DIAGNOSTIC IMAGING LIBRARY (Med)
3401 N. Broad St. Phone: (215)221-4226
Philadelphia, PA 19140 Nancy Washburne Haines, Libn./Dir.
Founded: 1960. **Staff:** Prof 1. **Subjects:** Diagnostic imaging, radiology, nuclear medicine. **Special Collections:** Radiological Teaching File Collection (10,000 films and scans). **Holdings:** 1000 books; 650 bound periodical volumes; 9000 radiologic teaching cases; 1000 transparencies; 18 departmental dissertations; 9 volumes of departmental publications; 80 videotapes; 20 slide/tape sets. **Subscriptions:** 45 journals and other serials. **Services:** Interlibrary loan; library open to health professionals on referral and by appointment. **Automated Operations:** Computerized serials. **Computerized Information Services:** BRS Information Technologies, NLM.

★14002★
TEMPLE UNIVERSITY - HEALTH SCIENCES CENTER - HEALTH SCIENCES LIBRARIES (Med)
Kresge Hall
3400 N. Broad St. Phone: (215)221-4502
Philadelphia, PA 19140 Mark-Allen Taylor, Dir.
Founded: 1901. **Staff:** Prof 9; Other 6. **Subjects:** Medicine, dentistry, pharmacy, basic sciences, nursing, allied health sciences. **Special Collections:** Medical History. **Holdings:** 92,340 volumes; audiotapes. **Subscriptions:** 1179 journals and other serials. **Services:** Interlibrary loan; copying; library open to the public. **Automated Operations:** Computerized cataloging. **Computerized Information Services:** NLM, BRS Information Technologies, DIALOG Information Services, RLIN. **Networks/Consortia:** Member of RLG. **Publications:** Periodicals Holdings List. **Remarks:** The Health Sciences Center holds the Dental-Allied Health-Pharmacy Library and the Medical Library. Each is housed separately. **Staff:** Virginia Lampson, Ref.Libn.; Marcelle Freyman, Ref.Libn.; Margaret Grzesiak, Cat.; Karen Burstein, Ref.Libn.; Maureen Smith, Cat.; Robert Rooney, Ref.Libn.; Jerry Holst, Circ.Libn.; Diana Zinnato, Asst.Dir., Tech.Serv..

★14003★
TEMPLE UNIVERSITY - LAW LIBRARY (Law)
N. Broad St. & Montgomery Ave. Phone: (215)787-7892
Philadelphia, PA 19122 John M. Lindsey, Law Prof./Law Libn.
Staff: Prof 7; Other 12. **Subjects:** Law, legal history. **Special Collections:** Justice of the Peace Manuals; Hirst Free Law Library. **Holdings:** 349,501 books; 13,000 bound periodical volumes; microforms. **Subscriptions:** 2627 journals and other serials. **Services:** Interlibrary loan; copying; library open to the public for reference use only. **Networks/Consortia:** Member of RLG.

★14004★
TEMPLE UNIVERSITY - TYLER SCHOOL OF FINE ARTS - SLIDE LIBRARY (Art, Aud-Vis)
Beech & Penrose Aves. Phone: (215)782-2848
Elkins Park, PA 19126 Edith Zuckerman, Hd. Slide Cur.
Founded: 1970. **Staff:** Prof 2; Other 2. **Subjects:** Art history - prehistoric to contemporary; decorative arts; ceramics; graphics; photography; film. **Holdings:** 307,000 slides. **Services:** Copying; library open to faculty and graduate students. **Automated Operations:** Computerized acquisitions. **Computerized Information Services:** Online systems. **Staff:** Diane Sarachman, Assoc.Cur..

ABE AND ESTHER TENENBAUM LIBRARY
See: Agudath Achim Synagogue (99)

TENNECO CANADA, INC. - ERCO
See: ERCO (4761)

★14005★
TENNECO, INC. - CORPORATE LIBRARY (Bus-Fin, Sci-Engr)
1010 Milam St., Suite 2449
Box 2511 Phone: (713)757-2788
Houston, TX 77252 Linda S. Bailey, Sr.Libn.
Staff: Prof 2; Other 1. **Subjects:** Business, technology, energy, engineering. **Holdings:** 5000 books; 1200 bound periodical volumes; government documents; corporate annual reports. **Subscriptions:** 176 journals and other serials; 6 newspapers. **Services:** Interlibrary loan; copying; library open to the public by appointment. **Computerized Information Services:** DIALOG Information Services, Pergamon ORBIT InfoLine, Inc., Dow Jones News/Retrieval, NEXIS, VU/TEXT Information Services, GEISCO (General Electric Information Services Company). **Staff:** Diane Lindenberger, Libn..

★14006★
TENNECO, INC. - NEWPORT NEWS SHIPBUILDING - LIBRARY (Biol Sci, Sci-Engr)
4101 Washington Ave. Phone: (804)380-2610
Newport News, VA 23067 Roberta M. Norton, Supv., Rec.Mgt.
Founded: 1947. **Staff:** Prof 3; Other 2. **Subjects:** Oceanography, management, naval architecture, marine engineering, mathematics. **Holdings:** 35,000 books; 9000 bound periodical volumes; 10,000 research reports and documents. **Subscriptions:** 1300 journals and other serials. **Services:** Interlibrary loan; library open to the public with security clearance.

TENNECO, INC. - NEWPORT NEWS SHIPBUILDING - SPERRY MARINE INC.
See: Sperry Marine Inc. (13550)

★14007★
TENNECO OIL EXPLORATION AND PRODUCTION - GEOLOGICAL RESEARCH LIBRARY (Sci-Engr)
Box 2511
Houston, TX 77252 Phone: (713)757-8832
Founded: 1958. **Staff:** 2. **Subjects:** Geology, geophysics, oceanology, petroleum exploration and production, mineral exploration, mining, natural resources. **Holdings:** 23,000 volumes; 5000 maps. **Subscriptions:** 250 journals and other serials. **Services:** Interlibrary loan; copying; library open to petroleum and mineral company librarians. **Computerized Information Services:** DIALOG Information Services, Pergamon ORBIT InfoLine, Inc. **Publications:** Bi-monthly Library Bulletin - for internal distribution only. **Remarks:** Library located at 1100 Milam Bldg., Rm. 1460, Houston, TX 77002. **Staff:** Olive Tyson, Libn.; Wilda Wiley, Libn..

★14008★
TENNESSEAN NEWSPAPER - LIBRARY (Publ)
1100 Broadway Phone: (615)259-8007
Nashville, TN 37202 Annette Morrison, Hd.Libn.
Founded: 1940. **Staff:** Prof 2; Other 5. **Subjects:** Newspaper reference topics. **Holdings:** 1550 books; 80 bound periodical volumes; 60 VF drawers of pamphlets; 1028 VF drawers of clippings; 160 VF drawers of photographs; 80 drawers of microfilm. **Subscriptions:** 30 journals and other serials. **Services:** Copying (limited); library open to journalists by appointment. **Automated Operations:** Computerized cataloging. **Special Indexes:** Files on people, reporter by-lines, criminals, lawsuit litigants, and businesses (card). **Staff:** Nancy St. Cyr, Asst.Libn..

★14009★
TENNESSEE BOTANICAL GARDENS & FINE ARTS CENTER - BOTANICAL GARDENS LIBRARY (Biol Sci)
Cheekwood-Forrest Park Dr. Phone: (615)356-3306
Nashville, TN 37205 Muriel H. Connell, Libn.
Founded: 1971. **Staff:** Prof 1; Other 2. **Subjects:** Horticulture, landscape architecture, plant science, ecology, wildflowers, garden design, botanical art, orchids, herbs, natural history. **Holdings:** 4300 books; 260 bound periodical volumes; 220 pamphlets; 82 slide programs; 3000 slides; flower and seed catalogs. **Subscriptions:** 130 journals and other serials. **Services:** Interlibrary loan; copying; library open to the public with restrictions.

★14010★
TENNESSEE BOTANICAL GARDENS & FINE ARTS CENTER - FINE ARTS CENTER LIBRARY (Art)
Cheekwood-Forrest Park Dr. Phone: (615)352-8632
Nashville, TN 37205 Mary N. Hernandez, Libn.
Staff: Prof 1. **Subjects:** Art, art history, decorative arts, contemporary American artists, photography. **Holdings:** 2000 volumes; 2000 slides. **Subscriptions:** 20 journals and other serials. **Services:** Interlibrary loan; copying; library open to the public for reference use only.

TENNESSEE EASTMAN COMPANY
See: Eastman Kodak Company - Eastman Chemicals Division - Business Library (4559)

★14011★
TENNESSEE STATE COMMISSION ON AGING - LIBRARY (Soc Sci)
706 Church St., Suite 201
Nashville, TN 37219-5573 Phone: (615)741-2056
Founded: 1963. **Staff:** 1. **Subjects:** Aging, geriatric psychology and sociology, retirement planning, community based health and social services. **Holdings:** 500 books; VF drawers. **Subscriptions:** 10 journals and other serials. **Services:** Copying; library open to the public for reference use only. **Staff:** Steve Canada, Prog.Spec.; Mason Rowe, Prog.Spec..

★14012★
TENNESSEE STATE DEPARTMENT OF AGRICULTURE - LOU WALLACE LIBRARY (Agri)
Ellington Agricultural Center
Melrose Sta., Box 40627 Phone: (615)360-0117
Nashville, TN 37204 Tom Womack, Adm.Asst., Pub.Aff.
Staff: Prof 2; Other 1. **Subjects:** Agriculture, statistics. **Holdings:** 1500 books. **Services:** Library open to the public for reference use only.

★14013★
TENNESSEE STATE DEPARTMENT OF CONSERVATION - RESOURCE CENTER
701 Broadway
Nashville, TN 37219-5237
Defunct

★14014★
TENNESSEE STATE DEPARTMENT OF ECONOMIC & COMMUNITY DEVELOPMENT - LIBRARY (Bus-Fin)
Rachel Jackson Bldg., 8th Fl. Phone: (615)741-1995
Nashville, TN 37219 Edith Snider, Libn.
Founded: 1973. **Staff:** Prof 1; Other 1. **Subjects:** Industrial development, economics, minority business enterprise. **Special Collections:** Department Archives. **Holdings:** 3000 books; 300 documents; 750 file folios of corporation annual reports from Fortune 500 companies and major Tennessee companies. **Subscriptions:** 210 journals and other serials. **Services:** Interlibrary loan; copying; library open to the public with restrictions.

★14015★
TENNESSEE STATE DEPARTMENT OF EMPLOYMENT SECURITY - RESEARCH & STATISTICS SECTION (Bus-Fin)
519 Cordell Hull Bldg. Phone: (615)741-2284
Nashville, TN 37219 Joe Cummings, Chf., Res. & Stat.
Staff: 1. **Subjects:** Data - labor market, census, economic. **Holdings:** Publications of the U.S. Bureau of Census, the U.S. Department of Labor, and the Department of Employment Security. **Services:** Copying; section open to the public for reference use only. **Publications:** Labor Market Information Directory.

★14016★
TENNESSEE STATE DEPARTMENT OF HEALTH AND ENVIRONMENT - CENTER FOR HEALTH STATISTICS - INFORMATION AND REFERRAL UNIT LIBRARY (Med, Plan)
C2-242 Cordell Hull Bldg. Phone: (615)741-1954
Nashville, TN 37219-5402 Ann Hogan, Stat.Anl.
Founded: 1976. **Staff:** Prof 1; Other 1. **Subjects:** Vital and health statistics, population. **Holdings:** 1200 books. **Subscriptions:** 13 journals and other serials. **Services:** Copying; library open to the public with restrictions. **Computerized Information Services:** Internal databases. **Publications:** List of publications - available on request. **Staff:** Gayle Casey, Statistician.

★14017★
TENNESSEE STATE DEPARTMENT OF HEALTH AND ENVIRONMENT - HEALTH PROMOTION SECTION - MEDIA RESOURCE CENTER (Aud-Vis, Med)
Old UT Bldg.
100 9th Ave., N. Phone: (615)741-7366
Nashville, TN 37219 Randall Brady, Dir.
Founded: 1950. **Staff:** Prof 2. **Subjects:** Health, safety, nutrition, drug abuse, allied health fields. **Special Collections:** Medical Self Help Series (5 sets). **Holdings:** 2000 films, filmstrips, slide series. **Services:** Materials available for free loan to Tennessee residents; library not open to the public. **Special Catalogs:** The Film Catalog and supplements.

★14018★
TENNESSEE STATE DEPARTMENT OF HEALTH AND ENVIRONMENT - RESOURCE CENTER (Med)
100 9th Ave., N. Phone: (615)741-7366
Nashville, TN 37219-5404 Randall Brady, Dir., Rsrc.Ctr.
Staff: Prof 1. **Subjects:** Maternal and child health, nursing, public health, health education. **Holdings:** 500 books. **Subscriptions:** 100 journals and other serials. **Services:** Center open to public health professionals. **Special Catalogs:** Media Resource Catalog (loose-leaf). **Formerly:** Tennessee State Department of Public Health.

★14019★
TENNESSEE STATE DEPARTMENT OF STATE - TENNESSEE STATE LIBRARY AND ARCHIVES (Hist, Law, Info Sci)
403 7th Ave. N., Main Fl. Phone: (615)741-2764
Nashville, TN 37219 Edwin S. Gleaves, Ph.D., Libn. & Archv.
Founded: 1854. **Staff:** Prof 37; Other 71. **Subjects:** Tennesseana, U.S. and local history, state and local government, law and public administration, genealogy. **Special Collections:** Papers of Jacob McGavock Dickinson, James Robertson, Andrew Jackson, George P. Buell, Henry Shelton Sanford, Richard Ewell; land records, 1777-1903 (600 volumes); state agency records and governors' papers, 1796 to present; legislative records and recordings, 1796 to present; state Supreme Court records, 1815-1955; ethics records, 1975-1976; county records on microfilm; prints and cartoons of Tennessee subjects; popular sheet music; 19th century broadsides; Tennessee newspapers. **Holdings:** 250,000 volumes; 2.7 million manuscript items; 800 original volumes; 15,000 reels of microfilm; 4000 hours of recordings; photographs. **Subscriptions:** 1400 journals and other serials; 200 newspapers. **Services:** Interlibrary loan; copying; library open to the public. **Automated Operations:** Computerized cataloging. **Computerized Information Services:** OCLC. **Networks/Consortia:** Member of SOLINET. **Publications:** List of Tennessee State Publications, quarterly; Writings on Tennessee Counties; Tennessee Newspapers on Microfilm; registers of manuscript materials; checklist of microfilm; Guide to the Processed Manuscripts of the Tennessee Historical Society; Guide to Microfilm Holdings of the Manuscripts Section. **Special Indexes:** Index to City Cemetery Records of Nashville; Index to Questionnaires of Civil War Veterans. **Staff:** Neal D. Harrell, Dir., TN State Lib. & Archv.; John McGlone, Dir., Pub.Serv.; Marylin Hughes, Hd., Res.Sect.; Fran Schell, Asst.Dir., Pub.Serv..

★14020★
TENNESSEE STATE DEPARTMENT OF TRANSPORTATION - LIBRARY (Trans)
James K. Polk Bldg., Suite 300 Phone: (615)741-2330
Nashville, TN 37219 Ruth S. Letson, Libn. II
Founded: 1973. **Staff:** Prof 1. **Subjects:** Transportation, Tennessee planning data, highways, road construction. **Special Collections:** Transportation Research Board publications. **Holdings:** 8000 books; 2000 local studies. **Subscriptions:** 100 journals and other serials. **Services:** Interlibrary loan; copying; library open to the public for reference use only. **Publications:** New Books, monthly - for internal distribution only.

★14021★
TENNESSEE (State) HUMAN RIGHTS COMMISSION - RESOURCE LIBRARY (Soc Sci)
Capitol Boulevard Bldg., Suite 602
226 Capitol Blvd.
Nashville, TN 37219 Phone: (615)741-5825
Staff: 1. **Subjects:** Race relations; discrimination in employment, housing, and public accommodations; legislation and decisions rendered in discrimination cases. **Holdings:** 60 books; 500 bound periodical volumes; commission-related materials. **Subscriptions:** 10 journals and other serials. **Services:** Library open to the public with restrictions. **Publications:** Annual Report.

★14022★
TENNESSEE STATE LAW LIBRARY (Law)
Supreme Court Bldg.
401 Seventh Ave., N. Phone: (615)741-2016
Nashville, TN 37219 G. Alvis Winstead, Dir./Libn.
Founded: 1937. **Staff:** Prof 2; Other 1. **Subjects:** Law. **Special Collections:** Depository Library. **Holdings:** 40,000 books; 1201 bound periodical volumes; 237 other cataloged items; 4 VF drawers; 200 cassettes of Supreme Court cases. **Subscriptions:** 116 journals and other serials. **Services:** Interlibrary loan; copying; library open to the public. **Remarks:** Maintains law libraries at Jackson, Knoxville, and Memphis.

★14023★
TENNESSEE STATE LEGISLATIVE LIBRARY (Law)
G-16 War Memorial Bldg. Phone: (615)741-3091
Nashville, TN 37219 Julie J. McCown, Leg.Libn.
Founded: 1977. **Staff:** Prof 1. **Subjects:** Tennessee law, legislative reference. **Holdings:** 12,000 volumes. **Subscriptions:** 70 journals and other serials. **Services:** Interlibrary loan; library open to the public for reference use only. **Remarks:** Maintained by Office of Legal Services for the Tennessee General Assembly.

★14024★
TENNESSEE STATE LIBRARY - LIBRARY FOR THE BLIND AND PHYSICALLY HANDICAPPED (Aud-Vis)
403 7th Ave., N. Phone: (615)741-3915
Nashville, TN 37219 Miss Francis H. Ezell, Dir.
Founded: 1970. **Staff:** Prof 2; Other 15. **Subjects:** General reading material for the blind and physically handicapped. **Holdings:** 23,000 titles of books recorded on disc and cassette, transcribed into braille; large print books. **Subscriptions:** 83 journals and other serials (45 disc, 35 braille, 3 cassette). **Services:** Free service to citizens of Tennessee who cannot read, hold, or turn the pages of a regular print book due to a visual or physical handicap. Playback equipment is provided. **Automated Operations:** Computerized cataloging, serials, and circulation. **Computerized Information Services:** BRS Information Technologies. **Networks/Consortia:** Member of National Library Service for the Blind & Physically Handicapped (NLS). **Remarks:** A toll-free telephone number in Tennessee is (800)342-3308.

TENNESSEE STATE LIBRARY AND ARCHIVES
See: Tennessee State Department of State (14019)

★14025★
TENNESSEE STATE MUSEUM - LIBRARY (Hist)
James K. Polk State Office Bldg. & Cultural Ctr.
505 Deaderick St. Phone: (615)741-2692
Nashville, TN 37219-5196 Evadine O. McMahan, Adm.Asst.
Founded: 1977. **Staff:** Prof 1; Other 1. **Subjects:** Tennessee history, American decorative arts, Southern U.S. history, weapons, anthropology, folklore. **Special Collections:** Official records of the War of the Rebellion (153 volumes); Weesner Collection (Indians; archeology); early Smithsonian Reports (22 volumes). **Holdings:** 1558 books; 148 bound periodical volumes; 22 videotapes; 21,000 slides. **Subscriptions:** 25 journals and other serials. **Services:** Copying; library open to the public for reference use only. **Special Catalogs:** Gallery exhibit catalogs (book).

★14026★
TENNESSEE STATE PLANNING OFFICE - LIBRARY (Plan)
John Sevier Bldg., Suite 310
500 Charlotte Ave. Phone: (615)741-2363
Nashville, TN 37219-5082 Eleanor J. Burt, Libn.
Founded: 1935. **Staff:** Prof 1; Other 1. **Subjects:** Planning, Tennessee, public affairs. **Special Collections:** Tennessee planning studies; state planning studies from other states; archives of planning office publications (3800 items); Tennessee state publications including departmental reports, Tennessee session laws, and the Tennessee Code. **Holdings:** 10,700 books and pamphlets; 1503 community planning color slides; 1980 Census Area Boundary Maps for Tennessee; 40 VF drawers; 10 cassettes; 1 film; 706 maps; 6858 microfiche; 50 binders of computer printouts. **Subscriptions:** 200 journals and other serials. **Services:** Interlibrary loan; copying; library open to the public. **Publications:** Acquisitions List, bimonthly; periodical list, irregular. **Remarks:** Reference collections of 9450 items and selected journal and newspaper subscriptions are maintained in six local planning field offices.

★14027★
TENNESSEE STATE PUBLIC SERVICE COMMISSION - LEGAL DEPARTMENT - LIBRARY (Law)
460 James Robertson Pkwy. Phone: (615)741-3191
Nashville, TN 37219 Henry Walker, Gen.Couns.
Founded: 1897. **Subjects:** Law, utility rates and service, transportation, tax assessments, railroads, transportation rates. **Holdings:** 2500 bound periodical volumes; docket files; transcripts; orders; court files. **Services:** Copying; library open to the public.

★14028★
TENNESSEE STATE SUPREME COURT - LAW LIBRARY (Law)
Supreme Court Bldg.
719 Locust St. Phone: (615)673-6128
Knoxville, TN 37902 Mamie H. Winstead, Libn.
Founded: 1937. **Staff:** Prof 1. **Subjects:** Law. **Holdings:** 81,000 volumes. **Subscriptions:** 150 journals and other serials. **Services:** Library open to the public with restrictions. **Automated Operations:** Computerized cataloging.

★14029★
TENNESSEE TECHNOLOGICAL UNIVERSITY - JERE WHITSON MEMORIAL LIBRARY (Bus-Fin, Sci-Engr)
Box 5066 Phone: (615)372-3326
Cookeville, TN 38505 Dr. Winston Walden, Dir., Lib.Serv.
Founded: 1915. **Staff:** Prof 15; Other 18. **Subjects:** Engineering. **Special Collections:** Tennessee and Upper Cumberland Region History Collection; archives; Congressman Joe Evins papers. **Holdings:** 242,835 books; 79,849 bound periodical volumes; 788,773 titles in microform; 129,262 government documents. **Subscriptions:** 3315 journals and other serials; 86 newspapers. **Services:** Interlibrary loan; SDI; library open to the public. **Automated Operations:** Computerized cataloging and acquisitions. **Computerized Information Services:** DIALOG Information Services, BRS Information Technologies, Pergamon ORBIT InfoLine, Inc. Performs searches on fee basis. Contact Person: David Gantt, Coord., Pub.Serv., 372-3958. **Staff:** Roger Jones, Coord., Coll.Mgt. & Dev.; Susan La Fever, Coord., Bibliog. Control; Carolyn Whitson, Coord., Media Serv..

★14030★
TENNESSEE VALLEY AUTHORITY - MAPPING SERVICES BRANCH (Geog-Map)
400 W. Summit Hill Dr. (WPA3) Phone: (615)632-2717
Knoxville, TN 37902 Jack L. Dodd, Civil Engr.
Founded: 1934. **Staff:** 2. **Subjects:** Tennessee Valley Region, planimetry, topography, water navigation, flood control, water power. **Holdings:** 12,000 sheet maps; navigation charts; geologic publications. **Services:** Reference and research services; sale of maps, charts, and engineering reproductions; services open to the public. **Publications:** Price Catalog - available upon request.

★14031★
TENNESSEE VALLEY AUTHORITY - MAPS AND SURVEYS BRANCH - MAP INFORMATION AND RECORDS UNIT (Geog-Map)
101 Haney Bldg. Phone: (615)751-5404
Chattanooga, TN 37401 J.L. Dodd, Civil Engr.
Founded: 1933. **Staff:** Prof 6; Other 1. **Subjects:** Mapping - land acquisition, land sales, special purpose; navigation charts and maps; control data; aerial photography; topography. **Holdings:** 1.2 million maps, charts, photographs, and control data. **Services:** Copying; unit open to the public. **Special Catalogs:** Price Catalog of Selected Maps and Data (book).

★14032★
TENNESSEE VALLEY AUTHORITY - NORRIS BRANCH LIBRARY (Biol Sci)
Norris, TN 37828 Phone: (615)632-1665
Colene H. Siler, Libn.
Founded: 1973. **Staff:** Prof 1; Other 1. **Subjects:** Forestry, fisheries, aquatic science, wildlife, waterfowl, recreation. **Holdings:** 7000 books; 15,000 documents. **Subscriptions:** 229 journals and other serials. **Services:** Interlibrary loan; copying; library open to the public. **Computerized Information Services:** DIALOG Information Services, BRS Information Technologies, Integrated Technical Information System (ITIS), OCLC.

★14033★
TENNESSEE VALLEY AUTHORITY - OGC LAW LIBRARY (Law)
400 W. Summit Hill Dr., E9C21 C-K Phone: (615)632-6645
Knoxville, TN 37902 Deborah A. Cherry, Supv., Legal Res.Ctr.
Staff: Prof 10; Other 11. **Subjects:** Law. **Holdings:** 20,000 volumes; 1 million documents. **Subscriptions:** 100 journals and other serials. **Services:** Interlibrary loan (limited); library not open to the public. **Automated Operations:** Computerized cataloging. **Computerized Information Services:** LEXIS, NEXIS, WESTLAW, ABA/net, ELSS (Electronic Legislative Search System), VU/TEXT Information Services, DIALOG Information Services. **Staff:** Robert Conrad, Ref./Indexer; Cheryl Dabbs, Ref./Cat.; Kim P. Kasten, Ref./Indexer; Teresa Scarlett, Ref./Thesaurus Coord.; Terry Hebb, Ref./Indexer; Ann C. Steffen, Ref./Indexer; Deborah H. Johnson, Ref./Indexer; Bessie Madison, Ref./Indexer; Michael Hamblin, Ref./Indexer.

★14034★
TENNESSEE VALLEY AUTHORITY - TECHNICAL LIBRARY (Sci-Engr, Agri)
National Fertilizer Development Center Phone: (205)386-2871
Muscle Shoals, AL 35660 Shirley G. Nichols, Lib.Mgr.
Founded: 1961. **Staff:** Prof 6; Other 5. **Subjects:** Agriculture, biomass energy, chemistry, chemical engineering, fertilizer, agricultural economics, environmental sciences, occupational health, waste management. **Special Collections:** One of the most complete collections on fertilizer in U.S.; history of fertilizer and agriculture. **Holdings:** 26,000 volumes; 2060 reels of microfilm; 400 VF drawers of pamphlets and documents. **Subscriptions:** 1310 journals and other serials; 8 newspapers. **Services:** Interlibrary loan; copying; reference services; library open to the public. **Automated Operations:** Computerized cataloging and serials. **Computerized Information Services:** DIALOG Information Services, Pergamon ORBIT InfoLine, Inc., STN International, BRS Information Technologies, Integrated Technical Information System (ITIS), NLM, OCLC; CATLIRS, TVAPUB (internal databases). Performs searches on fee basis. **Networks/Consortia:** Member of FEDLINK. **Publications:** Current Awareness and New Acquisitions, weekly; Calendar of Events, monthly; Fertilizer Publications with quarterly supplements; Bibliographies, semiannual. **Remarks:** Main library in Knoxville, Tennessee is in charge of cataloging. **Formerly:** National Fertilizer Library. **Staff:** Ra Nae Vaughn, Ref.Libn.; Drucilla Gambrell, Ref.Libn.; Wendolyn Clark, Ref.Libn.; Earline Pollard, Acq.Libn.; Kim Montgomery, Ref.Libn..

★14035★
TENNESSEE VALLEY AUTHORITY - TECHNICAL LIBRARY (Energy)
1101 Market St. Phone: (615)751-4913
Chattanooga, TN 37402 Dean Robinson, Supv.
Founded: 1957. **Staff:** Prof 4; Other 3. **Subjects:** Power, public utilities, environment. **Holdings:** 20,000 books; 16,000 government documents; 36,000 microfiche. **Subscriptions:** 400 journals and other serials. **Services:** Interlibrary loan; copying; SDI; library open to the public with restrictions. **Automated Operations:** Computerized cataloging. **Computerized Information Services:** DIALOG Information Services, OCLC; internal database. **Networks/Consortia:** Member of FEDLINK. **Publications:** Current Awareness Bulletins. **Special Indexes:** Index to electric utility statistical sources. **Remarks:** Main library in Knoxville, Tennessee is in charge of cataloging. **Staff:** Barbara Reavley, Ref.; Francis Bishop, Acq.Libn..

★14036★
TENNESSEE VALLEY AUTHORITY - TECHNICAL LIBRARY (Biol Sci, Sci-Engr, Env-Cons, Agri)
400 W. Summit Hill Dr. Phone: (615)632-3464
Knoxville, TN 37902 Margaret J. Bull, Chf.Libn.
Founded: 1933. **Staff:** Prof 22; Other 17. **Subjects:** Administration and finance; agriculture; chemistry; engineering - civil, mechanical, electrical, nuclear; environmental sciences and education; flood control and navigation; forestry and wildlife; recreation; resource development; energy research development. **Special Collections:** History and development of TVA and Tennessee River Valley; TVA printed archives. **Holdings:** 92,942 books; 16,000 bound periodical volumes; 450,000 clippings; 50,000 documents; 6500 reels of microfilm; 75,000 microfiche. **Subscriptions:** 2518 journals and other serials; 113 newspapers. **Services:** Interlibrary loan; copying; SDI; library open to the public. **Automated Operations:** Computerized cataloging and routing. **Computerized Information Services:** DIALOG Information Services, Pergamon ORBIT InfoLine, Inc., BRS Information Technologies, WILSONLINE, CAS ONLINE, Integrated Technical Information System (ITIS), OCLC; internal database. **Networks/Consortia:** Member of FEDLINK. **Publications:** TVA

Handbook, semiannual; Index of TVA News, weekly; Current Awareness List, semiweekly. **Remarks:** TVA maintains separate Technical Libraries in Knoxville, Norris, and Chattanooga, Tennessee and Muscle Shoals, Alabama. The central staff in Knoxville handles acquisitions and cataloging of materials for all libraries; figures above include holdings of the three libraries. **Staff:** Edwin J. Best, Jr., Supv., Serv.; Patricia Noonan, Cat.; Carolyn A. Thompson, Acq..

★14037★
TENNESSEE WESTERN HISTORY AND FOLKLORE SOCIETY - LIBRARY (Hist)
Box 60072
Nashville, TN 37206 Phone: (615)226-1890
Founded: 1979. **Staff:** Prof 2. **Subjects:** Tennessee and the Old West, Jesse and Frank James, the Seventh Cavalry (at Nashville), Ned Buntline, Clay Allison, Ambrose Bierce, Nat Love (black cowboy), J. Frank Dalton (Jesse James imposter), James Russell Davis (Cole Younger imposter), Butch Cassidy, John Wilkes Booth, Knights of the Golden Circle, filibusters, Western music. **Special Collections:** Jesse James, 1847-1882 (275 items); Western imposters (200 items). **Holdings:** 200 books; 100 letters; 300 miscellaneous items; articles and news clippings; photographs; affidavits; artifacts; maps. **Services:** Copying; research (both limited); library open to serious scholars by appointment. **Remarks:** The society is interested in acquiring any information about Western events or persons with Tennessee connections. It is affiliated with the Friends of the James Farm (Kearney, MO), Friends of the Youngers (Los Angeles, CA), and English Westerners Society (Westerners International). The society library is located at 1501 Eastland Ave., Nashville, TN 37206. **Staff:** Steve Eng, Cur.; Ted P. Yeatman, Cur..

★14038★
TERABYTE WETWARE INFOGURUS - LIBRARY
Box 356
Riverdale, MD 20737-0356
Founded: 1976. **Subjects:** Computer information systems. **Holdings:** 7500 books and bound periodical volumes.

★14039★
TERRA TEK RESEARCH - TECHNICAL LIBRARY (Sci-Engr, Energy)
University Research Park
420 Wakara Way
Salt Lake City, UT 84108 Phone: (801)584-2400
Founded: 1975. **Subjects:** Geothermal energy, rock mechanics, drilling, petroleum, materials testing. **Special Collections:** Technical reports. **Holdings:** Figures not available. **Services:** Interlibrary loan; copying; library open to the public.

★14040★
TERRELL STATE HOSPITAL - STAFF LIBRARY (Med)
Brin Ave.
Box 70 Phone: (214)563-6452
Terrell, TX 75160 Belinda K. Minahan, Libn.
Founded: 1964. **Staff:** 1. **Subjects:** Psychiatry, neurology, medicine, nursing, psychology, mental health and allied sciences. **Holdings:** 6775 books; 260 bound periodical volumes; 2145 unbound journals; 2369 pamphlets and nonbook materials. **Subscriptions:** 145 journals and other serials. **Services:** Interlibrary loan; copying; library open to the public for reference use only. **Networks/Consortia:** Member of TALON, Texas State Library Communications Network (TSLCN). **Publications:** Staff Library Handbook - to professional staff, hospital employees, and students of affiliated schools.

TERRORISM RESEARCH AND COMMUNICATION CENTER
See: Americans Combatting Terrorism (714)

SANDOR TESZLER LIBRARY
See: Wofford College (17984)

★14041★
TETON SCIENCE SCHOOL - MARDY MURIE LIBRARY (Biol Sci)
Box 68 Phone: (307)733-4765
Kelly, WY 83011 Roger Smith, Resident Instr.
Founded: 1967. **Staff:** 1. **Subjects:** Natural history, ecology, man and nature, zoology, botany, earth science. **Special Collections:** Greater Yellowstone ecosystem (articles; studies; papers). **Holdings:** 2500 books; 5000 other cataloged items. **Subscriptions:** 10 journals and other serials. **Services:** Library open to the public for reference use only. **Publications:** Biologue, 3/year - to secondary teachers.

★14042★
TEXACO CANADA RESOURCES - LIBRARY (Sci-Engr)
605 5th Ave., S.W.
Box 3333, Sta. M Phone: (403)267-0682
Calgary, AB, Canada T2P 2P8 Debbie Durie, Libn.
Staff: Prof 1; Other 1. **Subjects:** Geology, geophysics, petroleum engineering, business, management. **Holdings:** 3000 books; 300 bound periodical volumes; 2000 Geological Survey of Canada reports and government documents. **Subscriptions:** 150 journals and other serials; 5 newspapers. **Services:** Interlibrary loan; library not open to the public. **Automated Operations:** Computerized cataloging and circulation. **Computerized Information Services:** DIALOG Information Services, Pergamon ORBIT InfoLine, Inc., CAN/OLE, Info Globe; Envoy 100 (electronic mail service).

★14043★
TEXACO CHEMICAL COMPANY, INC. - TECHNICAL LITERATURE SECTION (Sci-Engr)
7114 N. Lamarr
Box 15730 Phone: (512)459-6543
Austin, TX 78761 Mary E. Reese, Sr.Res.Libn.
Founded: 1946. **Subjects:** Chemistry, chemical engineering. **Holdings:** 4000 books; 3725 bound periodical volumes; 400 other cataloged items; patents; reports. **Subscriptions:** 300 journals and other serials.

★14044★
TEXACO INC. - ARCHIVES (Bus-Fin)
2000 Westchester Ave. Phone: (914)253-7129
White Plains, NY 10650 Stafford Acher, Hist.
Subjects: Texaco Incorporated. **Holdings:** 200 volumes; 1500 cubic feet of records; Texaco Incorporated photographs and publications. **Services:** Copying; archives open to the public by appointment upon written request.

★14045★
TEXACO INC. - CORPORATE LIBRARY (Energy, Bus-Fin)
2000 Westchester Ave. Phone: (914)253-6382
White Plains, NY 10650 Holly J. Furman, Corp.Lib.Adm.
Founded: 1981. **Staff:** Prof 5; Other 3. **Subjects:** Business, energy, petroleum, area studies. **Holdings:** 11,300 volumes; 244,000 microfiche; 2400 reels of microfilm. **Subscriptions:** 450 journals and other serials. **Services:** Interlibrary loan; copying; SDI; library open to the public with restrictions. **Automated Operations:** Computerized public access catalog, cataloging, acquisitions, serials, and circulation. **Computerized Information Services:** Pergamon ORBIT InfoLine, Inc., DIALOG Information Services, Integrated Technical Information System (ITIS), NEXIS, OCLC, TEXTLINE, NewsNet, Inc., Dow Jones News/Retrieval, I.P. Sharp Associates Limited, Info Globe, INVESTEXT, Spectrum Ownership Profiles Online, WILSONLINE, Oil & Gas Journal Energy Database, VU/TEXT Information Services, DataTimes. **Networks/Consortia:** Member of New York Metropolitan Reference and Research Library Agency (METRO). **Publications:** The Source, monthly - for internal distribution only; Library brochures and bibliographies. **Staff:** Susan Feir, Info.Spec.; Nancy Williamson, Info.Spec.; Josephine Ndinyah, Info.Spec.; Kim Hibbard, Info.Spec..

★14046★
TEXACO INC. - DELAWARE CITY PLANT - LIBRARY
Delaware City, DE 19706
Defunct

★14047★
TEXACO INC. - HOUSTON RESEARCH CENTER LIBRARY (Energy)
3901 Briarpark Dr.
Box 770070 Phone: (713)953-6007
Houston, TX 77215-0070 Debra J. Clay, Lib.Supv.
Founded: 1960. **Staff:** Prof 3; Other 5. **Subjects:** Petroleum engineering, chemistry, geology, technology. **Holdings:** 40,000 books; 800 bound periodical volumes; AV programs; maps; company documents. **Subscriptions:** 300 journals and other serials. **Services:** Interlibrary loan; library not open to the public. **Automated Operations:** Computerized cataloging, serials, and circulation. **Computerized Information Services:** DIALOG Information Services, OCLC, BRS Information Technologies, STN International, Pergamon ORBIT InfoLine, Inc. **Networks/Consortia:** Member of AMIGOS Bibliographic Council, Inc.. **Publications:** Library Newsletter, quarterly; announcements of acquisitions and services, quarterly. **Staff:** Margy Walsh, Ref.Libn.; Marcene Goldman, Sr.Tech.Libn..

★14048★
TEXARKANA HISTORICAL SOCIETY & MUSEUM - LIBRARY (Hist)
219 State Line Ave.
Box 2343 Phone: (214)793-4831
Texarkana, TX 75504 Katy Caver, Cur.
Founded: 1971. **Staff:** Prof 2; Other 2. **Subjects:** Local history. **Special Collections:** Medical books of early local physicians; early school books and newspapers; local genealogy. **Holdings:** 1800 books; 15 scrapbooks of early residents; 40 Texarkana city directories; 44 annuals of local high schools. **Subscriptions:** 14 journals and newspapers. **Services:** Interlibrary loan; copying; library open to the public by request. **Staff:** Jeanette Winters, Educ.Coord..

★14049★
TEXAS A & M UNIVERSITY - ARCHIVES & MANUSCRIPTS COLLECTIONS (Hist)
Sterling C. Evans Library Phone: (409)845-1815
College Station, TX 77843-5000 Dr. Charles R. Schultz, Univ.Archv.
Founded: 1950. **Staff:** Prof 2; Other 2. **Subjects:** Texas A & M University, Texas agriculture, technology, modern politics, education. **Special Collections:** Papers of Congressmen Olin E. Teague, Robert Casey, John Young, and Graham Purcell; journalist Bascom N. Timmons; nuclear physicist Paul Aebersold; educator Tim M. Stinnett; author William A. Owens; Texas legislators Susan G. McBee, Tom Creighton, Will L. Smith, Bill Presnel, John Traeger, and Billy W. Clayton; real estate broker Owen Sherrill; animal scientist John McKinley Jones; engineer and highway administrator Thomas H. McDonald; political commentator Dan Smoot; electric utilities corporation executive J.B. Thomas; agricultural editors Eugene Butler and Charles Scruggs; oil and gas developers Michel T. Halbouty and Edgar B. Davis; political and religious activist Jonnie Mae Hackworth; maritime labor union organizer Joseph Curran; prison administrator W.J. Estelle, Jr.; military officer Brig. Gen. James F. Hollingsworth; photograph collection of Lt. Col. Noland Varley depicting the destruction caused by the atomic bombing of Hiroshima and Nagasaki, Japan in 1945; records of the Texas Cotton Association; records of the Texas section of the American Society of Civil Engineers. **Holdings:** 9661.25 linear feet of Texas A & M University records and historical manuscripts collections; photographs of campus; 675 hours of oral history interviews. **Services:** Copying; collections open to the public. **Publications:** Inventories of individual manuscript and archival collections; guides to all holdings, both irregular. **Staff:** David L. Chapman, Assoc.Archv..

★14050★
TEXAS A & M UNIVERSITY - CENTER FOR DREDGING STUDIES - OCEAN ENGINEERING LIBRARY (Sci-Engr)
Civil Engineering Department Phone: (409)845-4516
College Station, TX 77843-3136 Nell Bowden, Ck. III
Staff: Prof 1. **Subjects:** Dredging, coastal and ocean engineering. **Holdings:** 300 books; 60 bound periodical volumes; 3000 unbound reports; 3 VF drawers. **Subscriptions:** 40 journals and other serials. **Services:** Interlibrary loan; copying; library open to the public. **Publications:** Newsletter, 4/year; technical reports, 15/year; abstracts of articles relating to dredging technology - by subscription. **Staff:** John B. Herbich, Dir..

★14051★
TEXAS A & M UNIVERSITY - DEPARTMENTS OF OCEANOGRAPHY AND METEOROLOGY - WORKING COLLECTION (Sci-Engr)
Dept. of Oceanography Phone: (409)845-7327
College Station, TX 77843 Gloria Guffy, Rsrc.Ctr.Supv.
Staff: Prof 1; Other 1. **Subjects:** Oceanography, meteorology. **Holdings:** 1250 books; 850 technical reports; 620 theses and dissertations; 825 external reports and publications. **Services:** Copying; collection open to the public for reference use only. **Publications:** Contributions in Oceanography, annual - for exchange. **Special Catalogs:** Technical reports, 1947 to present.

TEXAS A & M UNIVERSITY - FOREST PEST CONTROL SECTION
See: Texas (State) Forest Service - Forest Pest Control Section (14105)

★14052★
TEXAS A & M UNIVERSITY - MAP DEPARTMENT (Geog-Map)
Sterling C. Evans Library Phone: (409)845-1024
College Station, TX 77843-5000 Julia Rholes, Map Libn.
Staff: Prof 1; Other 2. **Subjects:** Geology, soils, topography, energy resources, transportation. **Special Collections:** U.S. Geological Survey topographic maps; various Texas subjects (132 map cases). **Holdings:** 1600 titles; 45 bound periodical volumes; 116,000 maps; 212 slides; 318 microfiche. **Services:** Interlibrary loan; department open to the public.

★14053★
TEXAS A & M UNIVERSITY - MEDICAL SCIENCES LIBRARY (Med)
College Station, TX 77843-4462 Phone: (409)845-7410
Virginia L. Algermissen, Dir.
Staff: Prof 9; Other 16. **Subjects:** Pre-clinical science, clinical and research medicine, veterinary medicine. **Special Collections:** Ethnic medicine; veterinary medicine. **Holdings:** 29,000 books; 46,500 bound periodical volumes; 22,900 microforms. **Subscriptions:** 1979 journals and other serials; 10 newspapers. **Services:** Interlibrary loan; copying; SDI; library open to the public. **Automated Operations:** Computerized public access catalog, cataloging, acquisitions, serials, and circulation. **Computerized Information Services:** BRS Information Technologies, DIALOG Information Services, NLM, WILSONLINE; internal database; OnTyme Electronic Message Network Service (electronic mail service). **Networks/Consortia:** Member of South Central Academic Medical Libraries Consortium (SCAMEL), TALON, TAMU Consortium of Medical Libraries, AMIGOS Bibliographic Council, Inc.. **Publications:** Medical Sciences Library Newsletter; Annual Report. **Special Catalogs:** Union List of Serials (computer printout and microfiche). **Staff:** Esther Carrigan, Hd., Tech.Serv.; Naomi Fackler, Tech.Serv.Libn.; Ann Duyka, Ref./Online; Barbara Thomas, Circ./Res.; Cheryl Hanks, Academic Bus.Adm.; Kathrine MacNeil, Ref./Online; Ann Callaway, Comp.Proj.Mgr.; Karen Creacy, Res.Asst..

★14054★
TEXAS A & M UNIVERSITY - NAUTICAL ARCHAEOLOGY LIBRARY (Sci-Engr)
Dept. of Anthropology
College Station, TX 77843-4352 Phone: (409)845-6398
Staff: Prof 1. **Subjects:** Nautical archeology, maritime history, archeology, naval architecture, artifact conservation. **Special Collections:** G. Roger Edwards Collection (Greek, Hellenistic, Roman archeology and history; 550 volumes). **Holdings:** 2000 books; 250 bound periodical volumes; 4000 offprints and theses; 13 reels of microfilm; 13 microfiche. **Subscriptions:** 36 journals and other serials. **Services:** Library open to the public for reference use only.

★14055★
TEXAS A & M UNIVERSITY - REFERENCE DIVISION (Sci-Engr)
Sterling C. Evans Library Phone: (409)845-5741
College Station, TX 77843-5000 Katherine M. Jackson, Hd., Ref.Div.
Founded: 1876. **Staff:** Prof 17; Other 10. **Subjects:** Agriculture, engineering and technology, physical sciences, biology, transportation, petroleum geology. **Holdings:** 15,000 books. **Subscriptions:** 700 indexes and abstracts. **Services:** Interlibrary loan; copying; SDI; division open to the public. **Automated Operations:** Computerized cataloging, acquisitions, serials, and circulation. **Computerized Information Services:** DIALOG Information Services, BRS Information Technologies, WESTLAW, NLM, Pergamon ORBIT InfoLine, Inc., Mead Data Central, DataTimes, VU/TEXT Information Services, STN International, U.S. Patent Classification System, Chemical Information Systems, Inc. (CIS). **Staff:** Ann Moore, Sci.Ref.Libn.; Sue Charles, Sci.Libn.; Rosemary Loomis, Sci.Libn.; Nan Buctkovich, Sci.Ref.Libn.; Katherine Clark, Sci.Ref.Libn.; Vicki Anders, Hd., Automated Info.Ret.; Joe Jaros, Hd., Bibliog.Instr..

★14056★
TEXAS A & M UNIVERSITY - SPECIAL COLLECTIONS DIVISION (Hum)
Sterling C. Evans Library Phone: (409)845-1951
College Station, TX 77843-5000 Donald H. Dyal, Hd., Spec.Coll.Div.
Founded: 1968. **Staff:** Prof 2; Other 6. **Subjects:** Range livestock industry, science fiction, Texas, J. Frank Dobie, Western illustrators, Ku Klux Klan, W. Somerset Maugham, Matthew Arnold, P.G. Wodehouse, C.S. Forester, ornithology, early printing, 16th-18th century naval architecture, Joseph Conrad, William Faulkner, Ford Madox Ford, W.H. Auden, Henry James, E.M. Forster. **Special Collections:** Jeff Dykes Range Livestock Collection; Science Fiction Research Collection; J. Frank Dobie Collection; Great Western Illustrators Collection; architectural pattern books. **Holdings:** 65,000 books; 8000 bound periodical volumes; 14,000 reprints on developmental biology. **Subscriptions:** 40 journals and other serials. **Services:** Copying (limited); collections open to the public with restrictions. **Computerized Information Services:** OCLC. **Special Indexes:** Story index to science fiction anthologies.

★14057★
TEXAS A & M UNIVERSITY - TECHNICAL REPORTS DEPARTMENT (Sci-Engr)
Sterling C. Evans Library Phone: (409)845-2551
College Station, TX 77843-5000 Leslie Prather-Forbis, Tech.Rpts.Libn.
Founded: 1972. **Staff:** Prof 2; Other 3. **Subjects:** Oceanography, transportation, water resources. **Holdings:** 25,000 technical reports; 600,000 NASA, DOE, NTIS, and Atomic Energy Commission microfiche. **Services:** Interlibrary loan; copying; department open to the public. **Staff:** Eugenia Tang, Cat..

★14058★
TEXAS A & M UNIVERSITY - THERMODYNAMICS RESEARCH CENTER (Sci-Engr)
Texas Engineering Experiment Station Phone: (409)845-4940
College Station, TX 77843-3111 Dr. Kenneth N. Marsh, Dir.
Founded: 1942. **Staff:** Prof 9; Other 5. **Subjects:** Critically evaluated tables of physical and thermodynamic properties and spectral data in six categories (IR, UV, Raman, Mass, Proton NMR, C13 NMR) for hydrocarbons and related compounds and for other organic (non-hydrocarbon) and inorganic substances. **Holdings:** 1200 books; 1300 bound periodical volumes; 1000 data sets; 500,000 data cards on physical and thermodynamic properties; 200 government documents on microfiche. **Subscriptions:** 10 journals and other serials. **Services:** Center open to the public with permission. **Computerized Information Services:** CAS ONLINE; internal database. Performs searches on fee basis. **Publications:** Critically selected scientific data (loose-leaf); TRC Thermodynamics Tables - Hydrocarbons, semiannual; TRC Thermodynamics Tables - Non-hydrocarbons, semiannual; TRC Spectral Data, annual; Proton NMR and IR Data, semiannual; International Data Series, quarterly - all by subscription. **Staff:** Dr. Randolph C. Wilhoit, Assoc.Dir..

★14059★
TEXAS A & M UNIVERSITY AT GALVESTON - JACK K. WILLIAMS LIBRARY (Biol Sci)
Mitchell Campus
Pelican Island, Box 1675 Phone: (409)740-4566
Galveston, TX 77553 Natalie H. Wiest, Lib.Dir.
Founded: 1972. **Staff:** Prof 3; Other 5. **Subjects:** Marine biology, ecology, maritime systems engineering, maritime history, marine transportation and technology, maritime resources. **Holdings:** 33,000 books; 12,000 bound periodical volumes; 50,000 titles on microfiche. **Subscriptions:** 1130 journals and other serials; 9 newspapers. **Services:** Interlibrary loan; copying; library open to the public for reference use only. **Automated Operations:** Computerized cataloging, acquisitions, circulation, and ILL. **Networks/Consortia:** Member of AMIGOS Bibliographic Council, Inc.. **Publications:** Serials List, quarterly - free upon request. **Staff:** Alice Mongold, Tech.Serv.Libn.; Helene Shippington, Pub.Serv.Libn..

★14060★
TEXAS ADVISORY COMMISSION ON INTERGOVERNMENTAL RELATIONS - INFORMATION CENTER (Soc Sci)
Box 13206 Phone: (512)463-1812
Austin, TX 78711 Catherine K. Harris, Libn.
Founded: 1972. **Staff:** Prof 1. **Subjects:** Intergovernmental relations, local government finance, public health, regional planning. **Special Collections:** U.S. Advisory Commission on Intergovernmental Relations reports. **Holdings:** 3250 books; 330 unbound titles; current set of Texas statutes. **Subscriptions:** 160 journals and other serials. **Services:** Center open to the public for reference use only. **Publications:** Recent Aquisitions List, quarterly - to state government personnel; list of additional publications - available on request; Texistics: Law and Justice, 1984; Texistics: Business and Industry, 1986 - both for sale.

★14061★
TEXAS BAPTIST HISTORICAL MUSEUM - INDEPENDENCE HISTORICAL LIBRARY (Rel-Phil)
Rte. 5, Box 222 Phone: (409)836-5117
Brenham, TX 77833 Paul Sevar, Dir.
Staff: Prof 1. **Subjects:** Baptist history. **Special Collections:** Annuals of the Baptist General Convention of Texas (60 volumes); Southern Baptist Annuals (58 volumes); Link's Letters (bound in two volumes). **Holdings:** 502 books; 12 VF drawers of other cataloged items. **Services:** Library open to the public for reference use only.

★14062★
TEXAS BAPTIST INSTITUTE/SEMINARY - LIBRARY (Rel-Phil)
1300 Longview Dr.
Box 570 Phone: (214)657-6543
Henderson, TX 75652 Robert A. Brock, Libn.
Staff: Prof 1. **Subjects:** Religion, Baptist theology and history. **Holdings:** 7094 books; 230 dissertations. **Subscriptions:** 50 journals and other serials. **Services:** Interlibrary loan; library open to the public by special arrangement with librarian.

★14063★
TEXAS CATHOLIC HISTORICAL SOCIETY - CATHOLIC ARCHIVES OF TEXAS (Hist, Rel-Phil)
Capitol Sta., Box 13327 Phone: (512)476-4888
Austin, TX 78711 Michael E. Zilligen, Archv.
Founded: 1923. **Staff:** Prof 1; Other 1. **Subjects:** Spanish exploration and missionary period (1519-1836), Catholic Church history in Texas, immigration and emigration, colonization. **Special Collections:** Ecclesiastical records of the Catholic Church in Texas, 1836-1950; Texas Catholic Conference Papers, 1958-1979; Charles S. Taylor papers, 1829-1868 (over 2000 items); Bishop Odin papers, 1840-1870 (first Bishop of Texas; 400 letters); Knights of Columbus Collection; Papers of Volunteers for Educational & Social Services, 1958-1979. **Holdings:** 950 volumes; 70,000 pages of Spanish and Mexican documents, 1519-1880; 50 VF drawers of ecclesiastical records; 50 document cases of private collections; 58 shelves of Catholic newspapers; 120 reels of microfilm; 26 boxes of pamphlets; 36 boxes of photographs. **Subscriptions:** 31 journals and other serials. **Services:** Copying; library open to public; some materials require special permits for use; service fee for reference work. **Publications:** Our Catholic Heritage in Texas, 1519-1950 (7 volumes).

TEXAS CHILDREN'S HOSPITAL
See: St. Luke's Episcopal & Texas Children's Hospitals (12554)

★14064★
TEXAS CHIROPRACTIC COLLEGE - MAE HILTY MEMORIAL LIBRARY (Med)
5912 Spencer Hwy. Phone: (713)487-1170
Pasadena, TX 77505 Diane Watson, Lib.Dir.
Founded: 1954. **Staff:** 4. **Subjects:** Chiropractic, basic sciences, diagnosis, x-ray, public health, clinical sciences. **Special Collections:** C.S. Cooley and Carver Chiropractic College Collection; Willard Carver Collection. **Holdings:** 8000 books; 4000 bound periodical volumes; 4000 periodical volumes on microfiche; 8 VF drawers of pamphlets; 498 AV programs. **Subscriptions:** 204 journals. **Services:** Interlibrary loan; copying; library open to the public for reference use only. **Computerized Information Services:** MEDLARS. Performs searches on fee basis. **Networks/Consortia:** Member of Chiropractic Library Consortium (CLIBCON), TALON. **Special Catalogs:** Subject Catalog of AV Collection (book).

★14065★
TEXAS CHRISTIAN UNIVERSITY - MARY COUTS BURNETT LIBRARY - BRITE DIVINITY SCHOOL COLLECTION (Rel-Phil)
Fort Worth, TX 76129 Phone: (817)921-7106
Robert A. Olsen, Jr., Libn.
Founded: 1927. **Staff:** Prof 1; Other 1. **Subjects:** Religion, theology, biography, bibliography, literature by and about the Disciples of Christ. **Holdings:** 145,183 books; 21,701 bound periodical volumes; 17,664 volumes in microform. **Subscriptions:** 1068 journals and other serials. **Services:** Interlibrary loan; copying. **Computerized Information Services:** OCLC, DIALOG Information Services, Pergamon ORBIT InfoLine, Inc., BRS Information Technologies, MEDLINE; Management Systems through Texas Christian University Computer Center (internal database). **Networks/Consortia:** Member of Association for Higher Education of North Texas (AHE), AMIGOS Bibliographic Council, Inc..

★14066★
TEXAS CHRISTIAN UNIVERSITY - MARY COUTS BURNETT LIBRARY - MUSIC LIBRARY AND AUDIO CENTER (Mus)
Fort Worth, TX 76129 Phone: (817)921-7000
Sheila Madden, Mus.Libn.
Founded: 1945. **Staff:** Prof 1; Other 2. **Subjects:** Music. **Holdings:** 12,660 books; 20,776 scores; 8125 phonograph records; 3025 78rpm records; 135 titles on microcards; 120 reels of microfilm; 2893 reel-to-reel and cassette tapes. **Subscriptions:** 72 journals and other serials. **Services:** Interlibrary loan; copying; library open to the public with restrictions. **Automated Operations:** Computerized cataloging, serials, and circulation. **Computerized Information Services:** OCLC, Automated Information Retrieval Systems, Inc. (AIRS). **Networks/Consortia:** Member of

AMIGOS Bibliographic Council, Inc., Association for Higher Education of North Texas (AHE).

★14067★
TEXAS COLLEGE OF OSTEOPATHIC MEDICINE - HEALTH SCIENCES LIBRARY (Med)
3516 Camp Bowie Blvd. Phone: (817)735-2464
Fort Worth, TX 76107 Bobby R. Carter, Dir., Lib.Serv.
Founded: 1970. **Staff:** Prof 12; Other 24. **Subjects:** Health sciences, clinical and osteopathic medicine. **Special Collections:** Osteopathic medicine (1643 volumes); oral history collection (25 items); archives. **Holdings:** 36,888 books; 53,951 bound periodical volumes; 3504 AV programs; 4 VF drawers of pamphlets; 68 anatomical models. **Subscriptions:** 2671 journals and other serials. **Services:** Interlibrary loan; copying; SDI; library open to the public with restrictions. **Automated Operations:** Computerized public access catalog, cataloging, acquisitions, serials, and circulation. **Computerized Information Services:** MEDLINE, DIALOG Information Services, BRS Information Technologies, OCLC; OnTyme Electronic Message Network Service (electronic mail service). Performs searches on fee basis. Contact Person: Richard C. Wood, Assoc.Dir., Pub.Serv., 735-2591. **Networks/Consortia:** Member of AMIGOS Bibliographic Council, Inc., Association for Higher Education of North Texas (AHE), Dallas-Tarrant County Consortium of Health Science Libraries, South Central Academic Medical Libraries Consortium (SCAMEL). **Publications:** Health Sciences Library News, monthly - free upon request. **Staff:** Craig Elam, Assoc.Dir., Tech.Serv.; Paul Buchanan, Sys.Libn.; Sherry Porter, Ser.Libn.; Richard C. Wood, Dir, Pub.Serv.; Moira McInroy-Hocevar, AV Libn.; Timothy Mason, Cat./Acq.Libn.; Sue Raymond, Ref.Libn.; Ann Brooks, Ref.Libn.; Phyllis Muirhead, Ref.Libn.; Gay Taber, Ref.Libn.; Ray Stokes, Cur., Spec.Coll..

TEXAS CONFEDERATE MUSEUM LIBRARY
See: United Daughters of the Confederacy (14528)

★14068★
TEXAS EASTERN TRANSMISSION CORPORATION - CORPORATE LIBRARY (Energy, Bus-Fin)
One Houston Center
1221 McKinney
Box 2521
Houston, TX 77252 Phone: (713)759-3535
Founded: 1947. **Staff:** Prof 2. **Subjects:** Energy, oil and gas, economics, management. **Holdings:** 5000 books; 250 bound periodical volumes; 32 periodicals on microfilm. **Subscriptions:** 400 journals and other serials; 16 newspapers. **Services:** Interlibrary loan; copying; library available to public by telephone request. **Automated Operations:** Computerized acquisitions. **Computerized Information Services:** DIALOG Information Services, Pergamon ORBIT InfoLine, Inc., Dow Jones News/Retrieval, Occupational Health Services, Inc. **Staff:** Bob Kirtner, Libn.; Anne Lueckenhoff, Libn..

TEXAS EASTMAN COMPANY
See: Eastman Kodak Company (4568)

★14069★
TEXAS ELECTRIC SERVICE COMPANY - LIBRARY (Energy)
115 W. 7th St. Phone: (817)336-9454
Fort Worth, TX 76102 Melba Connelley, Libn.
Founded: 1954. **Subjects:** Business, management, electrical engineering. **Holdings:** 4500 books.

★14070★
TEXAS EMPLOYERS INSURANCE ASSOCIATION - ENGINEERING INFORMATION CENTER (Sci-Engr)
Box 2759 Phone: (214)760-6315
Dallas, TX 75221 Gay Bethel, Info.Res.Spec.
Founded: 1975. **Staff:** Prof 1; Other 1. **Subjects:** Safety engineering, industrial hygiene, traffic safety. **Holdings:** 400 books; 2400 technical reports and pamphlets; 195 films, filmstrips, slides, cassettes. **Subscriptions:** 35 journals and other serials. **Services:** Interlibrary loan; copying; center open to the public by appointment. **Automated Operations:** Computerized cataloging. **Computerized Information Services:** DIALOG Information Services; internal databases. **Special Indexes:** Information Center Index.

TEXAS FOREST PRODUCTS LABORATORY
See: Texas (State) Forest Service (14107)

★14071★
TEXAS GAS TRANSMISSION CORPORATION - LIBRARY (Energy)
Box 1160 Phone: (502)926-8686
Owensboro, KY 42302 Frieda Rhodes, Libn.
Staff: Prof 1; Other 1. **Subjects:** Natural gas technology, finance, petroleum, geology, economics. **Holdings:** 2500 books; 27 bound periodical titles. **Subscriptions:** 225 journals and other serials. **Services:** Library not open to the public.

TEXAS HERITAGE RESOURCE CENTER
See: San Antonio Conservation Society - Library & Archives (12741)

★14072★
TEXAS INSTRUMENTS, INC. - AUSTIN LIBRARY (Comp Sci, Bus-Fin)
Box 2909, MS/2207 Phone: (512)250-7421
Austin, TX 78769 Randy Lusk, Lib.Mgr.
Founded: 1978. **Staff:** Prof 2. **Subjects:** Computer technology, marketing, business management. **Holdings:** 2300 books; 125 marketing reports; industry standards and military specifications on microfilm. **Subscriptions:** 200 journals and other serials; 10 newspapers. **Services:** Interlibrary loan; library not open to the public. **Automated Operations:** Computerized cataloging. **Computerized Information Services:** DIALOG Information Services, BRS Information Technologies, NewsNet, Inc., OCLC; internal database. Performs searches on fee basis. **Staff:** Claudia F. Chidester, Libn..

★14073★
TEXAS INSTRUMENTS, INC. - CENTRAL RESEARCH DEVELOPMENT AND ENGINEERING LIBRARY (Sci-Engr)
Box 655936, MS 135 Phone: (214)995-2407
Dallas, TX 75265 Olga Paradis, Libn.
Staff: Prof 1; Other 1. **Subjects:** Physics, chemistry, mathematics, electronics, geophysics. **Holdings:** 10,000 books; 6000 bound periodical volumes; 40 VF drawers of theses and pamphlets. **Subscriptions:** 300 journals and other serials. **Services:** Interlibrary loan; library not open to the public. **Computerized Information Services:** OCLC, DIALOG Information Services. **Networks/Consortia:** Member of AMIGOS Bibliographic Council, Inc..

★14074★
TEXAS INSTRUMENTS, INC. - FOREST LANE TECHNICAL LIBRARY (Sci-Engr, Comp Sci)
8505 Forest Lane, MS 3132
Box 660246 Phone: (214)480-1117
Dallas, TX 75266 Charise F. Bell, Libn.
Founded: 1982. **Staff:** Prof 1; Other 1. **Subjects:** Optics, imaging, pattern recognition, personal and professional computers, military electronics. **Holdings:** 2000 books. **Subscriptions:** 201 journals and other serials. **Services:** Interlibrary loan; library not open to the public. **Automated Operations:** Computerized cataloging, acquisitions, serials, and circulation. **Computerized Information Services:** DIALOG Information Services, BRS Information Technologies, OCLC, NEXIS, DMS/ONLINE, DTIC; LIBS (internal database). **Networks/Consortia:** Member of AMIGOS Bibliographic Council, Inc.. **Publications:** Biblio-Tech, monthly - for internal distribution only.

★14075★
TEXAS INSTRUMENTS, INC. - HOUSTON SITE LIBRARY (Sci-Engr)
Box 1443, MS 695 Phone: (713)274-2981
Houston, TX 77001 Helen Manning, Libn.
Staff: Prof 1; Other 1. **Subjects:** Electronics, marketing, electrical engineering. **Holdings:** 2100 books. **Subscriptions:** 250 journals and other serials; 10 newspapers. **Services:** Interlibrary loan; library not open to the public. **Automated Operations:** Computerized cataloging, circulation, and serials. **Computerized Information Services:** OCLC, DIALOG Information Services; internal database. **Networks/Consortia:** Member of AMIGOS Bibliographic Council, Inc.. **Publications:** New at the Library, monthly.

★14076★
TEXAS INSTRUMENTS, INC. - INFORMATION SYSTEMS & SERVICES LIBRARY (Comp Sci, Info Sci)
Box 869305, MS 8429 Phone: (214)575-2852
Plano, TX 75086 Cecilia Tung, Libn.
Staff: Prof 1. **Subjects:** Computer science and graphics, data processing, information science. **Holdings:** 1500 books; 1000 IBM hardware and software manuals; industry reports. **Subscriptions:** 150 journals and other serials. **Services:** Interlibrary loan; library not open to the public. **Automated Operations:** Computerized cataloging. **Computerized**

Information Services: OCLC, DIALOG Information Services. **Networks/Consortia:** Member of AMIGOS Bibliographic Council, Inc.. **Special Indexes:** Keyword Index of IBM hardware and software manuals.

★14077★
TEXAS INSTRUMENTS, INC. - LEWISVILLE TECHNICAL LIBRARY (Sci-Engr, Comp Sci)
Box 405, M/S 3411 Phone: (214)462-5425
Lewisville, TX 75067 Cheryl Helmer, Libn.
Founded: 1980. **Staff:** Prof 1; Other 1. **Subjects:** Electronics, electrical and mechanical engineering, computer science, aerospace, defense industry and technology. **Holdings:** 3900 books; 10,500 microforms. **Subscriptions:** 300 journals and other serials. **Services:** Interlibrary loan; library not open to the public. **Automated Operations:** Computerized cataloging, serials, and circulation. **Computerized Information Services:** DIALOG Information Services, OCLC; internal database.

★14078★
TEXAS INSTRUMENTS, INC. - NORTH BUILDING LIBRARY (Sci-Engr)
Box 655474, MS 211 Phone: (214)995-2803
Dallas, TX 75265 Phyl Barrus, Libn.
Founded: 1950. **Staff:** Prof 1; Other 2. **Subjects:** Electronics, engineering, physics, mathematics. **Special Collections:** Institute of Electrical and Electronics Engineers (IEEE) periodicals (complete set); Stanford Computer Forum reports. **Holdings:** 5500 books; 3500 bound periodical volumes; 2500 technical reports. **Subscriptions:** 250 journals and other serials; 5 newspapers. **Services:** Interlibrary loan; library not open to the public. **Automated Operations:** Computerized cataloging, acquisitions, serials, and circulation. **Computerized Information Services:** DIALOG Information Services, BRS Information Technologies.

★14079★
TEXAS INSTRUMENTS, INC. - SEMICONDUCTOR BUILDING LIBRARY (Sci-Engr, Comp Sci)
Box 655012, MS 20 Phone: (214)995-2511
Dallas, TX 75265 Helen Manning, Coord.
Founded: 1957. **Staff:** Prof 1; Other 1. **Subjects:** Electronics, semiconductor technology, business management, computer science. **Holdings:** 8000 books; 3000 bound periodical volumes. **Subscriptions:** 200 journals and other serials; 9 newspapers. **Services:** Interlibrary loan; library not open to the public. **Computerized Information Services:** OCLC, DIALOG Information Services, NewsNet, Inc. **Networks/Consortia:** Member of AMIGOS Bibliographic Council, Inc..

TEXAS JAZZ ARCHIVE
See: Houston Public Library - Houston Metropolitan Research Center (6524)

★14080★
TEXAS MEDICAL ASSOCIATION - MEMORIAL LIBRARY (Med)
1801 Lamar Blvd. Phone: (512)477-6704
Austin, TX 78701 Betty Afflerbach, Lib.Dir.
Founded: 1922. **Staff:** Prof 5; Other 9. **Subjects:** Medicine. **Holdings:** 60,000 volumes; 15,000 reprints; 200 motion pictures; 1300 lecture tapes; 280 slide/tape programs; 330 video cassettes. **Subscriptions:** 1040 journals and other serials. **Services:** Interlibrary loan; copying; SDI; library open to nonmembers on fee basis. **Computerized Information Services:** MEDLARS. **Networks/Consortia:** Member of TALON. **Special Catalogs:** AV Catalog and supplements (book) - for sale; list of journals. **Staff:** Susan Michaelson; Susan Brock; Miriam Blum; Nancy Reynolds.

TEXAS MEDICAL CENTER LIBRARY
See: Houston Academy of Medicine - Texas Medical Center Library (6508)

★14081★
TEXAS MEMORIAL MUSEUM - LIBRARY
2400 Trinity St.
Austin, TX 78705
Founded: 1938. **Subjects:** Anthropology, archeology, museology, natural history, Texas history, geology, paleontology, arms and armor, art and antiquities. **Special Collections:** Material on pictographs and petroglyphs. **Holdings:** 3000 books; 15 VF drawers of reprints and photographic files. **Remarks:** Presently inactive.

★14082★
TEXAS MUNICIPAL LEAGUE - LIBRARY (Soc Sci)
211 E. 7th St., Suite 1020 Phone: (512)478-6601
Austin, TX 78701 Ted Willis, Exec.Dir.
Founded: 1913. **Staff:** Prof 1. **Subjects:** Municipal government. **Holdings:** 300 books; 2000 articles. **Subscriptions:** 75 journals and other serials. **Services:** Interlibrary loan; library not open to the public.

★14083★
TEXAS NATURAL RESOURCES INFORMATION SYSTEM (TNRIS) - LIBRARY (Biol Sci, Sci-Engr)
Box 13231, Capitol Sta. Phone: (512)463-8402
Austin, TX 78711 Charles Palmer, Mgr.
Founded: 1970. **Staff:** Prof 7; Other 1. **Subjects:** Remote sensing, natural resources, geology, hydrology, biology, census, meteorology, cartography. **Special Collections:** Aerial photography; Landsat and remote sensing imagery; computer compatible tapes. **Holdings:** Figures not available. **Services:** Copying; library open to the public. **Automated Operations:** Computerized cataloging. **Computerized Information Services:** NAWDEX (National Water Data Exchange), STORET, EROS Data Center. Performs searches on fee basis. **Publications:** File Description Report (newsletter), bimonthly - for sale. **Remarks:** Maintained by Texas (State) Water Development Board. An alternate telephone number is 463-8403.

TEXAS POWER & LIGHT COMPANY
See: TU Electric (14365)

★14084★
TEXAS RESEARCH LEAGUE - LIBRARY (Soc Sci)
1117 Red River Phone: (512)472-3127
Austin, TX 78701 Sarah L. Burka, Res.Libn.
Staff: Prof 1. **Subjects:** Texas state and local government, government finance, demographics, transportation policy, education, health care delivery. **Special Collections:** League archives (300 volumes). **Holdings:** 2000 books. **Subscriptions:** 134 journals and other serials. **Services:** Interlibrary loan; library open to the public with restrictions.

★14085★
TEXAS SCOTTISH RITE HOSPITAL FOR CRIPPLED CHILDREN - BRANDON CARRELL, M.D., MEDICAL LIBRARY (Med)
2222 Welborn St. Phone: (214)521-3168
Dallas, TX 75219-0567 Mary Peters, Med.Libn.
Founded: 1979. **Staff:** Prof 1. **Subjects:** Pediatric orthopedics and neurology. **Special Collections:** History of orthopedics. **Holdings:** 700 books; 525 bound periodical volumes. **Subscriptions:** 100 journals and other serials. **Services:** Interlibrary loan; library open to the public for reference use only; access to hospital departmental libraries can be requested. **Networks/Consortia:** Member of Dallas-Tarrant County Consortium of Health Science Libraries.

★14086★
TEXAS SOUTHERN UNIVERSITY - LAW LIBRARY (Law)
3100 Cleburne St. Phone: (713)527-7125
Houston, TX 77004 Walter T. Champion, Dir.
Founded: 1947. **Staff:** Prof 3; Other 6. **Subjects:** Law - American, English, African. **Holdings:** 80,000 books; 10,000 bound periodical volumes. **Subscriptions:** 360 journals and other serials. **Services:** Interlibrary loan; copying; library open to the public. **Computerized Information Services:** LEXIS, WESTLAW. **Staff:** Marguerite L. Butler, Assoc.Dir.; Shirley Lukan, Dir., Tech.Serv.; Faye Webster, Loose-leaf & Govt.Docs.Supv..

★14087★
TEXAS SOUTHERN UNIVERSITY - LIBRARY - HEARTMAN COLLECTION (Hist, Area-Ethnic)
3100 Cleburne St. Phone: (713)527-7149
Houston, TX 77004 Dorothy H. Chapman, Libn.
Staff: Prof 2. **Subjects:** Black culture and history, slavery. **Special Collections:** Barbara Jordan Archives (26 VF drawers); Texas Southern University Archives (8 VF drawers). **Holdings:** 25,000 books; 437 bound periodical volumes; 6000 pamphlets; 1 VF drawer of pictures; 1 VF drawer of sheet music. **Subscriptions:** 163 journals and other serials; 26 newspapers. **Services:** Interlibrary loan; copying; collection open to the public. **Automated Operations:** Computerized cataloging and acquisitions. **Staff:** Sandra Parham, Archv./Coord., Spec.Coll..

★14088★
TEXAS SOUTHERN UNIVERSITY - PHARMACY LIBRARY (Med)
3201 Wheeler Ave. Phone: (713)527-7160
Houston, TX 77004 Norma Bean, Assoc.Dir.
Founded: 1949. **Staff:** 1. **Subjects:** Pharmacology. **Holdings:** 4500 books; 2500 bound periodical volumes. **Subscriptions:** 177 journals and other serials. **Services:** Interlibrary loan; copying; SDI; library open to the public. **Computerized Information Services:** DIALOG Information Services. Performs searches on fee basis. **Networks/Consortia:** Member of Houston Area Research Library Consortium (HARLIC).

TEXAS SOUTHERN UNIVERSITY ARCHIVES
See: Texas Southern University - Library - Heartman Collection (14087)

★14089★
TEXAS STATE AERONAUTICS COMMISSION - LIBRARY & INFORMATION CENTER (Trans, Aud-Vis)
Capitol Sta., Box 12607 Phone: (512)476-9262
Austin, TX 78711 Nonie Mitchel, Libn.
Founded: 1945. **Staff:** Prof 1. **Subjects:** Aviation, aircraft, airports, planning, aviation education, flight safety. **Holdings:** 200 films; reports; government documents; 40 feet of Federal Aviation Administration, Civil Aeronautics Board, and National Transportation Safety Board regulations and publications; 2 bound volumes of clippings. **Subscriptions:** 50 journals and other serials. **Services:** Copying (limited); library open to the public for reference use only. **Networks/Consortia:** Member of Texas State Library Communications Network (TSLCN). **Publications:** List of Texas Aeronautics Commission Publications. **Special Catalogs:** Aviation Film Library Catalog; Aviation Video Library Catalog (book).

★14090★
TEXAS STATE AIR CONTROL BOARD - LIBRARY (Env-Cons)
6330 Hwy. 290, E. Phone: (512)451-5711
Austin, TX 78723 Kerry Williams, Libn.
Subjects: Air pollution, engineering, chemistry, physics, meteorology, law. **Special Collections:** Microfiche of technical subjects pertaining to air pollution (50,000). **Holdings:** 6000 books; 18 bound periodical volumes; 700 reprints. **Subscriptions:** 64 journals and other serials. **Services:** Copying; library open to the public for reference use only. **Publications:** Technical reports on air pollution in Texas.

★14091★
TEXAS STATE BUREAU OF ECONOMIC GEOLOGY - CORE RESEARCH CENTER (Sci-Engr)
Balcones Research Center
10100 Burnet Rd. Phone: (512)471-1534
Austin, TX 78758-4497 Allan Standen, Cur.
Founded: 1937. **Staff:** Prof 5; Other 20. **Subjects:** Well cores, borings, cuttings, and thin sections; oil scout tickets; drillers logs. **Special Collections:** John E. (Brick) Elliot Collection (5 VF drawers and 2 map cases of geological information, well data, maps, aerial photographs). **Holdings:** 5600 cored wells; 55,000 cuttings wells; 12,000 thin sections; 750,000 drillers logs; 400,000 scout tickets. **Services:** Library open to the public. **Automated Operations:** Computerized cataloging. **Special Indexes:** Computer printout listing of cuttings, cores, and thin sections.

★14092★
TEXAS STATE COURT OF APPEALS - 1ST SUPREME JUDICIAL DISTRICT - LAW LIBRARY (Law)
1307 San Jacinto, 10th Fl.
Houston, TX 77002 Phone: (713)655-2700
Founded: 1892. **Subjects:** Law. **Holdings:** 10,000 volumes. **Services:** Library not open to the public.

★14093★
TEXAS STATE COURT OF APPEALS - 3RD SUPREME JUDICIAL DISTRICT - LAW LIBRARY (Law)
Capitol Sta., Box 12547
Austin, TX 78711 Phone: (512)463-1733
Subjects: Law. **Holdings:** Figures not available. **Services:** Library not open to the public.

★14094★
TEXAS STATE COURT OF APPEALS - 5TH SUPREME JUDICIAL DISTRICT - LAW LIBRARY (Law)
Dallas County Courthouse
600 Commerce St.
Dallas, TX 75202 Phone: (214)653-7382
Subjects: Law. **Holdings:** 8340 volumes.

★14095★
TEXAS STATE COURT OF APPEALS - 6TH SUPREME JUDICIAL DISTRICT - LAW LIBRARY (Law)
Bi-State Justice Bldg.
100 N. State Line Ave.
Texarkana, TX 75501 Phone: (214)798-3046
Subjects; Law. **Holdings:** 15,000 volumes.

★14096★
TEXAS STATE COURT OF APPEALS - 11TH SUPREME JUDICIAL DISTRICT - LAW LIBRARY (Law)
Eastland, TX 76448 Phone: (817)629-2638
Founded: 1925. **Subjects:** Law. **Holdings:** 7000 volumes. **Services:** Library open to the public for reference use only.

TEXAS STATE COURT OF CIVIL APPEALS - 10TH JUDICIAL DISTRICT - LIBRARY
See: Mc Lennan County Law Library (8247)

★14097★
TEXAS STATE DEPARTMENT OF AGRICULTURE - LIBRARY (Agri)
Stephen F. Austin Bldg., Rm. 911
Box 12847 Phone: (512)463-7670
Austin, TX 78711 Virginia Hall, Libn.
Founded: 1975. **Staff:** Prof 1. **Subjects:** Agriculture, livestock, gardening, international trade, cooking. **Special Collections:** U.S. Department of Agriculture Yearbook of Agriculture, 1897 to present. **Holdings:** 5000 books; 1000 bound periodical volumes; 200 pamphlets. **Subscriptions:** 500 journals and other serials; 50 newspapers. **Services:** Copying; library open to the public.

★14098★
TEXAS (State) DEPARTMENT OF COMMERCE - LIBRARY (Bus-Fin)
Capitol Sta., Box 12728 Phone: (512)472-5059
Austin, TX 78711 Marilyn McCullough, Libn.
Staff: 1. **Subjects:** Industrial and economic development, local demographics. **Special Collections:** Texas State Data Center; U.S. Census Collection. **Holdings:** 1500 books. **Subscriptions:** 62 journals and other serials. **Services:** Copying; library open to the public. **Formerly:** Texas (State) Economic Development Commission.

★14099★
TEXAS STATE DEPARTMENT OF HEALTH - LIBRARY (Med)
1100 W. 49th St. Phone: (512)458-7559
Austin, TX 78756 John Burlinson, Libn.
Founded: 1958. **Staff:** Prof 2; Other 1. **Subjects:** Public health, infectious diseases, laboratory methods, environmental health, dental health, pediatrics, nursing, hospitals and nursing homes, heart, cancer. **Holdings:** 10,305 volumes; 1500 unbound items. **Subscriptions:** 325 journals and other serials. **Services:** Interlibrary loan; copying; SDI; library open to the public for reference use only. **Automated Operations:** Computerized cataloging, acquisitions, and circulation. **Computerized Information Services:** DIALOG Information Services, MEDLARS, BRS Information Technologies, Dialcom Inc., Chemical Information Systems, Inc. (CIS).

★14100★
TEXAS STATE DEPARTMENT OF HIGHWAYS AND PUBLIC TRANSPORTATION - RESEARCH & DEVELOPMENT SECTION - LIBRARY (Trans)
D10 Research
Box 5051 Phone: (512)465-7644
Austin, TX 78763-5051 Kevin Marsh, Res.Libn.
Subjects: Highway research, public transportation facilities. **Holdings:** 18,000 volumes. **Subscriptions:** 20 journals and other serials. **Services:** Library open to the public. **Computerized Information Services:** DIALOG Information Services. **Publications:** Catalog of Research Studies and Reports, annual.

★14101★
TEXAS STATE DEPARTMENT OF HUMAN SERVICES - LIBRARY (Soc Sci)
Box 2960 Phone: (512)450-3530
Austin, TX 78769 Diana Boardman Houston, Mgr., Lib.Serv.
Staff: Prof 2; Other 1. **Subjects:** Social work, child welfare, management, geriatrics, health services, human services, nutrition. **Holdings:** 16,000 books; 1500 AV programs. **Subscriptions:** 120 journals and other serials. **Services:** Interlibrary loan; SDI; library open to the public for reference use

only. **Computerized Information Services:** DIALOG Information Services. **Staff:** Holly Gordon, Ref.Libn..

★14102★
TEXAS STATE DEPARTMENT OF MENTAL HEALTH & MENTAL RETARDATION - CENTRAL OFFICE LIBRARY (Med)
Box 12668 Phone: (512)465-4621
Austin, TX 78711 Becky S. Renfro, Libn. II
Staff: Prof 1. **Subjects:** Mental health, mental retardation, alcoholism, drug abuse, rehabilitation. **Holdings:** 6000 books; 3000 bound periodical volumes; 20 file drawers of mental health files; 4 drawers of mental retardation files. **Subscriptions:** 50 journals and other serials. **Services:** Interlibrary loan; copying; library open to the public for reference use only. **Computerized Information Services:** DIALOG Information Services.

TEXAS STATE DEPARTMENT OF MENTAL HEALTH & MENTAL RETARDATION - SAN ANTONIO STATE HOSPITAL
See: San Antonio State Hospital (12749)

TEXAS (State) ECONOMIC DEVELOPMENT COMMISSION
See: Texas (State) Department of Commerce (14098)

★14103★
TEXAS (State) EDUCATION AGENCY - RESOURCE CENTER LIBRARY (Educ)
1701 N. Congress Ave. Phone: (512)463-9050
Austin, TX 78701-1494 Linda Kemp, Libn.
Staff: Prof 2; Other 1. **Subjects:** Public school education. **Special Collections:** Complete ERIC microfiche collection; Texas state-adopted textbook collection. **Holdings:** 10,000 volumes. **Subscriptions:** 355 journals and other serials. **Services:** Interlibrary loan; SDI; library open to Texas educators and state government personnel only. **Computerized Information Services:** BRS Information Technologies, DIALOG Information Services; Electric Pages (electronic mail service). **Staff:** Jan Anderson, Libn..

★14104★
TEXAS STATE EMPLOYMENT COMMISSION - TEC LIBRARY* (Bus-Fin)
15th & Congress Phone: (512)463-2426
Austin, TX 78778 Evelyn C. Houston, Adm.Techn.
Staff: 1. **Subjects:** Management, personnel management, human relations, communication, supervision. **Holdings:** 3500 books; 50 bound periodical volumes; TEC reports. **Services:** Interlibrary loan; library not open to the public.

★14105★
TEXAS (State) FOREST SERVICE - FOREST PEST CONTROL SECTION - LIBRARY (Biol Sci)
Box 310 Phone: (409)639-8170
Lufkin, TX 75901 Dr. Ronald F. Billings, Prin. Entomologist
Founded: 1967. **Staff:** Prof 1. **Subjects:** Forest insects and diseases in the South. **Special Collections:** Computerized records of southern pine beetle infestations in Texas, 1973-1987. **Holdings:** 500 books; 200 bound periodical volumes; 3000 color transparencies. **Subscriptions:** 12 journals and other serials. **Services:** Library open to the public with restrictions. **Remarks:** Jointly maintained with Texas A & M University.

★14106★
TEXAS (State) FOREST SERVICE - LIBRARY (Biol Sci)
Texas A & M University
College Station, TX 77843 Phone: (409)845-2641
Founded: 1919. **Subjects:** Forestry. **Holdings:** 625 books; 325 bound periodical volumes; 6000 pamphlets and reports on microfiche. **Subscriptions:** 60 journals and other serials. **Services:** Library open to the public for reference use only. **Automated Operations:** Computerized cataloging. **Computerized Information Services:** SourceMail, Dialcom, Inc. (electronic mail services). **Networks/Consortia:** Member of Forest Service Information Network/Forestry Online (FS INFO). **Special Catalogs:** Available publications of the Texas Forest Service (leaflet).

★14107★
TEXAS (State) FOREST SERVICE - TEXAS FOREST PRODUCTS LABORATORY - LIBRARY (Biol Sci)
Box 310 Phone: (409)639-8180
Lufkin, TX 75901 Susan Shockley, Libn.
Staff: Prof 1; Other 1. **Subjects:** Wood science, forest products technology and utilization. **Holdings:** 3025 books; 230 bound periodical volumes; 124,000 notebook articles; 36,400 articles in boxes. **Subscriptions:** 60 journals and other serials. **Services:** Interlibrary loan; copying; library open to the public. **Publications:** Directory of Forest Products Industries of Texas, biennial - for sale.

★14108★
TEXAS STATE LAW LIBRARY (Law)
Supreme Court Bldg.
Box 12367 Phone: (512)463-1722
Austin, TX 78711 Kay Schlueter, Dir.
Staff: Prof 3; Other 5. **Subjects:** Law. **Holdings:** 99,760 books; 3900 bound periodical volumes. **Subscriptions:** 215 journals and other serials. **Services:** Copying; library open to the public. **Automated Operations:** Computerized public access catalog. **Computerized Information Services:** Online systems. **Staff:** Tony Estrada, Acq.Libn.; Sally Harlow, Assoc.Libn..

★14109★
TEXAS STATE LEGISLATIVE REFERENCE LIBRARY (Soc Sci, Law)
Capitol Sta., Box 12488 Phone: (512)463-1252
Austin, TX 78711 Sally Reynolds, Dir.
Founded: 1969. **Staff:** Prof 11. **Subjects:** Law, Texas government and politics, legislative reference, political science, current events. **Special Collections:** Newspaper clipping file; legislative bill files. **Holdings:** 30,000 volumes; 726 shelves of Texas documents; 150,000 newspaper clippings; 1586 reels of microfilm; Texas and out-of-state agency reports. **Subscriptions:** 620 journals and other serials; 32 newspapers. **Services:** Copying; library open to the public for reference use only. **Automated Operations:** Computerized cataloging, acquisitions, and serials. **Computerized Information Services:** Legislative bill status and history (internal database). Performs searches free of charge. **Publications:** Chief Elected & Administrative Officials, biennial; bibliographies on state documents and new trade book acquisitions, monthly; Legislative Library Resources; Texas State Agency Publications, irregular. **Staff:** Brenda Olds, TX Docs.Libn.; Melissa Robinson, Libn. II; Carla Schuller, Libn. II; Joanne Ferguson, Paralegal.

★14110★
TEXAS STATE LIBRARY (Info Sci)
1201 Brazos
Box 12927 Phone: (512)463-5455
Austin, TX 78711 William D. Gooch, State Libn.
Founded: 1839. **Staff:** Prof 67; Other 143. **Subjects:** Texas history and government, genealogy, librarianship. **Special Collections:** Texana Collection. **Holdings:** 1.2 million books and bound periodical volumes; 196,394 microforms of newspapers and tax records. **Subscriptions:** 1314 journals and other serials; 30 newspapers. **Services:** Interlibrary loan; copying; library open to the public with restrictions. **Automated Operations:** Computerized cataloging. **Computerized Information Services:** OCLC; centralized storage and retrieval program for Texas state agency publications (internal database). **Networks/Consortia:** Member of AMIGOS Bibliographic Council, Inc.. **Publications:** Texas Libraries, quarterly; Checklist of Texas State Government Publications, monthly - all free upon request. **Special Indexes:** Index to state government publications, annual (book). **Staff:** Raymond W. Hitt, Asst. State Libn.; William H. Carlton, Dir., Adm.Div.; Edward Seidenberg, Dir., Lib.Dev.Div.; William Dyess, Dir., Rec.Mgt.Div.; Marilyn Von Kohl, Dir., Local Rec.Div.; Allan Quinn, Dir., Info.Serv.Div.; Christopher LaPlante, Dir., Archv.Div..

★14111★
TEXAS STATE LIBRARY - DIVISION FOR THE BLIND AND PHYSICALLY HANDICAPPED (Aud-Vis)
Box 12927 Phone: (512)463-5458
Austin, TX 78711 Dale W. Propp, Dir.
Founded: 1909. **Staff:** Prof 12; Other 40. **Subjects:** Visual impairment, physical handicaps, Texana, Spanish language, learning disabilities. **Holdings:** 533,004 books; 135 bound periodical volumes; cassettes. **Subscriptions:** 51 journals and other serials. **Services:** Interlibrary loan; copying; library open to the public with restrictions. **Automated Operations:** Computerized acquisitions, serials, and circulation. **Computerized Information Services:** BRS Information Technologies. Performs searches on fee basis. Contact Person: Linda Lindell. **Networks/Consortia:** Member of AMIGOS Bibliographic Council, Inc., National Library Service for the Blind & Physically Handicapped (NLS). **Publications:** In Touch (newsletter), quarterly - to registered patrons. **Special Catalogs:** Large Print Catalog (large type). **Staff:** Marta Westall, Mgr., Rsrc.Dev.; Jane Mullane, Mgr., Info.Sys.; Mike Conway, Patron Serv.Libn..

★14112★
TEXAS STATE LIBRARY - INFORMATION SERVICES DIVISION (Info Sci, Hist)
Box 12927 Phone: (512)463-5455
Austin, TX 78711 Allan S. Quinn, Div.Dir.
Staff: Prof 13; Other 15. **Subjects:** U.S. and Texas documents, genealogy, Texas history, biography, folklore. **Special Collections:** Texas State Publications Clearinghouse (the designated state office for the bibliographic control and distribution of Texas state documents). **Holdings:** 105,000 books; 1500 bound periodical volumes; 100,000 Texas state government documents; 1 million U.S. Government documents. **Subscriptions:** 1100 journals and other serials. **Services:** Interlibrary loan; copying; division open to the public. **Automated Operations:** Computerized cataloging. **Computerized Information Services:** DIALOG Information Services, DataTimes. **Publications:** Public Documents Highlights for Texas, quarterly - free upon request; Texas State Documents, monthly. **Special Indexes:** Texas State Documents title and subject index. **Staff:** Bonnie Grobar, Mgr., Pub.Serv.Dept.; Chris Fowler, Hd., State Docs. Unit; Jan Carter, Geneal. Unit.

★14113★
TEXAS STATE LIBRARY - LIBRARY SCIENCE COLLECTION (Info Sci)
Box 12927 Phone: (512)463-5494
Austin, TX 78711 Anne Ramos, Libn.
Founded: 1956. **Staff:** Prof 1; Other 1. **Subjects:** Library science, librarianship, information science. **Holdings:** 7000 books; 300 bound periodical volumes; 10,000 uncataloged ephemeral documents; 300 audio and video cassettes. **Subscriptions:** 120 journals and other serials. **Services:** Interlibrary loan; copying; collection open to the public. **Automated Operations:** Computerized cataloging. **Computerized Information Services:** DIALOG Information Services. **Publications:** Library Developments, bimonthly - free upon request.

★14114★
TEXAS STATE LIBRARY - LOCAL RECORDS DIVISION - SAM HOUSTON REGIONAL LIBRARY AND RESEARCH CENTER (Hist)
Box 310 Phone: (409)336-7097
Liberty, TX 77575 Robert L. Schaadt, Dir./Archv.
Founded: 1977. **Staff:** Prof 2; Other 5. **Subjects:** Southeast Texas history. **Special Collections:** Journal of Jean Laffite; Herbert Bolton's manuscript for Athanase de Mezieres & the Louisiana-Texas Frontier, 1768-1780; French Colony Champ D'Asile, 1819; Tidelands Papers; early Texas newspapers, 1846-1860; Congressman Martin Dies Papers, 1931-1960 (54 cubic feet); Jean Houston Baldwin Collection of Sam Houston (591 items); private executive record of President of the Republic of Texas Sam Houston, 1841-1844 (1 volume); early Texas maps; Trinity River papers (8 feet); H.O. Compton Surveyors Books; Captain William M. Logan Papers; O'Brien Papers; Hardin Papers (52 feet); Julia Duncan Welder Collection (150 feet); family photograph collections; original and microfilm material from the 10 counties of the old Atascosito District of Southeast Texas, 1826-1960; Encino Press Collection; Carl Hertzog books; many individual family papers and collections. **Holdings:** 4678 books; 451 reels of microfilm; 14,322 photographs; 16,000 cubic feet of manuscripts, government records, and archives; county records. **Subscriptions:** 17 journals and other serials; 9 newspapers. **Services:** Interlibrary loan; copying; center open to the public. **Publications:** Sam Houston Regional Library and Research Center News, 2/year. **Special Indexes:** Llerena B. Friend card index on Sam Houston; inventories of collections in books. **Staff:** Sally Rogers, Asst.Dir./Cur..

★14115★
TEXAS STATE LIBRARY - REGIONAL HISTORICAL RESOURCE DEPOSITORIES & LOCAL RECORDS DIVISION (Hist)
Capitol Sta., Box 12927 Phone: (512)463-5478
Austin, TX 78711 Marilyn Von Kohl, Dir.
Staff: Prof 9; Other 3. **Subjects:** Texas - vital statistics, judicial proceedings, education, economic development, politics, family history/biography. **Special Collections:** Tidelands Case Papers of Justice Price Daniel (130 cubic feet); congressional and other papers of Representative Martin Dies; early manuscripts and photographs of Sam Houston, David G. Burnet, and others (400 cubic feet); early Texas furniture; American Indian artifacts. **Holdings:** 3000 books; 13,000 cubic feet of local government records; vital statistics records of county and district clerks on microfilm. **Services:** Interlibrary loan; copying; depositories and division open to the public. **Publications:** Texas County Records Manual; Texas Municipal Records Manual; The Local Record (newsletter), quarterly; technical leaflets on local government records management.

★14116★
TEXAS STATE LIBRARY - STATE ARCHIVES DIVISION (Hist)
1201 Brazos St.
Box 12927 Phone: (512)463-5480
Austin, TX 78711 Christopher LaPlante, Dir.
Founded: 1876. **Staff:** Prof 9; Other 7. **Subjects:** Texas history. **Special Collections:** Archives of the Republic and State of Texas (25,000 linear feet). **Holdings:** 38,000 books; 3400 reels of microfilm; 2350 historical manuscript collections; 6000 maps; 70,000 photographic images. **Subscriptions:** 45 journals and other serials. **Services:** Copying; division open to the public. **Publications:** Historical publications, irregular.

★14117★
TEXAS (State) PARKS & WILDLIFE DEPARTMENT - LIBRARY (Biol Sci, Env-Cons, Rec)
4200 Smith School Rd. Phone: (512)479-4960
Austin, TX 78744 Debra E. Bunch, Libn.
Staff: Prof 1; Other 1. **Subjects:** Natural resources, wildlife and fishery management, recreation, parks and historic sites, game laws of Texas. **Special Collections:** Complete sets of Pittman-Robertson Federal Aid in Wildlife Restoration and Dingell-Johnson Federal Aid in Fish Restoration Acts, both for Texas, 1939 to present. **Holdings:** 12,000 books. **Subscriptions:** 120 journals and other serials. **Services:** Interlibrary loan; library open to the public for reference use only. **Special Indexes:** Index to Pittman-Robertson and Dingell-Johnson federal aid research reports.

★14118★
TEXAS (State) PARKS & WILDLIFE DEPARTMENT - MARINE LABORATORY LIBRARY (Biol Sci)
Box 1717 Phone: (512)729-2328
Rockport, TX 78382 T.L. Heffernan, Lab.Supv.
Staff: 1. **Subjects:** Marine biology. **Holdings:** 300 books; 1400 bound periodical volumes; 44 VF boxes of unbound reprints. **Subscriptions:** 31 journals and other serials. **Services:** Library open to the public for reference use only.

TEXAS STATE PUBLICATIONS CLEARINGHOUSE
See: Texas State Library - Information Services Division (14112)

★14119★
(Texas State) RAILROAD COMMISSION OF TEXAS - LIBRARY (Trans, Energy)
Capitol Sta., P.O. Drawer 12967 Phone: (512)463-7160
Austin, TX 78711-2967 Susan B. Rhyne, Libn.
Founded: 1985. **Staff:** Prof 1. **Subjects:** Oil and gas, law, transportation, gas utilities. **Holdings:** 10,000 books. **Subscriptions:** 52 journals and other serials. **Services:** Copying; library open to the public for reference use only. **Computerized Information Services:** WESTLAW.

★14120★
(Texas State) RAILROAD COMMISSION OF TEXAS - OIL AND GAS DIVISION - CENTRAL RECORDS (Bus-Fin, Trans)
William B. Travis Bldg.
1701 N. Congress Phone: (512)463-6882
Austin, TX 78711 Woody Ervin, Dir., Mapping & Rec. Retention
Founded: 1963. **Staff:** 33. **Subjects:** Railroad Commission - Oil and Gas Division business. **Holdings:** 20,000 reels of microfilm; plats; maps; logs. **Services:** Copying; research (limited); open to the public for reference use only. **Remarks:** The purpose of Central Records is to file division administrative decisions and all of the forms that the Railroad Commission requires for the drilling, operation, and maintenance of oil and gas wells in the State of Texas.

★14121★
TEXAS (State) REHABILITATION COMMISSION - LIBRARY (Med)
118 E. Riverside Dr. Phone: (512)445-8264
Austin, TX 78704 Laura F. Haneman, Libn.
Founded: 1975. **Staff:** Prof 1; Other 1. **Subjects:** Rehabilitation theory, disabilities, psychology of disability, caseload management, management skills, occupational therapy. **Holdings:** 12,000 books; 360 bound periodical volumes; videotapes; filmstrips; slide/tape sets; cassettes. **Subscriptions:** 52 journals and other serials. **Services:** Copying; library open to the public. **Automated Operations:** Computerized cataloging and acquisitions. **Computerized Information Services:** AVCAT (listing of audiovisuals), TXTEL (cross reference to all Texas telephone books; internal databases). **Publications:** Library Materials List, monthly; News & Views, monthly - for internal distribution only.

★14122★
TEXAS STATE TECHNICAL INSTITUTE, AMARILLO CAMPUS - LIBRARY (Educ)
Box 11117 Phone: (806)335-2316
Amarillo, TX 79111 Cynthia Sadler, Hd.Libn.
Founded: 1970. **Staff:** Prof 1; Other 3. **Holdings:** 15,800 books; 1740 AV programs; 746 microfiche of journals. **Subscriptions:** 296 journals and other serials; 10 newspapers. **Services:** Interlibrary loan; copying; library open to the public. **Computerized Information Services:** DIALOG Information Services. **Formerly:** Texas State Technical Institute, Mid-Continent Campus.

★14123★
TEXAS STATE TECHNICAL INSTITUTE, HARLINGEN CAMPUS - LIBRARY (Sci-Engr, Educ)
Harlingen, TX 78551-2628 Phone: (512)425-0630
David J. Diehl, Dir. of Lib.
Founded: 1970. **Staff:** Prof 2; Other 3. **Subjects:** Digital electronics, automotive mechanics, laser, instrumentation, dental laboratory, radio-TV repair, drafting and design, chemical technology, nuclear technology, data processing. **Holdings:** 17,000 books; 480 bound periodical volumes. **Subscriptions:** 420 journals and other serials; 20 newspapers. **Services:** Interlibrary loan; copying; library open to the public for reference use only. **Networks/Consortia:** Member of South Texas Library System, PAISANO Consortium of Libraries.

★14124★
TEXAS STATE TECHNICAL INSTITUTE, HARLINGEN CAMPUS - MC ALLEN EXTENSION LIBRARY (Comp Sci)
3201 W. Pecan Phone: (512)631-4922
McAllen, TX 78501-6661 Jose Alfonso Gamez, Libn.
Founded: 1984. **Staff:** Prof 1; Other 2. **Subjects:** Word processing, spreadsheet software. **Holdings:** 3000 books. **Subscriptions:** 85 journals and other serials; 6 newspapers. **Services:** Interlibrary loan; library open to the public for reference use only. **Automated Operations:** Computerized cataloging and acquisitions. **Networks/Consortia:** Member of PAISANO Consortium of Libraries.

★14125★
TEXAS STATE TECHNICAL INSTITUTE, WACO CAMPUS - LIBRARY (Sci-Engr, Educ)
Waco, TX 76705 Phone: (817)799-3611
Linda S. Koepf, Dir., Lib.
Founded: 1967. **Staff:** Prof 5; Other 9. **Subjects:** Horticulture-floriculture, automotive mechanics, electronics, computer science, animal technology, commercial art and advertising, food service administration, welding. **Special Collections:** Industrial Standards Collection (731 volumes); Deaf and Sign Language Collection (500 volumes). **Holdings:** 61,362 books and bound periodical volumes; 367,511 ERIC microfiche; 22,000 VF items; 2258 archival clippings. **Subscriptions:** 701 journals and other serials; 20 newspapers. **Services:** Interlibrary loan; copying; SDI; library open to the public with restrictions on circulation. **Automated Operations:** Computerized acquisitions and serials. **Computerized Information Services:** DIALOG Information Services. Performs searches on fee basis. **Publications:** What's New and Worth Reading, monthly; Library Newsletter, monthly - available on request. **Staff:** Mary Jenkins, Per.Libn.; Karen Wilson, Acq./Cat.Libn.; Bill Jackson, AV Techn..

★14126★
TEXAS (State) WATER COMMISSION - LIBRARY (Env-Cons)
Stephen F. Austin Bldg., Rm. 510
Capitol Sta., Box 13087 Phone: (512)463-7834
Austin, TX 78711-3087 Sylvia Von Fange, Hd.Libn.
Founded: 1965. **Staff:** Prof 1; Other 1. **Subjects:** Water resources. **Special Collections:** Publications of the commission and its predecessor agencies. **Holdings:** 55,000 books; 1700 bound periodical volumes; 8000 U.S. Geological Survey publications; 294 periodicals in microform; 2700 volumes of U.S. Environmental Protection Agency materials; 600 volumes of environmental impact statements; 3100 volumes of U.S. Army Corps of Engineers materials. **Subscriptions:** 555 journals and other serials. **Services:** Interlibrary loan; copying; library open to the public with restrictions. **Automated Operations:** Computerized cataloging, circulation, and serials. **Publications:** Library Bulletin, monthly; A Bibliography of State Agency Water Publications, 1986 (microfiche). **Remarks:** An alternate telephone number is 463-7837.

TEXAS (State) WATER DEVELOPMENT BOARD - TEXAS NATURAL RESOURCES INFORMATION SYSTEM (TNRIS)
See: Texas Natural Resources Information System (TNRIS) (14083)

★14127★
TEXAS TECH UNIVERSITY - HEALTH SCIENCES CENTER - LIBRARY OF THE HEALTH SCIENCES (Med)
Lubbock, TX 79430-0001 Phone: (806)743-2203
Charles W. Sargent, Ph.D., Dir.
Staff: Prof 14; Other 21. **Subjects:** Medicine, nursing, and allied health sciences. **Holdings:** 160,000 volumes; 100,000 slides, videotapes, and other AV programs. **Subscriptions:** 3000 journals and other serials. **Services:** Interlibrary loan; copying; SDI; library open to the public with restrictions. **Computerized Information Services:** LIS (internal database); OnTyme Electronic Message Network Service (electronic mail service). **Networks/Consortia:** Member of TALON, South Central Academic Medical Libraries Consortium (SCAMEL). **Publications:** Newsbriefs, monthly - to all full-time faculty and selected libraries. **Special Catalogs:** TALON Union List of Serials (microfiche); Media Catalog (computer). **Remarks:** Maintains branch libraries in Amarillo, Odessa, and El Paso, TX. **Staff:** Carolyn Patrick, Assoc.Dir., Tech.Serv.; Deborah Ward, Sr.Assoc.Dir.; Anne Thorton-Tromp, Hd., Cat.; Mary Moore, Assoc.Dir., Educ.; Donna Roush, Assoc.Dir., Info.Serv.; Steve Owen, Asst.Ref.Libn.; Judy Pedersen, Asst.Ref.Libn.; Teresa Knott, Assoc.Dir., El Paso; Dana Neeley, Assoc.Dir., Amarillo; Ursula Scott, Assoc.Dir., Odessa; Margaret Vugrin, Asst.Ref.Libn..

★14128★
TEXAS TECH UNIVERSITY - HEALTH SCIENCES CENTER - REGIONAL ACADEMIC HEALTH CENTER LIBRARY (Med)
4800 Alberta Ave. Phone: (915)533-3020
El Paso, TX 79905 Teresa L. Knott, Assoc.Dir.
Staff: Prof 1; Other 3. **Subjects:** Medicine. **Holdings:** 9929 books; 12,910 bound periodical volumes; 361 audiotapes; 65 slide/tape sets; 3 models; 2675 slides; 120 videotapes. **Subscriptions:** 398 journals and other serials. **Services:** Interlibrary loan; copying; SDI; library open to the public for reference use only. **Automated Operations:** Computerized cataloging, acquisitions, and serials. **Computerized Information Services:** NLM, DIALOG Information Services, BRS Information Technologies; OnTyme Electronic Message Network Service (electronic mail service). **Networks/Consortia:** Member of TALON. **Publications:** Newsbriefs, monthly - for internal distribution only. **Remarks:** Library is a branch of Texas Tech University - Library of the Health Sciences in Lubbock, TX.

★14129★
TEXAS TECH UNIVERSITY - LIBRARY (Sci-Engr, Hum)
Lubbock, TX 79409-0002 Phone: (806)742-2261
Dr. E. Dale Cluff, Dir. of Libs.
Founded: 1925. **Staff:** Prof 40; Other 56. **Subjects:** All major academic subjects, Spanish drama, Jewish and Hebrew literature, Turkish folk tales, Joseph Conrad, John Donne. **Holdings:** 1.1 million books and bound periodical volumes; 943,428 documents; 685,584 microforms; 16.6 million manuscripts. **Subscriptions:** 9346 journals and other serials; 70 newspapers. **Services:** Interlibrary loan; copying; library open to the public. **Automated Operations:** Computerized cataloging, acquisitions, serials, and circulation. **Computerized Information Services:** DIALOG Information Services, BRS Information Technologies; ALANET (electronic mail service). Performs searches on fee basis. Contact Person: Susan Larson Makar, Coord., CASS, 742-2236. **Networks/Consortia:** Member of AMIGOS Bibliographic Council, Inc.. **Staff:** David Murrah, Assoc.Dir./Spec.Coll.; Jennifer Cargill, Assoc.Dir./Info. Access & Sys..

★14130★
TEXAS TECH UNIVERSITY - LIBRARY - DOCUMENTS DEPARTMENT (Info Sci)
Lubbock, TX 79409 Phone: (806)742-2268
Mary Ann Higdon, Hd.
Founded: 1935. **Staff:** Prof 6; Other 4. **Subjects:** U.S. Government publications. **Holdings:** 78,299 bound volumes of U.S. documents; 476,947 unbound U.S. documents; 394,949 microforms; 117,000 CIS serials. **Services:** Interlibrary loan; copying; library open to the public. **Automated Operations:** Computerized cataloging and serials. **Networks/Consortia:** Member of AMIGOS Bibliographic Council, Inc.. **Remarks:** This is a regional depository for U.S. Government publications. **Staff:** Barbara Geyer, Maps/Ref.Libn.; Thomas K. Lindsey, Coord., Docs./Ref.; Mary Ann Higgins, Hd.; Theresa Trost, Doc./Ref.Libn.; Amy Chang, Doc./Ref.Libn.; Thomas Rohrig, Doc./Ref.Libn.; Teresa Blodgett, Doc./Ref.Libn.; Douglas Bates, Doc./Cat.Libn.; Lisa Spillers, Doc./Ref.Libn.; Janita Jobe, Doc./Ref.Libn..

★14131★
TEXAS TECH UNIVERSITY - SCHOOL OF LAW LIBRARY (Law)
Lubbock, TX 79409 Phone: (806)742-3794
Jane G. Olm, Dir.
Founded: 1966. **Staff:** Prof 4; Other 10. **Subjects:** Law. **Holdings:** 179,889 books and bound periodical volumes; 100,200 microfiche. **Subscriptions:** 3140 journals and other serials; 16 newspapers. **Services:** Interlibrary loan; copying; library open to the public for reference use only. **Automated Operations:** Computerized cataloging. **Computerized Information Services:** OCLC, LEXIS, WESTLAW. **Networks/Consortia:** Member of AMIGOS Bibliographic Council, Inc.. **Staff:** Carolie R. Mullan, Assoc.Libn.; Sherry K. Little, Tech.Serv.Libn.; Sharon Blackburn, Automated Res.Coord..

★14132★
TEXAS TECH UNIVERSITY - SOUTHWEST COLLECTION (Hist)
Box 4090 Phone: (806)742-3749
Lubbock, TX 79409 Dr. David Murrah, Dir.
Founded: 1955. **Staff:** Prof 6; Other 10. **Subjects:** Texas and Southwestern history and literature; history of Texas Tech University; social, economic, and religious affairs of West Texas; sociohistorical data pertaining to the area and its indigenous institutions; man-land confrontation in the arid and semi-arid Southwest including the struggle of the pioneer settlers, especially women; cattle industry; land colonization; mining; mechanized agriculture and the water problem. **Special Collections:** Ranching: Matador Land and Cattle Company, Spur Ranch, Pitchfork Land and Cattle Company, Bar S Ranch, Swenson Land and Cattle Company; Business: Itasca Cotton Manufacturing Company and Weavers Guild, Renfro Drug Company, Weatherby Motor Company, Cosden Petroleum Corporation, E.S. Graham Company, Higginbotham Brothers Company, John E. Morrison Company, records of the Quanah, Acme and Pacific, Fort Worth and Denver, Santa Fe railroads; Land Companies: Lone Star Land Company, Ripley Townsite Company, Yellow House Company, Texas Land and Development Company; Texas and Pacific Coal Company; Organizations: West Texas Chamber of Commerce, Texas Sheep and Goat Raisers Association, League of Women Voters; Individuals: R. Wright Armstrong, Clifford B. Jones, Carl Coke Rister, Ross Malone, William P. Soash, Preston Smith, Marvin Jones, George Mahon, Gordon McLendon. **Holdings:** 40,000 books; 16.5 million leaves of business and personal documents and university archives; 1500 maps; 3000 tape recordings; 6000 reels of microfilm; 300,000 photographs; 1200 reels of movie film. **Subscriptions:** 424 journals and other serials. **Services:** Interlibrary loan; copying; collection open to the public for reference use only. **Staff:** Dr. Doris Blaisdell, Assoc.Archv.; Janet Neugebauer, Asst.Archv.; Cindy Martin, Asst.Archv..

★14133★
TEXAS WOMAN'S UNIVERSITY - BLAGG-HUEY LIBRARY - SPECIAL COLLECTIONS (Soc Sci)
TWU Sta., Box 23715 Phone: (817)898-3751
Denton, TX 76204 Metta Nicewarner, Spec.Coll.Libn.
Founded: 1932. **Staff:** Prof 1; Other 2. **Subjects:** Women's biography, history, and literature; suffrage; cookery. **Special Collections:** Woman's Collection (30,600 books and bound periodical volumes, including the Madeleine Henrey Collection and the LaVerne Harrell Clark Collection); Sarah Weddington Collection; Texas Women: A Celebration of History collection; Texas Federation of Women's Clubs papers; Delta Kappa Gamma - Texas papers; Cookbook and Menu Collection (10,900 books and bound periodical volumes; 2000 menus, including the Julie Bennell Cookbook Collection and the Margaret Scruggs Cookbook Collection); The Ribbon Archives; Genevieve Dixon Collection (1038 books); university archives (2000 linear feet); manuscript collection (1900 linear feet). **Holdings:** 60,000 books and bound periodical volumes; 45,900 microforms; 600 AV programs. **Services:** Interlibrary loan; copying; collections open to the public. **Automated Operations:** Computerized public access catalog, cataloging, and circulation. **Computerized Information Services:** DIALOG Information Services, Geac Library Information System, OCLC, BRS Information Technologies, MEDLINE. **Networks/Consortia:** Member of AMIGOS Bibliographic Council, Inc., Association for Higher Education of North Texas (AHE). **Special Catalogs:** Finder's guide to Texas Women: A Celebration of History. **Remarks:** An alternate telephone number is 898-2665.

★14134★
TEXAS WOMAN'S UNIVERSITY - CENTER FOR THE STUDY OF LEARNING - LIBRARY (Educ)
Box 23029 Phone: (817)898-2045
Denton, TX 76204 Ruth M. Caswell, Dir.
Subjects: Reading - methodology, teaching, testing. **Holdings:** 1500 books; 150 other cataloged items. **Services:** Library open to the public by appointment for reference use. **Remarks:** An alternate telephone number is 898-2227.

★14135★
TEXAS WOMAN'S UNIVERSITY - LIBRARY SCIENCE LIBRARY (Info Sci)
School of Library and Information Studies Phone: (817)898-2621
Denton, TX 76204 Janice R. Franklin, Libn.
Founded: 1939. **Staff:** Prof 1; Other 13. **Subjects:** Library and information science, children's and young adult literature. **Holdings:** 18,483 books; 2910 bound periodical volumes; 291 reels of microfilm; 55 kits; 379 titles of library newsletters. **Subscriptions:** 148 journals. **Services:** Library open to the public. **Automated Operations:** Computerized public access catalog. **Computerized Information Services:** DIALOG Information Services, BRS Information Technologies, OCLC, Geac Library Information System.

★14136★
TEXAS WOMAN'S UNIVERSITY - LIBRARY SCIENCE LIBRARY - PROYECTO LEER (Educ)
School of Library and Information Studies Phone: (817)898-2615
Denton, TX 76204 Ivan E. Calimano, Coord.
Founded: 1967. **Subjects:** Spanish and bilingual (Spanish-English) materials. **Holdings:** 24,000 books, journals, and nonprint materials. **Services:** Research collection and advisory service available to TWU stuents and the public with restrictions; materials evaluated and reviewed; classes conducted for librarians, educators, and library school students. **Publications:** Proyecto LEER Bulletin, irregular. **Remarks:** Access to the collection is through OCLC and Geac Library Information System.

★14137★
TEXAS WOMAN'S UNIVERSITY, DALLAS CENTER - F.W. AND BESSIE DYE MEMORIAL LIBRARY (Med)
1810 Inwood Rd. Phone: (214)689-6580
Dallas, TX 75235 M. Virginia Kimzey, Coord., Hea.Sci.Lib.
Staff: Prof 1; Other 6. **Subjects:** Nursing, occupational therapy, medical records, health care administration, psychology, physical therapy. **Special Collections:** Nursing history collections. **Holdings:** 22,410 books; 8945 bound periodical volumes; 1065 bound theses, dissertations, and professional papers; 317 volumes on microfilm; 1674 volumes on microfiche; 172 volumes on microcard. **Subscriptions:** 380 journals and other serials. **Services:** Interlibrary loan; copying; library open to the public for reference use only. **Automated Operations:** Computerized public access catalog and cataloging. **Computerized Information Services:** DIALOG Information Services, Geac Library Information System, MEDLARS. **Networks/Consortia:** Member of Dallas-Tarrant County Consortium of Health Science Libraries, Association for Higher Education of North Texas (AHE), TALON.

★14138★
TEXTILE MUSEUM - ARTHUR D. JENKINS LIBRARY (Art, Hist)
2320 S St., N.W. Phone: (202)667-0441
Washington, DC 20008 Dolores E. Fairbanks, Libn./Pubns.Coord.
Staff: Prof 1. **Subjects:** Oriental rugs; ancient and ethnographic textiles - Islamic, Peruvian, Asian, Oriental, Central American, Southwest American. **Holdings:** 13,000 books and periodicals. **Subscriptions:** 144 journals and other serials. **Services:** Library open to the public on a limited schedule.

★14139★
TEXTILE RESEARCH INSTITUTE - LIBRARY (Sci-Engr)
601 Prospect Ave.
Box 625
Princeton, NJ 08540 Phone: (609)924-3150
Founded: 1945. **Staff:** 1. **Subjects:** Fibers, chemistry, textiles, polymers, physics, engineering, microscopy, cellulose. **Holdings:** 2000 books; 2500 bound periodical volumes; 50 VF drawers of reports, reprints, patents. **Subscriptions:** 100 journals and other serials. **Services:** Interlibrary loan (fee); copying; library open to the public by appointment. **Publications:** Books and journals received, semiannual.

★14140★
TEXTRON DEFENSE SYSTEMS - RESEARCH LIBRARY (Sci-Engr)
201 Lowell St. Phone: (617)657-2632
Wilmington, MA 01887 E. Cohen, Mgr.
Staff: Prof 3; Other 1. **Subjects:** Aerodynamics, chemistry, space technology, physics, instrumentation, electronics, missile technology. **Holdings:** 10,000 books; 8000 bound periodical volumes; 20,000 technical reports and documents in hardcopy and on microfiche. **Subscriptions:** 150 journals and other serials. **Services:** Interlibrary loan; library not open to the public. **Computerized Information Services:** DIALOG Information Services, DTIC; internal database. **Formerly:** AVCO Corporation - Systems Division. **Staff:** Chen-li Lee, Sr.Libn.; Robert Hall, Ref.Libn./ Info.Spec.; Shirley Levinson, Acq.Libn..

★14141★
TEXTRON, INC. - AEROSTRUCTURES DIVISION - ENGINEERING LIBRARY (Sci-Engr)
Box 210 Phone: (615)360-4043
Nashville, TN 37202 Jan L. Haley, Tech.Libn.
Staff: Prof 1. **Subjects:** Engineering, aircraft, aeronautics, chemistry, metallurgy. **Holdings:** 1242 books; 3100 pamphlets; 1300 reels of microfilm; military standards and specifications; industry standards; publications of NASA, National Advisory Committee for Aeronautics (NACA), Air Force Materials Laboratory (AFML), Air Force Wright Aeronautical Laboratories (FWAL), and Air Force Flight Dynamics Laboratory (AFFDL). **Subscriptions:** 37 journals and other serials. **Services:** Interlibrary loan (to local libraries); library open to the public with restrictions. **Computerized Information Services:** DIALOG Information Services. **Publications:** Newsletter, monthly. **Formerly:** AVCO Corporation.

★14142★
TEXTRON, INC. - LYCOMING DIVISION - LIBRARY & TECHNICAL INFORMATION CENTER (Sci-Engr, Bus-Fin)
550 Main St. Phone: (203)385-3429
Stratford, CT 06497 Lee G. Russell, Hd.Libn.
Founded: 1980. **Staff:** Prof 1; Other 1. **Subjects:** Aerospace, engineering, business planning, manufacturing, training and development. **Holdings:** 7500 books; 50 bound periodical volumes; 5000 NASA and National Advisory Committee for Aeronautics (NACA) reports; 5500 ASME papers, 1956 to present; Society of Automotive Engineers (SAE) papers, 1955 to present; AIAA and AHS technical papers; 100,000 company reports, proposals, papers on microfilm; training and development audio- and videotapes. **Subscriptions:** 600 journals and other serials; 20 newspapers. **Services:** Interlibrary loan; SDI; library open to the public by appointment. **Automated Operations:** Computerized cataloging, acquisitions, serials, and circulation. **Computerized Information Services:** DIALOG Information Services, DTIC, Pergamon ORBIT InfoLine, Inc., NASA/RECON; internal databases; Smart Communications, Inc. (electronic mail service). Performs searches free of charge. **Networks/ Consortia:** Member of Southwestern Connecticut Library Council (SWLC). **Publications:** Periodicals List, annual; accessions list, monthly - for internal distribution only; Monthly Newsletter, quarterly; user guide, annual. **Special Catalogs:** Microfilm holdings; research and development reports. **Formerly:** AVCO - Lycoming Textron Division.

★14143★
THACHER PROFFITT & WOOD - LIBRARY (Law)
2 World Trade Center, 39th Fl. Phone: (212)483-5844
New York, NY 10048 Elisabeth Tavss Ohman, Libn.
Staff: Prof 1; Other 2. **Subjects:** Law - admiralty, English, banking, corporate, real estate, tax. **Holdings:** 15,000 books; 1000 bound periodical volumes; 8 VF drawers. **Subscriptions:** 200 journals and other serials; 10 newspapers. **Services:** Interlibrary loan; library not open to the public. **Computerized Information Services:** LEXIS, WESTLAW, DIALOG Information Services.

THAYER ENGINEER LIBRARY
See: U.S. Army - TRADOC - Engineer School (14793)

THE DRUGSTORE INFORMATION CLEARINGHOUSE
See: South Carolina (State) Commission on Alcohol and Drug Abuse (13382)

★14144★
THEATRE HISTORICAL SOCIETY ARCHIVES (Theater)
2215 W. North Ave. Phone: (312)252-7200
Chicago, IL 60647 William T. Benedict, Adm.
Staff: Prof 1. **Subjects:** Theater architecture, theater. **Special Collections:** Chicago Architectural Photographing Co. (1000 negatives); Ben Hall Collection (photographs; clippings; memorabilia); blueprints. **Holdings:** 500 books; 8000 slides; 5000 negatives; index to 5000 U.S. theaters; antique postcards; artifacts. **Services:** Copying; library open to the public on a limited schedule and by appointment. **Publications:** Marquee, quarterly; annual publication on one theater or subject.

THEATRE INTIME ARCHIVES
See: Princeton University - William Seymour Theatre Collection (11595)

★14145★
THELEN, MARRIN, JOHNSON & BRIDGES - LAW LIBRARY (Law)
Two Embarcadero Center Phone: (415)392-6320
San Francisco, CA 94111 Marlene Harmon, Hd.Libn.
Staff: Prof 3; Other 2. **Subjects:** Law. **Holdings:** 30,000 volumes. **Subscriptions:** 320 journals and other serials. **Services:** Interlibrary loan; library not open to the public. **Computerized Information Services:** DIALOG Information Services, LEXIS, NEXIS, WESTLAW, DataTimes, RLIN. **Networks/Consortia:** Member of CLASS. **Staff:** Todd Bennett, Asst.Libn.; Lynn Zweifler, Asst.Libn..

★14146★
THEOSOPHICAL BOOK ASSOCIATION FOR THE BLIND, INC. (Aud-Vis)
Krotona 54 Phone: (805)646-2121
Ojai, CA 93023 Dennis Gottschalk, Dir.
Founded: 1910. **Staff:** 9. **Subjects:** Theosophy, science, healing, meditation, comparative religion, Yoga, philosophy, esoteric philosophy, spiritual awareness. **Holdings:** 1200 books; 600 tapes; magazines and pamphlets. **Services:** Library open to the public by mail. **Publications:** Braille Star Theosophist, bimonthly. **Remarks:** Library holdings are in braille and on tape.

★14147★
THEOSOPHICAL SOCIETY - HERMES LIBRARY (Rel-Phil)
2807 W. 16th Ave., Suite 2 Phone: (604)733-5684
Vancouver, BC, Canada V6K 3C5 Diana Cooper, Libn.
Founded: 1927. **Staff:** Prof 1; Other 1. **Subjects:** Theosophy, philosophy, mythology, psychology, religious studies. **Holdings:** 2500 books; 300 bound periodical volumes; 200 audio and video cassettes; reprints and originals of rare theosophical journals; pamphlet file. **Subscriptions:** 25 journals and other serials. **Services:** Interlibrary loan; library open to the public with restrictions.

★14148★
THEOSOPHICAL SOCIETY IN AMERICA - OLCOTT LIBRARY & RESEARCH CENTER (Rel-Phil)
1926 N. Main St.
Box 270 Phone: (312)668-1571
Wheaton, IL 60189-0270 Dorothy Abbenhouse, Natl.Pres.
Founded: 1926. **Staff:** 3. **Subjects:** Theosophy (wisdom traditions), comparative religions, metaphysics, parapsychology, mysticism. **Special Collections:** Boris DeZirkoff Collection (H.P. Blauatsky; 650 books); The Theosophical Society in America's National Archives (400 books; 32 reels of microfilm); rare works in subject areas; theosophical periodicals. **Holdings:** 12,000 books; 547 bound periodical volumes; 1000 pamphlets; 400 audio cassettes; 50 video cassettes; periodicals on microfilm. **Subscriptions:** 45 journals and other serials. **Services:** Interlibrary loan; copying; library open to the public. **Automated Operations:** Computerized circulation. **Networks/Consortia:** Member of Dupage Library System. **Publications:** Selected annotated bibliographies - for sale. **Special Catalogs:** Annotated reading lists of the library collection. **Staff:** Lewis Lucas, Libn.; Lakshmi Narayanswami, Tech.Serv.; Caroline Dauteuille, Circ.Serv..

★14149★
THEOSOPHICAL SOCIETY IN MIAMI - LIBRARY (Rel-Phil)
119 N.E. 62nd St. Phone: (305)754-4331
Miami, FL 33138 Carol L. Hurd, Libn.
Staff: Prof 1. **Subjects:** Theosophy; religion, especially eastern; yoga; philosophy; astrology; metaphysics. **Holdings:** 6000 books. **Services:** Library open to the public.

THEOSOPHICAL SOCIETY OF PASADENA - THEOSOPHICAL UNIVERSITY
See: Theosophical University - Library (14150)

★14150★
THEOSOPHICAL UNIVERSITY - LIBRARY (Rel-Phil)
2416 N. Lake Ave. Phone: (818)798-8020
Altadena, CA 91001 John P. Van Mater, Libn.
Founded: 1919. **Staff:** Prof 3; Other 3. **Subjects:** Theosophy, comparative religion and mythology, ancient and modern philosophy and science, occultism. **Special Collections:** Theosophical magazines, 1879 to present (nearly complete); first editions of theosophical books. **Holdings:** 50,000 books; 5000 bound periodical volumes; 1000 theosophical pamphlets. **Subscriptions:** 30 journals and other serials. **Services:** Interlibrary loan (limited); library open to the public for reference use. **Remarks:** Maintained by the Theosophical Society of Pasadena. **Staff:** I. Manuel Oderberg, Res.Libn.; Sarah B. Van Mater, Asst.Libn..

THEOSOPHY HALL - LIBRARY
See: United Lodge of Theosophists (14546)

★14151★
THERMARK CORPORATION - TECHNICAL INFORMATION SERVICES (Sci-Engr)
650 W. 67th Place
Schererville, IN 46375 Phone: (219)322-5030
Founded: 1973. **Staff:** Prof 1. **Subjects:** Coatings technology. **Special Collections:** Radiation curing technology. **Holdings:** 237 books; 58 bound periodical volumes; 450 other cataloged items; 2 VF drawers of technical reports; 66 audiotapes; microfilm; patents. **Subscriptions:** 106 journals and other serials. **Services:** Services not open to the public.

★14152★
THERMO KING CORPORATION - LIBRARY (Sci-Engr)
314 W. 90th St. Phone: (612)887-2336
Minneapolis, MN 55420 Julie Ann Ostrow, Corp.Libn.
Founded: 1973. **Staff:** Prof 1. **Subjects:** Refrigerated transport, air conditioning, refrigeration, heating, transportation, automotive engineering. **Special Collections:** International Institute of Refrigeration (61 volumes). **Holdings:** 1400 books; 2 VF drawers of patents; 10 VF drawers of documents; 1600 reports; 2000 vendor catalogs; 1 drawer of microfilm; 3 VF drawers of domestic and international standards. **Subscriptions:** 135 journals and other serials. **Services:** Library not open to the public. **Automated Operations:** Computerized cataloging. **Computerized Information Services:** DIALOG Information Services.

★14153★
THIELE KAOLIN COMPANY - RESEARCH & DEVELOPMENT LIBRARY (Sci-Engr)
Box 1056 Phone: (912)552-3951
Sandersville, GA 31082 Barbara W. Goodman, Tech.Sec.-Libn.
Staff: Prof 1; Other 1. **Subjects:** Clay beneficiation, kaolin, geology, mineralogy, applied chemistry. **Holdings:** 765 books; 70 bound periodical volumes; 13 VF drawers; 1116 patents. **Subscriptions:** 50 journals and other serials. **Services:** Interlibrary loan; library open to the public with restrictions. **Computerized Information Services:** CAS ONLINE, DIALOG Information Services; Paperchem, Agricola, Claims Patents (internal databases). Performs searches on fee basis.

★14154★
THIRD BAPTIST CHURCH - LIBRARY (Rel-Phil)
620 N. Grand Phone: (314)533-7340
St. Louis, MO 63103 Jim Wilson, Media Dir.
Founded: 1943. **Staff:** 10. **Subjects:** Bible, church doctrine, church history, church work, social sciences, literature, biography. **Holdings:** 6000 volumes; AV programs. **Subscriptions:** 40 journals and other serials. **Services:** Library open to the public with restrictions.

THIRD WORLD RESOURCE CENTRE
See: Ryerson Polytechnical Institute (12273)

★14155★
THIRD WORLD RESOURCE CENTER (Soc Sci)
125 Tecumseh, W. Phone: (519)252-1517
Windsor, ON, Canada N8X 1E8 Ellen Preuschat, Rsrc.Coord.
Staff: 3. **Subjects:** Aids to social action and development education, disarmament and arms trade, foreign relations, human rights, natural resources, Third World areas, native peoples, women's issues. **Holdings:** 1800 books; 194 reports and manuscripts; 40 vertical file boxes of articles; 32 simulation games; 150 videotapes, filmstrips, and slide shows; 70 kits. **Subscriptions:** 62 journals and other serials; 7 newspapers. **Services:** Copying; center open to the public. **Automated Operations:** Computerized cataloging. **Publications:** Newsletter, 5/year; bibliographies. **Special Catalogs:** AV Catalogue (booklet).

THIRTEEN RESEARCH LIBRARY
See: Educational Broadcasting Corporation (4616)

★14156★
THISTLETOWN REGIONAL CENTRE - LIBRARY (Soc Sci)
Rexdale Campus
51 Panorama Court Phone: (416)741-1210
Rexdale, ON, Canada M9V 4L8 Joy Shanfield, Supv. of Libs.
Founded: 1962. **Staff:** Prof 1; Other 2. **Subjects:** Child psychiatry and psychology, family therapy, special education, adolescent psychiatry and psychology, juvenile corrections. **Holdings:** 3150 books; 2200 bound periodical volumes; 300 audiotapes; 7 VF drawers; 2 drawers of legislation materials. **Subscriptions:** 104 journals and other serials. **Services:** Interlibrary loan; library open to the public for reference use only. **Automated Operations:** Computerized cataloging. **Computerized Information Services:** DIALOG Information Services. **Networks/Consortia:** Member of Ontario Government Libraries' Council (OGLC). **Publications:** Recent Acquisitions, quarterly - for internal distribution only. **Remarks:** Maintained by Ontario Ministry of Community and Social Services.

THODE LIBRARY OF SCIENCE & ENGINEERING
See: Mc Master University (8255)

CAREY S. THOMAS LIBRARY
See: Denver Conservative Baptist Seminary (4189)

★14157★
THOMAS COLLEGE - MARRINER LIBRARY (Bus-Fin)
W. River Rd. Phone: (207)873-0771
Waterville, ME 04901 Richard A. Boudreau, Libn.
Staff: Prof 1; Other 4. **Subjects:** Business. **Holdings:** 21,887 books and bound periodical volumes. **Subscriptions:** 230 journals and other serials; 12 newspapers. **Services:** Interlibrary loan; copying; library open to the public with restrictions.

★14158★
THOMAS COUNTY HISTORICAL SOCIETY - LIBRARY (Hist)
1525 W. Fourth Phone: (913)462-6972
Colby, KS 67701 Miriam R. Beck, Dir.
Founded: 1959. **Staff:** Prof 4; Other 4. **Subjects:** Local history. **Holdings:** 500 linear feet of microfilm, manuscripts, books, archives, photographs, slides, clippings, cassettes. **Subscriptions:** 42 journals and other serials. **Services:** Copying; library open to the public for reference use only. **Publications:** Newsletter, quarterly - to members; Golden Jubilee, 1935 reprint; Land of the Windmills, 1976; Golden Heritage of Thomas County, Kansas, 1979 (all books).

★14159★
HERBERT J. THOMAS MEMORIAL HOSPITAL - MEDICAL LIBRARY (Med)
4605 MacCorkle Ave., S.W. Phone: (304)768-3961
South Charleston, WV 25309 Barbara Rosen, Dir., Med.Rec.Dept.
Founded: 1946. **Subjects:** Medicine. **Holdings:** 300 books. **Subscriptions:** 80 journals and other serials. **Services:** Interlibrary loan; copying; library open to the public with director's permission. **Computerized Information Services:** Access to MEDLINE (through West Virginia University Library). **Staff:** Glenna Wolfe, ART, Libn..

THOMAS LIBRARY
See: Wittenberg University - Thomas Library (17983)

★14160★
THOMAS, SNELL, JAMISON, RUSSELL, AND ASPERGER ET AL - LIBRARY (Law)
2445 Capitol St.
Box 1461 Phone: (209)442-0600
Fresno, CA 93716 Tina Louise Marquez, Law Libn.
Staff: Prof 1; Other 1. **Subjects:** Law - corporate, tax, real estate, probate; civil litigation. **Holdings:** 5000 books; 500 bound periodical volumes; 350 cassette tapes. **Subscriptions:** 140 journals and other serials. **Services:** Library not open to the public. **Computerized Information Services:** LEXIS; ABA/net (electronic mail service).

★14161★
BOYCE THOMPSON INSTITUTE - LIBRARY (Biol Sci)
Cornell University
Tower Rd. Phone: (607)257-2030
Ithaca, NY 14853 Perry O. Dennis, Libn.
Staff: 1. **Subjects:** Plant physiology and pathology, biochemistry, microbiology, molecular biology, environmental biology, entomology, ecology. **Holdings:** 4000 books; 1500 bound periodical volumes. **Subscriptions:** 150 journals and other serials. **Services:** Copying; library open to the public.

C.Y. THOMPSON LIBRARY
See: University of Nebraska, Lincoln (16556)

★14162★
DAVID THOMPSON LIBRARY - SPECIAL COLLECTIONS (Hist)
1402 Fell St. Phone: (604)352-2241
Nelson, BC, Canada V1L 6A6 Roberta Griffiths, Mgr.
Founded: 1963. **Subjects:** Kootenaiana. **Holdings:** 1121 volumes; 946 photographs; clipping file. **Services:** Interlibrary loan (limited); copying; collections open to the public for reference use only. **Publications:** Kootenaiana: a listing of books, government publications, monographs, journals, pamphlets, etc. relating to the Kootenay area, 1976.

HAROLD W. THOMPSON FOLKLIFE ARCHIVES
See: New York State Historical Association - Library (10113)

J. THOMPSON PSYCHIATRY LIBRARY
See: Yeshiva University - Albert Einstein College of Medicine - Department of Psychiatry (18167)

★14163★
J. WALTER THOMPSON COMPANY - INFORMATION CENTER (Bus-Fin)
875 N. Michigan Ave. Phone: (312)951-4000
Chicago, IL 60611 Roberta Piccoli, V.P., Dir., Info.Serv.
Founded: 1921. **Staff:** Prof 3; Other 5. **Subjects:** Advertising, advertising research, market research, marketing, consumer products and services, consumer behavior. **Holdings:** 4000 books; 225 VF drawers; 20,000 research reports; 1 million print advertisements; 1000 reels of microfilm. **Subscriptions:** 600 journals and other serials; 5 newspapers. **Services:** Interlibrary loan; center open to the public by appointment. **Computerized Information Services:** DIALOG Information Services, NEXIS, Dun & Bradstreet Corporation, VU/TEXT Information Services, PRODUCTSCAN; internal databases. **Networks/Consortia:** Member of ILLINET. **Staff:** Sharon Kearney, Info.Spec.; Nancy Nichols, Info.Spec..

★14164★
J. WALTER THOMPSON COMPANY - INFORMATION CENTER (Bus-Fin)
466 Lexington Ave. Phone: (212)210-7267
New York, NY 10017 Carol Stankiewicz, Dir., Info.Serv.
Founded: 1918. **Staff:** Prof 2; Other 4. **Subjects:** Advertising, marketing, industry. **Special Collections:** Picture and art; consumer print advertisements. **Holdings:** 4000 books; 150 VF drawers; 1563 reels of microfilm; 2000 microfiche. **Subscriptions:** 300 journals and other serials. **Services:** Interlibrary loan; center open to SLA members and others by appointment. **Computerized Information Services:** DIALOG Information Services, NEXIS, NewsNet, Inc., Dow Jones News/Retrieval. **Staff:** Dana Peterson, Cat.; Nadine Bauman, Ref.Libn.; Joanne Scala, Ref.Libn.; Peggy Weiner, Ref.Libn..

★14165★
J. WALTER THOMPSON COMPANY - INFORMATION CENTRE (Bus-Fin)
160 Bloor St., E. Phone: (416)920-9171
Toronto, ON, Canada M4W 3P7 Rita Piazza, Mgr., Info.Serv.
Founded: 1984. **Staff:** Prof 1; Other 1. **Subjects:** Advertising, marketing, business. **Holdings:** 300 books; 15 drawers of reports and vertical files. **Subscriptions:** 178 journals and other serials. **Services:** Center not open to the public. **Automated Operations:** Computerized cataloging. **Computerized Information Services:** DIALOG Information Services, I.P. Sharp Associates Limited, Info Globe, Infomart, Canada Systems Group (CSG), WILSONLINE.

JOHN H. THOMPSON MEMORIAL LIBRARY
See: Torrington Historical Society, Inc. (14259)

★14166★
THOMPSON & KNIGHT - LIBRARY (Law)
3300 First City Center Phone: (214)969-1428
Dallas, TX 75201 Cindy Spano, Libn.
Staff: 5. **Subjects:** Law. **Holdings:** 20,000 volumes. **Subscriptions:** 75 journals and other serials. **Services:** Interlibrary loan; copying; library open to Dallas area law librarians only. **Computerized Information Services:** LEXIS, WESTLAW, Dow Jones News/Retrieval, DIALOG Information Services.

NANCY THOMPSON LIBRARY
See: Kean College of New Jersey (7382)

R.C. THOMPSON LIBRARY
See: Maryland Rehabilitation Center (8494)

W.F. THOMPSON MEMORIAL LIBRARY
See: U.S. Natl. Marine Fisheries Service (15226)

THOMSON COMPANY - ALTOONA MIRROR
See: Altoona Mirror - Library (349)

★14167★
THOMSON CONSUMER ELECTRONICS, INC. - ENGINEERING LIBRARY (Sci-Engr)
600 N. Sherman Dr., Bldg. 6-123 Phone: (317)267-5925
Indianapolis, IN 46201 Susan T. Crawley, Adm., Lib.Serv.
Founded: 1955. **Staff:** Prof 1. **Subjects:** Engineering, electronics, physics, chemistry, television, computers. **Holdings:** 2000 books; 800 bound periodical volumes. **Subscriptions:** 115 journals and other serials. **Services:** Interlibrary loan; library not open to the public. **Automated Operations:** Computerized cataloging. **Computerized Information Services:** DIALOG Information Services, WILSONLINE, OCLC. **Networks/Consortia:** Member of Central Indiana Area Library Services Authority (CIALSA), INCOLSA. **Publications:** The Elm, bimonthly - for internal distribution only. **Formerly:** RCA Corporation - RCA Consumer Electronics.

★14168★
THOMSON CONSUMER ELECTRONICS, INC. - PICTURE TUBE DIVISION - LIBRARY (Sci-Engr)
3301 S. Adams St. Phone: (317)662-5282
Marion, IN 46952 Marilyn Brown, Libn.
Founded: 1950. **Staff:** 1. **Subjects:** Vacuum tubes, television, electronics, physics, chemistry, glass, metals. **Holdings:** 2058 books; 1687 bound periodical volumes; 1200 pamphlets; 16 VF drawers of internal reports. **Services:** Library not open to the public. **Formerly:** RCA Corporation - Picture Tube Division.

★14169★
THOMSON, ROGERS, BARRISTERS & SOLICITORS - LIBRARY (Law)
390 Bay St., Suite 3100 Phone: (416)868-3100
Toronto, ON, Canada M5H 1W2 Dianne D. Sydij, Libn.
Staff: 1. **Subjects:** Law - commercial, motion picture, entertainment, copyright, insurance, aviation, taxation, real estate, municipal. **Holdings:** 10,000 volumes. **Services:** Library not open to the public.

★14170★
THOREAU SOCIETY, INC. - THOREAU LYCEUM - LIBRARY (Hum, Hist)
156 Belknap St. Phone: (617)369-5912
Concord, MA 01742 Anne McGrath, Cur.
Founded: 1967. **Staff:** Prof 1; Other 3. **Subjects:** Henry David Thoreau, American transcendentalism, natural history, Concord history, American literature. **Holdings:** 1500 volumes. **Services:** Library open to the public with restrictions.

DR. MAX THOREK LIBRARY AND MANUSCRIPT ROOM
See: International College of Surgeons Hall of Fame - Dr. Joseph Montague Proctologic Library (7002)

OLAF H. THORMODSGARD LAW LIBRARY
See: University of North Dakota (16657)

★14171★
THORNDIKE, DORAN, PAINE AND LEWIS INC. - RESEARCH LIBRARY (Bus-Fin)
233 Peachtree St., N.E., Suite 700 Phone: (404)688-2782
Atlanta, GA 30303 Linda Swann Austin, Libn.
Founded: 1970. **Staff:** Prof 1. **Subjects:** Investment information. **Holdings:** 100 volumes; 1000 company files on individual companies; 12 VF drawers of industry files. **Subscriptions:** 44 journals and other serials. **Services:** Library open to the public by appointment with restrictions. **Special Catalogs:** Catalog of company files (card); catalog of analyst reports published internally (card).

★14172★
THORNDIKE LIBRARY (Law)
1300 Court House Phone: (617)725-8078
Boston, MA 02108 Jean Roberts, Ed./Libn.
Founded: 1921. **Staff:** Prof 1. **Subjects:** Law. **Holdings:** 20,000 books; 525 bound periodical volumes. **Services:** Library is a private facility for court use only. **Remarks:** Chartered as Judges Library Corporation in 1921. Maintained by Massachusetts State Supreme Judicial Court.

★14173★
THORNE ERNST & WHINNEY - LIBRARY (Bus-Fin)
Bow Valley Square 2
205 5th Ave., S.W., Suite 1200 Phone: (403)262-0470
Calgary, AB, Canada T2P 4B9 Roxie De Ginnus, Libn.
Staff: Prof 1; Other 1. **Subjects:** Canadian and U.S. taxation, accounting, auditing, oil, gas. **Holdings:** 704 volumes; annual reports; prospectuses. **Subscriptions:** 105 journals and other serials; 6 newspapers. **Services:** Interlibrary loan; library open to clients and other libraries. **Automated Operations:** Computerized cataloging and serials. **Computerized Information Services:** DIALOG Information Services, Dow Jones News/Retrieval, QL Systems, WESTLAW, Info Globe, FP OnLine. Performs searches on fee basis. **Publications:** InSearch (newletter), quarterly - for internal distribution only. **Special Catalogs:** Score File. **Remarks:** Thorne Ernst & Whinney is a division of Ernst & Whinney.

★14174★
C.W. THORNTHWAITE ASSOCIATES LABORATORY OF CLIMATOLOGY - LIBRARY (Sci-Engr)
Rural Delivery 1
Elmer, NJ 08318 William J. Superior, Pres.
Subjects: Climatology, meteorology. **Holdings:** Figures not available. **Publications:** Publications in Climatology, irregular - for sale.

HARRY THORNTON MEMORIAL LIBRARY
See: Pensacola Museum of Art (11226)

THORPE MUSIC LIBRARY
See: Illinois Wesleyan University (6723)

THORVALDSON LIBRARY
See: University of Saskatchewan (16842)

★14175★
THOUSAND ISLANDS SHIPYARD MUSEUM, INC. - GILBART B. MERCIER MEMORIAL LIBRARY (Hist)
750 Mary St. Phone: (315)686-4104
Clayton, NY 13624 Phoebe Tritton, Libn.
Founded: 1983. **Staff:** 1. **Subjects:** Freshwater nautical history, St. Lawrence River and Seaway history, boat building and restoration. **Special Collections:** Sparkman and Stephens boat brokerage files (9331); Paul Malo Collection (Thousand Islands history; 3 linear feet); Homer Dodge Collection (canoeing; 3 boxes); permanently registered boat files (260). **Holdings:** 500 books; 2000 periodicals; 3200 photographs; 100 charts and maps; 20 oral history tapes; 6 VF drawers of boat plans, postcards, parts and equipment information, engine manuals, and boat manufacturers catalogs; 4 VF drawers of clippings; historic postcard file. **Subscriptions:** 25 journals and other serials; 15 newsletters. **Services:** Copying; library open to the public with restrictions on a limited schedule. **Special Indexes:** Index to Sparkman and Stephens brokerage files; index to photographs; index to periodicals (all on cards). **Remarks:** An alternate telephone number is 686-4127.

★14176★
THREE LIONS - PICTURE LIBRARY (Aud-Vis)
11 W. 19th St., 6th Fl.
New York, NY 10011-4214 Phone: (212)633-0200
Subjects: Fine art, religion, and general interest stock photography. **Holdings:** Figures not available.

★14177★
3M - 201 TECHNICAL LIBRARY (Sci-Engr)
3M Center, 201-2S-00 Phone: (612)733-2447
St. Paul, MN 55144 Karen L. Flynn, Supv.
Founded: 1955. **Staff:** Prof 5; Other 3. **Subjects:** Chemistry, physics, polymer science, electronics. **Holdings:** 30,000 books; 50,000 bound periodical volumes; 750 volumes of chemical trade literature; 60 VF; 250 audiotapes; 350 videotapes; 1000 bound documents; government documents on microfiche. **Subscriptions:** 905 journals and other serials; 20 newspapers. **Services:** Interlibrary loan; open to public with advance notice and a 3M visitor's pass. **Computerized Information Services:** DIALOG Information Services, NLM, BRS Information Technologies, STN International, Pergamon ORBIT InfoLine, Inc., Telesystemes Questel, PLASPEC. **Networks/Consortia:** Member of Twin Cities Standards Cooperators. **Publications:** Alert (acquisitions), biweekly - for internal distribution only; Bulletin Board. **Special Catalogs:** Computerized List of Serials. **Staff:** F. Bartow Culp; Jan M. Curtis; Mary E. Hansen; Elizabeth S. Smith.

★14178★
3M - 209 TECHNICAL LIBRARY (Sci-Engr)
3M Center, 209-BC-06 Phone: (612)733-6973
St. Paul, MN 55144 Alice Bresnahan, Libn.
Founded: 1959. **Staff:** Prof 1; Other 1. **Subjects:** Adhesives and adhesion, ceramics and glass, coatings, elastomers, imaging, organic chemistry, photographic chemistry, polymers, rubber technology, surface science. **Holdings:** 6000 books. **Subscriptions:** 270 journals and other serials. **Services:** Interlibrary loan; open to the public with advance notice and a 3M visitor's pass. **Computerized Information Services:** DIALOG Information Services, Pergamon ORBIT InfoLine, Inc., STN International, OCLC, BRS Information Technologies. **Publications:** 209 Library Bulletin (acquisitions list), monthly - for internal distribution only.

★14179★
3M - 230 TECHNICAL LIBRARY (Sci-Engr)
3M Center, 230-1S-12 Phone: (612)733-5017
St. Paul, MN 55144-1000 Elizabeth Sandness Smith, Libn.
Founded: 1935. **Staff:** Prof 1; Other 1. **Subjects:** Adhesives, elastomers, films, nonwovens, paper chemistry, rubber technology, packaging, plastics, polymers. **Holdings:** 3000 books; chemical trade literature. **Subscriptions:** 130 journals and other serials. **Services:** Interlibrary loan; open to the public with advance notice and a 3M visitor's pass. **Computerized Information Services:** DIALOG Information Services, STN International, Pergamon ORBIT InfoLine, Inc., BRS Information Technologies. **Publications:** Choice (acquisitions list) - for internal distribution only.

★14180★
3M - 235 TECHNICAL LIBRARY (Sci-Engr)
3M Center, 235-1A-25 Phone: (612)733-2592
St. Paul, MN 55144 Mariann Cyr, Libn.
Founded: 1966. **Staff:** Prof 1; Other 1. **Subjects:** Electronics, micrographics, optics, paper chemistry and technology, printing, reprographics, computer science. **Holdings:** 7200 books; 361 documents on microfilm. **Subscriptions:** 280 journals and other serials. **Services:** Interlibrary loan; open to the public with advance notice and a 3M visitor's pass. **Computerized Information Services:** DIALOG Information Services, STN International, Pergamon ORBIT InfoLine, Inc., WILSONLINE, BRS Information Technologies. **Publications:** Book Bin (acquisitions list), monthly; Information Link, quarterly - both for internal distribution only.

★14181★
3M - 236 TECHNICAL LIBRARY (Sci-Engr, Comp Sci)
3M Center, 236-1E-09 Phone: (612)733-5751
St. Paul, MN 55144 Paul Chrenka, Libn.
Founded: 1970. **Staff:** Prof 1; Other 1. **Subjects:** Chemistry, computers, electronics, electrical engineering, rubber. **Holdings:** 6000 books; 2 VF drawers of annual reports; 5 VF drawers of house organs; 15 VF drawers of trade literature. **Subscriptions:** 252 journals and other serials; 5 newspapers. **Services:** Interlibrary loan; open to the public with advance notice and a 3M visitor's pass. **Computerized Information Services:** DIALOG Information Services, STN International, Pergamon ORBIT InfoLine, Inc., Telesystemes Questel, DTIC, BRS Information Technologies. **Publications:** Recorder (acquisitions list), monthly - for internal distribution only.

★14182★
3M - 251 TECHNICAL LIBRARY (Sci-Engr)
3M Center, 251-2A-06 Phone: (612)733-5236
St. Paul, MN 55144 Ramona R. Huppert, Libn.
Founded: 1955. **Staff:** Prof 1; Other 1. **Subjects:** Abrasives, automotive technologies, chemistry, metallurgy, textiles, tribology. **Holdings:** 4050 books; 5900 microfiche; 105 reels of microfilm. **Subscriptions:** 230 journals and other serials. **Services:** Interlibrary loan; open to the public with advance notice and a 3M visitor's pass. **Computerized Information Services:** DIALOG Information Services, Pergamon ORBIT InfoLine, Inc., STN International. **Publications:** Focus (acquisitions list), bimonthly - for internal distribution only.

★14183★
3M - 270 TECHNICAL LIBRARY (Med)
3M Center, 270-4A-06 Phone: (612)733-1703
St. Paul, MN 55144 Eloise M. Jasken, Libn.
Founded: 1969. **Staff:** Prof 1; Other 1. **Subjects:** Biochemistry, medicine, physiology, chemistry, pharmacology, biomaterials. **Holdings:** 6500 books; 7200 bound periodical volumes. **Subscriptions:** 417 journals and other serials. **Services:** Interlibrary loan; open to the public with advance notice and a 3M visitor's pass. **Computerized Information Services:** DIALOG Information Services, NLM, Pergamon ORBIT InfoLine, Inc., BRS Information Technologies. **Publications:** Alembic (acquisitions list), monthly - for internal distribution only.

★14184★
3M - AUSTIN INFORMATION SERVICES (Sci-Engr)
Box 2963 Phone: (512)834-3236
Austin, TX 78769 Erika C. Mittag, Libn.
Founded: 1984. **Staff:** Prof 1; Other 2. **Subjects:** Business and technical information for the electronic and telecommunications industries. **Holdings:** 700 books; manufacturer's catalogs on microfilm. **Subscriptions:** 180 journals and other serials. **Services:** Interlibrary loan; library open to the public with advance notice and a 3M visitor's pass. **Automated Operations:** Computerized public access catalog and serials. **Computerized Information Services:** DIALOG Information Services, BRS Information Technologies, Data-Star, NEXIS, Dow Jones News/Retrieval, STN International, Pergamon ORBIT InfoLine, Inc., PLASPEC.

★14185★
3M - BUSINESS INFORMATION SERVICE (Bus-Fin)
3M Center, 220-1C-02 Phone: (612)733-9057
St. Paul, MN 55144 Aletta H. Moore, Supv.
Founded: 1952. **Staff:** Prof 5; Other 2. **Subjects:** Management, marketing, research and development, financial planning, personnel. **Holdings:** 3000 books; 60,000 microfiche of 10K reports for New York, American, and over the counter exchanges; 650 reels of microfilm; 50 VF. **Subscriptions:** 238 journals and other serials. **Services:** Interlibrary loan; open to the public with advance notice and a 3M visitor's pass. **Computerized Information Services:** DIALOG Information Services, NEXIS, TEXTLINE, Pergamon ORBIT InfoLine, Inc., Official Airline Guides, Inc. (OAG), WILSONLINE, BRS Information Technologies, Dow Jones News/Retrieval, VU/TEXT Information Services, DataTimes, INVESTEXT. **Publications:** Abbreviations, bimonthly - for internal distribution only.

★14186★
3M - ENGINEERING AND VENDOR LIBRARY (Sci-Engr)
Bldg. 21-BW
Box 3331 Phone: (612)778-4264
St. Paul, MN 55133 William T. Greene, Mgr.
Founded: 1956. **Staff:** Prof 4; Other 2. **Subjects:** Engineering. **Special Collections:** ANSI Standards Information. **Holdings:** 3000 books; 6000 vendor catalogs; 30,000 vendor catalogs on microfilm; 5 VF drawers of articles and pamphlets. **Subscriptions:** 212 journals and other serials. **Services:** Interlibrary loan; library open to the public with advance notice and a 3M visitor's pass. **Computerized Information Services:** DIALOG Information Services, NEXIS, BRS Information Technologies, OCLC, Dow Jones News/Retrieval, Pergamon ORBIT InfoLine, Inc., STN International, WILSONLINE, CompuServe, Inc. **Publications:** Spectrum, monthly - for internal distribution only. **Special Indexes:** Vendor Library Index (online). **Staff:** L.K. Hoekstra; K. Jursik; D.J. Willis.

★14187★
3M - INFORMATION SERVICES (Sci-Engr, Comp Sci, Med)
3M Center, 201-2S-09 Phone: (612)736-1943
St. Paul, MN 55144-1000 Barbara J. Peterson, Mgr.
Staff: Prof 34; Other 26. **Automated Operations:** Computerized cataloging, serials, and ILL. **Computerized Information Services:** DIALOG Information Services, Dow Jones News/Retrieval, TEXTLINE, NEXIS, OCLC, WILSONLINE, INVESTEXT, BRS Information Technologies, CompuServe Inc., Pergamon ORBIT InfoLine, Inc., Official Airline Guide (OAG), PLASPEC, Telesystemes Questel, STN International; internal databases. **Remarks:** 3M Information Services is comprised of the libraries whose listings follow. **Staff:** Ron Dueltgen, Current Awareness; Kristin K. Oberts, Mgr., Tech.Libs.; David Schrader, Mgr.Sys.Serv.; Thea Welsh, Supv.Tech.Serv..

★14188★
3M - LAW LIBRARY (Law)
Box 33428 Phone: (612)733-1460
St. Paul, MN 55133 C. Jean Johnson, Libn.
Staff: 2. **Subjects:** Law. **Holdings:** 10,000 volumes. **Services:** Library not open to the public.

★14189★
3M - PATENT AND TECHNICAL COMMUNICATIONS SERVICES (Sci-Engr)
3M Center, 201-2C-12 Phone: (612)733-7670
St. Paul, MN 55144 Victoria K. Veach, Mgr.
Founded: 1962. **Staff:** Prof 6; Other 6. **Subjects:** U.S. and foreign patents. **Special Collections:** Complete U.S. Patent collection, 1963 to present (microfilm). **Holdings:** 2700 bound periodical volumes; foreign patents on aperture cards; 110,000 3M reports on microfiche. **Services:** Executes patent searches and internal technical report searches for information on continuing basis for 3M's technical, engineering, and business staffs; open to the public with advance notice and 3M visitor's pass. **Staff:** John M. Dudinyak; Kent Kokko; F.B. Culp; Carla Moore; David R. Kaar; Margaret Hibberd.

★14190★
3M CANADA - TECHNICAL INFORMATION CENTRE (Sci-Engr)
Box 5757 Phone: (519)451-2500
London, ON, Canada N6A 4T1 Cheryl Stephenson, Tech.Libn.
Founded: 1973. **Staff:** Prof 1. **Subjects:** Polymer chemistry, plastics and rubber, adhesives, chemical technology. **Holdings:** 800 books; 200 items in vendor information file. **Subscriptions:** 150 journals and other serials. **Services:** Interlibrary loan; center not open to the public. **Computerized Information Services:** DIALOG Information Services, Info Globe, CAN/OLE, Dow Jones News/Retrieval, Occupational Health Services, Inc.; Envoy 100 (electronic mail service).

★14191★
THURBER CONSULTANTS LTD. - LIBRARY (Sci-Engr)
1445 W. Georgia St., Suite 200 Phone: (604)684-4384
Vancouver, BC, Canada V6G 2T3 Guy M. Robertson, Libn.
Founded: 1972. **Staff:** Prof 1; Other 3. **Subjects:** Geological engineering, geology, civil engineering. **Holdings:** 18,500 books; 5000 bound reports; 12,500 bound proposals; aerial photographs; maps. **Subscriptions:** 53 journals and other serials; 12 newspapers. **Services:** Copying; SDI; library open to the public upon approval of the president. **Computerized Information Services:** DIALOG Information Services.

I.N. THUT WORLD EDUCATION CENTER
See: University of Connecticut - School of Education (16103)

THYSSEN-BORNEMISZA, INC. - INFORMATION HANDLING SERVICES - GLOBAL ENGINEERING DOCUMENTATION
See: Global Engineering Documentation (5693)

TIBBY LIBRARY
See: University of Southern California - Catalina Marine Science Center (16866)

TICE MEMORIAL LIBRARY
See: Cook County Hospital (3730)

★14192★
TICONDEROGA HISTORICAL SOCIETY - LIBRARY (Hist)
Hancock House
Moses Circle Phone: (518)585-7868
Ticonderoga, NY 12883 Elizabeth E. McCaughin, Cur.
Subjects: Local and area history, 1609 to present. **Holdings:** 7000 volumes; correspondence; diaries; journals; logbooks; account books; business records; financial records; genealogical materials; public documents; maps; photographs. **Services:** Library open to the public.

★14193★
TIFFIN UNIVERSITY - RICHARD C. PFEIFFER LIBRARY (Bus-Fin)
139 Miami St. Phone: (419)447-6442
Tiffin, OH 44883 Frances A. Fleet, Libn.
Staff: Prof 1; Other 1. **Subjects:** Business. **Holdings:** 9800 books. **Subscriptions:** 98 journals and other serials; 8 newspapers. **Services:** Interlibrary loan; copying; library open to the public. **Computerized Information Services:** DIALOG Information Services. Performs searches on fee basis. **Networks/Consortia:** Member of Northwest Library District (NORWELD).

TILDERQUIST MEMORIAL MEDICAL LIBRARY
See: Miller-Dwan Medical Center (8986)

★14194★
TILLAMOOK COUNTY PIONEER MUSEUM - LIBRARY (Hist)
2106 Second St. Phone: (503)842-4553
Tillamook, OR 97141 M. Wayne Jensen, Jr., Dir.
Founded: 1935. **Subjects:** Northwest history and natural history, local history, genealogy. **Holdings:** Genealogy and county records; reference books; Tillamook Indian material; Tillamook County cemetery records; county newspapers. **Services:** Copying; library open to the public during museum hours.

★14195★
TIMBER PRODUCTS MANUFACTURERS - LIBRARY (Agri)
951 E. Third Ave. Phone: (509)535-4646
Spokane, WA 99202 Greg R. Tichy, Mgr.-Sec.
Founded: 1916. **Subjects:** Regional timber products manufacturing, wholesale lumber and building materials distribution. **Holdings:** 1500 volumes; biographical archives.

★14196★
TIME, INC. - LIBRARY (Publ)
Time & Life Bldg.
Rockefeller Center Phone: (212)556-3746
New York, NY 10020 Benjamin Lightman, Chf.Libn.
Founded: 1930. **Staff:** Prof 29; Other 74. **Subjects:** News reference topics. **Special Collections:** Reporting of Time, Inc. newsgathering services throughout the world. **Holdings:** 89,000 books; 500,000 folders of clippings and reports. **Subscriptions:** 1500 journals and other serials; 9 newspapers. **Services:** Library not open to the public. **Computerized Information Services:** DIALOG Information Services, Dow Jones News/Retrieval, Mead Data Central, BRS Information Technologies, INVESTEXT, VU/TEXT Information Services, Washington Alert Service, BASELINE, Warner Computer Systems, Inc. **Special Indexes:** Indexes to company magazines (card). **Staff:** Dorothy Paulsen, Hd. of Files; Patricia U. Rich, Hd. of Ref.; Robert Kassinger, Hd. of Index; Ellen Callahan, Hd. of Bk.Serv..

★14197★
TIME, INC. - SPORTS LIBRARY (Rec)
Radio City Sta., Box 614 Phone: (212)522-3397
New York, NY 10101 Peter Miller, Hd.Libn.
Founded: 1960. **Staff:** Prof 4; Other 6. **Subjects:** Sports. **Special Collections:** Olympic Games Collection. **Holdings:** 5000 books; 220 bound periodical volumes; 17,000 subject folders; 16,000 biographical folders. **Subscriptions:** 221 journals and other serials; 12 newspapers. **Services:** Library not open to the public. **Computerized Information Services:** DIALOG Information Services, VU/TEXT Information Services, DataTimes, NEXIS. **Publications:** Sports Source, quarterly - for internal distribution only. **Staff:** Charles Lampach; M. Catherine Smythe; Al Baman; Natasha Simon, Lib. Files Supv..

★14198★
TIME-LIFE BOOKS INC. - EDITORIAL REFERENCE LIBRARY (Hist, Rec, Publ)
777 Duke St., Suite 418 Phone: (703)838-7198
Alexandria, VA 22314 Louise D. Forstall, Hd.Libn.
Staff: Prof 2; Other 1. **Subjects:** History - United States Civil War, American West; photography; gardening; fantasy; culinary arts. **Special Collections:** Complete holdings of Time, Life, and Fortune magazines. **Holdings:** 20,000 books; 350 bound periodical volumes. **Subscriptions:** 175 journals and other serials. **Services:** Interlibrary loan; library not open to the public. **Staff:** Anne S. Heising, Libn..

★14199★
TIMEPLEX, INC. - TECHNICAL CENTER LIBRARY (Info Sci)
530 Chestnut Ridge Rd. Phone: (201)930-9888
Woodcliff Lake, NJ 07675 Margit Linforth, Libn.
Staff: Prof 1. **Subjects:** Data communications, telecommunications, electronic engineering. **Holdings:** 500 books. **Subscriptions:** 200 journals and other serials. **Services:** Interlibrary loan; library not open to the public. **Computerized Information Services:** DIALOG Information Services. **Publications:** Monthly Acquisitions Bulletin.

TIMES-MIRROR COMPANY - (Allentown) MORNING CALL
See: (Allentown) Morning Call (308)

★14200★
TIMES PUBLISHING COMPANY - NEWS LIBRARY (Publ)
490 First Ave., S.
Box 1121 Phone: (813)893-8111
St. Petersburg, FL 33704 Cary Kenney, Chf.Libn.
Founded: 1923. **Staff:** Prof 14; Other 10. **Subjects:** Newspaper reference topics. **Holdings:** 5000 books; 60 VF drawers of reports and pamphlets; newspaper clippings; news and historical photographs; original maps and artwork; newspapers on microfilm. **Services:** Library not open to the public. **Computerized Information Services:** NEXIS, DataTimes, VU/TEXT Information Services, Dialcom Inc., Washington Alert Service, DIALOG Information Services, CompuServe, Inc., Florida State Legislature Systems and Data Processing Division. **Networks/Consortia:** Member of Tampa Bay Library Consortium, Inc.. **Remarks:** Maintains a branch library in Tampa, FL. **Staff:** Barbara Hijek, Graphics Libn.; Peter Basofin, Asst.Libn.; Sammy Alzofon, Asst.Libn.; Jim Scofield, News Res.Coord..

★14201★
TIMES TRIBUNE - LIBRARY (Publ)
245 Lytton Ave.
Box 300 Phone: (415)853-5244
Palo Alto, CA 94302 Pam Allen, Hd.Libn.
Subjects: Newspaper reference topics. **Holdings:** 250 books; 200,000 file folders of clippings; 1404 reels of microfilm; 148,000 pictures; 200 state and county pamphlets and reports. **Subscriptions:** 5 newspapers. **Services:** Library not open to the public.

★14202★
TIMES-WORLD CORPORATION - NEWSPAPER LIBRARY (Publ)
Box 2491 Phone: (703)981-3279
Roanoke, VA 24010 Belinda Harris, Libn.
Founded: 1956. **Staff:** 3. **Subjects:** Newspaper reference topics. **Holdings:** 1500 books; newspaper clippings; pictures and biographical data; microfiche; by-line files; microfilm. **Subscriptions:** 18 journals and other serials. **Services:** Library not open to the public. **Computerized Information Services:** VU/TEXT Information Services, NEXIS. **Also Known As:** Roanoke Times & World-News.

★14203★
TIMKEN COMPANY - RESEARCH LIBRARY (Sci-Engr)
1835 Deuber Ave. Phone: (216)497-2049
Canton, OH 44706 Patricia A. Casey, Info.Anl.
Staff: Prof 1. **Subjects:** Research management and planning, steel process research, bearing design, engineering research, materials handling. **Holdings:** 30,000 volumes; microfilm. **Services:** Interlibrary loan; copying; SDI; library open to the public by appointment. **Automated Operations:** Computerized cataloging and acquisitions. **Computerized Information Services:** DIALOG Information Services, OCLC. **Networks/Consortia:** Member of OHIONET.

★14204★
TIMKEN MERCY MEDICAL CENTER - MEDICAL LIBRARY (Med)
1320 Timken Mercy Dr.
Canton, OH 44708 Phone: (216)489-1462
Staff: 1. **Subjects:** Medicine, nursing, allied health sciences. **Holdings:** 4000 books; 4100 bound periodical volumes; 400 AV programs. **Subscriptions:** 400 journals and other serials. **Services:** Interlibrary loan; copying; SDI; library open to the public with restrictions. **Automated Operations:** Computerized cataloging. **Computerized Information Services:** Online systems. **Networks/Consortia:** Member of NEOUCOM Council Associated Hospital Librarians.

TIMPANOGOS CAVE NATIONAL MONUMENT
See: U.S. Natl. Park Service (15357)

★14205★
TIN RESEARCH INSTITUTE, INC. - LIBRARY & INFORMATION CENTER (Sci-Engr)
1353 Perry St. Phone: (614)424-6200
Columbus, OH 43201 Daniel J. Maykuth, Mgr.
Founded: 1949. **Staff:** Prof 3; Other 2. **Subjects:** Tin and its uses. **Special Collections:** Information File (28 subjects including tinplate, solders, bronze, bearings). **Holdings:** 350 volumes; 28 VF drawers of reports, manuscripts, patents; slides; films; photographs. **Subscriptions:** 45 journals and other serials. **Services:** Interlibrary loan; copying; library open to the public. **Publications:** Tin and Its Uses, quarterly; research reports.

★14206★
CARRIE TINGLEY HOSPITAL - MEDICAL LIBRARY (Med)
1127 University Blvd., N.E.
Albuquerque, NM 87102 Phone: (505)841-5000
Staff: 1. **Subjects:** Orthopedics - pediatric, general; pediatric dysmorphology; pediatrics; rehabilitation. **Holdings:** 760 books; 250 bound periodical volumes; 200 resident research papers. **Subscriptions:** 12 journals and other serials. **Services:** Library not open to the public.

HELEN C. TINGLEY MEMORIAL LIBRARY
See: University of Maryland - School of Medicine - Department of Psychiatry (16363)

★14207★
ROBERT C. TINKER LIBRARY (Med)
3600 E. Harry Phone: (316)689-5377
Wichita, KS 67218 Carol Matulka, Med.Libn.
Founded: 1942. **Staff:** Prof 1; Other 2. **Subjects:** Medicine, nursing, allied health administration. **Holdings:** 4198 books; 1355 bound periodical volumes; 4247 books and journals in storage for recall; cassettes; records; AV programs and video cassettes. **Subscriptions:** 200 journals and other serials. **Services:** Interlibrary loan; copying; library open to hospital personnel and affiliated college/university students. **Computerized Information Services:** Online systems. Performs searches on fee basis. **Networks/Consortia:** Member of Wichita Area Health Science Libraries, Midcontinental Regional Medical Library Program.

★14208★
TINLEY PARK MENTAL HEALTH CENTER - INSTRUCTIONAL MEDIA LIBRARY (Med)
7400 W. 183rd St.
Tinley Park, IL 60477 Phone: (312)532-7000
Founded: 1962. **Staff:** Prof 1. **Subjects:** Psychiatry, psychology, community mental health, hospital administration. **Holdings:** 4100 books; 210 AV programs; 8 files of pamphlets and reprints; 210 reels of microfilm of professional journals. **Subscriptions:** 174 journals and other serials; 12 newspapers. **Services:** Interlibrary loan; copying; library open to the public for reference use only. **Networks/Consortia:** Member of Greater Midwest Regional Medical Library Network, Chicago and South Consortium, Illinois Department of Mental Health and Developmental Disabilities Library Services Network (LISN). **Publications:** Serials Holdings List; Monthly List of Acquisitions. **Remarks:** Maintained by Illinois State Department of Mental Health and Developmental Disabilities.

★14209★
TIOGA COUNTY HISTORICAL SOCIETY MUSEUM - LIBRARY (Hist)
110-112 Front St. Phone: (607)687-2460
Owego, NY 13827 Jean Winnie Neff, Dir.
Founded: 1914. **Staff:** Prof 3. **Subjects:** Tioga County, Owego, and Southern Tier (New York) history and genealogy. **Services:** Copying; library open to the public. **Staff:** Jean Winnie Neff, Dir..

★14210★
TIPPECANOE COUNTY HISTORICAL ASSOCIATION - ALAMEDA MC COLLOUGH RESEARCH & GENEALOGY LIBRARY (Hist)
909 South St. Phone: (317)742-8411
Lafayette, IN 47901 Nancy Weirich, Libn.
Founded: 1925. **Staff:** Prof 3. **Subjects:** Genealogy; Indiana; Tippecanoe and local history. **Holdings:** 6000 books; 150 bound periodical volumes; 125 VF drawers of manuscripts and clippings; 40 scrapbooks; 575 reels of microfilm; 10,000 negatives; 2000 photographs. **Subscriptions:** 21 journals and other serials. **Services:** Copying; library open to the public with restrictions. **Publications:** Weatenotes (newsletter), monthly - to members; historical booklets and leaflets, annual - for sale. **Staff:** Sarah E. Cooke, Archv..

TIREMAN LEARNING MATERIALS LIBRARY
See: University of New Mexico (16605)

TISHMAN LEARNING CENTER
See: Montefiore Medical Center - Health Sciences Library/Tishman Learning Center (9240)

★14211★
TITAN SYSTEMS, INC. - LIBRARY (Comp Sci)
1950 Old Gallows Rd., Suite 600 Phone: (703)883-9433
Vienna, VA 22180 Ines Siscoe, Libn.
Staff: Prof 1. **Subjects:** Artificial intelligence, advanced technology, defense systems, communications. **Holdings:** 200 monographs; 1000 reports. **Subscriptions:** 40 journals and other serials. **Services:** Interlibrary loan. **Computerized Information Services:** DIALOG Information Services, DTIC.

★14212★
TITANIUM METALS CORPORATION OF AMERICA - HENDERSON TECHNICAL LIBRARY (Sci-Engr)
Box 2128 Phone: (702)564-2544
Henderson, NV 89015 Sally Canada, Tech.Libn.
Founded: 1952. **Staff:** 1. **Subjects:** Metallurgy, chemistry, physics, aerospace. **Holdings:** 1500 books; technical reports and papers. **Subscriptions:** 30 journals and other serials. **Services:** Library not open to the public. **Automated Operations:** Computerized acquisitions.

PAUL TITUS MEMORIAL LIBRARY AND SCHOOL OF NURSING LIBRARY
See: St. Margaret Memorial Hospital (12575)

★14213★
TOBACCO INSTITUTE - INFORMATION CENTER (Biol Sci, Med)
1875 Eye St., N.W., Suite 800 Phone: (202)457-9325
Washington, DC 20006 Laura Picciano, Res./Ref.Libn.
Founded: 1958. **Staff:** Prof 4; Other 1. **Subjects:** Tobacco history, smoking/health controversy. **Holdings:** 2500 books; clippings; manuscripts; reports. **Subscriptions:** 200 journals and other serials; 10 newspapers. **Services:** Interlibrary loan; center not open to the public. **Automated Operations:** Computerized serials. **Computerized Information Services:** DIALOG Information Services, NEXIS, LEXIS, Dow Jones News/Retrieval. **Publications:** Tobacco state history series; Tobacco: Pioneer In American Industry; Tobacco Industry Profile; Tax Burden on Tobacco related smoking and health pamphlets.

TOBACCO LITERATURE SERVICE
See: North Carolina State University (10333)

★14214★
TOBACCO MERCHANTS ASSOCIATION OF THE U.S. - HOWARD S. CULLMAN LIBRARY (Agri)
Box 8019 Phone: (609)275-4900
Princeton, NJ 08543-8019 Thomas C. Slane, Ph.D., Dir., Res.
Founded: 1915. **Staff:** Prof 2. **Subjects:** Tobacco industry and products. **Special Collections:** Complete collections of Tobacco Leaf and U.S. Tobacco Journal; trademark and brand files of tobacco products; smokers' articles. **Holdings:** 2000 books; 296 bound periodical volumes; 150 VF drawers of pamphlets, archives, and clippings; 18 shelves of government reports; 135 drawers of trademark file cards; 25 drawers of brand file cards. **Subscriptions:** 99 journals and other serials; 10 newspapers. **Services:** Copying; library open to the public for reference use only by appointment only. **Publications:** List of publications - available upon request. **Special Indexes:** SYSTIM-INDEX (book); Cigarette Brand Directory (book). **Staff:** Eric J. Mathiason, Media Anl..

★14215★
TOBE COBURN SCHOOL FOR FASHION CAREERS - RESOURCE CENTER (Bus-Fin)
686 Broadway Phone: (212)460-9600
New York, NY 10012 Susan Cohan, Assoc. in Curric. & Dev.
Staff: Prof 1; Other 2. **Subjects:** Fashion history, textiles, and fabrics; designers and costumes; business; merchandising; international fashion forecasting. **Special Collections:** Vertical files on international fashion designers and businesses. **Holdings:** 2000 books; 300 bound periodical volumes; Tobe reports. **Subscriptions:** 33 journals and other serials; 5 newspapers. **Services:** Interlibrary loan; center open to the public with restrictions. **Networks/Consortia:** Member of New York Metropolitan Reference and Research Library Agency (METRO).

★14216★
TOBEY HOSPITAL - STILLMAN LIBRARY (Med)
High St. Phone: (508)295-0880
Wareham, MA 02571 Marion E. Miskinis, Libn.
Staff: Prof 1. **Subjects:** Medicine, surgery, nursing, hospital administration, basic sciences. **Holdings:** 1000 books; vertical files. **Subscriptions:** 50 journals and other serials; 5 newspapers. **Services:** Interlibrary loan; copying; library open to the public with restrictions. **Networks/Consortia:** Member of Southeastern Massachusetts Consortium of Health Science Libraries (SEMCO). **Publications:** Newsletter, quarterly - for internal distribution only.

TOBIN COLLECTION
See: Marion Koogler Mc Nay Art Museum (8262)

TOCANTINS MEMORIAL LIBRARY
See: Thomas Jefferson University - Cardeza Foundation (7180)

★14217★
TOCCOA FALLS COLLEGE - SEBY JONES LIBRARY (Rel-Phil)
Box 80038 Phone: (404)886-6831
Toccoa Falls, GA 30598 Ruth Good, Hd.Libn.
Staff: Prof 2; Other 1. **Subjects:** Religion, Bible, theology, Christian education, missiology, teacher education, sacred music, communications. **Holdings:** 77,000 books; 2900 bound periodical volumes; 8700 AV programs; 1500 vertical files; 1500 microforms. **Subscriptions:** 500 journals and other serials; 5 newspapers. **Services:** Interlibrary loan; copying; library open to the public. **Staff:** Teresa Smeltzer, Asst.Libn./Cat..

ERNST TOCH ARCHIVE
See: University of California, Los Angeles - Music Library (15981)

A.M. TODD RARE BOOK ROOM
See: Kalamazoo College - Upjohn Library (7327)

TODD LIBRARY
See: Rochester Museum and Science Center - Strasenburgh Planetarium (12116)

★14218★
TODMORDEN MILLS HISTORIC SITE - LIBRARY (Hist)
550 Mortimer Ave. Phone: (416)425-2250
Toronto, ON, Canada M4J 2H2 Lynda Scarrow, Cur.
Founded: 1967. **Staff:** Prof 2. **Subjects:** History of the Borough of East York, museology, 19th century history. **Special Collections:** Archives for the Borough of East York. **Holdings:** Figures not available. **Services:** Library open to the public with restrictions. **Remarks:** Maintained by the Borough of East York. **Staff:** Mary Austin.

ARNOLD B. TOFIAS INDUSTRIAL ARCHIVES
See: Stonehill College (13697)

★14219★
TOLEDO BLADE - LIBRARY (Publ)
541 Superior St. Phone: (419)245-6188
Toledo, OH 43660 Mary E. Reddington, Hd.Libn.
Founded: 1926. **Staff:** Prof 2; Other 2. **Subjects:** Newspaper reference topics. **Special Collections:** Movie Stills, 1980 to present. **Holdings:** 4 drawers of clippings on microfiche; 1200 bound volumes of newspapers; newspapers, 1835 to present, on microfilm; 500 drawers of clipping files. **Subscriptions:** 12 journals and other serials. **Services:** Library not open to the public.

★14220★
TOLEDO EDISON COMPANY - CORPORATE LIBRARY (Bus-Fin, Sci-Engr, Energy)
Edison Plaza Phone: (419)249-5126
Toledo, OH 43652 Barbara A. Bins, Rec.Serv.Supv.
Founded: 1953. **Staff:** Prof 1. **Subjects:** Electricity, electrical engineering, mechanical engineering, accounting, business management, personnel and industrial relations, nuclear energy. **Holdings:** 2000 books; 173 bound periodical volumes on microfilm; 10 VF drawers of pamphlets; 15 shelves of government documents; 26 shelves of reports; 246 audio cassettes. **Subscriptions:** 150 journals and other serials. **Services:** Interlibrary loan; copying; library open to the public with permission. **Computerized Information Services:** DIALOG Information Services. **Publications:** News From the Library - for internal distribution only.

★14221★
TOLEDO HOSPITAL - MEDICAL LIBRARY (Med)
2142 N. Cove Blvd. Phone: (419)471-5437
Toledo, OH 43606 Linda M. Tillman, Dir.
Staff: Prof 2; Other 5. **Subjects:** Medicine, nursing, allied health sciences. **Holdings:** 6687 books; 24,399 bound periodical volumes; video cassettes; audio cassettes; slides; filmstrips. **Subscriptions:** 610 journals and other serials. **Services:** Interlibrary loan; copying; SDI; library open to the public. **Automated Operations:** Computerized cataloging, circulation, and ILL. **Computerized Information Services:** BRS Information Technologies, MEDLARS. Performs searches on fee basis. **Networks/Consortia:** Member of Greater Midwest Regional Medical Library Network, Health Science Librarians of Northwest Ohio (HSLNO). **Special Catalogs:** Catalog for audiovisual materials (book). **Staff:** Debbie Lyons, Asst.Dir..

★14222★
TOLEDO LAW ASSOCIATION LIBRARY (Law)
Lucas County Court House Phone: (419)245-4747
Toledo, OH 43624 Brenda Woodruff, Libn./Dir.
Staff: Prof 1; Other 3. **Subjects:** Law. **Special Collections:** English and Canadian law. **Holdings:** 65,000 volumes. **Subscriptions:** 200 journals and other serials. **Services:** Interlibrary loan; library not open to the public. **Computerized Information Services:** WESTLAW, PHINet FedTax Database, VERALEX, ABA/net, Hannah Legislative Service; ABA/net, Hannah Legislative Service (electronic mail services). Performs searches on fee basis.

★14223★
TOLEDO-LUCAS COUNTY PLAN COMMISSIONS - LIBRARY
One Government Center, Suite 1620
Jackson Street
Toledo, OH 43604
Subjects: City planning, zoning, census, neighborhoods, historic preservation. **Remarks:** Presently inactive.

★14224★
TOLEDO-LUCAS COUNTY PUBLIC LIBRARY - BUSINESS DEPARTMENT (Bus-Fin)
325 Michigan St. Phone: (419)255-7055
Toledo, OH 43624 Susan B. Christoff, Dept.Mgr.
Staff: Prof 5; Other 2. **Subjects:** Business, economics, investment, trade. **Special Collections:** Phone directories (domestic and foreign); corporate annual reports representing 3500 companies; federal documents depository; import/export material; government procurement center (materials to help businesses win government contracts); career/vocational material center. **Holdings:** 41,000 books; 1710 file envelopes of pamphlets; house organs. **Subscriptions:** 762 journals and other serials. **Services:** Interlibrary loan; copying; department open to the public. **Automated Operations:** Computerized cataloging, circulation, and acquisitions. **Computerized Information Services:** DIALOG Information Services, Pergamon ORBIT InfoLine, Inc., Dow Jones News/Retrieval, BRS Information Technologies; internal database. Performs searches on fee basis. **Networks/Consortia:** Member of OHIONET. **Publications:** Business Briefs, semiannual - distributed internally and to members of Toledo Chamber of Commerce.

★14225★
TOLEDO-LUCAS COUNTY PUBLIC LIBRARY - FINE ARTS AND AUDIO SERVICE DEPARTMENT (Art, Mus, Rec)
325 Michigan St. Phone: (419)255-7055
Toledo, OH 43624 Dorcell Thrower-Dowdell, Dept.Mgr.
Staff: Prof 5; Other 2. **Subjects:** Art, music, sports, costume, architecture, photography, theater, dance, entertainment. **Special Collections:** Framed prints for borrowing (465); sheet music (organ, 550; piano and voice, 4200; violin, 410); picture collection loan file (107,500). **Holdings:** 63,300 books; 6987 phonograph records; 7132 cassettes; 1800 compact discs. **Subscriptions:** 241 journals; 385 serials. **Services:** Interlibrary loan; copying; department open to the public. **Automated Operations:** Computerized cataloging and circulation. **Computerized Information Services:** Online systems. **Networks/Consortia:** Member of OHIONET. **Special Catalogs:** Catalog of local artists and art, theater, and music (card; scrapbook).

★14226★
TOLEDO-LUCAS COUNTY PUBLIC LIBRARY - HISTORY-TRAVEL-BIOGRAPHY DEPARTMENT (Hist, Geog-Map)
325 Michigan St. Phone: (419)255-7055
Toledo, OH 43624 Donald C. Barnette, Jr., Dept.Mgr.
Staff: Prof 4; Other 1. **Subjects:** History, travel, geography, biography, archeology. **Holdings:** 101,647 books; 17,500 map sheets; duplicates of

Toledo and northwest Ohio Collection for circulation; travel pamphlets. **Subscriptions:** 76 journals and other serials. **Services:** Interlibrary loan; copying; department open to the public. **Automated Operations:** Computerized cataloging. **Networks/Consortia:** Member of OHIONET. **Publications:** Booklists, irregular - to branch libraries.

★14227★
TOLEDO-LUCAS COUNTY PUBLIC LIBRARY - LITERATURE/ FICTION DEPARTMENT (Hum)
325 Michigan St. Phone: (419)255-7055
Toledo, OH 43624 Susan I. Coburn, Dept.Mgr.
Staff: Prof 4; Other 1. **Subjects:** Literature, language. **Special Collections:** Large print materials; foreign language materials; Adult Literacy Center; criticism file. **Holdings:** 132,952 volumes. **Subscriptions:** 76 journals and other serials. **Services:** Interlibrary loan; copying; department open to the public. **Automated Operations:** Computerized cataloging. **Networks/ Consortia:** Member of OHIONET. **Publications:** Titles on Television, weekly - to local libraries.

★14228★
TOLEDO-LUCAS COUNTY PUBLIC LIBRARY - LOCAL HISTORY & GENEALOGY DEPARTMENT (Hist)
325 Michigan St. Phone: (419)255-7055
Toledo, OH 43624 James C. Marshall, Dept.Mgr.
Founded: 1941. **Staff:** Prof 5; Other 2. **Subjects:** Genealogy, local history, regional materials - Ohio, Indiana, Michigan, Illinois, and original 13 colonies. **Special Collections:** Manuscripts dealing with local urban history (100 boxes); local picture collection (12,000 items); map collection of Ohio and Toledo area, 1800 to present (350 items); oral history interviews (200). **Holdings:** 12,000 books; 1000 bound periodical volumes; 2000 reels of microfilm; 2000 microfiche; 300 scrapbooks relating to the local area; 700 reels of microfilm of Ohio census, at ten year intervals, 1820-1880, 1900, 1910; 800 reels of microfilm of Ohio Soundex census index, 1880, 1900, 1910; 230 reels of microfilm of Michigan census, at ten year intervals, 1820-1880, 1900; 172 reels of microfilm of Michigan census index, 1880 and 1900; 465 reels of microfilm of Toledo Blade, 1835 to present; 247 reels of microfilm of Toledo Times, 1900-1952; Toledo City Council and Committee Minutes, 1837-1899. **Subscriptions:** 121 journals and other serials. **Services:** Copying; department open to the public. **Automated Operations:** Computerized cataloging. **Networks/Consortia:** Member of OHIONET. **Special Indexes:** Toledo Blade Obituary Index, 1837 to present; manuscript index; map index; picture index; oral history index; architectural index (all on cards).

★14229★
TOLEDO-LUCAS COUNTY PUBLIC LIBRARY - SCIENCE AND TECHNOLOGY DEPARTMENT (Sci-Engr)
325 Michigan St. Phone: (419)255-7055
Toledo, OH 43624 Mary B. Hubbard, Dept.Mgr.
Staff: Prof 6; Other 1. **Subjects:** Physical and natural sciences, applied science and technology. **Special Collections:** Glass and glass technology. **Holdings:** 87,099 books; depository for federal documents; 11,118 bound patent specifications, 1871-1965; patent specifications, 1966 to present, on microfilm; 13 drawers of microforms; pamphlets; clippings. **Subscriptions:** 543 journals and other serials. **Services:** Interlibrary loan; copying; department open to the public. **Automated Operations:** Computerized cataloging and circulation. **Computerized Information Services:** DIALOG Information Services, BRS Information Technologies, Dow Jones News/ Retrieval, CAS ONLINE, U.S. Patent Classification System; TLM (internal database). **Networks/Consortia:** Member of OHIONET.

★14230★
TOLEDO-LUCAS COUNTY PUBLIC LIBRARY - SOCIAL SCIENCE DEPARTMENT (Soc Sci)
325 Michigan St. Phone: (419)255-7055
Toledo, OH 43624 Jane Pinkston, Dept.Mgr.
Staff: Prof 7; Other 2. **Subjects:** Religion, law, sociology, psychology, education, philosophy. **Special Collections:** Foundation Center Depository; Library and Information Science Collection. **Holdings:** 93,000 books; 15,785 bound periodical volumes; pamphlets; maps; federal and state documents; Toledo newspapers on microfilm. **Subscriptions:** 318 journals and other serials; 49 newspapers. **Services:** Interlibrary loan; copying; department open to the public. **Automated Operations:** Computerized cataloging. **Computerized Information Services:** DIALOG Information Services, BRS Information Technologies, Infotrac. **Networks/Consortia:** Member of OHIONET. **Publications:** Keeping Current, biennial - internal distribution and to local special and public libraries.

★14231★
TOLEDO MUSEUM OF ART - ART REFERENCE LIBRARY (Art)
Box 1013 Phone: (419)255-8000
Toledo, OH 43697 Anne O. Morris, Hd.Libn.
Founded: 1901. **Staff:** Prof 3. **Subjects:** History of art and decorative arts with special emphasis on glass, music. **Special Collections:** George W. Stevens Collection (history of writing). **Holdings:** 38,197 books; 5779 bound periodical volumes; 8974 collection catalogs; 104 VF drawers; sales catalogs; 75 reels of microfilm; 335 microfiche. **Subscriptions:** 295 journals and other serials. **Services:** Interlibrary loan; copying; library open to the public. **Staff:** Joan L. Sepessy, Assoc.Libn.; Sharon Scott, Cat..

★14232★
TOLEDO ZOOLOGICAL SOCIETY - LIBRARY AND ARCHIVES (Biol Sci)
2700 Broadway Phone: (419)385-5721
Toledo, OH 43609 Pam Bailey, Rrsc.Spec.
Founded: 1981. **Staff:** Prof 1. **Subjects:** Zoology, animal husbandry, endangered species, horticulture, natural history museums. **Holdings:** 1500 books; Toledo Zoo archives. **Subscriptions:** 120 journals and other serials. **Services:** Interlibrary loan; copying; library open to the public by appointment. **Publications:** Current Awareness Bulletin, monthly.

J. PENROD TOLES LEARNING CENTER
See: New Mexico Military Institute - J. Penrod Toles Learning Center (9977)

★14233★
TOLLAND PUBLIC LIBRARY ASSOCIATION - TOLLAND GENEALOGICAL LIBRARY (Hist)
Tolland Green
Box 47 Phone: (203)872-0138
Tolland, CT 06084 Prescott Libbey Brown, Chf.Libn.
Founded: 1986. **Staff:** 7. **Subjects:** Genealogy, local history. **Holdings:** 700 books; 300 pamphlets and magazines; 26 tapes. **Subscriptions:** 13 journals and other serials. **Services:** Library open to the public.

MELVIN B. TOLSON BLACK HERITAGE CENTER
See: Langston University (7657)

★14234★
TOLSTOY FOUNDATION INC. - ALEXANDRA TOLSTOY MEMORIAL LIBRARY (Hum)
200 Park Ave., S., Rm. 1612 Phone: (212)677-7770
New York, NY 10003-1503 Tatiana Kalinin, Act.Libn.
Founded: 1950. **Staff:** Prof 1. **Subjects:** Russia - language, history, memoirs, literature. **Special Collections:** Definitive edition of Tolstoy's works, 1919-1958 (90 volumes, in Russian); translations of Tolstoy's works (including Japanese, Chinese, Arabic); criticism of Tolstoy's works in Russian and other languages; complete sets of the Chekhov Publishing House; rare items published before 1917, all in Russian; Prof. N. Arseniev Collection (2000 volumes); Goltsoff Collection (1500 volumes); Russian books on loan from Rockland Community College (2000). **Holdings:** 30,000 Russian books; 5000 English and French books. **Services:** Library open to the public with restrictions. **Remarks:** Library located at the Tolstoy Foundation Center, Valley Cottage, NY 10989.

TOMLINSON LIBRARY
See: Arkansas Tech University (927)

★14235★
TOMPKINS COMMUNITY HOSPITAL - ROBERT BROAD MEDICAL LIBRARY (Med)
101 Dates Dr. Phone: (607)274-4407
Ithaca, NY 14850 Sally Van Idistine, Libn.
Subjects: Surgery, medicine, nursing. **Holdings:** 400 books; 800 bound periodical volumes. **Subscriptions:** 70 journals and other serials. **Services:** Copying.

★14236★
D.A. TOMPKINS MEMORIAL LIBRARY & ARCHIVES (Hist)
104 Courthouse Square
Box 468 Phone: (803)637-5652
Edgefield, SC 29824 Nancy C. Mims, Archv./Cur.
Founded: 1904. **Staff:** 1. **Subjects:** Antiquities of England, Ireland, Wales, and Normandy; history - American Colonial, South Carolina, Confederate. **Special Collections:** Antebellum home library of James Madison Abney. **Holdings:** 9000 volumes; Edgefield Advertiser, 1836-1902, on microfilm; 210 reels of microfilm of Edgefield County wills, probate records, equity,

and guardianships. **Services:** Copying; library open to the public for reference use only. **Publications:** The Quill, monthly; Annals of Edgefield District, S.C., semiannual - both by subscription.

TOMPKINS-MC CAW LIBRARY
See: Virginia Commonwealth University - Medical College of Virginia (17357)

★14237★
TONGASS HISTORICAL SOCIETY, INC. - TONGASS HISTORICAL MUSEUM - LIBRARY (Area-Ethnic)
629 Dock St. Phone: (907)225-5600
Ketchikan, AK 99901 Roxana Adams, Musm.Dir.
Staff: 4. **Subjects:** Alaska - forestry, mining, fishing, Indians. **Special Collections:** Ketchikan Spruce Mills manuscript collection (425 cubic feet); regional photographs of Alaskan industries and Indians (50,000). **Holdings:** 1000 books; 500 cubic feet of regional archives. **Services:** Copying; library open to the public for reference use only by request. **Remarks:** Library cooperates with Alaska State Historical Library, Pouch G, Juneau, AK 99801.

K. ROSS TOOLE ARCHIVES
See: University of Montana - Maureen & Mike Mansfield Library (16550)

TOPAZ MEMORIAL LIBRARY
See: Ohio State University (10707)

★14238★
TOPEKA STATE HOSPITAL - STAFF LIBRARY (Med)
2700 W. 6th St. Phone: (913)296-4411
Topeka, KS 66606 Laura E. Schafer, Libn.
Founded: 1950. **Staff:** Prof 1; Other 1. **Subjects:** Psychiatry, psychology, psychiatric nursing, social work, chaplaincy training. **Special Collections:** Rare books and journals on the history of psychiatry (150 volumes). **Holdings:** 6800 books; 2700 bound periodical volumes. **Subscriptions:** 50 journals and other serials. **Services:** Interlibrary loan; copying (limited); library open to the public with approval of Director of Research and Training. **Networks/Consortia:** Member of Midcontinental Regional Medical Library Program.

HELEN TOPPING ARCHITECTURE & FINE ARTS LIBRARY
See: University of Southern California (16873)

★14239★
TORONTO BOARD OF EDUCATION - EDUCATION CENTRE REFERENCE LIBRARY (Educ)
155 College St. Phone: (416)591-8183
Toronto, ON, Canada M5T 1P6 Joy Thomas, Mgr.
Founded: 1961. **Staff:** Prof 4; Other 10. **Subjects:** Education, psychology, Canadian studies, literary criticism, women's studies, business, economics, library science, science, technology. **Holdings:** 40,000 volumes; 5000 subject vertical files; ERIC, Ontario Education Resources Information System (ONTERIS), and MICROLOG microfiche. **Subscriptions:** 1200 journals and other serials. **Services:** Interlibrary loan; copying; library open to the public for reference use only. **Automated Operations:** Computerized public access catalog. **Computerized Information Services:** DIALOG Information Services, Info Globe, BRS Information Technologies, CAN/OLE, Infomart, WILSONLINE, Refcatss, UTLAS. **Networks/Consortia:** Member of Education Libraries Sharing of Resources Network (ELSOR). **Publications:** Additions and Accessions, 10/year; Conference Calendar, annual - both for internal distribution only; Library Fare, 3/year; Highlights, 3/year - to trustees; Journal Contents, 3/year. **Staff:** S. Nordien, ILL.

★14240★
TORONTO CITY PLANNING AND DEVELOPMENT DEPARTMENT - LIBRARY (Plan)
City Hall, 19th Fl., E. Phone: (416)392-7185
Toronto, ON, Canada M5H 2N2 Deborah Fowler, Lib./Info.Off
Founded: 1958. **Staff:** Prof 1; Other 2. **Subjects:** Planning, housing, urban design, transportation, economy. **Special Collections:** Planners' reports (microfiche). **Holdings:** 10,000 books. **Subscriptions:** 200 journals and other serials. **Services:** Copying; library open to the public with restrictions. **Publications:** Bibliography of Major Planning Publications.

★14241★
TORONTO DOMINION BANK - DEPARTMENT OF ECONOMIC RESEARCH - LIBRARY (Bus-Fin)
55 King St., W. Phone: (416)982-8068
Toronto, ON, Canada M5K 1A2 Ruth P. Smith, Libn.
Founded: 1960. **Staff:** Prof 1; Other 2. **Subjects:** Banking, finance, economics, trade, industry. **Holdings:** 7000 books; 5000 pamphlets; 24 VF drawers and 140 pamphlet boxes of weekly and monthly letters from financial institutions, associations, and government; 11 VF drawers and 900 pamphlet boxes of Statistics Canada publications; 13 VF drawers of newspaper clippings; 250 pamphlet boxes of annual reports from companies and banks. **Subscriptions:** 600 journals and other serials; 29 newspapers. **Services:** Interlibrary loan; library open to the public with librarian's permission. **Automated Operations:** Computerized serials. **Computerized Information Services:** The Financial Post Information Service, Info Globe. **Publications:** Recent Additions to the Library, monthly - for internal distribution only.

★14242★
TORONTO EAST GENERAL AND ORTHOPAEDIC HOSPITAL INC. - HEALTH SCIENCES LIBRARY (Med)
825 Coxwell Ave. Phone: (416)469-6011
Toronto, ON, Canada M4C 3E7 Roger Smithies, Libn.
Founded: 1960. **Staff:** Prof 1; Other 1. **Subjects:** Medicine, nursing, allied health sciences. **Holdings:** 1750 books. **Subscriptions:** 175 journals and other serials. **Services:** Interlibrary loan. **Computerized Information Services:** MEDLARS.

★14243★
TORONTO GENERAL HOSPITAL - FUDGER MEDICAL LIBRARY (Med)
200 Elizabeth St. Phone: (416)595-3429
Toronto, ON, Canada M5G 2C4 Jennifer Bayne, Chf.Libn.
Founded: 1964. **Staff:** Prof 1; Other 6. **Subjects:** Cardiovascular surgery, obstetrics and gynecology, psychiatry, dermatology, neurosurgery, family and community medicine. **Special Collections:** Drs. Brock, Delarue, and Morley Collections (neurosurgery; 1000 volumes). **Holdings:** 8000 books; 15,000 bound periodical volumes; cassettes; tapes. **Subscriptions:** 472 journals and other serials. **Services:** Interlibrary loan; copying; SDI; library open to the public by contacting chief librarian. **Publications:** Fudger Medical Library (flyer) - available on request; bibliographies.

★14244★
TORONTO GLOBE AND MAIL, LTD. - LIBRARY (Publ)
444 Front St., W. Phone: (416)585-5075
Toronto, ON, Canada M5V 2S9 Amanda Valpy, Chf.Libn.
Staff: Prof 3; Other 10. **Subjects:** Newspaper reference topics. **Holdings:** 8000 books; 7 million newspaper clippings; 1 million photographs; 40 VF drawers of pamphlets; 5 million clippings on microfiche; 1500 reels of microfilm of The Globe and Mail; 200,000 photographic negatives. **Subscriptions:** 200 journals and other serials; 20 newspapers. **Services:** Interlibrary loan; library not open to the public. **Automated Operations:** Computerized cataloging. **Computerized Information Services:** DIALOG Information Services, Dow Jones News/Retrieval, TEXTLINE, Canada Systems Group (CSG), World Reporter, Mead Data Central, Infomart, The Financial Post Information Service, Info Globe. **Staff:** Marilyn Grad, Assoc.Libn..

TORONTO HARBOUR COMMISSIONERS - WORLD TRADE CENTRE TORONTO
See: World Trade Centre Toronto (18064)

★14245★
TORONTO INSTITUTE OF MEDICAL TECHNOLOGY - LIBRARY (Med, Biol Sci)
222 St. Patrick St. Phone: (416)596-3123
Toronto, ON, Canada M5T 1V4 Kenneth Ladd, Libn.
Staff: Prof 1; Other 3. **Subjects:** Medical technology - laboratory, radiological, respiratory; nuclear medicine; cytotechnology; cytogenetics; cardiovascular perfusion. **Special Collections:** TIMT archives. **Holdings:** 15,000 books; 200 bound periodical volumes; 250 slide/tape programs; 96 slide programs; 30 16mm films; 250 videotapes; 73 filmstrips. **Subscriptions:** 127 journals and other serials. **Services:** Interlibrary loan; copying; library open to the public with restrictions. **Automated Operations:** Computerized cataloging, acquisitions, serials, and circulation. **Computerized Information Services:** MEDLARS, DIALOG Information Services.

TORONTO JEWISH CONGRESS
See: Canadian Jewish Congress (2575)

TORONTO JEWISH CONGRESS - ALBERT J. LATNER JEWISH PUBLIC LIBRARY
See: Albert J. Latner Jewish Public Library (7675)

★14246★
TORONTO PUBLIC LIBRARY - CANADIANA COLLECTION OF CHILDREN'S BOOKS (Hum)
Boys and Girls House
40 St. George St. Phone: (416)393-7753
Toronto, ON, Canada M5S 2E4 Margaret Crawford Maloney, Hd.
Staff: Prof 3; Other 3. **Subjects:** Children's literature written or illustrated by Canadians, about Canadians, or bearing a Canadian imprint. **Holdings:** 5000 books; 50 bound periodical volumes; manuscripts; original art. **Services:** Copying (limited); collection open to the public for research use only. **Special Indexes:** Chronological index; illustrators and engravers index; publishers, booksellers, and printers index (all on cards).**Staff:** Jill Shefrin, Libn.; Dana Tenny, Libn..

★14247★
TORONTO PUBLIC LIBRARY - LILLIAN H. SMITH COLLECTION OF CHILDREN'S BOOKS (Hum)
Boys and Girls House
40 St. George St. Phone: (416)393-7753
Toronto, ON, Canada M5S 2E4 Margaret Crawford Maloney, Hd.
Founded: 1962. **Staff:** Prof 3; Other 3. **Subjects:** Children's literature in English, 1910 to present. **Holdings:** 6000 books; manuscripts; original art. **Services:** Copying (limited); collection open to the public for research use only. **Special Indexes:** Chronological index; illustrators index; publishers and printers index (all on cards). **Remarks:** Books in this collection represent a qualitative selection of twentieth century publications. **Staff:** Jill Shefrin, Libn.; Dana Tenny, Libn..

★14248★
TORONTO PUBLIC LIBRARY - MARGUERITE G. BAGSHAW COLLECTION (Theater)
Boys and Girls House
40 St. George St. Phone: (416)393-7746
Toronto, ON, Canada M5S 2E4 Joanne Graham, Libn.
Founded: 1973. **Staff:** Prof 1; Other 1. **Subjects:** Puppetry, storytelling, creative drama, mime. **Holdings:** 850 books; 65 sets of puppets; 30 folders of reviews of Canadian groups; 35 posters on puppets; 12 toy theaters; 50 puppetry scripts. **Services:** Interlibrary loan; copying; collection open to the public for reference use only. **Publications:** Marguerite Bagshaw Newsletter, annual - to friends of the theater and by request.

★14249★
TORONTO PUBLIC LIBRARY - OSBORNE COLLECTION OF EARLY CHILDREN'S BOOKS (Rare Book)
Boys and Girls House
40 St. George St. Phone: (416)393-7753
Toronto, ON, Canada M5S 2E4 Margaret Crawford Maloney, Hd.
Founded: 1949. **Staff:** Prof 3; Other 3. **Subjects:** English children's literature, 14th century-1910; printing; book illustration; folklore; original art. **Special Collections:** Jean Thomson Collection of Original Art; Taylors of Ongar Collection; Queen Mary's Collection of Children's Books; Florence Nightingale Collection; G. A. Henty Collection. **Holdings:** 16,500 books; 800 bound periodical volumes; manuscripts; 600 original pictures; engraved wood blocks. **Services:** Copying (limited); collection open to the public for research use only. **Special Catalogs:** Osborne Collection of Early Children's Books: A Catalogue (2 volumes, 1975). **Special Indexes:** Chronological index (book and card); illustrators and engravers index (book and card); publishers, booksellers, and printers index (book and card). **Staff:** Jill Shefrin, Libn.; Dana Tenny, Libn..

★14250★
TORONTO PUBLIC LIBRARY - SPACED OUT LIBRARY - SCIENCE FICTION COLLECTION (Hum, Rec)
Phone: (416)393-7748
40 St. George St.
Toronto, ON, Canada M5S 2E4 Lorna Toolis, Coll.Hd.
Founded: 1970. **Staff:** Prof 2; Other 1. **Subjects:** Science fiction and fantasy. **Special Collections:** Specialty publishers collection, including Arkham House and Ace Double titles (complete run); Jules Verne Collection; UFO collection; philatelic collection; multilingual collection (primarily French, German, and Dutch with Eastern European and other languages). **Holdings:** 19,942 books; 13,500 periodicals; 1500 fanzine titles; 700 vertical file folders, including manuscripts; 320 tapes, phonograph records, cassettes; 6000 publications; 1.5 linear feet of manuscripts; 13 linear feet of French science fiction titles; 40 linear feet of science fiction and fantasy titles in Japanese, German, Chinese, Dutch, and Finnish. **Subscriptions:** 60 journals and other serials. **Services:** Copying; collection open to the public for reference use only. **Publications:** Sol Rising, semiannual - to members. **Remarks:** An alternate telephone number is 393-7749. **Staff:** John Dunham, AV Libn..

★14251★
TORONTO STAR NEWSPAPERS LTD. - LIBRARY (Publ)
One Yonge St. Phone: (416)367-2420
Toronto, ON, Canada M5E 1E6 Carol Lindsay, Chf.Libn.
Founded: 1923. **Staff:** Prof 6; Other 11. **Subjects:** Newspaper reference topics. **Special Collections:** Clipping files on subjects and personalities in the news; database of Toronto Star stories since 1986. **Holdings:** 3000 books; 400,000 photographs; reports; government documents. **Subscriptions:** 50 journals and other serials; 8 newspapers. **Services:** Library not open to the public. **Computerized Information Services:** Info Globe, VU/TEXT Information Services, Informart, LEXIS, NEXIS; internal database.

★14252★
TORONTO STOCK EXCHANGE - CORPORATE INFORMATION CENTRE (Bus-Fin)
The Exchange Tower
2 First Canadian Place, 3rd Fl. Phone: (416)947-4653
Toronto, ON, Canada M5X 1J2 Dani Juozapavicius, Mgr.
Founded: 1970. **Staff:** 2. **Subjects:** Securities industry, investment, economics, finance, stock exchanges. **Special Collections:** Stock exchange publications (Toronto, Canadian, U.S., and others); Toronto Stock Exchange archives. **Holdings:** 2000 books; 2000 unbound reports, speeches, and leaflets; 20 drawers of clippings. **Subscriptions:** 200 journals and other serials; 9 newspapers. **Services:** Interlibrary loan; library open to the public by appointment for unique materials only. **Automated Operations:** Computerized cataloging and serials. **Computerized Information Services:** DIALOG Information Services, Mead Data Central, Dow Jones News/Retrieval, QL Systems, Info Globe, I.P. Sharp Associates Limited, Canada Systems Group (CSG), Finsbury Data Services Ltd. **Publications:** Outlook, weekly; Information Exchange, monthly - both for internal distribution only.

★14253★
TORONTO SUN PUBLISHING COMPANY - LIBRARY (Publ)
333 King St., E. Phone: (416)947-2257
Toronto, ON, Canada M5A 3X5 Julie Kirsh, Chf.Libn.
Staff: Prof 1; Other 8. **Subjects:** Newspaper reference topics. **Holdings:** 200 books; newspaper clippings; Toronto Sun, 1971 to present, on microfilm; Toronto Telegram, 1887-1971, on microfilm. **Subscriptions:** 40 journals and other serials; 12 newspapers. **Services:** Library open to public at librarian's discretion. **Automated Operations:** Computerized cataloging, acquisitions, and serials. **Computerized Information Services:** Info Globe, Infomart, The Financial Post Information Service, DIALOG Information Services; SUNLIB (internal database).

★14254★
TORONTO TRANSIT COMMISSION - ENGINEERING & CONSTRUCTION LIBRARY (Sci-Engr, Trans)
1900 Yonge St. Phone: (416)393-4070
Toronto, ON, Canada M4S 1Z2 Frances Barnett, Lib.Techn.
Staff: Prof 1. **Subjects:** Transportation, construction, design. **Holdings:** 3900 books; standards from the American Society for Testing and Materials, Canadian Standards Association, and Canadian Government Specifications Board. **Subscriptions:** 49 journals and other serials. **Services:** Library open to the public with restrictions.

★14255★
TORONTO TRANSIT COMMISSION - HEAD OFFICE LIBRARY (Trans)
1900 Yonge St. Phone: (416)481-4252
Toronto, ON, Canada M4S 1Z2 Adrian Gehring, Lib.Techn.
Staff: Prof 1. **Subjects:** Transportation. **Special Collections:** Photograph collection; archival collection. **Holdings:** 3000 books. **Subscriptions:** 60 journals and other serials. **Services:** Library not open to the public.

★14256★
TORONTO WESTERN HOSPITAL - R.C. LAIRD HEALTH SCIENCES LIBRARY (Med)
399 Bathurst St. Phone: (416)369-5750
Toronto, ON, Canada M5T 2S8 Elizabeth A. Reid, Dir.
Founded: 1961. **Staff:** Prof 1; Other 6. **Subjects:** Medicine. **Holdings:** 2500 books; 10,000 bound periodical volumes; 100 AV kits. **Subscriptions:** 360 journals and other serials. **Services:** Interlibrary loan; library not open to the public. **Computerized Information Services:** MEDLARS, UTLAS,

CAN/OLE. **Publications:** Acquisitions list, quarterly - for internal distribution only.

★14257★
TORRANCE MEMORIAL HOSPITAL MEDICAL CENTER - HEALTH SCIENCES LIBRARY (Med)
3330 W. Lomita Blvd. Phone: (213)517-4720
Torrance, CA 90509 Anita N. Klecker, Med.Libn.
Founded: 1972. **Staff:** Prof 1; Other 2. **Subjects:** Medicine, surgery, cardiology, pediatrics, nursing, psychiatry, oncology. **Holdings:** 449 books; 221 Audio-Digest tapes; 56 videotapes. **Subscriptions:** 120 journals and other serials. **Services:** Interlibrary loan; copying; SDI; library open to health care professionals and students only. **Computerized Information Services:** MEDLARS, DIALOG Information Services. Performs searches on fee basis. **Networks/Consortia:** Member of Pacific Southwest Regional Medical Library Service.

★14258★
TORRINGTON COMMUNITY HOSPITAL - MEDICAL LIBRARY (Med)
2000 Campbell Dr. Phone: (307)532-4181
Torrington, WY 82240 Valerie Lamb, ART, DRG Coord./Libn.
Founded: 1978. **Staff:** Prof 1. **Subjects:** Medicine, nursing, patient care. **Holdings:** 150 books. **Subscriptions:** 25 journals and other serials. **Services:** Interlibrary loan; copying; library open to medical professionals and students. **Networks/Consortia:** Member of Southeast Wyoming Health Science Library Consortium. **Remarks:** Maintained by Lutheran Hospitals and Homes,

★14259★
TORRINGTON HISTORICAL SOCIETY, INC. - JOHN H. THOMPSON MEMORIAL LIBRARY (Hist)
192 Main St. Phone: (203)482-8260
Torrington, CT 06790 Mark McEachern, Exec.Dir.
Founded: 1944. **Staff:** Prof 2. **Subjects:** History - Torrington, Litchfield County, Connecticut. **Special Collections:** Connecticut Journal, 1782-1813; Litchfield Monitor, 1791-1795; Litchfield Enquirer, 1842-1941. **Holdings:** 5000 volumes; 200 boxes of microfilm; 8 file drawers containing 2500 newspapers; 800 sets of local architectural drawings. **Services:** Copying; library open to the public for reference use only. **Staff:** Gail Kruppa, Adm.Asst..

TORT LIABILITY RESEARCH LIBRARY
See: Defense Research Institute, Inc. - Brief Bank (4137)

★14260★
TORY, TORY, DESLAURIERS & BINNINGTON - LIBRARY (Law)
IBM Tower, 31st Fl.
Toronto Dominion Centre
P.O. Box 270 Phone: (416)865-0040
Toronto, ON, Canada M5K 1N2 Janet Darby, Libn.
Staff: Prof 2; Other 2. **Subjects:** Canadian law. **Holdings:** 5000 books; 1500 bound periodical volumes; 5000 bound volumes of law reports. **Subscriptions:** 200 journals; 90 law reports; 10 newspapers. **Services:** Interlibrary loan; copying; SDI; library open to the public by appointment. **Computerized Information Services:** QL Systems, Info Globe, DIALOG Information Services, Canada Systems Group (CSG), LEXIS, NEXIS, Infomart, CBA/NET, CAN/LAW, The Financial Post Information Service, CANADIAN TAX ONLINE, Dow Jones News/Retrieval; internal database. Performs searches on fee basis. Contact Person: Jan MacDonald, Libn., 865-7532.

TOSCANINI MEMORIAL ARCHIVES
See: New York Public Library - Performing Arts Research Center - Music Division (10081)

★14261★
TOTAL PETROLEUM CANADA LTD. - LIBRARY (Sci-Engr)
639 5th Ave., S.W., 6th Fl. Phone: (403)265-9080
Calgary, AB, Canada T2P 0M9 Cheryl Fishleigh, Libn.
Staff: Prof 1. **Subjects:** Geology, geophysics, petroleum engineering, business management. **Special Collections:** Annual reports from different companies (300). **Holdings:** 1500 books; 100 bound periodical volumes; 1000 government documents; 50 research reports; 50 theses. **Subscriptions:** 75 journals and other serials. **Services:** Interlibrary loan; copying; library open to the public by request. **Computerized Information Services:** Pergamon ORBIT InfoLine, Inc. **Publications:** Current News Letter, bimonthly - for internal distribution only.

★14262★
TOTEM HERITAGE CENTER (Area-Ethnic)
629 Dock St. Phone: (907)225-5900
Ketchikan, AK 99901 Roxana Adams, Musm.Dir.
Staff: Prof 3. **Subjects:** Northwest Coast Indian art, culture, and history. **Special Collections:** Northwest Coast totem poles (31). **Holdings:** 500 books; 150 bound periodical volumes; 2500 photographs; 50 manuscripts. **Services:** Copying; center open to the public for reference use only. **Remarks:** Maintained by the City of Ketchikan Museum Department. **Staff:** S. Liljeblad, Cur./Coll..

TOUCHE, ROSS
See: Charette, Fortier, Hawey/Touche, Ross (2980)

★14263★
TOUCHE ROSS AND COMPANY - INFORMATION CENTER (Bus-Fin)
1633 Broadway Phone: (212)489-1600
New York, NY 10019 Harold W. Miller, Mgr., Info.Serv.
Staff: Prof 2; Other 3. **Subjects:** Accounting, business, management. **Holdings:** 5000 books. **Subscriptions:** 300 journals and other serials; 10 newspapers. **Services:** Interlibrary loan; center open to SLA members. **Automated Operations:** Computerized cataloging, acquisitions, and serials. **Computerized Information Services:** DIALOG Information Services, NEXIS, VU/TEXT Information Services, Dow Jones News/Retrieval, TEXTLINE. **Networks/Consortia:** Member of SUNY/OCLC Library Network. **Staff:** Henry Hoyt, Ref.Libn..

★14264★
TOUCHE ROSS AND COMPANY - LIBRARY (Bus-Fin)
1000 Wilshire Blvd., 12th Fl. Phone: (213)381-3251
Los Angeles, CA 90017-2471 Kathy Tice, Libn.
Staff: Prof 1; Other 1. **Subjects:** Auditing, taxation, management services. **Holdings:** Figures not available. **Services:** Library not open to the public. **Automated Operations:** Computerized circulation. **Computerized Information Services:** LEXIS, The Reference Service (REFSRV), National Automated Accounting Research System (NAARS). **Publications:** Newsletters; booklets.

★14265★
TOUCHE ROSS AND COMPANY - LIBRARY (Bus-Fin)
333 Clay, Suite 2300 Phone: (713)750-4421
Houston, TX 77002 Tricia Schielack, Libn.
Staff: Prof 1; Other 1. **Subjects:** Taxation, accounting, auditing, management consulting. **Holdings:** 9000 books; 75 bound periodical volumes; 3 VF drawers of annual reports. **Services:** Interlibrary loan; copying; library open to the public by appointment. **Computerized Information Services:** LEXIS.

★14266★
TOUCHE ROSS AND COMPANY - LIBRARY (Bus-Fin)
Scotia Centre, Suite 3500
700 2nd St., S.W. Phone: (403)267-1783
Calgary, AB, Canada T2P 0S7 Anne Helgason, Libn.
Staff: Prof 1; Other 1. **Subjects:** Accounting, auditing, taxation. **Holdings:** 3500 books. **Subscriptions:** 140 journals and other serials; 6 newspapers. **Services:** Interlibrary loan; copying; SDI. **Automated Operations:** Computerized cataloging and serials. **Computerized Information Services:** Info Globe, DIALOG Information Services, Infomart, QL Systems; Envoy 100, Financial Post Electronic Edition (electronic mail services). **Remarks:** Maintains branch library at 1167 Kensington Crescent, N.W., Calgary, AB T2N 1X7.

★14267★
TOUCHE ROSS AND COMPANY - LIBRARY (Bus-Fin)
100 King St., W.
Box 12, First Canadian Place Phone: (416)364-4242
Toronto, ON, Canada M5X 1B3 Lilian Gilmour, Libn.
Founded: 1975. **Staff:** Prof 1; Other 2. **Subjects:** Accounting, management consulting, marketing, taxation, electronic data processing, public administration. **Holdings:** 4000 books; Statistics Canada material. **Subscriptions:** 170 journals and other serials; 5 newspapers. **Services:** Interlibrary loan; copying; SDI; center open to the public by appointment. **Computerized Information Services:** DIALOG Information Services, Pergamon ORBIT InfoLine, Inc., Info Globe, Dow Jones News/Retrieval, Infomart. Performs searches on fee basis.

★14268★
TOUCHE ROSS AND COMPANY - LIBRARY AND INFORMATION CENTER (Bus-Fin)
666 Burrard St., Suite 1700 Phone: (604)669-3343
Vancouver, BC, Canada V6E 3B3 C. Iona Douglas, Libn.
Staff: Prof 1. **Subjects:** Accounting, auditing, taxation, industry. **Holdings:** 2000 books; 2 VF drawers of clippings; annual reports; stock, exchange rate, and dividend records. **Subscriptions:** 65 journals and other serials; 6 newspapers. **Services:** Interlibrary loan; library open to the public with restrictions.

SAM TOUR LIBRARY
See: American Standards Testing Bureau, Inc. (692)

TOURISM REFERENCE AND DOCUMENTATION CENTRE
See: Canada - Department of Industry, Science & Technology (2353)

★14269★
TOURO INFIRMARY - HOSPITAL LIBRARY SERVICES (Med)
1401 Foucher St., 10th Fl., M Bldg. Phone: (504)897-8102
New Orleans, LA 70115 Patricia J. Greenfield, Libn.
Founded: 1947. **Staff:** Prof 1. **Subjects:** Clinical medicine, nursing. **Special Collections:** Elsie Waldhorn Cohn Memorial Collection (medical history); Jonas Rosenthal Memorial Ophthalmology Collection. **Holdings:** 2000 books; 5000 bound periodical volumes; 300 videotapes; 5 VF drawers of pamphlets; 100 Audio-Digest tapes. **Subscriptions:** 220 journals and other serials. **Services:** Interlibrary loan; copying; library open to the public for reference use only. **Automated Operations:** Computerized acquisitions. **Computerized Information Services:** NLM, BRS Information Technologies. **Networks/Consortia:** Member of TALON, New Orleans Area Health Science Libraries.

★14270★
TOWERS PERRIN - CORPORATE INFORMATION CENTER (Bus-Fin)
245 Park Ave. Phone: (212)309-3400
New York, NY 10167 Jack Borbely, Dir., Info.Serv.
Founded: 1925. **Staff:** Prof 7; Other 6. **Subjects:** Compensation, retirement/pensions, employee benefits, U.S. companies and industries, international business. **Holdings:** 3000 books; 125 VF drawers of clippings, reports, pamphlets; company annual reports and proxy statements on microfiche. **Subscriptions:** 600 journals and other serials. **Services:** Interlibrary loan; copying; center open to SLA members by appointment. **Computerized Information Services:** DIALOG Information Services, The Reference Service (REFSRV), NEXIS, INVESTEXT, VU/TEXT Information Services, BRS Information Technologies, NewsNet, Inc., DataTimes, Dow Jones News/Retrieval, TEXTLINE. **Special Indexes:** Coordinate index for reports. **Formerly:** Towers, Perrin, Forster & Crosby, Inc. **Staff:** Barbara Oliver, Info.Spec.; Helen Garvey, Info.Spec.; Regina Pichetti, Info.Spec.; Julia Blanchard, Info.Spec.; Mary Muenkel, Info.Spec.; Nancy Audino, Supv., Sys.; Amy Scowen, Supv., Network Sup.; Barbara Fiorillo, Indexing & Database Sup..

TOWERS PERRIN - CRESAP
See: Cresap (3883)

TOWERS PERRIN - TPF & C
See: TPF & C (14276)

★14271★
TOWERS, PERRIN, FORSTER & CROSBY, LTD. - INFORMATION CENTRE (Bus-Fin)
800 Dorchester W., Suite 2505
Montreal, PQ, Canada H3B 1X9 Phone: (514)866-7652
Staff: Prof 2. **Subjects:** Employee benefits, compensation, actuarial science, taxation, labor, social security. **Holdings:** 1000 books; 100 internal reports; 11 VF drawers of pamphlets and clippings; 1000 microfiche; AV programs. **Subscriptions:** 100 journals and other serials; 8 newspapers. **Services:** Center not open to the public. **Automated Operations:** Computerized cataloging. **Publications:** Communique, weekly - for internal distribution only. **Special Indexes:** Internal reports index (computerized). **Staff:** Dawn H. Chipps, Info.Spec.; Beverly J. Church, Info.Spec..

TOWNE LIBRARY
See: University of Pennsylvania - School of Engineering and Applied Science (16746)

★14272★
TOWNLEY & UPDIKE - LAW LIBRARY (Law)
405 Lexington Ave. Phone: (212)682-4567
New York, NY 10174 John S. Kostecky, Libn.
Staff: Prof 1; Other 2. **Subjects:** Law - labor, product liability, antitrust, securities, patent, trademark and copyright. **Holdings:** 20,000 volumes. **Subscriptions:** 50 journals and other serials; 10 newspapers. **Services:** Interlibrary loan; library not open to the public. **Computerized Information Services:** LEXIS, WESTLAW, DIALOG Information Services, Dow Jones News/Retrieval, ABA/net, NEXIS.

★14273★
TOWNSEND-GREENSPAN & COMPANY, INC. - LIBRARY (Bus-Fin)
Box 3663 Phone: (212)943-9515
New York, NY 10008-3663 Blanche Siegel, Libn.
Staff: Prof 1; Other 2. **Subjects:** National and international economic statistics, U.S. and foreign governments. **Holdings:** 1000 books; 1500 pamphlets. **Subscriptions:** 350 journals and other serials; 9 newspapers. **Services:** Interlibrary loan.

JOHN WILSON TOWNSEND ROOM
See: Eastern Kentucky University - John Grant Crabbe Library (4529)

TOWNSEND MEMORIAL LIBRARY
See: University of Mary Hardin-Baylor (16361)

★14274★
TOWSON STATE UNIVERSITY - GERHARDT LIBRARY OF MUSICAL INFORMATION (Mus)
Towson State University Phone: (301)321-2839
Towson, MD 21204 Edwin L. Gerhardt, Cur.
Staff: Prof 2. **Subjects:** Music literature. **Special Collections:** Thomas A. Edison and the phonograph; John Philip Sousa and bands. **Holdings:** Figures not available for books; phonograph records; pictures; artifacts. **Services:** Copying, library open to the public by appointment. **Remarks:** Library does not have a collection of scores or manuscripts. Direct all library correspondence to Edwin L. Gerhardt, 4926 Leeds Ave., Baltimore, MD 21227. Phone: (301)242-0328. **Staff:** Dale E. Rauschenberg, Coord..

★14275★
TOWSON STATE UNIVERSITY - GERHARDT MARIMBA & XYLOPHONE COLLECTION (Mus)
Towson State University Phone: (301)321-2839
Towson, MD 21204 Edwin L. Gerhardt, Cur.
Staff: Prof 2. **Subjects:** Marimbas and xylophones. **Holdings:** Figures not available for books; VF drawers of materials on assorted marimbas, xylophones, and artifacts. **Services:** Copying; colllection open to the public by appointment. **Remarks:** The collection is a unique and comprehensive accumulation of marimba and xylophone lore. It includes literature, phonograph recordings, tape recordings, catalogs, music, methods, pictures, correspondence, miscellaneous information. It is not a collection of instruments. Direct all library correspondence to Edwin L. Gerhardt, 4926 Leeds Ave., Baltimore, MD 21227. Phone: (301)242-0328. **Staff:** Dale E. Rauschenberg, Assoc.Prof., Mus./Coord..

TOZZER LIBRARY
See: Harvard University (6125)

★14276★
TPF & C - INFORMATION CENTRE (Bus-Fin)
250 Bloor St., E., Suite 1100 Phone: (416)960-2700
Toronto, ON, Canada M4W 3N3 Sari Bercovitch, Dir. of Info.Serv.
Staff: Prof 4; Other 1. **Subjects:** Employee benefits, compensation, communications, human resource management and information systems, insurance, management consulting, risk management. **Holdings:** 1300 books; 433 salary surveys; 372 Conference Board publications; 800 annual reports; 600 vertical files; 5000 internal reports on microfiche. **Subscriptions:** 200 journals and other serials. **Services:** Interlibrary loan; center not open to the public. **Automated Operations:** Computerized cataloging and serials. **Computerized Information Services:** DIALOG Information Services, Info Globe, Infomart, The Financial Post Information Service, Publinet Data Base; internal databases. **Publications:** Communique, weekly - for internal distribution only. **Special Indexes:** Index to internal reports (online). **Remarks:** TPF & C is a subsidiary of Towers Perrin. **Formerly:** Towers, Perrin, Forster & Crosby, Ltd. **Staff:** Rosemary Lindsay, Info.Serv.Spec.; Susan Clappison, Info.Serv.Anl.; Lorraine Flanigan, Info.Serv.Spec.; Maggie Fox, Info.Serv.Spec..

★14277★
TRA ARCHITECTURE ENGINEERING PLANNING INTERIORS - LIBRARY (Plan)
215 Columbia Phone: (206)682-1133
Seattle, WA 98104 Dan Trefethen, Libn.
Founded: 1979. **Staff:** Prof 1; Other 1. **Subjects:** Architecture, engineering, airport planning and design, interior design, planning, graphic design. **Special Collections:** Airport/Aircraft Data File (4 VF drawers). **Holdings:** 1500 books; 2000 reports; 2000 manufacturer's product catalogs; 10,000 slides. **Subscriptions:** 154 journals and other serials. **Services:** Interlibrary loan; library not open to the public. **Computerized Information Services:** DIALOG Information Services.

TRACE RESEARCH AND DEVELOPMENT CENTER ON COMMUNICATION, CONTROL & COMPUTER ACCESS FOR HANDICAPPED INDIVIDUALS
See: University of Wisconsin, Madison - Trace R & D Center (17156)

★14278★
TRACOR, INC. - TECHNICAL LIBRARY (Sci-Engr, Comp Sci)
6500 Tracor Ln. Phone: (512)926-2800
Austin, TX 78725-2070 Sara Jane Lee, Libn.
Founded: 1962. **Staff:** Prof 1; Other 1. **Subjects:** Electronics, aerospace engineering, environmental science, acoustics, computer mathematics, physics. **Holdings:** 8000 books; 500 bound periodical volumes; 300 microfiche; 2500 technical reports. **Subscriptions:** 245 journals and other serials; 5 newspapers. **Services:** Interlibrary loan; copying; library open to the public by appointment. **Automated Operations:** Computerized circulation. **Computerized Information Services:** DIALOG Information Services.

★14279★
TRACOR JITCO, INC. - RESEARCH RESOURCES INFORMATION CENTER (Biol Sci)
1601 Research Blvd. Phone: (301)984-2870
Rockville, MD 20850-3191 Edward Post, Dir.
Staff: Prof 6; Other 2. **Subjects:** Research - biomedical, animal, biotechnological, clinical. **Holdings:** Figures not available. **Services:** Center not open to the public. **Publications:** Research Resources Reporter, monthly; research resources directories, annual; DRR Program Highlights, annual. **Special Indexes:** Research Resources Reporter Index, annual. **Remarks:** Maintained by U.S. National Institutes of Health - Research Resources Division. **Staff:** Jude Langsam, Asst.Dir.; Ole Henriksen, Sci.Adv.; Andrea Clark, Sci. Correspondent; Dana Murphy, Sci. Correspondent; Barbara Proujan, Sci. Correspondent.

★14280★
TRACY-LOCKE ADVERTISING - INFORMATION SERVICES DEPARTMENT (Bus-Fin)
200 Crescent Ct., Suite 900 Phone: (214)969-9000
Dallas, TX 75201 Ellen Shapley, V.P./Mgr., Info.Serv.
Founded: 1967. **Staff:** Prof 2; Other 1. **Subjects:** Advertising, marketing, consumer products. **Holdings:** 2000 books, research reports, directories; 2 VF drawers of clippings on Texas subjects; 40 VF drawers of data on various industries and products. **Subscriptions:** 450 journals and other serials. **Services:** Interlibrary loan; copying; department open to the public by appointment. **Automated Operations:** Computerized routing. **Computerized Information Services:** DIALOG Information Services, Dow Jones News/Retrieval, NEXIS, Dun & Bradstreet Corporation, VU/TEXT Information Services, DataTimes. **Staff:** Susan Elam, Info.Spec..

★14281★
TRADE RELATIONS COUNCIL OF THE UNITED STATES - LIBRARY (Bus-Fin)
1001 Connecticut Ave., N.W., Suite 901 Phone: (202)785-4185
Washington, DC 20036 Eugene L. Stewart, Exec.Sec.
Subjects: Trade, tariff, and allied subjects. **Holdings:** Figures not available. **Services:** Library not open to the public.

★14282★
TRAFFIC INJURY RESEARCH FOUNDATION OF CANADA (TIRF) - TECHNICAL INFORMATION CENTRE (Med)
171 Nepean St., 6th Fl.
Ottawa, ON, Canada K2P 0B4 Phone: (613)238-5235
Staff: Prof 9; Other 2. **Subjects:** Road safety - behavioral, medical, pharmacological, statistical, engineering. **Holdings:** 800 books; 100 bound periodical volumes; 4500 technical reports, statistics reports, government publications, newsletters. **Subscriptions:** 53 journals and other serials. **Services:** Interlibrary loan; copying; center open to the public. **Computerized Information Services:** Road Safety Database (internal database). **Publications:** Acquisition List, monthly.

★14283★
TRAIN COLLECTORS ASSOCIATION - TOY TRAIN REFERENCE LIBRARY (Rec)
Paradise Lane
Box 248 Phone: (717)687-8623
Strasburg, PA 17579 Anne Kiscaden, Ref.Libn.
Founded: 1982. **Staff:** Prof 1; Other 3. **Subjects:** Toy and model trains. **Special Collections:** Manufacturer catalogs (1900); toy/model train serial publications (5000 issues of 180 titles). **Holdings:** 350 books; 80 bound periodical volumes; annual reports. **Subscriptions:** 27 journals and other serials. **Services:** Copying; library open to the public by appointment for reference use only.

★14284★
TRANET - LIBRARY (Soc Sci)
Box 567 Phone: (207)864-2252
Rangeley, ME 04970 William N. Ellis, Exec.Dir.
Founded: 1976. **Staff:** 4. **Subjects:** Appropriate technology, alternative energy, alternative economics, social humanism, new ruralism. **Holdings:** 2000 books; 900 unbound magazines; 200 reports; 200 papers. **Subscriptions:** 50 journals and other serials. **Services:** Library open to the public. **Publications:** Tranet, quarterly - to members.

★14285★
TRANS CANADA PIPELINES LTD. - LIBRARY (Energy)
Commerce Court West
Box 54 Phone: (416)869-2678
Toronto, ON, Canada M5L 1C2 Nancy L. Urbankiewicz, Supv., Lib.
Staff: Prof 1; Other 2. **Subjects:** Energy, pipelines, transmission, law. **Holdings:** 10,000 books. **Subscriptions:** 500 journals and other serials; 10 newspapers. **Services:** Interlibrary loan; copying; library open to the public with restrictions. **Automated Operations:** Computerized cataloging, acquisitions, serials, and circulation. **Computerized Information Services:** DIALOG Information Services, Pergamon ORBIT InfoLine, Inc., QL Systems, Info Globe, I.P. Sharp Associates Limited; A.G.A. GasNet (electronic mail service). **Publications:** New Books in the Library, bimonthly - for internal distribution only.

★14286★
TRANS QUEBEC & MARITIMES INC. - CENTRE DE DOCUMENTATION (Energy)
870 de Maisonneuve Blvd., E., 6th Fl. Phone: (514)286-5046
Montreal, PQ, Canada H2L 1Y6 Chantale Dion, Doc.
Staff: Prof 1; Other 1. **Subjects:** Pipeline construction, regulation, natural gas. **Holdings:** 5000 books; 200 bound periodical volumes; 2000 clippings; 1000 boxes of archival material. **Subscriptions:** 100 journals and other serials; 10 newspapers. **Services:** Interlibrary loan; copying; center open to the public by appointment. **Automated Operations:** Computerized cataloging.

★14287★
TRANS WORLD AIRLINES, INC. - CORPORATE LIBRARY (Trans)
605 Third Ave. Phone: (212)692-3521
New York, NY 10158 Esther L. Giles, Corp.Libn.
Founded: 1965. **Staff:** Prof 1. **Subjects:** Air transportation. **Holdings:** 7000 books and bound periodical volumes; 1100 pamphlets; 7 VF drawers of annual reports; 350 volumes of company reports; Civil Aeronautics Board statistics; travel surveys. **Subscriptions:** 210 journals and other serials. **Services:** Interlibrary loan; copying; library open to the public for reference use only on request. **Also Known As:** TWA.

TRANSACTION TECHNOLOGY INC.
See: Citicorp/Transaction Technology Inc. (3226)

★14288★
TRANSALTA UTILITIES CORPORATION - LIBRARY (Energy, Bus-Fin)
110 12th Ave., S.W.
P.O. Box 1900 Phone: (403)267-7388
Calgary, AB, Canada T2P 2M1 Shamim Kassam, Libn.
Staff: Prof 1; Other 2. **Subjects:** Electricity, management, reclamation. **Special Collections:** Electric Power Research Institute Research Reports. **Holdings:** 8000 books; 10 boxes of annual reports; 100 microfiche; 500 other cataloged items. **Subscriptions:** 600 journals and other serials; 50 newspapers. **Services:** Interlibrary loan; library open to the public at librarian's discretion. **Automated Operations:** Computerized cataloging,

serials, and circulation. **Computerized Information Services:** Pergamon ORBIT InfoLine, Inc., CAN/OLE, QL Systems, CANSIM, BRS Information Technologies, Info Globe.

★14289★
TRANSAMERICA OCCIDENTAL LIFE INSURANCE COMPANY - LAW LIBRARY (Law)
1150 S. Olive St., Suite T-2500 Phone: (213)742-3123
Los Angeles, CA 90015 Hellen A. Spear, Mgr.
Staff: 1. **Subjects:** Insurance law, general law. **Holdings:** 9000 volumes. **Subscriptions:** 11 journals and other serials. **Services:** Library not open to the public.

★14290★
TRANSCO ENERGY COMPANY - CORPORATE LIBRARY (Energy)
Box 1396 Phone: (713)871-2321
Houston, TX 77251 Cheryl L. Watson, Sr.Libn.
Founded: 1951. **Staff:** Prof 1. **Subjects:** Natural gas industry, petroleum industry. **Holdings:** 2000 books; 700 bound periodical volumes; 10 VF drawers of information files. **Subscriptions:** 300 journals and other serials. **Services:** Interlibrary loan; copying; library open to the public by appointment. **Computerized Information Services:** DIALOG Information Services, Dow Jones News/Retrieval. **Publications:** Library Lines (acquisitions list), monthly. **Remarks:** Library located at 2800 S. Post Oak Rd., Houston, TX 77056.

TRANSLAB LIBRARY
See: California State Department of Transportation - Laboratory Library (2198)

★14291★
TRANSLATORS' AND INTERPRETERS' EDUCATIONAL SOCIETY - LIBRARY (Info Sci)
Box 3027
Stanford, CA 94305 Etilvia Arjona, Exec.Dir.
Founded: 1982. **Subjects:** Translation and interpretation. **Holdings:** 400 volumes; biographical archives; oral history program with videotapes and cassettes.

TRANSPORT CANADA
See: Canada - Transport Canada (2505)

★14292★
TRANSPORTATION-COMMUNICATIONS UNION (TCU) - LIBRARY (Trans)
3 Research Place Phone: (301)948-4910
Rockville, MD 20850 Nancy Noechel, Asst.Dir./Libn.
Founded: 1980. **Staff:** Prof 1; Other 1. **Subjects:** Rail and airline industry; labor movement - law, history, statistics. **Special Collections:** Presidential Emergency Board documents (archival collection for disputes to which TCU was a party); historical collection of official union publications. **Holdings:** 2500 books; 30 VF drawers. **Subscriptions:** 170 journals and other serials; 5 newspapers. **Services:** Interlibrary loan; copying; SDI; library open to the public with restrictions. **Computerized Information Services:** DIALOG Information Services, LEGI-SLATE. **Networks/Consortia:** Member of Washington Area Labor Information Specialists (WALIS). **Publications:** Bracgrounder, 4-5/year - to TCU officers and by request. **Formerly:** Brotherhood of Railway and Airline Clerks (BRAC).

★14293★
TRANSPORTATION INSTITUTE - LIBRARY (Trans)
5201 Auth Way, 5th Fl. Phone: (301)423-3335
Camp Springs, MD 20746 Chung-Tai Shen, Chf.Libn.
Founded: 1968. **Staff:** Prof 1; Other 1. **Subjects:** Merchant marine, transportation, economics, statistics, labor management, manpower. **Holdings:** 1400 volumes; 4000 documents; 3000 newspaper clippings; 1000 Congressional documents; 1300 documents on microfiche. **Subscriptions:** 35 journals and other serials; 8 newspapers. **Services:** Interlibrary loan; library not open to the public. **Publications:** Transportation Institute Library Bulletin, monthly - for internal distribution only.

★14294★
TRANSPORTATION INSTITUTE - RESEARCH DOCUMENTATION CENTER
301-303 Merrick Bldg.
North Carolina Agricultural & Tech. State Univ.
Greensboro, NC 27411
Subjects: Urban public transit, freight transportation, transportation for the elderly and handicapped, rural public transit, public transit finance, motor carrier deregulation. **Holdings:** 4000 reports and books; 250 microfiche; unbound periodicals. **Remarks:** Presently inactive.

TRANSPORTATION RESEARCH BOARD LIBRARY
See: National Research Council (9772)

TRANSPORTATION RESEARCH INFORMATION CENTER (TRIC)
See: U.S. Urban Mass Transportation Administration (15511)

★14295★
TRAPHAGEN SCHOOL OF FASHION - ETHEL TRAPHAGEN LEIGH MEMORIAL LIBRARY (Art)
257 Park Ave., S. Phone: (212)673-0300
New York, NY 10010 Allyn Rice Bloeme, Chf.Libn.
Founded: 1923. **Staff:** Prof 1; Other 2. **Subjects:** Fashion design and illustration, history of costume, art, interior design, architecture. **Special Collections:** Old and rare bound fashion periodicals of France, England, Germany, and America; old German fine art books; Harper's Bazaar and Vogue, from their inception to the present; ethnic costumes (lithographs, original drawings). **Holdings:** 17,000 books; 716 bound periodical volumes; 40 VF drawers of clippings; 1130 lantern slides; 5000 color slides; black and white slides. **Subscriptions:** 14 journals and other serials. **Services:** Library open to the public by appointment for publication research. **Publications:** Library Newsletter.

TRASK LIBRARY
See: Andover Newton Theological School (774)

TRAVAIL CANADA
See: Canada - Labour Canada (2408)

TRAVAUX PUBLICS CANADA
See: Canada - Public Works Canada (2474)

TRAVEL INDUSTRY ASSOCIATION OF AMERICA - U.S. TRAVEL DATA CENTER
See: U.S. Travel Data Center (15508)

TRAVEL AND TOURISM RESEARCH ASSOCIATION - TRAVEL REFERENCE CENTER
See: University of Colorado, Boulder - Business Research Division - Travel Reference Center (16069)

TRAVEL WEEKLY LIBRARY
See: Murdock Magazines (9422)

★14296★
TRAVELERS INSURANCE COMPANIES - THE INFORMATION EXCHANGE (Bus-Fin)
One Tower Square Phone: (203)954-1990
Hartford, CT 06183 Lydia L. Ouellette, Info.Rsrc.Coord.
Staff: Prof 8; Other 11. **Subjects:** Insurance, law, management, actuarial science. **Special Collections:** Company history; mortality tables. **Holdings:** 55,000 books and unbound periodical volumes. **Subscriptions:** 1200 journals and other serials; 6 newspapers. **Services:** Interlibrary loan; SDI; open to the public by appointment. **Automated Operations:** Computerized public access catalog, cataloging, serials, and circulation. **Computerized Information Services:** DIALOG Information Services, BRS Information Technologies, Human Resource Information Network (HRIN), NewsNet, Inc., LEXIS, NEXIS, Dow Jones News/Retrieval, InfoMaster. **Networks/Consortia:** Member of Capitol Region Library Council (CRLC). **Publications:** Newsletter, quarterly. **Staff:** Harry Keiner, Archv.; Wendy Urciuoli, Info.Anl.; Judith Zanotta, Info.Serv.Cons.; Lucy Gangone, Info.Serv.Cons..

TRAVENOL LABORATORIES, INC.
See: Baxter Healthcare Corporation (1399)

★14297★
TRAVENOL LABORATORIES, INC. - INFORMATION RESOURCE CENTER - MORTON GROVE
6301 Lincoln Ave.
Morton Grove, IL 60053
Defunct

★14298★
TRAVERSE CITY REGIONAL PSYCHIATRIC HOSPITAL - PROFESSIONAL RESOURCE LIBRARY (Med)
Elmwood & 11th Sts.
Traverse City, MI 49684 Phone: (616)922-5238
Founded: 1885. **Staff:** Prof 1. **Subjects:** Psychiatry, psychology, neurology, medicine, nursing, social services. **Holdings:** 10,100 books; 3277 bound periodical volumes; 250 reprints; 41 films; 20 filmstrips; 26 tapes; 600 slides. **Subscriptions:** 53 journals and other serials. **Services:** Interlibrary loan; copying; library open to the public with restrictions.

TRAVERTINE NATURE CENTER LIBRARY
See: U.S. Natl. Park Service - Chickasaw Natl. Recreation Area (15269)

★14299★
TRAVIS AVENUE BAPTIST CHURCH - MAURINE HENDERSON LIBRARY (Rel-Phil)
3041 Travis Ave. Phone: (817)924-4266
Fort Worth, TX 76110 Mrs. S.H. Henderson, Libn.
Founded: 1954. **Staff:** 4. **Subjects:** Religion, biography, history, literature. **Holdings:** 16,712 books; AV programs. **Services:** Copying; library open to the public with restrictions.

★14300★
TRC ENVIRONMENTAL CONSULTANTS, INC. - LIBRARY
800 Connecticut Blvd.
East Hartford, CT 06108 Phone: (203)289-8631
Subjects: Environmental science, hazardous wastes, air and water pollution, meteorology. **Holdings:** 1300 books; 1200 documents, conference proceedings, meteorological data, U.S. Government documents, Environmental Protection Agency (EPA) documents, Air Pollution and Air Pollution Technical Data (APTD) documents, and Environmental Protection Research Institute (EPRI) documents. **Remarks:** Presently inactive.

★14301★
TREAD OF PIONEERS MUSEUM - ROUTT COUNTY COLLECTION (Hist)
Box 770768 Phone: (303)879-0240
Steamboat Springs, CO 80477 Sureva Towler, Archv.
Founded: 1981. **Staff:** Prof 1. **Subjects:** Local history and genealogy, skiing, ranching, mining. **Holdings:** 100 books; 8 file cabinets of manuscripts; photographs; scrapbooks; oral histories; clippings; 25 dissertations on microfilm; 1880 and 1890 census materials; maps. **Services:** Copying; searches; library open to the public with permission of librarian.

★14302★
TREASURE HUNTING RESEARCH AND INFORMATION CENTER (THRIC) (Rec)
Box 314
Gibson, LA 70356-0314 John Davis, Dir.
Founded: 1986. **Staff:** Prof 5; Other 4. **Subjects:** Treasure hunting, ship wrecks, exploration, prospecting, adventure. **Special Collections:** Latin American lost cities (10 vertical files); legendary Amazons of Latin America (5 vertical files). **Holdings:** 750 books; 350 bound periodical volumes; 250 vertical files. **Subscriptions:** 18 journals and other serials. **Services:** Center not open to the public. **Publications:** Treasure Hunting Research Bulletin, quarterly - by subscription. **Special Catalogs:** Catalog of treasure hunting clubs and organizations, periodicals, events, books, authors, and commercial enterprises (card). **Formerly:** Treasure Hunter Research and Information Center, located in Houston, TX.

★14303★
TREBAS INSTITUTE OF RECORDING ARTS - OTTAWA CAMPUS LIBRARY/RESOURCE CENTRE (Mus)
290 Nepean St. Phone: (613)232-7104
Ottawa, ON, Canada K1R 5G3 John Allen, Student Serv.
Founded: 1981. **Staff:** Prof 1; Other 2. **Subjects:** Audio engineering, music business and management, record and video production, music, communications. **Holdings:** 400 books; 25 videotapes; 100 audio cassettes. **Subscriptions:** 32 journals and other serials. **Services:** Center open to students and alumni. **Special Indexes:** Periodical table of contents (bound).

★14304★
TREBAS INSTITUTE OF RECORDING ARTS - RESOURCE CENTER (Mus)
1435 Bleury St., Suite 301 Phone: (514)845-4141
Montreal, PQ, Canada H3A 2H7 David P. Leonard, Pres.
Founded: 1979. **Staff:** Prof 1. **Subjects:** Music industry, recording arts and sciences, audio engineering, acoustics, electronic music synthesis. **Holdings:** 1000 books. **Subscriptions:** 25 journals and other serials. **Services:** Center not open to the public.

HARLEIGH B. TRECKER LIBRARY
See: University of Connecticut (16092)

★14305★
TREE OF LIFE PRESS - LIBRARY AND ARCHIVES (Publ)
420 N.E. Blvd.
Gainesville, FL 32601 Reva Pachefsky, Libn.
Founded: 1971. **Staff:** Prof 1; Other 1. **Subjects:** Infant language development, child development, graphic arts. **Special Collections:** Archives of the Tree of Life Press; Collection of the Art of Robert (Ishmael) Grabb, Jr. **Services:** Interlibrary loan; library open to the public by appointment. **Publications:** Newsletter; New Acquisitions; Listing of the Collection by Topic, all irregular.

★14306★
TREEHOUSE WILDLIFE CENTER, INC. - LIBRARY (Biol Sci)
R.R. 1, Box 125E Phone: (618)372-8092
Brighton, IL 62012 Richard D. Evans, D.V.M., Med.Dir.
Staff: 2. **Subjects:** Wildlife diseases, avian and mammalian natural history. **Special Collections:** Registry of Wildlife Pathology (1800 case histories). **Holdings:** 583 books; 1213 bound periodical volumes; 34,000 other cataloged items. **Subscriptions:** 31 journals and other serials. **Services:** Copying; library open to the public.

★14307★
TREEPEOPLE - ENVIRONMENTAL RESOURCES LIBRARY (Env-Cons)
12601 Mulholland Dr.
Beverly Hills, CA 90210 Phone: (818)769-2663
Staff: 1. **Subjects:** Forestry, air pollution, tropical rainforests, environmental issues. **Holdings:** Figures not available. **Services:** Library open to the public by appointment.

TRENDS PUBLISHING, INC.
See: Science Trends (12994)

★14308★
TRENTON FREE PUBLIC LIBRARY - ART & MUSIC DEPARTMENT (Art, Mus)
120 Academy St.
Box 2448 Phone: (609)392-7188
Trenton, NJ 08608 Shirley Michael, Dept.Hd.
Staff: Prof 2; Other 2. **Subjects:** Fine arts, music, applied arts, antiques, dance, photography. **Special Collections:** Collection of original oil and water color paintings (22 items); Archives of Trenton Area Music; Union List of Sacred Music. **Holdings:** 6400 books; 2650 bound periodical volumes; 4500 phonograph records; 30 VF drawers of pictures; 4 VF cabinets of orchestral scores and parts; 1 VF cabinet of choral parts; 300 pieces of sheet music; 205 16mm films. **Subscriptions:** 90 journals and other serials. **Services:** Interlibrary loan; copying; department open to the public. **Special Indexes:** Song index; paintings index; phonograph record index (all on cards); dance index; arias index. **Staff:** Greg Smith, Sr.Lib.Asst..

★14309★
TRENTON FREE PUBLIC LIBRARY - BUSINESS AND TECHNOLOGY DEPARTMENT (Bus-Fin, Sci-Engr)
120 Academy St. Phone: (609)392-7188
Trenton, NJ 08608 Richard D. Rebecca, Dept.Hd.
Founded: 1902. **Staff:** Prof 3; Other 1. **Subjects:** Business and finance, science and technology, labor. **Holdings:** 9000 books; 2000 bound periodical volumes; 600 annual reports; 350 telephone directories; 300 trade directories; 25 VF drawers; loose-leaf financial services. **Subscriptions:** 200 journals and other serials. **Services:** Interlibrary loan; copying; department open to the public. **Staff:** Nancy Leary, Sr.Libn.; Sharon Austin, Jr.Lib.Asst..

★14310★
TRENTON FREE PUBLIC LIBRARY - GOVERNMENT DOCUMENTS COLLECTION (Info Sci)
120 Academy St. Phone: (609)392-7188
Trenton, NJ 08608 Nan Wright, Hd., Ref.Dept.
Founded: 1910. **Staff:** Prof 1; Other 1. **Special Collections:** Federal, state, and local government documents; U.S. Government periodicals and serial sets. **Holdings:** 25,000 books; 1000 bound periodical volumes; 250,000 other cataloged items. **Subscriptions:** 150 journals and other serials. **Services:** Interlibrary loan; copying; SDI; collection open to the public.

Automated Operations: Computerized cataloging. **Computerized Information Services:** OCLC. Performs searches free of charge. Contact Person: James Kisthardt, Hd., Cat.Dept.. **Networks/Consortia:** Member of PALINET. **Staff:** Sharon Shrives, Jr.Asst.Libn..

★14311★
TRENTON FREE PUBLIC LIBRARY - TRENTONIANA COLLECTION (Hist)
120 Academy St. Phone: (609)392-7188
Trenton, NJ 08608 Nan Wright, Hd., Ref.Dept.
Staff: Prof 1; Other 1. **Subjects:** Local history, genealogy. **Special Collections:** Early Trenton Fire Department minutes and records; New Jersey books and documents; archives of local organizations; local maps. **Holdings:** 4000 books; 403 bound periodical volumes; 26 VF drawers of photographs; 34 VF drawers; 175 maps and atlases; 5 VF drawers of manuscripts; 28 reels of film; 35 audiotapes; 47 oral histories; Trenton newspapers on microfilm; 5 pieces of Lenox china; 3 VF drawers of memorabilia; 30 boxes of unspecified materials. **Subscriptions:** 45 journals and other serials; 5 newspapers. **Services:** Copying; collection open to the public. **Staff:** Richard Reeves, Sr.Asst.Libn..

★14312★
TRENTON PSYCHIATRIC HOSPITAL - PROFESSIONAL LIBRARY (Med)
Box 7500 Phone: (609)633-1572
West Trenton, NJ 08628 Elaine Scheuerer, Lib.Coord.
Founded: 1944. **Staff:** 1. **Subjects:** Psychiatry, psychotherapy, medicine, psychoanalysis, nursing. **Holdings:** 4250 books; 410 bound periodical volumes; 5 VF drawers of pamphlets; manuscripts; reports; clippings; 1 cabinet of phonograph records, tapes, filmstrips. **Subscriptions:** 89 journals and other serials. **Services:** Interlibrary loan; library open to the public for reference use only. **Networks/Consortia:** Member of Central Jersey Health Science Libraries Association, New Jersey Health Sciences Library Network (NJHSN), BHSL.

★14313★
TRENTON STATE COLLEGE - ROSCOE L. WEST LIBRARY - SPECIAL COLLECTIONS (Hist)
Hillwood Lakes, CN-4700 Phone: (609)771-2346
Trenton, NJ 08650-4700 Richard P. Matthews, Spec.Coll.Libn.
Founded: 1969. **Staff:** Prof 1. **Special Collections:** New Jersey (2820 volumes); Trenton State College Archives (1000 items); historic textbooks; Trenton State faculty author collection (670 volumes); Trenton State College masters' theses (250 volumes); autograph collection (100 volumes); historic children's books (78 volumes); Feinstone Collection of the American Revolution (50 items); oral history collection (31 cassettes); Trenton State College alumni author collection (14 volumes); special illustrators collection (6 volumes). **Holdings:** 50 unbound reports; 35 manuscripts; 20 magnetic tapes. **Services:** Interlibrary loan (limited); copying; collections open to the public for reference use only. **Automated Operations:** Computerized public access catalog, cataloging, and circulation. **Computerized Information Services:** BRS Information Technologies, OCLC, WILSONLINE, DIALOG Information Services, Dow Jones News/Retrieval; TOP CAT (internal database). **Networks/Consortia:** Member of PALINET, New Jersey Academic Library Network. **Publications:** Guide to the Library, annual; Previews, quarterly - both available on request; Periodical Holdings, biennial; Accessions List, monthly - both for internal distribution only. **Special Catalogs:** Catalog of the Feinstone Collection of the American Revolution (typed list).

★14314★
(Trenton) TIMES - LIBRARY (Publ)
500 Perry St.
Box 847 Phone: (609)396-3232
Trenton, NJ 08605 Marjorie Roseborough Carnevale, Hd.Libn.
Staff: Prof 1; Other 3. **Subjects:** Newspaper reference topics, state information on local political figures, highways. **Holdings:** Figures not available. **Subscriptions:** 16 journals and other serials; 6 newspapers. **Services:** Interlibrary loan; library not open to the public.

★14315★
RALPH TREVES WORKSHOP FEATURES - WORKSHOP PHOTOS (Aud-Vis, Rec)
311 Lake Evelyn Dr. Phone: (407)683-5167
West Palm Beach, FL 33411 Ralph Treves, Owner
Subjects: Manual crafts and skills, home improvements, hobby workshop projects, home security. **Special Collections:** Photographs illustrating techniques related to woodworking, home repair, and renovation. **Holdings:** 14,000 black/white photographs available for reproduction by magazines, public relations agencies, newspapers, book publishers. **Services:** Feature articles written on assignment.

★14316★
HARRY C. TREXLER MASONIC LIBRARY (Rec)
1524 Linden St. Phone: (215)432-2618
Allentown, PA 18102 Paul R. Breitenstein, Libn.
Staff: 1. **Subjects:** Freemasonry, Masonic history, Benjamin Franklin, George Washington. **Holdings:** 6000 books and bound periodical volumes. **Services:** Library open to the public with restrictions. **Remarks:** Maintained by five Masonic lodges in Allentown.

TREXLER NURSES' LIBRARY
See: St. Luke's Hospital of Bethlehem, Pennsylvania - School of Nursing (12564)

SCOTT ANDREW TREXLER II MEMORIAL LIBRARY
See: Lehigh County Historical Society (7750)

★14317★
TRI BROOK GROUP, INC. - LIBRARY (Med)
999 Oakmont Plaza Dr., Suite 600 Phone: (312)990-8070
Westmont, IL 60559-5504 Sandra Rumbyrt, Libn.
Staff: Prof 1. **Subjects:** Health care management, health statistics. **Holdings:** 4000 volumes including government publications and reports. **Subscriptions:** 85 journals and other serials. **Services:** Interlibrary loan; library; not open to the public. **Networks/Consortia:** Member of Fox Valley Health Science Library Consortium.

★14318★
TRI-CITY JEWISH CENTER - LIBRARY (Rel-Phil)
2715 30th St.
Box 679 Phone: (309)788-3426
Rock Island, IL 61201 Doris Greenblatt, Chm.
Founded: 1951. **Subjects:** Judaica. **Holdings:** 5500 books. **Services:** Library open to the public with restrictions.

★14319★
TRI-COUNTY METROPOLITAN DISTRICT OF OREGON (Tri-Met) - LIBRARY (Trans)
4012 S.E. 17th Ave. Phone: (503)238-4814
Portland, OR 97202 Julie Kawabata, Lib.Spec.
Founded: 1982. **Staff:** Prof 1; Other 1. **Subjects:** Public transit, urban transportation. **Holdings:** 3000 books. **Subscriptions:** 125 journals and other serials. **Services:** Interlibrary loan; copying; library open to the public by appointment. **Computerized Information Services:** DIALOG Information Services, LEXIS.

★14320★
TRI-COUNTY REGIONAL PLANNING COMMISSION - INFORMATION RESOURCE CENTER (Plan)
913 W. Holmes Rd., Suite 201 Phone: (517)393-0342
Lansing, MI 48910 Carrie Clinkscales, Exec.Asst.
Founded: 1956. **Subjects:** Urban and regional planning. **Holdings:** Figures not available. **Services:** Center open to the public for reference use only. **Computerized Information Services:** Internal databases; AutoMail (electronic mail service). **Publications:** Planning reports on Clinton, Eaton, and Ingham counties, continuous updates.

★14321★
TRI-COUNTY REGIONAL PLANNING COMMISSION - LIBRARY (Plan)
632 W. Jefferson St. Phone: (309)694-4391
Morton, IL 61550-1540 Robert L. Pinkerton, Exec.Dir.
Founded: 1958. **Subjects:** Land use, housing, open space and recreation, environment, transportation. **Special Collections:** Environmental Protection Agency (EPA) Special Environmental Technical Studies; depository for Federal Home Mortgage and Disclosure Act. **Holdings:** 450 books; 250 bound periodical volumes; 150 items of census information; transportation documents; local development codes; original of Standard Metropolitan Statistical Area maps; urban transportation planning package (special census tabulation). **Subscriptions:** 198 journals and other serials. **Services:** Interlibrary loan; copying; library open to the public for reference use only. **Computerized Information Services:** LINUS. **Networks/Consortia:** Member of Illinois State Data Center Cooperative (ISDCC). **Publications:** Annotated Bibliography of Agency Publications.

★14322★
TRI-COUNTY TECHNICAL COLLEGE - LEARNING RESOURCE CENTER (Sci-Engr, Educ)
Box 587 Phone: (803)646-8361
Pendleton, SC 29670 Dr. Stephen B. Walter, Dir.
Founded: 1963. **Staff:** Prof 2; Other 6. **Subjects:** Animal industry, industrial electronics, business administration, paramedicine, automotive technology, secretarial science, machine shop, marketing, management, radio and television broadcasting, electronics engineering. **Special Collections:** Black studies (300 items); Child Development (3000 items); Medical Lab Technicians (200 items). **Holdings:** 35,695 books; 4565 bound periodical volumes; 4709 AV programs. **Subscriptions:** 158 journals and other serials; 16 newspapers. **Services:** Interlibrary loan; copying; comprehensive audiovisual production services; center open to residents of Anderson, Oconee, and Pickens Counties, South Carolina. **Publications:** Quarterly and annual reports. **Special Catalogs:** Printed catalog of AV materials. **Staff:** Nancy C. Griese, Hd.Libn..

TRI-KAPPA COLLECTION OF AUBURN AUTOMOTIVE LITERATURE
See: Auburn-Cord-Duesenberg Museum (1144)

★14323★
TRI-STATE UNIVERSITY - GENERAL LEWIS B. HERSHEY MUSEUM (Hist)
Angola, IN 46703 Phone: (219)665-3141
John C. McBride, Dir.
Founded: 1970. **Subjects:** General Lewis B. Hershey. **Holdings:** Figures not available for books; memorabilia; articles. **Services:** Museum open to the public.

★14324★
TRI-STATE UNIVERSITY - PERRY T. FORD MEMORIAL LIBRARY (Sci-Engr, Bus-Fin)
S. Darling St. Phone: (219)665-3141
Angola, IN 46703 Mrs. Enriqueta G. Taboy, Lib.Dir.
Founded: 1962. **Staff:** Prof 2; Other 3. **Subjects:** Engineering, business, economics, elementary and secondary curricula. **Special Collections:** NACA and NASA publications; Smithsonian publications; NATO Advisory Group for Aerospace Research and Development (AGARD) publications. **Holdings:** 101,399 books; 12,891 bound periodical volumes; 2814 reels of microfilm; 710 phonograph records; 540 audio cassettes; 343 maps; 490 filmstrips; 31,665 other cataloged items. **Subscriptions:** 398 journals and other serials; 19 newspapers. **Services:** Interlibrary loan; copying; library open to the public with restrictions on circulation. **Automated Operations:** Computerized cataloging and periodical maintenance. **Computerized Information Services:** Access to DIALOG Information Services, OCLC. **Networks/Consortia:** Member of Tri-ALSA. **Publications:** Library Newsletter, monthly - for internal distribution only. **Staff:** Bruce Brinkley, Ref.Libn.; Carolyn Cripe, Cat..

TRIANGLE CLUB ARCHIVES
See: Princeton University - William Seymour Theatre Collection (11595)

★14325★
TRIANGLE PUBLICATIONS, INC. - TV GUIDE MICROFILM LIBRARY (Publ)
Four Radnor Corporate Center Phone: (215)293-8947
Radnor, PA 19088 Cathy Johnson, Microfilm Coord.
Staff: 2. **Subjects:** Television. **Holdings:** TV Guide, 1953-1985, on microfilm. **Services:** Library not open to the public. **Special Indexes:** TV Guide 25 Year Index, 1953-1977, with annual supplements.

TRIANON PRESS ARCHIVE
See: University of California, Santa Cruz - Dean E. Mc Henry Library (16021)

★14326★
TRICO-KOBE, INC. - ENGINEERING LIBRARY
3040 E. Slauson Ave.
Huntington Park, CA 90255
Defunct

★14327★
TRIDENT TECHNICAL COLLEGE - MAIN CAMPUS LEARNING RESOURCES CENTER (Sci-Engr, Educ)
LD/M Box 10367 Phone: (803)572-6089
Charleston, SC 29411 Marion L. Vogel, Dir., Lrng.Rsrcs.
Founded: 1964. **Staff:** Prof 6; Other 5. **Subjects:** Engineering technology, business and management, allied health, automotive and industrial crafts, horticulture, physical sciences, radio and television electronics, humanities. **Special Collections:** Archives; Sams Photofact Collection (Howard Sams Schematics for Radios and Televisions; complete collection); engineering and technical books (11,154). **Holdings:** 32,965 books; 39 bound periodical volumes; 325 government documents; 350 pamphlets in vertical file; 1536 reels of microfilm; 29,281 microfiche; 51 realia; 657 phonograph records; 3315 audiotapes; 214 videotapes; 292 films; 34,869 slides; 1575 overhead transparencies; 4 computer software programs; 42 boxes of archival materials. **Subscriptions:** 444 journals and other serials; 13 newspapers. **Services:** Interlibrary loan; copying; library open to the public for reference use only. **Computerized Information Services:** DIALOG Information Services. Performs searches on fee basis. Contact Person: Sylvia Hu, Pub.Serv.Libn.. **Networks/Consortia:** Member of Charleston Higher Education Consortium (CHEC). **Publications:** Annual Report - to administrators and administrative faculty; Audiovisual Bibliography, irregular; subject bibliographies. **Staff:** Rose Marie Huff, Acq.Libn.; Rosetta Martin, Ref.Libn.; Lisanne Hamilton, Tech.Serv.Libn..

TRIMBLE LIBRARY
See: Nazarene Bible College (9837)

★14328★
TRINITY BIBLE COLLEGE - FRED J. GRAHAM LIBRARY (Rel-Phil)
Ellendale, ND 58436 Phone: (701)349-5430
Esther Zink, Libn.
Staff: Prof 1; Other 4. **Subjects:** Bible, theology, church work, evangelism, Christian ministries, missions, clerical and secretarial education, elementary education. **Special Collections:** Pentecostal Works/Trinity Bible Institute archives. **Holdings:** 60,971 books; 6126 bound periodical volumes; 685 titles on microfiche; 50 VF drawers. **Subscriptions:** 404 journals and other serials. **Services:** Interlibrary loan; copying; library open to the public. **Automated Operations:** Computerized cataloging. **Networks/Consortia:** Member of MINITEX.

★14329★
TRINITY CHURCH - PARISH ARCHIVES (Rel-Phil, Hist)
74 Trinity Place Phone: (212)602-0848
New York, NY 10006 Phyllis Barr, Archv./Rec.Mgr./Cur.
Founded: 1980. **Staff:** Prof 1; Other 5. **Subjects:** Parish and diocesan history, New York City history, U.S. history. **Holdings:** 1000 books; 2500 linear feet of archival records; 10 cubic feet of microfilm. **Subscriptions:** 12 journals and other serials. **Services:** Copying; education programs; archives open to the public with restrictions. **Computerized Information Services:** MARCON.

★14330★
TRINITY COLLEGE - ARCHIVES (Hist)
Washington, DC 20017 Phone: (202)939-5005
Sr. Columba Mullaly, Ph.D., Archv.
Founded: 1965. **Staff:** Prof 1. **Subjects:** Trinity College archives. **Holdings:** 550 cubic feet of records, minutes, photographs, artifacts, college catalogs (1899 to present), and student yearbooks (1911-1982). **Services:** Archives open to the public with restrictions.

★14331★
TRINITY COLLEGE - WATKINSON LIBRARY (Hum)
300 Summit St. Phone: (203)527-3151
Hartford, CT 06106 Dr. Jeffrey H. Kaimowitz, Cur.
Founded: 1857. **Staff:** Prof 5; Other 2. **Subjects:** Americana (especially 19th century), American Indians, black history, U.S. Civil War, British history, folklore, witchcraft, graphic arts, history of printing, natural history, horology, philology (especially American Indian languages), early voyages and travels, maritime history. **Special Collections:** Incunabula and other early printed books; private press books (especially Ashendene Press); English and American first editions (especially Frost, E.A. Robinson, Walter Scott); 18th and 19th century English and American periodicals; ornithology (6000 volumes); Barnard Collection of early American school books; manuscripts of Charles Dudley Warner, Frost, E.A. Robinson, Walter Scott, Henry Barnard, Sibour, Nathan Allen, Watkinson family, Hartford families, and other historical and literary figures; American music (including jazz and blues and 18th and 19th century religious and secular works in printed and manuscript form; 1100 song sheets; 26,000 pieces of sheet music). **Holdings:** 165,000 books and bound periodical volumes; atlases; 500 maps; printed ephemera including 100 indexed scrapbooks, advertisements, fashion plates, music and theater programs, and valentines. **Subscriptions:** 40 journals and other serials. **Services:** Copying; library open to the public for reference use only. **Automated Operations:** Computerized cataloging. **Computerized Information Services:** OCLC. **Networks/Consortia:** Member of NELINET. **Publications:** Bibliographies,

irregular. **Special Catalogs:** Exhibition catalogs. **Staff:** Margaret F. Sax, Assoc.Cur.; Karen B. Clarke, Asst.Cur., Ornithology.

★14332★
TRINITY COUNTY LAW LIBRARY (Law)
Courthouse
101 Court St.
Box 1188 Phone: (916)623-1201
Weaverville, CA 96093 Carol Rose, Sec.
Subjects: Law. **Holdings:** 3326 volumes. **Services:** Library open to the public.

★14333★
TRINITY EPISCOPAL CHURCH - ASHTON LIBRARY (Rel-Phil)
128 W. Hardin St. Phone: (419)422-3214
Findlay, OH 45840 Kathryn J. Gambell, Libn.
Staff: 1. **Subjects:** Christianity, Episcopal Church. **Holdings:** 650 books. **Services:** Library

★14334★
TRINITY EPISCOPAL CHURCH - LIBRARY (Rel-Phil)
1500 State St. Phone: (805)965-7419
Santa Barbara, CA 93101 Liese Fajardo, Libn.
Staff: Prof 2; Other 10. **Subjects:** Religion. **Holdings:** 2450 books. **Services:** Library open to the public.

★14335★
TRINITY EVANGELICAL DIVINITY SCHOOL - ROLFING MEMORIAL LIBRARY (Rel-Phil)
2065 Half Day Rd. Phone: (312)945-8800
Deerfield, IL 60015 Dr. Brewster Porcella, Libn.
Staff: Prof 4; Other 17. **Subjects:** Biblical studies, evangelicalism and fundamentalism, theology, Christian education, church history. **Special Collections:** Evangelical Free Church of America Archives (books; periodicals; 8 VF drawers); Trinity Evangelical Divinity School Archives. **Holdings:** 107,512 books; 21,288 bound periodical volumes; 21,715 microfiche; 4862 reels of microfilm. **Subscriptions:** 1240 journals and other serials; 5 newspapers. **Services:** Interlibrary loan; copying; library open to the public. **Automated Operations:** Computerized cataloging. **Computerized Information Services:** OCLC. **Networks/Consortia:** Member of ILLINET, North Suburban Library System (NSLS), Association of Chicago Theological Schools. **Staff:** Keith Wells, Ref.Libn.; Jacquelyn Allen, Cat.; Debe Gordon, Adm.Assoc.; Cheryl Felmlee, Acq.; Eleanor Warner, ILL.

★14336★
TRINITY LUTHERAN CHURCH - LIBRARY (Rel-Phil)
210 S. 7th St.
Box 188 Phone: (218)236-1333
Moorhead, MN 56560 Rodney Erickson, Libn.
Founded: 1959. **Staff:** Prof 3; Other 4. **Subjects:** Biblical studies, personal growth, doctrine, missions, church history. **Special Collections:** Interpreters Bible and Dictionary. **Holdings:** 4226 books. **Services:** Library open to the public.

★14337★
TRINITY LUTHERAN CHURCH - LIBRARY (Rel-Phil)
2802 Belvedere Dr. Phone: (406)656-1021
Billings, MT 59102 Betty Koch
Founded: 1960. **Staff:** 1. **Subjects:** Bible, secular history. **Holdings:** Figures not available.

★14338★
TRINITY LUTHERAN CHURCH - LIBRARY (Rel-Phil)
1904 Winnebago St. Phone: (608)257-6781
Madison, WI 53704 Sharon Kenyon, Libn.
Founded: 1946. **Staff:** 5. **Subjects:** Religion, home and family, missions, juvenile and adult literature. **Special Collections:** Bible Study Aids (600). **Holdings:** 4800 books; 2 VF drawers of clippings; 80 pamphlets and tapes. **Subscriptions:** Interlibrary loan; copying; library open to area residents.

★14339★
TRINITY LUTHERAN CHURCH - LIBRARY & MEDIA CENTER (Rel-Phil)
5th & Chestnut Sts.
Box 231 Phone: (215)257-5801
Perkasie, PA 18944 Charles Snyder, Libn.
Staff: Prof 3; Other 5. **Subjects:** Bible, church history, prayer, mission and ministry, Lutheran Christian education. **Holdings:** 6000 books; 1000 AV programs. **Subscriptions:** 50 journals and other serials. **Services:** Interlibrary loan; copying; library open to the public.

★14340★
TRINITY LUTHERAN HOSPITAL - FLORENCE L. NELSON MEMORIAL LIBRARY (Med)
3030 Baltimore Phone: (816)753-4600
Kansas City, MO 64108 Cami L. Loucks, Dir.
Founded: 1970. **Staff:** Prof 2; Other 2. **Subjects:** Clinical medicine, preclinical medicine, nursing, hospital administration. **Special Collections:** Nelson Local History Collection (30 volumes); archival collection; media contacts. **Holdings:** 3500 books; 2500 bound periodical volumes; 12 VF drawers of pamphlets; 800 reels of microfilm; 180 filmstrips; 4000 slides; 450 audio cassettes; 10 16mm films; 450 video cassettes. **Subscriptions:** 425 journals and other serials; 8 newspapers. **Services:** Interlibrary loan; copying; library open to the public for reference use only. **Automated Operations:** Computerized cataloging. **Computerized Information Services:** MEDLINE, BRS Information Technologies, DIALOG Information Services; MEDNET (electronic mail service). **Networks/Consortia:** Member of Kansas City Library Network, Inc. (KCLN), Kansas City Metropolitan Library Network (KCMLN). **Publications:** Medical Library Informat, bimonthly - for internal distribution only. **Special Catalogs:** AV union list; serials union list. **Staff:** Kimberly A. Carter, Asst.Libn.; Paul Hagemaster, Media Techn..

★14341★
TRINITY LUTHERAN SEMINARY - HAMMA LIBRARY (Rel-Phil)
2199 E. Main St. Phone: (614)236-7116
Columbus, OH 43209 Donald L. Huber, Libn.
Founded: 1830. **Staff:** Prof 3; Other 3. **Subjects:** Theology. **Special Collections:** Hymnals; catechisms. **Holdings:** 95,000 books; 7500 bound periodical volumes. **Subscriptions:** 625 journals and other serials. **Services:** Interlibrary loan; copying; library open to the public for reference use only. **Automated Operations:** Computerized cataloging. **Networks/Consortia:** Member of OHIONET. **Staff:** Richard H. Mintel, Assoc.Libn.; Sucile Mellor, Asst.Libn..

★14342★
TRINITY MEDICAL CENTER - ANGUS L. CAMERON MEDICAL LIBRARY (Med)
Trinity Professional Bldg.
20 Burdick Expwy. Phone: (701)857-5435
Minot, ND 58701 Frances E. Cockrum, NW Campus Libn.
Founded: 1928. **Staff:** Prof 1. **Subjects:** Medicine, nursing. **Holdings:** 3000 books; 13.000 bound periodical volumes; 2000 AV programs. **Subscriptions:** 150 journals and other serials. **Services:** Interlibrary loan; copying; SDI; library open to the public for reference use only. **Computerized Information Services:** MEDLINE; EasyLink (electronic mail service). Performs searches on fee basis. **Networks/Consortia:** Member of Greater Midwest Regional Medical Library Network, Northwest Area Health Education Center Consortium. **Remarks:** This is the Northwest Campus Library of the University of North Dakota School of Medicine.

★14343★
TRINITY MEMORIAL HOSPITAL - LIBRARY (Med)
5900 S. Lake Dr. Phone: (414)769-9000
Cudahy, WI 53110 Mrs. Pat Cameron, Libn.
Founded: 1967. **Subjects:** Medicine, nursing. **Holdings:** 1050 books; 2100 bound periodical volumes; 8 VF drawers of pamphlets; Audio-Digest tapes; 100 slides. **Subscriptions:** 140 journals and other serials. **Services:** Interlibrary loan; copying; library open to the public for reference use only. **Computerized Information Services:** MEDLINE, BRS Information Technologies. **Networks/Consortia:** Member of Southeastern Wisconsin Health Science Library Consortium (SWHSL). **Publications:** Hospital Library Newsletter.

★14344★
TRINITY PRESBYTERIAN CHURCH - NORMAN E. HJORTH MEMORIAL LIBRARY (Rel-Phil)
Rte. 70 & W. Gate Dr. Phone: (609)428-2050
Cherry Hill, NJ 08034 Bernice R. Ahlquist, Chm., Lib.Comm.
Founded: 1961. **Staff:** Prof 1; Other 5. **Subjects:** Christian life and education, Bible study. **Holdings:** 2500 books; 25 phonograph records. **Services:** Library open to congregation members.

★14345★
TRINITY UNITED CHURCH OF CHRIST - EDITH L. STOCK MEMORIAL LIBRARY (Rel-Phil)
4700 S. Grand Blvd. Phone: (314)352-6645
St. Louis, MO 63111 Jean A. Allison, Chm., Lib.Comm.
Founded: 1960. **Subjects:** Religion. **Holdings:** 2500 books; 60 phonograph records; 125 filmstrips. **Services:** Library open to the public.

★14346★
TRINITY UNITED METHODIST CHURCH - LIBRARY (Rel-Phil)
2715 E. Jackson Blvd. Phone: (219)294-7602
Elkhart, IN 46514 Jodie Trimmer, Libn.
Staff: 1. **Subjects:** History of Methodism, United Methodist missions, religious study, social problems, devotions, United Methodist women. **Holdings:** 3900 books. **Services:** Library open to the public for reference use only.

★14347★
TRINITY UNITED METHODIST CHURCH - LIBRARY (Rel-Phil)
1920 N. 25th St. Phone: (817)754-1416
Waco, TX 76707 Mrs. R.L. Roberts, Jr., Libn.
Staff: Prof 1. **Subjects:** Religion, Bible, Christian doctrine, Jesus, devotional literature, religious art, worship, missions, religious education and leadership, career opportunities, evangelism, Methodism, social sciences, applied science, literature, history, travel, geography, biography. **Holdings:** 2000 books; hymnals; sheet music; conference and district reports; filmstrips; pamphlets; slides; AV maps. **Services:** Interlibrary loan; library not open to the public.

★14348★
TRINITY UNITED PRESBYTERIAN CHURCH - LIBRARY (Rel-Phil)
13922 Prospect Ave. Phone: (714)544-7850
Santa Ana, CA 92705 Patricia A. Veeh, Hd.Libn.
Founded: 1955. **Staff:** Prof 1; Other 6. **Subjects:** Bible, theology, psychology, church history, social concerns, missions, education, religions. **Special Collections:** Children's Library (2000 volumes). **Holdings:** 7500 books; 400 cassettes. **Subscriptions:** 25 journals and other serials. **Services:** Library open to the public with restrictions.

★14349★
TRINITY UNIVERSITY - ELIZABETH COATES MADDUX LIBRARY - SPECIAL COLLECTIONS (Soc Sci, Hum)
715 Stadium Dr.
Box 56 Phone: (512)736-7355
San Antonio, TX 78284 Katherine D. Pettit, Hd., Dept. of Archv./Spec.Coll
Founded: 1869. **Special Collections:** Beretta Texana Collection (includes Encino Press Collection and Nicholson Collection); Mr. and Mrs. Walter F. Brown Rare Book Collection; J.F. Buenz Collection; Paul A. Campbell International Library of Man and Space; Sir Henry Hardman Pamphlet Collection; Hilton Latin American Collection; George P. Isbell Collection of Works by and about Logan Pearsall Smith; Helen Miller Jones Collection of American Literature; Pola Negri Collection of World Literature and the Theatre; Malcolm Lowry Collection; Jim Maloney Aerospace Collection; C.W. Miller Collection of Manuscripts, Incunabula and Early Printed Books; Pat Ireland Nixon Texana Collection; Something Else Press/Avant-Garde Poetry Collection; Albert Steves, III, Collection of Works by and about Sir Winston Churchill; Decherd Turner Collection of William Morris' Kelmscott Press Editions; Trinity University Archives; U.S. and selected Texas Government document depository (total 200,000 items). **Services:** Interlibrary loan; copying. **Computerized Information Services:** DIALOG Information Services, BRS Information Technologies, OCLC, STN International, MARCIVE, Inc., LIBS 100 System. **Networks/Consortia:** Member of AMIGOS Bibliographic Council, Inc., Council of Research & Academic Libraries (CORAL).

★14350★
TRIODYNE CONSULTING ENGINEERS AND SCIENTISTS - SAFETY INFORMATION CENTER (Sci-Engr)
5950 W. Touhy Ave. Phone: (312)677-4730
Niles, IL 60648 Beth A. Hamilton, Sr.Info.Sci.
Founded: 1979. **Staff:** Prof 5; Other 2. **Subjects:** Engineering - forensic, mechanical, automotive, civil; industrial safety; chemistry; materials science. **Holdings:** 6650 books; 300 VF drawers of technical reports and patents; 143 VF drawers of manufacturers' literature; 45 VF drawers of engineering standards and specifications; 14 VF drawers of catalogs. **Subscriptions:** 212 journals and other serials. **Services:** Interlibrary loan; copying; SDI; center open to the public. **Automated Operations:** Computerized cataloging and acquisitions. **Computerized Information Services:** Pergamon ORBIT InfoLine, Inc., OCLC, DIALOG Information Services, BRS Information Technologies; POST, SAFE (internal databases). Performs searches on fee basis. **Networks/Consortia:** Member of ILLINET, North Suburban Library System (NSLS). **Special Indexes:** Permuted Index of Bibliographies on File (computer). **Remarks:** Jointly maintained with Institute for Advanced Safety Studies. **Staff:** Shirley W. Ruttenberg, Info.Anl.; Cheryl A. Hansen, Engr.Ref.Libn.; Meredith L. Hamilton, Engr.Ref.Libn.; Kimberly Last, Tech.Serv.Libn.; Norene Kramer, Acq.; Jackie Schwartz, Circ..

TRIPLER ARMY MEDICAL CENTER
See: U.S. Army Hospitals (14837)

★14351★
TRITON BIOSCIENCES INC. - LIBRARY (Biol Sci)
1501 Harbor Bay Pkwy. Phone: (415)769-5216
Alameda, CA 94501 Margaret N. Burnett, Supv., Lib. & Info.Serv.
Founded: 1984. **Staff:** Prof 1; Other 1. **Subjects:** Molecular biology, immunology, biochemistry, virology, genetics. **Holdings:** 900 books; 150 bound periodical volumes. **Subscriptions:** 234 journals and other serials. **Services:** Interlibrary loan; copying; SDI; library open to the public by appointment. **Computerized Information Services:** DIALOG Information Services, NLM, Mead Data Central, Data-Star, STN International, Pergamon ORBIT InfoLine, Inc., FYI News, OCLC; DIALMAIL (electronic mail service).

★14352★
TRITON MUSEUM OF ART - DRS. BEN AND A. JESS SHENSON LIBRARY (Art)
1505 Warburton Ave. Phone: (408)247-3754
Santa Clara, CA 95050 Bill Atkins, Dir.
Founded: 1965. **Subjects:** 19th and 20th century American art. **Special Collections:** Slide library of works of art in museum collection (400 slides). **Holdings:** 200 books; 300 exhibition catalogs and periodicals; 300 art newspapers; 300 art periodicals, 1919-1950; 12 volumes of news releases on Triton events. **Subscriptions:** 14 journals and other serials. **Services:** Library open to the public with restrictions.

TROLLEY PARK
See: Oregon Electric Railway Historical Society, Inc. (10888)

★14353★
TROTTING HORSE MUSEUM - PETER D. HAUGHTON MEMORIAL LIBRARY (Rec)
240 Main St. Phone: (914)294-6330
Goshen, NY 10924 Philip A. Pines, Dir.
Founded: 1951. **Staff:** Prof 4. **Subjects:** History of standard bred horses, history of harness racing, training horses, horses in literature, veterinary medicine. **Holdings:** 400 books; 200 bound periodical volumes; 4400 record books, sale catalogs, and racing records; videotapes; motion picture films. **Services:** Library open to the public with permission. **Automated Operations:** Computerized cataloging and acquisitions. **Computerized Information Services:** Internal database. **Special Catalogs:** Catalog of Books Available (online).

HARRY M. TROWBRIDGE RESEARCH LIBRARY
See: Wyandotte County Historical Society and Museum (18080)

★14354★
TROY PUBLIC LIBRARY - SPECIAL COLLECTIONS (Hist)
510 W. Big Beaver Rd. Phone: (313)524-3545
Troy, MI 48084 CoraEllen DeVinney, Dir.
Founded: 1963. **Special Collections:** White House Memorabilia; Fran Teasdale Collection (Civil War history); depository for Oakland County Genealogical Society material. **Services:** Interlibrary loan; copying; collections open to the public with restrictions. **Automated Operations:** Computerized public access catalog and circulation. **Networks/Consortia:** Member of Library Cooperative of Macomb (LCM). Inprint, quarterly; FYI, monthly. **Staff:** Sandra Arden, Asst.Dir..

★14355★
TROY TIMES RECORD - LIBRARY (Publ)
501 Broadway Phone: (518)272-2000
Troy, NY 12181 Susan A. Ness, Libn.
Staff: Prof 1; Other 1. **Subjects:** Newspaper reference topics. **Holdings:** 100 books; newspapers, 1884 to present, on microfilm; clippings. **Services:** Library not open to the public. **Special Indexes:** Index of clippings, 1977 to present.

★14356★
TRUDEAU INSTITUTE IMMUNOBIOLOGICAL RESEARCH LABORATORIES - LIBRARY (Med)
Algonquin Ave.
Box 59 Phone: (518)891-3080
Saranac Lake, NY 12983 Helen Jarvis, Libn.
Founded: 1900. **Staff:** 1. **Subjects:** Immunobiological research. **Holdings:** 13,000 books and bound periodical volumes. **Subscriptions:** 120 journals and other serials. **Services:** Interlibrary loan; copying; library open to the public with permission. **Publications:** Trudeau Institute Annual Report.

★14357★
TRUE VINE MISSIONARY BAPTIST CHURCH - LIBRARY (Rel-Phil)
831 Broadway Ave.
Box 1051 Phone: (318)445-6730
Alexandria, LA 71302 Hattie Shorter, Libn.
Founded: 1947. **Staff:** Prof 3; Other 5. **Subjects:** Religion - philosophy, history, doctrine. **Holdings:** 2000 books; AV programs. **Services:** Interlibrary loan; library open to other churches and the local community on a limited basis.

TRUE WEST ARCHIVES
See: University of Texas, Austin - Barker Texas History Center (16916)

GEORGE W. TRUETT MEMORIAL LIBRARY
See: First Baptist Church of Dallas - First Baptist Academy (5047)

HARRY S TRUMAN LIBRARY
See: U.S. Presidential Libraries (15484)

★14358★
TRUMBULL MEMORIAL HOSPITAL - SCHOOL OF NURSING LIBRARY (Med)
1350 East Market St. Phone: (216)841-9371
Warren, OH 44484 Dorothy Stambaugh, Libn.
Staff: Prof 1. **Subjects:** Nursing. **Holdings:** 3326 books; 169 bound periodical volumes; 15 VF drawers of pamphlets and other items. **Subscriptions:** 113 journals and other serials. **Services:** Interlibrary loan; copying; library open to the public for reference use only. **Networks/Consortia:** Member of Greater Midwest Regional Medical Library Network, NEOUCOM Council Associated Hospital Librarians. **Publications:** List of New Acquisitions, bimonthly - for internal distribution only.

★14359★
TRUMBULL MEMORIAL HOSPITAL - WEAN MEDICAL LIBRARY (Med)
1350 E. Market St. Phone: (216)841-9379
Warren, OH 44482 Bridget Lyden, Med.Libn.
Staff: Prof 1. **Subjects:** Medicine and allied health sciences. **Holdings:** 1441 books; 3439 bound periodical volumes. **Subscriptions:** 205 journals and other serials. **Services:** Interlibrary loan; copying; library open to college students. **Computerized Information Services:** MEDLINE. **Networks/Consortia:** Member of NEOUCOM Council Associated Hospital Librarians. **Publications:** Wean Library News, bimonthly - to medical staff and dental service.

★14360★
TRUNKLINE GAS COMPANY - EMPLOYEE RESOURCE CENTER
Box 1642
Houston, TX 77001
Defunct

SOJOURNER TRUTH LIBRARY
See: SUNY - College at New Paltz (13770)

SOJOURNER TRUTH ROOM
See: Prince George's County Memorial Library System (11565)

SOJOURNER TRUTH WOMEN'S RESOURCE LIBRARY
See: Women's Resource and Action Center (18000)

TRUXTUN-DECATUR NAVAL MUSEUM LIBRARY
See: U.S. Navy - Department Library (15369)

TRW, INC. - ELECTROMAGNETIC SYSTEMS LABORATORIES
See: ESL/Subsidiary of TRW, Inc. (4796)

★14361★
TRW, INC. - ELECTRONIC COMPONENTS - RESEARCH & DEVELOPMENT LIBRARY
401 N. Broad St.
Philadelphia, PA 19108
Defunct

★14362★
TRW, INC. - FEDERAL SYSTEMS GROUP - TECHNICAL LIBRARY (Sci-Engr)
Box 10400 Phone: (703)734-6243
Fairfax, VA 22031 Jill C. Mercury, Lib.Mgr.
Founded: 1965. **Staff:** Prof 1; Other 2. **Subjects:** Underwater acoustics, systems engineering, sonar and radar systems. **Holdings:** 5000 books and technical reports. **Subscriptions:** 76 journals and other serials. **Services:** Interlibrary loan; library open to the public by arrangement. **Computerized Information Services:** DIALOG Information Services, DTIC. **Networks/Consortia:** Member of Interlibrary Users Association (IUA). **Remarks:** Library located at 7600 Colshire Dr., McLean, VA 22102.

★14363★
TRW, INC. - INFORMATION CENTER/GOVERNMENT RELATIONS (Soc Sci)
1000 Wilson Blvd., Suite 2700 Phone: (703)276-5016
Arlington, VA 22209 Kathleen Galiher Ott, Mgr.
Founded: 1973. **Staff:** Prof 1; Other 1. **Subjects:** Congressional legislation, public policy, international affairs. **Special Collections:** Company photo catalog. **Holdings:** 1000 books. **Subscriptions:** 32 journals and other serials. **Services:** Interlibrary loan; copying; center not open to the public. **Computerized Information Services:** Mead Data Central, LEXIS, Washington Alert Service. **Publications:** Information Center Dataline, bimonthly - for internal distribution only.

★14364★
TRW, INC. - OPERATIONS & SUPPORT GROUP - SPACE & DEFENSE SECTOR - TECHNICAL INFORMATION CENTER (Sci-Engr, Comp Sci)
One Space Park, Bldg. S., Rm. 1930 Phone: (213)812-4194
Redondo Beach, CA 90278 Ann W. Ellington, Mgr.
Founded: 1954. **Staff:** Prof 9; Other 14. **Subjects:** Defense, space systems, electronics, energy, computer technology. **Special Collections:** Records Retention Center; American Institute of Aeronautics and Astronautics (AIAA) papers; SAE papers; NASA reports and microfiche. **Holdings:** 36,000 books; 9000 bound periodical volumes; 155,000 technical documents; 377,500 microfiche of documents. **Subscriptions:** 700 journals and other serials; 10 newspapers. **Services:** Interlibrary loan; center not open to the public. **Computerized Information Services:** BRS Information Technologies, DTIC, NASA/RECON, DIALOG Information Services, STN International, Pergamon ORBIT InfoLine, Inc., Mead Data Central. **Remarks:** An alternate telephone number is 812-4191. **Staff:** Gayle Berry, Ref.Supv.; Barbara Miyamoto, Supv.; Jerry Cao, Sys.Adm.; William Gammon; Hisao Matsumiya; Jeannine Marshall.

TRYON LIBRARY
See: University of Pittsburgh - Pymatuning Laboratory of Ecology (16777)

TRYON PALACE RESTORATION COMPLEX
See: North Carolina State Department of Cultural Resources (10311)

★14365★
TU ELECTRIC - LIBRARY (Energy, Bus-Fin)
Box 660268 Phone: (214)954-5966
Dallas, TX 75266 Ann S. Midgett, Corp.Libn.
Founded: 1983. **Staff:** Prof 1; Other 1. **Subjects:** Electrical engineering, energy industry, business administration, power transmission and distribution, finance, economics. **Special Collections:** Electric Power Research Institute reports; utility company annual reports. **Holdings:** 7000 books; 10 drawers of microfiche. **Subscriptions:** 425 journals and other serials; 8 newspapers. **Services:** Interlibrary loan; library not open to the public. **Automated Operations:** Computerized cataloging. **Computerized Information Services:** WILSONLINE, DataTimes, DIALOG Information Services; Utility Data Institute (UDI; electronic mail service). **Formerly:** Texas Power & Light Company.

★14366★
TUALITY COMMUNITY HOSPITAL - HEALTH SCIENCES LIBRARY (Med)
335 S.E. 8th Ave. Phone: (503)681-1121
Hillsboro, OR 97123 Natalie Zimmerman, Med.Libn.
Founded: 1980. **Staff:** Prof 1. **Subjects:** Clinical medicine, pharmacology, nursing, therapeutics, cardiovascular medicine. **Holdings:** 460 books; 109 bound periodical volumes. **Subscriptions:** 175 journals and other serials. **Services:** Interlibrary loan; copying; SDI; library open to local health professionals. **Computerized Information Services:** MEDLINE, DIALOG Information Services; OnTyme Electronic Message Network Service (electronic mail service). **Networks/Consortia:** Member of Oregon Health Information Network (OHIN), Washington County Cooperative Library Services (WCCLS), Portland Area Health Sciences Librarians, Oregon Health Sciences Libraries Association (OHSLA).

TUBISTS UNIVERSAL BROTHERHOOD ASSOCIATION (TUBA) RESOURCE LIBRARY
See: Ball State University - Music Library (1260)

TUCK MEMORIAL MUSEUM
See: Meeting House Green Memorial and Historical Association, Inc. (8629)

GERALD TUCKER MEMORIAL MEDICAL LIBRARY
See: National Jewish Center for Immunology and Respiratory Medicine (9717)

TUCKER LIBRARY OF THE HISTORY OF MEDICINE
See: University of Cincinnati - Medical Center Information and Communications - Historical, Archival and Museum Services (16054)

MOLLIE SUBLETT TUCKER MEMORIAL MEDICAL LIBRARY
See: Memorial Hospital (8644)

★14367★
TUCSON CITIZEN - LIBRARY (Publ)
Box 26767 Phone: (602)573-4570
Tucson, AZ 85726 Charlotte Kenan, Libn.
Staff: Prof 1; Other 4. **Subjects:** Newspaper reference topics. **Holdings:** 600 books; Tucson Citizen on microfilm; 1 million clippings; 1200 microfilm jackets; 20 drawers of pamphlets, photographs, negatives; clipping files. **Subscriptions:** 70 journals and other serials; 10 newspapers. **Services:** Library not open to the public. **Remarks:** Library located at 4850 S. Park Ave., Tucson, AZ 85714.

★14368★
TUCSON CITY PLANNING DEPARTMENT - LIBRARY (Plan)
Box 27210 Phone: (602)791-4234
Tucson, AZ 85726 Gloria June Crowe, Libn.
Founded: 1974. **Staff:** Prof 1. **Subjects:** Land use and development, planning, zoning, energy, environmental protection, economic development. **Special Collections:** City of Tucson planning reports, 1930 to present; local census reports, 1940 to present; zoning codes. **Holdings:** 5000 books; 150 bound periodical volumes; 300 microfiche; 3 VF drawers; slides; tapes; maps. **Subscriptions:** 72 journals and other serials. **Services:** Interlibrary loan; copying; SDI; library open to the public for reference use only. **Networks/Consortia:** Member of AMIGOS Bibliographic Council, Inc..

★14369★
TUCSON GENERAL HOSPITAL - MEDICAL LIBRARY (Med)
3838 N. Campbell Ave. Phone: (602)327-5431
Tucson, AZ 85719 Jacqueline Ford, Libn.
Founded: 1960. **Staff:** Prof 1. **Subjects:** Medicine, nursing, and allied health sciences. **Special Collections:** Osteopathic medicine; management. **Holdings:** 976 books; 122 bound periodical volumes; 296 videotapes; 210 audiotapes; 41 slide/tape sets. **Subscriptions:** 50 journals and other serials. **Services:** Interlibrary loan; copying; library open to the public. **Computerized Information Services:** MEDLINE; internal database. **Special Catalogs:** Book and AV holdings (printout).

★14370★
TUCSON MEDICAL CENTER - MEDICAL LIBRARY (Med)
Box 42195 Phone: (602)327-5461
Tucson, AZ 85733 Christee King, Mgr., Lib.Serv.
Founded: 1961. **Staff:** Prof 2; Other 1. **Subjects:** Clinical medicine and related sciences. **Holdings:** 2000 books; 10,000 bound periodical volumes; 750 AV programs. **Subscriptions:** 300 journals and other serials. **Services:** Interlibrary loan; library not open to the public. **Automated Operations:** Computerized cataloging and ILL. **Computerized Information Services:** MEDLARS, Dataderm, BRS Information Technologies; OnTyme Electronic Message Network Service, AMA/NET (electronic mail services). **Special Catalogs:** AV Catalog (book). **Staff:** Lynn Flance, Libn.; Dolores Canez, Ser..

★14371★
TUCSON MUSEUM OF ART - LIBRARY (Art)
140 N. Main Phone: (602)623-4881
Tucson, AZ 85701 Dorcas Worsley, Libn.
Founded: 1974. **Staff:** Prof 5; Other 5. **Subjects:** Art - pre-Columbian, primitive, African, other ethnic groups, Spanish-Colonial, U.S., European, Western, Oriental, contemporary. **Special Collections:** Pre-Columbian art (2000 books; 1500 pamphlets; 15,000 slides). **Holdings:** 6400 books; 700 unbound periodical volumes; 6500 slides; 3 VF drawers of local galleries and museums archives; 28 VF drawers of exhibition catalogs, newsletters, scrapbooks, minutes, and memorabilia of Tucson Museum archives, 1925 to present; 9 VF drawers of pamphlets by subject; 12 VF drawers of printed brochures, show announcements on artists; 3000 auction catalogs classified and arranged by subject; 14 VF drawers of archives on Arizona artists; 35 pamphlet boxes of publications from western states. **Subscriptions:** 36 journals and other serials. **Services:** Interlibrary loan; copying; library open to the public for reference use only. **Publications:** Brochure, 4th edition, 1984; Spanish Colonial Art: Books in the Tucson Museum of Art Library, 1985; bibliographic series. **Special Indexes:** Index to Arizona and Southwestern magazines on art; index to Arizona Artists (both on cards). **Staff:** Dorothy Siebecker, Cat.; Martha Lamont, Slide Libn.; Carol Elliott, Cat.; Elizabeth Franklin, Ser..

★14372★
TUCSON PUBLIC LIBRARY - STEINHEIMER COLLECTION OF SOUTHWESTERN CHILDREN'S LITERATURE (Hum)
200 S. 6th Ave.
Box 27470 Phone: (602)791-4393
Tucson, AZ 85701 Kris Hillier, Ch.Libn.
Staff: Prof 1; Other 1. **Subjects:** Southwestern children's literature, folklore, and nonfiction. **Holdings:** 2008 books, filmstrips, posters, teaching aids, phonograph records, activity books. **Services:** Copying; collection open to the public. **Automated Operations:** Computerized cataloging, acquisitions, and circulation.

★14373★
TUCSON PUBLIC LIBRARY - TUCSON GOVERNMENTAL REFERENCE LIBRARY (Soc Sci)
City Hall Annex
Box 27470 Phone: (602)791-4041
Tucson, AZ 85726-7470 Jo Riester, Mgr./Libn.
Founded: 1974. **Staff:** Prof 1; Other 1. **Subjects:** Local government, groundwater management, growth management, economic development, personnel. **Holdings:** 3287 books; 2200 periodical volumes; 800 local documents. **Subscriptions:** 175 journals and other serials; 8 newspapers. **Services:** Copying; SDI; library open to the public. **Automated Operations:** Computerized circulation and ILL. **Computerized Information Services:** DIALOG Information Services, LOGIN, Government Training News (GTN). Performs searches free of charge. **Publications:** GRL Update-New Arrivals, irregular - on request to other libraries.

★14374★
TUFTS UNIVERSITY - CENTER FOR THE STUDY OF DRUG DEVELOPMENT - LIBRARY (Med)
136 Harrison Ave. Phone: (617)956-0070
Boston, MA 02111 Betsy Morris, Rsrc.Assoc.
Founded: 1976. **Staff:** Prof 1. **Subjects:** Drug development and regulation, pharmaceutical industry. **Special Collections:** International drug development and regulation file (14,000 items). **Holdings:** 2000 books; 150 bound periodical volumes; 13,000 reports, manuscripts, reprints. **Subscriptions:** 20 journals and other serials. **Services:** Library open to researchers by appointment. **Computerized Information Services:** BRS Information Technologies; Drug Development File (internal database). Performs searches free of charge on internal database.

★14375★
TUFTS UNIVERSITY - FLETCHER SCHOOL OF LAW & DIPLOMACY - EDWIN GINN LIBRARY (Law, Soc Sci)
Medford, MA 02155 Phone: (617)628-5000
Natalie Schatz, Libn.
Founded: 1933. **Staff:** Prof 3; Other 7. **Subjects:** International law, world politics, economic development, foreign affairs, civilization. **Special Collections:** United Nations (80,000 microforms; 10,000 paper documents); Murrow Library (43,000 pieces of ephemera; 1600 books; 2 films;

audiotapes); Cabot papers (10,000 pieces of ephemera). **Holdings:** 93,000 books and bound periodical volumes. **Subscriptions:** 929 journals and other serials; 37 newspapers. **Services:** Interlibrary loan; copying; library open to the public. **Automated Operations:** Computerized public access catalog and circulation. **Computerized Information Services:** OCLC, DIALOG Information Services, NEXIS. **Networks/Consortia:** Member of NELINET, Boston Library Consortium.

★14376★
TUFTS UNIVERSITY - HEALTH SCIENCES LIBRARY (Med)
145 Harrison Ave. Phone: (617)956-7481
Boston, MA 02111 Elizabeth K. Eaton, Ph.D., Dir.
Founded: 1906. **Staff:** Prof 11; Other 12. **Subjects:** Medicine, dentistry, veterinary medicine, nutrition. **Special Collections:** History of Medicine. **Holdings:** 33,700 books; 67,500 bound periodical volumes; 108 audiotapes; 216 slide titles; 3223 reels of microfilm; 7027 microcards; 680 videotapes; 11 phonograph records; 7 video discs. **Subscriptions:** 1282 journals and other serials; 6 newspapers. **Services:** Interlibrary loan; copying; SDI; library open to the public by subscription. **Automated Operations:** Computerized public access catalog, cataloging, acquisitions, circulation, and ILL. **Computerized Information Services:** DIALOG Information Services, BRS Information Technologies, MEDIS, PaperChase, NLM; TAP-IN (internal database); MEDLINK, DOCLINE, OCLC (electronic mail services). Performs searches on fee basis. Contact Person: Linda VanHorn, Hd., Info.Serv., 956-6705. **Networks/Consortia:** Member of NELINET, Boston Library Consortium, Greater Northeastern Regional Medical Library Program. **Publications:** Library Guide; Brochures; New Acquisitions. **Staff:** Cora C. Ho, Assoc.Dir.; Carolyn Waite, Hd., Tech.Serv.; Frances Burke, Ser./Acq.Libn.; Judith Warnement, LRC Libn; Janet Holborow, Info.Serv.Libn.; Drusilla Raiford, Info.Serv.Libn.; Elizabeth J. Richardson, Info.Serv.Libn.; Anne Nou, Info.Serv.Libn.; Melinda Saffer-Marchand, Vet.Med.Libn.; Louise Goldstein, Circ./ Reserve Coord.; Connie Wong, ILL Coord..

★14377★
TUFTS UNIVERSITY - KNIPP PHYSICS LIBRARY (Sci-Engr, Comp Sci)
Robinson Hall, Rm. 251 Phone: (617)628-5000
Medford, MA 02155 Wayne B. Powell, Sci./Engr.Libn.
Founded: 1955. **Staff:** Prof 1. **Subjects:** High energy physics, nuclear physics, solid state physics, quantum mechanics, electricity and magnetism, general relativity, astronomy, astrophysics. **Holdings:** 6000 volumes; 135 dissertations; 1500 preprints. **Subscriptions:** 160 journals. **Services:** Interlibrary loan (through Wessell Library); library open to consortium members, others by permission. **Automated Operations:** public access catalog and circulation. **Computerized Information Services:** DIALOG Information Services, BRS Information Technologies, Pergamon ORBIT InfoLine, Inc., OCLC. **Networks/Consortia:** Member of Boston Library Consortium, NELINET. **Formerly:** Mathematics-Physics Library.

★14378★
TUFTS UNIVERSITY - MUSIC LIBRARY (Mus)
Talbot Ave. Phone: (617)381-3594
Medford, MA 02155 Brenda Chasen Goldman, Assoc.Libn., Mus.
Staff: Prof 1; Other 1. **Subjects:** Music theory and composition, musicology, ethnomusicology, music performance. **Holdings:** 13,000 books, scores, musical recordings. **Subscriptions:** 40 journals. **Services:** Interlibrary loan; copying; library open to the public by appointment. **Automated Operations:** Computerized public access catalog and circulation. **Networks/Consortia:** Member of Boston Library Consortium.

★14379★
TUFTS UNIVERSITY - RICHARD H. LUFKIN LIBRARY (Sci-Engr)
Anderson Hall Phone: (617)628-5000
Medford, MA 02155 Wayne B. Powell, Sci./Engr.Libn.
Founded: 1961. **Staff:** Prof 1; Other 1. **Subjects:** Engineering - civil, mechanical, electrical; engineering design; water resource control, mathematics. **Holdings:** 20,000 books; 24,000 bound periodical volumes; 600 dissertations; 11,000 technical reports; 4000 microforms. **Subscriptions:** 420 journals and other serials. **Services:** Interlibrary loan (through Wessell Library); copying; library open to consortium members, others by permission. **Automated Operations:** Computerized public access catalog and circulation. **Computerized Information Services:** DIALOG Information Services, BRS Information Technologies, Pergamon ORBIT InfoLine, Inc., OCLC. **Networks/Consortia:** Member of Boston Library Consortium, NELINET.

★14380★
TUFTS UNIVERSITY - ROCKWELL CHEMISTRY LIBRARY (Sci-Engr)
62 Talbot Ave. Phone: (617)628-5000
Medford, MA 02155 Wayne B. Powell, Sci./Engr.Libn.
Staff: Prof 1. **Subjects:** Chemistry, chemical engineering. **Holdings:** 6700 books; 7300 bound periodical volumes; 550 dissertations; 230 microforms. **Subscriptions:** 200 journals and other serials. **Services:** Interlibrary loan (through Wessell Library); copying; library open to consortium members, others by permission. **Automated Operations:** Computerized public access catalog and circulation. **Computerized Information Services:** DIALOG Information Services, BRS Information Technologies, Pergamon ORBIT InfoLine, Inc., OCLC. **Networks/Consortia:** Member of Boston Library Consortium, NELINET.

HAROLD B. TUKEY MEMORIAL LIBRARY
See: American Horticultural Society - Library (537)

★14381★
TULANE UNIVERSITY OF LOUISIANA - A.B. FREEMAN SCHOOL OF BUSINESS ADMINISTRATION - TURCHIN LIBRARY (Bus-Fin)
New Orleans, LA 70118 Phone: (504)865-5376
Dorothy Whittemore, Dir.
Founded: 1926. **Staff:** Prof 1; Other 3. **Subjects:** Accounting, finance, international business, marketing, behavioral analysis. **Special Collections:** Corporate financial history folders of annual reports and other documents (1000). **Holdings:** 35,500 volumes. **Subscriptions:** 500 journals and other serials. **Services:** Interlibrary loan; copying; library open to the public with restrictions. **Formerly:** Norman Mayer Library.

★14382★
TULANE UNIVERSITY OF LOUISIANA - ARCHITECTURE LIBRARY (Art, Plan)
Richardson Memorial Bldg. Phone: (504)865-5391
New Orleans, LA 70118 Frances E. Hecker, Hd.
Founded: 1948. **Staff:** 2. **Subjects:** Architecture, city planning, preservation, technology. **Holdings:** 9242 books; 928 bound periodical volumes. **Subscriptions:** 265 journals and other serials. **Services:** Interlibrary loan; copying; library open to the public.

★14383★
TULANE UNIVERSITY OF LOUISIANA - DELTA REGIONAL PRIMATE RESEARCH CENTER - SCIENCE INFORMATION SERVICE (Biol Sci, Med)
3 Rivers Rd. Phone: (504)892-2040
Covington, LA 70433 James L. Paysse, Ed.Asst.
Founded: 1963. **Staff:** 2. **Subjects:** Infectious diseases, acquired immune deficiency syndrome (AIDS), neurobiology, reproductive physiology, urology, veterinary science, immunology, parasitology, primatology. **Holdings:** 7671 books; 6896 bound periodical volumes; 5 dissertations; 126 microfiche; 23,398 reprints. **Subscriptions:** 62 journals and other serials. **Services:** Interlibrary loan; copying; SDI; service open to students, scientists, and researchers. **Automated Operations:** Computerized cataloging and ILL. **Computerized Information Services:** OCLC, MEDLINE, Louisiana Numerical Register (LNR). **Special Indexes:** Index of reprints by author.

★14384★
TULANE UNIVERSITY OF LOUISIANA - HOWARD-TILTON MEMORIAL LIBRARY - LOUISIANA COLLECTION (Hist, Art)
New Orleans, LA 70118 Phone: (504)865-5643
Gay Craft, Hd.
Staff: 3. **Subjects:** Louisiana - history and politics, art and architecture, literature, genealogy. **Holdings:** 30,700 books and bound periodical volumes; 64 VF drawers of clippings, pamphlets, and other material; 18 VF drawers of pictures, portraits; 5 cases of maps; 42 volumes of Louisiana sheet music. **Services:** Copying; collection open to the public with restrictions. **Automated Operations:** Computerized cataloging. **Computerized Information Services:** DIALOG Information Services, Pergamon ORBIT InfoLine, Inc., OCLC. **Special Indexes:** Indexes to books and periodicals, maps, sheet music (cards).

★14385★
TULANE UNIVERSITY OF LOUISIANA - LATIN AMERICAN LIBRARY (Area-Ethnic)
Howard-Tilton Memorial Library Phone: (504)865-5681
New Orleans, LA 70118 Thomas Niehaus, Dir.
Founded: 1924. **Staff:** Prof 1; Other 5. **Subjects:** Latin America - anthropology, archeology, art, history, economics, political science, sociology. **Special Collections:** Latin American Photographic Archive (15,000 photographs); Merle Greene Robertson Rubbings Collection (1400 rubbings of stone relief sculpture); William E. Gates Collections of Mexicana; Lewis Hanke Papers (18 VF drawers); France V. Scholes Collection (copies and notes of materials from the Archivo General de Indias of Seville and Archivo General de la Nacion of Mexico; 76 VF drawers); Nicolas Leon Collection; Ephraim George Squier Papers; Francisco Morazan Papers; George H. Pepper Papers on Indians of the American Southwest; Viceregal and Ecclesiastical Mexican Collection (3000 dossiers); William Walker Papers; Central American Printed Ephemera Collection; other collections relating to colonial and 19th century Mexico, Yucatan, and Chiapas. **Holdings:** 140,000 books; 125 cubic feet of manuscripts; 4000 pamphlets. **Subscriptions:** 1525 journals and other serials; 30 newspapers. **Services:** Interlibrary loan; copying; library open to the public. **Automated Operations:** Computerized cataloging and circulation. **Computerized Information Services:** DIALOG Information Services, Pergamon ORBIT InfoLine, Inc., OCLC. **Networks/Consortia:** Member of Center for Research Libraries (CRL) Consortia, SOLINET. **Publications:** Catalog of Latin American Library, 1970 (9 volumes); supplements, 1970, 1974, 1978. **Staff:** Ruth Olivera, Mss.Cat.; Martha Robertson, Rare Bks..

★14386★
TULANE UNIVERSITY OF LOUISIANA - LAW LIBRARY (Law)
School of Law Phone: (504)865-5952
New Orleans, LA 70118 David A. Combe, Libn.
Staff: Prof 10; Other 10. **Subjects:** Law - Roman, civil, maritime, comparative. **Holdings:** 340,000 volumes and microforms. **Subscriptions:** 3700 journals and other serials. **Services:** Interlibrary loan; library not open to the public. **Computerized Information Services:** DIALOG Information Services, OCLC, Pergamon ORBIT InfoLine, Inc., WESTLAW, DataTimes, ELSS (Electronic Legislative Search System), LEXIS, NEXIS. Performs searches on fee basis. Contact Person: Kathy Austin, Ref.Libn., 865-5856. **Networks/Consortia:** Member of SOLINET. **Staff:** Roy A. Lytle, Hd., Pub.Serv.; Mary McCorkle, Hd., Tech.Serv.; Katherine Nachod, Doc.Libn.; Mike Smith, Circ.Libn.; Sarah Churney, Cat.; Barbara Matthews, Cat.; Marian Drey, Cat.; Margareta Horiba, Acq.Libn..

★14387★
TULANE UNIVERSITY OF LOUISIANA - MANUSCRIPTS, RARE BOOKS, AND UNIVERSITY ARCHIVE (Rare Book, Hist)
Howard-Tilton Memorial Library Phone: (504)865-5685
New Orleans, LA 70118 Wilbur E. Meneray, Ph.D., Hd.
Founded: 1941. **Staff:** Prof 4; Other 6. **Subjects:** New Orleans and southern Louisiana history, politics, economics, religious and social history, 18th century to present; natural history; English county history; Romanov Russian history and travel; American Revolution; science fiction; 19th-20th century English language first editions. **Special Collections:** George W. Cable Collection; Favrot Family Papers (18th and early 19th century Louisiana); Charles Colcock Jones Papers (pre-Civil War minister and plantation owner in Georgia); Joseph Merrick Jones Steamboat Collection; Kuntz Collection (18th and early 19th century Louisiana); Albert Sidney and William Preston Johnston Papers; Louisiana Historical Association Collection (Civil War papers); papers of U.S. Representatives F. Edward Hebert, Dave Treen, and T. Hale Boggs, Governor Sam Jones, Mayor deLesseps S. Morrison; Political Ephemera Collection; William B. Wisdom Collections of William Faulkner and 19th and 20th century first editions; Lafcadio Hearn Collection; Colonial Americana Collection; Tulane University (theses; dissertations; 1000 titles of archival materials); Jules C. Alciatore Collections of Stendhal; Midlo Bookplate Collection; Rosel Brown Science Fiction Collection; Southern Jewish Archive. **Holdings:** 3 million manuscripts; 43,500 rare book titles. **Services:** Copying; archives open to the public with identification. **Automated Operations:** Computerized cataloging. **Computerized Information Services:** OCLC. **Networks/Consortia:** Member of SOLINET. **Publications:** Favrot Papers transcriptions. **Special Catalogs:** Catalogs of the Kuntz, Faulkner, and Hearn Collections; Favrot Library catalog; manuscript catalog; rare book catalog. **Staff:** Guillermo Nanez Falcon, Ph.D., Mss.Libn.; Sylvia V. Metzinger, Rare Bks.Libn.; Kennon Garofalo, Univ.Archv..

★14388★
TULANE UNIVERSITY OF LOUISIANA - MATHEMATICS RESEARCH LIBRARY (Sci-Engr)
Gibson Hall Phone: (504)865-5727
New Orleans, LA 70118 Dr. Terry Lawson, Prof., Math.
Founded: 1964. **Staff:** 1. **Subjects:** Graduate mathematics. **Holdings:** 11,500 books; 8500 bound periodical volumes; 133 Tulane math department dissertations. **Subscriptions:** 320 journals and other serials. **Services:** Interlibrary loan; copying; library open to the public with permission of librarian. **Publications:** Lecture Notes in Mathematics - for sale; conferences given by math department; list of lecture notes - available on request.

★14389★
TULANE UNIVERSITY OF LOUISIANA - MAXWELL MUSIC LIBRARY (Mus)
Howard-Tilton Memorial Library Phone: (504)865-5642
New Orleans, LA 70118 Robert Curtis, Ph.D., Libn.
Staff: Prof 1; Other 5. **Subjects:** Music. **Holdings:** 29,072 volumes; 16,200 phonograph records, tapes, compact discs. **Subscriptions:** 225 journals and other serials. **Services:** Interlibrary loan; copying; library open to the public for reference use only.

TULANE UNIVERSITY OF LOUISIANA - SCHOOL OF BUSINESS ADMINISTRATION - NORMAN MAYER LIBRARY
See: Tulane University of Louisiana - A.B. Freeman School of Business Administration - Turchin Library (14381)

★14390★
TULANE UNIVERSITY OF LOUISIANA - SCHOOL OF MEDICINE - RUDOLPH MATAS MEDICAL LIBRARY (Med, Biol Sci)
1430 Tulane Ave. Phone: (504)588-5155
New Orleans, LA 70112 William D. Postell, Jr., Med.Libn.
Founded: 1834. **Staff:** Prof 6; Other 8. **Subjects:** Medicine, biological sciences. **Special Collections:** Weinstein Collection (nonmedical books by and about doctors); Elizabeth Bass Collection (women in medicine). **Holdings:** 137,000 volumes. **Subscriptions:** 1200 journals and other serials. **Services:** Interlibrary loan; copying. **Computerized Information Services:** MEDLINE, DIALOG Information Services, Pergamon ORBIT InfoLine, Inc. **Networks/Consortia:** Member of TALON.

★14391★
TULANE UNIVERSITY OF LOUISIANA - SOUTHEASTERN ARCHITECTURAL ARCHIVE (Art)
7001 Freret St. Phone: (504)865-5697
New Orleans, LA 70118 William R. Cullison, Cur.
Staff: Prof 1; Other 2. **Subjects:** Architecture - general, Louisiana, Southeastern U.S. **Holdings:** 3 million items, including 200,000 architectural drawings; 15,000 photographs. **Services:** Copying; archive open to the public. **Publications:** Annual reports. **Special Catalogs:** Exhibit catalogs.

★14392★
TULANE UNIVERSITY OF LOUISIANA - WILLIAM RANSOM HOGAN JAZZ ARCHIVE (Mus)
Howard-Tilton Memorial Library Phone: (504)865-5688
New Orleans, LA 70118 Curtis D. Jerde, Cur.
Founded: 1958. **Staff:** Prof 2; Other 3. **Subjects:** Classic New Orleans jazz, with related background material and a limited amount of material relating to later developments in jazz; blues; rhythm and blues; gospel music. **Special Collections:** Nick LaRocca Collection (2644 items); Al Rose Collection (6500 items); John Robichaux Collection (7219 items); Herbert A. Otto Collection (20 tapes); Robert W. Greenwood Collection (345 items); Robert Bradley Collection (1179 items); Roger Gulbrandsen Collection (4372 items); George Blanchin Collection (920 items); Genevieve Pitot Collection (1000 items); Ted Demuth Collection (370 items); Gospel Music Collection (600 items); George Bing Collection (116 items); William Russell notes; Henry Kmen notes; Edmond Souchon Collection; Ralston Crawford Collection. **Holdings:** 2100 books; 6621 photographs; 1700 oral history tapes; 10,000 pages of oral history summaries; 37,600 phonograph records; 63 piano rolls; 24 cylinder recordings; 15,000 pieces of sheet music; 2272 magnetic tapes; 40 reels of motion picture film; 6 reels of microfilm; 21 videotapes; 25,655 miscellaneous notes, clippings, posters. **Subscriptions:** 461 journals and other serials. **Services:** Interlibrary loan; copying (copies of taped summaries and digests available); archive open to the public. **Automated Operations:** Computerized cataloging and circulation. **Computerized Information Services:** OCLC. **Publications:** List of publications - available

upon request. **Special Catalogs:** Catalog of 78 rpm recordings (card); catalog of popular music in print (computerized); name index of New Orleans musicians, past and present (card). **Staff:** Alma D. Williams, Asst. to Cur.; Bruce B. Raeburn, Assoc.Cur., Recorded Sound; Richard B. Allen, Cur., Oral Hist..

★14393★
TULARE COUNTY FREE LIBRARY - CALIFORNIA HISTORICAL RESEARCH COLLECTION - ANNIE R. MITCHELL ROOM (Hist)
200 W. Oak St. Phone: (209)733-8440
Visalia, CA 93277 Mary Anne Terstegge, Res.Rm.Libn.
Staff: 1. **Subjects:** Tulare county history, San Joaquin Valley history, Sequoia National Park, Kaweah Commonwealth Colony, Sierra Nevada Mountains. **Special Collections:** George W. Stewart Manuscript Collection on Sequoia/Kings Canyon National Parks and the California National Guard. **Holdings:** 3005 books; 29 bound periodical volumes; 39 VF drawers of pamphlets and pictures; 35 boxes. **Services:** Copying; research collection open to the public by appointment and on a limited schedule. **Networks/Consortia:** Member of San Joaquin Valley Library System (SJVLS).

★14394★
TULARE COUNTY LAW LIBRARY (Law)
County Civic Center, Rm. 1 Phone: (209)733-6395
Visalia, CA 93291 Sharon Borbon, Law Lib.Coord.
Founded: 1892. **Staff:** 1. **Subjects:** Law and related subjects. **Holdings:** 18,500 volumes. **Computerized Information Services:** WESTLAW.

★14395★
TULARE PUBLIC LIBRARY - INEZ L. HYDE MEMORIAL COLLECTION (Hist)
113 North F. St. Phone: (209)688-2001
Tulare, CA 93274 Ron Gallucci, Libn.
Subjects: Genealogy, local history. **Holdings:** 3836 volumes; 2982 reels of microfilm; 3084 titles on 16,400 microfiche. **Services:** Genealogy Room open to the public with restrictions.

ALICE TULLY LIBRARY
See: Temple University - Esther Boyer College of Music - New School Institute (13999)

★14396★
TULSA CITY-COUNTY LIBRARY SYSTEM - BUSINESS AND TECHNOLOGY DEPARTMENT (Sci-Engr, Trans, Energy, Bus-Fin)
400 Civic Center Phone: (918)592-7988
Tulsa, OK 74103 Karen S. Curtis, Dept.Hd.
Founded: 1920. **Staff:** Prof 9; Other 4. **Subjects:** Earth and petroleum sciences, energy technology, engineering, management, transportation, marketing. **Special Collections:** A.I. Levorsen Geology Collection (1600 books, serials, maps); General Land Office survey maps (18,000); C.R. Musgrave Transportation Library (700 items); local floodplain maps (50). **Holdings:** 130,000 books; 21,000 bound periodical volumes; 51,000 geologic and topographic maps; 1500 local government documents; 160,000 federal government documents; 2000 telephone and city directories; 8000 periodicals and newspapers in microform. **Subscriptions:** 770 journals and other serials; 10 newspapers. **Services:** Interlibrary loan; copying; fee-based research; department open to the public. **Automated Operations:** Computerized cataloging, acquisitions, and circulation. **Computerized Information Services:** DIALOG Information Services, BRS Information Technologies, Pergamon ORBIT InfoLine, Inc., WILSONLINE, DataTimes. **Networks/Consortia:** Member of Tulsa Area Library Cooperative (TALC), Oklahoma Telecommunications Interlibrary System (OTIS), AMIGOS Bibliographic Council, Inc.. **Publications:** INFO, bimonthly. **Remarks:** Department maintains Economic Development Information Center (EDIC). **Staff:** Robert Lieser, Libn.; Lisa Hansen, Libn.; Kathy Tappana, Libn.; Martha Gregory, EDIC Libn.; John Graham, Info. II Libn.; Mary Moore, Libn.; Sandy Hebermehl, Libn.; Robert Sears, Libn..

★14397★
TULSA COUNTY HISTORICAL SOCIETY - LIBRARY (Hist)
2501 W. Newton
Box 27303 Phone: (918)585-5520
Tulsa, OK 74149-0303 Robert Powers, Cur.
Subjects: State and local history. **Holdings:** 600 cubic feet of reminiscences of pioneers, oral history tapes, diaries, business records, public documents, manuscript maps, photographs. **Services:** Copying; library open to the public.

★14398★
TULSA COUNTY LAW LIBRARY (Law)
Tulsa County Court House, Rm. 242
500 S. Denver Phone: (918)584-0471
Tulsa, OK 74103 Rena C. Hanton, Libn.
Staff: Prof 1; Other 1. **Subjects:** Law. **Holdings:** 23,083 books and bound periodical volumes; 293 cassette tapes. **Services:** Copying; library open to the public. **Staff:** Beatrice Henderson, Asst.Libn..

TULSA MEDICAL COLLEGE
See: University of Oklahoma (16693)

★14399★
TULSA WORLD-TULSA TRIBUNE - LIBRARY DEPARTMENT (Publ)
315 S. Boulder Ave.
Box 1770 Phone: (918)581-8583
Tulsa, OK 74102 Austin Farley, Libn.
Founded: 1941. **Staff:** Prof 1; Other 8. **Subjects:** Newspaper reference topics. **Holdings:** 700 books; 220,000 file envelopes of clippings; 50,000 file envelopes of photographs; 1175 reels of microfilm. **Services:** Copying (limited); library open to the public, appointments preferred.

★14400★
TULSA ZOOLOGICAL PARK - LIBRARY (Biol Sci)
5701 E. 36th St., N. Phone: (918)835-9453
Tulsa, OK 74115 Carol Eames, Educ.Cur.
Founded: 1976. **Staff:** Prof 1. **Subjects:** Zoology, zoo animal husbandry. **Holdings:** 860 books; 1200 bound periodical volumes. **Subscriptions:** 14 journals and other serials. **Services:** Library open to members of zoo society.

TUNISON LABORATORY OF FISH NUTRITION
See: U.S. Fish & Wildlife Service (15089)

★14401★
TUOLUMNE COUNTY GENEALOGICAL SOCIETY - LIBRARY (Hist)
158 W. Bradford Ave.
Box 3956 Phone: (209)532-1317
Sonora, CA 95370 Delores Cole, Lib.Coord.
Founded: 1979. **Staff:** 6. **Subjects:** Genealogy, county and state history. **Special Collections:** Tuolumne County and central California census records, 1850-1910 (microfilm); Tuolumne County vital statistics records, 1850-1950 (microfilm); C.H. Burden burial records, 1862-1950; California pioneer file (100 microfiche); Newspapers of Early California Collection; photograph collections. **Holdings:** 700 books; 250 bound periodical volumes; 250 reels of microfilm; 300 other cataloged items, including mining, cemetery, and school records; ancestor charts. **Subscriptions:** 12 journals and other serials. **Services:** Interlibrary loan; copying; SDI; library open to the public. **Publications:** Golden Roots of the Mother Lode (newsletter). **Special Indexes:** Index to surnames being researched; index to photographs. **Remarks:** An alternate telephone number is 532-1918.

★14402★
TUOLUMNE COUNTY LAW LIBRARY (Law)
Court House
2 S. Green St. Phone: (209)533-5675
Sonora, CA 95370 Rose Engler, Law Libn.
Subjects: Law. **Holdings:** 18,000 volumes.

TURCHIN LIBRARY
See: Tulane University of Louisiana - A.B. Freeman School of Business Administration - Turchin Library (14381)

ROSALYN TURECK ARCHIVES
See: New York Public Library - Performing Arts Research Center - Rodgers & Hammerstein Archives of Recorded Sound (10082)

★14403★
TURKISH CULTURE AND INFORMATION OFFICE (Area-Ethnic)
821 United Nations Plaza Phone: (212)687-2194
New York, NY 10017 C. Kamil Muren, Dir.
Founded: 1960. **Subjects:** Travel in Turkey. **Holdings:** Films; slides; posters, brochures; maps. **Publications:** Sales Planning Guide, annual.

★14404★
TURNER, COLLIE & BRADEN, INC. - LIBRARY AND INFORMATION SERVICES (Sci-Engr, Energy)
Box 13089 Phone: (713)780-4100
Houston, TX 77219 Jean Steinhardt, Libn.
Founded: 1973. **Staff:** Prof 1, Other 1. **Subjects:** Hydraulic and sanitary engineering, water resources in Texas, transportation. **Special Collections:** Environmental Pollution and Control (2000 NTIS microfiche). **Holdings:** 10,000 books; 1500 bound periodical volumes; 2000 company reports. **Subscriptions:** 145 journals and other serials. **Services:** Interlibrary loan; copying; library open to the public by appointment. **Automated Operations:** Computerized cataloging and serials. **Computerized Information Services:** DIALOG Information Services, Pergamon ORBIT InfoLine, Inc. **Remarks:** Library located at 5757 Woodway, Houston, TX 77057.

★14405★
DON A. TURNER COUNTY LAW LIBRARY (Law)
401 N. Arrowhead Ave. Phone: (714)387-4960
San Bernardino, CA 92415-0015 Duncan C. Webb, Dir.
Founded: 1891. **Staff:** Prof 3; Other 9. **Subjects:** Law. **Holdings:** 65,874 books. **Subscriptions:** 460 journals and other serials; 5 newspapers. **Services:** Copying; library open to the public. **Automated Operations:** Computerized cataloging. **Computerized Information Services:** WESTLAW, OCLC, LIBS 100 System. Performs searches on fee basis. Contact Person: Carolyn Poston, Hd., Ref., 387-4957. **Networks/Consortia:** Member of San Bernardino, Inyo, Riverside Counties United Library Services (SIRCULS). **Staff:** Shannon H. Ng, Tech.Serv.Libn..

★14406★
DON A. TURNER COUNTY LAW LIBRARY, WEST END (Law)
8303 N. Haven Ave. Phone: (714)945-4300
Rancho Cucamonga, CA 91730-3848 Suzanne Oliver, Libn.
Staff: Prof 1; Other 1. **Subjects:** Law. **Special Collections:** California Continuing Education of the Bar Collection (117 hardbound volumes). **Holdings:** 11,296 books; 491 bound periodical volumes; 397 volumes on ultrafiche; 485 titles of program materials; 725 cassette tapes. **Subscriptions:** 30 journals and other serials. **Services:** Interlibrary loan; copying; library open to the public for reference use only. **Automated Operations:** Computerized cataloging. **Computerized Information Services:** WESTLAW, OCLC, LIBS 100 System. Performs searches on fee basis. Contact Person: Carolyn Poston, Hd., Ref., 387-4957.

J.A. TURNER PROFESSIONAL LIBRARY
See: Peel County Board of Education (11133)

TURNER MEMORIAL LIBRARY
See: Franklin Memorial Hospital (5356)

★14407★
TURNER MUSEUM - ARCHIVES (Art)
773 Downing St. Phone: (303)834-0924
Denver, CO 80218 Douglas Graham, Founder
Founded: 1966. **Staff:** Prof 1; Other 1. **Subjects:** Artists Joseph Mallord William Turner and Thomas Moran. **Special Collections:** Works by Turner and Moran. **Holdings:** 1000 books; folios; photographs; documents. **Services:** Interlibrary loan; copying. **Special Catalogs:** J.M.W. Turner catalog; Thomas Moran catalog.

TURPIN LIBRARY
See: Dallas Theological Seminary (4011)

★14408★
TURTLE BAY MUSIC SCHOOL - LIBRARY (Mus)
244 E. 52nd St. Phone: (212)753-8811
New York, NY 10022 Carmelo Ruta, Libn.
Founded: 1925. **Staff:** Prof 2; Other 6. **Subjects:** Music - piano, instrumental, chamber, popular, classical. **Holdings:** 590 books; 3414 scores and recordings. **Services:** Library open to enrolled students, faculty, and staff.

★14409★
TUSCARAWAS COUNTY GENEALOGICAL SOCIETY - LIBRARY (Hist)
Box 141
New Philadelphia, OH 44663 Doris Baker, Libn.
Staff: Prof 2; Other 23. **Subjects:** Genealogy, local history. **Special Collections:** Tuscarawas County records (55 volumes). **Holdings:** 357 books; 346 bound periodical volumes; 92 genealogical newsletters; 352 family histories; 85 cemetery records; 24 local histories; 22 city directories; 10 passenger and ship records; 39 state histories; 18 court records; 60 war records; 69 research guides; 88 church and sect histories; 259 city and county histories; 27 colonial records; 4 alien country histories; 29 land records and atlases; 25 printed census records; 27 phone books; 119 vital statistics records; 149 reels of microfilm of probate, census, war, marriage, birth, and death records. **Subscriptions:** 100 journals and other serials. **Services:** Copying; library open to the public on a limited schedule. **Publications:** Tuscarawas County Pioneer Footprints (newsletter), quarterly - to members. **Special Indexes:** List of indexes - available upon request.

★14410★
TUSCARAWAS COUNTY LAW LIBRARY ASSOCIATION (Law)
Court House Phone: (216)364-3703
New Philadelphia, OH 44663 Diana L. O'Meara, Libn.
Staff: 1. **Subjects:** Law. **Holdings:** 17,000 volumes. **Services:** Interlibrary loan; copying; library open to the public. **Computerized Information Services:** WESTLAW. Performs searches on fee basis.

★14411★
TUSCULUM COLLEGE - INSTRUCTIONAL MATERIALS CENTER (Educ)
Box 5028 Phone: (615)638-1111
Greeneville, TN 37743 Diana Wills, Supv., IMC
Founded: 1973. **Staff:** Prof 3. **Subjects:** Education - general, special, elementary, early childhood, physical; children's literature. **Holdings:** 2400 books; 300 pamphlets; 75 filmstrips; 100 educational kits; 15 phonograph records; 15 film loops; 15 cassettes; 45 puzzles; 55 tests; 90 games; 30 charts; curriculum guides. **Services:** Center open to the public. **Staff:** Dr. James T. Davis, Chm., Div. of Prof.Educ.; Dr. Carolyn Nave, Dir., Div. of Educ..

★14412★
TUSKEGEE UNIVERSITY - ARCHITECTURE LIBRARY (Art, Plan)
Tuskegee, AL 36088 Phone: (205)727-8351
Vinson E. McKenzie, Arch.Libn.
Founded: 1964. **Staff:** Prof 1; Other 6. **Subjects:** Architecture, construction, art, planning, historic preservation. **Special Collections:** Rare architectural book collection (520); African-American architects and architecture. **Holdings:** 8100 books; 525 bound periodical volumes; 89 theses; 22,678 slides; microfiche. **Subscriptions:** 125 journals and other serials. **Services:** Interlibrary loan; copying; SDI; library open to the public for reference use only. **Computerized Information Services:** Access to DIALOG Information Services. Performs searches on fee basis. Contact Person: Mrs. A.G. King, 727-8892. **Networks/Consortia:** Member of SOLINET. **Special Catalogs:** Library's Periodical Holdings (book). **Special Indexes:** Index to African-American architects and architecture collection.

★14413★
TUSKEGEE UNIVERSITY - DIVISION OF BEHAVIORAL SCIENCE RESEARCH - LIBRARY (Soc Sci)
Carnegie Hall, 4th Fl. Phone: (205)727-8575
Tuskegee, AL 36088 Dr. Paul L. Wall, Dir.
Founded: 1904. **Staff:** Prof 1; Other 3. **Subjects:** Race relations and problems of the South; student attitudes and aspirations; problems related to poverty and its alleviation; migration; informal adoption; gifted students; black oral history; patterns of individual and organizational adaptation; program evaluation; nutrition; sociocultural change; international rural development. **Holdings:** 5800 books; 400 bound journals; 14,000 pamphlets, brochures, reports. **Subscriptions:** 94 journals and other serials. **Services:** Copying; center open to the public for reference use only. **Computerized Information Services:** DIALOG Information Services. **Publications:** Papers of George Washington Carver at Tuskegee Institute, 1864-1943 (1975, on microfilm); Tuskegee Institute News Clippings File, 1899-1966 (1978, on microfilm); Census News (newsletter), quarterly. **Formerly:** Rural Development Resource Center. **Staff:** Louise E. Riley, Libn..

★14414★
TUSKEGEE UNIVERSITY - HOLLIS BURKE FRISSELL LIBRARY-ARCHIVES (Area-Ethnic, Hist)
Tuskegee, AL 36088 Phone: (205)727-8888
Daniel T. Williams, Archv.
Staff: Prof 1; Other 1. **Subjects:** African-American history, Tuskegee University history, civil rights, oral history. **Special Collections:** Washington Collection; Tuskegee University archives; Booker T. Washington papers (155 containers); George W. Carver papers (159 containers). **Holdings:** 25,000 books; 625 bound periodical volumes; 101 cabinets of Tuskegee University clipping files. **Subscriptions:** 39 journals and other serials; 19 newspapers. **Services:** Interlibrary loan; library open

to the public. **Computerized Information Services:** OCLC. **Networks/Consortia:** Member of Network of Alabama Academic Libraries (NAAL), CCLC. **Publications:** A Guide to the Special Collection and Archives of Tuskegee University (1974). **Staff:** Annie G. King, Hd.Libn..

★14415★
TUSKEGEE UNIVERSITY - SCHOOL OF ENGINEERING LIBRARY (Sci-Engr, Energy)
Tuskegee, AL 36088 Phone: (205)727-8901
Frances F. Davis, Libn.
Founded: 1962. **Staff:** Prof 1; Other 6. **Subjects:** Engineering - electrical, mechanical, chemical, aerospace. **Holdings:** 14,500 books; 3700 bound periodical volumes; 19,000 Atomic Energy Commission materials; Energy Research Abstracts and Indexes. **Subscriptions:** 205 journals and other serials. **Services:** Library open to the public with restrictions.

★14416★
TUSKEGEE UNIVERSITY - VETERINARY MEDICINE LIBRARY† (Med)
Patterson Hall Phone: (205)727-8307
Tuskegee, AL 36088 Carolyn W. Ford, Libn.
Founded: 1949. **Staff:** Prof 2; Other 3. **Subjects:** Anatomy, physiology, pathology, pharmacology, microbiology, radiology. **Special Collections:** Small and large animal medicine and surgery. **Holdings:** 13,565 volumes; 94 reels of microfilm; 447 slide programs; 478 video programs; 49 filmstrips; 20 tape programs. **Subscriptions:** 318 journals and other serials. **Services:** Interlibrary loan (fee); copying; library open to the public for reference use only. **Computerized Information Services:** DIALOG Information Services. Performs searches on fee basis. Contact Person: Gail A. Banks, Lib.Asst.. **Networks/Consortia:** Member of CCLC, Network of Alabama Academic Libraries (NAAL). **Publications:** Library Newsletter, semiannual - for internal distribution only. **Special Catalogs:** Tuskegee University School of Veterinary Medicine AV/AT Catalog of Programs. **Staff:** Dr. William E. Johnson, Dir., AV/AT Lab..

CHARLES LEAMING TUTT LIBRARY
See: Colorado College (3410)

★14417★
LYLE TUTTLE TATTOOING - TATTOO ART MUSEUM - LIBRARY (Art)
30 Seventh St. Phone: (415)864-9798
San Francisco, CA 94103 Lyle Tuttle, Dir.
Subjects: Tattooing and related arts. **Holdings:** 200 books; drawings; tattoo equipment; memorabilia. **Services:** Copying; library open to the public. **Publications:** Tattoo Historian, 2/year; Tattoo '70; Tattoo Calendar Book, annual - all for sale.

TUTWILER COLLECTION OF SOUTHERN HISTORY AND LITERATURE
See: Birmingham Public and Jefferson County Free Library - Linn-Henley Library for Southern Historical Research (1617)

★14418★
TUXEDO MEDICAL CENTER - HEALTH FACILITIES DIVISION/HAP - LIBRARY (Med)
1800 Tuxedo Ave. Phone: (313)252-1204
Detroit, MI 48206 Beth A. Salzwedel, Assoc.Libn.
Founded: 1955. **Staff:** Prof 1. **Subjects:** Medicine, nursing, alcohol, hospital administration. **Holdings:** 2010 books; 5000 bound periodical volumes; 945 audio cassettes. **Subscriptions:** 350 journals and other serials. **Services:** Interlibrary loan; copying; library open to the public for reference use only. **Automated Operations:** Computerized serials, circulation, and ILL. **Computerized Information Services:** DIALOG Information Services, VU/TEXT Information Services, BRS Information Technologies, NLM. **Networks/Consortia:** Member of Michigan Library Consortium (MLC). **Publications:** Newsletter - for internal distribution only.

TV GUIDE MICROFILM LIBRARY
See: Triangle Publications, Inc. (14325)

★14419★
TV ONTARIO - LIBRARY (Educ, Info Sci)
P.O. Box 200, Station Q Phone: (416)484-2600
Toronto, ON, Canada M4T 2T1 Ms. Rechilde Volpatti, Supv.
Founded: 1970. **Staff:** Prof 1; Other 2. **Subjects:** Educational television, television production, education, telecommunications, distance education, communications. **Holdings:** 10,500 books; TV Ontario documents, program guides, and newspaper clippings. **Subscriptions:** 160 journals and other serials. **Services:** Interlibrary loan; copying; library open to the public for reference use only. **Automated Operations:** Computerized cataloging. **Computerized Information Services:** DIALOG Information Services, BRS Information Technologies, Telesystemes Questel, Info Globe, QL Systems, MINISIS; Envoy 100 (electronic mail service). **Publications:** Journal articles, bimonthly - to staff and other libraries on request. **Remarks:** Distributes copies of its TV programs on videotape through its VIPS services to school boards, colleges, universities, and other educational institutions.

TWA
See: Trans World Airlines, Inc. (14287)

★14420★
MARK TWAIN BIRTHPLACE MUSEUM - RESEARCH LIBRARY (Hum)
Box 54 Phone: (314)565-3449
Stoutsville, MO 65283 John Cunning, Adm.
Founded: 1960. **Staff:** Prof 2. **Subjects:** Samuel L. Clemens (Mark Twain) - life and family. **Special Collections:** Manuscript used for the first British printing of The Adventures of Tom Sawyer and associated letters and documents. **Holdings:** 400 books. **Services:** Library open to the public for reference use only. **Remarks:** Maintained by Missouri State Department of Natural Resources.

★14421★
MARK TWAIN MEMORIAL - LIBRARY (Hum)
351 Farmington Ave. Phone: (203)247-0998
Hartford, CT 06105 Marianne J. Curling, Cur.
Founded: 1929. **Staff:** Prof 1. **Subjects:** Samuel L. Clemens and family. **Special Collections:** Samuel L. Clemens manuscript material, letters, clippings, pamphlets, documents. **Services:** Copying; library open to the public by appointment.

★14422★
MARK TWAIN MUSEUM - LIBRARY (Hum)
208 Hill St. Phone: (314)221-9010
Hannibal, MO 63401 Henry Sweets, Cur.
Founded: 1937. **Staff:** Prof 2; Other 3. **Subjects:** Mark Twain. **Special Collections:** Norman Rockwell paintings (15); first editions of Twain's works. **Holdings:** 400 books; 8 bound periodical volumes; booklets and pamphlets; scrapbooks of clippings; manuscript letters; 1 moving picture of Mark Twain. **Services:** Copying; library open only to special students with permission of curator. **Publications:** The Fence Painter, quarterly - by subscription; Hannibal: Mark Twain's Town. **Remarks:** Maintained by Mark Twain Home Board.

★14423★
MARK TWAIN RESEARCH FOUNDATION - LIBRARY (Hum)
Perry, MO 63462 Phone: (314)565-3570
Chester L. Davis, Exec.Sec.
Founded: 1939. **Subjects:** The life and writings of Mark Twain. **Holdings:** Figures not available. **Services:** Library open to foundation members only. **Publications:** The Twainian, bimonthly - by subscription.

★14424★
TWENTIETH CENTURY FOX FILM CORPORATION - RESEARCH LIBRARY (Art, Hist)
10201 W. Pico Blvd.
Box 900 Phone: (213)203-2782
Beverly Hills, CA 90213 Kenneth Kenyon, Hd. of Res.Dept.
Founded: 1924. **Staff:** Prof 2. **Subjects:** Architecture, house decoration, costume, travel, history, art. **Special Collections:** Wetzler and Tichy collections of World War II photographs (official U.S. and German Army photographs; 47 bound volumes). **Holdings:** 35,000 books; 5000 bound periodical volumes; 10,000 bound newspapers, pamphlets, plays; 345 VF drawers of photographs, clippings, maps; 600 research photographs bound in loose-leaf books. **Subscriptions:** 23 journals and other serials. **Services:** Interlibrary loan (fee); library not open to the public. **Special Catalogs:** Catalog of magazine articles and pictures (card). **Staff:** Carol Harrison, Res.Libn..

★14425★
TWENTIETH CENTURY FUND - LIBRARY (Soc Sci)
41 E. 70th St. Phone: (212)535-4441
New York, NY 10021 Nettie Gerduk, Libn.
Founded: 1935. **Staff:** Prof 1. **Subjects:** Economics, communications, international affairs, political science. **Holdings:** 1179 books. **Subscriptions:** 98 journals and other serials. **Services:** Interlibrary loan; library open to the public on request.

★14426★
TWENTIETH CENTURY TRENDS INSTITUTE, INC. - SOURCE LIBRARY (Soc Sci)
c/o Darien High School
Nutmeg Ln. Phone: (203)655-3981
Darien, CT 06820 George E. Emerson, Libn.
Subjects: Government, politics, economics, sociology, communications media, psychology. **Holdings:** 3194 books. **Subscriptions:** 175 journals and other serials. **Services:** Copying; library open to the public. **Special Indexes:** Articles index for subjects in library collection (card). **Staff:** Mrs. W. Cornwall, Pres..

★14427★
THE TWINS FOUNDATION - RESEARCH LIBRARY (Soc Sci)
Box 9487 Phone: (401)274-8946
Providence, RI 02940-9487 Kay Cassill, Pres.
Founded: 1983. **Staff:** Prof 1; Other 2. **Subjects:** Twins and other multiple births - research, literature, arts, mythology, history. **Special Collections:** National Twin Registry (20,000 persons). **Holdings:** Figures not available for books; bound periodical volumes; pamphlets; clippings; photographs; slides; correspondence; trivia; articles and scientific reprints. **Services:** Library not open to the public.

★14428★
TWIRLY BIRDS - LIBRARY (Trans, Hist)
Box 18029 Phone: (301)567-4407
Oxon Hill, MD 20745 John M. Slattery, Sec./Cur.
Subjects: Helicopter history. **Holdings:** Figures not available for books; 800 helicopter models. **Subscriptions:** 30 journals and other serials. **Publications:** Newsletter, 2/year - to members.

★14429★
TYLER COURIER-TIMES-TELEGRAPH - LIBRARY (Publ)
Box 2030 Phone: (214)597-8111
Tyler, TX 75710 Leoma Pratt, Libn.
Staff: Prof 1. **Subjects:** Newspaper reference topics. **Holdings:** Newspapers, December, 1910 to present, on microfilm. **Subscriptions:** 35 newspapers. **Services:** Library not open to the public.

TYLER SCHOOL OF FINE ARTS
See: Temple University - Central Library System (13995)

TYRRELL HISTORICAL LIBRARY
See: Beaumont Public Library System (1436)

★14430★
TYRRELL MUSEUM OF PALAEONTOLOGY - LIBRARY (Biol Sci, Sci-Engr)
Box 7500 Phone: (403)823-7707
Drumheller, AB, Canada T0J 0Y0 Connie L. Hall, Hd.Libn.
Founded: 1982. **Staff:** Prof 2; Other 1. **Subjects:** Paleontology, geology, palynology, comparative anatomy, museums. **Special Collections:** Vertebrate paleontology (1500 Ph.D. dissertations; 9500 reprints; 10,000 maps; 100 field notes; monographs; serials; periodicals). **Holdings:** 23,100 books; 2000 bound periodical volumes; 22 periodical titles on microform; 2000 reels of microfilm; 10,000 monographic serial titles. **Subscriptions:** 500 journals and other serials. **Services:** Interlibrary loan; copying; library open to the public for reference use only. **Automated Operations:** Computerized cataloging, serials, and document indexing. **Computerized Information Services:** DIALOG Information Services, CAN/OLE, UTLAS; internal database. **Publications:** Bibliosaurus (accession/current awareness newsletter), biweekly - for internal distribution only. **Remarks:** Maintained by Alberta Culture - Provincial Archives of Alberta.

SALLIE M. TYRRELL, M.D. MEMORIAL LIBRARY
See: St. Margaret Hospital (12574)

U

★14431★
U-HAUL INTERNATIONAL, INC. - CORPORATE LIBRARY
(Bus-Fin, Trans)
2727 N. Central Ave. Phone: (602)263-6606
Phoenix, AZ 85036 Meg Maher, Libn.
Staff: Prof 3. **Subjects:** Management, marketing, transportation, engineering, personnel, insurance, law. **Holdings:** 6600 books; 43 bound periodical volumes; 55 VF drawers of corporate archives; 70 VF drawers of internal publications; 4 boxes of microfiche. **Subscriptions:** 560 journals and other serials. **Services:** Interlibrary loan; library not open to the public. **Publications:** Information System List of Publications, quarterly - for internal distribution only. **Special Indexes:** Publication Index, quarterly - for internal distribution only.

★14432★
U.P.E.C. CULTURAL CENTER - J.A. FREITAS LIBRARY (Area-Ethnic, Hum)
1120-24 E. 14th St. Phone: (408)483-7676
San Leandro, CA 94577 Carlos Almeida, Dir.
Staff: Prof 1; Other 2. **Subjects:** Portuguese literature, history of Portuguese in California. **Holdings:** 5010 books; newspapers and historical documents. **Services:** Copying; translations of works from Portuguese to English; library open to the public.

U.S.
Filed as if spelled out United States

U.S.D.A.
Filed as if spelled out U.S. Department of Agriculture

UAW
See: United Automobile, Aerospace & Agricultural Implement Workers of America - Research Library (14511)

★14433★
UFO INFORMATION RETRIEVAL CENTER (Sci-Engr)
Points West No. 158
3131 W. Cochise Dr. Phone: (602)997-1523
Phoenix, AZ 85051 Thomas M. Olsen, Pres.
Staff: Prof 1. **Subjects:** UFO sighting reports and related topics. **Special Collections:** Computer-machine-readable text and data. **Holdings:** 151 books; 149 bound periodical volumes; 50 volumes of unbound reports; 1100 Library of Congress cards on UFO topics; 50 purported photographs of UFO; 3 volumes of lecture and symposia AV programs. **Services:** Center not open to the public; accepts written requests for information. **Computerized Information Services:** Internal databases. Performs searches on fee basis. **Publications:** The Reference for Outstanding UFO Sighting Reports, irregular - by mail order request. **Special Indexes:** Verbatim text of anecdotal reports (online); inverted index for 160 categories of reported characteristics. **Remarks:** Phone calls received 24 hours/day.

ROBERT UHLMANN MEDICAL LIBRARY
See: Menorah Medical Center (8701)

★14434★
UKRAINIAN CULTURAL AND EDUCATIONAL CENTRE - LIBRARY (Area-Ethnic)
184 Alexander Ave., E. Phone: (204)942-0218
Winnipeg, MB, Canada R3B 0L6 Tamara L. Chomenko, Libn.
Founded: 1944. **Staff:** Prof 1; Other 1. **Subjects:** Ukrainian history, literature, language, art, ethnography; Ukrainian settlement in Canada. **Special Collections:** Rare book collection (17th-19th century; 75 volumes); Koshetz Music Collection. **Holdings:** 38,000 books; 31,000 periodicals; 300 scores; 2000 slides. **Subscriptions:** 65 journals and other serials; 45 newspapers. **Services:** Interlibrary loan; copying; library open to the public for reference use only.

★14435★
UKRAINIAN ENGINEERS SOCIETY OF AMERICA - LIBRARY (Sci-Engr)
2 E. 79th St. Phone: (212)288-8660
New York, NY 10021 George Bazylevsky, Pres.
Subjects: Science and technology (in Ukrainian); development of the Ukraine. **Special Collections:** Engineering textbooks and handbooks in German and Russian; monographs, papers, reprints, theses, manuscripts authored by Ukrainian engineers and scientists in the U.S., Canada, and Germany, 1950 to present. **Holdings:** 400 volumes. **Subscriptions:** 15 journals and other serials; 5 newspapers. **Services:** Library not open to the public. **Publications:** Ukrainian Engineering News, quarterly; Bulletin, quarterly. **Remarks:** Branches of the society are located in Philadelphia, Chicago, and Detroit.

★14436★
UKRAINIAN MEDICAL ASSOCIATION OF NORTH AMERICA - UKRAINIAN MEDICAL ARCHIVES AND LIBRARY (Med)
2320 W. Chicago Ave. Phone: (312)237-2163
Chicago, IL 60622 Dr. Paul Pundy, Dir.
Staff: Prof 2. **Subjects:** Medicine. **Special Collections:** Russian Medical Encyclopedia (30 volumes); Ukrainian medical journals and books (originals; copies; microfilm); medical books and journals in English, Russian, German, and Polish. **Holdings:** 1800 books; 200 bound periodical volumes; 8 VF drawers of clippings, pamphlets, unbound reports, photograph albums. **Services:** Interlibrary loan; library open to the public with written or telephone request.

★14437★
UKRAINIAN MUSEUM-ARCHIVES, INC. (Area-Ethnic)
1202 Kenilworth Ave. Phone: (216)781-4329
Cleveland, OH 44113-4424 Stepan Malanczuk, Hd.Libn.
Founded: 1954. **Staff:** 4. **Subjects:** Ukrainian Revolution, post World War II immigration of Ukrainians, religion, linguistics. **Special Collections:** Taras Shevchenko Collection (816 volumes); publications from the Ukrainian Revolution, 1917-1921. **Holdings:** 13,500 books; 250 bound periodical volumes; 1000 unbound periodicals; archival materials in Ukrainian. **Subscriptions:** 40 journals and other serials. **Services:** Copying; archives open to the public for reference use only.

★14438★
UKRAINIAN MUSEUM OF CANADA - LIBRARY (Area-Ethnic)
7604 149th St. Phone: (403)424-1530
Edmonton, AB, Canada T5R 1A9 Mrs. J. Verchomin, Dir.
Staff: 1. **Subjects:** Ukrainian embroidery, ceramics, woodcraft, and Easter egg writing; folk art; historical costumes; composers. **Special Collections:** Ukrainian literature, history, religion, and biography. **Holdings:** 1500 books. **Subscriptions:** 120 journals and other serials. **Services:** Library open to the public by appointment.

★14439★
UKRAINIAN MUSEUM OF CANADA - LIBRARY (Area-Ethnic)
910 Spadina Crescent, E. Phone: (306)244-3800
Saskatoon, SK, Canada S7K 3H5 Irene Horhota-Ritch, Cur.
Staff: Prof 1; Other 3. **Subjects:** Art, history, literature, ethnography in Ukrainian and English. **Special Collections:** Archives. **Holdings:** 5000 volumes; 7000 slides. **Subscriptions:** 40 journals and other serials. **Services:** Copying; library open to the public by appointment. **Automated Operations:** Computerized cataloging. **Computerized Information Services:** UTLAS; UTLAS (electronic mail service). **Publications:** Ukrainian Embroidery Design; Pobut Art-Heritage Patterns; Pysanka: Icon of the Universe.

★14440★
UKRAINIAN NATIONAL FEDERATION - LIBRARY (Area-Ethnic)
297 College St.
Toronto, ON, Canada M5T 1S2 Nell Nakoneczny, Chf.Libn.
Founded: 1932. **Staff:** Prof 2. **Subjects:** Ukraine, Ukrainians. **Special Collections:** Z. Knysh Collection (organization of Ukrainian nationalists; 1000 volumes). **Holdings:** 15,000 books; 400 bound periodical volumes; 3 VF drawers. **Subscriptions:** 20 journals and other serials; 10 newspapers. **Services:** Library open to the public. **Staff:** Roma Yanchinski, Asst.Libn..

UKRAINIAN PUBLIC LIBRARY OF IVAN FRANKO
See: Ivan Franko Museum & Library Society, Inc. (5360)

★14441★
UKRAINIAN RESEARCH FOUNDATION - LIBRARY (Area-Ethnic)
6931 S. Yosemite Phone: (303)770-1220
Englewood, CO 80112 Bohdan Wynar, Pres.
Staff: Prof 1. **Subjects:** Ukrainian history and literature, economics, political science. **Holdings:** 7000 books; 2000 bound periodical volumes; manuscripts. **Subscriptions:** 150 journals and other serials; 15 newspapers. **Services:** Library not open to the public.

★14442★
EDWIN A. ULRICH MUSEUM - LIBRARY/ARCHIVES (Art)
"Wave Crest" On-The-Hudson
Albany Post Rd. Phone: (914)229-7107
Hyde Park, NY 12538 Edwin A. Ulrich, Dir./Owner
Staff: 1. **Subjects:** Art - three generations of the Waugh family of American painters. **Special Collections:** Materials related to Samuel Bell Waugh (1814-1884), Frederick Judd Waugh (1861-1940), and Coulton Waugh (1896-1973). **Holdings:** 200 books; other cataloged items. **Services:** Library open to the public.

★14443★
ULSTER COUNTY PLANNING BOARD - LIBRARY (Plan)
244 Fair St.
Box 1800 Phone: (914)331-9300
Kingston, NY 12401 Dennis Doyle, Plan.
Subjects: Planning, transportation, recreation, environmental management, energy conservation. **Holdings:** 500 books; 1000 bound periodical volumes; pamphlets; newsletters; maps. **Subscriptions:** 20 journals and other serials.

★14444★
JOHN UMSTEAD HOSPITAL - LEARNING RESOURCE CENTER (Med)
Twelfth St. Phone: (919)575-7259
Butner, NC 27509 Brenda M. Ellis, Libn.
Founded: 1979. **Staff:** 2. **Subjects:** Psychiatry, neurology, nursing, medicine, sociology, psychology, geriatrics, child psychiatry. **Holdings:** 2800 books; 3100 bound periodical volumes; 350 other cataloged items; 4 VF drawers of staff publications and reports. **Subscriptions:** 45 journals and other serials. **Services:** Interlibrary loan; copying; AV production; center open to the public. **Networks/Consortia:** Member of Resources for Health Information (REHI).

★14445★
UNCAP INTERNATIONAL, INC. - PROJECT COLLECTORS RESEARCH LIBRARY (Rec)
2613 Huron St. Phone: (213)222-2012
Los Angeles, CA 90065 James J. O'Connell, III, Cur.
Staff: 5. **Subjects:** Hobbies, history, culture. **Special Collections:** Numismatic and philatelic reference materials. **Holdings:** 6500 books; 500 bound periodical volumes; 32 books in microform; 10 slide sets; 200 periodicals and newsletters. **Services:** Library open to the public on fee basis. **Networks/Consortia:** Member of Southern California Answering Network (SCAN). **Publications:** Booklist, annual.

CAROLINE M. UNDERHILL RESEARCH LIBRARY
See: Andover Historical Society (773)

DANIEL UNDERHILL MUSIC LIBRARY
See: Swarthmore College (13827)

UNDERWOOD LAW LIBRARY
See: Southern Methodist University (13486)

★14446★
UNDERWOOD-MEMORIAL HOSPITAL - ANTHONY J.D. MARINO, M.D. MEMORIAL LIBRARY (Med)
N. Broad St. & W. Redbank Ave. Phone: (609)845-0100
Woodbury, NJ 08096 Ellen K. Tiedrich, Libn.
Founded: 1951. **Staff:** Prof 1. **Subjects:** Medicine, nursing, and allied health sciences. **Holdings:** 3500 books; 100 bound periodical volumes; 1500 reels of microfilm. **Subscriptions:** 125 journals and other serials. **Services:** Interlibrary loan; copying; library open to the public by appointment. **Computerized Information Services:** BRS Information Technologies, MEDLINE; DOCLINE (electronic mail service). Performs searches on fee basis. **Networks/Consortia:** Member of Greater Northeastern Regional Medical Library Program, Health Sciences Library Association of New Jersey, Pinelands Consortium, New Jersey Health Sciences Library Network (NJHSN), BHSL. **Remarks:** Underwood-Memorial Hospital has a teaching affiliation with Thomas Jefferson University.

★14447★
UNDERWOOD, NEUHAUS & COMPANY INC. - CORPORATE FINANCE LIBRARY (Bus-Fin)
724 Travis St.
Houston, TX 77002 Phone: (713)221-2200
Founded: 1975. **Staff:** Prof 1. **Subjects:** High technology companies, savings and loan associations. **Special Collections:** Fortune 1000, selected foreign and Southwest Companies. **Holdings:** 110 books. **Subscriptions:** 14 journals and other serials. **Services:** Library open to clients of Underwood, Neuhaus, and affiliated companies.

UNESCO - INTERGOVERNMENTAL OCEANOGRAPHIC COMMISSION - INTERNATIONAL TSUNAMI INFORMATION CENTER
See: International Tsunami Information Center (7076)

★14448★
UNEXPECTED WILDLIFE REFUGE - LIBRARY (Env-Cons)
Unexpected Rd.
Box 765
Newfield, NJ 08344 Hope Sawyer Buyukmihci, Sec.
Founded: 1968. **Staff:** 2. **Subjects:** Humane education, beavers, wildlife. **Special Collections:** Works of Grey Owl, Canadian naturalist. **Holdings:** Figures not available. **Services:** Library open to the public for reference use only by appointment. **Publications:** The Beaver Defenders, quarterly - to members and by subscription. **Also Known As:** The Beaver Defenders.

★14449★
UNI-BELL PVC PIPE ASSOCIATION - LIBRARY (Sci-Engr)
2655 Villa Creek, Suite 155 Phone: (214)243-3902
Dallas, TX 75234 Robert P. Walker, Exec.Dir.
Founded: 1971. **Subjects:** Pipe and pipe products design. **Holdings:** 1000 volumes.

UNICEF
See: U.S. Committee for UNICEF (14915)

★14450★
UNIDYNAMICS/PHOENIX, INC. - LIBRARY
Box 46100
Phoenix, AZ 85063-6100
Founded: 1963. **Subjects:** Chemistry, biology, pyrotechnics, aeronautical engineering. **Holdings:** 2000 books; 1500 technical reports; 800 patents; 400 technical abstracts. **Remarks:** Presently inactive.

★14451★
UNIDYNAMICS/ST. LOUIS, INC. - LIBRARY (Sci-Engr)
472 Paul Ave.
Box 11177 Phone: (314)522-6700
St. Louis, MO 63135 Barbara Schulik, Libn.
Staff: Prof 1. **Subjects:** Basic and applied sciences and technologies. **Holdings:** 2200 books; 4500 reports, patents, documents. **Subscriptions:** 153 journals and other serials. **Services:** Interlibrary loan; copying; library open to the public with approval of management.

★14452★
UNION OF AMERICAN HEBREW CONGREGATIONS - SYNAGOGUE ARCHITECTURAL AND ART LIBRARY (Art)
838 Fifth Ave. Phone: (212)249-0100
New York, NY 10021 Joseph C. Bernstein, Dir.
Founded: 1950. **Staff:** Prof 1; Other 1. **Subjects:** History of synagogue architecture, contemporary synagogue art and architecture, art of Jewish interest, ceremonial objects. **Holdings:** 200 books; 50 bound periodical volumes; 3000 slides; 1000 photographs. **Services:** Interlibrary loan; copying; slide rental service; library open to the public by appointment.

★14453★
UNION BANK - LIBRARY (Bus-Fin)
445 S. Figueroa St. Phone: (213)236-4040
Los Angeles, CA 90071 John D. Shea, Adm.Off.
Staff: Prof 1. **Subjects:** Economics, banking. **Holdings:** 2500 books; 75 bound periodical volumes; 52 VF drawers of economic statistics, newsletters, government documents. **Subscriptions:** 75 journals and other serials; 5 newspapers. **Services:** Interlibrary loan; library open to the public. **Computerized Information Services:** NEXIS.

★14454★
UNION BIBLE SEMINARY - LIBRARY (Rel-Phil)
434 S. Union St. Phone: (317)896-9324
Westfield, IN 46074 Steve Hickman, Academic Dean
Founded: 1951. **Subjects:** Bible, theology, Quaker history, general academic subjects. **Holdings:** 4000 volumes. **Subscriptions:** 32 journals and other serials.

★14455★
UNION CAMP CORP. - TECHNICAL INFORMATION SERVICE (Sci-Engr)
3401 Princeton Pike Phone: (609)896-1200
Lawrenceville, NJ 08648 Helen Lee, Libn.
Founded: 1963. **Staff:** Prof 1; Other 1. **Subjects:** Pulp and paper, chemistry, engineering. **Holdings:** 4000 books; 4000 bound periodical volumes. **Subscriptions:** 150 journals and other serials. **Services:** Interlibrary loan; copying; SDI; service open to the public by request. **Computerized Information Services:** Online systems.

UNION CARBIDE AGRICULTURAL PRODUCTS COMPANY, INC.
See: Rhone-Poulenc Ag Company (12034)

★14456★
UNION CARBIDE CANADA, LTD. - TECHNICAL CENTRE LIBRARY (Sci-Engr)
10555 Metropolitan Blvd., E.
C.P. 700, Sta. P.A.T. Phone: (514)640-6400
Montreal, PQ, Canada H1B 5K8 A.M. De Jesus, Libn.
Founded: 1963. **Staff:** Prof 1. **Subjects:** Chemistry, plastics technology. **Holdings:** 1400 volumes; R&D reports. **Subscriptions:** 86 journals and other serials. **Services:** Interlibrary loan; library not open to the public. **Computerized Information Services:** MEDLARS, Pergamon ORBIT InfoLine, Inc.

★14457★
UNION CARBIDE CORPORATION - BUSINESS RESEARCH & REFERENCE SERVICE (Bus-Fin)
Section N2, Old Ridgebury Rd. Phone: (203)794-5314
Danbury, CT 06817 Roger Miller, Mgr.
Staff: Prof 5; Other 2. **Subjects:** Management; marketing; medicine; health, safety, and environment; accounting; business; computers and information systems. **Special Collections:** Marketing Research reports; financial reports; government statistics. **Holdings:** 9000 books; 15 vertical files of pamphlets; 13 vertical files of statistics; 53 vertical files of financial reports. **Subscriptions:** 450 journals and other serials; 10 newspapers. **Services:** Interlibrary loan; library open to SLA and other selected library associations. **Computerized Information Services:** DIALOG Information Services, Pergamon ORBIT InfoLine, Inc., NEXIS, Telesystemes Questel, WILSONLINE, Dow Jones News/Retrieval, VU/TEXT Information Services, BRS Information Technologies, TEXTLINE, NLM.

★14458★
UNION CARBIDE CORPORATION - COATINGS SERVICE DEPARTMENT - LIBRARY (Sci-Engr)
1500 Polco St.
Box 24166 Phone: (317)240-2520
Indianapolis, IN 46224 Mary Ann Brady, Tech.Libn.
Founded: 1945. **Staff:** Prof 1; Other 1. **Subjects:** Metallurgy, mechanical engineering, advanced materials, high temperature coating technology. **Holdings:** 6700 books; 1800 bound periodical volumes. **Subscriptions:** 220 journals and other serials. **Services:** Interlibrary loan.

★14459★
UNION CARBIDE CORPORATION - ENGINEERING DEPARTMENT LIBRARY (Sci-Engr)
Box 8361
South Charleston, WV 25303 Phone: (304)747-4635
Founded: 1959. **Staff:** 2. **Subjects:** Engineering - chemical, mechanical, instrument, environmental, civil. **Holdings:** 8030 books; 815 bound periodical volumes; 48 reels of microfilm; 35 journal titles on microfilm. **Subscriptions:** 150 journals and other serials; 6 newspapers. **Services:** Interlibrary loan; copying; library open to the public with restrictions. **Publications:** Acquisition List and Book Reviews, biweekly - for internal distribution only. **Staff:** Helen Spangler, Ck..

★14460★
UNION CARBIDE CORPORATION - I.S. INFORMATION CENTER
100 Clearbrook
Saw Mill River Rd.
Tarrytown, NY 10591
Defunct. Holdings absorbed by Union Carbide Corporation - Library & Technical Information Service.

★14461★
UNION CARBIDE CORPORATION - LAW DEPARTMENT LIBRARY (Law)
Section N2, 39 Old Ridgebury Rd. Phone: (203)794-6396
Danbury, CT 06817 Carolyn A. Mariani, Mgr., Info.Res., Law Dept.
Founded: 1935. **Staff:** Prof 2; Other 1. **Subjects:** Law - antitrust, tax, patent, trademark, labor, corporation. **Holdings:** 30,000 volumes; 3 VF drawers; 7 titles in microform; Federal Register, 1970 to present, in microform. **Subscriptions:** 75 journals and other serials. **Services:** Interlibrary loan; library not open to the public. **Automated Operations:** Computerized acquisitions and serials. **Computerized Information Services:** LEXIS, WESTLAW, DIALOG Information Services. **Networks/Consortia:** Member of Southwestern Connecticut Library Council (SWLC).

★14462★
UNION CARBIDE CORPORATION - LIBRARY (Sci-Engr)
Bldg. 770
Box 8361 Phone: (304)747-5119
South Charleston, WV 25303 Alice S. Behr, Lib.Mgr.
Staff: Prof 1; Other 5. **Subjects:** Chemistry, chemical engineering, environmental sciences. **Holdings:** 100,000 books and bound periodical volumes. **Subscriptions:** 600 journals and other serials. **Services:** Interlibrary loan; copying; library open to the public with restrictions.

★14463★
UNION CARBIDE CORPORATION - LIBRARY & TECHNICAL INFORMATION SERVICE (Sci-Engr)
Tarrytown Technical Center
Old Sawmill Rd. Phone: (914)789-3703
Tarrytown, NY 10591 Joan Schechtman, Mgr.
Founded: 1971. **Staff:** Prof 3; Other 3. **Subjects:** Chemistry, chemical engineering, metals and materials, surface science, catalysis, industrial gases, physics. **Holdings:** 62,000 volumes; 200 VF drawers of patents, internal reports, vendors bulletins, and catalogs; 2800 reels of microfilm; 4000 microfiche; 5400 opaques. **Subscriptions:** 900 journals and other serials. **Services:** Interlibrary loan; library not open to the public. **Computerized Information Services:** CAS ONLINE, BRS Information Technologies, DIALOG Information Services, Pergamon ORBIT InfoLine, Inc. **Publications:** Newsletter, monthly; Union List, annual - both for internal distribution only. **Remarks:** Contains the holdings of Union Carbide Corporation - I.S. Information Center. **Staff:** Barry E. Galbraith, Tech.Info.Sci..

★14464★
UNION CARBIDE CORPORATION - LINDE DIVISION - TECHNICAL LIBRARY (Sci-Engr)
Box 44 Phone: (716)879-2031
Tonawanda, NY 14151 Sandra C. Anderson, Tech.Libn.
Founded: 1939. **Staff:** Prof 1; Other 1. **Subjects:** Engineering - cryogenic, chemical, mechanical; chemistry. **Holdings:** 8000 books; 4500 bound periodical volumes; 950 reels of microfilm. **Subscriptions:** 252 journals and other serials. **Services:** Interlibrary loan. **Networks/Consortia:** Member of Western New York Library Resources Council (WNYLRC).

★14465★
UNION CARBIDE CORPORATION - PARMA TECHNICAL CENTER - TECHNICAL INFORMATION SERVICE (Sci-Engr)
Box 6116 Phone: (216)676-2223
Cleveland, OH 44101 Linda Riffle, Mgr.
Founded: 1945. **Staff:** Prof 2; Other 3. **Subjects:** Manufactured carbon and graphite, high temperature chemistry, metallurgy. **Holdings:** 12,000 books; 15,000 bound periodical volumes; 20,000 U.S. and foreign patents; 30,000 government documents and contract reports. **Subscriptions:** 450 journals and other serials. **Services:** Interlibrary loan; SDI; service open to the public with special permission and limited access. **Automated Operations:** Computerized cataloging. **Computerized Information Services:** DIALOG Information Services, STN International, WILSONLINE, Pergamon ORBIT InfoLine, Inc.; INDOC, ACCESS (internal databases). **Publications:** Biweekly bulletin (listing of references to carbon and graphite) - for internal distribution only; bibliography of carbon and graphite technology, 1945 to present. **Special Indexes:** Literature of carbon and graphite; U.S. and foreign patent indexes. **Staff:** Mary D. Wood, Sr.Libn..

★14466★
UNION CARBIDE CORPORATION - TECHNICAL INFORMATION CENTER (Sci-Engr)
Bldg. 200
Box 670 Phone: (201)563-5730
Bound Brook, NJ 08805 Anna B. Coleman, Staff Coord.
Founded: 1957. **Staff:** Prof 4; Other 6. **Subjects:** Polymers, plastics, organic chemistry. **Holdings:** 10,000 books; 16,000 bound periodical volumes; U.S. patents on microfilm. **Subscriptions:** 600 journals and other serials. **Services:** Copying (limited); center open to the public by appointment. **Automated Operations:** Computerized cataloging and serials. **Computerized Information Services:** DIALOG Information Services, NEXIS, NLM, PLASPEC, Pergamon ORBIT InfoLine, Inc., STN International; internal database. Performs searches on fee basis. **Special Catalogs:** Serials and holdings locator (computer printout). **Special Indexes:** Literature Search Report Index (computer printout). **Staff:** Maria I.M. Lohse, Tech.Info.Spec./Patents.

★14467★
UNION CLUB - LIBRARY (Hist)
101 E. 69th St. Phone: (212)606-3413
New York, NY 10021 Helen M. Allen, Libn.
Founded: 1836. **Subjects:** New York City history. **Holdings:** Figures not available.

★14468★
UNION COLLEGE - ELLA JOHNSON CRANDALL MEMORIAL LIBRARY - SPECIAL COLLECTIONS (Rel-Phil)
3800 S. 48th St. Phone: (402)488-2331
Lincoln, NE 68506 Chloe Foutz, Lib.Dir. & Spec.Coll.
Staff: Prof 2; Other 3. **Special Collections:** Seventh-Day Adventism (early denominational books and periodicals); college archives. **Holdings:** 2600 books; 1000 bound periodical volumes; 60 VF drawers. **Services:** Interlibrary loan; copying; SDI; collections open to the public. **Automated Operations:** Computerized cataloging and circulation. **Computerized Information Services:** DIALOG Information Services; internal database. Performs searches on fee basis. Contact Person: DeForest Nesmith, Pub.Serv.Libn., ext. 403. **Networks/Consortia:** Member of NEBASE.

★14469★
UNION COLLEGE - SCHAFFER LIBRARY - SPECIAL COLLECTIONS† (Hist, Sci-Engr, Rare Book)
Schenectady, NY 12308 Phone: (518)370-6278
Ann M. Seeman, Libn.
Special Collections: Bailey Collection of North American Wit and Humor (2800 volumes); Kellert Microscopy Collection (400 volumes); rare books (2000); manuscript collections; college archives; Schenectady Archives of Science and Technology. **Services:** Interlibrary loan; copying; collections open to the public for reference use only. **Automated Operations:** Computerized cataloging, acquisitions, serials, and ILL. **Computerized Information Services:** DIALOG Information Services, OCLC, BRS Information Technologies; SINS-Serials Information System (internal database). Contact Person: David Gerhan, Hd., Info.Serv.. **Networks/Consortia:** Member of Capital District Library Council for Reference & Research Resources (CDLC). **Special Indexes:** Indexes to manuscripts in the Special Collections.

★14470★
UNION COUNTY HISTORICAL SOCIETY - JOHN B. DEANS MEMORIAL LIBRARY (Hist)
2nd & St. Louis Sts. Phone: (717)524-4461
Lewisburg, PA 17837 Gary W. Slear, Chm., Archv. & Musm.
Founded: 1963. **Staff:** 5. **Subjects:** Local history, genealogy. **Special Collections:** Oral traditions project (300 oral history tapes and transcripts; 10,000 slides and photographs). **Holdings:** 1500 books; 250 bound periodical volumes; 40 cubic feet of clippings; tax records on microfilm. **Services:** Copying; library open to the public. **Automated Operations:** Computerized cataloging and acquisitions. **Publications:** Biennial collection of manuscripts on local topics; regional studies of local crafts.

★14471★
UNION ELECTRIC COMPANY - LIBRARY (Sci-Engr, Bus-Fin)
1901 Gratiot St.
Box 149 Phone: (314)554-2913
St. Louis, MO 63166 Patricia F. Gatlin, Supv., Lib.Serv.
Founded: 1941. **Staff:** Prof 3; Other 1. **Subjects:** Engineering, nuclear and public utility regulation, financing, general business, public and private power. **Holdings:** 12,000 volumes; 15 VF drawers of annual reports; 85 VF drawers of pamphlets and scientific society papers. **Subscriptions:** 450 journals and other serials. **Services:** Interlibrary loan; copying; library open to the public by appointment. **Automated Operations:** Computerized serials. **Computerized Information Services:** DIALOG Information Services, BRS Information Technologies, WILSONLINE. **Publications:** What's New (bulletin), monthly; Library Clipping Service, daily - both for internal distribution only. **Staff:** Barbara G. Eglin-Robinson, Tech.Libn.; Alison Verbeck, Tech.Libn..

★14472★
UNION GAS, LTD. - LIBRARY SERVICE (Energy)
50 Keil Dr., N.
Box 2001 Phone: (519)352-3100
Chatham, ON, Canada N7M 5M1 Mrs. Alla Steen
Staff: Prof 1; Other 1. **Subjects:** Natural gas industry, public utility regulation, management, economics, energy, engineering. **Holdings:** 4500 books; 360 annual reports; 615 reels of microfilm; 220 microfiche. **Subscriptions:** 430 journals and other serials. **Services:** Interlibrary loan; copying; SDI; library open to the public with restrictions. **Automated Operations:** Computerized cataloging. **Computerized Information Services:** Online systems. **Publications:** Library acquisitions, monthly - for internal distribution only. **Special Indexes:** KWIC index to engineering standards.

★14473★
UNION HOSPITAL - MEDICAL LIBRARY (Med)
1000 Galloping Hill Rd. Phone: (201)687-1900
Union, NJ 07083 Aileen Z. Tannenbaum, Med.Libn.
Staff: Prof 1. **Subjects:** Medicine. **Holdings:** 800 monographs. **Subscriptions:** 121 journals and other serials. **Services:** Interlibrary loan; copying; library open to the public for reference use only. **Networks/Consortia:** Member of Cosmopolitan Biomedical Library Consortium (CBLC), Health Sciences Library Association of New Jersey, BHSL.

★14474★
UNION LEAGUE CLUB LIBRARY (Hist, Hum)
38 E. 37th St. Phone: (212)685-3800
New York, NY 10016 Jane Reed, Libn.
Founded: 1863. **Staff:** Prof 1. **Subjects:** Civil War; American history, art, biography; English literature. **Holdings:** 20,000 volumes. **Subscriptions:** 40 journals and other serials; 8 newspapers. **Services:** Library not open to the public. **Networks/Consortia:** Member of New York Metropolitan Reference and Research Library Agency (METRO). **Publications:** ULC Club Bulletin, monthly. **Special Indexes:** Index of paintings in Union League Club.

★14475★
UNION LEAGUE OF PHILADELPHIA - LIBRARY (Hist)
140 S. Broad St. Phone: (215)563-6500
Philadelphia, PA 19102 James G. Mundy, Jr., Libn.
Founded: 1862. **Staff:** Prof 1. **Subjects:** American Civil War; Lincoln; political history; Philadelphia and Pennsylvania history, biography. **Special Collections:** League archives (document cases). **Holdings:** 25,000 books. **Subscriptions:** 62 journals and other serials; 10 newspapers. **Services:** Library and archives open to researchers with proper introduction.

★14476★
UNION MEMORIAL HOSPITAL - LIBRARY & INFORMATION RESOURCES (Med)
201 E. University Pkwy. Phone: (301)554-2294
Baltimore, MD 21218 Martha Zimmerman, Dir.
Staff: Prof 2; Other 1. **Subjects:** Medicine, orthopedics. **Special Collections:** The hand (70 monographs; 17 journal subscriptions); sports medicine (50 monographs; 14 journal subscriptions). **Holdings:** 2500 books; 6600 bound periodical volumes; 1656 AV programs. **Subscriptions:** 300 journals and other serials. **Services:** Interlibrary loan; copying; SDI; literature searches; patient education; library open to health care professionals and outside users with restrictions. **Computerized Information Services:** MEDLARS, DIALOG Information Services, WILSONLINE, BRS Information Technologies; OnTyme Electronic Message Network Service, Maryland MED-SIG - Union Library (electronic mail services). **Networks/Consortia:** Member of Southeastern/Atlantic Regional Medical Library Services, Maryland Association of Health Science Librarians. **Staff:** Rena Sheffer, Clin.Ref.Libn..

★14477★
UNION MEMORIAL HOSPITAL - NURSING LIBRARY (Med)
3301 N. Calvert St. Phone: (301)554-2212
Baltimore, MD 21218 Carolyn M. Daugherty, Libn.
Founded: 1893. **Staff:** Prof 1; Other 7. **Subjects:** Nursing, medicine, sociology, psychology, life sciences. **Holdings:** 3000 books; 807 bound periodical volumes; 4 VF drawers of articles; 35 file boxes; 20 tapes; 50 cassettes. **Subscriptions:** 120 journals and other serials. **Services:**

Interlibrary loan; library not open to the public. **Publications:** Monthly Lists of Acquisitions.

★14478★
UNION NATIONAL BANK AND TRUST COMPANY - LIBRARY (Bus-Fin)
14 Main St. Phone: (215)721-2400
Souderton, PA 18964 Gladys Detweiler, Libn.
Founded: 1966. **Staff:** 1. **Subjects:** Banking, audit controls, commercial and installment lending, human resources, data processing. **Holdings:** 306 books; 295 other cataloged items; 200 tapes. **Subscriptions:** 50 journals and other serials; 7 newspapers. **Services:** Library

UNION PACIFIC CORPORATION - ROCKY MOUNTAIN ENERGY
See: Union Pacific Resources Company (14481)

★14479★
UNION PACIFIC RAILROAD COMPANY - LIBRARY (Trans, Bus-Fin)
1416 Dodge St. Phone: (402)271-4785
Omaha, NE 68179 K.E. Oyer, Hd.Libn.
Founded: 1976. **Staff:** Prof 1; Other 1. **Subjects:** Transportation, business. **Holdings:** 8500 books; 1000 annual reports. **Subscriptions:** 600 journals and other serials. **Services:** Interlibrary loan; copying; library open to the public with restrictions. **Automated Operations:** Computerized cataloging and serials. **Computerized Information Services:** DIALOG Information Services, Pergamon ORBIT InfoLine, Inc., Disclosure Information Group, NEXIS, VU/TEXT Information Services, Dow Jones News/Retrieval. **Publications:** Information Ties,

★14480★
UNION PACIFIC RESOURCES COMPANY - HOUSTON REGION LIBRARY (Energy)
1000 Louisiana, Suite 3000 Phone: (713)654-2749
Houston, TX 77002-5016 Deborah Arens, Libn.
Founded: 1984. **Staff:** Prof 1. **Subjects:** Petroleum geology, geophysical exploration, petroleum engineering. **Holdings:** 3600 books. **Subscriptions:** 48 journals and other serials. **Services:** Library not open to the public. **Automated Operations:** Computerized cataloging. **Computerized Information Services:** DIALOG Information Services, Pergamon ORBIT InfoLine, Inc. **Formerly:** Champlin Petroleum Company.

★14481★
UNION PACIFIC RESOURCES COMPANY - TECHNICAL INFORMATION CENTER (Sci-Engr)
5800 S. Quebec St. Phone: (303)721-2821
Denver, CO 80218 Rosemary R. Fair, Sci.Libn.
Founded: 1981. **Staff:** Prof 1; Other 1. **Subjects:** Geology, geophysics, engineering. **Holdings:** 12,000 volumes; **Subscriptions:** 150 journals and other serials; 50 newspapers. **Services:** Interlibrary loan; copying; center open to public at librarian's discretion. **Automated Operations:** Computerized cataloging, acquisitions, and circulation. **Computerized Information Services:** DIALOG Information Services, Pergamon ORBIT InfoLine, Inc. **Networks/Consortia:** Member of Central Colorado Library System (CCLS). **Publications:** Acquisitions, quarterly. **Formed by the merger of:** Champlin Petroleum Company and Union Pacific Corporation - Rocky Mountain Energy.

★14482★
UNION SAINT-JEAN-BAPTISTE - MALLET LIBRARY (Hist)
One Social St. Phone: (401)769-0520
Woonsocket, RI 02895-9987 Bro. Felician, S.C., Libn.
Founded: 1908. **Staff:** Prof 1. **Subjects:** Franco-American history, civilization, social life, and customs; biography; genealogy; French-Canadian civilization. **Special Collections:** Major Edmond Mallet's correspondence (600 letters). **Holdings:** 5042 books; 144 bound periodical volumes; 350 pamphlets; 30 sets of manuscript notes; 50 maps; 12 VF drawers; 33 dissertations; 17 drawers of photographs; 112 reels of microfilm; 850 French-Canadian and French phonograph records. **Services:** Library open to the public for reference use only. **Also Known As:** Bibliotheque Mallet.

★14483★
UNION TEXAS PETROLEUM CORPORATION - LIBRARY (Sci-Engr)
1330 Post Oak Rd.
Box 2120 Phone: (713)968-3282
Houston, TX 77252 Craig Wright, Supv., Lib.
Staff: Prof 1. **Subjects:** Geology, geophysics, business, engineering. **Holdings:** 4800 books. **Subscriptions:** 201 journals and other serials. **Services:** Interlibrary loan; copying; library open to the public with restrictions. **Computerized Information Services:** DIALOG Information Services, Pergamon ORBIT InfoLine, Inc.; Datatrieve (internal database).

★14484★
UNION THEOLOGICAL SEMINARY - BURKE LIBRARY (Rel-Phil)
3041 Broadway at Reinhold Niebuhr Place Phone: (212)662-7100
New York, NY 10027 Richard D. Spoor, Dir.
Founded: 1838. **Staff:** Prof 5; Other 12. **Subjects:** Bible, theology, sacred music, church history, missions, ecumenics. **Special Collections:** McAlpin Collection of British History and Theology; Van Ess Collection; sacred music collection (including hymnology); Bonhoeffer Collection; Auburn Collection; archives; Missionary Research Library Collection. **Holdings:** 565,000 volumes; 86,000 microforms; 1700 media items. **Subscriptions:** 1700 journals. **Services:** Interlibrary loan; copying; library open to the public upon application. **Computerized Information Services:** RLIN. **Networks/Consortia:** Member of New York State Interlibrary Loan Network (NYSILL), SUNY/OCLC Library Network, RLG, New York Metropolitan Reference and Research Library Agency (METRO). **Staff:** Seth E. Kasten, Hd., User Serv.; Paul A. Byrnes, Hd., Coll.Mgt.Serv.; John M. Cox, Hd., Tech.Serv.; Michael A. Bereza, Asst.Hd., Tech.Serv..

UNION THEOLOGICAL SEMINARY - HYMN SOCIETY OF AMERICA, INC.
See: Hymn Society of America, Inc. (6634)

★14485★
UNION THEOLOGICAL SEMINARY IN VIRGINIA - LIBRARY (Rel-Phil)
3401 Brook Rd. Phone: (804)355-0671
Richmond, VA 23227 Dr. John B. Trotti, Libn.
Founded: 1806. **Staff:** Prof 5; Other 21. **Subjects:** Bible, theology, church history. **Special Collections:** Presbyterian Church Archives (775 manuscript volumes); Human Relations Area Files (37,070 microfiche). **Holdings:** 248,534 volumes; 38,247 microfiche; 24,875 audio recordings; 2221 films; 2223 reels of microfilm; 706 microcards; 154 transparencies; 49 maps; 2080 phonograph records; 897 filmstrips; 205 videotapes; 26,675 slides; 556 kits and games. **Subscriptions:** 1502 journals and other serials. **Services:** Interlibrary loan; copying; library open to the public with restrictions on circulation. **Automated Operations:** Computerized cataloging. **Computerized Information Services:** OCLC, DIALOG Information Services, BRS Information Technologies. Performs searches on fee basis. Contact Person: Martha B. Aycock, Assoc.Libn.. **Networks/Consortia:** Member of SOLINET, Richmond Area Libraries Cooperative. **Publications:** Scholar's Choice, semiannual - for sale. **Special Catalogs:** Reigner Recording Library Catalog. **Staff:** Dorothy Thomason, Cat.; Linda Sue Quinn, Asst.Cat.; Eleanor Godfrey, Media Rsrcs.Dir..

★14486★
UNION UNIVERSITY - ALBANY LAW SCHOOL - SCHAFFER LAW LIBRARY (Law)
80 New Scotland Ave. Phone: (518)445-2340
Albany, NY 12208 Robert T. Begg, Dir.
Founded: 1851. **Staff:** Prof 8; Other 9. **Subjects:** Law. **Special Collections:** English and government law. **Holdings:** 258,500 volumes. **Subscriptions:** 4000 journals and other serials. **Services:** Interlibrary loan; copying; library open to alumni, attorneys, state and federal agencies. **Computerized Information Services:** LEXIS, DIALOG Information Services, VU/TEXT Information Services, WILSONLINE, WESTLAW, OCLC. **Publications:** Directory; acquisitions list, monthly. **Staff:** Robert Emery, Assoc.Dir.; Elizabeth Duncan, Tech.Serv.Libn.; Lauren Pinseley, Asst.Cat.; Mary Wood, Pub.Serv.Libn..

UNION UNIVERSITY - ALBANY MEDICAL COLLEGE
See: Albany Medical College (177)

UNION UNIVERSITY - ALBANY MEDICAL COLLEGE - CAPITAL DISTRICT PSYCHIATRIC CENTER
See: Capital District Psychiatric Center (2640)

★14487★
UNION UNIVERSITY - DUDLEY OBSERVATORY - LIBRARY (Sci-Engr)
69 Union Ave. Phone: (518)382-7583
Schenectady, NY 12308 Rita A. Spenser, Act.Libn.
Subjects: Astronomy, astrophysics, space science, physics, mathematics. **Special Collections:** Rare books in astronomy (250). **Holdings:** 5500 books; 10,000 bound periodical volumes; 8500 unbound serials; 6000 pamphlets, reports, specifications, and standards; 13 VF drawers of star atlases; 2 VF drawers of astronomical pictures. **Subscriptions:** 250 journals and other serials. **Services:** Interlibrary loan; copying; library open to the public. **Networks/Consortia:** Member of Capital District Library Council for Reference & Research Resources (CDLC). **Publications:** Dudley Observatory Reports, irregular - by exchange; Dudley Observatory Reprints - by request.

★14488★
UNIONTOWN HOSPITAL ASSOCIATION - MEDICAL LIBRARY (Med)
500 W. Berkeley St. Phone: (412)430-5178
Uniontown, PA 15401 Nina M. Stith, Med.Libn.
Staff: Prof 1. **Subjects:** Medicine and allied health sciences. **Holdings:** 1848 books; 1062 bound periodical volumes; 12 VF drawers; 120 videotapes; 380 cassettes and reels of tape. **Subscriptions:** 163 journals and other serials. **Services:** Interlibrary loan; copying; library open to the public with restrictions. **Networks/Consortia:** Member of Greater Northeastern Regional Medical Library Program, Pittsburgh Regional Medical Library Group.

★14489★
UNIONTOWN HOSPITAL ASSOCIATION - SCHOOL OF NURSING - LIBRARY (Med)
Annette Home
500 W. Berkeley St. Phone: (412)430-5348
Uniontown, PA 15401 Elizabeth A. Johnson, Libn.
Founded: 1904. **Staff:** Prof 1. **Subjects:** Nursing. **Holdings:** 4235 books; 214 bound periodical volumes; 555 audio cassettes; 24 charts; 20 computer disks; 13 filmloops; 224 filmstrips; 21 models; 15 motion pictures; 45 phonograph records; 2613 slides; 135 transparencies; 28 video cassettes. **Subscriptions:** 40 journals and other serials. **Services:** Interlibrary loan; copying; library open to the public with restrictions.

★14490★
UNIROYAL CHEMICAL COMPANY, INC. - MANAGEMENT & TECHNICAL INFORMATION SERVICES/LIBRARY (Sci-Engr)
Elm St. Phone: (203)723-3252
Naugatuck, CT 06770 Patricia Ann Harmon, Libn.
Staff: Prof 1; Other 2. **Subjects:** Agricultural chemicals, chemical engineering, organic chemistry, plastics and rubber technology. **Holdings:** 2000 books; 10,000 bound periodical volumes; 2200 reels of microfilm. **Subscriptions:** 300 journals and other serials. **Services:** Interlibrary loan; copying; library open to the public with restrictions. **Automated Operations:** Computerized serials and ILL. **Computerized Information Services:** DIALOG Information Services, NLM, Pergamon ORBIT InfoLine, Inc., CAS ONLINE, Dow Jones News/Retrieval. **Networks/Consortia:** Member of Region One Cooperating Library Service Unit, Inc., Region Four Cooperating Libraries Service Unit.

★14491★
UNIROYAL CHEMICAL COMPANY, INC. - TECHNICAL LIBRARY (Sci-Engr)
Box 117 Phone: (203)573-4509
Waterbury, CT 06720 Patrica Ann Harmon, Libn.
Staff: Prof 1. **Subjects:** Chemistry, physics, rubber, plastics. **Holdings:** 8000 books; 10,000 bound periodical volumes; patents; clippings; pamphlets; dissertations; documents. **Subscriptions:** 200 journals and other serials. **Services:** Library not open to the public.

★14492★
UNIROYAL CHEMICAL LTD. - RESEARCH LABORATORIES LIBRARY (Sci-Engr)
120 Huron St. Phone: (519)822-3790
Guelph, ON, Canada N1H 6N3 Lorna P. Cole, Mgr., Info.Serv.
Founded: 1943. **Staff:** Prof 1; Other 3. **Subjects:** Organic chemistry, plastics, rubber, composite materials. **Holdings:** 6000 books; 2555 bound periodical volumes; 44 drawers of reports, trade catalogs, patents, pamphlets; 900 reels of microfilm. **Subscriptions:** 350 journals and other serials. **Services:** Interlibrary loan; copying; SDI; library open to the public with restrictions. **Automated Operations:** Computerized serials. **Computerized Information Services:** DIALOG Information Services, QL Systems, CAS ONLINE, CAN/OLE, Pergamon ORBIT InfoLine, Inc., Info Globe; internal databases; Envoy 100 (electronic mail service). **Publications:** Library Bulletin, biweekly; Accessions List, monthly; Reports List, quarterly; Library Notes, irregular. **Special Catalogs:** Company research reports; periodical holdings (both computerized). **Formerly:** Uniroyal, Ltd.

★14493★
UNIROYAL GOODRICH TIRE COMPANY - AKRON INFORMATION CENTER (Sci-Engr)
600 S. Main St. Phone: (216)374-4368
Akron, OH 44397-0001 Virginia Gallicchio, Mgr.
Founded: 1971. **Staff:** Prof 1; Other 1. **Subjects:** Tires, rubber, polymers, elastomers, management. **Holdings:** 2500 books; 30 VF drawers of pamphlets. **Subscriptions:** 150 journals and other serials. **Services:** Interlibrary loan; center open to the public with advance clearance. **Computerized Information Services:** NEXIS, DIALOG Information Services, TOXLINE, MEDLINE, Pergamon ORBIT InfoLine, Inc., Dow Jones News/Retrieval. **Networks/Consortia:** Member of OHIONET. **Special Catalogs:** Tire pamphlet file; Journal Holdings.

★14494★
UNIROYAL, INC. - CORPORATE LIBRARY
World Headquarters
Middlebury, CT 06749
Defunct

★14495★
UNISYS CORPORATION - CORPORATE INFORMATION RESEARCH CENTER (Bus-Fin, Comp Sci)
Unisys Place, Rm. 4C51 Phone: (313)972-7350
Detroit, MI 48232 Jane E. Farraye, Mgr.
Founded: 1943. **Staff:** Prof 6; Other 4. **Subjects:** Computers, data processing, management, marketing, software. **Holdings:** 5000 books; 134 VF drawers of technical manuals and product information; 108 VF drawers of annual reports, Securities and Exchange Commission (SEC) documents, general files; 25 shelves of directories and loose-leaf services. **Subscriptions:** 500 journals and other serials. **Services:** Center open to the public with restrictions. **Computerized Information Services:** DIALOG Information Services, Dow Jones News/Retrieval, NEXIS, VU/TEXT Information Services, Info Globe, The Source Information Network, Wall Street Transcript Online Service; internal database.

★14496★
UNISYS CORPORATION - DEFENSE SYSTEMS OPERATIONS - COMPUTER SYSTEMS DIVISION - LIBRARY SERVICES (Sci-Engr, Comp Sci)
Box 64525, MSU0P25 Phone: (612)456-3468
St. Paul, MN 55164-0525 Linda M. Sellars, Supv.
Staff: Prof 4; Other 4. **Subjects:** Computers, electronics, data processing, management, physics, chemistry, mathematics. **Holdings:** 25,000 books; 15,000 technical reports. **Subscriptions:** 600 journals and other serials. **Services:** Interlibrary loan; copying; services open to the public with restrictions. **Automated Operations:** Computerized cataloging and circulation. **Computerized Information Services:** DIALOG Information Services, Pergamon ORBIT InfoLine, Inc., NEXIS. **Publications:** Bulletin (selected magazine articles and new book list), monthly. **Staff:** Virginia Van Horn, Libn.; Stephan Elfstrand, Libn.; Samira Saleh, Libn..

★14497★
UNISYS CORPORATION - INFORMATION CENTER (Sci-Engr, Comp Sci)
M.S. E2-112
Box 500 Phone: (215)542-2459
Blue Bell, PA 19424 John A. Fennell, Mgr., Info.Serv.
Founded: 1952. **Staff:** Prof 3; Other 2. **Subjects:** Business, computer science, electrical and electronic engineering, physics, telecommunications. **Holdings:** 20,000 books; 1500 bound periodical volumes; 600 audio cassettes; 5000 unbound items. **Subscriptions:** 525 journals and other serials; 25 newspapers. **Services:** Interlibrary loan; center open to the public by appointment. **Automated Operations:** Computerized acquisitions, serials, and circulation. **Computerized Information Services:** OCLC, DIALOG Information Services, NewsNet, Inc., Dow Jones News/Retrieval, Mead Data Central, NEXIS, LEXIS, Occupational Health Services, Inc. **Networks/Consortia:** Member of PALINET. **Staff:** E. Harris, Res.Anl.; Janet Discher, Lib.Spec..

★14498★
UNISYS CORPORATION - LAW LIBRARY (Law)
Unisys Place Phone: (313)972-7895
Detroit, MI 48232 Bernice C. Frank, Law Libn.
Staff: Prof 1; Other 1. **Subjects:** Law - labor, contract, patent, trademark, copyright. **Holdings:** 11,000 volumes.

★14499★
UNISYS CORPORATION - LIBRARY (Sci-Engr, Comp Sci)
322 North 2200 West Phone: (801)539-5222
Salt Lake City, UT 84116 Phyllis J. Nye, Libn.
Founded: 1956. **Staff:** Prof 1; Other 1. **Subjects:** Computer science, engineering, management, business. **Holdings:** 3000 books; 500 symposia proceedings; 5000 technical reports and manuals. **Subscriptions:** 250 journals and other serials. **Services:** Interlibrary loan; library not open to the public. **Computerized Information Services:** NEXIS, DIALOG Information Services. **Publications:** Acquisition list, monthly.

★14500★
UNISYS CORPORATION - PERIPHERALS PRODUCTS DIVISION - TECHNICAL INFORMATION CENTER (Sci-Engr, Comp Sci)
San Tomas at Central Expy., M/S14-05 Phone: (408)987-3599
Santa Clara, CA 95052 Lynne Szabo, Mgr.
Founded: 1977. **Staff:** Prof 2; Other 3. **Subjects:** Magnetism, disk drives, magnetic storage equipment, optics, computer equipment, peripherals, physics, management. **Holdings:** 15,000 volumes; 3000 patent files; 1000 annual reports. **Subscriptions:** 400 journals and other serials; 10 newspapers. **Services:** Interlibrary loan; copying; SDI; center open to the public with restrictions. **Automated Operations:** Computerized cataloging. **Computerized Information Services:** DIALOG Information Services, Pergamon ORBIT InfoLine, Inc., BRS Information Technologies, OCLC. **Networks/Consortia:** Member of Bay Area Reference Center (BARC), SOUTHNET. **Publications:** Acquisitions list; patent scan sheet; current awareness; specialized bibliographies. **Remarks:** An alternate telephone number is 987-2965. **Formerly:** Memorex Corporation. **Staff:** Kim Walters, Tech.Libn..

★14501★
UNISYS CORPORATION - RANCHO BERNARDO TECHNICAL INFORMATION CENTER (Sci-Engr)
10850 Via Frontera
Box 28810 Phone: (619)451-5142
San Diego, CA 92127 Marianna M. Seeley, Tech.Libn.
Founded: 1977. **Staff:** Prof 1. **Subjects:** Physics, semiconductors, electronics, statistics, quality control, management. **Special Collections:** Career education. **Holdings:** 800 books; 600 bound periodical volumes; 200 proceedings and specifications; 500 technical data tapes; AV programs. **Subscriptions:** 160 journals and other serials; 5 newspapers. **Services:** Interlibrary loan; not open to the public. **Automated Operations:** Computerized cataloging, acquisitions, and circulation. **Computerized Information Services:** DIALOG Information Services, TRAINET; Mail Manager (electronic mail service). **Networks/Consortia:** Member of CLASS.

★14502★
UNISYS CORPORATION - ROSEVILLE INFORMATION CENTER (Sci-Engr, Comp Sci)
Box 43942 Phone: (612)635-3003
St. Paul, MN 55164 Denise A. DeSota, Mgr.
Staff: Prof 3; Other 2. **Subjects:** Computers, electrical engineering, electronics, management, production methods. **Holdings:** 15,000 volumes; 22,000 technical reports; 1000 audio cassettes; 700 video cassettes; 6 VF drawers of microfiche. **Subscriptions:** 850 journals and other serials; 20 newspapers. **Services:** Interlibrary loan (limited); center not open to the public. **Automated Operations:** Computerized cataloging, acquisitions, serials, and circulation. **Computerized Information Services:** DIALOG Information Services; MAPPER (internal database). **Special Indexes:** Online indexes to internal documents. **Remarks:** Center is located at 2276 Highcrest Rd., Roseville, MN 55113. **Staff:** Barbara J. Randell, Sr.Info.Res.Anl..

★14503★
UNISYS CORPORATION - SYSTEM DEVELOPMENT GROUP - INFORMATION RETRIEVAL (Info Sci, Comp Sci)
5151 Camino Ruiz Phone: (805)987-6811
Camarillo, CA 93010 Mary King, Libn.
Founded: 1956. **Staff:** 1. **Subjects:** Computers, data processing, information science, computer programming, system analysis and design, management, education, energy, behavioral science, military. **Special Collections:** Computer Manufacturers Documents Collection; SDC Computer Program Library. **Holdings:** 15,000 books; 1000 bound periodical volumes; 250,000 internal reports; 50,000 external reports. **Subscriptions:** 250 journals and other serials; 6 newspapers. **Services:** Interlibrary loan; not open to the public. **Automated Operations:** Computerized cataloging and serials. **Computerized Information Services:** DIALOG Information Services, Pergamon ORBIT InfoLine, Inc.

★14504★
UNISYS CORPORATION - SYSTEM DEVELOPMENT GROUP - MC LEAN INFORMATION RETRIEVAL CENTER (Comp Sci)
7929 Westpark Dr. Phone: (703)847-4308
McLean, VA 22102 Alice Hill-Murray, Libn.
Subjects: Computers, software, information science. **Holdings:** Figures not available. **Services:** Interlibrary loan; center not open to the public. **Computerized Information Services:** DIALOG Information Services, Pergamon ORBIT InfoLine, Inc.

★14505★
UNISYS CORPORATION - TECHNICAL INFORMATION CENTER (Comp Sci)
25725 Jeronimo Rd., MS-260 Phone: (714)380-5061
Mission Viejo, CA 92691 M. Patricia Feeney, Sr.Tech.Libn.
Founded: 1974. **Staff:** Prof 1; Other 1. **Subjects:** Computer architecture, computer programming, software design, hardware engineering design, data communications, management. **Holdings:** 3500 books; 2700 technical reports; 3000 other cataloged items. **Subscriptions:** 160 journals and other serials. **Services:** Interlibrary loan; center open to public at librarian's discretion. **Automated Operations:** Computerized public access catalog, cataloging, and circulation. **Computerized Information Services:** DIALOG Information Services; DIALMAIL (electronic mail service). **Publications:** Acquisitions Bulletin, biweekly. **Special Indexes:** KWOC Index of Technical Reports.

★14506★
UNISYS CORPORATION - TECHNICAL INFORMATION CENTER (Sci-Engr, Comp Sci)
41100 Plymouth Rd. Phone: (313)451-4512
Plymouth, MI 48170 Carol Smith Feder, Info.Spec.
Founded: 1973. **Staff:** Prof 1. **Subjects:** Computer technology, engineering. **Holdings:** 1500 books; 75 bound periodical volumes. **Subscriptions:** 130 journals and other serials; 12 newspapers. **Services:** Interlibrary loan; center not open to the public. **Computerized Information Services:** DIALOG Information Services, NewsNet, Inc.; DIALMAIL (electronic mail service). **Networks/Consortia:** Member of Wayne Oakland Region of Interlibrary Cooperation. **Publications:** Plymouth Library News, every 3 weeks - for internal distribution only.

★14507★
UNISYS CORPORATION - TECHNICAL INFORMATION CENTER (Sci-Engr)
Lakeville Rd. & Marcus Ave. Phone: (516)574-1001
Great Neck, NY 11020 James Montalbano, Libn.
Staff: Prof 2. **Subjects:** Navigation, radar, electronics, telecommunications, optics, systems engineering. **Holdings:** 5600 books and bound periodical volumes. **Subscriptions:** 170 journals and other serials. **Services:** Interlibrary loan; center not open to the public. **Computerized Information Services:** DIALOG Information Services, DTIC, NEXIS. **Networks/Consortia:** Member of Long Island Library Resources Council, Inc. (LILRC). **Publications:** Acquisitions Bulletin, monthly - for internal distribution only.

★14508★
UNISYS CORPORATION - TECHNICAL INFORMATION RESOURCES CENTER (Comp Sci)
460 Sierra Madre Villa Phone: (818)351-6551
Pasadena, CA 91109 Nancy L. Olmstead, Libn.
Founded: 1956. **Staff:** Prof 1. **Subjects:** Computer science, mathematics, electronics. **Holdings:** 6000 books; 3000 bound periodical volumes; 1500 technical reports. **Subscriptions:** 300 journals and other serials. **Services:** Interlibrary loan; center not open to the public. **Automated Operations:** Computerized cataloging, acquisitions, circulation, and ILL. **Computerized Information Services:** DIALOG Information Services, OCLC.

★14509★
UNITARIAN-UNIVERSALIST ASSOCIATION - ARCHIVES (Rel-Phil)
25 Beacon St. Phone: (617)742-2100
Boston, MA 02108 Rev. Mark W. Harris, Dir. of Info.
Subjects: History, religion, biography, churches, ministers. **Special Collections:** Records of Unitarian-Universalist Ministers and Churches. **Holdings:** Clippings; manuscripts; pictures; maps; correspondence. **Services:** Copying; archives open to the public for research and reference.

★14510★
UNITARIAN AND UNIVERSALIST GENEALOGICAL SOCIETY - LIBRARY
10605 Lakespring Way
Hunt Valley, MD 21030
Defunct

★14511★
UNITED AUTOMOBILE, AEROSPACE & AGRICULTURAL IMPLEMENT WORKERS OF AMERICA - RESEARCH LIBRARY (Bus-Fin)
8000 E. Jefferson Ave. Phone: (313)926-5386
Detroit, MI 48214 Melba Kibildis, Libn.
Founded: 1947. **Staff:** Prof 2; Other 2. **Subjects:** Economics and collective bargaining in automobile, aerospace, and agricultural implement industries; labor economics; industrial relations; United Automobile Workers. **Special Collections:** Automation; plant closings; UAW collective agreements; testimonies and speeches of UAW officers and staff. **Holdings:** Figures not available for books and periodicals; U.S., state, and Canadian government documents; newspaper clippings; pamphlets; press releases; microforms. **Services:** Library not open to the public. **Automated Operations:** Computerized cataloging. **Computerized Information Services:** DIALOG Information Services, Pergamon ORBIT InfoLine, Inc., LEXIS, Dow Jones News/Retrieval, Info Globe, Bureau of Labor Statistics (BLS); internal database. **Also Known As:** UAW; International Union, United Automobile, Aerospace & Agricultural Implement Workers of America. **Staff:** Jane C. Murphey, Asst.Libn..

★14512★
UNITED BANK CENTER LAW LIBRARY (Law)
Two United Bank Center, Suite 1215
1700 Broadway Phone: (303)832-3335
Denver, CO 80290-1201 Kay Krodshen, Law Libn.
Staff: Prof 2; Other 1. **Subjects:** Law - tax, corporate, insurance, bankruptcy, real estate; estate planning. **Special Collections:** Code of Federal Regulations and Federal Register, 1975 to present; U.S. Government documents on taxes; U.S. Statutes at Large. **Holdings:** 15,220 books; 330 bound periodical volumes; 830 loose-leaf services; 7863 unbound reports. **Subscriptions:** 13 journals and other serials. **Services:** Interlibrary loan; library not open to the public. **Formerly:** Den-Cal Company. **Staff:** Colleen Kridle, Asst.Libn..

UNITED BIBLE SOCIETIES - ARCHIVES
See: American Bible Society - Library (422)

★14513★
UNITED CATALYSTS, INC. - TECHNICAL LIBRARY (Sci-Engr)
Box 32370 Phone: (502)634-7200
Louisville, KY 40232 Betty B. Simms, Tech.Libn.
Founded: 1943. **Staff:** Prof 1. **Subjects:** Catalysis, chemistry, physics, engineering, mathematics, clays, management. **Special Collections:** Catalysis. **Holdings:** 4000 books; 1300 bound periodical volumes; 18,000 patents; 18 VF drawers of indexed technical reports; microfilm. **Subscriptions:** 50 journals and other serials. **Services:** Interlibrary loan; reference service to comparable libraries; library open to the public by appointment. **Computerized Information Services:** DIALOG Information Services, Pergamon ORBIT InfoLine, Inc. **Publications:** Acquisition Bulletin; Patent Awareness Bulletin; Articles of Interest Bulletin. **Special Indexes:** Indexes to documents, pamphlets, and technical reports. **Remarks:** Library is located at 1227 S. 12th St., Louisville, KY 40210.

★14514★
UNITED CEREBRAL PALSY ASSOCIATION OF NORTHWESTERN CONNECTICUT, INC. - PROFESSIONAL RESOURCE CENTER (Med)
25 Hillside Ave. Phone: (203)274-9241
Oakville, CT 06779-1735 Thomas R. Briggs, Ph.D., Exec.Dir.
Subjects: Physically and severely handicapped, communication training, special education, parent training, therapeutic training. **Special Collections:** Severely physically handicapped. **Holdings:** 150 books; 100 other cataloged items. **Services:** Center open to the public with restrictions.

★14515★
UNITED CEREBRAL PALSY OF NEW YORK CITY, INC. - LIBRARY (Med)
122 E. 23rd St. Phone: (212)677-7400
New York, NY 10010 Richard Gordon, Lib.Adm.
Founded: 1959. **Staff:** Prof 2. **Subjects:** Cerebral palsy and allied subjects. **Holdings:** 524 books; 19 bound periodical volumes. **Subscriptions:** 13 journals and other serials; 5 newspapers. **Services:** Library open to the public. **Publications:** Update, quarterly. **Staff:** Peter Hollander, Adm.Asst..

★14516★
UNITED CHARITIES OF CHICAGO - LIBRARY (Soc Sci)
14 E. Jackson Blvd. Phone: (312)461-0800
Chicago, IL 60604 Eric B. Goodman, Libn./Rec.Mgr.
Staff: Prof 1; Other 1. **Subjects:** Social work, law. **Holdings:** 6700 books; 3000 pamphlets. **Subscriptions:** 111 journals and other serials. **Services:** Interlibrary loan; copying; library open to the public by appointment. **Networks/Consortia:** Member of Chicago Library System. **Publications:** New Acquisitions, monthly - for internal distribution only.

★14517★
UNITED CHURCH BOARD FOR WORLD MINISTRIES - LIBRARY (Rel-Phil)
475 Riverside Dr., 16th Fl. Phone: (201)567-5292
New York, NY 10115 Virginia Stowe, Libn.
Founded: 1820. **Staff:** Prof 1. **Subjects:** Missions of United Church Board for World Ministries and its predecessors (especially American Board of Commissioners for Foreign Ministries), third world areas. **Holdings:** 3000 books; 200 bound periodical volumes. **Subscriptions:** 50 journals and other serials. **Services:** Library open to the public by special permission. **Remarks:** Archival records are located in Houghton Library, Harvard University, Cambridge, MA 02138, and in the library of Lancaster Theological Seminary, Lancaster, PA 17603.

★14518★
UNITED CHURCH OF CANADA - ESSEX PRESBYTERY - RESOURCE CENTRE (Rel-Phil)
208 Sunset Ave. Phone: (519)253-4232
Windsor, ON, Canada N9B 3A7 Betsy Hanson
Staff: Prof 1; Other 1. **Subjects:** Religion. **Holdings:** Books; magazines; church and Sunday School material; filmstrip; records; cassettes; posters. **Subscriptions:** 14 journals and other serials. **Services:** Center open to the public.

★14519★
UNITED CHURCH OF CANADA - MARITIME CONFERENCE ARCHIVES (Hist, Rel-Phil)
Falconer Room
Atlantic School of Theology
640 Francklyn St. Phone: (902)429-4819
Halifax, NS, Canada B3H 3B5 Carolyn Earle, Act. Interim Archv.
Staff: Prof 1. **Subjects:** History of the Congregationalist, Methodist, Presbyterian, and United Churches in the Maritime provinces of Canada. **Special Collections:** McGregor Papers; Black-McColl Papers; Geddie Letters. **Holdings:** Several thousand books, pamphlets, manuscripts, photographs, microfilm, official church records. **Services:** Interlibrary loan; copying; assistance with research; archives open to the public. **Automated Operations:** Computerized cataloging and acquisitions.

UNITED CHURCH OF CANADA - ST. STEPHEN'S COLLEGE
See: St. Stephen's College (12672)

★14520★
UNITED CHURCH OF CANADA/VICTORIA UNIVERSITY ARCHIVES (Hist)
Birge-Carnegie Bldg.
73 Queen's Park Crescent, E. Phone: (416)585-4563
Toronto, ON, Canada M5S 1K7 Jean E. Dryden, Natl.Archv.
Founded: 1953. **Staff:** Prof 6; Other 3. **Subjects:** Religious and social history of the United Church of Canada and its antecedent churches, biography, Methodist and Presbyterian foreign missions activity, local church history, international religious organizations operating in Canada. **Special Collections:** Richard Green Collection of John Wesley's publications; Ryerson Press Book Collection; foreign mission manuscript collection of Canadian missionaries in China. **Holdings:** 13,000 books; 5000 bound periodical volumes; 600 yearbooks; 500 theses and documents; 9400 pamphlets; 8250 feet of manuscripts; 9351 pamphlets; 4700 reels of

microfilm; 2900 tapes. **Subscriptions:** 43 journals and other serials. **Services:** Interlibrary loan; copying; archives open to the public for reference use only. **Publications:** Bulletin, annual. **Special Indexes:** Indexes to the Christian Guardian, the Christian Advocate, other Methodist and Presbyterian serials, and local church records. **Formerly:** Central Archives. **Staff:** Dr. N.E. Semple, Sr.Archv.; Edythe A. Clapp, Libn.; Mrs. M. Tilley, Bus.Mgr.; Mark Van Stempvoort, Archv.; Rick Stapleton, Archv.; Susan Stanley, Sr.Archv.; Dr. Marilyn Whiteley, Indexer; Karen Banner, Libn..

UNITED CHURCH OF CHRIST - ARCHIVES
See: Evangelical and Reformed Historical Society - Lancaster Central Archives and Library (4833)

★14521★
UNITED CHURCH OF CHRIST - SOUTH DAKOTA CONFERENCE - ARCHIVES (Rel-Phil)
Center for Western Studies
Augustana College Phone: (605)336-4007
Sioux Falls, SD 57197 Harry F. Thompson, Archv.
Founded: 1980. **Staff:** Prof 4. **Subjects:** History - Congregational Church, Great Plains, American Indian; missionary work; American West. **Special Collections:** Oahe Industrial School; Santee Normal Training School; Steven R. Riggs; Alfred L. Riggs; Thomas L. Riggs; Louisa I. Riggs; Mary C. Collins. **Holdings:** 150 books; 30 bound periodical volumes; 170 linear feet of archival materials. **Services:** Copying; archives open to the public with restrictions. **Publications:** Buffalo Chips Newsletter, semiannual; Guide to the Archives of the South Dakota Conference of the United Church of Christ, 1986 (book).

★14522★
UNITED CHURCH OF CHRIST (Evangelical and Reformed) - CHURCH LIBRARY (Rel-Phil)
Grand & Ohio Sts.
850 Douglas St. Phone: (216)967-4539
Vermilion, OH 44089 Doris M. Feiszli, Chf.Libn.
Founded: 1954. **Staff:** Prof 1. **Subjects:** Religion, faith, devotions and prayer, Bible, biography, missions. **Holdings:** 5000 books; AV programs. **Services:** Library open to the public for reference use only.

★14523★
UNITED CHURCH OF LOS ALAMOS - LIBRARY (Rel-Phil)
2525 Canyon Rd.
Box 1286 Phone: (505)662-2971
Los Alamos, NM 87544 Martha C. MacMillan, Libn.
Founded: 1967. **Staff:** Prof 1; Other 3. **Subjects:** Religion, psychology, family, social problems, health, philosophy. **Holdings:** 3450 volumes. **Subscriptions:** 10 journals and other serials. **Services:** Library

★14524★
UNITED CHURCH OF RELIGIOUS SCIENCE - ERNEST HOLMES COLLEGE LIBRARY (Rel-Phil)
3251 W. Sixth St.
Box 75127 Phone: (213)388-2181
Los Angeles, CA 90075 Albert T. Wickham, Hd.Libn.
Founded: 1974. **Staff:** Prof 1. **Subjects:** "New Thought," science of mind, philosophy, religion, science, mental and spiritual healing. **Special Collections:** Science of mind (200 items); New Thought (500 items); church archives. **Holdings:** 8000 books; 300 audiotapes; 1000 metaphysical pamphlets and booklets; 16 VF drawers of clippings and archival materials; 200 file boxes of past metaphysical, scientific, and news magazines. **Subscriptions:** 40 journals and other serials. **Services:** Interlibrary loan; library open to the public for reference use only. **Special Indexes:** Index to Science of Mind Magazine.

★14525★
UNITED COOPERATIVES OF ONTARIO - HARMAN LIBRARY (Bus-Fin)
Sta. A, P.O. Box 527 Phone: (416)270-3560
Mississauga, ON, Canada L5A 3A4 Audrey Ferger, Libn.
Founded: 1964. **Staff:** 1. **Subjects:** History of cooperatives in Canada and the United States, finance and credit, personnel, training and management development, statistics. **Holdings:** 1800 books and bound periodical volumes; 2 VF drawers of archives; 150 pamphlets and annual reports. **Subscriptions:** 19 journals and other serials. **Services:** Interlibrary loan; copying (limited); library open to the public with restrictions.

★14526★
UNITED DAUGHTERS OF THE CONFEDERACY - CAROLINE MERIWETHER GOODLETT LIBRARY (Hist)
U.D.C. Headquarters Bldg.
328 North Blvd. Phone: (804)355-1636
Richmond, VA 23220 Annette E. Wetzel, Chm., Lib.Comm.
Founded: 1957. **Staff:** Prof 1; Other 1. **Subjects:** Civil War causes and Reconstruction. **Holdings:** 5000 books; diaries; letters; manuscripts; papers; clippings; memorabilia; photographs. **Services:** Library open to members and qualified historians by appointment.

★14527★
UNITED DAUGHTERS OF THE CONFEDERACY - SHROPSHIRE UPTON CHAPTER - CONFEDERATE MEMORIAL MUSEUM - LIBRARY (Hist)
Court House Square
Columbus, TX 78934 Phone: (409)732-3277
Founded: 1962. **Staff:** 5. **Subjects:** Civil War, local history. **Special Collections:** Antique local art (handwork; paintings); gun collection; 1913 Colorado River flood photographs; bound early newspapers; Civil War correspondence of George McCormick and John S. Shropshire. **Holdings:** 150 books; 100 bound periodical volumes. **Services:** Library open to the public by appointment. **Staff:** Millycent Tait Cranek, Cur.; Myrah Jane Draper, Cur..

★14528★
UNITED DAUGHTERS OF THE CONFEDERACY - TEXAS CONFEDERATE MUSEUM LIBRARY (Hist)
112 E. 11th Phone: (512)472-2596
Austin, TX 78701 Sharon Ann Hardin, Musm.Dir.
Founded: 1903. **Staff:** 1. **Subjects:** Southern history, Confederate States of America military records. **Holdings:** 600 books. **Services:** Library open to the public on a limited schedule.

UNITED ELECTRICAL, RADIO AND MACHINE WORKERS OF AMERICA ARCHIVES
See: University of Pittsburgh - Archives of Industrial Society (16756)

★14529★
UNITED EMPIRE LOYALISTS' ASSOCIATION OF CANADA - NATIONAL HEADQUARTERS - NATIONAL LOYALIST REFERENCE LIBRARY (Hist)
23 Prince Arthur Ave. Phone: (416)923-7921
Toronto, ON, Canada M5R 1B2 Dorothy Chisholm, Off.Adm.
Founded: 1968. **Staff:** Prof 2; Other 1. **Subjects:** Loyalist history, history of Loyalist families, genealogy, education. **Holdings:** Figures not available. **Services:** Copying; library open to the public. **Special Catalogs:** Catalog of holdings, 1963-1985 - for sale. **Remarks:** Library is said to be one of the best specialized collections in North America on United Empire Loyalists.

★14530★
UNITED ENGINEERING TRUSTEES, INC. - ENGINEERING SOCIETIES LIBRARY (Sci-Engr)
United Engineering Center
345 E. 47th St. Phone: (212)705-7611
New York, NY 10017 S.K. Cabeen, Dir.
Founded: 1913. **Staff:** Prof 11; Other 23. **Subjects:** Engineering - chemical, civil, electrical, mechanical, mining; history of engineering; fuels; metallurgy. **Holdings:** 125,000 books; 150,000 bound periodical volumes; 10,000 maps; 6500 searches. **Subscriptions:** 5500 journals and other serials. **Services:** Copying; library open to the public. **Computerized Information Services:** Online systems. **Publications:** Periodicals Currently Received, biennial; Selected Acquisitions List. **Staff:** Carmela Carbone, Dp.Dir.; Ari Cohen, Hd., Cat.Dept.; Dan Wood, Hd., Acq.Dept..

★14531★
UNITED ENGINEERS & CONSTRUCTORS INC. - LIBRARY (Sci-Engr, Energy)
100 Summer St. Phone: (617)338-6000
Boston, MA 02110 Margaret Preston, Libn.
Founded: 1908. **Staff:** Prof 1; Other 1. **Subjects:** Engineering - power, mechanical, civil, electrical, industrial, nuclear; environment; air and water pollution; architecture. **Holdings:** 8000 books; 400 bound periodical volumes; 1500 maps; standards; 9000 other cataloged items. **Subscriptions:** 230 journals and other serials. **Services:** Interlibrary loan; library open to the public with permission. **Computerized Information Services:** DIALOG Information Services, NASA/RECON, Integrated Technical Information System (ITIS). **Publications:** Library Bulletin, monthly - for internal distribution only.

★14532★
UNITED ENGINEERS & CONSTRUCTORS INC. - LIBRARY (Sci-Engr, Energy)
30 S. 17th St.
Box 8223 Phone: (215)422-3374
Philadelphia, PA 19101 Marie S. Knup, Hd.Libn.
Founded: 1928. **Staff:** Prof 1. **Subjects:** Heavy construction; design engineering and architecture; power plants; energy sources - nuclear, fossil fuels, solar, geothermal; wastewater; sanitary engineering; environmental protection; seismology; chemical process plants; iron and steel. **Special Collections:** Standards from voluntary standards organizations (10,000); Atomic Energy Commission, Nuclear Regulatory Commission, Energy Research and Development Administration, and Department of Energy licensing dockets on microfiche. **Holdings:** 7500 books; 16 VF drawers of technical material; 20,000 government documents. **Subscriptions:** 600 journals and other serials; 10 newspapers. **Services:** Interlibrary loan (by prior arrangement). **Automated Operations:** Computerized cataloging and serials. **Computerized Information Services:** DIALOG Information Services, Pergamon ORBIT InfoLine, Inc., BRS Information Technologies, VU/TEXT Information Services. **Special Indexes:** KWOC Index. **Remarks:** United Engineers & Constructors Inc. is a subsidiary of Raytheon Company.

★14533★
UNITED ENGINEERS & CONSTRUCTORS INC. - STEARNS-ROGER TECHNICAL LIBRARY (Sci-Engr)
700 S. Ash St.
Box 5888 Phone: (303)692-2943
Denver, CO 80217 Judy M. Oberg, Info.Spec.
Founded: 1971. **Staff:** Prof 1; Other 2. **Subjects:** Petroleum technology; engineering - chemical, mechanical, structural; mining; business. **Holdings:** 11,000 books; 250 bound periodical volumes; 1000 microfilm cartridges of vendor catalogs. **Subscriptions:** 350 journals and other serials; 5 newspapers. **Services:** Interlibrary loan; SDI; library open to the public by appointment. **Automated Operations:** Computerized cataloging. **Computerized Information Services:** Dun & Bradstreet Corporation, DIALOG Information Services, BRS Information Technologies, Crude Oil Analysis Data Bank, Pergamon ORBIT InfoLine, Inc., PASS; internal database. **Networks/Consortia:** Member of Engineering Information Network (EIN).

★14534★
UNITED FARM WORKERS OF AMERICA, AFL-CIO - I.C. LIBRARY (Agri)
Box 30
La Paz Phone: (805)822-5571
Keene, CA 93531 Sara Russell
Founded: 1973. **Staff:** Prof 1. **Subjects:** Agriculture, agricultural research, agribusiness, food industry, economics, pesticide research, farm labor, union law. **Special Collections:** Books about Cesar Chavez and the United Farm Workers Union. **Holdings:** Figures not available.

★14535★
UNITED FOOD AND COMMERCIAL WORKERS INTERNATIONAL UNION - LIBRARY (Bus-Fin)
Suffridge Bldg.
1775 K St., N.W. Phone: (202)223-3111
Washington, DC 20006 Ellen Newton, Libn.
Founded: 1975. **Staff:** Prof 1; Other 1. **Subjects:** Labor and trade union history, business, economics, agriculture, food industry, retail industry. **Holdings:** 1300 books; 300 Bureau of Labor Statistics Reports; 25 U.S.D.A. periodicals; 24 VF drawers of clippings and pamphlets. **Subscriptions:** 500 journals and other serials; 100 newspapers. **Services:** Interlibrary loan; copying; SDI; library open to researchers by appointment. **Automated Operations:** Computerized serials. **Computerized Information Services:** LEXIS, NEXIS, VU/TEXT Information Services, DataTimes, DIALOG Information Services. **Networks/Consortia:** Member of Washington Area Labor Information Specialists (WALIS).

★14536★
UNITED FRESH FRUIT AND VEGETABLE ASSOCIATION - INFORMATION CENTER (Food-Bev)
727 N. Washington Phone: (703)836-3410
Alexandria, VA 22314 Lisa Barmann, Mgr., Info.Serv.
Staff: Prof 1. **Subjects:** Marketing of fresh fruits and vegetables, nutrition, crop statistics. **Holdings:** 50,000 items; 20 VF drawers. **Subscriptions:** 150 journals and other serials; 15 newspapers. **Services:** Center open to the public by appointment only. **Computerized Information Services:** DIALOG Information Services. Performs searches on fee basis. Contact Person: Michelle C. Bing, Info.Spec..

★14537★
UNITED GRAIN GROWERS LTD. - LIBRARY (Agri)
433 Main St.
Box 6600 Phone: (204)944-5572
Winnipeg, MB, Canada R3C 3A7 Carole Rogers, Libn.
Staff: 1. **Subjects:** Grain handling and transportation, agricultural history, company archives. **Holdings:** 2000 books; 150 vertical file boxes; 10 Statistics Canada publications. **Subscriptions:** 150 journals and other serials; 15 newspapers. **Services:** Interlibrary loan; copying; library open to the public with restrictions. **Computerized Information Services:** iNet 2000 (electronic mail service).

UNITED GRAND IMPERIAL COUNCIL
See: Red Cross of Constantine - United Grand Imperial Council (11920)

★14538★
UNITED HEALTH SERVICES/BINGHAMTON GENERAL HOSPITAL - STUART B. BLAKELY MEMORIAL LIBRARY (Med)
Mitchell Ave. Phone: (607)771-2110
Binghamton, NY 13903 Maryanne Donnelly, Med.Libn.
Founded: 1940. **Staff:** Prof 1; Other 4. **Subjects:** Medicine and nursing. **Holdings:** 11,000 volumes; 400 audiotapes; 200 videotapes; 10 films; 500 slides; 10 VF drawers of pamphlets. **Subscriptions:** 208 journals and other serials. **Services:** Interlibrary loan; copying; library open to medical professionals. **Automated Operations:** cataloging cataloging. **Computerized Information Services:** DIALOG Information Services, WILSONLINE, BRS Information Technologies, MEDLINE, OCLC. Performs searches on fee basis. **Networks/Consortia:** Member of Greater Northeastern Regional Medical Library Program, South Central Research Library Council (SCRLC). **Remarks:** An alternate telephone number is 771-2109.

★14539★
UNITED HEALTH SERVICES/WILSON HOSPITAL - LEARNING RESOURCES DEPARTMENT (Med)
33-57 Harrison St. Phone: (607)770-6030
Johnson City, NY 13790 Shirley Edsall, Mgr.
Staff: Prof 3; Other 5. **Subjects:** Medicine, nursing, health sciences administration. **Holdings:** 4000 books; 5400 bound periodical volumes; 1800 video cassettes, slide/tape programs, models, films, charts. **Subscriptions:** 305 journals and other serials. **Services:** Interlibrary loan; copying; SDI; self instructional learning lab; department open to the public for reference use only. **Automated Operations:** Computerized cataloging, serials, and circulation. **Computerized Information Services:** MEDLINE, OCLC, BRS Information Technologies, DIALOG Information Services, WILSONLINE. Performs searches on fee basis. **Networks/Consortia:** Member of South Central Research Library Council (SCRLC). **Staff:** Marjorie Westerfield, Hea.Sci.Libn..

★14540★
UNITED HOSPITAL - LIBRARY (Med)
1200 S. Columbia Rd. Phone: (701)780-5187
Grand Forks, ND 58201 Patrice Conely, Med.Libn.
Founded: 1952. **Staff:** Prof 1; Other 2. **Subjects:** Medicine, nursing, allied health sciences. **Holdings:** 1000 books; 3 VF drawers of pamphlets and clippings. **Subscriptions:** 257 journals and other serials. **Services:** Interlibrary loan; copying; library open to the public. **Computerized Information Services:** MEDLARS, DIALOG Information Services; EasyLink (electronic mail service). Performs searches on fee basis. **Networks/Consortia:** Member of Greater Midwest Regional Medical Library Network, Valley Medical Network (VMN).

★14541★
UNITED HOSPITAL CENTER INC. - INFORMATION CENTER (Med)
3 Hospital Plaza Phone: (304)624-2230
Clarksburg, WV 26301 Karen H. Enderle, Med.Libn.
Staff: Prof 1. **Subjects:** Medicine, continuing education, health administration, health education. **Holdings:** 2520 books; 1400 bound periodical volumes; 260 microforms; 350 AV programs; 200 video cassettes; 500 audio cassettes. **Subscriptions:** 230 journals and other serials. **Services:** Interlibrary loan; copying; SDI; center open to the public. **Automated Operations:** Computerized serials. **Computerized Information Services:** MEDLARS, DIALOG Information Services. **Networks/Consortia:** Member of North-Central Area Consortium for Health Information Resources (NACHIR).

★14542★
UNITED HOSPITAL FUND OF NEW YORK - REFERENCE LIBRARY (Bus-Fin)
55 Fifth Ave., 16th Fl. Phone: (212)645-2500
New York, NY 10003 Kenneth H. Willer, Libn.
Founded: 1941. **Staff:** Prof 1; Other 1. **Subjects:** Hospital management, health services research, fund raising, volunteer services. **Holdings:** 5000 books; 90 VF drawers of reports, documents, pamphlets, clippings. **Subscriptions:** 100 journals and other serials. **Services:** Interlibrary loan; copying; library open to the public by appointment. **Networks/Consortia:** Member of Manhattan-Bronx Health Sciences Library Group, Medical & Scientific Libraries of Long Island (MEDLI), New York Metropolitan Reference and Research Library Agency (METRO).

★14543★
UNITED HOSPITALS MEDICAL CENTER - LIBRARY (Med)
15 S. 9th St. Phone: (201)268-8774
Newark, NJ 07107 Rosary S. Gilheany, Dir., Lib.Serv.
Founded: 1960. **Staff:** Prof 2; Other 1. **Subjects:** Medicine, nursing, ophthalmology, otorhinolaryngology, pediatrics, orthopedics, hospital administration. **Special Collections:** Learning Resource Center Collection. **Holdings:** 5500 books; 7000 bound periodical volumes; tapes; 6 VF drawers of pamphlets, clippings, reprints; 2 VF drawers and 3 shelves of archival materials; 650 AV programs; 7 audio cassette subscriptions. **Subscriptions:** 250 journals and other serials. **Services:** Interlibrary loan; copying; SDI (limited); library open to the public with restrictions. **Automated Operations:** Computerized serials and circulation. **Computerized Information Services:** DIALOG Information Services, MEDLINE, BRS Information Technologies; internal database; MESSAGES (electronic mail service). Performs searches on fee basis. **Networks/Consortia:** Member of Cosmopolitan Biomedical Library Consortium (CBLC), Health Sciences Library Association of New Jersey, Essex-Hudson Regional Library Cooperative. **Publications:** Library Informer (newsletter and acquisitions list), quarterly; bibliographies - to medical professionals. **Special Catalogs:** Children's Health Audiovisual Materials Project Catalog (pamphlet). **Remarks:** An alternate telephone number is 268-8776. **Staff:** Nancy Nagele, Pub.Serv.Libn..

★14544★
UNITED ILLUMINATING - LIBRARY (Sci-Engr, Energy)
80 Temple St. Phone: (203)787-7690
New Haven, CT 06506 Lynn Sabol, Libn.
Founded: 1979. **Staff:** Prof 1. **Subjects:** Electricity generation and distribution, energy resources, computer science, management, engineering. **Holdings:** 2400 books. **Subscriptions:** 448 journals and other serials. **Services:** Interlibrary loan; copying; library open to the public by appointment. **Computerized Information Services:** DIALOG Information Services, Utility Data Institute. **Publications:** Newsletter.

★14545★
UNITED LIBRARY OF GARRETT-EVANGELICAL AND SEABURY-WESTERN THEOLOGICAL SEMINARIES (Rel-Phil)
2121 Sheridan Rd.
Evanston, IL 60201 Phone: (312)866-3900
Founded: 1857. **Staff:** Prof 6; Other 5. **Subjects:** General theology, Wesleyana, British and American Methodism, Anglicana, Semitic languages and literature. **Special Collections:** Deering-Jackson Methodistica (500 titles); Keen Bible Collection; Hibbard Egyptian Collection. **Holdings:** 272,000 volumes. **Subscriptions:** 1900 journals and other serials. **Services:** Interlibrary loan; copying; library open to the public with restrictions with fee for borrowing. **Automated Operations:** Computerized cataloging, acquisitions, and serials. **Staff:** Alva Caldwell, Libn.; Newland Smith, III.

★14546★
UNITED LODGE OF THEOSOPHISTS - THEOSOPHY HALL - LIBRARY (Rel-Phil)
347 E. 72nd St.
New York, NY 10021 Phone: (212)535-2230
Founded: 1922. **Subjects:** Theosophy, comparative religion, Buddhism, Hinduism, philosophy, psychology, psychic research, mythology and symbolism, Christian church history, the heretics. **Special Collections:** Original editions of writings of H.P. Blavatsky and W.Q. Judge. **Holdings:** 6500 books; 325 bound periodical volumes. **Services:** Library open to the public.

UNITED MEDICAL STAFF OF BOULDER - BOULDER VALLEY MEDICAL LIBRARY
See: Boulder Valley Medical Library (1774)

★14547★
UNITED MERCHANTS AND MANUFACTURING COMPANY - RESEARCH CENTER LIBRARY (Sci-Engr)
Box 64A Phone: (803)593-4461
Langley, SC 29843-0009 Larry G. Smith, Mgr., Res.Serv.
Founded: 1962. **Staff:** Prof 1; Other 1. **Subjects:** Chemistry and chemical engineering, textiles. **Holdings:** 2500 books; 2200 bound periodical volumes; 500 other cataloged items. **Subscriptions:** 44 journals and other serials. **Services:** Library not open to the public.

UNITED METHODIST CHURCH - CALIFORNIA PACIFIC AND DESERT SOUTHWEST CONFERENCE - ARCHIVES
See: School of Theology at Claremont - Theology Library (12973)

★14548★
UNITED METHODIST CHURCH - CENTRAL ILLINOIS CONFERENCE - CONFERENCE HISTORICAL SOCIETY LIBRARY (Rel-Phil)
1211 N. Park
Box 515
Bloomington, IL 61702-0515
Staff: 2. **Subjects:** History of the Illinois Conference, 1824 to present; Methodism in Illinois; United Brethren and Evangelical Churches. **Holdings:** 1200 books and bound periodical volumes; local church histories; biographies; early conference journals on microfilm. **Services:** Library open to the public. **Publications:** Historical Messenger, quarterly.

★14549★
UNITED METHODIST CHURCH - EASTERN PENNSYLVANIA ANNUAL CONFERENCE - HISTORICAL SOCIETY LIBRARY (Hist, Rel-Phil)
326 New St. Phone: (215)925-7788
Philadelphia, PA 19106 Brian McCloskey, Adm.
Subjects: Methodist history and related subjects. **Special Collections:** Annual Conference Journals and Methodist Disciplines, 1784 to present; General Conference minutes of the United Methodist Church. **Holdings:** 7000 books and bound periodical volumes. **Services:** Library open to the public for reference use only.

★14550★
UNITED METHODIST CHURCH - GENERAL COMMISSION ON ARCHIVES AND HISTORY - LIBRARY AND ARCHIVES (Rel-Phil)
36 Madison Ave.
Box 127
Madison, NJ 07940 Kenneth E. Rowe, Libn.
Staff: Prof 3; Other 3. **Subjects:** Church records of Methodist Episcopal Church, Methodist Episcopal Church (South), Methodist Protestant Church, Methodist Church, Evangelical United Brethren Church, United Brethren in Christ Church, Evangelical Church, Evangelical Association, United Evangelical Church; United Methodist Church. **Special Collections:** Board of Mission correspondence from missionaries and overseas conference journals; private papers of Methodist leaders and bishops. **Holdings:** 70,000 books; 1600 bound periodical volumes; 4 million archival items; 100,000 feet of microfilm; 100 tubes of blueprints. **Subscriptions:** 600 journals and other serials. **Services:** Interlibrary loan; copying; library open to the public with restrictions. **Publications:** Historians' Digest (newsletter), quarterly; Methodist History, quarterly. **Remarks:** Includes the holdings of the Association of Methodist Historical Societies and the former E.U.B. Historical Society. **Staff:** William C. Beal, Jr., Archv..

★14551★
UNITED METHODIST CHURCH - HISTORICAL SOCIETY OF THE EASTERN PENNSYLVANIA CONFERENCE - ARCHIVES ROOM† (Rel-Phil)
Gossard Memorial Library
Lebanon Valley College Phone: (717)867-4411
Annville, PA 17003 Rev. Robert Curry, Archv.-Libn.
Founded: 1957. **Subjects:** Eastern Conference materials, general former Evangelical United Brethren Church materials. **Holdings:** 578 books; 42 bound periodical volumes; 463 conference proceedings; 53 VF drawers of unbound archival materials. **Services:** Archives open to the public by appointment. **Staff:** James O. Bemesderfer, Libn..

UNITED METHODIST CHURCH - KANSAS EAST CONFERENCE - COMMISSION ON ARCHIVES AND HISTORY
See: Baker University - Archives and Historical Library (1243)

★14552★
UNITED METHODIST CHURCH - KANSAS WEST CONFERENCE - ARCHIVES AND HISTORY DEPOSITORY (Rel-Phil)
Southwestern College Library Phone: (316)221-4150
Winfield, KS 67156 Joanne Black, Archv.
Founded: 1928. **Staff:** 1. **Subjects:** Methodism, especially Kansas Methodism. **Special Collections:** Journals of Kansas West Annual Conference and predecessor conferences; disciplines of United Methodist Church and predecessor denominations; unpublished histories of present and former United Methodist, Methodist, Methodist Episcopal, Evangelical, United Brethren in Christ, and Evangelical United Brethren churches in geographic area of Kansas West Annual Conference. **Holdings:** 1000 volumes; church records; newspapers; manuscripts; memoirs; obituaries. **Services:** Copying; archives open to the public by appointment.

★14553★
UNITED METHODIST CHURCH - NEBRASKA CONFERENCE - HISTORICAL CENTER (Rel-Phil, Hist)
Olin Hall of Science
Nebraska Wesleyan University
50th & St. Paul Phone: (402)465-2175
Lincoln, NE 68504 Bernice M. Boilesen, Cur.
Founded: 1942. **Staff:** Prof 1. **Subjects:** United Methodist history, Nebraska Conference. **Special Collections:** Bible Collection (200); Conference Journals - Methodist, 1856 to present, Evangelical United Brethren, 1880 to present; church histories; local church records. **Holdings:** 15,000 volumes. **Services:** Copying; research; center open to the public.

★14554★
UNITED METHODIST CHURCH - NORTHERN CALIFORNIA-NEVADA CONFERENCE - J.A.B. FRY RESEARCH LIBRARY (Rel-Phil)
University of the Pacific Phone: (209)946-2269
Stockton, CA 95211 Nadine Johnson
Staff: 1. **Subjects:** Methodism, church history, Western Americana. **Special Collections:** Hymnbooks (900). **Holdings:** 2700 books; 400 bound periodical volumes; 5000 archival items. **Subscriptions:** 30 journals and other serials. **Services:** Interlibrary loan; copying; library open to the public by appointment.

★14555★
UNITED METHODIST CHURCH - SOUTH DAKOTA CONFERENCE - COMMITTEE ON ARCHIVES AND HISTORY - LIBRARY (Rel-Phil, Hist)
1331 W. University Ave.
Box 460 Phone: (605)996-6552
Mitchell, SD 57301 Patricia A. Breidenbach, Archv.
Staff: Prof 1. **Subjects:** Religion, church history. **Holdings:** 2800 books; 300 bound periodical volumes; 350 slides and cassettes. **Services:** Copying; library open to the public.

★14556★
UNITED METHODIST CHURCH - SOUTHERN NEW ENGLAND CONFERENCE - HISTORICAL SOCIETY LIBRARY (Rel-Phil, Hist)
745 Commonwealth Ave. Phone: (617)353-3034
Boston, MA 02215 William E. Zimpfer, Libn.
Subjects: New England Methodist history, Wesleyana. **Holdings:** 12,375 books; 300 bound periodical volumes; 200 other cataloged items; 1000 pamphlets; 8000 letters; 30 VF drawers on local churches. **Subscriptions:** 10 journals and other serials. **Services:** Interlibrary loan; copying; library open to the public. **Automated Operations:** Computerized cataloging. **Remarks:** The library is housed in the library of the Boston University - School of Theology and serviced by that staff on a contract basis.

★14557★
UNITED METHODIST CHURCH - WISCONSIN CONFERENCE - ARCHIVES (Hist, Rel-Phil)
750 Windsor St., Suite 302 Phone: (608)837-7320
Sun Prairie, WI 53590 Mary E. Schroeder, Archv./Hist.Libn.
Staff: Prof 1. **Subjects:** Church history. **Special Collections:** Diaries of William Darwin Ames, 1857-1898. **Holdings:** 2000 books; 50 bound periodical volumes; 28 VF drawers of archival materials; 15 boxes of newspapers. **Services:** Copying; archives open to the public on a limited schedule. **Special Indexes:** Biographical indexes; church indexes.

★14558★
UNITED METHODIST CHURCH - YELLOWSTONE CONFERENCE - ARCHIVES (Hist, Rel-Phil)
531 Conway Phone: (406)656-8271
Billings, MT 59105-3353 Rev. Ruth Wight, Chair
Staff: 1. **Subjects:** History of ministers and churches. **Special Collections:** Personal papers of Brother Van Orsdel (Methodist circuit rider in Montana); papers of other early-day Methodist ministers. **Holdings:** Books of historical value; microfilm; church materials of historical importance; slides; photographs; tapes; Conference Journals. **Services:** Archives open to the public for reference use by appointment. **Special Catalogs:** List of United Methodist ministers who served within conference boundaries. **Remarks:** Archives located in Adams Library of Rocky Mountain College, Billings, MT 59102.

★14559★
UNITED METHODIST COMMISSION ON ARCHIVES & HISTORY - MINNESOTA ANNUAL CONFERENCE - ARCHIVES & HISTORICAL LIBRARY (Hist, Rel-Phil)
122 W. Franklin Ave., Rm. 400 Phone: (612)870-3657
Minneapolis, MN 55404 Thelma Boeder, Archv./Exec.Sec.
Founded: 1856. **Staff:** Prof 1. **Subjects:** United Methodist Church and Evangelical United Brethren history, particularly in the Minnesota Conference; Methodism. **Special Collections:** Records of many discontinued churches in Minnesota Conference; Church Disciplines; annual conference minutes; journals. **Holdings:** 2000 books; 100 bound periodical volumes; archival records. **Services:** Copying; library open to the public for reference use only.

★14560★
UNITED METHODIST COMMISSION ON ARCHIVES & HISTORY - NORTHWEST TEXAS ANNUAL CONFERENCE - ARCHIVES (Rel-Phil)
Jay-Rollins Library
McMurry College
Box 296 Phone: (915)691-2291
Abilene, TX 79697 Jewell Posey, Archv.
Staff: Prof 1; Other 1. **Subjects:** Church history. **Special Collections:** J.O. Haymes (6 boxes); O.P. Clark (1 box); Cal C. Wright (21 linear feet); Alsie H. Carleton (10 linear feet). **Holdings:** 459 books; 100 bound periodical volumes; 200 membership minutes; 2 VF drawers of local church histories; 25 boxes of unbound reports and publicity; 48 cases of sermon manuscripts; 2 boxes of videotapes and cassettes. **Services:** Copying; archives open to the public with restrictions.

★14561★
UNITED METHODIST COMMISSION ON ARCHIVES & HISTORY - SOUTH CAROLINA CONFERENCE - HISTORICAL SOCIETY LIBRARY (Rel-Phil)
Wofford College Phone: (803)585-4821
Spartanburg, SC 29301 Herbert Hucks, Jr., Cur.
Subjects: Methodist history with particular reference to South Carolina Methodism. **Holdings:** 1600 books and bound periodical volumes; minutes of the South Carolina conference; letters; notes; manuscripts. **Services:** Library open to the public for reference use only.

★14562★
UNITED METHODIST HISTORICAL SOCIETY - BALTIMORE ANNUAL CONFERENCE - LOVELY LANE MUSEUM LIBRARY (Rel-Phil, Hist)
2200 St. Paul St. Phone: (301)889-4458
Baltimore, MD 21218 Rev. Edwin Schell, Exec.Sec./Libn.
Founded: 1855. **Staff:** Prof 2; Other 1. **Subjects:** Religion, Wesleyana, American church history, higher education, Methodism. **Special Collections:** Baltimore Conference Journal and papers; letters of Bishop Asbury; journals of early Methodist preachers; letters and notes of Bishop Coke; E. Stanley Jones and John F. Goucher papers; Maryland church records. **Holdings:** 4518 books; 280 bound periodical volumes; 16,000 reports, personal papers, church histories, clippings. **Subscriptions:** 29 journals and other serials; 11 newspapers. **Services:** Interlibrary loan; copying; library open to qualified researchers. **Publications:** Third Century Methodism, triennial; annual reports. **Special Catalogs:** United Methodist Clergy - Baltimore and Vicinity, 1773-1986 (card). **Staff:** Betty Ammons, Asst.Libn..

★14563★
UNITED METHODIST PUBLISHING HOUSE - LIBRARY (Publ, Rel-Phil)
201 Eighth Ave., S., Rm. 122 Phone: (615)749-6437
Nashville, TN 37202 Rosalyn Lewis, Libn.
Staff: Prof 1; Other 2. **Subjects:** United Methodist Publishing House Archives, Methodist history, religion. **Special Collections:** Wesleyana (575 items). **Holdings:** 15,000 books; 4000 bound periodical volumes; 60 VF drawers; 1100 reels of microfilm; portraits; group pictures. **Subscriptions:** 263 journals and other serials; 62 newspapers. **Services:** Interlibrary loan; copying; library open to the public for research use only. **Automated Operations:** Computerized cataloging. **Computerized Information Services:** OCLC. **Networks/Consortia:** Member of SOLINET.

★14564★
UNITED MORTGAGE BANKERS OF AMERICA - LIBRARY (Bus-Fin)
800 Ivy Hill Rd. Phone: (215)242-6060
Philadelphia, PA 19150 Gene Hatton, Exec.Dir.
Founded: 1962. **Subjects:** Minority mortgage brokering and banking. **Holdings:** 2000 volumes.

★14565★
UNITED NATIONS - CENTRE FOR HUMAN SETTLEMENTS - INFORMATION OFFICE FOR NORTH AMERICA AND THE CARIBBEAN (Soc Sci)
Faculty of Environmental Studies
York University
4700 Keele St.
North York, ON, Canada M3J 1P3 Phone: (416)736-5377
Staff: Prof 1; Other 1. **Subjects:** Human settlements issues. **Special Collections:** Government documentation relating to the 1976 United Nations Conference on Human Settlements; government-produced films on human settlements issues (over 200). **Holdings:** 50 published works on human settlements; documents; reports; information directories; videotapes; films. **Subscriptions:** 28 journals and other serials. **Services:** Interlibrary loan; copying; office open to the public. **Publications:** Habitat News, 3/year; list of other publications - available on request. **Special Catalogs:** Film Catalog (English or French). **Remarks:** Center's headquarters is at Box 30030, Nairobi, Kenya. There are additional information offices in Amman, Bangkok, Budapest, Geneva, and Mexico City. **Also Known As:** Habitat.

★14566★
UNITED NATIONS - CENTRE ON TRANSNATIONAL CORPORATIONS - LIBRARY (Bus-Fin)
United Nations Phone: (212)963-3352
New York, NY 10017 Samuel K.B. Asante, Dir., Adv./Info.Serv.Div.
Founded: 1976. **Subjects:** Transnational corporations, foreign direct investment, foreign investment laws, contracts. **Special Collections:** Company directories; corporate reports; United Nations documents. **Holdings:** Figures not available. **Services:** Library open to public by written or telephone application. **Automated Operations:** Computerized cataloging. **Computerized Information Services:** DIALOG Information Services, Dow Jones News/Retrieval, Dun & Bradstreet Corporation, Pergamon ORBIT InfoLine, Inc.; internal databases. **Publications:** List of publications - available on request. **Staff:** Edith Ward, TNC Affairs Off.; Paul Dysenchuk, Res.Asst./Libn.; Sharon Brandstein, Res.Asst./Bibliog..

UNITED NATIONS - U.S. COMMITTEE FOR UNICEF
See: U.S. Committee for UNICEF (14915)

★14567★
UNITED NATIONS ASSOCIATION OF THE UNITED STATES OF AMERICA - GREATER ST. LOUIS CHAPTER - LIBRARY (Soc Sci)
7359 Forsyth Blvd. Phone: (314)721-1961
St. Louis, MO 63105 Alice W. Dunlop, Libn.
Staff: 1. **Subjects:** International culture, United Nations, peace, conservation, nutrition. **Holdings:** 1200 books; 143 files on U.N. member countries; U.N. publications; files on U.N. agencies. **Subscriptions:** 52 journals and other serials. **Services:** Interlibrary loan; copying; library open to the public. **Networks/Consortia:** Member of St. Louis Regional Library Network. **Publications:** UN Center Newsletter.

★14568★
UNITED NATIONS FUND FOR POPULATION ACTIVITIES - LIBRARY (Soc Sci)
220 E. 42nd St., Rm. DN-1710 Phone: (212)850-5809
New York, NY 10017 Avi Green, Chf.
Staff: Prof 2; Other 2. **Subjects:** Population, family planning, economic development. **Holdings:** 4500 books; 2500 reprints. **Subscriptions:** 400 journals and other serials; 5 newspapers. **Services:** Interlibrary loan; copying; SDI; library open to graduate students and professional researchers. **Automated Operations:** Computerized cataloging. **Computerized Information Services:** DIALOG Information Services, NEXIS, MEDLINE, POPLINE; internal database; Dialcom Inc., Dialnet (electronic mail services). **Networks/Consortia:** Member of APLIC International Census Network, Consortium of Foundation Libraries. **Publications:** UNFPA Project Publications Abstracts - for internal distribution only. **Staff:** David P. Rose, Tech.Serv. & Database Libn..

★14569★
UNITED NATIONS HEADQUARTERS - DAG HAMMARSKJOLD LIBRARY (Soc Sci)
United Nations Phone: (212)963-7412
New York, NY 10017 Lengvard Khitrov, Dir.
Founded: 1946. **Staff:** Prof 65; Other 86. **Subjects:** Political affairs, economics, national and international law, social affairs, international relations, science and technology, statistics, transnational corporations, history and activities of the United Nations. **Special Collections:** U.N. and specialized agencies documents; League of Nations documents; Woodrow Wilson Memorial Library (international affairs, 1918-1945); official gazettes of member states. **Holdings:** 400,000 volumes; 80,000 maps; 12,300 reels of microfilm; 50,000 microcards; 200,000 microfiche. **Subscriptions:** 8000 journals and other serials; 200 newspapers. **Services:** Interlibrary loan; library not open to the public. **Automated Operations:** Computerized cataloging and acquisitions. **Computerized Information Services:** NEXIS; UNBIS (internal database). **Publications:** List of publications - available on request. **Staff:** Joseph L. Fuchs, Chf., Users' Serv.; Frank Nakada, Act.Chf., Tech.Oper./Pubn.Serv.

★14570★
UNITED NATIONS INSTITUTE FOR TRAINING AND RESEARCH - LIBRARY (Soc Sci)
801 United Nations Plaza Phone: (212)754-8656
New York, NY 10017 Hideko Makiyama
Subjects: United Nations policy and efficacy; regional cooperation; policy choices and strategies for the future; energy and natural resources. **Special Collections:** Wilfred Jenks Memorial Collection (250 League of Nations documents). **Holdings:** 12,000 book titles; 105 periodical titles; 200,000 official and unofficial UN documents.

★14571★
UNITED NEGRO COLLEGE FUND, INC. - DEPARTMENT OF ARCHIVES AND HISTORY (Educ)
500 E. 62nd St. Phone: (212)326-1118
New York, NY 10021 Paula Williams, Asst.Archv.
Staff: Prof 3. **Subjects:** Higher education for blacks, history of philanthropy and fund raising. **Holdings:** 750 cubic feet. **Services:** Copying; department open to the public with restrictions.

UNITED OF OMAHA INSURANCE COMPANY
See: Mutual of Omaha/United of Omaha Insurance Company (9477)

★14572★
UNITED PAPERWORKERS INTERNATIONAL UNION - LIBRARY (Law, Soc Sci)
3340 Perimeter Hill Dr.
Box 1475 Phone: (615)834-8590
Nashville, TN 37202 Irene Glaus, Libn.
Founded: 1981. **Staff:** Prof 1. **Subjects:** Labor relations, law, and history; occupational safety and health. **Special Collections:** UPIU Oral History Series (50 audio- and videotapes). **Holdings:** 4343 books; 468 bound periodical volumes; 3200 microfiche; 38 audiotapes; 26 videotapes; 76 16mm films; 900 government documents. **Subscriptions:** 142 journals and other serials; 44 newspapers. **Services:** Interlibrary loan; library open to the public for reference use only. **Computerized Information Services:** LEXIS, NEXIS.

★14573★
UNITED SEAMAN'S SERVICE - AMERICAN MERCHANT MARINE LIBRARY ASSOCIATION - PUBLIC LIBRARY OF THE HIGH SEAS (Hum)
One World Trade Center, Suite 1365 Phone: (212)775-1038
New York, NY 10048 Vando Dell'Amico, Exec.Dir.
Founded: 1921. **Staff:** 4. **Special Collections:** William Bollman Collection (biography, history, travel). **Holdings:** 3500 volumes. **Services:** Library open to the public for reference use only. **Publications:** Annual report. **Remarks:** Bollman Collection is housed at the Seaman's Church Institute of New York - Joseph Conrad Library. Association solicits books from the public and prepares boxed libraries for placement aboard American-flag vessels.

★14574★
UNITED SERVICES AUTOMOBILE ASSOCIATION - CORPORATE LIBRARY C-1-E (Bus-Fin)
9800 Fredericksburg Rd. Phone: (512)498-1524
San Antonio, TX 78288 Sylvia Phillips, Mgr., Lib.Serv.
Founded: 1967. **Staff:** Prof 2; Other 3. **Subjects:** Insurance, business, management, computer science. **Holdings:** 4500 books; 10 drawers of pamphlets and maps. **Subscriptions:** 300 journals and other serials; 10 newspapers. **Services:** Interlibrary loan; copying; SDI; library open to the public by appointment. **Automated Operations:** Computerized cataloging. **Computerized Information Services:** DIALOG Information Services, Pergamon ORBIT InfoLine, Inc., OCLC, Dun & Bradstreet Corporation, Dow Jones News/Retrieval, NEXIS; internal database. **Networks/Consortia:** Member of AMIGOS Bibliographic Council, Inc., Council of Research & Academic Libraries (CORAL). **Staff:** Leslie Todd, Libn..

★14575★
UNITED SOCIETY OF BELIEVERS - THE SHAKER LIBRARY (Rel-Phil)
Shaker Village, Sabbathday Lake
Poland Spring, ME 04274 Phone: (207)926-4865
Staff: Prof 3; Other 2. **Subjects:** Shaker theology and history, biography, art, music, technology, herbology, historical agriculture, American communal societies. **Special Collections:** The Koreshan Unity; Christian Israelite Church; Religious Society of Friends. **Holdings:** 16,143 volumes; 8000 manuscripts; 20 VF drawers of catalogs, labels, broadsides; 8 VF drawers of tracts and pamphlets; 13 VF drawers of photographs, slides, maps; 200 reels of microfilm. **Subscriptions:** 106 journals and other serials. **Services:** Copying; library open to the public by appointment. **Automated Operations:** Computerized cataloging. **Publications:** The Shaker Quarterly. **Special Indexes:** Biographical index (card). **Staff:** Paige S. Lilly, Archv./Libn..

U.S. ADVISORY COMMISSION ON INTERGOVERNMENTAL RELATIONS
See: Advisory Commission on Intergovernmental Relations (71)

★14576★
U.S. AGENCY FOR INTERNATIONAL DEVELOPMENT - A.I.D. LIBRARY (Soc Sci, Sci-Engr)
320 21st St., N.W., Rm. 105, SA-18 Phone: (703)235-1000
Washington, DC 20523 Ardith M. Betts, Hd.
Founded: 1967. **Staff:** Prof 2; Other 4. **Subjects:** International economic development, foreign assistance administration, agricultural and rural development, education, health and population planning, science and technology, transportation, irrigation, energy. **Holdings:** 50,000 books and reports; 50,000 AID foreign assistance program documents and research reports on microfiche; FAO technical publications on microfiche. **Subscriptions:** 600 journals and other serials. **Services:** Interlibrary loan; library open to the public. **Automated Operations:** Computerized cataloging. **Computerized Information Services:** DIALOG Information Services, Pergamon ORBIT InfoLine, Inc., OCLC; AID Development Information System (internal database). Performs searches free of charge (internal database only). Contact Person: Ellen S. Nayeri, Ref.. **Networks/Consortia:** Member of FEDLINK. **Publications:** AID Research and Development Abstracts, quarterly - to government agencies, development organizations, research institutions, libraries. **Remarks:** Agency is part of the U.S. International Development Cooperation Agency. Library located at 1601 N. Kent St., Arlington, VA. **Staff:** Jim Harold, ILL; Margaret S. Pope, Res. & Ref.Serv.Coord..

U.S. AGENCY FOR INTERNATIONAL DEVELOPMENT - NITROGEN FIXATION BY TROPICAL AGRICULTURAL LEGUMES
See: Nitrogen Fixation by Tropical Agricultural Legumes (10253)

U.S. AGENCY FOR INTERNATIONAL DEVELOPMENT - POPULATION INFORMATION PROGRAM
See: Johns Hopkins University - Population Information Program (7242)

★14577★
U.S. AGENCY FOR INTERNATIONAL DEVELOPMENT - WATER & SANITATION FOR HEALTH PROJECT - INFORMATION CENTER (Env-Cons)
1611 N. Kent St., Rm. 1002 Phone: (703)243-8200
Arlington, VA 22209 Dan B. Campbell, Info.Dir.
Staff: Prof 2. **Subjects:** Water supply, sanitation, environmental health, technology transfer. **Special Collections:** Rainwater catchments; guineaworm control; women in development. **Holdings:** 5000 reports and texts focusing on rural and near-urban areas in developing countries; reports on 66 least-developed countries. **Subscriptions:** 35 journals and other serials; 50 newsletters. **Services:** Center open to the public. **Computerized Information Services:** DIALOG Information Services, Pergamon ORBIT InfoLine, Inc., BRS Information Technologies; internal databases. **Also Known As:** WASH Information Center.

★14578★
U.S. AIR FORCE - AEROSPACE AUDIOVISUAL SERVICE - RECORDS CENTER BRANCH (Aud-Vis, Mil)
1352 AVSQ/DOSR, Bldg. 248 Phone: (714)382-6315
Norton AFB, CA 92409 Lt. John Corry, Chf., Rec.Ctr.
Staff: 4. **Subjects:** Army, Navy, and Marine Corps documentary film and U.S. Department of Defense film productions, 1950 to present; Air Force in World Wars I and II; Korean War; Vietnam War. **Holdings:** 125 million feet of motion picture film and video records. **Services:** Center open to the public with clearance through appropriate military service public affairs office. **Remarks:** Records center is the depository for all motion pictures or video materials created or acquired by the U.S. military prior to their retirement to the national archives.

★14579★
U.S. AIR FORCE - AIR FORCE ACCOUNTING AND FINANCE CENTER - TECHNICAL LIBRARY (Bus-Fin)
AFAFC/FL7040 Phone: (303)370-7566
Denver, CO 80279-5000 Alreeta Eidson, Chf.Adm.Libn.
Founded: 1951. **Staff:** Prof 2; Other 2. **Subjects:** Accounting, data processing, business, management. **Holdings:** 9000 books; 148,500 Armed Forces and Department of Defense directives and other government documents. **Subscriptions:** 400 journals and other serials; 20 newspapers. **Services:** Interlibrary loan; library open to federal employees. **Automated Operations:** Computerized cataloging and ILL. **Computerized Information Services:** OCLC, DIALOG Information Services, Pergamon ORBIT InfoLine, Inc., BRS Information Technologies, WILSONLINE. **Networks/Consortia:** Member of FEDLINK. **Staff:** Judith D. Moisey, Ref.Libn..

★14580★
U.S. AIR FORCE - AIR FORCE COMMUNICATIONS COMMAND - TECHNICAL INFORMATION CENTER† (Info Sci)
HQ AFCC/DAPL
Bldg. 40, FL 3114
Scott AFB, IL 62225-6001 Phone: (618)256-4437
Staff: Prof 1; Other 3. **Subjects:** Communications, computers, electronics, engineering, mathematics, management. **Holdings:** 1400 technical reports; 3400 technical reports on microfilm. **Subscriptions:** 139 journals and other serials; 6 newspapers. **Services:** Center not open to the public. **Computerized Information Services:** DTIC, OCLC. **Networks/Consortia:** Member of Kaskaskia Library System. **Publications:** Library News, monthly - for internal distribution only.

★14581★
U.S. AIR FORCE - AIR FORCE ENGINEERING AND SERVICES CENTER - TECHNICAL LIBRARY (Sci-Engr)
Bldg. 1120, Stop 21
FL 7050 Phone: (904)283-6285
Tyndall AFB, FL 32403-6001 Andrew D. Poulis, Chf.Tech.Libn.
Founded: 1975. **Staff:** Prof 2; Other 2. **Subjects:** Engineering - civil, environmental, chemical; readiness; fire research; structural engineering. **Special Collections:** Rapid runway repair; centrifuges; bird air strike hazards; sonic boom research; groundwater contamination. **Holdings:** 5000 books; 525 bound periodical volumes; 30,000 hardcopy technical reports; 100,000 technical reports on microfiche; 150,000 military and commercial specifications and standards on microfilm; 30,000 engineering reports on microfilm; 3000 slides; 150 videotapes. **Subscriptions:** 525 journals and other serials; 10 newspapers. **Services:** Interlibrary loan; copying; SDI;

library open to Air Force, Department of Defense, other government agency personnel, and local residents. **Automated Operations:** Computerized public access catalog, cataloging, acquisitions, and serials. **Computerized Information Services:** DIALOG Information Services, BRS Information Technologies, OCLC, STN International, NASA/RECON, Pergamon ORBIT InfoLine, Inc., Integrated Technical Information System (ITIS), DTIC; LIB/INDEX (internal database). **Networks/ Consortia:** Member of FEDLINK. **Publications:** Databases Directory; Periodicals Directory, both annual - both for internal distribution only. **Remarks:** An alternate telephone number is 283-6270. **Staff:** Janet Davis, Ref.Libn..

★14582★
U.S. AIR FORCE - AIR FORCE LOGISTICS COMMAND - U.S. AIR FORCE MUSEUM - RESEARCH DIVISION LIBRARY (Mil)
Bldg. 489, Area B Phone: (513)255-3284
Wright-Patterson AFB, OH 45433 Charles G. Worman, Chf., Res.Div.
Staff: Prof 3; Other 4. **Subjects:** History and technology of the United States Air Force and its predecessor organizations. **Holdings:** 200,000 documents, including aircraft technical orders, manuscripts, photographs, and drawings. **Services:** Copying (documents); library open to the public by appointment.

★14583★
U.S. AIR FORCE - AIR FORCE MANPOWER & PERSONNEL CENTER - MORALE, WELFARE & RECREATION DIRECTORATE - LIBRARY SERVICES BRANCH
AFMPC/DPMSPL Phone: (512)652-3037
Randolph AFB, TX 78150-6001 Tony Dakan, Dir., USAF Libs.
Remarks: Section is administrative headquarters for Air Force library services throughout the world with a total of 340 library facilities and a book stock of more than 5 million volumes.

★14584★
U.S. AIR FORCE - AIR FORCE SYSTEMS COMMAND - AIR FORCE GEOPHYSICS LABORATORY - RESEARCH LIBRARY (Sci-Engr)
AFGL/SULL
FL 2807 Phone: (617)377-4895
Hanscom AFB, MA 01731 Ruth K. Seidman, Lib.Dir.
Staff: Prof 9; Other 8. **Subjects:** Physical and environmental sciences, geophysics, meteorology, math and computer science, astronomy and astrophysics, electronics and electrical engineering, chemical and materials sciences. **Special Collections:** Oriental Science Library (35,000 volumes); scientific manuscripts of 3rd and 4th Lords Rayleigh; early ballooning and aeronautics (200 volumes); rare books (2500 volumes). **Holdings:** 257,000 books and bound periodical volumes; 100,595 unbound technical reports; 1583 audio materials; 1548 reels of microfilm; 76,374 microfiche; 243 cassettes; 40 VF drawers of translations. **Subscriptions:** 2289 journals and other serials. **Services:** Interlibrary loan; copying; library open to the public with restrictions. **Automated Operations:** Computerized cataloging and serials. **Computerized Information Services:** DIALOG Information Services, BRS Information Technologies, OCLC, DTIC, NASA/RECON; LINX Courier, DIALMAIL (electronic mail services). **Networks/ Consortia:** Member of FEDLINK. **Publications:** Weekly Accessions List - for internal distribution only. **Staff:** John W. Armstrong, Sel.Libn.; Elfrieda L. Cavallari, Chf., Cat.; Ellen K. Dobi, Chf., Ref. & Circ.; Lee McLaughlin, Chf., Acq..

★14585★
U.S. AIR FORCE - AIR FORCE SYSTEMS COMMAND - AIR FORCE WEAPONS LABORATORY - TECHNICAL LIBRARY (Mil)
AFWL/SUL
FL 2809 Phone: (505)844-7449
Kirtland AFB, NM 87117-6008 Barbara I. Newton, Chf.
Founded: 1947. **Staff:** Prof 6; Other 6. **Subjects:** Advanced weapons development, civil engineering, aeronautical systems, lasers, missile and space systems, electromagnetic pulse. **Holdings:** 21,000 books; 10,000 bound periodical volumes; 8000 cartridges of microfilm of periodicals; 300,000 technical reports. **Subscriptions:** 870 journals and other serials. **Services:** Interlibrary loan; copying; SDI; library open to the public by permission of military authority. **Automated Operations:** Computerized cataloging, acquisitions, and serials. **Computerized Information Services:** DTIC, DIALOG Information Services, BRS Information Technologies, CAS ONLINE, STN International, Integrated Technical Information System (ITIS), NASA/RECON, OCLC. **Networks/Consortia:** Member of FEDLINK. **Staff:** Carol A. Cahn, Supv.Libn., Info.Serv.; Elizabeth Ybarra, Ref.Libn.; Janet Jourdain, Rpt.Cat..

★14586★
U.S. AIR FORCE - AIR FORCE SYSTEMS COMMAND - ARMAMENT DIVISION, AIR FORCE ARMAMENT LABORATORY - TECHNICAL LIBRARY (Sci-Engr)
AD/DOIL
FL 2825 Phone: (904)882-3212
Eglin AFB, FL 32542-5438 June C. Stercho, Chf.
Founded: 1955. **Staff:** Prof 3; Other 3. **Subjects:** Aeronautics, electronics, physics, mathematics, biology, chemistry. **Holdings:** 20,000 books; 4052 bound periodical volumes; 150,000 technical reports; 200,000 reports on microfiche; 15,000 reels of microfilm. **Subscriptions:** 731 journals and other serials. **Services:** Interlibrary loan; library open to qualified users. **Computerized Information Services:** DTIC, DIALOG Information Services, OCLC. **Networks/Consortia:** Member of FEDLINK. **Publications:** Accessions List, semimonthly - for internal distribution only. **Staff:** Mary A. Murphy, Open Lit.Libn.; Van M. Gandy, Doc.Libn..

★14587★
U.S. AIR FORCE - AIR FORCE SYSTEMS COMMAND - FLIGHT TEST CENTER - TECHNICAL LIBRARY (Sci-Engr)
6520 Test Group/ENXL
FL 2806 Phone: (805)277-3606
Edwards AFB, CA 93523-5000 Margaret O'Drobinak, Libn.
Founded: 1955. **Staff:** Prof 2; Other 2. **Subjects:** Aerodynamics, chemistry, physics, management, propulsion, mathematics. **Special Collections:** AFFTC technical reports; Air Force Astronautics Laboratory technical reports. **Holdings:** 27,000 books; 6000 bound periodical volumes; 10,000 society papers; 180,000 technical reports; 500 videotapes; audiotapes; periodicals on microfilm. **Subscriptions:** 500 journals and other serials. **Services:** Interlibrary loan; library not open to the public. **Computerized Information Services:** DIALOG Information Services, DTIC, OCLC. **Publications:** Current Contents of Periodicals; List of Books Received - both for internal distribution only. **Staff:** Jolaine Lamb, Br.Libn..

★14588★
U.S. AIR FORCE - AIR FORCE SYSTEMS COMMAND - HUMAN RESOURCES LABORATORY - LIBRARY (Soc Sci)
AFHRL/TSRL
FL 2870 Phone: (512)536-2651
Brooks AFB, TX 78235-5601 Orrine L. Woinowsk, Adm.Libn.
Founded: 1948. **Staff:** Prof 1; Other 1. **Subjects:** Psychology, mathematical statistics, computer sciences. **Holdings:** 12,604 volumes; 4701 technical reports; 2965 microforms. **Subscriptions:** 442 journals and other serials. **Services:** Interlibrary loan; copying; library open to the public by appointment for reference use only. **Automated Operations:** Computerized cataloging, serials, and ILL. **Computerized Information Services:** OCLC, DIALOG Information Services. **Networks/Consortia:** Member of Health Oriented Libraries of San Antonio (HOLSA), AMIGOS Bibliographic Council, Inc., Council of Research & Academic Libraries (CORAL), FEDLINK.

★14589★
U.S. AIR FORCE - AIR FORCE SYSTEMS COMMAND - HUMAN SYSTEMS DIVISION - SCHOOL OF AEROSPACE MEDICINE - STRUGHOLD AEROMEDICAL LIBRARY (Med)
Brooks AFB, TX 78235-5301 Phone: (516)536-3321
Fred W. Todd, Chf.Libn.
Founded: 1918. **Staff:** Prof 11; Other 6. **Subjects:** Aerospace medicine, bioastronautics, bionucleonics, clinical medicine, dentistry, life sciences. **Holdings:** 33,982 books; 101,131 bound periodical volumes; 47,800 microfiche; 100,367 technical reports. **Subscriptions:** 1983 journals and other serials; 11 newspapers. **Services:** Interlibrary loan; copying; SDI; library open by special permission. **Automated Operations:** Computerized cataloging. **Computerized Information Services:** DIALOG Information Services, DTIC, MEDLARS, NASA/RECON, OCLC, BRS Information Technologies, Chemical Information Systems, Inc. (CIS), National Technical Information Service (NTIS), Federal Research in Progress (FEDRIP), National Pesticide Information Retrieval System (NPIRS). **Networks/Consortia:** Member of TALON, Council of Research & Academic Libraries (CORAL), AMIGOS Bibliographic Council, Inc., Health Oriented Libraries of San Antonio (HOLSA). **Publications:** Library Accessions List, monthly. **Special Indexes:** KWIC index to current serials titles; Indexes to Aeromedical Reviews and Technical Reports for the School of Aerospace Medicine (book). **Staff:** Bonnie Fridley, Chf., Pub.Serv.; Olive N. Brewster, Chf., Tech.Proc.; Dewey A. Goff, Jr., Chf., Tech.Rpt.; Marion Green, Chf.Med.Ed.; Ena Shaw, Med.Ed.; John Glowacz, Med.Ed.; Marilyn Goff, Tech.Proc.Libn..

★14590★
U.S. AIR FORCE - AIR FORCE SYSTEMS COMMAND - LIBRARY DIVISION
AFSC/MPSL
FL 2865, Andrews AFB Phone: (301)981-2598
Washington, DC 20334 Frances Quinn Deel, Dir., Command Libs.
Staff: Prof 1; Other 1. **Remarks:** Director of Command Libraries is responsible for establishing plans and policies for library service in 20 Air Force Systems Command technical and base libraries.

★14591★
U.S. AIR FORCE - AIR FORCE SYSTEMS COMMAND - OFFICE OF SCIENTIFIC RESEARCH - LIBRARY (Sci-Engr)
AFOSR/XOTL
FL 2819, Bldg. 410, Bolling AFB Phone: (202)767-4910
Washington, DC 20332 Anthony G. Bialecki, Libn.
Founded: 1956. **Staff:** 1. **Subjects:** Physics, mathematics, solid state sciences, aerospace technology, chemistry, astronomy, life sciences, history and philosophy of science, information sciences. **Holdings:** 16,000 books; 2000 bound periodical volumes. **Subscriptions:** 280 journals and other serials; 5 newspapers. **Services:** Interlibrary loan; library open to researchers on a limited schedule.

★14592★
U.S. AIR FORCE - AIR FORCE SYSTEMS COMMAND - ROME AIR DEVELOPMENT CENTER - DATA & ANALYSIS CENTER FOR SOFTWARE (Comp Sci)
RADC/COED Phone: (315)336-0937
Griffiss AFB, NY 13441-5700 Stephen T. Kelly, DACS Prog.Mgr.
Staff: Prof 5; Other 5. **Subjects:** Software - engineering, technology, reliability, maintenance, productivity, research. **Holdings:** 100 books; 2190 conference proceedings papers; 1567 journal articles; 150 standards and regulations; 693 theses, dissertations, and technical reports. **Subscriptions:** 28 journals and other serials; 5 newspapers. **Services:** Center open to the public for reference use only. **Automated Operations:** Computerized cataloging and retrieval. **Computerized Information Services:** Software Engineering Bibliographic Database (internal database). Performs searches on fee basis. **Publications:** Annual Annotated Bibliography of Acquisitions; User's Guide to DACS Products & Services; DACS Newsletter. **Staff:** Christine C. Coit, Info.Spec..

★14593★
U.S. AIR FORCE - AIR FORCE SYSTEMS COMMAND - ROME AIR DEVELOPMENT CENTER - TECHNICAL LIBRARY (Sci-Engr)
RADC/DOL
FL 2810 Phone: (315)330-7607
Griffiss AFB, NY 13441-5700 Linda R. Evans, Chf.
Founded: 1942. **Staff:** Prof 2; Other 3. **Subjects:** Aeronautics, engineering, electronics, mathematics, computer science, artificial intelligence, radar, communications, electromagnetics, technology. **Holdings:** 17,300 books; 240,000 documents and technical reports. **Subscriptions:** 500 journals and other serials. **Services:** Interlibrary loan (limited). **Computerized Information Services:** DIALOG Information Services, DTIC, OCLC. **Networks/Consortia:** Member of Central New York Library Resources Council (CENTRO). **Publications:** Accessions List.

★14594★
U.S. AIR FORCE - AIR FORCE SYSTEMS COMMAND - TECHNICAL INFORMATION CENTER (Mil)
HQ AFSC/MPSLT
FL 2800, Andrews AFB Phone: (301)981-3551
Washington, DC 20334-5000 Yvonne A. Kinkaid, Chf.
Founded: 1952. **Staff:** Prof 1; Other 1. **Subjects:** Aerospace systems, management, energy, military affairs, operations research, government contracting, unconventional warfare, computer science. **Holdings:** 7700 books; 500 technical reports; 3000 reels of microfilm; 100 audio cassettes; 135 video cassettes. **Subscriptions:** 500 journals and other serials; 20 newspapers. **Services:** Interlibrary loan; center not open to the public. **Automated Operations:** Computerized cataloging. **Computerized Information Services:** DIALOG Information Services, DTIC. **Networks/Consortia:** Member of FEDLINK.

★14595★
U.S. AIR FORCE - AIR FORCE SYSTEMS COMMAND - WRIGHT AERONAUTICAL LABORATORIES - AEROSPACE STRUCTURES INFORMATION & ANALYSIS CENTER (Sci-Engr)
AFWAL/FIBRA/ASIAC Phone: (513)255-6688
Wright-Patterson AFB, OH 45433 Gordon R. Negaard, Dir.
Staff: Prof 5; Other 4. **Subjects:** Structures, computerized analysis, aircraft, stress (mechanics), mathematics, fatigue. **Special Collections:** Specialized and technical reports and publications dealing with aircraft structural design and analysis. **Holdings:** 11,000 technical reports; 36,000 reports on microfiche. **Services:** Interlibrary loan; copying; center open to government contractors. **Computerized Information Services:** DIALOG Information Services, DTIC, NASA/RECON. **Publications:** Newsletter, quarterly. **Staff:** Edward Malloy, Info.Spec.; Richard D. Scibetta, Info.Spec.; R. Rocky Arnold, Mgr..

★14596★
U.S. AIR FORCE - AIR FORCE SYSTEMS COMMAND - WRIGHT AERONAUTICAL LABORATORIES - TECHNICAL LIBRARY (Sci-Engr)
AFWAL/ISL
FL 2802, Bldg. 22 Phone: (513)255-3630
Wright-Patterson AFB, OH 45433 Carolyn Ray, Dir.
Founded: 1918. **Staff:** Prof 5; Other 7. **Subjects:** Aeronautics, astronautics, physics, chemistry, mathematics, electronics, engineering, logistics, propulsion, aerospace medicine, human-factors engineering, management. **Special Collections:** Lahm & Chandler Collection (aeronautics). **Holdings:** 56,000 books; 68,000 bound journals; 700,000 technical reports; microforms; military specifications; industry standards. **Subscriptions:** 1100 journals and other serials. **Services:** Interlibrary loan; library open to the public for reference use only. **Automated Operations:** Computerized cataloging, acquisitions, and circulation. **Computerized Information Services:** DIALOG Information Services, NASA/RECON, DTIC, MEDLARS, NEXIS, CIRC II. **Networks/Consortia:** Member of Southwest Ohio Council for Higher Education (SOCHE). **Staff:** Connie Wiley, Ser./Ref.; Frankie Schverak, Cat./Sys.Coord.; Ron Lundquist, Acq./Ref.; Elwood White, Rpt./Ref..

★14597★
U.S. AIR FORCE - AIR TRAINING COMMAND - KEESLER TECHNICAL TRAINING CENTER - ACADEMIC LIBRARY (Sci-Engr, Mil)
3396 TCHTG/TTEOL
FL 3011
McClelland Hall, Bldg. 2818 Phone: (601)377-4295
Keesler AFB, MS 39534 Verna Westerburg, Lib.Techn.
Founded: 1970. **Subjects:** Communications, electronics, management, military science, computer science, systems engineering. **Holdings:** 4100 books; 125 periodicals. **Services:** Interlibrary loan; library open to the public with restrictions. **Computerized Information Services:** DTIC.

★14598★
U.S. AIR FORCE - AIR TRAINING COMMAND - LIBRARY PROGRAM (Sci-Engr, Mil)
HQ ATC/DPSOL
FL 3000 Phone: (512)652-3410
Randolph AFB, TX 78150-5001 Duane A. Johnson, Command Libn.
Staff: Prof 28; Other 99. **Subjects:** Aeronautics, astronautics, engineering, leadership, military history, management, electronics. **Special Collections:** World War II; weather and instrument flying; survival training; education; vocational guidance; foreign affairs; foreign languages. **Holdings:** 428,904 books and bound periodical volumes; 6956 technical reports and documents; 255,957 microforms; 34,057 AV programs; 5910 maps. **Subscriptions:** 6376 journals and other serials; 608 newspapers. **Services:** Interlibrary loan; library not open to the public. **Automated Operations:** Computerized cataloging, acquisitions, and ILL. **Computerized Information Services:** OCLC, DTIC, The Reference Service (REFSRV). **Networks/Consortia:** Member of Council of Research & Academic Libraries (CORAL). **Remarks:** Command Librarian is responsible for the administration, development, and operation of 19 academic, technical, and base libraries in Air Training Command. Information represents all 19 libraries. An alternate telephone number is 652-2573.

★14599★
U.S. AIR FORCE - AIR TRAINING COMMAND - U.S. AIR FORCE SCHOOL OF HEALTH CARE SCIENCES - ACADEMIC LIBRARY (Med)
FL 3021, Bldg. 1900 Phone: (817)851-4471
Sheppard AFB, TX 76311-5465 Theodore C. Kennedy, Supv.Libn.
Founded: 1956. **Staff:** Prof 1; Other 2. **Subjects:** General medicine, biological science, nursing, dentistry, pharmacy, hospital administration, management. **Holdings:** 12,000 books; 1200 technical reports; 3000 pamphlets. **Subscriptions:** 250 journals and other serials. **Services:** Interlibrary loan; copying; library open to the public for reference use only.

★14600★
U.S. AIR FORCE - AIR UNIVERSITY - INSTITUTE OF TECHNOLOGY - LIBRARY (Sci-Engr)
FL 3319
Bldg. 640, Area B Phone: (513)255-5894
Wright-Patterson AFB, OH 45433 James T. Helling, Dir.
Founded: 1946. **Staff:** Prof 8; Other 8. **Subjects:** Aeronautics, astronautics, electrical engineering, computer engineering, management, logistics, physics. **Holdings:** 45,316 books; 34,121 bound periodical volumes; 800,103 technical reports on microfiche; 60,181 other uncataloged items; Rand reports. **Subscriptions:** 1231 journals and other serials; 26 newspapers. **Services:** Interlibrary loan; library not open to the public. **Automated Operations:** Computerized serials. **Computerized Information Services:** DIALOG Information Services, DTIC, NASA/RECON, OCLC. **Networks/Consortia:** Member of Southwest Ohio Council for Higher Education (SOCHE), FEDLINK. **Publications:** Computerized Journal Holdings List; Permuted Thesis Index - for internal distribution only. **Special Indexes:** Permuted Thesis Index print-out; serials listing; index to AFIT-owned AV materials. **Remarks:** Includes the holdings of the School of Systems and Logistics Library. **Staff:** Helen L. Helton, Chf., Tech.Serv.; Barry S. Boettcher, Chf., Rd.Serv.; Pam McCarthy, Chf., Rd.Serv., Engr.Div.; Chris Cupp, Br.Chf.; Lenore Pursch, Cat.; Kris Zobrowsky, Ref.Libn..

★14601★
U.S. AIR FORCE - AIR UNIVERSITY LIBRARY (Mil)
FL 3368 Phone: (205)293-2606
Maxwell AFB, AL 36112 Robert B. Lane, Dir.
Founded: 1946. **Staff:** Prof 30; Other 44. **Subjects:** Military science, aeronautics, political science, military affairs. **Special Collections:** Air Force Authority materials. **Holdings:** 267,000 books; 106,000 bound periodical volumes; 510,000 cataloged military documents; 850,000 maps and charts; 6600 reels of microfilm of serials and newspapers; 120,000 regulations and manuals; 9000 clippings and pamphlets. **Subscriptions:** 2500 journals and other serials; 50 newspapers. **Services:** Interlibrary loan; copying; library open to the public with restrictions. **Automated Operations:** Computerized cataloging, acquisitions, and serials. **Computerized Information Services:** DTIC, DIALOG Information Services, NEXIS, OCLC; internal database. **Networks/Consortia:** Member of SOLINET, FEDLINK, Network of Alabama Academic Libraries (NAAL). **Publications:** Air University Library Index to Military Periodicals, quarterly; Air University Abstracts of Student Research Reports, annual; Guide to Library Services, occasional; Roster of Subject Specialists, annual; Special Bibliographic Series, irregular; Selected Document Accession, weekly - all for limited distribution. **Remarks:** An alternate telephone number is 293-2888. **Staff:** Dallace L. Meehan, Exec.Off.; Helen N. Taliaferro, Chf., Rd.Serv.Div.; Donald B. Flournoy, Chf., Cart.; Regina A. Mayton, Chf., Sys.Div.; Gaye Byars, Chf.Bibliog.; Sue Goodman, Ed.; Gene Johnson, Chf., Adm.Serv..

U.S. AIR FORCE - ARMAMENT LABORATORY
See: U.S. Air Force - Air Force Systems Command - Armament Division, Air Force Armament Laboratory (14586)

U.S. AIR FORCE - ARNOLD ENGINEERING DEVELOPMENT CENTER
See: Arnold Engineering Development Center (946)

★14602★
U.S. AIR FORCE - ELECTRONIC SECURITY COMMAND - GENERAL LIBRARY (Sci-Engr, Comp Sci)
6923 SS/SSL
FL 7046 Phone: (512)925-2617
San Antonio, TX 78243 Dale T. Ogden, Libn.
Staff: Prof 3; Other 2. **Subjects:** Engineering, telecommunications, computers, electronics, management, recreation. **Holdings:** 20,000 books and bound periodical volumes; 8015 microforms; 3024 AV programs. **Subscriptions:** 475 journals and other serials; 17 newspapers. **Services:** Interlibrary loan; library open to the public with restrictions. **Staff:** Marilyn Wilson, Chf.Techn..

U.S. AIR FORCE - ENVIRONMENTAL TECHNICAL APPLICATIONS CENTER
See: U.S. Air Force - Military Airlift Command - Environmental Technical Applications Center (14604)

U.S. AIR FORCE - FLIGHT TEST CENTER
See: U.S. Air Force - Air Force Systems Command - Flight Test Center (14587)

U.S. AIR FORCE - GEOPHYSICS LABORATORY
See: U.S. Air Force - Air Force Systems Command - Air Force Geophysics Laboratory (14584)

★14603★
U.S. AIR FORCE - HEADQUARTERS USAF HISTORICAL RESEARCH CENTER (Mil)
HQ USAFHRC/HD Phone: (205)293-5723
Maxwell AFB, AL 36112-6678 Lloyd H. Cornett, Jr., Dir.
Founded: 1942. **Staff:** Prof 7; Other 9. **Subjects:** Army Air Force, U.S. Air Force history. **Special Collections:** Unit histories, 1942 to present; oral history tapes and transcripts; Air Corps Tactical School course materials, 1920s-1930s; materials relating to USAF activities in the Southeast Asian war; aircraft record card collection; End of Tour reports; Karlsruhe Collection on the German Air Force; papers of select Air Force personnel. **Holdings:** 3 million documents; 39,000 reels of microfilm; 1500 audiotapes. **Services:** Interlibrary loan (limited); copying; library open to the public for reference use on request, with restrictions on classified and some other selected documents. **Publications:** Bibliographies. **Special Catalogs:** Organizational catalogs reflecting the holdings by organization or special collection. **Remarks:** An alternate telephone number is 293-5733. **Staff:** Dr. Richard E. Morse, Chf., Ref.Div.; R. Cargill Hall, Chf., Res.Div.; Lt.Col. Lorenzo Crowell, Chf., Oral Hist.Div.; Barbara L. Hendry, Chf., Tech.Serv.Div.; Dr. Robert M. Johnson, II, Chf., Circ..

U.S. AIR FORCE - HUMAN RESOURCES LABORATORY
See: U.S. Air Force - Air Force Systems Command - Human Resources Laboratory (14588)

U.S. AIR FORCE - HUMAN SYSTEMS DIVISION
See: U.S. Air Force - Air Force Systems Command - Human Systems Division - School of Aerospace Medicine (14589)

U.S. AIR FORCE - INSTITUTE OF TECHNOLOGY
See: U.S. Air Force - Air University - Institute of Technology (14600)

★14604★
U.S. AIR FORCE - MILITARY AIRLIFT COMMAND - ENVIRONMENTAL TECHNICAL APPLICATIONS CENTER - AIR WEATHER SERVICE TECHNICAL LIBRARY (Sci-Engr)
FL 4414 Phone: (618)256-2625
Scott AFB, IL 62225-5458 Col. Kenneth P. Freeman, Commander
Founded: 1950. **Staff:** Prof 7; Other 9. **Subjects:** Meteorology, climatology. **Special Collections:** Meteorological and climatological data summarized for worldwide stations. **Holdings:** 9950 books; 2000 bound periodical volumes; 53,036 hardcopy technical reports; 117,000 technical reports on microfiche. **Subscriptions:** 348 journals and other serials. **Services:** Interlibrary loan; center open to agency personnel and their contractors. **Computerized Information Services:** DTIC, DIALOG Information Services, Pergamon ORBIT InfoLine, Inc., OCLC, BRS Information Technologies. **Networks/Consortia:** Member of FEDLINK, ILLINET. **Staff:** Walter S. Burgmann, Dir.; Kathryn E. Marshall, Hd.Libn.; Marianne Cavanaugh, Cat.Libn.; Wayne E. McCollom, Meteorologist.

★14605★
U.S. AIR FORCE - OFFICE OF THE JUDGE ADVOCATE GENERAL - LEGAL REFERENCE LIBRARY (Law)
Bldg. 5683 Phone: (202)767-1520
Bolling AFB, DC 20332-6128 William J. Zschunke, Libn.
Founded: 1949. **Subjects:** Law. **Special Collections:** Criminal law. **Holdings:** 16,000 volumes. **Services:** Library open to the public.

U.S. AIR FORCE - OFFICE OF SCIENTIFIC RESEARCH
See: U.S. Air Force - Air Force Systems Command - Office of Scientific Research (14591)

U.S. AIR FORCE - OFFICE OF THE SURGEON GENERAL
See: U.S. Army/U.S. Air Force - Offices of the Surgeons General (14864)

★14606★
U.S. AIR FORCE - OFFICER TRAINING SCHOOL - LIBRARY (Mil)
FL 3050, Bldg. 147 Phone: (512)671-4316
Lackland AFB, TX 78236-5000 Theresa B. Phillips, OTS Supv.Libn.
Staff: Prof 1; Other 2. **Subjects:** Military art and science, military history, leadership, management, communicative skills, physical fitness, defense studies. **Holdings:** 8000 books; 780 bound periodical volumes; 12,780 microfiche; 32 video recordings; 72 AV programs. **Subscriptions:** 96 journals and other serials; 9 newspapers. **Services:** Interlibrary loan; library not open to the public.

U.S. AIR FORCE - ROME AIR DEVELOPMENT CENTER
See: U.S. Air Force - Air Force Systems Command - Rome Air Development Center (14592)

U.S. AIR FORCE - SCHOOL OF AEROSPACE MEDICINE
See: U.S. Air Force - Air Force Systems Command - Human Systems Division - School of Aerospace Medicine (14589)

U.S. AIR FORCE - SCHOOL OF HEALTH CARE SCIENCES
See: U.S. Air Force - Air Training Command - U.S. Air Force School of Health Care Sciences (14599)

★14607★
U.S. AIR FORCE - STRATEGIC AIR COMMAND - LIBRARY HEADQUARTERS†
HQS SAC/DPSOL Phone: (402)294-2367
Offutt AFB, NE 68113-5001 Mary L. Sauer, Dir. of Libs., SAC
Remarks: Command Library Services Headquarters is responsible for direction and supervision of all 25 base libraries within Strategic Air Command (SAC).

U.S. AIR FORCE - WEAPONS LABORATORY
See: U.S. Air Force - Air Force Systems Command - Air Force Weapons Laboratory (14585)

★14608★
U.S. AIR FORCE - WESTERN SPACE AND MISSILE CENTER - WSMC/PMET TECHNICAL LIBRARY (Sci-Engr)
FL 2827 Phone: (805)866-9745
Vandenberg AFB, CA 93437-6021 Cheryl Zebrowski, Chf.Libn.
Founded: 1965. **Staff:** Prof 2; Other 2. **Subjects:** Aerospace vehicles, antennas, electronics, engineering, guided missiles, instrumentation, management, mathematics, propulsion. **Special Collections:** Radar; telemetry. **Holdings:** 10,000 books and bound periodical volumes; 2000 technical reports; 3400 maps; 41,000 microforms. **Subscriptions:** 410 journals and other serials; 24 newspapers. **Services:** Interlibrary loan; library not open to the public. **Automated Operations:** Computerized cataloging. **Computerized Information Services:** DIALOG Information Services, Pergamon ORBIT InfoLine, Inc., NASA/RECON, OCLC, DTIC. **Networks/Consortia:** Member of CLASS. **Publications:** Periodicals Holdings; New Acquisitions - both for internal distribution only. **Staff:** Suzanne Stanton, ILL Libn.; Cathy Andrejak, Ref.Libn..

★14609★
U.S. AIR FORCE ACADEMY - LAW LIBRARY (Law, Mil)
Colorado Springs, CO 80840 Phone: (719)472-3680
Col. M.E. Kinevan, Prof. of Law
Subjects: Law - general, constitutional, governmental contract, international. **Holdings:** 5617 volumes. **Subscriptions:** 126 journals and other serials. **Services:** Library open to faculty and students only. **Staff:** Capt. H. Manson.

★14610★
U.S. AIR FORCE ACADEMY - LIBRARY (Mil, Sci-Engr)
Colorado Springs, CO 80840-5701 Phone: (719)472-2590
Lt.Col. Reiner H. Schaeffer, Dir. of Libs.
Founded: 1955. **Staff:** Prof 16; Other 35. **Subjects:** Science, technology, humanities, social sciences, military art and science, aeronautics. **Special Collections:** Archival materials relating to the Air Force Academy; Colonel Richard Gimbel Aeronautics History Library (20,000 items); falconry. **Holdings:** 318,174 books; 98,136 bound periodical volumes; 4415 phonograph records; 156,328 U.S. Government documents; 14,915 reels of microfilm; 449,676 reports on microfiche; 2000 maps. **Subscriptions:** 3550 journals and other serials; 42 newspapers. **Services:** Interlibrary loan; copying; library open to the public with permission of the director. **Automated Operations:** Computerized public access catalog, cataloging, and circulation. **Computerized Information Services:** DIALOG Information Services, Pergamon ORBIT InfoLine, Inc., BRS Information Technologies, OCLC, NASA/RECON, MEDLARS, DTIC. **Networks/Consortia:** Member of FEDLINK, Plains and Peaks Regional Library Service System, Bibliographical Center for Research, Rocky Mountain Region, Inc. (BCR). **Publications:** New Books List, bimonthly; Handbook; special bibliographies, irregular. **Staff:** Donald J. Barrett, Asst.Dir., Pub.Serv.; Maj. James W. Hopkins, Asst.Dir., Tech.Serv.; Elisabeth J. Fleenor, Chf., Cat.Br.; Barbara Ivey, Chf., Acq.Br.; Elizabeth C. Kysely, Chf., Ref.Br.; Duane J. Reed, Spec.Coll.Libn.; M. Douglas Johnson, Chf., Sys.Br..

★14611★
U.S. AIR FORCE ACADEMY - MEDICAL LIBRARY (Med)
Colorado Springs, CO 80840-5300 Phone: (719)472-5107
Jeanne Entze, Libn.
Staff: 1. **Subjects:** Medicine. **Holdings:** 4313 books. **Subscriptions:** 355 journals and other serials. **Services:** Interlibrary loan; copying; library open to the public for reference use only. **Automated Operations:** Computerized cataloging and circulation. **Computerized Information Services:** DIALOG Information Services, MEDLARS. **Networks/Consortia:** Member of Colorado Council of Medical Librarians.

★14612★
U.S. AIR FORCE BASE - AIR TRAINING COMMAND - CHANUTE BASE TECHNICAL BRANCH LIBRARY (Sci-Engr)
FL 3018, Bldg. 95 Phone: (217)495-3191
Chanute AFB, IL 61868-5000 Esther Cornelius, Tech.Libn.
Founded: 1964. **Staff:** Prof 1. **Subjects:** Aerospace, electronics, metallurgy. **Holdings:** 2500 books. **Subscriptions:** 63 journals and other serials. **Services:** Interlibrary loan; library open to military personnel and their dependents.

★14613★
U.S. AIR FORCE BASE - ALTUS BASE LIBRARY (Mil)
FL 4419 Phone: (405)482-8670
Altus AFB, OK 73523-5985 Bruce Gaver, Libn.
Staff: Prof 1; Other 5. **Subjects:** Military sciences. **Holdings:** 29,000 books; sound recordings; cassettes. **Subscriptions:** 175 journals and other serials; 30 newspapers. **Services:** Interlibrary loan; copying; library open to military and government employees only.

★14614★
U.S. AIR FORCE BASE - ANDREWS BASE LIBRARY (Mil)
FL 4425, Andrews AFB Phone: (301)981-6454
Washington, DC 20331-5984 Linn Landis, Base Libn.
Staff: Prof 1; Other 3. **Subjects:** Aerospace, military history, ethnic literature. **Holdings:** 31,381 books; 180 bound periodical volumes; 300 video cassettes; 340 audio cassettes; microforms; war games. **Subscriptions:** 300 journals and other serials; 15 newspapers. **Services:** Interlibrary loan; copying; library open to military personnel and dependents and civilian base employees.

★14615★
U.S. AIR FORCE BASE - BARKSDALE BASE LIBRARY (Mil)
FL 4608 Phone: (318)456-4101
Barksdale AFB, LA 71110-5000 Sylvia J. Sefcik, Base Libn.
Staff: Prof 2; Other 5. **Subjects:** Aviation, management, business, history. **Special Collections:** Louisiana history. **Holdings:** 42,477 books; 33,055 microforms; 2102 phonograph records. **Subscriptions:** 261 journals and other serials; 23 newspapers. **Services:** Interlibrary loan; copying; library open to base community, military retirees and families.

★14616★
U.S. AIR FORCE BASE - BEALE BASE LIBRARY (Mil)
FL 4686 Phone: (916)634-2706
Beale AFB, CA 95903-5000 Sylvia J. Sefcik, Base Libn.
Staff: Prof 1; Other 2. **Subjects:** Military art and science. **Special Collections:** Framed art works; AV Collection. **Holdings:** 33,800 books; 315 reels of microfilm; 3115 phonograph records and tapes; 1564 microfiche. **Subscriptions:** 361 journals and other serials; 15 newspapers. **Services:** Interlibrary loan; copying; library open to the public for reference use only. **Special Indexes:** Periodical Holdings.

★14617★
U.S. AIR FORCE BASE - BERGSTROM BASE LIBRARY (Mil)
FL 4857 Phone: (512)479-3739
Bergstrom AFB, TX 78743-5000 Louise Saint-John, Base Libn.
Staff: Prof 1; Other 4. **Subjects:** Aeronautics, social sciences, mathematics, U.S. wars, U.S. and foreign history and travel, languages. **Holdings:** 30,255 books; 3 files of pamphlets on foreign countries; clippings file; 2104 phonograph records, tapes, filmstrips. **Subscriptions:** 260 journals and

other serials; 23 newspapers. **Services:** Interlibrary loan; library not open to the public.

★14618★
U.S. AIR FORCE BASE - BLYTHEVILLE BASE LIBRARY (Mil)
FL 4634, Bldg. 555
Blytheville AFB, AR 72317-5225 Bethey J. Becker, Lib.Mgr.
Staff: Prof 1; Other 3. **Subjects:** General collection. **Holdings:** 20,000 books. **Subscriptions:** 150 journals and other serials; 18 newspapers. **Services:** Interlibrary loan; library not open to the public.

★14619★
U.S. AIR FORCE BASE - BOLLING BASE LIBRARY (Mil)
FL 4400, Bolling AFB Phone: (202)767-4251
Washington, DC 20332-5000 Gloria Guffey, Libn.
Staff: Prof 1; Other 3. **Subjects:** General collection. **Special Collections:** Resource material for the deaf and hearing impaired. **Holdings:** 23,000 books. **Subscriptions:** 101 journals and other serials. **Services:** Interlibrary loan; copying; library open to the public on a limited schedule. **Special Indexes:** Index to college catalogs and telephone books; index to Monarch Notes (both on microfiche).

★14620★
U.S. AIR FORCE BASE - CANNON BASE LIBRARY (Mil)
FL 4855 Phone: (505)784-2786
Cannon AFB, NM 88103-5725 Carol J. Davidson, Base Libn.
Staff: Prof 1; Other 3. **Subjects:** U.S. Air Force history, New Mexico history, Southwest, general topics. **Holdings:** 35,000 books; 35,000 microfiche; 3030 AV programs. **Subscriptions:** 382 journals and other serials; 59 newspapers. **Services:** Interlibrary loan; library not open to the public. **Computerized Information Services:** OCLC, DIALOG Information Services.

★14621★
U.S. AIR FORCE BASE - CARSWELL BASE LIBRARY (Mil)
FL 4689 Phone: (817)735-5230
Carswell AFB, TX 76127-5000 Christine R. Lain, Libn.
Founded: 1943. **Staff:** Prof 1; Other 3. **Subjects:** General and technical collection. **Holdings:** 24,195 books; 20,462 other cataloged items. **Subscriptions:** 185 journals and other serials; 15 newspapers. **Services:** Interlibrary loan; copying; library open to the public with restrictions.

★14622★
U.S. AIR FORCE BASE - CASTLE BASE - BAKER LIBRARY (Mil)
FL 4672, Bldg. 422 Phone: (209)726-2630
Castle AFB, CA 95342-5200 D.L. Grinnell, Libn.
Founded: 1956. **Staff:** Prof 1; Other 4. **Subjects:** Management, defense management, United States and military history, sociology, aeronautics. **Holdings:** 30,046 books; 30 bound theses; 3059 phonograph records and tapes; 1000 pamphlets; 196 reels of microfilm. **Subscriptions:** 255 journals and other serials; 20 newspapers. **Services:** Interlibrary loan; copying; library open to the public for reference use only. **Publications:** Minorities bibliographies - for internal distribution only.

★14623★
U.S. AIR FORCE BASE - CHANUTE BASE LIBRARY (Mil)
FL 3018, Bldg. 95 Phone: (217)495-3191
Chanute AFB, IL 61868-5000 William R. Province, Base Libn.
Founded: 1925. **Subjects:** General and technical topics. **Holdings:** 27,000 volumes. **Subscriptions:** 308 journals and other serials. **Services:** Interlibrary loan; library open to active and retired military personnel and dependents and civilian base employees.

★14624★
U.S. AIR FORCE BASE - CHARLESTON BASE LIBRARY (Mil)
FL 4418 Phone: (803)554-3134
Charleston AFB, SC 29404-5225 William E. Darcy, Base Libn.
Staff: Prof 1; Other 5. **Holdings:** 24,800 books; 3200 phonograph records. **Subscriptions:** 125 journals and other serials; 12 newspapers. **Services:** Interlibrary loan; library not open to the public.

★14625★
U.S. AIR FORCE BASE - DOVER BASE LIBRARY (Mil)
436 ABG/SSL
FL 4497, Bldg. 443 Phone: (302)678-6246
Dover AFB, DE 19902-5225 Jean L. Hort, Base Libn.
Founded: 1953. **Staff:** Prof 1; Other 6. **Subjects:** Aviation, general topics. **Holdings:** 25,500 books; 20,000 microforms; college catalogs on microfiche. **Subscriptions:** 248 journals and other serials; 18 newspapers. **Services:** Interlibrary loan; copying; library open to the public for reference use only. **Networks/Consortia:** Member of Kent Library Network (KLN).

★14626★
U.S. AIR FORCE BASE - DYESS BASE LIBRARY (Mil)
FL 4661
Dyess AFB, TX 79607 Phone: (915)696-2618
Founded: 1957. **Staff:** 3. **Subjects:** Social science, Air Force history. **Special Collections:** Texas history and literature. **Holdings:** 21,000 books; 1500 phonograph records. **Subscriptions:** 225 journals and other serials; 12 newspapers. **Services:** Interlibrary loan; library open to the public for reference use only. **Publications:** Book List, monthly.

★14627★
U.S. AIR FORCE BASE - EDWARDS BASE LIBRARY (Mil)
6510th ABG/SSL, Stop 115
FL 2805, Bldg. 2665 Phone: (805)277-2375
Edwards AFB, CA 93523-5000 Orin M. Moyer, Libn.
Founded: 1942. **Staff:** Prof 1; Other 2. **Subjects:** Recreation, education. **Holdings:** 22,932 books; 319 bound periodical volumes; 608 phonograph records; 24 tapes; 694 reels of microfilm; 83 8mm films; 150 cassettes. **Subscriptions:** 350 journals and other serials. **Services:** Interlibrary loan; library not open to the public.

★14628★
U.S. AIR FORCE BASE - EGLIN BASE LIBRARY (Mil, Sci-Engr)
FL 2823 Phone: (904)882-5088
Eglin AFB, FL 32542 F.P. Morgan, Chf., Lib.Br.
Founded: 1942. **Staff:** Prof 2; Other 5. **Subjects:** Aeronautics, military art and science, counterinsurgency, aircraft and missile systems, mathematics, management. **Holdings:** 54,000 books; 1955 bound periodical volumes; 5983 reels of microfilm; 29,462 microfiche; 5944 recordings and tapes; 1728 video cassettes; 90 art prints; 1841 cassettes. **Subscriptions:** 479 journals and other serials; 33 newspapers. **Services:** Interlibrary loan; library not open to the public. **Automated Operations:** Computerized cataloging and ILL. **Computerized Information Services:** OCLC, DIALOG Information Services. **Networks/Consortia:** Member of FEDLINK. **Publications:** Accessions list, bimonthly. **Staff:** Carole B. Steele, Asst.Libn..

★14629★
U.S. AIR FORCE BASE - EIELSON BASE LIBRARY (Mil)
343 CSG/SSL
FL 5004 Phone: (907)377-3174
Eielson AFB, AK 99702-5000 Betty Galbraith, Adm.Libn.
Staff: Prof 1; Other 7. **Subjects:** Air Force professional and technical material, fiction and nonfiction. **Special Collections:** Alaska (463 books); children's collection. **Holdings:** 35,000 volumes; 600 reels of microfilm; 600 videotapes; 2000 phonograph records and audiotapes; 6 VF drawers. **Subscriptions:** 175 journals and other serials; 16 newspapers. **Services:** Interlibrary loan; copying; library open to military personnel and civilian base employees.

★14630★
U.S. AIR FORCE BASE - ENGLAND BASE LIBRARY (Mil)
FL 4805, Bldg. 1213 Phone: (318)448-5621
England AFB, LA 71311-5725 Rupert C. Thom, Libn.
Founded: 1952. **Staff:** Prof 1; Other 2. **Subjects:** Social and applied sciences, American history and literature. **Special Collections:** Louisiana. **Holdings:** 22,500 volumes; 2000 unbound periodicals; 1500 microfiche. **Subscriptions:** 115 journals and other serials; 12 newspapers. **Services:** Interlibrary loan; library not open to the public. **Publications:** Bibliographies, irregular.

★14631★
U.S. AIR FORCE BASE - FAIRCHILD BASE LIBRARY (Mil)
FL 4620 Phone: (509)247-5556
Fairchild AFB, WA 99011 Sherry Ann Hokanson, Libn.
Staff: Prof 2; Other 5. **Subjects:** General and technical topics, military science, Northwest, scouting, genealogy. **Special Collections:** Office collections (50). **Holdings:** 32,607 volumes; 3388 phonograph records and tapes; 15,724 microfiche; 715 reels of microfilm. **Subscriptions:** 272 journals and other serials; 12 newspapers. **Services:** Interlibrary loan; copying; library open to military personnel, dependents, and civilian base employees.

★14632★
U.S. AIR FORCE BASE - GEORGE BASE LIBRARY (Mil, Bus-Fin)
FL 4812 Phone: (714)269-3228
George AFB, CA 92394-5000 Celia Pamintuan, Base Libn.
Founded: 1941. **Staff:** Prof 1; Other 6. **Subjects:** Business and personnel management, public administration, World War II, social problems, Air Force history, California, foreign languages. **Holdings:** 24,670 books; 680 reels of microfilm of periodicals; 62 art reproductions; 491 popular music cassettes; 331 phonograph records. **Subscriptions:** 215 journals and other serials; 15 newspapers. **Services:** Interlibrary loan; copying (limited); library open to the public for reference use only. **Networks/Consortia:** Member of San Bernardino, Inyo, Riverside Counties United Library Services (SIRCULS). **Publications:** Booklists, irregular.

★14633★
U.S. AIR FORCE BASE - GOODFELLOW BASE LIBRARY (Mil)
FL 3030, Bldg. 712 Phone: (915)657-3045
Goodfellow AFB, TX 76908-5000 Elaine C. Penner, Libn.
Staff: Prof 1; Other 5. **Subjects:** Military science, cryptology, foreign language, general topics. **Holdings:** 28,000 books; 16,877 microfiche. **Subscriptions:** 102 journals and other serials; 19 newspapers. **Services:** Interlibrary loan; copying; library open to the public with restrictions. **Remarks:** An alternate telephone number is 657-3232.

★14634★
U.S. AIR FORCE BASE - GRAND FORKS BASE LIBRARY (Mil)
FL 4659
Grand Forks AFB, ND 58205-5000 Phone: (701)594-6725
Staff: Prof 1; Other 8. **Subjects:** Military science. **Holdings:** 30,000 books; 22 bound periodical volumes; 225 reels of microfilm. **Subscriptions:** 575 journals and other serials; 46 newspapers. **Services:** Interlibrary loan; copying; library open to the public.

★14635★
U.S. AIR FORCE BASE - GRISSOM BASE LIBRARY (Mil)
FL 4654, Bldg. 303 Phone: (317)689-2056
Grissom AFB, IN 46971-5000 John Kirwan, Libn.
Founded: 1956. **Staff:** Prof 1; Other 3. **Subjects:** Military science, business management. **Special Collections:** MacNaughton Booklease Plan (800 volumes). **Holdings:** 24,346 books; 8772 AV programs. **Subscriptions:** 115 journals and other serials; 15 newspapers. **Services:** Interlibrary loan; copying; SDI; library open to military personnel, dependents, and civilians employed on base. **Automated Operations:** Computerized cataloging. **Computerized Information Services:** MARCIVE, Inc. **Publications:** Library Brochure, irregular.

★14636★
U.S. AIR FORCE BASE - GUNTER BASE LIBRARY (Mil)
FL 3370 Phone: (205)279-3179
Gunter AFS, AL 36114 James Lee Clark, Base Libn.
Founded: 1950. **Staff:** Prof 1; Other 7. **Subjects:** Recreational materials, medicine, education, language, literature, history. **Holdings:** 29,000 books; 2000 recordings, 400 cassette recordings. **Subscriptions:** 100 journals and other serials. **Services:** Library open to military personnel, dependents, and civilian base employees.

★14637★
U.S. AIR FORCE BASE - HANSCOM BASE LIBRARY (Mil)
FL 2835 Phone: (617)861-2177
Hanscom AFB, MA 01731-5000 Ray Gerke, Base Libn.
Subjects: Military, technical, educational, and recreational topics. **Holdings:** 21,875 books; records; tapes. **Subscriptions:** 396 journals and other serials; 65 newspapers. **Services:** Interlibrary loan; copying; library open to the public for specific research. **Automated Operations:** Computerized cataloging. **Computerized Information Services:** OCLC. **Networks/Consortia:** Member of FEDLINK.

★14638★
U.S. AIR FORCE BASE - HICKAM BASE LIBRARY (Mil)
15 ABW/SSL, Bldg. 595
FL 5260 Phone: (808)449-2831
Hickam AFB, HI 96853-5000 William B. Hassler, Chf.Libn.
Staff: Prof 2; Other 7. **Subjects:** Military history, current foreign policy, U.S. Air Force, management, investments. **Holdings:** 61,291 volumes. **Subscriptions:** 407 journals and other serials; 60 newspapers. **Services:** Interlibrary loan; copying; library open to the public by appointment. **Computerized Information Services:** DIALOG Information Services. **Staff:** Mary K. Briggs, Asst.Libn..

★14639★
U.S. AIR FORCE BASE - HOLLOMAN BASE LIBRARY (Mil)
FL 4801 Phone: (505)479-3939
Holloman AFB, NM 88310 Kathleen E. Baumwart, Base Libn.
Staff: Prof 2; Other 7. **Subjects:** Military aerospace history, contemporary issues, the Southwest, business management, general topics. **Special Collections:** Southwest collection. **Holdings:** 30,000 books; 100 bound periodical volumes; 50 regional maps; 57,000 microfiche; 1800 phonograph records; 1500 cassettes; 2000 videotapes; 175 art prints; 3 VF drawers of pamphlets and clippings. **Subscriptions:** 500 journals and other serials; 28 newspapers. **Services:** Interlibrary loan; library not open to the public. **Automated Operations:** Computerized ILL. **Computerized Information Services:** OCLC, DIALOG Information Services. **Networks/Consortia:** Member of FEDLINK. **Staff:** Carol Austin, Lib.Techn..

★14640★
U.S. AIR FORCE BASE - HOMESTEAD BASE LIBRARY (Mil)
FL 4829 Phone: (305)257-8184
Homestead AFB, FL 33039-5000 Bettylou Rosen, Libn.
Staff: Prof 1; Other 9. **Subjects:** Aeronautics, Florida. **Holdings:** 31,000 books; 2000 records; 1004 audio and video cassettes; 11,000 microforms. **Subscriptions:** 388 journals and other serials; 33 newspapers. **Services:** Interlibrary loan; library not open to the public. **Automated Operations:** Computerized cataloging. **Computerized Information Services:** DIALOG Information Services, OCLC. **Networks/Consortia:** Member of FEDLINK.

★14641★
U.S. AIR FORCE BASE - HOWARD BASE LIBRARY (Mil)
FL 4810
APO Miami, FL 34001-5000 S.K. Murdoch, Base Libn.
Staff: Prof 2; Other 8. **Subjects:** Military arts and sciences, Latin America. **Holdings:** 35,544 books; 1710 records and tapes. **Subscriptions:** 243 journals and other serials; 31 newspapers. **Services:** Interlibrary loan; copying; library open to persons with government identification.

★14642★
U.S. AIR FORCE BASE - HURLBURT BASE LIBRARY (Mil)
Hurlburt Field, FL 32544-5000 Phone: (904)884-6947
Jimmie S. Norton, Libn.
Founded: 1945. **Staff:** Prof 1; Other 4. **Subjects:** General collection. **Holdings:** 27,276 books. **Subscriptions:** 200 journals and other serials; 9 newspapers. **Services:** Interlibrary loan; library not open to the public.

★14643★
U.S. AIR FORCE BASE - KEESLER BASE - MC BRIDE LIBRARY (Mil, Info Sci)
3380 MSS/SSL
FL 3010, Bldg. 2222 Phone: (601)377-2181
Keesler AFB, MS 39534-5225 Elizabeth A. DeCoux, Adm.Libn.
Staff: Prof 4; Other 15. **Subjects:** Telecommunications, computer science, military history, warfare, literature, management science, electronic and computer engineering. **Special Collections:** Professional military education and leadership. **Holdings:** 63,500 books; 1709 bound periodical volumes; 1700 AV programs; 2700 technical reports and documents; 500 maps; 53,000 microforms. **Subscriptions:** 865 journals and other serials; 55 newspapers. **Services:** Interlibrary loan; copying; SDI; library open to the public with commander's approval. **Automated Operations:** Computerized cataloging. **Computerized Information Services:** DTIC, NTIS, OCLC. **Networks/Consortia:** Member of FEDLINK. **Publications:** Direct Current (new acquisitions newsletter), irregular - for internal distribution only; Classified List of Periodicals; Guide to Use of Materials; special bibliographies. **Staff:** Joan I. Van Acker, Cat.Libn..

★14644★
U.S. AIR FORCE BASE - KELLY BASE LIBRARY (Mil)
FL 2050 Phone: (512)925-3214
Kelly AFB, TX 78241-5000 Elizabeth Louise Brown, Libn.
Founded: 1917. **Staff:** Prof 1; Other 7. **Subjects:** Aircraft, management, business, auto and home repair, logistics, Civil Service Test, American history, self-improvement, cooking. **Holdings:** 28,000 books; 510 reels of microfilm; 1420 phonograph records; 440 video cassettes; 6880 microfiche; 525 cassette tapes; 60 compact discs. **Subscriptions:** 135 journals and other serials; 11 newspapers. **Services:** Interlibrary loan; copying; library open to San Antonio area military personnel, civilian base employees, and dependents.

★14645★
U.S. AIR FORCE BASE - KIRTLAND BASE LIBRARY (Mil)
FL 4469 Phone: (505)844-0795
Kirtland AFB, NM 87117-5000 Martha K. Sumpter, Libn.
Founded: 1945. **Staff:** Prof 2; Other 6. **Subjects:** Military history and science, general education, Southwest. **Special Collections:** Project Warrior; Southwest. **Holdings:** 50,082 books; 11,127 microfiche of periodicals; 348 tapes; 1957 phonograph records; 50 language records and tapes. **Subscriptions:** 512 journals and other serials; 29 newspapers. **Services:** Interlibrary loan; copying; library open to active and retired military personnel, civilian base employees, and dependents for reference use only. **Computerized Information Services:** Access to DIALOG Information Services. **Publications:** New Acquisitions, monthly - for internal distribution only. **Staff:** Robert C. Mathews, Ref.Libn..

★14646★
U.S. AIR FORCE BASE - LANGLEY BASE LIBRARY (Mil)
FL 4800 Phone: (804)764-3078
Langley AFB, VA 23665 Margaret E. Whitehill, Base Libn.
Founded: 1942. **Staff:** Prof 2; Other 14. **Subjects:** Military history, sociology, foreign affairs. **Holdings:** 80,000 books; 16 mm films; video cassettes; phonograph records; tapes. **Subscriptions:** 600 journals and other serials. **Services:** Copying; document delivery service. **Automated Operations:** Computerized cataloging and ILL. **Computerized Information Services:** OCLC, DIALOG Information Services, Dun & Bradstreet Corporation, Faxon Company, Washington Alert Service.

★14647★
U.S. AIR FORCE BASE - LAUGHLIN BASE LIBRARY (Mil)
FL 3099 Phone: (512)298-5119
Laughlin AFB, TX 78840 Carlton Moyers, Base Libn.
Staff: Prof 1; Other 4. **Subjects:** Aviation; military history, art, and science; management. **Holdings:** 13,500 books; 200 microfiche; 3 VF drawers of pamphlets. **Subscriptions:** 120 journals and other serials; 6 newspapers. **Services:** Interlibrary loan; library open to the public with restrictions.

★14648★
U.S. AIR FORCE BASE - LITTLE ROCK BASE LIBRARY (Mil)
FL 4460, Bldg. 976 Phone: (501)988-6979
Little Rock AFB, AR 72099-5000 E. Ruth Godbey, Base Libn.
Founded: 1956. **Staff:** Prof 1; Other 6. **Subjects:** Military science, aeronautics, management, social science. **Holdings:** 24,000 books. **Subscriptions:** 150 journals and other serials; 10 newspapers. **Services:** Interlibrary loan; library not open to the public.

★14649★
U.S. AIR FORCE BASE - LORING BASE LIBRARY (Mil)
FL 4678 Phone: (207)999-2416
Loring AFB, ME 04751-5000 Mary E. Bushey, Lib.Dir.
Founded: 1958. **Staff:** Prof 1; Other 6. **Subjects:** General topics. **Special Collections:** Aeronautics. **Holdings:** 28,322 books; 2082 phonograph records; 826 tapes. **Subscriptions:** 248 journals and other serials; 12 newspapers. **Services:** Interlibrary loan; library not open to the public. **Automated Operations:** Computerized circulation.

★14650★
U.S. AIR FORCE BASE - LOWRY BASE LIBRARY (Mil)
Lowry Technical Training Ctr.
FL 3059, ABG/SSL Phone: (303)370-3093
Lowry AFB, CO 80230-5000 Helen C. McClaughry, Base Libn.
Founded: 1939. **Staff:** Prof 2; Other 5. **Subjects:** Electronics, missiles, photography, nuclear weapons, intelligence, special instruments, aeronautics, logistics, general collection with emphasis on military subjects and education. **Holdings:** 45,000 books; 2000 recordings; 500 framed and unframed pictures. **Subscriptions:** 350 journals and other serials. **Services:** Interlibrary loan; library not open to the public. **Networks/Consortia:** Member of Central Colorado Library System (CCLS). **Publications:** New Book List; Subject Bibliographies. **Remarks:** An alternate telephone number is 370-3836. **Staff:** Eileen Hogan, Asst.Libn..

★14651★
U.S. AIR FORCE BASE - LUKE BASE LIBRARY (Mil)
FL 4887 Phone: (602)856-6301
Luke AFB, AZ 85309-5725 Katheryn Kessler, Libn.
Founded: 1951. **Staff:** Prof 1; Other 8. **Subjects:** General collection with emphasis on aeronautics. **Special Collections:** Project Warrior; Arizona history. **Holdings:** 28,847 books; 1195 phonograph records; 530 audio cassettes; 689 video cassettes; 22,333 microfiche. **Subscriptions:** 398 journals and other serials; 23 newspapers. **Services:** Interlibrary loan; copying; library open to active duty and retired military personnel. **Automated Operations:** Computerized ILL. **Computerized Information Services:** DIALOG Information Services. Performs searches free of charge. **Networks/Consortia:** Member of FEDLINK.

★14652★
U.S. AIR FORCE BASE - MC CHORD BASE LIBRARY (Mil)
62 ABG/SSL
FL 4479 Phone: (206)984-3454
McChord AFB, WA 98438-5000 Margaret Ono, Base Libn.
Founded: 1940. **Staff:** Prof 1; Other 5. **Subjects:** Aeronautics, military history, fiction. **Holdings:** 28,000 books. **Subscriptions:** 198 journals and other serials. **Services:** Interlibrary loan; library not open to the public. **Computerized Information Services:** DIALOG Information Services.

★14653★
U.S. AIR FORCE BASE - MC CLELLAN BASE LIBRARY (Mil)
2852 ABG/SSL
FL 2040 Phone: (916)643-4640
McClellan AFB, CA 95652 Weldon B. Champneys, Libn.
Founded: 1941. **Staff:** Prof 1; Other 5. **Subjects:** Aeronautics, psychology, literature, government. **Special Collections:** Project Warrior (112 books); California description and travel (54 books). **Holdings:** 27,398 books; 4363 recordings; 157 reels of microfilm; 1378 microfiche; 131 video cassettes; 25 games; 12 cameras; 47 sculptures and framed art works. **Subscriptions:** 483 journals and other serials; 22 newspapers. **Services:** Interlibrary loan; copying; library open to military personnel and dependents and civilian base employees. **Publications:** New book list, bimonthly; bibliographies, monthly.

★14654★
U.S. AIR FORCE BASE - MC CONNELL BASE LIBRARY (Mil)
FL 4621 Phone: (316)652-4207
McConnell AFB, KS 67221-5000 Ann D. Moore, Libn.
Staff: Prof 1; Other 5. **Subjects:** General collection with emphasis on aeronautics. **Holdings:** 30,360 books; 350 bound periodical volumes; microforms; 5 VF drawers; art prints. **Subscriptions:** 399 journals and other serials; 30 newspapers. **Services:** Interlibrary loan; copying; library open to persons enrolled in education classes. **Networks/Consortia:** Member of South Central Kansas Library System (SCKLS). **Publications:** Flyleaf, irregular.

★14655★
U.S. AIR FORCE BASE - MAC DILL BASE LIBRARY (Mil)
FL 4814 Phone: (813)830-3607
MacDill AFB, FL 33608-5000 Jean Jacob Phillips, Base Libn.
Staff: Prof 1; Other 8. **Subjects:** Military history, Middle East, Latin America. **Holdings:** 23,594 books; 49,896 microforms; 3625 AV programs; 104 framed art prints; 23 technical reports; 146 maps. **Subscriptions:** 445 journals and other serials; 52 newspapers. **Services:** Interlibrary loan; copying; SDI; library open to military personnel and to civilians attending on-base university classes. **Automated Operations:** Computerized cataloging. **Computerized Information Services:** DIALOG Information Services, OCLC, LEXIS, NEXIS, BLDSC, Washington Alert Service. **Networks/Consortia:** Member of Tampa Bay Library Consortium, Inc..

★14656★
U.S. AIR FORCE BASE - MC GUIRE BASE LIBRARY (Mil)
FL 4484 Phone: (609)724-2079
McGuire AFB, NJ 08641-5225 Barbara-Ann Bomgardner, Base Libn.
Founded: 1948. **Staff:** Prof 1; Other 5. **Subjects:** General and technical topics. **Holdings:** 25,200 books. **Subscriptions:** 240 journals and other serials. **Services:** Interlibrary loan; copying; library open to the public for reference use only.

★14657★
U.S. AIR FORCE BASE - MALMSTROM BASE LIBRARY (Mil)
FL 4626 Phone: (406)731-2748
Malmstrom AFB, MT 59402-5000 Arden G. Hill, Libn.
Founded: 1957. **Staff:** 7. **Subjects:** General, aviation, alternative energy, and technical topics. **Holdings:** 27,528 books; 14 VF drawers; 1006 government publications; 3632 AV programs; 35,336 microforms. **Subscriptions:** 710 journals and other serials; 49 newspapers. **Services:** Interlibrary loan; library not open to the public.

★14658★
U.S. AIR FORCE BASE - MARCH BASE LIBRARY (Mil)
FL 4664 Phone: (714)655-2203
March AFB, CA 92518 Rose Moorhouse, Base Libn.
Staff: Prof 1; Other 5. **Subjects:** Aeronautics, education, political science, technology, general topics, children's literature. **Special Collections:** California Collection (250 items); International Relations (318 items); Caldecott/Newbery Collection; USC-SSMC Systems Management; Air War College. **Holdings:** 30,000 books; 203 maps; 604 reels of microfilm; 1686 phonograph records; 576 audiotapes; 100 video cassettes; 19 books on cassettes. **Subscriptions:** 180 journals and other serials; 13 newspapers. **Services:** Interlibrary loan (with other Armed Services libraries and the Inland Empire); library open to military personnel and to civilians enrolled in on-base education courses. **Networks/Consortia:** Member of San Bernardino, Inyo, Riverside Counties United Library Services (SIRCULS).

★14659★
U.S. AIR FORCE BASE - MATHER BASE LIBRARY (Mil)
FL 3067 Phone: (916)364-4759
Mather AFB, CA 95655-5000 Beatrice Alger, Libn.
Founded: 1943. **Staff:** Prof 1; Other 5. **Subjects:** Aviation, military history, World War II history. **Holdings:** 30,000 books; 3300 microfiche; 2400 records and tapes; 400 video cassettes. **Subscriptions:** 184 journals and other serials. **Services:** Interlibrary loan; library not open to the public.

★14660★
U.S. AIR FORCE BASE - MINOT BASE LIBRARY (Mil)
91 CSG/SSL
FL 4528
Minot AFB, ND 58705-5000 Phone: (701)727-4761
Staff: 7. **Subjects:** Aeronautics, electronics, ethnic studies, art and crafts, military history and science. **Special Collections:** Project Warrior (600 items); McNaughton Rental Collection; study guides; Air War College. **Holdings:** 28,648 books; 78 bound periodical volumes; 223 reels of microfilm; 2626 recordings; 4 VF drawers. **Subscriptions:** 672 journals and other serials; 41 newspapers. **Services:** Interlibrary loan; copying; library open to the public with restrictions.

★14661★
U.S. AIR FORCE BASE - MOODY BASE LIBRARY (Mil)
FL 4830
Moody AFB, GA 31699-5000 Phone: (912)333-3539
Founded: 1951. **Staff:** Prof 1; Other 4. **Subjects:** Aeronautics, science, history, general topics. **Holdings:** 21,768 books; 2251 phonograph records; 8000 microfiche; 223 videotapes; 105 filmstrips. **Subscriptions:** 337 journals and other serials; 21 newspapers. **Services:** Interlibrary loan; copying; library open to active and retired military personnel and dependents, Department of Defense personnel, and civilians enrolled in on-base educational programs. **Computerized Information Services:** OCLC, DIALOG Information Services.

★14662★
U.S. AIR FORCE BASE - MYRTLE BEACH BASE LIBRARY (Mil)
FL 4806 Phone: (803)238-7211
Myrtle Beach AFB, SC 29579-5000 Jean L. Cady, Base Libn.
Founded: 1956. **Staff:** Prof 1; Other 5. **Subjects:** Aeronautics, military science, electronics, business, general topics. **Special Collections:** Air War College Seminar books (military and political science). **Holdings:** 18,000 books; 1000 phonograph records and cassette tapes. **Subscriptions:** 200 journals and other serials. **Services:** Interlibrary loan; library not open to the public. **Remarks:** Maintains 43 office collections of 2500 books.

★14663★
U.S. AIR FORCE BASE - NELLIS BASE LIBRARY (Mil)
FL 4852, 554 CSG/SSL Phone: (702)643-2280
Nellis AFB, NV 89191-5000 Dorothy Hart, Base Libn.
Founded: 1949. **Staff:** Prof 1; Other 9. **Subjects:** Aeronautics, business, management, military history, political science, general reference. **Holdings:** 42,098 books; 44,000 microforms; 8091 tapes and phonograph records; 58 16mm films; 2600 video cassettes; 1378 slides; 253 art prints; 202 strategy games; 504 computer software items; 295 video games. **Subscriptions:** 458 journals and other serials; 11 newspapers. **Services:** Interlibrary loan; Dial-A-Story Program; library open to the public for reference use only. **Automated Operations:** Computerized public access catalog and circulation. **Computerized Information Services:** DIALOG Information Services, OCLC, U.S. Naval Institute (USNI).

★14664★
U.S. AIR FORCE BASE - NORTON BASE LIBRARY (Mil)
Bldg. 125 Phone: (714)382-7119
Norton AFB, CA 92409-5985 Carol Crowther, Base Libn.
Founded: 1943. **Staff:** Prof 1; Other 5. **Subjects:** Aeronautics, business and management, military history, general topics. **Holdings:** 23,500 books. **Subscriptions:** 250 journals and other serials; 15 newspapers. **Services:** Interlibrary loan; copying; library open to the public for reference use only. **Networks/Consortia:** Member of San Bernardino, Inyo, Riverside Counties United Library Services (SIRCULS).

★14665★
U.S. AIR FORCE BASE - OFFUTT BASE LIBRARY (Mil)
FL 4600 Phone: (402)294-2533
Offutt AFB, NE 68113-5000 Margaret A. Byrne, Libn.
Subjects: General collection. **Holdings:** 50,000 books and periodicals. **Services:** Library not open to the public.

★14666★
U.S. AIR FORCE BASE - PATRICK BASE LIBRARY (Mil)
FL 2829 Phone: (407)494-6881
Patrick AFB, FL 32925 Katheryn Kessler, Adm.Libn.
Staff: Prof 2; Other 4. **Subjects:** Social science, engineering technology, history. **Holdings:** 37,000 books; 2500 audio cassettes; 110 video cassettes. **Subscriptions:** 460 journals and other serials; 17 newspapers. **Services:** Interlibrary loan; library not open to the public.

★14667★
U.S. AIR FORCE BASE - PEASE BASE LIBRARY (Mil)
FL 4623 Phone: (603)430-3734
Pease AFB, NH 03803-5000 Teresa Hathaway, Libn.
Subjects: Military science. **Holdings:** 28,000 volumes.

★14668★
U.S. AIR FORCE BASE - POPE BASE LIBRARY (Mil)
317 CSG
Bldg. 370 Phone: (919)394-2791
Pope AFB, NC 28308 Karen L. Olender, Base Libn.
Staff: Prof 1; Other 4. **Subjects:** General and technical topics. **Holdings:** 21,000 books; 30 bound periodical volumes; 2500 phonograph records; 50 puzzles; 500 books in rental collection; 26,000 microfiche; 26 cassettes; 21 wargames; 42 computer software (wargames); 700 video cassettes; pamphlets; maps. **Subscriptions:** 302 journals and other serials; 24 newspapers. **Services:** Interlibrary loan; copying; preschool story service; library open to active and retired military personnel and dependents and to civilian base employees. **Automated Operations:** Computerized circulation. **Computerized Information Services:** DIALOG Information Services. **Networks/Consortia:** Member of FEDLINK.

★14669★
U.S. AIR FORCE BASE - RANDOLPH BASE LIBRARY (Mil)
FL 3089, Bldg. 584 Phone: (512)652-5578
Randolph AFB, TX 78150-5000 Ruth E. Francis, Act.Libn.
Staff: Prof 1; Other 2. **Subjects:** U.S. Air Force history, World War II, aeronautics, management, applied science, literature. **Special Collections:** Air War College Seminar Book Collection; Texas history. **Holdings:** 30,000 books. **Subscriptions:** 205 journals and other serials; 15 newspapers. **Services:** Interlibrary loan; copying; library open to the public with restrictions. **Automated Operations:** Computerized cataloging.

★14670★
U.S. AIR FORCE BASE - REESE BASE LIBRARY (Mil)
FL 3060 Phone: (806)885-3344
Reese AFB, TX 79489-5438 Mac Odom, Libn.
Founded: 1950. **Staff:** Prof 1; Other 5. **Subjects:** Aeronautics, management, travel, history, fiction. **Holdings:** 17,455 books. **Subscriptions:** 139 journals and other serials. **Services:** Interlibrary loan; library not open to the public.

★14671★
U.S. AIR FORCE BASE - ROBINS BASE LIBRARY (Mil)
2853 ABG/SSL
FL 2060 Phone: (912)926-5411
Robins AFB, GA 31098-5000 Carolyn M. Covington, Chf., Lib.Br.
Staff: Prof 2; Other 10. **Subjects:** General and technical topics. **Holdings:** 55,000 books. **Subscriptions:** 319 journals and other serials; 15 newspapers. **Services:** Interlibrary loan; library not open to the public. **Staff:** Joann B. Browning, Asst.Libn..

★14672★
U.S. AIR FORCE BASE - SHEPPARD BASE LIBRARY (Mil)
FL 3020 Phone: (817)851-2687
Sheppard AFB, TX 76311 Linda Fryar, Libn.
Staff: Prof 2; Other 8. **Subjects:** General and technical topics. **Holdings:** 38,000 books; 29,000 microforms; 3000 recordings. **Subscriptions:** 250 journals and other serials; 19 newspapers. **Services:** Interlibrary loan; copying; library open to the public with approval of base commander. **Networks/Consortia:** Member of Texas State Library Communications Network (TSLCN).

★14673★
U.S. AIR FORCE BASE - TINKER BASE LIBRARY (Mil)
2854 ABG/SSL
FL 2030, Bldg. 5702 Phone: (405)734-3083
Tinker AFB, OK 73145 Nellie K. Buffalomeat, Adm.Libn.
Founded: 1942. **Staff:** Prof 2; Other 6. **Subjects:** Aeronautics, engineering, management. **Special Collections:** Technical Mission Support publications. **Holdings:** 27,066 books; 1467 phonograph records. **Subscriptions:** 388 journals and other serials; 12 newspapers. **Services:** Interlibrary loan; library open to the public with permission. **Staff:** Ann Irby, Acq.; Dolores Loudermilk, Circ.Libn..

★14674★
U.S. AIR FORCE BASE - TRAVIS BASE LIBRARY (Mil)
Mitchell Memorial Library
60 ABG/SSL
FL 4427 Phone: (707)438-5254
Travis AFB, CA 94535 Nina Jacobs, Libn.
Founded: 1956. **Staff:** Prof 1; Other 9. **Subjects:** Military science and aviation, general topics. **Holdings:** 44,086 volumes. **Subscriptions:** 500 journals and other serials; 17 newspapers. **Services:** Interlibrary loan; library not open to the public. **Networks/Consortia:** Member of North Bay Cooperative Library System (NBCLS).

★14675★
U.S. AIR FORCE BASE - TYNDALL BASE LIBRARY (Mil)
325 CSG/SSL/45 Phone: (904)283-4287
Tyndall AFB, FL 32403-5725 Sheila Ray, Libn.
Staff: Prof 1; Other 5. **Subjects:** Aviation history, military science, business management. **Holdings:** 20,000 books. **Subscriptions:** 300 journals and other serials; 20 newspapers. **Services:** Interlibrary loan; library not open to the public. **Computerized Information Services:** DIALOG Information Services. **Publications:** Substance (newsletter), monthly - for internal distribution only.

★14676★
U.S. AIR FORCE BASE - VANCE BASE LIBRARY (Mil)
FL 3029 Phone: (405)249-7368
Vance AFB, OK 73705-5000 Tom L. Kirk, Chf.Libn.
Founded: 1941. **Staff:** Prof 1; Other 2. **Subjects:** General topics. **Holdings:** 14,500 books; 1300 volumes on pre-1900 American history/social life on microfiche; 3200 phonograph records; 4500 microforms. **Subscriptions:** 118 journals and other serials; 9 newspapers. **Services:** Interlibrary loan; library not open to the public. **Automated Operations:** Computerized cataloging.

★14677★
U.S. AIR FORCE BASE - VANDENBERG BASE LIBRARY (Mil)
FL 4610, Bldg. 13437-A Phone: (805)866-6414
Vandenberg AFB, CA 93437-5000 Joseph L. Buelna, Base Libn.
Founded: 1952. **Staff:** Prof 2; Other 10. **Subjects:** Military and general topics. **Special Collections:** Military science; books for War College students. **Holdings:** 36,000 books; 4000 nonbook items; 3600 reels of microfilm of technical periodicals, 1970 to present. **Subscriptions:** 236 journals and other serials; 8 newspapers. **Services:** Interlibrary loan; copying; library open to the public for reference use only.

★14678★
U.S. AIR FORCE BASE - WHEELER BASE LIBRARY (Mil)
FL 5296, 15 Air Base Squadron (SSL) Phone: (808)655-1867
Wheeler AFB, HI 96854-5000 Joanne M. Okuma, Base Libn.
Founded: 1960. **Staff:** Prof 1; Other 5. **Subjects:** Systems management, Air Force history, Hawaiiana, military history. **Holdings:** 28,000 books; 14 VF drawers; 68 periodicals on microfilm; maps; phonograph records. **Subscriptions:** 218 journals and other serials; 27 newspapers. **Services:** Interlibrary loan; copying; library open to military personnel and dependents.

★14679★
U.S. AIR FORCE BASE - WHITEMAN BASE LIBRARY (Mil)
FL 4625 Phone: (816)687-3089
Whiteman AFB, MO 65305-5000 Karen Highfill, Base Libn.
Founded: 1951. **Staff:** Prof 1; Other 5. **Subjects:** Military science, computer science, business and management, general fiction and nonfiction, children's literature. **Special Collections:** Project Warrior; office collections (51). **Holdings:** 22,000 volumes; 700 audiotapes; 7500 microforms; 3000 phonograph records; 250 video cassettes; 4 VF drawers of clippings and pamphlets. **Subscriptions:** 350 journals and other serials; 17 newspapers. **Services:** Interlibrary loan; library not open to the public.

★14680★
U.S. AIR FORCE BASE - WRIGHT-PATTERSON BASE LIBRARY (Mil)
2750 ABW/SSL
Kittyhawk Ctr., Bldg. 1044 Phone: (513)257-4815
Wright-Patterson AFB, OH 45433-5000 Mary E. Rinas, Chf., Lib.Br.
Staff: Prof 2; Other 11. **Subjects:** Military art and science, business management. **Special Collections:** Project Warrior (2176 items). **Holdings:** 55,000 books; AV programs. **Subscriptions:** 220 journals and other serials; 21 newspapers. **Services:** Interlibrary loan; copying; library open to the public for reference use only. **Staff:** David A. Ryans, Asst.Libn..

★14681★
U.S. AIR FORCE HOSPITAL - AIR UNIVERSITY REGIONAL HOSPITAL - MEDICAL LIBRARY (Med)
Maxwell AFB Phone: (205)293-5852
Montgomery, AL 36112-5304 Patricia A. Kuther, Med.Lib.Techn.
Founded: 1956. **Staff:** Prof 1. **Subjects:** General medicine, surgery, pathology, dentistry, nursing, veterinary medicine. **Holdings:** 4000 books and bound periodical volumes. **Subscriptions:** 200 journals and other serials. **Services:** Interlibrary loan; library not open to the public. **Formerly:** U.S. Air Force Hospital - Medical Library (AL-Maxwell AFB).

★14682★
U.S. AIR FORCE HOSPITAL - DAVID GRANT MEDICAL CENTER - MEDICAL LIBRARY (Med)
Travis AFB, CA 94535 Phone: (707)428-8556
V. Kay Hafner, Med.Libn./Dir.
Founded: 1958. **Staff:** Prof 1; Other 1. **Subjects:** Medicine, family practice, dentistry, nursing. **Holdings:** 4079 books; 10,987 bound periodical volumes. **Subscriptions:** 450 journals and other serials. **Services:** Interlibrary loan; library not open to the public. **Computerized Information Services:** MEDLARS, BRS Information Technologies, OCLC; OnTyme Electronic Message Network Service (electronic mail service). Performs searches free of charge. **Networks/Consortia:** Member of Pacific Southwest Regional Medical Library Service, Northern California and Nevada Medical Library Group (NCNMLG). **Publications:** Quarterly newsletter - to staff.

★14683★
U.S. AIR FORCE HOSPITAL - EHRLING BERGQUIST STRATEGIC HOSPITAL - MEDICAL LIBRARY (Med)
Offutt AFB, NE 68113-5300 Phone: (402)294-5499
Jan Hatcher, Lib.Mgr.
Founded: 1966. **Staff:** 1. **Subjects:** Surgery and allied health sciences. **Holdings:** 2000 books. **Subscriptions:** 260 journals and other serials. **Services:** Interlibrary loan; copying; library open to the public for reference use only. **Computerized Information Services:** MEDLINE; DOCLINE (electronic mail service).

★14684★
U.S. AIR FORCE HOSPITAL - MALCOLM GROW MEDICAL CENTER - LIBRARY (Med)
Box 3097
Andrews AFB, Stop 174 Phone: (202)981-2354
Washington, DC 20331 Mary Alice Zelinka, Med.Libn.
Staff: Prof 1; Other 2. **Subjects:** Internal medicine, nursing, cardiology, surgery, dentistry, food service. **Holdings:** 13,000 books; 4500 bound periodical volumes; clippings; maps; bibliographies; dissertations; reprints; pamphlets; tapes; phonograph records; slides; 8 VF drawers. **Subscriptions:** 408 journals and other serials. **Services:** Interlibrary loan; library not open to the public. **Computerized Information Services:** MEDLARS, OCLC. Performs searches free of charge. **Networks/Consortia:** Member of FEDLINK.

U.S. AIR FORCE HOSPITAL - MEDICAL LIBRARY (AL-Maxwell AFB)
See: **U.S. Air Force Hospital - Air University Regional Hospital - Medical Library** (14681)

★14685★
U.S. AIR FORCE HOSPITAL - MEDICAL LIBRARY (AK-Elmendorf AFB) (Med)
Elmendorf AFB, AK 99506-5300 Phone: (907)552-5325
Donna M. Hudson, Libn.
Founded: 1952. **Staff:** Prof 1; Other 3. **Subjects:** General and military medicine. **Holdings:** 4600 books; **Subscriptions:** 200 journals and other serials. **Services:** Interlibrary loan; copying; SDI; library open to the public for reference use only. **Computerized Information Services:** MEDLINE. **Networks/Consortia:** Member of National Library of Medicine (NLM), Alaska Library Network (ALN). **Publications:** Holdings List, annual.

★14686★
U.S. AIR FORCE HOSPITAL - MEDICAL LIBRARY (CA-Mather AFB) (Med)
Mather AFB, CA 95655 Phone: (916)364-3347
Willis J. Collick, Med.Libn.
Staff: 1. **Subjects:** Medicine. **Holdings:** 819 books. **Subscriptions:** 48 journals and other serials. **Services:** Interlibrary loan; library not open to the public.

★14687★
U.S. AIR FORCE HOSPITAL - MEDICAL LIBRARY (FL-Patrick AFB) (Med)
Patrick AFB, FL 32925-5300 Phone: (407)494-5501
Margaret A. Seifert, Lib.Cust.
Founded: 1968. **Staff:** Prof 1. **Subjects:** Medicine, psychiatry, nursing, allied health sciences. **Holdings:** 774 books; 361 bound periodical volumes; 150 other cataloged items. **Subscriptions:** 82 journals and other serials. **Services:** Interlibrary loan; copying; library open to medical students.

★14688★
U.S. AIR FORCE HOSPITAL - MEDICAL LIBRARY (IL-Chanute AFB) (Med)
Chanute AFB, IL 61868 Phone: (217)495-3068
Gordon P. Laumer, Libn.
Staff: 1. **Subjects:** Medicine. **Holdings:** 1734 books. **Subscriptions:** 90 journals and other serials. **Services:** Interlibrary loan; library not open to the public. **Networks/Consortia:** Member of Champaign-Urbana Consortium, Greater Midwest Regional Medical Library Network.

★14689★
U.S. AIR FORCE HOSPITAL - MEDICAL LIBRARY (NM-Kirtland AFB) (Med)
Kirtland AFB, NM 87117-5300 Phone: (505)844-1086
Alice T. Lee, Libn.
Founded: 1956. **Staff:** Prof 1. **Subjects:** Medicine, surgery, nursing, dentistry, environmental and radiological health. **Holdings:** 3100 books; 465 bound periodical volumes; 3 VF drawers of audiotapes, pamphlets, reports, guides, monographs; 150 filmstrips, video cassettes, 16mm films. **Subscriptions:** 103 journals and other serials. **Services:** Interlibrary loan; library not open to the public. **Computerized Information Services:** MEDLARS. **Networks/Consortia:** Member of New Mexico Consortium of Biomedical and Hospital Libraries.

★14690★
U.S. AIR FORCE HOSPITAL - MEDICAL LIBRARY (NY-Griffiss AFB) (Med)
Griffiss AFB, NY 13441-5300 Phone: (315)330-7713
Patty Sbaraglia, Med.Libn.
Staff: 1. **Subjects:** Nursing, dental services, mental and social health, surgery, internal medicine, food service. **Holdings:** 856 books. **Subscriptions:** 73 journals and other serials. **Services:** Interlibrary loan; library not open to the public. **Publications:** Newsletter. **Special Catalogs:** Union list.

★14691★
U.S. AIR FORCE HOSPITAL - MEDICAL LIBRARY (OK-Tinker AFB) (Med)
Tinker AFB, OK 73145 Phone: (405)734-8373
Mary B. Mills, Lib.Techn.
Staff: 1. **Subjects:** Pediatrics, internal medicine, surgery, nursing. **Holdings:** 1437 books. **Subscriptions:** 99 journals and other serials. **Services:** Interlibrary loan; copying; library open to the public with restrictions. **Networks/Consortia:** Member of Greater Oklahoma City Area Health Sciences Library Consortium (GOAL).

★14692★
U.S. AIR FORCE HOSPITAL - MEDICAL LIBRARY (TX-Carswell AFB) (Med)
Carswell AFB, TX 76127 Phone: (817)735-7579
Jean Robbins, Med.Libn.
Founded: 1956. **Staff:** Prof 1. **Subjects:** Medicine, surgery, nursing, psychiatry, dentistry, orthopedics, veterinary medicine. **Holdings:** 2600 books; 2300 bound periodical volumes. **Subscriptions:** 240 journals and other serials; 9 newspapers. **Services:** Interlibrary loan; library not open to the public.

★14693★
U.S. AIR FORCE HOSPITAL - MEDICAL LIBRARY (TX-Reese AFB) (Med)
SGAS/35
Reese AFB, TX 79489 Phone: (806)885-3543
Staff: 2. **Subjects:** Medicine and medical specialties, dentistry. **Holdings:** 780 books. **Subscriptions:** 40 journals and other serials. **Services:** Library open to USAF personnel.

★14694★
U.S. AIR FORCE HOSPITAL - MEDICAL LIBRARY (WA-Fairchild AFB) (Med)
Fairchild AFB, WA 99011-5300 Phone: (509)247-5353
Sgt. Richard B. Murphy, Med.Libn.
Staff: 1. **Subjects:** General internal medicine, pediatrics, orthopedics, obstetrics and gynecology, family practice. **Special Collections:** Hyperbaric medicine; aerospace medicine; bioenvironmental engineering; environmental health. **Holdings:** 1260 books; 54 bound periodical volumes. **Subscriptions:** 48 journals and other serials; 6 newspapers. **Services:** Library not open to the public. **Automated Operations:** Computerized cataloging, acquisitions, and circulation. **Computerized Information Services:** MEDLINE, MARCIVE, Inc.; internal database.

★14695★
U.S. AIR FORCE HOSPITAL - SHEPPARD REGIONAL HOSPITAL - MEDICAL LIBRARY (Med)
Sheppard AFB, TX 76311 Phone: (817)851-6647
Marilyn Lucas, Lib.Techn.
Staff: Prof 1. **Subjects:** Medicine, nursing, dentistry, pharmacy, hospital administration. **Holdings:** 4200 books; 2308 bound periodical volumes; 90 video cassettes; 1 VF drawer of pamphlets. **Subscriptions:** 160 journals and other serials. **Services:** Interlibrary loan; library open to the public for reference use only. **Automated Operations:** Computerized cataloging. **Computerized Information Services:** Access to MEDLINE. **Networks/Consortia:** Member of TALON.

★14696★
U.S. AIR FORCE HOSPITAL - WILFORD HALL U.S.A.F. MEDICAL CENTER - MEDICAL LIBRARY (SGEL) (Med)
Lackland AFB Phone: (512)670-7204
San Antonio, TX 78236-5300 Rita F. Smith, Med.Libn.
Staff: Prof 2; Other 4. **Subjects:** Medicine, nursing, dentistry, hospital administration, veterinary medicine. **Holdings:** 9800 books; 13,800 bound periodical volumes; 4900 AV programs; 1825 reels of microfilm of journals. **Subscriptions:** 900 journals and other serials. **Services:** Interlibrary loan; library not open to the public. **Computerized Information Services:** DIALOG Information Services, MEDLINE. **Staff:** Barbara Farwell, Asst.Libn..

★14697★
U.S. AIR FORCE HOSPITAL MEDICAL CENTER - MEDICAL LIBRARY (IL-Scott AFB) (Med)
Scott AFB, IL 62225 Phone: (618)256-7437
Blanche A. Savage, Hea.Sci.Libn.
Staff: Prof 1; Other 1. **Subjects:** Medicine, nursing, dentistry, allied health sciences. **Holdings:** 8000 books; 4633 bound periodical volumes; 1500 pamphlets and tapes. **Subscriptions:** 325 journals and other serials; 5 newspapers. **Services:** Interlibrary loan; library not open to the public. **Computerized Information Services:** Online systems. **Networks/Consortia:** Member of Areawide Hospital Library Consortium of Southwestern Illinois (AHLC).

★14698★
U.S. AIR FORCE HOSPITAL MEDICAL CENTER - MEDICAL LIBRARY (MS-Keesler AFB) (Med)
SGAL Phone: (601)377-6249
Keesler AFB, MS 39534-5300 Sherry N. Nave, Med.Libn.
Staff: Prof 1; Other 1. **Subjects:** Medicine, surgery, nursing, dentistry, allied health sciences. **Holdings:** 5000 books; 4000 bound periodical

volumes; 1100 volumes on microfilm. **Subscriptions:** 500 journals and other serials. **Services:** Interlibrary loan; library not open to the public. **Computerized Information Services:** NLM, DIALOG Information Services. **Networks/Consortia:** Member of Mississippi Biomedical Library Consortium.

★14699★
U.S. AIR FORCE HOSPITAL MEDICAL CENTER - MEDICAL LIBRARY (OH-Wright-Patterson AFB) (Med)
SGEL/Bldg. 830A Phone: (513)257-4506
Wright-Patterson AFB, OH 45433 Mert Adams, Biomed.Libn.
Staff: Prof 2; Other 3. **Subjects:** Clinical medicine, dentistry, veterinary medicine, hospital administration. **Special Collections:** Tropical medicine; plastic surgery; military and aerospace medicine. **Holdings:** 9000 books; 11,000 bound periodical volumes; 4000 AV programs; 45,000 microfiche. **Subscriptions:** 800 journals and other serials. **Services:** Interlibrary loan; copying; SDI; library open to members of affiliated institutions only. **Automated Operations:** Computerized cataloging, acquisitions, serials, and circulation. **Computerized Information Services:** MEDLINE, DIALOG Information Services, BRS Information Technologies. **Networks/Consortia:** Member of Greater Midwest Regional Medical Library Network, Southwest Ohio Council for Higher Education (SOCHE). **Staff:** Cathy Constance, Asst.Biomed.Libn..

U.S. AIR FORCE MUSEUM
See: U.S. Air Force - Air Force Logistics Command - U.S. Air Force Museum (14582)

U.S. ALCOHOL, DRUG ABUSE AND MENTAL HEALTH ADMINISTRATION - NATIONAL INSTITUTE ON DRUG ABUSE
See: National Institute on Drug Abuse - Addiction Research Center Library (9708)

★14700★
U.S. ARMED FORCES INSTITUTE OF PATHOLOGY - ASH LIBRARY (Med)
Walter Reed Army Medical Center
Bldg. 54, Rm. 4077 Phone: (202)576-2983
Washington, DC 20306-6000 Patricia C. Patel, Libn.
Founded: 1951. **Staff:** Prof 1; Other 4. **Subjects:** Pathology. **Special Collections:** Audiovisual Collection; microscopic slide sets (pathology); Yakolev Collection (brain pathology). **Holdings:** 6500 books; 18,000 bound periodical volumes; 10,000 documents, reports, pamphlets. **Subscriptions:** 410 journals and other serials. **Services:** Interlibrary loan; library open to the public. **Automated Operations:** Computerized cataloging and ILL. **Computerized Information Services:** OCLC, DIALOG Information Services. **Special Catalogs:** Audiovisual Catalog.

★14701★
U.S. ARMED FORCES RADIOBIOLOGY RESEARCH INSTITUTE (AFRRI) - LIBRARY SERVICES (Med)
National Naval Medical Ctr., Bldg.42 Phone: (301)295-1330
Bethesda, MD 20814 Ilse Vada, Adm.Libn.
Founded: 1962. **Staff:** Prof 2; Other 1. **Subjects:** Radiobiology, radiation physics, neurobiology, nuclear medicine, behavioral science, veterinary medicine. **Holdings:** 15,000 books; 20,000 bound periodical volumes; 6000 technical reports; Atomic Bomb Casualty Commission technical reports; 50,000 microfiche of U.S. Government-funded technical reports. **Subscriptions:** 200 journals and other serials; 6 newspapers. **Services:** Interlibrary loan; copying; library open to outside users who must register at reception desk of institute. **Automated Operations:** Computerized cataloging, acquisitions, and circulation. **Computerized Information Services:** BRS Information Technologies, MEDLINE, OCLC; Digital Datatrieve (internal database). **Networks/Consortia:** Member of FEDLINK, Southeastern/Atlantic Regional Medical Library Services, Interlibrary Users Association (IUA). **Publications:** Current Awareness, monthly. **Special Catalogs:** Union List of Serials-National Naval Medical Center (book). **Remarks:** Institute is part of the U.S. Defense Nuclear Agency. **Staff:** Sandra S. Matthews, Ref.; Myron K. Allman, Circ..

★14702★
U.S. ARMED FORCES SCHOOL OF MUSIC - REFERENCE LIBRARY (Mus)
NAVPHI Base, Little Creek Phone: (804)464-7501
Norfolk, VA 23521 Frank Felder, Chf.
Founded: 1941. **Staff:** Prof 1; Other 1. **Subjects:** Music - analysis, conducting, composition, counterpoint, harmony, theory, instruments; jazz; military music. **Holdings:** 3600 books; 4800 scores; 5600 phonograph records; 8500 instrumental methods; 7000 solos; 900 song books. **Subscriptions:** 30 journals and other serials. **Services:** Library open to the public with restrictions.

★14703★
U.S. ARMED FORCES STAFF COLLEGE - LIBRARY (Mil)
7800 Hampton Blvd. Phone: (804)444-5155
Norfolk, VA 23511-6097 Margaret J. Martin, Lib.Dir.
Founded: 1947. **Staff:** Prof 7; Other 11. **Subjects:** Military science, national and international affairs, history. **Special Collections:** Military administrative publications (3500). **Holdings:** 7900 bound periodical volumes; 90,000 other cataloged items; 10,000 microforms; 65 drawers and 716 boxes of archival materials; 24 drawers of pamphlets. **Subscriptions:** 670 journals and other serials; 20 newspapers. **Services:** Interlibrary loan; bibliographic and reference services to other U.S. government libraries; library not open to the public. **Computerized Information Services:** DIALOG Information Services, OCLC, DTIC, WILSONLINE. **Publications:** Library Accessions List, weekly; Current Periodical Review, weekly - both for internal distribution only. **Special Indexes:** Reference Information File; subject index to periodicals in defense area (card). **Remarks:** College operates under the direction of U.S. Department of Defense - Joint Chiefs of Staff. **Staff:** Sandra R. Byrn, Chf., Tech.Serv.; Janet Gail Nicula, Chf., Rd.Serv..

★14704★
U.S. ARMS CONTROL AND DISARMAMENT AGENCY - LIBRARY (Soc Sci)
Dept. of State Bldg., Rm. 5840
320 21st St., N.W. Phone: (202)647-5969
Washington, DC 20541 Diane A. Ferguson, Libn.
Staff: Prof 1. **Subjects:** Arms control, disarmament, nuclear proliferation, international peacekeeping. **Holdings:** 3000 volumes; documents of the Committee on Disarmament, 1962 to present; Congressional documents; ACDA research reports and publications. **Subscriptions:** 190 journals and other serials; 12 newspapers. **Services:** Interlibrary loan; copying; library open to the public by advance arrangement. **Computerized Information Services:** NEXIS, LEXIS, DTIC. **Publications:** Annual Report; World Military Expenditures and Arms Transfers; Documents on Disarmament, all annual. **Also Known As:** ACDA.

U.S. ARMY - AEROMEDICAL RESEARCH LABORATORY
See: U.S. Army - Medical Research & Development Command - Aeromedical Research Laboratory (14767)

U.S. ARMY - AIR DEFENSE ARTILLERY SCHOOL
See: U.S. Army - TRADOC - Air Defense Artillery School (14785)

★14705★
U.S. ARMY - ARMAMENT, MUNITIONS & CHEMICAL COMMAND - ARMAMENT RESEARCH, DEVELOPMENT & ENGINEERING CENTER - SCIENTIFIC & TECH.INFO. BRANCH - INFORMATION CENTER (Sci-Engr, Mil)
ARDEC, Bldg. 59 Phone: (201)724-2914
Picatinny Arsenal, NJ 07806-5000
Normand L. Varieur, Chf, Sci. & Tech.Info.Br.
Founded: 1929. **Staff:** Prof 7; Other 13. **Subjects:** Chemistry, engineering, ammunition, science, physics, explosives, fire control, optics, materials. **Special Collections:** Government-Industry Data Exchange Program Reports; Archive of Frankford Arsenal (Philadelphia, PA); Archive of Picatinny Arsenal; federal and military specifications and standards; commercial standards; vendor catalogs. **Holdings:** 70,000 books; 20,000 bound periodical volumes; 550,000 technical reports. **Subscriptions:** 1013 journals and other serials. **Services:** Interlibrary loan; copying (limited); center open to the public for reference use only on request. **Computerized Information Services:** DIALOG Information Services, DTIC, BRS Information Technologies, LS/2000, OCLC; ARPANET, LINX Courier (electronic mail services). **Networks/Consortia:** Member of FEDLINK. **Publications:** Technical Information Bulletin, biweekly - for internal distribution only. **Staff:** Ismail Haznedari, Supv.Libn.; Ruth Meredith, Supv.Libn..

★14706★
U.S. ARMY - ARMAMENT, MUNITIONS & CHEMICAL COMMAND - BENET LABORATORIES - TECHNICAL LIBRARY (Sci-Engr, Mil)
Watervliet Arsenal
Attn: SMCAR-CCB-TL Phone: (518)266-5613
Watervliet, NY 12189-5000 Susan A. Macksey, Chf., Sci./Tech.Info.
Staff: Prof 1; Other 6. **Subjects:** Metallurgy, physics, ordnance, artillery, cannon, mortars, composite materials, mechanics. **Holdings:** 9000 books; 5500 bound periodical volumes; 20,000 technical documents.

Subscriptions: 400 journals and other serials. **Services:** Interlibrary loan; copying; library open to the public on request subject to regulations. **Computerized Information Services:** DIALOG Information Services, OCLC, DTIC. **Networks/Consortia:** Member of FEDLINK, Capital District Library Council for Reference & Research Resources (CDLC). **Publications:** Library Accession List.

★14707★
U.S. ARMY - ARMAMENT, MUNITIONS & CHEMICAL COMMAND - CHEMICAL RESEARCH, DEVELOPMENT & ENGINEERING CENTER - TECHNICAL LIBRARY (Sci-Engr)
ATTN: SMCCR-MSI Phone: (301)671-2936
Aberdeen Proving Ground, MD 21010-5423
C.R. Anaclerio, Chf., Info.Serv.Div.
Founded: 1919. **Staff:** Prof 3; Other 7. **Subjects:** Chemistry, chemical engineering. **Holdings:** 4500 books; 8630 bound periodical volumes; 260,000 government reports; 10,000 film cartridges. **Subscriptions:** 350 journals and other serials. **Services:** Interlibrary loan; library not open to the public. **Automated Operations:** Computerized cataloging and serials. **Computerized Information Services:** OCLC, DIALOG Information Services. **Networks/Consortia:** Member of FEDLINK. **Publications:** Periodical Holding List, irregular. **Staff:** E.F. Gier, Ref.Libn.; D.C. Smith, Ref.Libn.; P.A. D'Eramo, Tech.Info.Spec..

★14708★
U.S. ARMY - ARMAMENT, MUNITIONS & CHEMICAL COMMAND - TECHNICAL LIBRARY (Sci-Engr, Mil)
HDQ AMCCOM
AMSMC-IMP-L Phone: (309)782-5031
Rock Island, IL 61299-6000 Cecelia J. Thorn
Founded: 1958. **Staff:** Prof 1; Other 3. **Subjects:** Weapons and ammunition, production engineering. **Holdings:** 11,736 books; 4010 bound periodical volumes; 13,300 technical reports; 72,458 reports on microfiche. **Subscriptions:** 182 journals and other serials; 7 newspapers. **Services:** Interlibrary loan; SDI; library open to the public with restrictions. **Computerized Information Services:** DIALOG Information Services, DTIC, OCLC; DDN Network Information Center (electronic mail service). **Networks/Consortia:** Member of River Bend Library System (RBLS), FEDLINK. **Publications:** Accession list, monthly - for internal distribution only. **Special Indexes:** Subject index of materiel status records (card).

U.S. ARMY - ARMOR SCHOOL
See: U.S. Army - TRADOC (14787)

★14709★
U.S. ARMY - AVIATION APPLIED TECHNOLOGY DIRECTORATE - TECHNICAL LIBRARY (Sci-Engr)
Aviation Applied Technology Directorate
U.S. Army Aviation Research & Development Activity
Phone: (804)878-4377
Ft. Eustis, VA 23604-5577 David J. Arola, Adm.Libn.
Founded: 1945. **Staff:** Prof 2; Other 1. **Subjects:** Aeronautical engineering, Army aircraft, composite structures, low speed aeronautics, aircraft flight control systems, flight safety and research, V/STOL aircraft, rotary wing aircraft. **Holdings:** 11,000 books and bound periodical volumes; 78,000 hard copy and microfiche technical reports; 1 million engineering drawings and technical data on Army aircraft. **Subscriptions:** 200 journals and other serials. **Services:** Interlibrary loan; library not open to the public. **Automated Operations:** Computerized cataloging and serials. **Computerized Information Services:** DIALOG Information Services, DTIC. **Networks/Consortia:** Member of FEDLINK, Shared Bibliographic Input Network. **Staff:** Edwin P. Knihnicki, Ref.Libn..

★14710★
U.S. ARMY - AVIATION SYSTEMS COMMAND - LIBRARY AND INFORMATION CENTER (Mil)
4300 Goodfellow Blvd. Phone: (314)263-2345
St. Louis, MO 63120-1798 Grace C. Feng, Supv.Libn.
Founded: 1954. **Staff:** Prof 5; Other 8. **Subjects:** Aircraft - systems, components, procurements, performance; aircraft/helicopter services; aeronautical engineering. **Holdings:** 10,000 books; 1300 bound periodical volumes; 2900 other cataloged items; 18,000 federal administrative publications; 109,000 specifications, standards, manuals, bulletins; 500 classified publications; 150,000 specifications, standards, cross reference lists on microfilm; 40,000 technical reports. **Subscriptions:** 400 journals and other serials. **Services:** Interlibrary loan (fee); copying; library open to the public with government authorization. **Automated Operations:** Computerized cataloging. **Computerized Information Services:** DIALOG Information Services, BRS Information Technologies, DTIC, Aerospace Online, Dun & Bradstreet Corporation. **Networks/Consortia:** Member of FEDLINK. **Publications:** Selected New Books; Selected New Technical Reports, both quarterly - both for internal distribution only; library bulletin. **Staff:** Thomas N. Tipsword, Tech.Serv.Libn.; W. Richard Schneider, Pub.Serv.Libn.; S. Faye Wilbur, Br.Libn.; Marie Wakefield, Cat./Ref..

U.S. ARMY - BELVOIR RESEARCH, DEVELOPMENT & ENGINEERING CENTER
See: U.S. Army - Troop Support Command - Belvoir Research, Development & Engineering Center (14811)

★14711★
U.S. ARMY - CENTER OF MILITARY HISTORY - 7TH INFANTRY DIVISION & FORT ORD MUSEUM - LIBRARY (Mil)
Attn: AF2W-DC-MUSEUM, DPT Phone: (408)242-4905
Fort Ord, CA 93941 Michael McGuire, Asst.Cur.
Founded: 1982. **Staff:** Prof 2. **Subjects:** History - Fort Ord, 7th Infantry Division, Army. **Holdings:** 100 books; 300 volumes on microfiche. **Services:** Library open to the public for reference use only by appointment only. **Staff:** Margaret B. Adams, Cur..

★14712★
U.S. ARMY - CENTER OF MILITARY HISTORY - U.S. ARMY MUSEUM, PRESIDIO OF MONTEREY - LIBRARY (Mil)
CDR, HQs, 7th Infantry Division & Fort Ord
ATTN: AFZW-DPT-P (Museum Library) Phone: (408)647-5414
Presidio of Monterey, CA 93944-5006 Margaret B. Adams, Cur.
Staff: Prof 1; Other 1. **Subjects:** Monterey County - local and military history, archeology; Presidio of Monterey history; U.S. Army history and equipment. **Holdings:** 100 books; 220 microfiche; 8 VF drawers of clippings and reports. **Services:** Library open to the public by appointment for reference use. **Remarks:** Museum and library located at Bldg. 113, Cpl. Ewing Rd.

U.S. ARMY - CHEMICAL RESEARCH, DEVELOPMENT & ENGINEERING CENTER
See: U.S. Army - Armament, Munitions & Chemical Command - Chemical Research, Development & Engineering Center (14707)

U.S. ARMY - CHEMICAL SCHOOL
See: U.S. Army - TRADOC - Chemical School (14790)

U.S. ARMY - COLD REGIONS RESEARCH & ENGINEERING LABORATORY
See: U.S. Army - Corps of Engineers - Cold Regions Research & Engineering Laboratory (14718)

U.S. ARMY - COMBAT DEVELOPMENTS EXPERIMENTATION COMMAND
See: U.S. Army - TRADOC - Combat Developments Experimentation Command (14791)

U.S. ARMY - COMMAND & GENERAL STAFF COLLEGE
See: U.S. Army - TRADOC - Command and General Staff College (14792)

★14713★
U.S. ARMY - COMMUNICATIONS-ELECTRONICS COMMAND - R & D TECHNICAL LIBRARY (Sci-Engr, Comp Sci)
Bldg. 2700, Attn: AMSEL-IM-L Phone: (201)544-2237
Ft. Monmouth, NJ 07703 William R. Werk, Chf.
Founded: 1942. **Staff:** Prof 3; Other 8. **Subjects:** Electronics, electrical engineering, chemistry, physics, computer science. **Holdings:** 49,000 books; 24,000 bound periodical volumes; 180,000 technical documents. **Subscriptions:** 390 journals and other serials. **Services:** Library not open to the public. **Automated Operations:** Computerized cataloging and acquisitions. **Computerized Information Services:** DIALOG Information Services, OCLC. **Networks/Consortia:** Member of FEDLINK. **Staff:** Margaret Borden, Libn..

★14714★
U.S. ARMY - COMMUNICATIONS-ELECTRONICS COMMAND - TECHNICAL LIBRARY (Sci-Engr)
AMSEL-ME-PSL Phone: (201)532-1298
Ft. Monmouth, NJ 07703 Regina Sieben, Libn.
Founded: 1940. **Staff:** Prof 2; Other 2. **Subjects:** Mathematics, electrical engineering, personnel management, physics, electronic engineering, chemistry, photography, test engineering. **Special Collections:** Historical file of official Signal Corps literature; complete collection of Department of

the Army literature on electronic equipment (cataloged by type designation). **Holdings:** 4000 books; 100,000 technical manuals and related publications; 1000 manufacturers' catalogs; 2500 pamphlets. **Subscriptions:** 300 journals and other serials. **Services:** Interlibrary loan; library not open to the public. **Staff:** Marion Clinton, Libn..

★14715★
U.S. ARMY - COMMUNICATIONS AND ELECTRONICS MUSEUM (Mil)
Bldg. 275, Kaplan Hall — Phone: (201)532-2445
Ft. Monmouth, NJ 07703 — Roger A. Godin, Musm.Cur.
Founded: 1975. **Staff:** Prof 2; Other 2. **Subjects:** History of communications and electronics developments at Fort Monmouth, 1917 to present. **Holdings:** 1200 volumes of out-of-print books, technical manuals, pamphlets. **Services:** Library open to qualified researchers. **Publications:** Fort Monmouth History and Place Names, 1917-1961.

★14716★
U.S. ARMY - COMMUNITY & FAMILY SUPPORT CENTER - LIBRARY DIVISION (Mil, Info Sci)
Hoffman Bldg. I, Rm. 1450 — Phone: (202)325-9700
Alexandria, VA 22331-0512 — Nellie B. Strickland, Div.Chf.
Staff: Prof 4; Other 2. **Computerized Information Services:** OCLC; OPTIMIS (electronic mail service). **Networks/Consortia:** Member of FEDLINK. **Publications:** Monthly newsletter; army regulations and directives pertaining to the Army Library Program. **Remarks:** Branch is administrative headquarters for the U.S. Army Morale, Welfare & Recreation Library Program, and establishes overall policy and procedures for the administration of over 278 general libraries, branches, bookmobiles, and technical processing centers. It also selects and purchases books for installation general libraries to supplement local acquisitions, and provides reading materials for isolated troop units and maneuver areas. **Staff:** Frances Perros, Chf.Acq.Libn.; Kathryn L. Earnest, Fld.Serv.Libn.; Barbara Christine, Asst.Acq.Libn..

★14717★
U.S. ARMY - CONCEPTS ANALYSIS AGENCY - LIBRARY (Comp Sci)
8120 Woodmont Ave. — Phone: (301)295-1530
Bethesda, MD 20814-2797 — Lynda Kuntz, Hd.Libn.
Founded: 1973. **Staff:** Prof 2; Other 1. **Subjects:** Computer science, military history. **Holdings:** 3000 books; 7500 government documents. **Subscriptions:** 210 journals and other serials. **Services:** Interlibrary loan; library not open to the public. **Computerized Information Services:** DIALOG Information Services, DTIC, OCLC, NEXIS. **Networks/Consortia:** Member of FEDLINK. **Staff:** Janice Beattie, Ref.Libn..

★14718★
U.S. ARMY - CORPS OF ENGINEERS - COLD REGIONS RESEARCH & ENGINEERING LABORATORY - LIBRARY (Sci-Engr)
72 Lyme Rd. — Phone: (603)646-4221
Hanover, NH 03755-1290 — Nancy C. Liston, Libn.
Founded: 1952. **Staff:** Prof 1; Other 3. **Subjects:** Civil engineering, physics, geology, hydrology, meteorology, geography, mathematics, engineering. **Special Collections:** Snow, ice, and frozen ground; cold regions environment and materials. **Holdings:** 15,000 books; 130,000 documents, reports, pamphlets, periodical articles; 30,000 articles on 460 reels of microfilm; 135,000 items on microfiche. **Subscriptions:** 550 journals and other serials. **Services:** Interlibrary loan; copying; SDI; library open to the public with restrictions. **Automated Operations:** Computerized cataloging. **Computerized Information Services:** DIALOG Information Services, Pergamon ORBIT InfoLine, Inc.; COLD (internal database); DIALMAIL (electronic mail service). **Networks/Consortia:** Member of Northern Libraries Colloquy, Corps of Engineers Network. **Publications:** Library accession bulletin; CRREL publications list; Bibliography on Cold Regions Science and Technology, irregular - by request. **Remarks:** An alternate telephone number is 646-4238.

★14719★
U.S. ARMY - CORPS OF ENGINEERS - CONSTRUCTION ENGINEERING RESEARCH LABORATORY - H.B. ZACKRISON MEMORIAL LIBRARY (Sci-Engr)
Interstate Research Park
Box 4005 — Phone: (217)373-7217
Champaign, IL 61820-1305 — Martha A. Blake, Libn.
Founded: 1969. **Staff:** Prof 1; Other 1. **Subjects:** Environmental and structural engineering, construction materials and management, computer applications, civil engineering. **Holdings:** 8000 books; 1000 bound periodical volumes; 10,000 technical reports. **Subscriptions:** 500 journals and other serials. **Services:** Interlibrary loan; copying; library open to the public for reference use only. **Computerized Information Services:** Pergamon ORBIT InfoLine, Inc., DIALOG Information Services, STN International, OCLC, DTIC. **Networks/Consortia:** Member of FEDLINK, ILLINET. **Publications:** New Acquisitions - for internal distribution only; library brochure. **Special Catalogs:** Catalog of laboratory reports (card).

★14720★
U.S. ARMY - CORPS OF ENGINEERS - DETROIT DISTRICT - TECHNICAL AND LEGAL LIBRARY (Sci-Engr)
Box 1027 — Phone: (313)226-6231
Detroit, MI 48231-1027 — Mary A. Auer, District Libn.
Staff: Prof 1; Other 1. **Subjects:** Engineering, environment, construction, water resources development, Great Lakes navigation, harbor structures, environmental and flood control. **Special Collections:** Detroit district technical reports and studies; district projects slide collection. **Holdings:** 3500 books; 5000 annual reports; government documents; climatological data. **Subscriptions:** 250 journals and other serials; 5 newspapers. **Services:** Interlibrary loan; copying; library open to the public by appointment. **Automated Operations:** Computerized cataloging. **Computerized Information Services:** OCLC, DIALOG Information Services; internal database. **Networks/Consortia:** Member of FEDLINK. **Formed by the merger of:** Legal and Technical Libraries.

★14721★
U.S. ARMY - CORPS OF ENGINEERS - ENGINEER TOPOGRAPHIC LABORATORIES - SCIENTIFIC & TECHNICAL INFORMATION CENTER (Sci-Engr)
Ft. Belvoir, VA 22060 — Phone: (202)355-2656
Mildred L. Stiger, Chf.
Staff: Prof 1; Other 5. **Subjects:** Geodesy, photogrammetry, remote sensing, robotics, mapping. **Holdings:** 8000 volumes; 260 bound periodical volumes; 1500 technical reports; 1000 microfiche. **Subscriptions:** 260 journals and other serials. **Services:** Interlibrary loan; copying; center open to government agencies and industry. **Automated Operations:** Computerized public access catalog, cataloging, and circulation. **Computerized Information Services:** DIALOG Information Services, DTIC, OCLC. **Networks/Consortia:** Member of FEDLINK.

U.S. ARMY - CORPS OF ENGINEERS - ENGINEER WATERWAY EXPERIMENT STATION
See: U.S. Army - Engineer Waterways Experiment Station (14747)

★14722★
U.S. ARMY - CORPS OF ENGINEERS - FORT WORTH DISTRICT - TECHNICAL LIBRARY (Sci-Engr, Law)
819 Taylor St.
Box 17300
Fort Worth, TX 76102 — Phone: (817)334-4820
Founded: 1950. **Staff:** Prof 1; Other 1. **Subjects:** Law; engineering - civil, electrical, mechanical, safety; finance; nuclear science; ecology; environment. **Special Collections:** Air and water pollution; water resources development. **Holdings:** 15,000 books; 20,000 technical reports; army regulations; congressional documents; industry standards and specifications on microfiche; Federal Register, 1969 to present. **Subscriptions:** 500 journals and other serials; 50 newspapers. **Services:** Interlibrary loan; library open to the public for reference use only. **Automated Operations:** Computerized cataloging. **Computerized Information Services:** DIALOG Information Services, LS/2000, OCLC. **Networks/Consortia:** Member of FEDLINK.

★14723★
U.S. ARMY - CORPS OF ENGINEERS - GALVESTON DISTRICT - LIBRARY (Sci-Engr)
Box 1229 — Phone: (409)766-3196
Galveston, TX 77553 — Esther Chavarria
Founded: 1945. **Staff:** 1. **Subjects:** Civil engineering, construction and operation of public works for navigation, flood control, environment, recreation, water resources, soil mechanics, law. **Special Collections:** Annual Reports of the Chief of Engineers, 1871 to present; Congressional documents, 1900-1978. **Holdings:** 8500 books; 2900 other cataloged items. **Subscriptions:** 170 journals and other serials; 19 newspapers. **Services:** Interlibrary loan; copying; library open to the public for reference use except for classified material. **Automated Operations:** Computerized cataloging, acquisitions, and serials. **Computerized Information Services:** DIALOG Information Services, OCLC; internal database. **Networks/Consortia:** Member of FEDLINK.

★14724★
U.S. ARMY - CORPS OF ENGINEERS - HUMPHREY'S ENGINEERING CENTER - TECHNICAL SUPPORT LIBRARY (Sci-Engr)
Kingman Bldg., Rm. 3C02 Phone: (202)325-2386
Ft. Belvoir, VA 22060 Bennie F. Maddox, Chf., Lib.Br.
Founded: 1940. **Staff:** Prof 3; Other 3. **Subjects:** Coastal engineering, hydraulics, shore protection, model studies, beach erosion, coastal ecology, navigation, coastal flood control. **Holdings:** 20,000 books; 40,000 technical reports; photographs; microforms; motion pictures. **Subscriptions:** 475 journals and other serials. **Services:** Interlibrary loan; copying; library open to the public. **Automated Operations:** Computerized cataloging. **Computerized Information Services:** OCLC, DIALOG Information Services; OnTyme Electronic Message Network Service (electronic mail service). **Networks/Consortia:** Member of FEDLINK. **Staff:** Lois J. Carey, Ref.Libn.; Areena Lowe, Acq.Libn.; Maryann Randall, Cat..

★14725★
U.S. ARMY - CORPS OF ENGINEERS - HUNTINGTON DISTRICT - LIBRARY (Sci-Engr, Env-Cons)
502 8th St. Phone: (304)529-5713
Huntington, WV 25701-2070 Sandra V. Morris, Libn.
Staff: Prof 1; Other 1. **Subjects:** Water resource development, environmental science, civil engineering, hydrology, water quality. **Special Collections:** Oral history collection (150 hours). **Holdings:** 11,800 books; 260 bound periodical volumes. **Subscriptions:** 80 journals and other serials; 10 newspapers. **Services:** Interlibrary loan; copying; SDI; library open to the public. **Automated Operations:** Computerized cataloging. **Computerized Information Services:** DIALOG Information Services, Washington Alert Service, OCLC, LEXIS, NEXIS; OnTyme Electronic Message Network Service, Email (electronic mail services). **Networks/ Consortia:** Member of FEDLINK. **Remarks:** An alternate telephone number is 529-5435.

★14726★
U.S. ARMY - CORPS OF ENGINEERS - HYDROLOGIC ENGINEERING CENTER - LIBRARY (Sci-Engr)
609 2nd St. Phone: (916)756-1104
Davis, CA 95616 Christie Ayala, Sec.
Staff: 1. **Subjects:** Hydrology, hydrologic modeling, hydrologic engineering, water resources planning and management, hydraulics. **Holdings:** 500 books; 500 unbound reports; 1000 documents. **Subscriptions:** 15 journals and other serials. **Services:** Interlibrary loan; copying; SDI; library open to the public with restrictions.

★14727★
U.S. ARMY - CORPS OF ENGINEERS - JACKSONVILLE DISTRICT - TECHNICAL LIBRARY (Biol Sci, Sci-Engr)
400 W. Bay St.
Box 4970 Phone: (904)791-3643
Jacksonville, FL 32232-0019 Oriana Brown West, District Libn.
Staff: Prof 2; Other 2. **Subjects:** Civil engineering, environmental resources, fish and wildlife, geology, coastal erosion, storms and hurricanes. **Special Collections:** Cross Florida Barge Canal; Central and Southern Florida Project for Flood Control and Other Purposes. **Holdings:** 4000 books; 8000 reports; Congressional documents, 1940-1970. **Subscriptions:** 150 journals and other serials. **Services:** Interlibrary loan; copying; library open to the public for reference use only. **Automated Operations:** Computerized cataloging and acquisitions. **Computerized Information Services:** DIALOG Information Services, Pergamon ORBIT InfoLine, Inc., BRS Information Technologies, OCLC, Institute for Scientific Information (ISI). **Networks/Consortia:** Member of FEDLINK. **Publications:** Corps of Engineers Project Reports. **Staff:** Linda Smith, Cons./Cat..

★14728★
U.S. ARMY - CORPS OF ENGINEERS - LOS ANGELES DISTRICT - TECHNICAL LIBRARY (Sci-Engr)
Box 2711 Phone: (213)894-5313
Los Angeles, CA 90053-2325 Connie Castillo, Libn.
Staff: Prof 1; Other 1. **Subjects:** Engineering, water resources, flood control, shoreline preservation, navigation, environmental studies. **Special Collections:** U.S. Army Corps of Engineers histories. **Holdings:** 8000 books; 2000 technical reports; Congressional materials on Rivers and Harbors Act. **Subscriptions:** 120 journals and other serials. **Services:** Interlibrary loan; library open to the public. **Automated Operations:** Computerized cataloging and acquisitions. **Computerized Information Services:** DIALOG Information Services. **Remarks:** Library located at 300 N. Los Angeles St., Los Angeles, CA 90012.

★14729★
U.S. ARMY - CORPS OF ENGINEERS - LOWER MISSISSIPPI VALLEY DIVISION - MISSISSIPPI RIVER COMMISSION - TECHNICAL LIBRARY (Sci-Engr)
1500 Bldg., Rm. G-1
1500 Walnut St.
Box 80 Phone: (601)634-5880
Vicksburg, MS 39180 Sherrie L. Moran, Libn.
Founded: 1943. **Staff:** Prof 1; Other 2. **Subjects:** Flood control, navigation, hydraulics. **Special Collections:** Mississippi River Commission historical documents (700). **Holdings:** 47,500 books; 200 bound periodical volumes; 700 reels of microfilm; 5000 microfiche. **Subscriptions:** 500 journals and other serials; 10 newspapers. **Services:** Interlibrary loan; library open to the public. **Automated Operations:** Computerized cataloging, acquisitions, circulation, and serials. **Computerized Information Services:** DIALOG Information Services, OCLC, LEXIS, NEXIS, LS/2000, LEGI-SLATE; OnTyme Electronic Message Network Service (electronic mail service). **Networks/Consortia:** Member of FEDLINK. **Publications:** List of publications received, monthly; Current Acquisitions, monthly; Technical Database Guide, annual; Library Handbook, biennial; Periodical Directory, annual.

★14730★
U.S. ARMY - CORPS OF ENGINEERS - MEMPHIS DISTRICT - LIBRARY (Sci-Engr)
B-202 Clifford Davis Federal Bldg. Phone: (901)521-3584
Memphis, TN 38103-1894 Rose Scott, Libn.
Founded: 1932. **Staff:** Prof 1. **Subjects:** Civil engineering, water resources, environmental concerns, economics. **Holdings:** 6000 books; 132 microforms. **Subscriptions:** 199 journals and other serials. **Services:** Interlibrary loan; copying; library open to the public for reference use only. **Automated Operations:** Computerized cataloging. **Computerized Information Services:** DIALOG Information Services, OCLC. **Networks/ Consortia:** Member of FEDLINK.

★14731★
U.S. ARMY - CORPS OF ENGINEERS - NEW ENGLAND DIVISION - TECHNICAL LIBRARY (Sci-Engr)
Bldg. 116N
424 Trapelo Rd. Phone: (617)647-8118
Waltham, MA 02254 Timothy P. Hays, Chf.
Staff: Prof 1; Other 1. **Subjects:** Water resources; hydrology; engineering - geotechnical, structural, civil; ecology. **Special Collections:** New England River Basin Collection. **Holdings:** 10,000 books; 50 bound periodical volumes; 7000 reports; 5000 Corps of Engineers reports including reports on dredged materials; 1000 hydrology reports. **Subscriptions:** 300 journals and other serials; 20 newspapers. **Services:** Interlibrary loan; copying; library open to the public with identification. **Automated Operations:** Computerized cataloging and serials. **Computerized Information Services:** DIALOG Information Services, Pergamon ORBIT InfoLine, Inc., OCLC, LEXIS, NEXIS; internal database. **Networks/Consortia:** Member of FEDLINK.

★14732★
U.S. ARMY - CORPS OF ENGINEERS - NORTH ATLANTIC DIVISION - TECHNICAL LIBRARY (Sci-Engr)
90 Church St. Phone: (212)264-7698
New York, NY 10007-9998 Susan Tu Lin, Engr.Div.Libn.
Founded: 1974. **Staff:** Prof 1; Other 2. **Subjects:** Flood, water development, locks and dams, civil engineering. **Special Collections:** Locks and Dams in Northeastern areas; History of the Corps of Engineers; Waterways Experiment Station Technical Reports. **Holdings:** 20,000 books; 2500 bound periodical volumes; microfiche; microfilm; 16mm film cartridges; government documents; technical reports. **Subscriptions:** 210 journals and other serials; 7 newspapers. **Services:** Interlibrary loan; library not open to the public. **Automated Operations:** Computerized cataloging. **Computerized Information Services:** OCLC, DIALOG Information Services, LEXIS, NEXIS, Congressional Quarterly Inc. (CQ). **Networks/ Consortia:** Member of FEDLINK. **Publications:** List of periodical subscriptions, annual.

★14733★
U.S. ARMY - CORPS OF ENGINEERS - OFFICE OF THE CHIEF OF ENGINEERS - LIBRARY (Sci-Engr)
20 Massachusetts Ave., N.W. Phone: (202)272-0455
Washington, DC 20314-1000 Sarah A. Mikel, Chf., Lib.Br.
Founded: 1941. **Staff:** Prof 4; Other 3. **Subjects:** Engineering - civil, environmental, military, mechanical; management. **Special Collections:** Early documents and reports of the Corps of Engineers; army explorations and surveys in the Middle and Far West, 1820-1890. **Holdings:** 40,000

books; 2000 bound periodical volumes; 22,000 Corps of Engineers reports; microforms; Congressional documents. **Subscriptions:** 750 journals and other serials; 5 newspapers. **Services:** Interlibrary loan; library not open to the public. **Automated Operations:** Computerized cataloging. **Computerized Information Services:** DIALOG Information Services, LEXIS, DTIC, OCLC, Washington Alert Service, LEGI-SLATE, LS/2000. **Networks/Consortia:** Member of FEDLINK. **Publications:** Acquisitions List, monthly - available on request; Periodicals Holdings List, annual; library brochure. **Special Indexes:** Index to Annual Report of the Chief of Engineers, 1775-1972 (book). **Staff:** James Dorsey, Chf., Ref.Sect.; Myra Craig, Chf., Cat..

★14734★
U.S. ARMY - CORPS OF ENGINEERS - OMAHA DISTRICT - LIBRARY (Sci-Engr)
6014 U.S. Post Office & Courthouse
215 N. 7th St. Phone: (402)221-3230
Omaha, NE 68102-4910 Karen S. SHafer, Lib.Techn.
Staff: 2. **Subjects:** Engineering, water resources, law. **Holdings:** Agency regulations and directives. **Services:** Interlibrary loan; library open to the public for reference use only. **Automated Operations:** Computerized cataloging. **Computerized Information Services:** DIALOG Information Services, OCLC. **Networks/Consortia:** Member of FEDLINK. **Remarks:** Library serves both the District Office and the Missouri River Division Office.

★14735★
U.S. ARMY - CORPS OF ENGINEERS - PHILADELPHIA DISTRICT - TECHNICAL LIBRARY (Sci-Engr)
2nd & Chestnut Sts. Phone: (215)597-3610
Philadelphia, PA 19106 Jeannemarie Faison, Libn.
Founded: 1974. **Staff:** Prof 1. **Subjects:** Engineering - civil, environmental, coastal. **Special Collections:** U.S. Army Corps of Engineers - Philadelphia District technical reports; U.S. Army Corps of Engineers Laboratory technical reports (3500). **Holdings:** 7000 books; 2 VF drawers of standards; 200 microfiche; 2 VF drawers of information files. **Subscriptions:** 115 journals and other serials. **Services:** Interlibrary loan; library open to the public with restrictions. **Automated Operations:** Computerized cataloging. **Computerized Information Services:** DIALOG Information Services, OCLC. **Networks/Consortia:** Member of FEDLINK. **Publications:** Accessions lists, monthly; bibliographies.

★14736★
U.S. ARMY - CORPS OF ENGINEERS - PORTLAND DISTRICT - LIBRARY (Sci-Engr)
319 S.W. Pine St.
Box 2946 Phone: (503)221-6016
Portland, OR 97208 Christian P. Hurd, District Libn.
Founded: 1938. **Staff:** Prof 1; Other 2. **Subjects:** Engineering, law. **Holdings:** 10,000 books. **Subscriptions:** 135 journals and other serials; 10 newspapers. **Services:** Interlibrary loan; library open to the public for reference use only. **Automated Operations:** Computerized cataloging and ILL. **Computerized Information Services:** DIALOG Information Services, Pergamon ORBIT InfoLine, Inc., BRS Information Technologies, OCLC.

★14737★
U.S. ARMY - CORPS OF ENGINEERS - ROCK ISLAND DISTRICT - TECHNICAL LIBRARY (Sci-Engr)
Clock Tower Bldg.
Box 2004 Phone: (309)788-6361
Rock Island, IL 61204-2004 Nancy J. Larson-Bloomer, Libn.
Staff: Prof 1. **Subjects:** Civil engineering, hydraulics/locks and dams, flood and plain management, construction, soil mechanics, environmental analysis. **Special Collections:** Hydraulics; Water Experiment Station technical reports; Water Resources Developments; construction. **Holdings:** 10,000 books; 15,000 technical reports; 5000 microfiche. **Subscriptions:** 100 journals and other serials. **Services:** Interlibrary loan; library open to the public by appointment. **Automated Operations:** Computerized cataloging and ILL. **Computerized Information Services:** DIALOG Information Services, OCLC, LS/2000, DTIC. **Networks/Consortia:** Member of FEDLINK, River Bend Library System (RBLS). **Publications:** Periodicals.

★14738★
U.S. ARMY - CORPS OF ENGINEERS - SACRAMENTO DISTRICT - TECHNICAL INFORMATION CENTER (Sci-Engr, Plan)
650 Capitol Mall Phone: (916)551-2456
Sacramento, CA 95814 Deborah A. Newton, District Libn.
Staff: Prof 1; Other 3. **Subjects:** Water, hydrology, hydraulics, environment, recreation planning, geology, architecture, construction. **Special Collections:** Annual Reports to the Chief of Engineers. **Holdings:** 25,000 volumes. **Subscriptions:** 220 journals and other serials; 5 newspapers. **Services:** Interlibrary loan; copying (limited); center open to the public with restrictions. **Automated Operations:** Computerized cataloging, acquisitions, and circulation. **Computerized Information Services:** DIALOG Information Services, FAR On-line; EasyLink, OnTyme Electronic Message Network Service (electronic mail services). **Networks/Consortia:** Member of FEDLINK. **Publications:** Library Bulletin, monthly - for internal distribution only.

★14739★
U.S. ARMY - CORPS OF ENGINEERS - ST. LOUIS DISTRICT - LIBRARY (Env-Cons, Sci-Engr)
210 Tucker Blvd., N.
St. Louis, MO 63101-1986 Phone: (314)263-5675
Staff: Prof 1; Other 1. **Subjects:** Civil engineering, water resources, environment, wildlife management, recreation. **Holdings:** 16,000 books; 6000 technical reports; microfilm. **Subscriptions:** 400 journals and other serials; 60 newspapers. **Services:** Interlibrary loan; copying; library open to the public. **Automated Operations:** Computerized cataloging, acquisitions, serials, and circulation. **Computerized Information Services:** OCLC, DIALOG Information Services, DTI Data Trek, Inc.; OnTyme Electronic Message Network Service (electronic mail service). **Networks/Consortia:** Member of FEDLINK. **Publications:** Periodical Holdings List, annual; Library Users Guide; New Books List, quarterly. **Special Catalogs:** Microfiche catalog of book and report collection.

★14740★
U.S. ARMY - CORPS OF ENGINEERS - ST. PAUL DISTRICT - MAP FILES (Geog-Map)
1122 U.S. Post Office & Custom House Phone: (612)725-7992
St. Paul, MN 55101-1479 Marianne D. Hageman, Tech.Info.Spec.
Staff: Prof 1; Other 1. **Subjects:** Engineering, water resources, flood control, inland waterways, environmental planning. **Special Collections:** Mississippi River Continuous Survey, 1937 to present (83 sheets); Mississippi River Commission Charts, 1898 and 1915 (278 sheets); Brown Surveys of the Mississippi River, 1930 (129 sheets). **Holdings:** 70,000 engineering drawings; 10,000 maps and charts; 50,000 aerial photographs; 1000 field books. **Services:** Copying; files open to the public with restrictions. **Automated Operations:** Computerized circulation.

★14741★
U.S. ARMY - CORPS OF ENGINEERS - ST. PAUL DISTRICT - TECHNICAL LIBRARY (Sci-Engr)
1135 U.S. Post Office & Custom House Phone: (612)725-5921
St. Paul, MN 55101 Jean Marie Schmidt, Libn.
Staff: Prof 1. **Subjects:** Engineering, hydrology, water resources, dam construction, environmental studies, military history. **Special Collections:** Chief of Engineers Annual Reports, 1867 to present; Army Technical Manuals; Waterborne Commerce Statistics. **Holdings:** 4810 books; 7350 government reports, including Waterway Experiment Station reports and U.S. Geological Survey reports. **Subscriptions:** 403 journals and other serials. **Services:** Interlibrary loan; library open to the public for reference use only. **Computerized Information Services:** DIALOG Information Services, OCLC, WILSONLINE, DunSprint, DATANET. **Networks/Consortia:** Member of FEDLINK, Metronet.

★14742★
U.S. ARMY - CORPS OF ENGINEERS - SAVANNAH DISTRICT - TECHNICAL LIBRARY (Sci-Engr)
Box 889 Phone: (912)944-5462
Savannah, GA 31402-0889 Joseph T. Page, Chf.
Founded: 1968. **Staff:** Prof 1. **Subjects:** Engineering, geology, legislation, environmental and architectural science. **Holdings:** 6000 books; 7000 technical reports; 16,920 microforms, including 3000 reels of microfilm; technical standards and specifications. **Subscriptions:** 897 journals and other serials; 32 journals and other serials. **Services:** Interlibrary loan; copying; SDI; library open to public at librarian's discretion. **Automated Operations:** Computerized cataloging. **Computerized Information Services:** DIALOG Information Services, LEGI-SLATE, Pergamon ORBIT InfoLine, Inc., OCLC. **Networks/Consortia:** Member of FEDLINK.

★14743★
U.S. ARMY - CORPS OF ENGINEERS - SEATTLE DISTRICT - LIBRARY (Sci-Engr)
Box C-3755 Phone: (206)764-3728
Seattle, WA 98124-2255 Pat J. Perry, District Libn.
Founded: 1940. **Staff:** Prof 2; Other 1. **Subjects:** Engineering, environment, hydraulics, hospital and marine construction, law. **Special Collections:** Army Field Law Library (8000 volumes); Eng/Tech Collection; Learning

Center (self-guided classes; 350 videotapes, audio cassettes, other AV programs). **Holdings:** 17,000 books and reports; 27,500 technical reports on microfiche; 20,000 35mm slides; 5 drawers of pamphlets. **Subscriptions:** 350 journals and other serials; 30 newspapers. **Services:** Interlibrary loan; library open to the public. **Automated Operations:** Computerized cataloging and circulation. **Computerized Information Services:** DIALOG Information Services, Pergamon ORBIT InfoLine, Inc., BRS Information Technologies, Integrated Technical Information System (ITIS), DTIC, OCLC, Environmental Technical Information System (ETIS); EasyLink, OnTyme Electronic Message Network Service (electronic mail services). **Publications:** New Titles; Periodical Holdings. **Special Indexes:** District slide file index; district regulations KWIC index. **Staff:** May Gin Carrell, Asst.Libn..

★14744★
U.S. ARMY - CORPS OF ENGINEERS - SOUTH ATLANTIC DIVISION - TECHNICAL LIBRARY (Sci-Engr)
426 Title Bldg.
30 Pryor St., S.W. Phone: (404)331-6620
Atlanta, GA 30335-6801 James D. Chestnut, Div.Libn.
Staff: Prof 1; Other 1. **Subjects:** Civil engineering, water resources, contract law. **Holdings:** 4123 books. **Subscriptions:** 164 journals and other serials. **Services:** Interlibrary loan; copying; library open to the public for reference use only. **Automated Operations:** Computerized cataloging. **Computerized Information Services:** OCLC, DIALOG Information Services. **Networks/Consortia:** Member of FEDLINK, Georgia Library Information Network (GLIN).

★14745★
U.S. ARMY - CORPS OF ENGINEERS - SOUTH PACIFIC DIVISION - LIBRARY (Sci-Engr)
630 Sansome St., Rm. 720 Phone: (415)556-5320
San Francisco, CA 94111-2206 Mary G. Anderson, Div.Libn.
Staff: Prof 1; Other 1. **Subjects:** Civil engineering, water resources. **Special Collections:** Corps of Engineers annual reports; Waterways Experiment Station Reports. **Holdings:** 4300 books; 7000 bound reports. **Subscriptions:** 182 journals and other serials. **Services:** Interlibrary loan; library open to the public for reference use only. **Automated Operations:** Computerized cataloging. **Computerized Information Services:** DIALOG Information Services, OCLC; OnTyme Electronic Message Network Service (electronic mail service). **Networks/Consortia:** Member of FEDLINK.

★14746★
U.S. ARMY - CORPS OF ENGINEERS - SOUTHWESTERN DIVISION - TECHNICAL LIBRARY (Sci-Engr)
1114 Commerce St.
Dallas, TX 75242-0216 Phone: (214)767-2325
Staff: 2. **Subjects:** Engineering, science, law, water resources. **Holdings:** 10,000 volumes; 20,000 pamphlets; Visual Search Microfilm File; 16mm cassettes. **Subscriptions:** 151 journals and other serials. **Services:** Interlibrary loan; copying; library open to the public for reference use only. **Automated Operations:** Computerized cataloging, acquisitions, and serials. **Computerized Information Services:** DIALOG Information Services, OCLC. **Networks/Consortia:** Member of FEDLINK. **Publications:** SWD Library Bookworm, bimonthly.

U.S. ARMY - DEPOT SYSTEM COMMAND - SPECIAL SERVICES DIVISION - SHARPE ARMY DEPOT - MORALE SUPPORT LIBRARY
See: U.S. Army - Materiel Command - Community Recreation Library (14763)

U.S. ARMY - DUGWAY PROVING GROUND
See: U.S. Army - Test & Evaluation Command (14781)

U.S. ARMY - ENGINEER SCHOOL
See: U.S. Army - TRADOC - Engineer School (14793)

U.S. ARMY - ENGINEER TOPOGRAPHIC LABORATORIES
See: U.S. Army - Corps of Engineers - Engineer Topographic Laboratories (14721)

★14747★
U.S. ARMY - ENGINEER WATERWAYS EXPERIMENT STATION - COASTAL ENGINEERING INFORMATION ANALYSIS CENTER (Sci-Engr)
Box 631 Phone: (601)634-2017
Vicksburg, MS 39180 Fred Camfield, Dir.
Subjects: Beach erosion, flood and storm protection, coastal and offshore structures, navigation structures. **Holdings:** Center acts as a central repository for the Corps of Engineers data collection under the field data collection program for coastal engineering. The data includes wave statistics, coastal currents, beach profiles, and aerial photographs. Center is supported by holdings in the Technical Information Division. **Services:** Interlibrary loan. **Publications:** CERCular (information bulletin), quarterly; annotated bibliography of publications of the Coastal Engineering Research Center. **Remarks:** Engineer Waterways Experiment Station is part of U.S. Army - Corps of Engineers.

★14748★
U.S. ARMY - ENGINEER WATERWAYS EXPERIMENT STATION - CONCRETE TECHNOLOGY INFORMATION ANALYSIS CENTER (Sci-Engr)
Box 631 Phone: (601)634-3264
Vicksburg, MS 39180 Bryant Mather, Dir.
Subjects: Concrete materials and properties, concrete tests and analysis, concrete construction, cements and pozzolans, reinforced concrete, waterstops and jointing materials, grouts and grouting, adhesives and coatings, corrosion in steel and concrete. **Holdings:** Center is supported by holdings of the Technical Information Division. **Services:** Interlibrary loan; copying. **Publications:** List of publications - available on request.

★14749★
U.S. ARMY - ENGINEER WATERWAYS EXPERIMENT STATION - HYDRAULIC ENGINEERING INFORMATION ANALYSIS CENTER (Sci-Engr)
Box 631 Phone: (601)634-3368
Vicksburg, MS 39180 Bobby J. Brown, Dir.
Subjects: Hydraulics - river, harbor, tidal, closed conduit; flood control structures; navigation structures; harbor protective structures; underwater shock effects. **Holdings:** Center is supported by holdings in the Technical Information Division. **Services:** Interlibrary loan; copying.

★14750★
U.S. ARMY - ENGINEER WATERWAYS EXPERIMENT STATION - PAVEMENTS & SOIL TRAFFICABILITY INFORMATION ANALYSIS CENTER (Sci-Engr)
Box 631 Phone: (601)634-2734
Vicksburg, MS 39180 Gerald W. Turnage, Dir.
Subjects: Soil trafficability, mobility, pavements, terrain evaluation. **Holdings:** Center is supported by the collection of holdings in the Technical Information Division. **Services:** Interlibrary loan; copying. **Publications:** List of publications - available on request.

★14751★
U.S. ARMY - ENGINEER WATERWAYS EXPERIMENT STATION - SOIL MECHANICS INFORMATION ANALYSIS CENTER (Sci-Engr)
Box 631 Phone: (601)634-3475
Vicksburg, MS 39180 Paul F. Hadala, Dir.
Subjects: Soil mechanics, soil dynamics, rock mechanics, foundation engineering, earthquake engineering, engineering geology, earth dams, subgrades. **Holdings:** Center is supported by holdings in the Technical Information Division. **Services:** Interlibrary loan; copying. **Publications:** Proceedings of Symposium on Applications of the Finite Element Method in Geotechnical Engineering; Microthesaurus of Soil Mechanics Terms; Evaluation Statements and Abstracts of Recent Acquisitions on Soil Mechanics and Related Subjects, bimonthly.

★14752★
U.S. ARMY - ENGINEER WATERWAYS EXPERIMENT STATION - TECHNICAL INFORMATION CENTER (Sci-Engr)
Box 631 Phone: (601)634-2533
Vicksburg, MS 39180 Al Sherlock, Chf., Tech.Info.Div.
Founded: 1933. **Staff:** Prof 13; Other 17. **Subjects:** Hydraulics, soil mechanics, concrete, weapons effects, mobility of vehicles, environmental studies, explosive excavation, pavements, geology. **Holdings:** 500,000 volumes, including microforms. **Subscriptions:** 1500 journals and other serials. **Services:** Interlibrary loan; copying; SDI; center open to the public with restrictions. **Automated Operations:** Computerized cataloging. **Computerized Information Services:** DTIC, DIALOG Information Services, OCLC. **Publications:** Recent Acquisitions Lists, monthly - to government agencies; List of Post Authorization Reports, annual; List of Translations of Waterways Experiment Station, irregular - both to Corps of Engineers; List of Publications of the U.S. Army Engineer Waterways Experiment Station, annual; List of Translations of Foreign Literature on Hydraulics, irregular; Bibliography on Tidal Hydraulics, irregular; WES Engineering Computer Programs Library Catalog, semiannual - to Corps of Engineers; bibliographies. **Remarks:** Supports the five Department of Defense Information Analysis Centers established at the Waterways

Experiment Station, which do not have separate collections. **Staff:** Carol McMillin, Act.Chf., Lib.Br.; Alfrieda Clark, Chf., Spec.Proj.; Hollis Landrum, Chf., Tech.Proc.Sect.; Don Kirby, Ref.Libn.; Jerry Griffith, Cat.; Helen Ingram, Ref.Libn.; Debbie Carpenter, Chf., Acq.Sect.; Carol McMillin, Chf., Ref.Sect.; Paul Taccarino, Libn.; Ernest Walton, Chf., Pub.Distr.Sect.; Katherine Kennedy, Libn.; Richard Hancock, Cat.; Marita Sanders, Cat.; Jimmie Perry, Ref.Libn..

U.S. ARMY - ENVIRONMENTAL HEALTH AGENCY
See: U.S. Army - Health Services Command - Environmental Hygiene Agency (14756)

U.S. ARMY - FIELD ARTILLERY SCHOOL
See: U.S. Army - TRADOC - Field Artillery School (14794)

U.S. ARMY - FIELD LAW LIBRARY
See: U.S. Army - Corps of Engineers - Seattle District - Library (14743)

★14753★
U.S. ARMY - FORCES COMMAND - FORT MEADE MUSEUM - LIBRARY (Mil)
Attn: AFZI-PTS-MU Phone: (301)677-7054
Ft. George G. Meade, MD 20755-5094 Robert S. Johnson, Cur.
Founded: 1963. **Subjects:** U.S. and foreign army material culture studies, general military history. **Special Collections:** Photographs of World Wars I and II; weapons, uniforms and accoutrements, and other memorabilia of the army. **Holdings:** 1000 books; 2000 Ft. Meade and 1st U.S. Army archival materials. **Services:** Copying; library open to the public by appointment. **Remarks:** An alternate telephone number is 677-6966.

★14754★
U.S. ARMY - FORCES COMMAND - LANGUAGE TRAINING FACILITY - LIBRARY (Hum)
Bldg. 2509
USA Education Center Phone: (301)677-7255
Ft. George G. Meade, MD 20755
Dorothy R. Kimball, Career Educ.Spec.
Staff: Prof 1; Other 1. **Subjects:** Foreign languages. **Holdings:** 8000 books; foreign language tapes, workbooks, dictionaries, encyclopedias. **Services:** Interlibrary loan; copying; library open to active, reserve, and retired military personnel, dependents, and staff. **Also Known As:** Fort Meade Army Education Center - Language Laboratory.

★14755★
U.S. ARMY - HEALTH SERVICES COMMAND - ACADEMY OF HEALTH SCIENCES - STIMSON LIBRARY (Med)
Bldg. 2840 Phone: (512)221-5932
Ft. Sam Houston, TX 78234-6100 Norma L. Sellers, Chf.Libn.
Founded: 1932. **Staff:** Prof 3; Other 6. **Subjects:** Military medicine, nursing, health care administration, management, psychiatry, veterinary medicine. **Holdings:** 35,828 books; 11,250 bound periodical volumes; 5800 technical reports; 2500 archival materials; 3500 items on microfilm; 1420 AV programs. **Subscriptions:** 560 journals and other serials. **Services:** Interlibrary loan; library open to the public for reference use only. **Computerized Information Services:** DIALOG Information Services, DTIC, MEDLINE. **Networks/Consortia:** Member of Council of Research & Academic Libraries (CORAL), Health Oriented Libraries of San Antonio (HOLSA). **Publications:** List of periodical holdings. **Staff:** Bertha Huber, Ref.Libn.; Kay D. Livingston, Tech.Serv..

★14756★
U.S. ARMY - HEALTH SERVICES COMMAND - ENVIRONMENTAL HYGIENE AGENCY - LIBRARY (Med)
Bldg. E1570 Phone: (301)671-4236
Aberdeen Proving Ground, MD 21010 Krishan S. Goel, Libn.
Founded: 1955. **Staff:** Prof 1; Other 2. **Subjects:** Occupational medicine, safety and health; chemistry and toxicology; audiology; medical entomology; laser, microwave, and radiological safety and health; air and water pollution; sanitary engineering. **Holdings:** 12,000 books; 8,000 bound periodical volumes; 8400 R&D reports; 3000 microfiche. **Subscriptions:** 450 journals and other serials. **Services:** Interlibrary loan; copying; SDI; library open to agency guests and researchers from accredited institutions. **Automated Operations:** Computerized serials. **Computerized Information Services:** OCLC, DIALOG Information Services, MEDLINE.

★14757★
U.S. ARMY - HEALTH SERVICES COMMAND - MEDICAL RESEARCH INSTITUTE OF CHEMICAL DEFENSE - WOOD TECHNICAL LIBRARY (Med)
Bldg. E3100 Phone: (301)671-4135
Aberdeen Proving Ground, MD 21010-5425
Patricia M. Pepin, Supv.Libn.
Staff: Prof 2; Other 2. **Subjects:** Pharmacology, biomedicine, psychology, biochemistry, medicine, toxicology. **Holdings:** 4000 books; 4416 bound periodical volumes; 10,956 reels of microfilm. **Subscriptions:** 832 journals and other serials. **Services:** Interlibrary loan; copying; SDI; library open to the public for reference use only. **Automated Operations:** Computerized cataloging. **Computerized Information Services:** OCLC. **Networks/Consortia:** Member of FEDLINK. **Publications:** New Acquisitions List, monthly - to branches.

U.S. ARMY - HYDROLOGIC ENGINEERING CENTER
See: U.S. Army - Corps of Engineers - Hydrologic Engineering Center (14726)

U.S. ARMY - INFANTRY SCHOOL
See: U.S. Army - TRADOC - Infantry School (14796)

★14758★
U.S. ARMY - INFORMATION SYSTEMS COMMAND - INFORMATION SYSTEMS ENGINEERING COMMAND - TECHNICAL LIBRARY (Comp Sci)
Stop H-9 Phone: (703)756-5872
Ft. Belvoir, VA 22060-5456 Grace C. Corbin, Tech.Info.Spec.
Founded: 1968. **Staff:** Prof 1; Other 1. **Subjects:** Data processing, computers, computer programming, operations research, functionally-oriented language, management information systems. **Holdings:** 2500 books; 3450 vendor manuals on computer hardware and programming; 1700 technical reports, hardcopy and microfiche; 1100 regulatory and standardization texts for federal and military ADP operations. **Subscriptions:** 190 journals and other serials. **Services:** Interlibrary loan; video self-study administration; library open to the public for reference use only.

U.S. ARMY - INFORMATION SYSTEMS COMMAND - SYSTEMS ACTIVITY - TECHNICAL LIBRARY
See: U.S. Army Garrison - Technical Library (14815)

U.S. ARMY - THE INSTITUTE OF HERALDRY
See: U.S. Army - Military Personnel Center - Personnel Service Support Directorate - The Institute of Heraldry (14775)

U.S. ARMY - INTELLIGENCE CENTER & SCHOOL
See: U.S. Army - TRADOC - Intelligence Center & School (14797)

U.S. ARMY - INTELLIGENCE SCHOOL, DEVENS
See: U.S. Army - TRADOC - Intelligence School, Devens (14798)

★14759★
U.S. ARMY - INTELLIGENCE & THREAT ANALYSIS CENTER - TECHNICAL INFORMATION FACILITY (Mil)
Attn: AIAIT-HI
Bldg. 213, Stop 314
Washington Navy Yard Phone: (202)863-3548
Washington, DC 20374-2136 Dean A. Burns, Chf., Info.Serv.Br.
Staff: Prof 11; Other 16. **Subjects:** Military intelligence. **Special Collections:** Army threat documents. **Holdings:** Figures not available. **Subscriptions:** 580 journals and other serials; 20 newspapers. **Services:** Interlibrary loan (limited); facility not open to the public. **Automated Operations:** Computerized public access catalog, cataloging, and circulation. **Computerized Information Services:** DIALOG Information Services, NEXIS, BRS Information Technologies. **Remarks:** Requests for classified documents should be submitted through channels. Contractors must submit requests through their contract monitors. All requests must include certification of need to know. **Staff:** Margaret Nicholas, Chf., Ref.Sect.; Anita Parins, Chf., Tech.Sect.; Holly Wilson, Libn.; Jamie Farriss, Tech.Info.Spec.; Carol Norton, Libn.; Carol Wong, Libn.; Richard Cooper, Libn.; Thomas Greene, Libn.; Betti Mack, Tech.Info.Spec.; Jeanne Razalon, Tech.Info.Spec..

★14760★
U.S. ARMY - JFK SPECIAL WARFARE CENTER & SCHOOL - MARQUAT MEMORIAL LIBRARY (Mil, Soc Sci)
Rm. 140, Kennedy Hall Phone: (919)432-9222
Ft. Bragg, NC 28307 Frank M. London, Supv.Libn.
Founded: 1952. **Staff:** Prof 2. **Subjects:** Military assistance, international studies, unconventional warfare, political science. **Holdings:** 45,000 volumes; pamphlets; documents; Human Relations Area Files on microfilm. **Subscriptions:** 350 journals and other serials; 20 newspapers. **Services:** Interlibrary loan; copying; library open to the public for reference use only. **Automated Operations:** Computerized cataloging and circulation. **Computerized Information Services:** DIALOG Information Services, OCLC, DTIC. **Networks/Consortia:** Member of FEDLINK. **Publications:** Accession List; Periodical Holdings List; library guide. **Remarks:** An alternate telephone number is 432-6503. **Staff:** Fred Fuller, Ref.Libn.; Mary Grooms, ILL.

★14761★
U.S. ARMY - LABORATORY COMMAND - INSTALLATION SUPPORT ACTIVITY - TECHNICAL INFORMATION BRANCH (Sci-Engr)
2800 Powder Mill Rd. (DELHD-TA-L) Phone: (202)394-2536
Adelphi, MD 20783-1145 Barbra L. McLaughlin, Chf.
Founded: 1959. **Staff:** Prof 4; Other 4. **Subjects:** Electronics, physics, engineering, chemistry, mathematics. **Holdings:** 34,900 books; 19,697 bound periodical volumes; 100,000 technical reports. **Subscriptions:** 726 journals and other serials. **Services:** Interlibrary loan; branch not open to the public. **Automated Operations:** Computerized cataloging. **Computerized Information Services:** DIALOG Information Services, OCLC, Pergamon ORBIT InfoLine, Inc., DTIC. **Publications:** Accession List.

★14762★
U.S. ARMY - LABORATORY COMMAND - MATERIALS TECHNOLOGY LABORATORY - TECHNICAL LIBRARY (Sci-Engr, Mil)
ATTN: SLCMT-IML Phone: (617)923-5460
Watertown, MA 02172-0001 Margaret M. Murphy, Chf., Tech.Lib.
Founded: 1920. **Staff:** Prof 3; Other 3. **Subjects:** Materials science, mechanics, composite materials, metallurgy, nondestructive testing, chemistry, engineering, ceramics, polymer chemistry, military science, physics. **Holdings:** 25,000 books; 20,000 bound periodical volumes; 33,000 documents; 47,000 documents on microfiche; 913 volumes on microfiche/microfilm. **Subscriptions:** 650 journals and other serials; 15 newspapers. **Services:** Interlibrary loan; library not open to the public. **Computerized Information Services:** DIALOG Information Services, NASA/RECON, BRS Information Technologies, DTIC, OCLC. **Networks/Consortia:** Member of NELINET, FEDLINK. **Publications:** Monographs, annotated bibliographies, both irregular. **Staff:** Dolores R. Allen, Libn.; Judy H. Kesserich, Libn..

U.S. ARMY - LANGUAGE TRAINING FACILITY
See: U.S. Army - Forces Command - Language Training Facility (14754)

U.S. ARMY - LANGUAGE TRAINING FACILITY
See: U.S. Army - TRADOC - Language Training Facility (14799)

U.S. ARMY - LOGISTICS LIBRARY
See: U.S. Army - TRADOC - Logistics Library (14800)

U.S. ARMY - MATERIEL COMMAND - ARMAMENT, MUNITIONS & CHEMICAL COMMAND
See: U.S. Army - Armament, Munitions & Chemical Command (14708)

U.S. ARMY - MATERIEL COMMAND - AUTOMATED LOGISTIC MANAGEMENT SYSTEM AGENCY
See: Automated Logistic Management Systems Agency (1188)

U.S. ARMY - MATERIEL COMMAND - AVIATION APPLIED TECHNOLOGY DIRECTORATE
See: U.S. Army - Aviation Applied Technology Directorate (14709)

U.S. ARMY - MATERIEL COMMAND - COMMUNICATIONS-ELECTRONICS COMMAND
See: U.S. Army - Communications-Electronics Command (14714)

★14763★
U.S. ARMY - MATERIEL COMMAND - COMMUNITY RECREATION LIBRARY (Mil, Geog-Map)
Sharpe Army Depot Phone: (209)982-2656
Lathrop, CA 95331-5214 Sheila A. White, Lib.Techn.
Staff: Prof 1. **Subjects:** Maps. **Holdings:** 5000 books. **Subscriptions:** 33 journals and other serials. **Services:** Interlibrary loan; copying; library open to active and retired military personnel and civilian depot employees. **Computerized Information Services:** OCLC. **Networks/Consortia:** Member of 49-99 Cooperative Library System. **Formerly:** U.S. Army - Depot System Command - Special Services Division - Sharpe Army Depot - Morale Support Library.

★14764★
U.S. ARMY - MATERIEL COMMAND - HEADQUARTERS - TECHNICAL LIBRARY (Mil)
Attn: AMCMP-L
5001 Eisenhower Ave. Phone: (202)274-8152
Alexandria, VA 22333-0001 M. Ann Parham, Chf.
Founded: 1973. **Staff:** Prof 3; Other 3. **Subjects:** Management, technology, mathematics and statistics, military affairs, data processing, social sciences and economics. **Holdings:** 17,000 volumes. **Services:** Interlibrary loan; library not open to the public. **Automated Operations:** Computerized cataloging. **Computerized Information Services:** DIALOG Information Services, DTIC, OCLC. **Networks/Consortia:** Member of FEDLINK.

U.S. ARMY - MATERIEL COMMAND - LABORATORY COMMAND
See: U.S. Army - Laboratory Command (14761)

U.S. ARMY - MATERIEL COMMAND - MISSILE COMMAND
See: U.S. Army - Missile Command & Marshall Space Flight Center (14776)

★14765★
U.S. ARMY - MATERIEL COMMAND - PLASTICS TECHNICAL EVALUATION CENTER (PLASTEC) - LIBRARY (Sci-Engr)
SMCAR-AET-O, Bldg. 355N
Armament Research, Development & Engineering Ctr.
Phone: (201)724-2778
Picatinny Arsenal, NJ 07806-5000 Suseela Chandrasekar, Tech.Info.Off.
Founded: 1960. **Staff:** Prof 1; Other 1. **Subjects:** Plastics, materials engineering, adhesives, organic matrix composites, compatibility of polymers with energetic materials, packaging materials. **Special Collections:** PLASTEC reports archives. **Holdings:** 2000 books; 200 bound periodical volumes; 45,000 technical reports; 20,000 reels of microfilm of military specifications and standards, commercial and foreign standards. **Subscriptions:** 50 journals and other serials. **Services:** Interlibrary loan; copying (limited); SDI; library open to the public by appointment. **Automated Operations:** Computerized cataloging. **Computerized Information Services:** DIALOG Information Services, DTIC, NASA/RECON; HAZARD, DETER, PLASTEC, COMPAT, MADPAC (internal databases). Performs searches on fee basis. **Networks/Consortia:** Member of FEDLINK. **Publications:** State-of-the Art reports; technical reports; technical notes; special bibliographies; evaluation reports - all released through the National Technical Information Service. **Special Catalogs:** Subject catalog for reports. **Staff:** Len Silver, Onsite Contract Mgr.; John Nardone, Chf..

★14766★
U.S. ARMY - MATERIEL COMMAND - SCHOOL OF ENGINEERING & LOGISTICS - TECHNICAL LIBRARY (Sci-Engr, Mil)
Red River Army Depot Phone: (214)838-3430
Texarkana, TX 75507-5000 Kathy Vollman, Lib.Serv.Spec.
Founded: 1970. **Staff:** Prof 1; Other 2. **Subjects:** Management; logistics; engineering - mechanical, electrical, safety, production, maintainability, industrial, software; computer management; quality and reliability. **Special Collections:** U.S. Military Regulations (3000); Intern Training Center Research Reports (600). **Holdings:** 18,900 books; 280 periodical volumes; 400 technical reports; 500 microfiche. **Subscriptions:** 189 journals and other serials; 10 newspapers. **Services:** Interlibrary loan; library not open to the public. **Automated Operations:** Computerized circulation. DTIC, OCLC, NTIS. **Publications:** Accessions list, quarterly. **Remarks:** An alternate telephone number is 838-2817.

U.S. ARMY - MATERIEL COMMAND - TANK-AUTOMOTIVE COMMAND
See: U.S. Army - Tank-Automotive Command (14779)

U.S. ARMY - MATERIEL COMMAND - TEST & EVALUATION COMMAND
See: U.S. Army - Test & Evaluation Command (14781)

U.S. ARMY - MATERIEL COMMAND - TROOP SUPPORT COMMAND
See: U.S. Army - Troop Support Command - Belvoir Research, Development & Engineering Center (14811)

★14767★
U.S. ARMY - MEDICAL RESEARCH & DEVELOPMENT COMMAND - AEROMEDICAL RESEARCH LABORATORY - SCIENTIFIC INFORMATION CENTER (Med)
Box 577 Phone: (205)255-6907
Ft. Rucker, AL 36362 Sybil H. Bullock, Libn.
Founded: 1963. **Staff:** Prof 3. **Subjects:** Aviation medicine, medicine, vision, audiology, aviation psychology, acoustics, optics. **Special Collections:** All Aeromedical Research Laboratory Reports. **Holdings:** 12,000 books; 5000 bound periodical volumes; 15,000 documents; 2500 reels of microfilm; 1500 VF items; 50 magnetic tapes. **Subscriptions:** 425 journals and other serials. **Services:** Interlibrary loan; copying; center open to the public. **Automated Operations:** Computerized cataloging and circulation. **Computerized Information Services:** DIALOG Information Services, OCLC, NASA/RECON, DTIC. Performs searches on fee basis. Contact Person: Diana Hemphill. **Networks/Consortia:** Member of SEASHEL Consortium. **Publications:** Monthly Acquisitions; Periodical List, annual; special bibliographies; union list; bibliography of USAARL technical reports and letter reports.

★14768★
U.S. ARMY - MEDICAL RESEARCH & DEVELOPMENT COMMAND - BIOMEDICAL RESEARCH & DEVELOPMENT LABORATORY - TECHNICAL REFERENCE LIBRARY (Biol Sci, Med)
Fort Detrick, Bldg. 568 Phone: (301)663-2502
Frederick, MD 21701-5010 Edna M. Snyder, Libn.
Founded: 1964. **Staff:** 2. **Subjects:** Field medical equipment; pest management systems; entomology; environmental protection in air, land, and water pollution; solid waste and pesticide disposal. **Holdings:** 5500 books; 1500 bound periodical volumes; 6100 technical reprints, patents, reports; 1000 photographs; 2200 slides. **Subscriptions:** 200 journals and other serials. **Services:** Interlibrary loan (limited); copying; library open to the public on special request. **Publications:** Reprints of journal publications - available on request; technical reports - available through DTIC. **Formerly:** Its Medical Bioengineering Research & Development Laboratory.

★14769★
U.S. ARMY - MEDICAL RESEARCH & DEVELOPMENT COMMAND - MEDICAL RESEARCH INSTITUTE OF INFECTIOUS DISEASES - MEDICAL LIBRARY (Med)
Fort Detrick Phone: (301)663-2720
Frederick, MD 21701 Denise M. Lupp, Libn.
Staff: Prof 1; Other 1. **Subjects:** Medicine, microbiology, biochemistry. **Holdings:** 7600 books; 6500 bound periodical volumes; 6 shelves of contract reports; 22 shelves of miscellaneous reports. **Subscriptions:** 190 journals and other serials. **Services:** Interlibrary loan; library open to the public with restrictions.

★14770★
U.S. ARMY - MEDICAL RESEARCH & DEVELOPMENT COMMAND - WALTER REED ARMY INSTITUTE OF RESEARCH - LIBRARY (Med)
Walter Reed Army Medical Center Phone: (202)576-3314
Washington, DC 20307-5100 V. Lynn Gera, Dir., Info.Rsrcs.Ctr./Lib.
Founded: 1946. **Staff:** Prof 4; Other 4. **Subjects:** Communicable diseases, immunology, dentistry, veterinary sciences, biochemistry, internal medicine, physiology, psychiatry, surgery. **Holdings:** 17,000 books; 13,000 bound periodical volumes. **Subscriptions:** 1000 journals and other serials. **Services:** Interlibrary loan; library open to the public for reference use only with authorization. **Computerized Information Services:** DIALOG Information Services, BRS Information Technologies, LS/2000. **Publications:** Union List of Biomedical Periodicals in the libraries of WRAIR, WRAMC and AFIP (Armed Forces Institute of Pathology), annual.

★14771★
U.S. ARMY - MILITARY ACADEMY - ARCHIVES (Hist)
West Point, NY 10996 Phone: (914)938-2017
Founded: 1954. **Staff:** Prof 2; Other 1. **Subjects:** History of the U.S. Military Academy and the Post of West Point; cadet personnel records, 1802 to present; alumni data on graduates, 1802-1905. **Holdings:** 30 cubic meters of archival materials, including 10 feet of sound recordings; 100,000 prints and negatives; official registers; yearbooks; catalogs. **Services:** Copying; archives open to the public by appointment.

★14772★
U.S. ARMY - MILITARY ACADEMY - LIBRARY (Mil, Hum, Sci-Engr)
West Point, NY 10966-1799 Phone: (914)938-3833
Egon A. Weiss, Libn.
Founded: 1802. **Staff:** Prof 25; Other 41. **Subjects:** Military arts and sciences, military history, history of the U.S. Army, history of U.S. Military Academy, engineering and technology, social sciences, modern American literature. **Special Collections:** Chess (350 items); early astronomy (170 items); military art and science (23,000 items); early atlases (200); Orientalia (3750 items); West Pointiana (3900 items); William Faulkner (600 first editions and criticisms). **Holdings:** 400,000 books; 49,000 bound periodical volumes; 27,000 other cataloged items; 135,000 documents; 375,000 microforms; 26,500 manuscripts; 8000 sound recordings. **Subscriptions:** 2300 journals; 56 newspapers. **Services:** Interlibrary loan; library open to the public by appointment. **Automated Operations:** Computerized cataloging and circulation. **Computerized Information Services:** DIALOG Information Services, OCLC; DDN Network Information Center (electronic mail service). **Networks/ Consortia:** Member of SUNY/OCLC Library Network, Southeastern New York Library Resources Council (SENYLRC). **Publications:** USMA Library Handbook/Reference Supplement, biennial; New Books, monthly; Periodical and Selective Serial Holdings; bibliography of military history (1978); USMA Library Bulletin, occasional; Friends of the West Point Library Newsletter, semiannual. **Special Catalogs:** Art Show Display Catalogs, irregular; Subject Catalog of the Military Art and Science Collection in the Library of the United States Military Academy with Selected Author and Added Entries, including a Preliminary Guide to the Manuscript Collection (1969; 4 volumes); Official Records of the American Civil War: a researcher guide (1977); Catalog of the Orientalia Collection of the USMA Library (1977). **Special Indexes:** Subject index to USMA serial publications; subject index to selected military periodicals, 1916-1960. **Staff:** Kenneth W. Hedman, Assoc.Libn.; Georgianna Watson, User Serv.Libn.; Joseph M. Barth, Coll.Dev.Libn.; Larry Randall, Sys.Libn.; Angela H. Kao, Orientalia Libn.; Alan C. Aimone, Mil.Hist.Libn.; Nicholas S. Battipaglia, Jr., Math/Sci.Libn.; Gladys T. Calvetti, Cur. of Rare Bks.; Susan M. Lintelmann, AV Libn.; Marie T. Capps, Maps & Mss.Libn.; Charles A. Ralston, Tech.Serv.Libn.; Robert D. Adamshick, Ref.Libn.; Rona N. Steindler, Cat.Libn.; Rose M. Robischon, Acq./ Ser.Libn.; Paul T. Nergelovic, Govt.Docs.Libn.; Judith A. Sibley, Ref.Libn.; Holbrooke W. York, Hum.Libn.; Linda E. Thompson, Circ.Libn.; Elizabeth J. Ince, Dir., Reading & Stud. Skill Ctr..

★14773★
U.S. ARMY - MILITARY DISTRICT OF WASHINGTON - PENTAGON LIBRARY (Mil)
The Pentagon, Rm. 1 A 518 Phone: (202)695-5346
Washington, DC 20310-6000 Dorothy A. Cross, Dir.
Founded: 1850. **Staff:** Prof 17; Other 22. **Subjects:** Military science, law, political science, history, computer science, international affairs, technology, social science, management, administration. **Special Collections:** Army studies; regulatory publications; legislative histories; army unit histories. **Holdings:** 120,000 volumes; 1 million documents. **Subscriptions:** 2000 journals and other serials. **Services:** Interlibrary loan; copying; SDI; library open to Department of Defense personnel only. **Automated Operations:** Computerized cataloging, acquisitions, serials, and circulation. **Computerized Information Services:** BRS Information Technologies, DIALOG Information Services, DMS/ONLINE, WESTLAW, LEXIS, NEXIS, DTIC, LEGI-SLATE, OCLC; PAILS, Integrated Library System (ILS; internal databases); OPTIMIS (electronic mail service). **Networks/Consortia:** Member of FEDLINK. **Publications:** Selected Current Acquisitions List, monthly; subject bibliographies, irregular; briefing guides, irregular; Checklist of Periodical Holdings, annual. **Staff:** Gene Kubal, Chf., Gen.Ref.Sect.; Irene Miner, Chf., Per.Sect.; Dexter Fox, Chf., Cat.Sect.; Gail Henderson, Chf., Army Stud.Sect.; Al Hardin, Chf., Law Sect.; Carol Bursik, Chf., ADP Sect.; Mary Bob Vick, Chf., Tech./Automated Serv.Br.; Menandra Whitmore, Chf., Acq.Sect..

★14774★
U.S. ARMY - MILITARY HISTORY INSTITUTE (Mil, Hist)
Carlisle Barracks, PA 17013-5008 Phone: (717)245-3611
Col. Rod Paschall, Dir.
Founded: 1967. **Staff:** Prof 19; Other 22. **Subjects:** Military history, U.S. and foreign history. **Special Collections:** Dyer Institute of Interdisciplinary Studies; Military Order of the Loyal Legion of the United States - Massachusetts Commandery Library. **Holdings:** 243,000 books; 12,000 bound periodical volumes; 466,000 military publications; 5500 military unit histories; 694,000 reports and studies; 2400 hours of taped oral history interviews; 12,500 boxes of manuscripts; 600,000 photographs; 12,000 reels of microfilm. **Subscriptions:** 221 journals and other serials. **Services:** Interlibrary loan; copying; institute open to the public. **Automated Operations:** Computerized public access catalog, cataloging, and ILL. **Computerized Information Services:** OCLC, LS/2000; CATS (internal database). Performs searches free of charge. Contact Person: Judy Meck. **Networks/Consortia:** Member of FEDLINK. **Publications:** Subject bibliographies. **Staff:** LTC Martin W. Andresen, Dp.Dir.; Nancy L. Gilbert, Asst.Dir./Lib.Serv.; James Williams, Asst.Dir./Ed.Serv. ; Mary Lou Harris, Asst.Dir./Adm.Serv.; John Slonaker, Chf., Hist.Ref.Br.; Richard Sommers, Chf., Archv.Br.; Michael Winey, Chf., Spec.Coll.Br.; Ruth E. Hodge, Chf., Tech.Serv.Br.; Kathryn E. Davis, Chf., Acq.Br.; Randall Rakers, Class.Archv.Techn..

★14775★
U.S. ARMY - MILITARY PERSONNEL CENTER - PERSONNEL SERVICE SUPPORT DIRECTORATE - THE INSTITUTE OF HERALDRY - LIBRARY (Mil)
Cameron Station, Bldg. 15 Phone: (202)274-6544
Alexandria, VA 22304-5050 Herbert M. Pastan, Libn.
Founded: 1962. **Staff:** Prof 1. **Subjects:** Heraldry, arts, colors, flags, lettering and decorations, history, medals, military history (chiefly U.S.), military insignia, military uniforms, seals, signs, symbolisms, weapons. **Special Collections:** Materials on uniforms, flags, and decorations of the U.S. Army, 1776 to present (1500 loose-leaf notebooks). **Holdings:** 12,200 volumes; 15 VF drawers. **Services:** Library open to the public by appointment.

U.S. ARMY - MILITARY POLICE SCHOOL
See: U.S. Army - TRADOC - Military Police School - Ramsey Library (14801)

★14776★
U.S. ARMY - MISSILE COMMAND & MARSHALL SPACE FLIGHT CENTER - REDSTONE SCIENTIFIC INFORMATION CENTER (Sci-Engr)
Redstone Arsenal, AL 35898-5241 Phone: (205)876-3251
Hollis T. Landrum, Dir.
Founded: 1949. **Staff:** Prof 19; Other 14. **Subjects:** Astronautics, astronomy, chemistry, engineering, management, mathematics, meteorology, physics. **Special Collections:** Rockets; missiles; space technology; lasers. **Holdings:** 220,000 books; 78,000 bound periodical volumes; 1.7 million documents and reports. **Subscriptions:** 3500 journals and other serials. **Services:** Interlibrary loan; copying; translations; center open to the public with restrictions on classified material. **Automated Operations:** Computerized cataloging, acquisitions, and circulation. **Computerized Information Services:** DTIC, NASA/RECON, BRS Information Technologies, DIALOG Information Services, Pergamon ORBIT InfoLine, Inc., The Reference Service (REFSRV). **Networks/ Consortia:** Member of Alabama Library Exchange, Inc. (ALEX). **Publications:** Literature surveys; data compilations. **Special Catalogs:** Periodicals Catalog, semiannual - by request; COM Book Catalog.

★14777★
U.S. ARMY - MUSEUM OF HAWAII - REFERENCE LIBRARY
Box 8064
Honolulu, HI 96830
Defunct

U.S. ARMY - OFFICE OF THE SURGEON GENERAL
See: U.S. Army/U.S. Air Force - Offices of the Surgeons General (14864)

★14778★
U.S. ARMY - OPERATIONAL TEST & EVALUATION AGENCY (OTEA) - TECHNICAL LIBRARY (Sci-Engr, Mil)
5600 Columbia Pike Phone: (202)756-2234
Falls Church, VA 22041-5115 Ava Dell Headley, Chf.
Staff: Prof 2; Other 1. **Subjects:** Test methodology, experimental/statistical design, instrumentation, reliability engineering, human engineering, combat arms/combat support weapon systems of U.S. Army. **Special Collections:** Army military publications (150 feet). **Holdings:** 4000 books; 2000 documents; 2000 microforms. **Subscriptions:** 225 journals and other serials; 9 newspapers. **Services:** Interlibrary loan; library not open to the public. **Computerized Information Services:** DIALOG Information Services, DTIC. **Publications:** Library accessions lists; Bibliography of USAOTEA Reports and Related Documents.

U.S. ARMY - ORDNANCE CENTER & SCHOOL
See: U.S. Army - TRADOC - Ordnance Center & School (14802)

U.S. ARMY - ORDNANCE MISSILE, MUNITIONS CENTER & SCHOOL
See: U.S. Army - TRADOC - Ordnance Missile, Munitions Center & School (14803)

U.S. ARMY - PATTON MUSEUM OF CAVALRY & ARMOR
See: U.S. Army - TRADOC - Patton Museum of Cavalry & Armor (14804)

U.S. ARMY - PENTAGON LIBRARY
See: U.S. Army - Military District of Washington - Pentagon Library (14773)

U.S. ARMY - PLASTICS TECHNICAL EVALUATION CENTER
See: U.S. Army - Materiel Command - Plastics Technical Evaluation Center (PLASTEC) (14765)

U.S. ARMY - SERGEANTS MAJOR ACADEMY
See: U.S. Army - TRADOC - Sergeants Major Academy (14806)

U.S. ARMY - SIGNAL CENTER & FORT GORDON
See: U.S. Army - TRADOC - Signal Center & Fort Gordon (14807)

★14779★
U.S. ARMY - TANK-AUTOMOTIVE COMMAND - TACOM SUPPORT ACTIVITY - GENERAL LIBRARY (Mil)
Bldg. 169 Phone: (313)466-5088
Selfridge Air Natl. Guard Base, MI 48045
JoAnn Bonnett, Chf., Lib.Br.
Founded: 1971. **Staff:** Prof 2; Other 6. **Subjects:** History, military affairs, management. **Holdings:** 25,000 books; cassettes; phonograph records; 5 VF drawers of pamphlets, maps, clippings. **Subscriptions:** 280 journals and other serials; 15 newspapers. **Services:** Interlibrary loan; copying; library serves military personnel and their dependents, retirees, and civilians employed at TACOM and Selfridge ANG Base. **Automated Operations:** Computerized cataloging and ILL. **Computerized Information Services:** DIALOG Information Services; DIALMAIL (electronic mail service). **Networks/Consortia:** Member of FEDLINK.

★14780★
U.S. ARMY - TANK-AUTOMOTIVE COMMAND - TECHNICAL LIBRARY SERVICE BRANCH (Sci-Engr, Mil)
28251 Van Dyke Phone: (313)574-6543
Warren, MI 48397-5000 Louis X. Barbalas, Chf.
Staff: Prof 2; Other 4. **Subjects:** Automotive mechanics, materials science, physical science, military science, engineering. **Holdings:** 7000 books; administrative and military publications; 28,000 technical reports; 52 drawers of microfiche. **Subscriptions:** 105 journals and other serials. **Services:** Interlibrary loan; library open to government contractors on special request. **Computerized Information Services:** DTIC.

★14781★
U.S. ARMY - TEST & EVALUATION COMMAND - DUGWAY PROVING GROUND - TECHNICAL LIBRARY (Mil, Sci-Engr)
Dugway, UT 84022 Phone: (801)831-3565
Duane Williamson, Chf.
Founded: 1950. **Staff:** Prof 1; Other 3. **Subjects:** Chemistry, biology, chemical/biological warfare. **Special Collections:** Classified and unclassified documents related to chemical/biological testing (access limited to U.S. Government agencies and their contractors). **Holdings:** 6000 books; 250 bound periodical volumes; 30,000 bound technical reports; 15,000 microforms. **Subscriptions:** 65 journals and other serials. **Services:** Interlibrary loan; library open to the public by appointment. **Automated Operations:** Computerized public access catalog, cataloging, serials, and circulation. **Computerized Information Services:** DIALOG Information Services, DTIC, OCLC.

★14782★
U.S. ARMY - TEST & EVALUATION COMMAND - TROPIC TEST CENTER - TECHNICAL INFORMATION CENTER (Sci-Engr)
Fort Clayton
Drawer 942
APO Miami, FL 34004-5000
Founded: 1969. **Staff:** Prof 2. **Subjects:** Tropical material research; scientific, engineering, and corrosion testing; meteorology; physics; chemistry. **Special Collections:** Tropical material test documents (6000); Tropical Test Center reports (500); material testing in the tropics (300). **Holdings:** 900 books; 40 VF drawers of maps; 1500 microfiche; 1200 test operations procedures documents; 2000 tropical testing documents; 2000 tropical regions reports; 15,000 microfiche. **Subscriptions:** 100 journals and other serials; 5 newspapers. **Services:** Interlibrary loan; copying; center open to the public with restrictions. **Automated Operations:** Computerized cataloging, serials, and circulation. **Computerized Information Services:** TICARS (Technical Information Center Automated Retrieval System; internal database). **Remarks:** The Technical Information Center is located in the Republic of Panama. The telephone number is 85-5910. **Staff:** Ann B. Guerriero, Tech.Info.Spec.; Arlene Sollas, Tech.Info.Spec..

★14783★
U.S. ARMY - TEST & EVALUATION COMMAND - WHITE SANDS MISSILE RANGE - TECHNICAL LIBRARY (Sci-Engr, Mil)
STEWS-IM-ST Phone: (505)678-1317
White Sands Missile Range, NM 88002-5030
Laurel B. Saunders, Chf.Libn.
Founded: 1955. **Staff:** Prof 5; Other 10. **Subjects:** Optics, guided missiles, electronics, mathematics, physics, computers. **Special Collections:** Military specifications and industrial standards. **Holdings:** 40,000 books; 2000 bound periodical volumes; 90,000 microforms; 120,000 research and development reports; 2.6 million engineering drawings. **Subscriptions:** 400 journals and other serials. **Services:** Interlibrary loan; library not open to the public. **Automated Operations:** Computerized cataloging and acquisitions. **Computerized Information Services:** DIALOG Information Services, DTIC, OCLC, TECH DATA, Government-Industry Data Exchange Program (GIDEP); WSDM (internal database); MISER (electronic mail service). **Publications:** Acquisitions of open literature and documents, annual; Bulletin, monthly; Periodical List, annual; GIDEP, monthly; Holdings Announcement List, irregular. **Staff:** Janice Haines, Chf., Doc.; Richard Farmer, Ref.Libn./Open Lit..

★14784★
U.S. ARMY - TEST & EVALUATION COMMAND - YUMA PROVING GROUND - TECHNICAL LIBRARY (Sci-Engr, Mil)
Attn: STEYP-IM-TL Phone: (602)328-2549
Yuma, AZ 85365-9103 Jean McCall, Chf.
Founded: 1965. **Staff:** Prof 1. **Subjects:** Research and development, test and evaluation, engineering and technology, U.S. Army materiel. **Holdings:** 2000 books; 100 bound periodical volumes; 35,000 other cataloged items; 200,000 documents in microform, including 16mm visual search microfilm service. **Subscriptions:** 140 journals and other serials. **Services:** Interlibrary loan (for material with limited control); library not open to the public. **Computerized Information Services:** DTIC.

★14785★
U.S. ARMY - TRADOC - AIR DEFENSE ARTILLERY SCHOOL - LIBRARY (Mil)
Bldg. 2, Wing E, Rm. 181 Phone: (915)568-5781
Ft. Bliss, TX 79916-7027 Dorothy R. LeBorious, Act.Chf.Libn.
Founded: 1944. **Staff:** Prof 2; Other 5. **Subjects:** Military art and science, air defense, military and world history, American history, education, human relations, psychology of management, technology, mathematics, science. **Special Collections:** Archival collection of military subjects; Southwest Collection. **Holdings:** 27,000 books; 500 bound periodical volumes; 95,000 reports and documents on microfiche; 2500 reels of microfilm; 32 VF drawers of pamphlets; 150 language recordings. **Subscriptions:** 188 journals and other serials; 20 newspapers. **Services:** Interlibrary loan; library not open to the public. **Automated Operations:** Computerized cataloging, acquisitions, and ILL. **Computerized Information Services:** DIALOG Information Services, OCLC, DTIC; OPTIMIS (electronic mail service). **Publications:** New books list. **Staff:** Donna Ramsay, Tech.Serv.Libn..

★14786★
U.S. ARMY - TRADOC - ANALYSIS COMMAND - TRAC-WSMR TECHNICAL LIBRARY (Mil, Sci-Engr)
Attn: ATRC-WSL Phone: (505)678-3135
White Sands Missile Range, NM 88002-5502
Julie A. Gibson, Adm.Libn.
Founded: 1977. **Staff:** Prof 1; Other 6. **Subjects:** Military science, ordnance, operations research, computer science, modelling. **Special Collections:** Defense Mapping Agency map collection. **Holdings:** 4400 books and bound periodical volumes; 57,000 technical reports. **Subscriptions:** 300 journals and other serials. **Services:** Interlibrary loan; library not open to the public. **Automated Operations:** Computerized cataloging, serials, and circulation. **Computerized Information Services:** DIALOG Information Services, BRS Information Technologies, DTIC, OCLC; Technical Library Information System database (internal database); OPTIMIS, LINX Courier (electronic mail services). **Networks/Consortia:** Member of TRALINET, FEDLINK. **Publications:** New Acquisitions.

★14787★
U.S. ARMY - TRADOC - ARMY ARMOR SCHOOL - LIBRARY (Mil)
Gaffey Hall, 2369
Old Ironsides Ave.
ATSB-DOTD-L Phone: (502)624-6231
Ft. Knox, KY 40121-5200 William H. Hansen, Chf.Libn.
Founded: 1941. **Staff:** Prof 2; Other 3. **Subjects:** Military science, history, political science, foreign affairs. **Holdings:** 20,000 books; 1000 bound periodical volumes; 14,092 Department of the Army publications; 138 reels of microfilm; 2432 student staff studies; 10,000 afteraction reports; 500,000 documents on microfiche. **Subscriptions:** 319 journals and other serials; 20 newspapers. **Services:** Interlibrary loan; library open to the public with restrictions on defense information. **Automated Operations:** Computerized cataloging and acquisitions. **Computerized Information Services:** DTIC, DIALOG Information Services, BRS Information Technologies. **Networks/Consortia:** Member of TRALINET, Kentucky Library Network, Inc. (KLN). **Staff:** Judy Stephenson, Cat. & Acq..

★14788★
U.S. ARMY - TRADOC - AVIATION MUSEUM - LIBRARY (Mil)
Bldg. 6007 Phone: (205)255-4507
Fort Rucker, AL 36362 Harford Edwards, Jr., Hist.
Subjects: U.S. Army aviation, 1942 to present; civilian aviation. **Holdings:** 500 documents, manuscripts, oral history tapes and manuscripts, sound recordings. **Services:** Copying; library open to serious researchers only.

★14789★
U.S. ARMY - TRADOC - AVIATION TECHNICAL LIBRARY (Mil, Sci-Engr)
Bldgs. 5906 & 5907
ATZQ-DAP-TL Phone: (205)255-4591
Ft. Rucker, AL 36362-5000 Beverly M. Hall, Dir.
Founded: 1955. **Staff:** Prof 4; Other 6. **Subjects:** Aviation, international affairs, sciences, military history and science, education, management. **Special Collections:** Documents on history and development of army aviation. **Holdings:** 23,077 books; 107,714 documents. **Services:** Interlibrary loan; copying; SDI; library open to the public with restrictions. **Automated Operations:** Computerized cataloging and acquisitions. **Computerized Information Services:** DTIC, NASA/RECON, NEXIS, LEXIS, DIALOG Information Services, OCLC. **Networks/Consortia:** Member of FEDLINK. **Publications:** Acquisitions lists; subject bibliographies; handbooks. **Special Indexes:** Periodical holdings lists. **Staff:** James Lee, Tech.Serv.Libn.; Sherry Miller, Ref.Libn.; Beverly McMaster, Ref.Libn..

★14790★
U.S. ARMY - TRADOC - CHEMICAL SCHOOL - FISHER LIBRARY (Sci-Engr, Mil)
Bldg. 2262 Phone: (205)238-4414
Fort McClellan, AL 36205-5020 Sybil P. Parker, Libn.
Founded: 1982. **Staff:** Prof 1; Other 4. **Subjects:** Chemical warfare, radiation protection, military history. **Special Collections:** Defense Department Technical Reports (2000); Defense Department documents (1500); rare books (150); Chemical School Archives (45 VF drawers). **Holdings:** 12,000 books; 10,000 documents; 200 periodical titles, 1977 to present, on microfilm. **Subscriptions:** 375 journals and other serials; 35 newspapers. **Services:** Interlibrary loan; library open to government agencies only. **Computerized Information Services:** DIALOG Information

Services, OCLC, BRS Information Technologies, DTIC. **Networks/Consortia:** Member of TRALINET.

★14791★
U.S. ARMY - TRADOC - COMBAT DEVELOPMENTS EXPERIMENTATION COMMAND - TECHNICAL INFORMATION CENTER (Mil, Sci-Engr)
HQ USACDEC
Bldg. 2925 Phone: (408)242-3618
Ft. Ord, CA 93941-7000 Carolyn I. Alexander, Chf.Libn.
Founded: 1966. **Staff:** Prof 2; Other 2. **Subjects:** Armor, behavioral sciences, experimental design, instrumentation, small arms, small unit organizations, helicopter warfare. **Holdings:** 5000 books and bound periodical volumes; 13,000 technical reports; 4000 publications; 50 pamphlets; 1000 microforms. **Subscriptions:** 400 journals and other serials; 10 newspapers. **Services:** Interlibrary loan; center not open to the public. **Publications:** Acquisitions List; Serials List, annual.

★14792★
U.S. ARMY - TRADOC - COMMAND AND GENERAL STAFF COLLEGE - COMBINED ARMS RESEARCH LIBRARY (Mil)
Bell Hall Phone: (913)684-4035
Ft. Leavenworth, KS 66027-6900 Martha Davis, Dir.
Founded: 1906. **Subjects:** Military art and science, military history, political science, management. **Holdings:** 116,000 books; 7750 bound periodical volumes; 175,000 documents; 1.4 million microforms. **Subscriptions:** 1300 journals and other serials; 32 newspapers. **Services:** Interlibrary loan; copying; library open to the public with restrictions. **Automated Operations:** Computerized public access catalog, cataloging, acquisitions, and circulation. **Computerized Information Services:** DIALOG Information Services, NEXIS, OCLC, U.S. Naval Institute (USNI), DTIC. **Networks/Consortia:** Member of TRALINET, FEDLINK. **Staff:** Bertina Byers, Chf., Info.Serv.; Dan Dorris, Chf., Sup.Serv.; Alice Blaser, Acq.Libn.; Carol Morrison, Archv..

★14793★
U.S. ARMY - TRADOC - ENGINEER SCHOOL - THAYER ENGINEER LIBRARY (Mil, Sci-Engr)
Bldg. 270 Phone: (703)664-2524
Ft. Belvoir, VA 22060-5261 William F. Tuceling, Supv.Libn.
Founded: 1935. **Subjects:** Civil and military engineering, military and American history. **Special Collections:** Corps of Engineers history; rare books on military engineering and history from 16th to 19th centuries; Fort Belvoir history; Army unit history. **Holdings:** 20,000 books; 5000 bound periodical volumes; 17,000 photographs; 60,000 military publications; 1000 AV programs. **Subscriptions:** 160 journals and other serials; 6 newspapers. **Services:** Interlibrary loan; copying; SDI; library open to the public by appointment. **Automated Operations:** Computerized acquisitions. **Computerized Information Services:** DIALOG Information Services, DTIC, OCLC, BRS Information Technologies; OPTIMIS (electronic mail service). **Networks/Consortia:** Member of TRALINET, FEDLINK. **Publications:** New Books List, quarterly; Periodicals List, annual; Periodicals Tables of Contents, monthly - all for internal distribution only. **Special Catalogs:** Author, title, and subject card catalogs to Engineer Magazine and staff studies/student papers; accession number cards for DTIC documents. **Staff:** Mary E. Reiman, Ref.Libn..

★14794★
U.S. ARMY - TRADOC - FIELD ARTILLERY SCHOOL - MORRIS SWETT TECHNICAL LIBRARY (Mil)
Snow Hall, Rm. 16, 19W Phone: (405)351-4525
Ft. Sill, OK 73503-0312 Lester L. Miller, Jr., Adm.Libn.
Founded: 1911. **Staff:** Prof 2; Other 4. **Subjects:** Military science and history, history of field artillery, political science, technology, management. **Special Collections:** U.S. Field Artillery Unit Histories; rare book collection. **Holdings:** 92,625 volumes; 45,000 other cataloged items; 138,713 microforms; 27,106 Department of the Army and Department of Defense publications. **Subscriptions:** 330 journals and other serials; 35 newspapers. **Services:** Interlibrary loan; copying; SDI; library open to the public for reference use only. **Computerized Information Services:** DTIC, BRS Information Technologies, DIALOG Information Services, OCLC. **Networks/Consortia:** Member of TRALINET, Oklahoma Telecommunications Interlibrary System (OTIS), Oklahoma Special Collections and Archives Network (OSCAN), Oklahoma Health Sciences Library Association (OHSLA). **Publications:** Special bibliographies; checklists - irregular; century series bibliographies; subject headings and "U" Military Science Classification List. **Special Indexes:** Card index to military periodicals dating to mid-1800s; internal military science and subject indexes. **Staff:** Matha H.C. Relph, Libn..

★14795★
U.S. ARMY - TRADOC - HQ/FORT MONROE LIBRARY & INTERN TRAINING CENTER (Mil)
ATLS-LT
Bldg. 133 Phone: (804)727-2821
Ft. Monroe, VA 23651-5000 Frances M. Doyle, Supv.Libn.
Staff: Prof 3; Other 4. **Subjects:** Military science and history, management, training and education. **Special Collections:** Department of the Army publications (60,000). **Holdings:** 11,000 books; 375 bound periodical volumes; 3000 technical documents. **Subscriptions:** 350 journals and other serials; 10 newspapers. **Services:** Interlibrary loan; library open to Department of Defense personnel. **Computerized Information Services:** DIALOG Information Services, BRS Information Technologies, DTIC, OCLC. **Networks/Consortia:** Member of TRALINET. **Publications:** Library Information Update, bimonthly - for internal distribution only. **Staff:** Janet M. Scheitle, Supv. of Intern Trng.; Fred L. Mathews, Res.Libn..

★14796★
U.S. ARMY - TRADOC - INFANTRY SCHOOL - DONOVAN TECHNICAL LIBRARY (Mil)
Infantry Hall, Bldg. 4 Phone: (404)544-4053
Ft. Benning, GA 31905-5452 Vivian S. Dodson, Chf., Lrng.Rsrcs.Div.
Founded: 1919. **Staff:** Prof 4; Other 5. **Subjects:** Military history, military art and science, political science, social science, national defense, foreign affairs, management, education. **Special Collections:** Map collection (12,000); rare military books (14,000). **Holdings:** 58,000 books and bound periodical volumes; 55,000 classified and unclassified documents. **Subscriptions:** 210 journals and other serials; 24 newspapers. **Services:** Interlibrary loan; library not open to the public. **Computerized Information Services:** DIALOG Information Services, DTIC. **Networks/Consortia:** Member of TRALINET.

★14797★
U.S. ARMY - TRADOC - INTELLIGENCE CENTER & SCHOOL - ACADEMIC LIBRARY (Mil)
Alvarado Hall Phone: (602)538-5930
Ft. Huachuca, AZ 85613 Esther A. Wruck, Act.Chf.
Founded: 1970. **Staff:** Prof 3; Other 1. **Subjects:** Military intelligence, military history, foreign affairs, political science, military geography, area studies of countries of the world. **Holdings:** 11,543 books; 4300 items in VF drawers; 2400 student research papers. **Subscriptions:** 300 journals and other serials; 20 newspapers. **Services:** Interlibrary loan; copying; SDI; library open to the public by appointment. **Automated Operations:** Computerized cataloging, acquisitions, serials, and ILL. **Computerized Information Services:** DIALOG Information Services, DTIC, WILSONLINE, OCLC; OPTIMIS (electronic mail service). **Networks/Consortia:** Member of TRALINET. **Staff:** Pauline Spanabel, Ref./Rd.Serv.Libn..

★14798★
U.S. ARMY - TRADOC - INTELLIGENCE SCHOOL, DEVENS - LIBRARY AND INFORMATION SERVICES DIVISION (Mil)
Commander USAISD Phone: (508)796-3413
Ft. Devens, MA 01433-6301 Ornella L. Pensyl, Chf.
Founded: 1951. **Subjects:** Military science, electronics, education. **Special Collections:** Cryptology; electronic warfare. **Holdings:** 5000 books; 844 bound periodical volumes; 13,000 microfiche; 12,200 technical reports; 18,600 military publications. **Subscriptions:** 203 journals and other serials; 22 newspapers. **Services:** Interlibrary loan; library not open to the public. **Automated Operations:** Computerized cataloging and acquisitions. **Computerized Information Services:** DIALOG Information Services, OCLC, BRS Information Technologies, DTIC; internal database; OPTIMIS (electronic mail service). **Networks/Consortia:** Member of TRALINET, FEDLINK. **Publications:** Monthly Acquisitions List -

★14799★
U.S. ARMY - TRADOC - LANGUAGE TRAINING FACILITY - LIBRARY (Hum)
Bldg. 829
Ft. Hood, TX 76544-5056
Founded: 1958. **Subjects:** Books and texts in 40 foreign languages, area studies of foreign nations. **Special Collections:** Bible collection in 56 languages and dialects. **Holdings:** 8000 books; 2000 magnetic tapes; 4 VF drawers of pamphlets, articles. **Subscriptions:** 35 journals and other serials; 11

★14800★
U.S. ARMY - TRADOC - LOGISTICS LIBRARY (Mil, Bus-Fin)
Bldg. P-12500 Phone: (703)734-4286
Ft. Lee, VA 23801-6047 Katherine P. Sites, Chf.Libn.
Founded: 1971. **Staff:** Prof 3; Other 3. **Subjects:** Logistics, military history, management, computer science, social sciences, business and finance, food and nutrition. **Holdings:** 40,000 books; 425 bound periodical volumes; 86,000 U.S. Government serial publications; 135,000 unbound periodicals; 19,500 periodicals in microform; 20,000 reports. **Subscriptions:** 260 journals and other serials; 8 newspapers. **Services:** Interlibrary loan; copying; library open to the public for reference use only. **Automated Operations:** Computerized cataloging and acquisitions. **Computerized Information Services:** BRS Information Technologies, DIALOG Information Services, DTIC, OCLC; OPTIMIS (electronic mail service). Performs searches free of charge. **Networks/Consortia:** Member of FEDLINK, TRALINET. **Publications:** Monthly newsletter; Library Handbook. **Staff:** Bernadette Schmidt, Asst.Libn.; Christine Baldwin, Ref.Libn.; Nola Parham, ILL.

★14801★
U.S. ARMY - TRADOC - MILITARY POLICE SCHOOL - RAMSEY LIBRARY (Mil, Law)
Bldg. 3181, Rm. 10 Phone: (205)238-3737
Ft. McClellan, AL 36205 Bernice Z. Parks, Supv.Libn.
Founded: 1941. **Staff:** Prof 2; Other 3. **Subjects:** Police science, education, military affairs, criminology, penology, military history. **Holdings:** 16,625 books; 2069 bound periodical volumes; 6500 paperbacks; 3675 reports; 1500 pamphlets; 30,000 military publications; 3537 microforms. **Subscriptions:** 248 journals and other serials; 23 newspapers. **Services:** Interlibrary loan; copying; library open to the public with restrictions. **Computerized Information Services:** DIALOG Information Services; OPTIMIS (electronic mail service). Performs searches on fee basis. Contact Person: Brenda Miller. **Networks/Consortia:** Member of TRALINET. **Publications:** New book list. **Remarks:** Includes holdings of the Women's Army Corps School Library. **Staff:** Martha M. Morgan, Libn..

★14802★
U.S. ARMY - TRADOC - ORDNANCE CENTER & SCHOOL - LIBRARY (Mil)
Attn: ATSL-SE-LI
Bldg. 3071, Simpson Hall Phone: (301)278-4991
Aberdeen Proving Ground, MD 21005-5201
Janice C. Weston, Chf.Libn.
Founded: 1940. **Subjects:** Military science, ordnance, management, educational technology, military history. **Special Collections:** U.S. Department of the Army publications. **Holdings:** Books; bound periodical volumes; reports; classified documents; tape recordings; microfiche; microfilm. **Services:** Interlibrary loan; copying; library open to the public for reference use only with prior approval. **Automated Operations:** Computerized cataloging and acquisitions. **Computerized Information Services:** DIALOG Information Services, OCLC, DTIC; OPTIMIS (electronic mail service). **Networks/Consortia:** Member of TRALINET. **Publications:** Monthly Acquisitions List; periodical listing, annual.

★14803★
U.S. ARMY - TRADOC - ORDNANCE MISSILE, MUNITIONS CENTER & SCHOOL - MMCS TECHNICAL LIBRARY (Sci-Engr)
Bldg. 3323 Phone: (205)876-7425
Redstone Arsenal, AL 35897-6280 Eleanore Zeman, Chf.Libn.
Founded: 1959. **Staff:** Prof 3; Other 4. **Subjects:** Guided missiles, electrical engineering, mathematics, physics, management, education. **Holdings:** 15,000 books; 420 bound periodical volumes; 20,000 reports; 720 AV programs; 3000 microfiche; 84,800 documents; 78,720 military publications. **Subscriptions:** 260 journals and other serials. **Services:** Interlibrary loan (limited); copying; library open to the public. **Computerized Information Services:** DIALOG Information Services, DTIC. **Networks/Consortia:** Member of TRALINET. **Publications:** Acquisitions Listings, bimonthly; Library Guide.

★14804★
U.S. ARMY - TRADOC - PATTON MUSEUM OF CAVALRY & ARMOR - EMERT L. DAVIS MEMORIAL LIBRARY (Hist)
4554 Fayette Ave.
Box 208 Phone: (502)624-6350
Ft. Knox, KY 40121-0208 David A. Holt, Libn.
Founded: 1975. **Staff:** Prof 1. **Subjects:** Armored fighting vehicles, General George S. Patton, Jr., armor warfare, Fort Knox history, unit histories. **Holdings:** 7800 books; 100 bound periodical volumes; 128 volumes of photographs; Fort Knox photographs and maps. **Subscriptions:** 15 journals and other serials. **Services:** Interlibrary loan; library open to researchers by appointment. **Publications:** Selected Bibliography: George S. Patton, Jr. (materials in library collection).

★14805★
U.S. ARMY - TRADOC - SCHOOL OF THE AMERICAS - LIBRARY (Mil)
Bldg. 35, Rm. 309
Attn: ATZL-SA-S-L Phone: (404)545-4631
Ft. Benning, GA 31905-6245 Lynda L. Kennedy, Libn.
Founded: 1961. **Staff:** Prof 1; Other 3. **Subjects:** Military science, Latin America. **Special Collections:** Irregular warfare (guerilla warfare and jungle warfare); terrorism (450 volumes). **Holdings:** 18,000 books; 20 VF drawers of pamphlets; 30 drawers of maps; 50 pamphlet files of Rand Studies; microfilm. **Subscriptions:** 183 journals and other serials. **Services:** Interlibrary loan; copying; library open to the public for reference use only. **Automated Operations:** Computerized cataloging and acquisitions. **Computerized Information Services:** Internal database. **Networks/Consortia:** Member of TRALINET. **Remarks:** 90% of the collection is in Spanish.

★14806★
U.S. ARMY - TRADOC - SERGEANTS MAJOR ACADEMY - OTHON O. VALENT LEARNING RESOURCES CENTER (Mil)
Bldg. 11294 Phone: (915)568-8176
Ft. Bliss, TX 79918-5000 Marijean Murray, Supv.Libn.
Founded: 1972. **Subjects:** Management, psychology, human relations, leadership, military studies. **Special Collections:** Collection of rare books on military history and the history of the Non-Commissioned Officer Corps (500 items). **Holdings:** 37,000 books; 1200 bound periodical volumes; 20 archival materials; 900 AV programs; 10,518 microfiche; 4192 reels of microfilm. **Subscriptions:** 350 journals and other serials; 26 newspapers. **Services:** Interlibrary loan; copying; center open to the public for reference use only. **Computerized Information Services:** DIALOG Information Services. **Networks/Consortia:** Member of TRALINET.

★14807★
U.S. ARMY - TRADOC - SIGNAL CENTER & FORT GORDON - CONRAD TECHNICAL LIBRARY (Mil, Sci-Engr)
Bldg. 29807 Phone: (404)791-3922
Ft. Gordon, GA 30905-5081 Margaret H. Novinger, Chf.
Staff: Prof 3; Other 3. **Subjects:** Communications-electronics, computer science, technology, military art and science, leadership, educational technology. **Holdings:** 11,228 books; 32 bound periodical volumes; 15,701 documents; 1016 periodical volumes on microfilm; 7751 microfiche; 8.9 linear feet of pamphlets and monographs. **Subscriptions:** 350 journals and other serials; 5 newspapers. **Services:** Interlibrary loan; library open to the public with restrictions. **Computerized Information Services:** DIALOG Information Services, BRS Information Technologies, DTIC, OCLC. **Networks/Consortia:** Member of TRALINET, Georgia Library Information Network (GLIN).

★14808★
U.S. ARMY - TRADOC - SOLDIER SUPPORT CENTER - MAIN LIBRARY (Mil, Info Sci)
Bldg. 400, Rm. 205 Phone: (317)542-3891
Ft. Benjamin Harrison, IN 46216 Mrs. Marina Griner, Supv.Libn.
Founded: 1957. **Staff:** Prof 4; Other 3. **Subjects:** Mass communications; journalism; management; military history, art, science; business; public relations. **Special Collections:** Silver Anvils; Department of Defense publications; law collection. **Holdings:** 55,000 volumes; 425 AV programs; 2000 reports; 210,000 documents; 2000 microforms; 151 VF drawers. **Subscriptions:** 450 journals and other serials; 100 newspapers. **Services:** Interlibrary loan; copying; SDI; library open to the public for reference use only. **Automated Operations:** Computerized cataloging, acquisitions, and ILL. **Computerized Information Services:** DIALOG Information Services, OCLC. **Networks/Consortia:** Member of FEDLINK, TRALINET. **Publications:** Library Guide; acquisition lists; newsletter, monthly; bibliographies; current awareness files. **Remarks:** Library serves U.S. Institute of Administration and Defense Information School. **Staff:** Thelma Shutt, Hd., Ref.Serv.; Eula Mallery, Hd., Tech.Serv.; Geneva Murphy, Hd., Pub.Serv..

★14809★
U.S. ARMY - TRADOC - TRANSPORTATION & AVIATION LOGISTICS SCHOOLS - INFORMATION CENTER (Mil, Trans)
Bldg. 705 Phone: (804)878-5563
Ft. Eustis, VA 23604-5450 Marion J. Knihnicki, Chf.Libn.
Founded: 1944. **Staff:** Prof 3; Other 3. **Subjects:** Military transportation, military history, instructional technology. **Special Collections:** U.S. Army Transportation School Materials. **Holdings:** 45,397 books, bound periodical volumes, documents; 26,163 unbound periodicals and newspapers; 54,107 official publications; 22,251 miscellaneous items. **Subscriptions:** 450 journals and other serials; 8 newspapers. **Services:** Interlibrary loan; copying; center open to the public for reference use only. **Computerized Information Services:** DIALOG Information Services, BRS Information Technologies, DTIC, OCLC. **Networks/Consortia:** Member of TRALINET. **Special Indexes:** Indexing Service for military transportation journals. **Staff:** Valerie Fashion-Dawson, Ref.Libn.; Richard Aubrey, Tech.Serv.Libn..

U.S. ARMY - TRAINING & DOCTRINE COMMAND
See: U.S. Army - TRADOC (14787)

★14810★
U.S. ARMY - TRANSPORTATION MUSEUM - LIBRARY (Trans)
Bldg. 300, Besson Hall Phone: (804)878-1115
Ft. Eustis, VA 23604-5260 Barbara A. Bower, Dir.
Subjects: History of transportation in the U.S. Army and the Transportation Corps, 1914 to present. **Holdings:** 2000 books; 250 films; 3600 photographs; 58 periodical titles. **Services:** Copying; library open to the public.

★14811★
U.S. ARMY - TROOP SUPPORT COMMAND - BELVOIR RESEARCH, DEVELOPMENT & ENGINEERING CENTER - TECHNICAL LIBRARY (Sci-Engr, Mil)
Bldg. 315 Phone: (703)664-5179
Ft. Belvoir, VA 22060 Gloria R. James, Chf., Tech.Lib.Div.
Staff: Prof 3; Other 9. **Subjects:** Vehicle drives, camouflage, amphibious vehicles, electric vehicles, detection and detectors, construction equipment, engineering, environmental control, gasahol, army equipment. **Holdings:** 15,000 books; 200 bound periodical volumes; 10,000 technical reports; 200 test reports. **Subscriptions:** 375 journals and other serials; 10 newspapers. **Services:** Interlibrary loan; library not open to the public. **Automated Operations:** Computerized cataloging. **Computerized Information Services:** DTIC, DIALOG Information Services, BRS Information Technologies, OCLC, DTIC. Performs searches on fee basis. Contact Person: Janice Pepper, Ref.Libn., Doc.Sect., 664-5339.

★14812★
U.S. ARMY - TROOP SUPPORT COMMAND - NATICK RESEARCH, DEVELOPMENT & ENGINEERING CENTER - TECHNICAL LIBRARY (Sci-Engr)
Natick, MA 01760-5000 Phone: (617)651-4542
M. Eileen Collins, Chf.
Founded: 1946. **Staff:** Prof 5; Other 5. **Subjects:** Food sciences and engineering, textile technology, environmental medicine, chemistry, packaging technology, physics. **Special Collections:** Bibliography on Physiological Effects of High Altitude (4000 references); U.S. Army Quartermaster research on clothing, 1942 to present (269 technical reports). **Holdings:** 40,000 books; 19,000 bound periodical volumes; 45,500 technical reports; 350 reels of microfilm. **Subscriptions:** 1100 journals and other serials; 10 newspapers. **Services:** Interlibrary loan; library open to the public for reference use only. **Automated Operations:** Computerized circulation. **Computerized Information Services:** DIALOG Information Services, Pergamon ORBIT InfoLine, Inc., OCLC, DTIC. **Networks/Consortia:** Member of FEDLINK, NELINET. **Publications:** Technical Library Accessions List, monthly - for internal distribution only.

U.S. ARMY - TROPIC TEST CENTER
See: U.S. Army - Test & Evaluation Command - Tropic Test Center (14782)

U.S. ARMY - WHITE SANDS MISSILE RANGE
See: U.S. Army - Test & Evaluation Command - White Sands Missile Range (14783)

U.S. ARMY - WOMEN'S ARMY CORPS SCHOOL - LIBRARY
See: U.S. Army - TRADOC - Military Police School - Ramsey Library (14801)

U.S. ARMY - YUMA PROVING GROUND
See: U.S. Army - Test & Evaluation Command - Yuma Proving Ground (14784)

★14813★
U.S. ARMY AND AIR FORCE EXCHANGE SERVICE (AAFES) - AD LIBRARY (Mil)
3911 S. Walton Walker Blvd.
Box 660202 Phone: (214)780-2110
Dallas, TX 75266-0202 Linda A. McVey, Lib.Techn.
Staff: Prof 1; Other 1. **Subjects:** Military regulations, business and management. **Special Collections:** Exchange Service manuals; military history (40 volumes). **Holdings:** 1150 books; 820 binders of regulations; Department of Defense publications. **Subscriptions:** 34 journals and other serials. **Services:** Library not open to the public. **Computerized Information Services:** DIALOG Information Services, Startext; internal database. **Remarks:** An alternate telephone number is 780-3337.

★14814★
U.S. ARMY IN EUROPE (USAREUR) - LIBRARY AND RESOURCE CENTER (Mil)
HQ USAREUR and Seventh Army
AEAIM-DL-L
APO New York, NY 09403-0106 Duane G. Nahley, Supv.Libn.
Founded: 1948. **Staff:** Prof 6; Other 12. **Subjects:** Military affairs, business, international relations, current events, political science, education. **Special Collections:** Evans Collection (early American imprints); Shaw-Shoemaker Collection; Western Americana; Gordon L. Cox Collection; Government Printing Office documents collection; World War II; genealogy and local history; unit histories; campaigns. **Holdings:** 86,000 books; 1.15 million microforms; 25,000 documents. **Subscriptions:** 1337 journals and other serials; 25 newspapers. **Services:** Interlibrary loan; copying; SDI; center open to the public. **Automated Operations:** Computerized public access catalog and cataloging. **Computerized Information Services:** DIALOG Information Services, OCLC; DDN Network Information Center (electronic mail service). **Publications:** Subject bibliographies, irregular; periodical holdings, annual; InfoBrief, quarterly - for internal distribution only. **Staff:** Eileen Diel, Supv., Ref.Serv.; Julia Foscue, Ref.Libn.; Barron Holland, Ref.Libn.; Phyllis Kelly, Lib.Techn., Circ.Serv.; Helen Gibson, Tech.Serv..

★14815★
U.S. ARMY GARRISON - TECHNICAL LIBRARY (Sci-Engr, Info Sci)
Greely Hall, Rm. 2102
Attn: ASH-CA-CRL Phone: (602)538-6304
Ft. Huachuca, AZ 85613 Dorothy C. Tompkins, Chf.Libn.
Staff: Prof 2; Other 4. **Subjects:** Telecommunication, electronic engineering, computer science, electrical engineering, mathematics, optics. **Special Collections:** Army technical manuals; field manuals; research and development documents; vendors' catalogs, engineering design file, standards, regulations (on microfilm). **Holdings:** 7000 books; 2000 bound periodical volumes; 110,000 hard copy reports; 200,000 documents in microform; 2550 VSMF (Visual Search Microfilm File) microfilms; 3000 periodicals on microfilm. **Subscriptions:** 350 journals and other serials; 5 newspapers. **Services:** Interlibrary loan; copying; library open to active and retired military and Department of Defense personnel. **Automated Operations:** Computerized cataloging and serials. **Computerized Information Services:** DIALOG Information Services, DTIC. **Networks/Consortia:** Member of FEDLINK. **Publications:** Weekly acquisition list - to interested patrons. **Formerly:** U.S. Army - Information Systems Command - Systems Command Activity - Technical Library. **Staff:** Chris Hurd, Ref.Libn..

★14816★
U.S. ARMY HOSPITALS - BASSETT ARMY COMMUNITY HOSPITAL - MEDICAL LIBRARY (Med)
Commander USA MEDDAC Phone: (907)353-5194
Ft. Wainwright, AK 99703-7300 George P. Kimmell, Lib.Techn.
Staff: Prof 1. **Subjects:** Surgery, obstetrics/gynecology, pediatrics, nursing, internal medicine, radiology. **Holdings:** 2450 books; 50 bound periodical volumes. **Subscriptions:** 110 journals and other serials. **Services:** Interlibrary loan; library open to the public for reference use only.

★14817★
U.S. ARMY HOSPITALS - BAYNE-JONES ARMY COMMUNITY HOSPITAL - MEDICAL LIBRARY (Med)
Ft. Polk, LA 71459-6000 Phone: (318)535-3725
Cecelia B. Higginbotham, Med.Libn.
Staff: Prof 1; Other 1. **Subjects:** Medicine, pathology, hospital administration, dentistry. **Holdings:** 2300 monographs; 3700 bound periodical volumes. **Subscriptions:** 136 serials. **Services:** Interlibrary loan; library open to the public by appointment. **Computerized Information Services:** MEDLINE, OCLC. **Networks/Consortia:** Member of TALON. **Staff:** Patricia A. Derrigo, Lib.Techn..

★14818★
U.S. ARMY HOSPITALS - BLANCHFIELD ARMY COMMUNITY HOSPITAL - MEDICAL LIBRARY (Med)
Ft. Campbell, KY 42223-1498 Phone: (502)798-8014
Lillian G. Graham, Med.Libn.
Founded: 1959. **Staff:** Prof 1; Other 1. **Subjects:** Medicine, allied health sciences. **Special Collections:** Ciba slide collection. **Holdings:** 4905 books; 4499 bound periodical volumes; video and audio cassettes. **Subscriptions:** 397 journals and other serials. **Services:** Interlibrary loan; copying; library open to medical personnel on limited basis. **Computerized Information Services:** MEDLARS, DIALOG Information Services. **Networks/Consortia:** Member of Greater Midwest Regional Medical Library Network, FEDLINK.

★14819★
U.S. ARMY HOSPITALS - BLISS ARMY HOSPITAL - MEDICAL LIBRARY (Med)
Ft. Huachuca, AZ 85613-7040 Phone: (602)538-5668
James H. Coffman, Lib.Off.
Staff: Prof 1. **Subjects:** Clinical medicine, nursing, hospital administration. **Special Collections:** Medicine in World War II (especially surgery). **Holdings:** 1124 books; unbound and bound periodical volumes; 646 audiovisual cassettes; 112 audio cassettes. **Subscriptions:** 125 journals and other serials. **Services:** Interlibrary loan; copying; library open to the public with approval of Library Officer. **Publications:** Quarterly Report - for internal distribution only. **Staff:** Ann E. Nichols, Libn..

★14820★
U.S. ARMY HOSPITALS - BROOKE ARMY MEDICAL CENTER - MEDICAL LIBRARY (Med)
Bldg. 1001 Phone: (512)221-4119
Ft. Sam Houston, TX 78234-6200 Kimmie Yu, Med.Libn.
Staff: Prof 1; Other 4. **Subjects:** Medicine, dentistry, nursing, allied health sciences, religion, social work. **Special Collections:** Institute of Surgical Research on Burns (8800 volumes). **Holdings:** 17,500 books; 22,500 bound periodical volumes. **Subscriptions:** 750 journals and other serials. **Services:** Interlibrary loan; library not open to the public. **Automated Operations:** Computerized cataloging. **Computerized Information Services:** MEDLINE, OCLC, DIALOG Information Services. **Networks/Consortia:** Member of Council of Research & Academic Libraries (CORAL), Health Oriented Libraries of San Antonio (HOLSA), TALON. **Remarks:** An alternate telephone number is 221-7182.

★14821★
U.S. ARMY HOSPITALS - COMMANDER SILAS B. HAYS ARMY COMMUNITY HOSPITAL - MEDICAL LIBRARY (Med)
Fort Ord, CA 93941-5800 Phone: (408)242-2023
Staff: Prof 1; Other 1. **Subjects:** Medicine, nursing, dentistry, veterinary medicine, hospital administration. **Holdings:** 3000 books; 7000 bound periodical volumes. **Subscriptions:** 310 journals and other serials. **Services:** Interlibrary loan; copying; library open to the public with restrictions. **Computerized Information Services:** MEDLINE; OPTIMIS (electronic mail service).

★14822★
U.S. ARMY HOSPITALS - CUTLER ARMY HOSPITAL - MEDICAL LIBRARY (Med)
Ft. Devens, MA 01433-6401 Phone: (508)796-6750
Leslie R. Seidel, Med.Libn.
Staff: Prof 1. **Subjects:** Medicine, surgery, nursing. **Holdings:** 1800 books; 1500 bound periodical volumes. **Subscriptions:** 130 journals and other serials. **Services:** Interlibrary loan; copying; library open to the public for reference use only.. **Networks/Consortia:** Member of Northeastern Consortium for Health Information (NECHI).

★14823★
U.S. ARMY HOSPITALS - D.D. EISENHOWER ARMY MEDICAL CENTER - MEDICAL LIBRARY (Med)
Ft. Gordon, GA 30905-5650 Phone: (404)791-6765
Judy M. Krivanek, Med.Libn.
Staff: Prof 2; Other 2. **Subjects:** Surgery, psychiatry, internal medicine, dentistry, nursing. **Holdings:** 6114 books; 8969 bound periodical volumes. **Subscriptions:** 500 journals and other serials. **Services:** Interlibrary loan; library not open to the public.

★14824★
U.S. ARMY HOSPITALS - DARNALL ARMY HOSPITAL - MEDICAL LIBRARY (Med)
Bldg. 36000 Phone: (817)288-8368
Ft. Hood, TX 76544-5063 Frank M. Norton, Adm.Libn.
Staff: Prof 2; Other 1. **Subjects:** Medicine and allied health sciences. **Holdings:** 2600 books; 3500 bound periodical volumes; 400 videotapes. **Subscriptions:** 750 journals and other serials. **Services:** Interlibrary loan; copying; library open to medical professionals. **Automated Operations:** Computerized cataloging, acquisitions, serials, and circulation. **Computerized Information Services:** MEDLINE, DIALOG Information Services, OCLC, AMA/NET. **Staff:** Jonella B. Lein, Tech.Info.Spec..

★14825★
U.S. ARMY HOSPITALS - EVANS ARMY COMMUNITY HOSPITAL - MEDICAL LIBRARY (Med)
Bldg. 7500 Phone: (719)579-7286
Ft. Carson, CO 80913 Alfreda H. Hanna, Med.Libn.
Staff: 2. **Subjects:** Medicine, nursing, allied health sciences, patient health education. **Holdings:** 3500 books; 13,000 bound periodical volumes; 546 AV programs; 9964 audiotapes. **Subscriptions:** 380 journals and other serials. **Services:** Interlibrary loan; copying; library open to the public with restrictions. **Computerized Information Services:** MEDLARS, OCLC, BRS Information Technologies, DIALOG Information Services; DOCLINE (electronic mail service). **Networks/Consortia:** Member of FEDLINK, Colorado Council of Medical Librarians, Peaks and Valleys (Medical) Library Consortium, UNISON, Plains and Peaks Regional Library Service System, Bibliographical Center for Research, Rocky Mountain Region, Inc. (BCR). **Publications:** Hippocrates hieroglyphics (newsletter) - for internal distribution only. **Remarks:** An alternate telephone number is 579-7285.

★14826★
U.S. ARMY HOSPITALS - FITZSIMONS ARMY MEDICAL CENTER - MEDICAL-TECHNICAL LIBRARY (Med)
Aurora, CO 80045-5000 Phone: (303)361-3378
Sue Coldren, Act.Adm.Libn.
Founded: 1947. **Staff:** Prof 2; Other 3. **Subjects:** Medicine and allied health sciences. **Holdings:** 13,400 books; 24,500 bound periodical volumes. **Subscriptions:** 700 journals and other serials. **Services:** Interlibrary loan; library not open to the public. **Automated Operations:** Computerized cataloging and serials. **Computerized Information Services:** BRS Information Technologies, MEDLINE; DOCLINE (electronic mail service).

★14827★
U.S. ARMY HOSPITALS - GENERAL LEONARD WOOD ARMY COMMUNITY HOSPITAL - MEDICAL LIBRARY (Med)
Ft. Leonard Wood, MO 65473-5700 Phone: (314)368-9110
Marian B. Strang, Med.Libn.
Founded: 1950. **Staff:** Prof 1. **Subjects:** Medicine. **Holdings:** 3500 books; 200 bound periodical volumes. **Subscriptions:** 200 journals and other serials. **Services:** Interlibrary loan; library not open to the public. **Computerized Information Services:** MEDLARS.

★14828★
U.S. ARMY HOSPITALS - IRWIN ARMY HOSPITAL - MEDICAL LIBRARY (Med)
Bldg. 485 Phone: (913)239-7874
Ft. Riley, KS 66442-5036 Phyllis J. Whiteside, Med.Libn.
Staff: Prof 1. **Subjects:** Medicine, surgery, dentistry, nursing. **Holdings:** 3729 books; 1146 bound periodical volumes; 455 reels of microfilm; 387 microfiche. **Subscriptions:** 250 journals and other serials. **Services:** Interlibrary loan; copying; library open to the public with restrictions. **Computerized Information Services:** DIALOG Information Services, NLM; OPTIMIS, Dialcom Inc. (electronic mail services). **Networks/Consortia:** Member of Midcontinental Regional Medical Library Program. **Publications:** Newsletter, monthly.

★14829★
U.S. ARMY HOSPITALS - KELLER ARMY HOSPITAL - LIBRARY (Med)
West Point, NY 10996-1197 Phone: (914)938-2722
Mary E. Stark, Libn.
Staff: Prof 2. **Subjects:** Orthopedics, medicine, surgery, nursing. **Holdings:** 2400 books; 2200 bound periodical volumes. **Subscriptions:** 173 journals and other serials. **Services:** Interlibrary loan; library not open to the public. **Computerized Information Services:** DIALOG Information Services, MEDLINE. **Networks/Consortia:** Member of Southeastern New York Library Resources Council (SENYLRC), Health Information Libraries of Westchester (HILOW). **Staff:** Manja Yirka, Libn.; Susan P. Walker, Libn..

★14830★
U.S. ARMY HOSPITALS - KENNER ARMY COMMUNITY HOSPITAL - MEDICAL LIBRARY (Med)
Ft. Lee, VA 23801-5260 Phone: (804)734-1339
Betty K. Lewis, Libn.
Subjects: Medicine. **Holdings:** 2200 volumes.

★14831★
U.S. ARMY HOSPITALS - LETTERMAN ARMY MEDICAL CENTER - MEDICAL LIBRARY (Med)
Bldg. 1100, Rm. 338 Phone: (415)561-2465
Presidio of San Francisco, CA 94129-6700 Dixie Meagher, Adm.Libn.
Founded: 1918. **Staff:** Prof 2; Other 3. **Subjects:** Medicine, nursing, psychology, hospital administration, military medical history. **Holdings:** 5000 books; 30,000 bound periodical volumes. **Subscriptions:** 600 journals and other serials. **Services:** Interlibrary loan; copying; SDI. **Automated Operations:** Computerized cataloging. **Computerized Information Services:** DIALOG Information Services, MEDLARS. **Networks/Consortia:** Member of San Francisco Biomedical Library Group, Northern California and Nevada Medical Library Group (NCNMLG).

★14832★
U.S. ARMY HOSPITALS - LYSTER ARMY COMMUNITY HOSPITAL - MEDICAL LIBRARY (Med)
Bldg. 301
U.S. Army Aeromedical Center Phone: (205)255-7350
Ft. Rucker, AL 36362-5333 Mary Fran Prottsman, Med.Libn.
Staff: 1. **Subjects:** Medicine, nursing, veterinary medicine, aviation medicine, dentistry. **Holdings:** 3800 books; 2500 bound and microform periodical volumes; 8 audio cassette subscriptions. **Subscriptions:** 130 journals and other serials. **Services:** Interlibrary loan; copying; SDI; library open to the public for reference use only. **Computerized Information Services:** MEDLARS; DOCLINE, Dialcom Inc. (electronic mail services). **Remarks:** An alternate telephone number is 255-7349.

★14833★
U.S. ARMY HOSPITALS - MC DONALD ARMY COMMUNITY HOSPITAL - MEDICAL LIBRARY (Med)
Ft. Eustis, VA 23604 Phone: (804)878-5800
Helen O. Hearn, Lib.Mgr.
Staff: 1. **Subjects:** Medicine, dentistry, nursing. **Holdings:** 1500 books; 1100 bound periodical volumes. **Subscriptions:** 100 journals and other serials. **Services:** Interlibrary loan; library open to the public.

★14834★
U.S. ARMY HOSPITALS - MADIGAN ARMY MEDICAL CENTER - MEDICAL LIBRARY (Med)
Box 375 Phone: (206)967-6782
Tacoma, WA 98431 Elizabeth C. Bolden, Libn.
Founded: 1944. **Staff:** Prof 2; Other 2. **Subjects:** Medicine, dentistry, nursing, hospital administration, pharmacology. **Holdings:** 12,000 books; 13,000 bound periodical volumes; 1000 reels of microfilm; 100 video cassettes; 4 VF drawers of pamphlets and reprints. **Subscriptions:** 600 journals and other serials. **Services:** Interlibrary loan; library not open to the public. **Computerized Information Services:** NLM, OCLC; OnTyme Electronic Message Network Service, OPTIMIS, Dialcom Inc. (electronic mail services). **Networks/Consortia:** Member of FEDLINK. **Publications:** Information Sources and Resources, irregular - to personnel at the center and local medical libraries. **Staff:** Robert L. Clark, Libn..

★14835★
U.S. ARMY HOSPITALS - MARTIN ARMY COMMUNITY HOSPITAL - MEDICAL LIBRARY (Med)
Bldg. 9200 HSXB-B-L Phone: (404)544-1341
Ft. Benning, GA 31905-6100 Elaine A. Tate, Med.Libn.
Founded: 1958. **Staff:** Prof 1; Other 1. **Subjects:** Medicine, allied health sciences. **Holdings:** 2300 books; 1700 bound periodical volumes; 500 audio cassette tapes. **Subscriptions:** 317 journals and other serials. **Services:** Interlibrary loan; library open to health care professionals for reference use only. **Computerized Information Services:** MEDLINE. **Networks/Consortia:** Member of Southeastern/Atlantic Regional Medical Library Services, Atlanta Health Science Libraries Consortium, Health Science Libraries of Central Georgia (HSLCG). **Publications:** Library Acquisitions; Internal News Bulletin, quarterly.

★14836★
U.S. ARMY HOSPITALS - NOBLE ARMY HOSPITAL - MEDICAL LIBRARY (Med)
HSXQ-DCS Phone: (205)238-2411
Ft. McClellan, AL 36205 Kathryn S. Aide, Lib.Techn.
Founded: 1951. **Staff:** 1. **Subjects:** Medicine and allied health sciences. **Holdings:** 2100 books; 855 bound periodical volumes. **Subscriptions:** 85 journals and other serials. **Services:** Interlibrary loan; copying; library open to the public for reference use only.

★14837★
U.S. ARMY HOSPITALS - TRIPLER ARMY MEDICAL CENTER - MEDICAL LIBRARY (Med)
Honolulu, HI 96859-5000 Phone: (808)433-6391
Linda Requena, Chf., Med.Lib.
Staff: Prof 2; Other 2. **Subjects:** Medicine, paramedical sciences, dentistry, nursing. **Holdings:** 15,000 books; 25,000 bound periodical volumes. **Subscriptions:** 500 journals and other serials. **Services:** Interlibrary loan; copying; SDI; library open to the public with restrictions. **Automated Operations:** Computerized cataloging. **Computerized Information Services:** MEDLINE, OCLC, DIALOG Information Services; OPTIMIS (electronic mail service). **Networks/Consortia:** Member of FEDLINK, Medical Library Group of Hawaii. **Special Indexes:** Union Lists.

★14838★
U.S. ARMY HOSPITALS - WALSON ARMY HOSPITAL - MEDICAL LIBRARY (Med)
Ft. Dix, NJ 08640-6734 Phone: (609)562-5741
Dale Eliasson, Med.Libn.
Founded: 1959. **Staff:** Prof 1; Other 1. **Subjects:** Medicine, dentistry, nursing, psychiatry. **Holdings:** Figures not available. **Services:** Interlibrary loan. **Networks/Consortia:** Member of Greater Northeastern Regional Medical Library Program.

★14839★
U.S. ARMY HOSPITALS - WALTER REED ARMY MEDICAL CENTER - MEDICAL LIBRARY (Med)
Bldg. 2, Rm. 2G Phone: (202)576-1238
Washington, DC 20307-5001 Hoyt W. Galloway, Lib.Dir.
Staff: Prof 4; Other 7. **Subjects:** Clinical medicine, allied health sciences. **Special Collections:** Fred C. Ainsworth Endowment Library (history of science and medicine). **Holdings:** 12,760 books; 16,215 bound periodical volumes. **Subscriptions:** 765 journals and other serials. **Services:** Interlibrary loan; library not open to the public. **Automated Operations:** Computerized public access catalog, cataloging, serials, and circulation. **Computerized Information Services:** DTIC, MEDLINE, OCLC, DIALOG Information Services, BRS Information Technologies; Integrated Library System (ILS; internal database); DIALMAIL, Dialcom Inc., DOCLINE, OPTIMIS, OnTyme Electronic Message Network Service (electronic mail services). **Networks/Consortia:** Member of FEDLINK. **Staff:** Judy Hartman, Chf., Tech.Serv.; Ann Dougherty, Chf., Pub.Serv..

★14840★
U.S. ARMY HOSPITALS - WILLIAM BEAUMONT ARMY MEDICAL CENTER - MEDICAL LIBRARY (Med)
Bldg. 7777 Phone: (915)569-2580
El Paso, TX 79920-5001 Merle I. Alexander, Med.Libn.
Founded: 1931. **Staff:** Prof 3; Other 2. **Subjects:** Surgery, medicine, nursing, dentistry, hospital administration. **Holdings:** 17,000 books; 12,000 bound periodical volumes; 20,000 periodical volumes on microfilm; 630 AV programs. **Subscriptions:** 600 journals and other serials. **Services:** Interlibrary loan; library not open to the public. **Computerized Information Services:** MEDLINE, DIALOG Information Services, OCLC. **Networks/Consortia:** Member of TALON. **Special Catalogs:** Catalog of Audiovisual Holdings (book). **Staff:** Holbrook W. Yorke, Med.Libn..

★14841★
U.S. ARMY HOSPITALS - WOMACK ARMY COMMUNITY HOSPITAL - MEDICAL LIBRARY (Med)
Walker, Med.Libn. Phone: (919)396-1819
Ft. Bragg, NC 28307-5000 Irene M.
Founded: 1958. **Staff:** 3. **Subjects:** Medicine, dentistry, allied health sciences. **Holdings:** 3800 books; 3363 bound periodical volumes; 2 VF drawers of clippings, pamphlets, documents. **Subscriptions:** 323 journals and other serials. **Services:** Interlibrary loan; library not open to the public. **Automated Operations:** Computerized cataloging. **Computerized Information Services:** MEDLINE; Dialcom Inc. (electronic mail service). Performs searches free of charge. **Networks/Consortia:** Member of FEDLINK, Cape Fear Health Sciences Information Consortium, Southeastern/Atlantic Regional Medical Library Services.

U.S. ARMY MUSEUM, PRESIDIO OF MONTEREY
See: U.S. Army - Center of Military History - U.S. Army Museum, Presidio of Monterey (14712)

★14842★
U.S. ARMY POST - ABERDEEN PROVING GROUND - MORALE SUPPORT ACTIVITIES DIVISION - POST LIBRARY (Mil)
Bldg. 3320 Phone: (301)278-3417
Aberdeen Proving Ground, MD 21005-5001
Robert Lee Hadden, Adm.Libn.
Staff: Prof 1; Other 15. **Subjects:** Biography, English and American literature, auto repair, military history. **Holdings:** 42,596 books; 4 drawers of information files; 28 drawers of microfilm. **Subscriptions:** 300 journals and other serials; 31 newspapers. **Services:** Interlibrary loan; copying; SDI; library open to the public with restrictions. **Automated Operations:** Computerized cataloging. **Computerized Information Services:** DIALOG Information Services; DDN Network Information Center, FEDLINK, DIALMAIL (electronic mail services). Performs searches free of charge.

★14843★
U.S. ARMY POST - FORT BELVOIR - VAN NOY LIBRARY (Mil)
Bldg. 1024 Phone: (703)664-6257
Ft. Belvoir, VA 22060 Madge J. Busey, Dir.
Founded: 1939. **Staff:** Prof 3; Other 9. **Subjects:** Military science, social sciences, management. **Holdings:** 116,590 books; 6527 pamphlets; 4943 phonograph records and tapes; 3243 periodical volumes on microfilm; 21,000 books in microform. **Subscriptions:** 530 journals and other serials; 43 newspapers. **Services:** Interlibrary loan; copying; library open to the public for reference use only. **Automated Operations:** Computerized cataloging. **Computerized Information Services:** DIALOG Information Services, OCLC, DTIC, LEXIS, NEXIS; OPTIMIS (electronic mail service). **Networks/Consortia:** Member of FEDLINK, TRALINET. **Publications:** Monthly acquisitions list; annual Christmas Book - both by request. **Special Catalogs:** Catalog of periodical holdings. **Staff:** Carolyn Graves, Chf., Tech.Serv.; Phyllis Cassler, Chf., Ref.Serv.; Delores Ostraco, Chf., Circ.Serv..

★14844★
U.S. ARMY POST - FORT BENNING - SAYERS MEMORIAL LIBRARY (Mil)
Bldg. 93 Phone: (404)545-4911
Ft. Benning, GA 31905 Gwendolyn I. Lewis, Supv.Libn.
Founded: 1920. **Staff:** Prof 3; Other 6. **Subjects:** Military science, art, education, business, general reference. **Holdings:** 112,000 books; 5000 bound and unbound periodicals; 1077 periodical volumes on microfilm; 24,000 pamphlets and clippings; 10,752 AV programs. **Subscriptions:** 452 journals and other serials; 75 newspapers. **Services:** Interlibrary loan; copying; library open to military personnel and civilian post employees. **Computerized Information Services:** DIALOG Information Services, BRS Information Technologies; OPTIMIS (electronic mail service). **Networks/Consortia:** Member of Georgia Library Information Network (GLIN), TRALINET.

★14845★
U.S. ARMY POST - FORT BRAGG - LIBRARY (Mil)
HQ, XVIII Airborne Corps & Fort Bragg
AFZA-PA-R Phone: (919)396-6919
Ft. Bragg, NC 28307-5000 Patricia J. Javaher, Chf.Libn.
Founded: 1941. **Subjects:** Military science, military history, education. **Holdings:** 111,308 books; 952,753 microforms, including periodicals and special collections. **Subscriptions:** 640 journals and other serials; 32 newspapers. **Services:** Interlibrary loan; copying.

★14846★
U.S. ARMY POST - FORT CARSON - LIBRARY (Mil)
Ft. Carson, CO 80913 Phone: (719)579-2350
Roger M. Miller, Lib.Dir.
Staff: Prof 3; Other 11. **Subjects:** General collection. **Holdings:** 47,595 books; 1500 phonograph records; 5400 pamphlets; 8168 microforms; 150 videotapes; 90 computer discs; 100 framed art prints. **Subscriptions:** 258 journals and other serials; 20 newspapers. **Services:** Interlibrary loan; copying; library open to Fort Carson community members. **Automated Operations:** Computerized cataloging and ILL. **Computerized Information Services:** DIALOG Information Services, DTIC; OPTIMIS (electronic mail service). **Networks/Consortia:** Member of Plains and Peaks Regional Library Service System, FEDLINK. **Remarks:** A bookmobile is also part of the Fort Carson library system.

★14847★
U.S. ARMY POST - FORT CLAYTON - COMMUNITY RECREATION DIVISION - LIBRARY (Mil)
P.O. Drawer 933
APO Miami, FL 34004-5000 John D. Paulding, Supv.Libn.
Staff: Prof 3; Other 6. **Subjects:** Military sciences, Latin America, Panama. **Holdings:** 60,000 books; 25,000 AV programs and reels of microfilm. **Subscriptions:** 300 journals and other serials; 30 newspapers. **Services:** Interlibrary loan; library not open to the public. **Publications:** Periodical holdings list. **Staff:** Mary G. Quintero, Ref.Libn.; David Hunter, Ref.Libn..

U.S. ARMY POST - FORT DIX
See: U.S. Army Post - Training Center & Fort Dix (14861)

U.S. ARMY POST - FORT GORDON
See: U.S. Army - TRADOC - Signal Center & Fort Gordon (14807)

★14848★
U.S. ARMY POST - FORT GREELY - LIBRARY (Mil)
Bldg. 663 Phone: (907)873-3217
APO Seattle, WA 98733 Bonnie Ricks, Adm.Libn.
Staff: Prof 1; Other 2. **Subjects:** Arctic region, war and history, technology, hunting, fishing, general fiction. **Special Collections:** Arctic. **Holdings:** 20,000 volumes; 2050 AV programs. **Subscriptions:** 100 journals and other serials; 8 newspapers. **Services:** Interlibrary loan; copying; library open to the public. **Networks/Consortia:** Member of Western Library Network (WLN). **Remarks:** An alternate telephone number is 873-4117. **Staff:** Betty Phillips, Lib.Techn.; Maxine Schmierer, Lib.Techn..

★14849★
U.S. ARMY POST - FORT HAMILTON - LIBRARY (Mil)
Bldg. 404 Phone: (718)630-4875
Brooklyn, NY 11252-5155 Amelia K. Sefton, Libn. I
Founded: 1942. **Staff:** Prof 1; Other 1. **Subjects:** Military history, science, and tactics. **Special Collections:** Newyorkana Collection. **Holdings:** 27,000 volumes; phonograph records. **Services:** Interlibrary loan; library not open to the public. **Computerized Information Services:** DIALOG Information Services, OCLC. **Networks/Consortia:** Member of TRALINET.

★14850★
U.S. ARMY POST - FORT HOOD - COMMUNITY RECREATION DIVISION - CASEY MEMORIAL LIBRARY (Mil)
Bldg. 18000 Phone: (817)287-5202
Ft. Hood, TX 76544 G.K. Cheatham, Chf.Libn.
Staff: Prof 6; Other 18. **Subjects:** General collection with emphasis on military science. **Holdings:** 69,000 books; 600 phonograph recordings; 400 video cassettes; 32,000 microforms. **Subscriptions:** 300 journals and other serials; 30 newspapers. **Services:** Interlibrary loan; copying; library open to military and Fort Hood employees. **Automated Operations:** Computerized cataloging and ILL. **Computerized Information Services:** DIALOG Information Services, OCLC; internal database. **Networks/Consortia:** Member of FEDLINK. **Publications:** Selected Subject Bibliographies, irregular. **Staff:** Mary F. Rogerson, Supv.Libn.; Pam Shelton, Ref.Libn.; Patsy Shields, Cat.; Alice Gadsden, Ext.Libn..

U.S. ARMY POST - FORT JACKSON
See: U.S. Army Post - Training Command & Fort Jackson (14862)

★14851★
U.S. ARMY POST - FORT LEWIS - LIBRARY SYSTEM (Mil)
Bldg. 2109 Phone: (206)967-7736
Ft. Lewis, WA 98433-5000 Patricia A. Louderback, Chf.Libn.
Founded: 1944. **Staff:** Prof 5; Other 11. **Subjects:** Military science, social sciences, psychology, mathematics, languages, education, literature. **Special**

Collections: Military affairs (8000 titles). **Holdings:** 110,000 books; 11,880 microforms; 12,671 phonograph records, cassettes, maps, art prints. **Subscriptions:** 425 journals and other serials. **Services:** Interlibrary loan; library not open to the public. **Networks/Consortia:** Member of Western Library Network (WLN). **Remarks:** Fort Lewis Library System consists of 1 main library, 3 branch libraries, and 1 field library. **Staff:** Bonnie Tucker, Main Post Libn.; Fay Robinson, Br.Libn.; Elsa Largen, Proc.Ctr.; Ute Jarasitis, ILL; Patrice Balliet, Ch.Serv..

★14852★
U.S. ARMY POST - FORT LEWIS - LIBRARY SYSTEM - MADIGAN COMMUNITY LIBRARY (Mil, Med)
Madigan Army Medical Center
Box 263 Phone: (206)967-6198
Tacoma, WA 98431-5263 Marganne Weathers, Libn.
Founded: 1944. **Staff:** Prof 1. **Special Collections:** Military affairs, patient education. **Holdings:** 20,000 books; 1800 phonograph records; 6 VF drawers of pamphlets. **Subscriptions:** 135 journals and other serials; 10 newspapers. **Services:** Interlibrary loan; copying; library open to the public for reference use only. **Automated Operations:** Computerized cataloging and circulation. **Networks/Consortia:** Member of Western Library Network (WLN). **Publications:** List of new books, monthly; annotated bibliographies of special collections subjects,

★14853★
U.S. ARMY POST - FORT MC PHERSON - LIBRARY SYSTEM (Mil)
Bldg. T-44 Phone: (404)752-3218
Ft. McPherson, GA 30330-5000 Helen T. Kiss, Chf.Libn.
Staff: Prof 3; Other 3. **Subjects:** Military history. **Holdings:** 44,000 books; 11,000 Army and Department of Defense documents. **Subscriptions:** 450 journals and other serials; 15 newspapers. **Services:** Interlibrary loan; library not open to the public. **Computerized Information Services:** DIALOG Information Services, DTIC, OCLC. **Networks/Consortia:** Member of Georgia Library Information Network (GLIN).

★14854★
U.S. ARMY POST - FORT RICHARDSON - LIBRARY (Mil)
Bldg. 636 Phone: (907)862-9188
Ft. Richardson, AK 99505 Doris A. Sheible, Lib.Dir.
Staff: Prof 2; Other 2. **Subjects:** Military science, Arctic regions, foreign languages. **Special Collections:** Military science; military history; Arctic region. **Holdings:** 40,000 books; 9300 microfiche; 7000 pamphlets. **Subscriptions:** 197 journals and other serials; 23 newspapers. **Services:** Interlibrary loan; copying; reader's advisory; library open to the public for reference use only. **Networks/Consortia:** Member of Western Library Network (WLN).

★14855★
U.S. ARMY POST - FORT RILEY - LIBRARIES (Mil)
Bldg. 405 Phone: (913)239-2323
Ft. Riley, KS 66442-6416 Jeanette Hoel, Chf.Libn.
Staff: Prof 2. **Subjects:** Military science. **Holdings:** 50,000 books; 3000 phonograph records; periodicals on microfilm; telephone books on microfiche; 500 video cassettes. **Subscriptions:** 200 journals and other serials; 25 newspapers. **Services:** Interlibrary loan; copying. **Automated Operations:** Computerized cataloging and ILL. **Computerized Information Services:** OCLC. **Networks/Consortia:** Member of FEDLINK. **Staff:** Barbara Eussen, Libn..

★14856★
U.S. ARMY POST - FORT STEWART/HUNTER AAF LIBRARY SYSTEM (Mil)
Bldg. 411 Phone: (912)767-2828
Ft. Stewart, GA 31314-3179 Richard D. Boyce, Chf.Libn.
Founded: 1942. **Subjects:** Military science, military history. **Special Collections:** Library of American Civilization (microfiche); Newsbank and Names in News; Korean language books and magazines; Library of English Literature (microfiche). **Holdings:** Figures not available for books; bound periodical volumes; microforms; phonograph records; cassettes; VF items; magnetic tapes. **Services:** Interlibrary loan; copying; library open to military personnel and dependents. **Computerized Information Services:** OCLC. **Networks/Consortia:** Member of Georgia Library Information Network (GLIN), FEDLINK. **Remarks:** The library system consists of the main post library, a branch library, and two bookmobiles. **Staff:** M. Malinda Johnson, Post Libn.; Fred Berg, Ref.Libn.; Hugh Thomas, Tech.Serv.Libn..

★14857★
U.S. ARMY POST - FORT STORY - LIBRARY (Mil)
Bldg. T-530 Phone: (804)422-7548
Ft. Story, VA 23459-5067 Leslie A. Smail, Chf.
Staff: Prof 1; Other 2. **Subjects:** Military science and general collection. **Holdings:** 20,000 books; 6 war games; 8 VF drawers of ephemera. **Subscriptions:** 110 journals and other serials; 10 newspapers. **Services:** Interlibrary loan; library open to military personnel, retirees, civil service, and dependents only. **Computerized Information Services:** OCLC, DIALOG Information Services; OPTIMIS (electronic mail service). Performs searches free of charge. **Networks/Consortia:** Member of FEDLINK, TRALINET. **Remarks:** An alternate telephone number is 422-7525.

★14858★
U.S. ARMY POST - FORT WAINWRIGHT - LIBRARY (Mil)
Bldg. 3717
Ft. Wainwright, AK 99703 Phone: (907)353-6114
Founded: 1951. **Staff:** Prof 2; Other 4. **Subjects:** General collection. **Special Collections:** Alaska and the Arctic; military. **Holdings:** 27,000 books; 2600 pamphlets, paintings; 6500 phonograph records, audio cassettes, compact discs; 2352 video cassettes. **Subscriptions:** 217 journals and other serials. **Services:** Interlibrary loan; copying; library open to the public for reference use only. **Networks/Consortia:** Member of Alaska Library Network (ALN), Western Library Network (WLN). **Staff:** Alfred Preston, Libn..

★14859★
U.S. ARMY POST - PRESIDIO OF SAN FRANCISCO - POST LIBRARY SYSTEM (Mil)
Bldg. 386 Phone: (415)561-3448
Presidio of San Francisco, CA 94129 Juanita Taylor, Chf.Libn.
Founded: 1944. **Staff:** Prof 4; Other 4. **Subjects:** Military science, military history, international relations, area studies. **Special Collections:** History of the Presidio of San Francisco; California and San Francisco history. **Holdings:** 50,000 volumes; 25 VF drawers of documents, pamphlets, and clippings. **Subscriptions:** 200 journals and other serials. **Services:** Interlibrary loan; copying; library open to the public for reference use only. **Staff:** Carolyn A. Garrett, Cat.Libn.; Joan R. Keller, Ext.Serv.Libn.; Andrew Minjiras, Post Libn..

★14860★
U.S. ARMY POST - TRAINING CENTER ENGINEER & FORT LEONARD WOOD - POST LIBRARY (Mil)
Bldg. 1607 Phone: (314)368-7169
Ft. Leonard Wood, MO 65473-5125 Christine M. Reser, Chf.Libn.
Founded: 1941. **Staff:** Prof 3; Other 7. **Subjects:** Military affairs, history, government, social sciences, sports and recreation. **Special Collections:** Children's collection; framed art reproductions; war games. **Holdings:** 44,000 books; magazines on microfilm; college catalogs on microfiche; video cassettes; Newsbank, 1970-1987, on microfiche. **Subscriptions:** 240 journals and other serials; 20 newspapers. **Services:** Interlibrary loan; copying; library open to the public. **Automated Operations:** Computerized cataloging, acquisitions, and ILL. **Computerized Information Services:** BRS Information Technologies, DTIC, DIALOG Information Services; OPTIMIS (electronic mail service). **Networks/Consortia:** Member of TRALINET. **Staff:** Belenda Wilkerson, Post Libn..

★14861★
U.S. ARMY POST - TRAINING CENTER & FORT DIX - GENERAL LIBRARY (Mil)
Pennsylvania Ave., Bldg. 6501 Phone: (609)562-4858
Fort Dix, NJ 08640-5111 Guy A. Marco, Chf.Libn.
Subjects: General collection with emphasis on military science. **Holdings:** 77,000 books; 2000 reels of microfilm. **Subscriptions:** 280 journals and other serials; 20 newspapers. **Services:** Interlibrary loan; copying; library open to the public for reference use only. **Automated Operations:** Computerized cataloging and acquisitions. **Computerized Information Services:** BRS Information Technologies, DIALOG Information Services, DTIC, OCLC; OPTIMIS (electronic mail service). **Networks/Consortia:** Member of TRALINET.

★14862★
U.S. ARMY POST - TRAINING COMMAND & FORT JACKSON - THOMAS LEE HALL POST LIBRARY (Mil)
U.S. Army Main Lib., Community Recreation Div.
Bldg. 4679 Phone: (803)751-5589
Ft. Jackson, SC 29207-5170 Marilyn M. Mancuso, Lib.Dir.
Founded: 1946. **Staff:** Prof 2. **Subjects:** Military history, business and management, auto repair, arts and crafts, children's literature. **Holdings:** 80,000 books; 130 framed art prints; 950 video cassettes; Newsbank, 1984-

1986; Phonefiche (Southeast Region). **Subscriptions:** 300 journals and other serials; 15 newspapers. **Services:** Interlibrary loan; copying; library open to the public for reference use only. **Automated Operations:** Computerized acquisitions. **Computerized Information Services:** DIALOG Information Services, BRS Information Technologies; OPTIMIS (electronic mail service). **Networks/Consortia:** Member of TRALINET. **Staff:** Fred Bush, Post Libn..

★14863★
U.S. ARMY RESEARCH OFFICE - TECHNICAL LIBRARY (Sci-Engr)
Box 12211 Phone: (919)549-0641
Research Triangle Park, NC 27709 Brenda Mann, Tech.Libn.
Staff: Prof 1; Other 2. **Subjects:** Physical sciences, engineering, materials, mathematics, geosciences, biology. **Holdings:** 2300 books. **Subscriptions:** 225 journals and other serials; 10 newspapers. **Services:** Library open to other government agencies. **Automated Operations:** Computerized cataloging.

★14864★
U.S. ARMY/U.S. AIR FORCE - OFFICES OF THE SURGEONS GENERAL - JOINT MEDICAL LIBRARY (Med)
5109 Leesburg Pike, Rm. 670 Phone: (703)756-8028
Falls Church, VA 22041-3258 Diane Zehnpfennig, Adm.Libn.
Founded: 1969. **Staff:** Prof 1; Other 2. **Subjects:** Military and general medicine, hospital administration. **Holdings:** 13,000 books; 8000 bound periodical volumes; 500 microfiche; 200 boxes of pamphlets. **Subscriptions:** 412 journals and other serials. **Services:** Interlibrary loan; library not open to the public. **Computerized Information Services:** DIALOG Information Services, DTIC, MEDLARS; OPTIMIS (electronic mail service). **Special Indexes:** Index to annual reports of army and air force surgeons general.

★14865★
U.S. ARMY WAR COLLEGE - LIBRARY (Mil)
Carlisle Barracks, PA 17013-5050 Phone: (717)245-3660
Louise Nyce, Dir.
Founded: 1951. **Subjects:** Military science, strategy, international relations, leadership and management, international law, area studies. **Holdings:** 109,499 books and documents; 7110 bound periodical volumes; 55,818 uncataloged documents and theses; 60,881 maps; 412,000 microforms; 769 AV programs. **Subscriptions:** 932 journals and other serials; 38 newspapers. **Services:** Interlibrary loan; library not open to the public. **Automated Operations:** Computerized cataloging, serials, and circulation. **Computerized Information Services:** DIALOG Information Services, LS/2000, DTIC; internal database; OPTIMIS (electronic mail service). **Networks/Consortia:** Member of FEDLINK. **Publications:** Periodicals Directory, annual; bibliographies, irregular; Library Acquisitions Bulletin. **Staff:** Iqbal Junaid, Sys.Libn.; Bohdan I. Kohutiak, Sys.Libn.; Lidwina J. Gole, Chf., Preparations Br.; Joan M. Hench, Chf., Coll.Dev.Br.; Margaret E. MacGregor, Chf., Circ.Br..

U.S. ATTORNEY
See: U.S. Dept. of Justice (15038)

★14866★
U.S. BANCORP - RESOURCE LIBRARY (Bus-Fin)
555 S.W. Oak St.
Portland, OR 97204 Phone: (503)225-5816
Staff: 1. **Subjects:** Banking and finance, management, personnel administration and supervision, education and training, computers, psychology and sociology. **Special Collections:** History of U.S. National Bank of Oregon. **Holdings:** 2500 books; 455 AV cassettes; 200 programmed instruction courses; 300 theses, speeches, reports. **Subscriptions:** 63 journals and other serials. **Services:** Library not open to the public. **Publications:** Resource Guide, annual update; Organization Directory, annual - both for internal distribution only.

★14867★
UNITED STATES BORAX RESEARCH CORPORATION - RESEARCH LIBRARY (Sci-Engr)
412 Crescent Way Phone: (714)774-2670
Anaheim, CA 92801 Betty J. Robson, Res.Libn.
Founded: 1956. **Staff:** Prof 2; Other 3. **Subjects:** Chemistry, agriculture, mining, metallurgy, glass, ceramics. **Holdings:** 4400 volumes; 2200 bound periodical volumes; 1500 government research reports; 6 VF drawers of patents; 1500 company research reports; 12 drawers of microcards; 120 reels of microfilm. **Subscriptions:** 200 journals and other serials. **Services:** Interlibrary loan; copying; library open to the public for reference use only on request. **Computerized Information Services:** DIALOG Information Services, DTIC; STAR (internal database). **Publications:** Library Bulletin, weekly - for internal distribution only. **Special Indexes:** Indexes to internal reports and patents (online).

★14868★
U.S. BUREAU OF ALCOHOL, TOBACCO AND FIREARMS - NATIONAL LABORATORY LIBRARY (Sci-Engr)
1401 Research Blvd. Phone: (301)294-0410
Rockville, MD 20850 Paula Deutsch, Lib.Techn.
Staff: 1. **Subjects:** Alcohol, analytical techniques, forensic sciences and photography, firearms, tobacco. **Holdings:** 6000 books; 4000 bound periodical volumes; 25 volumes of laboratory reports; government documents. **Subscriptions:** 75 journals and other serials. **Services:** Interlibrary loan; library not open to the public. **Automated Operations:** Computerized cataloging. **Computerized Information Services:** DIALOG Information Services, OCLC. **Networks/Consortia:** Member of FEDLINK. **Special Catalogs:** Technical publications of the ATF Laboratory System. **Remarks:** The Bureau of Alcohol, Tobacco and Firearms is part of the U.S. Department of the Treasury.

★14869★
U.S. BUREAU OF ALCOHOL, TOBACCO AND FIREARMS - REFERENCE LIBRARY (Sci-Engr)
1200 Pennsylvania Ave., N.W. Phone: (202)566-7557
Washington, DC 20226 Vicki R. Herrmann, Libn.
Staff: Prof 1. **Subjects:** Alcohol, tobacco, firearms, explosives. **Special Collections:** Tax and regulation history of the alcohol and tobacco industries in the United States (200 volumes). **Holdings:** 700 books; 100 bound periodical volumes; 200 linear feet of indexed hearings, projects, tasks, and correspondence; 2 drawers of microfiche of historical documents. **Subscriptions:** 250 journals and other serials. **Services:** Interlibrary loan; copying; SDI; library open to the public with written permission. **Automated Operations:** Computerized cataloging, serials, and circulation. **Computerized Information Services:** NEXIS, DataLinx; internal database. Performs searches free of charge. **Special Indexes:** Index to correspondence; indexes to internal and bureau publications, rulings and procedures, relevant Treasury Decisions, archival projects, and legal memoranda.

U.S. BUREAU OF THE CENSUS - CALIFORNIA STATE CENSUS DATA CENTER
See: California State Census Data Center (2173)

★14870★
U.S. BUREAU OF THE CENSUS - CENSUS AWARENESS AND PRODUCTS PROGRAM - BOSTON REGIONAL OFFICE - LIBRARY (Soc Sci)
441 Stuart St. Phone: (617)565-7078
Boston, MA 02116 Arthur G. Dukakis, Reg.Dir.
Staff: 4. **Subjects:** U.S. census reports. **Holdings:** 4000 books; 8 VF drawers; 1982 economic censuses, 1980 census reports (hard copy and microfiche); census maps. **Subscriptions:** 16 journals and other serials. **Services:** Copying; library open to the public. **Formerly:** Information Services Program. **Staff:** Janet Bryant-Scheir, Census Commun. Awareness Spec.; Karl S. Bynoe, Census Commun. Awareness Spec..

★14871★
U.S. BUREAU OF THE CENSUS - INFORMATION SERVICES PROGRAM - ATLANTA REGIONAL OFFICE (Soc Sci)
1365 Peachtree St., N.E., Rm. 621
Atlanta, GA 30309 Phone: (404)347-2274
Subjects: U.S. census reports. **Holdings:** Figures not available. **Services:** Office open to the public.

★14872★
U.S. BUREAU OF THE CENSUS - INFORMATION SERVICES PROGRAM - CHARLOTTE REGIONAL OFFICE - LIBRARY (Soc Sci)
222 S. Church St., Suite 505
Charlotte, NC 28202 Phone: (704)371-6144
Founded: 1977. **Staff:** Prof 2; Other 1. **Subjects:** U.S. census reports. **Holdings:** 4000 books; 60 bound periodical volumes; 4 drawers of microfiche. **Services:** Copying; library open to the public for reference use only. **Staff:** Ken Wright, Info.Serv.Spec.; Nancy Olson, Info.Serv.Asst..

★14873★
U.S. BUREAU OF THE CENSUS - INFORMATION SERVICES PROGRAM - CHICAGO REGIONAL OFFICE - REFERENCE CENTER (Soc Sci)
175 W. Jackson Blvd., Rm. 560 Phone: (312)353-0980
Chicago, IL 60604 Stanley D. Moore, Reg.Dir.
Founded: 1975. **Staff:** Prof 4; Other 1. **Subjects:** U.S. census - population, housing, manufacturers, retail trade, agriculture, wholesale/service trades. **Holdings:** 3500 books; 350 bound periodical volumes; 200 series; Census Bureau computer tape technical documentation; 1980 census data on microfiche; census tract maps; block maps of Illinois and Indiana. **Services:** Copying (limited); assistance with census data through telephone access services; free census data access and use workshops; consultations; center open to the public. **Networks/Consortia:** Member of Illinois State Data Center Cooperative (ISDCC), Indiana State Data Center. **Publications:** Census Information Digest - to Illinois and Indiana regional users of census data. **Staff:** Mary F. Grady, Info.Serv.Spec.; Stephen Laue, Info.Serv.Spec.; Norma Marti, Info.Serv.Spec..

★14874★
U.S. BUREAU OF THE CENSUS - INFORMATION SERVICES PROGRAM - DALLAS REGIONAL OFFICE - LIBRARY (Soc Sci)
6303 Harry Hines Blvd., Suite 103 Phone: (214)767-7105
Dallas, TX 75235 K. Brooks Sitton, Coord.
Founded: 1976. **Staff:** Prof 6; Other 2. **Subjects:** U.S. census reports. **Holdings:** 3500 volumes; 1980 census reports (hard copy and microfiche). **Subscriptions:** 12 journals and other serials. **Services:** Copying (limited); library open to the public. **Staff:** Willie DeBerry, Spec.; Linda Haralson, Spec.; Marisela Lopez, Spec.; Paula Wright, Spec.; Tomas Zuniga, Spec..

★14875★
U.S. BUREAU OF THE CENSUS - INFORMATION SERVICES PROGRAM - DENVER REGIONAL OFFICE - CENSUS PUBLICATION CENTER (Soc Sci)
7655 W. Mississippi Ave.
Box 26750
Denver, CO 80226 Phone: (303)234-5825
Staff: Prof 5; Other 1. **Subjects:** U.S. census reports. **Holdings:** Figures not available. **Services:** Copying; statistical assistance; center open to the public. **Staff:** Gina Valdez, Commun.Serv.Spec.; Vincent Lopez, Supv. Statistician; Jerry O'Donnell, Info.Serv.Spec.; Lance Hughes, Commun.Serv.Spec.; Jennifer Vallie, Commun.Serv.Spec..

★14876★
U.S. BUREAU OF THE CENSUS - INFORMATION SERVICES PROGRAM - DETROIT REGIONAL OFFICE - INFORMATION CENTER (Soc Sci)
231 W. Lafayette St., Rm. 565 Phone: (313)226-4675
Detroit, MI 48226 D. Ross Forbes, Coord., Info.Serv.
Founded: 1977. **Staff:** Prof 2; Other 1. **Subjects:** U.S. census reports. **Special Collections:** 1980 Census for Michigan and Ohio (microfiche). **Holdings:** 2550 volumes. **Services:** Copying; center open to the public. **Publications:** Great Lakes Data Highlights, quarterly; Census Users in Ohio and Michigan. **Staff:** Sandra Lucas, Commun.Serv.Spec.; Kurt Metzger, Info.Serv.Spec..

★14877★
U.S. BUREAU OF THE CENSUS - INFORMATION SERVICES PROGRAM - KANSAS CITY REGIONAL OFFICE - LIBRARY (Soc Sci)
10332 N.W. Prairie View Rd. Phone: (816)891-7562
Kansas City, MO 64117 Ben Arzu, Coord.
Staff: Prof 5; Other 1. **Subjects:** U.S. census reports - population, demographics. **Holdings:** Figures not available. **Services:** Copying; library open to the public. **Publications:** Midwest Messenger, quarterly - to selected mailing list. **Staff:** Cheryl Sorrell, Commun.Serv.Spec.; Bill Yates, Info.Spec.; Rachel Estrada, Commun.Serv.Spec.; Marietta Gumbel, Commun.Serv.Spec..

★14878★
U.S. BUREAU OF THE CENSUS - INFORMATION SERVICES PROGRAM - LOS ANGELES REGIONAL OFFICE - LIBRARY (Soc Sci)
16300 Roscoe Blvd.
Van Nuys, CA 91406 Phone: (818)892-3187
Staff: Prof 4; Other 1. **Subjects:** U.S. census reports - population, housing, economic, construction. **Holdings:** Figures not available. **Services:** Library open to the public. **Publications:** Data News, quarterly. **Staff:** Larry Hugg, Info.Serv.Spec.; Jerry Wong, Info.Serv.Spec.; Reina Ornelas, Commun.Serv.Spec.; Una Kuan, Info.Serv.Spec..

★14879★
U.S. BUREAU OF THE CENSUS - INFORMATION SERVICES PROGRAM - NEW YORK REGIONAL OFFICE - LIBRARY (Soc Sci)
26 Federal Plaza, Rm. 37-100 Phone: (212)264-4730
New York, NY 10278 Sheila H. Grimm, Reg.Dir.
Founded: 1976. **Subjects:** U.S. census reports. **Holdings:** 15,000 volumes. **Services:** SDI (limited); library open to the public.

★14880★
U.S. BUREAU OF THE CENSUS - INFORMATION SERVICES PROGRAM - PHILADELPHIA REGIONAL OFFICE - LIBRARY (Soc Sci)
Federal Bldg., Rm. 9244
600 Arch St. Phone: (215)597-8314
Philadelphia, PA 19106 David C. Lewis, Chf.
Subjects: U.S. census reports. **Holdings:** Census publications; 1980 census for Delaware, Maryland, New Jersey, and Pennsylvania on microfiche. **Services:** Library open to the public.

★14881★
U.S. BUREAU OF THE CENSUS - INFORMATION SERVICES PROGRAM - SEATTLE REGIONAL OFFICE - LIBRARY (Soc Sci)
101 Stewart St., No. 600 Phone: (206)442-7080
Seattle, WA 98101-1098 Sonya Steinke, Libn.
Staff: Prof 4. **Subjects:** U.S. decennial census reports, economic and agricultural census reports. **Special Collections:** Bureau of the Census Block Statistics and Census Tract Reports. **Holdings:** 5000 books; 100 bound periodical volumes; microfiche. **Services:** Interlibrary loan; copying; library open to the public. **Staff:** Alice Solomon, Census Coord.; Gary George, Commun. Awareness Spec.; Sumi Lee, Census Awareness Spec.; Andy Cortez, Census Awareness Spec.; Cam McIntosh, Info.Spec..

★14882★
U.S. BUREAU OF THE CENSUS - LIBRARY & INFORMATION SERVICES BRANCH (Soc Sci)
Federal Bldg. No. 3, Rm. 2455 Phone: (301)763-5042
Washington, DC 20233 Michelle ShaioLan Lee, Pgm.Mgr./Hd.Libn.
Founded: 1952. **Staff:** Prof 8; Other 7. **Subjects:** Economics, population, public finance, survey and statistical methodology, urban studies, data processing. **Special Collections:** U.S. Census publications, 1790-1985 (45,457); census volumes, statistical yearbooks, bulletins of foreign governments (21,101); publications on electronic data processing. **Holdings:** 135,000 books; 850 bound periodical volumes; 21,160 microfiche; 2245 corporation annual reports; 28 drawers of congressional materials; census staff papers; 590 college catalogs. **Subscriptions:** 2175 journals and other serials; 5 newspapers. **Services:** Interlibrary loan; copying; library open to the public by appointment. **Automated Operations:** Computerized cataloging, acquisitions, serials, and circulation. **Computerized Information Services:** DIALOG Information Services, LEXIS, NEXIS, OCLC, BRS Information Technologies, WILSONLINE, VU/TEXT Information Services, LEGI-SLATE, DunSprint. **Networks/Consortia:** Member of FEDLINK. **Publications:** Information Exchange, monthly - available on request. **Remarks:** The Bureau of the Census is part of the U.S. Department of Commerce. **Staff:** Rebecca Wolking, Hd.Ref.Libn.; Sherry Hart, Hd.Sys.Libn..

★14883★
U.S. BUREAU OF INDIAN AFFAIRS - SOUTHWESTERN INDIAN POLYTECHNIC INSTITUTE - LIBRARY (Educ)
9169 Coors Blvd., N.W.
Box 10146 Phone: (505)766-3266
Albuquerque, NM 87184 Paula M. Woodard, Educ.Spec./Libn.
Founded: 1972. **Staff:** Prof 2; Other 1. **Subjects:** Vocational-technical curriculum, American Indians, recreational reading. **Special Collections:** American Indian Collection (2240 volumes; 25-35 newspapers and newsletters). **Holdings:** 20,000 books; 100 bound periodical volumes; 500 filmstrips, audio cassettes, transparencies; 300 video cassettes. **Subscriptions:** 100 journals and other serials; 35 newspapers. **Services:** Interlibrary loan; copying; center open to the public for reference use only. **Publications:** Bibliographies. **Remarks:** The Bureau of Indian Affairs is part of the U.S. Department of the Interior. **Staff:** Helen F. Jojola, Hd.Techn..

★14884★
U.S. BUREAU OF LAND MANAGEMEMT - ALASKA STATE OFFICE - ALASKA RESOURCES LIBRARY (Biol Sci, Env-Cons)
701 C St.
Box 36 Phone: (907)271-5025
Anchorage, AK 99513 Martha L. Shepard, Chf.Libn.
Founded: 1972. **Staff:** Prof 4; Other 2. **Subjects:** Alaska - resources, wildlife, land management, forestry/vegetation; Arctic environment; pipelines; outer continental shelf; hydrology; pollution; engineering and geology. **Special Collections:** Alaskan map collection of original overlays; microfiche library of CRREL bibliography. **Holdings:** 45,000 volumes; 7000 maps. **Subscriptions:** 1200 journals and other serials. **Services:** Interlibrary loan; copying; library open to the public. **Computerized Information Services:** DIALOG Information Services, WLN, OCLC, Pergamon ORBIT InfoLine, Inc., LEXIS; Dialcom Inc., OnTyme Electronic Message Network Service (electronic mail services). **Networks/Consortia:** Member of FEDLINK, Alaska Library Network (ALN).

★14885★
U.S. BUREAU OF LAND MANAGEMENT - CALIFORNIA STATE OFFICE - LIBRARY (Env-Cons)
2800 Cottage Way, Rm. E-2841 Phone: (916)978-4713
Sacramento, CA 95825 Louise Tichy, Mgt.Asst.
Staff: 2. **Subjects:** Land resources, recreation, environmental statements, U.S. statutes, interior land decisions. **Holdings:** 3000 books; unbound periodicals; newspaper clippings. **Subscriptions:** 114 journals and other serials. **Services:** Interlibrary loan; copying; library open to the public for reference use only. **Computerized Information Services:** Raptor Management Research System (internal database). Performs searches on fee basis. Contact Person: Dr. Richard Olendorff, 978-4725.

★14886★
U.S. BUREAU OF LAND MANAGEMENT - CASPER DISTRICT OFFICE - LIBRARY (Env-Cons)
1701 East E St. Phone: (307)261-5591
Casper, WY 82601 Trudy Closson, Rec.Mgr.
Staff: 1. **Subjects:** Wildlife, fire, minerals, environmental impact statements, soil, hydrology. **Holdings:** Figures not available. **Subscriptions:** 12 journals and other serials. **Services:** Copying; library open to the public for reference use only. **Automated Operations:** Computerized cataloging.

★14887★
U.S. BUREAU OF LAND MANAGEMENT - EASTERN STATES OFFICE - LIBRARY (Env-Cons)
350 S. Pickett St.
Alexandria, VA 22304 M. Willette Proctor, Mgt.Asst.
Founded: 1975. **Staff:** Prof 1. **Subjects:** Land management and environmental assessment. **Holdings:** 10,000 books; BLM manuals; public lands law books; U.S. Department of the Interior manuals. **Subscriptions:** 50 journals and other serials. **Services:** Interlibrary loan; copying; library open to the public.

★14888★
U.S. BUREAU OF LAND MANAGEMENT - LIBRARY (Env-Cons)
Denver Federal Ctr., Bldg. 50
Box 25047 Phone: (303)236-6649
Denver, CO 80225-0047 Sandra L. Bowers, Chf., Lib.Sect.
Staff: Prof 2; Other 8. **Subjects:** Forestry, range and wildlife management, geology, minerals, oil shale. **Holdings:** 30,000 volumes. **Subscriptions:** 500 journals and other serials. **Services:** Interlibrary loan; copying; library open to the public for reference use only. **Automated Operations:** Computerized cataloging. **Computerized Information Services:** DIALOG Information Services, Pergamon ORBIT InfoLine, Inc., BRS Information Technologies. **Networks/Consortia:** Member of FEDLINK. **Remarks:** Library is headquarters library for the Bureau of Land Management, which is part of the U.S. Department of the Interior. An alternate telephone number is 236-6650.

★14889★
U.S. BUREAU OF LAND MANAGEMENT - MONTANA STATE OFFICE LIBRARY (Env-Cons)
222 N. 32nd St.
Box 36800 Phone: (406)657-6671
Billings, MT 59107 Patricia J. Koch, Lib.Techn.
Founded: 1972. **Staff:** 1. **Subjects:** Water resources, land use, range management, wildlife, coal, minerals. **Special Collections:** Missouri River Basin Reports. **Holdings:** 9000 books. **Subscriptions:** 175 journals and other serials; 8 newspapers. **Services:** Interlibrary loan; copying; library open to the public with restrictions. **Automated Operations:** Computerized cataloging and ILL. **Computerized Information Services:** OCLC. **Networks/Consortia:** Member of FEDLINK, National Natural Resources Library and Information System (NNRLIS).

★14890★
U.S. BUREAU OF LAND MANAGEMENT - NEW MEXICO STATE OFFICE LIBRARY (Env-Cons)
Box 1449 Phone: (505)988-6537
Santa Fe, NM 87504-1449 M. Ferne Bridgford, Mgt.Asst.
Founded: 1967. **Staff:** Prof 2; Other 1. **Subjects:** Management - land resource, wildlife, recreation, minerals, range; environmental protection. **Special Collections:** U.S. Statutes at Large; Interior Board of Land Appeals decisions; Lindley on Mines, Volumes I and II; Environmental Statements. **Holdings:** 7000 books; 500 bound periodical volumes. **Subscriptions:** 50 journals and other serials. **Services:** Interlibrary loan; copying; library open to the public for reference use only. **Computerized Information Services:** Dialcom Inc. (electronic mail service).

★14891★
U.S. BUREAU OF MINES - ALASKA FIELD OPERATIONS CENTER LIBRARY (Energy, Sci-Engr)
Box 020550 Phone: (907)364-2111
Juneau, AK 99802-0550 Helen Jacobson, Lib.Techn.
Staff: 1. **Subjects:** Mining, geology, engineering in Northern Regions, permafrost construction, mineral deposits of Alaska. **Special Collections:** U.S. Geological Survey publications on Alaska; U.S. Bureau of Mines publications; extensive publications on permafrost; state and territory of Alaska publications on mining and minerals. **Holdings:** 5500 volumes; 15,000 documents; 5500 titles on microfilm; 5000 maps. **Subscriptions:** 57 journals and other serials. **Services:** Interlibrary loan; copying; library open to the public. **Special Indexes:** Index of Bureau of Mines Publications on Alaska.

★14892★
U.S. BUREAU OF MINES - ALBANY RESEARCH CENTER LIBRARY (Sci-Engr)
1450 Queen Ave., S.W. Phone: (503)967-5864
Albany, OR 97321-2198 Harry Brooks, Libn.
Staff: Prof 1; Other 1. **Subjects:** Metallurgy, chemistry, physics, chemical engineering, thermodynamics, materials, environmental science. **Holdings:** 10,000 books; 17,000 bound periodical volumes; 16,000 technical reports; 11,000 microfiche. **Subscriptions:** 152 journals and other serials. **Services:** Interlibrary loan; library open to the public for reference use only. **Computerized Information Services:** DIALOG Information Services; internal databases. **Remarks:** An alternate telephone number is 967-5865. Fax: (503)967-5936.

★14893★
U.S. BUREAU OF MINES - AVONDALE RESEARCH CENTER LIBRARY† (Sci-Engr)
4900 La Salle Rd. Phone: (301)436-7552
Avondale, MD 20782 Hoor Siddiqui, Libn.
Founded: 1943. **Staff:** Prof 1; Other 1. **Subjects:** Chemistry, mineral industries, chemical engineering, corrosion, metallurgy, x-ray spectroscopy, recycling of solid wastes, asbestos. **Holdings:** 6751 books; 3835 bound periodical volumes; 179 reels of microfilm. **Subscriptions:** 148 journals and other serials. **Services:** Interlibrary loan; library open to the public. **Computerized Information Services:** DIALOG Information Services.

★14894★
U.S. BUREAU OF MINES - BOEING SERVICES INTERNATIONAL - LIBRARY (Sci-Engr, Energy)
Cochrans Mill Rd.
Box 18070 Phone: (412)675-4431
Pittsburgh, PA 15236 Kathleen M. Stabryla, Lead Libn.
Staff: Prof 3; Other 2. **Subjects:** Coal research, fossil fuels, mining, geology, chemistry. **Special Collections:** U.S. Bureau of Mines publications (complete set). **Holdings:** 165,000 books; 54,000 bound periodical volumes. **Subscriptions:** 250 journals and other serials. **Services:** Interlibrary loan; copying (limited); library open to the public for reference use only. **Computerized Information Services:** DIALOG Information Services. **Networks/Consortia:** Member of Pittsburgh Regional Library Center (PRLC). **Staff:** Bernard Kenney, Br.Libn.; Chia-ling Wu, Libn..

★14895★
U.S. BUREAU OF MINES - BRANCH OF OPERATIONS & SUPPORT - LIBRARY (Sci-Engr)
2401 E St., N.W., Rm. 127
Mail Stop 2150 Phone: (202)634-1116
Washington, DC 20241 Judy C. Jordan, Lib.Techn.
Founded: 1965. **Staff:** Prof 2. **Subjects:** Mineral industry, statistics, and economics. **Special Collections:** Mineral yearbooks, 1925-1984. **Holdings:** 22 VF drawers of clippings; 650 reels of microfilm. **Subscriptions:** 200 journals and other serials. **Services:** Library open to the public for reference use only on request. **Remarks:** The Bureau of Mines is part of the U.S. Department of the Interior.

★14896★
U.S. BUREAU OF MINES - CHARLES W. HENDERSON MEMORIAL LIBRARY (Sci-Engr)
Denver Federal Center, Bldg. 20 Phone: (303)236-0474
Denver, CO 80225 Ann Elizabeth Chapel, Libn.
Founded: 1963. **Staff:** Prof 1. **Subjects:** Mining engineering, economics, research, geology. **Holdings:** 21,000 books; 1380 bound periodical volumes; 2280 maps and charts; 11,100 bulletins; 2270 water supply papers. **Subscriptions:** 60 journals and other serials; 6 newspapers. **Services:** Interlibrary loan; copying; library open to the public with restrictions. **Computerized Information Services:** DIALOG Information Services, OCLC. **Networks/Consortia:** Member of FEDLINK.

★14897★
U.S. BUREAU OF MINES - COMMINUTION CENTER - REFERENCE CENTER (Sci-Engr)
115 EMRO
University of Utah Phone: (801)581-8283
Salt Lake City, UT 84112 Sam Asihene, Info.Off.
Founded: 1982. **Staff:** Prof 3. **Subjects:** Minerals - control, comminution, classification, models, wear. **Holdings:** 200 books and journals; 2000 scientific and technical papers; 2000 abstracts; 33 theses and dissertations on comminution and related subjects; 2 videotapes. **Services:** Copying; center open to the public. **Automated Operations:** Computerized cataloging. **Publications:** Master List; Book of Abstracts,

★14898★
U.S. BUREAU OF MINES - RENO RESEARCH CENTER - LIBRARY (Sci-Engr)
1605 Evans Ave. Phone: (702)784-5348
Reno, NV 89512 Sandy Crews, Lib.Techn.
Staff: Prof 1. **Subjects:** Chemistry, metallurgy, chemical engineering, physics, geology. **Holdings:** 3349 books; 1775 bound periodical volumes; 16,000 reports, manuscripts, documents. **Subscriptions:** 128 journals and other serials. **Services:** Interlibrary loan; copying; library open to the public for reference use only. **Automated Operations:** Computerized cataloging. **Computerized Information Services:** STN International, DIALOG Information Services.

★14899★
U.S. BUREAU OF MINES - ROLLA RESEARCH CENTER - LIBRARY (Sci-Engr)
1300 Bishop Ave.
Box 280
Rolla, MO 65401 Phone: (314)364-3169
Founded: 1921. **Staff:** 1. **Subjects:** Metallurgy and mining research. **Holdings:** 2000 books; 200 bound periodical volumes; 2000 reports; U.S. Bureau of Mines publications. **Subscriptions:** 33 journals and other serials. **Services:** Interlibrary loan; library open to the public for reference use only.

★14900★
U.S. BUREAU OF MINES - SALT LAKE CITY RESEARCH CENTER - LIBRARY (Env-Cons)
729 Arapeen Dr. Phone: (801)524-6112
Salt Lake City, UT 84108 Jean B. Beckstead, Libn.
Staff: 1. **Subjects:** Metallurgy research, natural resources conservation, environmental pollution, engineering, physical sciences. **Special Collections:** Bureau of Mines publications (1311 bound volumes). **Holdings:** 5108 books; 2199 bound periodical volumes; 39 notebooks of patents. **Subscriptions:** 56 journals and other serials. **Services:** Interlibrary loan; library open to the public for reference use only.

★14901★
U.S. BUREAU OF MINES - TUSCALOOSA RESEARCH CENTER - REFERENCE LIBRARY (Sci-Engr, Energy)
University of Alabama
Capstone Dr.
Box L Phone: (205)759-9400
Tuscaloosa, AL 35486-9777 Jean E. Daniel Moss, Ck./Typist
Founded: 1938. **Staff:** 1. **Subjects:** Chemistry, metallurgy, thermodynamics, physical chemistry, ceramics. **Special Collections:** Bureau of Mines publications. **Holdings:** 700 books; 100 bound periodical volumes; 3 drawers of photographs; 1 drawer of microfilm; 1 drawer of tapes. **Subscriptions:** 100 journals and other serials; 7 newspapers. **Services:** Interlibrary loan; library open to the public for reference use only.

★14902★
U.S. BUREAU OF MINES - TWIN CITIES RESEARCH CENTER - LIBRARY (Energy, Sci-Engr)
5629 Minnehaha Ave., S. Phone: (612)725-4503
Minneapolis, MN 55417 Marilynn R. Anderson, Libn.
Staff: Prof 1; Other 1. **Subjects:** Mining engineering, metallurgy, mineral industries, geology, industrial safety, conservation. **Holdings:** 7000 books; 2100 bound periodical volumes; 95 VF drawers of reports, documents, patents. **Subscriptions:** 220 journals and other serials. **Services:** Interlibrary loan; library open to the public. **Computerized Information Services:** FYI News.

★14903★
U.S. BUREAU OF RECLAMATION - ENGINEERING & RESEARCH CENTER - LIBRARY (Sci-Engr)
Denver Federal Center
Box 25007 Phone: (303)236-6963
Denver, CO 80225 Glada Costales, Proj.Mgr.
Founded: 1930. **Staff:** Prof 3; Other 6. **Subjects:** Water resources development; design, construction, and operation of dams, power plants, pumping plants, canals, transmission lines; water quality. **Holdings:** 15,000 books; 14,000 bound periodical volumes; 20,000 archival items; 10,000 specifications; 20,000 internal reports; 10,000 reports on microfilm; 20,000 external reports; Government Publications Office publications. **Subscriptions:** 1000 journals and other serials. **Services:** Interlibrary loan; copying; SDI; library open to the public for reference use only. **Automated Operations:** Computerized cataloging, acquisitions, circulation, and periodical routing. **Computerized Information Services:** DIALOG Information Services, Pergamon ORBIT InfoLine, Inc., Computer Intelligence. **Networks/Consortia:** Member of FEDLINK, Colorado Alliance of Research Libraries (CARL). **Publications:** Recent Library Additions - available on request; reclamation project histories. **Special Catalogs:** Specialized internal reports (online). **Remarks:** The Bureau of Reclamation is part of the U.S. Department of the Interior. **Staff:** Carolyn McNee, Ref.Libn.; Julie Clark, Ref.Libn..

★14904★
U.S. BUREAU OF RECLAMATION - LIBRARY (Sci-Engr)
2800 Cottage Way Phone: (916)978-5158
Sacramento, CA 95825-1898 Linda Lee Temple, Rec.Sect.Chf.
Founded: 1946. **Staff:** Prof 1; Other 1. **Subjects:** Water and water resources, power, agriculture. **Holdings:** 12,000 volumes. **Subscriptions:** 150 journals and other serials. **Services:** Interlibrary loan; copying; library open to the public for reference use only. **Publications:** Accession list, quarterly; magazine list, annual.

★14905★
U.S. BUREAU OF RECLAMATION - TECHNICAL LIBRARY
1404 Colorado St.
Box 427
Boulder City, NV 89005
Subjects: Water and resources development, hydrology, canals and other hydraulic structures, flood control, hydroelectric power, ecology, soils. **Special Collections:** Project histories for the lower Colorado region. **Holdings:** 5000 volumes. **Remarks:** Presently inactive.

★14906★
U.S. CAVALRY MUSEUM - LIBRARY (Mil)
Bldg. 30 Phone: (913)239-2737
Ft. Riley, KS 66442 Terry Van Meter, Musm.Dir.
Staff: 6. **Subjects:** United States cavalry. **Special Collections:** Complete black/white 16mm sound set of 12 cavalry training films, 1940. **Holdings:** Books; annual reports of Secretary of War; Cavalry Journal; photographs; documents. **Services:** Library open to researchers with restrictions.

★14907★
U.S. CENTERS FOR DISEASE CONTROL - CDC INFORMATION CENTER (Med)
1600 Clifton Rd., N.E. Phone: (404)329-3396
Atlanta, GA 30333 Louise W. Lewis, Act.Dir.
Founded: 1947. **Staff:** Prof 6; Other 9. **Subjects:** Communicable diseases, epidemiology, laboratory medicine, medical entomology, microbiology, biochemistry, public health, veterinary medicine, virology. **Holdings:** 84,597 volumes; 130 theses; 2600 U.S. Department of Health and Human Services publications; 82 serial titles on microfilm. **Subscriptions:** 1000 journals and other serials. **Services:** Interlibrary loan; copying; SDI; library open to the public with restrictions. **Automated Operations:** Computerized cataloging and serials. **Computerized Information Services:** BRS Information Technologies, DIALOG Information Services, LEXIS, NEXIS, MEDLINE; internal database. **Networks/Consortia:** Member of FEDLINK, Atlanta Health Science Libraries Consortium, Georgia Health Sciences Library Association (GHSLA). **Publications:** Library Up-Date, quarterly; Serial Holdings, annual. **Remarks:** Maintained by the U.S. Public Health Service. **Staff:** Carole Dean, Asst.Dir./Chf., Tech.Serv.; Susan Wilkin, Chf., Cat.Serv.; Jan Stansell, Chf., Pub.Serv.; Betty Cardell, Acq.; Harriette Morgan, Ser..

★14908★
U.S. CENTERS FOR DISEASE CONTROL - CHAMBLEE FACILITY LIBRARY (Biol Sci, Med)
1600 Clifton Rd., N.E., 30/1321 Phone: (404)452-4167
Atlanta, GA 30333 Pamela A. Martin, Libn.
Staff: Prof 1; Other 2. **Subjects:** Toxicology, clinical chemistry, vector biology and control, parasitic diseases, endocrinology, chronic diseases. **Holdings:** 3000 books; 6800 bound periodical volumes; 687 journal volumes on microfilm; 323 journal volumes on microfiche. **Subscriptions:** 300 journals and other serials. **Services:** Interlibrary loan; library open to the public by appointment. **Automated Operations:** Computerized cataloging, serials, and circulation. **Computerized Information Services:** DIALOG Information Services, BRS Information Technologies, MEDLARS.

U.S. CENTERS FOR DISEASE CONTROL - NATIONAL INSTITUTE FOR OCCUPATIONAL SAFETY & HEALTH
See: U.S. Natl. Institute for Occupational Safety & Health (15206)

★14909★
U.S. CENTERS FOR DISEASE CONTROL - OFFICE ON SMOKING AND HEALTH - TECHNICAL INFORMATION CENTER (Med)
Park Bldg., Rm. 1-16
5600 Fishers Lane Phone: (301)443-1690
Rockville, MD 20857 Susan Hawk, Tech.Info.Off.
Founded: 1965. **Staff:** Prof 3; Other 2. **Subjects:** Smoking and health, tobacco, nicotine, behavioral aspects of smoking, cessation techniques. **Holdings:** 55,000 books, reprints, journal articles, and technical reports. **Subscriptions:** 30 journals and other serials. **Services:** Copying; answers written and telephone requests for information; center open to the public. **Automated Operations:** Computerized cataloging. **Computerized Information Services:** DIALOG Information Services; internal database. **Publications:** Smoking and Health Bulletin, bimonthly; Health Consequences of Smoking, annual; Bibliography on Smoking and Health, annual; Directory of On-Going Research in Smoking and Health, biennial - all available to libraries and professionals. **Remarks:** Center houses the world's leading resource materials on smoking and its effects on health. Center is located at 12420 Parklawn Dr., Rockville, MD 20857. An alternate telephone number is 443-1575.

★14910★
U.S. COAST GUARD - RESEARCH AND DEVELOPMENT CENTER - TECHNICAL INFORMATION CENTER (Sci-Engr)
Avery Point Phone: (203)441-2648
Groton, CT 06340 Martha F. Kendall, Lib.Techn.
Founded: 1979. **Staff:** 1. **Subjects:** Ocean engineering, marine fire research, navigation aids, marine systems, physics and chemistry in marine environment, oil identification, search and rescue, ice technology, solar applications and science. **Holdings:** 1000 books; 1000 reports. **Subscriptions:** 170 journals and other serials; 6 newspapers. **Services:** Interlibrary loan; copying; SDI; center open to the public with permission. **Automated Operations:** Computerized cataloging. **Computerized Information Services:** DIALOG Information Services, NERAC, Inc. **Publications:** Library Update, bimonthly.

★14911★
U.S. COAST GUARD - SUPPORT CENTER LIBRARY (Mil)
Governors Island, Bldg. S251 Phone: (212)668-7394
New York, NY 10004 Bessie Seymour, Libn.
Founded: 1966. **Staff:** Prof 2; Other 1. **Subjects:** Military history, seamanship, U.S. Coast Guard. **Holdings:** 30,000 volumes; phonograph records. **Subscriptions:** 105 journals and other serials. **Services:** Interlibrary loan; library open to the public for reference use only. **Staff:** Anson Huang, Asst.Libn..

★14912★
U.S. COAST GUARD ACADEMY - LIBRARY (Mil)
New London, CT 06320-4195 Phone: (203)444-8510
Paul H. Johnson, Hd.Libn.
Founded: 1876. **Staff:** Prof 5; Other 3. **Subjects:** Coast Guard and Naval history, seafaring, piracy, marine subjects. **Special Collections:** U.S. documents depository. **Holdings:** 147,523 volumes; 20,221 government documents. **Subscriptions:** 533 journals and other serials. **Services:** Interlibrary loan; library open to the public by appointment. **Automated Operations:** Computerized cataloging, serials, and ILL. **Computerized Information Services:** DIALOG Information Services. Performs searches free of charge. **Networks/Consortia:** Member of FEDLINK. **Remarks:** The Coast Guard is part of the U.S. Department of Transportation. **Staff:** Mary A. McKenzie, Hd., Pub.Serv.; Patricia A. Daragan, Hd., Tech.Serv.; Pamela A. McNulty, Ref. & Docs.Libn.; Sheila Lamb, Asst.Tech.Serv. & Ref.Libn..

★14913★
U.S. COAST GUARD/AIR STATION - BASE LIBRARY (Mil)
Bldg. 5205 Phone: (508)968-5456
Otis ANGB, MA 02542 Lisa B. Martin, Libn.
Founded: 1974. **Staff:** Prof 1; Other 1. **Subjects:** U.S. and European history, American literature, military engineering, social sciences, aeronautics, children's literature. **Special Collections:** Air Forces (600 volumes); aeronautics (900 volumes); World War II history (2000 volumes). **Holdings:** 40,000 books; 200 bound periodical volumes; 6 VF drawers of military base information; 3 VF drawers of pamphlets; maps. **Subscriptions:** 60 journals and other serials; 5 newspapers. **Services:** Interlibrary loan; copying; library open to the public. **Publications:** New Books, monthly - for internal distribution only.

U.S. COMMISSION ON CIVIL RIGHTS
See: Commission on Civil Rights (3526)

★14914★
UNITED STATES COMMITTEE FOR REFUGEES - LIBRARY (Soc Sci)
1025 Vermont Ave., N.W. Phone: (202)347-3507
Washington, DC 20005 Roger Winter, Dir.
Subjects: Refugee matters. **Holdings:** Figures not available. **Services:** Telephone referral and response to inquiries; library open to researchers on a limited basis. **Publications:** Refugee Reports (newsletter), monthly - by subscription; World Refugee Survey, annual; periodic issue papers - free upon request. **Remarks:** United States Committee for Refugees is the publications and public information program of American Council for Nationalities Service, a private, nonprofit organization.

★14915★
U.S. COMMITTEE FOR UNICEF - INFORMATION CENTER ON CHILDREN'S CULTURES (Soc Sci)
331 E. 38th St. Phone: (212)686-5522
New York, NY 10016 Melinda Greenblatt, Chf.Libn.
Founded: 1968. **Staff:** Prof 2; Other 2. **Subjects:** Children in Asia, Africa, the Caribbean, the Pacific, the Middle East, and Latin America and their primary school texts, literature, education, social life, customs, festivals, games. **Holdings:** 18,000 books; 100 boxes of reports, booklists, pamphlets; 3500 pictures by children; 15,200 photographs of children; 445 phonograph records; 445 filmstrips; 110 films. **Subscriptions:** 50 journals and other serials. **Services:** Interlibrary loan; copying; center open to the public. **Publications:** Bibliographies of children's books about countries in Asia, Africa, Latin America, the Pacific, the Caribbean, and the Middle East. **Staff:** Janet Smith, Adm.Asst..

★14916★
U.S. COMPTROLLER OF THE CURRENCY - LIBRARY (Bus-Fin)
490 L'Enfant Plaza, S.W., 5th Fl. Phone: (202)447-1843
Washington, DC 20219 Robert A. Updegrove, Adm.Libn.
Founded: 1974. **Staff:** Prof 2; Other 4. **Subjects:** Law, banking, economics. **Holdings:** 43,500 volumes. **Subscriptions:** 500 journals and other serials; 12

newspapers. **Services:** Interlibrary loan; library open to the public with restrictions. **Automated Operations:** Computerized cataloging and serials. **Computerized Information Services:** DIALOG Information Services, WESTLAW, NEXIS, OCLC. **Networks/Consortia:** Member of FEDLINK. **Publications:** Recent Acquisitions and Journal Articles, monthly - to other banking libraries. **Remarks:** The Comptroller of the Currency is part of the U.S. Department of the Treasury. **Staff:** Kristine Klein, Asst.Libn..

U.S. CONGRESS - CONGRESSIONAL BUDGET OFFICE
See: Congressional Budget Office (3636)

U.S. CONGRESS - HOUSE OF REPRESENTATIVES
See: U.S. House of Representatives (15137)

U.S. CONGRESS - OFFICE OF TECHNOLOGY ASSESSMENT
See: U.S. Office of Technology Assessment (15477)

U.S. CONGRESS - SENATE
See: U.S. Senate (15493)

U.S. CONSUMER PRODUCT SAFETY COMMISSION
See: Consumer Product Safety Commission (3703)

★14917★
U.S. COUNCIL FOR ENERGY AWARENESS - LIBRARY (Energy)
1776 I St., N.W., Suite 400 Phone: (202)872-1280
Washington, DC 20006 Patricia J. Goldman, Mgr.
Founded: 1954. **Staff:** Prof 1; Other 1. **Subjects:** Nuclear energy, environment, waste management, nuclear regulation. **Holdings:** 2500 books; 5000 technical reports. **Subscriptions:** 200 journals and other serials; 5 newspapers. **Services:** Interlibrary loan; library open to association members. **Computerized Information Services:** FYI News. **Formerly:** Atomic Industrial Forum.

★14918★
U.S. COURT OF APPEALS, 1ST CIRCUIT - LIBRARY (Law)
1208 U.S. Post Office & Courthouse Phone: (617)223-9044
Boston, MA 02109 Karen M. Moss, Circuit Libn.
Founded: 1927. **Staff:** Prof 3; Other 2. **Subjects:** Federal law, administrative material. **Special Collections:** Selective U.S. Government depository; slip opinions of all U.S. Courts of Appeals. **Holdings:** 50,000 books; 3000 bound periodical volumes; 2000 unbound reports; 26 drawers of microfilm; 40 drawers of microfiche; Code of Federal Regulations; Federal Register and Congressional Record in microform. **Subscriptions:** 136 journals and other serials; 5 newspapers. **Services:** Interlibrary loan (to Boston area law libraries); library open to members of the bar. **Automated Operations:** Computerized cataloging. **Computerized Information Services:** WESTLAW, LEXIS, DIALOG Information Services, OCLC. **Networks/Consortia:** Member of NELINET, FEDLINK. **Staff:** Susan Lee, Tech.Serv.Libn.; Kristie Randall, Ref.Libn..

★14919★
U.S. COURT OF APPEALS, 2ND CIRCUIT - LIBRARY (Law)
U.S. Court House, Rm. 2501, Foley Square
40 Centre St. Phone: (212)791-1052
New York, NY 10007 Margaret J. Evans, Circuit Libn.
Founded: 1917. **Staff:** Prof 5; Other 6. **Subjects:** Law. **Special Collections:** Legislative and judiciary history. **Holdings:** 100,000 books; 4500 bound periodical volumes. **Subscriptions:** 138 journals and other serials; 5 newspapers. **Services:** Library open to the public with librarian's permission. **Automated Operations:** Computerized cataloging. **Computerized Information Services:** LEXIS, DIALOG Information Services, OCLC, WESTLAW. **Networks/Consortia:** Member of FEDLINK. **Publications:** Acquisitions List and Comments; Library Report Letter. **Special Indexes:** Index to Second Circuit Slip Opinions (looseleaf). **Staff:** John F. Necci, Dp. Circuit Libn.; Stephanie Jones, CALR Coord.; Philip Becker, Ref.Libn..

★14920★
U.S. COURT OF APPEALS, 3RD CIRCUIT - BRANCH LIBRARY (Law)
U.S. Courthouse
844 King St.
Box 43 Phone: (302)573-6178
Wilmington, DE 19801 Shirley C. Harrison, Libn.
Founded: 1974. **Staff:** Prof 2. **Subjects:** Law. **Holdings:** 15,000 books and bound periodical volumes. **Staff:** Judith F. Ambler, Asst.Libn..

★14921★
U.S. COURT OF APPEALS, 3RD CIRCUIT - BRANCH LIBRARY (Law)
U.S. Post Office & Court House
Box 1068 Phone: (201)645-3034
Newark, NJ 07101 Andrea Battel, Libn.
Founded: 1975. **Staff:** Prof 2; Other 1. **Subjects:** Law. **Holdings:** 22,000 volumes. **Subscriptions:** 30 journals and other serials. **Services:** Copying; library open to members of the bar and pro se litigants. **Computerized Information Services:** LEXIS, WESTLAW. **Special Catalogs:** Case name files for slip opinions from the U.S. Court of Appeals, 3rd Circuit and the U.S. District Court for the District of New Jersey. **Staff:** Dorothy Cordo, Lib.Techn..

★14922★
U.S. COURT OF APPEALS, 3RD CIRCUIT - LIBRARY (Law)
22409 U.S. Court House
601 Market St. Phone: (215)597-2009
Philadelphia, PA 19106 Dorothy A. Cozzolino, Circuit Libn.
Staff: Prof 4; Other 3. **Subjects:** Law. **Holdings:** 70,000 books; 4000 bound periodical volumes. **Subscriptions:** 80 journals and other serials. **Services:** Interlibrary loan (limited); copying; library open to the public with approval of librarian. **Staff:** Katherine Cater, Deputy Circuit Libn..

★14923★
U.S. COURT OF APPEALS, 3RD CIRCUIT - PITTSBURGH BRANCH LIBRARY (Law)
512 U.S. Courthouse Phone: (412)644-6485
Pittsburgh, PA 15219 Linda Schneider, Libn.
Staff: Prof 2; Other 1. **Subjects:** Law - U.S., Pennsylvania, New Jersey, Virgin Islands, Delaware. **Holdings:** 22,000 books; 1100 bound periodical volumes. **Subscriptions:** 85 journals and other serials; 6 newspapers. **Services:** Interlibrary loan; copying; library open to the public. **Computerized Information Services:** LEXIS, WESTLAW. **Special Indexes:** Western District of Pennsylvania Opinions (by case name and subject; card); Middle District of Pennsylvania Opinions (by case name and subject; card). **Staff:** Barbara Alexander, Asst.Libn..

★14924★
U.S. COURT OF APPEALS, 4TH CIRCUIT - LIBRARY (Law)
U.S. Courthouse, Rm. 424
Tenth & Main Sts. Phone: (804)771-2219
Richmond, VA 23219 Peter A. Frey, Circuit Libn.
Founded: 1891. **Staff:** Prof 4; Other 4. **Subjects:** Law. **Holdings:** 60,000 volumes. **Services:** Interlibrary loan; copying; library open to judiciary and members of the bar. **Computerized Information Services:** LEXIS, WESTLAW. **Staff:** Elaine H. Woodward, Tech.Serv.Libn.; Alyene H. McClure, Asst.Libn.; Elizabeth Bilyeu, Asst.Libn..

★14925★
U.S. COURT OF APPEALS, 5TH CIRCUIT - LIBRARY (Law)
600 Camp St., Rm. 106 Phone: (504)589-6510
New Orleans, LA 70130 Kay E. Duley, Circuit Libn.
Staff: Prof 3; Other 5. **Subjects:** Law. **Holdings:** 50,000 books; 200 bound periodical volumes; microfiche. **Services:** Interlibrary loan; copying; library open to the public. **Automated Operations:** Computerized cataloging. **Computerized Information Services:** OCLC, LEXIS, WESTLAW, DIALOG Information Services. Performs limited searches free of charge. **Networks/Consortia:** Member of FEDLINK. **Staff:** Cassandra Dover, Asst.Libn.; Vic Buccola, Asst.Libn..

★14926★
U.S. COURT OF APPEALS, 6TH CIRCUIT - LIBRARY (Law)
617 U.S. Court House & Post Office Bldg. Phone: (513)684-2678
Cincinnati, OH 45202 Kathy Joyce Welker, Circuit Libn.
Founded: 1894. **Staff:** Prof 3; Other 3. **Subjects:** Law. **Holdings:** 60,000 volumes. **Services:** Library open to attorneys only. **Automated Operations:** Computerized cataloging and acquisitions. **Computerized Information Services:** WESTLAW, DIALOG Information Services, BRS Information Technologies, NEXIS, LEXIS. **Special Indexes:** Index of Sixth Circuit Published Opinions. **Staff:** Pamela Schaffner, Dp.Libn.; James Voelker, Ref.Libn..

★14927★
U.S. COURT OF APPEALS, 8TH CIRCUIT - BRANCH LIBRARY (Law)
Post Office and Courthouse
600 W. Capitol, Rm. 224 Phone: (501)378-5039
Little Rock, AR 72201 Allison P. Mays, Br.Libn.
Founded: 1981. **Staff:** Prof 1. **Subjects:** Law. **Holdings:** 10,000 books; 500 bound periodical volumes; 100 other cataloged items. **Subscriptions:** 50 journals and other serials. **Services:** Interlibrary loan; copying; library open to members of the federal bar. **Automated Operations:** Computerized cataloging. **Computerized Information Services:** WESTLAW, LEXIS.

★14928★
U.S. COURT OF APPEALS, 8TH CIRCUIT - LIBRARY (Law)
U.S. Court House
811 Grand Ave., Rm. 805 Phone: (816)374-2937
Kansas City, MO 64106 Margaret Tranne Pearce, Libn.
Subjects: Law. **Holdings:** 20,000 volumes. **Services:** Library open to members of the bar.

★14929★
U.S. COURT OF APPEALS, 8TH CIRCUIT - LIBRARY (Law)
U.S. Court & Customs House, Rm. 503
1114 Market St. Phone: (314)425-4930
St. Louis, MO 63101 Ann T. Fessenden, Circuit Libn.
Staff: Prof 4; Other 3. **Subjects:** Law. **Holdings:** 25,000 books; 1000 bound periodical volumes. **Subscriptions:** 91 journals and other serials. **Services:** Interlibrary loan; copying; library open to government attorneys, members of the federal bar, and to the public with permission. **Automated Operations:** Computerized cataloging. **Computerized Information Services:** WESTLAW, LEXIS, NEXIS, OCLC. **Networks/Consortia:** Member of FEDLINK. **Remarks:** Branch libraries are located in Little Rock, AR; St. Paul, MN; Omaha, NE; Des Moines, IA; Kansas City, MO; Minneapolis, MN; Fargo, ND. **Staff:** Mary Kay Jung, Dp. Circuit Libn.; Kirk Gregory, Ref.Libn.; Mary Fulghum, Comp.Res.Libn..

★14930★
U.S. COURT OF APPEALS, 8TH CIRCUIT - RESEARCH LIBRARY (Law)
590 Federal Bldg.
316 N. Robert St. Phone: (612)290-3177
St. Paul, MN 55101 Kathryn C. Kratz, Br.Libn.
Staff: 1. **Subjects:** Legal research topics. **Holdings:** 14,000 volumes. **Services:** Interlibrary loan; copying; library open to the public. **Computerized Information Services:** WESTLAW, NEXIS.

★14931★
U.S. COURT OF APPEALS, 9TH CIRCUIT - LIBRARY (Law)
709 W. 9th St.
Box 020349
Juneau, AK 99802 Phone: (907)586-7458
Subjects: Law. **Holdings:** 7000 volumes. **Services:** Library open to attorneys and law students.

★14932★
U.S. COURT OF APPEALS, 9TH CIRCUIT - LIBRARY (Law)
U.S. Courthouse, Rm. 6434
230 N. First Ave. Phone: (602)261-3879
Phoenix, AZ 85025-0074 Delores E. Daniels, Libn.
Staff: Prof 2; Other 2. **Subjects:** Law. **Special Collections:** U.S. Government documents depository. **Holdings:** 24,000 books; 1400 bound periodical volumes. **Subscriptions:** 900 journals and other serials; 7 newspapers. **Services:** Interlibrary loan; library open to the public. **Computerized Information Services:** OCLC, LEXIS, WESTLAW. **Networks/Consortia:** Member of FEDLINK. **Publications:** Library Guide, annual - for internal distribution only. **Staff:** Richard Wiebelhaus, Asst.Libn.; Evelyn Rayburn, Govt.Docs..

★14933★
U.S. COURT OF APPEALS, 9TH CIRCUIT - LIBRARY (Law)
1702 U.S. Courthouse
312 N. Spring St. Phone: (213)894-3636
Los Angeles, CA 90012 Joanne Mazza, Libn.
Staff: Prof 2; Other 2. **Subjects:** Law. **Holdings:** 34,000 books; 51,330 microfiche. **Services:** Interlibrary loan; library open to the public for reference use only. **Computerized Information Services:** WESTLAW, LEXIS, OCLC.

★14934★
U.S. COURT OF APPEALS, 9TH CIRCUIT - LIBRARY (Law)
125 S. Grand Ave. Phone: (818)405-7020
Pasadena, CA 91105 Evelyn K. Brandt, Libn.
Founded: 1985. **Staff:** Prof 1; Other 1. **Subjects:** Law. **Holdings:** 16,852 books; 1521 bound periodical volumes; 46,518 microfiche and ultrafiche. **Subscriptions:** 498 journals and other serials; 7 newspapers. **Services:** Library open to the public with restrictions. **Computerized Information Services:** WESTLAW, LEXIS. **Publications:** BiblioVista, quarterly - for internal distribution only. **Special Indexes:** Index to the Published Decisions & Orders of the Ninth Circuit (card).

★14935★
U.S. COURT OF APPEALS, 9TH CIRCUIT - LIBRARY (Law)
Box 5731 Phone: (415)556-6129
San Francisco, CA 94101 Francis Gates, Circuit Libn.
Staff: Prof 5; Other 3. **Subjects:** Law. **Holdings:** 66,099 volumes; 150,669 microforms. **Subscriptions:** 430 journals and other serials. **Services:** Interlibrary loan; library open to the public with restrictions. **Automated Operations:** Computerized cataloging. **Computerized Information Services:** LEXIS, WESTLAW, InfoTrac, NEXIS, DIALOG Information Services. **Special Indexes:** Index to current 9th Circuit opinions. **Staff:** Sue Welsh, Dp. Circuit Libn.; Deborah Celle, Hd., Tech.Serv.; Emily Matteucci, Asst.Libn..

★14936★
U.S. COURT OF APPEALS, 9TH CIRCUIT - LIBRARY (Law)
Pioneer Courthouse Phone: (503)221-6042
Portland, OR 97204 Scott M. McCurdy, Libn.
Staff: Prof 2. **Subjects:** Law. **Holdings:** 13,000 books; 400 bound periodical volumes. **Services:** Interlibrary loan; copying; library open to attorneys on day of court proceedings. **Computerized Information Services:** WESTLAW, LEXIS. **Staff:** Dianne Schauer, Asst.Libn..

★14937★
U.S. COURT OF APPEALS, 9TH CIRCUIT - LIBRARY (Law)
1018 U.S. Courthouse
1010 5th Ave. Phone: (206)442-4475
Seattle, WA 98104 Deborah Norwood
Founded: 1939. **Staff:** Prof 2; Other 2. **Subjects:** Law. **Holdings:** 19,900 books; 65,000 microfiche. **Subscriptions:** 1000 journals and other serials. **Services:** Library open to the public for reference use only. **Computerized Information Services:** WESTLAW, LEXIS.

★14938★
U.S. COURT OF APPEALS, 10TH CIRCUIT - LIBRARY (Law)
U.S. Court House, Rm. C 411 Phone: (303)844-3591
Denver, CO 80294 J. Terry Hemming, Circuit Libn.
Staff: Prof 4; Other 2. **Subjects:** Law. **Holdings:** 28,000 volumes. **Services:** Interlibrary loan; copying; library open to the public. **Automated Operations:** Computerized cataloging. **Computerized Information Services:** LEXIS, WESTLAW. **Staff:** Loretta Nolin, CALR Libn.; Catherine McGuire Eason, Dp. Circuit Libn.; Carol Minor, Tech.Serv.Libn..

★14939★
U.S. COURT OF APPEALS, 10TH CIRCUIT - OKLAHOMA CITY GENERAL LIBRARY (Law)
200 N.W. 4th St. Phone: (405)231-4866
Oklahoma City, OK 73102 Sharon Watts, Sec.
Staff: Prof 1. **Subjects:** Law. **Special Collections:** Unpublished opinions of the Tenth Circuit. **Holdings:** U.S. code and statutes at large; law reviews and digests. **Services:** Library open to the public for reference use only.

★14940★
U.S. COURT OF APPEALS, 11TH CIRCUIT - LIBRARY (Law)
56 Forsyth St., N.W. Phone: (404)331-2510
Atlanta, GA 30303 Elaine P. Fenton, Circuit Libn.
Staff: Prof 4; Other 2. **Subjects:** Law. **Holdings:** 25,000 books; 5000 bound periodical volumes; 15 cabinets of microforms. **Subscriptions:** 200 journals and other serials; 6 newspapers. **Services:** Interlibrary loan; library open to attorneys only. **Automated Operations:** Computerized cataloging. **Computerized Information Services:** WESTLAW, LEXIS, NEXIS, DIALOG Information Services, VU/TEXT Information Services, OCLC. **Networks/Consortia:** Member of FEDLINK. **Staff:** Sara M. Straub, Dp. Circuit Libn.; Sue T. Lee, Ref.Libn.; Judith F. Newsom, Tech.Serv.Libn..

★14941★
U.S. COURT OF APPEALS, DISTRICT OF COLUMBIA CIRCUIT - LIBRARY (Law)
5518 U.S. Court House
3rd & Constitution Ave., N.W. Phone: (202)535-3400
Washington, DC 20001 Nancy Lazar, Circuit Libn.
Staff: Prof 4. **Subjects:** Law. **Holdings:** 120,000 volumes. **Subscriptions:** 200 journals and other serials; 7 newspapers. **Services:** Copying; library open to the public with permission of librarian. **Staff:** Theresa Santella, Dp. Circuit Libn.; William Stockey, Asst.Libn., Tech.Serv.; Linda Baltrusch, Asst.Libn..

★14942★
U.S. COURT OF APPEALS FOR THE FEDERAL CIRCUIT - NATIONAL COURTS' LIBRARY (Law)
717 Madison Pl., N.W., Rm. 218 Phone: (202)633-5871
Washington, DC 20439 Patricia M. McDermott, Libn.
Staff: Prof 2; Other 2. **Subjects:** Law, taxation, government contracts, patents and trademarks, customs, international trade. **Holdings:** 36,263 books. **Subscriptions:** 90 journals and other serials; 6 newspapers. **Services:** Interlibrary loan; copying; library open to members of the Courts' Bar. **Automated Operations:** Computerized cataloging. **Computerized Information Services:** WESTLAW, LEXIS, NEXIS, LEGI-SLATE, VERALEX. **Networks/Consortia:** Member of FEDLINK. **Staff:** David J. Lockwood, Asst.Libn..

★14943★
U.S. COURT OF INTERNATIONAL TRADE - LAW LIBRARY (Law)
One Federal Plaza Phone: (212)264-2816
New York, NY 10007 Simone-Marie Kleckner, Law Libn.
Founded: 1926. **Staff:** Prof 2; Other 3. **Subjects:** Law, customs, tariff, international trade, science and technology. **Special Collections:** Customs laws and procedures (3000 volumes); legislative histories of custom and trade laws; tariff schedules. **Holdings:** 50,000 volumes; 8700 bound periodical volumes; 8000 government documents; 12 VF drawers of pamphlets; microfiche. **Subscriptions:** 100 journals and other serials; 9 newspapers. **Services:** Interlibrary loan; copying; library open to the public by appointment. **Automated Operations:** Computerized cataloging. **Computerized Information Services:** LEXIS, NEXIS, OCLC. **Networks/Consortia:** Member of FEDLINK. **Publications:** U.S. Court of International Trade reports, annual - for sale; Test Case List. **Staff:** Ella Lidsky, Asst.Libn..

★14944★
U.S. COURT OF MILITARY APPEALS - LIBRARY (Law, Mil)
450 E St., N.W. Phone: (202)272-1466
Washington, DC 20442 Mary S. Kuck, Libn.
Founded: 1952. **Staff:** Prof 2. **Subjects:** Law - military, criminal, evidence, international. **Special Collections:** Air Force, Army, Navy, and Marine Corps regulations pertaining to military justice. **Holdings:** 19,000 volumes. **Subscriptions:** 60 journals and other serials. **Services:** Interlibrary loan; library open to the public for reference use only on request. **Staff:** Agnes Kiang, Asst.Libn..

★14945★
U.S. CUSTOMS SERVICE - LIBRARY AND INFORMATION CENTER (Law)
1301 Constitution Ave., N.W., Rm. 3340 Phone: (202)566-5642
Washington, DC 20229 Patricia M. Dobrosky, Dir.
Founded: 1975. **Staff:** Prof 5; Other 4. **Subjects:** Law, law enforcement, economics, international trade, drugs. **Holdings:** 42,000 volumes. **Subscriptions:** 600 journals and other serials. **Services:** Interlibrary loan; copying; SDI; library open to the public for reference use only. **Automated Operations:** Computerized cataloging and acquisitions. **Computerized Information Services:** DIALOG Information Services, LEXIS, NEXIS, LEGI-SLATE, WESTLAW, OCLC. **Networks/Consortia:** Member of FEDLINK, Metropolitan Washington Library Council. **Publications:** Media Varia. **Remarks:** The Customs Service is part of the U.S. Department of the Treasury. **Staff:** Martha Glock, User Serv.Libn.; Cecilia Hlatshwayo, Bus. & Econ.Libn..

★14946★
U.S. DEFENSE COMMUNICATIONS AGENCY - TECHNICAL AND MANAGEMENT INFORMATION CENTER (Comp Sci, Info Sci)
Headquarters, DCA, Code H396 Phone: (202)692-2468
Washington, DC 20305 Donald A. Guerriero, Lib.Dir.
Founded: 1974. **Staff:** Prof 6. **Subjects:** Telecommunications, computer science, systems analysis, operations research, management. **Holdings:** 10,000 books; 1500 technical reports. **Subscriptions:** 500 journals and other serials. **Services:** Interlibrary loan (limited); center not open to the public. **Automated Operations:** Computerized cataloging, acquisitions, and serials. **Computerized Information Services:** OCLC, DIALOG Information Services, DTIC, Pergamon ORBIT InfoLine, Inc., BRS Information Technologies. **Networks/Consortia:** Member of FEDLINK. **Remarks:** Serves headquarters and field agencies of the Defense Communications Agency (DCA). Center located in Arlington, VA with a branch in Reston, VA. The Defense Communications Agency is part of the U.S. Department of Defense. **Staff:** Grace Aitel, Libn.; Margaret Martinez, Libn.; Joan Brassfield, Libn.; Mary Jane Steele, Libn.; Roberta Babbitt, Libn.; Marilyn Valone, Libn..

★14947★
U.S. DEFENSE INTELLIGENCE AGENCY - LIBRARY RTS-2A (Mil)
Washington, DC 20340-3342 Phone: (202)373-3775
W. Crislip, Chf.Libn.
Founded: 1963. **Staff:** Prof 21; Other 19. **Subjects:** Intelligence - armed forces, transportation, political, scientific and technical, economic, sociological; communications and electronics. **Special Collections:** Intelligence reports, documents, periodicals, video cassettes. **Holdings:** 85,000 books; 100,000 reports; 50,000 translations; 1.5 million microfiche; 2.5 million unbound reports; 1000 video cassettes. **Subscriptions:** 1500 journals and other serials. **Services:** Interlibrary loan; library not open to the public but public information act requests are satisfied. **Automated Operations:** Computerized cataloging, acquisitions, serials, and circulation. **Computerized Information Services:** DIALOG Information Services, Pergamon ORBIT InfoLine, Inc., NEXIS, OCLC, NewsNet, Inc. **Networks/Consortia:** Member of FEDLINK. **Remarks:** The Defense Intelligence Agency is part of the U.S. Department of Defense.

★14948★
U.S. DEFENSE LOGISTICS AGENCY - DEFENSE CONSTRUCTION SUPPLY CENTER (Sci-Engr)
Box 3990
ATTN: DCSC-SDA Phone: (614)238-3549
Columbus, OH 43216-5000 Norma J. Watkins, Chf.
Staff: 16. **Holdings:** Specifications; manufacturers' catalogs; government specifications and standards. **Services:** Center not open to the public.

★14949★
U.S. DEFENSE LOGISTICS AGENCY - DEFENSE CONTRACT ADMINISTRATION SERVICES OF MILWAUKEE AREA - LIBRARY (Mil)
310 W. Wisconsin Ave., Suite 340 Phone: (414)291-4327
Milwaukee, WI 53203 Nancy J. Slowinski, QA Data Ck.
Founded: 1965. **Staff:** 2. **Holdings:** Microfilm library of military standards; QPL qualified products lists; manufacturers' code books and miscellaneous publications. **Services:** Library open to the public for reference use only. **Automated Operations:** Computerized cataloging. **Computerized Information Services:** Online systems. Performs searches free of charge.

★14950★
U.S. DEFENSE LOGISTICS AGENCY - DEFENSE GENERAL SUPPLY CENTER - CENTER LIBRARY (Mil)
Richmond, VA 23297 Phone: (804)275-3215
Yvonne H. Oakley, Ctr.Libn.
Staff: Prof 1. **Subjects:** Management, military science, economics, political science. **Holdings:** 6228 volumes; 280 boxes of unbound magazines; operating regulations and manuals. **Subscriptions:** 38 journals and other serials; 9 newspapers. **Services:** Interlibrary loan; library open to the public with restrictions. **Computerized Information Services:** OCLC, BRS Information Technologies. **Special Catalogs:** Library shelf list handbook.

★14951★
U.S. DEFENSE LOGISTICS AGENCY - DEFENSE INDUSTRIAL SUPPLY CENTER - TECHNICAL DATA MANAGEMENT DIVISION (Sci-Engr)
700 Robbins Ave. Phone: (215)697-2757
Philadelphia, PA 19111 Nancy J. Popson, Chf.
Founded: 1961. **Staff:** 80. **Subjects:** Industrial metals, plastics, and synthetic rubbers; engineering; management; industrial and general hardware. **Holdings:** 2000 books; 1.7 million aperture cards of manufacturers' drawings; 20,000 manufacturers' catalogs; 30,000 industry standards; 35,000 government specifications and standards; cartridge film file. **Services:** Division not open to the public.

★14952★
U.S. DEFENSE LOGISTICS AGENCY - DEFENSE LOGISTICS SERVICES CENTER - LIBRARY (Mil, Comp Sci)
Federal Ctr.
74 N. Washington St. Phone: (616)961-4957
Battle Creek, MI 49017-3084 Anna K. Winger, Libn.
Founded: 1962. **Staff:** Prof 1. **Subjects:** Electronic data processing, adult education, management. **Holdings:** 3700 books; 363 government documents. **Subscriptions:** 174 journals and other serials. **Services:** Interlibrary loan; library open to the public for reference use only. **Automated Operations:** Computerized cataloging. **Computerized Information Services:** OCLC, BRS Information Technologies. **Networks/ Consortia:** Member of FEDLINK.

★14953★
U.S. DEFENSE LOGISTICS AGENCY - DEFENSE PERSONNEL SUPPORT CENTER - DIRECTORATE OF MEDICAL MATERIEL TECHNICAL LIBRARY (Med, Sci-Engr)
2800 S. 20th St., Bldg. 9-3-F Phone: (215)952-2110
Philadelphia, PA 19101-8419 Ann Cline Tobin, Libn.
Founded: 1952. **Staff:** Prof 1. **Subjects:** Medicine, pharmacy, engineering. **Holdings:** 5875 books; 1500 bound periodical volumes; 1500 manufacturers' catalogs; 300 documents; 45 reels of microfilm of periodicals; 40 pharmaceutical tapes; military and federal specifications and American Society for Testing and Materials (ASTM) standards on microfilm. **Subscriptions:** 55 journals and other serials. **Services:** Interlibrary loan; library not open to the public. **Publications:** Directorate of Medical Materiel, monthly - for internal distribution only. **Special Catalogs:** Document file holdings; manufacturers' catalogs holdings (both on cards).

★14954★
U.S. DEFENSE LOGISTICS AGENCY - HEADQUARTERS LIBRARY (Mil, Comp Sci)
Cameron Sta., Rm. 4D120 Phone: (202)274-6055
Alexandria, VA 22304-6100 Barbara Federline, Chf.Libn.
Founded: 1962. **Subjects:** Management, automatic data processing. **Special Collections:** Military regulations (5000 items). **Holdings:** 8300 books; 300,000 microforms. **Subscriptions:** 290 journals and other serials. **Services:** Interlibrary loan; library open to the public by permission. **Automated Operations:** Computerized cataloging, serials, and circulation. **Computerized Information Services:** OCLC, FYI News, EasyNet, DIALOG Information Services, WESTLAW, LEGI-SLATE, Dun & Bradstreet Corporation, EBSCO Subscription Services, The Faxon Company, University Microfilms International (UMI), DTIC, Haystack. **Networks/Consortia:** Member of FEDLINK. **Remarks:** The Defense Logistics Agency is part of the U.S. Department of Defense. **Staff:** Barbara Sable, Asst.Libn..

★14955★
U.S. DEFENSE MAPPING AGENCY - AEROSPACE CENTER - TECHNICAL LIBRARY (Sci-Engr, Comp Sci)
3200 S. Second St. Phone: (314)263-4267
St. Louis, MO 63118-3399 Margaret Mechanic, Chf.
Founded: 1943. **Subjects:** Geodesy, computer science, earth sciences, astronomy, mathematics, management. **Holdings:** 17,000 books; 8000 scientific-technical reports. **Subscriptions:** 520 journals and other serials. **Services:** Interlibrary loan; library not open to the public. **Computerized Information Services:** DTIC, OCLC, DIALOG Information Services. **Staff:** Barbara Bick, Acq..

★14956★
U.S. DEFENSE MAPPING AGENCY - HYDROGRAPHIC/ TOPOGRAPHIC CENTER - SUPPORT DIVISION - SCIENTIFIC DATA DEPARTMENT (Geog-Map)
6500 Brookes Lane Phone: (301)227-2080
Washington, DC 20315 Frank Lozupone, Chf., Sup.Div.
Founded: 1871. **Staff:** Prof 65; Other 30. **Subjects:** Topography, cartography, hydrography, bathymetry, geodesy, toponomy. **Special Collections:** Department of Defense libraries of maps, geodetic data, foreign place names, nautical charts, bathymetric data. **Holdings:** 80,000 books, periodicals, documents; 500,000 maps; 25,000 charts; 4.5 million place names; 50,000 bathymetric surveys. **Services:** Interlibrary loan (limited); library not open to the public. **Automated Operations:** Computerized cataloging. **Computerized Information Services:** DIALOG Information Services, Pergamon ORBIT InfoLine, Inc.; internal databases. **Publications:** Biweekly accessions listings. **Remarks:** The Defense Mapping Agency is part of the U.S. Department of Defense. **Staff:** Maurice S. Stuckey, Chf., Sci. Data Dept..

U.S. DEFENSE NUCLEAR AGENCY - ARMED FORCES RADIOBIOLOGY RESEARCH INSTITUTE (AFRRI)
See: U.S. Armed Forces Radiobiology Research Institute (AFRRI) (14701)

★14957★
U.S. DEFENSE NUCLEAR AGENCY - TECHNICAL LIBRARY (Sci-Engr)
Washington, DC 20305-1000 Phone: (202)325-7780
Sandra E. Young, Asst.Dir., Tech.Info.
Founded: 1947. **Staff:** Prof 4; Other 6. **Subjects:** Nuclear science and technology, nuclear weapons effects. **Holdings:** 10,000 volumes; 125,000 technical reports. **Subscriptions:** 300 journals and other serials. **Services:** Interlibrary loan; library not open to the public. **Automated Operations:** Computerized cataloging and circulation. **Computerized Information Services:** NEXIS, DIALOG Information Services, DTIC. **Remarks:** The Defense Nuclear Agency is part of the U.S. Department of Defense. **Staff:** Ethel D. Scaccio, Hd., Doc.Anl.; Albert G. West, Hd., Tech.Lib.Serv..

★14958★
U.S. DEFENSE TECHNICAL INFORMATION CENTER (Sci-Engr, Info Sci)
Cameron Sta. Phone: (202)274-7633
Alexandria, VA 22304-6145 Kurt N. Molholm, Adm.
Staff: 450. **Subjects:** All areas of science and technology. **Holdings:** 1.7 million reports of Department of Defense research, development, testing, and evaluation. **Services:** Document announcement; secondary distribution of paper and microform copies of documents; specialized bibliographies; current awareness; cumulated indexes; defense management information databases (current work and program planning summaries). **Computerized Information Services:** Operates the Defense Research, Development, Test and Evaluation Online System (DROLS). **Publications:** Technical Reports Awareness Circular (TRAC), monthly; DROLS News, irregular; Defense Technical Information Center Digest, quarterly; bibliographies. **Remarks:** Services of the center are available only to Department of Defense activities, other federal government organizations, their contractors, subcontractors, and grantees. Center is sponsored by the U.S. Department of Defense. Further information available from Reference Services Branch or Office of User Services and Marketing. An alternate telephone number is 274-6434. **Also Known As:** DTIC.

★14959★
U.S. DEFENSE TECHNICAL INFORMATION CENTER - DTIC ON-LINE SERVICE FACILITY (Mil)
222 N. Sepulveda Blvd. Phone: (213)335-4170
El Segundo, CA 90245-4320 Carol D. Finney, Mgr.
Staff: Prof 2. **Subjects:** Research and development funded by the U.S. Department of Defense. **Special Collections:** Information Analysis Center collections. **Holdings:** 2 million documents. **Services:** Facility open to government agencies and U.S. Department of Defense registered and potential registered contractors. **Computerized Information Services:** DTIC. **Publications:** Technical Reports Announcement Circular (TRAC), bimonthly. **Special Indexes:** TRAC Indexes, bimonthly and annual (microfiche). **Staff:** L.A. Ames, Tech.Info.Spec..

★14960★
U.S. DEFENSE TECHNICAL INFORMATION CENTER - TECHNICAL LIBRARY (Sci-Engr, Comp Sci)
Cameron Sta., Bldg. 5 Phone: (202)274-6833
Alexandria, VA 22304-6145 Dominic N.C. Bui, Libn.
Founded: 1958. **Staff:** Prof 1; Other 1. **Subjects:** Computer and information sciences, physical sciences, engineering, life sciences. **Holdings:** 5500 books. **Subscriptions:** 264 journals and other serials. **Services:** Interlibrary loan; library not open to the public. **Automated Operations:** Computerized cataloging and serials. **Computerized Information Services:** DIALOG Information Services, Pergamon ORBIT InfoLine, Inc., BRS Information Technologies, NEXIS, DTIC, NASA/RECON, OCLC; internal database. **Networks/Consortia:** Member of FEDLINK. **Remarks:** This is an internal support library primarily for DTIC personnel.

★14961★
U.S.D.A. - AGRICULTURAL RESEARCH SERVICE - ARIDLAND WATERSHED MANAGEMENT RESEARCH UNIT (Env-Cons)
2000 E. Allen Rd. Phone: (602)629-6381
Tucson, AZ 85719 E. Sue Anderson, Libn.
Staff: 1. **Subjects:** Water and soil conservation, sediment, runoff, erosion, rainfall, arid land ecosystems improvement, watershed protection. **Holdings:** 400 books; 150 bound periodical volumes; 1700 theses and papers. **Subscriptions:** 35 journals and other serials. **Services:** Interlibrary

loan; center open to the public with restrictions. **Publications:** Bibliography of abstracts and papers, annual - to mailing list.

★14962★
U.S.D.A. - AGRICULTURAL RESEARCH SERVICE - ARTHROPOD-BORNE ANIMAL DISEASES RESEARCH LABORATORY LIBRARY (Med)
University Sta., Box 3965
Laramie, WY 82071-3965 Phone: (307)721-0304
Founded: 1954. **Subjects:** Arthropod-borne virus diseases of domestic animals. **Holdings:** 2000 volumes.

U.S.D.A. - AGRICULTURAL RESEARCH SERVICE - BEE BIOLOGY AND SYSTEMATICS LABORATORY
See: Bee Biology and Systematics Laboratory (1464)

★14963★
U.S.D.A. - AGRICULTURAL RESEARCH SERVICE - CENTRAL GREAT PLAINS RESEARCH STATION - LIBRARY (Agri)
Box K Phone: (303)345-2259
Akron, CO 80720 Dr. D.E. Smika, Res.Ldr.
Founded: 1907. **Staff:** Prof 6; Other 11. **Subjects:** Agronomy, soils, water, plants, hydrology. **Holdings:** 250 books. **Subscriptions:** 26 journals and other serials. **Services:** Library open to the public.

★14964★
U.S.D.A. - AGRICULTURAL RESEARCH SERVICE - CEREAL CROPS RESEARCH UNIT - LIBRARY (Agri)
501 N. Walnut St.
Madison, WI 53705 Phone: (608)262-3355
Founded: 1948. **Subjects:** Malting, brewing, cereal chemistry. **Holdings:** 500 volumes. **Remarks:** Center is jointly operated with University of Wisconsin, Madison.

★14965★
U.S.D.A. - AGRICULTURAL RESEARCH SERVICE - EASTERN REGIONAL RESEARCH CENTER LIBRARY (Sci-Engr, Food-Bev)
600 E. Mermaid Lane Phone: (215)233-6602
Philadelphia, PA 19118 Wendy H. Kramer, Adm.Libn.
Founded: 1940. **Staff:** Prof 1; Other 3. **Subjects:** Chemistry, biochemistry, chemical engineering, food sciences, leather research, plant sciences, microbiology. **Holdings:** Figures not available. **Subscriptions:** 350 journals and other serials. **Services:** Interlibrary loan; library open to the public. **Automated Operations:** Computerized cataloging, acquisitions, circulation, and ILL. **Computerized Information Services:** DIALOG Information Services, Pergamon ORBIT InfoLine, Inc., OCLC. **Networks/Consortia:** Member of FEDLINK, Interlibrary Delivery Service of Pennsylvania (IDS), Greater Northeastern Regional Medical Library Program. **Publications:** Accession List, monthly. **Remarks:** Alternate telephone numbers are 233-6604 and 233-6660. Fax: (215)233-6606.

★14966★
U.S.D.A. - AGRICULTURAL RESEARCH SERVICE - HONEY BEE RESEARCH LABORATORY - LIBRARY (Biol Sci)
509 W. 4th St. Phone: (512)968-3150
Weslaco, TX 78596 W.T. Wilson, Res. Entomologist
Staff: Prof 3; Other 5. **Subjects:** Apiculture, pesticides, beekeeping, honey bees, bee diseases, acarine parasites, insect pathology, entomology. **Holdings:** 480 books and bound periodical volumes; bulletins and reprints. **Services:** Library open to graduate students in apiculture research.

★14967★
U.S.D.A. - AGRICULTURAL RESEARCH SERVICE - HORTICULTURAL CROPS RESEARCH LABORATORY - LIBRARY (Biol Sci)
2021 S. Peach Ave. Phone: (209)487-5334
Fresno, CA 93727-5999 Marya Salmu, Libn.
Staff: Prof 1. **Subjects:** Botany, horticulture, plant and insect pathology, stored-product entomology, food science. **Holdings:** 1200 books; 600 bound periodical volumes; government documents. **Subscriptions:** 74 journals and other serials. **Services:** Library open to the public for reference use only. **Computerized Information Services:** Internal database.

★14968★
U.S.D.A. - AGRICULTURAL RESEARCH SERVICE - HORTICULTURAL RESEARCH LABORATORY - LIBRARY (Biol Sci, Agri)
2120 Camden Rd. Phone: (407)897-7301
Orlando, FL 32803 Denise A. Bergman, Libn.
Founded: 1970. **Staff:** 1. **Subjects:** Citrus - culture, breeding, processing, insects; nematology; plant pathology and physiology; biochemistry; transportation, storage, and marketing of fruits and vegetables. **Special Collections:** Publications and reprints on citrus and related topics. **Holdings:** 1500 books; 1000 bound periodical volumes; reprints; slides and photographs. **Subscriptions:** 100 journals and other serials. **Services:** Interlibrary loan; copying; library open to the staff and students of nearby universities and experiment stations.

★14969★
U.S.D.A. - AGRICULTURAL RESEARCH SERVICE - MEAT ANIMAL RESEARCH CENTER (Biol Sci, Food-Bev)
Box 166 Phone: (402)762-3241
Clay Center, NE 68933 Patricia L. Sheridan, Libn.
Staff: Prof 1. **Subjects:** Animals - science, breeding and reproduction, nutrition; agricultural engineering; meats; production systems. **Holdings:** 1600 books; 2700 bound periodical volumes. **Subscriptions:** 153 journals and other serials. **Services:** Interlibrary loan; copying; center open to the public with restrictions. **Computerized Information Services:** OCLC, DIALOG Information Services. **Networks/Consortia:** Member of FEDLINK. **Also Known As:** Roman L. Hruska U.S. Meat Animal Research Center.

★14970★
U.S.D.A. - AGRICULTURAL RESEARCH SERVICE - NATIONAL ANIMAL DISEASE CENTER - LIBRARY (Biol Sci, Med)
Box 70 Phone: (515)239-8271
Ames, IA 50010 Janice K. Eifling, Libn.
Founded: 1961. **Staff:** Prof 1; Other 1. **Subjects:** Biomedicine, microbiology, veterinary science. **Holdings:** 8000 books; 18,000 bound periodical volumes. **Subscriptions:** 350 journals and other serials. **Services:** Interlibrary loan; copying; ARS Current Awareness Literature Service; library open to qualified researchers. **Computerized Information Services:** DIALOG Information Services. **Publications:** Library Notes, monthly - for internal distribution only; Periodical Holdings List, annual; NADC Publications List, annual - available on request. **Special Catalogs:** Catalog of literature references on animal diseases, 1800-1940 (microfilm).

★14971★
U.S.D.A. - AGRICULTURAL RESEARCH SERVICE - NATIONAL SOIL DYNAMICS LABORATORY - LIBRARY (Agri)
Box 792 Phone: (205)887-8596
Auburn, AL 36831-0792 L.W. Larson, Dir.
Staff: 1. **Subjects:** Tillage, traction, soil-machine relations, soil reactions, earth-moving. **Special Collections:** Translations of foreign technical publications (60 bound volumes; 7000 other cataloged items). **Holdings:** 400 books; 500 bound periodical volumes; 7000 other cataloged items; 18,000 reports; 130 theses; 50 technical films; 5000 slides; 5000 photographs. **Subscriptions:** 30 journals and other serials. **Services:** Interlibrary loan; library not open to the public.

★14972★
U.S.D.A. - AGRICULTURAL RESEARCH SERVICE - NORTHERN REGIONAL RESEARCH CENTER LIBRARY (Sci-Engr, Biol Sci)
1815 N. University St. Phone: (309)685-4011
Peoria, IL 61604 Donald L. Blevins, Libn.
Founded: 1940. **Staff:** Prof 1; Other 2. **Subjects:** Organic chemistry, chemical engineering, biochemistry, microbiology, fermentation. **Holdings:** 40,000 volumes; 200 reels of microfilm. **Subscriptions:** 320 journals and other serials. **Services:** Interlibrary loan; copying; SDI; library open to the public. **Automated Operations:** Computerized cataloging. **Computerized Information Services:** DIALOG Information Services, STN International, OCLC. **Networks/Consortia:** Member of FEDLINK, Heart of Illinois Library Consortium (HILC), Illinois Valley Library System.

★14973★
U.S.D.A. - AGRICULTURAL RESEARCH SERVICE - PLUM ISLAND ANIMAL DISEASE CENTER - LIBRARY (Agri, Med)
Box 848 Phone: (516)323-2500
Greenport, NY 11944-0848 Stephen Perlman, Libn.
Founded: 1954. **Staff:** Prof 1. **Special Collections:** Virology, microbiology, immunology, molecular biology, veterinary medicine, laboratory animal sciences. **Special Collections:** Foreign animal diseases exotic to the U.S.

Holdings: 12,000 books; 16,000 bound periodical volumes; 12,645 reprints; 85 VF drawers of pamphlets and reprints. **Subscriptions:** 166 journals and other serials. **Services:** Interlibrary loan; library not open to the public. **Computerized Information Services:** DIALOG Information Services, OCLC, EMERPRO; SCIENCEREF (internal database). **Networks/ Consortia:** Member of FEDLINK. **Special Catalogs:** Card catalog on foreign animal diseases; subject catalog (computerized).

★14974★
U.S.D.A. - AGRICULTURAL RESEARCH SERVICE - SNAKE RIVER CONSERVATION RESEARCH CENTER - LIBRARY (Agri)
Route 1, Box 186 Phone: (208)423-5582
Kimberly, ID 83341 D. Easterday, Libn.
Staff: Prof 2; Other 1. **Subjects:** Agriculture, agronomy, entomology, computers, plant and crop science, soil science, meteorology, ecology and environment, water and hydrology. **Holdings:** 1300 books; 1500 bound periodical volumes. **Subscriptions:** 45 journals and other serials. **Services:** Interlibrary loan; library open to the public for reference use only. **Publications:** New Book List - for internal distribution only.

★14975★
U.S.D.A. - AGRICULTURAL RESEARCH SERVICE - SOUTH ATLANTIC AREA - RICHARD B. RUSSELL AGRICULTURAL RESEARCH CENTER LIBRARY (Agri)
College Station Rd., Box 5677 Phone: (404)546-3314
Athens, GA 30613 Benna Brodsky Thompson, Libn.
Staff: Prof 1; Other 2. **Subjects:** Agriculture, toxicology, food safety. **Holdings:** 6000 volumes. **Subscriptions:** 340 journals and other serials. **Services:** Interlibrary loan; copying; SDI; library open to the public. **Automated Operations:** Computerized cataloging and ILL. **Computerized Information Services:** DIALOG Information Services, OCLC, Integrated Technical Information System (ITIS), CAS ONLINE, MEDLARS, Pergamon ORBIT InfoLine, Inc. **Networks/Consortia:** Member of FEDLINK. **Publications:** Newsletter.

★14976★
U.S.D.A. - AGRICULTURAL RESEARCH SERVICE - SOUTHERN REGIONAL RESEARCH CENTER (Sci-Engr, Food-Bev, Biol Sci)
1100 Robert E. Lee Blvd.
Box 19687 Phone: (504)589-7072
New Orleans, LA 70179 Dorothy B. Skau, Libn.
Founded: 1941. **Staff:** Prof 2; Other 1. **Subjects:** Chemistry, textiles, food processing, plant sciences, aquaculture, mechanical and chemical engineering, microscopy, electron microscopy, vegetable fats and oils, microbiology, statistics. **Special Collections:** Trade literature; U.S. and foreign patents in laboratory's fields of interest. **Holdings:** 35,000 volumes; 59 VF drawers of pamphlets, foreign patents, trade literature, reprints, translations and manuscripts; 68 shelves of U.S. patents. **Subscriptions:** 2000 journals and other serials. **Services:** Interlibrary loan; center open to the public for reference use only. **Automated Operations:** Computerized cataloging. **Computerized Information Services:** DIALOG Information Services, OCLC. **Networks/Consortia:** Member of FEDLINK. **Publications:** Accession List, monthly; bibliography on Aflatoxin and Byssinosis (card). **Staff:** Marguerite R. Florent, Asst.Libn..

★14977★
U.S.D.A. - AGRICULTURAL RESEARCH SERVICE - STORED-PRODUCT INSECTS RESEARCH & DEVELOPMENT LABORATORY - LIBRARY (Biol Sci, Sci-Engr)
3401 Edwin St.
Box 22909 Phone: (912)233-7981
Savannah, GA 31403 M. Harriet Winiger, Lib.Techn.
Staff: Prof 1. **Subjects:** Stored-product insect control, entomology, chemistry, biology, insect-resistant packaging, mothproofing, insect rearing. **Holdings:** 4000 books; 9000 bound periodical volumes; 15 VF drawers of U.S.D.A. publications; 2000 slides; 3500 unbound journals; 17,000 reprints; 200 microfiche. **Subscriptions:** 220 journals and other serials. **Services:** Interlibrary loan; library open to the public with director's permission.

★14978★
U.S.D.A. - AGRICULTURAL RESEARCH SERVICE - U.S. LIVESTOCK INSECTS LABORATORY - LIBRARY (Biol Sci)
Box 232
Kerrville, TX 78029-0232 Phone: (512)257-3566
Founded: 1946. **Subjects:** Veterinary entomology. **Holdings:** 1000 books; 2000 bound periodical volumes. **Subscriptions:** 61 journals and other serials. **Services:** Interlibrary loan; library open to the public. **Computerized Information Services:** DIALOG Information Services.

★14979★
U.S.D.A. - AGRICULTURAL RESEARCH SERVICE - U.S. WATER CONSERVATION LABORATORY - LIBRARY (Agri)
4331 E. Broadway Rd.
Phoenix, AZ 85040 Phone: (602)261-4356
Founded: 1961. **Staff:** Prof 1. **Subjects:** Agricultural and irrigation engineering, hydraulics, hydrology, soils, plant physiology, chemistry, meteorology, instrumentation, wastewater renovation, infrared remote sensing, plant stress. **Holdings:** 1300 books; 200 bound periodical volumes; laboratory annual reports; reports of Geological Survey and ARS Series. **Subscriptions:** 85 journals and other serials. **Services:** Library open to the public for reference use only. **Publications:** Listing of publications of laboratory staff members, annual.

★14980★
U.S.D.A. - AGRICULTURAL RESEARCH SERVICE - WESTERN REGIONAL RESEARCH CENTER LIBRARY (Agri, Food-Bev)
Berkeley, CA 94710 Phone: (415)486-3351
Rena Schonbrun, Libn.
Founded: 1940. **Staff:** Prof 1; Other 2. **Subjects:** Cereals, fruits and vegetables, field crops, food technology, pharmacology, chemistry, nutrition. **Holdings:** Figures not available. **Subscriptions:** 320 journals. **Services:** Interlibrary loan; copying; SDI; library open to the public by appointment. **Automated Operations:** Computerized cataloging. **Computerized Information Services:** DIALOG Information Services, OCLC. **Networks/Consortia:** Member of FEDLINK.

★14981★
U.S.D.A. - ANIMAL AND PLANT INSPECTION SERVICE - ANIMAL DAMAGE CONTROL PROGRAM - DENVER WILDLIFE RESEARCH CENTER - LIBRARY (Biol Sci, Env-Cons, Sci-Engr)
Federal Center, Bldg. 16
Box 25266 Phone: (303)236-7873
Denver, CO 80225-0266 Diana L. Dwyer, Libn.
Staff: Prof 2; Other 3. **Subjects:** Wildlife biology, zoology, ornithology, mammalogy, ecology, pesticides, animal damage control, analytical chemistry, statistics, land use and energy in relation to wildlife. **Special Collections:** Fish and Wildlife Service publications; wildlife reprints and technical reports. **Holdings:** 15,000 books; 600 bound periodical volumes; 1500 technical reports and reprints; 500 unbound periodical volumes. **Subscriptions:** 271 journals and other serials. **Services:** Interlibrary loan; copying; library open to the public with restrictions. **Automated Operations:** Computerized cataloging and ILL. **Computerized Information Services:** DIALOG Information Services, BRS Information Technologies, Chemical Information Systems, Inc. (CIS), STN International, OCLC; Predator Database, Urban Mammal, Bird Damage (internal databases). **Networks/Consortia:** Member of FEDLINK. **Publications:** Acquisitions list, quarterly; Serials Holdings, irregular; publications list, annual.

★14982★
U.S.D.A. - ECONOMIC RESEARCH SERVICE - ERS REFERENCE CENTER (Bus-Fin)
1301 New York Ave., Rm. B28 Phone: (202)786-1724
Washington, DC 20005-4788 Donna Jean Fusonie, Dir.
Staff: Prof 2; Other 2. **Subjects:** Agricultural economics. **Special Collections:** Comprehensive collection of the U.S.D.A. - Economic Research Service and U.S.D.A. - Economics and Statistics Service publications (unbound and/or on microfiche). **Holdings:** 350 bound periodical volumes. **Subscriptions:** 400 journals and other serials. **Services:** Copying (limited); center open to the public by appointment for reference use. **Automated Operations:** Computerized ILL. **Computerized Information Services:** DIALOG Information Services. **Networks/ Consortia:** Member of FEDLINK. **Publications:** Newsletter, irregular. **Special Catalogs:** Catalog to book collection; catalog to vertical file collection of articles (online and book); catalog to journal holdings. **Staff:** Joan Carabell, Tech.Info.Spec..

U.S.D.A. - FOREST SERVICE
See: U.S. Forest Service (15097)

★14983★
U.S.D.A. - NATIONAL AGRICULTURAL LIBRARY (Biol Sci, Agri, Sci-Engr)
10301 Baltimore Blvd. Phone: (301)344-3755
Beltsville, MD 20705 Joseph H. Howard, Dir.
Founded: 1862. **Staff:** Prof 96; Other 94. **Subjects:** Plant science, forestry, horticulture, animal industry, veterinary medicine, aquaculture, entomology, soils and fertilizers, alternative farming, agricultural engineering, rural development, agricultural products, food and nutrition, home economics, biotechnology, agricultural trade and marketing. **Special Collections:** Layne R. Beaty papers (farm radio and television broadcasting); foreign and domestic nursery and seed trade catalogs; flock, herd, and stud books; rare book collection; AV collection on food and nutrition; apiculture; Forest Service Photo Collection; M. Truman Fossum Collection (floriculture); James M. Gwin Collection (poultry); Charles E. North Collection (milk sanitation); Pomology Collection (original pomological art); Charles Valentine Riley Collection (entomology); plant exploration photo collection; food and nutrition microcomputer software; MAPP collection of family life education materials. **Holdings:** 1.9 million volumes; 637,406 microforms; 13,000 maps. **Subscriptions:** 25,000 journals and newspapers. **Services:** Interlibrary loan; copying; SDI; library open to the public. **Automated Operations:** Computerized cataloging and serials. **Computerized Information Services:** DIALOG Information Services, BRS Information Technologies, OCLC; internal databases; Dialcom Inc. (electronic mail service). **Networks/Consortia:** Member of FLICC. **Publications:** Agricultural Libraries Information Notes, monthly; Quick Bibliography, irregular; AGRICOLA (computerized tape service), monthly - for sale. **Staff:** Samuel T. Waters, Assoc.Dir.; Pamela Andre, Chf., Info.Sys.Div.; Sarah Thomas, Chf., Tech.Serv.Div.; Keith Russell, Chf., Pub.Serv.Div..

★14984★
U.S.D.A. - NATIONAL AGRICULTURAL LIBRARY - FOOD AND NUTRITION INFORMATION CENTER (Food-Bev)
10301 Baltimore Blvd., Rm. 304 Phone: (301)344-3719
Beltsville, MD 20705 Robyn C. Frank, Dir.
Founded: 1971. **Staff:** Prof 4; Other 1. **Subjects:** Human nutrition research and education, food service management and food technology. **Special Collections:** Audiovisual materials (1700 AV programs). **Holdings:** 7500 books; 2 drawers of pamphlets; games; posters. **Subscriptions:** 150 journals and other serials. **Services:** Interlibrary loan; copying; center open to the public with restrictions. **Automated Operations:** Computerized cataloging. **Computerized Information Services:** DIALOG Information Services; Dialcom Inc. (electronic mail service). Performs searches on fee basis. **Publications:** Food and Nutrition Quarterly Index.

U.S.D.A. - NATIONAL AGRICULTURAL LIBRARY - NATIONAL ARBORETUM
See: U.S. Natl. Arboretum (15190)

★14985★
U.S.D.A. - OFFICE OF GENERAL COUNSEL - LAW LIBRARY (Law)
Independence Ave. at 12th St., S.W.
Rm. 1406, S Bldg. Phone: (202)447-7751
Washington, DC 20250 Edward S. Billings, Law Libn.
Founded: 1910. **Staff:** Prof 2; Other 2. **Subjects:** Law, legislative histories of federal acts of interest to the Department of Agriculture, federal administrative decisions (selective). **Holdings:** 116,277 books; 2404 bound periodical volumes; 49 reels of microfilm of Congressional Globe; 192,748 microfiche of the CIS microfiche library of the working papers of the U.S. Congress; 328 reels of microfilm of Federal Register, March 1936-December 1979; 615 reels of microfilm. **Subscriptions:** 115 journals and other serials. **Services:** Interlibrary loan (within metropolitan area); copying; library open to the public for reference use only. **Computerized Information Services:** LEXIS, WESTLAW, DIALOG Information Services. **Staff:** Denis Konouck.

★14986★
U.S.D.A. - OFFICE OF GOVERNMENTAL AND PUBLIC AFFAIRS - PHOTOGRAPHY DIVISION - PHOTOGRAPH LIBRARY (Aud-Vis, Agri)
14th & Independence Ave., S.W. Phone: (202)447-6633
Washington, DC 20250 Theodosia Thomas, Chf., Photo.Div.
Staff: Prof 2; Other 4. **Subjects:** Agriculture, food production and marketing, land use. **Holdings:** 70,000 black/white photographs; 20,000 color slides. **Services:** Library open to the public by appointment. **Publications:** Filmstrips and Slide Sets of the USDA - free upon request. **Special Catalogs:** Catalog of USDA Photos. **Staff:** Robert Hailstock, Vis.Info.Spec.; June Davidek, Vis.Info.Spec..

U.S.D.A. - SOIL CONSERVATION SERVICE
See: U.S. Soil Conservation Service (15497)

U.S. DEPT. OF COMMERCE - BUREAU OF THE CENSUS
See: U.S. Bureau of the Census (14882)

U.S. DEPT. OF COMMERCE - COMMERCE PRODUCTIVITY CENTER
See: U.S. Dept. of Commerce - Office of Productivity, Technology and Innovation - Commerce Productivity Center (14991)

★14987★
U.S. DEPT. OF COMMERCE - ECONOMIC DEVELOPMENT ADMINISTRATION - LIBRARY (Soc Sci)
Main Commerce Bldg., Rm. 7866 Phone: (202)377-5111
Washington, DC 20230 Venita Pettus, Prog.Asst.
Founded: 1981. **Subjects:** Economic development. **Holdings:** Figures not available.

U.S. DEPT. OF COMMERCE - INTERNATIONAL TRADE ADMINISTRATION
See: U.S. International Trade Administration (15143)

★14988★
U.S. DEPT. OF COMMERCE - LAW LIBRARY (Law)
14th & E St., N.W., Rm. 1894 Phone: (202)377-5517
Washington, DC 20230 Billie J. Grey, Dir.
Staff: Prof 2; Other 2. **Subjects:** International law, antitrust, government procurement. **Special Collections:** Congressional documents, circa 1930 to present. **Holdings:** 30,000 books; 10,000 bound periodical volumes; 100,000 uncataloged items. **Subscriptions:** 200 journals and other serials. **Services:** Interlibrary loan (limited); library open to the public. **Automated Operations:** Computerized cataloging. **Computerized Information Services:** LEXIS, LEGI-SLATE, WESTLAW, NEXIS. **Networks/Consortia:** Member of FEDLINK. **Remarks:** Library is accessible to the deaf through TTY at (202)377-5588.

★14989★
U.S. DEPT. OF COMMERCE - LIBRARY (Bus-Fin)
14th & Constitution Ave., N.W. Phone: (202)377-3611
Washington, DC 20230 Anthony J. Steinhauser, Dir.
Founded: 1913. **Staff:** Prof 7; Other 5. **Subjects:** Economics, export-import, foreign trade, business, economic theory, economic conditions, statistics, marketing, industry, finance, legislation, management, telecommunications. **Special Collections:** U.S. Census; Department of Commerce publications; telecommunications. **Holdings:** 50,000 books and bound periodical volumes; 4300 reels of microfilm; 250,000 volumes of microfiche. **Subscriptions:** 1600 journals and other serials. **Services:** Interlibrary loan; copying; library open to the public for reference use only. **Automated Operations:** Computerized cataloging. **Computerized Information Services:** DIALOG Information Services, OCLC, Pergamon ORBIT InfoLine, Inc., BRS Information Technologies, LEXIS, LEGI-SLATE, The Reference Service (REFSRV). **Networks/Consortia:** Member of FEDLINK. **Publications:** Directory of Libraries in the U.S. Dept. of Commerce (COM 72-11147); Library Bulletin. **Special Catalogs:** Law catalog. **Remarks:** Contains the holdings of the U.S. Dept. of Commerce - National Telecommunications and Information Administration Library. **Staff:** Vera Whisenton, Chf., Rd.Serv.; Willene J. Gaines, Chf., Tech.Serv.; Marie Scroggs, Adm.Asst.; Lee Ruffin, ILL; Mary S. Hardison, Acq.Libn.; Uko Villemi, Cat..

U.S. DEPT. OF COMMERCE - NATIONAL BUREAU OF STANDARDS
See: U.S. Natl. Bureau of Standards (15203)

U.S. DEPT. OF COMMERCE - NATIONAL OCEANIC & ATMOSPHERIC ADMINISTRATION
See: U.S. Natl. Oceanic & Atmospheric Administration (15233)

U.S. DEPT. OF COMMERCE - NATIONAL OCEANIC & ATMOSPHERIC ADMINISTRATION - NATIONAL MARINE FISHERIES SERVICE
See: U.S. Natl. Marine Fisheries Service (15211)

U.S. DEPT. OF COMMERCE - NATIONAL OCEANIC & ATMOSPHERIC ADMINISTRATION - NATIONAL WEATHER SERVICE
See: U.S. Natl. Weather Service (15367)

★14990★
U.S. DEPT. OF COMMERCE - NATIONAL TECHNICAL INFORMATION SERVICE (Info Sci)
5285 Port Royal Rd.
Springfield, VA 22161 Phone: (703)487-4600
Holdings: 1.8 million titles of non-classified U.S. government-sponsored and foreign research, development, and engineering reports, and other analyses prepared by federal agencies, their contractors, or grantees. **Services:** Current summaries (abstracts) of NTIS documents sold in paper or microform copy; microfiche service; bibliographic databases are available on magnetic tapes; source data files and software are available on magnetic tape and diskette. **Computerized Information Services:** DIALOG Information Services, BRS Information Technologies, Pergamon ORBIT InfoLine, Inc., STN International, Data-Star. **Publications:** Abstract newsletters; journals, biweekly; published searches. **Special Catalogs:** Annual catalog of holdings. **Special Indexes:** Indexes to current abstracts published in weekly journals. **Remarks:** The service is a central source for the public sale of government-sponsored reports, software, and database services. NTIS has agreements with several hundred federal research-sponsoring organizations and foreign government sources to provide the most complete list of publications possible. **Also Known As:** NTIS.

★14991★
U.S. DEPT. OF COMMERCE - OFFICE OF PRODUCTIVITY, TECHNOLOGY AND INNOVATION - COMMERCE PRODUCTIVITY CENTER (Bus-Fin)
14th St. & Constitution Ave., N.W., Rm. 7413 Phone: (202)377-0940
Washington, DC 20230 Carol Ann Meares, Mgr.
Founded: 1978. **Staff:** Prof 1; Other 1. **Subjects:** Technology and innovation, productivity, quality of working life, economics, management, labor relations, public administration. **Holdings:** 5580 volumes; 2000 microfiche; 2000 clippings. **Subscriptions:** 60 journals and other serials. **Services:** Interlibrary loan; copying (both limited); center open to the public. **Publications:** Publications on productivity and quality of working life.

U.S. DEPT. OF COMMERCE - PATENT & TRADEMARK OFFICE
See: U.S. Patent & Trademark Office (15479)

★14992★
U.S. DEPT. OF DEFENSE - ARMED FORCES PEST MANAGEMENT BOARD - DEFENSE PEST MANAGEMENT INFORMATION ANALYSIS CENTER (Biol Sci, Sci-Engr)
Walter Reed Army Medical Center
Forest Glen Section Phone: (202)427-5365
Washington, DC 20307-5001 LTC Alan R. Gillogly, Chf.
Founded: 1963. **Staff:** Prof 5; Other 6. **Subjects:** Vector biology and control, vector-borne disease, arthropods of economic importance, stored product insects, pesticides, pesticide application equipment, pest vertebrates, pest management, agronomy. **Holdings:** 119,894 volumes. **Subscriptions:** 134 journals and other serials. **Services:** Copying; SDI; center open to employees of the Department of Defense and other federal agencies. **Automated Operations:** Computerized cataloging. **Computerized Information Services:** DIALOG Information Services; internal database; SEANET (electronic mail service). **Publications:** Bibliographies; Technical Information Bulletin, bimonthly; Disease Vector Ecology Profiles (foreign countries).

★14993★
U.S. DEPT. OF DEFENSE - COMPUTER INSTITUTE - TECHNICAL LIBRARY (Comp Sci)
National Defense University Library
Bldg. 175, Rm. 37
Washington Navy Yard Phone: (202)433-3653
Washington, DC 20374 Ms. Johnsie A. Smalls, Lib.Techn.
Staff: 1. **Subjects:** Automated information systems, computer hardware and software management. **Holdings:** 1780 books; 250 other cataloged items. **Subscriptions:** 100 journals and other serials; 14 newspapers. **Services:** Interlibrary loan; copying (limited). **Computerized Information Services:** Internal database. Performs searches free of charge.

U.S. DEPT. OF DEFENSE - DEFENSE ADVANCED RESEARCH PROJECTS AGENCY - TACTICAL TECHNOLOGY CENTER
See: Battelle-Columbus Laboratories - Tactical Technology Center (1378)

U.S. DEPT. OF DEFENSE - DEFENSE COMMUNICATIONS AGENCY
See: U.S. Defense Communications Agency (14946)

★14994★
U.S. DEPT. OF DEFENSE - DEFENSE INDUSTRIAL PLANT EQUIPMENT CENTER - TECHNICAL DATA REPOSITORY & LIBRARY (Sci-Engr)
2163 Airways Blvd. Phone: (901)775-6549
Memphis, TN 38114 Tom Dumser, Chf., Lib.
Founded: 1963. **Staff:** Prof 1; Other 1. **Holdings:** 580 volumes; 20,000 administrative, manufacturers', and military technical publications; 2050 feet of manufacturers' commercial technical data. **Subscriptions:** 23 journals and other serials. **Services:** Interlibrary loan; library not open to the public. **Automated Operations:** Computerized serials.

U.S. DEPT. OF DEFENSE - DEFENSE INTELLIGENCE AGENCY
See: U.S. Defense Intelligence Agency (14947)

U.S. DEPT. OF DEFENSE - DEFENSE LOGISTICS AGENCY
See: U.S. Defense Logistics Agency (14954)

U.S. DEPT. OF DEFENSE - DEFENSE MAPPING AGENCY
See: U.S. Defense Mapping Agency (14956)

U.S. DEPT. OF DEFENSE - DEFENSE NUCLEAR AGENCY
See: U.S. Defense Nuclear Agency (14957)

U.S. DEPT. OF DEFENSE - DEFENSE SYSTEMS MANAGEMENT COLLEGE (DSMC)
See: Defense Systems Management College (DSMC) (4139)

U.S. DEPT. OF DEFENSE - DEFENSE TECHNICAL INFORMATION CENTER
See: U.S. Defense Technical Information Center (14958)

U.S. DEPT. OF DEFENSE - INFRARED INFORMATION AND ANALYSIS CENTER (IRIA)
See: Environmental Research Institute of Michigan - Infrared Information and Analysis Center (IRIA) (4747)

U.S. DEPT. OF DEFENSE - JOINT CHIEFS OF STAFF - ARMED FORCES STAFF COLLEGE
See: U.S. Armed Forces Staff College (14703)

U.S. DEPT. OF DEFENSE - JOINT CHIEFS OF STAFF - NATIONAL DEFENSE UNIVERSITY
See: U.S. Natl. Defense University (15204)

★14995★
U.S. DEPT. OF DEFENSE - LANGUAGE INSTITUTE - ACADEMIC LIBRARY (Area-Ethnic, Hum)
Presidio, Bldg. 618 Phone: (408)647-5572
Monterey, CA 93944-5007 Gary D. Walter, Libn.
Founded: 1944. **Staff:** Prof 6; Other 7. **Subjects:** Foreign languages, linguistics, history and culture of foreign countries. **Holdings:** 100,000 books; 650 bound periodical volumes; 8 VF drawers of pamphlets and clippings; 65 reels of microfilm; 5000 video cassettes. **Subscriptions:** 600 journals and other serials; 150 newspapers. **Services:** Interlibrary loan; copying; library open to the public for reference use only on request. **Computerized Information Services:** DIALOG Information Services. **Staff:** Carl Chan, Cat.; Rosemary Canfield, Ref..

U.S. DEPT. OF DEFENSE - RELIABILITY ANALYSIS CENTER
See: IIT Research Institute - Reliability Analysis Center (6682)

★14996★
U.S. DEPT. OF DEFENSE - STILL MEDIA RECORDS CENTER (Aud-Vis, Mil)
Bldg. 168, NDW Phone: (202)433-2166
Washington, DC 20374-1681 Linda Letchworth, Proj.Mgr.
Founded: 1980. **Staff:** Prof 20; Other 9. **Subjects:** Military activities, equipment, weapons, operations, personalities, history of military aviation, aircraft, ships, World War II, Korean War, Vietnam. **Holdings:** Over 2 million color and black and white photographs. **Services:** Copying; reprints available on fee basis to unofficial requestors, free of charge to government agencies; center open to the public. **Staff:** Michael Rusnak, Hd., Rec.Ctr.Mgt.Div..

U.S. DEPT. OF DEFENSE - UNDER SECRETARY OF DEFENSE FOR RESEARCH AND ENGINEERING - NONDESTRUCTIVE TESTING INFORMATION ANALYSIS CENTER
See: Southwest Research Institute - Nondestructive Testing Information Analysis Center (13517)

U.S. DEPT. OF DEFENSE - U.S. UNIFORMED SERVICES UNIVERSITY OF THE HEALTH SCIENCES
See: U.S. Uniformed Services University of the Health Sciences (15510)

U.S. DEPT. OF EDUCATION - EAST CENTRAL NETWORK FOR CURRICULUM COORDINATION
See: Sangamon State University - East Central Network for Curriculum Coordination (12854)

★14997★
U.S. DEPT. OF EDUCATION - EDUCATION RESEARCH LIBRARY (Educ)
555 New Jersey Ave., N.W. Phone: (202)357-6884
Washington, DC 20208 Dr. Milbrey L. Jones, Chf.
Staff: Prof 5; Other 4. **Subjects:** Education, psychology, management, educational statistics, library and information science. **Special Collections:** Rare Book Collection (education); American Textbook Collection, 1786-1940; William S. Gray Reading Collection (on microfiche); U.S. Office of Education Historical Collection, 1870-1980; Elaine Exton's papers; historical foreign language periodicals. **Holdings:** 200,000 books; 42,000 bound periodical volumes; 300,000 ERIC microfiche; 500 National Institute of Education archives reports collection; 2000 reels of microfilm; 35,000 microfiche. **Subscriptions:** 1500 journals and other serials. **Services:** Interlibrary loan; copying; library open to the public with restrictions. **Automated Operations:** Computerized public access catalog and cataloging. **Computerized Information Services:** OCLC. **Networks/Consortia:** Member of FEDLINK. **Publications:** Acquisitions list, monthly; Periodical Holdings List. **Special Catalogs:** Catalog of Rare Books on Education; Early American Textbook Catalog; NIE Products Catalog. **Staff:** Jo Anne S. Cassell, Asst.Libn..

U.S. DEPT. OF EDUCATION - ERIC PROCESSING AND REFERENCE FACILITY
See: ERIC Processing and Reference Facility (4777)

★14998★
U.S. DEPT. OF EDUCATION - REFUGEE MATERIALS CENTER
10220 N. Executive Hills Blvd.
Kansas City, MO 64153
Defunct

U.S. DEPT. OF EDUCATION - WESTERN CURRICULUM COORDINATION CENTER
See: Western Curriculum Coordination Center (WCCC) (17701)

★14999★
U.S. DEPT. OF ENERGY - ALASKA POWER ADMINISTRATION - LIBRARY (Energy)
Box 020050 Phone: (907)586-7405
Juneau, AK 99802-0050 Marie Parfitt, Power Div.Asst.
Subjects: Water and power resources, Alaska natural resources, engineering. **Special Collections:** Alaskan utilities. **Holdings:** Figures not available. **Subscriptions:** 34 journals and other serials. **Services:** Interlibrary loan; copying; library open to the public with restrictions.

★15000★
U.S. DEPT. OF ENERGY - ALBUQUERQUE OPERATIONS OFFICE - NATIONAL ATOMIC MUSEUM - LIBRARY AND PUBLIC DOCUMENT ROOM (Energy)
Box 5400
Albuquerque, NM 87113 Phone: (505)844-4378
Founded: 1975. **Staff:** Prof 1; Other 1. **Subjects:** Nuclear waste management, nuclear weapons history, energy. **Special Collections:** Waste Isolation Pilot Project (400 items). **Holdings:** 1700 books; 1500 reports; 3900 microfiche. **Subscriptions:** 22 journals and other serials. **Services:** Interlibrary loan; copying; library open to the public with restrictions on borrowing. **Computerized Information Services:** DIALOG Information Services. Performs searches on fee basis.

U.S. DEPT. OF ENERGY - AMES LABORATORY
See: Ames Laboratory (719)

U.S. DEPT. OF ENERGY - ARGONNE NATIONAL LABORATORY
See: Argonne National Laboratory (870)

U.S. DEPT. OF ENERGY - ATMOSPHERIC TURBULENCE & DIFFUSION DIVISION
See: U.S. Natl. Oceanic & Atmospheric Administration - Atmospheric Turbulence & Diffusion Division (15228)

U.S. DEPT. OF ENERGY - BATTELLE-NORTHWEST - PACIFIC NORTHWEST LABORATORY
See: Battelle-Northwest - Pacific Northwest Laboratory (1384)

U.S. DEPT. OF ENERGY - BENDIX FIELD ENGINEERING CORPORATION
See: Bendix Field Engineering Corporation - Grand Junction Office - Technical Library (1504)

U.S. DEPT. OF ENERGY - BETTIS ATOMIC POWER LABORATORY
See: Westinghouse Electric Corporation - Bettis Atomic Power Laboratory (17765)

★15001★
U.S. DEPT. OF ENERGY - BONNEVILLE POWER ADMINISTRATION - LIBRARY (Energy, Sci-Engr)
905 N.E. 11th Ave.
Box 3621 Phone: (503)230-4171
Portland, OR 97232 Karen L. Hadman, Chf., Lib.Br.
Founded: 1939. **Staff:** Prof 5; Other 5. **Subjects:** Electrical engineeering, law, conservation, natural resources, mathematics, basic sciences, mechanical and civil engineering, personnel administration. **Special Collections:** Western SUN (Solar Utilization Network) Collection (3000 volumes); Bonneville Power Administration publications and reports. **Holdings:** 33,700 volumes; 75,000 microfiche. **Subscriptions:** 1200 journals and other serials. **Services:** Interlibrary loan; library open to the public. **Automated Operations:** Computerized cataloging and serials. **Computerized Information Services:** DIALOG Information Services, BRS Information Technologies, LEXIS, NEXIS; OnTyme Electronic Message Network Service (electronic mail service). **Publications:** Library Bulletin, quarterly; new book list, monthly; research guides, irregular - all distributed internally and by request. **Staff:** Monte J. Gittings, Engr.Libn.; Jean Connors, Law Libn.; Brenda E. Bonnell, Power Mgt.Libn.; Linda L. Kuriger, Tech.Serv.Supv..

★15002★
U.S. DEPT. OF ENERGY - BONNEVILLE POWER ADMINISTRATION - ROSS LIBRARY-ER (Energy)
Box 491 Phone: (206)690-2617
Vancouver, WA 98666 John A. Fenker, Libn.
Founded: 1982. **Subjects:** Energy. **Special Collections:** Internal technical and laboratory reports; federal, military, and industry standards; EPRI reports depository. **Holdings:** Figures not available. **Services:** Interlibrary loan; library open to the public for reference use only. **Computerized Information Services:** DIALOG Information Services, BRS Information Technologies, TOXNET, Chemical Information Systems, Inc. (CIS); OnTyme Electronic Message Network Service (electronic mail service). **Special Catalogs:** Catalog of internal technical and laboratory reports. **Special Indexes:** Index to internal technical and laboratory reports.

U.S. DEPT. OF ENERGY - BROOKHAVEN NATIONAL LABORATORY
See: Brookhaven National Laboratory (1924)

U.S. DEPT. OF ENERGY - CONSERVATION AND RENEWABLE ENERGY INQUIRY AND REFERRAL SERVICE
See: Conservation and Renewable Energy Inquiry and Referral Service (3682)

★15003★
U.S. DEPT. OF ENERGY - DALLAS SUPPORT OFFICE - LIBRARY (Energy)
1440 W. Mockingbird Ln., Suite 400 Phone: (214)767-7203
Dallas, TX 75247 Nancy Holley
Subjects: Nuclear waste management. **Holdings:** DOE Energy Information Administration (EIA) publications. **Services:** Library open to the public by permission for reference use only.

U.S. DEPT. OF ENERGY - EG&G IDAHO, INC. - IDAHO NATIONAL ENGINEERING LABORATORY
See: EG&G Idaho, Inc. - Idaho National Engineering Laboratory (4624)

★15004★
U.S. DEPT. OF ENERGY - ENERGY INFORMATION ADMINISTRATION - NATIONAL ENERGY INFORMATION CENTER (Energy)
Forrestal Bldg., Rm. 1F-048 Phone: (202)586-8800
Washington, DC 20585 John H. Weiner, Dir., Info./Adm.Serv.Div.
Staff: Prof 32; Other 2. **Subjects:** Energy - petroleum, electric power, nuclear power, coal and synthetic fuels, renewable energy resources, natural gas; energy statistics. **Services:** Center open to the public; responds to telephone and letter inquiries. **Publications:** EIA (Energy Information Administration) Publications: New Releases; Energy Facts; EIA Publications Directory: A User's Guide; Energy Information Directory. **Staff:** Mary Ellen Golby, Chf., Natl. Energy Info.Ctr.; Nancy Nicoletti, Chf., Pubns.Serv..

★15005★
U.S. DEPT. OF ENERGY - ENERGY LIBRARY (Energy)
MA 232 Phone: (202)586-9534
Washington, DC 20585 Denise B. Diggin, Libn.
Founded: 1947. **Staff:** Prof 10; Other 10. **Subjects:** Energy resources and technologies; economic, environmental, and social effects of energy; energy regulation; water resources; management. **Special Collections:** International Atomic Energy Agency (IAEA) Publications; legislative histories relating to Atomic Energy Commission (AEC) and Energy Research and Development Administration (ERDA); ERDA, Federal Energy Administration (FEA), and DOE technical reports. **Holdings:** 1 million volumes of books, journals, technical reports, government documents. **Subscriptions:** 1600 journals and other serials. **Services:** Interlibrary loan; copying; SDI; library open to DOE headquarters staff and authorized contractors. **Automated Operations:** Computerized cataloging, acquisitions, serials, and circulation. **Computerized Information Services:** DIALOG Information Services, Pergamon ORBIT InfoLine, Inc., NEXIS, Integrated Technical Information System (ITIS), MEDLARS, Chase Econometrics, BRS Information Technologies, Telesystemes Questel, TEXTLINE, Value Line Data Services, NASA/RECON, STN International, I.P. Sharp Associates Limited, LEXIS, NewsNet, Inc, OCLC. **Networks/Consortia:** Member of FEDLINK, FLICC. **Publications:** Data Bases Available at the Energy Library, irregular; Energy Library Guide to Services.

★15006★
U.S. DEPT. OF ENERGY - ENVIRONMENTAL MEASUREMENTS LABORATORY LIBRARY (Energy, Sci-Engr)
376 Hudson St. Phone: (212)620-3606
New York, NY 10014 Rita D. Rosen, Tech.Libn.
Founded: 1947. **Staff:** Prof 1. **Subjects:** Physics, chemistry, environmental science, radiation physics. **Holdings:** 2000 books; 1800 bound periodical volumes; 30,000 technical reports; 35,000 reports in microform. **Subscriptions:** 125 journals and other serials. **Services:** Interlibrary loan; library not open to the public. **Computerized Information Services:** DIALOG Information Services.

U.S. DEPT. OF ENERGY - FEDERAL ENERGY REGULATORY COMMISSION
See: Federal Energy Regulatory Commission (4948)

U.S. DEPT. OF ENERGY - INHALATION TOXICOLOGY RESEARCH INSTITUTE
See: Lovelace Biomedical & Environmental Research Institute, Inc. - Inhalation Toxicology Research Institute (8074)

U.S. DEPT. OF ENERGY - KNOLLS ATOMIC POWER LABORATORY
See: Knolls Atomic Power Laboratory (7529)

U.S. DEPT. OF ENERGY - LABORATORY OF BIOMEDICAL AND ENVIRONMENTAL SCIENCES
See: University of California, Los Angeles - Laboratory of Biomedical and Environmental Sciences (15976)

U.S. DEPT. OF ENERGY - LAWRENCE BERKELEY LABORATORY
See: Lawrence Berkeley Laboratory (7703)

U.S. DEPT. OF ENERGY - LAWRENCE LIVERMORE NATIONAL LABORATORY
See: Lawrence Livermore National Laboratory - Technical Information Department Library (7711)

U.S. DEPT. OF ENERGY - LOS ALAMOS NATIONAL LABORATORY
See: University of California - Los Alamos National Laboratory (15892)

U.S. DEPT. OF ENERGY - MARTIN MARIETTA ENERGY SYSTEMS INC.
See: Martin Marietta Energy Systems Inc. - Libraries (8475)

U.S. DEPT. OF ENERGY - MASON & HANGER-SILAS MASON COMPANY, INC.
See: Mason & Hanger-Silas Mason Company, Inc. (8511)

★15007★
U.S. DEPT. OF ENERGY - MORGANTOWN ENERGY TECHNOLOGY CENTER - LIBRARY (Energy)
Box 880 Phone: (304)291-4184
Morgantown, WV 26505 S. Elaine Pasini, Info.Spec. II
Founded: 1953. **Staff:** Prof 2; Other 1. **Subjects:** Coal and fossil fuel, petroleum, chemistry, chemical engineering, geology, coal gasification. **Special Collections:** U.S. Office of Coal Research reports (100); U.S. Dept. of Energy publications; U.S. Bureau of Mines publications (complete). **Holdings:** 10,000 books; 7000 bound periodical volumes; 1500 reports; 20 VF drawers of patents. **Subscriptions:** 300 journals and other serials. **Services:** Interlibrary loan; copying; library open to the public. **Computerized Information Services:** OCLC, Pergamon ORBIT InfoLine, Inc., DIALOG Information Services, BRS Information Technologies. **Publications:** Annual publications list.

★15008★
U.S. DEPT. OF ENERGY - NEVADA OPERATIONS OFFICE - TECHNICAL LIBRARY (Sci-Engr, Energy)
Mail Stop 505
Box 98518 Phone: (702)295-1274
Las Vegas, NV 89193-8518 Cynthia Ortiz, Tech.Libn. II
Founded: 1969. **Staff:** Prof 2; Other 1. **Subjects:** Nuclear explosives, radiation bioenvironmental effects, geology, hydrology, alternate energy sources, radioactive waste storage. **Special Collections:** Peaceful uses of nuclear explosions. **Holdings:** 2630 books; 51,940 technical reports; 75,980 microfiche of technical reports; 7 file drawers of clippings; 400 maps. **Subscriptions:** 220 journals and other serials. **Services:** Interlibrary loan; copying; library open to the public by prior arrangement. **Computerized Information Services:** Integrated Technical Information System (ITIS), DIALOG Information Services, LEXIS, NEXIS.

U.S. DEPT. OF ENERGY - OAK RIDGE NATIONAL LABORATORY
See: Oak Ridge National Laboratory (10582)

★15009★
U.S. DEPT. OF ENERGY - OFFICE OF GENERAL COUNSEL LAW LIBRARY (Law)
1000 Independence Ave., S.W., Rm. 6A 156 Phone: (202)252-4848
Washington, DC 20585 Oscar E. Strothers, Chf. Law Libn.
Founded: 1975. **Staff:** Prof 2. **Subjects:** Law - energy, environmental, contract, administrative, patents; statutes. **Holdings:** 40,000 volumes; microfiche. **Subscriptions:** 270 journals and other serials. **Services:** Interlibrary loan; copying (limited); library open to the public for reference use only. **Computerized Information Services:** LEXIS, JURIS, WESTLAW. **Staff:** Paula Lipman, Asst.Libn..

★15010★
U.S. DEPT. OF ENERGY - OFFICE OF SCIENTIFIC AND TECHNICAL INFORMATION (OSTI) - TECHNICAL INFORMATION CENTER (Energy, Info Sci)
Box 62 Phone: (615)576-6299
Oak Ridge, TN 37831 Joseph G. Coyne, Mgr.
Founded: 1947. **Subjects:** Energy. **Special Collections:** Information science (4000 items). **Holdings:** 8000 books; 100 bound periodical volumes; 600,000 technical reports; 5000 conference proceedings; 2500 engineering drawing packages. **Subscriptions:** 1000 journals and other serials. **Services:** Center not open to the public. **Automated Operations:** Computerized cataloging. **Computerized Information Services:** Integrated Technical Information System (ITIS), DIALOG Information Services, STN International. **Publications:** Energy Research Abstracts, semimonthly; Energy Abstracts for Policy Analysis; Energy Meetings, monthly; Buildings Energy

Technologies; Energy from Biomass; Direct Energy Conversion; Nuclear Fuel Cycle; Nuclear Reactor Safety; Radioactive Waste Management; Acid Precipitation; Solar Thermal Energy Technology; Geothermal Energy Technology; Transportation Energy Research. **Remarks:** This is a centralized R&D Information Management center for the U.S. Dept. of Energy. Requests for information and publications, including interlibrary loan, should be directed to Request Section, (615)576-2413. **Staff:** Elizabeth Buffurn, Dp.Mgr.; Dora H. Moneyhun, Dir.,Tech.Info.Div..

U.S. DEPT. OF ENERGY - PLANT RESEARCH LABORATORY
See: Michigan State University - Plant Research Laboratory (8922)

U.S. DEPT. OF ENERGY - REYNOLDS ELECTRICAL AND ENGINEERING COMPANY, INC.
See: Reynolds Electrical and Engineering Company, Inc. - Coordination and Information Center (12004)

★15011★
U.S. DEPT. OF ENERGY - SAN FRANCISCO OPERATIONS OFFICE - ENERGY INFORMATION CENTER (Energy)
1333 Broadway Phone: (415)273-4428
Oakland, CA 94612 Norma DelGaudio, Info.Coord.
Subjects: Energy. **Holdings:** Figures not available for books; Energy Research Abstracts; Energy Information Administration (EIA) publications, analyses, energy data reports, statistics, and forecasts; educational materials for students and teachers; pamphlets. **Services:** Interlibrary loan; center open to the public for reference use only. **Remarks:** Center serves as the DOE's Public Reading Room in northern California.

U.S. DEPT. OF ENERGY - SANDIA NATIONAL LABORATORIES
See: Sandia National Laboratories (12843)

U.S. DEPT. OF ENERGY - SAVANNAH RIVER LABORATORY
See: Savannah River Laboratory (12940)

U.S. DEPT. OF ENERGY - SOLAR ENERGY RESEARCH INSTITUTE
See: Solar Energy Research Institute (13350)

U.S. DEPT. OF ENERGY - STANFORD LINEAR ACCELERATOR CENTER
See: Stanford Linear Accelerator Center (13604)

U.S. DEPT. OF ENERGY - WESTINGHOUSE MATERIALS CO. OF OHIO
See: Westinghouse Materials Co. of Ohio (17779)

U.S. DEPT. OF ENERGY HISTORIAN ARCHIVES OFFICE
See: Reynolds Electrical and Engineering Company, Inc. - Coordination and Information Center (12004)

U.S. DEPT. OF HEALTH AND HUMAN SERVICES - FAMILY SUPPORT ADMINISTRATION - PROJECT SHARE
See: Berul Associates, Ltd. - Project SHARE (1536)

★15012★
U.S. DEPT. OF HEALTH AND HUMAN SERVICES - LIBRARY AND INFORMATION CENTER (Soc Sci, Med)
330 Independence Ave., S.W., Rm. G-400
Washington, DC 20201 Phone: (202)245-6791
Founded: 1953. **Staff:** Prof 4; Other 5. **Subjects:** Social welfare, social sciences, education, health, medicine, law and legislation, administration and management. **Special Collections:** Departmental archives. **Holdings:** 200,000 volumes; 450,000 microforms. **Subscriptions:** 3500 journals and other serials. **Services:** Interlibrary loan; copying; library open to the public. **Computerized Information Services:** OCLC, BRS Information Technologies, MEDLINE, JURIS, Mead Data Central, DIALOG Information Services, LEGI-SLATE. **Staff:** Violet L. Carter, Adm.Off.; Daniel Beam, Ref.Libn..

U.S. DEPT. OF HEALTH AND HUMAN SERVICES - NATIONAL ARTHRITIS AND MUSCULOSKELETAL AND SKIN DISEASES INFORMATION CLEARINGHOUSE
See: National Arthritis and Musculoskeletal and Skin Diseases Information Clearinghouse (9561)

U.S. DEPT. OF HEALTH AND HUMAN SERVICES - NATIONAL CENTER ON CHILD ABUSE AND NEGLECT (NCCAN) - CLGHSE. ON CHILD ABUSE & NEGLECT INFO.
See: Clearinghouse on Child Abuse and Neglect Information (3283)

U.S. DEPT. OF HEALTH AND HUMAN SERVICES - NATIONAL DIGESTIVE DISEASES INFORMATION CLEARINGHOUSE
See: National Digestive Diseases Information Clearinghouse (9652)

★15013★
U.S. DEPT. OF HEALTH AND HUMAN SERVICES - POLICY INFORMATION CENTER (Soc Sci, Med)
200 Independence Ave., S.W. Phone: (202)245-6445
Washington, DC 20201 Carolyn Solomon, Tech.Info.Spec.
Founded: 1974. **Staff:** Prof 2; Other 1. **Subjects:** Health, income maintenance and support, program inspections, social services. **Special Collections:** Department of Health and Human Services Program Evaluation Reports; reports of CBO, GAO, OTA, and the Health and Human Services Inspector General. **Holdings:** 1850 books; 2000 General Accounting Office (GAO) reports; Executive Summaries; 2000 other cataloged items. **Services:** Copying; center open to the public for reference use only. **Automated Operations:** Computerized cataloging and circulation. **Computerized Information Services:** Software AG of North America, Inc; PIC On-line, EDC Database (internal databases). Performs searches free of charge. **Publications:** Compendium of Health and Human Services Evaluations and Other Relevant Studies, annual; Users Guide to the EDC. **Special Indexes:** Indexes of program names, sponsoring agencies, and subject names. **Remarks:** Evaluation reports are made available to the public through the National Technical Information Service (NTIS), U.S. Dept. of Commerce, Springfield, VA. **Staff:** Joan Turek-Brezina, Dir., Div. of Tech.Sup..

★15014★
U.S. DEPT. OF HEALTH AND HUMAN SERVICES - REGION I - OFFICE OF THE REGIONAL DIRECTOR
John F. Kennedy Bldg., Rm. 2411
Boston, MA 02203
Defunct

U.S. DEPT. OF HEALTH AND HUMAN SERVICES - SOCIAL SECURITY ADMINISTRATION
See: U.S. Social Security Administration (15494)

★15015★
U.S. DEPT. OF HOUSING AND URBAN DEVELOPMENT - LIBRARY (Soc Sci, Plan)
451 Seventh St., S.W., Rm. 8141 Phone: (202)755-6376
Washington, DC 20410 Carol A. Johnson, Proj.Mgr.
Founded: 1934. **Subjects:** Housing, community development, urban planning, sociology, law, mortgage and construction finance, architecture, land use, intergovernmental relations. **Special Collections:** HUD publications; HUD-sponsored reports including Comprehensive Planning (701) and Model Cities (50,000 reports). **Holdings:** 600,000 items. **Subscriptions:** 2100 journals and other serials. **Services:** Interlibrary loan; copying (limited); SDI; library open to the public for reference use only. **Automated Operations:** Computerized cataloging, acquisitions, serials, circulation, and ILL. **Computerized Information Services:** Online systems. **Networks/Consortia:** Member of FEDLINK. **Publications:** Recent Library Acquisitions; Library Periodicals List. **Special Catalogs:** Computer printout for Comprehensive Planning Reports. **Remarks:** The HUD Library is operated by Aspen Systems Corporation under contract to the U.S. Department of Housing and Urban Development.

★15016★
U.S. DEPT. OF HOUSING AND URBAN DEVELOPMENT - PHOTOGRAPHY LIBRARY (Aud-Vis)
451 7th St., S.W., Rm. B-120 Phone: (202)755-7305
Washington, DC 20410 Rowena M. Sanders, Visual Info.Spec.
Staff: Prof 1. **Subjects:** Housing, urban development, housing for the elderly, housing renewal. **Special Collections:** Instant Rehab (Core) in New York City (500 color slides; 150 black/white negatives); Operation Breakthrough; Johnstown Flood Disaster. **Holdings:** 200,000 black/white negatives; 40,000 color slides; 10,000 black/white prints. **Services:** Interlibrary loan; library open to the public by appointment only.

★15017★
U.S. DEPT. OF HOUSING AND URBAN DEVELOPMENT - REGION I - LIBRARY (Plan)
J.F.K. Federal Bldg. Phone: (617)223-4674
Boston, MA 02203 Christine A. Fraser, Libn.
Staff: Prof 1. **Subjects:** Housing, planning, urban development, law. **Holdings:** 1500 books; 3500 microfiche. **Subscriptions:** 100 journals and other serials; 10 newspapers. **Services:** Interlibrary loan; copying; SDI; library open to the public. **Automated Operations:** Computerized cataloging. **Computerized Information Services:** OCLC, JURIS, HUD USER; internal database. **Networks/Consortia:** Member of FEDLINK. **Publications:** Information-Information, monthly - free to mailing list.

★15018★
U.S. DEPT. OF HOUSING AND URBAN DEVELOPMENT - REGION III - LIBRARY
105 S. 7th St.
Liberty Square Bldg.
Philadelphia, PA 19106-3392
Defunct

★15019★
U.S. DEPT. OF HOUSING AND URBAN DEVELOPMENT - REGION IV - LIBRARY (Soc Sci)
Richard B. Russell Fed. Bldg., Rm. 722
75 Spring St., S.W. Phone: (404)331-3367
Atlanta, GA 30303 Mrs. Davide B. Williams, Reg.Libn.
Founded: 1968. **Staff:** Prof 1; Other 2. **Subjects:** Housing, planning, urban development, economic analysis, law, statistics. **Special Collections:** Housing and Urban Affairs (2700 microfiche; 1000 titles). **Holdings:** 17,000 books; 87 bound periodical volumes; Federal Register, 1967 to present, on microfilm; 12 VF drawers. **Subscriptions:** 83 journals and other serials. **Services:** Interlibrary loan; copying; library open to the public. **Publications:** Instructions on maintaining field collections - for internal distribution only.

★15020★
U.S. DEPT. OF HOUSING AND URBAN DEVELOPMENT - REGION VI - LIBRARY
1600 Throckmorton
Box 2905
Fort Worth, TX 76113-2905
Founded: 1966. **Subjects:** Law - Arkansas, Texas, Oklahoma, Louisiana, New Mexico; housing; economics; community development; management. **Holdings:** 6500 books; city charters for states listed above. **Remarks:** Presently inactive.

★15021★
U.S. DEPT. OF HOUSING AND URBAN DEVELOPMENT - REGION IX - LIBRARY
450 Golden Gate Ave.
Box 36003
San Francisco, CA 94102
Defunct

U.S. DEPT. OF THE INTERIOR - BUREAU OF INDIAN AFFAIRS
See: U.S. Bureau of Indian Affairs (14883)

U.S. DEPT. OF THE INTERIOR - BUREAU OF LAND MANAGEMENT
See: U.S. Bureau of Land Management (14888)

U.S. DEPT. OF THE INTERIOR - BUREAU OF MINES
See: U.S. Bureau of Mines (14895)

U.S. DEPT. OF THE INTERIOR - BUREAU OF RECLAMATION
See: U.S. Bureau of Reclamation (14903)

U.S. DEPT. OF THE INTERIOR - FISH & WILDLIFE SERVICE
See: U.S. Fish & Wildlife Service (15078)

U.S. DEPT. OF THE INTERIOR - GEOLOGICAL SURVEY
See: U.S. Geological Survey (15119)

★15022★
U.S. DEPT. OF THE INTERIOR - INDIAN ARTS AND CRAFTS BOARD (Art)
18th & C Sts., N.W., Rm. 4004-MIB Phone: (202)343-2773
Washington, DC 20240 Robert G. Hart, Gen.Mgr.
Founded: 1935. **Subjects:** Contemporary Native American arts and crafts. **Services:** Prepares answers or makes referrals for inquiries concerning contemporary Native American arts and crafts of the U.S.; no facilities maintained for researchers. **Publications:** Source Directory of Indian, Eskimo and Aleut Owned and Operated Arts and Crafts Businesses. **Remarks:** The Indian Arts and Crafts Board serves Indians, Eskimos, Aleuts, and the general public as an information, promotional, and advisory clearinghouse for all matters pertaining to the development of authentic Native American arts and crafts. **Staff:** Myles Libhart, Dir. of Pubn.; Geoffrey Stamm, Dir., Advisory Serv..

★15023★
U.S. DEPT. OF THE INTERIOR - INFORMATION AND LIBRARY SERVICES DIVISION - LAW BRANCH (Law)
18th & C Sts., N.W., Rm. 7100W Phone: (202)343-4571
Washington, DC 20240 Carl Kessler, Chf.
Founded: 1975. **Staff:** Prof 2; Other 2. **Subjects:** Law - public land, Indian, natural resources, administrative, environmental. **Special Collections:** Pre-Federal Register regulations of the Department of the Interior (1000 pieces); Native American Legal Materials (500 microfiche). **Holdings:** 30,000 books; 2000 bound periodical volumes; 10,000 microfiche; 1000 reels of microfilm; 3000 microfiche of Indian Claims Commission materials; 10 reels of microfilm of executive orders; 1000 microfiche of Council of State Governments publications; 150 legislative histories. **Subscriptions:** 801 journals and other serials. **Services:** Library open to the public for reference use only. **Automated Operations:** Computerized cataloging and acquisitions. **Computerized Information Services:** Online systems; Public Land Order Status System (internal database). **Networks/Consortia:** Member of FEDLINK. **Publications:** Law Library Update, monthly - for internal distribution only; Selected List of Federal Register Items of Interest to the Department of the Interior, weekly. **Special Indexes:** Statutory Index to the Legislative History Collection; Index to Microfilmed Public Lands Withdrawal Orders; Index to the Files on the Passage of PL96-487, Alaska National Interest Lands Conservation Act. **Staff:** Ocedell Barnes, Ref.Libn..

★15024★
U.S. DEPT. OF THE INTERIOR - MINERALS MANAGEMENT SERVICE - ALASKA OUTER CONTINENTAL SHELF REGIONAL LIBRARY (Env-Cons)
949 E. 36th Ave., Rm. 110 Phone: (907)261-2409
Anchorage, AK 99508-4435 Christine R. Huffaker, Libn.
Founded: 1976. **Staff:** 5. **Subjects:** Environmental science, geophysics, geology, socioeconomic assessment. **Holdings:** 6000 books; 1500 bound periodical volumes. **Subscriptions:** 100 journals and other serials; 10 newspapers. **Services:** Library not open to the public. **Automated Operations:** Computerized cataloging. **Computerized Information Services:** LEXIS, NEXIS, OCLC, DIALOG Information Services. **Networks/Consortia:** Member of FEDLINK.

U.S. DEPT. OF THE INTERIOR - NATIONAL PARK SERVICE
See: U.S. Natl. Park Service (15242)

★15025★
U.S. DEPT. OF THE INTERIOR - NATURAL RESOURCES LIBRARY (Env-Cons, Energy)
18th & C Sts., N.W. Phone: (202)343-5815
Washington, DC 20240 Gail L. Kohlhorst, Asst.Chf., Info./Lib.Serv.Dir.
Founded: 1949. **Staff:** Prof 13; Other 9. **Subjects:** Conservation, energy and power, land use, parks, American Indians, fish and wildlife, mining, law, management. **Special Collections:** Archival collection of materials published by Department of Interior (150,000 items). **Holdings:** 600,000 books; 90,000 bound periodical volumes; 7000 reels of microfilm; 40,000 unbound periodical volumes; 300,000 microfiche. **Subscriptions:** 10,000 journals and other serials. **Services:** Interlibrary loan; copying; library open to the public with restrictions. **Automated Operations:** Computerized cataloging, acquisitions, serials, circulation, and ILL. **Computerized Information Services:** DIALOG Information Services, NEXIS, OCLC. **Networks/Consortia:** Member of FEDLINK. **Publications:** Departmental Manual Subject Index: FPM, FAR, and IPMR Additions; Law Library Update; Selected List of Federal Register Items of Interest to the Department of Interior. **Staff:** Robert Uskavitch, Chf., Info.Serv.; Sue Ellen Sloca, Chf., Info. Products.

★15026★
U.S. DEPT. OF JUSTICE - ANTITRUST BRANCH LIBRARY (Law)
10th & Pennsylvania Ave., N.W., Rm. 3310 Phone: (202)633-2431
Washington, DC 20530 Mary E. Clarity, Libn.
Staff: Prof 2; Other 2. **Subjects:** Antitrust law, administrative law, business. **Special Collections:** Legislative histories. **Holdings:** 18,000 volumes. **Subscriptions:** 350 journals and other serials. **Services:** Interlibrary loan; library not open to the public. **Computerized Information Services:** DIALOG Information Services, Pergamon ORBIT InfoLine, Inc., MEDLINE, NEXIS, LEXIS, JURIS, LEGI-SLATE, Dow Jones News/Retrieval, Dun & Bradstreet Corporation, WESTLAW, VU/TEXT Information Services, DataTimes, WILSONLINE, Washington Alert Service, BRS Information Technologies, OCLC, DATALIB.

★15027★
U.S. DEPT. OF JUSTICE - BUREAU OF PRISONS - LIBRARY (Law)
320 First St., N.W. Phone: (202)724-3029
Washington, DC 20534 Lloyd W. Hooker, Libn.
Founded: 1960. **Staff:** Prof 1; Other 1. **Subjects:** Criminology, corrections, criminal psychology. **Special Collections:** Archival material of the bureau (100 items). **Holdings:** 2523 books and bound periodical volumes; 65 periodicals; 1200 items in information file; 100 annual reports. **Subscriptions:** 62 journals and other serials. **Services:** Interlibrary loan; library open to those in correctional work and related fields, including graduate students doing research in corrections. **Computerized Information Services:** OCLC. **Publications:** Correctional Bookshelf, a bibliography, 1977.

★15028★
U.S. DEPT. OF JUSTICE - BUREAU OF PRISONS - NATIONAL INSTITUTE OF CORRECTIONS - NIC INFORMATION CENTER (Law)
1790 30th St., Suite 130 Phone: (303)444-1101
Boulder, CO 80301 Coralie Whitmore, Dir.
Subjects: Prisons, jails, probation, parole, community corrections. **Holdings:** 10,000 documents. **Services:** Interlibrary loan; copying; center open to the public. **Automated Operations:** Computerized cataloging, acquisitions, serials, and circulation. **Computerized Information Services:** DIALOG Information Services; internal database. **Networks/Consortia:** Member of Criminal Justice Information Exchange Group. **Publications:** Corrections Information Series. **Staff:** Eileen Conway, Rsrc.Coord.; Barbara Sudol, Libn.; Brian Bemus, Corrections Spec.; Kathy Black-Dennis, Corrections Spec.; Bob Greene, Corrections Spec..

★15029★
U.S. DEPT. OF JUSTICE - CIVIL BRANCH LIBRARY (Law)
10th & Pennsylvania Ave., N.W., Rm. 3344 Phone: (202)633-3523
Washington, DC 20530 Roger N. Kerr, Libn.
Staff: Prof 3; Other 2. **Subjects:** Law, customs, bankruptcy, government contracts, commercial law, admiralty, aviation, patents, trademarks, copyright. **Special Collections:** Legislative histories. **Holdings:** 45,000 volumes. **Subscriptions:** 300 journals and other serials. **Services:** Interlibrary loan; library not open to the public. **Computerized Information Services:** DIALOG Information Services, Pergamon ORBIT InfoLine, Inc., LEXIS, NEXIS, JURIS, LEGI-SLATE, Dow Jones News/Retrieval, WESTLAW, MEDLINE, DataTimes, WILSONLINE, Washington Alert Service, DATALIB, BRS Information Technologies, OCLC; Email (electronic mail service). **Networks/Consortia:** Member of FEDLINK.

★15030★
U.S. DEPT. OF JUSTICE - CIVIL RIGHTS BRANCH LIBRARY (Soc Sci, Law)
10th & Pennsylvania Ave., N.W., Rm. 7618 Phone: (202)633-4098
Washington, DC 20530 Catherine D. Harman, Libn.
Staff: Prof 2; Other 1. **Subjects:** Civil rights, constitutional law, demographics. **Holdings:** 10,000 volumes. **Subscriptions:** 150 journals and other serials. **Services:** Interlibrary loan; library not open to the public. **Computerized Information Services:** JURIS, WESTLAW, LEXIS, NEXIS, DIALOG Information Services, Pergamon ORBIT InfoLine, Inc., LEGI-SLATE, Dow Jones News/Retrieval, MEDLINE, VU/TEXT Information Services, DataTimes, WILSONLINE, Washington Alert Service, DATALIB, BRS Information Technologies, OCLC; Email (electronic mail service). **Networks/Consortia:** Member of FEDLINK. **Staff:** Gertrude Dennis, Asst.Libn..

★15031★
U.S. DEPT. OF JUSTICE - CRIMINAL BRANCH LIBRARY (Law)
1400 New York Ave., N.W.
Bond Bldg., Rm. 7100 Phone: (202)724-6934
Washington, DC 20530 Diane L. Smith, Libn.
Staff: Prof 2; Other 1. **Subjects:** Federal criminal law, procedure and evidence. **Special Collections:** White collar, computer, and organized crime; espionage and terrorism. **Holdings:** 25,000 books. **Subscriptions:** 51 journals and other serials. **Services:** Interlibrary loan; library not open to the public. **Automated Operations:** Computerized cataloging. **Computerized Information Services:** JURIS, LEXIS, NEXIS, WESTLAW, DIALOG Information Services, Pergamon ORBIT InfoLine, Inc., LEGI-SLATE, Dow Jones News/Retrieval, MEDLINE, BRS Information Technologies, VU/TEXT Information Services; Email (electronic mail service). **Networks/Consortia:** Member of FEDLINK.

U.S. DEPT. OF JUSTICE - DRUG ENFORCEMENT ADMINISTRATION
See: U.S. Drug Enforcement Administration (15066)

U.S. DEPT. OF JUSTICE - FEDERAL BUREAU OF INVESTIGATION
See: U.S. Federal Bureau of Investigation (15075)

U.S. DEPT. OF JUSTICE - FOREIGN CLAIMS SETTLEMENT COMMISSION OF THE UNITED STATES
See: Foreign Claims Settlement Commission of the United States (5251)

★15032★
U.S. DEPT. OF JUSTICE - LAND AND NATURAL RESOURCES BRANCH LIBRARY (Law)
10th & Pennsylvania Ave., N.W., Rm. 2333 Phone: (202)633-2768
Washington, DC 20530 Cynthia R. Plisch, Libn.
Staff: Prof 2; Other 1. **Subjects:** Civil cases regarding lands, titles, water rights, Indian claims, hazardous waste, public works, pollution control, marine resources, fish and wildlife, environment. **Special Collections:** Legislative histories. **Holdings:** 13,000 volumes. **Subscriptions:** 160 journals and other serials. **Services:** Interlibrary loan; library not open to the public. **Computerized Information Services:** JURIS, DIALOG Information Services, Pergamon ORBIT InfoLine, Inc., LEXIS, NEXIS, LEGI-SLATE, Dow Jones News/Retrieval, MEDLINE, OCLC, VU/TEXT Information Services, DataTimes, WILSONLINE, Washington Alert Service, DATALIB, BRS Information Technologies; Email (electronic mail service). **Networks/Consortia:** Member of FEDLINK. **Staff:** Edward Wolff, Asst.Libn..

★15033★
U.S. DEPT. OF JUSTICE - MAIN LIBRARY (Law, Bus-Fin)
10th & Pennsylvania Ave., N.W., Rm. 5400 Phone: (202)633-2133
Washington, DC 20530 Daphne B. Sampson, Dir.
Founded: 1831. **Staff:** Prof 15; Other 4. **Subjects:** Law, business, and allied subjects. **Special Collections:** Legislative histories; Department of Justice publications. **Holdings:** 200,000 volumes; 1 million microforms. **Subscriptions:** 800 journals. **Services:** Interlibrary loan; library open to the public by appointment. **Automated Operations:** Computerized cataloging and acquisitions. **Computerized Information Services:** DIALOG Information Services, OCLC, Pergamon ORBIT InfoLine, Inc., LEXIS, JURIS, NEXIS, LEGI-SLATE, Dow Jones News/Retrieval, MEDLINE, WESTLAW, VU/TEXT Information Services, WILSONLINE, Washington Alert Service, Washington On-Line, BRS Information Technologies, DataTimes, DATALIB, BRS Information Technologies; Email (electronic mail service). **Networks/Consortia:** Member of FEDLINK. **Publications:** Consolidated Periodicals Guide; Database Guide; Library Handbook. **Staff:** Kristina Kelley, Chf., Res.; Winifred Hart, Chf., Coll.; Richard Shrout, Asst.Dir., Tech.Serv.; Daire McCabe, Chf., Acq.; Camille Simmons, Chf., Cat..

U.S. DEPT. OF JUSTICE - NATIONAL INSTITUTE OF CORRECTIONS
See: U.S. Dept. of Justice - Bureau of Prisons - National Institute of Corrections (15028)

★15034★
U.S. DEPT. OF JUSTICE - NATIONAL INSTITUTE OF JUSTICE - LIBRARY (Soc Sci, Law)
633 Indiana Ave., N.W., Rm. 900 Phone: (202)724-5884
Washington, DC 20531 Denise W. Lomax, Libn.
Founded: 1970. **Staff:** 1. **Subjects:** Law enforcement, police science, criminology, juvenile delinquency, courts, corrections, white collar crime,

spouse and child abuse, victims. **Holdings:** 5500 books; 1000 U.S. Government documents. **Subscriptions:** 130 journals and other serials. **Services:** Interlibrary loan; copying; library open to the public for reference use only. **Computerized Information Services:** DIALOG Information Services, OCLC, WESTLAW.

★15035★
U.S. DEPT. OF JUSTICE - NATIONAL INSTITUTE OF JUSTICE - NATIONAL CRIMINAL JUSTICE REFERENCE SERVICE (Soc Sci, Law)
1600 Research Blvd.
Box 6000 Phone: (301)251-5500
Rockville, MD 20850 Richard S. Rosenthal, Prog.Dir.
Founded: 1972. **Subjects:** Law enforcement, criminal and juvenile justice, white collar crime, public corruption, courts, corrections, crime prevention/security, evaluations and research, criminology, victim/witness assistance, dispute resolution. **Holdings:** 90,000 books, research reports, articles; 40,000 documents on microfiche. **Subscriptions:** 200 journals and other serials. **Services:** Interlibrary loan; referrals; service open to the public. **Computerized Information Services:** DIALOG Information Services, JURIS; internal database. Performs searches on fee basis. **Networks/Consortia:** Member of Criminal Justice Information Exchange Group. **Publications:** NIJ Reports (research and abstract bulletin), bimonthly - free upon request; Monthly Accessions List; Microfiche Packages; Directory of Criminal Justice Information Sources; DIALOG User's Manual. **Special Indexes:** Document Retrieval Index (microfiche); index to microfiche collection. **Remarks:** Outside of Maryland, Washington, D.C., and Alaska, call (800)851-3420.

★15036★
U.S. DEPT. OF JUSTICE - TAX BRANCH LIBRARY (Bus-Fin, Law)
10th & Pennsylvania Ave., N.W., Rm. 4335 Phone: (202)633-2819
Washington, DC 20530 Jacqueline Lee, Libn.
Staff: Prof 2; Other 1. **Subjects:** Taxation, bankruptcy. **Holdings:** 30,000 volumes. **Services:** Interlibrary loan; library not open to the public. **Computerized Information Services:** JURIS, LEXIS, NEXIS, WESTLAW, DIALOG Information Services, PHINet FedTax Database, Pergamon ORBIT InfoLine, Inc., LEGI-SLATE, Dow Jones News/Retrieval, MEDLINE, VU/TEXT Information Services, DataTimes, WILSONLINE, Washington Alert Service, DATALIB, BRS Information Technologies, OCLC; Email (electronic mail service). **Networks/Consortia:** Member of FEDLINK.

★15037★
U.S. DEPT. OF JUSTICE - UNITED STATES ATTORNEY, CENTRAL DISTRICT OF CALIFORNIA - LIBRARY (Law)
1214 U.S. Court House
312 N. Spring St.
Los Angeles, CA 90012 Phone: (213)688-2419
Staff: Prof 1; Other 1. **Subjects:** Law. **Holdings:** 13,000 volumes. **Services:** Library not open to the public.

★15038★
U.S. DEPT. OF JUSTICE - UNITED STATES ATTORNEY, DISTRICT OF NEW JERSEY - LAW LIBRARY (Law)
970 Broad St. Phone: (201)621-2951
Newark, NJ 07102 Roberta D. Klotz, Libn.
Staff: Prof 1. **Subjects:** Law. **Holdings:** 6000 volumes. **Services:** Library not open to the public. **Computerized Information Services:** JURIS.

★15039★
U.S. DEPT. OF JUSTICE - UNITED STATES ATTORNEY, EASTERN DISTRICT OF PENNSYLVANIA - LIBRARY (Law)
3310 U.S. Courthouse
601 Market St. Phone: (215)597-2161
Philadelphia, PA 19106 Susan J. Falken, Libn.
Staff: Prof 1; Other 2. **Subjects:** Criminal law. **Holdings:** 7600 books; 40 bound periodical volumes. **Subscriptions:** 12 journals and other serials; 10 newspapers. **Services:** Interlibrary loan; copying; library open to the public with restrictions. **Computerized Information Services:** NEXIS, VU/TEXT Information Services, WESTLAW, JURIS. **Special Indexes:** Briefs of the Third Circuit.

★15040★
U.S. DEPT. OF JUSTICE - UNITED STATES ATTORNEY, NORTHERN DISTRICT OF ILLINOIS - LIBRARY (Law)
1500 Dirksen Federal Bldg.
219 S. Dearborn St. Phone: (312)353-5338
Chicago, IL 60604 Mary Alice Stack, Libn.
Staff: Prof 1. **Subjects:** Federal law. **Holdings:** 12,000 volumes. **Services:** Interlibrary loan; library not open to the public. **Computerized Information Services:** JURIS, WESTLAW, LEXIS.

★15041★
U.S. DEPT. OF JUSTICE - UNITED STATES ATTORNEY, SOUTHERN DISTRICT OF NEW YORK - LIBRARY (Law)
One St. Andrew's Plaza, 6th Fl. Phone: (212)791-0029
New York, NY 10007 Barbara J. Zelenko, Hd.Libn.
Staff: Prof 1; Other 3. **Subjects:** Law. **Holdings:** 20,000 books; law memoranda; manuscripts; 12 VF drawers of clippings; sample indictment file; 6 VF drawers of sample charge files. **Subscriptions:** 91 journals and other serials. **Services:** Interlibrary loan; library not open to the public. **Computerized Information Services:** JURIS, LEXIS.

★15042★
U.S. DEPT. OF LABOR - BUREAU OF LABOR STATISTICS - INFORMATION AND ADVISORY SECTION (Bus-Fin)
1515 Broadway, Rm. 3400
New York, NY 10036 Phone: (212)944-3121
Founded: 1949. **Subjects:** Labor force, employment, productivity, industrial relations, occupational outlook, occupational health and safety statistics, consumer and producer price indexes. **Holdings:** 500 books; 1500 bound periodical volumes; 5000 pamphlets. **Subscriptions:** 100 journals and other serials. **Services:** Copying; library open to the public. **Remarks:** Maintains 24-hour recordings providing information on national and regional Consumer Price Indexes, Producer Price Indexes, unemployment rates, and weekly research findings. **Staff:** Patricia Bommicino; Lillian Kohlrieser; Robert Okell.

★15043★
U.S. DEPT. OF LABOR - BUREAU OF LABOR STATISTICS - NORTH CENTRAL REGIONAL OFFICE REFERENCE LIBRARY (Bus-Fin)
230 S. Dearborn St., 9th Fl. Phone: (312)353-1880
Chicago, IL 60604 Ronald M. Guzicki, Supv. Economist
Staff: Prof 3; Other 3. **Subjects:** Labor force, price indexes, productivity, occupational safety and health, compensation, industrial relations. **Holdings:** Bureau of Labor Statistics bulletins, reports, and monthly labor reviews. **Services:** Library open to the public for reference use only. **Computerized Information Services:** LABSTAT (internal database). **Staff:** Roger Sanzenbacher, Economist; Gerald Jaecks, Economist.

★15044★
U.S. DEPT. OF LABOR - EMPLOYMENT & TRAINING ADMINISTRATION - REGION IV RESOURCE CENTER (Bus-Fin)
1371 Peachtree St., N.E., Rm. 419 Phone: (404)347-3534
Atlanta, GA 30367 Toussaint Hayes, Trng.Dir.
Staff: Prof 1; Other 1. **Subjects:** Employment and training programs, labor statistics, training packages, management development. **Holdings:** 3500 volumes. **Services:** Interlibrary loan; center open to the public. **Automated Operations:** Computerized cataloging and acquisitions. **Computerized Information Services:** Internal database.

★15045★
U.S. DEPT. OF LABOR - EMPLOYMENT & TRAINING ADMINISTRATION - REGION X RESOURCE CENTER
909 First Ave., No. 1136
Seattle, WA 98174
Defunct

★15046★
U.S. DEPT. OF LABOR - LIBRARY (Bus-Fin)
200 Constitution Ave., N.W. Phone: (202)523-6988
Washington, DC 20210 Sabina Jacobson, Lib.Dir.
Founded: 1917. **Staff:** Prof 9; Other 11. **Subjects:** Economics, labor. **Special Collections:** Trade union constitutions, proceedings, and journals. **Holdings:** 535,000 volumes; labor papers on microfilm. **Subscriptions:** 3200 journals; 9 newspapers. **Services:** Interlibrary loan (limited); copying; library open to the public for reference use only. **Automated Operations:** Computerized cataloging, acquisitions, and circulation. **Computerized Information Services:** OCLC, DIALOG Information Services, The Reference Service (REFSRV), BRS Information Technologies, Pergamon

ORBIT InfoLine, Inc., LEXIS, NEXIS, JURIS. **Networks/Consortia:** Member of FEDLINK. **Publications:** Periodicals Currently Received by the U.S. Department of Labor Library, irregular.

★15047★
U.S. DEPT. OF LABOR - LIBRARY - LAW LIBRARY DIVISION (Law)
200 Constitution Ave., N.W., Rm. N-2439 Phone: (202)523-7991
Washington, DC 20210 Donald L. Martin, Law Libn.
Founded: 1940. **Staff:** Prof 2; Other 2. **Subjects:** Labor law. **Holdings:** 25,000 volumes. **Services:** Library open to the public. **Automated Operations:** Computerized acquisitions.

★15048★
U.S. DEPT. OF LABOR - MINE SAFETY & HEALTH ADMINISTRATION - INFORMATIONAL SERVICES LIBRARY (Sci-Engr)
Box 25367 Phone: (303)236-2729
Denver, CO 80225 James A. Greenhalgh, Libn.
Founded: 1979. **Staff:** Prof 1; Other 1. **Subjects:** Mine safety and health, mining industry. **Special Collections:** Federal standards. **Holdings:** 1200 books and bound periodical volumes; 5400 government documents on microfiche; 4500 Bureau of Mines reports; 7200 Mines Safety & Health Administration reports; 4 CD-ROMs on chemical information. **Subscriptions:** 117 journals and other serials. **Services:** Interlibrary loan; copying; library open to the public. **Automated Operations:** Computerized cataloging and serials. **Computerized Information Services:** DIALOG Information Services, NLM, Integrated Technical Information System (ITIS), Occupational Health Services, Inc. (OHS), OCLC. **Publications:** New Publications List, quarterly; occasional bibliographies.

★15049★
U.S. DEPT. OF LABOR - MINE SAFETY & HEALTH ADMINISTRATION - NATIONAL MINE HEALTH AND SAFETY ACADEMY - LEARNING RESOURCE CENTER (Bus-Fin, Sci-Engr)
Airport Rd.
Box 1166 Phone: (304)256-3100
Beckley, WV 25802-1166 Stephen J. Hoyle, Chf., LRC
Staff: Prof 1; Other 4. **Subjects:** Mine and industrial safety, industrial health, management, education. **Special Collections:** Audiovisual materials on mine safety; government publications on mine safety. **Holdings:** 8800 books; 723 films; 600 video cassettes; 115,000 microfiche; 740 reels of microfilm; 300 audio cassettes; 400 slide/tape sets; 200 slide sets. **Subscriptions:** 125 journals and other serials; 5 newspapers. **Services:** Copying; SDI; center open to the public for reference use only. **Automated Operations:** Computerized cataloging. **Computerized Information Services:** DIALOG Information Services, Pergamon ORBIT InfoLine, Inc.; Accident Data Analysis, Training Materials Database, Educational Materials Search System (internal databases). Performs searches free of charge. Contact Person: Becky Farley, Lib.Techn., 265-3226. **Publications:** News clips; acquisitions list, both irregular.

U.S. DEPT. OF LABOR - OCCUPATIONAL SAFETY AND HEALTH ADMINISTRATION
See: U.S. Dept. of Labor - OSHA (15054)

★15050★
U.S. DEPT. OF LABOR - OSHA - BILLINGS AREA OFFICE LIBRARY (Med)
19 N. 25th St. Phone: (406)657-6649
Billings, MT 59101 Marilyn J. Dillon, Ck.
Founded: 1974. **Staff:** 1. **Subjects:** Safety and health in the workplace. **Holdings:** 500 books; microfilm. **Services:** Library open to the public. **Automated Operations:** Computerized cataloging.

★15051★
U.S. DEPT. OF LABOR - OSHA - IDAHO AREA OFFICE - LIBRARY (Med)
550 W. Fort St., Rm. 324
Box 007 Phone: (208)334-1867
Boise, ID 83724 Ryan Kuehmichel, Area Dir.
Staff: 1. **Subjects:** Safety, health, industrial hygiene, chemistry, fire codes. **Holdings:** 500 books; 90 bound periodical volumes. **Services:** Library not open to the public.

★15052★
U.S. DEPT. OF LABOR - OSHA - REGION III LIBRARY (Med)
3535 Market St., Suite 2100 Phone: (215)596-1201
Philadelphia, PA 19104 Barbara Goodman, Libn.
Staff: Prof 1. **Subjects:** Occupational health and safety, industrial hygiene, toxic substances. **Special Collections:** National Institute of Occupational Safety and Health (NIOSH) documents; OSHA standards; industry standards. **Holdings:** 1500 books. **Services:** Interlibrary loan; library open to the public. **Computerized Information Services:** DIALOG Information Services, OCLC, MEDLARS; OCIS (internal database). **Networks/Consortia:** Member of FEDLINK.

★15053★
U.S. DEPT. OF LABOR - OSHA - REGION X LIBRARY (Med)
6003 Federal Office Bldg.
909 First Ave. Phone: (206)442-5930
Seattle, WA 98174 Donna M. Hoffman, Libn.
Staff: Prof 1. **Subjects:** Industrial hygiene, toxic substances, industrial safety, toxicology, safety, engineering. **Special Collections:** ANSI Standards; NIOSH documents. **Holdings:** 1000 titles. **Subscriptions:** 10 journals and other serials. **Services:** Interlibrary loan; copying; library open to the public for reference use only. **Computerized Information Services:** NLM, DIALOG Information Services. **Networks/Consortia:** Member of FEDLINK.

★15054★
U.S. DEPT. OF LABOR - OSHA - TECHNICAL DATA CENTER (Sci-Engr, Med)
200 Constitution Ave., N.W.
Rm. N-2439 Rear Phone: (202)523-9700
Washington, DC 20210 Thomas A. Towers, Dir.
Founded: 1972. **Staff:** Prof 7; Other 3. **Subjects:** Occupational safety, industrial hygiene, toxicology, control technology, hazardous materials, fire safety, electrical safety, noise, carcinogens, material safety. **Holdings:** 8000 books and bound periodical volumes; 150,000 microfiche; 2000 technical documents; 3000 standards and codes. **Subscriptions:** 250 journals and other serials. **Services:** Interlibrary loan; copying; center open to the public for reference use only. **Computerized Information Services:** DIALOG Information Services, Pergamon ORBIT InfoLine, Inc., BRS Information Technologies, Chemical Information Systems, Inc. (CIS), NLM; NIOSHTIC, OCIS, TIRS (internal databases). **Networks/Consortia:** Member of FEDLINK. **Publications:** TDC User Reference Guide; Information and Insight Bulletin, quarterly - for internal and limited external distribution. **Staff:** Shirley Marshall, Tech.Info.Spec.; Denise E. Hayes, Tech.Info.Spec.; Daniel Marsick, Tech.Info.Spec.; Elaine C. Johnson, Tech.Info.Spec.; James Towles, Tech.Info.Spec.; Robert Turnage, Tech.Info.Spec.; Elaine G. Bynum, Docket Off..

★15055★
U.S. DEPT. OF STATE - LIBRARY (Soc Sci, Hist, Law)
Washington, DC 20520 Phone: (202)647-1062
Conrad P. Eaton, Libn.
Founded: 1789. **Staff:** Prof 11; Other 10. **Subjects:** International relations, diplomatic history, international law, treaties and agreements, political history, economic conditions, social and cultural developments, ideologies and trends, law. **Holdings:** 650,000 books. **Subscriptions:** 1100 journals and other serials. **Services:** Interlibrary loan; library may be consulted by special arrangement. **Automated Operations:** Computerized cataloging and circulation. **Computerized Information Services:** DIALOG Information Services, Pergamon ORBIT InfoLine, Inc., BRS Information Technologies, Mead Data Central, TEXTLINE, LEGI-SLATE, Dow Jones News/Retrieval, RLIN, WILSONLINE, VU/TEXT Information Services, DataTimes, G.CAM, Data Resources (DRI), Dialcom Inc. **Networks/Consortia:** Member of FEDLINK. **Staff:** Dan O. Clemmer, Chf., Rd.Serv..

★15056★
U.S. DEPT. OF STATE - OFFICE OF THE LEGAL ADVISER LAW LIBRARY (Law)
Dept. of State, Rm. 6422
Washington, DC 20520 Helena P. Von Pfeil, Intl.Law Libn./Law Lib.Adm.
Founded: 1920. **Staff:** Prof 1; Other 1. **Subjects:** Law - international, foreign, comparative, U.S. **Holdings:** 90,000 volumes, 5000 other cataloged items. **Subscriptions:** 500 journals and other serials. **Services:** Library not open to the public. **Automated Operations:** Computerized cataloging and serials. **Computerized Information Services:** LEXIS, WESTLAW, DIALOG Information Services, JURIS. **Networks/Consortia:** Member of FEDLINK. **Special Catalogs:** International Court of Justice, Arbitration, and International Law Treatises catalogs.

U.S. DEPT. OF TRANSPORTATION - COAST GUARD
See: U.S. Coast Guard (14912)

U.S. DEPT. OF TRANSPORTATION - FEDERAL AVIATION ADMINISTRATION
See: U.S. Federal Aviation Administration (15070)

U.S. DEPT. OF TRANSPORTATION - FEDERAL HIGHWAY ADMINISTRATION
See: U.S. Federal Highway Administration (15076)

★15057★
U.S. DEPT. OF TRANSPORTATION - LIBRARY AND DISTRIBUTION SERVICES DIVISION (Trans)
400 7th St., S.W. Phone: (202)366-0746
Washington, DC 20590 Lawrence E. Leonard, Lib.Dir.
Founded: 1969. **Staff:** Prof 16; Other 11. **Subjects:** Highways, aviation, marine transportation, law, urban mass transit, railroads. **Special Collections:** Aviation reports (50,000 volumes); aviation technical publications (4600 titles). **Holdings:** 384,935 books; 51,360 bound periodical volumes; 80 pamphlet boxes of state highway department maps; 40,000 pamphlets in VF drawers; 533,067 microforms. **Subscriptions:** 2683 journals and other serials; 5 newspapers. **Services:** Interlibrary loan; copying; division open to the public for limited reference use. **Automated Operations:** Computerized cataloging, acquisitions, serials, and ILL. **Computerized Information Services:** DIALOG Information Services, BRS Information Technologies, DTIC, JURIS, NEXIS, LEXIS, OCLC, WESTLAW, DunSprint. **Networks/Consortia:** Member of FEDLINK. **Publications:** Selected Library Acquisitions, quarterly - for official distribution. **Special Indexes:** Periodicals Index File on transportation, 1921-1982 (card). **Remarks:** The 10-A Services Section, M-493.2, library is located at 800 Independence Ave., S.W., Washington, DC 20591 and the telephone number is 267-3113. The library director can be reached at 366-2565. The telephone number for law is 366-0749. Subject scope of the 10-A library stresses air transportation, aviation, and related subjects. There is also a Coast Guard law collection located at 2100 2nd St., S.W., Washington, DC 20593, telephone 267-2536. **Staff:** Dorothy Poehlman, Chf., Info.Serv.Br.; Cecily V. Wood, Chf., Tech.Serv.Br.; William Mills, Chf., Acq.Sect.; Mon-hua Mona Kuo, Chf., Cat.Sect.; Loretta A. Norris, Chf., Law Serv.Sect.; Thomas M. Haggerty, Chf., 10A Serv.Sect.; Mary Jo Burke, Chf., HQ Serv.Sect..

U.S. DEPT. OF TRANSPORTATION - MARITIME ADMINISTRATION
See: U.S. Maritime Administration (15188)

U.S. DEPT. OF TRANSPORTATION - MARITIME ADMINISTRATION - U.S. MERCHANT MARINE ACADEMY
See: U.S. Merchant Marine Academy (15189)

U.S. DEPT. OF TRANSPORTATION - NATIONAL HIGHWAY TRAFFIC SAFETY ADMINISTRATION
See: U.S. Natl. Highway Traffic Safety Administration (15205)

★15058★
U.S. DEPT. OF TRANSPORTATION - RESEARCH AND SPECIAL PROGRAMS ADMINISTRATION - TRANSPORTATION SYSTEMS CENTER - TECHNICAL REFERENCE CENTER (Trans)
Kendall Square Phone: (617)494-2306
Cambridge, MA 02142 Susan C. Dresley, Lib.Dir.
Founded: 1970. **Staff:** Prof 6; Other 2. **Subjects:** Transportation. **Holdings:** 30,000 books; 650 bound periodical volumes; 350,000 microfiche; 36 VF drawers of maps. **Subscriptions:** 150 journals and other serials; 5 newspapers. **Services:** Interlibrary loan; center open to the public for reference use only. **Automated Operations:** Computerized cataloging. **Computerized Information Services:** OCLC, DIALOG Information Services, Aviation Online, LEGI-SLATE. **Networks/Consortia:** Member of FEDLINK. **Staff:** Robert Perreault, ILL.

U.S. DEPT. OF TRANSPORTATION - URBAN MASS TRANSPORTATION ADMINISTRATION
See: U.S. Urban Mass Transportation Administration (15511)

★15059★
U.S. DEPT. OF THE TREASURY - AUTOMATED SYSTEMS - INFORMATION SERVICES - TREASURY DEPARTMENT LIBRARY (Bus-Fin, Law)
Main Treasury Bldg., Rm. 5030 Phone: (202)566-2777
Washington, DC 20220 Elisabeth S. Knauff, Mgr., Info.Serv.
Founded: 1789. **Staff:** Prof 7; Other 5. **Subjects:** Taxation, public finance, law, domestic and international economics and economic conditions. **Holdings:** 85,100 books and bound periodical volumes; 307,500 microfiche; 6800 reels of microfilm. **Services:** Interlibrary loan; copying; library open to the public by appointment for reference use only. **Automated Operations:** Computerized acquisitions and serials. **Computerized Information Services:** DIALOG Information Services, LEXIS, NEXIS, OCLC, TEXTLINE, Dow Jones News/Retrieval, Washington Alert Service. **Networks/Consortia:** Member of FEDLINK, Metropolitan Washington Library Council. **Staff:** Christine R. Rudy, Chf., Rd.Serv.Br.; Linda Trout, Legal Ref.Libn.; Betty Elmore, Ser.Cat.; Mary Pope, Chf., Tech.Serv.Br..

U.S. DEPT. OF THE TREASURY - BUREAU OF ALCOHOL, TOBACCO AND FIREARMS
See: U.S. Bureau of Alcohol, Tobacco and Firearms (14868)

U.S. DEPT. OF THE TREASURY - COMPTROLLER OF THE CURRENCY
See: U.S. Comptroller of the Currency (14916)

U.S. DEPT. OF THE TREASURY - CUSTOMS SERVICE
See: U.S. Customs Service (14945)

U.S. DEPT. OF THE TREASURY - INTERNAL REVENUE SERVICE
See: U.S. Internal Revenue Service (15142)

★15060★
U.S. DISTRICT COURT - EASTERN DISTRICT OF NEW YORK - LIBRARY (Law)
225 Cadman Plaza E. Phone: (718)330-7483
Brooklyn, NY 11201 John T. Saiz, Law Libn.
Founded: 1965. **Staff:** Prof 1. **Subjects:** Federal and state law. **Holdings:** 21,500 books; 500 bound periodical volumes; 600 other cataloged items; 3500 items of Congressional Record; 3000 items of Federal Register; 85 reels of microfilm. **Subscriptions:** 110 journals and other serials. **Services:** Library not open to the public. **Computerized Information Services:** WESTLAW, LEXIS.

★15061★
U.S. DISTRICT COURT - LAW LIBRARY (Law)
701 C St.
Box 31 Phone: (907)271-5655
Anchorage, AK 99513 Rita Dursi, Libn.
Staff: Prof 1; Other 1. **Subjects:** Law. **Holdings:** 15,708 books; 833 bound periodical volumes; 530 pamphlets. **Subscriptions:** 94 journals and other serials. **Services:** Library open to the public with restrictions. **Computerized Information Services:** WESTLAW, LEXIS.

★15062★
U.S. DISTRICT COURT - LEGAL LIBRARY (Law)
Box 3671 Phone: (809)725-9229
San Juan, PR 00904 Ana Milagros Rodriguez, Libn.
Staff: 1. **Subjects:** Law. **Holdings:** 15,000 volumes. **Subscriptions:** 250 journals and other serials. **Services:** Copying; library open to the public with written permission.

★15063★
U.S. DISTRICT COURT - LIBRARY (Law)
U.S. Court House
300 Ala Moana Blvd.
Box 50128 Phone: (808)541-1797
Honolulu, HI 96850 Isabel T. Anduha, Libn.
Staff: 1. **Subjects:** Law. **Holdings:** 22,700 volumes; 14 tapes in Nita Younger Cassette Series. **Services:** Library serves U.S. Court personnel, supporting staff, federal and state agencies, and attorneys practicing before the court.

★15064★
U.S. DISTRICT COURT - LIBRARY (Law)
213 U.S. Courthouse
620 S.W. Main Phone: (503)221-6042
Portland, OR 97205-3080 Scott McCurdy, Libn.
Staff: Prof 2. **Subjects:** Law. **Holdings:** 12,000 volumes. **Services:** Interlibrary loan; library open to attorneys on day of hearing. **Computerized Information Services:** WESTLAW, LEXIS. **Staff:** Diane Schauer, Asst.Libn..

★15065★
U.S. DISTRICT COURT - NORTHERN CALIFORNIA DISTRICT - LOUIS E. GOODMAN MEMORIAL LIBRARY (Law)
450 Golden Gate Ave.
Box 36060 Phone: (415)556-7979
San Francisco, CA 94102 Lynn E. Lundstrom, Libn.
Founded: 1964. **Staff:** Prof 1; Other 2. **Subjects:** Federal and state law. **Holdings:** 28,600 books; 2000 bound periodical volumes. **Subscriptions:** 265 journals and other serials; 6 newspapers. **Services:** Library serves attorneys before the court and judges. **Computerized Information Services:** LEXIS, WESTLAW.

★15066★
U.S. DRUG ENFORCEMENT ADMINISTRATION - LIBRARY (Law)
1405 Eye St., N.W. Phone: (202)633-1369
Washington, DC 20537 Morton S. Goren, Libn.
Staff: Prof 3; Other 1. **Subjects:** Narcotic addiction, dangerous drug abuse, law and legislation, law enforcement, drug abuse education, international control. **Holdings:** 10,000 books; 24 VF drawers. **Subscriptions:** 300 journals and other serials. **Services:** Interlibrary loan; copying; library open to the public. **Publications:** Accession list, monthly. **Computerized Information Services:** DIALOG Information Services, LEXIS, NEXIS, OCLC. **Remarks:** The Drug Enforcement Administration is part of the U.S. Department of Justice.

U.S. ELECTROMAGNETIC COMPATIBILITY ANALYSIS CENTER
See: IIT Research Institute (6678)

★15067★
U.S. ELECTROPHORESIS SOCIETY - LIBRARY (Sci-Engr)
Box 956 Phone: (803)792-3694
Mt. Pleasant, SC 29464 Robert C. Allen, Sec.
Founded: 1980. **Subjects:** Electrophoretic methods in biological sciences. **Holdings:** Historical and archival materials.

★15068★
U.S. ENGLISH - LIBRARY† (Hum)
1424 16th St., N.W., Suite 714 Phone: (202)232-5200
Washington, DC 20036 Gerda Bikales, Exec.Dir.
Founded: 1983. **Staff:** Prof 2; Other 2. **Subjects:** English language, bilingual education, immigrant assimilation, language segregation and discrimination, illiteracy. **Holdings:** 500 books; 500 bound periodical volumes; reports; manuscripts; monographs; testimonies; editorials; news clippings. **Subscriptions:** 29 journals and other serials. **Services:** Interlibrary loan; copying; library open to the public with restrictions. **Publications:** UPDATE, 6/year.

U.S. ENVIRONMENTAL PROTECTION AGENCY
See: Environmental Protection Agency (4721)

U.S. EQUAL EMPLOYMENT OPPORTUNITY COMMISSION
See: Equal Employment Opportunity Commission (4756)

★15069★
U.S. EXECUTIVE OFFICE OF THE PRESIDENT - LIBRARY (Soc Sci)
726 Jackson Place, N.W., Rm. G-102 Phone: (202)395-3654
Washington, DC 20503
Adrienne Kosciusko Gillen, Dir., Lib. & Info.Serv.
Founded: 1978. **Staff:** Prof 7; Other 5. **Subjects:** Public administration, political science, Presidency, economics, federal legislation, policymaking. **Special Collections:** Federal government reorganization; World War II administrative history; federal government appropriations. **Holdings:** 100,000 books; 4000 bound periodical volumes; 750,000 microfiche of Congressional materials; 20,000 microfiche of periodicals; 4200 reels of microfilm of periodicals. **Subscriptions:** 710 journals and other serials; 15 newspapers. **Services:** Interlibrary loan; copying; SDI; library open to the public with special permission. **Automated Operations:** Computerized cataloging, acquisitions, serials, and circulation. **Computerized Information Services:** DIALOG Information Services, Pergamon ORBIT InfoLine, Inc., VU/TEXT Information Services, WESTLAW, LEXIS, NEXIS, BRS Information Technologies, LEGI-SLATE, Dialcom Inc., OCLC, CompuServe, Inc. **Networks/Consortia:** Member of FEDLINK, Metropolitan Washington Library Council. **Staff:** Mary H. Anton, Dp.Dir..

★15070★
U.S. FEDERAL AVIATION ADMINISTRATION - AERONAUTICAL CENTER LIBRARY, AAC-64D (Sci-Engr)
6500 S. MacArthur
Box 25082 Phone: (405)686-4709
Oklahoma City, OK 73125 Virginia C. Hughes, Libn.
Staff: Prof 1. **Subjects:** Aeronautics, airplanes, mathematics, avionics, electronics, management. **Holdings:** Books; periodicals; technical reports. **Subscriptions:** 52 journals and other serials. **Services:** Interlibrary loan; library open to the public. **Automated Operations:** Computerized cataloging. **Computerized Information Services:** OCLC; EasyNet (electronic mail service). **Networks/Consortia:** Member of FEDLINK. **Remarks:** The Federal Aviation Administration is part of the U.S. Department of Transportation. **Also Known As:** FAA.

★15071★
U.S. FEDERAL AVIATION ADMINISTRATION - CIVIL AEROMEDICAL INSTITUTE LIBRARY, AAM-100 (Med, Biol Sci)
6500 S. MacArthur Blvd.
Box 25082 Phone: (405)686-4398
Oklahoma City, OK 73125 Janice Varner Nakagawara, Med.Libn.
Founded: 1963. **Staff:** Prof 1. **Subjects:** Aviation medicine, biochemistry, psychology, human factors, toxicology, occupational hygiene. **Special Collections:** Aviation medicine. **Holdings:** 4000 books; 9146 bound periodical volumes; 7500 unbound reports. **Subscriptions:** 104 journals and other serials. **Services:** Interlibrary loan; copying; library open to the public with restrictions.

★15072★
U.S. FEDERAL AVIATION ADMINISTRATION - EASTERN REGION LIBRARY (Trans)
Fitzgerald Federal Bldg., AEA-61
J.F. Kennedy Intl. Airport Phone: (718)917-0984
Jamaica, NY 11430 Eric Andrews, Mgt.Asst.
Founded: 1965. **Staff:** Prof 1. **Subjects:** Aeronautics, aviation, transportation, management. **Holdings:** 2000 books; 800 pamphlets; 15,000 NASA reports on microfiche; 8000 National Advisory Committee for Aeronautics (NACA) and NASA reports; 1500 FAA research and development reports; 8 VF drawers of clippings and pamphlets. **Subscriptions:** 50 journals and other serials. **Services:** Interlibrary loan; library not open to the public.

★15073★
U.S. FEDERAL AVIATION ADMINISTRATION - LAW LIBRARY (Trans, Law)
800 Independence Ave., S.W. Phone: (202)267-3174
Washington, DC 20591 Jane Elliott Braucher, Law Libn.
Staff: Prof 2; Other 3. **Subjects:** Law and legislation - aviation, medical, labor, administrative, international, environmental; government contracts. **Holdings:** 80,000 books; 300,000 films; 200,000 congressional documents. **Services:** Interlibrary loan; copying (both limited); library open to the public with permission. **Computerized Information Services:** DIALOG Information Services, LEXIS, NEXIS, OCLC.

★15074★
U.S. FEDERAL AVIATION ADMINISTRATION - TECHNICAL CENTER - INFORMATION RESEARCH FACILITY (ACT-65A) (Trans)
Atlantic City International Airport, NJ 08405 Phone: (609)484-5772
Harry Kemp, Supv.
Founded: 1958. **Staff:** Prof 4; Other 1. **Subjects:** Air traffic control, collision avoidance, aviation safety, radar, navigation, configuration management. **Special Collections:** Addison B. Johnson Air Traffic Control Resource Center; Air Traffic Safety Information Center. **Holdings:** 7000 books; 3500 bound periodical volumes; 2000 technical reports; 80,000 unbound, uncataloged technical reports. **Subscriptions:** 400 journals and other serials. **Services:** Interlibrary loan; copying; SDI; facility open to the public. **Automated Operations:** Computerized cataloging, acquisitions, serials and circulation. **Computerized Information Services:** DIALOG Information Services, DTIC, NASA/RECON, OCLC; internal databases. Performs searches free of charge and on fee basis. **Networks/Consortia:**

Member of FEDLINK. **Publications:** Acquisitions List; custom bibliographies. **Special Catalogs:** NAS Documents Catalog. **Staff:** Dr. Nancy Boylan, Tech.Info.Spec.; Ruta Farrel, Cat..

★15075★
U.S. FEDERAL BUREAU OF INVESTIGATION - F.B.I. ACADEMY - LIBRARY (Law)
Quantico, VA 22135 Phone: (703)640-1135
Edward J. Tully, Unit Chf.
Founded: 1972. **Staff:** Prof 2; Other 11. **Subjects:** Law enforcement, police, criminal justice. **Holdings:** 35,000 books; 1300 bound periodical volumes; 11,000 government documents; 6800 vertical file materials; 12,050 items in law library; 2400 AV programs; 22,000 microfiche. **Subscriptions:** 525 journals and other serials; 6 newspapers. **Services:** Interlibrary loan; SDI; library open to the public by special permission only. **Computerized Information Services:** DIALOG Information Services, NEXIS, OCLC, JURIS, WESTLAW. **Publications:** Subject bibliographies - available upon request. **Special Catalogs:** Periodicals holdings list, annual; training films and videotapes catalog, annual. **Remarks:** The Federal Bureau of Investigation is part of the U.S. Department of Justice. **Staff:** Sandra Coupe, Libn.; Bertha Scott, Libn..

U.S. FEDERAL COMMUNICATIONS COMMISSION
See: Federal Communications Commission (4944)

U.S. FEDERAL DEPOSIT INSURANCE CORPORATION
See: Federal Deposit Insurance Corporation (4945)

U.S. FEDERAL ELECTION COMMISSION
See: Federal Election Commission (4946)

★15076★
U.S. FEDERAL HIGHWAY ADMINISTRATION - OFFICE OF THE CHIEF COUNSEL - LEGISLATIVE/REFERENCE LIBRARY (Trans, Law)
400 Seventh St., S.W., Rm. 4205 Phone: (202)366-1388
Washington, DC 20590 Sherie A. Abbasi, Law Libn.
Staff: Prof 1. **Subjects:** Highways and roads. **Special Collections:** Legislative histories of highways, 1909 to present. **Holdings:** Figures not available. **Services:** Library open to the public by appointment. **Computerized Information Services:** WESTLAW, LEXIS, NEXIS; internal databases; OnTyme Electronic Message Network Service (electronic mail service). Performs searches on fee basis. **Publications:** Federal laws and material relating to the Federal Highway Administration, biennial. **Remarks:** The Federal Highway Administration is part of the U.S. Department of Transportation.

U.S. FEDERAL HOME LOAN BANK BOARD
See: Federal Home Loan Bank Board (4950)

★15077★
U.S. FEDERAL JUDICIAL CENTER - INFORMATION SERVICES (Law)
1520 H St., N.W.
Washington, DC 20005 Phone: (202)633-6365
Staff: Prof 2; Other 2. **Subjects:** Judicial administration, court management, crime and criminals, probation, constitutional law. **Special Collections:** Dolley Madison Collection (life of Mrs. Madison; 60 volumes). **Holdings:** 4500 books; 60 bound periodical volumes; 80 volumes of seminar materials; 9 drawers of article files; 3 file drawers of court rules and local rules of federal courts; 150 volumes of Federal Reporter 2d on ultrafiche. **Subscriptions:** 70 journals and other serials. **Services:** Interlibrary loan; copying; services open to the public. **Computerized Information Services:** DIALOG Information Services, The Reference Service (REFSRV); internal database. **Special Catalogs:** Catalog of Publications.

U.S. FEDERAL MARITIME COMMISSION
See: Federal Maritime Commission (4953)

U.S. FEDERAL TRADE COMMISSION
See: Federal Trade Commission (4973)

★15078★
U.S. FISH & WILDLIFE SERVICE - ABERNATHY SALMON CULTURE TECHNOLOGY CENTER - RESEARCH AND INFORMATION CENTER (Biol Sci)
1440 Abernathy Rd. Phone: (206)425-6072
Longview, WA 98632 David A. Leith, Dir.
Founded: 1942. **Staff:** 10. **Subjects:** Fish culture, feeding salmonids, water reuse, diseases of fish, temperature, hatchery techniques. **Holdings:** 125 books; 175 bound periodical volumes; 2125 other cataloged items; 5 drawers of reprints. **Services:** Interlibrary loan; center not open to the public. **Remarks:** The Fish & Wildlife Service is part of the U.S. Department of the Interior.

★15079★
U.S. FISH & WILDLIFE SERVICE - FISH FARMING EXPERIMENTAL STATION - LIBRARY (Biol Sci)
Box 860 Phone: (501)673-8761
Stuttgart, AR 72160 Harry K. Dupree, Dir.
Founded: 1962. **Subjects:** Freshwater fisheries, parasites and diseases, physiology, nutrition, aquaculture. **Holdings:** 900 volumes; 8700 reprints. **Subscriptions:** 146 journals and other serials. **Services:** Interlibrary loan; library open to the public. **Staff:** Joyce Cooper, Lib.Techn..

★15080★
U.S. FISH & WILDLIFE SERVICE - LIBRARY (Biol Sci)
1011 E. Tudor Rd. Phone: (907)786-3358
Anchorage, AK 99503 Cathy Vitale, Libn.
Staff: Prof 1. **Subjects:** Alaska fisheries and wildlife. **Special Collections:** U.S. Fish and Wildlife Service publications; Alaska Department of Fish and Game publications. **Holdings:** 1600 books; 2700 monographs. **Subscriptions:** 80 journals and other serials. **Services:** Interlibrary loan; copying; library open to the public. **Computerized Information Services:** OCLC.

★15081★
U.S. FISH & WILDLIFE SERVICE - NATIONAL FISHERIES CONTAMINANT RESEARCH CENTER - LIBRARY (Env-Cons, Agri)
Route 1 Phone: (314)875-5399
Columbia, MO 65201 Dr. Richard Shoettger, Dir.
Founded: 1959. **Staff:** Prof 2. **Subjects:** Pesticides, agricultural chemicals, pollution, environmental contaminants. **Holdings:** 3000 books; 1100 bound periodical volumes; 3000 monographs; 18,000 reprints. **Subscriptions:** 200 journals and other serials. **Services:** Interlibrary loan; copying; library open to the public. **Computerized Information Services:** Online systems. **Staff:** Ell-Piret Multer, Tech.Info.Spec.; Axie Hindman, Libn..

★15082★
U.S. FISH & WILDLIFE SERVICE - NATIONAL FISHERIES RESEARCH CENTER - GREAT LAKES - JOHN VAN OOSTEN LIBRARY (Biol Sci, Env-Cons)
1451 Green Rd. Phone: (313)994-3331
Ann Arbor, MI 48105 Eileen K. Bartels, Libn.
Staff: Prof 1; Other 1. **Subjects:** Fishery biology, aquatic ecology, pesticide, mercury and water pollution, Great Lakes. **Holdings:** 3000 books; 2100 bound periodical volumes; 40,000 reprints. **Subscriptions:** 163 journals and other serials. **Services:** Interlibrary loan; copying; library open to the public. **Automated Operations:** Computerized cataloging. **Computerized Information Services:** DIALOG Information Services, BRS Information Technologies. **Networks/Consortia:** Member of FEDLINK, Michigan Library Consortium (MLC).

★15083★
U.S. FISH & WILDLIFE SERVICE - NATIONAL FISHERIES RESEARCH CENTER - LIBRARY (Biol Sci, Agri)
Box 818 Phone: (608)783-6451
La Crosse, WI 54602-0818 Rosalie A. Schnick, Tech.Info.Spec.
Founded: 1959. **Staff:** Prof 1; Other 1. **Subjects:** Fish management, toxicology, pharmacology, fish culture and physiology, limnology. **Special Collections:** Complete sets of volumes of early studies on fish culture, fish diseases, and fishery biology. **Holdings:** 4000 books; 300 bound periodical volumes; 15,000 reprints; 10,000 leaflets and pamphlets. **Subscriptions:** 200 journals and other serials. **Services:** Interlibrary loan; library open to the public for reference use only on request. **Computerized Information Services:** DIALOG Information Services, OCLC. **Publications:** List of Serials - available on request.

★15084★
U.S. FISH & WILDLIFE SERVICE - NATIONAL FISHERIES RESEARCH CENTER - TECHNICAL INFORMATION SERVICES (Biol Sci, Sci-Engr, Agri)
Box 700 Phone: (304)725-8461
Kearneysville, WV 25430 Joyce A. Mann, Tech.Info.Off.
Founded: 1959. **Staff:** Prof 3; Other 3. **Subjects:** Aquaculture; fish - diseases, nutrition, pathology, physiology, bacteriology, virology, parasitology, culture, immunology, chemotherapy, freshwater biology. **Special Collections:** Fish diseases (16,500 reprints); benthic organisms and plankton, water quality monitoring, and biological assessment

methodology (3000 reports and reprints); fish culture (8000 reports and reprints); clearinghouse for all Fish & Wildlife Service aquacultural materials. **Holdings:** 25,300 books; 27,500 reprints; government depository for Fish Disease Leaflets; 13 VF drawers of staff publications. **Subscriptions:** 786 journals and other serials. **Services:** Interlibrary loan; copying; services open to the public with restrictions. **Automated Operations:** Computerized cataloging. **Computerized Information Services:** DIALOG Information Services, OCLC. **Networks/Consortia:** Member of FEDLINK. **Remarks:** Statistics include the holdings of the Fish Farming Experimental Station in Stuttgart, Arkansas; the National Fishery Research and Development Laboratory in Wellsboro, Pennsylvania; the Southeastern Fish Cultural Laboratory in Marion, Alabama; the Tunison Laboratory of Fish Nutrition in Cortland, New York and its Field Station in Hagerman, Idaho. **Staff:** Vi Catrow, Libn..

★15085★
U.S. FISH & WILDLIFE SERVICE - NORTHERN PRAIRIE WILDLIFE RESEARCH CENTER - LIBRARY (Biol Sci, Env-Cons)
Box 2096 Phone: (701)252-5363
Jamestown, ND 58402 Ann Zimmerman, Libn.
Founded: 1965. **Staff:** Prof 1. **Subjects:** Wildlife management and research, avian biology, plant and animal ecology. **Holdings:** 3000 books; 700 bound periodical volumes. **Subscriptions:** 150 journals and other serials. **Services:** Interlibrary loan; copying; library open to qualified persons by permission. **Computerized Information Services:** DIALOG Information Services, OCLC. **Networks/Consortia:** Member of FEDLINK, MINITEX.

★15086★
U.S. FISH & WILDLIFE SERVICE - OFFICE OF AUDIO-VISUAL - LIBRARY (Aud-Vis)
Dept. of the Interior, Rm. 8070 Phone: (202)343-8770
Washington, DC 20240 Craig A. Koppie, Visual Info.Spec.
Staff: 1. **Subjects:** Wildlife, especially birds and endangered species. **Holdings:** 15,000 still photographs and color transparencies. **Services:** Photographs may be consulted by authors, editors, publishers, and conservationists.

★15087★
U.S. FISH & WILDLIFE SERVICE - PATUXENT WILDLIFE RESEARCH CENTER - LIBRARY (Biol Sci, Env-Cons)
Laurel, MD 20708 Phone: (301)498-0235
Lynda Garrett, Libn.
Founded: 1942. **Staff:** Prof 1; Other 1. **Subjects:** Wildlife, especially birds; environmental pollution - pesticides, heavy metals, oil; biostatistics. **Holdings:** 8200 books; 35,000 reprints and pamphlets. **Subscriptions:** 400 journals and other serials. **Services:** Interlibrary loan; copying; library open to the public for reference use only. **Automated Operations:** Computerized cataloging and ILL. **Computerized Information Services:** DIALOG Information Services, OCLC. **Networks/Consortia:** Member of National Natural Resources Library and Information System (NNRLIS), Maryland Interlibrary Organization (MILO), FEDLINK.

★15088★
U.S. FISH & WILDLIFE SERVICE - SCIENCE REFERENCE LIBRARY (Biol Sci, Sci-Engr, Env-Cons)
Federal Bldg., Fort Snelling Phone: (612)725-3576
Twin Cities, MN 55111 Lisa Mandell, Libn.
Founded: 1964. **Staff:** Prof 1. **Subjects:** Wildlife, fish, river basin development and water pollution, environmental quality, forestry, outdoor recreation, soils, engineering. **Special Collections:** U.S. Fish and Wildlife Service publications (5000). **Holdings:** 15,000 books; 450 bound periodical volumes; 2000 reprints and reports. **Subscriptions:** 60 journals and other serials. **Services:** Interlibrary loan; library open to the public for reference use only on request. **Computerized Information Services:** DIALOG Information Services, OCLC. **Networks/Consortia:** Member of FEDLINK, MINITEX.

★15089★
U.S. FISH & WILDLIFE SERVICE - TUNISON LABORATORY OF FISH NUTRITION - LIBRARY (Biol Sci, Agri)
3075 Gracie Rd. Phone: (607)753-9391
Cortland, NY 13045 Gary L. Rumsey, Dir.
Founded: 1932. **Staff:** 1. **Subjects:** Fish nutrition and physiology, fishery biology, general nutrition and physiology. **Holdings:** 700 books; 500 bound periodical volumes; 5200 reprints. **Services:** Interlibrary loan; copying; library open to the public for reference use only. **Remarks:** Library is part of the National Fisheries Research Center, Kearneysville, WV.

★15090★
U.S. FOOD & DRUG ADMINISTRATION - CENTER FOR DEVICES & RADIOLOGICAL HEALTH - LIBRARY (Med)
5600 Fishers Lane Phone: (301)443-1038
Rockville, MD 20857 Harriet Aldershein, Chf.Libn.
Founded: 1962. **Staff:** Prof 2; Other 2. **Subjects:** Radiology, radiobiology, radiation, nuclear medicine, radiological health, radiation hazards, emission, microwaves, ultrasonics, lasers. **Special Collections:** Radiological health; radiation protection; medical use of x-rays. **Holdings:** 4500 books; 2500 bound periodical volumes. **Subscriptions:** 400 journals and other serials. **Services:** Interlibrary loan; library open to qualified users for research in subject field. **Automated Operations:** Computerized cataloging. **Publications:** Acquisitions List, quarterly - to other libraries. **Remarks:** Library located at 12720 Twin Brook Pkwy., Rm. 408-T, Rockville, MD 20852.

★15091★
U.S. FOOD & DRUG ADMINISTRATION - CENTER FOR DEVICES & RADIOLOGICAL HEALTH - LIBRARY (Med)
8757 Georgia Ave., HFZ-46 Phone: (301)427-7755
Silver Spring, MD 20910 Harriet Albersheim, Libn.
Staff: Prof 1; Other 2. **Subjects:** Medicine, medical devices, biomedical engineering, biomaterials, polymer science. **Special Collections:** Medical Equipment Devices and Supplies Service (MEDS) collection (16,000 medical and in vitro diagnostic manufacturers catalogs on microfilm). **Holdings:** 8000 books; 100 bound periodical volumes. **Subscriptions:** 600 journals and other serials. **Services:** Interlibrary loan; copying; library open to the public for reference use only. **Automated Operations:** Computerized cataloging. **Computerized Information Services:** DIALOG Information Services, OCLC, MEDLINE. **Networks/Consortia:** Member of FEDLINK. **Publications:** CDRH Library Information Bulletin - for internal distribution only.

★15092★
U.S. FOOD & DRUG ADMINISTRATION - CENTER FOR DRUGS AND BIOLOGICS - MEDICAL LIBRARY/HFN-98 (Med)
5600 Fishers Lane, Rm. 11B-07 Phone: (301)443-3180
Rockville, MD 20857 Elizabeth C. Kelly, Dir., Med.Lib.
Staff: Prof 10; Other 7. **Subjects:** Pharmacology, pharmacy and pharmaceutical technology, drug therapy, adverse reactions, toxicology, carcinogenicity, food and drug law, clinical and veterinary medicine, chemistry and biochemistry, microbiology, biotechnology, epidemiology, biostatistics. **Special Collections:** FDA Archival Collection (6200 archival materials); U.S. and foreign drug compendia. **Holdings:** 25,000 books; 30,000 bound periodical volumes; 210 VF drawers of drug literature card services; 325 journal titles on microfilm; 1500 folders of pamphlets and reprints. **Subscriptions:** 2000 journals and other serials. **Services:** Interlibrary loan; SDI; translations; library open to nongovernment personnel for official study or research. **Automated Operations:** Computerized cataloging. **Computerized Information Services:** NLM, BRS Information Technologies, Pergamon ORBIT InfoLine, Inc., DIALOG Information Services, OCLC, Chemical Information Systems, Inc. (CIS), WILSONLINE, CAS ONLINE. **Networks/Consortia:** Member of FEDLINK, Southeastern/Atlantic Regional Medical Library Services. **Publications:** FDA Medical Library Information Update (newsletter) - for internal distribution only; FDA Medical Library Serials Holdings. **Staff:** Carol S. Assouad, Dp.Dir.; Kathy Kruse, Br.Chf., Lib.Serv.; Joan Crisp, Br.Chf., Tech.Serv..

★15093★
U.S. FOOD & DRUG ADMINISTRATION - CENTER FOR FOOD SAFETY & APPLIED NUTRITION - LIBRARY (Food-Bev, Sci-Engr)
200 C St., S.W., Rm. 3321, HFF-37 Phone: (202)245-1235
Washington, DC 20204 Michele R. Chatfield, Dir.
Staff: Prof 5; Other 3. **Subjects:** Chemistry, analytical chemistry, toxicology, food technology, nutrition, medicine, biology, cosmetics. **Holdings:** 12,000 books; 1500 reports, documents, pamphlets; 18,000 cartridges of microfilm. **Subscriptions:** 900 journals and other serials. **Services:** Interlibrary loan; SDI; library open to the public. **Automated Operations:** Computerized cataloging and serials. **Computerized Information Services:** DIALOG Information Services, MEDLARS, Pergamon ORBIT InfoLine, Inc., BRS Information Technologies, CAS ONLINE, OCLC, JOURNALINK. **Networks/Consortia:** Member of FEDLINK. **Special Catalogs:** Union List of Periodicals in conjunction with other federal libraries. **Remarks:** The Food & Drug Administration is part of the U.S. Public Health Service. **Also Known As:** FDA. **Staff:** Lee Bernstein, Ref.Libn.; Carol Smalls, Ser.Libn.; Anna McGowan, Beltsville Research Complex Libn.; Lydia Beyerlan, Ref.Libn..

★15094★
U.S. FOOD & DRUG ADMINISTRATION - FISHERY RESEARCH BRANCH - LIBRARY (Biol Sci)
Box 158 Phone: (205)861-2962
Dauphin Island, AL 36528 Patsy C. Purvis, Sec./Libn.
Staff: Prof 12; Other 7. **Subjects:** Microbiology, marine biology, chemistry. **Holdings:** 400 books. **Subscriptions:** 20 journals and other serials. **Services:** Library open to the public by special arrangement.

★15095★
U.S. FOOD & DRUG ADMINISTRATION - NATIONAL CENTER FOR TOXICOLOGICAL RESEARCH - LIBRARY (Biol Sci)
Jefferson, AR 72079 Phone: (501)541-4322
Susan Laney-Sheehan, Supv.Libn.
Founded: 1972. **Staff:** Prof 1; Other 2. **Subjects:** Toxicology, chemistry, teratogenesis, carcinogenesis, mutagenesis, biochemistry. **Special Collections:** Bacteriology. **Holdings:** 15,000 books; 500 bound periodical volumes. **Subscriptions:** 250 journals and other serials. **Services:** Interlibrary loan; SDI; library open to the public for reference use only. **Automated Operations:** Computerized cataloging. **Computerized Information Services:** Pergamon ORBIT InfoLine, Inc., DIALOG Information Services, BRS Information Technologies, MEDLARS, OCLC. **Networks/Consortia:** Member of FEDLINK, AMIGOS Bibliographic Council, Inc..

★15096★
U.S. FOOD AND DRUG ADMINISTRATION - WINCHESTER ENGINEERING & ANALYTICAL CENTER - LIBRARY (Med)
109 Holton St.
Winchester, MA 01890 Phone: (617)729-5700
Founded: 1961. **Staff:** 1. **Subjects:** Radiology, medical roentgenology, chemistry, physics, nuclear science, oceanography, statistics, medicine, electronics. **Holdings:** 1000 books; 710 bound periodical volumes; technical documents; miscellaneous reports; 20 VF drawers of unbound materials. **Subscriptions:** 109 journals and other serials. **Services:** Interlibrary loan; copying; library open to the public for reference use only upon request.

U.S. AND FOREIGN COMMERCIAL SERVICE
See: U.S. International Trade Administration (15143)

★15097★
U.S. FOREST SERVICE - FOREST PRODUCTS LABORATORY LIBRARY (Sci-Engr, Agri, Biol Sci)
One Gifford Pinchot Dr. Phone: (608)264-5712
Madison, WI 53705-2398 Roger Scharmer, Libn.
Founded: 1910. **Staff:** Prof 2; Other 5. **Subjects:** Forest products utilization, energy from wood, paper and pulp, wood engineering, wood process and protection, timber, wood products economics. **Special Collections:** Forest products utilization. **Holdings:** 56,300 books and bound periodical volumes; 30,300 technical reports; 20,000 bulletins, reports, reprints; 6100 patents; 5900 microforms. **Subscriptions:** 550 journals. **Services:** Interlibrary loan; copying (limited); library open to the public. **Computerized Information Services:** DIALOG Information Services; internal database. **Remarks:** The Forest Service is part of the U.S. Department of Agriculture. **Staff:** Cynthia Provow, Asst.Libn..

★15098★
U.S. FOREST SERVICE - FOREST SERVICE INFORMATION NETWORK-NORTHWEST (Biol Sci)
Mail Stop AQ-15 Phone: (206)543-7484
Seattle, WA 98195 Kay F. Denfeld, Libn.
Founded: 1976. **Staff:** Prof 2; Other 2. **Subjects:** Forestry. **Holdings:** Forest Service Database. **Services:** Interlibrary loan; not open to the public. **Automated Operations:** Computerized cataloging. **Computerized Information Services:** DIALOG Information Services, OCLC; internal database. **Networks/Consortia:** Member of Forest Service Information Network/Forestry Online (FS INFO), Western Library Network (WLN). **Publications:** Monthly Alert (library bibliography) - to network members. **Remarks:** Jointly maintained with University of Washington. **Also Known As:** U.S. Forest Service - FS-INFO-NW.

★15099★
U.S. FOREST SERVICE - FOREST SERVICE INFORMATION NETWORK-PACIFIC SOUTHWEST - SERVICE CENTER (Biol Sci, Agri, Env-Cons)
1960 Addison St.
Box 245 Phone: (415)486-3686
Berkeley, CA 94701-0245 Dennis Galvin, Sta.Libn.
Founded: 1960. **Staff:** Prof 1; Other 4. **Subjects:** Forest management, silviculture, watershed management, computers and statistics, wildlife management, environmental protection. **Holdings:** 40,000 volumes, documents, offprints, reprints, preprints, bulletins, research notes. **Subscriptions:** 602 journals and other serials. **Services:** Interlibrary loan; copying; center open to the public for reference use only. **Automated Operations:** Computerized public access catalog and cataloging. **Computerized Information Services:** DIALOG Information Services, RLIN, OCLC; internal databases. **Networks/Consortia:** Member of Forest Service Information Network/Forestry Online (FS INFO). **Publications:** WESTFORNET Monthly Alert. **Special Indexes:** FAMULUS-based indexes and abstract collections. **Formerly:** WESTFORNET Berkeley Service Center. **Also Known As:** U.S. Forest Service - FS-INFO-PSW. **Staff:** Ellen Dreibelbis, Doc. Delivery/ILL; Richard Kimball, Ser./Acq..

★15100★
U.S. FOREST SERVICE - FORESTRY SCIENCES LABORATORY - LIBRARY (Biol Sci)
5985 Hwy. K
Box 898 Phone: (715)362-7474
Rhinelander, WI 54501 Betty J. Coates, Libn.
Founded: 1957. **Subjects:** Biotechnology, biology, botany, genetics, silviculture, horticulture. **Holdings:** 3000 books; 2300 bound periodical volumes. **Subscriptions:** 33 journals and other serials. **Services:** Interlibrary loan; library open to the public for reference use only.

U.S. FOREST SERVICE - GILA NATL. FOREST
See: U.S. Natl. Park Service - Gila Cliff Dwellings Natl. Monument (15297)

★15101★
U.S. FOREST SERVICE - INTERMOUNTAIN FOREST & RANGE EXPERIMENT STATION - LIBRARY (Env-Cons, Agri)
Forest Service Bldg.
324 25th St. Phone: (801)625-5444
Ogden, UT 84401 Carol A. Ayer, Tech.Info.Off.
Founded: 1962. **Staff:** Prof 2; Other 2. **Subjects:** Management - forest, range, watershed; forest fires; wildlife; forest disease, economics, utilization, and insects. **Holdings:** 7000 books; 2500 bound periodical volumes; 29,000 reprints, pamphlets, translations; 6 files of microfiche; 4 drawers of microfilm. **Subscriptions:** 450 journals and other serials. **Services:** Interlibrary loan; library open to the public. **Computerized Information Services:** DIALOG Information Services, Pergamon ORBIT InfoLine, Inc., LS/2000, OCLC; Forestry Online (internal database); Dialcom Inc. (electronic mail service). Performs searches free of charge on internal databases only. Contact Person: Ruth Hyland, Tech.Info.Spec., 625-5446. **Networks/Consortia:** Member of FEDLINK. **Publications:** FS INFO Monthly Alert.

★15102★
U.S. FOREST SERVICE - NORTH CENTRAL FOREST EXPERIMENT STATION LIBRARY (Biol Sci, Agri)
1992 Folwell Ave. Phone: (612)649-5273
St. Paul, MN 55108 Floyd L. Henderson, Libn.
Founded: 1923. **Staff:** Prof 1; Other 2. **Subjects:** Forestry, forest management, forest botany, silviculture, forest protection, forest economics, watershed management, forest recreation, associated use of forests. **Holdings:** 3400 volumes; 20,000 pamphlets; 27 drawers of maps. **Subscriptions:** 270 journals and other serials. **Services:** Interlibrary loan; copying; library open to the public. **Computerized Information Services:** DIALOG Information Services, OCLC, BRS Information Technologies; Dialcom Inc. (electronic mail service). **Networks/Consortia:** Member of FEDLINK, MINITEX. **Publications:** Accessions to the Reference Collection, irregular - to station and field unit personnel.

★15103★
U.S. FOREST SERVICE - NORTHEASTERN FOREST EXPERIMENT STATION LIBRARY (Biol Sci)
359 Main Rd. Phone: (614)369-4471
Delaware, OH 43015 Sheryl A. Dew, Lib.Techn.
Founded: 1961. **Staff:** 1. **Subjects:** Economics; silviculture; forest botany, mensuration, utilization, management, entomology and pathology,

resources and conservation; watershed management. **Holdings:** Figures not available.

★15104★
U.S. FOREST SERVICE - PACIFIC NORTHWEST RESEARCH STATION - FORESTRY SCIENCES LABORATORY LIBRARY (Agri, Biol Sci)
653 Federal Bldg.
Box 020909 Phone: (907)586-8811
Juneau, AK 99802 Kate Munson, Biol.Libn.
Founded: 1961. **Staff:** 2. **Subjects:** Boreal forestry, fisheries, wildlife, entomology, recreation. **Holdings:** 2500 books; 3000 bound periodical volumes; 24,000 pamphlets, reprints, and reports; 15,000 government serial documents; 250 maps and charts; 1500 photographs; 150 reels of microfilm and microfiche. **Subscriptions:** 224 journals and other serials. **Services:** Interlibrary loan; library open to the public with restrictions on circulation. **Computerized Information Services:** DIALOG Information Services. **Networks/Consortia:** Member of Forest Service Information Network/ Forestry Online (FS INFO). **Publications:** Accession Lists, monthly; Periodicals and Serials Holdings Lists; Station Publication Lists; special subject bibliographies, all irregular.

★15105★
U.S. FOREST SERVICE - RECREATION, WILDERNESS, & CULTURAL RESOURCES (Hist)
630 Sansome St.
San Francisco, CA 94111 Phone: (415)556-4175
Subjects: History of the National Forests in California - logging, mining, grazing, forestry, recreation, subsistence uses; history of California Indians, Euro-Americans, Chinese, other cultural and ethnic groups in the National Forests, 1800 to present. **Holdings:** 1700 manuscripts, records, oral history materials. **Services:** Copying; center open to the public during business hours. **Formerly:** Recreation Resource Management - Cultural Resource Management - Research & Archives Center.

★15106★
U.S. FOREST SERVICE - ROCKY MOUNTAIN FOREST & RANGE EXPERIMENT STATION - LIBRARY (Biol Sci, Agri)
240 W. Prospect St. Phone: (303)224-1268
Fort Collins, CO 80526 Frances J. Barney, Libn.
Founded: 1966. **Staff:** Prof 2; Other 2. **Subjects:** Forest management, shelterbelts, wildland valuation, resource economics, snow and watershed management, forest entomology and pathology, wildlife habitats, disturbed site reclamation, atmospheric deposition, nematology, ecology of arid lands, history of forestry in Rocky Mountains. **Special Collections:** World Mistletoe Literature (on Famulus retrieval system; 7000 references); Boyce Index to Forest Pathology Literature (30 card file drawers). **Holdings:** 15,000 books; 5000 bound periodical volumes; 20,000 unbound serials; 10 VF drawers of reprints; 150 reels of microfilm of Oxford Catalog and periodicals; 800 dissertations; 2 VF drawers of Rocky Mountain Station historical material. **Subscriptions:** 650 journals and other serials. **Services:** Interlibrary loan; copying; library open to the public for reference use only. **Computerized Information Services:** DIALOG Information Services, BRS Information Technologies, RLIN, OCLC, LS/2000. **Networks/Consortia:** Member of Forest Service Information Network/Forestry Online (FS INFO). **Staff:** Robert W. Dana, Tech.Info.Spec..

★15107★
U.S. FOREST SERVICE - SOUTHERN FOREST EXPERIMENT STATION - INSTITUTE OF TROPICAL FORESTRY - LIBRARY (Biol Sci, Env-Cons)
Call Box 25000 Phone: (809)763-3939
Rio Piedras, PR 00928-2500 JoAnne Feheley, Tech.Info.Spec.
Subjects: Tropical forestry and ecology, wildlife management. **Holdings:** 50,000 cataloged items. **Services:** Interlibrary loan; copying; library open to the public for reference use only. **Automated Operations:** Computerized mailing list for dissemination of institute's publications. **Computerized Information Services:** DIALOG Information Services, CAB Abstracts, Pergamon ORBIT InfoLine, Inc. **Publications:** ITF Annual Letter.

★15108★
U.S. FOREST SERVICE - SOUTHERN FOREST EXPERIMENT STATION LIBRARY (Agri, Biol Sci)
Postal Service Bldg., Rm. T-10210
701 Loyola Ave. Phone: (504)589-6800
New Orleans, LA 70113 Aleta Ryder, Ed.Asst.
Founded: 1921. **Staff:** 1. **Subjects:** Forest management, economics, and utilization; range and watershed management; forest disease, fire, and insects; wildlife habitat. **Holdings:** Figures not available. **Services:** Interlibrary loan; copying; library open to the public. **Networks/Consortia:** Member of FEDLINK.

★15109★
U.S. GENERAL ACCOUNTING OFFICE - BOSTON REGIONAL OFFICE - TECHNICAL INFORMATION SERVICES (Bus-Fin)
10 Causeway St., Rm. 575 Phone: (617)223-6536
Boston, MA 02222-1030 Jennifer Arns, Tech.Info.Spec.
Staff: Prof 1. **Subjects:** Auditing, public administration, health care financing, environmental protection, procurement, major weapons systems. **Special Collections:** All GAO publications (20 VF drawers); Comptroller General Decisions (published and unpublished); legislative histories. **Holdings:** Public laws; appropriation hearings; technical reports; Congressional documents; U.S. Code; Code of Federal Regulations. **Subscriptions:** 71 journals and other serials. **Services:** Interlibrary loan; services open to the public by appointment for reference use only. **Computerized Information Services:** Library of Congress Information System (LOCIS), DMS/ONLINE, VU/TEXT Information Services, LEXIS, NEXIS, DIALOG Information Services; internal database. **Networks/Consortia:** Member of FEDLINK.

★15110★
U.S. GENERAL ACCOUNTING OFFICE - OFFICE OF LIBRARY SERVICES (Law, Bus-Fin)
441 G St., N.W., Rm. 6430 Phone: (202)275-5180
Washington, DC 20548 Phyllis Christenson, Dir.
Founded: 1949. **Staff:** Prof 23; Other 32. **Subjects:** Law, accounting and auditing, management, public policy, program evaluation, energy. **Special Collections:** Federal departmental regulatory material; legislative history collection; GAO Historical Collection; GAO reports (in microform). **Holdings:** 95,000 volumes; 1 million microfiche. **Subscriptions:** 1700 journals; 2529 serials; 7 newspapers. **Services:** Interlibrary loan; library open to the public for reference use only. **Automated Operations:** Computerized cataloging and acquisitions. **Computerized Information Services:** DIALOG Information Services, Pergamon ORBIT InfoLine, Inc., VU/TEXT Information Services, BRS Information Technologies, JURIS, LEXIS, LEGIS, NEXIS, Data Resources (DRI), Library of Congress Information System (LOCIS), DDN Network Information Center, WESTLAW, OCLC; internal databases. **Networks/Consortia:** Member of FEDLINK. **Publications:** Library Focus, monthly; Library & Information Services Handbook; subject bibliographies, irregular; GAO Library Periodicals. **Also Known As:** GAO. **Staff:** Maureen Canick, Mgr., Tech.Lib.; Larry Boyer, Mgr., Law Lib.; Bonita Mueller, Mgr., Tech.Serv..

★15111★
U.S. GENERAL ACCOUNTING OFFICE - PHILADELPHIA REGIONAL RESOURCE CENTER (Bus-Fin)
841 Chestnut St., Suite 760 Phone: (215)597-7360
Philadelphia, PA 19107 Linda Carnevale Skale, Tech.Info.Spec.
Founded: 1979. **Staff:** Prof 1. **Subjects:** Accounting, U.S. legislation. **Special Collections:** Decisions of the U.S. Comptroller General, 1921 to present; GAO Legislative History Microfiche Collection (through 96th Congress); Congressional agencies' material. **Holdings:** 500 books; 25 General Accounting Office annual reports, 1961 to present; complete set of Public Laws from 90th Congress to present; U.S. House Committee on Appropriations hearings records. **Subscriptions:** 64 journals and other serials. **Services:** Interlibrary loan; copying; SDI; center open to the public by appointment. **Computerized Information Services:** DIALOG Information Services, Library of Congress Information System (SCORPIO), Mead Data Central, OCLC, VU/TEXT Information Services; internal database.

★15112★
U.S. GENERAL ACCOUNTING OFFICE - SAN FRANCISCO REGIONAL OFFICE - LIBRARY (Bus-Fin)
1275 Market St. Phone: (415)556-6200
San Francisco, CA 94103 Linda F. Sharp, Tech.Info.Spec.
Founded: 1976. **Staff:** Prof 1; Other 1. **Subjects:** Auditing, program evaluation, legislation. **Special Collections:** U.S. General Accounting Office Audit Reports; annual reports. **Holdings:** 10 VF drawers of reports on microfiche. **Subscriptions:** 30 journals and other serials. **Services:** Interlibrary loan; SDI; library open to the public by appointment. **Computerized Information Services:** Online systems.

U.S. GENERAL SERVICES ADMINISTRATION
See: General Services Administration (5571)

★15113★
U.S. GEOLOGICAL SURVEY - EARTH RESOURCES OBSERVATION SYSTEMS (EROS) DATA CENTER - TECHNICAL REFERENCE UNIT (Sci-Engr)
EROS Data Center Phone: (605)594-6102
Sioux Falls, SD 57198 K.C. Wehde, Tech.Ref. Unit Rep.
Founded: 1974. **Staff:** Prof 1. **Subjects:** Remote sensing, natural resources. **Special Collections:** ERTS reports (microfiche). **Holdings:** 3000 books; 200 bound periodical volumes; 6000 microfiche; 12,000 reports; 2000 periodicals. **Subscriptions:** 55 journals and other serials. **Services:** Interlibrary loan; unit open to the public. **Automated Operations:** Computerized cataloging.

★15114★
U.S. GEOLOGICAL SURVEY - FLAGSTAFF FIELD CENTER - BRANCH LIBRARY (Sci-Engr, Geog-Map)
2255 N. Gemini Dr. Phone: (602)527-7008
Flagstaff, AZ 86001 James R. Nation, Libn.
Founded: 1964. **Staff:** Prof 1; Other 1. **Subjects:** Earth sciences, space sciences. **Holdings:** 19,530 volumes; 27,300 maps. **Subscriptions:** 134 journals and other serials. **Services:** Interlibrary loan; library open to the public for reference use only.

★15115★
U.S. GEOLOGICAL SURVEY - ICE AND CLIMATE PROJECT - GLACIER INVENTORY PHOTO LIBRARY (Sci-Engr, Aud-Vis)
University of Puget Sound Phone: (206)593-6516
Tacoma, WA 98416 David R. Hirst, Photo.
Founded: 1960. **Staff:** 1. **Subjects:** Glaciers, glacier features, mountainous regions, conterminous U.S. **Special Collections:** Aerial photographs of glaciated areas in western U.S., Canada, and Alaska (75,000 black/white images, 1960 to present). **Holdings:** Figures not available. **Services:** Copying; library open to the public with restrictions.

★15116★
U.S. GEOLOGICAL SURVEY - LIBRARY (Sci-Engr)
345 Middlefield Rd., MS955
Menlo Park, CA 94025 Phone: (415)329-5090
Founded: 1953. **Staff:** Prof 3; Other 10. **Subjects:** Geology, geophysics, oceanography. **Holdings:** 400,000 volumes; 50 drawers of microforms; 35,000 maps; 30 drawers of photographs. **Subscriptions:** 1200 journals and other serials. **Services:** Interlibrary loan; SDI; library open to the public for reference use only. **Automated Operations:** Computerized public access catalog, cataloging, serials, and circulation. **Computerized Information Services:** DIALOG Information Services, Pergamon ORBIT InfoLine, Inc., OCLC. **Staff:** Nancy Blair, Ref.Libn.; Ellen White, Ref.Libn.; J. Freeberg, Ref.Libn..

★15117★
U.S. GEOLOGICAL SURVEY - LIBRARY (Sci-Engr)
Box 25046
Mail Stop 914 Phone: (303)236-1000
Denver, CO 80225 Robert A. Bier, Jr., Chf.Libn.
Founded: 1948. **Staff:** Prof 6; Other 3. **Subjects:** Geology, mineral and water resources, mineralogy, physics, paleontology, petrology, chemistry, soil and environmental sciences. **Special Collections:** Photographic Library (300,000 items); Field Records Library (80,000 items). **Holdings:** 175,000 books; 60,000 bound periodical volumes; 75,000 other cataloged items; 15,000 microforms; 65,000 topographic maps of U.S.; 1500 geologic world maps; 7000 USGS maps in series (complete); 20,000 reports and pamphlets. **Subscriptions:** 1600 journals and other serials. **Services:** Interlibrary loan; library open to the public for reference use only. **Automated Operations:** Computerized cataloging and circulation. **Computerized Information Services:** DIALOG Information Services, Pergamon ORBIT InfoLine, Inc.; DIALMAIL (electronic mail service). **Networks/Consortia:** Member of Central Colorado Library System (CCLS). **Staff:** Jane Bonn, Ref./Circ.Libn.; M. Elaine Watson, ILL Libn.; Deborah F. Rowen, Fld.Rec.Libn..

★15118★
U.S. GEOLOGICAL SURVEY - LIBRARY (Sci-Engr)
Federal Bldg.
300 E. 8th St. Phone: (512)482-5520
Austin, TX 78701 Julie Menard, Libn.
Staff: Prof 1; Other 1. **Subjects:** Hydrology, hydrogeology, hydrologic and environmental engineering, water quality. **Special Collections:** U.S.G.S Professional Papers (complete collection); U.S.G.S. Water Supply Papers (complete collection). **Holdings:** 3000 books; 5000 technical reports. **Subscriptions:** 15 journals and other serials. **Services:** Interlibrary loan; library open to the public for reference use only. **Automated Operations:** Computerized cataloging. **Computerized Information Services:** DIALOG Information Services.

★15119★
U.S. GEOLOGICAL SURVEY - LIBRARY SYSTEM (Sci-Engr)
12201 Sunrise Valley Dr.
National Center, Mail Stop 950 Phone: (703)648-4302
Reston, VA 22092 Elizabeth J. Yeates, Chf.Libn.
Founded: 1882. **Staff:** Prof 26; Other 25. **Subjects:** Geology, mineralogy, mineral resources, water resources, petrology, paleontology. **Special Collections:** George F. Kunz Collection of Gems and Precious Stones; Douglas C. Alverson Collection of Russian Geological Books. **Holdings:** 755,000 volumes; 307,500 maps; 267,000 pamphlets; 318,000 microforms; doctoral dissertations on microfilm and microfiche; NTIS report literature on microfiche. **Subscriptions:** 10,000 journals and other serials. **Services:** Interlibrary loan; copying; SDI; library open to the public with borrowing restricted to interlibrary loan. **Automated Operations:** Computerized cataloging, serials, and circulation. **Computerized Information Services:** DIALOG Information Services, Pergamon ORBIT InfoLine, Inc., Integrated Technical Information System (ITIS), LS/2000, UMI, OCLC; Geoindex (internal database). **Networks/Consortia:** Member of FEDLINK. **Publications:** New Information Resources. **Remarks:** The Geological Survey is part of the U.S. Department of the Interior. **Staff:** Edward H. Liszewski, Assoc.Chf.Libn.; Barbara A. Chappell, Hd., Ref./Circ.; Emily Jane Perry, Automated Sys.Mgr.; Virginia L. Major, Hd., Geologic Inquiries; Bruce Keck, Asst.Libn., Coll.Mgt. & Access.

★15120★
U.S. GEOLOGICAL SURVEY - NATIONAL CARTOGRAPHIC INFORMATION CENTER (NCIC) (Geog-Map)
Federal Ctr., Stop 511
Box 25046 Phone: (303)236-5829
Denver, CO 80225 Rudolph Hildebrandt, Cart.
Founded: 1947. **Staff:** 15. **Subjects:** Topographic maps, aerial photography, space imagery, orthophotoquads, digital data, land use. **Special Collections:** Out of print topographic quadrangles (266 reels of microfilm). **Holdings:** 480 VF drawers of maps; 1 million aerial photographs. **Services:** Copying; center open to the public for reference use only. **Computerized Information Services:** Internal database. **Special Indexes:** Topographic and orthophotoquad advance material index (map indexes available for each state).

★15121★
U.S. GEOLOGICAL SURVEY - NATIONAL CARTOGRAPHIC INFORMATION CENTER (NCIC) (Geog-Map)
507 National Center Phone: (703)860-6045
Reston, VA 22092 John T. Wood, Chf.
Founded: 1974. **Staff:** 26. **Subjects:** Maps and charts, aerial and space photos, satellite and radar imagery, geodetic control, digital cartographic/geographic data (tapes), related cartographic data. **Holdings:** Cartographic Catalog (78,000 entries); Aerial Photo Summary Record System (489,000 air photo project records); Map and Chart Information System (221,000 map records). **Publications:** NCIC Newsletter, quarterly; technical user guides, as needed. **Special Indexes:** Indexes to numerous scaled U.S. map products, semiannual. **Remarks:** NCIC provides information on cartographic and geographic data produced by federal agencies, states, and commercial organizations.

★15122★
U.S. GEOLOGICAL SURVEY - NATIONAL CARTOGRAPHIC INFORMATION CENTER (NCIC) - WESTERN BRANCH (Geog-Map)
345 Middlefield Rd., MS 532 Phone: (415)323-8111
Menlo Park, CA 94025 Richard Zorker, Chf., NCIC - W.
Founded: 1977. **Staff:** 20. **Subjects:** Maps and charts, aerial photography, geodetic control, satellite imagery. **Special Collections:** Original map reproduction material on separate data plates. **Holdings:** 25 million photographs and images; 11,200 square feet of records. **Subscriptions:** 10 journals and other serials. **Services:** Copying; photograph reproduction; cartographic research, reference, and technical advice; center open to the public. **Automated Operations:** Computerized cataloging, acquisitions, and circulation. **Computerized Information Services:** Internal database. Performs searches free of charge. Contact Person: Dennis Cole, Chf., User Serv., 329-4357. **Publications:** Topographic, geologic, water resources, and conservation brochures; directories. **Special Catalogs:** Microform catalogs. **Special Indexes:** Published map and advanced materials indexes. **Staff:** Gerald Greenberg, Chf., Data Acq..

★15123★
U.S. GEOLOGICAL SURVEY - NATIONAL MAPPING DIVISION ASSISTANCE FACILITY - LIBRARY (Geog-Map)
National Space Technology Laboratories Phone: (601)688-3541
NSTL Station, MS 39529 Frank Beatty, Libn.
Founded: 1973. **Staff:** Prof 1; Other 1. **Subjects:** Remote sensing, mapping, platforms and sensors, electromagnetic energy, cultural features and other man-related aspects of remote sensing, animal and plant life, geology and meteorology, hydrology and astronomy, data processing and management. **Special Collections:** Photo interpretation keys (87). **Holdings:** 1200 books; 183 bound periodical volumes; 15,000 documents on microfiche; 4000 maps. **Subscriptions:** 45 journals and other serials. **Services:** Interlibrary loan; copying; microfiche loan service; library open to the public. **Publications:** Remote Sensing and Mapping Source List.

★15124★
U.S. GEOLOGICAL SURVEY - PUBLIC INQUIRIES OFFICE - LIBRARY (Energy, Sci-Engr)
4230 University Dr., Rm. 101 Phone: (907)561-5555
Anchorage, AK 99508-4664
Elizabeth C. Behrendt, Supv.Tech.Info.Spec.
Founded: 1951. **Staff:** Prof 1; Other 2. **Subjects:** Geology, water resources, oil and gas, minerals. **Special Collections:** U.S. Geological Survey (USGS) open-file reports on Alaska (1000); all USGS topographic and thematic maps for Alaska; USGS world and U.S. maps. **Holdings:** 8000 books; departmental publications; State of Alaska publications. **Subscriptions:** 10 journals and other serials. **Services:** Copying; library open to the public for reference use only. **Computerized Information Services:** Earth Science Information Network (internal database). **Special Catalogs:** Lists of all U.S.G.S. publications on Alaska (card).

★15125★
U.S. GEOLOGICAL SURVEY - WATER RESOURCES DIVISION - COLORADO DISTRICT LIBRARY (Env-Cons)
Federal Center
Box 25046, Stop 415 Phone: (303)236-4895
Denver, CO 80225 Barbara J. Condron, Libn.
Founded: 1973. **Staff:** Prof 1. **Subjects:** Water resources, limnology, coal, oil shale. **Special Collections:** Annual reports of the Colorado River Basin, Arkansas River Basin, Missouri River, and Rio Grande River; U.S. Geological Survey Water Supply Papers (complete set); oil shale material. **Holdings:** 1000 books; 5000 pamphlets and serials; 2000 microfiche; 10 videotapes; 5 VF drawers of clippings and small pamphlets. **Subscriptions:** 35 journals and other serials. **Services:** Interlibrary loan; copying (limited); library open to the public for reference use only. **Automated Operations:** Computerized cataloging. **Computerized Information Services:** OCLC. **Remarks:** Branch libraries located at Lakewood, Pueblo, Grand Junction, and Meeker, Colorado.

★15126★
U.S. GEOLOGICAL SURVEY - WATER RESOURCES DIVISION - INFORMATION RESOURCE CENTER
5957 Lakeside Blvd.
Indianapolis, IN 46278
Founded: 1977. **Subjects:** Hydrology, water resources in Indiana, geology, water pollution. **Holdings:** 7000 books; 225 reports on microfiche; 600 maps; 1000 reprints. **Remarks:** Presently inactive.

★15127★
U.S. GEOLOGICAL SURVEY - WATER RESOURCES DIVISION - LIBRARY (Env-Cons)
Federal Bldg., Rm. 428
301 S. Park
Drawer 10076 Phone: (406)449-5263
Helena, MT 59626-0076 Cynthia J. Diamond, Libn.
Staff: Prof 1. **Subjects:** Water resources and development, water quality, floods. **Special Collections:** U.S. Geological Survey water supply papers, bulletins, professional papers. **Holdings:** 10,000 items. **Subscriptions:** 10 journals and other serials. **Services:** Interlibrary loan; copying; library open to the public for reference use only. **Computerized Information Services:** OCLC. **Automated Operations:** Computerized cataloging. **Networks/ Consortia:** Member of FEDLINK.

★15128★
U.S. GEOLOGICAL SURVEY - WATER RESOURCES DIVISION - LIBRARY (Env-Cons)
6417 Normandy Ln. Phone: (608)262-2488
Madison, WI 53719-1133 Rachel A. Lansing, Adm.Oper.Asst.
Staff: 1. **Subjects:** Surface and ground water, water quality. **Special Collections:** Complete set of WRD Wisconsin publications. **Holdings:** 2500 books; 550 water supply papers; 475 professional papers; 140 bulletins; 180 circulars. **Services:** Library open to the public for reference use only.

★15129★
U.S. GEOLOGICAL SURVEY - WATER RESOURCES DIVISION - NATIONAL WATER DATA STORAGE & RETRIEVAL SYSTEM (Sci-Engr)
National Center, Mail Stop 409 Phone: (703)648-5687
Reston, VA 22092 Philip Cohen, Chf. Hydrologist
Founded: 1889. **Staff:** Prof 16; Other 9. **Subjects:** Surface water stage and discharge, chemical quality parameters, radiochemistry, sedimentology, pesticide and biological concentrations in water, ground and surface water levels, flood frequency and flood inundation mapping. **Holdings:** Observations from 16,600 streamflow gauging stations, 6230 water quality measuring stations, 900,000 wells and springs; historical data, 1890 to present. **Services:** Data collection and analysis; data from computerized files is available on magnetic tape or cards; system open to the public on fee basis. **Publications:** List of publications - available on request. **Also Known As:** WATSTORE.

★15130★
U.S. GEOLOGICAL SURVEY - WATER RESOURCES DIVISION - NEW YORK DISTRICT - LIBRARY (Sci-Engr)
343 Court House
Box 1669 Phone: (518)472-3107
Albany, NY 12201 Margaret L. Phillips, Act.Libn.
Subjects: Geochemistry, hydrology, geology, climatology. **Special Collections:** Acid Precipitation Collection (reprints and documents). **Holdings:** 6500 books; 250 pamphlet boxes of periodicals; 1000 maps; climatological data; 950 hydrologic investigations; atlases.

★15131★
U.S. GEOLOGICAL SURVEY - WATER RESOURCES DIVISION - NEW YORK SUBDISTRICT - LIBRARY
5 Aerial Way
Syosset, NY 11791
Subjects: Water resources, geology of Long Island. **Special Collections:** U.S. Geological Survey's professional papers; water supply papers; water resources investigations. **Holdings:** 300 books; 27 bound periodical volumes. **Remarks:** Presently inactive.

★15132★
U.S. GEOLOGICAL SURVEY - WATER RESOURCES DIVISION - READING ROOM (Sci-Engr, Geog-Map)
4501 Indian School Rd., N.E., Suite 200 Phone: (505)262-6697
Albuquerque, NM 87110 Arsilia Alvarez
Founded: 1958. **Staff:** Prof 1. **Subjects:** Hydrology, geology of New Mexico. **Special Collections:** Topographic and geologic maps. **Holdings:** 1427 books; 10,012 bound periodical volumes; 19,965 unbound periodicals and reports; 855 microfiche. **Subscriptions:** 374 journals and other serials. **Services:** Interlibrary loan; copying; room open to the public for reference use only.

★15133★
U.S. GEOLOGICAL SURVEY - WATER RESOURCES LIBRARY (Env-Cons)
W. Aspinall Federal Bldg., Rm. 201
4th & Rood Ave.
Box 2027 Phone: (303)245-5257
Grand Junction, CO 815012 Dannie L. Collins, Subdistrict Chf.
Staff: Prof 2. **Subjects:** Water resources, water quality, geological and atmospheric conditions as they pertain to water. **Holdings:** 1534 books; 1014 bound periodical volumes; 669 volumes of basic data reports; 3880 maps; 110 decisions on names in the U.S.; 55 reels of microfilm of well log data for Colorado; 179 volumes of professional papers. **Services:** Interlibrary loan; copying; library open to the public with restrictions. **Publications:** Water Resources Data, Colorado; Water Year 1987; Missouri River Basin; Rio Grande River Basin.

★15134★
U.S. GEOLOGICAL SURVEY - WESTERN MINERAL RESOURCES LIBRARY (Sci-Engr)
656 U.S. Court House
920 W. Riverside Ave. Phone: (509)456-4677
Spokane, WA 99201 Anita W. Tarbert, Lib.Techn.
Founded: 1948. **Staff:** 1. **Subjects:** Geology and allied sciences. **Special Collections:** U.S. Geological Survey publications (almost complete run). **Holdings:** Figures not available for books and bound periodical volumes; 1200 shelf feet of topographic maps of Pacific Northwest states and Alaska;

state publications related to geology of Idaho, Washington, Montana, and Oregon. **Services:** Library open to the public with restrictions.

★15135★
UNITED STATES GOLF ASSOCIATION - GOLF HOUSE LIBRARY (Rec)
Golf House — Phone: (201)234-2300
Far Hills, NJ 07931 — Janet Seagle, Libn./Musm.Cur.
Staff: Prof 1. **Subjects:** Golf. **Holdings:** 7000 books; 440 bound periodical volumes; 52 scrapbooks of newspaper clippings. **Subscriptions:** 25 journals and other serials. **Services:** Library open to the public for reference use only.

★15136★
U.S. HOCKEY HALL OF FAME - LIBRARY (Rec)
Hat Trick Ave..
Box 657
Eveleth, MN 55734 — Phone: (218)749-5167
Founded: 1973. **Subjects:** Ice hockey. **Special Collections:** College hockey rulebooks. **Holdings:** Unbound periodicals; newspapers; guide books; programs; scrapbooks. **Services:** Library open to serious researchers only. **Staff:** Archie J. Rauzi, Co-Dir.; Mitch Batinich, Co.-Dir..

★15137★
U.S. HOUSE OF REPRESENTATIVES - LIBRARY (Law)
B-18 Cannon Bldg. — Phone: (202)225-0462
Washington, DC 20515 — E. Raymond Lewis, Libn.
Founded: 1792. **Staff:** 4. **Subjects:** Legislation, law. **Special Collections:** Congressional documents, Continental Congress to present. **Holdings:** 225,000 volumes. **Services:** Use of library restricted to members and committees of Congress and their staffs, except by special permission. **Publications:** Index to Congressional Committee Hearings in the House.

U.S. INDUSTRIAL CHEMICALS COMPANY - RESEARCH DEPARTMENT LIBRARY
See: USI Chemicals Company - CRL Library (17222)

★15138★
U.S. INFORMATION AGENCY - LIBRARY PROGRAM DIVISION† (Info Sci)
301 4th St., S.W., Rm. 314 — Phone: (202)485-1511
Washington, DC 20547 — Richard B. Fitz, Chf.
Holdings: 828,255 books; periodicals; documents; microforms; AV programs. **Remarks:** Agency functions as service headquarters for 131 I.A. libraries in 81 countries abroad, and also provides support to library programs in 27 Binational Centers. Holdings listed above represent combined resources.

★15139★
U.S. INFORMATION AGENCY - USIA LIBRARY (Soc Sci)
301 4th St., S.W. — Phone: (202)485-8947
Washington, DC 20547 — Richard B. Fitz, Chf., Lib.Prog.Div.
Founded: 1955. **Staff:** Prof 29; Other 16. **Subjects:** International affairs, Americana, area studies, communication. **Special Collections:** Agency historical collection (5500 volumes). **Holdings:** 70,000 books; 27,000 bound periodical volumes; 85 VF drawers of clippings and documents; 90,500 microforms. **Subscriptions:** 840 journals and other serials; 12 newspapers. **Services:** Interlibrary loan; copying; SDI; library open to the public by appointment. **Automated Operations:** Computerized cataloging. **Computerized Information Services:** DIALOG Information Services, OCLC, NEXIS, VU/TEXT Information Services, DataTimes, LEGI-SLATE, WILSONLINE; internal database; DIALMAIL (electronic mail service). **Networks/Consortia:** Member of FEDLINK. **Publications:** USIA Library Bulletin, monthly; Calendar of Coming Events and Anniversaries, quarterly; Periodical Holdings, annual - all for internal distribution only. **Special Indexes:** Program Materials Index (PMI; online); index to government documents (online). **Staff:** Helen Amabile, Dp.Chf., Lib.Prog.; Suzanne Dawkins, Cat.; Janet M. Gilligan, Chf., Tech.Serv.; Sara Strom, Chf., Ref.Br..

U.S. INFORMATION CENTER FOR THE UNIVERSAL DECIMAL CLASSIFICATION
See: University of Maryland, College Park - College of Library & Information Services (16368)

★15140★
UNITED STATES INFORMATION SERVICE - LIBRARY (Soc Sci)
150 Wellington St., 3rd Fl. — Phone: (613)238-5335
Ottawa, ON, Canada K1P 5A4 — Brenda Brady, Lib.Dir.
Founded: 1960. **Staff:** Prof 2; Other 1. **Subjects:** United States - politics and government, legislation and policy; Canadian/American relations. **Special Collections:** United States Code Annotated; Code of Federal Regulations; selected U.S. Government publications; current speeches. **Holdings:** 3000 books and government documents; 14 VF drawers of clippings; telephone directories of major U.S. cities. **Subscriptions:** 93 journals and other serials. **Services:** Interlibrary loan; locates addresses and backgrounds of U.S. departments and institutions; provides information on U.S. laws, legislation, and documents; library open to the public with restrictions. **Computerized Information Services:** DIALOG Information Services, Info Globe, Public Diplomacy Query (PDQ), LEGI-SLATE; DIALMAIL (electronic mail service). **Networks/Consortia:** Member of FEDLINK. **Publications:** Library News, quarterly; Article Alert, bimonthly; V/F, weekly. **Special Catalogs:** U.S. Official Publications in Selected Canadian Libraries. **Staff:** Kyle Ward, Ref.Libn..

U.S. INSTITUTE OF ADMINISTRATION AND DEFENSE INFORMATION SCHOOL
See: U.S. Army - TRADOC - Soldier Support Center - Main Library (14808)

★15141★
U.S. INTERAGENCY ADVANCED POWER GROUP - POWER INFORMATION CENTER (Sci-Engr, Energy)
1400 Eye St., N.W., Suite 600 — Phone: (202)842-7600
Washington, DC 20005 — Judi Decker, Prog.Coord.
Founded: 1960. **Staff:** Prof 4. **Subjects:** Electrical engineering; power conditioning; pulse power; mechanical engineering; heat engines and auxiliary components; thermoelectrics; chemical, nuclear, and solar energy; magnetohydrodynamics; systems. **Holdings:** 4008 project briefs and project reports. **Services:** Center open to government employeees. **Publications:** Project Briefs, monthly; meeting proceedings; roster, semiannual. **Special Indexes:** Indexes to briefs, monthly and semiannual indexes. **Staff:** Marion Millhouse, Proj.Mgr.; Judi Decker, Prog.Coord./Meeting Coord.; Christopher Moore, Asst.Prog.Coord..

★15142★
U.S. INTERNAL REVENUE SERVICE - LAW LIBRARY (Law)
Internal Revenue Service Bldg., Rm. 4324
1111 Constitution Ave., N.W. — Phone: (202)566-6342
Washington, DC 20224 — Geraldine F. Katz, Chf.
Founded: 1917. **Staff:** Prof 8; Other 9. **Subjects:** Federal tax law, international taxation, accounting, management, economics. **Special Collections:** Historical collection of Internal Revenue publications and tax forms; legislative histories of all Internal Revenue acts and related statutes. **Holdings:** 100,000 volumes. **Subscriptions:** 1200 journals and other serials; 8 newspapers. **Services:** Interlibrary loan (to government agencies only); library open to government employees on official business. **Automated Operations:** Computerized cataloging, acquisitions, and serials. **Computerized Information Services:** LEXIS, DIALOG Information Services, PHINet FedTax Database, WESTLAW, VU/TEXT Information Services, WILSONLINE, OCLC. **Networks/Consortia:** Member of FEDLINK. **Publications:** Library Bulletin, monthly. **Remarks:** The Internal Revenue Service is part of the U.S. Department of the Treasury. **Also Known As:** IRS. **Staff:** Susan N. Cushing, Cat.; Jill H. Klein, Acq.; Minnie Sue Ripy, Ref.; Luanne Karr, Digest Group; Jule McCartney, Ref.; Catherine Duffy, Leg.Res.; Brenda Cape, Leg.Res..

U.S. INTERNATIONAL DEVELOPMENT COOPERATING AGENCY - AGENCY FOR INTERNATIONAL DEVELOPMENT
See: U.S. Agency for International Development (14576)

★15143★
U.S. INTERNATIONAL TRADE ADMINISTRATION - U.S. AND FOREIGN COMMERCIAL SERVICE - ALBUQUERQUE DISTRICT OFFICE LIBRARY (Bus-Fin)
517 Gold, S.W., Rm. 4303
Albuquerque, NM 87102 — Phone: (505)766-2386
Staff: 1. **Holdings:** Foreign country directories. **Services:** Provides international marketing services for U.S. Dept. of Commerce.

★15144★
U.S. INTERNATIONAL TRADE ADMINISTRATION - U.S. AND FOREIGN COMMERCIAL SERVICE - ANCHORAGE DISTRICT OFFICE LIBRARY (Bus-Fin)
701 C St., Box 32 Phone: (907)271-5041
Anchorage, AK 99513 Richard M. Lenahan, Dir.
Holdings: 1000 volumes, including Census Bureau publications, Alaska and international commerce reference files. **Services:** Copying; library open to the public. **Publications:** Alaska World Trade U.S.A., monthly. **Special Indexes:** Alaska International Trade Directory.

★15145★
U.S. INTERNATIONAL TRADE ADMINISTRATION - U.S. AND FOREIGN COMMERCIAL SERVICE - ATLANTA DISTRICT OFFICE LIBRARY (Bus-Fin)
1365 Peachtree St., N.E., Suite 504
Atlanta, GA 30309 Christine B. Brown, Trade Ref.Asst.
Staff: Prof 1. **Subjects:** Demographic and economic statistics, foreign trade, patents, copyrights. **Holdings:** 600 books; 32 bound periodical volumes. **Subscriptions:** 31 journals and other serials. **Services:** Copying; library open to the public. **Computerized Information Services:** DIALOG Information Services, Pergamon ORBIT InfoLine, Inc., BRS Information Technologies. **Publications:** Census and foreign trade publications.

★15146★
U.S. INTERNATIONAL TRADE ADMINISTRATION - U.S. AND FOREIGN COMMERCIAL SERVICE - BALTIMORE DISTRICT OFFICE MARKETING INFORMATION CENTER (Bus-Fin)
413 U.S. Customhouse
Gay & Lombard Sts. Phone: (301)962-3560
Baltimore, MD 21202 LoRee P. Silloway, Dir.
Staff: Prof 4; Other 2. **Subjects:** International trade, export expansion, domestic economic growth. **Holdings:** 10 VF drawers; 3 bookcases; trade directories for 20 countries. **Services:** Center open to the public.

★15147★
U.S. INTERNATIONAL TRADE ADMINISTRATION - U.S. AND FOREIGN COMMERCIAL SERVICE - BIRMINGHAM DISTRICT OFFICE LIBRARY (Bus-Fin)
Berry Bldg., 3rd Fl.
2015 2nd Ave., N., Rm. 302 Phone: (205)731-1331
Birmingham, AL 35203 Gayle C. Shelton, Jr., Dir.
Holdings: 170 books; reports; departmental and Census Bureau publications. **Services:** Library open to the public.

★15148★
U.S. INTERNATIONAL TRADE ADMINISTRATION - U.S. AND FOREIGN COMMERCIAL SERVICE - BOSTON DISTRICT OFFICE LIBRARY (Bus-Fin)
World Trade Center, Boston
Commonwealth Pier, Suite 307 Phone: (617)565-8573
Boston, MA 02210 Frank J. O'Connor, Dir.
Founded: 1930. **Staff:** 14. **Subjects:** Business, commerce, foreign and domestic trade. **Holdings:** 960 linear feet of reference files. **Services:** Library open to the public. **Publications:** Commerce New England Newsletter, irregular.

★15149★
U.S. INTERNATIONAL TRADE ADMINISTRATION - U.S. AND FOREIGN COMMERCIAL SERVICE - BUFFALO DISTRICT OFFICE LIBRARY
1312 Federal Bldg.
111 W. Huron St.
Buffalo, NY 14202
Holdings: 3000 volumes, including Census Bureau and departmental publications. **Remarks:** Presently inactive.

★15150★
U.S. INTERNATIONAL TRADE ADMINISTRATION - U.S. AND FOREIGN COMMERCIAL SERVICE - CHARLESTON DISTRICT OFFICE LIBRARY (Bus-Fin)
Federal Office Bldg.
500 Quarrier St. Phone: (304)347-5123
Charleston, WV 25301 Roger L. Fortner, Dir.
Subjects: Exporting, patents, copyright. **Holdings:** 4400 volumes, including departmental publications, International Trade Administration directories, West Virginia state pamphlets and studies, . **Services:** Library open to the public.

★15151★
U.S. INTERNATIONAL TRADE ADMINISTRATION - U.S. AND FOREIGN COMMERCIAL SERVICE - CHICAGO DISTRICT OFFICE LIBRARY (Bus-Fin)
Mid-Continental Plaza Bldg., Rm. 1406
55 E. Monroe Phone: (312)353-4450
Chicago, IL 60603 Bernadine C. Roberson, Libn.
Founded: 1940. **Staff:** 1. **Subjects:** Business economics, population (census), foreign trade statistics. **Special Collections:** Census materials; foreign trade directories. **Holdings:** 5000 books; 5000 pamphlets; 500 bibliographies. **Subscriptions:** 30 journals and other serials. **Services:** Library open to the public.

★15152★
U.S. INTERNATIONAL TRADE ADMINISTRATION - U.S. AND FOREIGN COMMERCIAL SERVICE - CINCINNATI DISTRICT OFFICE LIBRARY (Bus-Fin)
9504 Federal Office Bldg.
550 Main St. Phone: (513)684-2944
Cincinnati, OH 45202 Gordon B. Thomas, Dir.
Subjects: Domestic and international trade. **Holdings:** 16 bookcase sections of statistical data, catalogs, trade journals, industry reports, department publications, directories, Census Bureau materials; 10 VF drawers. **Services:** Library open to the public.

★15153★
U.S. INTERNATIONAL TRADE ADMINISTRATION - U.S. AND FOREIGN COMMERCIAL SERVICE - CLEVELAND DISTRICT OFFICE - INFORMATION CENTER (Bus-Fin)
668 Euclid Ave., Rm. 600 Phone: (216)522-4755
Cleveland, OH 44114 Toby T. Zettfer, Dist.Dir.
Founded: 1947. **Staff:** Prof 4; Other 2. **Subjects:** International trade, marketing, economic trends, business. **Holdings:** 200 volumes; 15 VF drawers. **Services:** Professional consultations by international trade specialists; center open to the public with restrictions. **Publications:** Trade World Ohio, bimonthly.

★15154★
U.S. INTERNATIONAL TRADE ADMINISTRATION - U.S. AND FOREIGN COMMERCIAL SERVICE - DALLAS DISTRICT OFFICE LIBRARY (Bus-Fin)
1100 Commerce St., Rm. 7A5 Phone: (214)767-0542
Dallas, TX 75242 C. Carmon Stiles, Dir.
Subjects: Domestic and foreign commerce. **Holdings:** 3725 volumes. **Services:** Library open to the public.

★15155★
U.S. INTERNATIONAL TRADE ADMINISTRATION - U.S. AND FOREIGN COMMERCIAL SERVICE - DES MOINES DISTRICT OFFICE LIBRARY (Bus-Fin)
817 Federal Bldg.
210 Walnut St. Phone: (515)284-4222
Des Moines, IA 50309 Jesse N. Durden, Dir.
Subjects: Foreign trade and census statistics. **Holdings:** Figures not available. **Services:** Library open to the public.

★15156★
U.S. INTERNATIONAL TRADE ADMINISTRATION - U.S. AND FOREIGN COMMERCIAL SERVICE - DETROIT DISTRICT OFFICE LIBRARY (Bus-Fin)
477 Michigan Ave., Suite 1140 Phone: (313)226-3650
Detroit, MI 48226 William R. Dahlin, Act.Dir.
Subjects: Economics, marketing, trade, census. **Holdings:** 100 volumes; 4 drawers of international trade statistics on microfiche. **Subscriptions:** 10 journals and other serials. **Services:** Library open to the public. **Computerized Information Services:** DIALOG Information Services; internal database. **Publications:** Business America - Michigan Newsletter, monthly; Bugs, Bytes & Glitches (newsletter), quarterly.

★15157★
U.S. INTERNATIONAL TRADE ADMINISTRATION - U.S. AND FOREIGN COMMERCIAL SERVICE - GREENSBORO DISTRICT OFFICE LIBRARY (Bus-Fin)
Box 1950 Phone: (919)333-5345
Greensboro, NC 27402 Jack F. Whiteley, Dp.Dir.
Subjects: Domestic and foreign commerce. **Holdings:** 1400 volumes. **Subscriptions:** 15 journals and other serials. **Services:** Library open to the public. **Computerized Information Services:** DIALOG Information Services; Automatic Information Transfer System (internal database).

★15158★
U.S. INTERNATIONAL TRADE ADMINISTRATION - U.S. FOREIGN AND COMMERCIAL SERVICE - HARTFORD DISTRICT OFFICE LIBRARY (Bus-Fin)
450 Main St., Rm. 610B Phone: (203)240-3530
Hartford, CT 06103 Eric B. Outwater, Dir.
Subjects: Census statistics. **Holdings:** Figures not available. **Services:** Library open to the public.

★15159★
U.S. INTERNATIONAL TRADE ADMINISTRATION - U.S. AND FOREIGN COMMERCIAL SERVICE - HOUSTON DISTRICT OFFICE LIBRARY (Bus-Fin)
515 Rusk Ave., Rm. 2625 Phone: (713)229-2578
Houston, TX 77002 James D. Cook, Dir.
Subjects: Commerce, business. **Holdings:** 600 volumes, including departmental publications. **Services:** Library open to the public.

★15160★
U.S. INTERNATIONAL TRADE ADMINISTRATION - U.S. AND FOREIGN COMMERCIAL SERVICE - LITTLE ROCK DISTRICT OFFICE LIBRARY (Bus-Fin)
320 W. Capitol, Suite 811 Phone: (501)378-5794
Little Rock, AR 72201 Mary Hayward, Sec.
Founded: 1979. **Staff:** Prof 1. **Subjects:** International trade. **Holdings:** 1000 books; 35 bound periodical volumes; departmental and Census Bureau publications. **Subscriptions:** 25 journals and other serials; 5 newspapers. **Services:** Library open to the public for reference use only. **Computerized Information Services:** DIALOG Information Services; CompuServe Information Service (CIS; electronic mail service).

★15161★
U.S. INTERNATIONAL TRADE ADMINISTRATION - U.S. AND FOREIGN COMMERCIAL SERVICE - MIAMI DISTRICT OFFICE LIBRARY (Bus-Fin)
Federal Bldg., Rm. 224
51 S.W. First Ave. Phone: (305)536-5267
Miami, FL 33130 Ivan A. Cosimi, Dir.
Subjects: Business, foreign and domestic trade. **Holdings:** Foreign directories; government reports. **Services:** Library open to the public.

★15162★
U.S. INTERNATIONAL TRADE ADMINISTRATION - U.S. AND FOREIGN COMMERCIAL SERVICE - MILWAUKEE DISTRICT OFFICE LIBRARY (Bus-Fin)
Federal Bldg., Rm. 606
517 E. Wisconsin Ave. Phone: (414)291-3473
Milwaukee, WI 53202 Patrick A. Willis, Dir.
Subjects: Economic and market research, technology, foreign trade statistics. **Holdings:** 6000 volumes. **Services:** Library open to the public.

★15163★
U.S. INTERNATIONAL TRADE ADMINISTRATION - U.S. AND FOREIGN COMMERCIAL SERVICE - MINNEAPOLIS DISTRICT OFFICE LIBRARY (Bus-Fin)
108 Federal Bldg.
110 S. Fourth St. Phone: (612)348-1638
Minneapolis, MN 55401 Mary Hobbs, Trade Spec.
Staff: Prof 1. **Subjects:** Census, marketing, government statistics, foreign trade, area development. **Special Collections:** Directories. **Holdings:** Figures not available. **Services:** Interlibrary loan; library open to the public.

★15164★
U.S. INTERNATIONAL TRADE ADMINISTRATION - U.S. AND FOREIGN COMMERCIAL SERVICE - NASHVILLE DISTRICT OFFICE LIBRARY (Bus-Fin)
404 James Robertson Pkwy., Rm. 1114 Phone: (615)736-5161
Nashville, TN 37219-1505 Jim Charlet, Dir.
Founded: 1930. **Staff:** Prof 4; Other 2. **Subjects:** International trade, economic studies, foreign trade regulations, customs procedures. **Holdings:** 1000 books; 77 bound periodical volumes; 3000 other cataloged items. **Subscriptions:** 27 journals and other serials; 6 newspapers. **Services:** Interlibrary loan; copying; library open to the public for reference use only. **Computerized Information Services:** DIALOG Information Services, Foreign Traders Index (FTI); internal database. Performs searches on fee basis.

★15165★
U.S. INTERNATIONAL TRADE ADMINISTRATION - U.S. AND FOREIGN COMMERCIAL SERVICE - NEW ORLEANS DISTRICT OFFICE LIBRARY (Bus-Fin)
World Trade Center, Rm. 432
2 Canal St. Phone: (504)589-6546
New Orleans, LA 70130 Paul L. Guidry, Dir.
Subjects: Census and foreign trade statistics. **Holdings:** Foreign phone books and commercial directories. **Services:** Library open to the public.

★15166★
U.S. INTERNATIONAL TRADE ADMINISTRATION - U.S. AND FOREIGN COMMERCIAL SERVICE - NEW YORK DISTRICT OFFICE MARKET INFORMATION CENTER (Bus-Fin)
26 Federal Plaza Phone: (212)264-0630
New York, NY 10278 Stuart Werner, Tech.Info.Spec.
Founded: 1925. **Staff:** Prof 2; Other 1. **Subjects:** Census, economics, business, technology, foreign trade, marketing. **Special Collections:** Foreign and domestic trade directories. **Holdings:** 3000 books; 65 VF drawers of economic and business information. **Subscriptions:** 75 journals and other serials; 10 newspapers. **Services:** Copying; center open to the public. **Computerized Information Services:** DIALOG Information Services. **Staff:** Elisa Colas, Tech.Info.Spec..

★15167★
U.S. INTERNATIONAL TRADE ADMINISTRATION - U.S. AND FOREIGN COMMERCIAL SERVICE - PHILADELPHIA DISTRICT OFFICE LIBRARY (Bus-Fin)
9448 Federal Bldg.
600 Arch St. Phone: (215)597-2866
Philadelphia, PA 19106 Robert Kistler, Dir.
Subjects: Industry, foreign business, international marketing. **Holdings:** 800 volumes; Department of Commerce publications. **Services:** Library open to the public.

★15168★
U.S. INTERNATIONAL TRADE ADMINISTRATION - U.S. AND FOREIGN COMMERCIAL SERVICE - PHOENIX DISTRICT OFFICE LIBRARY (Bus-Fin)
230 N. 1st Ave., Rm. 3412 Phone: (602)254-3285
Phoenix, AZ 85025 Donald W. Fry, Dir.
Founded: 1946. **Staff:** Prof 5. **Subjects:** Technology, census, agriculture, business, education, transportation, Indians, importing and exporting, Arizona statistics. **Holdings:** 6000 books; 1500 other volumes. **Services:** Library open to the public.

★15169★
U.S. INTERNATIONAL TRADE ADMINISTRATION - U.S. AND FOREIGN COMMERCIAL SERVICE - PITTSBURGH DISTRICT OFFICE LIBRARY (Bus-Fin)
2002 Federal Bldg.
1000 Liberty Ave. Phone: (412)644-2850
Pittsburgh, PA 15222 John A. McCartney, Dir.
Subjects: Foreign commerce, census, international trade. **Holdings:** 1000 volumes; 140 VF drawers of government pamphlets, reports, and statistics. **Subscriptions:** 30 journals and other serials. **Services:** Library open to the public.

★15170★
U.S. INTERNATIONAL TRADE ADMINISTRATION - U.S. AND FOREIGN COMMERCIAL SERVICE - RICHMOND DISTRICT OFFICE LIBRARY (Bus-Fin)
8010 Federal Bldg.
400 N. 8th St. Phone: (804)771-2246
Richmond, VA 23240 Philip A. Ouzts, Dir.
Subjects: Census, business economics, foreign trade. **Holdings:** 1300 volumes. **Services:** Library open to the public.

★15171★
U.S. INTERNATIONAL TRADE ADMINISTRATION - U.S. AND FOREIGN COMMERCIAL SERVICE - ST. LOUIS DISTRICT OFFICE LIBRARY (Bus-Fin)
7911 Forsyth Blvd., Suite 610
St. Louis, MO 63105 Phone: (314)425-3302
Subjects: Exports, foreign trade. **Holdings:** 1500 volumes. **Services:** Interlibrary loan; library open to the public.

★15172★
U.S. INTERNATIONAL TRADE ADMINISTRATION - U.S. AND FOREIGN COMMERCIAL SERVICE - SALT LAKE CITY DISTRICT OFFICE LIBRARY (Bus-Fin)
340 U.S. Post Office Bldg.
350 S. Main St. Phone: (801)524-5116
Salt Lake City, UT 84101 Stephen P. Smoot, Dir.
Founded: 1945. **Subjects:** Business economics. **Holdings:** 200 books. **Services:** Library open to the public.

★15173★
U.S. INTERNATIONAL TRADE ADMINISTRATION - U.S. AND FOREIGN COMMERCIAL SERVICE - SAN JUAN DISTRICT OFFICE - BUSINESS LIBRARY (Bus-Fin)
Federal Office Bldg., Rm. G-55 Phone: (809)753-4555
Hato Rey, PR 00918 Enrique Vilella, Dir.
Staff: 4. **Subjects:** Market statistics, international economics and marketing, export/import. **Holdings:** 1000 volumes; international manufacturers' directories. **Services:** Copying; library open to the public.

★15174★
U.S. INTERNATIONAL TRADE ADMINISTRATION - U.S. AND FOREIGN COMMERCIAL SERVICE - SAVANNAH DISTRICT OFFICE LIBRARY (Bus-Fin)
120 Barnard St., A-107 Phone: (912)944-4204
Savannah, GA 31401 James W. McIntire, Dir.
Subjects: Census and other department publications, foreign and domestic trade directories, market research, foreign trade and tariff regulations. **Holdings:** 1800 volumes. **Services:** Library open to the public.

★15175★
U.S. INTERNATIONAL TRADE COMMISSION - LAW LIBRARY (Law)
500 E St., S.W. Phone: (202)523-0333
Washington, DC 20436 Steven J. Kover, Hd.
Founded: 1972. **Staff:** Prof 2; Other 1. **Subjects:** U.S. trade and patent law. **Special Collections:** Legislative histories of U.S. trade and tariff acts; U.S. International Trade Commission reports. **Holdings:** 10,000 books; 700 bound periodical volumes. **Subscriptions:** 70 journals and other serials. **Services:** Interlibrary loan; copying; library open to the public. **Automated Operations:** Computerized cataloging. **Computerized Information Services:** WESTLAW, LEGI-SLATE, OCLC. **Publications:** Bibliography of Law Journal Articles on Statutes Administered by the U.S.I.T.C. and Related Subjects. **Staff:** Maureen Bryant, Law Libn.

★15176★
U.S. INTERNATIONAL TRADE COMMISSION - LIBRARY (Soc Sci)
500 E St., N.W. Phone: (202)252-1626
Washington, DC 20024 Barbara J. Pruett, Chf., Lib.Div.
Founded: 1917. **Staff:** Prof 6; Other 7. **Subjects:** U.S. trade policy, international trade, foreign trade statistics, tariffs. **Holdings:** 77,500 volumes. **Subscriptions:** 2200 journals and other serials. **Services:** Interlibrary loan except for legislative histories; copying; library open to the public with restrictions. **Automated Operations:** Computerized cataloging, acquisitions, serials, and circulation. **Computerized Information Services:** OCLC, DIALOG Information Services, LEGI-SLATE, The Reference Service (REFSRV). **Networks/Consortia:** Member of FEDLINK. **Publications:** Selected current acquisitions, monthly - to staff and by request; Our Library Presents ... - for internal distribution only. **Staff:** Hennie R. Schneider, Ref.Libn.; Beth Root, Tech.Serv..

U.S. INTERSTATE COMMERCE COMMISSION
See: Interstate Commerce Commission (7082)

★15177★
U.S. LEAGUE OF SAVINGS INSTITUTIONS - LIBRARY (Bus-Fin)
1709 New York Ave., N.W. Phone: (202)637-8920
Washington, DC 20006 Katherine Harahan, Libn.
Staff: Prof 1; Other 2. **Subjects:** Savings and loans, economics. **Special Collections:** Savings and loan congressional materials; general historical data. **Holdings:** 8000 books. **Subscriptions:** 200 journals and other serials; 15 newspapers. **Services:** Interlibrary loan; library open to public at librarian's discretion. **Computerized Information Services:** LEGI-SLATE, Congressional Quarterly Inc. (CQ).

★15178★
U.S. LEAGUE OF SAVINGS INSTITUTIONS - LIBRARY (Bus-Fin)
111 E. Wacker Dr. Phone: (312)644-3100
Chicago, IL 60601 Charlotte Wilson, Chf.Libn.
Staff: Prof 3; Other 2. **Subjects:** Savings and loans, housing finance and mortgages, savings banks, banking services, electronic funds transfer. **Holdings:** 2500 books; 300 bound periodical volumes; 70 VF drawers. **Subscriptions:** 150 journals and other serials; 7 newspapers. **Services:** Interlibrary loan; copying; library open to the public with restrictions. **Automated Operations:** Computerized cataloging. **Computerized Information Services:** DIALOG Information Services, Mead Data Central, Dow Jones News/Retrieval, OCLC. **Staff:** Ronald Stoner, Tech.Serv.Libn.; Sandra Engram, Res.Libn..

U.S. LIBRARY OF CONGRESS
See: Library of Congress (7807)

★15179★
UNITED STATES LIFESAVING ASSOCIATION - LIBRARY & INFORMATION CENTER (Med)
425 E. McFetridge Dr.
Chicago, IL 60605 Joe Pecoraro, Pres.
Founded: 1964. **Staff:** Prof 1. **Subjects:** Open-water lifeguarding, rescue procedures, first aid and resuscitation, ocean environment, marine safety, flood rescue procedures. **Special Collections:** Films and photographs of open-water lifeguard subjects; lifeguard manuals from United States and World Lifesaving. **Holdings:** 1000 U.S. Lifesaving Magazines; 1000 lifesaving photographs. **Services:** Library not open to the public. **Automated Operations:** Computerized acquisitions. **Publications:** Annual Reports; Emergency Services, annual; Lifeguarding and Marine Safety; Beach Information; Guidelines for Open-Water Lifeguard Training. **Remarks:** Sponsors the American Lifesaving Emergency Response Team (A.L.E.R.T.) to respond to floods and water disasters throughout the United States.

U.S. LIVESTOCK INSECTS LABORATORY
See: U.S.D.A. - Agricultural Research Service (14978)

★15180★
U.S. MARINE CORPS - CAMP H.M. SMITH LIBRARY (Mil)
Bldg. 27 Phone: (808)477-6348
Honolulu, HI 96861 Evelyn Mau, Libn.
Founded: 1966. **Staff:** Prof 1; Other 2. **Subjects:** Marine Corps. **Holdings:** 10,000 books. **Subscriptions:** 60 journals and other serials; 8 newspapers. **Services:** Interlibrary loan; library not open to the public.

★15181★
U.S. MARINE CORPS - CAMP PENDLETON LIBRARY SYSTEM (Mil)
Marine Corps Base
1122 E St. Phone: (619)725-5104
Camp Pendleton, CA 92055 Patrick J. Carney, Lib.Dir.
Founded: 1950. **Staff:** Prof 3; Other 17. **Subjects:** Military art and science. **Holdings:** 111,481 books and bound periodical volumes; 22 VF drawers of pamphlets; 49,058 microforms; 115 films; 1897 phonograph records. **Subscriptions:** 636 journals and other serials; 27 newspapers. **Services:** Interlibrary loan; copying; library open to the public for reference use only on request. **Automated Operations:** Computerized cataloging. **Publications:** Library Bulletin, irregular - for internal distribution only. **Remarks:** Maintains base branch libraries and a bookmobile. **Staff:** Lorna Dodt, Asst.Dir.; Mrs. Vernese B. Thompson, Cons..

★15182★
U.S. MARINE CORPS - COMMANDING GENERAL (856) - LOGISTICS BASE - TECHNICAL SUPPORT LIBRARY (Sci-Engr, Mil)
Albany, GA 31704-5000 Phone: (912)439-6470
Dennis L. Gay, Jr., Tech.Libn.
Founded: 1966. **Staff:** 1. **Subjects:** Physical science, engineering, ordnance, electronics, military science. **Special Collections:** Marine Corps publications. **Holdings:** 25,000 books; 40,000 military specifications and standards on microfilm; 200 Army handbooks and bulletins. **Subscriptions:** 40 journals and other serials. **Services:** Interlibrary loan; library not open to the public. **Automated Operations:** Computerized acquisitions.

★15183★
U.S. MARINE CORPS - EDUCATION CENTER (Code E038) - JAMES CARSON BRECKINRIDGE LIBRARY (Mil, Soc Sci)
Marine Corps Development & Education Command
Phone: (703)640-2248
Quantico, VA 22134-5050 David C. Brown, Adm.Libn.
Founded: 1928. **Staff:** Prof 3; Other 5. **Subjects:** Military art and science, history, naval art and science, political and social science. **Special Collections:** Amphibious operations; Marine Corps; federal documents depository, 1967 to present. **Holdings:** 77,000 books and bound periodical volumes; 4500 unbound periodicals; 3600 reels of microfilm; 4000 documents. **Subscriptions:** 254 journals and other serials; 6 newspapers. **Services:** Interlibrary loan; copying; library open to the public by permission. **Automated Operations:** Computerized cataloging. **Computerized Information Services:** OCLC. **Networks/Consortia:** Member of FEDLINK. **Publications:** New Acquisitions List, quarterly; Current Contents of Selected Military Periodicals, bimonthly - both for limited distribution. **Staff:** Mary J. Porter, Ref.Libn.; JoAnn H. Payne, Acq..

★15184★
U.S. MARINE CORPS - EL TORO AIR STATION LIBRARY (Mil)
Bldg. 280 Phone: (714)651-3474
Santa Ana, CA 92709-5007 Karen L. Hayward, Lib.Dir.
Staff: Prof 2; Other 5. **Subjects:** Military history and science, biography, social science. **Special Collections:** Early California history; Marine Corps and military aviation history; Library of American Civilization (microfiche). **Holdings:** 55,000 books and bound periodical volumes; 1 file cabinet of maps; 2 file cabinets of pamphlets; 19,000 volumes in microform; microfiche. **Subscriptions:** 200 journals and other serials; 13 newspapers. **Services:** Interlibrary loan; library not open to the public. **Automated Operations:** Computerized cataloging, acquisitions, and circulation.

★15185★
U.S. MARINE CORPS - HISTORICAL CENTER LIBRARY (Mil)
Washington Navy Yard, Bldg. 58 Phone: (202)433-4253
Washington, DC 20374-0580 Evelyn A. Englander, Libn.
Staff: Prof 1; Other 1. **Subjects:** U.S. Marine Corps history, history of amphibious warfare, general naval and military history. **Special Collections:** Marine-published periodicals and newspapers; Marine Corps doctrinal publications; personal papers of famous figures in Marine Corps history. **Holdings:** 30,000 books; 500 bound periodical volumes; 6500 pamphlets; 5000 maps; 4000 reels of microfilm; 1987 linear feet of research papers. **Subscriptions:** 50 journals and other serials; 18 newspapers. **Services:** Interlibrary loan; copying; library open to the public. **Automated Operations:** Computerized cataloging and ILL. **Computerized Information Services:** DIALOG Information Services, OCLC. **Networks/Consortia:** Member of FEDLINK. **Publications:** Fontitudine (newsletter of Marine Corps history), quarterly. **Special Catalogs:** Marine Corps Historical Publications Catalog. **Remarks:** An alternate telephone number is 433-3447.

★15186★
U.S. MARINE CORPS - KANEOHE AIR STATION LIBRARY (Mil)
Bldg. 219 Phone: (808)257-3583
Kaneohe Bay, HI 96863-5010 Lola K. Todd, Supv.Libn.
Founded: 1951. **Staff:** Prof 1; Other 5. **Subjects:** Military history, U.S. Marine Corps. **Special Collections:** Hawaiiana; children's literature. **Holdings:** 35,199 books; 30,036 microforms; 3196 paperback books; 897 VF items; 1900 phonograph records. **Subscriptions:** 159 journals and other serials; 14 newspapers. **Services:** Interlibrary loan; copying; library open to military dependents and to civilians who work on base. **Special Indexes:** Leatherneck index, 1962-1980; Marine Corps Gazette Index, 1952-1980.

★15187★
U.S. MARINE CORPS - MARINE BAND LIBRARY (Mil, Mus)
Marine Barracks
8th & I Sts., S.E. Phone: (202)433-4298
Washington, DC 20390-5000 Frank P. Byrne, Jr., Chf.Libn.
Staff: Prof 6. **Subjects:** Band music, orchestra music, instrumental ensembles, national anthems, piano music, dance band. **Special Collections:** History of the Marine Band archives (photographs, 1863 to present; program files, 1898 to present; daily activities logs, 1918 to present; published material; tour and biographical information and memorabilia of former Marine Bandsmen); Military Music Collection (John Philip Sousa Collection; Victor Grabel/John Philip Sousa Music Library; The Sousa Band Encore Books; personal items of Sousa Band members John J. Heney, Sr., Walter F. Smith, Earle Polling, and Rudolph Becker). **Holdings:** 600 books; 40,000 pieces of sheet music. **Services:** Library open to the public by appointment.

★15188★
U.S. MARITIME ADMINISTRATION - NATIONAL MARITIME RESEARCH CENTER - MARITIME TECHNICAL INFORMATION FACILITY (Sci-Engr, Trans)
Kings Point, NY 11024-1699 Phone: (516)773-5577
Rayma Feldman, Mgr.
Founded: 1973. **Staff:** Prof 3; Other 5. **Subjects:** Ship operations and structures, ship simulation, navigation safety, maritime training, mariner performance, bridge design, shipping economics. **Holdings:** 1260 books; 1875 periodical volumes; 12,000 reports and serials. **Subscriptions:** 250 journals and other serials. **Services:** Copying; SDI; facility open to the public with restrictions. **Computerized Information Services:** STAR (internal database). Performs searches on fee basis. **Publications:** Acquisitions List; Maritime Abstracts Journal, both monthly; Maritime Thesaurus. **Remarks:** The Maritime Administration is part of the U.S. Department of Transportation. **Staff:** Barbara Ehrlich, Info.Spec.; Herb Loewenthal, Info.Spec..

★15189★
U.S. MERCHANT MARINE ACADEMY - SCHUYLER OTIS BLAND MEMORIAL LIBRARY (Trans)
Steamboat Rd. Phone: (516)773-5501
Kings Point, NY 11024 Dr. George J. Billy, Chf.Libn.
Founded: 1944. **Staff:** Prof 4; Other 3. **Subjects:** Marine engineering, nautical science, maritime history and economics. **Special Collections:** William Bollman Collection (maritime history). **Holdings:** 160,000 books; 5032 bound periodical volumes, 85,700 microfiche; 3520 reels of microfilm; 50 films; 12 VF drawers of maritime research reports; 300 maps; 15,000 other cataloged items. **Subscriptions:** 1246 journals and other serials; 8 newspapers. **Services:** Interlibrary loan; copying; library open to the public for reference use only. **Automated Operations:** Computerized cataloging. **Computerized Information Services:** DIALOG Information Services, OCLC; internal databases. **Networks/Consortia:** Member of Long Island Library Resources Council, Inc. (LILRC). **Publications:** Acquisitions List, monthly; Library Handbook, annual; Periodicals Holdings List, annual; Oil Spills and Tanker Regulations bibliographies. **Remarks:** The Academy is operated by the Maritime Administration of the U.S. Department of Transportation. **Staff:** Stephen R. Wiist, Tech.Serv.Libn.; Esther W. Bovarnick, Rd.Serv.Libn.; Martin M. Goldberg, Hd., Instr. Media.

U.S. NASA
See: NASA (9500)

★15190★
U.S. NATL. ARBORETUM - LIBRARY (Biol Sci)
3501 New York Ave., N.E. Phone: (202)475-4828
Washington, DC 20002 Susan C. Whitmore, Libn.
Staff: Prof 1. **Subjects:** Botany, taxonomy, floristics, horticulture, gardening, genetics, plant breeding. **Special Collections:** Nursery and seed trade catalogs (3 VF drawers); Mary Cokely Wood Ikebana Collection (75 volumes); floral prints; early photographs of U.S. Department of Agriculture Plant Exploration trips; U.S. Department of Agriculture photographs of agricultural practices of early 20th century; Bonsai; U.S. Plant Patent File (5400); Carlton R. Ball Collection on Salix (25 volumes); Arie F. den Boer manuscripts on crabapples (967 folders). **Holdings:** 5500 books; 500 periodical titles; 4 VF drawers of pamphlets and clippings. **Subscriptions:** 175 journals and other serials. **Services:** Interlibrary loan (through National Agricultural Library only); SDI; library open to the public for on-site research by appointment. **Computerized Information Services:** DIALOG Information Services. **Remarks:** A branch of the National Agricultural Library of the U.S. Department of Agriculture.

★15191★
U.S. NATL. BUREAU OF STANDARDS - ALLOY PHASE DIAGRAM DATA CENTER (Sci-Engr)
Bldg. 223, Rm. B-150 Phone: (301)921-2917
Gaithersburg, MD 20899 J.B. Clark, Dir.
Staff: Prof 2; Other 2. **Subjects:** Alloy phase stability and phase diagrams, metallurgy, metal physics, magnetism, electronic structures, density of states, physical properties of alloys. **Holdings:** Collection of alloy phase diagram evaluations and related compilations. **Subscriptions:** 10 journals and other serials. **Services:** Center open to the public with restrictions. **Publications:** List of publications - available on request. **Special Indexes:** Compilations of Binary Ti- Al- and Fe-based alloy phase diagrams. **Staff:** Dr. Ben Burton.

★15192★
U.S. NATL. BUREAU OF STANDARDS - ATOMIC ENERGY LEVELS DATA CENTER (Energy)
Physics Bldg., Rm. A155 Phone: (301)975-3221
Gaithersburg, MD 20899 Dr. William C. Martin, Physicist
Staff: Prof 3. **Subjects:** Atomic energy levels and spectra. **Holdings:** 7000 reprints of pertinent papers on atomic energy levels and spectra. **Services:** Copying; center open to the public. **Automated Operations:** Computerized cataloging. **Publications:** Bibliography on Atomic Energy Levels and Spectra, quadrennial - to users of the Data Center; Compilations of Atomic Energy Levels, 1-2/year. **Special Catalogs:** Current card catalog on atomic spectra which covers information not yet published in bibliographies. **Staff:** Dr. J. Sugar, Physicist; Arlene F. Musgrove, Tech.Info.Spec..

★15193★
U.S. NATL. BUREAU OF STANDARDS - CHEMICAL THERMODYNAMICS DATA CENTER (Sci-Engr)
Chemistry Bldg., Rm. A158 Phone: (301)975-2526
Gaithersburg, MD 20899 Malcolm W. Chase, Supv.Chem.
Subjects: Chemical thermodynamics, molecular parameters, correlation of physical properties. **Holdings:** 250 books; 117 bound periodical volumes; 33 reels of microfilm; 26.5 meters of unbound journals; microfilm file of 50,000 papers on experiments. **Services:** Center open to the public. **Automated Operations:** Computerized acquisitions. **Computerized Information Services:** DIALOG Information Services, Pergamon ORBIT InfoLine, Inc. **Publications:** NBS Tables of Chemical Thermodynamic Properties; bibliography of papers on thermochemical and related measurements (60,000 entries); JANAF Thermochemical Tables (3rd edition). **Special Indexes:** Index to thermochemical measurements coded by substance and property measured (card, 250,000 entries, with computer tape backup). **Staff:** David Neumann, Data Sys.; T.L. Jobe, Info.Spec.; D. Garvin, Sr. Data Anl..

★15194★
U.S. NATL. BUREAU OF STANDARDS - DATA CENTER ON ATOMIC TRANSITION PROBABILITIES (Sci-Engr)
Physics Bldg., Rm. A267 Phone: (301)975-3204
Gaithersburg, MD 20899 Dr. W.L. Wiese, Dir.
Founded: 1960. **Staff:** Prof 2. **Subjects:** Atomic transition probabilities. **Holdings:** Complete and up-to-date files of publications on atomic transition probabilities (5200 articles). **Services:** Numerical data provided on atomic transition probabilities; center open to the public. **Automated Operations:** Computerized cataloging. **Publications:** Bibliographies and critically-evaluated data tables. **Staff:** J.R. Fuhr, Physicist; M. Suskin, Physicist.

★15195★
U.S. NATL. BUREAU OF STANDARDS - FIRE RESEARCH INFORMATION SERVICES (Sci-Engr)
Bldg. 224, Rm. A252 Phone: (301)975-6862
Gaithersburg, MD 20899 Nora H. Jason, Proj.Ldr.
Founded: 1971. **Staff:** 2. **Subjects:** Fire research and safety, combustion, combustion toxicology, arson, fabric flammability, fire modeling and suppression, building fires. **Holdings:** 400 books and bound periodical volumes; 30,000 technical reports and conference proceedings. **Subscriptions:** 90 journals and other serials. **Services:** Interlibrary loan; services open to the public. **Computerized Information Services:** Online systems; FIREDOC (internal database). **Publications:** Fire Research Publications, annual.

★15196★
U.S. NATL. BUREAU OF STANDARDS - FUNDAMENTAL CONSTANTS DATA CENTER (Sci-Engr)
Bldg. 220, Rm. B258 Phone: (301)975-4220
Gaithersburg, MD 20899 Dr. Barry N. Taylor, Chf., Electricity Div.
Founded: 1970. **Staff:** Prof 1. **Subjects:** Fundamental constants, precision measurement. **Holdings:** 10,000 journal article reprints, late 1960s to present. **Services:** Center not open to the public. **Publications:** Periodic compilation of sets of recommended values of the fundamental physical constants.

★15197★
U.S. NATL. BUREAU OF STANDARDS - ION KINETICS AND ENERGETICS DATA CENTER (Sci-Engr)
Chemistry Bldg., Rm. A265 Phone: (301)921-2783
Gaithersburg, MD 20899 Dr. Sharon G. Lias, Dir.
Founded: 1963. **Staff:** 2. **Subjects:** Ionization potentials, appearance potentials, heats of formation of positive ions, proton affinity, electron affinity, ion-molecule reaction rate constants. **Holdings:** 6000 reprints. **Services:** Center open to the public. **Publications:** A Bibliography on Ion-Molecule Reactions, NBS Technical Note 291; Ionization Potentials, Appearance Potentials, and Heats of Formation of Gaseous Positive Ions, NSRDS-NBS 26; Energetics of Gaseous Ions, J. Phys. Chem. Ref. 6, Suppl. 1 (1977); The Measurement of Ionization and Appearance Potentials, International J. Mass Spectro. Ion Phys 20, 139 (1976); Ionization Potential and Appearance Potential Measurements, NSRDS-NBS 71 (1971-1981); Evaluated Gas Basicities and Proton Affinities (1984); Gas-phase Ion and Neutral Thermochemistry (1988).

U.S. NATL. BUREAU OF STANDARDS - JOINT INSTITUTE FOR LABORATORY ASTROPHYSICS (JILLA)
See: University of Colorado, Boulder - Joint Institute for Laboratory Astrophysics (JILLA) (16077)

★15198★
U.S. NATL. BUREAU OF STANDARDS - METALLURGY DIVISION - DIFFUSION IN METALS DATA CENTER (Sci-Engr)
Bldg. 223, Rm. A153 Phone: (301)975-6157
Gaithersburg, MD 20899 John R. Manning, Dir.
Staff: Prof 1. **Subjects:** Solid-state and liquid diffusion, diffusion coatings, oxidation, permeation, electromigration, thermomigration. **Special Collections:** Atomic motion in solids (25,000 documents). **Holdings:** 500 books; 10,000 reports on microfilm. **Services:** Center open to the public for reference use only. **Publications:** Diffusion in Copper and Copper Alloys; The Metallurgy of Copper.

★15199★
U.S. NATL. BUREAU OF STANDARDS - NATIONAL CENTER FOR STANDARDS AND CERTIFICATION INFORMATION (Sci-Engr)
Administration Bldg., Rm. A629 Phone: (301)975-4040
Gaithersburg, MD 20899 JoAnne R. Overman, Supv.Tech.Info.Spec.
Founded: 1965. **Staff:** 4. **Subjects:** Engineering and product standards, specifications, test methods, analytical methods, codes, and recommended practices; certification rules and programs; standardization; international, foreign, U.S., and state government standards and regulations. **Holdings:** Figures not available for books; U.S. national and industry standards; U.S. Government standards; foreign national standards; international standards; unbound articles; pamphlets; reports; monographs; microform files. **Services:** Information and referral services; center open to the public for reference use only. **Automated Operations:** Computerized indexing. **Computerized Information Services:** Internal databases. **Publications:** List of publications - available on request. **Special Indexes:** KWIC Index of the U.S. voluntary engineering standards. **Remarks:** This collection of standards and related information is the largest and most comprehensive of its kind in the United States. It is located at Quince Orchard Rd. & Rte. 270, Gaithersburg, MD. **Staff:** Ann Rothgeb, Tech.Info.Spec.; Brenda Umberger, Tech.Info.Asst..

★15200★
U.S. NATL. BUREAU OF STANDARDS - OFFICE OF STANDARD REFERENCE DATA - REFERENCE CENTER (Sci-Engr)
Physics Bldg., Rm. A320 Phone: (301)975-2208
Gaithersburg, MD 20899 Joan Sauerwein, Tech.Info.Spec.
Founded: 1963. **Staff:** Prof 1. **Subjects:** Physical and chemical properties data of substances and systems, thermodynamics and transport data, chemical kinetics, mechanical properties, solid state data, atomic and molecular data, nuclear data. **Holdings:** 2800 books, bound periodical volumes, and loose-leaf services; 2000 other cataloged items; 150 volumes of Russian materials. **Subscriptions:** 25 journals and other serials. **Services:** Referral services; center open to the public. **Computerized Information Services:** Internal database. **Publications:** Journal of Physical and Chemical Reference Data (JPCRD), quarterly; US NSRDS-NBS Series; NBS Special Publications; Technical Notes; Handbooks; Monographs; Russian Translations - all available to government and private publishers; NSRDS Publications List, 1964-1984 (NBS SP708).

★15201★
U.S. NATL. BUREAU OF STANDARDS - PHASE DIAGRAMS FOR CERAMISTS - DATA CENTER (Sci-Engr)
Gaithersburg, MD 20899 Phone: (301)975-6121
Camden R. Hubbard, Supv.
Staff: Prof 3. **Subjects:** Chemical phase equilibria data - phase diagrams of nonmetallic, inorganic substances. **Services:** Inquiries about phase diagrams are answered. **Publications:** Phase Diagrams for Ceramists, irregular - for sale by American Ceramic Society. **Remarks:** Jointly sponsored by the U.S. National Bureau of Standards and the American Ceramic Society. **Staff:** Helen Ondik, Oper.Mgr..

★15202★
U.S. NATL. BUREAU OF STANDARDS - PHOTON AND CHARGED PARTICLE DATA CENTER (Sci-Engr)
Radiation Physics Bldg., Rm. C311 Phone: (301)975-5551
Gaithersburg, MD 20899 Martin J. Berger, Mgr.
Founded: 1952. **Staff:** Prof 5. **Subjects:** Electrons, positrons, protons, and other charged particles; photons; bremsstrahlung; stopping power and range tables; photon cross sections: Compton scattering atomic and nuclear photoeffect, pair production, and atomic form factors; x-ray attenuation coefficients; critical evaluations; radiation dosimetry. **Holdings:** 5 VF drawers of x-ray and Gamma ray total cross section reprints and reports; 20 VF drawers of partial cross sections, applications to shielding, radiometric gauging, x-ray crystallography, and other related reprints; 5 VF drawers of photonuclear data reprints. **Services:** Will answer inquiries; library open to the public with professional interest in the field. **Publications:** Evaluation of Collision Stopping Power of Elements and Compounds for Electrons and Positrons, 1982; Bremsstrahlung Energy Spectra from Electrons with Kinetic Energy 1 keV - 10 GeV Incident on Screened Nuclei and Orbital Electrons of Neutral Atoms with Z=1-100, 1986; Pair, Triplet and Total Atomic Cross Sections (and Mass Attenuation Coefficients) for 1 MeV - 100 GeV Photons in Elements Z=1-100, 1980; Bibliography of Photon Total Cross Section (Attenuation Coefficient) Measurements 10 eV - 13.5 GeV and Comparison with Theoretical Values 0.1 - 100 keV, 1986; Photonuclear Data-Abstract Sheets, 1955-1982 (Z=1-95). **Special Indexes:** Photonuclear Data Index, 1955-1972, 1973-1981. **Remarks:** An alternate telephone number is 975-5550. **Staff:** J.H. Hubbell; S.M. Seltzer; E.B. Saloman.

★15203★
U.S. NATL. BUREAU OF STANDARDS - RESEARCH INFORMATION CENTER (Sci-Engr)
E106 Administration Bldg. Phone: (301)975-3052
Gaithersburg, MD 20899 Patricia W. Berger, Chf., Info.Rsrcs. & Serv.
Founded: 1901. **Staff:** Prof 10; Other 21. **Subjects:** Physical sciences, chemistry, metrology, engineering, computer science, technology, statistics, mathematics. **Special Collections:** Museum collection of scientific apparatus and other memorabilla of the past work of the National Bureau of Standards; oral history collection; history of metrology and standardization; intergovernmental affairs. **Holdings:** 210,000 books and bound periodical volumes; scientific artifacts and historical files, AV collection. **Subscriptions:** 2500 journals and other serials. **Services:** Interlibrary loan; copying (limited); center open to the public for reference use only. **Automated Operations:** Computerized cataloging, acquisitions, serials, and circulation. **Computerized Information Services:** DIALOG Information Services, Pergamon ORBIT InfoLine, Inc., BRS Information Technologies, NLM, LEXIS, NEXIS, Chemical Information Systems, Inc. (CIS), NASA/RECON, Integrated Technical Information System (ITIS), Institute for Scientific Information (ISI), The Reference Service (REFSRV), OCLC, Government-Industry Data Exchange Program (GIDEP). **Networks/Consortia:** Member of FEDLINK, Interlibrary Users Association (IUA). **Publications:** Monthly bulletin; special catalogs; finding aids. **Remarks:** Contains information holdings of the Office of Standard Reference Data. The National Bureau of Standards is part of the U.S. Department of Commerce. **Staff:** Karma A. Beal, Hist.Info.Spec.; Marvin A. Bond, Chf., Res.Dev.; Sami Klein, Chf., Res.Info.Serv..

★15204★
U.S. NATL. DEFENSE UNIVERSITY - LIBRARY (Mil)
Fort Lesley J. McNair
4th & P Sts., S.W. Phone: (202)475-1905
Washington, DC 20319-6000 J. Thomas Russell, Dir.
Founded: 1976. **Staff:** Prof 16; Other 17. **Subjects:** Military history and science, manpower and industrial mobilization, political science, national security affairs, international relations, management of resources, joint and combined operations, strategic studies, wargaming. **Special Collections:** Personal papers of Maxwell D. Taylor, Lyman L. Lemnitzer, George S. Brown, Andrew J. Goodpaster, Paul D. Adams, and Frank S. Besson, Jr.; speeches on industrial mobilization by J. Carlton Ward, Jr.; Hudson Institute Papers; early editions of Marshal de Saxe; Libraries of Arthur W. Radford, Hoffman Nickerson (both on military history), Roland H. del Mar (Latin America), and Ralph L. Powell (China). **Holdings:** 220,000 books and bound periodical volumes; 15 VF drawers; 2600 nonprint items; 600 linear feet of local history materials. **Subscriptions:** 1000 journals and newspapers. **Services:** Interlibrary loan; library open to the public by appointment. **Automated Operations:** Computerized public access catalog, cataloging, serials, and circulation. **Computerized Information Services:** DIALOG Information Services, Pergamon ORBIT InfoLine, Inc., LS/2000, LEXIS, NEXIS, OCLC, Washington Alert Service, DTIC. **Networks/Consortia:** Member of FLICC. **Publications:** New acquisitions listing, monthly - distributed locally and on request; Handbook, biennial; subject pathfinders and bibliographies, irregular. **Remarks:** The National Defense University operates under the direction of the Joint Chiefs of Staff of the U.S. Department of Defense. **Staff:** Julia Mayo, Chf., Res. & Info.Serv.; Ann Sullivan, Ref.Libn.; Teresa Hodge, Doc.Libn.; Johanna De Onis, Ref.Libn.; Ruby Ramer, Ref.Libn.; Mary Ann Varoutsos, Ref.Libn.; Lily Waters, Ref.Libn.; Mary T. Quintero, Ref.Libn.; Howard Hume, Dp.Dir./Chf., Automation & Tech.Serv.; Elizabeth Slawson, Chf., Tech.Serv.; Eunice White, Ser.Cat.; Mary-Ruth Duncan, Monograph Cat.; Alta Davis, Sys.Libn.; Susan Lemke, Chf., Spec.Coll. & Hist.; Mary-Stuart Taylor, Coll. Control Libn..

★15205★
U.S. NATL. HIGHWAY TRAFFIC SAFETY ADMINISTRATION - TECHNICAL REFERENCE DIVISION (Sci-Engr, Trans)
400 7th St., S.W., Rm. 5108 Phone: (202)366-2768
Washington, DC 20590 Jerome A. Holiber, Chf.
Founded: 1967. **Staff:** Prof 9; Other 2. **Subjects:** Motor vehicle safety, highway safety, alcohol countermeasures for driving safety, automobile occupant protection, emergency medical services. **Special Collections:** NHTSA Research Reports; Federal Motor Vehicle Standards Docket; Compliance Test Reports; Defects Investigation Reports; Recall Campaigns; Crash Test Reports. **Holdings:** 2100 books; 35,000 reports; 500,000 microfiche. **Subscriptions:** 100 journals and other serials. **Services:** Interlibrary loan (limited); copying; division open to the public for reference use only. **Computerized Information Services:** Manufacturer's Service Bulletins, Consumer Complaints, Recall Campaigns, Defects Investigation (internal databases). Performs searches on fee basis. **Remarks:** The National Highway Traffic Safety Administration is part of the U.S. Department of Transportation. **Staff:** Dawn Gordy, Tech.Info.Spec.; Clara Wampler, Tech.Info.Spec.; Paulette Twine, Tech.Info.Spec.; Frances Bean, Tech.Info.Spec.; Grace Ogden, Tech.Info.Spec.; Robert Hornickle, Tech.Info.Spec.; David Doernberg, Tech.Info.Spec.; Constance Connolly, Tech.Info.Spec..

★15206★
U.S. NATL. INSTITUTE FOR OCCUPATIONAL SAFETY & HEALTH - TECHNICAL INFORMATION BRANCH (Med)
Robert A. Taft Laboratory
4676 Columbia Pkwy. Phone: (513)533-8321
Cincinnati, OH 45226 Debbie Perrhan, Sect.Chf.
Founded: 1960. **Staff:** Prof 3; Other 2. **Subjects:** Occupational safety and health, industrial hygiene and toxicology. **Holdings:** 10,000 books; 10,000 bound periodical volumes; 1000 other cataloged items. **Subscriptions:** 800 journals and other serials. **Services:** Interlibrary loan; branch open to the public. **Automated Operations:** Computerized ILL. **Computerized Information Services:** OCLC. **Networks/Consortia:** Member of FEDLINK. **Remarks:** Institute is a branch of U.S. Centers for Disease Control. **Staff:** Roberta Andrews, Libn.; Lawrence Q. Foster, Tech.Info.Spec.; Barbara J. Sternad, Libn..

★15207★
U.S. NATL. INSTITUTES OF HEALTH - COMPUTER RESEARCH & TECHNOLOGY DIVISION - LIBRARY (Comp Sci, Sci-Engr)
9000 Rockville Pike
Bldg. 12A, Rm. 3018 Phone: (301)496-1658
Bethesda, MD 20892 Ellen Moy Chu, Libn.
Founded: 1966. **Staff:** Prof 2; Other 1. **Subjects:** Computer science, mathematics, statistics, medical information systems, information science. **Holdings:** 6000 books and reports; 800 bound periodical volumes; 9 drawers of microfilm. **Subscriptions:** 200 journals and other serials. **Services:** Interlibrary loan; SDI; library open to the public by special permission. **Automated Operations:** Computerized public access catalog, cataloging, acquisitions, serials, and circulation. **Computerized Information Services:** DIALOG Information Services, MEDLARS, NEXIS, OCLC; Ethernet (electronic mail service). **Networks/Consortia:** Member of FEDLINK, Interlibrary Users Association (IUA).

U.S. NATL. INSTITUTES OF HEALTH - HIGH BLOOD PRESSURE INFORMATION CENTER
See: National High Blood Pressure Education Program - High Blood Pressure Information Center (9692)

★15208★
U.S. NATL. INSTITUTES OF HEALTH - LIBRARY (Med, Biol Sci)
9000 Rockville Pike
Bldg. 10, Rm. 1L-25 Phone: (301)496-2447
Bethesda, MD 20892 Carolyn P. Brown, Chf.Libn.
Founded: 1903. **Staff:** Prof 26; Other 30. **Subjects:** Medicine, health sciences, chemistry, pathology, physiology, biology. **Holdings:** 85,000 books; 155,000 bound periodical volumes; 17,000 microforms. **Subscriptions:** 6000 journals and other serials. **Services:** Interlibrary loan; copying; SDI; library open to the public for reference use only. **Automated Operations:** Computerized cataloging, acquisitions, serials and circulation. **Computerized Information Services:** DIALOG Information Services, BRS Information Technologies, STN International, NLM, OCLC, PHILSOM, Pergamon ORBIT InfoLine, Inc. **Networks/Consortia:** Member of FEDLINK. **Publications:** Recent Additions to the NIH Library, monthly. **Remarks:** Institutes are a part of the U.S. Public Health Service. **Staff:** Maxine Hanke, Dp.Chf.; Jennylind C. Boggess, Sys.Libn.; Rosalie H. Stroman, Chf., Rd.Serv.Sect.; Lisa C. Wu, Chf., Tech.Serv.; Elsie Cerutti, Chf., Ref. & Bibliog.Serv.; Jean Soong, Hd., Cat.; Patricia A. Barnes, ILL Libn.; Joan Daghita, Hd., Circ.; Margaret Kunz, Hd., Acq..

U.S. NATL. INSTITUTES OF HEALTH - NATIONAL ARTHRITIS AND MUSCULOSKELETAL AND SKIN DISEASE INFORMATION CLEARINGHOUSE
See: National Arthritis and Musculoskeletal and Skin Diseases Information Clearinghouse (9561)

★15209★
U.S. NATL. INSTITUTES OF HEALTH - NATIONAL CANCER INSTITUTE - FREDERICK CANCER RESEARCH FACILITY - SCIENTIFIC LIBRARY (Med)
Box B - Bldg. 549 Phone: (301)698-1093
Frederick, MD 21701-1013 Susan W. Wilson, Mgr.
Founded: 1972. **Subjects:** Cancer biology, biological and chemical carcinogenesis, acquired immunodeficiency syndrome, biomedical research. **Holdings:** 16,000 books; 24,000 bound periodical volumes; 2600 reels of microfilm of periodicals. **Subscriptions:** 718 journals and other serials. **Services:** Interlibrary loan; SDI; library open to the public with restrictions. **Automated Operations:** Computerized serials. **Computerized Information Services:** Online systems. **Networks/Consortia:** Member of FEDLINK. **Publications:** Accessions list, monthly; Serial holdings list, annual.

U.S. NATL. INSTITUTES OF HEALTH - NATIONAL DIGESTIVE DISEASES INFORMATION CLEARINGHOUSE
See: National Digestive Diseases Information Clearinghouse (9652)

U.S. NATL. INSTITUTES OF HEALTH - NATIONAL INSTITUTE ON AGING
See: National Institute on Aging (9703)

★15210★
U.S. NATL. INSTITUTES OF HEALTH - NATIONAL INSTITUTE OF ALLERGY & INFECTIOUS DISEASES - ROCKY MOUNTAIN LABORATORY LIBRARY (Med, Biol Sci)
Hamilton, MT 59840 Phone: (406)363-3211
Liza Serha Hamby, Med.Libn.
Founded: 1932. **Staff:** Prof 1. **Subjects:** Medicine, virology, bacteriology, immunology, entomology, chemistry, parasitology, pathology, microbiology, biochemistry, biology, sexually transmitted disease. **Holdings:** 11,000 books; 27,000 bound periodical volumes. **Subscriptions:** 285 journals and other serials. **Services:** Interlibrary loan (limited); library not open to the public. **Computerized Information Services:** WLN, MEDLARS; OnTyme Electronic Message Network Service (electronic mail service).

U.S. NATL. INSTITUTES OF HEALTH - NATIONAL INSTITUTE OF ARTHRITIS AND MUSKULOSKELETAL AND SKIN DISEASES
See: National Institute of Arthritis and Muskuloskeletal and Skin Diseases (9704)

U.S. NATL. INSTITUTES OF HEALTH - NATIONAL INSTITUTE OF DENTAL RESEARCH
See: National Institute of Dental Research (9706)

U.S. NATL. INSTITUTES OF HEALTH - NATIONAL INSTITUTE OF ENVIRONMENTAL HEALTH SCIENCES
See: National Institute of Environmental Health Sciences (9709)

U.S. NATL. INSTITUTES OF HEALTH - NATIONAL LIBRARY OF MEDICINE
See: National Library of Medicine (9738)

U.S. NATL. INSTITUTES OF HEALTH - RESEARCH RESOURCES DIVISION - TRACOR JITCO, INC.
See: Tracor Jitco, Inc. (14279)

U.S. NATL. LABOR RELATIONS BOARD
See: National Labor Relations Board (9721)

★15211★
U.S. NATL. MARINE FISHERIES SERVICE - AUKE BAY FISHERIES LABORATORY - FISHERIES RESEARCH LIBRARY (Biol Sci, Env-Cons)
Box 210155 Phone: (907)789-6010
Auke Bay, AK 99821 Paula Johnson, Libn.
Founded: 1960. **Staff:** Prof 1; Other 1. **Subjects:** Biological sciences, fisheries, oceanography, water pollution. **Special Collections:** Scandinavian fisheries periodicals; International North Pacific Fisheries Commission documents; Pribiloff Island Log Books. **Holdings:** 11,500 books; 2700 bound periodical volumes; 500 manuscripts; 1500 reprints; 2000 translations; 105 reels of microfilm; 40 microfiche and microcard titles; 1500 slides. **Subscriptions:** 202 journals and other serials. **Services:** Interlibrary loan; copying; library open to the public. **Computerized Information Services:** DIALOG Information Services; Learn Alaska Network (electronic mail service). **Publications:** Accession List, quarterly. **Remarks:** An alternate telephone number is 789-6009. The National Marine Fisheries Service is part of the National Oceanic & Atmospheric Administration of the U.S. Department of Commerce.

★15212★
U.S. NATL. MARINE FISHERIES SERVICE - CHARLESTON LABORATORY - LIBRARY (Biol Sci, Food-Bev)
217 Fort Johnson Rd.
Box 12607 Phone: (803)762-1200
Charleston, SC 29412 Lois F. Winemiller, Chf., Tech.Info.Serv.
Subjects: Chemistry, food science and technology, nutrition, microbiology, biology. **Holdings:** 7000 volumes.

★15213★
U.S. NATL. MARINE FISHERIES SERVICE - HONOLULU LABORATORY - LIBRARY (Biol Sci)
2750 Dole St.
Box 3830 Phone: (808)943-1221
Honolulu, HI 98612 Hazel S. Nishimura, Libn.
Founded: 1950. **Staff:** Prof 1. **Subjects:** Marine biology, ichthyology, tuna, oceanography. **Holdings:** 3800 books. **Subscriptions:** 200 journals and other serials. **Services:** Interlibrary loan; copying; library open to qualified researchers for reference only.

★15214★
U.S. NATL. MARINE FISHERIES SERVICE - MILFORD LABORATORY LIBRARY (Biol Sci, Env-Cons)
212 Rogers Ave. Phone: (203)783-4234
Milford, CT 06460 Barbara D. Gibson, Libn.
Staff: Prof 1. **Subjects:** Fisheries, marine biology, aquaculture, cytology, genetics, ecology, microbiology, physiology, biochemistry, microscopy, statistics, marine pollution. **Special Collections:** Reprints (primarily fisheries and related subjects); U.S. Bureau of Fisheries and NOAA/NMFS documents, 1874 to present. **Holdings:** 3300 books; 1500 bound periodical volumes; 1800 slides. **Subscriptions:** 100 journals and other serials. **Services:** Interlibrary loan; library open to the public for reference use only with permission. **Automated Operations:** Computerized cataloging. **Computerized Information Services:** OCLC, DIALOG Information Services.

★15215★
U.S. NATL. MARINE FISHERIES SERVICE - MISSISSIPPI LABORATORIES - LIBRARY (Biol Sci)
3209 Frederic St.
Drawer 1207 Phone: (601)762-4591
Pascagoula, MS 39568 Jon Martin, Libn.
Staff: Prof 1. **Subjects:** Marine biology, fishery and fishing gear research, marine resources, microbiology, chemistry. **Holdings:** 2000 books; 1800 bound periodical volumes; 3000 reprints. **Subscriptions:** 150 journals and other serials. **Services:** Interlibrary loan; copying; library open to the public. **Computerized Information Services:** DIALOG Information Services, OCLC. **Networks/Consortia:** Member of FEDLINK, U.S. Natl.

Oceanic & Atmospheric Administration Southeastern Area Resources Cooperative (NOAASARC).

★15216★
U.S. NATL. MARINE FISHERIES SERVICE - NATIONAL MARINE MAMMAL LABORATORY - LIBRARY (Biol Sci)
7600 Sand Point Way N.E., Bldg. 4 Phone: (206)526-4013
Seattle, WA 98115-0070 Sherry Pearson, Tech.Info.Spec.
Staff: 1. **Subjects:** Marine mammals. **Holdings:** 1500 books and bound periodical volumes; 72 VF drawers of reprints. **Subscriptions:** 90 journals and other serials. **Services:** Interlibrary loan.

★15217★
U.S. NATL. MARINE FISHERIES SERVICE - NORTHEAST FISHERIES CENTER - LIBRARY (Biol Sci, Env-Cons)
Woods Hole, MA 02543 Phone: (508)548-5123
Judith Brownlow, Libn.
Founded: 1893. **Staff:** Prof 2; Other 1. **Subjects:** Fishery biology, marine biology, oceanography, management and law of fisheries. **Special Collections:** Research documents of the former International Commission for the Northwest Atlantic Fisheries (ICNAF) and the current Northwest Atlantic Fisheries Organization (NAFO); annual meeting documents of the International Council for the Exploration of the Sea (I.C.E.S.). **Holdings:** 7000 bound periodicals and other cataloged items; 50 films; 2000 slides; scrapbooks of newspaper clippings and photographs, 1940-1967; archives. **Subscriptions:** 40 journals and other serials. **Services:** Interlibrary loan; copying; library open to the public. **Automated Operations:** Computerized cataloging. **Computerized Information Services:** DIALOG Information Services, OCLC. Performs searches on fee basis. **Networks/Consortia:** Member of FEDLINK. **Special Catalogs:** Collected Reprints of the Northeast Fisheries Center, 1977 to present; Serials List.

★15218★
U.S. NATL. MARINE FISHERIES SERVICE - NORTHEAST FISHERIES CENTER - OXFORD LABORATORY LIBRARY (Biol Sci, Env-Cons)
Oxford, MD 21654 Phone: (301)226-5193
Susie K. Hines, Libn.
Founded: 1961. **Staff:** Prof 1. **Subjects:** Marine shellfish and fish pathology, marine resource investigations. **Special Collections:** U.S. government publications on fisheries. **Holdings:** 4350 books; 4700 bound periodical volumes; 40,000 reprints and pamphlets. **Subscriptions:** 125 journals and other serials. **Services:** Interlibrary loan; copying; library open to the public for reference use only. **Computerized Information Services:** DIALOG Information Services, OCLC. **Networks/Consortia:** Member of FEDLINK. **Publications:** Annual Publications List; Serials Holding List, annual; Dissertations and Theses Collection of the Oxford Laboratory Library.

★15219★
U.S. NATL. MARINE FISHERIES SERVICE - NORTHWEST & ALASKA FISHERIES CENTER - LIBRARY (Biol Sci, Env-Cons)
2725 Montlake Blvd., E. Phone: (206)442-7795
Seattle, WA 98112 Patricia Cook, Libn.
Staff: Prof 2. **Subjects:** Fisheries, oceanography, chemistry, biochemistry, food technology, statistics. **Holdings:** 32,000 volumes; 4000 files of reprints; 3000 files of translations. **Subscriptions:** 220 journals and other serials. **Services:** Interlibrary loan; library open to the public for reference use only. **Computerized Information Services:** OCLC; internal database. **Networks/Consortia:** Member of FEDLINK. **Staff:** Marilyn Magnuson, Libn..

★15220★
U.S. NATL. MARINE FISHERIES SERVICE - SANDY HOOK LABORATORY - LIONEL A. WALFORD LIBRARY (Biol Sci, Env-Cons)
Highlands, NJ 07732 Phone: (201)872-0200
Claire L. Steimle, Libn.
Founded: 1961. **Staff:** Prof 1; Other 1. **Subjects:** Fisheries, environmental problems, marine invertebrates, biological and chemical oceanography, plankton behavior, microbiology, New York Bight. **Special Collections:** Fishery Bulletins and Reports to Commissioner of Fisheries; Benedict Collection of Sportfishing (131 volumes); Special Pollution Collection (150 volumes). **Holdings:** 6000 books; 4500 bound periodical volumes; 14,000 documents. **Subscriptions:** 300 journals and other serials. **Services:** Interlibrary loan; copying (limited); library open to the public by appointment. **Publications:** Bibliographies.

★15221★
U.S. NATL. MARINE FISHERIES SERVICE - SOUTHEAST FISHERIES CENTER - MIAMI LABORATORY LIBRARY (Biol Sci)
75 Virginia Beach Dr. Phone: (305)361-4229
Miami, FL 33149 Julianne Josiek, Hd.Libn.
Founded: 1965. **Staff:** Prof 1; Other 1. **Subjects:** Marine biology, fish, fisheries. **Special Collections:** Reprint collection (7000 concerning fish, fish eggs, and larvae). **Holdings:** 20,500 books and bound periodical volumes. **Subscriptions:** 350 journals and other serials. **Services:** Interlibrary loan; copying; library open to the public with restrictions. **Automated Operations:** Computerized cataloging, acquisitions, and serials. **Computerized Information Services:** DIALOG Information Services, OCLC. Performs searches on fee basis. **Networks/Consortia:** Member of FEDLINK.

★15222★
U.S. NATL. MARINE FISHERIES SERVICE - SOUTHEAST FISHERIES CENTER - PANAMA CITY LABORATORY - LIBRARY (Biol Sci, Env-Cons)
3500 Delwood Beach Rd. Phone: (904)234-6541
Panama City, FL 32407 Rosalie Vaught, Libn.
Founded: 1972. **Staff:** Prof 1. **Subjects:** Fishery science, marine and fresh water biology, oceanography, zoology, ecology. **Holdings:** 2500 books and bound periodical volumes; 8500 technical reports; 10,000 unbound periodicals and technical reports; 125 dissertations; 8000 reprints. **Subscriptions:** 200 journals and other serials. **Services:** Interlibrary loan; copying; library open to the public. **Computerized Information Services:** DIALOG Information Services. **Networks/Consortia:** Member of U.S. Natl. Oceanic & Atmospheric Administration Library & Information Network. **Publications:** List of contributions, annual; serials holdings list.

★15223★
U.S. NATL. MARINE FISHERIES SERVICE - SOUTHEAST FISHERIES CENTER - RICE LIBRARY (Biol Sci, Env-Cons)
Beaufort, NC 28516-9722 Phone: (919)728-3595
Ann Bowman Manooch, Libn.
Founded: 1949. **Staff:** Prof 1. **Subjects:** Fish, fisheries, marine biology, radioecology, oceanography. **Holdings:** 15,000 books and bound periodical volumes; 200 linear feet of unbound materials. **Subscriptions:** 380 journals and other serials. **Services:** Interlibrary loan; library open to the public with restrictions. **Automated Operations:** Computerized cataloging. **Computerized Information Services:** DIALOG Information Services, Pergamon ORBIT InfoLine, Inc., BRS Information Technologies. **Publications:** List of Serials. **Remarks:** Alternate telephone numbers are 728-8713 and 728-8714.

★15224★
U.S. NATL. MARINE FISHERIES SERVICE - SOUTHWEST FISHERIES CENTER - LIBRARY (Biol Sci, Env-Cons)
8604 La Jolla Shores Dr.
Box 271 Phone: (619)546-7038
La Jolla, CA 92038-0271 Debra A. Losey, Libn.
Founded: 1965. **Staff:** Prof 1; Other 1. **Subjects:** Fisheries, oceanography, marine biology and ecology. **Holdings:** 2500 books; 12,000 periodical volumes; 9000 pamphlets. **Subscriptions:** 280 journals and other serials. **Services:** Interlibrary loan; copying; SDI; library open to the public for reference use only. **Automated Operations:** Computerized cataloging. **Computerized Information Services:** DIALOG Information Services, BRS Information Technologies, OCLC; NALIS (internal database); DIALMAIL (electronic mail service). **Networks/Consortia:** Member of FEDLINK. **Remarks:** Figures include Inter-American Tropical Tuna Commission Collection.

★15225★
U.S. NATL. MARINE FISHERIES SERVICE - TIBURON LABORATORY LIBRARY (Biol Sci, Env-Cons)
3150 Paradise Dr. Phone: (415)435-3149
Tiburon, CA 94920 Maureen Leet, Libn.
Founded: 1962. **Staff:** Prof 1. **Subjects:** Marine biology, fishery science, commercial fishing, sport fisheries, oceanography. **Special Collections:** Collection of W.H. Rich on Salmon; Dr. Victor L. Loosanoff Reprint Collection (commercial mollusks); Susumu Kato Shark Reprint Collection (shark taxonomy). **Holdings:** 2800 books; 2700 bound periodical volumes; 12,000 reprints. **Subscriptions:** 250 journals and other serials. **Services:** Interlibrary loan; library open to the public for reference use only. **Automated Operations:** Computerized cataloging and ILL. **Computerized Information Services:** DIALOG Information Services, Pergamon ORBIT InfoLine, Inc., BRS Information Technologies; OCLC. **Networks/Consortia:** Member of FEDLINK. **Publications:** Occasional reprints.

★15226★
U.S. NATL. MARINE FISHERIES SERVICE - W.F. THOMPSON MEMORIAL LIBRARY (Biol Sci, Env-Cons)
Box 1638 Phone: (907)487-4961
Kodiak, AK 99615 Cheryl Elmer, Lib.Techn.
Founded: 1971. **Staff:** 1. **Subjects:** Fisheries, biology, chemistry, fishery food science, Alaska fishing research. **Special Collections:** Collection of W.F. Thompson, leader in Alaska fishery research. **Holdings:** 2500 books; 3300 bound periodical volumes; leaflets; circulars; reports; biological reports. **Subscriptions:** 90 journals and other serials; 5 newspapers. **Services:** Interlibrary loan; copying; library open to the public by permission. **Computerized Information Services:** DIALOG Information Services; access to NOAA internal database.

★15227★
U.S. NATL. OCEANIC & ATMOSPHERIC ADMINISTRATION - ASSESSMENT AND INFORMATION SERVICES CENTER (Env-Cons)
Federal Bldg., Rm. 200
608 E. Cherry St. Phone: (314)875-5263
Columbia, MO 65201 Rita B. Terry, Libn.
Staff: 1. **Subjects:** Climatology, ecology, crop production, world food supply, energy consumption. **Holdings:** 100 volumes; raw climatological data; reprint/report file. **Subscriptions:** 75 journals and other serials. **Services:** Center open to the public for reference use only. **Automated Operations:** Computerized cataloging.

★15228★
U.S. NATL. OCEANIC & ATMOSPHERIC ADMINISTRATION - ATMOSPHERIC TURBULENCE & DIFFUSION DIVISION - LIBRARY (Sci-Engr, Energy)
Box 2456 Phone: (615)576-1236
Oak Ridge, TN 37831 Ruth A. Green, Adm.Off.
Staff: 1. **Subjects:** Energy production, air pollution, forest meteorology, climatic studies. **Holdings:** 2500 volumes; 6000 technical reports and reprints. **Subscriptions:** 60 journals and other serials. **Services:** Library open to the public for reference use only. **Remarks:** Laboratory is operated for the Department of Energy as a division of the National Oceanic & Atmospheric Administration's Air Resources Laboratory.

★15229★
U.S. NATL. OCEANIC & ATMOSPHERIC ADMINISTRATION - GEOPHYSICAL FLUID DYNAMICS LABORATORY - LIBRARY (Sci-Engr)
Box 308 Phone: (609)452-6550
Princeton, NJ 08542 Mae E. Blessing, Libn.
Founded: 1968. **Staff:** Prof 1. **Subjects:** Meteorology, climatology, oceanography, fluid dynamics. **Special Collections:** Russian monographs on meteorology and climatology (200 volumes); atmospheric sciences collection. **Holdings:** 7500 books; 1500 bound periodical volumes; 3000 technical reports; 50 atlases; 30 films. **Subscriptions:** 120 journals and other serials. **Services:** Interlibrary loan; copying; library open to the public. **Automated Operations:** Computerized cataloging and serials. **Computerized Information Services:** DIALOG Information Services, OCLC; internal database. **Networks/Consortia:** Member of FEDLINK. **Publications:** GFDL Activities and Plans, annual; bibliography of the works of L.S. Gantin, Russian scientist.

★15230★
U.S. NATL. OCEANIC & ATMOSPHERIC ADMINISTRATION - GEORGETOWN CENTER
3300 Whitehaven
Washington, DC 20235
Defunct. Holdings absorbed by U.S. Natl. Oceanic & Atmospheric Administration - Library and Information Services Division - Main Library.

★15231★
U.S. NATL. OCEANIC & ATMOSPHERIC ADMINISTRATION - GREAT LAKES ENVIRONMENTAL RESEARCH LABORATORY LIBRARY (Sci-Engr)
2205 Commonwealth Blvd. Phone: (313)668-2242
Ann Arbor, MI 48105 Barbara J. Carrick, Libn.
Staff: Prof 1; Other 2. **Subjects:** Great Lakes - hydraulics, hydrology, limnology, limnologic systems, meteorological weather data, physical oceanography, water characteristics, modeling, water quality control; information analysis. **Holdings:** 9000 books; 200 bound periodical volumes; 217 reels of microfilm of Great Lakes Archives, 1841-1952; 12 VF drawers of pamphlets; 124 agency publications. **Subscriptions:** 210 journals and other serials. **Services:** Interlibrary loan; copying; library open to the public for reference use only. **Computerized Information Services:** Online systems. **Publications:** List of publications - available on request.

★15232★
U.S. NATL. OCEANIC & ATMOSPHERIC ADMINISTRATION - LIBRARY AND INFORMATION SERVICES DIVISION (Sci-Engr)
7600 Sand Point Way, N.E., Bin C-15700, Bldg. 3
Phone: (206)526-6241
Seattle, WA 98115-0070 Martha B. Thayer, Libn.
Founded: 1980. **Staff:** Prof 1; Other 1. **Subjects:** Physical and chemical oceanography, marine pollution, geochemistry, meteorology, atmospheric physics, ocean engineering, mathematics, statistics, climatology. **Holdings:** 5500 books and technical reports. **Subscriptions:** 220 journals and other serials. **Services:** Interlibrary loan; copying; SDI; center open to the public for reference use only. **Automated Operations:** Computerized cataloging, acquisitions, and serials. **Computerized Information Services:** DIALOG Information Services, BRS Information Technologies, NEXIS, OCLC; NALIS (internal database). **Networks/Consortia:** Member of FEDLINK.

★15233★
U.S. NATL. OCEANIC & ATMOSPHERIC ADMINISTRATION - LIBRARY AND INFORMATION SERVICES DIVISION - MAIN LIBRARY† (Geog-Map, Sci-Engr)
6009 Executive Blvd.
Rockville, MD 20852 Phone: (301)443-8330
Founded: 1846. **Staff:** Prof 15; Other 16. **Subjects:** Geodesy, surveying, oceanography, geophysics, geodetic and hydrographic surveying, photogrammetry, nautical and aeronautical cartography, fisheries, geodetic astronomy, meteorology, climatology, hydrology, atmospheric physics, ocean engineering, mathematics, computer science. **Special Collections:** Rare book collection (includes scientific treatises from the 16th and 17th centuries). **Holdings:** 654,000 volumes; 100,100 bound periodical volumes; 100,400 bound documents; 19,500 microfiche; 34,000 reports, maps, charts, data publications. **Subscriptions:** 9040 journals and other serials. **Services:** Interlibrary loan; copying; SDI; library open to the public for reference use only. **Automated Operations:** Computerized cataloging, serials, and acquisitions. **Computerized Information Services:** DIALOG Information Services, Pergamon ORBIT InfoLine, Inc., BRS Information Technologies, NEXIS, NLM, LEGI-SLATE, OCLC. **Networks/Consortia:** Member of FEDLINK. **Publications:** Acquisitions list; list of other publications - available on request. **Remarks:** The National Oceanic & Atmospheric Administration is part of the U.S. Department of Commerce. Provides consultative and technical guidance to 37 NOAA libraries and information centers with highly specialized collections in meteorology, climatology, hydrology, marine biology, fisheries science located throughout the U.S. Maintains branches in Miami, FL and Seattle, WA. **Also Known As:** NOAA. **Staff:** Frances F. Swim, Reg.Libs.Coord..

★15234★
U.S. NATL. OCEANIC & ATMOSPHERIC ADMINISTRATION - MOUNTAIN ADMINISTRATIVE SUPPORT CENTER - LIBRARY (Sci-Engr, Comp Sci)
325 Broadway MC5 Phone: (303)497-3271
Boulder, CO 80303 John J. Welsh, Chf., Lib.Div.
Founded: 1954. **Staff:** Prof 5; Other 10. **Subjects:** Mathematics, electronics engineering, atmospheric science, aeronomy, computer science, telecommunications, radio physics, oceanography, marine sciences, astrophysics, cryogenics, radio engineering, physics, astronomy. **Holdings:** 42,095 books; 25,000 bound periodical volumes; 29,763 technical reports; 283,966 titles on microfiche; 175 audio cassettes; 50 video cassettes. **Subscriptions:** 1446 journals and other serials. **Services:** Interlibrary loan; copying; library open to the public for reference use only. **Automated Operations:** Computerized cataloging, acquisitions, and circulation. **Computerized Information Services:** DIALOG Information Services, Pergamon ORBIT InfoLine, Inc., BRS Information Technologies, Integrated Technical Information System (ITIS), NASA/RECON, DTIC, OCLC. **Networks/Consortia:** Member of Bibliographical Center for Research, Rocky Mountain Region, Inc. (BCR), FEDLINK. **Publications:** TRAC Sheet, monthly; Library Notes, weekly - both for internal distribution only. **Staff:** Jean Bankhead, Hd., Ref.Serv./ILL; Sara Martin, Cat.Libn.; Jane Watterson, Hd., Circ.Serv.; Katherine Day, Ref.Libn..

★15235★
U.S. NATL. OCEANIC & ATMOSPHERIC ADMINISTRATION - NATIONAL ENVIRONMENTAL SATELLITE, DATA, & INFORMATION SERVICE - NATIONAL OCEANOGRAPHIC DATA CENTER (Biol Sci, Sci-Engr)
Washington, DC 20235 Phone: (202)673-5549
Gregory W. Withee, Dir.
Founded: 1961. **Staff:** 86. **Subjects:** Oceanography - physical, chemical, biological. **Holdings:** Digital oceanographic data: oceanographic station and bathythermograph data covering the world's oceans; marine pollution and marine biological data from selected offshore areas of the U.S.; surface and subsurface current data; wind/wave data from environmental buoys offshore of the U.S.; global wind/wave data derived from altimeter measurements of the U.S. Navy GEOSAT; data from special projects such as the Climatological Atlas of the World Ocean. **Services:** Data inventory searches; selective retrieval and output of data; referral services; center open to the public. **Automated Operations:** Computerized data retrieval and presentation. **Publications:** List of publications - available on request; NODC User's Guide (which describes data holdings, products, and services) - free upon request. **Remarks:** Center located at Universal South Bldg., 1825 Connecticut Ave., N.W., Washington, DC 20235. **Staff:** Robert Lockerman, User Serv..

★15236★
U.S. NATL. OCEANIC & ATMOSPHERIC ADMINISTRATION - NATIONAL ENVIRONMENTAL SATELLITE, DATA, & INFORMATION SERVICES - NATIONAL CLIMATIC DATA CENTER - LIBRARY (Sci-Engr)
Federal Bldg., MC16.5 Phone: (704)259-0677
Asheville, NC 28801-2696 Linda D. Preston, Libn.
Founded: 1962. **Staff:** 1. **Subjects:** Climatology, meteorology, oceanography, weather records. **Special Collections:** Past weather records. **Holdings:** 10,455 books; 700 bound periodical volumes; 29 reels of microfilm; 2000 microfiche; 94,000 pamphlets; 8 atmospheric models. **Subscriptions:** 300 journals and other serials. **Services:** Interlibrary loan; copying; library open to the public with restrictions. **Computerized Information Services:** DIALOG Information Services, Pergamon ORBIT InfoLine, Inc., DTIC, BRS Information Technologies, OCLC.

★15237★
U.S. NATL. OCEANIC & ATMOSPHERIC ADMINISTRATION - NATIONAL GEODETIC INFORMATION CENTER - GEODETIC REFERENCE SERVICES (Sci-Engr)
11400 Rockville Pike Phone: (301)443-8316
Rockville, MD 20852 Grace C. Sollers, Tech.Info.Spec.
Founded: 1975. **Staff:** Prof 5. **Subjects:** Geodesy. **Holdings:** 50,000 books; 10,000 bound periodical volumes; reports; manuscripts; agency records, publications, surveys. **Services:** Copying; services open to the public for reference use only. **Computerized Information Services:** Social Science Data Libraries.

★15238★
U.S. NATL. OCEANIC & ATMOSPHERIC ADMINISTRATION - NATIONAL HURRICANE CENTER - LIBRARY (Sci-Engr)
Gables 1 Tower, 6th Fl.
1320 S. Dixie Hwy. Phone: (305)666-0413
Coral Gables, FL 33146 Robert Ting, Chf.Libn.
Staff: Prof 1. **Subjects:** Meteorology - tropical, hurricane, satellite. **Special Collections:** Films of clouds and rainband as planes penetrate hurricanes. **Holdings:** 5000 volumes; contractor reports; college, government, and private meteorological reports; maps and hemispheric information on microfilm; films of reconnaissance and research flights into hurricanes; photopanel films of instrument panel of planes in hurricane flight; film of radar in planes; printouts of processed data on information from hurricane flights. **Subscriptions:** 30 journals and other serials. **Services:** Interlibrary loan; copying; library open to the public for reference use only. **Also Known As:** Technical Library for Tropical and Hurricane Meteorology.

★15239★
U.S. NATL. OCEANIC & ATMOSPHERIC ADMINISTRATION - NATIONAL OCEAN SERVICE - MAP LIBRARY (Geog-Map)
6501 Lafayette Ave. Phone: (301)436-5766
Riverdale, MD 20737 Samuel Walinsky, Chf.
Founded: 1938. **Subjects:** Cartographic information, U.S. nautical and aeronautical charts, U.S. and Canadian topographical maps, special maps. **Special Collections:** Civil War maps (800); early city plans; 19th century nautical charts; 16th, 17th, and 18th century historical expedition maps; Great Lakes nautical charts (6500). **Holdings:** 138,000 cartographic publications of the 19th century; 8000 aeronautical charts, 1927 to present; 22 atlases; 214 American Revolution maps; 500,000 other cataloged items. **Services:** Copying; library open to the public for reference use only. **Staff:** Elaine S. Downs, Tech.Info.Spec..

★15240★
U.S. NATL. OCEANIC AND ATMOSPHERIC ADMINISTRATION - NATIONAL SEVERE STORMS LABORATORY - LIBRARY (Sci-Engr)
1313 Halley Circle Phone: (405)366-0421
Norman, OK 73069 Mary Meacham, Libn.
Founded: 1972. **Staff:** Prof 1. **Subjects:** Meteorology, climatology. **Holdings:** 1500 volumes. **Subscriptions:** 50 journals and other serials. **Services:** Interlibrary loan; library open to the public.

★15241★
U.S. NATL. OCEANIC & ATMOSPHERIC ADMINISTRATION - NOAA/AOML LIBRARY (Sci-Engr)
4301 Rickenbacker Causeway Phone: (305)361-4428
Miami, FL 33149 Elizabeth A. Goonan, Lib.Techn.
Founded: 1970. **Staff:** 1. **Subjects:** Oceanography, tropical meteorology, marine geology, ocean chemistry, applied mathematics, physics. **Special Collections:** U.S. Coast and Geodetic Survey Report, 1866-1982. **Holdings:** 12,000 volumes; 19,000 technical reports; 750 atlases and symposia; 12,000 microforms; 4000 charts and maps. **Subscriptions:** 180 journals and other serials. **Services:** Interlibrary loan; copying; library open to the public for reference use only. **Automated Operations:** Computerized cataloging. **Computerized Information Services:** OCLC. **Networks/Consortia:** Member of U.S. Natl. Oceanic & Atmospheric Administration Southeastern Area Resources Cooperative (NOAASARC). **Publications:** New acquisitions list, monthly.

★15242★
U.S. NATL. PARK SERVICE - ABRAHAM LINCOLN BIRTHPLACE NATL. HISTORIC SITE - LIBRARY (Hist)
Rte. 1, Box 94 Phone: (502)358-3874
Hodgenville, KY 42748 Gary V. Talley, Chf., Interp.
Founded: 1916. **Staff:** 4. **Subjects:** Abraham Lincoln. **Special Collections:** Thomas Lincoln Land Records (microfilm; photostats); Lincoln Farm Association Collection (photographs; documents). **Holdings:** 200 books and bound periodical volumes. **Services:** Library open to the public with restrictions. **Remarks:** The National Park Service is part of the U.S. Department of the Interior.

★15243★
U.S. NATL. PARK SERVICE - ACADIA NATL. PARK - ISLESFORD HISTORICAL MUSEUM (Geog-Map, Hist)
Islesford, ME 04646
Subjects: History of old Acadia, eastern Maine, and the Canadian Maritime Provinces, 1640-1933. **Special Collections:** Schooner trade from Cranberry Isles, 1796-1890 (ships' logs; freight slips; pilot slips; papers; documents); Cranberry Isles and Mount Desert real estate and town papers; early history of Acadia National Park. **Holdings:** 1500 archival items including papers, manuscripts, genealogical data, maps, photographs. **Services:** Museum open to the public during the summer months.

★15244★
U.S. NATL. PARK SERVICE - ALLEGHENY PORTAGE RAILROAD NATL. HISTORIC SITE - LIBRARY (Trans, Hist)
Lemon House
Box 247 Phone: (814)886-8176
Cresson, PA 16630 Paul B. Cole, III, Chf.
Founded: 1964. **Staff:** Prof 4; Other 4. **Subjects:** Railroad, 1834-1854; transportation and canals of Pennsylvania, 1830-1850; Johnstown Flood of 1889. **Holdings:** 120 volumes; 12 rare documents; old newspaper files. **Services:** Library open to the public for reference use only. **Staff:** Lawrence Trombello, Pk. Ranger; Ingrid Peterec, Pk. Ranger.

★15245★
U.S. NATL. PARK SERVICE - ANDREW JOHNSON NATL. HISTORIC SITE - LIBRARY (Hist)
College & Depot Sts.
Box 1088 Phone: (615)638-3551
Greeneville, TN 37744-1088 Kent R. Cave, Supv.Pk. Ranger
Special Collections: Andrew Johnson (65 volumes); The Presidency (21 volumes); Tennessee history (50 volumes); Civil War and Reconstruction history (22 volumes). **Holdings:** 200 books, periodicals, pamphlets, Park Service documents and publications. **Services:** Library open to the public for reference use only. **Remarks:** An alternate telephone number is 638-1326.

★15246★
U.S. NATL. PARK SERVICE - ANTIETAM NATL. BATTLEFIELD - VISITOR CENTER LIBRARY (Hist)
Box 158
Sharpsburg, MD 21782 Phone: (301)432-5125
Staff: 2. **Subjects:** Civil War, especially the Battles of South Mountain and Antietam; regimental histories; park history. **Special Collections:** Henry Kyd Douglas Collection; Park Service and Washington County publications. **Holdings:** 980 books; 3 VF drawers of periodicals; 6 VF drawers of reports, manuscripts, transcripts, and copies of diaries, slides, photographs, news articles, and park history; 16mm films; microfilms; tapes; maps. **Services:** Copying; library open to the public by appointment for reference use only.

★15247★
U.S. NATL. PARK SERVICE - APOSTLE ISLANDS NATL. LAKESHORE - LIBRARY (Hist)
Old Courthouse Bldg.
Rte. 1, Box 4 Phone: (715)779-3397
Bayfield, WI 54814 Diane Chalfant, Park Naturalist
Founded: 1970. **Staff:** 1. **Subjects:** Apostle Islands natural and cultural history, Great Lakes region, National Park Service history. **Special Collections:** Research reports on the natural and cultural history of Apostle Islands National Lakeshore (200). **Holdings:** 500 books; 150 bound periodical volumes; 4000 VF items; 60 oral history tapes; 40 reels of microfilm; 150 microfiche; 300 planning documents. **Subscriptions:** 42 journals and other serials. **Services:** Library not open to the public. **Networks/Consortia:** Member of Northwest Wisconsin Library System (NWLS). **Special Indexes:** Index to research reports.

★15248★
U.S. NATL. PARK SERVICE - APPOMATTOX COURT HOUSE NATL. HISTORICAL PARK - LIBRARY (Hist)
Box 218 Phone: (804)352-8987
Appomattox, VA 24522 Ronald G. Wilson, Pk.Hist.
Staff: Prof 2; Other 2. **Subjects:** Civil War, history of Park and Village of Appomattox. **Holdings:** 1000 books; 3700 artifacts and maps. **Services:** Library open to the public for reference use only. **Special Indexes:** Confederate enlisted men who surrendered at Appomattox (card). **Staff:** Jon Montgomery, Supt..

★15249★
U.S. NATL. PARK SERVICE - ARLINGTON HOUSE, THE ROBERT E. LEE MEMORIAL - LIBRARY (Hist)
Turkey Run Park Phone: (703)557-0613
McLean, VA 22101 Agnes Downey Mullins, Cur.
Staff: 1. **Subjects:** Robert E. Lee, George W.P. Custis, Arlington House. **Special Collections:** 19th century sheet music. **Holdings:** 500 books; 100 pamphlets; 70 Custis and Lee family and associated family manuscripts. **Services:** Library open to the public by appointment. **Remarks:** Library located in the Arlington National Cemetery, Arlington, VA.

★15250★
U.S. NATL. PARK SERVICE - ASSATEAGUE ISLAND NATL. SEASHORE - LIBRARY (Biol Sci)
Rte. 2, Box 294 Phone: (301)641-1441
Berlin, MD 21811 Larry G. Points, Chf., Interp.
Staff: 2. **Subjects:** Marine biology, botanical sciences, zoological sciences, geography. **Special Collections:** Research documents and reprint abstracts of seashore environments (250). **Holdings:** 500 books; 6500 color slides of Assateague Island and environs. **Services:** Library open to the public with restrictions.

★15251★
U.S. NATL. PARK SERVICE - AZTEC RUINS NATL. MONUMENT - LIBRARY (Hist)
Box 640
Aztec, NM 87410 Phone: (505)334-6174
Founded: 1923. **Staff:** Prof 1. **Subjects:** Archeology, natural history, National Park Service history. **Holdings:** 500 books; 5 VF drawers of maps; pamphlets; 16 volumes of ruins stabilization reports. **Services:** Interlibrary loan; library open to the public with restrictions.

★15252★
U.S. NATL. PARK SERVICE - BADLANDS NATL. PARK - LIBRARY (Hist)
Box 6 Phone: (605)433-5361
Interior, SD 57750 Midge Johnston, Bus.Mgr.
Founded: 1961. **Staff:** 1. **Subjects:** Natural history, paleontology, geology, National Park Service. **Holdings:** 1000 books; 500 bound periodical volumes. **Services:** Interlibrary loan; copying; library open to the public for reference use only. **Remarks:** Maintained by Badlands Natural History Association.

★15253★
U.S. NATL. PARK SERVICE - BANDELIER NATL. MONUMENT - LIBRARY (Hist)
Los Alamos, NM 87544 Phone: (505)672-3861
Edward J. Greene, Supv.Pk. Ranger
Staff: 2. **Subjects:** Bandelier National Monument excavations and stabilization; archeology, ethnology, and natural history of the Southwest. **Holdings:** 1400 books; 100 pamphlets; 11 VF drawers of early correspondence; 1 box of cassette tapes of guest speakers and oral history; annual and monthly reports of Southwest monuments, 1933-1940; monthly report of superintendent, 1941-1978; unpublished excavation and stabilization reports; excavation maps. **Subscriptions:** 25 journals and other serials. **Services:** Library open to researchers by request. **Publications:** Trail Guides for Frijoles Canyon and Tsankawi - for sale.

★15254★
U.S. NATL. PARK SERVICE - BIG HOLE NATL. BATTLEFIELD - LIBRARY (Hist)
Box 237 Phone: (406)689-3155
Wisdom, MT 59761 Jimmy D. Taylor, Supt.
Subjects: Nez Perce War of 1877. **Holdings:** 100 books. **Services:** Library open to researchers.

★15255★
U.S. NATL. PARK SERVICE - BIGHORN CANYON NATL. RECREATION AREA - LIBRARY (Hist)
Box 458 Phone: (406)666-2412
Fort Smith, MT 59035 James E. Staebler, Pk. Ranger
Founded: 1967. **Staff:** Prof 1. **Subjects:** Local history, Crow Indian history, ethnology, wildlife, geology, botany, archeology. **Special Collections:** Government reports on Crow Indians of Montana. **Holdings:** 1100 books. **Subscriptions:** 14 journals and other serials. **Services:** Interlibrary loan; library open to the public.

★15256★
U.S. NATL. PARK SERVICE - BOOKER T. WASHINGTON NATL. MONUMENT - LIBRARY (Hist)
Rte. 3, Box 310 Phone: (703)721-2094
Hardy, VA 24101 Richard Saunders, Chf.Interp. & Rsrcs.Mgt.
Subjects: Booker T. Washington, black history, local agriculture in the mid-19th century, Appalachian culture. **Special Collections:** Correspondence and documents relating to Burroughs plantation, birthplace of Booker T. Washington. **Holdings:** 600 books; photographs. **Services:** Interlibrary loan; copying (limited); library open to the public.

★15257★
U.S. NATL. PARK SERVICE - BRANCH OF CULTURAL RESEARCH - LIBRARY (Sci-Engr)
1220 S. St. Francis Dr. Phone: (505)988-6778
Santa Fe, NM 87501 Judith Miles, Archeo.
Staff: Prof 1; Other 2. **Subjects:** North American and Southwestern archeology. **Special Collections:** R.G. Vivian Archive (3047 professional papers, manuscripts, field notes, and other materials). **Holdings:** 970 books; 1455 institutional publications; 1200 unpublished manuscripts; 41,850 photographs and negatives; 9000 color slides; 850 maps. **Services:** Library open to the public for reference use only. **Computerized Information Services:** ORACLE Teletext Ltd.; internal databases. Performs searches free of charge. **Publications:** Chaco Canyon Studies in archeology, 2 volumes, annual - free upon request. **Special Indexes:** Subject and proper name indexes to holdings. **Remarks:** An alternate telephone number is 988-6832.

★15258★
U.S. NATL. PARK SERVICE - CABRILLO NATL. MONUMENT - LIBRARY & INFORMATION CENTER (Hist, Env-Cons)
Box 6670
San Diego, CA 92106 Phone: (619)557-5450
Founded: 1966. **Subjects:** History - California, Mexico, San Diego; conservation; ecology; lighthouses; marine life; California gray whale. **Holdings:** 1550 books; photographs; slides. **Subscriptions:** 10 journals and other serials. **Services:** Copying; library open to the public for reference use only.

★15259★
U.S. NATL. PARK SERVICE - CAPE COD NATL. SEASHORE - LIBRARY (Env-Cons, Hist)
Marconi Station Site Phone: (508)349-3785
South Wellfleet, MA 02663 G. Franklin Ackerman, Chf., Interp.
Founded: 1961. **Staff:** 1. **Subjects:** Ecology, local history, botany, earth sciences. **Special Collections:** U.S. Life Saving Service annual reports, 1879-1914; Rhodora Journal of the New England Botanical Club (26 volumes). **Holdings:** 2300 books. **Subscriptions:** 15 journals and other serials. **Services:** Interlibrary loan; library open to the public for reference use only.

★15260★
U.S. NATL. PARK SERVICE - CAPE HATTERAS NATL. SEASHORE - LIBRARY (Hist, Biol Sci)
Rte. 1, Box 675 Phone: (919)473-2111
Manteo, NC 27954 Penny Ambrose, Sec./Libn.
Founded: 1955. **Staff:** Prof 1. **Subjects:** History and natural history of North Carolina Outer Banks. **Special Collections:** Records and annual reports of U.S. Life-Saving Service. **Holdings:** 3500 books; 100 bound periodical volumes; 4000 items in technical reference file; 200 microforms. **Subscriptions:** 30 journals and other serials. **Services:** Interlibrary loan; library open to the public by appointment.

★15261★
U.S. NATL. PARK SERVICE - CAPE LOOKOUT NATL. SEASHORE - LIBRARY (Env-Cons)
415 Front St.
Box 690 Phone: (919)728-2121
Beaufort, NC 28516 Chuck Harris, Chf., Pk.Oper.
Founded: 1976. **Staff:** 2. **Subjects:** Seashore ecology, geology, Outer Banks history, marine natural history, barrier island ecology, lighthouses and life-saving, local history. **Holdings:** 2000 volumes. **Subscriptions:** 18 journals and other serials. **Services:** Library open to the public for reference use only with permission of park superintendent. **Remarks:** Library located at the District Office, Harkers Island, NC. **Staff:** Robert Patton, Interp.Spec..

★15262★
U.S. NATL. PARK SERVICE - CAPULIN VOLCANO NATL. MONUMENT - LIBRARY (Sci-Engr, Biol Sci)
Capulin, NM 88414 Phone: (505)278-2201
George R. West, Chf.
Founded: 1968. **Staff:** Prof 4; Other 2. **Subjects:** Geology, national parks and monuments, birds, plants, wildlife, history. **Holdings:** 662 books. **Services:** Library open to the public.

★15263★
U.S. NATL. PARK SERVICE - CARL SANDBURG HOME NATL. HISTORIC SITE - MUSEUM/LIBRARY (Hum, Hist)
1928 Little River Rd. Phone: (704)693-4178
Flat Rock, NC 28731 Kenneth Hulick, Supt.
Founded: 1969. **Staff:** Prof 2. **Subjects:** Carl Sandburg, local history. **Holdings:** 9000 books. **Services:** Library open to the public as a museum only. **Remarks:** This historic house contains part of Carl Sandburg's personal working library. **Staff:** Warren R. Weber, Cur..

★15264★
U.S. NATL. PARK SERVICE - CARLSBAD CAVERNS NATL. PARK - LIBRARY (Biol Sci, Sci-Engr)
3225 National Parks Hwy.
Carlsbad, NM 88220 Phone: (505)885-8884
Staff: 1. **Subjects:** Geology, botany, zoology, paleontology, parks and conservation, regional history. **Holdings:** 3500 books; 100 bound periodical volumes; 850 reprints; 63 boxes. **Subscriptions:** 25 journals and other serials. **Services:** Library open to the public for reference use only on request.

★15265★
U.S. NATL. PARK SERVICE - CASTILLO DE SAN MARCOS NATL. MONUMENT & FORT MATANZAS NATL. MONUMENT - LIBRARY (Hist)
1 Castillo Dr. Phone: (904)829-6506
St. Augustine, FL 32084-3699 Luis R. Arana, Hist.
Subjects: Florida's colonial history, 1518-1833, especially the construction and repair of Castillo de San Marcos and Fort Matanzas. **Special Collections:** Spanish and British records concerning Florida's colonial history; East Florida Papers (Spanish military, administrative, ecclesiastical, financial, and personal records of the territory; 175 reels of microfilm total). **Services:** Library open to the public by appointment.

★15266★
U.S. NATL. PARK SERVICE - CHACO CULTURE NATL. HISTORICAL PARK - STUDY LIBRARY (Sci-Engr, Hist)
Star Rte. 4, Box 6500 Phone: (505)988-6727
Bloomfield, NM 87413 Bonnie Sue Winslow, Pk. Ranger
Staff: 1. **Subjects:** Chaco and Southwest archeology, Southwest cultural and natural history, park planning. **Special Collections:** Unpublished records of park administrative history, early explorations; historic photographs. **Holdings:** 2000 books; 500 bound periodical volumes. **Subscriptions:** 12 journals and other serials. **Services:** Library open to the public with approval of superintendent.

★15267★
U.S. NATL. PARK SERVICE - CHAMIZAL NATL. MEMORIAL - LIBRARY (Hist)
Federal Bldg., Suite D-301
700 E. San Antonio Phone: (915)534-6277
El Paso, TX 79901 Elias B. Valencia, Interp.Spec.
Founded: 1967. **Staff:** 1. **Subjects:** Border disputes between U.S. and Mexico, Mexican and Spanish drama, political evolution in Mexico, U.S. and Mexican history, biology. **Holdings:** 1200 books; historic documents and manuscripts on border disputes. **Subscriptions:** 10 journals and other serials. **Services:** Library open to the public for reference use only.

★15268★
U.S. NATL. PARK SERVICE - CHEROKEE STRIP LAND RUSH MUSEUM - DOCKING RESEARCH CENTER ARCHIVES LIBRARY (Hist)
S. Summit Street Rd.
Box 230 Phone: (316)442-6750
Arkansas City, KS 67005 Sharon Olmstead, Dir.
Founded: 1981. **Staff:** Prof 1; Other 1. **Subjects:** Local history, genealogy. **Special Collections:** Speeches and pictures of Governor Robert Docking (5 filing cabinets). **Holdings:** 325 books; 1018 bound periodical volumes; 50 pamphlets on historical events; 20 unbound reports; newspapers; 15 patents; maps; pictures; letters; manuscripts; clippings; dissertations; 6 reels of microfilm; 10 tapes. **Services:** Copying; research upon request; library open to the public for reference use only. **Remarks:** Library contains the holdings of the Cowley County Genealogical Society.

★15269★
U.S. NATL. PARK SERVICE - CHICKASAW NATL. RECREATION AREA - TRAVERTINE NATURE CENTER LIBRARY (Biol Sci)
Box 201 Phone: (405)622-3165
Sulphur, OK 73086 Bert L. Speed, Chf.Pk.Interp.
Staff: 4. **Subjects:** Biological sciences, botany, zoology, American Indians, U.S. history, astronomy, geology, natural resources. **Holdings:** 800 books; 5 boxes of pamphlets; 80 boxes of periodicals. **Subscriptions:** 31 journals and other serials. **Services:** Library open to the public.

★15270★
U.S. NATL. PARK SERVICE - CORONADO NATL. MEMORIAL - ARCHIVES (Hist, Area-Ethnic)
R.R. 2, Box 126 Phone: (602)366-5515
Hereford, AZ 85615 Joseph L. Sewell, Supt.
Subjects: Coronado expedition, history and cultural contributions of the Spanish Empire, history of Spanish-Mexican movement into the United States and northwestern Mexico, 1500 to present. **Special Collections:** Formation and development of the Coronado National Memorial (8 linear feet). **Holdings:** Figures not available. **Services:** Archives open to the public.

★15271★
U.S. NATL. PARK SERVICE - COULEE DAM NATL. RECREATION AREA - FORT SPOKANE VISITOR CENTER (Hist)
H.C.R. 11, Box 51 Phone: (509)725-2715
Davenport, WA 99122-0051 Steve Shrader, Dist. Ranger
Founded: 1966. **Staff:** 2. **Subjects:** Military history, 1880-1900; Colville Indian Agency, 1900-1930; history and natural sciences of the Upper Columbia River Valley. **Special Collections:** Artifactual study collection of Fort Spokane. **Holdings:** 5 volumes of copies of historical news articles and diaries; 9 volumes of professional research reports. **Services:** Center open to the public for reference use only. **Automated Operations:** Computerized cataloging.

★15272★
U.S. NATL. PARK SERVICE - CRATER LAKE NATL. PARK - LIBRARY (Hist, Biol Sci)
Box 7 Phone: (503)594-2211
Crater Lake, OR 97604 Henry Tanski, Asst.Chf., Interp.
Founded: 1930. **Staff:** Prof 1. **Subjects:** Geology, botany, zoology, human and natural history. **Special Collections:** Crater Lake Nature Notes. **Holdings:** 1500 books; 100 bound periodical volumes; 6 VF drawers of journal articles and similar material. **Subscriptions:** 10 journals and other serials. **Services:** Library open to the public for reference use only by appointment only.

★15273★
U.S. NATL. PARK SERVICE - CUMBERLAND GAP NATL. HISTORICAL PARK - LIBRARY (Hist)
Box 1848 Phone: (606)248-2817
Middlesboro, KY 40965 Wesley D. Leishman, Chf., Interp.
Founded: 1959. **Staff:** 1. **Subjects:** History, folklife, natural history, transportation. **Special Collections:** Hensly Settlement Oral History Collection (on local Appalachian culture; 87 tapes). **Holdings:** 1250 books; 200 bound periodical volumes; 50 documents. **Services:** Library open to the public by appointment for research.

★15274★
U.S. NATL. PARK SERVICE - CUSTER BATTLEFIELD NATL. MONUMENT - LIBRARY (Hist)
Box 39 Phone: (406)638-2622
Crow Agency, MT 59022-0039 Neil C. Mangum, Pk.Hist.
Founded: 1952. **Staff:** 2. **Subjects:** Battle of Little Big Horn, George Custer, Western history, Indian wars. **Special Collections:** Elizabeth B. Custer Correspondence Collection; Walter M. Camp papers. **Holdings:** 2000 books; 500 bound periodical volumes; 15,000 artifacts, relics, and correspondences; 19 reels of microfilm; rare book and manuscript collection. **Subscriptions:** 10 journals and other serials. **Services:** Copying; library open to the public for reference use only by appointment. **Special Indexes:** Photographic Index of Sioux, Cheyenne, Crow, and 7th Cavalry.

★15275★
U.S. NATL. PARK SERVICE - DE SOTO NATL. MEMORIAL - LIBRARY (Hist)
75th St., N.W. Phone: (813)792-0458
Bradenton, FL 34209-9656 Elias Ramirez-Diaz, Pk. Ranger
Staff: Prof 1; Other 1. **Subjects:** Spanish exploration; general exploration; American, Florida, and natural history. **Holdings:** 1128 volumes. **Services:** Library open to the public.

★15276★
U.S. NATL. PARK SERVICE - DEATH VALLEY NATL. MONUMENT - REFERENCE AND RESEARCH LIBRARY (Biol Sci, Sci-Engr)
Death Valley, CA 92328 Phone: (714)786-2331
Shirley A. Harding, Libn.
Founded: 1933. **Staff:** Prof 1; Other 2. **Subjects:** Death Valley geology, history, and research; biological sciences. **Special Collections:** Graduate theses in the natural sciences prepared from Death Valley data (50 volumes). **Holdings:** 4200 books; 50 bound periodical volumes; 60 boxes of pamphlets and reprints; 55 boxes of unbound periodicals; 3 VF drawers of folders on National Park System areas. **Subscriptions:** 14 journals and other serials; 7 newspapers. **Services:** Interlibrary loan; copying; library open to the public on written request.

★15277★
U.S. NATL. PARK SERVICE - DENALI NATL. PARK - LIBRARY (Biol Sci, Hist)
Box 9 Phone: (907)683-2294
Denali Park, AK 99755 George Wagner, Chf. Naturalist
Subjects: Natural history, history. **Holdings:** 1800 books. **Subscriptions:** 10 journals and other serials. **Services:** Library open to the public by appointment.

★15278★
U.S. NATL. PARK SERVICE - DINOSAUR NATL. MONUMENT - DINOSAUR QUARRY - LIBRARY (Sci-Engr, Biol Sci)
Box 128
Jensen, UT 84035 Phone: (801)789-2115
Founded: 1962. **Subjects:** Paleontology, geology, area history, wildlife management, natural history. **Holdings:** 3500 volumes. **Subscriptions:** 15 journals and other serials. **Services:** Library open to the public by appointment.

★15279★
U.S. NATL. PARK SERVICE - EDISON NATL. HISTORIC SITE - ARCHIVES (Sci-Engr, Hist)
Main St. and Lakeside Ave. Phone: (201)736-0550
West Orange, NJ 07052 Mary Bowling, Archv.
Founded: 1887. **Staff:** Prof 1; Other 2. **Subjects:** Invention, science, electricity, botanic research, chemistry, geology. **Holdings:** 10,000 volumes; 3.5 million pages of Edison's personal and laboratory correspondence and documents; business records of Edison Industries and Thomas Alva Edison, Inc.; 3000 notebooks kept by Edison and his workers; 60,000 photographic images. **Services:** Copying (limited); archives open to the public by appointment.

★15280★
U.S. NATL. PARK SERVICE - EFFIGY MOUNDS NATL. MONUMENT - LIBRARY (Sci-Engr, Biol Sci)
R.R. 1, Box 25A Phone: (319)873-3491
Harpers Ferry, IA 52146 Thomas A. Munson, Supt.
Founded: 1949. **Staff:** Prof 1. **Subjects:** Archeology, anthropology, ethnology, local history, natural sciences. **Special Collections:** Ellison Orr manuscripts and library (1000 items). **Holdings:** 2600 books. **Subscriptions:** 17 journals and other serials. **Services:** Library open to the public for reference use only.

★15281★
U.S. NATL. PARK SERVICE - EVERGLADES NATL. PARK - REFERENCE LIBRARY (Biol Sci)
Box 279 Phone: (305)245-5266
Homestead, FL 33030 Glenna R. McCowan, Libn.
Founded: 1964. **Staff:** Prof 1. **Subjects:** Birds, botany, marine biology and ecology, wildlife biology, aquatic ecology, hydrology, national parks, South Florida natural history and water resources. **Holdings:** 6525 books and bound periodical volumes; 10,500 pamphlets and reprints; 635 maps; 945 microforms. **Subscriptions:** 110 journals and other serials. **Services:** Interlibrary loan; copying (limited); library open to the public.

★15282★
U.S. NATL. PARK SERVICE - FIRE ISLAND NATL. SEASHORE - HEADQUARTERS LIBRARY (Hist, Sci-Engr)
120 Laurel St. Phone: (516)289-4810
Patchogue, NY 11772 Neal Bullington, Asst.Chf. Ranger
Staff: 1. **Subjects:** Barrier Island geology, marine biology, oceanography, history. **Holdings:** 5000 books; 1000 other cataloged items. **Services:** Copying; library open to the public for reference use only.

★15283★
U.S. NATL. PARK SERVICE - FLORISSANT FOSSIL BEDS NATL. MONUMENT - LIBRARY (Sci-Engr)
Box 185 Phone: (719)748-3253
Florissant, CO 80816 Duncan Rollo, Chf., Visitor Serv.
Subjects: Geology, paleontology, natural history. **Holdings:** 500 books. **Services:** Library open to the public upon request.

★15284★
U.S. NATL. PARK SERVICE - FORT DAVIS NATL. HISTORIC SITE - LIBRARY (Hist)
Box 1456 Phone: (915)426-3224
Fort Davis, TX 79734 Stephen T. Miller, Supt.
Founded: 1963. **Subjects:** Frontier military history. **Special Collections:** Colonel Benjamin H. Grierson Manuscript Collection (10,000 letters and documents, 1840-1920, on microfilm). **Holdings:** 1300 books; 100 pamphlets and magazines; 60 copies of frontier military maps; 10 manuscripts and theses; 100 reels of microfilm of records of Fort Davis. **Services:** Library open to the public for reference use only.

★15285★
U.S. NATL. PARK SERVICE - FORT LARAMIE NATL. HISTORIC SITE - LIBRARY (Hist)
Box 86 Phone: (307)837-2221
Fort Laramie, WY 82212 Steven R. Fullmer, Pk. Ranger
Founded: 1955. **Staff:** 1. **Subjects:** Frontier military history, Western history, Oregon-California-Mormon trails, Plains Indians. **Holdings:** 3500 books; 160 reels of microfilm. **Services:** Copying; library open to scholars for reference use only.

★15286★
U.S. NATL. PARK SERVICE - FORT LARNED NATL. HISTORIC SITE - LIBRARY (Hist)
Rte. 3, Box 69 Phone: (316)285-6911
Larned, KS 67550-9803 John B. Arnold, Supt.
Founded: 1966. **Staff:** 1. **Subjects:** Fort Larned, 1859-1878; Plains Indians; Santa Fe Trail; military history; Indian Wars, 1848-1890; museum conservation and preservation. **Holdings:** 775 books; 110 reels of microfilm; 10 binders of national archives. **Subscriptions:** 10 journals and other serials. **Services:** Library open to the public by appointment.

★15287★
U.S. NATL. PARK SERVICE - FORT MC HENRY NATL. MONUMENT - HISTORICAL & ARCHEOLOGICAL RESEARCH PROJECT (HARP) (Mil, Hist)
Baltimore, MD 21230 Phone: (301)962-4290
Scott S. Sheads, Pk. Ranger/Hist.
Subjects: War of 1812, Star-Spangled Banner, Civil War, Battle of Baltimore, World War I, U.S. Army General Hospital Number 2. **Special Collections:** Register of over 20,000 political prisoners and prisoners of war held at Fort McHenry during the Civil War. **Holdings:** 50,000 copies of documents from the National Archives; 150 reels of microfilm; maps, 1775-1912. **Services:** Library open to the public by appointment.

★15288★
U.S. NATL. PARK SERVICE - FORT NECESSITY NATL. BATTLEFIELD - LIBRARY (Hist)
The National Pike
RD 2, Box 528 Phone: (412)329-5512
Farmington, PA 15437 William Fink, Supt.
Founded: 1962. **Staff:** 2. **Subjects:** Battle of Great Meadows (July 3, 1754), French and Indian War, 19th century transportation in western Pennsylvania, fauna and flora of the region. **Holdings:** 800 books. **Services:** Library open to the public by appointment.

★15289★
U.S. NATL. PARK SERVICE - FORT PULASKI NATL. MONUMENT - LIBRARY (Hist)
Box 98 Phone: (912)786-5787
Tybee Island, GA 31328 John Beck, Chf., Visitor Serv.
Founded: 1924. **Staff:** Prof 3. **Subjects:** Siege of Fort Pulaski, 1862; Civil War; Fort Pulaski restoration, 1933-1940; American historic preservation; Colonial history of Georgia; Siege of Savannah, 1779. **Special Collections:** Complete set of War of the Rebellion, Official Records of the Union and Confederate Armies and Navies. **Holdings:** 920 books; 300 other cataloged items; 20 linear feet of VF on Civilian Conservation Corps research on historic sites in Florida, Georgia, and South Carolina, 1934-1940; 2600 photographs, 1862-1866 and 1930-1960. **Services:** Interlibrary loan; copying (limited); library open to the public with restrictions.

★15290★
U.S. NATL. PARK SERVICE - FORT SUMTER NATL. MONUMENT - LIBRARY (Hist)
1214 Middle St. Phone: (803)883-3123
Sullivan's Island, SC 29482 Brien Varnado, Supt.
Founded: 1948. **Staff:** 2. **Subjects:** Civil War, Revolutionary War, Fort Sumter, Fort Moultrie, U.S. Seacoast fortifications, artillery, South Carolina, firearms, conservation. **Special Collections:** War of the Rebellion, Official Records of the Union and Confederate Armies (128 volumes); Naval Records (30 volumes); American Revolution naval documents. **Holdings:** 700 books; 200 bound periodical volumes; 250 maps; 650 pamphlets. **Subscriptions:** 10 journals and other serials. **Services:** Library open to the public for reference use only by reservation. **Staff:** David R. Ruth, Hist.; Tyrone Brandyburg, Libn..

★15291★
U.S. NATL. PARK SERVICE - FORT UNION NATL. MONUMENT - LIBRARY (Hist)
Watrous, NM 87753 Phone: (505)425-8025
Douglas C. McChristian, Supt.
Founded: 1956. **Staff:** 2. **Subjects:** Santa Fe Trail and Fort Union history, military history, Western Americana. **Special Collections:** Rare books on the Santa Fe Trail and Fort Union; Fort Union documents (on microcards and microfilm). **Holdings:** 3000 books. **Subscriptions:** 10 journals and other serials. **Services:** Library open to the public for reference use only.

★15292★
U.S. NATL. PARK SERVICE - FORT VANCOUVER NATL. HISTORIC SITE - LIBRARY (Hist)
612 E. Reserve St. Phone: (206)696-7655
Vancouver, WA 98661 Robert D. Appling, Supv./Pk. Ranger
Founded: 1948. **Staff:** Prof 2. **Subjects:** Hudson's Bay Company, fur trade, Western expansion. **Special Collections:** Archeological and historical reports on old Fort Vancouver. **Holdings:** 1300 books; 200 bound periodical volumes; historical pamphlets; 60 historic documents. **Services:** Library open to the public for reference use only. **Automated Operations:** Computerized cataloging. **Remarks:** Jointly maintained with Pacific Northwest National Parks Association.

★15293★
U.S. NATL. PARK SERVICE - FREDERICK LAW OLMSTED NATL. HISTORIC SITE - ARCHIVES (Plan)
99 Warren St. Phone: (617)566-1689
Brookline, MA 02146 Elizabeth S. Banks, Coll.Mgr.
Staff: Prof 3; Other 4. **Subjects:** Landscape architecture, urban design, city planning. **Special Collections:** 19th and early 20th century photographic prints of parks, landscapes, estates, urban design in European cities and towns (25 linear feet). **Holdings:** 1000 books; 650 bound periodical volumes; 150,000 landscape architectural drawings, 1860-1979; 60,000 photographic prints of Olmsted landscape jobs in the U.S. and Canada; 30 linear feet of landscape job planting lists. **Services:** Copying; archives open to scholars by appointment.

★15294★
U.S. NATL. PARK SERVICE - FREDERICKSBURG & SPOTSYLVANIA NATL. MILITARY PARK - LIBRARY (Hist)
Box 679 Phone: (703)373-4461
Fredericksburg, VA 22404 Robert K. Krick, Chf.Hist.
Founded: 1927. **Staff:** 3. **Subjects:** Civil War in Virginia. **Holdings:** 5500 books; 250 bound periodical volumes; 1400 manuscript items; 1100 reels of microfilm; 10 drawers of maps. **Services:** Copying; library open to the public by appointment.

★15295★
U.S. NATL. PARK SERVICE - GEORGE WASHINGTON CARVER NATL. MONUMENT - LIBRARY (Hist)
Box 38 Phone: (417)325-4151
Diamond, MO 64840 Walter Tegge, Chf. Ranger
Staff: Prof 1. **Subjects:** George Washington Carver, black history, national parks. **Special Collections:** Carver Collection (3019 archives and artifacts); original Carver letters (97 items). **Holdings:** 246 books; 130 documents and technical reports; 50 maps and charts; 1505 pictures and study prints; 16 VF drawers of park administrative records. **Subscriptions:** 14 journals and other serials. **Services:** Interlibrary loan; copying; library open to the public for historic research. **Publications:** Monumental News (newsletter), quarterly - free upon request. **Special Catalogs:** Carver Collection.

★15296★
U.S. NATL. PARK SERVICE - GETTYSBURG NATL. MILITARY PARK - CYCLORAMA CENTER LIBRARY (Hist)
Gettysburg, PA 17325 Phone: (717)334-1124
Kathleen G. Harrison, Hist.
Staff: 2. **Subjects:** Battle of Gettysburg, Civil War, Lincoln, Eisenhower at Gettysburg, 19th century life, environment. **Special Collections:** Eisenhower oral history (100 tapes); William H. Tipton photographs (2500). **Holdings:** 3800 books; 20 VF drawers; 1700 maps and plans; 180 reels of microfilm. **Subscriptions:** 20 journals and other serials. **Services:** Copying (limited); library open to the public for reference use only.

★15297★
U.S. NATL. PARK SERVICE - GILA CLIFF DWELLINGS NATL. MONUMENT - VISITOR CENTER LIBRARY (Hist)
Rte. 11, Box 100 Phone: (505)536-9461
Silver City, NM 88061 Annamarie Hoge
Founded: 1967. **Staff:** 1. **Subjects:** Archeology, natural history, Mogollon Indians. **Special Collections:** Mogollon Indian artifacts. **Holdings:** 300 books. **Services:** Library open to the public for reference use only. **Remarks:** Consolidated with U.S. Forest Service to serve Gila National Forest.

★15298★

U.S. NATL. PARK SERVICE - GLACIER NATL. PARK - GEORGE C. RUHLE LIBRARY (Env-Cons, Biol Sci)
West Glacier, MT 59936 Phone: (406)888-5441
Beth Dunagan, Pk.Libn.
Founded: 1975. **Staff:** 1. **Subjects:** Glacier Park history, environment, geology, glaciology, mammals, Plains Indians. **Special Collections:** Schultz books on the Plains Indians. **Holdings:** 10,000 books; 2000 reprints; 10,000 museum specimens. **Subscriptions:** 27 journals and other serials; 6 newspapers. **Services:** Library open to the public for reference use only.

U.S. NATL. PARK SERVICE - GOLDEN GATE NATL. RECREATION AREA - NATL. MARITIME MUSEUM
See: National Maritime Museum (9742)

★15299★

U.S. NATL. PARK SERVICE - GRAND CANYON RESEARCH LIBRARY (Biol Sci, Sci-Engr)
Grand Canyon Natl. Park
Box 129 Phone: (602)638-7768
Grand Canyon, AZ 86023 Julie Russell, Libn.
Founded: 1931. **Staff:** 2. **Subjects:** Grand Canyon region - geology, zoology, botany, ethnology, archeology, anthropology, history. **Holdings:** 9000 books and bound periodical volumes; river journals; clippings; reprints; oral histories. **Subscriptions:** 42 journals and other serials. **Services:** Interlibrary loan; library open to the public by appointment.

★15300★

U.S. NATL. PARK SERVICE - GRAND PORTAGE NATL. MONUMENT - LIBRARY (Hist)
Box 666 Phone: (218)387-2788
Grand Marais, MN 55604 Donald W. Carney, Supv.Pk. Ranger
Subjects: American-Canadian fur trade, Chippewa Indian culture, Canadian-Minnesota exploration and history. **Special Collections:** Wisconsin Historical Collection (21 volumes); journals of the Hudson's Bay Company (24 volumes); works of Samuel De Champlain (6 volumes). **Holdings:** 900 books; 100 bound periodical volumes. **Services:** Library open to the public with restrictions.

★15301★

U.S. NATL. PARK SERVICE - GRAND TETON NATL. PARK - LIBRARY (Biol Sci)
Drawer 170
Moose, WY 83012 Phone: (307)733-2880
Founded: 1929. **Subjects:** Grand Teton National Park - fauna, flora, history, geology; Western history. **Holdings:** 1500 books; pamphlets; 1000 historic photographs. **Subscriptions:** 15 journals and other serials. **Services:** Library open to the public for reference use only.

★15302★

U.S. NATL. PARK SERVICE - GRANT-KOHRS RANCH NATL. HISTORIC SITE (Hist)
Box 790 Phone: (406)846-2070
Deer Lodge, MT 59722 Neysa Dickey, Supv.Pk. Ranger
Subjects: History - ranching, local, Western U.S., natural; interpretation. **Special Collections:** Frontier cattle era collection; oral histories. **Holdings:** 1200 volumes. **Services:** Library open to the public for reference use only.

★15303★

U.S. NATL. PARK SERVICE - GREAT SMOKY MOUNTAINS NATL. PARK - SUGARLANDS VISITOR CENTER (Biol Sci, Hist)
Gatlinburg, TN 37738 Phone: (615)436-1296
Annette Evans, Libn.
Staff: Prof 1. **Subjects:** Natural sciences, area history, pioneer and oral history, environment, geology, park history. **Special Collections:** Naturalists' journals; historic maps; memorabilia of early settlers; archival collection (18,000 black and white photographs; 250 linear feet of files); Research/Resource Management Report Series (66). **Holdings:** 3000 books; bound periodical volumes; theses and dissertations; VF drawers of technical papers and clippings; 123 tapes and transcriptions; records; films. **Subscriptions:** 45 journals and other serials. **Services:** Interlibrary loan (limited); center open to the public for reference use only.

★15304★

U.S. NATL. PARK SERVICE - HALEAKALA NATL. PARK - LIBRARY (Biol Sci)
Box 369 Phone: (808)572-9306
Makawao, HI 96768 Jim Boll, Pk. Ranger, Interp.
Staff: 1. **Subjects:** Botany, zoology, Hawaiiania, geology, ecology, parks, archeology. **Special Collections:** IBP-Island Ecosystems (of Hawaii; 75). **Holdings:** 560 books; 18 file boxes of pertinent subject material. **Services:** Library open to the public for reference use only on request.

★15305★

U.S. NATL. PARK SERVICE - HARPERS FERRY CENTER - OFFICE OF GRAPHICS RESEARCH - PICTURE LIBRARY (Aud-Vis)
5508 Port Royal Rd. Phone: (703)756-6138
Springfield, VA 22151-2393 Thomas A. DuRant, Pict.Libn.
Founded: 1982. **Staff:** Prof 1. **Subjects:** National Park Service. **Special Collections:** George A. Grant Collection (circa 1929-1954); E.B. Thompson Collection (circa 1900-1940); George Wright/Joseph Dixon Collection (natural science, circa 1930-1950); National Park Service photographs, 1929-1980. **Holdings:** 700,000 images, including 39 file cabinets of prints, 12 file cabinets of negatives, and 400 3-ring binders of slides. **Services:** Interlibrary loan; library open to the public with restrictions.

★15306★

U.S. NATL. PARK SERVICE - HARPERS FERRY CENTER LIBRARY (Hist, Mil)
Harpers Ferry, WV 25425 Phone: (304)535-6371
David Nathanson, Chf.Libn.
Staff: Prof 3; Other 3. **Subjects:** American history, natural history, museology, decorative arts, photography, American military history. **Special Collections:** U.S. National Park Service Research Reports (15,000 items); Historic Furnishings Library (4000 volumes); Harold L. Peterson Collection (military art and science, firearms; 4000 volumes); Vera Craig Pictorial Archive of American Interiors (250 items); National Park Service History Collection (2000 books; 200 bound periodical volumes; 500 boxes of archival/manuscript materials; 100 films; 750 museum artifacts; 1000 hours of oral history tapes); National Park Service Historical Photograph Library (1.2 million items). **Holdings:** 26,000 books; 500 bound periodical volumes; 120 shelf feet of unbound periodicals; 25 VF drawers of pamphlets; 220 reels of microfilm; 12,500 microfiche; 1100 trade catalogs. **Subscriptions:** 250 journals and other serials. **Services:** Interlibrary loan; copying; library open to the public for reference use only. **Automated Operations:** Computerized cataloging and ILL. **Computerized Information Services:** DIALOG Information Services, BRS Information Technologies, OCLC, WILSONLINE. **Networks/Consortia:** Member of FEDLINK. **Publications:** New Accessions at HFC Library, monthly. **Special Catalogs:** Guide to the Trade Catalog Collection, 1984; Guide to the NPS Reports Collection; Collecting, Using and Preserving Oral History in the National Park Service (1984); Reprint File; NPS Oral History Survey, 1981; Sunshine and Shadows: A Catalog of Civil War Regimental Histories and Personal Narratives in NPS Libraries, 1986. **Special Indexes:** Inventories of archival/manuscript collections; index to The Courier: The National Park Service Newsletter, 1983-1987. **Staff:** Ruthanne Heriot, Spec.Coll.Libn.; Nancy L. Potts, ILL Off..

★15307★

U.S. NATL. PARK SERVICE - HARPERS FERRY NATL. HISTORICAL PARK - LIBRARY (Hist)
Box 65 Phone: (304)535-6371
Harpers Ferry, WV 25425 Hilda E. Staubs, Musm.Techn.
Founded: 1962. **Staff:** 1. **Subjects:** John Brown, Armory, Civil War, Negro education, local and general history, natural science, military science. **Holdings:** 1917 books; 230 historical newspapers; 224 research reports on historic structures, sites, archeology, and related histories; 53 college catalogs; 58 binders of unpublished correspondence and papers; booklet and document file; historic and modern photographs; 165 reels of microfilm. **Services:** Interlibrary loan; library open to the public for reference use only.

★15308★

U.S. NATL. PARK SERVICE - HAWAII VOLCANOES NATL. PARK - LIBRARY (Biol Sci, Sci-Engr)
Hawaii National Park, HI 96718 Phone: (808)967-7311
John Wise, Chf.Pk.Interp.
Founded: 1916. **Staff:** 1. **Subjects:** Volcanology, zoology, botany, ancient culture of Hawaiians. **Holdings:** 2300 books; 460 bound periodical volumes; 1560 pamphlets; 2000 black/white photographs; 3000 slides. **Subscriptions:**

17 journals and other serials. **Services:** Library open to the public by appointment for reference use only.

★15309★
U.S. NATL. PARK SERVICE - HOMESTEAD NATL. MONUMENT - RESEARCH LIBRARY (Hist)
R.R. 3, Box 47 Phone: (402)223-3514
Beatrice, NE 68310-9416 Randall K. Baynes, Supt.
Founded: 1936. **Staff:** Prof 1; Other 5. **Subjects:** U.S. public lands policy and Western expansion, U.S. agricultural history, Nebraska history, ecology and natural history. **Special Collections:** Museum Study Collection on the homesteading experience and the local area of Nebraska (189 books). **Holdings:** 1000 books; 60 bound periodical volumes; 40 park archives. **Services:** Library open to the public for reference use only.

★15310★
U.S. NATL. PARK SERVICE - HOPEWELL FURNACE NATL. HISTORIC SITE - LIBRARY (Hist)
R.D. 1, Box 345 Phone: (215)582-8773
Elverson, PA 19520 Elizabeth E. Disrude, Supt.
Founded: 1938. **Staff:** 1. **Subjects:** 18th and 19th century ironmaking. **Special Collections:** Hopewell Furnace Records (80 items); name file for persons associated with the Hopewell Furnace during its 113 years of operation. **Holdings:** 500 books; 100 unpublished reports; 10,000 furnace documents; microfilm. **Services:** Library open to the public by appointment for reference use only. **Special Indexes:** Hopewell Source Material Index.

★15311★
U.S. NATL. PARK SERVICE - HORSESHOE BEND NATL. MILITARY PARK - LIBRARY (Hist)
Route 1
Box 103 Phone: (205)234-7111
Daviston, AL 36256 Marilyn H. Parris, Supt.
Staff: Prof 4; Other 5. **Subjects:** Battle of Horseshoe Bend, Creek Indians, War of 1812. **Holdings:** 400 books; 35 bound periodical volumes; letters; maps; documents. **Services:** Copying; library open to the public by appointment.

★15312★
U.S. NATL. PARK SERVICE - INDEPENDENCE NATL. HISTORICAL PARK - LIBRARY (Hist)
313 Walnut St. Phone: (215)597-8047
Philadelphia, PA 19106 Shirley A. Mays, Lib.Techn.
Founded: 1951. **Staff:** Prof 1. **Subjects:** American history, Philadelphia and Pennsylvania history, arts and crafts. **Special Collections:** Independence Hall Association Papers; Judge Edwin O. Lewis Papers. **Holdings:** 8500 books; 800 bound periodical volumes; 200 manuscripts; 600 reels of microfilm; 150 resource studies reports; 150,000 research note cards; 15,000 photographs; 60,000 slides. **Subscriptions:** 34 journals and other serials. **Services:** Interlibrary loan; library open to the public for reference use only. **Remarks:** Library is located at 120 S. Third St., Philadelphia, PA. **Staff:** David C.G. Dutcher, Chf., Div. of Hist. & Hist.Archv..

★15313★
U.S. NATL. PARK SERVICE - JEFFERSON NATL. EXPANSION MEMORIAL - LIBRARY (Hist)
11 N. Fourth St. Phone: (314)425-6023
St. Louis, MO 63102 Kathleen E. Moenster, Cur.Asst.
Founded: 1959. **Staff:** 1. **Subjects:** Westward expansion, St. Louis and Missouri history, fur trade, steamboats, Thomas Jefferson, Lewis & Clark. **Special Collections:** Grace Lewis Miller Collection on Meriwether Lewis. **Holdings:** 3800 books; 175 linear feet of archival material on park history; 450 other cataloged items; research reports. **Subscriptions:** 25 journals and other serials. **Services:** Copying; library open to the public for reference use only by appointment.

★15314★
U.S. NATL. PARK SERVICE - KENNESAW MOUNTAIN NATL. BATTLEFIELD PARK - LIBRARY (Hist)
Box 1167 Phone: (404)427-4686
Marietta, GA 30061 Emmet A. Nichols, Chf.Interp. & Rsrcs.Mgr.
Founded: 1939. **Staff:** 2. **Subjects:** Civil War, 19th century American history, Georgia history. **Holdings:** 1000 books; 20 diaries; 25 reels of microfilm; 20 manuscripts and letters; 6 films. **Services:** Library open to serious researchers for reference use only.

★15315★
U.S. NATL. PARK SERVICE - KINGS MOUNTAIN NATL. MILITARY PARK - LIBRARY (Hist)
Box 40 Phone: (803)936-7921
Kings Mountain, NC 28086 James J. Anderson, Chf. Ranger
Founded: 1941. **Subjects:** Revolutionary War history. **Holdings:** Figures not available. **Services:** Library open to the public with restrictions.

★15316★
U.S. NATL. PARK SERVICE - LAKE MEAD NATL. RECREATION AREA - LIBRARY (Biol Sci)
601 Nevada Hwy. Phone: (702)293-8907
Boulder City, NV 89005-2426 Robinett Hourie, Libn.
Founded: 1962. **Staff:** Prof 2. **Subjects:** Lake Mead - history, geology, plants, animals, archeology; National Park Service. **Holdings:** 800 books; 1000 other cataloged items. **Services:** Interlibrary loan; copying; library open to the public. **Automated Operations:** Computerized cataloging and acquisitions. **Computerized Information Services:** Internal database.

★15317★
U.S. NATL. PARK SERVICE - LAVA BEDS NATL. MONUMENT - LIBRARY (Sci-Engr, Hist)
Box 867 Phone: (916)667-2282
Tulelake, CA 96134 Gary Hathaway, Chf., Div. of Interp.
Founded: 1933. **Staff:** Prof 1; Other 1. **Subjects:** History of Modoc War, 1872-1873; geology and volcanology; natural history; Indian ethnography; archeology. **Holdings:** 1800 books. **Services:** Copying; library open to the public by appointment for reference use only. **Automated Operations:** Computerized cataloging.

★15318★
U.S. NATL. PARK SERVICE - LIBRARY (Rec, Hist)
12795 W. Alameda Pkwy.
Box 25287
Denver, CO 80225-0287 Phone: (303)969-2715
Founded: 1971. **Staff:** Prof 1; Other 1. **Subjects:** National parks and monuments, outdoor recreation, ecology, landscape and historic architecture, American history. **Special Collections:** Brochures and pamphlets on individual national parks and monuments (3000 items). **Holdings:** 25,000 books, reports, documents, and dissertations. **Subscriptions:** 300 journals and other serials; 10 newspapers. **Services:** Interlibrary loan; copying; library open to the public for reference use only. **Automated Operations:** Computerized cataloging and ILL. **Computerized Information Services:** OCLC. **Networks/Consortia:** Member of FEDLINK, National Natural Resources Library and Information System (NNRLIS).

★15319★
U.S. NATL. PARK SERVICE - LINCOLN BOYHOOD NATL. MEMORIAL - LIBRARY (Hist)
Lincoln City, IN 47552 Phone: (812)937-4541
Norman D. Hellmers, Supt.
Founded: 1962. **Staff:** 1. **Subjects:** Abraham Lincoln, pioneer life, state and local history. **Special Collections:** Interpretive Museum for the 1816-1830 period of Lincoln's life. **Holdings:** 1000 books; 25 bound periodical volumes; pamphlets; maps; documents. **Subscriptions:** 16 journals and other serials. **Services:** Copying; library open to the public for reference use only. **Publications:** Handout copies of information about Lincoln.

★15320★
U.S. NATL. PARK SERVICE - LONGFELLOW NATL. HISTORIC SITE - LIBRARY (Hum)
105 Brattle St. Phone: (617)876-4491
Cambridge, MA 02138 Elizabeth Banks, Act.Cur.
Staff: Prof 1; Other 2. **Subjects:** European literature and languages, American literature, H.W. Longfellow's works, Dante, Scandinavian literature. **Holdings:** 10,000 books, bound periodical volumes, pamphlets; 175 linear feet of Longfellow-Wadsworth-Appleton-Dana family papers. **Services:** Library open to the public for bona fide scholarly use only.

★15321★
U.S. NATL. PARK SERVICE - LYNDON B. JOHNSON NATL. HISTORICAL PARK - LIBRARY (Hist)
Box 329 Phone: (512)868-7128
Johnson City, TX 78636 John T. Tiff, Pk. Ranger/Hist.
Founded: 1970. **Staff:** Prof 1; Other 1. **Subjects:** Lyndon B. Johnson and his family, Texas hill country history, local natural history. **Special Collections:** Oral history collection on life and times of LBJ (500 tapes). **Holdings:** 2000 books; 750 slides; 20 VF drawers of pamphlets; artifacts; 125 reels of 35mm microfilm of historic newspapers. **Subscriptions:** 15

journals and other serials. **Services:** Copying (limited); library open to the public for reference use only for approved research.

★15322★
U.S. NATL. PARK SERVICE - MANASSAS NATL. BATTLEFIELD PARK - LIBRARY (Hist)
Box 1830 Phone: (703)754-7107
Manassas, VA 22110 Rolland Swain, Supt.
Founded: 1940. **Staff:** Prof 3. **Subjects:** Civil War - history, biographies, medicine, surgery, uniforms, equipment; campaigns and battles of First and Second Manassas (Bull Run); general military works. **Special Collections:** Fitz-John Porter Collection; James Brewerton Ricketts Collection; T.C.H. Smith Papers (photostat); journal of Abner Doubleday, 1862 (photocopy); Franklin B. Hough Papers (photostat). **Holdings:** 1500 books; 92 bound periodical volumes; 200 contemporary photographs; 100 photostats of Civil War-related newspapers; 1000 photostats of documents, diaries, and memoirs; 100 maps; bibliography files on First and Second Manassas. **Services:** Copying; library open to the public by appointment. **Staff:** James Burgess, Cur./Archv.; Edmund Raus, Chf.Hist.; Keith Snyder, Pk. Ranger.

★15323★
U.S. NATL. PARK SERVICE - MESA VERDE NATL. PARK - MUSEUM LIBRARY (Hist)
Box 38 Phone: (303)529-4475
Mesa Verde Natl. Park, CO 81330 Beverly J. Cunningham, Libn.
Staff: Prof 1. **Subjects:** Archeology, ethnology, anthropology, history. **Special Collections:** Early historical and archeological documents of Mesa Verde Natl. Park. **Holdings:** 6221 books; 150 bound periodical volumes; 42 filing boxes of unbound documents. **Subscriptions:** 42 journals and other serials. **Services:** Interlibrary loan; library not open to the public. **Networks/Consortia:** Member of Southwest Regional Library Service System (SWRLSS).

★15324★
U.S. NATL. PARK SERVICE - MIDWEST ARCHEOLOGICAL CENTER - RESEARCH LIBRARY (Soc Sci)
Federal Bldg., Rm. 474
100 Centennial Mall N. Phone: (402)471-5392
Lincoln, NE 68508-3873 Ellen Dubas, Lib.Techn.
Founded: 1969. **Staff:** Prof 1. **Subjects:** Archeology of the mid-continental United States, National Park Service, American Indians. **Holdings:** 400 books; 5600 bound periodical volumes; 1900 volumes of manuscripts; 100 volumes of government publications. **Subscriptions:** 45 journals and other serials. **Services:** Library not open to the public.

★15325★
U.S. NATL. PARK SERVICE - MIDWEST REGIONAL OFFICE LIBRARY* (Hist)
1709 Jackson St. Phone: (402)221-3471
Omaha, NE 68102 Elizabeth Lane, Pub.Info.Asst.
Founded: 1935. **Staff:** 1. **Subjects:** Western Americana, ethnology, and anthropology. **Special Collections:** Pacific railroad surveys; early Western travel; Westerners brand book. **Holdings:** 6000 books; special historical research, interpretive planning, historic structures, and salvage archeology reports. **Subscriptions:** 15 journals and other serials. **Services:** Library open to the public for limited use.

★15326★
U.S. NATL. PARK SERVICE - MOORES CREEK NATL. BATTLEFIELD - LIBRARY (Hist)
Box 69 Phone: (919)283-5591
Currie, NC 28435 Fred Boyles, Supt.
Founded: 1960. **Staff:** Prof 2; Other 1. **Subjects:** North Carolina history, American Revolution, national parks, environment, Highland Scots. **Holdings:** 325 books; 100 bound volumes of periodicals and historical papers. **Services:** Library open to the public for reference use only.

★15327★
U.S. NATL. PARK SERVICE - MORRISTOWN NATL. HISTORICAL PARK - LIBRARY (Hist)
Washington Place Phone: (201)539-2016
Morristown, NJ 07960 Alan Stein, Libn.
Founded: 1955. **Staff:** Prof 1. **Subjects:** History of the American Revolution, Colonial Americana, George Washington, New Jersey local history. **Holdings:** 15,000 books; 300 bound periodical volumes; 500 pamphlets; 46,000 manuscripts; 252 reels of microfilm. **Subscriptions:** 25 journals and other serials. **Services:** Copying; library open to the public. **Special Catalogs:** Guide to the Manuscript Collection.

★15328★
U.S. NATL. PARK SERVICE - MOUND CITY GROUP NATL. MONUMENT - LIBRARY (Hist)
16062 State Rte. 104 Phone: (614)774-1125
Chillicothe, OH 45601 Kenneth Apschnikat, Supt.
Staff: Prof 1. **Subjects:** Archeology, Hopewell and other prehistoric Indian cultures of Ohio, environment and environmental education, Ohio history. **Special Collections:** Reports of archeological research on Hopewell and Adena cultures conducted at monument; Hopewell Archeological Conference papers, 1978. **Holdings:** 1800 books; 650 magazines, reports, unbound articles. **Services:** Copying; library open to the public for reference use only by request. **Staff:** Jean M. Schaeppi, Pk. Ranger.

★15329★
U.S. NATL. PARK SERVICE - MOUNT RUSHMORE NATL. MEMORIAL - LIBRARY (Hist)
Box 268 Phone: (605)574-4145
Keystone, SD 57751 Larry G. Asher, Lead Pk. Ranger
Founded: 1964. **Staff:** 3. **Subjects:** American history, Mount Rushmore history, natural history of the Black Hills, history of South Dakota, national parks. **Special Collections:** Development of Mount Rushmore (documents on administrative history). **Holdings:** 750 books; 5 VF drawers of subject files; 6 VF drawers of black and white photo files. **Services:** Library open to the public by appointment.

★15330★
U.S. NATL. PARK SERVICE - NATCHEZ TRACE PARKWAY - LIBRARY & VISITOR CENTER (Hist)
R.R. 1, NT-143
Tupelo, MS 38801 Phone: (601)842-1572
Founded: 1963. **Staff:** 1. **Subjects:** History, natural history, national parks. **Special Collections:** Papers and letters related to Choctaw and Chickasaw Indians (200 items). **Holdings:** 2300 books; 200 bound periodical volumes; 1000 color slides; 10,000 negatives. **Subscriptions:** 10 journals and other serials. **Services:** Interlibrary loan; copying; library open to the public.

★15331★
U.S. NATL. PARK SERVICE - NATIONAL CAPITAL REGION - FREDERICK DOUGLASS HOME AND VISITOR CENTER - LIBRARY (Hist)
1411 W St., S.E. Phone: (202)426-5962
Washington, DC 20020 Tyra S. Walker, Musm.Cur.
Founded: 1877. **Staff:** 1. **Subjects:** History, biography, science, geography, philosophy. **Special Collections:** History of Women's Suffrage (4 volumes); Executive Documents, 1820-1895. **Holdings:** 2000 books. **Subscriptions:** 14 journals and other serials. **Services:** Library open to researchers by appointment for reference use only. **Computerized Information Services:** Internal database. **Also Known As:** National Capital Park-East - Douglass Private Collection.

★15332★
U.S. NATL. PARK SERVICE - NATIONAL CAPITAL REGION - ROCK CREEK NATURE CENTER LIBRARY (Biol Sci)
5200 Glover Rd., N.W. Phone: (202)426-6829
Washington, DC 20015 Clark Dixon, Supv.Pk. Ranger
Subjects: Birds, mammals, reptiles, astronomy, park and milling history, environment and environmental education. **Holdings:** 1000 books; 32 boxes of clippings and photographs; unbound journals. **Services:** Library open to the public for reference use only. **Publications:** Mimeographed nature leaflets.

★15333★
U.S. NATL. PARK SERVICE - NEZ PERCE NATL. HISTORICAL PARK - LIBRARY (Hist)
Box 93 Phone: (208)843-2261
Spalding, ID 83551 Roy Weaver, Supt.
Founded: 1965. **Staff:** 12. **Subjects:** Nez Perce Indians, Nez Perce War, Indian ethnology, history of the Northwest and Idaho, Western history. **Holdings:** 850 books; 300 historical photographs; 1000 photographs. **Services:** Library open to the public with restrictions on reference and archival materials.

★15334★
U.S. NATL. PARK SERVICE - OLYMPIC NATL. PARK - PIONEER MEMORIAL MUSEUM - LIBRARY (Biol Sci)
3002 Mount Angeles Rd. Phone: (206)452-4501
Port Angeles, WA 98362 Henry C. Warren, Chf.Pk. Naturalist
Staff: 1. **Subjects;** Natural history, Northwest Coast Indians, Olympic National Park. **Special Collections:** Manuscript material and reports relating to exploration and settlement of the Olympic Peninsula;

correspondence, memoranda, reports, and photographs relating to the establishment and administration of Olympic National Park. **Holdings:** 2000 books; 6 VF drawers of clippings and articles relating to natural and human history of Olympic National Park. **Services:** Copying; library open to the public by appointment.

★15335★
U.S. NATL. PARK SERVICE - ORGAN PIPE CACTUS NATL. MONUMENT - LIBRARY (Hist)
Rte. 1, Box 100
Ajo, AZ 85321 Caroline Wilson, Interp.Spec.
Staff: 1. **Subjects:** Natural and cultural history, ecology of the Sonora Desert and the Southwest, U.S. Natl. Park Service history and policies. **Holdings:** 1500 books and bound periodical volumes; research reports and manuscripts. **Services:** Library open to park employees and approved researchers.

★15336★
U.S. NATL. PARK SERVICE - PEA RIDGE NATL. MILITARY PARK - LIBRARY (Hist)
Pea Ridge, AR 72751 Phone: (501)451-8122
Billy D. Stout, Hist.
Founded: 1960. **Subjects:** Battle of Pea Ridge, Civil War west of the Mississippi, regimental histories, Indians of the Civil War, arms and equipment, medicine. **Special Collections:** Battle of Pea Ridge (30 reels of microfilm; 15 reports). **Holdings:** 450 books; letters; clippings. **Services:** Library open to the public for reference use only.

★15337★
U.S. NATL. PARK SERVICE - PERRY'S VICTORY & INTERNATIONAL PEACE MEMORIAL - LIBRARY (Hist)
Box 549 Phone: (419)285-2184
Put-In-Bay, OH 43456 Harry C. Myers, Supt.
Subjects: Naval victory of Oliver H. Perry over British at the Battle of Lake Erie, War of 1812; Lake Erie Islands. **Special Collections:** Construction of memorial designed by Freedlander and Seymour. **Holdings:** 700 books; 2 VF drawers of reports and correspondence from Centennial Commission and subsequent organizations; 2 VF drawers of pamphlets; 1200 photographs. **Services:** Library open to the public by appointment.

★15338★
U.S. NATL. PARK SERVICE - PETERSBURG NATL. BATTLEFIELD - LIBRARY (Hist)
Box 549 Phone: (804)732-3531
Petersburg, VA 23803 Christopher M. Calkins, Hist./Pk. Ranger
Founded: 1926. **Staff:** Prof 2. **Subjects:** Civil War, Petersburg. **Holdings:** 1900 books; 200 bound periodical volumes; 500 maps; 200 letters and documents. **Subscriptions:** 10 journals and other serials. **Services:** Copying (limited); library open to the public by appointment. **Staff:** John R. Davis, Chf., Interp..

★15339★
U.S. NATL. PARK SERVICE - PETRIFIED FOREST NATL. PARK - LIBRARY (Sci-Engr, Hist)
Petrified Forest Natl. Park, AZ 86028 Phone: (602)524-6228
Terry E. Maze, Dist. Ranger
Subjects: Petrified wood, geology, paleontology, natural and cultural history. **Special Collections:** Paleontology library (papers and reports on continental Tirassic deposits of the world). **Holdings:** 2190 books and bound periodical volumes. **Subscriptions:** 19 journals and other serials. **Services:** Library open to the public by appointment; paleontology library open to bona fide researchers by appointment only.

★15340★
U.S. NATL. PARK SERVICE - PIPESTONE NATL. MONUMENT - LIBRARY & ARCHIVES (Hist)
Box 727 Phone: (507)825-5463
Pipestone, MN 56164 Vincent J. Halvorson, Supt.
Subjects: Archeology, history, ethnology of the early Indian occupation of the Northern Plains; white exploration and settlement of the region. **Special Collections:** Publications relating to ceremonial pipes and Indian smoking customs. **Holdings:** 430 volumes; manuscripts; reports; clippings; microfilm; photographs; slides. **Services:** Library open to the public for reference use only.

★15341★
U.S. NATL. PARK SERVICE - POINT REYES NATL. SEASHORE - LIBRARY (Biol Sci)
Point Reyes, CA 94956 Phone: (415)663-1092
Armando Quintero, Supv.Pk. Ranger
Subjects: Natural history, Indians, environmental education, geology, California history, sea life, mammals, botany, National Park Service. **Holdings:** 2500 books; 2075 bound periodical volumes; 425 other cataloged items; reports. **Services:** Library open to the public for reference use only by special arrangement.

★15342★
U.S. NATL. PARK SERVICE - PU'UHONUA O HONAUNAU NATL. HISTORICAL PARK - LIBRARY (Hist)
Box 129 Phone: (808)328-2288
Honaunau, HI 96726 Blossom Sapp, Pk. Ranger
Founded: 1961. **Staff:** Prof 1. **Subjects:** Hawaiian culture and history; National Park Service. **Holdings:** 300 books; 87 manuscripts. **Services:** Library open to the public for reference use only.

★15343★
U.S. NATL. PARK SERVICE - RICHMOND NATL. BATTLEFIELD PARK - LIBRARY (Hist)
3215 E. Broad St. Phone: (804)226-1981
Richmond, VA 23223
Keithel C. Morgan, Chf., Interp. & Cultural Rsrcs
Founded: 1966. **Staff:** 3. **Subjects:** Civil War, national parks, museums. **Holdings:** 900 books. **Services:** Library open to the public for reference use only by appointment.

★15344★
U.S. NATL. PARK SERVICE - ROCKY MOUNTAIN NATIONAL PARK - LIBRARY (Biol Sci, Hist)
Estes Park, CO 80517 Phone: (303)586-2371
Helen M. Burgener, Lib.Techn.
Staff: Prof 1. **Subjects:** Rocky Mountain National Park - history, geology, plant and animal ecology; Western history. **Special Collections:** Enos Mills collection; William Allen White collection. **Holdings:** 2225 books; 208 bound periodical volumes; 112 theses; 75 boxes of clippings and reports; 4 volumes of maps; 52 oral history tapes and cassettes. **Subscriptions:** 28 journals and other serials. **Services:** Copying; library open to the public with restrictions.

★15345★
U.S. NATL. PARK SERVICE - ROOSEVELT-VANDERBILT NATL. HISTORIC SITES - MUSEUMS (Hist)
Hyde Park, NY 12538 Phone: (914)229-9115
Beverly Kane, Site Libn.
Staff: 1. **Subjects:** Franklin and Eleanor Roosevelt, National Park Service, Vanderbilt families, architecture, antiques, historic houses. **Holdings:** 1200 books and bound periodical volumes. **Services:** House museums open to the public. **Remarks:** There are three historic house museums, consisting of the homes of Franklin D. Roosevelt, Eleanor Roosevelt, and the Frederick W. Vanderbilt family. The small library in the park headquarters is open to the public with restrictions.

★15346★
U.S. NATL. PARK SERVICE - RUSSELL CAVE NATL. MONUMENT - LIBRARY (Sci-Engr)
Rte. 1, Box 175 Phone: (205)495-2672
Bridgeport, AL 35740 Dorothy Marsh, Supt.
Staff: 6. **Subjects:** Archeology of Russell Cave and related sites. **Special Collections:** Miscellaneous points and shards (1500). **Holdings:** 382 books; 4 unbound manuscripts. **Services:** Library open to the public for reference use only.

★15347★
U.S. NATL. PARK SERVICE - SALEM MARITIME NATL. HISTORIC SITE - LIBRARY (Hist)
Custom House, Derby St. Phone: (617)744-4323
Salem, MA 01970 John M. Frayler, Hist.
Founded: 1937. **Staff:** 1. **Subjects:** Maritime history, Essex County and local history, recreation and conservation. **Holdings:** 806 books; 250 periodicals; 3 VF drawers of Custom House records; pamphlets; clippings; historic prints. **Services:** Copying (limited); library open to the public by appointment.

★15348★
U.S. NATL. PARK SERVICE - SARATOGA NATL. HISTORICAL PARK - LIBRARY (Hist)
R.D. 2, Box 33 Phone: (518)664-9821
Stillwater, NY 12170 S. Paul Okey, Pk.Hist.
Founded: 1948. **Subjects:** Battles of Saratoga, military campaign of 1777, American Revolution, National Park System. **Special Collections:** Primary source materials (microfilm). **Holdings:** 500 books; 500 maps; 500 photographs; 1000 slides; 100 unbound reports and primary source transcript groupings. **Services:** Library open to the public by appointment.

★15349★
U.S. NATL. PARK SERVICE - SAUGUS IRON WORKS NATL. HISTORIC SITE - LIBRARY (Hist)
244 Central St. Phone: (617)233-0050
Saugus, MA 01906 Frank Studinski, Supv.Pk. Ranger
Founded: 1969. **Staff:** Prof 2; Other 1. **Subjects:** Early iron technology, 17th century life, natural history, Americana. **Holdings:** 500 books. **Services:** Library open to the public for reference use only.

★15350★
U.S. NATL. PARK SERVICE - SCOTTS BLUFF NATL. MONUMENT - LIBRARY (Hist)
Box 427
Gering, NE 69341 Phone: (308)436-4340
Staff: 1. **Subjects:** Westward movement, Oregon Trail. **Holdings:** 850 books and diaries. **Services:** Library open to members.

★15351★
U.S. NATL. PARK SERVICE - SHILOH NATL. MILITARY PARK - LIBRARY (Hist)
Box 61 Phone: (901)689-5275
Shiloh, TN 38376 George A. Reaves, Chf.Interp. & Rsrcs.Mgt.
Founded: 1894. **Subjects:** Battle of Shiloh, American Civil War, military arms and equipment. **Holdings:** 1000 books; 200 unbound periodicals; 150 monographs; 200 letters from Civil War personnel. **Services:** Library open to the public for reference use only.

★15352★
U.S. NATL. PARK SERVICE - SITKA NATL. HISTORICAL PARK - LIBRARY (Hist)
Box 738 Phone: (907)747-6281
Sitka, AK 99835 Gary Candelaria, Chf.Pk. Ranger
Founded: 1965. **Staff:** Prof 1. **Subjects:** Pacific Northwest Coast Indians, arts and crafts, ethnology, archeology, Southeast Alaska history, natural history, Russian American history. **Holdings:** 1150 books; 200 clippings and special papers; 55 tapes; 14 films. **Services:** Library open to the public with permission and by advance request.

★15353★
U.S. NATL. PARK SERVICE - SPRINGFIELD ARMORY NATL. HISTORIC SITE - LIBRARY AND ARCHIVES (Mil)
One Armory Square Phone: (413)734-8551
Springfield, MA 01105 Barbara Higgins Aubrey, Libn.
Staff: Prof 2. **Subjects:** Small armaments, military science, industrial history. **Special Collections:** Manuscript papers of 20th century inventors John C. Garand and John D. Pedersen. **Holdings:** 2000 books; 36 bound periodical volumes; 1300 periodicals; 4 VF drawers of papers, reports, histories, memorabilia; 22 theses; 8000 maps and drawings; 214 reels of microfilm; 181 films; 18,000 photographic images; oral history tapes. **Services:** Copying (limited); library open to the public for reference use only. **Staff:** Stanislaus Skarzynski, Photo.Archv..

★15354★
U.S. NATL. PARK SERVICE - STATUE OF LIBERTY NATL. MONUMENT - LIBRARY (Hist)
Liberty Island
New York, NY 10004 Phone: (212)363-3200
Founded: 1972. **Staff:** Prof 1; Other 2. **Subjects:** Statue of Liberty, Ellis Island, history of American immigration. **Special Collections:** Augustus F. Sherman Collection of Ellis Island photographs (141 prints); Statue of Liberty and Ellis Island Collection (8 VF drawers; 1302 prints); immigrant oral history (400 tapes; 350 transcripts); American Museum of Immigration, Inc. papers (20 boxes). **Holdings:** 1300 books; 6102 photographs; 2141 negatives; 16,400 slides; 3300 aperture cards; 165 microfiche; 65 reports; 20 manuscripts; 30 films; 3 VF drawers of research papers. **Services:** Interlibrary loan; copying; tape and photograph duplication; library open to the public by appointment.

★15355★
U.S. NATL. PARK SERVICE - STONES RIVER NATL. BATTLEFIELD - LIBRARY (Hist)
Old Nashville Hwy.
Rte. 10, Box 495 Phone: (615)893-9501
Murfreesboro, TN 37130 Donald E. Magee, Pk.Supt.
Founded: 1932. **Staff:** 2. **Subjects:** American history, Civil War history, environmental education, National Park Service. **Special Collections:** Regimental files on units participating in battle of Stones River (250). **Holdings:** 400 books; 124 bound periodical volumes; 10 Civil War manuscripts. **Services:** Interlibrary loan; copying; library open to bona fide researchers. **Special Indexes:** Regimental index; map index. **Staff:** Charles Spearman, Hist..

★15356★
U.S. NATL. PARK SERVICE - THEODORE ROOSEVELT NATL. PARK - LIBRARY (Hist)
Medora, ND 58645 Phone: (701)623-4466
Susan Snow, Libn.
Founded: 1947. **Staff:** 2. **Subjects:** Theodore Roosevelt, open range cattle industry, environment and ecology, natural sciences of the area, Fort Union, Knife River Indian Villages. **Holdings:** 2000 books; 57 boxes of unbound pamphlets and manuscripts; 57 boxes of unbound periodicals. **Subscriptions:** 30 journals and other serials. **Services:** Library open to the public for reference use only.

★15357★
U.S. NATL. PARK SERVICE - TIMPANOGOS CAVE NATL. MONUMENT - LIBRARY (Sci-Engr)
R.R. 3, Box 200 Phone: (801)756-5239
American Fork, UT 84003 Scott W. Isaacson, Supv.Pk. Ranger
Founded: 1922. **Subjects:** Speleology, biology, geography, history, natural science, environmental conservation. **Holdings:** 600 books; 300 unbound periodicals. **Services:** Library open to the public for reference use only. **Automated Operations:** Computerized public access catalog. **Staff:** William E. Wellman, Supt..

★15358★
U.S. NATL. PARK SERVICE - VICKSBURG NATL. MILITARY PARK - LIBRARY (Hist)
3201 Clay St. Phone: (601)636-0583
Vicksburg, MS 39180 Mary Davis, Musm.Cur.
Staff: 1. **Subjects:** Vicksburg campaign, U.S.S. Cairo. **Special Collections:** Vicksburg campaign manuscript collections (100). **Holdings:** 600 books; 300 folders of other cataloged items. **Services:** Interlibrary loan; library open to the public by appointment for reference use.

★15359★
U.S. NATL. PARK SERVICE - WALNUT CANYON NATL. MONUMENT - LIBRARY (Biol Sci)
Walnut Canyon Rd.
Flagstaff, AZ 86004 Phone: (602)526-3367
Founded: 1935. **Staff:** 1. **Subjects:** National parks, archeology and natural history of the Southwest. **Holdings:** 700 books. **Services:** Library open to the public for reference use only.

★15360★
U.S. NATL. PARK SERVICE - WESTERN ARCHEOLOGICAL AND CONSERVATION CENTER - MUSEUM COLLECTION REPOSITORY LIBRARY AND ARCHIVES (Biol Sci, Soc Sci)
1415 N. 6th Ave.
Box 41058 Phone: (602)629-6995
Tucson, AZ 85717 W. Richard Horn, Chf.Libn.
Founded: 1953. **Staff:** Prof 2; Other 4. **Subjects:** Archeology, ethnology, and history of the Southwest; natural history - geology, botany, biology. **Special Collections:** Ruins Stabilization reports; George Grant Photograph Collection; unpublished archeological reports. **Holdings:** 17,000 books; 5000 bound periodical volumes; 100 VF drawers of reports, manuscripts, clippings, pamphlets, documents; 170,000 photographic images. **Subscriptions:** 100 journals and other serials. **Services:** Interlibrary loan; copying; library open to the public for reference use only. **Automated Operations:** Computerized cataloging. **Computerized Information Services:** DIALOG Information Services, OCLC. **Networks/Consortia:** Member of FEDLINK. **Staff:** Lynn M. Mitchell, Photo.Archv.; Phil Heikinen, Sys.Spec..

★15361★
U.S. NATL. PARK SERVICE - WESTERN REGIONAL OFFICE - REGIONAL RESOURCES LIBRARY (Hist)
450 Golden Gate Ave., Rm. 14009
Box 36063 Phone: (415)556-4165
San Francisco, CA 94102 Gordon Chappell, Reg.Hist.
Subjects: History, archeology, historic architecture of National Park Service areas in California, Nevada, Arizona, Hawaii, and Guam. **Holdings:** 3500 books; 50 VF drawers of manuscripts, photographs, research files, clippings, and archival materials. **Services:** Copying; library open to the public for reference use only.

★15362★
U.S. NATL. PARK SERVICE - WILLIAM HOWARD TAFT NATL. HISTORIC SITE - LIBRARY (Hist)
2038 Auburn Ave.
Cincinnati, OH 45219
Founded: 1969. **Subjects:** William Howard Taft, National Park Service. **Holdings:** 300 books; William Howard Taft Memorial Association papers. **Services:** Library open to the public with restrictions.

★15363★
U.S. NATL. PARK SERVICE - WUPATKI NATL. MONUMENT - LIBRARY (Hist)
HC 33, Box 444A Phone: (602)527-7040
Flagstaff, AZ 86001 Patricia Crowley, Pk. Ranger/Libn.
Staff: 1. **Subjects:** Archeology, ethnology, natural history. **Holdings:** 1000 books; 200 bound periodical volumes; 800 pamphlets. **Services:** Library open to the public for reference use only.

★15364★
U.S. NATL. PARK SERVICE - YELLOWSTONE ASSOCIATION - RESEARCH LIBRARY (Hist, Sci-Engr)
Box 117 Phone: (307)344-7381
Yellowstone Park, WY 82190 Patricia Eisenbise, Bus.Mgr.
Founded: 1931. **Staff:** 2. **Subjects:** History of Yellowstone area, science. **Special Collections:** Haynes Guides to Yellowstone, 1894-1966; superintendents' reports, 1872 to present. **Holdings:** 11,000 books; 15,000 reprints; 4 drawers of manuscripts; 36 drawers of reprint material and clippings; maps. **Subscriptions:** 65 journals and other serials. **Services:** Interlibrary loan; copying; library open to the public with restrictions. **Staff:** Beverly Whitman, Lib.Techn.; Mary A. Davis, Lib.Techn..

★15365★
U.S. NATL. PARK SERVICE - YOSEMITE NATL. PARK - RESEARCH LIBRARY (Hist, Biol Sci)
Box 577 Phone: (209)372-4461
Yosemite National Park, CA 95389 Mary Vocelka, Res.Libn.
Founded: 1923. **Staff:** 2. **Subjects:** History and natural history of Yosemite National Park. **Holdings:** 9000 books; 900 bound periodical volumes; 36 VF drawers; 150 boxes of historical documents; maps; black and white photographs. **Subscriptions:** 100 journals and other serials. **Services:** Interlibrary loan; library open to the public.

★15366★
U.S. NATL. PARK SERVICE - ZION NATL. PARK - LIBRARY (Biol Sci)
Springdale, UT 84767 Phone: (801)772-3256
Founded: 1930. **Staff:** Prof 1. **Subjects:** Natural sciences, Utah history. **Holdings:** 2700 books. **Services:** Library open to the public for reference use only. **Remarks:** The interpretive, scientific, and historical programs of the park are assisted by the Zion Natural History Association.

★15367★
U.S. NATL. WEATHER SERVICE - CENTRAL REGION HEADQUARTERS - LIBRARY (Sci-Engr)
601 E. 12th St., Rm. 1836 Phone: (816)374-5672
Kansas City, MO 64106 Beverly D. Lambert, Meteorological Techn.
Staff: 1. **Subjects:** Meteorology, climatology, hydrology. **Holdings:** 1708 volumes. **Subscriptions:** 10 journals and other serials. **Services:** Interlibrary loan; copying (limited); library open to the public for reference use only. **Remarks:** The National Weather Service is part of the National Oceanic & Atmospheric Administration of the U.S. Department of Commerce.

U.S. NATL. WEATHER SERVICE - INTERNATIONAL TSUNAMI INFORMATION CENTER
See: International Tsunami Information Center (7076)

★15368★
U.S. NATL. WEATHER SERVICE - WEATHER SERVICE NUCLEAR SUPPORT OFFICE - LIBRARY (Sci-Engr)
2753 S. Highland
Box 14985 Phone: (702)295-1235
Las Vegas, NV 89114 Linda C. Schmith, Off.Serv.Asst.
Founded: 1956. **Staff:** 1. **Subjects:** Meteorology, nuclear science. **Holdings:** 300 volumes. **Subscriptions:** 17 journals and other serials. **Services:** Library not open to the public.

U.S. NAVAL...
See: U.S. Navy - Naval (15375)

U.S. NAVY - DAVID W. TAYLOR NAVAL SHIP RESEARCH AND DEVELOPMENT CENTER
See: David Taylor Research Center (13896)

★15369★
U.S. NAVY - DEPARTMENT LIBRARY (Mil)
Bldg. 44
Washington Navy Yard Phone: (202)433-2386
Washington, DC 20374-0571 Stanley Kalkus, Dir.
Founded: 1800. **Staff:** Prof 6; Other 4. **Subjects:** Naval history, naval art and science, polar studies, naval and military biography, maritime law, naval ordnance, voyages. **Special Collections:** Congressional documents; Reports of the Secretary of the Navy; manuscripts; American Revolution maps and charts; rare books (10,000); Truxtun-Decatur Naval Museum Library. **Holdings:** 200,000 books; 32,000 bound periodical volumes; 10,000 pamphlets; 10,000 reels of microfilm. **Subscriptions:** 400 journals and other serials. **Services:** Interlibrary loan; copying; library open to the public. **Automated Operations:** Computerized cataloging. **Computerized Information Services:** DIALOG Information Services, DTIC, BRS Information Technologies, Faxon, OCLC. **Networks/Consortia:** Member of FEDLINK. **Publications:** Accession List; Subject Bibliographies, both monthly. **Staff:** John E. Vajda, Asst.Libn.; Janice Beattie, Ref.Libn..

★15370★
U.S. NAVY - FLEET ANALYSIS CENTER (FLTAC) - LIBRARY (Sci-Engr)
Naval Weapons Sta., Bldg. 512
Seal Beach
Corona Annex Phone: (714)736-4467
Corona, CA 91720-5000 Carol Stevenson, Libn.
Founded: 1953. **Staff:** Prof 1; Other 1. **Subjects:** Electronics, computers, mathematics, management. **Holdings:** 6000 books; 1400 bound periodical volumes; 450 reels of microfilm. **Subscriptions:** 120 journals and other serials; 5 newspapers. **Services:** Interlibrary loan; library not open to the public. **Computerized Information Services:** Online systems. **Publications:** Accessions List, biweekly - for internal distribution only.

★15371★
U.S. NAVY - FLEET ANTI-SUBMARINE WARFARE TRAINING CENTER, ATLANTIC - TECHNICAL LIBRARY (Sci-Engr, Mil)
Norfolk, VA 23511-6495 Phone: (804)444-1660
D.S. Kolick, Libn.
Founded: 1956. **Staff:** Prof 1; Other 3. **Subjects:** Antisubmarine warfare, equipment, vehicles, oceanography, tactics, antisubmarine warfare foreign capabilities. **Holdings:** 10,000 books; 200 bound periodical volumes. **Subscriptions:** 22 journals and other serials. **Services:** Maintains operation orders and post exercise results on major ASW exercises; maintains retrieval system compatible with similar library in San Diego; U.S. government clearance for secret and cognizant, bureau "Need to Know" certification for individual user within the Department of Defense only. **Publications:** Quarterly Accession List - to military commands.

★15372★
U.S. NAVY - FLEET COMBAT DIRECTION SYSTEMS SUPPORT ACTIVITY - DATA RESOURCE CENTER (Comp Sci)
200 Catalina Blvd.
Point Loma Phone: (619)553-9488
San Diego, CA 92147 Marilyn Soldwisch, Tech.Info.Serv.Spec.
Founded: 1961. **Staff:** 1. **Subjects:** Computer technology, software, hardware, tactical data systems. **Holdings:** 9165 documents and technical reports; 1400 microfiche. **Subscriptions:** 23 journals and other serials. **Automated Operations:** Computerized cataloging. **Publications:** Accessions list.

U.S. NAVY - MARINE CORPS
See: U.S. Marine Corps (15180)

★15373★
U.S. NAVY - NAUTILUS MEMORIAL - SUBMARINE FORCE LIBRARY AND MUSEUM (Mil)
Box 571 Phone: (203)449-3174
Groton, CT 06349-5000 Robert M. Banas, Dir.
Founded: 1964. **Staff:** Prof 4. **Subjects:** Submarine history and memorabilia. **Special Collections:** Submarines and their inventors prior to 1900; U.S. Navy and foreign submarines; biographical file of submariners; U.S. submarine patrol reports of World War II and the Korean War; German submarine patrol reports and war diaries of World War II; histories of General Dynamics/Electric Boat, 1915-1964, and Naval Submarine Base, Groton, 1868 to present; J.P. Holland and Simon Lake papers; U.S. submarine cachets; submarine paintings and photographs. **Holdings:** 8000 books; 50,000 photographs; blueprints; technical manuals; memorabilia. **Subscriptions:** 20 journals and other serials. **Services:** Memorial and museum open to the public on a limited schedule; library open to the public by appointment through curator. **Publications:** Museum brochure. **Staff:** Theresa M. Cass, Archv.Techn..

★15374★
U.S. NAVY - NAVAL ACADEMY - NIMITZ LIBRARY (Mil)
Annapolis, MD 21402 Phone: (301)267-2194
Prof. Richard A. Evans, Lib.Dir.
Founded: 1845. **Staff:** Prof 20; Other 31. **Subjects:** Naval science, naval history, history, international relations, biography, technology, science. **Special Collections:** Benjamin Collection (1150 volumes of early works on electricity); Weidorn Collection (900 volumes containing colorplates); Guggenheim Collection (2950 volumes, including literary first editions); Steichen Collection (10,000 photographs). **Holdings:** 327,000 books; 90,300 bound periodical volumes; 16,000 reels of microfilm; 97,000 government documents. **Subscriptions:** 1778 journals and other serials; 39 newspapers. **Services:** Interlibrary loan; copying; library open to the public with restrictions. **Automated Operations:** Computerized public access catalog, cataloging, and circulation. **Computerized Information Services:** DIALOG Information Services, Pergamon ORBIT InfoLine, Inc., BRS Information Technologies, OCLC. **Networks/Consortia:** Member of FEDLINK. **Publications:** Nimitz Library Newsletter and Guide to the Nimitz Library, both irregular; Serials Holdings List, biennial. **Staff:** John P. Cummings, Assoc.Dir.; Robert A. Lambert, Assoc.Libn., Tech.Serv.; Alice S. Creighton, Asst.Libn., Spec.Coll..

★15375★
U.S. NAVY - NAVAL AEROSPACE MEDICAL INSTITUTE - LIBRARY (Med)
Bldg. 1953, Code 03L Phone: (904)452-2256
Pensacola, FL 32508-5600 Ruth T. Rogers, Adm.Libn.
Founded: 1940. **Staff:** Prof 1; Other 2. **Subjects:** Aviation and aerospace medicine, medical specialties, basic sciences. **Holdings:** 10,000 books; 10,000 bound periodical volumes. **Subscriptions:** 300 journals and other serials. **Services:** Interlibrary loan; library not open to the public.

★15376★
U.S. NAVY - NAVAL AIR DEVELOPMENT CENTER - TECHNICAL INFORMATION BRANCH (Sci-Engr)
Technical Services Dept. Phone: (215)441-3380
Warminster, PA 18974-5000 Dora Huang, Br.Hd.Libn.
Founded: 1944. **Subjects:** Naval aviation, air and ship navigation, aerospace medicine, systems engineering, computer science, crew systems. **Special Collections:** Defense reports; NASA reports. **Holdings:** 30,000 books; 20,000 bound periodical volumes; 400,000 technical reports including microfiche. **Subscriptions:** 650 journals. **Services:** Interlibrary loan; library open to Department of Defense personnel and approved government contractors. **Automated Operations:** Computerized cataloging. **Computerized Information Services:** DIALOG Information Services, DTIC, NASA/RECON, OCLC. **Networks/Consortia:** Member of FEDLINK.

★15377★
U.S. NAVY - NAVAL AIR ENGINEERING CENTER - TECHNICAL LIBRARY, CODE 1115 (Sci-Engr)
Naval Air Engineering Center Phone: (201)323-2893
Lakehurst, NJ 08733 Linda M. Hayes, Adm. & Tech.Sup.Div.Hd.
Founded: 1917. **Staff:** 2. **Subjects:** Aerodynamics, aeronautics, astronautics, aviation medicine, electronics, mechanical engineering, guided missiles, ground support equipment, mathematics. **Special Collections:** NASA reports. **Holdings:** 6000 books; 4000 unbound periodical volumes; 56,000 technical reports. **Subscriptions:** 150 journals and other serials. **Services:** Interlibrary loan; library not open to the public. **Publications:** List of Accessions Received by NAEC Library, bimonthly - for internal distribution only.

★15378★
U.S. NAVY - NAVAL AIR PROPULSION CENTER - TECHNICAL DATA CENTER (Sci-Engr)
Box 7176 Phone: (609)896-5609
Trenton, NJ 08628 Eleanor Reilly, Data Techn.
Founded: 1955. **Staff:** 1. **Subjects:** Aircraft engines and fuels. **Holdings:** 1000 books; 1000 unbound periodical volumes; 7500 technical reports; 1000 government specifications; 1000 microcards. **Subscriptions:** 104 journals and other serials. **Services:** Interlibrary loan; center open to outside users by appointment. **Publications:** Accessions list, 5/year - limited distribution.

★15379★
U.S. NAVY - NAVAL AIR STATION (CA-Alameda) - LIBRARY (Mil)
Bldg. 2, Wing 3 Phone: (415)869-2519
Alameda, CA 94501 Barbara A. Arnott, Adm.Libn.
Founded: 1940. **Staff:** Prof 1; Other 6. **Subjects:** Navy and other military branches, California, careers and education, women and minorities. **Holdings:** 29,200 volumes; 200 bound periodical volumes; 10 VF drawers of pamphlets and clippings; 20 shelves of periodicals; 1200 phonograph records/tapes (mainly popular music). **Subscriptions:** 105 journals and other serials; 10 newspapers. **Services:** Interlibrary loan; copying; library open to the public with visitor permit.

★15380★
U.S. NAVY - NAVAL AIR STATION (CA-Lemoore) - LIBRARY (Mil)
Bldg. 821 Phone: (209)998-3144
Lemoore, CA 93246-5001 Lois C. Gruntorad, Libn.
Founded: 1961. **Staff:** Prof 1; Other 2. **Subjects:** U.S. Navy, biography, history, science. **Holdings:** 20,000 books. **Subscriptions:** 55 journals and other serials; 8 newspapers. **Services:** Interlibrary loan; copying; library open to students, civil employees, and active duty military personnel. **Networks/Consortia:** Member of San Joaquin Valley Library System (SJVLS).

★15381★
U.S. NAVY - NAVAL AIR STATION (CA-North Island) - LIBRARY (Mil, Sci-Engr)
Bldg. 650
Box 29 Phone: (619)437-7041
San Diego, CA 92135 Sharon Nelson, Adm.Libn.
Staff: Prof 1; Other 3. **Subjects:** Naval aviation and history. **Holdings:** 22,000 books; 12 drawers of pamphlets. **Subscriptions:** 100 journals and other serials; 8 newspapers. **Services:** Interlibrary loan; copying; library open to the public by appointment.

★15382★
U.S. NAVY - NAVAL AIR STATION (FL-Jacksonville) - LIBRARY (Mil, Sci-Engr)
Bldg. 620, Box 52 Phone: (904)772-3415
Jacksonville, FL 32212-0052 Paula K. Alston, Libn.
Staff: Prof 1; Other 2. **Subjects:** World War II, naval history and aviation. **Holdings:** 28,000 books; 200 bound periodical volumes; 1200 records; 5 drawers of microfiche. **Subscriptions:** 100 journals and other serials; 12 newspapers. **Services:** Interlibrary loan; library not open to the public.

★15383★
U.S. NAVY - NAVAL AIR STATION (FL-Key West) - LIBRARY (Mil)
Bldg. 514 Phone: (305)292-2116
Key West, FL 33040-5000 Nancy Lee Cannon, Lib.Techn.-in-Charge
Staff: 1. **Subjects:** Naval air history, naval history. **Holdings:** 4000 books. **Subscriptions:** 60 journals and other serials. **Services:** Library not open to the public.

★15384★
U.S. NAVY - NAVAL AIR STATION (FL-Pensacola) - LIBRARY (Mil, Sci-Engr)
Bldg. 633 Phone: (904)452-4362
Pensacola, FL 32508 C.R. Moreland, Hd.Libn.
Staff: Prof 2; Other 4. **Subjects:** Aviation, Navy, military training. **Special Collections:** Historical archives for naval installations in the area. **Holdings:** 25,000 books; 500 bound periodical volumes; 500 reels of microfilm of periodical backfiles; 8 VF drawers of clippings and pamphlets on local history. **Subscriptions:** 135 journals and other serials; 18 newspapers. **Services:** Interlibrary loan (limited); library open to the public by appointment. **Staff:** Judy Walker, Cat..

★15385★
U.S. NAVY - NAVAL AIR STATION (FL-Whiting Field) - LIBRARY (Mil)
Bldg. 1417
Milton, FL 32570 Dawn M. Smith, Libn.
Staff: Prof 1. **Subjects:** Naval aviation, U.S. Navy, United States history. **Holdings:** 13,000 books. **Subscriptions:** 58 journals and other serials; 6 newspapers. **Services:** Interlibrary loan; library not open to the public. **Publications:** Naval Education and Training Program Development Center General Library News Memorandum, monthly - for internal distribution only.

★15386★
U.S. NAVY - NAVAL AIR STATION (ME-Brunswick) - LIBRARY (Mil)
Bldg. 20
Box 21 Phone: (207)921-2639
Brunswick, ME 04011 Judy A. Schwartz, Libn.
Staff: Prof 1; Other 1. **Subjects:** Navy, World War II. **Holdings:** 18,476 books; 283 phonograph records; 67 films. **Subscriptions:** 102 journals and other serials; 13 newspapers. **Services:** Interlibrary loan; library open to the public for reference use only.

★15387★
U.S. NAVY - NAVAL AIR STATION (TN-Memphis) - LIBRARY (Mil, Sci-Engr)
Bldg. S-78 Phone: (901)872-5683
Millington, TN 38054 Jo Ann Rosas, Sr.Lib.Techn.
Staff: Prof 1; Other 5. **Subjects:** Electronics, avionics, aeronautics, navigation, military history and biography, geography. **Special Collections:** "Welcome Aboard" (packets from worldwide military installations). **Holdings:** 49,000 books; 450 bound periodical volumes; 400 phonograph records. **Subscriptions:** 75 journals and other serials; 11 newspapers. **Services:** Interlibrary loan; library open to active and retired military personnel and dependents and civilian employees.

★15388★
U.S. NAVY - NAVAL AIR STATION (TX-Corpus Christi) - LIBRARY (Mil)
Station Library, Bldg. 5 Phone: (512)939-3574
Corpus Christi, TX 78419 Eugene V. Lopez, Libn.
Founded: 1941. **Staff:** 4. **Subjects:** U.S. Navy, World War II, aeronautics. **Holdings:** 22,000 books; 8 VF drawers of clippings, pamphlets, pictures, maps. **Subscriptions:** 140 journals and other serials. **Services:** Interlibrary loan; copying; library open to the public by permission.

★15389★
U.S. NAVY - NAVAL AIR SYSTEMS COMMAND - TECHNICAL INFORMATION & REFERENCE CENTER AIR-5004 (Sci-Engr)
Washington, DC 20361 Phone: (202)692-9006
Pat Stone, Hd.
Founded: 1922. **Staff:** Prof 5; Other 5. **Subjects:** Aeronautics, weapon systems, management, mathematics, materials, electronics. **Special Collections:** Technical manuals; naval aviation. **Holdings:** 14,000 books; 1600 bound periodical volumes; 300,000 technical reports. **Subscriptions:** 300 journals and other serials. **Services:** Interlibrary loan; copying; library serves government agencies and contractors only. **Automated Operations:** Computerized cataloging. **Computerized Information Services:** DIALOG Information Services, DTIC, OCLC. **Networks/Consortia:** Member of FEDLINK. **Publications:** Accessions list, monthly. **Staff:** Marilynn Harned, Ref.Libn..

★15390★
U.S. NAVY - NAVAL AIR TEST CENTER - CENTRAL LIBRARY (Mil, Sci-Engr)
Bldg. 407 Phone: (301)863-1927
Patuxent River, MD 20670 Suzanne M. Ryder, Dir.
Founded: 1943. **Staff:** Prof 2; Other 4. **Subjects:** Engineering, aviation, military science and history, management, computer science, science. **Holdings:** 60,000 books; 15,000 government documents. **Subscriptions:** 400 journals and other serials; 25 newspapers. **Services:** Interlibrary loan; copying; department open only to base personnel and retired military with the exception of a government documents depository that serves all residents of Southern Maryland. **Automated Operations:** Computerized cataloging. **Computerized Information Services:** DIALOG Information Services, BRS Information Technologies, DTIC, NASA/RECON, Government-Industry Data Exchange Program (GIDEP). **Networks/Consortia:** Member of FEDLINK. **Staff:** Carol Sullivan, Libn..

★15391★
U.S. NAVY - NAVAL AMPHIBIOUS BASE (CA-Coronado) - LIBRARY (Mil)
San Diego, CA 92155 Phone: (619)522-4939
Nadine Bangsberg, Adm.Libn.
Founded: 1950. **Staff:** Prof 1; Other 2. **Subjects:** Naval history, amphibious operations, guerrilla warfare, Vietnam, World War II. **Holdings:** 25,000 books; 159 bound periodical volumes; 3000 tapes and phonograph records; 2000 paperbacks. **Subscriptions:** 125 journals and other serials; 8 newspapers. **Services:** Interlibrary loan; library not open to the public. **Publications:** Subject bibliographies; Book List, monthly - for internal distribution only.

★15392★
U.S. NAVY - NAVAL AMPHIBIOUS SCHOOL - JOHN SIDNEY MC CAIN AMPHIBIOUS WARFARE LIBRARY (Mil)
Bldg. 3504 Phone: (804)464-7467
Norfolk, VA 23521-5290 Bernice S. Martin, Dir., Lib.Serv.
Founded: 1965. **Staff:** Prof 2. **Subjects:** Amphibious warfare, military arts and sciences. **Holdings:** 2500 books; 3000 documents. **Subscriptions:** 70 journals and other serials. **Services:** Interlibrary loan; library open to qualified researchers.

★15393★
U.S. NAVY - NAVAL AVIONICS CENTER - TECHNICAL LIBRARY (Sci-Engr)
6000 E. 21st St. Phone: (317)353-7765
Indianapolis, IN 46219-2189 Louise Boyd, Supv.
Founded: 1945. **Subjects:** Mathematics, electronics, electrical engineering, physics, metallurgy, avionics equipment. **Holdings:** 11,000 books; 2000 microfiche; 30,000 technical reports. **Subscriptions:** 450 journals and other serials. **Services:** Interlibrary loan; library not open to the public.

★15394★
U.S. NAVY - NAVAL CIVIL ENGINEERING LABORATORY - LIBRARY (Sci-Engr)
Code L08A Phone: (805)982-4788
Port Hueneme, CA 93043-5003 Bryan Thompson, Adm.Libn.
Founded: 1948. **Staff:** Prof 2; Other 3. **Subjects:** Engineering, ocean engineering, construction materials, environmental protection, energy, soil mechanics. **Holdings:** 16,000 books; 7000 bound periodical volumes; 20,000 technical reports. **Subscriptions:** 485 journals and other serials. **Services:** Interlibrary loan; library open to the public by appointment. **Automated Operations:** Computerized cataloging, acquisitions, serials, and circulation. **Computerized Information Services:** DIALOG Information Services, DTIC. **Networks/Consortia:** Member of FEDLINK, Total Interlibrary Exchange (TIE). **Publications:** NCEL Newsletter - for internal distribution only. **Remarks:** An alternate telephone number is 982-4252.

★15395★
U.S. NAVY - NAVAL COASTAL SYSTEMS CENTER - TECHNICAL INFORMATION SERVICES BRANCH (Sci-Engr, Mil)
Panama City, FL 32407 Phone: (904)234-4381
Myrtle J. Rhodes, Supv.Libn.
Founded: 1945. **Staff:** Prof 4; Other 4. **Subjects:** Mine and ordnance countermeasures, acoustic countermeasures, amphibious operations support, naval diving and salvage support, inshore warfare, coastal technology. **Holdings:** 16,000 books; 5000 bound periodical volumes; 80,000 technical reports; 15,000 microforms. **Subscriptions:** 414 journals and other serials; 5 newspapers. **Services:** Interlibrary loan; copying; SDI; library open to outside users cleared by Security Office. **Automated Operations:** Computerized cataloging, acquisitions, serials, and circulation. **Computerized Information Services:** DIALOG Information Services, DTIC, Integrated Technical Information System (ITIS); internal databases. **Publications:** OFFLINE, monthly. **Special Catalogs:** Computer-generated subject catalogs. **Staff:** B. Householder, Ref./NWPL; Nadine Iferd, Acq./Ser.; D. Hines, Doc.Cat./DTIC; Angelia Whatley, Bk.Cat./INTEL; Schurron Finklea, Circ..

★15396★
U.S. NAVY - NAVAL CONSTRUCTION BATTALION CENTER - LIBRARY (Sci-Engr, Mil)
Code 31L Phone: (805)982-4411
Port Hueneme, CA 93043 Nancy R. Thorne, Libn.
Staff: Prof 1; Other 2. **Subjects:** Naval history, construction, building trades, guerilla warfare, engineering, survival. **Holdings:** 25,000 books; 1000 phonograph records; 52 8mm films. **Subscriptions:** 100 journals and other serials. **Services:** Interlibrary loan; copying; library open to the public

with restrictions. **Publications:** Bibliographies on ethnic groups and women.

★15397★
U.S. NAVY - NAVAL DENTAL RESEARCH INSTITUTE - LIBRARY (Med)
Naval Training Center, Bldg. 1-H Phone: (312)688-5647
Great Lakes, IL 60088-5259 Myra J. Rouse, Libn.
Staff: Prof 1; Other 1. **Subjects:** Clinical dentistry, basic sciences, oral biology, dental research. **Holdings:** 450 books; 1550 bound periodical volumes. **Subscriptions:** 74 journals and other serials. **Services:** Interlibrary loan; library not open to the public.

★15398★
U.S. NAVY - NAVAL EDUCATION AND TRAINING CENTER - LIBRARY SYSTEM (Mil)
Main Library Bldg. 114 Phone: (401)841-3044
Newport, RI 02841-5002 James F. Aylward, Adm.
Founded: 1917. **Staff:** Prof 3; Other 4. **Subjects:** Military and naval science, naval history, technology, curriculum background. **Holdings:** 85,560 books; 250 bound periodical volumes; 10 VF drawers; 1895 microforms; 2500 NAV manuals; 1700 audio programs; military documents. **Subscriptions:** 274 journals and other serials; 28 newspapers. **Services:** Interlibrary loan; copying; library open to the public with Naval Command permission. **Computerized Information Services:** DTIC. **Remarks:** The NETC Library System includes the main library, Officer Candidate School Library, Chaplains School Library, Brig Library, and the Naval Hospital Patients' Library. An alternate telephone number is 841-4352. **Staff:** Robert S. Wessells, Asst.Libn.; Paul Cotsoridis, Hd., Circ. Control.

★15399★
U.S. NAVY - NAVAL ELECTRONICS SYSTEMS ENGINEERING CENTER - SAN DIEGO LIBRARY (Sci-Engr)
4297 Pacific Hwy.
Box 80337 Phone: (619)260-2482
San Diego, CA 92138 C.E. Larsen, Hd.
Founded: 1967. **Staff:** Prof 1; Other 2. **Subjects:** Electronics, engineering, antennas, finance, computers, business administration. **Special Collections:** U.S. Navy Electronic Equipment; DOD Electronic Equipment. **Holdings:** 6000 books; 5000 reports; 11,000 other cataloged items. **Subscriptions:** 123 journals and other serials. **Services:** Interlibrary loan; library open to Department of Defense contractors. **Special Catalogs:** Subject; Equipment nomenclature.

★15400★
U.S. NAVY - NAVAL ENVIRONMENTAL PREDICTION RESEARCH FACILITY - TECHNICAL LIBRARY (Sci-Engr)
Naval Postgraduate School
Annex Bldg. 22
Monterey, CA 93942 Joanne M. May, Libn.
Founded: 1971. **Staff:** Prof 1. **Subjects:** Meteorology. **Holdings:** 2900 books; 3000 bound periodical volumes; 7560 technical reports; 30,000 microfiche. **Subscriptions:** 125 journals and other serials. **Services:** Interlibrary loan; copying; SDI; library open to Department of Defense only. **Computerized Information Services:** DIALOG Information Services. **Publications:** Library Bulletin, biweekly - for internal distribution only.

★15401★
U.S. NAVY - NAVAL EXPLOSIVE ORDNANCE DISPOSAL TECHNOLOGY CENTER - TECHNICAL LIBRARY (Sci-Engr)
Indian Head, MD 20640-5070 Phone: (301)743-4738
Marie O'Mara, Hd.Libn.
Staff: Prof 3; Other 4. **Subjects:** U.S. and foreign ordnance, explosives, underwater equipment, diving. **Special Collections:** Explosive ordnance disposal procedures, tools, and equipment. **Holdings:** 15,000 books; 140,000 documents; 48,000 engineering drawings; 700 photographs; 25,000 microfiche; 60 reels of microfilm. **Subscriptions:** 250 journals and other serials. **Services:** Interlibrary loan; copying; library open to outside users with permission of the head librarian. **Automated Operations:** Computerized cataloging, acquisitions, serials, and circulation. **Computerized Information Services:** DIALOG Information Services, BRS Information Technologies. **Publications:** Accession List, monthly.

★15402★
U.S. NAVY - NAVAL FACILITIES ENGINEERING COMMAND - NORTHERN DIVISION - DESIGN DIVISION LIBRARY (Sci-Engr)
Bldg. 77-L
Philadelphia Naval Base Phone: (215)897-6069
Philadelphia, PA 19112-5094 Patti Ray, Engr.Libn.
Staff: Prof 1; Other 2. **Subjects:** Civil engineering, architectural design, mechanical and electrical engineering, management. **Special Collections:** Navy manuals (200). **Holdings:** 2000 books; 500 unbound reports and documents. **Subscriptions:** 64 journals and other serials. **Services:** Library not open to the public. **Automated Operations:** Computerized cataloging. **Computerized Information Services:** Internal database. **Publications:** Design Library Newsletter, quarterly - for internal distribution only.

★15403★
U.S. NAVY - NAVAL FACILITIES ENGINEERING COMMAND - TECHNICAL LIBRARY (Sci-Engr)
Hoffman Bldg. 2, Stop 14
200 Stovall St. Phone: (202)325-8507
Alexandria, VA 22332-2300 Cynthia K. Neyland, Libn.
Founded: 1941. **Staff:** Prof 1. **Subjects:** Engineering, architecture, management, general science and mathematics. **Holdings:** 15,000 books; 5000 technical reports. **Subscriptions:** 200 journals and other serials. **Services:** Interlibrary loan (excludes NAVFAC publications); copying; library open to Department of Defense personnel. **Automated Operations:** Computerized cataloging. **Computerized Information Services:** DIALOG Information Services, OCLC. **Networks/Consortia:** Member of FEDLINK.

★15404★
U.S. NAVY - NAVAL FACILITIES ENGINEERING COMMAND HISTORIAN (Hist, Mil)
Naval Construction Battalion Ctr. Phone: (805)982-5563
Port Hueneme, CA 93043 Vincent A. Transano, Command Hist.
Subjects: History of the Naval Facilities Engineering Command, the Naval Construction Force (Seabees), and the Navy's Civil Engineering Corps, 1940 to present. **Special Collections:** Records of the Naval Facilities Engineering Command (acquisition, construction, and maintenance of the naval shore establishment in the U.S. and abroad); Naval Construction Force records (operational accomplishments of the combat construction branch of the U.S. Navy); Civil Engineers Corps records (the evolving role of the civil engineer in the U.S. Navy). **Holdings:** 12,000 cubic feet of records. **Services:** Copying; open to the public during business hours.

★15405★
U.S. NAVY - NAVAL HEALTH RESEARCH CENTER - WALTER L. WILKINS BIO-MEDICAL LIBRARY (Med)
Box 85122 Phone: (619)225-6640
San Diego, CA 92138-9174 Mary Aldous, Libn.
Founded: 1959. **Staff:** Prof 1; Other 1. **Subjects:** Environmental and stress medicine, psychiatry, medical information systems, work physiology, biological sciences, social medicine, enhanced performance, sleep research. **Special Collections:** Prisoners of War studies. **Holdings:** 8854 books; 6944 bound periodical volumes; 8670 technical reports; 410 audiotapes. **Subscriptions:** 250 journals and other serials. **Services:** Interlibrary loan; library open to the public with restrictions. **Automated Operations:** Computerized cataloging. **Computerized Information Services:** DIALOG Information Services, BRS Information Technologies, MEDLARS, OCLC, DTIC; OnTyme Electronic Message Network Service (electronic mail service). **Publications:** Periodicals holding list.

★15406★
U.S. NAVY - NAVAL HISTORICAL CENTER - OPERATIONAL ARCHIVES (Mil, Hist)
Bldg. 57, Washington Navy Yard Phone: (202)433-3170
Washington, DC 20374 Bernard F. Cavalcante, Dir.
Staff: Prof 8; Other 2. **Subjects:** U.S. Naval history, naval operations, naval archives, naval biography. **Special Collections:** CNO records; oral history interview transcripts; China repository; aviation histories; materials relating to World War II and post-war operations. **Holdings:** 10,000 feet of records and documents, including 1200 feet of action and operational reports, 1941-1953; 900 feet of naval command war diaries, 1941-1953; 570 feet of miscellaneous records and publications, 1931-1950. **Services:** Copying (limited); reading room open to the public. **Publications:** List of open collections and publications - available on request. **Staff:** Regina T. Akers, Archv.; Ariana A. Jacob, Archv.; Kathleen M. Lloyd, Archv.; George W. Pryce, III, Archv.; Kathleen L. Rohr, Archv.; Judith W. Short, Archv.; Richard M. Walker, Archv..

★15407★
U.S. NAVY - NAVAL HISTORICAL CENTER - PHOTOGRAPHIC SECTION (Aud-Vis)
Washington Navy Yard
Washington, DC 20374-0571 Phone: (202)433-2765
Staff: Prof 2. **Subjects:** Visual aspects of naval history, including weapons, wars, U.S. and foreign naval ships. **Holdings:** 200,000 photographs, prints, drawings, posters. **Services:** Copying; section open to the public.

★15408★
U.S. NAVY - NAVAL HOSPITAL (CA-Camp Pendleton) - MEDICAL LIBRARY (Med)
Camp Pendleton, CA 92055 Phone: (619)725-1322
Deborah G. Batey, Med.Libn.
Founded: 1949. **Staff:** Prof 1; Other 1. **Subjects:** General medicine, nursing, family practice. **Holdings:** 1000 books; 4800 bound periodical volumes; 350 AV programs. **Subscriptions:** 200 journals and other serials. **Services:** Interlibrary loan; copying; library open to the public for reference use only. **Computerized Information Services:** NLM. **Networks/Consortia:** Member of Pacific Southwest Regional Medical Library Service. **Publications:** Medical Library News, bimonthly - for internal distribution only.

★15409★
U.S. NAVY - NAVAL HOSPITAL (CA-Oakland) - MEDICAL LIBRARY (Med)
8750 Mountain Blvd. Phone: (415)639-2031
Oakland, CA 94627-5000 Harriet V. Cohen, Adm.Libn.
Staff: Prof 2; Other 2. **Subjects:** Medicine, nursing, paramedical sciences, psychiatry. **Holdings:** 8000 books; 10,000 bound periodical volumes. **Subscriptions:** 400 journals and other serials. **Services:** Interlibrary loan; library not open to the public. **Computerized Information Services:** MEDLINE, BRS Information Technologies. **Networks/Consortia:** Member of Pacific Southwest Regional Medical Library Service. **Publications:** Serials List, annual; New Book List, monthly - to department heads. **Staff:** Robin L. Holloway, Med.Libn..

★15410★
U.S. NAVY - NAVAL HOSPITAL (CA-San Diego) - MEDICAL AND GENERAL LIBRARIES (Med)
San Diego, CA 92134 Phone: (619)532-7950
Marilyn Schwartz, Chf.Libn.
Founded: 1923. **Staff:** Prof 3; Other 2. **Subjects:** Medicine, nursing, dentistry, hospital administration. **Special Collections:** Meyer Wiener Collection on Ophthalmology. **Holdings:** 13,792 books; 13,198 bound periodical volumes. **Subscriptions:** 573 journals. **Services:** Interlibrary loan; copying; SDI; library open to military personnel. **Computerized Information Services:** DIALOG Information Services, MEDLINE, BRS Information Technologies; OnTyme Electronic Message Network Service (electronic mail service). **Networks/Consortia:** Member of Pacific Southwest Regional Medical Library Service. **Publications:** List of journal subscriptions, annual; recent acquisitions, quarterly; Library Newsletter, quarterly. **Formed by the merger of:** Thompson Medical Library and General Library. **Staff:** Jan B. Dempsey, Ref.Libn..

★15411★
U.S. NAVY - NAVAL HOSPITAL (FL-Jacksonville) - MEDICAL LIBRARY† (Med)
Jacksonville, FL 32214 Bettye W. Stilley, Med.Libn.
Founded: 1942. **Staff:** Prof 1. **Subjects:** Medicine. **Holdings:** 1500 books; 2400 bound periodical volumes; 500 other cataloged items; 1500 cassette tapes. **Subscriptions:** 162 journals and other serials. **Services:** Interlibrary loan; library not open to the public. **Computerized Information Services:** MEDLARS.

★15412★
U.S. NAVY - NAVAL HOSPITAL (FL-Orlando) - MEDICAL LIBRARY (Med)
Orlando, FL 32813 Phone: (407)646-4959
Nancy B. Toole, Med.Libn.
Staff: Prof 1. **Subjects:** Clinical medicine. **Holdings:** 800 books; 500 bound periodical volumes. **Subscriptions:** 86 journals and other serials. **Services:** Interlibrary loan; library not open to the public.

★15413★
U.S. NAVY - NAVAL HOSPITAL (FL-Pensacola) - MEDICAL LIBRARY (Med)
Pensacola, FL 32512-5000 Phone: (904)452-6635
Juan E. Terry, Med.Libn.
Staff: Prof 1; Other 1. **Subjects:** Medicine, allied health sciences. **Holdings:** 5000 books; 15,000 bound periodical volumes. **Subscriptions:** 228 journals and other serials. **Services:** Interlibrary loan; library not open to the public.

★15414★
U.S. NAVY - NAVAL HOSPITAL (Guam) - MEDICAL LIBRARY (Med)
Box 7747 Phone: (671)344-9250
FPO San Francisco, CA 96630-1649 Alice E. Hadley, Med.Libn.
Founded: 1954. **Staff:** Prof 1. **Subjects:** Medicine, nursing, dentistry, surgery, obstetrics. **Holdings:** 1800 books; 1300 bound periodical volumes. **Subscriptions:** 115 journals and other serials. **Services:** Interlibrary loan; copying; library open to medical professionals.

★15415★
U.S. NAVY - NAVAL HOSPITAL (IL-Great Lakes) - MEDICAL LIBRARY (Med)
Bldg. 200-H Phone: (312)688-4601
Great Lakes, IL 60088 Susan L. Thompson, Med.Libn.
Founded: 1945. **Staff:** Prof 1. **Subjects:** Medicine, surgery, dentistry, nursing. **Holdings:** 2150 books; 5075 bound periodical volumes. **Subscriptions:** 185 journals and other serials. **Services:** Interlibrary loan; library not open to the public. **Computerized Information Services:** BRS Information Technologies. **Networks/Consortia:** Member of Greater Midwest Regional Medical Library Network.

★15416★
U.S. NAVY - NAVAL HOSPITAL (MD-Bethesda) - EDWARD RHODES STITT LIBRARY (Med)
Bethesda, MD 20814-5011 Phone: (202)295-1184
Jerry Meyer, Adm.Libn.
Founded: 1902. **Staff:** Prof 2; Other 2. **Subjects:** Medicine and allied health sciences. **Special Collections:** Pastoral Counseling Collection (500 volumes); Video Cassette Collection (950 tapes). **Holdings:** 65,000 volumes; 800 audiotapes. **Subscriptions:** 650 journals and other serials. **Services:** Interlibrary loan; library not open to the public. **Automated Operations:** Computerized cataloging. **Computerized Information Services:** MEDLINE, BRS Information Technologies.

★15417★
U.S. NAVY - NAVAL HOSPITAL (NC-Camp Lejeune) - MEDICAL LIBRARY (Med)
Camp Lejeune, NC 28542 Phone: (919)451-4076
Betty Frazelle, Lib.Techn.
Founded: 1941. **Staff:** 1. **Subjects:** Medicine and allied health sciences. **Holdings:** 2110 books; 4964 bound periodical volumes. **Subscriptions:** 151 journals and other serials. **Services:** Interlibrary loan; library not open to the public.

★15418★
U.S. NAVY - NAVAL HOSPITAL (PA-Philadelphia) - MEDICAL LIBRARY (Med)
17th & Pattison Aves.
Philadelphia, PA 19145-5199 Giovina Cavacini, Libn.
Founded: 1917. **Staff:** Prof 1. **Subjects:** Medicine, allied health sciences. **Holdings:** 6000 books; 8000 bound periodical volumes; Audio-Digest tapes. **Subscriptions:** 275 journals and other serials. **Services:** Interlibrary loan; copying; library open to the public with restrictions. **Computerized Information Services:** NLM. **Networks/Consortia:** Member of Greater Northeastern Regional Medical Library Program.

★15419★
U.S. NAVY - NAVAL HOSPITAL (RI-Newport) - MEDICAL LIBRARY (Med)
Cypress & Third Sts. Phone: (401)841-4512
Newport, RI 02840 Winifred M. Jacome, Med.Lib.Techn.
Staff: 1. **Subjects:** Medicine and allied health sciences, dentistry. **Holdings:** 1500 books; Audio-Digest tapes, 1984 to present. **Subscriptions:** 159 journals and other serials. **Services:** Interlibrary loan; copying; library open to the public for reference use only. **Networks/Consortia:** Member of Association of Rhode Island Health Sciences Librarians (ARIHSL), North Atlantic Health Science Libraries (NAHSL).

★15420★
U.S. NAVY - NAVAL HOSPITAL (TN-Memphis) - GENERAL AND MEDICAL LIBRARY (Med)
Millington, TN 38054 Phone: (901)872-5846
G.R. Counts, Libn.
Founded: 1942. **Staff:** Prof 1. **Subjects:** Dentistry, medicine, nursing. **Holdings:** 5511 volumes. **Subscriptions:** 62 journals and other serials. **Services:** Library open to staff and their dependents. **Computerized Information Services:** Access to online systems. **Networks/Consortia:** Member of Association of Memphis Area Health Sciences Libraries (AMAHSL).

★15421★
U.S. NAVY - NAVAL HOSPITAL (TX-Corpus Christi) - MEDICAL LIBRARY (Med)
Corpus Christi, TX 78419 Phone: (512)939-3863
Dorothy Reichenstein, Med.Libn.
Founded: 1941. **Staff:** 2. **Subjects:** Medicine, surgery, nursing, allied health sciences. **Holdings:** Figures not available. **Subscriptions:** 74 journals and other serials. **Services:** Interlibrary loan; library not open to the public. **Networks/Consortia:** Member of Coastal Bend Health Sciences Library Consortium.

★15422★
U.S. NAVY - NAVAL HOSPITAL (VA-Portsmouth) - MEDICAL LIBRARY (Med)
Portsmouth, VA 23708 Phone: (804)398-5385
Suad Jones, Med.Libn.
Staff: Prof 1; Other 2. **Subjects:** Medicine, dentistry, nursing, allied health sciences. **Holdings:** 6751 books; 13,846 bound periodical volumes; 1126 cartridges of microfilm. **Subscriptions:** 573 journals and other serials. **Services:** Interlibrary loan; copying; SDI; library open to the public for reference use only on request. **Computerized Information Services:** MEDLINE, OCLC, BRS Information Technologies; OnTyme Electronic Message Network Service (electronic mail service). **Networks/Consortia:** Member of Tidewater Health Sciences Libraries (THSL). **Publications:** Medical Library/News/Acquisitions/Publications, irregular - for internal distribution only.

★15423★
U.S. NAVY - NAVAL HOSPITAL (WA-Bremerton) - MEDICAL LIBRARY (Med)
Bremerton, WA 98314 Phone: (206)478-9316
Jane Easley, Libn.
Founded: 1947. **Staff:** 1. **Subjects:** Medicine, nursing, administration. **Holdings:** 1300 books; 2700 bound periodical volumes. **Subscriptions:** 185 journals and other serials. **Services:** Interlibrary loan; copying; library open to qualified medical personnel. **Computerized Information Services:** NLM. **Publications:** Bibliographies.

★15424★
U.S. NAVY - NAVAL INSTITUTE - ORAL HISTORY OFFICE (Mil, Hist)
Annapolis, MD 21402 Phone: (301)268-6110
Paul Stillwell, Dir., Oral Hist.
Founded: 1969. **Staff:** Prof 3. **Subjects:** Naval biography, Coast Guard biography, naval aviation. **Special Collections:** Admiral Nimitz Collection; POLARIS interviews; WAVE interviews; early black naval officers. **Holdings:** 160 bound volumes containing 85,000 pages of transcripts; tapes of 200 individual memoirs. **Services:** Library open to researchers. **Remarks:** Copies of some volumes available for loan by mail; copies of all bound volumes are also available in the special collections at the Nimitz Library of the U.S. Naval Academy, Annapolis, MD and the Naval Historical Center, Washington Navy Yard, Washington, DC.

★15425★
U.S. NAVY - NAVAL INSTITUTE - REFERENCE & PHOTOGRAPHIC LIBRARY (Mil)
Annapolis, MD 21402 Phone: (301)268-6110
Patty M. Maddocks, Dir.
Staff: 4. **Subjects:** U.S. Navy - ships, aircraft, personalities; American Revolution; Vietnam War; foreign ships and personalities. **Special Collections:** James C. Fahey Ship and Aircraft Collection of U.S. Navy; "Our Navy" collection. **Holdings:** 4000 books; 100 bound periodical volumes; 100 oral history materials; 100 bound volumes of proceedings. **Subscriptions:** 103 journals and other serials. **Services:** Copying; library open to the public. **Publications:** U.S. Naval Institute Proceedings; Naval History Magazine. **Special Indexes:** Proceedings Index; Navy Oral History Index.

★15426★
U.S. NAVY - NAVAL INTELLIGENCE SUPPORT CENTER - INFORMATION SERVICES DIVISION (Mil)
4301 Suitland Rd.
Code 63 Phone: (202)763-1606
Washington, DC 20390 Stephanie V. Williams, Hd.
Founded: 1944. **Staff:** Prof 5; Other 20. **Subjects:** Military intelligence, science and technology. **Special Collections:** Russian Language technical book and manual collection (4500). **Holdings:** 5000 books; 50,000 reports; 50,000 documents. **Subscriptions:** 1000 journals and other serials; 30 newspapers. **Services:** Interlibrary loan; division not open to the public. **Automated Operations:** Computerized cataloging, acquisitions, serials, and circulation. **Computerized Information Services:** DIALOG Information Services, Pergamon ORBIT InfoLine, Inc., BRS Information Technologies. **Publications:** Weekly Accession Bulletin; Library Happenings, irregular; Periodicals Collection, updated annually.

★15427★
U.S. NAVY - NAVAL MEDICAL COMMAND - NAVAL DENTAL SCHOOL - NAVAL DENTAL CLINIC - WILLIAM L. DARNALL LIBRARY (Med)
Bethesda, MD 20814-5077 Phone: (202)295-0080
Patricia A. Evans, Chf., Lrng.Rsrc.Div.
Staff: Prof 1. **Subjects:** Dentistry, medicine. **Holdings:** 8500 books. **Subscriptions:** 85 journals and other serials. **Services:** Interlibrary loan; copying (limited); library open to command personnel and others with authorization from the director of the Naval Dental School.

★15428★
U.S. NAVY - NAVAL MEDICAL RESEARCH INSTITUTE - INFORMATION SERVICES DIVISION (Med)
Bethesda, MD 20814-5055 Phone: (202)295-2186
Rosemary B. Coskey, Adm.Libn.
Founded: 1942. **Staff:** Prof 1; Other 2. **Subjects:** Infectious diseases, casualty care, hyperbaric medicine, experimental surgery, transplantation, military medicine. **Special Collections:** Naval Medical Research Institute Reports, 1943 to present. **Holdings:** 5000 books. **Subscriptions:** 250 journals and other serials. **Services:** Interlibrary loan; copying; SDI; division open to the public for reference use only. **Automated Operations:** Computerized cataloging. **Computerized Information Services:** DIALOG Information Services, OCLC, BRS Information Technologies; internal database. **Networks/Consortia:** Member of FEDLINK, Interlibrary Users Association (IUA). **Publications:** Summaries of Research; Union List of Serials, both annual.

★15429★
U.S. NAVY - NAVAL MILITARY PERSONNEL COMMAND - TECHNICAL LIBRARY (Bus-Fin, Mil)
NMPC-013DD
Arlington Annex, Rm. 1403 Phone: (202)694-2073
Washington, DC 20370 Rufus E. Lassiter, Libn.
Founded: 1946. **Staff:** Prof 2. **Subjects:** Military personnel administration, education, psychology, management, statistics. **Holdings:** 4000 books; 146 VF drawers of technical reports. **Subscriptions:** 350 journals and other serials. **Services:** Interlibrary loan; copying; library open to naval personnel and other government agencies. **Staff:** Steven E. Norris, Asst.Libn..

★15430★
U.S. NAVY - NAVAL OBSERVATORY - MATTHEW FONTAINE MAURY MEMORIAL LIBRARY (Sci-Engr)
34th and Massachusetts Ave., N.W. Phone: (202)653-1499
Washington, DC 20392-5100 Brenda G. Corbin, Libn.
Founded: 1843. **Staff:** Prof 1; Other 1. **Subjects:** Astronomy, astrophysics, celestial mechanics, geophysics, mathematics, physics. **Special Collections:** Rare books, 1482-1800 (astronomy, navigation, mathematics; 800 volumes). **Holdings:** 75,000 volumes; slides; microfiche; maps; manuscripts; archives. **Subscriptions:** 200 journals and other serials. **Services:** Interlibrary loan; copying (both limited); library open to graduate students. **Automated Operations:** Computerized cataloging. **Computerized Information Services:** OCLC, DIALOG Information Services. **Networks/Consortia:** Member of FEDLINK. **Publications:** Naval Observatory Publications - restricted distribution; Acquisitions List, quarterly.

★15431★
U.S. NAVY - NAVAL OCEAN SYSTEMS CENTER - TECHNICAL LIBRARIES (Sci-Engr)
Code 964 Phone: (619)225-6171
San Diego, CA 92152-5000 Joan Buntzen, Hd., Tech.Libs.Br.
Founded: 1977. **Staff:** Prof 7; Other 15. **Subjects:** Electronics, physics, ocean engineering, underwater ordnance, marine biology, the Arctic,

communications, oceanography, artificial intelligence, robotics. **Special Collections:** Scientific Datalink (technical reports on artificial intelligence; microfiche). **Holdings:** 60,000 books; 60,000 bound periodical volumes; 100,000 technical reports. **Subscriptions:** 1500 journals and other serials. **Services:** Interlibrary loan; copying; SDI; libraries open to the public on a need-to-know basis. **Automated Operations:** Computerized cataloging, acquisitions, circulation, and serials. **Computerized Information Services:** DIALOG Information Services, BRS Information Technologies, Pergamon ORBIT InfoLine, Inc., DATALIB, OCLC, VU/TEXT Information Services, NASA/RECON, WILSONLINE, TECH DATA, DTIC. **Networks/Consortia:** Member of FEDLINK. **Publications:** List of periodical holdings, annual; New Publications, biweekly; Current Awareness, monthly. **Remarks:** Technical libraries include holdings of the Topside Technical Library Branch, the Bayside Technical Library Branch, and the Hawaii library. **Staff:** Kathy Wright, Hd., Bayside Br..

★15432★
U.S. NAVY - NAVAL OCEANOGRAPHIC OFFICE - MATTHEW FONTAINE MAURY OCEANOGRAPHIC LIBRARY (Sci-Engr)
NSTL Phone: (601)688-4017
Bay St. Louis, MS 39522 Kay Miller, Supv.Libn.
Founded: 1871. **Staff:** Prof 2; Other 3. **Subjects:** Oceanography - biological, chemical, geological, physical; ocean engineering; cartography; photogrammetry; meteorology. **Special Collections:** Domestic and foreign sailing directions; International Hydrographic Bureau publications and oceanographic expeditions; Naval Oceanographic Office publications. **Holdings:** 100,000 books, bound periodical volumes, documents, translations, pamphlets; 10,000 microforms. **Subscriptions:** 550 journals and other serials. **Services:** Interlibrary loan; copying; library open to qualified research workers. **Automated Operations:** Computerized cataloging. **Computerized Information Services:** BRS Information Technologies, Pergamon ORBIT InfoLine, Inc., DTIC, NASA/RECON, DIALOG Information Services. **Networks/Consortia:** Member of FEDLINK. **Publications:** Accessions List, monthly - for internal distribution only. **Staff:** Ann Loomis, Libn..

★15433★
U.S. NAVY - NAVAL ORDNANCE STATION - LIBRARY BRANCH (Sci-Engr)
Indian Head, MD 20640-5000 Phone: (301)743-4742
Charles F. Gallagher, Libn.
Staff: Prof 1; Other 5. **Subjects:** Explosives and propellants, missiles and rockets, aerospace technology, chemistry, chemical engineering, management. **Holdings:** 24,000 books; 5500 bound periodical volumes; 60,000 domestic and foreign research reports; 7400 microcards; microfiche. **Subscriptions:** 400 journals and other serials. **Services:** Interlibrary loan; branch not open to the public. **Automated Operations:** Computerized cataloging and serials. **Computerized Information Services:** DTIC, DIALOG Information Services, LS/2000; LINX Courier (electronic mail service). **Networks/Consortia:** Member of FEDLINK. **Publications:** Accessions Bulletin - for internal distribution only.

★15434★
U.S. NAVY - NAVAL ORDNANCE STATION - TECHNICAL LIBRARY (Sci-Engr, Mil)
50 D, MDS 50 Phone: (502)364-5662
Louisville, KY 40214-5001 Elizabeth T. Miles, Libn.
Staff: 2. **Subjects:** Naval ordnance, engineering. **Holdings:** 1900 books; 27 bound periodical volumes; 1945 technical reports; 45,500 government specifications. **Services:** Interlibrary loan; library open to the public with restrictions. **Remarks:** An alternate telephone number is 364-5667.

★15435★
U.S. NAVY - NAVAL POSTGRADUATE SCHOOL - DUDLEY KNOX LIBRARY (Sci-Engr, Mil)
Monterey, CA 93943-5002 Phone: (408)646-2341
Paul Spinks, Dir. of Libs.
Staff: Prof 15; Other 18. **Subjects:** Engineering, physical sciences, naval science, operations research, administrative sciences, international affairs. **Special Collections:** Christopher Buckley, Jr. Library (naval and maritime history; 8000 volumes). **Holdings:** 180,000 books; 84,500 bound periodical volumes; 230 videtapes; programs; 188,000 research reports; 19,500 pamphlets; 422,500 microforms. **Subscriptions:** 1807 journals and other serials; 20 newspapers. **Services:** Interlibrary loan; copying; SDI; library open to the public with some facilities limited to authorized personnel. **Automated Operations:** Computerized cataloging, acquisitions, and serials. **Computerized Information Services:** DIALOG Information Services, BRS Information Technologies, RLIN, NEXIS, NASA/RECON, CIRC II, DTIC; SABIRS III (internal database); OnTyme Electronic Message Network Service (electronic mail service). **Networks/Consortia:** Member of CLASS, Monterey Bay Area Cooperative Library System (MOBAC), SOUTHNET. **Publications:** New on the Shelf, monthly; Library Periodicals: Current Subscriptions and Earlier Holdings, annual; This is Your Library, annual - all for internal distribution only. **Staff:** Terry Britt, Assoc.Dir. of Libs.; Sharon Serzan, Hd., Acq.Div.; Bobbie Carr, Hd., Bibliog. Control Div.; Roger Martin, Hd., Rd.Serv.Div.; Norma Dobay, Hd., Res.Rpt.Div..

★15436★
U.S. NAVY - NAVAL REGIONAL MEDICAL CLINIC - MEDICAL LIBRARY (Med)
Quantico, VA 22134 Phone: (703)640-2887
Mrs. A.D. Walker, Libn.
Staff: 2. **Subjects:** Medicine. **Holdings:** 54 books; 63 medical and nursing journals. **Subscriptions:** 45 journals and other serials. **Services:** Library not open to the public.

★15437★
U.S. NAVY - NAVAL RESEARCH LABORATORY - RUTH H. HOOKER TECHNICAL LIBRARY (Sci-Engr)
Code 2620 Phone: (202)767-2357
Washington, DC 20375-5000 Laurie E. Stackpole, Libn.
Founded: 1927. **Staff:** Prof 9; Other 22. **Subjects:** Physics, chemistry, electronics, materials, systems. **Holdings:** 150,000 books and bound periodical volumes; 650,000 reports on microfiche; 350,000 paper reports. **Subscriptions:** 2000 journals and other serials. **Services:** Interlibrary loan; copying; library open to the public with prior arrangement. **Automated Operations:** Computerized cataloging and circulation. **Computerized Information Services:** DIALOG Information Services, STN International. **Networks/Consortia:** Member of FEDLINK. **Publications:** Your Library as a Research Tool; Holdings List of Periodicals in the Ruth H. Hooker Library of the Naval Research Laboratory (book). **Remarks:** An alternate telephone number is 767-2354. **Staff:** Fred Rettenmaier, Ref.Libn.; Eileen Pickenpaugh, Res.Cons.; Doris Folen, Hd., Doc.Sect.; Patricia Cook, ILL.

★15438★
U.S. NAVY - NAVAL RESEARCH LABORATORY - UNDERWATER SOUND REFERENCE DETACHMENT - TECHNICAL LIBRARY (Sci-Engr)
755 Gatlin Ave.
Box 568337 Phone: (407)857-5238
Orlando, FL 32856-8337 Marge Tarnowski, Libn.
Founded: 1947. **Staff:** 1. **Subjects:** Underwater sound, electroacoustics, electronics, mathematics, physics. **Holdings:** 5100 books; 1200 bound periodical volumes; 10,165 documents; 1500 documents on microfiche. **Subscriptions:** 80 journals and other serials. **Services:** Library not open to the public. **Publications:** USRD Library Bulletin - for internal distribution only.

★15439★
U.S. NAVY - NAVAL SCHOOL - CIVIL ENGINEER CORPS OFFICERS - MOREELL LIBRARY (Sci-Engr)
Port Hueneme, CA 93043 Phone: (805)982-3241
Deborah Gunia, Lib.Dir.
Founded: 1946. **Staff:** Prof 1; Other 2. **Subjects:** Engineering and construction management, economic analysis, PERT and CPM, civil engineering. **Special Collections:** Admiral Ben Moreell Collection (1100 volumes and correspondence). **Holdings:** 7982 books; 370 bound periodical volumes; 7468 reports and 7500 texts; 4500 course materials; 300 microfiche. **Subscriptions:** 209 journals and other serials; 8 newspapers. **Services:** Interlibrary loan; copying; library open to the public upon written request. **Networks/Consortia:** Member of Total Interlibrary Exchange (TIE).

★15440★
U.S. NAVY - NAVAL SCHOOL OF HEALTH SCIENCES - LIBRARY (Bus-Fin)
Bldg. 141
Bethesda, MD 20814-5033 Phyllis R. Blum, Libn.
Subjects: Accounting, business management, health care administration, personnel management, medical sociology. **Holdings:** 4000 books; 1000 bound periodical volumes; 165 American Hospital Association publications. **Subscriptions:** 130 journals and other serials. **Services:** Interlibrary loan; library not open to the public. **Computerized Information Services:** MEDLINE, BRS Information Technologies, OCLC.

★15441★
U.S. NAVY - NAVAL SEA SYSTEMS COMMAND - LIBRARY DOCUMENTATION BRANCH (SEA 09B31) (Sci-Engr)
Rm. 1S28, National Center, Bldg. 3 Phone: (202)692-3349
Washington, DC 20362 Claudia M. Devlin, Hd.Libn.
Founded: 1976. **Staff:** Prof 2; Other 6. **Subjects:** Engineering - marine, electrical, mechanical, nuclear; naval architecture and ordnance; marine propulsion; acoustics; shipbuilding. **Special Collections:** Complete sets of RINA Transactions and U.S. Naval Institute Proceedings. **Holdings:** 25,000 books; 7000 bound periodical volumes; 500,000 research and development reports; 110,000 technical manuals; 60,000 microforms. **Subscriptions:** 500 journals and other serials. **Services:** Interlibrary loan; copying; SDI; library open to navy contractors, authorized Department of Defense components, and federal libraries. **Automated Operations:** Computerized cataloging. **Computerized Information Services:** OCLC, DIALOG Information Services, BRS Information Technologies, Pergamon ORBIT InfoLine, Inc., NEXIS. **Networks/Consortia:** Member of FEDLINK. **Publications:** FOCUS (list of acquisitions), monthly - to authorized Department of Defense components. **Staff:** Elmer Long, Hd., Tech.Rpt., Indexing, Doc.Sect..

★15442★
U.S. NAVY - NAVAL SHIP SYSTEMS ENGINEERING STATION HEADQUARTERS - TECHNICAL LIBRARY (Sci-Engr)
Bldg. 619, Naval Base Phone: (215)897-7078
Philadelphia, PA 19112 Kathleen Gross, Libn.
Founded: 1979. **Staff:** Prof 1; Other 4. **Subjects:** Engineering - marine, mechanical, electrical; chemistry; metallurgy. **Holdings:** 125,000 books and Navy manuals; microforms. **Subscriptions:** 250 journals and other serials. **Services:** Interlibrary loan; library not open to the public. **Computerized Information Services:** Information Handling Services (IHS).

★15443★
U.S. NAVY - NAVAL SHIPYARD (CA-Long Beach) - TECHNICAL LIBRARY (Sci-Engr)
Code 202.4, Bldg. 300, Rm. 358 Phone: (213)547-6515
Long Beach, CA 90822-5099 Mari S. Zeoli, Libn.
Staff: Prof 1; Other 5. **Subjects:** Naval architecture, ship repair and maintenance, electronic equipment, mechanical equipment, industrial management, occupational safety. **Special Collections:** Naval Sea Systems Command Technical Publications. **Holdings:** 8000 books; 110,000 technical manuals and reports; 150,000 microfilm copies of military specifications and standards; 1000 microfiche; 1500 manufacturers' catalogs; 4000 American Society for Testing and Materials (ASTM) specifications; government reports relating to U.S. Fleet. **Subscriptions:** 107 journals and other serials. **Services:** Interlibrary loan; library open to Department of Defense contractors. **Publications:** Acquisitions list, irregular.

★15444★
U.S. NAVY - NAVAL SHIPYARD (CA-Mare Island) - SCIENCE AND TECHNOLOGY LIBRARY (Sci-Engr)
Code 202.13, Stop T-4 Phone: (707)646-4306
Vallejo, CA 94592-5100 Jane Oswitt, Supv.Libn.
Founded: 1945. **Staff:** Prof 2; Other 1. **Subjects:** Naval shipbuilding and repair; occupational safety and health; chemistry; engineering - nuclear, civil, mechanical, electrical; materials science; physics. **Holdings:** 11,000 books; 1200 bound periodical volumes; 6800 technical reports; 12,000 specifications and standards. **Subscriptions:** 200 journals and other serials. **Services:** Interlibrary loan; copying (limited); library open to the public by appointment. **Automated Operations:** Computerized cataloging. **Computerized Information Services:** BRS Information Technologies, DIALOG Information Services, DTIC, OCLC; DOCLINE, OPTIMIS (electronic mail services). **Networks/Consortia:** Member of FEDLINK, Pacific Southwest Regional Medical Library Service. **Publications:** Accessions list, monthly; periodical list, irregular. **Remarks:** An alternate telephone number is 646-2532.

★15445★
U.S. NAVY - NAVAL SHIPYARD (HI-Pearl Harbor) - TECHNICAL LIBRARY (Sci-Engr)
Code 244.5, Box 400 Phone: (808)474-0023
Pearl Harbor, HI 96860-5350 Lincoln H.S. Yu, Libn.
Founded: 1951. **Staff:** Prof 1; Other 9. **Subjects:** Engineering, naval shipbuilding. **Holdings:** 40,000 volumes. **Services:** Library not open to the public.

★15446★
U.S. NAVY - NAVAL SHIPYARD (NH-Portsmouth) - TECHNICAL LIBRARY (Sci-Engr)
Code 863 Phone: (603)438-2769
Portsmouth, NH 03801 Josephine Rafferty, Tech.Libn.
Founded: 1947. **Staff:** Prof 1; Other 1. **Subjects:** Submarines, naval architecture, marine and nuclear engineering, mathematics, noise and vibration, electrical engineering, materials, management. **Special Collections:** Society of Naval Architects and Marine Engineers Transactions, 1893 to present (complete set). **Holdings:** 20,000 books and bound periodical volumes; 13,000 technical reports; 4 VF drawers of reprints and pamphlets; 350 reels of microfilm; videotapes. **Subscriptions:** 180 journals and other serials. **Services:** Interlibrary loan; copying; library open to the public with restrictions.

★15447★
U.S. NAVY - NAVAL SHIPYARD (PA-Philadelphia) - TECHNICAL LIBRARY (Sci-Engr)
Philadelphia Naval Base Phone: (215)897-2568
Philadelphia, PA 19112 Alice R. Murray, Tech.Libn.
Founded: 1946. **Staff:** Prof 1. **Subjects:** Naval science and architecture; engineering - marine, electrical, mechanical; electronics; mathematics. **Special Collections:** Shipbuilding; naval engineering. **Holdings:** 10,000 books; 100 bound periodical volumes; 61,000 technical reports; 5000 microfiche; 2000 cartridges of microfilm. **Subscriptions:** 203 journals and other serials. **Services:** Interlibrary loan (limited to Department of Defense); library not open to the public.

★15448★
U.S. NAVY - NAVAL SHIPYARD (SC-Charleston) - TECHNICAL LIBRARY (Sci-Engr)
Naval Base Phone: (803)743-4071
Charleston, SC 29408 Leola Gadsden, Lib.Techn.
Founded: 1946. **Staff:** 4. **Subjects:** Naval engineering and architecture, electronics, management, ordnance, mathematics. **Holdings:** 1000 books; 100,000 technical manuals; 1000 reports and pamphlets. **Subscriptions:** 60 periodicals. **Services:** Interlibrary loan; library not open to the public.

★15449★
U.S. NAVY - NAVAL SHIPYARD (VA-Norfolk) - TECHNICAL LIBRARY (Sci-Engr)
Code 202.3, Bldg. 29, 2nd Fl. Phone: (804)396-5674
Portsmouth, VA 23709-5000 Patsy J. Scott, Supv.Lib.Techn.
Subjects: Engineering, management, mathematics, physics, chemistry, mechanical trades. **Holdings:** 6000 books; 2500 reports; 50,000 technical manuals; 40 reels of magnetic tape. **Subscriptions:** 200 journals and other serials. **Services:** Interlibrary loan; library not open to the public.

★15450★
U.S. NAVY - NAVAL STATION LIBRARY (CA-San Diego) (Mil)
Naval Station, Box 224
San Diego, CA 92135-5224 Phone: (619)235-1403
Staff: Prof 2; Other 2. **Subjects:** Naval history, World War II. **Special Collections:** Auxiliary Library Service Collection for Naval Officers (professional reading). **Holdings:** 27,000 books; 400 bound periodical volumes. **Subscriptions:** 169 journals and other serials; 19 newspapers. **Services:** Interlibrary loan; copying; library open to the public for reference use only, circulation limited to active or retired military and Station staff civilians and their authorized dependents. **Publications:** Current Subscriptions & Periodicals Holdings List, annual; Classified List of Periodicals, annual; Selected Acquistions List/Naval Station General Library Bulletin, bimonthly; bibliographies; reading lists. **Remarks:** An alternate telephone number is 235-2420. **Staff:** Marion N. Steele, Asst.Libn..

★15451★
U.S. NAVY - NAVAL STATION LIBRARY (FL-Mayport) (Mil)
Box 235 Phone: (904)246-5393
Mayport, FL 32228 Elizabeth K. Fahnert, Dir.
Staff: Prof 2; Other 1. **Subjects:** Naval history, military art and science, navigation, fiction and nonfiction. **Holdings:** 13,000 books. **Subscriptions:** 57 journals and other serials; 8 newspapers. **Services:** Interlibrary loan; library not open to the public. **Staff:** Joseph Pickett, Sr., Asst.Libn..

★15452★
U.S. NAVY - NAVAL SUBMARINE MEDICAL RESEARCH LABORATORY - MEDICAL LIBRARY (Med)
Naval Submarine Base New London
Box 900 Phone: (203)449-3629
Groton, CT 06340 Elaine M. Gaucher, Libn.
Founded: 1945. **Staff:** Prof 1; Other 1. **Subjects:** Submarine medicine, diving, physiology, psychology. **Holdings:** 5300 books; 8000 bound periodical volumes; 7000 documents; 1400 microforms; 1200 internal reports. **Subscriptions:** 165 journals and other serials. **Services:** Interlibrary loan; copying; library open to doctors, hospital staff, corpsmen, and researchers. **Automated Operations:** Computerized circulation. **Computerized Information Services:** BRS Information Technologies. **Networks/Consortia:** Member of Connecticut Association of Health Science Libraries (CAHSL). **Publications:** Submarine Medical Research Laboratory Reports.

★15453★
U.S. NAVY - NAVAL SUPPLY CENTER - TECHNICAL DIVISION - TECHNICAL LIBRARY (Sci-Engr, Mil)
Bldg. 322
937 North Harbor Dr., Code 103 Phone: (619)235-2450
San Diego, CA 92132-5068 Ivy Seaberry, Lib.Techn.
Founded: 1950. **Staff:** 1. **Subjects:** Electronics; ordnance; weapons; fire control systems; engineering - automotive, electrical, mechanical. **Holdings:** 25,355 books and bound periodical volumes; 3136 reels of microfilm; 550,600 aperture cards; 35,700 microfiche. **Subscriptions:** 10 journals and other serials. **Services:** Library open to the public.

★15454★
U.S. NAVY - NAVAL SUPPORT ACTIVITY - LIBRARY (Hum)
Bldg. 47
7500 Sand Point Way, N.E. Phone: (206)526-3577
Seattle, WA 98115 Bob Kinsedahl, Libn.
Founded: 1932. **Staff:** Prof 1. **Subjects:** Nonfiction, fiction, science, art, mystery, science fiction. **Holdings:** 10,000 volumes; pamphlets. **Subscriptions:** 22 journals and other serials. **Services:** Library serves station personnel, retired military personnel, and dependents.

★15455★
U.S. NAVY - NAVAL SURFACE WARFARE CENTER - TECHNICAL LIBRARY (Sci-Engr, Mil)
Mail Code E23 Phone: (703)663-8994
Dahlgren, VA 22448 Dr. J. Marshal Hughes, II, Hd.
Founded: 1953. **Staff:** Prof 14; Other 19. **Subjects:** Mathematics, electronics, physics, weapons systems, management, chemistry, materials. **Special Collections:** Independent Research and Development Navy/Industry Collection. **Holdings:** 220,000 books; 8000 bound periodical volumes; 11,200 periodical volumes on microfilm; 250,000 documents. **Subscriptions:** 553 journals and other serials. **Services:** Interlibrary loan; copying; SDI; translations; library open to government agencies and contractors. **Automated Operations:** Computerized cataloging. **Computerized Information Services:** DIALOG Information Services, NASA/RECON, Integrated Technical Information System (ITIS), DTIC; internal database. **Publications:** Accession Lists, biweekly; SDI, daily. **Remarks:** The Technical Library is composed of the Dahlgren, VA and Silver Spring, MD libraries. Figures represent the combined holdings of the libraries. **Formerly:** Naval Surface Weapons Center - Center Library.

★15456★
U.S. NAVY - NAVAL SURFACE WARFARE CENTER - WHITE OAK LIBRARY (Sci-Engr, Mil)
10901 New Hampshire Ave. Phone: (202)394-1922
Silver Spring, MD 20903-5000 Katharine R. Wallace, Supv.Libn.
Founded: 1944. **Staff:** Prof 11; Other 10. **Subjects:** Naval ordnance, explosives, aerodynamics, plastics, magnetic materials, optics, mathematics. **Holdings:** 50,000 books; 750 periodical titles; 160 periodical titles on microfilm. **Services:** Interlibrary loan; copying (limited); library open to other government agencies and contractors. **Automated Operations:** Computerized cataloging. **Computerized Information Services:** DIALOG Information Services, Pergamon ORBIT InfoLine, Inc., BRS Information Technologies, NASA/RECON, Integrated Technical Information System (ITIS), DTIC; internal database. **Staff:** Charlotte Mullinix, Libn.; Catherine Lee, Libn.; Elizabeth Tucker, Libn..

★15457★
U.S. NAVY - NAVAL TEST PILOT SCHOOL - RESEARCH LIBRARY (Sci-Engr, Mil)
Naval Air Test Center Phone: (301)863-4411
Patuxent River, MD 20670 Robert B. Richards, Hd. of Academics
Founded: 1950. **Staff:** Prof 1; Other 1. **Subjects:** Aeronautical engineering, aircraft flight testing, propulsion, aircraft systems, space engineering. **Special Collections:** Aero engineering; flight testing; atmospheric propulsion. **Holdings:** 750 books; 5500 reports. **Subscriptions:** 10 journals and other serials. **Services:** Library open to U.S. government agencies.

★15458★
U.S. NAVY - NAVAL TRAINING CENTER - LIBRARY (Mil)
Bldg. 177 Phone: (619)225-5470
San Diego, CA 92133-3000 Raul P. Fernandez, Jr., Lib.Supv.
Founded: 1924. **Staff:** Prof 1; Other 3. **Subjects:** Naval art and science. **Special Collections:** Naval history; U.S. Naval Institute Proceedings, 1800 to present. **Holdings:** 36,000 books; 18,180 microforms. **Subscriptions:** 127 journals and other serials; 11 newspapers. **Services:** Interlibrary loan; copying; library open to the public with restrictions.

★15459★
U.S. NAVY - NAVAL TRAINING SYSTEMS CENTER - TECHNICAL INFORMATION CENTER (Mil, Sci-Engr)
TIC, Bldg. 2068
Orlando, FL 32813-7100 Phone: (407)646-5637
Founded: 1946. **Staff:** Prof 2; Other 3. **Subjects:** Training simulation technology, military training methodology, human factors, engineering, equipment and systems, mathematics and computers, ordnance, physics. **Special Collections:** Technical reports and handbooks for simulators and training devices (13,000); human factors reports relating to theory, design, and use of training devices. **Holdings:** 4800 books; 1100 bound periodical volumes; 28,000 documents and manuals; 1100 microforms; specifications; standards. **Subscriptions:** 200 journals and other serials. **Services:** Interlibrary loan (limited); center not open to the public. **Computerized Information Services:** BRS Information Technologies, DTIC. **Networks/Consortia:** Member of FEDLINK. **Publications:** Technical Spotlight, monthly; annual periodical list - both for internal distribution only. **Remarks:** Center operated by University of Central Florida. **Staff:** T.R. Pfarrer, Asst.Libn..

★15460★
U.S. NAVY - NAVAL UNDERWATER SYSTEMS CENTER - NEW LONDON TECHNICAL LIBRARY (Sci-Engr, Mil)
Bldg. 80
New London, CT 06320 David L. Hanna, Hd.Libn.
Founded: 1970. **Staff:** Prof 5; Other 3. **Subjects:** Underwater acoustics, ordnance, surveillance; antisubmarine warfare. **Holdings:** 35,000 volumes; 425,000 technical documents; 425,000 government reports on microfiche. **Subscriptions:** 505 journals and other serials. **Services:** Interlibrary loan; library not open to the public. **Automated Operations:** Computerized cataloging. **Computerized Information Services:** DIALOG Information Services, Pergamon ORBIT InfoLine, Inc., DTIC, BRS Information Technologies, Library Management & Retrieval System (LMARS). **Networks/Consortia:** Member of FEDLINK. **Publications:** Periodical holding list. **Staff:** J. Ned Shaw, Libn.; Charles Logan, Cat.; Jerome Barner, Ref.; Barbara Campbell, Bks. & Per..

★15461★
U.S. NAVY - NAVAL UNDERWATER SYSTEMS CENTER - NEWPORT TECHNICAL LIBRARY (Sci-Engr, Mil)
Bldg. 103 Phone: (401)841-4338
Newport, RI 02841-4421 Mary N. Barravecchia, Hd.Libn.
Staff: Prof 3. **Subjects:** Antisubmarine warfare, undersea warfare and surveillance, underwater ordnance, target detection. **Holdings:** 14,000 books; 425,000 technical documents. **Subscriptions:** 525 journals and other serials. **Services:** Interlibrary loan; library not open to the public. **Automated Operations:** Computerized cataloging. **Computerized Information Services:** DIALOG Information Services, Pergamon ORBIT InfoLine, Inc., DTIC, BRS Information Technologies, Library Management & Retrieval System (LMARS). **Publications:** Technical reports. **Staff:** Philip Tomposki, Ref.Libn.; Carolyn Prescott, Libn..

★15462★
U.S. NAVY - NAVAL WAR COLLEGE - LIBRARY (Mil, Hist)
Newport, RI 02841-5010 Phone: (401)841-2641
Robert E. Schnare, Dir.
Founded: 1884. **Staff:** Prof 13; Other 19. **Subjects:** Military art and science, naval art and science, international relations, international law, economics, history. **Holdings:** 159,000 books and bound periodical volumes; 82,000

classified documents; 16,000 periodical volumes in microform. **Subscriptions:** 514 journals and other serials. **Services:** Interlibrary loan; library open to the public with permission. **Automated Operations:** Computerized cataloging and ILL. **Computerized Information Services:** OCLC, WILSONLINE, DTIC, DIALOG Information Services. **Networks/Consortia:** Member of FEDLINK, NELINET, Consortium of Rhode Island Academic and Research Libraries, Inc. (CRIARL). **Publications:** Faculty Guide; Research Guide, both annual. **Staff:** Marilyn D. Curtis, Hd., Tech.Serv.; Murray L. Bradley, Hd., Rd.Serv.; Doris B. Ottaviano, Hd., Ref.Br.; Ann H. Hall, Hd., Cat.Br./On-line Proj.Mgr.; Robin Lima, ILL.

★15463★
U.S. NAVY - NAVAL WEAPONS CENTER - LIBRARY DIVISION (Sci-Engr, Mil)
Mail Code 3433 Phone: (619)939-2507
China Lake, CA 93555 Elizabeth Babcock, Hd., Lib.Div.
Founded: 1946. **Staff:** Prof 8; Other 13. **Subjects:** Rockets, missiles, propellants, explosives, chemistry, physics, electronics, aerodynamics, parachutes. **Holdings:** 30,000 books; 50,000 bound periodical volumes; 180,000 reports; 600,000 microfiche of technical reports. **Subscriptions:** 900 journals and other serials. **Services:** Interlibrary loan; restricted access to library. **Automated Operations:** Computerized serials, document retrieval, and catalog production. **Computerized Information Services:** DIALOG Information Services, DTIC, RLIN, NASA/RECON. **Networks/Consortia:** Member of FEDLINK, CLASS. **Publications:** Accession List of Technical Reports, bimonthly; Periodicals Table of Contents List, weekly; Periodicals List, annual; Guide to the Use of NWC Technical Library; Accession List of Books, monthly. **Staff:** Craig Pelz, Hd., Info.Serv.Br.; Elizabeth Shanteler, Hd., Ctr.Lib.; Mary Coraggio, Hd., Tech.Serv.Br..

★15464★
U.S. NAVY - NAVAL WEAPONS STATION - LIBRARY (Sci-Engr, Mil)
Bldg. 705 Phone: (804)887-4726
Yorktown, VA 23691-5000 Eleanor Lacy Sorokatch, Libn.
Founded: 1961. **Staff:** Prof 1. **Subjects:** Naval mines, missiles, torpedoes, corrosion, depth charges, explosives, underwater weapons, engineering. **Holdings:** 10,000 books; 5000 technical reports. **Subscriptions:** 135 journals and other serials. **Services:** Interlibrary loan; copying; library open to qualified persons by permission. **Publications:** Accession Lists, monthly.

★15465★
U.S. NAVY - NAVAL WEAPONS SUPPORT CENTER - LIBRARY (Sci-Engr, Mil)
Code 016 Phone: (812)854-3143
Crane, IN 47522 Aaron Pettiford, Supv.Tech.Info.Spec.
Founded: 1958. **Staff:** Prof 1; Other 8. **Subjects:** Explosives, ammunition, pyrotechnics, engineering, military science, electronics. **Special Collections:** History file (2000). **Holdings:** 21,000 books; 360,000 aperture cards; 1500 reels of microfilm; 1350 technical reports. **Subscriptions:** 520 journals and other serials; 15 newspapers. **Services:** Interlibrary loan; library not open to the public. **Computerized Information Services:** DTIC, BRS Information Technologies, DIALOG Information Services, OCLC. **Networks/Consortia:** Member of Four Rivers Area Library Services Authority.

★15466★
U.S. NAVY - NAVY PERSONNEL RESEARCH & DEVELOPMENT CENTER - LIBRARY (Soc Sci)
Code 231 Phone: (619)553-7841
San Diego, CA 92152-6800 Barbara Busch, Libn.
Founded: 1953. **Staff:** Prof 1; Other 3. **Subjects:** Industrial and social psychology, education, computer technology, human factors, management science. **Holdings:** 8500 books; 3700 bound periodical volumes; 30,000 technical reports; 6000 microfiche. **Subscriptions:** 450 journals and other serials. **Services:** Interlibrary loan; copying; SDI; library open to public at librarian's discretion. **Automated Operations:** Computerized cataloging and circulation. **Computerized Information Services:** DIALOG Information Services, OCLC; internal database. **Networks/Consortia:** Member of FEDLINK. **Publications:** Accessions list, weekly; periodical list, annual. **Remarks:** Alternate telephone numbers are 553-7842 and 553-7846.

★15467★
U.S. NAVY - OFFICE OF THE CHIEF OF NAVAL RESEARCH - LIBRARY (Biol Sci, Sci-Engr, Mil)
Ballston Tower, No. 1
800 N. Quincy St. Phone: (202)696-4415
Arlington, VA 22217 Dorcas E. Tabor, Lib.Techn.
Founded: 1948. **Staff:** 2. **Subjects:** Biological and medical sciences, physical and chemical sciences, naval and marine sciences, social sciences. **Holdings:** 20,000 periodicals; reference books. **Subscriptions:** 483 journals and other serials; 5 newspapers. **Services:** Interlibrary loan; library not open to the public. **Computerized Information Services:** DIALOG Information Services, OCLC. **Networks/Consortia:** Member of FEDLINK. **Remarks:** Library is a branch of the Naval Research Laboratory Library.

★15468★
U.S. NAVY - OFFICE OF THE GENERAL COUNSEL - LAW LIBRARY (Law, Mil)
Crystal Plaza 5, Rm. 450 Phone: (202)692-7378
Washington, DC 20360-5110 Mary Kathryn Wilson, Hd.Libn.
Founded: 1949. **Staff:** Prof 2. **Subjects:** Government contracts, civilian personnel law. **Holdings:** 30,000 books; 1400 bound periodical volumes. **Services:** Interlibrary loan; copying (both limited); library open to federal government employees. **Automated Operations:** Computerized cataloging. **Computerized Information Services:** JURIS, WESTLAW. **Networks/Consortia:** Member of FEDLINK. **Staff:** Mary Williams, Asst.Libn..

★15469★
U.S. NAVY - OFFICE OF THE JUDGE ADVOCATE GENERAL - LAW LIBRARY (Law, Mil)
Code 64.3
Hoffman Bldg. No. 2
200 Stovall St. Phone: (202)325-9565
Alexandria, VA 22332-2400 Richard S. Barrows, Libn.
Staff: Prof 3; Other 2. **Subjects:** Law - military, international, criminal. **Special Collections:** Opinions of the Judge Advocate General (unpublished); Decisions of the U.S. Navy Court of Military Review (unpublished). **Holdings:** 50,000 volumes; 29 VF drawers. **Subscriptions:** 95 journals and other serials. **Services:** Interlibrary loan; library open to the public by appointment. **Computerized Information Services:** OCLC, WESTLAW; OPTIMIS (electronic mail service). **Remarks:** Supports 300 field libraries. **Staff:** Sue Roach, Hd., Ref./Tech.Serv.; Erika Teal, Hd., Fld.Lib. Procurement.

★15470★
U.S. NAVY - PACIFIC MISSILE TEST CENTER - TECHNICAL LIBRARY (Sci-Engr)
Code 1018 Phone: (805)989-8156
Point Mugu, CA 93042 JoAnn Van Reenan, Libn.
Founded: 1948. **Staff:** Prof 1; Other 1. **Subjects:** Aeronautics, mathematics, electronics, astronautics, meteorology, oceanography, naval history, physics, radar technology. **Holdings:** 20,000 books; 9000 bound periodical volumes; 1000 reels of microfilm. **Subscriptions:** 100 journals and other serials. **Services:** Interlibrary loan; library open to Department of Defense personnel and others with librarian's permission. **Networks/Consortia:** Member of Total Interlibrary Exchange (TIE). **Publications:** Bibliographies.

★15471★
U.S. NAVY - PACIFIC SUBMARINE MUSEUM - LIBRARY (Mil)
Naval Submarine Base Phone: (808)423-1341
Pearl Harbor, HI 96860 Harvey Gray, Exec.Dir.
Founded: 1979. **Staff:** 1. **Subjects:** Submarine history and warfare, World Wars I and II, oceanographic studies, salvage and rescue. **Special Collections:** World War II patrol reports for U.S. submarines; special files on all U.S. submarines and related vessels. **Holdings:** 1000 books; 500 bound periodical volumes; reports; manuscripts and investigations; film; microfilm. **Services:** Library open to the public by appointment for reference use only.

★15472★
U.S. NAVY - PUGET SOUND NAVAL SHIPYARD - ENGINEERING LIBRARY (Mil)
Code 202-5 Phone: (206)476-2767
Bremerton, WA 98314-5000 Carol Campbell, Libn.
Founded: 1936. **Staff:** Prof 1. **Subjects:** Engineering, naval architecture, management, computer science, Navy ships and history. **Holdings:** 12,000 books; 10,000 industry standards. **Subscriptions:** 281 journals and other serials. **Services:** Interlibrary loan; library not open to the public. **Computerized Information Services:** DIALOG Information Services.

★15473★
U.S. NAVY - REGIONAL DATA AUTOMATION CENTER - TECHNICAL LIBRARY (Sci-Engr, Comp Sci)
Bldg. 143, Washington Navy Yard Phone: (202)433-5700
Washington, DC 20374 Joanne H. Johnson, Libn.
Founded: 1964. **Staff:** 1. **Subjects:** Electronic data processing, management, data communications, mathematics, naval science. **Holdings:**

5400 books; 218 bound periodical volumes; 3006 technical documents; 113 microfiche. **Subscriptions:** 186 journals and other serials. **Services:** Interlibrary loan; copying; library open to Department of Defense employees. **Automated Operations:** Computerized circulation. **Special Catalogs:** Catalog of project documentation (computer printout).

★15474★
U.S. NAVY - STRATEGIC SYSTEMS PROJECT OFFICE - TECHNICAL LIBRARY (Sci-Engr, Mil)
Washington, DC 20376-5002 Phone: (202)697-2852
June R. Gable, Tech.Lib.Br.Hd.
Staff: Prof 1; Other 2. **Subjects:** Missile technology, mathematics, electronics, solid propellants, management. **Holdings:** 2500 books; 40,000 technical reports; 4 VF drawers of pamphlets. **Subscriptions:** 175 journals and other serials. **Services:** Interlibrary loan; library open to persons with appropriate security clearance and need-to-know. **Automated Operations:** Computerized cataloging. **Computerized Information Services:** DIALOG Information Services, OCLC. **Networks/Consortia:** Member of FEDLINK.

★15475★
U.S. NAVY - SUPERVISOR OF SHIPBUILDING, CONVERSION AND REPAIR - TECHNICAL LIBRARY (Sci-Engr, Mil)
U.S. Naval Station, Code 253
32nd St. & Harbor Dr.
Box 119 Phone: (619)235-2455
San Diego, CA 92136-5119 Patricia Parker, Lib.Techn.
Founded: 1960. **Staff:** Prof 2; Other 2. **Subjects:** Ship systems, ordnance, electronics, engineering. **Holdings:** 100,000 books and bound periodical volumes; 500 reels of microfilm of military and federal specifications; 300 reels of microfilm of design information files; manuals and textbooks. **Subscriptions:** 10 journals and other serials. **Services:** Interlibrary loan; library open to federal personnel and government contractors.

★15476★
U.S. NEWS & WORLD REPORT - LIBRARY (Publ)
2400 N St., N.W. Phone: (202)955-2350
Washington, DC 20037 Kathleen Trimble, Lib.Dir.
Staff: Prof 14; Other 6. **Subjects:** Government, politics, history, economics, law. **Holdings:** 10,000 books; 4000 volumes of congressional hearings and reports; 10,000 vertical files; 6600 newspaper clipping files; 9000 biographical files; 50 drawers of microforms of newspapers and periodicals. **Subscriptions:** 300 journals and other serials; 30 newspapers. **Services:** Interlibrary loan; library not open to the public. **Computerized Information Services:** DIALOG Information Services, VU/TEXT Information Services, DataTimes, Dow Jones News/Retrieval, BRS Information Technologies, WILSONLINE, Washington Alert Service, Finsbury Data Services Ltd., Datasolve Ltd., NEXIS. **Publications:** Library guide with periodicals list (online) - for internal distribution only. **Special Indexes:** Index to U.S. News & World Report (printed, through 1979; card, 1980-1986; online, 1987 to present). **Staff:** Kate Forsyth, Asst.Dir.; Judith Katzung, Newspaper File Mgr..

U.S. NUCLEAR REGULATORY COMMISSION
See: Nuclear Regulatory Commission (10558)

U.S. OFFICE OF EDUCATION - REGION VI - EDUCATIONAL RESOURCES INFORMATION CENTER
See: Dallas Public Library - J. Erik Jonsson Central Library - History and Social Sciences Division (4007)

U.S. OFFICE OF PERSONNEL MANAGEMENT
See: Office of Personnel Management (10639)

★15477★
U.S. OFFICE OF TECHNOLOGY ASSESSMENT - INFORMATION CENTER (Plan, Sci-Engr)
Congress of the United States Phone: (202)226-2160
Washington, DC 20510 Martha M. Dexter, Mgr., Info.Serv.
Staff: Prof 2; Other 3. **Subjects:** Technology assessment, future, science policy. **Holdings:** 6000 books; 300,000 microfiche; 1000 documents in VF drawers. **Subscriptions:** 500 journals and other serials; 6 newspapers. **Services:** Interlibrary loan; copying; SDI; center open to the public with restrictions. **Automated Operations:** Computerized cataloging, acquisitions, serials, and circulation. **Computerized Information Services:** DIALOG Information Services, MEDLINE, Library of Congress Information System (LOCIS), House Information Systems (HIS); OnTyme Electronic Message Network Service (electronic mail service). **Networks/Consortia:** Member of FEDLINK. **Publications:** FOCUS (newsletter), biweekly. **Special Indexes:** Quotation, a computerized index of Office of Technology Assessment publications. **Remarks:** The Office of Technology Assistance is under the direction of the U.S. Congress. **Staff:** Gail M. Kouril, Asst.Mgr., Info.Serv..

★15478★
U.S. OLYMPIC COMMITTEE - SPORTS MEDICINE AND SCIENCE INFORMATION CENTER (Med)
Sports Medicine Div.
Dept. of Education Services
1750 E. Boulder St. Phone: (719)632-5551
Colorado Springs, CO 80909 Mary Margaret Newsom, Dir., Educ.Serv.
Staff: Prof 2; Other 2. **Subjects:** Sports medicine - exercise physiology, biomechanics, sports psychology, vision and dental screening, athletic training, injury prevention and treatment, health maintenance and conditioning, coaching science. **Holdings:** 3500 books; unbound periodicals; 2000 reprints; sports rulebooks; U.S. Olympic Committee central files of photographs, slides, and 16mm films; N.G.B. constitutions and by-laws. **Subscriptions:** 300 journals and other serials; 5 newspapers. **Services:** Interlibrary loan; copying; SDI; center open to the public for reference use only. **Automated Operations:** Computerized cataloging, serials, ILL, and indexes. **Computerized Information Services:** Pergamon ORBIT InfoLine, Inc., DIALOG Information Services, BRS Information Technologies; SMILE (internal database). **Networks/Consortia:** Member of Bibliographical Center for Research, Rocky Mountain Region, Inc. (BCR), Colorado Council of Medical Librarians, Peaks and Valleys (Medical) Library Consortium. **Publications:** SportsMediscope (newsletter), quarterly. **Staff:** Kristine M. Golian, Libn..

★15479★
U.S. PATENT & TRADEMARK OFFICE - SCIENTIFIC LIBRARY (Sci-Engr)
Crystal Plaza Bldg. 3
2021 Jefferson Davis Hwy. Phone: (703)557-2955
Arlington, VA 22202 Henry Rosicky, Prog.Mgr.
Founded: 1836. **Staff:** Prof 19; Other 37. **Subjects:** Technology, applied science. **Special Collections:** Foreign patents (12 million in numerical arrangement). **Holdings:** 250,000 books; 87,800 bound periodical volumes; 58,790 titles on microfiche; 430 titles on microfilm; U.S. Government documents depository (selective). **Subscriptions:** 1200 journals and other serials. **Services:** Interlibrary loan; copying; library open to the public for reference use only. **Automated Operations:** Computerized cataloging, serials, and circulation. **Computerized Information Services:** DIALOG Information Services, OCLC, Pergamon ORBIT InfoLine, Inc., BRS Information Technologies, MEDLINE, Integrated Technical Information System (ITIS), DTIC. **Networks/Consortia:** Member of FEDLINK. **Remarks:** The Patent & Trademark Office is part of the U.S. Department of Commerce. **Staff:** Kay H. Melvin, Chf., Sci.Lit.Div.; Barry Balthrop, Hd., Foreign Patents.

U.S. PEACE CORPS
See: Peace Corps (11127)

U.S. PHARMACEUTICAL & NUTRITION GROUP
See: Bristol-Myers Company - U.S. Pharmaceutical & Nutrition Group (1855)

★15480★
U.S. POSTAL SERVICE - LIBRARY (Bus-Fin)
475 L'Enfant Plaza, S.W. Phone: (202)245-4021
Washington, DC 20260 Jane F. Kennedy, Gen.Mgr.
Founded: 1955. **Staff:** Prof 5; Other 7. **Subjects:** Management, law, engineering, economics, marketing, electronic data processing. **Special Collections:** History and operation of U.S. Postal Service. **Holdings:** 57,000 volumes; 12,000 microforms; 44,000 government documents; pictures on 263 subjects; VF material on 673 subjects. **Subscriptions:** 850 journals and other serials. **Services:** Interlibrary loan; copying; library open to the public for reference use only. **Computerized Information Services:** DIALOG Information Services, LEXIS, BRS Information Technologies, WESTLAW, National Planning Data Corporation (NPDC), RLIN, NEXIS, Dun & Bradstreet Corporation, Dow Jones News/Retrieval. **Staff:** Catherine Turner, Sr.Libn..

★15481★
U.S. PRESIDENTIAL LIBRARIES - DWIGHT D. EISENHOWER LIBRARY (Hist)
S.E. Fourth St. Phone: (913)263-4751
Abilene, KS 67410 Dr. John E. Wickman, Dir.
Founded: 1961. **Staff:** Prof 25; Other 10. **Subjects:** Dwight D. Eisenhower - life, presidency, military career; World War II. **Special Collections:** Papers of Dwight D. Eisenhower and his associates. **Holdings:** 24,000 books; 19

million pages of manuscripts; 12,000 government documents; 23,000 items in VF drawers; 250,000 photographs; 2205 hours of sound recordings; 4055 reels of microfilm; 675,000 feet of motion picture film. **Subscriptions:** 75 journals and other serials. **Services:** Interlibrary loan (limited); copying; library open to the public on written application to the director. **Publications:** Overview (newsletter), quarterly - available on request; Dwight D. Eisenhower: A Selected Bibliography of Periodical and Dissertation Literature. **Special Catalogs:** List of Holdings, biennial - available on request; registers to manuscript collections. **Remarks:** Maintained by the National Archives & Records Administration. **Staff:** James W. Leyerzapf, Supv.Archv..

★15482★
U.S. PRESIDENTIAL LIBRARIES - FRANKLIN D. ROOSEVELT LIBRARY (Hist)
259 Albany Post Rd. Phone: (914)229-8114
Hyde Park, NY 12538 William R. Emerson, Dir.
Founded: 1941. **Staff:** Prof 12; Other 10. **Subjects:** The New Deal, 1933-1940; World War II; Franklin D. Roosevelt; American naval history, 1775-1945; American political and social history, 1900-1950. **Special Collections:** Papers of Franklin and Eleanor Roosevelt and various associates; American children's books, 18th-19th centuries; Franklin D. Roosevelt's naval history library, manuscripts, and ship models; Americana and Hudson Valley local history books and manuscripts; Archives of the Livingston Family, 1680-1880; papers of Henry Morgenthau Jr. **Holdings:** 45,000 books; 87,000 pamphlets and serials; 16 million manuscripts; 130,000 photographs; 21,000 museum objects; 1850 reels of microfilm; 500 microfiche; 300,000 feet of motion picture film; 1100 phonograph records; 1000 audiotapes. **Subscriptions:** 25 journals and other serials. **Services:** Interlibrary loan; copying; library open to the public upon application. **Networks/Consortia:** Member of Southeastern New York Library Resources Council (SENYLRC). **Publications:** Franklin D. Roosevelt and Conservation, 1911-1945, 2 volumes, 1957; Calendar of Speeches and Other Published Statements of Franklin D. Roosevelt, 1910-1920; Franklin D. Roosevelt and Foreign Affairs, 10 volumes, 1979; Era of Franklin D. Roosevelt: A Selected Bibliography of Periodical, Essay, and Dissertation Literature, 1945-1971; The Roosevelt-Churchill Messages (microfilm); The Press Conferences of Franklin D. Roosevelt, 1933-1945 (microfilm). **Remarks:** Maintained by National Archives & Records Administration. **Staff:** Sheryl Griffith, Supv.Libn.; Frances M. Seeber, Sr.Supv.Archv.; Raymond Teichman, Supv.Archv.; Mark Renovitch, AV Archv.; Alycia Vivona, Musm.Reg..

★15483★
U.S. PRESIDENTIAL LIBRARIES - GERALD R. FORD LIBRARY (Hist)
1000 Beal Ave. Phone: (313)668-2218
Ann Arbor, MI 48109 Dr. Don W. Wilson, Dir.
Founded: 1981. **Staff:** Prof 11; Other 2. **Subjects:** Gerald R. Ford; U.S. Presidency, government, and politics, 1974-1977; U.S. Congress, 1948-1977. **Special Collections:** Papers of Gerald R. Ford, 1948 to present; papers of individuals and records of agencies and organizations associated with Gerald Ford's career. **Holdings:** 8500 books; 50 bound periodical volumes; 8500 linear feet of archival records and manuscripts; 310,000 photographs; 1049 hours of audiotape; 778,000 feet of film; 1068 hours of videotape. **Subscriptions:** 34 journals and other serials. **Services:** Copying; library open to the public. **Publications:** Newsletter, quarterly; list of holdings - both free upon request. **Special Indexes:** Inventory of each archivally processed collection (typescript); keyword index to public statements by President Ford (card). **Remarks:** Maintained by the National Archives and Records Administration. **Staff:** David A. Horrocks, Supv.Archv.; Richard L. Holzhausen, AV Archv.; William J. Stewart, Dp.Dir..

★15484★
U.S. PRESIDENTIAL LIBRARIES - HARRY S TRUMAN LIBRARY (Hist)
Independence, MO 64050 Phone: (816)833-1400
Dr. Benedict K. Zobrist, Dir.
Founded: 1957. **Staff:** Prof 9; Other 20. **Subjects:** Career and administration of former President Harry S Truman. **Holdings:** 40,683 books; 2264 bound periodical volumes; 13.4 million manuscripts on paper; 91,158 other printed items; 424 oral history interviews; 25 VF drawers. **Subscriptions:** 75 journals and other serials. **Services:** Interlibrary loan; copying; library open to the public by written application. **Publications:** Harry S Truman Library/Institute Newsletter; Whistlestop, quarterly. **Special Catalogs:** Historical Materials in the Harry S Truman Library (book). **Remarks:** Maintained by National Archives & Records Administration. **Staff:** Dr. George H. Curtis, Asst.Dir..

★15485★
U.S. PRESIDENTIAL LIBRARIES - HERBERT HOOVER LIBRARY (Hist)
West Branch, IA 52358 Phone: (319)643-5301
Richard Norton Smith, Dir.
Staff: 16. **Subjects:** Herbert Hoover, 20th century history with special emphasis on the period 1920-1960. **Special Collections:** Manuscripts of George Akerson, American Child Health Association, Arthur A. Ballantine, Harriet C. Brown, Herbert D. Brown, Delph E. Carpenter, William R. Castle, Kenneth W. Colegrove, Colorado River Commission, George C. Drescher, Ralph Evans, Frederick M. Feiker, James P. Goodrich, Harold R. Gross, George Hastings, Bourke B. Hickenlooper, Herbert Hoover, Lou Henry Hoover, Hoover Commissions of 1947 and 1953, Theodore G. Joslin, Rose Wilder Lane, Irwin B. Laughlin, Robert H. Lucas, Nathan W. MacChesney, William P. MacCracken, Hanford MacNider, Verne Marshall, Ferdinand L. Mayer, John F. Meck, Felix Morley, William C. Mullendore, Bradley Nash, Gerald Nye, Maurice Pate, Westbrook Pegler, John F. Shafroth, Truman Smith, Oscar C. Stine, Lewis H. Strauss, French Strother, Charles C. Tansill, Henry J. Taylor, Walter Trohan, Ray Lyman Wilbur, Hugh R. Wilson, Richard L. Wilson, Robert E. Wood. **Holdings:** 24,500 volumes; 34,280 photographs; 151,591 feet of motion picture film; 2767 reels of microfilm; 81 microfiche; 11,245 pages of oral history transcripts; 239 hours of sound recordings. **Subscriptions:** 46 journals and other serials. **Services:** Interlibrary loan (limited); copying; library open to researchers who apply in writing. **Special Catalogs:** Book catalog; photographs; finding aids and selected indexes for manuscript collections; Historical Materials in the Herbert Hoover Presidential Library - free upon request. **Remarks:** Maintained by National Archives & Records Administration. **Staff:** Mildred Mather, Archv.-Libn..

★15486★
U.S. PRESIDENTIAL LIBRARIES - JIMMY CARTER LIBRARY (Hist)
One Copenhill Ave. Phone: (404)331-3942
Atlanta, GA 30307 Dr. Donald B. Schewe, Dir.
Founded: 1985. **Staff:** Prof 8; Other 20. **Subjects:** Presidency of Jimmy Carter. **Holdings:** Papers of Jimmy Carter during his presidency (27 million pages). **Services:** Copying; library open to the public. **Automated Operations:** Computerized cataloging and acquisitions. **Computerized Information Services:** DIALOG Information Services, WILSONLINE. **Networks/Consortia:** Member of FEDLINK. **Remarks:** Maintained by National Archives & Records Administration. **Staff:** Dr. David E. Alsobrook, Supv.Archv.; Dr. Martin I. Elzy, Asst.Dir.; James R. Kratsas, Musm.Cur..

★15487★
U.S. PRESIDENTIAL LIBRARIES - JOHN F. KENNEDY LIBRARY (Hist, Hum)
Columbia Point on Dorchester Bay Phone: (617)929-4500
Boston, MA 02125 John F. Stewart, Act.Dir.
Staff: Prof 8; Other 34. **Subjects:** John F. Kennedy and his administration, mid-20th century American politics and government. **Special Collections:** Oral history; Robert Kennedy papers; Ernest Hemingway papers; Seymour Harris Economics Collection. **Holdings:** 35,000 volumes; 28 million manuscript pages; 2.2 million pages of records of the Democratic National Committee; 500,000 pages of collections of personal papers; 40,000 pages of oral history interviews; 12,500 museum objects; 2500 reels of records and papers; 100,000 photographs; 4500 sound recordings; 6.5 million feet of motion picture film. **Subscriptions:** 12 journals and other serials. **Services:** Interlibrary loan; copying; library open to the public. **Special Catalogs:** Historical Materials in the John F. Kennedy Library. **Remarks:** Maintained by National Archives & Records Administration. **Staff:** E. William Johnson, Chf.Archv.; Ronald E. Whealan, Libn.; David F. Powers, Musm.Cur.; Allan B. Goodrich, AV Archv..

★15488★
U.S. PRESIDENTIAL LIBRARIES - LYNDON B. JOHNSON LIBRARY AND MUSEUM (Hist)
2313 Red River St. Phone: (512)482-5137
Austin, TX 78705 Harry J. Middleton, Dir.
Founded: 1971. **Staff:** Prof 21; Other 6. **Subjects:** Lyndon B. Johnson - career, administration, family, papers; U.S. Presidency; American political, social, and economic history, 1937 to present. **Special Collections:** Oral history interviews; individual personal papers. **Holdings:** 15,352 books; 3938 unbound periodicals; 4926 transcripts of Congressional hearings; 38 million archives-manuscript pages; 608,122 photographs; 6736 video recordings; 12,566 sound recordings; 35,870 museum items; 824,746 feet of motion picture film; 8 VF drawers of periodical articles; 4 VF drawers of papers and dissertations; 8 VF drawers of newspaper clippings. **Subscriptions:** 10 journals and other serials. **Services:** Interlibrary loan

(limited); copying; library open to the public. **Publications:** The Lyndon B. Johnson Library - to visitors. **Special Catalogs:** Finding aids to papers of Lyndon B. Johnson as President, Congressman, Senator, and Vice President (notebook form); finding aids to oral histories. **Remarks:** Maintained by National Archives & Records Administration. **Staff:** Charles W. Corkran, Asst.Dir.; Christina Houston, Supv.Archv.; Gary Yarrington, Musm.Cur.; Michael Gillette, Chf., Oral Hist.Sect.; Frank Wolfe, Chf., Tech.Serv.; Barbara Jensen, Adm.Off..

★15489★
U.S. PRESIDENTIAL MUSEUM - LIBRARY OF THE PRESIDENTS (Hist)
622 N. Lee St. Phone: (915)332-7123
Odessa, TX 79761 D'Aun McGonagill, Cur.
Founded: 1964. **Staff:** Prof 1; Other 10. **Subjects:** U.S. Presidents, presidential candidates, Vice Presidents, First Ladies, political parties, campaigns. **Holdings:** 4000 volumes; 500 volumes of rare and first edition books; unbound periodicals. **Subscriptions:** 53 journals and other serials. **Services:** Library open to the public for reference use only by appointment on a limited schedule.

U.S. PUBLIC HEALTH SERVICE - CENTERS FOR DISEASE CONTROL
See: U.S. Centers for Disease Control (14907)

U.S. PUBLIC HEALTH SERVICE - FOOD & DRUG ADMINISTRATION
See: U.S. Food & Drug Administration (15093)

U.S. PUBLIC HEALTH SERVICE - MESCALERO PUBLIC HEALTH SERVICE HOSPITAL
See: Mescalero Public Health Service Hospital (8786)

U.S. PUBLIC HEALTH SERVICE - NATIONAL CENTER FOR HEALTH STATISTICS
See: National Center for Health Statistics (9613)

U.S. PUBLIC HEALTH SERVICE - NATIONAL INSTITUTES OF HEALTH
See: U.S. Natl. Institutes of Health (15208)

U.S. PUBLIC HEALTH SERVICE - NAVAJO AREA INDIAN HEALTH SERVICE - GALLUP INDIAN MEDICAL CENTER
See: Gallup Indian Medical Center (5458)

★15490★
U.S. PUBLIC HEALTH SERVICE - OFFICE OF DISEASE PREVENTION AND HEALTH PROMOTION - ODPHP NATIONAL HEALTH INFORMATION CENTER (OHIC) (Med)
Box 1133 Phone: (202)429-9091
Washington, DC 20013-1133 Linda M. Malcolm, Proj.Dir.
Staff: Prof 10; Other 3. **Subjects:** Health, nutrition, health promotion. **Holdings:** 800 books; 50 bound periodical volumes; 44 VF drawers of pamphlets and clippings. **Subscriptions:** 75 journals and other serials. **Services:** Copying; center open to the public by appointment. **Automated Operations:** Computerized inventory control. **Computerized Information Services:** DIALOG Information Services, BRS Information Technologies, MEDLARS; internal database. **Publications:** Healthfinder series, irregular; resource guides to health topics of current interest. **Special Catalogs:** Address and contact information for over 1000 health-related organizations (machine-readable format). **Remarks:** Center located at 1010 Wayne Ave., Suite 300, Silver Spring, MD 20910. A toll-free telephone number is (800)336-4797. **Staff:** Roger Buker, Info.Serv.Mgr..

U.S. PUBLIC HEALTH SERVICE - OFFICE FOR SUBSTANCE ABUSE PREVENTION - NATIONAL CLEARINGHOUSE FOR ALCOHOL AND DRUG INFORMATION
See: National Clearinghouse for Alcohol and Drug Information (9625)

★15491★
U.S. PUBLIC HEALTH SERVICE - PARKLAWN HEALTH LIBRARY (Med, Soc Sci)
5600 Fishers Ln., Rm. 13-12 Phone: (301)443-2665
Rockville, MD 20857 Bruce N. Yamasaki, Lib.Dir.
Founded: 1969. **Staff:** Prof 5; Other 9. **Subjects:** Delivery of health services, drug abuse, health planning, health care statistics, health services research, mental health, social aspects of health care, emergency medical services. **Special Collections:** Public Health Service Numbered Report Series; Vital Statistics of the U.S.; Public Health Service Contract Reports. **Holdings:** 20,000 books; 2000 bound periodical volumes; 10,000 NTIS reports on microfiche. **Subscriptions:** 1100 journals and other serials. **Services:** Interlibrary loan; copying; SDI; library open to the public for reference use only. **Automated Operations:** Computerized cataloging. **Computerized Information Services:** DIALOG Information Services, MEDLINE, OCLC; Emergency Medical Services Database (internal database). **Publications:** Current Awareness; Parklawn Health Library Bulletin, monthly - both to mailing list; Periodical List - free upon request. **Special Indexes:** KWIC index. **Staff:** Karen Stakes, Dp.Dir.; Angela Sirrocco, Spec.Asst. to Dir.; Marge Szawlewicz, Ref.Libn..

U.S. PUBLIC HEALTH SERVICE ARCHIVE
See: Reynolds Electrical and Engineering Company, Inc. - Coordination and Information Center (12004)

★15492★
U.S. PUBLIC HEALTH SERVICE HOSPITAL - GILLIS W. LONG HANSEN'S DISEASE CENTER - MEDICAL LIBRARY (Med)
Carville, LA 70721 Phone: (504)642-4748
Marilyn P. McManus, Med.Libn.
Staff: Prof 2; Other 1. **Subjects:** Hansen's disease, dermatology, ophthalmology, bone and joint surgery, plastic surgery, rehabilitation, physical therapy, dentistry, nursing. **Special Collections:** Leprosy Archives (all material published in English about leprosy, 1958 to present). **Holdings:** 8000 books; 10,000 unbound items; films; slides; tapes. **Subscriptions:** 130 journals and other serials. **Services:** Interlibrary loan; copying; SDI; library open to the public for reference use only. **Computerized Information Services:** MEDLARS. **Networks/Consortia:** Member of TALON, Health Sciences Library Association of Louisiana. **Special Indexes:** Hansen's Disease Index (card). **Staff:** AnnaBelle Steinbach, Libn..

U.S. RAILROAD RETIREMENT BOARD
See: Railroad Retirement Board (11864)

U.S. REFRACTORIES
See: General Refractories Company (5568)

U.S. SECURITIES AND EXCHANGE COMMISSION
See: Securities and Exchange Commission (13046)

★15493★
U.S. SENATE - LIBRARY (Soc Sci)
Capitol Bldg., Suite S-332 Phone: (202)224-7106
Washington, DC 20510 Roger K. Haley, Senate Libn.
Founded: 1871. **Staff:** Prof 9; Other 11. **Subjects:** Legislation, government, political science, history, biography, economics. **Special Collections:** House and Senate bills and resolutions; committee hearings; legislative proceedings and debates. **Holdings:** 100,000 volumes; 500,000 microforms. **Subscriptions:** 200 journals and other serials; 10 newspapers. **Services:** Library not open to the public. **Automated Operations:** Computerized cataloging. **Computerized Information Services:** NEXIS, LEXIS, DIALOG Information Services, VU/TEXT Information Services, DataTimes, Dow Jones News/Retrieval, OCLC, House Information System (HIS), Library of Congress Information System (LOCIS); SLCC (internal database). Performs searches free of charge. **Networks/Consortia:** Member of FEDLINK. **Publications:** Presidential Vetoes. **Staff:** Ann C. Womeldorf, Asst.Libn.; Gregory C. Harness, Hd.Ref.Libn.; Thea Koehler, Ref.Libn.; Leona Pfund, Hd.Cat./Automated Sys.Coord.; Jean Winslow, Ref.Libn.; Thomas McCray, Doc.Libn.; Laura Macqueen, Congressional Pubns.Cat..

U.S. SMALL BUSINESS ADMINISTRATION
See: Small Business Administration (13232)

★15494★
U.S. SOCIAL SECURITY ADMINISTRATION - BRANCH LIBRARY (Bus-Fin, Med)
Universal N. Bldg., Rm. 320-0
1875 Connecticut Ave. N.W. Phone: (202)673-5624
Washington, DC 20009 Octavio Alvarez, Libn.
Founded: 1972. **Staff:** Prof 1; Other 2. **Subjects:** Social Security programs, disability insurance, income maintenance, pension benefits, health insurance, medical care. **Special Collections:** Research Grant Reports and Contract Reports of SSA and Office of Research and Statistics. **Holdings:** 9000 books; 100 bound periodical volumes; 200 pamphlets; 500 microforms. **Subscriptions:** 260 journals and other serials. **Services:** Interlibrary loan; copying; library open to the public with permission. **Automated Operations:** Computerized circulation.

★15495★
U.S. SOCIAL SECURITY ADMINISTRATION - COMPARATIVE STUDIES STAFF REFERENCE ROOM (Law)
1875 Connecticut Ave., N.W.
Universal North Bldg., Rm. 940 Phone: (202)673-5713
Washington, DC 20009 Concepcion McNeace, Lib.Techn.
Staff: Prof 1. **Subjects:** Social security, disability, work injuries, and health care laws in foreign countries. **Special Collections:** Foreign annual yearbooks, 1965 to present; International Labor Organization, Organization for Economic Cooperation and Development (OECD), and International Social Security Association publications. **Holdings:** 25,000 volumes; 38 VF drawers of clippings on international subjects. **Subscriptions:** 153 journals and other serials. **Services:** Room open to the public by appointment. **Publications:** Social Security Bulletin; Social Security Programs throughout the World, biennial.

★15496★
U.S. SOCIAL SECURITY ADMINISTRATION - INFORMATION RESOURCES BRANCH - LIBRARY SERVICES SECTION (Soc Sci, Bus-Fin, Med)
6401 Security Blvd.
Altmeyer Bldg., Rm. 570
Baltimore, MD 21235 Phone: (301)594-1650
Founded: 1942. **Staff:** Prof 7; Other 7. **Subjects:** Social insurance, medical and hospital economics, operations research, management, personnel administration, supervision and training, electronic data processing, law, health insurance, business and management. **Holdings:** 83,280 books; 1250 bound periodical volumes; 600,000 microfiche; 4700 ultrafiche. **Subscriptions:** 1447 journals and other serials. **Services:** Interlibrary loan; copying (limited); library open to the public for reference use only on request. **Automated Operations:** Computerized cataloging, acquisitions, and circulation. **Computerized Information Services:** DIALOG Information Services, BRS Information Technologies, LEXIS, NEXIS, LEGI-SLATE, JURIS, OCLC. **Publications:** SSA Library Notes, monthly; Bibliographic Quick Lists; Legislative Notes (guide to particular Social Security laws) - all free upon request. **Special Indexes:** Index to legislative information (card). **Remarks:** The Social Security Administration is part of the U.S. Department of Health and Human Services. **Staff:** Leo Hollenbeck, Ref.Libn.; Dorothy Dougherty, Ref.Libn.; Joyce Donohue, Supv. Law Libn.; Barbara Giersch, Supv.Tech.Serv.Libn..

★15497★
U.S. SOIL CONSERVATION SERVICE - NATIONAL PHOTOGRAPHIC LIBRARY (Aud-Vis, Env-Cons)
Box 2890 Phone: (202)447-7547
Washington, DC 20013 Katherine C. Gugulis, Br.Chf.
Founded: 1935. **Staff:** Prof 2. **Subjects:** Soil erosion, conservation practices, agricultural scenes. **Holdings:** 10,000 photographs. **Services:** Library open to the public with restrictions. **Remarks:** The Soil Conservation Service operates under the jurisdiction of the U.S. Department of Agriculture. **Staff:** Jodell Choate, Visual Info.Spec..

★15498★
UNITED STATES SPACE EDUCATION ASSOCIATION - G.L. BORROWMAN ASTRONAUTICS LIBRARY (Sci-Engr)
P.O. Box 1032
Weyburn, SK, Canada S4H 2L3 Gerald L. Borrowman, Chf.Libn.
Staff: Prof 2. **Subjects:** Astronautics, American and Soviet space programs, Apollo and Gemini projects, space shuttle. **Holdings:** 2000 books; 2000 bound periodical volumes; press kits and photographs. **Subscriptions:** 32 journals and other serials. **Services:** Library not open to the public.

★15499★
UNITED STATES SPACE EDUCATION ASSOCIATION - USSEA MEDIA CENTER (Sci-Engr)
746 Turnpike Rd. Phone: (717)367-3265
Elizabethtown, PA 17022-1161 Stephen M. Cobaugh, Intl.Pres.
Founded: 1973. **Staff:** 7. **Subjects:** NASA space program, space sciences, solar power, UFOs, science fiction. **Special Collections:** NASA Technical Publications (1000 documents); Solar Power Abstracts (250 documents). **Holdings:** 1500 books; 500 bound periodical volumes; 5000 slides, photographs, and cassettes; 1000 brochures and reports; 5000 clippings. **Subscriptions:** 30 journals and other serials. **Services:** Copying; center open to the public with restrictions. **Publications:** Space Age Times, bimonthly; USSEA Update, monthly.

★15500★
UNITED STATES SPORTS ACADEMY - LIBRARY (Rec)
One Academy Dr. Phone: (205)626-3303
Daphne, AL 36526 Betty Dance, Hd.Libn.
Staff: 2. **Subjects:** Sports, including medicine, research and management; fitness; coaching. **Holdings:** 2353 books; 8 VF drawers of clippings; 271 cassette tapes; films; slides; periodicals on microfiche. **Subscriptions:** 390 journals and other serials. **Services:** Interlibrary loan; copying; library open to the public for reference use only. **Computerized Information Services:** Pergamon ORBIT InfoLine, Inc., BRS Information Technologies, MEDLARS. Performs searches on fee basis. **Publications:** Handbook; Shelflist (acquisitions list), monthly. **Special Catalogs:** Books by discipline (computer printout).

UNITED STATES STEEL CORPORATION
See: USX Corporation - USS Division (17225)

★15501★
UNITED STATES STUDENT ASSOCIATION - INFORMATION SERVICES (Educ)
1012 14th St., N.W., No. 207 Phone: (202)347-8772
Washington, DC 20005 Circe Dajunen, Pres.
Staff: Prof 3. **Subjects:** PSE governance, history of student activism, women and minorities, collective bargaining, educational innovation, funding PSE. **Special Collections:** National Student Association Publications, 1947 to present. **Holdings:** 1200 books; 250 file sleeves of data; 500 unbound reports and periodicals. **Subscriptions:** 30 journals and other serials; 200 newspapers. **Services:** Copying; services open to members with restrictions depending on nature of request. **Publications:** Research Periodicals on topics of interest to members - for sale. **Staff:** Fred Azcurate, V.P..

★15502★
U.S. SUPREME COURT - LIBRARY (Law)
One First St., N.E. Phone: (202)252-3000
Washington, DC 20543 Stephen G. Margeton, Libn.
Staff: Prof 11; Other 11. **Subjects:** Law, legislative histories. **Special Collections:** Records and briefs of the Supreme Court, 1832 to present; Gerry Collection (26,000 volumes). **Holdings:** 250,000 books; 50,000 microforms; 15,000 bound periodical volumes. **Subscriptions:** 4050 journals and other serials. **Services:** Copying; library open to members of Supreme Court Bar and government attorneys. **Automated Operations:** Computerized cataloging, acquisitions, serials, and circulation. **Computerized Information Services:** DIALOG Information Services, NEXIS, OCLC, LEXIS, WESTLAW, Library of Congress Information System (LOCIS). **Networks/Consortia:** Member of FEDLINK. **Staff:** Martha C. Byrnes, Asst.Libn., Res.; Rosalie Sherwin, Asst.Libn., Tech.Serv.; Kimberly Allen, Asst.Libn., Circ..

★15503★
U.S. TAX COURT - LIBRARY (Law)
400 Second St., N.W. Phone: (202)376-2707
Washington, DC 20217 Jeanne R. Bonynge, Libn.
Founded: 1924. **Staff:** Prof 3; Other 3. **Subjects:** Federal tax law - income, estate, gift. **Holdings:** 40,000 books; 7900 bound periodical volumes; 380,000 Index-Digest card file of federal tax cases; 1000 reels of microfilm of Congressional Record and Federal Register; 5000 microfiche of tax legislation. **Subscriptions:** 90 journals and other serials. **Services:** Interlibrary loan (limited); library not open to the public. **Automated Operations:** Computerized serials. **Computerized Information Services:** Washington Alert Service, LEXIS, OCLC, PHINet FedTax Database, VERALEX, WESTLAW; ABA/net (electronic mail service). **Networks/Consortia:** Member of FEDLINK. **Publications:** Library Memorandum, monthly - to Tax Court personnel. **Special Indexes:** File of tax cases arranged by case name, Internal Revenue code section, and subject (card). **Staff:** Elsa B. Silverman, Asst.Libn.; Tania Andreeff, Paralegal Spec..

★15504★
U.S. TEAM HANDBALL FEDERATION - ADMINISTRATIVE OFFICE LIBRARY (Rec)
1750 E. Boulder St. Phone: (719)632-5551
Colorado Springs, CO 80909 Dr. Peter Buehning, Pres.
Staff: 1. **Subjects:** Team handball - rules, equipment, technique. **Holdings:** Films; videotapes. **Services:** Library open to the public with restrictions. **Publications:** Team Handball USA.

★15505★
UNITED STATES TESTING COMPANY, INC. - LIBRARY (Sci-Engr)
1415 Park Ave. Phone: (201)792-2400
Hoboken, NJ 07030 Dorothy M. Campbell, Libn.
Founded: 1930. **Staff:** Prof 1; Other 1. **Subjects:** Biology; chemistry; consumer research; engineering - materials, physical, electronics, product, nuclear; environmental testing; paper; plastics; textiles. **Holdings:** 5000 military and government specifications. **Subscriptions:** 150 journals and other serials. **Services:** Library not open to the public.

★15506★
U.S. TOBACCO - R & D LIBRARY (Sci-Engr)
800 Harrison St. Phone: (615)244-5270
Nashville, TN 37203 Barbara Borrelli, Libn.
Staff: Prof 1. **Subjects:** Tobacco. **Holdings:** 1300 books; 600 bound periodical volumes. **Subscriptions:** 101 journals and other serials. **Services:** Library not open to the public. **Computerized Information Services:** DIALOG Information Services, STN International.

★15507★
UNITED STATES TRADEMARK ASSOCIATION - LAW LIBRARY (Law)
6 E. 45th St. Phone: (212)986-5880
New York, NY 10017 Charlotte Jones, Mng.Ed./Libn.
Founded: 1878. **Staff:** 16. **Subjects:** Trademarks. **Holdings:** 1800 books; 73 bound periodical volumes. **Subscriptions:** 40 journals and other serials. **Services:** Library open to the public.

★15508★
U.S. TRAVEL DATA CENTER - LIBRARY (Bus-Fin)
2 Lafayette Centre
1133 21st St., N.W. Phone: (202)293-1040
Washington, DC 20036 Suzanne D. Cook, Dir.
Founded: 1973. **Staff:** 14. **Subjects:** Travel and tourism. **Holdings:** 3000 research documents; 3800 government documents; 250 unpublished travel research reports; 15,000 clippings; 20 tapes. **Subscriptions:** 27 journals and other serials. **Services:** Library not open to the public. **Special Catalogs:** Publications Catalog, annual - free upon request. **Remarks:** Affiliated with Travel Industry Association of America. **Staff:** Ida Simmons, Mgr.Commun..

★15509★
UNITED STATES TRUST COMPANY - INVESTMENT LIBRARY (Bus-Fin)
45 Wall St.
New York, NY 10005 Phone: (212)806-4478
Founded: 1958. **Staff:** Prof 1; Other 2. **Subjects:** Finance, investments, banking, securities. **Holdings:** 300 volumes; 1000 unbound periodicals; 2750 corporate files. **Subscriptions:** 80 journals and other serials; 7 newspapers. **Services:** Interlibrary loan; copying; library open to clients and employees. **Automated Operations:** Computerized cataloging, acquisitions, and serials. **Computerized Information Services:** DIALOG Information Services, NEXIS, FINSTAT.

★15510★
U.S. UNIFORMED SERVICES UNIVERSITY OF THE HEALTH SCIENCES - LEARNING RESOURCE CENTER (Med)
4301 Jones Bridge Rd. Phone: (301)295-3356
Bethesda, MD 20814-4799 Chester J. Pletzke, Assoc.Prof. & Dir.
Staff: Prof 5; Other 15. **Subjects:** Medicine, military medicine. **Holdings:** 72,818 books and journals; 50,000 bound periodical volumes. **Subscriptions:** 1470 journals and other serials; 10 newspapers. **Services:** Interlibrary loan; copying; center open to the public. **Automated Operations:** Computerized cataloging, acquisitions, serials, and circulation. **Computerized Information Services:** DIALOG Information Services, NLM, OCLC; USUHS Information System (internal database). **Networks/Consortia:** Member of FEDLINK, Southeastern/Atlantic Regional Medical Library Services. **Publications:** Research Series Guide; Exhibit Bibliographies, both irregular - both for internal distribution only. **Remarks:** The University is under the direction of the U.S. Department of Defense. **Staff:** Janice Powell Muller, Hd., Tech.Serv.; Judith Torrence, Hd., Ref. & Info.Serv..

★15511★
U.S. URBAN MASS TRANSPORTATION ADMINISTRATION - TRANSPORTATION RESEARCH INFORMATION CENTER (TRIC) (Trans)
400 7th St., S.W. Phone: (202)366-9157
Washington, DC 20590 Ronald J. Fisher, Dir., Info.Serv.
Staff: Prof 3. **Subjects:** Urban transportation - bus and paratransit systems, rail and construction technology, new systems and technology, service and methods, planning and analysis, management resources. **Holdings:** 4000 reports. **Services:** Copying; SDI; center open to the public by appointment; responds to inquiries. **Computerized Information Services:** DIALOG Information Services. **Publications:** UMTA Abstracts, biennial - for sale. **Remarks:** The Urban Mass Transportation Administration is part of the U.S. Department of Transportation and sponsors the Urban Mass Transportation Research Information Service (UMTRIS), a computer-based information system operated by the Transportation Research Board (TRB) of the National Academy of Sciences. UMTRIS contains transportation information from domestic and international sources and is available as DIALOG File 63. **Staff:** Helen Tann, Tech.Info.Spec.; Marina Drancsak, Tech.Info.Spec..

★15512★
U.S. VETERANS ADMINISTRATION (AL-Birmingham) - MEDICAL CENTER LIBRARY (Med)
700 S. 19th St. Phone: (205)933-8101
Birmingham, AL 35233 Mary Ann Knotts, Chf., Lib.Serv.
Founded: 1953. **Staff:** Prof 4; Other 1. **Subjects:** Medicine, dentistry, nursing, hospital administration. **Holdings:** 1000 books; 2487 bound periodical volumes; 1000 AV programs. **Subscriptions:** 300 journals and other serials. **Services:** Interlibrary loan; copying; SDI; library open to the public with restrictions. **Computerized Information Services:** NLM, BRS Information Technologies, DIALOG Information Services; VALOR (internal database); OnTyme Electronic Message Network Service (electronic mail service). **Networks/Consortia:** Member of VALNET, Jefferson County Hospital Librarians' Association. **Staff:** Henrietta Mims, Med.Libn.; Nelle Williams, Med.Libn.; Gail Frey, Med.Libn..

★15513★
U.S. VETERANS ADMINISTRATION (AL-Montgomery) - MEDICAL CENTER LIBRARY (142D) (Med)
215 Perry Hill Rd. Phone: (205)272-4670
Montgomery, AL 36193 Marie Johnette Cummins, Chf., Lib.Serv.
Founded: 1940. **Staff:** Prof 2. **Subjects:** Medicine, allied health sciences. **Holdings:** 700 books; 839 bound periodical volumes; 156 audio cassettes; 50 AV programs. **Subscriptions:** 100 journals. **Services:** Interlibrary loan; library open to the public for reference use only. **Automated Operations:** Computerized cataloging. **Computerized Information Services:** MEDLINE. **Networks/Consortia:** Member of VALNET. **Publications:** Bibliographies. **Staff:** Susan Helms, Asst.Libn..

★15514★
U.S. VETERANS ADMINISTRATION (AL-Tuscaloosa) - MEDICAL CENTER LIBRARY (Med)
Loop Rd. Phone: (205)553-3760
Tuscaloosa, AL 35404 Olivia S. Maniece, Chf.Libn.
Founded: 1932. **Staff:** Prof 2; Other 1. **Subjects:** Psychiatry, nursing, geriatrics and gerontology, community mental health. **Special Collections:** Psychiatry; geriatrics and gerontology; community mental health. **Holdings:** 2333 books; 1560 bound periodical volumes; 150 other cataloged items; 200 manuscripts, reports, clippings. **Subscriptions:** 177 journals and other serials; 24 newspapers. **Services:** Interlibrary loan; copying; SDI; library open to the public. Performs searches free of charge. **Computerized Information Services:** MEDLINE; OnTyme Electronic Message Network Service, MAILMAN (electronic mail services). Performs searches free of charge. **Networks/Consortia:** Member of VALNET, Tuscaloosa Health Science Library Association (THeSLA). **Publications:** News-O-Gram. **Staff:** Betsy S. Pertzog, Med.Libn..

★15515★
U.S. VETERANS ADMINISTRATION (AL-Tuskegee) - MEDICAL CENTER LIBRARY (Med)
Tuskegee, AL 36083 Phone: (205)727-0550
Artemisia J. Junier, Chf., Lib.Serv.
Founded: 1948. **Staff:** Prof 3; Other 2. **Subjects:** Medicine, patient education. **Holdings:** 28,000 books; 9500 bound periodical volumes; 2300 AV programs. **Subscriptions:** 586 journals and other serials. **Services:** Interlibrary loan; copying; library open to the public with restrictions. **Automated Operations:** Computerized cataloging, acquisitions, serials, and circulation. **Computerized Information Services:** NLM; MAILMAN

(electronic mail service). **Networks/Consortia:** Member of VALNET. **Staff:** Inez C. Pinkard, Med.Libn.; Elaine P. McGee, Libn..

★15516★
U.S. VETERANS ADMINISTRATION (AZ-Phoenix) - HOSPITAL LIBRARY (Med)
Seventh St. & Indian School Rd. Phone: (602)277-5551
Phoenix, AZ 85012 Susan Harker, Chf., Lib.Serv.
Founded: 1946. **Staff:** Prof 2; Other 1. **Subjects:** Medicine, nursing, allied health sciences. **Special Collections:** Staff development; patient education. **Holdings:** 3161 books; 2953 bound periodical volumes; AV programs. **Subscriptions:** 300 journals and other serials. **Services:** Interlibrary loan; copying; library open to the public for reference use only. **Computerized Information Services:** BRS Information Technologies, MEDLINE, TOXLINE, International Cancer Research Data Bank Program. **Networks/Consortia:** Member of VALNET. **Publications:** Acquisitions List, quarterly; Journal Holdings, annual - to staff and other libraries. **Remarks:** Patients' library contains additional volumes. **Staff:** Jean Crosier, Med.Libn..

★15517★
U.S. VETERANS ADMINISTRATION (AZ-Prescott) - HEALTH SCIENCES LIBRARY (Med)
Prescott, AZ 86313 Phone: (602)445-4860
Carol Clark, Chf., Lib.Serv.
Staff: Prof 1; Other 1. **Subjects:** Medicine, nursing, surgery, dentistry, allied health sciences, administration. **Holdings:** 600 books; 300 AV programs; 30 titles on microfilm. **Subscriptions:** 140 journals and other serials; 10 newspapers. **Services:** Interlibrary loan; library not open to the public. **Computerized Information Services:** MEDLARS, BRS Information Technologies. **Networks/Consortia:** Member of VALNET.

★15518★
U.S. VETERANS ADMINISTRATION (AZ-Tucson) - MEDICAL CENTER LIBRARY (142D) (Med)
3601 S. 6th Ave. Phone: (602)792-1450
Tucson, AZ 85723 William E. Azevedo, Chf., Lib.Serv.
Staff: 2. **Subjects:** Medicine, nursing, surgery, neurology, psychiatry, radiology. **Holdings:** 3204 books; 7802 bound periodical volumes; 968 volumes on microfilm. **Subscriptions:** 320 journals and other serials; 5 newspapers. **Services:** Interlibrary loan; copying; library open to qualified reseachers. **Computerized Information Services:** MEDLINE. **Networks/Consortia:** Member of VALNET, Medical Library Group of Southern California and Arizona (MLGSCA).

★15519★
U.S. VETERANS ADMINISTRATION (AR-Fayetteville) - MEDICAL CENTER LIBRARY (Med)
1100 N. College Phone: (501)443-4301
Fayetteville, AR 72701 Kimberly Megginson, Chf., Lib.Serv.
Founded: 1946. **Staff:** Prof 1; Other 2. **Subjects:** Medicine, nursing, allied health sciences. **Holdings:** 2300 books; 1700 bound and unbound periodical volumes. **Subscriptions:** 200 journals and other serials. **Services:** Interlibrary loan; copying; SDI; library open to the public for reference use only. **Automated Operations:** Computerized cataloging and acquisitions. **Computerized Information Services:** MEDLARS, BRS Information Technologies. Performs searches free of charge. **Networks/Consortia:** Member of VALNET. **Remarks:** Patients' library contains an additional 3500 volumes.

★15520★
U.S. VETERANS ADMINISTRATION (AR-Little Rock) - HOSPITAL LIBRARIES (Med)
4300 W. 7th St. Phone: (501)660-2044
Little Rock, AR 72205 George M. Zumwalt, Chf., Lib.Serv.
Founded: 1950. **Staff:** Prof 3; Other 1. **Subjects:** Medicine, surgery, nursing, psychiatry, psychology, social work, dietetics. **Holdings:** 3506 books; 7500 bound periodical volumes; 20 16mm motion pictures; 360 video cassettes; 145 audio cassettes; 193 slides and filmstrips. **Subscriptions:** 292 journals and other serials. **Services:** Interlibrary loan; copying; library open to professionals and health science students. **Computerized Information Services:** BRS Information Technologies, MEDLINE. **Remarks:** Above data includes the holdings of the U.S. Veterans Administration Hospital Library in North Little Rock, which has consolidated its library service with the Little Rock Hospital Library. Patients' libraries contain an additional 8000 volumes. **Staff:** Jack W. Griffith, Libn., NLR Div.; Michael M. Blarton, Hea.Sci.Libn., LR Div..

★15521★
U.S. VETERANS ADMINISTRATION (CA-Fresno) - HOSPITAL MEDICAL LIBRARY (Med)
2615 E. Clinton Ave. Phone: (209)225-6100
Fresno, CA 93703 Cynthia K. Meyer, Chf., Lib.Serv.
Founded: 1950. **Staff:** Prof 2; Other 2. **Subjects:** Medicine, nursing, allied health sciences. **Holdings:** 4250 books; 7527 bound periodical volumes. **Subscriptions:** 362 journals and other serials. **Services:** Interlibrary loan; copying; SDI; library open to the public for reference use only. **Computerized Information Services:** MEDLARS, DIALOG Information Services. **Networks/Consortia:** Member of VALNET, Areawide Library Network (AWLNET), Northern California and Nevada Medical Library Group (NCNMLG), Pacific Southwest Regional Medical Library Service. **Staff:** Paul L. Connor, Med.Libn..

★15522★
U.S. VETERANS ADMINISTRATION (CA-Livermore) - MEDICAL LIBRARY (Med)
Arroyo Rd. Phone: (415)447-2560
Livermore, CA 94550 Jane H. Levie, Chf.Libn.
Founded: 1925. **Staff:** Prof 1; Other 1. **Subjects:** Medicine, nursing, allied health sciences. **Holdings:** 1300 books; 2365 bound periodical volumes; 128 AV programs; 204 boxes of microfilm. **Subscriptions:** 188 journals and other serials. **Services:** Interlibrary loan; copying; library open to the public for reference use only. **Networks/Consortia:** Member of VALNET.

★15523★
U.S. VETERANS ADMINISTRATION (CA-Loma Linda) - HOSPITAL LIBRARY SERVICE (Med)
11201 Benton St. Phone: (714)825-7084
Loma Linda, CA 92357 Kathleen M. Puffer, Chf.
Staff: Prof 2; Other 2. **Subjects:** Medicine. **Holdings:** 2500 books. **Subscriptions:** 500 journals and other serials. **Services:** Interlibrary loan; copying; SDI; library open to the public. **Automated Operations:** Computerized cataloging. **Computerized Information Services:** DIALOG Information Services, MEDLINE, BRS Information Technologies. **Networks/Consortia:** Member of VALNET, San Bernardino, Inyo, Riverside Counties United Library Services (SIRCULS), Inland Empire Medical Library Cooperative. **Staff:** Deborah Mayers, Clin.Libn..

★15524★
U.S. VETERANS ADMINISTRATION (CA-Long Beach) - MEDICAL CENTER LIBRARY (Med)
5901 E. Seventh St. Phone: (213)494-5465
Long Beach, CA 90822 Betty F. Connolly, Chf., Lib.Serv.
Founded: 1946. **Staff:** Prof 5; Other 2. **Subjects:** Medicine and allied health sciences, patient education. **Holdings:** 6100 books; 9000 bound periodical volumes; 1141 other volumes; AV programs. **Subscriptions:** 650 journals and other serials. **Services:** Interlibrary loan; copying; library open to the public for reference use only. **Automated Operations:** Computerized acquisitions, circulation, serials, and AV holdings. **Computerized Information Services:** DIALOG Information Services, BRS Information Technologies, MEDLARS; OnTyme Electronic Message Network Service (electronic mail service). **Networks/Consortia:** Member of VALNET. **Remarks:** Patients' library contains an additional 3050 volumes. **Staff:** Patti Flynn, Patient Libn.; Meredith Mitchell, Med.Libn.; Eileen Wakiji, Rsrc.Libn..

★15525★
U.S. VETERANS ADMINISTRATION (CA-Los Angeles) - MEDICAL RESEARCH LIBRARY (Med)
Wilshire & Sawtelle Blvds. Phone: (213)478-3711
Los Angeles, CA 90073 Sandra L. Schonlau, Chf., Med.Res.Lib.Sect.
Staff: Prof 1; Other 1. **Subjects:** Biochemistry, immunology, microbiology, molecular biology, physiology, ultrastructural research, metabolism. **Holdings:** 3400 books; 6200 bound periodical volumes. **Subscriptions:** 125 journals and other serials. **Services:** Interlibrary loan; library not open to the public. **Automated Operations:** Computerized acquisitions and serials. **Computerized Information Services:** MEDLARS; Checkmate (internal database). **Networks/Consortia:** Member of VALNET, CLASS, Pacific Southwest Regional Medical Library Service. **Publications:** Library Bulletin, bimonthly; Library Acquisitions List - for internal distribution only; Quarterly Newsletter - for internal distribution only.

★15526★
U.S. VETERANS ADMINISTRATION (CA-Los Angeles) - WADSWORTH MEDICAL LIBRARY 691W/142D (Med)
Wilshire & Sawtelle Blvds.
Los Angeles, CA 90073
Staff: Prof 5; Other 4. **Subjects:** Clinical medicine, surgery, dentistry, nursing, epilepsy, geriatrics, nutrition, social work. **Special Collections:** Patient Education Resource Library (500 volumes); AV collection (400 programs). **Holdings:** 6044 books; 12,557 bound periodical volumes; pamphlet file of monographs. **Subscriptions:** 480 journals and other serials; 12 newspapers. **Services:** Interlibrary loan; SDI; library open to the public for reference use only. **Automated Operations:** Computerized cataloging. **Computerized Information Services:** MEDLINE; Checkmate (internal database). **Networks/Consortia:** Member of VALNET, CLASS, Pacific Southwest Regional Medical Library Service, Metropolitan Cooperative Library System (MCLS). **Publications:** Library Newsletter, quarterly - for internal distribution and to VALNET members.

★15527★
U.S. VETERANS ADMINISTRATION (CA-Martinez) - HOSPITAL LIBRARY (Med)
150 Muir Rd. Phone: (415)228-6800
Martinez, CA 94553 Dorothea E. Bennett, Chf., Lib.Serv.
Founded: 1947. **Staff:** Prof 2; Other 1. **Subjects:** Medicine. **Holdings:** 6127 books; 8550 bound periodical volumes; 945 audiotapes. **Subscriptions:** 530 journals and other serials. **Services:** Interlibrary loan; library open to health care personnel for reference use only. **Networks/Consortia:** Member of VALNET. **Staff:** R.W. Phillips, Asst.Libn..

★15528★
U.S. VETERANS ADMINISTRATION (CA-Palo Alto) - MEDICAL CENTER - MEDICAL LIBRARIES (Med)
3801 Miranda Ave. Phone: (415)493-5000
Palo Alto, CA 94304 C.R. Gallimore, Chf., Lib.Serv.
Founded: 1922. **Staff:** Prof 4; Other 2. **Subjects:** Medicine, behavioral sciences. **Holdings:** 13,000 books; 13,000 bound periodical volumes; 5000 recreational books. **Subscriptions:** 690 journals and other serials; 6 newspapers. **Services:** Interlibrary loan; copying; libraries open to the public by appointment. **Networks/Consortia:** Member of VALNET.

★15529★
U.S. VETERANS ADMINISTRATION (CA-San Diego) - MEDICAL CENTER LIBRARY (142D) (Med)
3350 La Jolla Village Dr. Phone: (619)453-7500
San Diego, CA 92161 Barbara W. Huckins, Chf., Lib.Serv.
Staff: Prof 3; Other 2. **Subjects:** Medicine, patient education, management, self development. **Holdings:** 11,000 bound periodical volumes; 427 reels of microfilm; AV programs. **Subscriptions:** 520 journals and other serials. **Services:** Interlibrary loan; copying; SDI; library open to the public with restrictions. **Computerized Information Services:** DIALOG Information Services, MEDLARS; VALOR (internal database). Performs searches free of charge. Contact Person: Deborah Batey, Med.Libn., 453-7500, ext. 3422. **Networks/Consortia:** Member of VALNET, CLASS. **Publications:** Medical Library Update, monthly - for internal distribution only; Journal Holdings List, annual - internal and Southern California VA hospitals; AV Holdings List, annual - selective distribution. **Remarks:** Patients' Health Information Collection contains an additional 2000 items. **Staff:** Joanne Metcalf, Med.Libn..

★15530★
U.S. VETERANS ADMINISTRATION (CA-San Francisco) - MEDICAL CENTER LIBRARY SERVICE (142D) (Med)
4150 Clement St. Phone: (415)221-4810
San Francisco, CA 94121 William Koch, Chf., Lib.Serv.
Founded: 1947. **Staff:** Prof 3; Other 1. **Subjects:** Health sciences. **Special Collections:** Patient education. **Holdings:** 5500 books; 20,000 bound periodical volumes. **Subscriptions:** 400 journals and other serials. **Services:** Interlibrary loan; library not open to the public. **Computerized Information Services:** BRS Information Technologies, DIALOG Information Services, MEDLARS; MAILMAN, OnTyme Electronic Message Network Service (electronic mail services). **Networks/Consortia:** Member of VALNET, San Francisco Biomedical Library Group. **Remarks:** Includes a Patient Education Resource Center. **Staff:** Sen Yee, Patient Educ.Libn.; Sara Gouveia, Med.Libn..

★15531★
U.S. VETERANS ADMINISTRATION (CO-Denver) - LIBRARY SERVICE (142D) (Med)
1055 Clermont St. Phone: (303)393-2821
Denver, CO 80220 Deborah A. Thompson, Chf., Lib.Serv.
Founded: 1947. **Staff:** Prof 2; Other 2. **Subjects:** Medicine and allied clinical sciences. **Holdings:** 3000 books; 5000 bound periodical volumes; 200 pamphlets. **Subscriptions:** 250 journals and other serials. **Computerized Information Services:** MEDLARS, BRS Information Technologies; DOCLINE, ABACUS (electronic mail services). **Networks/Consortia:** Member of VALNET, Denver Area Health Sciences Library Consortium. **Remarks:** Patients' library contains an additional 4000 volumes. **Staff:** Helen Eaton, Gen.Libn..

★15532★
U.S. VETERANS ADMINISTRATION (CO-Fort Lyon) - MEDICAL LIBRARY (Med)
VA Medical Center (567/142D) Phone: (303)456-1260
Fort Lyon, CO 81038 Helen S. Bradley, Chf., Lib.Serv.
Founded: 1922. **Staff:** Prof 1; Other 3. **Subjects:** Psychiatry, nursing, geriatrics, medicine, allied health sciences. **Holdings:** Figures not available. **Services:** Interlibrary loan; copying; library open to the public. **Computerized Information Services:** MEDLARS, BRS Information Technologies; internal database; MAILMAN (electronic mail service). Performs searches free of charge. **Networks/Consortia:** Member of Arkansas Valley Regional Library Service System, Plains and Peaks Regional Library Service System, VALNET.

★15533★
U.S. VETERANS ADMINISTRATION (CO-Grand Junction) - MEDICAL CENTER MEDICAL LIBRARY (Med)
2121 North Ave. Phone: (303)242-0731
Grand Junction, CO 81501 Lynn L. Bragdon, Chf., Lib.Serv.
Founded: 1948. **Staff:** Prof 1; Other 1. **Subjects:** Medicine, surgery. **Holdings:** 1200 books; 900 bound periodical volumes. **Subscriptions:** 130 journals and other serials. **Services:** Interlibrary loan; library open to health care professionals. **Computerized Information Services:** MEDLARS, BRS Information Technologies; VALOR (internal database). **Networks/Consortia:** Member of VALNET, Midcontinental Regional Medical Library Program. **Remarks:** Patients' library contains an additional 1600 volumes.

★15534★
U.S. VETERANS ADMINISTRATION (CT-Newington) - HOSPITAL HEALTH SCIENCES LIBRARY (Med)
555 Willard Ave. Phone: (203)666-6951
Newington, CT 06111 Julie A. Lueders, Chf., Lib.Serv.
Founded: 1938. **Staff:** Prof 1; Other 1. **Subjects:** Medicine, surgery, psychiatry, nursing, hospital administration. **Holdings:** 2279 books; 1700 bound periodical volumes. **Subscriptions:** 210 journals and other serials. **Services:** Interlibrary loan; copying; library open to the public for reference use only. **Computerized Information Services:** MEDLINE, BRS Information Technologies. **Networks/Consortia:** Member of VALNET, Connecticut Association of Health Science Libraries (CAHSL). **Remarks:** Patients' library contains an additional 4550 volumes.

★15535★
U.S. VETERANS ADMINISTRATION (CT-West Haven) - MEDICAL CENTER LIBRARY (Med)
West Spring St. Phone: (203)932-5711
West Haven, CT 06516 Fran Bernstein, Chf., Lib.Serv.
Staff: Prof 2; Other 1. **Subjects:** Medicine, psychiatry, psychology. **Holdings:** 6500 books; 9000 bound periodical volumes; AV programs. **Subscriptions:** 360 journals and other serials. **Services:** Interlibrary loan; copying; library open to area health professionals for reference use only. **Automated Operations:** Computerized cataloging and serials. **Computerized Information Services:** DIALOG Information Services, MEDLARS, BRS Information Technologies. **Networks/Consortia:** Member of VALNET, Connecticut Association of Health Science Libraries (CAHSL). **Remarks:** Patients' library contains an additional 5426 volumes.

★15536★
U.S. VETERANS ADMINISTRATION (DE-Wilmington) - CENTER MEDICAL LIBRARY (Med)
1601 Kirkwood Hwy. Phone: (302)994-2511
Wilmington, DE 19805 Donald A. Passidomo, Chf.Libn.
Founded: 1940. **Staff:** Prof 2; Other 1. **Subjects:** General medicine, surgery, dentistry, nursing. **Holdings:** 4500 books; 6000 bound periodical volumes; 2000 AV programs; medical journals on microfilm. **Subscriptions:** 325 journals and other serials. **Services:** Interlibrary loan; copying (for ILL);

SDI; library open to medical staff and affiliated students only. **Automated Operations:** Computerized cataloging. **Computerized Information Services:** MEDLINE. **Networks/Consortia:** Member of VALNET, Wilmington Area Biomedical Library Consortium (WABLC). **Publications:** Acquisitions List, quarterly - to hospital staff. **Special Catalogs:** AV Holdings List (cataloged by title and subject). **Staff:** Helen Post, Med.Libn..

★15537★
U.S. VETERANS ADMINISTRATION (DC-Washington) - GENERAL COUNSEL'S LAW LIBRARY (026H) (Law)
810 Vermont Ave., N.W., Rm. 1039 Phone: (202)233-2159
Washington, DC 20420 Nina Kahn, Law Libn.
Staff: Prof 2; Other 2. **Subjects:** Law, with emphasis on veterans' laws. **Holdings:** 25,000 volumes. **Services:** Interlibrary loan; library is for official use of the Veterans Administration and other government agencies. **Computerized Information Services:** WESTLAW. **Staff:** Kenneth E. Nero, Asst. Law Libn..

★15538★
U.S. VETERANS ADMINISTRATION (DC-Washington) - HEADQUARTERS CENTRAL OFFICE LIBRARY (142D) (Med)
810 Vermont Ave., N.W. Phone: (202)233-2430
Washington, DC 20420 Karen Renninger, Chf., Lib.Div.
Founded: 1930. **Staff:** Prof 7; Other 3. **Subjects:** Medicine, health care administration, veterans affairs, management. **Special Collections:** Historical material relating to Veterans Administration. **Holdings:** 13,000 books; 11,000 bound periodical volumes; 700 AV programs; slides. **Subscriptions:** 700 journals and other serials; 6 newspapers. **Services:** Interlibrary loan; copying; SDI; library open to the public for reference use only. **Computerized Information Services:** DIALOG Information Services, BRS Information Technologies, MEDLARS, NEXIS, PaperChase, NEXIS, EdVent (Educational Events) Data Base; VALOR (internal database); MAILMAN, OnTyme Electronic Message Network Service (electronic mail services). **Networks/Consortia:** Member of VALNET, District of Columbia Health Sciences Information Network (DOCHSIN), FLICC. **Publications:** Acquisitions List, quarterly; Journal Holdings List, annual; fact sheets, annual; brochure, biennial. **Special Catalogs:** AV catalog, annual. **Remarks:** An alternate telephone number is 233-3085. **Staff:** Diane Wiesenthal, Asst./Lib.Oper.; Wendy N. Carter, Rd.Serv.Spec.; Jean McVoy, Rsrcs.Coord., Spec.; Mary Ann Tatman, Sr.Tech.Serv.Spec.; Susan Gaudet, AV Lib.Techn.; Mary Kay Massay, Ref.Libn..

★15539★
U.S. VETERANS ADMINISTRATION (DC-Washington) - HEADQUARTERS LIBRARY DIVISION (142D) (Med)
810 Vermont Ave., N.W. Phone: (202)233-2711
Washington, DC 20420 Karen Renninger, Chf., Lib.Div.
Founded: 1930. **Subjects:** Medicine, allied health sciences, health care administration, veterans affairs, management, medical education. **Special Collections:** Veterans Administration archival materials. **Holdings:** 695,000 books; 155,000 AV programs; pamphlets; microforms; government documents. **Subscriptions:** 3400 journals and other serials. **Services:** Interlibrary loan; copying; SDI; library open to the public. **Automated Operations:** Computerized cataloging and ILL. **Computerized Information Services:** BRS Information Technologies, DIALOG Information Services, MEDLARS, NEXIS, Edvent (Educational Events) Data Base, OCLC; VALOR (internal database); MAILVAN, OnTyme Electronic Message Network Service (electronic mail services). **Publications:** List of publications - available on request. **Special Catalogs:** Union List of Periodicals Held in the VA Library Network; Union List of Monographs and Audiovisuals Held in the VA Library Network. **Remarks:** The division administers the libraries in 175 VA facilities throughout the U.S. with a combined staff of 350 library professionals and 350 nonprofessionals. Figures given represent combined holdings. Division is headquarters of VALNET. **Staff:** Diane Wiesenthal, Asst./Lib.Oper.; Wendy Carter, Rd.Serv.Spec.; Jean McVoy, Rsrcs.Coord./Spec.; Mary Ann Tatman, Tech.Serv.Spec.; Mary Kay Massay, Ref.Libn..

★15540★
U.S. VETERANS ADMINISTRATION (DC-Washington) - MEDICAL CENTER LIBRARY (Med)
50 Irving St., N.W. Phone: (202)745-8262
Washington, DC 20422 Mary Netzow, Chf.Libn.
Staff: Prof 3. **Subjects:** General medicine, surgery. **Holdings:** 2000 books; 4300 bound periodical volumes. **Subscriptions:** 200 journals and other serials. **Services:** Interlibrary loan. **Computerized Information Services:** Online systems. **Staff:** Ginny DuPont, Med.Libn.; Gayle Rockelli, Libn..

★15541★
U.S. VETERANS ADMINISTRATION (DC-Washington) - OFFICE OF TECHNOLOGY TRANSFER (110A1) - RESOURCE CENTER (Med)
VA Prosthetics Research & Development Center
103 S. Gay St. Phone: (301)962-1800
Baltimore, MD 21202 Helen Nowatarski, Libn.
Founded: 1949. **Staff:** Prof 1; Other 1. **Subjects:** Prosthetics, sensory aids, orthotics, spinal cord injury, rehabilitation, automotive adaptive equipment, biomechanics. **Holdings:** 3600 books; 80 motion pictures; 15 video cassettes; 2500 technical and contractor reports. **Subscriptions:** 150 journals and other serials. **Services:** Center open to the public for reference use only with permission. **Computerized Information Services:** BRS Information Technologies, DIALOG Information Services, AMA/NET. **Special Indexes:** Index to Journal of Rehabilitation Research and Development.

★15542★
U.S. VETERANS ADMINISTRATION (FL-Bay Pines) - MEDICAL LIBRARY (142D) (Med)
Bay Pines, FL 33504 Phone: (813)398-9366
Ann A. Conlan, Chf., Lib.Serv.
Staff: Prof 3; Other 1. **Subjects:** Medicine, surgery, psychiatry, nursing, radiology, dentistry. **Special Collections:** Gerontology. **Holdings:** 5000 books; 2000 bound periodical volumes. **Subscriptions:** 451 journals and other serials. **Services:** Interlibrary loan; library not open to the public. **Computerized Information Services:** DIALOG Information Services, BRS Information Technologies, MEDLINE. **Networks/Consortia:** Member of VALNET, Tampa Bay Medical Library Network. **Staff:** Arnold Jasen, AV Libn.; Jacqueline Rahman, PHE Libn..

★15543★
U.S. VETERANS ADMINISTRATION (FL-Gainesville) - HOSPITAL LIBRARY (Med)
Archer Rd. Phone: (904)376-1611
Gainesville, FL 32602 Marylyn E. Gresser, Chf., Lib.Serv.
Founded: 1967. **Staff:** Prof 2; Other 1. **Subjects:** Health education, neurology, surgery, internal medicine, nursing, pathology, pharmacology, ophthalmology, psychiatry, radiology. **Holdings:** 6657 books; 2500 periodical volumes; journal volumes on microfilm. **Subscriptions:** 358 journals and other serials; 9 newspapers. **Services:** Interlibrary loan; copying; library open to those in the medical or paramedical fields. **Computerized Information Services:** BRS Information Technologies, MEDLINE. **Networks/Consortia:** Member of VALNET. **Publications:** New Books List, quarterly; Medical Library Policies & Journal Holdings, annual.

★15544★
U.S. VETERANS ADMINISTRATION (FL-Lake City) - MEDICAL CENTER - LEARNING RESOURCE CENTER (Med)
Baya & Marion Sts. Phone: (904)755-3016
Lake City, FL 32055 Shirley Mabry, Chf., Lib.Serv.
Staff: Prof 2; Other 2. **Subjects:** Medicine, surgery, nursing, and allied health sciences; hospital administration; patient education. **Holdings:** 3900 books; 2800 bound periodical volumes; 550 AV programs; 550 patient health education pamphlets and handouts; 300 patient education talking books; 10 VF drawers; 2500 volumes on microfilm. **Subscriptions:** 478 journals and other serials; 8 newspapers. **Services:** Interlibrary loan; copying; SDI; transparencies; center open for reference use to professionals and lay persons requiring health information. **Computerized Information Services:** BRS Information Technologies, MEDLINE; VALOR (internal database); MAILMAN (electronic mail service). **Networks/Consortia:** Member of VALNET. **Publications:** Acquisitions Bulletin, bimonthly; Patients' Library Booklist, bimonthly; Annual Journal List; Health Education List, annual. **Remarks:** Patients' library contains an additional 4000 volumes and 3000 paperbacks.

★15545★
U.S. VETERANS ADMINISTRATION (FL-Miami) - MEDICAL LIBRARY (Med)
1201 N.W. 16th St. Phone: (305)324-3187
Miami, FL 33125 Raissa Maurin, Chf.Libn.
Founded: 1947. **Staff:** Prof 2; Other 3. **Subjects:** Medicine, nursing, psychology, allied health sciences. **Holdings:** 3032 books; 5328 bound periodical volumes; Audio-Digest tapes; 392 AV programs. **Subscriptions:** 650 journals and other serials. **Services:** Interlibrary loan; library not open to the public. **Computerized Information Services:** MEDLINE, BRS Information Technologies; OnTyme Electronic Message Network Service, MAILMAN (electronic mail services). **Networks/Consortia:** Member of

VALNET. **Publications:** Serials Holding List; Acquisitions List bimonthly. **Staff:** Charles D. Garrett, Med.Libn.; Cecy Rowen, ILL Techn..

★15546★
U.S. VETERANS ADMINISTRATION (FL-Tampa) - MEDICAL LIBRARY (Med)
James A. Haley Veterans Hospital
13000 N. Bruce B. Downs Blvd. Phone: (813)972-2000
Tampa, FL 33612 Iris A. Renner, Chf., Lib.Serv.
Staff: Prof 2; Other 1. **Subjects:** Internal medicine, psychiatry, nursing, geriatrics. **Holdings:** 3441 books; 1650 bound periodical volumes. **Subscriptions:** 350 journals and other serials. **Services:** Interlibrary loan; library not open to the public. **Computerized Information Services:** MEDLARS, BRS Information Technologies. **Networks/Consortia:** Member of VALNET, Tampa Bay Medical Library Network. **Staff:** Nancy Bernal, Med.Libn..

★15547★
U.S. VETERANS ADMINISTRATION (GA-Atlanta) - HOSPITAL MEDICAL LIBRARY (Med)
1670 Clairmont Rd. Phone: (404)321-6111
Decatur, GA 30033 Eugenia H. Abbey, Chf.Libn.
Founded: 1945. **Staff:** Prof 2; Other 3. **Subjects:** Medicine, health and social sciences. **Holdings:** 4666 books; 7000 bound periodical volumes; 253 AV programs. **Subscriptions:** 461 journals and other serials. **Services:** Interlibrary loan; copying; SDI; library open to the public for reference use only. **Computerized Information Services:** MEDLINE; MAILMAN (electronic mail service). **Networks/Consortia:** Member of VALNET, Atlanta Health Science Libraries Consortium, Georgia Library Information Network (GLIN). **Remarks:** Patients' library contains an additional 5613 volumes. **Staff:** Rita Clifton, Patients' Libn..

★15548★
U.S. VETERANS ADMINISTRATION (GA-Augusta) - HOSPITAL LIBRARY (Med)
2460 Wrightsboro Rd. Phone: (404)724-5116
Augusta, GA 30910 Elizabeth Northington, Chf., Lib.Serv.
Founded: 1937. **Staff:** Prof 3; Other 3. **Subjects:** Medicine, nursing, psychiatry, allied health sciences. **Holdings:** 4801 books; 2497 bound periodical volumes; 3 VF drawers. **Subscriptions:** 299 journals and other serials; 30 newspapers. **Services:** Interlibrary loan; copying; SDI; library open to the public for reference use only. **Computerized Information Services:** OCLC, BRS Information Technologies, MEDLARS, MEDLINE; VALOR (internal database); MAILMAN (electronic mail service). **Networks/Consortia:** Member of VALNET. **Remarks:** Patients' library contains an additional 17,706 volumes. **Staff:** Anita Bell, Asst.Chf., Lib.Serv.; Robert Schnick, Med.Libn..

★15549★
U.S. VETERANS ADMINISTRATION (GA-Dublin) - CENTER LIBRARY (Med)
Carl Vinson VA Medical Center Phone: (912)272-1210
Dublin, GA 31021 Mrs. Kodell M. Thomas, Chf., Lib.Serv.
Founded: 1948. **Staff:** Prof 1; Other 2. **Subjects:** Medicine, nursing and allied health sciences. **Holdings:** 3708 books; AV programs; microfilm. **Subscriptions:** 280 journals and other serials. **Services:** Interlibrary loan; copying; library open to medical professionals only. **Computerized Information Services:** MEDLINE. **Networks/Consortia:** Member of VALNET, Health Science Libraries of Central Georgia (HSLCG). **Remarks:** Patients' library contains an additional 9447 volumes.

★15550★
U.S. VETERANS ADMINISTRATION (ID-Boise) - MEDICAL CENTER LIBRARY (142D) (Med)
500 W. Fort St. Phone: (208)338-7206
Boise, ID 83702-4598 Gordon Carlson, Chf.Libn.
Founded: 1929. **Staff:** Prof 1; Other 1. **Subjects:** Clinical medicine. **Holdings:** 1800 books; 2894 bound periodical volumes; 450 AV programs. **Subscriptions:** 220 journals and other serials. **Services:** Interlibrary loan; library open to health science professionals and students. **Computerized Information Services:** BRS Information Technologies; OnTyme Electronic Message Network Service, MESSAGES (electronic mail service). **Networks/Consortia:** Member of VALNET, Boise Valley Health Sciences Library Consortium. **Publications:** New Acquisitions List, quarterly - available on request.

★15551★
U.S. VETERANS ADMINISTRATION (IL-Chicago) - LAKESIDE HOSPITAL MEDICAL LIBRARY (Med)
333 E. Huron St. Phone: (312)943-6600
Chicago, IL 60611 Lydia Tkaczuk, Chf., Lib.Serv.
Founded: 1954. **Staff:** Prof 2; Other 1. **Subjects:** Medicine and allied health sciences. **Special Collections:** Patient education; management/employee development collection. **Holdings:** 5000 books; 3500 bound periodical volumes; 200 other cataloged items; 2 VF drawers of pamphlets. **Subscriptions:** 250 journals and other serials. **Services:** Interlibrary loan; copying. **Computerized Information Services:** MEDLINE. **Networks/Consortia:** Member of Greater Midwest Regional Medical Library Network, VALNET, Metropolitan Consortium of Chicago. **Publications:** Medical Library Quarterly. **Staff:** Cheryl Kinnaird, Med.Libn..

★15552★
U.S. VETERANS ADMINISTRATION (IL-Chicago) - WESTSIDE HOSPITAL LIBRARY (Med)
820 S. Damen Ave. Phone: (312)666-6500
Chicago, IL 60612 Christine M. Mitchell, Chf., Lib.Serv.
Founded: 1953. **Staff:** Prof 3; Other 3. **Subjects:** Medicine and allied health sciences. **Holdings:** 6000 books; 3497 bound periodical volumes; 9 linear feet of VF materials; 2300 AV programs. **Subscriptions:** 350 journals and other serials. **Services:** Interlibrary loan; SDI; library open to the public. **Computerized Information Services:** MEDLINE, BRS Information Technologies. **Networks/Consortia:** Member of VALNET, Illinois Health Libraries Consortium, Chicago Library System. **Remarks:** Patients' library contains an additional 2000 volumes. **Staff:** Janette Trofimuk, Med.Libn.; Bryan Parhad, Patients' Libn..

★15553★
U.S. VETERANS ADMINISTRATION (IL-Danville) - MEDICAL CENTER LIBRARY (Med)
Danville, IL 61832 Phone: (217)442-8000
Edward J. Poletti, Chf., Lib.Serv.
Staff: Prof 3; Other 2. **Subjects:** Psychiatry, psychology, medicine, allied health sciences. **Holdings:** 2900 books; 2275 bound periodical volumes; 342 reels of microfilm. **Subscriptions:** 190 journals and other serials. **Services:** Interlibrary loan; library open to health care community for reference use. **Computerized Information Services:** MEDLINE, BRS Information Technologies. **Networks/Consortia:** Member of VALNET, Metropolitan Consortium of Chicago. **Publications:** New Titles List, quarterly - for internal distribution only. **Remarks:** Patients' library contains an additional 3000 volumes.

★15554★
U.S. VETERANS ADMINISTRATION (IL-Hines) - LIBRARY SERVICES (142D) (Med)
Edward Hines, Jr. Medical Center Phone: (312)343-7200
Hines, IL 60141 Bill Leavens, Chf.Libn.
Staff: Prof 4; Other 4. **Subjects:** Hospital administration, medicine, nursing, allied health sciences. **Holdings:** 8000 books; 23,000 bound periodical volumes. **Subscriptions:** 950 journals and other serials. **Services:** Interlibrary loan; copying; library open to the public. **Automated Operations:** Computerized acquisitions. **Computerized Information Services:** VALOR (internal database). **Networks/Consortia:** Member of VALNET, Greater Midwest Regional Medical Library Network, Suburban Library System (SLS). **Remarks:** Patients' libraries contain an additional 9000 volumes. **Staff:** John Cline, Med.Libn.; Ann Novacich, Libn.; Marian Daley, Libn..

★15555★
U.S. VETERANS ADMINISTRATION (IL-Marion) - HOSPITAL LIBRARY (Med)
W. Main St. Phone: (618)997-5311
Marion, IL 62959 Arlene M. Dueker, Chf., Lib.Serv.
Staff: Prof 1; Other 1. **Subjects:** Medicine, surgery. **Holdings:** 956 books. **Subscriptions:** 156 journals and other serials. **Services:** Interlibrary loan; library open to the public with restrictions. **Automated Operations:** Computerized cataloging. **Computerized Information Services:** MEDLARS; MAILMAN (electronic mail service). **Networks/Consortia:** Member of VALNET. **Remarks:** Affiliated with Southern Illinois University Medical School.

★15556★
U.S. VETERANS ADMINISTRATION (IL-North Chicago) - HOSPITAL LIBRARY (Med)
North Chicago, IL 60064 Phone: (312)688-1900
Lou Ann Moore, Act.Chf., Lib.Serv.
Staff: Prof 4; Other 1. **Subjects:** Psychiatry, psychology, medicine, allied health sciences. **Holdings:** 4600 books; 4100 bound periodical volumes; 2 VF drawers; 700 AV programs. **Subscriptions:** 450 journals and other serials; 5 newspapers. **Services:** Interlibrary loan; copying; library open to health science professionals. **Computerized Information Services:** BRS Information Technologies, MEDLINE. **Networks/Consortia:** Member of VALNET. **Publications:** Newsletter; New Book List; bibliographies. **Staff:** Sylvia Ryan, Media Libn..

★15557★
U.S. VETERANS ADMINISTRATION (IN-Fort Wayne) - MEDICAL CENTER LIBRARY SERVICE (Med)
1600 Randallia Dr. Phone: (219)426-5431
Fort Wayne, IN 46805 Enolia L. Stalnaker, Chf., Lib.Serv.
Founded: 1950. **Staff:** Prof 1; Other 1. **Subjects:** Medicine, nursing, patient education. **Holdings:** 954 books; 169 volumes of unbound periodicals; 210 AV programs; 138 microforms. **Subscriptions:** 165 journals and other serials; 10 newspapers. **Services:** Interlibrary loan; copying; SDI; library open to the public with restrictions. **Computerized Information Services:** MEDLARS. **Networks/Consortia:** Member of VALNET, Tri-ALSA, Northeast Indiana Health Sciences Libraries. **Remarks:** Patients' library contains an additional 2442 volumes.

★15558★
U.S. VETERANS ADMINISTRATION (IN-Indianapolis) - MEDICAL CENTER LIBRARY (Med)
1481 W. Tenth St. Phone: (317)635-7401
Indianapolis, IN 46202 Lori L. Klein, Chf., Lib.Serv.
Founded: 1952. **Staff:** Prof 3; Other 2. **Subjects:** General medicine, surgery, nursing, psychiatry, allied health sciences. **Holdings:** 4000 books; 4400 bound periodical volumes; 3000 reels of microfilm; 800 AV programs. **Subscriptions:** 400 journals and other serials. **Services:** Interlibrary loan; copying; SDI; library open to the public. **Automated Operations:** Computerized cataloging. **Computerized Information Services:** MEDLINE, BRS Information Technologies; MESSAGES (electronic mail service). Performs searches free of charge. Contact Person: Linda Bennett, Med.Libn.. **Networks/Consortia:** Member of VALNET, Central Indiana Health Science Library Consortium. **Publications:** New Book List, quarterly; AV list; serials list.

★15559★
U.S. VETERANS ADMINISTRATION (IN-Marion) - HOSPITAL MEDICAL LIBRARY (Med)
E. 38th St. at Home Ave. Phone: (317)674-3321
Marion, IN 46952 Karen A. Davis, Chf., Lib.Serv.
Founded: 1930. **Staff:** Prof 2; Other 2. **Subjects:** Medicine, with special emphasis on psychiatry and psychology. **Special Collections:** NCME video cassette library; Patient Health Education Collection (140 books). **Holdings:** 3720 books; 6648 bound periodical volumes (also in microform); government documents; slides; audio and video cassettes; microforms. **Subscriptions:** 468 journals and other serials; 40 newspapers. **Services:** Interlibrary loan; copying; library open to local health care community. **Automated Operations:** Computerized cataloging, serials, and ILL. **Computerized Information Services:** MEDLARS, BRS Information Technologies; VALOR Interlibrary loan; MAILMAN (electronic mail service). **Networks/Consortia:** Member of VALNET, Eastern Indiana Area Library Services Authority (EIALSA), Greater Midwest Regional Medical Library Network. **Remarks:** Patients' library contains an additional 5983 volumes, with emphasis on patient health education. **Staff:** Alice Clouser, Patient Libn..

★15560★
U.S. VETERANS ADMINISTRATION (IA-Des Moines) - HOSPITAL LIBRARY (Med)
30th & Euclid Ave. Phone: (515)271-5824
Des Moines, IA 50310 Clare M. Jergens, Chf., Lib.Serv.
Founded: 1934. **Staff:** Prof 2; Other 1. **Subjects:** Medicine, nursing, psychology, audiology, surgery, patient education. **Holdings:** 3824 books; 4227 bound periodical volumes; Network for Continuing Medical Education video cassettes. **Subscriptions:** 405 journals and other serials. **Services:** Interlibrary loan; copying; library open to the public for reference use only. **Computerized Information Services:** DIALOG Information Services, MEDLINE; MAILMAN (electronic mail service). **Networks/Consortia:** Member of VALNET, Greater Midwest Regional Medical Library Network, Polk County Biomedical Consortium (PCBC). **Publications:** Source (newsletter), quarterly - for internal distribution only; periodicals holdings list, annual - for internal distribution and to consortia and VALNET members. **Staff:** Geraldine Rees, Libn..

★15561★
U.S. VETERANS ADMINISTRATION (IA-Iowa City) - MEDICAL CENTER LIBRARY (Med)
Iowa City, IA 52241 Phone: (319)338-0581
Jeanine B. Brown, Chf., Lib.Serv.
Founded: 1952. **Staff:** Prof 2. **Subjects:** Medicine, allied health sciences. **Holdings:** 2415 books; 2736 bound periodical volumes; 455 AV programs. **Subscriptions:** 209 journals and other serials. **Services:** Interlibrary loan; copying; SDI; library open to the public. **Automated Operations:** Computerized ILL. **Computerized Information Services:** NLM, BRS Information Technologies; VALOR (internal database); MAILMAN (electronic mail service). **Networks/Consortia:** Member of VALNET.

★15562★
U.S. VETERANS ADMINISTRATION (IA-Knoxville) - MEDICAL CENTER LIBRARY (Med)
Knoxville, IA 50138 Phone: (515)842-3101
R.B. Sayers, Chf.Libn.
Founded: 1921. **Staff:** Prof 2; Other 3. **Subjects:** Psychiatry, psychology, medicine. **Holdings:** 10,500 books; 3000 bound periodical volumes; 400 other cataloged items. **Subscriptions:** 400 journals and other serials; 20 newspapers. **Services:** Interlibrary loan; SDI. **Computerized Information Services:** MEDLINE. **Networks/Consortia:** Member of VALNET. **Staff:** Wanda F. Kincaid, Med.Libn..

★15563★
U.S. VETERANS ADMINISTRATION (KS-Leavenworth) - CENTER MEDICAL LIBRARY (Med)
Leavenworth, KS 66048 Phone: (913)682-2000
Bennett F. Lawson, Chf., Lib.Serv.
Staff: Prof 2; Other 1. **Subjects:** Medicine, allied health sciences. **Holdings:** 3535 books; 4743 bound periodical volumes; 1400 periodical volumes on microfilm. **Subscriptions:** 230 journals and other serials. **Services:** Interlibrary loan; copying; library open to the public for reference use only. **Computerized Information Services:** MEDLINE, BRS Information Technologies, DIALOG Information Services; OnTyme Electronic Message Network Service (electronic mail service). **Networks/Consortia:** Member of VALNET. **Remarks:** Patients' library contains an additional 15,006 volumes. **Staff:** Judith Guttshail, Med.Libn..

★15564★
U.S. VETERANS ADMINISTRATION (KS-Topeka) - DR. KARL A. MENNINGER MEDICAL LIBRARY (Med)
2200 Gage Blvd. Phone: (913)272-3111
Topeka, KS 66622 Norma R. Torkelson, Chf., Lib.Serv.
Founded: 1946. **Staff:** Prof 3; Other 3. **Subjects:** Psychiatry, internal medicine, pathology, neurology, surgery, rehabilitation medicine, psychology, social service, fine arts. **Holdings:** 19,000 books; 5800 bound periodical volumes; 13 VF drawers of clippings, reprints, original papers. **Subscriptions:** 340 journals and other serials. **Services:** Interlibrary loan; library open to the public for reference use only. **Computerized Information Services:** MEDLINE, BRS Information Technologies. **Networks/Consortia:** Member of VALNET. **Publications:** Recent Acquisitions, quarterly - free upon request. **Remarks:** Holdings include patients' library of approximately 9200 volumes. **Staff:** Nancy Vaughn, Med.Libn.; Rosemarie Adkins, Tech.Serv.Libn..

★15565★
U.S. VETERANS ADMINISTRATION (KS-Wichita) - MEDICAL CENTER LIBRARY (Med)
5500 E. Kellogg St. Phone: (316)685-2221
Wichita, KS 67208 Alice H. Schad, Chf., Lib.Serv.
Founded: 1933. **Staff:** Prof 1; Other 1. **Subjects:** Medicine, nursing, allied health sciences, social sciences, patient health education, veterans affairs. **Holdings:** 2000 books; 1155 bound periodical volumes; 1306 reels of microfilm; 4 VF drawers of pamphlets; 414 AV programs. **Subscriptions:** 233 journals and other serials. **Services:** Interlibrary loan; copying; SDI; library open to the public for reference use only. **Automated Operations:** Computerized cataloging and serials. **Computerized Information Services:** BRS Information Technologies, DOCLINE, MEDLARS, MEDLINE; VALOR, Checkmate (internal databases); OnTyme Electronic Message Network Service, FORUM-80 (electronic mail services). **Networks/Consortia:** Member of VALNET. **Publications:** Journal holdings list, annual; acquisitions list, quarterly. **Remarks:** Patients' library contains an additional 5000 volumes.

★15566★
U.S. VETERANS ADMINISTRATION (KY-Lexington) - MEDICAL CENTER LIBRARY (Med)
142D
Leestown Rd.
Lexington, KY 40511 Phone: (606)233-4511
Staff: Prof 3; Other 2. **Subjects:** Psychology, psychiatry, nursing, medicine, surgery, social sciences. **Holdings:** 7000 books; 5000 bound periodical volumes. **Subscriptions:** 260 journals and other serials; 60 newspapers. **Services:** Interlibrary loan; copying; SDI; library open to the public with restrictions. **Computerized Information Services:** MEDLINE. **Networks/Consortia:** Member of VALNET, Kentucky Health Sciences Library Consortium. **Staff:** Deborah Kessler, Med.Libn..

★15567★
U.S. VETERANS ADMINISTRATION (KY-Louisville) - HOSPITAL LIBRARY (Med)
800 Zorn Ave. Phone: (502)895-3401
Louisville, KY 40202 James F. Kastner, Chf.Libn.
Founded: 1946. **Staff:** Prof 3; Other 1. **Subjects:** Clinical medicine, surgery, nursing, psychiatry, social work. **Holdings:** 3250 books; 8000 bound periodical volumes; 8690 volumes of journals in microform; 1325 AV programs. **Subscriptions:** 445 journals and other serials. **Services:** Interlibrary loan; library not open to the public. **Automated Operations:** Computerized cataloging. **Computerized Information Services:** MEDLINE, BRS Information Technologies; MAILMAN (electronic mail service). **Networks/Consortia:** Member of VALNET, Kentucky Health Sciences Library Consortium, State Assisted Academic Library Council of Kentucky (SAALCK), Kentucky Library Network, Inc. (KLN). **Staff:** Alice Briggs, Med.Libn.; Donna White, Med.Libn..

★15568★
U.S. VETERANS ADMINISTRATION (LA-Alexandria) - MEDICAL CENTER MEDICAL LIBRARY (Med)
Alexandria, LA 71301 Phone: (318)473-0010
Nancy M. Guillet, Chf., Lib.Serv.
Founded: 1930. **Staff:** Prof 1; Other 3. **Subjects:** Medicine, employee development, patient education and recreation. **Holdings:** 1478 books; 2475 bound periodical volumes; 61 maps and atlases; 389 AV programs. **Subscriptions:** 184 journals and other serials; 8 newspapers. **Services:** Interlibrary loan; copying (limited); SDI; library open to medical and health professionals. **Computerized Information Services:** MEDLARS, BRS Information Technologies. Performs searches free of charge. **Networks/Consortia:** Member of VALNET, TALON, Health Sciences Library Association of Louisiana. **Remarks:** Patients' library contains an additional 4037 volumes.

★15569★
U.S. VETERANS ADMINISTRATION (LA-New Orleans) - MEDICAL CENTER LIBRARY (Med)
1601 Perdido St. Phone: (504)589-5272
New Orleans, LA 70146 Wilma B. Neveu, Chf., Lib.Serv.
Founded: 1945. **Staff:** Prof 2; Other 1. **Subjects:** Medicine, nursing, dentistry, surgery, allied health sciences. **Holdings:** 3966 books; 2482 bound periodical volumes. **Subscriptions:** 185 journals and other serials; 12 newspapers. **Services:** Interlibrary loan; library not open to the public. **Computerized Information Services:** BRS Information Technologies, MEDLINE. **Networks/Consortia:** Member of VALNET. **Remarks:** Patients' library contains an additional 4190 volumes. **Staff:** Charles Bagnerise, Asst.Libn..

★15570★
U.S. VETERANS ADMINISTRATION (LA-Shreveport) - MEDICAL CENTER LIBRARY (Med)
510 E. Stoner Phone: (318)424-6036
Shreveport, LA 71101 Shirley B. Hegenwald, Chf., Lib.Serv.
Founded: 1950. **Staff:** Prof 2. **Subjects:** General medicine. **Holdings:** 1920 books; 1497 bound periodical volumes; 2 VF drawers of pamphlets. **Subscriptions:** 221 journals and other serials; 6 newspapers. **Services:** Interlibrary loan; library not open to the public. **Computerized Information Services:** MEDLINE; DOCLINE (electronic mail service). **Networks/Consortia:** Member of VALNET. **Remarks:** Patients' library contains an additional 3600 volumes.

★15571★
U.S. VETERANS ADMINISTRATION (ME-Togus) - MEDICAL & REGIONAL OFFICE CENTER - LIBRARY (Med)
Togus, ME 04330 Phone: (207)623-8411
Melda W. Page, Chf.Libn.
Founded: 1933. **Staff:** Prof 3; Other 3. **Subjects:** Social sciences/psychiatry, medicine, alcoholism, nursing, dentistry, hospital administration. **Special Collections:** Patient health education (1000 items). **Holdings:** 4000 books; 3800 bound periodical volumes; 2000 AV programs; 400 serial titles in microform; 3100 other cataloged items. **Subscriptions:** 570 journals and other serials; 50 newspapers. **Services:** Interlibrary loan; copying; SDI; library open to the public. **Automated Operations:** Computerized acquisitions and serials. **Computerized Information Services:** DIALOG Information Services, NLM, BRS Information Technologies, WILSONLINE; MAILMAN, MEDLINK, DOCLINE (electronic mail services). Performs searches on fee basis. Contact Person: Christopher Bovie, Med.Libn.. **Networks/Consortia:** Member of VALNET, Health Science Library and Information Cooperative of Maine (HSLIC). **Publications:** Medical Library Newsletter, quarterly; Patients' Library Newssheet, weekly. **Staff:** June C. Roullard, Med.Libn.; Judy Littlefield, Supv.Lib.Techn.; Christopher Bovie, Med.Libn..

★15572★
U.S. VETERANS ADMINISTRATION (MD-Baltimore) - MEDICAL CENTER LIBRARY SERVICE (142D) (Med)
3900 Loch Raven Blvd. Phone: (301)467-9932
Baltimore, MD 21218 Deborah A. Stout, Chf., Lib.Serv.
Staff: Prof 2. **Subjects:** Medicine, surgery, nursing. **Holdings:** 2000 books; 4000 bound periodical volumes; 200 AV programs; staff and VA publications; pamphlets. **Subscriptions:** 290 journals and other serials. **Services:** Interlibrary loan; copying; SDI; library open to the public for reference use only. **Computerized Information Services:** BRS Information Technologies, NLM; DOCLINE, MAILMAN (electronic mail services). **Networks/Consortia:** Member of VALNET. **Publications:** Acquisitions List, monthly - for internal distribution only. **Remarks:** Patients' library contains an additional 2000 volumes including AV programs, vocational and patient health education collections.

★15573★
U.S. VETERANS ADMINISTRATION (MD-Fort Howard) - HOSPITAL LIBRARY (Med)
Fort Howard, MD 21052 Phone: (301)687-8729
Betty A. Withrow, Chf.Libn.
Founded: 1941. **Staff:** Prof 1; Other 1. **Subjects:** Medicine. **Holdings:** 1800 books; 2262 bound periodical volumes. **Subscriptions:** 160 journals and other serials. **Services:** Interlibrary loan; copying; library open to the public by permission. **Computerized Information Services:** MEDLINE. **Networks/Consortia:** Member of VALNET.

★15574★
U.S. VETERANS ADMINISTRATION (MD-Perry Point) - MEDICAL CENTER MEDICAL LIBRARY (Med)
Perry Point, MD 21902 Phone: (301)642-2411
Barbara A. Schultz, Chf., Lib.Serv.
Founded: 1947. **Staff:** Prof 3; Other 2. **Subjects:** Psychiatry, nursing, geriatrics. **Holdings:** 3800 books; 4298 bound periodical volumes; 660 cassettes; 12 VF drawers of clippings, pamphlets, reprints. **Subscriptions:** 200 journals and other serials. **Services:** Interlibrary loan; copying; library open to the public for reference use only. **Computerized Information Services:** BRS Information Technologies, NLM. **Networks/Consortia:** Member of VALNET, Maryland Association of Health Science Librarians. **Remarks:** Patients' library contains an additional 11,000 volumes. **Staff:** Vikki Cecere, Med.Libn..

★15575★
U.S. VETERANS ADMINISTRATION (MA-Bedford) - EDITH NOURSE ROGERS MEMORIAL VETERANS HOSPITAL - MEDICAL LIBRARY (Med)
200 Springs Rd. Phone: (617)275-7500
Bedford, MA 01730 Sanford S. Yagendorf, Chf., Lib.Serv.
Founded: 1928. **Staff:** Prof 3; Other 3. **Subjects:** Psychiatry, geriatrics. **Holdings:** 6855 books; 3488 bound periodical volumes; 1702 boxes of microfilm; 776 tapes. **Subscriptions:** 270 journals and other serials. **Services:** Interlibrary loan; SDI; library open to the public for reference use only. **Computerized Information Services:** DIALOG Information Services, BRS Information Technologies, MEDLINE; OnTyme Electronic Message Network Service (electronic mail service). **Networks/Consortia:** Member of Boston Biomedical Library Consortium, WELEXACOL, Northeastern Consortium for Health Information (NECHI). **Publications:** Medical Library Newsletter, quarterly; acquisition list, monthly - to hospital staff.

Remarks: Patients' library contains an additional 10,000 volumes. **Staff:** Irmeli Kilburn, Libn., Med.Lib.; Kimberly Megginson, Libn., Patients' Lib..

★15576★
U.S. VETERANS ADMINISTRATION (MA-Boston) - HOSPITAL MEDICAL LIBRARY (142D) (Med)
150 S. Huntington Ave. Phone: (617)739-3434
Boston, MA 02130 John F. Connors, Chf., Lib.Serv.
Founded: 1952. **Staff:** Prof 3; Other 3. **Subjects:** General medicine, surgery, allied health sciences, patient education. **Holdings:** 4500 books; 12,000 bound periodical volumes. **Subscriptions:** 450 journals and other serials. **Services:** Interlibrary loan; copying; SDI; library open to the public with restrictions. **Computerized Information Services:** MEDLINE, BRS Information Technologies; OnTyme Electronic Message Network Service, MEDLINK (electronic mail services). **Networks/Consortia:** Member of VALNET, Boston Biomedical Library Consortium. **Remarks:** Patients' library contains an additional 5344 volumes. **Staff:** Ann Samson, Patients' Libn.; Olga Lyczmanenko, Med.Libn..

★15577★
U.S. VETERANS ADMINISTRATION (MA-Boston) - OUTPATIENT CLINIC LIBRARY SERVICE (142D) (Med)
17 Court St.
Boston, MA 02108 Carolyn B. Mathes, Chf., Lib.Serv.
Founded: 1975. **Staff:** Prof 2; Other 3. **Subjects:** Health sciences, consumer health, U.S. military, management. **Holdings:** 2500 books; 1836 periodical volumes on microfilm; 1000 patient education pamphlets. **Subscriptions:** 182 journals and other serials. **Services:** Interlibrary loan; copying; SDI; library open to the public. **Automated Operations:** Computerized ILL. **Computerized Information Services:** DIALOG Information Services, BRS Information Technologies; OnTyme Electronic Message Network Service (electronic mail service). Performs searches free of charge. **Networks/Consortia:** Member of VALNET, Massachusetts Health Sciences Library Network (MAHSLIN), Greater Northeastern Regional Medical Library Program. **Publications:** Newsletter, 4/year; bibliographies; new acquisitions list, monthly. **Staff:** Lucy Butler, Libn..

★15578★
U.S. VETERANS ADMINISTRATION (MA-Brockton) - MEDICAL CENTER LIBRARY (Med)
940 Belmont St. Phone: (617)583-4500
Brockton, MA 02401 Suzanne Noyes, Chf., Lib.Serv.
Founded: 1953. **Staff:** Prof 2; Other 3. **Subjects:** Psychiatry, psychology, hospital administration, nursing, medicine, alcoholism, drug abuse. **Holdings:** 5200 books; 7000 bound periodical volumes; 400 other cataloged items. **Subscriptions:** 450 journals and other serials. **Services:** Interlibrary loan; copying; library open to the public. **Computerized Information Services:** MEDLINE, DIALOG Information Services, BRS Information Technologies; MAILMAN, OnTyme Electronic Message Network Service, MEDLINK (electronic mail services). **Networks/Consortia:** Member of VALNET, Greater Northeastern Regional Medical Library Program, Southeastern Massachusetts Cooperating Libraries (SMCL), Southeastern Massachusetts Consortium of Health Science Libraries (SEMCO). **Publications:** Medical Library Newsletter, monthly. **Remarks:** Patients' library contains an additional 10,000 volumes. **Staff:** Bruce Thornlow, Ref./AV Libn..

★15579★
U.S. VETERANS ADMINISTRATION (MA-Northampton) - MEDICAL CENTER LIBRARY (Med)
N. Main St. Phone: (413)584-4040
Northampton, MA 01060 Marjorie C. Dewey, Chf., Lib.Serv.
Founded: 1935. **Staff:** Prof 2; Other 5. **Subjects:** Neurology, psychiatry, psychology, nursing, medicine. **Holdings:** 3122 books; 273 bound periodical volumes; 3823 volumes on microfilm; 812 unbound periodical volumes. **Subscriptions:** 249 journals and other serials. **Services:** Interlibrary loan; library open to the public for reference use only. **Computerized Information Services:** BRS Information Technologies. **Networks/Consortia:** Member of VALNET, Western Massachusetts Health Information Consortium, Massachusetts Health Sciences Library Network (MAHSLIN). **Remarks:** Patients' library contains an additional 10,141 volumes.

★15580★
U.S. VETERANS ADMINISTRATION (MI-Allen Park) - MEDICAL CENTER LIBRARY SERVICE (142D) (Med)
Southfield and Outer Dr. Phone: (313)562-6000
Allen Park, MI 48101 Arlene Devlin, Chf., Lib.Serv.
Founded: 1939. **Staff:** Prof 2; Other 3. **Subjects:** Surgery, oncology, internal medicine, psychiatry, psychology, health management. **Special Collections:** Health information for patients; patient record slide collection; complete works of Sigmund Freud; Armed Forces Institute of Pathology (AFIP) Pathology Series. **Holdings:** 8000 books; 10,000 bound periodical volumes; 1500 reels of microfilm. **Subscriptions:** 450 journals and other serials; 10 newspapers. **Services:** Interlibrary loan; copying; SDI; library open to the public with restrictions. **Automated Operations:** Computerized acquisitions. **Computerized Information Services:** DIALOG Information Services, BRS Information Technologies, MEDLARS; internal database; OnTyme Electronic Message Network Service (electronic mail service). **Networks/Consortia:** Member of VALNET, Metropolitan Detroit Medical Library Group (MDMLG). **Publications:** Acquisitions list, quarterly; journal list, annual. **Staff:** Mary Jo Durivage, Med.Libn..

★15581★
U.S. VETERANS ADMINISTRATION (MI-Ann Arbor) - HOSPITAL LIBRARY (Med)
2215 Fuller Rd. Phone: (313)769-7100
Ann Arbor, MI 48105 Vickie Smith, Act.Chf.Libn.
Founded: 1953. **Staff:** Prof 1; Other 1. **Subjects:** Medicine, patient education. **Holdings:** 4610 books; 3610 bound periodical volumes. **Subscriptions:** 345 journals and other serials. **Services:** Interlibrary loan; copying; SDI; library open to the public with restrictions. **Computerized Information Services:** MEDLINE, BRS Information Technologies; VALOR (internal database). **Networks/Consortia:** Member of VALNET, Washtenaw-Livingston Library Network (WLLN), Metropolitan Detroit Medical Library Group (MDMLG).

★15582★
U.S. VETERANS ADMINISTRATION (MI-Battle Creek) - MEDICAL CENTER LIBRARY (Med)
Battle Creek, MI 49016 Phone: (616)966-5600
Thomas Pyles, Jr., Chf., Lib.Serv.
Founded: 1925. **Staff:** Prof 2; Other 3. **Subjects:** Psychiatry, neurology. **Holdings:** 2554 books; 913 bound periodical volumes; 1856 volumes of journals on microfilm. **Subscriptions:** 423 journals and other serials; 21 newspapers. **Services:** Interlibrary loan; copying; library open to the public. **Automated Operations:** Computerized cataloging. **Computerized Information Services:** BRS Information Technologies, MEDLINE; MAILMAN (electronic mail service). Performs searches free of charge. Contact Person: Barbara Burhans, Biomed.Libn., 966-5600, ext. 4280. **Networks/Consortia:** Member of VALNET. **Remarks:** Patients' library contains an additional 9380 books and 138 bound periodical volumes.

★15583★
U.S. VETERANS ADMINISTRATION (MI-Iron Mountain) - MEDICAL CENTER LIBRARY (Med)
East H St. Phone: (906)774-3300
Iron Mountain, MI 49801 Jeanne M. Durocher, Chf., Lib.Serv.
Founded: 1950. **Staff:** Prof 1; Other 1. **Subjects:** Internal medicine, surgery, nursing. **Holdings:** 1474 books; 2318 bound periodical volumes; 15 files of patient education materials; 87 video cassettes; 365 audio cassettes; 592 filmstrips and slide/tape kits. **Subscriptions:** 253 journals and other serials; 29 newspapers. **Services:** Interlibrary loan; SDI; library open to the public for reference use only. **Automated Operations:** Computerized cataloging. **Computerized Information Services:** MEDLINE; MAILMAN (electronic mail service). **Networks/Consortia:** Member of VALNET, UP Health Sciences Libraries Consortium, Michigan Health Sciences Libraries Association (MHSLA), Mid-Peninsula Library Cooperative. **Remarks:** Patients' library contains an additional 5700 volumes.

★15584★
U.S. VETERANS ADMINISTRATION (MI-Saginaw) - MEDICAL CENTER LIBRARY (Med)
1500 Weiss St. Phone: (517)793-2340
Saginaw, MI 48602 Nancy R. Dingman, Chf., Lib.Serv.
Founded: 1950. **Staff:** Prof 2; Other 1. **Subjects:** Medicine, surgery, nursing, health education. **Special Collections:** Respiratory, coronary, and intensive care; computer information and management. **Holdings:** 2000 books; periodicals in microform; 1000 AV programs; health education pamphlets. **Subscriptions:** 150 journals and other serials; 6 newspapers. **Services:** Interlibrary loan; copying; SDI; library open to hospital personnel only. **Automated Operations:** Access to computerized cataloging, acquisitions, serials, and ILL. **Computerized Information Services:** MEDLINE, DIALOG Information Services, BRS Information Technologies; internal databases. **Networks/Consortia:** Member of VALNET, Greater Midwest Regional Medical Library Network, Michigan Health Sciences Libraries Association (MHSLA). **Remarks:** Patients' library contains an additional 2000 volumes and a large collection of health educational AV, print, and pamphlet materials.

★15585★
U.S. VETERANS ADMINISTRATION (MN-Minneapolis) - MEDICAL CENTER LIBRARY SERVICE (Med)
54th St. & 48th Ave., S. Phone: (612)725-6767
Minneapolis, MN 55417 Margery MacNeill, Chf., Lib.Serv.
Founded: 1946. **Staff:** Prof 4; Other 6. **Subjects:** General medicine, psychology, pre-clinical sciences. **Holdings:** 5500 books; 11,000 bound periodical volumes; 1500 volumes on microfilm; 1000 AV programs. **Subscriptions:** 530 journals and other serials; 5 newspapers. **Services:** Interlibrary loan; SDI; patient education; library not open to the public. **Computerized Information Services:** MEDLINE, DIALOG Information Services, BRS Information Technologies; OnTyme Electronic Message Network Service, MAILMAN (electronic mail services). **Networks/Consortia:** Member of VALNET, Greater Midwest Regional Medical Library Network, Twin Cities Biomedical Consortium (TCBC). **Publications:** Acquisitions list, quarterly; special bibliographies; list of journal holdings, annual; patient education publications. **Remarks:** Patient Education Center/Library has print and nonprint collections in health care field for patients, families, and staff. **Staff:** Kathy Mackay, Libn., Patient Educ.Ctr.; Dorothy Sinha, Med.Libn.; Judith Stanke, Med.Libn..

★15586★
U.S. VETERANS ADMINISTRATION (MN-St. Cloud) - MEDICAL CENTER LIBRARY (Med)
St. Cloud, MN 56301 Phone: (612)252-1670
Sanford J. Banker, Chf., Lib.Serv.
Founded: 1924. **Staff:** Prof 3; Other 1. **Subjects:** General medicine, psychology, nursing, geriatrics. **Holdings:** 2000 books; 1000 bound periodical volumes; microfilm. **Subscriptions:** 325 journals and other serials. **Services:** Interlibrary loan; copying; library open to health care professionals, students, and local residents for reference use only. **Computerized Information Services:** MAILMAN, OnTyme Electronic Message Network Service (electronic mail services). **Networks/Consortia:** Member of VALNET. **Remarks:** Patients' library contains an additional 8000 volumes.

★15587★
U.S. VETERANS ADMINISTRATION (MS-Jackson) - CENTER LIBRARY (Med)
1500 E. Woodrow Wilson Dr. Phone: (601)364-1273
Jackson, MS 39216 Carol Sistrunk, Chf.Libn.
Founded: 1946. **Staff:** Prof 2; Other 1. **Subjects:** Medicine and allied health sciences. **Holdings:** 1800 books; 2750 bound periodical volumes; 2000 volumes of journals on microfilm; 275 AV software programs. **Subscriptions:** 200 journals and other serials; 5 newspapers. **Services:** Interlibrary loan; copying; SDI; library open to the public by permission. **Automated Operations:** Computerized circulation. **Computerized Information Services:** MEDLINE, BRS Information Technologies; VALOR (internal database); MAILMAN (electronic mail service). **Networks/Consortia:** Member of VALNET, Central Mississippi Council of Medical Libraries, Mississippi Biomedical Library Consortium. **Remarks:** Patients' library contains an additional 500 volumes.

★15588★
U.S. VETERANS ADMINISTRATION (MO-Columbia) - HOSPITAL LIBRARY (Med)
800 Stadium Rd. Phone: (314)443-2511
Columbia, MO 65201 Ray Starke, Chf., Lib.Serv.
Founded: 1972. **Staff:** Prof 2; Other 3. **Subjects:** Medicine, surgery. **Special Collections:** Patient education (267 books; 67 AV programs). **Holdings:** 4400 books; 2000 bound periodical volumes. **Subscriptions:** 300 journals and other serials; 14 newspapers. **Services:** Interlibrary loan; copying; SDI; library open to the public for reference use only. **Automated Operations:** Computerized cataloging and serials. **Computerized Information Services:** MEDLARS, BRS Information Technologies, DIALOG Information Services; MAILMAN, OnTyme Electronic Message Network Service (electronic mail services). **Networks/Consortia:** Member of VALNET, Mid-Missouri Library Network (MMLN). **Staff:** Mark Fleetwood, Med.Libn..

★15589★
U.S. VETERANS ADMINISTRATION (MO-Kansas City) - MEDICAL CENTER LIBRARY (Med)
4801 Linwood Blvd. Phone: (816)861-4700
Kansas City, MO 64128 Shirley C. Ting, Chf., Lib.Serv.
Founded: 1952. **Staff:** Prof 2; Other 1. **Subjects:** Medicine, surgery, neurology, nursing, psychology, psychiatry. **Special Collections:** Patient education. **Holdings:** 4730 books; 6278 bound periodical volumes; 550 AV programs. **Subscriptions:** 364 journals and other serials. **Services:** Interlibrary loan; copying; SDI; library open to the public for reference use only. **Automated Operations:** Computerized cataloging, acquisitions, serials, and ILL. **Computerized Information Services:** MEDLINE, BRS Information Technologies, Octanet, Mednet, DIALOG Information Services; internal database; OnTyme Electronic Message Network Service, MESSAGES, Mednet (electronic mail services). **Networks/Consortia:** Member of VALNET, Midcontinental Regional Medical Library Program, Kansas City Library Network, Inc. (KCLN). **Remarks:** Patients' library contains an additional 4669 volumes. **Staff:** Valerie Smith, Med.Libn..

★15590★
U.S. VETERANS ADMINISTRATION (MO-Poplar Bluff) - LIBRARY SERVICE (142D) (Med)
John J. Pershing Veterans Administration Medical Center
1500 N. Westwood Blvd. Phone: (314)686-4151
Poplar Bluff, MO 63901 Wilfrid S. Akiyama, Chf., Lib.Serv.
Founded: 1951. **Staff:** Prof 1. **Subjects:** Medicine. **Holdings:** 944 books; AV equipment and programs. **Subscriptions:** 154 journals and other serials; 9 newspapers. **Services:** Interlibrary loan; copying; SDI; library open to the public. **Computerized Information Services:** MEDLARS. **Networks/Consortia:** Member of VALNET. **Remarks:** Patients' library contains an additional 4029 books and 56 periodicals.

★15591★
U.S. VETERANS ADMINISTRATION (MO-St. Louis) - LIBRARY SERVICE (142D) (Med)
Jefferson Barracks Division Phone: (314)487-0400
St. Louis, MO 63125 Larry Weitkemper, Chf., Lib.Serv.
Staff: Prof 5; Other 3. **Subjects:** Medicine and allied health sciences. **Special Collections:** Geriatrics. **Holdings:** 5500 books; 5000 bound periodical volumes; 8000 reels of microfilm; 1200 AV programs. **Subscriptions:** 750 journals and other serials. **Services:** Interlibrary loan; copying; SDI; library open to the public. **Computerized Information Services:** Philnet, DIALOG Information Services, MEDLARS; MAILMAN (electronic mail service). **Networks/Consortia:** Member of VALNET, Saint Louis Medical Librarians Consortia. **Remarks:** Patients' libraries contain an additional 4000 volumes. **Staff:** John Chesmelewski, Libn.; Ann Repetto, Libn.; Alfreida Keeling, Libn..

★15592★
U.S. VETERANS ADMINISTRATION (MT-Fort Harrison) - MEDICAL CENTER LIBRARY (Med)
Fort Harrison, MT 59636 Phone: (406)442-6410
Charles Grasmick, Chf., Lib.Serv.
Staff: Prof 1. **Subjects:** Medicine, internal medicine, surgery. **Holdings:** 1484 books. **Subscriptions:** 268 journals and other serials; 10 newspapers. **Services:** Interlibrary loan; library open to the public with restrictions. **Computerized Information Services:** MEDLARS. **Networks/Consortia:** Member of VALNET, Helena Area Health Sciences Library Consortium (HAHSLC). **Remarks:** Patients' library contains an additional 6013 volumes.

★15593★
U.S. VETERANS ADMINISTRATION (MT-Miles City) - MEDICAL CENTER LIBRARY (Med)
Miles City, MT 59301 Phone: (406)232-3060
Elizabeth J. Alme, Chf., Lib.Serv.
Founded: 1951. **Staff:** 1. **Subjects:** Medicine. **Holdings:** 1288 volumes. **Subscriptions:** 131 journals and other serials. **Services:** Interlibrary loan; library not open to the public. **Automated Operations:** Computerized ILL. **Computerized Information Services:** MEDLARS. **Networks/Consortia:** Member of VALNET. **Remarks:** Patients' library contains an additional 1229 volumes.

★15594★
U.S. VETERANS ADMINISTRATION (NE-Grand Island) - HOSPITAL LIBRARY (Med)
2201 N. Broadwell St.
Grand Island, NE 68803 Phone: (308)382-3660
Founded: 1950. **Staff:** Prof 1. **Subjects:** Medicine, surgery, nursing. **Holdings:** 1074 books. **Subscriptions:** 110 journals and other serials. **Services:** Interlibrary loan; copying; loan services from Library of Congress and regional libraries for blind and physically handicapped; library open to the public by permission. **Remarks:** Patients' library contains an additional 1000 volumes, 12 journal subscriptions, and large print books.

★15595★
U.S. VETERANS ADMINISTRATION (NE-Lincoln) - MEDICAL CENTER LIBRARY (142D) (Med)
600 S. 70th St.
Lincoln, NE 68510 Phone: (402)489-3802
Staff: Prof 1; Other 1. **Subjects:** Medicine and allied health sciences. **Holdings:** 1555 titles; 3800 bound periodical volumes; 700 journals on microfilm; 700 AV programs. **Subscriptions:** 253 journals and other serials. **Services:** Interlibrary loan; copying; library open to qualified medical personnel. **Computerized Information Services:** NLM. **Networks/Consortia:** Member of VALNET, Lincoln Health Science Library Group. **Remarks:** Patients' library contains an additional 3000 volumes.

★15596★
U.S. VETERANS ADMINISTRATION (NE-Omaha) - HOSPITAL LIBRARY (Med)
4101 Woolworth Ave. Phone: (402)346-8800
Omaha, NE 68105 Lois J. Inskeep, Chf., Lib.Serv.
Founded: 1950. **Staff:** Prof 1; Other 1. **Subjects:** Medicine and allied health sciences. **Holdings:** 2000 books; 3800 bound periodical volumes; 2000 AV programs. **Subscriptions:** 250 journals and other serials; 25 newspapers. **Services:** Interlibrary loan; copying; library open to the public by request. **Networks/Consortia:** Member of VALNET.

★15597★
U.S. VETERANS ADMINISTRATION (NV-Reno) - MEDICAL CENTER - LEARNING CENTER (Med)
1000 Locust St. Phone: (702)786-7200
Reno, NV 89509 Christine J. Simpson, Chf., Lib.Serv.
Staff: Prof 2; Other 1. **Subjects:** Clinical medicine, gerontology. **Holdings:** 2300 books. **Subscriptions:** 210 journals and other serials. **Services:** Interlibrary loan; copying; SDI; library open to the public with referral. **Automated Operations:** Computerized cataloging. **Computerized Information Services:** DIALOG Information Services, MEDLARS; MAILMAN, OnTyme Electronic Message Network Service (electronic mail services). **Networks/Consortia:** Member of VALNET, Northern California and Nevada Medical Library Group (NCNMLG). **Staff:** Ester Robles, Libn..

★15598★
U.S. VETERANS ADMINISTRATION (NH-Manchester) - MEDICAL CENTER LIBRARY (Med)
718 Smyth Rd. Phone: (603)624-4366
Manchester, NH 03104 Joan McGinnis, Chf., Lib.Serv.
Founded: 1950. **Staff:** Prof 1; Other 1. **Subjects:** Medicine, surgery, nursing. **Holdings:** 1650 books; 1500 bound periodical volumes. **Subscriptions:** 168 journals and other serials; 12 newspapers. **Services:** Interlibrary loan; copying; SDI; library open to the public with restrictions. **Computerized Information Services:** BRS Information Technologies, NLM; MAILMAN, DOCLINE, OnTyme Electronic Message Network Service (electronic mail services). **Networks/Consortia:** Member of VALNET, Health Science Libraries of New Hampshire and Vermont. **Remarks:** Patients' library contains an additional 2500 volumes.

★15599★
U.S. VETERANS ADMINISTRATION (NJ-East Orange) - MEDICAL CENTER LIBRARY (142D) (Med)
Tremont & S. Centre Phone: (201)676-1000
East Orange, NJ 07019 Calvin A. Zamarelli, Chf., Lib.Serv.
Founded: 1952. **Staff:** Prof 3; Other 3. **Subjects:** General medicine. **Holdings:** 11,000 books; 16,000 bound periodical volumes; 900 AV programs. **Subscriptions:** 400 journals and other serials. **Services:** Interlibrary loan; library not open to the public. **Automated Operations:** Computerized acquisitions and serials. **Computerized Information Services:** BRS Information Technologies, DIALOG Information Services, MEDLINE. **Networks/Consortia:** Member of VALNET. **Staff:** David Madden, Med.Libn.; Judith Grace, AV Libn./ILL.

★15600★
U.S. VETERANS ADMINISTRATION (NJ-Lyons) - HOSPITAL LIBRARY (Med)
Knollcroft Rd. Phone: (201)647-0180
Lyons, NJ 07939 James G. Delo, Chf., Lib.Serv.
Founded: 1930. **Staff:** Prof 2; Other 1. **Subjects:** Psychiatry, neurology, psychology, medicine, nursing, patient health education. **Holdings:** 9000 books; 5200 bound periodical volumes; 500 AV programs; 14 newspapers. **Services:** Interlibrary loan; copying; library open to the public for reference use only. **Computerized Information Services:** BRS Information Technologies, MEDLINE; MUMPS (internal database). **Networks/Consortia:** Member of VALNET, Medical Resources Consortium of Central New Jersey (MEDCORE). **Remarks:** Patients' library contains an additional 13,329 volumes. **Staff:** Marian Krugman, Patients' Libn..

★15601★
U.S. VETERANS ADMINISTRATION (NM-Albuquerque) - MEDICAL CENTER LIBRARY (Med)
2100 Ridgecrest Dr., S.E. Phone: (505)265-1711
Albuquerque, NM 87108 Nancy Myer, Chf., Lib.Serv.
Founded: 1932. **Staff:** Prof 2; Other 2. **Subjects:** Medicine, surgery, nursing, psychiatry. **Holdings:** 1530 books; 8537 bound periodical volumes; 500 reels of microfilm of journals. **Subscriptions:** 393 journals and other serials; 10 newspapers. **Services:** Interlibrary loan; copying; library open to the public by special permission. **Computerized Information Services:** MEDLINE, DIALOG Information Services. **Networks/Consortia:** Member of VALNET, New Mexico Consortium of Biomedical and Hospital Libraries. **Remarks:** Patients' library contains an additional 1225 volumes. **Staff:** Phyllis L. Kregstein, Biomed.Libn..

★15602★
U.S. VETERANS ADMINISTRATION (NY-Albany) - MEDICAL CENTER LIBRARY (142D) (Med)
113 Holland Ave. Phone: (518)462-3311
Albany, NY 12208 Carolyn B. Mathes, Chf., Lib.Serv.
Founded: 1951. **Staff:** Prof 2; Other 2. **Subjects:** Medicine, social services, nursing, mental health. **Holdings:** 2500 books; 1920 bound periodical volumes; 210 AV programs. **Subscriptions:** 302 journals and other serials. **Services:** Interlibrary loan; copying; SDI; library open to the public for reference use only. **Automated Operations:** Computerized acquisitions and ILL. **Computerized Information Services:** MEDLINE, BRS Information Technologies; MAILMAN (electronic mail service). **Networks/Consortia:** Member of VALNET, Capital District Library Council for Reference & Research Resources (CDLC). **Publications:** Medical Library Handbook; Patient Library Handbook; Journal Holdings List; New Book List. **Staff:** Diane Kiefer, Med.Libn..

★15603★
U.S. VETERANS ADMINISTRATION (NY-Batavia) - MEDICAL CENTER LIBRARY (Med)
Redfield Pkwy. Phone: (716)343-7500
Batavia, NY 14020 Madeline A. Coco, Chf.Libn.
Founded: 1934. **Staff:** Prof 1; Other 1. **Subjects:** General medicine, surgery, nursing, pathology, radiology. **Holdings:** 1700 books; 1700 bound periodical volumes. **Subscriptions:** 99 journals and other serials. **Services:** Interlibrary loan; copying; library open to medical professionals and students. **Computerized Information Services:** MEDLINE. **Networks/Consortia:** Member of VALNET, Western New York Library Resources Council (WNYLRC). **Remarks:** Patients' library contains an additional 4500 volumes.

★15604★
U.S. VETERANS ADMINISTRATION (NY-Bath) - MEDICAL CENTER LIBRARY (Med)
Bath, NY 14810 Phone: (607)776-2111
Founded: 1930. **Staff:** Prof 2; Other 1. **Subjects:** Geriatrics, chronic diseases, general internal medicine, long term care. **Holdings:** 1479 books; 450 bound periodical volumes; 482 video cassettes; 600 periodical volumes on microfilm. **Subscriptions:** 123 journals and other serials; 23 newspapers. **Services:** Interlibrary loan; library not open to the public. **Automated Operations:** Computerized cataloging and acquisitions. **Computerized Information Services:** MEDLINE, BRS Information Technologies; MAILMAN (electronic mail service). **Networks/Consortia:** Member of VALNET, South Central Research Library Council (SCRLC). **Publications:** Newsletter. **Remarks:** Patients' library contains an additional 12,521 volumes. **Staff:** Sally Ann Hillegas, Med.Libn..

★15605★
U.S. VETERANS ADMINISTRATION (NY-Bronx) - MEDICAL CENTER LIBRARY (Med)
130 W. Kingsbridge Rd.
Bronx, NY 10468 Margaret M. Kinney, Chf.Libn.
Staff: Prof 3; Other 3. **Subjects:** Medicine and allied health sciences. **Holdings:** 20,244 volumes. **Services:** Interlibrary loan; library open to the public with restrictions. **Computerized Information Services:** Online systems. **Networks/Consortia:** Member of VALNET. **Remarks:** Patients' library contains an additional 5000 volumes.

★15606★
U.S. VETERANS ADMINISTRATION (NY-Brooklyn) - MEDICAL CENTER LIBRARY (Med)
800 Poly Place
Brooklyn, NY 11209 Phone: (718)836-6600
Founded: 1947. **Staff:** Prof 3; Other 3. **Subjects:** Medicine, surgery, psychiatry, psychology, nursing, social work. **Holdings:** 6685 books; 7226 bound periodical volumes; 106 video cassettes; 138 slide sets; 6 films. **Subscriptions:** 477 journals and other serials. **Services:** Interlibrary loan; library not open to the public. **Automated Operations:** Computerized cataloging. **Computerized Information Services:** MEDLINE, DIALOG Information Services, BRS Information Technologies; DOCLINE, OnTyme Electronic Message Network Service (electronic mail services). **Networks/Consortia:** Member of VALNET, Medical Library Center of New York (MLCNY), Brooklyn-Queens-Staten Island Health Sciences Librarians (BQSI), New York Metropolitan Reference and Research Library Agency (METRO). **Staff:** Halyna Liszczynskyj, Med.Libn..

★15607★
U.S. VETERANS ADMINISTRATION (NY-Buffalo) - MEDICAL CENTER LIBRARY SERVICE (Med)
3495 Bailey Ave. Phone: (716)834-9200
Buffalo, NY 14215 Betty A. Withrow, Chf.Libn.
Founded: 1950. **Staff:** Prof 3; Other 1. **Subjects:** Medicine, surgery, nursing, management, patient education. **Holdings:** 2700 books; 9000 bound periodical volumes; 700 AV programs. **Subscriptions:** 389 journals and other serials. **Services:** Interlibrary loan; copying; SDI; library open to the public for reference use only. **Computerized Information Services:** BRS Information Technologies, NLM, DIALOG Information Services. Performs searches free of charge for graduate students. **Networks/Consortia:** Member of VALNET, Western New York Library Resources Council (WNYLRC), Greater Northeastern Regional Medical Library Program, Library Consortium of Health Institutions in Buffalo (LCHIB). **Publications:** Newsletter, quarterly; Serial Holdings List, annual; AV Holdings List, annual; Patient Education Bibliography; Management Bibliography; Geriatrics Bibliography; Nursing Bibliography. **Remarks:** Patients' library contains an additional 5000 volumes. **Staff:** Russell Hall, Med.Libn.; James Mendola, Med.Libn..

★15608★
U.S. VETERANS ADMINISTRATION (NY-Canandaigua) - MEDICAL CENTER LIBRARY (142D) (Med)
Canandaigua, NY 14424 Phone: (716)396-3649
Peter Fleming, Chf., Lib.Serv.
Founded: 1933. **Staff:** Prof 2; Other 3. **Subjects:** Psychiatry, psychology, medicine, nursing, alcoholism, geriatrics. **Holdings:** 4000 books; 612 bound periodical volumes; 2488 other volumes. **Subscriptions:** 200 journals and other serials. **Services:** Interlibrary loan; SDI; library open to the public for reference use only. **Automated Operations:** Computerized cataloging. **Computerized Information Services:** NLM, BRS Information Technologies. **Networks/Consortia:** Member of Rochester Regional Library Council (RRLC). **Remarks:** Patients' library contains an additional 7270 volumes.

★15609★
U.S. VETERANS ADMINISTRATION (NY-Castle Point) - DEPARTMENT OF MEDICINE AND SURGERY - LIBRARY SERVICE (Med)
Castle Point, NY 12511 Phone: (914)831-2000
Kimberly Megginson, Chf., Lib.Serv.
Staff: Prof 1; Other 2. **Subjects:** Spinal cord injuries, surgery, nursing education, geriatric medicine, dentistry. **Holdings:** 1966 books; 649 periodicals on microfilm; 286 audio cassettes; 37 video cassettes. **Subscriptions:** 250 journals and other serials; 10 newspapers. **Services:** Interlibrary loan; copying; SDI; library open to the public for reference use only. **Computerized Information Services:** MEDLINE, BRS Information Technologies; VALOR (internal database). **Networks/Consortia:** Member of VALNET, Southeastern New York Library Resources Council (SENYLRC).

★15610★
U.S. VETERANS ADMINISTRATION (NY-Montrose) - MEDICAL LIBRARY (Med)
Franklin Delano Roosevelt Veterans Medical Ctr. Phone: (914)737-4400
Montrose, NY 10548 Bruce S. Delman, Ph.D., Chf., Lib.Serv.
Founded: 1950. **Staff:** Prof 4; Other 2. **Subjects:** Psychiatry, psychology, orthopedics, medicine, sociology, nursing. **Special Collections:** Patient Education Collection. **Holdings:** 7422 books; 1600 bound periodical volumes; 2800 boxes of microfilm; 15 VF drawers of pamphlets and clippings; 436 AV programs. **Subscriptions:** 615 journals and other serials; 8 newspapers. **Services:** Interlibrary loan; copying; SDI; library open to the public by permission. **Computerized Information Services:** MEDLARS; MAILMAN (electronic mail service). Performs searches on fee basis. Contact Person: Mark Simmons, Med.Libn.. **Networks/Consortia:** Member of VALNET, Health Information Libraries of Westchester (HILOW), New York Metropolitan Reference and Research Library Agency (METRO). **Publications:** Medical Library News, bimonthly - to staff members and VA hospitals. **Remarks:** Patients' library contains an additional 5067 volumes. **Staff:** Timothy Galvin, AV Libn..

★15611★
U.S. VETERANS ADMINISTRATION (NY-New York) - MEDICAL LIBRARY (Med)
408 First Ave. Phone: (212)686-7500
New York, NY 10010 Erich Meyerhoff, Chf.Libn.
Founded: 1955. **Staff:** Prof 4; Other 5. **Subjects:** Medicine, surgery, neurology, psychiatry, nursing. **Holdings:** 5000 books; 5684 bound periodical volumes. **Subscriptions:** 500 journals and other serials; 10 newspapers. **Services:** Interlibrary loan; library open to affiliated medical professionals. **Computerized Information Services:** MEDLINE. **Networks/Consortia:** Member of VALNET, Medical Library Center of New York (MLCNY), Manhattan-Bronx Health Sciences Library Group. **Remarks:** Patients' library contains an additional 5344 volumes. **Staff:** Karin Wiseman, Asst.Chf.Libn.; Lily Hom, Gen.Libn..

★15612★
U.S. VETERANS ADMINISTRATION (NY-Northport) - HEALTH SCIENCE LIBRARY (Med)
Middleville Rd. Phone: (516)261-4400
Northport, NY 11768 Deborah Sher, Chf., Lib.Serv.
Staff: Prof 4; Other 3. **Subjects:** Medicine, allied health sciences, psychiatry, dentistry. **Special Collections:** Geriatrics; hospital administration. **Holdings:** 5000 books; 2000 AV programs. **Subscriptions:** 600 journals and other serials. **Services:** Interlibrary loan; library open to the public for reference use only. **Computerized Information Services:** MEDLINE, BRS Information Technologies, DIALOG Information Services. **Networks/Consortia:** Member of VALNET, Medical & Scientific Libraries of Long Island (MEDLI), Long Island Library Resources Council, Inc. (LILRC). **Publications:** Library Line, quarterly. **Staff:** Caryl Kazan, Asst.Chf.; Marc Horowitz, AV Libn.; Robert Toronto, Libn..

★15613★
U.S. VETERANS ADMINISTRATION (NY-Syracuse) - MEDICAL CENTER LIBRARY (Med)
Irving Ave. & University Pl. Phone: (315)476-7461
Syracuse, NY 13210 June M. Mitchell, Chf., Lib./LRC Serv.
Founded: 1953. **Staff:** Prof 3. **Subjects:** Clinical medicine, surgery, nursing, psychology, social work. **Holdings:** 4000 books; 2625 bound and microform periodical volumes; 700 pamphlets. **Subscriptions:** 190 journals and other serials. **Services:** Library open to the public for reference use only. **Computerized Information Services:** MEDLINE. **Networks/Consortia:** Member of VALNET, Central New York Library Resources Council (CENTRO). **Remarks:** Patients' library contains an additional 10,000 volumes, including management and patient education collections. Learning Resources Center, established in 1975, contains many AV programs in patient education, staff instruction and training. **Staff:** Kay A.W. Root, Med.Libn.; E. Nancy Hellwig, AV Libn..

★15614★
U.S. VETERANS ADMINISTRATION (NC-Asheville) - MEDICAL CENTER LIBRARY (Med)
Riceville & Tunnel Rds. Phone: (704)298-7911
Asheville, NC 28805 Jane Lambermont, Chf.Libn.
Staff: Prof 1; Other 1. **Subjects:** General and cardiopulmonary medicine, thoracic surgery, nursing. **Holdings:** 2000 books; 3000 bound periodical volumes. **Subscriptions:** 275 journals and other serials. **Services:** Interlibrary loan; copying; library open to medical professionals. **Automated Operations:** Computerized serials. **Computerized Information Services:** NLM, BRS Information Technologies, DIALOG Information Services. **Networks/Consortia:** Member of VALNET.

★15615★
U.S. VETERANS ADMINISTRATION (NC-Durham) - MEDICAL CENTER LIBRARY (Med)
508 Fulton St. Phone: (919)286-0411
Durham, NC 27705 Leola H. Jenkins, Chf., Lib.Serv.
Founded: 1953. **Staff:** Prof 2; Other 1. **Subjects:** Clinical medicine, pre-clinical sciences, allied health sciences, management, research, patient health education. **Holdings:** 4311 books; 9000 bound periodical volumes; 2500 reels of microfilm; 70 microfiche; 1256 AV programs. **Subscriptions:**

443 journals and other serials; 13 newspapers. **Services:** Interlibrary loan; SDI; library open to the public with restrictions. **Computerized Information Services:** MEDLINE, BRS Information Technologies, Net-Search; MAILMAN, OnTyme Electronic Message Network Service (electronic mail services). **Networks/Consortia:** Member of VALNET. **Publications:** Medical Library Journal Holdings, annual; Library Guide, irregular; PERC Update, quarterly; Library Communique, quarterly. **Staff:** Margaret F. Clifton, Med.Libn.; Sheila H. Thompson, Per./ILL Libn..

★15616★
U.S. VETERANS ADMINISTRATION (NC-Fayetteville) - HOSPITAL LIBRARY (Med)
Fayetteville, NC 28301 Phone: (919)488-2120
Diana Akins, Chf., Lib.Serv.
Founded: 1940. **Staff:** Prof 1; Other 1. **Subjects:** Medicine, nursing, dentistry. **Holdings:** 2900 books; 3978 periodicals; 467 AV programs. **Subscriptions:** 420 journals and other serials. **Services:** Interlibrary loan; copying; SDI; library open to students and physicians. **Computerized Information Services:** MEDLINE, BRS Information Technologies; MAILMAN, DOCLINE (electronic mail services). **Networks/Consortia:** Member of VALNET, Cape Fear Health Sciences Information Consortium. **Remarks:** Patients' library contains an additional 3900 volumes and patient health education resource center.

★15617★
U.S. VETERANS ADMINISTRATION (NC-Salisbury) - MEDICAL CENTER LIBRARY (Med)
1601 Brenner Ave. Phone: (704)636-2351
Salisbury, NC 28144 Mara R. Wilhelm, Chf., Lib.Serv.
Founded: 1953. **Staff:** Prof 3; Other 3. **Subjects:** Psychology, psychiatry, nursing, internal medicine, alcoholism, surgery, gerontology, dentistry. **Holdings:** 2700 books; 1500 AV programs. **Subscriptions:** 274 journals and other serials. **Services:** Interlibrary loan; library open to health science professionals. **Computerized Information Services:** BRS Information Technologies, MEDLINE; DOCLINE (electronic mail service). **Networks/Consortia:** Member of VALNET. **Publications:** Newsletter, monthly - for internal distribution only. **Remarks:** Patients' library contains an additional 2300 books. **Staff:** Lucile Owsley, Libn.; Glenna McCowan, Libn..

★15618★
U.S. VETERANS ADMINISTRATION (ND-Fargo) - CENTER LIBRARY (Med)
Fargo, ND 58102 Phone: (701)232-3241
James Robbins, Chf., Lib.Serv.
Founded: 1945. **Staff:** Prof 3. **Subjects:** Medicine, dentistry, nursing, social work, hospital administration. **Holdings:** 2700 books; 5605 bound periodical volumes; 2 VF drawers of reprints, pamphlets, bibliographies. **Subscriptions:** 290 journals and other serials. **Services:** Interlibrary loan; copying; library open to the public with restrictions. **Computerized Information Services:** MEDLINE, BRS Information Technologies. Performs searches on fee basis. **Networks/Consortia:** Member of VALNET, Valley Medical Network (VMN), Prairie Library Network. **Remarks:** Patients' library services and patient education material available. **Staff:** Jane Borland, SE Campus Libn..

★15619★
U.S. VETERANS ADMINISTRATION (OH-Brecksville) - MEDICAL LIBRARY (142D) (Med)
10000 Brecksville Rd. Phone: (216)526-3030
Brecksville, OH 44141 Nancy S. Tesmer, Chf., Lib.Serv.
Founded: 1961. **Staff:** Prof 3; Other 3. **Subjects:** Psychology, nursing, psychiatry, social work, neurology. **Holdings:** 4807 volumes; 20 dissertations; 1900 AV programs. **Subscriptions:** 285 journals and other serials. **Services:** Interlibrary loan; SDI; library open to the public. **Computerized Information Services:** MEDLINE, DIALOG Information Services, BRS Information Technologies, EdVent (Educational Events) Data Base. **Networks/Consortia:** Member of VALNET. **Special Catalogs:** Subject coded reference catalog on suicide (card). **Remarks:** Patients' library contains an additional 2000 volumes. **Staff:** Mary Conway, Med.Libn.; John C. White, AV Libn..

★15620★
U.S. VETERANS ADMINISTRATION (OH-Chillicothe) - HOSPITAL LIBRARY (Med)
Chillicothe, OH 45601 Phone: (614)773-1141
John A. Package, Chf.Libn.
Founded: 1947. **Staff:** Prof 2; Other 2. **Subjects:** Psychiatry, medicine, allied health sciences. **Holdings:** 4525 volumes; 4 VF drawers. **Subscriptions:** 220 journals and other serials. **Services:** Interlibrary loan; copying; SDI. **Computerized Information Services:** MEDLARS, BRS Information Technologies. **Networks/Consortia:** Member of VALNET. **Remarks:** Patients' library contains an additional 7050 volumes.

★15621★
U.S. VETERANS ADMINISTRATION (OH-Cincinnati) - MEDICAL CENTER LIBRARY (Med)
3200 Vine St. Phone: (513)861-3100
Cincinnati, OH 45220 Judith Alfred, Chf., Lib.Serv.
Staff: Prof 2. **Subjects:** Medicine, mental health, nursing, surgery. **Holdings:** 10,036 volumes. **Subscriptions:** 218 journals and other serials. **Services:** Interlibrary loan; SDI; library open to the public. **Automated Operations:** Computerized cataloging. **Computerized Information Services:** NLM, BRS Information Technologies; MAILMAN (electronic mail service). **Networks/Consortia:** Member of VALNET. **Staff:** Robert Mohrman, Med.Libn..

★15622★
U.S. VETERANS ADMINISTRATION (OH-Cleveland) - HOSPITAL LIBRARY (Med)
10701 East Blvd. Phone: (216)791-3800
Cleveland, OH 44106 Nancy S. Tesmer, Chf., Lib.Serv.
Founded: 1946. **Staff:** Prof 5; Other 5. **Subjects:** Clinical and pre-clinical medicine. **Holdings:** 9664 books; 7915 bound periodical volumes. **Subscriptions:** 485 journals and other serials. **Services:** Interlibrary loan; copying; library open to the public by permission. **Computerized Information Services:** DIALOG Information Services, BRS Information Technologies, MEDLINE. **Networks/Consortia:** Member of VALNET. **Remarks:** Patients' library contains an additional 7495 volumes. The library also serves the Brecksville unit, 10000 Brecksville Rd., Brecksville, OH 44141. **Staff:** Mary Nourse, Med.Libn.; Mary Conway, Med.Libn.; John C. White, AV Libn..

★15623★
U.S. VETERANS ADMINISTRATION (OH-Dayton) - CENTER LIBRARY SERVICE (142D) (Med)
4100 W. Third St. Phone: (513)268-6511
Dayton, OH 45428 Lendell Beverly, Chf., Lib.Serv.
Founded: 1867. **Staff:** Prof 4; Other 3. **Subjects:** Medicine, nursing, hospital administration, patient education, military history. **Special Collections:** U.S. Military History (1200 volumes); patient education. **Holdings:** 7000 books; 4840 bound periodical volumes. **Subscriptions:** 500 journals and other serials; 22 newspapers. **Services:** Interlibrary loan; copying; SDI; library open to the public for reference use only. **Automated Operations:** Computerized cataloging. **Computerized Information Services:** BRS Information Technologies, NLM, DIALOG Information Services; OnTyme Electronic Message Network Service, DOCLINE (electronic mail services). **Networks/Consortia:** Member of VALNET. **Publications:** Fact Sheet; new book list, monthly. **Remarks:** Patients' library contains an additional 9000 volumes. **Staff:** Robert Mohrman, AV Libn.; Mert Adams, Patient Educ.Rsrc.Ctr.Libn..

★15624★
U.S. VETERANS ADMINISTRATION (OK-Muskogee) - MEDICAL CENTER LIBRARY (Med)
1101 Honor Height Dr. Phone: (918)683-3261
Muskogee, OK 74401 Larry L. Shea, Chf., Lib.Serv.
Staff: Prof 2; Other 3. **Subjects:** Medicine, nursing, allied health sciences. **Holdings:** 3269 books; 4584 bound periodical volumes; 737 AV programs. **Subscriptions:** 251 medical journals; 12 newspapers. **Services:** Interlibrary loan; copying; SDI; library open to hospital staff and health professionals in the community. **Automated Operations:** Computerized cataloging and acquisitions. **Computerized Information Services:** MEDLARS. **Networks/Consortia:** Member of VALNET, Oklahoma Health Sciences Library Association (OHSLA), South Central Academic Medical Libraries Consortium (SCAMEL). **Publications:** Library Newsletter, quarterly; journals holdings list, annual; AV holdings list, annual. **Remarks:** Patients' library contains an additional 3076 volumes and 172 patient education programs. **Staff:** Carolyn Gutierrez, Med.Libn..

★15625★
U.S. VETERANS ADMINISTRATION (OK-Oklahoma City) - MEDICAL CENTER LIBRARY (Med)
921 N.E. 13th St. Phone: (405)272-9876
Oklahoma City, OK 73104 Verlean Delaney, Chf.Libn.
Founded: 1946. **Staff:** 3. **Subjects:** Medicine, patient health education, consumer information. **Holdings:** 1553 books; 4372 bound periodical volumes; 426 AV programs. **Subscriptions:** 310 journals and other serials. **Services:** Interlibrary loan; SDI; library open to the public for reference use only. **Computerized Information Services:** NLM. **Networks/Consortia:**

Member of VALNET, Greater Oklahoma City Area Health Sciences Library Consortium (GOAL). **Publications:** Medical Media Newsbreak, biweekly - for internal distribution.

★15626★
U.S. VETERANS ADMINISTRATION (OR-Portland) - MEDICAL LIBRARY (Med)
Box 1035 Phone: (503)220-8262
Portland, OR 97207 Mrs. Nymah L. Trued, Chf., Lib.Serv.
Staff: Prof 3; Other 3. **Subjects:** Medicine, nursing, allied health sciences, psychology, basic sciences. **Special Collections:** Patient Health Information. **Holdings:** 5900 books; 6010 bound periodical volumes; journals on microfilm. **Subscriptions:** 590 journals; 95 administrative serials. **Services:** Interlibrary loan; copying; SDI; library open to the public for reference use only. **Computerized Information Services:** MEDLARS, BRS Information Technologies; OnTyme Electronic Message Network Service (electronic mail service). **Networks/Consortia:** Member of VALNET. **Publications:** Acquisitions List - for internal distribution only.

★15627★
U.S. VETERANS ADMINISTRATION (OR-Portland) - VANCOUVER DIVISION - MEDICAL LIBRARY (Med)
Box 1035 Phone: (206)696-4061
Portland, OR 97207 Mrs. Nymah L. Trued, Chf., Lib.Serv.
Founded: 1946. **Subjects:** Medicine. **Special Collections:** Patient Health Information. **Holdings:** Figures not available. **Services:** Interlibrary loan; copying; SDI; library open to the public for reference use only. **Computerized Information Services:** MEDLARS, BRS Information Technologies; OnTyme Electronic Message Network Service (electronic mail service). **Networks/Consortia:** Member of VALNET.

★15628★
U.S. VETERANS ADMINISTRATION (OR-Roseburg) - MEDICAL CENTER LIBRARY SERVICE (Med)
Garden Valley Blvd. Phone: (503)440-1000
Roseburg, OR 97470 Cathryn M. Jordan, Chf., Lib.Serv.
Staff: Prof 1; Other 1. **Subjects:** Medicine, patient education, management, nursing. **Holdings:** 4400 books; 500 AV programs; 60 journals on microfilm. large-print materials. **Subscriptions:** 340 journals and other serials; 15 newspapers. **Services:** Interlibrary loan; copying; SDI; library open to the public when referred by another librarian. **Automated Operations:** Computerized circulation. **Computerized Information Services:** NLM, BRS Information Technologies, DIALOG Information Services; MAILMAN, OnTyme Electronic Message Network Service (electronic mail services). Performs searches free of charge. **Networks/Consortia:** Member of VALNET, Oregon Health Information Network (OHIN), Oregon Health Sciences Libraries Association (OHSLA), Substance Abuse Librarians and Information Specialists (SALIS). **Publications:** Newsletter, bimonthly - for internal distribution and to other librarians.

★15629★
U.S. VETERANS ADMINISTRATION (OR-White City) - LIBRARY (Med)
VA Domiciliary Phone: (503)826-2111
White City, OR 97503 Sarah Fitzpatrick, Chf., Lib.Serv.
Staff: Prof 2; Other 1. **Subjects:** Medicine. **Holdings:** 10,662 books; 101 bound periodical volumes. **Subscriptions:** 379 journals and other serials; 22 newspapers. **Services:** Interlibrary loan; library not open to the public. **Computerized Information Services:** MAILMAN (electronic mail service). **Networks/Consortia:** Member of VALNET. **Staff:** Margaret C. Rose, Libn..

★15630★
U.S. VETERANS ADMINISTRATION (PA-Altoona) - JAMES E. VAN ZANDT MEDICAL CENTER - LIBRARY SERVICE (142D) (Med)
27th St. & Robin Ave. Phone: (814)943-8164
Altoona, PA 16603 Linda Knerr, Chf., Lib.Serv.
Founded: 1950. **Staff:** Prof 1; Other 1. **Subjects:** Medicine, patient education, management. **Holdings:** 5089 books; 500 periodical volumes; 1355 reels of microfilm and AV programs. **Subscriptions:** 220 journals and other serials; 43 newspapers. **Services:** Interlibrary loan; copying; SDI; library open to the public with restrictions. **Automated Operations:** Computerized cataloging. **Computerized Information Services:** BRS Information Technologies, Sterling Software; FILEMAN (internal database); MAILMAN (electronic mail service). **Networks/Consortia:** Member of Central Pennsylvania Health Sciences Library Association (CPHSLA). **Publications:** Orientation booklets for patients and medical staff.

★15631★
U.S. VETERANS ADMINISTRATION (PA-Butler) - MEDICAL CENTER LIBRARY (Med)
Butler, PA 16001 Phone: (412)287-4781
Dianne Hohn, Chf., Lib.Serv.
Founded: 1946. **Staff:** Prof 2; Other 1. **Subjects:** Nursing, general medicine. **Holdings:** 2000 books; 3000 periodical volumes, bound and in microform. **Subscriptions:** 100 journals and other serials; 10 newspapers. **Services:** Interlibrary loan; copying; library open to the public for reference use only. **Computerized Information Services:** BRS Information Technologies. **Networks/Consortia:** Member of VALNET. **Remarks:** Patients' library contains an additional 5623 volumes. **Staff:** Donna D. Blose, Libn..

★15632★
U.S. VETERANS ADMINISTRATION (PA-Coatesville) - MEDICAL CENTER LIBRARY (Med)
Coatesville, PA 19320 Phone: (215)383-0245
Mary Lou Burton, Chf., Lib.Serv.
Founded: 1930. **Staff:** Prof 3; Other 3. **Subjects:** Psychiatry, neurology, medicine, nursing, psychology. **Holdings:** 7200 books; 8000 bound periodical volumes; 10 VF drawers of information files; 1500 AV programs. **Subscriptions:** 450 journals and other serials; 10 newspapers. **Services:** Interlibrary loan; copying; library open to health service personnel only. **Automated Operations:** Computerized serials. **Computerized Information Services:** Informatics Inc., MEDLINE, BRS Information Technologies. **Networks/Consortia:** Member of VALNET, Consortium for Health Information & Library Services (CHI). **Remarks:** Patients' library contains an additional 5000 volumes. **Staff:** Frances De Million, Libn.; Mary L. Walters, Libn..

★15633★
U.S. VETERANS ADMINISTRATION (PA-Erie) - MEDICAL CENTER - MEDICAL LIBRARY (Med)
135 E. 38th St. Phone: (814)868-6207
Erie, PA 16504 Jeff Kager, Chf., Lib.Serv.
Founded: 1951. **Staff:** Prof 1; Other 1. **Subjects:** Medicine, nursing, geriatrics, quality assurance. **Special Collections:** The classics of medicine library (70 volumes). **Holdings:** 3000 books; 4000 boxes of microfilm. **Subscriptions:** 220 journals and other serials; 15 newspapers. **Services:** Interlibrary loan; copying; SDI; library open to the public for reference use only. **Automated Operations:** Computerized cataloging. **Computerized Information Services:** MEDLARS; FILEMAN (internal database); MAILMAN (electronic mail service). Performs searches free of charge. **Networks/Consortia:** Member of VALNET, Erie Area Health Information Library Cooperative (EAHILC), Northwest Interlibrary Cooperative of Pennsylvania (NICOP). **Publications:** Periodicals holdings list, annual - for internal distribution only.

★15634★
U.S. VETERANS ADMINISTRATION (PA-Lebanon) - MEDICAL CENTER LIBRARY (Med)
State Drive Phone: (717)272-6621
Lebanon, PA 17042 David E. Falger, Chf., Lib.Serv.
Founded: 1947. **Staff:** Prof 3; Other 3. **Subjects:** Medicine, aging and geriatrics, psychiatry. **Holdings:** 2093 books; 1000 periodical volumes on microfilm. **Subscriptions:** 259 journals and other serials; 37 newspapers. **Services:** Interlibrary loan; copying (limited); library open to the public with restrictions. **Computerized Information Services:** DIALOG Information Services, MEDLINE, BRS Information Technologies; MAILMAN, DOCLINE (electronic mail services). **Networks/Consortia:** Member of VALNET, Greater Northeastern Regional Medical Library Program, Central Pennsylvania Health Sciences Library Association (CPHSLA). **Publications:** Quarterly newsletter. **Remarks:** Patients' library contains an additional 5000 books. **Staff:** Barbara E. Deaven, Med.Libn.; Michelle Clark, Patients' Libn..

★15635★
U.S. VETERANS ADMINISTRATION (PA-Philadelphia) - MEDICAL CENTER LIBRARY (Med)
University & Woodland Aves. Phone: (215)823-5860
Philadelphia, PA 19104 Robert S. Lyle, Chf., Lib.Serv.
Founded: 1953. **Staff:** Prof 2; Other 1. **Subjects:** Medicine and allied health sciences. **Holdings:** 3010 books; 7100 bound periodical volumes. **Subscriptions:** 415 journals and other serials. **Services:** Interlibrary loan; copying; SDI; library open to the public by permission. **Computerized Information Services:** BRS Information Technologies, MEDLINE; MAILMAN (electronic mail service). **Networks/Consortia:** Member of VALNET, Delaware Valley Information Consortium (DEVIC). **Staff:** Cynthia Burhans, Libn..

★15636★
U.S. VETERANS ADMINISTRATION (PA-Pittsburgh) - MEDICAL CENTER LIBRARY SERVICE (142D) (Med)
Highland Dr. Phone: (412)363-4900
Pittsburgh, PA 15206 Sandra Mason, Chf.
Founded: 1953. **Staff:** Prof 2; Other 1. **Subjects:** Psychiatry, general medicine, neurology, nursing, social work. **Holdings:** 3319 books; 8 VF drawers of pamphlets; 458 video cassettes. **Subscriptions:** 298 journals and other serials; 6 newspapers. **Services:** Interlibrary loan; library not open to the public. **Computerized Information Services:** MEDLARS, BRS Information Technologies. **Networks/Consortia:** Member of VALNET. **Publications:** Bibliographies. **Remarks:** Patients' library contains an additional 6310 volumes.

★15637★
U.S. VETERANS ADMINISTRATION (PA-Pittsburgh) - MEDICAL CENTER LIBRARY SERVICE (142D) (Med)
University Dr. C Phone: (412)683-3000
Pittsburgh, PA 15240 Tuula Beazell, Chf., Lib.Serv.
Founded: 1946. **Staff:** Prof 3; Other 2. **Subjects:** Medicine and allied health sciences. **Holdings:** 2200 books; 12,400 bound periodical volumes. **Subscriptions:** 400 journals and other serials. **Services:** Interlibrary loan; copying; SDI. **Computerized Information Services:** BRS Information Technologies; VALOR (internal database); MAILMAN (electronic mail service). **Networks/Consortia:** Member of VALNET.

★15638★
U.S. VETERANS ADMINISTRATION (PA-Wilkes-Barre) - MEDICAL CENTER LIBRARY (Med)
1111 E. End Blvd. Phone: (717)824-3521
Wilkes-Barre, PA 18711 Bruce D. Reid, Chf., Lib.Serv.
Founded: 1950. **Staff:** Prof 2; Other 1. **Subjects:** Medicine, allied health sciences. **Holdings:** 6299 books; 2600 bound periodical volumes; journals on microfilm. **Subscriptions:** 234 journals and other serials. **Services:** Interlibrary loan; library open to the public with restrictions. **Computerized Information Services:** Online systems. **Networks/Consortia:** Member of VALNET, Northeastern Pennsylvania Bibliographic Center (NEPBC), Health Information Library Network of Northeastern Pennsylvania (HILNNEP). **Remarks:** Patients' library contains an additional 4800 volumes.

★15639★
U.S. VETERANS ADMINISTRATION (PR-San Juan) - HOSPITAL LIBRARY (Med)
VA Medical & Regional Office Center
Barrio Monacillos
Box 4867 Phone: (809)758-7575
San Juan, PR 00936 Raquel A. Walters, Chf., Lib.Serv.
Founded: 1947. **Staff:** Prof 2; Other 2. **Subjects:** Medicine and specialties, nursing, surgery and specialties, dietetics and nutrition. **Holdings:** 8598 books and bound periodical volumes; AV programs. **Subscriptions:** 610 journals and other serials. **Services:** Interlibrary loan; library open to the public through sharing agreements with community institutions. **Computerized Information Services:** NLM. **Publications:** Annual Periodical Holding List; Quarterly New Medical Books List; Annual Library Orientation Guide. **Remarks:** Patients' library contains an additional 8745 volumes with special collections on the Caribbean, management, talking books. **Staff:** Virginia E. Budet, Patients' Libn..

★15640★
U.S. VETERANS ADMINISTRATION (RI-Providence) - HEALTH SCIENCES LIBRARY (Med)
Davis Park Phone: (401)457-3001
Providence, RI 02908 Lynn A. Lloyd, Chf., Lib.Serv.
Founded: 1949. **Staff:** Prof 2. **Subjects:** Medicine, nursing, psychology, allied health sciences, social work, management. **Holdings:** 3500 books; 4000 bound periodical volumes; AV programs. **Subscriptions:** 307 journals and other serials. **Services:** Interlibrary loan; copying; SDI; library open to the public for reference use only. **Computerized Information Services:** MEDLINE, BRS Information Technologies; OnTyme Electronic Message Network Service (electronic mail service). **Networks/Consortia:** Member of North Atlantic Health Science Libraries (NAHSL), Association of Rhode Island Health Sciences Librarians (ARIHSL). **Publications:** Bibliographies. **Remarks:** Patients' library contains consumer health education collection.

★15641★
U.S. VETERANS ADMINISTRATION (SC-Columbia) - WILLIAM JENNINGS BRYAN-DORN VETERANS HOSPITAL - LIBRARY (Med)
Garners Ferry Rd. Phone: (803)776-4000
Columbia, SC 29201 Charletta P. Felder, Chf., Lib.Serv.
Founded: 1933. **Staff:** Prof 2. **Subjects:** Medicine, surgery, nursing, dentistry, psychiatry. **Holdings:** 3817 books; 3200 bound periodical volumes; 15 drawers of microfilm; 800 AV programs. **Subscriptions:** 250 journals and other serials; 12 newspapers. **Services:** Interlibrary loan; copying; SDI; library open to the public. **Computerized Information Services:** MEDLINE; OnTyme Electronic Message Network Service (electronic mail service). **Networks/Consortia:** Member of VALNET, Columbia Area Medical Librarians' Association (CAMLA). **Remarks:** Patients' library contains an additional 6500 volumes. **Staff:** Emily E. Clyburn, Staff Libn..

★15642★
U.S. VETERANS ADMINISTRATION (SD-Fort Meade) - MEDICAL CENTER LIBRARY SERVICE (142D) (Med)
Fort Meade, SD 57741 Phone: (605)347-2511
Gene Stevens, Chf., Lib.Serv.
Founded: 1942. **Staff:** Prof 1; Other 1. **Subjects:** Medicine and allied health sciences. **Holdings:** 1180 books; 1158 volumes of journals on microfilm; 301 AV programs. **Subscriptions:** 128 journals and other serials. **Services:** Interlibrary loan; copying; library open to the public. **Computerized Information Services:** MEDLINE; MAILMAN (electronic mail service). Performs searches free of charge. **Networks/Consortia:** Member of VALNET. **Remarks:** Patients' library contains an additional 3599 titles.

★15643★
U.S. VETERANS ADMINISTRATION (SD-Hot Springs) - CENTER LIBRARY (Med)
Hot Springs, SD 57747 Phone: (605)745-4101
Carole W. Miles, Chf., Lib.Serv.
Staff: Prof 1; Other 1. **Subjects:** Geriatrics, surgery. **Holdings:** 845 books; 781 bound periodical volumes. **Subscriptions:** 108 journals and other serials. **Services:** Interlibrary loan; library open to the medical community. **Remarks:** Patients' library contains an additional 10,135 volumes.

★15644★
U.S. VETERANS ADMINISTRATION (SD-Sioux Falls) - MEDICAL & REGIONAL OFFICE CENTER - MEDICAL LIBRARY (Med)
2501 W. 22nd St.
Box 5046 Phone: (605)336-3230
Sioux Falls, SD 57117 Steve Cole, Act.Chf., Lib.Serv.
Staff: Prof 2; Other 2. **Subjects:** General medicine and allied health sciences. **Special Collections:** AV medical collection (1200 programs). **Holdings:** 4600 books; 4631 bound periodical volumes; 4968 reels of microfilm; 1168 AV programs. **Subscriptions:** 400 journals and other serials; 50 newspapers. **Services:** Interlibrary loan; copying; SDI; library open to medical and allied health professionals. **Computerized Information Services:** NLM, BRS Information Technologies; OnTyme Electronic Message Network Service, EasyLink (electronic mail services). **Networks/Consortia:** Member of VALNET. **Remarks:** Patients' library contains an additional 2984 volumes.

★15645★
U.S. VETERANS ADMINISTRATION (TN-Johnson City) - MEDICAL CENTER LIBRARY (Med)
Mountain Home, TN 37684 Phone: (615)926-1171
Nancy Dougherty, Chf., Lib.Serv.
Staff: Prof 2; Other 1. **Subjects:** Medicine and allied health sciences. **Holdings:** 2925 books; 3681 bound periodical volumes. **Subscriptions:** 315 journals and other serials. **Services:** Interlibrary loan; library open to the public with restrictions. **Computerized Information Services:** MEDLARS, BRS Information Technologies; MAILMAN (electronic mail service). **Networks/Consortia:** Member of VALNET, Tri-Cities Area Health Sciences Libraries Consortium. **Remarks:** Patients' library contains an additional 18,000 volumes. **Staff:** Joan Warden, Libn.; Peggy Patterson, Libn..

★15646★
U.S. VETERANS ADMINISTRATION (TN-Memphis) - MEDICAL CENTER LIBRARY (Med)
1030 Jefferson Ave. Phone: (901)523-8990
Memphis, TN 38104 Mary Virginia Taylor, Chf., Lib.Serv.
Founded: 1941. **Staff:** Prof 2; Other 2. **Subjects:** Medicine, dentistry, nursing. **Holdings:** 4650 books; 3377 bound periodical volumes; microfilm.

Subscriptions: 250 journals and other serials. **Services:** Interlibrary loan; SDI; library open to the public for reference use only. **Computerized Information Services:** MEDLINE; MAILMAN (electronic mail service). **Networks/Consortia:** Member of VALNET, Association of Memphis Area Health Sciences Libraries (AMAHSL). **Remarks:** Patients' library contains an additional 6000 volumes. **Staff:** Mari Lyn Melin, MEDLINE Libn..

★15647★
U.S. VETERANS ADMINISTRATION (TN-Murfreesboro) - MEDICAL CENTER LIBRARY (Med)
Murfreesboro, TN 37130 Phone: (615)893-1360
Joy W. Hunter, Chf., Lib.Serv.
Staff: Prof 3; Other 1. **Subjects:** Psychiatry, medicine, nursing. **Holdings:** 2800 books; 1200 bound periodical volumes; 1072 AV programs. **Subscriptions:** 280 journals and other serials. **Services:** Interlibrary loan; library not open to the public. **Automated Operations:** Computerized cataloging. **Computerized Information Services:** BRS Information Technologies, MEDLINE. **Networks/Consortia:** Member of VALNET. **Publications:** Libragram, quarterly - for internal distribution only. **Remarks:** Patients' library contains an additional 4600 volumes. **Staff:** Marie Eubanks, Med.Libn.; Ruby H. Nichols, Patients' Libn..

★15648★
U.S. VETERANS ADMINISTRATION (TN-Nashville) - MEDICAL CENTER LIBRARY SERVICE (Med)
1310 24th Ave., S. Phone: (615)327-4751
Nashville, TN 37203 Barbara A. Meadows, Chf., Lib.Serv.
Founded: 1946. **Staff:** Prof 2; Other 1. **Subjects:** Medicine, nursing, psychology, nuclear medicine, hospital administration, dentistry. **Holdings:** 2050 books; 4202 bound periodical volumes; 294 AV programs. **Subscriptions:** 263 journals and other serials. **Services:** Interlibrary loan; copying; library open to the public for reference use only. **Automated Operations:** Computerized cataloging and serials. **Computerized Information Services:** MEDLINE. **Networks/Consortia:** Member of VALNET.

★15649★
U.S. VETERANS ADMINISTRATION (TX-Amarillo) - HOSPITAL LIBRARY (Med)
Amarillo, TX 79106 Phone: (806)355-9703
Cheryl A. Latham, Chf., Lib.Serv.
Founded: 1941. **Staff:** Prof 1; Other 1. **Subjects:** General medicine, surgery, nursing, dentistry. **Special Collections:** Staff and patient education collection (550 AV programs; 150 pamphlet titles). **Holdings:** 3894 books; periodicals on microfilm. **Subscriptions:** 235 journals and other serials. **Services:** Interlibrary loan; copying; library open to area medical personnel only. **Computerized Information Services:** MEDLINE. **Networks/Consortia:** Member of VALNET. **Publications:** Medical Newsletter, quarterly; serials listing. **Special Catalogs:** Patient Education Materials Catalog.

★15650★
U.S. VETERANS ADMINISTRATION (TX-Big Spring) - HOSPITAL LIBRARY (Med)
2400 S. Gregg St.
Big Spring, TX 79720 Phone: (915)263-7361
Founded: 1950. **Staff:** Prof 1. **Subjects:** General medicine, surgery. **Holdings:** 947 books; 1149 bound periodical volumes. **Subscriptions:** 63 journals and other serials. **Services:** Interlibrary loan; library open to qualified health personnel only. **Remarks:** Patients' library contains an additional 3112 volumes.

★15651★
U.S. VETERANS ADMINISTRATION (TX-Bonham) - SAM RAYBURN MEMORIAL VETERANS CENTER - MEDICAL LIBRARY (Med)
9th & Lipscomb Sts. Phone: (214)583-2111
Bonham, TX 75418 Donna S. Locke, Chf., Lib.Serv.
Founded: 1951. **Staff:** Prof 1; Other 1. **Subjects:** Medicine and allied health sciences. **Holdings:** 713 books; 248 bound periodical volumes; 110 Audio-Digest tapes. **Subscriptions:** 152 journals and other serials. **Services:** Interlibrary loan; copying; SDI; library open to the public with restrictions. **Computerized Information Services:** MEDLARS, BRS Information Technologies; MAILMAN (electronic mail service). Performs searches free of charge. **Networks/Consortia:** Member of VALNET. **Remarks:** Patients' library contains an additional 4819 books.

★15652★
U.S. VETERANS ADMINISTRATION (TX-Dallas) - LIBRARY SERVICE (142D) (Med)
4500 S. Lancaster Rd. Phone: (214)372-7025
Dallas, TX 75216 Nancy A. Clark, Chf., Lib.Serv.
Founded: 1940. **Staff:** Prof 2; Other 2. **Subjects:** Medicine, surgery, allied health sciences, management. **Special Collections:** Patient health information. **Holdings:** 4500 books; 10,000 bound periodical volumes; 4500 volumes on microfilm; 1000 AV programs. **Subscriptions:** 480 journals and other serials. **Services:** Interlibrary loan; SDI; library open to health care personnel. **Automated Operations:** Computerized cataloging. **Computerized Information Services:** MEDLARS, BRS Information Technologies; MAILMAN (electronic mail service). **Networks/Consortia:** Member of VALNET, Dallas-Tarrant County Consortium of Health Science Libraries. **Staff:** Shirley A. Campbell, Med.Libn..

★15653★
U.S. VETERANS ADMINISTRATION (TX-Houston) - MEDICAL CENTER LIBRARY (Med)
2002 Holcombe Blvd. Phone: (713)795-4411
Houston, TX 77211 Jerry E. Barrett
Staff: Prof 3; Other 2. **Subjects:** Medicine. **Holdings:** 2864 books; 7500 periodical volumes. **Subscriptions:** 235 journals and other serials. **Services:** Interlibrary loan; library open to qualified users. **Computerized Information Services:** MEDLINE. **Networks/Consortia:** Member of VALNET.

★15654★
U.S. VETERANS ADMINISTRATION (TX-Kerrville) - HEALTH SCIENCES LIBRARY (Med)
Memorial Blvd. Phone: (512)896-2020
Kerrville, TX 78028 Elsie B. Branton, Chf., Lib.Serv.
Founded: 1922. **Staff:** Prof 1; Other 1. **Subjects:** Medicine and allied health sciences. **Holdings:** 2300 books; journals, 1967 to present, on microfilm; 400 video cassettes and 16mm films. **Subscriptions:** 125 journals and other serials. **Services:** Interlibrary loan; copying; SDI; AV loans; library open to the public for reference use only. **Automated Operations:** Computerized circulation. **Computerized Information Services:** MEDLINE; OnTyme Electronic Message Network Service (electronic mail service). **Networks/Consortia:** Member of TALON, Health Oriented Libraries of San Antonio (HOLSA), VALNET. **Publications:** Library Newsletters; Guide to New Media Titles; New Book List, all quarterly; Guide to the Use of the Health Sciences Library.

★15655★
U.S. VETERANS ADMINISTRATION (TX-Marlin) - MEDICAL CENTER LIBRARY SERVICE (142D) (Med)
1016 Ward St. Phone: (817)883-3511
Marlin, TX 76661 Edwina M. Hubbard, Chf., Lib.Serv.
Founded: 1950. **Staff:** Prof 1. **Subjects:** Medicine, nursing, allied health sciences, health care administration. **Holdings:** 835 books; 1000 periodical volumes on microfilm; unbound reports; pamphlets. **Subscriptions:** 100 journals and other serials. **Services:** Interlibrary loan; library open to the public. **Networks/Consortia:** Member of VALNET.

★15656★
U.S. VETERANS ADMINISTRATION (TX-San Antonio) - MEDICAL CENTER LIBRARY SERVICE (142D) (Med)
7400 Merton Minter Blvd. Phone: (512)696-9660
San Antonio, TX 78284 Marsha White, Chf.
Founded: 1973. **Staff:** Prof 2; Other 2. **Subjects:** Medicine, allied health sciences. **Holdings:** 4790 books; 4500 bound periodical volumes; 250 AV programs. **Subscriptions:** 400 journals and other serials; 21 newspapers. **Services:** Interlibrary loan; library not open to the public. **Computerized Information Services:** NLM, BRS Information Technologies. **Networks/Consortia:** Member of CLASS, VALNET, Health Oriented Libraries of San Antonio (HOLSA), Council of Research & Academic Libraries (CORAL). **Publications:** Library Newsletter, quarterly; Library Handbook, annual; subject bibliographies - for internal distribution only.

★15657★
U.S. VETERANS ADMINISTRATION (TX-Temple) - MEDICAL CENTER MEDICAL LIBRARY (Med)
Olin E. Teague Veterans Adm. Ctr.
1901 S. First St. Phone: (817)778-4811
Temple, TX 76501 Barbara D. Coronado, Chf., Lib.Serv.
Founded: 1942. **Staff:** Prof 3; Other 3. **Subjects:** Medicine, surgery, nursing, dentistry. **Special Collections:** Patient education. **Holdings:** 3500 books; 9038 bound periodical volumes; 8 VF drawers of clippings and pamphlets; 17 VF drawers of audio cassettes; 260 video cassette tapes.

Subscriptions: 500 journals and other serials; 12 newspapers. **Services:** Interlibrary loan; copying; library open to the public with restrictions. **Computerized Information Services:** NLM, BRS Information Technologies; OnTyme Electronic Message Network Service (electronic mail service). **Networks/Consortia:** Member of VALNET, TAMU Consortium of Medical Libraries. **Staff:** Mary Kay Massay, Med.Libn.; Ruth Hempel, Med.Libn..

★15658★
U.S. VETERANS ADMINISTRATION (TX-Waco) - MEDICAL CENTER LIBRARY (Med)
Memorial Dr. Phone: (817)752-6581
Waco, TX 76703 Barbara H. Hobbs, Chf., Lib.Serv.
Founded: 1932. **Staff:** Prof 4; Other 2. **Subjects:** Psychiatry, neurology, psychology, nursing, gerontology. **Holdings:** 4475 volumes; 1219 volumes on microfilm; 760 AV programs; 8 VF drawers. **Subscriptions:** 272 journals and other serials. **Services:** Interlibrary loan; copying; library open to the public with restrictions. **Computerized Information Services:** MEDLINE. **Networks/Consortia:** Member of VALNET, TALON. **Publications:** Medical Library Newsletter, bimonthly - for internal distribution only. **Staff:** JoAnn Greenwood, Med.Libn..

★15659★
U.S. VETERANS ADMINISTRATION (UT-Salt Lake City) - HOSPITAL MEDICAL LIBRARY (Med)
500 Foothill Dr. Phone: (801)584-1209
Salt Lake City, UT 84148 Carl Worstell, Chf.Libn.
Staff: Prof 3; Other 3. **Subjects:** Medicine, surgery, psychiatry, emergency medicine, research, allied health sciences. **Special Collections:** Hospital Satellite Network Collection (170 videotapes). **Holdings:** 2670 books; 11,262 bound periodical volumes; 1696 reels of microfilm; 85 video cassettes; 240 pamphlets; 1830 other cataloged items. **Subscriptions:** 297 journals and other serials. **Services:** Interlibrary loan; copying; SDI; library open to the public for reference use only. **Computerized Information Services:** DIALOG Information Services, BRS Information Technologies, MEDLARS; MAILMAN, OnTyme Electronic Message Network Service, INFONET (electronic mail services). **Networks/Consortia:** Member of VALNET, Midcontinental Regional Medical Library Program, Utah Health Sciences Library Consortium. **Publications:** Book, journal, & audiovisual holdings lists, annual. **Remarks:** Patients' library contains an additional 5699 volumes. **Staff:** Kirk L. Davis, Libn.; Barbara B. Windley, Libn..

★15660★
U.S. VETERANS ADMINISTRATION (VT-White River Junction) - MEDICAL & REGIONAL OFFICE CENTER - LIBRARY SERVICE (Med)
White River Junction, VT 05001 Phone: (802)295-9363
Richard Haver, Chf., Lib.Serv.
Staff: Prof 1; Other 1. **Subjects:** Medicine, surgery, psychiatry, nursing. **Holdings:** 1000 books. **Subscriptions:** 240 journals and other serials. **Services:** Interlibrary loan; library not open to the public. **Automated Operations:** Computerized cataloging. **Computerized Information Services:** NLM, BRS Information Technologies; MAILMAN (electronic mail service). **Networks/Consortia:** Member of VALNET, Vermont/New Hampshire Health Science Libraries.

★15661★
U.S. VETERANS ADMINISTRATION (VA-Hampton) - MEDICAL CENTER LIBRARY (Med)
Hampton, VA 23667 Phone: (804)722-9961
Jacqueline Bird, Chf., Lib.Serv.
Staff: Prof 3; Other 1. **Subjects:** Surgery, medicine, nursing, psychology, patient education. **Holdings:** 4000 books; 800 bound periodical volumes; 7500 unbound periodicals. **Subscriptions:** 544 journals and other serials. **Services:** Interlibrary loan (limited); library not open to the public. **Computerized Information Services:** BRS Information Technologies, MEDLINE. **Networks/Consortia:** Member of VALNET, Tidewater Health Sciences Libraries (THSL). **Publications:** Book lists, quarterly; special bibliographies. **Remarks:** Patients' library contains an additional 14,000 volumes. **Staff:** Lori Beudoin, Med.Libn.; Sharon Durio, Med.Libn..

★15662★
U.S. VETERANS ADMINISTRATION (VA-Richmond) - HOSPITAL LIBRARY (Med)
1201 Broad Rock Blvd. Phone: (804)230-0001
Richmond, VA 23249 Eleanor Rollins, Chf., Lib.Serv.
Founded: 1945. **Staff:** Prof 2; Other 2. **Subjects:** Medicine, psychology, sociology. **Holdings:** 4000 books; 6000 bound periodical volumes; 1000 AV programs; 1000 volumes on microfilm. **Subscriptions:** 830 journals and other serials. **Services:** Interlibrary loan; copying; library open to the public with restrictions.

★15663★
U.S. VETERANS ADMINISTRATION (VA-Salem) - MEDICAL CENTER LIBRARY (Med)
1970 Roanoke Blvd. Phone: (703)982-2463
Salem, VA 24153 Jean A. Kennedy, Chf.Libn.
Staff: Prof 3; Other 2. **Subjects:** Medicine, psychiatry, nursing, allied health sciences. **Holdings:** 5270 books; 1141 AV programs. **Subscriptions:** 265 journals and other serials. **Services:** Interlibrary loan; SDI; library open to community health professionals. **Computerized Information Services:** MEDLARS, BRS Information Technologies. **Networks/Consortia:** Member of VALNET, Southwestern Virginia Health Information Librarians. **Publications:** Medical Library Books and AVs Bulletin, quarterly. **Remarks:** Patients' library contains an additional 8606 volumes. **Staff:** Jacqueline S. Cahill, Med.Libn.; Susan B. DuGrenier, Patients' Libn..

★15664★
U.S. VETERANS ADMINISTRATION (WA-Seattle) - HOSPITAL MEDICAL LIBRARY (Med)
1660 S. Columbian Way Phone: (206)764-2065
Seattle, WA 98108 Mary Jo Harbold, Chf., Lib.Serv.
Staff: Prof 3; Other 1. **Subjects:** Medicine. **Special Collections:** Health education program. **Holdings:** 1620 books; 4000 bound periodical volumes; 570 AV programs. **Subscriptions:** 405 journals and other serials. **Services:** Interlibrary loan; SDI; library open to the public for reference use only. **Computerized Information Services:** MEDLINE, BRS Information Technologies. **Networks/Consortia:** Member of VALNET, Seattle Area Hospital Library Consortium (SAHLC). **Publications:** Medical Library Newsletter, irregular - for internal distribution only. **Staff:** Jeanyce Almgren, Med.Libn.; Mia Hannula, Med.Libn..

★15665★
U.S. VETERANS ADMINISTRATION (WA-Spokane) - MEDICAL CENTER LIBRARY (Med)
N. 4815 Assembly St. Phone: (509)328-4521
Spokane, WA 99205 Ruth A. Jones, Chf., Lib.Serv.
Founded: 1950. **Staff:** Prof 1; Other 2. **Subjects:** Medicine and allied health sciences. **Special Collections:** Health Information Center. **Holdings:** 175 books; 924 bound periodical volumes; 205 video cassettes; 15 models; pamphlets; patient teaching charts. **Subscriptions:** 323 journals and other serials. **Services:** Interlibrary loan; library not open to the public. **Computerized Information Services:** OnTyme Electronic Message Network Service (electronic mail service). **Networks/Consortia:** Member of VALNET. **Remarks:** Patients' library contains an additional 100 volumes.

★15666★
U.S. VETERANS ADMINISTRATION (WA-Tacoma) - MEDICAL CENTER LIBRARY (Med)
American Lake Phone: (206)582-8440
Tacoma, WA 98493 Dennis L. Levi, Chf., Lib.Serv.
Founded: 1924. **Staff:** Prof 2; Other 1. **Subjects:** Psychiatry, psychology, general medicine, nursing. **Holdings:** 1893 books; 2 VF drawers of pamphlets. **Subscriptions:** 241 journals and other serials; 33 newspapers. **Services:** Interlibrary loan; SDI; library open to the public for reference use only. **Computerized Information Services:** MEDLARS, BRS Information Technologies; MIALMAN, DOCLINE, OnTyme Electronic Message Network Service (electronic mail services). **Networks/Consortia:** Member of VALNET. **Remarks:** Patients' library contains an additional 4631 volumes.

★15667★
U.S. VETERANS ADMINISTRATION (WA-Walla Walla) - HOSPITAL LIBRARY (Med)
77 Wainwright Dr. Phone: (509)525-5200
Walla Walla, WA 99362 Max J. Merrell, Chf.Libn.
Staff: Prof 1. **Subjects:** Medicine, surgery, nursing, allied health sciences. **Holdings:** 900 books; 700 volumes of journals. **Subscriptions:** 130 journals and other serials. **Services:** Interlibrary loan; copying; SDI; library open to the public for reference use only; borrowing by special permission of librarian. **Computerized Information Services:** MEDLINE. **Networks/Consortia:** Member of VALNET, Western Library Network (WLN). **Special Catalogs:** VA Medical District Union List of Audiovisuals in Walla Walla. **Remarks:** Patients' library contains an additional 1000 volumes.

★15668★
U.S. VETERANS ADMINISTRATION (WV-Beckley) - MEDICAL CENTER LIBRARY (Med)
200 Veterans Ave. Phone: (304)255-2121
Beckley, WV 25801 Shelley C. Doman, Chf., Lib.Serv.
Founded: 1951. **Staff:** Prof 1. **Subjects:** Medicine, nursing, surgery. **Holdings:** 1004 volumes; 973 journal volumes; 2 VF drawers of patient education pamphlets; Audio-Digest tapes; microfilm. **Subscriptions:** 117 journals and other serials. **Services:** Interlibrary loan; copying; library open to the public with restrictions. **Networks/Consortia:** Member of VALNET. **Remarks:** Patients' library contains an additional 1911 volumes.

★15669★
U.S. VETERANS ADMINISTRATION (WV-Clarksburg) - MEDICAL CENTER LIBRARY SERVICE (Med)
Clarksburg, WV 26301 Phone: (304)623-3461
Joanne M. Bennett, Chf., Lib.Serv.
Founded: 1950. **Staff:** Prof 1; Other 1. **Subjects:** Medicine. **Holdings:** 1181 books; 2301 bound periodical volumes. **Subscriptions:** 138 journals and other serials; 25 newspapers. **Services:** Interlibrary loan; copying; library open to the public for reference use only. **Computerized Information Services:** NLM, BRS Information Technologies. **Networks/Consortia:** Member of VALNET. **Remarks:** Patients' library contains an additional 3448 volumes.

★15670★
U.S. VETERANS ADMINISTRATION (WV-Huntington) - MEDICAL CENTER LIBRARY (Med)
1540 Spring Valley Dr. Phone: (304)429-6741
Huntington, WV 25704 Hope Reenstjeine, Chf., Lib.Serv.
Founded: 1931. **Staff:** Prof 2; Other 1. **Subjects:** Clinical medicine. **Holdings:** 1200 books; Audio-Digest tapes; microfilm. **Subscriptions:** 213 journals and other serials. **Services:** Interlibrary loan; SDI; library open to the public with restrictions. **Computerized Information Services:** MEDLINE. **Networks/Consortia:** Member of VALNET, West Virginia Biomedical Information Network, Huntington Health Science Library Consortium.

★15671★
U.S. VETERANS ADMINISTRATION (WV-Martinsburg) - CENTER MEDICAL LIBRARY (Med)
Martinsburg, WV 25401 Phone: (304)263-0811
Barbara S. Adams, Chf.Libn.
Founded: 1945. **Staff:** Prof 2; Other 2. **Subjects:** Medicine, surgery, allied health sciences. **Holdings:** 3000 books; 5435 bound periodical volumes; 996 AV programs; 53 titles on microfilm. **Subscriptions:** 300 journals and other serials. **Services:** Interlibrary loan; copying. **Computerized Information Services:** MEDLINE; MAILMAN (electronic mail service). **Networks/Consortia:** Member of VALNET. **Remarks:** Patients' library contains an additional 6400 volumes. **Staff:** Geraldine Meyer, Med.Lib.Techn..

★15672★
U.S. VETERANS ADMINISTRATION (WI-Madison) - WILLIAM S. MIDDLETON MEMORIAL VETERANS HOSPITAL - LIBRARY (Med)
2500 Overlook Terrace Phone: (608)256-1901
Madison, WI 53705 Phyllis E. Goetz, Chf., Lib.Serv.
Founded: 1951. **Staff:** Prof 1; Other 2. **Subjects:** General medicine. **Holdings:** 7094 books; 15,700 bound periodical volumes; 2566 journal volumes on microfilm. **Subscriptions:** 218 journals and other serials. **Services:** Interlibrary loan; library not open to the public. **Computerized Information Services:** MEDLINE; MAILMAN, DOCLINE (electronic mail services). **Networks/Consortia:** Member of South Central Wisconsin Health Planning Area Cooperative.

★15673★
U.S. VETERANS ADMINISTRATION (WI-Milwaukee) - MEDICAL CENTER LIBRARY (Med)
5000 W. National Ave. Phone: (414)384-2000
Milwaukee, WI 53295 Jeanne A. Holcomb, Chf., Lib.Serv.
Founded: 1946. **Staff:** Prof 2; Other 2. **Subjects:** Medicine, nursing, dentistry, allied health sciences. **Holdings:** 5100 books; 5000 bound periodical volumes; 1400 AV programs. **Subscriptions:** 485 journals and other serials. **Services:** Interlibrary loan; SDI; library open to the public with restrictions. **Automated Operations:** Computerized serials. **Computerized Information Services:** MEDLARS, BRS Information Technologies, DIALOG Information Services; internal database. **Networks/Consortia:** Member of VALNET, Southeastern Wisconsin Health Science Library Consortium (SWHSL). **Remarks:**. Patients' library contains an additional 20,000 volumes. **Staff:** Maureen Farmer, Med.Libn..

★15674★
U.S. VETERANS ADMINISTRATION (WI-Tomah) - MEDICAL CENTER LIBRARY (142D) (Med)
Tomah, WI 54660 Phone: (608)372-1716
Xena C. Kenyon, Chf., Lib.Serv.
Founded: 1947. **Staff:** Prof 4; Other 1. **Subjects:** Psychiatry, neurology, general medicine, psychology, nursing, aging. **Holdings:** 2349 books; 505 bound periodical volumes; 100 volumes of unbound journals; AV programs. **Subscriptions:** 200 journals and other serials. **Services:** Interlibrary loan; copying; library open to the public. **Computerized Information Services:** MEDLINE; DOCLINE (electronic mail service). Performs searches free of charge. **Networks/Consortia:** Member of VALNET. **Publications:** Acquisitions List; special bibliographies. **Remarks:** Patients' library contains an additional 7182 volumes.

★15675★
U.S. VETERANS ADMINISTRATION (WY-Cheyenne) - MEDICAL AND REGIONAL OFFICE CENTER - LIBRARY (Med)
2360 E. Pershing Blvd. Phone: (307)778-7550
Cheyenne, WY 82001 Eris J. Kirby, Chf., Lib.Serv.
Staff: Prof 1. **Subjects:** Medicine, nursing. **Holdings:** 759 books; 2063 volumes of journals, bound and on microfilm. **Subscriptions:** 119 journals and other serials; 15 newspapers. **Services:** Interlibrary loan; copying; SDI; library open to the public. **Computerized Information Services:** MEDLINE; internal database; OnTyme Electronic Message Network Service, Octanet (electronic mail services). **Networks/Consortia:** Member of VALNET. **Remarks:** Patients' library contains an additional 2577 volumes.

★15676★
U.S. VETERANS ADMINISTRATION (WY-Sheridan) - MEDICAL CENTER LIBRARY† (Med)
Sheridan, WY 82801 Mary Curtis Kellett, Chf., Lib.Serv.
Staff: Prof 1; Other 2. **Subjects:** Psychiatry, psychology, medicine, nursing, administration. **Holdings:** 2250 books; 250 bound periodical volumes; 1620 periodical volumes on microfilm; 2000 AV programs. **Subscriptions:** 300 journals and other serials. **Services:** Interlibrary loan; copying; library open to the public. **Computerized Information Services:** MEDLARS, BRS Information Technologies; MAILMAN (electronic mail service). **Networks/Consortia:** Member of VALNET, Health Sciences Information Network (HSIN), Northeastern Wyoming Medical Library Consortium. **Remarks:** Patients' library contains an additional 5000 volumes.

UNITED STATES VOLLEYBALL ASSOCIATION ARCHIVES
See: Ball State University - Bracken Library - Special Collections (1256)

U.S. WATER CONSERVATION LABORATORY
See: U.S.D.A. - Agricultural Research Service (14979)

★15677★
U.S.S. MASSACHUSETTS MEMORIAL COMMITTEE, INC. - ARCHIVES & TECHNICAL LIBRARY (Sci-Engr, Hist)
Battleship Cove Phone: (508)678-1100
Fall River, MA 02721 Mark Newton, Educ.Coord./Cur.
Founded: 1982. **Staff:** Prof 1. **Subjects:** Naval engineering and ordnance, naval radio and radar, shipboard ephemera, World War II naval history, battleship systems. **Holdings:** 300 books; 200 bound periodical volumes; films; videotapes; 75 shelf feet of blueprints; 35 reels of microfilm; voice recordings of first U.S. fleet raids on Japan; 250 pages of correspondence. **Services:** Copying; library open to the public by appointment with one-time research fee. **Publications:** Bibliographies.

★15678★
UNITED STEELWORKERS OF AMERICA - LIBRARY (Law, Bus-Fin)
234 Eglinton Ave., E., 7th Fl. Phone: (416)487-1571
Toronto, ON, Canada M4P 1K7 Leslie Stodart, Libn.
Founded: 1963. **Staff:** Prof 1. **Subjects:** Canadian law, labor law, economics; health and safety; labor; business. **Special Collections:** Current and archival USWA collective agreements (20,000); Steelabour magazine, January 1946 to present; Royal Commission reports, 1930s to present. **Holdings:** 10,000 books; 2000 bound periodical volumes; local union publications; government documents. **Subscriptions:** 120 journals and other serials; 6 newspapers. **Services:** Copying; library open to the public by appointment. **Computerized Information Services:** Canada Systems Group (CSG), Info Globe, Canadian Centre for Occupational Health & Safety.

UNITED TECHNOLOGIES CORPORATION - CARRIER CORPORATION
See: Carrier Corporation (2699)

★15679★
UNITED TECHNOLOGIES CORPORATION - CHEMICAL SYSTEMS DIVISION - LIBRARY (Sci-Engr)
Box 49028 Phone: (408)365-5794
San Jose, CA 95161-9028 Eric Kristofferson, Lib.Supv.
Founded: 1959. **Staff:** Prof 2. **Subjects:** Chemical propulsion and technology, mechanical and aeronautical engineering. **Special Collections:** National Advisory Committee for Aeronautics (NACA) Annual Reports, 1915-1959. **Holdings:** 5500 books; 2000 bound periodical volumes; 1850 microfilm cartridges; 6700 microfiche; 25,000 other cataloged items. **Subscriptions:** 153 journals and other serials. **Services:** Interlibrary loan; library not open to the public. **Computerized Information Services:** NASA/RECON, DIALOG Information Services, DTIC, CAS ONLINE. **Networks/Consortia:** Member of CLASS. **Publications:** Library Bulletins, irregular - for internal distribution only. **Staff:** Mary Lou Hall, Ref./Info.Spec..

★15680★
UNITED TECHNOLOGIES CORPORATION - ELLIOTT COMPANY - LIBRARY (Sci-Engr)
N. Fourth St. Phone: (412)527-8054
Jeannette, PA 15644 Geri K. Keitzer, Libn.
Staff: Prof 1. **Subjects:** Turbines, compressors. **Holdings:** 2300 books; 4200 pamphlets; 900 company technical reports and memoranda; 300 microfiche. **Subscriptions:** 50 journals and other serials. **Services:** Interlibrary loan; library not open to the public.

★15681★
UNITED TECHNOLOGIES CORPORATION - LIBRARY & INFORMATION SERVICES (Sci-Engr)
United Technologies Research Center Phone: (203)727-7478
East Hartford, CT 06108 Jean G. Mayhew, Mgr.
Founded: 1939. **Staff:** Prof 24; Other 22. **Subjects:** Aerospace sciences and engineering, business, power plants and energy conversion, metals and materials, electronics, lasers, optics, physics, chemistry. **Holdings:** 55,000 book titles; 15,000 bound periodical volumes; 105,000 technical reports and preprint titles; 500,000 microfiche. **Subscriptions:** 1200 journals and other serials. **Services:** Interlibrary loan (limited); library not open to the public. **Automated Operations:** Computerized cataloging and circulation. **Computerized Information Services:** DIALOG Information Services, Pergamon ORBIT InfoLine, Inc., Dow Jones News/Retrieval, BRS Information Technologies, DTIC, LEXIS, NEXIS, NewsNet, Inc., NLM, TEXTLINE, VU/TEXT Information Services, STN International, WILSONLINE, NASA/RECON, Integrated Technical Information System (ITIS), Electronic Materials Information Service (EMIS); UTOC (internal database). **Publications:** UTLIS Bulletin; Technical Contents, both biweekly; Business Contents, semimonthly - all for internal distribution only. **Staff:** Rita Yeh, Supv., Lib.Sys.; John Goncar, Supv., Tech.Serv..

UNITED TECHNOLOGIES CORPORATION - NORDEN SYSTEMS, INC.
See: Norden Systems, Inc. (10272)

UNITED TECHNOLOGIES CORPORATION - PRATT AND WHITNEY CANADA INC.
See: Pratt and Whitney Canada Inc. (11518)

★15682★
UNITED TECHNOLOGIES CORPORATION - PRATT & WHITNEY INFORMATION SERVICES (Sci-Engr)
400 Main St., MS 169-31 Phone: (203)344-5138
East Hartford, CT 06108 Noreen O. Steele, Sr.Libn.
Founded: 1961. **Staff:** Prof 2; Other 2. **Subjects:** Materials, aerospace technology, chemistry, engineering, computers, business, gas turbine engines, manufacturing. **Holdings:** 5000 books; 1500 bound periodical volumes; 4500 technical reports. **Subscriptions:** 225 journals and other serials. **Services:** Interlibrary loan; services not open to the public. **Automated Operations:** Computerized public access catalog and circulation. **Computerized Information Services:** DIALOG Information Services, NEXIS, Pergamon ORBIT InfoLine, Inc., ESA-QUEST, BRS Information Technologies, CAS ONLINE, Aerospace Online, VU/TEXT Information Services, EdVent (Educational Events) Data Base, WILSONLINE.

★15683★
UNITED TECHNOLOGIES CORPORATION - SIKORSKY AIRCRAFT DIVISION - LIBRARY AND INFORMATION SERVICES S339A (Sci-Engr)
6900 Main St. Phone: (203)386-4713
Stratford, CT 06601-1381 Carol A. Stiles, Sr.Libn.
Founded: 1945. **Staff:** Prof 2; Other 1. **Subjects:** Aeronautics, engineering, management. **Special Collections:** Helicopter and vertical takeoff and landing (VTOL) aircraft data. **Holdings:** 3300 books; 90,000 technical government reports. **Subscriptions:** 125 journals and other serials. **Services:** Interlibrary loan; copying; library open to the public with restrictions. **Automated Operations:** Computerized public access catalog, cataloging, acquisitions, and circulation. **Computerized Information Services:** BRS Information Technologies, Pergamon ORBIT InfoLine, Inc., DIALOG Information Services, NEXIS, NewsNet, Inc., DTIC, WILSONLINE. **Publications:** Library Bulletin of new materials - for internal distribution only. **Staff:** Jim Smallwood, Libn.; Noreen Sherman, Assoc.Libn..

★15684★
UNITED TELECOMMUNICATIONS, INC. - CORPORATE RESEARCH CENTER (Info Sci)
2330 Shawnee Mission Pkwy. Phone: (913)676-3014
Shawnee Mission, KS 66205 Kathleen S. Mobley, Mgr.
Founded: 1980. **Staff:** Prof 2; Other 1. **Subjects:** Telecommunications, data communications, telephone engineering, information management, office automation. **Holdings:** 700 books; 4 cases of conference proceedings; 2 cases of government documents; 10 cases of market studies; 20 VF drawers of annual reports; 9 VF drawers of standards. **Subscriptions:** 323 journals and other serials. **Services:** Center not open to the public. **Automated Operations:** Computerized cataloging. **Computerized Information Services:** DIALOG Information Services, BRS Information Technologies, The Source, VU/TEXT Information Services, Telescope, Dow Jones News/Retrieval, NewsNet, Inc.; internal database. **Publications:** Information Newsletter, monthly - for internal distribution only.

★15685★
UNITED THEOLOGICAL SEMINARY - LIBRARY (Rel-Phil)
1810 Harvard Blvd. Phone: (513)278-5817
Dayton, OH 45406 Elmer J. O'Brien, Libn./Prof.
Founded: 1872. **Staff:** Prof 2; Other 3. **Subjects:** Theology. **Special Collections:** Evangelical United Brethren Church Collection (8000 items). **Holdings:** 108,275 volumes. **Subscriptions:** 453 journals and other serials; 5 newspapers. **Services:** Interlibrary loan; copying; library open to the public by application with references. **Automated Operations:** Computerized cataloging and serials. **Computerized Information Services:** DIALOG Information Services, BRS Information Technologies, OCLC; PRESBYNET (internal database). **Networks/Consortia:** Member of Southwest Ohio Council for Higher Education (SOCHE). **Staff:** Richard R. Berg, Asst.Libn..

★15686★
UNITED THEOLOGICAL SEMINARY OF THE TWIN CITIES - LIBRARY (Rel-Phil)
3000 Fifth St., N.W. Phone: (612)633-4311
New Brighton, MN 55112 Arthur L. Merrill, Dir.
Founded: 1962. **Staff:** Prof 3; Other 4. **Subjects:** Theology, church history, education, sociology, psychology, philosophy. **Holdings:** 64,000 volumes; 318 films and filmstrips; 491 microforms; 92 videotapes; 772 cassettes and tapes. **Subscriptions:** 282 journals and other serials. **Services:** Interlibrary loan; copying; library open to the public. **Computerized Information Services:** Joint consortium catalog (internal database). **Networks/Consortia:** Member of Minnesota Theological Libraries Association (MTLA), MINITEX. **Staff:** Susan Ebbers, Asst.Libn.; Janet Weiss, Cat..

★15687★
UNITED VIRGINIA BANK - INFORMATION CENTER (Bus-Fin)
Box 26665 Phone: (804)782-7452
Richmond, VA 23261 Sue N. Miller, Mgr., Info.Serv.
Founded: 1970. **Staff:** Prof 3; Other 1. **Subjects:** Banking, finance, economics, statistics, accounting, management, economic statistics of Southeastern U.S., international banking and economic data. **Holdings:** 10,000 books; 50 VF drawers of annual reports of banks and bank holding companies; 5 drawers of international economic and financial data; 20 drawers of banking-related subjects. **Subscriptions:** 600 journals and other serials; 10 newspapers. **Services:** Interlibrary loan; copying; center open to students and customers by appointment. **Automated Operations:** Computerized cataloging and serials. **Computerized Information Services:** DIALOG Information Services, Dow Jones News/Retrieval, TEXTLINE, NEXIS. **Publications:** Books 'n Things (informational sheet), monthly - to

banks and holding company management personnel. **Staff:** Linda F. Weeks, Tech.Serv.Spec.; Tina Schmitt, Info.Ctr.Asst..

★15688★
UNITED WAY OF AMERICA - INFORMATION CENTER (Soc Sci)
701 N. Fairfax St.
Alexandria, VA 22314-2088 Phone: (703)836-7100
Founded: 1934. **Staff:** 2. **Subjects:** History and management of social and human services, fund raising, information and referral, voluntarism. **Holdings:** 600 books; 5000 monographs and research reports. **Subscriptions:** 253 journals and other serials. **Services:** Interlibrary loan; copying; center open to area researchers and human service professionals by appointment. **Automated Operations:** Computerized cataloging, acquisitions, and serials. **Computerized Information Services:** FYI News, DIALOG Information Services; Human Care Network (internal database). **Publications:** Digest of Selected Reports - to members and others by subscription; Where Can You Look for Help (brochure).

★15689★
UNITED WAY/CRUSADE OF MERCY - LIBRARY (Soc Sci)
125 S. Clark St. Phone: (312)580-2697
Chicago, IL 60603-4012 Sally J. Barnum, Mgr.
Founded: 1977. **Staff:** Prof 1; Other 2. **Subjects:** Social services, fund raising, social statistics, nonprofit management. **Special Collections:** United Way/Crusade of Mercy and predecessor agency archives (United Way of Chicago, Welfare Council of Metropolitan Chicago, Community Fund of Chicago, Council for Community Services, Crusade of Mercy; 225 titles); United Way/Crusade of Mercy and United Way of Chicago central files. **Holdings:** 10,000 books; 300 reports on microfiche. **Subscriptions:** 200 journals and other serials; 5 newspapers. **Services:** Interlibrary loan; SDI; library open to the public by appointment. **Automated Operations:** Computerized cataloging. **Computerized Information Services:** OCLC. **Networks/Consortia:** Member of ILLINET, Greater Midwest Regional Medical Library Network, Chicago Library System. **Publications:** Recent Acquisitions, bimonthly - to staff and local libraries by request.

★15690★
UNITED WAY OF THE LOWER MAINLAND - SOCIAL PLANNING AND RESEARCH DEPARTMENT LIBRARY (Soc Sci)
1625 W. 8th Ave. Phone: (604)731-7781
Vancouver, BC, Canada V6J 1T9 Beverley Scott, Libn.
Founded: 1965. **Staff:** 1. **Subjects:** Family violence, income security, housing, social problems, child abuse and child sexual abuse, social services planning. **Special Collections:** United Way of the Lower Mainland publications (200 titles). **Holdings:** 3000 books and bound reports; 2500 unbound reports, pamphlets, and ephemera. **Subscriptions:** 75 journals and other serials. **Services:** Interlibrary loan; copying; library open to the public for reference use only.

UNITED WORLD COLLEGES - LESTER B. PEARSON COLLEGE OF THE PACIFIC
See: Lester B. Pearson College of the Pacific (11130)

★15691★
UNITY OF FAIRFAX - LIBRARY (Rel-Phil)
2854 Hunter Mill Rd. Phone: (703)281-1767
Oakton, VA 22124 Lorna Barnes, Libn.
Staff: Prof 1; Other 2. **Subjects:** Religion, metaphysics. **Holdings:** 1000 books. **Services:** Library open to the public.

★15692★
UNITY MEDICAL CENTER - LIBRARY (Med)
550 Osborne Rd. Phone: (612)786-2200
Fridley, MN 55432 Janet M. Joerger, Med.Libn.
Founded: 1973. **Staff:** Prof 1. **Subjects:** Medicine, nursing, and allied health sciences. **Holdings:** 800 books; 3000 bound periodical volumes. **Subscriptions:** 105 journals and other serials. **Services:** Interlibrary loan (to network members); copying; SDI; library open to public at librarian's discretion. **Automated Operations:** Computerized cataloging. **Computerized Information Services:** MEDLARS, MEDLINE. **Networks/Consortia:** Member of Twin Cities Biomedical Consortium (TCBC).

★15693★
UNIVERSAL CITY STUDIOS - RESEARCH DEPARTMENT LIBRARY (Art, Hist)
100 Universal City Plaza Phone: (818)777-2493
Universal City, CA 91608 Robert A. Lee, Hd., Res.Dept.
Founded: 1916. **Staff:** Prof 2; Other 2. **Subjects:** American West, Americana, costume, literature, art and architecture, wars, film history, history, biography. **Holdings:** 23,000 books; 700 bound periodical volumes; 6000 files of clippings, stills, brochures, pictures, illustrations, slides and transparencies for background research on film and television projects. **Subscriptions:** 90 journals and other serials. **Services:** Library not open to the public. **Special Indexes:** Clipping file index; pictorial magazine index. **Staff:** Sherri Seeling, Res.Spec.; Margaret Ross, Res.Spec..

UNIVERSAL FLAVOR CORPORATION - HURTY-PECK LIBRARY OF BEVERAGE LITERATURE
See: Hurty-Peck Library of Beverage Literature (6621)

★15694★
UNIVERSAL FOODS CORPORATION - TECHNICAL INFORMATION CENTER (Biol Sci, Food-Bev)
6143 N. 60th St. Phone: (414)535-4307
Milwaukee, WI 53218 Aileen Mundstock, Tech.Info.Spec.
Founded: 1951. **Staff:** Prof 1. Fermentation industry, biotechnology, biochemistry, microbiology, chemistry, quality control, product development, engineering. **Holdings:** 4000 books and bound periodical volumes; patents; internal reports. **Subscriptions:** 60 journals and other serials. **Services:** Copying (limited); center open to the public with restrictions. **Automated Operations:** Computerized public access catalog, acquisitions, circulation, and budget. **Computerized Information Services:** DIALOG Information Services, Pergamon ORBIT InfoLine, Inc. **Networks/Consortia:** Member of Library Council of Metropolitan Milwaukee, Inc. (LCOMM).

★15695★
UNIVERSAL SERIALS & BOOK EXCHANGE, INC. - DUPLICATE EXCHANGE CLEARINGHOUSE & INFORMATION CENTER (Info Sci)
3335 V St., N.E. Phone: (202)636-8723
Washington, DC 20018 Claude Hooker, Mng.Dir.
Founded: 1948. **Staff:** Prof 6; Other 36. **Subjects:** U.S. and foreign publications, library science. **Holdings:** 4 million items, including bound and unbound journals, books, microforms, and government documents. **Services:** Document delivery; copying; center open to the public on fee basis. **Computerized Information Services:** OCLC, BRS Information Technologies, UTLAS, DIALOG Information Services. Performs searches on fee basis. Contact Person: H.Gerald Phillips, Dir. of Member Serv.. **Networks/Consortia:** Member of CAPCON. **Publications:** USBE/NEWS (catalog and newsletter), monthly - to members and by subscription. **Remarks:** USBE is a nonprofit library cooperative, organized to facilitate the redistribution of library resources and to extend the availability of publications. **Also Known As:** USBE, Inc. **Staff:** Robert Hodges, Bus.Mgr.; H. Gerald Phillips, Dir., Member Serv..

★15696★
UNIVERSITE LAVAL - BIBLIOTHEQUE (Area-Ethnic, Hum, Sci-Engr, Energy, Biol Sci)
Cite Universitaire Phone: (418)656-3344
Ste. Foy, PQ, Canada G1K 7P4 Celine R. Cartier, Dir.
Founded: 1852. **Staff:** Prof 70; Other 208. **Subjects:** French Canadian and Quebec studies; French Canadian folklore; Quebec geography; ethnic groups from Quebec and Canada; French and French Canadian literature; 19th century French musical press; law; philosophy of science; philosophy - Aristotelian, Thomist, and French modern; food and nutrition; wood science technology and forest ecology (mycories); animal science; soils; phytopathology; electrochemistry and corrosion; noise pollution; wind energy. **Holdings:** 1.16 million books; 433,006 bound periodical volumes; 105,186 maps; 126,728 aerial photographs; 176,307 transparencies; 9745 phonograph records; 6500 films; 718,667 microforms. **Subscriptions:** 14,142 journals and other serials; 111 newspapers. **Services:** Interlibrary loan; SDI. **Automated Operations:** Computerized cataloging, acquisitions, serials, and circulation. **Computerized Information Services:** DIALOG Information Services, QL Systems, CAN/OLE, RESORS (Remote Sensing On-Line Retrieval System), BADADUQ, WILSONLINE, International Development Research Centre (IDRC), SOQUIJ, LaborLine, MEDLINE, BRS Information Technologies, Telesystemes Questel, UTLAS, CANSIM, Info Globe, Pergamon ORBIT InfoLine, Inc. **Publications:** Guides bibliographiques; Repertoire de vedettes-matieres; Guide du lecteur; Liste de periodiques par sujet; Liste des commandes permanentes; Liste de nouvelles acquisitions. **Special Catalogs:** Film catalog; Catalogue des

Manuels Scolaires Quebecois. **Staff:** Claude Bonnelly, Assoc.Chf.Libn.; Philippe Houyoux, Chf., Soc.Sci./Hum.Coll.; Alain Bourque, Chf., Sci.Coll.; Denis Kronstrom, Chf., Circ.; Agathe Garon, Chf., Spec.Coll.; Doris Dufour, Online/SDI Serv.; Helene Genest, Online/SDI Serv..

★15697★
UNIVERSITE LAVAL - BIBLIOTHEQUE SCIENTIFIQUE (Sci-Engr, Med, Agri)
Quebec, PQ, Canada GlK 7P4 — Phone: (418)656-3967
Alain Bourque, Hd.
Founded: 1973. **Staff:** Prof 10; Other 24. **Subjects:** Science, technology, medical and paramedical sciences, agriculture, forestry. **Holdings:** 100,000 books; 200,000 bound periodical volumes; 16,153 reels of microfilm; 18,526 microfiches. **Subscriptions:** 2738 journals and other serials; 30 newspapers. **Services:** Interlibrary loan; copying; library open to the public. **Automated Operations:** Computerized cataloging, acquisitions, serials, and circulation. **Computerized Information Services:** DIALOG Information Services, BRS Information Technologies, QL Systems, Telesystemes Questel, MEDLARS, RESORS (Remote Sensing On-line Retrieval System), Info Globe, WILSONLINE, UTLAS, International Development Research Centre (IDRC), CAN/OLE, Pergamon ORBIT InfoLine, Inc. **Staff:** Claude Busque, Subj.Spec., Sci.; Louise DeLisle, Subj.Spec., Tech.; Philippe LeMay, Subj.Spec., Forestry; Jean Morel, Subj.Spec., Med.Sci.; Yolande Taillon, Subj.Spec., Agri.; Robert Giroux, Subj.Spec., Agri.; Lorraine V. Berube, Subj.Spec., Med.Sci.; Michel Dagenais, Subj.Spec., Sci.; Doris Dufour, Subj.Spec., Med.Sci..

★15698★
UNIVERSITE LAVAL - INTERNATIONAL CENTRE FOR RESEARCH ON BILINGUALISM (Hum)
Pavillon Casault, 6th Fl. — Phone: (418)656-3232
Ste. Foy, PQ, Canada G1K 7P4 — France Methot, Lib.Techn.
Founded: 1967. **Staff:** 12. **Subjects:** Bilingualism; bilingual education; language - teaching, learning, rights, contact. **Special Collections:** Commission on Bilingualism and Biculturalism; Commission Gendron; Commission Bibeau; Report of the Bilingual Districts Advisory Board. **Holdings:** 5000 books; 30,000 documents; 250 reels of microfilm. **Subscriptions:** 50 journals and other serials. **Services:** Copying; center open to the public. **Automated Operations:** Computerized cataloging and acquisitions. **Computerized Information Services:** BIBELO (internal database). **Publications:** List of publications - available upon request.

★15699★
UNIVERSITE DE MONCTON - BIBLIOTHEQUE DE DROIT (Law)
Moncton, NB, Canada E1A 3E9 — Phone: (506)858-4547
Simonne Clermont, Law Libn.
Founded: 1978. **Staff:** Prof 2; Other 7. **Subjects:** Law. **Holdings:** 37,391 books; 41,500 bound periodical volumes; 24,316 AV programs. **Subscriptions:** 915 journals and other serials. **Services:** Interlibrary loan; copying; library open to the public for reference use only. **Computerized Information Services:** QL Systems. Performs searches on fee basis. **Publications:** Liste selective des nouvelles acquisitions. **Staff:** Carmel Allain, Cat..

★15700★
UNIVERSITE DE MONCTON - CENTRE D'ETUDES ACADIENNES (Area-Ethnic)
Moncton, NB, Canada E1A 3E9 — Phone: (506)858-4085
Ronald Leblanc, Libn.
Staff: Prof 5; Other 3. **Subjects:** Acadian history, genealogy, and folklore. **Holdings:** 9849 books and pamphlets; 3596 reels of microfilm; 450 feet of manuscripts; 2000 reels of magnetic tape of Acadian folk tales and songs. **Services:** Interlibrary loan (limited); copying; center open to the public. **Publications:** Contact-Acadie, irregular.

★15701★
UNIVERSITE DE MONCTON - FACULTE DES SCIENCES DE L'EDUCATION - CENTRE DE RESSOURCES PEDAGOGIQUES (Educ)
Moncton, NB, Canada E1A 3E9 — Phone: (506)858-4356
Berthe Boudreau, Dir.
Founded: 1973. **Staff:** Prof 2; Other 2. **Subjects:** Education: instructional material on the subject studies in public schools. **Holdings:** 28,000 books, kits, and tests; 28,172 slides; 1052 filmstrips; 1577 pictures; 1992 transparencies. **Services:** Copying; center open to teachers. **Automated Operations:** Computerized cataloging and circulation. **Staff:** Leonard Gallant, Ref.Libn..

UNIVERSITE DE MONCTON - GULF FISHERIES CENTER
See: Canada - Fisheries & Oceans - Fisheries Research Branch, Gulf Region - Gulf Fisheries Center (2383)

★15702★
UNIVERSITE DE MONTREAL - AMENAGEMENT-BIBLIOTHEQUE (Art, Plan)
C.P. 6128, Succursale A — Phone: (514)343-7177
Montreal, PQ, Canada H3C 3J7 — Vesna Blazina, Libn.
Founded: 1964. **Staff:** Prof 3; Other 10. **Subjects:** Architecture, landscape architecture, design, city planning, urbanism. **Holdings:** 33,794 books; 8805 bound periodical volumes; 34,628 slides; 857 microforms; 16,448 clippings; 3289 AV programs and other documents; 3928 reports. **Subscriptions:** 669 journals and other serials. **Services:** Interlibrary loan; copying; library open to the public with restrictions. **Automated Operations:** Computerized cataloging and acquisitions. **Computerized Information Services:** DIALOG Information Services, Pergamon ORBIT InfoLine, Inc., CAN/OLE, Telesystemes Questel, QL Systems. **Publications:** Acquisitions list, monthly - limited distribution.

★15703★
UNIVERSITE DE MONTREAL - AUDIOVIDEOTHEQUE (Aud-Vis)
C.P. 6128, Succursale A — Phone: (514)343-7344
Montreal, PQ, Canada H3C 3J7 — Ginette Gagnier, Libn.
Staff: Prof 1; Other 4. **Holdings:** 10,000 AV programs. **Services:** Interlibrary loan; library open to the public with restrictions. **Automated Operations:** Computerized cataloging and acquisitions.

★15704★
UNIVERSITE DE MONTREAL - BIBLIOTHECONOMIE-BIBLIOTHEQUE (Info Sci)
C.P. 6128, Succursale A — Phone: (514)343-6047
Montreal, PQ, Canada H3C 3J7 — Myloan Duong, Libn.
Founded: 1961. **Staff:** Prof 1; Other 3. **Subjects:** Library science, information science, records management. **Holdings:** 22,347 books; 16,972 bound periodical volumes; 4457 microforms; 7410 reports. **Subscriptions:** 717 journals and other serials. **Services:** Interlibrary loan; copying; library open to the public with restrictions. **Automated Operations:** Computerized cataloging, acquisitions, and circulation. **Publications:** Acquisitions list, monthly - limited distribution. **Special Catalogs:** Periodicals list.

★15705★
UNIVERSITE DE MONTREAL - BIBLIOTHEQUE DES LETTRES ET SCIENCES HUMAINES (Soc Sci, Hum)
C.P. 6128, Succursale A — Phone: (514)343-7430
Montreal, PQ, Canada H3C 3J7 — Richard Greene, Libn.
Founded: 1968. **Staff:** Prof 16; Other 44. **Subjects:** Anthropology, criminology, demography, history, French studies, linguistics, philosophy, industrial relations, political science, economics, social service, sociology, science history, science policy, comparative literature, art history, African studies, theology. **Holdings:** 734,810 books; 156,983 bound periodical volumes; 264,949 microforms; 22,273 AV programs (Mediatheque). **Subscriptions:** 3523 journals and other serials. **Services:** Interlibrary loan; copying; library open to the public with restrictions. **Automated Operations:** Computerized cataloging, acquisitions, and circulation. **Computerized Information Services:** DIALOG Information Services, BRS Information Technologies, Pergamon ORBIT InfoLine, Inc., CAN/OLE, Telesystemes Questel, QL Systems. Performs searches on fee basis. Contact Person: Marc Joanis. **Publications:** Bibliographic guides. **Special Catalogs:** Journals and periodicals list (on microfilm); Preliminary Inventory of Landmarks of Science Collection. **Formed by the merger of:** Sciences Humaines et Sociales-Bibliotheque and Theologie-Philosophie Bibliotheque.

★15706★
UNIVERSITE DE MONTREAL - BIBLIOTHEQUE PARA-MEDICALE (Med)
C.P. 6128, Succursale A — Phone: (514)343-7490
Montreal, PQ, Canada H3C 3J7 — Johanne Hopper, Libn.
Founded: 1963. **Staff:** Prof 3; Other 10. **Subjects:** Nursing, health administration, nutrition, epidemiology, environmental health, audiology, ergotherapy, orthophonics, physiotherapy, social and preventive medicine, gerontology and geriatrics. **Holdings:** 48,188 books; 16,862 bound periodical volumes; 10,934 microforms; 1673 slides; 1190 AV programs. **Subscriptions:** 1439 journals and other serials. **Services:** Interlibrary loan; copying; library open to the public with restrictions. **Automated Operations:** Computerized cataloging and acquisitions. **Computerized Information Services:** DIALOG Information Services, MEDLINE. **Publications:** Acquisitions list, monthly - limited distribution.

★15707★
UNIVERSITE DE MONTREAL - BIBLIOTHEQUE DE LA SANTE (Med)
C.P. 6128, Succursale A Phone: (514)343-6826
Montreal, PQ, Canada H3C 3J7 Therese Peternell, Libn.
Founded: 1962. **Staff:** Prof 7; Other 22. **Subjects:** Medicine, dentistry, pharmacy. **Holdings:** 79,000 books; 101,000 bound periodical volumes; 3011 microforms; 13,000 slides. **Subscriptions:** 2539 journals and other serials. **Services:** Interlibrary loan; copying; library open to the public with restrictions. **Automated Operations:** Computerized cataloging and acquisitions. **Computerized Information Services:** DIALOG Information Services, Pergamon ORBIT InfoLine, Inc., BRS Information Technologies, CAN/OLE, MEDLINE, Telesystemes Questel, QL Systems. **Publications:** Acquisitions list - limited distribution. **Special Catalogs:** Periodicals list.

★15708★
UNIVERSITE DE MONTREAL - BIOLOGIE-BIBLIOTHEQUE (Biol Sci)
C.P. 6128, Succursale A Phone: (514)343-6801
Montreal, PQ, Canada H3C 3J7 Robert Gauthier, Libn.
Founded: 1962. **Staff:** Prof 2; Other 7. **Subjects:** Biology, zoology. **Holdings:** 17,620 books; 17,859 bound periodical volumes; 2223 microforms; 452 reports; 276 AV programs. **Subscriptions:** 534 journals and other serials. **Services:** Interlibrary loan; copying; library open to the public with restrictions. **Automated Operations:** Computerized cataloging and acquisitions. **Computerized Information Services:** DIALOG Information Services, BRS Information Technologies, Pergamon ORBIT InfoLine, Inc., CAN/OLE, MEDLINE, Telesystemes Questel, QL Systems. **Publications:** Acquisitions list, irregular - limited distribution; User Guide, annual.

★15709★
UNIVERSITE DE MONTREAL - BOTANIQUE-BIBLIOTHEQUE (Biol Sci)
4101 est, rue Sherbrooke Phone: (514)256-9441
Montreal, PQ, Canada H1X 2B2 Robert Gauthier, Libn.
Founded: 1925. **Staff:** 1. **Subjects:** General botany, taxonomy, genetics, evolution, paleobotany, ecology, plant physiology, mycology, algology, bryology. **Holdings:** 9163 books; 12,068 bound periodical volumes; 27,580 microforms; 15,127 slides; 6300 photographs; 17,197 reports. **Subscriptions:** 241 journals and other serials. **Services:** Interlibrary loan; copying; library open to the public with restrictions. **Automated Operations:** Computerized acquisitions. **Publications:** Acquisitions list, monthly - limited distribution; User Guide, annual.

★15710★
UNIVERSITE DE MONTREAL - CENTRE DE DOCUMENTATION DE CRIMINOLOGIE (Soc Sci)
3150, rue Jean-Brillant Phone: (514)343-6534
Montreal, PQ, Canada H3C 3J7 Aniela Belina, Resp.
Founded: 1964. **Staff:** Prof 2; Other 1. **Subjects:** Criminology, corrections, law enforcement, juvenile delinquency. **Holdings:** 2000 books; 7000 documents, theses, research reports, government reports, and statistics. **Subscriptions:** 80 journals and other serials. **Services:** Copying; center open to the public with restrictions. **Computerized Information Services:** Internal database. **Publications:** List of publications; acquisitions list - by subscription.

★15711★
UNIVERSITE DE MONTREAL - CENTRE DE RECHERCHE SUR LES TRANSPORTS - DOCUMENTATION CENTRE (Trans)
C.P. 6128, Succursale A Phone: (514)343-6949
Montreal, PQ, Canada H3C 3J7 Sylvie Hetu, Libn.
Founded: 1971. **Staff:** Prof 1; Other 1. **Subjects:** Transportation, road safety. **Holdings:** 200 books; 40 bound periodical volumes; 7300 technical reports; 300 microfiche. **Subscriptions:** 80 journals and other serials. **Services:** Interlibrary loan; copying; SDI; center open to the public for reference use only. **Automated Operations:** Computerized cataloging. **Computerized Information Services:** DIALOG Information Services, Telesystemes Questel, CAN/OLE. Performs searches on fee basis. **Publications:** Bulletin du C.R.T., quarterly - free upon request.

★15712★
UNIVERSITE DE MONTREAL - CENTRE DE RECHERCHES CARAIBES - BIBLIOTHEQUE
C.P. 6128
Montreal, PQ, Canada H3C 3J7
Founded: 1968. **Subjects:** West Indies - anthropology, sociology, history, geography, languages, literature, social and economic studies, natural sciences. **Holdings:** 3000 books and bound periodical volumes; 2000 reprints; 90 dissertations and theses; 100 maps. **Remarks:** Presently inactive.

★15713★
UNIVERSITE DE MONTREAL - CHIMIE-BIBLIOTHEQUE (Sci-Engr)
C.P. 6128, Succursale A Phone: (514)343-6459
Montreal, PQ, Canada H3C 3J7 Corinne Haumont, Libn.
Founded: 1963. **Staff:** Prof 1; Other 4. **Subjects:** Chemistry. **Holdings:** 7401 books; 14,350 bound periodical volumes; 8138 microforms. **Subscriptions:** 290 journals and other serials. **Services:** Interlibrary loan; copying; library open to the public with restrictions. **Automated Operations:** Computerized cataloging and acquisitions. **Computerized Information Services:** DIALOG Information Services, Pergamon ORBIT InfoLine, Inc., BRS Information Technologies, CAN/OLE, Telesystemes Questel, QL Systems. **Publications:** Acquisitions list, monthly - limited distribution; User Guide, annual. **Special Catalogs:** Periodicals catalog (book).

UNIVERSITE DE MONTREAL - CLINICAL RESEARCH INSTITUTE OF MONTREAL
See: Clinical Research Institute of Montreal (3330)

★15714★
UNIVERSITE DE MONTREAL - COLLECTIONS SPECIALES (Hist, Rare Book)
C.P. 6128, Succursale A Phone: (514)343-7753
Montreal, PQ, Canada H3C 3J7 Genevieve Bazin, Libn.
Founded: 1984. **Staff:** Prof 2; Other 1. **Subjects:** Canadian history, rare books. **Special Collections:** The Louis Melzack Collection of Canadian Books (4000 volumes); The L.F. Georges Baby Collection of Canadian Books (1250 volumes). **Holdings:** 54,000 books. **Services:** Copying; collection open to the public. **Automated Operations:** Computerized cataloging and acquisitions.

★15715★
UNIVERSITE DE MONTREAL - DEPARTEMENT DE DEMOGRAPHIE - CENTRE DE DOCUMENTATION (Soc Sci)
C.P. 6128, Succursale A Phone: (514)343-7567
Montreal, PQ, Canada H3C 3J7 Micheline Frechette, Doc.
Founded: 1966. **Staff:** Prof 1. **Subjects:** Census, vital statistics, mortality, marriages, fertility, population theory and policy, migration, geographical distribution and ethnic groups, historical demography. **Special Collections:** Census of Canada, 1850 to present; vital statistics of Canada, 1921 to present; Canadian Yearbook, 1900 to present; Quebec Yearbook, 1914 to present. **Holdings:** 5000 books; 3000 bound periodical volumes; 4200 reprints, dissertations, and unbound reports. **Subscriptions:** 200 journals and other serials. **Services:** Interlibrary loan; copying; center open to the public.

★15716★
UNIVERSITE DE MONTREAL - DROIT-BIBLIOTHEQUE (Law)
Pavillon Maximilien Caron
3101, chemin de la Tour
C.P. 6206, Succursale A Phone: (514)343-6132
Montreal, PQ, Canada H3C 3T6 Paquerette Ranger, Dir.
Founded: 1942. **Staff:** Prof 5; Other 16. **Subjects:** Law. **Special Collections:** Public law; civil law; history of law. **Holdings:** 65,500 books; 72,100 bound periodical volumes; 26,900 microforms. **Subscriptions:** 1400 journals and other serials. **Services:** Interlibrary loan; copying; library open to the public with restrictions. **Automated Operations:** Computerized cataloging and acquisitions. **Computerized Information Services:** DIALOG Information Services, Pergamon ORBIT InfoLine, Inc., BRS Information Technologies, CAN/OLE, QL Systems, Societe Quebecoise d'Information Juridique (SOQUIJ). **Publications:** Reader's Guide.

UNIVERSITE DE MONTREAL - ECOLE DES HAUTES ETUDES COMMERCIALES DE MONTREAL
See: Ecole des Hautes Etudes Commerciales de Montreal (4580)

UNIVERSITE DE MONTREAL - ECOLE POLYTECHNIQUE DE MONTREAL
See: Ecole Polytechnique de Montreal (4581)

★15717★
UNIVERSITE DE MONTREAL - EDUCATION PHYSIQUE-BIBLIOTHEQUE (Educ, Rec)
C.P. 6128, Succursale A Phone: (514)343-6765
Montreal, PQ, Canada H3C 3J7 Lise Mayrand, Libn.
Founded: 1966. **Staff:** Prof 1; Other 6. **Subjects:** Physical education, sports, physiology, psychology, education. **Holdings:** 18,140 books; 7500 bound periodical volumes; 16,631 microforms; 1971 reports. **Subscriptions:** 409 journals and other serials. **Services:** Interlibrary loan; copying; library open to the public with restrictions. **Automated Operations:** Computerized cataloging and acquisitions. **Publications:** Acquisitions list; periodicals list - both limited distribution.

★15718★
UNIVERSITE DE MONTREAL - EDUCATION/PSYCHOLOGIE/COMMUNICATION-BIBLIOTHEQUE (Educ)
C.P. 6128, Succursale A Phone: (514)343-6638
Montreal, PQ, Canada H3C 3J7 Marielle Durand, Libn.
Founded: 1965. **Staff:** Prof 4; Other 18. **Subjects:** Education, pedagogy, psychology, communication, school administration. **Special Collections:** Rey-Herme Collection (3500 volumes); Villeneuve Collection (8150 volumes). **Holdings:** 70,000 books; 27,000 bound periodical volumes; 297,435 microforms. **Subscriptions:** 1351 journals and other serials. **Services:** Interlibrary loan; copying; library open to the public with restrictions. **Automated Operations:** Computerized cataloging and acquisitions. **Computerized Information Services:** DIALOG Information Services, BRS Information Technologies, Pergamon ORBIT InfoLine, Inc., CAN/OLE, Telesystemes Questel, QL Systems. **Publications:** Acquisitions list; list of serials; list of reference works; list of dissertations - all limited distribution. **Special Catalogs:** Rey-Herme Collection Catalog.

★15719★
UNIVERSITE DE MONTREAL - GEOGRAPHIE-BIBLIOTHEQUE (Geog-Map)
C.P. 6128, Succursale A Phone: (514)270-3727
Montreal, PQ, Canada H3C 3J7 Denis Harpin, Libn.
Staff: 1. **Subjects:** Geography. **Holdings:** 5958 books; 660 bound periodical volumes; 85 microforms. **Subscriptions:** 340 journals and other serials. **Services:** Interlibrary loan; copying; library open to the public with restrictions. **Automated Operations:** Computerized cataloging, acquisitions, and circulation.

★15720★
UNIVERSITE DE MONTREAL - GEOLOGIE-BIBLIOTHEQUE (Sci-Engr)
C.P. 6128, Succursale A Phone: (514)343-6831
Montreal, PQ, Canada H3C 3J7 Clement Arwas, Libn.
Founded: 1965. **Staff:** Prof 1; Other 1. **Subjects:** Geology. **Holdings:** 6782 books; 15,750 bound periodical volumes; 1019 microforms; 3636 reports. **Subscriptions:** 307 journals and other serials. **Services:** Interlibrary loan; copying; library open to the public with restrictions. **Automated Operations:** Computerized cataloging and acquisitions. **Publications:** Acquisitions list; periodicals list - both have limited distribution; Users Guide, annual.

★15721★
UNIVERSITE DE MONTREAL - INFORMATIQUE-BIBLIOTHEQUE (Info Sci, Comp Sci)
C.P. 6128, Succursale A Phone: (514)343-6819
Montreal, PQ, Canada H3C 3J7 Louis Sarrasin, Libn.
Founded: 1966. **Staff:** Prof 1; Other 4. **Subjects:** Computer science, applied linguistics, operations research, systems theory. **Holdings:** 10,970 books; 5057 bound periodical volumes; 3535 microforms; 8936 reports; 479 slides; 27 AV programs. **Subscriptions:** 308 journals and other serials. **Services:** Interlibrary loan; copying; library open to the public with restrictions. **Automated Operations:** Computerized acquisitions. **Computerized Information Services:** DIALOG Information Services, Pergamon ORBIT InfoLine, Inc., BRS Information Technologies, CAN/OLE, Telesystemes Questel, QL Systems. **Publications:** Acquisitions list, monthly - limited distribution; periodicals list; User Guide, annual.

★15722★
UNIVERSITE DE MONTREAL - MATHEMATIQUES-BIBLIOTHEQUE (Sci-Engr)
C.P. 6128, Succursale A Phone: (514)343-6703
Montreal, PQ, Canada H3C 3J7 Jules Giroux, Libn.
Founded: 1966. **Staff:** 3. **Subjects:** Mathematics. **Holdings:** 18,472 books; 13,440 bound periodical volumes; 2554 microforms; 3080 reports; 119 AV programs. **Subscriptions:** 348 journals and other serials. **Services:** Interlibrary loan; copying; library open to the public with restrictions. **Automated Operations:** Computerized acquisitions. **Computerized Information Services:** DIALOG Information Services, BRS Information Technologies, Pergamon ORBIT InfoLine, Inc., CAN/OLE, Telesystemes Questel, QL Systems. **Publications:** Reports of Higher Mathematics Seminars, 3/year; acquisitions list, monthly - limited distribution; User Guide, annual.

★15723★
UNIVERSITE DE MONTREAL - MEDECINE VETERINAIRE-BIBLIOTHEQUE (Med)
C.P. 5000 Phone: (514)773-8521
St. Hyacinthe, PQ, Canada J2S 7C6 Jean-Paul Jette, Libn.
Founded: 1948. **Staff:** Prof 1; Other 4. **Subjects:** Veterinary medicine, animal science. **Special Collections:** French veterinary theses (13,722). **Holdings:** 14,071 books; 12,424 bound periodical volumes; 325 reports; 1942 microforms; 3190 government publications; 387 AV programs. **Subscriptions:** 500 journals and other serials. **Services:** Interlibrary loan; copying; library open to the public. **Automated Operations:** Computerized cataloging and acquisitions. **Computerized Information Services:** DIALOG Information Services, MEDLINE; TELUM (internal database). **Publications:** Liste de Nouvelles Acquisitions, irregular - limited distribution; User Guide, annual; publications lists on veterinary information.

★15724★
UNIVERSITE DE MONTREAL - MUSIQUE-BIBLIOTHEQUE (Mus)
C.P. 6128, Succursale A Phone: (514)343-6432
Montreal, PQ, Canada H3C 3J7 Monique Lecavalier, Libn.
Founded: 1952. **Staff:** Prof 2; Other 7. **Subjects:** Music. **Holdings:** 9900 books; 2700 bound periodical volumes; 9947 phonograph records; 2012 slides; 16,572 scores; 6015 microforms; 2843 audiotapes; 111 cassettes; 139 compact discs; 91 AV programs. **Subscriptions:** 165 journals and other serials. **Services:** Interlibrary loan; copying; library open to the public with restrictions. **Automated Operations:** Computerized cataloging and acquisitions. **Publications:** Acquisitions list - for internal distribution only. **Special Catalogs:** Periodicals list.

★15725★
UNIVERSITE DE MONTREAL - OPTOMETRIE-BIBLIOTHEQUE (Med)
C.P. 6128, Succursale A Phone: (514)343-7674
Montreal, PQ, Canada H3C 3J7 Diane Clerk, Libn.
Founded: 1964. **Staff:** 1. **Subjects:** Optometry. **Holdings:** 4000 books; 4963 bound periodical volumes. **Subscriptions:** 130 journals and other serials. **Services:** Interlibrary loan; copying; library open to the public with restrictions. **Automated Operations:** Computerized cataloging and acquisitions. **Publications:** Acquisitions list, monthly - limited distribution.

★15726★
UNIVERSITE DE MONTREAL - PHYSIQUE-BIBLIOTHEQUE (Sci-Engr)
C.P. 6128, Succursale A Phone: (514)343-6613
Montreal, PQ, Canada H3C 3J7 Janine Cadet, Libn.
Founded: 1966. **Staff:** Prof 1; Other 3. **Subjects:** Physics, astrophysics, astronomy, biophysics. **Holdings:** 12,404 books; 16,113 bound periodical volumes; 1456 reports; 83 microforms. **Subscriptions:** 224 journals and other serials. **Services:** Interlibrary loan; copying; library open to the public with restrictions. **Automated Operations:** Computerized cataloging and acquisitions. **Computerized Information Services:** DIALOG Information Services, BRS Information Technologies, Pergamon ORBIT InfoLine, Inc., CAN/OLE, Telesystemes Questel, QL Systems. **Publications:** Acquisitions list, monthly - limited distribution. **Special Catalogs:** Periodicals list.

★15727★
UNIVERSITE DE MONTREAL - PSYCHO-EDUCATION-BIBLIOTHEQUE (Educ)
750 est, blvd. Gouin Phone: (514)382-0951
Montreal, PQ, Canada H2C 1A6 Yolande Beaudoin, Libn.
Founded: 1970. **Staff:** Prof 1; Other 3. **Subjects:** Child psychology, rehabilitation of maladjusted children. **Holdings:** 9400 books; 2600 bound periodical volumes; 76 microforms; 110 slides. **Subscriptions:** 141 journals and other serials. **Services:** Interlibrary loan; library open to the public with restrictions. **Automated Operations:** Computerized cataloging and acquisitions. **Publications:** Acquisitions list; periodical list - both for internal distribution only.

★15728★
UNIVERSITE DE MONTREAL - THEOLOGIE-PHILOSOPHIE BIBLIOTHEQUE
Pavillon Maximilien Caron C.P. 6128, Succursale A
3101, chemin de la Tour Montreal, PQ, Canada H3C 3T6
Defunct. Merged with Sciences Humaines et Sociales-Bibliotheque to form Bibliotheque des Lettres et Sciences Humaines.

★15729★
UNIVERSITE DU QUEBEC - ECOLE NATIONALE D'ADMINISTRATION PUBLIQUE - CENTRE DE DOCUMENTATION (Soc Sci, Bus-Fin)
945, ave. Wolfe Phone: (418)657-2485
Ste. Foy, PQ, Canada G1V 3J9 Michel Gelinas, Libn.
Founded: 1969. **Staff:** Prof 3; Other 8. **Subjects:** Public administration, management, economics, political science. **Holdings:** 39,300 books; 8300 pamphlets; 680 dissertations; 250 theses. **Subscriptions:** 719 journals and other serials; 7 newspapers. **Services:** Interlibrary loan; copying; center open to the public. **Automated Operations:** Computerized cataloging and circulation. **Computerized Information Services:** DIALOG Information Services, Telesystemes Questel, MINISIS, BADADUQ. **Publications:** Vient de paraitre; Bulletin signaletique des acquisitions; Guide bibliographique en administration publique; Administration publique canadienne, bibliographie; Thesaurus multilingue en administration publique. **Staff:** Jean-Marc Alain, Dir. of Commun..

★15730★
UNIVERSITE DU QUEBEC - ECOLE NATIONALE D'ADMINISTRATION PUBLIQUE - CENTRE DE DOCUMENTATION ENAP-MONTREAL (Bus-Fin)
4835, rue Christophe Colomb Phone: (514)522-3641
Montreal, PQ, Canada H2J 3G8 Carole Urbain, Libn.
Founded: 1976. **Staff:** Prof 1; Other 2. **Subjects:** Public and urban administration, management, international studies. **Holdings:** 10,000 volumes; 300 annual reports of federal and provincial government and international organizations; 2500 microfiche. **Subscriptions:** 330 journals and other serials; 9 newspapers. **Services:** Interlibrary loan; copying; SDI; center open to the public. **Automated Operations:** Computerized cataloging and circulation. **Computerized Information Services:** DIALOG Information Services, Telesystemes Questel, DOBIS, BADADUQ; POSTE, Envoy 100 (electronic mail services).

UNIVERSITE DU QUEBEC - INSTITUT ARMAND-FRAPPIER
See: Institut Armand-Frappier (6859)

★15731★
UNIVERSITE DU QUEBEC - MEDIATHEQUE (Educ)
2875, blvd. Laurier Phone: (418)657-3551
Ste. Foy, PQ, Canada G1V 2M3 Pierre Naudeau, Dir.
Founded: 1972. **Staff:** Prof 2; Other 1. **Subjects:** Higher education, administration, information processing. **Holdings:** 2000 books; 1000 Quebec and federal publications; 200 Quebec statutes. **Subscriptions:** 153 journals and other serials. **Services:** Interlibrary loan; copying; library open to the public on request. **Automated Operations:** Computerized cataloging and serials. **Computerized Information Services:** Online systems. **Staff:** Jean-Pierre Roy, Libn..

★15732★
UNIVERSITE DU QUEBEC EN ABITIBI-TEMISCAMINGUE - BIBLIOTHEQUE (Educ)
446, rue Gagne
Box 8000 Phone: (819)762-0971
Rouyn-Noranda, PQ, Canada J9X 5M5 Serge Allard, Dir.
Founded: 1971. **Staff:** Prof 3; Other 14. **Subjects:** Education, administration. **Special Collections:** Northwest Quebec (Abitibi-Temiscamingue; 6608 documents; 4 newspaper titles; 10,622 slides and AV programs); Societe du Developpement de la Baie James documents (20,000). **Holdings:** 44,622 books; 318,390 microforms; 8207 AV programs. **Subscriptions:** 739 journals and other serials. **Services:** Interlibrary loan; copying; library open to the public with restrictions. **Computerized Information Services:** DIALOG Information Services, BADADUQ. **Publications:** Liste des nouveaux titres catalogues et classifies. **Staff:** Levis Tremblay, Tech.Serv.; Andre Beland, Ref.Libn.; Gisele Neas, ILL.

★15733★
UNIVERSITE DU QUEBEC A CHICOUTIMI - BIBLIOTHEQUE - CARTOTHEQUE (Geog-Map)
555, blvd. de l'Universite Phone: (418)545-5623
Chicoutimi, PQ, Canada G7H 2B1 Paul-Emile Boulet, Dir.
Founded: 1969. **Subjects:** Regional studies. **Holdings:** 15,414 topographical maps; 9544 thematic maps; 31,083 aerial photographs; 88 satellite photographs; 16 atlases. **Services:** Interlibrary loan; SDI; library open to the public. **Automated Operations:** Computerized cataloging, acquisitions, and circulation. **Computerized Information Services:** DIALOG Information Services, Pergamon ORBIT InfoLine, Inc., BRS Information Technologies, CAN/OLE, CAN/SDI, MEDLINE, Telesystemes Questel, FRI Information Services Ltd., DOBIS Canadian Online Library System, BADADUQ; DOMYNO (internal database); Envoy 100 (electronic mail service). Performs searches on fee basis.

★15734★
UNIVERSITE DU QUEBEC A HULL - BIBLIOTHEQUE (Soc Sci, Hum)
C.P. 1250, Succursale B Phone: (819)595-2370
Hull, PQ, Canada J8X 3X7 Andre Chenier, Dir.
Founded: 1972. **Staff:** Prof 5; Other 13. **Subjects:** Administration, education, social sciences, nursing, computer science, art, linguistics and literature. **Holdings:** 70,377 books; 12,377 bound periodical volumes; 2228 microforms; 10,000 other cataloged items. **Subscriptions:** 1614 journals and other serials; 5 newspapers. **Services:** Interlibrary loan; SDI; library open to the public. **Automated Operations:** Computerized public access catalog, cataloging, acquisitions, serials, and circulation. **Computerized Information Services:** DIALOG Information Services, BRS Information Technologies, Telesystemes Questel, BADADUQ; Envoy 100, Biblioposte (electronic mail services). Performs searches on fee basis. Contact Person: Danielle Boisvert, Ref.Libn., 595-2374. **Staff:** Gilles Bergeron, Pub.Serv.Libn.; Louise Grondines, Cat.Libn.; Monique Dion, Cat.Libn.; Jacques Cloutier, Acq..

★15735★
UNIVERSITE DU QUEBEC A MONTREAL - AUDIOVIDEOTHEQUE (Aud-Vis)
C.P. 8889, Succursale A Phone: (514)282-4332
Montreal, PQ, Canada H3C 3P3 Huguette Tanguay, AV Libn.
Staff: Prof 1; Other 1. **Subjects:** Sexology, administration, earth sciences, psychology, education. **Holdings:** 1800 films and videotapes. **Services:** Library open to the public with restrictions.

★15736★
UNIVERSITE DU QUEBEC A MONTREAL - BIBLIOTHEQUE DES ARTS (Art)
C.P. 8889, Succursale A Phone: (514)282-6134
Montreal, PQ, Canada H3C 3P3 Daphne Dufresne, Hd.Libn.
Founded: 1944. **Staff:** Prof 1; Other 8. **Subjects:** Painting, sculpture, art history, Canadian art, design, engraving, dance. **Holdings:** 60,000 books; 5000 bound periodical volumes; 130,000 slides; 1600 microforms; 15 drawers of clippings on Canadian art. **Subscriptions:** 350 journals and other serials. **Services:** Interlibrary loan; copying; library open to university students. **Automated Operations:** Computerized cataloging, circulation, and acquisitions. **Computerized Information Services:** BADADUQ, DIALOG Information Services, DOBIS Canadian Online Library System, Telesystemes Questel, RLIN.

★15737★
UNIVERSITE DU QUEBEC A MONTREAL - BIBLIOTHEQUE DE MUSIQUE (Mus)
C.P. 8889, Succursale A Phone: (514)282-3934
Montreal, PQ, Canada H3C 3P3 Gerald Parker, Libn.
Staff: Prof 1; Other 3. **Subjects:** Music education and therapy, musicology. **Special Collections:** Canadian Broadcasting Corporation (CBC) Music Program archives, 1940-1983. **Holdings:** 6314 books; 355 bound periodical volumes; 13,700 scores; 8945 phonograph records; 8000 tape records. **Subscriptions:** 95 journals and other serials. **Services:** Interlibrary loan; copying; library open to the public. **Automated Operations:** Computerized cataloging, circulation, and acquisitions. **Computerized Information Services:** BADADUQ.

★15738★
UNIVERSITE DU QUEBEC A MONTREAL - BIBLIOTHEQUE DES SCIENCES (Sci-Engr)
C.P. 8889, Succursale A Phone: (514)282-6164
Montreal, PQ, Canada H3C 3P3 Conrad Corriveau, Dir.
Staff: Prof 5; Other 8. **Subjects:** Chemistry, biology, mathematics, physics, geology, technology, psychology. **Holdings:** 53,200 books; 35,100 bound

periodical volumes; 2500 microforms; 500 dissertations. **Services:** Interlibrary loan; copying; library open to the public with restrictions. **Automated Operations:** Computerized cataloging, acquisitions, and circulation. **Computerized Information Services:** DIALOG Information Services, BADADUQ, CAN/OLE, BRS Information Technologies, Pergamon ORBIT InfoLine, Inc., MEDLINE, INFO/tek, QL Systems, International Development Research Centre (IDRC). **Special Catalogs:** Lists of periodical and monograph holdings (computer printout). **Staff:** Jean Juneau, Ref.Libn.; Mychelle Boulet, Ref.Libn.; Lise Chabot, Libn.; Bibiane Dostie, Libn..

★15739★
UNIVERSITE DU QUEBEC A MONTREAL - BIBLIOTHEQUE DES SCIENCES DE L'EDUCATION (Educ)
C.P. 8889, Succursale A Phone: (514)282-6174
Montreal, PQ, Canada H3C 3P3 Andre Champagne, Dir.
Staff: Prof 3; Other 8. **Subjects:** Continuing teacher education, elementary and secondary education, physical education, disadvantaged and exceptional child education, hearing and learning disabilities, professional and vocational information. **Special Collections:** ERIC documents. **Holdings:** 48,000 books; 8000 bound periodical volumes; 258,000 ERIC microfiche; 3900 microcards; 750 reels of microfilm; 225 film loops; 1550 slides. **Subscriptions:** 425 journals and other serials. **Services:** Interlibrary loan; copying; SDI; library open to the public for reference use only. **Automated Operations:** Computerized public access catalog, cataloging, acquisitions, and circulation. **Computerized Information Services:** BRS Information Technologies, DIALOG Information Services, Pergamon ORBIT InfoLine, Inc., MEDLINE, CAN/OLE, BADADUQ, IST-Informatheque Inc., WILSONLINE, International Development Research Centre (IDRC); SIGIRD (Systeme integre de gestion des ressources documentaires) (internal database). Performs searches on fee basis. **Special Catalogs:** Lists of periodical holdings (printout). **Staff:** Lucie Verreault, Ref.Libn.; Danielle Mallette, Ref.Libn.; Monique Gaucher, Libn..

★15740★
UNIVERSITE DU QUEBEC A MONTREAL - BIBLIOTHEQUE DES SCIENCES JURIDIQUES (Law, Soc Sci)
C.P. 8889, Succursale A
Local T-2600 Phone: (514)282-6184
Montreal, PQ, Canada H3C 3P3 Micheline Drapeau, Dir.
Founded: 1974. **Staff:** Prof 3; Other 7. **Subjects:** Jurisprudence; social security; law - consumer and environmental protection, constitutional, family, fiscal, health, housing, labor, poverty, public education, social; immigration and civil rights. **Holdings:** 30,481 volumes; 6 VF drawers of microfiche; 101 magnetic tapes; 434 reels of microfilm. **Subscriptions:** 444 journals and other serials. **Services:** Interlibrary loan; copying; library open to the public with restrictions. **Automated Operations:** Computerized cataloging, acquisitions, and circulation. **Computerized Information Services:** BADADUQ. **Staff:** Claudio Antonelli, Ref.Libn.; Jean-Paul Reid, Ref.Libn..

★15741★
UNIVERSITE DU QUEBEC A MONTREAL - CARTOTHEQUE (Geog-Map)
C.P. 8889, Succursale A Phone: (514)282-3133
Montreal, PQ, Canada H3C 3P8 Leon-Pierre Sciamma, Cart.
Staff: Prof 2; Other 2. **Subjects:** Cartography, aerial photography. **Holdings:** 9000 books; 600 bound periodical volumes; 442,000 aerial photographs; 65,800 maps. **Services:** Library open to the public. **Computerized Information Services:** BADADUQ.

★15742★
UNIVERSITE DU QUEBEC A MONTREAL - CENTRE DE DOCUMENTATION ECONOMIE-ADMINISTRATION (Soc Sci)
C.P. 8889, Succursale A Phone: (514)282-6136
Montreal, PQ, Canada H3C 3P8 Monique Cote, Libn.
Founded: 1971. **Staff:** Prof 1; Other 1. **Subjects:** Economics, administration, urban studies. **Holdings:** 43,809 corporation reports, public documents, university studies; 21,346 microforms. **Subscriptions:** 1262 journals and other serials. **Services:** Center open to the public. **Automated Operations:** Computerized acquisitions. **Computerized Information Services:** BADADUQ, MINISIS. **Publications:** Nouveautes and periodical highlights, monthly.

★15743★
UNIVERSITE DU QUEBEC A MONTREAL - CENTRE DE DOCUMENTATION EN SCIENCES HUMAINES (Soc Sci)
C.P. 8889, Succursale A Phone: (514)282-6138
Montreal, PQ, Canada H3C 3P3 Louis LeBorgne, Doc.
Staff: Prof 1; Other 1. **Subjects:** Political parties, labor unions, feminism, urban movements, Latin America, Eastern Europe, ethnic studies. **Special Collections:** Quebec labor union archives; Quebec and Canadian political party archives; Quebec feminist movement archives. **Holdings:** 1021 books; 72 boxes of archives; 365 linear feet of bound periodical volumes; 25 VF drawers; 320 reels of microfilm; 12 linear feet of microfilm; 900 maps. **Subscriptions:** 58 journals and other serials. **Services:** Interlibrary loan; copying; center open to the public. **Automated Operations:** Computerized cataloging and acquisitions. **Computerized Information Services:** BADADUQ.

★15744★
UNIVERSITE DU QUEBEC A MONTREAL - INSTITUT NATIONAL DE LA RECHERCHE SCIENTIFIQUE-URBANISATION - BIBLIOTHEQUE (Plan)
3465 Durocher Phone: (514)842-4191
Montreal, PQ, Canada H2X 2C6 Helene Houde, Libn.
Founded: 1970. **Staff:** Prof 20; Other 18. **Subjects:** Urban and regional planning, demography, sociology, economics. **Holdings:** 5000 books. **Subscriptions:** 300 journals and other serials. **Services:** Interlibrary loan; copying; library open to the public. **Automated Operations:** Computerized cataloging and circulation. **Publications:** Etudes et documents; rapports de recherche, both irregular. **Also Known As:** INRS-Urbanisation.

★15745★
UNIVERSITE DU QUEBEC A MONTREAL - INSTITUT NATIONAL DE LA RECHERCHE SCIENTIFIQUE-URBANISATION - CARTOTHEQUE (Geog-Map)
3465 Durocher, Local 225 Phone: (514)842-4191
Montreal, PQ, Canada H2X 2C6 Christiane Desmarais, Cart.
Founded: 1973. **Staff:** Prof 1. **Subjects:** Cartography - urban and topographic. **Special Collections:** Land-use plans for Montreal, 1964-1986; fire insurance plans of Quebec, 1885-1973. **Holdings:** 117 atlases; 78 bound periodical volumes; 12,200 topographic maps; 17,780 urban maps; 17 reels of microfilm. **Services:** Interlibrary loan; copying; library open to the public. **Networks/Consortia:** Member of Association des Cartotheques Canadiennes. **Special Catalogs:** Catalogs by area and subject.

★15746★
UNIVERSITE DU QUEBEC A RIMOUSKI - CARTOTHEQUE (Geog-Map)
300, ave. des Ursulines Phone: (418)724-1669
Rimouski, PQ, Canada G5L 3A1 Yves Michaud, Map Libn.
Founded: 1971. **Staff:** Prof 1. **Subjects:** Cartography, aerial photography. **Special Collections:** Canadian, Quebec, East Quebec, lower St. Lawrence, and Gaspesia region maps. **Holdings:** 700 books; 700 atlases; 25,000 maps; 20,000 aerial photographs; 100 other cataloged items. **Services:** Library open to the public. **Publications:** Information cartologique, irregular.

★15747★
UNIVERSITE DU QUEBEC A TROIS-RIVIERES - CARTOTHEQUE (Geog-Map)
Pavillon Leon-Provancher
C.P. 500 Phone: (819)376-5099
Trois-Rivieres, PQ, Canada G9A 5H7 Marie Lefebvre, Cart.
Staff: Prof 1. **Subjects:** Cartography, aerial photography. **Special Collections:** Maps of the Trois-Rivieres region. **Holdings:** 1881 books and bound periodical volumes; 39,050 maps; 209 atlases; 3 globes; 5 relief models; 49,592 aerial photographs. **Services:** Library open to the public. **Networks/Consortia:** Member of Association des Cartotheques Canadiennes. **Publications:** Repertoire des documents cartographiques et photographiques sur la region de Trois-Rivieres, 1985; Guide de l'usager, 1987 - both for sale. **Remarks:** The map collection is administered by the Department of Humanities.

★15748★
UNIVERSITE DE SHERBROOKE - BIBLIOTHEQUE DES SCIENCES (Sci-Engr)
2500, blvd. Universite Phone: (819)821-7099
Sherbrooke, PQ, Canada J1K 2R1 Roger B. Bernier, Resp.
Founded: 1960. **Staff:** Prof 1; Other 6. **Subjects:** Biology; mathematics; chemistry; physics; engineering - chemical, civil, mechanical, electrical. **Holdings:** 52,600 books; 68,800 bound periodical volumes. **Subscriptions:** 1006 journals and other serials. **Services:** Interlibrary loan; copying; SDI; library open to the public. **Automated Operations:** Computerized

cataloging and circulation. **Computerized Information Services:** DIALOG Information Services, BRS Information Technologies, MEDLARS, QL Systems, Telesystemes Questel, Pergamon ORBIT InfoLine, Inc., ESA/IRS, IST-Informatheque Inc; CEDBOBUS (internal database); Envoy 100 (electronic mail service). **Publications:** Liste des Periodiques, annual.

★15749★
UNIVERSITE DE SHERBROOKE - FACULTE DE MEDECINE - BIBLIOTHEQUE DES SCIENCES DE LA SANTE (Med)
Centre Hospitalier Universitaire Phone: (819)565-2096
Sherbrooke, PQ, Canada J1H 5N4 Germain Chouinard, Dir.
Founded: 1965. **Staff:** Prof 1; Other 6. **Subjects:** Health sciences. **Holdings:** 75,337 volumes. **Subscriptions:** 1300 journals and other serials. **Services:** Interlibrary loan; copying; SDI; library open to the public with restrictions. **Automated Operations:** Computerized cataloging and circulation. **Computerized Information Services:** NLM, DIALOG Information Services, BRS Information Technologies, Pergamon ORBIT InfoLine, Inc., MEDLINE, CAN/OLE. Performs searches on fee basis.

★15750★
UNIVERSITE ST-PAUL - BIBLIOTHEQUE (Rel-Phil)
223 Main Phone: (613)236-1393
Ottawa, ON, Canada K1S 1C4 Barbara Hicks, Chf.Libn.
Founded: 1937. **Staff:** Prof 4; Other 13. **Subjects:** Religious sciences, philosophy, canon law, medieval sciences, theology, Bible, church history. **Holdings:** 350,000 books; 70,000 bound periodical volumes; 5000 reels of microfilm; 85,000 microfiche; 3000 manuscripts on microfilm. **Subscriptions:** 1200 journals and other serials. **Services:** Interlibrary loan; copying; library open to the public with restrictions. **Remarks:** Maintained by Oblate Fathers.

UNIVERSITE DE SUDBURY
See: University of Sudbury (16898)

★15751★
UNIVERSITIES FIELD STAFF INTERNATIONAL - INFORMATION CENTER (Soc Sci)
620 Union Dr. Phone: (317)274-4122
Indianapolis, IN 46202 Aaron Miller, Exec.Dir.
Founded: 1951. **Staff:** Prof 1. **Subjects:** International politics, economics, and organizations; Third World development. **Holdings:** 500 books; 500 bound periodical volumes; UFSI Reports, 1970 to present, on microfiche; United Nations publications. **Services:** Center open to the public for reference use only.

★15752★
UNIVERSITY AFFILIATED CINCINNATI CENTER FOR DEVELOPMENTAL DISORDERS - RESEARCH LIBRARY (Med, Educ)
Pavilion Bldg.
3300 Elland Ave. Phone: (513)559-4626
Cincinnati, OH 45229 Dorothy A. Gilroy, Chf.Res.Libn.
Founded: 1960. **Staff:** Prof 3; Other 1. **Subjects:** Developmental disabilities, mental retardation, learning disabilities, special education, pediatrics, neurology, nutrition, rehabilitation, psychology, social work, vocational counseling. **Special Collections:** Library for parents of exceptional children (1000 books and 500 pamphlet titles for distribution); Toy Library for Special Children; bibliotherapy collection. **Holdings:** 16,000 books; 2000 bound periodical volumes; 100 AV programs; 175,000 reprint articles relating to developmental disorders and pediatrics; 4 VF drawers of staff publications; 10,000 slides. **Subscriptions:** 240 journals and other serials. **Services:** Interlibrary loan; copying; SDI; library open to the public with restrictions and for reference only. **Computerized Information Services:** BRS Information Technologies, MEDLINE. **Networks/Consortia:** Member of Greater Midwest Regional Medical Library Network, U.S.A. Toy Library Association. **Publications:** Library Bulletin, quarterly - for internal distribution and limited outside distributicn. **Special Indexes:** Card index to reprint file. **Remarks:** Affiliated with University of Cincinnati and Cincinnati Children's Hospital. **Staff:** Jennie Swerdlow, Cat..

★15753★
UNIVERSITY OF AKRON - AMERICAN HISTORY RESEARCH CENTER (Hist)
Bierce Library Phone: (216)375-7670
Akron, OH 44325 John V. Miller, Jr., Dir.
Founded: 1970. **Staff:** Prof 1; Other 2. **Subjects:** State and local history, business, labor, politics, religion, social services. **Special Collections:** Records and papers of Akron Area Chamber of Commerce, Akron Mayors John Ballard and Roy Ray, Canal Society of Ohio, General Tire and Rubber Company, B.F. Goodrich Company, John S. Knight, Lighter-than-Air Society, Ohio Edison Company, Congressman John F. Seiberling. **Holdings:** 4100 cubic feet of historical documents. **Services:** Center open to the public. **Networks/Consortia:** Member of Ohio Network of American History Research Centers.

★15754★
UNIVERSITY OF AKRON - ARCHIVES OF THE HISTORY OF AMERICAN PSYCHOLOGY (Soc Sci)
Simmons Hall Phone: (216)375-7285
Akron, OH 44325 John A. Popplestone, Dir.
Founded: 1965. **Staff:** Prof 2; Other 10. **Subjects:** American psychology. **Special Collections:** Papers of E.A. Doll, H.H. Goddard, H.S. Hollingworth, Leta Hollingworth, K. Koffka, A. Maslow, M. Scheerer, W. Shipley, E.C. Tolman; historical laboratory equipment (600 items). **Holdings:** 18,000 books; 2000 linear feet of documents; 70 linear feet of ephemeral and fugitive material; 5000 tests; 3000 photographs; 5500 films; 350 audiotapes. **Services:** Copying; archives open to the public by appointment. **Staff:** Marion White McPherson, Assoc.Dir..

★15755★
UNIVERSITY OF AKRON - ART SLIDE LIBRARY (Art)
150 E. Exchange St. Phone: (216)375-5962
Akron, OH 44325 Ivy Carter, Slide Libn.
Founded: 1978. **Staff:** Prof 1; Other 3. **Subjects:** Art history, textile, fiber art, photography, museums, advertising, architecture. **Holdings:** 868 books; 40,000 slides. **Subscriptions:** 13 journals and other serials. **Services:** Library not open to the public.

★15756★
UNIVERSITY OF AKRON - CENTER FOR PEACE STUDIES - LIBRARY (Soc Sci)
Akron, OH 44325 Phone: (216)375-7008
Martha C. Leyden, Dir.
Staff: 1. **Subjects:** Peace movements and their history; internationalism; human rights; peace education. **Special Collections:** Library of World Peace Studies (5000 microfiche). **Holdings:** 400 books; 2 VF drawers of peace societies and organizations; 2 VF drawers of academic peace programs. **Subscriptions:** 15 journals and other serials. **Services:** Copying; library open to the public. **Publications:** International Peace Studies Newsletter, 3/year - to mailing list; Human Rights bibliography (card).

★15757★
UNIVERSITY OF AKRON - HERMAN MUEHLSTEIN RARE BOOK COLLECTION (Rare Book)
Bierce Library
Akron, OH 44325 Phone: (216)375-7670
Staff: Prof 1. **Subjects:** American and English literature, American history. **Holdings:** 1500 volumes. **Services:** Collection open to the public. **Computerized Information Services:** OCLC; VTLS (internal database). Performs searches on fee basis.

★15758★
UNIVERSITY OF AKRON - MEDIA RESOURCE CENTER (Aud-Vis)
63 Bierce Library Phone: (216)375-6102
Akron, OH 44325 Frank Leyda
Founded: 1983. **Staff:** 1. **Subjects:** Foreign languages, music, literature, history, mathematics, elementary and higher education, art, communication, nursing, business, manufacturing, physical sciences, recreation. **Special Collections:** Government propaganda films, 1933-1948 (32). **Holdings:** 4723 phonograph records; 112 audiotapes; 2172 cassettes; 850 8mm films; 1080 16mm films; 613 slide sets; 24 computer programs. **Services:** Tape duplication; transparency production; center open to the public.

★15759★
UNIVERSITY OF AKRON - MEDIA SERVICES (Aud-Vis)
63 Bierce Library Phone: (216)375-7811
Akron, OH 44325 Stanley W. Akers, Asst.Dir., ULLR
Founded: 1952. **Staff:** Prof 3; Other 1. **Holdings:** Media equipment, university-produced and general media software. **Services:** Center open to campus and nonprofit groups.

★15760★
UNIVERSITY OF AKRON - SCHOOL OF LAW - C. BLAKE MC DOWELL LAW LIBRARY (Law)
Law Center
302 E. Buchtel Ave. Phone: (216)375-7447
Akron, OH 44325 Paul Richert, Law Libn.
Founded: 1965. **Staff:** Prof 5; Other 6. **Subjects:** Anglo-American law. **Holdings:** 190,000 volumes. **Subscriptions:** 1073 periodicals. **Services:** Interlibrary loan; copying; library open to the public. **Computerized Information Services:** LEXIS, OCLC, WESTLAW. **Publications:** Acquisition List, monthly - for internal distribution only. **Staff:** Robbie Robertson, Acq.Coord..

★15761★
UNIVERSITY OF AKRON - SCIENCE AND TECHNOLOGY LIBRARY (Sci-Engr, Biol Sci, Comp Sci)
104 Auburn Science Center Phone: (216)375-7195
Akron, OH 44325 Norma Pearson, Hd.
Founded: 1967. **Staff:** Prof 2; Other 3. **Subjects:** Biology; chemistry; physics; mathematics; computer science; geology; polymer science; nursing and allied health sciences; engineering - biomedical, chemical, civil, computer, electrical, mechanical, polymer. **Holdings:** 65,000 volumes. **Subscriptions:** 2000 journals and other serials. **Services:** Copying; library open to the public. **Automated Operations:** Computerized public access catalog, cataloging, serials, and circulation. **Computerized Information Services:** DIALOG Information Services, BRS Information Technologies, Pergamon ORBIT InfoLine, Inc., CAS ONLINE, OCLC; VTLS (internal database). Performs searches on fee basis. **Networks/Consortia:** Member of Center for Research Libraries (CRL) Consortia, OHIONET, NOEMARL. **Staff:** Ann Bolek, Physical Sci.Libn.

★15762★
UNIVERSITY OF AKRON - UNIVERSITY ARCHIVES (Hist)
Bierce Library Phone: (216)375-7670
Akron, OH 44325 John V. Miller, Jr., Dir. of Archv.Serv.
Founded: 1965. **Staff:** Prof 1; Other 2. **Subjects:** University of Akron. **Holdings:** 4000 cubic feet of archival materials, 1870 to present. **Services:** Archives open to the public.

★15763★
UNIVERSITY OF ALABAMA - BUSINESS LIBRARY (Bus-Fin)
Box S Phone: (205)348-6096
Tuscaloosa, AL 35487-9784 Kathy Field, Act.Hd.
Founded: 1925. **Staff:** Prof 2; Other 4. **Subjects:** Accounting, banking, economics, finance, human resource management, marketing, international business, real estate, transportation, business law, insurance. **Special Collections:** Corporate reports (90,000). **Holdings:** 134,200 books; 42,437 bound periodical volumes; 1150 reels of microfilm; 223,900 microfiche. **Subscriptions:** 2600 journals and other serials. **Services:** Interlibrary loan; copying; library open to the public. **Automated Operations:** Computerized public access catalog, cataloging, and circulation. **Computerized Information Services:** DIALOG Information Services, Pergamon ORBIT InfoLine, Inc., BRS Information Technologies, OCLC. Performs searches on fee basis. **Networks/Consortia:** Member of Network of Alabama Academic Libraries (NAAL), SOLINET. **Special Catalogs:** Corporate report catalog (card).

★15764★
UNIVERSITY OF ALABAMA - COLLEGE OF COMMUNITY HEALTH SCIENCES - HEALTH SCIENCES LIBRARY (Med)
Box 6331 Phone: (205)348-1360
Tuscaloosa, AL 35487 Lisa Rains Russell, Chf.Med.Libn.
Founded: 1973. **Staff:** Prof 2; Other 11. **Subjects:** Medicine, nursing, pharmacy, medical sociology. **Special Collections:** AV programs on clinical medicine (2000). **Holdings:** 9000 books; 16,000 bound periodical volumes; 16 VF drawers of pamphlets and clippings. **Subscriptions:** 475 journals and other serials. **Services:** Interlibrary loan; copying; library open to health care professionals. **Computerized Information Services:** MEDLARS, DIALOG Information Services, OCLC. Performs searches on fee basis. Contact Person: Barbara Doughty, Med.Ref.Libn., 348-1364. **Special Catalogs:** Audiovisuals Catalog of the Health Sciences Library, annual - for internal distribution only. **Staff:** Bobby Selwyn, Mgr., AV; Greg Ledet, Circ.Mgr..

★15765★
UNIVERSITY OF ALABAMA - ENGINEERING LIBRARY (Sci-Engr, Comp Sci)
Box S Phone: (205)348-6551
Tuscaloosa, AL 35487-9784 Aydan Kalyoncu, Sr.Libn.
Founded: 1963. **Staff:** Prof 2; Other 2. **Subjects:** Engineering - aerospace, industrial, mechanical, minerals, electrical, chemical, metallurgical, civil; computer science. **Holdings:** 72,000 books, bound periodical volumes, and technical reports; 4000 microforms; standards and specifications. **Subscriptions:** 650 journals and other serials. **Services:** Interlibrary loan; copying; library open to the public. **Automated Operations:** Computerized public access catalog, cataloging, and circulation. **Computerized Information Services:** DIALOG Information Services, Pergamon ORBIT InfoLine, Inc., BRS Information Technologies, OCLC, CAS ONLINE, NASA/RECON, Association of Research Libraries (ARL), WILSONLINE. Performs searches on fee basis. **Networks/Consortia:** Member of Network of Alabama Academic Libraries (NAAL), SOLINET.

UNIVERSITY OF ALABAMA - GAS RESEARCH INSTITUTE
See: University of Alabama - School of Mines and Energy Development (15769)

★15766★
UNIVERSITY OF ALABAMA - MC LURE EDUCATION LIBRARY (Educ)
Box S Phone: (205)348-6055
Tuscaloosa, AL 35487-9784 Sharon Lee Stewart, Sr.Libn.
Founded: 1928. **Staff:** Prof 2; Other 4. **Subjects:** Higher education; special education; curriculum and instruction; health, physical education, and recreation; behavioral studies; fine arts education. **Special Collections:** Curriculum Laboratory; Children's Collection; history of education in America. **Holdings:** 134,145 books; 13,508 bound periodical volumes; 479,404 microforms; 3 VF drawers of newsletters; 6 VF drawers of additional material. **Subscriptions:** 901 journals and other serials. **Services:** Interlibrary loan; copying; microfiche-to-microfiche copying; library open to the public. **Automated Operations:** Computerized public access catalog, cataloging, and circulation. **Computerized Information Services:** DIALOG Information Services, OCLC, BRS Information Technologies, Pergamon ORBIT InfoLine, Inc., Association of Research Libraries (ARL). **Networks/Consortia:** Member of SOLINET, Network of Alabama Academic Libraries (NAAL). **Publications:** Education Library Resources. **Staff:** Helga Visscher, Ref.Libn..

★15767★
UNIVERSITY OF ALABAMA - SCHOOL OF LAW - ALABAMA LAW REVIEW - LIBRARY (Law)
Box 1976 Phone: (205)348-5300
Tuscaloosa, AL 35487-1976 Gary Farris, Ed.-in.-Chf.
Staff: 1. **Subjects:** Federal and state law. **Holdings:** 3366 books; 361 bound periodical volumes. **Subscriptions:** 25 journals and other serials. **Services:** Library not open to the public. **Publications:** Alabama Law Review, 3/year - by subscription.

★15768★
UNIVERSITY OF ALABAMA - SCHOOL OF LAW LIBRARY (Law)
Box 6205 Phone: (205)348-5925
Tuscaloosa, AL 35487-6205 Cherry L. Thomas, Law Lib.Dir./Asst.Prof.
Founded: 1872. **Staff:** Prof 6; Other 6. **Subjects:** Law. **Special Collections:** U.S. Supreme Court Justice Hugo L. Black Book Collection. **Holdings:** 195,175 books; 27,347 bound periodical volumes; 42,500 microforms. **Subscriptions:** 2387 journals and other serials; 10 newspapers. **Services:** Interlibrary loan; copying; library open to the public. **Computerized Information Services:** LEXIS, DIALOG Information Services, WESTLAW. **Networks/Consortia:** Member of Consortium of Southeast Law Libraries. **Staff:** David Lowe, Comp.Serv.Ref.; Ruth Weeks, Cat.; Robert Marshall, Ref.; Paul Pruitt, Ref./Coll.Dev.; Penny C. Gibson, Pub.Serv.Libn..

★15769★
UNIVERSITY OF ALABAMA - SCHOOL OF MINES AND ENERGY DEVELOPMENT - COALBED METHANE RESOURCE CENTER (Energy)
Farrah Hall
Box 1982 Phone: (205)348-2839
Tuscaloosa, AL 35487 Eve E. Conaway, Ref.Coll.Mgr.
Founded: 1985. **Staff:** Prof 1; Other 1. **Subjects:** Coalbed methane; coal, gas, and petroleum industries; alternative energy sources. **Holdings:** 300 books; 12 coalbed basin reports; 415 petrophysical well logs; 600 technical

reports; 400 vertical files and ephemera; 60 maps; unbound periodicals. **Subscriptions:** 28 journals and other serials. **Services:** Copying; SDI; center open to the public. **Automated Operations:** Computerized cataloging and acquisitions. **Computerized Information Services:** COMET (internal database). Performs searches free of charge. **Publications:** Bibliographies, irregular. **Special Indexes:** Index to well logs; index to vertical files. **Formerly:** Gas Research Institute.

★15770★
UNIVERSITY OF ALABAMA - SCIENCE LIBRARY (Sci-Engr, Biol Sci)
Box S Phone: (205)348-5959
Tuscaloosa, AL 35487-9784 John S. Langen, Sr.Libn.
Founded: 1963. **Staff:** Prof 1; Other 2. **Subjects:** Chemistry, physics, biology, geology, astronomy, mathematics, microbiology. **Special Collections:** Alabama Museum of Natural History (1500 volumes). **Holdings:** 35,000 books; 60,000 bound periodical volumes; 900 theses; 315 science dissertations; 229 reels of microfilm. **Subscriptions:** 1350 journals and other serials. **Services:** Interlibrary loan; copying; library open to the public. **Automated Operations:** Computerized public access catalog, cataloging, and circulation. **Computerized Information Services:** DIALOG Information Services, Pergamon ORBIT InfoLine, Inc., BRS Information Technologies, OCLC. **Networks/Consortia:** Member of Network of Alabama Academic Libraries (NAAL), Southeast Idaho Health Information Consortium.

★15771★
UNIVERSITY OF ALABAMA - UNIVERSITY MAP LIBRARY (Geog-Map)
Box 1982 Phone: (205)348-6028
Tuscaloosa, AL 35487 Thomas J. Kallsen, Map Lib.Supv.
Founded: 1971. **Staff:** Prof 1; Other 1. **Subjects:** Maps - U.S., Alabama, geology, natural resources, world, Europe. **Special Collections:** Winn-Dixie Atlas Collection (110 thematic atlases). **Holdings:** 300 books; 175,000 maps; 65,500 aerial photographs; 65 relief models. **Services:** Interlibrary loan; SDI; library open to the public with restrictions on circulation. **Publications:** Map Library: University of Alabama (brochure).

★15772★
UNIVERSITY OF ALABAMA - WILLIAM STANLEY HOOLE SPECIAL COLLECTIONS LIBRARY (Hum, Rare Book)
Box S Phone: (205)348-5512
Tuscaloosa, AL 35487-9784 Joyce H. Lamont, Asst. Dean, Spec.Coll.
Staff: Prof 5; Other 2. **Subjects:** Alabamiana, travels in the South East, southern Americana, early imprints, state documents. **Special Collections:** Rare books (12,500); manuscripts (14 million); university archives (4 million items); Alabamiana (35,000 volumes); black folk music (250 magnetic tapes); oral history (875 magnetic tapes); maps (15,000). **Holdings:** 46,000 books; 10,000 theses, dissertations, and pamphlets. **Subscriptions:** 135 journals and other serials. **Services:** Interlibrary loan; copying; library open to the public. **Computerized Information Services:** OCLC; AMELIA (internal database). **Networks/Consortia:** Member of SOLINET, Network of Alabama Academic Libraries (NAAL). **Special Indexes:** Finding aids for manuscripts and archival collections.

★15773★
UNIVERSITY OF ALABAMA IN BIRMINGHAM - COMPUTER AND INFORMATION SCIENCES RESEARCH LIBRARY (Comp Sci)
Campbell Hall, Rm. 122 Phone: (205)934-2213
Birmingham, AL 35294 Barrett Bryant, Fac.Lib.Rep.
Founded: 1982. **Staff:** 2. **Subjects:** Computer science, parallel processing, artificial intelligence, programming languages. **Holdings:** 500 books; 2000 unbound periodicals; 200 technical reports; 500 manuscripts. **Subscriptions:** 20 journals and other serials; 10 newspapers. **Services:** Library not open to the public. **Automated Operations:** Computerized cataloging, acquisitions, and serials. **Publications:** Department of Computer and Information Sciences Technical Report Series, 15-25/year - free upon request.

★15774★
UNIVERSITY OF ALABAMA IN BIRMINGHAM - LISTER HILL LIBRARY OF THE HEALTH SCIENCES (Med)
University Sta. Phone: (205)934-5460
Birmingham, AL 35294 Lynn M. Fortney, Act.Dir.
Founded: 1945. **Staff:** Prof 12; Other 39. **Subjects:** Medicine, dentistry, nursing, public health, optometry, allied health fields. **Special Collections:** Lawrence Reynolds Collection (rare medical books and manuscripts; 9202 items); Alabama Museum of the Health Sciences (medical history; 10,700 items); Multi-Media Health Library (1755 AV programs). **Holdings:** 83,167 books; 118,530 bound periodical volumes; 13,433 microfiche; 126 reels of microfilm; 3285 slides; 30 phonograph records. **Subscriptions:** 2950 journals and other serials. **Services:** Interlibrary loan; copying; SDI; library open to the public. **Automated Operations:** Computerized public access catalog, cataloging, acquisitions, serials, and circulation. **Computerized Information Services:** OCLC, MEDLINE, BRS Information Technologies, DIALOG Information Services, Pergamon ORBIT InfoLine, Inc., AMA/NET; internal database; OnTyme Electronic Message Network Service (electronic mail service). Performs searches on fee basis. Contact Person: Nancy Clemmons, Hd., Ref.Serv., 934-2230. **Networks/Consortia:** Member of SOLINET, Network of Alabama Academic Libraries (NAAL). **Publications:** Rare Books and Collections of the Reynolds Historical Library: A Bibliography, 1968; Alabama Medicus (newsletter); Reynolds Library Associates Newsletter.

★15775★
UNIVERSITY OF ALABAMA IN BIRMINGHAM - SCHOOL OF MEDICINE - ANESTHESIOLOGY LIBRARY (Med)
Dept. of Anesthesiology
619 19th St., S. Phone: (205)934-6500
Birmingham, AL 35233-1924 A.J. Wright, Clin.Libn.
Founded: 1980. **Staff:** Prof 1; Other 1. **Subjects:** Anesthesia, pain management. **Special Collections:** Closed Circuit Anesthesia Archives (300 articles and monographs); Anesthesia History Collection (400 articles and monographs). **Holdings:** 1065 books; 705 bound periodical volumes; 100 cassettes; 110 videotapes. **Subscriptions:** 102 journals and other serials. **Services:** Interlibrary loan; copying; SDI; library open to the public for reference use only. **Automated Operations:** Computerized cataloging. **Computerized Information Services:** NLM, DIALOG Information Services; CSAR (Closed Circuit Archives Index; internal database). Performs searches on fee basis. **Networks/Consortia:** Member of Jefferson County Hospital Librarians' Association. **Publications:** ANESTHESIA ALERT: A Selection of Recent Articles in Non-Specialty Journals; A Core List of Anesthesia Monographs and Serials. **Special Indexes:** Journal Holdings List.

★15776★
UNIVERSITY OF ALABAMA IN HUNTSVILLE - ARCHIVES AND SPECIAL COLLECTIONS (Hist, Sci-Engr)
Library Phone: (205)895-6540
Huntsville, AL 35899 Jean M. Perreault
Staff: Prof 1; Other 4. **Special Collections:** Congressman Robert E. Jones papers (correspondence, office files, personal papers); university archives, 1947 to present; Willy Ley Collection (space sciences, ballistics, science fiction, paleontology); Saturn history documentation; Peenemunde documents; Rudolf Herrmann Collection (space science reprints, personal papers). **Holdings:** 897 linear feet of books, journals, and file boxes. **Services:** Copying; collections open to the public. **Computerized Information Services:** Internal databases. **Staff:** Lelon Oliver, Asst.Libn.; Richard A. Gayton, Asst.Libn..

★15777★
UNIVERSITY OF ALASKA - INSTITUTE OF MARINE SCIENCE - SEWARD MARINE STATION LIBRARY (Biol Sci, Sci-Engr)
Box 730 Phone: (907)224-5261
Seward, AK 99664 Dwight Ittner, Libn.
Staff: 1. **Subjects:** Physical and chemical oceanography, aquaculture, marine biology, marine botany. **Special Collections:** Aquaculture reprint collection. **Holdings:** 3000 books; 400 bound periodical volumes; 10,200 reprints; 2300 technical reports; 2000 hydrographic charts. **Subscriptions:** 100 journals and other serials. **Services:** Interlibrary loan; library open to the public with restrictions.

★15778★
UNIVERSITY OF ALASKA, ANCHORAGE - ARCTIC ENVIRONMENTAL INFORMATION AND DATA CENTER (Env-Cons, Energy)
707 A St. Phone: (907)257-2734
Anchorage, AK 99501 Barbara J. Sokolov, Supv., Info.Serv. Group
Founded: 1972. **Staff:** Prof 2. **Subjects:** Alaska - environment, geology, fisheries, glaciology, land use planning, oil pollution, energy resources, coastal zone management; Arctic research; Alaska climate records. **Special Collections:** Depository for Arctic Petroleum Operators Association and Alaska Oil and Gas Association (AOGA) reports. **Holdings:** 8000 books; 2000 photographs of Alaska; 10,000 microfiche; reports; pamphlets; maps. **Subscriptions:** 50 journals and other serials. **Services:** Center not open to the public. **Automated Operations:** Computerized cataloging. **Computerized Information Services:** Internal databases. **Publications:** List of publications - available on request.

★15779★
UNIVERSITY OF ALASKA, ANCHORAGE - ENERGY EXTENSION SERVICE - ALASKA ENERGY LIBRARY (Energy)
949 E. 36th St., Suite 403 Phone: (907)563-1955
Anchorage, AK 99508 Ginny Moore, Libn.
Founded: 1984. **Staff:** Prof 1. **Subjects:** Energy - conservation, renewable sources and applications, building construction, management, education; indoor air quality. **Holdings:** 2000 books; 56 films and videotapes; reports and studies. **Subscriptions:** 35 journals and other serials. **Services:** Interlibrary loan; copying; library open to the public. **Automated Operations:** Computerized cataloging and acquisitions. **Publications:** Energy for Alaskans Resource Directory. **Remarks:** Jointly maintained with State of Alaska.

★15780★
UNIVERSITY OF ALASKA, ANCHORAGE - LIBRARY - ARCHIVES & MANUSCRIPTS DEPARTMENT (Hist)
3211 Providence Dr. Phone: (907)786-1849
Anchorage, AK 99508 Dennis F. Walle, Archv./Mss.Cur.
Founded: 1979. **Staff:** Prof 1; Other 3. **Special Collections:** University archives (300 record series) and historical manuscripts (300 collections); social, political, and cultural organizations, business records, papers of individuals and families (1550 cubic feet). **Services:** Department open to the public with restrictions. **Publications:** Annual Report; Guide to R.T. Harris Family Collection, 1981; Guide to the Fred Wildon Fickett Collection, 1985; Guide to the Victor C. Rivers Family Collection, 1986; occasional guides to specific collections. **Special Catalogs:** Unpublished internal guide containing collection and university record inventories.

★15781★
UNIVERSITY OF ALASKA, ANCHORAGE - LIBRARY - GOVERNMENT DOCUMENTS (Info Sci)
3211 Providence Dr. Phone: (907)786-1874
Anchorage, AK 99508 Alden Rollins, Gov.Docs.Libn.
Founded: 1973. **Special Collections:** Government documents. **Holdings:** 170,000 volumes. **Services:** Interlibrary loan; copying; library open to the public. **Computerized Information Services:** DIALOG Information Services, WILSONLINE. **Networks/Consortia:** Member of Alaska Library Network (ALN), Western Library Network (WLN). **Publications:** Census Alaska: Number of Inhabitants, 1792-1970. **Special Indexes:** Anchorage Documents File, 1970-1979.

★15782★
UNIVERSITY OF ALASKA, ANCHORAGE - LIBRARY - SPECIAL COLLECTIONS (Hist, Mus)
3211 Providence Dr. Phone: (907)786-1873
Anchorage, AK 99508 John Summerhill, Supv., Spec.Coll.
Founded: 1973. **Special Collections:** Alaskana Collection; sheet music collection; rare books; maps. **Holdings:** Figures not available. **Services:** Interlibrary loan; copying; collections open to the public. **Computerized Information Services:** DIALOG Information Services, Pergamon ORBIT InfoLine, Inc.; University of Alaska Computer Network (internal database). **Networks/Consortia:** Member of Alaska Library Network (ALN), Western Library Network (WLN). **Special Catalogs:** Catalog of Sheet Music at the UAA Library.

★15783★
UNIVERSITY OF ALASKA, FAIRBANKS - AGRICULTURAL & FORESTRY EXPERIMENT STATION - PALMER RESEARCH CENTER (Agri)
533 E. Fireweed Phone: (907)745-3257
Palmer, AK 99645 G. Allen Mitchell, Assoc.Dir.
Founded: 1950. **Staff:** Prof 1; Other 1. **Subjects:** Agriculture, soil science, crop science, animal science, statistics, plant pathology. **Holdings:** 1800 books; 3000 bound periodical volumes; 40,500 abstracts on cards. **Subscriptions:** 124 journals and other serials. **Services:** Interlibrary loan; copying (limited); library open to the public.

★15784★
UNIVERSITY OF ALASKA, FAIRBANKS - ALASKA NATIVE LANGUAGE CENTER - RESEARCH LIBRARY (Area-Ethnic)
Box 900111 Phone: (907)474-7874
Fairbanks, AK 99775-0120 Michael Krauss, Dir.
Founded: 1972. **Staff:** Prof 7; Other 2. **Subjects:** Alaskan native, Athabaskan, Eyak, Thingit, and Eskimo languages; Amerindian linguistics. **Holdings:** 7000 books, journals, unpublished papers, field notes, and archival materials. **Services:** Copying (limited); library open to the public for reference use only with permission. **Publications:** List of publications - available on request. **Special Catalogs:** Annotated catalog of Indian languages of Alaska - for sale.

★15785★
UNIVERSITY OF ALASKA, FAIRBANKS - ALASKA AND POLAR REGIONS DEPARTMENT (Hist)
Elmer E. Rasmuson Library Phone: (907)479-7261
Fairbanks, AK 99701 Paul H. McCarthy, Archv./Hd.
Founded: 1965. **Staff:** Prof 8; Other 39. **Subjects:** Alaska - history, business, anthropology, sciences, university; Arctic; Antarctic. **Special Collections:** Alaska historical photograph collection (200,000 items); rare books (3200); rare maps (450); oral history; Alaska Book Collection; Alaska Congressional papers of Anthony Dimond, 1933-1945; Ernest Gruening, 1959-1974; Ralph J. Rivers, 1959-1966; E.L. Bartlett, 1944-1968; Howard Pollock, 1966-1970; Nick Begich, 1970-1972; Mike Gravel, 1957-1980. **Holdings:** 75,800 books and bound periodical volumes; 10,996 microforms; 2800 Alaska historical and university audiotapes; 300 videotapes; 730 reels of archival movie film; 2000 cubic feet of university archives; 4200 cubic feet of manuscripts; 158,350 U.S. Government documents. **Subscriptions:** 935 journals and other serials; 50 newspapers. **Services:** Copying; department open to the public. **Networks/Consortia:** Member of Western Library Network (WLN). **Publications:** Published Guide to the Holdings in the University Archives and Manuscript Collections (microfiche); Bibliography of Alaskana (microfiche). **Special Indexes:** Alaska Commercial Co. Records, 1868-1911; Anthony J. Dimond Papers, 1933-1945, an inventory; Guide to the Mike Gravel Papers, 1957-1980; Ralph J. Rivers Papers, 1959-1966, an inventory; Howard W. Pollock Papers, 1967-1971, an inventory; unpublished indexes for all processed collections; translations of historic Alaskan documents in foreign languages.

★15786★
UNIVERSITY OF ALASKA, FAIRBANKS - BIO-MEDICAL LIBRARY (Med, Biol Sci)
Fairbanks, AK 99775-0300 Phone: (907)474-7442
Dwight Ittner, Libn.
Staff: Prof 1; Other 3. **Subjects:** Health sciences, veterinary medicine, fish biology and fisheries, animal physiology, microbiology. **Holdings:** 25,000 books; 17,000 bound periodical volumes; 2000 volumes in microform. **Subscriptions:** 536 journals and other serials. **Services:** Interlibrary loan; copying; library open to the public. **Automated Operations:** Computerized cataloging. **Computerized Information Services:** DIALOG Information Services, BRS Information Technologies, QL Systems, Pergamon ORBIT InfoLine, Inc. **Networks/Consortia:** Member of Pacific Northwest Regional Health Sciences Library Service, Western Library Network (WLN), Alaska Library Network (ALN). **Remarks:** Includes the holdings of the Institute of Marine Science - Library.

★15787★
UNIVERSITY OF ALASKA, FAIRBANKS - COLLEGE OF HUMAN AND RURAL DEVELOPMENT - RESOURCE CENTER (Educ)
Gruening Bldg., Rm. 505 Phone: (907)474-6633
Fairbanks, AK 99775 Meredith Ottenheimer, Contact Person
Founded: 1974. **Staff:** Prof 1; Other 1. **Subjects:** Cross-cultural education, psychology, and sociology; Alaska native studies; rural development. **Special Collections:** Small High School Project curriculum materials (1000 items). **Holdings:** 5000 books; 150 unpublished theses and research reports; 4000 VF items; 3500 government publications. **Subscriptions:** 45 journals and other serials; 5 newspapers. **Services:** Interlibrary loan; copying; center open to the public. **Special Catalogs:** Catalog of the Small High Schools Project (book).

★15788★
UNIVERSITY OF ALASKA, FAIRBANKS - GEOPHYSICAL INSTITUTE LIBRARY (Sci-Engr)
Fairbanks, AK 99775-0800 Phone: (907)479-7503
Julia H. Triplehorn, Libn.
Founded: 1949. **Staff:** Prof 1; Other 2. **Subjects:** Physics, astronomy, geophysics, geology, mathematics, electronic engineering, meteorology, solar terrestrial science, geothermal energy, glaciology, solid earth sciences, oceanography, remote sensing, polar phenomena. **Special Collections:** Alaska Earthquake Photographs; International Geophysical Year materials; Alaska Climate Data. **Holdings:** 21,000 books and bound periodical volumes; technical reports and data. **Subscriptions:** 374 journals and other serials. **Services:** Interlibrary loan; copying; library open to the public. **Computerized Information Services:** DIALOG Information Services, Pergamon ORBIT InfoLine, Inc., NASA/RECON, RESORS (Remote Sensing On-line Retrieval System), QL Systems. **Networks/Consortia:** Member of Western Library Network (WLN).

★15789★
UNIVERSITY OF ALASKA, FAIRBANKS - INSTITUTE OF MARINE SCIENCE - LIBRARY
Fairbanks, AK 99701
Defunct. Holdings absorbed by Bio-Medical Library.

★15790★
UNIVERSITY OF ALASKA, FAIRBANKS - WILDLIFE LIBRARY (Biol Sci)
Division of Life Sciences Phone: (907)474-7174
Fairbanks, AK 99701 Carol Button, Lib. Aide
Staff: 1. **Subjects:** Wildlife management, animal ecology, mammalogy, plant ecology, wildlife economics, outdoor recreation, Arctic ecology. **Special Collections:** Government reports. **Holdings:** 300 volumes; 10,000 reprints. **Subscriptions:** 31 journals and other serials. **Services:** Interlibrary loan; copying; library open to the public. **Computerized Information Services:** Reprint collection emphasizing Alaskan, arctic-sub-arctic birds and mammals (internal database). **Special Catalogs:** Termatrex cataloging of reprints (taxonomy, geographic area, date).

UNIVERSITY OF ALBERTA - ALBERTA LAW FOUNDATION - HEALTH LAW INSTITUTE
See: Health Law Institute (6199)

★15791★
UNIVERSITY OF ALBERTA - BRUCE PEEL SPECIAL COLLECTIONS LIBRARY (Rare Book, Hum, Hist)
Rutherford South Phone: (403)432-5998
Edmonton, AB, Canada T6G 2J4 John W. Charles, Spec.Coll.Libn./Hd.
Founded: 1964. **Staff:** Prof 2; Other 4. **Subjects:** Western Canadiana; English literature, 1600-1940; Canadian drama; European drama, 17th-18th centuries; California history; European history, 1500-1900; book arts. **Special Collections:** John Bunyan (early editions; 245 volumes); Milton (early editions; 165 volumes); Salzburg (16th-18th century editions of canon law and ecclesiastical works; 700 volumes); Cuala Press (250 items including broadsides); D.H. Lawrence (early editions; 290 volumes); Grabhorn Press (600 volumes); 19th century English theater playbills (900); Curwen Press (Curwen's own in-house collection of their publications, 1920-1956; 1000 volumes, 3000 ephemera, scrapbooks, posters); Gregory Javitch Collection on North and South American Indians (emphasis on treaties, warfare, language, and ceremonial dances; 900 volumes); 19th and 20th century book arts (emphasis on Victorian chromo-lithography, Canadian fine printing, contemporary book works, and artists' books; 1500 volumes); Georg Kaiser archiv (39 boxes and photocopies of manuscripts); Ariel Benson Collection (Sephardic manuscripts and texts; 10 volumes; 350 manuscripts); Wordsworth (153 volumes of facsimiles of Dove Cottage manuscripts); Black Sparrow Press archives, 1966-1970 (archives for first 94 publications). **Holdings:** 75,000 volumes; 12,500 volumes of University of Alberta dissertations and theses; 700 volumes of Rutherford pamphlets on Canadiana; 48 volumes of diaries and typescripts on Alberta early settlers and local history. **Services:** Interlibrary loan; copying (both limited); library open to the public. **Automated Operations:** Computerized cataloging. **Computerized Information Services:** DIALOG Information Services, Pergamon ORBIT InfoLine, Inc., QL Systems, CAN/OLE, UTLAS. **Publications:** News from the Rare Book Room, irregular; University of Alberta Theses, semiannual - both available on request. **Staff:** Jeannine Green, Spec.Coll.Libn.; Carolynne Poon, Conservator.

★15792★
UNIVERSITY OF ALBERTA - COMPUTING SCIENCE READING ROOM (Sci-Engr, Comp Sci)
604 General Services Bldg. Phone: (403)432-3977
Edmonton, AB, Canada T6G 2H1 Linda Needham, Lib.Techn.
Founded: 1968. **Staff:** 1. **Subjects:** Computing science, mathematics, statistics, engineering. **Holdings:** 4500 books; 500 bound periodical volumes; 3500 technical reports; 1000 IBM manuals; 200 theses. **Subscriptions:** 200 journals and other serials. **Services:** Interlibrary loan; room open to the public. **Automated Operations:** Computerized public access catalog.

★15793★
UNIVERSITY OF ALBERTA - COMPUTING SERVICES - DATA LIBRARY (Info Sci)
352 General Services Bldg. Phone: (403)432-5212
Edmonton, AB, Canada T6G 2H1 Jana M. Lamont, Data Libn.
Founded: 1977. **Staff:** Prof 2. **Subjects:** Social sciences, literature. **Holdings:** 3500 files of machine-readable statistical and textual data on magnetic tapes and disks. **Services:** Interlibrary loan; SDI; library open to the public. **Automated Operations:** Computerized cataloging and acquisitions. **Computerized Information Services:** ICPSR Guide, SMIS Database (internal databases); NetNorth (electronic mail service). Performs searches on fee basis. **Special Catalogs:** Data Library Catalogue (online and book), biennial. **Remarks:** Library located at Torey Bldg., Rm. 1-56, Edmonton, AB T6G 2H1. An alternate telephone number is 432-2462. **Staff:** Charles Humphrey, Data Lib.Anl..

★15794★
UNIVERSITY OF ALBERTA - DEPARTMENT OF GEOGRAPHY - UNIVERSITY MAP COLLECTION (Geog-Map)
B-7 H.M. Tory Bldg. Phone: (403)432-4760
Edmonton, AB, Canada T6G 2H4 Ronald Whistance-Smith, Map Cur.
Staff: Prof 1; Other 2. **Subjects:** Topography, geology, geography, cartography, history, soils, aerial photography, Canada, Eastern Europe. **Holdings:** 2500 atlases; 439 gazetteers; 2100 reference books; 45 titles of bound periodicals; 3000 unbound reports; 12 reels of microfilm of maps; 281 reels of microfilm of air photographs; 32 cartobibliographies on microfilm; 1200 map and air photo index titles on microfiche; 280,000 map titles; 1 million air photographs; 72 relief models. **Subscriptions:** 181 journals and other serials. **Services:** Interlibrary loan; copying; collection open to the public with restrictions. **Publications:** Accessions list, bimonthly - available upon request.

★15795★
UNIVERSITY OF ALBERTA - DEVELOPMENTAL DISABILITIES CENTRE - LIBRARY (Med)
6-123A Education II Phone: (403)432-4439
Edmonton, AB, Canada T6G 2G5 Fran Russell, Adm.Asst.
Founded: 1967. **Subjects:** Biology, medicine, neurology, psychology, education. **Holdings:** 250 books and bound periodical volumes; 50 other cataloged items. **Services:** Interlibrary loan; library not open to the public.

★15796★
UNIVERSITY OF ALBERTA - DIVISION OF EDUCATIONAL RESEARCH SERVICES - TECHNICAL LIBRARY (Educ, Comp Sci)
3-104 Education Bldg. North Phone: (403)432-3762
Edmonton, AB, Canada T6G 2G5 R. Perez, Libn.
Staff: Prof 1; Other 1. **Subjects:** Computers, computer-based instruction, statistics and research design. **Holdings:** 4000 books and bound periodical volumes; 1 VF drawer; Educational Testing Service Research Bulletins, 1963 to present. **Subscriptions:** 46 journals and other serials. **Services:** Interlibrary loan; copying; library open to the public with restrictions. **Automated Operations:** Computerized cataloging.

★15797★
UNIVERSITY OF ALBERTA - FACULTE ST-JEAN - BIBLIOTHEQUE (Area-Ethnic, Hum)
8406 91st St. Phone: (403)468-1254
Edmonton, AB, Canada T6C 4G9 Juliette J. Henley, Hd.Libn.
Founded: 1910. **Staff:** Prof 4; Other 5. **Subjects:** French-Canadian and Western Canadian history, ethnology, French and French-Canadian literature, French language resources in education, arts, humanities, social sciences, and science. **Special Collections:** French government documents (7920 items). **Holdings:** 72,239 books (mainly in French); 2577 bound periodical volumes; 1234 reels of microfilm; 11,298 microfiche. **Subscriptions:** 231 journals and other serials; 8 newspapers. **Services:** Interlibrary loan; SDI; library open to the public for reference use only. **Automated Operations:** Computerized cataloging and acquisitions. **Computerized Information Services:** IST-Informatheque Inc., BRS Information Technologies, Termium, INFOPUQ, Banque de Terminologie du Quebec (BTQ), UTLAS. Performs searches on fee basis. Contact Person: Michel Boucher, Ref.Libn.. **Staff:** Danielle Bugeaud, Hd., Tech.Serv.; Jacqueline Girouard, Cat..

★15798★
UNIVERSITY OF ALBERTA - H.T. COUTTS LIBRARY (Educ)
Faculty of Education Bldg. Phone: (403)432-5759
Edmonton, AB, Canada T6G 2J8 Madge MacGown, Area Coord.
Founded: 1945. **Staff:** Prof 9; Other 33. **Subjects:** Education, teaching materials, children's literature. **Special Collections:** Historical Textbook Collection; William Gray Reading Collection (on microfiche). **Holdings:** 224,596 volumes; 310,278 titles on microfiche; 6917 reels of microfilm; 28,368 nonbook titles; 6612 newspaper clippings; 3019 theses; ERIC, ONTERIS, and MICROLOG education collection microfiche. **Subscriptions:** 914 journals. **Services:** Interlibrary loan; copying; library open to the public for reference use only. **Automated Operations:** Computerized cataloging, acquisitions, and circulation. **Computerized Information Services:** DIALOG Information Services, Pergamon ORBIT

InfoLine, Inc., BRS Information Technologies, SPIRES. **Special Indexes:** Alberta Education Index; Index to Faculty of Education theses held by library (computer printout); picture and art slide indexes; index to record collection; index to curriculum guides. **Staff:** Josie Tong, Curric.Libn.; Kathleen De Long, Hd., Ref./Info.Serv.; Leslie LaFleur, Coll.Coord.; Grant Kayler, Hd., Access Serv..

★15799★
UNIVERSITY OF ALBERTA - HUMANITIES AND SOCIAL SCIENCES LIBRARY (Hum, Soc Sci)
Rutherford North Phone: (403)432-3794
Edmonton, AB, Canada T6G 2J4 B.J. Busch, Area Coord.
Founded: 1972. **Staff:** Prof 14; Other 47. **Subjects:** Humanities, social sciences, business and commerce, physical education, library science. **Holdings:** 1.3 million volumes; 130,000 bound periodical volumes; 2.25 million microforms. **Subscriptions:** 7500 journals and other serials; 115 newspapers. **Services:** Interlibrary loan; copying; SDI; library open to the public for reference use only. **Automated Operations:** Computerized cataloging, acquisitions, serials and circulation. **Computerized Information Services:** DIALOG Information Services, Pergamon ORBIT InfoLine, Inc., BRS Information Technologies, International Development Research Centre (IDRC), Info Globe; internal database. Performs searches on fee basis. **Publications:** Library Guide. **Special Indexes:** Business Annual Reports Index. **Staff:** B. Champion, Ref.Libn.; G. Olson, Ref.Libn.; W. Quoika-Stanka, Ref.Libn.; K. West, Bus.Libn.; K. Wikeley, Ref.Libn.; M. McClary, Per./Microforms Libn.; Deborah Dancik, Pub.Serv.Coord.; F. Ziegler, Tech.Serv.Libn.; C.D. Sharplin, Ref.Libn.; S. Powelson, Asst.Bus.Libn.; S. Manwaring, Govt.Pubns.Libn..

★15800★
UNIVERSITY OF ALBERTA - HUMANITIES AND SOCIAL SCIENCES LIBRARY - GOVERNMENT PUBLICATIONS (Soc Sci)
Edmonton, AB, Canada T6G 2J8 Phone: (403)432-3776
Sally Manwaring, Hd., Govt.Pubn.Lib.
Staff: Prof 2; Other 5. **Subjects:** Economics, political science, business, history, sociology. **Holdings:** 290,000 books and bound periodical volumes; 900,000 microforms. **Subscriptions:** 4050 journals and other serials. **Services:** Interlibrary loan; copying; open to the public. **Automated Operations:** Computerized cataloging and serials. **Computerized Information Services:** DIALOG Information Services; SPIRES (internal database). Performs searches free of charge. Contact Person: David Sharplin, Asst.Govt.Pubns.Libn.. **Publications:** Statistical sources in the library, a selected bibliography, 1974; Descriptive guide to government publications of Canada, Great Britain, the United States and international bodies, 1977; Selected Accessions List, bimonthly - for internal distribution and by request. **Special Indexes:** KWOC index to uncataloged acquisitions.

★15801★
UNIVERSITY OF ALBERTA - HUMANITIES AND SOCIAL SCIENCES LIBRARY - WINSPEAR READING ROOM (Bus-Fin)
1-18 Business Bldg. Phone: (403)432-5652
Edmonton, AB, Canada T6G 2R6 Kathy West, Bus. & Econ.Libn.
Staff: Prof 2; Other 3. **Subjects:** Business. **Special Collections:** Canadian annual reports, 1975 to present; Canadian prospectuses, 1981 to present; U.S. annual reports, 1981 to present; 10K reports, 1975 to present; Statistical Reference Index; corporate and industry research reports. **Holdings:** 1000 books; 64 drawers of microfiche; 50 lateral file drawers of annual reports. **Services:** Interlibrary loan; copying; room open to the public. **Computerized Information Services:** DIALOG Information Services, BRS Information Technologies, Info Globe, Mead Data Central, Dunserve II, Canadian Financial Database (C.F.D.); internal database. Performs searches on fee basis. Contact Person: Susan Powelson, Asst.Bus.Libn.. **Also Known As:** Business Reference Center.

★15802★
UNIVERSITY OF ALBERTA - JOHN A. WEIR MEMORIAL LAW LIBRARY (Law)
Law Centre Phone: (403)432-5560
Edmonton, AB, Canada T6G 2H5 Lillian MacPherson, Area Coord.
Founded: 1951. **Staff:** Prof 6; Other 12. **Subjects:** Anglo-American law. **Holdings:** 72,813 books; 105,037 bound periodical volumes; 66,098 microforms; 735 AV programs. **Subscriptions:** 4963 journals and other serials. **Services:** Interlibrary loan; copying; library open to the public with restrictions. **Automated Operations:** Computerized cataloging and acquisitions. **Computerized Information Services:** LEXIS, WESTLAW, CAN/LAW, WILSONLINE, Info Globe, DIALOG Information Services, QL Systems; internal databases; Envoy 100, QL Mail, NETNORTH (electronic mail services). Performs searches free of charge. Contact Person: M. Lefebvre or A. Sunahara, 421-8660. **Special Indexes:** Alberta Case Locator; index of all Alberta Queen's Bench, Court of Appeal and written Provincial Court decisions (online). **Staff:** A. Eikeland, Ref.Libn./Adm.Asst.; M. Storozuk, Coll.Mgt.Libn.; S. Wilkins, Ref.Libn.; S. Hebditch, Ref.Libn.; J. Parkinson, Ref.Libn.; B. Burrows, Cat.Libn..

★15803★
UNIVERSITY OF ALBERTA - JOHN W. SCOTT HEALTH SCIENCES LIBRARY (Med)
Edmonton, AB, Canada T6G 2B7 Phone: (403)432-3791
Sylvia R. Chetner, Area Coord.
Staff: Prof 7; Other 18. **Subjects:** Medicine, nursing, dentistry, pharmacy, rehabilitation medicine, health services administration. **Special Collections:** Rawlinson Historical Collection (1000 volumes). **Holdings:** 157,910 books and bound periodical volumes; 2230 microfiche. **Subscriptions:** 2092 journals and other serials. **Services:** Interlibrary loan; copying; SDI; library open to the public with restrictions. **Automated Operations:** Computerized cataloging, acquisitions, and circulation. **Computerized Information Services:** DIALOG Information Services, Pergamon ORBIT InfoLine, Inc., BRS Information Technologies, CAN/OLE, MEDLINE. **Special Indexes:** Index to Alberta Medical Bulletin (card). **Staff:** L. Starr, Coord., Ref.Serv.; J. Buckingham, Coord., Coll.Mgt.; J. Irving, Supv., Circ.Serv. & Doc. Delivery; S. Shores, Libn.; M. Dorgan, Libn.; P. Schoenberg, Libn.; L. Sutherland, Libn..

★15804★
UNIVERSITY OF ALBERTA - LEGAL RESOURCE CENTRE - LIBRARY (Law)
Faculty of Extension
10049 81st Ave. Phone: (403)432-5732
Edmonton, AB, Canada T6E 1W7 Elaine Hutchinson, Libn.
Staff: Prof 1; Other 3. **Subjects:** Law for the layperson, criminal law, public legal education, family and juvenile law, business law, native rights. **Holdings:** 24,000 books and AV programs. **Subscriptions:** 454 journals and other serials. **Services:** Interlibrary loan; copying; SDI; library open to the public. **Automated Operations:** Computerized cataloging. **Computerized Information Services:** Info Globe, QL Systems, SPIRES; LRCDATA (internal database). **Publications:** Resource News, monthly; Bibliography of Law-Related AV Materials (book); Legal Resource Centre Pamphlet List (book). **Special Indexes:** Index of Holdings on Microfiche - limited distribution.

★15805★
UNIVERSITY OF ALBERTA - NUCLEAR PHYSICS LIBRARY (Sci-Engr)
Nuclear Research Center Phone: (403)432-3637
Edmonton, AB, Canada T6G 2N5 Llanca Letelier, Sec.
Staff: Prof 1. **Subjects:** Sub-atomic physics. **Holdings:** 760 books; 1849 bound periodical volumes; 106 theses; 543 preprints and reprints of internal research reports; 1222 external reports. **Services:** Library open to the public. **Publications:** Progress Report, annual.

★15806★
UNIVERSITY OF ALBERTA - SCIENCE AND TECHNOLOGY LIBRARY (Sci-Engr)
Edmonton, AB, Canada T6G 2J8 Phone: (403)432-2728
Margo Young, Area Coord.
Founded: 1963. **Staff:** Prof 7; Other 20. **Subjects:** Pure sciences, engineering, agriculture, forestry, household economics. **Special Collections:** Solar and wind energy; UFO's. **Holdings:** 400,000 books and bound periodical volumes. **Subscriptions:** 5000 journals and other serials. **Services:** Interlibrary loan; copying; SDI; library open to the public. **Automated Operations:** Computerized cataloging, acquisitions, serials, and circulation. **Computerized Information Services:** DIALOG Information Services, Pergamon ORBIT InfoLine, Inc., CAN/OLE, QL Systems, BRS Information Technologies, Info Globe, STN International; Envoy 100, DIALMAIL, NETNORTH (electronic mail services). Performs searches on fee basis. **Staff:** David Jones, Coll.Coord.; Vera Kunda, Ref.Coord.; Susan Moysa, Ref.Libn.; John Miletich, Ref.Libn.; Sandra Campbell, Ref.Libn.; Marianne Jamieson, Ref.Libn.; Randy Reichardt, Ref.Libn..

★15807★
UNIVERSITY OF ALBERTA - STANLEY TAYLOR SOCIOLOGY READING ROOM (Soc Sci)
Dept. of Sociology Phone: (403)432-3916
Edmonton, AB, Canada T6G 2H4 Kerri Calvert, Lib.Asst.
Staff: Prof 1; Other 1. **Subjects:** Demography, criminology, statistics and methodology. **Special Collections:** Canada, U.S., and International census. **Holdings:** 9353 books; 521 bound periodical volumes; 262 dissertations; 10 unbound reports; 2000 reprints and conference papers; 300 maps.

Subscriptions: 182 journals and other serials. **Services:** Room open to the public for reference use only. **Publications:** List of publications - available upon request.

★15808★
UNIVERSITY OF ARIZONA - ARID LANDS INFORMATION CENTER (Sci-Engr)
845 N. Park Ave. Phone: (602)621-1955
Tucson, AZ 85719 Barbara Hutchinson, Mgr.
Staff: Prof 5; Other 3. **Subjects:** Deserts of the world - international research, economic crops, remote sensing. **Special Collections:** MUSAT:sra (Summer Rainfall Agriculture; 14,000 items); West Africa Collection (1500 items); Dryland Forestry (1500 items); Jojoba, Guayule (1300 items). **Holdings:** 30,000 volumes; 100 environmental impact statements. **Subscriptions:** 100 journals and other serials. **Services:** Copying; SDI; center open to the public with restrictions. **Computerized Information Services:** DIALOG Information Services, BRS Information Technologies; Dialcom Inc. (electronic mail service). Performs searches on fee basis. **Publications:** List of publications - available on request. **Staff:** Deirdre Campbell, Libn..

UNIVERSITY OF ARIZONA - ARIZONA BUREAU OF GEOLOGY & MINERAL TECHNOLOGY LIBRARY
See: Arizona Geological Survey - Library (881)

★15809★
UNIVERSITY OF ARIZONA - ARIZONA HEALTH SCIENCES CENTER LIBRARY (Med)
1501 N. Campbell Ave. Phone: (602)626-6121
Tucson, AZ 85724 Thomas D. Higdon, Dir.
Founded: 1967. **Staff:** Prof 15; Other 20. **Subjects:** Medicine and allied health sciences; preclinical sciences. **Special Collections:** Hugh H. Smith Collection/Public Health (300 volumes). **Holdings:** 66,047 books; 88,420 bound periodical volumes; 3316 AV program titles; 20 drawers of microforms. **Subscriptions:** 3626 journals and other serials. **Services:** Interlibrary loan; copying; SDI; library open to the public. **Automated Operations:** Computerized public access catalog, cataloging, acquisitions, serials, and circulation. **Computerized Information Services:** DIALOG Information Services, BRS Information Technologies; OnTyme Electronic Message Network Service (electronic mail service). Performs searches on fee basis. Contact Person: Fred Heidenreich, Hd., Ref.Serv., 626-7724. **Networks/Consortia:** Member of AMIGOS Bibliographic Council, Inc., Pacific Southwest Regional Medical Library Service. **Publications:** Media Software Titles (subject list); Bulletin, bimonthly. **Staff:** Jeanette C. McCray, Assoc.Dir.; Bertha R. Almagro, Asst.Dir./Proc.; Anita T. Glassmeyer, Media Libn.; Marilyn Martam, Hd., Loan Serv.; Mary Rhoads, Fld.Libn.; Frances Chen, Ser.Libn.; Nancy Condit, Cat.Libn.; Catherine Wolfson, Acq.Libn..

★15810★
UNIVERSITY OF ARIZONA - ARIZONA STATE MUSEUM LIBRARY (Hist)
Tucson, AZ 85721 Phone: (602)621-4695
Founded: 1958. **Staff:** Prof 1; Other 2. **Subjects:** Southwestern and Mesoamerican anthropology, museum studies. **Special Collections:** Kelemen Collection of Latin American art and architecture (1000 items). **Holdings:** 43,000 volumes; 500 bound periodical volumes. **Subscriptions:** 150 journals and other serials. **Services:** Interlibrary loan; copying; library open to the public.

★15811★
UNIVERSITY OF ARIZONA - CENTER FOR CREATIVE PHOTOGRAPHY (Art)
843 E. University Blvd. Phone: (602)621-4636
Tucson, AZ 85719 Amy Stark, Photo.Archv.Libn.
Founded: 1975. **Staff:** Prof 5; Other 9. **Subjects:** Photography. **Holdings:** 10,000 books; 1000 bound periodical volumes; 600 reels of microfilm; 36 feet of biographical files; 400 oral history videotapes; photographic archives, including those of Ansel Adams. **Subscriptions:** 50 journals and other serials. **Services:** Interlibrary loan; copying; center open to the public. **Automated Operations:** Computerized cataloging. **Computerized Information Services:** OCLC. **Publications:** The Archive, irregular. **Staff:** Nancy Solomon, Pubns.Coord.; James Enyeart, Dir.; Terence Pitts, Cur..

★15812★
UNIVERSITY OF ARIZONA - COLLEGE OF ARCHITECTURE LIBRARY (Art, Plan)
Tucson, AZ 85721 Phone: (602)621-2498
Kathryn Wayne, Libn.
Founded: 1961. **Staff:** Prof 1; Other 2. **Subjects:** Architecture, urban planning, building technology, historic preservation. **Holdings:** 12,000 books; 1700 bound periodical volumes; 24,500 slides. **Subscriptions:** 140 journals and other serials. **Services:** Copying; library open to the public for reference use only. **Publications:** College of Architecture Library Newsletter/Booklist, bimonthly - free.

★15813★
UNIVERSITY OF ARIZONA - COLLEGE OF LAW LIBRARY (Law)
Tucson, AZ 85721 Phone: (602)621-1413
Ronald L. Cherry, Dir.
Founded: 1915. **Staff:** Prof 8; Other 6. **Subjects:** Law. **Special Collections:** Natural resources; law relating to American Indians; Latin American law. **Holdings:** 169,845 volumes; 55,149 volumes in microform. **Subscriptions:** 3129 journals and other serials; 12 newspapers. **Services:** Interlibrary loan; copying; library open to the public for reference use only. **Automated Operations:** Computerized cataloging. **Computerized Information Services:** LEXIS, WESTLAW. **Staff:** Robert Genovese, Asst.Libn., Tech.Serv.; Edward White, Asst.Libn., Pub.Serv.; Francisco Avalos, Asst.Libn., Spec.Coll.; Carol G. Elliott, Ref.Libn.; Arturo Torres, Ref.Libn.; Patricia Taylor, Acq.Libn..

★15814★
UNIVERSITY OF ARIZONA - DIVISION OF ECONOMIC AND BUSINESS RESEARCH - LIBRARY (Bus-Fin, Soc Sci)
College of Business & Public Administration Phone: (602)621-2109
Tucson, AZ 85721 Holly A. Penix, Lib.Asst.
Staff: Prof 1; Other 2. **Subjects:** Economic, demographic, and industrial data for Arizona; energy; employment; labor and productivity; travel and tourism. **Special Collections:** Regional econometric models for Pima and Maricopa counties and state of Arizona. **Holdings:** 8000 items. **Subscriptions:** 359 journals and other serials; 6 newspapers. **Services:** Library open to the public for reference use only. **Computerized Information Services:** Arizona Economic Indicators Database (internal database). **Remarks:** An alternate telephone number is 621-2155.

★15815★
UNIVERSITY OF ARIZONA - DIVISION OF MEDIA & INSTRUCTIONAL SERVICES - FILM LIBRARY (Aud-Vis)
Audiovisual Bldg. Phone: (602)621-3282
Tucson, AZ 85721 Katherine Holsinger, Mgr.
Founded: 1919. **Staff:** Prof 1; Other 6. **Special Collections:** Archive Film Collection (2500 16mm film titles); archive collection of television commercials; Gallagher Memorial Film Collection. **Holdings:** 7500 16mm motion pictures in active collection. **Services:** Films available for rental; library open to the public. **Networks/Consortia:** Member of Consortium of University Film Centers (CUFC). **Publications:** Newsletter. **Special Catalogs:** Film rental catalog.

★15816★
UNIVERSITY OF ARIZONA - ENVIRONMENTAL PSYCHOLOGY PROGRAM - LIBRARY (Soc Sci)
Department of Psychology Phone: (602)626-2921
Tucson, AZ 85721 Robert B. Bechtel, Dir., Env.Psych.
Founded: 1980. **Staff:** Prof 3; Other 1. **Subjects:** Environmental psychology, behavior and environment, post occupancy evaluations. **Special Collections:** Edward T. Hall Library (2529 items). **Holdings:** 1200 books; 100 bound periodical volumes; 3500 other cataloged items. **Services:** Interlibrary loan; copying; library open to the public with permission from psychology office. **Special Catalogs:** Environmental Research and Development Foundation and Hall Library card catalogs.

★15817★
UNIVERSITY OF ARIZONA - ENVIRONMENTAL RESEARCH LABORATORY - LIBRARY (Biol Sci)
Tucson International Airport
2601 E. Airport Rd. Phone: (602)621-7962
Tucson, AZ 85706 Susan Lake, Info.Spec.
Staff: Prof 1. **Subjects:** Aquaculture, seawater irrigation, controlled environment agriculture, solar energy, controlled ecological systems. **Holdings:** 1500 books. **Subscriptions:** 80 journals and other serials. **Services:** Interlibrary loan; copying; library open to the public for reference use only. **Automated Operations:** Computerized cataloging. **Computerized Information Services:** DIALOG Information Services.

★15818★
UNIVERSITY OF ARIZONA - GOVERNMENT DOCUMENTS DEPARTMENT (Info Sci)
University Library Phone: (602)621-4871
Tucson, AZ 85721 Cynthia E. Bower, Hd.Docs.Libn.
Founded: 1907. **Staff:** Prof 3; Other 6. **Subjects:** U.S. business and economics, environmental studies, American history, politics and government, foreign relations, health care, education, law enforcement and criminal justice. **Special Collections:** Selected holdings of National Archives microfilm (5000 reels); U.S. Congressional hearings and committee prints, 1869-1981 (100,000 microfiche); current Arizona documents. **Holdings:** 900,000 printed documents; 300,000 ERIC microfiche; 650,000 other microfiche; 6200 reels of microfilm. **Subscriptions:** 3200 journals and other serials. **Services:** Interlibrary loan; copying; department open to the public. **Automated Operations:** Computerized circulation. **Computerized Information Services:** DIALOG Information Services, OCLC. **Publications:** Documents Despatch, bimonthly - free upon request. **Special Indexes:** Geographic index to environmental impact statements (card file). **Staff:** Robert P. Mitchell, Govt.Docs.Libn.; Atifa Rawan, Govt.Docs.Libn..

★15819★
UNIVERSITY OF ARIZONA - INSTITUTE OF ATMOSPHERIC PHYSICS LIBRARY (Sci-Engr)
PAS Bldg., Rm. 542
Tucson, AZ 85721 Cynthia Coan, Libn.
Staff: 1. **Subjects:** Physical and dynamical meteorology, cloud physics, atmospheric dynamics, thunderstorm electricity, micrometeorology. **Special Collections:** Manuscripts, publications, and library of Dr. James E. McDonald. **Holdings:** 3000 volumes. **Subscriptions:** 55 journals and other serials. **Services:** Copying; library open to the public for reference use only.

★15820★
UNIVERSITY OF ARIZONA - LIBRARY SCIENCE COLLECTION (Info Sci)
Graduate Library School
1515 E. First Phone: (602)621-3383
Tucson, AZ 85721 Cecil W. Wellborn, Hd.Libn.
Staff: Prof 1; Other 3. **Subjects:** Libraries, library organization, books, book binding and printing, cataloging, children's literature. **Special Collections:** Historical Children's Collection. **Holdings:** 13,800 books; 2400 bound periodical volumes; 12 drawers of pamphlets and newsletters; 1 drawer of library school catalogs, library guides and handbooks, masters' theses. **Subscriptions:** 325 journals and other serials. **Services:** Interlibrary loan; copying; collection open to the public.

★15821★
UNIVERSITY OF ARIZONA - MAP COLLECTION (Geog-Map)
University Library Phone: (602)621-2596
Tucson, AZ 85721 James O. Minton, Hd. Map Libn.
Founded: 1955. **Staff:** Prof 3; Other 5. **Subjects:** Geology, mines and mineral resources, history, topography, climate, water resources, Arizona and Southwestern U.S., Mexico, Latin America, arid lands. **Special Collections:** Frank A. Schilling Military Collection (military post of the Southwest; 60 maps); Maurice Garland Fulton Collection (history of the Southwest; 59 maps). **Holdings:** 5000 books; 300 bound periodical volumes; 200,000 sheet maps; 17,000 aerial photographs; 13 globes; 10,000 microfiche; 60 relief models; 11 reels of microfilm. **Subscriptions:** 39 journals and other serials. **Services:** Interlibrary loan; copying; collection open to the public. **Automated Operations:** Computerized cataloging, acquisitions, and circulation. **Computerized Information Services:** OCLC, Geac Library Information System, INNOVACQ Automated Library System, DIALOG Information Services. **Publications:** UA Map News Monthly - free upon request. **Staff:** Linda D. Cottrell, Map Cat.Libn.; Jack Mount, Map Ref.Libn..

★15822★
UNIVERSITY OF ARIZONA - MEDIA CENTER (Aud-Vis, Educ)
Library - B104 Phone: (602)621-6409
Tucson, AZ 85721 Bonnie L. Travers, Hd. Media Ctr.Libn.
Founded: 1977. **Staff:** Prof 2; Other 6. **Subjects:** Nonprint materials for elementary through college levels, K-12 textbooks, juvenile trade books. **Holdings:** 22,000 juvenile trade books; 10,700 textbooks; 12,450 nonprint titles; 1100 reference books and serials. **Services:** Center open to the public. **Automated Operations:** Computerized cataloging and circulation. **Computerized Information Services:** DIALOG Information Services. Performs searches on fee basis. **Publications:** Visuals (newsletter), semiannual - free upon request. **Special Indexes:** Media Center videotape catalog and index (book); Media Center Archival Radio Program List (book).

★15823★
UNIVERSITY OF ARIZONA - MUSIC COLLECTION (Mus)
Tucson, AZ 85721 Phone: (602)621-7009
Dorman H. Smith, Hd.Mus.Libn.
Founded: 1959. **Staff:** Prof 2; Other 4. **Subjects:** Music - classical, ethnic, folk, popular. **Special Collections:** National Flute Association Music Library; International Trombone Association Resource Library; Arizona and Southwest; historical popular sheet music. **Holdings:** 52,000 scores; 30,000 pieces of classical sheet music; 38,000 pieces of popular sheet music; 30,000 phonograph records and tapes; microforms. **Subscriptions:** 300 journals and other serials. **Services:** Interlibrary loan; copying; collection open to the public. **Automated Operations:** Computerized circulation. **Computerized Information Services:** Internal databases. **Special Catalogs:** National Flute Association Music Library Catalog, 1987 - to members and for sale to libraries. **Special Indexes:** Song, piano and jazz indexes (card); band music and children's songs indexes (online). **Remarks:** Music books and journals housed separately.

★15824★
UNIVERSITY OF ARIZONA - OFFICE OF ARID LANDS STUDIES - BIORESOURCES RESEARCH LIBRARY (Energy)
250 E. Valencia Phone: (602)621-7928
Tucson, AZ 85706 Jan Taylor, Lib.Asst.
Staff: Prof 1; Other 2. **Subjects:** Energy - resource development, research, biomass production and conversion, solar. **Holdings:** 100 books; 700 other cataloged items. **Subscriptions:** 12 journals and other serials. **Services:** Copying; library open to the public for reference use only. **Computerized Information Services:** DIALOG Information Services. Performs searches on fee basis. Contact Person: Deirdre Campbell, Libn., 621-7897.

★15825★
UNIVERSITY OF ARIZONA - OPTICAL SCIENCES CENTER - READING ROOM (Sci-Engr)
Tucson, AZ 85721 Phone: (602)621-4479
Cathy Smith
Founded: 1968. **Staff:** 1. **Subjects:** Optics, optical physics, optical engineering. **Holdings:** 3300 books; 400 bound periodical volumes; 350 theses and dissertations. **Subscriptions:** 50 journals and other serials. **Services:** Interlibrary loan; copying; room open to the public with prior approval. **Remarks:** An alternate telephone number is 621-4479.

★15826★
UNIVERSITY OF ARIZONA - ORIENTAL STUDIES COLLECTION (Area-Ethnic)
University Library Phone: (602)621-6380
Tucson, AZ 85721 Ju-Yen Teng, Hd.Libn.
Founded: 1964. **Staff:** Prof 3; Other 2. **Subjects:** Social studies and humanities of China, Japan, and Middle East; vernacular language materials - Chinese, Japanese, Arabic, Persian, Turkish. **Holdings:** 162,310 books and bound periodical volumes; 1141 reels of microfilm. **Subscriptions:** 870 journals and other serials; 75 newspapers. **Services:** Interlibrary loan; copying; collection open to the public. **Automated Operations:** Computerized circulation. **Staff:** Gene Hsiao, Cat.Libn.; Lucia Hu, Oriental Stud.Libn..

★15827★
UNIVERSITY OF ARIZONA - POETRY CENTER (Hum)
1086 N. Highland Ave. Phone: (602)621-7941
Tucson, AZ 85719 Lois Shelton, Dir.
Founded: 1960. **Staff:** Prof 1; Other 1. **Subjects:** Poetry. **Holdings:** 18,500 books and periodicals; 650 phonograph records and audiotapes; 16 videotapes. **Subscriptions:** 200 journals and other serials. **Services:** Center open to the public; sponsors a series of poetry readings annually. **Publications:** Poetry Center Newsletter, 4/year; 25th Anniversary Anthology, 1985.

★15828★
UNIVERSITY OF ARIZONA - SCIENCE-ENGINEERING LIBRARY (Sci-Engr, Agri)
Tucson, AZ 85721 Phone: (602)621-6394
Donald G. Frank, Hd.Libn.
Founded: 1963. **Staff:** Prof 8; Other 7. **Subjects:** Agriculture, astronomy, biology, chemistry, computer science, engineering, forestry, geology, hydrology, mathematics, mining and metallurgy, optical science, physics. **Special Collections:** Arid lands. **Holdings:** 425,000 volumes; 1.2 million microforms; 26,000 government documents; 2900 pamphlets. **Subscriptions:** 9000 journals and other serials. **Services:** Interlibrary loan; copying; SDI; library open to the public. **Automated Operations:** Computerized circulation. **Computerized Information Services:** DIALOG Information Services, BRS Information Technologies, Pergamon ORBIT

InfoLine, Inc., OCLC, Telesystemes Questel, STN International, CAS ONLINE. Performs searches on fee basis. **Networks/Consortia:** Member of AMIGOS Bibliographic Council, Inc.. **Publications:** SEL News; CAS Online News; New Accessions List - to interested faculty. **Remarks:** An alternate telephone number is 621-6384. **Staff:** Charlene Baldwin, Sci.Engr.Ref.Libn.; Robert Mautner, Sci.Engr.Ref.Libn.; Douglas Jones, Sci.Engr.Ref.Libn. & Asst.Hd.; Jeanne Pfander, Sci.Engr.Ref.Libn.; Kathy Whitley, Sci.Engr.Ref.Libn.; Janet Fore, Sci.Engr.Ref.Libn./Cat .; Jill Newby, Sci.Engr.Ref.Libn..

★15829★
UNIVERSITY OF ARIZONA - SPACE IMAGERY CENTER (Sci-Engr)
Lunar & Planetary Laboratory
Tucson, AZ 85721 Phone: (602)621-4861
Founded: 1977. **Staff:** Prof 1; Other 2. **Subjects:** Space photography, planetary sciences. **Holdings:** 750,000 images of planets and satellites taken from spacecraft and earth-based telescopes; 1000 maps; 23 atlases; 3000 35mm slides. **Services:** Center open to the public with restrictions. **Automated Operations:** Computerized cataloging. **Computerized Information Services:** Internal database.

★15830★
UNIVERSITY OF ARIZONA - SPECIAL COLLECTIONS DEPARTMENT (Hist, Hum)
University Library Phone: (602)621-6423
Tucson, AZ 85721 Louis A. Hieb, Hd.Spec.Coll.Libn.
Founded: 1958. **Staff:** Prof 3; Other 3. **Subjects:** Arizona, University of Arizona archives, Southwest, science fiction, history of science. **Special Collections:** Frank Holme Collection; Thomas Wood Stevens Collection; Lewis W. Douglas Papers; War Relocation Authority Papers; Hubbell Trading Post Papers; Bukowski and Wakoski Poetry Collections; Black Sparrow Press Archives. **Holdings:** 150,000 volumes; 700 manuscript collections. **Services:** Copying; department open to the public. **Staff:** David P. Robrock, Act.Hd.Spec.Coll.Libn..

★15831★
UNIVERSITY OF ARKANSAS, FAYETTEVILLE - CHEMISTRY LIBRARY (Sci-Engr, Comp Sci)
Chemistry Bldg. Phone: (501)575-2028
Fayetteville, AR 72701 Carolyn DeLille, Chem.Libn.
Staff: Prof 1; Other 4. **Subjects:** Chemistry, mathematics, physics, chemical technology, computer science, biochemistry, biology, medicine. **Holdings:** 10,111 books; 14,471 bound periodical volumes. **Subscriptions:** 254 journals and other serials. **Services:** Interlibrary loan; copying; library open to the public.

★15832★
UNIVERSITY OF ARKANSAS, FAYETTEVILLE - FINE ARTS LIBRARY (Art, Plan)
Fayetteville, AR 72701 Phone: (501)575-4708
Joyce M. Clinkscales, Assoc.Libn./Fine Arts Libn.
Staff: Prof 1; Other 18. **Subjects:** Art, architecture, music, city planning, interior design, landscape architecture. **Special Collections:** Edward Durell Stone papers; William Grant Still papers. **Holdings:** 40,500 books; 7300 bound periodical volumes; 225 reels of microfilm; 1500 microfiche; 15 slide sets. **Subscriptions:** 200 journals and other serials. **Services:** Interlibrary loan; copying; SDI; library open to the public. **Computerized Information Services:** OCLC. **Networks/Consortia:** Member of AMIGOS Bibliographic Council, Inc.. **Remarks:** The special collections, recordings, and some rare books are housed in Mullins Library.

★15833★
UNIVERSITY OF ARKANSAS, FAYETTEVILLE - MAP COLLECTION (Geog-Map)
University Library Phone: (501)575-3176
Fayetteville, AR 72701 Janet B. Dixon, Map Rsrcs.Coord.
Staff: 3. **Subjects:** Maps - U.S. topography and geology and world topography, transportation, and geology. **Special Collections:** Historical maps of Arkansas and region and Sanborn Fire Insurance maps of Arkansas towns (9500). **Holdings:** 107,000 map sheets. **Services:** Copying; collection open to the public. **Computerized Information Services:** DIALOG Information Services, BRS Information Technologies, NASA/RECON, STN International, Pergamon ORBIT InfoLine, Inc. Performs searches on fee basis. Contact reference department, 575-6645. **Networks/Consortia:** Member of AMIGOS Bibliographic Council, Inc..

★15834★
UNIVERSITY OF ARKANSAS, FAYETTEVILLE - SCHOOL OF LAW - ROBERT A. AND VIVIAN YOUNG LAW LIBRARY (Law)
Fayetteville, AR 72701 Phone: (501)575-5604
George E. Skinner, Dir.
Founded: 1924. **Staff:** Prof 4; Other 4. **Subjects:** Law. **Special Collections:** Selective government depository. **Holdings:** 210,000 books; 30,000 bound periodical volumes. **Subscriptions:** 550 journals and other serials. **Services:** Copying; library open to the public for reference use only. **Computerized Information Services:** LEXIS, WESTLAW. **Staff:** Lou Lindsey, Assoc.Libn.; Cathy Chick, Asst.Libn.; Marcia Baker, Asst.Libn..

★15835★
UNIVERSITY OF ARKANSAS, FAYETTEVILLE - SPECIAL COLLECTIONS DIVISION (Hist, Hum)
Fayetteville, AR 72701 Phone: (501)575-4101
Michael J. Dabrishus, Cur.
Staff: Prof 3; Other 8. **Subjects:** Arkansas - history, literature, politics, culture, and folklore; Ozark folklore; international education. **Special Collections:** John Gould Fletcher Collection (1983 volumes); Otto Ernest Rayburn Library of Folklore (838 volumes); Dime Novel Collection (1630 items); Haldeman-Julius Little Blue Books (2404 items); Robert Owen Collection. **Holdings:** 41,000 books; 11,980 bound periodical volumes; 6000 linear feet of manuscripts; 225 linear feet of university archives; 40,000 photographs; 350 rare maps. **Subscriptions:** 425 journals and other serials. **Services:** Interlibrary loan; copying; division open to the public with restrictions. **Computerized Information Services:** OCLC. **Networks/Consortia:** Member of AMIGOS Bibliographic Council, Inc.. **Publications:** A Guide to Selected Manuscripts Collections in the University of Arkansas Library, 1976. **Special Catalogs:** Card catalog of published titles; unpublished finding aids to manuscript collections. **Special Indexes:** Index to Arkansas periodicals (card). **Staff:** Andrea C. Cantrell, Asst.Libn.; Ethel C. Simpson, Assoc.Libn..

★15836★
UNIVERSITY OF ARKANSAS, FAYETTEVILLE - TECHNOLOGY CAMPUS LIBRARY (Sci-Engr)
1201 McAlmont St.
Box 3017 Phone: (501)373-2754
Little Rock, AR 72203 Brent A. Nelson, Libn.
Founded: 1958. **Staff:** Prof 1; Other 1. **Subjects:** Electronics, engineering, chemistry, physics. **Holdings:** 13,144 books; 8200 bound periodical volumes; 7 VF drawers of pamphlets, documents, and clippings. **Subscriptions:** 225 journals and other serials. **Services:** Interlibrary loan; copying; library open to the public. **Computerized Information Services:** DIALOG Information Services. Performs searches on fee basis.

UNIVERSITY OF ARKANSAS, LITTLE ROCK - MIDSOUTH ASTRONOMICAL RESEARCH SOCIETY, INC.
See: Midsouth Astronomical Research Society, Inc. (8966)

★15837★
UNIVERSITY OF ARKANSAS, LITTLE ROCK - PULASKI COUNTY LAW LIBRARY (Law)
400 W. Markham Phone: (501)371-1071
Little Rock, AR 72201 Lynn Foster, Dir.
Founded: 1965. **Staff:** Prof 5; Other 6. **Subjects:** Law. **Holdings:** 170,000 books; 1200 audio cassettes. **Subscriptions:** 2300 journals and other serials. **Services:** Interlibrary loan; copying; library open to the public. **Computerized Information Services:** LEXIS, NEXIS, WESTLAW. **Networks/Consortia:** Member of AMIGOS Bibliographic Council, Inc.. **Staff:** Kathryn Fitzhugh, Ref.Libn.; Pauline Ghidotti, Asst.Dir.; Jada Aitchison, Acq..

★15838★
UNIVERSITY OF ARKANSAS, LITTLE ROCK - RESEARCH & PUBLIC SERVICE LIBRARY (Soc Sci, Bus-Fin)
2801 S. University Phone: (501)371-2999
Little Rock, AR 72204 Crata Castleberry, Res.Libn.
Founded: 1960. **Staff:** Prof 1; Other 2. **Subjects:** Business and economics, industrial development, labor statistics, resources for Arkansas, demographics, government and taxes. **Holdings:** 9500 books; 230 bound periodical volumes; census data for U.S. and Arkansas, 1900 to present. **Subscriptions:** 150 journals and other serials; 5 newspapers. **Services:** Copying; library open to the public for reference use only. **Computerized Information Services:** DIALOG Information Services, Dun & Bradstreet Corporation. Performs searches on fee basis. **Remarks:** Contains the holdings of the Arkansas State Data Center.

★15839★
UNIVERSITY OF ARKANSAS, MONTICELLO - LIBRARY - SPECIAL COLLECTIONS (Hist)
Box 3599 Phone: (501)367-6811
Monticello, AR 71655 William F. Droessler, Libn.
Special Collections: Arkansas Collection (1000 items and miscellaneous pamphlets); government documents (75,000). **Services:** Interlibrary loan; copying; collections open to the public. **Automated Operations:** Computerized cataloging and ILL.

★15840★
UNIVERSITY OF ARKANSAS, PINE BLUFF - JOHN BROWN WATSON MEMORIAL LIBRARY (Soc Sci)
N. University Blvd.
U.S. Hwy. 79 Phone: (501)541-6825
Pine Bluff, AR 71601 E.J. Fontenette, Libn.
Founded: 1938. **Staff:** 1. **Subjects:** History and biography, emigration, sociology, literature, slavery and emancipation, education, music, religion, economics. **Special Collections:** Afro-American Literature; Paul Laurence Dunbar papers (9 reels of microfilm). **Holdings:** 4615 books; 65 bound periodical volumes; 73 reels of microfilm of the Pittsburgh Courier; 4 recordings; 4 films; 18 overhead transparencies; periodicals on microfilm. **Subscriptions:** 41 journals and other serials; 10 newspapers. **Services:** Interlibrary loan; copying; library open to the public. **Computerized Information Services:** OCLC. **Networks/Consortia:** Member of AMIGOS Bibliographic Council, Inc..

★15841★
UNIVERSITY OF ARKANSAS FOR MEDICAL SCIENCES - LIBRARY (Med)
Slot 586
4301 W. Markham Phone: (501)661-5980
Little Rock, AR 72205-7186 Rose Hogan, Dir.
Founded: 1879. **Staff:** Prof 13; Other 27. **Subjects:** Medical sciences. **Holdings:** 139,294 books and bound periodical volumes; 2000 AV programs. **Subscriptions:** 2500 journals and other serials. **Services:** Interlibrary loan; copying; library open to the public for reference use only. **Automated Operations:** Computerized cataloging, circulation, and serials. **Computerized Information Services:** OCLC, BRS Information Technologies. **Networks/Consortia:** Member of AMIGOS Bibliographic Council, Inc., TALON, South Central Academic Medical Libraries Consortium (SCAMEL). **Staff:** Neil Kelley, Assoc.Dir./Hd., Pub.Serv.; Mary Ryan, Asst.Dir./Hd., Tech.Serv.; Sally Kasalko, Hd., Ref.Div.; Jean Ann Moles, Hd., Ser.Div.; Edwina Walls, Hd., Hist. of Med.Div./Archv.; Margaret Ann Johnson, Hd., ILL Div.; Amanda Saar, Hd., Circ.Div.; Mary Hawks, Hd., Monographs Div.; Jan North, Assoc.Proj.Dir., Integrated Online Lib.Sys.; Leo Clougherty, Ref./Ext.Libn.; Patricia Lee, Ref.Libn..

★15842★
UNIVERSITY OF ARKANSAS FOR MEDICAL SCIENCES - NORTHWEST ARKANSAS HEALTH EDUCATION CENTER - LIBRARY (Med)
1125 N. College Phone: (501)521-7615
Fayetteville, AR 72701 Connie M. Wilson, Libn.
Founded: 1975. **Staff:** Prof 1; Other 1. **Subjects:** Medicine, nursing, and allied health sciences. **Holdings:** 1500 books; 3260 bound periodical volumes. **Subscriptions:** 168 journals and other serials. **Services:** Interlibrary loan; copying; SDI; library open to the public for reference use only. **Automated Operations:** Computerized cataloging. **Computerized Information Services:** MEDLINE, BRS Information Technologies, OCLC; OnTyme Electronic Message Network Service (electronic mail service). **Publications:** From the Shelf, irregular - to mailing list. **Special Catalogs:** Library Guide. **Remarks:** Library has been designated as the regional information center for the Northwest Arkansas area and serves health professionals in an eleven county area. It is located at Washington Regional Medical Center.

★15843★
UNIVERSITY OF THE ARTS - AUDIOVISUAL DEPARTMENT - FILM LIBRARY (Theater)
Broad & Pine Sts. Phone: (215)875-1017
Philadelphia, PA 19102 Brian Feeney, Dir., AV Serv.
Founded: 1968. **Staff:** Prof 1; Other 4. **Subjects:** Silent films - early experimental and comedy, black and white feature films. **Holdings:** 300 films. **Services:** Library open to the public for reference use only. **Networks/Consortia:** Member of Tri-County Library Consortium. **Formerly:** Philadelphia Colleges of the Arts.

★15844★
UNIVERSITY OF THE ARTS - LIBRARIES (Art, Theater, Mus)
Broad & Pine Sts. Phone: (215)875-1111
Philadelphia, PA 19102 Janice J. Powell, Dir.
Staff: Prof 4; Other 9. **Subjects:** Visual arts, theater, dance, music. **Holdings:** 65,819 books; 6951 bound periodical volumes; 1500 reproductions; 13,138 phonograph records; 128,000 pictures; 155,000 slides; 240 volumes of archival materials; 462 cassettes; 233 boxes of microfilm; 50 videotapes. **Subscriptions:** 211 journals and other serials. **Services:** Interlibrary loan; copying; library open to the public for reference use only. **Automated Operations:** Computerized cataloging. **Networks/Consortia:** Member of PALINET. **Remarks:** Includes the holdings of the music and slide libraries. **Formerly:** Philadelphia Colleges of the Arts - Albert M. Greenfield Library. **Staff:** Carol Homan Graney, Hd., Tech.Serv.; Martha Hall, Hd., Br.Libs.Supv.; John Caldwell, Slide Coord..

UNIVERSITY AVENUE CHURCH OF CHRIST LIBRARY AND INSTITUTE FOR CHRISTIAN STUDIES LIBRARY
See: Institute for Christian Studies - Library (6894)

★15845★
UNIVERSITY OF BALTIMORE - LANGSDALE LIBRARY - SPECIAL COLLECTIONS DEPARTMENT (Plan, Soc Sci)
1420 Maryland Ave. Phone: (301)625-3135
Baltimore, MD 21201 Gerry Yeager, Hd. of Spec.Coll.
Staff: Prof 2; Other 5. **Subjects:** Baltimore - history, planning, urban renewal, housing, community development, social welfare, family planning, business, church activities; accounting. **Special Collections:** Oral histories; records of organizations and associations important to the economic, political, and social development of the Baltimore region (55 collections); Abell TV Newsfilm Collection; WMAR-TV Newsfilm Collection; Herwood Accounting Collection (2000 volumes); Steamship Historical Society of America Library; U.S. and Maryland Document Depository; corporate annual and 10K reports (5000 editions for 1000 companies). **Holdings:** 10,000 books; 9000 cubic feet of manuscripts and archives. **Services:** Interlibrary loan; copying; department open to the public. **Automated Operations:** Computerized cataloging and circulation. **Computerized Information Services:** Internal database. Performs searches on fee basis. **Publications:** Urban Information Thesaurus; The Records of Baltimore's Private Organizations. **Staff:** Laura Brown, Archv.; Jorma Sjoblom, Libn.; Ann House, Libn..

★15846★
UNIVERSITY OF BALTIMORE - LAW LIBRARY (Law)
1415 Maryland Ave. Phone: (301)625-3400
Baltimore, MD 21201 Emily R. Greenberg, Libn.
Founded: 1925. **Staff:** Prof 6; Other 8. **Subjects:** Anglo-American law. **Holdings:** 110,000 books; 95,000 microforms. **Subscriptions:** 2500 journals and other serials. **Services:** Interlibrary loan; copying; SDI; library open to members of Maryland Bar. **Computerized Information Services:** OCLC, WESTLAW, LEXIS. **Networks/Consortia:** Member of CAPCON. **Staff:** Will Tress, Assoc.Libn.; Patricia Behles, Govt.Doc.Libn.; Jane Cupit, Ref.Libn.; Jean Berard, Tech.Serv.Libn.; Anne Bunja, Ref.Libn.; Robin Klein, Circ.Libn..

★15847★
UNIVERSITY OF BRIDGEPORT - MAGNUS WAHLSTROM LIBRARY - SPECIAL COLLECTIONS (Hum)
126 Park Ave. Phone: (203)576-4740
Bridgeport, CT 06601 Judith Lin Hunt, Univ.Libn.
Staff: Prof 9; Other 10. **Subjects:** Exploration, literature, graphic arts, Socialist-Labor movement, political science, history, health sciences. **Special Collections:** McKew Parr Memorial Collection (exploration); Starr Collection (English literature); Lincolniana (manuscripts; clippings; photographs). **Holdings:** 300,000 books. **Services:** Interlibrary loan; collections open to the public. **Automated Operations:** Computerized cataloging and ILL. **Computerized Information Services:** BRS Information Technologies, DIALOG Information Services, OCLC. Performs searches on fee basis. Contact Person: Carol Harker, Hd., Database Serv., 576-4747. **Networks/Consortia:** Member of Southwestern Connecticut Library Council (SWLC), NELINET.

★15848★
UNIVERSITY OF BRIDGEPORT - SCHOOL OF LAW - LAW LIBRARY (Law)
126 Park Ave. Phone: (203)576-4056
Bridgeport, CT 06601 Madeleine J. Wilken, Prof./Dir., Law Info.Serv.
Staff: Prof 8; Other 5. **Subjects:** Law - federal, state, international. **Holdings:** 200,000 volumes; legal treatises; journals; government documents. **Services:** Interlibrary loan; library open to the public.

Automated Operations: Computerized cataloging and acquisitions. **Computerized Information Services:** WESTLAW, LEXIS, NEXIS, DIALOG Information Services; internal databases. **Networks/Consortia:** Member of NELINET, New England Law Library Consortium (NELLCO). **Staff:** Ann DeVeaux, Assoc.Libn.; Tina Delucia, Ref.Libn.; Theresa Fu, Asst.Libn., Tech.Serv.; Lisa Satterlund, Ref.Libn.; Judith Parisi, Rsrc.Libn.; Michael Hughes, Asst.Libn., Pub.Serv..

★15849★
UNIVERSITY OF BRITISH COLUMBIA - ASIAN STUDIES LIBRARY (Area-Ethnic)
1871 West Mall — Phone: (604)228-2427
Vancouver, BC, Canada V6T 1W5 — Linda Joe, Hd.
Founded: 1960. **Staff:** Prof 3; Other 3. **Subjects:** East Asia (mainly China and Japan) - history, classics, language, literature, philosophy, Buddhism, fine arts, archeology, economics, political science, sociology, anthropology, education. **Special Collections:** P'u-pan Collection (45,000 volumes in Chinese, including 320 editions of the 12th-17th centuries and 270 gazetteers). **Holdings:** 273,550 volumes in East Asian languages; 31,000 volumes in Indic languages; 2756 periodical titles of Japanese government publications; 4474 reels of microfilm; 14,000 microfiche. **Subscriptions:** 1128 journals and other serials; 23 newspapers. **Services:** Interlibrary loan; copying; library open to the public for reference use only; annual fee required for circulation. **Publications:** Reference lists, irregular; Bibliography on the History of the Chinese Book & Calligraphy, 1970; a descriptive catalog of valuable manuscripts and rare books from China (P'u-pan Collection) by Dr. Yi-t'ung Wang, 1959 (book form, mimeographed). **Special Indexes:** Title index to P'u-pan Collection (in Chinese, on cards); Periodicals in Asian Studies (book form; revised edition 1971; 3rd edition, 1979). **Staff:** Tsuneharu Gonnami, Ref.Libn. (Japanese); Shui-Yim Tse, Ref.Libn. (Chinese).

★15850★
UNIVERSITY OF BRITISH COLUMBIA - BIOMEDICAL BRANCH LIBRARY (Med)
Vancouver General Hospital
700 W. 10th Ave. — Phone: (604)875-4505
Vancouver, BC, Canada V5Z 1L5
George C. Freeman, Hd., Biomed.Br.
Founded: 1952. **Staff:** Prof 2; Other 4. **Subjects:** Clinical medicine. **Holdings:** 12,149 books; 17,762 bound periodical volumes. **Subscriptions:** 554 journals and other serials. **Services:** Interlibrary loan (through Woodward Biomedical Library); copying; library open to the public for reference use only. **Automated Operations:** Computerized circulation. **Computerized Information Services:** NLM, BRS Information Technologies, DIALOG Information Services. **Staff:** Nancy Forbes, Ref.Libn..

★15851★
UNIVERSITY OF BRITISH COLUMBIA - CHARLES CRANE MEMORIAL LIBRARY (Aud-Vis)
1874 East Mall — Phone: (604)228-6111
Vancouver, BC, Canada V6T 1W5 — Paul E. Thiele, Libn. & Hd.
Founded: 1968. **Subjects:** University and college texts, reference materials, literature, research, and reports for the blind, visually impaired, and handicapped nonprint readers. **Special Collections:** Electronic, optical, and mechanical reading aids for the blind; Crane ABC - Alternate Book Centre. **Holdings:** 40,000 talking books on cassette and reel tapes; 25,000 braille volumes; 300 large print books; 500 printed books on blindness and disability. **Subscriptions:** 12 journals and other serials (recorded, braille, large print, and ordinary print). **Services:** Interlibrary loan; search and location service of books and materials for the blind and handicapped; sales of duplicate copies of talking books; recordings of books on demand (Crane Library Recording Centre has nine sound studios, high speed duplicating and mixing facilities). **Computerized Information Services:** BRS Information Technologies, ABLEDATA, CANUC:H, DOBIS; Envoy 100 (electronic mail service). Performs searches on fee basis. **Publications:** Crane Works in Progress, monthly (computer-produced); FUNSTUFF: Recreational and Leisure Materials in the Crane Collection, 1982. **Staff:** Judith C. Thiele, Ref. & Coll.Libn..

★15852★
UNIVERSITY OF BRITISH COLUMBIA - CURRICULUM LABORATORY (Educ)
Scarfe Bldg.
2125 Main Mall — Phone: (604)228-5378
Vancouver, BC, Canada V6T 1Z5 — Howard Hurt, Hd.Libn.
Staff: Prof 3; Other 11. **Subjects:** Educational theory and methods, children's literature. **Special Collections:** Historical textbooks (4000); French Collection (12,000 volumes). **Holdings:** 100,000 books; 6000 bound periodical volumes; 500 slide sets; 36 drawers of pamphlets; 1000 kits; 10,000 pictures; 200 jackdaws; 1500 posters; 2000 transparencies; 100 maps; 1461 films; 3000 filmstrips; 3000 audiotapes; 430 videotapes. **Subscriptions:** 600 journals and other serials. **Services:** Interlibrary loan; copying; SDI; open to the public for reference use only. **Automated Operations:** Computerized cataloging, acquisitions, serials, and circulation. **Computerized Information Services:** DIALOG Information Services, Pergamon ORBIT InfoLine, Inc., BRS Information Technologies, ERIC. **Publications:** Orientation brochure; bibliographies. **Special Catalogs:** Film Catalog of UBC Films (book). **Staff:** Beth Anholt, Ref.Libn.; Jo-Anne Naslund, Ref.Libn..

★15853★
UNIVERSITY OF BRITISH COLUMBIA - DATA LIBRARY (Info Sci, Comp Sci)
6356 Agricultural Rd., Rm. 206 — Phone: (604)228-5587
Vancouver, BC, Canada V6T 1W5 — Ms. Laine Ruus, Hd., Data Lib.
Founded: 1972. **Staff:** Prof 2; Other 1. **Subjects:** Social sciences, humanities, sciences. **Special Collections:** Canada census, 1961, 1966, 1971, 1976, 1981; Canadian Institute of Public Opinion surveys, 1945-1985 (400 subfiles of data). **Holdings:** 1000 books; 4600 files and subfiles of machine-readable data; 1500 codebooks. **Subscriptions:** 86 journals and other serials. **Services:** Copying of data files where contracts allow; library open to the public with restrictions on some files. **Computerized Information Services:** I.P. Sharp Associates Limited, DIALOG Information Services; DATALIB, DIRECTORY, BIBLIO (internal databases); BITNET, MAILNET (electronic mail services). **Special Catalogs:** Data Library Catalogue (COM) - free upon request. **Remarks:** The Data Library, jointly operated by the UBC Library and the UBC Computing Centre, acquires, organizes, and services a collection of nonbibliographic data in computer-readable form. **Staff:** Matthew Kruk, Data Lib.Prog..

★15854★
UNIVERSITY OF BRITISH COLUMBIA - DEPARTMENT OF CHEMICAL ENGINEERING - CHEMICAL ENGINEERING READING ROOM (Sci-Engr, Energy)
Chemical Engineering Bldg.
2216 Main Mall
Vancouver, BC, Canada V6T 1W5 — Phone: (604)228-3238
Staff: 1. **Subjects:** Biochemical and biomedical engineering, oil and gas, pulp and paper, heat transfer, fluidized and spouted beds. **Holdings:** 1907 books; departmental bachelors', masters', and Ph.D. theses; fourth year summer essays. **Subscriptions:** 27 journals and other serials. **Services:** Room open to the public. **Automated Operations:** Computerized cataloging. **Special Catalogs:** Union catalog of books and serials held by the six engineering reading rooms. **Special Indexes:** Indexes to fourth year summer essays and bachelors' theses (card).

★15855★
UNIVERSITY OF BRITISH COLUMBIA - DEPARTMENT OF CIVIL ENGINEERING - CIVIL ENGINEERING READING ROOM (Sci-Engr)
CEME Bldg., Rm. 2050
2324 Main Mall
Vancouver, BC, Canada V6T 1W5 — Phone: (604)228-2120
Staff: 1. **Subjects:** Engineering - geotechnical, coastal, ocean; structures; construction; management; water resources; hydrology; environmental pollution. **Holdings:** 1785 books; departmental masters' and Ph.D. theses and other publications. **Subscriptions:** 54 journals and other serials. **Services:** Room open to the public. **Automated Operations:** Computerized cataloging. **Special Catalogs:** Union catalog of books and serials held by the six engineering reading rooms. **Special Indexes:** Index to theses (card).

★15856★
UNIVERSITY OF BRITISH COLUMBIA - DEPARTMENT OF ELECTRICAL ENGINEERING - ELECTRICAL ENGINEERING READING ROOM (Sci-Engr)
2356 Main Mall
Vancouver, BC, Canada V6T 1W5 — Phone: (604)228-2872
Staff: 1. **Subjects:** Applied electromagnetics, biomedical engineering, solid state microelectronics, communications and signal processing, systems and control, digital system design, software engineering. **Holdings:** 670 books; departmental masters' and Ph.D. theses. **Subscriptions:** 74 journals and other serials. **Services:** Room open to the public. **Automated Operations:** Computerized cataloging. **Special Catalogs:** Union catalog of books and serials held by the six engineering reading rooms. **Special Indexes:** Index to departmental theses (card).

★15857★
UNIVERSITY OF BRITISH COLUMBIA - DEPARTMENT OF GEOGRAPHY - MAP AND AIR PHOTO CENTRE (Geog-Map)
1984 West Mall Phone: (604)228-3048
Vancouver, BC, Canada V6T 1W5 Rosemary J. Cann, Map Libn.
Staff: Prof 1. **Subjects:** Maps, air photography. **Special Collections:** Tri-Met air photo coverage of British Columbia; provincial/federal air photo indexes for British Columbia. **Holdings:** 187,257 air photos; 11,187 air photo index maps; 86,270 maps. **Services:** Interlibrary loan (limited); center open to the public.

★15858★
UNIVERSITY OF BRITISH COLUMBIA - DEPARTMENT OF MECHANICAL ENGINEERING - MECHANICAL ENGINEERING READING ROOM (Sci-Engr)
CEME Bldg., Rm. 2050
2324 Main Mall
Vancouver, BC, Canada V6T 1W5 Phone: (604)228-2120
Staff: 1. **Subjects:** Engineering - wind, design, industrial; solid mechanics; vibration; fluid mechanics; aerodynamics; bioengineering; applied statistics; space dynamics; energy conversion; nuclear safety. **Holdings:** 1291 books; departmental masters' and Ph.D. theses and other departmental publications. **Subscriptions:** 25 journals and other serials. **Services:** Room open to the public. **Automated Operations:** Computerized cataloging. **Special Catalogs:** Union catalog of books and serials held by the six engineering reading rooms.

★15859★
UNIVERSITY OF BRITISH COLUMBIA - DEPARTMENT OF METALS AND MATERIALS ENGINEERING - METALS AND MATERIALS ENGINEERING READING ROOM (Sci-Engr)
Metallurgy Bldg., Rm. 319
6350 Stores Rd.
Vancouver, BC, Canada V6T 1W5 Phone: (604)228-2676
Staff: 1. **Subjects:** Mathematical modeling, ceramics, hydrometallurgy, composites, welding, metallurgical kinetics. **Holdings:** 1499 books; departmental masters' and Ph.D. theses. **Subscriptions:** 44 journals and other serials. **Services:** Room open to the public. **Automated Operations:** Computerized cataloging. **Special Catalogs:** Union catalog of books and serials held by the six engineering reading rooms. **Special Indexes:** Index to theses (card).

★15860★
UNIVERSITY OF BRITISH COLUMBIA - DEPARTMENT OF MINING AND MINERAL PROCESS ENGINEERING - MINING AND MINERAL PROCESS ENGINEERING READING ROOM (Sci-Engr)
Forward Bldg., Rm. 319
6350 Stores Rd.
Vancouver, BC, Canada V6T 1W5 Phone: (604)228-2540
Staff: 1. **Subjects:** Mining, mineral processing, geology. **Holdings:** 1137 books; departmental masters' and Ph.D. theses. **Subscriptions:** 17 journals and other serials. **Services:** Room open to the public. **Automated Operations:** Computerized cataloging. **Special Catalogs:** Union catalog of books and serials held by the six engineering reading rooms. **Special Indexes:** Index to theses.

★15861★
UNIVERSITY OF BRITISH COLUMBIA - ERIC W. HAMBER LIBRARY (Med)
Children's Hospital
4480 Oak St. Phone: (604)875-2154
Vancouver, BC, Canada V6H 3V4 Ann M.A. Nelson, Libn.
Founded: 1982. **Staff:** Prof 1; Other 5. **Subjects:** Clinical medicine, pediatrics, obstetrics and gynecology. **Holdings:** 3335 books; 1528 bound periodical volumes. **Subscriptions:** 406 journals and other serials. **Services:** Interlibrary loan; copying; SDI; library open to the public. **Automated Operations:** Computerized cataloging, acquisitions, serials, and circulation. **Computerized Information Services:** DIALOG Information Services, BRS Information Technologies, NLM; internal databases. **Networks/Consortia:** Member of Health Sciences Library Network.

★15862★
UNIVERSITY OF BRITISH COLUMBIA - FACULTY OF COMMERCE & BUSINESS ADMINISTRATION - DAVID LAM MANAGEMENT RESEARCH LIBRARY (Bus-Fin)
HA No. 307
2053 Main Mall Phone: (604)224-8470
Vancouver, BC, Canada V6T 1Y8 Diana Chan, Adm.Libn.
Founded: 1985. **Staff:** Prof 2; Other 4. **Subjects:** Finance, accounting, marketing, sales management, industrial relations, Asia-Pacific business, urban land economics, transportation. **Holdings:** 3000 books; 6000 bound periodical volumes; 6000 corporate annual reports; 3000 microfiche; 6 file cabinets of working papers; 2 file cabinets of arbitration cases and Labour Board decisions; Canadian Government publications. **Subscriptions:** 600 journals and other serials; 10 newspapers. **Services:** Copying; library open to the public. **Automated Operations:** Computerized cataloging, acquisitions, and serials. **Computerized Information Services:** DIALOG Information Services, I.P. Sharp Associates Limited, Info Globe, Financial Post Information Service, BNA Executive Day. Performs searches on fee basis. **Publications:** Directory of Business Computerized Databases, annual - for sale; Library Source Guides 1-9, irregular - for internal distribution only; management bibliographies on various topics, irregular - for sale. **Special Indexes:** Working Paper Quarterly Checklist (printout); index to corporate annual reports (printout). **Staff:** Hazel Cameron, Libn..

★15863★
UNIVERSITY OF BRITISH COLUMBIA - FILM LIBRARY (Aud-Vis)
316 Library Processing Centre
2206 East Mall Phone: (604)228-4400
Vancouver, BC, Canada V6T 1Z8 Howard Hurt, Hd.Libn.
Founded: 1940. **Staff:** 3. **Subjects:** Post-secondary and general education. **Holdings:** 2000 16mm films; 1000 videotapes. **Services:** Library open to the public on fee basis. **Automated Operations:** Computerized public access catalog, cataloging, and acquisitions. **Computerized Information Services:** Envoy 100 (electronic mail service). **Special Collections:** Film/video catalog.

★15864★
UNIVERSITY OF BRITISH COLUMBIA - FINE ARTS LIBRARY (Art)
University Library
1956 Main Mall Phone: (604)228-2720
Vancouver, BC, Canada V6T 1Y3 Hans Burndorfer, Hd.
Founded: 1948. **Staff:** Prof 3; Other 6. **Subjects:** Fine arts, architecture, community and regional planning, history of costume and dance, artistic photography, fashion design. **Holdings:** 125,000 books; 25,000 bound periodical volumes; 30,000 pamphlets; 4000 photographs; 50,000 pictures; 40,000 exhibition catalogs; 40,000 clippings; 8000 microforms. **Subscriptions:** 400 journals and other serials. **Services:** Interlibrary loan; copying; library open to the public with restrictions. **Automated Operations:** Computerized cataloging, serials, and circulation. **Computerized Information Services:** DIALOG Information Services, UTLAS. **Special Catalogs:** Catalogs of exhibitions, pictures, planning pamphlets and clippings, Canadian art and artists, fashion design, and designers. **Staff:** Diana Cooper, Fine Arts Ref.Libn.; Peggy McBride, Plan.Ref.Libn..

★15865★
UNIVERSITY OF BRITISH COLUMBIA - GOVERNMENT PUBLICATIONS & MICROFORMS DIVISIONS (Info Sci)
University Library Phone: (604)228-2584
Vancouver, BC, Canada V6T 1Y3 Suzanne Dodson, Hd.
Founded: 1964. **Staff:** Prof 5; Other 8. **Subjects:** Publications from all levels of government and from all parts of the world; varied subjects on microforms. **Holdings:** 3.3 million microforms; 560,000 uncataloged government publications. **Subscriptions:** 10,000 government publications. **Services:** Interlibrary loan; copying; divisions open to the public. **Automated Operations:** Computerized acquisitions, serials and processing. **Special Catalogs:** Union list of all government publications in the library system. **Remarks:** Although the Microforms Division is administered by the same staff as the Government Publications Division, the microform collection covers every possible subject and is not limited to government publications. **Staff:** Theresa Iverson, Proc.Libn.; Constance Fitzpatrick, Ref.Libn.; Mary Luebbe, Ref.Libn.; Lee Ann Bryant, Ref.Libn..

★15866★
UNIVERSITY OF BRITISH COLUMBIA - HUMANITIES AND SOCIAL SCIENCES DIVISION (Soc Sci, Hum)
University Library Phone: (604)228-2725
Vancouver, BC, Canada V6T 1Y3 Jocelyn Foster, Hd.
Founded: 1984. **Staff:** Prof 9; Other 6. **Subjects:** Religion, language and literature, philosophy, history, linguistics, classical studies, theater, film, sociology, business administration, anthropology, commerce, economics, psychology, geography, political science, education, physical education, library science. **Holdings:** 59,100 books and bound periodical volumes; annual reports of 850 companies. **Subscriptions:** 10,743 journals and other serials. **Services:** Interlibrary loan; copying; division open to the public. **Automated Operations:** Computerized cataloging, acquisitions, and serials. **Computerized Information Services:** DIALOG Information Services, Pergamon ORBIT InfoLine, Inc., CAN/OLE, QL Systems, Infomart, The Financial Post Information Service, Canada Systems Group (CSG), LaborLine, Telesystemes Questel, Info Globe, I.P. Sharp Associates Limited, BRS Information Technologies; SDIProfiles, Canadian Politics Bibliography (internal databases). Performs searches on fee basis. **Publications:** Reference bibliographies and "Start Here" guides, irregular - on request. **Staff:** Helene Redding, Libn.; Elizabeth Caskey, Libn.; Seonaid Lamb, Libn.; Lois Carrier, Libn.; Iza Laponce, Libn.; Dorothy Martin, Libn.; Pia Christensen, Libn.; Joseph Jones, Libn.; Ture Erickson, Libn..

★15867★
UNIVERSITY OF BRITISH COLUMBIA - LAW LIBRARY (Law)
1822 East Mall Phone: (604)228-2275
Vancouver, BC, Canada V6T 1Y3 Thomas J. Shorthouse, Law Libn.
Founded: 1945. **Staff:** Prof 3; Other 12. **Subjects:** Law. **Holdings:** 150,000 books and bound periodical volumes; law reports; statutes; legal journals; monographs. **Subscriptions:** 2900 journals and other serials. **Services:** Interlibrary loan; copying; library open to the public with restrictions. **Automated Operations:** Computerized acquisitions and circulation. **Computerized Information Services:** QL Systems, DIALOG Information Services, WESTLAW. **Staff:** Allen H. Soroka, Asst.Libn., Ref.; Mary E. Mitchell, Ref.Libn..

★15868★
UNIVERSITY OF BRITISH COLUMBIA - MAC MILLAN FORESTRY/AGRICULTURE LIBRARY (Agri, Biol Sci)
MacMillan Bldg.
2357 Main Mall Phone: (604)228-3445
Vancouver, BC, Canada V6T 2A2 Lore Brongers, Hd.
Founded: 1967. **Staff:** Prof 2; Other 4. **Subjects:** Agricultural sciences, aquaculture, food science, forestry, forest products. **Holdings:** 55,000 books and bound periodical volumes; 75,400 unbound government publications; 200 annual reports; 37,500 microfiche; 281 reels of microfilm. **Subscriptions:** 1300 journals. **Services:** Interlibrary loan; copying; SDI; library open to the public. **Automated Operations:** Computerized serials and circulation. **Computerized Information Services:** CAN/SDI, CAN/OLE, DIALOG Information Services; Document Retrieval System (internal database). Performs searches on fee basis. **Staff:** Marjorie Nelles, Ref.Libn..

★15869★
UNIVERSITY OF BRITISH COLUMBIA - MAP LIBRARY (Geog-Map)
University Library
1956 Main Mall Phone: (604)228-2231
Vancouver, BC, Canada V6T 1Y3 Maureen F. Wilson, Hd.
Founded: 1964. **Staff:** Prof 1; Other 3. **Subjects:** Maps, cartography, map librarianship. **Holdings:** 2408 books; 2949 atlases; 472 gazetteers; 148,524 maps; 131 pamphlet boxes of tourist literature and city guides; 6300 microfiche. **Services:** Copying; library open to the public. **Publications:** Acquisitions list, quarterly; bibliographies, occasional; guide to collections. **Remarks:** An alternate telephone number is 228-6191.

★15870★
UNIVERSITY OF BRITISH COLUMBIA - MARJORIE SMITH LIBRARY (Soc Sci)
School of Social Work
6201 Cecil Green Park Rd. Phone: (604)228-2242
Vancouver, BC, Canada V6T 1W5 Judith Frye, Hd.
Founded: 1965. **Staff:** Prof 1; Other 2. **Subjects:** Social work, public welfare, social policy, community organization, human behavior. **Holdings:** 17,800 books; 1300 bound periodical volumes; 28 VF drawers of pamphlets and annual reports. **Subscriptions:** 125 journals and other serials. **Services:** Interlibrary loan; copying; library open to the public. **Staff:** Pia Christensen, Act.Hd.Libn..

★15871★
UNIVERSITY OF BRITISH COLUMBIA - MATHEMATICS LIBRARY (Comp Sci, Sci-Engr)
1984 Main Mall Phone: (604)228-2667
Vancouver, BC, Canada V6T 1W5 Reinder J. Brongers, Hd.
Founded: 1966. **Staff:** Prof 1; Other 2. **Subjects:** Mathematics, computer science. **Holdings:** 29,000 books and bound periodical volumes. **Subscriptions:** 325 journals and other serials. **Services:** Interlibrary loan; library open to the public.

★15872★
UNIVERSITY OF BRITISH COLUMBIA - MUSIC LIBRARY (Mus)
6361 Memorial Rd. Phone: (604)228-3589
Vancouver, BC, Canada V6T 1W5 Hans Burndorfer, Hd.
Staff: Prof 2; Other 2. **Subjects:** Music. **Holdings:** 60,000 books and scores; 3000 reels of microfilm; 10,000 recordings. **Subscriptions:** 150 journals and other serials. **Services:** Interlibrary loan; copying; library open to the public. **Staff:** Kirsten Walsh, Mus.Ref.Libn..

★15873★
UNIVERSITY OF BRITISH COLUMBIA - ST. PAUL'S HOSPITAL HEALTH SCIENCES LIBRARY (Med)
1081 Burrard St. Phone: (604)682-2344
Vancouver, BC, Canada V6Z 1Y6 Barbara J. Saint, Hd.
Founded: 1950. **Staff:** Prof 1; Other 4. **Subjects:** Health sciences. **Special Collections:** St. Paul's Hospital Museum and Archives (200 books; 25 audiotapes; 5 videotapes; 10 filing cabinets of documents; photographs; artifacts; archives administered separately). **Holdings:** 5000 books; 1 VF drawer of pamphlets. **Subscriptions:** 225 journals and other serials. **Services:** Interlibrary loan; copying; SDI; library open to the public. **Automated Operations:** Computerized cataloging, acquisitions, serials, and circulation. **Computerized Information Services:** DIALOG Information Services, BRS Information Technologies, NLM, CAN/OLE, QL Systems; OnTyme Electronic Message Network Service, Envoy 100 (electronic mail services). Performs searches on fee basis. **Publications:** Newsletter, irregular - for internal distribution only. **Special Catalogs:** Periodical holdings (book), annual.

★15874★
UNIVERSITY OF BRITISH COLUMBIA - SCHOOL OF LIBRARY, ARCHIVAL AND INFORMATION STUDIES READING ROOM (Info Sci)
1956 Main Mall, Rm. 831 Phone: (604)228-2704
Vancouver, BC, Canada V6T 1Y3 Lynne Lighthall, Libn./Instr.II
Founded: 1961. **Staff:** Prof 1; Other 1. **Subjects:** Librarianship, archival studies, information science, publishing and book trade. **Holdings:** 3000 cataloged books and bound periodical volumes; uncataloged annual reports, newsletters, publishers' catalogs, course materials. **Subscriptions:** 130 journals and other serials. **Services:** Room open to the public with restrictions. **Computerized Information Services:** Envoy 100 (electronic mail service).

★15875★
UNIVERSITY OF BRITISH COLUMBIA - SCIENCE DIVISION (Sci-Engr)
University Library Phone: (604)228-3295
Vancouver, BC, Canada V6T 1Y3 Reinder J. Brongers, Hd.
Staff: Prof 4; Other 2. **Subjects:** Chemistry, physics, engineering, mathematics, geology, astronomy. **Special Collections:** Rand Corporation Depository, 1970 to present. **Holdings:** 230,000 volumes. **Subscriptions:** 3000 journals and other serials. **Services:** Interlibrary loan; copying; division open to the public. **Computerized Information Services:** CAN/OLE, DIALOG Information Services, QL Systems, CAS ONLINE. **Staff:** Helen Mayoh, Ref.Libn.; Sundaram Venkataraman, Ref.Libn.; Jack McIntosh, Ref.Libn.; Janice Kreider, Ref.Libn..

★15876★
UNIVERSITY OF BRITISH COLUMBIA - SPECIAL COLLECTIONS DIVISION (Hist)
University Library
1956 Main Mall Phone: (604)228-2521
Vancouver, BC, Canada V6T 1Y3 Anne Yandle, Hd., Spec.Coll.
Founded: 1960. **Staff:** Prof 5; Other 4. **Subjects:** Canadian history, travel, and literature; Pacific Northwest; early children's literature; historical cartography; 19th century English and Anglo-Irish literature; University of British Columbia; labor and business history; Arctic explorations. **Special Collections:** Colbeck Collection (English and Anglo-Irish belles lettres; 20,000 books); Robert Burns Collection (700 books); Thomas J. Wise Collection (200 books); University Archives and Historical Manuscripts

Collections (7000 linear feet). **Holdings:** 75,000 books and bound periodical volumes; 6000 pamphlets; 25,000 maps; 70,000 photographs; 2000 audiotapes; 86 films. **Subscriptions:** 140 journals and other serials. **Services:** Copying; division open to the public. **Automated Operations:** Computerized cataloging, acquisitions, and serials. **Staff:** Charles Forbes, Thesis & Colbeck Libn.; Laurenda Daniells, Univ.Archv.; George Brandak, Mss.Cur.; Frances Woodward, Ref.Libn..

★15877★
UNIVERSITY OF BRITISH COLUMBIA - SPENCER ENTOMOLOGICAL MUSEUM - LIBRARY (Biol Sci)
Dept. of Zoology — Phone: (604)228-3379
Vancouver, BC, Canada V6T 2A9 — G.G.E. Scudder, Dir.
Founded: 1953. **Staff:** Prof 2. **Subjects:** Entomology. **Holdings:** 350 books; 8000 reprints; 50 series of unbound journals. **Services:** Copying; library open to the public at the discretion of the director. **Special Catalogs:** Subject catalog for reprints. **Staff:** S. Cannings, Cur..

★15878★
UNIVERSITY OF BRITISH COLUMBIA - WILSON RECORDINGS COLLECTION (Aud-Vis)
1958 Main Mall — Phone: (604)228-2534
Vancouver, BC, Canada V6T 1W5 — Douglas Kaye, Hd.
Founded: 1941. **Staff:** Prof 1; Other 3. **Subjects:** Literature, music. **Holdings:** 33,000 phonograph records; 3200 compact discs. **Services:** Interlibrary loan; collection open to the public. **Automated Operations:** Computerized public access catalog, cataloging, and circulation. **Computerized Information Services:** Internal database. **Special Indexes:** Author/composer, number, performer/conductor, distinctive title (microfiche).

★15879★
UNIVERSITY OF BRITISH COLUMBIA - WOODWARD BIOMEDICAL LIBRARY (Med, Biol Sci)
2198 Health Sciences Mall — Phone: (604)228-2762
Vancouver, BC, Canada V6T 1W5 — Anna R. Leith, Hd.
Founded: 1950. **Staff:** Prof 12; Other 29. **Subjects:** Medicine, zoology, botany, dentistry, pharmacy, nursing, rehabilitation medicine, nutrition. **Special Collections:** Historical Collection in Science and Medicine (5000 volumes; pictures; manuscripts; letters; reprints; artifacts). **Holdings:** 150,000 books; 130,000 bound periodical volumes; 14,025 microforms. **Subscriptions:** 4350 journals and other serials. **Services:** Interlibrary loan; copying; SDI; library open to the public for reference use only. **Automated Operations:** Computerized acquisitions, serials, and circulation. **Computerized Information Services:** NLM, DIALOG Information Services, CAN/OLE, BRS Information Technologies, QL Systems, STN International; Envoy 100, OnTyme Electronic Message Network Service (electronic mail services). Performs searches on fee basis. **Networks/Consortia:** Member of Health Sciences Library Network. **Remarks:** Alternate telephone numbers are 228-4440 and 228-5461. **Staff:** Elsie De Bruijn, Assoc.Libn.; Lynne Hallonquist, Life Sci.Bibliog.; Lee Perry, Hist.Coll.; Stephanie Dykstra, Ser.Libn.; Diana Kent, Ref.Libn.; John Cole, Ref.Libn.; Pat Lysyk, Ref.Libn.; William Parker, Ref.Libn.; Florence Doidge, Circ.Libn.; Jim Henderson, Ref.Libn.; Margaret Price, Ref.Libn..

★15880★
UNIVERSITY OF CALGARY - ARTS AND HUMANITIES LIBRARY (Art, Hum)
2500 University Dr., N.W. — Phone: (403)220-7272
Calgary, AB, Canada T2N 1N4 — Marnie C. Swanson, Area Hd./Arts & Hum.Libn.
Founded: 1966. **Staff:** Prof 7; Other 16. **Subjects:** Literature; art; drama; philosophy; religious studies; Germanic, Slavic, and Romance languages. **Special Collections:** Canadian Authors Manuscripts; Canadian Architectural Archives. **Holdings:** Figures not available. **Services:** Interlibrary loan; copying; SDI; library open to the public. **Automated Operations:** Computerized cataloging, acquisitions, and circulation. **Computerized Information Services:** DIALOG Information Services, CAN/OLE, QL Systems; internal databases; Envoy 100, NETNORTH (electronic mail services). Performs searches on fee basis. Contact Person: Saundra Lipton, Hum.Libn., 220-3793. **Staff:** Nora Robins, Hum.Libn.; Rita Vine, Mus.Libn.; Joanne Henning; Kathy Zimon, Fine Arts Libn.; Polly Steele, Spec.Coll.Libn..

★15881★
UNIVERSITY OF CALGARY - CANADIAN INSTITUTE OF RESOURCES LAW - LIBRARY (Law, Energy)
BioSciences Bldg., Rm. 430M — Phone: (403)282-2569
Calgary, AB, Canada T2N 1N4 — Evangeline S. Case, Pubn.Off.
Subjects: Canadian energy regulation, oil and gas law. **Holdings:** 200 books; 5 book shelves and 2 VF drawers of Canadian regulatory tribunal publications. **Subscriptions:** 25 journals and other serials. **Services:** Copying; library open to the public with permission.

★15882★
UNIVERSITY OF CALGARY - EDUCATION MATERIALS CENTRE (Educ)
Education Tower, Rm. 402
2500 University Dr., N.W. — Phone: (403)220-5637
Calgary, AB, Canada T2N 1N4 — David Brown, Dir.
Founded: 1963. **Staff:** Prof 2; Other 6. **Subjects:** Teaching methods, elementary and secondary curriculum, school libraries, children's literature. **Special Collections:** Archive collection of Alberta curriculum guides and texts. **Holdings:** 55,000 books; 5000 pictures; 1500 sound recordings; 300 video cassettes; 4000 filmstrips; 2500 kits; 3000 slides. **Subscriptions:** 170 journals and other serials. **Services:** Copying; center open to the public for reference use only. **Remarks:** Maintained by Faculty of Education. **Staff:** Pearl Herscovitch, Curric.Libn..

★15883★
UNIVERSITY OF CALGARY - ENVIRONMENT-SCIENCE-TECHNOLOGY LIBRARY (Sci-Engr, Env-Cons)
2500 University Dr., N.W. — Phone: (403)220-5966
Calgary, AB, Canada T2N 1N4 — Michael Brydges, Act. Area Hd.
Staff: Prof 6; Other 9. **Subjects:** Physical and biological sciences, engineering, geology and geophysics, northern studies, environment and architecture, urban and regional planning, mathematics and computing science, nursing. **Special Collections:** Arctic Institute of North America Collection; maps and aerial photographs. **Holdings:** Figures not available for books and bound periodical volumes; maps; aerial photographs; microforms. **Subscriptions:** 3800 journals and other serials. **Services:** Interlibrary loan (fee); copying; SDI; library open to the public. **Automated Operations:** Computerized public access catalog, cataloging, acquisitions, and circulation. **Computerized Information Services:** DIALOG Information Services, BRS Information Technologies, CAN/SDI, DOBIS, CAN/OLE, QL Systems, SPIRES, STN International, Pergamon ORBIT InfoLine, Inc.; NOMADS (internal database); Envoy 100 (electronic mail service). Performs searches on fee basis. Contact Person: Kathleen Robertson, EST Online Coord., 220-3734. **Staff:** Midge King, Geol.Libn.; Yvonne Hinks, Asst. Area Hd.; Sharon Neary, Engr.Libn.; Helen Clark, Map/Airphoto Libn.; Kathleen Robertson, Nurs./Comp.Sci.Libn..

★15884★
UNIVERSITY OF CALGARY - GALLAGHER LIBRARY OF GEOLOGY & GEOPHYSICS (Sci-Engr)
2500 University Dr., N.W., — Phone: (403)220-6042
Calgary, AB, Canada T2N 1N4 — Midge King, Libn.
Founded: 1974. **Staff:** Prof 1; Other 2. **Subjects:** Sedimentary and petroleum geology, geophysics. **Holdings:** 19,000 books; 15,000 bound periodical volumes; 10,000 government publications; 2300 maps; 550 microforms; 52 slide sets. **Subscriptions:** 100 journals and other serials. **Services:** Interlibrary loan; copying; library open to the public. **Automated Operations:** Computerized cataloging, acquisitions, and circulation. **Computerized Information Services:** CAN/OLE, SPIRES Data Base Management, DIALOG Information Services; NETNORTH, BITNET, Envoy 100 (electronic mail services). Performs searches on fee basis. **Publications:** Newsline (newsletter) - for internal distribution only. **Special Catalogs:** University of Calgary Theses in Geology and Geophysics (printout).

★15885★
UNIVERSITY OF CALGARY - KANANASKIS CENTRE FOR ENVIRONMENTAL RESEARCH - LIBRARY (Env-Cons, Biol Sci)
Calgary, AB, Canada T2N 1N4 — Phone: (403)220-5271
Grace LeBel, Libn.
Staff: 1. **Subjects:** Chemistry, biology, environmental research. **Special Collections:** Environmental collection. **Holdings:** 4000 books; 3000 unpublished reports and theses. **Subscriptions:** 40 journals and other serials. **Services:** Library not open to the public.

★15886★
UNIVERSITY OF CALGARY - LAW LIBRARY (Law)
2500 University Dr., N.W. Phone: (403)220-5090
Calgary, AB, Canada T2N 1N4 Olga Margaret Kizlyk, Law Libn.
Founded: 1975. **Staff:** Prof 4; Other 10. **Subjects:** Law. **Holdings:** 91,000 volumes; 44,000 microforms. **Subscriptions:** 2200 journals and other serials. **Services:** Interlibrary loan; copying; library open to the public. **Automated Operations:** Computerized public access catalog, cataloging, acquisitions, and circulation. **Computerized Information Services:** QL Systems, DIALOG Information Services, WESTLAW; Envoy 100, QL/MAIL (electronic mail services). **Staff:** Don Sanders; Umesh Vyas; Marilyn Nasserden.

★15887★
UNIVERSITY OF CALGARY - MAC KIMMIE LIBRARY - ARTS AND HUMANITIES AREA LIBRARY - SPECIAL COLLECTIONS DIVISION (Hum)
2500 University Dr., N.W. Phone: (403)220-5972
Calgary, AB, Canada T2N 1N4 Apollonia Lang Steele, Spec.Coll.Libn.
Founded: 1966. **Staff:** Prof 1; Other 3. **Subjects:** Canadian literature. **Special Collections:** Papers of Hugh MacLennan, Alice Munro, Mordecai Richler, Brian Moore, W.O. Mitchell, Christie Harris, Robert Kroetsch, Rudy Weibe, George Ryga, Gwen Ringwood, Len Peterson, Michael Cook, Joanna Glass, Aritha van Herk, Sharon Pollock, John Murrell, Grant MacEwan, James Gray, Bruce Hutchison, Alden Nowlan, Clark Blaise, John Metcalf, Lois Kerr; Morris Surdin (papers; musical scores; Canadian Broadcasting Corporation scripts); E.C.W. Press. **Holdings:** 30,000 books and bound periodical volumes; 875 meters of manuscripts and archives. **Subscriptions:** 10 journals and other serials. **Services:** Copying; collections open to the public. **Automated Operations:** Computerized cataloging and acquisitions. **Publications:** Published inventories of The Hugh MacLennan Papers; The Rudy Wiebe Papers: First Accession; The Robert Kroetsch Papers: First Accession; The Alice Munro Papers: First Accession; The Joanna M. Glass Papers; The W.O. Mitchell Papers; The Alice Munro Papers: Second Accession; The Brian Moore Papers: First Accession and Second Accession; The Mordecai Richler Papers; The Gwen Pharis Ringwood Papers.

★15888★
UNIVERSITY OF CALGARY - MEDIA UTILIZATION UNIT & FILM LIBRARY (Aud-Vis)
2500 University Dr., N.W. Phone: (403)220-6231
Calgary, AB, Canada T2N 1N4 Jennie Paine, Mgr.
Founded: 1969. **Staff:** Prof 2; Other 4. **Subjects:** Social sciences. **Special Collections:** Film study collection (392 titles); University of Calgary Public Service programs (72 titles). **Holdings:** 2724 16mm film titles; 1753 videotape titles; 41 slide sets; 8 videodisc titles; 9 VF drawers of distributors' catalogs. **Subscriptions:** 65 journals and other serials. **Services:** Interlibrary loan; rental service; library open to the public with restrictions. **Automated Operations:** Computerized cataloging. **Publications:** Media Methods, bimonthly - to faculty members. **Special Catalogs:** Catalog of film and videotape holdings (book). **Staff:** Douglas Coughlin, Film Libn..

★15889★
UNIVERSITY OF CALGARY - MEDICAL LIBRARY (Med)
Health Sciences Centre
3330 Hospital Dr., N.W. Phone: (403)220-6858
Calgary, AB, Canada T2N 4N1 Andras Kirchner, Med.Libn.
Founded: 1968. **Staff:** Prof 3; Other 20. **Subjects:** Health sciences with special emphasis on family practice. **Holdings:** 87,919 volumes; 14,635 microforms; 67 films; 469 videotapes; 332 slide/tape programs; 2538 cassettes. **Subscriptions:** 1580 journals and other serials. **Services:** Interlibrary loan; copying; SDI; library open to the public. **Automated Operations:** Computerized cataloging and acquisitions. **Computerized Information Services:** DIALOG Information Services, CAN/OLE, AMA/NET, MEDLARS; Envoy 100 (electronic mail service). Performs searches on fee basis. Contact Person: William Maes, Asst.Med.Libn., 220-6857. **Special Catalogs:** Union list of serials of Calgary area hospital libraries. **Staff:** G.E. Zizka, Coll.Dev.Libn..

★15890★
UNIVERSITY OF CALGARY - SOCIAL SCIENCES LIBRARY (Soc Sci)
2500 University Dr., N.W. Phone: (403)220-6097
Calgary, AB, Canada T2N 1N4 Gretchen Ghent, Area Hd.
Founded: 1966. **Staff:** Prof 8; Other 10. **Subjects:** History, archeology and classics, management and economics, education, sociology and anthropology, social welfare, psychology, physical education, geography, communication studies. **Holdings:** Figures not available. **Subscriptions:** 2400 journals and other serials; 50 newspapers. **Services:** Interlibrary loan; copying; SDI; library open to the public. **Automated Operations:** Computerized cataloging, acquisitions, and circulation. **Computerized Information Services:** DIALOG Information Services, Pergamon ORBIT InfoLine, Inc., CAN/OLE, QL Systems, Info Globe, Dow Jones News/Retrieval, SPIRES; NOMADS (internal database); Envoy 100, AOSS (electronic mail services). Performs searches on fee basis. **Remarks:** Library maintains the Government Publications Division, Microforms Division, Management Resources Centre, and newspapers for all University of Calgary libraries. **Staff:** Laureen Moffat, Asst. Area Hd.; Shelagh Mikulak, Mgt.Rsrcs.Ctr.; Maurice Lepper; Rhys Williams; Alane Jeffery; Debbie DeBruijn; Sharon Stevelman.

★15891★
UNIVERSITY OF CALIFORNIA - KEARNEY AGRICULTURAL CENTER (Agri)
9240 S. Riverbend Ave. Phone: (209)646-2794
Parlier, CA 93648 Dr. Donald W. Grimes, Ctr.Dir.
Staff: Prof 20; Other 60. **Subjects:** Agronomy, agricultural economics, entomology, nematology, plant pathology, pomology, viticulture, vegetable crops, water science, biological control. **Holdings:** 1000 books; 1000 reprints. **Services:** Center open to the public by permission. **Staff:** Dr. Larry Williams, Chm., Lib.Comm..

★15892★
UNIVERSITY OF CALIFORNIA - LOS ALAMOS NATIONAL LABORATORY - LIBRARY (Sci-Engr)
MS-P362 Phone: (505)667-4448
Los Alamos, NM 87545 J. Arthur Freed, Hd.Libn.
Founded: 1943. **Staff:** Prof 16; Other 28. **Subjects:** Military and peaceful uses of nuclear energy, physics, chemistry, materials science, engineering, earth sciences, mathematics and computers. **Special Collections:** Biomedicine (40,000 volumes). **Holdings:** 110,000 books; 200,000 bound periodical volumes; 1 million technical reports; 500 reels of motion picture film. **Services:** Interlibrary loan; copying; internal translation; library open to the public on a limited schedule. **Automated Operations:** Computerized cataloging, acquisitions, serials, and circulation. **Computerized Information Services:** DIALOG Information Services, Pergamon ORBIT InfoLine, Inc., Geac Library Information System, BRS Information Technologies, Integrated Technical Information System (ITIS), RLIN, NLM, NASA/RECON, DTIC, NEXIS, STN International, CompuServe, Inc., WILSONLINE. **Publications:** What's New; Publications of Los Alamos Research. **Special Catalogs:** Card catalog for technical reports; computer listing of laboratory sponsored unclassified publications. **Remarks:** Affiliated with the U.S. Department of Energy. **Staff:** Karen Stoll, Dp.Hd.Libn.; Lois Godfrey, Asst.Hd.Libn.; Theresa Connaughton, Info. Access Libn.; Carol Nielson, Ref.Libn.; Donna Berg, Ref.Libn.; Ann Beyer, Ref.Libn.; Jacqueline Stack, Ref.Libn.; Carroll Sue Wagner, Ref.Libn.; Betty Burnett; Viola Salazar; Dan Baca, Supv., Rpt.Lib.; Jackson Carter; Kathryn Gursky, Cat.; Sharon Smith, Acq.Libn.; Irma Holtkamp, Cat.Libn.; Kathryn Varjabedian, Subj.Cat.Coord..

★15893★
UNIVERSITY OF CALIFORNIA, BERKELEY - ANTHROPOLOGY LIBRARY (Soc Sci)
230 Kroeber Hall Phone: (415)642-2400
Berkeley, CA 94720 Dorothy A. Koenig, Libn.
Founded: 1956. **Staff:** Prof 1; Other 2. **Subjects:** Anthropology. **Holdings:** 60,601 volumes; 605 microforms; 1598 pamphlets. **Subscriptions:** 1003 journals and other serials. **Services:** Interlibrary loan (through 307 General Library); copying; library open for reference use with restrictions on circulation. **Remarks:** An alternate telephone number is 642-2419.

★15894★
UNIVERSITY OF CALIFORNIA, BERKELEY - ASIAN AMERICAN STUDIES LIBRARY (Area-Ethnic)
3407 Dwinelle Hall Phone: (415)642-2218
Berkeley, CA 94720 Mrs. Wei Chi Poon, Hd.Libn.
Founded: 1970. **Staff:** Prof 1; Other 4. **Subjects:** Asians in the U.S., past and present. **Special Collections:** Chinese American Research Collection (archival materials in English and Chinese; 38,113 items). **Holdings:** 63,579 volumes; 5000 slides; 106 videotapes; 26 16mm films. **Subscriptions:** 167 journals and other serials; 134 newspapers. **Services:** Library open to the public with restrictions on circulation.

★15895★
UNIVERSITY OF CALIFORNIA, BERKELEY - ASTRONOMY-MATHEMATICS-STATISTICS LIBRARY (Sci-Engr, Comp Sci)
100 Evans Hall Phone: (415)642-3381
Berkeley, CA 94720 Kimiyo T. Hom, Libn.
Founded: 1959. **Staff:** Prof 1; Other 3. **Subjects:** Astronomy, pure and applied mathematics, statistics, mathematics and theory of computer science. **Holdings:** 66,966 volumes; 3510 photographic plates; 53 manuscripts; 149 microforms; 1472 pamphlets; 3 sound recordings. **Subscriptions:** 1217 journals and other serials. **Services:** Interlibrary loan (through 307 General Library); copying; library open to the public for reference use with restricted circulation.

★15896★
UNIVERSITY OF CALIFORNIA, BERKELEY - BANCROFT LIBRARY (Hist, Rare Book)
Berkeley, CA 94720 Phone: (415)642-3781
James D. Hart, Dir.
Founded: 1859. **Staff:** Prof 19; Other 27. **Special Collections:** Bancroft Collection (history of western North America, especially western plains states to the Pacific Coast and from Panama to Alaska with greatest emphasis on California and Mexico); Rare Books (incunabula; 403); rare European, English, U.S., and South American imprints; fine printing of all periods and places (emphasis on modern English and American typography, medieval manuscript books and documents, papyri); University Archives; Regional Oral History Office (recollections of persons who have contributed to the development of the West and the nation); Mark Twain Papers (collection of the author's manuscripts, correspondence, related documentary material, and the editorial program to publish it); history of science and technology, especially in California. **Holdings:** 343,000 volumes; 51.6 million manuscripts; 21,300 maps and atlases; 2.34 million pictures and portraits; 47,000 microforms; 8500 recordings; 108,500 pamphlets; 1000 motion pictures. **Subscriptions:** 1926 journals and other serials. **Services:** Interlibrary loan (limited to microfilm; through 307 General Library); copying (limited); library open to the public. **Automated Operations:** Computerized cataloging. **Publications:** A Guide to the Manuscripts of the Bancroft Library, Volumes 1 and 2, Berkeley, 1963 and 1972; Bancroftiana (newsletter), 3/year - to Friends of The Bancroft Library. **Special Catalogs:** A Catalog of the Bancroft Collection, 1964, and supplements (book).

★15897★
UNIVERSITY OF CALIFORNIA, BERKELEY - BIOCHEMISTRY LIBRARY (Biol Sci)
430 Biochemistry Bldg.
Berkeley, CA 94720 Phone: (415)642-5112
Founded: 1950. **Staff:** 1. **Subjects:** Biochemistry. **Holdings:** 9395 volumes. **Subscriptions:** 148 journals and other serials. **Services:** Copying; library open for reference use with limited circulation.

★15898★
UNIVERSITY OF CALIFORNIA, BERKELEY - BIOLOGY LIBRARY (Biol Sci)
3503 Life Sciences Bldg. Phone: (415)642-2531
Berkeley, CA 94720 Beth Weil, Libn.
Founded: 1930. **Staff:** Prof 3; Other 7. **Subjects:** Anatomy, biochemistry, botany, physiology, microbiology, molecular biology, biology, immunology, zoology. **Special Collections:** Rare Book Collection (17th-19th century natural history; 12,000 volumes). **Holdings:** 220,000 volumes; 44,432 pamphlets and reprints; 8547 reels of microfilm; 5072 microfiche. **Subscriptions:** 3700 journals and other serials. **Services:** Interlibrary loan (through 307 General Library); copying; library open to the public for reference use with restricted circulation. **Computerized Information Services:** DIALOG Information Services, BRS Information Technologies, NLM, RLIN, STN International.

★15899★
UNIVERSITY OF CALIFORNIA, BERKELEY - BOTANICAL GARDEN - LIBRARY (Biol Sci)
Centennial Dr. Phone: (415)643-8040
Berkeley, CA 94720 Dr. James Affolter, Cur.
Staff: Prof 1. **Subjects:** Horticulture, plant taxonomy, botanical gardens. **Holdings:** 1000 books; 30 feet of other cataloged items. **Subscriptions:** 20 journals and other serials. **Services:** Library not open to the public.

★15900★
UNIVERSITY OF CALIFORNIA, BERKELEY - BUSINESS/SOCIAL SCIENCE LIBRARY (Soc Sci, Bus-Fin)
30 Stephens Hall Phone: (415)642-0400
Berkeley, CA 94720 Milt Ternberg, Libn.
Founded: 1964. **Staff:** Prof 2; Other 7. **Subjects:** Economics, business administration, labor, public policy. **Special Collections:** Labor union publications. **Holdings:** 106,000 volumes; 800,000 microforms; 37,218 pamphlets. **Subscriptions:** 2747 journals and other serials. **Services:** Interlibrary loan (through 307 General Library); copying; library open to the public, special borrowers' card required. **Computerized Information Services:** DIALOG Information Services, WILSONLINE, Dow Jones News/Retrieval, BRS Information Technologies, RLIN. **Publications:** Berkeley Business Guides, annual - free upon request.

★15901★
UNIVERSITY OF CALIFORNIA, BERKELEY - CENTER FOR CHINESE STUDIES - LIBRARY (Area-Ethnic)
2223 Fulton St. Phone: (415)642-6510
Berkeley, CA 94720 Chi-Ping Chen, Libn.
Founded: 1959. **Staff:** Prof 1; Other 2. **Subjects:** Social sciences and humanities of Peoples' Republic of China. **Special Collections:** KEIO Collection (29 reels of microfilm); Hatano Collection (41 reels of microfilm); Union Research Institute Classified File on Contemporary China, 1949-1975 (650 microfiche); Chen Cheng Collection (20 reels of microfilm); Wen Shih Tzu Liao Collection (675 volumes); videotape collection of television programs from the People's Republic of China (62 videotapes); People's University Reprint Series of selected articles published in the People's Republic of China (social science; 50 serial titles). **Holdings:** 40,500 volumes; 40 drawers of microfilm; 4250 items in VF drawers; newspaper clippings. **Subscriptions:** 325 journals and other serials; 48 newspapers. **Services:** Interlibrary loan (through 307 General Library); copying; library open to the public.

★15902★
UNIVERSITY OF CALIFORNIA, BERKELEY - CHEMISTRY LIBRARY (Sci-Engr)
100 Hildebrand Hall Phone: (415)642-3753
Berkeley, CA 94720 Alison Howard, Act.Hd.
Founded: 1948. **Staff:** Prof 1; Other 1. **Subjects:** Chemistry - inorganic, organic, physical; chemical kinetics, thermodynamics, and engineering; electrochemistry; transport and mass transfer; polymer chemistry. **Special Collections:** Russian monographs and serials obtained on exchange; U.S. chemical patents (20,000). **Holdings:** 47,078 volumes; 31,300 microforms; 322 pamphlets. **Subscriptions:** 790 journals and other serials. **Services:** Interlibrary loan (through 307 General Library); copying; library open for reference use with restricted circulation. **Automated Operations:** Computerized public access catalog. **Computerized Information Services:** DIALOG Information Services, BRS Information Technologies, CAS ONLINE.

★15903★
UNIVERSITY OF CALIFORNIA, BERKELEY - CHICANO STUDIES LIBRARY (Area-Ethnic)
3404 Dwinelle Hall Phone: (415)642-3859
Berkeley, CA 94720 Lillian Castillo-Speed, Coord.
Founded: 1970. **Staff:** Prof 2; Other 6. **Subjects:** Chicano, Mexican American, Spanish speaking/surname people in U.S.; Raza; farmworkers; bilingual and biculturalgroups. **Special Collections:** Retrospective Newspaper Collection, 1844-1943; Chicano Art Color Transparencies (4000); Chicano Posters (800). **Holdings:** 5000 volumes; 150 bound periodical volumes; 4300 other cataloged items; 1500 microforms; 350 audiotapes; 10 videotapes; 5 films; 5000 slides; 20 maps; 1000 noncurrent journal titles; 150 linear feet of archives. **Subscriptions:** 400 journals and other serials; 75 newspapers. **Services:** Interlibrary loan; library open to the public. **Computerized Information Services:** Internal database. **Networks/Consortia:** Member of Chicano Information Management Consortium of California. **Publications:** List of publications - available on request. **Special Indexes:** Chicano Periodical Index. **Remarks:** Library located at 104 Wheeler Hall.

★15904★
UNIVERSITY OF CALIFORNIA, BERKELEY - EARTH SCIENCES LIBRARY (Sci-Engr)
230 Earth Sciences Bldg. Phone: (415)642-2997
Berkeley, CA 94720 Julie Rinaldi, Hd.Libn.
Founded: 1961. **Staff:** Prof 1; Other 2. **Subjects:** Geology, geophysics, seismology, physical geography, climatology, paleontology. **Holdings:** 93,000 volumes; 15,000 microforms; 2500 pamphlets; 50,000 maps. **Subscriptions:** 2700 journals and other serials. **Services:** Interlibrary loan

(through 307 General Library); copying; library open for reference use with limited circulation. **Computerized Information Services:** Online systems. Performs searches on fee basis.

★15905★
UNIVERSITY OF CALIFORNIA, BERKELEY - EARTHQUAKE ENGINEERING RESEARCH CENTER LIBRARY (Sci-Engr)
1301 S. 46th St. Phone: (415)231-9401
Richmond, CA 94804 Shirley Joy Svihra, Libn.
Founded: 1972. **Staff:** Prof 2; Other 2. **Subjects:** Engineering - earthquake, civil, geotechnical, structural; geology; seismology; natural hazards mitigation. **Holdings:** 32,000 items including 2380 nonbook materials. **Subscriptions:** 296 journals and other serials. **Services:** Interlibrary loan; copying; SDI; library open to the public. **Computerized Information Services:** DIALOG Information Services; MELVYL (internal database). Performs searches on fee basis. Contact Person: Helen Tseng, Asst.Libn., 231-9523. **Publications:** Abstract Journal in Earthquake Engineering, semiannual - by subscription; UCB/EERC reports, irregular - by subscription or single issues; Library Acquisitions Alert - free upon request; EERC News - free upon request. **Remarks:** Library materials are in English, Asian, and other Indo-European languages. An alternate telephone number is 231-9403.

★15906★
UNIVERSITY OF CALIFORNIA, BERKELEY - EAST ASIATIC LIBRARY (Area-Ethnic)
208 Durant Hall Phone: (415)642-2556
Berkeley, CA 94720 Donald H. Shively, Hd.
Founded: 1947. **Staff:** Prof 11; Other 14. **Subjects:** Publications in Chinese, Korean, and Japanese languages, primarily in the humanities and social sciences. **Special Collections:** Asami Library of Yi dynasty Korean books and manuscripts; Murakami Library of Meiji literature, 1868-1911; Chohyo-kaku collection of Chinese stone and bronze rubbings (2104); Japanese woodblock and lithograph maps, 17th to early 20th centuries; Doi Gakken collection of Chinese poetry and prose by Japanese writers; Soshin and Motoori collections of xylographic editions of Tokugawa and early Meiji periods and the Kihon section containing publications of the 100 years prior to World War II; Rare Books Room collection devoted to pre-1644 Chinese and pre-1660 Japanese imprints. **Holdings:** 513,728 volumes; 6892 manuscripts; 7108 microforms; 2298 old maps; 5051 prints and photographs. **Subscriptions:** 4625 journals and other serials; 28 newspapers. **Services:** Interlibrary loan (through 307 General Library); copying; library open to the public with restrictions. **Networks/Consortia:** Member of RLG. **Publications:** Newly Cataloged Books in the East Asiatic Library, monthly. **Special Catalogs:** Book Catalog, 1968, first supplement, 1973; Asami Library, 1969.

★15907★
UNIVERSITY OF CALIFORNIA, BERKELEY - EDUCATION/ PSYCHOLOGY LIBRARY (Educ)
2600 Tolman Hall Phone: (415)642-4208
Berkeley, CA 94720 Barbara Kornstein, Libn.
Founded: 1924. **Staff:** Prof 3; Other 5. **Subjects:** Education, psychology, and allied subjects. **Special Collections:** Children's and young adult collection. **Holdings:** 114,000 volumes; 297,000 microforms; ERIC microfiche. **Subscriptions:** 1842 journals and other serials. **Services:** Interlibrary loan (through 307 General Library); copying; library open to the public. **Computerized Information Services:** DIALOG Information Services, BRS Information Technologies, NLM. **Remarks:** An alternate telephone number is 642-2475. **Staff:** Sonya Kaufman, Hd., Ref.Serv..

★15908★
UNIVERSITY OF CALIFORNIA, BERKELEY - ENTOMOLOGY LIBRARY (Biol Sci)
Wellman Hall, Rm. 210 Phone: (415)642-2030
Berkeley, CA 94720 Nancy Axelrod, Hd.
Founded: 1943. **Staff:** 1. **Subjects:** Entomology, parasitology, helminthology, biological control, insect pathology, and allied subjects. **Holdings:** 14,737 volumes; 17,050 pamphlets and reprints; 4 sound recordings. **Subscriptions:** 324 journals and other serials. **Services:** Interlibrary loan (through 307 General Library); copying; library open to the public for reference use with restricted circulation.

★15909★
UNIVERSITY OF CALIFORNIA, BERKELEY - ENVIRONMENTAL DESIGN LIBRARY (Art, Plan)
210 Wurster Hall Phone: (415)642-4818
Berkeley, CA 94720 Elizabeth Byrne, Libn.
Founded: 1964. **Staff:** Prof 3; Other 4. **Subjects:** Architecture, city and regional planning, landscape architecture. **Special Collections:** Beatrix Jones Farrand Collection (early and rare landscape architectural history). **Holdings:** 160,000 volumes; 9600 microforms. **Subscriptions:** 1400 journals and other serials. **Services:** Interlibrary loan (through 307 General Library); copying; library open to the public for reference use with restricted circulation. **Computerized Information Services:** DIALOG Information Services, RLIN. Performs searches on fee basis.

★15910★
UNIVERSITY OF CALIFORNIA, BERKELEY - EXTENSION MEDIA CENTER (Aud-Vis)
2176 Shattuck Ave. Phone: (415)642-0460
Berkeley, CA 94704 Olga Knight, Dir.
Founded: 1915. **Staff:** Prof 2; Other 14. **Subjects:** Anthropology, sciences, social studies and social issues, futures studies, education, arts. **Special Collections:** Documentaries; anthropology; education; ecology; ethnic studies; film studies; women. **Holdings:** 4000 films in rental collection; 350 films and videotapes for sale. **Services:** Film rental and preview before purchase; center open to the public; rental film distribution limited to continental U.S. **Automated Operations:** Computerized cataloging and film reservation system. **Networks/Consortia:** Member of Educational Film Library Association, Consortium of University Film Centers (CUFC). **Publications:** Brochures; newsletters; books; study guides. **Special Catalogs:** Rental catalogs; sales catalogs.

★15911★
UNIVERSITY OF CALIFORNIA, BERKELEY - FOREST PRODUCTS LIBRARY (Sci-Engr)
1301 S. 46th St. Phone: (415)231-9549
Richmond, CA 94804 Peter A. Evans, Libn.
Founded: 1963. **Staff:** Prof 1; Other 1. **Subjects:** Wood chemistry, pulp and paper technology, adhesives, wood preservation, timber physics, identification and anatomy of wood. **Holdings:** 8790 volumes; 4616 pamphlets; 668 microforms. **Subscriptions:** 322 journals and other serials. **Services:** Interlibrary loan (through 307 General Library); copying; SDI; library open to the public. **Computerized Information Services:** DIALOG Information Services; MELVYL (internal database). **Special Catalogs:** List of FPL staff publications, biennial.

★15912★
UNIVERSITY OF CALIFORNIA, BERKELEY - FORESTRY LIBRARY (Env-Cons, Biol Sci)
260 Mulford Hall Phone: (415)642-2936
Berkeley, CA 94720 Peter A. Evans, Libn.
Founded: 1948. **Staff:** Prof 1; Other 2. **Subjects:** Forestry, conservation, wildlife management, and related subjects. **Special Collections:** Rudy Grah Agroforestry Collection; Metcalf-Fritz Photograph Collection (6400 photographs of western forestry, 1910-1960). **Holdings:** 30,500 volumes; 85 manuscripts; 1500 maps; microforms; 8000 unbound pamphlets. **Subscriptions:** 1355 journals and other serials. **Services:** Interlibrary loan (through 307 General Library); copying; library open to the public for reference use with restricted circulation. **Automated Operations:** Computerized public access catalog. **Computerized Information Services:** DIALOG Information Services; MELVYL, GLADIS (internal databases). Performs searches on fee basis.

★15913★
UNIVERSITY OF CALIFORNIA, BERKELEY - GIANNINI FOUNDATION OF AGRICULTURAL ECONOMICS - RESEARCH LIBRARY (Agri)
248 Giannini Hall Phone: (415)642-7121
Berkeley, CA 94720 Grace Dote, Libn.
Founded: 1930. **Staff:** Prof 1; Other 2. **Subjects:** Agriculture - economics, labor, land utilization, valuation and tenure, marketing and transportation problems, cost of production and marketing studies; agricultural economic developments in Lesser Developed Countries; water resources economics; conservation of natural resources. **Special Collections:** Federal state market news reports from most major U.S. cities, 1920-1982. **Holdings:** 19,000 volumes; 132,000 pamphlets; 3800 microforms; 140 maps. **Subscriptions:** 3000 journals and other serials. **Services:** Copying; library open to qualified researchers for reference use only. **Publications:** Economic research of interest to agriculture, triennial - to mailing list; Material Added to the Giannini Foundation Library, 10/year - by subscription.

★15914★
UNIVERSITY OF CALIFORNIA, BERKELEY - GOVERNMENT DOCUMENTS LIBRARY (Info Sci)
General Library Phone: (415)642-2568
Berkeley, CA 94720 Gary R. Peete, Hd.
Founded: 1938. **Staff:** Prof 5; Other 14. **Subjects:** U.S., state, and foreign governmental affairs and politics; economics; demography; history;

industry and commerce; international organizations. **Holdings:** 348,003 volumes; 579,444 microforms. **Subscriptions:** 17,472 journals and other serials. **Services:** Interlibrary loan (through Interlibrary Lending Division); copying; department open to the public. **Computerized Information Services:** DIALOG Information Services, BRS Information Technologies; MELVYL, GLADIS (internal databases). **Staff:** Suzanne Gold, Libn.; Jo Ann Brock, Assoc.Libn..

★15915★
UNIVERSITY OF CALIFORNIA, BERKELEY - GRADUATE SCHOOL OF JOURNALISM - LIBRARY (Info Sci)
140 North Gate Hall — Phone: (415)642-0415
Berkeley, CA 94720 — David Martinez, Hd.
Founded: 1977. **Staff:** Prof 1; Other 1. **Subjects:** Print journalism, photojournalism, broadcasting. **Special Collections:** Major authors collection (225 volumes). **Holdings:** 2525 books; 500 bound periodical volumes; 480 theses; 4 VF drawers of pamphlets; unbound periodicals; newspapers. **Subscriptions:** 75 journals and other serials; 25 newspapers. **Services:** Copying; library open to the public with restrictions.

★15916★
UNIVERSITY OF CALIFORNIA, BERKELEY - INSTITUTE OF GOVERNMENTAL STUDIES - LIBRARY (Soc Sci)
Moses Hall, Rm. 109 — Phone: (415)642-1472
Berkeley, CA 94720 — Jack Leister, Libn.
Founded: 1920. **Staff:** Prof 4; Other 8. **Subjects:** Administration, metropolitan problems, planning, finance, taxation, welfare, criminology, personnel, transportation, local government. **Holdings:** 411,175 pamphlets and documents; 20,864 microforms. **Subscriptions:** 2129 journals and other serials. **Services:** Interlibrary loan; copying; library open to the public. **Automated Operations:** Computerized cataloging. **Computerized Information Services:** OCLC; OnTyme Electronic Message Network Service (electronic mail service). **Networks/Consortia:** Member of CLASS. **Staff:** Terry Dean, Libn.; Ronald Heckart, Libn.; Marc Levin, Libn..

★15917★
UNIVERSITY OF CALIFORNIA, BERKELEY - INSTITUTE OF INDUSTRIAL RELATIONS - LABOR OCCUPATIONAL HEALTH PROGRAM LIBRARY (Bus-Fin, Med)
2521 Channing Way — Phone: (415)642-5507
Berkeley, CA 94720 — Susan J. Salisbury, Lib.Asst.
Staff: 1. **Subjects:** Chemical and physical occupational hazards, medical and industrial hygiene, standards and regulations, workers' compensation and education. **Special Collections:** Papers and pamphlets on occupational health topics; resource center for information on the hazards of video display terminals; special files on indoor air quality; new technology; hazardous waste; workers' compensation; AIDS in the Workplace. **Holdings:** 2200 books; 180 unbound periodicals; newspaper clipping file. **Subscriptions:** 50 journals and other serials; 110 newspapers. **Services:** Copying; library open to the public for reference use only. **Publications:** Labor Occupational Health Program Monitor (newsletter), bimonthly - by subscription; Getting the Facts (guidebook on setting up a health and safety library, includes an extensive occupational health bibliography) - available on request. **Special Indexes:** Occupational health and safety and labor-related issues index (card).

★15918★
UNIVERSITY OF CALIFORNIA, BERKELEY - INSTITUTE OF INDUSTRIAL RELATIONS - LIBRARY (Soc Sci, Bus-Fin)
2521 Channing Way, Rm. 110 — Phone: (415)642-1705
Berkeley, CA 94720 — Nanette O. Sand, Libn.
Founded: 1948. **Staff:** Prof 2; Other 2. **Subjects:** Industrial relations, labor, and allied social science topics. **Special Collections:** Tenth Regional War Labor Board Collection (World War II). **Holdings:** 40,000 cataloged items; 3000 uncataloged items. **Subscriptions:** 800 journals and other serials. **Services:** Interlibrary loan; library open for reference use with restricted circulation.

★15919★
UNIVERSITY OF CALIFORNIA, BERKELEY - INSTITUTE OF INTERNATIONAL STUDIES LIBRARY (Soc Sci)
340 Stephens Hall — Phone: (415)642-3633
Berkeley, CA 94720 — Colette Myles, Hd.Libn.
Founded: 1921. **Staff:** Prof 1; Other 2. **Subjects:** International politics, international organizations, economic development, political and social change, technology and society, area studies. **Special Collections:** Current political and economic newsletters from Latin America, Africa, and the Middle East; collection of journals on Francophone Africa. **Holdings:** 12,300 volumes; 8100 pamphlets. **Subscriptions:** 250 journals and other serials; 5 newspapers. **Services:** Interlibrary loan; library open to the public.

★15920★
UNIVERSITY OF CALIFORNIA, BERKELEY - INSTITUTE OF TRANSPORTATION STUDIES LIBRARY (Trans)
412 McLaughlin Hall — Phone: (415)642-3604
Berkeley, CA 94720 — Michael Kleiber, Hd.Libn.
Founded: 1948. **Staff:** Prof 3; Other 4. **Subjects:** Transportation. **Holdings:** 121,000 volumes; 15 VF drawers of newspaper clippings; visual aids; 775 maps; 56,000 microfiche. **Subscriptions:** 2697 journals and other serials. **Services:** Interlibrary loan; copying; library open to the public for reference use only. **Automated Operations:** Computerized cataloging. **Computerized Information Services:** DIALOG Information Services, OCLC; MELVYL (internal database). **Networks/Consortia:** Member of Transportation Research Services Information Network (TRISNET). **Publications:** Recent Transportation Literature, monthly; Library References, irregular. **Special Indexes:** Index to 50,000 articles (card and online). **Staff:** Daniel Krummes, Tech.Serv.Libn.; Catherine Cortelyou, Pub.Serv.Libn..

★15921★
UNIVERSITY OF CALIFORNIA, BERKELEY - LAW LIBRARY (Law)
230 Boalt Hall — Phone: (415)642-4044
Berkeley, CA 94720 — Robert Berring, Libn.
Founded: 1907. **Staff:** Prof 16; Other 17. **Subjects:** Law - Anglo-American, foreign, international. **Special Collections:** Robbins Collection (canon and ecclesiastical law); Colby Collection (mining law); Robbins Collection (civil and medieval law). **Holdings:** 495,000 volumes; 512,166 microforms; 857 sound recordings; 175 manuscripts; 290,000 court briefs and theses. **Subscriptions:** 8105 journals and other serials. **Services:** Interlibrary loan; library open to the public for reference use only. **Computerized Information Services:** LEXIS, NEXIS, DIALOG Information Services, INNOPAC, RLIN, OCLC, INNOVACQ Library System, WESTLAW. **Networks/Consortia:** Member of RLG. **Remarks:** The Graduate Theological Union Library works cooperatively with the Canon Law Collection. **Also Known As:** Garret W. McEnerney Law Library.

UNIVERSITY OF CALIFORNIA, BERKELEY - LAWRENCE BERKELEY LABORATORY
See: Lawrence Berkeley Laboratory (7703)

★15922★
UNIVERSITY OF CALIFORNIA, BERKELEY - LIBRARY SCHOOL LIBRARY (Info Sci)
2 South Hall — Phone: (415)642-2253
Berkeley, CA 94720 — Virginia Pratt, Libn.
Founded: 1946. **Staff:** Prof 1; Other 2. **Subjects:** Library science and history of libraries; printing, publishing, and book trade; information storage, retrieval, policy, and services; archives and records management; bibliographical organization, theory, and methods; bibliography, history, and criticism of children's literature. **Holdings:** 46,321 volumes; 1920 microforms; 4609 pamphlets; 500 sound recordings. **Subscriptions:** 1712 journals and other serials. **Services:** Interlibrary loan (through 307 General Library); copying; library open to the public. **Publications:** Selected Additions to the Library School Library, bimonthly - free.

★15923★
UNIVERSITY OF CALIFORNIA, BERKELEY - MAP ROOM (Geog-Map)
137 General Library — Phone: (415)642-4940
Berkeley, CA 94720 — Philip Hoehn, Libn.
Founded: 1917. **Staff:** Prof 1; Other 2. **Subjects:** Worldwide maps, national and regional atlases. **Holdings:** 3224 volumes; 279,672 maps; 33,368 aerial photographs; 818 pamphlets; 29,707 microforms. **Subscriptions:** 150 journals and other serials. **Services:** Interlibrary loan (through Interlibrary Lending Service); copying; room open to the public. **Automated Operations:** Computerized public access catalog and cataloging. **Networks/Consortia:** Member of RLG.

★15924★
UNIVERSITY OF CALIFORNIA, BERKELEY - MUSIC LIBRARY (Mus)
240 Morrison Hall — Phone: (415)642-2623
Berkeley, CA 94720 — John H. Roberts, Hd.
Founded: 1947. **Staff:** Prof 4; Other 4. **Subjects:** History of Western music; history of opera; 18th century instrumental music; contemporary American and European music; ethnomusicology; Afro-American, Indic, Indonesian, and Japanese music; historiography of music. **Special Collections:** Connick and Romberg Opera Collections (10,000 scores); music manuscripts of the 11th-15th centuries (1200 titles); music manuscripts of the 20th century (200 titles); Chambers Campanology Collection; archival collections (60 collections); Cortot Opera Collection (400 scores); Italian instrumental

music (1000 manuscripts); opera libretti (5000). **Holdings:** 128,570 volumes; 37,401 sound recordings; 5191 early music manuscripts; 8139 microforms; 6459 pamphlets; 565 slides. **Subscriptions:** 1651 journals and other serials. **Services:** Interlibrary loan (through 307 General Library); copying; library open to the public for reference use; circulation available to users with valid borrower's cards. **Automated Operations:** Computerized cataloging. **Computerized Information Services:** RLIN; internal database. **Networks/Consortia:** Member of RLG. **Publications:** Cum Notis Variorum (newsletter), 10/year. **Special Catalogs:** Duckles and Elmer Thematic Catalog of a Manuscript Collection of Italian Instrumental Music of the 18th Century, 1963; Early Music Printing in Music Library. **Staff:** Ann P. Basart; Keith Stetson; Leah Emdy; Elisabeth Aurelle; Linda Foy; Ruth Tucker.

★15925★
UNIVERSITY OF CALIFORNIA, BERKELEY - NATIVE AMERICAN STUDIES LIBRARY (Area-Ethnic)
3415 Dwinelle Hall — Phone: (415)642-2793
Berkeley, CA 94720 — Rosalie McKay-Want, Libn.
Staff: 3. **Subjects:** Native Americans. **Special Collections:** Annual Reports of the Commissioner of Indian Affairs, 1849-1949; Survey of the Conditions of the Indians of the U.S., 1929-1944; Records of the Bureau of Indian Affairs, Record Group 75: Indian Census, 1885-1941; Harvard University Peabody Museum papers and memoirs, 1896-1957; Indian Rights Association papers, 1864-1973; Bureau of American Ethnology annual reports and bulletins; Indian Claims Commission reports; water rights; special collection on California Indians. **Holdings:** 30,000 cataloged items; 7800 monographs; dissertations on microfilm; 150 phonograph records; 100 cassettes; 67 reel-to-reel tapes; 90 videotapes; newsclipping files. **Subscriptions:** 200 Indian newsletters and journals. **Services:** Library open to the public for reference use only, circulation available for University of California students, faculty, and staff.

★15926★
UNIVERSITY OF CALIFORNIA, BERKELEY - NATURAL RESOURCES LIBRARY (Env-Cons, Agri)
40 Giannini Hall — Phone: (415)642-4493
Berkeley, CA 94720 — Norma Kobzina, Libn.
Founded: 1963. **Staff:** Prof 2; Other 3. **Subjects:** Agriculture, environmental sciences, pest management, nutrition. **Special Collections:** Holl Collection of Cookbooks. **Holdings:** 111,939 volumes; 6032 pamphlets; 745 microforms. **Subscriptions:** 3816 journals and other serials. **Services:** Interlibrary loan (through 307 General Library); copying; library open to public for reference use with restricted circulation. **Computerized Information Services:** DIALOG Information Services, BRS Information Technologies, NTIS, RLIN, OCLC. **Special Indexes:** California Index - Publications of the California Agricultural Experiment Station (card).

★15927★
UNIVERSITY OF CALIFORNIA, BERKELEY - OPTOMETRY LIBRARY (Med)
490 Minor Hall — Phone: (415)642-1020
Berkeley, CA 94720 — Alison Howard, Hd.
Founded: 1949. **Staff:** Prof 1; Other 1. **Subjects:** Optometry, physiological optics, ophthalmology. **Holdings:** 8041 volumes; 668 pamphlets; 414 microforms; 251 sound recordings; 3300 slides; 120 video recordings; 30 motion pictures. **Subscriptions:** 188 journals and other serials. **Services:** Interlibrary loan (through 307 General Library); copying; library open to the public for reference use only. **Computerized Information Services:** DIALOG Information Services, BRS Information Technologies. **Publications:** Acquisition lists, monthly - to local and related libraries.

★15928★
UNIVERSITY OF CALIFORNIA, BERKELEY - PHYSICS LIBRARY (Sci-Engr)
Berkeley, CA 94720 — Phone: (415)642-3122
Camille Wanat, Hd.
Founded: 1948. **Staff:** Prof 1; Other 3. **Subjects:** Physics and allied sciences. **Holdings:** 37,739 volumes; 1429 microforms; 358 pamphlets; 20 sound recordings. **Subscriptions:** 463 journals and other serials. **Services:** Interlibrary loan (through 307 Main Library); copying; library open to the public. **Automated Operations:** Computerized public access catalog, cataloging, and acquisitions. **Computerized Information Services:** DIALOG Information Services, STN International, BRS Information Technologies; MELVYL (internal database). Performs searches on fee basis. **Networks/Consortia:** Member of RLG. **Publications:** Acquisitions List, monthly.

★15929★
UNIVERSITY OF CALIFORNIA, BERKELEY - PROGRAM IN POPULATION RESEARCH - LIBRARY (Soc Sci)
2234 Piedmont Ave. — Phone: (415)642-9800
Berkeley, CA 94720 — Magali Barbieri, Lib.Asst.
Founded: 1978. **Subjects:** Demography - historical, statistical, mathematical, ethnographic, economic. **Holdings:** 2000 volumes. **Services:** Library open to the public for reference use only. **Computerized Information Services:** Internal database.

★15930★
UNIVERSITY OF CALIFORNIA, BERKELEY - PUBLIC HEALTH LIBRARY (Med)
42 Earl Warren Hall — Phone: (415)642-2511
Berkeley, CA 94720 — Thomas J. Alexander, Libn.
Founded: 1947. **Staff:** Prof 6; Other 6. **Subjects:** Public health, epidemiology, biostatistics, hospital administration, environmental health, maternal and child health, biomedical science (laboratory), occupational health, toxicology. **Holdings:** 80,121 volumes; 10,000 pamphlets; 1100 microforms. **Subscriptions:** 2151 journals and other serials. **Services:** Interlibrary loan (through 307 General Library); copying; library open to the public for reference use only. **Computerized Information Services:** DIALOG Information Services, BRS Information Technologies, Pergamon ORBIT InfoLine, Inc., NLM, CAS ONLINE. Performs searches on fee basis. **Staff:** Patricia Stewart, Ref.Libn.; Charleen Kubota, Ref.Libn.; Sharon Brunzel, Ref.Libn.; Juta Savage, Ref.Libn.; Beth Sibley, Ref.Libn.; Cris Campbell, Asst.Hd..

★15931★
UNIVERSITY OF CALIFORNIA, BERKELEY - SCIENCE & MATHEMATICS EDUCATION LIBRARY (Educ, Sci-Engr)
Lawrence Hall of Science
Centennial Dr. — Phone: (415)642-1334
Berkeley, CA 94720 — Ann M. Jensen, Libn.
Founded: 1970. **Staff:** Prof 1. **Subjects:** Teaching aids in math, science, and environmental education; teacher education; curriculum development; juvenile and adult science, math, and environmental education trade books. **Holdings:** 8000 volumes. **Subscriptions:** 60 journals and other serials. **Services:** Copying; library open to the public.

★15932★
UNIVERSITY OF CALIFORNIA, BERKELEY - SEBASTIAN S. KRESGE ENGINEERING LIBRARY (Sci-Engr, Comp Sci)
Stephen D. Bechtel Engineering Center — Phone: (415)642-3339
Berkeley, CA 94720 — Camille Wanat, Act.Hd.
Staff: Prof 3; Other 6. **Subjects:** Engineering - civil, mineral, mechanical, nuclear, electrical, industrial; computer science; operations research; naval architecture; materials science; mining and metallurgy. **Special Collections:** IHS industry standard reports. **Holdings:** 133,372 books; 550,000 technical reports on paper and in microform. **Subscriptions:** 4600 journals and other serials. **Services:** Interlibrary loan (through 307 General Library); copying; library open to the public for reference use only. **Automated Operations:** Computerized cataloging and acquisitions. **Computerized Information Services:** DIALOG Information Services, RLIN, OCLC; GLADIS, MELVYL (internal databases). Performs searches on fee basis. Contact Person: Diane Brown, Ref./Database Serv.Libn., 642-3532.

★15933★
UNIVERSITY OF CALIFORNIA, BERKELEY - SOCIAL WELFARE LIBRARY (Soc Sci)
227 Haviland Hall — Phone: (415)642-4432
Berkeley, CA 94720 — Lora L. Graham, Supv.
Founded: 1963. **Staff:** 2. **Subjects:** Social welfare. **Holdings:** 20,702 volumes; 1095 pamphlets; 9 microforms. **Subscriptions:** 265 journals and other serials. **Services:** Interlibrary loan (through 307 General Library); copying; library open to the public for reference use only. **Staff:** Geraldine Scalzo, Libn..

★15934★
UNIVERSITY OF CALIFORNIA, BERKELEY - SOUTH/ SOUTHEAST ASIA LIBRARY SERVICE (Area-Ethnic)
438 General Library — Phone: (415)642-3095
Berkeley, CA 94720 — Peter Ananda, Libn.
Staff: Prof 2; Other 3. **Subjects:** South and Southeast Asia - history, political science, language and literature (especially strong in Hindi, Urdu, Tamil, Sanskrit, Nepal, Indonesian, Malay, Thai, and Vietnamese), art and art history, sociology, education, philosophy and religion, anthropology, geography. **Special Collections:** Ghadar Party Collection; Nepal Collection; Thai Collection; modern Hindi, Indonesian, and Malay literature; government publications on India and Indonesia. **Holdings:**

305,000 books; 62,000 bound periodical volumes; 5500 other cataloged items; 2500 dissertations; 1000 reels of microfilm; pamphlets; manuscripts; videotapes; sound recordings; maps; monographs. **Subscriptions:** 1550 journals and other serials; 75 newspapers. **Services:** Interlibrary loan; copying; service open to the public. **Automated Operations:** Computerized cataloging, acquisitions, and serials. **Computerized Information Services:** DIALOG Information Services, OCLC, BRS Information Technologies, RLIN; GLADIS (internal database). Performs searches on fee basis. **Special Catalogs:** Catalog of South Asia by language; catalog of Southeast Asia by country (both on cards). **Staff:** Kenneth R. Logan, Asst.Hd..

★15935★
UNIVERSITY OF CALIFORNIA, BERKELEY - STATE DATA PROGRAM LIBRARY (Soc Sci)
Survey Research Center
2538 Channing Way
Berkeley, CA 94720 Phone: (415)642-6571
Founded: 1958. **Staff:** Prof 2; Other 2. **Subjects:** Sociology, political science, psychology, survey research methods, statistics, opinion polls, U.S. Census, economics, health, vital statistics. **Special Collections:** Unpublished reports on social science, topics employing survey research methods. **Holdings:** 1000 volumes; 2000 studies on computer tapes; questionnaires, interview forms, codebooks, and data sets of past U.S. and foreign surveys; news releases of Gallup, Harris, L.A. Times, and California polls. **Subscriptions:** 40 journals and other serials. **Services:** Copying; magnetic tape reproduction of data sets from past surveys; library open to the public for reference use only. **Computerized Information Services:** BITNET (electronic mail service). **Publications:** State Data Program Research Reports. **Special Catalogs:** Catalog of available material, annual - by subscription. **Staff:** Ilona Einowski, Data Archv.; Ann Gerken, Data Archv..

★15936★
UNIVERSITY OF CALIFORNIA, BERKELEY - UNIVERSITY EXTENSION - CONTINUING EDUCATION OF THE BAR - LIBRARY (Law)
2300 Shattuck Ave. Phone: (415)642-5343
Berkeley, CA 94704 Virginia Polak, Libn.
Founded: 1960. **Staff:** Prof 1; Other 2. **Subjects:** Law. **Holdings:** 15,000 volumes. **Subscriptions:** 221 journals and other serials; 7 newspapers. **Services:** Interlibrary loan; library; not open to the public. **Publications:** Recent Acquisitions, bimonthly - for internal distribution only.

★15937★
UNIVERSITY OF CALIFORNIA, BERKELEY - UNIVERSITY HERBARIUM - LIBRARY (Biol Sci)
Department of Botany Phone: (415)642-2465
Berkeley, CA 94720 Thomas Duncan, Dir.
Subjects: Botany. **Special Collections:** History of the University Herbarium, 1870s to present (field books kept by collectors; correspondence; transactions information; photographs of persons and events related to the Herbarium). **Holdings:** 100 linear feet of archival materials. **Services:** Copying; library open to the public during business hours.

★15938★
UNIVERSITY OF CALIFORNIA, BERKELEY - WATER RESOURCES CENTER ARCHIVES (Env-Cons)
410 O'Brien Hall Phone: (415)642-2666
Berkeley, CA 94720 Gerald J. Giefer, Libn.
Founded: 1956. **Staff:** Prof 1; Other 2. **Subjects:** Water as a natural resource, water resources development and management, municipal and industrial water uses and problems, reclamation and irrigation, flood control, waste disposal, coastal engineering, water quality, water law. **Special Collections:** Ocean engineering (20,000 pieces); manuscript collection of papers of men prominent in western water development (4290). **Holdings:** 102,840 volumes; 5188 maps; 1104 microforms; 7985 manuscripts. **Subscriptions:** 1800 journals and other serials. **Services:** Interlibrary loan; copying; archives open to the public. **Automated Operations:** Computerized cataloging. **Computerized Information Services:** OCLC, DIALOG Information Services. Performs searches on fee basis. **Publications:** Selected Recent Accessions, bimonthly; Archives series (monographs), irregular; list of other publications - available upon request.

★15939★
UNIVERSITY OF CALIFORNIA, DAVIS - AGRICULTURAL ECONOMICS BRANCH LIBRARY (Agri)
Voorhies Hall Phone: (916)752-1540
Davis, CA 95616 Susan Casement, Hd.
Founded: 1950. **Staff:** Prof 1; Other 2. **Subjects:** Agricultural economics; agricultural business; land, resource, and consumer economics; international agriculture. **Holdings:** 7036 volumes; 245,977 pamphlets. **Services:** Copying; library open to the public for reference use only.

★15940★
UNIVERSITY OF CALIFORNIA, DAVIS - INSTITUTE OF GOVERNMENTAL AFFAIRS - LIBRARY (Soc Sci, Plan)
Davis, CA 95616 Phone: (916)752-2045
Jean Stratford, Hd.Libn.
Founded: 1962. **Staff:** Prof 1; Other 2. **Subjects:** Macroeconomics; public policy; East Asian business and economics; administration; planning - city, regional, state; politics, political parties, elections, and campaign literature. **Holdings:** 5000 books; 140,000 clippings; 96,000 other cataloged items. **Subscriptions:** 750 journals and other serials. **Services:** Interlibrary loan; library open to researchers, students, and public. **Automated Operations:** Computerized cataloging and circulation. **Computerized Information Services:** DIALOG Information Services, BRS Information Technologies; Dialcom Inc. (electronic mail service). **Publications:** Accessions list, monthly - university distribution.

★15941★
UNIVERSITY OF CALIFORNIA, DAVIS - LOREN D. CARLSON HEALTH SCIENCES LIBRARY (Med)
Davis, CA 95616 Phone: (916)752-1214
Jo Anne Boorkman, Hd.Libn.
Founded: 1966. **Staff:** Prof 9; Other 30. **Subjects:** Medicine, veterinary medicine, primatology. **Special Collections:** Veterinary historical collection. **Holdings:** 48,425 books; 148,275 bound periodical volumes; 12,412 microforms; 4069 foreign veterinary theses; 477 AV programs; 5285 government documents. **Subscriptions:** 4221 journals and other serials. **Services:** Interlibrary loan; copying; SDI; library open to the public with fee card. **Automated Operations:** Computerized cataloging and circulation. **Computerized Information Services:** NLM, BRS Information Technologies, DIALOG Information Services, STN International, VETNET; OnTyme Electronic Message Network Service (electronic mail service). Performs searches on fee basis. **Networks/Consortia:** Member of Pacific Southwest Regional Medical Library Service. **Publications:** HSL News, bimonthly - to library clientele. **Staff:** David C. Anderson, Tech.Serv.Libn.; Carolyn Kopper, Hd.Ref.Serv.; Rebecca Davis, Coord. Online Serv.; Judy Welsh, Ref.Libn.; Karleen Darr, Hd.Cat.Serv..

★15942★
UNIVERSITY OF CALIFORNIA, DAVIS - MEDICAL CENTER LIBRARY (Med)
4301 X St., Rm. 1005 Phone: (916)453-3529
Sacramento, CA 95817 Terri L. Malmgren, Hd.Libn.
Staff: Prof 2; Other 4. **Subjects:** Medicine, nursing, and allied health sciences. **Holdings:** 9000 books; 13,934 bound periodical volumes; 4707 AV programs. **Subscriptions:** 783 journals and other serials. **Services:** Copying; library open to the public for reference use only. **Computerized Information Services:** MEDLINE, DIALOG Information Services; OnTyme Electronic Message Network Service (electronic mail service). **Networks/Consortia:** Member of Mountain Valley Library System, Pacific Southwest Regional Medical Library Service, Sacramento Area Health Sciences Librarians Group (SAHSL). **Publications:** Monthly Newsletter/Acquisitions List - for internal distribution only. **Staff:** Dena Sehr, Asst.Libn..

★15943★
UNIVERSITY OF CALIFORNIA, DAVIS - MICHAEL AND MARGARET B. HARRISON WESTERN RESEARCH CENTER (Hist)
Department of Special Collections
Shields Library Phone: (916)752-1621
Davis, CA 95616 Michael Harrison, Dir.
Founded: 1981. **Staff:** Prof 1. **Subjects:** History and development of the trans-Mississippi West, mid-19th century to present; American Indians; ethnic studies; military, local, and economic history; sociology; folklore; exploration and travel; geography; religious studies, especially the Catholic and Mormon churches; literature; art and architecture; history of printing. **Special Collections:** Books from Western fine presses; correspondence with 20th century artists, writers, and enthusiasts of the American West; original works of art. **Holdings:** 15,000 volumes. **Services:** Center open to the public by appointment only.

★15944★
UNIVERSITY OF CALIFORNIA, DAVIS - PHYSICAL SCIENCES LIBRARY (Sci-Engr)
University Library Phone: (916)752-1627
Davis, CA 95616 Marlene Tebo, Hd.Libn.
Founded: 1971. **Staff:** Prof 5; Other 8. **Subjects:** Chemistry, engineering, physics, geology, mathematics, statistics. **Special Collections:** Depository for DOE documents and selected NASA documents. **Holdings:** 126,463 books; 95,987 bound periodical volumes; 812,030 DOE and NASA microforms and Nuclear Regulatory Commission dockets; 9223 maps; 119,643 additional microforms; 31,629 research reports; 1430 vertical files. **Subscriptions:** 4869 journals and other serials. **Services:** Interlibrary loan; copying; library open to the public. **Automated Operations:** Computerized public access catalog, cataloging, and circulation. **Computerized Information Services:** DIALOG Information Services, Pergamon ORBIT InfoLine, Inc., BRS Information Technologies, STN International. **Networks/Consortia:** Member of Center for Research Libraries (CRL) Consortia, RLG. **Staff:** Johanna Ross, Libn.; Glee Willis, Assoc.Libn.; Edward Jestes, Libn.; Carol LaRussa, Asst.Libn..

★15945★
UNIVERSITY OF CALIFORNIA, DAVIS - SCHOOL OF LAW - LAW LIBRARY (Law)
Davis, CA 95616 Phone: (916)752-3322
Mortimer D. Schwartz, Law Libn.
Founded: 1963. **Staff:** Prof 5; Other 13. **Subjects:** Law - U.S., California, international, comparative, and foreign; common law countries. **Special Collections:** Depository for federal and California documents. **Holdings:** 225,000 volumes; 55,000 volumes in microform. **Subscriptions:** 5300 journals and other serials. **Services:** Interlibrary loan; copying; library open to the public. **Computerized Information Services:** LEXIS, RLIN, WESTLAW; MELVYL (internal database). **Staff:** Alfred J. Lewis, Assoc. Law Libn.; Judy C. Janes, Asst. Law Libn..

★15946★
UNIVERSITY OF CALIFORNIA, DAVIS - TOXICOLOGY DOCUMENTATION CENTER (Env-Cons)
Davis, CA 95616 Phone: (916)752-2587
Dr. Ming-Yu Li, Doc.Spec.
Founded: 1966. **Staff:** Prof 1; Other 2. **Subjects:** Pesticides, environmental pollutants, toxic metals, PCBs, air and water pollutants, food additives and toxicants, hazardous wastes management. **Special Collections:** Pesticide chemical and subject files. **Holdings:** 5000 books; 3500 bound periodical volumes; 65,000 classified abstract cards; 36,000 items on pesticides in VF drawers; 41,000 items in subject files on environmental pollutants, toxic metals and elements, hazardous substances, and waste management. **Subscriptions:** 100 journals and other serials. **Services:** Center open to the public for reference use only with special permission. **Computerized Information Services:** NLM, BRS Information Technologies, DIALOG Information Services, STN International, Chemical Information Systems, Inc. (CIS); MELVYL, Pesticide Data Bank (internal databases). **Publications:** Chlorinated Hydrocarbon Pesticides, 1974-1978.

★15947★
UNIVERSITY OF CALIFORNIA, DAVIS - UNIVERSITY LIBRARIES - SPECIAL COLLECTIONS (Agri, Biol Sci, Hum)
Davis, CA 95616 Phone: (916)752-1621
Donald Kunitz, Hd., Spec.Coll.
Special Collections: American literature (18th, 19th, and 20th centuries); agricultural technology (450,000 pieces); alternative energy (126,500 pieces); animal science (137,500 pieces); apiculture (55,000 archival records and ephemera); Avant-Garde Poetry: Gary Snyder Papers (17,000 pieces), Steve Sanfield Papers (6500 pieces); botany; brewing and fermentation; California artists and architecture (9300 pieces); California citrus industry-advertising art (3600 pieces); California historical manuscripts-pioneering and mining (6500 pieces); California promotional materials (2600 pieces); contemporary issues (14,200 pieces); English history, literature, and religion (16th-20th centuries); enology, viticulture, and wine (363,000 archival records and ephemera); Ferry-Morse Archives (5900 pieces); fine printing (1000 volumes); foods and food science and industry (2400 archive boxes); performing arts (180,000 pieces); plant culture and pomology (27,500 archival records, nursery catalogs, photographs, and ephemera); radical groups (13,800 pamphlets). **Holdings:** 25,000 volumes. **Services:** Interlibrary loan; copying; collections open to the public. **Automated Operations:** Computerized cataloging. **Computerized Information Services:** MELVYL (internal database). **Networks/Consortia:** Member of RLG. **Staff:** John Skarstad, Archv..

★15948★
UNIVERSITY OF CALIFORNIA, DAVIS - WOMEN'S RESOURCES & RESEARCH CENTER - LIBRARY (Soc Sci)
10 Lower Freeborn Hall Phone: (916)752-3373
Davis, CA 95616 Joy Fergoda, Libn.
Staff: 1. **Subjects:** Women's issues, concerns, and research. **Special Collections:** Native and Pioneer Women in Yolo and Solano Counties, California (oral history collection; 28 tapes; 2 photograph albums). **Holdings:** 4000 books; 6500 vertical file materials; 600 audiotapes. **Subscriptions:** 130 journals and other serials; 14 newspapers. **Services:** Copying; library open to the public for reference use only.

★15949★
UNIVERSITY OF CALIFORNIA, IRVINE - BIOLOGICAL SCIENCES LIBRARY (Biol Sci)
Irvine, CA 92717 Phone: (714)856-6730
Margaret Aguirre, Lib.Asst. IV
Staff: 7. **Subjects:** Biological sciences. **Holdings:** 26,000 volumes. **Subscriptions:** 1100 journals and other serials. **Services:** Interlibrary loan; copying; library open to the public with restrictions. **Automated Operations:** Computerized serials. **Remarks:** A branch of the Biomedical Library. An alternate telephone number is 856-7515.

★15950★
UNIVERSITY OF CALIFORNIA, IRVINE - BIOMEDICAL LIBRARY (Med)
Box 19556 Phone: (714)856-6652
Irvine, CA 92713 Cynthia Butler, Act.Biomed.Libn.
Founded: 1969. **Staff:** Prof 7; Other 10. **Subjects:** Medicine. **Special Collections:** Bibliotheca Neurologica Courville (special book collection featuring aspects of medical history and research in neurology). **Holdings:** 135,000 volumes; 5485 audio cassettes; 475 microfiche; pamphlet file. **Subscriptions:** 2086 journals and other serials. **Services:** Interlibrary loan; copying; SDI; library open to the public. **Automated Operations:** Computerized cataloging, serials, and circulation. **Computerized Information Services:** MEDLINE, BRS Information Technologies, DIALOG Information Services; OnTyme Electronic Message Network Service (electronic mail service). Performs searches on fee basis. **Networks/Consortia:** Member of Nursing Information Consortium of Orange County (NICOC), Pacific Southwest Regional Medical Library Service. **Special Catalogs:** Catalog of Works in the Neurological Sciences Collected by Cyril Brian Courville, M.D., Representative of Clinical Neurology, Neuroanatomy, and Neuropathology with Particular Reference to Head Trauma (book); Serial Holdings, 1980, with periodic updates (book). **Staff:** Herbert Ahn, Ref.Libn.; Rochelle Clary, Sr.Ref.Libn.; Judith Bube, Acq.Libn.; Stephen Clancy, Ref.Libn.; Joyce Loepprich, Ser.Libn.; Jae Hwi Myong, Cat.Libn..

★15951★
UNIVERSITY OF CALIFORNIA, IRVINE - INSTITUTE OF TRANSPORTATION STUDIES - INFORMATION CENTER (Trans)
Irvine, CA 92717 Phone: (714)856-5985
Lynn Sirignano, Libn.
Staff: Prof 1. **Subjects:** Urban transportation. **Holdings:** 10,000 books and reports; 800 bound periodical volumes; 6700 NTIS technical reports on microfiche; 600 dissertations. **Subscriptions:** 55 journals and other serials. **Services:** Interlibrary loan; SDI; center open to the public. **Computerized Information Services:** DIALOG Information Services. **Networks/Consortia:** Member of Transportation Research Services Information Network (TRISNET).

★15952★
UNIVERSITY OF CALIFORNIA, IRVINE - MEDICAL CENTER LIBRARY (Med)
101 City Dr., S. Phone: (714)634-5585
Orange, CA 92668 Susan Russell, Hd.Libn.
Staff: Prof 2; Other 5. **Subjects:** Clinical medicine. **Holdings:** 28,000 volumes; 4 VF drawers; 10 filmstrips; 100 slide and cassette programs; 130 videotapes; 200 software diskettes. **Subscriptions:** 825 journals and other serials. **Services:** Interlibrary loan; copying; SDI; library open to the public. **Automated Operations:** Computerized serials and circulation. **Computerized Information Services:** DIALOG Information Services, Pergamon ORBIT InfoLine, Inc., BRS Information Technologies, MEDLINE. **Networks/Consortia:** Member of Nursing Information Consortium of Orange County (NICOC). **Remarks:** The Medical Center Library is a branch of the Biomedical Library.

★15953★
UNIVERSITY OF CALIFORNIA, IRVINE - UNIVERSITY LIBRARY - DEPARTMENT OF SPECIAL COLLECTIONS (Hum, Hist)
Box 19557 Phone: (714)856-7227
Irvine, CA 92713 Roger B. Berry, Hd., Spec.Coll.
Founded: 1965. **Staff:** Prof 4; Other 2. **Subjects:** Californiana, dance, literary criticism and theory, 16th-18th century French literature, British naval history, orchids, book illustration. **Special Collections:** Meadows Collection of California history (5000 volumes); Menninger Collection in Horticulture (1800 volumes); Rene Wellek Collection of the History of Criticism (4000 volumes); Hans Waldmuller Thomas Mann Collection (2000 volumes); contemporary small press poetry collection (6000 titles); 20th century political pamphlets (2500 titles); books and manuscripts of Ross Macdonald and Kathleen Raine. **Holdings:** 53,000 books; 1500 bound periodical volumes; 103,000 manuscripts; 300 maps; 12,000 photographs. **Subscriptions:** 25 journals and other serials. **Services:** Copying (limited); department open to qualified researchers. **Automated Operations:** Computerized cataloging. **Staff:** Sylvester E. Klinicke, Spec.Coll.Cat.; Eddie Yeghiayan, Cur., Lit. Theory/Criticism Colls.; Sharon G. Pugsley, Reg.Hist.Mss.Libn..

★15954★
UNIVERSITY OF CALIFORNIA, LOS ANGELES - AFRICAN STUDIES CENTER - LIBRARY
10244 Bunche Hall
Los Angeles, CA 90024
Founded: 1959. **Staff:** 1. **Subjects:** Africa. **Holdings:** 100 bound periodical volumes; 100 pamphlets; 160 monographs; 75 bibliographies. **Remarks:** Presently inactive.

★15955★
UNIVERSITY OF CALIFORNIA, LOS ANGELES - AMERICAN INDIAN STUDIES CENTER - LIBRARY (Area-Ethnic)
3220 Campbell Hall Phone: (213)825-4591
Los Angeles, CA 90024-1548 Velma S. Salabiye, Libn.
Staff: Prof 1; Other 1. **Subjects:** American Indians - government relations, history, literature, art, language; Indians in California; works of Indian authorship. **Special Collections:** Dissertations and theses by and about American Indians; Indian newspapers and journals. **Holdings:** 6500 volumes; 381 reels of microfilm; 4805 pamphlets. **Subscriptions:** 150 serials. **Services:** Copying; library open to the public with restrictions.

★15956★
UNIVERSITY OF CALIFORNIA, LOS ANGELES - ARCHITECTURE & URBAN PLANNING LIBRARY (Art, Plan)
1302 Architecture Bldg. Phone: (213)825-2747
Los Angeles, CA 90024-1467 Anne M. Hartmere, Libn.
Staff: Prof 1; Other 2. **Subjects:** Architecture, urban planning. **Holdings:** 25,441 volumes; 60 reels of microfilm; 136 microfiche; 4 sound recordings; 173 maps. **Subscriptions:** 750 journals and other serials. **Services:** Interlibrary loan; copying; library open to the public. **Automated Operations:** Computerized cataloging, acquisitions, and serials. **Computerized Information Services:** Internal database.

★15957★
UNIVERSITY OF CALIFORNIA, LOS ANGELES - ART DEPARTMENT - VISUAL RESOURCE COLLECTION & SERVICES (Art)
3239 Dickson Art Center
405 Hilgard Ave. Phone: (213)825-3725
Los Angeles, CA 90024 David K. Ziegler, Slide Cur./Musm.Sci.
Founded: 1958. **Staff:** Prof 3; Other 7. **Subjects:** Painting, sculpture, applied art, and architecture - European, Islamic, Japanese, Indian, American, Chinese, African; Pre-Columbian, Oceanic, and American Indian art; contemporary art forms. **Special Collections:** The Burton Holmes Collection (hand-tinted lantern slides, 1886-1937; 19,000) **Holdings:** 260,000 slides. **Services:** Collection not open to the public. **Automated Operations:** Computerized cataloging and acquisitions. **Computerized Information Services:** Internal database. **Special Indexes:** Artists and architects index to slide collection and manuscript index by title and location (both punched cards). **Staff:** Susan Rosenfeld, Asst. Slide Cur.; Ron Reimers, Photo..

★15958★
UNIVERSITY OF CALIFORNIA, LOS ANGELES - ART LIBRARY (Art)
2250 Dickson Art Center Phone: (213)825-3817
Los Angeles, CA 90024 Joyce Pellerano Ludmer, Art Libn.
Founded: 1952. **Staff:** Prof 2; Other 5. **Subjects:** Art, and architectural history, design. **Special Collections:** Judith A. Hoffberg Collection of Bookworks and Artists' Publications (2500 volumes). **Holdings:** 91,371 volumes; 166 VF drawers of uncataloged serials, clippings, museum catalogs, one-person exhibition catalogs, and announcements; 65 manuscripts; 655 reels of microfilm; 11,000 microfiche; 75,000 pamphlets; 350,000 pictorial items. **Subscriptions:** 3100 journals and other serials. **Services:** Interlibrary loan; copying; library open to the public for reference use only. **Automated Operations:** Computerized cataloging, acquisitions, and serials. **Computerized Information Services:** BRS Information Technologies, OCLC; ORION, MELVYL (internal databases). **Special Indexes:** Princeton Index of Christian Art; Decimal Index to the Art of the Low Countries (DIAL); Index of Jewish Art; Marburger Index. **Staff:** Patricia Moore, Hd., Tech.Serv./Acq.; Raymond Reece, Pub.Serv.Libn..

★15959★
UNIVERSITY OF CALIFORNIA, LOS ANGELES - ART LIBRARY - ELMER BELT LIBRARY OF VINCIANA (Art)
Dickson Art Center Phone: (213)825-3817
Los Angeles, CA 90024 Joyce Pellerano Ludmer, Art Libn.
Founded: 1971. **Subjects:** Italian Renaissance, Leonardo da Vinci, Renaissance technology. **Special Collections:** Archives of Dr. Elmer Belt and Kate Trauman Steinitz; graphics collection; Renaissance furniture and objects. **Holdings:** 9000 books; 500 unbound and bound periodical volumes; 8 VF drawers of pamphlets and clippings; 22 file boxes of clippings; documents; 19 file boxes of articles arranged by author; 30 file boxes of magazines. **Services:** Copying; library open to the public by appointment. **Special Catalogs:** Catalogue of the Incunabula in the Elmer Belt Library of Vinciana, 1971 (book). **Special Indexes:** Leonardo Subject Index (card).

★15960★
UNIVERSITY OF CALIFORNIA, LOS ANGELES - ASIAN AMERICAN STUDIES CENTER READING ROOM (Area-Ethnic)
2230 Campbell Hall Phone: (213)825-5043
Los Angeles, CA 90024-1546 Marjorie Lee, Coord.
Staff: 3. **Subjects:** Asian American studies. **Holdings:** 4000 volumes; 450 slides; 8 multimedia kits; 150 sound recordings; 2 filmstrips; 10 maps; 160 manuscripts; 3000 pamphlets; 60 government documents; 5 video recordings. **Subscriptions:** 30 journals and other serials; 25 newspapers. **Services:** Room open to the public. **Publications:** Asian American Library Resources at University of California, Los Angeles - available upon request.

★15961★
UNIVERSITY OF CALIFORNIA, LOS ANGELES - BRAIN INFORMATION SERVICE (Med)
Center for Health Sciences, No. 43-367 Phone: (213)825-3417
Los Angeles, CA 90024 Michael H. Chase, Dir.
Founded: 1964. **Staff:** Prof 1. **Subjects:** Neurosciences, alcohol and driving, sleep. **Holdings:** Figures not available. **Services:** Service open to researchers. **Publications:** Sleep Research, annual; Alcohol, Drugs and Driving, quarterly.

★15962★
UNIVERSITY OF CALIFORNIA, LOS ANGELES - CENTER FOR AFRO-AMERICAN STUDIES - LIBRARY (Area-Ethnic)
3111 Campbell Hall
405 Hilgard Ave. Phone: (213)825-6060
Los Angeles, CA 90024-1545 Claudia Mitchell-Kernan, Dir.
Founded: 1969. **Staff:** Prof 1; Other 4. **Subjects:** Afro-American studies. **Special Collections:** Black history photograph collection (250 items). **Holdings:** 4200 books; 80 bound periodical volumes; 550 VF items; 150 newsletters; 500 35mm slides; 260 photographs; 53 videotapes; 300 audio cassettes; 1000 pamphlets. **Subscriptions:** 62 journals and other serials; 6 newspapers. **Services:** Copying; library open to the public. **Publications:** Afro-American Library Resources at UCLA, 1980; Graduate Research in Afro-American Studies, 1942-1980. **Staff:** Jerry Wright, Libn..

★15963★
UNIVERSITY OF CALIFORNIA, LOS ANGELES - CENTER FOR INTERNATIONAL AND STRATEGIC AFFAIRS (CISA) - LIBRARY (Mil)
11383 Bunche Hall Phone: (213)825-0604
Los Angeles, CA 90024-1486 Brett Henry, Prog.Asst.
Founded: 1978. **Staff:** 1. **Subjects:** Arms control, nuclear strategy and proliferation, international and regional security, U.S.-Soviet relations. **Special Collections:** NTIS reports (Soviet journals in translation); Current News (U.S. Air Force publication); Rand Corporation documents. **Holdings:** 2500 books; 200 monographs and reports. **Subscriptions:** 50 journals and other serials; 10 newspapers. **Services:** Library open to the public for reference use only. **Computerized Information Services:** ORION

★15964★
UNIVERSITY OF CALIFORNIA, LOS ANGELES - CHEMISTRY LIBRARY (Sci-Engr)
4238 Young Hall Phone: (213)825-3342
Los Angeles, CA 90024-1569 Marion C. Peters, Hd.Libn.
Founded: 1947. **Staff:** Prof 1; Other 2. **Subjects:** Chemistry - organic, inorganic, analytical, physical; biochemistry. **Special Collections:** Morgan Memorial Collection (history of chemistry). **Holdings:** 59,591 volumes; 1275 reels of microfilm; 37,720 microcards; U.S. chemical patents, 1952 to present, in microform. **Subscriptions:** 794 journals and other serials. **Services:** Interlibrary loan; copying; SDI; library open to the public. **Automated Operations:** Computerized cataloging, acquisitions, and serials. **Computerized Information Services:** DIALOG Information Services, BRS Information Technologies, CAS ONLINE, Institute for Scientific Information (ISI); ORION, MELVYL (internal databases); BITNET (electronic mail service). Performs searches on fee basis.

★15965★
UNIVERSITY OF CALIFORNIA, LOS ANGELES - CHICANO STUDIES RESEARCH LIBRARY (Area-Ethnic)
1112 Campbell Hall
405 Hilgard Ave. Phone: (213)206-6052
Los Angeles, CA 90024-1544 Richard Chabran, Assoc.Libn./Coord.
Founded: 1969. **Staff:** Prof 1; Other 2. **Subjects:** Immigration, labor, higher education, school desegregation, Raza women, Chicano literature, U.S.-Mexico relations. **Special Collections:** Ron Lopez papers; Latino Community Development Archive; Casa Collection; Mexico-U.S. Relations Archive; Magdalena Mora Archive; Jose Ortiz papers; Grace Montanas Davis Papers. **Holdings:** 8150 books; 200 bound periodical volumes; 1100 manuscripts; 1680 theses and dissertations; 51 16mm films; 5100 clippings and pamphlets; 100 student papers; 658 reels of microfilm; 136 posters; 3 multimedia kits; 319 pictorial items; 333 sound recordings; 140 cassettes; 54 audiotapes; 8 filmstrips; 50 motion pictures; 800 volumes of newspapers; 22 realia; 30 maps; 106 video recordings; 335 slides. **Subscriptions:** 30 journals and other serials; 20 newspapers. **Services:** Interlibrary loan; copying; library open to the public for reference use only. **Automated Operations:** Computerized cataloging. **Computerized Information Services:** ORION (internal database). **Publications:** Early Childhood Education: A Selected Bibliography (1972); The Chicana: A Comprehensive Bibliographic Study (1976); Quien Sabe A Preliminary List of Chicano Reference Materials (1981).

★15966★
UNIVERSITY OF CALIFORNIA, LOS ANGELES - COMPUTER SCIENCE DEPARTMENT - ARCHIVES (Comp Sci)
3440 Boelter Hall Phone: (213)825-4317
Los Angeles, CA 90024-1596 Doris Sublette, Libn.
Staff: Prof 1. **Subjects:** Computer science. **Special Collections:** Institute of Electrical and Electronics Engineers Repository Collection. **Holdings:** 3000 books; 181 bound periodical volumes; 10,000 technical reports; 3000 dissertations, theses, and microfiche. **Subscriptions:** 150 journals. **Services:** Interlibrary loan; archives not open to the public. **Automated Operations:** Computerized circulation. **Publications:** CSD Newsletter, monthly.

★15967★
UNIVERSITY OF CALIFORNIA, LOS ANGELES - DEPARTMENT OF SPECIAL COLLECTIONS (Hist, Hum)
University Research Library, Fl. A Phone: (213)825-4988
Los Angeles, CA 90024-1575 David Zeidberg, Hd.
Founded: 1946. **Staff:** Prof 5; Other 16. **Subjects:** Californiana; motion pictures; radio; television; dance; blacks in entertainment and literature; Japanese in America; history of photography; folklore, including broadside ballads, songsters, hymnals, American almanacs; university archives; popular culture, including pulp magazines and comic books. **Special Collections:** Michael Sadleir Collection of 19th century English fiction; Ahmanson-Murphy Collections of Aldines and Early Italian Printing; Sir Maurice Holmes Collection of Captain Cook; English and American auction catalogs; early children's books; Bodoni imprints; Spinoza Collection; 1500 manuscript collections, including papers of William Starke Rosecrans, Franz Werfel, Henry Stevens, John Houseman, Ralph Bunche; oral history interviews; Near Eastern manuscripts (Arabic, Turkish, Persian, Armenian); books and manuscripts of Henry Miller, Norman Douglas, Aldous Huxley, Edward Gordon Craig, Gertrude Stein, Maria Edgeworth, Raymond Chandler. **Holdings:** 171,570 volumes; 19.4 million manuscripts; 632 volumes of newspapers; 238,409 pieces of ephemera and clippings; 46,715 pamphlets; 663,680 pictorial items; 2188 historical maps; 12,344 reels of microfilm; 3203 sound recordings; 4719 slides. **Subscriptions:** 319 journals and other serials. **Services:** Copying (limited); department open to the public for reference use only. **Automated Operations:** Computerized cataloging, acquisitions, serials, and circulation. **Computerized Information Services:** OCLC; ORION (internal database). Performs searches free of charge. **Publications:** Bibliographies of Henry Miller, Kenneth Rexroth, and Lawrence Durrell. **Remarks:** An alternate telephone number is 825-4879. **Staff:** James Davis, Rare Bks.Libn.; Anne Caiger, Mss.Libn.; Philip Bantin, Univ.Archv.; Dale Treleven, Dir., Oral Hist.Prog..

★15968★
UNIVERSITY OF CALIFORNIA, LOS ANGELES - EDUCATION & PSYCHOLOGY LIBRARY (Educ, Med)
390 Powell Library Bldg. Phone: (213)825-4081
Los Angeles, CA 90024-1516 Barbara Duke, Hd.
Founded: 1965. **Staff:** Prof 4; Other 5. **Subjects:** Education; psychology - general, experimental, cognitive, abnormal, social, developmental; English as a second language; applied linguistics. **Holdings:** 147,000 volumes; 560,000 microfiche; 328 audiotapes; 2062 reels of microfilm; ERIC microfiche. **Subscriptions:** 2800 journals and other serials. **Services:** Interlibrary loan; copying; library open to the public. **Automated Operations:** Computerized cataloging, acquisitions, and serials. **Computerized Information Services:** DIALOG Information Services, BRS Information Technologies. **Publications:** Recent Acquisitions: A Selected List; INFO 390 (newsletter). **Staff:** San Oak Kim, Coll.Dev./Ref.; Diane Pezzullo, Coll.Dev./Ref.; Joan Kaplowiltz, Pub.Serv./Ref.; Cathy Brown, Ref.Serv./Ref..

★15969★
UNIVERSITY OF CALIFORNIA, LOS ANGELES - ENGINEERING & MATHEMATICAL SCIENCES LIBRARY (Sci-Engr)
8270 Boelter Hall Phone: (213)825-3982
Los Angeles, CA 90024-1600 Kate S. Herzog, Hd.
Founded: 1945. **Staff:** Prof 4; Other 7. **Subjects:** Astronomy, atmospheric science, mathematics, computer science, engineering. **Special Collections:** Technical Reports Collection (including depository items from DOE, NASA, NTIS, Rand Corporation). **Holdings:** 208,000 volumes; 3499 reels of microfilm; 1.7 million technical reports on microfiche; 70,000 hard copy technical reports; **Subscriptions:** 4500 journals and other serials. **Services:** Interlibrary loan; copying; library open to the public. **Automated Operations:** Computerized cataloging, acquisitions, and serials. **Computerized Information Services:** DIALOG Information Services, BRS Information Technologies; ORION (internal database); BITNET, DDN Network Information Center (electronic mail services). Performs searches on fee basis. Contact Person: Aggi Raeder, Ref.Libn., 825-2649. **Staff:** Bruce E. Pelz, Ref.Libn.; Karen L. Andrews, Ref.Libn.; Charlene Silverstein, Hd., Circ.; Germaine Nagaraja, Hd., Acq..

★15970★
UNIVERSITY OF CALIFORNIA, LOS ANGELES - ENGLISH READING ROOM (Hum)
1120 Rolfe Hall Phone: (213)825-4511
Los Angeles, CA 90024-1528 Tim Strawn, Hd.
Founded: 1950. **Staff:** 1. **Subjects:** English and American literature, literary criticism, composition. **Special Collections:** Josephine Miles Poetry Collection (contemporary poetry; 700 volumes). **Holdings:** 23,590 volumes. **Subscriptions:** 149 journals and other serials. **Services:** Copying; library open to the public.

★15971★
UNIVERSITY OF CALIFORNIA, LOS ANGELES - ENVIRONMENTAL SCIENCE AND ENGINEERING - LIBRARY
2066 Engineering I Bldg.
Los Angeles, CA 90024
Founded: 1970. **Subjects:** Environmental sciences, air quality, energy sources, ecology, urban studies. **Holdings:** 2000 technical, governmental,

and environmental impact reports and monographs; 500 periodicals. **Remarks:** Presently inactive.

★15972★
UNIVERSITY OF CALIFORNIA, LOS ANGELES - GEOLOGY-GEOPHYSICS LIBRARY (Sci-Engr)
Geology Bldg., Rm. 4697 Phone: (213)825-1055
Los Angeles, CA 90024-1567 Michael M. Noga, Hd.
Founded: 1940. **Staff:** Prof 1; Other 2. **Subjects:** Geology, geophysics, planetary sciences, paleontology, geochemistry, space physics. **Special Collections:** California geology; UCLA geology theses and dissertations. **Holdings:** 95,732 volumes; 189 reels of microfilm; 16,651 microfiche; 1048 maps; 12,592 microcards; 3 globes. **Subscriptions:** 2175 journals and other serials. **Services:** Interlibrary loan; copying; library open to the public. **Automated Operations:** Computerized acquisitions and serials. **Computerized Information Services:** DIALOG Information Services, STN International, BRS Information Technologies; MELVYL, ORION (internal databases).

★15973★
UNIVERSITY OF CALIFORNIA, LOS ANGELES - HOUSING, REAL ESTATE & URBAN LAND STUDIES PROGRAM COLLECTION (Plan)
405 Hilgard
Graduate School of Management 4274 Phone: (213)825-3977
Los Angeles, CA 90024-1481 Frank G. Mittelbach, Dir./Prof.
Founded: 1952. **Staff:** Prof 2; Other 2. **Subjects:** Transportation, housing and real estate, land use, environment, planning, urban sociology. **Special Collections:** Reprints; journals; articles; Council of Planning Libraries bibliographies 1-176; Housing and Urban Development (miscellaneous reports). **Holdings:** 3450 books; 30,500 pamphlets; 41 maps; 6000 government pamphlets and census materials; clippings; 1 volume of bound newspapers. **Subscriptions:** 178 journals and other serials. **Services:** Interlibrary loan; copying; collection open to the public. **Publications:** Real Estate Indicators, quarterly.

★15974★
UNIVERSITY OF CALIFORNIA, LOS ANGELES - INSTITUTE FOR SOCIAL SCIENCE RESEARCH - SOCIAL SCIENCE DATA ARCHIVE (Soc Sci)
405 Hilgard Ave. Phone: (213)825-0711
Los Angeles, CA 90024-1484 Elizabeth Stephenson, Data Archv.
Staff: Prof 2; Other 1. **Subjects:** Social science. **Special Collections:** California Polls; Los Angeles Metropolitan Area Surveys; National Center for Health Statistics data repository; Southern California Social Surveys. **Holdings:** 1204 volumes. **Subscriptions:** 18 serials. **Services:** Interlibrary loan; archive open to the public with restrictions. **Automated Operations:** Computerized cataloging. **Computerized Information Services:** ORION (internal database). **Publications:** ISSR, quarterly. **Special Indexes:** Index of women's studies machine-readable data files; Index of the Southern California Social Surveys.

★15975★
UNIVERSITY OF CALIFORNIA, LOS ANGELES - JOHN E. ANDERSON GRADUATE SCHOOL OF MANAGEMENT - LIBRARY (Bus-Fin)
Los Angeles, CA 90024-1460 Phone: (213)825-3138
Robert Bellanti, Hd.
Founded: 1961. **Staff:** Prof 5; Other 7. **Subjects:** All fields of management and business administration, accounting-information systems, business economics, computers and information systems, finance and investments, personnel and industrial relations, international and comparative management studies, arts management, marketing, operations research, sociotechnical systems/behavioral science, urban land economics. **Special Collections:** Robert E. Gross Collection of Rare Books in Business and Economics; James R. Pattillo Library of Banking and Finance; Dean Emeritus Neil H. Jacoby Collection; Goldsmiths'-Kress Collection of Rare Books in Business and Economics. **Holdings:** 134,340 volumes; 85,873 hardcopy annual and 10K reports of corporations; 234,807 microcards and microfiche; 988 pamphlets; 7007 reels of microfilm of journals and newspapers. **Subscriptions:** 2810 journals and other serials. **Services:** Interlibrary loan; copying; library open to the public for reference use only. **Automated Operations:** Computerized cataloging, acquisitions, and serials. **Computerized Information Services:** DIALOG Information Services, OCLC, BRS Information Technologies; ORION (internal database). Performs searches on fee basis. Contact Person: Karen Sternheim, Ref.Libn., 825-3047. **Networks/Consortia:** Member of CLASS. **Publications:** GSM Library Guides. **Staff:** Eloisa G. Yeargain, Ref.Libn.; Rita Costello, Coll.Dev./Ref.; Peter Kaatrude, Coll.Dev./Ref.; Lerleen Costa, Tech.Serv.Sect.; Arturo Esparza, Circ.Sect..

★15976★
UNIVERSITY OF CALIFORNIA, LOS ANGELES - LABORATORY OF BIOMEDICAL AND ENVIRONMENTAL SCIENCES - LIBRARY (Env-Cons, Med)
900 Veteran Ave. Phone: (213)825-8741
Los Angeles, CA 90024-1786 Janet D. Carter, Libn.
Founded: 1955. **Staff:** Prof 1; Other 1. **Subjects:** Biochemistry, nuclear medicine, environmental science, energy, cell biology. **Special Collections:** Depository for U.S. Atomic Energy Commission reports. **Holdings:** 1750 books; 7000 bound periodical volumes; 1280 government documents; 425 reels of microfilm; 100,000 reports on microfiche; 500 technical reports. **Subscriptions:** 115 journals and other serials. **Services:** Library open to the public with restrictions. **Computerized Information Services:** Integrated Technical Information System (ITIS), MEDLINE, DIALOG Information Services, Pergamon ORBIT InfoLine, Inc., BRS Information Technologies. **Publications:** Annual reports. **Remarks:** The Laboratory of Biomedical and Environmental Sciences operates under contract to the U.S. Department of Energy.

★15977★
UNIVERSITY OF CALIFORNIA, LOS ANGELES - LAW LIBRARY (Law)
School of Law Bldg.
405 Hilgard Ave. Phone: (213)825-3960
Los Angeles, CA 90024-1458 Myra Saunders, Act. Law Libn.
Founded: 1949. **Staff:** Prof 9; Other 16. **Subjects:** Law. **Special Collections:** Anglo-American legal materials; David Bernard Memorial Aviation Law Library. **Holdings:** 322,327 volumes; 151,694 microcards and microfiche; 1156 sound recordings; 42,270 government documents; 182 manuscripts; 2 maps; 1631 reels of microfilm. **Subscriptions:** 6505 journals and other serials. **Services:** Interlibrary loan; library open to the public for reference use only. **Computerized Information Services:** LEXIS, WESTLAW, Legaltrac; ORION, MELVYL (internal databases). **Staff:** Adrienne Adan, Assoc. Law Libn. for Tech.Serv..

★15978★
UNIVERSITY OF CALIFORNIA, LOS ANGELES - LOUISE DARLING BIOMEDICAL LIBRARY (Med, Biol Sci)
Center for Health Sciences Phone: (213)825-5781
Los Angeles, CA 90024-1798 Alison Bunting, Biomed.Libn.
Founded: 1947. **Staff:** Prof 15; Other 25. **Subjects:** Medicine, dentistry, nursing, public health, biology, microbiology, botany, zoology. **Special Collections:** Japanese medical books and prints; classics in ornithology and mammalogy from the Donald R. Dickey Library of Vertebrate Zoology; S. Weir Mitchell Collection (history of medical science); Dr. M.N. Beigelman Collection (classics in ophthalmology); Florence Nightingale Collection; John A. Benjamin Collection of Medical History. **Holdings:** 454,129 volumes; 42 manuscripts; 472 maps; 1176 reels of microfilm; 17,085 microfiche; 3500 sound recordings; 7592 pamphlets; 39,208 slides; 9492 pictorial items; 5 filmstrips; 5 motion pictures; 1551 video recordings; 13 videodiscs. **Subscriptions:** 4214 journals and other serials. **Services:** Interlibrary loan; copying; SDI; library open to the public. **Automated Operations:** Computerized cataloging, acquisitions, serials, and circulation. **Computerized Information Services:** NLM, BRS Information Technologies, DIALOG Information Services; ORION (internal database); OnTyme Electronic Message Network Service (electronic mail service). Performs searches on fee basis. **Publications:** Recent Acquisitions in the Biomedical Library, monthly; Serials Holdings List, annual - both for sale; UCLA Biomedical Library: Brief Guide to Its Facilities, Policies and Services, annual - free upon request. **Remarks:** Library is headquarters of the Pacific Southwest Regional Medical Library Service (PSRMLS). An alternate telephone number is 825-6098. **Staff:** Gail Yokote, Assoc.Biomed.Libn.-Pub.Serv. ; Pat L. Walter, Assoc.Biomed.Libn.-Tech.Serv.; Elaine Graham, Assoc.Dir., PSRMLS.

★15979★
UNIVERSITY OF CALIFORNIA, LOS ANGELES - MAP LIBRARY (Geog-Map)
Bunche Hall, Rm. A-253 Phone: (213)825-3526
Los Angeles, CA 90024-1468 Carlos B. Hagen-Lautrup, Hd.
Founded: 1957. **Staff:** Prof 1; Other 3. **Subjects:** Nautical and aeronautical charts, map intelligence materials, topographic maps, city plans. **Special Collections:** Latin America and Pacific Ocean materials. **Holdings:** 6857 books; 469,133 maps; 1200 technical reports; 47,757 VF of city plans and road maps; 2822 atlases; 12,330 aerial photographs; 12,033 microcards; 38 slides; 943 pictorial items. **Subscriptions:** 334 journals and other serials. **Services:** Interlibrary loan; copying; library open to the public for reference use only. **Publications:** Newsletter & Selected Acquisitions, irregular; technical reports.

★15980★
UNIVERSITY OF CALIFORNIA, LOS ANGELES - MATHEMATICS READING ROOM (Sci-Engr)
Mathematics Science Bldg., Rm. 5379 Phone: (213)825-4930
Los Angeles, CA 90024 Sharon Marcus, Libn.
Founded: 1948. **Staff:** Prof 1; Other 2. **Subjects:** Mathematics. **Holdings:** 8650 books; 9166 bound periodical volumes; reports and reprints; preprints of faculty and students; 240 departmental dissertations. **Subscriptions:** 141 journals and other serials. **Services:** Reading room open to the public for reference use only.

★15981★
UNIVERSITY OF CALIFORNIA, LOS ANGELES - MUSIC LIBRARY (Mus)
1102 Schoenberg Hall
405 Hilgard Ave. Phone: (213)825-4881
Los Angeles, CA 90024-1490 Stephen M. Fry, Mus.Libn.
Founded: 1942. **Staff:** Prof 5; Other 4. **Subjects:** Music, musicology, ethnomusicology, music education. **Special Collections:** Ethnomusicology Archive (telephone: 825-1695); Ernst Toch Archive; Erich Zeisl Archive; Archive of Popular American Music (800,000 popular song sheets and folios; telephone: 825-1665); John Vincent Archive; Clarence V. Mader Archive; 17th and 18th century Venetian libretti (11,000); film and TV recordings and manuscript score collection. **Holdings:** 52,000 volumes; 60,000 scores; 150,000 manuscripts; 12,647 reels of microfilm; 36,874 sound recordings; 1919 slides; 42 video recordings; 366 pictorial items; 65 cartons of manuscripts and documents of American composers; 10,387 pamphlets; 115 filmstrips; 1 multimedia kit. **Subscriptions:** 1155 journals and other serials. **Services:** Interlibrary loan; copying; library open to the public. **Automated Operations:** Computerized acquisitions and text editing. **Publications:** The Full Score (newsletter), monthly; UCLA Music Library Bibliography Series, irregular; UCLA Music Library Discography Series, irregular; Guide to UCLA Music Library, annual - all free upon request. **Special Catalogs:** Exhibit catalogs - free upon request. **Special Indexes:** Tune-dex/song-dex (10,000 song cards). **Staff:** Marsha Berman, Assoc.Mus.Libn.; Gordon Theil, Asst.Mus.Libn.; Louise Spear, Ethnomusicology Archv..

★15982★
UNIVERSITY OF CALIFORNIA, LOS ANGELES - ORAL HISTORY PROGRAM LIBRARY (Hist)
136 Powell Library Phone: (213)825-4932
Los Angeles, CA 90024-1575 Dale Treleven, Dir.
Staff: Prof 4; Other 12. **Subjects:** Arts in southern California, architecture, civil liberties, printing and bookselling, politics and government, university history, Los Angeles black leadership. **Holdings:** 350 volumes of tape transcriptions. **Services:** Copying; library open to the public. **Special Catalogs:** Catalog of holdings (bound). **Staff:** Richard Candida Smith, Prin.Ed.; Alva Moore Stevenson, Adm.Asst..

★15983★
UNIVERSITY OF CALIFORNIA, LOS ANGELES - PHYSICAL SCIENCES & TECHNOLOGY LIBRARIES
8251 Boelter Hall Phone: (213)825-6515
Los Angeles, CA 90024-1600 Michael Sullivan, Hd.Libn.
Founded: 1975. **Staff:** Prof 11; Other 20. **Holdings:** 500,000 books; 1.7 million microfiche; 8492 pamphlets; 6 sound recordings; 68,246 government documents; 945 maps; 8 videotapes. **Subscriptions:** 11,177 journals and other serials. **Remarks:** Administrative unit for Chemistry, Engineering and Mathematical Sciences, Geology/Geophysics, and Physics Libraries including centralized cataloging and interlibrary loan service. **Staff:** Dorothy McGarry, Hd.Cat.; Sara Shatford Layne, Hd., ILL.

★15984★
UNIVERSITY OF CALIFORNIA, LOS ANGELES - PHYSICS LIBRARY (Sci-Engr)
213 Kinsey Hall Phone: (213)825-4792
Los Angeles, CA 90024-1500 J. Wally Pegram, Libn.
Founded: 1947. **Staff:** Prof 1; Other 2. **Subjects:** Physics - solid state, high energy and particle, plasma, condensed matter, low temperature, mathematical; elementary particles; acoustics; astrophysics and applied fields. **Special Collections:** SLAC High Energy Preprint Library (8294). **Holdings:** 41,632 volumes; 66 microforms. **Subscriptions:** 614 journals and other serials. **Services:** Interlibrary loan; copying; library open to the public for reference use only. **Automated Operations:** Computerized acquisitions and serials. **Computerized Information Services:** DIALOG Information Services, Pergamon ORBIT InfoLine, Inc., BRS Information Technologies; BITNET (electronic mail service). Performs searches on fee basis.

★15985★
UNIVERSITY OF CALIFORNIA, LOS ANGELES - PUBLIC AFFAIRS SERVICE (Soc Sci, Plan)
405 Hilgard Phone: (213)825-3135
Los Angeles, CA 90024-1575 Lauri Sebo, Hd.
Staff: Prof 6; Other 9. **Subjects:** Government, social and economic problems and development, local and regional planning, industrial relations, ethnic studies, social welfare, politics and political parties. **Holdings:** 327,284 volumes; 33 reels of microfilm; 560,968 microfiche and microcards; 23,516 pamphlets. **Subscriptions:** 16,067 serials. **Services:** Interlibrary loan; copying; service open to the public with restrictions. **Automated Operations:** Computerized acquisitions and serials. **Computerized Information Services:** DIALOG Information Services, Pergamon ORBIT InfoLine, Inc., BRS Information Technologies. Performs searches on fee basis. Contact Person: Chere Negaard, Ref.Serv.Coord.. **Staff:** Eudora Loh, Docs.Libn.; Roberta Medford, Docs.Libn.; Barbara Silvernail, Docs.Libn.; Dorothy Wells, Docs.Libn.; Claudia Baldwin, Asst.Docs.Libn..

★15986★
UNIVERSITY OF CALIFORNIA, LOS ANGELES - RICHARD C. RUDOLPH ORIENTAL LIBRARY (Area-Ethnic)
405 Hilgard Ave. Phone: (213)825-4836
Los Angeles, CA 90024-1575 James K.M. Cheng, Hd.
Founded: 1948. **Staff:** Prof 4; Other 10. **Subjects:** East Asia - art, archeology, history, literature, Buddhism, linguistics, political science, religion, sociology, humanities, social science (in the Chinese, Japanese, and Korean languages). **Holdings:** 270,000 volumes; 4100 reels of microfilm; 1790 microcards; 1937 newspaper volumes; 719 pamphlets. **Subscriptions:** 1400 journals and other serials; 45 newspapers. **Services:** Interlibrary loan; copying; library open to the public.

★15987★
UNIVERSITY OF CALIFORNIA, LOS ANGELES - THEATER ARTS LIBRARY (Theater)
22478 University Research Library Phone: (213)825-4880
Los Angeles, CA 90024-1575 Brigitte Kueppers, Hd.Libn.
Founded: 1947. **Staff:** Prof 2; Other 2. **Subjects:** Theater, film, television, radio. **Special Collections:** RKO Pictures Archive, 1929-1956 (2000 linear feet of scripts, production information and story submission files, dance and music material); Terrence O'Flaherty Collection (history of television; 200 linear feet of publicity stills and network kits); Walter Lantz Collection of Animation Cels; papers of screenwriters Waldo Scott, Michael Wilson, and Emmet Lavery. Jessen Collection (2169 stills and 901 portraits from the silent era through 1940); Twentieth Century-Fox Motion Picture Still Collection, 1950-1960 (3 million production stills; 3178 proof sheets; 658 proof sheet books; 71 keysets and 164 color transparencies); Universal Studios Keybooks (645); papers of Mark Robson, William Wyler, Allan Joslyn, Stanley Kramer; Columbia Pictures Still Collection, 1950-1960 (80,000 production stills; 188 keysets); Metro-Goldwyn-Mayer Screenplay Collection, 1924-1960 (1270 screenplays); Film Poster Collection, 1915 to present (2500 rare and early posters of American, Polish, and Czechoslovakian productions); Richard Dix Collection (5217 stills). **Holdings:** 31,000 volumes; 44,000 manuscripts; 3.2 million production stills and portraits, 1905 to present; 13,000 screenplays and television scripts; 45,000 slides; 102,000 clippings; 2500 motion picture programs; 670 film festival programs; 177,000 pamphlets; 181,000 pictorial items. **Subscriptions:** 317 journals and other serials. **Services:** Copying (limited); library open to the public. **Automated Operations:** Computerized cataloging, acquisitions, and serials. **Special Catalogs:** Motion Pictures: A Catalog of Books, Periodicals, Screen Plays, and Productions, 1 volume, 1976. **Staff:** Ray Soto, Ref.Libn..

★15988★
UNIVERSITY OF CALIFORNIA, LOS ANGELES - UCLA FILM AND TELEVISION ARCHIVES (Aud-Vis)
Melnitz Hall, Rm. 1438 Phone: (213)206-8013
Los Angeles, CA 90024 Robert Rosen, Dir.
Founded: 1965. **Staff:** Prof 19; Other 26. **Subjects:** U.S. theatrical films and broadcast television programs, theatrical newsreels, films of recognized importance in world film history, television news programs, animated films. **Special Collections:** Paramount Collection (740 prints); Twentieth Century-Fox Collection (750 prints); Warner Brothers Collection (1200 prints and negatives); Republic Pictures Collection (3000 prints and negatives); Universal Pictures Collection (100 prints); Columbia Pictures Collection (300 prints); RKO Pictures Collection (700 prints); Animated Film Study Collection (1000 prints); China Film Study Collection (100 prints); Exploitation Film Study Collection (1000 prints); Hearst Newsreel Library (15 million feet); Collection of Television Technology and Design (300 pieces); Television News and Public Affairs Collection (60,000

programs); Hallmark Hall of Fame Collection (150 programs); Alcoa Collection (150 programs); Paramount Telefilm Collection (500 prints); Jack Benny Radio and Television Collection (1200 programs); Los Angeles Area Emmy Awards Nominees and Winners, 1965 to present (2000 programs); National Emmy Awards Nominees and Winners (1000 programs). **Holdings:** 40,000 motion picture prints and negatives; 25,000 television films and tapes. **Services:** Interlibrary loan (limited); archives open to the public for scholarly and project-oriented research only. **Automated Operations:** Computerized public access catalog and cataloging. **Publications:** Film calendar, monthly; special program brochures. **Staff:** Claire Aguilar, Asst. Film Prog.; William Ault, Paper Print Presrv.; Blaine Bartell, Newsreel Presrv.; Daniel Einstein, Television Archv.; Geoffrey Gilmore, Hd., Prog.; Robert Gitt, Presrv.Supv.; Jere Guldin, Vault Mgr.; Howard Hays, Commercial Serv.Mgr.; Charles Hopkins, Motion Pict.Archv.; Eric Jerstad, Asst. Commercial Serv.Mgr.; Jane Dunbar Johnson, Cat.; Deborah Miller, Admin.Coord.; Edward Richmond, Cur.; Ronald Staley, Radio Coll.Spec.; Geoffrey Stier, Asst. to Dir.; Eleanore Tanin, Res.Ctr.Supv.; John Tirpak, Fiction Film Presrv.; Martha Yee, Cat.Supv..

★15989★
UNIVERSITY OF CALIFORNIA, LOS ANGELES - UNIVERSITY ELEMENTARY SCHOOL LIBRARY (Hum)
1017 Seeds U.E.S. Bldg. Phone: (213)825-4928
Los Angeles, CA 90024-1619 Judith Kantor, Hd.Libn.
Founded: 1920. **Staff:** Prof 1; Other 1. **Subjects:** Children's literature. **Special Collections:** Folk literature; poetry collection. **Holdings:** 17,800 books; 59 bound periodical volumes. **Subscriptions:** 43 journals and other serials. **Services:** Interlibrary loan; library open to the public with restrictions. **Automated Operations:** Computerized cataloging and acquisitions. **Staff:** Jenifer S. Abramson, Libn..

★15990★
UNIVERSITY OF CALIFORNIA, LOS ANGELES - WATER RESOURCES CENTER ARCHIVES (Env-Cons)
2081 Engineering I Phone: (213)825-7734
Los Angeles, CA 90024-1600 Beth R. Willard, Assoc.Libn.
Founded: 1967. **Staff:** Prof 1; Other 1. **Subjects:** Water - resources, reclamation, pollution, supply, quality, and economics; wastes disposal; irrigation; flood control; water law; environment; energy; soils; water-based recreation. **Holdings:** 78,900 volumes; 8500 microcards; 11,520 pamphlets. **Subscriptions:** 595 serials. **Services:** Interlibrary loan; archives open to the public with restrictions on circulation. **Computerized Information Services:** Integrated Technical Information System (ITIS).

★15991★
UNIVERSITY OF CALIFORNIA, LOS ANGELES - WAYLAND D. HAND LIBRARY OF FOLKLORE AND MYTHOLOGY (Hist)
Los Angeles, CA 90024 Phone: (213)825-4242
Staff: Prof 1; Other 2. **Subjects:** Folklore and folk literature, mythology, folk music and folk song, folklife, material culture, folk arts, ethnology. **Special Collections:** Western European folklore atlases; Ralph Steele Boggs Collection of Latin American folklore. **Holdings:** 3060 books; 867 bound periodical volumes; 173 boxes and 3 VF drawers of reprints, pamphlets, and clippings; 946 reels of microfilm; 222 cassettes; 2046 tapes; 11,000 phonograph records. **Subscriptions:** 108 journals and other serials. **Services:** Library open to visiting scholars. **Publications:** American Ethnic Bibliography; Bibliography of Games and Other Play Activities. **Special Catalogs:** Ralph Steele Boggs Collection of Latin American Folklore (card). **Remarks:** Maintained by the Center for the Study of Comparative Folklore and Mythology.

★15992★
UNIVERSITY OF CALIFORNIA, LOS ANGELES - WILLIAM ANDREWS CLARK MEMORIAL LIBRARY (Hum)
2520 Cimarron St. Phone: (213)731-8529
Los Angeles, CA 90018-2098 John Brewer, Dir.
Staff: Prof 4; Other 6. **Subjects:** English civilization, 1640-1750; Eric Gill; John Dryden; Oscar Wilde; Montana history; modern graphic arts. **Holdings:** 80,000 volumes; 14,500 manuscripts. **Services:** Copying; library open to the public for research purposes. **Computerized Information Services:** OCLC, RLIN, Eighteenth Century Short Title Catalogue (ESTC); ORION, MELVYL (internal databases). **Publications:** Seminar papers, 3-4/year; Augustan Reprint Society, 6/year - both by subscription. **Staff:** Thomas F. Wright, Libn.; John Bidwell, Ref.Libn..

★15993★
UNIVERSITY OF CALIFORNIA, RIVERSIDE - BIO-AGRICULTURAL LIBRARY (Biol Sci, Agri)
Riverside, CA 92521 Phone: (714)787-3238
Myra Russell, Hd.Libn.
Staff: Prof 4; Other 9. **Subjects:** Biochemistry, biology, biomedical sciences, citrus and desert horticulture, entomology, environmental sciences, nematology, pest management, plant pathology, plant sciences, soil sciences-agricultural engineering. **Special Collections:** Citrus Collection (citrus fruits and citrus industry in California); desert ecology; arid land research; collections on jojoba, guayule, and dates. **Holdings:** 151,000 volumes. **Subscriptions:** 2200 journals and other serials. **Services:** Interlibrary loan; copying; SDI; library open to the public. **Automated Operations:** Computerized acquisitions and circulation. **Computerized Information Services:** DIALOG Information Services, Pergamon ORBIT InfoLine, Inc., BRS Information Technologies, NLM, STN International. **Networks/Consortia:** Member of Inland Empire Academic Libraries Cooperative (IEALC), San Bernardino, Inyo, Riverside Counties United Library Services (SIRCULS).

★15994★
UNIVERSITY OF CALIFORNIA, RIVERSIDE - CALIFORNIA MUSEUM OF PHOTOGRAPHY (Art)
Riverside, CA 92521 Phone: (714)787-4787
Charles Desmarais, Dir.
Founded: 1973. **Staff:** Prof 4; Other 6. **Subjects:** Photography, art. **Special Collections:** Keystone-Mast Collection (major world events and sites, 1880-1930; 350,000 stereo photographs); University Print Collection (10,000 photographs of extraordinary artistic and historical value); Bingham Collection, 1851 to present (4000 cameras). **Services:** Copying; museum open to the public. **Computerized Information Services:** Internal database. **Publications:** CMP Bulletin, quarterly - to members; calendar, bimonthly - to members and others on request. **Staff:** Edward W. Earle, Cur., Keystone-Mast Coll.; Deborah Klochko, Cur.; Dan Meinwald, Cur. of Coll..

★15995★
UNIVERSITY OF CALIFORNIA, RIVERSIDE - DEEP CANYON DESERT RESEARCH CENTER - LIBRARY (Biol Sci)
Box 1738 Phone: (619)341-3655
Palm Desert, CA 92261 Allan Muth, Ph.D., Resident Dir.
Subjects: Desert - biology, climatology, archeology, geology; ecology; hydrology. **Special Collections:** Rare books about the desert. **Holdings:** 350 books; 392 bound periodical volumes; 240 dissertations, theses, and professional reports; maps; aerial photographs; slides. **Services:** Library open to scientists by appointment with prior approval of Resident Director.

★15996★
UNIVERSITY OF CALIFORNIA, RIVERSIDE - EDUCATION SERVICES LIBRARY (Educ)
Box 5900 Phone: (714)787-3715
Riverside, CA 92517 Peter Bliss, Hd., Educ.Serv.
Founded: 1970. **Staff:** 2. **Subjects:** Education. **Holdings:** 27,000 volumes, including textbooks, children's literature, kits with cassettes and tapes, curriculum guides, study prints, software, and educational tests. **Services:** Library open to the public. **Special Catalogs:** Children's literature collection, textbook collection, curriculum guides, nonbook materials, and test collection.

★15997★
UNIVERSITY OF CALIFORNIA, RIVERSIDE - ENGLISH DEPARTMENT LIBRARY (Hum)
Humanities Bldg. Phone: (714)787-5301
Riverside, CA 92521 Elizabeth Lang, Hd.
Founded: 1965. **Staff:** 1. **Subjects:** English literary bibliography, literary reference and criticism. **Special Collections:** Olga W. Vickery Collection of Southern Literature (100 volumes); Mortimer Proctor Memorial Collection (700 volumes). **Holdings:** 3600 volumes; 300 pamphlets; 60 recordings; 100 offprints. **Subscriptions:** 45 journals and other serials. **Services:** Library open to the university community.

★15998★
UNIVERSITY OF CALIFORNIA, RIVERSIDE - GOVERNMENT PUBLICATIONS DEPARTMENT - LIBRARY (Info Sci, Law)
Box 5900 Phone: (714)787-3226
Riverside, CA 92517 James Rothenberger, Dept.Hd.
Staff: Prof 2; Other 6. **Subjects:** U.S. and California governments, international organizations. **Special Collections:** Law Collection (National Reporter System; federal and California statutory and administrative law). **Holdings:** 30,000 volumes; 400,000 government documents; 60,000

microforms. **Services:** Interlibrary loan; copying; library open to the public. **Computerized Information Services:** DIALOG Information Services, BRS Information Technologies. Performs searches on fee basis. Contact Person: Margaret Mooney, Assoc.Libn..

★15999★
UNIVERSITY OF CALIFORNIA, RIVERSIDE - MAP SECTION - LIBRARY (Geog-Map)
Box 5900 Phone: (714)787-3226
Riverside, CA 92517 James Rothenberger, Dept.Hd.
Founded: 1963. **Staff:** Prof 1; Other 1. **Subjects:** All areas of the world with emphasis on the western hemisphere. **Special Collections:** U.S. Geological Survey topographic maps (depository); Defense Mapping Agency Topographic Center maps (depository). **Holdings:** 65,000 sheet maps; 2000 folded maps; 1500 atlases. **Subscriptions:** 10 journals and other serials. **Services:** Library open to the public. **Automated Operations:** Computerized cataloging.

★16000★
UNIVERSITY OF CALIFORNIA, RIVERSIDE - MEDIA RESOURCES (Aud-Vis)
University Library
Box 5900 Phone: (714)787-3041
Riverside, CA 92517 Jerry A. Gordon, Hd.
Staff: 3. **Subjects:** Foreign languages, film study, biomedical sciences, music, biology, history. **Holdings:** 184 16mm films; 765 video cassettes; 2500 sound recordings; 250 audio cassettes; 110 slide sets; 23 videodiscs. **Services:** Resources open to the public for reference use only. **Computerized Information Services:** Internal database. Performs searches on fee basis. Contact Person: Jim Glenn, Hd., Media Lib.. **Publications:** Media Resources Newsletter, quarterly - for internal distribution only. **Remarks:** An alternate telephone number is 787-5606.

★16001★
UNIVERSITY OF CALIFORNIA, RIVERSIDE - MUSIC LIBRARY (Mus)
Riverside, CA 92521 Phone: (714)787-3137
John W. Tanno, Assoc.Univ.Libn.
Founded: 1963. **Staff:** Prof 1; Other 2. **Subjects:** Musicology, composition and theory, organology, performance practice. **Special Collections:** Books on bells and carillons (200 titles); Niels Wilhelm Gade Collection (all editions and arrangements of his works); Oswald Jonas Memorial Archive, incorporating the Heinrich Schenker Archive; Harry and Grace James Recorded Sound Archive (15,000 78rpm phonograph records); Works Progress Administration (WPA) Southern California Music Project Collection (750 scores and parts). **Holdings:** 20,000 volumes; 18,000 scores; 11,000 phonograph records; 120 reels of microfilm. **Subscriptions:** 300 journals and other serials. **Services:** Interlibrary loan; copying; library open to the public.

★16002★
UNIVERSITY OF CALIFORNIA, RIVERSIDE - PHYSICAL SCIENCES LIBRARY (Sci-Engr)
Riverside, CA 92517 Phone: (714)787-3511
Carol S. Resco, Hd.Libn.
Founded: 1961. **Staff:** Prof 3; Other 5. **Subjects:** Chemistry, physics, energy science, geology, geophysics, physical geography, mathematics and computer science, soil and environmental science, pre-engineering studies. **Special Collections:** Weaver and Putnam Collections (geology); geologic maps (10,123); Sadtler, Coblentz, and API/MCA spectra; U.S. Geological Survey open file reports; American Society for Testing and Materials (ASTM) and American National Standards Institute (ANSI) standards. **Holdings:** 100,000 volumes; 10,000 microforms; 1000 reels of microfilm. **Subscriptions:** 1200 journals and other serials. **Services:** Interlibrary loan; copying; library open to the public. **Automated Operations:** Computerized acquisitions, serials, and circulation. **Computerized Information Services:** DIALOG Information Services, BRS Information Technologies, Chemical Information Systems, Inc. (CIS), Pergamon ORBIT InfoLine, Inc., STN International, WILSONLINE. **Networks/Consortia:** Member of Inland Empire Academic Libraries Cooperative (IEALC), San Bernardino, Inyo, Riverside Counties United Library Services (SIRCULS). **Special Catalogs:** Map catalog (online). **Staff:** Richard Vierich, Ref.Libn..

★16003★
UNIVERSITY OF CALIFORNIA, RIVERSIDE - SPECIAL COLLECTIONS (Hum)
Box 5900 Phone: (714)787-3233
Riverside, CA 92517 Clifford R. Wurfel, Hd., Spec.Coll.
Staff: Prof 3; Other 1. **Special Collections:** 20th century English literature; Ezra Pound (700 volumes); Juan Silvano Godoi Collection (45 volumes; 57 boxes); Eaton Collection of Fantasy and Science Fiction (43,000 volumes; 5600 periodicals); historical collection of children's literature (2000 volumes); Thomas Hardy Theater Collection; Skinner-Ropes Collection (7000 manuscripts, 1843-1917, including 5 Civil War diaries and extensive Californiana); Sadakichi Hartmann Collection (47 boxes); Oswald Jonas/ Heinrich Schenker Collection (71 boxes); Jack Hirschman poetry (2700 sheets of manuscripts); William Blake Collection (900 volumes); Niels Gade Collection (600 volumes); German National Socialism (5000 volumes); photography (3000 volumes); utopias (500 volumes); women (5000 volumes); history of citriculture; date growing; Paraguay (1000 volumes); B. Traven (240 volumes; 1 box of manuscripts); William Walker (75 volumes); manuscripts and papers of Robert L. Forward and Gregory Benford; university archives (1300 items; 52 tapes). **Holdings:** 52,000 books; 100 bound periodical volumes; 2500 volumes of dissertations. **Services:** Interlibrary loan; copying; collections open to the public.

★16004★
UNIVERSITY OF CALIFORNIA, SAN DIEGO - BIOMEDICAL LIBRARY (Biol Sci, Med)
La Jolla, CA 92093 Phone: (619)534-3253
Mary Horres, Libn.
Founded: 1963. **Staff:** Prof 7; Other 22. **Subjects:** Clinical and pre-clinical medicine, biology. **Holdings:** 181,985 volumes. **Subscriptions:** 3707 journals and other serials. **Services:** Interlibrary loan; copying; library open to the public. **Automated Operations:** Computerized acquisitions and serials. **Computerized Information Services:** NLM, BRS Information Technologies, OCLC, DIALOG Information Services. Performs searches on fee basis. **Networks/Consortia:** Member of Pacific Southwest Regional Medical Library Service. **Staff:** Susan Starr, Hd., Pub.Serv.; Thomas Morton, Hd., Tech.Serv..

★16005★
UNIVERSITY OF CALIFORNIA, SAN DIEGO - CENTER FOR MAGNETIC RECORDING RESEARCH - INFORMATION CENTER (Sci-Engr)
R-001 Phone: (619)534-6213
La Jolla, CA 92093 Dawn E. Talbot, Info.Mgr.
Founded: 1984. **Staff:** Prof 1; Other 1. **Subjects:** Magnetic recording technology, magnetic media, optical recording technology. **Holdings:** 650 books. **Subscriptions:** 60 journals and other serials. **Services:** Interlibrary loan; copying; SDI; center open to the public. **Automated Operations:** Computerized cataloging and acquisitions. **Computerized Information Services:** DIALOG Information Services, CAS ONLINE, NewsNet, Inc., Pergamon ORBIT InfoLine, Inc.; OnTyme Electronic Message Network Service (electronic mail service). Performs searches on fee basis. **Publications:** CMRR Information Bulletin - to sponsoring companies; CMRR Report - free upon request. **Remarks:** An alternate telephone number is 534-6199.

UNIVERSITY OF CALIFORNIA, SAN DIEGO - CENTER FOR U.S.-MEXICAN STUDIES
See: Center for U.S.-Mexican Studies (2884)

★16006★
UNIVERSITY OF CALIFORNIA, SAN DIEGO - MEDICAL CENTER LIBRARY (Med)
225 Dickinson St. Phone: (619)534-6520
San Diego, CA 92103 Christine Chapman, Hd.Libn.
Staff: Prof 2; Other 5. **Subjects:** Medicine, nursing. **Holdings:** 23,786 volumes; 9777 slides; 1517 cassettes. **Subscriptions:** 796 journals and other serials. **Services:** Interlibrary loan; copying; SDI; library open to the public. **Automated Operations:** Computerized acquisitions and serials. **Computerized Information Services:** NLM, BRS Information Technologies, DIALOG Information Services; OnTyme Electronic Message Network Service (electronic mail service). Performs searches on fee basis. **Networks/Consortia:** Member of Pacific Southwest Regional Medical Library Service. **Remarks:** Library is a branch of the Biomedical Library. **Staff:** Barbara Slater, Ref.Libn.; Jill Rowe, Br.Mgr..

★16007★
UNIVERSITY OF CALIFORNIA, SAN DIEGO - SCIENCE & ENGINEERING LIBRARY (Sci-Engr, Comp Sci)
C-075E Phone: (619)534-3257
La Jolla, CA 92093-0175 Karen Feeney, Act.Hd.
Founded: 1965. **Staff:** Prof 5; Other 9. **Subjects:** Mathematics, chemistry, physics, computer science, engineering, astronomy. **Holdings:** 153,202 volumes; 156,114 reports on microfiche. **Subscriptions:** 2492 journals and other serials. **Services:** Interlibrary loan; copying; library open to the public. **Computerized Information Services:** DIALOG Information

Services, CAS ONLINE, STN International. **Staff:** Karen Feeney, Ref.Libn.; Mara Sprain, Ref.Libn.; Sherry Willhite, Chem.Spec..

★16008★
UNIVERSITY OF CALIFORNIA, SAN DIEGO - SCRIPPS INSTITUTION OF OCEANOGRAPHY LIBRARY (Sci-Engr, Biol Sci)
C-075C — Phone: (619)534-3274
La Jolla, CA 92093-0175 — William J. Goff, Libn.
Founded: 1913. **Staff:** Prof 4; Other 15. **Subjects:** Oceanography, marine biology, geological sciences. **Special Collections:** Expedition literature; rare books; SIO archives. **Holdings:** 201,745 volumes; 56,639 maps and charts; 32,712 microforms. **Subscriptions:** 3857 journals and other serials. **Services:** Interlibrary loan; copying; library open to the public. **Automated Operations:** Computerized cataloging, acquisitions, and serials. **Computerized Information Services:** DIALOG Information Services, STN International, Aquatic Sciences and Fisheries Abstracts (ASFA), BRS Information Technologies; MELVYL (internal database). Performs searches on fee basis. Contact Person: Peter Brueggeman, Hd., Pub.Serv.. **Networks/Consortia:** Member of CLASS, OCLC Pacific Network. **Publications:** Newsletter/Acquisitions List, bimonthly; Technical Reports Accessions List, monthly; SIO Contributions, annual; Serials List, quarterly. **Special Indexes:** KWIC Index to Technical Report Collection (COM); finding aids for archival collections (online). **Staff:** Deborah Day, Archv..

★16009★
UNIVERSITY OF CALIFORNIA, SAN DIEGO - UNIVERSITY LIBRARIES (Hum, Sci-Engr, Biol Sci)
La Jolla, CA 92093 — Phone: (619)534-3336
Dorothy Gregor, Univ.Libn.
Staff: Prof 76; Other 198. **Subjects:** Marine sciences, Latin American studies, Melanesian studies, magnetic recording, medicine. **Special Collections:** Baja California Collection; Pacific voyages; Spanish Civil War; Archive for New Poetry. **Holdings:** 1.8 million volumes. **Subscriptions:** 29,586 journals and other serials. **Services:** Interlibrary loan; copying; libraries open to the public. **Automated Operations:** Computerized cataloging and serials. **Computerized Information Services:** DIALOG Information Services, OCLC, Pergamon ORBIT InfoLine, Inc., BRS Information Technologies, Association of Research Libraries (ARL). **Networks/Consortia:** Member of Center for Research Libraries (CRL) Consortia, Learning Resources Cooperative, CLASS. **Remarks:** Figures given include holdings of the Central University Library and five branch libraries. **Staff:** Phyllis S. Mirsky, Assoc.Univ.Libn.; George J. Soete, Assoc.Univ.Libn.; Mary M. Horres, Asst.Univ.Libn.; R. Bruce Miller, Asst.Univ.Libn.; Jacqueline Coolman, Asst.Univ.Libn.; Garrett Bowles, Mus.Libn.; Chris D. Ferguson, Undergraduate Libn.; M. Sharon Anderson, Doc.Dept.Libn.; Marilyn J. Wilson, Acq.Libn.; Barbara Tillett, Cat.Libn.; Brigid Welch, Ref.Libn.; Virginia Steel, Circ.Libn.; Lynda Claassen, Spec.Coll.Libn..

★16010★
UNIVERSITY OF CALIFORNIA, SAN FRANCISCO - CENTER ON DEAFNESS - LIBRARY (Soc Sci)
3333 California St., Suite 10
San Francisco, CA 94143-1208 — Phone: (415)476-4980
Subjects: Psychosocial and linguistic aspects of deafness. **Holdings:** 200 volumes. **Remarks:** TDD number is 476-7600.

★16011★
UNIVERSITY OF CALIFORNIA, SAN FRANCISCO - HASTINGS COLLEGE OF THE LAW - LEGAL INFORMATION CENTER (Law)
200 McAllister St. — Phone: (415)565-4750
San Francisco, CA 94102 — Dan F. Henke, Dir.
Founded: 1878. **Staff:** Prof 11; Other 9. **Subjects:** Law. **Special Collections:** U.S. and California Documents Depository. **Holdings:** 312,853 volumes; 140,332 volumes in microform; 2436 audio cassettes. **Subscriptions:** 3869 journals and other serials. **Services:** Interlibrary loan; copying; center open to the public. **Automated Operations:** Computerized public access catalog, cataloging, acquisitions, and serials. **Computerized Information Services:** WESTLAW, OCLC, LEXIS, NEXIS, DIALOG Information Services, RLIN, ELSS (Electronic Legislative Search System), BRS Information Technologies, BILLTRAK, DataTimes, Dow Jones News/Retrieval, Finsbury Data Services, Ltd., Information for Public Affairs, Inc. (IPA), VU/TEXT Information Services, Western Library Network (WLN), WILSONLINE; Innovacq, STAR (internal databases); ALANET, ABA/net (electronic mail services). **Networks/Consortia:** Member of Bay Area Library and Information System (BALIS), CLASS. **Publications:** Hastings Library Newsletter, 2/year; New Acquisitions, monthly - both available on request; Hastings Library Guide, annual. **Remarks:** An alternate telephone number is 565-4761. **Staff:** Gail Winson, Assoc. Law Libn.; Linda Weir, Pub.Serv.Libn.; Janice Kelly, Hd.Ref.Libn.; Anne Bock, Circ.Libn.; Mary Glennon, Tech.Serv.Libn.; Laura Peritore, Ref./CA Docs.Libn.; Veronica Maclay, U.S. Docs.Libn.; Rebecca Holland, Ser.Libn./Hd.Cat.; Leigh Donley, Cat.; Dorothy Mackay-Collins, Cur./Archv..

★16012★
UNIVERSITY OF CALIFORNIA, SAN FRANCISCO - LIBRARY (Med)
257 Medical Sciences Bldg.
Parnassus Ave. — Phone: (415)476-2334
San Francisco, CA 94143-0840 — David Bishop, Univ.Libn.
Founded: 1864. **Staff:** Prof 19; Other 52. **Subjects:** Health sciences, medicine, dentistry, pharmacy, nursing. **Special Collections:** History of Health Sciences; Oriental Medicine; homeopathy; Osleriana; California medicine; university archives. **Holdings:** 641,780 volumes. **Subscriptions:** 4059 journals and other serials. **Services:** Interlibrary loan; copying; library open to public with restricted circulation. **Automated Operations:** Computerized cataloging, acquisitions, and serials. **Computerized Information Services:** MEDLINE, OCLC, BRS Information Technologies, DIALOG Information Services; MELVYL (internal database); OnTyme Electronic Message Network Service, BITNET (electronic mail services). Performs searches on fee basis. Contact Person: Elisabeth Bell, Hd., Ref.Div., 476-8253. **Networks/Consortia:** Member of Pacific Southwest Regional Medical Library Service, San Francisco Consortium. **Publications:** Journals Title List. **Staff:** Richard S. Cooper, Assoc.Univ.Libn.; Mary P. Barr, Hd., Pub.Serv.; Steven I. Tarczy, Hd., Tech.Serv..

★16013★
UNIVERSITY OF CALIFORNIA, SANTA BARBARA - ARTS LIBRARY (Art, Mus)
Santa Barbara, CA 93106 — Phone: (805)961-3613
William R. Treese, Hd./Art Libn.
Staff: Prof 4; Other 9. **Subjects:** Art, music, history of photography. **Special Collections:** Art Exhibition Catalog Collection (60,000); Archive of Art Auction Catalogs (42,000); Archive of Recorded Vocal Music (22,000 78rpm discs). **Holdings:** 120,000 volumes; 26,000 phonograph records; 11,500 microforms; 68 videotapes; 2000 audiotapes. **Subscriptions:** 750 journals and other serials. **Services:** Interlibrary loan; copying; library open to the public. **Automated Operations:** Computerized cataloging and circulation. **Computerized Information Services:** DIALOG Information Services, BRS Information Technologies, OCLC, RLIN; internal database. **Networks/Consortia:** Member of RLG. **Special Indexes:** Art Exhibition Catalog Subject Index (1978); catalog of Archive of Recorded Vocal Music (online). **Staff:** Martin Silver, Asst.Hd./Mus.Libn.; Susan Bower, Asst.Mus.Libn.; Lyn Korenic, Asst. Arts Libn..

★16014★
UNIVERSITY OF CALIFORNIA, SANTA BARBARA - BLACK STUDIES LIBRARY UNIT (Area-Ethnic)
Santa Barbara, CA 93106 — Phone: (805)961-2922
Sylvia Y. Curtis, Act.Libn.
Founded: 1971. **Staff:** Prof 1; Other 1. **Subjects:** Afro-American studies, African area studies, Caribbean studies, black literature and history. **Holdings:** 5500 books; 5 VF drawers of newspaper clippings; 5 VF drawers of pamphlets; catalogs from black colleges and universities. **Subscriptions:** 101 journals and other serials. **Services:** Interlibrary loan; SDI; library open to the public. **Automated Operations:** Computerized cataloging, acquisitions, serials, and circulation. **Computerized Information Services:** DIALOG Information Services, BRS Information Technologies, Pergamon ORBIT InfoLine, Inc. **Publications:** The AfroAmerican, quarterly - to staff, patrons, and on request.

★16015★
UNIVERSITY OF CALIFORNIA, SANTA BARBARA - DEPARTMENT OF SPECIAL COLLECTIONS (Rare Book, Hum)
University Library — Phone: (805)961-3420
Santa Barbara, CA 93106 — Christian Brun, Dept.Hd.
Staff: Prof 1; Other 2. **Subjects:** Printing; Abraham Lincoln; Civil War; antislavery; U.S. westward expansion; Aldous Huxley; Samuel Beckett; Henry James; Robinson Jeffers; Charles Bukowski; W. Somerset Maugham; avant-garde literature; illustrated books; birth control; circus; Californiana; Bibles; Colombian novels; Mauritius; Spanish Inquisition; French revolutionary pamphlets; Christmas books; press books; trade catalogs; evolution; Edmund Burke; Pear Tree Press; Rudge Press; Mme. Lotte Lehman Archive; Pearl Chase Collection; Donald Culross Peattie Collection; George Tebbetts Collection; Stuart L. Bernath Collection;

Morris Ernst Banned Book Collection. **Holdings:** 100,000 books; 385,000 manuscripts; 2400 theses; 1600 reels of microfilm; 12,000 microcards. **Subscriptions:** 63 journals and other serials. **Services:** Interlibrary loan; copying; collections open to qualified individuals.

UNIVERSITY OF CALIFORNIA, SANTA BARBARA - DEPARTMENT OF SPECIAL COLLECTIONS - THE AMERICAN INSTITUTE OF WINE AND FOOD
See: The American Institute of Wine and Food (561)

★16016★
UNIVERSITY OF CALIFORNIA, SANTA BARBARA - GOVERNMENT PUBLICATIONS DEPARTMENT (Info Sci)
University Library Phone: (805)961-2863
Santa Barbara, CA 93106 Herbert Linville, Hd.
Staff: Prof 5; Other 6. **Subjects:** Federal, state, and international government publications. **Holdings:** 585,000 hard copy government publications; 280,000 government publications in microform. **Subscriptions:** 5900 journals and other serials. **Services:** Interlibrary loan; copying; department open to the public. **Staff:** Gary Peete, Foreign Docs.Libn.; Lucia Snowhill, U.S. Docs.Libn.; Janet Martorana, Local Docs.Libn..

★16017★
UNIVERSITY OF CALIFORNIA, SANTA BARBARA - LIBRARY - CHICANO STUDIES COLLECTION (Area-Ethnic)
University Library Phone: (805)961-2756
Santa Barbara, CA 93106 Sal Guerena, Assoc.Libn./Unit Hd.
Staff: Prof 1; Other 1. **Subjects:** Chicano literature and history, social sciences, bibliography, bilingual education. **Special Collections:** Chicano Studies Serial Collection (300 titles on microfilm); Chicano Studies Literary Videotape Series (38 videotapes). **Holdings:** 6500 books; 200 bound periodical volumes; 6500 files of pamphlets and clippings; 200 posters. **Subscriptions:** 65 journals and other serials. **Services:** Interlibrary loan; copying; collection open to the public for reference use only. **Automated Operations:** Computerized cataloging. **Computerized Information Services:** OCLC. **Networks/Consortia:** Member of Center for Research Libraries (CRL) Consortia, Chicano Information Management Consortium of California. **Publications:** Chicanos: A Checklist of Current Materials, biennial - free upon request; list of additional publications - free upon request. **Also Known As:** Coleccion Tloque Nahuaque.

★16018★
UNIVERSITY OF CALIFORNIA, SANTA BARBARA - MAP AND IMAGERY LABORATORY - LIBRARY (Geog-Map)
Santa Barbara, CA 93106 Phone: (805)961-2779
Larry Carver, Dept.Hd.
Founded: 1967. **Staff:** Prof 1; Other 5. **Subjects:** Remotely sensed imagery, topographic maps, physical and biological science mapping, land use mapping, nautical charts. **Special Collections:** U.S. Geological Survey historic backfiles of topographic maps; Corps of Engineers historic backfiles of topographic mapping. **Holdings:** 2 million frames of satellite imagery; 2400 atlases and gazetteers; 305,000 maps; EROS microforms. **Services:** Interlibrary loan (limited); training on cartographic/remote sensing interpretation/information transfer lab equipment by prior arrangement. **Computerized Information Services:** Earth Resources Observation System (EROS), OCLC; internal database. **Networks/Consortia:** Member of Total Interlibrary Exchange (TIE). **Special Catalogs:** EROS Data Center's MicroCatalog.

★16019★
UNIVERSITY OF CALIFORNIA, SANTA BARBARA - ORIENTAL COLLECTION (Area-Ethnic)
University Library Phone: (805)961-2365
Santa Barbara, CA 93106 Henry H. Tai, Oriental Libn.
Staff: Prof 2; Other 1. **Subjects:** East Asia - humanities, social sciences. **Holdings:** 65,000 books; 9000 bound periodical volumes; 360 microforms. **Subscriptions:** 297 journals and other serials; 17 newspapers. **Services:** Interlibrary loan; collection open to the public. **Computerized Information Services:** OCLC. **Networks/Consortia:** Member of RLG. **Staff:** Sung In Ch'oe, Asst.Libn..

★16020★
UNIVERSITY OF CALIFORNIA, SANTA BARBARA - SCIENCES-ENGINEERING LIBRARY (Biol Sci, Sci-Engr)
Santa Barbara, CA 93106 Phone: (805)961-2765
Robert Sivers, Hd.
Founded: 1966. **Staff:** Prof 6; Other 9. **Subjects:** Geography; physical sciences; life sciences; geology; military science; marine science; mathematics; computer science; linguistics; speech and communication; environmental studies; engineering - chemical, nuclear, electrical, mechanical. **Special Collections:** Oil Spill Information Center Archives (contains materials of the Santa Barbara oil spill of January 24, 1969; 3000 documents). **Holdings:** 375,000 volumes; 625,000 technical and contract reports; 3500 pamphlets; 2000 uncataloged items. **Subscriptions:** 5900 journals and other serials. **Services:** Interlibrary loan; copying; library open to the public. **Computerized Information Services:** DIALOG Information Services, Pergamon ORBIT InfoLine, Inc., BRS Information Technologies, MEDLINE, Chemical Information Systems, Inc. (CIS), RLIN, NLM, Earth Resources Observation System (EROS); Instructional Improvement Information Data Base (internal database). **Publications:** Laboratory workbook on information resources in science and engineering; literature guides in chemistry, geography, botany, ergonomics and general biology - distributed through office of University Librarian. **Staff:** Norma Claussen, Engr./Math Libn.; Virginia Weiser, Life Sci.Libn.; Albert Krichmar, Linguistics/Commun.Libn.; Al Hodina, Physics Libn.; Charles Huber, Chem.Libn..

★16021★
UNIVERSITY OF CALIFORNIA, SANTA CRUZ - DEAN E. MC HENRY LIBRARY (Hist, Hum)
Santa Cruz, CA 95064 Phone: (408)429-2801
Allan J. Dyson, Univ.Libn.
Staff: Prof 29; Other 83. **Subjects:** Literature, local history. **Special Collections:** Thomas Carlyle; Kenneth Patchen; Gregory Bateson; Robert Heinlein; South Pacific; Santa Cruz local history including pre-statehood and Mexican local government archives; Trianon Press Archive; fine printing; Californiana. **Holdings:** 850,049 volumes; 898,252 manuscripts; 144,316 maps; 17,535 reels of microfilm; 348,791 microfiche, 75,311 microprints; 11,632 pamphlets; 61,075 government documents; 11,755 phonograph records; 9963 audiotapes; 336 videotapes; 21 multi-media kits; 615 motion pictures; 24 filmstrips; 13,791 pictures; 170,578 slides. **Services:** Interlibrary loan; copying; library open to the public. **Automated Operations:** Computerized public access catalog, cataloging, acquisitions, and circulation. **Computerized Information Services:** DIALOG Information Services, BRS Information Technologies, OCLC; Performs searches free of charge. Contact Person: Al Eickhoff, Comp.Ref.Coord., 429-4974. **Networks/Consortia:** Member of Monterey Bay Area Cooperative Library System (MOBAC). **Special Catalogs:** Catalog of the South Pacific Collection. **Staff:** Margaret Gordon, Hd., Ref.; Rita Bottoms, Hd., Spec.Coll.; Wayne Mullin, Hd., Access Serv.; Marion Taylor, Hd., Coll.Plan..

★16022★
UNIVERSITY OF CALIFORNIA, SANTA CRUZ - MAP COLLECTION (Geog-Map)
Dean E. McHenry Library Phone: (408)429-2364
Santa Cruz, CA 95064 Stanley D. Stevens, Map Libn.
Staff: Prof 1; Other 1. **Subjects:** Cartography, aerial photography. **Special Collections:** The Hihn Archive (land ownership maps and records of Frederick Augustus Hihn, F.A. Hihn Company, Capitola-Hihn Company, Santa Cruz Water Company, and Valencia-Hihn Company); Sanborn maps on color film of Monterey Bay area cities; historical maps of Santa Cruz County and the four adjacent counties; depository library for complete topographical coverage of the United States. **Holdings:** 145,000 maps; 27,000 aerial photographs; 28,000 microfiche; 4000 Sanborn maps on film mounted into slides. **Services:** Interlibrary loan (limited); copying; collection open to the public. **Computerized Information Services:** OCLC. **Special Catalogs:** Catalog of Aerial Photos in the Map Collection of the University Library, May, 1979 to present (loose-leaf binder).

★16023★
UNIVERSITY OF CALIFORNIA, SANTA CRUZ - REGIONAL HISTORY PROJECT (Hist)
Dean E. McHenry Library Phone: (408)429-2847
Santa Cruz, CA 95064 Randall Jarrell, Dir.
Founded: 1965. **Staff:** Prof 1; Other 1. **Subjects:** California and central California Coast area: social, economic, agricultural and governmental history, transportation, principal industries. **Holdings:** Transcripts of interviews; photographs of interviewees. **Services:** Project open to researchers on request, for reference use only. **Publications:** Bibliography - available on request. **Special Indexes:** Master regional history index. **Remarks:** Transcripts are also on deposit in the Bancroft Library of University of California, Berkeley; some are available on microfilm through the New York Times Oral History Program.

★16024★
UNIVERSITY OF CALIFORNIA, SANTA CRUZ - SCIENCE LIBRARY (Biol Sci, Sci-Engr)
Santa Cruz, CA 95064 Phone: (408)429-2866
Carolyn Miller, Sci.Libn.
Founded: 1969. **Staff:** Prof 5; Other 4. **Subjects:** Astronomy, biology, chemistry, earth sciences, mathematics, physics. **Special Collections:** Lick Observatory Library (40,000 volumes; 750 serials). **Holdings:** 200,000 volumes. **Subscriptions:** 3500 journals and other serials. **Services:** Interlibrary loan; copying; library open to the public. **Automated Operations:** Computerized public access catalog and cataloging. **Computerized Information Services:** DIALOG Information Services, BRS Information Technologies, CAS ONLINE. Performs searches free of charge. **Staff:** George Keller, Sci.Ref.Libn.; Pamela Wilkes, Sci.Ref.Libn.; Robert Fessenden, Sci.Ref.Libn.; Axel Borg, Sci.Ref.Libn..

UNIVERSITY OF CENTRAL ARKANSAS - MIDSOUTH ASTRONOMICAL RESEARCH SOCIETY, INC.
See: Midsouth Astronomical Research Society, Inc. (8966)

UNIVERSITY OF CENTRAL FLORIDA - FLORIDA SOLAR ENERGY CENTER
See: Florida Solar Energy Center (5162)

UNIVERSITY OF CENTRAL FLORIDA - NAVAL TRAINING SYSTEMS CENTER
See: U.S. Navy - Naval Training Systems Center (15459)

UNIVERSITY OF CHICAGO - ARGONNE NATIONAL LABORATORY
See: Argonne National Laboratory (870)

★16025★
UNIVERSITY OF CHICAGO - ART AND ARCHITECTURE COLLECTION (Art)
Joseph Regenstein Library, Rm. 420
1100 E. 57th St. Phone: (312)702-8439
Chicago, IL 60637 Katherine Haskins, Art Bibliog.
Founded: 1938. **Staff:** Prof 1; Other 10. **Subjects:** Art and architecture - ancient through modern; history of photography. **Holdings:** 60,000 volumes. **Subscriptions:** 500 journals and other serials. **Services:** Collection open to the public with restrictions. **Computerized Information Services:** OCLC. **Networks/Consortia:** Member of Center for Research Libraries (CRL) Consortia, ILLINET. **Special Catalogs:** Union Art Catalog (includes the holdings of major Chicago art libraries, through 1980).

★16026★
UNIVERSITY OF CHICAGO - BUSINESS AND ECONOMICS COLLECTION (Bus-Fin)
Joseph Regenstein Library
1100 E. 57th St. Phone: (312)702-8716
Chicago, IL 60637 Jennette S. Rader, Bus./Econ.Libn.
Staff: Prof 2; Other 1. **Subjects:** Economics, economic and business history, finance, management, accounting. **Holdings:** 375,000 books. **Subscriptions:** 4000 journals and other serials. **Services:** Interlibrary loan; copying; collection open to the public with restrictions. **Automated Operations:** Computerized public access catalog, cataloging, acquisitions, and circulation. **Computerized Information Services:** DIALOG Information Services, VU/TEXT Information Services, WILSONLINE, OCLC. **Networks/Consortia:** Member of Center for Research Libraries (CRL) Consortia, ILLINET.

★16027★
UNIVERSITY OF CHICAGO - DEPARTMENT OF ART - MAX EPSTEIN ARCHIVE (Art)
Joseph Regenstein Library, Rm. 420
1100 E. 57th St.
Chicago, IL 60637 Phone: (312)702-7080
Founded: 1938. **Staff:** 4. **Subjects:** General art. **Special Collections:** Photographs of medals in the Courtauld Institute and the British Museum; Armenian Architectural Collection. **Holdings:** 550,000 mounted photographs. **Services:** Archive open to the public by appointment. **Special Indexes:** Decimal Index of Arts in the Lowlands (DIAL).

★16028★
UNIVERSITY OF CHICAGO - EAST ASIAN COLLECTION (Area-Ethnic, Hum)
Joseph Regenstein Library
1100 E. 57th St. Phone: (312)702-8436
Chicago, IL 60637 Tai-loi Ma, Cur.
Founded: 1936. **Staff:** Prof 7; Other 23. **Subjects:** Chinese classics, philosophy, history, archeology, biography, social sciences, literature, and art; Japanese history, social sciences, and literature; Korean history, social sciences, and literature. **Special Collections:** Chinese classics; Chinese local gazetteers; rare books. **Holdings:** 280,000 volumes in Chinese; 129,000 volumes in Japanese; 4100 volumes in Korean; 6400 volumes in Tibetan, Mongol, and Manchu; 7700 volumes of Western language reference works; 18,800 microforms. **Subscriptions:** 3980 journals and other serials. **Services:** Interlibrary loan; copying; collection open to qualified visitors. **Networks/Consortia:** Member of Center for Research Libraries (CRL) Consortia, RLG, ILLINET. **Publications:** Reference List: Chinese Local Histories, 1969; Far Eastern Serials, 1977; Daisaku Ikeda Collection of Japanese Religion and Culture, 1977. **Special Catalogs:** Author-title catalog of Chinese Collection (8 volumes); author-title catalog of Japanese Collection (4 volumes); classified catalog and subject index of the Chinese and Japanese Collections (6 volumes), 1974; 12 volume First Supplement to above catalogs, 1981. **Formerly:** Far Eastern Collection. **Staff:** Wen-Pai Tai, Chinese Libn.; Eizaburo Okuizumi, Japanese Libn.; On-sook Lee, Korean Libn..

★16029★
UNIVERSITY OF CHICAGO - JOHN CRERAR LIBRARY (Biol Sci, Sci-Engr, Med)
5730 S. Ellis Phone: (312)702-7715
Chicago, IL 60637 Patricia K. Swanson, Asst.Dir. for Sci.Libs.
Staff: Prof 9; Other 26. **Subjects:** Astronomy; astrophysics; biological sciences, including botany, physiology, and zoology; chemistry; clinical medicine; computer science; geophysical sciences, including geology, meteorology, and oceanography; history of medicine; history of science; mathematics; physics; statistics; technology. **Special Collections:** National Translations Center; John Crerar Collection of Rare Books (history of science, medicine, and technology). **Holdings:** 375,000 books; 585,000 bound periodical volumes. **Subscriptions:** 8000 journals and other serials. **Services:** Interlibrary loan; copying; library open to the public. **Automated Operations:** Computerized cataloging, acquisitions, and circulation. **Computerized Information Services:** BRS Information Technologies, DIALOG Information Services, CAS ONLINE, MEDLARS, Pergamon ORBIT InfoLine, Inc., OCLC; LDMS (University of Chicago Library Data Management System; internal database). Performs searches on fee basis. Contact Person: Ammiel Prochovnick, Asst.Libn., 702-8337. **Networks/Consortia:** Member of Center for Research Libraries (CRL) Consortia, ILLINET, Greater Midwest Regional Medical Library Network. **Publications:** Consolidated Index of Translations into English, 1st edition 1953-1967, 2nd edition 1968-1984 (microfiche). **Remarks:** Telephone number for the National Translations Center is 702-7060. An alternate telephone number is 702-7437. John Crerar Collection of Rare Books is housed in the Joseph Regenstein Library. **Staff:** Kathleen Zar, Hd., Ref. & Subj.Serv.; James Vaughan, Hd., Access Serv.; Ildiko Nowak, Hd., Natl.Transl.Ctr..

★16030★
UNIVERSITY OF CHICAGO - LAW SCHOOL LIBRARY (Law)
1121 E. 60th St. Phone: (312)753-3425
Chicago, IL 60637 Judith M. Wright, Dir.
Founded: 1902. **Staff:** Prof 8; Other 13. **Subjects:** Law - Anglo-American, foreign, international. **Special Collections:** U.S. Supreme Court Briefs and Records. **Holdings:** 464,157 volumes. **Subscriptions:** 6733 journals and other serials. **Services:** Interlibrary loan; library not open to the public. **Automated Operations:** Computerized cataloging and acquisitions. **Computerized Information Services:** LEXIS, OCLC, WESTLAW; internal database. **Networks/Consortia:** Member of Center for Research Libraries (CRL) Consortia, ILLINET. **Publications:** Selected List of Recent Publications Added to the Library, bimonthly; Law Library Handbook, annual. **Staff:** Charles Ten Brink, Hd., Pub.Serv.; Lorna Tang, Hd., Tech.Serv.; Jane Strable, Docs.Libn.; Adolf Sprudz, Foreign Law Libn..

★16031★
UNIVERSITY OF CHICAGO - MAP COLLECTION (Geog-Map)
Joseph Regenstein Library
1100 E. 57th St. Phone: (312)702-8761
Chicago, IL 60637 Christopher Winters, Map Bibliog.
Founded: 1929. **Staff:** Prof 1; Other 3. **Subjects:** Maps, atlases, charts, aerial photographs. **Special Collections:** 19th century county atlases (500); 19th and 20th century topographic maps of Europe and America; 19th and

20th century urban plans (American and foreign); depository for maps of the U.S. Geological Survey, the U.S. Defense Mapping Agency, the Superintendent of Documents, U.S. National Oceanic and Atmospheric Administration, and Central Intelligence Agency. **Holdings:** 2000 books; 325,000 maps; 9000 aerial photographs. **Subscriptions:** 20 journals and other serials. **Services:** Interlibrary loan (contingent on condition of materials); copying; collection open to the public with restrictions. **Publications:** Cumulative New Maps List; Maps of the Soviet Union at the University of Chicago Map Collection; Maps of Chicago at the University of Chicago Map Collection; The University of Chicago Map Collection: A Brief Guide; Cartographic Materials at the University of Chicago Library.

★16032★
UNIVERSITY OF CHICAGO - MIDDLE EASTERN COLLECTION (Area-Ethnic)
Joseph Regenstein Library, Rm. 560
1100 E. 57th St. Phone: (312)702-8425
Chicago, IL 60637 Bruce D. Craig, Bibliog.
Founded: 1924. **Staff:** Prof 5; Other 7. **Subjects:** Middle Eastern and Islamic studies. **Special Collections:** Middle Eastern Documentation Center (government documents; medieval archives and manuscripts). **Holdings:** 250,000 books; 100,000 bound periodical volumes. **Subscriptions:** 2000 journals and other serials; 50 newspapers.

★16033★
UNIVERSITY OF CHICAGO - MUSIC COLLECTION (Mus)
Joseph Regenstein Library
1100 E. 57th St. Phone: (312)702-8451
Chicago, IL 60637 Hans Lenneberg, Mus.Libn.
Founded: 1940. **Staff:** Prof 1; Other 5. **Subjects:** Music, musicology, theory. **Special Collections:** Chicago Jazz Archive (1700 hours of recordings). **Holdings:** 100,000 books; 6000 reels of microfilm; 10,000 recordings. **Subscriptions:** 400 journals and other serials. **Services:** Interlibrary loan; copying; collection open to the public with restrictions. **Automated Operations:** Computerized cataloging, acquisitions, and circulation. **Computerized Information Services:** OCLC. **Networks/Consortia:** Member of Center for Research Libraries (CRL) Consortia, ILLINET. **Staff:** Edna Christopher, Cat..

★16034★
UNIVERSITY OF CHICAGO - NATIONAL OPINION RESEARCH CENTER - PAUL B. SHEATSLEY LIBRARY (Soc Sci)
1155 E. 60th St. Phone: (312)702-1213
Chicago, IL 60637 Patrick Bova, Libn.
Founded: 1941. **Staff:** Prof 1; Other 1. **Subjects:** Sociology, public opinion research, statistics, political science, education, health and medicine. **Special Collections:** Current domestic and foreign public opinion polls; U.S. International Communication Agency Research Reports. **Holdings:** 3000 books; 24 VF drawers; NORC numbered research reports; data and materials from NORC studies; NORC field materials. **Subscriptions:** 100 journals and other serials. **Services:** Interlibrary loan; copying; library open to qualified users. **Computerized Information Services:** DIALOG Information Services, WILSONLINE, VU/TEXT Information Services. **Networks/Consortia:** Member of Chicago Library System. **Publications:** Bibliography of publications, annual - free to mailing list.

★16035★
UNIVERSITY OF CHICAGO - ORIENTAL INSTITUTE - ARCHIVES (Area-Ethnic, Hist)
1155 E. 58th St. Phone: (312)702-9520
Chicago, IL 60637-1569 John A. Larson, Musm.Archv.
Staff: Prof 1; Other 4. **Subjects:** Ancient Near East, Near Eastern archeology, Egyptology, Assyriology, Syro-Palestinian archeology, Achaemenid Persian art. **Special Collections:** The Director's Files, 1919 to present; the personal papers of James Henry Breasted, Harold H. Nelson, William F. Edgerton, Keith C. Seele, Nabia Abbott, Wilhelm Spiegelberg, W. Max Muller, and Raymond O. Bowman; field records and publication materials of the institute's archeological field expeditions in the Near East: The Epigraphic and Architectural Survey in Egypt, The Anatolian Expedition (Alishar Huyuk), The Megiddo Expedition, The Persepolis Expedition, The Nippur Expedition, The Iraq Expedition (Khorsabad, Tell Asmar, Tell Agrab, Khafajah), and The Prehistoric Expedition. **Holdings:** 200 VF drawers; 100,000 black and white photographic images, 1905 to present. **Services:** Copying; archives open to qualified scholars by appointment. **Special Catalogs:** The 1905-1907 Breasted Expeditions to Egypt and the Sudan: A Photographic Study (2 volumes); Persepolis and Ancient Iran; The 1919/1920 Expedition to the Near East; Ptolemais Cyrenaica (all on microfiche).

★16036★
UNIVERSITY OF CHICAGO - ORIENTAL INSTITUTE - RESEARCH ARCHIVES (Area-Ethnic)
1155 E. 58th St. Phone: (312)962-9537
Chicago, IL 60637 Charles E. Jones, Res.Archv.
Founded: 1973. **Staff:** Prof 1; Other 2. **Subjects:** Egyptology, Cuneiform studies, Near Eastern archeology, Northwest Semitic languages. **Holdings:** 12,523 books; 6800 bound periodical volumes; 8300 pamphlets; 9000 other cataloged items; 2000 maps. **Subscriptions:** 616 journals and other serials. **Services:** Archives open to members of the institute.

★16037★
UNIVERSITY OF CHICAGO - SOCIAL SERVICES ADMINISTRATION LIBRARY (Soc Sci, Med)
969 E. 60th St. Phone: (312)702-1199
Chicago, IL 60637 Eileen Libby, Libn.
Founded: 1965. **Staff:** Prof 1; Other 3. **Subjects:** Social services, American and foreign social work, public welfare, mental health, urban policy, social problems, child welfare, health care, aged, psychotherapy. **Holdings:** 21,100 books; 1500 bound periodical volumes; 5800 pamphlets; 6510 microforms. **Subscriptions:** 400 journals and other serials. **Services:** Interlibrary loan (through main university library); copying; library open to the public with restrictions. **Automated Operations:** Computerized public access catalog, cataloging, and acquisitions. **Computerized Information Services:** DIALOG Information Services, Pergamon ORBIT InfoLine, Inc., OCLC. **Networks/Consortia:** Member of Center for Research Libraries (CRL) Consortia, ILLINET. **Publications:** Selected List of New Acquisitions, monthly.

★16038★
UNIVERSITY OF CHICAGO - SOUTHERN ASIA COLLECTION (Area-Ethnic)
Joseph Regenstein Library
1100 E. 57th St. Phone: (312)702-8430
Chicago, IL 60637 James H. Nye, Bibliog./Hd.
Founded: 1959. **Staff:** Prof 1; Other 3. **Subjects:** Humanities and social sciences in thirty South Asian and many Western languages; Indology; regional history and culture; economics; geography; art history. **Special Collections:** Albert Mayer papers; Gitel Steed papers; Bhubaneshwar Archive on Modern Orissa. **Holdings:** 198,480 books; 116,600 bound periodical volumes; 50 VF drawers of pamphlets and ephemera. **Subscriptions:** 4400 journals and other serials; 15 newspapers. **Services:** Interlibrary loan (through main university library); copying; collection open to the public with restrictions. **Automated Operations:** Computerized cataloging, acquisitions, and circulation. **Computerized Information Services:** DIALOG Information Services, Pergamon ORBIT InfoLine, Inc., OCLC. **Networks/Consortia:** Member of Center for Research Libraries (CRL) Consortia, ILLINET. **Publications:** Guide to the Albert Mayer Papers. **Special Catalogs:** Pamphlet Collection Card Catalog.

★16039★
UNIVERSITY OF CHICAGO - SPECIAL COLLECTIONS (Rare Book, Hum)
Joseph Regenstein Library
1100 E. 57th St. Phone: (312)702-8705
Chicago, IL 60637 Robert Rosenthal, Cur.
Special Collections: Ludwig Rosenberger Collection of Judaica; Donnelley Collection (fine printing and the history of printing); Grant Collection of English Bibles; William E. Barton Collection of Lincolniana; Frank Collection (anatomical illustration); Durrett Collection (history of Kentucky and the Ohio River Valley); Encyclopaedia Britannica Collection (books for children, particularly of the nineteenth century); Croue Collection of Balzac's Works; American Bible Union and Hengstenberg Collections (early theology and Biblical criticism); Littlefield Collection (early American schoolbooks); Samuel Harper Collection (Russian political pamphlets, 1902-1946); Lincke Collection (German popular fiction, 1790-1850); Hirsch-Bernays Collection (Continental literature); Celia and Delia Austrian Collection (English drama to 1800); Eckels Collection of Cromwelliana; Heinemann Goethe Collection; Helen and Ruth Regenstein Collection (rare books on English and American literature); personal papers of William Beaumont, Saul Bellow, Stephen A. Douglas, William H. English, Elijah Grant, John Gunther, Salmon O. Levinson, Fielding Lewis, Frank O. Lowden, Wyndham Robertson, Julius Rosenwald, Joel T. Hart, Joshua Lacy Wilson, George Nicholas, Michael Polanyi, and others; Sir Nicholas Bacon Collection (papers and manorial records relating to estates in Norfolk and Suffolk); office files of Poetry: A Magazine of Verse, including the personal papers of Harriet Monroe; life records of Geoffrey Chaucer; The Canterbury Tales transcripts and photostats of manuscripts; Samuel R. and Marie-Louise Rosenthal Collection (northern Italian documents); Wieboldt-Rosenwald Collection (photostats of German

folksongs); Edgar J. Goodspeed Collection (New Testament manuscripts); University of Chicago Archives, including papers of George Herbert Mead, Robert M. Hutchins, S. Chandrusekhar, Enrico Fermi, Robert Herrick, William Vaughn Moody, Howard Taylor Ricketts, Thomas C. Chamberlin, Hermann E. von Holst, William F. Ogburn, Ernest W. Burgess, Charles E. Merriam, James Franck, and other members of the faculty. **Holdings:** 250,000 volumes; 6 million manuscripts and archival materials. **Computerized Information Services:** OCLC. **Networks/Consortia:** Member of Center for Research Libraries (CRL) Consortia, ILLINET. **Staff:** Daniel Meyer, Asst.Cur., Mss. & Archv.; Gary Van Zante, Chf.Bibliog.Asst..

★16040★
UNIVERSITY OF CHICAGO - YERKES OBSERVATORY LIBRARY (Sci-Engr)
Williams Bay, WI 53191 Phone: (414)245-5555
J.A. Bausch, Asst. in Chg.
Founded: 1897. **Staff:** 1. **Subjects:** Astronomy, astrophysics. **Holdings:** 15,000 books; 10,000 bound periodical volumes. **Subscriptions:** 150 journals and other serials. **Services:** Interlibrary loan; copying; library open to the public by appointment.

★16041★
UNIVERSITY OF CHICAGO HOSPITALS - PHARMACEUTICAL SERVICES - DRUG INFORMATION SERVICE (Med)
5841 S. Maryland Ave. Phone: (312)702-1388
Chicago, IL 60637 Maureen E. Savitsky, Pharm.D., Dir.
Founded: 1975. **Staff:** Prof 2. **Subjects:** Pharmacy, biopharmaceutics, clinical pharmacology. **Holdings:** 300 books; 50 bound periodical volumes; 100 boxes of journals; Drugdex; Iowa Drug Information System. **Subscriptions:** 28 journals and other serials. **Services:** Service not open to the public. **Automated Operations:** Computerized formulary maintenance. **Computerized Information Services:** NLM. **Publications:** Topics in Drug Therapy, monthly - by subscription. **Special Indexes:** Formulary.

★16042★
UNIVERSITY OF CINCINNATI - ARCHIVES AND RARE BOOKS DEPARTMENT (Hum, Rare Book)
Carl Blegen Library, 8th Fl. Phone: (513)475-6459
Cincinnati, OH 45221 Alice M. Cornell, Hd.
Founded: 1973. **Staff:** Prof 2; Other 3. **Subjects:** University of Cincinnati, Southwestern Ohio, 18th century English literature, travel and exploration, North American Indians, baseball history. **Holdings:** Rare Book Collection (15,000); University Archives (5550 linear feet); Urban Studies Collection (2500 linear feet); Ohio Network Collection (2150 linear feet); Medical History Collection (700 linear feet); Baseball Research Collection (15 linear feet); History of Design Collection; University Biographical File (40 linear feet); university theses and dissertations; Southwest Ohio Public Records (167 reels of microfilm). **Services:** Copying; department open to the public with restrictions. **Automated Operations:** Computerized public access catalog and cataloging. **Networks/Consortia:** Member of Greater Cincinnati Library Consortium (GCLC), Ohio Network of American History Research Centers, OHIONET. **Staff:** Kevin Grace, Asst.Hd.; Anne J. Guilland, Staff Archv..

★16043★
UNIVERSITY OF CINCINNATI - COLLEGE CONSERVATORY OF MUSIC - GORNO MEMORIAL MUSIC LIBRARY (Mus)
Carl Blegen Library, Rm. 417 Phone: (513)475-4471
Cincinnati, OH 45221 Robert O. Johnson, Hd.
Founded: 1967. **Staff:** Prof 3; Other 3. **Subjects:** Music performance, history, and theory; musicology; dance; broadcasting; theater arts; music education. **Special Collections:** Everett Helm Collection (1500 items); Leigh Harline Collection (500 items); Anatole Chujoy Memorial Dance Collection (700 items). **Holdings:** 26,000 volumes; 32,000 scores; 25,000 phonograph records; 6000 microforms. **Subscriptions:** 600 journals and other serials. **Services:** Interlibrary loan; copying; library open to the public for reference use only. **Automated Operations:** Computerized public access catalog and cataloging. **Networks/Consortia:** Member of Greater Cincinnati Library Consortium (GCLC), OHIONET. **Staff:** Mark Palkovic, Rec.Libn..

★16044★
UNIVERSITY OF CINCINNATI - CURRICULUM RESOURCES CENTER (Educ, Aud-Vis)
Carl Blegen Library, Rm. 600 Phone: (513)475-2161
Cincinnati, OH 45221 Dr. Gary Lare, Libn.
Founded: 1971. **Staff:** Prof 1; Other 4. **Subjects:** Curriculum resources, primary and secondary education and teaching. **Holdings:** 25,983 books; 655 tests; 2000 microfiche; 8776 AV programs; elementary and secondary school textbooks; children's books; curriculum guides; teaching activities books. **Subscriptions:** 75 journals and other serials. **Services:** Center open to the public for reference use only. **Automated Operations:** Computerized public access catalog and cataloging.

★16045★
UNIVERSITY OF CINCINNATI - DEPARTMENT OF ENVIRONMENTAL HEALTH LIBRARY (Med)
Kettering Laboratory Library
3223 Eden Ave. Phone: (513)872-5771
Cincinnati, OH 45267 Sherrie Kline, Sr.Res.Assoc.
Founded: 1930. **Staff:** Prof 1; Other 3. **Subjects:** Environmental health, toxicology, physiology, analytical chemistry, statistics. **Special Collections:** Industrial health. **Holdings:** 7000 books; 3700 bound periodical volumes; 78 VF drawers of reprints, reports, translations; 850 microfiche and reels of microfilm; 565 unpublished reports. **Subscriptions:** 185 journals and other serials. **Services:** Interlibrary loan; copying; SDI; library open to professional personnel. **Automated Operations:** Computerized cataloging. **Computerized Information Services:** BRS Information Technologies, DIALOG Information Services, MEDLARS, Chemical Information Systems, Inc. (CIS), STN International, NLM. Performs searches on fee basis.

★16046★
UNIVERSITY OF CINCINNATI - DESIGN, ARCHITECTURE, ART & PLANNING LIBRARY (Art)
800 Alms Bldg.
Cincinnati, OH 45221-0016 Phone: (513)475-3238
Founded: 1929. **Staff:** Prof 1; Other 3. **Subjects:** Architecture, art history, art education, planning, interior design, industrial design, fine arts, fashion design, urban studies, health planning, graphic design. **Special Collections:** Ladislas Segoe Collection (city planning; 200 volumes); artists' publications. **Holdings:** 38,217 books; 9965 serial volumes; 2448 microforms; 100 planning reports. **Subscriptions:** 500 journals and other serials. **Services:** Interlibrary loan; copying; library open to the public with fee card required for nonuniversity persons to check out materials. **Automated Operations:** Computerized public access catalog and cataloging. **Computerized Information Services:** DIALOG Information Services, RLIN; MIQ (internal database). Performs searches on fee basis. **Networks/Consortia:** Member of Greater Cincinnati Library Consortium (GCLC), OHIONET. **Special Catalogs:** Planning reports catalog; artists' publications catalog (both card).

★16047★
UNIVERSITY OF CINCINNATI - ENGINEERING LIBRARY (Sci-Engr)
880 Baldwin Hall Phone: (513)475-3761
Cincinnati, OH 45221 Dorothy F. Byers, Hd.
Staff: Prof 2; Other 3. **Subjects:** Engineering - environmental, nuclear, civil, mechanical, aerospace, chemical, metallurgical, electrical, industrial, computer; material science; engineering mechanics. **Holdings:** 30,000 books; 30,000 bound periodical volumes; 2 cabinets of journals on microfilm; 1 cabinet of NASA on microfiche; 26 cabinets of AEC/DOE on microfiche; technical reports. **Subscriptions:** 750 journals and other serials. **Services:** Interlibrary loan; copying; library open to the public. **Automated Operations:** Computerized public access catalog and cataloging. **Computerized Information Services:** DIALOG Information Services, Pergamon ORBIT InfoLine, Inc., BRS Information Technologies. Performs searches on fee basis. Contact Person: Margaret Lippert, Ref.Libn.. **Networks/Consortia:** Member of Greater Cincinnati Library Consortium (GCLC), OHIONET. **Staff:** Ann Ridgway, Lib.Assoc..

★16048★
UNIVERSITY OF CINCINNATI - GEOLOGY LIBRARY (Sci-Engr, Geog-Map)
103 Old Tech Bldg.
ML 13 Phone: (513)475-4332
Cincinnati, OH 45221 Richard A. Spohn, Hd.
Staff: Prof 1; Other 1. **Subjects:** Geology. **Special Collections:** S.V. Hrabar - Exxon Guidebook Collection (1500 guidebooks of U.S. and Canada). **Holdings:** 29,434 books; 7441 bound periodical volumes; 100,000 maps. **Subscriptions:** 650 journals and other serials. **Services:** Interlibrary loan; library open to the public. **Automated Operations:** Computerized public access catalog and cataloging. **Networks/Consortia:** Member of Greater Cincinnati Library Consortium (GCLC), OHIONET.

★16049★
UNIVERSITY OF CINCINNATI - GEORGE ELLISTON POETRY COLLECTION (Hum)
646 Central Library Phone: (513)475-4709
Cincinnati, OH 45221 James Cummins, Cur.
Staff: Prof 1. **Subjects:** 20th century poetry. **Special Collections:** Rare book collection (300 titles). **Holdings:** 7264 books; 434 bound periodical volumes; 413 phonograph records. **Subscriptions:** 88 journals and other serials. **Services:** Collection open to the public for reference use only. **Automated Operations:** Computerized cataloging. **Publications:** Calendar of events, 3/year.

★16050★
UNIVERSITY OF CINCINNATI - GERMAN-AMERICANA COLLECTION (Area-Ethnic)
Langsam Library, Mail Location 33 Phone: (513)475-2411
Cincinnati, OH 45221 Don Heinrich Tolzmann, Sr.Libn.
Founded: 1974. **Staff:** Prof 1; Other 1. **Subjects:** German-American literature, history, and culture. **Special Collections:** Fick Collection; Goebel Collection; Niers Collection; Wolff Collection; Helmecke Collection. **Holdings:** 2000 books; 250 bound periodical volumes; 1000 other cataloged items. **Services:** Copying; collection open to the public for reference use only. **Special Catalogs:** Catalog of the German-Americana Collection, University of Cincinnati, 1987. **Remarks:** An alternate telephone number is 475-6459.

★16051★
UNIVERSITY OF CINCINNATI - JOHN MILLER BURNAM CLASSICAL LIBRARY (Hum)
Carl Blegen Library, Rm. 320 Phone: (513)475-6724
Cincinnati, OH 45221 Jean Susorney Wellington, Hd.
Founded: 1900. **Staff:** Prof 2; Other 4. **Subjects:** Classical and bronze age Greek archeology, Greek and Latin languages and literature, Greek and Latin paleography and epigraphy, Byzantine and modern Greece, modern Greek language and literature, ancient history. **Special Collections:** Paleography Collection (1500 volumes); Modern Greek Collection (34,000 volumes). **Holdings:** 115,000 volumes; 13,500 Programmschriften and dissertations; 2000 offprints; 3500 microforms; 200 sound recordings; 732 maps. **Subscriptions:** 2000 journals and other serials. **Services:** Interlibrary loan; copying; library open to the public for reference use only. **Automated Operations:** Computerized public access catalog and cataloging. **Networks/Consortia:** Member of Greater Cincinnati Library Consortium (GCLC), OHIONET. **Special Catalogs:** Catalog of the Modern Greek Collection, University of Cincinnati, 5 volumes (1980); The Modern Greek Collection in the Library of the University of Cincinnati, by Niove Kyparissiotis (1960). **Staff:** Eugenia Foster, Cur., Modern Greek Coll.; Michael Braunlin, Asst.Hd..

★16052★
UNIVERSITY OF CINCINNATI - MATHEMATICS LIBRARY (Sci-Engr, Comp Sci)
840 Old Chemistry Bldg. Phone: (513)475-4449
Cincinnati, OH 45221 Joyce Pons, Hd.
Founded: 1973. **Staff:** 2. **Subjects:** Pure and applied mathematics, including complex analysis, functional analysis, mathematical logic, topology, differential geometry, probability, and statistics; computer science. **Holdings:** 16,000 books; 11,882 bound periodical volumes. **Subscriptions:** 384 journals and other serials. **Services:** Interlibrary loan; copying; library open to the public. **Automated Operations:** Computerized public access catalog and cataloging. **Computerized Information Services:** DIALOG Information Services. **Networks/Consortia:** Member of Greater Cincinnati Library Consortium (GCLC), OHIONET.

★16053★
UNIVERSITY OF CINCINNATI - MEDICAL CENTER INFORMATION AND COMMUNICATIONS - HEALTH SCIENCES LIBRARY (Med)
231 Bethesda Ave. Phone: (513)872-5627
Cincinnati, OH 45267-0574 Roger Verny, Dir.
Founded: 1974. **Staff:** Prof 12; Other 12. **Subjects:** Medicine, biomedical sciences, pharmacy. **Holdings:** 46,000 books; 77,000 bound periodical volumes. **Subscriptions:** 2776 journals and other serials. **Services:** Interlibrary loan; copying; SDI; library open to the public. **Automated Operations:** Computerized public access catalog, cataloging, and ILL. **Computerized Information Services:** DIALOG Information Services, BRS Information Technologies, MEDLINE, NLM; MIQ (Medical Information Quick; internal database); OnTyme Electronic Message Network Service (electronic mail service). Performs searches on fee basis. **Networks/Consortia:** Member of Greater Midwest Regional Medical Library Network. **Publications:** New from the MCIC Libraries, monthly - to library patrons. **Special Catalogs:** Media Resources Center Catalog; Medical Union List of Serials (both book). **Remarks:** An alternate telephone number is 872-5541.

★16054★
UNIVERSITY OF CINCINNATI - MEDICAL CENTER INFORMATION AND COMMUNICATIONS - HISTORICAL, ARCHIVAL AND MUSEUM SERVICES (Hist, Med)
121 Wherry Hall
Eden & Bethesda Aves. Phone: (513)872-5120
Cincinnati, OH 45267-0574 Billie Broaddus, Dir.
Staff: Prof 3. **Subjects:** History of medicine and pharmacy. **Special Collections:** Tucker Library of the History of Medicine (1500 items); Mussey Collection (19th century medicine; 4000 items); Daniel Drake Historical Collection (60 items; 30 manuscripts); hospital records, 1837-1900. **Holdings:** 28,450 books; 3782 bound periodical volumes; 10,000 pamphlets; 1000 linear feet of archives; 5000 photographs; 31 oral history videotapes; 150 diplomas and certificates; 2000 medical instruments; 109 pharmacy jars (Cantagalli 15th century replicas produced in 1890s). **Subscriptions:** 15 journals and other serials. **Services:** Interlibrary loan; copying; services open to the public with restrictions. **Automated Operations:** Computerized public access catalog. **Computerized Information Services:** NLM, BRS Information Technologies. **Special Catalogs:** Tucker Library of the History of Medicine (book); Guide to the Mussey Medical and Scientific Library. **Staff:** Susanne Gilliam, Cat.; Cory Oysler, Cons..

★16055★
UNIVERSITY OF CINCINNATI - MEDICAL CENTER INFORMATION AND COMMUNICATIONS - NURSING EDUCATIONAL RESOURCES (Med)
College of Nursing & Health
Vine St. & St. Clair Ave. Phone: (513)872-5543
Cincinnati, OH 45219 Ava Fried, Info.Spec.
Staff: Prof 2; Other 3. **Subjects:** Nursing, clinical medicine, gerontology, education, sociology. **Special Collections:** Phoebe Kandel Historical Collection (history of nursing). **Holdings:** 12,000 volumes; 500 AV programs. **Subscriptions:** 450 journals and other serials. **Services:** Interlibrary loan; open to the public by permission. **Computerized Information Services:** Online systems. **Remarks:** Includes holdings of the Levi Memorial Library. **Staff:** Leslie Schick, Dir., Lib.Serv..

★16056★
UNIVERSITY OF CINCINNATI - OBSERVATORY LIBRARY
Observatory Place
High Park
Cincinnati, OH 45208
Subjects: Astronomy. **Special Collections:** Rare books. **Holdings:** 13,000 volumes. **Remarks:** Maintained by University of Cincinnati - Physics Library. Presently inactive.

★16057★
UNIVERSITY OF CINCINNATI - OESPER CHEMISTRY-BIOLOGY LIBRARY (Sci-Engr, Biol Sci)
Brodie A-3, Rm. 503 (151) Phone: (513)475-4524
Cincinnati, OH 45221 Dorice Des Chene, Hd.
Staff: Prof 1; Other 2. **Subjects:** Chemistry, biology. **Holdings:** 35,500 books; 37,400 bound periodical volumes; 236 reels of microfilm; 2117 microfiche. **Subscriptions:** 985 journals and other serials. **Services:** Interlibrary loan; copying; library open to the public, ID card required for check out of materials. **Automated Operations:** Computerized public access catalog and cataloging. **Computerized Information Services:** DIALOG Information Services, NLM, Pergamon ORBIT InfoLine, Inc., BRS Information Technologies, OCLC. **Networks/Consortia:** Member of Greater Cincinnati Library Consortium (GCLC), OHIONET.

★16058★
UNIVERSITY OF CINCINNATI - OMI COLLEGE OF APPLIED SCIENCE - TIMOTHY C. DAY TECHNICAL LIBRARY (Sci-Engr)
100 E. Central Pkwy. Phone: (513)475-6553
Cincinnati, OH 45210 Rosemary Young, Libn.
Founded: 1828. **Staff:** Prof 1; Other 2. **Subjects:** Computer science, electrical and mechanical engineering technology, chemical technology, construction science, fire science technology. **Holdings:** 31,200 books; 1100 bound periodical volumes; 300 senior design theses; 1050 reels of microfilm; 700 microfiche; 30 videotapes. **Subscriptions:** 168 journals and other serials; 8 newspapers. **Services:** Interlibrary loan; copying; SDI; library open to the public for reference use only. **Automated Operations:** Computerized public access catalog and cataloging. **Computerized**

Information Services: DIALOG Information Services. Performs searches on fee basis. **Networks/Consortia:** Member of Greater Cincinnati Library Consortium (GCLC), OHIONET.

★16059★
UNIVERSITY OF CINCINNATI - PHYSICS LIBRARY (Sci-Engr)
406 Braunstein Hall — Phone: (513)475-2331
Cincinnati, OH 45221 — Marianna Wells, Hd.
Founded: 1929. **Staff:** Prof 1; Other 2. **Subjects:** Physics - classical and modern, condensed matter, high-energy, nuclear and particle, atmospheric and terrestrial; biophysics. **Special Collections:** High-energy preprint library. **Holdings:** 18,009 books; 15,334 bound periodical volumes; 231 dissertations. **Subscriptions:** 324 journals and other serials. **Services:** Interlibrary loan; copying; library open to the public. **Automated Operations:** Computerized public access catalog and cataloging. **Computerized Information Services:** Online systems. **Networks/Consortia:** Member of Greater Cincinnati Library Consortium (GCLC), OHIONET.

★16060★
UNIVERSITY OF CINCINNATI - RAYMOND WALTERS COLLEGE - LIBRARY (Med)
9555 Plainfield Rd. — Phone: (513)745-5710
Cincinnati, OH 45236 — Lucy Wilson, Coll.Libn.
Staff: Prof 5; Other 6. **Subjects:** Dental hygiene. **Holdings:** 50,000 books; 2500 government documents; 12,000 microforms; 1500 pamphlets; newspapers. **Subscriptions:** 671 journals and other serials; 16 newspapers. **Services:** Interlibrary loan; copying; SDI; library open to the public. **Automated Operations:** Computerized public access catalog and cataloging. **Computerized Information Services:** DIALOG Information Services. Performs searches on fee basis. Contact Person: Gerald Nidich, Ref.Libn.. **Networks/Consortia:** Member of OHIONET, Greater Cincinnati Library Consortium (GCLC). **Publications:** New & Novel, quarterly - to college faculty. **Staff:** Janice Sankot, Ref.Libn.; Mike Sander, Media Libn.; Rose Neyhouse, Microcomputer Lab.Supv..

★16061★
UNIVERSITY OF CINCINNATI - ROBERT S. MARX LAW LIBRARY (Law)
Law School — Phone: (513)472-3016
Cincinnati, OH 45221 — Taylor Fitchett, Hd.Libn.
Founded: 1832. **Staff:** Prof 5; Other 4. **Subjects:** Law - general, comparative, international; government documents. **Special Collections:** Morgan Collection on Human Rights (800 volumes). **Holdings:** 194,000 volumes. **Subscriptions:** 3000 journals and other serials; 20 newspapers. **Services:** Interlibrary loan; copying; library open to the public for reference use only. **Automated Operations:** Computerized cataloging. **Computerized Information Services:** LEXIS, WESTLAW, NEXIS. **Staff:** Janice W. Smith, Hd., Pub.Serv.; Patricia Denham, Acq.; Janice Platt, Hd., Tech.Serv.; Mark Dinkelacker, ILL; Charles Parsons, Govt.Doc.; Betsy Wood, Ref.Libn.; Harold Parker, Circ.; Swarn Varma, Asst.Cat..

UNIVERSITY OF CINCINNATI - UNIVERSITY AFFILIATED CINCINNATI CENTER FOR DEVELOPMENTAL DISORDERS
See: University Affiliated Cincinnati Center for Developmental Disorders (15752)

★16062★
UNIVERSITY CITY PUBLIC LIBRARY - RECORD COLLECTION (Mus)
6701 Delmar Blvd.
University City, MO 63130 — Robert L. Miller, Libn.
Subjects: Music - classical, popular, jazz, folk. **Holdings:** 12,300 music and spoken word phonograph records; 190 art prints; 200 8mm films; scores. **Services:** Collection open to the public.

★16063★
UNIVERSITY CLUB LIBRARY (Hum)
1 W. 54th St. — Phone: (212)572-3418
New York, NY 10019 — Andrew J. Berner, Dir.
Founded: 1879. **Staff:** Prof 3; Other 2. **Subjects:** Literature; history - Civil War, World Wars I and II; collegiana; biography. **Special Collections:** Tinker, Darrow, Rudge Collections (printing and printing history); Bicklehaupt Collection of Sporting Books; Southern Society Collection of Books about the South; George Cruikshank. **Holdings:** 100,000 books; 1500 bound periodical volumes; 15 VF drawers of New York newspapers in microform; 25 VF drawers of University Club Archives. **Subscriptions:** 150 journals and other serials; 20 newspapers. **Services:** Copying; library open to serious scholars with written application. **Automated Operations:** Computerized cataloging and circulation. **Publications:** The University Club Library Quarterly - limited distribution. **Staff:** Katherine Richards, Asst.Libn.; William Watson, Tech.Serv.Libn..

★16064★
UNIVERSITY COLLEGE OF CAPE BRETON - BEATON INSTITUTE - EACHDRAIDH ARCHIVES (Hist, Area-Ethnic)
Box 5300 — Phone: (902)564-6343
Sydney, NS, Canada B1P 6L2 — Dr. R.J. Morgan, Dir.
Founded: 1957. **Staff:** Prof 3; Other 3. **Subjects:** Cape Breton Island - history, labor history, Gaelic literature, folklore, political history; traditional Scottish music of Cape Breton Island; genealogy. **Special Collections:** John Parker Nautical Collection (8.7 meters); Gaelic and Scottish collection (3000 volumes); political papers; Micmac Indian, Acadian, and other ethnic collections (manuscripts; audio- and videotapes). **Holdings:** 5000 books; 200 bound periodical volumes; 200 unbound reports; 20,000 photographs; 800 maps; 115 meters of manuscripts; 5 VF drawers of clippings; 600 reels of microfilm; 150 large scrapbooks; 3500 tapes; 600 slides; 50 videotapes. **Subscriptions:** 10 journals and other serials. **Services:** Copying; archives open to the public. **Computerized Information Services:** QL Systems; K-MAN (internal database). **Staff:** Dr. Mary K. Macleod, Asst.Dir.; Elizabeth Planetta, Cur..

★16065★
UNIVERSITY OF COLORADO, BOULDER - ACADEMIC MEDIA SERVICES (Aud-Vis)
Stadium Bldg., Rm. 361
Campus Box 379 — Phone: (303)492-7341
Boulder, CO 80309 — Dr. Daniel Niemeyer, Dir.
Founded: 1923. **Staff:** Prof 1; Other 3. **Subjects:** Social studies, science, arts and humanities, language, general areas. **Special Collections:** 16mm educational films and videotapes covering most subject areas for primary, elementary, junior, senior, and adult groups. **Holdings:** 6000 16mm films; 500 videotapes. **Services:** Interlibrary loan; audio- and videotape duplication; services open to the public. **Special Catalogs:** University of Colorado Instructional Film Video Catalog. **Staff:** Jan Sichel, Supv., Film & Video Lib..

★16066★
UNIVERSITY OF COLORADO, BOULDER - ART AND ARCHITECTURE LIBRARY (Art)
Norlin Library
Campus Box 184 — Phone: (303)492-7955
Boulder, CO 80309 — Liesel Nolan, Libn.
Founded: 1966. **Staff:** Prof 1; Other 2. **Subjects:** Fine arts, art history, photography, landscape architecture, urban design and planning. **Special Collections:** Art exhibition catalogs, 1962 to present. **Holdings:** 66,500 volumes. **Subscriptions:** 380 journals and other serials. **Services:** Interlibrary loan; library open to the public.

★16067★
UNIVERSITY OF COLORADO, BOULDER - AUDIOVISUAL/ MICROFORMS DEPARTMENT (Aud-Vis)
Norlin Library
Campus Box 184
Boulder, CO 80309 — Phone: (303)492-6930
Founded: 1968. **Staff:** 2. **Subjects:** Literature, social science, art, science. **Holdings:** 2082 audiotapes; 4389 phonograph records; 395 filmstrips; 125 film loops; 189 videotapes; 11,613 slides; 583,970 microforms. **Services:** Department open to the public.

★16068★
UNIVERSITY OF COLORADO, BOULDER - BUSINESS RESEARCH DIVISION - BUSINESS & ECONOMIC COLLECTION (Bus-Fin)
Campus Box 420 — Phone: (303)492-8227
Boulder, CO 80309 — C.R. Goeldner, Dir.
Founded: 1915. **Subjects:** National and Colorado economic data, finance, marketing, real estate, insurance, management. **Holdings:** 4500 volumes. **Subscriptions:** 65 journals and other serials. **Services:** Copying; collection open to the public.

★16069★
UNIVERSITY OF COLORADO, BOULDER - BUSINESS RESEARCH DIVISION - TRAVEL REFERENCE CENTER (Bus-Fin)
Campus Box 420 — Phone: (303)492-8227
Boulder, CO 80309 — C.R. Goeldner, Dir.
Founded: 1969. **Staff:** 2. **Subjects:** Travel, tourism, recreation, leisure. **Holdings:** 40 books; 2 VF drawers of travel papers, speeches, and miscellaneous publications; 8000 other cataloged items. **Subscriptions:** 20

journals and other serials. **Services:** Copying; center open to the public. **Remarks:** Jointly maintained with Travel and Tourism Research Association.

★16070★
UNIVERSITY OF COLORADO, BOULDER - CENTER FOR ECONOMIC ANALYSIS - LIBRARY (Bus-Fin)
Economics Bldg. 208
Campus Box 257 Phone: (303)492-7413
Boulder, CO 80309 Michael Greenwood
Founded: 1964. **Staff:** Prof 3; Other 1. **Subjects:** Economics. **Holdings:** 500 volumes. **Subscriptions:** 15 journals and other serials. **Services:** Interlibrary loan (limited); library not open to the public.

★16071★
UNIVERSITY OF COLORADO, BOULDER - EARTH SCIENCES LIBRARY (Sci-Engr)
Campus Box 184 Phone: (303)492-6133
Boulder, CO 80309 Terrie O'Neal, Lib.Techn.
Founded: 1876. **Staff:** 2. **Subjects:** Physical geology, historical geology, mineralogy, paleontology, stratigraphy, geophysics, geochemistry, oceanography, structural geology. **Holdings:** 28,000 volumes. **Subscriptions:** 325 journals and other serials. **Services:** Interlibrary loan; copying; SDI; library open to the public. **Computerized Information Services:** DIALOG Information Services, BRS Information Technologies.

★16072★
UNIVERSITY OF COLORADO, BOULDER - ENGINEERING LIBRARY (Sci-Engr)
Campus Box 184 Phone: (303)492-5396
Boulder, CO 80309 Sharon Gause, Libn.
Founded: 1965. **Staff:** Prof 1; Other 2. **Subjects:** Engineering. **Holdings:** 94,356 volumes; 500 titles on microfilm and microfiche. **Subscriptions:** 830 journals. **Services:** Interlibrary loan; copying; library open to the public. **Computerized Information Services:** Online systems. Performs searches on fee basis. **Publications:** Acquisitions list, monthly.

★16073★
UNIVERSITY OF COLORADO, BOULDER - GOVERNMENT PUBLICATIONS DIVISION (Info Sci)
Norlin Library
Campus Box 184 Phone: (303)492-8834
Boulder, CO 80309 Timothy Byrne, Hd., Govt.Pubn.
Staff: Prof 3; Other 5. **Subjects:** Government publications - federal, state, foreign, international. **Holdings:** 200,000 volumes; 10,500 reels of microfilm; 2.2 million microcards and microfiche; 169,900 microprints. **Services:** Interlibrary loan; copying; division open to the public.

★16074★
UNIVERSITY OF COLORADO, BOULDER - INSTITUTE OF ARCTIC & ALPINE RESEARCH - READING ROOM (Sci-Engr)
Rose M. Litman Research Lab.
Campus Box 450 Phone: (303)492-1867
Boulder, CO 80309 Martha Andrews, Prof.Res.Asst.
Staff: 1. **Subjects:** Arctic and Alpine environments, meteorology, climatology, geomorphology, hydrology, palynology, Quaternary geology, glaciology, plant and animal ecology. **Holdings:** 2100 books; 225 unbound periodical volumes; 4200 reports; 300 maps; 200 microfiche; 250 theses. **Subscriptions:** 60 journals and other serials. **Services:** Room open to serious researchers for reference use only.

★16075★
UNIVERSITY OF COLORADO, BOULDER - INSTITUTE OF BEHAVIORAL SCIENCE - NATURAL HAZARDS RESEARCH AND APPLICATIONS INFORMATION CENTER (Soc Sci)
IBS Bldg. 6
Campus Box 482 Phone: (303)492-6818
Boulder, CO 80309 Dave Morton, Lib.Techn.
Founded: 1972. **Staff:** 1. **Subjects:** Natural hazards and disasters, technological hazards, socioeconomic and psychological effects of disasters. **Holdings:** 3000 volumes; 100 departmental publications; VF drawers. **Services:** Interlibrary loan; copying (both limited); center open to the public by appointment. **Computerized Information Services:** Internal database.

★16076★
UNIVERSITY OF COLORADO, BOULDER - JOINT INSTITUTE FOR LABORATORY ASTROPHYSICS (JILLA) - ATOMIC COLLISION CROSS SECTION DATA CENTER (Sci-Engr)
Campus Box 440 Phone: (303)492-7801
Boulder, CO 80309 J.W. Gallagher, Mgr.
Founded: 1963. **Staff:** Prof 3; Other 1. **Subjects:** Low-energy atomic collision; collisions of low-energy electrons and photons with atoms and simple molecules; low-energy heavy-particle collisions. **Holdings:** 21,000 documents on microfiche. **Services:** Center open to the public for reference use only. **Computerized Information Services:** Internal database. **Publications:** Annotated bibliographies on time-share disk files and hard copies.

★16077★
UNIVERSITY OF COLORADO, BOULDER - JOINT INSTITUTE FOR LABORATORY ASTROPHYSICS (JILLA) - READING ROOM (Sci-Engr)
Campus Box 440 Phone: (303)492-5097
Boulder, CO 80309 Kevin McInery, Libn.
Founded: 1962. **Subjects:** Nuclear physics, astronomy. **Holdings:** 600 volumes. **Subscriptions:** 60 journals and other serials. **Remarks:** Institute jointly maintained with the U.S. National Bureau of Standards.

★16078★
UNIVERSITY OF COLORADO, BOULDER - LAW LIBRARY (Law)
Campus Box 402 Phone: (303)492-7534
Boulder, CO 80309 Oscar J. Miller, Law Libn.
Founded: 1892. **Staff:** Prof 5; Other 5. **Subjects:** Law, international law. **Holdings:** 184,000 volumes; 50,075 volumes in microform. **Subscriptions:** 520 journals and other serials. **Services:** Interlibrary loan; copying; library open to the public with restrictions. **Computerized Information Services:** WESTLAW, LEXIS. **Staff:** Barbara Bintliff, Assoc. Law Libn.; Leanne Kunkle Walther, Asst.Libn.; Jane Hames, Asst.Libn.; Richard Jost, Ref.Libn..

★16079★
UNIVERSITY OF COLORADO, BOULDER - MAP LIBRARY (Geog-Map)
Norlin Library
Campus Box 184 Phone: (303)492-7578
Boulder, CO 80309 Susan Anthes, Asst.Sci.Libn. & Map Cur.
Staff: 1. **Holdings:** General map collection (150,000 sheets). **Services:** Interlibrary loan; copying; library open to the public.

★16080★
UNIVERSITY OF COLORADO, BOULDER - MATH/PHYSICS LIBRARY (Sci-Engr)
Duane Physical Laboratories G140
Campus Box 184 Phone: (303)492-8231
Boulder, CO 80309 Allen Wynne, Dept.Hd.
Founded: 1963. **Staff:** Prof 1; Other 2. **Subjects:** Mathematics, astrogeophysics, physics, computer theory and programming languages, astrophysics. **Special Collections:** High Energy Physics (5000 preprints and reports). **Holdings:** 35,568 books; 33,535 bound periodical volumes; 2280 microforms; 150 linear feet of government publications. **Subscriptions:** 750 journals and other serials. **Services:** Interlibrary loan; copying; library open to the public. **Automated Operations:** Computerized cataloging and circulation. **Computerized Information Services:** DIALOG Information Services, Pergamon ORBIT InfoLine, Inc., BRS Information Technologies, The Reference Service (REFSRV). **Publications:** Bi-weekly Acquisitions - on request. **Special Indexes:** Index to physics, astronomy, and computer science book reviews; index to the library's documents collection (both punched card).

★16081★
UNIVERSITY OF COLORADO, BOULDER - MUSIC LIBRARY (Mus)
N-290 Warner Imig Music Bldg.
Campus Box 184 Phone: (303)492-8093
Boulder, CO 80309 Karl Kroeger, Mus.Libn.
Founded: 1959. **Staff:** Prof 2; Other 3. **Subjects:** Music. **Special Collections:** Lumpkin Folk Song Collection (research collection); manuscripts of composers Cecil Effinger and Normand Lockwood; papers of musicologist Erich Katz; popular sheet music collection (10,000 items). **Holdings:** 50,000 volumes; 30,000 phonograph records and phonotapes; 40,000 scores. **Subscriptions:** 250 journals and other serials. **Services:** Interlibrary loan; copying; library open to the public.

★16082★
UNIVERSITY OF COLORADO, BOULDER - SCIENCE LIBRARY (Sci-Engr, Biol Sci)
Norlin Library
Campus Box 184 Phone: (303)492-5136
Boulder, CO 80302 David M. Fagerstrom, Libn.
Founded: 1939. **Staff:** Prof 2; Other 2. **Subjects:** Chemistry; biology - molecular, cellular, developmental, environmental, organismic, population; psychology; pharmacy; speech pathology; audiology; artificial intelligence; exercise physiology. **Holdings:** 170,000 volumes; 17,000 microforms. **Subscriptions:** 2000 journals and other serials. **Services:** Interlibrary loan; copying; SDI; library open to the public. **Computerized Information Services:** DIALOG Information Services, BRS Information Technologies, STN International, NASA/RECON. **Staff:** Susan Anthes, Asst.Sci.Libn..

★16083★
UNIVERSITY OF COLORADO, BOULDER - SPECIAL COLLECTIONS DEPARTMENT (Rare Book)
Norlin Library
Campus Box 184 Phone: (303)492-6144
Boulder, CO 80309 Nora Quinlan, Hd.
Founded: 1939. **Staff:** Prof 2; Other 2. **Special Collections:** Photography; Bibles in many languages; Epsteen Collection (children's literature); Willard Collection (17th-19th century pamphlets); Aileen Fisher Manuscripts; Gene Fowler Manuscripts; Bowen Collection (French Revolution); Aldous Huxley; David Lavender Manuscripts; Hugh MacDiarmid; John Masefield; Florence Crannell Means Manuscripts; Tour Collection (history of metallurgy); mountaineering; Samuel French Plays; Dickson Leavens Collection (silver money); Pettit Collection (Edward Young); 18th century English literature; 20th century English and American literature; Ashendene Press; Doves Press; Kelmscott Press; Limited Editions Club; Nonesuch Press; Vale Press; Jean Stafford Manuscripts; history of meteorology; John D. MacDonald Collection; Leon Uris Manuscripts; M. Creighton Collection (Renaissance Papacy); Florence Becker Lennon Collection (20th century poetry); Franklin Folsom and Mary Elting Manuscripts; Craemer Collection (19th century English literature); Kempner Collection (history of mathematics); Veazie Collection (philosophy); Camille Cummings Collection (Elliot Paul); Feldman Collection (Mark Twain; medieval manuscripts); Eaker Collection (20th century photography). **Holdings:** 40,000 volumes. **Services:** Interlibrary loan; department open to the public.

★16084★
UNIVERSITY OF COLORADO, BOULDER - WESTERN HISTORICAL COLLECTION & UNIVERSITY ARCHIVES (Hist)
Norlin Library
Campus Box 184 Phone: (303)492-7242
Boulder, CO 80309 Dr. John A. Brennan, Cur.
Founded: 1918. **Staff:** Prof 1; Other 2. **Subjects:** Colorado history, 19th and 20th century American West, political leadership, organized labor, professional organizations, business and industry. **Special Collections:** Women's International League for Peace and Freedom Papers; National Farmers Union Archives; Edward P. Costigan Papers; Western Federation of Miners Archives; James G. Patton Papers; Herrick Roth Papers; Elwood Brooks Papers; Western History Association Papers. **Holdings:** 15,000 linear feet of historical manuscripts; 3000 linear feet of university archives; 2000 linear feet of newspapers; 12,000 volumes; pamphlets; maps; photographs; microfilm. **Services:** Copying; collection open to the public. **Publications:** A Guide to Manuscript Collections (1982); guides to individual manuscript collections - for sale.

★16085★
UNIVERSITY OF COLORADO, BOULDER - WILLIAM M. WHITE BUSINESS LIBRARY (Bus-Fin, Info Sci)
Business Bldg.
Campus Box 184 Phone: (303)492-8367
Boulder, CO 80309 Carol Krismann, Hd.
Founded: 1970. **Staff:** Prof 3; Other 2. **Subjects:** Information systems, management and organization, finance, accounting, marketing, transportation, management science, banking, real estate, insurance. **Special Collections:** Douglas H. Buck Financial Records Collection (71,000 annual and 10K reports on microfiche). **Holdings:** 60,000 volumes; 1700 serials on microfilm. **Subscriptions:** 600 journals; 12 newspapers. **Services:** Copying; library open to the public. **Computerized Information Services:** DIALOG Information Services, BRS Information Technologies, Pergamon ORBIT InfoLine, Inc. **Publications:** Acquisitions list, monthly.

★16086★
UNIVERSITY OF COLORADO HEALTH SCIENCES CENTER - DENISON MEMORIAL LIBRARY (Med)
4200 E. 9th Ave. Phone: (303)270-5125
Denver, CO 80262 Charles Bandy, Dir.
Founded: 1924. **Staff:** Prof 10; Other 25. **Subjects:** Medicine, nursing, dentistry, allied health sciences. **Special Collections:** James J. Waring History of Medicine Collection. **Holdings:** 80,803 books; 120,607 bound periodical volumes; 2633 AV programs. **Subscriptions:** 2267 journals and other serials. **Services:** Interlibrary loan (fee); copying; SDI; library open to the public. **Automated Operations:** Computerized cataloging, acquisitions, serials, and circulation. **Computerized Information Services:** OCLC, DIALOG Information Services, Pergamon ORBIT InfoLine, Inc., BRS Information Technologies, NLM; OnTyme Electronic Message Network Service, EasyLink, OCLC (electronic mail services). Performs searches on fee basis. Contact Person: Carol VerValin, Hd., Info.Serv., 270-5128. **Networks/Consortia:** Member of Midcontinental Regional Medical Library Program, Denver Area Health Sciences Library Consortium. **Publications:** Currents, bimonthly. **Staff:** Jim Bothmer, Assoc.Dir., Pub.Serv.; Pat Nelson, Hd., Coll.Dev.; Rick Forsman, Assoc.Dir., Tech.Sys.; Betty Schaetzel, Hd., Cat.; Peggy Edwards, Coord., Ed.Serv..

★16087★
UNIVERSITY OF COLORADO HEALTH SCIENCES CENTER - RENE A. SPITZ PSYCHIATRIC LIBRARY (Med)
4200 E. 9th Ave., C-249 Phone: (303)394-7039
Denver, CO 80262 Irwin Berry, Libn.
Founded: 1967. **Staff:** Prof 1. **Subjects:** Psychiatry, psychoanalysis. **Holdings:** 2900 books; 350 bound periodical volumes; 2550 unbound journals; 100 cassettes. **Subscriptions:** 15 journals and other serials. **Services:** Interlibrary loan; copying; library open to the public with restrictions. **Networks/Consortia:** Member of Colorado Council of Medical Librarians.

★16088★
UNIVERSITY COMMUNITY HOSPITAL - MEDICAL LIBRARY (Med)
3100 E. Fletcher Ave. Phone: (813)972-7236
Tampa, FL 33613 Gwen E. Walters, Lib.Dir.
Founded: 1974. **Staff:** Prof 2; Other 1. **Subjects:** Medicine, nursing, allied health sciences, health care delivery and administration. **Holdings:** 1740 books; 715 bound periodical volumes; 168 periodicals in microform; 28 file drawers of microfilm; 8 file drawers of microfiche; slides; audiotapes. **Subscriptions:** 431 journals and other serials. **Services:** Interlibrary loan; copying; SDI; library open to the public by appointment. **Automated Operations:** Computerized cataloging, acquisitions, and serials. **Computerized Information Services:** DIALOG Information Services, MEDLARS, OCLC, BRS Information Technologies; DOCLINE, OnTyme Electronic Message Network Service (electronic mail services). **Networks/Consortia:** Member of Tampa Bay Medical Library Network, Tampa Bay Library Consortium, Inc.. **Staff:** Jo Ann W. Tibbs, Med.Libn..

★16089★
UNIVERSITY OF CONNECTICUT - BARTLETT ARBORETUM - LIBRARY (Biol Sci, Agri)
151 Brookdale Rd. Phone: (203)322-6971
Stamford, CT 06903 Gaye P. Mote, Adm.Asst.
Founded: 1965. **Staff:** Prof 1. **Subjects:** Horticulture, plant science, botany, arboriculture. **Special Collections:** Materials on conifers and U.S. floras. **Holdings:** 2500 books; 1000 bound periodical volumes; 30 VF drawers. **Subscriptions:** 25 journals and other serials. **Services:** Library open to the public.

★16090★
UNIVERSITY OF CONNECTICUT - CENTER FOR REAL ESTATE & URBAN ECONOMIC STUDIES - REFERENCE & DOCUMENTS ROOM (Bus-Fin, Plan)
U-41-RE, Rm. 426
368 Fairfield Rd. Phone: (203)486-3227
Storrs, CT 06268 Judith B. Paesani, Asst.Dir.
Staff: Prof 6; Other 4. **Subjects:** Real estate, urban studies, housing, finance, land use. **Holdings:** 4000 volumes. **Subscriptions:** 65 journals and other serials. **Services:** Interlibrary loan; room open to the public with restrictions. **Publications:** List of publications - available on request.

★16091★
UNIVERSITY OF CONNECTICUT - FRANK B. COOKSON MUSIC LIBRARY (Mus)
U-12 Phone: (203)486-2502
Storrs, CT 06268 Dorothy McAdoo Bognar, Hd.Mus.Libn.
Staff: Prof 2; Other 2. **Subjects:** Music. **Holdings:** 9500 books; 1900 bound periodical volumes; 10,500 scores; 16,500 phonograph records; 200 compact discs; 570 reels of microfilm. **Subscriptions:** 100 journals and other serials. **Services:** Interlibrary loan; library open to the public for reference use only. **Automated Operations:** Computerized cataloging. **Computerized Information Services:** OCLC. **Networks/Consortia:** Member of NELINET. **Publications:** Guide to the Music Library, irregular - for internal distribution only. **Special Catalogs:** Catalog of piano music and vocal music in collections (card). **Staff:** Joseph Scott.

★16092★
UNIVERSITY OF CONNECTICUT - HARLEIGH B. TRECKER LIBRARY (Soc Sci, Bus-Fin)
1800 Asylum Ave. Phone: (203)241-4906
West Hartford, CT 06117 Richard Bradberry, Lib.Dir.
Founded: 1985. **Staff:** Prof 11; Other 1. **Subjects:** Business, insurance, data processing, economics, child study, psychoanalysis, psychology, social work, sociology, social security, social welfare, psychiatry, social research, criminology and corrections, recreation. **Holdings:** 93,000 volumes; 60 drawers of pamphlets; 60 drawers of annual reports and company histories; 3700 reels of microfilm of business and insurance periodicals and newspapers and social science materials. **Subscriptions:** 897 journals and other serials; 17 newspapers. **Services:** Interlibrary loan; copying; library open to the public for reference use only. **Automated Operations:** Computerized cataloging and circulation. **Computerized Information Services:** DIALOG Information Services, BRS Information Technologies, Disclosure Information Group, OCLC. Performs searches on fee basis. Contact Person: Sue Marsh, Bus.Ref.Libn., 241-4905. **Networks/Consortia:** Member of NELINET, Capitol Region Library Council (CRLC). **Remarks:** An alternate telephone number is 241-4869. **Staff:** Hong-Chan Li, Soc. Work Ref.Libn..

★16093★
UNIVERSITY OF CONNECTICUT - HEALTH CENTER - LYMAN MAYNARD STOWE LIBRARY (Med)
Farmington, CT 06032-9984 Phone: (203)679-2547
Ralph Arcari, Dir.
Founded: 1966. **Staff:** Prof 11; Other 24. **Subjects:** Medicine, dentistry, nursing, allied health sciences. **Special Collections:** Learning Resources Center collection of audiovisuals (5000 items in health sciences). **Holdings:** 50,761 books; 100,754 bound periodical volumes; 189 computer software programs; 5 drawers of pamphlets. **Subscriptions:** 3561 journals and other serials. **Services:** Interlibrary loan; copying; SDI; library open to the public. **Automated Operations:** Computerized cataloging, acquisitions, serials, circulation, and ILL. **Computerized Information Services:** MEDLINE, DIALOG Information Services, OCLC, LS/2000, BRS Information Technologies. **Networks/Consortia:** Member of Capitol Region Library Council (CRLC), Connecticut Association of Health Science Libraries (CAHSL), NELINET, Greater Northeastern Regional Medical Library Program. **Publications:** Newsletter, bimonthly; Serials Holdings, annual; Health Sciences Audiovisual Resources List, biennial. **Staff:** Marion Levine, Assoc.Dir.; Malcolm Brantz, AV Libn.; Jacqueline Lewis, Circ./ ILL Libn.; Barbara J. Frey, Hd.Ref.Libn.; Lorna Wright, Cat./ Automation Libn.; Eugene Cseh, Coll.Mgt.Libn..

★16094★
UNIVERSITY OF CONNECTICUT - HOMER BABBIDGE LIBRARY - SPECIAL COLLECTIONS (Soc Sci, Hum)
Storrs, CT 06268 Phone: (203)486-2524
Richard H. Schimmelpfeng, Dir., Spec.Coll.
Founded: 1881. **Staff:** Prof 4; Other 2. **Special Collections:** Charles Olson Archives; Turkish language collection; Puerto Rican Collection; Madrid Collection; Spanish periodicals and newspapers; Gaines Americana Collection; Kays Horse Collection; Alternative Press Collection; little magazines; Edwin Way Teale Archives; Chilean history and literature; Jose Toribio Medina Collection; modern German drama; French language and dialects; Luis Camoens; Powys Brothers; American socialist and communist pamphlets and periodicals. **Holdings:** Figures not available. **Services:** Interlibrary loan; copying; collections open to the public. **Automated Operations:** Computerized circulation. **Computerized Information Services:** BRS Information Technologies, OCLC. **Publications:** Bibliography series, irregular; HARVEST, irregular.

★16095★
UNIVERSITY OF CONNECTICUT - INSTITUTE OF MATERIALS SCIENCE - READING ROOM (Sci-Engr)
Storrs, CT 06268 Phone: (203)486-4623
Mary Roche, Adm.Asst.
Staff: 1. **Subjects:** Metallurgy, polymer science, materials science. **Holdings:** 50 books; 200 bound periodical volumes. **Subscriptions:** 95 journals and other serials. **Services:** Copying; room open to the public.

★16096★
UNIVERSITY OF CONNECTICUT - INSTITUTE OF PUBLIC AND URBAN AFFAIRS - LIBRARY (Soc Sci)
421 Whitney Rd.
Box U-106 Phone: (203)486-4518
Storrs, CT 06268 Jean W. Gosselin, Prog.Asst.
Founded: 1963. **Staff:** Prof 1; Other 1. **Subjects:** State and local urban affairs. **Special Collections:** Connecticut town and city materials; special reports from Connecticut agencies; New Cities. **Holdings:** 145 books; 1000 pamphlets. **Subscriptions:** 11 journals and other serials. **Services:** Copying, library open to the public with restrictions.

★16097★
UNIVERSITY OF CONNECTICUT - INSTITUTE FOR SOCIAL INQUIRY (Soc Sci)
Box U-164 Phone: (203)486-4440
Storrs, CT 06268 Everett C. Ladd, Jr., Exec.Dir.
Founded: 1968. **Staff:** Prof 24; Other 6. **Subjects:** Public opinion surveys, election data, U.S. and foreign census data. **Holdings:** Over 10,000 surveys. **Subscriptions:** Poll releases, journals, and serials. **Services:** Provides instruction in the use of social data; engages in original data collection, including the Connecticut Poll; conducts workshops and seminars; assists in the administration of special research projects involving social data for public-service agencies in Connecticut. **Remarks:** The institute is a local archive of survey and aggregate data in machine readable form and serves as a multipurpose research and teaching facility for the social sciences. It also hosts the archival development component, user services, and Office of the Executive Director of the Roper Center (see the description of the Roper Center for further information). **Staff:** Marilyn Potter, Asst.Dir./ User Serv.; Jack Davis, Asst.Dir./Tech.Serv.; G. Donald Ferree, Assoc.Dir..

★16098★
UNIVERSITY OF CONNECTICUT - LABOR EDUCATION CENTER - INFORMATION CENTER (Bus-Fin)
One Bishop Circle, Rm. 204
Box U-13 Phone: (203)486-3417
Storrs, CT 06268 Morris L. Fried, Dir.
Founded: 1946. **Subjects:** Labor studies, industrial relations. **Holdings:** 300 volumes. **Subscriptions:** 20 journals and other serials. **Services:** Center open to the public with restrictions.

★16099★
UNIVERSITY OF CONNECTICUT - LAW SCHOOL LIBRARY† (Law)
120 Sherman St.
Hartford, CT 06105-2289 Dennis J. Stone, Law Libn.
Founded: 1942. **Staff:** Prof 7; Other 10. **Subjects:** Law. **Holdings:** 267,564 books; AV programs; microfiche. **Subscriptions:** 4288 serials. **Services:** Interlibrary loan; copying; library open to the public for reference use only. **Automated Operations:** Computerized cataloging. **Computerized Information Services:** LEXIS, WESTLAW, OCLC, RLIN. **Networks/Consortia:** Member of New England Law Library Consortium (NELLCO), NELINET. **Staff:** Judith F. Anspach, Assoc.Libn.; Robert Connell, Asst. Law Libn./Tech.Serv.; Dennis Benamati, Hd., Cat.; David Voisinet, Ref.Libn.; Andrea Joseph, Ref.Libn., ILL/Microforms.

★16100★
UNIVERSITY OF CONNECTICUT - MAP LIBRARY (Geog-Map)
Homer Babbidge Library Phone: (203)486-4589
Storrs, CT 06268 Thornton P. McGlamery, Map Libn.
Founded: 1976. **Staff:** Prof 1; Other 1. **Subjects:** Maps, cartography, history of cartography, computer cartography, remote sensing, travel. **Special Collections:** Petersen Collection; photostat collection of 19th century New England towns; enlarged photostats of manuscript working charts of the U.S. Coast Survey. **Holdings:** 130,000 maps; 8 VF drawers of aerial photographs; 12 VF drawers of U.S. Geological Survey reports; 6 VF drawers of map publisher and dealer catalogs; Sanborn Fire Insurance Maps for Connecticut on microfilm. **Services:** Interlibrary loan; copying; library open to the public. **Automated Operations:** Computerized cataloging, acquisitions, serials, and circulation. **Computerized Information**

Services: National Cartographic Information Center (NCIC); internal databases.

★16101★
UNIVERSITY OF CONNECTICUT - PHARMACY LIBRARY AND LEARNING CENTER (Med)
Box U-92 Phone: (203)486-2218
Storrs, CT 06268 Georgia Scura, Dir.
Staff: Prof 2. **Subjects:** Pharmaceutics, pharmacology, pharmacognosy, pharmaceutical chemistry, health care services. **Holdings:** 5000 books; 14,000 bound periodical volumes; 5 VF drawers of pamphlets and clippings; 300 AV programs; 299 reels of microfilm of periodicals. **Subscriptions:** 282 journals and other serials. **Services:** Interlibrary loan; copying; library open to the public for reference use only. **Computerized Information Services:** BRS Information Technologies, NLM, DIALOG Information Services. **Staff:** David Keighley, Media Spec..

★16102★
UNIVERSITY OF CONNECTICUT - ROPER CENTER FOR PUBLIC OPINION RESEARCH (Soc Sci)
Box 440 Phone: (203)486-4440
Storrs, CT 06268-0440 Everett C. Ladd, Exec.Dir.
Founded: 1946. **Staff:** Prof 24; Other 4. **Subjects:** Survey data contributed by the world's major survey organizations. **Special Collections:** Gallup opinion surveys, 1936 to present; Yankelovich, Clancy Shulman surveys for Time magazine; CBS/New York Times; ABC/Washington Post; NBC/Associated Press; Los Angeles Times; National Opinion Research Center (NORC); Roper Organization; international surveys conducted by United States Information Agency, International Research Associates, Gallup Affiliates, Brulle Ville, and Commission of European Communities (Eurobarometer). **Services:** Data set reproduction; data analysis; search and retrieval; duplication of questionnaires and codebooks; copying; center open to the public. **Computerized Information Services:** POLL (Public Opinion Location Library; internal database). Performs searches on fee basis. Contacts: Lois Times-Ferrara, John M. Barry, Mgr., User Serv., Marilyn Potter. **Publications:** Study listings organized by country; Data Set News (announcements of data sets of special interest to the research community); Data Aquisitions, biennial; Profiles of the American Collection, annual. **Remarks:** Since 1977, the Roper Center has operated through a formal partnership of the University of Connecticut and Williams College. The University of Connecticut branch of the Roper Center, which has primary operating responsibilities, is housed administratively within the Institute for Social Inquiry. **Staff:** Anne-Marie Mercure, Mgr., Archv.; Cheryl Handley, Asst.Mgr., Archv..

★16103★
UNIVERSITY OF CONNECTICUT - SCHOOL OF EDUCATION - I.N. THUT WORLD EDUCATION CENTER (Educ)
Box U-32
Storrs, CT 06268 Phone: (203)486-3321
Staff: Prof 2; Other 2. **Subjects:** Education - multicultural, international, global, bilingual-bicultural, urban; education for development. **Special Collections:** The Peoples of Connecticut oral histories (150); artifacts collection for teaching about other cultures and nations. **Holdings:** 800 books; 1000 documents; 110 sets of slides; 20 videotapes. **Subscriptions:** 40 journals and other serials. **Services:** Interlibrary loan; copying; center open to the public. **Automated Operations:** Computerized cataloging, acquisitions, serials, and circulation. **Computerized Information Services:** Online systems. **Publications:** Annual report; publications list; annotated bibliography on Peace Studies; Tootline: Newsletter of The Isaac N. Thut World Education Center, semiannual. **Special Catalogs:** Catalog of Asian and Middle Eastern Studies resources in Connecticut; curriculum guides for the Peoples of Connecticut, World Education Monograph Series, Multicultural Educational Research Methodologies Series. **Staff:** Dr. Patricia Snyder Weibust, Co-Dir.; Dr. Frank A. Stone, Co-Dir..

★16104★
UNIVERSITY OF DAYTON - LAW SCHOOL LIBRARY (Soc Sci, Law)
300 College Park Phone: (513)229-2314
Dayton, OH 45469 Prof. Thomas L. Hanley, Dir.
Founded: 1974. **Staff:** Prof 4; Other 8. **Subjects:** Law, political science, social sciences. **Holdings:** 192,000 volumes; government documents. **Subscriptions:** 702 journals and other serials; 15 newspapers. **Services:** Interlibrary loan; copying; library open to the public for reference use only. **Automated Operations:** Computerized cataloging and ILL. **Computerized Information Services:** LEXIS, WESTLAW, OCLC. **Networks/Consortia:** Member of Southwest Ohio Council for Higher Education (SOCHE). **Publications:** Recent Acquisitions List, monthly; Annual Report. **Staff:** Theodora Artz, Hd., Acq.Dept.; Geraldine Wernersbach, Hd., Ref./Circ.Dept.; Michael Krieger, Hd., Cat.Dept..

★16105★
UNIVERSITY OF DAYTON - MARIAN LIBRARY (Rel-Phil)
300 College Park Phone: (513)229-4214
Dayton, OH 45469 Rev. Thomas A. Thompson, S.M., Dir.
Founded: 1943. **Staff:** Prof 4; Other 4. **Subjects:** Virgin Mary in theology, devotions, belles lettres, art, music. **Special Collections:** Clugnet Collection (Marian shrines; 8000 items); religious art (300 volumes). **Holdings:** 67,000 volumes; 50,300 clippings; 200 reels of microfilm; 2 boxes of American bishops' pastoral letters; 2200 slides; 4 manuscripts; 5000 pictures; 10,000 holy cards; postcards of Marian shrine and art; 10 albums of postage stamps; 1000 photographs; 300 medals; 80 phonograph records; 250 cassettes. **Subscriptions:** 110 journals and other serials; 10 newspapers. **Services:** Interlibrary loan; copying; library open to the public. **Publications:** Marian Library Studies, annual - by subscription; Marian Library Newsletter, 2/year - free upon request. **Special Catalogs:** Union catalog of Marian holdings in selected North American libraries. **Special Indexes:** Author/title indexes to proceedings of International Mariological Congresses: 1950, 1954, 1958, 1965, 1971, 1975; indexes to selected journals. **Staff:** William Fackovec, S.M., Cat./Bibliog.; Helen Nykolyshyn, Cat.; Donald Fahrig, S.M., Asst.Cat..

★16106★
UNIVERSITY OF DAYTON - ROESCH LIBRARY - RARE BOOKS (Rare Book)
300 College Park Ave., 7th Fl. Phone: (513)229-3669
Dayton, OH 45469 Raymond H. Nartker, Rare Bks.Libn.
Founded: 1965. **Staff:** Prof 1. **Subjects:** First editions of 19th and early 20th century English and American literature; works of Paul Laurence Dunbar, Booth Tarkington, Charles Craddock, George Bar McCutcheon; Lincoln and the Civil War; theology; church history; canon law. **Holdings:** 7200 volumes; limited editions books. **Services:** Copying; library open to the public by appointment.

★16107★
UNIVERSITY OF DAYTON - ROESCH LIBRARY - UNIVERSITY ARCHIVES/SPECIAL COLLECTIONS (Hum)
300 College Park Ave., 3rd Fl. Phone: (513)229-4221
Dayton, OH 45469 Cecilia Mushenheim, Archv./Spec.Coll.Libn.
Founded: 1970. **Staff:** Prof 1. **Subjects:** University of Dayton, science fiction, Dayton Performing Arts. **Special Collections:** University archives (706 linear feet); Science Fiction Writers of America (SFWA) Collection (785 books); Urban Schnurr Collection; Victory Theatre Papers; Charles W. Whalen Congressional Papers, 1966-1978 (464 boxes); Michael Polanyi Papers; Catholic Council on Civil Liberties (CCCL) Papers; Association for Creative Change Papers. **Holdings:** 342 linear feet. **Services:** Copying; collections open to the public. **Automated Operations:** Computerized cataloging and circulation. **Computerized Information Services:** DIALOG Information Services, BRS Information Technologies. **Networks/Consortia:** Member of Southwest Ohio Council for Higher Education (SOCHE). **Special Catalogs:** Catalogs of archives and SWFA Collection (card). **Special Indexes:** Inventories of Schnurr, Whalen, Polanyi, and CCCL Collections.

★16108★
UNIVERSITY OF DAYTON - SCHOOL OF EDUCATION - CURRICULUM MATERIALS CENTER (Educ)
Chaminade Hall
300 College Park Phone: (513)229-3140
Dayton, OH 49469 Dr. Peggy Leahy, Dir.
Founded: 1955. **Staff:** Prof 3; Other 4. **Subjects:** Elementary and secondary textbooks, children's literature, teacher education. **Holdings:** 20,046 books; 215 bound periodical volumes; 81 sets of transparencies; 2200 filmstrips; 600 records; 57 models; 400 material kits; 223 cartridges; 470 sets of charts and posters; 1500 other teaching aids; 56 VF drawers. **Subscriptions:** 64 journals and other serials. **Services:** Center open to the public. **Publications:** Monthly News Bulletin, bimonthly during academic year - to faculty and students. **Special Catalogs:** Book and material catalogs. **Staff:** Ann Raney, Cat..

★16109★
UNIVERSITY OF DELAWARE, NEWARK - ARCHIVES (Hist)
78 E. Delaware Ave. Phone: (302)451-2750
Newark, DE 19716 John M. Clayton, Jr., Archv./Dir., Rec.Mgt
Founded: 1969. **Staff:** Prof 2; Other 2. **Subjects:** University of Delaware history. **Holdings:** 9463 theses and dissertations; 320 bound periodical volumes; 3618 cubic feet of records; 950 reels of AV programs; 8000 photographs and negatives. **Services:** Copying; archives open to the public

for approved research projects. **Automated Operations:** Computerized cataloging. **Staff:** Jean K. Brown, Rec.Mgt.Adm..

★16110★
UNIVERSITY OF DELAWARE, NEWARK - CENTER FOR COMPOSITE MATERIALS - COMPOSITE MATERIALS REFERENCE ROOM (Sci-Engr)
201 Spencer Laboratory Phone: (302)451-8149
Newark, DE 19716 Carolyn Ryan, Libn.
Staff: 1. **Subjects:** Engineering mechanics, materials science, polymer science. **Special Collections:** Composite materials (2000 volumes). **Holdings:** 400 books; 100 bound periodical volumes; 1500 other cataloged items. **Subscriptions:** 22 journals and other serials. **Services:** Copying; room open to the public for reference use only.

★16111★
UNIVERSITY OF DELAWARE, NEWARK - CENTER FOR INTERDISCIPLINARY RESEARCH IN COMPUTER-BASED LEARNING (CIRCLe) - LIBRARY (Educ, Comp Sci)
College of Education
Willard Hall Education Bldg., Rm. 105 Phone: (302)451-2927
Newark, DE 19716 Jimmie Lee, Libn.
Subjects: Artificial intelligence, computer-based education and learning. **Holdings:** 2000 books and papers; 300 microfiche. **Subscriptions:** 30 journals and other serials. **Services:** Interlibrary loan; collection open to the public for reference use only. **Automated Operations:** Computerized cataloging.

★16112★
UNIVERSITY OF DELAWARE, NEWARK - COLLEGE OF URBAN AFFAIRS AND PUBLIC POLICY - LIBRARY (Soc Sci)
Graham Hall Phone: (302)451-2394
Newark, DE 19716 Mary Helen Callahan, Adm.
Staff: 1. **Subjects:** Government, economics, and sociology (primarily Delaware); census information on all school districts in New Castle County. **Holdings:** 2000 books. **Subscriptions:** 40 journals and other serials. **Services:** Students and others may borrow items with special permission. **Publications:** Bibliography of staff publications.

★16113★
UNIVERSITY OF DELAWARE, NEWARK - DEPARTMENT OF MUSIC - MUSIC RESOURCE CENTER (Mus)
Newark, DE 19716 Phone: (302)451-8130
J. Michael Foster, Supv.
Founded: 1979. **Staff:** Prof 1. **Subjects:** Music. **Holdings:** 2600 books; 4500 scores; 4300 phonograph records; 800 tape recordings. **Services:** Center open to the public.

★16114★
UNIVERSITY OF DELAWARE, NEWARK - DISASTER RESEARCH CENTER - LIBRARY (Soc Sci)
Newark, DE 19716 Phone: (302)451-6618
Founded: 1963. **Staff:** Prof 4. **Subjects:** Disaster research, sociology of disaster and mass emergencies. **Holdings:** 5000 books; 14,000 reports and articles; 250 dissertations and theses; documents. **Subscriptions:** 125 journals and other serials. **Services:** Copying; library open to the public. **Publications:** Publications List, semiannual - free upon request.

★16115★
UNIVERSITY OF DELAWARE, NEWARK - EDUCATION RESOURCE CENTER (Educ)
013 Willard Hall Education Bldg. Phone: (302)451-2335
Newark, DE 19716 Beth G. Anderson, Coord.
Founded: 1972. **Staff:** Prof 2. **Subjects:** Curriculum materials in elementary science and mathematics, elementary language arts, occupational education, special education, elementary social studies, reading, marine studies. **Holdings:** 15,000 books; AV programs and kits; microcomputer laboratory; videodiscs. **Subscriptions:** 10 education journals. **Services:** Center open to the public. **Computerized Information Services:** Special Education Mini Center (internal database). **Networks/Consortia:** Member of Delaware Learning Resource System (DLRS).

★16116★
UNIVERSITY OF DELAWARE, NEWARK - LIBRARY - AGRICULTURE LIBRARY (Agri)
002 Townsend Hall Phone: (302)451-2530
Newark, DE 19717-1303 Frederick B. Getze, Assoc.Libn.
Founded: 1888. **Staff:** Prof 1; Other 1. **Subjects:** Agriculture and related areas in biology and chemistry, veterinary medicine. **Special Collections:** State agricultural experiment station documents; Unidel History of Horticultural Landscape Architecture (housed at Morris Library). **Holdings:** 15,900 books; 18,300 bound periodical volumes; 3850 microforms. **Subscriptions:** 428 journals and other serials; 6 newspapers. **Services:** Interlibrary loan; copying; library open to the public. **Automated Operations:** Computerized public access catalog, cataloging, acquisitions, serials, circulation, and ILL. **Computerized Information Services:** DIALOG Information Services, Association of Research Libraries (ARL), RLIN, BRS Information Technologies, OCLC. Performs searches on fee basis. **Networks/Consortia:** Member of Center for Research Libraries (CRL) Consortia, PALINET.

★16117★
UNIVERSITY OF DELAWARE, NEWARK - LIBRARY - CHEMISTRY/CHEMICAL ENGINEERING LIBRARY (Sci-Engr)
202 Brown Laboratory Phone: (302)451-2993
Newark, DE 19716 Grace Vattilano, Chem.Lib.Supv.
Founded: 1938. **Staff:** 1. **Subjects:** Chemistry and chemical engineering. **Special Collections:** Unidel History of Chemistry Collection (housed at Morris Library). **Holdings:** 9990 books; 10,268 bound periodical volumes; 1035 reels of microfilm; Sadtler Spectra. **Subscriptions:** 445 journals and other serials. **Services:** Interlibrary loan; copying; library open to the public. **Automated Operations:** Computerized cataloging, acquisitions, serials, circulation, and ILL. **Computerized Information Services:** BRS Information Technologies, Association of Research Libraries (ARL), STN International, CAS ONLINE, DIALOG Information Services, RLIN, OCLC. **Networks/Consortia:** Member of Center for Research Libraries (CRL) Consortia, PALINET.

★16118★
UNIVERSITY OF DELAWARE, NEWARK - LIBRARY - MARINE STUDIES LIBRARY (Biol Sci, Sci-Engr)
Harry L. Cannon Marine Studies Laboratory Phone: (302)645-4290
Lewes, DE 19958 Dorothy Allen, Lib.Supv.
Founded: 1973. **Staff:** Prof 1; Other 1. **Subjects:** Marine biology and geology, physical and chemical oceanography. **Special Collections:** All publications of Delaware College of Marine Studies; Sea Grant publications. **Holdings:** 7200 books; 4100 bound periodical volumes; 5300 reprints. **Subscriptions:** 175 journals and other serials. **Services:** Interlibrary loan; copying; library open to the public. **Automated Operations:** Computerized public access catalog, cataloging, acquisitions, serials, and circulation. **Computerized Information Services:** DIALOG Information Services, OCLC, RLIN, BRS Information Technologies. **Networks/Consortia:** Member of Center for Research Libraries (CRL) Consortia, PALINET. **Formerly:** College of Marine Studies - Marine Studies Complex Library.

★16119★
UNIVERSITY OF DELAWARE, NEWARK - LIBRARY - PHYSICS LIBRARY (Sci-Engr)
221 Sharp Laboratory Phone: (302)451-2323
Newark, DE 19716 Andrea Gould, Lib.Supv.
Staff: 1. **Subjects:** Physics, astronomy, astrophysics, mathematics, engineering. **Holdings:** 3100 books; 2700 bound periodical volumes. **Subscriptions:** 80 journals and other serials. **Services:** Interlibrary loan; library open to the public. **Automated Operations:** Computerized cataloging, acquisitions, serials, circulation, and ILL. **Computerized Information Services:** DIALOG Information Services, RLIN, BRS Information Technologies, Association of Research Libraries (ARL), OCLC. **Networks/Consortia:** Member of Center for Research Libraries (CRL) Consortia, PALINET. **Formerly:** Hugh M. Morris Library - Physics Branch Library.

★16120★
UNIVERSITY OF DELAWARE, NEWARK - RALPH MAYER CENTER FOR ARTISTS' TECHNIQUES (Art)
303 Old College Phone: (302)451-8236
Newark, DE 19716 Hilton Brown, Coord.
Founded: 1984. **Staff:** 1. **Subjects:** Artists' materials and techniques. **Special Collections:** Archives of Ralph and Bena Mayer. **Holdings:** 200 books; 5 filing boxes of manuscripts, letters, reports. **Services:** Center not open to the public.

★16121★
UNIVERSITY OF DENVER - COLLEGE OF LAW - WESTMINSTER LAW LIBRARY (Law)
1900 Olive St. - LTLB Phone: (303)871-6190
Denver, CO 80220 Alfred J. Coco, Libn.
Founded: 1898. **Staff:** Prof 8; Other 8. **Subjects:** Law. **Holdings:** 215,648 books, bound periodical volumes, microforms, government documents. **Subscriptions:** 2406 journals and other serials. **Services:** Interlibrary loan; copying; library open to lawyers on payment of annual fee. **Automated Operations:** Computerized cataloging, acquisitions, and circulation. **Computerized Information Services:** DIALOG Information Services, WESTLAW, LEXIS. **Networks/Consortia:** Member of Colorado Alliance of Research Libraries (CARL). **Staff:** Gary Alexander, Hd., Pub.Serv.; Mary Wilder, Pub.Serv.Libn.; David Burrows, Pub.Serv.Libn.; Cindy Scott, Pub.Serv.Libn.; Barbara Allen, Cat.Libn.; Hollace Westfeldt, Acq./Ser.Libn..

★16122★
UNIVERSITY OF DENVER - PENROSE LIBRARY - SPECIAL COLLECTIONS (Hist)
2150 E. Evans Ave. Phone: (303)871-3428
Denver, CO 80208-0287 Steven Fisher, Cur.
Founded: 1864. **Special Collections:** Judaica (17,000 volumes); Husted Culinary Collection (8000 items); Miller Civil War Collection (1000 items); Davidson Folklore Collection (1000 items). **Services:** Interlibrary loan; copying; collections open to the public. **Automated Operations:** Computerized cataloging, acquisitions, serials, and circulation. **Computerized Information Services:** Online systems. **Networks/Consortia:** Member of Colorado Alliance of Research Libraries (CARL).

★16123★
UNIVERSITY OF DENVER AND DENVER RESEARCH INSTITUTE - SOCIAL SYSTEMS RESEARCH AND EVALUATION LIBRARY
2135 E. Wesley
Denver, CO 80210
Defunct

★16124★
UNIVERSITY OF DETROIT - EVENING BUSINESS AND ADMINISTRATION LIBRARY (Bus-Fin)
651 E. Jefferson Phone: (313)927-1525
Detroit, MI 48226 JoAnn Chalmers, Libn.
Founded: 1961. **Staff:** Prof 1; Other 1. **Subjects:** Accounting, economics, finance, management, marketing, statistics. **Holdings:** 11,500 books; 2200 bound periodical volumes; 500 corporate annual reports. **Subscriptions:** 100 journals and other serials. **Services:** Interlibrary loan; copying; library open to the public for reference use only. **Computerized Information Services:** OCLC. **Networks/Consortia:** Member of Michigan Library Consortium (MLC).

★16125★
UNIVERSITY OF DETROIT - LIBRARY MEDIA CENTER (Aud-Vis)
4001 W. McNichols Rd. Phone: (313)927-1075
Detroit, MI 48221 Maris L. Cannon, Hd., Lib. Media Serv.
Founded: 1961. **Staff:** Prof 4. **Subjects:** History, literature, language arts, fine arts, education, business and management, sociology, psychology, science, mathematics, religious studies, philosophy, economics, political science. **Holdings:** 2001 phonograph records and sets; 1520 filmstrips and filmstrip sets with sound; 155 slides and slide sets with sound; 646 models and games; 92 video cassettes and 16mm films; 320 audio cassettes and sets; 1740 transparencies and sets; 275 testing materials titles; reference materials. **Services:** Interlibrary loan; copying; AV equipment pool; AV aids for the visually impaired; projection rooms; group study rooms; photography; AV software production; audio cassette duplication; graphic design, production, and duplication; punch binding; center open to the public with restrictions. **Networks/Consortia:** Member of Michigan Library Consortium (MLC). **Publications:** Bibliography of Recent Acquisitions, annual. **Staff:** Ann Walaskay, Hd., Ref..

★16126★
UNIVERSITY OF DETROIT - SCHOOL OF DENTISTRY LIBRARY (Med)
2931 E. Jefferson Ave. Phone: (313)446-1817
Detroit, MI 48207 M. Agnes Shoup, Dir.
Founded: 1932. **Staff:** Prof 2; Other 3. **Subjects:** Dentistry. **Holdings:** 13,000 books; 15,000 bound periodical volumes. **Subscriptions:** 450 journals and other serials. **Services:** Interlibrary loan; copying; SDI; library open to the public for reference use only. **Automated Operations:** Computerized cataloging. **Computerized Information Services:** MEDLINE, DIALOG Information Services. Performs searches on fee basis. **Networks/Consortia:** Member of Michigan Library Consortium (MLC). **Publications:** Acquisitions, quarterly. **Staff:** Beverly Dorrah, Libn..

★16127★
UNIVERSITY OF DETROIT - SCHOOL OF LAW LIBRARY (Law)
651 E. Jefferson Ave. Phone: (313)961-5444
Detroit, MI 48226 Byron D. Cooper, Dir.
Founded: 1912. **Staff:** Prof 5; Other 7. **Subjects:** Law - United States, Canada, England. **Holdings:** 198,000 volumes; 50,000 volumes in microform. **Subscriptions:** 1800 journals and other serials; 10 newspapers. **Services:** Interlibrary loan; copying; library open to the public. **Automated Operations:** Computerized cataloging. **Computerized Information Services:** LEXIS, NEXIS, DIALOG Information Services, WESTLAW, VU/TEXT Information Services, BRS Information Technologies, (ELSS) Electronic Legislative Search System. **Networks/Consortia:** Member of Michigan Library Consortium (MLC). **Publications:** Law Library Guide, annual - to students; Current Acquisitions List, monthly. **Staff:** Colleen M. Hickey, S.S.J., Assoc.Dir.; Mary E. Hayes, Ref.Libn.; Gene P. Moy, Docs./Circ.Libn.; Katherine A. Cooper, Res.Spec.; Lida Keem, Tech.Serv..

★16128★
UNIVERSITY OF THE DISTRICT OF COLUMBIA - GEORGIA/HARVARD CAMPUS - HARVARD STREET LIBRARY (Educ)
1100 Harvard St., N.W. Phone: (202)673-7018
Washington, DC 20009 Melba Broome, Supv.
Staff: Prof 3; Other 1. **Subjects:** Education, human ecology. **Special Collections:** Trevor Arnett Library of Black Culture (8000 reels of microfilm); Miner-Wilson Collection (2000 rare books); legislative history of Federal City College. **Holdings:** 111,000 books; 10,000 bound periodical volumes; 150,000 microforms; archives. **Subscriptions:** 500 journals and other serials; 6 newspapers. **Services:** Interlibrary loan; copying; library open to the public with restrictions. **Networks/Consortia:** Member of Consortium of Universities of the Washington Metropolitan Area. **Special Catalogs:** Catalog of Miner-Wilson Collection; District of Columbia Teachers College Library (book catalog). **Staff:** Taro G. Gehani, Acq.Libn.; Elizabeth M. Thompson, Media Serv.Libn.; Anne Robinson, Media Serv.Libn..

★16129★
UNIVERSITY OF THE DISTRICT OF COLUMBIA - LEARNING RESOURCES DIVISION (Soc Sci, Hist)
4200 Connecticut Ave., N.W. Phone: (202)282-7536
Washington, DC 20008 Albert J. Casciero, Dir.
Holdings: Human Relations Area File (65 cabinets of 5" x 8" slips); African/Afro-Hispanic/American Media Collection (25 films; 97 books; 2 VF drawers of clippings); Atlanta University Black Culture Collection; Water Resources (625 items); University of D.C. archives (513 linear feet); slavery source materials (962 microfiche). **Subscriptions:** 1863 journals and other serials; 25 newspapers. **Services:** Interlibrary loan; copying; SDI; division open to the public with restrictions. **Automated Operations:** Computerized cataloging and circulation. **Computerized Information Services:** DIALOG Information Services, OCLC, Pergamon ORBIT InfoLine, Inc. Performs searches on fee basis. Contact Person: Chet Sarangapani, 282-3091. **Networks/Consortia:** Member of CAPCON, Consortium of Universities of the Washington Metropolitan Area. **Publications:** Library Newsletter.

UNIVERSITY OF FLORIDA - AGRICULTURAL RESEARCH CENTER - LIBRARY
See: University of Florida - Central Florida Research and Education Center - Leesburg Library (16140)

★16130★
UNIVERSITY OF FLORIDA - AGRICULTURAL RESEARCH & EDUCATION CENTER - LIBRARY (Agri)
Box 728 Phone: (904)692-1792
Hastings, FL 32045 M.J. Campbell, Staff Asst.
Staff: 1. **Subjects:** Agriculture, vegetable production. **Holdings:** 300 books; 240 bound periodical volumes; 100 unbound periodicals; 1400 unbound agricultural bulletins and pamphlets. **Subscriptions:** 28 journals and other serials. **Services:** Library open to the public for reference use only.

★16131★
UNIVERSITY OF FLORIDA - AQUATIC PLANT INFORMATION RETRIEVAL CENTER (Biol Sci)
2183 McCarty Hall Phone: (904)392-1799
Gainesville, FL 32611 Victor Ramey, Res.Ed.
Staff: Prof 2; Other 2. **Subjects:** Aquatic plants - biology, control, utilization, ecology. **Holdings:** 500 books; 25,000 other cataloged items. **Services:** Interlibrary loan; copying; center open to the public for reference use only. **Automated Operations:** Computerized cataloging, acquisitions, and document indexing. **Computerized Information Services:** DIALOG Information Services; Aquatic Weed Program (internal database). Performs searches free of charge. **Publications:** Aquaphyte, biennial - free upon request; bibliographic current-awareness service (computer printout); retrospective database searches (computer printout). **Formerly:** Aquatic Weed Program - Information and Retrieval Center. **Staff:** Karen Brown, Info.Spec..

★16132★
UNIVERSITY OF FLORIDA - ARCHITECTURE & FINE ARTS LIBRARY (Art)
201 FAA Phone: (904)392-0222
Gainesville, FL 32611 Edward H. Teague, AFA Libn.
Staff: Prof 2; Other 2. **Subjects:** Architecture, fine arts, interior design, building construction, landscape architecture, urban design. **Holdings:** 72,500 volumes; 12 VF drawers; 20 drawers of Historic American Buildings Survey drawings and pictures; 3715 microforms. **Subscriptions:** 431 journals and other serials. **Services:** Interlibrary loan; copying; library open to the public. **Publications:** New Books Received, monthly. **Staff:** Deirdre Spencer, Asst.Univ.Libn..

★16133★
UNIVERSITY OF FLORIDA - BALDWIN LIBRARY (Hum)
308 Library East
Gainesville, FL 32611 Dr. Ruth Baldwin
Staff: Prof 1; Other 1. **Subjects:** Historical children's literature. **Holdings:** 82,500 books, periodicals, and manuscripts.

★16134★
UNIVERSITY OF FLORIDA - BELKNAP COLLECTION FOR THE PERFORMING ARTS (Mus, Theater)
512 Library W. Phone: (904)392-0322
Gainesville, FL 32611 Sidney Ives, Libn.
Founded: 1953. **Staff:** Prof 1; Other 2. **Subjects:** Dance, opera, music, theater, film. **Special Collections:** Ringling Collection (early playbills; engravings; prints; photographs); 20th century American playbills; Florida performing arts files; popular sheet music collection; Sarah Belknap Correspondence and Guide to the Performing Arts. **Holdings:** 4200 books; 912 bound periodicals; 912 scores; 200,000 souvenir programs, prints and photographs, clippings, correspondence, posters. **Subscriptions:** 60 journals and other serials. **Services:** Copying; collection open to the public.

★16135★
UNIVERSITY OF FLORIDA - BORLAND HEALTH SCIENCES LIBRARY (Med)
580 W. 8th St. Phone: (904)359-6516
Jacksonville, FL 32209 Carolyn G. Hall, Dir.
Founded: 1964. **Staff:** Prof 3; Other 4. **Subjects:** Medicine, psychiatry, public health, nursing, allied health sciences, dentistry. **Holdings:** 3400 books; 23,000 bound periodical volumes. **Subscriptions:** 580 journals and other serials. **Services:** Interlibrary loan; copying. **Computerized Information Services:** MEDLINE, DIALOG Information Services. **Formerly:** Jacksonville Health Education Programs, Inc.

★16136★
UNIVERSITY OF FLORIDA - CENTER FOR CLIMACTERIC STUDIES - ROBERT B. GREENBLATT LIBRARY
901 N.W. 8th Ave., Suite B1
Gainesville, FL 32601
Defunct

★16137★
UNIVERSITY OF FLORIDA - CENTER FOR HEALTH POLICY RESEARCH - LIBRARY (Med)
Box J-177, Health Science Center Phone: (904)392-2571
Gainesville, FL 32610 Michael K. Miller, Ph.D., Dir.
Founded: 1981. **Staff:** Prof 2; Other 2. **Subjects:** Medical care regulation and administration, health economics. **Holdings:** 1500 volumes. **Services:** Library not open to the public.

★16138★
UNIVERSITY OF FLORIDA - CENTER FOR LATIN AMERICAN AND TROPICAL ART - LIBRARY (Art)
University Art Gallery
Gainesville, FL 32611
Subjects: Art - Latin American, African, Asian, Indian. **Holdings:** Figures not available. **Remarks:** Presently inactive.

★16139★
UNIVERSITY OF FLORIDA - CENTER FOR WETLANDS REFERENCE LIBRARY (Env-Cons)
Phelps Laboratory Phone: (904)392-2424
Gainesville, FL 32611 G. Ronnie Best, Assoc.Dir.
Staff: 6. **Subjects:** Wetlands research, ecosystems modeling, energy analysis, reclamation. **Holdings:** 900 books; 16 VF drawers of unbound reports; 100 theses and dissertations; 70 technical reports. **Services:** Library open to the public.

★16140★
UNIVERSITY OF FLORIDA - CENTRAL FLORIDA RESEARCH AND EDUCATION CENTER - LEESBURG LIBRARY (Biol Sci, Agri)
Inst. of Food & Agricultural Sciences
5336 University Ave. Phone: (904)787-3423
Leesburg, FL 32748 Dr. Gary W. Elmstrom, Asst.Ctr.Dir.
Founded: 1930. **Staff:** 2. **Subjects:** Plant pathology, vegetable crops, fruit crops, entomology. **Holdings:** 1267 volumes; 5335 indexed reprints; 109 unbound journals; 4250 abstract cards; 21,345 index cards. **Subscriptions:** 51 journals and other serials. **Services:** Library not open to the public. **Formerly:** Agricultural Research Center - Library.

★16141★
UNIVERSITY OF FLORIDA - CENTRAL SCIENCE LIBRARY (Sci-Engr)
Gainesville, FL 32611 Phone: (904)392-0342
Founded: 1987. **Staff:** Prof 10; Other 12. **Subjects:** Science, engineering, chemistry, physics, astronomy, food and agricultural sciences. **Holdings:** 446,000 books; 791,000 microforms. **Services:** Interlibrary loan; library open to the public. **Automated Operations:** Computerized cataloging, acquisitions, serials, and circulation. **Computerized Information Services:** DIALOG Information Services, OCLC, Pergamon ORBIT InfoLine, Inc., RLIN, WILSONLINE, TECH-NET, CAS ONLINE; FOCUS (internal database). Performs searches on fee basis. **Networks/Consortia:** Member of SOLINET.

★16142★
UNIVERSITY OF FLORIDA - CITRUS RESEARCH & EDUCATION CENTER - LAKE ALFRED LIBRARY (Agri, Biol Sci)
Inst. of Food & Agricultural Sciences
700 Experiment Station Rd. Phone: (813)956-1151
Lake Alfred, FL 33850 Pamela K. Russ, Assoc.Univ.Libn.
Founded: 1935. **Staff:** Prof 1. **Subjects:** Chemistry, botany, entomology, nematology, agronomy. **Special Collections:** Yothers Rare Book Collection (citrus). **Holdings:** 4635 books; 8145 bound periodical volumes; 850 documents; 24 VF drawers of citrus reprints; 1595 Florida Geological Survey maps. **Subscriptions:** 150 journals and other serials. **Services:** Copying; library open to the public for reference use only. **Automated Operations:** Computerized ILL. **Computerized Information Services:** DIALOG Information Services. **Special Indexes:** Citrus card file (author and subject).

★16143★
UNIVERSITY OF FLORIDA - COASTAL & OCEANOGRAPHIC ENGINEERING DEPARTMENT - COASTAL ENGINEERING ARCHIVES (Sci-Engr)
433 Weil Hall Phone: (904)392-2710
Gainesville, FL 32611 Judith J. Foxworth, Archv.
Staff: Prof 1; Other 1. **Subjects:** Florida beaches, beach erosion, sediment transport, coastal vegetation, nearshore oceanography, estuarine circulation. **Holdings:** 350 books; 360 microforms; 7500 other cataloged items. **Subscriptions:** 17 journals and other serials. **Services:** Interlibrary loan; copying; archives open to the public for reference use only.

★16144★
UNIVERSITY OF FLORIDA - COLLEGE OF EDUCATION LIBRARY (Educ)
1500 Norman Hall Phone: (904)392-0707
Gainesville, FL 32611 Myra Suzanne Brown, Chm./Assoc.Libn.
Staff: Prof 3; Other 2. **Subjects:** Education, child development, higher education, psychology, counseling, children's literature. **Holdings:** 74,800 books; 9000 bound periodical volumes; 322,034 ERIC microfiche; 725 reels of microfilm. **Services:** Interlibrary loan; copying; library open to the public. **Automated Operations:** Computerized cataloging. **Computerized Information Services:** RLIN, DIALOG Information Services, BRS Information Technologies, WILSONLINE. Performs searches on fee basis. **Staff:** Linda Sparks, Assoc.Libn.; Bruce Emerton, Asst.Libn..

★16145★
UNIVERSITY OF FLORIDA - DATA TAPE LIBRARY (Info Sci)
513 Library West Phone: (904)392-0796
Gainesville, FL 32611 Bill Covey
Founded: 1970. **Staff:** Prof 4; Other 2. **Subjects:** Census data, business data. **Holdings:** 4134 machine readable data tapes; 1995 computer disks. **Services:** Library open to the public with restrictions. **Automated Operations:** Computerized cataloging, acquisitions, circulation, and serials. **Computerized Information Services:** DIALOG Information Services, BRS Information Technologies, RLIN, Pergamon ORBIT InfoLine, Inc., OCLC, Northwestern Online Total Integrated System (NOTIS); LUIS (internal database). Performs searches on fee basis. Contact Person: Colleen Seale, Ref.Dept., 392-0361.

★16146★
UNIVERSITY OF FLORIDA - DOCUMENTS LIBRARY (Info Sci)
254 Library West Phone: (904)392-0367
Gainesville, FL 32611 Sally Cravens, Chm./Univ.Libn.
Staff: Prof 4; Other 4. **Subjects:** Government publications - United States, foreign, international, Florida, and other states. **Holdings:** 620,114 documents; 522,950 microfiche; 19 reels of microfilm; 28 VF drawers of Florida material. **Subscriptions:** 165 journals and other serials. **Services:** Interlibrary loan; copying; library open to the public. **Automated Operations:** Computerized cataloging. **Computerized Information Services:** OCLC, DIALOG Information Services, Pergamon ORBIT InfoLine, Inc.; Focus (internal database). **Staff:** Gary Cornwell, Assoc.Libn./U.S., Fed.Docs.; Bonnie Konop, Asst.Libn./State Docs..

★16147★
UNIVERSITY OF FLORIDA - EVERGLADES RESEARCH & EDUCATION CENTER - BELLE GLADE LIBRARY (Biol Sci, Agri)
Inst. of Food & Agricultural Sciences
Drawer A Phone: (407)996-3062
Belle Glade, FL 33430 Dr. Jones, Lib.Comm.Chm.
Staff: 1. **Subjects:** Agriculture, soils science, rice, vegetables, sugarcane, tropical botany, animal science, crops science, horticulture science. **Holdings:** 5000 books; 3700 bound periodical volumes. **Subscriptions:** 171 journals and other serials. **Services:** Interlibrary loan; copying; library open to the public for reference use only. **Publications:** AREC Research Reports EES. **Formerly:** Agricultural Research & Education Center.

★16148★
UNIVERSITY OF FLORIDA - FLORIDA STATE MUSEUM - SIMPSON LIBRARY OF PALEONTOLOGY (Sci-Engr, Biol Sci)
Museum Rd. Phone: (904)392-1721
Gainesville, FL 32611 Dr. S. David Webb, Dir.
Founded: 1971. **Subjects:** Vertebrate and invertebrate paleontology, geology, natural history, ecology. **Special Collections:** G.G. Simpson's personal collection of books and reprints. **Holdings:** 4000 books; 2000 bound periodical volumes; 50,000 reprints and separates; 30 dissertations. **Subscriptions:** 20 journals and other serials. **Services:** Library open to visiting scientists for reference use only. **Staff:** Graig D. Shaak, Assoc.Dir..

★16149★
UNIVERSITY OF FLORIDA - GULF COAST RESEARCH & EDUCATION CENTER - BRADENTON LIBRARY (Biol Sci)
Inst. of Food & Agricultural Sciences
5007 60th St., E. Phone: (813)755-1568
Bradenton, FL 34203 Tracey Revels, Libn.
Staff: 1. **Subjects:** Plant pathology, entomology, vegetable crops, horticulture. **Holdings:** 550 books; 900 bound periodical volumes. **Subscriptions:** 40 journals and other serials. **Services:** Library not open to the public.

★16150★
UNIVERSITY OF FLORIDA - HEALTH SCIENCE LIBRARY (Med)
Box J-206 Phone: (904)392-4016
Gainesville, FL 32611 Ted F. Srygley, Dir.
Founded: 1956. **Staff:** Prof 11; Other 30. **Subjects:** Medicine, basic medical sciences, nursing, pharmacy, veterinary medicine, allied health sciences, dentistry. **Holdings:** 215,000 volumes; 2317 films and tapes; 1289 microfiche; 24 microcards; 183 reels of microfilm; Ciba collection of slides. **Subscriptions:** 4470 journals and other serials. **Services:** Interlibrary loan (fee); copying; library open to the public by permission. **Computerized Information Services:** MEDLINE, DIALOG Information Services, Pergamon ORBIT InfoLine, Inc., OCLC. **Networks/Consortia:** Member of SOLINET. **Publications:** New Book List; annual periodical list. **Staff:** Esther Jones, Pub.Serv.Libn.; Leonard Rhine, Tech.Serv.Libn..

★16151★
UNIVERSITY OF FLORIDA - ISSER AND RAE PRICE LIBRARY OF JUDAICA (Hist, Rel-Phil)
18 Library East Phone: (904)392-0308
Gainesville, FL 32611 Robert Singerman, Libn.
Founded: 1977. **Staff:** Prof 1; Other 1. **Subjects:** Judaism, Jewish history, Hebrew and Yiddish language and literature, Israel and Zionism, Rabbinic literature, Hebrew scriptures. **Special Collections:** Mishkin Collection (30,000 volumes). **Holdings:** 52,500 books; 2200 bound periodical volumes; 375 reels of microfilm; 303 microfiche. **Subscriptions:** 350 journals and other serials. **Services:** Interlibrary loan; copying; library open to the public for reference use only. **Automated Operations:** Computerized cataloging. **Computerized Information Services:** OCLC. **Networks/Consortia:** Member of SOLINET. **Publications:** Isser and Rae Price Library of Judaica Report, semiannual - free upon request. **Special Catalogs:** Catalog to pre-1881 Hebrew and Yiddish imprints (card).

★16152★
UNIVERSITY OF FLORIDA - LATIN AMERICAN COLLECTION (Area-Ethnic)
4th Fl., Library East Phone: (904)392-0360
Gainesville, FL 32611 Dr. Rosa Q. Mesa, Dir.
Founded: 1967. **Staff:** Prof 2; Other 10. **Subjects:** Latin America, Caribbean and Circum-Caribbean, Brazil. **Special Collections:** Caribbean Collection (45,880 books; 203 current periodicals; 13,494 reels of microfilm); Latin American Collection (177,254 books; 1103 periodicals; 19,370 reels of microfilm; 6806 microcards; 12,255 microfiche). **Holdings:** 6200 dissertations on microfilm; 123 atlases; Latin American vertical file. **Subscriptions:** 1334 journals and other serials; 38 newspapers. **Services:** Interlibrary loan; collection open to the public.

★16153★
UNIVERSITY OF FLORIDA - LEGAL INFORMATION CENTER (Law)
Gainesville, FL 32611 Phone: (904)392-0418
Dr. Betty W. Taylor, Dir./Prof.
Founded: 1909. **Staff:** Prof 9; Other 13. **Subjects:** Law - tax, labor, statutory, water resources, property and public, international, admiralty, Latin American. **Holdings:** 278,450 volumes; 703,650 microforms; 3850 computer disks. **Subscriptions:** 6301 journals and other serials. **Services:** Interlibrary loan; copying; library open to the public by permission. **Automated Operations:** Computerized cataloging and serials. **Computerized Information Services:** LEXIS, WESTLAW, OCLC, DIALOG Information Services, InfoTrac, Legaltrak, RLIN. **Networks/Consortia:** Member of SOLINET. **Staff:** A.R. Donnelly, Act. & Assoc.Dir.; Robert Munro, Law Libn.; Carol Feltz, Asst.Libn., Acq.; Pamela D. Williams, Assoc.Libn., Ref.; Carole Grooms, Assoc.Libn., Cat.; Susy B. Gilman, Asst.Libn., Circ.; James Flavin, Asst.Libn., AV; Scott Rawnsley, Asst.Libn., Ref.; Randall Coorough, Asst.Libn., AV.

★16154★
UNIVERSITY OF FLORIDA - MAP LIBRARY (Geog-Map)
Central Science Library Phone: (904)392-0803
Gainesville, FL 32611 Dr. HelenJane Armstrong, Map Libn.
Staff: Prof 1; Other 4. **Subjects:** Maps, aerial photographs and remote sensing images including the specialized areas of Latin America, Africa, and Southeastern United States. **Special Collections:** Erwin Raisz Collection of Maps and Cartographic Papers; Sanborn Historical Maps of Florida Cities (6000). **Holdings:** 350,400 maps; 150,224 aerial photographs; 1300 remote sensing images; 110 relief models; 150 transparencies; 925 microforms. **Services:** Library open to the public. **Automated Operations:** Computerized cataloging. **Computerized Information Services:** OCLC, RLIN, FOCUS. **Publications:** Acquisitions List, irregular.

★16155★
UNIVERSITY OF FLORIDA - MUSIC LIBRARY (Mus)
231 Music Bldg. Phone: (904)392-6678
Gainesville, FL 32611 Robena Eng Cornwell, Assoc.Univ.Libn.
Founded: 1972. **Staff:** Prof 1; Other 1. **Subjects:** Music. **Special Collections:** Claude Murphree Collection (10 VF drawers). **Holdings:** 17,500 books; 7000 scores; 2000 bound periodical volumes; 1442 microfiche; 15,000 phonograph records; 3057 tapes; 775 VF titles; 476 reels of microfilm. **Subscriptions:** 141 journals and other serials. **Services:** Interlibrary loan; copying; library open to the public with restrictions. **Automated Operations:** Computerized cataloging.

★16156★
UNIVERSITY OF FLORIDA - NORTH FLORIDA RESEARCH & EDUCATION CENTER - QUINCY LIBRARY
Rte. 3, Box 4370
Quincy, FL 32351
Subjects: Agriculture. **Holdings:** Figures not available. **Remarks:** Presently inactive.

★16157★
UNIVERSITY OF FLORIDA - P.K. YONGE LABORATORY SCHOOL - MEAD LIBRARY (Educ)
1080 S.W. 11th St. Phone: (904)391-1506
Gainesville, FL 32611 Iona Malanchuk, Hd.Libn.
Founded: 1934. **Staff:** Prof 2; Other 2. **Subjects:** Curriculum materials for grades K-12. **Holdings:** 19,000 volumes; 253 maps; 520 recordings; 1052 filmstrips; 126 tapes; 122 slide-tape sets; 42 cassettes; 93 film loops; 40 games; 400 kits; 13 reels of microfilm; 124 posters; 506 slides; 300 transparencies. **Subscriptions:** 102 journals and other serials. **Services:** Interlibrary loan; library open to qualified persons.

★16158★
UNIVERSITY OF FLORIDA - P.K. YONGE LIBRARY OF FLORIDA HISTORY (Hist)
404 Library West Phone: (904)392-0319
Gainesville, FL 32611 Elizabeth Alexander, Libn.
Founded: 1944. **Staff:** Prof 1; Other 2. **Subjects:** Florida history and prehistory. **Special Collections:** Stetson Collection (photostats of documents from the Archivo General de Indias, Sevilla, relating to Spanish activity in the Southeastern borderlands, 1518-1819; 150,000); East Florida Papers (archives of the Second Spanish Administration of East Florida, 1784-1821; 178 reels of microfilm); Papeles de Cuba (Spanish West and East Florida, 1784-1819; 761 reels of microfilm). **Holdings:** 25,000 books and bound periodical volumes; 2500 maps; 19th and 20th century Florida newspapers on microfilm; miscellaneous manuscripts; microfilm and photocopies of Colonial British and Spanish Florida materials. **Services:** Library open to adults for reference use only.

★16159★
UNIVERSITY OF FLORIDA - RARE BOOKS & MANUSCRIPTS (Rare Book, Hum)
531 Library West Phone: (904)392-0321
Gainesville, FL 32611 Sidney Ives, Libn.
Staff: Prof 1; Other 1. **Subjects:** 17th, 18th, and 19th century English and American literature; English theology (especially 17th century); modern English and American poetry; history of ideas; Irish literary revival. **Special Collections:** Printing and graphic arts; Rochambeau papers; John Wilson Croker papers; Margaret Dreier Robins papers; Bromsen-Medina and Harrisse collections of Latin American bibliography; Jeremie papers (Haiti); Sir Walter Scott; Florida authors: papers of Alden Hatch, Zora Neale Hurston, John D. MacDonald, Edith Pope, Marjorie Kinnan Rawlings, and Lillian Smith; manuscripts of Lady Gregory; P.D. Howe Collection (New England authors' first printings and manuscripts; 6000 volumes); Kohler Collection of Victorian Theology. **Holdings:** 62,000 books; 350 unbound periodicals; 560 linear feet of manuscripts; 99 linear feet of pamphlets. **Subscriptions:** 74 journals and other serials. **Services:** Copying (limited); library open to the public. **Computerized Information Services:** OCLC, RLIN. **Networks/Consortia:** Member of SOLINET. **Special Catalogs:** Descriptive author catalogs (Howe Library I-IV in print). **Special Indexes:** Manuscript collection index (loose-leaf).

★16160★
UNIVERSITY OF FLORIDA - RESEARCH & EDUCATION CENTER - FORT LAUDERDALE LIBRARY (Agri, Biol Sci)
Inst. of Food & Agricultural Sciences
3205 College Ave.
Fort Lauderdale, FL 33314 Phone: (305)475-8990
Staff: Prof 1. **Subjects:** Ornamental horticulture, entomology, turf science, plant pathology, soils, aquatic weeds science, environmental quality, urban entomology. **Holdings:** 1200 books; 360 bound periodical volumes. **Subscriptions:** 65 serials. **Services:** Library open to the public with restrictions. **Computerized Information Services:** Access to online systems. **Publications:** Conference proceedings; Library Bulletin. **Formerly:** Agricultural Research & Education Center.

★16161★
UNIVERSITY OF FLORIDA - SPACE ASTRONOMY LABORATORY - LIBRARY (Sci-Engr)
1810 N.W. 6th St. Phone: (904)392-5450
Gainesville, FL 32609 Ms. P. Perkins, Libn.
Founded: 1973. **Subjects:** Atmospheric physics, astronomy, space astronomy, spacecraft environments, space instrumentation, nuclear physics/astrophysics. **Special Collections:** Magnetic tapes of observations from Skylab, Space Shuttle Mission 3, Pioneer 10 and 11; ESA GIOTTO Halley Mission; ground observations of zodiacal light and background starlight. **Holdings:** 200 volumes. **Subscriptions:** 25 journals and other serials. **Services:** Interlibrary loan; library open to the public for reference use only.

★16162★
UNIVERSITY OF FLORIDA - TRANSPORTATION RESEARCH CENTER (Trans)
Civil Engineering Dept.
245 Weil Hall Phone: (904)392-6656
Gainesville, FL 32611 Deborah Reaves, Assoc. in Engr.
Subjects: Transportation engineering and planning, traffic engineering. **Holdings:** 100 books; 2000 government and private reports. **Subscriptions:** 10 journals and other serials. **Services:** Copying; center open to the public by appointment. **Publications:** Research publications, 12/year.

★16163★
UNIVERSITY OF FLORIDA - TROPICAL RESEARCH & EDUCATION CENTER - HOMESTEAD LIBRARY (Biol Sci, Agri)
Inst. of Food & Agricultural Sciences
18905 S.W. 280th St. Phone: (305)247-4624
Homestead, FL 33031 R.M. Baranowski, Dir.
Staff: 14. **Subjects:** Plant pathology, entomology, plant nutrition, horticulture, tropical foliage plants, soil science, tropical exotics, tissue culture. **Special Collections:** Collection on all aspects of mango culture and tropical and subtropical fruits. **Holdings:** 3200 books; 750 bound periodical volumes. **Subscriptions:** 75 journals and other serials. **Services:** Library not open to the public. **Staff:** C.M. Sullivan, Libn..

★16164★
UNIVERSITY OF FLORIDA - UNIVERSITY ARCHIVES AND UNIVERSITY COLLECTION (Hist)
303 Library East Phone: (904)392-6547
Gainesville, FL 32611 Carla Kemp, Univ.Archv./Assoc.Libn.
Founded: 1951. **Staff:** Prof 1; Other 2. **Subjects:** University history. **Holdings:** 25,000 volumes; 1300 cubic feet of manuscripts from faculty, staff, alumni; 1566 linear feet of university publications, theses, dissertations, newspapers, yearbooks, ephemera, and photographs. **Services:** Copying; archives open to the public.

★16165★
UNIVERSITY OF FLORIDA - URBAN AND REGIONAL PLANNING DOCUMENTS COLLECTION (Plan)
Library West Phone: (904)392-0317
Gainesville, FL 32611 Margaret S. LeSourd, Assoc.Univ.Libn.
Staff: Prof 1; Other 1. **Subjects:** Planning. **Special Collections:** HUD 701 planning reports; Florida Local Government Comprehensive Planning Reports. **Holdings:** 30,800 documents; 10,200 Rand Corporation publications; 2 VF drawers of census maps. **Services:** Interlibrary loan; collection open to the public with courtesy card required for borrowing.

★16166★
UNIVERSITY OF GEORGIA - COLLEGE OF EDUCATION - CURRICULUM MATERIALS CENTER (Educ)
Aderhold Hall Phone: (404)542-2996
Athens, GA 30602 Janet Lawrence, Libn.
Staff: Prof 1; Other 5. **Subjects:** Juvenile and young adult literature, education. **Special Collections:** The Osborne Collection: Toronto Public Library Early English Children's Books (30 volumes). **Holdings:** 19,000 books; 5 VF drawers; 6 cabinet drawers of microfiche; Kraus Curriculum Guides on microfiche, 1970 to present; phonograph records; videotapes; posters; maps; charts; slides. **Subscriptions:** 70 journals and other serials. **Services:** Center open to the public with restrictions. **Automated Operations:** Computerized public access catalog. **Computerized**

Information Services: BITNET; internal database. **Publications:** Acquisitions lists, quarterly; information brochure and resource lists.

★16167★
UNIVERSITY OF GEORGIA - DATA SERVICES (Soc Sci)
University of Georgia Libraries Phone: (404)542-0727
Athens, GA 30602 Hortense L. Bates, Hd.
Founded: 1986. **Staff:** Prof 1; Other 2. **Subjects:** Census, social and political sciences, public opinion polls. **Holdings:** 800 books; 900 reels of magnetic tape. **Services:** Services open to the public with restrictions. **Automated Operations:** Computerized cataloging, acquisitions, and circulation.

★16168★
UNIVERSITY OF GEORGIA - DEPARTMENT OF RECORDS MANAGEMENT & UNIVERSITY ARCHIVES (Hist)
4th Fl., Old Section
Ilah Dunlap Little Memorial Library Phone: (404)542-8151
Athens, GA 30602 Dr. John Carver Edwards, Rec.Off./Archv.
Founded: 1972. **Staff:** 4. **Subjects:** Presidential papers, administrative records, student records, fiscal records. **Special Collections:** Ecological Society of America Collection; Institute of Ecology Archives. **Holdings:** 9500 cubic feet of university archival material. **Services:** Archives open to the public.

★16169★
UNIVERSITY OF GEORGIA - GEORGIA AGRICULTURAL EXPERIMENT STATION LIBRARY (Agri)
Experiment, GA 30212 Phone: (404)228-7238
Carole L. Ledford, Libn.
Staff: Prof 1; Other 2. **Subjects:** Agriculture and related sciences. **Holdings:** 36,000 volumes. **Subscriptions:** 557 journals and other serials. **Services:** Interlibrary loan; library open to the public with restrictions. **Computerized Information Services:** DIALOG Information Services, BRS Information Technologies.

★16170★
UNIVERSITY OF GEORGIA - GEORGIA CENTER FOR CONTINUING EDUCATION - LIBRARY (Educ)
Athens, GA 30602 Phone: (404)542-6663
Deanna L. Roberts, Act.Hd.Libn.
Founded: 1957. **Staff:** Prof 1; Other 2. **Subjects:** Adult and continuing education, conference programming and management. **Holdings:** 1865 books; 162 bound periodical volumes. **Subscriptions:** 224 journals and other serials; 7 newspapers. **Services:** Interlibrary loan; copying; library open to the public. **Automated Operations:** Computerized public access catalog.

★16171★
UNIVERSITY OF GEORGIA - GEORGIA COASTAL PLAIN EXPERIMENT STATION LIBRARY (Agri)
Tifton, GA 31793 Phone: (912)386-3447
Founded: 1924. **Staff:** 2. **Subjects:** Agricultural research. **Holdings:** 16,500 volumes; 300 theses and dissertations; 20 VF drawers of reprints and pamphlets. **Subscriptions:** 300 journals and other serials. **Services:** Interlibrary loan; copying; library primarily for use of research personnel at the station.

★16172★
UNIVERSITY OF GEORGIA - GOVERNMENT DOCUMENTS DEPARTMENT (Info Sci)
University of Georgia Libraries Phone: (404)542-8949
Athens, GA 30602 Susan C. Field, Hd., Govt.Docs.Dept.
Founded: 1907. **Staff:** Prof 4; Other 4. **Special Collections:** U.S. Government publications; Georgia state and United Nations documents; British Parliamentary debates and papers; official gazettes of France and West Germany; regional U.S. Government document depository, 1977 to present; selective depository for Canadian documents. **Holdings:** Figures not available. **Services:** Interlibrary loan; department open to the public. **Publications:** Documents in Georgia. **Special Indexes:** U.S. agency and shelflist; Georgia shelflist, keyword, and title; U.N. shelflist and title; Canada shelflist and series title.

★16173★
UNIVERSITY OF GEORGIA - HARGRETT RARE BOOK AND MANUSCRIPT LIBRARY (Rare Book, Hist)
University of Georgia Libraries Phone: (404)542-7123
Athens, GA 30602 Thomas E. Camden, Hd.
Staff: Prof 5; Other 6. **Subjects:** Georgiana, Civil War, small press and fine printing, theater arts, southern culture, English and American literature, British local history, music, photography. **Special Collections:** Georgiana (100,000 volumes); DeRenne Collection (Georgiana); Egmont papers; Charles Coburn Collection; Charles C. Jones Collection; Telamon Cuyler Collection; Olin Downes Collection; Ward Morehouse Collection; Paris Music Hall Collection; Keith Read Collection; Margaret Mitchell Marsh papers; Lillian Smith papers. **Holdings:** 100,000 rare books; 4 million manuscripts. **Services:** Department open to the public. **Special Catalogs:** Unpublished guides to manuscripts. **Staff:** Joseph Cote, Georgiana; Mary Ellen Brooks, Rare Bks.; Nancy Stamper, Rare Bks.; Larry Gulley, Mss..

★16174★
UNIVERSITY OF GEORGIA - LAW LIBRARY (Law)
Athens, GA 30602 Phone: (404)542-8480
Erwin C. Surrency, Dir.
Staff: Prof 7; Other 11. **Subjects:** Law. **Holdings:** 322,173 volumes; 4379 reels of microfilm; 231,310 microfiche. **Subscriptions:** 1190 journals and other serials; 11 newspapers. **Services:** Interlibrary loan; copying; library open to the public. **Computerized Information Services:** LEXIS, WESTLAW, OCLC. **Publications:** List of Acquisitions. **Special Indexes:** Index to legal publications in the state of Georgia (cards). **Staff:** Jose R. Pages, Acq.Libn.; Carol Ramsey, Cat.Libn.; Martha N. Hampton, Law Ser.Libn.; Jose F. Rodriguez, Circ. & Ref.Libn.; Diana Duderwicz, Asst.Cat.Libn.; Sally Curtis Askew, Asst.Pub.Serv.Libn.; James M. Whitehead, Asst.Pub.Serv.Libn..

★16175★
UNIVERSITY OF GEORGIA - RICHARD B. RUSSELL MEMORIAL LIBRARY (Soc Sci)
University of Georgia Libraries Phone: (404)542-5788
Athens, GA 30602 Sheryl B. Vogt, Dept.Hd.
Founded: 1974. **Staff:** 5. **Subjects:** 20th century Georgia politics; U.S. Congress; civil rights; agriculture, defense, and armed services legislation. **Holdings:** 5708 linear feet. **Services:** Interlibrary loan; copying; library open to the public; visiting scholars should write for application to do research. **Staff:** Lenore Richey, Archv.Assoc.; James Greve, Libn..

★16176★
UNIVERSITY OF GEORGIA - SCIENCE LIBRARY (Sci-Engr)
Athens, GA 30602 Phone: (404)542-4535
Arlene E. Luchsinger, Hd.
Staff: Prof 13; Other 22. **Subjects:** Science, technology, agriculture, home economics, medicine, veterinary medicine. **Holdings:** 600,000 books. **Subscriptions:** 5000 journals and other serials. **Services:** Interlibrary loan; copying; library open to the public. **Automated Operations:** Computerized public access catalog, acquisitions, and circulation. **Computerized Information Services:** DIALOG Information Services, BRS Information Technologies, OCLC, Pergamon ORBIT InfoLine, Inc.; ALANET (electronic mail service). **Networks/Consortia:** Member of SOLINET.

★16177★
UNIVERSITY OF GEORGIA - SCIENCE LIBRARY - MAP COLLECTION (Geog-Map)
University of Georgia Libraries Phone: (404)542-4535
Athens, GA 30602 John Sutherland, Map Cur.
Staff: Prof 1; Other 1. **Subjects:** Topography, geology, natural resources, climate, population. **Special Collections:** Sanborn Atlas Sheets of Georgia (7100). **Holdings:** 208,000 aerial photographs; 315,000 maps; 1400 atlases. **Services:** Interlibrary loan; copying; collection open to the public. **Computerized Information Services:** OCLC. **Publications:** Selected Acquisitions, quarterly; Sanborn Fire Insurance Maps of Georgia Held by the Map Collection; Atlases in the Map Collection; Aerial Photograph coverage of Georgia Held by the Map Collection.

★16178★
UNIVERSITY OF GEORGIA - SKIDAWAY INSTITUTE OF OCEANOGRAPHY - LIBRARY (Sci-Engr, Biol Sci)
Box 13687 Phone: (912)356-2474
Savannah, GA 31406-0687 Tom A. Turner, Libn.
Staff: Prof 1. **Subjects:** Oceanography, marine resources, fisheries, marine pollution, geochemistry, marine research. **Special Collections:** Climatological data for Georgia and adjacent states; sea surface isotherm records, 1960 to 1979; Gulf Stream data, 1966 to present; marine science reprints (11,000). **Holdings:** 3600 books; 6500 bound periodical volumes; 8000 reports, documents, and unbound serials. **Subscriptions:** 260 journals and other serials; 35 newsletters. **Services:** Interlibrary loan; copying; library open to the public with restrictions. **Automated Operations:** Computerized cataloging, acquisitions, and serials (through University of Georgia Libraries). **Computerized Information Services:** DIALOG Information Services, Association of Research Libraries (ARL). **Networks/Consortia:** Member of Center for Research Libraries (CRL) Consortia. **Publications:** Serials holdings list. **Remarks:** The library is a

branch of the University of Georgia Libraries but the Skidaway Institute of Oceanography is a separate research unit of the University System of Georgia.

★16179★
UNIVERSITY OF GUAM - MICRONESIAN AREA RESEARCH CENTER - PACIFIC COLLECTION (Area-Ethnic)
U.O.G. Sta. Phone: (717)734-2921
Mangilao, GU 96923 Albert L. Williams, Libn.
Founded: 1967. **Staff:** Prof 3. **Subjects:** Micronesia - history, marine biology, anthropology, missions, languages, World War II. **Special Collections:** Spanish manuscripts; South Pacific Commission depository; Guam Constitutional Convention Papers; A.B. Won Pat Papers (300 boxes). **Holdings:** 20,000 volumes; 80 VF drawers of clippings and pamphlets; 1000 slides; 30 VF drawers containing 12,000 photographs; 58 boxes of microfiche; 1300 reels of microfilm; 150 boxes of archives; 2000 sheets of maps and charts; 220 tapes. **Subscriptions:** 300 journals and other serials. **Services:** Copying (limited); collection open to the public for reference use only. **Computerized Information Services:** DIALOG Information Services; internal database. Performs searches free of charge. Contact Person: Dr. Kenneth Carriveau, Libn.. **Publications:** Bibliographies; special publications; MARC Working Papers; Newsletter. **Special Indexes:** Indexes for photographs, Pacific Islands, ships, personalities; tables of contents and subject indexes for manuscripts. **Staff:** Marjorie G. Driver, Spanish Period Spec..

★16180★
UNIVERSITY OF GUELPH - HUMANITIES AND SOCIAL SCIENCES DIVISION - MAP COLLECTION (Geog-Map)
McLaughlin Library Phone: (519)824-4120
Guelph, ON, Canada N1G 2W1 Flora Francis, Ref.Libn.
Staff: Prof 2; Other 2. **Subjects:** Cartography, agriculture, climatology, economics, geology, historiology, hydrology, land use, population, soils, topography, transportation. **Holdings:** 68,000 maps; 1150 atlases; 100 gazetteers; indexes; cartobibliographies; cartographic equipment. **Services:** Interlibrary loan (limited); copying; collection open to the public. **Automated Operations:** Computerized public access catalog, cataloging, acquisitions, serials, and circulation. **Computerized Information Services:** BRS Information Technologies, CAN/OLE, DIALOG Information Services, Info Globe, QL Systems, International Development Research Center (IDRC); ALANET, Envoy 100, BITNET (electronic mail services). Performs searches on fee basis.

★16181★
UNIVERSITY OF GUELPH - UNIVERSITY LIBRARY (Soc Sci, Agri, Hum)
Guelph, ON, Canada N1G 2W1 Phone: (519)824-4120
Dr. John B. Black, Chf.Libn.
Founded: 1964. **Staff:** Prof 35; Other 110. **Subjects:** Agriculture; veterinary medicine; arts; humanities; social sciences; pure, natural, and applied sciences. **Special Collections:** Theatre Archives; Bernard Shaw Collection; Scottish Collection; L.M. Montgomery; Apiculture. **Holdings:** 2.4 million volumes. **Subscriptions:** 8500 journals and other serials. **Services:** Interlibrary loan; copying; SDI; library open to the public. **Automated Operations:** Computerized public access catalog, cataloging, acquisitions, serials, circulation, documents, and maps. **Computerized Information Services:** QL Systems, CAN/OLE, BRS Information Technologies, WILSONLINE, MEDLARS, Info Globe, International Development Research Centre (IDRC), RESORS (Remote Sensing On-Line Retrieval System), DIALOG Information Services; internal databases; ALANET, BITNET, NETNORTH, CoSy, Envoy 100 (electronic mail services). Performs searches on fee basis. Contact Person: Ellen M. Pearson, Assoc.Libn., Info.Serv.. **Networks/Consortia:** Member of Ontario Council of University Libraries (OCUL). **Publications:** Reports, irregular; Library Newsletter; bibliography series, irregular; Collection Update, annual. **Staff:** E.M. Pearson, Assoc.Libn., Info.Sys.; L.T. Porter, Assoc.Libn., Sys./Tech.Proc.; V.A. Gillham, Asst.Libn., Rd.Serv.; F.J. Stewart, Hd., Bus.Off.; P.L. Hock, Hd., Circ.Div.; J.M. Kaufman, Hd., Doc. & Media Rsrc.Ctr.; B.M.L. Katz, Hd., Hum. & Soc.Sci.Div.; D.C. Hull, Hd., Sci. & Vet.Sci.Div.; E.L. Tom, Hd., Tech.Proc.Div.; E.M. Wiegand, Asst.Hd., Tech.Proc.Div.; N.C. Sadek, Archv. & Spec.Coll.; T.D. Sauer, Hd., Acq. & Coll.Div.; C.P. Pawley, Info. Desk/ILL Serv.; R.A. Logan, Liaison/Info.Serv.; W.R. Halahan, Lib.Sys..

★16182★
UNIVERSITY OF HARTFORD - ANNE BUNCE CHENEY LIBRARY (Art)
200 Bloomfield Ave. Phone: (203)243-4397
West Hartford, CT 06117 Jean J. Miller, Art Libn.
Founded: 1963. **Staff:** Prof 1; Other 1. **Subjects:** Art history, art education, applied art, decorative arts, crafts, photography, typography. **Holdings:** 10,817 books; 1533 bound periodical volumes; 14,517 mounted reproductions; 3005 pamphlets; 17 VF drawers of exhibition catalogs. **Subscriptions:** 95 journals and other serials. **Services:** Interlibrary loan; library open to the public. **Computerized Information Services:** OCLC. **Networks/Consortia:** Member of NELINET, Capitol Region Library Council (CRLC), Hartford Consortium for Higher Education.

★16183★
UNIVERSITY OF HARTFORD - HARTT SCHOOL OF MUSIC - ALLEN MEMORIAL LIBRARY (Mus)
200 Bloomfield Ave. Phone: (203)243-4491
West Hartford, CT 06117 Linda Solow Blotner, Mus.Libn.
Staff: Prof 1; Other 3. **Subjects:** Music and performing arts. **Special Collections:** Robert E. Smith Record Collection (30,000 phonograph records); Kalmen Opperman Collection (clarinet). **Holdings:** 13,500 books; 1200 bound periodical volumes; 30,000 pieces of music; 20,000 phonograph records; 2000 audiotapes; 160 reels of microfilm; 300 compact discs; 100 video cassettes. **Subscriptions:** 200 journals and other serials. **Services:** Interlibrary loan; copying; library open to the public for reference use only. **Automated Operations:** Computerized cataloging. **Computerized Information Services:** OCLC. **Networks/Consortia:** Member of NELINET, Hartford Consortium for Higher Education, Capitol Region Library Council (CRLC).

★16184★
UNIVERSITY OF HARTFORD - WILLIAM H. MORTENSEN LIBRARY - DANA SCIENCE & ENGINEERING LIBRARY (Sci-Engr)
200 Bloomfield Ave., Dana Bldg. Phone: (203)243-4404
West Hartford, CT 06117 Frances T. Libbey, Sci./Engr.Libn.
Founded: 1967. **Staff:** Prof 2; Other 15. **Subjects:** Chemistry, biology, physiological psychology, mathematics, physics, earth sciences, engineering. **Special Collections:** History of Science (300 volumes). **Holdings:** 15,000 books; 16,000 bound periodical volumes; microforms; 90 masters' theses. **Subscriptions:** 750 journals and other serials. **Services:** Interlibrary loan; copying; library open to the public for reference use only. **Automated Operations:** Computerized cataloging. **Computerized Information Services:** DIALOG Information Services, OCLC. **Networks/Consortia:** Member of Hartford Consortium for Higher Education, Capitol Region Library Council (CRLC), NELINET. **Publications:** Listing of Periodical Holdings - to consortium members. **Staff:** Jenny Wong, Asst.Libn..

★16185★
UNIVERSITY OF HAWAII - ASIA COLLECTION (Area-Ethnic)
Hamilton Library
2550 The Mall Phone: (808)948-8116
Honolulu, HI 96822 Alan Kamida, Hd.
Founded: 1962. **Staff:** Prof 11; Other 1. **Subjects:** East, Southeast, and South Asia. **Special Collections:** Sakamaki Collection (Ryukyus); Kajiyama Collection (Japanese language). **Holdings:** 536,000 volumes; 35,500 reels of microfilm; 74,500 microfiche. **Subscriptions:** 9500 journals and other serials; 115 newspapers. **Services:** Interlibrary loan; copying; collection open to the public. **Automated Operations:** Computerized public access catalog, cataloging, serials, and circulation. **Computerized Information Services:** RLIN. **Networks/Consortia:** Member of RLG. **Staff:** Masato Matsui, Japanese Lang.; Sam Suk Hahn, Korean Lang.; Tomoyoshi Kurokawa, E. Asian Ser.; Chau Mun Lau, Chinese Bibliog.; Lynette Wageman, S. Asia Spec.; Lan Char, S.E. Asia Spec.; Katherine Yoshimura, Asia Ser.Libn.; Alice Mak, Philippines; Shiro Saito, Philippines; Patricia Polansky, Russian Bibliog..

★16186★
UNIVERSITY OF HAWAII - CENTER FOR KOREAN STUDIES - LIBRARY (Area-Ethnic)
1881 East-West Rd. Phone: (808)948-7041
Honolulu, HI 96822 Ki-Ae Ch'oi, Libn.
Staff: Prof 2. **Subjects:** Korea. **Special Collections:** Archival collection of Tongjihoe organization (Honolulu); George and Evelyn McCune Library; Doo Soo Suh Collection; Eugene I. Knez Collection. **Holdings:** 22,500 items (6500 titles), including 700 serial titles; 825 reels of microfilm of doctoral dissertations; 71 16mm films; 226 reels of microfilm of newspapers; 91 lectures and 11 conference/workshops on audio cassette; 12

cassette-slide sets; sound recordings. **Subscriptions:** 105 journals and other serials; 11 newspapers. **Services:** Copying; film showings; library open to the public with restrictions. **Publications:** The Tongjihoe Collection: A List of Archival Materials; informal acquisitions lists; bibliographies. **Remarks:** An alternate telephone number is 948-6391. **Staff:** Charlotte Oser, Adm.Off..

★16187★
UNIVERSITY OF HAWAII - DEPARTMENT OF HISTORY - PACIFIC REGIONAL ORAL HISTORY PROGRAM - LIBRARY (Hist, Area-Ethnic)
2530 Dole St. Phone: (808)948-8486
Honolulu, HI 96822 Edward Beechert, Prof.
Staff: Prof 1. **Subjects:** Hawaiian labor, agricultural, and ethnic history. **Holdings:** 126 interview transcripts. **Services:** Copying; library open to the public with restrictions. **Special Catalogs:** Catalog of interviews.

★16188★
UNIVERSITY OF HAWAII - JOHN A. BURNS SCHOOL OF MEDICINE - REHABILITATION RESEARCH & TRAINING CENTER LIBRARY (Med)
Rehabilitation Hospital of the Pacific
226 N. Kuakini St., Rm. 233 Phone: (808)537-5986
Honolulu, HI 96817 Clara A. Abe, Off.Mgr.
Subjects: Disabled, handicapped, independent living, community education, rehabilitation, manpower development training, communications. **Holdings:** 140 books. **Subscriptions:** 64 journals and other serials.

★16189★
UNIVERSITY OF HAWAII - MAUNA KEA OBSERVATORY - SUPPORT SERVICES LIBRARY (Sci-Engr)
177 Makaala Phone: (808)935-3371
Hilo, HI 96720 Gaila Vidunas, Libn.
Staff: Prof 1. **Subjects:** Astronomy, astrophysics. **Holdings:** 400 books; 300 bound periodical volumes; 2 VF drawers of preprints and reprints; 20 map drawers of sky surveys. **Subscriptions:** 52 journals and other serials. **Services:** Interlibrary loan; library not open to the public.

UNIVERSITY OF HAWAII - NITROGEN FIXATION BY TROPICAL AGRICULTURAL LEGUMES
See: Nitrogen Fixation by Tropical Agricultural Legumes (10253)

★16190★
UNIVERSITY OF HAWAII - PACIFIC BIO-MEDICAL RESEARCH CENTER - LIBRARY (Biol Sci)
41 Ahui St. Phone: (808)531-3538
Honolulu, HI 96813 Dr. Barbara H. Gibbons, Res.
Founded: 1967. **Staff:** 1. **Subjects:** Biochemistry, cell biology, developmental morphology, molecular biology. **Special Collections:** Reprints of papers by C.F.W. McClure. **Holdings:** 700 bound periodical volumes. **Subscriptions:** 15 journals and other serials. **Services:** Copying; library open to the public with restrictions.

★16191★
UNIVERSITY OF HAWAII - PUBLIC SERVICES - GOVERNMENT DOCUMENTS, MAPS & MICROFORMS (Info Sci, Geog-Map)
Hamilton Library
2550 The Mall Phone: (808)948-8230
Honolulu, HI 96822 Virginia Richardson, Hd.
Founded: 1945. **Staff:** Prof 3; Other 5. **Holdings:** 62,193 volumes; public documents of official U.S. agencies, including U.S. Geological Survey, Defense Mapping Agency, and National Ocean Service (regional depository), state agricultural departments and experiment stations, United Nations and its affiliated agencies (including UNESCO, Food and Agriculture Organization, World Bank, World Health Organization), European Economic Community (EEC), and selected British, Australian, and New Zealand parliamentary documents; 560,194 unbound parts; 1.2 million microforms; 125,000 maps; 80,000 aerial photographs. **Services:** Interlibrary loan; copying; collection open to the public. **Staff:** Patricia Shelden, Docs.Libn.; Janet Morrison, Docs.Libn..

★16192★
UNIVERSITY OF HAWAII - SCHOOL OF PUBLIC HEALTH - LIBRARY (Med)
1960 East-West Rd.
Court D., Rm. 207 Phone: (808)948-8666
Honolulu, HI 96822 Carol W. Arnold, Hd.Libn.
Founded: 1968. **Staff:** Prof 2; Other 2. **Subjects:** Public health, health services planning and administration, environmental health, population studies, quantitative health sciences, health education, maternal and child health, public health nutrition, international health, population and family planning studies, gerontology. **Special Collections:** Kaiser-Hawaii Health Care Microfiche Collection (organization and delivery of health care; 22,000 microfiche). **Holdings:** 14,000 books; 1200 bound periodical volumes; 1500 theses and dissertations; 1000 VF items. **Subscriptions:** 427 journals and other serials. **Services:** Interlibrary loan; copying; library open to the public with permission of librarian. **Computerized Information Services:** MEDLARS; DOCLINE (electronic mail service). Performs searches on fee basis. **Networks/Consortia:** Member of Pacific Southwest Regional Medical Library Service. **Special Indexes:** Index to the School of Public Health Collection of Student Papers (book).

★16193★
UNIVERSITY OF HAWAII - SOCIAL SCIENCE RESEARCH INSTITUTE (Soc Sci)
Porteus Hall 704
Maile Way Phone: (808)948-8930
Honolulu, HI 96822 Donald M. Topping, Dir.
Founded: 1974. **Subjects:** Research in the social sciences with emphasis on Hawaii and the Pacific; anthropology; language acquisition; oral history; linguistics; telecommunications; health and social sciences; development studies; cognitive studies. **Holdings:** Figures not available. **Publications:** Asian Perspectives, semiannual; Oceanic Linguistics, semiannual; Asian and Pacific Archeology Series; Hawaii Series (annotated bibliographies); Oceanic Linguistics: Special Publications (monographs); PALI Language Texts.

★16194★
UNIVERSITY OF HAWAII - SPECIAL COLLECTIONS - ARCHIVES AND MANUSCRIPTS (Hist)
Sinclair Library
2425 Campus Rd. Phone: (808)948-6673
Honolulu, HI 96822 Nancy Morris, Asst.Lib.Spec.
Founded: 1968. **Staff:** 2. **Subjects:** University of Hawaii. **Holdings:** Noncurrent official records of the university, faculty, and staff; miscellaneous historical material about the university; manuscript material related to Hawaii and the Pacific. **Services:** Copying; archives open to the public. **Publications:** Guides to holdings; specialized finding aids.

★16195★
UNIVERSITY OF HAWAII - SPECIAL COLLECTIONS - HAWAII WAR RECORDS DEPOSITORY (Hist)
Hamilton Library
2550 The Mall Phone: (808)948-8473
Honolulu, HI 96822 Eleanor Au, Hd., Spec.Coll.
Founded: 1943. **Subjects:** Hawaii in World War II. **Holdings:** 200 linear feet of books, transcripts, microfilm, letters, memoranda, diaries, narratives, pamphlets, articles, government documents. **Services:** Depository open to the public.

★16196★
UNIVERSITY OF HAWAII - SPECIAL COLLECTIONS - HAWAIIAN COLLECTION (Area-Ethnic)
Hamilton Library
2550 The Mall Phone: (808)948-8264
Honolulu, HI 96822 Dr. Chieko Tachihata, Asst.Lib.Spec.
Founded: 1927. **Staff:** Prof 2. **Subjects:** Hawaiian Islands, Captain Cook, state and county government documents, children's literature, Hawaiian language materials, ethnic materials. **Special Collections:** Rare Hawaiiana; 19th century Hawaiian business and literary manuscripts (15 linear feet). **Holdings:** 84,000 volumes; microfilm; 19 file cabinets of newspaper clippings; 39 linear feet of pamphlets; audiotapes of oral history. **Subscriptions:** 1988 journals and other serials. **Services:** Interlibrary loan; copying; collection open to the public. **Publications:** Acquisitions list; Dissertations and Theses, University of Hawaii at Manoa, annual. **Special Catalogs:** Union catalog of Hawaiian holdings of several Honolulu libraries (card); file of theses by fields of study (card). **Staff:** Dr. Michaelyn Chou, Assoc.Lib.Spec..

★16197★
UNIVERSITY OF HAWAII - SPECIAL COLLECTIONS - JEAN CHARLOT COLLECTION (Art, Hum)
Hamilton Library, Rm. 501
2550 The Mall Phone: (808)948-8473
Honolulu, HI 96822 Nancy Morris, Asst.Lib.Spec.
Staff: 1. **Subjects:** French artist and writer Jean Charlot, 1898-1979. **Holdings:** Art works, documents, and working papers of and relating to Charlot: oil paintings, mural drawings, sketchbooks, and prints by Charlot; published and unpublished writings by Charlot; private documents, including Charlot's daily journal; tape-recorded interviews; correspondence; reminiscences; Charlot's personal library of over 1500 items; works by other artists, including Orozco, Siquieros, Rivera, Edward Weston, Ben Shahn, Louis Elshemius, and Hawaiian artists; prints by Posada and Daumier; Mexican folk art; documents by or relating to other artists and scholars.

★16198★
UNIVERSITY OF HAWAII - SPECIAL COLLECTIONS - PACIFIC COLLECTION (Area-Ethnic)
Hamilton Library
2550 The Mall Phone: (808)948-8264
Honolulu, HI 96822 Karen Peacock, Cur.
Founded: 1959. **Staff:** Prof 3. **Subjects:** Pacific Islands - government, economics, law, linguistics, vernacular texts, art, literature, anthropology, history, geography, business; Melanesia; Micronesia; Polynesia. **Special Collections:** Depository for microfilm issued by PAMBU (Pacific Manuscripts Bureau), Canberra; out-of-state theses; depository for South Pacific Commission documents; Trust Territory Archives (microfilm); rare Pacific materials. **Holdings:** 57,000 volumes. **Subscriptions:** 1125 journals and other serials. **Services:** Interlibrary loan; copying; collection open to the public. **Publications:** Acquisitions List. **Staff:** Renee Heyum, Assoc.Lib.Spec.; Lynette Furuhashi, Jr.Lib.Spec..

★16199★
UNIVERSITY OF HAWAII - SPECIAL COLLECTIONS - RARE BOOKS (Rare Book)
Hamilton Library
2550 The Mall Phone: (808)948-7923
Honolulu, HI 96822 Eleanor C. Au, Hd., Spec.Coll.
Staff: Prof 1. **Holdings:** Authors - Jack London, Mark Twain, Herman Melville, C.W. Stoddard; Book Arts Collection; juvenile books; historical text books; Social Movement Collection. **Services:** Collection open to the public for reference use only.

★16200★
UNIVERSITY OF HAWAII - WAIKIKI AQUARIUM - LIBRARY (Biol Sci)
2777 Kalakaua Ave. Phone: (808)923-9741
Honolulu, HI 96815 Doreen W. Grant, Libn.
Founded: 1980. **Staff:** Prof 1; Other 1. **Subjects:** Hawaii-South Pacific region - marine aquarium technology, zoology, oceanography, vertebrata, invertebrata, mollusca, sharks, ichthyology. **Special Collections:** Collection of out-of-print aquarium magazines. **Holdings:** 1000 books; 75 journals and newsletters; 10 VF drawers of reprints; reports. **Services:** Copying; SDI; library open to the public for reference use only by request. **Automated Operations:** Computerized acquisitions. **Computerized Information Services:** DIALOG Information Services. **Publications:** Directory of Public Aquaria of the World; Directory of Aquarium Specialists; Directory of Aquarium Libraries of the U.S., irregular; nature pamphlets; Kilo i'a Looking at the Sea (newsletter), monthly; acquisitions list and "Current Contents" (contains tables of contents of journals of professional interest to the staff) - both for internal distribution only. **Special Catalogs:** Subject catalog (selected subjects only) for reprints, journals, and newsletters received (card).

★16201★
UNIVERSITY OF HAWAII - WILLIAM S. RICHARDSON SCHOOL OF LAW - LIBRARY (Law)
2525 Dole St. Phone: (808)948-7583
Honolulu, HI 96822 John E. Pickron, Law Libn.
Founded: 1973. **Staff:** Prof 4; Other 3. **Subjects:** Anglo-American and Hawaiian law. **Holdings:** 180,000 volumes. **Subscriptions:** 2400 journals and other serials. **Services:** Interlibrary loan; copying; library open to the public. **Automated Operations:** Computerized cataloging. **Computerized Information Services:** LEXIS; internal database. **Staff:** Crys Kauka, Pub.Serv.Libn.; Martha Laxson, Tech.Serv.Libn.; Swee Berkey, Ref.Libn..

★16202★
UNIVERSITY OF HEALTH SCIENCES - MAZZACANO HALL LIBRARY (Med)
2105 Independence Blvd. Phone: (816)283-2451
Kansas City, MO 64124 Marilyn J. DeGeus, Dir. of Libs.
Staff: Prof 4; Other 3. **Subjects:** Medicine, osteopathy. **Holdings:** 50,000 books; 16,000 bound periodical volumes; 142 cassette tape titles; 3000 slide titles; 3100 videotapes; 1 microfiche; 2 transparencies; 24 teaching models; 24 three-dimensional disc titles; 156 computer programs; 891 x-ray radiographs; 67 16mm films. **Subscriptions:** 1820 journals and other serials. **Services:** Interlibrary loan; copying; library open to the public for reference use only. **Automated Operations:** Computerized cataloging. **Computerized Information Services:** MEDLINE, TOXLINE, OCLC, BRS Information Technologies, DIALOG Information Services, Mednet; DOCLINE, OCLC (electronic mail services). Performs searches on fee basis. Contact Person: Madonna Hunt, Ref.Libn., 283-2213. **Networks/Consortia:** Member of Kansas City Library Network, Inc. (KCLN), Midcontinental Regional Medical Library Program. **Publications:** Mazzacano Hall Library Handbook. **Staff:** Eleanor Sanders, Cat.; Kathleen Horton, AV.

★16203★
UNIVERSITY OF HEALTH SCIENCES/CHICAGO MEDICAL SCHOOL - LEARNING RESOURCES CENTER (Med)
3333 Green Bay Rd. Phone: (312)578-3242
North Chicago, IL 60064 Nancy W. Garn, Dir.
Founded: 1912. **Staff:** Prof 6; Other 17. **Subjects:** Medicine, psychology, and allied health sciences. **Special Collections:** Grants Resource Center. **Holdings:** 19,775 books; 72,076 bound periodical volumes; 20,000 volumes on 2800 reels of microfilm; 3 drawers of residency catalogs; 150 dissertations; 3 drawers of elective catalogs; 8 drawers of pamphlets. **Subscriptions:** 1301 journals and other serials; 7 newspapers. **Services:** Interlibrary loan; copying; center open to the public with letter of introduction. **Automated Operations:** Computerized cataloging, serials, and ILL. **Computerized Information Services:** BRS Information Technologies, DIALOG Information Services, OCLC. **Publications:** Calendar of Events, weekly; Grants Resource Center Report, bimonthly; Current Monographs and Serials Newsletter, monthly; LRC Guide, annual; Journal Holdings List, annual; bibliographies, irregular; subject guides, irregular. **Special Catalogs:** AV Catalog, annual. **Remarks:** Center is a supplemental resource institute of the Greater Midwest Regional Medical Library Network (Region 3). **Staff:** Sharyn Fradin, Hd., Ref. & Online Serv.; Maryann Brennan, Asst.Libn.; Kevin Robertson, ILL & Ser.Libn.; Rob Schmid, Assoc.Dir.; Gary Dandurand, AV Libn..

★16204★
UNIVERSITY HOSPITAL - HEALTH SCIENCES LIBRARY (Med)
1350 Walton Way Phone: (404)722-9011
Augusta, GA 30910-3599 Jane B. Wells, Libn.
Staff: Prof 1; Other 1. **Subjects:** Medicine, nursing, allied health sciences. **Holdings:** 5000 books; 450 bound periodical volumes. **Subscriptions:** 300 journals and other serials. **Services:** Interlibrary loan; library not open to the public.

★16205★
UNIVERSITY HOSPITAL AND CLINIC - HERBERT L. BRYANS MEMORIAL LIBRARY (Med)
1200 W. Leonard St. Phone: (904)436-9187
Pensacola, FL 32501 Ms. Sammie Campbell, Libn.
Staff: Prof 1. **Subjects:** Medicine, dentistry, nursing, dietetics, hospital administration. **Holdings:** 200 books. **Subscriptions:** 37 journals and other serials. **Services:** Interlibrary loan; copying; library open to the public with restrictions. **Remarks:** AV programs are available through the Pensacola Education Program.

★16206★
UNIVERSITY HOSPITALS OF CLEVELAND & CASE WESTERN RESERVE UNIVERSITY - DEPARTMENT OF PATHOLOGY - LIBRARY (Med)
2085 Adelbert Rd. Phone: (216)368-2482
Cleveland, OH 44106 Jeanette W. Nagy, Dir.
Founded: 1930. **Staff:** Prof 1. **Subjects:** Pathology, biochemistry, obstetrics, gynecology, surgery, neuropathology, immunology, histology, cytology. **Holdings:** 2000 books; 7000 bound periodical volumes; reprints; theses; dissertations. **Subscriptions:** 75 journals and other serials. **Services:** Library open to the public with restrictions.

★16207★
UNIVERSITY OF HOUSTON - ALLIED GEOPHYSICAL LABORATORIES - MILTON B. DOBRIN LIBRARY (Sci-Engr)
Allied Geophysical Laboratories Bldg.
4800 Calhoun Phone: (713)749-7336
Houston, TX 77004 Gloria Bellis, Libn.
Founded: 1984. **Staff:** Prof 1. **Subjects:** Geophysics, geology. **Holdings:** 2200 books; 132 bound periodical volumes. **Services:** Copying; library open to members of the Allied Geophysical Laboratories Consortium. **Automated Operations:** Computerized cataloging. **Publications:** The Milton B. Dobrin Geophysical Library Newsletter, irregular - available on request.

★16208★
UNIVERSITY OF HOUSTON - ARCHITECTURE AND ART LIBRARY (Art, Plan)
4800 Calhoun Phone: (713)749-7551
Houston, TX 77004 Margaret Culbertson, Libn.
Founded: 1961. **Staff:** Prof 1; Other 2. **Subjects:** Architecture, art, urban design, photography. **Holdings:** 45,000 books and bound periodical volumes. **Subscriptions:** 300 journals and other serials. **Services:** Interlibrary loan; library open to the public for reference use only. **Automated Operations:** Computerized cataloging, acquisitions, and circulation. **Computerized Information Services:** DIALOG Information Services, Pergamon ORBIT InfoLine, Inc., BRS Information Technologies, RLIN. **Networks/Consortia:** Member of AMIGOS Bibliographic Council, Inc., Houston Area Research Library Consortium (HARLIC).

★16209★
UNIVERSITY OF HOUSTON - AUDIOVISUAL SERVICES (Aud-Vis)
4800 Calhoun Phone: (713)749-2361
Houston, TX 77004 Joe Schroeder, Dir.
Founded: 1927. **Staff:** Prof 6; Other 11. **Holdings:** 2570 films, videotapes, and AV modules. **Services:** Full audiovisual services to administration, research, and instructional programs: television, photographic, audio, and graphic production; media distribution; media supplies; electronic maintenance; instruction development; Instructional Television Fixed Service (ITFS) broadcast studio/classroom. **Staff:** James Joplin, Asst.Dir., Prod.Serv.; Umesh Kapur, Asst.Dir., Tech.Serv.; Betty Bishop, Coord., Educ. LRC.

★16210★
UNIVERSITY OF HOUSTON - COLLEGE OF OPTOMETRY LIBRARY (Med)
4800 Calhoun Phone: (713)749-2411
Houston, TX 77004 Suzanne Ferimer, Dir., Lrng.Rsrcs.
Staff: Prof 1; Other 3. **Subjects:** Ocular diagnosis, public health services, contact lenses, history of optometry, pediatric optometry, optics, physiological optics. **Holdings:** 6000 books and bound periodical volumes; 350 audio cassettes; 3 drawers of vertical files, bibliographies, reports; 65 video cassettes; 50 slide-tape presentations; 310 pamphlets. **Subscriptions:** 125 journals and other serials. **Services:** Interlibrary loan; copying; library open to the public with restrictions. **Automated Operations:** Computerized cataloging, acquisitions, and circulation. **Computerized Information Services:** DIALOG Information Services, Pergamon ORBIT InfoLine, Inc., NLM, BRS Information Technologies. **Networks/Consortia:** Member of AMIGOS Bibliographic Council, Inc., Houston Area Research Library Consortium (HARLIC).

★16211★
UNIVERSITY OF HOUSTON - COLLEGE OF PHARMACY LIBRARY (Med)
4800 Calhoun Phone: (713)749-1566
Houston, TX 77004 Derral Parkin, Libn.
Founded: 1947. **Staff:** Prof 1; Other 4. **Subjects:** Chemistry, pharmacy, pharmaceuticals, toxicology, pharmacognosy, pharmacology. **Special Collections:** History and biography of pharmacy and medicine. **Holdings:** 14,300 books and bound periodical volumes; pharmaceutical catalogs. **Subscriptions:** 195 journals and other serials. **Services:** Interlibrary loan; copying; library open to the public with permission. **Automated Operations:** Computerized cataloging, acquisitions, and circulation. **Computerized Information Services:** Pergamon ORBIT InfoLine, Inc., BRS Information Technologies, DIALOG Information Services, NLM, STN International. **Networks/Consortia:** Member of AMIGOS Bibliographic Council, Inc., Houston Area Research Library Consortium (HARLIC). **Publications:** Quarterly acquisitions list - for internal distribution only.

★16212★
UNIVERSITY OF HOUSTON - LAW LIBRARY (Law)
4800 Calhoun Phone: (713)749-3191
Houston, TX 77004 Jon S. Schultz, Dir.
Staff: Prof 9; Other 6. **Subjects:** Law. **Holdings:** 194,106 volumes; 5000 Texas Supreme Court briefs; 5000 microcards; 451,872 microfiche. **Subscriptions:** 3606 journals and other serials. **Services:** Interlibrary loan; copying; library open to the public with permission. **Automated Operations:** Computerized cataloging, acquisitions, and serials. **Computerized Information Services:** LEXIS, WESTLAW. **Networks/Consortia:** Member of AMIGOS Bibliographic Council, Inc..

★16213★
UNIVERSITY OF HOUSTON - LIBRARIES - SPECIAL COLLECTIONS (Hist, Hum)
4800 Calhoun Phone: (713)749-2726
Houston, TX 77004 Pat Bozeman, Hd. of Spec.Coll.
Staff: Prof 1; Other 3. **Subjects:** Texana; Western history; Houston, British, and American authors; Latin drama. **Special Collections:** George Fuermann City of Houston Collection; W.B. Bates Collection of Texana; James E. & Miriam A. Ferguson Papers (3 boxes); Jones Drama Collection (1500 volumes); Israel Shreve papers (25); James V. Allred papers (100 linear feet); Larry McMurtry manuscripts (60 boxes); Beverly Lowry manuscripts (5 boxes); Jan de Hartog manuscripts (19 boxes); Aldous Huxley manuscripts (3 boxes); historical railroad and Western hemisphere maps; Kenneth Patchen Collection (188 items); university archives. **Holdings:** 50,000 books; 2000 bound periodical volumes. **Subscriptions:** 11 journals and other serials. **Services:** Collections open to the public with supervision. **Special Catalogs:** W.B. Bates Collection Catalog; Robinson Jeffers Collection Catalog; John Updike Catalog; Luyet Memorial Collection in Cryobiology Catalog.

★16214★
UNIVERSITY OF HOUSTON - MUSIC LIBRARY (Mus)
4800 Calhoun Phone: (713)749-2534
Houston, TX 77004 Samuel R. Hyde, Libn.
Founded: 1975. **Staff:** Prof 1; Other 1. **Subjects:** Music. **Holdings:** 35,543 books, bound periodical volumes, scores. **Subscriptions:** 138 journals and other serials. **Services:** Interlibrary loan; copying; library open to the public for reference use only. **Automated Operations:** Computerized cataloging, acquisitions, and circulation. **Computerized Information Services:** DIALOG Information Services. **Networks/Consortia:** Member of AMIGOS Bibliographic Council, Inc., Houston Area Research Library Consortium (HARLIC).

UNIVERSITY OF HOUSTON, VICTORIA
See: Victoria College/University of Houston, Victoria (17330)

★16215★
UNIVERSITY OF IDAHO - BUREAU OF PUBLIC AFFAIRS RESEARCH - LIBRARY (Soc Sci)
Moscow, ID 83843 Phone: (208)885-6563
Sid Duncombe, Dir.
Founded: 1959. **Staff:** Prof 1; Other 1. **Subjects:** State and local politics and administration. **Holdings:** Reference books, pamphlets, reports, periodicals, newsletters, and other publications of governmental research bureaus and state and local agencies throughout the nation. **Services:** Research and training services for state and local government agencies in Idaho.

★16216★
UNIVERSITY OF IDAHO - HUMANITIES LIBRARY (Hum)
Moscow, ID 83843 Phone: (208)885-6584
Ron Force, Libn.
Staff: Prof 2; Other 2. **Subjects:** Literature, music, language, art, philosophy, architecture. **Holdings:** 127,666 books; 31,397 bound periodical volumes; 127,389 volumes in microform. **Subscriptions:** 2575 journals and other serials; 117 newspapers. **Services:** Interlibrary loan; copying; library open to the public. **Networks/Consortia:** Member of Western Library Network (WLN). **Publications:** The Bookmark, 2/year; The Idaho, annual - both for sale.

★16217★
UNIVERSITY OF IDAHO - IDAHO GEOLOGICAL SURVEY - LIBRARY (Sci-Engr)
Morrill Hall, Rm. 332 Phone: (208)885-7991
Moscow, ID 83843 Earl Bennett, Dir.
Founded: 1984. **Staff:** Prof 1; Other 1. **Subjects:** Geology, mineral resources. **Holdings:** 3000 volumes. **Services:** Copying. **Publications:** List of publications - available on request.

★16218★
UNIVERSITY OF IDAHO - IDAHO WATER RESOURCES RESEARCH INSTITUTE - TECHNICAL INFORMATION CENTER & READING ROOM (Env-Cons)
Moscow, ID 83843 Phone: (208)885-6429
George Bloomsburg, Dir.
Staff: Prof 2; Other 2. **Subjects:** Water resources, resource economics, outdoor recreation, groundwater, irrigation, wild and scenic rivers, water seepage, agriculture, water law, precipitation distribution, small hydroelectric developments. **Holdings:** 4000 books and bound periodical volumes. **Services:** Interlibrary loan; center open to the public. **Publications:** Newsletter and information bulletins; Completion Report series.

★16219★
UNIVERSITY OF IDAHO - LAW LIBRARY (Law)
College of Law Phone: (208)885-6521
Moscow, ID 83843 James Heller, Libn.
Founded: 1911. **Staff:** Prof 4; Other 5. **Subjects:** Law. **Holdings:** 122,273 volumes. **Subscriptions:** 2077 journals and other serials. **Services:** Interlibrary loan; copying. **Networks/Consortia:** Member of Western Library Network (WLN).

★16220★
UNIVERSITY OF IDAHO - MARTIN INSTITUTE OF HUMAN BEHAVIOR - LIBRARY (Soc Sci)
Moscow, ID 83843 Phone: (208)885-6527
Boyd A. Martin, Dir.
Staff: Prof 3; Other 1. **Subjects:** Causes of war, violence, and terrorism; conditions of peace; conflict resolution and prevention; conflicts which lead to war. **Special Collections:** Nuclear war, armament, disarmament, and arms races (films). **Holdings:** 2000 books. **Services:** Library open to the public for reference use only.

★16221★
UNIVERSITY OF IDAHO - PACIFIC NORTHWEST ANTHROPOLOGICAL ARCHIVES (Hist)
Dept. of Sociology/Anthropology Phone: (208)885-6123
Moscow, ID 83843 Roderick Sprague, Dir.
Staff: Prof 1; Other 1. **Subjects:** Pacific Northwest - archeology, ethnography, ethnohistory, historical archeology, physical anthropology. **Holdings:** 7000 complete photocopies of all materials relating to the archeology and physical anthropology of the Pacific Northwest. **Services:** Copying; archives open to the public.

★16222★
UNIVERSITY OF IDAHO - SCIENCE AND TECHNOLOGY LIBRARY (Biol Sci, Sci-Engr)
Moscow, ID 83843 Phone: (208)885-6235
Donna Hanson, Libn.
Staff: Prof 3; Other 1. **Subjects:** Forestry, agriculture, mining and geology, entomology, engineering, physical sciences, biological sciences. **Holdings:** 140,673 books; 110,233 bound periodical volumes; 4727 microforms. **Subscriptions:** 6439 journals and other serials. **Services:** Interlibrary loan; copying; library open to the public. **Networks/Consortia:** Member of Western Library Network (WLN).

★16223★
UNIVERSITY OF IDAHO - SOCIAL SCIENCE LIBRARY (Soc Sci)
Moscow, ID 83843 Phone: (208)885-6344
Dennis Baird, Libn.
Staff: Prof 3; Other 2. **Subjects:** History, education, political science, sociology, business and economics. **Holdings:** 180,446 books; 40,086 bound periodical volumes; 640,018 government publications; 184,714 volumes in microform and ERIC microfiche; 139,692 sheet maps. **Subscriptions:** 3222 journals and other serials. **Services:** Interlibrary loan; copying; library open to the public. **Networks/Consortia:** Member of Western Library Network (WLN).

★16224★
UNIVERSITY OF IDAHO - SPECIAL COLLECTIONS LIBRARY (Hum)
Moscow, ID 83843 Phone: (208)885-7951
Terry Abraham, Libn.
Staff: Prof 3; Other 2. **Subjects:** Pacific Northwest, Idaho publications, University of Idaho archives, Sir Walter Scott, Basques, Ezra Pound. **Holdings:** 36,538 volumes; 274 cubic feet of prints and photographs; 3522 cubic feet of manuscripts; 811 cubic feet of archives; 106 cubic feet of maps, vertical files, oral history materials, and other cataloged items. **Subscriptions:** 643 journals and other serials. **Services:** Interlibrary loan; copying; library open to the public for reference use only. **Networks/Consortia:** Member of Western Library Network (WLN).

★16225★
UNIVERSITY OF ILLINOIS - AGRICULTURE LIBRARY (Agri)
226 Mumford Hall
1301 W. Gregory Phone: (217)333-2416
Urbana, IL 61801 Carol Boast, Libn.
Founded: 1915. **Staff:** Prof 5; Other 5. **Subjects:** Agricultural economics, animal science, agricultural engineering, crops, horticulture, food science and technology, agricultural history, forestry, soils. **Holdings:** 70,000 volumes; 600 microforms. **Subscriptions:** 2850 journals and other serials. **Services:** Interlibrary loan; copying; library open to the public. **Automated Operations:** Computerized cataloging, acquisitions, serials, and circulation. **Computerized Information Services:** BRS Information Technologies, DIALOG Information Services; internal database. **Publications:** Selected New Acquisitions List, bimonthly. **Staff:** Nancy Davis, Asst.Libn.; Maria Porta, Asst.Libn.; Ken Carlborg, Sr.Proj.Cat.; Dave Hoogakker, Asst.Proj.Cat..

★16226★
UNIVERSITY OF ILLINOIS - APPLIED LIFE STUDIES LIBRARY (Educ, Rec)
Main Library, Rm. 146
1408 W. Gregory Dr. Phone: (217)333-3615
Urbana, IL 61801 Patricia McCandless, Libn.
Founded: 1949. **Staff:** Prof 1; Other 2. **Subjects:** Leisure studies; education - physical, health, safety, driver; sport science - biomechanics, medicine, psychology, sociology, history; dance. **Special Collections:** Avery Brundage Collection (1600 volumes). **Holdings:** 21,074 volumes; 1100 theses; 6 VF drawers of pamphlets; 10,536 microcards; 7304 microfiche. **Subscriptions:** 517 journals and other serials. **Services:** Interlibrary loan; copying. **Automated Operations:** Computerized circulation. **Computerized Information Services:** Online systems. Performs searches on fee basis. **Publications:** Acquisition list, quarterly - to faculty, students, and others on request.

★16227★
UNIVERSITY OF ILLINOIS - ASIAN LIBRARY (Area-Ethnic)
325 Main Library
1408 W. Gregory Dr. Phone: (217)333-1501
Urbana, IL 61801 William S. Wong, Asst.Dir.
Founded: 1965. **Staff:** Prof 5; Other 6. **Subjects:** East Asia, South Asia, Middle East - history, literature, linguistics, economics, sociology. **Holdings:** 240,000 books. **Subscriptions:** 900 journals and other serials. **Services:** Interlibrary loan; copying; library open to the public. **Remarks:** The University of Illinois Rare Book Room contains a collection of Japanese rare books. **Staff:** Narindar K. Aggarwal, Assoc. Asian Libn.; Yasuko Makino, Japanese Libn.; Sachie Noguchi, Asst. Japanese Libn.; Karen Wei, Asst. Chinese Libn..

★16228★
UNIVERSITY OF ILLINOIS - ASIAN LIBRARY - SOUTH AND WEST ASIAN DIVISION (Area-Ethnic)
325 Main Library
1408 W. Gregory Dr. Phone: (217)333-2492
Urbana, IL 61801 Narindar K. Aggarwal, Assoc. Asian Libn.
Founded: 1964. **Staff:** Prof 1; Other 2. **Subjects:** South and West Asia - languages, literature, history, culture. **Holdings:** 95,000 books; 150 bound periodical volumes. **Services:** Interlibrary loan; division open to the public.

★16229★
UNIVERSITY OF ILLINOIS - BIOLOGY LIBRARY (Biol Sci)
101 Burrill Hall
407 S. Goodwin Phone: (217)333-3654
Urbana, IL 61801 Elisabeth B. Davis, Libn.
Founded: 1884. **Staff:** Prof 2; Other 12. **Subjects:** Biology, botany, entomology, biophysics, genetics, ecology, microbiology, physiology, zoology. **Special Collections:** Oberholser reprint collection on ornithology; microfiche collection of vascular plant types from botanical gardens and herbaria. **Holdings:** 110,978 volumes. **Subscriptions:** 2058 journals and other serials. **Services:** Interlibrary loan; copying; SDI; library open to the public by permit. **Automated Operations:** Computerized cataloging, acquisitions, and circulation. **Computerized Information Services:** DIALOG Information Services, NLM, BRS Information Technologies. Performs searches on fee basis. Contact Person: Mitsuko Williams, Asst.Libn.. **Publications:** List of New Acquisitions, monthly; Guides to the Literature Held in the Biology Library.

★16230★
UNIVERSITY OF ILLINOIS - CHEMISTRY LIBRARY (Sci-Engr)
257 Noyes Laboratory
505 S. Matthews Phone: (217)333-3737
Urbana, IL 61801 Tina E. Chrzastowski, Chem.Libn.
Founded: 1892. **Staff:** Prof 1; Other 3. **Subjects:** Chemistry - analytical, inorganic, organic, physical; biochemistry; chemical engineering. **Holdings:** 70,000 volumes; 925 films and microfiche. **Subscriptions:** 840 journals and other serials. **Services:** Interlibrary loan; copying; library open to the public. **Automated Operations:** Computerized public access catalog and circulation. **Computerized Information Services:** DIALOG Information Services, BRS Information Technologies, CAS ONLINE, OCLC. **Publications:** List of Acquisitions, monthly; Chemistry Library Communications.

★16231★
UNIVERSITY OF ILLINOIS - CITY PLANNING AND LANDSCAPE ARCHITECTURE LIBRARY (Plan)
203 Mumford Hall
1301 W. Gregory Dr. Phone: (217)333-0424
Urbana, IL 61801 Mary D. Ravenhall, Libn.
Founded: 1912. **Staff:** Prof 1; Other 1. **Subjects:** City and regional planning, landscape architecture, urban studies. **Holdings:** 21,706 volumes; 14,000 pamphlets. **Subscriptions:** 544 journals and other serials. **Services:** Interlibrary loan; copying; library open to the public by permit from Main Library. **Automated Operations:** Computerized public access catalog and circulation. **Publications:** Acquisitions List, irregular - to mailing list.

★16232★
UNIVERSITY OF ILLINOIS - CLASSICS LIBRARY (Hum)
419A Main Library
1408 W. Gregory Dr. Phone: (217)333-1124
Urbana, IL 61801 Suzanne Griffiths, Libn.
Subjects: Classical languages and literatures, Roman and Greek history and civilizations, classical archeology. **Special Collections:** Dittenberger-Vahlen Collection. **Holdings:** 46,901 volumes. **Subscriptions:** 375 journals and other serials. **Services:** Interlibrary loan; library open to the public.

★16233★
UNIVERSITY OF ILLINOIS - COLLEGE OF ENGINEERING - ENGINEERING DOCUMENTS CENTER (Sci-Engr)
112 Engineering Hall
1308 W. Green St. Phone: (217)244-6271
Urbana, IL 61801 Mu-chin Cheng, Doc.Libn.
Staff: Prof 1. **Subjects:** Engineering. **Holdings:** 9000 technical reports. **Services:** Interlibrary loan; copying; center open to the public. **Automated Operations:** Computerized cataloging. **Special Indexes:** Engineering Documents Center Index, annual.

★16234★
UNIVERSITY OF ILLINOIS - COMMERCE LIBRARY (Bus-Fin)
Rm. 101, Main Library
1408 W. Gregory Dr. Phone: (217)333-3619
Urbana, IL 61801 M. Balachandran, Libn.
Staff: Prof 3; Other 5. **Subjects:** Economics, business administration, accounting, finance. **Holdings:** 46,855 volumes; 90,360 company annual and 10K reports on microfiche. **Subscriptions:** 2205 journals and other serials. **Services:** Interlibrary loan; library open to the public by permit. **Automated Operations:** Computerized circulation. **Computerized Information Services:** BRS Information Technologies, DIALOG Information Services. Performs searches on fee basis. **Publications:** Acquisitions List, 10/year - for internal distribution only. **Staff:** J. Phillips, Asst.Libn.; K. Chapman, Asst.Libn..

★16235★
UNIVERSITY OF ILLINOIS - COMMUNICATIONS LIBRARY (Info Sci)
122 Gregory Hall Phone: (217)333-2216
Urbana, IL 61801 Diane Carothers, Commun.Libn.
Founded: 1933. **Staff:** Prof 1; Other 2. **Subjects:** Advertising, broadcasting, magazines, newspapers, public relations, communication theory, mass communications, photography, publishing, typography, motion pictures. **Special Collections:** D'Arcy Collection (advertising clippings from magazines and newspapers, 1890-1970; 2 million clippings). **Holdings:** 16,000 volumes. **Subscriptions:** 774 journals and other serials; 30 newspapers. **Services:** Interlibrary loan; copying; library open to the public with permit from Main Library. **Automated Operations:** Computerized public access catalog and circulation. **Publications:** Acquisition List (annotated), quarterly.

★16236★
UNIVERSITY OF ILLINOIS - COORDINATED SCIENCE LABORATORY LIBRARY (Sci-Engr)
1101 W. Springfield, Rm. 269 A Phone: (217)333-4368
Urbana, IL 61801 Ms. Marty North, Info.Spec.
Founded: 1951. **Staff:** Prof 1. **Subjects:** Electrical engineering, computers and control, physics, systems theory, artificial intelligence. **Holdings:** 3000 books; 2200 bound periodical volumes; 250 technical reports and dissertations. **Subscriptions:** 137 journals and other serials. **Services:** Copying; SDI; library open to the public for reference use only.

★16237★
UNIVERSITY OF ILLINOIS - DEPARTMENT OF COMPUTER SCIENCE LIBRARY (Comp Sci)
260 Digital Computer Laboratory Phone: (217)333-6777
Urbana, IL 61801 Prof. S. Muroga, Lib.Mgr.
Founded: 1961. **Staff:** Prof 1; Other 2. **Subjects:** Computer science, electrical engineering, applied mathematics. **Holdings:** 11,600 books; 3200 bound periodical volumes; 4000 technical reports; 2225 departmental reports. **Subscriptions:** 120 journals and other serials. **Services:** Library not open to the public.

★16238★
UNIVERSITY OF ILLINOIS - DOCUMENTS LIBRARY (Info Sci)
200D Main Library
1408 W. Gregory Dr. Phone: (217)333-1056
Urbana, IL 61801 Susan E. Bekiares, Hd.
Founded: 1980. **Staff:** Prof 4; Other 3. **Subjects:** Statistics, legislation, regulation, historical bibliography. **Special Collections:** U.S. Government and Illinois state research and development reports. **Holdings:** 72,000 volumes; 1 million microfiche. **Subscriptions:** 6000 journals and other serials. **Services:** Interlibrary loan; copying; library open to the public for reference use only. **Automated Operations:** Computerized public access catalog, cataloging, acquisitions, serials, and circulation. **Computerized Information Services:** BRS Information Technologies, OCLC, DIALOG Information Services; internal databases. Performs searches on fee basis. Contact Person: Mary Gassmann, Docs.Libn.. **Networks/Consortia:** Member of ILLINET. **Staff:** John Littlewood, Docs.Libn.; Mary Mallory, Docs.Libn..

★16239★
UNIVERSITY OF ILLINOIS - EDUCATION AND SOCIAL SCIENCE LIBRARY (Soc Sci)
100 Main Library
1408 W. Gregory Dr. Phone: (217)333-2305
Urbana, IL 61801 Susan Klingberg, Educ. & Soc.Sci.Libn.
Staff: Prof 5; Other 9. **Subjects:** Education, anthropology, psychology, political science, social work, sociology, speech and hearing science. **Special Collections:** C.W. Odell Test Collection (7600 educational and psychological tests); children's literature collection; Human Relations Area Files; U.N. official records; parapsychology and the occult; curriculum collection. **Holdings:** 131,000 volumes; ERIC microfiche. **Subscriptions:** 2249 journals and other serials. **Services:** Interlibrary loan; copying; library open to the public on a limited basis. **Automated Operations:** Computerized circulation. **Computerized Information Services:** BRS Information Technologies. **Publications:** Bibliographies, occasional. **Staff:** J. Williams, Asst.Libn.; S. Atkins, Asst.Libn.; N. O'Brien, Assoc.Libn..

★16240★
UNIVERSITY OF ILLINOIS - ENGINEERING LIBRARY (Sci-Engr)
221 Engineering Hall
1308 W. Green St. Phone: (217)333-3576
Urbana, IL 61801 William Mischo, Engr.Libn.
Staff: Prof 4; Other 5. **Subjects:** Engineering - aeronautical, agricultural, astronautical, ceramic, civil, computer, electrical, materials, mechanical, metallurgical, nuclear; bioengineering; computer science; theoretical and applied mechanics. **Special Collections:** U.S. National Advisory Committee for Aeronautics (NACA) Depository Sets, 1915-1958; U.S. NASA Depository Sets, 1978 to present. **Holdings:** 175,000 volumes. **Subscriptions:** 3000 journals and other serials. **Services:** Interlibrary loan; copying; library open to the public with permit. **Automated Operations:** Computerized public access catalog, serials, and circulation. **Computerized Information Services:** DIALOG Information Services, BRS Information Technologies, STN International. Performs searches on fee basis. **Remarks:** An alternate telephone number is 333-7497. **Staff:** Melvin G. DeSart, Asst.Engr.Libn..

★16241★
UNIVERSITY OF ILLINOIS - ENGLISH LIBRARY (Hum)
321 Library
1408 W. Gregory Dr. Phone: (217)333-2220
Urbana, IL 61801 Robert M. Jones, Act.Hd.
Founded: 1908. **Staff:** Prof 2. **Subjects:** English literature - early, medieval, Renaissance, 17th-20th centuries; American literature; philology; folk tales; worldwide cinema and theater. **Holdings:** 24,676 volumes. **Subscriptions:** 514 journals and other serials. **Services:** Interlibrary loan; copying.

★16242★
UNIVERSITY OF ILLINOIS - GEOLOGY LIBRARY (Sci-Engr)
223 Natural History Bldg.
1301 W. Green St. Phone: (217)333-1266
Urbana, IL 61801 Dederick C. Ward, Libn.
Founded: 1959. **Staff:** Prof 1; Other 3. **Subjects:** Geology, mineralogy, paleontology, geomorphology, geophysics, geochemistry, oceanography, stratigraphy, petrology. **Special Collections:** History of Geology (early and rare items in geology); biographies of geologists. **Holdings:** 80,000 volumes; 54,000 geological maps. **Subscriptions:** 2000 journals and other serials. **Services:** Interlibrary loan; copying; library not open to the public. **Automated Operations:** Computerized public access catalog. **Computerized Information Services:** Online systems. Performs searches on fee basis.

★16243★
UNIVERSITY OF ILLINOIS - HISTORY AND PHILOSOPHY LIBRARY (Rel-Phil, Hist)
424 Main Library
1408 W. Gregory Dr. Phone: (217)333-1091
Urbana, IL 61801 Martha Friedman, Libn.
Founded: 1918. **Staff:** Prof 2; Other 3. **Subjects:** Medieval and modern philosophy; religious studies; history - American, European, Far Eastern, Latin American. **Special Collections:** Horner Lincoln Collection (10,000 books, pamphlets, broadsides; manuscripts; microfilm). **Holdings:** 21,311 volumes. **Subscriptions:** 1500 journals and other serials. **Services:** Interlibrary loan (through Main Library). **Automated Operations:** Computerized circulation. **Staff:** Priscilla Yu, Asst.Libn..

★16244★
UNIVERSITY OF ILLINOIS - HOME ECONOMICS LIBRARY (Agri, Food-Bev)
905 S. Goodwin Ave. Phone: (217)333-0748
Urbana, IL 61801 Barbara C. Swain, Libn.
Founded: 1957. **Staff:** Prof 1; Other 1. **Subjects:** Family and consumer economics, foods and nutrition, home economics education, human development and family ecology, textiles, apparel, interior design, food science. **Holdings:** 18,000 volumes; 2608 slides. **Subscriptions:** 256 journals and other serials. **Services:** Interlibrary loan; library open to the public by permit from Main Library. **Computerized Information Services:** DIALOG Information Services, BRS Information Technologies, WILSONLINE. Performs searches on fee basis. **Publications:** Selected List of New Books, quarterly.

★16245★
UNIVERSITY OF ILLINOIS - HOUSING RESEARCH & DEVELOPMENT PROGRAM - LIBRARY (Plan)
1204 W. Nevada Phone: (217)333-7330
Urbana, IL 61801 Trudy Patton, Libn./Res.Assoc.
Staff: Prof 1; Other 1. **Subjects:** Housing design, community development, housing for the elderly, low-income housing, environmental psychology, government programs. **Holdings:** 2000 books; 20 bound periodical volumes; 8 VF drawers of clippings, reports, pamphlets, brochures, maps. **Subscriptions:** 37 journals and other serials. **Services:** Library open to the public for reference use only.

★16246★
UNIVERSITY OF ILLINOIS - ILLINOIS HISTORICAL SURVEY LIBRARY (Hist)
346 Main Library
1408 W. Gregory Dr. Phone: (217)333-1777
Urbana, IL 61801 John Hoffmann, Libn.
Founded: 1910. **Staff:** Prof 1; Other 1. **Subjects:** Regional history - Mississippi Valley and subsidiary areas. **Special Collections:** Religious Society of Friends; communitarianism; Illinois labor; German immigration. **Holdings:** 12,000 volumes; 1750 maps; 800 linear feet of archives and manuscripts; 700 reels of microfilm of manuscripts; 3500 VF items. **Subscriptions:** 30 journals and other serials. **Services:** Interlibrary loan; copying; library open to the public for reference and research only. **Publications:** Manuscripts guide to collections at the University of Illinois at Urbana-Champaign; Guide to the Heinrich A. Rattermann Collection of German-American Manuscripts; Guide to the Papers in the John Hunter Walker Collection, 1911-1953.

★16247★
UNIVERSITY OF ILLINOIS - ILLINOIS STATE NATURAL HISTORY SURVEY - LIBRARY (Biol Sci)
196 Natural Resources Bldg.
607 E. Peabody Phone: (217)333-6892
Champaign, IL 61820 Carla G. Heister, Libn.
Founded: 1858. **Staff:** Prof 1; Other 1. **Subjects:** Economic entomology, faunistic survey and insect identification, aquatic biology, applied botany and plant pathology, wildlife research, environmental quality. **Holdings:** 36,000 volumes. **Subscriptions:** 1003 journals and other serials. **Services:** Interlibrary loan; copying; SDI; library open to the public for reference use only. **Automated Operations:** Computerized cataloging, acquisitions, and circulation. **Computerized Information Services:** BRS Information Technologies, DIALOG Information Services, OCLC. Performs searches on fee basis. **Networks/Consortia:** Member of ILLINET.

★16248★
UNIVERSITY OF ILLINOIS - INSTITUTE OF LABOR AND INDUSTRIAL RELATIONS LIBRARY (Bus-Fin)
504 E. Armory Phone: (217)333-2380
Champaign, IL 61820 Margaret A. Chaplan, Libn.
Founded: 1947. **Staff:** Prof 1; Other 2. **Subjects:** Labor and industrial relations. **Holdings:** 11,502 volumes; 30,000 VF items; 809 reels of microfilm; 1500 microfiche; 53 audio cassettes. **Subscriptions:** 457 journals and other serials. **Services:** Interlibrary loan; copying; library open to the public. **Automated Operations:** Computerized public access catalog, cataloging, and circulation. **Computerized Information Services:** DIALOG Information Services, BRS Information Technologies, Pergamon ORBIT InfoLine, Inc.; DIALMAIL (electronic mail service). Performs searches on fee basis. **Publications:** ILIR Library Selected Recent Acquisitions, weekly -for internal distribution only.

★16249★
UNIVERSITY OF ILLINOIS - LAW LIBRARY (Law)
104 Law Bldg.
504 E. Pennsylvania Ave. Phone: (217)333-2914
Champaign, IL 61820 Richard Surles, Dir.
Founded: 1897. **Staff:** Prof 7; Other 10. **Subjects:** Law and related social sciences. **Special Collections:** Depository for U.S., Illinois State, and European Economic Community documents; Archives of the American Association of Law Libraries. **Holdings:** 453,000 volumes; 33,856 microcards; 1330 reels of microfilm; 177,900 microfiche; 2957 pamphlets. **Subscriptions:** 5637 journals and other serials. **Services:** Interlibrary loan; copying; library open to the public. **Computerized Information Services:** LEXIS, WESTLAW, OCLC; LCS (internal database). **Publications:** Research Aids. **Staff:** Fred Mansfield, Bibliog.; Timothy Kearley, Assoc.Dir.; Cheryl Nyberg, Docs./Ref.Libn.; Jane Williams, Ref.; Patricia Norcott, Records/Ref.Libn..

★16250★
UNIVERSITY OF ILLINOIS - LIBRARY AND INFORMATION SCIENCE LIBRARY (Info Sci)
306 Main Library
1408 W. Gregory Dr. Phone: (217)333-3804
Urbana, IL 61801 Patricia F. Stenstrom, Libn.
Founded: 1906. **Staff:** Prof 1; Other 2. **Subjects:** Library and information science. **Holdings:** 19,775 volumes; 1423 microfiche. **Subscriptions:** 1181 journals and other serials. **Services:** Interlibrary loan; copying; library open to the public with permit from Main Library. **Automated Operations:** Computerized public access catalog and circulation. **Computerized Information Services:** WILSONLINE. Performs searches on fee basis. **Remarks:** An alternate telephone number is 333-4456.

★16251★
UNIVERSITY OF ILLINOIS - MAP AND GEOGRAPHY LIBRARY (Geog-Map)
418 Main Library
1408 W. Gregory Dr. Phone: (217)333-0827
Urbana, IL 61801 David A. Cobb, Map & Geog.Libn.
Founded: 1944. **Staff:** Prof 2; Other 1. **Subjects:** Maps, geography, Illinois aerial photography, atlases, gazetteers. **Special Collections:** Sanborn fire insurance maps for Illinois cities; Cavagna Library (16th-19th century maps of Italy); 19th century U.S. coastal charts. **Holdings:** 15,000 volumes; 150,000 aerial photographs; 370,000 maps; 475 reels of microfilm. **Subscriptions:** 700 journals and other serials. **Services:** Interlibrary loan; copying; library open to the public. **Automated Operations:** Computerized cataloging. **Computerized Information Services:** OCLC. **Networks/**

Consortia: Member of ILLINET. **Publications:** Biblio, quarterly; Acquisition Policy Statement. **Special Catalogs:** Catalog of Aerial Photographs in the Map and Geography Library; Sanborn Maps; State Atlases in the University of Illinois Library; List of Illinois County Atlases; List of Illinois Topographic Maps; List of Gazetteers in the Map and Geography Library. **Staff:** Nancy Vick, Asst. Map & Geog.Libn..

★16252★
UNIVERSITY OF ILLINOIS - MATHEMATICS LIBRARY (Sci-Engr, Comp Sci)
216 Altgeld Hall
1409 W. Green St. Phone: (217)333-0258
Urbana, IL 61801 Nancy D. Anderson, Libn.
Staff: Prof 2; Other 2. **Subjects:** Pure and applied mathematics, mathematical physics, statistics, computer sciences. **Holdings:** 69,000 volumes; 750 microforms; AV programs. **Subscriptions:** 965 journals and other serials. **Services:** Interlibrary loan; copying; library open to the public with permit from Main Library. **Automated Operations:** Computerized public access catalog and circulation. **Publications:** List of Acquisitions, bimonthly - to mailing list. **Staff:** Lois Pausch, Asst.Libn..

★16253★
UNIVERSITY OF ILLINOIS - MODERN LANGUAGES AND LINGUISTICS LIBRARY (Hum)
425 Main Library
1408 W. Gregory Dr. Phone: (217)333-0076
Urbana, IL 61801 Sara de Mundo Lo, Libn.
Founded: 1911. **Staff:** Prof 5; Other 3. **Subjects:** Romance and Germanic language and literature, linguistics. **Special Collections:** Linguistic atlases; International Cinema Collection; Proust Collection; Chicano Collection. **Holdings:** 17,000 books; 800 bound periodical volumes. **Subscriptions:** 400 journals and other serials; 40 newspapers. **Services:** Interlibrary loan; copying; library open to the public. **Automated Operations:** Computerized circulation. **Publications:** The Stentor, irregular - to faculty; user's guide - free upon request.

★16254★
UNIVERSITY OF ILLINOIS - MUSIC LIBRARY (Mus)
Music Bldg. Phone: (217)333-1173
Urbana, IL 61801 William M. McClellan, Mus.Libn.
Founded: 1943. **Staff:** Prof 4; Other 8. **Subjects:** Music performance and research. **Special Collections:** Pre-1800 music manuscripts and editions (emphasis on medieval and Renaissance vocal music, lute and keyboard music sources; 2000 titles on microfilm); American popular sheet music, 1830-1970 (vocal; 100,000 titles); Rafael Joseffy Collection (19th century piano music; 2000 titles); Joseph Szigeti Collection (19th-20th century violin music manuscripts and editions; 700 titles); choral reference collection (single copies of octavos; 40,000 titles); recorded concerts and programs of the School of Music, 1950 to present (3000 reels of tape). **Holdings:** 37,000 volumes; 140,000 scores and parts; 9000 reels of microfilm; 2422 microcards; 2000 microfiche; 80,000 phonograph records; 4 VF drawers of pamphlets; audio cassettes; compact discs; video cassettes. **Subscriptions:** 1300 journals and other serials. **Services:** Interlibrary loan; copying; library open to the public. **Automated Operations:** Computerized public access catalog and circulation. **Networks/Consortia:** Member of ILLINET. **Staff:** Jean Geil, Mus.Spec.Coll.Coord.; Richard Burbank, Mus.Cat.Coord.; Leslie Troutman, Mus. User Serv.Coord..

UNIVERSITY OF ILLINOIS - NATIONAL CLEARINGHOUSE ON MARITAL AND DATE RAPE
See: National Clearinghouse on Marital and Date Rape (9627)

★16255★
UNIVERSITY OF ILLINOIS - NEWSPAPER LIBRARY (Info Sci)
Main Library, Rm. 1
1408 W. Gregory Dr. Phone: (217)333-1509
Urbana, IL 61801 Victoria L. Jaeger, Hd.
Staff: 2. **Subjects:** Newspapers. **Holdings:** 11,018 volumes; 77,078 reels of microfilm; 8810 microcards. **Subscriptions:** 55 journals and other serials; 670 newspapers. **Services:** Interlibrary loan; copying; library open to the public. **Publications:** Holdings of Subject Classified Newspapers; general newspapers in microform - backfiles; Foreign Newspapers Currently Received; U.S. Newspapers Currently Received; Labor Newspapers Currently Received; Labor Newspapers on Microfilm and Other Special Listings, revised and reissued biennially.

★16256★
UNIVERSITY OF ILLINOIS - PHYSICS/ASTRONOMY LIBRARY (Sci-Engr)
204 Loomis Laboratory
1110 W. Green St. Phone: (217)333-2101
Urbana, IL 61801 David Stern, Physics/Astronomy Libn.
Founded: 1948. **Staff:** Prof 1; Other 2. **Subjects:** Physics - solid state, nuclear, theoretical, medical; fluorescence dynamics; complex systems; astronomy and astrophysics; magnetism; optics. **Holdings:** 34,300 volumes. **Subscriptions:** 400 journals and other serials. **Services:** Interlibrary loan; copying; library open to the public with permit. **Automated Operations:** Computerized public access catalog and circulation. **Computerized Information Services:** BRS Information Technologies, DIALOG Information Services, STN International, OCLC; BITNET (electronic mail service). **Publications:** Acquisitions list; dedicated issues of journals list, both monthly. **Special Catalogs:** Conference file keyword index (card).

★16257★
UNIVERSITY OF ILLINOIS - RARE BOOK AND SPECIAL COLLECTIONS LIBRARY (Rare Book)
346 Main Library
1408 W. Gregory Dr. Phone: (217)333-3777
Urbana, IL 61801 Nancy Romero, Hd.
Staff: Prof 4; Other 1. **Subjects:** Sixteenth and seventeenth century editions of classical authors, Bibles, catechisms and sermons, grammars, and dictionaries; English and American literature and history; Italian drama, history, and biography; history of science. **Special Collections:** Milton Collection (3000 volumes); Ingold Shakespeare Collection; Clayton Papers, 1579-1744 (3020 original letters and documents); Cobbett Collection; 17th century newsletters; Proust correspondence; Meine Collection of American Humor; Harwell Collection of Confederate Imprints; Hollander Collection on Economics; Baskette Collection on Freedom of Expression; Nickell Collection of 18th Century English Literature; Winston S. Churchill Collection; Carl Sandburg Collection; H.G. Wells Collection; emblem books of Germany and low countries, 16th and 17th centuries; Japanese rare books; W.S. Merwin Archives; Motley Theater Design Collection. **Holdings:** 141,535 books, manuscripts, pamphlets, and early periodicals; 26,870 reels of microfilm. **Subscriptions:** 55 journals and other serials. **Services:** Interlibrary loan; copying (limited); room open to the public. **Special Catalogs:** Book catalog (1972, 11 volumes; Supplement, 1978, 2 volumes). **Formerly:** Rare Book Room.

UNIVERSITY OF ILLINOIS - REHABILITATION EDUCATION CENTER - NATIONAL PUBLICATIONS LIBRARY
See: National Publications Library (9761)

★16258★
UNIVERSITY OF ILLINOIS - RICKER LIBRARY OF ARCHITECTURE AND ART (Art)
208 Architecture Bldg. Phone: (217)333-0224
Urbana, IL 61801 Judith C. Surles, Act.Hd.Libn.
Founded: 1873. **Staff:** Prof 3; Other 3. **Subjects:** Architecture, fine arts, applied arts, art education, art history, history of photography, industrial design, graphic design. **Holdings:** 59,100 volumes. **Subscriptions:** 668 journals and other serials. **Services:** Interlibrary loan; library open to the public. **Automated Operations:** Computerized circulation. **Staff:** Joan Wells, Asst.Libn..

★16259★
UNIVERSITY OF ILLINOIS - SLAVIC AND EAST EUROPEAN LIBRARY (Area-Ethnic)
225 Main Library Phone: (217)333-1349
Urbana, IL 61801 Marianna Tax Choldin, Hd.
Staff: Prof 9; Other 17. **Subjects:** Slavic languages, social sciences, humanities. **Holdings:** 520,000 books and bound periodical volumes; 80,000 volumes in microform. **Subscriptions:** 3000 journals and other serials. **Services:** Interlibrary loan; copying; library open to the public with permit from Main Library. **Automated Operations:** Computerized circulation. **Computerized Information Services:** DIALOG Information Services, BRS Information Technologies, RLIN, OCLC, InfoTrac; internal databases; EasyLink (electronic mail service). Performs searches on fee basis. **Remarks:** Maintains Slavic Reference Service which handles bibliographic and reference questions in the humanities and social sciences. **Staff:** Robert H. Burger, Slavic Acq.Libn.; Dmytro Shtohryn, Slavic Cat.Libn.; Helen Sullivan, Slavic Ref.Serv..

★16260★
UNIVERSITY OF ILLINOIS - SURVEY RESEARCH LABORATORY - SRL LIBRARY (Soc Sci)
1005 W. Nevada St. Phone: (217)333-7109
Urbana, IL 61801 Mary A. Spaeth, Survey Res.Info.Coord.
Founded: 1967. **Staff:** Prof 1; Other 1. **Subjects:** Survey research, consumer behavior. **Holdings:** 1400 books; 2000 unbound periodicals; 72 VF drawers of government publications, reprints, newsletters, reports, pamphlets, catalogs. **Subscriptions:** 32 journals and other serials. **Services:** Library open to researchers for reference use only. **Computerized Information Services:** SRLLIST (keyword file to SRL studies; internal database). **Publications:** Survey Research (newsletter), quarterly - to supporting organizations and qualified researchers.

★16261★
UNIVERSITY OF ILLINOIS - UNIVERSITY ARCHIVES (Educ)
University Library, Rm. 19
1408 W. Gregory Dr. Phone: (217)333-0798
Urbana, IL 61801 Maynard Brichford, Univ.Archv.
Founded: 1963. **Staff:** Prof 2; Other 1. **Subjects:** Higher education, graduate education, teaching, research, public service, science and technology, humanities, extracurricular activities, business archives, agriculture, fraternities, library science, librarianship, athletics, physical education. **Holdings:** 7630 cubic feet of office records; 3337 cubic feet of faculty papers; 1183 cubic feet of publications; 1308 cubic feet of American Library Association (ALA) archives; 10.9 million historical manuscripts; scrapbooks; clippings; pamphlets; microfilm; videotapes; photographs; sound recordings. **Services:** Copying; archives open to the public. **Publications:** Annual Report; Guide to University Archives; Manuscripts Guide to Collections at the University of Illinois at Urbana-Champaign; Guide to ALA Archives. **Special Catalogs:** Recorded series control (4900 cards); supplementary finding aids (lists, publications, narrative descriptions, file guides); PARADIGM online series and subject control and data processing listings. Series are arranged by source and record groups and subgroups are described in the University Archives Classification Guide. **Staff:** William Maher, Asst.Archv..

★16262★
UNIVERSITY OF ILLINOIS - VETERINARY MEDICINE LIBRARY (Med)
1257 Vet. Med. Basic Sciences Bldg.
2001 S. Lincoln Ave.
Urbana, IL 61801 Phone: (217)333-2193
Founded: 1952. **Staff:** Prof 2; Other 2. **Subjects:** Pathology, physiology, pharmacology, bacteriology, veterinary science, parasitology. **Holdings:** 33,746 volumes; 10 VF drawers of pamphlets. **Subscriptions:** 838 journals and other serials. **Services:** Interlibrary loan; copying; library open to the public. **Automated Operations:** Computerized circulation. **Computerized Information Services:** DIALOG Information Services, BRS Information Technologies, NLM. **Staff:** Priscilla Smiley, Asst.Libn..

★16263★
UNIVERSITY OF ILLINOIS AT CHICAGO - COLLEGE OF MEDICINE AT PEORIA - LIBRARY OF THE HEALTH SCIENCES (Med)
Box 1649 Phone: (309)671-8490
Peoria, IL 61656 Trudy Landwirth, Br.Libn.
Founded: 1971. **Staff:** Prof 2; Other 6. **Subjects:** Medicine, basic sciences, nursing. **Holdings:** 23,871 books; 23,031 bound periodical volumes; 1926 AV programs; 5767 government documents. **Subscriptions:** 731 journals and other serials. **Services:** Interlibrary loan; library open to the public with restrictions. **Automated Operations:** Computerized circulation. **Computerized Information Services:** NLM, BRS Information Technologies, DIALOG Information Services, NOTIS, Statewide Library Computer System (LCS). **Networks/Consortia:** Member of Greater Midwest Regional Medical Library Network, Heart of Illinois Library Consortium (HILC), Illinois Valley Library System. **Publications:** Library Guide; Current List of Serials; Subject List of Current Serials. **Special Catalogs:** Subject Guide to Audiovisual Holdings (book). **Remarks:** Library located at One Illini Dr., Peoria, IL 61605.

★16264★
UNIVERSITY OF ILLINOIS AT CHICAGO - COLLEGE OF MEDICINE AT ROCKFORD - WOODRUFF L. CRAWFORD BRANCH LIBRARY OF THE HEALTH SCIENCES (Med)
1601 Parkview Ave. Phone: (815)987-7377
Rockford, IL 61107 Prudence W. Dalrymple, Hea.Sci.Libn.
Founded: 1941. **Staff:** Prof 3; Other 11. **Subjects:** Medicine, biomedical sciences, consumer health. **Holdings:** 26,000 books; 21,982 bound periodical volumes; 2031 pamphlets; 2550 slides; 512 reels of microfilm; 1900 magnetic tapes. **Subscriptions:** 642 journals and other serials; 7 newspapers. **Services:** Interlibrary loan; copying; SDI; library open to the public. **Automated Operations:** Computerized cataloging, acquisitions, serials, circulation, and ILL. **Computerized Information Services:** NLM, BRS Information Technologies, OCLC, WILSONLINE, PHILSOM, DIALOG Information Services, Statewide Library Computer System (LCS); DOCLINE (electronic mail service). Performs searches on fee basis. Contact Person: Christine Rouze, Ref.Libn., 987-7494. **Networks/Consortia:** Member of Greater Midwest Regional Medical Library Network, Northern Illinois Library System (NILS). **Publications:** Library Guide, annual - free upon request. **Staff:** Ellani Abate, Circ./Ser.Libn..

★16265★
UNIVERSITY OF ILLINOIS AT CHICAGO - ENERGY RESOURCES CENTER - DOCUMENTS CENTER (Energy)
412 S. Peoria St.
Box 4348 Phone: (312)996-4490
Chicago, IL 60680 Donald R. Bless, Res.Libn.
Staff: Prof 1; Other 1. **Subjects:** Energy - resources, policy, conservation, technology; alternative energy technologies; electric utility statistics. **Special Collections:** Heat and mass transfer (225 monographs; 15 journal subscriptions). **Holdings:** 4000 books; 100 bound periodical volumes; 2 VF drawers of clippings; 3 VF drawers of pamphlets; 100 maps; 100 reports on microfiche. **Subscriptions:** 120 journals and other serials. **Services:** Interlibrary loan; copying; SDI; center open to the public. **Computerized Information Services:** DIALOG Information Services, BRS Information Technologies. **Networks/Consortia:** Member of Chicago Library System. **Publications:** Illinois Energy Newsletter - free upon request.

★16266★
UNIVERSITY OF ILLINOIS AT CHICAGO - HEALTH SCIENCES CENTER - LIBRARY OF THE HEALTH SCIENCES (Med)
1750 W. Polk St. Phone: (312)996-8974
Chicago, IL 60612 Irwin H. Pizer, Univ.Libn. for the Hea.Sci.
Founded: 1890. **Staff:** Prof 30; Other 65. **Subjects:** Medicine, dentistry, nursing, pharmacy, public health, behavioral sciences, allied health professions. **Special Collections:** Kiefer Collection (urology; 2000 volumes); herbals and pharmacopoeias (500 volumes); Bailey Collection (neurology and psychiatry; 1000 volumes); medical center archives. **Holdings:** 542,843 volumes; 35,030 document titles; 222,512 AV programs; 725 linear feet of archives. **Subscriptions:** 6590 journals and other serials. **Services:** Interlibrary loan; SDI; library open to the public for reference use only. **Automated Operations:** Computerized cataloging, serials, and circulation; online regional catalog of monographs and AV programs. **Computerized Information Services:** MEDLINE, BRS Information Technologies, Pergamon ORBIT InfoLine, Inc., DIALOG Information Services, OCLC, NOTIS, Statewide Library Computer System (LCS). **Networks/Consortia:** Member of ILLINET, Greater Midwest Regional Medical Library Network. **Publications:** News Notes, monthly; Annual Report; Library Guides for Chicago, Peoria, Rockford, and Urbana branches, annual; Information Services Department guides to various special segments of the literature of the health sciences; Media Software Holdings catalog; Proceedings of the Dedication of the Library; Subject List of Current Serials; Bibliographiti, quarterly. **Special Catalogs:** Percival Bailey Catalog of Neurology and Psychiatry; Joseph Kiefer Catalog of Urology; Dental Literature Collection; Pharmacopoeias, Formularies, and Dispensatories; Warren Henry Cole - a bibliography; Catalog of pre-fire Chicago imprints (1844-1873) - all for sale. **Remarks:** Library is the Region 3 Medical Library of the National Library of Medicine. **Staff:** John N. Theall, Assoc.Univ.Libn., Pub.Serv.; Robert Adelsperger, Hd., Spec.Coll./Archv.; Stephen Van Houten, Hd.Cat.; Ann Weller, Hd., Ser.; Kathryn Hammell, Hd., Acq.; Ruby S. May, Assoc.Dir., Greater Midwest Reg.Med.Lib. Network; Kim Goldman, Prog.Coord..

★16267★
UNIVERSITY OF ILLINOIS AT CHICAGO - LIBRARY OF THE HEALTH SCIENCES, URBANA (Med)
506 S. Mathews
102 Medical Sciences Bldg.
Urbana, IL 61801 Phone: (217)333-4893
Founded: 1971. **Staff:** Prof 4; Other 4. **Subjects:** Medicine, gerontology, nursing, rehabilitation, basic sciences. **Holdings:** 22,763 books; 7769 bound periodical volumes; 2763 pamphlets; 2921 AV programs; 2815 other cataloged items. **Subscriptions:** 886 journals and other serials. **Services:** SDI; library open to the public. **Automated Operations:** Computerized cataloging, acquisitions, serials, and circulation. **Computerized Information Services:** BRS Information Technologies, NLM, DIALOG Information Services. Performs searches on fee basis. **Networks/Consortia:** Member of Greater Midwest Regional Medical Library Network, ILLINET.

★16268★
UNIVERSITY OF ILLINOIS AT CHICAGO - PACIFIC/ASIAN AMERICAN MENTAL HEALTH RESEARCH CENTER - DOCUMENTATION CENTER (Area-Ethnic)
1033 W. Van Buren Phone: (312)996-2964
Chicago, IL 60607 Phyllis Flattery, Dir., Pub.Info.
Founded: 1974. **Staff:** Prof 1; Other 1. **Subjects:** Asian, Oceanic, and Pacific Islander Americans. **Holdings:** 150 books; 28 VF drawers of unbound reports and papers. **Subscriptions:** 25 journals and other serials. **Services:** Copying; center open to the public for reference use only. **Automated Operations:** Computerized cataloging. **Computerized Information Services:** Internal database. **Publications:** Research Review, quarterly - free; list of recent acquisitions, quarterly; Pacific/Asian American Research: An Annotated Bibliography, 1981; The Pacific/Asian Americans: A Selected and Annotated Bibliography of Recent Materials.

★16269★
UNIVERSITY OF ILLINOIS AT CHICAGO - SCIENCE LIBRARY (Sci-Engr)
Science & Engineering South Bldg.
Box 7565
Chicago, IL 60680 Phone: (312)996-5396
Founded: 1970. **Staff:** Prof 2; Other 4. **Subjects:** Chemistry, biology, geology, astronomy, physics. **Special Collections:** Sadtler Research Laboratories Standard Collections of Spectra; industry standards and codes. **Holdings:** 53,900 books; 64,650 bound periodical volumes; 83,830 technical reports, hard copy and microform. **Subscriptions:** 1673 journals and other serials. **Services:** Interlibrary loan; copying; library open to the public for reference use only. **Automated Operations:** Computerized cataloging. **Computerized Information Services:** OCLC, DIALOG Information Services, STN International, WILSONLINE, Northwestern Online Total Integrated Systems (NOTIS), BRS Information Technologies, Statewide Library Computer System (LCS). **Staff:** Gladys Odegaard, Asst.Sci.Libn.; Helen Badawi, Circ.Supv..

★16270★
UNIVERSITY OF ILLINOIS AT CHICAGO - UNIVERSITY LIBRARY - MAP SECTION (Geog-Map)
Box 8198 Phone: (312)996-5277
Chicago, IL 60680 Marsha L. Selmer, Map Libn.
Staff: Prof 1; Other 1. **Subjects:** Maps, atlases, aerial photographs. **Special Collections:** Historic Urban Plans (complete set); 16th-19th century maps of the Russian Empire and Eastern Europe; 19th century maps of Illinois; 17th-18th century maps of the Great Lakes; aerial photographs and photomaps of Chicago and northeastern Illinois. **Holdings:** 141,242 maps; 747 atlases; 3850 aerial photographs. **Services:** Interlibrary loan; section open to the public. **Publications:** Chicago in Maps; information brochure, both irregular - both free upon request.

★16271★
UNIVERSITY OF IOWA - ART LIBRARY (Art)
Art Bldg. Phone: (319)335-3089
Iowa City, IA 52242 Harlan Sifford, Libn.
Staff: Prof 1; Other 1. **Subjects:** Art. **Holdings:** 67,566 volumes. **Services:** Interlibrary loan; copying.

★16272★
UNIVERSITY OF IOWA - BIOLOGY LIBRARY (Biol Sci)
301 Zoology Bldg. Phone: (319)335-3083
Iowa City, IA 52242 Stephen Mackey, Act.Libn.
Staff: Prof 1; Other 1. **Subjects:** Zoology. **Holdings:** 34,939 volumes. **Services:** Interlibrary loan; copying.

★16273★
UNIVERSITY OF IOWA - BOTANY-CHEMISTRY LIBRARY (Biol Sci, Sci-Engr)
Iowa City, IA 52242 Phone: (319)335-3085
Stephen Mackey, Act.Libn.
Staff: Prof 1; Other 1. **Subjects:** Botany, chemistry, and related fields. **Holdings:** 73,868 volumes. **Services:** Interlibrary loan; copying.

★16274★
UNIVERSITY OF IOWA - BUSINESS LIBRARY (Bus-Fin)
College of Business Administration
Phillips Hall Phone: (319)335-3077
Iowa City, IA 52242 David Martin, Bus.Libn.
Founded: 1965. **Staff:** Prof 2; Other 1. **Subjects:** Management, labor relations, labor unions, accounting, finance. **Special Collections:** Major labor union periodicals. **Holdings:** 21,522 volumes. **Services:** Interlibrary loan; copying.

★16275★
UNIVERSITY OF IOWA - COLLEGE OF EDUCATION - CURRICULUM RESOURCES LABORATORY (Educ)
N140 Lindquist Center Phone: (319)335-5616
Iowa City, IA 52242 Paula O. Brandt, Coord.
Staff: Prof 2; Other 2. **Subjects:** Children's books; adolescent novels; special, elementary, and secondary education curriculum materials. **Special Collections:** K-12 textbooks (15,000); curriculum guides (5000). **Holdings:** 29,000 books; 4000 AV programs, games, computer diskettes, picture sets, and other nonprint materials. **Services:** Copying; laboratory open to the public. **Publications:** Newsletter, irregular. **Staff:** Carol Vogt, Ref.Libn..

★16276★
UNIVERSITY OF IOWA - COLLEGE OF PHARMACY - IOWA DRUG INFORMATION SERVICE (Med)
Westlawn, Box 330 Phone: (319)335-8913
Iowa City, IA 52242 C. David Butler, Pharm.D., Dir.
Staff: Prof 17; Other 17. **Subjects:** Drugs and drug therapy. **Holdings:** 230,000 articles on microfilm; Drug and Disease Indexes with internal descriptor-index, 1966 to present, on microfilm. **Subscriptions:** 160 journals and other serials. **Services:** SDI; service open to subscribers. **Computerized Information Services:** DIALOG Information Services, NLM; Drug Literature Microfilm File (internal database); BITNET, EasyLink (electronic mail services). Performs searches on fee basis. **Publications:** Drug Literature Microfilm File (DLMF), monthly; Procedure Manual, annual. **Special Indexes:** Drug Cross Reference Index, quarterly; Disease Cross Reference Index, quarterly.

★16277★
UNIVERSITY OF IOWA - ENGINEERING LIBRARY (Sci-Engr)
106 Engineering Bldg. Phone: (319)335-6047
Iowa City, IA 52242 John W. Forys, Libn.
Staff: Prof 1; Other 1. **Subjects:** Engineering, science, technology. **Holdings:** 77,664 volumes. **Services:** Interlibrary loan.

★16278★
UNIVERSITY OF IOWA - GEOLOGY LIBRARY (Sci-Engr)
136 Trowbridge Hall Phone: (319)335-3084
Iowa City, IA 52242 Louise Zipp, Libn.
Staff: Prof 1; Other 1. **Subjects:** Sedimentology, crystallography, mineralogy, structural geology, petrology, geochemistry, geophysics, engineering geology. **Holdings:** 40,851 volumes. **Services:** Interlibrary loan.

★16279★
UNIVERSITY OF IOWA - HEALTH SCIENCES LIBRARY (Med)
Health Sciences Library Bldg. Phone: (319)335-9871
Iowa City, IA 52242 David S. Curry, Libn.
Founded: 1870. **Staff:** Prof 8; Other 7. **Subjects:** Medicine, speech pathology, dentistry, nursing, pharmacy. **Special Collections:** John Martin History of Medicine Collection. **Holdings:** 211,038 volumes. **Services:** Interlibrary loan; copying. **Automated Operations:** Computerized cataloging and serials. **Computerized Information Services:** MEDLINE. **Networks/Consortia:** Member of Greater Midwest Regional Medical Library Network.

★16280★
UNIVERSITY OF IOWA - IOWA URBAN COMMUNITY RESEARCH CENTER - REFERENCE LIBRARY (Soc Sci)
W170 Seashore Hall Phone: (319)353-4119
Iowa City, IA 52242 Lyle W. Shannon, Dir.
Founded: 1958. **Subjects:** U.S. Census, vital statistics and public health, population and demography, minority groups, juvenile delinquency and crime. **Special Collections:** Selected series of U.S. Census, 1910 to present. **Holdings:** 1000 books; 25 drawers of reprints, publications; punched cards and tapes on all studies conducted, 1958 to present. **Subscriptions:** 30 journals and other serials. **Services:** Library open to the public. **Publications:** Monograph series - for sale.

★16281★
UNIVERSITY OF IOWA - LABORATORY FOR POLITICAL RESEARCH (Soc Sci)
345A Schaeffer Hall Phone: (319)353-3103
Iowa City, IA 52242 Prof. Arthur Miller, Dir.
Founded: 1968. **Staff:** Prof 3; Other 1. **Subjects:** Political science, sociology, history, geography, economics, law. **Special Collections:** Des Moines Register and Tribune public opinion polls; machine-readable bibliographies on legislative behavior and communist political systems. **Holdings:** 450 data sets. **Services:** Copying; laboratory open to the public. **Publications:** Laboratory for Political Research Report Series; Reprint Series; SSDA Codebooks. **Special Indexes:** Listing of archive holdings;

index of survey items on legislative behavior; Annual Report. **Remarks:** Includes the Social Science Data Archive. **Staff:** John Kolp, Prog.Assoc.; C.H. Lu, Tech.Dir.; James R. Grifhorst, Data Archv.Mgr..

★16282★
UNIVERSITY OF IOWA - LAW LIBRARY (Law)
Law Center Phone: (319)353-5968
Iowa City, IA 52242 Arthur Bonfield, Dir.
Founded: 1865. **Staff:** Prof 11; Other 14. **Subjects:** Anglo-American law. **Holdings:** 135,076 books; 315,176 bound periodical volumes; U.S. Supreme Court records and briefs in microform. **Subscriptions:** 1809 journals and other serials; 10 newspapers. **Services:** Interlibrary loan; copying; library open to the public with restrictions on circulation. **Computerized Information Services:** LEXIS, WESTLAW, RLIN; ABA/net (electronic mail service). Performs searches on fee basis. Contact Person: Tom Eicher, Ref., 335-9038. **Networks/Consortia:** Member of RLG. **Staff:** Katherine Belgum, Exec. Law Libn.; Caitlin Robinson, Tech.Serv.; Virginia Melroy, Cat.; Mary Ertl, Acq.; Sue Emde, Docs.; Karen Nobbs, Hd.Cat.; John Bengstrom; Ted Mahr, Ref.; Sandra Keller, Ref..

★16283★
UNIVERSITY OF IOWA - LIBRARY SCIENCE LIBRARY
Main Library
Iowa City, IA 52242
Defunct. Absorbed by general library.

★16284★
UNIVERSITY OF IOWA - MATHEMATICS LIBRARY (Sci-Engr)
MacLean Hall Phone: (319)335-3076
Iowa City, IA 52242 Katherine Kjaer, Libn.
Staff: Prof 1; Other 1. **Subjects:** Mathematics. **Holdings:** 42,420 volumes. **Services:** Interlibrary loan; copying.

★16285★
UNIVERSITY OF IOWA - MUSIC LIBRARY (Mus)
Music Bldg. Phone: (319)335-3086
Iowa City, IA 52242 Joan O. Falconer, Libn.
Founded: 1957. **Staff:** Prof 1; Other 2. **Subjects:** Music. **Holdings:** 69,288 volumes. **Services:** Interlibrary loan; copying; library open to the public. **Special Catalogs:** Annotated catalog of rare music items in the libraries of the University of Iowa.

★16286★
UNIVERSITY OF IOWA - OFFICE OF THE STATE ARCHAEOLOGIST - DOCUMENT COLLECTION (Sci-Engr, Hist)
317 Eastlawn Phone: (319)335-2395
Iowa City, IA 52242 Martin Kurth, Docs.Cur.
Staff: Prof 1. **Subjects:** Archeology, anthropology, geomorphology, soil surveys, ethnology, physical anthropology. **Special Collections:** All published and unpublished archeological surveys and excavations performed in Iowa; office archives. **Holdings:** 2000 books; 15,000 other items. **Subscriptions:** 45 journals and other serials. **Services:** Copying; SDI; collection open to the public for reference use only. **Computerized Information Services:** Internal database of site records and catalog sheets. **Publications:** Bibliography on Mesquakie Indians. **Special Indexes:** Index to the Journal of the Iowa Archeological Society and Newsletter.

★16287★
UNIVERSITY OF IOWA - PHYSICS LIBRARY (Sci-Engr)
Physics Research Center Phone: (319)335-3082
Iowa City, IA 52242 Kathy Kjaer, Libn.
Staff: Prof 1; Other 1. **Subjects:** Physics. **Holdings:** 40,328 volumes. **Services:** Interlibrary loan; copying.

★16288★
UNIVERSITY OF IOWA - PSYCHOLOGY LIBRARY (Soc Sci)
Iowa City, IA 52242 Phone: (319)335-2405
Dorothy M. Persson, Libn.
Staff: Prof 1; Other 2. **Subjects:** Psychology. **Holdings:** 48,566 volumes. **Services:** Interlibrary loan; copying.

★16289★
UNIVERSITY OF IOWA - SPECIAL COLLECTIONS DEPARTMENT (Rare Book)
Main Library Phone: (319)335-5921
Iowa City, IA 52242 Robert A. McCown, Hd.
Staff: Prof 4; Other 3. **Special Collections:** Brewer-Leigh Hunt Collection (2200 volumes; 3520 leaves of manuscript; 1635 manuscript letters); Iowa Authors Collection (10,000 volumes; 3000 manuscripts); Bollinger-Lincoln Collection (4600 volumes; 480 pamphlets); History of Hydraulics Collection (550 volumes); map collection (190,000 maps and aerial photographs; 3300 atlases); university archives (4000 linear feet of papers; 4000 volumes); French medals, 1848 (842); original Ding Darling cartoons (6000); right-wing ephemeral publications (1100 titles). **Holdings:** 26,000 rare books; 450 manuscript collections of personal and corporate records. **Services:** Department open to the public. **Publications:** Books at Iowa, semiannual - to members of the Friends of the University of Iowa Libraries. **Special Indexes:** The Wallace Papers: An Index to the Microfilm Editions of the Henry A. Wallace Papers (1975), 2 volumes; A Guide for the Study of the Recent History of the U.S. (1977). **Staff:** Earl M. Rogers, Cur. of Archv.; Richard Green, Map Libn.; David E. Schoonover, Cur. of Rare Bks..

★16290★
UNIVERSITY OF IOWA - TRANSLATION LABORATORY (Hum)
W 615 Seashore Hall Phone: (319)335-2002
Iowa City, IA 52242 Gertrud G. Champe, Dir.
Founded: 1982. **Staff:** Prof 1; Other 3. **Subjects:** Translation, interpreting, international research, subtitling. **Special Collections:** Completed translations (1000). **Holdings:** 100 books. **Services:** Laboratory open to the public.

★16291★
UNIVERSITY OF KANSAS - DEPARTMENT OF SPECIAL COLLECTIONS (Hist, Hum)
Spencer Research Library Phone: (913)864-4334
Lawrence, KS 66045-2800 Alexandra Mason, Spencer Libn.
Founded: 1953. **Staff:** Prof 7; Other 2. **Subjects:** 17th and 18th century English history, economics, literature; history of ornithology; European Renaissance and early modern history, economics, politics; discovery and exploration; Latin America; history of botany; Anglo-Irish literature. **Special Collections:** Summerfield Collection of Renaissance and Early Modern Books (7400 volumes including 130 incunabula); Roger Clubb Memorial Collection of Books in Anglo-Saxon Types (300 books); Brodie of Brodie Collection of 17th to 19th century pamphlets (1200 items); Edmund Curll Collection (750 books); English Poetical Miscellanies, 18th century (500 books); Melvin French Revolutionary Collection (9000 items); Realey Collection of Walpoliana (500 items); Robert Horn Collection of Panegyrics on the Duke of Marlborough (200 items); 18th century English Pamphlet Collection (15,000 items); James Joyce Collection (900 books); Rainer Maria Rilke Collection (1700 items); W.B. Yeats Collection (650 items); New American Poetry Collection (6000 items); Ellis Ornithology Collection (15,000 volumes, pamphlets, letters, drawings, and manuscripts); Linnaeus Collection (1750 volumes); Children's Literature, 18th to 20th century (6500 volumes); H.L. Mencken (780 volumes, scrapbooks, manuscripts); Science Fiction (7000 items); O'Hegarty Anglo-Irish Literature and History (12,000 volumes); manuscripts and documents in medieval, early modern, and modern literature, history, and science (480,000 items); Bond Collection of 18th century English newspapers and periodicals; paleography and manuscript studies; Frank Lloyd Wright Collection (books; blueprints; clippings; photographs; manuscripts); Griffith Collection on Guatemala; W.D. Paden Collection of Tennyson; World Science Fiction Depository; Howey Collection of Economics and Economic History to 1850 (3500 volumes). **Holdings:** 186,537 books and periodicals; 887 rare maps; 2092 photographs; 1377 linear feet of manuscripts. **Services:** Copying; department open to the public for reference use only. **Automated Operations:** Computerized cataloging and serials. **Computerized Information Services:** OCLC, RLIN. **Networks/Consortia:** Member of Bibliographical Center for Research, Rocky Mountain Region, Inc. (BCR). **Publications:** A Guide to the Collections, 1987. **Special Catalogs:** Catalog of manuscripts (loose-leaf); exhibit catalogs, irregular - available on request. **Special Indexes:** Indexes of provenance, printers, methods of illustration (card); Boys-Mizener first-line index to English poetical miscellanies (card); chronological indexes to books and manuscripts. **Staff:** William L. Mitchell, Consrv.Libn.; Ann Hyde, Mss.Libn.; Sarah E. Haines, Botany Libn.; L.E.J. Helyar, Cur. in Graphics; Robert Melton, Asst.Libn.; Richard Clement, Asst.Libn..

★16292★
UNIVERSITY OF KANSAS - DOCUMENTS COLLECTION (Info Sci)
117 Spencer Research Library Phone: (913)864-4662
Lawrence, KS 66045-2800 Donna Koepp, Doc./Maps Libn.
Founded: 1869. **Staff:** Prof 2; Other 4. **Subjects:** Census, U.S. legislative history, British parliamentary history. **Special Collections:** Regional depository for U.S. documents; United Nations depository; official publications of the United Kingdom; Organization for Economic Cooperation and Development and European Community publications;

Kansas State census on microfilm; Joint Publications Research Service (JPRS) publications in microform. **Holdings:** 775,767 documents; 572,000 microforms. **Subscriptions:** 2817 journals and other serials. **Services:** Interlibrary loan; copying; collection open to the public. **Computerized Information Services:** OCLC. **Networks/Consortia:** Member of Bibliographical Center for Research, Rocky Mountain Region, Inc. (BCR), Kansas Library Network. **Publications:** Duplicate List of Regional Depository, monthly - to other depository libraries. **Staff:** Dan Barkley, Asst.Libn..

★16293★
UNIVERSITY OF KANSAS - EAST ASIAN LIBRARY (Area-Ethnic)
Watson Library Phone: (913)864-4669
Lawrence, KS 66045-2800 Eugene Carvalho, Libn.
Founded: 1964. **Staff:** Prof 1; Other 1. **Subjects:** Chinese and Japanese history, literature, language, culture; contemporary China; contemporary Japan. **Holdings:** 116,343 books and bound periodical volumes. **Subscriptions:** 722 journals and other serials; 15 newspapers. **Services:** Interlibrary loan; copying; library open to the public. **Automated Operations:** Computerized cataloging, serials, and circulation. **Computerized Information Services:** OCLC. **Networks/Consortia:** Member of Bibliographical Center for Research, Rocky Mountain Region, Inc. (BCR), Kansas Library Network. **Remarks:** Materials primarily in Chinese, Japanese, and Korean languages.

★16294★
UNIVERSITY OF KANSAS - ENGINEERING LIBRARY (Sci-Engr)
1012 Learned Hall Phone: (913)864-3866
Lawrence, KS 66045-2800 LeAnn Weller, Libn.
Staff: Prof 1; Other 3. **Subjects:** Engineering. **Holdings:** 44,176 books and bound periodical volumes. **Subscriptions:** 1239 journals and other serials. **Services:** Interlibrary loan; copying; library open to the public. **Automated Operations:** Computerized cataloging and serials. **Computerized Information Services:** DIALOG Information Services, Pergamon ORBIT InfoLine, Inc., OCLC, BRS Information Technologies. **Networks/Consortia:** Member of Bibliographical Center for Research, Rocky Mountain Region, Inc. (BCR), Kansas Library Network.

★16295★
UNIVERSITY OF KANSAS - INSTITUTE FOR PUBLIC POLICY AND BUSINESS RESEARCH (Soc Sci)
607 Blake Hall Phone: (913)864-3701
Lawrence, KS 66045-2800 Thelma Helyar, Libn.
Founded: 1985. **Staff:** Prof 1. **Subjects:** Survey research; economic indicators; economic, community, and rural development; census data; data processing; econometric models; demographics; policy studies; statistics. **Holdings:** 9000 volumes. **Subscriptions:** 200 journals and other serials. **Services:** Interlibrary loan; copying; institute open to the public. **Publications:** Kansas Statistical Abstract and the Kansas Business Review, quarterly. **Remarks:** Institute is affiliated with the Kansas State Data Center.

★16296★
UNIVERSITY OF KANSAS - JOURNALISM READING ROOM (Info Sci)
William Allen White School of Journalism
210 Flint Hall Phone: (913)864-4755
Lawrence, KS 66045-2800 Ethel Stewart, Libn.
Founded: 1955. **Staff:** Prof 1. **Subjects:** Newspaper journalism, mass communications, broadcasting, graphic arts, advertising. **Holdings:** Figures not available. **Services:** Copying; room open to the public.

★16297★
UNIVERSITY OF KANSAS - KANSAS COLLECTION (Hist)
220 Spencer Research Library Phone: (913)864-4274
Lawrence, KS 66045-2800 Sheryl K. Williams, Cur.
Founded: 1892. **Staff:** Prof 3; Other 3. **Subjects:** Kansas and Great Plains - social movements, business and economic history, social and cultural history, politics, travel; regional African-American history. **Special Collections:** Overland diaries; depository of Kansas State Printer; J.J. Pennell Collection of photographs and negatives, 1891-1923 (40,000 items); Wilcox Collection of Contemporary Political Movements, 1960 to present (5000 books; 4000 serials; 80,000 pieces of ephemera); Jules Bourquin Collection of photographs, 1898-1959 (30,000); J.B. Watkins Land Mortgage Company Records, 1864-1946 (627 linear feet). **Holdings:** 95,598 volumes; 6444 linear feet of manuscripts; 1.1 million photographs; 79,576 glass negatives; 9365 sheets and volumes of maps; 4259 cartoons. **Subscriptions:** 1575 journals and other serials; 50 newspapers. **Services:** Interlibrary loan; copying; collection open to the public. **Automated Operations:** Computerized cataloging and serials. **Computerized Information Services:** OCLC. **Networks/Consortia:** Member of Bibliographical Center for Research, Rocky Mountain Region, Inc. (BCR), Kansas Library Network. **Staff:** Nicolette Bromberg, Photoarchv.; Rebecca Schulte, Asst.Libn..

★16298★
UNIVERSITY OF KANSAS - LATIN AMERICAN COLLECTION (Area-Ethnic)
Watson Library Phone: (913)864-3351
Lawrence, KS 66045-2800 Rachel Miller, Bibliog.
Staff: Prof 1; Other 1. **Subjects:** Latin America - literature, history, social sciences. **Special Collections:** Central America; 19th century Guatemala; Costa Rica; Paraguay. **Holdings:** 175,000 volumes in Spanish and Portuguese. **Services:** Interlibrary loan; copying; collection open to the public. **Automated Operations:** Computerized cataloging, serials, and circulation.

★16299★
UNIVERSITY OF KANSAS - MAP LIBRARY (Geog-Map)
110 Spencer Research Library Phone: (913)864-4420
Lawrence, KS 66045-2800 Donna Koepp, Doc./Maps Libn.
Founded: 1950. **Staff:** Staff: 1. **Subjects:** Cartography, geography, topography, Kansas aerial photography. **Holdings:** 2771 volumes; 258,850 maps; photographic film. **Subscriptions:** 93 journals and other serials. **Services:** Interlibrary loan; copying; library open to the public. **Automated Operations:** Computerized cataloging and serials. **Computerized Information Services:** OCLC. **Networks/Consortia:** Member of Bibliographical Center for Research, Rocky Mountain Region, Inc. (BCR), Kansas Library Network.

★16300★
UNIVERSITY OF KANSAS - MURPHY LIBRARY OF ART AND ARCHITECTURE (Art)
Helen Foresman Spencer Museum of Art Phone: (913)864-3020
Lawrence, KS 66045-2800 Susan V. Craig, Art & Arch.Libn.
Founded: 1970. **Staff:** Prof 1; Other 3. **Subjects:** Art, design, photography, architecture, art history. **Special Collections:** Ephemeral collection of museum and gallery publications. **Holdings:** 77,564 volumes; pamphlet files on artists. **Subscriptions:** 770 journals and other serials. **Services:** Interlibrary loan; copying; library open to the public. **Automated Operations:** Computerized cataloging, serials, and circulation. **Computerized Information Services:** OCLC, RLIN, DIALOG Information Services (through Watson Library). **Networks/Consortia:** Member of Bibliographical Center for Research, Rocky Mountain Region, Inc. (BCR), Kansas Library Network.

★16301★
UNIVERSITY OF KANSAS - OFFICE OF GRADUATE STUDIES AND RESEARCH - LIBRARY (Med)
University of Kansas Medical Center
39th & Rainbow
Kansas City, KS 66103 Phone: (913)588-5237
Subjects: Medical research, funding. **Holdings:** Figures not available.

★16302★
UNIVERSITY OF KANSAS - SCHOOL OF LAW LIBRARY (Law)
Green Hall Phone: (913)864-3025
Lawrence, KS 66045-2800 Peter C. Schanck, Dir.
Founded: 1904. **Staff:** Prof 5; Other 7. **Subjects:** Law. **Special Collections:** Basic collection in the law of Great Britain, Canada, and other common law countries; Russian law (includes complete code of the Russian Empire, 1801-1894). **Holdings:** 165,000 bound volumes; 35,000 government documents; 40,000 volumes in microform. **Subscriptions:** 3700 journals and other serials. **Services:** Interlibrary loan; copying; library open to the public. **Automated Operations:** Computerized cataloging. **Computerized Information Services:** LEXIS, WESTLAW, NEXIS, DIALOG Information Services, WILSONLINE. **Networks/Consortia:** Member of Kansas Library Network, Northeast Kansas Library System (NEKL), Mid-America Law School Library Consortium. **Publications:** Weekly List of Acquisitions - for internal distribution only; Readers' Handbook; Guide for Readers No. 14: University of Kansas Law Library. **Staff:** Fritz Snyder, Assoc.Dir. for Pub.Serv.; Mary D. Burchill, Assoc.Dir. for Adm.; Mon Yin Lung, Hd., Tech.Serv..

★16303★
UNIVERSITY OF KANSAS - SCIENCE LIBRARY (Sci-Engr, Biol Sci)
6040 Malott Hall Phone: (913)864-4928
Lawrence, KS 66045-2800 Kathleen Neeley, Sci.Libn.
Founded: 1954. **Staff:** Prof 3; Other 6. **Subjects:** Chemistry, physics, pharmacy, biology, geology, medicine, astronomy, history of science, general science. **Holdings:** 220,661 volumes; 18,471 government documents; 89,966 microforms. **Subscriptions:** 4745 journals and other serials. **Services:** Interlibrary loan; library open to the public. **Automated Operations:** Computerized cataloging, serials, and circulation. **Computerized Information Services:** DIALOG Information Services, Pergamon ORBIT InfoLine, Inc., BRS Information Technologies, NLM, OCLC. **Networks/Consortia:** Member of Bibliographical Center for Research, Rocky Mountain Region, Inc. (BCR), Kansas Library Network. **Staff:** Janice Franklin, Asst.Sci.Libn.; Judith Emde, Asst.Sci.Libn..

★16304★
UNIVERSITY OF KANSAS - SLAVIC COLLECTION (Area-Ethnic)
Watson Library Phone: (913)864-3957
Lawrence, KS 66045-2800 Gordon Anderson, Dir.
Founded: 1954. **Staff:** Prof 3; Other 1. **Subjects:** Slavic literature, languages, linguistics, history, social sciences. **Special Collections:** 16th-18th century Slavic imprints, especially Polish; World War II materials, especially Ukrainian and Polish memoirs; Yugoslav literature and languages; Russian and Polish emigre literature. **Holdings:** 177,500 volumes in Slavic languages; 66,000 volumes in translation or in West European languages; 90,000 bound periodical volumes. **Services:** Interlibrary loan; collection open to authorized users. **Automated Operations:** Computerized public access catalog, cataloging, acquisitions, serials, and circulation. **Computerized Information Services:** OCLC. **Networks/Consortia:** Member of Bibliographical Center for Research, Rocky Mountain Region, Inc. (BCR), Kansas Library Network. **Staff:** Priscilla Howe, Exchange & Cat.Libn.; George Jerkovich, Soviet & S. Slavic Bibliog..

★16305★
UNIVERSITY OF KANSAS - THOMAS GORTON MUSIC LIBRARY (Mus)
448 Murphy Hall Phone: (913)864-3496
Lawrence, KS 66045-2800 Susan Hitchens, Libn.
Founded: 1953. **Staff:** Prof 2; Other 1. **Subjects:** Music. **Holdings:** 41,319 books and scores; 84,615 sound recordings; 7514 microforms. **Services:** Interlibrary loan; copying; library open to the public. **Automated Operations:** Computerized cataloging and serials. **Computerized Information Services:** OCLC. **Networks/Consortia:** Member of Bibliographical Center for Research, Rocky Mountain Region, Inc. (BCR), Kansas Library Network. **Staff:** Ellen Johnson, Assoc.Libn..

★16306★
UNIVERSITY OF KANSAS - UNIVERSITY ARCHIVES (Hist)
422 Spencer Research Library Phone: (913)864-4188
Lawrence, KS 66045-2800 John M. Nugent, Univ.Archv.
Founded: 1969. **Staff:** Prof 2; Other 1. **Subjects:** University of Kansas. **Special Collections:** University records, 1866 to present; faculty papers; D'Ambra photographs, 1925-1970. **Holdings:** 21,978 volumes; 576,254 negatives; 207,098 photographs; 2234 tapes; 14,051 linear feet of university records; 3558 reels of 16mm film; 528 reels of microfilm; 1028 videotapes. **Services:** Interlibrary loan; copying; archives open to the public with restrictions. **Computerized Information Services:** OCLC. **Networks/Consortia:** Member of Bibliographical Center for Research, Rocky Mountain Region, Inc. (BCR), Kansas Library Network. **Staff:** Edward Kehde, Archv..

★16307★
UNIVERSITY OF KANSAS - UNIVERSITY INFORMATION CENTER (Hist)
Burge Union Phone: (913)864-3506
Lawrence, KS 66045 Patricia C. Kehde, Coord.
Founded: 1970. **Staff:** Prof 1; Other 15. **Subjects:** University of Kansas; Lawrence/Kansas City area. **Holdings:** 100 volumes; university papers. **Services:** Copying; center open to the public. **Publications:** Lecture List; Travel and Transportation Information; Bank Guide; Abbreviation and Acronym Directory for University of Kansas - all for internal distribution only.

★16308★
UNIVERSITY OF KANSAS - WEALTHY BABCOCK MATHEMATICS AND COMPUTER SCIENCE LIBRARY (Sci-Engr, Comp Sci)
209 Strong Hall Phone: (913)864-3440
Lawrence, KS 66045-2800 Ruth D. Fauhl, Lib.Asst.
Staff: 1. **Subjects:** Mathematics, computer science. **Holdings:** 29,980 volumes. **Subscriptions:** 543 journals and other serials. **Services:** Interlibrary loan; copying; library open to the public. **Automated Operations:** Computerized cataloging and serials. **Computerized Information Services:** OCLC. **Networks/Consortia:** Member of Bibliographical Center for Research, Rocky Mountain Region, Inc. (BCR), Kansas Library Network.

★16309★
UNIVERSITY OF KANSAS MEDICAL CENTER - ARCHIE R. DYKES LIBRARY OF THE HEALTH SCIENCES (Med)
2100 W. 39th St. Phone: (913)588-7166
Kansas City, KS 66103 James L. Bingham, Dir.
Founded: 1906. **Staff:** Prof 10; Other 28. **Subjects:** Basic sciences, clinical medicine, allied health sciences, nursing, social work. **Special Collections:** Educational Resource Center. **Holdings:** 55,947 books; 77,658 bound periodical volumes. **Subscriptions:** 1950 journals and other serials. **Services:** Interlibrary loan; copying; library open to the public with restrictions. **Automated Operations:** Computerized cataloging, serials, and circulation. **Computerized Information Services:** BRS Information Technologies, NLM, OCLC, DIALOG Information Services. Performs searches on fee basis. **Networks/Consortia:** Member of Kansas City Library Network, Inc. (KCLN), Midcontinental Regional Medical Library Program. **Publications:** New Titles, monthly - for internal distribution only.

★16310★
UNIVERSITY OF KANSAS REGENTS CENTER - LIBRARY (Educ, Bus-Fin)
9900 Mission Rd. Phone: (913)341-4554
Shawnee Mission, KS 66206 Nancy J. Burich, Libn.
Founded: 1976. **Staff:** Prof 1; Other 3. **Subjects:** Education, business, history, literature, engineering management, journalism management, architecture management, urban planning, public administration, computer science, social welfare, health services administration. **Special Collections:** Reavis Reading Room. **Holdings:** 11,392 books; 6310 microforms. **Subscriptions:** 420 journals and other serials; 8 newspapers. **Services:** Interlibrary loan; copying; library open to the public with restrictions. **Automated Operations:** Computerized serials. **Computerized Information Services:** DIALOG Information Services, BRS Information Technologies. **Networks/Consortia:** Member of Kansas City Metropolitan Library Network (KCMLN).

★16311★
UNIVERSITY OF KENTUCKY - AGRICULTURE LIBRARY (Biol Sci, Agri)
N 24 Agricultural Science Ctr., N. Phone: (606)257-2758
Lexington, KY 40546-0091 Antoinette P. Powell, Dir.
Founded: 1905. **Staff:** Prof 3; Other 5. **Subjects:** Agriculture, forestry, veterinary medicine, food, nutrition, entomology, horticulture, botany, landscape architecture. **Holdings:** 32,067 books; 56,022 bound periodical volumes; 3160 reels of microfilm; 30,325 microfiche; 8641 U.S. Department of Agriculture publications; 2144 unbound materials. **Subscriptions:** 2587 journals and other serials; 10 newspapers. **Services:** Interlibrary loan; copying; library open to the public. **Automated Operations:** Computerized cataloging and circulation. **Computerized Information Services:** OCLC, DIALOG Information Services, BRS Information Technologies, ANSER. Performs searches on fee basis. **Networks/Consortia:** Member of SOLINET. **Publications:** Monthly Acquisitions List - available upon request. **Staff:** Agnes McDowell, Selection; Lillian Mesner, Cat..

★16312★
UNIVERSITY OF KENTUCKY - ART LIBRARY (Art, Theater)
2 King Library N. Phone: (606)257-3938
Lexington, KY 40506-0039 Meg Shaw, Libn.
Staff: Prof 1; Other 1. **Subjects:** Art, theater arts. **Holdings:** 24,666 books; 6253 bound periodical volumes; 68 reels of microfilm; 812 microfiche; 36 VF drawers of pamphlets and catalogs. **Subscriptions:** 176 journals and other serials. **Automated Operations:** Computerized cataloging and circulation. **Services:** Interlibrary loan; copying; library open to the public.

★16313★
UNIVERSITY OF KENTUCKY - BIOLOGICAL SCIENCES LIBRARY (Biol Sci)
313 Thomas Hunt Morgan Bldg. Phone: (606)257-5889
Lexington, KY 40506-0225 Mildred A. Moore, Biol.Sci.Libn.
Founded: 1963. **Staff:** Prof 1; Other 1. **Subjects:** Microbiology, biology, botany, zoology, virology, endocrinology. **Holdings:** 18,425 books; 22,096 bound periodical volumes; 1425 microforms. **Subscriptions:** 445 journals and other serials. **Services:** Interlibrary loan; copying; library open to the public. **Automated Operations:** Computerized cataloging and circulation. **Computerized Information Services:** OCLC. **Networks/Consortia:** Member of SOLINET. **Publications:** Acquisitions List, 8/year.

★16314★
UNIVERSITY OF KENTUCKY - CHEMISTRY-PHYSICS LIBRARY (Sci-Engr)
150 Chemistry-Physics Bldg. Phone: (606)257-5954
Lexington, KY 40506-0055 Kerry Kresse, Libn.
Founded: 1963. **Staff:** Prof 1; Other 1. **Subjects:** Chemistry, physics, astronomy. **Holdings:** 9586 books; 36,846 bound periodical volumes; 231 reels of microfilm. **Subscriptions:** 489 journals and other serials. **Services:** Interlibrary loan; copying; library open to the public. **Automated Operations:** Computerized cataloging and circulation. **Computerized Information Services:** CAS ONLINE, DIALOG Information Services. Performs searches on fee basis.

★16315★
UNIVERSITY OF KENTUCKY - EDUCATION LIBRARY (Educ)
205 Dickey Hall Phone: (606)257-7977
Lexington, KY 40503 Mary Vass, Libn.
Staff: Prof 1; Other 8. **Subjects:** Education, juvenile literature, counseling. **Special Collections:** Juvenile and young adult collection (15,841 volumes). **Holdings:** 62,326 volumes; 8564 bound periodical volumes; 340,000 ERIC microfiche; 24,215 other microfiche; 228 reels of microfilm. **Subscriptions:** 316 journals and other serials. **Services:** Interlibrary loan; copying; SDI; library open to the public with restrictions. **Automated Operations:** Computerized public access catalog, cataloging, acquisitions, and circulation. **Computerized Information Services:** DIALOG Information Services, BRS Information Technologies. Performs searches on fee basis. **Networks/Consortia:** Member of SOLINET. **Publications:** Newsletter/Acquisitions List, irregular - for internal distribution only. **Remarks:** An alternate telephone number is 257-1351.

★16316★
UNIVERSITY OF KENTUCKY - GEORGE W. PIRTLE GEOLOGICAL SCIENCES LIBRARY (Sci-Engr)
100 Bowman Hall Phone: (606)257-5730
Lexington, KY 40506-0059 Phil Stoffer, Libn.
Founded: 1923. **Staff:** Prof 1; Other 1. **Subjects:** Petroleum geology and paleontology, mining geology, hydrogeology, tectonics, geophysics, volcanology, remote sensing, mineralogy, petrology, geochemistry, all aspects of geology including regional and economic. **Special Collections:** Depository for all U.S. Geological Survey publications; paleontology; Repository of Black Shale Documents by U.S. Department of Energy researchers. **Holdings:** 13,405 books; 29,628 bound periodical volumes; 112,356 maps; 405 reels of microfilm; 12,614 microfiche. **Subscriptions:** 1150 journals and other serials. **Services:** Interlibrary loan; copying; library open to the public. **Automated Operations:** Computerized cataloging and circulation. **Computerized Information Services:** DIALOG Information Services, Pergamon ORBIT InfoLine, Inc., The Reference Service (REFSRV), OCLC; Info-Ky News Retrieval System (internal database). **Networks/Consortia:** Member of SOLINET. **Publications:** Acquisition list, monthly; theses listing; periodicals list, both annual.

★16317★
UNIVERSITY OF KENTUCKY - HUNTER M. ADAMS ARCHITECTURE LIBRARY (Plan, Art)
College of Architecture
200 Pence Hall Phone: (606)257-1533
Lexington, KY 40506-0041 Harry Gilbert, Libn.
Founded: 1962. **Staff:** Prof 1; Other 1. **Subjects:** Architecture, landscape architecture, city and urban planning, historic preservation, alternative energy sources, photography, interior design. **Special Collections:** Rare books; Le Corbusier (300 volumes); Kentucky architecture. **Holdings:** 20,065 books; 7873 bound periodical volumes; 600 sheets of architectural plans and drawings; 600 reels of microfilm; 1804 microfiche; 7924 VF items; 48 cassettes. **Subscriptions:** 150 journals and other serials. **Services:** Interlibrary loan; copying; library open to the public. **Automated Operations:** Computerized cataloging, acquisitions, and circulation. **Computerized Information Services:** DIALOG Information Services, Pergamon ORBIT InfoLine, Inc., OCLC. **Networks/Consortia:** Member of SOLINET. **Publications:** Periodic Acquisitions List; Library Guide.

★16318★
UNIVERSITY OF KENTUCKY - LAW LIBRARY (Law)
College of Law Phone: (606)257-8346
Lexington, KY 40506-0048 William James, Dir.
Founded: 1908. **Staff:** Prof 4. **Subjects:** Law. **Special Collections:** Kocourek Collection on Jurisprudence; Records and Briefs on U.S. Supreme Court (full opinions, 1897 to present). **Holdings:** 193,695 books; 167,746 U.S. Government publications (partial depository); 463,624 microforms; 1786 audiotapes and cassettes. **Subscriptions:** 980 journals and other serials; 10 newspapers. **Services:** Interlibrary loan; copying; Kentucky Legal Information; library open to the public. **Automated Operations:** Computerized cataloging, acquisitions, and circulation. **Computerized Information Services:** OCLC, LEXIS, WESTLAW. **Networks/Consortia:** Member of SOLINET, Center for Research Libraries (CRL) Consortia. **Publications:** Acquisitions List, monthly; table of contents for periodicals received, weekly; Users Manual, annual. **Staff:** Cheryl Jones, Pub.Serv.Libn.; Gary Stottlemyer, Circ./Ref.Libn.; Ebba Jo Sexton, Tech.Serv.Libn..

★16319★
UNIVERSITY OF KENTUCKY - MARGARET I. KING LIBRARY - GOVERNMENT PUBLICATIONS/MAP DEPARTMENT (Info Sci)
Lexington, KY 40506 Phone: (602)257-3139
Sandra McAninch, Hd., Govt.Pubns.
Staff: Prof 2; Other 5. **Subjects:** Government publications - U.S., Canada, Great Britain, Kentucky, and other states of the U.S.; United Nations documents; European Communities documents; technical reports. **Holdings:** 1.1 million hard copy documents; 2200 linear feet of microfiche; 303 linear feet of microfilm; 700 linear feet of microprint; 120 linear feet of microcards. **Subscriptions:** 8140 journals and other serials. **Services:** Interlibrary loan; copying; department open to the public. **Publications:** Let's Talk Documents. **Staff:** Barbara Hale, Asst.Docs.Libn..

★16320★
UNIVERSITY OF KENTUCKY - MARGARET I. KING LIBRARY - GOVERNMENT PUBLICATIONS/MAP DEPARTMENT - MAP COLLECTION (Geog-Map)
Lexington, KY 40506-0039 Phone: (606)257-1853
Gwen Curtis, Hd.
Staff: 1. **Subjects:** Cartography. **Special Collections:** Kentucky maps, 1875 to present; Southeastern U.S. maps, 1800 to present; Sanborn Insurance Maps of Kentucky cities (7895 sheets; 3000 maps on microfilm); Defense Mapping Agency Depository (19,600 sheets). **Holdings:** 1400 books and atlases; 10,760 cataloged maps; 63,300 uncataloged maps and aerial photographs. **Services:** Interlibrary loan; copying; collection open to the public with limited circulation. **Automated Operations:** Computerized cataloging. **Computerized Information Services:** OCLC. **Networks/Consortia:** Member of SOLINET. **Publications:** Selected Acquisitions Bulletin, quarterly - to faculty and other libraries. **Remarks:** Kentucky maps published before 1875 are housed in the Special Collections Department of the King Library; geology and hydrology maps are housed in the Geology Library.

★16321★
UNIVERSITY OF KENTUCKY - MARGARET I. KING LIBRARY - SPECIAL COLLECTIONS AND ARCHIVES (Hist)
11 King Library N. Phone: (606)257-8611
Lexington, KY 40506-0039 William Marshall, Libn.
Staff: Prof 7; Other 8. **Subjects:** Kentuckiana, 20th century politics, Appalachia, English Romantic and Victorian literature, Miltoniana, history of printing, typography and the fine press. **Holdings:** 120,972 volumes; 9059 linear feet of manuscripts; 8868 linear feet of archives; 351,650 photographs; 11,673 reels of microfilm; 2207 oral history interviews; 3686 audiotapes; 616 videotapes. **Subscriptions:** 850 journals and other serials. **Services:** Interlibrary loan; copying; collections open to the public. **Automated Operations:** Computerized cataloging. **Computerized Information Services:** OCLC. **Networks/Consortia:** Member of SOLINET. **Special Catalogs:** Applied Anthropology Documentation Project; catalogs to Dime Novel collection, Science Fiction Collection, Milton Collection, Cortot Collection, Kentucky Imprint Collection; theses catalog; catalogs to photographic archives, microfilm, and manuscripts (all on cards).

★16322★
UNIVERSITY OF KENTUCKY - MATHEMATICAL SCIENCES LIBRARY (Sci-Engr, Comp Sci)
OB-9 Patterson Office Tower Phone: (606)257-8365
Lexington, KY 40506-0027 Joanne Goode, Libn.
Staff: Prof 1. **Subjects:** Mathematics, computer science, statistics. **Holdings:** 17,100 books; 12,521 bound periodical volumes. **Subscriptions:** 470 journals and other serials. **Services:** Interlibrary loan; copying; library open to the public. **Automated Operations:** Computerized cataloging and circulation. **Computerized Information Services:** DIALOG Information Services, BRS Information Technologies, OCLC; BITNET (electronic mail service). Performs searches on fee basis. **Publications:** Monthly acquisitions list; newsletter, irregular; annual report.

★16323★
UNIVERSITY OF KENTUCKY - MEDICAL CENTER LIBRARY (Med)
Lexington, KY 40536-0084 Phone: (606)233-5300
Omer Hamlin, Jr., Dir.
Founded: 1957. **Staff:** Prof 9; Other 17. **Subjects:** Medicine, dentistry, nursing, pharmacy, allied health sciences. **Special Collections:** Harvey Collection; Servetus Collection. **Holdings:** 70,609 books; 90,335 bound periodical volumes; 1058 reels of microfilm; 2424 AV programs. **Subscriptions:** 1818 journals and other serials. **Services:** Interlibrary loan (fee); copying; SDI; library open to health science personnel. **Automated Operations:** Computerized cataloging, circulation, and ILL. **Computerized Information Services:** MEDLINE, DIALOG Information Services, BRS Information Technologies, OCLC. **Networks/Consortia:** Member of Greater Midwest Regional Medical Library Network, SOLINET, Kentucky Library Network, Inc. (KLN). **Staff:** Janet Stith, Asst.; Karl Heinz-Boewe, Circ.Libn.; Bev Hilton, AV Libn.; Lynn Bowman, Cat.Libn.; Florence Jones, Ser.Libn.; Bernadette Baldini, Asst.; Stephanie Allen, Ref.Libn.; Edwina Thierl, ILL Libn..

★16324★
UNIVERSITY OF KENTUCKY - MUSIC LIBRARY/LISTENING CENTER (Mus)
116 Fine Arts Bldg. Phone: (606)257-2800
Lexington, KY 40506-0022 Cathy S. Hunt, Mus.Libn.
Staff: Prof 1; Other 2. **Subjects:** Music - history, theory, education; applied music. **Special Collections:** Alfred Cortot Collection (265 early theory books). **Holdings:** 42,532 books and scores; 3346 bound periodical volumes; 10,251 phonograph records; 81 compact discs; 7000 microforms; 1551 cassettes. **Subscriptions:** 210 journals and other serials. **Services:** Interlibrary loan; copying; library open to the public with check-out privileges for residents of Kentucky. **Automated Operations:** Computerized cataloging, acquisitions, and circulation. **Computerized Information Services:** OCLC. **Networks/Consortia:** Member of SOLINET.

★16325★
UNIVERSITY OF KENTUCKY - ROBERT E. SHAVER LIBRARY OF ENGINEERING (Energy, Sci-Engr)
355 Anderson Hall Phone: (606)257-2965
Lexington, KY 40506-0046 Russell H. Powell, Libn.
Founded: 1965. **Staff:** Prof 1; Other 1. **Subjects:** Environment; coal mining and processing; transportation; engineering mechanics; energy; engineering - civil, mechanical, electrical, chemical, metallurgical. **Holdings:** 55,460 volumes; 1862 reels of microfilm; 63,926 microfiche. **Subscriptions:** 550 journals and other serials. **Services:** Interlibrary loan; copying; library open to the public with restrictions on borrowing. **Automated Operations:** Computerized cataloging and circulation. **Computerized Information Services:** DIALOG Information Services, OCLC. **Networks/Consortia:** Member of SOLINET.

UNIVERSITY OF KENTUCKY - TECHNOLOGY APPLICATIONS PROGRAM
See: NASA/University of Kentucky - Technology Applications Program (9512)

★16326★
UNIVERSITY OF KING'S COLLEGE - KING'S COLLEGE LIBRARY (Rel-Phil, Hum)
Halifax, NS, Canada B3H 2A1 Phone: (902)422-1271
Dr. W.J. Hankey, Chf.Libn.
Staff: Prof 2; Other 3. **Subjects:** Theology, Canadiana, philosophy, history, classics, journalism. **Special Collections:** Incunabula and rare books (20,000 volumes); William Inglis Morse Canadiana Collection; Journalism Resource Collection; Weldon China Collection. **Holdings:** 78,000 books and bound periodical volumes; college archives. **Subscriptions:** 335 journals and other serials; 25 newspapers. **Services:** Interlibrary loan; library open to the public with restrictions. **Special Catalogs:** Incunabula. **Staff:** Jane Trimble, Asst.Libn., Spec.Proj.; Elaine Galey, Asst.Libn.; Drake Petersen, Cat..

★16327★
UNIVERSITY OF LA VERNE - COLLEGE OF LAW AT SAN FERNANDO VALLEY - LAW LIBRARY (Law)
1950 3rd St. Phone: (714)593-7184
La Verne, CA 91750 Gay Toltl Kinman, Dir. of Law Libs.
Founded: 1978. **Staff:** Prof 1; Other 4. **Subjects:** Law. **Special Collections:** Juvenile Law (3080 volumes). **Holdings:** 43,181 volumes; 6473 bound periodical volumes; 3458 government documents; 320 audio cassettes; 1961 volumes on microfilm; 35,796 volumes on microfiche. **Subscriptions:** 451 journals and other serials. **Services:** Interlibrary loan; copying; library open to the public. **Automated Operations:** Computerized cataloging. **Computerized Information Services:** WESTLAW.

★16328★
UNIVERSITY OF LA VERNE - COLLEGE OF LAW AT SAN FERNANDO VALLEY - LAW LIBRARY (Law)
8353 Sepulveda Blvd. Phone: (818)894-5711
Sepulveda, CA 91343-6577 Harold R. Stokes, Lib.Dir.
Founded: 1962. **Staff:** Prof 2; Other 3. **Subjects:** Law. **Holdings:** 71,082 volumes; 27,639 microforms; 16,310 other cataloged items. **Subscriptions:** 200 journals and other serials. **Services:** Copying; library open to the public with restrictions. **Staff:** Jon Portera, Asst. Law Libn..

★16329★
UNIVERSITY OF LOUISVILLE - ALLEN R. HITE ART INSTITUTE - MARGARET M. BRIDWELL ART LIBRARY (Art)
Belknap Campus Phone: (502)588-6741
Louisville, KY 40292 Gail R. Gilbert, Hd.
Founded: 1956. **Staff:** Prof 1; Other 1. **Subjects:** Art - Renaissance, medieval, ancient, American; modern architecture; landscape architecture; German sculpture; art history; photography; textiles; graphic design; interior design. **Special Collections:** Robert J. Doherty Typography Collection; Ainslie Hewett Bookplate Collection. **Holdings:** 46,000 volumes; 820 posters; 11,000 folders of artists' files and information files. **Subscriptions:** 264 journals and other serials. **Services:** Interlibrary loan; library open to the public for reference use only. **Automated Operations:** Computerized public access catalog.

★16330★
UNIVERSITY OF LOUISVILLE - DEPARTMENT OF RARE BOOKS AND SPECIAL COLLECTIONS (Rare Book, Hum)
Belknap Campus Phone: (502)588-6762
Louisville, KY 40292 Delinda S. Buie, Cur.
Founded: 1837. **Staff:** Prof 2; Other 1. **Subjects:** Astronomy-mathematics, World War I, literary first editions, popular culture, Irish Literary Renaissance literature, American humor, Louisvilliana. **Special Collections:** Bullitt Collection (rare astronomy and mathematics; 400 items); Arthur Rackham Collection (500 books, manuscripts, original art); Edgar Rice Burroughs Collection (20,000 items); H.L. Mencken Collection (500 items); Graham Greene Collection (250 items); Lawrence Durrell Collection (200 items); J.D. Salinger Collection (200 items); American Humor (3000 items); Lafcadio Hearn Collection (200 items); World War I Collection (2000 items); Mosher Press (1000 volumes); Roger Manvell Collection of Theater & Film History (20,000 items); Irish Literary Renaissance Collection (2000 volumes, manuscripts, and ephemera). **Holdings:** 70,000 books and periodicals; 160 linear feet of manuscripts. **Services:** Interlibrary loan; copying; department open to the public for reference use only. **Also Known As:** University of Louisville - John L. Patterson Room. **Staff:** George McWhorter, Cur., Burroughs Coll..

★16331★
UNIVERSITY OF LOUISVILLE - DWIGHT ANDERSON MEMORIAL MUSIC LIBRARY (Mus)
2301 S. 3rd St. Phone: (502)588-5659
Louisville, KY 40292 Marion Korda, Libn.
Founded: 1947. **Staff:** Prof 2; Other 4. **Subjects:** Music. **Special Collections:** Early American Sheet Music; Kentucky imprints; Kentucky composers; music archival collection; Louisville Orchestra Commissioning Project materials; Jean Thomas "Traipsin' Woman" Collection; Isidore Philipp Archive and Memorial Library. **Holdings:** 19,000 books; 4700 bound periodical volumes; 26,000 scores; 822 microtext and microfilm titles; 2000 music tapes; 15,000 sound recordings; 20,000 uncataloged items. **Subscriptions:** 500 journals and other serials. **Services:** Interlibrary loan; copying; library open to the public, registration required for borrowing purposes. **Automated Operations:** Computerized cataloging and

circulation. **Computerized Information Services:** OCLC. **Networks/Consortia:** Member of SOLINET.

UNIVERSITY OF LOUISVILLE - JOHN L. PATTERSON ROOM
See: University of Louisville - Department of Rare Books and Special Collections (16330)

★16332★
UNIVERSITY OF LOUISVILLE - KENTUCKY ENERGY CABINET LABORATORY - KEC LIBRARY (Energy)
Iron Works Pike, Box 11888 Phone: (606)252-5535
Lexington, KY 40578-1916 Theresa K. Wiley, Lib.Mgr.
Founded: 1974. **Staff:** Prof 1; Other 1. **Subjects:** Coal, oil shale, mining, reclamation. **Holdings:** 8200 books; 846 bound periodical volumes; 44,000 technical reports in microform. **Subscriptions:** 150 journals and other serials. **Services:** Interlibrary loan; library open to the public for reference use only. **Automated Operations:** Computerized cataloging. **Computerized Information Services:** DIALOG Information Services, OCLC, Pergamon ORBIT InfoLine, Inc. Performs searches on fee basis. **Publications:** Research Reports - for sale.

★16333★
UNIVERSITY OF LOUISVILLE - KERSEY LIBRARY (Sci-Engr)
Belknap Campus Phone: (502)588-6297
Louisville, KY 40292 Carol S. Brinkman, Hd.Libn.
Staff: Prof 2; Other 7. **Subjects:** Applied mathematics; computer science; engineering - chemical, electrical, mechanical, civil, industrial, nuclear, environmental; physics; chemistry; mathematics; statistics; astronomy; history of science and technology; general science. **Holdings:** 79,830 volumes; 29,139 microforms. **Subscriptions:** 1306 journals and other serials. **Services:** Interlibrary loan; copying; library open to the public. **Computerized Information Services:** Online systems.

★16334★
UNIVERSITY OF LOUISVILLE - KORNHAUSER HEALTH SCIENCES LIBRARY (Med)
Louisville, KY 40292 Phone: (502)588-5771
Leonard M. Eddy, Dir.
Staff: Prof 10; Other 14. **Subjects:** Medicine, dentistry, nursing, allied health sciences, medical history. **Special Collections:** Horine Anesthesia Collection; Gardner Collection in the History of Psychiatry; Charles Caldwell Collection. **Holdings:** 53,688 books; 95,424 bound periodical volumes; 3972 AV programs. **Subscriptions:** 1514 journals. **Services:** Interlibrary loan; copying; library open to the public. **Automated Operations:** Computerized public access catalog, cataloging, acquisitions, and circulation. **Computerized Information Services:** BRS Information Technologies, MEDLINE, DIALOG Information Services, OCLC. **Networks/Consortia:** Member of Greater Midwest Regional Medical Library Network. **Publications:** Bio-Echo, monthly. **Staff:** Nancy Craig Lee, Hd., Tech.Serv.; Parthenia Durrett, Circ.; Mary S. Barber, Asst. to Dir.; Diane Nichols, Ref.Libn.; Nancy Utterback, Hd., Pub.Serv.; Virginia Leightly, Acq.; Mary Grant, ILL; Sherrill Redmon, Archv.; Neal Nixon, Cat.; Maura Ellison, Ser.; Gwen Snodgrass, Ref.Libn..

★16335★
UNIVERSITY OF LOUISVILLE - PHOTOGRAPHIC ARCHIVES (Hist)
Belknap Campus Phone: (502)588-6752
Louisville, KY 40292 James C. Anderson, Cur. & Hd.
Staff: Prof 2; Other 2. **Subjects:** History of Louisville; 20th century social history; American industry; oil industry; photography - historic, artistic, documentary, commercial. **Special Collections:** Antique media and equipment; Lou Block Collection; Will Bowers Collection; Bradley Studio/Georgetown Collection; Theodore M. Brown/Robert J. Doherty Collection; Caldwell Tank Company Collection; Cooper Collection; erotic photography; Fine Print Collection; Arthur Y. Ford albums; Forensic Photography Collection; U.S. Corps of Engineers (Louisville District) Collection; Vida Hunt Francis Collection; Mary D. Hill Collection; Joseph Krementz Collection; Macauley Collection; Manvell Collection (film stills); Boyd Martin Collection; Kate Matthews Collection; Metropolitan Sewer District Collection; R.G. Potter Collection; J.C. Rieger Collection; Royal Photo Studio Collection; Jean Thomas Collection; World Wars I and II photographs; Caufield and Shook of Louisville Collection; Roy E. Stryker Collections, including Standard Oil Company of New Jersey Collection. **Holdings:** 1000 books; 10,000 pages of manuscripts; 1 million photographs and photograph-related items. **Subscriptions:** 20 journals and other serials. **Services:** Interlibrary loan; copying; photographic print service; library open to the public. **Automated Operations:** Computerized cataloging. **Computerized Information Services:** Internal databases. **Publications:** Exhibition catalogs, irregular; Guide to Collections - for sale. **Staff:** David Horvath, Cur., Coll..

★16336★
UNIVERSITY OF LOUISVILLE - SCHOOL OF LAW LIBRARY (Law)
Belknap Campus Phone: (502)588-6392
Louisville, KY 40292 Patricia E. Anderson, Law Libn.
Founded: 1926. **Staff:** Prof 5; Other 4. **Subjects:** Law. **Special Collections:** Correspondence of Mr. Justice Brandeis (250,000 items) and Mr. Justice Harlan, 1833-1911 (1500 items). **Holdings:** 150,000 volumes. **Subscriptions:** 3313 journals and other serials. **Services:** Interlibrary loan; library open to the public with restrictions.

★16337★
UNIVERSITY OF LOUISVILLE - UNIVERSITY ARCHIVES AND RECORDS CENTER (Hist)
Ekstrom Library Phone: (502)588-6674
Louisville, KY 40292 William J. Morison, Dir./Univ.Archv.
Founded: 1973. **Staff:** Prof 7; Other 2. **Subjects:** History of the university and its predecessor schools; political, social, economic, and cultural history of Louisville and the geographic region; regional business. **Special Collections:** Louis D. Brandeis papers (184 reels of microfilm); Louisville and Nashville Railroad Company records (155 linear feet; 39 reels of microfilm; 46 oral history interviews); Louisville Orchestra records (150 linear feet; 19 oral history interviews); Louisville Defender records and Frank L. Stanley papers (13.75 linear feet; 13 reels of microfilm; 2 oral history interviews); Presbyterian Community Center records (8 linear feet); Louisville YWCA records (51.5 linear feet); Simmons University records (5 linear feet); Isaac W. Bernheim papers. **Holdings:** 5149 linear feet of archives and personal papers; 1550 linear feet of local government archives; 1860 linear feet of Kentuckiana Historical Collections, records of local organizations, and personal papers of area individuals and families; 1027 reels of microfilm; 77 microfiche; oral history materials. **Services:** Copying; microfilming; archives open to the public with restrictions. **Publications:** A Place Where Historical Research May Be Pursued: Selected Primary Sources in the University of Louisville Archives; Papers of Louis D. Brandeis at the University of Louisville, Microfilm Edition, 1981; D.W. Griffith Papers 1897-1954: Guide to the Microfilm Edition, 1982. **Staff:** Thomas Owen, Assoc.Archv.; Janet Hodgson, Assoc.Archv.; Sherrill Redmon, Assoc.Archv.; Margaret Merrick, Assoc.Archv.; L. Dale Patterson, Assoc.Archv.; Larry Raymond, Hd., Microform Lab.; Cynthia Stevenson, Proj.Archv..

★16338★
UNIVERSITY OF LOUISVILLE - UNIVERSITY ARCHIVES AND RECORDS CENTER - ORAL HISTORY CENTER (Hist)
Ekstrom Library
Louisville, KY 40292 Phone: (502)588-6674
Founded: 1968. **Staff:** Prof 2. **Subjects:** History of Louisville, Kentucky, including the Louisville Orchestra; prominent citizens; university history; local and regional journals; the Louisville and Nashville Railroad; photography; Jewish history; local government; black history; Kentucky distilling industry; Bernheim Forest. **Holdings:** 1100 cassette tapes. **Services:** Copying; copies of tapes, finding aids, and selected transcripts available; center open to the public. **Staff:** L. Dale Patterson, Co-Dir.; Carl G. Ryant, Co-Dir..

★16339★
UNIVERSITY OF LOUISVILLE - URBAN STUDIES CENTER - LIBRARY (Soc Sci)
College of Urban and Public Affairs Phone: (502)588-6626
Louisville, KY 40292 Shirley Demos, Mgr., State Data Ctr.
Staff: Prof 1; Other 1. **Subjects:** Demography of Kentucky, housing needs assessment, public opinion surveys, public administration, municipal planning, criminal justice surveys and statistics. **Special Collections:** Census maps for Kentucky, 1970 and 1980 (1000). **Holdings:** 5000 books; 200 computer tapes; computer printouts; maps; microfiche. **Subscriptions:** 37 journals and other serials. **Services:** Copying; library open to the public. **Computerized Information Services:** Internal database. **Remarks:** The Urban Studies Center operates the State Data Center of Kentucky which answers questions concerning census data with information from the population, housing, and economic censuses. Also operates, with the attorney general's office, the Criminal Justice Statistical Analysis Center.

★16340★
UNIVERSITY OF LOWELL - CENTER FOR LOWELL HISTORY (Hist)
Mogan Cultural Center
French St. Phone: (508)454-7811
Lowell, MA 01854 Martha Mayo, Dir.
Founded: 1971. **Staff:** Prof 1; Other 4. **Subjects:** Middlesex Canal; Lowell, Massachusetts; hydraulics; women in industry; textile manufacturing; Warren H. Manning. **Special Collections:** Lowell Historical Society Collection; Middlesex Canal Collection; Proprietors of Locks & Canals Collection; Manning Collection; University Archives; Olney Collection (textile books); Boston & Maine Railroad Historical Society Collection; Lowell Museum Collection; Greater Lowell Chapter of the American Association of University Women Records; Coggeshall Collection; Davis Collection; Tsongas Collection. **Holdings:** 28,750 volumes; 936 linear feet of records and manscripts; 4420 maps and plans; 240 hours of oral histories; 22,000 photographs; 25 paintings; 1552 reels of microfilm. **Services:** Copying; collections open to the public. **Special Indexes:** Index of VF material; index of photographs; inventories of most records and manuscript collections. **Formerly:** University of Lowell, North Campus - University Libraries - Special Collections.

★16341★
UNIVERSITY OF MAINE, ORONO - IRA C. DARLING CENTER LIBRARY (Biol Sci, Sci-Engr)
Walpole, ME 04573 Phone: (207)563-3146
Louise M. Dean, Libn.
Founded: 1967. **Staff:** Prof 1. **Subjects:** Marine biology; oceanography - biological, physical, chemical, geological; fisheries; aquaculture. **Holdings:** 6700 books; 3029 bound periodical volumes; 8000 reprints; 1500 microforms. **Subscriptions:** 190 journals and other serials. **Services:** Interlibrary loan; copying; library open to the public.

★16342★
UNIVERSITY OF MAINE, ORONO - NORTHEAST ARCHIVES OF FOLKLORE AND ORAL HISTORY (Hist)
Dept. of Anthropology
S. Stevens Hall Phone: (207)581-1891
Orono, ME 04469 Edward D. Ives, Dir.
Founded: 1964. **Staff:** Prof 1; Other 1. **Subjects:** Folklore, oral history. **Special Collections:** Folksong; lumbering and river driving; folklife of Maine and the Maritime Provinces. **Holdings:** 1900 cataloged accessions; 6000 photographs of lumbering and other aspects of folklife. **Services:** Copying; archives open to the public. **Publications:** Northeast Folklore, annual. **Special Indexes:** Place names, personal names, song titles, subjects. **Staff:** Alicia Rouverol, Archv.Mgr..

★16343★
UNIVERSITY OF MAINE, ORONO - RAYMOND H. FOGLER LIBRARY - SPECIAL COLLECTIONS DEPARTMENT (Hist)
Orono, ME 04469 Phone: (207)581-1686
Eric S. Flower, Hd., Spec.Coll.
Founded: 1970. **Staff:** Prof 2; Other 2. **Subjects:** State of Maine, maritime history. **Special Collections:** State of Maine Collection (16,000 volumes); Maine State Documents Collection (8200 titles); University Collection (13,500 items); Clinton L. Cole Marine Library (4550 volumes); O'Brien Collection of American Negro History and Culture (1600 items); Philip H. Taylor Collection of Modern History, War, and Diplomacy (1200 volumes); Thoreau Fellowship Papers. **Holdings:** 31,500 books; 450 bound periodical volumes; 1450 archive boxes of manuscripts on Maine; 2325 maps of Maine; 5550 reels of microfilm. **Subscriptions:** 75 journals and other serials; 36 Maine newspapers. **Services:** Interlibrary loan; copying; library open to the public. **Automated Operations:** Computerized acquisitions, serials, and indexing. **Special Catalogs:** A Catalog of the Clinton L. Cole Collection (1972). **Special Indexes:** Maine Times Index; Down East Magazine Index; Maine Campus Index; Maine Townsman Index; Maine Teacher Index; Elderberry Times Index; Habitat: Journal of the Maine Audubon Society Index; Maine Fish and Wildlife Index (each in card or book form); Shaker Quarterly Index; Maine Life Index. **Staff:** Muriel A. Sanford, Spec.Coll.Libn..

★16344★
UNIVERSITY OF MAINE, ORONO - RAYMOND H. FOGLER LIBRARY - TRI-STATE REGIONAL DOCUMENT DEPOSITORY (Info Sci)
Orono, ME 04469 Phone: (207)581-1680
Francis R. Wihbey, Hd., Govt.Docs./Microforms Dep
Founded: 1907. **Staff:** Prof 1; Other 5. **Subjects:** Government, Canada, New Brunswick, Agricultural Experiment Stations, maps and atlases, forestry. **Special Collections:** Regional depository of U.S. documents; selective depository of U.S. National Oceanic and Atmospheric Administration and Canadian documents; Army Map Service; Defense Mapping Agency; U.S. Department of Agriculture Soil Survey and U.S. Geological Survey maps. **Holdings:** 1.4 million documents; 425,000 microforms; maps - 57,000 sheet, 120,000 bound, 26,000 in microform. **Subscriptions:** 7000 journals and other serials. **Services:** Interlibrary loan; copying; SDI; depository open to the public. **Computerized Information Services:** BRS Information Technologies, OCLC, DIALOG Information Services, Integrated Technical Information System (ITIS); internal databases. Performs searches on fee basis. Contact Person: Thomas Patterson, 581-1673. **Publications:** Newsletter to U.S. Government Document Depositories in Tri-State Region, irregular. **Special Catalogs:** Maine Agricultural Experiment Station publications (card); Canadian Forest Service and Forest Research Centres publications (card). **Special Indexes:** Index guide to 1980 census microfiche set (Maine tables).

★16345★
UNIVERSITY OF MAINE, PRESQUE ISLE - LIBRARY AND LEARNING RESOURCES CENTER - SPECIAL COLLECTIONS (Hist)
181 Main St. Phone: (207)764-0311
Presque Isle, ME 04769 Anna McGrath, Spec.Coll.Libn.
Founded: 1980. **Staff:** Prof 2; Other 1. **Subjects:** Maine - authors, town and city histories, Aroostook County. **Special Collections:** Aroostook County, Maine Collection (1700 volumes); Maine Collection (1200 volumes). **Holdings:** 300 rare books; 10 bound periodical volumes; 336 Maine maps; 20 reels of microfilm; 30 tapes; 1500 Maine documents; 8 VF drawers; 3 boxes of photographs; scrapbooks; Civil War memorabilia. **Services:** Interlibrary loan; copying; collections open to the public. **Automated Operations:** Computerized cataloging. **Computerized Information Services:** BRS Information Technologies, OCLC, DIALOG Information Services. Performs searches on fee basis. Performs searches free of charge. **Networks/Consortia:** Member of NELINET. **Staff:** Nancy Roe, Cat..

★16346★
UNIVERSITY OF MAINE SCHOOL OF LAW - DONALD L. GARBRECHT LAW LIBRARY (Law)
246 Deering Ave. Phone: (207)780-4350
Portland, ME 04102 William Wells, Law Libn.
Founded: 1961. **Staff:** Prof 9; Other 6. **Subjects:** Law. **Holdings:** 230,000 books and books in microform. **Subscriptions:** 2600 journals and other serials. **Services:** Interlibrary loan; copying; SDI; library open to the public with restrictions. **Automated Operations:** Computerized cataloging, acquisitions, and ILL. **Computerized Information Services:** WESTLAW, DIALOG Information Services, RLIN. **Networks/Consortia:** Member of CLASS, New England Law Library Consortium (NELLCO). **Staff:** Anne K. Myers, Asst. Law Libn.; Ramona L. Moore, Ser.Libn.; Tom French, Asst. Law Libn.; Patricia M. Milligan, Sr.Cat.; Fran Rice, Cat.; Suzanne I. Parent, Acq.Libn.; Robin Meisner, Ref.Libn.; Hugh Hill, Ref.Libn..

★16347★
UNIVERSITY OF MANITOBA - AGRICULTURE LIBRARY (Biol Sci, Agri)
W212 Agriculture Bldg. Phone: (204)474-9457
Winnipeg, MB, Canada R3T 2N2 Judith Harper, Hd.
Founded: 1906. **Staff:** Prof 1; Other 2. **Subjects:** Agriculture, animal science, plant science, entomology, agricultural economics, soil science, food science. **Holdings:** 17,700 volumes. **Subscriptions:** 300 journals and other serials. **Services:** Interlibrary loan; SDI; library open to the public. **Automated Operations:** Computerized cataloging, acquisitions, serials, circulation, and ILL. **Computerized Information Services:** DIALOG Information Services, CAN/OLE, UTLAS; Envoy 100 (electronic mail service). Performs searches on fee basis.

★16348★
UNIVERSITY OF MANITOBA - ALBERT D. COHEN MANAGEMENT LIBRARY (Bus-Fin)
207 Drake Centre Bldg. Phone: (204)474-8440
Winnipeg, MB, Canada R3T 2N2 Dennis Felbel, Hd.Libn.
Founded: 1971. **Staff:** Prof 1; Other 6. **Subjects:** Accounting, finance, marketing, business administration, actuarial and business mathematics, public policy, business law, industrial relations. **Holdings:** 19,200 volumes; annual reports for 800 companies (past 5 years). **Subscriptions:** 425 journals and other serials. **Services:** Interlibrary loan; library open to the public. **Automated Operations:** Computerized cataloging, acquisitions, serials, circulation, and ILL. **Computerized Information Services:** DIALOG Information Services, MEDLARS, CAN/OLE, BRS Information Technologies, UTLAS; Envoy 100 (electronic mail service). Performs searches on fee basis. **Special Indexes:** KWIC Index to Working Papers.

★16349★
UNIVERSITY OF MANITOBA - ARCHITECTURE & FINE ARTS LIBRARY (Art, Plan)
206 Architecture Bldg. Phone: (204)474-9216
Winnipeg, MB, Canada R3T 2N2 Michele Laing, Hd.Libn.
Founded: 1916. **Staff:** Prof 2; Other 8. **Subjects:** Architecture, interior design, fine arts, city planning, photography, graphics, design, landscape architecture, environmental studies. **Holdings:** 59,000 volumes; 1200 maps; 28 VF drawers of art reproductions; 600 large art reproductions; 500 student projects; 1100 product catalogs; 40 VF drawers of miscellaneous material. **Subscriptions:** 450 journals and other serials. **Services:** Interlibrary loan. **Automated Operations:** Computerized cataloging, acquisitions, serials, circulation, and ILL. **Computerized Information Services:** DIALOG Information Services, UTLAS, CAN/OLE, BRS Information Technologies; Envoy 100 (electronic mail service). Performs searches on fee basis. Contact Person: Sharon Tully, 474-9844. **Special Indexes:** KWIC Index to Product Catalogs.

★16350★
UNIVERSITY OF MANITOBA - D.S. WOODS EDUCATION LIBRARY (Educ)
228 Education Bldg. Phone: (204)474-9976
Winnipeg, MB, Canada R3T 2N2 David Thirlwall, Act.Hd.
Staff: Prof 3; Other 11. **Subjects:** Education, child development, guidance, physical education. **Special Collections:** Manitoba school textbooks (18,000 volumes). **Holdings:** 61,000 volumes; 394,000 ERIC microfiche. **Subscriptions:** 610 journals and other serials. **Services:** Interlibrary loan; library open to the public. **Automated Operations:** Computerized cataloging, acquisitions, serials, circulation, and ILL. **Computerized Information Services:** UTLAS, DIALOG Information Services, CAN/OLE, BRS Information Technologies; Envoy 100 (electronic mail service). Performs searches on fee basis. **Special Catalogs:** Catalog of instructional materials (card). **Special Indexes:** KWIC Indexes to Records, Adolescent Literature, Paperback Collection, Educational Foundations Readings, Standardized Tests. **Staff:** Richard Ellis, Ref.Libn..

★16351★
UNIVERSITY OF MANITOBA - E.K. WILLIAMS LAW LIBRARY (Law)
401 Robson Hall Phone: (204)474-9995
Winnipeg, MB, Canada R3T 2N2 Denis Marshall, Hd.Libn.
Founded: 1922. **Staff:** Prof 3; Other 11. **Subjects:** Law. **Holdings:** 127,000 volumes; 57,000 microfiche. **Subscriptions:** 1500 journals and other serials. **Services:** Interlibrary loan; reference service for members of legal profession residing in Manitoba. **Automated Operations:** Computerized cataloging, serials, circulation, and ILL. **Computerized Information Services:** QL Systems, UTLAS, WESTLAW, DIALOG Information Services; Envoy 100 (electronic mail service). Performs searches on fee basis. Contact Person: Gordon Russell, Ref.Libn.. **Publications:** Bibliographies - to legal professionals. **Special Indexes:** KWIC Index to unreported Manitoba case laws. **Staff:** Debra Bedford Benson, Cat..

★16352★
UNIVERSITY OF MANITOBA - ELIZABETH DAFOE LIBRARY (Hum, Soc Sci, Area-Ethnic)
Winnipeg, MB, Canada R3T 2N2 Phone: (204)474-9211
Michael Angel, Hd.
Founded: 1885. **Staff:** Prof 32; Other 98. **Subjects:** Humanities, social sciences, nursing, social work, human ecology. **Special Collections:** Slavic collection (55,000 volumes); Icelandic collection (24,000 volumes); rare books (35,000 volumes); archives (1500 linear feet); manuscript collection (1300 linear feet). **Holdings:** 756,000 volumes; 400,000 government publications; 478,000 microfiche; 46,000 reels of microfilm; 91,000 maps; theses. **Subscriptions:** 4500 journals and other serials. **Services:** Interlibrary loan; SDI; library open to the public with restrictions. **Automated Operations:** Computerized cataloging, acquisitions, serials, circulation, and ILL. **Computerized Information Services:** DIALOG Information Services, CAN/OLE, BRS Information Technologies, UTLAS, MEDLARS; internal databases; Envoy 100 (electronic mail service). Performs searches on fee basis. Contact Person: Sharon Tully, 474-9844. **Special Indexes:** KWIC Indexes to Microform Collections, Uncataloged Collections, Photographs, Theses, University Publications, Patents. **Staff:** Nicole Michaud-Oystryk, Hd., Ref.; June Dutka, Hd., Govt.Pubns.; R.E. Bennett, Univ.Archv./Hd., Spec.Coll.; John Muchin, Hd., Slavic Coll.; S. Johnson, Icelandic Coll..

★16353★
UNIVERSITY OF MANITOBA - ENGINEERING LIBRARY (Sci-Engr)
351 Engineering Bldg. Phone: (204)474-6360
Winnipeg, MB, Canada R3T 2N2 Norma Godavari, Hd.
Founded: 1907. **Staff:** Prof 2; Other 5. **Subjects:** Engineering - civil, electrical, agricultural, geological, mechanical. **Holdings:** 43,500 volumes; 30,000 government publications; 19,000 microfiche. **Subscriptions:** 675 journals and other serials. **Services:** Interlibrary loan; SDI; library open to the public. **Automated Operations:** Computerized cataloging, acquisitions, serials, circulation, and ILL. **Computerized Information Services:** CAN/OLE, Infomart, DIALOG Information Services, QL Systems, MEDLINE, UTLAS, BRS Information Technologies; Envoy 100 (electronic mail service). Performs searches on fee basis. Contact Person: Patricia Routledge, Ref.Libn.. **Special Indexes:** KWIC Index to Standards.

★16354★
UNIVERSITY OF MANITOBA - MEDICAL LIBRARY (Med)
Medical College Bldg.
770 Bannatyne Ave. Phone: (204)788-6342
Winnipeg, MB, Canada R3T 0W3 Audrey M. Kerr, Hd.Med.Libn.
Founded: 1895. **Staff:** Prof 5; Other 18. **Subjects:** Medicine and basic medical sciences. **Special Collections:** History of Medicine. **Holdings:** 97,000 volumes. **Subscriptions:** 1450 journals and other serials. **Services:** Interlibrary loan; reference services for members of the medical profession residing in Manitoba; library open to qualified users. **Automated Operations:** Computerized cataloging, acquisitions, serials, circulation, and ILL. **Computerized Information Services:** UTLAS, MEDLINE, DIALOG Information Services, BRS Information Technologies, MEDLARS, CAN/OLE, PaperChase; Envoy 100 (electronic mail service). Performs searches on fee basis. Contact Person: Michael Tennenhouse, Pub.Serv.Libn.. **Publications:** Bibliographies - to medical professionals. **Staff:** Beverly Brown, Cat.; Natalia Pohorecky, Ref.Libn.; Helene Proteau, Ext.Libn..

★16355★
UNIVERSITY OF MANITOBA - MUSIC LIBRARY (Mus)
223 Music Bldg. Phone: (204)474-9567
Winnipeg, MB, Canada R3T 2N2 Vladimir Simosko, Hd.
Founded: 1965. **Staff:** Prof 1; Other 2. **Subjects:** Music reference and research, historical musicology, instruments and voice, theory and analysis of music. **Holdings:** 17,000 volumes; 6000 phonograph records; 32,000 items of performance music; composers' works and scores. **Subscriptions:** 150 journals and other serials. **Services:** Interlibrary loan; library open to the public with restrictions on borrowing. **Automated Operations:** Computerized cataloging, acquisitions, serials, circulation, and ILL. **Computerized Information Services:** UTLAS, DIALOG Information Services, CAN/OLE; Envoy 100 (electronic mail service). Performs searches on fee basis. Contact Person: Sharon Tully, 474-9844. **Special Indexes:** KWIC Indexes to Performance Tapes, Sound Recordings, Performance Music.

★16356★
UNIVERSITY OF MANITOBA - NEILSON DENTAL LIBRARY (Med)
780 Bannatyne Ave. Phone: (204)788-6635
Winnipeg, MB, Canada R3E 0W3 Doris Pritchard, Hd.Libn.
Founded: 1958. **Staff:** Prof 1; Other 4. **Subjects:** Dentistry. **Holdings:** 22,300 volumes; 1500 pamphlets. **Subscriptions:** 380 journals and other serials. **Services:** Interlibrary loan; library open to medical and dental professionals. **Automated Operations:** Computerized circulation. **Computerized Information Services:** UTLAS, MEDLARS, DIALOG Information Services, BRS Information Technologies, CAN/OLE, PaperChase; Envoy 100 (electronic mail service). Performs searches on fee basis. Contact Person: Michael Tennenhouse, 788-6342. **Publications:** Dental Library News, 6/year; Selected Book List, 6/year; Suggested Readings from the Current Literature, quarterly.

★16357★
UNIVERSITY OF MANITOBA - ST. JOHN'S COLLEGE - LIBRARY (Hum, Rel-Phil)
400 Dysart Rd. Phone: (204)474-8542
Winnipeg, MB, Canada R3T 2M5 Patrick D. Wright, Libn.
Founded: 1849. **Staff:** Prof 1; Other 2. **Subjects:** Religion, Canadian studies, humanities. **Holdings:** 49,000 volumes. **Subscriptions:** 135 journals and other serials. **Services:** Interlibrary loan; library open to the public. **Automated Operations:** Computerized cataloging, acquisitions, circulation, and ILL. **Computerized Information Services:** UTLAS, DIALOG Information Services, BRS Information Technologies, CAN/OLE; Envoy 100 (electronic mail service). Performs searches on fee basis. Contact Person: Sharon Tully, 474-9844.

★16358★
UNIVERSITY OF MANITOBA - ST. PAUL'S COLLEGE - LIBRARY (Rel-Phil)
119 St. Paul's College Phone: (204)474-8585
Winnipeg, MB, Canada R3T 2M6 Fr. Harold Drake, Hd.
Founded: 1931. **Staff:** Prof 1; Other 3. **Subjects:** Religion, theology. **Special Collections:** Vatican archives on microfilm (transactions and correspondence pertaining to Canada, 1668 to present; in progress). **Holdings:** 64,000 volumes. **Subscriptions:** 240 journals and other serials. **Services:** Interlibrary loan; library open to the public. **Automated Operations:** Computerized circulation. **Computerized Information Services:** UTLAS, DIALOG Information Services, CAN/OLE, BRS Information Technologies; Envoy 100 (electronic mail service). Performs searches on fee basis. Contact Person: Sharon Tully, 474-9844. **Publications:** List of new acquisitions.

★16359★
UNIVERSITY OF MANITOBA - SCIENCE LIBRARY (Biol Sci, Sci-Engr)
211 Machray Hall Phone: (204)474-8171
Winnipeg, MB, Canada R3T 2N2 H.J. William Westelaken, Hd.
Founded: 1906. **Staff:** Prof 3; Other 9. **Subjects:** Physical, mathematical, earth, and biological sciences; computer science; pharmacy; statistics; botany; chemistry; astronomy. **Holdings:** 125,800 volumes. **Subscriptions:** 1230 journals and other serials. **Services:** Interlibrary loan; library open to the public with restrictions. **Automated Operations:** Computerized cataloging, acquisitions, serials, circulation, and ILL. **Computerized Information Services:** CAN/OLE, MEDLARS, DIALOG Information Services, UTLAS, BRS Information Technologies; Envoy 100 (electronic mail service). Performs searches on fee basis. Contact Person: M. Speare, Ref.Libn.. **Staff:** B. Carstens, Ref.Libn..

★16360★
UNIVERSITY OF MARY - LIBRARY (Rel-Phil)
7500 University Dr. Phone: (701)255-4681
Bismarck, ND 58504 Cheryl M. Bailey, Dir.
Founded: 1959. **Staff:** Prof 2; Other 3. **Subjects:** Theology, philosophy, education, music, history, nursing, business. **Holdings:** 45,000 books; 3000 bound periodical volumes; 7000 records, films, tapes, maps, AV programs; 1600 reels of microfilm of back files of magazines. **Subscriptions:** 450 journals and other serials; 12 newspapers. **Services:** Interlibrary loan; copying; library open to the public with restrictions. **Computerized Information Services:** OCLC. **Networks/Consortia:** Member of North Dakota Network for Knowledge, Northwest Area Health Education Center Consortium, MINITEX.

★16361★
UNIVERSITY OF MARY HARDIN-BAYLOR - TOWNSEND MEMORIAL LIBRARY (Educ)
9th & Wells
UMHB Sta., Box 439 Phone: (817)939-5811
Belton, TX 76513 Robert Strong, Libn.
Founded: 1845. **Staff:** Prof 3; Other 2. **Subjects:** Education, religion, nursing. **Special Collections:** McFadden-Texas Collection. **Holdings:** 79,232 books; 11,700 bound periodical volumes; 21,676 microforms. **Subscriptions:** 600 journals and other serials; 8 newspapers. **Services:** Interlibrary loan; copying; library open to the public for reference use only. **Automated Operations:** Computerized cataloging and ILL. **Computerized Information Services:** OCLC. **Networks/Consortia:** Member of AMIGOS Bibliographic Council, Inc.. **Staff:** Izoro Daphane Kerley, Asst.Libn.; Denise Karimkhani, Asst.Libn..

★16362★
UNIVERSITY OF MARYLAND - CENTER FOR ENVIRONMENTAL & ESTUARINE STUDIES - CHESAPEAKE BIOLOGICAL LABORATORY - LIBRARY (Biol Sci)
Box 38 Phone: (301)326-4281
Solomons, MD 20688 Kathleen A. Heil, Libn.
Founded: 1925. **Staff:** Prof 1. **Subjects:** Fisheries research; marine research, biology, zoology; oceanography; aquatic microbiology; ecosystems studies; environmental chemistry and toxicology. **Special Collections:** Freshwater sponge reprints; shellfish reprints (1200); larvel fishes reprints (7000). **Holdings:** 4500 books; 25,000 bound periodical volumes; 3500 reports and documents; 2000 manuscripts; 1000 archival items; 17,000 reprints; 55 VF drawers of laboratory publications; 600 retrospective titles. **Subscriptions:** 202 journals and other serials. **Services:** Interlibrary loan; copying; SDI; library open to the public for reference use only. **Computerized Information Services:** DIALOG Information Services. **Networks/Consortia:** Member of Maryland Interlibrary Organization (MILO). **Publications:** Newsletter, monthly; annual bibliography of serials - both for internal distribution only.

★16363★
UNIVERSITY OF MARYLAND - SCHOOL OF MEDICINE - DEPARTMENT OF PSYCHIATRY - HELEN C. TINGLEY MEMORIAL LIBRARY (Med)
Maryland Psychiatric Research Ctr.
Box 21247 Phone: (301)747-1071
Catonsville, MD 21228 Edward D. French, Libn.
Staff: Prof 1. **Subjects:** Psychiatry, allied health sciences. **Holdings:** 400 volumes; 50 bound periodical volumes; 50 audio cassettes; 50 reference works. **Subscriptions:** 15 journals and other serials. **Services:** Interlibrary loan; library not open to the public.

★16364★
UNIVERSITY OF MARYLAND, BALTIMORE - HEALTH SCIENCES LIBRARY (Med)
111 S. Greene St. Phone: (301)328-7545
Baltimore, MD 21201 Cyril C.H. Feng, Libn.
Founded: 1813. **Staff:** Prof 26; Other 36. **Subjects:** Medicine, dentistry, pharmacy, nursing, social work. **Special Collections:** Crawford Medical Historical Collection; Cordell Medical Historical Collection; Grieves Dental Historical Collection; historical book collections in pharmacy, social work, and nursing. **Holdings:** 132,948 books; 138,238 bound periodical volumes; University of Maryland archives. **Subscriptions:** 4726 journals and other serials. **Services:** Interlibrary loan; copying; library open to qualified public for reference use only. **Automated Operations:** Computerized cataloging, serials, and circulation. **Computerized Information Services:** OCLC, DIALOG Information Services, BRS Information Technologies, MEDLINE. Performs searches on fee basis. Contact Person: Marjorie Simon, Hd., Ref., 328-3773. **Networks/Consortia:** Member of Southeastern/Atlantic Regional Medical Library Services, PALINET, Maryland Interlibrary Organization (MILO). **Staff:** Frieda Weise, Dp.Dir.; Diana Cunningham, Asst.Dir., Pub.Serv..

★16365★
UNIVERSITY OF MARYLAND, BALTIMORE - SCHOOL OF LAW - MARSHALL LAW LIBRARY (Law)
20 N. Paca St. Phone: (301)528-7270
Baltimore, MD 21201 Barbara S. Gontrum, Dir.
Founded: 1843. **Staff:** Prof 7; Other 16. **Subjects:** Law. **Special Collections:** U.S. Government document depository. **Holdings:** 221,219 volumes; microforms. **Subscriptions:** 4025 journals and other serials. **Services:** Interlibrary loan; copying; library open to the public. **Automated Operations:** Computerized public access catalog, cataloging, and circulation. **Computerized Information Services:** LEXIS, OCLC, DIALOG Information Services, WESTLAW. **Networks/Consortia:** Member of PALINET. **Staff:** David Grahek, Assoc.Dir.; Pamela Bluh, Asst.Libn., Tech.Serv.; Maxine Grosshans, Asst.Libn., Info.Serv.; Laura Orr, Res.Libn.; Dennis Guion, Coll.Dev..

★16366★
UNIVERSITY OF MARYLAND, CAMBRIDGE - CENTER FOR ENVIRONMENTAL AND ESTUARINE STUDIES - LIBRARY (Biol Sci, Env-Cons)
Box 775 Phone: (301)228-9250
Cambridge, MD 21613 Darlene Windsor, Libn.
Founded: 1973. **Staff:** Prof 1. **Subjects:** Aquaculture, water quality, wildlife information, water resources. **Holdings:** 31,697 volumes.

★16367★
UNIVERSITY OF MARYLAND, COLLEGE PARK - COLLEGE OF LIBRARY & INFORMATION SERVICES - LIBRARY (Info Sci)
Hornbake Library Bldg., Rm. 4105 Phone: (301)454-6003
College Park, MD 20742 William G. Wilson, Libn.
Founded: 1965. **Staff:** Prof 2; Other 5. **Subjects:** Organization of knowledge, bibliography, administration, information science, computer applications for libraries, juvenile books, communication. **Holdings:** 45,000 books; 6000 bound periodical volumes; 2300 pamphlets; 154 VF drawers of pamphlets and reports; 21,000 microforms; 1500 nonprint items (540 titles); 100 software programs. **Subscriptions:** 425 journals and other serials. **Services:** Interlibrary loan; copying; library open to the public with limited circulation. **Automated Operations:** Computerized cataloging, acquisitions, and serials. **Publications:** Orientation handouts. **Staff:** William B. Pitt, Assoc.Libn..

★16368★
UNIVERSITY OF MARYLAND, COLLEGE PARK - COLLEGE OF LIBRARY & INFORMATION SERVICES - U.S. INFORMATION CENTER FOR THE UNIVERSAL DECIMAL CLASSIFICATION (Info Sci)
College Park, MD 20742 Phone: (301)454-3785
Hans H. Wellisch, Dir.
Staff: Prof 1. **Subjects:** Universal Decimal Classification (UDC). **Special Collections:** UDC schedules in English and in the major languages of Europe and Asia. **Holdings:** 500 books. **Services:** Interlibrary loan; copying; center open to the public.

★16369★
UNIVERSITY OF MARYLAND, COLLEGE PARK - COMPUTER SCIENCE CENTER - PROGRAM LIBRARY (Info Sci, Comp Sci)
College Park, MD 20742 Phone: (301)454-4261
Barbara Rush, Mgr., Lib.Serv.
Founded: 1963. **Staff:** Prof 2; Other 2. **Subjects:** Computer science, information science, mathematics, statistics. **Special Collections:** System Reference Libraries for UNIVAC 1100 series; reference manuals for IBM 4300; Maryland State Data Center (500 U.S. census publications and magnetic tapes of census statistics). **Holdings:** 3500 books; 750 bound periodical volumes; 5000 technical reports; 1000 computer usage reports; 3081 computer programs; 1450 computer programs on magnetic tape; 150 computer programs on disks; 30 computer newsletters from universities; 100 software packages. **Subscriptions:** 150 journals and other serials. **Services:** Copying; library open to the public for reference use only. **Automated Operations:** Computerized cataloging. **Computerized Information Services:** BITNET (electronic mail service). **Publications:** Program Library Bulletin, monthly. **Special Indexes:** KWOC Index for all computer programs; KWOC Index of library's holdings of proceedings. **Staff:** Mai-leng Ong, Asst.Libn..

★16370★
UNIVERSITY OF MARYLAND, COLLEGE PARK - M. LUCIA JAMES CURRICULUM LABORATORY (Educ)
College of Education Phone: (301)454-5466
College Park, MD 20742 Dr. Charles Brand, Dir.
Staff: Prof 1; Other 3. **Subjects:** Education - elementary, secondary, teacher, special, art, early childhood, curriculum development; guidance and counseling. **Special Collections:** Curriculum guides from many states and major U.S. (5900); Microcomputer Courseware (95); special subject collections by subject/name. **Holdings:** 18,500 volumes; reports of curriculum projects; 1200 filmstrips; 184 slides; 1040 transparencies; 1860 multimedia kits and manipulative teaching aids; 77 maps; 705 tapes; 48 VF drawers; 28 VF drawers of resource materials; 745 standardized test specimen sets. **Subscriptions:** 105 journals and other serials. **Services:** Copying; transparency making; laboratory open to the public for reference use only. **Publications:** Bibliographies; recent acquisitions and special reports on curriculum materials - to students, staff, and faculty of the College of Education; Tabs on the Lab (newsletter), bimonthly.

★16371★
UNIVERSITY OF MARYLAND, COLLEGE PARK - MARYLAND CENTER FOR PRODUCTIVITY AND QUALITY OF WORKING LIFE - LIBRARY (Bus-Fin)
College of Business and Management Phone: (301)454-6688
College Park, MD 20742
Jan R. Lawrence, Mgr., Commun. & Policy Prog.
Founded: 1977. **Staff:** Prof 4; Other 3. **Subjects:** Productivity, productivity measurement, management development, participative management, labor-management cooperation, gainsharing. **Holdings:** 1100 books. **Subscriptions:** 30 journals and other serials. **Services:** Library open to the public. **Publications:** Maryland Workplace (newsletter), bimonthly - free upon request.

★16372★
UNIVERSITY OF MARYLAND, COLLEGE PARK - NATIONAL CLEARINGHOUSE FOR COMMUTER PROGRAMS (Soc Sci, Trans)
1195 Adele H. Stamp Union Phone: (301)454-5274
College Park, MD 20742 Dr. Barbara Jacoby, Dir.
Staff: Prof 1; Other 2. **Subjects:** Student commuters, housing, transportation, tenant/landlord relations, orientation. **Holdings:** 8 VF drawers of manuscripts, reports, handbooks. **Services:** Copying; clearinghouse open to the public by appointment. **Publications:** The Commuter, quarterly - to members; Serving Commuter Students: Examples of Good Practice; Commuter Students: References & Resources.

★16373★
UNIVERSITY OF MARYLAND, COLLEGE PARK LIBRARIES - ARCHITECTURE LIBRARY (Art, Plan)
College Park, MD 20742 Phone: (301)454-4316
Berna E. Neal, Hd.
Founded: 1967. **Staff:** Prof 2; Other 2. **Subjects:** Architecture, urban design. **Special Collections:** Collection on world expositions, 1851-1937 (500 volumes, pamphlets, clippings, engravings, and memorabilia). **Holdings:** 22,000 books; 6000 bound periodical volumes. **Subscriptions:** 150 journals and other serials. **Services:** Interlibrary loan; copying; library open to the public for reference use only. **Automated Operations:** Computerized cataloging and circulation.

★16374★
UNIVERSITY OF MARYLAND, COLLEGE PARK LIBRARIES - ARCHITECTURE LIBRARY - NATIONAL TRUST FOR HISTORIC PRESERVATION LIBRARY (Plan)
College Park, MD 20742 Phone: (301)454-4316
Sally R. Sims, Hist.Presrv.Libn.
Staff: Prof 1; Other 1. **Subjects:** All aspects of historic preservation including architecture, maritime preservation, tax incentives, urban renewal, building restoration. **Special Collections:** Postcards, 1903-1914 (18,500). **Holdings:** 11,000 books; 200 bound periodical volumes; 25 films; 100 audio- and videotapes; 13,000 vertical files; 600 microfiche of newspaper clippings. **Subscriptions:** 400 journals and other serials. **Services:** Interlibrary loan; copying; library open to the public for reference use only. **Automated Operations:** Computerized cataloging, acquisitions, and circulation. **Computerized Information Services:** OCLC. **Publications:** Accessions list, monthly - for internal distribution only. **Special Indexes:** Index to articles in periodicals acquired (card). **Remarks:** An alternate telephone number is 454-3979.

★16375★
UNIVERSITY OF MARYLAND, COLLEGE PARK LIBRARIES - ART LIBRARY (Art)
College Park, MD 20742 Phone: (301)454-2065
Courtney A. Shaw, Hd.Libn.
Founded: 1979. **Staff:** Prof 2; Other 2. **Subjects:** Art history, studio art, art education, decorative and applied arts. **Special Collections:** Decimal Index to the Art of the Low Countries; Index photographique d'art de France; emblem books; Marburg Index; Alinari; picture collection. **Holdings:** 64,000 books; 10 VF drawers; 27,000 art reproduction files. **Subscriptions:** 210 journals. **Services:** Interlibrary loan; copying; library open to the public for reference use only. **Automated Operations:** Computerized public access catalog, cataloging, acquisitions, and circulation. **Computerized Information Services:** DIALOG Information Services, RLIN, OCLC. Performs searches on fee basis. Contact Person: Julie Dabbs, Asst. Art Libn..

★16376★
UNIVERSITY OF MARYLAND, COLLEGE PARK LIBRARIES - CHARLES E. WHITE MEMORIAL LIBRARY (Sci-Engr)
College Park, MD 20742 Phone: (301)454-2609
Elizabeth W. McElroy, Hd.
Staff: Prof 2; Other 2. **Subjects:** Chemistry, biochemistry, spectroscopy, microbiology, nuclear chemistry. **Holdings:** 27,000 books; 25,000 bound periodical volumes; 2000 cartridges of microfilm; 1250 dissertations. **Subscriptions:** 540 journals and other serials. **Services:** Interlibrary loan; copying; library open to the public for reference use only. **Automated Operations:** Computerized cataloging and circulation. **Computerized Information Services:** OCLC, DIALOG Information Services, MEDLINE, CAS ONLINE. Performs searches on fee basis.

★16377★
UNIVERSITY OF MARYLAND, COLLEGE PARK LIBRARIES - ENGINEERING & PHYSICAL SCIENCES LIBRARY (Sci-Engr)
College Park, MD 20742 Phone: (301)454-3037
Herbert N. Foerstel, Hd., Br.Libs.
Founded: 1953. **Staff:** Prof 6; Other 13. **Subjects:** Aeronautics and astronautics; astronomy; computer science; engineering - chemical, civil, electrical, industrial, mechanical; geology; materials science; mathematics; oceanography; physics; transportation. **Special Collections:** Patent Depository Library (complete patent backfile, 1789 to present); R. von Mises Collection (1100 titles; 217 boxes of reprints); Max Born Collection (theoretical mathematics and physics; 650 titles; 6 boxes of reprints). **Holdings:** 125,000 books; 120,000 bound periodical volumes; 125,000 hardcopy reports; 1.1 million reports on microfiche; 90,460 reports on microcard; 5100 reels of microfilm. **Subscriptions:** 3128 journals and other serials. **Services:** Interlibrary loan; copying; library open to the public for reference use only. **Automated Operations:** Computerized cataloging,

acquisitions, an circulation. **Computerized Information Services:** DIALOG Information Services, BRS Information Technologies, DTIC, U.S. Patent Classification System, OCLC. **Publications:** New Books List, monthly - to departments and library representatives.

★16378★
UNIVERSITY OF MARYLAND, COLLEGE PARK LIBRARIES - MC KELDIN LIBRARY - EAST ASIA COLLECTION (Area-Ethnic)
College Park, MD 20742-7011 Phone: (301)454-5459
Frank Joseph Shulman, Cur.
Founded: 1963. **Staff:** Prof 3; Other 2. **Subjects:** Social sciences (Japanese, Chinese, and Korean languages); modern Japanese, Chinese, and Korean history and literature; World War II (Pacific area). **Special Collections:** Gordon W. Prange Collection: Allied Occupation of Japan, 1945-1952 (50,000 Japanese-language monographs; 13,000 titles of Japanese magazines; 17,000 titles of Japanese newspapers; 24 file cabinets of unique censored materials from Supreme Commander, Allied Powers' Censorship Detachment); papers of Justin Williams, Sr. (69 filing boxes of material relating to political aspects of the Allied Occupation of Japan). **Holdings:** 55,000 books; 10,000 bound periodical volumes; 1492 reels of microfilm; 232 filing boxes of U.S. Army, Allied Translator, and Interpreter Service documents and transcripts of International Military Tribunal for the Far East; 100 photograph albums relating to Japanese history and naval affairs; U.S. Office of Strategic Bombing Survey materials on the interrogation of Japanese officials. **Subscriptions:** 800 journals and other serials; 29 newspapers. **Services:** Interlibrary loan; collection open to the public for reference use only. **Publications:** Microfilm Edition of Censored Periodicals, 1945-1949 (User's Guide to the Gordon W. Prange Collection, I). **Special Catalogs:** Newspapers and periodicals from period of Allied Occupation of Japan (card files); guide to Justin Williams papers. **Remarks:** An alternate telephone number is 454-2819.

★16379★
UNIVERSITY OF MARYLAND, COLLEGE PARK LIBRARIES - MC KELDIN LIBRARY - GOVERNMENT DOCUMENTS/MAP ROOM (Info Sci, Geog-Map)
College Park, MD 20742 Phone: (301)454-3034
Lola N. Warren, Hd., Govt.Docs/Maps
Staff: Prof 3; Other 3. **Subjects:** U.S. Government documents, maps, international agency and state agriculture publications. **Special Collections:** U.S. Government documents regional depository (900,000); United Nations documents (25,000); topographic maps (70,000); state agriculture documents (20,000). **Holdings:** 1 million documents; 100,000 maps; 2000 reels of microfilm; 29 cabinets of microfiche. **Services:** Interlibrary loan; copying; room open to the public. **Computerized Information Services:** DIALOG Information Services, OCLC. Performs searches on fee basis. Contact Person: Ray Foster, 454-2983. **Networks/Consortia:** Member of Maryland Interlibrary Organization (MILO). **Staff:** Robert A. Staley, Map Libn.; Elizabeth A. Robertson, Ref.Libn., Intl..

★16380★
UNIVERSITY OF MARYLAND, COLLEGE PARK LIBRARIES - MC KELDIN LIBRARY - HISTORICAL MANUSCRIPTS AND ARCHIVES DEPARTMENT (Hist)
College Park, MD 20742 Phone: (301)454-2318
Lauren R. Brown, Cur.
Staff: Prof 2; Other 1. **Special Collections:** Personal and organizational papers related to the Maryland region (Thomas Bray papers; Maryland Division/American Association of University Women Archives); papers of leading Maryland political leaders and organizations (Millard Tydings papers; Maryland League of Women Voters Archives); archives of trade unions (Cigar Makers; Marine & Shipbuilding Workers; Tobacco Workers; Bakery & Confectionery Workers); Cuba Company Archives; Association for Childhood Education International Archives; Association for Intercollegiate Athletics for Women Archives; Maryland Sheet Music Collection; University of Maryland, College Park archives (archival record groups; university publications; faculty papers; photographs; memorabilia). **Holdings:** 10,000 cubic feet. **Services:** Department open to the public for reference use only. **Publications:** Personal and Organizational Papers Relating to Maryland, 1978; Greenbelt: A Guide to Further Sources, 1981; University Fact Book, 1981.

★16381★
UNIVERSITY OF MARYLAND, COLLEGE PARK LIBRARIES - MC KELDIN LIBRARY - KATHERINE ANNE PORTER ROOM (Hum)
College Park, MD 20742 Phone: (301)454-4020
Donald Farren, Assoc.Dir., Spec.Coll.
Staff: Prof 1; Other 1. **Subjects:** The personal library and memorabilia of author Katherine Anne Porter. **Holdings:** 2000 books. **Services:** Room open to the public for reference use only.

★16382★
UNIVERSITY OF MARYLAND, COLLEGE PARK LIBRARIES - MC KELDIN LIBRARY - MARYLANDIA DEPARTMENT (Rare Book)
College Park, MD 20742 Phone: (301)454-3035
Peter H. Curtis, Cur.
Staff: Prof 2; Other 3. **Subjects:** Maryland history - political, social, economic, industrial, agricultural. **Special Collections:** Maryland state, county, and municipal documents (400 linear feet); maps of Maryland and Chesapeake Bay region; University of Maryland, College Park theses and dissertations. **Holdings:** 60,000 volumes; 50 drawers of maps. **Subscriptions:** 300 journals and other serials. **Services:** Department open to the public for reference use only.

★16383★
UNIVERSITY OF MARYLAND, COLLEGE PARK LIBRARIES - MC KELDIN LIBRARY - PERIODICALS/MICROFORMS COLLECTION (Info Sci)
College Park, MD 20742 Phone: (301)454-3032
Paula Hayes, Hd., Ref.
Special Collections: Statistical Reference Index; Early English Books, 1475-1640 and 1641-1701; American Culture Series and Periodical Series, 1493-1875; Q-File; Early American Imprints; English Literary Periodicals; History of Women; Human Relations Area File; Landmarks of Science; Eighteenth-Century Short-Title Catalogue; Underground Newspaper ollection; Goldsmith-Kress Library of Economic Literature; U.S. Supreme Court records and briefs; International Population Census publications; Wright American Fiction Collection; Great Britain Parliament records and papers; U.S. Joint Publications Research Service; selected papers of U.S. presidents; CIRR/Corporate and Industry Research Reports; American Public Opinion Data; ERIC reports; U.S. National Criminal Justice Reference Service (all in microform). **Holdings:** 2.6 million microforms. **Services:** Collection open to the public with restrictions.

★16384★
UNIVERSITY OF MARYLAND, COLLEGE PARK LIBRARIES - MC KELDIN LIBRARY - RARE BOOKS AND LITERARY MANUSCRIPTS DEPARTMENT (Rare Book)
College Park, MD 20742 Phone: (301)454-3035
Blanche T. Ebeling-Koning, Cur.
Staff: Prof 1; Other 1. **Subjects:** Rare books and manuscripts in a wide range of scholarly fields. **Special Collections:** Djuna Barnes Collection; Katherine Anne Porter Collection; manuscripts of contemporary American and British authors, including T.S. Eliot, Robert Frost, William Faulkner, John Dos Passos, Thom Gunn, and Ernest Hemingway; history of books, typography, and printing; William Morris and the Kelmscott Press; German Expressionism; Mazarinades; 19th and 20th century American and British literature; Savoy regional history; 16th-19th century French politics and economics; French and Spanish drama; pamphlets on slavery. **Holdings:** 60,000 books. **Services:** Department open to the public for reference use only. **Special Indexes:** Guide to the William Morris Collection (typescript); inventory of the Barnes and Porter manuscript collections (typescript).

★16385★
UNIVERSITY OF MARYLAND, COLLEGE PARK LIBRARIES - MUSIC LIBRARY (Mus)
College Park, MD 20742 Phone: (301)454-3036
Neil Ratliff, Hd.
Founded: 1958. **Staff:** Prof 4. **Subjects:** Music, dance. **Special Collections:** American Bandmasters Association Research Center; Music Educators National Conference Historical Center; College Band Directors National Association Archives; National Association of College Wind and Percussion Instructors Research Center; International Clarinet Society Research Center; Archives of the Music Library Association; Archives of the United States Branch of the International Association of Music Libraries, Archives, and Documentation Centers; The Irving and Margery Lowens Collection of Musical Americana and Music Criticism; Jacob Coopersmith Collection of Handeliana; Wallenstein Collection of Orchestra Music (29,628 items); Contemporary Music Project (CMP)

Lending Service; Archives of the American Society of University Composers; Archives of the International Society for Music Education. **Holdings:** 40,000 volumes; 80,000 scores; 45,000 phonograph records; 671 VF drawers. **Subscriptions:** 324 journals and other serials. **Services:** Interlibrary loan; copying; library open to the public for reference use only. **Automated Operations:** Computerized cataloging, acquisitions, serials, and circulation. **Computerized Information Services:** DIALOG Information Services, Pergamon ORBIT InfoLine, Inc. **Publications:** Guide to the Coopersmith Collection of Handeliana at the University of Maryland.

★16386★
UNIVERSITY OF MARYLAND, COLLEGE PARK LIBRARIES - MUSIC LIBRARY - INTERNATIONAL PIANO ARCHIVES AT MARYLAND (Mus)
Hornbake Library, 3210 Phone: (301)454-6479
College Park, MD 20742 Morgan Cundiff, Libn.
Founded: 1965. **Staff:** Prof 2. **Subjects:** Music, performance practice, piano, harpsichord. **Special Collections:** Archival papers and recordings of Gary Graffman, Josef Hofmann, Jan Holcman, William Kapell, Arthur Loesser, Jerome Lowenthal, Nadia Reisenberg, David Barnett, Erno Balogh, and Inga Hoegsbro Christensen. **Holdings:** 1800 books and pamphlets; 75 manuscripts; 8000 reproducing piano rolls; 8500 78rpm phonograph records; 6000 piano scores; 1600 audiotapes. **Services:** Copying; archives open to the public with restrictions. **Publications:** IPAM Newsletter, irregular - free upon request. **Special Catalogs:** Catalog of the Reproducing Piano Roll Collection. **Remarks:** An alternate telephone number is 454-6903.

★16387★
UNIVERSITY OF MARYLAND, COLLEGE PARK LIBRARIES - NONPRINT MEDIA SERVICES (Aud-Vis)
Hornbake Library Phone: (301)454-4723
College Park, MD 20742 Allan C. Rough, Hd.
Founded: 1972. **Staff:** Prof 2; Other 8. **Subjects:** Physical sciences, sociology, history, English literature and theater, women's studies, business and management. **Special Collections:** Video cassettes of Watergate hearings (162); NOVA (series) video cassettes (350); BBC Shakespeare Series (complete plays on video cassette); U.S. Air Force Film Collection (600); U.S.D.A. Food and Nutrition Information Center's Deposit AV Collection (3250 items); Pioneers in Science and Technology (30 video cassettes). **Holdings:** 100 laser videodiscs; 48 slide sets; 1200 16mm films; 3600 video cassettes; 3200 audio cassettes. **Services:** Services open to public by arrangement with department head. **Automated Operations:** Computerized circulation. **Publications:** Subject "Mediagraphies" (media bibliographies, 102). **Staff:** Angela Domanico, Oper.Supv.; Linda Sarigol, Film Unit Supv.; Jeffrey Bonar, Electronic Media Sys.Engr..

★16388★
UNIVERSITY OF MASSACHUSETTS - CRANBERRY EXPERIMENT STATION (Agri)
Glen Charlie Rd.
Box 569 Phone: (508)295-2213
East Wareham, MA 02538 Irving E. Demoranville, Dept.Hd.
Subjects: Cranberry culture and history. **Holdings:** Figures not available. **Services:** Station open to the public.

★16389★
UNIVERSITY OF MASSACHUSETTS, AMHERST - LABOR RELATIONS & RESEARCH CENTER LIBRARY (Bus-Fin)
Draper Hall Phone: (413)545-2884
Amherst, MA 01003 Janice Tausky, Libn.
Founded: 1965. **Staff:** 2. **Subjects:** Industrial relations. **Holdings:** 5000 books; 10,000 pamphlets. **Subscriptions:** 400 journals and other serials. **Services:** Interlibrary loan; copying; library open to the public with restrictions.

★16390★
UNIVERSITY OF MASSACHUSETTS, AMHERST - LIBRARY - DEPARTMENT OF ARCHIVES AND MANUSCRIPTS (Hist, Area-Ethnic)
Amherst, MA 01003 Phone: (413)545-2780
Kenneth Fones-Wolf, Archv.
Staff: Prof 2; Other 3. **Subjects:** Massachusetts, Afro-American studies, labor history. **Special Collections:** Papers of W.E.B. Du Bois, Horace Mann Bond, Erasmus Darwin Hudson, John Haigis, Maurice Donahue, Sol Barkin, J. William Belanger, Kenyon Butterfield, Harvey Swados, Robert Francis, Joseph Obrebski, Thomas Copeland; Records of American Writing Paper Co., Northampton Cutlery Co., George H. Gilbert Co., Granite Cutters International Association, Carpenters unions of Western Massachusetts, New England Joint Board of Amalgamated Clothing and Textile Workers Union, Northampton Labor Council, New Bedford Joint Board of Textile Workers Union of America, American Dialect Society, Renaissance Diplomatic Documents, University of Massachusetts. **Holdings:** 5000 linear feet of records, manuscripts, clippings, photographs, maps, building plans, microfilm, audiotapes, and books. **Services:** Copying; department open to the public. **Special Catalogs:** The Papers of W.E.B. Du Bois: A Guide; The Horace Mann Bond Papers; Major Manuscript Collections by Subject in the Archives and Manuscripts Department.

★16391★
UNIVERSITY OF MASSACHUSETTS, AMHERST - LIBRARY - SPECIAL COLLECTIONS AND RARE BOOKS (Rare Book)
Amherst, MA 01003 Phone: (413)545-0274
John D. Kendall, Hd.
Staff: Prof 2; Other 1. **Subjects:** History of botany and entomology to 1900; historical geography and cartography of Northeastern United States to 1900; history of Massachusetts and New England; antislavery movement in New England; travel and tourism in New England, New York, and eastern Canada. **Special Collections:** Alspach Yeats Collection (600 items); Federal Land Bank Collection (cartography, county atlases; 270 items); Robert Francis Collection (100 items); Binet French Revolution Collection (1524 items); Massachusetts Pamphlet Collection (985); Benjamin Smith Lyman Collection (Japan; 2000 items). **Holdings:** 19,000 books. **Services:** Copying; collections open to the public. **Automated Operations:** Computerized cataloging, acquisitions, serials, and circulation (through main library). **Computerized Information Services:** OCLC. **Networks/Consortia:** Member of NELINET, HILC, Inc..

★16392★
UNIVERSITY OF MASSACHUSETTS, AMHERST - MORRILL BIOLOGICAL & GEOLOGICAL SCIENCES LIBRARY (Biol Sci, Sci-Engr)
214 Morrill Science Center Phone: (413)545-2674
Amherst, MA 01003 Laurence M. Feldman, Libn.
Founded: 1963. **Staff:** Prof 3; Other 6. **Subjects:** Botany, zoology, geography, forestry, wildlife and fisheries biology, geology, microbiology. **Special Collections:** Arthur Cleveland Bent (ornithology); Guy Chester Crampton (entomology and evolutionary biology). **Holdings:** 100,000 volumes; 125,000 maps. **Subscriptions:** 1200 journals and other serials. **Services:** Interlibrary loan; copying; library open to the public for reference use only; borrowing privileges upon application. **Networks/Consortia:** Member of Boston Library Consortium, NELINET. **Publications:** New Acquisitions List, weekly - for internal and limited external distribution; Literature Guides, irregular - for internal distribution only. **Staff:** Alena Chadwick, Br.Libn.; James' L. Craig, Biol.Sci.Libn..

★16393★
UNIVERSITY OF MASSACHUSETTS, AMHERST - MUSIC LIBRARY (Mus)
Fine Arts Center, Rm. 149 Phone: (413)545-2870
Amherst, MA 01003 Pamela Juengling, Mus.Libn.
Staff: Prof 1; Other 3. **Subjects:** Music. **Special Collections:** Alma Werfel Collection; Howard LeBow Collection; Philip Bezanson papers. **Holdings:** 13,000 books; 3000 bound periodical volumes; 9000 scores; 11,000 sound recordings; 600 other cataloged items. **Subscriptions:** 250 journals and other serials. **Services:** Interlibrary loan; copying; listening facilities; library open to the public. **Automated Operations:** Computerized cataloging and acquisitions. **Computerized Information Services:** DIALOG Information Services, BRS Information Technologies, NLM, OCLC. Performs searches on fee basis. Contact Person: Virginia Craig, 545-0150. **Networks/Consortia:** Member of NELINET. **Special Catalogs:** Catalog of recording analytics (card).

★16394★
UNIVERSITY OF MASSACHUSETTS, AMHERST - PHYSICAL SCIENCES LIBRARY (Sci-Engr)
Graduate Research Center Phone: (413)545-1370
Amherst, MA 01003 Eric Esau, Libn.
Founded: 1971. **Staff:** Prof 3; Other 7. **Subjects:** Engineering - chemical, civil, electrical, industrial, mechanical; chemistry; physics and astronomy; mathematics and statistics; aeronautics and astronautics; computer science; food technology; polymer science; wood technology. **Holdings:** 97,000 books; 58,000 bound periodical volumes; 800,000 technical reports on microfiche; U.S. patents, 1950 to present. **Subscriptions:** 1900 journals and other serials. **Services:** Interlibrary loan; copying; library open to the public for reference use only; borrowing privileges on application. **Automated Operations:** Computerized public access catalog, cataloging, acquisitions, and circulation. **Computerized Information Services:** DIALOG Information Services, U.S. Patent Classification System. **Networks/**

Consortia: Member of Boston Library Consortium. **Staff:** Linda Arny, Ref./Asst.Br.Libn.; Selma Etter, Ref.Libn..

★16395★
UNIVERSITY OF MASSACHUSETTS MEDICAL SCHOOL & WORCESTER DISTRICT MEDICAL SOCIETY - LIBRARY (Med)
55 N. Lake Ave. Phone: (508)856-2511
Worcester, MA 01605 Donald J. Morton, Lib.Dir.
Founded: 1966. **Staff:** Prof 9; Other 13. **Subjects:** Medicine, health sciences, human biology. **Special Collections:** Scientific government publications depository; history of medicine. **Holdings:** 30,000 books; 81,000 bound periodical volumes. **Subscriptions:** 2700 journals and other serials. **Services:** Interlibrary loan; copying; SDI; library open to the public. **Automated Operations:** Computerized cataloging and serials. **Computerized Information Services:** MEDLINE, BRS Information Technologies, DIALOG Information Services, Pergamon ORBIT InfoLine, Inc., MEDLARS, OCLC. **Networks/Consortia:** Member of Worcester Area Cooperating Libraries (WACL), Boston Library Consortium, Central Massachusetts Consortium of Health Related Libraries (CMCHRL), Massachusetts Conference of Chief Librarians in Public Higher Educational Institutions, Greater Northeastern Regional Medical Library Program, C/W MARS, Inc.. **Staff:** Beverly Shattuck, Asst.Dir., Pub.Serv.; Jean M. Conelley, Asst.Dir., Tech.Serv..

★16396★
UNIVERSITY MEDICAL CENTER OF SOUTHERN NEVADA - MEDICAL LIBRARY (Med)
2040 W. Charleston Blvd., Suite 500 Phone: (702)383-2368
Las Vegas, NV 89102 Aldona Jonynas, Dir., Lib.Serv.
Founded: 1964. **Staff:** Prof 1; Other 2. **Subjects:** Medicine, nursing. **Holdings:** 4641 books; 6446 bound periodical volumes; 276 bound indexes; 115 vertical files; 5 boxes of staff publications; 580 symposia; 620 cassettes. **Subscriptions:** 182 journals and other serials. **Services:** Interlibrary loan; copying; bibliographic searches (limited); library open to the public for reference use only. **Computerized Information Services:** MEDLINE; OnTyme Electronic Message Network Service, DOCLINE (electronic mail services). **Publications:** Medical Library Bulletin - to medical and allied health professionals, hospital personnel, and consortium members.

★16397★
UNIVERSITY OF MEDICINE AND DENTISTRY OF NEW JERSEY - GEORGE F. SMITH LIBRARY (Med)
30 Twelfth Ave. Phone: (201)456-4580
Newark, NJ 07103-2706 Philip Rosenstein, Dir. of Libs.
Staff: Prof 15; Other 15. **Subjects:** Health sciences. **Special Collections:** Rare book collection; archival collection. **Holdings:** 60,000 books; 75,000 bound periodical volumes; AV programs. **Subscriptions:** 2500 journals and other serials. **Services:** Interlibrary loan; copying; SDI; library open to the public for reference use only. **Automated Operations:** Computerized cataloging, acquisitions, serials, and circulation. **Computerized Information Services:** BRS Information Technologies, NLM, OCLC. Performs searches on fee basis. Contact Person: Sushila Kapadia, Info.Sys.Supv., 456-5318. **Networks/Consortia:** Member of Greater Northeastern Regional Medical Library Program, Essex-Hudson Regional Library Cooperative. **Publications:** Periodicals holdings, biennial; Library Newsletter, 4/year. **Special Catalogs:** Media Catalog (book); Rare Book Catalog (book). **Staff:** Reginald W. Smith, Assoc.Dir. of Libs.; Victor Basile, Asst.Libn.; Madeline Taylor, Asst.Libn.; George Sprung, Ref.Libn.; Melvin White, Chf., Circ.; Jackie K. Bush, Asst.Chf., Circ.; Valentine Allen, ILL; Laura Barrett, AV Libn.; Janice Rettino, Mgr., Univ.Lib.Sys.; Robert Cupryk, Ref.Libn.; Daria Gorman, Cat.; Barbara Packard, Chf.Cat.; Beth Lapow, Acq.Libn.; Barbara Irwin, Oral Hist. Archv..

★16398★
UNIVERSITY OF MEDICINE AND DENTISTRY OF NEW JERSEY - ROBERT WOOD JOHNSON LIBRARY OF THE HEALTH SCIENCES (Med)
CN 19 Phone: (201)937-7606
New Brunswick, NJ 08903 Mary R. Scanlon, Lib.Dir.
Founded: 1982. **Staff:** Prof 3; Other 5. **Subjects:** Clinical medicine, hospital administration, nursing. **Holdings:** 4611 books; 12,770 bound periodical volumes; 310 AV programs. **Subscriptions:** 461 journals and other serials. **Services:** Interlibrary loan; copying; library open to the public for reference use only. **Automated Operations:** Computerized serials and circulation. **Computerized Information Services:** MEDLINE, BRS Information Technologies, DIALOG Information Services; DOCLINE, MESSAGES (electronic mail services). Performs searches on fee basis. Contact Person: Kerry O'Rourke, Ref.Libn., 937-7604. **Networks/Consortia:** Member of Medical Resources Consortium of Central New Jersey (MEDCORE), Health Sciences Library Association of New Jersey. **Publications:** Library Notes, bimonthly - available upon request. **Staff:** Robert Gessner, Asst.Ref.Libn..

★16399★
UNIVERSITY OF MEDICINE AND DENTISTRY OF NEW JERSEY - ROBERT WOOD JOHNSON MEDICAL SCHOOL - MEDIA LIBRARY (Med)
675 Hoes Ln. Phone: (201)463-4460
Piscataway, NJ 08854-5635 Zana Early, Media Libn.
Staff: Prof 1; Other 2. **Subjects:** Medicine, allied health sciences. **Holdings:** 750 books; 2200 AV programs; 400 tapes of lectures; 18 VF drawers; 35 software programs. **Services:** Interlibrary loan; copying; SDI; library open to the public for reference use only. **Networks/Consortia:** Member of Medical Resources Consortium of Central New Jersey (MEDCORE).

★16400★
UNIVERSITY OF MEDICINE AND DENTISTRY OF NEW JERSEY - SCHOOL OF OSTEOPATHIC MEDICINE - HEALTH SCIENCES LIBRARY (Med)
Ambulatory Health Care Center
301 S. Central Plaza, Suite 1100
Laurel Rd. Phone: (609)346-6800
Stratford, NJ 08084 Judith Schuback Cohn, Lib.Dir.
Founded: 1974. **Staff:** Prof 3; Other 4. **Subjects:** Medicine, nursing, hospital administration, allied health sciences. **Special Collections:** Osteopathy. **Holdings:** 2500 books; 8000 bound periodical volumes; 300 AV programs; 250 government documents; 2 vertical files; 200 reels of microfilm. **Subscriptions:** 530 journals and other serials. **Services:** Interlibrary loan; copying; SDI; library open to the public by appointment. **Automated Operations:** Computerized cataloging. **Computerized Information Services:** MEDLARS, BRS Information Technologies, DIALOG Information Services; MESSAGES, Email, OnTyme Electronic Message Network Service (electronic mail services). Performs searches on fee basis. Contact Person: Janice K. Skica, Pub.Serv.Libn., 346-6810. **Networks/Consortia:** Member of BHSL, New Jersey Health Sciences Library Network (NJHSN), Pinelands Consortium. **Publications:** News Bulletin, monthly - for internal distribution only. **Staff:** Micki McIntyre, Info.Mgt.Libn.; Marianne Ryan, ILL; Martha Lawrence, Ser.; Christina Branyan, Circ..

★16401★
UNIVERSITY OF MIAMI - DOROTHY & LEWIS ROSENSTIEL SCHOOL OF MARINE & ATMOSPHERIC SCIENCES - LIBRARY (Biol Sci, Sci-Engr)
4600 Rickenbacker Causeway Phone: (305)361-4007
Miami, FL 33149 Kay K. Hale, Libn.
Staff: Prof 2; Other 3. **Subjects:** Marine sciences (especially tropical), biology, fisheries, marine geology and geophysics, ocean engineering, physical and chemical oceanography, atmospheric sciences, marine affairs. **Holdings:** 45,000 volumes; 25,000 reprints; 600 reels of microfilm; 1000 microfiche; 1242 microcards; 45 sets of oceanographic expedition reports; 400 atlases; 2500 nautical charts. **Subscriptions:** 1100 journals and other serials. **Services:** Interlibrary loan; copying; library open to the public for reference use only. **Computerized Information Services:** DIALOG Information Services, OCLC. **Networks/Consortia:** Member of SOLINET.

★16402★
UNIVERSITY OF MIAMI - INTELLIGENT COMPUTER SYSTEMS RESEARCH INSTITUTE - LIBRARY (Comp Sci)
Box 248235
Coral Gables, FL 33124 Phone: (305)284-5195
Founded: 1983. **Subjects:** Computer systems. **Holdings:** 2000 volumes. **Services:** Library not open to the public. **Computerized Information Services:** Internal database.

★16403★
UNIVERSITY OF MIAMI - LOWE ART MUSEUM LIBRARY (Art)
1301 Stanford Dr. Phone: (305)284-3535
Coral Gables, FL 33146 Ira Licht, Dir.
Founded: 1971. **Subjects:** Art and art history. **Holdings:** 4000 books; 2500 unbound periodical volumes; 4000 museum exhibition catalogs; 27,000 slides. **Subscriptions:** 12 journals and other serials. **Services:** Library open to the public by appointment.

★16404★
UNIVERSITY OF MIAMI - MORTON COLLECTANEA (Biol Sci)
Box 8204 Phone: (305)284-3741
Coral Gables, FL 33124 Dr. Julia F. Morton, Dir.
Founded: 1932. **Staff:** Prof 1; Other 2. **Subjects:** Economic botany. **Special Collections:** Tropical fruits and vegetables; poisonous plants; medicinal plants; edible wild plants; aquatic plants; honeybee plants; horticulture. **Holdings:** 5800 books; 3500 unbound journals; 186 VF drawers of plant species subject files; field investigations; lectures. **Subscriptions:** 25 journals and other serials. **Services:** Copying; consultations; library open to scientists and students from other institutions. **Publications:** Communications.

★16405★
UNIVERSITY OF MIAMI - OTTO G. RICHTER LIBRARY - ARCHIVES & SPECIAL COLLECTIONS DIVISION (Hist)
Coral Gables, FL 33124 Phone: (305)284-3247
Helen C. Purdy, Hd., Archv. & Spec.Coll.
Founded: 1926. **Staff:** Prof 3; Other 4. **Subjects:** University history, Floridiana, Cuba and Cuban exiles, Jamaica, Colombia, Latin America. **Holdings:** University Collection (1680 linear feet); Mark F. Boyd Collection (Florida; 31 linear feet); Minnie Moore Willson Collection (Florida; 28.38 linear feet); American Literary Agency Collection, 1980-1983 (10 linear feet); Latin America, 1948-1980 (10 linear feet); Bernhardt E. Muller Collection (Opalocka, FL; 19.8 cubic feet); A. Curtis Wilgus Collection (Latin America; 174.73 linear feet); 35,687 books; 10,979 volumes of periodicals; 849 manuscripts; 1658 dissertations; 3033 masters' theses; 854 audiotapes; 101 audio and video cassettes; 20 16mm films. **Services:** Interlibrary loan; copying; department open to the public for serious research. **Automated Operations:** Computerized cataloging. **Staff:** Esperanza B. Varona, Asst.Libn.; John McMinn, Cat..

★16406★
UNIVERSITY OF MIAMI - SCHOOL OF LAW LIBRARY (Law)
Box 248087 Phone: (305)284-2250
Coral Gables, FL 33124 Westwell R. Daniels, Law Libn.
Staff: Prof 13; Other 22. **Subjects:** Law - Anglo-American, Latin American, Caribbean area, European, international. **Holdings:** 264,150 volumes; 271,512 microforms. **Subscriptions:** 6017 journals and other serials. **Services:** Interlibrary loan; library open to those doing legal research. **Automated Operations:** Computerized cataloging, acquisitions, and serials. **Computerized Information Services:** LEXIS, NEXIS, WESTLAW, DIALOG Information Services, OCLC. **Networks/Consortia:** Member of SOLINET. **Staff:** Felice K. Lowell, Asst.Libn.; Warren Rosmarin, Assoc.Libn.; Roberta F. Studwell, Ref.; Amber Lee Smith, Foreign and Intl. Law Libn.; Beth Gwynn, Ref.Libn.; Leila Mestrits, Cat.; Michael Petit, Acq.Libn.; Emerita Cuesta, Circ.Libn.; Linda Golian, Ser.Libn.; E.J. Yera, Ref..

★16407★
UNIVERSITY OF MIAMI - SCHOOL OF MEDICINE - BASCOM PALMER EYE INSTITUTE - LIBRARY (Med)
Ann Bates Leach Eye Hospital
900 N.W. 17th St.
Box 016880 Phone: (305)326-6078
Miami, FL 33101 Reva Hurtes, Libn.
Founded: 1962. **Staff:** Prof 1; Other 2. **Subjects:** Ophthalmology, visual optics, visual physiology and anatomy. **Special Collections:** Historical and rare books (3000 volumes). **Holdings:** 15,000 volumes; AV programs. **Subscriptions:** 200 journals and other serials. **Services:** Interlibrary loan; copying; SDI; library open to the public on a limited basis. **Automated Operations:** Computerized cataloging. **Computerized Information Services:** BRS Information Technologies.

★16408★
UNIVERSITY OF MIAMI - SCHOOL OF MEDICINE - LOUIS CALDER MEMORIAL LIBRARY (Med)
Box 016950 Phone: (305)547-6441
Miami, FL 33101 Henry L. Lemkau, Jr., Dir.
Founded: 1952. **Staff:** Prof 10; Other 25. **Subjects:** Medicine, nursing. **Special Collections:** Weinstein Collection (paramedical sciences; 461 volumes); Ophthalmology Collection (8852 volumes); History of Medicine Collection (3832 volumes); Florida Collection (429 volumes); rare books (1036 volumes). **Holdings:** 56,254 books; 90,497 bound periodical volumes; 620 Florida pamphlets; 257 linear feet of archives; 20 linear feet of clipping files; 1821 illustrations; 212 medallions; 1151 portraits; 339 dissertations; 318 volumes of faculty publications. **Subscriptions:** 2154 journals and other serials. **Services:** Interlibrary loan; copying; SDI; library open to health science personnel and institutions of Southern Florida. **Computerized Information Services:** MEDLINE, DIALOG Information Services, BRS Information Technologies, Pergamon ORBIT InfoLine, Inc., OCLC; DOCLINE, OnTyme Electronic Message Network Service (electronic mail services). Performs searches on fee basis. Contact Person: David Ginn, Hd., Ref., 547-6648. **Networks/Consortia:** Member of Southeastern/Atlantic Regional Medical Library Services, Miami Health Sciences Library Consortium (MHSLC), SOLINET. **Publications:** Bulletin; guide; Fee Structure; Periodicals Currently Received; Annual Report. **Staff:** August La Rocco, Hea.Info. Network; Erica Powell, Hd., LRC; Teresita D. Sayus, Circ.Libn.; Yanira Garcia, Ref.Libn.; Isabel Caballero, Ref.Libn.; Van Afes, Hd., Tech.Serv.; James Clark, Hd., ILL; Frank Yanes, Mgr., Auto.Sys.; Amalia De La Vega, Hd., Acq. & Ser.; Suzetta C. Burrows, Vice Chair; Mary P. Dillon, Assoc.Dir./Database Creation; Thomas Williams, Assoc.Dir./Educ. & Info.Serv..

★16409★
UNIVERSITY OF MIAMI - SCHOOL OF MUSIC - ALBERT PICK MUSIC LIBRARY (Mus)
Coral Gables, FL 33124 Phone: (305)284-2429
Nancy Kobialka, Mus.Libn.
Founded: 1957. **Staff:** Prof 2; Other 4. **Subjects:** Music. **Special Collections:** Autographed recordings (composers and performers); ethnic recordings, especially Latin American, Yiddish, jazz; Inter-American Music Archive; Handleman Institute of Recorded Sound Archives (25,000 uncataloged recordings); Yiddish music scores and recordings. **Holdings:** 32,500 scores; 22,000 recordings. **Subscriptions:** 180 journals and other serials. **Services:** Interlibrary loan; library open to the public for reference use only. **Automated Operations:** Computerized cataloging. **Computerized Information Services:** OCLC. **Networks/Consortia:** Member of SOLINET. **Special Catalogs:** Inter-American Music Archive (card). **Staff:** Cheryl Gowing, Mus.Cat..

★16410★
UNIVERSITY OF MICHIGAN - AEROSPACE ENGINEERING DEPARTMENTAL LIBRARY (Sci-Engr)
221 Aerospace Engineering Bldg. Phone: (313)764-7200
Ann Arbor, MI 48109 Debbie Birdsall, Libn.
Staff: 1. **Subjects:** Aerospace science, plasma physics, fluid mechanics, aerodynamics, mathematics, structures and elasticity. **Holdings:** 1000 books; 6000 NASA reports and departmental dissertations. **Subscriptions:** 20 journals and other serials. **Services:** Library open to the public with permission of the department chairman.

★16411★
UNIVERSITY OF MICHIGAN - ALFRED TAUBMAN MEDICAL LIBRARY (Med)
1135 E. Catherine Phone: (313)764-1210
Ann Arbor, MI 48109-0726 Dottie Eakin, Act.Hd.Libn.
Founded: 1920. **Staff:** Prof 9; Other 26. **Subjects:** Basic medical sciences, clinical medicine, nursing, pharmacy, history of medicine. **Special Collections:** Crummer Collection (History of Medicine); Warthin Collection (Dance of Death). **Holdings:** 275,743 volumes. **Subscriptions:** 2334 journals and other serials. **Services:** Interlibrary loan; copying; SDI; library open to health science professionals only. **Automated Operations:** Computerized cataloging, acquisitions, and circulation. **Computerized Information Services:** DIALOG Information Services, BRS Information Technologies, Pergamon ORBIT InfoLine, Inc., NLM, RLIN. **Networks/Consortia:** Member of Greater Midwest Regional Medical Library Network. **Staff:** Helen F. Meranda, Rare Bks.Coord.; Diane G. Schwartz, Act.Pub.Serv.Coord.; Sandra C. Dow, Ref.Libn.; Whitney K. Field, Circ.Hd.; Nancy J. Rosenzweig, Reserve Supv.; Doris M. Mahony, Ref.Libn.; Barbara L. Shipman, Database Coord.; Marilynn Simpson, ILL Hd.; Carole Weber, Hd., Tech.Proc..

★16412★
UNIVERSITY OF MICHIGAN - ART & ARCHITECTURE LIBRARY (Art, Plan)
2106 Art & Architecture Bldg. Phone: (313)764-1303
Ann Arbor, MI 48109 Peggy Ann Kusnerz, Libn.
Staff: Prof 2; Other 4. **Subjects:** Architecture, art history, urban and regional planning, landscape architecture, applied art, art education, photography. **Special Collections:** Jens Jensen landscape drawings. **Holdings:** 55,000 books; 82 VF drawers of pamphlets; 1500 photographs; 50,000 slides; 1000 maps; 477 prints; 2000 drawings; microcomputer software programs. **Subscriptions:** 500 journals and other serials. **Services:** Interlibrary loan; copying; library open to the public with restrictions. **Automated Operations:** Computerized cataloging, acquisitions, and circulation. **Computerized Information Services:** RLIN. Performs searches on fee basis. **Networks/Consortia:** Member of RLG. **Publications:** Guide Series - available upon request. **Staff:** Dorothy Shields, Asst.Libn..

★16413★
UNIVERSITY OF MICHIGAN - ASIA LIBRARY (Area-Ethnic)
Hatcher Graduate Library, 4th Fl. Phone: (313)764-0406
Ann Arbor, MI 48109-1205 Weiying Wan, Hd.
Founded: 1947. **Staff:** Prof 7; Other 6. **Subjects:** East Asian humanities and social sciences, including anthropology, archeology, calligraphy, communism, drama, theater, economics, education, ethics, fine arts, geography, history, journalism, linguistics, phonology, library science, military history, military science, music, political science, religion, sociology. **Special Collections:** Union Research Institute Classified Files on China; Red Guards materials and classified files on the Cultural Revolution; rare editions of Chinese fiction in Japanese collections; Ming local gazetteers and literary collections; National Peking Library Rare Book Collection on microfilm; British Public Record Office Archives on China; non-Buddhist Tun-huang materials from the British Museum and the Bibliotheque Nationale; Japanese local history; materials on the Occupation of Japan; Japanese literature; Japanese Diet Proceedings; Bartlett Collection of Botanical Works and Materia Medica; Kamada Collection of Pre-war Japanese Works. **Holdings:** 235,256 volumes in Chinese; 194,027 volumes in Japanese; 3132 volumes in Korean; 18,010 reels of microfilm and 16,701 sheets of microfiche in Chinese; 6459 reels of microfilm and 5041 sheets of microfiche in Japanese. **Subscriptions:** 1654 journals and other serials; 31 newspapers. **Services:** Interlibrary loan; copying. **Publications:** Selective List of New Acquisitions, bimonthly. **Staff:** Choo Won Suh, Sr. Japanese Libn.; Sharon Ying, Chinese Cat.Supv.; Wei-Yi Ma, Chinese Bibliog.; Mei-Ying Lin, Chinese Cat.; Takaharu Yamakawa, Japanese Cat..

★16414★
UNIVERSITY OF MICHIGAN - BIOLOGICAL STATION LIBRARY (Biol Sci)
Pellston, MI 49769 Phone: (616)539-8408
Patricia B. Yocum, Hd.
Subjects: Zoology, botany, ichthyology, parisitology, limnology, ornithology. **Holdings:** 11,500 volumes; 1950 station papers. **Subscriptions:** 69 journals and other serials. **Services:** Library open only during summer. **Computerized Information Services:** Internal databases. **Remarks:** Telephone number in Ann Arbor, MI is (313)764-1494.

★16415★
UNIVERSITY OF MICHIGAN - BURN CENTER - LIBRARY (Med)
c/o Feller
1500 E. Medical Center Dr.
Box 0033 1B401 Phone: (313)936-9671
Ann Arbor, MI 48109 Julia L. Casa, Libn.
Staff: Prof 1. **Subjects:** Burns - research, care, prevention; rehabilitation; reconstructive surgery. **Holdings:** 125 books; 42,000 articles; 4 films. **Services:** Interlibrary loan; copying; library open to the public by appointment. **Publications:** International Bibliography on Burns, 1969 with annual supplements - for sale.

★16416★
UNIVERSITY OF MICHIGAN - CENTER FOR CONTINUING EDUCATION OF WOMEN - LIBRARY (Soc Sci)
350 S. Thayer Phone: (313)763-7080
Ann Arbor, MI 48104-1608 Deb Biggs, Info. & Rsrc.Coord.
Founded: 1965. **Staff:** Prof 1; Other 1. **Subjects:** Women - employment, education, status, counseling. **Special Collections:** Women's organizations collection (3 cubic feet); women in science series (20 audio- and videotapes). **Holdings:** 600 books; 2500 dissertations, manuscripts, unpublished papers, articles, and government publications; 200 bibliographies classified by subject; 3 cubic feet of vocational files; 1 cubic foot of clippings; Michigan Occupational Information System microfiche. **Subscriptions:** 65 journals and other serials. **Services:** Copying; library open to the public. **Computerized Information Services:** BRS Information Technologies. Performs searches on fee basis. **Publications:** Acquisition List, quarterly; library brochure; The Job Search, a selected annotated bibliography - all free upon request; Directory of Special Collections/Libraries Independent of the University of Michigan Library System, irregular; Joint Project with the University of Michigan Center for Afro-American/African Studies Library - for internal distribution only.

★16417★
UNIVERSITY OF MICHIGAN - CHEMISTRY LIBRARY (Sci-Engr)
2000 Chemistry Bldg. Phone: (313)764-7337
Ann Arbor, MI 48109-1055 Grace Baysinger, Chem.Libn.
Staff: Prof 1; Other 2. **Subjects:** Chemistry. **Special Collections:** Beilstein; Sadtler Proton NMR Spectra. **Holdings:** 53,000 volumes; Chemical Abstracts. **Subscriptions:** 400 journals and other serials. **Services:** Interlibrary loan; copying; library open to the public for reference use only. **Automated Operations:** Computerized cataloging and acquisitions. **Computerized Information Services:** DIALOG Information Services, RLIN, STN International.

★16418★
UNIVERSITY OF MICHIGAN - DENTISTRY LIBRARY (Med)
1100 Dentistry Phone: (313)764-1526
Ann Arbor, MI 48109-1078 Susan I. Seger, Hd.Libn.
Founded: 1908. **Staff:** Prof 2; Other 6. **Subjects:** Dentistry. **Special Collections:** Rare Book Collection (850). **Holdings:** 48,850 volumes; 25 VF drawers of pamphlets. **Subscriptions:** 636 journals and other serials. **Services:** Interlibrary loan; copying; library open to the public for reference use only. **Automated Operations:** Computerized cataloging, acquisitions, and circulation. **Computerized Information Services:** BRS Information Technologies, MEDLINE. **Networks/Consortia:** Member of Greater Midwest Regional Medical Library Network, RLG. **Publications:** Library Information Guide; Special Subject Bibliographies. **Special Indexes:** Index of M.S. theses (card).

★16419★
UNIVERSITY OF MICHIGAN - DEPARTMENT OF GEOLOGICAL SCIENCES - SUBSURFACE LABORATORY LIBRARY (Sci-Engr)
1006 C.C. Little Bldg. Phone: (313)764-2434
Ann Arbor, MI 48109-1063 Joyce M. Budai, Dir.
Staff: Prof 1; Other 5. **Subjects:** Geology, stratigraphy, sedimentary rocks, sedimentation, sedimentary geochemistry. **Special Collections:** Michigan well history central system file; subsurface geology materials and information. **Holdings:** 500 well cores; cuttings for 4000 wells; petrophysical logs for 2300 wells. **Services:** Interlibrary loan; copying; library open to the public. **Automated Operations:** Computerized cataloging and acquisitions. **Computerized Information Services:** MICRO Data Management System (internal database). Performs searches on fee basis. **Special Catalogs:** Core, mounted strip log, unmounted cuttings, electric log, and descriptive log catalogs.

★16420★
UNIVERSITY OF MICHIGAN - DEPARTMENT OF RARE BOOKS AND SPECIAL COLLECTIONS - LIBRARY (Rare Book)
711 Hatcher Graduate Library
Ann Arbor, MI 48109-1205 Phone: (313)764-9377
Staff: Prof 4; Other 5. **Subjects:** Rare books on all branches of knowledge. **Special Collections:** Worcester Philippine Collection; imaginary voyages; history of science; English and American drama; incunabula; manuscripts - biblical, medieval, renaissance, modern, Islamic; papyri (7000 items); theater collections; Shakespeare; information science and micrographics; military art and science; documents of the Weimar Republic and Nazi periods; Labadie Collection (social protest movements; 105 linear feet of vertical files; 45,488 other items). **Holdings:** 170,000 books, bound periodical volumes, pamphlets, nonbook materials; 105 linear feet of vertical files; 650 linear feet of modern manuscripts. **Services:** Interlibrary loan; copying (both limited); collection open to qualified researchers. **Automated Operations:** Computerized cataloging, acquisitions, and circulation. **Computerized Information Services:** Labadie Database (internal database); MTS (electronic mail service). Performs searches free of charge. Contact Person: R. Anne Okey, Asst. Labadie Coll.Libn.. **Networks/Consortia:** Member of RLG. **Special Catalogs:** Exhibition checklists and occasional catalogs. **Staff:** Helen S. Butz, Rare Bk.Libn.; Karla Vandersypen, Asst. Rare Bk.Libn.; Kathryn L. Beam, Ms.Libn.; Edward C. Weber, Labadie Coll.Libn.; David R. Whitesell, Supv..

★16421★
UNIVERSITY OF MICHIGAN - ENGINEERING-TRANSPORTATION LIBRARY (Trans, Sci-Engr)
312 Undergraduate Library Bldg. Phone: (313)764-7494
Ann Arbor, MI 48109-1185 Maurita Peterson Holland, Hd.
Founded: 1903. **Staff:** Prof 4; Other 10. **Subjects:** All divisions and aspects of engineering except nuclear engineering; all divisions and aspects of transportation. **Special Collections:** Early U.S. canals and railroads; Currier and Ives prints. **Holdings:** 450,000 volumes. **Subscriptions:** 2600 journals and other serials. **Services:** Interlibrary loan; copying. **Computerized Information Services:** DIALOG Information Services, Pergamon ORBIT InfoLine, Inc., Integrated Technical Information System (ITIS), NASA/RECON, QL Systems, CAS ONLINE, BRS Information Technologies, DTIC, VU/TEXT Information Services, U.S. Patent Classification System; BITNET, EDUNET (electronic mail services). **Publications:** Library News, monthly - free upon request. **Staff:**

Sharon Balius, Asst.Hd.; Joe Badics, Hd., Ser.; Charles Curtiss, Hd., Circ.; Theresa Lee, Asst.Libn..

★16422★
UNIVERSITY OF MICHIGAN - ENGLISH LANGUAGE INSTITUTE AND LINGUISTICS LIBRARY (Educ)
3003 North University Bldg. Phone: (313)764-2413
Ann Arbor, MI 48109 Patricia M. Aldridge, Libn.
Founded: 1960. **Staff:** 2. **Subjects:** Teaching English as a foreign language, teaching modern foreign language, English grammar, linguistics, psycholinguistics, sociolinguistics, bilingual education, language laboratories, foreign students in the U.S. **Holdings:** 6750 books and pamphlets; 400 boxed volumes of periodicals; 32 VF drawers; 15 series of Working Papers; 60 videotapes; audiotapes; microfiche; microfilm. **Subscriptions:** 105 journals and other serials. **Services:** Interlibrary loan; copying; library open to the public for reference use only on request. **Remarks:** Includes the holdings of the Linguistics Department Library.

★16423★
UNIVERSITY OF MICHIGAN - FINE ARTS LIBRARY (Art)
260 Tappan Hall Phone: (313)764-5405
Ann Arbor, MI 48109 Margaret P. Jensen, Hd.
Staff: Prof 1; Other 2. **Subjects:** History of art and architecture. **Holdings:** 61,040 volumes; 32 VF drawers. **Subscriptions:** 285 journals and other serials. **Services:** Interlibrary loan; library open to the public for reference use only.

★16424★
UNIVERSITY OF MICHIGAN - HISTORY OF ART DEPARTMENT - ARCHIVES OF ASIAN ART (Art)
519 S. State
Tappan Hall, Rm. 50 Phone: (313)764-5555
Ann Arbor, MI 48109-1357 Wendy Holden, Cur.
Staff: Prof 2; Other 4. **Subjects:** Art - Chinese, Japanese, South and Southeast Asian. **Special Collections:** Photographs of paintings from the National Palace Museum, Taiwan; Indian Buddhist cave sites; Thai art; Islamic manuscripts. **Holdings:** 80,000 photographs and mounted reproductions. **Services:** Archives open to the public for reference use only; slides and photographs of Chinese and Japanese paintings available for sale to institutions.

★16425★
UNIVERSITY OF MICHIGAN - HISTORY OF ART DEPARTMENT - COLLECTION OF SLIDES AND PHOTOGRAPHS (Art)
20A Tappan Hall Phone: (313)764-5404
Ann Arbor, MI 48109 Joy Alexander, Cur.
Founded: 1946. **Staff:** Prof 6; Other 35. **Subjects:** History of art. **Holdings:** 240,000 35mm transparencies; 30,000 lantern slides; 190,000 photographs and mounted reproductions. **Services:** Illustrative material provided to history of art faculty for lectures and research.

★16426★
UNIVERSITY OF MICHIGAN - HOPWOOD ROOM (Hum)
1006 Angell Hall Phone: (313)764-6296
Ann Arbor, MI 48109 Andrea Beauchamp, Prog.Assoc.
Subjects: Contemporary literature. **Special Collections:** Hopwood Awards manuscripts. **Holdings:** Figures not available.

★16427★
UNIVERSITY OF MICHIGAN - INFORMATION AND LIBRARY STUDIES LIBRARY (Info Sci)
300 Hatcher Graduate Library Phone: (313)764-9375
Ann Arbor, MI 48109-1205 Judith C. Avery, Libn.
Staff: Prof 1; Other 2. **Subjects:** Library science, history of libraries, history of publishing, history of bookselling, history of the book, bibliography, children's literature, online information services, information storage and retrieval, micrographics. **Holdings:** 52,000 books; 460 dissertations; 453 reels of microfilm; 2608 sheets of microfiche; 100 AV programs. **Subscriptions:** 474 journals and other serials. **Services:** Interlibrary loan; library open to the public. **Automated Operations:** Computerized cataloging, acquisitions, and circulation. **Computerized Information Services:** DIALOG Information Services, RLIN, BRS Information Technologies, WILSONLINE. **Networks/Consortia:** Member of RLG. **Staff:** Ann Thomas, Lib.Supv..

★16428★
UNIVERSITY OF MICHIGAN - INSTITUTE FOR SOCIAL RESEARCH - INTER-UNIVERSITY CONSORTIUM FOR POLITICAL AND SOCIAL RESEARCH (Info Sci)
Box 1248 Phone: (313)764-2570
Ann Arbor, MI 48106 Dr. Jerome M. Clubb, Exec.Dir.
Staff: Prof 13; Other 27. **Subjects:** International and national social, economic, and political data: elections, census; international relations; aging and the aging process; crime, deviance, and criminal justice; recreation and leisure. **Holdings:** 1500 collections of machine-readable data representing 24,000 discrete data files. **Services:** Services open to the public on a fee basis. **Automated Operations:** Computerized public access catalog, cataloging, and acquisitions. **Computerized Information Services:** CDNet; ICPSR Guide, ICPSR Variables, ICPSR Rollcalls, (internal databases); BITNET, InterNet Corporation (electronic mail services). **Publications:** Guide to Resources and Services, annual; annual report; ICPSR's Bulletin, quarterly; codebooks. **Also Known As:** ICPSR. **Remarks:** An alternate telephone number is 763-5010. **Staff:** Erik W. Austin, Dir., Arch.Dev.; Janet K. Vaura, Tech.Dir.; Robert J. Adler, Data Libn..

★16429★
UNIVERSITY OF MICHIGAN - INSTITUTE FOR SOCIAL RESEARCH - LIBRARY (Soc Sci)
426 Thompson St.
Box 1248 Phone: (313)764-8513
Ann Arbor, MI 48109 Mrs. Adye Bel Evans, Libn.
Staff: Prof 1; Other 1. **Subjects:** Social psychology, industrial psychology, mental health, economic behavior. **Holdings:** 3000 books, monographs, unpublished papers, and research reports comprising publications of institute staff; 1000 research reports produced by other survey institutions. **Subscriptions:** 100 journals and other serials. **Services:** Interlibrary loan; copying; library open to the public for reference use only. **Publications:** Bibliography of institute-authored publications, annual with five-year cumulations.

★16430★
UNIVERSITY OF MICHIGAN - KRESGE BUSINESS ADMINISTRATION LIBRARY (Bus-Fin)
School of Business Administration
Tappan & Monroe Sts. Phone: (313)764-7356
Ann Arbor, MI 48109-1234 Dr. Elaine K. Didier, Dir.
Founded: 1925. **Staff:** Prof 6; Other 10. **Subjects:** General business, accounting, finance, marketing, statistics, international banking and finance, human resource management, organizational behavior. **Special Collections:** Career Resources Center (files of 500 companies). **Holdings:** 208,000 volumes; government documents; corporate financial reports; 10K reports; loose-leaf services; working papers. **Subscriptions:** 1200 journals and 1500 other serials. **Services:** Library open to the public with restrictions. **Automated Operations:** Computerized cataloging. **Computerized Information Services:** DIALOG Information Services, BRS Information Technologies, Dow Jones News/Retrieval, InfoTrac, Disclosure Information Group, RLIN; internal databases; MTS (electronic mail service). **Networks/Consortia:** Member of RLG, Michigan Library Consortium (MLC).

★16431★
UNIVERSITY OF MICHIGAN - LAW LIBRARY (Law)
Legal Research Bldg. Phone: (313)764-9322
Ann Arbor, MI 48109-1210 Margaret A. Leary, Dir.
Founded: 1859. **Staff:** Prof 14; Other 27. **Subjects:** Anglo-American law, foreign law, international law, international organizations, Roman law, legal bibliography. **Holdings:** 650,000 volumes. **Subscriptions:** 9783 journals and other serials. **Services:** Interlibrary loan; copying; library open to the public. **Automated Operations:** Computerized cataloging and circulation. **Computerized Information Services:** LEXIS, WESTLAW, DIALOG Information Services. **Networks/Consortia:** Member of RLG. **Remarks:** Fax: (313)936-3884. **Staff:** Linda Maslow, Chf.Ref.Libn.; Bobbie Snow, Chf.Circ.Libn.; Evelyn L. Smith, Chf., Tech.Serv.Libn..

★16432★
UNIVERSITY OF MICHIGAN - MAP LIBRARY (Geog-Map)
825 Hatcher Graduate Library Phone: (313)764-0407
Ann Arbor, MI 48109-1205 Kathleen M. Bergen, Map Libn.
Staff: Prof 1; Other 2. **Subjects:** Maps - topographic, geologic, political, thematic; nautical charts; history of cartography. **Holdings:** 280,000 sheet maps; 5000 pre-1900 maps; 7000 monographs, serials, atlases, gazetteers; cartobibliographies; 2400 aerial photographs; satellite images. **Services:** Copying; map-o-graph; library open to the public. **Automated Operations:** Computerized cataloging, acquisitions, serials, and circulation. **Computerized Information Services:** Map Publishers Database (internal

database); ALANET (electronic mail service). **Staff:** Tim Utter, Supv.; Jerry Thornton, Cat..

★16433★
UNIVERSITY OF MICHIGAN - MATHEMATICS LIBRARY (Sci-Engr)
3027 Angell Hall Phone: (313)764-7266
Ann Arbor, MI 48109-1003 Jack W. Weigel, Libn.
Founded: 1930. **Staff:** Prof 1; Other 2. **Subjects:** Mathematics, statistics, history of mathematics, actuarial insurance. **Holdings:** 52,500 volumes; 700 reels of microfilm; 550 dissertations. **Subscriptions:** 720 journals and other serials. **Services:** Interlibrary loan; library open to the public for reference use only. **Computerized Information Services:** DIALOG Information Services, BRS Information Technologies, STN International. Performs searches on fee basis.

★16434★
UNIVERSITY OF MICHIGAN - MATTHAEI BOTANICAL GARDENS - LIBRARY (Biol Sci)
1800 N. Dixboro Rd. Phone: (313)763-7060
Ann Arbor, MI 48105-9741 Laurianne L. Hannan, Interp. Botanist
Staff: Prof 1. **Subjects:** Botany, horticulture. **Holdings:** 1700 volumes; 8 VF drawers of brochures and clippings. **Subscriptions:** 34 journals and other serials. **Services:** Library open to the public for reference use only.

★16435★
UNIVERSITY OF MICHIGAN - MICHIGAN HISTORICAL COLLECTIONS - BENTLEY HISTORICAL LIBRARY (Hist)
1150 Beal Phone: (313)764-3482
Ann Arbor, MI 48109-2113 Francis X. Blouin, Jr., Dir.
Staff: Prof 10; Other 6. **Subjects:** Michigan - history, religion, urban affairs, education, business; University of Michigan; politics and government of Michigan and United States; ethnic groups. **Special Collections:** Philippine Islands; Sino-American relations; printed and manuscript holdings on temperance and prohibition in the U.S. **Holdings:** 45,000 volumes; 20,000 linear feet of manuscripts and archives; 6500 collections; 1700 maps; 350 reels of microfilm of newspapers; 32 VF drawers; 500,000 photographs. **Subscriptions:** 176 journals and other serials. **Services:** Interlibrary loan (limited); copying; library open to the public. **Automated Operations:** Computerized cataloging and serials. **Computerized Information Services:** RLIN. **Networks/Consortia:** Member of RLG. **Publications:** Annual Report; Bulletins, annual; Michigan Gazette, annual; Bibliographical series, irregular; Guide to the Michigan Historical Collections. **Staff:** William K. Wallach, Asst.Dir.; Thomas Powers, Archv.; Nancy Bartlett, Ref.Archv.; James Craven, Consrv.; Kenneth Scheffel, Assoc.Archv.; Leonard Coombs, Assoc.Archv.; Marjorie Barritt, Asst.Archv.; Frank Boles, Asst.Archv.; Kathleen Koehler, Asst.Archv..

★16436★
UNIVERSITY OF MICHIGAN - MICHIGAN INFORMATION TRANSFER SOURCE (MITS) (Info Sci)
106 Hatcher Graduate Library Phone: (313)763-5060
Ann Arbor, MI 48109-1205 Anne K. Beaubien, Dir.
Founded: 1980. **Staff:** Prof 2; Other 7. **Services:** Interlibrary loan; SDI; organization of materials, patents, translations. **Computerized Information Services:** DIALOG Information Services, BRS Information Technologies, Pergamon ORBIT InfoLine, Inc., VU/TEXT Information Services, WILSONLINE. **Networks/Consortia:** Member of RLG. **Publications:** Brochure; bibliographies. **Remarks:** MITS provides research and information services to business, industry, and individuals on a cost recovery basis. Fee schedule available upon request.

★16437★
UNIVERSITY OF MICHIGAN - MUSEUMS LIBRARY (Biol Sci)
2500 Ruthven Museums Bldg. Phone: (313)764-0467
Ann Arbor, MI 48109 Patricia B. Yocum, Hd.
Founded: 1928. **Staff:** Prof 1; Other 2. **Subjects:** Natural history with emphasis on systematic and taxonomic works. **Special Collections:** Anthropology; paleontology; botany; birds; herpetology; fish; insects; mammals; mollusks. **Holdings:** 104,000 volumes. **Subscriptions:** 1400 journals and other serials. **Automated Operations:** Computerized public access catalog. **Computerized Information Services:** DIALOG Information Services, RLIN, BRS Information Technologies. **Networks/Consortia:** Member of RLG.

★16438★
UNIVERSITY OF MICHIGAN - MUSIC LIBRARY (Mus)
3250 Earl V. Moore Bldg., N. Campus Phone: (313)764-2512
Ann Arbor, MI 48109-2085 Peggy E. Daub, Mus.Libn.
Founded: 1942. **Staff:** Prof 2; Other 4. **Subjects:** Music. **Special Collections:** Rare book collection; women's music collection (1800 scores). **Holdings:** 77,500 books and scores; 3000 reels of microfilm; 22,000 recordings. **Subscriptions:** 400 journals and other serials. **Services:** Interlibrary loan; copying; library open to the public for reference use only. **Automated Operations:** Computerized circulation. **Computerized Information Services:** DIALOG Information Services, BRS Information Technologies, RLIN. Performs searches on fee basis. Contact Person: W. Bjorke, Asst.Hd.. **Networks/Consortia:** Member of RLG.

★16439★
UNIVERSITY OF MICHIGAN - NATURAL SCIENCE LIBRARY (Sci-Engr, Biol Sci)
3140 Natural Science Bldg. Phone: (313)764-1494
Ann Arbor, MI 48109-1048 Patricia B. Yocum, Hd.
Founded: 1917. **Staff:** Prof 3; Other 5. **Subjects:** Biology, geology, natural resources. **Special Collections:** Masters' theses. **Holdings:** 165,000 volumes; 2100 masters' theses. **Subscriptions:** 1800 journals and other serials. **Services:** Copying; library open to the public for reference use only. **Automated Operations:** Computerized public access catalog and circulation. **Computerized Information Services:** DIALOG Information Services, BRS Information Technologies, RLIN. **Networks/Consortia:** Member of RLG.

★16440★
UNIVERSITY OF MICHIGAN - NORTH ENGINEERING LIBRARY (Energy, Biol Sci)
1100 Dow Phone: (313)764-5298
Ann Arbor, MI 48109 Maurita Peterson Holland, Hd.
Founded: 1974. **Staff:** Prof 1; Other 2. **Subjects:** Nuclear power, reactor design and construction, radiation utilization and effects, natural science aspect of the Great Lakes, limnology, biophysics, biochemistry. **Holdings:** 70,000 volumes; 40,000 hardcopy Atomic Energy Commission and DOE reports; 80,000 AEC microcards; 600,000 AEC and DOE microfiche. **Subscriptions:** 300 journals and other serials. **Services:** Interlibrary loan; copying; library open to the public. **Computerized Information Services:** DIALOG Information Services, BRS Information Technologies, Pergamon ORBIT InfoLine, Inc., Integrated Technical Information System (ITIS), NASA/RECON, QL Systems; BITNET, EDUNET (electronic mail services).

★16441★
UNIVERSITY OF MICHIGAN - PHYSICS-ASTRONOMY LIBRARY (Sci-Engr)
290 Dennison Bldg. Phone: (313)764-3442
Ann Arbor, MI 48109-1090 Jack W. Weigel, Libn.
Founded: 1924. **Staff:** Prof 1; Other 2. **Subjects:** Astronomy, history of astronomy, physics, applied mathematics. **Holdings:** 60,000 volumes; 108 reels of microfilm; 578 technical reports; 750 dissertations. **Subscriptions:** 880 journals and other serials. **Services:** Interlibrary loan; library open to the public for reference use only. **Computerized Information Services:** DIALOG Information Services, BRS Information Technologies, STN International. Performs searches on fee basis.

★16442★
UNIVERSITY OF MICHIGAN - SCHOOL OF EDUCATION & SCHOOL OF INFORMATION AND LIBRARY STUDIES - INSTRUCTIONAL STRATEGY SERVICES (Educ, Info Sci, Comp Sci)
3012 School of Education
Corner East and South University Avenues Phone: (313)764-0519
Ann Arbor, MI 48109 Claire Sandler, Dir.
Founded: 1979. **Staff:** Prof 4; Other 35. **Subjects:** Elementary and secondary education, library science, higher education, microcomputers, media services. **Special Collections:** Resource Center (microcomputers; textbooks; curriculum guides; teaching aids; AV programs); Media Services; Graphics Services. **Holdings:** 1000 books; 6500 textbooks; 2300 dissertations; 1200 AV programs; 2000 microcomputer programs; 36 VF drawers of curriculum guides; 32 VF drawers of information files; 1500 tests. **Subscriptions:** 40 journals and other serials. **Services:** Copying; demonstration and evaluation of curriculum materials, microcomputers, and software; consultation; workshops; services open to the public. **Computerized Information Services:** BRS Information Technologies, DIALOG Information Services; internal databases. Performs searches on fee basis. **Networks/Consortia:** Member of Michigan Library Consortium (MLC). **Special Catalogs:** Software catalog (computerized). **Formerly:**

School of Education & School of Library Science. **Staff:** Jennifer Marquardt, Rsrc.Ctr.; Ronald Miller, Media Serv.; Stephan Burdick, Graphics Serv..

★16443★
UNIVERSITY OF MICHIGAN - SCHOOL OF PUBLIC HEALTH - DEPARTMENT OF POPULATION PLANNING AND INTERNATIONAL HEALTH - REFERENCE COLLECTION (Soc Sci, Med)
Ann Arbor, MI 48109 Phone: (313)763-5732
Staff: Prof 2. **Subjects:** National and international population policy and family planning; educational and medical aspects of family planning; family planning systems; demography. **Holdings:** 500 books; 6000 unbound reports and documents; 1000 country files representing 70 countries; family planning program data; reprints; documents; conference proceedings. **Subscriptions:** 100 journals and other serials. **Services:** Collection open to the public for reference use only. **Automated Operations:** Computerized cataloging. **Computerized Information Services:** POPLINE, DIALOG Information Services. **Special Catalogs:** Holdings lists of country files, journals, and serials. **Staff:** June Grube, Libn.; Harriet Phinney, Libn..

★16444★
UNIVERSITY OF MICHIGAN - SCHOOL OF PUBLIC HEALTH - PUBLIC HEALTH LIBRARY (Med)
M2030 School of Public Health Phone: (313)764-5473
Ann Arbor, MI 48109 Mary Townsend, Hd.Libn.
Founded: 1943. **Staff:** Prof 2; Other 3. **Subjects:** Public health, environmental and industrial health, epidemiology, population planning, health services management and policy, biostatistics, health behavior, health education. **Holdings:** 60,000 volumes; 581 pamphlet boxes. **Subscriptions:** 500 journals and other serials. **Services:** Interlibrary loan; library open to other state university faculty and students in Michigan. **Automated Operations:** Computerized cataloging, acquisitions, and circulation. **Computerized Information Services:** DIALOG Information Services, BRS Information Technologies, NLM. **Networks/Consortia:** Member of RLG. **Staff:** Kirsten I. Lietz, Ref.Libn.; Kathleen Dow, Circ.Supv..

★16445★
UNIVERSITY OF MICHIGAN - SOCIAL WORK LIBRARY (Soc Sci)
1548 Frieze Bldg. Phone: (313)764-5169
Ann Arbor, MI 48109 Christina W. Neal, Hd.
Staff: Prof 1; Other 3. **Subjects:** Social work. **Special Collections:** Minority content in the curriculum; National Assessment of Juvenile Corrections (NAJEC); reprints; case studies. **Holdings:** 37,000 books; 200 boxes of pamphlets; 10 cassettes. **Subscriptions:** 500 journals and other serials. **Services:** Interlibrary loan; copying; consultation; library open to the public with restrictions. **Computerized Information Services:** BRS Information Technologies. **Publications:** Accessions list, semiannual - for internal distribution only; information leaflets, annual - available on request.

★16446★
UNIVERSITY OF MICHIGAN - SUMNER & LAURA FOSTER LIBRARY (Soc Sci)
Lorch Hall, Rm. 265 Phone: (313)763-6609
Ann Arbor, MI 48109-1220 Carol R. Wilson, Info.Rsrcs.Coord.
Founded: 1985. **Staff:** Prof 2; Other 6. **Subjects:** Economics, international development, public policy. **Special Collections:** African government documents (10,500 items); Sharfman Collection (economics); Livestock in Africa documentation (500 items). **Holdings:** 500 books; 400 series of working papers and research reports. **Subscriptions:** 403 journals and other serials. **Services:** Interlibrary loan; copying; SDI; library open to the public with restrictions. **Computerized Information Services:** Internal databases. **Publications:** Working Papers Acquisition Bulletin, monthly - for internal distribution only. **Staff:** Margo Williams, Asst. to Libn..

★16447★
UNIVERSITY OF MICHIGAN - TRANSPORTATION RESEARCH INSTITUTE - LIBRARY (Trans)
2901 Baxter Rd. Phone: (313)764-2171
Ann Arbor, MI 48109-2150 Ann C. Grimm, Hd.Libn.
Founded: 1966. **Staff:** Prof 2; Other 3. **Subjects:** Highway safety, accident investigation, biomechanics, driver behavior and characteristics, vehicle dynamics, shipbuilding, automotive industry. **Holdings:** 67,000 documents. **Subscriptions:** 200 journals and other serials. **Services:** Copying; library open to the public for reference use only. **Computerized Information Services:** DIALOG Information Services. **Publications:** UMTRI Research Review, bimonthly - by subscription; Transportation Research Information (acquisitions list), weekly - available on exchange or by subscription. **Staff:** R. Guy Gattis, Asst.Libn..

★16448★
UNIVERSITY OF MICHIGAN - TRANSPORTATION RESEARCH INSTITUTE - PUBLIC INFORMATION MATERIALS CENTER
2901 Baxter Rd.
Ann Arbor, MI 48109-2150
Founded: 1972. **Subjects:** Public information campaigns, program evaluation. **Holdings:** 900 journal articles/research reports; 250 radio and television commercials; 400 radio and television scripts; 750 pamphlets; 30 films and filmstrips; 350 print advertisements; 50 posters; 500 promotional gimmicks used in advertising campaigns. **Remarks:** Presently inactive.

★16449★
UNIVERSITY OF MICHIGAN - WILLIAM L. CLEMENTS LIBRARY (Hist)
S. University Ave. Phone: (313)764-2347
Ann Arbor, MI 48109 John C. Dann, Dir.
Founded: 1923. **Staff:** Prof 6; Other 3. **Subjects:** Rare Americana to 1877 - discovery and exploration, early settlement, Indian relations, colonial wars, American Revolution, beginnings of federal government, Northwest Territory, War of 1812, early reforms, Westward movement, Civil War, arts and crafts. **Holdings:** 60,000 volumes; 350 manuscript collections, 1740-1900; 36,000 printed and manuscript maps; 40,000 pieces of sheet music, 1790-1920. **Services:** Library open to the public with interview. **Computerized Information Services:** RLIN. **Networks/Consortia:** Member of RLG. **Publications:** American Magazine; Historical Chronicle, both 2/year - to members of Clement Library Associates. **Special Catalogs:** Guide to Manuscript Collections; Division of Maps; Guide to Manuscript Maps; Author/Title Catalog of Americana 1493-1860 in The William L. Clements Library (book, 7 volumes). **Staff:** Richard W. Ryan, Cur. of Bks.; Galen Wilson, Mss.Libn.; Arlene P. Shy, Hd., Rd.Serv.; David Bosse, Cur. of Maps.

★16450★
UNIVERSITY MICROFILMS INTERNATIONAL - LIBRARY (Publ)
300 N. Zeeb Rd. Phone: (313)761-4700
Ann Arbor, MI 48106 Joseph J. Fitzsimmons, Pres.
Founded: 1938. **Staff:** Prof 5. **Subjects:** Early English printed books, incunabula, early American printed books, early English and American periodicals, out-of-print books. **Holdings:** 800,000 dissertations; 113,000 out-of-print books; 175 major research collections; 13,000 periodicals on microfilm. **Services:** Library not open to the public. **Computerized Information Services:** DATRIX (doctoral research information; internal database). **Publications:** UMI Newsletter; Collections Guides and Indexes; Special Bibliographies; Dissertation Abstracts International; Masters Abstracts; Monograph Abstracts; American Doctoral Dissertations. **Special Catalogs:** Serials in Microform Catalog; Books on Demand Catalog. **Special Indexes:** Comprehensive Dissertation Index; Japanese Technical Abstracts and Japanese Current Research.

★16451★
UNIVERSITY OF MINNESOTA - AMES LIBRARY OF SOUTH ASIA (Area-Ethnic)
Wilson Library, S-10
309 19th Ave., S. Phone: (612)624-4857
Minneapolis, MN 55455 Donald Johnson, Hd.
Founded: 1908. **Staff:** Prof 1. **Subjects:** South Asia - history, economics, political science, art, literature, philology, philosophy, religion, music. **Special Collections:** French India (400 volumes); Portuguese India (includes the Trois Johnson Collection; 1500 volumes); Sanskrit series (4000 volumes). **Holdings:** 112,049 volumes; 8924 microforms; 17 feet of manuscripts; 1162 AV programs; 248 maps. **Subscriptions:** 81 journals and other serials. **Services:** Interlibrary loan; copying; library open to the public for reference use only. **Networks/Consortia:** Member of MINITEX, RLG. **Special Indexes:** Author-subject index of the Journal of Indian History; author-subject index of 19th century pamphlet collection.

★16452★
UNIVERSITY OF MINNESOTA - ARCHITECTURE LIBRARY (Art, Plan)
160 Architecture Bldg.
89 Church St., S.E. Phone: (612)624-6383
Minneapolis, MN 55455 A. Kristine Johnson, Hd.
Founded: 1913. **Staff:** Prof 1; Other 1. **Subjects:** Architecture, planning, landscape architecture, design methodology, energy conservation, interior design, environmental psychology. **Holdings:** 35,048 volumes; 381 AV

programs; 244 microforms; pamphlets; theses. **Subscriptions:** 232 journals and other serials. **Services:** Interlibrary loan; copying; library open to the public for reference use only. **Networks/Consortia:** Member of MINITEX, RLG. **Special Catalogs:** Thesis, video cassette, and pamphlet catalogs (card).

★16453★
UNIVERSITY OF MINNESOTA - BELL MUSEUM OF NATURAL HISTORY - LIBRARY (Biol Sci)
10 Church St., S.E. Phone: (612)624-1639
Minneapolis, MN 55455 Tom English, Hd.
Staff: Prof 1. **Subjects:** Ornithology, ethology, mammalogy, herpetology, animal behavior, taxonomy. **Holdings:** 11,658 volumes; 56 AV programs. **Subscriptions:** 297 journals and other serials. **Services:** Interlibrary loan; library open to the public for reference only. **Networks/Consortia:** Member of MINITEX, RLG.

★16454★
UNIVERSITY OF MINNESOTA - BIOMEDICAL LIBRARY (Med, Biol Sci)
Diehl Hall
505 Essex St., S.E. Phone: (612)626-3260
Minneapolis, MN 55455 Sherrilynne Fuller, Dir.
Founded: 1892. **Staff:** Prof 13; Other 16. **Subjects:** Medicine and allied health sciences, nursing, dentistry, pharmacy, public health, biology. **Holdings:** 344,473 volumes; 1781 AV programs. **Subscriptions:** 4330 journals and other serials. **Services:** Interlibrary loan; copying; library open to the public for reference use only. **Automated Operations:** Computerized cataloging, acquisitions, and serials. **Computerized Information Services:** BRS Information Technologies, MEDLARS, Pergamon ORBIT InfoLine, Inc., DIALOG Information Services. Performs searches on fee basis. **Networks/Consortia:** Member of Greater Midwest Regional Medical Library Network, MINITEX, RLG. **Publications:** Bio-Medical Library Bulletin.

★16455★
UNIVERSITY OF MINNESOTA - BIOMEDICAL LIBRARY - OWEN H. WANGENSTEEN HISTORICAL LIBRARY OF BIOLOGY AND MEDICINE (Biol Sci, Med)
505 Essex St., S.E. Phone: (612)626-6881
Minneapolis, MN 55455 Judith Overmier, Ph.D., Cur.
Founded: 1967. **Staff:** Prof 1. **Subjects:** Health sciences, surgery, nursing, tuberculosis, pharmacy, medicine. **Special Collections:** Burch Ophthalmology Collection; Mackall Mushroom Collection; Cole Collection of Orthopedic Surgery; College of American Pathology Manuscripts and Archives; Minnesota Association of Public Health Archives; Spink Brucellosis Collection; Minnesota Health Science Libraries Association Archives; medical and pharmaceutical artifacts. **Holdings:** 44,195 books. **Services:** Copying; library open to the public. **Automated Operations:** Computerized cataloging, acquisitions, and serials. **Networks/Consortia:** Member of MINITEX, RLG. **Special Indexes:** Index to author presentation copies.

★16456★
UNIVERSITY OF MINNESOTA - BUSINESS REFERENCE SERVICE (Bus-Fin)
Wilson Library, 2nd Fl.
309 19th Ave., S. Phone: (612)624-9066
Minneapolis, MN 55455 Judy Wells, Hd.
Staff: Prof 1; Other 2. **Subjects:** Business, finance and investments, marketing, accounting, management information systems, computer hardware and software, insurance, management science, transportation. **Holdings:** 5301 volumes; 80,410 microforms. **Subscriptions:** 562 journals and other serials. **Services:** Interlibrary loan; copying; service open to the public for reference use only. **Computerized Information Services:** DIALOG Information Services, BRS Information Technologies, Disclosure Information Group. **Networks/Consortia:** Member of MINITEX, RLG.

★16457★
UNIVERSITY OF MINNESOTA - CENTER FOR YOUTH DEVELOPMENT AND RESEARCH - RESOURCE ROOM (Soc Sci)
386 McNeal Hall
1985 Buford Ave.
St. Paul, MN 55108 Phone: (612)624-3700
Subjects: Youth. **Holdings:** 1000 books; 1000 clippings; 100 county reports. **Subscriptions:** 18 journals and other serials. **Services:** Center open to the public. **Publications:** Occasional papers and reports. **Special Catalogs:** Youth-related materials in the University of Minnesota libraries (card).

★16458★
UNIVERSITY OF MINNESOTA - CHARLES BABBAGE INSTITUTE COLLECTION (Comp Sci)
103 Walter Library
117 Pleasant St., S.E. Phone: (612)624-5050
Minneapolis, MN 55455 Bruce Bruemmer, Archv.
Staff: Prof 1. **Subjects:** History of information processing, computers and computing. **Holdings:** 588 volumes; 1250 linear feet of documents, oral interview transcripts, records, papers, computer manuals, reports; 222 AV programs. **Services:** Copying; collection open to researchers. **Publications:** Newsletter, quarterly - free upon request.

★16459★
UNIVERSITY OF MINNESOTA - CHILDREN'S LITERATURE RESEARCH COLLECTIONS (Hum)
109 Walter Library
117 Pleasant St., S.E. Phone: (612)624-4576
Minneapolis, MN 55455 Karen Nelson Hoyle, Cur.
Founded: 1949. **Staff:** Prof 1; Other 1. **Subjects:** Children's books - first editions, manuscripts, illustrations; children's periodicals; American and British dime novels, periodicals, story papers, pulps; Big Little Books; comic books. **Special Collections:** Kerlan Collection (39,000 books; manuscript materials for 2487 titles; illustration materials for 3223 titles; correspondence); Hess Collection (47,583 dime novels; 25,000 periodicals, story papers, pulps; 561 Big Little Books; 1200 comic books); Wanda Gag Collection (33 books; manuscript and illustration materials for 8 titles); Gustaf Tenggren Collection (150 books; illustration materials for 78 titles); Children's Periodicals Collection (64 19th century American titles; 26 19th century British titles); Series Books Collection (7859 books); Beulah Counts Rudolph Collection of Figurines, Wall Hangings and Book Marks (400 figurines; 68 wall hangings; 700 book marks); Paul Bunyan Collection (138 books; 8 linear feet of related materials); Ethnicity in Children's Literature; The Immigration Experience; Translation of Classics to English; Non-English Language books (3600 titles). **Holdings:** 47,330 volumes; 689.4 feet of manuscripts; 2511 illustrations; 127 microforms. **Subscriptions:** 29 journals and other serials. **Services:** Copying (limited); collections open for research upon application. **Networks/Consortia:** Member of RLG. **Publications:** List of brochures and bibliographies - available on request. **Special Catalogs:** The Kerlan Collection: Manuscripts and Illustrations, 1985 (book).

★16460★
UNIVERSITY OF MINNESOTA - CLASSICAL STUDIES DEPARTMENT - SEMINAR LIBRARY (Hum)
311 Folwell Hall
9 Pleasant St., S.E. Phone: (612)625-5353
Minneapolis, MN 55455 Prof. Eva C. Keuls, Libn.
Staff: Prof 1. **Subjects:** Latin, Greek, classical civilization. **Special Collections:** Classics Curriculum Library of elementary and intermediate texts. **Holdings:** 2000 volumes. **Services:** Copying; library open to the public with restrictions.

★16461★
UNIVERSITY OF MINNESOTA - DELOITTE HASKINS & SELLS TAX RESEARCH ROOM (Bus-Fin)
Wilson Library, 2nd Fl.
309 19th Ave., S. Phone: (612)624-9066
Minneapolis, MN 55455 Judy Wells, Hd.
Founded: 1978. **Subjects:** Taxation. **Holdings:** 1207 volumes; 1907 tax pamphlets. **Services:** Copying; room open to the public for reference use only. **Networks/Consortia:** Member of RLG.

★16462★
UNIVERSITY OF MINNESOTA - DEPARTMENT OF LINGUISTICS - LINGUISTICS LIBRARY (Hum)
146 Klaeber Court
320 16th Ave., S.E. Phone: (612)624-3528
Minneapolis, MN 55455 Karen Frederickson, Prin.Sec.
Subjects: Linguistics. **Holdings:** 400 books. **Subscriptions:** 67 journals and other serials. **Services:** Library not open to the public.

★16463★
UNIVERSITY OF MINNESOTA - DRUG INFORMATION SERVICES (Med)
3-106 Health Science Unit F
308 Harvard St., S.E. Phone: (612)624-6492
Minneapolis, MN 55455 Martha E. Joy, Dir.
Founded: 1970. **Staff:** Prof 3; Other 1. **Subjects:** Social aspects and research findings of drugs of abuse, alternatives to drug abuse, school curricula, drug abuse in business, treatment and prevention of drug abuse,

alcoholism. **Holdings:** 24,000 books, bound periodical volumes, reprints; pamphlets. **Subscriptions:** 90 journals and other serials. **Services:** Interlibrary loan; copying; services open to the public. **Computerized Information Services:** BRS Information Technologies, NLM; DRUGINFO (internal database). Performs searches on fee basis. Contact Person: Gail Weinberg, Libn.. **Networks/Consortia:** Member of Twin Cities Biomedical Consortium (TCBC). **Publications:** DIS Update, 4/year. **Special Catalogs:** Thesaurus for DRUGINFO database. **Remarks:** The center is part of the College of Pharmacy and the University of Minnesota Hospital's Department of Pharmacy. **Also Known As:** DIS.

★16464★
UNIVERSITY OF MINNESOTA - EAST ASIAN LIBRARY (Area-Ethnic)
Wilson Library, S-30
309 19th Ave., S. Phone: (612)624-9833
Minneapolis, MN 55455 Emiko Weeks, Act.Hd.
Staff: Prof 1; Other 1. **Subjects:** China and Japan - language and literature, history and politics, philosophy and religion; Asian art history. **Holdings:** 87,833 volumes; 1064 microforms; 6 maps. **Subscriptions:** 435 journals and other serials. **Services:** Interlibrary loan; copying; library open to the public for reference use only. **Networks/Consortia:** Member of MINITEX, RLG.

★16465★
UNIVERSITY OF MINNESOTA - ECONOMICS RESEARCH LIBRARY (Bus-Fin)
525 Science Classroom Bldg.
222 Pleasant St., S.E. Phone: (612)625-2307
Minneapolis, MN 55455 Wendy Williamson, Libn.
Founded: 1969. **Staff:** 1. **Subjects:** Economics, econometrics, mathematics. **Holdings:** 3000 books; 18,000 working papers; 1500 documents; 4500 reprints. **Subscriptions:** 50 journals and other serials. **Services:** Library open to university faculty and students on a limited schedule. **Publications:** Recent Acquisitions, monthly.

★16466★
UNIVERSITY OF MINNESOTA - ERIC SEVAREID JOURNALISM LIBRARY (Info Sci)
121 Murphy Hall
206 Church St., S.E. Phone: (612)625-7892
Minneapolis, MN 55455 Kathleen Hansen, Assoc.Prof./Libn.
Founded: 1941. **Staff:** Prof 1; Other 1. **Subjects:** Mass communications, newspaper journalism, broadcasting, magazine journalism, graphic arts, advertising, international communication, public relations, behavioral research, media management. **Special Collections:** Thomas Heggen Memorial Library (creative writing; 1000 items); Eric Sevareid Papers (29 reels of microfilm). **Holdings:** 6200 books; 1300 bound periodical volumes; 1000 pamphlets; 120 theses. **Subscriptions:** 160 journals and other serials; 40 newspapers. **Services:** Interlibrary loan; copying; library open to the public. **Automated Operations:** Computerized cataloging. **Computerized Information Services:** DIALOG Information Services. Performs searches on fee basis. **Networks/Consortia:** Member of RLG.

★16467★
UNIVERSITY OF MINNESOTA - GOVERNMENT PUBLICATIONS LIBRARY (Info Sci)
409 Wilson Library
309 19th Ave., S. Phone: (612)624-5073
Minneapolis, MN 55455 William LaBissoniere, Hd.
Staff: Prof 1; Other 5. **Subjects:** Government publications. **Special Collections:** Regional depository for U.S. documents; Minnesota state documents depository; United Nations depository; European Community documents; Organization for Economic Cooperation and Development (OECD) documents; Organization of American States (OAS) documents; ASI microfiche (complete). **Holdings:** 1.97 million documents; 819,768 microforms. **Subscriptions:** 1307 journals and other serials. **Services:** Interlibrary loan; copying; library open to the public for reference use only; loans made with acceptable borrowing cards. **Networks/Consortia:** Member of MINITEX, RLG, Center for Research Libraries (CRL) Consortia.

★16468★
UNIVERSITY OF MINNESOTA - HORMEL INSTITUTE - LIBRARY (Sci-Engr)
801 16th Ave., N.E. Phone: (507)433-8804
Austin, MN 55912 Jacqueline Budde, Libn.
Founded: 1948. **Staff:** Prof 1. **Subjects:** Lipid and membrane chemistry and biochemistry. **Holdings:** 1800 books; 8000 bound periodical volumes. **Subscriptions:** 100 journals and other serials. **Services:** Interlibrary loan; copying; library open to the public with permission. **Automated Operations:** Computerized cataloging. **Computerized Information Services:** DIALOG Information Services, OCLC, MEDLARS. **Networks/Consortia:** Member of MINITEX, Southeast Library System (SELS).

★16469★
UNIVERSITY OF MINNESOTA - HUMANITIES/SOCIAL SCIENCES LIBRARY - LEARNING RESOURCES CENTER - NON-PRINT LIBRARY (Aud-Vis)
15 Walter Library
117 Pleasant St., S.E. Phone: (612)624-1584
Minneapolis, MN 55455 Daniel Donnelly, Hd.
Staff: 3. **Subjects:** Foreign languages, liberal arts, science, agriculture, ethnic materials, graphic materials. **Holdings:** 18,700 sound recordings; 2000 video programs; 15,000 slides. **Services:** Center open to the public for reference use only.

★16470★
UNIVERSITY OF MINNESOTA - HUMANITIES/SOCIAL SCIENCES LIBRARY, EAST BANK (Educ, Info Sci)
110 Walter Library
117 Pleasant St., S.E.
Minneapolis, MN 55455 Phone: (612)624-4185
Founded: 1962. **Staff:** Prof 4; Other 3. **Subjects:** Education, psychology, library science. **Special Collections:** Educational Testing Service; tests (microfiche); psychological tests. **Holdings:** 207,258 volumes; 465,397 microforms; college catalogs on microfiche; ERIC microfiche; annual reports from college and university libraries. **Subscriptions:** 2440 journals and other serials. **Services:** Interlibrary loan; copying; SDI; library open to the public for reference use only. **Computerized Information Services:** DIALOG Information Services, BRS Information Technologies, Pergamon ORBIT InfoLine, Inc. **Networks/Consortia:** Member of MINITEX, RLG.

★16471★
UNIVERSITY OF MINNESOTA - IMMIGRATION HISTORY RESEARCH CENTER (Area-Ethnic)
826 Berry St. Phone: (612)627-4208
St. Paul, MN 55114 Joel Wurl, Cur.
Staff: Prof 1; Other 1. **Subjects:** East, Central, and South European and Near Eastern immigration and ethnic groups in the United States, 1880 to present, with emphasis on Finns, Italians, and Slavic peoples; ethnic labor and political movement; ethnic churches, presses, and fraternal organizations; resettlement of refugees after World War II; immigrant welfare agencies; Ukraine and Ukrainians. **Special Collections:** Records of the American Council for Nationalities Service, Jugoslav Socialist Federation, American Latvian Association, Tyomies Society, National Slovak Society, United Ukrainian American Relief Committee, and other ethnic organizations; papers of Anthony Capraro, Alexander A. Granovsky, Philip K. Hitti, Karol T. Jaskolski, Joseph C. Roucek, Theodore Saloutos, and other ethnic scholars and leaders; publications of ethnic presses and organizations. **Holdings:** 46,615 volumes, including 3000 serial titles and files of 900 newspapers; 1685 AV programs; 65 maps; 3161 feet of manuscripts; 5403 microforms. **Subscriptions:** 488 journals and other serials. **Services:** Interlibrary loan (microfilm only); copying (limited); collection open for research upon application. **Networks/Consortia:** Member of RLG. **Publications:** IHRC Ethnic Collections Series (9 volumes) - for sale; Spectrum (IHRC newsletter), 3/year - by subscription; conference proceedings; reprints; preservation manuals; survey guides; microfilm guides - all for sale; publications brochure - available upon request. **Staff:** Rudolph J. Vecoli, Dir..

★16472★
UNIVERSITY OF MINNESOTA - INDUSTRIAL RELATIONS CENTER - REFERENCE ROOM (Bus-Fin)
Management & Economics, West Campus
271 19th Ave., S. Phone: (612)624-7011
Minneapolis, MN 55455 Georgianna Herman, Libn. & Supv.
Founded: 1945. **Staff:** Prof 2; Other 3. **Subjects:** Personnel administration, labor relations, human resource management, collective bargaining, management theory, industrial sociology, labor economics, industrial psychology. **Special Collections:** Publications from industrial relations centers in the U.S. (6000). **Holdings:** 14,000 books; 5000 bound periodical volumes; 120 VF drawers of subject files; 5500 government documents; 570 volumes of court cases, labor arbitration awards, and other loose-leaf reporting services. **Subscriptions:** 140 journals and other serials; 60 labor union newspapers. **Services:** Copying; reference room open to the public. **Staff:** Mariann Nelson, Lib.Asst..

★16473★
UNIVERSITY OF MINNESOTA - INFORM (Info Sci)
179 Wilson Library
309 19th Ave., S. Phone: (612)624-5516
Minneapolis, MN 55455 Christopher B. Loring, Hd.
Staff: Prof 1; Other 5. **Computerized Information Services:** DIALOG Information Services, OCLC, BRS Information Technologies. Performs searches on fee basis. **Networks/Consortia:** Member of Center for Research Libraries (CRL) Consortia, RLG, MINITEX. **Remarks:** INFORM is a service unit which provides fee-based document delivery for business, industry, and individuals. Scope includes literature in business, law, government, education, psychology, humanities, and social sciences. Services include photocopying of articles, book loans, and database searching. Interlibrary loan service provided for material within scope as well as science and technology literature. Referrals of requests are made to other campus fee-based services as appropriate. Fee schedule available on request.

★16474★
UNIVERSITY OF MINNESOTA - INSTITUTE OF INTERNATIONAL STUDIES - HAROLD SCOTT QUIGLEY LIBRARY (Soc Sci)
214 Social Sciences Bldg.
267 19th Ave., S.
Minneapolis, MN 55455 Phone: (612)624-9007
Staff: 1. **Subjects:** Foreign policy; international studies - politics, organizations, law, economics. **Holdings:** 400 books; 300 bound periodical volumes. **Services:** Library open to the public with restrictions.

★16475★
UNIVERSITY OF MINNESOTA - JAMES FORD BELL LIBRARY (Hist)
462 Wilson Library
309 19th Ave., S. Phone: (612)624-1528
Minneapolis, MN 55455 John Parker, Cur.
Founded: 1953. **Staff:** Prof 2. **Subjects:** History of European overseas expansion to 1800. **Holdings:** 13,512 volumes; 200 AV programs; 200 reels of microfilm. **Services:** Copying; collection open to the public for reference use only. **Networks/Consortia:** Member of RLG. **Publications:** The Merchant Explorer, annual - on request and to selected libraries. **Special Catalogs:** The James Ford Bell Library: an annotated catalog of original source materials relating to the history of European expansion, 1400-1800 (1981).

★16476★
UNIVERSITY OF MINNESOTA - LANDSCAPE ARBORETUM - ELMER L. & ELEANOR J. ANDERSEN HORTICULTURAL LIBRARY (Biol Sci)
3675 Arboretum Dr. Phone: (612)443-2440
Chaska, MN 55317 Richard T. Isaacson, Hd.
Founded: 1973. **Staff:** Prof 1; Other 2. **Subjects:** Horticulture, botany, natural science, landscape architecture. **Special Collections:** Wildflowers (botanical illustrations); Frances R. Williams Collection (publications on the genus Hosta); seed and nursery catalogs. **Holdings:** 8766 volumes; 555 AV programs; 9 manuscripts; 840 microforms. **Subscriptions:** 383 journals and other serials. **Services:** Library open to the public for reference use only; arboretum plant locater. **Networks/Consortia:** Member of RLG.

★16477★
UNIVERSITY OF MINNESOTA - LAW LIBRARY (Law)
120 The Law Center Phone: (612)625-6821
Minneapolis, MN 55455 Kathleen Price, Dir.
Founded: 1888. **Staff:** Prof 9; Other 12. **Subjects:** Law - Anglo-American, foreign. **Special Collections:** Scandinavian law; American Indians; British Commonwealth legal materials, including Indian and Pakistani legal materials. **Holdings:** 472,893 volumes; 460,320 microforms. **Subscriptions:** 9032 journals and other serials. **Services:** Interlibrary loan; copying; library open to the public for reference use only. **Automated Operations:** Computerized cataloging. **Computerized Information Services:** LEXIS, WESTLAW, ELSS (Electronic Legislative Search System), LEGI-SLATE, DIALOG Information Services, NEXIS, RLIN, OCLC. **Networks/Consortia:** Member of MINITEX. **Publications:** Newsletter, bimonthly; Law Library Guide, irregular. **Staff:** Gail M. Daly, Asst.Dir./Tech.Serv.; Tom Woxland, Asst.Dir./Pub.Serv.; Milagros R. Rush, Cat.; Susanne Nevin, Cat.; Nancy McCormick, Circ.; Lyonette Louis-Jacques, Ref.; Warren Rees, Ref..

★16478★
UNIVERSITY OF MINNESOTA - LITZENBERG-LUND LIBRARY (Med)
Box 395, Mayo Memorial Bldg.
420 Delaware St., S.E.
Minneapolis, MN 55455 Phone: (612)626-5998
Founded: 1977. **Staff:** 1. **Subjects:** Obstetrics, gynecology, endocrinology, oncology. **Special Collections:** Historical medical and obstetrics-gynecology books. **Holdings:** 450 books; 530 bound periodical volumes. **Subscriptions:** 32 journals and other serials. **Services:** Interlibrary loan; copying; library open to the public with restrictions. **Special Indexes:** Index of obstetrics-gynecology journals. **Remarks:** The Litzenberg-Lund Library is sponsored by the University of Minnesota Obstetrics & Gynecology Associates and donations.

★16479★
UNIVERSITY OF MINNESOTA - MANUSCRIPTS DIVISION (Hist)
826 Berry St. Phone: (612)627-4199
St. Paul, MN 55114 Alan K. Lathrop, Cur.
Founded: 1970. **Staff:** Prof 1. **Special Collections:** Literary Manuscripts Collections - papers of Gordon R. Dickson (63 linear feet), Clifford D. Simak (10 linear feet), John Berryman (55 linear feet), Frederick Manfred (84 linear feet), H.P. Lovecraft (87 items), Thomas Disch (6 linear feet), Arthur Motley (195 linear feet); Performing Arts Archives - records of Guthrie Theater (300 linear feet), Minnesota Orchestra (350 linear feet); Twin Cities scenic design studios scenic backdrop renderings (1100 items); Northwest Architectural Archives - records of American Terra Cotta Company, Purcell and Elmslie, architects (100,000 items), Morrel and Nichols Landscape Architects (48 linear feet), Ellerbe Architects (20 linear feet), Liebenberg and Kaplan Architects (840 linear feet), L.S. Buffington Drawings Collection (2200 items), Close Associates architects (40 linear feet); trade catalog collection (6000 items). **Holdings:** 100 volumes of stock plan books; 9625.8 feet of manuscripts; 393 microforms; 27,886 AV programs. **Services:** Copying; division open for research upon application. **Networks/Consortia:** Member of RLG. **Publications:** Newsletter, 5/year. **Special Indexes:** Index to architectural archives by building name, identifying media, and type of documentation (card).

★16480★
UNIVERSITY OF MINNESOTA - MAP LIBRARY (Geog-Map)
Wilson Library, S-76
309 19th Ave., S. Phone: (612)624-4549
Minneapolis, MN 55455 Brent Allison, Hd.
Founded: 1940. **Staff:** Prof 1; Other 1. **Special Collections:** Ames Library of South Asia Map Collection of India; early maps of Minnesota. **Holdings:** 4816 books, atlases, bound periodical volumes; 360,304 documents; 232,559 maps; 55 microforms; 167,293 AV programs; pamphlets. **Subscriptions:** 35 journals and other serials. **Services:** Interlibrary loan (limited); copying; library open to the public with restrictions. **Networks/Consortia:** Member of MINITEX, RLG. **Special Indexes:** Address file of map and atlas publishers and dealers, by subject (card).

★16481★
UNIVERSITY OF MINNESOTA - MATHEMATICS LIBRARY (Sci-Engr)
Vincent Hall, Rm. 310
206 Church St., S.E. Phone: (612)624-6075
Minneapolis, MN 55455 Gregg Hoffman, Act.Hd.
Staff: 1. **Subjects:** Pure mathematics, theoretical statistics. **Holdings:** 29,574 volumes. **Subscriptions:** 366 journals and other serials. **Services:** Interlibrary loan; copying; library open to the public for reference use only. **Computerized Information Services:** DIALOG Information Services, Pergamon ORBIT InfoLine, Inc., BRS Information Technologies. **Networks/Consortia:** Member of MINITEX, RLG.

★16482★
UNIVERSITY OF MINNESOTA - MIDDLE EAST LIBRARY (Area-Ethnic)
Wilson Library, S-50
309 19th Ave., S. Phone: (612)624-1012
Minneapolis, MN 55455 Nassif Youssif, Hd.
Founded: 1967. **Staff:** Prof 1; Other 1. **Subjects:** Arabic, Hebrew, Persian, and Turkish languages, literature, and history. **Special Collections:** Middle Eastern vernaculars (32,000 volumes). **Holdings:** 43,633 volumes; 111 AV programs; 18 microforms. **Subscriptions:** 126 journals and other serials; 32 newspapers. **Services:** Interlibrary loan; library open to the public for reference use only. **Networks/Consortia:** Member of MINITEX, RLG.

★16483★
UNIVERSITY OF MINNESOTA - MINNESOTA CENTER FOR PHILOSOPHY OF SCIENCE - DEPARTMENTAL LIBRARY
309 Ford Hall
224 Church St., S.E.
Minneapolis, MN 55455
Subjects: Philosophy of science, physics, psychology; theoretical physics; psychology; logic (mathematical). **Holdings:** 1000 books; reprints; manuscripts. **Remarks:** Presently inactive.

★16484★
UNIVERSITY OF MINNESOTA - MINNESOTA EXTENSION SERVICE - DIAL-U INSECT AND PLANT INFORMATION CLINIC (Biol Sci)
145 Alderman Hall
1970 Folwell Ave.
St. Paul, MN 55108 Dr. Mark Ascerno, Dial-U Coord.
Founded: 1983. **Staff:** Prof 4; Other 8. **Subjects:** Horticulture, plant pathology, entomology. **Holdings:** 200 books; 400 extension fact sheets and bulletins. **Subscriptions:** 15 journals and other serials. **Remarks:** This is a telephone information service that can be reached by metropolitan area residents calling 1-976-0200. Caller is automatically charged a special fee when information number is used. **Staff:** Deborah Brown, Horticulture Ext.Spec.; Jeff Hahn, Entomology Ext.Educ.; Cynthia Ash, Plant Pathology Ext.Educ..

★16485★
UNIVERSITY OF MINNESOTA - MINNESOTA EXTENSION SERVICE - MINNESOTA ANALYSIS & PLANNING SYSTEM (Soc Sci)
475 Coffey Hall
1420 Eckles Ave. Phone: (612)624-7767
St. Paul, MN 55108 David M. Nelson, Dir.
Founded: 1967. **Staff:** Prof 2; Other 2. **Subjects:** U.S. census of population, 1960-1980; agricultural and economic census. **Holdings:** 150 volumes; 300 computer tapes; 500 other cataloged items. **Subscriptions:** 20 journals and other serials. **Services:** Copying; system open to the public by appointment. **Computerized Information Services:** CENDATA. Performs searches on fee basis. Contact Person: Phil Smith-Cunnien, Census Info.Spec.. **Publications:** MAPS Newsletter, bimonthly - free upon request. **Special Indexes:** Data File Inventory. **Also Known As:** MAPS.

★16486★
UNIVERSITY OF MINNESOTA - MUSIC LIBRARY (Mus)
70 Ferguson Hall
2106 4th St., S. Phone: (612)624-5890
Minneapolis, MN 55455 Katharine Holum, Hd.
Founded: 1947. **Staff:** Prof 2; Other 1. **Subjects:** Musicology; music history; opera; theory and composition; vocal, instrumental, and orchestra music; ethnomusicology; folk music; music therapy; music education; keyboard music. **Special Collections:** Donald N. Ferguson Collection of Rare Books and Scores (336 volumes); Operas of 18th & early 19th centuries (175 volumes); Ritzen Collection of Sound Recordings (2200 phonograph records); Latin American music scores (450 volumes); Berger Band Library (335 volumes). **Holdings:** 56,925 books, bound periodical volumes, scores; 29,533 AV programs; 1493 microforms. **Subscriptions:** 302 journals and other serials. **Services:** Interlibrary loan; copying; library open to the public for reference use only. **Computerized Information Services:** DIALOG Information Services, BRS Information Technologies, Pergamon ORBIT InfoLine, Inc. **Networks/Consortia:** Member of MINITEX, RLG.

★16487★
UNIVERSITY OF MINNESOTA - NEWMAN CENTER LIBRARY (Rel-Phil)
1701 University Ave., S.E. Phone: (612)331-3437
Minneapolis, MN 55414 Christine Cundall, Libn.
Staff: Prof 1; Other 1. **Subjects:** Theology, philosophy, humanities, ethics, medical ethics, social issues. **Special Collections:** Newman Center history. **Holdings:** 10,000 books and bound periodical volumes; 195 tapes; 1 box of Newman publications; pamphlets; clippings. **Subscriptions:** 37 journals and other serials. **Services:** Library open to the public.

★16488★
UNIVERSITY OF MINNESOTA - PUBLIC AFFAIRS LIBRARY (Soc Sci)
50 Humphrey Ctr.
301 19th Ave., S. Phone: (612)625-3038
Minneapolis, MN 55455 Eunice Bisbee Johnson, Hd.
Founded: 1936. **Staff:** 2. **Subjects:** Public administration, local government, policy analysis and evaluation, human services, planning, land use. **Holdings:** 45,450 volumes; 320 documents; 28 AV programs; 1181 microforms. **Subscriptions:** 343 journals and other serials. **Services:** Interlibrary loan (limited); library open to the public for reference use only. **Networks/Consortia:** Member of MINITEX, RLG.

★16489★
UNIVERSITY OF MINNESOTA - ST. ANTHONY FALLS HYDRAULIC LABORATORY - LORENZ G. STRAUB MEMORIAL LIBRARY (Sci-Engr)
Mississippi River at Third Ave., S.E. Phone: (612)627-4010
Minneapolis, MN 55414 Jody Lin Mason, Libn.
Founded: 1964. **Staff:** 1. **Subjects:** Hydraulics, hydrology, fluid mechanics, water resources. **Holdings:** 2000 books; 10,000 other cataloged items. **Subscriptions:** 15 journals and other serials. **Services:** Copying; library open to the public. **Remarks:** An alternate telephone number is 627-4011.

★16490★
UNIVERSITY OF MINNESOTA - SCANDINAVIAN COLLECTION (Area-Ethnic)
Wilson Library
309 19th Ave., S. Phone: (612)624-5860
Minneapolis, MN 55455 Mariann Tiblin, Bibliog.
Subjects: Scandinavian humanities and social sciences. **Special Collections:** Jeppe Aakjaer Collection (110 volumes); Scandinavian Children's Literature Collection (700 volumes); Scandinavian Government Documents Collection; Par Lagerkvist Collection (158 volumes); Finnish-American Collection; Scandinavian maps; Scandinavian Travels Collection; August Strindberg Collection (800 volumes); Swedish Royal Decrees, 1649-1824 (2655); Tell G. Dahllof Collection of Swedish-Americana. **Holdings:** 150,000 volumes (in general Wilson Library collection). **Services:** Interlibrary loan; copying; collection open to the public. **Computerized Information Services:** DIALOG Information Services, BRS Information Technologies, Pergamon ORBIT InfoLine, Inc. **Networks/Consortia:** Member of MINITEX, RLG. **Remarks:** Materials in the Scandinavian Collection are located in various departments of the university libraries.

★16491★
UNIVERSITY OF MINNESOTA - SCIENCE AND ENGINEERING LIBRARY (Sci-Engr)
206 Walter Library
117 Pleasant St., S.E. Phone: (612)624-0224
Minneapolis, MN 55455 Cynthia A. Steinke, Dir.
Founded: 1985. **Staff:** Prof 7; Other 2. **Subjects:** Engineering, chemistry, physics, geology, astronomy, history of science and technology. **Special Collections:** Archive for the History of Quantum Physics. **Holdings:** 322,729 books and bound periodical volumes; 89,604 maps; 29,905 microfiche; 2191 reels of microfilm. **Subscriptions:** 3537 journals and other serials. **Services:** Interlibrary loan; copying; SDI (fee); library open to the public. **Automated Operations:** Computerized cataloging. **Computerized Information Services:** DIALOG Information Services, BRS Information Technologies, Pergamon ORBIT InfoLine, Inc. Performs searches on fee basis. Contact Person: Donna Rubens, ESTIS Coord., 624-2356. **Networks/Consortia:** Member of MINITEX, RLG. **Remarks:** Maintained by Institute of Technology Libraries. An alternate telephone number is 624-3366.

★16492★
UNIVERSITY OF MINNESOTA - SOCIAL AND ADMINISTRATIVE PHARMACY READING ROOM (Med)
7-159 Health Sciences Unit F
308 Harvard St., S.E. Phone: (612)624-5900
Minneapolis, MN 55455 Dr. Albert I. Wertheimer, Dir.
Staff: 2. **Subjects:** Pharmacy, drugs, health service. **Holdings:** 260 books; 290 bound periodical volumes; 3100 NTIS reports on microfiche; government publications; Ph.D. dissertations. **Subscriptions:** 51 journals and other serials. **Services:** Room open to the public with permission.

★16493★
UNIVERSITY OF MINNESOTA - SOCIAL WELFARE HISTORY ARCHIVES (Soc Sci)
101 Walter Library
117 Pleasant St., S.E. Phone: (612)624-6394
Minneapolis, MN 55455 David Klaassen, Cur./Archv.
Staff: Prof 2; Other 3. **Subjects:** Social welfare, settlement movement, professional social work, voluntary associations, recreation, health. **Special Collections:** Records and files of Survey Associates, National Federation of Settlements, Young Men's Christian Association (YMCA) of the U.S.A., National Association of Social Workers, United Neighborhood Houses of New York, and others; social service organization materials (600 linear feet); contemporary feminist periodicals and pamphlets (100 linear feet).

Holdings: 10,134 books; 7060 feet of manuscripts; 1491 microforms; 20,044 AV programs. **Subscriptions:** 61 journals and other serials. **Services:** Interlibrary loan (limited); copying; archives open for research upon application. **Publications:** Guide to Holdings, 1979; Descriptive Inventories of Collections in the Social Welfare History Archives. **Networks/ Consortia:** Member of RLG.

★16494★
UNIVERSITY OF MINNESOTA - SPECIAL COLLECTIONS AND RARE BOOKS LIBRARY (Rare Book)
466 Wilson Library
309 19th Ave. S. Phone: (612)624-3855
Minneapolis, MN 55455 Austin J. McLean, Cur.
Staff: Prof 2; Other 1. **Subjects:** History, literature, philosophy, astronomy, 17th century England and Holland, private press books, fortification, Scandinavian travel. **Special Collections:** Walter de la Mare; Henry Miller; John Galsworthy; Franklin Delano Roosevelt; Sinclair Lewis; John Steinbeck; Sherlock Holmes; Charles Dickens - Edwin Drood; modern Greek literature; Thomas Wolfe; World War I pamphlets (6000); black literature (3000 volumes). **Holdings:** 89,554 books and bound periodical volumes. **Subscriptions:** 21 journals and other serials. **Services:** Copying; library open to the public for reference use only. **Networks/Consortia:** Member of RLG. **Special Indexes:** Card indexes to places, dates, printers of books before 1700; card index to private press books by press, printer, designers; card indexes of provenance, manuscripts, signed bindings.

★16495★
UNIVERSITY OF MINNESOTA - STATISTICS LIBRARY (Sci-Engr)
270a Vincent Hall
206 Church St., S.E. Phone: (612)625-7300
Minneapolis, MN 55455 Seymour Geisser, Dir.
Staff: 4. **Subjects:** Statistics. **Holdings:** 368 books; 235 bound periodical volumes; 23 bound theses; 482 School of Statistics technical reports. **Subscriptions:** 10 journals and other serials. **Services:** Library open to the public for reference use only.

★16496★
UNIVERSITY OF MINNESOTA - UNDERGROUND SPACE CENTER - LIBRARY (Energy)
790 Civil and Mineral Engr. Bldg.
500 Pillsbury Dr., S.E. Phone: (612)624-0066
Minneapolis, MN 55455 Andrea M. Spartz, Sec.
Founded: 1977. **Staff:** Prof 1. **Subjects:** Earth sheltered housing, energy, underground space use, rock and soil mechanics, alternative energy financing and legislation, building codes. **Holdings:** 150 books; 200 technical papers; 600 documents; 900 clippings. **Subscriptions:** 20 journals and other serials. **Services:** Library open to the public for reference use only. **Publications:** Underline (newsletter), annual - free upon request. **Special Indexes:** Professionals involved in underground construction (computer listings). **Staff:** Dr. Ray Sterling, Dir..

★16497★
UNIVERSITY OF MINNESOTA - UNIVERSITY ARCHIVES (Hist)
10 Walter Library
117 Pleasant St., S.E. Phone: (612)624-0562
Minneapolis, MN 55455 Penelope Krosch, Hd.
Staff: Prof 2; Other 1. **Subjects:** University of Minnesota archives. **Special Collections:** Papers of people and organizations connected with the university. **Holdings:** 68,549 books, bound periodical volumes, dissertations; 12,175 linear feet of manuscripts; 40 VF drawers of ready reference material; 924 microforms; 40,716 AV programs. **Subscriptions:** 671 journals and other serials. **Services:** Copying; archives open for research upon application. **Networks/Consortia:** Member of RLG. **Special Indexes:** Indexes for 7 major university publications (card); index of photograph collection.

★16498★
UNIVERSITY OF MINNESOTA - UNIVERSITY COUNSELING SERVICES - CAREER RESOURCE CENTER (Educ)
302 Eddy Hall
192 Pillsbury Dr., S.E. Phone: (612)624-3323
Minneapolis, MN 55455 Georgia Loughren, Supv.
Staff: 2. **Subjects:** Educational and career opportunities. **Holdings:** 100 books; 600 school catalogs; 300 occupational files based on Dictionary of Occupational Titles; 36 cassette tapes on careers; career guidance systems (online). **Subscriptions:** 12 journals and other serials. **Services:** Center open to the public with restrictions.

★16499★
UNIVERSITY OF MINNESOTA - UNIVERSITY FILM AND VIDEO (Aud-Vis)
3300 University Ave., S.E. Phone: (612)373-3810
Minneapolis, MN 55414 Judith A. Gaston, Dir.
Founded: 1913. **Staff:** Prof 2; Other 16. **Subjects:** Education, training, entertainment, health, film study. **Holdings:** 9750 16mm films; 13,500 prints. **Subscriptions:** 20 journals and other serials. **Services:** Library open to the public. **Automated Operations:** Computerized circulation.

★16500★
UNIVERSITY OF MINNESOTA, CROOKSTON - KIEHLE LIBRARY - MEDIA RESOURCES (Agri, Bus-Fin)
Crookston, MN 56716-9998 Phone: (218)281-6510
Harold J. Opgrand, Dir., Media Rsrcs.
Staff: Prof 4. **Subjects:** Agriculture, horsemanship, business, foods. **Special Collections:** Minnesota State Depository materials. **Holdings:** 24,348 books; 119 periodicals on microfilm; 1691 AV programs. **Subscriptions:** 845 journals and other serials; 53 newspapers. **Services:** Interlibrary loan; copying; resources open to the public, AV materials available for on-site use only. **Automated Operations:** Computerized cataloging and ILL. **Computerized Information Services:** OCLC. **Networks/Consortia:** Member of MINITEX, Northern Lights Library Network (NLLN). **Staff:** Owen Williams, Ref.Libn.; Berneil Nelson, Libn.; Krista Proulx, Per./AV Libn..

★16501★
UNIVERSITY OF MINNESOTA, DULUTH - HEALTH SCIENCE LIBRARY† (Med)
10 University Dr. Phone: (218)726-8585
Duluth, MN 55812 Diane C.P. Ebro, Dir.
Founded: 1971. **Staff:** Prof 4; Other 2. **Subjects:** Medicine, dentistry, veterinary medicine, forensic medicine, nursing, biology, behavioral science, geology, chemistry, computer science, mathematics, physics, engineering. **Holdings:** 16,382 books; 58,320 bound periodical volumes; 2000 pamphlets; 3782 reels of microforms. **Subscriptions:** 668 journals and other serials. **Services:** Interlibrary loan; copying; SDI; library open to the public. **Automated Operations:** Computerized cataloging and serials. **Computerized Information Services:** DIALOG Information Services, Pergamon ORBIT InfoLine, Inc., NLM, BRS Information Technologies, OCLC; EasyLink (electronic mail service). **Networks/Consortia:** Member of Greater Midwest Regional Medical Library Network, MINITEX, Arrowhead Professional Libraries Association (APLA). **Special Catalogs:** Serials Holding List. **Staff:** Martha Eberhart, Ref./Online Serv.; Pamela Enrici, Ref./Online Serv.; Thomas Zogg, Ref./Online Ser.; Mary Lundgren, ILL.

★16502★
UNIVERSITY OF MINNESOTA, DULUTH - NATURAL RESOURCES RESEARCH INSTITUTE (NRRI) - LIBRARY (Biol Sci)
3151 Miller Trunk Hwy. Phone: (218)720-4228
Duluth, MN 55811 John H. Sandy, Libn.
Founded: 1985. **Staff:** Prof 1; Other 2. **Subjects:** Forest products, minerals, peat, aquatic ecosystems. **Holdings:** 2067 books; 2075 microfiche. **Subscriptions:** 203 journals and other serials. **Services:** Interlibrary loan; copying; library open to the public. **Computerized Information Services:** DIALOG Information Services, Pergamon ORBIT InfoLine, Inc., DATANET, OCLC. **Networks/Consortia:** Member of MINITEX. **Publications:** New Acquisitions, irregular - available upon request.

UNIVERSITY OF MINNESOTA, DULUTH - NORTHEAST MINNESOTA HISTORICAL CENTER
See: Northeast Minnesota Historical Center (10391)

★16503★
UNIVERSITY OF MINNESOTA, DULUTH - SOCIOLOGY-ANTHROPOLOGY-GEOGRAPHY DEPARTMENT - MAP LIBRARY (Geog-Map)
228 Cina Hall Phone: (218)726-7552
Duluth, MN 55812 Gordon L. Levine, Asst.Prof., Geog.
Subjects: Topography - Minnesota, North Dakota, South Dakota, Iowa, Wisconsin, Michigan, Illinois. **Special Collections:** Great Lakes nautical maps; world map series. **Holdings:** 1000 books; 30,000 maps. **Services:** Copying; library open to the public.

UNIVERSITY OF MINNESOTA, MORRIS - WEST CENTRAL MINNESOTA HISTORICAL CENTER
See: West Central Minnesota Historical Center (17644)

★16504★
UNIVERSITY OF MINNESOTA, ST. PAUL - BIOCHEMISTRY LIBRARY (Biol Sci, Sci-Engr)
406 Biological Sciences Ctr.
1445 Gortner Ave. Phone: (612)624-1292
St. Paul, MN 55108 Jeffrey Dains, Lib.Asst.
Staff: 1. **Subjects:** Biochemistry, plant biochemistry, animal biochemistry, chemistry of cereals and cereal products, genetics, cell biology. **Holdings:** 19,303 volumes; 8188 microforms. **Subscriptions:** 275 journals and other serials. **Services:** Interlibrary loan (through Central Library, St. Paul Campus); copying; library open to the public for reference use. **Networks/Consortia:** Member of MINITEX, RLG.

★16505★
UNIVERSITY OF MINNESOTA, ST. PAUL - CENTRAL LIBRARY (Biol Sci, Agri)
1984 Buford Ave. Phone: (612)624-1212
St. Paul, MN 55108 Richard L. Rohrer, Dir.
Founded: 1890. **Staff:** Prof 7; Other 16. **Subjects:** Agricultural economics and engineering, agricultural and home economics education, home economics, agronomy and plant genetics, animal science, horticultural sciences, biological sciences, applied statistics, food science and nutrition, plant pathology, soil science. **Special Collections:** U.S.D.A. Depository materials; agricultural experiment station, extension, and international agricultural exchange publications; Ruth Jenson Collection (family relations; 55,000 volumes). **Holdings:** 152,678 volumes; 378,066 documents; 1177 AV programs; 26,621 microforms. **Subscriptions:** 2891 journals and other serials. **Services:** Interlibrary loan; copying; BASIS (fee-based services); library open to the public for reference use. **Computerized Information Services:** BRS Information Technologies, DIALOG Information Services, Pergamon ORBIT InfoLine, Inc.

★16506★
UNIVERSITY OF MINNESOTA, ST. PAUL - DEPARTMENT OF VOCATIONAL & TECHNICAL EDUCATION - LEARNING RESOURCE CENTER (Educ)
Vocational & Technical Educ. Bldg.
1954 Buford Ave. Phone: (612)624-1214
St. Paul, MN 55108 Dr. George Copa, Dir.
Founded: 1965. **Staff:** 2. **Subjects:** Vocational and technical education, research and development materials, SOM instructional materials. **Special Collections:** All documents available on microfiche from AIM and ARM. **Holdings:** 20,000 documents; 10 drawers of microfiche; 7 drawers of microfilm; 5000 hardcopy items. **Services:** Microfiche to microfiche duplication; center open to the public for reference use only. **Publications:** Bibliographies (computerized).

★16507★
UNIVERSITY OF MINNESOTA, ST. PAUL - ENTOMOLOGY, FISHERIES AND WILDLIFE LIBRARY (Biol Sci)
1980 Folwell Ave.
375 Hodson Hall Phone: (612)624-9288
St. Paul, MN 55108 Barbara A. Kautz, Hd.
Founded: 1905. **Staff:** Prof 1; Other 1. **Subjects:** Entomology, fisheries, wildlife, pesticides, water pollution, limnology, aquatic biology. **Special Collections:** Bee collection (800 monographs; 87 journal titles). **Holdings:** 34,055 books and bound periodical volumes; 35,395 documents; 85 maps; 1824 AV programs; 4410 microforms. **Subscriptions:** 973 journals and other serials. **Services:** Interlibrary loan; copying; library open to the public for reference use only. **Computerized Information Services:** DIALOG Information Services, BRS Information Technologies. **Networks/Consortia:** Member of MINITEX, RLG.

★16508★
UNIVERSITY OF MINNESOTA, ST. PAUL - FORESTRY LIBRARY (Biol Sci, Env-Cons)
203 Green Hall
1530 N. Cleveland Ave. Phone: (612)624-3222
St. Paul, MN 55108 Jean Albrecht, Hd.
Founded: 1899. **Staff:** Prof 1; Other 1. **Subjects:** Forestry, forest products, outdoor recreation, conservation of natural resources, hydrology, range management, aerial photogrammetry, remote sensing, pulp and paper. **Holdings:** 23,874 books and bound periodical volumes; 64,194 documents; 3746 maps; 618 AV programs; 2110 microforms. **Subscriptions:** 1069 journals and other serials. **Services:** Interlibrary loan (through Central Library, St. Paul Campus); copying; library open to the public for reference use only. **Computerized Information Services:** Pergamon ORBIT InfoLine, Inc., DIALOG Information Services. **Networks/Consortia:** Member of MINITEX, RLG. **Publications:** Social Sciences in Forestry: A Current Selected Bibliography and Index, quarterly - free upon request.

★16509★
UNIVERSITY OF MINNESOTA, ST. PAUL - HERBARIUM COLLECTION (Biol Sci)
St. Paul Campus Library
1984 Buford Ave.
St. Paul, MN 55108 Phone: (612)624-1212
Special Collections: Special subject collection of botanical taxonomic materials (2130 volumes; 1500 reprints and pamphlets). **Holdings:** Figures not available. **Subscriptions:** 12 journals and other serials. **Services:** Collection open to faculty and graduate students only.

★16510★
UNIVERSITY OF MINNESOTA, ST. PAUL - PLANT PATHOLOGY LIBRARY (Biol Sci)
395 Borlaug Hall
1991 Upper Buford Circle Phone: (612)625-9777
St. Paul, MN 55108 Erik Biever, Lib.Asst.
Founded: 1909. **Staff:** 1. **Subjects:** Phytopathology, mycology, air pollution effects on vegetation. **Holdings:** 7749 books and bound periodical volumes; 66 AV programs; 215 microforms. **Subscriptions:** 120 journals and other serials. **Services:** Interlibrary loan (through Central Library, St. Paul Campus); copying; library open to the public for reference use. **Networks/Consortia:** Member of MINITEX, RLG.

★16511★
UNIVERSITY OF MINNESOTA, ST. PAUL - VETERINARY MEDICAL LIBRARY (Med)
450 Veterinary Science Bldg.
1971 Commonwealth Ave. Phone: (612)624-4281
St. Paul, MN 55108 Livija Carlson, Hd.
Staff: Prof 1; Other 1. **Subjects:** Veterinary medicine. **Special Collections:** German veterinary theses. **Holdings:** 38,782 books and bound periodical volumes; 16,638 documents; 83 AV programs; 933 microforms; dissertations. **Subscriptions:** 918 journals and other serials. **Services:** Interlibrary loan; copying; library open to the public for reference use only. **Networks/Consortia:** Member of MINITEX, RLG. **Special Catalogs:** Pamphlet and documents catalogs.

★16512★
UNIVERSITY OF MINNESOTA TECHNICAL COLLEGE, WASECA - UMW LIBRARY (Agri)
1000 University Dr., S.W. Phone: (507)835-1000
Waseca, MN 56093 Nan Wilhelmson, Dir.
Founded: 1971. **Staff:** Prof 3; Other 1. **Subjects:** Agricultural business, production, industries, and services; animal health technology; food industry and technology; home and family services; horticulture technology. **Holdings:** 24,000 books; 490 bound periodical volumes; 3500 AV programs; 7320 government documents; 2320 microforms; 7600 pamphlets. **Subscriptions:** 830 journals and other serials; 40 newspapers. **Services:** Interlibrary loan; copying; library open to the public. **Automated Operations:** Computerized cataloging. **Computerized Information Services:** DIALOG Information Services, OCLC. **Networks/Consortia:** Member of MINITEX, Southcentral Minnesota Inter-Library Exchange (SMILE), Waseca Interlibrary Resource Exchange (WIRE). **Publications:** Monthly Bibliography - free upon request. **Special Catalogs:** KWIT catalog to AV programs. **Staff:** Kathryn Rynders, Ref.Libn.; Kathleen Ashe, Tech.Serv.Libn..

★16513★
UNIVERSITY OF MISSISSIPPI - ARCHIVES & SPECIAL COLLECTIONS/MISSISSIPPIANA (Hum, Hist)
University, MS 38677 Phone: (601)232-7408
Dr. Thomas M. Verich, Univ.Archv.
Founded: 1975. **Staff:** Prof 2; Other 3. **Subjects:** Mississippi and Southern subjects and authors, Afro-American fiction. **Special Collections:** Lumber archives of lumber industry of southern Mississippi (268 linear feet); William Faulkner Collection (2000 volumes); Wynn Collection of Faulkner editions; Senator Pat Harrison Collection (51 linear feet including photographs); Arthur Palmer Hudson Folklore Collection (5 linear feet); David L. Cohn Collection (12 linear feet); Stark Young Collection (3.5 linear feet); Revolutionary War Letters (1 linear foot); Rayburn Collection of Paper Americana (36 linear feet); Herschel Brickell Collection (4000 manuscript items; 3400 volumes; 150 linear feet); William Faulkner Rowan Oak Literary Manuscript Collection; James Silver papers (20 linear feet); Aldrich Collection (10 linear feet); William R. Ferris Collection (350 linear feet). **Holdings:** 32,000 books; 3000 bound periodical volumes; 2000 manuscripts; 525 linear feet of University of Mississippi archival materials; 221 linear feet of Thomas G. Abernathy papers; 67 linear feet of Carroll Gartin papers, 1913-1966; 485 linear feet of John E. Rankin papers, 1882-1960; 164 linear feet of William M. Whittington papers, 1878-1962; 180

linear feet of William M. (Fishbait) Miller papers (all papers are unprocessed); 9.5 linear feet of Henry H. Bellamann papers, 1882-1945; 80 linear feet of James W. Garner papers. **Subscriptions:** 150 journals and other serials. **Services:** Copying; archives open to the public. **Staff:** Elise Winter Gillespie, Sr.Lib.Asst.; Sharron Eve Sarthou, Sr.Lib.Asst..

★16514★
UNIVERSITY OF MISSISSIPPI - BUREAU OF BUSINESS & ECONOMIC RESEARCH LIBRARY (Bus-Fin)
School of Business Administration
University, MS 38677 Phone: (601)232-7481
Subjects: Economics, business, public finance, government. **Holdings:** 5000 documents; Mississippi documents. **Subscriptions:** 300 journals and other serials. **Services:** Interlibrary loan; library open to the public for reference use only.

★16515★
UNIVERSITY OF MISSISSIPPI - JOHN DAVIS WILLIAMS LIBRARY - AUSTIN A. DODGE PHARMACY LIBRARY (Med)
University, MS 38677 Phone: (601)232-7381
Nancy F. Fuller, Libn.
Founded: 1965. **Staff:** Prof 1; Other 1. **Subjects:** Pharmacy, medicine, organic chemistry, health care administration, botany (pharmacognosy). **Holdings:** 27,997 books, bound periodical volumes, reels of microfilm, AV programs; 34 VF drawers of pamphlets; 127 dissertations and graduate theses from School of Pharmacy. **Subscriptions:** 442 journals and other serials; 5 newspapers. **Services:** Interlibrary loan; copying; library open to the public for reference use only. **Computerized Information Services:** BRS Information Technologies, DIALOG Information Services, NLM, MEDLINE, CAS ONLINE, OCLC. **Networks/Consortia:** Member of Association of Memphis Area Health Sciences Libraries (AMAHSL), Mississippi Biomedical Library Consortium.

★16516★
UNIVERSITY OF MISSISSIPPI - JOHN DAVIS WILLIAMS LIBRARY - BLUES ARCHIVE (Mus)
Farley Hall Phone: (601)232-7753
University, MS 38677 Suzanne Flandreau Steel, Libn.
Founded: 1984. **Staff:** Prof 2; Other 1. **Subjects:** Music - blues, gospel, American traditional; folklore. **Special Collections:** Goldstein Folklore Collection (10,000 volumes; 5600 recordings); B.B. King Collection (9100 recordings); Living Blues Archival Collection (18 feet of archives; 17,000 recordings); Trumpet Record Company (10 feet of archives). **Holdings:** 11,000 books; 200 bound periodical volumes; 35,000 phonograph records; 30 feet of manuscripts and archives; 500 posters; 4 feet of photographs; 100 audio cassettes; 50 video cassettes; 2000 pamphlets; 150 feet of unbound periodicals. **Subscriptions:** 40 journals and other serials. **Services:** Copying; archive open to the public. **Automated Operations:** Computerized cataloging. **Computerized Information Services:** OCLC. **Networks/Consortia:** Member of SOLINET. **Special Catalogs:** Finding aids to manuscript and archival collections. **Staff:** Elaine Raybon White, Cat.; Walter Liniger, Fld.Res..

★16517★
UNIVERSITY OF MISSISSIPPI - PUBLIC POLICY RESEARCH CENTER (Soc Sci)
University, MS 38677 Phone: (601)232-7401
Carol M. Hopkins, Libn.
Founded: 1945. **Staff:** Prof 1. **Subjects:** State, local, and national government; public administration and regional governance. **Special Collections:** Mississippi Collection (500 volumes). **Holdings:** 5500 volumes; 10 VF drawers of publications and clippings; 85 dissertations and masters' theses. **Subscriptions:** 200 journals and other serials. **Services:** Library open to qualified researchers.

★16518★
UNIVERSITY OF MISSISSIPPI - SCHOOL OF LAW LIBRARY (Law)
University, MS 38677 Phone: (601)232-7361
J. Wesley Cochran, Law Libn.
Founded: 1854. **Staff:** Prof 5; Other 6. **Subjects:** American and international law. **Special Collections:** Papers of Senator Eastland (1600 linear feet), Senator Cochran (75 linear feet), Congressman Lott (40 linear feet), Judge Smith (20 linear feet); space law (500 volumes). **Holdings:** 150,000 volumes; 200,000 microforms. **Subscriptions:** 2200 journals and other serials. **Services:** Interlibrary loan; copying; library open to the public with restrictions. **Automated Operations:** Computerized cataloging. **Computerized Information Services:** LEXIS, WESTLAW, OCLC. **Networks/Consortia:** Member of SOLINET. **Staff:** Ellis Tucker, Pub.Serv.Libn.; Nancy North, Ref.Libn..

★16519★
UNIVERSITY OF MISSISSIPPI - UNIVERSITY MUSEUMS - LIBRARY (Hist)
University, MS 38677 Phone: (601)232-7073
Lucy Turnbull, Dir. of Musms.
Subjects: Local history. **Holdings:** 800 books. **Services:** Library open to the public with supervision.

UNIVERSITY OF MISSOURI - WESTERN HISTORICAL MANUSCRIPT COLLECTION
See: Western Historical Manuscript Collection/State Historical Society of Missouri Manuscripts Joint Collection (17708)

★16520★
UNIVERSITY OF MISSOURI, COLUMBIA - ANTHROPOLOGY MUSEUM - ARCHIVES (Soc Sci)
Dept. of Anthropology
104 Swallow Hall
Columbia, MO 65211 Phone: (314)882-3764
Founded: 1973. **Staff:** Prof 1. **Subjects:** Guatemalan colonial manuscripts; publications from Thailand; travels of Missourians abroad in the early 20th century, especially Francis Pearl Mitchell; oral history; photograph collection; motion pictures. **Holdings:** 41 archival boxes; tapes; videotapes; slides. **Subscriptions:** 27 journals and other serials. **Services:** Archives open to the public at director's discretion.

★16521★
UNIVERSITY OF MISSOURI, COLUMBIA - CENTER FOR ECONOMIC EDUCATION - LIBRARY (Bus-Fin)
Dept. of Economics
Professional Bldg. Phone: (314)882-3803
Columbia, MO 65211 Dr. Elizabeth Dickhaus, Dir.
Founded: 1970. **Subjects:** Economic education. **Holdings:** 2000 volumes. **Publications:** Newsletters, quarterly.

UNIVERSITY OF MISSOURI, COLUMBIA - COLLEGE OF VETERINARY MEDICINE - OFA HIP DISPLASIA REGISTRY
See: Orthopedic Foundation for Animals - OFA Hip Dysplasia Registry (10938)

★16522★
UNIVERSITY OF MISSOURI, COLUMBIA - COLUMBIA MISSOURIAN - NEWSPAPER REFERENCE LIBRARY (Publ)
Box 917 Phone: (314)882-4876
Columbia, MO 65205 Robert Stevens, Newspaper Ref.Libn.
Staff: Prof 1; Other 6. **Subjects:** Newspaper reference topics, Columbia, Boone County, Missouri, University of Missouri. **Holdings:** 95 books; 37,800 biographical clippings files; 10,800 subject clippings files; 13,200 photograph and illustration files; 560 pamphlet files. **Services:** Interlibrary loan; copying; SDI; library open to the public for reference use only. **Computerized Information Services:** Dow Jones News/Retrieval, CompuServe, Inc., VU/TEXT Information Services, The Source Information Network; internal database. Performs searches on fee basis. **Special Indexes:** Subject index to file cards and clippings; references to Columbia Missourian, Columbia Missourian Weekly, and Columbia Daily Tribune, 1977-1981. **Remarks:** Library located at 9th and Elm, Columbia, MO 65201.

★16523★
UNIVERSITY OF MISSOURI, COLUMBIA - DEPARTMENT OF GEOGRAPHY - MAP COLLECTION (Geog-Map)
8 Stewart Hall Phone: (314)882-8370
Columbia, MO 65211 Walter A. Schroeder, Chm.
Founded: 1950. **Subjects:** Missouri, Anglo-America. **Special Collections:** Maps and state agency documents on Missouri. **Holdings:** 4200 maps; 166 atlases; 480 wall maps. **Services:** Collection open to the public.

★16524★
UNIVERSITY OF MISSOURI, COLUMBIA - ENGINEERING LIBRARY (Sci-Engr)
2017 Engineering Bldg. Phone: (314)882-2379
Columbia, MO 65211 Alfred H. Jones, Engr.Libn.
Founded: 1906. **Staff:** Prof 1; Other 2. **Subjects:** Engineering - chemical, civil, electrical, industrial, mechanical, aerospace, agricultural, nuclear. **Holdings:** 65,065 volumes. **Subscriptions:** 606 journals and other serials. **Services:** Interlibrary loan; copying; library open to the public with

restrictions on borrowing. **Automated Operations:** Computerized cataloging and acquisitions. **Computerized Information Services:** DIALOG Information Services, Pergamon ORBIT InfoLine, Inc., BRS Information Technologies, OCLC. **Networks/Consortia:** Member of Center for Research Libraries (CRL) Consortia, Missouri Library Network (MLNC). **Publications:** New Book List, monthly - to engineering faculty.

★16525★
UNIVERSITY OF MISSOURI, COLUMBIA - FREEDOM OF INFORMATION CENTER (Info Sci)
20 Walter Williams Hall
Box 858 Phone: (314)882-4856
Columbia, MO 65205 M. Kathleen Edwards, Mgr.
Founded: 1959. **Subjects:** Governmental, societal, and economic controls on information. **Holdings:** 171 volumes; pamphlets; clippings; reprints; government documents; professional newsletters. **Subscriptions:** 150 journals and other serials. **Services:** Collecting, indexing, and disseminating information on the public's right to know; copying; reference and referral on over 1000 subjects on demand; center open to the public.

★16526★
UNIVERSITY OF MISSOURI, COLUMBIA - GEOLOGY LIBRARY (Sci-Engr)
201 Geology Bldg. Phone: (314)882-4860
Columbia, MO 65211 Robert Heidlage, Lib.Asst.
Staff: 5. **Subjects:** Paleontology, stratigraphy, sedimentology, geochemistry, geomorphology, hydrology. **Holdings:** 39,000 volumes; 100,000 maps. **Subscriptions:** 500 journals and other serials. **Services:** Interlibrary loan; copying; library open to the public for reference use; materials circulate to library card holders only. **Automated Operations:** Computerized cataloging and acquisitions. **Computerized Information Services:** OCLC, DIALOG Information Services, Pergamon ORBIT InfoLine, Inc., BRS Information Technologies. **Networks/Consortia:** Member of Center for Research Libraries (CRL) Consortia.

★16527★
UNIVERSITY OF MISSOURI, COLUMBIA - INFORMATION SCIENCE GROUP - INFORMATION CENTER (Med)
605 Lewis Hall Phone: (314)882-6966
Columbia, MO 65211 Joyce A. Mitchell, Ph.D., Dir.
Founded: 1977. **Staff:** Prof 3; Other 2. **Subjects:** Health care technology, health services research, computer applications in medicine. **Special Collections:** Medical Information Systems (2600 entries), includes Drug Information Systems (290 entries) and Hospital Information Systems (600 entries); Microprocessors (200 entries); Medical Imaging (2000 entries), including Computerized Tomography (1200 entries) and Ultrasound (600 entries); End-Stage Renal Disease (460 entries); Medical Competency Examination (290 entries); Hospital Technology Costs (500 entries); Mental Health Information Systems (1200 entries). **Holdings:** 1200 books; 2000 unbound periodicals; 6000 reprints; 800 pamphlets, clippings, manuscripts, and reports. **Subscriptions:** 70 journals and other serials. **Services:** Copying; center open to the public through HCTC Project Staff. **Computerized Information Services:** DIALOG Information Services, MEDLARS; HSRC/HCTC Special Collections database (internal database). **Staff:** Beatrice Engley, Info.Spec.; Jody Neikirk, Info.Asst..

★16528★
UNIVERSITY OF MISSOURI, COLUMBIA - J. OTTO LOTTES HEALTH SCIENCES LIBRARY (Med)
Health Sciences Center Phone: (314)882-8086
Columbia, MO 65212 Dean Schmidt, Dir.
Founded: 1903. **Staff:** Prof 9; Other 13. **Subjects:** Medicine, nursing, hospital administration. **Holdings:** 167,216 volumes; 230 microforms; 500 tapes; 150 motion pictures; 200 AV programs; 25 phonograph records; 2000 slides. **Subscriptions:** 1930 journals and other serials. **Services:** Interlibrary loan; copying; SDI; library open to the public. **Automated Operations:** Computerized cataloging, acquisitions, serials, and ILL. **Computerized Information Services:** WILSONLINE, AMA/NET, MEDLINE, BRS Information Technologies, DIALOG Information Services, Pergamon ORBIT InfoLine, Inc.; LUMIN (internal database). Performs searches on fee basis. Contact Person: Diane Johnson, Hd., Info.Serv., 882-6141. **Networks/Consortia:** Member of Midcontinental Regional Medical Library Program. **Staff:** Richard Rexroat, Hd., Tech.Serv.; Alice Edwards, Hd., Access Serv.; Shelley Worden, Hd., Coll.Mgt.; Isabel Pinto, Ref.Libn.; Ruth Riley, Ref.Libn.; Ming Luh, Hd., ILL.

★16529★
UNIVERSITY OF MISSOURI, COLUMBIA - JOURNALISM LIBRARY (Info Sci)
117 Walter Williams Hall Phone: (314)882-7502
Columbia, MO 65202 Mary E. Allcorn, Libn.
Founded: 1908. **Staff:** Prof 1; Other 4. **Subjects:** Advertising, broadcasting, journalism, magazines, news writing and management, newspaper publishing, photography, public relations, semantics, typography, linotype. **Holdings:** 21,696 books; 5590 bound periodical volumes. **Subscriptions:** 350 journals and other serials. **Computerized Information Services:** DIALOG Information Services, BRS Information Technologies.

★16530★
UNIVERSITY OF MISSOURI, COLUMBIA - MATH SCIENCES LIBRARY (Sci-Engr, Comp Sci)
206 Math Sciences Bldg. Phone: (314)882-7286
Columbia, MO 65211 Dixie L. Fingerson, Lib.Asst.
Founded: 1968. **Staff:** 2. **Subjects:** Mathematics, computer science, statistics. **Holdings:** 33,380 volumes. **Subscriptions:** 462 journals and other serials. **Services:** Interlibrary loan; library open to the public with restrictions. **Automated Operations:** Computerized cataloging, acquisitions, and circulation. **Computerized Information Services:** DIALOG Information Services, Pergamon ORBIT InfoLine, Inc., BRS Information Technologies, OCLC. **Networks/Consortia:** Member of Center for Research Libraries (CRL) Consortia.

★16531★
UNIVERSITY OF MISSOURI, COLUMBIA - MISSOURI INSTITUTE OF PSYCHIATRY LIBRARY (Med)
5400 Arsenal St. Phone: (314)644-8838
St. Louis, MO 63139-1494 Mary E. Johnson, Lib.Dir.
Founded: 1962. **Staff:** Prof 1; Other 4. **Subjects:** Psychiatry, neurology, psychology, biochemistry, nursing. **Holdings:** 9760 books; 10,000 bound periodical volumes; 7 VF drawers; 125 films and video cassettes; 450 audio cassettes; 50 microforms. **Subscriptions:** 400 journals and other serials. **Services:** Interlibrary loan; copying; SDI; library open to the public. **Automated Operations:** Computerized cataloging, serials, circulation, and ILL. **Computerized Information Services:** DIALOG Information Services, BRS Information Technologies, OCLC, Philnet, PHILSOM. Performs searches on fee basis. **Networks/Consortia:** Member of St. Louis Regional Library Network, Midcontinental Regional Medical Library Program. **Publications:** Missouri Institute of Psychiatry Faculty Publications. **Remarks:** An alternate telephone number is 644-8860.

★16532★
UNIVERSITY OF MISSOURI, COLUMBIA - MUSEUM OF ART AND ARCHAEOLOGY - LIBRARY (Art)
1 Pickard Hall Phone: (314)882-3591
Columbia, MO 65211 Forrest McGill, Dir. of Musm.
Subjects: Art history, archeology. **Holdings:** 560 books; 5160 exhibition and sales catalogs. **Services:** Library open to the public with restrictions.

★16533★
UNIVERSITY OF MISSOURI, COLUMBIA - SCHOOL OF LAW LIBRARY (Law)
Tate Hall Phone: (314)882-4597
Columbia, MO 65211 Susan D. Csaky, Prof./Law Libn.
Staff: Prof 5; Other 7. **Subjects:** Law. **Special Collections:** Lawson Collection (criminal law and criminology); U.S. and state government document depository. **Holdings:** 181,714 volumes; 270,464 microforms. **Subscriptions:** 3576 journals and other serials. **Services:** Interlibrary loan; copying; library open to the public with restrictions. **Automated Operations:** Computerized cataloging. **Computerized Information Services:** LEXIS, NEXIS, OCLC, WESTLAW; ABA/net (electronic mail service). Performs searches on fee basis. Contact Person: JoAnn Humphreys, Comp.Serv./Law Libn., 882-4597. **Networks/Consortia:** Member of Mid-America Law School Library Consortium, Libraries of the University of Missouri Information Network (LUMIN), Missouri Library Network (MLNC), CLASS. **Publications:** Law Library Guide; Selected Acquisitions List; Information Services; bibliographies. **Staff:** Needra Jackson, Pub.Serv./Law Libn.; Connie Fennewald, Tech.Serv./Law Libn.; Wilma Gulstad, Cat./Law Libn..

★16534★
UNIVERSITY OF MISSOURI, COLUMBIA - SPECIAL COLLECTIONS (Hist)
9th St. and Lowry Mall Phone: (314)882-7461
Columbia, MO 65201 Margaret A. Howell, Hd., Spec.Coll.
Staff: Prof 1; Other 4. **Subjects:** American and church history, history of printing. **Special Collections:** Rare book collection; Thomas Moore

Johnson Collection of Philosophy; Frank Luther Mott Collection of American Best Sellers; University of Missouri Collection; Anthony C. DeBellis Collection of Italian Literature; 19th century British pamphlets. **Holdings:** 41,000 books; 1650 bound periodical volumes; 2.8 million microforms. **Subscriptions:** 270 journals and other serials; 23 newspapers. **Services:** Interlibrary loan; copying (both limited); collections open to the public. **Automated Operations:** Computerized cataloging, acquisitions, and serials.

★16535★
UNIVERSITY OF MISSOURI, COLUMBIA - VETERINARY MEDICAL LIBRARY (Med)
W218 Veterinary Medicine — Phone: (314)882-2461
Columbia, MO 65211 — Trenton Boyd, Libn.
Founded: 1951. **Staff:** Prof 1; Other 2. **Subjects:** Veterinary medicine. **Holdings:** 18,789 books; 19,477 bound periodical volumes; 740 microforms. **Subscriptions:** 615 journals and other serials; 5 newspapers. **Services:** Interlibrary loan; copying; library open to the public. **Automated Operations:** Computerized cataloging, acquisitions, and serials. **Computerized Information Services:** MEDLINE, DIALOG Information Services, Pergamon ORBIT InfoLine, Inc., BRS Information Technologies.

★16536★
UNIVERSITY OF MISSOURI, KANSAS CITY - CONSERVATORY LIBRARY (Mus)
General Library
5100 Rockhill Rd. — Phone: (816)276-1675
Kansas City, MO 64110 — Peter Munstedt, Mus.Libn.
Founded: 1906. **Staff:** Prof 1; Other 1. **Subjects:** Music. **Special Collections:** Archives of the Institute for Studies in American Music (manuscripts of regional and national composers, including Amy Beach and Paul Creston; 10 collections); popular American sheet music (30,000 items); Warner Brothers Film Music Collection (12,000 scores). **Holdings:** 50,143 volumes; 18,005 recordings; music sheets. **Subscriptions:** 288 journals and other serials. **Services:** Interlibrary loan; library not open to the public.

★16537★
UNIVERSITY OF MISSOURI, KANSAS CITY - HEALTH SCIENCES LIBRARY (Med)
2411 Holmes — Phone: (816)474-4100
Kansas City, MO 64108 — Marilyn Sullivan, Chf.Libn.
Founded: 1967. **Staff:** Prof 7; Other 7. **Subjects:** Medicine, nursing. **Holdings:** 17,073 books; 47,365 serial volumes; 2645 AV titles. **Subscriptions:** 1031 journals and other serials. **Services:** Interlibrary loan; copying; SDI; library open to members of the health sciences community. **Computerized Information Services:** DIALOG Information Services, Pergamon ORBIT InfoLine, Inc., BRS Information Technologies, MEDLARS; internal database. **Networks/Consortia:** Member of Kansas City Library Network, Inc. (KCLN). **Publications:** Current References, monthly - free to UMKC School of Medicine and affiliated institutions. **Remarks:** Contains the archives of the American Nurses' Association. **Staff:** Amrita Burdick, Asst.Chf.Libn.; Ruth Shipley, Clin.Med.Libn.; Marlene Smith, AV Med.Libn.; Roberta Munsterman, ILL.

★16538★
UNIVERSITY OF MISSOURI, KANSAS CITY - LAW LIBRARY (Law)
School of Law
5100 Rockhill Rd.
Kansas City, MO 64110 — Phone: (816)276-1650
Staff: Prof 5; Other 6. **Subjects:** Law. **Holdings:** 144,647 volumes; 183,145 microfiche; 351 reels of microfilm. **Subscriptions:** 4714 journals and other serials. **Services:** Interlibrary loan; copying; library open to the public. **Automated Operations:** Computerized cataloging, acquisitions, and serials. **Computerized Information Services:** LEXIS, WESTLAW, INNOVACQ Automated Library System, OCLC; LUMIN (internal database). **Staff:** Patricia Court, Rd.Serv.Libn.; Margaret Hohenstein, Tech.Serv.Libn.; Claudia Dansby, Acq.Libn.; William Draper, Ref.Libn..

★16539★
UNIVERSITY OF MISSOURI, KANSAS CITY - SCHOOL OF DENTISTRY LIBRARY (Med)
650 E. 25th St. — Phone: (816)234-0494
Kansas City, MO 64108 — Ann Marie Corry, Dental Libn.
Founded: 1920. **Staff:** Prof 2; Other 3. **Subjects:** Dentistry. **Holdings:** 11,504 books; 9998 bibliographic volumes of periodicals. **Subscriptions:** 385 journals and other serials. **Services:** Interlibrary loan; copying; library open to the public for reference use only. **Computerized Information Services:** BRS Information Technologies, MEDLINE, Octanet. **Networks/Consortia:** Member of Kansas City Library Network, Inc. (KCLN). **Staff:** Carol Doms, Asst. Dental Libn..

★16540★
UNIVERSITY OF MISSOURI, KANSAS CITY - SNYDER COLLECTION OF AMERICANA (Hist)
General Library
5100 Rockhill Rd.
Kansas City, MO 64110 — Phone: (816)276-1534
Founded: 1937. **Subjects:** Political campaign literature; Civil War; Indians of North America; Kansas and Missouri - history, travel, biography, fiction, poetry; 19th century Americana; early Missouri and Kansas imprints. **Holdings:** 25,000 volumes. **Services:** Interlibrary loan; copying (both limited).

★16541★
UNIVERSITY OF MISSOURI, KANSAS CITY - TEDROW TRANSPORTATION COLLECTION
General Library
5100 Rockhill Rd.
Kansas City, MO 64110
Defunct. Holdings absorbed by general library.

★16542★
UNIVERSITY OF MISSOURI, ROLLA - CURTIS LAWS WILSON LIBRARY (Sci-Engr)
Rolla, MO 65401 — Phone: (314)341-4227
Ronald Bohley, Libn.
Founded: 1871. **Staff:** Prof 8; Other 19. **Subjects:** Mining, metallurgy, engineering, geology, earth sciences. **Special Collections:** U.S. Geological Survey publications; U.S. Bureau of Mines publications. **Holdings:** 391,000 volumes; 330,000 titles on microform. **Subscriptions:** 2000 journals and other serials; 20 newspapers. **Services:** Interlibrary loan; copying; library open to the public. **Automated Operations:** Computerized cataloging and serials. **Computerized Information Services:** DIALOG Information Services, OCLC; LUMIN (internal database). **Networks/Consortia:** Member of Missouri Library Network (MLNC), Southwest Missouri Library Network. **Staff:** Jean Eisenman, Asst.Dir., Pub.Serv.; Bruce Gilbert, Asst.Dir., Tech.Serv.; Gloria Ho, Cat.; Susan Singleton, Ref.; Andy Stewart, Ref..

★16543★
UNIVERSITY OF MISSOURI, ST. LOUIS - EDUCATION LIBRARY (Educ)
8001 Natural Bridge Rd. — Phone: (314)553-5572
St. Louis, MO 63121 — Virginia Workman, Hd.
Founded: 1976. **Staff:** Prof 1; Other 15. **Subjects:** Education, children's literature. **Special Collections:** Children's literature (6498 books). **Holdings:** 27,017 books; 5141 bound periodical volumes; 12,426 K-12 textbooks; 12,735 curriculum guides (4481 hardcopy; 8254 on microfiche); 351,596 ERIC microfiche; 1702 tests (840 standardized; 862 unpublished). **Subscriptions:** 404 journals and other serials. **Services:** Interlibrary loan; library open to the public with restrictions. **Automated Operations:** Computerized cataloging. **Computerized Information Services:** BRS Information Technologies; LUMIN (internal database). Performs searches on fee basis. **Networks/Consortia:** Member of St. Louis Regional Library Network. **Remarks:** An alternate telephone number is 553-5188. **Staff:** Leta Webster, Tech.Serv.Supv.; Diane Burnett, Pub.Serv.Supv..

★16544★
UNIVERSITY OF MISSOURI, ST. LOUIS - HEALTH SCIENCES LIBRARY (Med)
8001 Natural Bridge Rd. — Phone: (314)553-5909
St. Louis, MO 63121 — Cheryle J. Cann, Hd.Libn.
Founded: 1981. **Staff:** Prof 1; Other 2. **Subjects:** Optometry, ophthalmology, nursing, public health, medicine. **Holdings:** 4500 books; 2400 bound periodical volumes; 600 AV programs; 215 reels of microfilm; 1000 microfiche. **Subscriptions:** 190 journals and other serials. **Services:** Interlibrary loan; copying; SDI (upon written request); library open to the public. **Automated Operations:** Computerized cataloging. **Computerized Information Services:** OCLC, BRS Information Technologies; LUMIN (internal database). **Networks/Consortia:** Member of St. Louis Regional Library Network, Libraries of the University of Missouri Information Network (LUMIN), Association of Visual Science Librarians (AVSL). **Publications:** Self-Guided Tour of the Health Sciences Library - to students, faculty, and staff; recent acquisitions list, irregular - to faculty, staff, and Association of Visual Science Librarians members.

★16545★
UNIVERSITY OF MISSOURI, ST. LOUIS - THOMAS JEFFERSON LIBRARY - SPECIAL COLLECTIONS (Soc Sci, Hum)
8001 Natural Bridge Rd. Phone: (314)553-5053
St. Louis, MO 63121 Barbara Lehocky, Act.Dir.
Special Collections: Colonial Latin American history; Utopian literature and science fiction; U.S. Government Depository Library. **Services:** Interlibrary loan; copying; collections open to the public. **Automated Operations:** Computerized cataloging. **Computerized Information Services:** DIALOG Information Services, BRS Information Technologies, OCLC; LUMIN (internal database). Performs searches on fee basis. Contact Person: Mark Scheu, 553-5060. **Networks/Consortia:** Member of St. Louis Regional Library Network, Missouri Library Network (MLNC).

★16546★
UNIVERSITY OF MISSOURI, ST. LOUIS - WOMEN'S CENTER (Soc Sci)
107A Benton Hall
8001 Natural Bridge Rd. Phone: (314)553-5380
St. Louis, MO 63121 Cathy Burack, Dir.
Staff: 3. **Subjects:** Women - politics, psychology, medicine; male sex roles. **Holdings:** 450 books; 500 unbound periodicals; 8 VF drawers of clippings and reports. **Subscriptions:** 6 newspapers. **Services:** Center open to the public with permission.

★16547★
UNIVERSITY OF MONTANA - BUREAU OF BUSINESS AND ECONOMIC RESEARCH - LIBRARY (Bus-Fin)
School of Business Administration Phone: (406)243-5113
Missoula, MT 59812 James Sylvester, Statistician
Staff: 1. **Subjects:** Economic indicators in the United States and Montana; regional economics with emphasis on Montana and northern Rocky Mountain area; wood products industry. **Special Collections:** Montana, Idaho, and Wyoming Forest Industry Data Systems; County Data Packages, Montana. **Holdings:** Figures not available. **Subscriptions:** 52 journals and other serials. **Services:** Copying; library open to the public with restrictions. **Publications:** List of publications - available on request.

★16548★
UNIVERSITY OF MONTANA - ENVIRONMENTAL LIBRARY
Jeanette Rankin Hall
Missoula, MT 59812
Defunct

★16549★
UNIVERSITY OF MONTANA - INSTRUCTIONAL MATERIALS SERVICE (Aud-Vis)
Missoula, MT 59812 Phone: (406)243-4070
Devon Chandler, Dir.
Staff: Prof 6; Other 10. **Subjects:** Audio-visual materials. **Holdings:** 63,937 AV programs; 1400 films; 900 videotapes; 7725 sound recordings; 2500 slides, filmstrips, art prints, study prints, transparencies, kits, computer files. **Services:** Interlibrary loan; copying; service open to the public with restrictions. **Automated Operations:** Computerized cataloging and acquisitions. **Computerized Information Services:** AVLINE; internal databases. Performs searches free of charge. Contact Person: Linda Harris, 243-2859. **Networks/Consortia:** Member of Western Library Network (WLN). **Special Catalogs:** Film catalog, annual - to Consortium of University Film Centers members; IMS Review - for internal distribution only. **Staff:** Karen Driessen; Robert Wachtel.

★16550★
UNIVERSITY OF MONTANA - MAUREEN & MIKE MANSFIELD LIBRARY - K. ROSS TOOLE ARCHIVES (Hist)
Missoula, MT 59812 Phone: (406)243-2053
Dale L. Johnson, Archv.
Staff: Prof 1. **Subjects:** Montana - business history, forest industries; politics and government. **Special Collections:** James W. Gerard Collection; Mike Mansfield Collection; James E. Murray Collection; Joseph M. Dixon Collection; Dorothy M. Johnson Collection; Chet Huntley Collection. **Holdings:** 800 oral histories; 30,000 photographs; 8000 feet of manuscripts. **Services:** Copying; archives open to the public.

★16551★
UNIVERSITY OF MONTANA - MAUREEN & MIKE MANSFIELD LIBRARY - SCIENCE DIVISION (Sci-Engr, Env-Cons)
Missoula, MT 59812 Phone: (406)243-6411
Robert Schipf, Sci.Libn.
Staff: Prof 1; Other 1. **Subjects:** Forestry sciences, conservation, range management, public administration, wildlife management, wood science and technology, recreation. **Holdings:** 40,000 cataloged items. **Subscriptions:** 50 journals and other serials. **Services:** Collection open to the public. **Computerized Information Services:** DIALOG Information Services, BRS Information Technologies. **Networks/Consortia:** Member of Western Library Network (WLN). **Formerly:** School of Forestry - Oxford Collection. **Staff:** Irene Evers, Asst.Sci.Libn..

★16552★
UNIVERSITY OF MONTANA - OFFICE OF CAREER SERVICES - CAREER RESOURCE CENTER (Educ)
Lodge 006 Phone: (406)243-5460
Missoula, MT 59812 Richard McDonough, Career Couns.
Founded: 1974. **Staff:** Prof 1; Other 4. **Subjects:** Career information. **Holdings:** 200 books; 1200 reports, monographs, pamphlet files; state and national job vacancy listings; state and federal government career information; corporate literature; undergraduate and graduate school information. **Subscriptions:** 12 journals and other serials. **Services:** Center open to the public for reference use only.

UNIVERSITY OF MONTANA - SCHOOL OF FORESTRY - OXFORD COLLECTION
See: University of Montana - Maureen & Mike Mansfield Library - Science Division (16551)

★16553★
UNIVERSITY OF MONTANA - SCHOOL OF LAW - LAW LIBRARY (Law)
Missoula, MT 59812 Phone: (406)243-6171
Maurice M. Michel, Dir.
Founded: 1911. **Staff:** Prof 2; Other 3. **Subjects:** Law. **Special Collections:** Indian law (156 treatises). **Holdings:** 110,200 books. **Subscriptions:** 783 journals and other serials. **Services:** Interlibrary loan; copying; library open to the public for reference use only. **Computerized Information Services:** WESTLAW.

★16554★
UNIVERSITY OF NEBRASKA, LINCOLN - ARCHITECTURE LIBRARY (Art, Plan)
308 Architectural Hall Phone: (402)472-1208
Lincoln, NE 68588-0108 Kay Logan-Peters, Arch.Libn.
Staff: Prof 1; Other 2. **Subjects:** Architecture, community and regional planning. **Holdings:** 20,122 books; 9442 bound periodical volumes; 988 volumes on microfilm; 4103 volumes on microfiche; 48 VF drawers; 10,000 slides. **Subscriptions:** 756 journals and other serials. **Services:** Interlibrary loan; library open to the public. **Automated Operations:** Computerized circulation. **Computerized Information Services:** DIALOG Information Services, BRS Information Technologies (through Love Library). **Networks/Consortia:** Member of NEBASE.

★16555★
UNIVERSITY OF NEBRASKA, LINCOLN - BIOLOGICAL SCIENCES LIBRARY (Biol Sci)
Manter Hall 402 Phone: (402)472-2756
Lincoln, NE 68588-0118 Richard E. Voeltz, Assoc.Prof.
Founded: 1895. **Staff:** Prof 1; Other 2. **Subjects:** Botany, zoology, microbiology. **Holdings:** 30,344 books; 37,670 bound periodical volumes; 505 microforms. **Subscriptions:** 2001 journals and other serials. **Services:** Interlibrary loan; copying; library open to the public. **Automated Operations:** Computerized cataloging, acquisitions, and circulation. **Computerized Information Services:** DIALOG Information Services. **Publications:** Acquisitions list, monthly - for internal distribution only.

★16556★
UNIVERSITY OF NEBRASKA, LINCOLN - C.Y. THOMPSON LIBRARY (Biol Sci, Sci-Engr, Agri)
East Campus Phone: (402)472-2802
Lincoln, NE 68583-0717 Lyle Schreiner, Prof.
Staff: Prof 3; Other 4. **Subjects:** Agriculture, home economics, textiles, wildlife conservation, human development, nutrition, applied sciences, speech pathology. **Special Collections:** Entomology collection containing many rare volumes. **Holdings:** 121,143 books; 119,673 bound periodical volumes; 15,890 microforms. **Subscriptions:** 4586 journals and other

serials; 9 newspapers. **Services:** Interlibrary loan; copying; library open to the public. **Automated Operations:** Computerized cataloging, acquisitions, and circulation. **Computerized Information Services:** DIALOG Information Services, WILSONLINE; internal database. Performs searches on fee basis. **Publications:** Acquisitions list, biweekly - for internal distribution only. **Staff:** Richard Jizba, Asst.Prof.; Vicki Eastman, Lib.Techn.; B.J. Kacena, Asst.Prof..

★16557★
UNIVERSITY OF NEBRASKA, LINCOLN - CENTER FOR GREAT PLAINS STUDIES (Hist, Art)
205 Love Library Phone: (402)472-6220
Lincoln, NE 68588-0475 Jon Nelson, Cur.
Founded: 1980. **Staff:** Prof 1; Other 5. **Subjects:** Western Americana. **Special Collections:** William Henry Jackson Photographs; Patricia J. and Stanley H. Broder Collection of Indian Painting. **Holdings:** 2500 books; 500 photographs; 300 paintings; 200 sculptures; 100 drawings and graphics. **Services:** Copying; center open to the public. **Automated Operations:** Computerized public access catalog and cataloging. **Publications:** Great Plains Quarterly.

★16558★
UNIVERSITY OF NEBRASKA, LINCOLN - CHEMISTRY LIBRARY (Sci-Engr)
Hamilton Hall 427 Phone: (402)472-2739
Lincoln, NE 68588-0305 Richard E. Voeltz, Assoc.Prof.
Founded: 1930. **Staff:** Prof 1; Other 1. **Subjects:** Chemistry, chemical engineering. **Holdings:** 14,591 books; 23,091 bound periodical volumes; 1498 microforms. **Subscriptions:** 839 journals and other serials. **Services:** Interlibrary loan; copying; library open to the public. **Automated Operations:** Computerized cataloging, acquisitions, and circulation. **Computerized Information Services:** DIALOG Information Services. **Publications:** Acquisitions list, monthly - for internal distribution only.

★16559★
UNIVERSITY OF NEBRASKA, LINCOLN - COLLEGE OF LAW LIBRARY (Law)
East Campus Phone: (402)472-3548
Lincoln, NE 68583-0902 Sally H. Wise, Law Libn./Asst.Prof. of Law
Founded: 1891. **Staff:** Prof 4; Other 6. **Subjects:** Anglo-American law. **Special Collections:** U.S. taxation. **Holdings:** 163,770 volumes; 39,278 volumes in microform. **Subscriptions:** 3974 journals and other serials. **Services:** Interlibrary loan; copying; library open to the public for reference use only. **Automated Operations:** Computerized cataloging. **Computerized Information Services:** LEXIS, WESTLAW. **Staff:** Richard A. Leiter, Pub.Serv.Libn.; Brian D. Striman, Tech.Serv.Libn.; Mitchell J. Fontenot, Ref.Libn..

★16560★
UNIVERSITY OF NEBRASKA, LINCOLN - DENTISTRY LIBRARY (Med)
College of Dentistry, East Campus, Rm. 8 Phone: (402)472-1323
Lincoln, NE 68583-0740 Alice McIntosh, Assoc.Prof., Libs.
Staff: Prof 1; Other 5. **Subjects:** Dentistry, dental hygiene, anatomy, histology, oral surgery and biology. **Holdings:** 5224 books; 5124 bound periodical volumes; 360 masters' theses; 340 AV programs. **Subscriptions:** 200 journals and other serials. **Services:** Interlibrary loan; copying; library open to the public. **Automated Operations:** Computerized circulation. **Computerized Information Services:** DIALOG Information Services, MEDLINE. Performs searches on fee basis. **Publications:** Acquisitions list, monthly - for internal distribution only.

★16561★
UNIVERSITY OF NEBRASKA, LINCOLN - ENGINEERING LIBRARY (Sci-Engr)
Nebraska Hall, 2nd Fl. W. Phone: (402)472-3411
Lincoln, NE 68588-0516 Alan V. Gould, Asst.Prof.
Founded: 1973. **Staff:** Prof 1; Other 3. **Subjects:** Engineering. **Special Collections:** Government Printing Office depository; patent depository. **Holdings:** 36,849 books; 47,194 bound periodical volumes; 238,476 microfiche; 4033 reels of microfilm. **Subscriptions:** 2841 journals and other serials. **Services:** Interlibrary loan; copying; library open to the public. **Automated Operations:** Computerized cataloging, acquisitions, and circulation. **Computerized Information Services:** DIALOG Information Services. Performs searches on fee basis. **Publications:** Acquisitions list, monthly - for internal distribution only.

★16562★
UNIVERSITY OF NEBRASKA, LINCOLN - GEOLOGY LIBRARY (Sci-Engr)
Bessey Hall, Rm. 10 Phone: (402)472-2653
Lincoln, NE 68588-0341 Agnes Adams, Assoc.Prof.
Founded: 1895. **Staff:** Prof 1; Other 1. **Subjects:** Geology. **Special Collections:** Geological and topographic maps (75,000). **Holdings:** 12,328 books; 25,653 bound periodical volumes. **Subscriptions:** 1771 journals and other serials. **Services:** Interlibrary loan; copying; library open to the public. **Automated Operations:** Computerized cataloging, acquisitions, and circulation. **Computerized Information Services:** DIALOG Information Services. **Publications:** Acquisitions list, monthly - for internal distribution only.

★16563★
UNIVERSITY OF NEBRASKA, LINCOLN - MATHEMATICS LIBRARY (Sci-Engr)
Oldfather Hall, Rm. 907 Phone: (402)472-6900
Lincoln, NE 68588-0361 Richard E. Voeltz, Assoc.Prof.
Founded: 1966. **Staff:** Prof 1; Other 1. **Subjects:** Mathematics, statistics. **Holdings:** 7871 books; 9037 bound periodical volumes. **Subscriptions:** 446 journals and other serials. **Services:** Interlibrary loan; copying; library open to the public. **Automated Operations:** Computerized cataloging, acquisitions, and circulation. **Computerized Information Services:** DIALOG Information Services. **Publications:** Acquisitions list, monthly - for internal distribution only.

★16564★
UNIVERSITY OF NEBRASKA, LINCOLN - MUSIC LIBRARY (Mus)
30 Westbrook Music Bldg. Phone: (402)472-6300
Lincoln, NE 68588-0101 Susan Messerli, Mus.Libn.
Founded: 1980. **Staff:** Prof 1; Other 3. **Subjects:** Music - history, literature, theory, performance. **Special Collections:** Guenther Collection of Passion Music (313 items); Ruth Etting Collection (707 scores, recordings, photographs, scrapbooks). **Holdings:** 22,286 journals and other serials; 2975 bound periodical volumes; 8328 sound recordings; 222 volumes on microfilm; 178 volumes on microfiche. **Subscriptions:** 176 journals and other serials. **Services:** Interlibrary loan; copying; library open to the public. **Automated Operations:** Computerized cataloging and circulation. **Computerized Information Services:** DIALOG Information Services, Pergamon ORBIT InfoLine, Inc., OCLC. **Networks/Consortia:** Member of NEBASE.

★16565★
UNIVERSITY OF NEBRASKA, LINCOLN - NEBRASKA CAREER INFORMATION SYSTEM (Educ)
519 Nebraska Hall Phone: (402)472-2570
Lincoln, NE 68588-0552 Fay G. Larson, Dir.
Founded: 1978. **Staff:** Prof 4; Other 2. **Special Collections:** Occupational briefs (557); Nebraska School and Program Information; military occupations; programs of study. **Special Collections:** State information on employment and education. **Services:** System open to the public by special request. **Computerized Information Services:** Internal database. Performs searches on fee basis. **Remarks:** This is a career information system available by lease agreement to schools and social agencies for career guidance support.

★16566★
UNIVERSITY OF NEBRASKA, LINCOLN - PHYSICS LIBRARY (Sci-Engr)
Behlen Laboratory, Rm. 263 Phone: (402)472-1209
Lincoln, NE 68588-0112 Richard E. Voeltz, Assoc.Prof.
Founded: 1965. **Staff:** Prof 1; Other 1. **Subjects:** Physics, astronomy. **Holdings:** 8126 books; 13,400 bound periodical volumes; 20 microforms. **Subscriptions:** 685 journals and other serials. **Services:** Interlibrary loan; copying; library open to the public. **Automated Operations:** Computerized cataloging, acquisitions, and circulation. **Computerized Information Services:** DIALOG Information Services. **Publications:** Acquisitions list, weekly - for internal distribution only.

★16567★
UNIVERSITY OF NEBRASKA, LINCOLN - STATE MUSEUM - HAROLD W. MANTER LABORATORY - LIBRARY (Biol Sci)
W-529 Nebraska Hall
16th and W Sts. Phone: (402)472-3334
Lincoln, NE 68588-0514 Mary Hanson Pritchard, Prof. & Cur.
Staff: 5. **Subjects:** Parasitology. **Special Collections:** Collection of articles on parasitology (50,000 reprints). **Holdings:** 1000 books; 525 bound periodical volumes; 1750 other cataloged items. **Services:** Library open to

the public by appointment for reference use. **Publications:** Contributions from the Harold W. Manter Laboratory, irregular; University Library exchange list and request; Technical Bulletins, irregular. **Remarks:** The laboratory is a research unit encompassing specimen collections, a specialized library for parasitological research, and a National Resource Center for Parasitology.

★16568★
UNIVERSITY OF NEBRASKA, LINCOLN - UNIVERSITY ARCHIVES AND SPECIAL COLLECTIONS (Hist, Hum)
308 Love Library Phone: (402)472-2531
Lincoln, NE 68588-0410 Joseph G. Svoboda, Prof./Hd.
Staff: Prof 3; Other 1. **Subjects:** Nebraskana, World Wars I and II, ethnicity, French Revolution, railroads, American folklore, university archives. **Special Collections:** Mari Sandoz Collection (210 feet); Benjamin A. Botkin Collection (500 feet; 10,000 volumes); Charles E. Bessey papers (45 feet); Charles M. Russell Collection (50 feet; 500 volumes); Czech Heritage Collection (300 feet of manuscripts, newspapers, periodicals; 6000 volumes; 200 reels of microfilm of newspapers); Christlieb Collection of Western Americana (3000 volumes); Mazour Collection of Russian History and Culture (5200 volumes); Latvian Collection (5 feet; 2000 volumes); Frank H. Shoemaker Collection. **Holdings:** 44,000 books; 1000 bound periodical volumes; 5000 cubic feet of university archives; 20,000 volumes of university theses and dissertations; 20 linear feet of manuscripts; 20 linear feet of glass negative plates and prints. **Services:** Interlibrary loan; copying; collections open to the public. **Staff:** Gerald A. Rudolph, Prof.; Elsie Thomas, Assoc.Prof..

★16569★
UNIVERSITY OF NEBRASKA, OMAHA - CENTER FOR APPLIED URBAN RESEARCH - LIBRARY (Soc Sci)
60th & Dodge Streets Phone: (402)554-8311
Omaha, NE 68182 Gloria Ruggiero, Pubns.Mgr.
Founded: 1972. **Staff:** 3. **Subjects:** Census, community development and planning, economics, employment, government, public administration. **Holdings:** 1000 books; 250 manuscripts. **Subscriptions:** 24 journals and other serials. **Services:** Copying; library open to the public for reference use only. **Publications:** Newsletter, semiannual; research monographs; Nebraska Policy Choices series. **Special Catalogs:** Publications catalog. **Staff:** Betty Young, Libn.; Sharon Delauben Fels, Ed. & Asst.Libn..

★16570★
UNIVERSITY OF NEBRASKA, OMAHA - UNIVERSITY LIBRARY - SPECIAL COLLECTIONS (Hist, Publ)
Omaha, NE 68182-0237 Phone: (402)554-2640
Robert S. Runyon, Lib.Dir.
Founded: 1908. **Special Collections:** Arthur Paul Afghanistan Collection; Mary L. Richmond Cummington Press Collection; Edna Cole Postcard Collection; Icarian Collection; Wright Morris; Weldon Kees; Wayne C. Lee; Seven Anderton; WPA Historical Manuscripts on Omaha; Nebraska writers; Omaha history; fine presses. **Services:** Copying; collections open to the public by appointment. **Automated Operations:** Computerized cataloging and circulation. **Computerized Information Services:** DIALOG Information Services, BRS Information Technologies, The Source Information Network, WILSONLINE. Performs searches on fee basis. Contact Person: Robert Nash, 554-2884. **Publications:** Bibliography on Afghanistan (in progress).

★16571★
UNIVERSITY OF NEBRASKA MEDICAL CENTER - MC GOOGAN LIBRARY OF MEDICINE (Med)
42nd & Dewey Ave. Phone: (402)559-4006
Omaha, NE 68105-1065 Nancy N. Woelfl, Ph.D., Dir.
Founded: 1902. **Staff:** Prof 17; Other 32. **Subjects:** Medicine, nursing, pharmacy, psychiatry, allied health sciences. **Special Collections:** History of medicine; Nebraska Archives of Medicine; H. Winnett Orr Historical Collection (American College of Surgeons). **Holdings:** 79,713 books; 134,901 bound periodical volumes; 681 microforms; 25 VF drawers of archives. **Subscriptions:** 2376 journals and other serials. **Services:** Interlibrary loan (fee); copying; SDI; library open to the public. **Automated Operations:** Computerized cataloging, circulation, serials, and ILL. **Computerized Information Services:** DIALOG Information Services, NLM, BRS Information Technologies, WILSONLINE, PaperChase. **Remarks:** Contains the holdings of Eppley Institute for Research in Cancer & Allied Diseases - Library. Library serves as headquarters for Midcontinental Regional Medical Library Program. **Staff:** Audrey P. Newcomer, Assoc.Dir., Tech.Serv.; Marie A. Reidelbach, Hd., Ref.; Suzanne Kehm, Hd., LRC; Joan L. Konecky, Ref.; Joan Stark, Ref.; Leslee B. Shell, Ref.; Helen Yam, Hd., Hist. of Med.; Bernice M. Hetzner, Hist. of NE Med.; Claire E. Gadzikowski, Spec.Proj.Coord., MCRMLP; Dorothy B. Willis, Reg.Dev.Coord., MCRMLP; Helen-Ann Brown, Online Serv.Coord., MCRMLP; Dorothy A. Earley, Online Serv.Instr., MCRMLP.

★16572★
UNIVERSITY OF NEVADA, LAS VEGAS - GAMING RESEARCH CENTER (Rec)
4505 Maryland Pkwy. Phone: (702)739-3252
Las Vegas, NV 89154 Susan Jarvis, Spec.Coll.Libn.
Founded: 1966. **Staff:** Prof 2; Other 2. **Subjects:** Gambling, horse racing, lotteries, cards. **Holdings:** 5000 books; 250 bound periodical volumes; 600 clippings. **Subscriptions:** 205 journals and other serials; 10 newspapers. **Services:** Copying; center open to the public. **Automated Operations:** Computerized cataloging, acquisitions, serials, and circulation. **Publications:** A Gambling Bibliography, 1972 (based on the collection, listing over 1700 items). **Special Catalogs:** Gambling Catalog, a list of monographs from the research collection at the University of Nevada, Las Vegas, 1978.

★16573★
UNIVERSITY OF NEVADA, RENO - BASQUE STUDIES PROGRAM (Area-Ethnic)
Library Phone: (702)784-4854
Reno, NV 89557 William A. Douglass, Coord.
Staff: Prof 4; Other 2. **Subjects:** Basque culture, history, language, literature. **Holdings:** 20,000 books; 1600 bound periodical volumes; 64 boxes of archives; 140 reels of microfilm; 15,500 slides; 500 cassettes and phonograph records. **Subscriptions:** 70 journals and other serials; 6 newspapers. **Services:** Interlibrary loan; copying; collection open to the public. **Computerized Information Services:** DIALOG Information Services, BRS Information Technologies, RLIN, WILSONLINE (through main library). Performs searches on fee basis. Contact Person: Maria Otero-Boisvert, Basque Stud.Libn.. **Networks/Consortia:** Member of Information Nevada. **Publications:** Basque Studies Program Newsletter, semiannual - free upon request; Basque Studies Program Occasional Papers Series - for sale.

★16574★
UNIVERSITY OF NEVADA, RENO - DESERT RESEARCH INSTITUTE - DANDINI PARK LIBRARY
Box 60220
Reno, NV 89506
Defunct. Holdings absorbed by University of Nevada, Reno - Desert Research Institute - Library.

★16575★
UNIVERSITY OF NEVADA, RENO - DESERT RESEARCH INSTITUTE - LIBRARY (Sci-Engr)
Box 60220
Reno, NV 89506 Phone: (702)972-1676
Staff: Prof 1; Other 2. **Subjects:** Atmospheric physics, meteorology, weather modification, Antarctic studies, air pollution. **Holdings:** 5955 books; 2636 bound periodical volumes; 2183 bound government publications; 21,371 unbound government publications; 714 technical reports; 2530 microforms. **Subscriptions:** 221 journals and other serials. **Services:** Interlibrary loan; copying; library open to the public. **Computerized Information Services:** BRS Information Technologies, STN International, DIALOG Information Services. **Networks/Consortia:** Member of CLASS.

★16576★
UNIVERSITY OF NEVADA, RENO - ENGINEERING LIBRARY (Sci-Engr)
Scrugham Engineering Bldg., Rm. 228
Reno, NV 89557 Phone: (702)784-6945
Founded: 1962. **Staff:** Prof 1; Other 2. **Subjects:** Engineering - civil, electrical, mechanical; computer science. **Holdings:** 19,128 books; 11,054 bound periodical volumes; 608 government reports; 500 pamphlets; 622 microfiche. **Subscriptions:** 429 journals. **Services:** Interlibrary loan; copying; library open to the public. **Automated Operations:** Computerized public access catalog, acquisitions, serials, and circulation. **Computerized Information Services:** DIALOG Information Services, BRS Information Technologies. Performs searches on fee basis. Contact Person: Lois Smyres. **Networks/Consortia:** Member of Information Nevada, CLASS. **Publications:** New Book List, monthly - free upon request.

★16577★
UNIVERSITY OF NEVADA, RENO - FILM & VIDEO LIBRARY (Aud-Vis)
Getchell Library Phone: (702)784-6037
Reno, NV 89557 Ruth Hart, Film Libn.
Founded: 1955. **Staff:** Prof 1; Other 2. **Subjects:** Education, child development, anthropology, psychology, political science, business. **Special Collections:** Nevada films and videos; BBC productions of Shakespeare plays (37); Civilisation, Ascent of Man, Tribal Eye, In Search of Alexander the Great, Elizabeth R, Connections, The Long Search, Cosmos, and Six Wives of Henry VIII series. **Holdings:** 2960 16mm films; 459 video cassettes. **Services:** Interlibrary loan; library open to the public on fee basis. **Networks/Consortia:** Member of Consortium of University Film Centers (CUFC). **Publications:** Film and video catalogs and addenda. **Staff:** Michael Simons, Educ. Media Libn..

★16578★
UNIVERSITY OF NEVADA, RENO - GOVERNMENT PUBLICATIONS DEPARTMENT (Info Sci)
Library Phone: (702)784-6579
Reno, NV 89557 Duncan M. Aldrich, Act.Hd.
Founded: 1907. **Staff:** Prof 2; Other 3. **Subjects:** Government - Nevada, federal; United Nations. **Special Collections:** Patents, 1964 to present. **Holdings:** 1.05 million documents; 1.5 million microforms. **Services:** Interlibrary loan; copying; department open to the public. **Computerized Information Services:** DIALOG Information Services, BRS Information Technologies, RLIN, U.S. Patent Classification System, LIBS 100 System; Nevada Documents Online (internal database). Performs searches on fee basis. **Publications:** Selected List of Publications Received..., monthly.

★16579★
UNIVERSITY OF NEVADA, RENO - LIFE AND HEALTH SCIENCES LIBRARY (Sci-Engr, Med)
Fleischmann College of Agriculture Bldg. Phone: (702)784-6616
Reno, NV 89557 Susan Stewart, Libn.
Founded: 1958. **Staff:** Prof 1; Other 2. **Subjects:** Biology, agriculture, nursing, health resources, speech pathology and audiology, medical technology. **Special Collections:** Bankofier Collection on horses. **Holdings:** 26,811 books; 22,215 bound periodical volumes; 7699 bound government reports; 68,623 unbound government reports; 414 reels of microfilm; 9378 microfiche. **Subscriptions:** 560 journals. **Services:** Interlibrary loan; copying; library open to the public. **Automated Operations:** Computerized cataloging, acquisitions, serials, and circulation. **Computerized Information Services:** DIALOG Information Services, BRS Information Technologies. Performs searches on fee basis. **Networks/Consortia:** Member of Information Nevada. **Publications:** New Book List, quarterly - free upon request. **Staff:** Dorothy Good, Sr.Supv..

★16580★
UNIVERSITY OF NEVADA, RENO - MINES LIBRARY (Sci-Engr)
Getchell Library, Rm. 2 Phone: (702)784-6596
Reno, NV 89557-0044 Linda P. Newman, Libn.
Founded: 1908. **Staff:** Prof 2; Other 3. **Subjects:** Earth science; engineering - mining, chemical, metallurgical; physical geography. **Special Collections:** Theses on the geology of Nevada. **Holdings:** 13,600 books; 14,380 bound periodical volumes; 712 reels of microfilm; 113,000 maps; 23,200 microfiche; 8200 bound government reports; 13,300 unbound government reports. **Subscriptions:** 351 journals; 5 newspapers. **Services:** Interlibrary loan; copying; library open to the public with restrictions on borrowing. **Automated Operations:** Computerized public access catalog, acquisitions, serials, and circulation. **Computerized Information Services:** DIALOG Information Services, BRS Information Technologies. Performs searches on fee basis. **Networks/Consortia:** Member of Information Nevada. **Publications:** New Books and Maps List, quarterly - free upon request; Mackay School of Mines Thesis List, 1908-1983 - for sale; Mineral Waste and Recovery Bibliography. **Special Indexes:** Nevada Mining and Geology File (41,000 cards).

★16581★
UNIVERSITY OF NEVADA, RENO - PHYSICAL SCIENCES LIBRARY (Sci-Engr)
Chemistry Bldg., Rm. 316 Phone: (702)784-6716
Reno, NV 89557 Susan Stewart, Physical Sci.Libn.
Founded: 1965. **Staff:** Prof 1; Other 1. **Subjects:** Chemistry, physics. **Holdings:** 9895 books; 17,136 bound periodical volumes; 75 reels of microfilm; 1789 microfiche. **Subscriptions:** 305 journals and other serials. **Services:** Interlibrary loan; copying; SDI; library open to the public. **Automated Operations:** Computerized public access catalog, acquisitions, serials, and circulation. **Computerized Information Services:** DIALOG Information Services, BRS Information Technologies, CAS ONLINE. Performs searches on fee basis. **Networks/Consortia:** Member of CLASS, Information Nevada. **Publications:** New Book List, bimonthly.

★16582★
UNIVERSITY OF NEVADA, RENO - RESEARCH AND EDUCATIONAL PLANNING CENTER (Educ)
College of Education, Rm. 201 Phone: (702)784-4921
Reno, NV 89557 Daniel Cline, Dir.
Staff: Prof 10; Other 4. **Subjects:** Legal education, Nevada and world history, school facility planning, bilingual education, Western community studies, risk reduction, socio-demographic impact studies, organization and curriculum development in schools, personnel development. **Special Collections:** M-X publications. **Holdings:** 2000 books, documents, journals, unbound fugitive material; ERIC publications. **Services:** Interlibrary loan; center open to the public.

★16583★
UNIVERSITY OF NEVADA, RENO - SAVITT MEDICAL LIBRARY (Med)
Savitt Medical Sciences Bldg. Phone: (702)784-4625
Reno, NV 89557 Joan S. Zenan, Dir.
Founded: 1978. **Staff:** Prof 3; Other 6. **Subjects:** Medicine and allied health sciences. **Special Collections:** Medical archives of Nevada. **Holdings:** 33,000 volumes. **Subscriptions:** 497 journals and other serials. **Services:** Interlibrary loan; copying; library open to the public. **Automated Operations:** Computerized public access catalog and cataloging. **Computerized Information Services:** Online systems. **Networks/Consortia:** Member of Pacific Southwest Regional Medical Library Service. **Staff:** Mary Ellen Lemon, Ref. & Online Searching; Rosalyn Casey, Ser. & Sys.; Elizabeth McDonald, ILL; Jeannine Funk, Cat.; Donna Packard, Acq..

★16584★
UNIVERSITY OF NEVADA, RENO - SPECIAL COLLECTIONS DEPARTMENT/UNIVERSITY ARCHIVES (Hist)
University Library Phone: (702)784-6538
Reno, NV 89557-0044 Robert E. Blesse, Hd.
Founded: 1963. **Staff:** Prof 1; Other 4. **Subjects:** Nevada history, 20th century poetry and fiction, anthropology, ethnography, architecture, women in the trans-Mississippi West, magic, witchcraft, history of printing, university archives, mining, water and land use. **Special Collections:** Nevada Collection; Great Basin Anthropological Collection; Nevada fiction; Women in the West; Modern Authors Collection (170 English and American writers prominent after 1910); University of Nevada, Reno archives; History of Printing and the Book Arts Collection; Nevada Architectural Archives; Senator Alan Bible papers; Virginia & Truckee Railroad Collection; Samuel Johnson; Robert Burns; George Stewart. **Holdings:** 43,000 books; 600 bound periodical volumes; 4000 linear feet of manuscripts; 100,000 photographs; 1500 maps; 15,000 architectural drawings. **Subscriptions:** 120 journals and other serials. **Services:** Copying; department open to the public for reference use only. **Special Catalogs:** Specialized subject and form catalogs (card); guides to manuscript collections.

★16585★
UNIVERSITY OF NEW BRUNSWICK - EDUCATION RESOURCE CENTRE (Educ)
D'Avray Hall
P.O. Box 7500 Phone: (506)453-3516
Fredericton, NB, Canada E3B 5H5 Andrew Pope, Hd.
Founded: 1973. **Staff:** Prof 2; Other 4. **Subjects:** Education, home economics. **Special Collections:** Micmac-Maliseet Institute (1070 volumes). **Holdings:** 22,113 books; 2873 bound periodical volumes; 362,211 microfiche; 28 VF drawers of pamphlets; 17,449 AV and instructional programs. **Subscriptions:** 305 journals and other serials. **Services:** Interlibrary loan; copying; center open to the public. **Automated Operations:** Computerized cataloging. **Computerized Information Services:** BRS Information Technologies; PHOENIX (internal database). Performs searches free of charge on PHOENIX; BRS searches on fee basis. **Staff:** Helen Craig, Asst.Libn..

★16586★
UNIVERSITY OF NEW BRUNSWICK - ENGINEERING LIBRARY (Sci-Engr)
P.O. Box 440 Phone: (506)453-4747
Fredericton, NB, Canada E3B 3J7 Everett Dunfield, Hd.
Founded: 1967. **Staff:** Prof 2; Other 6. **Subjects:** Engineering - civil, mechanical, geological, electrical, forestry, surveying, chemical; computer science; transportation; bioengineering. **Holdings:** 25,200 books; 14,000 bound periodical volumes; 86,000 reports on microfiche and microfilm;

1350 theses; 142 films and slide sets; 15,000 reports, pamphlets, and clippings. **Subscriptions:** 735 journals and other serials; 5 newspapers. **Services:** Interlibrary loan; copying; SDI; library open to the public. **Automated Operations:** Computerized cataloging. **Computerized Information Services:** CAN/OLE, DIALOG Information Services, BRS Information Technologies, STN International; ENLIST, PHOENIX (internal databases); Envoy 100 (electronic mail service). Performs searches on fee basis. **Publications:** Bibliographies and manuals - for internal and patron use only.

★16587★
UNIVERSITY OF NEW BRUNSWICK - HARRIET IRVING LIBRARY - ARCHIVES AND SPECIAL COLLECTIONS (Hum, Hist)
P.O. Box 7500 Phone: (506)453-4748
Fredericton, NB, Canada E3B 5H5 Mary Flagg, Mgr./Res.Off.
Founded: 1931. **Staff:** 6. **Subjects:** University and New Brunswick history, Canadian literature. **Special Collections:** Hathaway Collection of Canadian Literature (3500 volumes); maritime history (3400 volumes); Beaverbrook Special Collections (1981 volumes). **Holdings:** 25,000 books; 4500 linear feet of bound periodical volumes; 2561 linear feet of university archives; 1000 linear feet of historical and literary manuscripts; 2100 photographs; personal papers. **Services:** Interlibrary loan; copying; collections open to the public. **Automated Operations:** Computerized cataloging and acquisitions. **Computerized Information Services:** Envoy 100, Datapac (electronic mail services). **Special Catalogs:** Maritime Pamphlet Catalogue (online).

★16588★
UNIVERSITY OF NEW BRUNSWICK - LAW LIBRARY (Law)
Ludlow Hall
Bag Service No. 44999 Phone: (506)453-4734
Fredericton, NB, Canada E3B 6C9 C. Anne Crocker, Law Libn.
Founded: 1933. **Staff:** 8. **Subjects:** Law and common law. **Special Collections:** Lord Beaverbrook Legal Collection. **Holdings:** 80,000 books and bound periodical volumes; 15,396 volumes in microform; 57 AV titles. **Subscriptions:** 1527 journals and other serials. **Services:** Interlibrary loan; copying; library open to the public. **Automated Operations:** Computerized cataloging. **Computerized Information Services:** WESTLAW, QL Systems, UTLAS; PHOENIX (internal database); QL/Mail (electronic mail service). **Publications:** Acquisitions List, monthly - on exchange.

★16589★
UNIVERSITY OF NEW BRUNSWICK - SCIENCE LIBRARY (Biol Sci, Sci-Engr)
P.O. Box 7500 Phone: (506)453-4601
Fredericton, NB, Canada E3B 5H5 Eszter L.K. Schwenke, Hd.
Staff: Prof 1; Other 5. **Subjects:** Forestry, biology, chemistry, geology, physics. **Special Collections:** Forestry Collection (11,000 pamphlets). **Holdings:** 41,532 books; 41,600 bound periodical volumes; 800 theses; 435 reels of microfilm; 11,620 microcards; 51,065 microfiche. **Subscriptions:** 880 journals and other serials. **Services:** Interlibrary loan; copying; SDI; library open to the public. **Computerized Information Services:** DIALOG Information Services, CAN/OLE, QL Systems, CAS ONLINE, STN International, Information Retrieval System for the Sociology of Leisure and Sport (SIRLS), MEDLINE; PHOENIX (internal database). Performs searches on fee basis. **Special Indexes:** ENLIST, forestry pamphlet file (online and printout); GEOSCAN, New Brunswick mineral assessment file (microfiche). **Remarks:** An alternate telephone number is 453-4602.

★16590★
UNIVERSITY OF NEW HAMPSHIRE - BIOLOGICAL SCIENCES LIBRARY (Biol Sci, Agri)
Kendall Hall Phone: (603)862-1018
Durham, NH 03824 David Lane, Br.Libn.
Staff: Prof 1; Other 2. **Subjects:** General biology, agriculture, forestry, botany, microbiology, zoology, entomology, animal science, plant science, nutrition, biochemistry, genetics. **Holdings:** 70,000 volumes. **Subscriptions:** 800 journals and other serials. **Services:** Interlibrary loan; copying; library open to limited public use. **Automated Operations:** Computerized cataloging and serials list. **Computerized Information Services:** DIALOG Information Services, BRS Information Technologies, OCLC. **Networks/Consortia:** Member of NELINET, New Hampshire College & University Council Library Policy Committee (NHCUC).

★16591★
UNIVERSITY OF NEW HAMPSHIRE - CHEMISTRY LIBRARY (Sci-Engr)
Parsons Hall Phone: (603)862-1083
Durham, NH 03824 Edward J. Dauphinais, Libn.
Staff: Prof 1; Other 1. **Subjects:** Chemistry. **Holdings:** 21,027 volumes. **Subscriptions:** 160 journals and other serials. **Services:** Interlibrary loan; copying; library open to the public. **Automated Operations:** Computerized serials. **Computerized Information Services:** OCLC, DIALOG Information Services, Pergamon ORBIT InfoLine, Inc. **Networks/Consortia:** Member of NELINET, New Hampshire College & University Council Library Policy Committee (NHCUC).

★16592★
UNIVERSITY OF NEW HAMPSHIRE - DAVID G. CLARK MEMORIAL PHYSICS LIBRARY (Sci-Engr)
DeMeritt Hall Phone: (603)862-2348
Durham, NH 03824 Edward J. Dauphinais, Libn.
Founded: 1965. **Staff:** Prof 1; Other 1. **Subjects:** Physics. **Holdings:** 17,798 books; 11,382 bound periodical volumes; 120 theses; 70 film loops. **Subscriptions:** 160 journals and other serials. **Services:** Interlibrary loan; copying; library open to the public. **Automated Operations:** Computerized cataloging and acquisitions. **Computerized Information Services:** DIALOG Information Services, Pergamon ORBIT InfoLine, Inc., OCLC. **Networks/Consortia:** Member of NELINET, New Hampshire College & University Council Library Policy Committee (NHCUC).

★16593★
UNIVERSITY OF NEW HAMPSHIRE - DEPARTMENT OF MEDIA SERVICES - FILM LIBRARY (Aud-Vis)
Dimond Library Phone: (603)862-2240
Durham, NH 03824 Norman Bourque, Supv., Film Dist.
Staff: Prof 10; Other 8. **Special Collections:** Lotte Jacobi Photo Archive. **Holdings:** 3000 educational films for all ages. **Services:** Films available for rent; library open to New England area residents. **Special Catalogs:** Instructional Film Catalog (book); NMDC Catalog of French Publications. **Staff:** Joann Brady, Graphic Designer; Bill Howe, TV Producer-Dir.; Gary Samson, Filmmaker-Photog.; Dorothy Ahlgren, TV Producer-Supv..

★16594★
UNIVERSITY OF NEW HAMPSHIRE - ENGINEERING-MATH LIBRARY (Sci-Engr, Comp Sci)
Kingsbury Hall Phone: (603)862-1196
Durham, NH 03824 Edward J. Dauphinais, Libn.
Staff: Prof 1; Other 2. **Subjects:** Engineering - mechanical, civil, electrical, chemical; mathematics; materials science; computer science. **Holdings:** 43,319 volumes; 700 reels of microfilm of journals. **Subscriptions:** 750 journals and other serials. **Services:** Interlibrary loan; copying; library open to the public. **Automated Operations:** Computerized serials. **Computerized Information Services:** DIALOG Information Services, Pergamon ORBIT InfoLine, Inc., OCLC. **Networks/Consortia:** Member of NELINET, New Hampshire College & University Council Library Policy Committee (NHCUC).

★16595★
UNIVERSITY OF NEW HAMPSHIRE - NEW HAMPSHIRE WATER RESOURCE RESEARCH CENTER - LIBRARY (Env-Cons)
224 Science/Engineering Research Bldg. Phone: (603)862-2144
Durham, NH 03824 Thomas P. Ballestero, Dir.
Founded: 1965. **Staff:** Prof 1; Other 2. **Subjects:** Theoretical, analytical, and practical evaluation of hydrologic phenomena including evaporation and transpiration, watershed management, groundwater, water law and economics, interbasin transfers, water conservation, radon, aquifer remediation, and stream hydraulics. **Holdings:** 520 books and bound periodical volumes; 6361 pamphlets; 7500 reports and documents. **Subscriptions:** 16 journals and newsletters. **Services:** Library open to the public. **Publications:** Research reports and associated publications. **Special Catalogs:** Keyterm and title catalogs; shelf list; publication catalog.

★16596★
UNIVERSITY OF NEW HAMPSHIRE - SPECIAL COLLECTIONS (Hist, Hum)
Dimond Library
Durham, NH 03824 Phone: (603)862-2714
Staff: Prof 1; Other 2. **Subjects:** New Hampshire. **Special Collections:** Archives of the University of New Hampshire, including dissertations (10,000 volumes); Robert Frost (250 volumes); angling (2500 volumes); New Hampshire (21,000 volumes); Early New Hampshire Imprints (850 volumes); historical juvenile books (1200). **Holdings:** 45,000 books; 2155

cubic feet of manuscripts. **Services:** Copying; collections open to the public. **Publications:** Friends of the University of New Hampshire Library Notes, annual - to Friends of the Library; Guide to Special Collections, 1983. **Special Catalogs:** Robert Frost New Hampshire, 1976 (printed catalog).

★16597★
UNIVERSITY OF NEW MEXICO - ART MUSEUM - RAYMOND JONSON ARCHIVES (Art)
1909 Las Lomas Rd., N.E. Phone: (505)277-4967
Albuquerque, NM 87131 Tiska Blankenship, Asst.Cur.
Founded: 1950. **Staff:** Prof 1; Other 1. **Subjects:** Modernism, transcendentalism, Dame Rudhyar, Hilaire Hiler, music, poetry. **Special Collections:** Jonson's personal books, correspondence, manuscripts, photographs, news clippings, diaries. **Holdings:** 800 books. **Services:** Copying; archives open to the public by appointment. **Formerly:** Jonson Gallery - Library.

★16598★
UNIVERSITY OF NEW MEXICO - BUNTING MEMORIAL SLIDE LIBRARY (Aud-Vis)
Fine Arts Center Phone: (505)277-6415
Albuquerque, NM 87131 A. Zelda Richardson, Dir.
Staff: Prof 3. **Subjects:** Art, architecture. **Holdings:** 295,000 slides. **Services:** Library serves faculty only.

★16599★
UNIVERSITY OF NEW MEXICO - BUREAU OF BUSINESS & ECONOMIC RESEARCH DATA BANK (Soc Sci, Bus-Fin)
1920 Las Lomas Blvd., N.E. Phone: (505)277-6626
Albuquerque, NM 87131 Kevin Kargacin, Hd., Info.Serv.
Founded: 1945. **Staff:** Prof 3; Other 4. **Subjects:** New Mexico - economics, income, employment, demographics, census. **Special Collections:** Census of Population and Housing for New Mexico, 1940-1980. **Holdings:** 12,000 cataloged publications. **Subscriptions:** 400 journals and other serials. **Services:** Copying; bureau open to the public. **Automated Operations:** Computerized cataloging. **Publications:** New Mexico Business, monthly - by subscription. **Staff:** Julianna Boyle, Asst. Economist.

★16600★
UNIVERSITY OF NEW MEXICO - FINE ARTS LIBRARY (Art, Mus)
Albuquerque, NM 87131 Phone: (505)277-2357
James B. Wright, Hd.
Founded: 1963. **Staff:** Prof 4; Other 5. **Subjects:** Art, music, architecture, photography. **Special Collections:** Archives of Southwestern Music; art exhibition catalogs; Gigante Collection (orchestra bowing markings). **Holdings:** 100,124 books; 21,000 records and tapes. **Subscriptions:** 350 journals and other serials. **Services:** Listening center; copying; library open to the public. **Automated Operations:** Computerized circulation. **Staff:** Nancy Pistorius, Asst.Libn..

UNIVERSITY OF NEW MEXICO - JONSON GALLERY - LIBRARY
See: University of New Mexico - Art Museum - Raymond Jonson Archives (16597)

★16601★
UNIVERSITY OF NEW MEXICO - MEDICAL CENTER LIBRARY (Med)
North Campus Phone: (505)277-2548
Albuquerque, NM 87131 Erika Love, Dir.
Founded: 1963. **Staff:** Prof 12; Other 31. **Subjects:** Medicine, basic sciences, nursing, pharmacy, Indian health, dental hygiene, allied health sciences. **Special Collections:** New Mexico medical history and public health; Medical Center archives; Indian health papers; oral histories of New Mexico physicians. **Holdings:** 44,674 books; 81,434 bound periodical volumes; 5434 AV programs. **Subscriptions:** 2286 journals and other serials. **Services:** Interlibrary loan; SDI; outreach programs for New Mexico health personnel; library open to the public. **Automated Operations:** Computerized cataloging and circulation. **Computerized Information Services:** OCLC, NLM, BRS Information Technologies, DIALOG Information Services, Pergamon ORBIT InfoLine, Inc.; OnTyme Electronic Message Network Service (electronic mail service). Performs searches on fee basis. Contact Person: Andrea Testi, Online Serv.Coord., 277-2311. **Networks/Consortia:** Member of TALON, AMIGOS Bibliographic Council, Inc., South Central Academic Medical Libraries Consortium (SCAMEL), CLASS. **Publications:** Adobe Medicus; New Books, both bimonthly - both to user community and selected U.S. medical libraries; Medical Center Faculty Publications list. **Special Catalogs:** Media Catalog. **Special Indexes:** Serials List (computer printout) - campus and local distribution only. **Remarks:** Fax: (505)277-5351. **Staff:** Cecile C. Quintal, Assoc.Dir.; Susan Anderson, Asst.Dir., Educ. & Instr.Serv.; Jon Eldredge, Chf., Coll.Dev.; Julie Kesti, Asst.Dir., Biomed.Info.Serv..

★16602★
UNIVERSITY OF NEW MEXICO - SCHOOL OF LAW LIBRARY (Law)
1117 Stanford, N.E. Phone: (505)277-6236
Albuquerque, NM 87106 Anita Morse, Libn.
Founded: 1950. **Staff:** Prof 5; Other 16. **Subjects:** Law. **Special Collections:** American Indian law; Community Land Grant Law; Mexican and Latin American legal materials. **Holdings:** 188,960 volumes; 591,405 microforms (114,684 volume equivalents); 12,000 New Mexico Supreme Court records and briefs. **Subscriptions:** 4300 journals and other serials; 21 newspapers. **Services:** Interlibrary loan; copying; library open to the public. **Automated Operations:** Computerized cataloging, acquisitions, serials, and circulation. **Computerized Information Services:** LEXIS, DIALOG Information Services, OCLC, WESTLAW. **Networks/Consortia:** Member of AMIGOS Bibliographic Council, Inc.. **Publications:** A Guide to the School of Law Library; Annual New Acquisitions List - both to members of the New Mexico State Bar, judicial offices, patrons; New Titles Received. **Special Catalogs:** Catalog of American Indian Law. **Staff:** Lorraine Lester, Adm.Libn.; Ken Shoemaker, Hd., Circ.; Elizabeth Scherer, Hd., Tech.Serv.; Tom Huesemann, Acq..

★16603★
UNIVERSITY OF NEW MEXICO - SPECIAL COLLECTIONS DEPARTMENT (Hist)
General Library Phone: (505)277-6451
Albuquerque, NM 87131 William E. Tydeman, Hd.
Staff: Prof 1; Other 6. **Subjects:** History of the American West, New Mexico history, history of Mexico and Latin America, Indians of the Southwest, southwestern architectural history. **Special Collections:** Doris Duke Collection (982 oral history tapes); Pioneer Foundation (527 tapes). **Holdings:** 35,000 volumes; 2000 tape recordings; 3000 linear feet of manuscript material; 17,000 photographs; 250 videocassettes. **Subscriptions:** 121 journals and other serials. **Services:** Copying (limited); department open to the public. **Publications:** Annual report. **Remarks:** The Special Collections Department consists of five divisions: the Anderson Room, containing Western Americana; the Coronado Room collection on the history and culture of New Mexico; the Bell Room, housing the rare book collection; and the manuscript collections and architectural records, which are also housed separately. **Staff:** Kathlene Ferris, Archv.; Stella De Sa Rego, Cur., Photo.; Jan Barnhart, Cur., John Gaw Meem Archv. of SW Arch..

★16604★
UNIVERSITY OF NEW MEXICO - TECHNOLOGY APPLICATION CENTER (Sci-Engr)
Albuquerque, NM 87131 Phone: (505)277-3622
Stanley A. Morain, Dir.
Founded: 1965. **Staff:** Prof 14; Other 7. **Subjects:** Remote sensing, earth photography, geographic information systems. **Special Collections:** Remote sensing bibliography (citations). **Holdings:** 10K slides of earth-oriented photography. **Services:** Image processing; short courses; visiting scientist program; photograph search service. **Computerized Information Services:** NASA/RECON, EROS Data Center; Dialcom Inc., NASAMAIL (electronic mail services). Performs searches on fee basis. **Publications:** Remote Sensing of Natural Resources Quarterly Literature Review. **Remarks:** Center is a NASA Industrial Applications Center (NIAC). **Also Known As:** TAC. **Staff:** Mike Inglis, Assoc.Dir.; Amy Budge, Photo. Search Serv..

★16605★
UNIVERSITY OF NEW MEXICO - TIREMAN LEARNING MATERIALS LIBRARY (Educ)
Albuquerque, NM 87131 Phone: (505)277-3854
Bernice Martinez-Comstock, Br.Libn.
Founded: 1965. **Staff:** Prof 1; Other 2. **Subjects:** Children's and young adult's literature; curriculum materials for kindergarten through high school. **Special Collections:** Anita Osuna Carr Bicultural Bilingual Collection; Microcomputer Preview Laboratory. **Holdings:** 13,000 books; 102 bound periodical volumes; 900 filmstrips, sound filmstrips, kits, and games; 552 cassette tapes; 75 film loops; 80 study prints; 344 phonograph records; 36 VF drawers; 8 VF drawers of curriculum guides; 4 VF drawers of pictures; curriculum microfiche. **Services:** Interlibrary loan; library open to the public with borrower's card. **Automated Operations:** Computerized cataloging, acquisitions, serials, and circulation. **Remarks:** Library is a regional evaluation center for state textbooks.

★16606★
UNIVERSITY OF NEW MEXICO - WILLIAM J. PARISH MEMORIAL LIBRARY (Bus-Fin)
Albuquerque, NM 87131 Phone: (505)277-5912
Judith Bernstein, Hd.
Founded: 1969. **Staff:** Prof 3; Other 7. **Subjects:** Economics, management, accounting, finance, personnel, marketing, international management, travel and tourism, real estate, management information systems. **Holdings:** 90,000 books and bound periodical volumes; 40,000 10K and annual reports. **Subscriptions:** 1400 journals and other serials. **Services:** Interlibrary loan; copying; library open to the public with limited circulation. **Automated Operations:** Computerized cataloging, acquisitions, serials, and circulation. **Computerized Information Services:** DIALOG Information Services, Pergamon ORBIT InfoLine, Inc., BRS Information Technologies, OCLC. Performs searches on fee basis. **Networks/Consortia:** Member of AMIGOS Bibliographic Council, Inc.. **Publications:** Annual report; monthly new books list - for internal distribution only; guides to the collection. **Staff:** Peter Ives, Ref.Libn..

★16607★
UNIVERSITY OF NEW MEXICO, LOS ALAMOS - LEARNING RESOURCE CENTER/LIBRARY (Sci-Engr)
4000 University Dr. Phone: (505)662-5919
Los Alamos, NM 87544 Linda G. Schappert, Dir.
Founded: 1984. **Staff:** Prof 1; Other 3. **Subjects:** Technology, science, mathematics, southwestern United States. **Holdings:** 6200 books. **Subscriptions:** 106 journals and other serials; 6 newspapers. **Services:** Interlibrary loan; copying; center open to New Mexico residents. **Automated Operations:** Computerized cataloging and ILL.

★16608★
UNIVERSITY OF NEW ORLEANS - CENTER FOR ECONOMIC DEVELOPMENT - LIBRARY (Soc Sci)
BA 368, Lakefront Campus Phone: (504)286-6663
New Orleans, LA 70148 Kay Chapoton, Libn.
Founded: 1978. **Subjects:** Housing, trade, real estate, development, small business, international trade. **Holdings:** 500 volumes. **Services:** Library not open to the public.

★16609★
UNIVERSITY OF NEW ORLEANS - EARL K. LONG LIBRARY - ARCHIVES & MANUSCRIPTS/SPECIAL COLLECTIONS DEPARTMENT (Hist)
Lake Front Phone: (504)286-7273
New Orleans, LA 70148 D. Clive Hardy, Archv.
Founded: 1968. **Staff:** Prof 4; Other 16. **Subjects:** New Orleans - ethnic groups, labor unions, legal records, businesses, history, culture. **Special Collections:** Crabites Collection of Egyptology (printed materials, mainly books); Frank Von der Haar Collection of William Faulkner (printed materials, mainly books); Orleans Parish School Board Collection; Chamber of Commerce of New Orleans Collection; Louisiana Supreme Court Collection; Marcus Christian Collection; Audubon Park Commission Collection; National Association for the Advancement of Colored People, New Orleans Branch Collection; Jean Lafitte National Historical Park Collection. **Holdings:** 4800 volumes; 11,000 linear feet of manuscripts and archival records. **Subscriptions:** 12 journals and other serials. **Services:** Interlibrary loan (limited); copying; department open to the public. **Special Catalogs:** Special Collections at the University of New Orleans; The Frank A. Von der Haar Collection. **Staff:** Dr. Raymond O. Nussbaum, Lib.Asst. II; Marie E. Windell, Lib.Asst. II; Beatrice R. Owsley, Lib.Asst. II.

★16610★
UNIVERSITY OF NORTH CAROLINA, ASHEVILLE - SOUTHERN HIGHLANDS RESEARCH CENTER (Hist)
Asheville, NC 28814 Phone: (704)251-6414
Dr. Milton Ready, Dir.
Subjects: Western North Carolina, 1833 to present; Appalachia. **Special Collections:** Asheville and Buncombe County photograph collection; papers of U.S. Representative Roy A. Taylor concerning the proposed Mount Mitchell National Park; oral history recordings of mountaineers (200); collections of black, Jewish, Greek, and other ethnic groups in Appalachia; Tom Wolfe Collection. **Holdings:** 50 linear feet of records and photographs. **Services:** Copying; center open to the public. **Remarks:** An alternate telephone number is 251-6415.

★16611★
UNIVERSITY OF NORTH CAROLINA, CHAPEL HILL - ALFRED T. BRAUER LIBRARY (Sci-Engr, Comp Sci)
Phillips Hall, CB 3250 Phone: (919)962-2323
Chapel Hill, NC 27599 Dana M. Sally, Math/Physics Libn.
Founded: 1920. **Staff:** Prof 1; Other 4. **Subjects:** Mathematics, physics, statistics, computer science, operations research, astronomy. **Holdings:** 76,511 volumes; 571 technical reports; 992 microfiche; 139 audiotapes. **Subscriptions:** 964 journals and other serials. **Services:** Interlibrary loan; copying; library open to the public. **Automated Operations:** Computerized cataloging. **Computerized Information Services:** OCLC, DIALOG Information Services. **Networks/Consortia:** Member of SOLINET. **Publications:** List of new books received, monthly; special subject bibliographies, irregular - both available on request.

★16612★
UNIVERSITY OF NORTH CAROLINA, CHAPEL HILL - CENTER FOR ALCOHOL STUDIES - LIBRARY (Med)
335 Wing B
Medical School Bldg. 207H Phone: (919)966-5678
Chapel Hill, NC 27514 Patricia B. Fogleman, Adm.Mgr.
Staff: Prof 1. **Subjects:** Alcohol research, alcoholism. **Holdings:** 550 books; 36 bound periodical volumes; 3000 reprints; clippings. **Subscriptions:** 30 journals and other serials. **Services:** Interlibrary loan; copying; library open to the public. **Publications:** Activities Report, annual - free upon request.

★16613★
UNIVERSITY OF NORTH CAROLINA, CHAPEL HILL - CENTER FOR EARLY ADOLESCENCE - INFORMATION SERVICES DIVISION (Educ)
Carr Mill Mall, Suite 223 Phone: (919)966-1148
Carrboro, NC 27510 Susan Rosenzweig, Dir., Info.Serv.
Staff: Prof 2; Other 1. **Subjects:** Young adolescents - biological, cognitive, psychological, and social development; middle schools and junior high schools; youth advocacy/services; sexuality and sex education; nutrition; after-school care; literacy. **Holdings:** 7000 books and articles; statistics. **Subscriptions:** 150 journals and other serials. **Services:** Phone and mail reference; copying; center open to the public. **Publications:** Common Focus (newsletter), irregular - free upon request; assorted bibliographies, resource lists, monographs, curricula, and AV materials on early adolescence - for sale; thesaurus of subject descriptors. **Remarks:** Center is part of the School of Medicine.

★16614★
UNIVERSITY OF NORTH CAROLINA, CHAPEL HILL - F. STUART CHAPIN, JR. PLANNING LIBRARY (Plan)
New East, CB 3140 Phone: (919)962-3985
Chapel Hill, NC 27599 Charlotte Slocum, City & Reg.Plan.Libn.
Founded: 1949. **Staff:** Prof 1; Other 4. **Subjects:** Urban planning, land use, housing and community development, transportation, environmental planning, regional economics. **Special Collections:** Planning document collection; John Nolan Collection. **Holdings:** 16,500 books; 1600 bound periodical volumes; 10,000 documents; 5800 microforms; 457 audio cassettes; 3651 slides. **Subscriptions:** 275 journals and other serials. **Services:** Interlibrary loan; copying; library open to the public. **Automated Operations:** Computerized cataloging. **Computerized Information Services:** DIALOG Information Services, BRS Information Technologies. Performs searches on fee basis. **Publications:** Acquisitions list, monthly; Library Notes - for internal distribution only.

★16615★
UNIVERSITY OF NORTH CAROLINA, CHAPEL HILL - GEOLOGY LIBRARY (Sci-Engr)
Mitchell Hall, CB 3315 Phone: (919)962-2386
Chapel Hill, NC 27599 Miriam L. Sheaves, Libn.
Staff: Prof 1; Other 1. **Subjects:** Geology, geophysics, paleontology, oceanography. **Holdings:** 43,282 volumes; 36,720 map sheets; 12,411 microforms; partial depository of U.S. Geological Survey topographic and geologic maps. **Subscriptions:** 780 journals and other serials. **Services:** Interlibrary loan; copying; library open to the public. **Computerized Information Services:** DIALOG Information Services; BITNET (electronic mail service).

★16616★
UNIVERSITY OF NORTH CAROLINA, CHAPEL HILL - HEALTH SCIENCES LIBRARY (Med)
Chapel Hill, NC 27514 Phone: (919)966-2111
Carol G. Jenkins, Dir.
Founded: 1952. **Staff:** Prof 24; Other 38. **Subjects:** Medicine, nursing, dentistry, public health, pharmacy, allied health sciences. **Special**

Collections: History of Health Sciences. **Holdings:** 78,000 books; 156,000 bound periodical volumes; 3900 AV programs. **Subscriptions:** 4590 journals and other serials. **Services:** Interlibrary loan; copying; SDI; microcomputer learning center; library open to the public. **Automated Operations:** Computerized public access catalog, cataloging, acquisitions, and serials. **Computerized Information Services:** BRS Information Technologies, DIALOG Information Services, Pergamon ORBIT InfoLine, Inc., NLM, OCLC; OnTyme Electronic Message Network Service (electronic mail service). Performs searches on fee basis. **Networks/Consortia:** Member of Southeastern/Atlantic Regional Medical Library Services, SOLINET, North Carolina Area Health Education Centers Program Library and Information Services Network. **Publications:** Recent Acquisitions, monthly; Annual Report; News & Views, semimonthly - to mailing list. **Special Catalogs:** Audiovisual union catalogs (online). **Staff:** Gary Byrd, Assoc.Dir.; Marjory Waite, Hd., Acq.Serv.; Susan Lyon, Hd., Circ.Serv.; Carmela DiDomenico, Hd., Cat.Serv.; Diane Futrelle, Hd., Lrng.Rsrcs.Serv.; Nidia Scharlock, Hd., Info.Serv.; Francesca Allegri, Hd., Info.Mgt.Educ.; Carolyn Lipscomb, Coord., Staff Dev./Pubn.; Lynne Siemers, AHEC Liaison.

★16617★
UNIVERSITY OF NORTH CAROLINA, CHAPEL HILL - HIGHWAY SAFETY RESEARCH CENTER - LIBRARY (Trans)
Craige Trailer Park, CB 3430 Phone: (919)962-8701
Chapel Hill, NC 27599 Emma G. Stupp, Libn.
Founded: 1970. **Staff:** Prof 1; Other 1. **Subjects:** Highway safety, accident and investigation analysis, driver education and licensing, restraint systems usage and effectiveness, traffic records, evaluation of highway safety programs. **Special Collections:** North Carolina traffic data (traffic accidents, arrest/disposition reports, driver licensing, and driver improvement programs). **Holdings:** 16,000 books, documents, technical reports; 575 bound periodical volumes; 38,000 research reports on microfiche. **Subscriptions:** 125 journals and other serials. **Services:** Interlibrary loan; copying; library open to the public for reference use only. **Computerized Information Services:** DIALOG Information Services.

★16618★
UNIVERSITY OF NORTH CAROLINA, CHAPEL HILL - INSTITUTE OF GOVERNMENT - LIBRARY (Soc Sci)
Knapp Bldg., CB 3330 Phone: (919)966-4130
Chapel Hill, NC 27599-3330 Rebecca S. Ballentine, Libn.
Founded: 1930. **Staff:** Prof 1; Other 2. **Subjects:** Public administration, state and local government, public law. **Holdings:** 7850 books; 6800 bound periodical volumes; 24,490 pamphlets. **Subscriptions:** 510 journals and other serials; 12 newspapers. **Services:** Interlibrary loan; copying; library open to the public. **Automated Operations:** Computerized public access catalog and acquisitions. **Computerized Information Services:** LEXIS; internal database. Performs searches free of charge (limited). **Networks/Consortia:** Member of Triangle Research Libraries Network (TRLN). **Publications:** Acquisitions List, bimonthly. **Special Catalogs:** Publications of the Institute of Government, biennial cumulation.

★16619★
UNIVERSITY OF NORTH CAROLINA, CHAPEL HILL - INSTITUTE OF MARINE SCIENCES - LIBRARY (Biol Sci)
3407 Arendell St. Phone: (919)726-6841
Morehead City, NC 28557 Brenda B. Bright, Libn.
Founded: 1948. **Staff:** Prof 1; Other 1. **Subjects:** Biological oceanography, marine ecology, malacology, ichthyology, mycology, carcinology, sedimentology, microbiology. **Holdings:** 1415 books; 3150 bound periodical volumes; 100 dissertations. **Subscriptions:** 297 journals and other serials. **Services:** Interlibrary loan; copying; library open to the public for reference use only. **Publications:** Separates of research staff publications, annual - on exchange basis.

★16620★
UNIVERSITY OF NORTH CAROLINA, CHAPEL HILL - INSTITUTE OF OUTDOOR DRAMA - ARCHIVES (Theater)
202 Graham Memorial Hall Phone: (919)962-1328
Chapel Hill, NC 27514 Mark R. Sumner, Dir.
Founded: 1963. **Staff:** Prof 1; Other 2. **Subjects:** Architecture, lighting, scripts, organization, finance, personnel, promotion and publicity, production, planning. **Holdings:** 21 VF drawers of documents, souvenir programs, articles, manuscripts, dissertations, photographs, theses, clippings. **Services:** Archives not open to the public. **Publications:** Newsletter, quarterly; assorted bulletins on phases of outdoor drama.

★16621★
UNIVERSITY OF NORTH CAROLINA, CHAPEL HILL - INSTITUTE FOR RESEARCH IN SOCIAL SCIENCE - DATA LIBRARY (Soc Sci)
Manning Hall, CB 3355, Rm. 10 Phone: (919)966-3346
Chapel Hill, NC 27599 Diana McDuffee, Dir.
Founded: 1969. **Staff:** Prof 5; Other 2. **Subjects:** Census data, election data, student attitude data, mass political behavior, political systems, socioeconomic data, social systems/socialization, international and cross-national public opinion polls. **Special Collections:** Public Opinion Poll conducted by Louis Harris & Associates, Inc., 1963 to present. **Holdings:** 2000 machine-readable data files. **Services:** Data sets can be disseminated for a fee; library open to the public. **Automated Operations:** Computerized cataloging. **Computerized Information Services:** DIALOG Information Services; Harris Question Retrieval System (internal database). **Publications:** List of publications - available upon request. **Also Known As:** Louis Harris Data Center. **Staff:** Sue A. Dodd, Libn.; Josephine Marsh, Data.Proc.; David Sheaves, Libn.; Jack Beggs, Census Cons..

★16622★
UNIVERSITY OF NORTH CAROLINA, CHAPEL HILL - JOHN N. COUCH LIBRARY (Biol Sci)
301 Coker Hall, CB 3280 Phone: (919)962-3783
Chapel Hill, NC 27599 William R. Burk, Botany Libn.
Founded: 1926. **Staff:** Prof 1; Other 1. **Subjects:** Mycology, plant physiology, genetics, economic botany, algae, world floras, horticulture, cytology, ecology, plant taxonomy, paleobotany, molecular biology. **Special Collections:** Rare books in mycology (1000 volumes); collected papers of university botanists (reprints and photocopies; 20 volumes containing 862 published works). **Holdings:** 24,938 books; 12,344 bound periodical volumes; 1672 maps; 15,174 microforms; 9000 mycological reprints. **Subscriptions:** 676 journals and other serials. **Services:** Interlibrary loan; copying; library open to the public. **Computerized Information Services:** DIALOG Information Services. **Publications:** Library Literature Guides on botanical topics, irregular - for internal distribution only. **Special Indexes:** Index to mycological pamphlet collection (card).

★16623★
UNIVERSITY OF NORTH CAROLINA, CHAPEL HILL - KENAN CHEMISTRY LIBRARY (Sci-Engr)
269 Venable Hall, CB 3290 Phone: (919)962-1188
Chapel Hill, NC 27599 Jimmy Dickerson, Chem.Libn.
Staff: Prof 1; Other 2. **Subjects:** All branches of chemistry. **Special Collections:** Venable History of Science Collection (850 volumes). **Holdings:** 50,000 volumes; 2391 microforms. **Subscriptions:** 735 journals and other serials. **Services:** Interlibrary loan; copying; library open to the public with restrictions. **Computerized Information Services:** DIALOG Information Services, CAS ONLINE, Chemical Information Systems, Inc. (CIS). **Publications:** Monthly new book list - free upon request.

★16624★
UNIVERSITY OF NORTH CAROLINA, CHAPEL HILL - LAW LIBRARY (Law)
Van Hecke-Wettach Bldg. 064A Phone: (919)962-1321
Chapel Hill, NC 27514 Laura N. Gasaway, Dir.
Staff: Prof 8; Other 12. **Subjects:** Law. **Special Collections:** Native American law. **Holdings:** 245,159 volumes; 355,140 microforms. **Subscriptions:** 5387 journals and other serials. **Services:** Copying; library open to the public. **Computerized Information Services:** WESTLAW, LEXIS, DIALOG Information Services, PHINet FedTax Database, WILSONLINE, OCLC. **Staff:** Timothy L. Coggins, Assoc.Dir.; Martha Barefoot, Circ.Libn.; Carol Nicholson, Tech.Serv.Libn.; Terri Saye, Cat.Libn.; Deborah Webster, Ref.Libn.; Doina Massey, Acq.Libn.; Janice Hammett, Asst.Ref.Libn..

★16625★
UNIVERSITY OF NORTH CAROLINA, CHAPEL HILL - MAPS COLLECTION (Geog-Map)
Wilson Library 024A Phone: (919)962-3028
Chapel Hill, NC 27514 Celia D. Pratt, Map Libn.
Staff: Prof 1; Other 1. **Subjects:** Cartography. **Holdings:** 156,400 maps, including maps from the Defense Mapping Agency, National Ocean Survey, and U.S. Geological Survey; 1275 atlases; 650 reference works and cartobibliographies; 365 gazetteers. **Subscriptions:** 26 journals and other serials. **Services:** Interlibrary loan (limited); copying; collection open to the public.

★16626★
UNIVERSITY OF NORTH CAROLINA, CHAPEL HILL - MUSIC LIBRARY (Mus)
Hill Hall, CB 3320 Phone: (919)966-1113
Chapel Hill, NC 27599 Ida Reed, Mus.Libn.
Founded: 1935. **Staff:** Prof 3; Other 3. **Subjects:** Music, music literature, musicology. **Special Collections:** Opera; history of music theory; the sonata; early American music collection; American shape-note tunebook collection. **Holdings:** 34,500 volumes; 58,000 volumes of music; 25,500 phonograph records; 4700 reels of microfilm; 2300 microcards; 500 microfiche. **Subscriptions:** 724 journals and other serials. **Services:** Interlibrary loan; copying. **Computerized Information Services:** OCLC. **Networks/Consortia:** Member of SOLINET. **Special Indexes:** Song anthology index; record anthology vocal index; music biography index; early American music index; American shape-note tunebook collection index; place/date/publisher index for rare materials. **Staff:** Alan Gregory, Mus.Cat..

★16627★
UNIVERSITY OF NORTH CAROLINA, CHAPEL HILL - NORTH CAROLINA COLLECTION (Hist, Rare Book)
Wilson Library 024A Phone: (919)962-1172
Chapel Hill, NC 27514 H.G. Jones, Cur.
Founded: 1844. **Staff:** Prof 6; Other 5. **Subjects:** North Caroliniana; books by and about North Carolinians. **Special Collections:** Sir Walter Raleigh Collection (by and about Raleigh); Thomas Wolfe Collection (by and about Wolfe); Bruce Cotten Collection (fine and rare North Caroliniana). **Holdings:** 175,899 volumes; 4294 maps; 3850 broadsides; 12,667 manuscripts; 12,221 reels of microfilm; 45,000 pictures; 165,000 mounted newspaper clippings. **Subscriptions:** 3000 journals and other serials. **Services:** Copying; collection open to the public with identification. **Publications:** Annual Report; North Caroliniana Society Imprints, irregular. **Staff:** Alice R. Cotten, Ref.Hist.; Robert G. Anthony, Jr., Coll.Dev.Libn.; Eileen McGrath, Cat.; Sue W. Lithgo, Cat.; R. Neil Fulgham, Kpr., NC Gallery.

★16628★
UNIVERSITY OF NORTH CAROLINA, CHAPEL HILL - OCCUPATIONAL SAFETY & HEALTH EDUCATIONAL RESOURCE CENTER - OSHERC LIBRARY (Med)
109 Conner Dr., Suite 1101 Phone: (919)962-2101
Chapel Hill, NC 27514 Mary Ellen Tucker, Libn.
Founded: 1979. **Staff:** Prof 1; Other 1. **Subjects:** Industrial hygiene; occupational medicine, health nursing, and safety. **Special Collections:** Audiovisual training materials (150); research reports, theses, and dissertations of UNC Environmental Sciences graduate students; UNC Rubber Industry Study research reports (50). **Holdings:** 2500 books. **Subscriptions:** 18 journals and other serials. **Services:** Copying; library open to the public with restrictions. **Computerized Information Services:** DIALOG Information Services, NIOSH Data Base. Performs searches on fee basis.

★16629★
UNIVERSITY OF NORTH CAROLINA, CHAPEL HILL - RARE BOOK COLLECTION (Rare Book)
Wilson Library 024A Phone: (919)962-1143
Chapel Hill, NC 27514 Charles B. McNamara, Cur.
Staff: Prof 4; Other 2. **Subjects:** History of the book, incunabula, English and American literature, French history, Americana. **Special Collections:** Bernard J. Flatow Collection of Early Latin American Cronistas; George Baer Collection of Fine Bindings; Jacques Barzun and Wendell Hertig Taylor Collection of Crime and Detection; Mary Shore Cameron Collection of Sherlock Holmes; Confederate Imprint Collection; Preston Davie Collection of Early Americana; Annette Duchein Collection of Ornithology; Burton Emmett Collection of First Editions and Fine Typography; Eton College Collection; Bowman Gray Collection Relating to World Wars I and II; Hanes Collection of Estienne Imprints; Hanes Incunabula Collection; Dannie N. Heineman Collection of Hebraica and Judaica; Archibald Henderson Collection of George Bernard Shaw; Roland Holt Collection of American Theater; Walter Hooper Collection of C.S. Lewis; William Henry Hoyt Collection of French History; Richard Jente Collection of Proverbs; Kellam Collection of "The Night Before Christmas"; Clifford and Glady Lyons Collection of Robert Frost; Mazarinades Collection; John Murray and Smith-Elder Imprints Collection; Shedd Collection of Aphorisms; Southern Pamphlets Collection; Samuel A. Tannenbaum Collection of William Shakespeare; Ticknor and Fields Collection; Leslie Weil Collection of Science; William A. Whitaker Collections of Charles Dickens, Costume Plate Books, George Cruikshank, Samuel Johnson and His Circle, and William Makepeace Thackeray; Victorian Bindings; Richard H. Wilmer, Jr. Collection of Civil War Novels. **Holdings:** 87,000 books; 16,000 graphics; 1170 manuscripts. **Subscriptions:** 20 journals and other serials. **Services:** Interlibrary loan; copying; collection open to the public with restrictions. **Automated Operations:** Computerized cataloging. **Publications:** Hanes Lectures. **Staff:** Roberta Engleman, Rare Bks.Cat.; Elizabeth Chenault, Pub.Serv.Libn..

★16630★
UNIVERSITY OF NORTH CAROLINA, CHAPEL HILL - SCHOOL OF INFORMATION AND LIBRARY SCIENCE LIBRARY (Info Sci)
114 Manning Hall, CB 3360 Phone: (919)962-8361
Chapel Hill, NC 27599 Elizabeth J. Laney, Libn.
Founded: 1931. **Staff:** 2. **Subjects:** Librarianship, documentation, communication, publishing, automation, information, management, education. **Special Collections:** Historical collection of children's literature in the United States; annual reports and newsletters of libraries and related institutions. **Holdings:** 66,852 books and bound periodical volumes; 1492 reels of microfilm; 2105 microcards and microfiche; 1600 documents in report literature collection; 3480 AV programs; 27,879 pamphlet and VF materials. **Subscriptions:** 1550 journals and other serials. **Services:** Interlibrary loan; copying; library open to the public. **Computerized Information Services:** DIALOG Information Services, WILSONLINE. **Publications:** Acquisitions list, monthly; annual report.

★16631★
UNIVERSITY OF NORTH CAROLINA, CHAPEL HILL - SLOANE ART LIBRARY (Art)
Hanes Art Center, CB 3405 Phone: (919)962-2397
Chapel Hill, NC 27599 Philip A. Rees, Art Libn.
Founded: 1958. **Staff:** Prof 1; Other 1. **Subjects:** Art. **Holdings:** 61,500 volumes; 12,200 microfiche; 315 reels of microfilm. **Subscriptions:** 425 journals and other serials. **Services:** Interlibrary loan; copying; library open to the public with limited circulation.

★16632★
UNIVERSITY OF NORTH CAROLINA, CHAPEL HILL - SOUTHERN HISTORICAL COLLECTION & MANUSCRIPTS DEPARTMENT (Hist)
Wilson Library 024A Phone: (919)962-1345
Chapel Hill, NC 27514 Richard A. Shrader, Act.Dir./Cur.
Founded: 1930. **Staff:** Prof 4; Other 3. **Subjects:** Southern history and culture, university history, American and English literature. **Holdings:** Over 8 million manuscript items organized into over 4400 collections; 1.5 million items in University of North Carolina archives; 3071 microforms; 492 AV programs; 1953 audio recordings. **Services:** Copying; department open to the public for reference use only. **Publications:** The Southern Historical Collection: A Guide to Manuscripts, 1970 (supplement, 1976). **Staff:** Michael G. Martin, Jr., Univ.Archv.; Tim West, Tech.Serv.Archv.; Frances A. Weaver, Asst.Univ.Archv..

★16633★
UNIVERSITY OF NORTH CAROLINA, CHAPEL HILL - ZOOLOGY LIBRARY (Biol Sci)
213 Wilson Hall, CB 3280 Phone: (919)962-2264
Chapel Hill, NC 27599 John B. Darling, Zoology Libn.
Founded: 1940. **Staff:** Prof 1; Other 1. **Subjects:** Invertebrate and vertebrate zoology, cell biology, genetics, physiology, evolution, molecular biology, embryology, behavior, ecology. **Holdings:** 38,450 volumes. **Subscriptions:** 652 journals and other serials. **Services:** Interlibrary loan; copying; library open to the public. **Computerized Information Services:** DIALOG Information Services.

★16634★
UNIVERSITY OF NORTH CAROLINA, GREENSBORO - DANCE COLLECTION (Hum)
Jackson Library, Special Collections Phone: (919)334-5246
Greensboro, NC 27412 Emilie Mills, Spec.Coll.Libn.
Staff: Prof 1; Other 2. **Subjects:** History of the dance, modern dance, dance notation. **Special Collections:** Early dance books, 16th-18th centuries (100 volumes). **Holdings:** 3000 volumes. **Subscriptions:** 40 journals and other serials. **Services:** Collection open to the public for research.

★16635★
UNIVERSITY OF NORTH CAROLINA, GREENSBORO - EUGENIE SILVERMAN BAIZERMAN ARCHIVE (Art)
Jackson Library, Special Collections
Greensboro, NC 27412 Phone: (919)334-5246
Staff: Prof 1; Other 2. **Subjects:** Art. **Holdings:** 2000 items. **Services:** Archive open to the public but manuscript materials are not available.

Special Catalogs: Catalog of Special Collections' Manuscripts and Archives.

★16636★
UNIVERSITY OF NORTH CAROLINA, GREENSBORO - GEORGE HERBERT COLLECTION (Hum)
Jackson Library, Special Collections
Greensboro, NC 27412 Phone: (919)334-5246
Staff: Prof 2; Other 1. **Special Collections:** George Herbert Collection of books, 17th-20th centuries; Cross-Bias Newsletter, 1975 to present; Friends of Bemerton miscellanea (50 items). **Holdings:** 270 books; 4 dissertations on Herbert on microfilm. **Services:** Copying; collection open to the public for research.

★16637★
UNIVERSITY OF NORTH CAROLINA, GREENSBORO - GIRLS BOOKS IN SERIES (Hum)
Jackson Library, Special Collections
Greensboro, NC 27412 Phone: (919)334-5246
Staff: Prof 1; Other 2. **Subjects:** Children's literature. **Holdings:** 600 books. **Services:** Collection open to the public for research.

★16638★
UNIVERSITY OF NORTH CAROLINA, GREENSBORO - LOIS LENSKI COLLECTION (Hum, Rare Book)
Jackson Library, Special Collections
Greensboro, NC 27412 Phone: (919)334-5246
Subjects: Children's literature. **Holdings:** Lois Lenski Collection (5000 books, manuscripts, original drawings, correspondence, photographs, clippings, and ephemera); early children's books, 18th-19th centuries (1500). **Services:** Copying (limited); collection open to public for research.

★16639★
UNIVERSITY OF NORTH CAROLINA, GREENSBORO - LUIGI SILVA COLLECTION (Mus)
Jackson Library, Special Collections
Greensboro, NC 27412 Phone: (919)334-5246
Staff: Prof 1; Other 2. **Subjects:** History and teaching of the cello. **Special Collections:** Luigi Silva Library of the History and Teaching of the Cello. **Holdings:** 200 books; 20 bound periodical volumes; 73 boxes of manuscripts and printed scores; 80 bound volumes of chamber music. **Services:** Copying; collection open to the public for research. **Special Catalogs:** Catalog of the cello collections at University of North Carolina at Greensboro: Part I: The Luigi Silva Collection (1978).

★16640★
UNIVERSITY OF NORTH CAROLINA, GREENSBORO - PHYSICAL EDUCATION HISTORY COLLECTION (Educ)
Jackson Library, Special Collections
Greensboro, NC 27412 Phone: (919)334-5246
Subjects: Physical activity, training, theory; gymnastics; dance history. **Special Collections:** Gymnastics books dating from the 16th century; early dance books and landmark works on all types of physical activity, training, and theory, 16th century-early 1900s in English and several foreign languages. **Holdings:** 1500 books and pamphlets. **Services:** Collection open to the public for research.

★16641★
UNIVERSITY OF NORTH CAROLINA, GREENSBORO - PRINTING COLLECTION (Rare Book)
Jackson Library, Special Collections
Greensboro, NC 27412 Phone: (919)334-5246
Staff: Prof 1; Other 2. **Subjects:** Private presses, history of printing, 20th century illustrated books. **Special Collections:** Modern fine printing and the art of the book; 19th century American publishers' trade bindings; American publishers' cloth, early period. **Holdings:** 1000 volumes. **Services:** Collection open to the public for research.

★16642★
UNIVERSITY OF NORTH CAROLINA, GREENSBORO - RANDALL JARRELL COLLECTION (Hum)
Jackson Library, Special Collections
Greensboro, NC 27412 Phone: (919)334-5246
Staff: Prof 1; Other 2. **Subjects:** Randall Jarrell. **Holdings:** 300 books; over 3000 manuscript items; 10 films and tapes; 6 recordings. **Services:** Copying; collection open to the public for research.

★16643★
UNIVERSITY OF NORTH CAROLINA, GREENSBORO - SAUL BAIZERMAN ARCHIVE (Art)
Jackson Library, Special Collections
Greensboro, NC 27412 Phone: (919)334-5246
Staff: Prof 2; Other 1. **Subjects:** Saul Baizerman, sculptor (1889-1957). **Holdings:** Drawings, sketches, photographs of sculptures completed and in progress; exhibition catalogs, reviews, journals, personal memorabilia (2100 items). **Services:** Archive open to the public with restrictions on unpublished material. **Special Indexes:** Special Collections' Manuscripts and Archives (description with box listings).

★16644★
UNIVERSITY OF NORTH CAROLINA, GREENSBORO - WAY & WILLIAMS COLLECTION (Publ)
Jackson Library, Special Collections
Greensboro, NC 27412 Phone: (919)334-5246
Holdings: Way & Williams Collection (100 books, manuscripts, correspondence, and original drawings of a Chicago literary publishing firm, 1895-1898). Important associations include Will Bradley, Maxfield Parrish, William Allen White. **Services:** Collection open to public for research.

★16645★
UNIVERSITY OF NORTH CAROLINA, GREENSBORO - WOMAN'S COLLECTION (Soc Sci)
Jackson Library, Special Collections
Greensboro, NC 27412 Phone: (919)334-5246
Staff: Prof 1; Other 2. **Subjects:** Women - education, history, suffrage; history of costume; women authors; manners and morals; child raising and family life. **Special Collections:** Women in the 17th-19th centuries. **Holdings:** 5000 books; 254 bound periodical volumes. **Services:** Copying; collection open to the public for research. **Publications:** The Woman's Collection, A Check-list of Holdings, 1975.

★16646★
UNIVERSITY OF NORTH CAROLINA, GREENSBORO - WOMAN'S DETECTIVE FICTION COLLECTION (Hum)
Jackson Library, Special Collections
Greensboro, NC 27412 Phone: (919)334-5246
Staff: Prof 2; Other 1. **Subjects:** Women detectives in American fiction, 1890 to present. **Holdings:** 900 books. **Services:** Copying (limited); collection open to the public for research.

★16647★
UNIVERSITY OF NORTH CAROLINA, WILMINGTON - INSTITUTE OF MARINE BIOMEDICAL RESEARCH - LIBRARY (Env-Cons, Biol Sci)
601 S. College Rd.
Wilmington, NC 28406 Phone: (919)256-3721
Founded: 1962. **Subjects:** Environmental physiology, deep sea oceanography. **Holdings:** 10,000 volumes.

★16648★
UNIVERSITY OF NORTH CAROLINA, WILMINGTON - WILLIAM MADISON RANDALL LIBRARY - HELEN HAGAN RARE BOOK ROOM (Rare Book)
601 S. College Rd. Phone: (919)395-3276
Wilmington, NC 28403-3297 Sue Hiatt, Hd., Ref./Spec.Coll.Libn.
Subjects: History of the lower Cape Fear area of North Carolina (including Brunswick, Columbus, New Hanover, and Pender counties), 1700 to present. **Special Collections:** Papers of Congressmen Alton Lennon and Thomas J. Armstrong; local history collection (including land grants from George II and property documents); collection of ephemera about North Carolina artists and art institutions. **Holdings:** 480 linear feet of archival material. **Services:** Copying; room open to the public. **Publications:** Descriptive inventory of the Armstrong papers.

★16649★
UNIVERSITY OF NORTH DAKOTA - CHEMISTRY LIBRARY (Sci-Engr)
224 Abbott Hall Phone: (701)777-2741
Grand Forks, ND 58202 Evelyn Cole, Sec.
Staff: 1. **Subjects:** Chemistry - electrochemistry, environmental, inorganic, organometallic, medicinal. **Holdings:** 4600 books; 7700 bound periodical volumes; 611 microfiche; 21,510 microcards; 24 reels of microfilm. **Subscriptions:** 170 journals and other serials. **Services:** Interlibrary loan; library open to the public. **Networks/Consortia:** Member of MINITEX, North Dakota Network for Knowledge.

★16650★
UNIVERSITY OF NORTH DAKOTA - ELWYN B. ROBINSON DEPARTMENT OF SPECIAL COLLECTIONS (Hist)
Chester Fritz Library Phone: (701)777-4625
Grand Forks, ND 58202 Dan Rylance, Coord. of Spec.Coll.
Founded: 1963. **Staff:** Prof 3; Other 2. **Subjects:** History - North and South Dakota, Northern Great Plains, Plains Indian, women, environmental; agrarian radicalism; Nonpartisan League (North Dakota); genealogy; oral history. **Special Collections:** North Dakota Book Collection (8000 volumes); Fred G. Aandahl Book Collection (1350 volumes); Family History/Genealogy Collection (1700 volumes); North Dakota State Documents (40,000); university archives (1000 linear feet); Orin G. Libby Manuscript Collection (5700 linear feet). **Holdings:** 11,000 books; 6700 linear feet of manuscript material; 3725 reels of microfilm. **Services:** Copying; department open to the public. **Automated Operations:** Computerized acquisitions. **Publications:** University of North Dakota Theses and Dissertations on North Dakota, 1895-1971, 1972; Reference Guide to North Dakota History and Literature, 1979; Reference Guide to the Orin G. Libby Manuscript Collection (Volume 1, 1975; Volume 2, 1983; Volume 3, 1985). **Special Catalogs:** Subject Guide to the Orin G. Libby Manuscript Collection, 1979; Guide to Genealogical/Family History Sources, 1984; Guide to Norwegian Bygdeboker, 1985. **Special Indexes:** Index to the Dakota Student (newspaper); index to the Alumni Review (newspaper). **Staff:** Sandra Beidler, Asst.Coord..

★16651★
UNIVERSITY OF NORTH DAKOTA - ENERGY AND MINERAL RESEARCH CENTER - ENERGY LIBRARY (Energy)
University Sta., Box 8213 Phone: (701)777-5132
Grand Forks, ND 58202 Lorraine Knox, Sci.Bibliog.
Founded: 1951. **Staff:** Prof 1. **Subjects:** Fossil energy conversion, coal, lignite. **Holdings:** 3500 books; 760 bound periodical volumes; U.S. Department of Energy reports; 229 periodical titles. **Subscriptions:** 108 journals and other serials. **Services:** Interlibrary loan (through Chester Fritz Library); copying; SDI; library open to the public. **Automated Operations:** Computerized cataloging. **Computerized Information Services:** DIALOG Information Services, Pergamon ORBIT InfoLine, Inc., BRS Information Technologies, Performs searches on fee basis. **Networks/Consortia:** Member of MINITEX.

★16652★
UNIVERSITY OF NORTH DAKOTA - ENGINEERING LIBRARY (Sci-Engr)
Harrington Hall, University Sta. Phone: (701)777-3040
Grand Forks, ND 58202 Kay Olesen, Libn.
Staff: 1. **Subjects:** Engineering - chemical, civil, electrical, industrial, mechanical. **Holdings:** 12,700 books; 8440 bound periodical volumes; 4600 microfiche; 715 reels of microfilm. **Subscriptions:** 406 journals and other serials. **Services:** Interlibrary loan; copying; library open to the public. **Computerized Information Services:** DIALOG Information Services, Pergamon ORBIT InfoLine, Inc. **Networks/Consortia:** Member of MINITEX, North Dakota Network for Knowledge.

★16653★
UNIVERSITY OF NORTH DAKOTA - GEOLOGY LIBRARY (Sci-Engr)
Leonard Hall, University Sta. Phone: (701)777-3221
Grand Forks, ND 58202 Mary Sand, Ref.Libn.
Staff: 1. **Subjects:** Geology, paleontology, petroleum engineering, North Dakota geology. **Special Collections:** Depository for state geological surveys publications; U.S. Geological Survey and U.S. Bureau of Mines publications; U.S.G.S. open-file reports for North Dakota. **Holdings:** 11,748 books; 18,622 bound periodical volumes; 86 microfiche; 210 reels of microfilm; 130,000 U.S. Geological Survey topographic maps; 7700 other maps; air photograph collection for North Dakota. **Subscriptions:** 756 journals and other serials. **Services:** Interlibrary loan; copying; library open to the public. **Computerized Information Services:** DIALOG Information Services, Pergamon ORBIT InfoLine, Inc. **Networks/Consortia:** Member of MINITEX, North Dakota Network for Knowledge. **Remarks:** An alternate telephone number is 777-2408.

★16654★
UNIVERSITY OF NORTH DAKOTA - INSTITUTE FOR ECOLOGICAL STUDIES - ENVIRONMENTAL RESOURCE CENTER - LIBRARY (Env-Cons)
Box 8278 Phone: (701)777-2851
Grand Forks, ND 58202 Rod Sayler, Dir.
Founded: 1972. **Staff:** 2. **Subjects:** Ecology, land use, water and air pollution, chemical and biological contaminants, wildlife, environmental education, energy, nonrenewable resources. **Holdings:** 1000 books; 600 research reports; 1000 environmental impact statements; 12 drawers of pamphlets; 600 maps. **Services:** Interlibrary loan; copying; SDI; center open to the public.

★16655★
UNIVERSITY OF NORTH DAKOTA - MATH-PHYSICS LIBRARY (Sci-Engr)
211 Witmer Hall Phone: (701)777-2911
Grand Forks, ND 58202 Debra Streifel, Sec.
Staff: 1. **Subjects:** Field theory, solid state physics, mathematical physics, thin films, mathematical analysis, mathematical models. **Holdings:** 9275 books; 8250 bound periodical volumes. **Subscriptions:** 230 journals and other serials. **Services:** Interlibrary loan; library open to the public. **Networks/Consortia:** Member of MINITEX, North Dakota Network for Knowledge.

★16656★
UNIVERSITY OF NORTH DAKOTA - MUSIC LIBRARY (Mus)
Hughes Fine Arts Center Phone: (701)777-2817
Grand Forks, ND 58202 Beth Nienow, Libn.
Founded: 1974. **Staff:** 2. **Subjects:** Music. **Holdings:** 4000 phonograph records; 4000 scores. **Services:** Interlibrary loan; copying; library open to the public, phonograph records do not circulate.

★16657★
UNIVERSITY OF NORTH DAKOTA - OLAF H. THORMODSGARD LAW LIBRARY (Law)
Grand Forks, ND 58201 Phone: (701)777-2204
Gary D. Gott, Dir.
Founded: 1899. **Staff:** Prof 6; Other 3. **Subjects:** Law. **Holdings:** 135,276 bound volumes; 50,000 volumes in microform; 296,985 microfiche; 793 reels of microfilm; 280 AV programs. **Subscriptions:** 3900 journals and other serials. **Services:** Interlibrary loan; copying; library open to the public with restrictions. **Automated Operations:** Computerized cataloging. **Computerized Information Services:** LEXIS, WESTLAW; ALANET (electronic mail service). Performs searches on fee basis. Contact Person: Ted Smith, Dir., Att.Serv., 777-3354. **Networks/Consortia:** Member of MINITEX. **Staff:** Donald D. Olson, Tech.Serv.Libn.; Patricia Folkestad, Ser.Libn.; Dennis Fossum, Monograph Libn.; James R. Carlson, Pub.Serv./Ref.Libn.; Kaaren Pupino, ILL; Kim Balow, Looseleaf Libn.; Sarah Scheuring, Bus.Mgr..

★16658★
UNIVERSITY OF NORTH DAKOTA - SCHOOL OF MEDICINE - HARLEY E. FRENCH LIBRARY OF THE HEALTH SCIENCES (Med)
Grand Forks, ND 58202-9002 Phone: (701)777-3993
David Boilard, Dir.
Founded: 1949. **Staff:** Prof 5; Other 5. **Subjects:** Medicine, nursing, physical therapy. **Special Collections:** Dr. French Collection (books by and about doctors; history of medicine); human nutrition research and trace elements. **Holdings:** 27,000 books; 38,000 bound periodical volumes; 1300 AV programs; 720 volumes on microfiche. **Subscriptions:** 1150 journals and other serials. **Services:** Interlibrary loan; copying; SDI; library open to the public for reference use only. **Automated Operations:** Computerized cataloging and ILL. **Computerized Information Services:** OCLC, MEDLINE, TOXLINE, BRS Information Technologies; EasyLink, OnTyme Electronic Message Network Service, DOCLINE (electronic mail services). Performs searches on fee basis. Contact Person: Lorraine Ettl, Pub.Serv.. **Networks/Consortia:** Member of Greater Midwest Regional Medical Library Network, MINITEX. **Publications:** Biomedia Report, quarterly. **Special Catalogs:** Audiovisual catalog (book); serials list, annual. **Staff:** Lila Pedersen, Asst.Dir., Coll.Dev.; Michael Strahan, Comp.Serv./ILL; Zoltan Tomory, Cat.; Michael Safratowich, Cat..

UNIVERSITY OF NORTH DAKOTA - SCHOOL OF MEDICINE - NORTHWEST CAMPUS LIBRARY
See: Trinity Medical Center - Angus L. Cameron Medical Library (14342)

★16659★
UNIVERSITY OF NORTH TEXAS LIBRARIES - MEDIA LIBRARY (Aud-Vis)
Box 12898 Phone: (817)565-2691
Denton, TX 76203-2898 George D. Mitchell, III, Media Lib.Dir.
Staff: Prof 2; Other 12. **Subjects:** Gerontology, education, psychology, business, sciences, film studies. **Special Collections:** Gerontological Film Collection (420 titles). **Holdings:** 1958 reels of motion picture film; 990 video cassettes; 67 laser discs; 2129 filmstrips; 2450 phonograph records; 3192 phonotapes; 25,586 slides; 231 transparencies; 65 kits; 184

microcomputer discs. **Subscriptions:** 12 journals and other serials. **Services:** Library open to the public for reference use only; qualified outside users may rent materials. **Automated Operations:** Computerized cataloging. **Networks/Consortia:** Member of Consortium of University Film Centers (CUFC), Association for Higher Education of North Texas (AHE). **Special Catalogs:** Gerontological Film Collection catalog, bimonthly; Title Catalog of Motion Picture and Video Collection with Supplements of Media Acquired in all Formats since 1980. **Formerly:** North Texas State University Libraries. **Staff:** Mark Withers, Serv.Coord..

★16660★
UNIVERSITY OF NORTH TEXAS LIBRARIES - ORAL HISTORY COLLECTION (Hist)
University Sta., Box 5188
Denton, TX 76203 Dr. Ronald E. Marcello, Coord.
Founded: 1963. **Staff:** Prof 1; Other 1. **Subjects:** Texas governors and legislators, World War II, New Deal, integration, business history, institutional history, politics. **Holdings:** 800 books; 900 oral history tapes. **Services:** Copying; collection open to the public with restrictions. **Publications:** Bulletin, Oral History Collection. **Formerly:** North Texas State University Libraries.

★16661★
UNIVERSITY OF NORTH TEXAS LIBRARIES - RARE BOOK ROOM (Rare Book)
North Texas Sta., Box 5188 Phone: (817)565-2769
Denton, TX 76203 Dr. Kenneth Lavender, Univ.Bibliog.
Founded: 1981. **Staff:** Prof 1; Other 3. **Subjects:** Travel, children's literature, Texana, 18th century English literature. **Special Collections:** Larry McMurtry (63 typescripts; proof copies; signed editions); Mary Webb (38 editions; photographs); Anson Jones (133 volumes); Willa Cather (49 first editions). **Holdings:** 6826 books; 75 manuscripts. **Services:** Room open to the public with restrictions. **Networks/Consortia:** Member of AMIGOS Bibliographic Council, Inc., Association for Higher Education of North Texas (AHE). **Special Catalogs:** Catalogue of Webb Collection; Printers' File; catalog of children's literature; catalog of 18th century holdings (all on cards). **Formerly:** North Texas State University Libraries.

★16662★
UNIVERSITY OF NORTHERN COLORADO - UNIVERSITY ARCHIVES† (Hist)
James A. Michener Library Phone: (303)351-2632
Greeley, CO 80639-9986 Suzanne Schulze, Archv.Libn.
Staff: Prof 1; Other 1. **Subjects:** University archives, including faculty publications. **Special Collections:** Papers and manuscripts of James A. Michener and other authors. **Holdings:** 2000 books; 500 other cataloged items; 200 boxes of papers and manuscripts. **Services:** Interlibrary loan; copying; SDI; archives open to the public. **Automated Operations:** Computerized cataloging, acquisitions, serials, circulation, and holdings. **Networks/Consortia:** Member of Colorado Alliance of Research Libraries (CARL). **Publications:** List of publications - available on request. **Special Indexes:** Index of old slides; faculty index.

★16663★
UNIVERSITY OF NORTHERN IOWA - ROD LIBRARY - SPECIAL COLLECTIONS (Hist)
Cedar Falls, IA 50613 Phone: (319)273-6307
Gerald L. Peterson, Spec.Coll.Libn.
Staff: Prof 1; Other 1. **Subjects:** Education, Iowa history. **Special Collections:** American fiction first editions, proofs, and manuscripts (5000 volumes); university archives. **Holdings:** 7500 books; 1000 cubic feet of manuscripts. **Services:** Interlibrary loan; copying; collections open to the public.

★16664★
UNIVERSITY OF NOTRE DAME - ARCHITECTURE LIBRARY (Art, Plan)
210 Architectural Bldg. Phone: (219)239-6654
Notre Dame, IN 46556 Robert Havlik, Libn.
Staff: Prof 1; Other 3. **Subjects:** Architecture, allied art and design, city planning, environment, landscape architecture. **Holdings:** 14,132 volumes; 8 VF drawers; 25,000 slides. **Subscriptions:** 84 journals and other serials. **Services:** Interlibrary loan; copying; library open to the public for reference use only. **Computerized Information Services:** DIALOG Information Services, WILSONLINE. **Staff:** Linda Messersmith, Supv..

★16665★
UNIVERSITY OF NOTRE DAME - ARCHIVES (Hist)
607 Memorial Library Phone: (219)239-6447
Notre Dame, IN 46556 Dr. Wendy Clauson Schlereth, Univ.Archv.
Founded: 1875. **Staff:** Prof 5; Other 12. **Subjects:** American Catholicism, University of Notre Dame. **Holdings:** 4000 linear feet of manuscripts and archival material. **Services:** Copying; archives open to the public. **Publications:** Guides to microfilmed collections - for sale.

★16666★
UNIVERSITY OF NOTRE DAME - CHEMISTRY/PHYSICS LIBRARY (Sci-Engr)
231 Nieuwland Science Hall Phone: (219)239-7203
Notre Dame, IN 46556 Shirley Scott, Phys. & Math.Sci.Libn.
Founded: 1963. **Staff:** Prof 1; Other 2. **Subjects:** Chemistry - analytical, biochemistry, environmental, inorganic, organic, photochemistry, polymer, solid-state, stereo, theoretical; physics - acoustical, astrophysics, biophysics, computer, cryogenics, elementary particle, high energy, mathematical, nuclear, radio, solid-state, technical. **Holdings:** 41,095 volumes. **Subscriptions:** 350 journals. **Services:** Interlibrary loan; copying; library open to the public for reference use only. **Computerized Information Services:** DIALOG Information Services, BRS Information Technologies, CAS ONLINE. Performs searches on fee basis.

★16667★
UNIVERSITY OF NOTRE DAME - DEPARTMENT OF SPECIAL COLLECTIONS (Hum, Rare Book)
102 Memorial Library Phone: (219)239-6489
Notre Dame, IN 46556 David E. Sparks, Hd.
Staff: Prof 2; Other 2. **Subjects:** Theology, philosophy, language and literature, sports and games, botany. **Special Collections:** John Augustine Zahm Collection on Dante (5000 items); John Bennett Shaw Collection on Chesterton (2000 items); Rare Books Collection (25,000 items); International Sports/Games Research Collection (500,000 items); Jeremiah D.M. Ford Collection on Romance Languages and Literature (3000 items); Edward L. Greene Collection on Botany (4000 items); Notre Dame Collection (8000 items). **Subscriptions:** 100 journals and other serials. **Services:** Interlibrary loan (limited); copying; department open to the public. **Special Catalogs:** Exhibit catalogues; Incunabula Typographica, 1979; Catalogue of Medieval and Renaissance Manuscripts, 1978.

★16668★
UNIVERSITY OF NOTRE DAME - ENGINEERING LIBRARY (Sci-Engr)
149 Fitzpatrick Hall of Engineering Phone: (219)239-6665
Notre Dame, IN 46556 Robert J. Havlik, Engr.Libn.
Staff: Prof 1; Other 3. **Subjects:** Engineering - civil, aerospace, mechanical, electrical, environmental, metallurgical, chemical. **Holdings:** 28,780 books; 17,500 bound periodical volumes; 12,500 microfiche; 2800 microforms. **Subscriptions:** 625 journals and other serials. **Services:** Interlibrary loan; copying; library open to the public for reference use only. **Computerized Information Services:** DIALOG Information Services, BRS Information Technologies. **Staff:** John Harlan, Supv..

★16669★
UNIVERSITY OF NOTRE DAME - INTERNATIONAL STUDIES RESOURCE CENTER (Soc Sci)
213 Memorial Library
Box 517 Phone: (219)239-6587
Notre Dame, IN 46556 Susan Saavedra, Supv.
Founded: 1986. **Staff:** Prof 2; Other 1. **Subjects:** International relations, foreign policy, diplomacy, Latin America. **Holdings:** 860 boxes of newspaper clippings; 140 files of pamphlets. **Services:** Center open to the public.

★16670★
UNIVERSITY OF NOTRE DAME - LAW SCHOOL LIBRARY (Law)
Kresge Library
Box 535 Phone: (219)239-7024
Notre Dame, IN 46556 Roger F. Jacobs, Dir.
Founded: 1869. **Staff:** Prof 7; Other 6. **Subjects:** Law. **Holdings:** 180,000 volumes. **Subscriptions:** 697 journals; 3000 serials. **Services:** Interlibrary loan; copying; library open to the public. **Automated Operations:** Computerized cataloging. **Computerized Information Services:** LEXIS, WESTLAW, DIALOG Information Services, NEXIS. **Networks/Consortia:** Member of INCOLSA. **Staff:** Granville Cleveland, Asst.Dir., Stud.Empl.; Nanette Moegerle, Cat.Libn.; David Boeck, Res.Libn.; Michael Slinger, Assoc.Dir., Rd.Serv.; Dwight King, Res.Libn.; Janis Johnston, Assoc.Dir., Tech.Serv..

★16671★
UNIVERSITY OF NOTRE DAME - LIFE SCIENCES RESEARCH LIBRARY (Biol Sci)
B146 Galvin Life Sciences Bldg. Phone: (219)239-7209
Notre Dame, IN 46556 Dorothy Coil, Libn.
Founded: 1938. **Staff:** Prof 1; Other 2. **Subjects:** Biology, genetics, microbiology, entomology, parasitology, gnotobiology. **Holdings:** 26,500 volumes. **Subscriptions:** 580 journals and other serials. **Services:** Interlibrary loan; copying; library open to the public for reference use only. **Computerized Information Services:** DIALOG Information Services, BRS Information Technologies. **Staff:** Judy Mahoney, Supv..

★16672★
UNIVERSITY OF NOTRE DAME - MATHEMATICS LIBRARY (Sci-Engr)
200 Computing Center Phone: (219)239-7278
Notre Dame, IN 46556 Shirley Scott, Phys. & Math.Sci.Libn.
Founded: 1962. **Staff:** Prof 1; Other 1. **Subjects:** Pure mathematics. **Holdings:** 21,859 volumes. **Subscriptions:** 260 journals and other serials. **Services:** Interlibrary loan; copying; library open to the public for reference use only. **Staff:** Jennifer Helmen, Supv..

★16673★
UNIVERSITY OF NOTRE DAME - MEDIEVAL INSTITUTE LIBRARY (Hist)
715 Memorial Library Phone: (219)239-7420
Notre Dame, IN 46556 Dr. Louis Jordan, Hd.
Staff: Prof 1; Other 1. **Subjects:** Medieval studies. **Special Collections:** Frank M. Folsom Ambrosiana; Microfilm & Photograph Collection; medieval education; medieval manuscripts; medieval seals. **Holdings:** 50,000 volumes; 15,000 microforms; 12 VF drawers. **Subscriptions:** 300 journals and other serials. **Services:** Interlibrary loan; copying; library open to the public for reference use only.

★16674★
UNIVERSITY OF NOTRE DAME - RADIATION LABORATORY - RADIATION CHEMISTRY DATA CENTER (Sci-Engr)
Notre Dame, IN 46556 Phone: (219)239-6527
Dr. Alberta B. Ross, Supv.
Founded: 1965. **Staff:** Prof 4; Other 3. **Subjects:** Radiation chemistry, photochemistry. **Holdings:** 96,000 data files. **Services:** Center open to scientists on request. **Computerized Information Services:** RCDC Bibliographic Database (internal database). **Publications:** Biweekly List of Papers on Radiation Chemistry and Photochemistry with indexed annual cumulation; Thesaurus for Radiation Chemistry. **Staff:** Dr. W.P. Helman; Dr. Gordon Hug; Dr. Ian Carmichael.

★16675★
UNIVERSITY OF NOTRE DAME - SNITE MUSEUM OF ART - LIBRARY (Art)
Notre Dame, IN 46556 Phone: (219)239-5466
Mary V. Weidler, Libn.
Staff: Prof 1. **Subjects:** Art. **Holdings:** 2500 books; 3000 unbound periodicals. **Services:** Copying; library open to the public with restrictions.

★16676★
UNIVERSITY OF OKLAHOMA - BIOLOGICAL STATION LIBRARY (Biol Sci)
Star Route B
Kingston, OK 73439 Phone: (405)564-2463
Founded: 1947. **Staff:** Prof 3. **Subjects:** Aquatic ecology, fisheries, reservoir limnology. **Special Collections:** Lake Texoma Collection (1200 items); Riggs Collection (fishes and fisheries; 5550 items); Greenbank Collection (fishes and fisheries; 2081 items). **Holdings:** 3238 volumes; 4927 reprints. **Subscriptions:** 30 journals and other serials. **Services:** Library open to qualified persons. **Special Indexes:** Indexes to Lake Texoma Collection and reprints.

★16677★
UNIVERSITY OF OKLAHOMA - CARL ALBERT CENTER CONGRESSIONAL ARCHIVES (Hist, Soc Sci)
630 Parrington Oval, Rm. 202 Phone: (405)325-5401
Norman, OK 73019 John M. Caldwell, Archv.
Founded: 1986. **Staff:** Prof 2; Other 2. **Subjects:** U.S. Congress, Oklahoma, American Southwest. **Special Collections:** Archival collection of 50 members of U.S. Congress. **Holdings:** 4500 cubic feet of manuscripts, photographs, audio- and videotapes, political ephemera. **Services:** Copying; archives open to the public with restrictions. **Automated Operations:** Computerized cataloging. **Special Indexes:** University of Oklahoma Congressional Record Series. **Staff:** Judy D. Day, Asst.Archv..

★16678★
UNIVERSITY OF OKLAHOMA - CENTER FOR ECONOMIC AND MANAGEMENT RESEARCH - LIBRARY (Bus-Fin)
307 W. Brooks St., Rm. 4 Phone: (405)325-2931
Norman, OK 73019 Deanna Osburn, Libn.
Staff: 2. **Subjects:** Statistics on Oklahoma business and economic conditions; economic aspects of energy. **Holdings:** 600 books; 50 bound periodical volumes; 1600 government documents; 24 VF drawers of reports. **Subscriptions:** 150 journals and other serials; 8 newspapers. **Services:** Copying; library open to the public with restrictions. **Publications:** Oklahoma Business Bulletin, monthly; Statistical Abstract of Oklahoma, biennial.

★16679★
UNIVERSITY OF OKLAHOMA - CHEMISTRY-MATHEMATICS LIBRARY (Sci-Engr)
Physical Sciences Center, 207 Phone: (405)325-5628
Norman, OK 73019 Jeanne G. Howard, Chem.-Math.Libn.
Founded: 1921. **Staff:** Prof 1; Other 1. **Subjects:** Chemistry, mathematics. **Holdings:** 50,000 volumes; 12,787 microforms. **Subscriptions:** 586 journals and other serials. **Services:** Interlibrary loan; copying; library open to the public for reference use only. **Automated Operations:** Computerized circulation. **Computerized Information Services:** DIALOG Information Services, Pergamon ORBIT InfoLine, Inc., BRS Information Technologies, OCLC. Performs searches on fee basis. **Networks/Consortia:** Member of AMIGOS Bibliographic Council, Inc., RLG.

★16680★
UNIVERSITY OF OKLAHOMA - ENGINEERING LIBRARY (Sci-Engr)
Norman, OK 73019 Phone: (405)325-2941
Jimmie L. Lee, Act.Hd.
Staff: Prof 1; Other 1. **Subjects:** Engineering - electrical, mechanical, chemical, geological, industrial, nuclear, petroleum, civil, aerospace, metallurgy; computer science; environmental science. **Holdings:** 55,000 volumes; 12,000 microforms. **Subscriptions:** 600 journals and other serials. **Services:** Interlibrary loan; copying; library open to the public. **Automated Operations:** Computerized circulation. **Computerized Information Services:** DIALOG Information Services, Pergamon ORBIT InfoLine, Inc., BRS Information Technologies. **Networks/Consortia:** Member of AMIGOS Bibliographic Council, Inc..

★16681★
UNIVERSITY OF OKLAHOMA - FINE ARTS LIBRARY (Mus, Art)
007 Catlett Music Center
Jacobson Hall, Rm. 203 Phone: (405)325-2841
Norman, OK 73019 Jan Seifert, Fine Arts Libn.
Founded: 1986. **Staff:** Prof 1; Other 3. **Subjects:** Music, art, dance. **Special Collections:** Spencer Norton Collection; Joseph Benton Collection; Bixler Files. **Holdings:** 42,845 books, bound periodical volumes, and scores; 424 reels of microfilm; 108 microcards; 1937 microfiche. **Subscriptions:** 114 journals. **Services:** Interlibrary loan; copying; SDI; library open to the public. **Automated Operations:** Computerized cataloging and circulation. **Computerized Information Services:** DIALOG Information Services, Pergamon ORBIT InfoLine, Inc., BRS Information Technologies, OCLC, WILSONLINE, DataTimes, PHINet FedTax Database; RLG (electronic mail service). Performs searches on fee basis. **Networks/Consortia:** Member of AMIGOS Bibliographic Council, Inc., RLG. **Remarks:** An alternate telephone number is 325-4243. **Staff:** Dennis Mosser, Supv..

★16682★
UNIVERSITY OF OKLAHOMA - GEOLOGY LIBRARY (Sci-Engr)
830 Van Vleet Oval, Rm. 103 Phone: (405)325-6451
Norman, OK 73019 Claren M. Kidd, Libn.
Staff: Prof 1; Other 1. **Subjects:** Geology, paleontology, mineralogy, palynology, petroleum geology, geochemistry, geophysics, oceanography, hydrology. **Special Collections:** Herndon Map Service (Oklahoma); theses on Oklahoma geology. **Holdings:** 86,541 volumes; 110,640 maps; 218,760 PI completion cards for Oklahoma. **Subscriptions:** 1000 journals and other serials. **Services:** Interlibrary loan; copying; library open to the public. **Automated Operations:** Computerized circulation. **Computerized Information Services:** DIALOG Information Services. **Networks/Consortia:** Member of RLG, AMIGOS Bibliographic Council, Inc..

★16683★
UNIVERSITY OF OKLAHOMA - HARRY W. BASS COLLECTION IN BUSINESS HISTORY (Bus-Fin, Hist)
401 W. Brooks Phone: (405)325-3941
Norman, OK 73019 Dr. Daniel A. Wren, Cur.
Founded: 1955. **Staff:** Prof 1; Other 2. **Subjects:** History - business, economic, management. **Special Collections:** Sears Roebuck catalogs on microfilm; rare books in economic history; archives of the J. & W. Seligman & Co., Inc. (76 bound letter books, 19th and early 20th centuries; 23,000 pages and 6 linear feet of modern archival material; 325 engraved stock certificates). **Holdings:** 20,400 books; 1460 bound periodical volumes; 1750 pamphlets; 382 reels of microfilm; 10,000 microfiche; 30 magnetic tapes. **Subscriptions:** 23 journals and other serials. **Services:** Collection open to the public. **Special Catalogs:** Catalogs of the Collection, irregular. **Staff:** Sydona Baroff, Libn..

★16684★
UNIVERSITY OF OKLAHOMA - HEALTH SCIENCES CENTER - DEAN A. MC GEE EYE INSTITUTE - LIBRARY (Med)
Department of Ophthalmology
608 Stanton L. Young Blvd. Phone: (405)271-6085
Oklahoma City, OK 73104 Sheri Greenwood, Med.Libn.
Staff: Prof 1. **Subjects:** Ophthalmology. **Holdings:** 1200 books; 1000 bound periodical volumes; 30 slide sets; 84 video cassettes. **Subscriptions:** 34 journals and other serials. **Services:** Interlibrary loan; SDI; library open to medical personnel only. **Computerized Information Services:** MEDLARS, BRS Information Technologies. **Networks/Consortia:** Member of Greater Oklahoma City Area Health Sciences Library Consortium (GOAL).

★16685★
UNIVERSITY OF OKLAHOMA - HEALTH SCIENCES CENTER - DEPARTMENT OF SURGERY LIBRARY (Med)
Box 26307 Phone: (405)271-5506
Oklahoma City, OK 73126 Linda R. O'Rourke, Med.Libn.
Staff: Prof 1. **Subjects:** Surgery - general, plastic, neurosurgery, thoracic and cardiovascular, oral; emergency medicine and trauma. **Holdings:** 3349 volumes. **Subscriptions:** 90 journals and other serials. **Services:** Interlibrary loan; copying; SDI; library open to affiliated surgical personnel. **Computerized Information Services:** DIALOG Information Services, MEDLARS. **Networks/Consortia:** Member of Greater Oklahoma City Area Health Sciences Library Consortium (GOAL).

★16686★
UNIVERSITY OF OKLAHOMA - HEALTH SCIENCES CENTER LIBRARY (Med)
1000 Stanton L. Young Blvd.
Box 26901 Phone: (405)271-2285
Oklahoma City, OK 73190 C.M. Thompson, Jr., Dir.
Founded: 1928. **Staff:** Prof 10; Other 25. **Subjects:** Medicine, dentistry, nursing, public health, pharmacy, allied health subjects. **Holdings:** 63,886 books; 124,541 bound periodical volumes. **Subscriptions:** 2500 journals and other serials. **Services:** Interlibrary loan; copying; SDI; library open to the public for reference use only. **Automated Operations:** Computerized cataloging. **Computerized Information Services:** DIALOG Information Services, MEDLARS, OCLC; OnTyme Electronic Message Network Service (electronic mail service). Performs searches on fee basis. **Networks/Consortia:** Member of AMIGOS Bibliographic Council, Inc., Oklahoma Telecommunications Interlibrary System (OTIS), TALON. **Publications:** Guide, annual; Footnote, bimonthly. **Remarks:** An alternate telephone number is 271-2670. **Staff:** Barbara B. Peshel, Monograph Serv.; Virgil L. Jones, Ref.Libn.; Ilse Von Brauchitsch, Ref.Libn.; Joanne Callard, Assoc. to Dir.; Sally Shrout, Ser.Serv.; Jack Wagner, Cat..

★16687★
UNIVERSITY OF OKLAHOMA - HISTORY OF SCIENCE COLLECTIONS (Sci-Engr, Hist)
401 W. Brooks, Rm. 521 Phone: (405)325-2741
Norman, OK 73019 Duane H.D. Roller, Cur.
Founded: 1951. **Staff:** Prof 2; Other 4. **Subjects:** History of science and technology. **Special Collections:** DeGolyer, Klopsteg, Crew, Sally Hall, Nielsen, Lacy, ADF, and Harlow Collections. **Holdings:** 75,000 volumes; 881 photographs, prints, pictures; 4378 volumes on microfilm; 671 volumes on microcards; 19,617 volumes in microprint; 232 volumes on microfiche; 18.15 cubic feet of manuscripts; 2848 pamphlets. **Subscriptions:** 83 journals and other serials. **Services:** Copying (limited); microfilming; collections open to the public by permission. **Automated Operations:** Computerized cataloging and circulation. **Computerized Information Services:** Association of Research Libraries (ARL), DIALOG Information Services, Pergamon ORBIT InfoLine, Inc., OCLC, BRS Information Technologies. **Networks/Consortia:** Member of AMIGOS Bibliographic Council, Inc., RLG. **Special Catalogs:** Short-title Catalog (online and microfiche). **Special Indexes:** Alphabetical and chronological index to journal articles (card). **Staff:** Marcia M. Goodman, Hist. of Sci.Libn..

★16688★
UNIVERSITY OF OKLAHOMA - LAW LIBRARY (Law)
300 Timberdell Rd. Phone: (405)325-4311
Norman, OK 73019 Mickie A. Voges, Dir.
Founded: 1909. **Staff:** Prof 7; Other 7. **Subjects:** Law. **Special Collections:** Law - Indian, water, agriculture, natural resources; Indian land titles. **Holdings:** 156,019 volumes; 105,929 volumes in microform. **Subscriptions:** 2981 journals and other serials; 25 newspapers. **Services:** Interlibrary loan; copying; library open to legal researchers, law students, faculty. **Automated Operations:** Computerized cataloging and acquisitions. **Computerized Information Services:** LEXIS, WESTLAW, DIALOG Information Services, ELSS (Electronic Legislative Search System), DataTimes. **Networks/Consortia:** Member of AMIGOS Bibliographic Council, Inc., Mid-America Law School Library Consortium. **Publications:** Law Library Newsletter, monthly; User's Guide; Research Guide. **Staff:** Marilyn K. Nicely, Tech.Serv.Libn.; Maria E. Protti, Pub.Serv.Libn..

★16689★
UNIVERSITY OF OKLAHOMA - LIMITED ACCESS COLLECTION (Hum)
401 W. Brooks, Rm. 509 Phone: (405)325-2048
Norman, OK 73019 Duane H.D. Roller, Cur.
Staff: Prof 2; Other 1. **Subjects:** Literature, history. **Special Collections:** Lois Lenski Children's Literature Collection; Bizzell Bible Collection. **Holdings:** 12,199 volumes. **Services:** Copying (limited); collection open to the public by permission. **Automated Operations:** Computerized cataloging and circulation. **Computerized Information Services:** DIALOG Information Services, Association of Research Libraries (ARL), Pergamon ORBIT InfoLine, Inc., OCLC. **Networks/Consortia:** Member of AMIGOS Bibliographic Council, Inc., RLG, Center for Research Libraries (CRL) Consortia. **Staff:** Marcia M. Goodman, Libn..

★16690★
UNIVERSITY OF OKLAHOMA - PHYSICS-ASTRONOMY LIBRARY (Sci-Engr)
219 Nielsen Hall Phone: (405)325-3961
Norman, OK 73019 Jeanne Howard, Chem.-Math.Libn.
Staff: Prof 1; Other 1. **Subjects:** Quantum mechanics, high energy physics, astronomy, astrophysics, classical physics. **Special Collections:** Atlases of the northern and southern skies. **Holdings:** 9000 books; 11,000 bound periodical volumes. **Subscriptions:** 205 journals and other serials. **Services:** Interlibrary loan; library open to the public for reference use only. **Computerized Information Services:** DIALOG Information Services, Pergamon ORBIT InfoLine, Inc., BRS Information Technologies. Performs searches on fee basis. **Networks/Consortia:** Member of AMIGOS Bibliographic Council, Inc., RLG. **Remarks:** An alternate telephone number is 325-5628.

★16691★
UNIVERSITY OF OKLAHOMA - SCHOOL OF ARCHITECTURE LIBRARY (Plan)
Oklahoma Memorial Stadium 285 Phone: (405)325-5521
Norman, OK 73019 Ilse Davis, Lib.Techn.
Founded: 1929. **Subjects:** Architecture; landscape architecture; design - urban, environmental, interior; construction science. **Special Collections:** Lt. Orville S. Witt Memorial Collection. **Holdings:** 11,275 books; 340 manufacturers' catalogs. **Subscriptions:** 93 journals and other serials. **Services:** Interlibrary loan.

★16692★
UNIVERSITY OF OKLAHOMA - SCIENCE AND PUBLIC POLICY PROGRAM - LIBRARY (Env-Cons, Sci-Engr)
601 Elm Ave., Rm. 431 Phone: (405)325-2554
Norman, OK 73019 Elizabeth Choinski, Libn.
Staff: Prof 1. **Subjects:** Energy policy, impact assessment, environmental policy, regional studies, technology assessment, information transfer, science policy. **Holdings:** 7000 books and documents; unbound periodicals; 3 cabinets of information files. **Subscriptions:** 24 journals and other serials. **Services:** Copying; library open to the public for reference use only. **Computerized Information Services:** Catalog of acquisitions, 1984 to present (internal database).

★16693★
UNIVERSITY OF OKLAHOMA - TULSA MEDICAL COLLEGE - LIBRARY (Med)
2808 S. Sheridan Phone: (918)838-4616
Tulsa, OK 74129 Janet Minnerath, Lib.Dir.
Staff: Prof 1; Other 5. **Subjects:** Medicine. **Holdings:** 5914 books; 21,076 bound periodical volumes. **Subscriptions:** 674 journals and other serials. **Services:** Interlibrary loan; copying; SDI; library open to the public. **Automated Operations:** Computerized cataloging. **Computerized Information Services:** NLM, BRS Information Technologies; OnTyme Electronic Message Network Service (electronic mail service). Performs searches on fee basis. **Networks/Consortia:** Member of AMIGOS Bibliographic Council, Inc., South Central Academic Medical Libraries Consortium (SCAMEL), Tulsa Area Library Cooperative (TALC).

★16694★
UNIVERSITY OF OKLAHOMA - WESTERN HISTORY COLLECTIONS (Hist)
630 Parrington Oval, Rm. 452 Phone: (405)325-3641
Norman, OK 73019 Donald L. DeWitt, Cur.
Founded: 1927. **Staff:** Prof 5; Other 4. **Subjects:** American Indian, Oklahoma, American Southwest, American Trans-Mississippi West, recent U.S. history. **Special Collections:** Cherokee Nation Papers; Patrick J. Hurley papers; E.E. Dale papers; Frank E. Phillips Collections; Alan Farley Collection; Henry B. Bass Collection; Norman Brillhart Collection. **Holdings:** 50,000 books; 8000 linear feet of manuscripts; 250,000 items in photographic archives; 20,000 microforms; 6000 maps; 1400 transcripts, tapes, and discs of oral history; 5000 pamphlets and documents; 1500 linear feet of University of Oklahoma archives; newspapers, posters, broadsides. **Services:** Copying (limited); collections open to the public. **Automated Operations:** Computerized cataloging. **Computerized Information Services:** RLIN, OCLC. **Networks/Consortia:** Member of RLG. **Publications:** Guide to Regional Manuscripts in Division of Manuscripts of University of Oklahoma Library, 1960. **Special Catalogs:** Calendars and catalogs of individual collections; catalog of microform holdings. **Staff:** Bradford Koplowitz, Asst.Cur.; Nathan Bender, Libn.; John R. Lovett, Photo Archv..

★16695★
UNIVERSITY OF OREGON - ARCHITECTURE AND ALLIED ARTS LIBRARY (Art, Plan)
277 Lawrence Hall Phone: (503)686-3637
Eugene, OR 97403-1206 Sheila M. Klos, Hd.Libn.
Staff: Prof 3; Other 3. **Subjects:** Architecture, fine and applied arts, interior architecture, landscape design, urban planning, art history and education, historic preservation, computer graphics. **Holdings:** 41,255 volumes; 20,000 prints and photographs; 200,000 slides; 4200 pamphlets; 500 original architectural drawings; 200 sets of blueprints. **Subscriptions:** 330 journals and other serials. **Services:** Interlibrary loan (through Main Library); copying; library open to the public. **Computerized Information Services:** RLIN, DIALOG Information Services, OCLC, BRS Information Technologies. Performs searches on fee basis.

★16696★
UNIVERSITY OF OREGON - CAREER INFORMATION CENTER (Educ)
221 Hendricks Hall
Box 3257 Phone: (503)686-3235
Eugene, OR 97403 Lawrence H. Smith, Dir.
Founded: 1972. **Staff:** 1. **Subjects:** Career awareness and planning, job search, interview techniques, resume and cover-letter writing. **Holdings:** 250 books; 150 feet and shelves of pamphlets from professional organizations; 1 VF drawer of training information sources. **Services:** Center not open to the public but will answer mail or phone questions from others interested in career planning.

★16697★
UNIVERSITY OF OREGON - CAREER INFORMATION SYSTEM (Educ)
1787 Agate St. Phone: (503)686-3872
Eugene, OR 97403 Bruce McKinlay, Dir.
Founded: 1971. **Staff:** Prof 12; Other 15. **Subjects:** Occupations, study and training programs, education, financial aid, career development, computer systems for guidance. **Holdings:** 3000 volumes; occupational information in 300 areas; 130 programs of study and training. **Subscriptions:** 30 journals and other serials. **Services:** Copying; open to the public. **Publications:** Updated issues of printouts, annual - by subscription. **Remarks:** Provides technical assistance, research, and development for operators of the Career Information System nationwide. Operates the Career Information System for schools, colleges, and agencies in Oregon. Operates a clearinghouse for the National Association of Computer-Based Systems for Career Information.

★16698★
UNIVERSITY OF OREGON - CENTER FOR ADVANCED TECHNOLOGY IN EDUCATION - CATE RESOURCE CENTER (Educ, Comp Sci)
1787 Agate St., Rm. 104 Phone: (503)686-3640
Eugene, OR 97403 Tom Walter, Rsrc.Ctr.Coord.
Staff: Prof 1; Other 1. **Subjects:** Computers in education, instructional technology, educational software, media production. **Special Collections:** International Council for Computers in Education (1200 volumes); Instructional Technology (630 volumes). **Holdings:** 1830 books; 1000 titles of educational computer software. **Subscriptions:** 87 journals and other serials; 5 newspapers. **Services:** Copying; center open to the public. **Automated Operations:** Computerized cataloging and serials. **Computerized Information Services:** Internal database.

★16699★
UNIVERSITY OF OREGON - COMPUTING CENTER - LIBRARY (Comp Sci)
Eugene, OR 97403 Phone: (503)686-4406
Betsy Shaw, Lib.Mgr.
Founded: 1965. **Staff:** Prof 1; Other 2. **Subjects:** Computer science, microcomputers, educational computing. **Special Collections:** Newsletters from academic computing centers and computing organizations (200); collection of public domain software. **Holdings:** 1000 books; 500 computer manuals; university catalogs; hardware/software directories; vertical files of pamphlets and brochures. **Subscriptions:** 125 journals; 200 newsletters. **Services:** Interlibrary loan; SDI; library open to the public. **Automated Operations:** Computerized cataloging, serials, and routing of periodicals and newsletters. **Publications:** Quarterly reports - for internal distribution only; accessions lists, irregular; series of specialized bibliographies - both available on request.

★16700★
UNIVERSITY OF OREGON - DEPARTMENT OF ENGLISH - RANDALL V. MILLS ARCHIVES OF NORTHWEST FOLKLORE (Hist)
Eugene, OR 97403 Phone: (503)686-3925
Tim Miller, Archv.
Staff: Prof 1. **Subjects:** Folksongs, Bigfoot lore, logger lore, oral history, folklore and folklife. **Special Collections:** Robert Winslow Gordon Collection (folksongs and ballads); Randall V. Mills Collection (dialect studies, proverbs, place names, railroad and steamship lore); Otillie Seybolt Dialect Studies; Webfoots and Bunchgrassers Oregon Folk Art Slide Collection. **Holdings:** 200 books; 300 bound periodical volumes; 3500 unbound fieldwork projects; 9 dissertations/theses. **Services:** Copying; archives open to researchers with interview.

★16701★
UNIVERSITY OF OREGON - ENVIRONMENTAL STUDIES CENTER (Env-Cons, Energy)
Eugene, OR 97403 Phone: (503)686-5006
Kathryn Harnden, Dir.
Founded: 1971. **Staff:** Prof 1; Other 3. **Subjects:** Ecology, environmental issues, energy. **Holdings:** 8000 books; 100 bound periodical volumes; environmental impact statements; 250 clipping and article folders; maps. **Subscriptions:** 100 journals and other serials. **Services:** Center open to the public with restrictions. **Publications:** Resource Lists, irregular - free upon request; bibliographies and reading lists. **Special Catalogs:** Catalog of Environmental Studies of University.

★16702★
UNIVERSITY OF OREGON - GOVERNMENT DOCUMENTS COLLECTION (Info Sci)
University Library Phone: (503)686-3070
Eugene, OR 97403 Thomas A. Stave, Hd.
Staff: Prof 2; Other 2. **Subjects:** U.S., Canadian, and British Government documents; international intergovernmental organizations. **Holdings:** 362,000 documents; 310,000 microforms. **Subscriptions:** 2900 journals and other serials. **Services:** Interlibrary loan; copying; collection open to the public. **Computerized Information Services:** DIALOG Information Services, BRS Information Technologies.

★16703★
UNIVERSITY OF OREGON - INSTITUTE OF RECREATION RESEARCH & SERVICE (Rec)
Esslinger Hall, Rm. 133
Eugene, OR 97403 Mary-Faeth Chenery, Ph.D., Dir.
Subjects: Leisure services management, therapeutic recreation, basic and applied leisure research. **Special Collections:** L.S. Rodney Collection. **Holdings:** 200 books; 2000 bound periodical volumes; 700 studies; 1000 park and recreation materials; clippings. **Publications:** Technical report series; monographs.

★16704★
UNIVERSITY OF OREGON - INSTRUCTIONAL MEDIA CENTER (Aud-Vis)
University Library Phone: (503)686-3091
Eugene, OR 97403 George E. Bynon, Dir.
Staff: Prof 2; Other 12. **Subjects:** Instructional media. **Holdings:** 1403 films and film loops; 826 filmstrips; 264 media kits; 399 videotapes. **Services:** Center open to the public for reference use only. **Networks/Consortia:** Member of Consortium of University Film Centers (CUFC). **Publications:** IMC Newsletter, quarterly - to faculty and staff. **Special Catalogs:** IMC Film Videotape and Catalog. **Staff:** William C. Leonard, Hd., Graphic Arts Serv..

★16705★
UNIVERSITY OF OREGON - LAW LIBRARY (Law)
Eugene, OR 97403-1221 Phone: (503)686-3088
Dennis R. Hyatt, Libn.
Founded: 1884. **Staff:** Prof 4; Other 5. **Subjects:** Law. **Holdings:** 123,853 volumes; 502,383 microforms. **Subscriptions:** 2916 journals and other serials. **Services:** Interlibrary loan; copying. **Automated Operations:** Computerized cataloging and acquisitions. **Computerized Information Services:** OCLC, LEXIS, DIALOG Information Services, WESTLAW, Oregon Legislative Information Service.

★16706★
UNIVERSITY OF OREGON - MAP LIBRARY (Geog-Map)
165 Condon Hall Phone: (503)686-3051
Eugene, OR 97403-1218 Peter L. Stark, Hd.
Staff: Prof 1; Other 1. **Subjects:** Cartographic materials, aerial photography. **Holdings:** 1912 volumes, including atlases; 247,000 maps; 384,000 aerial photographs. **Services:** Interlibrary loan; copying; library open to the public for reference use only. **Publications:** Acquisitions list, semiannual - by exchange. **Special Indexes:** Index to maps (card).

★16707★
UNIVERSITY OF OREGON - MATHEMATICS LIBRARY† (Sci-Engr, Comp Sci)
University Library Phone: (503)686-3023
Eugene, OR 97403-1229 Isabel A. Stirling, Hd.Libn.
Staff: 1. **Subjects:** Mathematics, computer science. **Holdings:** 22,524 volumes. **Subscriptions:** 400 journals and other serials. **Services:** Copying.

★16708★
UNIVERSITY OF OREGON - MICROFORMS AND RECORDINGS DEPARTMENT (Aud-Vis)
University Library Phone: (503)686-3080
Eugene, OR 97403-1299 Rory A. Funke, Hd.
Founded: 1980. **Staff:** 4. **Holdings:** 1 million microforms; 24,603 phonograph records; 2402 tapes; 70 compact discs. **Services:** Interlibrary loan; copying; department open to the public. **Publications:** Oregon Newspapers on Microfilm, 1980.

UNIVERSITY OF OREGON - NEPAL/USAID PROJECT ARCHIVES
See: American Nepal Education Foundation - Wood Nepal Library (618)

★16709★
UNIVERSITY OF OREGON - OREGON INSTITUTE OF MARINE BIOLOGY - LIBRARY (Biol Sci)
Charleston, OR 97420 Phone: (503)888-5534
Jean Hanna, Lib.Asst.
Staff: 1. **Subjects:** Marine biology, ecology, environmental research, comparative physiology of blood pigments of vertebrates and invertebrates. **Special Collections:** Student reports. **Holdings:** 3000 books; 300 maps; 150 topographic maps; 2500 reprints; 2000 slides; herbarium collection of local flora. **Subscriptions:** 30 journals and other serials. **Services:** Interlibrary loan; copying; library open to the public for reference use only. **Automated Operations:** Computerized cataloging and acquisitions. **Computerized Information Services:** DIALOG Information Services, BRS Information Technologies, CAS ONLINE. Performs searches on fee basis. Contact Person: Isabel Stirling, Hd., Sci.Lib., 686-3075.

★16710★
UNIVERSITY OF OREGON - ORIENTALIA COLLECTION (Hist, Area-Ethnic)
University Library Phone: (503)686-3096
Eugene, OR 97403 William Z. Schenck, Coll.Dev.Libn.
Staff: Prof 1. **Subjects:** East Asia - history, language, literature, Buddhism, humanities, social sciences. **Holdings:** 42,000 volumes; 220 reels of film. **Subscriptions:** 495 journals and other serials. **Services:** Interlibrary loan; copying; collection open to the public. **Staff:** Katsuko Hotelling, Cat.; Daphne Wang, Cat..

★16711★
UNIVERSITY OF OREGON - PUBLIC AFFAIRS LIBRARY (Soc Sci, Plan)
130 Hendricks Hall Phone: (503)686-3048
Eugene, OR 97403-1221 John A. Shuler, Libn.
Staff: Prof 1. **Subjects:** Public administration - finance, planning, lands; intergovernmental relations; social services; transportation; environment; welfare. **Holdings:** 30,000 books, government documents, and reports. **Subscriptions:** 125 serials. **Services:** Interlibrary loan; library open to the public. **Publications:** Monthly accessions list. **Special Indexes:** Index to thesis projects of School of Community Service & Public Affairs and Department of Planning, Public Policy and Management.

★16712★
UNIVERSITY OF OREGON - SCIENCE LIBRARY (Biol Sci, Sci-Engr)
University Library Phone: (503)686-3075
Eugene, OR 97403-5201 Isabel A. Stirling, Hd.Libn.
Staff: Prof 2; Other 5. **Subjects:** Basic sciences, physics, chemistry, biological sciences, neuroscience, geology. **Holdings:** 146,036 volumes. **Subscriptions:** 3000 journals and other serials. **Services:** Interlibrary loan (through Main Library); copying. **Computerized Information Services:** DIALOG Information Services, BRS Information Technologies, CAS ONLINE, STN International.

★16713★
UNIVERSITY OF OREGON - SPECIAL COLLECTIONS DEPARTMENT (Hist)
University Library Phone: (503)686-3068
Eugene, OR 97403 Kenneth Duckett, Cur.
Staff: Prof 3; Other 2. **Subjects:** Political, social, economic, and literary history of the United States in the 19th and 20th centuries, with emphasis on Oregon and the Pacific Northwest. **Special Collections:** Manuscript Collection (materials of political conservatives, authors and illustrators of children's literature, writers of western fiction, missionaries to the Far East, 20th century artists and illustrators; Pacific Northwest authors, architects, politicians, and business figures); Photograph Collection (largely negatives of the Pacific Northwest, Alaska, Appalachia, and Far East); Rare Book Collection (western Americana, Bodoni Imprints, early European imprints, travels and voyages, pulp magazines, Esperanto language books and journals); Oregon Collection (circulating collection of books and journals on all phases and periods of Oregon history, life, and letters). **Holdings:** 70,000 volumes; 12 million manuscripts; 125,000 photographic images; 75,000 architectural drawings. **Subscriptions:** 880 journals and other serials. **Services:** Interlibrary loan (from the Oregon Collection); copying (limited). **Special Catalogs:** Catalogue of Manuscripts in the University of Oregon Library, 1971 (book); Catalog of the George Alan Connor Esperanto Collection, 1978 (pamphlet); Inventory of the Papers of Senator Wayne L. Morse, 1974 (book); Inventory of the Papers of T. Coleman Andrews, 1967 (pamphlet); Catalog of the Louis Conrad Rosenberg Collection, 1978 (pamphlet); Jane C. Grant Papers: A Collection of the University of Oregon Library, 1985 (pamphlet).

★16714★
UNIVERSITY OF ORIENTAL STUDIES - LIBRARY (Rel-Phil, Area-Ethnic)
309 S. Saltair Ave.
Los Angeles, CA 90049 Phone: (213)472-2462
Staff: Prof 2; Other 1. **Subjects:** Buddhist literature; Far Eastern languages; East and West - philosophy, psychology, history, literature. **Special Collections:** Buddhism (holdings in Chinese, Japanese, Pali, and Sanskrit languages). **Holdings:** 45,000 books. **Subscriptions:** 80 journals and other serials; 10 newspapers. **Services:** Library open to scholars with qualifications.

★16715★
UNIVERSITY OF OSTEOPATHIC MEDICINE AND HEALTH SCIENCES - LIBRARY (Med)
3200 Grand Ave. Phone: (515)271-1430
Des Moines, IA 50312 Larry D. Marquardt, Lib.Dir.
Founded: 1898. **Staff:** Prof 1; Other 5. **Subjects:** Osteopathic and podiatric medicine, allied health sciences. **Holdings:** 26,200 volumes. **Subscriptions:** 450 journals and other serials. **Services:** Interlibrary loan; copying; SDI; library open to the public for reference use only. **Automated Operations:** Computerized cataloging. **Computerized Information Services:** MEDLARS, BRS Information Technologies, American Osteopathic Network (AONET). **Networks/Consortia:** Member of Polk County Biomedical Consortium (PCBC), Greater Midwest Regional Medical Library Network. **Publications:** Annual report - for internal distribution only.

★16716★
UNIVERSITY OF OTTAWA - HEALTH SCIENCES LIBRARY (Med)
451 Smyth Rd. Phone: (613)737-6521
Ottawa, ON, Canada K1H 8M4 Myra Owen, Dir.
Staff: Prof 3; Other 7. **Subjects:** Medicine, nursing, kinanthropology, physiotherapy. **Holdings:** 44,225 books; 42,132 bound periodical volumes; 608 filmstrips; 190 video cassettes; 685 audio cassettes. **Subscriptions:** 1448 journals and other serials. **Services:** Interlibrary loan; copying; library open to the public with limited borrowing privileges. **Automated Operations:** Computerized circulation. **Computerized Information Services:** Infomart, BRS Information Technologies, MEDLINE, CAN/OLE. **Staff:** Helena Wybenga, Ref./Tech.Serv.; Michelle LeBlanc, Ref..

★16717★
UNIVERSITY OF OTTAWA - LAW LIBRARY (Law)
Fauteux Hall
57 Copernicus St. Phone: (613)231-4943
Ottawa, ON, Canada K1N 6N5 Raymond Dicaire, Dir.
Staff: Prof 4; Other 16. **Subjects:** Civil law (Quebec), common law. **Holdings:** 149,950 books; 16,402 microfiche; 292 reels of microfilm; 523 cassettes. **Subscriptions:** 1500 journals and other serials; 12 newspapers. **Services:** Interlibrary loan; copying; library open to the public for reference use only. **Staff:** Ophelia Meza, Ref. (Civil Law); Mr. Chin-Shih Tang, Ref. (Common Law); Marcel Joanisse, Cat.; Marilyn Rennick, Tech.Serv..

★16718★
UNIVERSITY OF OTTAWA - MAP LIBRARY (Geog-Map)
Morisset Library
65 Hastey St., Rm. 353 Phone: (613)231-6830
Ottawa, ON, Canada K1N 9A5 Aileen Desbarats, Hd.
Founded: 1968. **Staff:** Prof 1; Other 3. **Subjects:** Geography - general, physical, urban; urban planning; map coverage of Ottawa and the national capital region, Northern Canada, Bolivia, Chile, Colombia, Ecuador, Peru, French-speaking Africa. **Holdings:** 124,642 sheet maps; 462 wall maps; 2009 atlases; 15 globes; 249,759 aerial photographs; 1099 diapositive mapping plates; 7914 reference books; 500 bound periodical volumes. **Subscriptions:** 57 journals and other serials. **Services:** Interlibrary loan; copying; library open to the public.

★16719★
UNIVERSITY OF OTTAWA - MORISSET LIBRARY (Hum, Soc Sci)
65 Hastey St. Phone: (613)231-6880
Ottawa, ON, Canada K1N 9A5 Yvon Richer, Univ.Chf.Libn.
Founded: 1904. **Staff:** Prof 35; Other 150. **Subjects:** Humanities and social sciences. **Special Collections:** Rare book collection. **Holdings:** 974,375 volumes; 3557 dissertations; 743,909 microfiche; 129,430 slides; 1384 films; 352,230 government documents. **Subscriptions:** 9600 journals and other serials. **Services:** Interlibrary loan; copying; library open to the public. **Automated Operations:** Computerized cataloging and circulation. **Computerized Information Services:** DIALOG Information Services, QL Systems, Infomart, CAN/OLE, BRS Information Technologies, MEDLINE, UTLAS. **Publications:** Subject bibliographies. **Remarks:** Library is a depository for publications of the Canadian federal government, the province of Ontario, and the United Nations and its affiliates. **Staff:** Jean LeBlanc, Dir.; Dorothy Thomson, Asst.Libn., Coll.; Suzanne St-Jacques, Hd., Ref.Serv.; Agnes Sulyok, Hd., Circ.; Marie Duhamel, Govt.Pubn.; David Holmes, Sys..

★16720★
UNIVERSITY OF OTTAWA - MUSIC LIBRARY (Mus)
One Stewart St. Phone: (613)231-5717
Ottawa, ON, Canada K1N 6H7 Debra Begg, Libn.
Founded: 1970. **Staff:** Prof 1; Other 2. **Subjects:** Music. **Holdings:** 19,426 scores; 6415 phonograph records; 790 tapes; 240 cassettes. **Services:** Interlibrary loan (through Morisset Library). **Remarks:** Book collection and journals housed at Morisset Library.

★16721★
UNIVERSITY OF OTTAWA - TEACHER EDUCATION LIBRARY (Educ)
651 Cumberland St. Phone: (613)231-5986
Ottawa, ON, Canada K2P 1L3 Jan Kolaczek, Libn.
Staff: Prof 1; Other 4. **Subjects:** Teacher education, elementary and secondary teaching in both French and English languages, education theory. **Holdings:** 41,039 volumes; 1095 filmstrips and film loops; 80 slide carousels; 568 multimedia kits; 3000 mounted photographs; 678 sound recordings; 213 video cassettes; 100 videotapes. **Subscriptions:** 200 journals and other serials. **Services:** Interlibrary loan; copying; SDI; library open to the public with restrictions on borrowing. **Also Known As:** Bibliotheque de la Formation a l'Enseignement.

★16722★
UNIVERSITY OF OTTAWA - VANIER SCIENCE & ENGINEERING LIBRARY (Sci-Engr)
11 Somerset St., E. Phone: (613)231-2324
Ottawa, ON, Canada K1N 9A4 Blanca Stead, Dir.
Staff: Prof 3; Other 8. **Subjects:** Science, engineering. **Special Collections:** Academic dissertations in science and technology accepted by the university. **Holdings:** 67,716 books; 84,537 bound periodical volumes; 19,341 microfiche. **Subscriptions:** 1640 journals and other serials. **Services:** Interlibrary loan; copying; library open to the public with restrictions on borrowing. **Computerized Information Services:** Online systems. **Staff:** Maurice Alarie, Ref.; Edith Arbach, Ref.; Lynette Ng, Ref. & Tech.Serv..

★16723★
UNIVERSITY OF THE PACIFIC - HOLT-ATHERTON CENTER FOR WESTERN STUDIES (Hist)
Stockton, CA 95211 Phone: (209)946-2404
Thomas W. Leonhardt, Dir.
Founded: 1947. **Staff:** Prof 2; Other 1. **Subjects:** Californiana, Western Americana, Pacific Northwest, Western authors, Native Americans, economic development of the West. **Special Collections:** Early California exploration; fur trade; John Muir papers; Jack London family collection. **Holdings:** 20,000 books; 2928 bound periodical volumes; 75 linear feet of VF pamphlets; 30,000 photographs; 700 maps; 1500 linear feet of manuscripts. **Subscriptions:** 116 journals and other serials. **Services:** Interlibrary loan (limited); copying; library open to the public. **Automated Operations:** Computerized cataloging. **Computerized Information Services:** RLIN. **Networks/Consortia:** Member of 49-99 Cooperative Library System. **Publications:** Monographs; Bibliographic Guides to Archives. **Also Known As:** Stuart Library of Western Americana. **Staff:** Ms. Daryl Morrison, Spec.Coll..

★16724★
UNIVERSITY OF THE PACIFIC - SCIENCE LIBRARY (Sci-Engr, Med)
Stockton, CA 95211 Phone: (209)946-2940
Judith K. Andrews, Sci.Libn.
Founded: 1955. **Staff:** Prof 1; Other 4. **Subjects:** Pharmacy and pharmacology, medicine, chemistry, drug information. **Special Collections:** Iowa Drug Literature Information Service. **Holdings:** 13,168 books; 13,996 bound periodical volumes; 82,745 index cards; 1468 reels of microfilm; 9478 microcards; 9822 microfiche. **Subscriptions:** 371 journals and other serials. **Services:** Interlibrary loan; copying; library open to the public with restrictions. **Automated Operations:** Computerized cataloging, acquisitions, and serials. **Computerized Information Services:** DIALOG Information Services, RLIN, INNOVACQ Automated Library System; OnTyme Electronic Message Network Service (electronic mail service). Performs searches on fee basis. **Networks/Consortia:** Member of 49-99 Cooperative Library System, Central Association of Libraries (CAL), Northern California Medical Library Group, North San Joaquin Health Sciences Library Consortium.

★16725★
UNIVERSITY OF PENNSYLVANIA - ANNENBERG SCHOOL OF COMMUNICATIONS - LIBRARY (Info Sci)
3620 Walnut St. Phone: (215)898-7027
Philadelphia, PA 19104-6220 Sandra B. Grilikhes, Hd.Libn.
Founded: 1962. **Staff:** Prof 3; Other 4. **Subjects:** Theory and research of communications; public communications; mass media communication; interpersonal communications; social psychology of communication; communications economics; sound communication; history and technology of communication. **Special Collections:** Annenberg Faculty Publications; 16mm film catalogs; annual reports of leading U.S. communications companies and U.S. public television stations; Sol Worth Ethnographic Film Archive; Television Script Archive. **Holdings:** 22,000 volumes; 40 VF drawers of pamphlets and clippings; 400 theses and dissertations; 600 colloquium tapes and disc recordings; 650 reels of microfilm; 7000 microfiche. **Subscriptions:** 450 journals and other serials; 10 newspapers. **Services:** Interlibrary loan; library open to the public for reference use only. **Computerized Information Services:** RLIN. **Networks/Consortia:** Member of PALINET, RLG. **Publications:** Selected New Acquisitions, quarterly; Selected Reference Sources in Communications - free upon request. **Staff:** Joan Bernstein, Asst.Libn.; Sharon Black, TV Scripts Libn..

★16726★
UNIVERSITY OF PENNSYLVANIA - ARCHIVE OF FOLKLORE & FOLKLIFE (Area-Ethnic)
417 Logan Hall Phone: (215)898-7352
Philadelphia, PA 19104 Dr. Kenneth Goldstein, Dir.
Subjects: Folklore, music, New Foundland folksong, West Indies, Virginia and Pennsylvania, American Folklore Society. **Special Collections:** Mac Edward Leach Collections from New Foundland, Nova Scotia, and Jamaica; Kenneth Goldstein Collection (New Foundland, Labrador, North Carolina, Great Britain, and Ireland); Horace and Jane Beck Collection (West Indies); Samuel Bayard recordings; Jacob Elder Collection (Trinidad); American Folklore Society letters, 1918-1943; Ray Birdwhistell Collection of Americana and American Humor; Niles C. Geerhold Popular Music Collection; John Diamond Record Collection. **Holdings:** 251 volumes; 4000 phonograph records; 30 dissertations; files of student papers and other items. **Subscriptions:** 28 journals and other serials; 10 newspapers. **Services:** Copying; archive open to the public by appointment. **Remarks:** Archives are open on a limited schedule during the summer months.

★16727★
UNIVERSITY OF PENNSYLVANIA - ARCHIVES AND RECORDS CENTER (Hist)
North Arcade, Franklin Field Phone: (215)898-7024
Philadelphia, PA 19104-6320 Mark Frazier Lloyd, Dir.
Staff: Prof 6; Other 4. **Subjects:** University history. **Holdings:** 135 linear feet of books; 200 linear feet of bound periodical volumes; 8017 cubic feet of manuscripts; 22,000 photographs, drawings, prints, paintings; 79 cubic feet of memorabilia. **Subscriptions:** 12 journals and other serials. **Services:** Interlibrary loan; copying; microfilming; archives open to the public. **Computerized Information Services:** RLIN. **Publications:** Report, biennial; Guide to the Archives of the University of Pennsylvania from 1740 to 1820; The University Archives and Records Center: A Guide to Records Management. **Staff:** Hamilton Y. Elliott, Assoc.Dir.; Laura G. Thomforde, Univ.Rec.Mgr.; Louise S. Chaney, Asst.Rec.Mgr.; Wanda W. Johnson, Asst.Rec.Mgr.; Karen D. Stevens, Tech.Serv.Archv..

★16728★
UNIVERSITY OF PENNSYLVANIA - THE ARNOLD AND MABEL BECKMAN CENTER FOR THE HISTORY OF CHEMISTRY (Sci-Engr)
3401 Walnut St., Suite 460B Phone: (215)898-4896
Philadelphia, PA 19104-6228 Dr. Arnold W. Thackray, Dir.
Staff: Prof 5; Other 7. **Subjects:** History of chemistry, chemical engineering, chemical process industries. **Holdings:** Figures not available. **Services:** Copying; center open to the public. **Computerized Information Services:** RLIN, OCLC. **Networks/Consortia:** Member of RLG. **Publications:** Beckman Center News. **Remarks:** The purpose of this center is to locate, preserve, catalog, and make available records of chemistry, chemical engineering, and the chemical industry. It is jointly sponsored by the American Chemical Society, the American Institute of Chemical Engineers, and the University of Pennsylvania. **Staff:** Dr. Jeffrey L. Sturchio, Assoc.Dir.; Colleen Wickey, Archv.; J.J. Bohning, Oral Hist..

★16729★
UNIVERSITY OF PENNSYLVANIA - BIDDLE LAW LIBRARY (Law)
3400 Chestnut St. Phone: (215)898-7478
Philadelphia, PA 19104-6279 Prof. Elizabeth Slus Kelly, Libn.
Founded: 1886. **Staff:** Prof 13; Other 15. **Subjects:** American and foreign legislation; reports of Anglo-American and other judicial decisions; administrative regulations and decisions; law - Anglo-American, foreign, canon, Roman, international. **Holdings:** 380,626 volumes; 284,394 microfiche; 3095 reels of microfilm. **Subscriptions:** 5036 journals and other serials. **Services:** Interlibrary loan; copying; library open to the public for reference use only. **Computerized Information Services:** DIALOG Information Services, ELSS (Electronic Legislative Search System), VU/TEXT Information Services, RLIN, LEXIS, WESTLAW, OCLC, InfoTrac. **Networks/Consortia:** Member of RLG, PALINET, Mid-Atlantic Law Library Cooperative (MALLCO). **Staff:** Cynthia Arkin, Assoc.Libn.; Patricia Callahan, Hd., Tech.Serv.; Marta Tarnawsky, Asst.Libn., Intl. Law; Ronald Day, Ref.; Merle Slyhoff, Ref./Media; David Batista, Ref./Docs.; Nancy Whitmer, Ref.; Ralph Gaebler, Ref.; Judith Vaughan-Sterling, Cat.; Maria Smolka-Day, Intl. Law.

★16730★
UNIVERSITY OF PENNSYLVANIA - BIOMEDICAL LIBRARY (Med)
Johnson Pavilion
36th & Hamilton Walk Phone: (215)898-5817
Philadelphia, PA 19104-6060 Valerie A. Pena, Libn.
Founded: 1916. **Staff:** Prof 11; Other 16. **Subjects:** Medicine, biology, nursing, health care, basic sciences. **Holdings:** 154,887 volumes; 1997 AV programs. **Subscriptions:** 2510 journals and other serials. **Services:** Interlibrary loan; copying; orientations; workshops; library open to the public for reference use only. **Automated Operations:** Computerized cataloging, acquisitions, serials, and ILL. **Computerized Information Services:** DIALOG Information Services, BRS Information Technologies, NLM, RLIN, PaperChase, OCLC; internal database; DOCLINE (electronic mail service). **Networks/Consortia:** Member of RLG, Greater Northeastern Regional Medical Library Program, PALINET, Health Sciences Library Consortium. **Publications:** Newsletter, quarterly - for internal distribution only. **Staff:** Judie Malamud, Asst.Libn., Pub.Serv.; Linda Rosenstein, Asst.Libn., Tech.Serv..

★16731★
UNIVERSITY OF PENNSYLVANIA - CHEMISTRY LIBRARY (Sci-Engr)
231 S. 34th St. Phone: (215)898-5627
Philadelphia, PA 19104-6323 Carol Carr, Libn.
Staff: Prof 1; Other 1. **Subjects:** Biochemistry; chemistry - inorganic, organic, physical. **Holdings:** 20,616 books. **Subscriptions:** 254 journals and other serials. **Services:** Interlibrary loan; copying; library open to the public. **Computerized Information Services:** STN International, DIALOG Information Services, BRS Information Technologies, RLIN, OCLC. Performs searches on fee basis. **Networks/Consortia:** Member of RLG, PALINET.

★16732★
UNIVERSITY OF PENNSYLVANIA - EDGAR FAHS SMITH MEMORIAL COLLECTION IN THE HISTORY OF CHEMISTRY (Sci-Engr, Med)
Van Pelt Library Phone: (215)898-7088
Philadelphia, PA 19104-6206 Dr. Arnold W. Thackray, Cur.
Founded: 1931. **Subjects:** History of chemistry, alchemy, chemical biography, chemical engineering, chemical industry, early medicine, metallurgy, mineralogy, pharmacy, pyrotechnics. **Holdings:** 3000 portraits, prints, engravings; Robert Boyle and Joseph Priestley; imprints; 300 late 19th century German chemical dissertations; 8 boxes of Archives of the Division of Chemical Education, American Chemical Society; assorted manuscript collections (inventories available upon request). **Subscriptions:** 18 journals and other serials. **Services:** Interlibrary loan; copying; collection open to the public. **Computerized Information Services:** RLIN. **Networks/Consortia:** Member of RLG. **Special Catalogs:** Catalog of the Edgar Fahs Smith Memorial Collection in the History of Chemistry, 1960; Catalog of Manuscripts in the Libraries of the University of Pennsylvania to 1800, 1965. **Staff:** Christine A. Ruggere, Libn..

★16733★
UNIVERSITY OF PENNSYLVANIA - FINE ARTS LIBRARY (Art, Plan)
Van Pelt Library
3400 Walnut St. Phone: (215)898-8325
Philadelphia, PA 19104-6206 Alan E. Morrison, Libn.
Founded: 1890. **Staff:** Prof 2; Other 10. **Subjects:** Architecture, city planning, history of art, landscape architecture, regional planning, urban design, historic preservation, appropriate technology. **Special Collections:** Rare architectural books, 16th to 20th century. **Holdings:** 92,500 volumes; 59,000 mounted photographs; 282,000 35mm slides. **Subscriptions:** 750 journals and other serials. **Services:** Interlibrary loan; copying; library open to the public for reference use only. **Networks/Consortia:** Member of RLG, PALINET. **Remarks:** Library is temporarily located in the Van Pelt Library during renovation of the Furness Bldg. **Staff:** Micheline Nilsen, Slide Libn..

★16734★
UNIVERSITY OF PENNSYLVANIA - HENRY CHARLES LEA LIBRARY (Hist)
Van Pelt Library
3420 Walnut St. Phone: (215)898-7088
Philadelphia, PA 19104-6206 Edward M. Peters, Hon.Cur.
Founded: 1924. **Subjects:** Medieval and Renaissance history, church history, canon law, the Inquisition, magic, witchcraft. **Special Collections:** Manuscripts, 12th-18th centuries (600 volumes). **Holdings:** 18,000 volumes. **Services:** Interlibrary loan; copying; library open to the public. **Networks/Consortia:** Member of RLG, PALINET. **Special Catalogs:** Catalog of Manuscripts in the Libraries of the University of Pennsylvania to 1800 (book). **Remarks:** Holdings available through Christine A. Ruggere, Curator of Special Collections, Van Pelt Library.

★16735★
UNIVERSITY OF PENNSYLVANIA - HORACE HOWARD FURNESS MEMORIAL LIBRARY (Hum)
Van Pelt Library
3420 Walnut St. Phone: (215)898-7552
Philadelphia, PA 19104-6206 Georgianna Ziegler, Cur.
Founded: 1932. **Staff:** Prof 1. **Subjects:** Shakespeare, medieval to 17th century English drama, theater history. **Special Collections:** Playbills, promptbooks, and pictures; dissertations on Shakespeare and his contemporaries (2000 reels of microfilm); STC Collection. **Holdings:** 20,000 volumes. **Services:** Library open to qualified scholars and students. **Computerized Information Services:** RLIN, ESTC. **Networks/Consortia:** Member of RLG, PALINET.

★16736★
UNIVERSITY OF PENNSYLVANIA - INSTITUTE FOR STRUCTURAL AND FUNCTIONAL STUDIES - LIBRARY (Biol Sci)
University City Science Center
3401 Market St., Suite 320 Phone: (215)386-1912
Philadelphia, PA 19104 Ellen Kim, Libn.
Founded: 1949. **Staff:** 1. **Subjects:** Biochemistry, biophysics, physiology. **Holdings:** 650 books; 1000 bound periodical volumes. **Subscriptions:** 40 journals and other serials. **Services:** Library open to the public.

★16737★
UNIVERSITY OF PENNSYLVANIA - JOHN PENMAN WOOD LIBRARY OF NATIONAL DEFENSE (Mil)
516 Hollenback Center
3000 South St. Phone: (215)898-7757
Philadelphia, PA 19104-6325 Loretta Miller, Adm.Asst.
Founded: 1928. **Staff:** 1. **Subjects:** Officer education and production; leadership, organization, and management; operations, tactics, and strategy; logistics, supply, and transportation; military biography and history; principles of war, weaponry, and war gaming; medical services. **Holdings:** 15,500 books; 66 bound periodical volumes. **Services:** Interlibrary loan; library open to the public for reference use only. **Remarks:** An alternate telephone number is 898-7756.

★16738★
UNIVERSITY OF PENNSYLVANIA - LIPPINCOTT LIBRARY (Bus-Fin)
3420 Walnut St. Phone: (215)898-5924
Philadelphia, PA 19104-6207 Michael Halperin, Hd.Libn.
Founded: 1927. **Staff:** Prof 9; Other 13. **Subjects:** Applied economics, econometrics, business, management, finance, multinational enterprises, marketing, accounting, insurance, labor, industrial relations, transportation, statistics, regional science, operations research, real estate. **Holdings:** 198,000 volumes; 2900 reels of microfilm; 79,000 microfiche and microcards. **Subscriptions:** 4800 journals and other serials. **Services:** Interlibrary loan; copying; library open to the public. **Automated Operations:** Computerized circulation. **Computerized Information Services:** DIALOG Information Services, BRS Information Technologies, NEXIS, VU/TEXT Information Services, WILSONDISC, Disclosure Information Group, RLIN, OCLC, Dow Jones News/Retrieval. **Networks/Consortia:** Member of RLG, PALINET. **Staff:** Ruth Pagell, Assoc.Libn..

★16739★
UNIVERSITY OF PENNSYLVANIA - MAP LIBRARY (Geog-Map)
Hayden Hall
240 S. 33rd St. Phone: (215)898-5156
Philadelphia, PA 19104-6316 Carol Faul, Map Libn.
Staff: Prof 1; Other 1. **Subjects:** Regional, U.S., and international maps. **Special Collections:** Depository for U.S. Geological Survey, National Ocean Survey Charts, Defense Mapping Agency, and Canadian Geological Survey. **Holdings:** 120,000 maps. **Services:** Copying; map enlarger; library open to the public.

★16740★
UNIVERSITY OF PENNSYLVANIA - MATHEMATICS-PHYSICS-ASTRONOMY LIBRARY (Sci-Engr)
Rittenhouse Laboratory
Philadelphia, PA 19104-6317 Phone: (215)898-8173
Founded: 1948. **Staff:** Prof 1; Other 1. **Subjects:** Astronomy, mathematics, physics. **Holdings:** 53,198 volumes. **Subscriptions:** 522 journals and other serials. **Services:** Interlibrary loan; copying; library open to the public for reference use only. **Computerized Information Services:** DIALOG Information Services, SPIRES, RLIN, OCLC. **Networks/Consortia:** Member of RLG, PALINET.

★16741★
UNIVERSITY OF PENNSYLVANIA - MORRIS ARBORETUM LIBRARY (Biol Sci)
9414 Meadowbrook Ave.
Philadelphia, PA 19118 Phone: (215)247-5777
Founded: 1932. **Subjects:** Ornamental horticulture, garden history (especially Victorian period), floristic botany, urban forestry and silviculture, plant exploration. **Holdings:** 5000 books; 2500 bound periodical volumes. **Subscriptions:** 100 journals and other serials. **Services:** Interlibrary loan; library open to the public for reference use only. **Staff:** Timothy R. Tomlinson, Assoc.Dir.; Ann F. Rhoads, Dir. of Botany.

★16742★
UNIVERSITY OF PENNSYLVANIA - NEW BOLTON CENTER - JEAN AUSTIN DU PONT LIBRARY (Med)
382 W. Street Rd. Phone: (215)444-5800
Kennett Square, PA 19348 Lillian D. Bryant, Libn.
Founded: 1963. **Staff:** 1. **Subjects:** Veterinary medicine, with emphasis on large animal medicine. **Special Collections:** Fairman Rogers Rare Book Collection (horsemanship and equitation; 1201 volumes). **Holdings:** 2334 books; 2945 bound periodical volumes. **Subscriptions:** 65 journals and other serials. **Services:** Interlibrary loan; copying; library open to the public for reference use only. **Networks/Consortia:** Member of RLG, PALINET, Greater Northeastern Regional Medical Library Program. **Special Catalogs:** Catalog of Fairman Rogers Rare Book Collection (book).

★16743★
UNIVERSITY OF PENNSYLVANIA - POPULATION STUDIES CENTER - DEMOGRAPHY LIBRARY (Soc Sci)
3718 Locust Walk Phone: (215)898-5375
Philadelphia, PA 19104-6298 Lisa A. Newman, Libn.
Staff: Prof 1; Other 2. **Subjects:** Foreign and United States census, population organizations, demographic surveys, statistics. **Special Collections:** Foreign censuses for 50 countries (varying years); statistical materials for 113 countries; United Nations repository; World Fertility Survey repository; John D. Durand Collection (historical demography). **Holdings:** 5000 books; 600 bound periodical volumes; reprints; dissertations. **Subscriptions:** 60 journals and other serials. **Services:** Interlibrary loan; library not open to the public but special requests will be taken from related interest institutions. **Automated Operations:** Computerized cataloging and acquisitions. **Computerized Information Services:** NLM. **Networks/Consortia:** Member of APLIC International Census Network. **Publications:** Acquisitions List, monthly - to related interest institutions.

★16744★
UNIVERSITY OF PENNSYLVANIA - SCHOOL OF DENTAL MEDICINE - LEON LEVY LIBRARY (Med)
4001 Spruce St. Phone: (215)898-8969
Philadelphia, PA 19104-6041 Sherry L. Montgomery, Libn.
Founded: 1914. **Staff:** Prof 2; Other 4. **Subjects:** Dentistry, oral biology, history of dentistry. **Special Collections:** Rare dental books (1400). **Holdings:** 12,000 books; 27,000 bound periodical volumes. **Subscriptions:** 435 journals and other serials. **Services:** Interlibrary loan; copying; SDI; library open to the public for reference use only. **Automated Operations:** Computerized cataloging. **Computerized Information Services:** RLIN, NLM, DIALOG Information Services. Performs searches on fee basis. **Networks/Consortia:** Member of RLG, PALINET, Health Sciences Library Consortium, Greater Northeastern Regional Medical Library Program. **Remarks:** An alternate telephone number is 898-8978. **Staff:** Elizabeth Jendryk, Libn..

★16745★
UNIVERSITY OF PENNSYLVANIA - SCHOOL OF ENGINEERING AND APPLIED SCIENCE - MOORE LIBRARY (Sci-Engr)
200 South 33rd St. Phone: (215)898-8135
Philadelphia, PA 19104-6314 Charles J. Myers, Libn.
Founded: 1926. **Staff:** Prof 1; Other 2. **Subjects:** Electrical engineering, electronics, computers, information science, optics, systems engineering. **Special Collections:** Robotics. **Holdings:** 21,000 volumes. **Subscriptions:** 419 journals and other serials. **Services:** Interlibrary loan; copying; library open to the public for reference use only. **Computerized Information Services:** RLIN, OCLC, DIALOG Information Services, BRS Information Technologies. **Networks/Consortia:** Member of RLG, PALINET.

★16746★
UNIVERSITY OF PENNSYLVANIA - SCHOOL OF ENGINEERING AND APPLIED SCIENCE - TOWNE LIBRARY (Sci-Engr)
220 S. 33rd St. Phone: (215)898-7266
Philadelphia, PA 19104-6315 Charles J. Myers, Libn.
Founded: 1947. **Staff:** Prof 2; Other 2. **Subjects:** Engineering - chemical, civil, metallurgical, mechanical, aeronautical, transportation, environmental; engineering science; materials science; bioengineering. **Special Collections:** Depository for NASA reports; robotics; heat transfer; fluid mechanics. **Holdings:** 73,695 volumes; 165,500 microfiche; 100 videotapes. **Subscriptions:** 700 journals and other serials. **Services:** Interlibrary loan; copying; library open to the public for reference use only. **Computerized Information Services:** DIALOG Information Services, BRS Information Technologies, RLIN, OCLC. **Networks/Consortia:** Member of RLG, PALINET.

★16747★
UNIVERSITY OF PENNSYLVANIA - SCHOOL OF MEDICINE - CLINICAL EPIDEMIOLOGY UNIT - LIBRARY (Med)
2L NEB/S2
Philadelphia, PA 19104 Phone: (215)898-4623
Founded: 1978. **Subjects:** Medicine, clinical epidemiology, public health, statistics. **Holdings:** Figures not available. **Services:** Library not open to the public. **Staff:** Dr. Paul Stolley, Co-Dir.; Brian L. Strom, M.D., Co-Dir..

★16748★
UNIVERSITY OF PENNSYLVANIA - SCHOOL OF SOCIAL WORK - SMALLEY LIBRARY OF SOCIAL WORK
Caster Bldg.
3701 Locust Walk
Philadelphia, PA 19104-6214
Defunct. Holdings absorbed by Van Pelt Library.

★16749★
UNIVERSITY OF PENNSYLVANIA - SCHOOL OF VETERINARY MEDICINE - C.J. MARSHALL MEMORIAL LIBRARY (Med)
3800 Spruce St. Phone: (215)898-8874
Philadelphia, PA 19104-6008 Lillian D. Bryant, Libn.
Founded: 1908. **Staff:** Prof 1; Other 2. **Subjects:** Veterinary and comparative medicine, animal husbandry. **Holdings:** 9751 books; 24,475 bound periodical volumes; 18 VF drawers of pamphlets, bulletins, annual reports. **Subscriptions:** 362 journals and other serials. **Services:** Interlibrary loan; copying; library open to the public for reference use only. **Computerized Information Services:** DIALOG Information Services, MEDLINE, RLIN, OCLC; DOCLINE (electronic mail service). **Networks/Consortia:** Member of RLG, PALINET, Greater Northeastern Regional Medical Library Program, Health Sciences Library Consortium. **Remarks:** Figures include holdings of the New Bolton Center Library in Kennett Square.

★16750★
UNIVERSITY OF PENNSYLVANIA - SPECIAL COLLECTIONS (Hum, Rare Book)
Van Pelt Library
3420 Walnut St. Phone: (215)898-7088
Philadelphia, PA 19104-6206
Daniel H. Traister, Asst.Dir. of Libs., Spec.Coll.
Staff: Prof 5. **Subjects:** Literature - English, American, Spanish, Italian, German, classical, neo-Latin; French drama; history of agriculture; cryptography; ancient and early modern philosophy. **Special Collections:** Jonathan Swift (1400 volumes); English novel to 1820 (3000 volumes); Torquato Tasso, 16th and 17th centuries (350 volumes); Aristotle editions and commentaries before 1750 (1200 manuscript and printed volumes); Elzevir imprints (2500 volumes); Latin American history and religion, 17th-19th centuries (1500 volumes); Benjamin Franklin imprints (200 volumes); Philadelphia Society for the Promotion of Agriculture (1500 manuscript and printed volumes); French Revolution (25,000 items in 1460 volumes); Roman Catholic and Anglo-Catholic theology and liturgy (1000 volumes); University of Pennsylvania medical dissertations, 18th and 19th centuries (800 volumes); Indic manuscripts (50 volumes); collections of manuscripts by and about authors, artists, and public figures: Marian Anderson; Berchtesgaden interrogations, 1945; Robert Montgomery Bird; Van Wyck Brooks; Carey & Lea, Publishers; Theodore Dreiser; James T. Farrell; Howard Fast; Waldo Frank; John Haviland; Francis Hopkinson; William C. Lengel; Horace Liveright; H.L. Mencken; S. Weir Mitchell; Lewis Mumford; John Rowe Parker; Francis Daniel Pastorius; William Pepper; Ezra Pound; Arthur Hobson Quinn; Samuel J. Randall; Burton Rascoe; Ada Rehan; Agnes Repplier; Jurgis Saulys; George Seldes; Gilbert Seldes; May Sinclair; Robert E. Spiller and the Archive of the Literary History of the United States; Alma Mahler Werfel; Franz Werfel; Samuel Wetherill and Wetherill business records; Walt Whitman; Carl Zigrosser. **Holdings:** 300,000 books; 3500 linear feet of manuscripts. **Services:** Interlibrary loan; copying; collections open to the public by appointment. **Computerized Information Services:** RLIN. **Networks/Consortia:** Member of RLG, PALINET. **Special Catalogs:** Catalogs to: European manuscripts to 1800, 1965; 16th century imprints, 1976; English 17th century imprints, 1978; Spanish drama of the Golden Age, 1971; Aristotle collection, 1961; Maclure Collection of the French Revolution, 1966; Marian Anderson Collection, 1981 (all in book form). **Staff:** Christine A. Ruggere, Cur., Spec.Coll.; Nancy M. Shawcross, Cur., Mss.; Dr. Georgianna Ziegler, Asst.Cur., Spec.Coll.; Elizabeth Mosimann, Hd., Rd.Serv..

★16751★
UNIVERSITY OF PENNSYLVANIA - UNIVERSITY HOSPITAL LIBRARY
3400 Spruce St.
Philadelphia, PA 19104-4283
Defunct

★16752★
UNIVERSITY OF PENNSYLVANIA - THE UNIVERSITY MUSEUM OF ARCHAEOLOGY/ANTHROPOLOGY - MUSEUM LIBRARY (Soc Sci)
33rd & Spruce Sts. Phone: (215)898-7840
Philadelphia, PA 19104-6324 Jean S. Adelman, Libn.
Founded: 1887. **Staff:** Prof 1; Other 2. **Subjects:** Archeology, anthropology, ethnology. **Special Collections:** Brinton Collection of 19th century American Indian linguistics and ethnology (2000 titles). **Holdings:** 87,435 volumes; 4500 pamphlets; 60 reels of microfilm. **Subscriptions:** 900 journals and other serials. **Services:** Interlibrary loan; copying; library open to the public for reference use only. **Computerized Information Services:** BRS Information Technologies, RLIN, OCLC. **Networks/Consortia:** Member of RLG, PALINET.

UNIVERSITY OF PENNSYLVANIA MEDICAL CENTER
See: Presbyterian-University of Pennsylvania Medical Center (11531)

UNIVERSITY OF PHILADELPHIA - MARRIAGE COUNCIL OF PHILADELPHIA
See: Marriage Council of Philadelphia (8457)

★16753★
UNIVERSITY OF PITTSBURGH - AFRO-AMERICAN LIBRARY (Area-Ethnic)
120 Hillman Library Phone: (412)648-7713
Pittsburgh, PA 15260 Ida M. Lewis, Hd.
Founded: 1969. **Staff:** Prof 1; Other 1. **Subjects:** History, political science, literature, literary criticism, social sciences, culture and the arts, blacks in Western Pennsylvania. **Special Collections:** Atlanta University Black Culture Collection (microfilm); W.E.B. Dubois Papers (microfilm); papers of the Congress of Racial Equity (microfilm); black history and landmarks in Western Pennsylvania (80 slides). **Holdings:** 14,606 volumes; 6 VF drawers of clippings, pamphlets. **Subscriptions:** 77 journals and other serials; 27 newspapers. **Services:** Interlibrary loan; library open to the public for reference use only. **Automated Operations:** Computerized cataloging. **Computerized Information Services:** DIALOG Information Services, BRS Information Technologies, The Reference Service (REFSRV). **Networks/Consortia:** Member of Pittsburgh Regional Library Center (PRLC).

★16754★
UNIVERSITY OF PITTSBURGH - ALLEGHENY OBSERVATORY - LIBRARY (Sci-Engr)
159 Riverview Airway
Pittsburgh, PA 15260 Phone: (412)321-2400
Founded: 1868. **Staff:** 1. **Subjects:** Astronomy, astrometry. **Special Collections:** British and French Astronomical Association publications, 1800 to present; exchange publications from over 500 observatories throughout the world. **Holdings:** 3717 volumes. **Subscriptions:** 21 journals and other serials. **Services:** Interlibrary loan; library open to the public for reference use only. **Publications:** Allegheny Observatory reports, irregular - to other observatories on exchange, free to libraries upon request. **Remarks:** All inquiries concerning this library should be directed to Paul Kobulnicky, Physics Library, 208 Engineering Hall; telephone: 624-8770.

★16755★
UNIVERSITY OF PITTSBURGH - ARCHIVES (Hist)
363 Hillman Library
Pittsburgh, PA 15260 Phone: (412)648-8190
Founded: 1966. **Staff:** Prof 1. **Subjects:** University of Pittsburgh history and records. **Special Collections:** Thomas Parron papers (Surgeon General of the U.S., 1936-1946, and a founder of the World Health Organization). **Holdings:** 14,180 books; 310 bound periodical volumes; 2008 linear feet of manuscripts; 25,641 microforms; 742 films; 11,363 photographs; 653 sound recordings; 772 slides; 437 drawings and prints. **Subscriptions:** 58 journals and other serials. **Services:** Copying; archives open to the public. **Staff:** Julie Suni.

★16756★
UNIVERSITY OF PITTSBURGH - ARCHIVES OF INDUSTRIAL SOCIETY (Hist)
363-H Hillman Library Phone: (412)648-8190
Pittsburgh, PA 15260 Frank A. Zabrosky, Cur.
Founded: 1963. **Staff:** Prof 2; Other 2. **Subjects:** History - urban, labor, ethnic. **Special Collections:** 441 collections (primarily manuscripts) of individuals, businesses, churches, institutions, organizations, labor unions, ethnic groups; municipal records of Pittsburgh, Allegheny, Allegheny County; United Electrical, Radio and Machine Workers of America Archives; Pittsburgh City Photographer Collection; oral history tapes. **Holdings:** 880 volumes; 10,012 linear feet of manuscripts; 1737 reels of microfilm; 4875 reels of 16mm film; 82 phonograph records; 723 tape cassettes; 615 maps; 788 architectural drawings, plans, sketches; 75,061 photographic images: glass plates, negatives, prints. **Subscriptions:** 14 journals and other serials. **Services:** Copying; use of collections may be subject to conditions of owner/donor; access to archives is conditional. **Publications:** Inventories to specific collections - for sale. **Special Catalogs:** Resources on the Ethnic and the Immigrant in the Pittsburgh Area, 1979 (book). **Special Indexes:** Indexes to the microfilmed correspondence of directors, acting directors, and selected astronomers. **Staff:** Mark McColloch, Archv..

★16757★
UNIVERSITY OF PITTSBURGH - BEVIER ENGINEERING LIBRARY (Sci-Engr)
126 Benedum Hall Phone: (412)624-9620
Pittsburgh, PA 15261 Sandra S. Kerbel, Hd.
Founded: 1956. **Staff:** Prof 1; Other 2. **Subjects:** Engineering - chemical, civil, electrical, industrial, mechanical, metallurgical, petroleum, environmental, mining, materials; bioengineering; energy resources. **Special Collections:** Selected depository for U.S. Department of Energy, Environmental Protection Agency, and selected National Bureau of Standards documents; Advisory Group for Aerospace Research and Development depository set. **Holdings:** 51,721 volumes; 46,507 microfiche; 3060 reels of microfilm; 3880 U.S. documents; 100 nonprint items. **Subscriptions:** 890 journals and other serials. **Services:** Interlibrary loan; copying; library open to the public. **Computerized Information Services:** DIALOG Information Services, OCLC, STN International, Integrated Technical Information System (ITIS); internal database. **Networks/ Consortia:** Member of Pittsburgh Regional Library Center (PRLC), Center for Research Libraries (CRL) Consortia.

★16758★
UNIVERSITY OF PITTSBURGH - BIOLOGICAL SCIENCES AND PSYCHOLOGY LIBRARY (Biol Sci)
A-217 Langley Hall Phone: (412)624-4490
Pittsburgh, PA 15260 Drynda L. Johnston, Hd.
Founded: 1961. **Staff:** Prof 1; Other 2. **Subjects:** Biological sciences, biophysics, biochemistry, psychology. **Holdings:** 52,530 books; 23,100 bound periodical volumes; 4300 microfiche. **Subscriptions:** 697 journals and other serials. **Services:** Interlibrary loan; copying; library open to the public for reference use only. **Automated Operations:** Computerized circulation. **Computerized Information Services:** DIALOG Information Services. **Networks/Consortia:** Member of Pittsburgh Regional Library Center (PRLC).

★16759★
UNIVERSITY OF PITTSBURGH - CHEMISTRY LIBRARY (Sci-Engr)
200 Alumni Hall Phone: (412)624-8294
Pittsburgh, PA 15260 Paul J. Kobulnicky, Libn.
Staff: Prof 1; Other 1. **Subjects:** Chemistry - organic, physical, analytical; chemistry of natural products; spectroscopy. **Holdings:** 24,686 books; 13,000 bound periodical volumes; 151 government documents; 627 microforms; spectral files and indices. **Subscriptions:** 151 journals and other serials. **Services:** Interlibrary loan; copying; library open to the public. **Computerized Information Services:** OCLC, DIALOG Information Services, STN International. Performs searches on fee basis. **Publications:** Monthly Acquisitions List.

★16760★
UNIVERSITY OF PITTSBURGH - CIOCCO LIBRARY (Med)
130 DeSoto St. Phone: (412)624-3016
Pittsburgh, PA 15261 Suzanne O. Paul, Hd.
Founded: 1949. **Staff:** Prof 2; Other 2. **Subjects:** Public health, industrial hygiene, biostatistics, epidemiology, microbiology, public health administration, radiation health, toxicology. **Special Collections:** Parran Collection; Wilson G. Smillie Collection; Autism Collection. **Holdings:** 46,242 volumes; 545 government documents; 195 microforms; 86 maps. **Subscriptions:** 217 journals and other serials. **Services:** Interlibrary loan; copying; SDI; library open to the public for reference use only. **Computerized Information Services:** DIALOG Information Services, BRS Information Technologies, NLM. Performs searches on fee basis. **Networks/Consortia:** Member of Pittsburgh Regional Library Center (PRLC). **Publications:** Bi-monthly List of Books Acquired.

★16761★
UNIVERSITY OF PITTSBURGH - COMPUTER SCIENCE LIBRARY (Comp Sci)
200 Alumni Hall Phone: (412)624-8294
Pittsburgh, PA 15260 Paul Kobulnicky, Libn.
Founded: 1956. **Staff:** Prof 1; Other 1. **Subjects:** Computer science - theory, programming languages, operating systems, database theory, graphics, networking, software engineering, artificial intelligence, computer management. **Holdings:** 9240 books; 3000 bound periodical volumes; 6000 technical reports; 65 microforms. **Subscriptions:** 294 journals and other serials. **Services:** Interlibrary loan; copying; library open to the public. **Computerized Information Services:** OCLC, DIALOG Information Services. **Special Indexes:** KWIC index to technical report literature.

★16762★
UNIVERSITY OF PITTSBURGH - DARLINGTON MEMORIAL LIBRARY (Hist)
Cathedral of Learning Phone: (412)624-4491
Pittsburgh, PA 15260 Charles E. Aston, Jr., Coord., Spec.Coll.
Founded: 1918. **Staff:** Prof 1; Other 1. **Subjects:** Colonial Americana, pre-1870 Pennsylvania and Ohio Valley history. **Special Collections:** O'Hara Darlington Collection (first editions of 19th century English novels). **Holdings:** 17,846 books; 1507 bound periodical volumes; 273 bound volumes of newspapers; 4570 pamphlets; 290 prints; 901 maps; 45 linear feet of manuscripts. **Services:** Copying; library open to the public for reference use only by appointment. **Publications:** Guide to Manuscripts

Collection; Women in Historical Perspective: Guide to the Resources in the Darlington Memorial Library - for sale.

★16763★
UNIVERSITY OF PITTSBURGH - EAST ASIAN LIBRARY (Area-Ethnic)
201 Hillman Library Phone: (412)648-8185
Pittsburgh, PA 15260 Dr. Thomas C. Kuo, Cur.
Founded: 1960. **Staff:** Prof 4; Other 3. **Subjects:** Chinese, Japanese, and Korean humanities and social sciences. **Special Collections:** Complete Sets of Ku chin t'u shu chi ch'eng (800 volumes of the 1934 photolithographic edition of the 1728 original collection); Yuan chien lei han (Imperial Palace block print edition of 1710); Shigaku zasshi, 1889 to present; Rekishi-Gaku Kenkyu, 1928 to present. **Holdings:** 121,333 volumes; 11,571 bound periodical volumes; 1223 microfiche; 3549 reels of microfilm. **Subscriptions:** 678 journals and other serials. **Services:** Interlibrary loan; open to the public with restrictions; library open to the public. **Automated Operations:** Computerized circulation. **Networks/Consortia:** Member of Pittsburgh Regional Library Center (PRLC). **Publications:** A Selected List of Outstanding New Acquisitions, quarterly. **Special Catalogs:** East Asian Periodicals and Serials (1970); Catalog of Microfilms of the East Asian Library of the University of Pittsburgh (1971); The Chinese Local History - Descriptive Holding List (1969). **Staff:** Agnes Wen, Tech.Serv.Libn.; Yumi Nishibu, Japanese Bibliog./Cat.; Lisa Woo, Chinese Bibliog./Cat..

★16764★
UNIVERSITY OF PITTSBURGH - ECONOMICS/COLLECTION IN REGIONAL ECONOMICS (Soc Sci, Bus-Fin)
4P56 Forbes Quadrangle Phone: (412)648-7375
Pittsburgh, PA 15260 Patricia Suozzi, Hd.
Staff: Prof 1; Other 3. **Subjects:** Regional economics, econometrics, economic theory, international trade and finance, money and banking, demography, statistics, comparative systems. **Holdings:** 22,474 books; 6500 bound periodical volumes; 6147 working papers; 160 doctoral dissertations; 1500 government documents. **Subscriptions:** 411 journals and other serials. **Services:** Interlibrary loan; collection open to the public. **Computerized Information Services:** I.P. Sharp Associates Limited, DIALOG Information Services, OCLC, VU/TEXT Information Services. Performs searches on fee basis. **Networks/Consortia:** Member of Pittsburgh Regional Library Center (PRLC). **Publications:** Economics Books: Current Selections, quarterly - by subscription; Bimonthly Acquisitions Letter - free upon request.

★16765★
UNIVERSITY OF PITTSBURGH - FALK LIBRARY OF THE HEALTH SCIENCES (Med)
Scaife Hall, 2nd Fl. Phone: (412)648-9020
Pittsburgh, PA 15261 P. Mickelson, Dir.
Founded: 1957. **Staff:** Prof 11; Other 15. **Subjects:** Medicine, biology, dentistry, nursing, pharmacy, allied health professions. **Special Collections:** History of medicine and dental medicine (12,000 items); history of anesthesia (400 items). **Holdings:** 227,079 books; 5823 government documents; 107 microforms; 60 films; 1556 audio recordings; 578 video recordings; 19,483 slides; 199 linear feet of manuscripts. **Subscriptions:** 2305 journals and other serials. **Services:** Interlibrary loan; copying; library open to the public for reference use only. **Computerized Information Services:** MEDLINE, BRS Information Technologies, DIALOG Information Services; OnTyme Electronic Message Network Service (electronic mail service). **Networks/Consortia:** Member of Greater Northeastern Regional Medical Library Program. **Publications:** Recent List of Acquisitions and Newsletter, monthly. **Special Catalogs:** Title and subject list of serials; union list of serials. **Staff:** Mary Ann Englert, Cat.; Esther Waldron, Hd., Cat.Dept.; Margaret Norden, Ref.Libn.; Jonathon Erlen, Ph.D., Cur., Hist.Coll.; Sally Wilson, Ser.Libn.; Jeremy Shellhase, Acq.Libn.; Elizabeth Geltz, Nursing Libn.; June E. Bandemeir, Asst.Dir.; Charles Wessel, Ref..

★16766★
UNIVERSITY OF PITTSBURGH - FOSTER HALL COLLECTION (Mus)
Stephen Foster Memorial
Forbes Ave. Phone: (412)624-4100
Pittsburgh, PA 15260 Dr. Deane L. Root, Cur.
Founded: 1931. **Staff:** Prof 1; Other 6. **Subjects:** Life and works of Stephen Collins Foster; American music history. **Holdings:** 1200 books; 100 bound periodical volumes; 7000 pieces of 19th century sheet music; 3000 uncataloged pieces of music; 2000 20th century scores and collections for vocal and instrumental ensembles; 2500 magazine and newspaper articles; 200 music manuscripts; 1700 photographs; 400 broadsides; 900 78rpm phonograph records; 75 cylinders; 60 music-box discs; 19 organ cylinders; 1080 songbooks; Foster instruments and artifacts; collection archives. **Services:** Interlibrary loan; copying; collection open to the public by appointment. **Publications:** Songs of Stephen Foster; research monographs - both for sale. **Special Indexes:** Partial index with files for arrangers, broadsides, derivata, magazines, recordings, pictures, scores, and songbooks (card).

★16767★
UNIVERSITY OF PITTSBURGH - GRADUATE SCHOOL OF BUSINESS LIBRARY (Bus-Fin)
1501 Cathedral of Learning Phone: (412)648-1669
Pittsburgh, PA 15260 Dr. Susan Neuman, Hd.
Founded: 1961. **Staff:** Prof 2; Other 4. **Subjects:** Econometrics, economics, business, management, accounting, industrial labor relations, behavioral science in business, business and society, marketing, finance. **Holdings:** 42,014 books; 4000 bound periodical volumes; 1509 reels of microfilm; 70,411 microfiche; annual reports of companies listed on New York and American Stock Exchanges on microfiche; 12 VF drawers of pamphlets. **Subscriptions:** 698 journals and other serials. **Services:** Interlibrary loan; copying; library open to the public for reference use only. **Computerized Information Services:** DIALOG Information Services, BRS Information Technologies, I.P. Sharp Associates Limited, NEXIS, VU/TEXT Information Services. **Networks/Consortia:** Member of Pittsburgh Regional Library Center (PRLC). **Publications:** Bimonthly Acquisitions List. **Staff:** Dennis Smith, Ref.Libn..

★16768★
UNIVERSITY OF PITTSBURGH - GRADUATE SCHOOL OF PUBLIC & INTERNATIONAL AFFAIRS LIBRARY (Soc Sci)
Forbes Quadrangle, 1st Fl. West Phone: (412)648-7575
Pittsburgh, PA 15260 Patricia Suozzi, Hd.
Founded: 1958. **Staff:** Prof 3; Other 1. **Subjects:** Public administration, urban affairs, economic and social development, international affairs. **Holdings:** 98,566 books; 4785 bound periodical volumes; 3000 pamphlets; 3500 microforms. **Subscriptions:** 538 journals and other serials. **Services:** Interlibrary loan; library open to the public for reference use only. **Automated Operations:** Computerized cataloging. **Computerized Information Services:** DIALOG Information Services, Pergamon ORBIT InfoLine, Inc.; internal databases. **Networks/Consortia:** Member of Pittsburgh Regional Library Center (PRLC). **Publications:** Accessions list. **Staff:** Mary Lois Kepes, Libn..

★16769★
UNIVERSITY OF PITTSBURGH - HENRY CLAY FRICK FINE ARTS LIBRARY (Art)
Pittsburgh, PA 15260 Phone: (412)648-2410
Ray Ann Lockard, Hd.
Founded: 1927. **Staff:** Prof 1; Other 3. **Subjects:** Art of the Western World, with emphasis on Byzantine, early Christian, Medieval, Renaissance, and modern periods; Oriental art; studio arts. **Special Collections:** Medieval illuminated manuscript facsimiles. **Holdings:** 63,544 volumes; 29 microforms; 1518 pamphlets; 89 facsimiles of Oriental scrolls. **Subscriptions:** 316 journals and other serials. **Services:** Interlibrary loan; library open to the public for reference use only. **Networks/Consortia:** Member of Pittsburgh Regional Library Center (PRLC). **Special Catalogs:** Exhibitions Catalog File; Art Sales Catalog File.

★16770★
UNIVERSITY OF PITTSBURGH - HUMAN RELATIONS AREA FILES (Soc Sci)
G16 Hillman Library Phone: (412)648-7722
Pittsburgh, PA 15260 Anne W. Gordon, Access Serv.Libn.
Staff: Prof 1; Other 2. **Subjects:** Anthropology and related behavioral sciences. **Holdings:** 20,656 microfiche. **Services:** Files open to the public for reference use only.

★16771★
UNIVERSITY OF PITTSBURGH - LATIN AMERICAN COLLECTION (Area-Ethnic)
171 Hillman Library Phone: (412)648-7730
Pittsburgh, PA 15260 Eduardo Lozano, Libn., Latin Amer.Stud.
Staff: Prof 4; Other 2. **Subjects:** Latin America - humanities, social sciences. **Special Collections:** Cuban Collection (12,800 volumes); Bolivian Collection (10,500 volumes; 1050 Bolivian political pamphlets); Human Relations Area File (1166 sources). **Holdings:** 210,000 books; 40,000 bound periodical volumes; 4560 reels of microfilm; 20,656 microfiche; 13,157 microcards; 1500 maps; 550 dissertations. **Subscriptions:** 4530 journals and other serials; 13 newspapers. **Services:** Interlibrary loan; copying; collection open to the public. **Automated Operations:** Computerized cataloging, acquisitions, serials, and circulation. **Computerized Information Services:**

DIALOG Information Services, BRS Information Technologies, NEXIS, VU/TEXT Information Services, OCLC. Performs searches on fee basis. Contact Person: Fern Brody, 624-4438. **Publications:** Cuban Periodicals in the University of Pittsburgh Libraries, 4th edition, 1985. **Special Catalogs:** Catalog of Latin American Periodicals (indexed by country and subject); Catalog of the Bolivian Collection (author and subject indexes).

★16772★
UNIVERSITY OF PITTSBURGH - LAW LIBRARY (Law)
3900 Forbes Ave. Phone: (412)648-1330
Pittsburgh, PA 15260 Jenni Parrish, Dir.
Founded: 1895. **Staff:** Prof 5; Other 11. **Subjects:** Law. **Holdings:** 133,401 volumes; 351,245 microforms; 177 nonprint recordings. **Subscriptions:** 3662 journals and other serials. **Services:** Interlibrary loan; copying; library open to the public for reference use only. **Automated Operations:** Computerized cataloging. **Computerized Information Services:** LEXIS, BRS Information Technologies, WESTLAW, DIALOG Information Services. **Networks/Consortia:** Member of Pittsburgh Regional Library Center (PRLC), Mid-Atlantic Law Library Cooperative (MALLCO). **Staff:** Nickie Singleton, Assoc. Law Libn.; Cynthia Larter, Asst. Law Libn.; Marc Silverman, Asst. Law Libn.; Elizabeth Bedford, Cat.Libn.; Spencer Clough, Pub.Serv.Libn..

★16773★
UNIVERSITY OF PITTSBURGH - MATHEMATICS LIBRARY (Sci-Engr)
430 Thackeray Hall Phone: (412)624-8205
Pittsburgh, PA 15260 Sandra S. Kerbel, Hd.
Founded: 1963. **Staff:** Prof 1. **Subjects:** Mathematics - pure, applied, numerical; statistics. **Holdings:** 17,798 volumes; 83 reels of microfilm; 868 microfiche. **Subscriptions:** 223 journals and other serials. **Services:** Interlibrary loan; copying; library open to the public. **Computerized Information Services:** DIALOG Information Services; internal database. **Networks/Consortia:** Member of Pittsburgh Regional Library Center (PRLC), Center for Research Libraries (CRL) Consortia.

★16774★
UNIVERSITY OF PITTSBURGH - NASA INDUSTRIAL APPLICATIONS CENTER (NIAC) (Sci-Engr, Info Sci, Comp Sci)
823 William Pitt Union Phone: (412)648-7000
Pittsburgh, PA 15260 Paul A. McWilliams, Exec.Dir.
Founded: 1963. **Staff:** Prof 12; Other 13. **Subjects:** Science and technology, business and marketing, computer and information sciences. **Holdings:** Figures not available. **Services:** Center provides full consulting and information brokerage activities; computer retrieval services; engineering services; database system development; database creation; special multidisciplinary studies and international projects; document procurement; center open to the public for reference use only. **Computerized Information Services:** DIALOG Information Services, Pergamon ORBIT InfoLine, Inc., NASA/RECON; internal databases. **Publications:** United States Political Science Documents (USPSD) annual reference guide (hardcopy and online); Economic Books (review), quarterly. **Staff:** Jan P. Miller, Sr.Mgr., Sys. & Oper..

★16775★
UNIVERSITY OF PITTSBURGH - PHYSICS LIBRARY (Sci-Engr)
208 Engineering Hall Phone: (412)624-8770
Pittsburgh, PA 15260 Paul J. Kobulnicky, Libn.
Founded: 1953. **Staff:** Prof 1; Other 1. **Subjects:** Physics - nuclear, high energy, atomic, molecular, solid state, quantum optics, atmospheric, low temperature; relativity; astrophysics; earth and planetary sciences. **Holdings:** 30,310 books; 15,000 bound periodical volumes; 1096 microforms. **Subscriptions:** 308 journals and other serials. **Services:** Interlibrary loan; copying; library open to the public. **Computerized Information Services:** OCLC, DIALOG Information Services, STN International. Performs searches on fee basis. **Networks/Consortia:** Member of Pittsburgh Regional Library Center (PRLC). **Publications:** Monthly Acquisitions List.

★16776★
UNIVERSITY OF PITTSBURGH - PRESBYTERIAN-UNIVERSITY HOSPITAL - MEDICAL STAFF LIBRARY (Med)
DeSoto at O'Hara Sts. Phone: (412)647-3287
Pittsburgh, PA 15213 Bianka M. Hesz, Med.Libn.
Founded: 1943. **Staff:** Prof 1; Other 3. **Subjects:** Clinical medicine, cancer, hematology, neurology, surgery. **Holdings:** 1500 books; 2875 bound periodical volumes; 639 Audio-Digest tapes. **Subscriptions:** 158 journals and other serials. **Services:** Interlibrary loan; copying; library open to the public. **Publications:** Newsletter, 2/year.

★16777★
UNIVERSITY OF PITTSBURGH - PYMATUNING LABORATORY OF ECOLOGY - TRYON LIBRARY (Env-Cons)
R.R. 1, Box 7 Phone: (814)683-5813
Linesville, PA 16424 Dolores E. Smith, Sec./Libn.
Founded: 1949. **Staff:** 1. **Subjects:** Ecology, field biology, limnology, animal behavior. **Holdings:** 2100 books; 200 bound periodical volumes. **Subscriptions:** 11 journals and other serials. **Services:** Copying; library open to the public with restrictions. **Publications:** Special publications of Pymatuning Laboratory, irregular.

★16778★
UNIVERSITY OF PITTSBURGH - SCHOOL OF LIBRARY & INFORMATION SCIENCE - INTERNATIONAL LIBRARY INFORMATION CENTER (Info Sci)
135 N. Bellefield Ave. Phone: (412)624-3394
Pittsburgh, PA 15260 Dr. Richard Krzys, Dir.
Founded: 1964. **Holdings:** 23,000 volumes. **Services:** Library open to the public. **Remarks:** This library maintains a special collection of materials relating to libraries, librarianship, documentation, and book production and distribution abroad. Resources are primarily of a nonbook nature including library reports, studies resulting from assignments by American librarians, and data on overseas book and library activities of governmental, philanthropic, and industrial agencies. Noteworthy collections within the center include those relating to Australia, Canada, Germany, Great Britain, India, Italy, Latin America and Pakistan. **Staff:** Jean Kindlin, Dir., Lib. & Media Serv..

★16779★
UNIVERSITY OF PITTSBURGH - SCHOOL OF LIBRARY & INFORMATION SCIENCE - LIBRARY (Info Sci)
135 N. Bellefield Ave. Phone: (412)624-5238
Pittsburgh, PA 15260 Elizabeth T. Mahoney, Hd.
Founded: 1966. **Staff:** Prof 3; Other 3. **Subjects:** Library and information science. **Special Collections:** Historical children's literature; Clifton Fadiman Collection of 20th Century Children's Literature; children's television archives, including archives of Mr. Roger's Neighborhood. **Holdings:** 91,852 books; 3467 microforms; 7 linear feet of manuscripts; 1112 pamphlets; 665 videotapes. **Subscriptions:** 943 journals and other serials. **Services:** Interlibrary loan; copying; library open to the public with restrictions. **Computerized Information Services:** DIALOG Information Services, BRS Information Technologies; ALANET (electronic mail service). **Networks/Consortia:** Member of Pittsburgh Regional Library Center (PRLC). **Staff:** Amira Al-Sadat, Hd., Tech.Serv..

★16780★
UNIVERSITY OF PITTSBURGH - SCHOOL OF SOCIAL WORK - BUHL LIBRARY (Soc Sci)
113 Hillman Library Phone: (412)648-7716
Pittsburgh, PA 15260 Patricia Miles Carle, Libn.
Founded: 1938. **Staff:** Prof 1; Other 1. **Subjects:** Social work, social policy research, community studies, family interaction, child welfare, gerontology, juvenile justice. **Special Collections:** Classified Abstract Archive of Alcohol Literature (19,000 cards). **Holdings:** 16,244 volumes; 22 VF drawers. **Subscriptions:** 139 journals and other serials. **Services:** Interlibrary loan; library open to the public with restrictions. **Automated Operations:** Computerized cataloging. **Computerized Information Services:** DIALOG Information Services, BRS Information Technologies, OCLC. **Networks/Consortia:** Member of Pittsburgh Regional Library Center (PRLC).

★16781★
UNIVERSITY OF PITTSBURGH - SPECIAL COLLECTIONS DEPARTMENT (Rare Book, Hum)
363 Hillman Library Phone: (412)648-8190
Pittsburgh, PA 15260 Charles E. Aston, Jr., Coord.
Founded: 1966. **Staff:** Prof 3; Other 3. **Subjects:** Incunabula, early printed books, little presses, English and American first editions, 20th century poetry, early American textbooks, 20th century Spanish literature, theater programs and playbills, detective and mystery stories, modern dance, popular culture, science fiction, history and philosophy of science. **Special Collections:** Hervey Allen Collection; Mary Roberts Rinehart Collection; Ramon Gomez de la Serna Collection; Curtis Theater Collection; Nietz Old Textbook Collection; Bernard S. Horne Memorial-Izaak Walton Compleat Angler Collection; Anna Pavlowa-Karl G. Heinrich Collection; Archive of Popular Culture; Rudolf Carnap Collection; Hans Reichenbach papers; Frank P. Ramsey papers; Walter and Martha Leuba Collection;

Bollingen Foundation Collection; Cooperative Movement Collection; Tomas G. Masaryk papers; Lawrence Lee Collection. **Holdings:** 52,423 volumes; 606 feet of manuscripts and archives; 1557 broadsides and dealer catalogs; 760 photographs; 343 posters; 505,166 theater programs; 52,750 theater history clippings; 442 sheet music scores; 1411 pamphlets; 1640 microforms; 11,914 prints; 355 slides; 34 recordings; 3715 acting editions and scripts. **Subscriptions:** 91 journals and other serials; 15 newspapers. **Services:** Copying; department open to the public for reference use only. **Computerized Information Services:** Internal database. **Special Catalogs:** Card files on printers, book designers, typography, paper, book illustration.

★16782★
UNIVERSITY OF PITTSBURGH - THEODORE M. FINNEY MUSIC LIBRARY (Mus)
Music Bldg. Phone: (412)624-4130
Pittsburgh, PA 15260 Norris L. Stephens, Libn.
Founded: 1966. **Staff:** Prof 1; Other 3. **Subjects:** Music. **Special Collections:** Pre-1800 music and music literature (1000 items); Fidelis Zitterbart (1000 manuscripts); Adolph Foerster (290 manuscripts and printed music); Ethelbert Nevin (100 manuscripts and printed music); William Steinberg (800 items). **Holdings:** 37,104 books; 1500 bound periodical volumes; 1094 microforms; 19,300 pieces of sheet music; 100 photographs and prints; 14,717 sound recordings; 754 slides; 6 linear feet of manuscripts and archives. **Subscriptions:** 172 journals and other serials. **Services:** Interlibrary loan; copying; library open to the public. **Automated Operations:** Computerized cataloging, acquisitions, and serials. **Computerized Information Services:** DIALOG Information Services, BRS Information Technologies, OCLC. Performs searches on fee basis. **Networks/Consortia:** Member of Pittsburgh Regional Library Center (PRLC).

★16783★
UNIVERSITY OF PITTSBURGH - UNIVERSITY CENTER FOR INSTRUCTIONAL RESOURCES (Aud-Vis)
G-20 Hillman Library Phone: (412)648-7220
Pittsburgh, PA 15260 Dr. J. Fred Gage, Dir.
Founded: 1968. **Staff:** Prof 18; Other 17. **Subjects:** Education, psychology, anthropology, history, life sciences, sociology, women's studies, black studies, film studies, administration of justice, labor history. **Special Collections:** Faces of Change (25 film series produced by American Universities' field staff; anthropological films on five countries); Maurice Falk Medical Fund (20 films); Ascent of Man series; Civilisation series; Europe the Mighty Continent series; World at War series; growing collections of films on aging, labor history, and film studies. **Holdings:** 1338 16mm films; reference books on nonprint media; 79 games; 39 kits; 20 transparency sets; 58 slide sets; 147 filmstrips; 423 video recordings; 870 audio recordings; 27 manipulatives. **Subscriptions:** 30 journals and other serials. **Services:** Free loan for university classroom use; video duplication; center open to the public with restrictions. **Automated Operations:** Computerized cataloging. **Computerized Information Services:** OCLC. **Networks/Consortia:** Member of Consortium of University Film Centers (CUFC). **Special Catalogs:** University of Pittsburgh Film Catalog, 1978, supplement, 1979, 1981, 1982, 1984; various mediagraphies; video recording catalog, January 1985. **Staff:** Scott Koziol, Non-Print Cat..

★16784★
UNIVERSITY OF PITTSBURGH - WESTERN PSYCHIATRIC INSTITUTE AND CLINIC - LIBRARY (Med)
3811 O'Hara St. Phone: (412)624-2378
Pittsburgh, PA 15213 Barbara A. Epstein, Dir.
Founded: 1942. **Staff:** Prof 4; Other 6. **Subjects:** Psychiatry, behavioral science, neurology, marriage and family, clinical psychology, child development. **Special Collections:** Rare books in the History of Psychiatry (2300 volumes housed in Falk Library of the Health Professions, University of Pittsburgh). **Holdings:** 52,956 volumes; 2400 audio- and videotapes; 8 VF drawers of ephemera. **Subscriptions:** 519 journals and other serials. **Services:** Interlibrary loan; copying; SDI; library open to the public for reference use only; borrowers must be affiliated with a university hospital or mental health center. **Automated Operations:** Computerized cataloging. **Computerized Information Services:** MEDLINE, DIALOG Information Services, BRS Information Technologies. Performs searches on fee basis. Contact Person: Ester Saghafi, Ref. & Cat.Libn.. **Networks/Consortia:** Member of Health Sciences Library Consortium, Pittsburgh Regional Library Center (PRLC), Greater Northeastern Regional Medical Library Program. **Publications:** Booklist of New Books Cataloged - general distribution; Current Awareness Series - for internal distribution only. **Special Catalogs:** Media Catalog. **Staff:** Patricia Reavis, AV & Ref.Libn.; Meliza Jackson, Patients' Libn..

★16785★
UNIVERSITY OF PORTLAND - WILSON W. CLARK MEMORIAL LIBRARY - SPECIAL COLLECTIONS (Hist, Agri)
5000 N. Willamette Blvd.
Box 03017 Phone: (503)283-7111
Portland, OR 97203 Rev. Joseph P. Browne, C.S.C., Dir.
Founded: 1901. **Staff:** Prof 6; Other 7. **Subjects:** Abraham Lincoln, forestry. **Special Collections:** Salvador J. Macias Collection of Spanish Literature (750 volumes); David W. Hazen Collection in American History (4000 volumes); Daniel Buckley Forestry Collection (500 volumes). **Holdings:** 1500 volumes; 5000 government documents. **Services:** Interlibrary loan; copying; collections open to the public for reference use only. **Automated Operations:** Computerized cataloging, acquisitions, and serials. **Computerized Information Services:** DIALOG Information Services, BRS Information Technologies, OCLC; OnTyme Electronic Message Network Service (electronic mail service). **Publications:** Philobiblon, monthly - for internal distribution only.

★16786★
UNIVERSITY OF PRINCE EDWARD ISLAND - ROBERTSON LIBRARY (Area-Ethnic)
Charlottetown, PE, Canada C1A 4P3 Phone: (902)566-0460
C.M. Crockett, Chf.Libn.
Founded: 1975. **Staff:** Prof 9; Other 17. **Special Collections:** Prince Edward Island collection. **Holdings:** 7400 books; 104 bound periodical volumes; clippings; pamphlets; government documents; microforms. **Subscriptions:** 18 journals and other serials; 6 newspapers. **Services:** Library open to the public with restrictions. **Staff:** F.L. Pigot, Ref.Libn..

★16787★
UNIVERSITY PUBLICATIONS OF AMERICA, INC. - LIBRARY (Publ)
44 N. Market St. Phone: (301)694-0100
Frederick, MD 21701 Robert E. Lester, Media Spec./Res.Coord.
Staff: 1. **Subjects:** History - U.S. diplomatic, social, economic, political, Anglo-American, science, legal. **Holdings:** 450 books; 50,000 reels of microfilm. **Services:** Library not open to the public.

★16788★
UNIVERSITY OF PUERTO RICO - AGRICULTURAL EXPERIMENT STATION - LIBRARY (Agri, Biol Sci)
Box 25000 Phone: (809)763-3939
Rio Piedras, PR 00928 Joan P. Hayes, Libn.
Founded: 1915. **Staff:** Prof 1; Other 2. **Subjects:** Agriculture, biology, botany, animal production, chemistry, food technology, rum research. **Holdings:** 33,124 volumes; 273,413 pamphlets, technical reports, annual reports. **Subscriptions:** 895 journals and other serials. **Services:** Interlibrary loan; copying; library open to the public for reference use only. **Publications:** Book List, irregular; Monthly Library List - to staff members and government libraries. **Special Indexes:** Index to the Journal of Agriculture of the University of Puerto Rico (book and card); indexes to Revista de Agricultura de Puerto Rico and Caribbean Journal of Science (both on cards).

★16789★
UNIVERSITY OF PUERTO RICO - COLLEGE OF EDUCATION - SELLES SOLA MEMORIAL COLLECTION (Educ)
Rio Piedras, PR 00931 Phone: (809)764-0000
Lina Bauza, Hd.Libn.
Staff: Prof 2; Other 1. **Subjects:** Education, psychology, educational philosophy. **Special Collections:** Public school textbook collection, 1900 to present (2488 textbooks). **Holdings:** 17,229 books; 1677 bound periodical volumes; 500 pamphlets; 28 VF drawers of clippings; 200 unbound reports; 425 pictures. **Subscriptions:** 45 journals and other serials. **Services:** Interlibrary loan; copying; collection open to the public for reference use only. **Special Indexes:** Indexes to local educational periodicals. **Remarks:** The Selles Sola documents are housed in the university's General Library. **Staff:** Rafael Melendez, Libn..

★16790★
UNIVERSITY OF PUERTO RICO - GENERAL LIBRARY - ZENOBIA Y JUAN RAMON JIMENEZ COLLECTION (Hum, Soc Sci)
Box 22933 - UPR Sta. Phone: (809)764-0000
Rio Piedras, PR 00931 Raquel Sarraga, Libn.
Founded: 1955. **Staff:** Prof 1; Other 2. **Subjects:** Spanish literature, modernism. **Special Collections:** Zenobia y Juan Ramon Jimenez Collection (89,788 items); Caribbean collection (115,668 items); documents depository for the U.S. Government, United Nations, Organization of

American States, AEC; Army map serial collection (1,479,540 items); Room for the Blind (872 items). **Services:** Interlibrary loan; copying; library open to the public with restrictions. **Automated Operations:** Computerized cataloging, acquisitions, serials, and circulation. **Computerized Information Services:** Internal database. **Publications:** Anuario Bibliografico Puertorriqueno, annual. **Special Catalogs:** Union Catalog of University Libraries of Puerto Rico. **Special Indexes:** Index of Spanish poetry (card). **Remarks:** Houses Caribbean Regional Library.

★16791★
UNIVERSITY OF PUERTO RICO - GRADUATE SCHOOL OF PLANNING - LIBRARY (Plan)
UPR Sta., Box BE Phone: (809)764-0000
Rio Piedras, PR 00931 Martha Torres, Libn.
Founded: 1965. **Staff:** Prof 1; Other 1. **Subjects:** Planning - general, urban, regional, agricultural, educational, environmental; economics; sociology. **Holdings:** 13,935 books; 1931 bound periodical volumes; 5148 volumes of Puerto Rican and Latin American Government publications; 11,061 pamphlets; 474 maps; 113 microfiche; 5 reels of microfilm; 456 student monographs. **Subscriptions:** 261 journals and other serials. **Services:** Interlibrary loan; copying; library open to the public for reference use only on request, circulation with special permit. **Special Indexes:** Author, title, subject index to PLERUS (journal published by the school), volume 1 to present; index to Revista Interamericana de Planificacion, volume 1 to present; author and title index to planning periodicals in Spanish (all on cards).

★16792★
UNIVERSITY OF PUERTO RICO - HISTORICAL RESEARCH CENTER (Hist)
University Sta., Box 22802 Phone: (809)764-0000
Rio Piedras, PR 00931 Maria de los Angeles Castro, Dir.
Staff: Prof 5; Other 2. **Subjects:** Puerto Rican, Caribbean, Latin America. **Special Collections:** Personal documents. **Holdings:** 3837 books; 4862 bound periodical volumes; 76 theses; 7122 reprints; 6472 translations; 14,210 reels of microfilm; 11,563 microfiche. **Services:** Center open to the public. **Publications:** Boletin del Centro de Investigaciones Historicas, annual - by subscription; Los primeros pasos: Una bibliografia para empezara investigar la historia de Puerto Rico (book). **Special Indexes:** Guia descriptiva de los fondos existentes en el Centro de Investigaciones Historicas (pamphlet). **Also Known As:** Centro de Investigaciones Historicas (CIH). **Staff:** Maria Dolores Luque de Sanchez, Assoc.Dir..

★16793★
UNIVERSITY OF PUERTO RICO - HUMACAO UNIVERSITY COLLEGE - LIBRARY (Sci-Engr, Hum)
Bo. Tejas, CUH-Sta. Phone: (809)852-2525
Humacao, PR 00661 Ileana D. Martinez, Dir.
Founded: 1962. **Staff:** Prof 8; Other 18. **Subjects:** Natural sciences, applied sciences, electronics, social sciences, social welfare, special education. **Special Collections:** Puerto Rican collection (4227 books; 121 periodicals). **Holdings:** 72,854 volumes; 3257 bound periodical volumes; 6108 unbound periodicals; 752 phonograph records; 1495 reels of microfilm; 68 cassettes; 4375 documents; 128 maps. **Subscriptions:** 672 journals and other serials; 21 newspapers. **Services:** Interlibrary loan; copying; library open to the public. **Publications:** List of New Acquisitions; Desde la Biblioteca, irregular; Mundo Bibliografico, quarterly. **Staff:** Laura C. Garcia, Pub.Serv.Coord.; Ramon Budet, Ref.Libn.; Carlos Perez, CPR Libn.; Violeta Guzman, Per.Libn.; Angela M. Ruiz de Nieves, Cat..

★16794★
UNIVERSITY OF PUERTO RICO - LAW LIBRARY (Law)
Box L Phone: (809)764-9777
San Juan, PR 00931 Carmelo Delgado Cintron, Law Libn.
Founded: 1903. **Staff:** Prof 10; Other 32. **Subjects:** Law - common, civil, international. **Special Collections:** Rare Puerto Rican Law Books Collection. **Holdings:** 130,789 books; bound periodical volumes. **Subscriptions:** 3508 journals and other serials; 8 newspapers. **Services:** Interlibrary loan; copying; library open to the public. **Computerized Information Services:** LEXIS. **Publications:** Boletin Bibliografico, irregular - free upon request. **Staff:** Altagracia Miranda, Dp.Libn.; Marta E. Perez, Hd., Doc.Dept.; Enriqueta Marcano, Hd.Cat.; Idalia Chinea, Cat.; Josefina Bulerin, Hd., Circ. & Reserve; Carmen M. Melendez, Circ.; Miguel A. Rivera, Circ.; Orietta Ayala, Hd., Acq.Dept.; Esther Villarino, Cat..

★16795★
UNIVERSITY OF PUERTO RICO - LIBRARY AND INFORMATION SCIENCE LIBRARY (Info Sci)
Box 21906 Phone: (809)764-0000
San Juan, PR 00931 Haydee Munoz-Soln, Hd.Libn.
Staff: Prof 1; Other 3. **Subjects:** Libraries - school, public, special, university; library administration; history of books and libraries; cataloging and classification; juvenile literature; information science. **Special Collections:** Juvenile collection. **Holdings:** 23,886 books; 4459 bound periodical volumes; 1141 other cataloged items; 1547 AV programs. **Subscriptions:** 596 journals and other serials. **Services:** Interlibrary loan; copying; library open to the public. **Automated Operations:** Computerized acquisitions. **Computerized Information Services:** DIALOG Information Services. **Publications:** Bibliografia Bibliotecologia Puertorriquena. **Special Indexes:** Boletin de la UNESCO para las Bibliotecas (book); SALALM Working Papers (card); Indice de Articulos de Periodicos de Bibliotecologia Puertorriquena (book).

★16796★
UNIVERSITY OF PUERTO RICO - MAYAGUEZ CAMPUS LIBRARY - MARINE SCIENCES COLLECTION (Biol Sci)
Mayaguez, PR 00709 Phone: (809)834-4040
Sheila Dunstan, Hd.
Founded: 1954. **Staff:** Prof 2; Other 1. **Subjects:** Marine biology; marine invertebrates; fish biology; marine botany; aquaculture; oceanography - chemical, physical, geological, biological. **Special Collections:** Reprints on Marine Sciences (11,373). **Holdings:** 1341 books; 3932 bound and unbound periodicals; 7042 documents; 170 theses; 17 reels of microfilm; 361 microfiche; 2 tapes. **Subscriptions:** 208 journals and other serials. **Services:** Interlibrary loan; copying; collection open to the public for reference use only on request. **Computerized Information Services:** OCLC, DIALOG Information Services. Performs searches on fee basis. Contact Person: Ada C. Ramgolam or Jeanette Valentin, 834-4040, ext. 2209. **Publications:** Department of Marine Sciences Contributions, annual - on exchange. **Staff:** Tomasita Martinez de Hernandez, Asst.Libn..

★16797★
UNIVERSITY OF PUERTO RICO - MAYAGUEZ CAMPUS LIBRARY - SPECIAL COLLECTIONS (Sci-Engr, Hum)
Main Library Phone: (809)834-4040
Mayaguez, PR 00708 Grace Quinones-Seda, Act.Lib.Dir.
Founded: 1911. **Special Collections:** Theses (1250) and books written by professors and alumni; Nuclear Science Collection; Puerto Rican Collection (9500 items); Center for Energy and Environmental Research (4980 items); Music (6844 phonograph records). **Services:** Interlibrary loan; copying; SDI; collections open to the public for external use of material with special permission. **Automated Operations:** Computerized cataloging. **Computerized Information Services:** DIALOG Information Services, OCLC. Performs searches on fee basis. Contact Person: Ada C. Ramgolam. **Networks/Consortia:** Member of SOLINET. **Publications:** Documents holdings, monthly; list of theses, semiannual. **Staff:** Isaura Gonzalez, Hd., Puerto Rican Coll.; Eneida M. Vicente, Hd., Mus.Coll.; Sandra Alameda, Hd., Ctr. for Energy and Environ.Res..

★16798★
UNIVERSITY OF PUERTO RICO - MEDICAL SCIENCES CAMPUS - LIBRARY (Med)
Box 5067 Phone: (809)758-2525
San Juan, PR 00936 Ana Isabel Moscoso, Dir.
Founded: 1950. **Staff:** Prof 7; Other 23. **Subjects:** Medicine, dentistry, public health, pharmacy, allied health sciences, nursing. **Special Collections:** History of Health Sciences; Puerto Rican Medical Collection; Dr. Bailey K. Ashford Collection. **Holdings:** 29,985 books; 70,720 bound periodical volumes; 5000 clippings; 700 reprints; 1000 pamphlets. **Subscriptions:** 1407 journals and other serials. **Services:** Interlibrary loan; copying; library open to the public with restrictions. **Computerized Information Services:** MEDLINE. Performs searches on fee basis. Contact Person: Margarita Jiminez, Ref.Libn.. **Networks/Consortia:** Member of Greater Northeastern Regional Medical Library Program. **Special Indexes:** Author index to Boletin de la Asociacion Medica de Puerto Rico (card); Saludhos; Revista de Educadores en Salud; Homines; Boletin del Colegio de Profesionales de la Enfermeria; Revista de Adminstracion Publica; Revista de Psiquiatria y Salud Mental; Superacion; Informe Epidemiologico. **Staff:** Elsa M. Lopez, Tech.Serv.Libn.; Leticia Perez, Ser.Libn.; Nilca I. Parrilla, AV Libn..

★16799★
UNIVERSITY OF PUERTO RICO - PUBLIC ADMINISTRATION LIBRARY (Bus-Fin, Soc Sci)
UPR Sta., Box C Phone: (809)764-0000
Rio Piedras, PR 00931 Martha Torres-Irizarry, Libn.
Founded: 1949. **Staff:** Prof 1; Other 4. **Subjects:** Public administration, government personnel administration, organization and management, budgeting, public relations, administrative law. **Holdings:** 13,789 books; 1596 bound periodical volumes; 1000 Puerto Rican Government documents; 4190 readings. **Subscriptions:** 84 journals and other serials. **Services:** Interlibrary loan; copying; library open to the public for reference use only. **Automated Operations:** Computerized public access catalog. **Computerized Information Services:** DIALOG Information Services. **Special Indexes:** Index to Revista de Administracion Publica UPF, 1974 to present (card).

★16800★
UNIVERSITY OF PUERTO RICO - PUERTO RICAN COLLECTION (Area-Ethnic)
UPR Sta., Box C Phone: (809)764-0000
Rio Piedras, PR 00931 Ms. Noris J. Vazquez, Hd.Libn.
Founded: 1940. **Staff:** Prof 3; Other 8. **Subjects:** Puerto Rican humanities and social sciences. **Special Collections:** Rare books (19th century books printed in or dealing with Puerto Rico); 19th century newspapers; Puerto Rican posters; manuscripts; photographs. **Holdings:** 87,891 books; 51,857 bound periodical volumes; 77,507 government documents and pamphlets; 5831 reels of microfilm; 468 maps; 725 posters; 154 tapes; vertical files. **Services:** Interlibrary loan; copying; bibliographic instruction; collection open to the public for reference use only. **Automated Operations:** Computerized acquisitions and serials. **Computerized Information Services:** DIALOG Information Services. Performs searches on fee basis. Contact Person: Maria Otero. **Special Indexes:** Indexes to Puerto Rican short stories, illustrations, El Mundo Newspaper (card and online), book reviews, biographies, and magazines. **Staff:** Maria E. Ordonez; Elisa Vazquez; Maria P. Soto.

★16801★
UNIVERSITY OF PUERTO RICO - SCIENCE LIBRARY (Sci-Engr, Biol Sci)
Box 22446 Phone: (809)764-0000
Rio Piedras, PR 00931 Giovanna Del Pilar-Barber, Hd.Libn.
Founded: 1954. **Staff:** Prof 2; Other 6. **Subjects:** Chemistry, biology, ecology, physics, mathematics, biochemistry. **Special Collections:** Environmental Sciences (760 volumes); Center for Resources in Science and Engineering Applied Sciences (598 volumes). **Holdings:** 39,321 books; 34,979 bound periodical volumes; 2 videotapes; 207 films; 155 filmstrips; 254 pamphlets; 1553 reels of microfilm; 28,779 microfiche and microcards; 3992 astronomical photographs; 21,554 other cataloged items. **Subscriptions:** 1401 journals and other serials. **Services:** Interlibrary loan; copying; library open to the public for reference use only. **Automated Operations:** Computerized cataloging and acquisitions. **Computerized Information Services:** DIALOG Information Services. Performs searches on fee basis. Contact Person: Daniel Ortiz-Zapata, Libn., 764-0000, ext. 2359. **Publications:** Biblionotas Cientificas, monthly; List of Journals; List of Serials, both annual - all free upon request. **Special Catalogs:** Card catalog of Environmental Management Program. **Special Indexes:** Index to the Caribbean Journal of Science (card).

★16802★
UNIVERSITY OF PUGET SOUND - SCHOOL OF LAW - LAW LIBRARY (Law)
Norton Clapp Law Center
950 Broadway Plaza Phone: (206)591-2970
Tacoma, WA 98402-4470 Anita M. Steele, Dir.
Staff: Prof 7; Other 9. **Subjects:** Law. **Holdings:** 110,393 books; 13,503 bound periodical volumes; 107,054 volumes in microform. **Subscriptions:** 3275 journals and other serials; 10 newspapers. **Services:** Interlibrary loan; copying; library open to the public with limited circulation. **Automated Operations:** Computerized cataloging, acquisitions, and serials. **Computerized Information Services:** InfoTrac, RLIN, LEXIS, WESTLAW, DIALOG Information Services, BRS Information Technologies, WILSONLINE; DIALMAIL, OnTyme Electronic Message Network Service (electronic mail services). **Networks/Consortia:** Member of Western Library Network (WLN), Northwest Consortium of Law Libraries. **Publications:** UPS Law Library Newsletter; Student Library Handbook. **Staff:** Faye Jones, Asst.Law Libn.; Betty Warner, Acq. & Fin.Rec.; Suzanne Harvey, Bibliog.Sys.Libn. (Cat.); Bob Menanteaux, Info.Serv.Libn. (Ref.); Roger Becker, Sys. Strategist Law Libn.; Kelly Kunsch, Ref.Libn..

★16803★
UNIVERSITY OF REGINA - BILINGUAL CENTRE - LIBRARY (Hum)
College West No. 218
Regina, SK, Canada S4S 0A2 Phone: (306)584-4177
Subjects: Bilingualism, translation. **Holdings:** 2579 books. **Subscriptions:** 10 journals and other serials; 10 newspapers. **Services:** Library open to the public.

★16804★
UNIVERSITY OF REGINA - CANADIAN PLAINS RESEARCH CENTER INFORMATION SYSTEM
Regina, SK, Canada S4S 0A2
Defunct

★16805★
UNIVERSITY OF REGINA - EDUCATION BRANCH LIBRARY (Educ)
Regina, SK, Canada S4S 0A2 Phone: (306)584-4642
Del Affleck, Hd.
Staff: Prof 4; Other 6. **Subjects:** Education, children's literature. **Holdings:** 127,500 books; 15,500 bound periodical volumes; 380,700 ERIC and CANEDEX microfiche; 23,200 AV programs; 21,600 study prints; 20,700 VF items; 34,700 games and kits. **Subscriptions:** 757 journals and other serials. **Services:** Interlibrary loan; copying; library open to the public with restrictions. **Automated Operations:** Computerized cataloging, acquisitions, and serials. **Staff:** Marianne Thauberger, Libn.; Sue Allen, Libn.; Gary Lamoureux, Libn..

★16806★
UNIVERSITY OF REGINA - MAP LIBRARY (Geog-Map)
Regina, SK, Canada S4S 0A2 Phone: (306)584-4401
Founded: 1968. **Staff:** 2. **Subjects:** Cartography. **Special Collections:** Historical urban plans and aerial photographs (15,000). **Holdings:** 5000 volumes; 65,000 maps; 15,000 aerial photographs; 800 microforms; 15 globes. **Subscriptions:** 28 journals and other serials. **Services:** Copying; library open to the public with restrictions. **Publications:** List of special acquisitions; list of atlases; list of wall maps; list of class-sets; Map Library Resources; Map Library Brochure.

★16807★
UNIVERSITY RESEARCH CORPORATION - LIBRARY (Soc Sci)
5530 Wisconsin Ave. Phone: (301)654-8338
Chevy Chase, MD 20815 Kathleen A. Skapik, Dir., Adm.Serv.
Subjects: International health, criminal justice, housing rehabilitation, management and evaluation. **Special Collections:** Alcohol and drug abuse (300 volumes and VF materials). **Holdings:** 3000 books; 3500 other cataloged items; 30 VF drawers. **Subscriptions:** 25 journals and other serials; 20 newspapers. **Services:** Interlibrary loan; library not open to the public. **Computerized Information Services:** DIALOG Information Services, MEDLARS.

★16808★
UNIVERSITY OF RHODE ISLAND - ART DEPARTMENT - SLIDE LIBRARY (Art)
Fine Arts Center Phone: (401)792-2771
Kingston, RI 02881 Linda Mugica, Cur.
Subjects: Arts - fine, graphic, applied; architecture; photography. **Holdings:** 65,000 slides.

★16809★
UNIVERSITY OF RHODE ISLAND - INTERNATIONAL CENTER FOR MARINE RESOURCE DEVELOPMENT - LIBRARY (Sci-Engr, Biol Sci)
Main Library Phone: (401)792-2938
Kingston, RI 02881 Mary Jane Beardsley, Libn.
Founded: 1973. **Staff:** Prof 2; Other 1. **Subjects:** Fisheries, aquaculture, coastal zone management in developing countries. **Holdings:** 13,000 books and documents. **Subscriptions:** 200 journals and other serials. **Services:** Interlibrary loan; copying (limited); library open to the public. **Computerized Information Services:** DIALOG Information Services, BRS Information Technologies. **Publications:** Titles on artisanal fisheries; list of other publications - available on request.

★16810★
UNIVERSITY OF RHODE ISLAND - RHODE ISLAND ORAL HISTORY PROJECT (Hist)
Library - Special Collections Phone: (401)792-2594
Kingston, RI 02881 David C. Maslyn, Hd., Spec.Coll.
Founded: 1972. **Subjects:** Millworkers of Rhode Island and their social milieu, 1900 to present; Narragansett Indians; university history; local Franco-American community; state jewelry industry; Rhode Island's Islands (Block, Prudence, Conanicut); Galilee fisherman; immigrants; women's suffrage; town government (Yankee ingenuity). **Holdings:** 311 tapes of interviews; typescripts of some taped interviews; 70 tapes and transcripts of interviews on 1938 hurricane. **Services:** Project open to the public.

★16811★
UNIVERSITY OF RHODE ISLAND - SPECIAL COLLECTIONS (Rare Book)
Library Phone: (401)792-2594
Kingston, RI 02881 David C. Maslyn, Hd.
Founded: 1966. **Staff:** Prof 1; Other 1. **Special Collections:** Rare books (6200 volumes); Rhode Island Collection (3088 volumes); Whitman (289 volumes); Pound (474 volumes); Millay (163 volumes); Robinson (150 volumes); herbals; fine press books; printing presses, 1830-1840; working presses - Albion, Adams, Washington. **Holdings:** 9585 volumes; theses; 1729 linear feet of university archives; 2669 linear feet of personal papers; 12,425 maps; 16 VF drawers of ephemera. **Services:** Copying; collections open to the public with restrictions. **Computerized Information Services:** OCLC. **Networks/Consortia:** Member of Rhode Island Interrelated Library Network, NELINET, Consortium of Rhode Island Academic and Research Libraries, Inc. (CRIARL). **Publications:** Internal finding aids; New Leaves Press - Library Keepsakes.

★16812★
UNIVERSITY OF RHODE ISLAND, NARRAGANSETT BAY - PELL MARINE SCIENCE LIBRARY (Biol Sci, Sci-Engr)
Narragansett, RI 02882 Phone: (401)792-6161
Janice F. Sieburth, Hd.
Founded: 1959. **Staff:** Prof 2; Other 3. **Subjects:** Oceanography, marine biology and technology, fisheries. **Special Collections:** Marine and polar expeditionary reports (123 shelf feet); Paul S. Galtsoff Reprint Collection on the American Oyster (230 pamphlet boxes). **Holdings:** 8537 books; 14,075 bound periodical volumes; 1342 sheets of U.S. nautical charts; 16,000 reprints of scientific papers. **Subscriptions:** 970 journals and other serials. **Services:** Interlibrary loan; copying; library open to the public. **Computerized Information Services:** DIALOG Information Services, OCLC. Performs searches on fee basis. **Publications:** Graduate School of Oceanography, University of Rhode Island, Collected Reprints, annual - by exchange. **Staff:** Judith B. Barnett, Asst.Libn..

★16813★
UNIVERSITY OF RICHMOND - E. CLAIBORNE ROBINS SCHOOL OF BUSINESS - BUSINESS INFORMATION CENTER (Bus-Fin)
Boatwright Library Phone: (804)289-8666
Richmond, VA 23173 Littleton M. Maxwell, Dir.
Staff: Prof 1; Other 2. **Subjects:** Business administration, accounting, economics, finance, management, marketing. **Holdings:** 30,000 books; 5600 bound periodical volumes; 300 cassettes; 20 file cabinets of annual reports; 6 file cabinets of vertical files. **Subscriptions:** 1020 journals and other serials; 18 newspapers. **Services:** Interlibrary loan; copying; SDI; library open to the public. **Automated Operations:** Computerized cataloging. **Computerized Information Services:** DIALOG Information Services, Pergamon ORBIT InfoLine, Inc., BRS Information Technologies, OCLC, InfoTrac, Standard & Poor's Corporation, Disclosure Information Group, Dun & Bradstreet Corporation, Dow Jones News/Retrieval. Performs searches on fee basis. **Networks/Consortia:** Member of SOLINET, Richmond Area Libraries Cooperative. **Publications:** E. Claiborne Robins School of Business Information Center Briefs. **Special Indexes:** Business and Economic update (card); Marketing Proceedings (online).

★16814★
UNIVERSITY OF RICHMOND - MUSIC LIBRARY (Mus)
Richmond, VA 23173 Phone: (804)289-8286
Bonlyn G. Hall, Mus.Libn.
Founded: 1955. **Staff:** Prof 1; Other 7. **Subjects:** Music. **Holdings:** 370 books; 8110 phonograph records; 7530 scores. **Subscriptions:** 50 journals and other serials. **Services:** Interlibrary loan; copying; library open to the public. **Automated Operations:** Computerized cataloging.

★16815★
UNIVERSITY OF RICHMOND - WILLIAM T. MUSE MEMORIAL LAW LIBRARY (Law)
Richmond, VA 23173 Phone: (804)289-8225
Susan B. English, Law Libn.
Staff: Prof 6; Other 7. **Subjects:** Law. **Special Collections:** Environmental law. **Holdings:** 98,151 books; 38,425 volumes in microform. **Subscriptions:** 2240 journals and other serials; 10 newspapers. **Services:** Interlibrary loan; library open to the public for reference use only. **Automated Operations:** Computerized cataloging and serials. **Computerized Information Services:** LEXIS, OCLC, WESTLAW, DIALOG Information Services, NEXIS, VU/TEXT Information Services. **Networks/Consortia:** Member of SOLINET. **Publications:** The Museletter (newsletter), quarterly; Selected List of Recent Acquisitions, quarterly - both for internal distribution only. **Staff:** Joyce Manna Janto, Acq.Libn.; Sally H. Wambold, Cat.Libn.; Anne H. Cresap, Cat.Libn.; Steven D. Hinckley, Assoc. Law Libn.; Lucinda D. Harrison, Ref.Libn..

★16816★
UNIVERSITY OF RICHMOND/VIRGINIA INSTITUTE - UR/VISR SCIENCE LIBRARY (Biol Sci, Sci-Engr)
Richmond, VA 23173 Phone: (804)289-8261
Melanie M. Hillner, Dir.
Staff: Prof 1; Other 2. **Subjects:** Chemistry, biology, physics, mathematics. **Holdings:** 22,258 books; 28,590 bound periodical volumes. **Subscriptions:** 553 journals and other serials. **Services:** Interlibrary loan; copying; SDI; library open to the public. **Computerized Information Services:** BRS Information Technologies, DIALOG Information Services. Performs searches on fee basis. **Networks/Consortia:** Member of Richmond Area Libraries Cooperative.

★16817★
UNIVERSITY OF ROCHESTER - ASIA LIBRARY (Area-Ethnic)
Rush Rhees Library
River Campus Phone: (716)275-4489
Rochester, NY 14627 Datta S. Kharbas, Libn.
Staff: Prof 1; Other 1. **Subjects:** Chinese, Japanese, and Indian history and philosophy; Japanese, Chinese, Sanskrit, Hindi, and Marathi language and literature. **Special Collections:** Asahi Shinbum on microfilm; Times of India, 1861-1889 (Indian gazetteers on microfilm); India census, 1881-1971. **Holdings:** 97,000 books; 12,000 bound periodical volumes. **Subscriptions:** 420 journals and other serials; 12 newspapers. **Services:** Interlibrary loan; copying; library open to the public on written request. **Computerized Information Services:** DIALOG Information Services, BRS Information Technologies. **Special Catalogs:** Catalog of the East Asia Collection.

★16818★
UNIVERSITY OF ROCHESTER - CARLSON LIBRARY (Biol Sci, Sci-Engr)
Computer Studies Bldg.
River Campus Phone: (716)275-4465
Rochester, NY 14627 Arleen Somerville, Libn.
Founded: 1987. **Staff:** Prof 3; Other 5. **Subjects:** Chemistry, biology, mathematics, statistics, computer science, engineering. **Holdings:** 64,000 books; 48,000 bound periodical volumes; 12,700 computer science technical reports; computer software. **Subscriptions:** 1600 journals and other serials. **Services:** Interlibrary loan; copying; library open to the public for reference use only. **Computerized Information Services:** DIALOG Information Services, Pergamon ORBIT InfoLine, Inc., BRS Information Technologies, STN International, OCLC, RLIN, WILSONLINE; internal database. **Remarks:** Includes the holdings of the Engineering Library.

★16819★
UNIVERSITY OF ROCHESTER - CHARLOTTE WHITNEY ALLEN LIBRARY (Art)
Memorial Art Gallery
500 University Ave. Phone: (716)473-7227
Rochester, NY 14607 Stephanie Frontz, Libn.
Staff: Prof 1; Other 1. **Subjects:** Art history, architecture, museology. **Holdings:** 17,000 books; 2000 bound periodical volumes; 2600 unbound museum bulletins and annual reports; 12,000 slides; 24 VF drawers of clippings, exhibition catalogs, pamphlets; gallery archives; Sotheby Parke-Bernet auction sales catalogs, 1952 to present; historical scrapbooks of Memorial Art Gallery. **Subscriptions:** 85 journals and other serials. **Services:** Interlibrary loan; copying; library open to the public.

★16820★
UNIVERSITY OF ROCHESTER - DEPARTMENT OF RARE BOOKS AND SPECIAL COLLECTIONS (Hist, Rare Book)
River Campus Phone: (716)275-4477
Rochester, NY 14627 Peter Dzwonkoski, Hd.
Founded: 1930. **Staff:** Prof 4; Other 4. **Subjects:** Rare books; literary and historical manuscripts; university archives; local history; Restoration and 19th century British theater and drama; history of law and political theory; 19th century American political history. **Special Collections:** Thomas E. Dewey papers; William Henry Seward papers; Thurlow Weed papers; Guzzetta Collection of Leonardo da Vinci; Ellwanger & Barry Horticultural Library; Upstate New York Historical Collection; Susan B. Anthony; Lewis Henry Morgan; Robert Southey; Arthur Wing Pinero; Henry James; John Masefield; Claude Bragdon; Berlove Collection of Christopher Morley; Ross Collection of John Ruskin (400 volumes); Victoriana; Markiewicz Collection of Children's Books; Frederick Exley archive; John Gardner archive; Thomas McGuane manuscripts; Jerre Mangione archive; John A. Williams archive; Hubbell Collection (books illustrated with mounted photographs); 19th and 20th century trade-bindings; Tauchnitz Editions; Roycroft Press; local imprints through 1860. **Holdings:** 75,000 volumes; 2.5 million manuscripts; 500,000 archival items; 8 VF drawers of ephemera. **Subscriptions:** 20 journals and other serials. **Services:** Copying; department open to qualified scholars. **Automated Operations:** Computerized cataloging. **Computerized Information Services:** OCLC, RLIN. **Publications:** Library Bulletin, annual - to friends and institutions. **Special Catalogs:** Exhibition catalogs, irregular. **Special Indexes:** Registers and letter writer/recipient index to manuscript collections. **Staff:** Karl S. Kabelac, Mss.Libn.; Mary Huth, Asst.Hd.; Evelyn Walker, Rare Bk.Libn..

★16821★
UNIVERSITY OF ROCHESTER - EASTMAN SCHOOL OF MUSIC - SIBLEY MUSIC LIBRARY (Mus)
26 Gibbs St. Phone: (716)275-3018
Rochester, NY 14604 Mary Wallace Davidson, Libn.
Founded: 1904. **Staff:** Prof 7; Other 12. **Subjects:** Music. **Special Collections:** Pougin Collection (books on music and theater); Krehbiel Collection (folk music); Gordon Collection (chamber music). **Holdings:** 375,000 volumes; 60,000 phonograph records; 1400 manuscripts, autograph letters; 85,000 pieces of early American sheet music; 22,000 items in the choral octavo collection; 750 volumes of clippings. **Subscriptions:** 525 journals and other serials. **Services:** Interlibrary loan; copying; library open to the public for reference use only. **Automated Operations:** Computerized cataloging and ILL. **Networks/Consortia:** Member of SUNY/OCLC Library Network, RLG. **Publications:** The Sibley Muse (newsletter), quarterly - free upon request. **Special Catalogs:** Catalog of Sound Recordings, 1977 (14 volumes). **Special Indexes:** Pre-1949 Periodical Index (card). **Staff:** Charles Lindahl, Ref.Libn.; Joan Swanekamp, Hd., Tech.Proc.; Dr. Iva Buff, Acq.Libn.; Dr. Louise Goldberg, Rare Bks.Libn.; Pamela Jones, Cat.; Ann McCollough, Cat.; Jane Nowakowski, Cat..

★16822★
UNIVERSITY OF ROCHESTER - ENGINEERING LIBRARY
Gavett Hall
Rochester, NY 14627
Defunct. Holdings absorbed by Carlson Library.

★16823★
UNIVERSITY OF ROCHESTER - FINE ARTS LIBRARY (Art)
Rush Rhees Library
River Campus Phone: (716)275-4476
Rochester, NY 14627 Stephanie Frontz, Libn.
Staff: Prof 1; Other 1. **Subjects:** Architecture, sculpture, painting, photography, graphic arts, decorative arts. **Holdings:** 37,500 books; 8500 bound periodical volumes; 3000 exhibition catalogs and pamphlets; 28 VF drawers of clippings and ephemera. **Subscriptions:** 220 journals and other serials. **Services:** Interlibrary loan; copying; library open to the public for reference use only. **Computerized Information Services:** OCLC, RLIN. **Networks/Consortia:** Member of Rochester Regional Library Council (RRLC), RLG.

★16824★
UNIVERSITY OF ROCHESTER - GEOLOGY/MAP LIBRARY (Geog-Map, Sci-Engr)
Rush Rhees Library
Rochester, NY 14627 Mary Strife, Libn.
Founded: 1960. **Staff:** Prof 1; Other 1. **Subjects:** Environment, geological sciences, paleontology, mineralogy, sedimentation, geochemistry, maps and atlases. **Holdings:** 18,000 books; 17,000 bound periodical volumes; U.S. Geological Survey microfiche; 90,000 maps. **Subscriptions:** 680 journals and other serials. **Services:** Interlibrary loan; copying; library open to the public for reference use only. **Automated Operations:** Computerized cataloging. **Computerized Information Services:** DIALOG Information Services, Pergamon ORBIT InfoLine, Inc., BRS Information Technologies, WILSONLINE, OCLC, RLIN.

★16825★
UNIVERSITY OF ROCHESTER - GOVERNMENT DOCUMENTS AND MICROTEXT CENTER (Info Sci)
Rush Rhees Library Phone: (716)274-4484
Rochester, NY 14627 Kathleen E. Wilkinson, Govt.Docs.Libn.
Staff: Prof 1; Other 4. **Subjects:** Documents - U.S. Congress, U.S. Bureau of the Census, New York State, women's studies, black studies, North American Indians, American and British literature. **Special Collections:** Goldsmiths'-Kress Collection (economic literature); slavery; papers of William Henry Seward and the National Association for the Advancement of Colored People (NAACP); early English books; American fiction; history of women; early British periodicals. **Holdings:** 380 books; 2800 shelves of unbound documents; 70 drawers of microfiche of documents; 1.9 million microforms. **Services:** Interlibrary loan; copying; center open to the public. **Computerized Information Services:** DIALOG Information Services, BRS Information Technologies.

★16826★
UNIVERSITY OF ROCHESTER - LABORATORY FOR LASER ENERGETICS - LIBRARY (Sci-Engr)
250 E. River Rd. Phone: (716)275-5768
Rochester, NY 14623 Mary Strife, Libn.
Founded: 1976. **Staff:** Prof 1. **Subjects:** Plasma physics, inertial fusion, high energy lasers, x-ray diffraction, optical materials and coatings. **Holdings:** 2000 books; 1000 bound periodical volumes; 25,000 DOE Contractor Reports. **Subscriptions:** 80 journals and other serials. **Services:** Interlibrary loan; copying; SDI; library open to the public by appointment. **Automated Operations:** Computerized cataloging. **Computerized Information Services:** DIALOG Information Services, Pergamon ORBIT InfoLine, Inc., BRS Information Technologies, Integrated Technical Information System (ITIS), NEXIS, WILSONLINE, STN International, OCLC, RLIN. **Networks/Consortia:** Member of RLG, Rochester Regional Library Council (RRLC), New York State Interlibrary Loan Network (NYSILL). **Publications:** New Books List; New Reports, both irregular.

★16827★
UNIVERSITY OF ROCHESTER - MANAGEMENT LIBRARY (Bus-Fin)
Rush Rhees Library
River Campus Phone: (716)275-4482
Rochester, NY 14627 Violanda Burns, Libn.
Founded: 1962. **Staff:** Prof 3; Other 2. **Subjects:** Management, accounting, economics, finance, marketing, operations research and management, quantitative business methods, computer and information science, behavioral science in industry. **Holdings:** Annual reports of 7000 companies in hardcopy and microform; 56 VF drawers of pamphlets on industry statistics and economic conditions; 3500 working papers; 153,900 microforms. **Services:** Interlibrary loan; library open to the public. **Automated Operations:** Computerized cataloging. **Computerized Information Services:** DIALOG Information Services, NEXIS, TEXTLINE, Dow Jones News/Retrieval, BRS Information Technologies, OCLC, RLIN, Pergamon ORBIT InfoLine, Inc., InfoTrac, WILSONLINE, CompuServe, Inc.; internal database. **Networks/Consortia:** Member of RLG. **Publications:** Bulletin and list of recent acquisitions, 10/year; Rochester Management Bibliographies, irregular. **Staff:** Janet Prentice, Libn.; Datta Kharbas, Libn..

★16828★
UNIVERSITY OF ROCHESTER - MICROCOMPUTER INFORMATION CENTER (Comp Sci)
Rush Rhees Library Phone: (716)275-8470
Rochester, NY 14627 Michael Robertson, Mgr.
Founded: 1985. **Staff:** Prof 2. **Subjects:** Microcomputers. **Holdings:** 250 books; 76 bound periodical volumes; 2000 software titles. **Subscriptions:** 122 journals and other serials. **Services:** Interlibrary loan; center not open to the public. **Computerized Information Services:** DIALOG Information Services, OCLC, RLIN, BRS Information Technologies; BITNET (electronic mail service). Performs searches on fee basis. **Publications:** PerCeptions; FindUR, both monthly - both for internal distribution only. **Special Indexes:** Index to software titles (computer printout). **Staff:** Phil Harriman, Lib.Microcomp.Serv..

★16829★
UNIVERSITY OF ROCHESTER - PHYSICS-OPTICS-ASTRONOMY LIBRARY (Sci-Engr)
374 Bausch & Lomb Bldg. Phone: (716)275-4469
Rochester, NY 14627 Julie Kreunen, Libn.
Founded: 1960. **Staff:** Prof 1; Other 1. **Subjects:** Astronomy and astrophysics; physics - condensed matter, biological, high energy/particle, nuclear; optics. **Special Collections:** Preprints in High Energy Physics (5000). **Holdings:** 12,500 books; 11,500 bound periodical volumes; 500 patents; 950 theses; preprints and reports. **Subscriptions:** 375 journals and other serials. **Services:** Interlibrary loan; copying; SDI; library open to the public. **Automated Operations:** Computerized public access catalog, cataloging, and circulation. **Computerized Information Services:** DIALOG Information Services, BRS Information Technologies, STN International, WILSONLINE, Standard Public Information Retrieval System (SPIRES); internal database. **Networks/Consortia:** Member of New York State Interlibrary Loan Network (NYSILL), RLG, Rochester Regional Library Council (RRLC). **Publications:** New Books List, quarterly.

★16830★
UNIVERSITY OF ROCHESTER - SCHOOL OF MEDICINE & DENTISTRY - EDWARD G. MINER LIBRARY (Med)
601 Elmwood Ave. Phone: (716)275-3364
Rochester, NY 14642 Lucretia McClure, Med.Libn.
Founded: 1923. **Staff:** Prof 9; Other 15. **Subjects:** Medicine, nursing, psychiatry, dental research. **Special Collections:** Edward W. Mulligan History of Medicine Collection; Edward G. Miner Yellow Fever Collection. **Holdings:** 200,000 volumes. **Subscriptions:** 3074 journals and other serials. **Services:** Interlibrary loan; copying. **Automated Operations:** Computerized cataloging. **Computerized Information Services:** DIALOG Information Services, BRS Information Technologies, OCLC, MEDLINE. **Networks/Consortia:** Member of Rochester Regional Library Council (RRLC), Greater Northeastern Regional Medical Library Program. **Publications:** Bulletin, monthly - to medical personnel and institutions. **Remarks:** Also serves the School of Nursing and Strong Memorial Hospital.

★16831★
UNIVERSITY OF ST. MARY OF THE LAKE - MUNDELEIN SEMINARY - FEEHAN MEMORIAL LIBRARY (Rel-Phil)
Mundelein, IL 60060 Phone: (312)566-6401
Gloria Sieben, Libn.
Founded: 1929. **Staff:** Prof 1; Other 2. **Subjects:** Ancient Christian literature, medieval theology, Catholic theology. **Special Collections:** Irish history, language, literature. **Holdings:** 140,000 books; 25,000 bound periodical volumes; 610 reels of microfilm; 401 microcards. **Subscriptions:** 450 journals and other serials; 5 newspapers. **Services:** Interlibrary loan; copying.

★16832★
UNIVERSITY OF SAN DIEGO - MARVIN & LILLIAN KRATTER LAW LIBRARY (Law)
Alcala Park Phone: (619)260-4541
San Diego, CA 92110 Nancy C. Carter, Dir.
Founded: 1954. **Staff:** Prof 8; Other 12. **Subjects:** Law. **Special Collections:** Selective government documents depository. **Holdings:** 240,000 volumes. **Subscriptions:** 1150 journals and other serials; 50 newspapers. **Services:** Interlibrary loan; copying; library open to the public. **Automated Operations:** Computerized cataloging. **Computerized Information Services:** LEXIS, WESTLAW, DIALOG Information Services, OCLC. **Staff:** Robert Giblin, Assoc. Law Libn.; Georgia Briscoe, Hd., Tech.Serv./Doc.; Mary Lynn Hyde, Govt.Doc.; Annette Felman, Ref.; Diane Garcia, Ref.; Elizabeth Carrol, Cat.; Kathy Whistler, Cat..

★16833★
UNIVERSITY OF SAN FRANCISCO - SCHOOL OF LAW LIBRARY (Law)
Kendrick Hall Phone: (415)666-6679
San Francisco, CA 94117-1080 Virginia Kelsh, Law Libn./Assoc.Prof.
Founded: 1912. **Staff:** Prof 5; Other 5. **Subjects:** Anglo-American law. **Holdings:** 102,791 volumes; 652 reels of microfilm; 590,511 microfiche; 364 audio cassettes. **Subscriptions:** 2096 journals and other serials; 10 newspapers. **Services:** Interlibrary loan; library open to the public with restrictions. **Automated Operations:** Computerized cataloging. **Computerized Information Services:** LEXIS, WESTLAW. **Networks/Consortia:** Member of CLASS. **Staff:** Eleanor Covalesky, Cat.Libn.; Jean Stefancic, Acq. & Ser.Libn.; Marian Shostrom, Pub.Serv.Libn.; Lee Ryan, Ref.Libn..

★16834★
UNIVERSITY OF SAN FRANCISCO - SPECIAL COLLECTIONS DEPARTMENT/DONOHUE RARE BOOK ROOM (Rare Book)
Richard A. Gleeson Library
2130 Fulton St. Phone: (415)666-6718
San Francisco, CA 94117 D. Steven Corey, Spec.Coll.Libn.
Staff: Prof 1. **Subjects:** 16th and 17th century English religious history; graphic arts; San Francisco area private press books; English and American literature of the 19th and 20th centuries. **Special Collections:** St. Thomas More and English Contemporaries; recusant literature; Robert Graves (first editions; translations; manuscripts; letters); Charles Carroll of Carrollton (books; letters; account books; ephemera); Robinson Jeffers (first editions; manuscripts; letters); Madeline Gleason Poetry Archive and Collection of San Francisco Poets; A.E. Housman (first editions); Laurence Housman (first editions and letters); 1890s collection, including Arthur Symons, Oscar Wilde, Norman Gale, George Moore, and William Watson (1 box of manuscripts); Max Beerbohm Collection; Norman and Charlotte Strouse Collection of Richard Le Gallienne (first editions; manuscripts; letters); collections of other authors, including Mary Webb, James Hanley, and Vincent Starrett; Mr. and Mrs. S. Gale Herrick Collection of the Gregynog Press; William P. Barlow, Jr. Collection of the Daniel Press; M. Wallace Friedman Collection of L. Frank Baum and Oziana; Norman and Charlotte Strouse Collections of: The Book Club of California, Allen Press, Victor Hammer, Hammer Creek Press, John Henry Nash, Officina Bodoni, and the Peregrine Press; Theodore M. and Frances B. Lilienthal Grabhorn Press Collection; R.S. Speck Collection of the Kennedy Press; Overbrook Press; Albert Sperisen Collection of Eric Gill (books; prints; woodblocks; drawings; letters; ephemera); The Colt Press, Toyon Press, Black Vine Press, and James McNeill Whistler; Chauncey D. Leake, Jr. Collection of Abattoir Press and Prairie Press; William Everson (books; letters; ephemera); Tamalpais Press of Roger Levenson (complete archive); Scholartis Press; Poltroon Press; Plantin Press; Cranium Press (complete archive); Five Trees Press (archive); Black Stone Press (complete collection); Two Windows Press (complete collection); John De Poh; Turkey Press; Mallette Dean Archive; James E. Beard of St. Helena Archive; Grace Hoper Press Archive; Clark Pamphlet File (political, social, and military literature, 1914-1939); Van Houten Collection (Spanish manuscripts, correspondence of Jose de Piedade, 1784-1818, and Marie Guadalupe de Lencastre, 1679-1691, relating to missions in Mexico and South America); Adolph Sutro Archive-Sutro Baths and Sutro Tunnel (6 boxes); George Poultney Theatre typescripts, 19th and 20th century drama (273 items); Ernest Born Collection; Rev. Peter C. Yorke Collection; George Tyrell-Modernist controversy, 1890-1910; Winterburn Bookplate Collection; W. Phillip Barrett (bookplate designer); Eidenmuller Collection of American Women's Suffrage; Kenneth Ball Collection of Christmas Literature; Dorothy Payne (bookplate designer); The Reed O. Hunt Archive of President Nixon's Commission on Financial Structure & Regulation, 1970-1972 (6 boxes); Dr. David Hyatt and the National Conference of Christians and Jews, 1973 to present (8 boxes); San Francisco and California Fiction Collection (1300 volumes); Monsignor George Lacombe Archive of Medieval Philosophy (6 boxes); The V.C.C. Collum Carnac and Mother-Goddess Research Archive (7 boxes); incunabula (53); Albrecht Durer prints (87); Mihail Chemiakin art works. **Holdings:** 15,000 volumes; photographs; prints; letters; manuscripts. **Services:** Copying; collections open to the public. **Computerized Information Services:** OCLC. **Publications:** Occasional keepsakes; announcements of exhibitions; brochure briefly describing collections is available upon request. **Special Catalogs:** Files of presses, prints, manuscripts, letters, provenance, bindings, bookplates, chronology (card). **Remarks:** The special collections were started in 1951; the Donohue Room was dedicated in 1972. **Also Known As:** University of San Francisco - Countess Bernardine Murphy Donohue Rare Book Room.

★16835★
UNIVERSITY OF SASKATCHEWAN - EDUCATION BRANCH LIBRARY (Educ)
Saskatoon, SK, Canada S7N 0W0 Phone: (306)966-5973
Founded: 1970. **Staff:** Prof 2; Other 6. **Subjects:** Education, school librarianship, music, curriculum materials for grades K-12. **Holdings:** 141,359 volumes; 419,385 microforms; 9632 AV programs; 5126 pamphlets; 245 maps; 38,480 pictures; music scores and recordings. **Subscriptions:** 663 journals and other serials. **Services:** Interlibrary loan; copying; library open to the public with courtesy card. **Computerized Information Services:** DIALOG Information Services, BRS Information Technologies; Envoy 100 (electronic mail service).

★16836★
UNIVERSITY OF SASKATCHEWAN - ENGINEERING BRANCH LIBRARY (Sci-Engr)
Saskatoon, SK, Canada S7N 0W0 Phone: (306)966-5976
D. Salt, Sci. & Engr.Libn.
Staff: Prof 2; Other 4. **Subjects:** Engineering - mechanical, electrical, civil, agricultural; computational science. **Holdings:** 60,000 volumes; 2800 pamphlets; 3800 documents; 6000 microforms. **Subscriptions:** 950 journals and other serials. **Services:** Library open to the public with courtesy card. **Automated Operations:** Computerized public access catalog and circulation. **Computerized Information Services:** DIALOG Information Services, Pergamon ORBIT InfoLine, Inc., BRS Information Technologies, CAN/OLE; Envoy 100 (electronic mail service). Performs searches on fee basis. **Remarks:** An alternate telephone number is 966-5978. **Staff:** E. Wilson, Br.Supv..

★16837★
UNIVERSITY OF SASKATCHEWAN - GEOLOGY/PHYSICS LIBRARY (Sci-Engr)
Saskatoon, SK, Canada S7N 0W0 Phone: (306)966-6047
G.D. Armstrong, Sci.Ref.Libn.
Staff: Prof 1; Other 3. **Subjects:** Geological sciences, physics. **Holdings:** 42,000 volumes; 9000 bound periodical volumes; 600 reels of microfilm; 300 maps. **Subscriptions:** 500 journals and other serials. **Services:** Interlibrary loan; SDI; library open to the public with courtesy card. **Automated Operations:** Computerized public access catalog, cataloging, acquisitions, serials, and circulation. **Computerized Information Services:** DIALOG Information Services, CAN/OLE, BRS Information Technologies. **Formed by the merger of:** Geology and Physics Branch Libraries. **Remarks:** Alternate telephone numbers are 966-6048 and 966-6049.

★16838★
UNIVERSITY OF SASKATCHEWAN - HEALTH SCIENCES LIBRARY (Med)
Saskatoon, SK, Canada S7N 0W0 Phone: (306)966-5991
Dr. Wilma P. Sweaney, Libn.
Founded: 1951. **Staff:** Prof 2; Other 6. **Subjects:** Medicine, clinical and basic sciences, nursing, dentistry, biochemistry, microbiology, pharmacology, physiology, physical therapy, cancer research. **Holdings:** 95,630 volumes; 11,045 slides; 171 cassettes; 45 kits; 20 realia. **Subscriptions:** 1454 journals and other serials. **Services:** Interlibrary loan; copying; library open to medical professionals. **Automated Operations:** Computerized public access catalog and circulation. **Computerized Information Services:** MEDLARS, BRS Information Technologies, DIALOG Information Services, QL Systems, Pergamon ORBIT InfoLine, Inc.; Envoy 100 (electronic mail service). Performs searches on fee basis. **Staff:** Joan MacLaine, Ref.Libn..

★16839★
UNIVERSITY OF SASKATCHEWAN - LAW LIBRARY (Law)
College of Law Bldg. Phone: (306)966-5999
Saskatoon, SK, Canada S7N 0W0 E. Stanek, Law Libn.
Founded: 1915. **Staff:** Prof 2; Other 6. **Subjects:** Law. **Holdings:** 115,325 volumes; 12,048 microforms; 16,199 documents; 34,364 pamphlets; 118 AV programs. **Subscriptions:** 1392 journals and other serials. **Services:** Interlibrary loan; copying; library open to the public with courtesy card. **Computerized Information Services:** QL Systems. **Staff:** Ken Whiteway, Rd.Serv.Libn..

UNIVERSITY OF SASKATCHEWAN - LUTHERAN THEOLOGICAL SEMINARY
See: Lutheran Theological Seminary (8137)

★16840★
UNIVERSITY OF SASKATCHEWAN - NATIVE LAW CENTRE - LIBRARY (Law)
159 Diefenbaker Centre Phone: (306)966-6195
Saskatoon, SK, Canada S7N 0W0 Linda Fritz, Libn.
Founded: 1979. **Staff:** Prof 1; Other 1. **Subjects:** Law, native studies. **Special Collections:** Mackenzie Valley Pipeline Inquiry (archival materials); Canadian native rights cases (reported and unreported, relating to aboriginal, treaty, and Indian Act issues). **Holdings:** 15,000 books; cases. **Subscriptions:** 40 journals and other serials; 35 newspapers. **Services:** Interlibrary loan; copying; library open to the public. **Publications:** Acquisitions list; Native Law Bibliography.

UNIVERSITY OF SASKATCHEWAN - ST. ANDREW'S COLLEGE
See: St. Andrew's College (12312)

UNIVERSITY OF SASKATCHEWAN - ST. THOMAS MORE COLLEGE
See: St. Thomas More College (12678)

★16841★
UNIVERSITY OF SASKATCHEWAN - SPECIAL COLLECTIONS (Hist)
University Library Phone: (306)966-6030
Saskatoon, SK, Canada S7N 0W0 Shirley Martin, Hd.
Staff: Prof 1; Other 1. **Subjects:** Prairie provinces, pre-Confederation history, Canadian church history. **Special Collections:** Shortt Library of Canadiana; P.A. Sorokin Papers and Library; Morton Manuscripts on Rupert's Land and North-West Territories to 1940 (45 linear feet). **Holdings:** 40,398 volumes; 5338 pamphlets; 51.3 million manuscripts; 4677 photographs. **Services:** Copying; collections open to the public. **Automated Operations:** Computerized public access catalog, cataloging, acquisitions, and circulation. **Computerized Information Services:** GEAC Library Information System.

★16842★
UNIVERSITY OF SASKATCHEWAN - THORVALDSON LIBRARY (Sci-Engr)
Thorvaldson Bldg. Phone: (306)966-6038
Saskatoon, SK, Canada S7N 0W0 G.D. Armstrong, Sci.Ref.Libn.
Staff: Prof 1; Other 3. **Subjects:** Chemistry, pharmacy, chemical engineering, home economics. **Holdings:** 16,000 books; 5000 bound periodical volumes. **Subscriptions:** 400 journals and other serials. **Services:** Interlibrary loan; SDI; library open to the public with courtesy card. **Automated Operations:** Computerized public access catalog, cataloging, acquisitions, serials, and circulation. **Computerized Information Services:** DIALOG Information Services, BRS Information Technologies, CAN/OLE. Performs searches on fee basis. **Remarks:** An alternate telephone number is 966-4681. **Staff:** Lilly Chin, Supv.; Connie Fendelet, Supv..

★16843★
UNIVERSITY OF SASKATCHEWAN - VETERINARY MEDICAL LIBRARY (Med)
Western College of Veterinary Medicine Phone: (306)966-7206
Saskatoon, SK, Canada S7N 0W0 John V. James, Vet.Med.Libn.
Founded: 1965. **Staff:** Prof 1; Other 2. **Subjects:** Veterinary medicine, animal science. **Holdings:** 32,000 books; 30,000 bound periodical volumes. **Subscriptions:** 556 journals and other serials. **Services:** Interlibrary loan; library open to the public. **Computerized Information Services:** DIALOG Information Services, MEDLINE, CAN/OLE, GEAC Library Information System. Performs searches on fee basis. **Publications:** New Acquisitions, monthly; Bulletin, quarterly. **Remarks:** An alternate telephone number is 966-7205.

★16844★
UNIVERSITY OF THE SOUTH - ARCHIVES (Hist)
duPont Library Phone: (615)598-5931
Sewanee, TN 37375 Anne Armour, Dir., Univ.Archv./Spec.Coll.
Staff: Prof 1; Other 2. **Subjects:** University history, Protestant Episcopal Church in the South, local and regional history. **Special Collections:** Papers of Leonidas Polk (850 items); correspondence and diaries of Charles T. Quintard (1200 items); sermons of Walter Dakin (100 items). **Holdings:** 1500 books; 500,000 manuscripts and photographs. **Services:** Interlibrary loan; copying; archives open to the public. **Computerized Information Services:** OCLC. **Networks/Consortia:** Member of SOLINET.

★16845★
UNIVERSITY OF THE SOUTH - SCHOOL OF THEOLOGY LIBRARY (Rel-Phil)
Sewanee, TN 37375-4006 Phone: (615)598-5931
Thomas Edward Camp, Libn.
Staff: Prof 3; Other 1. **Subjects:** Theology, Biblical studies, church music and art, church history, religious biography, liturgy and ritual, Episcopal Church in the U.S.A. **Special Collections:** Bayard H. Jones Liturgical Library; journals of Diocesan Conventions of the Episcopal Church; journals of General Convention of Episcopal Church, 1790s to present. **Holdings:** 98,000 books; 6500 bound periodical volumes; 2000 pamphlets. **Subscriptions:** 500 journals and other serials. **Services:** Interlibrary loan; copying; library open to the public. **Automated Operations:** Computerized cataloging and acquisitions. **Computerized Information Services:** DIALOG Information Services; internal database. Performs searches on fee basis. **Networks/Consortia:** Member of SOLINET. **Staff:** Anne Flint, Tech.Serv.Libn.; Don Haymes, Asst.Libn. for Pub.Serv..

★16846★
UNIVERSITY OF SOUTH ALABAMA - COLLEGE OF MEDICINE - BIOMEDICAL LIBRARY (Med)
Library 312 Phone: (205)460-7043
Mobile, AL 36688 Robert M. Donnell, Dir.
Founded: 1972. **Staff:** Prof 8; Other 13. **Subjects:** Medicine, nursing, allied health sciences. **Holdings:** 29,256 books; 48,140 bound periodical volumes; 612 reels of microfilm of periodicals; 7282 microfiche; AV programs. **Subscriptions:** 2238 journals and other serials. **Services:** Interlibrary loan (fee); copying; SDI; library open to the public with restrictions. **Automated Operations:** Computerized cataloging, acquisitions, serials, and ILL. **Computerized Information Services:** BRS Information Technologies, NLM, OCLC, Northwestern Online Total Integrated System (NOTIS); OnTyme Electronic Message Network Service (electronic mail service). **Networks/Consortia:** Member of SOLINET. **Publications:** Acquisitions & Information Letter, quarterly - free upon request. **Staff:** Patricia M. Rodgers, Assoc.Dir., Tech.Serv.; Sr. Mary Giles Peresich, Cat.; Geneva Bush, Info.Serv.; Barbara Shearer, Coord., Pub.Serv., Med.Ctr.; Virginia Vail, Info.Serv.Libn., Med.Ctr..

★16847★
UNIVERSITY OF SOUTH ALABAMA - LIBRARY - SPECIAL COLLECTIONS (Hist)
Mobile, AL 36688 Phone: (205)460-7028
Founded: 1964. **Subjects:** Local history, Alabama authors. **Holdings:** 942 books; university archival materials; masters' theses. **Services:** Library open to the public for reference use only. **Computerized Information Services:** OCLC, Northwestern Online Total Integrated System (NOTIS), DIALOG Information Services, BRS Information Technologies.

★16848★
UNIVERSITY OF SOUTH CAROLINA - BUREAU OF GOVERNMENTAL RESEARCH AND SERVICE - LIBRARY (Soc Sci)
Columbia, SC 29208 Phone: (803)777-8156
Sandra T. Cowen, Chf., Info.Serv.
Founded: 1947. **Staff:** Prof 1. **Subjects:** State and local government, public finance, public personnel administration. **Special Collections:** State of South Carolina reference materials and U.S. census information. **Holdings:** 300 books; 1500 South Carolina documents; 5000 federal and state documents. **Subscriptions:** 203 journals and other serials. **Services:** Library open to the public for reference use only. **Automated Operations:** Computerized cataloging. **Publications:** Bibliography of bureau publications.

★16849★
UNIVERSITY OF SOUTH CAROLINA - COLEMAN KARESH LAW LIBRARY (Law)
Law Center Phone: (803)777-5942
Columbia, SC 29208 Bruce S. Johnson, Law Libn.
Founded: 1867. **Staff:** Prof 7; Other 7. **Subjects:** Law. **Holdings:** 194,951 volumes; 485,876 microfiche; 2716 reels of microfilm; 1661 audio cassettes; 87 video cassettes. **Subscriptions:** 4061 journals and other serials; 11 newspapers. **Services:** Interlibrary loan; copying; library open to the public. **Automated Operations:** Computerized cataloging. **Computerized Information Services:** LEXIS, WESTLAW, OCLC. **Networks/Consortia:** Member of SOLINET. **Staff:** Steve Huang, Assoc. Law Libn.; Joseph R. Cross, Jr., Hd., Rd.Serv.; Paula G. Benson, Ref.Libn.; Melissa M. Surber, Acq./Ser.Libn.; Diana Osbaldiston, Cat.Libn.; Cassandra S. Gissendanner, Cat.Libn..

★16850★
UNIVERSITY OF SOUTH CAROLINA - COMPUTER SERVICES DIVISION REFERENCE ROOM (Comp Sci)
1244 Blossom St. Phone: (803)777-6015
Columbia, SC 29208 Pam Shanley, Mgr.
Founded: 1982. **Staff:** Prof 1; Other 4. **Subjects:** Computer hardware and software. **Holdings:** 200 books. **Subscriptions:** 40 journals and other serials. **Services:** Copying; SDI; room open to the public. **Automated Operations:** Computerized cataloging. **Computerized Information Services:** CompuServe, Inc. **Publications:** Network, monthly - for internal distribution only.

★16851★
UNIVERSITY OF SOUTH CAROLINA - SCHOOL OF MEDICINE LIBRARY (Med)
Columbia, SC 29208 Phone: (803)733-3344
R. Thomas Lange, Dir.
Founded: 1975. **Staff:** Prof 5; Other 16. **Subjects:** Medicine. **Holdings:** 15,000 books; 46,000 bound periodical volumes; 815 AV programs; 4100 reels of microfilm. **Subscriptions:** 1103 journals and other serials. **Services:** Interlibrary loan; copying; SDI; library open to the public with services to medical professionals only. **Automated Operations:** Computerized public access catalog, cataloging, acquisitions, serials, circulation, and ILL. **Computerized Information Services:** OCLC, DIALOG Information Services, Pergamon ORBIT InfoLine, Inc., Library and Information Services (LIS), BRS Information Technologies, MEDLARS; OnTyme Electronic Message Network Service (electronic mail service). **Networks/Consortia:** Member of SOLINET, Columbia Area Medical Librarians' Association (CAMLA), South Carolina Health Information Network (SCHIN). **Special Catalogs:** Southeastern Medical Periodicals Union List; South Carolina Union List of Medical Periodicals, annual - free to participating libraries, for sale to individuals. **Staff:** Julie Johnson McGowan, Assoc.Dir.; Felicia Yeh-Lin, Cat.Libn.; Karen Warren, Ser.Libn.; Sarah Gable, Ref.Libn..

★16852★
UNIVERSITY OF SOUTH CAROLINA - SOUTH CAROLINIANA LIBRARY (Hist)
Columbia, SC 29208 Phone: (803)777-3131
Allen H. Stokes, Libn.
Staff: Prof 4; Other 5. **Subjects:** South Caroliniana. **Holdings:** 83,558 books and pamphlets; 2.1 million manuscripts; 500,000 issues of South Carolina newspapers; 2067 maps; 12,428 reels of microfilm; 14,000 pictures; 400 pieces of sheet music. **Subscriptions:** 254 journals and other serials; 96 newspapers. **Services:** Interlibrary loan; copying; library open to the public for reference use only. **Publications:** A Guide to the Manuscript Collection of the South Caroliniana Library. **Staff:** Eleanor Richardson, Ref.Libn.; Herbert Hartsook, Mss.Libn.; Thomas L. Johnson, Asst.Libn..

★16853★
UNIVERSITY OF SOUTH CAROLINA - THOMAS COOPER LIBRARY - MAP LIBRARY (Geog-Map)
Columbia, SC 29208 Phone: (803)777-2802
David C. McQuillan, Map Libn.
Staff: Prof 1. **Subjects:** Maps. **Holdings:** 182,350 maps; 1746 atlases; 76,434 aerial photographs; U.S. Geological Survey depository. **Services:** Copying; library open to the public for reference use only.

★16854★
UNIVERSITY OF SOUTH CAROLINA - THOMAS COOPER LIBRARY - RARE BOOKS & SPECIAL COLLECTIONS DEPARTMENT (Rare Book)
Columbia, SC 29208 Phone: (803)777-8154
Roger Mortimer, Hd., Spec.Coll.
Staff: Prof 1; Other 2. **Subjects:** English and American literature, ornithology, history of science, travel, theology. **Special Collections:** American Civil War; Left Bank Club Collection; papers of Lord Allen of Hurtwood (2000 manuscripts); Robert Bridges; Historical Children's Literature; Muggletonianism. **Holdings:** 30,000 books; 1000 bound periodical volumes. **Services:** Interlibrary loan; copying; department open to the public for reference use only. **Publications:** A Load of Gratitude: Audubon and South Carolina; Aspects of the Western Religious Heritage.

★16855★
UNIVERSITY OF SOUTH CAROLINA - UNIVERSITY ARCHIVES (Hist)
McKissick Museum Phone: (803)777-7251
Columbia, SC 29208 George D. Terry, Dir./Archv.
Founded: 1976. **Staff:** Prof 2; Other 2. **Subjects:** University history. **Special Collections:** 19th century library records; photographs (20 cubic feet). **Holdings:** 3500 cubic feet of archives; student yearbooks, 1899 to present; minutes of faculty senate and board of trustees meetings, 1803-1962. **Services:** Copying; archives open to the public. **Publications:** University Archives Preliminary Guide; Guide to University Archives Photographic Collection.

UNIVERSITY OF SOUTH DAKOTA - CENTER FOR THE STUDY OF THE HISTORY OF MUSICAL INSTRUMENTS - SHRINE TO MUSIC MUSEUM
See: Shrine to Music Museum (13163)

★16856★
UNIVERSITY OF SOUTH DAKOTA - CHEMISTRY LIBRARY (Sci-Engr)
Pardee Laboratory
Vermillion, SD 57069 Phone: (605)677-5487
Subjects: Chemistry, chemical physics, history and philosophy of science. **Special Collections:** A.M. Pardee Historical Book Collection (420 volumes). **Holdings:** 1029 books; 3771 bound periodical volumes.

Subscriptions: 109 journals and other serials. Services: Interlibrary loan; copying; library open to the public with restrictions on circulation.

★16857★
UNIVERSITY OF SOUTH DAKOTA - CHRISTIAN P. LOMMEN HEALTH SCIENCES LIBRARY (Med)
School of Medicine
414 E. Clark Phone: (605)677-5347
Vermillion, SD 57069-2390 David A. Hulkonen, Dir.
Founded: 1907. **Staff:** Prof 3; Other 7. **Subjects:** Anatomy, physiology, pharmacology, microbiology, pathology, biochemistry, nursing, dental hygiene, medical technology, clinical medicine. **Special Collections:** History of Medicine; medical school archives. **Holdings:** 36,000 books; 40,000 bound periodical volumes; 900 AV programs. **Subscriptions:** 1042 journals and other serials. **Services:** Interlibrary loan; copying; SDI; reference; consultation services for hospitals; library open to the public. **Automated Operations:** Computerized cataloging and serials. **Computerized Information Services:** OCLC, BRS Information Technologies, MEDLINE, PHILSOM; EasyLink, DOCLINE (electronic mail services). Performs searches on fee basis. Contact Person: Rita Sieracki, Hd., User Serv.. **Networks/Consortia:** Member of Greater Midwest Regional Medical Library Network, MINITEX. **Publications:** Accessions list, monthly; bibliographies. **Special Catalogs:** AV Union Catalog; South Dakota Union List of Health Science Serials. **Special Indexes:** Index to faculty publications (computer printout). **Staff:** Gene Sederstrom, Hd., Tech.Serv.; Mary Craig, ILL.

★16858★
UNIVERSITY OF SOUTH DAKOTA - GOVERNMENTAL RESEARCH LIBRARY (Soc Sci)
Vermillion, SD 57069 Phone: (605)677-5702
Steven H. Feimer, Dir.
Founded: 1939. **Subjects:** State and local government, public administration, South Dakota government, political behavior, public finance, Missouri Valley development, American Indians, public law, legislative apportionment. **Special Collections:** Missouri River Basin Commission publications (complete set). **Holdings:** 6000 books; 400 bound periodical volumes; 20,000 newspaper clippings from South Dakota dailies, 1950 to present. **Subscriptions:** 47 journals and other serials. **Services:** Copying; library open to the public for reference use only. **Publications:** Public Affairs, quarterly; Reports, irregular; Special Projects, irregular.

★16859★
UNIVERSITY OF SOUTH DAKOTA - I.D. WEEKS LIBRARY - RICHARDSON ARCHIVES (Hist)
Vermillion, SD 57069 Phone: (605)677-5371
Karen Zimmerman, Act.Archv.
Staff: Prof 1. **Subjects:** History - Western U.S., frontier, South Dakota; American Indians. **Special Collections:** Herman P. Chilson Western Americana Collection. **Holdings:** 10,500 books; 2066 linear feet of manuscripts. **Services:** Copying; archives open to the public with permission. **Automated Operations:** Computerized cataloging and acquisitions. **Computerized Information Services:** OCLC, BRS Information Technologies, Pergamon ORBIT InfoLine, Inc., DIALOG Information Services, Telesystemes Questel, WILSONLINE. Performs searches on fee basis. Contact Person: Miriam Kahn, 677-6087. **Networks/Consortia:** Member of MINITEX.

★16860★
UNIVERSITY OF SOUTH DAKOTA - MC KUSICK LAW LIBRARY (Law)
414 E. Clark Phone: (605)677-5259
Vermillion, SD 57069 John F. Hagemann, Law Libn.
Founded: 1901. **Staff:** Prof 7; Other 1. **Subjects:** Law - U.S., English, Canadian. **Special Collections:** Law - agricultural, Indian, family, water, tax, professional responsibility; arts and the law; South Dakota Supreme Court briefs (60 VF drawers); U.S. Circuit Court, 8th Circuit slip opinions. **Holdings:** 103,753 books; 13,503 bound periodical volumes; 4 VF drawers of pamphlets; 11,679 volumes in microform; 4 VF drawers of archives. **Subscriptions:** 1640 journals and other serials; 11 newspapers. **Services:** Interlibrary loan (fee); copying; SDI; library open to the public. **Automated Operations:** Computerized cataloging and acquisitions. **Computerized Information Services:** LEXIS, WESTLAW. Performs searches on fee basis. Contact Person: Mary Brandt Jensen, Asst. Law Libn.. **Networks/Consortia:** Member of MINITEX. **Publications:** Selective list of acquisitions, quarterly; surveys of library holdings in specialized areas of law, 3/year - to South Dakota Clerks of Court, legal services, selected South Dakota attorneys, and libraries; Guide to the Law Library; Locator Guide. **Special Indexes:** List of Periodicals; Survey of Bibliographies and Indexes. **Staff:** Candice Spurlin, Circ./ILL Libn.; Delores Jorgenson, Cat.Libn.; Shirley Bridge, Acq.Libn./Accounting; Karyl Knodel, Ser.Libn.; Barbara Heisinger, Lib.Techn..

★16861★
UNIVERSITY OF SOUTH FLORIDA - DIVISION OF LEARNING TECHNOLOGIES - FILM LIBRARY (Aud-Vis)
4202 Fowler Ave. Phone: (813)974-2874
Tampa, FL 33620 Jacqueline D. Langer, Film Lib.Coord.
Staff: Prof 4; Other 1. **Subjects:** Education, special education, social studies, literature, fine arts, management. **Special Collections:** Physical Education for the Handicapped (19 titles); Mid-Life and Pre-Retirement (30 titles); Protocol Materials for Teacher Training (76 titles). **Holdings:** 3000 16mm films; 100 video cassettes. **Services:** Library open to the public with rental fee for film usage. **Networks/Consortia:** Member of Consortium of University Film Centers (CUFC). **Special Catalogs:** Triennial book catalog of currently available film titles, updated with annual supplements - on request. **Formerly:** Division of Educational Resources.

★16862★
UNIVERSITY OF SOUTH FLORIDA - FLORIDA MENTAL HEALTH INSTITUTE - LIBRARY (Med, Soc Sci)
13301 Bruce B. Downs Blvd. Phone: (813)974-4533
Tampa, FL 33612 Josephine King Evans, Asst.Univ.Libn./Dir.
Founded: 1974. **Staff:** Prof 1; Other 2. **Subjects:** Psychology and psychiatry; epidemiology; aging, child, and family programs; forensics; community mental health; social work. **Special Collections:** Florida Mental Health Institute Archives (800 items). **Holdings:** 9192 books; 62 bound periodical volumes; 3000 unbound periodicals; 1373 state and government documents; 73 microforms; 176 audio and video cassettes. **Subscriptions:** 194 journals and other serials. **Services:** Interlibrary loan; copying; SDI; library open to the public with restrictions. **Computerized Information Services:** Internal database.

★16863★
UNIVERSITY OF SOUTH FLORIDA - LIBRARY - SPECIAL COLLECTIONS DEPARTMENT (Hum, Hist)
Tampa, FL 33620 Phone: (813)974-2732
Mr. J.B. Dobkin, Spec.Coll.Libn.
Staff: Prof 2; Other 4. **Subjects:** Floridiana, 19th and early 20th century American literature with emphasis on juvenile fiction. **Special Collections:** Florida Collection (20,000 volumes; maps; photographs; other items); Hudson Collection of Hard Cover Boys and Girls Series Books (9000 volumes); Dime Novel Collection (9000 items); Early American Textbook Collection (1000 volumes); 19th Century American Literature Collection (25,000 volumes); American Toybook Collection (600 items); Cigar Box Art (cigar labels and progressive proof books); 19th century American Almanacs (800); 19th century American Printed Ephemera (10,000 advertising and greeting cards); Florida Postcards (6000); G.A. Henty Collection (500 volumes); Mosher Press Publications (700 volumes). **Services:** Interlibrary loan (limited); copying; collections open to public. **Automated Operations:** Computerized cataloging and serials. **Computerized Information Services:** OCLC. **Networks/Consortia:** Member of SOLINET. **Publications:** Ex Libris, irregular - internal distribution and to other libraries. **Staff:** Paul Eugen Camp, Assoc.Libn..

★16864★
UNIVERSITY OF SOUTH FLORIDA - MEDICAL CENTER LIBRARY (Med)
Box 31 Phone: (813)974-2399
Tampa, FL 33612 Maxyne M. Grimes, Act.Dir.
Founded: 1971. **Staff:** Prof 7; Other 14. **Subjects:** Medicine, nursing, public health, allied health sciences. **Holdings:** 25,267 books; 65,426 bound periodical volumes. **Subscriptions:** 1502 journals and other serials. **Services:** Interlibrary loan; copying; SDI; library open to the public for health related research. **Automated Operations:** Computerized cataloging and serials. **Computerized Information Services:** Online systems; OnTyme Electronic Message Network Service (electronic mail service). Performs searches on fee basis. **Networks/Consortia:** Member of Tampa Bay Medical Library Network. **Publications:** Occasional papers. **Staff:** Judy Johnston, Asst.Dir., Pub.Serv.; Larry Chrisman, Cat.; Sarah Harmon, Hd., Ref.Dept.; Paul Cadby, Ref./Search Anl..

★16865★
UNIVERSITY OF SOUTHERN CALIFORNIA - ALLAN HANCOCK FOUNDATION - HANCOCK LIBRARY OF BIOLOGY & OCEANOGRAPHY (Biol Sci)
University Park Phone: (213)743-6005
Los Angeles, CA 90089-0372 Jean E. Crampon, Hd.Libn.
Founded: 1944. **Staff:** Prof 2; Other 3. **Subjects:** Marine biology, geology, zoology, botany, paleontology. **Special Collections:** Early scientific

expeditions; natural history. **Holdings:** 31,000 books; 70,000 bound periodical volumes; scientific reprints and pamphlets. **Subscriptions:** 2330 journals and other serials. **Services:** Interlibrary loan; copying; library open to researchers. **Automated Operations:** Computerized cataloging. **Computerized Information Services:** OCLC, DIALOG Information Services, BRS Information Technologies. **Staff:** Melinda Hayes, Tech.Serv.Libn..

UNIVERSITY OF SOUTHERN CALIFORNIA - ARNOLD SCHOENBERG INSTITUTE
See: Arnold Schoenberg Institute (12963)

★16866★
UNIVERSITY OF SOUTHERN CALIFORNIA - CATALINA MARINE SCIENCE CENTER - TIBBY LIBRARY (Biol Sci)
Big Fisherman Cove
Box 398 Phone: (213)743-6792
Avalon, CA 90704 Elzbet Diaz de Leon, Staff Biol.
Founded: 1969. **Staff:** Prof 1. **Subjects:** Marine biology, oceanography, marine ecology, invertebrate zoology. **Holdings:** 700 books; 100 bound periodical volumes. **Subscriptions:** 10 journals and other serials. **Services:** Interlibrary loan; copying; library open to the public by permission. **Remarks:** Alternate telephone numbers are 743-6793 and 743-7882.

★16867★
UNIVERSITY OF SOUTHERN CALIFORNIA - CROCKER BUSINESS AND ACCOUNTING LIBRARIES (Bus-Fin)
University Park - MC 1421 Phone: (213)743-7348
Los Angeles, CA 90089-1421 Judith A. Truelson, Dir.
Staff: Prof 3; Other 7. **Subjects:** Accounting and taxation, finance, marketing, decision systems, organizational behavior, business economics, management, investments, multinational business. **Holdings:** 71,000 books; 12,500 bound periodical volumes; 15,000 reels of microfilm; 500,000 microfiche, including annual reports. **Subscriptions:** 1650 journals and other serials; 50 newspapers. **Services:** Library open to the public. **Computerized Information Services:** DIALOG Information Services, BRS Information Technologies, Pergamon ORBIT InfoLine, Inc. **Publications:** Selected subject bibliographies - for internal distribution only; Top Fifty Acquisitions, monthly - for internal distribution only. **Staff:** Lillian Yang, Accounting Lib.Libn.; Deborah Bryson, Tech.Serv./Ref.Libn..

★16868★
UNIVERSITY OF SOUTHERN CALIFORNIA - DENTISTRY LIBRARY (Med)
DEN 201
University Park - MC 0641 Phone: (213)743-2870
Los Angeles, CA 90089-0641 Frank O. Mason, Dental Libn.
Founded: 1897. **Staff:** Prof 2; Other 3. **Subjects:** Dentistry, medicine, allied sciences. **Special Collections:** History of Dentistry (400 volumes). **Holdings:** 17,325 books; 11,500 bound periodical volumes; 2300 test files; 2519 AV programs and filmstrips; 1142 reading files. **Subscriptions:** 532 journals and other serials. **Services:** Interlibrary loan (fee); copying; SDI; library open to the public with Library card. **Automated Operations:** Computerized public access catalog, cataloging, acquisitions, serials, and circulation. **Computerized Information Services:** DIALOG Information Services, Compact Cambridge, RLIN, MEDLARS, MEDLINE; OnTyme Electronic Message Network Service, DOCLINE (electronic mail services). Performs searches on fee basis. Contact Person: John Glueckert, Ref.Libn., 743-2884. **Networks/Consortia:** Member of Pacific Southwest Regional Medical Library Service, CLASS. **Publications:** List of Recently Acquired Titles, bimonthly - for internal distribution only.

★16869★
UNIVERSITY OF SOUTHERN CALIFORNIA - EAST ASIAN COLLECTION (Area-Ethnic)
University Park - MC 0182 Phone: (213)743-6055
Los Angeles, CA 90089-0182 Ken Klein, Libn.
Staff: Prof 1; Other 1. **Subjects:** East Asian social sciences and humanities with emphasis on Korean language. **Holdings:** 33,000 volumes. **Subscriptions:** 300 journals and other serials. **Services:** Interlibrary loan; copying; library open to the public for reference use only.

★16870★
UNIVERSITY OF SOUTHERN CALIFORNIA - EMERY STOOPS AND JOYCE KING-STOOPS EDUCATION LIBRARY (Educ)
University Park Phone: (213)743-6249
Los Angeles, CA 90089-0182 Susan R. Gibberman, Act.Hd.
Staff: Prof 2; Other 4. **Subjects:** Education and related subjects, instructional technology, educational psychology, international education, sociology of education, higher education, early childhood education. **Special Collections:** Curriculum Collection (7839 texts and 6532 courses); juvenile books (6500 volumes); tests (1815); Donald E. Wilson Collection of Old Textbooks (200 volumes); Jean Burton Clark Higher Education Browsing Area (400 volumes). **Holdings:** 120,000 books; 7000 bound periodical volumes; 140 AV programs; 31 films; 390,000 microfiche; 12 VF drawers of pamphlets; 5000 reels of microfilm. **Subscriptions:** 466 journals and other serials. **Services:** Interlibrary loan; copying; library open to the public for reference use only. **Automated Operations:** Computerized cataloging, acquisitions, and circulation. **Computerized Information Services:** DIALOG Information Services,

★16871★
UNIVERSITY OF SOUTHERN CALIFORNIA - GERONTOLOGY LIBRARY (Soc Sci)
120 Gerontology - MC 0191 Phone: (213)743-5990
Los Angeles, CA 90089-0191 Jeanne E. Miller, Dept.Hd.
Founded: 1966. **Staff:** Prof 1; Other 2. **Subjects:** Gerontology. **Special Collections:** Doctoral dissertations on aging and gerontology, 1934-1976 (microfilm); reprints collection (2000 items); Leonard Davis School of Gerontology Masters' Theses Collection; SCAN microfiche collection. **Holdings:** 8500 books; 750 bound periodical volumes; 1500 reels of microfilm of dissertations. **Subscriptions:** 100 journals; 200 newsletters and other serials. **Services:** Interlibrary loan; copying; center open to the public for reference use only. **Automated Operations:** Computerized public access catalog, cataloging, acquisitions, and circulation. **Computerized Information Services:** RLIN, DIALOG Information Services, BRS Information Technologies. **Networks/Consortia:** Member of RLG. **Publications:** A Bibliography of Doctoral Dissertations on Aging from American Institutions of Higher Learning, 1934-1969 through 1976-1978; Journal of Gerontology, 1971-1987, annual.

★16872★
UNIVERSITY OF SOUTHERN CALIFORNIA - HEALTH SCIENCES CAMPUS - NORRIS MEDICAL LIBRARY (Med)
2003 Zonal Ave. Phone: (213)224-7231
Los Angeles, CA 90033 Nelson J. Gilman, Libn./Dir.
Founded: 1928. **Staff:** Prof 14; Other 26. **Subjects:** Medicine, pharmacy. **Special Collections:** History of Medicine; Ethnopharmacology of American Indians; Far West Medicine. **Holdings:** 48,086 books; 83,799 bound periodical volumes; 39,012 slides; 7514 microfiche; 105 reels of microfilm; 3528 audio cassettes; 886 video cassettes; 101 films; 48 filmstrips; 26 discs; 385 floppy discs. **Subscriptions:** 2368 journals and other serials. **Services:** Interlibrary loan; copying; SDI; library open to the public for reference use only. **Automated Operations:** Computerized cataloging, acquisitions, serials, and circulation. **Computerized Information Services:** DIALOG Information Services, RLIN, MEDLARS, Pergamon ORBIT InfoLine, Inc., BRS Information Technologies; OnTyme Electronic Message Network Service (electronic mail service). Performs searches on fee basis. **Networks/Consortia:** Member of CLASS, Pacific Southwest Regional Medical Library Service, RLG, Health Information to Community Hospitals (HITCH). **Publications:** A Guide to Drug Information and Literature: An Annotated Bibliography; Learning Resources Newsletter; Library Newsletter; New Books, all bimonthly; Information, irregular; Computerized Acquisitions Tracking System (CATS); occasional papers. **Special Catalogs:** Union List of Health Sciences Serials, annual. **Remarks:** An alternate telephone number is 224-7400. **Staff:** Karen Hollister, Ref.Libn.; Teresa Manthey, Ref.Libn.; Bill Clintworth, Assoc.Dir., Info.Serv.; Christina Bell, Ref.Libn.; Elizabeth Wood, Ref.Libn.; Melanie Wilson, Ref.Libn.; Janis Brown, Assoc.Dir., Educ.Rsrcs.; Alice Karasick, Acq./Ser.Libn.; Margaret Wineburgh-Freed, Cat.Libn.; David Morse, Assoc.Dir., Coll.Rsrcs.; Louise Adams, Circuit-Rider Libn.; Pamela Corley, Circuit-Rider Libn.; Judy Sherman, Circuit-Rider Libn.; Joan Mircheff, AV Acq.Libn..

★16873★
UNIVERSITY OF SOUTHERN CALIFORNIA - HELEN TOPPING ARCHITECTURE & FINE ARTS LIBRARY (Art, Plan)
University Park - MC 0292 Phone: (213)743-2798
Los Angeles, CA 90089-0292 Nancy A. Smith, Act.Hd.
Founded: 1925. **Staff:** Prof 3; Other 6. **Subjects:** Art history, history of architecture, architectural design, studio arts, photography, museum studies, city planning. **Special Collections:** Primary source material in architectural history of Southern California; contemporary art. **Holdings:** 55,000 books; 5500 bound periodical volumes; 28 VF drawers of architecture and fine arts materials; 8 VF drawers of city planning materials; 160,000 slides; 10 VF drawers of exhibition catalogs. **Subscriptions:** 250 journals and other serials. **Services:** Interlibrary loan; copying; library open to the public. **Automated Operations:** Computerized

cataloging, acquisitions, and circulation. **Computerized Information Services:** RLIN, DIALOG Information Services. **Networks/Consortia:** Member of RLG. **Special Catalogs:** East Asian Art catalog (card). **Special Indexes:** Guide to Indexes in the Architecture & Fine Arts Library; Guide to Vertical File. **Staff:** Lindy Narver, Slide Cur.; Una Kim, Lib.Asst..

★16874★
UNIVERSITY OF SOUTHERN CALIFORNIA - INFORMATION SCIENCES INSTITUTE - TECHNICAL LIBRARY (Comp Sci)
4676 Admiralty Way — Phone: (213)822-1511
Marina Del Rey, CA 90292 — Annie Chen, Libn.
Founded: 1972. **Staff:** Prof 1; Other 1. **Subjects:** Computer science, mathematics, electronics, cognitive psychology, linguistics. **Holdings:** 2100 books; 200 bound periodical volumes; 4000 technical reports. **Subscriptions:** 101 journals and other serials. **Services:** Interlibrary loan; library not open to the public. **Automated Operations:** Computerized cataloging, acquisitions, serials, and circulation. **Computerized Information Services:** DIALOG Information Services. **Publications:** Newsletter, monthly.

★16875★
UNIVERSITY OF SOUTHERN CALIFORNIA - INSTITUTE OF SAFETY AND SYSTEMS MANAGEMENT - LIBRARY (Sci-Engr)
SSM Library
University Park - MC 0021 — Phone: (213)743-6253
Los Angeles, CA 90089-0021 — Monir Ziaian, Hd.Libn.
Founded: 1966. **Staff:** Prof 1; Other 8. **Subjects:** Safety, systems, and decision science; systems management; human factors; biomechanics. **Special Collections:** Safety and Systems Management. **Holdings:** 10,000 books; 1270 bound periodical volumes; annual reports; proceedings; indexes; abstracts; safety newsletters and related serials. **Subscriptions:** 350 journals and other serials; 10 newspapers. **Services:** Interlibrary loan; copying; library open to the public with restrictions. **Automated Operations:** Computerized cataloging. **Computerized Information Services:** Access to DIALOG Information Services, OCLC. Performs searches on fee basis. **Publications:** List of acquisitions, bimonthly - for internal distribution only. **Remarks:** The library serves 67 ISSM study centers in the U.S., Japan, and West Germany in addition to the USC campus. An alternate telephone number is 743-6999.

★16876★
UNIVERSITY OF SOUTHERN CALIFORNIA - LAW LIBRARY (Law)
University Park - MC 0072 — Phone: (213)743-6487
Los Angeles, CA 90089-0072 — Albert Brecht, Dir.
Founded: 1896. **Staff:** Prof 8; Other 10. **Subjects:** Anglo-American law, legal history, legal literature, taxation, law and social sciences. **Special Collections:** Legislative history of Internal Revenue Acts; depository of Copyright Office publications. **Holdings:** 212,897 books; 305,265 microforms; 230 shelves of documents; 718 audiotapes and video cassettes. **Subscriptions:** 3418 journals and other serials. **Services:** Interlibrary loan; copying; SDI; library open to the public. **Automated Operations:** Computerized cataloging. **Computerized Information Services:** LEXIS, WESTLAW, DIALOG Information Services, NEXIS, DataQuick Information Network, ORION, Legaltrac, RLIN; RLG, ABA/net (electronic mail services). **Networks/Consortia:** Member of RLG. **Publications:** Acquisition list, monthly; library guide, irregular; newsletter, semiannual; subject guide to secondary sources, irregular. **Staff:** Victoria K. Trotta, Asst.Dir.; Leonette Williams, Hd., Tech.Serv.; Janet Nelson, Access Serv.; Paul George, Ref.; Sue Burkhart, Cat.; Delsie Stayner, Acq.; Pauline Aranas, Hd., Pub.Serv..

★16877★
UNIVERSITY OF SOUTHERN CALIFORNIA - LIBRARY - CINEMA/TELEVISION LIBRARY (Theater)
Doheny Memorial Library — Phone: (213)743-6058
Los Angeles, CA 90089-0182 — Don K. Thompson, Act.Hd.
Founded: 1964. **Staff:** Prof 2; Other 2. **Subjects:** Motion pictures, television, radio. **Special Collections:** MGM Collection, 1918-1958 (1900 titles, including screenplay drafts, synopses, and treatments); Warner Brothers Collection (all files from Burbank studio through 1967); Twentieth Century-Fox Script Collection, 1919-1967 (900 titles); Universal Pictures Collection (800 boxes); motion picture clippings and ephemera (175 feet); U.S. theater programs (50 feet); motion picture stills (135 feet); over 150 collections of memorabilia from directors, writers, producers, actors. **Holdings:** 18,000 volumes; 250 reels of microfilm; 427 cartridges of videotape of David Wolper productions; teleplay collection; screenplay collection; 1700 reels and cartridges of audiotape; 1200 soundtracks and original cast recordings. **Subscriptions:** 220 journals and other serials. **Services:** Interlibrary loan; copying; library open to the public for reference use only. **Special Catalogs:** Catalog of Screenplays; Catalog of Audiotapes; Catalog of Theater Programs (all on cards). **Special Indexes:** Index of Collections (loose-leaf); An Index to Screenplays, Interviews and Special Collections (1975); An Index to Warner Bros. Collection; An Index to Universal Pictures Collection.

★16878★
UNIVERSITY OF SOUTHERN CALIFORNIA - LIBRARY - DEPARTMENT OF SPECIAL COLLECTIONS (Hist)
University Park - MC 0182 — Phone: (213)743-0966
Los Angeles, CA 90089-0182 — Loss Glazier, Act.Hd.
Founded: 1940. **Staff:** Prof 2; Other 1. **Subjects:** History - general, western, aeronautical; bibliography; fine printing; evolution. **Special Collections:** 120 special collections including Admiral William H. Standley Collection (47 document boxes); Library of Aeronautical History (100 document boxes); Lion Feuchtwanger Oral History Collection; collections of Charles Leonard Bagley, Amy Ransome, Irving Schulman, Women's International Association of Aeronautics, German Theater Programs, American revolutionary pamphlets, Darwin. **Holdings:** 51,000 volumes; 50,000 manuscripts; 12,000 clippings. **Subscriptions:** 54 journals and other serials. **Services:** Interlibrary loan; department open to researchers for reference use only. **Publications:** Guide to Special Collections (loose-leaf).

★16879★
UNIVERSITY OF SOUTHERN CALIFORNIA - LIBRARY - DEPARTMENT OF SPECIAL COLLECTIONS - AMERICAN LITERATURE COLLECTION (Hum)
University Park - MC 0182 — Phone: (213)743-0914
Los Angeles, CA 90089-0182 — Loss Glazier, Cur./Act.Hd., Spec.Coll.
Founded: 1940. **Staff:** Prof 1. **Subjects:** American literature, especially 1850 to present. **Special Collections:** Hamlin Garland papers (12,000 items); Jack London Collection (300 items); Willard S. Morse Collections of Ambrose Bierce, William Dean Howells, Sinclair Lewis, and Frank Norris; Paul Bowles Collection; Kenneth Rexroth Collection; archives of Charles Bukowski, Lawrence Ferlinghetti, Lawrence Lipton, Jack Hirschman, and Tom Clark. **Holdings:** 38,000 books; 19,000 manuscripts; 10,000 clippings. **Subscriptions:** 20 journals and other serials. **Services:** Interlibrary loan; copying; collection open to researchers for reference use only. **Special Indexes:** Index to Hamlin Garland Collection (book); List of Manuscript Collections (loose-leaf).

★16880★
UNIVERSITY OF SOUTHERN CALIFORNIA - LIBRARY - REGIONAL CULTURAL HISTORY COLLECTION (Hist)
University Park — Phone: (213)743-3147
Los Angeles, CA 90089-0182 — L. Glazier, Act.Hd.
Founded: 1940. **Staff:** Prof 2; Other 1. **Subjects:** Southern California politics. **Special Collections:** Hearst Collection (4000 bound volumes of newspapers; 1.2 million photographs; 220,000 negatives, metal plates, clippings); Edmund G. Brown, Jr. Collection (2000 boxes); Craig Hosmer Collection (248 boxes); Thomas Rees Collection (117 boxes); Alphonzo Bell Collection (200 boxes); Yvonne Burke Collection (410 boxes). **Services:** Interlibrary loan; copying; collection open to the public by appointment. **Automated Operations:** Computerized cataloging, acquisitions, serials, and circulation. **Computerized Information Services:** RLIN, OCLC. **Publications:** Guide to the Regional Cultural History Collection (loose-leaf). **Special Indexes:** Governor Edmund G. Brown, Jr. Collection: An Inventory. **Staff:** Gary Bryson, Archv..

★16881★
UNIVERSITY OF SOUTHERN CALIFORNIA - MUSIC LIBRARY (Mus)
University Park - MC 0182 — Phone: (213)743-2525
Los Angeles, CA 90089-0182 — Rodney D. Rolfs, Mus.Libn.
Staff: Prof 1; Other 2; **Subjects:** Music. **Holdings:** 15,000 volumes; 18,000 phonograph records; 4000 cassettes; 40,000 scores. **Subscriptions:** 145 journals and other serials. **Services:** Interlibrary loan; copying.

★16882★
UNIVERSITY OF SOUTHERN CALIFORNIA - NASA INDUSTRIAL APPLICATION CENTER (NIAC) (Sci-Engr)
3716 S. Hope St., Rm. 200 — Phone: (213)743-6132
Los Angeles, CA 90007-4344 — Radford King, Dir.
Founded: 1967. **Staff:** 10. **Subjects:** Aerodynamics; aircraft; auxiliary systems; biosciences; biotechnology; chemistry; communications; computers; electronic equipment; electronics; facilities research and support; fluid mechanics; geophysics; instrumentation and photography; machine elements and processes; masers; metallic and nonmetallic materials; mathematics; meteorology; navigation; nuclear engineering;

physics - general, atomic, molecular, nuclear, plasma, solid state; propellants; propulsion systems; space - radiation, sciences, vehicles; structural mechanics; thermodynamics and combustion. **Holdings:** Figures not available. **Services:** Technology services include Current Awareness Information Services (current awareness search; standard interest profile; monthly manual search of any source) and Retrospective Information Services (retrospective search; one time search of any source for period desired). **Computerized Information Services:** NASA/USC has at its disposal the data banks of NASA, the Department of Defense, DIALOG Information Services, Pergamon ORBIT InfoLine, Inc., MEDLINE. **Remarks:** NASA/USC is a nonprofit organization whose purpose is to disseminate technological information to U.S. industry and to implement NASA's Technology Utilization Program in the Western U.S. **Staff:** Herbert Asbury, Prog.Mgr.; Martin Zeller, Mgr., Info.Serv.; Suzanne French, Doc.Ret.Libn.; Walter Goldenrath, Ph.D., Tech.Couns.; Deborah J. Swift, Info.Spec..

★16883★
UNIVERSITY OF SOUTHERN CALIFORNIA - PHILOSOPHY LIBRARY (Hum)
University Park - MC 0182 Phone: (213)743-2634
Los Angeles, CA 90089-0182 Bridget Molloy, Libn.
Founded: 1930. **Staff:** Prof 1; Other 1. **Subjects:** Philosophy. **Special Collections:** W.T. Harris Collection; Gomperz Collection (11,000 volumes; 2000 pamphlets). **Holdings:** 60,000 books; 4200 bound periodical volumes. **Subscriptions:** 160 journals and other serials. **Services:** Interlibrary loan; copying; library open to the public for reference use only.

★16884★
UNIVERSITY OF SOUTHERN CALIFORNIA - POPULATION RESEARCH LABORATORY - LIBRARY (Soc Sci)
University Park, Research Annex 385 Phone: (213)743-2950
Los Angeles, CA 90007 Prof. Maurice D. Van Arsdol, Jr., Dir.
Founded: 1960. **Subjects:** Population, demography, census, human ecology, urban sociology. **Special Collections:** U.S. Census of Population and Housing, 1940, 1950, 1960, 1970, 1980; Latin American census. **Holdings:** 6000 U.S. Bureau of Census reports, vital statistics reports, United Nations reports, maps, computer tapes, journals, books, reprints, dissertations, newsletters, pamphlets, bibliographies. **Subscriptions:** 30 journals and other serials. **Services:** Library open to the public upon request.

UNIVERSITY OF SOUTHERN CALIFORNIA - SCHOOL OF ARCHITECTURE - GREENE AND GREENE LIBRARY
See: Greene and Greene Library (5869)

★16885★
UNIVERSITY OF SOUTHERN CALIFORNIA - SCIENCE & ENGINEERING LIBRARY (Sci-Engr)
University Park - MC 0481 Phone: (213)743-2118
Los Angeles, CA 90089-0481 Kimberly Douglas, Dept.Hd.
Founded: 1970. **Staff:** Prof 4; Other 6. **Subjects:** Chemistry, physics, biological sciences, engineering, mathematics, geology, astronomy, computer science. **Special Collections:** David Spence Library (rubber technology). **Holdings:** 110,000 books; 120,000 bound periodical volumes; 25,000 technical reports; 1200 pamphlets; 14,000 microforms; rubber formulary on 15,000 punched cards. **Subscriptions:** 2500 journals. **Services:** Interlibrary loan; copying; library open to the public for reference use only. **Computerized Information Services:** DIALOG Information Services. **Staff:** Hazel Wetts, Tech.Serv./Engr.Libn.; Linda Weber, Circ.Libn.; Bruce Bennion, Hd.Ref.Libn..

★16886★
UNIVERSITY OF SOUTHERN CALIFORNIA - SOCIAL WORK LIBRARY (Soc Sci)
University Park - MC 0411 Phone: (213)743-7932
Los Angeles, CA 90089-0411 Ruth Britton, Soc. Work Libn.
Founded: 1971. **Staff:** Prof 1; Other 1. **Subjects:** Social work, social welfare, child welfare, mental health, community organizations, social problems. **Special Collections:** California Social Welfare History Archives; Hispanic Mental Health Collection (200 volumes); unpublished masters' research papers (500). **Holdings:** 35,000 books; 2300 bound periodical volumes; 300 linear feet of other uncataloged items. **Services:** Interlibrary loan; copying; library open to the public for reference use only. **Automated Operations:** Computerized cataloging, acquisitions, and circulation. **Computerized Information Services:** DIALOG Information Services, BRS Information Technologies; Email (electronic mail service). **Publications:** New Acquisitions; Current Contents of Selected Journals, both monthly - both for internal distribution only.

★16887★
UNIVERSITY OF SOUTHERN CALIFORNIA - VON KLEINSMID LIBRARY (Soc Sci)
University Park - MC 0182 Phone: (213)743-7347
Los Angeles, CA 90089-0182 Janice Hanks, Dept.Hd.
Founded: 1928. **Staff:** Prof 4; Other 4. **Subjects:** International relations, political science, public administration, urban and regional planning, economic development, international economic relations. **Special Collections:** International documents collection; planning documents collection. **Holdings:** 180,200 books; 5900 reels of microfilm; 73,800 microfiche. **Subscriptions:** 1850 journals and other serials; 72 newspapers. **Services:** Interlibrary loan; copying; library open to the public for reference use only. **Automated Operations:** Computerized circulation. **Computerized Information Services:** BRS Information Technologies, DIALOG Information Services. **Publications:** Newsletter; Selected Recent Acquisitions, monthly - local distribution. **Special Indexes:** International & Public Affairs Index (card). **Staff:** Annelore Stern, Asst.Libn.; Anthony Anderson, Asst.Libn..

UNIVERSITY OF SOUTHERN CALIFORNIA MEDICAL CENTER
See: Los Angeles County/University of Southern California Medical Center (8004)

★16888★
UNIVERSITY OF SOUTHERN COLORADO - LIBRARY - SPECIAL COLLECTIONS (Area-Ethnic)
2200 Bonforte Blvd. Phone: (719)549-2361
Pueblo, CO 81001 Metoda Mencin, Slavic Heritage Coll.Libn.
Founded: 1933. **Special Collections:** Slavic Heritage Collection (2000 volumes and uncataloged items); U.S. Government publications depository (250,000 documents). **Services:** Interlibrary loan; copying; collections open to the public with restrictions. **Automated Operations:** Computerized cataloging, acquisitions, serials, circulation, and ILL. **Computerized Information Services:** DIALOG Information Services. **Networks/Consortia:** Member of Arkansas Valley Regional Library Service System, Bibliographical Center for Research, Rocky Mountain Region, Inc. (BCR), Peaks and Valleys (Medical) Library Consortium.

★16889★
UNIVERSITY OF SOUTHERN INDIANA - SPECIAL COLLECTIONS AND UNIVERSITY ARCHIVES (Hist)
8600 University Blvd. Phone: (812)464-1896
Evansville, IN 47712-3595 Gina R. Walker, Act.Archv.
Founded: 1972. **Staff:** Prof 1; Other 1. **Subjects:** Regional and university history, communal societies, petroleum, geology, theater and film, children's literature. **Special Collections:** University Archives (70 cubic feet); Center for Communal Studies (560 volumes; 70 tapes; 25 linear feet); Sun Oil Geology Collection (130 VF drawers); Mead Johnson Archives (75 linear feet); Indiana labor history (18 linear feet). **Holdings:** 3500 books; 1100 linear feet of manuscripts; 300 oral history tapes; archives; maps; photographs; slides. **Services:** Interlibrary loan; copying; collections open to the public. **Automated Operations:** Computerized cataloging and circulation. **Computerized Information Services:** OCLC. **Networks/Consortia:** Member of Area 2 Library Services Authority (ALSA 2), INCOLSA. **Publications:** A Preliminary Guide to the Special Collections of Indiana State University Evansville, 1975. **Special Catalogs:** Guides to collections (typescript, loose-leaf), with updates; selected holdings of USI and other area repositories.

★16890★
UNIVERSITY OF SOUTHERN MAINE - OFFICE OF SPONSORED RESEARCH - LIBRARY (Soc Sci)
96 Falmouth St. Phone: (207)780-4411
Portland, ME 04103 Janet F. Brysh, Libn.
Founded: 1973. **Staff:** Prof 1. **Subjects:** Maine - state, county, economic, and social data; economic and environmental resources; health/social welfare; population/housing; manpower; taxes; education. **Special Collections:** Regional collection for Foundation Center of New York (open collection). **Holdings:** 1500 books; 300 other cataloged items; 44 VF drawers of state and federal agency reports and documents, data compilations; 95 newsletters and bulletins; microfiche aperture cards of IRS tax exempt foundations for Maine. **Subscriptions:** 65 journals and other serials; 5 newspapers. **Services:** Interlibrary loan; copying; library open to the public. **Publications:** A Directory of Maine Foundations; list of other publications - available on request. **Remarks:** Library houses all research reports produced by the Human Services Development Institute, Health Policy Unit, and Child Welfare Research Center. **Formerly:** Center for Research & Advanced Study - Research Center Library.

★16891★
UNIVERSITY OF SOUTHERN MAINE - SMALL BUSINESS DEVELOPMENT CENTER - BUSINESS INFORMATION SERVICE (Bus-Fin)
246 Deering Ave. Phone: (207)780-4420
Portland, ME 04102 Janice E. Tisdale, Libn.
Subjects: Business. **Special Collections:** Starting a Business collection (books; pamphlets). **Holdings:** 1000 volumes; 12 VF drawers of clippings; telephone directories for Maine, Massachusetts, and major U.S. cities. **Subscriptions:** 104 journals and other serials. **Services:** Copying; service open to the public. **Formerly:** New Enterprise Institute - Enterprise Information Service.

★16892★
UNIVERSITY OF SOUTHERN MISSISSIPPI - GEOLOGY DEPARTMENT - LIBRARY (Sci-Engr)
Southern Sta., Box 5044 Phone: (601)266-4526
Hattiesburg, MS 39406 Dr. Maurice A. Meylan, Assoc.Prof.
Founded: 1972. **Staff:** 2. **Subjects:** Geology. **Special Collections:** State geological publications; government geological publications; foreign geological publications; publications related to nuclear waste storage; oil well logs (50,000). **Holdings:** 20,000 volumes. **Subscriptions:** 10 journals and other serials. **Services:** Library open to the public with permission of Geology Department.

★16893★
UNIVERSITY OF SOUTHERN MISSISSIPPI - MC CAIN LIBRARY AND ARCHIVES (Hist)
Southern Sta., Box 5148 Phone: (601)266-4345
Hattiesburg, MS 39406-5148 Terry S. Latour, Dir.
Founded: 1976. **Staff:** Prof 7; Other 3. **Subjects:** Mississippiana, genealogy, Civil War, Confederate States of America, children's literature, British and American literary criticism, political cartoons. **Special Collections:** Papers of Theodore G. Bilbo, William M. Colmer, Governor Paul B. Johnson; Cleanth Brooks Literature Collection; de Grummond Children's Literature Research Collection; Ernest A. Walen Collection of Confederate Literature; Collection of Rare Books; Association of American Editorial Cartoonists Collection; genealogy collection; University Archives; Association of American Railroads Collection; Gulf, Mobile & Ohio Railroad Collection. **Holdings:** 58,000 volumes; 6000 linear feet of manuscripts and illustrations. **Subscriptions:** 220 journals and other serials; 64 newspapers. **Services:** Interlibrary loan; copying (both limited); library open to the public for reference use only. **Automated Operations:** Computerized cataloging and serials. **Computerized Information Services:** OCLC. **Networks/Consortia:** Member of SOLINET. **Publications:** Juvenile Miscellany, quarterly - by subscription. **Staff:** Sandra E. Boyd, Asst.Archv.; Alexandra S. Gressitt, Asst.Archv.; Betty S. Drake, Geneal.Libn.; Dolores A. Jones, Cur.; Anne H. Lundin, Asst.Cur.; Henry L. Simmons, Cur..

★16894★
UNIVERSITY OF SOUTHWESTERN LOUISIANA - CENTER FOR LOUISIANA STUDIES (Hist)
Box 4-0831 Phone: (318)231-6027
Lafayette, LA 70504 Glenn R. Conrad, Dir.
Staff: Prof 5; Other 2. **Subjects:** Louisiana history. **Special Collections:** Louisiana Colonial Records; Women in Louisiana Collection; folklore and folklife. **Holdings:** Photographs; magnetic tapes; documents; microfilm. **Services:** Copying; center open to the public with restrictions. **Publications:** USL History Series; USL Architecture Series; Louisiana Language and Life Series. **Staff:** Carl A. Brasseaux, Asst.Dir.; Jane B. Chaillot, Res.Asst.; Rebecca Batiste, Ed.Asst..

★16895★
UNIVERSITY OF SOUTHWESTERN LOUISIANA - JEFFERSON CAFFERY LOUISIANA ROOM - SOUTHWESTERN ARCHIVES AND MANUSCRIPTS COLLECTION (Hist, Area-Ethnic)
Dupre Library
302 E. St. Mary Blvd. Phone: (318)231-6031
Lafayette, LA 70503 Dr. I. Bruce Turner, Hd., Archv. & Spec.Coll.
Founded: 1962. **Staff:** Prof 2; Other 2. **Subjects:** Cajun and Creole culture; history - state, local, university; horticulture; Louisiana politics; agriculture; petroleum; genealogy. **Special Collections:** USL Oral History Program (50 tapes); Robert and Edwin Broussard papers (35 feet); Louisiana state documents; Zimmer papers (State Conservation Commission hearing reports); Jefferson Caffery Collection; David R. Williams papers; Ollie Tucker Osborne papers; Ernest J. Gaines papers; Edwin W. Willis papers; John M. Parker papers; Freeland Collection (photographic plates); Acadian Folklore Collection (taped interviews); Rice Millers Association Archives; university archives (500 linear feet); rare books (emphasis on Renaissance architecture, horticulture, and French literature). **Holdings:** 20,000 volumes; 36 VF drawers of clippings and pamphlets; 1700 theses; 250 manuscript collections (1500 linear feet); 500 audiotapes; microforms. **Services:** Copying; microfilming; collection open to the public. **Automated Operations:** Computerized cataloging and circulation. **Special Indexes:** Unpublished guides to manuscript collections. **Remarks:** An alternate telephone number is 231-5702. **Staff:** Jean Schmidt, LA Rm.Libn..

★16896★
UNIVERSITY OF SOUTHWESTERN LOUISIANA - ORNAMENTAL HORTICULTURE LIBRARY
Dept. of Agricultural Sciences
Box 44333
Lafayette, LA 70504
Defunct. Holdings absorbed by Dupre Library.

★16897★
UNIVERSITY OF SUDBURY - JESUIT ARCHIVES (Hist, Rel-Phil)
Sudbury, ON, Canada P3E 2C6 Phone: (705)673-5661
Robert Toupin, S.J., Prof. of Hist.
Founded: 1913. **Staff:** Prof 1. **Subjects:** French-Canadian and Catholic institutions in the Sudbury area, Manitoulin Island, Indians, Jesuit missionaries in Northern Ontario, Ste. Anne parish, St. Ignace/Sault Ste. Marie parish, French education in Ontario, Manitoulin Ojibway missions, Detroit and Windsor 18th century missions among the French and Hurons, Thunder Bay missions. **Special Collections:** Societe historique du Nouvel-Ontario (85 volumes); College du Sacre-Coeur Archives; papers of Romanet, Racette, and Hurtubise (10 boxes each). **Holdings:** 350 books; 200 bound periodical volumes; 150 pamphlets; 18 cassettes; 60 maps; 300 photographic portraits; 60 photograph albums; 450 boxes of archival material. **Services:** Copying; archives open to the public on request. **Remarks:** Most of the holdings are in French.

★16898★
UNIVERSITY OF SUDBURY - LIBRARY (Rel-Phil, Area-Ethnic)
Sudbury, ON, Canada P3E 2C6 Phone: (705)673-5661
Olga Beaulieu, Dir. of Lib.
Founded: 1960. **Staff:** 3. **Subjects:** Religion, philosophy, Native studies, folklore. **Holdings:** 37,300 books; 4600 bound periodical volumes. **Subscriptions:** 127 journals and other serials; 8 newspapers. **Services:** Interlibrary loan; copying; library open to the public. **Also Known As:** Universite de Sudbury.

★16899★
UNIVERSITY OF TENNESSEE - AGRICULTURE-VETERINARY MEDICINE LIBRARY (Agri, Med)
Veterinary Medicine Teaching Hospital Phone: (615)974-7338
Knoxville, TN 37996-4500 Don Jett, Libn.
Staff: Prof 2; Other 4. **Subjects:** Agriculture, veterinary medicine. **Holdings:** 103,628 volumes. **Subscriptions:** 2505 journals and other serials. **Services:** Interlibrary loan; library open to the public for reference use only. **Computerized Information Services:** DIALOG Information Services, MEDLINE, Integrated Technical Information System (ITIS), Pergamon ORBIT InfoLine, Inc.

★16900★
UNIVERSITY OF TENNESSEE - ARBORETUM SOCIETY - LIBRARY (Biol Sci)
Univ. of Tenn. Experiment Station & Arboretum
901 Kerr Hollow Rd. Phone: (615)483-3571
Oak Ridge, TN 37830 Richard M. Evans, Supv., Forestry Sta.
Staff: 2. **Subjects:** Botany, horticulture, trees and shrubs, landscaping, floriculture. **Holdings:** 200 books; bulletins, journals, and plant lists from all major arboreta in the United States and abroad. **Services:** Copying (limited); library open to the public for reference use only.

★16901★
UNIVERSITY OF TENNESSEE - COLLEGE OF LAW - PUBLIC LAW INSTITUTE LIBRARY (Law)
1505 W. Cumberland Ave. Phone: (615)974-6691
Knoxville, TN 37996 Julia P. Hardin, Assoc. Dean
Founded: 1973. **Staff:** Prof 1; Other 2. **Subjects:** Judicial and law-related education, Tennessee law. **Holdings:** 500 volumes; Tennessee statutes. **Services:** Library not open to the public. **Publications:** Tennessee Judicial Newsletter, 6/year - by subscription.

★16902★
UNIVERSITY OF TENNESSEE - COLLEGE OF LAW LIBRARY (Law)
1505 W. Cumberland Ave. Phone: (615)974-4381
Knoxville, TN 37996-1800 William J. Beintema, Dir.
Founded: 1890. **Staff:** Prof 4; Other 9. **Subjects:** Law. **Special Collections:** Depository of U.S. documents (10,000); constitutional law books and materials in braille (948 volumes). **Holdings:** 275,387 volumes. **Subscriptions:** 3569 journals and other serials; 16 newspapers. **Services:** Interlibrary loan; copying; library open to the public. **Automated Operations:** Computerized cataloging. **Computerized Information Services:** LEXIS, WESTLAW. Performs searches on fee basis. **Staff:** Reba A. Best, Asst.Libn., Tech.Serv.; D. Cheryn Picquet, Assoc. Law Libn., Adm.; Ruth J. Hill, Asst.Libn., Ref..

★16903★
UNIVERSITY OF TENNESSEE - ENERGY, ENVIRONMENT & RESOURCES CENTER - JOINT RESEARCH CENTERS' LIBRARY (Trans, Energy)
327 S. Stadium Hall Phone: (615)974-4251
Knoxville, TN 37996-0710 Joyce L. Finney, Libn.
Founded: 1981. **Staff:** Prof 1. **Subjects:** Energy conservation, solar energy, coal, waste management, transportation, water resources. **Holdings:** 10,000 books; 14,000 technical reports. **Subscriptions:** 120 journals and other serials. **Services:** Interlibrary loan; copying; library open to the public. **Publications:** Quarterly acquisitions list; bibliographies.

UNIVERSITY OF TENNESSEE - INSTITUTE FOR PUBLIC SERVICE - MUNICIPAL TECHNICAL ADVISORY SERVICE
See: Municipal Technical Advisory Service (9419)

★16904★
UNIVERSITY OF TENNESSEE - MEDICAL CENTER, KNOXVILLE - PRESTON MEDICAL LIBRARY (Med)
1924 Alcoa Hwy. Phone: (615)544-9525
Knoxville, TN 37920 Martha C. Watkins, Libn.
Founded: 1966. **Staff:** Prof 2; Other 3. **Subjects:** Medicine, hematology, biochemistry, immunology. **Holdings:** 2600 books; 20,000 bound periodical volumes. **Subscriptions:** 420 journals and other serials. **Services:** Interlibrary loan; copying; library open to the public with limited circulation. **Computerized Information Services:** DIALOG Information Services, BRS Information Technologies, MEDLARS. Performs searches on fee basis. **Networks/Consortia:** Member of Knoxville Area Health Sciences Library Consortium (KAHSLC). **Staff:** Lynne Yeomans Gard, Libn..

★16905★
UNIVERSITY OF TENNESSEE - MUSIC LIBRARY (Mus)
Music Bldg., Rm. 301 Phone: (615)974-3474
Knoxville, TN 37796-2600 Pauline S. Bayne, Libn.
Founded: 1971. **Staff:** Prof 1; Other 2. **Subjects:** Music. **Special Collections:** Galston-Busoni Music Collection (manuscripts; photographs; memorabilia; 2000 scores for piano); Grace Moore memorabilia, photographs, autographed and annotated scores; David Van Vactor Collection (manuscripts; sketchbooks; first editions; original recordings). **Holdings:** 29,447 volumes; 15,956 recordings. **Subscriptions:** 329 journals and other serials. **Services:** Interlibrary loan; copying; library open to the public. **Computerized Information Services:** DIALOG Information Services, BRS Information Technologies, RLIN, Pergamon ORBIT InfoLine, Inc. (through Main Library).

★16906★
UNIVERSITY OF TENNESSEE - SPACE INSTITUTE - LIBRARY (Sci-Engr)
Tullahoma, TN 37388-8897 Phone: (615)455-0631
Mary M. Lo, Hd.Libn.
Founded: 1965. **Staff:** Prof 2; Other 1. **Subjects:** Engineering - aeronautical, mechanical, electrical, metallurgical; fluid mechanics; MHD power generation; lasers; propulsion; physics; artificial intelligence; mathematics; aerodynamics; propulsion; space science and technology; computer science. **Holdings:** 16,200 books; 700 bound periodical volumes; 40,000 reports; 165,000 microforms; 180 dissertations; 30 patents. **Subscriptions:** 184 journals and other serials. **Services:** Interlibrary loan; copying; library open to the public by appointment. **Automated Operations:** Computerized cataloging and ILL. **Computerized Information Services:** DIALOG Information Services, NASA/RECON. Performs searches on fee basis. **Networks/Consortia:** Member of SOLINET. **Staff:** Marjorie Joseph, Libn..

★16907★
UNIVERSITY OF TENNESSEE - SPECIAL COLLECTIONS (Hist)
Knoxville, TN 37996-1000 Phone: (615)974-4480
Dr. James Lloyd, Spec.Coll.Libn.
Founded: 1959. **Staff:** Prof 1; Other 3. **Subjects:** Tennesseana, 19th century American fiction, Southern Indians, early imprints. **Special Collections:** Estes Kefauver Collection (political papers and memorabilia; 1204 feet); Radiation Research Archives (300,000 items); William Congreve Collection; University of Tennessee Archives (1200 feet). **Holdings:** 33,324 books; 3 million manuscripts. **Services:** Copying; collection open to the public with restrictions. **Publications:** Occasional publication. **Special Catalogs:** Rare books catalog (card); unpublished registers and calendars to manuscript collections.

★16908★
UNIVERSITY OF TENNESSEE, MEMPHIS - HEALTH SCIENCES LIBRARY (Med)
800 Madison Ave. Phone: (901)528-5638
Memphis, TN 38163 Jess A. Martin, Dir.
Founded: 1913. **Staff:** Prof 13; Other 22. **Subjects:** Medicine, dentistry, nursing, pharmacy, allied health sciences, social work. **Special Collections:** Wallace Collection (books authored by University of Tennessee personnel). **Holdings:** 40,010 books; 114,999 bound periodical volumes; 130 microforms; 306 slide programs; 403 filmstrips; 220 films; 1185 video and audio cassettes. **Subscriptions:** 2142 journals and other serials. **Services:** Interlibrary loan; copying; library open to the public for reference use only. **Automated Operations:** Computerized cataloging and ILL. **Computerized Information Services:** OCLC, DIALOG Information Services, MEDLINE; internal database; OnTyme Electronic Message Network Service, DOCLINE (electronic mail services). Performs searches on fee basis. Contact Person: Janet Smith, Ref.Libn., 528-5406. **Networks/Consortia:** Member of SOLINET. **Publications:** Library Guide, annual; Periodicals Holdings List, annual; Library Bulletin, bimonthly. **Staff:** Susan Selig, Hd., Educ. & Rd.Serv.Dept.; Anne Carroll Bunting, Hd., Tech.Serv.Dept.; Ellen Cooper, Acq./Ser.Libn.; Wilma R. Lasslo, Circ.Libn.; Frances Verble, Cat.; Mary K. Givens, Assoc.Dir.; Glenda Mendina, Ref.Libn.; Ronald R. Sommer, Spec.Asst. to Dir.; Janet Smith, Ref.Libn.; Nelda Burroughs, Br.Libn.; Lois Bellamy, Sys.Libn.; Richard Nollen, Ref.Libn..

★16909★
UNIVERSITY OF TEXAS - INSTITUTE OF TEXAN CULTURES AT SAN ANTONIO - LIBRARY (Area-Ethnic)
801 S. Bowie St.
Box 1226 Phone: (512)226-7651
San Antonio, TX 78294 James C. McNutt, Ph.D., Dir., Lib.Serv.
Founded: 1968. **Staff:** Prof 1; Other 3. **Subjects:** Texas ethnic history and regional folklore. **Special Collections:** Photograph collection (35,000 indexed copy negatives on Texas subjects); San Antonio Light negative collection (48,000 negatives made from 1924 to 1940 and retired from the newspaper morgue). **Holdings:** 4500 books; 80 bound periodical volumes; 100 VF drawers. **Services:** Interlibrary loan; copying; reproduction of photographs; library open to the public by appointment for reference use. **Networks/Consortia:** Member of Council of Research & Academic Libraries (CORAL). **Publications:** The Texians and the Texans (series of ethnic pamphlets); slides and filmstrips useful for teaching; books on Texas history and institute exhibits. **Special Indexes:** Subject index to photographs.

★16910★
UNIVERSITY OF TEXAS - M.D. ANDERSON HOSPITAL AND TUMOR INSTITUTE - RESEARCH MEDICAL LIBRARY (Med)
Texas Medical Center Phone: (713)792-2282
Houston, TX 77030 Sara Jean Jackson, Dir.
Founded: 1945. **Staff:** Prof 5; Other 9. **Subjects:** Cancer, radiological physics, cell biology. **Special Collections:** Rare books and early treatises on cancer (375 volumes). **Holdings:** 45,000 volumes. **Subscriptions:** 1200 journals and other serials. **Services:** Interlibrary loan; copying; library open to the public for reference use only. **Automated Operations:** Computerized cataloging and circulation. **Computerized Information Services:** Online systems. **Networks/Consortia:** Member of AMIGOS Bibliographic Council, Inc., TALON. **Also Known As:** University of Texas System Cancer Center.

★16911★
UNIVERSITY OF TEXAS, ARLINGTON - LIBRARY - DIVISION OF SPECIAL COLLECTIONS AND ARCHIVES (Hist)
Box 19497 Phone: (817)273-3393
Arlington, TX 73109 Dr. Gerald D. Saxon, Asst.Dir., Spec.Coll.
Founded: 1974. **Staff:** Prof 9; Other 6. **Subjects:** Texana; Mexican war; history - cartographic, Meso-American, Texas labor and politics. **Special Collections:** Jenkins Garrett Library (Texana and Mexican war; 12,000 items); Cartographic History Library (3500 items); Fort Worth Star-Telegram Photographic Archive (750,000 items); Basil Clemons Photographic Collection (20,000 items); UTA Press Collection; Robertson Colony Collection of Historic Texana. **Holdings:** 15,000 books; 134 bound periodical volumes; 3500 maps, pieces of sheet music, lithographs; 600 linear feet of manuscripts; 1000 folders of newspapers; 4 VF drawers of clippings. **Subscriptions:** 27 journals and other serials. **Services:** Copying; division open to the public. **Networks/Consortia:** Member of AMIGOS Bibliographic Council, Inc.. **Publications:** Papers Concerning Robertson's Colony in Texas UTA Press, annual; Compass Rose (newsletter), semiannual. **Staff:** Dr. Malcolm D. McLean, Hd., Robertson Colony Coll.; Jane Boley, Univ.Archv.; Ms. Marcelle Hull, Adm.Asst., Spec.Coll.; Maritza Arrigunaga, Meso-American Coll.; Lisa Davis-Allen, Cart.Hist.Spec.; Shirley Rodnitzky, Spec. in Hist.Photo. & Nonbook Mtls.; Kathy Rankin, Cat.; Betsy Hudson, Fort Worth Star-Telegram Photo.Archv..

★16912★
UNIVERSITY OF TEXAS, AUSTIN - ARCHITECTURE & PLANNING LIBRARY (Art, Plan)
General Libraries, BTL 200 Phone: (512)471-1844
Austin, TX 78713-7330 Eloise E. McDonald, Arch. & Plan.Libn.
Staff: Prof 1; Other 2. **Subjects:** Architecture, architectural history, landscape architecture, city and regional planning. **Special Collections:** Architectural Drawings Collection (99,547 drawings). **Holdings:** 22,164 books; 7402 bound periodical volumes; 17,810 HUD 701 depository items; 385 reels of microfilm; 7266 microfiche. **Subscriptions:** 375 journals and other serials. **Services:** Interlibrary loan; copying; library open to the public. **Publications:** Library Guide. **Staff:** Lila Stillson, Cur., Arch. Drawings Coll..

★16913★
UNIVERSITY OF TEXAS, AUSTIN - ARTIFICIAL INTELLIGENCE LABORATORY - INFORMATION CENTER (Comp Sci)
Computer Sciences Dept.
Painter Hall 3.28 Phone: (512)471-4353
Austin, TX 78712 Christine Sawyer, Tech.Sec.
Founded: 1985. **Staff:** 3. **Subjects:** Artificial intelligence, system documentation, computer science. **Special Collections:** Reports from 9 University of Texas research centers, 1959 to present. **Holdings:** 250 volumes; 5000 technical reports on microfiche; 275 technical reports. **Subscriptions:** 20 journals and other serials. **Services:** Center open to the public with special permission. **Automated Operations:** Computerized cataloging, acquisitions, serials, and circulation. **Computerized Information Services:** Internal database; ARPAnet (electronic mail service). **Publications:** Artificial Intelligence Laboratory Technical Report Series, quarterly.

★16914★
UNIVERSITY OF TEXAS, AUSTIN - ASIAN COLLECTION (Area-Ethnic)
General Libraries, MAI 316 Phone: (512)471-3135
Austin, TX 78713-7330 Kevin Lin, Libn.
Staff: Prof 1; Other 2. **Subjects:** China and Japan; art; history, especially of Meiji Period in Japan; politics; economics and statistics; anthropology; philosophy; literature; Chinese and Japanese linguistics; India, Bangladesh, and Sri Lanka - language, literature, history, philosophy, religion, economics, government, education (in Hindi, Pali, Prakrit, Sanskrit, Urdu). **Special Collections:** Selected South Asian research materials in English (census of India, 1872-1951 (on microfiche); bound censuses of India and Pakistan; district gazetteers; 20,196 uncataloged items). **Holdings:** 107,534 volumes; 12,405 microfiche; 778 reels of microfilm. **Subscriptions:** 746 journals and other serials; 15 newspapers. **Services:** Interlibrary loan; copying; collection open to the public. **Publications:** Library Guide. **Remarks:** Materials in Indian languages other than those stated above are in the Collections Deposit Library. **Staff:** Merry Burlingham, South Asian Studies Bibliog..

★16915★
UNIVERSITY OF TEXAS, AUSTIN - AUDIO VISUAL LIBRARY (Aud-Vis)
Peter T. Flawn Academic Center 101
General Libraries Phone: (512)471-5222
Austin, TX 78713-7330 Marcia Parsons, Libn.
Staff: Prof 1; Other 5. **Subjects:** Audiovisual materials for instructional use and research, all subjects. **Holdings:** 988 cassettes; 270 filmstrips; 9600 phonograph records; 175 phonotapes; 6443 slides; 575 video cassettes. **Services:** Library open to the public. **Publications:** Library Guide.

★16916★
UNIVERSITY OF TEXAS, AUSTIN - BARKER TEXAS HISTORY CENTER (Hist)
General Libraries, SRH 2.109 Phone: (512)471-5961
Austin, TX 78713-7330 Dr. Don E. Carleton, Dir.
Staff: Prof 8; Other 15. **Subjects:** Texas history, literature, and folklore; Texas state documents; University of Texas publications and history; Southern and Western history. **Special Collections:** Sound archives (1006 audio cassettes; 8122 phonograph records; 4023 audiotapes; 82 video cassettes; 66 videotapes); dime novel collection; Kell Frontier Collection; Austin papers; Bexar Archives; Bryan papers; T.S. Henderson papers; James S. Hogg papers; Ashbel Smith papers; John Henry Faulk papers; Pompeo Coppini-Waldine Tauch papers; Jesse Jones papers; James Wells papers; Martin M. Crane papers; Luther M. Evans Collection; James Harper Starr papers; True West archives; Natchez Trace Collection; Russell Lee Photograph Collection; R.C. Hickman Photograph Collection. **Holdings:** 140,077 volumes; 3000 linear feet of university records; 22,500 linear feet of nonuniversity records; 29,066 maps; 2000 titles of historic Texas newspapers; 500,000 photographs; 3529 slides; 100 VF drawers of clippings; 1500 scrapbooks; 15,393 reels of microfilm; 1138 tapes of oral recordings. **Subscriptions:** 1182 journals and other serials. **Services:** Interlibrary loan; copying; center open to the public. **Publications:** Newsletter; Archives Guide; Library Guide. **Staff:** Katherine Adams, Asst.Dir.; Ralph Elder, Pub.Serv.; Alison Beck, Archv. & Mss..

★16917★
UNIVERSITY OF TEXAS, AUSTIN - BENSON LATIN AMERICAN COLLECTION (Area-Ethnic)
General Libraries, SRH 1.108 Phone: (512)471-3818
Austin, TX 78713-7330 Laura Gutierrez-Witt, Hd.Libn.
Staff: Prof 5; Other 19. **Subjects:** Latin American anthropology, art, culture, economics, education, geography, government, history, law, literature, music, philology, philosophy, religion, science; Mexican American history, social sciences, and literature; studies on Hispanics in the U.S. **Special Collections:** Genaro Garcia; Joaquin Garcia Icazbalceta; Luis Garcia Pimentel; Alejandro Prieto; W.B. Stephens; Diego Munoz; Manuel Gondra; Hernandez y Davalos; Sanchez Navarro family; Simon Lucuix Rio de La Plata Library (21,000 volumes); Arturo Taracena Flores Library (Guatemala; 10,000 titles); Pedro Martinez Reales Gaucho Collection; Pablo Salce Arredondo Collection of Mexican Manuscripts and Imprints; Julio Cortazar Literary Papers; St. John del Rey Mining Company Archives from Brazil; Chicano Writers Manuscript Collection (21 linear feet); Archive of the League of United Latin American Citizens (70 linear feet); Raza Unida Party Archive (5 linear feet); Economy Furniture Company Strike Collection (3 linear feet); Carlos Castaneda Collection (35 linear feet); Eleuterio Escobar Collection (15 linear feet); Carlos Villalongin Dramatic Company Archives (247 playscripts; 32 photographs; 15 playbills and notices). **Holdings:** 526,085 volumes; 4 million pages of manuscripts; 19,516 reels of microfilm; 18,500 maps; 15,393 microfiche; 20,086 pages of broadsides; 22,100 prints and photographs; 10,000 volumes of newspapers; 1561 phonograph records; 3281 slides. **Subscriptions:** 22,321 journals and other serials. **Services:** Interlibrary loan; copying; collection open to the public for reference use only. **Publications:** Bibliographic Guide to Latin American Studies; Benson Latin American Serials List (microfiche); Mexican American Archives in the Benson Collection: A Supplement for Educators; Chicano Film Guide, 2nd edition; Archives and Manuscripts on Microfilm in the Nettie Lee Benson Latin American Collection: A Checklist; Mexican American Archives in the Benson Collection: A Guide for Users; Inventory of the Records of the Cuban Consulate, Key West, Florida, 1886-1961, on microfilm; Revolution and Counterrevolution in Guatemala, 1944-1963: An Annotated Bibliography of Materials in the Benson Latin American Collection. **Special Catalogs:** Catalog of the Benson Latin American Collection. **Remarks:** Includes the holdings of University of Texas, Austin - Mexican American Library Program. **Staff:** Ann Hartness, Asst.Hd.Libn.; Jane Garner, Archv.; Donald Gibbs, Bibliog.; Anne Jordan, Rare Bks.Libn.; Margo Gutierrez, Mexican Amer.Stud.Libn..

★16918★
UNIVERSITY OF TEXAS, AUSTIN - BUREAU OF BUSINESS RESEARCH - INFORMATION SERVICES (Bus-Fin)
Box 7459, University Sta. Phone: (512)471-5180
Austin, TX 78713 Rita J. Wright, Libn.
Founded: 1926. **Staff:** Prof 1; Other 1. **Subjects:** Texas - demographics, economics, industries. **Holdings:** 1200 books; Texas and U.S. Government documents; 1980 Census tapes and microfiche; other states' manufacturing directories. **Subscriptions:** 700 journals and other serials. **Services:** Copying; services open to the public. **Computerized Information Services:** Directory of Texas Manufacturers (internal database). Performs searches on fee basis. **Publications:** Texas Trade and Professional Associations, biennial; Texas Fact Book, irregular.

★16919★
UNIVERSITY OF TEXAS, AUSTIN - BUREAU OF ECONOMIC GEOLOGY - READING ROOM/DATA CENTER (Sci-Engr)
University Sta., Box X
Austin, TX 78713-7508 Jeffrey Thurwachter, Data Ctr.Supv.
Staff: Prof 2; Other 3. **Subjects:** Texas geology, mineral resources, nuclear waste repositories, Texas water resources, petroleum industry, general geology. **Special Collections:** Maps (100 VF drawers); aerial photographs (200,000 frames); well logs (70,000); well data (2000 notebooks). **Holdings:** 13,000 books. **Subscriptions:** 50 journals and other serials. **Services:** Copying; room open to the public for reference use only.

★16920★
UNIVERSITY OF TEXAS, AUSTIN - CENTER FOR ENERGY STUDIES - ENERGY INFORMATION SERVICE
Balcones Research Center
10100 Burnet Rd.
Austin, TX 78758
Founded: 1974. **Subjects:** Energy resources - petroleum, natural gas, solar, geothermal, electric, nuclear, coal; energy conservation, policy, and technology. **Holdings:** 2500 books; 150 bound periodical volumes; 4 VF drawers of clippings; 33,000 reports on microfiche; 300 pamphlets. **Remarks:** Presently inactive.

★16921★
UNIVERSITY OF TEXAS, AUSTIN - CENTER FOR FUSION ENGINEERING - LIBRARY
10100 Burnet Rd.
Austin, TX 78758
Subjects: Fusion science and engineering. **Holdings:** 2000 volumes. **Remarks:** Presently inactive.

★16922★
UNIVERSITY OF TEXAS, AUSTIN - CENTER FOR INTERCULTURAL STUDIES IN FOLKLORE AND ETHNOMUSICOLOGY - LIBRARY (Hist)
Student Services Bldg., Rm. 3.106 Phone: (512)471-1288
Austin, TX 78712 Dr. Steven Feld, Dir.
Founded: 1970. **Staff:** 1. **Subjects:** Folklore, anthropology, sociology, ethnomusicology. **Holdings:** 900 books; 540 bound periodical volumes; 600 articles. **Subscriptions:** 18 journals and other serials.

★16923★
UNIVERSITY OF TEXAS, AUSTIN - CENTER FOR TRANSPORTATION RESEARCH (Trans)
3208 Red River St. Phone: (512)472-8875
Austin, TX 78705 Brenda Ziser, Libn.
Staff: Prof 1. **Subjects:** Transportation planning, transportation and highway engineering. **Holdings:** 50 books; 2000 reports. **Subscriptions:** 25 journals and other serials. **Services:** Interlibrary loan; center not open to the public. **Computerized Information Services:** DIALOG Information Services.

★16924★
UNIVERSITY OF TEXAS, AUSTIN - CHEMISTRY LIBRARY (Sci-Engr)
General Libraries, WEL 2.132 Phone: (512)471-1303
Austin, TX 78713-7330 Christine Johnston, Libn.
Staff: Prof 1; Other 2. **Subjects:** Chemistry, biochemistry, nutrition, chemical engineering. **Holdings:** 25,070 books; 25,520 bound periodical volumes; 144 reels of microfilm; 3383 microfiche. **Subscriptions:** 630 journals and other serials. **Services:** Interlibrary loan; copying; library open to the public. **Publications:** Library Guide. **Also Known As:** John W. Mallet Chemistry Library.

★16925★
UNIVERSITY OF TEXAS, AUSTIN - CLASSICS LIBRARY (Hum)
General Libraries, WAG 1 Phone: (512)471-9174
Austin, TX 78713-7330 Cynthia Cash, Lib.Asst.
Staff: 1. **Subjects:** Greek and Latin literature, classical civilization, Greek and Latin languages, classical archeology, Greek and Roman history, epigraphy, numismatics. **Holdings:** 19,723 books; 1858 bound periodical volumes; 79 reels of microfilm. **Subscriptions:** 161 journals and other serials. **Services:** Interlibrary loan; copying; library open to the public. **Publications:** Library Guide.

★16926★
UNIVERSITY OF TEXAS, AUSTIN - DOCUMENTS COLLECTION (Info Sci)
General Libraries, PCL 2.400 Phone: (512)471-3813
Austin, TX 78713-7330 Paul Rascoe, Libn.
Staff: Prof 1; Other 5. **Subjects:** U.S. Government documents, U.N. documents. **Holdings:** 201,517 U.S. documents; 95,210 U.N. documents; 22,522 microfiche. **Services:** Interlibrary loan; copying; collection open to the public.

★16927★
UNIVERSITY OF TEXAS, AUSTIN - ENGINEERING LIBRARY (Sci-Engr)
General Libraries, ECJ 1.300 Phone: (512)471-1610
Austin, TX 78713-7330 Susan B. Ardis, Libn.
Staff: Prof 3; Other 6. **Subjects:** Engineering - aerospace, civil, electrical, computer, mechanical, petroleum; engineering mechanics. **Holdings:** 57,280 books; 56,515 bound periodical volumes; 523,268 microfiche of DOE technical reports, industry standards, product catalogs, military specifications; 3500 reels of microfilm; 82,025 microcards; U.S. Patent Depository Library. **Subscriptions:** 2374 journals and other serials. **Services:** Interlibrary loan; copying; library open to the public. **Publications:** Library Guide. **Also Known As:** Richard W. McKinney Engineering Library. **Staff:** Larayne Dallas, Asst.Libn.; Molly White, Balcones Lib.Serv.Ctr.Libn..

★16928★
UNIVERSITY OF TEXAS, AUSTIN - FILM LIBRARY (Aud-Vis)
General Libraries, EDA G-12
Box W Phone: (512)471-3572
Austin, TX 78713-7448 Jane Hazelton, Media Coord.
Staff: 6. **Special Collections:** Films of University of Texas football games, 1937 to present. **Holdings:** 2504 16mm educational films; 382 video cassettes; 39 audiotapes. **Services:** Interlibrary loan; rentals; library open to the public. **Networks/Consortia:** Member of Consortium of University Film Centers (CUFC). **Special Catalogs:** Learning Resource Guide (film catalog).

★16929★
UNIVERSITY OF TEXAS, AUSTIN - FINE ARTS LIBRARY (Art, Mus, Theater)
General Libraries, FAB 3.200 Phone: (512)471-4777
Austin, TX 78713-7330 Carole Cable, Hd.Libn.
Staff: Prof 4; Other 12. **Subjects:** Art history, aesthetics, studio art, philosophy of art, art education, play production, drama education, theatrical designing, playwriting, dance, music, performance, composition, ethnomusicology, music education, music theory, musicology. **Special Collections:** Historical Music Recordings Collection. **Holdings:** 138,945 books; 12,664 bound periodical volumes; 24,473 phonograph records; 1145 compact discs; 2262 tapes; 1818 audio cassettes; 247 video cassettes; 74 videodiscs; 1644 slides; 4227 reels of microfilm; 23,379 microfiche; 992 microcards; prints; mounted photographs; VF drawers of pamphlets, clippings. **Subscriptions:** 1309 journals and other serials. **Services:** Interlibrary loan; copying; library open to the public. **Publications:** Library Guide. **Staff:** Karl F. Miller, AV Libn..

★16930★
UNIVERSITY OF TEXAS, AUSTIN - GEOLOGY LIBRARY (Sci-Engr)
General Libraries, GEO 302 Phone: (512)471-1257
Austin, TX 78713-7330 Dennis Trombatore, Libn.
Staff: Prof 1; Other 2. **Subjects:** Geology, paleontology, mineralogy, geophysics, petroleum and marine geology, volcanology. **Holdings:** 76,111 volumes; 248 reels of microfilm; 11,080 microfiche; 35,772 geological maps. **Subscriptions:** 1224 journals and other serials. **Services:** Interlibrary loan; copying; library open to the public. **Publications:** Library Guide. **Also Known As:** Joseph C. Walter, Jr. and Elizabeth C. Walter Geology Library.

★16931★
UNIVERSITY OF TEXAS, AUSTIN - HARRY RANSOM HUMANITIES RESEARCH CENTER (Hum)
Box 7219 Phone: (512)471-9111
Austin, TX 78713 Decherd Turner, Dir.
Staff: Prof 13; Other 51. **Subjects:** American, English, and French literature; photography; theater arts; book arts. **Special Collections:** Norman Bel Geddes (250,000 items); Alfred A. and Blanche Knopf Library and Publishing Archives (100,000 items); David O. Selznick Film Archives (1 million items); Robert Lee Wolff Collection (19th century fiction; 18,000 volumes); Miriam Lutcher Stark Library (10,000 items); John Henry Wrenn Library (6000 items); Pforzheimer Library of English Literature to 1700 (1010 items); Giorgio Uzielli Aldine Collection (287 items). **Holdings:** 9 million pages of manuscripts; 800,000 volumes; 5 million photographic images; 3000 linear feet of clippings, playbills, and miscellaneous files; 80,000 pieces of literary iconography. **Services:** Copying; use of unique materials requires approval of faculty committee. **Computerized Information Services:** OCLC. **Networks/Consortia:** Member of AMIGOS Bibliographic Council, Inc.. **Publications:** The Library Chronicle, 4/year; bibliographies; bibliographical monographs. **Special Catalogs:** Exhibition catalogs; catalogs of collections. **Remarks:** An alternate telephone number is 471-9119. **Staff:** Sally Leach, Asst. to the Dir.; Catherine Henderson, Res.Libn.; John P. Chalmers, Libn.; W.H. Crain, Cur., Theater Arts; Roy Flukinger, Cur., Photog.; Maria X. Wells, Cur., Italian Coll..

★16932★
UNIVERSITY OF TEXAS, AUSTIN - HOGG FOUNDATION FOR MENTAL HEALTH - LIBRARY (Soc Sci)
W.C. Hogg Bldg., Rm. 301 Phone: (512)471-5041
Austin, TX 78712 Anita Faubion, Libn.
Staff: 2. **Subjects:** Psychology, psychiatry, gerontology, learning disabilities, parenting, social work, sociology, education, family life. **Special Collections:** Regional Foundation Library (depository of the Foundation Center in N.Y.; Internal Revenue Service tax returns from foundations in Texas); collection on foundations and philanthropy, grant seeking, proposal writing, and fund-raising information. **Holdings:** 1500 books; 300 foundation annual reports. **Subscriptions:** 16 journals and newsletters. **Services:** Library open to the public.

★16933★
UNIVERSITY OF TEXAS, AUSTIN - HUMANITIES RESEARCH CENTER - THEATRE ARTS COLLECTIONS (Theater)
Box 7219 Phone: (512)471-9122
Austin, TX 78713 Decherd Turner, Dir.
Staff: Prof 3; Other 5. **Special Collections:** Gloria Swanson Collection (20,000 photographs; 500,000 other cataloged items); David O. Selznick Collection (scenarios; music; artwork; photographs; correspondence; contracts and other legal papers); Ernest Lehman Collection (screenplays; production notes; correspondence); MGM Matte Drawings (1400); Albert Davis Collection (theatrical artifacts, including posters, programs, and photographs collected between 1874-1942); Messmore Kendall Collection (theatrical materials, including letters, engravings, programs, opera liberetti, and extra-illustrated books); Robert Downing Collection on the History and Theory of the Theatre (books; photographs; typescripts of plays; Lacy acting editions; American plays inscribed by their authors; sketches, floor plans, lightplots, and prompt scripts from productions for which Mr. Downing was stage manager); Hoblitzelle Interstate Circuit Collection (450,000 cinema artifacts, 1900-1973, including photographs, publicity materials, lobbby cards, and records of the circuits movie houses); John Gassner Collection (3000 books; typescripts and holograph manuscripts; pamphlets; reviews; clippings; play manuscripts; letters; photographs; magazines; personal memorabilia); Stanley Marcus Collection of Sicilian Marionettes (60); papers of Edith Evans, Marie Tempest, Pat Rooney, Frances Starr, Lucy Barton, B. Iden Payne, E.P. Conkle; Jule Styne Musical Collection (original manuscript scores of individual songs and entire productions; libretti; typed manuscripts and published versions of musicals; publicity materials; correspondence; stage directions); W.H. Crain Collection (original designs of costumes and scenery; posters; scrapbooks; sheet music, including that from the Ziegfield Follies; Marquis de Cuevas Archive; film stills and posters; music hall sheet music; prompt scripts); Joe E. Ward Collection (19th and 20th century circus memorabilia, including photographs, letters, programs, playbills, route books, costumes); Donald Albery Collection (correspondence; legal papers; minutes; financial records; designs; notes of telephone conversations and other materials); B.J. Simmons Collection (29,000 costume designs and documentation, 1880-1960); Fred Fehl Collection of Theatre and Dance Photographs (200,000 photographs; 250,000 negatives; programs). **Holdings:** 15,000 books; 40,000 bound periodical volumes; 100 films and videotapes. **Subscriptions:** 50 journals and other serials. **Services:** Copying; library open to the public by appointment for reference use. **Staff:** Dr. William H. Crain, Cur.; Charles Bell, Assoc.Cur..

★16934★
UNIVERSITY OF TEXAS, AUSTIN - INSTITUTE FOR GEOPHYSICS - LIBRARY (Sci-Engr)
8701 Mopac Blvd. Phone: (512)471-0499
Austin, TX 78759-8345 Josefa A. York, Libn.
Founded: 1973. **Staff:** Prof 1. **Subjects:** Geophysics, marine geology, seismology. **Special Collections:** Caribbean; Central America; Gulf of Mexico; Data Archive/Library: Multichannel Seismic Film Master Library; Multichannel Seismic Digital Tape Library (20,000); Underway Geophysical (Analog Data) Data Base; Underway Geophysical Digital Data Base; Worldwide Underway Geophysical Data Base (digital); Global Digital Seismograph Network Database. **Holdings:** 4254 books; 2463 bound periodical volumes; 65 VF drawers of reprints; 185 theses; 2348 maps. **Subscriptions:** 279 journals and other serials. **Services:** Interlibrary loan; copying; library open to the public for reference use only. **Automated Operations:** Computerized serials. **Computerized Information Services:** DIALOG Information Services. **Publications:** List of scientific publications and papers - available upon request. **Special Indexes:** Caribbean region (online; in preparation).

★16935★
UNIVERSITY OF TEXAS, AUSTIN - LIBRARY AND INFORMATION SCIENCE COLLECTION (Info Sci)
General Libraries, PCL 6.102 Phone: (512)471-7598
Austin, TX 78713-7330 Amy Mollberg, Libn.
Staff: Prof 1; Other 1. **Subjects:** Library functions, organization, and administration; information science; children's and young adult literature. **Holdings:** 40,485 volumes; 993 reels of microfilm; 548 microfiche; 536 microcards; 298 cassettes; 386 slides. **Subscriptions:** 486 journals and other serials. **Services:** Interlibrary loan; copying; collection open to the public.

★16936★
UNIVERSITY OF TEXAS, AUSTIN - MAP COLLECTION (Geog-Map)
General Libraries, PCL 1.306 Phone: (512)471-5944
Austin, TX 78713-7330 Dennis Dillon, Map Libn.
Staff: Prof 1; Other 1. **Subjects:** Maps. **Special Collections:** Depository for U.S. Geological Survey topographic quadrangles; maps from U.S. Defense Mapping Agency, Special Foreign Currency Program, U.S. Air Force, and U.S. National Ocean Survey. **Holdings:** 778 volumes; 224,509 maps; 11 globes; 390 microfiche. **Subscriptions:** 16 journals and other serials. **Services:** Interlibrary loan; copying; collection open to the public.

★16937★
UNIVERSITY OF TEXAS, AUSTIN - MARINE SCIENCE INSTITUTE - LIBRARY (Biol Sci)
Port Aransas, TX 78373-1267 Phone: (512)749-6723
Ruth Grundy, Libn.
Founded: 1941. **Staff:** Prof 1; Other 2. **Subjects:** Marine science in the areas of botany, chemistry, ecology, geology, zoology. **Holdings:** 12,000 books; 45,000 bound periodical volumes; documents; maps; 900 exchange journals. **Subscriptions:** 160 journals and other serials. **Services:** Interlibrary loan; copying; library open to the public. **Computerized Information Services:** DIALOG Information Services. **Publications:** Contributions in Marine Science, irregular.

UNIVERSITY OF TEXAS, AUSTIN - MEXICAN AMERICAN LIBRARY PROGRAM
See: University of Texas, Austin - Benson Latin American Collection (16917)

★16938★
UNIVERSITY OF TEXAS, AUSTIN - MIDDLE EAST COLLECTION (Area-Ethnic)
General Libraries, MAI 316 Phone: (512)471-4675
Austin, TX 78713-7330 Abazar Sepehri, Libn.
Staff: Prof 1; Other 4. **Subjects:** Arabic, Persian, and Turkish language and literature; general Middle East studies in the vernacular. **Holdings:** 56,530 books; 4348 bound periodical volumes; 898 reels of microfilm; 5183 microfiche; 34 audio cassettes; 51 phonograph records; 43 slides. **Subscriptions:** 486 journals and other serials. **Services:** Interlibrary loan; copying; collection open to the public. **Publications:** Library Guide (introductory brochure); Middle East Collection: A Guide for Faculty and Students; Arabic and Persian Periodicals in the Middle East Collection; The Z Note.

★16939★
UNIVERSITY OF TEXAS, AUSTIN - NATURAL FIBERS INFORMATION CENTER (Agri)
University Sta., Box 7459 Phone: (512)471-1616
Austin, TX 78713 Margaret Herring, Res.Assoc.
Staff: 2. **Subjects:** Agricultural and economic statistics; export and import statistics; natural fibers - cotton, wool, mohair; oilseeds; production; climatological data. **Holdings:** 500 books; 100 bound periodical volumes; 10,000 pamphlets, circulars; climatological summaries; fiber and fabric educational resources. **Subscriptions:** 100 journals and other serials. **Services:** Minor statistical searches; copying; center open to the public for reference use only. **Publications:** The Climates of the Texas Counties.

★16940★
UNIVERSITY OF TEXAS, AUSTIN - PHYSICS-MATHEMATICS-ASTRONOMY LIBRARY (Sci-Engr)
General Libraries, RLM 4.200 Phone: (512)471-7539
Austin, TX 78713-7330 Karen Croneis, Libn.
Staff: Prof 1; Other 2. **Subjects:** Astronomy, physics, mathematics. **Holdings:** 32,141 books; 32,008 bound periodical volumes; 235 reels of microfilm; 186 microfiche; 1500 strips of 35mm microfilm. **Subscriptions:** 720 journals and other serials. **Services:** Interlibrary loan; copying; library open to the public. **Publications:** Library Guide. **Also Known As:** John M. Kuehne Physics-Math-Astronomy Library.

★16941★
UNIVERSITY OF TEXAS, AUSTIN - POPULATION RESEARCH CENTER LIBRARY (Soc Sci)
1800 Main Bldg. Phone: (512)471-5514
Austin, TX 78712 Doreen S. Goyer, Dir., Lib. Core
Founded: 1960. **Staff:** Prof 2; Other 1. **Subjects:** Population and census data, human ecology and fertility. **Special Collections:** International census publications (covers 80% of all bona fide national population censuses taken; 25,000 items). **Holdings:** 7000 books; 27 file drawers of reprints, unbound reports, and other ephemera; 440 linear feet of periodicals; 200 microfiche; 1042 reels of microfilm. **Subscriptions:** 80 journals and other serials. **Services:** Interlibrary loan; copying; library open to qualified researchers. **Computerized Information Services:** NLM. Performs searches on fee basis. **Networks/Consortia:** Member of APLIC International Census Network. **Publications:** International Population Census Bibliography; Handbook of National Population Censuses (1983).

★16942★
UNIVERSITY OF TEXAS, AUSTIN - SCHOOL OF LAW - TARLTON LAW LIBRARY (Law)
727 E. 26th St. Phone: (512)471-7726
Austin, TX 78705 Roy M. Mersky, Prof./Dir. of Res.
Founded: 1883. **Staff:** Prof 17; Other 23. **Subjects:** Law - Anglo-American, foreign, international. **Special Collections:** U.S. Government depository; rare books; European communities depository; U.N. documents; papers of Tom C. Clark, U.S. Supreme Court Assoc. Justice; briefs of U.S. Supreme Court, 5th Circuit Court of Appeals (Texas cases) and Texas courts. **Holdings:** 650,000 books and bound periodical volumes; 19,610 microcards; 7241 reels of microfilm; 494,056 microfiche. **Subscriptions:** 12,978 journals and other serials. **Services:** Interlibrary loan; SDI; library open to the public. **Automated Operations:** Computerized cataloging, acquisitions, and ILL. **Computerized Information Services:** LEXIS, WESTLAW, DIALOG Information Services, BRS Information Technologies, ELSS (Electronic Legislative Search System), RLIN. **Networks/Consortia:** Member of RLG. **Publications:** Tarlton Law Library Legal Bibliography Series; Notes from the Tarlton Law Library, both irregular; Contents Pages of Legal Periodicals, weekly. **Special Indexes:** Index to Periodical Articles Related to Law. **Staff:** Gary R. Hartman, Assoc. Law Libn.; Gwyn Anderson, Assoc., Lib.Oper.; Andy Barnes, Hd., Cat.; Barbara Bridges, Docs.Libn.; E. Leslie Kanter, Act.Hd., Ref.; Jon Pratter, Foreign & Intl. Law Libn.; David Burch, Ref.Libn.; David Gunn, Reserve Libn.; Pierrette Moreno, Circ./Reserve Libn.; Adrienne DeVergie, Cat.Libn.; Julia Ashworth, Archv.; John Petesch, Cat.Libn.; Evan Quenon, Ref.Libn..

★16943★
UNIVERSITY OF TEXAS, AUSTIN - SCIENCE LIBRARY (Biol Sci)
General Libraries, MAI 220 Phone: (512)471-1475
Austin, TX 78713-7330 Nancy Elder, Libn.
Staff: Prof 1; Other 4. **Subjects:** Botany, microbiology, zoology, genetics, molecular biology, ecology, marine biology, pharmacy, pharmacology, pharmacognosy, pharmaceutical administration. **Special Collections:** Gray Herbarium Index. **Holdings:** 64,378 volumes; 58,206 bound periodical volumes; 1616 reels of microfilm; 19,546 microfiche; 1032 microcards; 105 cassettes. **Subscriptions:** 1874 journals and other serials. **Services:** Interlibrary loan; copying; library open to the public. **Publications:** Library Guide.

★16944★
UNIVERSITY OF TEXAS, AUSTIN - TEXTBOOK AND CURRICULUM COLLECTION (Educ)
General Libraries, PCL 2.430 Phone: (512)471-5944
Austin, TX 78713-7330 Philip Schwartz, Educ.Bibliog.
Staff: Prof 1. **Special Collections:** Textbooks submitted for adoption by the state, grades K-12; curriculum guides of Texas Education Agency and other school districts; textbooks published prior to 1900; bilingual education materials. **Holdings:** 12,555 textbooks; 320 currriculum guides; 39,113 uncataloged items. **Services:** Interlibrary loan; copying; collection open to the public.

★16945★
UNIVERSITY OF TEXAS, AUSTIN - WASSERMAN PUBLIC AFFAIRS LIBRARY (Soc Sci)
General Libraries
Sid Richardson Hall, 3.243 Phone: (512)471-4486
Austin, TX 78713-7330 Olive Forbes, Hd.Libn.
Staff: Prof 2; Other 10. **Subjects:** Politics and government, public administration and finance, social problems and policy, civil rights, discrimination, public welfare, pollution and environmental policy, education, regional and municipal planning, public health, evaluation research. **Special Collections:** Budgets and financial reports for selected cities, counties, and states; Henry David Manpower Policy Collection; state documents; selective U.S. documents depository, 1968 to present and Canadian documents depository, 1985 to present (23,000 documents). **Holdings:** 56,260 volumes; 122,565 uncataloged documents; 223 phonotapes; 146 cassettes; 193 video cassettes; 137 videotapes; 2000 reels of microfilm; 77,000 microfiche. **Subscriptions:** 1761 journals and other serials. **Services:** Copying; library open to the public.

UNIVERSITY OF TEXAS, AUSTIN - WINEDALE HISTORICAL CENTER
See: Winedale Historical Center (17924)

UNIVERSITY OF TEXAS, DALLAS - GEOLOGICAL INFORMATION LIBRARY OF DALLAS (GILD)
See: Geological Information Library of Dallas (GILD) (5585)

★16946★
UNIVERSITY OF TEXAS, EL PASO - INSTITUTE OF ORAL HISTORY (Hist)
Liberal Arts 339 Phone: (915)747-5508
El Paso, TX 79968 Rebecca Craver, Prog.Dir.
Staff: Prof 1; Other 2. **Subjects:** History - El Paso and Ciudad Juarez, Chihuahua, University of Texas, El Paso; Mexican Americans; the Border; the Mexican Revolution; Border Labor History. **Holdings:** 550 manuscripts; 900 magnetic tapes. **Services:** Institute open to the public. **Special Catalogs:** Catalog of Oral History Program; interviewee and subject files (card).

★16947★
UNIVERSITY OF TEXAS, EL PASO - LIBRARY - DOCUMENTS/MAPS DEPARTMENT (Info Sci, Geog-Map)
Main Library Phone: (915)747-5685
El Paso, TX 79968 Louise M. Tenner, Hd.
Founded: 1974. **Staff:** Prof 1; Other 4. **Subjects:** Economics and business, political science, geology, history, sociology, sciences. **Special Collections:** U.S. documents depository (124,602 items); Texas documents depository (12,581 items); U.S. Geological Survey maps depository; National Oceanic and Atmospheric Administration maps; Defense Mapping Agency (total map collection 89,271 items). **Holdings:** 241,663 volumes; 213,632 microfiche; 155,500 microprints. **Services:** Interlibrary loan; copying; SDI; department open to the public with restrictions. **Computerized Information Services:** DIALOG Information Services, BRS Information Technologies, OCLC (through University Library). **Networks/Consortia:** Member of AMIGOS Bibliographic Council, Inc.. **Publications:** Government Documents (newsletter), bimonthly - campus distribution; Carto-points, quarterly - to map libraries in the U.S. and interested faculty. **Special Indexes:** Subject index to microforms (card); subject and area index to maps (card).

★16948★
UNIVERSITY OF TEXAS, EL PASO - LIBRARY - S.L.A. MARSHALL MILITARY HISTORY COLLECTION (Mil, Hist)
Rm. 602 Phone: (915)747-5697
El Paso, TX 79968-0582 Thomas F. Burdett, Cur.
Founded: 1974. **Staff:** 1. **Subjects:** Military history from antiquity to the present with emphasis on World Wars I and II, British colonial wars, Vietnamese conflict, Israeli wars, Korean War. **Special Collections:** Brigadier General S.L.A. Marshall papers (69 linear feet of papers; 42 linear feet of memorabilia); Rear Admiral Edwin C. Parsons papers (10 linear feet); Major General Frank S. Ross papers (2 linear feet); Colonel Kimbrough S. Brown papers (20 linear feet); Major Edward F. Hinkle papers (1 linear foot). **Holdings:** 9000 books; 35 bound periodical volumes; miscellaneous collections of military papers. **Services:** Copying; collection open to the public for reference use only. **Publications:** Newsletter of the S.L.A. Marshall Military History Collection, irregular - to mailing list.

★16949★
UNIVERSITY OF TEXAS, EL PASO - LIBRARY - SPECIAL COLLECTIONS (Hum)
El Paso, TX 79968 Phone: (915)747-5684
Cesar Caballero, Hd.
Founded: 1913. **Special Collections:** Southwest and Border Studies (8746 books); rare books (5957); western fiction (1701 books); art (6280 books); Judaica (1863 books); Hertzog (1389 books); Mexican Archives on microfilm (2147 reels); oral history (391 reels; 227 transcripts); manuscripts (470 collections); military history (7801 books); Chicano studies (1531 books; 45 films and other AV programs). **Services:** Interlibrary loan (limited); copying; collections open to the public. **Automated Operations:** Computerized cataloging. **Computerized Information Services:** DIALOG Information Services, BRS Information Technologies, OCLC. **Networks/Consortia:** Member of AMIGOS Bibliographic Council, Inc.. **Special Catalogs:** Mexico and the Southwest: Microfilm Holdings of Historical Documents and Rare books at the University of Texas at El Paso Library; The Border Finder: The Border Studies Bibliography. **Staff:** Juan A. Sandoval, Ref./Chicano Serv.Libn.; S.H. Newman, Asst.Hd..

★16950★
UNIVERSITY OF TEXAS, EL PASO - NURSING/MEDICAL LIBRARY
El Paso, TX 79968
Defunct. Holdings absorbed by main library.

★16951★
UNIVERSITY OF TEXAS, EL PASO - TEACHING MATERIALS CENTER (Educ)
Main Library Phone: (915)747-5417
El Paso, TX 79968 Jean Stevens, Hd.
Founded: 1972. **Staff:** Prof 1; Other 2. **Subjects:** Education - elementary, secondary, special, physical. **Holdings:** 13,267 state adopted textbooks; 9500 children's books; 1331 AV programs; 4500 curriculum guides; 350 subject folders of pamphlets. **Services:** Copying; center open to the public with restrictions. **Automated Operations:** Computerized cataloging. **Computerized Information Services:** OCLC. **Networks/Consortia:** Member of AMIGOS Bibliographic Council, Inc..

★16952★
UNIVERSITY OF TEXAS HEALTH CENTER, TYLER - LIBRARY AND BIOMEDICAL INFORMATION RESOURCES CENTER (Med)
Box 2003 Phone: (214)877-3451
Tyler, TX 75710 Elaine Wells, Dir.
Founded: 1978. **Staff:** Prof 2; Other 4. **Subjects:** Lung and heart diseases, biochemistry, oncology, nursing, surgery. **Holdings:** 2606 books; 6000 bound periodical volumes; 1000 AV programs; 600 reels of microfilm. **Subscriptions:** 502 journals and other serials. **Services:** Interlibrary loan; copying; SDI; library open to the public. **Automated Operations:** Computerized cataloging and acquisitions. **Computerized Information Services:** OCLC, DIALOG Information Services, NLM. Performs searches on fee basis. **Networks/Consortia:** Member of TALON, East Texas Health Sciences Consortium. **Staff:** Thomas B. Craig, Asst. to Dir..

★16953★
UNIVERSITY OF TEXAS HEALTH SCIENCE CENTER, HOUSTON - DENTAL BRANCH LIBRARY (Med)
6516 John Freeman Ave. Phone: (713)792-4094
Houston, TX 77225 Lorrayne Beth Webb, Dir.
Founded: 1943. **Staff:** Prof 3; Other 3. **Subjects:** Dentistry. **Special Collections:** History of dentistry. **Holdings:** 13,675 books; 12,856 bound periodical volumes; 525 videotapes; theses. **Subscriptions:** 375 journals and other serials. **Services:** Interlibrary loan; copying; library open to the public for reference use only. **Automated Operations:** Computerized public access catalog, cataloging, circulation, and ILL. **Computerized Information Services:** BRS Information Technologies, OCLC, LS/2000. **Staff:** Ann T. Williams, Asst.Libn.; Robert C. Park, Cat.Libn..

★16954★
UNIVERSITY OF TEXAS HEALTH SCIENCE CENTER, SAN ANTONIO - DOLPH BRISCOE, JR. LIBRARY (Med)
7703 Floyd Curl Dr. Phone: (512)691-6271
San Antonio, TX 78284 Virginia M. Bowden, Lib.Dir.
Founded: 1968. **Staff:** Prof 18; Other 34. **Subjects:** Health related sciences, nursing, dentistry. **Special Collections:** History of medicine (4894 volumes). **Holdings:** 93,931 books; 85,642 bound periodical volumes; 3827 AV programs. **Subscriptions:** 3315 journals and other serials. **Services:** Interlibrary loan; copying; SDI; film booking; library open to the public for reference use only. **Automated Operations:** Computerized cataloging, acquisitions, serials, and circulation. **Computerized Information Services:** DIALOG Information Services, OCLC, PHILSOM, BRS Information Technologies, NLM; LIS, mini Medline (internal databases); OnTyme Electronic Message Network Service, DOCLINE (electronic mail services). **Networks/Consortia:** Member of AMIGOS Bibliographic Council, Inc., Council of Research & Academic Libraries (CORAL), South Central Academic Medical Libraries Consortium (SCAMEL), Health Oriented Libraries of San Antonio (HOLSA). **Publications:** Library Acquisitions; Library Bibliography Series; UTHSCSA Publications; Library News. **Special Catalogs:** Videotape Catalog; Multimedia Catalog. **Staff:** Rajia Tobia, Asst.Dir., Pub.Serv.; Sallieann Swanner, Asst.Dir., Sys.Tech.Serv.; Daniel Jones, Circ. & Coll.Dev.; Nancy Bierschenk, ILL/User Educ.; Evelyn Olivier, Adm.Serv.; Barbara Greene, Asst.Dir., Instr.Serv.; Martha Knott, Tchg.Lrng.Ctr.; Susan Beck, Cat.; Wayne Pedersen, Ref.; Patricia Riley, Online Serv.; Patti Martin, Ref.; Anne Comeaux, Sys.; Ellen Hanks, Ref.; Nancy Morrow, Ref..

★16955★
UNIVERSITY OF TEXAS HEALTH SCIENCE CENTER, SAN ANTONIO - DOLPH BRISCOE, JR. LIBRARY - BRADY/GREEN LIBRARY (Med)
527 N. Leona St. Phone: (512)270-3938
San Antonio, TX 78207 Wayne A. Pedersen, Brady/Green Libn.
Founded: 1958. **Staff:** Prof 1; Other 2. **Subjects:** Obstetrics, pediatrics, family practice, ambulatory care, general medicine. **Holdings:** 1350 books; 4225 bound periodical volumes. **Subscriptions:** 121 journals. **Services:** Interlibrary loan; copying; SDI; library open to the public. **Automated Operations:** Computerized public access catalog, cataloging, acquisitions, and serials. **Computerized Information Services:** DIALOG Information Services, WILSONLINE, BRS Information Technologies, MEDLARS; LIS (internal database). Performs searches on fee basis. **Networks/Consortia:** Member of Health Oriented Libraries of San Antonio (HOLSA). **Publications:** Brady/Green Library Newsletter, monthly - for internal distribution only. **Remarks:** Alternate telephone numbers are 270-3939 and 270-3940.

★16956★
UNIVERSITY OF TEXAS MEDICAL BRANCH - MOODY MEDICAL LIBRARY (Med)
Galveston, TX 77550-2782 Phone: (409)761-1971
Emil F. Frey, Dir.
Founded: 1891. **Staff:** Prof 17; Other 40. **Subjects:** Medicine, nursing, history of medicine, allied health sciences. **Special Collections:** History of medicine; medical prints and portraits. **Holdings:** 95,008 books; 114,703 bound periodical volumes; 33,200 other cataloged items; 1130 AV programs. **Subscriptions:** 3952 journals and other serials; 15 newspapers. **Services:** Interlibrary loan; copying; SDI; library open to the public. **Automated Operations:** Computerized public access catalog, cataloging, serials, and circulation. **Computerized Information Services:** MEDLINE, BRS Information Technologies, DIALOG Information Services, OCLC; MEDICAT (internal database); OnTyme Electronic Message Network Service (electronic mail service). Performs searches on fee basis. Contact Person: Carol B. Phillips, Asst.Dir., Pub.Serv., 761-2375. **Networks/Consortia:** Member of AMIGOS Bibliographic Council, Inc., TALON, Houston Area Research Library Consortium (HARLIC). **Publications:** The Truman G. Blocker, Jr., History of Medicine Collections (book). **Staff:** Larry J. Wygant, Assoc.Dir., Pub.Serv.; Mary M. Asbell, Clin.Libn.; Alexander C. Bienkowski, Ref./AV Libn.; Dr. Inci A. Bowman, Cur., Hist./Med.; Gary C. Rasmussen, Assoc.Dir., Automated Serv.; William F. Sherwood, Prog.Anl.; Alice C. Wygant, Ref./Info.Mgt.Coord.; Christine L. Foster, Ref./Educ.Spec.; Patricia A. Ciejka, Chf.Clin.Libn.; Lynn Burke, Clin.Libn.; Deirdre R. Becker, Ref./ILL Libn.; Robert A. Want,

Ref./Database Libn.; Ellen C. Wong, Med.Cat.; Mary Vaughn, Ref./ Educ.Spec..

★16957★
UNIVERSITY OF TEXAS MENTAL SCIENCES INSTITUTE - UT PSYCHIATRY LIBRARY (Med)
1300 Moursund Ave. Phone: (713)792-7711
Houston, TX 77030 Felicia S. Chuang, Libn.
Founded: 1959. **Staff:** Prof 2; Other 2. **Subjects:** Psychiatry, psychopharmacology, clinical psychology, gerontology, drug abuse. **Holdings:** 9900 books; 4200 bound periodical volumes; 64 dissertations on microfilm; 735 journal volumes on microfilm. **Subscriptions:** 230 journals and other serials. **Services:** Interlibrary loan; copying; SDI; library open to the public. **Computerized Information Services:** DIALOG Information Services, MEDLARS. **Networks/Consortia:** Member of TALON. **Staff:** Marilyn Howe, Asst.Libn..

★16958★
UNIVERSITY OF TEXAS SOUTHWESTERN MEDICAL CENTER, DALLAS - LIBRARY (Med)
5323 Harry Hines Blvd. Phone: (214)688-3368
Dallas, TX 75235 Jean K. Miller, Dir.
Founded: 1943. **Staff:** Prof 23; Other 35. **Subjects:** Medicine, biochemistry, biological science, medical specialities. **Special Collections:** Medical history. **Holdings:** 224,732 volumes; 2941 AV programs; 20,860 microforms. **Subscriptions:** 2255 journals and other serials; 5 newspapers. **Services:** Interlibrary loan; copying; SDI; library open to the public. **Automated Operations:** Computerized public access catalog, cataloging, serials, and circulation. **Computerized Information Services:** DIALOG Information Services, Pergamon ORBIT InfoLine, Inc., OCLC, BRS Information Technologies, Litton Computer Services (LCS), PHILSOM. **Networks/Consortia:** Member of TALON, Association for Higher Education of North Texas (AHE), AMIGOS Bibliographic Council, Inc.. **Publications:** Library Acquisitions and Library Update (newsletter) - to faculty and by request; Annual Report - by request. **Staff:** Patricia Armes, Assoc.Dir.; Spencer Marsh, Asst.Dir., Pub.Serv.; Patricia McKeown, Online Rsrcs.Libn.; Regina Lee, Assoc.Dir., TALON; Janet Cowen, Hd., LRC; Helen Mayo, Hd., Info.Serv.; Laura Wilder, Asst.Hd., Info.Serv.; Kathryn Connell, Hd., Circ./ILL; Leslie Dworkin, Info.Serv.Libn.; Bill Maina, Hd., Coll.Dev./Acq.; Glenn Bunton, Info.Serv.Libn.; Penny Billings, Info.Serv.Libn.; Marilyn McKay, AV Libn.; Margie Steele-Fuller, Hd., Cat.; Judy Wilkerson, Hd., Ser.; Marty Adamson, Sys.Libn.; Alan Carr, Info.Serv.Libn.; Le Anthony, Cat.; Janis Bandelin, Circ.; Nancy Camacho, TALON; Elaine Jones, TALON.

UNIVERSITY OF TEXAS SYSTEM CANCER CENTER
See: University of Texas - M.D. Anderson Hospital and Tumor Institute (16910)

★16959★
UNIVERSITY OF TOLEDO - COLLEGE OF LAW LIBRARY (Law)
2801 W. Bancroft St. Phone: (419)537-2733
Toledo, OH 43606 Janet L. Wallin, Law Libn.
Staff: Prof 5; Other 6. **Subjects:** Law. **Special Collections:** Josef L. Kunz Collection (international and comparative law; 1000 volumes). **Holdings:** 140,936 books and bound periodical volumes; 30,842 volumes in microform. **Subscriptions:** 2808 journals and other serials. **Services:** Interlibrary loan; library open to the public. **Automated Operations:** Computerized cataloging and ILL. **Computerized Information Services:** LEXIS, OCLC. **Publications:** Recent Acquisitions List, monthly - available upon request. **Staff:** P. Michael Whipple, Assoc. Law Libn.; Diane S. Bitter, Cat.; Theodore A. Potter, Acq.; Clara Smith, Circ.; Joseph Fugere, Evening Supv..

★16960★
UNIVERSITY OF TOLEDO - WARD M. CANADAY CENTER (Hum)
William S. Carlson Library Phone: (419)537-2443
Toledo, OH 43606 Richard W. Oram, Dir.
Staff: Prof 3; Other 2. **Subjects:** 20th century American poetry, Southern authors, and black American literature; university history; history of books and printing. **Special Collections:** Ezra Pound Collection (400 volumes); William Faulkner Collection (500 volumes); Black American Poetry, 1945 to present (1000 volumes); William Dean Howells Collection (150 volumes); Herbert W. Martin Collection (15 feet); Etheridge Knight Collection (10 feet); Richard T. Gosser Collection (20 feet); Jean Gould Collection (11 feet); university archives (900 feet); J.H. Leigh Hunt (100 volumes); Scott Nearing (50 volumes); T.S. Eliot (200 volumes); William Carlos Williams (75 volumes); Marianne Moore (75 volumes); Broadside Press (200 items); Women's Social History, 1840-1920 (1000 volumes). **Holdings:** 20,000 books; 2000 linear feet of archives and manuscripts. **Services:** Copying; center open to the public. **Automated Operations:** Computerized cataloging. **Publications:** Friends of The University of Toledo Libraries. **Special Catalogs:** Exhibition catalogs; card catalogs to 20th Century Black Authors Collection, William Faulkner Collection, University of Toldeo Theses and Dissertations Collection, and 20th century American poetry. **Staff:** Barbara Floyd, Univ.Archv.; Nola Skousen, Mss.Proc..

★16961★
UNIVERSITY OF TORONTO - A.E. MACDONALD OPHTHALMIC LIBRARY (Med)
1 Spadina Crescent Phone: (416)978-2635
Toronto, ON, Canada M5S 2J5 Eva Wong, Res.Sec.
Staff: 1. **Subjects:** Ophthalmology. **Special Collections:** Historical collection. **Holdings:** 1000 bound periodical volumes; reprints of publications by Ophthalmology Department members, 1950 to present. **Subscriptions:** 25 journals and other serials. **Services:** Interlibrary loan; library not open to the public.

★16962★
UNIVERSITY OF TORONTO - ANTHROPOLOGY READING ROOM (Soc Sci)
Sidney Smith Hall, Rm. 560A
100 St. George St. Phone: (416)978-3028
Toronto, ON, Canada M5S 1A1
Prof. Krystyna Sieciechowicz, Chm., Dept.Lib.Comm.
Founded: 1967. **Staff:** 1. **Subjects:** Archeology; anthropology - physical, social, cultural; linguistics. **Special Collections:** Human Relations Area Files. **Holdings:** 2478 volumes; 61,900 microforms. **Services:** Reading room open to the public with restrictions. **Publications:** Accession list, monthly - for internal distribution only. **Special Catalogs:** Department of Anthropology publications; International Biological Program reports.

★16963★
UNIVERSITY OF TORONTO - ASTRONOMY LIBRARY (Sci-Engr)
60 St. George St., Rm. 1306 Phone: (416)978-4268
Toronto, ON, Canada M5S 1A7 Marlene Cummins, Libn.
Founded: 1935. **Staff:** Prof 1. Other 1. **Subjects:** Astronomy, astrophysics. **Holdings:** 20,000 books, bound periodical volumes, observatory publications. **Subscriptions:** 480 journals and other serials. **Services:** Interlibrary loan; copying; library open to the public for reference use only. **Publications:** Acquisitions list, weekly. **Special Indexes:** Preprint index; Selected Astronomy Book Reviews.

★16964★
UNIVERSITY OF TORONTO - AUDIO-VISUAL LIBRARY (Aud-Vis)
9 King's College Circle Phone: (416)978-6520
Toronto, ON, Canada M5S 2E8 Liz Avison, Hd.Libn.
Staff: Prof 3; Other 7. **Subjects:** Media, broadcasting. **Holdings:** 312 books; 1085 films; 1476 video cassettes; 505 sound recordings. **Subscriptions:** 41 journals and other serials. **Services:** Interlibrary loan; copying; videotape dubbing; library open to the public.

★16965★
UNIVERSITY OF TORONTO - BANTING & BEST DEPARTMENT OF MEDICAL RESEARCH - LIBRARY (Med)
Best Institute, Rm. 304
112 College St. Phone: (416)978-2588
Toronto, ON, Canada M5G 1L6 Colin Savage
Founded: 1953. **Staff:** 1. **Subjects:** Medicine, physiology, diabetes, insulin, anticoagulants, lipid metabolism. **Holdings:** 7669 volumes. **Subscriptions:** 31 journals and other serials.

★16966★
UNIVERSITY OF TORONTO - CENTRE OF CRIMINOLOGY - LIBRARY (Law, Soc Sci)
130 St. George St., Suite 8055 Phone: (416)978-7068
Toronto, ON, Canada M5S 1A5 Catherine J. Matthews, Libn.
Founded: 1963. **Staff:** Prof 2; Other 2. **Subjects:** Criminology. **Holdings:** 21,717 volumes; 250 files of newspaper clippings (by subject); 2100 reprints. **Subscriptions:** 215 journals and other serials. **Services:** Interlibrary loan; copying; library open to the public with deposit required for borrowing. **Publications:** Criminology Library Acquisitions List, 3/ year.

★16967★
UNIVERSITY OF TORONTO - CENTRE FOR INDUSTRIAL RELATIONS - JEAN & DOROTHY NEWMAN LIBRARY (Bus-Fin)
123 St. George St. Phone: (416)978-2928
Toronto, ON, Canada M5S 2E8 Elizabeth Perry, Libn.
Founded: 1968. **Staff:** Prof 2; Other 2. **Subjects:** Labor relations, labor economics, personnel administration, industrial psychology, industrial sociology, labor law, manpower training. **Special Collections:** Labor union archives (constitutions; newspapers; proceedings; clippings). **Holdings:** 10,065 volumes; 950 linear feet of clippings, reprints, photocopies, reports, pamphlets, statistics, documents. **Subscriptions:** 550 journals and other serials. **Services:** Copying; library open to the public for reference use only.

★16968★
UNIVERSITY OF TORONTO - CENTRE FOR URBAN AND COMMUNITY STUDIES - RESOURCE ROOM (Plan)
455 Spadina Ave. Phone: (416)978-4478
Toronto, ON, Canada M5S 2G8 Judith Kjellberg, Info.Off.
Staff: 1. **Subjects:** Urban studies. **Holdings:** 500 books; 4000 documents, manuscripts, research papers. **Services:** Interlibrary loan; library open to the public with restrictions. **Publications:** Newsletter, 5/year.

★16969★
UNIVERSITY OF TORONTO - DEPARTMENT OF BOTANY LIBRARY (Biol Sci)
Botany Bldg., Rm. 202
6 Queen's Park Phone: (416)978-3538
Toronto, ON, Canada M5S 1A1 Ellen Chamberlain, Sec.
Founded: 1932. **Staff:** 1. **Subjects:** Botany, bacteriology, biology, agriculture, paleobotany, horticulture, biochemistry. **Holdings:** 12,659 volumes. **Subscriptions:** 208 journals and other serials. **Services:** Interlibrary loan.

★16970★
UNIVERSITY OF TORONTO - DEPARTMENT OF CHEMISTRY LIBRARY (Sci-Engr)
Lash-Miller Bldg., Rms. 429-433
80 St. George St. Phone: (416)978-3587
Toronto, ON, Canada M5S 2T4 Mary Power, Sec.
Founded: 1938. **Staff:** 2. **Subjects:** Chemistry - analytical, inorganic, organic, physical. **Holdings:** 29,863 volumes; 2671 microforms. **Subscriptions:** 254 journals and other serials. **Services:** Interlibrary loan.

★16971★
UNIVERSITY OF TORONTO - DEPARTMENT OF COMPUTER SCIENCE - COMPUTER LIBRARY (Comp Sci)
Engineering Annex, Rm. 206
11 King's College Rd. Phone: (416)978-2987
Toronto, ON, Canada M5S 2E7 Stephanie Johnston, Libn.
Founded: 1950. **Staff:** Prof 1; Other 1. **Subjects:** Computers, information retrieval, numerical analysis, automatic translation. **Special Collections:** Abstracts on cards. **Holdings:** 11,542 volumes; 281 microforms. **Subscriptions:** 162 journals and other serials. **Services:** Interlibrary loan. **Special Catalogs:** Punched card title listings.

★16972★
UNIVERSITY OF TORONTO - DEPARTMENT OF GEOLOGY - COLEMAN LIBRARY (Sci-Engr)
Mining Bldg., Rm. 316
170 College St. Phone: (416)978-3024
Toronto, ON, Canada M5S 1A1 Deborah Green, Libn.
Staff: Prof 1. **Subjects:** Geology. **Holdings:** 25,268 volumes; 937 microforms.

★16973★
UNIVERSITY OF TORONTO - DEPARTMENT OF PHYSICS LIBRARY (Sci-Engr)
McLennan Physical Labs., Rm. 211
60 St. George St. Phone: (416)978-5188
Toronto, ON, Canada M5S 1A7 B. Chu, Libn.
Founded: 1910. **Staff:** Prof 1; Other 1. **Subjects:** Physics, geophysics. **Holdings:** 28,179 volumes. **Subscriptions:** 210 journals and other serials. **Services:** Interlibrary loan.

★16974★
UNIVERSITY OF TORONTO - DEPARTMENT OF ZOOLOGY LIBRARY (Biol Sci)
Ramsey-Wright Bldg., Rm. 225
25 Harbord St. Phone: (416)978-3515
Toronto, ON, Canada M5S 1A1 Kim Jallant
Staff: 1. **Subjects:** Zoology, aquatic biology. **Holdings:** 86,359 volumes; 71,101 indexed reprints and articles. **Subscriptions:** 214 journals and other serials.

★16975★
UNIVERSITY OF TORONTO - EAST ASIAN LIBRARY (Area-Ethnic)
Robarts Library, Rm. 8049
130 St. George St. Phone: (416)928-3300
Toronto, ON, Canada M5S 1A5 Anna U, Libn.
Staff: Prof 3. **Subjects:** East Asia. **Special Collections:** Mu Collection (Chinese rare books); Chinese local histories; modern Japanese literature (13,000 volumes). **Holdings:** 198,476 volumes; 9004 microforms. **Subscriptions:** 732 journals and other serials. **Services:** Interlibrary loan; copying; library open to the public for reference use only. **Staff:** Teresa Hsieh; David Chang.

★16976★
UNIVERSITY OF TORONTO - FACULTY OF APPLIED SCIENCE AND ENGINEERING - CENTRE FOR BUILDING SCIENCE - LIBRARY (Sci-Engr)
35 St. George St. Phone: (416)978-5053
Toronto, ON, Canada M5S 1A4 Mr. A. Seskus, Res.Off.
Subjects: Air infiltration, moisture movement, materials, energy conservation, retrofit, construction. **Holdings:** 500 books; 2000 other cataloged items. **Subscriptions:** 10 journals and other serials. **Services:** Library open to the public with chairman's approval.

★16977★
UNIVERSITY OF TORONTO - FACULTY OF ARCHITECTURE AND LANDSCAPE ARCHITECTURE - LIBRARY (Plan)
230 College St. Phone: (416)978-2649
Toronto, ON, Canada M5S 1A1 Pamela Manson-Smith, Libn.
Founded: 1922. **Staff:** Prof 1; Other 1. **Subjects:** Architecture, urban and regional planning. **Holdings:** 17,226 volumes; 4.5 meters of VF materials. **Subscriptions:** 119 journals and other serials. **Services:** Interlibrary loan; copying; library open to the public for reference use only.

★16978★
UNIVERSITY OF TORONTO - FACULTY OF DENTISTRY LIBRARY (Med)
124 Edward St., Rm. 267 Phone: (416)979-4560
Toronto, ON, Canada M5G 1G6 Susan Goddard, Fac.Libn.
Founded: 1925. **Staff:** Prof 2; Other 2. **Subjects:** Dentistry, medicine, health sciences. **Special Collections:** Phyllis M. Smith Collection (rare books and catalogs). **Holdings:** 23,445 volumes; 298 microforms; 45 videotapes; 128 slide/tape sets; 10.5 linear feet of clippings, pamphlets, and other vertical file materials. **Subscriptions:** 190 journals and other serials. **Services:** Interlibrary loan; copying; library open to the public with restrictions. **Computerized Information Services:** MEDLINE, CAN/OLE. Performs searches on fee basis. **Publications:** Filling the Gap, quarterly - to faculty and dental libraries. **Special Catalogs:** The Rare Books Collection of the Dental Library, University of Toronto and the Harry R. Abbott Memorial Library, 1978; staff articles file (cards). **Staff:** Susan Murray, Libn..

★16979★
UNIVERSITY OF TORONTO - FACULTY OF EDUCATION LIBRARY (Educ)
371 Bloor St., W. Phone: (416)978-3224
Toronto, ON, Canada M5S 2R7 Diana George, Chf.Libn.
Founded: 1906. **Staff:** Prof 3; Other 6. **Subjects:** Education - history, philosophy, psychology, administration, general methodology. **Special Collections:** Authorized school textbooks from the 19th century. **Holdings:** 40,426 volumes; 8403 microforms; government documents; picture collection. **Subscriptions:** 247 journals and other serials. **Services:** Interlibrary loan; copying; library open to the public. **Publications:** Bibliographic aids for teachers.

★16980★
UNIVERSITY OF TORONTO - FACULTY OF ENGINEERING LIBRARY (Sci-Engr)
Sandford Fleming Bldg., Rm 2402
10 King's College Rd. Phone: (416)978-6494
Toronto, ON, Canada M5S 1A4 Elaine Granatstein, Libn.
Staff: Prof 2; Other 6. **Subjects:** Engineering - civil, mechanical, industrial, chemical, electrical; engineering science and technology; metallurgy; aerospace science. **Holdings:** 101,963 volumes; 16,245 microforms. **Subscriptions:** 1586 journals and other serials. **Services:** Interlibrary loan; copying.

★16981★
UNIVERSITY OF TORONTO - FACULTY OF FORESTRY LIBRARY (Biol Sci)
Forestry Bldg., Rm. 102
45 St. George St.
Toronto, ON, Canada M5S 1A1
Founded: 1907. **Staff:** 2. **Subjects:** Forestry. **Holdings:** 29,316 volumes; 5891 microforms. **Subscriptions:** 434 journals and other serials. **Services:** Interlibrary loan; copying.

★16982★
UNIVERSITY OF TORONTO - FACULTY OF LAW LIBRARY (Law)
78 Queen's Park Crescent Phone: (416)978-8580
Toronto, ON, Canada M5S 1A1 Ann Rae, Libn.
Staff: Prof 3; Other 11. **Subjects:** Law. **Special Collections:** Raoul Collection in International Law (4500 volumes). **Holdings:** 128,302 volumes. **Subscriptions:** 2951 journals and other serials. **Services:** Interlibrary loan; library open to the public with restrictions on borrowing.

★16983★
UNIVERSITY OF TORONTO - FACULTY OF LIBRARY AND INFORMATION SCIENCE LIBRARY (Info Sci)
140 St. George St. Phone: (416)978-7060
Toronto, ON, Canada M5S 1A1 Diane Henderson, Chf.Libn.
Founded: 1928. **Staff:** Prof 4; Other 5. **Subjects:** Library and information science, Canadian bibliography, printing, history of libraries and publishing. **Special Collections:** Library-related annual reports and calendars; subject analysis; systems. **Holdings:** 102,012 volumes; 29 meters of pamphlets and newspaper clippings; 26,624 microforms; 25 drawers of reprint files. **Subscriptions:** 1450 journals and other serials. **Services:** Interlibrary loan; copying; library open to the public. **Automated Operations:** Computerized cataloging, serials, and indexes. **Computerized Information Services:** UTLAS, DIALOG Information Services, CAN/SDI; Envoy 100 (electronic mail service). Performs searches on fee basis. Contact Person: Ellen Jones, Pub.Serv.Libn.. **Publications:** Library and Information Science Update, monthly - by subscription. **Special Indexes:** Automated index to ERIC and NTIS reports; KWOC index to reprint files.

★16984★
UNIVERSITY OF TORONTO - FACULTY OF MANAGEMENT STUDIES LIBRARY (Bus-Fin)
246 Bloor St., W. Phone: (416)978-3421
Toronto, ON, Canada M5S 1V4 Ruth Tolmie, Libn.
Founded: 1950. **Staff:** Prof 1; Other 4. **Subjects:** Accounting, marketing, finance, organizational behavior, statistics, management science, administration, industrial relations, business mathematics. **Special Collections:** Working papers of North American and European business schools. **Holdings:** 37,273 volumes; 7396 microforms; 51 meters of VF materials. **Subscriptions:** 466 journals and other serials. **Services:** Interlibrary loan; copying; library open to the public for reference use only. **Publications:** Business Research: Basic Reference Sources; Selected List of Recent Acquisitions, every six weeks. **Special Indexes:** Index to working paper collection (list file). **Remarks:** The Faculty of Management Studies Library is affiliated with the university's Centre for Industrial Relations Information Service.

★16985★
UNIVERSITY OF TORONTO - FACULTY OF MUSIC LIBRARY (Mus)
Edward Johnson Bldg. Phone: (416)978-3734
Toronto, ON, Canada M5S 1A1 Kathleen McMorrow, Libn.
Founded: 1945. **Staff:** Prof 4; Other 10. **Subjects:** Music - theory, history, biography. **Special Collections:** Creighton Collection of Violin Recordings; rare book room; Cobbett Chamber Music Collection; Fisher Collection (historical books, music, and instruments). **Holdings:** 125,579 volumes; 36,378 pieces of sheet music; 166,820 sound recordings. **Subscriptions:** 582 journals and other serials. **Services:** Interlibrary loan; copying; library open to the public for music-related research. **Staff:** S.M. Sawa, Asst.Libn.; Steven Pallay, Cat.Libn.; James Creighton, Recordings Archv..

★16986★
UNIVERSITY OF TORONTO - FACULTY OF PHARMACY - R.O. HURST LIBRARY (Med)
25 Russell St. Phone: (416)978-2872
Toronto, ON, Canada M5S 1A1 Barbara A. Gallivan, Libn.
Staff: Prof 1; Other 1. **Subjects:** Pharmacy, chemistry, history of pharmacy and medicine. **Special Collections:** R.O. Hurst Collection of Pharmacopoeias; history of pharmacy. **Holdings:** 8767 volumes. **Subscriptions:** 175 journals and other serials. **Services:** Interlibrary loan.

★16987★
UNIVERSITY OF TORONTO - FINE ARTS LIBRARY (Art)
100 St. George St. Phone: (416)978-5006
Toronto, ON, Canada M5S 1A1 Andrea Retfalvi, Libn.
Founded: 1934. **Staff:** Prof 1; Other 1. **Subjects:** History and techniques of fine arts. **Special Collections:** Photographs of illustrated Bibles of the 12th and 13th centuries (8500); exhibition and sales catalogs. **Holdings:** 23,272 books; 91,234 photographs. **Services:** Library not open to the public. **Special Indexes:** Subject index to Bible illustrations.

★16988★
UNIVERSITY OF TORONTO - GENERAL LIBRARY - SCIENCE AND MEDICINE DEPARTMENT (Sci-Engr, Med, Food-Bev)
Toronto, ON, Canada M5S 1A5 Phone: (416)978-2284
Ms. G. Heaton, Hd.
Staff: Prof 12; Other 29. **Subjects:** Technology (excluding engineering), science, medicine, nursing, anatomy, food sciences, bacteriology, industrial hygiene. **Holdings:** 615,417 volumes; 74,472 microforms. **Subscriptions:** 3324 journals and other serials. **Services:** Interlibrary loan; copying; department open to the public with restrictions.

★16989★
UNIVERSITY OF TORONTO - INSTITUTE FOR AEROSPACE STUDIES - LIBRARY (Sci-Engr)
4925 Dufferin St. Phone: (416)667-7712
Downsview, ON, Canada M3H 5T6 Judy Mills, Libn.
Founded: 1950. **Staff:** Prof 1; Other 1. **Subjects:** Aeronautical and aerospace engineering, gas dynamics, materials science, laser technology. **Special Collections:** UTIAS reviews, technical notes, reports, and theses. **Holdings:** 77,000 monographs and reports. **Subscriptions:** 113 journals and other serials. **Services:** Interlibrary loan (fee); copying; library open to the public. **Automated Operations:** Computerized public access catalog and cataloging. **Computerized Information Services:** CAN/OLE, DIALOG Information Services; UTIAS Catalog (internal database).

★16990★
UNIVERSITY OF TORONTO - INSTITUTE OF CHILD STUDY - LIBRARY (Educ)
45 Walmer Rd. Phone: (416)978-4897
Toronto, ON, Canada M5R 2X2 Miriam Herman, Admin.Asst.
Staff: 1. **Subjects:** Child psychology and development, assessment and counselling, early childhood education. **Holdings:** 5568 volumes; 1200 pamphlets. **Subscriptions:** 40 journals and other serials. **Services:** Library open to the public for reference use only.

★16991★
UNIVERSITY OF TORONTO - INSTITUTE FOR POLICY ANALYSIS - LIBRARY (Soc Sci)
150 St. George St. Phone: (416)928-8623
Toronto, ON, Canada M5S 2E9 U. Gutenburg, Lib.Techn.
Staff: 1. **Subjects:** Economics. **Holdings:** 4423 volumes. **Services:** Copying; library open to the public.

★16992★
UNIVERSITY OF TORONTO - KNOX COLLEGE - CAVEN LIBRARY (Rel-Phil)
59 St. George St. Phone: (416)978-4504
Toronto, ON, Canada M5S 2E6 A. Burgess, Libn.
Founded: 1845. **Staff:** Prof 2; Other 1. **Subjects:** Theology (Presbyterian), philosophy, social ethics, Reformation era church history. **Special Collections:** Reproductions of Biblical codices; early editions of Bibles and commentaries; reproductions of medieval illuminated manuscripts; John Calvin Collection. **Holdings:** 66,986 volumes; 1397 microforms. **Subscriptions:** 201 journals and other serials. **Services:** Interlibrary loan; copying; library open to the public.

★16993★
UNIVERSITY OF TORONTO - MAP LIBRARY (Geog-Map)
130 St. George St., Rm. 1001 Phone: (416)978-3372
Toronto, ON, Canada M5S 1A5 Joan Winearls, Map Libn.
Staff: Prof 2; Other 3. **Subjects:** Geography, cartography. **Holdings:** 12,044 books and atlases; 201,693 maps; 252,958 aerial photographs. **Subscriptions:** 42 journals and other serials. **Services:** Interlibrary loan; copying; library open to the public. **Publications:** Accessions list, bimonthly.

★16994★
UNIVERSITY OF TORONTO - MATHEMATICS LIBRARY (Sci-Engr)
Sidney Smith Hall, Rm. 2124
100 St. George St. Phone: (416)978-8624
Toronto, ON, Canada M5S 1A1 Chibeck Graham, Libn.
Founded: 1970. **Staff:** Prof 1; Other 1. **Subjects:** Mathematics. **Holdings:** 22,716 volumes. **Subscriptions:** 556 journals and other serials. **Services:** Interlibrary loan; library not open to the public.

★16995★
UNIVERSITY OF TORONTO - PATHOLOGY LIBRARY (Med)
Banting Institute, Rms. 108-109
100 College St. Phone: (416)978-2558
Toronto, ON, Canada M5G 1L5 Sophia Duda, Libn.
Founded: 1923. **Staff:** 1. **Subjects:** Pathology, immunology, bacteriology. **Holdings:** 3974 volumes. **Subscriptions:** 65 journals and other serials. **Services:** Interlibrary loan; copying.

★16996★
UNIVERSITY OF TORONTO - PONTIFICAL INSTITUTE OF MEDIAEVAL STUDIES - LIBRARY (Hist)
113 St. Joseph St. Phone: (416)926-7146
Toronto, ON, Canada M5S 1J4 Rev. D.F. Finlay, Libn.
Founded: 1929. **Staff:** Prof 3; Other 2. **Subjects:** Medieval life and thought. **Special Collections:** Gordon Taylor Microfilm Collection; Etienne Gilson Collection; Gerald B. Phelan Archives. **Holdings:** 56,000 books; 11,600 bound periodical volumes; 2.5 million pages on microfilm. **Subscriptions:** 150 journals and other serials. **Services:** Interlibrary loan; copying; library open to bona fide scholars with letters of introduction.

★16997★
UNIVERSITY OF TORONTO - ST. MICHAEL'S COLLEGE - JOHN M. KELLY LIBRARY (Rel-Phil)
113 St. Joseph St. Phone: (416)926-7111
Toronto, ON, Canada M5S 1J4 Rev. Donald Finlay, Libn.
Founded: 1929. **Staff:** Prof 9; Other 14. **Subjects:** Humanities, medieval studies, theology. **Special Collections:** Counter Reformation; G.K. Chesterton; J.H. Newman; Roy Campbell; Stathas Collection (Spain); Etienne Gilson Archive. **Holdings:** 236,000 volumes; 6 linear feet of VF material; 7250 microforms; 16,417 slides. **Subscriptions:** 1600 journals and other serials; 25 newspapers. **Services:** Interlibrary loan; copying; library open to the public. **Automated Operations:** Computerized cataloging. **Computerized Information Services:** UTLAS. **Publications:** Pamphlets on the Counter Reformation and Newman collections. **Special Catalogs:** Catalog of the Pontifical Institute Library (book). **Remarks:** St. Michael's College Library is affiliated with the University of Toronto's Pontifical Institute of Mediaeval Studies Library. **Staff:** Louise H. Girard, Assoc.Libn.; Evelyn Collins, Hd., Ref.; Bea Lawford, Circ..; Margaret Ivor, Circ.; Andrew West, Hd., Tech.Serv..

★16998★
UNIVERSITY OF TORONTO - THOMAS FISHER RARE BOOK LIBRARY (Rare Book, Hist, Hum)
120 St. George St. Phone: (416)978-5285
Toronto, ON, Canada M5S 1A5 Richard G. Landon, Dept.Hd.
Founded: 1955. **Staff:** Prof 10; Other 11. **Subjects:** English literature, Canadian literature, European literature, theater history, history, Canadian history, philosophy and theology, science, history of medicine, art, book arts and bibliography, rare books. **Special Collections:** Fisher Collection (Shakespeare editions and Shakespeareana; 3000 volumes); Endicott Collection (works by British authors whose careers fall between 1880 and 1930; 4500 volumes); DeLury Collection of Anglo-Irish Literature (5000 volumes); Duncan Collection (editions of D.H. Lawrence, Richard Aldington, Max Beerbohm, Norman Douglas, and Aldous Huxley; 800 volumes); Yellowback Collection (popular Victorian reading, fiction and nonfiction; 400 volumes); manuscript collections of Canadian authors, including Earle Birney, Margaret Atwood, Mazo De La Roche, Duncan Campbell Scott, Ernest Buckler, Leonard Cohen, Mavis Gallant, Dennis Lee, Gwendolyn McEwan, John Newlove, Raymond Souster, Josef Skvorecky, W.A. Deacon; Canadian literary periodicals; Rousseau Collection (700 volumes); Voltaire Collection (900 volumes); Italian play collection (especially Renaissance period; 6500 volumes); Rime Collection (Italian lyric verse; 700 volumes); Buchanan Collection (Spanish and Italian literature and historical works; 1700 volumes); Petlice Collection (Czechoslovakian works not allowed to be published in Czechoslovakia; 200 volumes); Bagnani Collection (editions of Petronius Arbiter; 200 volumes); Juvenile Drama Collection (6000 sheets; 150 volumes); papers of Dora Mavor Moore, Canadian director and founder of the New Play Society; French Revolution pamphlets (900); Spanish Civil War Collection (650 volumes); Shelden Collection of Australiana (1500 volumes); Czechoslovakia '68 Collection and Czechoslovakian History and Politics Collection (2500 volumes); Radio Free Europe Collection (3000 items); NSZZ Solidarnosc Collection (materials relating to the Solidarity movement in Poland; 1500 items); 17th and 18th century British history; Canadian history, discovery, and exploration (30,000 manuscripts; 1200 maps, plans, and insurance plans of Canadian towns); Kenny Collection (socialist and radical Canadian material; 2500 volumes); Woodsworth Collection of Co-operative Commonwealth Federation Material (700 items); Maclean Hunter and Southam Press Collections (periodicals and trade journals; 310 titles); papers of Mark Gayn, Canadian foreign correspondent, 1909-1981; historical manuscript collections and papers of eminent Canadians, including J.B. Tyrrell, James Mavor, Sir Alan MacNab, Sir Edmund Walker; James Forbes Collection (17th century theological works; 1600 volumes); Aristotle Collection (300 volumes); Bacon Collection (250 volumes); Hobbes Collection (500 volumes); Locke Collection (170 volumes); Bertrand Russell Collection (published works by and about Russell; 10,000 volumes); Science Collection (emphasis on Renaissance astronomy, physics, mechanics, and on English experimental science of the 17th and 18th centuries; 4500 volumes); Galileo Collection (300 volumes); James L. Baillie Collection of (ornithology; 3000 items); Darwin Collection (2000 volumes); Einstein Collection (300 volumes); Bronowski Collection (books and papers); Simcoe Collection (military science; 360 volumes); Victorian Natural History Collection (1700 volumes); Jason A. Hannah Collection (first and significant editions of medical works from classical times to the 20th century; 6000 volumes); Sir Frederick Banting Collection (books and manuscripts, including records of experiments leading to insulin); Fisher Hollar Collection (etchings by Wenceslaus Hollar, 1607-1677; 100 volumes; 3500 etchings); John E. Langdon Collection (silver and silversmiths; 1000 volumes); G.M. Miller Collection (architectural plans for buildings in Toronto region, 1888-1952; 1300 plans); L.B. Duff Collection and reference collections (arts of the books, collectors, bibliography; 1500 volumes); Stanbrook Abbey Press Collection (125 volumes); Middle Hill Press Collection (325 volumes); Thoreau MacDonald Collection (illustrator; 300 volumes); Birdsall Collection (binders' finishing tools, 18th and 19th centuries; 3000); booksellers' catalogs. **Holdings:** 244,820 books; 3166 linear feet of manuscripts. **Services:** Interlibrary loan; copying (both limited); library open to the public. **Automated Operations:** Computerized cataloging. **Computerized Information Services:** UTLAS. **Publications:** A Brief Guide to the Collections - free upon request. **Special Catalogs:** Manuscript collection finding aids; chronological file for Canadiana holdings (card); autograph, bookplate, association, binding, and printers' files (all card); exhibition catalogs, 5-6/year - free upon request. **Staff:** Katharine Martyn, Asst.Hd.; Katharine Martyn, Mss.Libn.; E. Anne Jocz, Hd.Cat.; Emrys Evans, Cons. & Binder.

★16999★
UNIVERSITY OF TORONTO - UNIVERSITY ARCHIVES (Hist)
Fisher Library
120 St. George St. Phone: (416)978-2277
Toronto, ON, Canada M5S 1A5 Kent Haworth, Univ.Archv.
Founded: 1965. **Staff:** Prof 2; Other 3. **Subjects:** University of Toronto, higher education. **Holdings:** 13,000 linear feet of publications of and about the university, theses, manuscripts, clippings, photographs, plans, tape recordings, motion picture films. **Services:** Interlibrary loan; copying; archives open to the public. **Special Catalogs:** Finding aids in typescript.

★17000★
UNIVERSITY OF TORONTO - UNIVERSITY OF TRINITY COLLEGE - LIBRARY (Rel-Phil, Hum)
6 Hoskin Ave. Phone: (416)978-2653
Toronto, ON, Canada M5S 1H8 Linda Wilson Corman, Hd.Libn.
Staff: Prof 3; Other 7. **Subjects:** Anglican theology, English Literature, classics, philosophy, French and German literature. **Special Collections:** Bishop Strachan Collection (500 volumes); S.P.C.K. Collection (400 volumes). **Holdings:** 116,737 books and bound periodical volumes. **Subscriptions:** 259 journals and other serials. **Services:** Interlibrary loan; copying; library open to the public for reference use only. **Automated**

Operations: Computerized cataloging. **Computerized Information Services:** BRS Information Technologies. **Staff:** Lesie Del Bianco, Asst.Libn..

★17001★
UNIVERSITY OF TORONTO - VICTORIA UNIVERSITY - LIBRARY (Hum, Soc Sci)
71 Queen's Park Crescent, E. Phone: (416)978-3821
Toronto, ON, Canada M5S 1K7 Dr. Robert C. Brandeis, Chf.Libn.
Staff: Prof 5; Other 14. **Subjects:** Humanities, social sciences, theology. **Special Collections:** E.J. Pratt Manuscript Collection; Coleridge Collection (350 books and manuscripts); Tennyson Collection (500 books and periodical articles); Wesleyana Collection (800 books); Woolf/ Bloomsbury/Hogarth Press Collection (500 books); Church of Christ Disciples Archives; Hymnology (500 hymn books). **Holdings:** 216,116 volumes; 150 Emmanuel College theses. **Subscriptions:** 796 journals and other serials. **Services:** Interlibrary loan; copying; library open to the public registration. **Automated Operations:** Computerized cataloging. **Remarks:** Victoria University Library houses its Arts College Collection in the E.J. Pratt Library, which also houses the Centre for Reformation and Renaissance Studies Collection (14,000 volumes). Victoria's Theological Collection is housed in the Emmanuel College Library.

★17002★
UNIVERSITY OF TORONTO - WYCLIFFE COLLEGE - LEONARD LIBRARY (Rel-Phil)
Hoskin Ave. Phone: (416)979-2870
Toronto, ON, Canada M5S 1H7 Adrienne Taylor, Coll.Libn.
Founded: 1880. **Staff:** Prof 1; Other 1. **Subjects:** Theology. **Special Collections:** Cody Memorial Library (mainly homiletics). **Holdings:** 43,634 volumes; 2200 pamphlets; maps. **Subscriptions:** 93 journals and other serials. **Services:** Interlibrary loan; copying; library open to the public by permission. **Automated Operations:** Computerized cataloging.

UNIVERSITY OF TRINITY COLLEGE
See: University of Toronto (17000)

★17003★
UNIVERSITY OF TULSA - COLLEGE OF LAW LIBRARY (Law)
3120 E. Fourth Place Phone: (918)592-6000
Tulsa, OK 74104 Richard E. Ducey, Dir./Asst.Prof.
Founded: 1923. **Staff:** Prof 5; Other 7. **Subjects:** Law. **Special Collections:** American Indian law; Energy Law and Policy Collection. **Holdings:** 217,000 volumes, including 92,879 microfiche. **Subscriptions:** 3368 journals and other serials; 8 newspapers. **Services:** Interlibrary loan; copying; library open to members, excluding government documents. **Automated Operations:** Computerized cataloging, acquisitions, circulation, and ILL. **Computerized Information Services:** DIALOG Information Services, LEXIS, NEXIS, OCLC, WESTLAW, Library Information Access System (LIAS). Performs limited searches on fee basis. Contact Person: Melanie Nelson, Pub.Serv./Circ.. **Networks/Consortia:** Member of AMIGOS Bibliographic Council, Inc., Mid-America Law School Library Consortium. **Remarks:** Includes holdings of the University of Tulsa Law Research Center. **Staff:** Sue Sark, Asst.Libn./Coll.Dev.; Katherine J. Tooley, Tech.Serv.; Kathy Kane, Pub.Serv./Gov.Docs..

★17004★
UNIVERSITY OF TULSA - MC FARLIN LIBRARY - SPECIAL COLLECTIONS (Hum, Hist)
600 S. College Ave. Phone: (918)592-6000
Tulsa, OK 74104 Sidney F. Huttner, Cur.
Staff: Prof 2; Other 4. **Subjects:** 20th century British and American literature; Indian history, law, and policy; World War I; Proletarian literature; American fiction regarding Vietnam; performing arts. **Special Collections:** Cyril Connolly Library; Edmund Wilson Library; Rebecca West papers; Stevie Smith papers; Shleppey Indian Collection; Indian Claims Commission Archives; University Archives. **Holdings:** 100,000 books; 1000 bound periodical volumes; 55 boxes of Alice Robertson papers; 75,000 British and American 20th century literary manuscripts; 300 pieces of 20th century American Indian art; 150 territorial maps. **Subscriptions:** 20 journals and other serials; 10 newspapers. **Services:** Interlibrary loan; copying; collections open to the public with written permission. **Automated Operations:** Computerized cataloging, acquisitions, and serials. **Computerized Information Services:** DIALOG Information Services, Library Information Access System (LIAS). **Networks/Consortia:** Member of Tulsa Area Library Cooperative (TALC), Oklahoma Special Collections and Archives Network (OSCAN), AMIGOS Bibliographic Council, Inc.. **Publications:** Women Writers in McFarlin Special Collections; The Paul and Lucie Leon/James Joyce Collection; keepsake series; guides to manuscript collections - available on request; finding aids. **Staff:** Lori N. Curtis, Asst.Cur..

★17005★
UNIVERSITY OF UTAH - AUDIO-VISUAL SERVICES (Aud-Vis)
Marriott Library, 4th Fl. Phone: (801)581-6283
Salt Lake City, UT 84112 Ralph E. Kranz, AV Libn.
Staff: Prof 1; Other 25. **Subjects:** Music, drama, poetry, art, dance, social sciences, sciences, architecture. **Holdings:** 2054 audio cassettes; 19,000 phonograph records; 21,118 slides; 491 filmstrips; 121 films; 7361 audiotapes; 3500 video cassettes; 124 videotapes. **Services:** Division open to the public with restrictions. **Computerized Information Services:** OCLC; WANGNET (electronic mail service). **Networks/Consortia:** Member of Bibliographical Center for Research, Rocky Mountain Region, Inc. (BCR). **Remarks:** Division maintains a microcomputer center with 150 computers. **Publications:** Music and video bibliographies. **Staff:** Reid Sondrup, AV Assoc.; Joni Clayton, AV Asst.; Ken Tuddenham, Comp.Ctr.Coord.; Pete Johnson, Comp.Ctr.Assoc.Coord.; Behzad Moaddeli, Comp.Ctr.Asst.Coord.

★17006★
UNIVERSITY OF UTAH - DOCUMENTS DIVISION (Info Sci)
Marriott Library Phone: (801)581-8394
Salt Lake City, UT 84112 Julianne P. Hinz, Hd.
Staff: Prof 4; Other 8. **Subjects:** Energy research and development, business and economics, statistics, geological and earth sciences, legislative documents, presidential materials, patents. **Special Collections:** Energy research and development reports, 1950 to present; Congressional committee prints on microfiche (15,100 prints); Congressional committee hearings on microfiche (29,400 hearings); American Statistics Index Nondepository Collection on microfiche (complete set); United Nations Depository Collection; Federal Documents Depository Collection. **Holdings:** 350,000 volumes. **Subscriptions:** 1050 journals and other serials. **Services:** Interlibrary loan; copying; division open to the public. **Computerized Information Services:** DIALOG Information Services, Pergamon ORBIT InfoLine, Inc., BRS Information Technologies. **Staff:** Maxine R. Haggerty, Doc.Acq.Libn.; David L. Morrison, Patents Docs.Libn..

★17007★
UNIVERSITY OF UTAH - HUMAN RELATIONS AREA FILES (Soc Sci)
Marriott Library Phone: (801)581-7024
Salt Lake City, UT 84112 Mark W. Emery, Ref.Libn.
Founded: 1950. **Staff:** Prof 1. **Subjects:** Anthropology, behavioral sciences, geography, history, psychology, sociology, political science. **Holdings:** 5000 books; 3.5 million records on microfiche. **Services:** Files open to the public for reference use only.

★17008★
UNIVERSITY OF UTAH - INSTRUCTIONAL MEDIA SERVICES (Educ)
207 Milton Bennion Hall Phone: (801)581-6112
Salt Lake City, UT 84112 James R. Baird, Dir.
Founded: 1952. **Staff:** 27. **Subjects:** Social and behavioral sciences, literature, history, science, mathematics. **Holdings:** 4500 film titles. **Services:** T.V. distribution/production; photography and graphics; AV equipment service; instructional design; services open to the public on a fee basis. **Special Catalogs:** University of Utah Film Library Catalog and Supplement. **Staff:** Jan Bruckman, Supv., Film Lib..

★17009★
UNIVERSITY OF UTAH - LAW LIBRARY (Law)
College of Law Phone: (801)581-6438
Salt Lake City, UT 84112 Rita Reusch, Dir.
Staff: Prof 6; Other 11. **Subjects:** Law. **Holdings:** 200,000 volumes; 350,000 microfiche; 1500 reels of microfilm; 350 cassettes. **Subscriptions:** 1841 journals and other serials; 10 newspapers. **Services:** Interlibrary loan; copying; library open to the public. **Automated Operations:** Computerized public access catalog, cataloging, and circulation. **Computerized Information Services:** RLIN, WESTLAW, LEXIS, LegalTrac, Northwestern Online Total Integrated System (NOTIS). **Networks/Consortia:** Member of RLG. **Publications:** Acquisitions, monthly; miscellaneous bibliographies. **Staff:** Lee Warthen, Asst.Dir./Hd. of Pub.Serv.; Ellen Ouyang, Tech.Serv.Libn.; Linda Stephenson, Ref.Libn.; Eileen Allen, Circ.Libn..

★17010★
UNIVERSITY OF UTAH - MAP LIBRARY (Geog-Map)
158 Marriott Library Phone: (801)581-7533
Salt Lake City, UT 84112 Barbara Cox, Map Libn.
Staff: Prof 1. **Subjects:** Maps. **Holdings:** 400 books; 125,000 maps; 100 photographs. **Services:** Interlibrary loan; copying; library open to the public. **Automated Operations:** Computerized cataloging and circulation.

★17011★
UNIVERSITY OF UTAH - MATHEMATICS LIBRARY (Sci-Engr)
121 JWB Phone: (801)581-6208
Salt Lake City, UT 84112 Cindy Rabey, Math.Lib.Supv.
Founded: 1965. **Staff:** 2. **Subjects:** Mathematics. **Holdings:** 7000 books; 8500 bound periodical volumes; 1400 technical reports. **Subscriptions:** 255 journals and other serials. **Services:** Interlibrary loan; copying; library open to the public.

★17012★
UNIVERSITY OF UTAH - MIDDLE EAST LIBRARY (Area-Ethnic)
Marriott Library Phone: (801)581-6311
Salt Lake City, UT 84112 Mr. Ragai N. Makar, Hd.
Staff: Prof 1; Other 3. **Subjects:** Humanities; language and literature; political science; social sciences; Islamic studies and history; Arabic, Hebrew, Persian, and Turkish culture and civilization. **Special Collections:** Arabic papyrus and paper documents (9th-11th centuries; 1560 items; 3400 rare books); Arabic, Persian, and Turkish manuscripts (250 items); Fayez Sayegh Collection; Zaki Abushadi Collection; Martin Levey Collection on the history of Arabic science (10,000 items); Arabic and Greek manuscripts (2255 reels of microfilm); illustrated history of Rashid al-Din; Arab League manuscripts collection (470 reels of microfilm); manuscript Qurans; Iranian newspapers on microfilm, 1978-1984; Kabbalah manuscripts collection (65 reels of microfilm); U.S. Department of State, Affairs of Turkey documents, 1910-1929 (125 reels of microfilm); Hebrew journals on microfiche (19th and early 20th centuries). **Holdings:** 116,000 books; 11,200 periodical volumes; 3500 reels of microfilm and microfiche. **Subscriptions:** 504 journals and other serials; 40 newspapers and newsletters. **Services:** Interlibrary loan; copying (limited); library open to the public for reference use only. **Automated Operations:** Computerized cataloging, acquisitions, and circulation. **Computerized Information Services:** Association of Research Libraries (ARL), DIALOG Information Services, Pergamon ORBIT InfoLine, Inc., Performs searches on fee basis. Contact Person: Ruth Frear, 581-7533. **Networks/Consortia:** Member of Utah College Library Council, Bibliographical Center for Research, Rocky Mountain Region, Inc. (BCR). **Publications:** Aziz S. Atiya Library for Middle East Studies Arabic Collection, 3 volumes; Middle East Bibliographic Bulletin, triennial. **Staff:** Judy Jarrow, Asst.Libn..

★17013★
UNIVERSITY OF UTAH - SPECIAL COLLECTIONS DEPARTMENT (Hist)
Marriott Library Phone: (801)581-8863
Salt Lake City, UT 84112 Gregory C. Thompson, Asst.Dir., Spec.Coll.
Staff: Prof 5; Other 35. **Subjects:** Utah, Mountain West, Mormons, Indians. **Holdings:** 83,000 books; 5411 periodical titles; 27,115 theses and dissertations; 1679 federal documents; 4827 folders of clippings; 6301 folders of pamphlets; 5600 linear feet of manuscripts; 112,000 photographs; 2200 linear feet of archives. **Subscriptions:** 1717 journals and other serials; 143 newspapers. **Services:** Interlibrary loan; copying (both limited); department open to the public for reference use only. **Automated Operations:** Computerized public access catalog, cataloging, acquisitions, serials, and circulation. **Publications:** Registers to manuscript collections; Annie Clark Tanner Memorial Trust Fund, Utah, the Mormons and the West Series. **Special Indexes:** Analytic index for serials and pamphlets; newspaper clip file; Arizona index; Chronicle index; review index; university contracts index; manuscript inventories; manuscript name and subject index. **Staff:** Ruth Yeaman, Libn.; Walter Jones, Libn.; Clint Bailey, Archv.Rec.Mgr.; Nancy Young, Libn..

★17014★
UNIVERSITY OF UTAH - SPENCER S. ECCLES HEALTH SCIENCES LIBRARY (Med)
Bldg. 89
10 N. Medical Dr. Phone: (801)581-8771
Salt Lake City, UT 84112 Wayne J. Peay, Dir.
Founded: 1906. **Staff:** Prof 9; Other 36. **Subjects:** Medicine, pharmacy, nursing, basic sciences, health. **Special Collections:** Hope Fox Eccles Clinical Library (300 books; 1250 bound periodical volumes); selective documents depository for health sciences (23,845 items). **Holdings:** 34,000 books; 70,923 bound periodical volumes; 2862 AV programs. **Subscriptions:** 2107 journals and other serials. **Services:** Interlibrary loan; copying; SDI; AV loans; CAI; library open to the public with annual permit. **Automated Operations:** Computerized cataloging, acquisitions, serials, circulation, and ILL. **Computerized Information Services:** BRS Information Technologies, INFONET, Octanet, MEDLINE, OCLC, PHILSOM. **Networks/Consortia:** Member of Midcontinental Regional Medical Library Program, Utah Health Sciences Library Consortium. **Publications:** Synapse (newsletter and acquisitions list), bimonthly; IMS Newsletter, quarterly. **Special Indexes:** MEDOC: Index to U.S. Government Documents in the Health Sciences, quarterly. **Staff:** Elena Eyzaguirre, Assoc.Dir.; Nina Dougherty, Asst.Dir, Info.Serv.; Joan Stoddart, Asst.Dir., Pub.Serv.; Linda Newman, Asst.Dir., Tech.Serv.; Kathleen McCloskey, Hd., Clin.Lib.; Mary Youngkin, Ref.Serv.; Joan Marcotte, Hd., Comp. & Media Serv.; Maureen Carleton, Ref.Libn..

★17015★
UNIVERSITY OF VERMONT - CHEMISTRY/PHYSICS LIBRARY (Sci-Engr)
Cook Physical Sciences Bldg. Phone: (802)656-2268
Burlington, VT 05405 Craig A. Robertson, Chem./Physics Libn.
Staff: Prof 1; Other 1. **Subjects:** Chemistry, physics. **Holdings:** 8500 books; 16,000 bound periodical volumes; 350 reels of microfilm; 1700 microfiche. **Subscriptions:** 351 journals and other serials. **Services:** Interlibrary loan; copying; SDI; library open to the public with restrictions on circulation. **Automated Operations:** Computerized cataloging, acquisitions, and circulation. **Computerized Information Services:** DIALOG Information Services, BRS Information Technologies, CAS ONLINE. Performs searches on fee basis. **Publications:** Library Handbook; acquisitions list, monthly - both for internal distribution only.

★17016★
UNIVERSITY OF VERMONT - DEPARTMENT OF SPECIAL COLLECTIONS (Hist)
Bailey/Howe Library Phone: (802)656-2138
Burlington, VT 05405 John Buechler, Asst.Dir., Spec.Coll.
Staff: Prof 3; Other 3. **Subjects:** Vermontiana, English printer Charles Whittingham, illustrated editions of Ovid, English poet John Masefield, history of books and printing and photography. **Special Collections:** Wilbur Collection of Vermontiana: manuscripts of Dorothy Canfield Fisher, Warren Austin, John Spargo, Ira Allen, Champlain Transportation Company, Vermont governors Roswell Farnham and James Hartness, General William Wells, Henry Stevens and family, George P. Marsh; papers of Senators Winston Prouty and George D. Aiken, Governor Philip H. Hoff, Congressmen Richard Mallary and William Meyer, and several other Vermont public figures and companies. **Holdings:** 85,000 books; 900 bound periodical volumes; 7500 linear feet of manuscripts; 7500 maps; census reports, 1810-1880, 1900, on microfilm; 225,000 photographs; university archives. **Subscriptions:** 110 journals and other serials. **Services:** Interlibrary loan; copying; department open to the public. **Publications:** Periodic lists of manuscript holdings; oral history lists; Liber (newsletter) - to members. **Special Catalogs:** Catalogs of type and paper specimens, binding samples, and imprints by place and date; catalog of illustrated books by types of illustrations (all on cards); exhibit catalogs; Guides to Manuscripts Collection (card and loose-leaf); Guide to Canadian research collections, 1986. **Staff:** J. Kevin Graffagnino, Cur., Wilbur Coll.; Connell Gallagher, Archv. & Cur. of Mss.; Nadia Smith, Ref.Spec..

★17017★
UNIVERSITY OF VERMONT - DIVISION OF HEALTH SCIENCES - CHARLES A. DANA MEDICAL LIBRARY (Med)
Given Bldg. Phone: (802)656-2200
Burlington, VT 05405 Ellen Nagle, Med.Libn.
Founded: 1917. **Staff:** Prof 8; Other 17. **Subjects:** Medicine, nursing, and allied health sciences. **Special Collections:** Historical collection, emphasizing Vermont and U.S. history of medicine. **Holdings:** 24,453 books; 59,486 bound periodical volumes; 7279 AV programs. **Subscriptions:** 1481 journals and other serials. **Services:** Interlibrary loan; copying; library open to the public. **Automated Operations:** Computerized public access catalog, cataloging, acquisitions, serials, and circulation. **Computerized Information Services:** DIALOG Information Services, BRS Information Technologies, NLM, MEDLINE, OCLC; internal database. Performs searches on fee basis. Contact Person: Joanna Weinstock, Ref.Hd.. **Networks/Consortia:** Member of Greater Northeastern Regional Medical Library Program. **Publications:** Resource Library News, bimonthly - to participating hospital librarians; Dana Medical Library Newsletter, monthly - to user groups. **Staff:** Amy Cooper, Hd., Tech.Serv.; Robert J. Sekerak, Plan.Libn.; Tamara Durfee, Ref.Libn.; Donna Lee, Ref.Libn.; Carolyn Fox, Ref.Libn.; Janet Reit, Media Libn.; Lida Douglas, Circ.Supv..

★17018★
UNIVERSITY OF VERMONT - PRINGLE HERBARIUM - LIBRARY (Biol Sci)
Botany Dept. Phone: (802)656-3221
Burlington, VT 05405 David S. Barrington, Cur.
Subjects: Plant taxonomy, botany, genetics. **Special Collections:** Memorabilia and collection of Cyrus Guernsey Pringle and Nellie Flynn. **Holdings:** 500 books; 120 bound periodical volumes; 6000 reprints; 331,000 dried plants. **Services:** Interlibrary loan; library not open to the public.

★17019★
UNIVERSITY OF VICTORIA - DEPARTMENT OF GEOGRAPHY - UNIVERSITY MAP COLLECTION (Geog-Map)
P.O. Box 1700 Phone: (604)721-7348
Victoria, BC, Canada V8W 2Y2 June Whitmore, Map Cur.
Founded: 1967. **Staff:** 1. **Subjects:** General reference map collection, with emphasis on Western North America, the Pacific Basin, Oceania, East Asia, Western Europe; aerial photographs, mainly of Vancouver Island. **Holdings:** 3400 books; 315 atlases; 55,000 maps; 83,000 aerial photographs. **Subscriptions:** 57 journals and other serials. **Services:** Interlibrary loan; copying; collection open to persons engaged in scholarly research.

★17020★
UNIVERSITY OF VICTORIA - KATHARINE MALTWOOD COLLECTION (Art)
P.O. Box 1700 Phone: (604)477-6911
Victoria, BC, Canada V8W 2Y2 Martin Segger, Dir.
Founded: 1944. **Staff:** Prof 1; Other 1. **Subjects:** Art. **Special Collections:** Personal papers and writings of Katharine Maltwood (3000 items); 19th and 20th century architectural plans of regional significance (5000 sheets). **Holdings:** 1000 books; 50 bound periodical volumes. **Services:** Library open to the public. **Special Indexes:** Client index to architectural plans; index to Maltwood papers; index to artifact collection.

★17021★
UNIVERSITY OF VICTORIA - LAW LIBRARY (Law)
P.O. Box 2300 Phone: (604)721-8562
Victoria, BC, Canada V8W 3B1 John N. Davis, Law Libn.
Staff: Prof 3; Other 13. **Subjects:** Law - Canada, U.S., England, Ireland, Scotland, Australia, New Zealand. **Holdings:** 129,224 volumes; 3157 reels of microfilm; 48,020 microfiche.

★17022★
UNIVERSITY OF VICTORIA - MC PHERSON LIBRARY - CURRICULUM LABORATORY (Educ)
P.O. Box 1800 Phone: (604)721-7900
Victoria, BC, Canada V8W 3H5 Donald E. Hamilton, Educ.Libn.
Founded: 1964. **Staff:** Prof 1; Other 5. **Subjects:** Curriculum-support material, education. **Holdings:** 30,000 volumes; 4500 AV programs; 9 VF drawers of pamphlets; elementary and secondary school textbooks. **Subscriptions:** 90 journals and other serials. **Services:** Interlibrary loan; copying; laboratory open to the public with restrictions. **Automated Operations:** Computerized circulation. **Publications:** Information sheets; resource guide to community for teachers.

★17023★
UNIVERSITY OF VICTORIA - MC PHERSON LIBRARY - MUSIC & AUDIO COLLECTION (Mus)
P.O. Box 1800 Phone: (604)721-8232
Victoria, BC, Canada V8W 3H5 Sandra Benet Acker, Mus.Libn.
Staff: Prof 1; Other 4. **Subjects:** Music history and literature, music performance, recorded sound. **Special Collections:** William F. Tickle Collection (theater and dance orchestra music, 1919-1960); Charles Haywood Shakespeare Music Collection; Bernard Naylor Archives; University of Victoria Audio Archives. **Holdings:** 44,000 books and scores; 39,000 sound recordings; music publisher's catalogs; unbound sheet music. **Subscriptions:** 272 journals and other serials. **Services:** Interlibrary loan; copying; listening facilities; collection open to the public for reference use only. **Automated Operations:** Computerized cataloging, serials, and circulation. **Computerized Information Services:** UTLAS, DIALOG Information Services, BRS Information Technologies, MEDLINE, CAN/OLE, QL Systems, Info Globe; Envoy 100 (electronic mail service). Performs searches on fee basis. Contact Person: Dorothy Grieve or Marilyn Berry, 721-8269. **Publications:** Information sheet. **Special Indexes:** Index to record collection by manufacturer's number (card); index to Audio Archives (COM); index to ethnic recordings (card).

★17024★
UNIVERSITY OF VICTORIA - MC PHERSON LIBRARY - SPECIAL COLLECTIONS (Hum, Hist)
Box 1800 Phone: (604)477-6911
Victoria, BC, Canada V8W 3H5 Howard B. Gerwing, Rare Bks.Libn.
Staff: Prof 2; Other 2. **Subjects:** Modern British literature, Vancouver Island studies, Western Canadiana, North American anthropology, Canadian military history, Pacific Rim studies. **Special Collections:** Sir Herbert Read Archives (400 books; 6 drawers of manuscripts); Sir John Betjeman (250 books; 45 drawers of manuscripts); Robert Graves Archives (300 books; 3 drawers of manuscripts); University of Victoria Archives (1000 books; 175 meters of manuscripts). **Holdings:** 40,000 volumes; 1000 pieces of sheet music; 10 VF drawers of military maps; 100 drawers of literary manuscripts. **Subscriptions:** 30 journals and other serials. **Services:** Interlibrary loan; copying; SDI; collections open to the public for reference use only. **Automated Operations:** Computerized cataloging and serials. **Computerized Information Services:** Online systems. **Special Indexes:** Indexes to Sir Herbert Read and Robert Graves Archives. **Staff:** Christopher Petter, Archv..

★17025★
UNIVERSITY OF THE VIRGIN ISLANDS - CARIBBEAN RESEARCH INSTITUTE - LIBRARY (Env-Cons)
St. Thomas, VI 00801 Phone: (809)774-1252
Elba Richardson, Asst.
Staff: Prof 1; Other 1. **Subjects:** Water resources, economics, social sciences, ecology, marine sciences, education, energy. **Special Collections:** Maps of the Caribbean, with emphasis on the Virgin Islands (50); Caribbean Shipwreck and other archeological documents (3 VF drawers); Reference/AV Working Paper Series (Numbers 1 and 2); Microstate Studies Journal (Numbers 1, 2, 3 and 4). **Holdings:** 700 books; 500 documents on energy; 400 pieces of Caribbeana. **Subscriptions:** 53 journals and other serials. **Services:** Copying; library open to the public with restrictions. **Publications:** Covicrier (newsletter), quarterly - free upon request. **Formerly:** Research/Land Grant Library St. Thomas.

★17026★
UNIVERSITY OF THE VIRGIN ISLANDS - RALPH M. PAIEWONSKY LIBRARY - FOUNDATION CENTER REGIONAL COLLECTION (Bus-Fin)
St. Thomas, VI 00802 Phone: (809)774-9200
F. Keith Bingham, Assoc.Libn.
Founded: 1979. **Staff:** Prof 1. **Subjects:** Foundations, grants, fund-raising. **Holdings:** 65 books; 90 microfiche; 50 aperture cards; 165 annual reports and information brochures; 2 VF drawers. **Services:** Interlibrary loan; collection open to the public. **Computerized Information Services:** DIALOG Information Services.

★17027★
UNIVERSITY OF VIRGINIA - ARTHUR J. MORRIS LAW LIBRARY (Law)
School of Law Phone: (804)924-3384
Charlottesville, VA 22901 Larry B. Wenger, Law Libn.
Staff: Prof 14; Other 16. **Subjects:** Law - Anglo-American, international, foreign. **Special Collections:** John Bassett Moore Collection of International Law. **Holdings:** 144,555 books; 280,607 bound periodical volumes; 161,769 microforms; 63,079 government documents. **Subscriptions:** 8448 journals and other serials; 18 newspapers. **Services:** Interlibrary loan; copying; library open to the public with restrictions. **Automated Operations:** Computerized cataloging. **Computerized Information Services:** LEXIS, WESTLAW, OCLC. **Networks/Consortia:** Member of SOLINET. **Staff:** Barbara G. Murphy, Assoc. Law Libn.; Mary Cooper Gilliam, Tech.Serv.Libn.; Susan Tulis, Docs.Libn.; Anne Mustain, Cat.Libn.; Michael Klepper, Media Serv.Libn.; Margaret Aycock, Oceans/Intl. Law Libn.; Kent Olson, Hd., Ref.; Katherine Malmquist, Circ.Libn..

★17028★
UNIVERSITY OF VIRGINIA - BIOLOGY/PSYCHOLOGY LIBRARY (Biol Sci)
Gilmer Hall Phone: (804)924-3529
Charlottesville, VA 22903 Sandra Dulaney, Libn.
Staff: 2. **Subjects:** Biological sciences, psychology. **Holdings:** 20,290 volumes. **Subscriptions:** 467 journals and other serials. **Services:** Interlibrary loan; copying; library open to the public.

★17029★
UNIVERSITY OF VIRGINIA - BLANDY EXPERIMENTAL FARM LIBRARY (Biol Sci)
Box 175 Phone: (703)837-1758
Boyce, VA 22620 Edward F. Connor, Dir.
Founded: 1926. **Subjects:** Plant science, genetics, botany, plant taxonomy, plant collecting, horticulture. **Special Collections:** Manuals of plants of the world; genetic reprint collection. **Holdings:** 2000 books; 1400 bound periodical volumes; 6000 reprints. **Subscriptions:** 50 journals and other serials. **Services:** Interlibrary loan; library open to the public with prior permission.

★17030★
UNIVERSITY OF VIRGINIA - CHEMISTRY LIBRARY (Sci-Engr)
Chemistry Bldg.
McCormick Rd. Phone: (804)924-3159
Charlottesville, VA 22903 Christine Denton, Libn.
Staff: 1. **Subjects:** Chemistry. **Holdings:** 18,351 volumes. **Subscriptions:** 305 journals and other serials. **Services:** Interlibrary loan; copying; library open to the public.

★17031★
UNIVERSITY OF VIRGINIA - CLIFTON WALLER BARRETT LIBRARY (Hum)
Alderman Library Phone: (804)924-3366
Charlottesville, VA 22901 Joan S. Crane, Cur., Amer.Lit.
Subjects: American literature from American Revolution to present. **Holdings:** 40,770 books; 180,000 manuscripts. **Services:** Copying; library open to the public for advanced research only. **Publications:** Exhibition Catalogs, occasional.

★17032★
UNIVERSITY OF VIRGINIA - COLGATE DARDEN GRADUATE SCHOOL OF BUSINESS ADMINISTRATION - LIBRARY (Bus-Fin)
Box 6550 Phone: (804)924-7321
Charlottesville, VA 22906 Henry Wingate, Libn.
Founded: 1957. **Staff:** Prof 1; Other 5. **Subjects:** Business, management, finance, accounting, economics, marketing, organization behavior. **Special Collections:** Corporation annual and 10K reports (200,000 microfiche). **Holdings:** 50,000 books; 5000 bound periodical volumes; 2000 reels of microfilm of periodicals. **Subscriptions:** 900 journals and other serials; 10 newspapers. **Services:** Interlibrary loan; copying; library open to the public. **Computerized Information Services:** DIALOG Information Services, Pergamon ORBIT InfoLine, Inc., BRS Information Technologies, The Reference Service (REFSRV), Dow Jones News/Retrieval.

★17033★
UNIVERSITY OF VIRGINIA - EDUCATION LIBRARY (Educ)
Ruffner Hall
405 Emmet St.
Charlottesville, VA 22903 Betsy Anthony, Educ.Libn.
Staff: Prof 1; Other 4. **Subjects:** Education. **Holdings:** 40,000 books; 1300 bound periodical volumes; ERIC microfiche. **Subscriptions:** 700 journals and other serials. **Services:** Interlibrary loan; copying.

★17034★
UNIVERSITY OF VIRGINIA - FISKE KIMBALL FINE ARTS LIBRARY (Art)
Bayly Dr. Phone: (804)924-7024
Charlottesville, VA 22903 Jack Robertson, Libn.
Founded: 1970. **Staff:** Prof 3; Other 5. **Subjects:** Architecture, art, archeology, city planning, theater, landscape architecture, film, photography, costume. **Special Collections:** Frances Benjamin Johnson Photograph Collection of Virginia Architecture (1000); William Morris Library on Forgery of Works of Art, 15th century to present (700 items); drawings of Charles F. Gillette (landscape architect). **Holdings:** 103,000 volumes; 135,000 architecture slides; 875 reels of microfilm; 14,800 microfiche. **Subscriptions:** 787 journals and other serials. **Services:** Interlibrary loan; copying; library open to the public with circulation restrictions on some holdings. **Automated Operations:** Computerized cataloging. **Computerized Information Services:** OCLC. **Networks/Consortia:** Member of SOLINET. **Staff:** Christie D. Stephenson, Asst. Fine Arts Libn.; Lynda S. White, Asst. Fine Arts Libn..

★17035★
UNIVERSITY OF VIRGINIA - LIBRARY - MANUSCRIPTS DEPARTMENT AND UNIVERSITY ARCHIVES (Hum, Area-Ethnic)
Charlottesville, VA 22901 Phone: (804)924-4971
Edmund Berkeley, Jr., Cur. of Mss./Univ.Archv.
Subjects: Virginia and southeastern U.S. history and literature, 20th century Virginia and U.S. politics and government, American literature, Afro-Americans, university archives. **Holdings:** 10 million manuscripts; 1.6 million archival items. **Services:** Interlibrary loan (limited); copying; department open to the public.

★17036★
UNIVERSITY OF VIRGINIA - LIBRARY - RARE BOOK DEPARTMENT (Rare Book, Hum, Hist)
Charlottesville, VA 22901 Phone: (804)924-3366
Julius P. Barclay, Cur. of Rare Bks.
Staff: Prof 5; Other 5. **Subjects:** American literature and history, voyages and travels, typography, Gothic novel in British literature, railroads, evolution; 19th century British literature, books design and illustration; French renaissance literature. **Special Collections:** Stone Collection of Typography; Sadleir-Black Gothic Novel Collection; Streeter Railroad Collection; Victorius Evolution Collection; Marion DuPont Scott Collection. **Holdings:** 200,000 volumes; 30 VF drawers of Virginiana; 115 drawers of maps; 65 boxes of broadsides; 950 bound volumes of newspapers; 30 drawers of posters. **Subscriptions:** 126 journals and other serials. **Services:** Copying; department open to the public with restrictions. **Automated Operations:** Computerized cataloging and circulation. **Computerized Information Services:** DIALOG Information Services, BRS Information Technologies, Pergamon ORBIT InfoLine, Inc., Telesystemes Questel, RLIN (through main library). Performs searches on fee basis. Contact Person: Carol M. Pfeiffer, Dir. of Adm.Serv., 924-0502. **Publications:** Chapter and Verse, irregular - to members of the Library Associates and other libraries in the U.S. and Canada. **Staff:** Clinton Sisson, Asst. to Cur.; Mildred K. Abraham, Libn., Rd.Serv.; Joan St.C. Crane, Cur., Amer.Lit.Coll.; William H. Runge, Cur., McGregor Lib.; Roger M. Leachman, Rare Bks.Coll.Dev.Libn..

★17037★
UNIVERSITY OF VIRGINIA - MATHEMATICS-ASTRONOMY LIBRARY (Sci-Engr)
Mathematics-Astronomy Bldg. Phone: (804)924-7806
Charlottesville, VA 22903 Roma Reed, Libn.
Staff: 1. **Subjects:** Mathematics, astronomy. **Holdings:** 31,387 volumes. **Subscriptions:** 350 journals and other serials. **Services:** Interlibrary loan; copying; library open to the public.

★17038★
UNIVERSITY OF VIRGINIA - MEDICAL CENTER - CLAUDE MOORE HEALTH SCIENCES LIBRARY (Biol Sci, Med)
Box 234 Phone: (804)924-5464
Charlottesville, VA 22908 Terry A. Thorkildson, Dir. & Assoc.Prof.
Founded: 1825. **Staff:** Prof 14; Other 32. **Subjects:** Biological and medical sciences, nursing, allied health sciences. **Special Collections:** Walter Reed Archives. **Holdings:** 147,984 volumes; 3054 AV programs. **Subscriptions:** 2842 journals and other serials. **Services:** Interlibrary loan; copying; SDI; library open to the public with restrictions. **Computerized Information Services:** DIALOG Information Services, Pergamon ORBIT InfoLine, Inc., ISI/BIOMED, BRS Information Technologies, NLM; OnTyme Electronic Message Network Service (electronic mail service). Performs searches on fee basis. **Publications:** Claude Moore Health Sciences Library News, monthly. **Special Catalogs:** Virginia Union List of Biomedical Serials, annual. **Staff:** Gretchen Naisawald, Asst.Dir., Pub.Serv.; John Patruno, Jr., Assoc.Dir.; Lenore Schnaitman, Ref.Libn.; Richard A. Peterson, Automated Serv.Libn.; Marylin James, Asst.Cat.; Joan Echtenkamp, Hist.Coll.Libn.; Frank Sadowski, Asst.Dir., Tech.Serv.; Allison Sleeman, Hd., Cat.; Judith Robinson, Coll.Dev.Libn.; Susan G. Bader, User Educ.Libn.; Gary Ives, Access Serv.; Anne Humphries, Hd.Ref.Libn.; Jonquil Feldman, Ref.Libn..

★17039★
UNIVERSITY OF VIRGINIA - MEDICAL CENTER - DEPARTMENT OF NEUROLOGY - ELIZABETH J. OHRSTROM LIBRARY (Med)
Box 394 Phone: (804)924-8378
Charlottesville, VA 22908 Wendy-Marie Goodman, Lib.Asst.
Staff: 2. **Subjects:** General and pediatric neurology, cardiovascular systems, neuroscience. **Special Collections:** Rare and original neurological texts. **Holdings:** 3000 books; 2000 bound periodical volumes. **Subscriptions:** 35 journals and other serials. **Services:** Library not open to the public.

Computerized Information Services: DIALOG Information Services, Sci-Mate. **Staff:** Lawrence H. Phillips, II, Chm., Lib.Comm..

★17040★
UNIVERSITY OF VIRGINIA - MUSIC LIBRARY (Mus)
Old Cabell Hall Phone: (804)924-7041
Charlottesville, VA 22903-3298 Diane Parr Walker, Mus.Libn.
Staff: Prof 2; Other 3. **Subjects:** Music. **Special Collections:** Mackay-Smith Collection (18th century imprints); Monticello Music Collection; printed and manuscript collection of the music of John Powell; 19th century American sheet music. **Holdings:** 45,000 volumes; 6054 microfiche; 1371 reels of microfilm; 3120 microcards; 3000 magnetic tapes; 22,000 phonograph records; 533 compact discs. **Subscriptions:** 576 journals and other serials. **Services:** Interlibrary loan; copying; library open to the public. **Special Catalogs:** Computer Catalog of Nineteenth-Century American-Imprint Sheet Music (microfiche). **Staff:** Karen R. Little, Asst.Mus.Libn..

★17041★
UNIVERSITY OF VIRGINIA - PHYSICS LIBRARY (Sci-Engr)
Physics Bldg. Phone: (804)924-6589
Charlottesville, VA 22903 James Shea, Libn.
Staff: 2. **Subjects:** Physics. **Holdings:** 23,846 volumes. **Subscriptions:** 273 journals and other serials. **Services:** Interlibrary loan; copying; library open to the public.

★17042★
UNIVERSITY OF VIRGINIA - SCIENCE & ENGINEERING LIBRARY (Sci-Engr)
Clark Hall Phone: (804)924-7209
Charlottesville, VA 22903-3188 Edwina H. Pancake, Dir.
Staff: Prof 4; Other 13. **Subjects:** General science and engineering including reference materials. **Special Collections:** Government technical reports from Atomic Energy Commission, Department of Defense, and NASA. **Holdings:** 220,309 volumes; 162,836 titles of hard copy technical reports; 939,693 technical reports on microfiche. **Subscriptions:** 1564 journals and other serials. **Services:** Interlibrary loan; copying; library open to the public. **Automated Operations:** Computerized cataloging, acquisitions, and circulation. **Computerized Information Services:** DIALOG Information Services, Pergamon ORBIT InfoLine, Inc., BRS Information Technologies, Telesystemes Questel, CAS ONLINE, National Environmental Data Referral Service (NEDRES). **Staff:** Jean L. Cooper, Tech.Serv.Libn.; Tran Ton-nu, Pub.Serv.Libn.; Fred O'Bryant, Sci.Bibliog..

★17043★
UNIVERSITY OF VIRGINIA - TRACY W. MC GREGOR LIBRARY (Hist)
Alderman Library Phone: (804)924-3366
Charlottesville, VA 22901 William H. Runge, Cur.
Subjects: American history, especially Southeastern United States, 1607 through the 19th century. **Holdings:** 21,000 books; 10,000 manuscripts. **Services:** Copying; library open to the public for advanced research only. **Special Catalogs:** Exhibition catalogs, occasional.

UNIVERSITY OF VIRGINIA - VIRGINIA TRANSPORTATION RESEARCH COUNCIL
See: Virginia Transportation Research Council - Library (17389)

★17044★
UNIVERSITY OF WASHINGTON - ALCOHOL & DRUG ABUSE INSTITUTE - LIBRARY (Med)
3937 15th Ave., N.E., NL-15 Phone: (206)543-0937
Seattle, WA 98105 Nancy Sutherland, Dir. of Lib.
Founded: 1975. **Staff:** Prof 1; Other 1. **Subjects:** Alcohol and drug abuse. **Holdings:** 1500 books; 2500 reprints. **Subscriptions:** 80 journals and other serials. **Services:** Interlibrary loan; SDI; library open to the public. **Automated Operations:** Computerized cataloging and serials. **Computerized Information Services:** DIALOG Information Services, NLM; ADAI Library database (internal database). Performs searches free of charge. **Networks/Consortia:** Member of Substance Abuse Librarians and Information Specialists (SALIS). **Publications:** Current Literature on Alcohol and Drug Abuse, 10/year - limited distribution; subject bibliographies (online).

★17045★
UNIVERSITY OF WASHINGTON - ARCHITECTURE-URBAN PLANNING LIBRARY (Art, Plan)
334 Gould Hall, JO-30 Phone: (206)543-4067
Seattle, WA 98195 Betty L. Wagner, Libn.
Founded: 1923. **Staff:** Prof 1; Other 2. **Subjects:** Architecture, urban planning, landscape architecture, building construction. **Holdings:** 31,699 volumes; 4430 ephemeral items; 2258 HUD reports; 5246 microfiche. **Subscriptions:** 311 journals and other serials. **Services:** Interlibrary loan; copying; library open to the public for reference use only. **Computerized Information Services:** OCLC. **Networks/Consortia:** Member of Western Library Network (WLN).

★17046★
UNIVERSITY OF WASHINGTON - ART LIBRARY (Art)
101 Art Bldg., DM-10 Phone: (206)543-0648
Seattle, WA 98195 Connie T. Okada, Libn.
Founded: 1949. **Staff:** Prof 1; Other 2. **Subjects:** Painting, ceramics, printmaking, sculpture, industrial design, fiber arts, metal design, graphic design, photography, history of art. **Holdings:** 38,938 volumes; 25 drawers of pamphlets and clippings; 7500 mounted reproductions. **Subscriptions:** 413 journals and other serials. **Services:** Interlibrary loan; copying; library open to the public for reference use only. **Computerized Information Services:** OCLC. **Networks/Consortia:** Member of Western Library Network (WLN).

★17047★
UNIVERSITY OF WASHINGTON - ART SLIDE COLLECTION (Aud-Vis)
120 Art Bldg., DM-10 Phone: (206)543-0649
Seattle, WA 98195 Joan Nilsson, Dir. of Visual Serv.
Staff: 2. **Subjects:** Fine arts and related material. **Holdings:** 195,231 slides. **Services:** Open to faculty in other campus departments and local museum personnel.

★17048★
UNIVERSITY OF WASHINGTON - BUSINESS ADMINISTRATION LIBRARY (Bus-Fin)
100 Balmer Hall, DJ-10 Phone: (206)543-4360
Seattle, WA 98195 Anne B. Passarelli, Hd.Libn.
Founded: 1951. **Staff:** Prof 2; Other 5. **Subjects:** Management, marketing, personnel and labor, accounting, finance, international business, transportation, insurance, real estate, business law. **Holdings:** 47,539 volumes; 195,268 microfiche of U.S. corporation records. **Subscriptions:** 1035 journals and other serials; 11 newspapers. **Services:** Interlibrary loan; copying; library open to the public for reference use only. **Computerized Information Services:** DIALOG Information Services, Pergamon ORBIT InfoLine, Inc., BRS Information Technologies, Knowledge Index, Disclosure Information Group, OCLC. **Networks/Consortia:** Member of Western Library Network (WLN). **Publications:** Bibliographies, irregular. **Staff:** Gordon J. Aamot, Asst.Libn..

★17049★
UNIVERSITY OF WASHINGTON - CENTER FOR LAW & JUSTICE - CLJ/NCADBIP INFORMATION SERVICE (Law, Soc Sci)
DK-40 Phone: (206)543-1485
Seattle, WA 98195 Janette H. Schueller, Info.Spec.
Staff: Prof 1; Other 1. **Subjects:** Juvenile delinquency and its prevention, juvenile justice, school-based delinquency prevention strategies, criminal justice, social science methodology, violent behavior. **Special Collections:** Juvenile delinquency prevention program questionnaire responses, descriptions, evaluations. **Holdings:** 3000 books; 1000 evaluative reports; 300 microfiche. **Subscriptions:** 89 journals and other serials. **Services:** Interlibrary loan; copying; SDI; service open to the public for reference use only. **Automated Operations:** Computerized cataloging. **Computerized Information Services:** DIALOG Information Services; NCADBIP literature database, Prevention Programs (internal databases). **Networks/Consortia:** Member of Criminal Justice Information Exchange Group. **Publications:** New Acquisitions List, monthly - to staff and interested parties. **Remarks:** NCADBIP stands for National Center for the Assessment of Delinquency Behavior and Its Prevention, which is a federally funded project at the center.

★17050★
UNIVERSITY OF WASHINGTON - CENTER FOR STUDIES IN DEMOGRAPHY AND ECOLOGY - LIBRARY (Soc Sci)
102 Savery Hall, DK-40 Phone: (206)543-9525
Seattle, WA 98195 Melanie Lightbody, Libn.
Staff: Prof 1. **Subjects:** Census, vital statistics, demography, ecology. **Holdings:** 2000 books; 1000 U.S. Government periodicals; 200 publications on family planning. **Subscriptions:** 36 journals and other serials. **Automated Operations:** Computerized cataloging, acquisitions, and serials.

★17051★
UNIVERSITY OF WASHINGTON - CHEMISTRY LIBRARY AND INFORMATION SERVICES (Sci-Engr)
192 Bagley Hall, BG-10 Phone: (206)543-1603
Seattle, WA 98195 Susanne Redalje, Hd.
Staff: Prof 1; Other 2. **Subjects:** Chemistry, chemical engineering, pharmaceuticals, medicinal chemistry. **Holdings:** 48,031 volumes; 3223 microfiche. **Subscriptions:** 905 journals and other serials. **Services:** Interlibrary loan; copying; library open to the public for reference use only. **Computerized Information Services:** DIALOG Information Services, Pergamon ORBIT InfoLine, Inc., CAS ONLINE, Chemical Information Systems, Inc. (CIS), BRS Information Technologies, OCLC. **Networks/Consortia:** Member of Western Library Network (WLN).

★17052★
UNIVERSITY OF WASHINGTON - COMPUTING INFORMATION CENTER (Comp Sci)
Academic Computing Services, HG-45 Phone: (206)543-8519
Seattle, WA 98195 Darlene Myers Hildebrandt, Comp.Info.Serv.Adm.
Founded: 1967. **Staff:** Prof 3; Other 5. **Subjects:** Computing, programming languages, hardware, software, programming, electronic music, data communications. **Special Collections:** Collection of computer produced art; conferences/symposia in the computer science field. **Holdings:** 8600 books; 1600 bound periodical volumes; 8500 technical reports; computer manuals. **Subscriptions:** 1200 journals and other serials. **Services:** Interlibrary loan; copying; SDI; center open to the public; user's fee required for borrowing. **Computerized Information Services:** CIRIX (internal database). **Publications:** Computing Resources for the Professional, bimonthly - by subscription; list of additional publications - available upon request. **Staff:** Richard E. Obert, Lib.Spec.; Kim Lafferty, Lib.Spec..

★17053★
UNIVERSITY OF WASHINGTON - CURRICULUM MATERIALS SECTION (Educ)
Suzzallo Library, FM-25 Phone: (206)543-2725
Seattle, WA 98195 Loretta Lopez, Ref./Educ.Libn.
Founded: 1960. **Staff:** Prof 1; Other 2. **Subjects:** Children's literature, elementary and secondary curriculum and instruction, educational and psychological testing, educational games/simulations. **Special Collections:** Children's Literature Archive; Resource Center for Gifted Education. **Holdings:** 54,434 books, textbooks, and curriculum guides; 8000 children's literature book jackets, 1920-1965, arranged by author; 3206 standardized tests; 258 games and simulations; 8276 curriculum guides on microfiche. **Subscriptions:** 72 journals and other serials. **Services:** Interlibrary loan (limited); copying; section open to the public for reference use only. **Computerized Information Services:** OCLC. **Networks/Consortia:** Member of Western Library Network (WLN).

★17054★
UNIVERSITY OF WASHINGTON - DRAMA LIBRARY (Theater)
145 Hutchinson Hall, DX-20 Phone: (206)543-5148
Seattle, WA 98195 Elizabeth Fugate, Libn.
Founded: 1931. **Staff:** Prof 1; Other 1. **Subjects:** Drama history, dramatic literature, theater history, acting, children's theater, costume, make-up, scene design, creative dramatics, directing, lighting, playwriting, mime, theater buildings and architecture. **Special Collections:** 19th Century Acting Editions (2807). **Holdings:** 20,079 volumes; unbound play collection (14,000 acting editions); 360 phonograph records; 323 tapes. **Subscriptions:** 144 journals and other serials. **Services:** Interlibrary loan; copying; library open to the public for reference use only. **Computerized Information Services:** OCLC. **Networks/Consortia:** Member of Western Library Network (WLN). **Special Catalogs:** Catalog of 19th Century Acting Editions and theses (card). **Special Indexes:** Index of anthologies; sound effects.

★17055★
UNIVERSITY OF WASHINGTON - EAST ASIA LIBRARY (Area-Ethnic)
322 Gowen Hall, DO-27 Phone: (206)543-4490
Seattle, WA 98195 Karl Lo, Hd.
Founded: 1947. **Staff:** Prof 5; Other 10. **Subjects:** Social sciences, humanities, literature and language, history, religion and philosophy, arts. **Special Collections:** Works in Chinese, Japanese, Korean, Tibetan, Thai, Vietnamese, Mongolian, Manchu, and Indonesian. **Holdings:** 315,183 volumes; 10,619 reels of microfilm; 6681 microfiche; 4433 pamphlets. **Subscriptions:** 2849 journals and other serials; 96 newspapers. **Services:** Interlibrary loan; copying; library open to the public for reference use only. **Computerized Information Services:** OCLC. **Networks/Consortia:** Member of Western Library Network (WLN). **Staff:** Yeen-Mei Wu Chang, China Libn.; Elise Chin, Hd., Cat.Sect.; Teruko Kyuma Chin, Japan Libn.; Yoon-Whan Choe, Korea Libn..

★17056★
UNIVERSITY OF WASHINGTON - ENGINEERING LIBRARY AND INFORMATION SERVICES (Sci-Engr, Comp Sci)
Engineering Library Bldg., FH-15 Phone: (206)543-0740
Seattle, WA 98195 Harold N. Wiren, Hd.
Founded: 1947. **Staff:** Prof 3; Other 5. **Subjects:** Applied mathematics, applied physics, computer science, energy, engineering, environment, social management of technology, theoretical and applied mechanics. **Holdings:** 116,724 volumes; 45,935 paper copy technical reports; 1 million technical reports in microform; patent specifications, 1966 to present, on microfilm. **Subscriptions:** 2689 journals and other serials. **Services:** Interlibrary loan; copying; library open to the public for reference use only. **Computerized Information Services:** DIALOG Information Services, STN International, Pergamon ORBIT InfoLine, Inc., BRS Information Technologies, OCLC. **Networks/Consortia:** Member of Western Library Network (WLN). **Special Catalogs:** Technical report catalog (card). **Staff:** Charles Lord, Engr.Libn.; Pamela Yorks, Asst.Engr.Libn..

★17057★
UNIVERSITY OF WASHINGTON - ETHNOMUSICOLOGY ARCHIVES (Mus)
School of Music, DN-10 Phone: (206)543-0974
Seattle, WA 98195 Laurel Sercombe, Archv.
Founded: 1962. **Staff:** Prof 1. **Subjects:** World music, including classical and indigenous forms. **Special Collections:** Field recordings of Robert Garfias (Burma, Korea, Romania, Mexico, Philippines) and Melville Jacobs (Pacific Northwest Indians); Joe Heaney Collection (Irish songs, stories). **Holdings:** 50 books; 5000 hours of audiotape; 150 videotapes; 150 films; 250 phonograph records; 200 photographs and slides; 300 musical instruments. **Subscriptions:** 10 journals and other serials. **Services:** Interlibrary loan; copying; archives open to researchers. **Automated Operations:** Computerized cataloging. **Computerized Information Services:** Internal database.

★17058★
UNIVERSITY OF WASHINGTON - FISHERIES-OCEANOGRAPHY LIBRARY (Biol Sci, Sci-Engr)
151 Oceanography Teaching Bldg., WB-30 Phone: (206)543-4279
Seattle, WA 98195 Pamela A. Mofjeld, Hd.
Founded: 1950. **Staff:** Prof 1; Other 3. **Subjects:** Fisheries science, marine biology, oceanography, food science and technology, marine policy. **Special Collections:** Canadian translations of fisheries and aquatic sciences on microfiche; Pacific Salmon Literature Compilation. **Holdings:** 55,054 volumes; 57,113 reprints, translations, reports; 339 reels of microfilm; 5976 microcards; 14,367 microfiche; 1750 maps. **Subscriptions:** 1258 journals and other serials. **Services:** Interlibrary loan; copying; library open to the public for reference use only. **Computerized Information Services:** DIALOG Information Services, Pergamon ORBIT InfoLine, Inc., BRS Information Technologies, STN International, OCLC. **Networks/Consortia:** Member of Western Library Network (WLN). **Special Catalogs:** Selected References to Literature on Marine Expeditions, 1700-1960 (1972).

★17059★
UNIVERSITY OF WASHINGTON - FISHING VESSEL SAFETY CENTER - LIBRARY (Sci-Engr)
326 Mechanical Engineering Bldg.
Mail Stop FU-10 Phone: (206)543-7446
Seattle, WA 98195 Bruce H. Adee, Dir.
Staff: 1. **Subjects:** Fishing vessels and their safety. **Holdings:** 100 books; 500 other cataloged items. **Subscriptions:** 12 journals and other serials. **Services:** Library open to the public. **Publications:** Occasional reports.

★17060★
UNIVERSITY OF WASHINGTON - FOREST RESOURCES LIBRARY (Biol Sci, Sci-Engr)
60 Bloedel Hall, AQ-15 Phone: (206)543-2758
Seattle, WA 98195 Carol Green, Hd.
Founded: 1947. **Staff:** Prof 1; Other 2. **Subjects:** Forestry; wood science, technology, chemistry, and anatomy; paper and pulp technology; logging engineering; forest management, economics, soils, pathology, hydrology, and entomology; fire control; silvics and silviculture; recreation. **Holdings:** 47,732 volumes. **Subscriptions:** 1690 journals and other serials. **Services:** Interlibrary loan; copying; library open to the public for reference use only. **Computerized Information Services:** DIALOG Information Services, Pergamon ORBIT InfoLine, Inc., BRS Information Technologies, STN International, OCLC. **Networks/Consortia:** Member of Western Library Network (WLN).

UNIVERSITY OF WASHINGTON - FOREST SERVICE INFORMATION - FS-INFO-NW
See: U.S. Forest Service (15098)

★17061★
UNIVERSITY OF WASHINGTON - FRIDAY HARBOR LABORATORIES - LIBRARY (Biol Sci)
NJ-22 Phone: (206)378-2501
Friday Harbor, WA 98250 Kathy M. Carr, Libn.
Founded: 1921. **Staff:** Prof 1. **Subjects:** Marine biology, invertebrate embryology, invertebrate zoology, algology; fish biology. **Holdings:** 16,162 volumes; 946 microfiche; 242 maps. **Subscriptions:** 147 journals and other serials. **Services:** Interlibrary loan; copying; library open to the public by permission. **Computerized Information Services:** DIALOG Information Services, Pergamon ORBIT InfoLine, Inc., BRS Information Technologies. **Remarks:** Librarian is available at the Friday Harbor Library only during summer quarter; September through May contact Kathy M. Carr in the Natural Sciences Library at (206)543-1243.

★17062★
UNIVERSITY OF WASHINGTON - GEOGRAPHY LIBRARY (Geog-Map)
415 Smith Hall, DP-10 Phone: (206)543-5244
Seattle, WA 98195 Robert D. Bjoring, Libn.
Founded: 1952. **Staff:** Prof 1; Other 1. **Subjects:** Geography, cartography, regional science. **Holdings:** 14,528 volumes. **Subscriptions:** 368 journals and other serials. **Services:** Interlibrary loan; library open to the public for reference use only. **Computerized Information Services:** OCLC. **Networks/Consortia:** Member of Western Library Network (WLN).

★17063★
UNIVERSITY OF WASHINGTON - GOVERNMENT PUBLICATIONS DIVISION (Info Sci)
Suzzallo Library, FM-25 Phone: (206)543-1937
Seattle, WA 98195 Eleanor L. Chase, Hd.Libn.
Founded: 1890. **Staff:** Prof 4; Other 3. **Subjects:** Demography and population, energy resources, forestry, international trade and relations, U.S. Government. **Special Collections:** Depository for U.S. documents; publications of United Nations, Food and Agriculture Organization, UNESCO, European Communities, General Agreement on Tariffs and Trade (GATT); Canada; Washington; Alaska; California; New York. **Holdings:** 1.09 million volumes of government publications; 238,500 microforms. **Services:** Interlibrary loan; copying; division open to the public. **Computerized Information Services:** DIALOG Information Services, Pergamon ORBIT InfoLine, Inc., BRS Information Technologies, OCLC. **Networks/Consortia:** Member of Western Library Network (WLN). **Staff:** Andrew F. Johnson, State/Local Docs.Libn.; David Maack, Intl.Docs.Libn.; Cynthia Fugate, Foreign Docs.Libn..

★17064★
UNIVERSITY OF WASHINGTON - HEALTH SCIENCES LIBRARY AND INFORMATION CENTER (Med)
T-227 Health Sciences, SB-55 Phone: (206)543-5530
Seattle, WA 98195 Gerald J. Oppenheimer, Dir.
Founded: 1949. **Staff:** Prof 18; Other 35. **Subjects:** Medicine, dentistry, nursing, pharmacy, public health. **Special Collections:** Biomedical history (2283 volumes). **Holdings:** 84,000 books; 179,000 bound periodical volumes; 25,345 microcards; 49,277 microfiche. **Subscriptions:** 3766 journals and other serials. **Services:** Interlibrary loan; copying; SDI; library open to the public for reference use only. **Computerized Information Services:** DIALOG Information Services, Pergamon ORBIT InfoLine, Inc., NLM, BRS Information Technologies, PaperChase, OCLC; OnTyme Electronic Message Network Service (electronic mail service). Performs searches on fee basis. **Networks/Consortia:** Member of Western Library Network (WLN). **Publications:** The Supplement (newsletter of the Pacific Northwest Regional Health Sciences Library Service), quarterly - to libraries in the Pacific Northwest. **Remarks:** Headquarters of Pacific Northwest Regional Health Sciences Library Service (PNRHSLS). **Staff:** Carolyn Weaver, Assoc.Dir.; Siew-Choo Poh, Hd., Info.Serv.; Colleen Weum, Coll.Dev.Libn.; Lorraine Raymond, Hd., Tech.Serv.; Ellen Howard, Hd., Pub.Serv.; Leroy Chadwick, Ser.Libn.; Debra Ketchell, Info.Sys./State Rsrc.Libn.; Dale Middleton, Assoc.Dir., PNRHSLS; Linda Milgrom, Rsrc.Libn., PNRHSLS; Nancy Press, Educ.Coord., PNRHSLS; Jan Schueller, Spec.Proj.Libn..

★17065★
UNIVERSITY OF WASHINGTON - HEALTH SCIENCES LIBRARY AND INFORMATION CENTER - K.K. SHERWOOD LIBRARY (Med)
Harborview Medical Center
325 9th Ave., ZA-43 Phone: (206)223-3360
Seattle, WA 98104 Sharon Babcock, Lib.Supv.
Staff: 2. **Subjects:** Core medical collection. **Holdings:** 1050 books; 3210 bound periodical volumes. **Subscriptions:** 175 journals and other serials. **Services:** Interlibrary loan; copying; library open to the public for reference use only.

★17066★
UNIVERSITY OF WASHINGTON - INSTITUTE ON AGING - INFORMATION CLEARINGHOUSE
University of Washington JM-20
Seattle, WA 98195
Defunct. Holdings absorbed by Northwest Geriatric Education Center - Resource Center.

★17067★
UNIVERSITY OF WASHINGTON - MANUSCRIPTS AND UNIVERSITY ARCHIVES DIVISION - MANUSCRIPT COLLECTION (Hist)
Suzzallo Library, FM-25 Phone: (206)543-1879
Seattle, WA 98195 Karyl Winn, Mss.Libn.
Staff: Prof 1; Other 2. **Subjects:** Washington politics and government, congressional papers, public power, labor, forest products, fisheries and mining, American literature, Pacific Northwest art, urban affairs, ethnic history, education. **Holdings:** 21,069 linear feet of manuscripts. **Services:** Interlibrary loan (limited); copying; collection open to researchers with restrictions. **Publications:** Guide to the Wilbert McLeod Chapman Collection; Manual for Accessioning, Arrangement and Description of Manuscripts and Archives. **Special Catalogs:** Comprehensive Guide to the Manuscripts Collections and to the Personal Papers in the University Archives. **Special Indexes:** Inventories, name and subject indexes for each accession.

★17068★
UNIVERSITY OF WASHINGTON - MANUSCRIPTS AND UNIVERSITY ARCHIVES DIVISION - UNIVERSITY ARCHIVES (Hist)
3902 Cowlitz Rd., HO-10 Phone: (206)543-6509
Seattle, WA 98195 Kerry Bartels, Univ.Archv.
Founded: 1967. **Staff:** Prof 1; Other 1. **Subjects:** University history and administration. **Holdings:** 9616 linear feet of archives; records of major administrative offices and academic departments; personal papers of faculty, administrators, students, and faculty organizations; university publications. **Services:** Copying; archives open to the public; private papers open to researchers with restrictions. **Special Indexes:** Inventories of individual accessions.

★17069★
UNIVERSITY OF WASHINGTON - MAP COLLECTION AND CARTOGRAPHIC INFORMATION SERVICES (Geog-Map)
Suzzallo Library, FM-25 Phone: (206)543-9392
Seattle, WA 98195 Steven Z. Hiller, Hd.
Staff: Prof 2; Other 1. **Subjects:** Geologic and topographic maps, nautical charts, aerial photographs, atlases. **Special Collections:** Braille maps and atlases (300). **Holdings:** 2081 books and atlases; 218,971 maps; 50,219 aerial photographs; 253 reels of microfilm; 2746 microfiche. **Services:** Interlibrary loan; copying; collection open to the public for reference use only. **Computerized Information Services:** OCLC. **Networks/Consortia:** Member of Western Library Network (WLN). **Staff:** Robert Bjoring, Asst.Libn..

★17070★
UNIVERSITY OF WASHINGTON - MARIAN GOULD GALLAGHER LAW LIBRARY (Law)
School of Law
1100 N.E. Campus Pkwy., JB-20 Phone: (206)543-4089
Seattle, WA 98105 Penny A. Hazelton, Law Libn.
Founded: 1899. **Staff:** Prof 10; Other 21. **Subjects:** Law. **Special Collections:** Japanese legal material; Washington State Bench and Bar biographies (15 file drawers of pictures and biographical sketches). **Holdings:** 423,842 volumes; 135 bound volumes of clippings. **Subscriptions:** 7104 journals and other serials. **Services:** Interlibrary loan; copying; library open to the public for reference use only. **Automated Operations:** Computerized cataloging. **Computerized Information Services:** LEXIS, DIALOG Information Services, OCLC, ELSS (Electronic Legislative Search System), WESTLAW, NEXIS. **Networks/Consortia:** Member of Western Library Network (WLN), Northwest Consortium of Law Libraries. **Publications:** Current Index to Legal Periodicals, weekly; List of Books Cataloged, monthly - both on exchange. **Staff:** Melissa Landers, Asst.Libn.; Reba Turnquist, Asst.Libn.; Marjan Wazeka, Circ.Libn.; David Rudman, Ref.Libn.; Grace Malson, Docs.Libn..

★17071★
UNIVERSITY OF WASHINGTON - MATHEMATICS RESEARCH LIBRARY (Sci-Engr)
C306 Padelford, GN-50 Phone: (206)543-7296
Seattle, WA 98195 Martha Tucker Murdoch, Hd.
Staff: Prof 1; Other 1. **Subjects:** Pure and theoretical mathematics and statistics. **Holdings:** 30,382 volumes. **Subscriptions:** 530 journals and other serials. **Services:** Interlibrary loan; copying; library open to the public for reference use only. **Computerized Information Services:** DIALOG Information Services, Pergamon ORBIT InfoLine, Inc., BRS Information Technologies, STN International, OCLC. **Networks/Consortia:** Member of Western Library Network (WLN).

★17072★
UNIVERSITY OF WASHINGTON - MUSIC LIBRARY (Mus)
113 Music Bldg., DN-10 Phone: (206)543-1168
Seattle, WA 98195 David A. Wood, Hd.Libn.
Founded: 1950. **Staff:** Prof 3; Other 2. **Subjects:** Music. **Special Collections:** American music center (Kinscella Collection); opera scores, 17th-19th century; Eric Offenbacher Mozart Collection (recordings); Melvin Harris Collection of Wind Recordings. **Holdings:** 53,035 volumes; 34,006 scores; 1505 reels of microfilm; 38,139 sound recordings; 27 video discs. **Subscriptions:** 499 journals and other serials. **Services:** Interlibrary loan; copying; library open to the public for reference use only. **Computerized Information Services:** OCLC. **Networks/Consortia:** Member of Western Library Network (WLN). **Staff:** John R. Gibbs, Asst.Libn.; Deborah L. Pierce, Mus.Cat./Ref.Libn..

★17073★
UNIVERSITY OF WASHINGTON - NATURAL SCIENCES LIBRARY (Biol Sci, Sci-Engr)
Suzzallo Library, FM-25 Phone: (206)543-1243
Seattle, WA 98195 Nancy G. Blase, Hd.
Founded: 1935. **Staff:** Prof 3; Other 3. **Subjects:** Zoology, geology, geophysics, botany, atmospheric sciences, general science, history of science, biology. **Holdings:** 202,082 volumes. **Subscriptions:** 2429 journals and other serials. **Services:** Interlibrary loan; copying; library open to the public for reference use only. **Computerized Information Services:** DIALOG Information Services, Pergamon ORBIT InfoLine, Inc., BRS Information Technologies, STN International, OCLC. **Networks/Consortia:** Member of Western Library Network (WLN). **Staff:** Jackie Pritchard, Asst.Libn.; Kathy Carr, Ref.Libn..

★17074★
UNIVERSITY OF WASHINGTON - PHILOSOPHY LIBRARY (Rel-Phil)
331 Savery, DK-50 Phone: (206)543-5856
Seattle, WA 98195 Linda P. Di Biase, Libn.
Founded: 1948. **Staff:** Prof 1; Other 1. **Subjects:** Philosophy, aesthetics, political and legal philosophy. **Holdings:** 19,239 volumes. **Subscriptions:** 230 journals and other serials. **Services:** Interlibrary loan; copying; library open to the public for reference use only. **Computerized Information Services:** OCLC. **Networks/Consortia:** Member of Western Library Network (WLN).

★17075★
UNIVERSITY OF WASHINGTON - PHYSICS-ASTRONOMY LIBRARY (Sci-Engr)
219 Physics Bldg., FM-15 Phone: (206)543-2988
Seattle, WA 98195 Martha Austin, Hd.
Founded: 1935. **Staff:** Prof 1; Other 1. **Subjects:** Physics, astronomy, astrophysics. **Holdings:** 24,377 volumes; sky atlases. **Subscriptions:** 332 journals and other serials. **Services:** Interlibrary loan; copying; library open to the public for reference use only. **Computerized Information Services:** DIALOG Information Services, Pergamon ORBIT InfoLine, Inc., BRS Information Technologies, STN International, OCLC. **Networks/Consortia:** Member of Western Library Network (WLN).

★17076★
UNIVERSITY OF WASHINGTON - POLITICAL SCIENCE LIBRARY (Soc Sci)
220 Smith Hall, DP-25 Phone: (206)543-2389
Seattle, WA 98195 Al Fritz, Libn.
Founded: 1945. **Staff:** Prof 1; Other 3. **Subjects:** Political science, public administration. **Holdings:** 57,638 volumes. **Subscriptions:** 575 journals and other serials; 5 newspapers. **Services:** Interlibrary loan; copying; library open to the public for reference use only. **Computerized Information Services:** DIALOG Information Services, Pergamon ORBIT InfoLine, Inc., BRS Information Technologies, OCLC. **Networks/Consortia:** Member of Western Library Network (WLN).

★17077★
UNIVERSITY OF WASHINGTON - REGIONAL PRIMATE RESEARCH CENTER - PRIMATE INFORMATION CENTER (Biol Sci, Med)
SJ-50 Phone: (206)543-4376
Seattle, WA 98195 Jackie Lee Pritchard, Mgr.
Founded: 1963. **Subjects:** Nonhuman primates, biomedical research, behavioral sciences. **Services:** SDI. **Publications:** Current Primate References (listing of citations), monthly - by subscription; retrospective bibliographies from extensively indexed reference files - for sale; recurrent bibliographies, monthly - by subscription; list of other publications - available on request. **Remarks:** The Primate Information Center is an indexing service providing literature-based information to scientists throughout the world. Its staff offers special assistance to those with information needs not met by its services.

★17078★
UNIVERSITY OF WASHINGTON - SOCIAL WORK LIBRARY (Soc Sci)
Social Work/Speech-Hearing Bldg., JH-30 Phone: (206)545-2180
Seattle, WA 98195 Guela G. Johnson, Libn.
Founded: 1954. **Staff:** Prof 1; Other 2. **Subjects:** Social work; health care; social welfare, policy, and services; human growth and behavior; agency administration and supervision; community organizations; social research. **Holdings:** 25,906 volumes; 5108 pamphlets. **Subscriptions:** 217 journals and other serials. **Services:** Interlibrary loan; copying; reading room with adaptive equipment for disabled persons; library open to the public for reference use only. **Computerized Information Services:** DIALOG Information Services, Pergamon ORBIT InfoLine, Inc., BRS Information Technologies, OCLC. **Networks/Consortia:** Member of Western Library Network (WLN).

★17079★
UNIVERSITY OF WASHINGTON - TRI-CITIES UNIVERSITY CENTER - LIBRARY (Bus-Fin, Sci-Engr, Educ)
100 Sprout Rd. Phone: (509)943-3176
Richland, WA 99352 Beverly Jane Cooper, Lib.Dir.

★17080★
UNIVERSITY OF WASHINGTON - TRI-CITIES UNIVERSITY CENTER - LIBRARY (Bus-Fin, Sci-Engr, Educ)
100 Sprout Rd. Phone: (509)943-3176
Richland, WA 99352 Beverly Jane Cooper, Lib.Dir.
Staff: Prof 1; Other 1. **Subjects:** Business, science, technology, education. **Holdings:** 20,000 volumes. **Subscriptions:** 300 journals and other serials. **Services:** Interlibrary loan; copying; library open to the public. **Computerized Information Services:** DIALOG Information Services; OnTyme Electronic Message Network Service (electronic mail service). Performs searches on fee basis. **Networks/Consortia:** Member of Western Library Network (WLN).

UNIVERSITY OF WATERLOO - CANADIAN INDUSTRIAL INNOVATION CENTRE/WATERLOO
See: Canadian Industrial Innovation Centre/Waterloo (2567)

★17081★
UNIVERSITY OF WATERLOO - DANA PORTER LIBRARY (Hum, Soc Sci)
Waterloo, ON, Canada N2L 3G1 Phone: (519)885-1211
Murray C. Shepherd, Univ.Libn.
Staff: Prof 31; Other 111. **Subjects:** Humanities, social and behavioral sciences, leisure studies, environmental studies, architecture. **Special Collections:** Works of Eric Gill; Euclid's Elements and History of Mathematics; private presses (Dolmen, Nonesuch, Golden Cockerel); Santayana Collection; D.R. Davis "Southey" Collection; rare materials from Lady Aberdeen Library of the History of Women; Crapo Dance Collection. **Holdings:** 884,000 volumes; 569,000 government publications; 500,000 microforms. **Subscriptions:** 3450 journals and other serials. **Services:** Interlibrary loan; copying; facilities for the print-handicapped; library open to the public. **Automated Operations:** Computerized cataloging, acquisitions, serials, and circulation. **Computerized Information Services:** DIALOG Information Services, BRS Information Technologies, CAN/OLE, MEDLINE, Pergamon ORBIT InfoLine, Inc., International Research Development Centre, QL Systems; ALANET, Envoy 100, CoSy, NETNORTH (electronic mail services). Performs searches on fee basis. Contact Person: Faye Abrams, Coord./Indus. & Bus.Info.Serv., 888-4517. **Networks/Consortia:** Member of Ontario Council of University Libraries (OCUL), Canadian Association of Research Libraries (CARL). **Publications:** Focus, Aids, Research Guide, irregular - for internal distribution only; Bibliographies and Occasional Papers, irregular - external distribution; Library Handbook, annual - for internal distribution only. **Staff:** Bruce MacNeil, Assoc.Libn./Pub.Serv.; C. David Emery, Assoc.Libn./Coll.; Lorraine Beattie, Coord./Adm.Serv.; Carolynne Presser, Assoc.Libn./Plan. & Sys.; Lois Claxton, Coord./Info.Serv..

★17082★
UNIVERSITY OF WATERLOO - DAVIS CENTRE LIBRARY (Sci-Engr)
Waterloo, ON, Canada N2L 3G1 Phone: (519)885-1211
Murray C. Shepherd, Univ.Libn.
Staff: Prof 11; Other 23. **Subjects:** Engineering, mathematics, sciences, health studies, kinesiology, optometry. **Holdings:** 317,500 volumes; 34,000 microforms; 95,400 government publications. **Subscriptions:** 2530 journals and other serials. **Services:** Interlibrary loan; copying; library open to the public. **Automated Operations:** Computerized cataloging, acquisitions, serials, and circulation. **Computerized Information Services:** DIALOG Information Services, BRS Information Technologies, CAN/OLE, MEDLINE, Pergamon ORBIT InfoLine, Inc., International Development Research Centre (IDRC), QL Systems; internal database; Envoy 100, CoSy, ALANET, NETNORTH (electronic mail services). Performs searches on fee basis. Contact Person: Faye Abrams, Coord./Indus. & Bus.Info.Serv., 888-4517. **Networks/Consortia:** Member of Ontario Council of University Libraries (OCUL), Canadian Association of Research Libraries (CARL). **Publications:** Focus, Aids, Research Guide & Checklist Series, irregular - for internal distribution only. **Special Indexes:** KWOC Index to IEEE and ACM Conference proceedings (card). **Formerly:** Engineering, Mathematics & Science Divisional Library. **Staff:** Lois Claxton, Coord./Info.Serv.; D. Morton, Coord., Online Ref..

★17083★
UNIVERSITY OF WATERLOO - SIRLS - SPORT & LEISURE DATABASE/COLLECTION (Soc Sci, Rec)
Waterloo, ON, Canada N2L 3G1 Phone: (519)885-1211
Betty Millman, Database Mgr./Cons.
Founded: 1971. **Staff:** Prof 1; Other 2. **Subjects:** Sociology and social psychology of leisure, sport, and recreation. **Holdings:** 15,000 documents, articles, conference papers, theses, dissertations, unpublished papers, and reports in hardcopy and microfiche. **Services:** Online access by external users; user-request searches; document duplication. **Publications:** SIRLS Sport & Leisure Database/Collection Brochure - free upon request; Sociology of Leisure and Sport Abstracts (journal). **Remarks:** Maintained by the University's Faculty of Human Kinetics and Leisure Studies, SIRLS provides online access to 17,000 abstracted citations in its Sport & Leisure database.

★17084★
UNIVERSITY OF WATERLOO - UNIVERSITY MAP AND DESIGN LIBRARY (Geog-Map, Art)
Environmental Studies Bldg., Rm. 246 Phone: (519)885-1211
Waterloo, ON, Canada N2L 3G1 Murray C. Shepherd, Univ.Libn.
Founded: 1965. **Staff:** Prof 2; Other 3. **Subjects:** Cartography, architectural design. **Special Collections:** Environmental Studies Honours Essays. **Holdings:** 12,500 books, atlases, and bound periodical volumes; 77,800 maps; 30,300 aerial photographs. **Subscriptions:** 95 journals and other serials. **Services:** Interlibrary loan; copying; library open to the public. **Automated Operations:** Computerized cataloging, acquisitions, serials, and circulation. **Computerized Information Services:** DIALOG Information Services, BRS Information Technologies, CAN/OLE, MEDLINE, Pergamon ORBIT InfoLine, Inc., QL Systems; ALANET, Envoy 100, CoSy, NETNORTH (electronic mail services). Performs searches on fee basis. Contact Person: Faye Abrams, Coord./Indus. & Bus.Info.Serv., 885-4517. **Publications:** Checklist. **Special Indexes:** Map index (microfiche). **Staff:** Richard H. Pinnell, Libn..

★17085★
UNIVERSITY OF WEST FLORIDA - HUMAN RESOURCE VIDEOTAPE LIBRARY (Aud-Vis)
Dept. of Social Work
College of Arts & Sciences
11000 University Pkwy. Phone: (904)474-2381
Pensacola, FL 32514-5751 Prof. Bonnie Bedics
Founded: 1978. **Staff:** Prof 1; Other 20. **Subjects:** Addiction, child abuse, mental illness and therapy. **Holdings:** 500 videotapes. **Services:** Copying; library open to the public. **Publications:** VRL Connection newsletter, semiannual. **Special Catalogs:** Video Resource Library Catalog, annual. **Formerly:** University of Wisconsin, Madison - School of Social Work - Videotape Resource Library.

★17086★
UNIVERSITY OF WEST FLORIDA - JOHN C. PACE LIBRARY - CURRICULUM MATERIALS LIBRARY (Educ)
Pensacola, FL 32514 Phone: (904)474-2439
Ron Toifel, Coord., Educ.Serv.
Staff: Prof 1; Other 1. **Subjects:** Elementary, secondary, and special education textbooks; teaching aids; nonprint media for all subjects, K-12. **Holdings:** 12,000 books; 500 filmstrips; 2600 slides; 370 transparencies; 1200 kits and games; 1300 cassette tapes and phonograph records; 200 publishers' catalogs; 7 VF drawers of pamphlets and ephemera; 2700 curriculum guides; 2100 curricula on microfiche; 85 education reference books; 7 global maps; 1600 prints, photographs, posters, charts. **Services:** Library open to the public with restrictions. **Automated Operations:** Computerized public access catalog and cataloging. **Computerized Information Services:** DIALOG Information Services.

★17087★
UNIVERSITY OF WEST FLORIDA - JOHN C. PACE LIBRARY - SPECIAL COLLECTIONS (Hist)
Pensacola, FL 32504-0101 Phone: (904)474-2213
Dean DeBolt, Spec.Coll.Libn.
Staff: Prof 1; Other 2. **Subjects:** West Florida, 1559 to present, including Florida under Spanish, British, American, and Confederate governments; Pensacola, 1559 to present; Florida Panhandle, southern Alabama and Mississippi; university archives. **Special Collections:** George Washington Sully watercolors, 1833-1839; Governor Sidney Catts papers (5000 items); Eudora Welty Collection; Langston Hughes Collection; James Dickey Collection. **Holdings:** 5000 rare books and monographs; 500,000 manuscript and archival documents, including personal and family papers, church and business records, and records of organizations; 3000 maps; 10,000 photographs; 300 newspapers. **Services:** Copying; collections open to the public. **Publications:** Bibliography of West Florida, 1535-1986 (4 volumes). **Special Catalogs:** Separate collection inventories; Guide to the Manuscripts, 1979.

★17088★
UNIVERSITY OF WEST LOS ANGELES - KELTON LAW LIBRARY (Law)
12201 Washington Place Phone: (213)313-1011
Los Angeles, CA 90066 Arlen Bristol, Univ.Libn.
Founded: 1967. **Staff:** Prof 1; Other 12. **Subjects:** Law. **Holdings:** 28,000 books; 3000 bound periodical volumes; 6000 microfiche. **Subscriptions:** 300 journals and other serials. **Services:** Copying; library open to the public. **Computerized Information Services:** WESTLAW.

★17089★
UNIVERSITY OF WESTERN ONTARIO - CENTRE FOR AMERICAN STUDIES - LIBRARY (Soc Sci)
Social Science Centre Phone: (519)661-2122
London, ON, Canada N6A 5C2 D.H. Flaherty, Dir.
Subjects: Canadian perspective on American history, literature, society, and politics. **Holdings:** Figures not available for books, pamphlets, and files.

★17090★
UNIVERSITY OF WESTERN ONTARIO - D.B. WELDON LIBRARY - DEPARTMENT OF SPECIAL COLLECTIONS (Hist, Hum)
London, ON, Canada N6A 3K7 Phone: (519)679-2111
John Lutman, Libn.
Staff: Prof 1. **Subjects:** Canadiana - literature from pre-1867 to present, history, voyages and travel, black studies; Edwardian writers, 1889-1918; British history, 16th and 17th centuries; history of science and medicine; Napoleonic era and the French Revolution. **Special Collections:** G. William Stuart Collection of Milton and Miltonia (850 volumes); 19th century plays of manners and morals (578 volumes); John Galt Collection (150 volumes); Richard Maurice Bucke Collection (515 volumes; 12 linear feet of scrapbooks and pamphlets; 300 items in picture files; diaries; letters; documents); Beatrice Hitchins Memorial Collection of Aviation History (1500 volumes; 91 picture files; 350 vertical files; 50 manuscripts; 15,000 card files). **Holdings:** 27,492 volumes; 400 British and American pamphlets of Edwardian era; 250 contemporary Canadian pamphlets. **Services:** Interlibrary loan; copying (both limited); department open to the public. **Automated Operations:** Computerized cataloging and acquisitions. **Special Catalogs:** G.W. Stuart Collection of Milton and Miltonia; Canadian Chronological Imprints; Private Press Holdings; British/American Pamphlets; Canadian Pamphlets; Juvenilia.

★17091★
UNIVERSITY OF WESTERN ONTARIO - D.B. WELDON LIBRARY - REGIONAL COLLECTION (Hist)
London, ON, Canada N6A 3K7 Phone: (519)679-2111
Edward Phelps, Libn.
Founded: 1942. **Staff:** Prof 1; Other 2. **Subjects:** Canadiana, Ontario regional and local history, historical geography, archives. **Special Collections:** County records (local public archives; business archives; private papers); Ontario textbook collection (3000); A. Scott Garrett Collection (historical material including scrapbooks, pamphlets, and negatives). **Holdings:** 39,049 books, bound periodical volumes, U.W.O. dissertations, boxes and volumes of manuscripts and archives, maps, and pictures. **Subscriptions:** 10 journals and other serials. **Services:** Interlibrary loan; copying; collection open to the public with restrictions. **Automated Operations:** Computerized cataloging. **Publications:** Western Ontario Historical Notes, annual - free to libraries. **Remarks:** Genealogical inquiries are forwarded to the London, ON Genealogical Society.

★17092★
UNIVERSITY OF WESTERN ONTARIO - DEPARTMENT OF GEOGRAPHY - MAP LIBRARY (Geog-Map)
London, ON, Canada N6A 5C2 Phone: (519)661-3424
Serge A. Sauer, Map Cur.
Founded: 1966. **Staff:** Prof 2; Other 3. **Subjects:** World, Great Lakes, Canadiana, geography, planning, natural resources. **Holdings:** 210,000 maps; 20,000 aerial photographs; 2050 atlases; 1562 theses. **Services:** Interlibrary loan; copying; library open to the public. **Publications:** Theses Bibliography, annual; Newsletter, irregular; facsimile reproductions of historical maps and charts. **Special Catalogs:** Atlas listing (online). **Remarks:** This is regarded as the largest university map collection in Canada. The Great Lakes Cartographic Resource Centre is located in the Map Library.

★17093★
UNIVERSITY OF WESTERN ONTARIO - DR. JOSEPH POZSONYI MEMORIAL LIBRARY (Med)
CPRI
Box 2460, Terminal A Phone: (519)471-2540
London, ON, Canada N6A 4G6 Asta Hansen, Lib.Supv.
Staff: Prof 1; Other 1. **Subjects:** Administration; audiology; behavior modification; biochemistry; clinical chemistry; cytogenetics; electroencephalography; therapy - music, physical, occupational, speech; neurology; nursing; pathology; nutrition; pediatrics; psychiatry; psychology; public health; recreation; social work; sociology; special education. **Holdings:** 2800 books; 3800 bound periodical volumes; 400 staff papers; 6000 reprints; 60 government directories and acts. **Subscriptions:** 125 journals and other serials. **Services:** Interlibrary loan; copying; library open to professionals, university and community college faculty, and students. **Publications:** CPRI Annual Symposium Monographs. **Also Known As:** Children's Psychiatric Research Institute.

★17094★
UNIVERSITY OF WESTERN ONTARIO - ENGINEERING LIBRARY (Sci-Engr)
London, ON, Canada N6A 5B9 Phone: (519)679-2111
Lorraine Busby, Libn.
Founded: 1959. **Staff:** Prof 1; Other 4. **Subjects:** Engineering - chemical, civil, electrical, materials, mechanical. **Holdings:** 19,342 books; 19,445 bound periodical volumes; 4076 government documents; 757 pamphlets; 1454 microforms. **Subscriptions:** 812 journals and other serials. **Services:** Interlibrary loan; copying; SDI; library open to the public. **Automated Operations:** Computerized cataloging, acquisitions, serials, and circulation. **Computerized Information Services:** CAN/OLE, DIALOG Information Services, BRS Information Technologies, WILSONLINE.

★17095★
UNIVERSITY OF WESTERN ONTARIO - FACULTY OF EDUCATION LIBRARY (Educ)
Althouse College
1137 Western Rd. Phone: (519)679-2111
London, ON, Canada N6G 1G7 Anna Holman, Libn.
Founded: 1965. **Staff:** Prof 2; Other 6. **Subjects:** Education. **Holdings:** 87,372 volumes; 392,765 microfiche; 110,897 AV programs; 3861 pamphlets; 458 government documents; 12 VF drawers of clippings; 202 computer programs; 2051 curriculum guidelines. **Subscriptions:** 756 journals and other serials. **Services:** Interlibrary loan; copying; library open to the public excluding school and community college students. **Automated Operations:** Computerized cataloging, acquisitions, serials, and circulation. **Special Catalogs:** Audiovisual catalog (card).

★17096★
UNIVERSITY OF WESTERN ONTARIO - FACULTY OF LAW LIBRARY (Law)
London, ON, Canada N6A 3K7 Phone: (519)679-2111
Dr. Margaret A. Banks, Libn.
Staff: Prof 3; Other 10. **Subjects:** Law. **Holdings:** 131,367 volumes; 675 cassettes; 18,720 microforms; 195 pamphlets. **Subscriptions:** 2903 journals and other serials. **Services:** Interlibrary loan; copying; library open to the public with restrictions. **Automated Operations:** Computerized cataloging, acquisitions, serials, and circulation. **Computerized Information Services:** QL Systems.

★17097★
UNIVERSITY OF WESTERN ONTARIO - MUSIC LIBRARY (Mus)
London, ON, Canada N6A 3K7 Phone: (519)679-2111
William Guthrie, Libn.
Founded: 1963. **Staff:** Prof 4; Other 6. **Subjects:** Music theory, music history, applied music, music education. **Special Collections:** Mahler-Rose Collection (scores by Gustav Mahler, Alfred Rose, and Bruno Walter; 675 letters and documents related to Mahler, including 300 letters written by Mahler); The Opera Collection (200 musical manuscripts; 1900 volumes of contemporary printed scores and librettos of opera titles, 1600-early 20th century). **Holdings:** 77,447 volumes and scores; 344,410 choral, band, and orchestral scores; 25,216 sound recordings; 8640 microforms; 1461 pamphlets. **Subscriptions:** 430 journals and other serials. **Services:** Interlibrary loan; copying; disc and tape recording listening facilities; library open to the public. **Automated Operations:** Computerized cataloging, acquisitions, serials, and circulation. **Computerized Information Services:** DIALOG Information Services.

★17098★
UNIVERSITY OF WESTERN ONTARIO - SCHOOL OF BUSINESS ADMINISTRATION - BUSINESS LIBRARY & INFORMATION CENTRE (Bus-Fin)
London, ON, Canada N6A 3K7 Phone: (519)679-2111
Jerry Mulcahy, Libn.
Founded: 1960. **Staff:** Prof 1; Other 4. **Subjects:** International business, finance, marketing, operations research, labor relations, accounting. **Special Collections:** Microfiche collection of Canadian and U.S. company data (120,000 items). **Holdings:** 38,048 books; 11,368 bound periodical volumes; 7911 government documents (coded); 206,963 microforms; 468 pamphlets; 117 cassettes; 19,553 items on companies, industries, and business conditions in Canada. **Subscriptions:** 1929 journals and other serials. **Services:** Interlibrary loan; copying; reference service to academic and business community; library open to the public with borrowing restrictions. **Automated Operations:** Computerized cataloging, acquisitions, serials, and circulation. **Computerized Information Services:** QL Systems, BRS Information Technologies, DIALOG Information Services, Info Globe.

★17099★
UNIVERSITY OF WESTERN ONTARIO - SCHOOL OF LIBRARY & INFORMATION SCIENCE - LIBRARY (Info Sci, Comp Sci)
London, ON, Canada N6G 1H1 Phone: (519)661-3542
Daniel Dorner, Academic Sup.Serv.Coord.
Founded: 1967. **Staff:** Prof 5; Other 6. **Subjects:** Library and information science, computers and electronic data processing, children's literature, communications. **Special Collections:** Pre-1800 handprinted books (10,000 volumes); dictionaries (500); private press books (600). **Holdings:** 60,000 books; 24,000 bound periodical volumes; 10,000 microforms; 300 tapes. **Subscriptions:** 402 journals. **Services:** Interlibrary loan; copying; library open to the public. **Automated Operations:** Computerized public access catalog, cataloging, acquisitions, and circulation. **Computerized Information Services:** DIALOG Information Services; Envoy 100 (electronic mail service). **Special Catalogs:** Serials list; special collections catalog. **Special Indexes:** KWOC index to technical reports and ERIC documents on microfiche. **Staff:** Hanna Marti, Cat.Sys.Libn.; John Fracasso, Automated Sys. & Serv.; Martie Grof-Ianelli, Asst.Libn.; Charles McClellan, Prog..

★17100★
UNIVERSITY OF WESTERN ONTARIO - SCIENCES LIBRARY (Biol Sci, Sci-Engr, Med)
Natural Sciences Centre Phone: (519)679-2111
London, ON, Canada N6A 5B7 Larry C. Lewis, Sci.Libn.
Founded: 1881. **Staff:** Prof 6; Other 31. **Subjects:** Anesthesia, anatomy, applied mathematics, astronomy, biochemistry, biology, biophysics, chemistry, clinical neurological sciences, communicative disorders, computer science, dentistry, epidemiology, family medicine, genetics, geology, geophysics, history of medicine and science, mathematics, medicine, microbiology, nursing, obstetrics and gynecology, occupational therapy, ophthalmology, otolaryngology, pediatrics, pathology, pharmacology, physical medicine, physical therapy, physics, physiology, plant sciences, psychiatry, radiation oncology, radiology, statistics, surgery, zoology. **Holdings:** 167,673 books; 238,693 bound periodical volumes; 37,523 microforms; 9023 AV programs; 1040 pamphlets. **Subscriptions:** 4505 journals and other serials. **Services:** Interlibrary loan; copying; library open to the public with restrictions. **Automated Operations:** Computerized cataloging, acquisitions, serials, and circulation. **Computerized Information Services:** BRS Information Technologies, CAN/OLE, DIALOG Information Services, NLM, WILSONLINE, Institute for Scientific Information (ISI); internal database.

★17101★
UNIVERSITY OF WESTERN ONTARIO - SCIENCES LIBRARY - NORTHERN OUTREACH LIBRARY SERVICE (Med)
London, ON, Canada N6A 5B7 Phone: (519)661-3169
Sylvia Katzer, Libn.
Founded: 1983. **Staff:** Prof 1; Other 1. **Subjects:** Medicine, allied health sciences, biological sciences, chemistry. **Holdings:** Figures not available. **Services:** Interlibrary loan; copying; SDI; library open to health care professionals in Northern Ontario only. **Computerized Information Services:** BRS Information Technologies, MEDLARS. Performs searches on fee basis.

UNIVERSITY OF WESTERN ONTARIO - WESTMINSTER INSTITUTE FOR ETHICS AND HUMAN VALUES
See: Westminster Institute for Ethics and Human Values (17785)

★17102★
UNIVERSITY OF WINDSOR - FACULTY OF EDUCATION LIBRARY (Educ)
600 Third Concession Rd. Phone: (519)969-0520
Windsor, ON, Canada N9E 1A5 Thomas J. Robinson, Educ.Libn.
Founded: 1962. **Staff:** Prof 1; Other 3. **Subjects:** Education. **Special Collections:** School texts; Montessori Memorial Collection. **Holdings:** 58,530 books; 2588 bound periodical volumes; 1173 filmstrips; 15,200 mounted pictures; 2433 unmounted pictures and charts; 420 cassettes; 643 kits; 272 phonograph records; 12 drawers of pamphlets; 4284 public documents; ERIC microfiche, 1966 to present; ONTERIS microfiche, 1972 to present. **Subscriptions:** 199 journals and other serials. **Services:** Interlibrary loan; copying; library open to the public with restrictions. **Automated Operations:** Computerized cataloging and serials. **Computerized Information Services:** Online systems (through Leddy Library).

★17103★
UNIVERSITY OF WINDSOR - PAUL MARTIN LAW LIBRARY (Law)
Windsor, ON, Canada N9B 3P4 Phone: (519)253-4232
Paul T. Murphy, Law Libn.
Staff: Prof 3; Other 9. **Subjects:** Law. **Holdings:** 68,000 books; 126,750 bound periodical volumes. **Subscriptions:** 2700 journals and other serials. **Services:** Interlibrary loan; copying; library open to the public with restrictions. **Computerized Information Services:** QL Systems, DIALOG Information Services, CAN/OLE, UTLAS, WESTLAW; Envoy 100 (electronic mail service). **Staff:** Daniel K.L. Boen, Cat.Libn.; Huey-Min Soong, Ref.Libn..

★17104★
UNIVERSITY OF WINNIPEG - LIBRARY - SPECIAL COLLECTIONS (Area-Ethnic, Rel-Phil)
515 Portage Ave. Phone: (204)786-9801
Winnipeg, MB, Canada R3B 2E9 Dr. W.R. Converse, Chf.Libn.
Special Collections: Ashdown Collection of Canadian Studies; Newcombe Collection of Theology; Mary Iris Atchison Collection; Conference of Manitoba and Northwestern Ontario Archives; United Church of Canada; University of Winnipeg Archives; George H. Reavis Reading Collection. **Holdings:** Figures not available. **Services:** Interlibrary loan; copying; SDI; collections open to the public for reference use only. **Automated Operations:** Computerized cataloging, acquisitions, serials, and circulation. **Computerized Information Services:** DIALOG Information Services, Info Globe, QL Systems, UTLAS, Canada Institute for Scientific and Technical Information (CISTI); Envoy 100 (electronic mail service). Performs searches on fee basis. Contact Person: William Pond, Hd., Pub.Serv., 786-9812. **Staff:** Coreen Koz, Asst.Chf.Libn.; Sandra Zuk, Spec.Proj.Libn.; Linwood DeLong, Ref.Libn. (Coll.Dev.); Joan Scanlon, Hd., Tech.Serv.; Linda Dixon, Ref.Libn. (Govt.Docs.); Kam Lee, Cat.Libn..

★17105★
UNIVERSITY OF WISCONSIN, EAU CLAIRE - SIMPSON GEOGRAPHIC RESEARCH CENTER - MAP LIBRARY (Geog-Map)
Department of Geography Phone: (715)836-3244
Eau Claire, WI 54701 Adam Cahow, Dir.
Staff: Prof 1; Other 5. **Subjects:** Complete topographic coverage of North America. **Holdings:** 250,000 maps; Eau Claire weather data for last 30 years; 200 atlases; 1500 aerial photographs. **Services:** Interlibrary loan; copying; library open to the public. **Publications:** New Listings - to interested faculty.

★17106★
UNIVERSITY OF WISCONSIN, EAU CLAIRE - SPECIAL COLLECTIONS - AREA RESEARCH CENTER, UNIVERSITY ARCHIVES, RARE BOOKS (Hist)
McIntyre Library Phone: (715)836-2739
Eau Claire, WI 54701 Richard L. Pifer, Archv.
Staff: Prof 1; Other 2. **Subjects:** History of western Wisconsin, lumbering history, genealogy, university history. **Special Collections:** Historical atlases and plat books of Wisconsin (44 reels of microfilm). **Holdings:** 1000 linear feet and 40 reels of microfilm of historical manuscripts; 330 maps and atlases; 620 linear feet and 350 reels of microfilm of university records; 19,000 photographs/negatives. **Services:** Interlibrary loan; copying; center open to the public for reference use only. **Networks/Consortia:** Member of Wisconsin Area Research Center Network.

★17107★
UNIVERSITY OF WISCONSIN, GREEN BAY - AREA RESEARCH CENTER (Hist, Soc Sci)
2420 Nicolet Dr. Phone: (414)465-2539
Green Bay, WI 54301-7001 Thomas F. Reitz, Dir., Spec.Coll.
Staff: Prof 1; Other 1. **Subjects:** Local history, genealogy, radical literature. **Special Collections:** Belgian American research material; Leon Kramer Collection of Communist, Socialist and Anarchist Literature (10,000 pamphlets). **Holdings:** 7600 books; 4000 linear feet of local governmental records and private papers. **Services:** Interlibrary loan; copying; center open to the public. **Networks/Consortia:** Member of Wisconsin Area Research Center Network. **Special Indexes:** Belgian American Research Materials; Guide to Archives and Manuscripts in the University of Wisconsin, Green Bay Area Research Center.

★17108★
UNIVERSITY OF WISCONSIN, GREEN BAY - WOMEN'S EDUCATIONAL PROGRAMS - WOMEN'S STUDIES RESOURCE LIBRARY (Soc Sci)
IS 1008 Phone: (414)465-2582
Green Bay, WI 54302 Patricia Maguire, Spec.
Staff: Prof 1; Other 2. **Subjects:** Women's history, women's movement, biography, resources available to women. **Holdings:** 200 books; 50 bound periodical volumes; information files. **Subscriptions:** 15 journals and other serials. **Services:** Library open to the public.

★17109★
UNIVERSITY OF WISCONSIN, LA CROSSE - ALICE HAGAR CURRICULUM RESOURCE CENTER (Educ)
213 Morris Hall Phone: (608)785-8651
La Crosse, WI 54601 Dr. E.J. Zeimet, Dir.
Founded: 1972. **Staff:** Prof 2; Other 8. **Subjects:** Curriculum materials for English, mathematics, science, social studies, music; literature for children and young adults. **Special Collections:** Standardized test files; district curriculum guides. **Holdings:** 15,000 books; nonprint items; 10 curriculum files; 5 standard test files; 24 vertical files. **Subscriptions:** 50 journals and other serials. **Services:** Interlibrary loan; copying; center open to the public with valid identification. **Formerly:** Curriculum and Instruction Center. **Staff:** Mary Esten, Libn..

★17110★
UNIVERSITY OF WISCONSIN, LA CROSSE - AUDIOVISUAL CENTER - FILM LIBRARY (Aud-Vis)
Phone: (800)362-8323
1705 State St.
La Crosse, WI 54601 Gary Goorough, Coord., Film Lib.
Founded: 1961. **Staff:** Prof 5; Other 23. **Holdings:** 6761 film titles. **Services:** Library open to the public on a rental basis. **Automated Operations:** Computerized cataloging, acquisitions, and circulation. **Networks/Consortia:** Member of Consortium of University Film Centers (CUFC). **Special Catalogs:** 1985 Film Rental catalog. **Remarks:** A toll-free telephone number outside Wisconsin is (800)831-9504.

★17111★
UNIVERSITY OF WISCONSIN, LA CROSSE - CENTER FOR CONTEMPORARY POETRY (Hum)
Murphy Library
1631 Pine St. Phone: (608)785-8511
La Crosse, WI 54601 Edwin L. Hill, Spec.Coll.Libn.
Founded: 1970. **Staff:** Prof 1; Other 1. **Subjects:** Contemporary poetry, with emphasis on Midwestern poetry. **Special Collections:** August Derleth (107 volumes); private presses: Prairie, Trovillion, Sumac, Perishable Press, Bieler Press, Penumbra Press, Sea Pen Press, Meadow Press, Coffee House Press, Toothpaste Press, Crepuscular Press, Arkham House (120 volumes); Skeeters Collection of Gothic, Fantasy, and Science Fiction (1046 volumes). **Holdings:** 4500 books. **Subscriptions:** 65 journals and other serials. **Services:** Copying (limited); center open to the public; persons seeking particular information should call in advance. **Special Indexes:** Index to manuscripts (card).

★17112★
UNIVERSITY OF WISCONSIN, LA CROSSE - MURPHY LIBRARY (Hum, Hist)
1631 Pine St. Phone: (608)785-8505
La Crosse, WI 54601 Dale Montgomery, Dir., Instr.Serv.
Founded: 1909. **Staff:** Prof 11; Other 15. **Subjects:** Humanities, business administration, education, physical education, science, medical technology. **Special Collections:** Local and regional history (4159 volumes; 895 tapes; 67,000 photographs; maps); rare books (10,000); oral history collection (2500 hours of interviews). **Holdings:** 357,267 books; 52,949 bound periodical volumes; 161,778 government documents; 32,509 reels of microfilm; 689,324 microforms. **Subscriptions:** 1959 journals and other serials; 43 newspapers. **Services:** Interlibrary loan; copying; library open to students, faculty, and local community for reference use only. **Automated Operations:** Computerized cataloging, acquisitions, and serials. **Computerized Information Services:** OCLC, DIALOG Information Services, BRS Information Technologies, Knowledge Index. Performs searches on fee basis. Contact Person: Anita Evans, Online Search Serv., 785-8395. **Networks/Consortia:** Member of Wisconsin Interlibrary Services (WILS), West Central Wisconsin Library Consortium. **Remarks:** Local cooperative lending with Viterbo College and Western Wisconsin Technical Institute. **Staff:** S. Sechrest, Doc.; Cristine Berg, Circ.; C. Marx, Cat.; O. Thompson, Microforms; Dale Gresseth, Ser.; Karin Sandvik, Acq.; Ruth Roby, Coord., Tech.Serv./Automation.

★17113★
UNIVERSITY OF WISCONSIN, LA CROSSE - STEAMBOAT COLLECTION (Hist)
Murphy Library
1631 Pine St. Phone: (608)785-8511
La Crosse, WI 54601 Edwin L. Hill, Spec.Coll.Libn.
Founded: 1973. **Staff:** Prof 1; Other 1. **Subjects:** Inland river steamboats, Mississippi River, river towns. **Holdings:** 350 books; 150 bound periodical volumes; 35,000 photographs. **Services:** Copying; collection open to the public. **Special Indexes:** Index to inland river steamboat names. **Remarks:** Copy prints of photographs are available for educational and research purposes, and for commercial use with some restrictions. Inquiries before visiting or ordering are recommended.

★17114★
UNIVERSITY OF WISCONSIN, MADISON - AFRICAN STUDIES INSTRUCTIONAL MATERIALS CENTER (Area-Ethnic)
1334 Van Hise Hall Phone: (608)262-9689
Madison, WI 53706 Patricia S. Kuntz, Outreach Coord.
Founded: 1971. **Staff:** Prof 1; Other 3. **Subjects:** Social studies, music, literature, French, art, anthropology, science, economics, African languages, mathematics, education, history, geography, global issues. **Special Collections:** Life in African countries slide collection (7000). **Holdings:** 2700 books; 200 maps; cassettes; discs; filmstrips; transparencies; 73 vertical files. **Subscriptions:** 10 journals and other serials. **Services:** Center open to the public. **Networks/Consortia:** Member of Multitype Advisory Library Committee (MALC). **Special Catalogs:** Catalog of 35mm slide collection, 1985. **Remarks:** Maintained by University of Wisconsin, Madison - African Studies Program. An alternate telephone number is 262-2380.

★17115★
UNIVERSITY OF WISCONSIN, MADISON - ARCHIVES (Hist)
B134 Memorial Library
728 State St. Phone: (608)262-3290
Madison, WI 53706 J. Frank Cook, Dir.
Staff: Prof 6. **Subjects:** University archives. **Holdings:** 1000 books; 200 bound periodical volumes; 20,000 cubic feet of archival materials, photographs, microfilm. **Services:** Interlibrary loan; copying; archives open to the public with restrictions. **Staff:** Bernard Schermetzler, Archv./Iconographer; Nancy Kunde, Archv./Rec.Mgr.; James Liebig, Archv./Assoc.Dir.; Steve Masar, Archv./Proc.; Laura Smail, Spec./Oral Hist..

★17116★
UNIVERSITY OF WISCONSIN, MADISON - ARTHUR H. ROBINSON MAP LIBRARY (Geog-Map)
310 Science Hall
550 N. Park St. Phone: (608)262-1471
Madison, WI 53706 Mary Galneder, Map Libn.
Staff: Prof 1; Other 3. **Subjects:** Worldwide coverage of topographic, thematic, and general maps; aerial photographs; nautical charts. **Holdings:** 500 books; 228,600 maps; 136,507 aerial photographs; 2470 air photo mosaic indexes. **Services:** Interlibrary loan; library open to the public for reference use only.

★17117★
UNIVERSITY OF WISCONSIN, MADISON - BIOLOGY LIBRARY (Biol Sci)
Birge Hall
430 Lincoln Dr.
Madison, WI 53706 Phone: (608)262-2740
Founded: 1907. **Staff:** Prof 1; Other 1. **Subjects:** Botany, zoology. **Holdings:** 42,000 volumes. **Subscriptions:** 750 journals and other serials. **Services:** Library open to the public for reference use. **Computerized Information Services:** BRS Information Technologies, WILSONLINE. Performs searches on fee basis. **Publications:** Acquisitions list, quarterly; library use aids. **Special Catalogs:** Serials file (card).

★17118★
UNIVERSITY OF WISCONSIN, MADISON - BOTANY DEPARTMENT - HERBARIUM LIBRARY (Biol Sci)
158 Birge Hall
430 Lincoln Dr. Phone: (608)262-2792
Madison, WI 53706 H.H. Iltis, Dir. of Herbarium
Founded: 1849. **Subjects:** Taxonomy of flowering plants, corn, lichens, mosses; Wisconsin, United States, Latin American, and world flora, biogeography, and evolution. **Special Collections:** Specimens of pressed dried plants from all over the world (850,000); C.R. Huskins and D.C. Cooper reprint collections on cytology; man's need for nature; topographic

and vegetation maps (10,000). **Holdings:** 2000 volumes; 490 bound periodical volumes; 50,000 reprints; 67 dissertations; 155 boxes of microcards. **Subscriptions:** 13 journals and other serials. **Services:** Copying; library open to the public with restrictions. **Publications:** Atlas of the Vascular Flora of Wisconsin Plants; 60 papers on selected Wisconsin plant families; books on lichens. **Staff:** Ted Cochrane, Cur. III; Mark Wetter, Coll.Mgr..

★17119★
UNIVERSITY OF WISCONSIN, MADISON - BUREAU OF AUDIOVISUAL INSTRUCTION - LIBRARY (Aud-Vis)
1327 University Ave.
Box 2093 Phone: (608)262-1644
Madison, WI 53701 Bruce E. Dewey, Dir.
Staff: Prof 3; Other 15. **Special Collections:** Cooperative Extension Media Collection (agricultural and home economics extension programs; 1200 titles of videotapes and slide/tape sets). **Holdings:** 12,000 prints of video cassettes and 16mm motion picture films (7000 titles). **Services:** Library open to the public. **Automated Operations:** Computerized cataloging, acquisitions, and circulation. **Networks/Consortia:** Member of Consortium of University Film Centers (CUFC). **Special Catalogs:** Bound book catalog, every 2-3 years; interim catalog, annual; special catalogs and lists, irregular. **Remarks:** Maintained by University of Wisconsin Extension.

★17120★
UNIVERSITY OF WISCONSIN, MADISON - CAST METALS LABORATORY - LIBRARY (Sci-Engr)
1509 University Ave. Phone: (608)262-2562
Madison, WI 53706 Carl R. Loper, Hd., Lab.
Founded: 1946. **Subjects:** Cast metals, sand molding. **Holdings:** 5000 volumes; technical reports. **Services:** Library not open to the public.

★17121★
UNIVERSITY OF WISCONSIN, MADISON - CENTER FOR DEMOGRAPHY - LIBRARY (Soc Sci)
4457 Social Science Bldg.
1180 Observatory Dr. Phone: (608)262-2182
Madison, WI 53706 Ruth Sandor, Dir.
Founded: 1962. **Staff:** Prof 1; Other 1. **Subjects:** Demography. **Holdings:** 10,000 books; 200 bound periodical volumes; 200 U.S. census reports; international population censuses, 1945-1967, on microfilm; reprints; documents. **Subscriptions:** 200 journals and other serials. **Services:** Library open to the public with restrictions. **Computerized Information Services:** Internal database; BITNET (electronic mail service). **Networks/Consortia:** Member of APLIC International Census Network. **Publications:** Acquisition List, monthly - free upon request; List of Periodical Holdings.

★17122★
UNIVERSITY OF WISCONSIN, MADISON - CENTER FOR HEALTH SCIENCES LIBRARIES (Med)
1305 Linden Dr. Phone: (608)262-6594
Madison, WI 53706 Virginia Holtz, Dir.
Staff: Prof 19; Other 19. **Subjects:** Health sciences and health care administration. **Special Collections:** History of medicine (15,000 volumes). **Holdings:** 105,500 books; 110,000 bound periodical volumes; 5000 AV programs; 3660 pamphlets and government documents. **Subscriptions:** 4000 journals and other serials. **Services:** Interlibrary loan; copying; SDI; center open to the public. **Automated Operations:** Computerized cataloging, acquisitions, and serials. **Computerized Information Services:** MEDLINE, BRS Information Technologies, TOXLINE; internal database. Performs searches on fee basis. **Networks/Consortia:** Member of Greater Midwest Regional Medical Library Network, Wisconsin Interlibrary Services (WILS). **Remarks:** The Center for Health Sciences Libraries includes the holdings of the William S. Middleton Health Sciences Library at the above address and the Weston Clinical Science Center Library, 600 Highland Ave., Rm. J5120, Madison, WI 53792. **Staff:** Dorothy Whitcomb, Hist.Coll.Libn.; Patricia Wilcox, Weston Lib.; Dorothy Kanter, Coll.Dev.; Lowell Ransom, Cat.; Barbara Schmiechen, Weston Lib.; Judith Hathway, Cat.; Terrance Jones, Cat.; Susan Kirkbride, Ref.Libn.; Wanda Auerbach, Ref.Libn.; Blanche Singer, Ref.Libn.; Diana Slater, Assoc.Dir.; Phyllis Kauffman, Ref.Libn.; Jacqueline Pratt, Ref.Libn.; Michele Jacques, ILL; Josephine Crawford, Automation Mgr.; James Markiewicz, AV Libn..

★17123★
UNIVERSITY OF WISCONSIN, MADISON - CENTER FOR LIMNOLOGY - READING ROOM (Biol Sci)
680 N. Park Phone: (608)262-3304
Madison, WI 53706 Diane Poplawsky, Libn.
Staff: Prof 1. **Subjects:** Limnology, freshwater ecology, zoology, fishes, oceanography, environmental studies. **Holdings:** 2400 books; 500 bound periodical volumes; 20,000 reprints; 5000 government documents; 100 microfiche; 300 unbound volumes of journals. **Subscriptions:** 45 journals and other serials. **Services:** Library open to the public for reference use only. **Automated Operations:** Computerized cataloging.

UNIVERSITY OF WISCONSIN, MADISON - CEREAL CROPS RESEARCH UNIT
See: U.S.D.A. - Agricultural Research Service - Cereal Crops Research Unit (14964)

★17124★
UNIVERSITY OF WISCONSIN, MADISON - CHEMISTRY LIBRARY (Sci-Engr)
Chemistry Bldg. Phone: (608)262-2942
Madison, WI 53706 Kendall Rouse, Hd.
Founded: 1947. **Staff:** Prof 1; Other 1. **Subjects:** Chemistry - analytical, inorganic, organic, physical, theoretical. **Holdings:** 14,211 books; 22,082 bound periodical volumes. **Subscriptions:** 400 journals and other serials. **Services:** Interlibrary loan; copying; library open to the public. **Computerized Information Services:** CAS ONLINE, Institute for Scientific Information (ISI). **Publications:** New Acquisitions List, monthly.

★17125★
UNIVERSITY OF WISCONSIN, MADISON - CLINICAL RESEARCH LABORATORIES - LIBRARY* (Med)
Clinical Science Center, Rm. B4/249
600 Highland Ave.
Madison, WI 53792 Phone: (608)263-7507
Subjects: Clinical laboratories - instrument design and applications, test development and applications, quality control techniques, computer system design, clinical evaluation of cancer markers. **Holdings:** Figures not available.

★17126★
UNIVERSITY OF WISCONSIN, MADISON - COOPERATIVE CHILDREN'S BOOK CENTER (CCBC) (Educ)
Helen C. White Hall, Rm. 4290
600 N. Park St. Phone: (608)263-3720
Madison, WI 53706 Ginny Moore Kruse, Dir.
Founded: 1963. **Staff:** Prof 2; Other 12. **Subjects:** Children's and young adult literature - current trade titles, selected and recommended titles in print, 19th and early 20th century titles; publishing of children's and young adult books; intellectual freedom and book censorship; book reviewing and evaluation; book illustration; biography. **Special Collections:** Edgar Rice Burroughs Collection (60 titles); Mother Goose Collection (80 titles); Thornton Burgess Collection (150 titles); Alternative Press Children's Books Collection (1000 titles); Newbery and Caldecott Medal books, including first printings and significant editions; historical and contemporary children's books by Wisconsin authors and illustrators; historical and contemporary pop-up books. **Holdings:** 25,000 volumes; 12 VF drawers; manuscripts. **Subscriptions:** 44 journals; 22 newsletters. **Services:** Offers lectures, workshops, conferences, speeches, courses, and special events; open to adult public for reference use only. **Publications:** CCBC Choices, annual; bibliographies - free to Wisconsin residents and for sale to nonresidents; The Book in a Technological Society, 1986; A Directory of Alternative Press Publishers of Children's Books (3rd edition, 1988) - for sale. **Remarks:** Supported by the Wisconsin Department of Public Instruction through the Division for Library Services and by the University of Wisconsin, Madison through the School of Education. An alternate telephone number is 263-3721. **Staff:** Kathleen Horning, Spec.Coll.Coord..

★17127★
UNIVERSITY OF WISCONSIN, MADISON - DATA AND PROGRAM LIBRARY SERVICE (Info Sci)
3308 Social Science Bldg. Phone: (608)262-7962
Madison, WI 53706 Laura A. Guy, Hd.
Founded: 1966. **Staff:** Prof 4. **Subjects:** Political science, sociology, economics, history, census/demography. **Special Collections:** Slave trade to the Americas; Florentine census and property survey of 1428; American fertility surveys; occupational and social mobility. **Holdings:** 300 books; 3500 data files; 80 bound periodical volumes; 1750 codebooks for data; 70 guides to data archival holdings; 2000 magnetic tapes. **Subscriptions:** 32

journals and other serials. **Services:** Interlibrary loan; copying; service open to the public. **Publications:** Directory of the Machine Readable Data and Program Holdings of the Data and Program Library Service. **Staff:** Laura Campbell, Data Libn. & Archv.; Patrick Wenzel, Automation Libn.; Dennis Nara, Data Proc.Spec..

★17128★
UNIVERSITY OF WISCONSIN, MADISON - DEPARTMENT OF PSYCHIATRY - LITHIUM INFORMATION CENTER (Med)
600 Highland Ave. Phone: (608)263-6171
Madison, WI 53792 Margaret G. Baudhuin, Libn./Info.Spec.
Founded: 1975. **Staff:** Prof 5; Other 3. **Subjects:** Medical uses of lithium. **Holdings:** 15,000 articles, books, abstracts, miscellaneous items stored online. **Services:** Copying; SDI; center open to the public; direct access to holdings through a compatible computer terminal. **Automated Operations:** Computerized cataloging. **Computerized Information Services:** Lithium Library. Performs searches on fee basis. **Publications:** Lithium and Manic Depression: A Guide; Lithium and the Kidney: A Bibliography; Depression and Its Treatment; Lithium Encyclopedia for Clinical Practice - all for sale. **Special Indexes:** Lithium Index. **Staff:** James W. Jefferson, M.D., Co-Dir.; John H. Greist, M.D., Co-Dir.; Bette L. Hartley, Libn..

★17129★
UNIVERSITY OF WISCONSIN, MADISON - DEPARTMENT OF RURAL SOCIOLOGY - APPLIED POPULATION LABORATORY - LIBRARY (Soc Sci)
Agriculture Hall, Rm. 316 Phone: (608)262-1515
Madison, WI 53706 Karen Daramola, Adm.Asst.
Staff: 1. **Subjects:** Demographic material on fertility, mortality, migration. **Holdings:** 2000 books; 24 VF drawers of pamphlets. **Services:** Copying; library open to the public by appointment. **Computerized Information Services:** WISPOP (internal database).

★17130★
UNIVERSITY OF WISCONSIN, MADISON - DEPARTMENT OF URBAN AND REGIONAL PLANNING - GRADUATE RESEARCH CENTER (Plan)
Music Hall
925 Bascom Mall Phone: (608)262-1004
Madison, WI 53706 Irwin Weintraub, Libn.
Founded: 1965. **Staff:** Prof 1; Other 1. **Subjects:** Urban and regional planning, land and water resources, zoning, social services planning, planning in developing areas. **Holdings:** 7000 books; 25,000 planning reports and documents; 100 theses and dissertations. **Subscriptions:** 120 journals and other serials. **Services:** Interlibrary loan; copying; center open to the public.

★17131★
UNIVERSITY OF WISCONSIN, MADISON - EAST ASIAN COLLECTION (Area-Ethnic, Rel-Phil)
728 State St. Phone: (608)262-0344
Madison, WI 53706 Chester Wang, Bibliog.
Founded: 1964. **Staff:** Prof 4; Other 5. **Subjects:** Chinese and Japanese literature and history. **Special Collections:** Buddhist studies. **Holdings:** 150,000 books; 2000 bound periodical volumes. **Subscriptions:** 250 journals and other serials; 6 newspapers. **Services:** Interlibrary loan; collection open to the public. **Automated Operations:** Computerized cataloging and serials.

★17132★
UNIVERSITY OF WISCONSIN, MADISON - F.B. POWER PHARMACEUTICAL LIBRARY (Med)
School of Pharmacy
425 N. Charter St. Phone: (608)262-2894
Madison, WI 53706 Dolores Nemec, Libn.
Founded: 1883. **Staff:** Prof 1; Other 1. **Subjects:** Pharmacy and related subjects. **Special Collections:** Catalogs of drugs and pharmaceutical equipment, 1860 to present; Kremers Reference Files, 1870 to present (pamphlets; correspondence; manuscripts; pictures; broadsides; clippings); Iowa Drug Information Service. **Holdings:** 12,568 books; 22,630 bound periodical volumes. **Subscriptions:** 404 journals; 311 serials. **Services:** Interlibrary loan; copying; library open to the public for reference use only. **Computerized Information Services:** DIALOG Information Services, BRS Information Technologies. Performs searches on fee basis.

★17133★
UNIVERSITY OF WISCONSIN, MADISON - GEOGRAPHY LIBRARY (Geog-Map)
280 Science Hall Phone: (608)262-1706
Madison, WI 53706 Miriam E. Kerndt, Hd.
Staff: Prof 1; Other 1. **Subjects:** Geography, cartography. **Holdings:** 45,000 volumes. **Subscriptions:** 600 journals and other serials. **Services:** Interlibrary loan; library open to the public. **Automated Operations:** Computerized cataloging. **Networks/Consortia:** Member of Wisconsin Interlibrary Services (WILS). **Publications:** Acquisitions list, 3/year.

★17134★
UNIVERSITY OF WISCONSIN, MADISON - GEOLOGY-GEOPHYSICS LIBRARY (Sci-Engr)
440 Weeks Hall
1215 W. Dayton St. Phone: (608)262-8956
Madison, WI 53706 Marie Dvorzak, Libn.
Staff: Prof 1; Other 1. **Subjects:** Geology, geophysics, oceanography. **Holdings:** 16,000 books; 33,000 bound periodical volumes; 700 department theses, 1970 to present; 2300 maps. **Subscriptions:** 1250 journals and other serials. **Services:** Interlibrary loan; copying; library open to the public. **Automated Operations:** Computerized public access catalog, acquisitions, and serials. **Computerized Information Services:** DIALOG Information Services. **Publications:** Acquisitions list, monthly.

★17135★
UNIVERSITY OF WISCONSIN, MADISON - INSTITUTE ON AGING - TOPIC FILE ON AGING
425 Henry Mall
Madison, WI 53706
Defunct

★17136★
UNIVERSITY OF WISCONSIN, MADISON - INSTITUTE FOR RESEARCH IN THE HUMANITIES - LIBRARY (Hum)
Old Observatory
1401 Observatory Dr. Phone: (608)262-3855
Madison, WI 53706 Loretta Freiling, Prog.Asst.
Founded: 1959. **Staff:** 1. **Subjects:** Humanities - Ancient to Renaissance. **Special Collections:** Works by Benedetto Croce (500 volumes). **Holdings:** 1100 books. **Services:** Library open to the public with restrictions.

★17137★
UNIVERSITY OF WISCONSIN, MADISON - KOHLER ART LIBRARY (Art)
General Library System
800 University Ave. Phone: (608)263-2256
Madison, WI 53706 William C. Bunce, Dir. & Hd.Libn.
Founded: 1970. **Staff:** Prof 1; Other 2. **Subjects:** Art, architecture, decorative arts, photography. **Holdings:** 102,000 volumes; 28 VF drawers of exhibition catalogs; theses and dissertations; 14,500 microforms. **Subscriptions:** 297 journals and other serials. **Services:** Interlibrary loan; copying; library open to the public with restrictions on circulation. **Automated Operations:** Computerized public access catalog, cataloging, and acquisitions. **Computerized Information Services:** DIALOG Information Services, BRS Information Technologies, WILSONLINE. Performs searches on fee basis. **Remarks:** Alternate telephone numbers are 263-2257 and 263-2258.

★17138★
UNIVERSITY OF WISCONSIN, MADISON - LAND TENURE CENTER - LIBRARY (Agri)
434 Steenbock Memorial Library
550 Babcock Dr. Phone: (608)262-1240
Madison, WI 53706 Beverly R. Phillips, Libn.
Founded: 1962. **Staff:** Prof 1; Other 3. **Subjects:** Land tenure, agrarian reform, agricultural economics, Latin America, Asia, Africa, rural development, underdeveloped areas. **Holdings:** 25,000 books; 1200 bound periodical volumes; 36,000 unbound reports, manuscripts, clippings, pamphlets, documents; 8 VF drawers of microfilm; 100 titles of Economic Development Plans; 250 titles of dissertations. **Subscriptions:** 350 journals and other serials. **Services:** Interlibrary loan; copying; library open to the public. **Automated Operations:** Computerized cataloging. **Computerized Information Services:** OCLC; NLS (Network Library System; internal database). **Publications:** Accessions List, irregular - free upon request; irregular bibliographies; annotated bibliography on land tenure and reform in Latin America, Africa, and Asia.

★17139★
UNIVERSITY OF WISCONSIN, MADISON - LAW SCHOOL LIBRARY (Law)
Madison, WI 53706 Phone: (608)262-1128
Founded: 1868. **Staff:** Prof 9; Other 5. **Subjects:** Law, criminal justice, foreign law. **Holdings:** 278,885 volumes; 330,181 microforms. **Subscriptions:** 4440 serials; 20 newspapers. **Services:** Interlibrary loan; copying; library open to the public. **Automated Operations:** Computerized cataloging. **Computerized Information Services:** OCLC, LEXIS, WESTLAW; MCI Mail (electronic mail service). **Networks/Consortia:** Member of Wisconsin Interlibrary Services (WILS). **Publications:** Selected Recent Acquisitions; Current Criminal Justice Literature. **Staff:** Nancy Paul, Asst.Dir., Tech.Serv.; Cindy May, Cat.Libn.; Gloria Holz, Circ./Reserve Libn.; William Ebbott, Asst.Dir., Info.Serv.; Telle Zoller, Foreign Law Libn.; Virginia Meier, Cat.Libn.; Barbara Meyer, Pub.Serv.Libn.; Sue Center, Asst.Dir., Pub.Serv..

★17140★
UNIVERSITY OF WISCONSIN, MADISON - LAW SCHOOL LIBRARY - CRIMINAL JUSTICE REFERENCE & INFORMATION CENTER (Law, Soc Sci)
L140 Law Library Phone: (608)262-1499
Madison, WI 53706 Sue L. Center, Asst.Dir.
Founded: 1969. **Staff:** Prof 3; Other 2. **Subjects:** Criminal justice system, police science, corrections, drug abuse, delinquency, alcoholism. **Special Collections:** Penal Press Publications. **Holdings:** 29,000 volumes. **Subscriptions:** 755 journals and other serials. **Services:** Interlibrary loan; copying; center open to the public with restrictions. **Publications:** Current Criminal Justice Literature, bimonthly - to agencies in Wisconsin. **Staff:** Virginia Meier, Libn.; Barbara Meyer, Libn..

★17141★
UNIVERSITY OF WISCONSIN, MADISON - MATHEMATICS LIBRARY (Sci-Engr, Comp Sci)
B224 Van Vleck Hall Phone: (608)262-3596
Madison, WI 53706 Shirley Shen, Assoc.Libn.-Spec.
Founded: 1938. **Staff:** Prof 1. **Subjects:** Mathematics, statistics, computer sciences, mathematical physics. **Holdings:** 37,000 volumes. **Subscriptions:** 392 journals and other serials. **Services:** Interlibrary loan; copying; library open to the public for reference use only. **Automated Operations:** Computerized cataloging. **Computerized Information Services:** BRS Information Technologies; NLS (Network Library System; internal database). Performs searches on fee basis.

★17142★
UNIVERSITY OF WISCONSIN, MADISON - MEMORIAL LIBRARY - DEPARTMENT OF RARE BOOKS & SPECIAL COLLECTIONS (Rare Book, Hum)
728 State St. Phone: (608)262-3243
Madison, WI 53706 John Tedeschi, Cur.
Staff: Prof 2; Other 4. **Subjects:** History of science, 19th and 20th century American literature, English literature, Socialistica, Russian history, 16th-18th century European history and literature. **Special Collections:** Thordarson Collection (history of science; 5000 volumes); Duveen Collection (history of chemistry; 2900 titles); Cole Collection (history of chemistry; 700 titles); Bassett-Brownell Mark Twain Collection (500 volumes; periodicals; manuscripts); Sukov Collection of Little Magazines (4800 titles); Russian Underground Collection (1800 items); French pamphlet collection (2500 titles); Cairns Collection (American women writers; 3700 titles); Tank Collection (Dutch culture, 16th-18th centuries; 4800 volumes); medieval manuscripts. **Holdings:** 100,000 books; 29,000 periodical volumes. **Subscriptions:** 1200 journals and other serials. **Services:** Department open to the public with restrictions. **Special Catalogs:** Exhibit catalogs, irregular. **Special Indexes:** Chronological and geographical files (book and card); literature in translation and interview indexes.

★17143★
UNIVERSITY OF WISCONSIN, MADISON - MILLS MUSIC LIBRARY (Mus)
B162 Memorial Library
728 State St. Phone: (608)263-1884
Madison, WI 53706 William Bunce, Act.Mus.Libn.
Staff: Prof 3; Other 7. **Subjects:** Music. **Special Collections:** American music before 1900 (3000 items); Wisconsin Music Archives (2000 items); Stratman-Thomas Collection (Wisconsin folk songs); Civil War band books; Tams-Witmark Collection (American musical theater). **Holdings:** 78,000 scores; 35,000 volumes; 120,000 recordings; 800 reels of microfilm. **Subscriptions:** 418 journals and other serials. **Services:** Interlibrary loan; library open to the public for reference use only. **Automated Operations:** Computerized cataloging. **Special Catalogs:** Catalog of American music collection (card). **Special Indexes:** Indexes to Stratman-Thomas Collection and Tams-Witmark Collection (online).

★17144★
UNIVERSITY OF WISCONSIN, MADISON - NIEMAN-GRANT JOURNALISM READING ROOM (Info Sci)
2130 Vilas Communication Hall
821 University Ave. Phone: (608)263-3387
Madison, WI 53706 Geri Cupery, Libn.
Founded: 1953. **Staff:** Prof 3. **Subjects:** Journalism and reporting, law of mass communications, mass communications methodology and research, mass media in the U.S., public opinion and propaganda, public relations, international communications, advertising, photojournalism and photography. **Special Collections:** Thayer Law of Mass Communications Collection (350). **Holdings:** 5000 books; 800 bound periodical volumes; 4 VF drawers of pamphlets and clippings. **Subscriptions:** 120 journals and other serials; 70 newspapers. **Services:** Room open to the public for research projects. **Computerized Information Services:** Network Library System (NLS; internal database). **Remarks:** Reading Room is part of the School of Journalism and Mass Communications. **Staff:** Beth Duncan, Asst.Libn.; Susan Soden, Asst.Libn..

★17145★
UNIVERSITY OF WISCONSIN, MADISON - PHYSICS LIBRARY (Sci-Engr)
1150 University Ave. Phone: (608)262-9500
Madison, WI 53706 John J. Wanserski, Assoc. Academic Libn.
Founded: 1974. **Staff:** Prof 1; Other 3. **Subjects:** Experimental and theoretical physics. **Holdings:** 16,000 books; 20,000 bound periodical volumes; 6000 microforms. **Subscriptions:** 450 journals and other serials. **Services:** Interlibrary loan; library open to the public. **Automated Operations:** Computerized public access catalog. **Computerized Information Services:** BRS Information Technologies, STN International. Performs searches on fee basis. **Publications:** Acquisitions List and Information Letter, monthly.

★17146★
UNIVERSITY OF WISCONSIN, MADISON - PLANT PATHOLOGY MEMORIAL LIBRARY (Biol Sci)
1630 Linden Dr. Phone: (608)262-8698
Madison, WI 53706 Patricia J. Herrling, Libn.
Staff: Prof 1. **Subjects:** Phytopathology, plant virology, plant physiology. **Special Collections:** Johnson-Hoggan Memorial Collection of Plant Virus Literature. **Holdings:** 2646 books; 2301 bound periodical volumes; 65,000 reprints; 400 theses and dissertations. **Subscriptions:** 90 journals and other serials. **Services:** Interlibrary loan; library open to the public for reference use only. **Special Catalogs:** Catalogs of abstracts of virus and reprint materials in all branches of plant pathology (card).

★17147★
UNIVERSITY OF WISCONSIN, MADISON - POULTRY SCIENCE DEPARTMENT - HALPIN MEMORIAL LIBRARY (Agri)
Animal Science Bldg., Rm. 214
1675 Observatory Dr. Phone: (608)262-1243
Madison, WI 53706 Louis C. Arrington, Prof.
Founded: 1960. **Staff:** 2. **Subjects:** Poultry science. **Special Collections:** Radford Collection of poultry literature. **Holdings:** 840 books; 600 bound periodical volumes; 12,000 reprints and pamphlets. **Subscriptions:** 30 journals and other serials. **Services:** Library open to the public.

★17148★
UNIVERSITY OF WISCONSIN, MADISON - SCHOOL OF EDUCATION - INSTRUCTIONAL MATERIALS CENTER (Educ)
Teacher Education Bldg.
225 N. Mills St. Phone: (608)263-4750
Madison, WI 53706 Jo Ann Carr, Dir.
Founded: 1950. **Staff:** Prof 3; Other 13. **Subjects:** Education, print and nonprint instructional materials, children's literature. **Special Collections:** Standardized tests; curriculum guides on microfiche. **Holdings:** 55,000 books and AV programs; 1460 bound periodical volumes; microfiche; ERIC microfiche with indexes; ERIC CD-ROM. **Subscriptions:** 300 journals and other serials. **Services:** Interlibrary loan; copying; center open to the public with borrower's card. **Automated Operations:** Computerized cataloging. **Computerized Information Services:** DIALOG Information Services, BRS Information Technologies; NLS (Network Library System; internal database); Email (electronic mail service). Performs searches on fee basis. Contact Person: Nancy McClements, Pub.Serv.Libn., 263-4934.

Networks/Consortia: Member of Wisconsin Interlibrary Services (WILS). **Publications:** Bibliographies on topics of current interest in education. **Staff:** Lisa Baures, Tech.Serv.Libn..

★17149★
UNIVERSITY OF WISCONSIN, MADISON - SCHOOL OF LIBRARY AND INFORMATION STUDIES - LIBRARY (Info Sci)
600 N. Park St. Phone: (608)263-2960
Madison, WI 53706 Sally Davis, Libn.
Founded: 1906. **Staff:** Prof 2; Other 3. **Subjects:** Library science, information science, children's literature, young adult literature. **Holdings:** 60,000 books; 5000 bound periodical volumes; 8800 pamphlets; 1800 microforms; 2500 AV programs. **Subscriptions:** 550 journals and other serials. **Services:** Interlibrary loan; copying; library open to the public. **Automated Operations:** Computerized cataloging. **Computerized Information Services:** NLS (Network Library System; internal database). **Networks/Consortia:** Member of Wisconsin Interlibrary Services (WILS). **Staff:** Peggy Green, Asst.Libn..

UNIVERSITY OF WISCONSIN, MADISON - SCHOOL OF SOCIAL WORK - VIDEO RESOURCE LIBRARY
See: University of West Florida - Human Resource Videotape Library (17085)

★17150★
UNIVERSITY OF WISCONSIN, MADISON - SCHOOL OF SOCIAL WORK - VIRGINIA L. FRANKS MEMORIAL LIBRARY (Soc Sci)
425 Henry Mall, Rm. 230 Phone: (608)263-3840
Madison, WI 53706 Mary Crompton, Libn.
Founded: 1972. **Staff:** 8. **Subjects:** Social work - education and administration, psychotherapy and behavior modification, corrections, alcoholism and drug abuse, adoption and foster care. **Special Collections:** Unpublished theses and research projects (500); social gerontology books. **Holdings:** 12,773 books; 1323 bound periodical volumes; VF items; pamphlets; AV programs. **Subscriptions:** 217 journals and other serials. **Services:** Interlibrary loan; copying; library open to the public with restrictions. **Computerized Information Services:** BRS Information Technologies, DIALOG Information Services.

★17151★
UNIVERSITY OF WISCONSIN, MADISON - SEMINARY OF MEDIEVAL SPANISH STUDIES - LIBRARY (Area-Ethnic)
1120 Van Hise Hall Phone: (608)262-2529
Madison, WI 53706 Lloyd Kasten, Prof.
Founded: 1931. **Subjects:** Alfonso X of Castille, Old Spanish and Aragonese, Old Spanish literature. **Special Collections:** Photostatic reproduction of works of Alfonso X; vocabulary files of works of Alfonso X and Juan Fernandez de Heredia; Old Spanish dictionaries. **Holdings:** 8500 books; 550 bound periodical volumes; 274 volumes of photostats; 4500 pamphlets and reprints; 38 drawers of notes and research materials; 50 dissertations; 450 reels of microfilm. **Subscriptions:** 25 journals and other serials. **Services:** Copying; library open to the public with restrictions.

★17152★
UNIVERSITY OF WISCONSIN, MADISON - SMALL BUSINESS DEVELOPMENT & RECREATION CENTER - LIBRARY
Extension Bldg., Rm. 104
432 N. Lake St.
Madison, WI 53703
Defunct. Holdings absorbed by Extension Library.

★17153★
UNIVERSITY OF WISCONSIN, MADISON - STEENBOCK MEMORIAL LIBRARY (Agri, Biol Sci)
550 Babcock Dr. Phone: (608)262-9990
Madison, WI 53706 Kenneth Frazier, Act.Dir.
Founded: 1904. **Staff:** Prof 10; Other 9. **Subjects:** Life sciences, agriculture, veterinary medicine, biotechnology, food and dairy science, family studies, consumer science, agricultural economics. **Special Collections:** Miller Beekeeping Collection; Swanton Cooperative Collection; Levitan Cookbook Collection. **Holdings:** 101,567 monographs; 56,937 bound periodical volumes; 413,749 documents; 48,215 microforms; 539 AV programs. **Subscriptions:** 3370 journals and other serials. **Services:** Interlibrary loan; copying; document delivery; SDI; library open to the public. **Automated Operations:** Computerized cataloging, acquisitions, and serials. **Computerized Information Services:** OCLC, DIALOG Information Services, BRS Information Technologies, STN International, NLM. **Networks/Consortia:** Member of Center for Research Libraries (CRL) Consortia, Wisconsin Interlibrary Services (WILS). **Publications:** New Book List, monthly; library guide series, irregular. **Staff:** Jean Gilbertson, Act.Asst.Dir.; Lois Komai, Ref.Libn.; Robert Sessions, Ref.Libn./Vet.Med.; Mary Lou Stursa, Hd., Tech.Serv. & Docs.; Terri Anderson, Hd., Circ.; Barbara Lazewski, Ref.Libn.; John Koch, Ref.Libn.; Gordon Luce, Ref.Libn..

★17154★
UNIVERSITY OF WISCONSIN, MADISON - STUDY IN HEALTH CARE FISCAL MANAGEMENT ORGANIZATION AND CONTROL - LIBRARY (Bus-Fin)
1155 Observatory Dr., Rm. 301 Phone: (608)262-1943
Madison, WI 53706 Belle Oswald-Heberling, Prog.Asst.
Founded: 1972. **Staff:** Prof 1; Other 1. **Subjects:** Health care fiscal management, financial management, accounting and internal auditing, sources of funding, reimbursement and related subjects, information systems. **Holdings:** 813 books; 17 bound periodical volumes. **Subscriptions:** 14 journals and other serials. **Services:** Library not open to the public.

★17155★
UNIVERSITY OF WISCONSIN, MADISON - THEORETICAL CHEMISTRY INSTITUTE - LIBRARY (Sci-Engr)
1101 University Ave., Rm. 8326 Phone: (608)262-1511
Madison, WI 53706 Sherry Naffz, Prog.Asst.
Founded: 1962. **Staff:** 1. **Subjects:** Quantum and statistical mechanics, scattering theory, transport phenomena, thermodynamics. **Special Collections:** University of Wisconsin Naval Research Laboratory Reports; Theoretical Chemistry Institute Reports. **Holdings:** 2264 books; 12,273 bound periodical volumes; 65,000 other cataloged items. **Services:** Library open to the public by permission. **Special Indexes:** Complete indexes of University of Wisconsin Theoretical Chemistry Institute Reports and publications.

★17156★
UNIVERSITY OF WISCONSIN, MADISON - TRACE R & D CENTER - INFORMATION AREA (Soc Sci)
S157 Waisman Center
1500 Highland Ave. Phone: (608)263-5408
Madison, WI 53705-2280 Peter Borden, Proj.Dir.
Staff: Prof 1; Other 1. **Subjects:** Nonvocal communication, computer access for the disabled, rehabilitation engineering, software/hardware for the disabled. **Holdings:** 12 linear feet and 2 filing cabinets of research materials; directories; newsletters; conference proceedings. **Subscriptions:** 10 journals and other serials. **Computerized Information Services:** Trace Base (internal database). Performs searches on fee basis. Contact Person: Ann Devine. **Publications:** Rehab/Education Resource Book Series (Volume 1 - Communication Aids; Volume 2 - Switches & Environmental Controls; Volume 3 - Computer Hardware and Software). **Special Catalogs:** Resource lists. **Also Known As:** Trace Research and Development Center on Communication, Control & Computer Access for Handicapped Individuals.

★17157★
UNIVERSITY OF WISCONSIN, MADISON - UNIVERSITY CENTER FOR COOPERATIVES - COOPERATIVE LIBRARY (Bus-Fin)
Lowell Hall, Rm. 526
610 Langdon St. Phone: (608)262-3251
Madison, WI 53703 MaryJean McGrath, Act.Libn.
Founded: 1962. **Staff:** Prof 1; Other 1. **Subjects:** Cooperatives. **Special Collections:** Rochdale Collection (900 early U.S. and English co-op books, European cooperative federations' annual reports); Shaars Collection. **Holdings:** 7000 books; 16 VF drawers of research working papers of Works Progress Administration (WPA) research on cooperatives; 45 VF drawers of information on all aspects and types of cooperatives worldwide. **Subscriptions:** 350 journals and other serials. **Services:** Interlibrary loan; copying; library open to the public with restrictions.

★17158★
UNIVERSITY OF WISCONSIN, MADISON - WASHBURN OBSERVATORY - WOODMAN ASTRONOMICAL LIBRARY (Sci-Engr)
6521 Sterling Hall
475 N. Charter St. Phone: (608)262-1320
Madison, WI 53706 Diane Poplawsky, Libn.
Founded: 1882. **Staff:** Prof 1. **Subjects:** Astronomy, astrophysics. **Special Collections:** Noncommercial astronomical (Society and/or Observatory) publications (800 titles). **Holdings:** 4800 books; 2000 bound periodical volumes; 3500 volumes of noncommercial serials; 4670 charts, plates, photographs; 1065 microfiche. **Subscriptions:** 40 journals and other serials.

Services: Interlibrary loan; library not open to the public. **Networks/Consortia:** Member of Multitype Advisory Library Committee (MALC), Wisconsin Interlibrary Services (WILS).

★17159★
UNIVERSITY OF WISCONSIN, MADISON - WATER RESOURCES CENTER - LIBRARY (Env-Cons)
1975 Willow Dr. Phone: (608)262-3069
Madison, WI 53706 Sarah L. Calcese, Libn.
Founded: 1965. **Staff:** Prof 1; Other 2. **Subjects:** Water resources - pollution sources, abatement and control, waste water treatment, limnology, resources management, research and planning. **Special Collections:** Eutrophication (7000 reprints and documents); Water Resources Economics Collection (800 reprints). **Holdings:** 22,000 books and technical reports. **Subscriptions:** 22 journals and other serials; 80 newsletters. **Services:** Interlibrary loan; library open to the public. **Automated Operations:** Computerized cataloging. **Networks/Consortia:** Member of South Central Library System. **Publications:** Monthly Acquisitions List - available upon request.

★17160★
UNIVERSITY OF WISCONSIN, MADISON - WILLIAM A. SCOTT BUSINESS LIBRARY (Bus-Fin)
Bascom Hall Phone: (608)262-5935
Madison, WI 53706 Marilyn A. Hicks, Hd.
Founded: 1955. **Staff:** Prof 1; Other 1. **Subjects:** Accounting, finance, management, marketing, real estate, insurance, international business. **Special Collections:** Corporate annual reports; Johnson Foundation Collection (productivity). **Holdings:** 20,000 books; 7000 periodical volumes; 104,037 microfiche; 298 reels of microfilm; 970 masters' papers. **Subscriptions:** 500 journals and other serials; 5 newspapers. **Services:** Interlibrary loan; copying; library open to the public. **Networks/Consortia:** Member of Wisconsin Interlibrary Services (WILS).

★17161★
UNIVERSITY OF WISCONSIN, MADISON - WISCONSIN CENTER FOR FILM AND THEATER RESEARCH (Theater)
6040 Vilas Hall
821 University Ave. Phone: (608)262-9706
Madison, WI 53706 Donald Crafton, Dir.
Founded: 1960. **Staff:** Prof 2; Other 3. **Subjects:** Film, television, theater, radio. **Holdings:** Over 200 manuscript collections of individuals and organizations in the performing arts, including scripts, correspondence, production and promotional materials, legal files, financial records; 14,000 films; 2 million photographs. The largest collection is the United Artists Corporation Collection which contains the corporate records of United Artists from its founding in 1919 through 1951, and includes: 1750 feature films from Warner Brothers, RKO, and Monogram film libraries with related manuscripts; 2000 episodes from the ZIV Library of Television Programs with related manuscripts; 1500 Vitaphone short subjects and 600 Warner and Popeye cartoons with related manuscripts. **Services:** Copying and photoduplication of stills; center open to the public; original material does not circulate; film archive open to qualified researchers by appointment only. **Publications:** Brochure; guide to collections; feature film list. **Special Catalogs:** Detailed inventories for each processed collection. **Special Indexes:** Production title index for films, stills, and scripts (card). **Staff:** Maxine Fleckner-Ducey, Film Archv..

★17162★
UNIVERSITY OF WISCONSIN, MADISON - WISCONSIN REGIONAL PRIMATE RESEARCH CENTER - PRIMATE CENTER LIBRARY (Biol Sci, Med)
1223 Capitol Court Phone: (608)263-3512
Madison, WI 53715-1299 Lawrence Jacobsen, Hd.Libn.
Founded: 1973. **Staff:** Prof 2; Other 2. **Subjects:** Primatology, neurosciences, reproductive physiology, behavioral endocrinology, animal behavior. **Special Collections:** Primate vocalizations, videotapes, slides, and other nonprint media; Neurosciences Research Program Collection; rare books. **Holdings:** 5000 books; 10,000 bound periodical volumes; 500 unbound volumes; 12,000 topical reprints; 3400 AV programs; 100 masters' and Ph.D. theses. **Subscriptions:** 275 journals and other serials. **Services:** Interlibrary loan; copying; SDI; library open to the public. **Automated Operations:** Computerized cataloging and serials. **Computerized Information Services:** MEDLINE, OCLC, BRS Information Technologies; Network Library System (NLS; internal database). **Networks/Consortia:** Member of Wisconsin Interlibrary Services (WILS). **Publications:** Primate Library Report: Print Acquisitions, bimonthly; Primate Library Report: Audio-Visual Acquisitions, biennial. **Staff:** Amy Kindschi, Tech.Serv.Libn.; Raymond Hamel, Spec.Coll.Libn..

★17163★
UNIVERSITY OF WISCONSIN, MADISON - ZOOLOGICAL MUSEUM LIBRARY (Biol Sci)
L.E. Noland Bldg.
250 N. Mills St. Phone: (608)262-3766
Madison, WI 53706 John A.W. Kirsch, Dir.
Founded: 1887. **Staff:** Prof 1. **Subjects:** Zoology. **Holdings:** 5000 volumes; 20,000 reprints; monographs; original field data. **Services:** Interlibrary loan; copying; library open to the public with restrictions.

UNIVERSITY OF WISCONSIN, MILWAUKEE - AMERICAN GEOGRAPHICAL SOCIETY COLLECTION
See: American Geographical Society Collection of the University of Wisconsin, Milwaukee - Golda Meir Library (519)

★17164★
UNIVERSITY OF WISCONSIN, MILWAUKEE - CENTER FOR ECONOMIC EDUCATION - LIBRARY (Educ)
Bolton Hall 824 Phone: (414)963-4678
Milwaukee, WI 53201 Dr. Leon M. Schur, Dir.
Founded: 1964. **Subjects:** Economic education. **Holdings:** 2000 volumes.

★17165★
UNIVERSITY OF WISCONSIN, MILWAUKEE - GOLDA MEIR LIBRARY - ALBERT CAMUS ARCHIVES (Rare Book)
2311 E. Hartford Ave. Phone: (414)229-6119
Milwaukee, WI 53201 Robert F. Roeming
Staff: 1. **Subjects:** Albert Camus. **Holdings:** 20 VF drawers; 6 cases of books and reference materials; 175 reels of microfilm of dissertations and manuscripts; 24 card file drawers of investigators' notes and references to personal contacts abroad; newspapers edited by Camus and in which he was published. **Services:** Archives open to the public with restrictions. **Computerized Information Services:** Internal database. **Publications:** Camus: A Bibliography (7th edition), 1987 - free upon request.

★17166★
UNIVERSITY OF WISCONSIN, MILWAUKEE - GOLDA MEIR LIBRARY - AREA RESEARCH CENTER (Hist)
2311 E. Hartford Ave. Phone: (414)229-5402
Milwaukee, WI 53201 Allan Kovan, Cur.
Founded: 1965. **Staff:** Prof 1; Other 1. **Subjects:** Private papers, county documents of Milwaukee, Ozaukee, Sheboygan, Washington, and Waukesha counties; local history, businesses, associations, and churches. **Holdings:** 425 manuscript collections; 142 state, county, and local government record series. **Services:** Copying; center open to the public. **Networks/Consortia:** Member of Wisconsin Area Research Center Network. **Publications:** John A. Fleckner and Stanley Mallach, Guide to Historical Resources in Milwaukee Area Archives, 1976.

★17167★
UNIVERSITY OF WISCONSIN, MILWAUKEE - GOLDA MEIR LIBRARY - CURRICULUM COLLECTION (Educ, Aud-Vis)
Box 604 Phone: (414)229-4074
Milwaukee, WI 53201 Marianna Markowetz, Educ.Libn.
Founded: 1956. **Staff:** Prof 1; Other 3. **Subjects:** Children's literature, elementary and secondary textbooks and AV media. **Special Collections:** Children's Literature and Textbook Historical Collection (1121). **Holdings:** 19,877 books; 450 bound periodical volumes; 1986 curriculum guides; 7672 K-12 textbooks; 1970 AV programs; 735 seminar papers; 237 tests; ERIC microfiche collection. **Subscriptions:** 28 journals and other serials. **Services:** Interlibrary loan (limited); copying; collection open to the public under rules and regulations of the University Library. **Automated Operations:** Computerized cataloging. **Computerized Information Services:** Internal database. **Networks/Consortia:** Member of Wisconsin Interlibrary Services (WILS), Library Council of Metropolitan Milwaukee, Inc. (LCOMM).

★17168★
UNIVERSITY OF WISCONSIN, MILWAUKEE - GOLDA MEIR LIBRARY - SEVENTEENTH-CENTURY COLLECTION (Rare Book)
Box 604 Phone: (414)229-4345
Milwaukee, WI 53201 Ellen M. Murphy, Spec.Coll.Libn.
Founded: 1976. **Staff:** Prof 1; Other 1. **Subjects:** 17th century rare books. **Holdings:** 685 books. **Services:** Copying; collection open to the public.

★17169★
UNIVERSITY OF WISCONSIN, MILWAUKEE - GOLDA MEIR LIBRARY - SHAKESPEARE RESEARCH COLLECTION (Theater)
Box 604 Phone: (414)229-6436
Milwaukee, WI 53201 Dr. Virginia Haas, Cur.
Founded: 1970. **Staff:** Prof 2. **Subjects:** Shakespeare, Elizabethan and Jacobean theater. **Holdings:** 3000 books. **Subscriptions:** 18 journals and other serials. **Services:** Interlibrary loan; copying; collection open to the public.

★17170★
UNIVERSITY OF WISCONSIN, MILWAUKEE - GRADUATE SCHOOL - OFFICE OF RESEARCH - INFORMATION LIBRARY (Bus-Fin)
Box 340 Phone: (414)229-4063
Milwaukee, WI 53201 Victor J. Larson, Info.Spec.
Founded: 1967. **Staff:** Prof 1; Other 2. **Special Collections:** Federal and foundation extramural support program information (program announcements; guideline documents; general information items; reference books relating to sources of funds; information and proposal writing guides). **Holdings:** 8000 documents; 2 VF drawers of Senate and House bills and laws; 9 VF drawers of federal program information; 4 VF drawers of foundation and corporate program information; 100 program application kits. **Subscriptions:** 125 journals and other serials. **Services:** Copying; library open to the public by appointment. **Computerized Information Services:** Online systems. Performs searches on fee basis. **Publications:** Acquisitions List, quarterly; Application Deadline List, bimonthly.

★17171★
UNIVERSITY OF WISCONSIN, MILWAUKEE - GREENE MEMORIAL MUSEUM - LIBRARY
3367 N. Downer Ave.
Milwaukee, WI 53201
Founded: 1913. **Subjects:** Paleontology, mineralogy, geology. **Holdings:** 300 volumes. **Remarks:** This is the personal reference library of Thomas A. Greene, a 19th century collector whose fossil and mineral collections make up the bulk of the museum collection. Presently inactive.

★17172★
UNIVERSITY OF WISCONSIN, MILWAUKEE - INSTITUTE OF WORLD AFFAIRS - RESOURCE CENTER (Soc Sci)
Mitchell 141
Box 413 Phone: (414)229-4251
Milwaukee, WI 53201 Gary Shellman, Asst.Dir.
Founded: 1960. **Staff:** Prof 1. **Subjects:** United States foreign policy, United Nations, regional organizations, international relations, current world problems, international trade and finance, international energy, arms control. **Holdings:** 300 books; 100 bound periodical volumes; 50 other cataloged items. **Subscriptions:** 13 journals and other serials. **Services:** Center not open to the public.

★17173★
UNIVERSITY OF WISCONSIN, MILWAUKEE - MORRIS FROMKIN MEMORIAL COLLECTION (Soc Sci)
2311 E. Hartford Ave. Phone: (414)229-5402
Milwaukee, WI 53201 Stanley Mallach, Bibliog.
Founded: 1969. **Staff:** Prof 1. **Subjects:** Socialism in the U.S., 1890-1940; communism in the U.S., 1920-1940; labor movement in the U.S., 1865-1940; social insurance in the U.S. to 1940; reform movements in the U.S., 1865-1940; housing and city planning in the U.S., 1890-1940; materials on European movements and events that affected American Left and Reform movements. **Holdings:** 4150 books; 2000 pamphlets. **Services:** Interlibrary loan; copying; library open to the public for reference use only.

★17174★
UNIVERSITY OF WISCONSIN, MILWAUKEE - MUSIC COLLECTION (Mus)
2311 E. Hartford Ave.
Box 604 Phone: (414)229-5529
Milwaukee, WI 53201 Linda B. Hartig, Mus.Libn.
Staff: Prof 2; Other 2. **Subjects:** Music - history, criticism, theory, instruction and study; music bibliography; music librarianship; music sociology; chamber music. **Special Collections:** American Arriaga Archive (52 items); Slovenian Music Collection (1500 items); European-Tradition Music Catalog & Bibliography Collection (4000 items); John Dale Owen Jazz Recordings Collection (10,000 items). **Holdings:** 15,090 books; 1890 bound periodical volumes; 15,000 scores and parts; 43,000 recordings and tapes; 5100 catalogs, pamphlets, bibliographies; 4200 microforms. **Subscriptions:** 109 journals and other serials. **Services:** Interlibrary loan; copying; collection open to the public with restrictions. **Automated Operations:** Computerized cataloging, serials, and circulation. **Computerized Information Services:** OCLC. **Networks/Consortia:** Member of Wisconsin Interlibrary Services (WILS), Library Council of Metropolitan Milwaukee, Inc. (LCOMM). **Staff:** Lynn Gullickson, Mus.Cat.; Patricia Wiese, Aud.Ctr.Supv..

★17175★
UNIVERSITY OF WISCONSIN, OSHKOSH - UNIVERSITY LIBRARIES AND LEARNING RESOURCES - SPECIAL COLLECTIONS (Educ)
800 Algoma Blvd. Phone: (414)424-3334
Oshkosh, WI 54901 Dr. Norma L. Jones, Act.Exec.Dir.
Founded: 1871. **Special Collections:** Rowland Collection (Limited Editions Club); Pare Lorentz Collection (16mm films); archives of the Wisconsin Area Research Center; children's literature collection; A.F. Neumann Collection; J.R. Putney Collection (Wisconsin); government documents depository; Defense Agency map depository. **Services:** Interlibrary loan; copying; collections open to the public. **Automated Operations:** Computerized cataloging, acquisitions, and circulation. **Computerized Information Services:** OCLC, DIALOG Information Services, BRS Information Technologies, Pergamon ORBIT InfoLine, Inc., LS/2000; PULL (internal database). Performs searches on fee basis. Contact Person: Susheela Rao, Act.Coord., Online Database Searching, 424-2206. **Networks/Consortia:** Member of Council of Wisconsin Libraries, Inc. (COWL), Fox Valley Library Council, Wisconsin Interlibrary Services (WILS), Fox River Valley Area Library Consortium.

★17176★
UNIVERSITY OF WISCONSIN, PARKSIDE - UNIVERSITY ARCHIVES AND AREA RESEARCH CENTER (Hist)
Box 2000 Phone: (414)553-2411
Kenosha, WI 53141 Rebecca Mitchell, Archv.
Staff: Prof 1; Other 1. **Subjects:** History - local, state, university; genealogy. **Special Collections:** Irving Wallace; Norman Mailer; David Kherdian; H.O. Teisberg; Collection of American Plays; Black Sparrow Collection; Perishable Press Collection. **Holdings:** 1234 books; 36 bound periodical volumes; 2600 cubic feet of manuscripts and archives; 2000 reels of microfilm of censuses and local newspapers. **Services:** Interlibrary loan; copying; archives open to the public. **Automated Operations:** Computerized cataloging. **Special Catalogs:** Guide to Archives & Manuscripts in the University of Wisconsin-Parkside Area Research Center.

★17177★
UNIVERSITY OF WISCONSIN, PLATTEVILLE - KARRMANN LIBRARY - SPECIAL COLLECTIONS (Hist)
725 W. Main St. Phone: (608)342-1688
Platteville, WI 53818 Jerome P. Daniels, Dir.
Founded: 1866. **Staff:** Prof 1; Other 1. **Subjects:** History - local, state, university; genealogy; mining. **Special Collections:** Southwest Wisconsin History and Southwestern Wisconsin Area Research Center (history of the Upper Mississippi Valley lead and zinc mining region). **Holdings:** 2254 books; 585 bound periodical volumes; 678 linear feet of unbound reports, manuscripts, and archival materials; 1409 linear feet of county documents; 7 cubic feet of photographs and negatives; 1538 reels of microfilm; 446 magnetic tapes; 17 films/videotapes; 125 maps; 8 VF drawers. **Subscriptions:** 25 journals and other serials. **Services:** Interlibrary loan; copying; collections open to the public. **Networks/Consortia:** Member of Wisconsin Interlibrary Services (WILS), Wisconsin Area Research Center Network. **Special Indexes:** Southwest Wisconsin Surname index, 1815-1860 (card).

★17178★
UNIVERSITY OF WISCONSIN, RIVER FALLS - AREA RESEARCH CENTER (Hist)
Chalmer Davee Library Phone: (715)425-3567
River Falls, WI 54022 Timothy D. Cary, Dir.
Founded: 1960. **Staff:** Prof 1; Other 10. **Subjects:** History of Western Wisconsin (Pierce, Polk, St. Croix, Washburn, and Burnett Counties); Civil War history; genealogy; university history. **Special Collections:** Oral History (250 tapes); Wisconsin Census Records, 1832-1910. **Holdings:** 1000 books; 1500 linear feet of manuscript collections; 2250 reels of microfilm; 1200 pamphlets; 10,000 photographs; maps; newspaper collection. **Services:** Interlibrary loan; copying; center open to the public for reference use only. **Networks/Consortia:** Member of Wisconsin Area Research Center Network. **Special Indexes:** Voices of the St. Croix Valley (bound index to Oral History Collections); biographical index for Burnett, Pierce,

Polk, Washburn, and St. Croix counties, 1850-1910 (60,000 card entries); university alumni index (25,000 card entries).

★17179★
UNIVERSITY OF WISCONSIN, RIVER FALLS - CHALMER DAVEE LIBRARY (Hist)
120 E. Cascade Ave. Phone: (715)425-3222
River Falls, WI 54022 Don Sweet, Dir.
Founded: 1875. **Staff:** Prof 7; Other 10. **Subjects:** Education. **Special Collections:** Western Americana and frontier history; Pierce and St. Croix county history. **Holdings:** 204,177 books; 36,002 bound periodical volumes; 8733 AV programs; 149,867 government documents; 471,438 microfiche and microcards; 7879 reels of microfilm. **Subscriptions:** 1620 journals and other serials; 51 newspapers. **Services:** Interlibrary loan; copying; library open to the public, deposit required for borrowing. **Automated Operations:** Computerized cataloging, acquisitions, and serials. **Computerized Information Services:** DIALOG Information Services, BRS Information Technologies, WILSONLINE, OCLC. **Networks/Consortia:** Member of Wisconsin Interlibrary Services (WILS). **Staff:** Herman Storm, Cat.; Harriet Barry, Automation Libn.; Jane Peirce, Ref.; Tony Adam, Coll.Dev.; Ann Gilson, Asst.Dir..

★17180★
UNIVERSITY OF WISCONSIN, STEVENS POINT - DEPARTMENT OF GEOGRAPHY & GEOLOGY - MAP COLLECTION (Geog-Map)
2100 Main St. Phone: (715)346-2629
Stevens Point, WI 54481 William M. McKinney, Cur.
Founded: 1964. **Staff:** Prof 2; Other 3. **Subjects:** Maps - U.S. topographic, urban Wisconsin, geologic/oceanographic, aeronautic, Latin America, road. **Holdings:** 100 books; 103,000 maps; drawers of aerial photographs. **Services:** Collection open to the public.

★17181★
UNIVERSITY OF WISCONSIN, STEVENS POINT - UNIVERSITY ARCHIVES & PORTAGE COUNTY HISTORICAL SOCIETY (Hist)
Learning Resources Center, 5th Fl. S. Phone: (715)346-2586
Stevens Point, WI 54481 William G. Paul, Univ.Archv.
Subjects: History and development of the University of Wisconsin, Stevens Point, 1894 to present; individuals and institutions of Stevens Point and central Wisconsin. **Holdings:** 800 linear feet of manuscripts, photographs, tapes, catalogs, bulletins, tapes of events and activities, faculty committee minutes, yearbooks, administrative correspondence and reports, personnel records; 1300 linear feet of county records and manuscripts; Portage County Historical Society records, papers, and photographs. **Services:** Copying; archives open to the public.

★17182★
UNIVERSITY OF WISCONSIN, STEVENS POINT - UNIVERSITY LIBRARY (Educ)
Stevens Point, WI 54481 Phone: (715)346-2540
Arne J. Arneson, Dir.
Staff: Prof 16; Other 17. **Subjects:** Natural resources, communicative disorders, home economics, education, communication. **Special Collections:** Federal government document depository; Wisconsin State document depository. **Holdings:** 251,483 books; 52,995 bound periodical volumes; 422,026 microforms; 40,292 AV programs; 526,910 volumes of government documents. **Subscriptions:** 5517 journals and other serials; 22 newspapers. **Services:** Interlibrary loan; copying; library open to the public. **Automated Operations:** Computerized cataloging. **Computerized Information Services:** OCLC, Faxon, ERIC, LS/2000, DIALOG Information Services, BRS Information Technologies, WILSONLINE. **Networks/Consortia:** Member of Wisconsin Interlibrary Services (WILS). **Staff:** Fred M. Buehler, Asst.Ref.Libn.; Theresa Chao, Per.Libn.; Marg Whalen, Doc.Libn.; John D. Gillesby, Hd.Ref.Libn.; Kathleen Halsey, ILL Libn.; James Belz, Lib.Instr.; Lois Huizar, Instr.Mtls.Ctr.Libn.; Patricia Paul, Hd.Cat.; Alice L. Randlett, Acq.Libn.; Carole Van Horn, Data Base Libn..

★17183★
UNIVERSITY OF WISCONSIN, STOUT - LIBRARY LEARNING CENTER (Bus-Fin, Educ)
Menomonie, WI 54751 Phone: (715)232-1215
John J. Jax, Dir.
Staff: Prof 11; Other 17. **Subjects:** Industrial technology, hotel and restaurant management, home economics, business, vocational rehabilitation, tourism, hospitality, early childhood education. **Holdings:** 200,000 books; 67,000 volumes on industrial, technical, and vocational education; 1100 16mm films; 500,000 microfiche. **Subscriptions:** 1450 journals and other serials; 34 newspapers. **Services:** Interlibrary loan; copying; SDI; center open to the public for reference use only. **Automated Operations:** Computerized public access catalog, cataloging, acquisitions, and circulation. **Computerized Information Services:** DIALOG Information Services, BRS Information Technologies, OCLC. **Networks/Consortia:** Member of Wisconsin Interlibrary Services (WILS). **Special Indexes:** KWOC indexes to theses and AV media. **Staff:** Brooke B. Anson, Coord., Pub.Serv.; Mary R. Donley, Coord., Tech.Serv.; Philip Sawin, Jr., Coll.Dev.Off.; Mary Richards, Hd., Cat.; Philip J. Schwarz, Automation; Gayle J. Martinson, Archv..

★17184★
UNIVERSITY OF WISCONSIN, WHITEWATER - ARTS MEDIA CENTER (Art, Mus)
College of the Arts, CA16 Phone: (414)472-1756
Whitewater, WI 53190 Kirby H. Bock, Libn.
Staff: Prof 1; Other 4. **Subjects:** Music, art, theater. **Holdings:** 1000 books; 3000 scores (bound and unbound); 5300 phonograph records; 3010 cassettes; 101,060 art slides. **Services:** Copying; center open to the public.

★17185★
UNIVERSITY OF WYOMING - AMERICAN HERITAGE CENTER - LIBRARY (Hist)
William Robertson Coe Library
Univ. Sta., Box 3924 Phone: (307)766-4114
Laramie, WY 82071 Dr. Lewis Dabney, Act.Dir.
Founded: 1945. **Staff:** Prof 3; Other 26. **Subjects:** Western Americana. **Special Collections:** Range cattle industry history; business; conservation; petroleum; mining; performing arts; mountaineering; water resources; transportation history. **Holdings:** 26,000 books; 1500 bound periodical volumes; 64 file cases of clippings and pamphlets; 6000 linear feet of manuscripts; 1500 reels of microfilm; 39,485 maps; 110,000 photographs. **Subscriptions:** 62 journals and other serials; 53 newspapers. **Services:** Interlibrary loan; copying; library open to the public. **Publications:** News releases. **Formerly:** Western History Research Center.

★17186★
UNIVERSITY OF WYOMING - ANIMAL SCIENCE DIVISION - WOOL LIBRARY (Biol Sci)
University Sta., Box 3354 Phone: (307)766-5212
Laramie, WY 82071 Robert Stobart, Dir.
Founded: 1908. **Staff:** Prof 1; Other 2. **Subjects:** Wool science, wool textiles, sheep husbandry. **Special Collections:** W.T. Ritch Collection. **Holdings:** 830 books; 275 bound periodical volumes; 9850 bulletins, articles, and reprints; 900 containers of various specimens of animal and other textile fibers. **Subscriptions:** 18 journals and other serials. **Services:** Library open to the public upon request.

★17187★
UNIVERSITY OF WYOMING - COLLEGE OF HUMAN MEDICINE - FAMILY PRACTICE RESIDENCY PROGRAM - LANGE LIBRARY (Med)
1522 East A St. Phone: (307)266-3076
Casper, WY 82601 Lydia Miller, Med.Libn.
Staff: Prof 1. **Subjects:** Medicine - clinical, family practice, behavioral. **Holdings:** 800 books; 300 video cassettes; 675 audio cassettes; 42 slide/tape programs; 16 slide programs. **Subscriptions:** 26 journals and other serials. **Services:** Interlibrary loan; copying; SDI; center open to the public with restrictions on borrowing. **Computerized Information Services:** MEDLARS. **Networks/Consortia:** Member of Muddy Mountain Health Sciences Library Consortium, Health Sciences Information Network (HSIN).

★17188★
UNIVERSITY OF WYOMING - GEOLOGY LIBRARY (Sci-Engr)
S.H. Knight Bldg.
University Station, Box 3006 Phone: (307)766-3374
Laramie, WY 82071 Linda R. Zellmer, Geol. & Maps Libn.
Founded: 1956. **Staff:** Prof 1; Other 6. **Subjects:** Geology, geophysics, paleontology, Wyoming and Rocky mountain geology, remote sensing. **Special Collections:** UMI geology dissertations, 1981 to present (microfiche); Wyoming infrared photographs (58,000); Wyoming Geological Survey publications. **Holdings:** 50,684 books; 11,500 bound periodical volumes; 16,000 government documents; 26,000 maps; 17,520 titles in microform. **Subscriptions:** 629 journals and other serials. **Services:** Interlibrary loan; copying; library open to the public with restrictions. **Automated Operations:** Computerized public access catalog and serials. **Computerized Information Services:** CAS ONLINE, DIALOG Information Services. Performs searches on fee basis. **Networks/Consortia:** Member of Bibliographical Center for Research, Rocky Mountain Region,

Inc. (BCR). **Publications:** Map Projections: Newsletter and Acquisitions List of the University Libraries' Map Collections, quarterly.

★17189★
UNIVERSITY OF WYOMING - LAW LIBRARY (Law)
College of Law
University Sta., Box 3035 Phone: (307)766-2210
Laramie, WY 82071 Catherine Mealey, Law Libn./Prof.
Founded: 1920. **Staff:** Prof 3; Other 5. **Subjects:** Law. **Special Collections:** Blume Collection (Roman law). **Holdings:** 102,430 volumes; 239,955 microfiche. **Subscriptions:** 2710 journals and other serials. **Services:** Interlibrary loan; copying; library open to the public for reference use. **Automated Operations:** Computerized public access catalog and cataloging. **Computerized Information Services:** LEXIS, NEXIS, WESTLAW, DIALOG Information Services, OCLC; internal database. **Networks/Consortia:** Member of Bibliographical Center for Research, Rocky Mountain Region, Inc. (BCR), Northwest Consortium of Law Libraries. **Staff:** Joan Binder, Tech.Serv.Libn.; Marilyn Burman, Ref.Libn..

★17190★
UNIVERSITY OF WYOMING - PETROLEUM HISTORY AND RESEARCH CENTER LIBRARY (Hist)
William Robertson Coe Library
Univ. Sta., Box 3924 Phone: (307)766-4114
Laramie, WY 82071 Dr. Lewis Dabney, Act.Dir.
Founded: 1956. **Subjects:** Petroleum history. **Holdings:** Figures not available. **Services:** Library open to the public.

★17191★
UNIVERSITY OF WYOMING - SCIENCE AND TECHNOLOGY LIBRARY (Sci-Engr)
University Sta., Box 3262 Phone: (307)766-5165
Laramie, WY 82071 Diana W. Shelton, Asst.Dir. of Libs.
Founded: 1970. **Staff:** Prof 6; Other 7. **Subjects:** Natural, physical, and health sciences; engineering; mathematics; agriculture; psychology. **Holdings:** 275,000 volumes; 10,600 reels of microfilm; 144,500 microfiche. **Subscriptions:** 5000 journals. **Services:** Interlibrary loan; copying; library open to the public. **Automated Operations:** Computerized public access catalog and serials. **Computerized Information Services:** DIALOG Information Services, BRS Information Technologies, MEDLARS, CAS ONLINE, WILSONLINE. Performs searches on fee basis. Contact Person: Larry Jansen, 766-6538. **Networks/Consortia:** Member of Bibliographical Center for Research, Rocky Mountain Region, Inc. (BCR). **Remarks:** Houses Wyoming Health Sciences Information Network, representing Region IV in the National Library of Medicine's Biomedical Communications Network. **Staff:** Bonnie Mack, Hd., HSIN; Alice Collins, Hd., Circ.; Tedine Roos, Ref.Libn.; Deborah Dawson, Ref./Coll.Dev.; Gail Chance, Ref..

★17192★
UNIVERSITY OF WYOMING - WATER RESEARCH CENTER - LIBRARY (Sci-Engr)
Laramie, WY 82071 Phone: (307)766-2143
Pam Murdock, Adm.Asst.
Subjects: Water resources, evaporation, snow and ice, conservation, irrigation, water law, river basins and water planning, sanitary and civil engineering. **Special Collections:** U.S. Geological Survey water supply papers relating to Wyoming. **Holdings:** 1000 books; 14,000 reports, articles, reprints. **Services:** Copying; library open to the public for reference use only.

★17193★
UNOCAL CANADA LIMITED - LIBRARY (Sci-Engr)
335 8th Ave., S.W.
P.O. Box 999 Phone: (403)268-0303
Calgary, AB, Canada T2P 2K6 Julie MacInnis, Libn.
Staff: Prof 1. **Subjects:** Geology, geophysics, law. **Holdings:** 1350 books; 325 bound periodical volumes; 1075 Geological Survey of Canada papers; 1050 reprints; 600 miscellaneous provincial papers. **Subscriptions:** 140 journals and other serials. **Services:** Interlibrary loan; copying; library open to employees and other libraries.

★17194★
UNOCAL CORPORATION - CORPORATE PLANNING LIBRARY (Energy, Bus-Fin)
461 S. Boylston, Rm. 1042
Box 7600 Phone: (213)977-7725
Los Angeles, CA 90051 Millie Chong-Dillon, Libn.
Founded: 1974. **Staff:** Prof 1; Other 1. **Subjects:** Petroleum and natural gas industries, business and finance. **Special Collections:** J.S. Herold Oil Industry Comparative Appraisals, 1956 to present; annual reports for major oil companies, 1970 to present. **Holdings:** 1570 books; annual and 10K reports for 1150 companies. **Subscriptions:** 56 journals and other serials; 5 newspapers. **Services:** Interlibrary loan; library not open to the public. **Automated Operations:** Computerized cataloging, acquisitions, and serials. **Computerized Information Services:** DIALOG Information Services, NEXIS, Dow Jones News/Retrieval, I.P. Sharp Associates Limited.

★17195★
UNOCAL CORPORATION - INTERNATIONAL EXPLORATION LIBRARY (Sci-Engr)
1201 W. 5th St. Phone: (213)977-6381
Los Angeles, CA 90017 Mary Stecheson, Lib.Mgr.
Founded: 1960. **Staff:** Prof 1; Other 1. **Subjects:** Geology, petroleum geology, oceanography, geophysics. **Holdings:** 9000 books; 800 bound periodical volumes. **Subscriptions:** 100 journals and other serials. **Services:** Interlibrary loan; library not open to the public. **Automated Operations:** Computerized cataloging, acquisitions, serials, and circulation. **Computerized Information Services:** NEXIS, DIALOG Information Services. **Networks/Consortia:** Member of CLASS.

★17196★
UNOCAL CORPORATION - LIBRARY-FILE ROOM (Sci-Engr)
2323 Knoll Dr.
Box 6176 Phone: (805)656-7600
Ventura, CA 93006 Ruth Neumann, Libn.
Staff: Prof 1. **Subjects:** Geology, geophysics, paleontology. **Holdings:** 620 books; 250 maps; 180 linear feet of company reports; 575 reprints. **Subscriptions:** 10 journals and other serials. **Services:** Library not open to the public.

★17197★
UNOCAL CORPORATION - MOLYCORP, INC. - LIBRARY
Box 54945
Los Angeles, CA 90054
Subjects: Geology, mineralogy, mining, metallurgy. **Holdings:** 3300 books; 200 bound periodical volumes; 19,000 government documents. **Remarks:** Presently inactive.

★17198★
UNOCAL CORPORATION - SCIENCE & TECHNOLOGY DIVISION - TECHNICAL INFORMATION CENTER (Sci-Engr, Energy)
376 S. Valencia Ave. Phone: (714)528-7201
Brea, CA 92621 Barbara J. Orosz, Supv., Tech.Comm.Serv.
Staff: Prof 3; Other 5. **Subjects:** Petroleum technology, chemistry, geosciences, oceanography, physics, chemical engineering, mathematics, agriculture, geology. **Holdings:** 24,000 books; 23,500 bound periodical volumes; 29,000 documents; 18,000 government documents; 35 shelves of maps. **Subscriptions:** 850 journals and other serials. **Services:** Interlibrary loan; copying; center open to students by appointment for reference use only. **Computerized Information Services:** Internal database. **Publications:** List of books and documents, semimonthly - to research center personnel. **Staff:** Gloria Okasako-Oshiro, Sr.Info.Chem.; Robert Powers, Libn..

★17199★
UNUM LIFE INSURANCE CO. - CORPORATE INFORMATION CENTER (Bus-Fin)
2211 Congress St. Phone: (207)780-2347
Portland, ME 04105 Phillip C. Kalloch, Jr., Mgr., Info.Serv.
Founded: 1958. **Staff:** Prof 4; Other 3. **Subjects:** Life and health insurance, management, economics, business. **Special Collections:** Corporate archives; legal library; investments library. **Holdings:** 5000 books; 10 VF drawers. **Subscriptions:** 360 journals and other serials; 10 newspapers. **Services:** Interlibrary loan; center open to the public by appointment. **Automated Operations:** Computerized serials. **Computerized Information Services:** DIALOG Information Services, Pergamon ORBIT InfoLine, Inc., WESTLAW, BRS Information Technologies, VU/TEXT Information Services, LEXIS, NEXIS, Datacenter, Dow Jones News/Retrieval, INVESTEXT, Donnelly Marketing Information Services (DMIS). **Publications:** CIC Review, weekly - for internal distribution only. **Staff:** Sandra Shryock, Sr.Info.Spec.; Ann Madigan, Sr.Info.Spec..

★17200★
UP FRONT DRUG INFORMATION - LIBRARY (Med)
5701 Biscayne Blvd., Suite 602 Phone: (305)757-2566
Miami, FL 33137 James N. Hall, Dir.
Founded: 1973. **Staff:** Prof 3. **Subjects:** Drug information. **Holdings:** 1000 books; 900 unbound periodicals; 12 VF drawers and 100 pamphlet files of

drug information. **Subscriptions:** 27 journals and other serials; 5 newspapers. **Services:** Copying; library open to the public. **Automated Operations:** Computerized cataloging, acquisitions, and serials. **Publications:** Street Pharmacologist, monthly - by subscription; drug abuse brochures. **Staff:** Roman Dominguez, Adm.Dir..

★17201★
UPDATA PUBLICATIONS, INC. - LIBRARY (Publ)
1746 Westwood Blvd. Phone: (213)474-5900
Los Angeles, CA 90024 Susan Rydquist, Libn.
Founded: 1973. **Staff:** Prof 1. **Subjects:** Micropublishing, publishing, optical discs, information retrieval. **Special Collections:** National Advisory Committee for Aeronautics Collection, 1915-1958 (13,914 microfiche); U.S. Bureau of Mines Collection, 1910 to present (15,500 microfiche); Mine Safety and Health (400 microfiche); Central Intelligence Agency (1671 microfiche); U.S. Army Area Handbooks (527 microfiche); U.S. Geological Survey Water Supply Papers (8000 microfiche); U.S. Department of Agriculture (30,000 microfiche); U.S. Bureau of Fisheries (3000 microfiche); U.S. Government Indexes of various departments (400 microfiche). **Holdings:** 2000 books; 76,000 microfiche; 60 reels of microfilm. **Subscriptions:** 40 journals and other serials. **Services:** SDI; library open to the public on request. **Computerized Information Services:** DIALOG Information Services, Pergamon ORBIT InfoLine, Inc.; UPDATALINE (internal database). Performs searches on fee basis. Contact Person: Herbert Sclar, Pres..

★17202★
UPJOHN COMPANY - BUSINESS LIBRARY 88-91 (Bus-Fin, Med)
Kalamazoo, MI 49001 Phone: (616)323-6351
Valerie Noble, Mgr.
Founded: 1960. **Staff:** Prof 1; Other 3. **Subjects:** Business and finance, management and supervision, marketing, microcomputer applications, clinical medicine, pharmaceuticals and drugs. **Holdings:** 5000 books; SRI-BIP reports; annual reports; microfiche; cassettes; IBM PC-compatible software; road maps to major U.S. cities. **Subscriptions:** 250 journals and other serials. **Services:** Interlibrary loan; copying; SDI; library open to the public by appointment. **Automated Operations:** Computerized acquisitions, circulation, and subscriptions systems. **Computerized Information Services:** DIALOG Information Services, BRS Information Technologies, Dow Jones News/Retrieval, OCLC, DataStar, Finsbury Data Services Ltd., Mead Data Central, Dun & Bradstreet Corporation, Nikkei Telecom, WILSONLINE. **Publications:** Monthly List of New Materials. **Special Catalogs:** Selective author-subject catalog, biennial. **Special Indexes:** KWIC index to Corporate Archives. **Staff:** Jan Dommer, Sr.Info.Spec..

★17203★
UPJOHN COMPANY - CORPORATE PATENTS AND TRADEMARKS - LIBRARY (Law)
Unit 1920-32-1
301 Henrietta St. Phone: (616)385-7012
Kalamazoo, MI 49001 Sandra Williams
Founded: 1950. **Staff:** 1. **Subjects:** U.S. patent, trademark, and copyright law; licensing and unfair competition. **Special Collections:** U.S. chemical patents; U.S. Official Gazette (microform). **Holdings:** 2000 books; 1500 bound periodical volumes. **Subscriptions:** 75 journals and other serials. **Services:** Library not open to the public. **Computerized Information Services:** LEXIS, DIALOG Information Services.

★17204★
UPJOHN COMPANY - CORPORATE TECHNICAL LIBRARY (Sci-Engr, Med)
7284-267-21 Phone: (616)385-6414
Kalamazoo, MI 49001 Lorraine Schulte, Dir.
Founded: 1941. **Staff:** Prof 20; Other 21. **Subjects:** Chemistry, biotechnology, biochemistry, pharmacology, biomedical and pharmaceutical sciences, statistics, computer science. **Holdings:** 21,700 books; 53,000 bound periodical volumes. **Subscriptions:** 1600 journals and other serials. **Services:** Current awareness; library open to the public with prior approval. **Automated Operations:** Computerized public access catalog, cataloging, acquisitions, serials, and circulation. **Computerized Information Services:** Library Information System (LIS), DIALOG Information Services, Pergamon ORBIT InfoLine, Inc., BRS Information Technologies, NLM, OCLC, CAS ONLINE, WILSONLINE, Telesystemes Questel, Pergamon ORBIT InfoLine, Inc., Chemical Information Systems, Inc. (CIS); Product Information Retrieval System (PIRSU), Technical Report Electronic Knowledge Base (TREK), TUCO Database (internal databases); OnTyme Electronic Message Network Service (electronic mail service). **Networks/Consortia:** Member of Michigan Library Consortium (MLC), Southwest Michigan Library Cooperative (SMLC). **Publications:** Library Additions, weekly; CTL News, bimonthly; Brief Guide to the Corporate Technical Library, annual; Brief Guide to Using LIS, irregular. **Special Catalogs:** Upjohn Scientific Publications, annual. **Staff:** Ruth C.T. Morris, Hd., Tech.Serv./Lib.Sys.; Dorian Martyn, Tech.Serv.Libn.; Michael Homan, Hd., Info.Serv./Ctrl.Tech.Doc.; Susan Fierke, Info.Spec.; Paula Allred, Info.Spec.; Janet Everitt, Info.Spec.; Rein Virkhaus, Info.Sci.; Geneva Williams, Info.Sci.; James Powell, Info.Sci.; June Slach, Info.Sci.; L. Pauline Sattler, PIRSU Proj.Ldr.; Suzanne Dankert, Coll.Dev.Spec.; Elin Shallcross, Supv., Ctrl.Tech.Doc.; Susan Cooke, Tech.Rpt. Index Spec.; Diane Worden, Info.Spec..

★17205★
UPJOHN COMPANY - MEDICAL LIBRARY SERVICES (Med)
Division of Medical Affairs
9184-243-129 Phone: (616)323-6238
Kalamazoo, MI 49001 Gale G. Hannigan, Mgr.
Founded: 1985. **Staff:** Prof 3; Other 5. **Subjects:** Clinical medicine, drug information, clinical trials. **Holdings:** 700 books; 550 microfilm cartridges. **Subscriptions:** 412 journals and other serials. **Services:** Interlibrary loan; services not open to the public. **Automated Operations:** Computerized public access catalog, serials, and circulation. **Computerized Information Services:** BRS Information Technologies, DIALOG Information Services, Pergamon ORBIT InfoLine, Inc., NLM; Product Information Retrieval Service (internal database). **Publications:** Medical Information Newsletter, monthly - for internal distribution only. **Staff:** Mary Kay Snider, Info.Spec..

UPJOHN LIBRARY
See: Kalamazoo College - Upjohn Library (7327)

UPLANDS FARM ENVIRONMENTAL CENTER
See: Nature Conservancy - Long Island Chapter (9832)

★17206★
UPPER CANADA RAILWAY SOCIETY, INC. - LIBRARY (Trans)
Box 122, Sta. A
Toronto, ON, Canada M5W 1A2
Founded: 1941. **Subjects:** Canadian railways and street railways. **Special Collections:** Canadian, U.S., British, Belgian, and Australian railroad club publications. **Holdings:** Books; maps; timetables; artifacts. **Services:** Library open to the public by prior arrangement.

UPPER CANADA VILLAGE REFERENCE LIBRARY
See: Ontario St. Lawrence Parks Commission (10866)

★17207★
UPPER COLORADO RIVER COMMISSION - LIBRARY (Env-Cons)
355 S. Fourth East St. Phone: (801)531-1150
Salt Lake City, UT 84111 Gerald R. Zimmerman, Exec.Dir.
Staff: 5. **Subjects:** Water and related resource development. **Holdings:** 9000 volumes. **Services:** Library open to the public for reference use only.

★17208★
THE UPPER ROOM - DEVOTIONAL LIBRARY, MUSEUM AND ARCHIVES (Rel-Phil)
1908 Grand Ave.
Box 189 Phone: (615)340-7204
Nashville, TN 37202 Sarah Linn, Libn.
Founded: 1955. **Staff:** Prof 1. **Subjects:** Devotions, prayers, meditations, spiritual formation, hymns, Methodism. **Special Collections:** Original letters of John Wesley (66 items). **Holdings:** 14,000 books; 200 other cataloged items; 150 feet of archival materials of The Upper Room. **Subscriptions:** 50 journals and other serials. **Services:** Library open to the public for reference use only.

★17209★
UPPER SAVANNAH AREA HEALTH EDUCATION CONSORTIUM - LIBRARY (Med)
Self Memorial Hospital
1325 Spring St. Phone: (803)227-4851
Greenwood, SC 29646 Thomas W. Hill, Libn.
Founded: 1977. **Staff:** Prof 1; Other 2. **Subjects:** Medicine. **Holdings:** 1000 books; 800 audio and video cassettes, 16mm films, sound recordings. **Subscriptions:** 154 journals and other serials. **Services:** Interlibrary loan; copying; library open to the public. **Computerized Information Services:** NLM. Performs searches on fee basis. **Networks/Consortia:** Member of South Carolina Health Information Network (SCHIN).

★17210★
UPPER SNAKE RIVER VALLEY HISTORICAL SOCIETY - LIBRARY (Hist)
49 North Center
Box 244
Rexburg, ID 83440 Jerry Glenn, Libn.
Founded: 1965. **Staff:** Prof 1; Other 3. **Subjects:** Idaho history. **Special Collections:** Oral history (300 tapes). **Holdings:** 300 books; 50 tapes; 18 videotapes; 12 maps. **Subscriptions:** 10 journals and other serials. **Services:** Copying; library open to the public by appointment. **Publications:** Snake River Echoes, quarterly.

★17211★
URBAN INSTITUTE - LIBRARY (Soc Sci, Plan)
2100 M St., N.W. Phone: (202)857-8688
Washington, DC 20037 Camille A. Motta, Dir. of Lib./Archv.
Founded: 1968. **Staff:** Prof 2; Other 3. **Subjects:** Public policy and economics, housing and urban development, health policy, public finance, human resources research, productivity and economic development, state and local government policy, income security. **Special Collections:** Urban Institute archival materials. **Holdings:** 28,000 books and documents; 650 periodical titles; 4600 reels of microfilm. **Subscriptions:** 650 journals. **Services:** Interlibrary loan (fee); SDI; library open to the public by appointment. **Automated Operations:** Computerized cataloging. **Computerized Information Services:** DIALOG Information Services, VU/TEXT Information Services, WILSONLINE, MEDLARS, BRS Information Technologies; Urban Institute Publications Database (internal database). Performs searches on fee basis, 857-8686. **Networks/Consortia:** Member of Metropolitan Washington Library Council, Interlibrary Users Association (IUA), CAPCON. **Publications:** Books, Bytes and Bits (acquisitions list), monthly - for internal distribution only; Urban Institute Project Reports and Research Papers - for sale. **Staff:** Catherine Selden, Asst.Dir..

★17212★
URBAN LAND INSTITUTE - LIBRARY (Plan)
1090 Vermont Ave., N.W. Phone: (202)289-3500
Washington, DC 20005 Ann Benson, Libn.
Founded: 1958. **Staff:** Prof 1. **Subjects:** Land use, real estate, urban planning, housing, environment. **Holdings:** 6000 books; U.S. census publications, 1960; ULI publications. **Subscriptions:** 200 journals and other serials. **Services:** Interlibrary loan; copying; library open to the public by appointment.

URBAN MASS TRANSPORTATION ADMINISTRATION
See: U.S. Urban Mass Transportation Administration (15511)

★17213★
URBAN TRANSPORTATION DEVELOPMENT CORPORATION - METRO CANADA LIBRARY (Trans)
Sta. A, Box 70 Phone: (613)384-3100
Kingston, ON, Canada K7M 6P9 Theresa Brennan, Mgr., Rec./Off.Sys.
Founded: 1974. **Staff:** Prof 1; Other 1. **Subjects:** Urban transportation, engineering, marketing, business. **Special Collections:** Engineering standards and specifications (150 items). **Holdings:** 2000 books; 1200 technical reports; 200 documents. **Subscriptions:** 100 journals and other serials. **Services:** Interlibrary loan; library open to the public by appointment with restrictions. **Publications:** Accession List, quarterly; Annual Report.

★17214★
URBANA MUNICIPAL DOCUMENTS CENTER (Soc Sci)
The Urbana Free Library
201 S. Race St. Phone: (217)384-0092
Urbana, IL 61801-3283 Jean E. Koch, Dir.
Founded: 1979. **Staff:** Prof 1; Other 1. **Subjects:** Urbana city government. **Holdings:** 29,242 documents on 10,164 microfiche. **Services:** Copying; center open to the public with restrictions. **Automated Operations:** Computerized indexing. **Special Indexes:** Alphabetical, geographical, numerical, and citation indexes (COM).

★17215★
URBANA UNIVERSITY - SWEDENBORG MEMORIAL LIBRARY - SPECIAL COLLECTIONS (Rel-Phil)
College Way Phone: (513)652-1301
Urbana, OH 43078 Carol Ann Sabella, Dir.
Special Collections: Swedenborgian Collection (2035 titles). **Services:** Copying; collection open to the public. **Automated Operations:** Computerized cataloging. **Networks/Consortia:** Member of Southwest Ohio Council for Higher Education (SOCHE), OHIONET. **Staff:** Jeanne Gamble, Hd., Cat.; Jennifer Midgley, Circ.Supv..

URIS LIBRARY AND RESOURCE CENTER
See: Metropolitan Museum of Art (8829)

★17216★
URS CONSULTANTS - RESOURCE CENTER (Art, Sci-Engr)
3605 Warrensville Center Rd. Phone: (216)283-4000
Cleveland, OH 44122 Cheryl L. Spahr, Mgr.
Staff: Prof 1; Other 2. **Subjects:** Architecture, engineering, interior design, environment. **Special Collections:** Structural, civil, electrical, mechanical, and environmental engineering; health care. **Holdings:** 5720 books; 50 bound periodical volumes; 15 file cabinets of internal proposals and reports; blueprints on microfiche. **Subscriptions:** 122 journals and other serials. **Services:** Interlibrary loan; copying; center open to the public through ILL. **Automated Operations:** Computerized cataloging, acquisitions, serials, and circulation. **Computerized Information Services:** Mapper (internal database). **Networks/Consortia:** Member of OHIONET. **Formerly:** URS Dalton.

★17217★
URSINUS COLLEGE - MYRIN LIBRARY - SPECIAL COLLECTIONS (Area-Ethnic)
Collegeville, PA 19426-9989 Phone: (215)489-4111
Subjects: Pennsylvania German culture; German Reformed Church; Francis Mairs Huntington Wilson diplomatic papers, 1897-1913. **Holdings:** 179,500 manuscripts; photographs; oral histories; videotapes. **Services:** Copying; collections open to the public.

★17218★
US WEST COMMUNICATIONS - LEARNING SYSTEMS LIBRARY (Info Sci)
1005 17th St., Rm. 330
Box 1976 Phone: (303)896-4607
Denver, CO 80201-1976 Ellis B. McFadden, Data Adm.
Founded: 1953. **Staff:** Prof 1; Other 1. **Subjects:** Communications, management and economics. **Holdings:** 8000 books; 500 bound periodical volumes; pamphlets; Bell Laboratory records; Bell technical journals; maps. **Subscriptions:** 84 journals and other serials. **Services:** Interlibrary loan; library open to the public for reference use only. **Computerized Information Services:** DIALOG Information Services.

★17219★
USAFIC INTERNATIONAL - LIBRARY (Law)
Box 136
Wyncote, PA 19095 Phone: (215)657-3976
Founded: 1975. **Subjects:** Security, law enforcement, firearms education and training. **Holdings:** 400 volumes. **Services:** Library open to researchers and other approved users.

★17220★
USG CORPORATION - BUSINESS LIBRARY (Sci-Engr)
101 S. Wacker Dr. Phone: (312)606-5810
Chicago, IL 60606 Suzanne Gerrity, Corp.Libn.
Staff: Prof 1; Other 2. **Subjects:** Business, building and construction, architecture. **Holdings:** 1550 books; 30 VF drawers. **Subscriptions:** 200 journals and other serials; 5 newspapers. **Services:** Interlibrary loan; copying; SDI; library open to the public by appointment. **Automated Operations:** Computerized cataloging. **Computerized Information Services:** DIALOG Information Services, LEXIS, NEXIS, VU/TEXT Information Services, Dow Jones News/Retrieval. **Networks/Consortia:** Member of ILLINET, Chicago Library System. **Publications:** Off-the-Shelf, quarterly - for internal distribution only.

★17221★
USG CORPORATION - GRAHAM J. MORGAN RESEARCH LIBRARY (Sci-Engr)
700 N. Hwy. 45 Phone: (312)362-9797
Libertyville, IL 60048 Sylvia Beardsley, Res.Libn.
Founded: 1961. **Staff:** Prof 2; Other 2. **Subjects:** Building materials, gypsum products, engineering, plastics and adhesives, lime, coatings, chemistry, mineral fibers, paper, fertilizers, acoustical products. **Holdings:** 5483 books; 2452 bound periodical volumes; 1619 pamphlets; 32,700 laboratory reports; 987 reels of microfilm; 970 microfiche; 15 VF drawers of unbound reports, articles, documents. **Subscriptions:** 381 journals and other serials. **Services:** Library open to the public with the approval of the director of research. **Automated Operations:** Computerized serials. **Computerized Information Services:** DIALOG Information Services, NERAC, Inc., CAS ONLINE; IRMAS (internal database). **Networks/**

Consortia: Member of North Suburban Library System (NSLS). **Publications:** For Your Information, monthly - for internal distribution only. **Special Indexes:** Gypsum references (computerized).

★17222★
USI CHEMICALS COMPANY - CRL LIBRARY (Sci-Engr)
1275 Section Rd. Phone: (513)761-4130
Cincinnati, OH 45222-1809 Michelle M. Rudy, Tech.Libn.
Staff: Prof 1. **Subjects:** Organometallic chemistry, catalysis, polymers and polymerization. **Holdings:** 5100 books; 7300 bound periodical volumes; U.S. chemical patents, 1966 to present, in microform. **Subscriptions:** 165 journals and other serials; 10 newspapers. **Services:** Interlibrary loan; library not open to the public. **Automated Operations:** Computerized serials. **Computerized Information Services:** DIALOG Information Services, Pergamon ORBIT InfoLine, Inc., CAS ONLINE. **Publications:** New Acquisitions, monthly - for internal distribution only; Journals Holdings List - free to requesting libraries. **Remarks:** USI Chemicals Company is a subsidiary of Quantum Chemical Corporation. **Formerly:** U.S. Industrial Chemicals Company - Research Department Library.

USI CHEMICALS CO. - ENRON CHEMICAL COMPANY
See: Quantum Chemical Corporation - USI Division (11754)

★17223★
USX CORPORATION - MARATHON OIL COMPANY - EXPLORATION AND PRODUCTION TECHNOLOGY - TECHNICAL INFORMATION LIBRARY (Energy)
Box 269 Phone: (303)794-2601
Littleton, CO 80160 Clarence A. Sturdivant, Supv.
Founded: 1956. **Staff:** Prof 4; Other 1. **Subjects:** Petroleum - exploration, refining, production, transportation, conservation. **Holdings:** 15,000 books; 20,000 bound periodical volumes; 40,000 hardcopy and microfiche technical reports, dissertations, meeting papers; 20,000 patents; 10,000 maps and charts. **Subscriptions:** 750 journals and other serials; 10 newspapers. **Services:** Library not open to the public. **Automated Operations:** Computerized cataloging and serials. **Computerized Information Services:** RLIN, OCLC. **Special Catalogs:** Catalog for books, maps, and technical reports (online). **Formerly:** Marathon Oil Company - Exploration and Production Technology Library.

★17224★
USX CORPORATION - MARATHON OIL COMPANY - LAW LIBRARY (Law, Energy)
539 S. Main St., Rm. 854-M Phone: (419)422-2121
Findlay, OH 45840 Connie S. Whipple, Law Libn.
Staff: Prof 1; Other 1. **Subjects:** Law, petroleum industry. **Holdings:** 19,300 books; 16 drawers of microfiche; 16 drawers of microfilm. **Subscriptions:** 250 journals and other serials. **Services:** Interlibrary loan; copying; library open to the public by permission. **Computerized Information Services:** LEXIS.

★17225★
USX CORPORATION - USS DIVISION - INFORMATION RESOURCE CENTER (Sci-Engr)
4000 Tech Center Dr.
MS 88 Phone: (412)825-2344
Monroeville, PA 15146 Angela R. Pollis, Staff Supv.
Founded: 1928. **Staff:** Prof 3; Other 1. **Subjects:** Metallurgy, materials science, steel manufacture and finishing, chemistry and physics, coal and coke technology, physical chemistry, business. **Holdings:** 25,000 books; 1500 dissertations; 30,000 translations; 10,000 government and university reports; U.S. patents and chemical abstracts on microfilm. **Subscriptions:** 400 journals and other serials; 5 newspapers. **Services:** Interlibrary loan; center not open to the public. **Automated Operations:** Computerized cataloging and serials. **Computerized Information Services:** DIALOG Information Services, NEXIS, Dow Jones News/Retrieval, Dun & Bradstreet Corporation, Inforonics, Inc.; internal database. Performs searches on fee basis. **Publications:** Newsletter, monthly. **Special Indexes:** KWIC and KWOC listings of technical reports. **Remarks:** An alternate telephone number is 825-2345. **Staff:** L.W. Berger, Sr.Info.Spec.; J.A. Richardson, Info.Spec..

★17226★
UTAH FIELD HOUSE OF NATURAL HISTORY STATE PARK - REFERENCE LIBRARY (Biol Sci, Sci-Engr)
235 E. Main St. Phone: (801)789-3799
Vernal, UT 84078 Alden H. Hamblin, Park Mgr.
Founded: 1948. **Staff:** Prof 3; Other 3. **Subjects:** Natural history, geology, paleontology, archeology. **Holdings:** 4000 books. **Services:** Library open to the public.

★17227★
UTAH STATE ARCHIVES (Hist)
Archives Bldg.
State Capitol
Salt Lake City, UT 84114 Phone: (801)533-5250
Founded: 1951. **Staff:** Prof 11; Other 29. **Subjects:** Public records of the State of Utah and its political subdivisions. **Special Collections:** Military burial records. **Holdings:** 60,000 cubic feet of semi-active and historically valuable records; 60,000 cubic feet of records in paper copy; 68,000 reels of microfilm; 90,000 microfiche. **Services:** Copying; archives open to the public. **Computerized Information Services:** RLIN. **Publications:** Records Retention Schedule; Guide to Official Records of Genealogical Value in the State of Utah. **Special Catalogs:** Preliminary Inventory of County Microfilm (microfiche); Inventory - Military Department, Record Group 027. **Staff:** Loretta L. Hefner, Bur.Archv./Rec.Anl.; Jeffery O. Johnson, Bur.Archv./Ref..

★17228★
UTAH STATE BOARD OF EDUCATION - TECHNOLOGY ASSISTANCE CENTER (Educ, Comp Sci)
250 E. Fifth, S. Phone: (801)533-4774
Salt Lake City, UT 84111 Robert Ives, Dir.
Staff: Prof 6; Other 12. **Subjects:** All school subjects. **Special Collections:** ERIC collection; public domain software. **Holdings:** 30,000 software titles. **Services:** Interlibrary loan; copying; SDI; center open to the public. **Computerized Information Services:** CompuServe, Inc., DIALOG Information Services, BRS Information Technologies, Pergamon ORBIT InfoLine, Inc., Dow Jones News/Retrieval; Project Resources (internal database); electronic mail service. **Remarks:** The center tests and evaluates software and hardware and provides training for state educators.

UTAH STATE DEPARTMENT OF NATURAL RESOURCES AND ENERGY - UTAH STATE GEOLOGICAL AND MINERAL SURVEY
See: Utah State Geological and Mineral Survey (17230)

★17229★
UTAH STATE DEPARTMENT OF SOCIAL SERVICES - ALCOHOLISM AND DRUG DIVISION - LIBRARY (Med)
Box 45500 Phone: (801)533-6532
Salt Lake City, UT 84145-0500 Launi Snyder
Subjects: Alcoholism, drug abuse. **Holdings:** 2600 books. **Remarks:** Library located at 150 West North Temple, Salt Lake City, UT 84103-1594.

★17230★
UTAH STATE GEOLOGICAL AND MINERAL SURVEY - LIBRARY (Sci-Engr)
606 Black Hawk Way Phone: (801)581-6831
Salt Lake City, UT 84108 Mage Yonetani, Libn.
Subjects: Geology, mineral deposits. **Holdings:** 5000 books. **Remarks:** Maintained by Utah State Department of Natural Resources and Energy.

★17231★
UTAH STATE HISTORICAL SOCIETY - RESEARCH LIBRARY (Hist)
300 Rio Grande Phone: (801)533-5808
Salt Lake City, UT 84101 Jay M. Haymond, Libn.
Founded: 1952. **Staff:** Prof 5; Other 1. **Subjects:** History - Utah, Mormon, Western. **Special Collections:** Utah water records (200 linear feet); Works Progress Administration records (124 linear feet). **Holdings:** 23,000 books; 18,000 bound periodical volumes; 300,000 photographs; 22,000 pamphlets; 30,000 maps; 1500 oral history tapes; 3500 linear feet of manuscripts; 5000 reels of microfilm; 160 feet of clippings files. **Subscriptions:** 220 journals and other serials. **Services:** Copying; library open to the public. **Automated Operations:** Computerized cataloging. **Computerized Information Services:** OCLC; internal database. **Publications:** Guide to Unpublished Materials; Guide to the Women's History Holdings at the USHS Library. **Special Indexes:** Utah History Index (card). **Staff:** Linda Thatcher, Acq. & Ref.Libn.; Gary Topping, Mss.Cur.; Susan Mortenson, Map & Photo.Libn..

★17232★
UTAH STATE HOSPITAL - LIBRARY (Med)
1300 East Center St.
Box 270 Phone: (801)373-4400
Provo, UT 84601 Janina Chilton, Libn.
Staff: Prof 1. **Subjects:** Medicine, psychology. **Holdings:** 900 volumes; records; tapes. **Subscriptions:** 54 journals and other serials. **Services:** Library not open to the public. **Computerized Information Services:**

DIALOG Information Services. **Remarks:** Maintains a patients' collection of 1500 volumes and 14 journal subscriptions.

★17233★
UTAH STATE LAW LIBRARY (Law)
125 State Capitol Bldg. Phone: (801)538-1045
Salt Lake City, UT 84114 Russell E. Van Allen, Law Libn.
Staff: Prof 1; Other 2. **Subjects:** Law. **Holdings:** 42,000 volumes.

★17234★
UTAH STATE LEGISLATURE - OFFICE OF LEGISLATIVE RESEARCH AND GENERAL COUNSEL - INFORMATION CENTER (Law)
436 State Capitol Phone: (801)538-1032
Salt Lake City, UT 84114 Jane A. Peterson, Info.Coord.
Subjects: State legislature, state and local government. **Holdings:** 3000 books. **Subscriptions:** 82 journals and other serials. **Services:** Center open to the public. **Automated Operations:** Computerized public access catalog and cataloging. **Computerized Information Services:** DIALOG Information Services, WESTLAW, LEGISNET; Utah Code (internal database). **Staff:** Sarah Gray, Pub.Info.Spec..

★17235★
UTAH STATE LIBRARY (Info Sci)
2150 South 300 West, Suite 16 Phone: (801)466-5888
Salt Lake City, UT 84115 Amy Owen, Dir.
Founded: 1957. **Staff:** Prof 15; Other 20. **Subjects:** State and federal government. **Holdings:** 36,284 volumes; 49,486 federal documents; 23,982 state documents. **Subscriptions:** 105 journals and other serials. **Services:** Interlibrary loan; copying; library open to the public with restrictions. **Automated Operations:** Computerized cataloging and acquisitions. **Computerized Information Services:** DIALOG Information Services, Pergamon ORBIT InfoLine, Inc., BRS Information Technologies, The Reference Service (REFSRV). **Networks/Consortia:** Member of Bibliographical Center for Research, Rocky Mountain Region, Inc. (BCR). **Publications:** Horsefeathers, monthly - free upon request; Utah Undercover, annual; Directory of Public Libraries in Utah, annual; Annual Report. **Staff:** Douglas Abrams, Dp.Dir.; Gerald Buttars, Dp.Dir.; Edith Blankenship, Prog.Dir., Info.Serv..

★17236★
UTAH STATE LIBRARY - BLIND AND PHYSICALLY HANDICAPPED PROGRAM - REGIONAL LIBRARY (Aud-Vis)
2150 South 300 West, Suite 16 Phone: (801)533-5855
Salt Lake City, UT 84115 Gerald A. Buttars, Prog.Dir.
Founded: 1934. **Staff:** Prof 6; Other 10. **Holdings:** 384,771 talking books and braille books; cassettes; open reel tapes; large print books. **Subscriptions:** 120 journals and other serials. **Services:** Interlibrary loan; copying; radio reading service; library open to blind and physically handicapped. **Automated Operations:** Computerized circulation. **Networks/Consortia:** Member of National Library Service for the Blind & Physically Handicapped (NLS). **Publications:** The Ensign, monthly. **Remarks:** This Regional Library for the Blind is the Multi-State Center for 16 Western states. **Staff:** Karnell Parry, Multi-State Libn.; Michael Sweeney, Circ.Libn.; Bessie Oakes, Braille Libn.; Rex Wallgren, Radio Prog.Mgr.; Bob Wall, Radio Prog..

★17237★
UTAH STATE UNIVERSITY - DEVELOPMENTAL CENTER FOR HANDICAPPED PERSONS - PARENT RESOURCE LIBRARY (Educ)
UMC 68 Phone: (801)752-0238
Logan, UT 84332 Julia Burnham, Lib.Coord.
Founded: 1972. **Subjects:** Parent resources about handicapping conditions and training of the handicapped. **Holdings:** 900 volumes.

★17238★
UTAH VALLEY REGIONAL MEDICAL CENTER - MEDICAL LIBRARY (Med)
1034 N. 500 W. Phone: (801)373-7850
Provo, UT 84603 Gregory R. Patterson, Dir.
Staff: Prof 2. **Subjects:** Medicine. **Special Collections:** Pediatrics (500 books); history of medicine, 1870-1975. **Holdings:** 3400 books; 110,000 bound periodical volumes; 3 drawers of manuscripts; 88 drawers of microfilm and microfiche. **Subscriptions:** 1225 journals and other serials; 15 newspapers. **Services:** Interlibrary loan; copying; library open to the public. **Automated Operations:** Computerized cataloging, serials, and circulation. **Computerized Information Services:** MEDLINE, DIALOG Information Services, INFONET; DOCLINE (electronic mail service). Performs searches on fee basis. **Networks/Consortia:** Member of Midcontinental Regional Medical Library Program, Utah Health Sciences Library Consortium, Health Sciences Consortium. **Publications:** Exchange List; Excess Journal List - both free upon request. **Staff:** Alan Grosbeck, Media Spec..

★17239★
UTAH WATER RESEARCH LABORATORY - LIBRARY (Sci-Engr)
Utah State University Phone: (801)752-4100
Logan, UT 84322-8200 Clarice W. Reese, Asst.Libn.
Founded: 1965. **Staff:** Prof 1; Other 2. **Subjects:** Water resources planning, water quality, hydrology, hydraulics. **Special Collections:** UWRL Project Report Series, occasional papers, and proceedings. **Holdings:** 25,000 books. **Subscriptions:** 11 journals and other serials; 6 newspapers. **Services:** Interlibrary loan; copying; library open to the public. **Special Catalogs:** Special catalog of UWRL publications.

★17240★
UTICA MUTUAL INSURANCE COMPANY - RESOURCE CENTER (Bus-Fin)
180 Genesee St. Phone: (315)735-3321
New Hartford, NY 13413 Brenda Krol, Rsrc.Coord.
Staff: Prof 1. **Subjects:** Law, insurance, business management, history. **Holdings:** 9200 books. **Subscriptions:** 89 journals and other serials. **Services:** Interlibrary loan; copying; center open to the public with approval. **Automated Operations:** Computerized cataloging. **Computerized Information Services:** DIALOG Information Services; internal database.

★17241★
(Utica) OBSERVER DISPATCH - LIBRARY (Publ)
221-3 Oriskany Plaza Phone: (315)792-5000
Utica, NY 13501 Virginia Malecki, Libn.
Founded: 1922. **Staff:** 1. **Subjects:** Newspaper reference topics. **Holdings:** 172 VF drawers of clippings; microfilm, 1952 to present. **Services:** Library open to scholars and journalists with permission from executive editor.

V

★17242★
VALDEZ HISTORICAL SOCIETY, INC. N-P - VALDEZ HERITAGE ARCHIVES ALIVE (Hist)
Royal Center Egan Drive
Box 6 Phone: (907)835-4367
Valdez, AK 99686 Dorothy I. Clifton, Dir.
Founded: 1959. **Staff:** 2. **Subjects:** Alaska, Valdez, poetry, philately, religion. **Holdings:** 3300 square feet of archival materials; films; slides. **Services:** Copying; free film and slide showings; archives open to the public.

OTHON O. VALENT LEARNING RESOURCES CENTER
See: U.S. Army - TRADOC - Sergeants Major Academy (14806)

CURT VALENTIN ARCHIVE
See: Museum of Modern Art - Department of Rights and Reproductions - Photographic Archives (9451)

H.A. VALENTINE MEMORIAL LIBRARY
See: High Street Christian Church (6283)

★17243★
VALENTINE MUSEUM - LIBRARY (Hist)
1015 E. Clay St.
Richmond, VA 23219 Phone: (804)649-0711
Staff: Prof 2. **Subjects:** Life and history of Richmond, fine arts and photography. **Special Collections:** Cook Collection of Photographs (10,000); advertising (chromolithographs, especially tobacco); Hibb's Collection (580 prints); rare book collection (includes parts of the libraries of John Wickham and Valentine family members); manuscripts collection (personal and business papers of Richmond, 1760 to present; papers of the Valentine family, 1786-1920; papers of William James Hubard, artist, 1807-1862; papers of Daniel Call, lawyer, 1772-1844; records of the Richmond Exchange for Women's Work, 1883-1952; minute books of the Richmond Chamber of Commerce, 1867-1980; serials collection (19th century Richmond imprints; 250 volumes); Richmond City directories; Richmond City and Henrico county maps (200); theater collection (19th and 20th century playbills; 100 broadsides); ephemera collection (programs; holiday cards; invitations; miscellaneous printed material); correspondence of Edgar Allan Poe, James Chaffin, and others. **Holdings:** 7000 books; 104 bound periodical volumes; 32 VF drawers; 300 bound volumes of manuscripts; 70 major manuscript collections; 40,000 photographs. **Subscriptions:** 10 journals and other serials. **Services:** Copying; library open to the public by appointment. **Staff:** Gregg Kimball, Cur.; Lacy Dick, Supv., Reading Rm..

★17244★
VALERO ENERGY CORPORATION - CORPORATE RESOURCE CENTER (Energy)
530 McCullough
Box 500 Phone: (512)246-2869
San Antonio, TX 78292 Judith L. Anilosky, Supv.
Staff: Prof 2; Other 3. **Subjects:** Natural gas, petroleum refining, exploration, management, business. **Holdings:** 3000 books; 1000 bound periodical volumes; 1000 reports on microfiche; 45 VF drawers. **Subscriptions:** 354 journals and other serials. **Services:** Interlibrary loan; copying; SDI; library open to the public by appointment. **Automated Operations:** Computerized cataloging and serials. **Computerized Information Services:** DIALOG Information Services, Pergamon ORBIT InfoLine, Inc., BRS Information Technologies, Dow Jones News/Retrieval, APILIT, Petroleum Abstracts Information Services (PAIS). **Networks/Consortia:** Member of Council of Research & Academic Libraries (CORAL). **Publications:** Newsletter, monthly - for internal distribution only. **Special Indexes:** Geology holdings; serials list; oil field index (all printouts).

★17245★
VALLEJO NAVAL AND HISTORICAL MUSEUM - LIBRARY (Hist)
734 Marin St. Phone: (707)643-0077
Vallejo, CA 94590 Dorothy E. Marsden, Libn.
Founded: 1980. **Staff:** Prof 1. **Subjects:** Local history; maritime history - general and of the Bay Area; Mare Island Naval Shipyard; naval philately. **Holdings:** 5000 books; Solano County Articles of Incorporation, 1852-1958; marriage records, 1895-1977; wills, 1856-1922; Solano County Historical Society notebooks; 3000 photographs. **Services:** Library open to the public by appointment. **Networks/Consortia:** Member of Bay Area Reference Center (BARC).

★17246★
VALLEY DAILY NEWS - LIBRARY (Publ)
600 S. Washington St.
Box 130 Phone: (206)872-6674
Kent, WA 98031 Frances Wright, Libn.
Founded: 1970. **Staff:** 1. **Subjects:** Newspaper reference topics. **Special Collections:** Bound volumes of Daily Record Chronicle, Daily News Journal, Daily Globe News, and their predecessors. **Holdings:** Books; microfilm; newspaper clippings; news photos; government documents; maps. **Subscriptions:** 6 newspapers. **Services:** Library not open to the public.

★17247★
VALLEY FORGE CHRISTIAN COLLEGE - LIBRARY (Rel-Phil)
Phoenixville, PA 19460 Phone: (215)935-0450
Dorsey Reynolds, Libn.
Staff: Prof 1; Other 2. **Subjects:** Bible, theology (emphasis on Evangelical and Pentecostal doctrines), church history, Christian education. **Special Collections:** Pentecostalism. **Holdings:** 39,065 books. **Subscriptions:** 260 journals and other serials. **Services:** Interlibrary loan; copying; library open to the public.

★17248★
VALLEY FORGE HISTORICAL SOCIETY - WASHINGTON MEMORIAL LIBRARY (Hist)
Box 122
Valley Forge, PA 19481 Phone: (215)783-0535
Founded: 1918. **Staff:** Prof 1; Other 1. **Subjects:** Revolutionary War, Washingtoniana, American history. **Special Collections:** Writings of Washington; Pennsylvania archives; Library of Reverend Andrew Hunter, Chaplain in Continental Army. **Holdings:** 2000 books; 300 manuscripts. **Services:** Library open to the public by appointment.

★17249★
VALLEY HOSPITAL - MEDICAL LIBRARY (Med)
Linwood & N. Van Dien Aves. Phone: (201)447-8285
Ridgewood, NJ 07451 Claudia Allocco, Dir., Lib.Serv.
Founded: 1963. **Staff:** Prof 1; Other 2. **Subjects:** Medicine, nursing, hospital management, allied health sciences. **Holdings:** 1000 books; 3000 bound periodical volumes; 2 VF drawers of pamphlets. **Subscriptions:** 160 journals and other serials. **Services:** Interlibrary loan; library not open to the public. **Computerized Information Services:** MEDLARS. Performs searches on fee basis. **Networks/Consortia:** Member of Bergen-Passaic Health Sciences Library Consortium.

★17250★
VALLEY MEDICAL CENTER - LIBRARY (Med)
400 S. 43rd St.
Renton, WA 98055 Phone: (206)251-5194
Founded: 1969. **Staff:** Prof 1. **Subjects:** Medicine, surgery, allied health sciences. **Holdings:** 1050 books; 200 bound periodical volumes. **Subscriptions:** 200 journals and other serials; 5 newspapers. **Services:** Interlibrary loan. **Computerized Information Services:** MEDLINE, DIALOG Information Services. **Networks/Consortia:** Member of Seattle Area Hospital Library Consortium (SAHLC). **Publications:** Library News, quarterly. **Staff:** Teresa Y. Lu, Libn.; Lynne B. Graber, Libn..

★17251★
VALLEY MEDICAL CENTER OF FRESNO - MEDICAL LIBRARY (Med)
445 S. Cedar Ave. Phone: (209)453-5030
Fresno, CA 93702 Vicky Christianson, Hosp.Libn.
Staff: Prof 1; Other 1. **Subjects:** Medicine, dentistry, nursing, hospital administration. **Holdings:** 5000 volumes. **Subscriptions:** 150 journals and other serials. **Services:** Interlibrary loan; copying; library open to the public with restrictions.

★17252★
VALLEY NATIONAL BANK - LIBRARY/INFORMATION CENTER (Bus-Fin)
Box 71, A-315 Phone: (602)261-2456
Phoenix, AZ 85001 J.F. Gorman, Mgr.
Founded: 1948. **Staff:** Prof 1. **Subjects:** Banking, business, economics, management. **Holdings:** 1000 volumes. **Subscriptions:** 250 journals and other serials. **Services:** Library not open to the public. **Computerized**

Information Services: DIALOG Information Services, VU/TEXT Information Services, Dow Jones News/Retrieval.

★17253★
VALLEY PRESBYTERIAN HOSPITAL - RICHARD O. MYERS LIBRARY (Med)
15107 Vanowen St.
Box 9102 Phone: (818)902-2973
Van Nuys, CA 91409-9102 Francine Kubrin, Dir.Lib.Serv.
Founded: 1959. **Staff:** Prof 1; Other 1. **Subjects:** General medicine, general surgery, nursing, hospital administration. **Holdings:** 5000 volumes; 500 audio cassettes; 1 VF drawer of pamphlets, bibliographies, and reprints; 1 VF drawer of AV catalogs. **Subscriptions:** 365 journals and other serials. **Services:** Interlibrary loan; library not open to the public. **Computerized Information Services:** MEDLINE, BRS Information Technologies.

★17254★
VALPARAISO UNIVERSITY - LAW LIBRARY (Law)
School of Law Phone: (219)465-7838
Valparaiso, IN 46383 Mary G. Persyn, Law Libn.
Founded: 1879. **Staff:** Prof 5; Other 6. **Subjects:** Law. **Special Collections:** Indiana Supreme Court and Court of Appeals briefs, 1977 to present. **Holdings:** 90,627 books; 6000 bound periodical volumes; 75,000 volumes in microform; CIS legislative histories, 1974 to present, on microfiche; Supreme Court records and briefs, 1978 to present, on microfiche. **Subscriptions:** 2541 journals and other serials. **Services:** Interlibrary loan; copying; library open to lawyers. **Automated Operations:** Computerized cataloging. **Computerized Information Services:** LEXIS, WESTLAW, DIALOG Information Services, VU/TEXT Information Services, ELSS (Electronic Legislative Search System), LegalTrac; ABA/net (electronic mail service). **Networks/Consortia:** Member of INCOLSA, CLASS. **Staff:** Sally Holterhoff, Doc.Libn.; Tim Watts, Ref.Libn.; Rich Mills, Asst. Law Libn.; Naomi Goodman, Ref.Libn..

★17255★
VALUATION RESEARCH CORPORATION - CORPORATE RESEARCH AND REFERENCE LIBRARY (Bus-Fin)
411 E. Wisconsin Ave. Phone: (414)271-8662
Milwaukee, WI 53202 Don F. Schwamb, Corp.Libn.
Staff: Prof 1; Other 2. **Subjects:** Appraisal/valuation, property assessment, real estate, accounting, taxation, industrial technology. **Special Collections:** Price indexes; machinery and equipment pricing files; real estate transactions; financial statements of corporations. **Holdings:** 2500 books; 200 bound periodical volumes; catalogs and price lists; annual and 10K reports for over 3500 firms. **Subscriptions:** 100 journals and other serials. **Services:** Interlibrary loan; copying; library open to the public with restrictions. **Automated Operations:** Computerized cataloging. **Networks/Consortia:** Member of Library Council of Metropolitan Milwaukee, Inc. (LCOMM).

★17256★
VALUE LINE INC. - LIBRARY (Bus-Fin)
711 Third Ave., 8th Fl. Phone: (212)687-3965
New York, NY 10017 Kathleen Clancy, Hd.Libn./Dept.Mgr.
Staff: Prof 1; Other 4. **Subjects:** Finance and economics. **Holdings:** Figures not available. **Subscriptions:** 200 journals and other serials. **Services:** Information provided by written request only; library not open to the public. **Automated Operations:** Computerized circulation. **Formerly:** Arnold Bernhard and Company, Inc. - Business Library.

★17257★
VALVE MANUFACTURERS ASSOCIATION OF AMERICA - LIBRARY (Sci-Engr)
1050 17th St., N.W., Suite 701 Phone: (202)331-8105
Washington, DC 20036 Malcolm E. O'Hagan, Pres.
Subjects: Industrial and distribution valves, actuators. **Holdings:** 300 volumes of technical and industrial data.

VAN EVERA LIBRARY
See: Human Resources Research Organization (6590)

VAN GORDEN-WILLIAMS LIBRARY
See: Museum of Our National Heritage (9461)

★17258★
VAN HORNESVILLE COMMUNITY CORPORATION - LIBRARY (Hist)
Box 15 Phone: (315)858-0030
Van Hornesville, NY 13475 Josephine Young Case, Pres.
Subjects: Local and regional New York State history. **Holdings:** Books; rare maps. **Services:** Copying; library open to graduate students holding letters of recommendation. **Remarks:** Owen D. Young Collection transferred to St. Lawrence University - Owen D. Young Library.

ROBERT W. VAN HOUTEN LIBRARY
See: New Jersey Institute of Technology (9960)

VAN NOORD HEALTH SCIENCES LIBRARY
See: Pine Rest Christian Hospital (11347)

VAN NOY LIBRARY
See: U.S. Army Post - Fort Belvoir (14843)

JOHN VAN OOSTEN LIBRARY
See: U.S. Fish & Wildlife Service - National Fisheries Research Center - Great Lakes (15082)

JOHN VAN PUFFELEN LIBRARY
See: Appalachian Bible College (821)

VAN STEENBERG LEARNING RESOURCE CENTER
See: Kendall College of Art & Design (7399)

E.A. VAN STEENWYK MEMORIAL LIBRARY
See: Blue Cross of Greater Philadelphia (1666)

JAMES D. VAN TRUMP LIBRARY
See: Pittsburgh History & Landmarks Foundation (11367)

JOSSELYN VAN TYNE MEMORIAL LIBRARY
See: Wilson Ornithological Society (17912)

VAN VOORHIS LIBRARY
See: Poetry Society of America (11413)

JARED VAN WAGENEN, JR. LEARNING RESOURCE CENTER
See: SUNY (13758)

★17259★
VAN WERT COUNTY LAW LIBRARY (Law)
Court of Common Pleas, 3rd Fl. Phone: (419)238-6935
Van Wert, OH 45891 Richard L. Atwood, Sec./Treas.
Staff: 1. **Subjects:** Law. **Holdings:** 14,000 volumes; Ohio law publications. **Services:** Library open to members of the bar.

★17260★
VAN WYCK HOMESTEAD MUSEUM - LIBRARY (Hist)
Rte. 9, Box 133 Phone: (914)896-9560
Fishkill, NY 12524 Ruth B. Polhill, Libn.
Founded: 1973. **Staff:** Prof 1. **Subjects:** Local and American history, early American crafts, genealogy, American Indian, biography. **Special Collections:** Holland Society of New York yearbooks, 1888-1931. **Holdings:** 700 books; 80 bound periodical volumes; 100 early military documents; clippings and early local newspapers; early business ledgers and schoolbooks. **Services:** Interlibrary loan; library open to the public for research. **Publications:** Newsletter, monthly. **Remarks:** Maintained by Fishkill Historical Society, Inc.

JAMES E. VAN ZANDT MEDICAL CENTER
See: U.S. Veterans Administration (PA-Altoona) (15630)

★17261★
VANCOUVER ART GALLERY - LIBRARY (Art)
750 Hornby St. Phone: (604)682-4668
Vancouver, BC, Canada V6Z 2H7 Cheryl A. Siegel, Libn.
Founded: 1931. **Staff:** Prof 1; Other 1. **Subjects:** Painting, sculpture, prints, drawings. **Special Collections:** Canadian exhibition catalogs, artists files, and museum collection catalogs. **Holdings:** 8900 books; 500 bound periodical volumes; 14,500 exhibition catalogs. **Subscriptions:** 125 journals and other serials. **Services:** Interlibrary loan; copying; library open to the public for reference use only. **Publications:** Members Calendar; annual report. **Special Catalogs:** Checklist of biographical files (Canadian artists and artists working in Canada); artists exhibiting at the Vancouver Art Gallery.

★17262★
VANCOUVER BOARD OF TRADE/WORLD TRADE CENTRE VANCOUVER - INFORMATION SERVICES DEPARTMENT (Bus-Fin)
999 Canada Place, Suite 400 Phone: (604)681-2111
Vancouver, BC, Canada V6E 3C1 Karen Marotz, Info.Serv.Mgr.
Staff: Prof 1; Other 1. **Subjects:** Business, economics, international trade. **Special Collections:** International trade. **Holdings:** 350 books; 4 VF drawers of newspapers and pamphlets; 7 VF drawers of Statistics Canada publications; 5 VF drawers of annual reports and official publications; Business Opportunities Sourcing System (BOSS) of Canadian manufacturers and trading houses on microfiche. **Subscriptions:** 100 journals and other serials; 10 newspapers. **Services:** Copying; SDI; library open to the public if material is not available elsewhere. **Computerized Information Services:** DIALOG Information Services, Infomart, The Financial Post Information Service, Info Globe, I.P. Sharp Associates Limited; Network (electronic mail service). **Networks/Consortia:** Member of Central Vancouver Library Group. **Publications:** Annual Clerical Salary Survey; Laws in the Making (summary of provincial government bills introduced in the legislature), irregular; Business Barometer, biweekly; Facts and Trends (digest of current industrial relations), biweekly - by subscription.

★17263★
VANCOUVER BOTANICAL GARDENS ASSOCIATION - VANDUSEN GARDENS LIBRARY (Biol Sci)
5251 Oak St. Phone: (604)266-7194
Vancouver, BC, Canada V6M 4H1 Charlaine Corbett, Libn.
Staff: Prof 1; Other 20. **Subjects:** Horticulture, botany, gardening, plant exploration. **Holdings:** 2600 books; 6 VF drawers of documents. **Subscriptions:** 50 journals and other serials. **Services:** Copying; library open to the public for reference use only.

VANCOUVER COMMUNITY COLLEGE - VANCOUVER VOCATIONAL INSTITUTE
See: Vancouver Vocational Institute (17271)

★17264★
VANCOUVER MEMORIAL HOSPITAL - R.D. WISWALL MEMORIAL LIBRARY (Med)
3400 Main St.
Box 1600 Phone: (206)696-5143
Vancouver, WA 98668 Sylvia E. MacWilliams, Lib.Coord.
Founded: 1965. **Staff:** Prof 1. **Subjects:** Medicine, nursing. **Holdings:** Figures not available. **Services:** Interlibrary loan; library not open to the public. **Automated Operations:** Computerized statistics. **Computerized Information Services:** MEDLARS. **Remarks:** Maintained by Southwest Washington Hospitals.

★17265★
VANCOUVER MUSEUM - LIBRARY AND RESOURCE CENTRE (Hist)
1100 Chestnut St. Phone: (604)736-4431
Vancouver, BC, Canada V6J 3J9 Norah J. McLaren, Libn.
Founded: 1968. **Staff:** Prof 1; Other 3. **Subjects:** Local history, decorative arts, ethnology, archeology, natural history. **Holdings:** 5900 books; maps. **Subscriptions:** 30 journals and other serials. **Services:** Library open to the public by appointment.

★17266★
VANCOUVER PUBLIC AQUARIUM - LIBRARY (Biol Sci)
Box 3232 Phone: (604)685-3364
Vancouver, BC, Canada V6B 3X8 Treva Ricou, Libn.
Staff: Prof 1; Other 3. **Subjects:** Marine mammals, fish, reptiles, amphibians, invertebrates, birds. **Holdings:** 3800 books; 850 bound periodical volumes. **Subscriptions:** 124 journals and other serials. **Services:** Copying; library open to the public by appointment for reference use only.

★17267★
VANCOUVER PUBLIC LIBRARY - BUSINESS & ECONOMICS DIVISION (Bus-Fin)
750 Burrard St. Phone: (604)665-3365
Vancouver, BC, Canada V6Z 1X5 Sheila Thompson, Hd.
Founded: 1951. **Staff:** Prof 6; Other 13. **Subjects:** Industrial economics, transportation, management, marketing, labor, real estate. **Holdings:** 72,000 volumes; 1500 trade directories; 20,000 corporation reports; 20,000 pamphlets; 51 cases of clippings. **Subscriptions:** 900 journals and other serials; 10 newspapers. **Services:** Interlibrary loan; division open to the public. **Automated Operations:** Computerized cataloging and circulation. **Networks/Consortia:** Member of Central Vancouver Library Group. **Special Indexes:** Corporation card file; periodical indexing card file. **Staff:** Nancy Clegg, Libn.; Glenda Guttman, Libn.; Shelagh Flaherty, Libn.; Helen Russell, Libn.; Nancy Stubbs, Libn..

★17268★
VANCOUVER SCHOOL OF THEOLOGY - LIBRARY (Rel-Phil)
6050 Chancellor Blvd. Phone: (604)228-9031
Vancouver, BC, Canada V6T 1X3 Elizabeth Hart, Libn.
Staff: Prof 1; Other 5. **Subjects:** Biblical studies, Christianity, doctrinal and practical theology, denominations and sects, Judaism. **Holdings:** 73,043 books; 4155 bound periodical volumes; 83 kits; 793 microfiche titles; 685 reels of microfilm; 39 phonograph records; 1642 audio cassettes and tapes; 74 filmstrips; 5312 slides; 17 maps; 62 video cassettes. **Subscriptions:** 358 journals and other serials. **Services:** Interlibrary loan; copying; library open to the public. **Publications:** Acquisitions list, monthly; periodical abstracts, monthly.

★17269★
VANCOUVER TALMUD TORAH SCHOOL - LIBRARY (Rel-Phil)
998 W. 26th Ave. Phone: (604)736-7307
Vancouver, BC, Canada V5Z 2G1 Marylile Gill, Teacher/Libn.
Staff: Prof 1. **Subjects:** Hebraica and Judaica. **Holdings:** 5000 books; phonograph records; filmstrips; audio cassettes; kits; transparencies; study prints. **Subscriptions:** 50 journals and other serials. **Services:** Interlibrary loan; library open to the public with restrictions.

★17270★
VANCOUVER TEACHERS' PROFESSIONAL LIBRARY (Educ)
Teacher Centre
123 E. 6th Ave. Phone: (604)874-2617
Vancouver, BC, Canada V5T 1J6 Linda Dunbar, Lib.Techn.
Founded: 1921. **Staff:** 2. **Subjects:** Education. **Holdings:** 15,000 books; 500 pamphlets; 650 microfiche. **Subscriptions:** 282 journals and other serials. **Services:** Interlibrary loan; library open to the public for reference use only. **Computerized Information Services:** DIALOG Information Services.

★17271★
VANCOUVER VOCATIONAL INSTITUTE - LIBRARY (Educ)
250 West Pender St. Phone: (604)681-8111
Vancouver, BC, Canada V6B 1S9 Frieda Wiebe, Campus Libn.
Founded: 1974. **Staff:** Prof 2; Other 8. **Subjects:** Business, allied health sciences, drafting, electricity and electronics, food trades, hairdressing, building construction, printing production, power engineering, tourism and hospitality. **Holdings:** 16,000 books; 600 pamphlet files; 3000 AV programs; 3000 microfiche. **Subscriptions:** 250 journals and other serials; 7 newspapers. **Services:** Interlibrary loan; copying; library open to the public with restrictions. **Automated Operations:** Computerized cataloging. **Computerized Information Services:** DIALOG Information Services, UTLAS, BRS Information Technologies; Envoy 100 (electronic mail service). Performs searches on fee basis. **Remarks:** Maintained by Vancouver Community College. **Staff:** Elizabeth Devakos, Pub.Serv.Libn..

★17272★
VANDALIA HISTORICAL SOCIETY - JAMES HALL LIBRARY (Hist)
Little Brick House
621 St. Clair St. Phone: (618)283-0024
Vandalia, IL 62471 Mary Burtschi, Dir.
Staff: Prof 3. **Subjects:** Illinois and local history. **Special Collections:** James Hall Collection, 1793-1868; Abraham Lincoln Collection, 1834-1839; National Road in Illinois Collection (photographs; essays; articles); biographies of Vandalia authors, artists, and statesmen; Joseph Charles Burtschi Collection; Mary Burtschi Collection; Burtschi family archives, 1775-1975; History of the Fayette County Bicentennial of the American Revolution, 1974-1976; Memory Book of the Fayette County Bicentennial of the American Revolution, 1974-1976 (includes photographs of commission members and events; newspaper and magazine articles; printed programs); Badger Collection Featuring Vandalia, Illinois, 1985 (sketches of residences and churches of architectural quality, 1836-1913); Vandalia Historical Society Memory Book, 1954-1987 (photographs; newspaper articles; printed programs); Inventory File of Fifty Old Buildings, 1820-1913 (photographs; sketches; architectural, cultural, and historical research survey sheets); Walking Tour A (booklet on the original town of Vandalia, 1819); old Vandalia residences photographs. **Holdings:** 10 books; photographs; manuscripts; reports; letters; scrapbooks. **Services:** Library open to the public by appointment. **Publications:** List of publications - available on request. **Staff:** Josephine Burtschi, Archv./Act.Libn.; Dr. Charles Koch, Supv..

★17273★
R.T. VANDERBILT COMPANY, INC. - LIBRARY
33 Winfield St.
East Norwalk, CT 06855
Founded: 1956. **Subjects:** Organic chemistry, rubber, plastics, ceramics, paint, mineralogy. **Holdings:** 10,000 books; 4800 bound periodical volumes; 1500 technical reports; 1000 reprints; 22 VF drawers of technical data; 1200 reels of microfilm; Chemical Abstracts and Official Patent Gazette on microfilm. **Remarks:** Presently inactive.

★17274★
VANDERBILT UNIVERSITY - ALYNE QUEENER MASSEY LAW LIBRARY (Law)
School of Law — Phone: (615)322-2568
Nashville, TN 37203 — Igor I. Kavass, Dir.
Staff: Prof 8; Other 10. **Subjects:** Law. **Special Collections:** James Cullen Looney Medico-Legal Collection. **Holdings:** 220,057 volumes; microforms; 80,036 documents. **Subscriptions:** 3902 journals and other serials. **Services:** Interlibrary loan; copying; library open to the public for reference use only. **Automated Operations:** Computerized cataloging and acquisitions. **Computerized Information Services:** OCLC, LEXIS, WESTLAW, Information Access Company (IAC). **Networks/Consortia:** Member of SOLINET. **Publications:** Selected bibliographies - available on request. **Staff:** Howard A. Hood, Legal Info.Spec..

VANDERBILT UNIVERSITY - GEORGE PEABODY COLLEGE FOR TEACHERS
See: George Peabody College for Teachers of Vanderbilt University - Kennedy Center (11123)

★17275★
VANDERBILT UNIVERSITY - JEAN AND ALEXANDER HEARD LIBRARY - ARTS LIBRARY (Art)
419 21st Ave., S. — Phone: (615)322-3485
Nashville, TN 37240 — Sigrid Docken Mount, Arts Libn.
Founded: 1973. **Staff:** Prof 1; Other 1. **Subjects:** Art - history, biography, theory, criticism; architectural history; photography; landscape design. **Special Collections:** The Norman L. and Roselea J. Goldberg Research Library (18th and 19th century British landscape art; 400 volumes). **Holdings:** 40,000 books; 5500 bound periodical volumes; 37 VF drawers of art ephemera; 8000 items in arts picture file. **Subscriptions:** 335 journals and other serials. **Services:** Interlibrary loan; library open to the public on a fee basis. **Automated Operations:** Computerized cataloging, acquisitions, serials, and circulation. **Computerized Information Services:** DIALOG Information Services, OCLC, BRS Information Technologies. **Networks/Consortia:** Member of Association for Library Information (AFLI), Center for Research Libraries (CRL) Consortia. **Publications:** Bibliography of art bibliographies.

★17276★
VANDERBILT UNIVERSITY - JEAN AND ALEXANDER HEARD LIBRARY - DIVINITY LIBRARY (Rel-Phil)
419 21st Ave., S. — Phone: (615)322-2865
Nashville, TN 37240 — William J. Hook, Dir.
Founded: 1894. **Staff:** Prof 2; Other 2. **Subjects:** Biblical studies, church history, worship and preaching, theology, ethics, history of religion, religion and personality. **Special Collections:** Judaica (7000 volumes); memorabilia. **Holdings:** 140,000 volumes; microforms. **Subscriptions:** 1073 journals and other serials. **Services:** Interlibrary loan; copying; library open to the public on a fee basis. **Automated Operations:** Computerized public access catalog, cataloging, acquisitions, serials, and circulation. **Computerized Information Services:** BRS Information Technologies, OCLC; ALANET (electronic mail service). **Networks/Consortia:** Member of Association for Library Information (AFLI). **Publications:** Library Guide, annual; subject bibliographies for each graduate area in the Divinity School. **Staff:** Anne Womack, Circ.Supv.; Dorothy Parks, Coll.Libn..

★17277★
VANDERBILT UNIVERSITY - JEAN AND ALEXANDER HEARD LIBRARY - DIVINITY LIBRARY - KESLER CIRCULATING LIBRARY (Rel-Phil)
419 21st Ave., S. — Phone: (615)322-2865
Nashville, TN 37240 — William J. Hook, Dir.
Founded: 1940. **Staff:** Prof 1; Other 1. **Subjects:** Religion. **Services:** Mail circulation of books to ordained ministry; library open to the public with restrictions. **Publications:** Recent Acquisition Lists, irregular - to members. **Remarks:** Kesler Circulating Library is a continuing education service of the Divinity Library and utilizes its holdings. Membership is open to clergy engaged in ministry (except those based in academic institutions whose needs are met by interlibrary loan) in the continental United States and Canada; nondenominational; free membership upon application. **Staff:** Anne Womack, Circ.Supv..

★17278★
VANDERBILT UNIVERSITY - JEAN AND ALEXANDER HEARD LIBRARY - DYER OBSERVATORY (Sci-Engr)
Sta. B
Box 1803 — Phone: (615)373-4897
Nashville, TN 37235 — Ellen Ellis, Libn.
Founded: 1953. **Staff:** Prof 1. **Subjects:** Astronomy, astrophysics. **Holdings:** 4600 books; 6500 bound periodical volumes; 9000 unbound reprints; 43 theses; 1100 slides; 5000 photographs of star fields. **Subscriptions:** 345 journals and other serials. **Services:** Interlibrary loan; observatory open to the public by appointment. **Publications:** Arthur J. Dyer Observatory Reprints, irregular. **Remarks:** The observatory is located at 1000 Oman Dr., Brentwood, TN 37027.

★17279★
VANDERBILT UNIVERSITY - JEAN AND ALEXANDER HEARD LIBRARY - EDUCATION LIBRARY (Educ, Info Sci)
Box 325 — Phone: (615)322-8095
Nashville, TN 37203 — Mary Beth Blalock, Dir.
Staff: Prof 3; Other 6. **Subjects:** Education, psychology, special education, child study, physical education, library and information science, curriculum materials. **Holdings:** 216,710 books; 670 reels of microfilm; 388,725 microfiche; 10,641 microcards; 899 cassettes; 1559 games and kits. **Subscriptions:** 1378 journals and other serials. **Services:** Interlibrary loan; copying; library open to visiting scholars for reference use only. **Automated Operations:** Computerized public access catalog, cataloging, acquisitions, and circulation. **Computerized Information Services:** OCLC, DIALOG Information Services. **Networks/Consortia:** Member of Association for Library Information (AFLI). **Staff:** Jean Reese, Pub.Serv.Libn..

★17280★
VANDERBILT UNIVERSITY - JEAN AND ALEXANDER HEARD LIBRARY - EDUCATION LIBRARY - PEABODY COLLECTION OF BOOKS ON CHILDREN
Box 325
Nashville, TN 37203
Defunct. Holdings absorbed by Education Library.

★17281★
VANDERBILT UNIVERSITY - JEAN AND ALEXANDER HEARD LIBRARY - MUSIC LIBRARY (Mus)
2400 Blakemore Ave. — Phone: (615)322-7696
Nashville, TN 37212 — Shirley Marie Watts, Dir.
Founded: 1948. **Staff:** Prof 1; Other 3. **Subjects:** Music. **Special Collections:** Seminar in piano teaching (lectures, master classes, recitals, 1970-1976; cassette tapes). **Holdings:** 12,500 volumes; 13,000 scores; 12,300 phonograph records; 112 reels of tapes; 500 cassette tapes; microforms. **Subscriptions:** 170 journals and other serials. **Services:** Interlibrary loan; copying; library open to visiting scholars for reference use only. **Automated Operations:** Computerized public access catalog, cataloging, acquisitions, serials, and circulation.

★17282★
VANDERBILT UNIVERSITY - JEAN AND ALEXANDER HEARD LIBRARY - SCIENCE LIBRARY (Biol Sci, Sci-Engr)
419 21st Ave., S. — Phone: (615)322-2775
Nashville, TN 37240 — Timothy F. Richards, Dir.
Staff: Prof 5; Other 5. **Subjects:** Biology, chemistry, engineering, geology, mathematics, physics, astronomy. **Special Collections:** Foreign and State Geological Survey Collections. **Holdings:** 225,000 volumes; 385 boxes of microcards of Landmarks of Science I and II; 96 drawers of microfiche of AEC Reports through February 1971; 8 drawers of microfiche of NASA Reports, 1976 to present; 708 reels of microfilm of U.S. Patent Official Gazette, 1872 to present; 39 reels of microfilm of U.S. Patent Official Gazette Trademarks, 1971 to present; 20 reels of microfilm of U.S. Annual Report of the Commissioner of Patents, 1790-1871; 3190 reels of microfilm of U.S. patents, January 1965 to present; 24 drawers of microfiche of miscellaneous materials. **Subscriptions:** 2980 journals and other serials. **Services:** Interlibrary loan; copying; SDI; library open to the public on fee basis. **Automated Operations:** Computerized cataloging, acquisitions, serials, and circulation. **Computerized Information Services:** DIALOG Information Services, OCLC, BRS Information Technologies, CAS ONLINE, U.S. Patent Classification System. Performs searches on fee basis. **Networks/Consortia:** Member of Association for Library Information (AFLI), Center for Research Libraries (CRL) Consortia. **Staff:** Paul Murphy, Info.Serv.Libn.; Kathy Shelby, Info.Serv.Libn.;

Cynthia Shabb, Info.Serv.Libn.; Godlind Johnson, Info.Serv.Libn.; Laurie Allen, Info.Serv.Libn..

★17283★
VANDERBILT UNIVERSITY - JEAN AND ALEXANDER HEARD LIBRARY - SPECIAL COLLECTIONS DEPARTMENT (Hum)
419 21st Ave., S. Phone: (615)322-2807
Nashville, TN 37240-0007 Marice Wolfe, Hd.
Founded: 1965. **Staff:** Prof 3; Other 4. **Subjects:** Southern literature, history, and politics; 19th and 20th century French literature; performing arts. **Special Collections:** Sevier and Rand Collections (fine bindings, rare books; 10,000 volumes); Jesse E. Wills Fugitive/Agrarian Collection (American literature and criticism, 1920 to present; 1000 volumes; 2500 cubic feet of manuscripts); W.T. Bandy Center for Baudelaire Studies (6000 volumes; 40 cubic feet of manuscripts); Pascal Pia Collection (20th century French literature; 3000 volumes); Francis Robinson Collection of Theatre, Music and Dance (4000 volumes; 100 cubic feet of manuscripts). **Holdings:** 40,000 books; Vanderbilt theses and dissertations; 1300 cubic feet of manuscripts; 3000 cubic feet of archival materials. **Services:** Copying; department open to the public for reference use only. **Automated Operations:** Computerized cataloging and acquisitions. **Computerized Information Services:** OCLC; Baudelaire Ephemera, University Archives CIS (internal databases). Performs searches on fee basis. Contact Person: Sara Harwell, Libn./Archv..

★17284★
VANDERBILT UNIVERSITY - JEAN AND ALEXANDER HEARD LIBRARY - TELEVISION NEWS ARCHIVE (Info Sci)
419 21st Ave., S. Phone: (615)322-2927
Nashville, TN 37240 Julie M. Strickland, Adm.Asst.
Founded: 1968. **Staff:** Prof 1; Other 9. **Subjects:** Television news, 1968 to present. **Special Collections:** Network evening news programs (videotape); Presidential speeches and press conferences; Democratic and Republican National Conventions; Watergate hearings; impeachment debates and more recent events. **Holdings:** 14,000 hours of videotape. **Services:** Interlibrary loan; copying; archives open to the public. **Publications:** Television News Index and Abstracts, monthly.

★17285★
VANDERBILT UNIVERSITY - JEAN AND ALEXANDER HEARD LIBRARY - WALKER MANAGEMENT LIBRARY (Bus-Fin)
401 21st Ave., S. Phone: (615)322-2970
Nashville, TN 37203 Carol Dickerson, Dir.
Founded: 1970. **Staff:** Prof 6; Other 7. **Subjects:** Management and business, corporate information. **Special Collections:** Career planning and placement resources. **Holdings:** 22,376 volumes; 500 AV programs; 145,710 microfiche; 2016 reels of microfilm. **Subscriptions:** 1140 journals and other serials; 8 newspapers. **Services:** Interlibrary loan; copying; SDI; library open to the public on fee basis. **Automated Operations:** Computerized cataloging and serials. **Computerized Information Services:** DIALOG Information Services, NEXIS, OCLC, BRS Information Technologies, DataTimes, WILSONLINE, Datext, Inc., Dow Jones News/Retrieval; ACORN (internal database). Performs searches on fee basis. Contact Person: Vicki Watkins, Mgr., Bus.Info.Serv.. **Networks/Consortia:** Member of Association for Library Information (AFLI). **Publications:** Newsletter - for internal distribution only. **Staff:** Sylvia Graham, Asst.Dir.; Danny Sulkin, Media Spec.; Rosemary Madill, Supv., Lib.Oper.; William Taylor, Coord., Info.Serv.; Joan Quinn, Info.Serv.Libn.; Cindy Boin, Info.Serv.Libn..

★17286★
VANDERBILT UNIVERSITY - MEDICAL CENTER LIBRARY (Med)
Nashville, TN 37232 Phone: (615)322-2292
T. Mark Hodges, Dir.
Founded: 1906. **Staff:** Prof 10; Other 21. **Subjects:** Health sciences. **Special Collections:** History of Medicine; History of Nutrition (Goldberger-Sebrell Pellagra Collection; Lydia J. Roberts Collection; Helen S. Mitchell Collection; E. Neige Todhunter Collection); Moll Hypnosis Collection; Vanderbilt Medical Faculty Manuscripts; Archives of Vanderbilt University Medical Center. **Holdings:** 50,262 books and theses; 89,272 bound periodical volumes; 6486 government publications; 1928 AV programs; 4597 microforms; 390 linear feet of manuscripts. **Subscriptions:** 1871 journals and other serials. **Services:** Interlibrary loan (fee); copying; SDI; library open to the public with restrictions on borrowing. **Automated Operations:** Computerized cataloging, acquisitions, serials, circulation, and ILL. **Computerized Information Services:** MEDLINE, BRS Information Technologies, DIALOG Information Services; OnTyme Electronic Message Network Service (electronic mail service). Performs searches on fee basis. Contact Person: Judy Orr, Hd., Ref. & Res.Serv., 322-2291. **Networks/Consortia:** Member of Southeastern/Atlantic Regional Medical Library Services. **Publications:** Catalist, quarterly; Nutrition History Notes, quarterly; Current Serials List, annual. **Staff:** Byrd S. Helguera, Assoc.Dir.; Frances H. Lynch, Asst.Dir., Tech.Serv.; Mary H. Teloh, Spec.Coll.Libn.; Deborah Broadwater, Cat.Libn.; Mary Charles Lasater, Monographs Libn.; Mari Stoddard, Outreach Libn.; Judy Rieke, Ser.Libn.; Carol E. Lewis, Ref.Libn.; Beverly Carlton, Ref.Libn.; Gayle Grantham, Circ.Supv.; Marilyn Eckert, ILL Supv.; Dr. William J. Darby, Hon.Cur.; Dr. Harry S. Shelley, Hon.Cur..

★17287★
VANDERBURGH COUNTY LAW LIBRARY (Law)
City-County Courts Bldg., Rm. 207 Phone: (812)426-5175
Evansville, IN 47708 Helen S. Reed, Libn.
Founded: 1900. **Staff:** Prof 1. **Subjects:** Law. **Holdings:** 12,000 volumes. **Services:** Copying; library open to the public with restrictions. **Computerized Information Services:** Online systems. **Remarks:** Maintained by Vanderburgh County, Evansville Bar Association, and Vanderburgh Law Library Foundation.

★17288★
VANDERCOOK COLLEGE OF MUSIC - RUPPEL MEMORIAL LIBRARY (Mus)
3209 S. Michigan Ave. Phone: (312)225-6288
Chicago, IL 60616 Dean P. Jensen, Lib.Dir.
Founded: 1967. **Staff:** Prof 1; Other 2. **Subjects:** Music and music education, education. **Special Collections:** Performance Library (12,000 items). **Holdings:** 18,898 books; 1874 phonograph records; 3157 scores; 8 VF drawers of pamphlets; 1841 reels of microfilm. **Subscriptions:** 68 journals and other serials. **Services:** Interlibrary loan; copying; library open to the public with restrictions. **Automated Operations:** Computerized cataloging. **Computerized Information Services:** OCLC. **Networks/Consortia:** Member of Chicago Library System, ILLINET.

VANDUSEN GARDENS LIBRARY
See: Vancouver Botanical Gardens Association (17263)

GEORGES P. VANIER LIBRARY
See: Concordia University - Loyola Campus - Georges P. Vanier Library (3587)

★17289★
VANIER INSTITUTE OF THE FAMILY - RESOURCE & INFORMATION CENTRE (Soc Sci)
120 Holland Ave., Suite 300 Phone: (613)722-4007
Ottawa, ON, Canada K1Y 0X6 Susan L. Campbell, Res./Pub.Info.Asst.
Founded: 1968. **Staff:** Prof 1. **Subjects:** Family, communications, learning, informal economy, social work, social services, social policy, women's issues, lifestyles. **Holdings:** 5000 books; 20 VF drawers of pamphlets, dissertations, and documents. **Subscriptions:** 125 journals and other serials. **Services:** Interlibrary loan; copying; center open to the public with restrictions. **Publications:** A Selected Bibliography on Family Violence; Every Family is a Working Family: A Reading List.

VANIER SCIENCE & ENGINEERING LIBRARY
See: University of Ottawa (16722)

VIDA B. VAREY LIBRARY
See: Plymouth Congregational Church (11408)

★17290★
VARIAN ASSOCIATES - EIMAC DIVISION - TECHNICAL LIBRARY (Sci-Engr)
301 Industrial Way
San Carlos, CA 94070 Phone: (415)592-1221
Founded: 1955. **Subjects:** Electronics, electron devices, metals, ceramics, chemistry. **Holdings:** 5700 books; 2350 bound periodical volumes; 5800 pamphlets; 6300 technical reports. **Subscriptions:** 170 journals and other serials. **Services:** Interlibrary loan; library not open to the public. **Computerized Information Services:** DIALOG Information Services.

★17291★
VARIAN ASSOCIATES - TECHNICAL LIBRARY (Sci-Engr)
611 Hansen Way
Box 10800 Phone: (415)493-4000
Palo Alto, CA 94303-0883 Joan Murphy, Lib.Mgr.
Founded: 1961. **Staff:** Prof 3; Other 2. **Subjects:** Electronics, chemistry, instrumentation, applied mathematics, physics. **Holdings:** 13,000 books; 30,000 bound periodical volumes; 7000 technical reports; microcomputer software; videotapes. **Subscriptions:** 708 journals and other serials; 12 newspapers. **Services:** Interlibrary loan; copying; SDI; library open to the public by appointment for reference. **Computerized Information Services:** STN International, DIALOG Information Services, RLIN, VU/TEXT Information Services, Dow Jones News/Retrieval, BRS Information Technologies, DataTimes, DTIC, Socrates; internal database. **Networks/Consortia:** Member of SOUTHNET. **Publications:** Technical Library Bulletin, bimonthly. **Staff:** Donna Barranti, Libn.; Donna Farmer, Libn..

★17292★
VARIAN ASSOCIATES - TECHNICAL LIBRARY (Sci-Engr)
8 Salem Rd. Phone: (617)922-6000
Beverly, MA 01915 Gunta Vittands, Libn.
Founded: 1961. **Staff:** Prof 1. **Subjects:** Microwave engineering, semiconductors. **Holdings:** 1200 books; 355 bound periodical volumes; government reports. **Subscriptions:** 75 journals and other serials. **Services:** Interlibrary loan; library not open to the public. **Automated Operations:** Computerized cataloging and circulation. **Computerized Information Services:** DIALOG Information Services. **Networks/Consortia:** Member of North of Boston Library Exchange (NOBLE). **Publications:** Newsletter, semimonthly - for internal distribution only.

★17293★
VARIAN CANADA INC. - TECHNICAL LIBRARY (Sci-Engr)
45 River Dr.
Georgetown, ON, Canada L7G 2J4 Phone: (416)877-0161
Founded: 1958. **Staff:** Prof 2. **Subjects:** Microwave electronics, metallurgy, chemical analysis, metal working, tool design, management. **Holdings:** 530 books. **Subscriptions:** 60 journals and other serials; 5 newspapers. **Services:** Interlibrary loan; library not open to the public. **Staff:** Harry V. Haylock, Supv..

★17294★
VASSAR BROTHERS HOSPITAL - MEDICAL LIBRARY (Med)
Reade Place Phone: (914)454-8500
Poughkeepsie, NY 12601 Mrs. Howard A. Wilson, Med.Libn.
Founded: 1951. **Staff:** Prof 1. **Subjects:** Internal medicine, surgery, cardiology, pulmonary medicine, orthopedics. **Holdings:** 1425 books; 450 bound periodical volumes; 8 VF drawers of pamphlets, flyers, and reports. **Subscriptions:** 72 journals and other serials. **Services:** Interlibrary loan; copying (limited); library open to students by appointment. **Networks/Consortia:** Member of Southeastern New York Library Resources Council (SENYLRC).

★17295★
VASSAR COLLEGE - ART LIBRARY (Art)
Poughkeepsie, NY 12601 Phone: (914)452-7000
Thomas E. Hill, Art Libn.
Staff: Prof 1; Other 1. **Subjects:** Western European art and architecture, ancient through contemporary; American art. **Holdings:** 40,000 books and bound periodical volumes. **Subscriptions:** 200 journals and other serials. **Services:** Interlibrary loan; library open to the public with restrictions. **Automated Operations:** Computerized cataloging, acquisitions, and serials. **Computerized Information Services:** DIALOG Information Services, BRS Information Technologies, WILSONLINE, SCIPIO, Avery Index to Architectural Periodicals. **Networks/Consortia:** Member of Southeastern New York Library Resources Council (SENYLRC).

★17296★
VASSAR COLLEGE - GEORGE SHERMAN DICKINSON MUSIC LIBRARY (Mus)
Poughkeepsie, NY 12601 Phone: (914)452-7000
Sabrina L. Weiss, Mus.Libn.
Founded: 1908. **Staff:** Prof 2; Other 3. **Subjects:** Music. **Special Collections:** Chittenden Pianoforte Library; historical editions and collected works. **Holdings:** 16,529 books and bound periodical volumes; 30,000 scores; 25,000 phonograph records. **Services:** Interlibrary loan; library open to the public with restrictions. **Computerized Information Services:** OCLC. **Staff:** Sarah B. Ransom, Mus.Cat..

★17297★
VASSAR COLLEGE - LIBRARY - DEPARTMENT OF SPECIAL COLLECTIONS (Hum, Hist)
Box 20 Phone: (914)452-7000
Poughkeepsie, NY 12601 Nancy S. MacKechnie, Act.Cur., Rare Bks./Mss.
Staff: Prof 2; Other 2. **Subjects:** College history, women's history, American and British literature, etiquette and household, fine printing, early atlases and maps. **Special Collections:** Papers of Elizabeth Bishop, Ruth Benedict, Mary McCarthy, John Burroughs, Mark Twain, Maria Mitchell, Lucy Maynard Salmon, Alma Lutz, Elizabeth Cady Stanton, Susan B. Anthony, Robert Owens; women's suffrage collection; household manuals; cookbooks; Courtesy Books; children's literature; gardening and herbal books; Village Press Collection; Jean Webster McKinney Collection of Mark Twain Manuscripts. **Holdings:** 16,000 books; 1125 linear feet of documents. **Services:** Copying; collection open to the public. **Networks/Consortia:** Member of SUNY/OCLC Library Network, Southeastern New York Library Resources Council (SENYLRC). **Special Indexes:** Manuscript registers for some collections (book).

JOHN VAUGHAN LIBRARY/LRC
See: Northeastern Oklahoma State University (10405)

VAUGHAN LIBRARY
See: Acadia University (25)

VEDDER MEMORIAL LIBRARY
See: Greene County Historical Society - Vedder Memorial Library (5866)

★17298★
VEGETARIAN INFORMATION SERVICE, INC. - INFORMATION CENTER (Food-Bev)
Box 5888 Phone: (301)530-1737
Bethesda, MD 20814 Dr. Alex Hershaft, Libn.
Founded: 1976. **Staff:** 4. **Subjects:** Vegetarianism, diet and health, treatment of farm animals, animal rights. **Holdings:** 100 volumes; clipping files. **Subscriptions:** 20 journals and other serials. **Services:** Center open to serious scholars of vegetarianism and animal rights.

★17299★
VENABLE BAETJER & HOWARD - LIBRARY (Law)
2 Hopkins Plaza Phone: (301)244-7502
Baltimore, MD 21201 John S. Nixdorff, Libn.
Staff: Prof 1; Other 3. **Subjects:** Law - tax, labor, corporate, securities, environmental, trusts and estates, health care, real estate; litigation. **Holdings:** 33,000 books; 1000 bound periodical volumes. **Subscriptions:** 100 journals and other serials; 5 newspapers. **Services:** Interlibrary loan; library not open to the public. **Computerized Information Services:** NEXIS, LEXIS, DIALOG Information Services, VU/TEXT Information Services, PHINet FedTax Database. **Remarks:** Maintains branch libraries in Washington, DC, Arlington, VA, and McLean, VA.

★17300★
VENANGO COUNTY LAW LIBRARY (Law)
Court House
Corner 12th & Liberty Sts.
Franklin, PA 16323 Phone: (814)437-6871
Founded: 1922. **Staff:** Prof 4. **Subjects:** Pennsylvania and United States laws and court reports. **Holdings:** 30,000 volumes. **Services:** Library open to the public for reference use only.

★17301★
VENTURA COUNTY HISTORICAL SOCIETY - LIBRARY & ARCHIVES (Hist)
100 E. Main St. Phone: (805)653-0323
Ventura, CA 93001 Alberta Word, Libn.
Founded: 1913. **Staff:** Prof 1. **Subjects:** Local history. **Holdings:** 2000 volumes; 12,000 photographs; 150 oral histories. **Subscriptions:** 45 journals and other serials. **Services:** Copying; photograph reproduction; library open to the public. **Publications:** Newsletter, monthly.

★17302★
VENTURA COUNTY LAW LIBRARY (Law)
800 S. Victoria Ave. Phone: (805)654-2695
Ventura, CA 93009 Naydean L. Baker, Law Libn.
Founded: 1891. **Staff:** Prof 1; Other 9. **Subjects:** Law. **Holdings:** 51,244 volumes; 105 reels of microfilm of U.S. Statutes; 1319 cassettes; 8848 volumes on microfiche. **Subscriptions:** 337 journals and other serials. **Services:** Library open to the public for reference use only.

★17303★
VENTURA COUNTY RESOURCE MANAGEMENT AGENCY - TECHNICAL LIBRARY (Env-Cons, Plan)
800 S. Victoria Ave. Phone: (805)654-2480
Ventura, CA 93009 Evelyn Adams, Tech.Libn.
Staff: 1. **Subjects:** Environment, planning, air and water pollution, sanitation, public health, building and safety, transportation. **Holdings:** 7500 reports and documents. **Subscriptions:** 80 journals and other serials. **Services:** Library open to the public for reference use only.

★17304★
VENTURA COUNTY STAR-FREE PRESS - LIBRARY (Publ)
Box 6711 Phone: (805)655-5803
Ventura, CA 93006 Kelly Baker, Libn.
Staff: Prof 2. **Subjects:** Newspaper reference topics. **Holdings:** 100 books; newspapers, 1897 to present, on microfilm; county government documents; photograph files; clippings. **Subscriptions:** 13 journals and other serials. **Services:** Copying; library open to the public with restrictions. **Special Catalogs:** Divided card file: subject and byline, crime/law suits, accidents. **Special Indexes:** Index to county news items. **Remarks:** Library located at 5250 Ralston, Ventura, CA 93003. **Staff:** Sara Bobson, Libn..

★17305★
VERMONT CENTER FOR INDEPENDENT LIVING (VCIL) - INFORMATION AND REFERRAL SYSTEM (Med)
174 River St. Phone: (802)229-0501
Montpelier, VT 05602 Erica Garfin, Dir.
Founded: 1979. **Staff:** 4. **Subjects:** Disability, adaptive equipment. **Holdings:** 628 books; 24 VF drawers. **Subscriptions:** 22 journals and other serials; 256 newspapers and newsletters. **Services:** Copying; center open to the public. **Computerized Information Services:** BRS Information Technologies. Performs searches free of charge for Vermont residents. **Publications:** Newsletter, quarterly - to the public; fact sheets; bibliographies, both irregular.

VERMONT EDUCATIONAL RESOURCE CENTER (VERC)
See: Vermont State Department of Education (17310)

VERMONT ENVIRONMENTAL CENTER
See: Vermont Institute of Natural Sciences - Library (17307)

★17306★
VERMONT HISTORICAL SOCIETY - LIBRARY (Hist)
Pavilion Bldg.
109 State St. Phone: (802)828-2291
Montpelier, VT 05602 Mrs. Reidun D. Nuquist, Libn.
Staff: Prof 2; Other 1. **Subjects:** Vermont history and Vermontiana, New England state and local history, genealogy. **Special Collections:** Vermont imprints; Harold G. Rugg Collection of Vermontiana. **Holdings:** 40,000 books and bound periodical volumes; 1000 maps; 30,000 photographs; 200 reels of microfilm; 700 cubic feet of manuscripts; pamphlets; 7000 broadsides. **Subscriptions:** 220 journals and other serials. **Services:** Interlibrary loan (limited); copying; library open to the public. **Publications:** Vermont History, quarterly; Vermont History News, 6/year; Green Mountaineer, 3/year - to members. **Staff:** Karl B. Bloom, Asst.Libn..

★17307★
VERMONT INSTITUTE OF NATURAL SCIENCES - LIBRARY (Biol Sci)
Church Hill Rd. Phone: (802)457-2779
Woodstock, VT 05091 Sarah B. Laughlin, Dir.
Staff: Prof 14. **Subjects:** Environmental research, natural history. **Special Collections:** Natural history slides (60,000); Billings-Kittredge Herbarium Collection. **Holdings:** 3500 books; 90 bound periodical volumes; 2000 pamphlets in vertical file. **Subscriptions:** 55 journals and other serials. **Services:** Library open to the public for reference use only. **Publications:** Vermont Natural History, annual; newsletter, quarterly; Bird Records, quarterly. **Remarks:** Includes the holdings of Vermont Environmental Center. **Staff:** Cassie Horner, Rsrcs.Ctr.Dir..

★17308★
VERMONT LAW SCHOOL - LIBRARY (Law)
Box 60 Phone: (802)763-8303
South Royalton, VT 05068 W. Leslie Peat, Law Libn.
Founded: 1973. **Staff:** Prof 4; Other 5. **Subjects:** Law. **Special Collections:** Environmental law (5200 volumes); Historic Preservation (1100 volumes); Alternative Dispute Resolution (300 volumes). **Holdings:** 67,300 books; 12,200 bound periodical volumes; 52,300 volumes in microform; government document depository. **Subscriptions:** 1400 journals and other serials; 10 newspapers. **Services:** Interlibrary loan; copying; library open to the public for reference use only. **Automated Operations:** Computerized cataloging, acquisitions, and ILL. **Computerized Information Services:** WESTLAW, OCLC. **Networks/Consortia:** Member of New England Law Library Consortium (NELLCO), NELINET. **Staff:** Lisa Meyer, Asst.Libn./Pub.Serv.; Victoria Weber, Asst.Libn./Acq.; Susan Zeigfinger, Asst.Libn./Tech.Serv..

★17309★
VERMONT STATE AGENCY OF ADMINISTRATION - PUBLIC RECORDS DIVISION (Hist)
State Administrative Bldg. Phone: (802)828-3288
Montpelier, VT 05602 A. John Yacavoni, Dir.
Staff: Prof 1; Other 16. **Subjects:** Vermont town and city land records prior to 1850, Vermont town vital records prior to 1850, Vermont probate record volumes prior to 1850. **Special Collections:** Field forms and draft material of Historical Records Survey inventories of Vermont town records and church records; Vermont Vital Record File, 1760-1954 (939 cubic feet). **Holdings:** 887 boxes of archival holdings; 23,071 reels of microfilm; 32,139 boxes of semiactive records center material. **Services:** Copying; division open to the public. **Publications:** Information Bulletin, monthly - to Vermont town and city clerks and treasurers.

★17310★
VERMONT STATE DEPARTMENT OF EDUCATION - VERMONT EDUCATIONAL RESOURCE CENTER (VERC) (Educ)
120 State St. Phone: (802)828-3352
Montpelier, VT 05602 David D. Joslyn, Rsrc.Libn.
Staff: Prof 1; Other 1. **Subjects:** Education. **Special Collections:** ERIC microfiche (complete set); Vermont Educational Resource Base (VERB; 450 educational materials on microfiche). **Holdings:** 1200 books, pamphlets, and newsletters. **Subscriptions:** 30 journals and other serials. **Services:** Interlibrary loan; copying; SDI; center open to the public. **Computerized Information Services:** BRS Information Technologies. Performs searches on fee basis. **Publications:** Occasional newsletters. **Special Catalogs:** RAP (Resource Agent Program) catalog of free workshops, annual. **Special Indexes:** VERB Index (with abstracts to collection holdings). **Staff:** Joyce Dann, Educ.Rsrc.Coord..

★17311★
VERMONT STATE DEPARTMENT OF LIBRARIES (Info Sci)
State Office Bldg. Post Office Phone: (802)828-3261
Montpelier, VT 05602 Patricia E. Klinck, State Libn.
Founded: 1970. **Staff:** Prof 16; Other 41. **Subjects:** Law, Vermontiana, general subjects. **Holdings:** 547,000 books; films; filmstrips; microfilm; records; tapes; state and federal documents. **Services:** Interlibrary loan; copying; department open to the public. **Computerized Information Services:** DIALOG Information Services, Pergamon ORBIT InfoLine, Inc., BRS Information Technologies, ERIC, OCLC. **Networks/Consortia:** Member of NELINET, Vermont Resource Sharing Network. **Publications:** Biennial Report; Department of Libraries News; Checklist of Available Vermont State Publications. **Special Catalogs:** Union Catalog of total holdings of libraries throughout the state, including colleges and universities (author-title card catalog). **Remarks:** The Department of Libraries maintains regional libraries in Dummerston, Berlin, Rutland, Georgia, and St. Johnsbury. Located at 111 State St., Montpelier, VT 05602.

★17312★
VERMONT STATE HOSPITAL - AGENCY OF HUMAN SERVICES - RESEARCH LIBRARY (Med)
103 S. Main St. Phone: (802)241-2248
Waterbury, VT 05676 James Jatkevicius, Libn.
Staff: Prof 1. **Subjects:** Psychiatry, public health, psychology, medicine, alcohol and drug abuse, corrections. **Holdings:** 10,000 books; 2000 bound periodical volumes; 30 cassettes; 60 cases of pamphlets; 45 boxes of government documents. **Subscriptions:** 200 journals and other serials. **Services:** Interlibrary loan; library open to hospital affiliates with restrictions. **Special Catalogs:** Union lists of books and journals.

★17313★
VERMONT STATE OFFICE OF THE SECRETARY OF STATE - VERMONT STATE PAPERS (Hist)
Redstone Bldg.
26 Terrace St. Phone: (802)828-2363
Montpelier, VT 05602 D. Gregory Sanford, State Archv.
Founded: 1777. **Staff:** Prof 2. **Subjects:** Governors' official papers, surveyors' general papers, municipal corporations charter records, legislative committee records, original acts and resolves, Vermont state

papers, 1744-1920, election records. **Special Collections:** Vermont/New Hampshire Boundary Case (30 feet); Vermont Bicentennial Commission (30 feet); Order of Women Legislators (2 feet); Records of the Governor's Commission on the Status of Women (20 feet); Houston Studio/Country Camera Photograph Collection; Agency and Department Photograph and Film Collection (35 feet); various state officers' papers (20 feet). **Holdings:** 500 books; 250 volumes of bound manuscripts; 60 volumes of maps, surveys, and charters; 500 cartons of manuscript material; 60 boxes of original acts and resolutions; 57 boxes of legislative committee records. **Services:** Copying; material is available for research; will answer correspondence pertaining to archival material; open to the public. **Publications:** State Papers of Vermont. **Special Catalogs:** Inventories for manuscript collections. **Staff:** Julie P. Cox, Asst. State Archv..

★17314★
VERMONT TECHNICAL COLLEGE - HARTNESS LIBRARY (Sci-Engr, Agri)
Randolph Center, VT 05061 Phone: (802)728-3391
Dewey F. Patterson, Lib.Dir.
Staff: Prof 1; Other 4. **Subjects:** Dairy management; agribusiness; engineering - civil, electrical, electronics, electromechanical, mechanical; surveying; architecture and building. **Holdings:** 50,000 books. **Subscriptions:** 396 journals and other serials; 8 newspapers. **Services:** Copying; library open to the public with restrictions.

★17315★
VERMONT YANKEE NUCLEAR POWER CORPORATION - ENERGY INFORMATION CENTER (Energy)
Governor Hunt Rd.
Box 157 Phone: (802)257-1416
Vernon, VT 05354 Barbara V.E. Martocci, Mgr.
Founded: 1981. **Staff:** Prof 2. **Subjects:** Energy. **Holdings:** 500 books; 300 bound periodical volumes; technical reports. **Services:** Interlibrary loan; center open to the public. **Publications:** Energy Educators' Newsletter, 3/year - to teachers. **Staff:** Linda Zinn, Educ.Asst..

★17316★
VERNER, LIIPFERT, BERNHARD & MC PHERSON - LIBRARY (Law)
1660 L St., N.W., Suite 1000 Phone: (202)775-1000
Washington, DC 20036 Donald W. Crandall, Law Libn.
Staff: Prof 3; Other 2. **Subjects:** Law - international, administrative, commercial; legislation. **Special Collections:** Aviation collection; surface transportation collection. **Holdings:** 10,000 books; 129 audio cassettes; 455 microforms; work/product collection. **Subscriptions:** 254 journals and other serials; 30 newspapers. **Services:** Interlibrary loan; copying; library open to the public by appointment. **Computerized Information Services:** LEXIS, Mead Data Central, Disclosure Online Database, Accountants' Index, The Reference Service (REFSRV). **Networks/Consortia:** Member of Metropolitan Washington Library Council. **Publications:** VLBM Weekly; Inside VLBM, biweekly - both for internal distribution only. **Staff:** Christopher Hays, Asst.Libn.; Michael Hill, Asst.Libn..

★17317★
VERRILL AND DANA - LAW LIBRARY (Law)
2 Canal Plaza Phone: (207)774-4000
Portland, ME 04112 Anne M. Reiman, Libn.
Founded: 1970. **Subjects:** Law. **Holdings:** 11,500 books. **Subscriptions:** 60 journals and other serials. **Services:** Library not open to the public. **Computerized Information Services:** LEXIS, WESTLAW.

★17318★
VERSAR INC. - CORPORATE LIBRARY (Env-Cons)
6850 Versar Center
Box 1549
Springfield, VA 22151 Phone: (703)750-3000
Founded: 1981. **Staff:** Prof 1. **Subjects:** Environmental research and engineering, asbestos, PCBs, coal cleaning. **Holdings:** 2000 books; 85 periodical titles; government publications. **Subscriptions:** 105 journals and other serials. **Services:** Interlibrary loan; copying; SDI; library open to the public by appointment. **Computerized Information Services:** DIALOG Information Services, BRS Information Technologies, NLM. **Publications:** Journal Holdings, annual; Library News and Notes, monthly - both for internal distribution only.

★17319★
VERSATEC - TECHNICAL INFORMATION CENTER (Sci-Engr)
2805 Bowers Ave. Phone: (408)988-2800
Santa Clara, CA 95051 Sharon Tyler, Tech.Info.Spec.
Founded: 1982. **Staff:** Prof 1. **Subjects:** Electronics, computer graphics, paper. **Holdings:** 2000 books. **Subscriptions:** 150 journals and other serials. **Services:** Interlibrary loan; center not open to the public. **Automated Operations:** Computerized cataloging and serials. **Computerized Information Services:** Pergamon ORBIT InfoLine, Inc., DIALOG Information Services, RLIN; OnTyme Electronic Message Network Service (electronic mail service). **Publications:** Periodical holdings; NEWSCAN (current awareness bulletin). **Remarks:** Versatec is a division of Xerox Corporation.

A.S. VESIC ENGINEERING LIBRARY
See: Duke University (4433)

★17320★
VESTAVIA ALLIANCE CHURCH - ALLIANCE CHRISTIAN SCHOOLS - RONALD JOHNSON MEMORIAL LIBRARY
1289 Montgomery Highway
Birmingham, AL 35216
Defunct

★17321★
VESTERHEIM GENEALOGICAL CENTER/NORWEGIAN-AMERICAN MUSEUM - LIBRARY (Area-Ethnic)
4909 Sherwood Rd. Phone: (608)271-8826
Madison, WI 53711 Gerhard B. Naeseth, Dir.
Founded: 1975. **Staff:** Prof 2. **Subjects:** Norwegian-American genealogy and history. **Holdings:** 935 books; 1100 reels of microfilm; 60 notebooks. **Services:** Copying; library open to the public by appointment. **Publications:** Norwegian Tracks, quarterly - to members.

★17322★
VESTIGIA - LIBRARY (Rel-Phil)
56 Brookwood Rd. Phone: (201)347-3638
Stanhope, NJ 07874 Robert Jones, Pres.
Staff: 2. **Subjects:** Unexplained phenomena. **Holdings:** 400 volumes. **Subscriptions:** 53 journals and other serials; 6 newspapers. **Services:** Library open to the public with restrictions. **Publications:** Vestigia Newsletter, annual. **Staff:** Dorothy Larkin, Libn./Exec.Sec.; Susan Balsley, Libn..

★17323★
VETCO GRAY, INC. - TECHNICAL LIBRARY (Sci-Engr)
7135 Ardmore
Box 2291 Phone: (713)747-1240
Houston, TX 77054 Paul Kohlmier, Tech.Libn.
Founded: 1982. **Staff:** Prof 1. **Subjects:** Engineering - offshore, mechanical, petroleum; metallurgy; welding; nondestructive examination. **Special Collections:** National Standards Association vendor catalogs (9000 on microfiche). **Holdings:** 500 books; 5 VF drawers of industrial and governmental engineering standards; 7 VF drawers of U.S. mechanical and design patents; 5 VF drawers of engineering periodical reprints (arranged by subject); 70 VF drawers of internal engineering reports and project files. **Subscriptions:** 150 journals and other serials. **Services:** Interlibrary loan; copying; library open to the public by appointment with restrictions. **Automated Operations:** Computerized cataloging, acquisitions, and serials. **Computerized Information Services:** DIALOG Information Services, BRS Information Technologies, Pergamon ORBIT InfoLine, Inc., RLIN, LEXIS, NEXIS. **Networks/Consortia:** Member of CLASS, Total Interlibrary Exchange (TIE). **Special Catalogs:** Government and Industry Codes, Regulations, Standards and Specifications Held in the Technical Library (computer printout). **Formerly:** Located in Ventura, CA.

VETERANS ADMINISTRATION
See: U.S. Veterans Administration (15512)

VETERANS AFFAIRS CANADA
See: Canada - Veterans Affairs Canada (2512)

★17324★
VETERANS HOME OF CALIFORNIA - LINCOLN MEMORIAL LIBRARY (Mil)
Yountville, CA 94599 Phone: (707)944-4915
Cynthia Hegedus, Libn.
Founded: 1886. **Staff:** Prof 3; Other 16. **Subjects:** Spanish American War, World Wars I and II. **Special Collections:** Spanish American War papers. **Holdings:** 37,265 books; 353 bound periodical volumes. **Subscriptions:** 160

journals and other serials; 55 newspapers. **Services:** Interlibrary loan; copying; library open to the public for reference use only. **Staff:** Phyllis Bush, Asst.Libn.; Suzel Ho, Asst.Libn..

★17325★
VETERANS HOME OF CALIFORNIA - WILLIAM K. MURPHY MEMORIAL HEALTH SCIENCE LIBRARY (Med)
Yountville, CA 94599 Phone: (707)944-4545
Cynthia Hegedus, Libn.
Founded: 1978. **Staff:** Prof 1; Other 2. **Subjects:** Medicine. **Holdings:** 800 books; 210 bound periodical volumes. **Subscriptions:** 128 journals and other serials. **Services:** Interlibrary loan; copying; library open to the public for reference use only. **Networks/Consortia:** Member of North Bay Health Sciences Library Group, Northern California and Nevada Medical Library Group (NCNMLG).

★17326★
VIA RAIL CANADA INC. - RESOURCE CENTER (Trans)
P.O. Box 8116, Sta. A Phone: (514)871-6442
Montreal, PQ, Canada H3C 3N3 Barbara Downey, Lib.Adm.
Founded: 1982. **Staff:** Prof 3; Other 1. **Subjects:** Engineering, transportation, management, railroad history, law, public affairs. **Holdings:** 4000 books; 500 reels of microfilm; 1000 microfiche; 30 VF drawers; specifications; slides; photographs; video cassettes. **Subscriptions:** 130 journals and other serials. **Services:** Interlibrary loan; copying; SDI; library open to the public by appointment. **Automated Operations:** Computerized cataloging and circulation. **Computerized Information Services:** DIALOG Information Services, CAN/OLE; internal database. **Staff:** Anne Metras, Info.Res.Anl.; Nicole DuSablon, Info.Res.Anl..

★17327★
VIBRATION INSTITUTE - LIBRARY (Sci-Engr)
115 W. 55th St., Suite 401 Phone: (312)654-2254
Clarendon Hills, IL 60514 Dr. Ronald L. Eshleman, Dir.
Founded: 1972. **Subjects:** Vibration technology, balancing, rotor/bearing dynamics, torsional vibrations, turbomachinery blading, shaft vibrations. **Holdings:** 800 books and journals.

VICK MEMORIAL LIBRARY
See: Baptist Bible College (1310)

VICKS RESEARCH CENTER
See: Procter & Gamble Company - Vicks Research Center (11605)

★17328★
VICKSBURG MEDICAL CENTER - MEDICAL LIBRARY (Med)
3311 I-20 Frontage Rd. Phone: (601)636-2611
Vicksburg, MS 39180 Linda Stephenson, Med.Rec.Mgr.
Founded: 1975. **Staff:** Prof 1. **Subjects:** Medicine, surgery, nursing, patient education. **Holdings:** 534 books; 1610 bound periodical volumes; 60 VF folders; 45 cassettes; 9 slide sets; 20 microforms; 2 video cassettes. **Subscriptions:** 70 journals and other serials. **Services:** Interlibrary loan; copying; library open to the public with approval of hospital administrator. **Networks/Consortia:** Member of Central Mississippi Council of Medical Libraries.

VICKSBURG NATIONAL MILITARY PARK
See: U.S. Natl. Park Service (15358)

★17329★
VICKSBURG & WARREN COUNTY HISTORICAL SOCIETY - MC CARDLE LIBRARY (Hist)
Old Court House Museum Phone: (601)636-0741
Vicksburg, MS 39180 Blanche Terry, Res.Dir.
Founded: 1948. **Staff:** Prof 2. **Subjects:** Confederacy, local history, genealogy. **Holdings:** 2000 volumes. **Services:** Copying; library open to the public with restrictions.

MICHAEL VICTOR II ART LIBRARY
See: Springfield Art Association (13566)

★17330★
VICTORIA COLLEGE/UNIVERSITY OF HOUSTON, VICTORIA - LIBRARY - SPECIAL COLLECTIONS (Hist)
2602 N. Ben Jordan Phone: (512)576-3157
Victoria, TX 77901 Dr. S. Joe McCord, Lib.Dir.
Holdings: Local history (6500 volumes; 10,000 slides; photographs); Regional Historical Resource Depository (180 feet of archival materials; 280 reels of microfilm); 220 cubic feet of other archival materials. **Services:** Interlibrary loan; copying; collections open to the public with restrictions. **Automated Operations:** Computerized cataloging and circulation. **Computerized Information Services:** DIALOG Information Services, MEDLARS; DataPhase Automated Library Information System (internal database). Performs searches on fee basis. Contact Person: Karen Locker, Govt.Doc.Libn.. **Networks/Consortia:** Member of AMIGOS Bibliographic Council, Inc., Circuit Rider Health Information Service (CRHIS), PAISANO Consortium of Libraries.

★17331★
VICTORIA CONSERVATORY OF MUSIC - LEON AND THEA KOERNER FOUNDATION - MUSIC LIBRARY (Mus)
839 Academy Close Phone: (604)386-5311
Victoria, BC, Canada V8R 2L1 Larry De La Haye, Libn.
Founded: 1969. **Staff:** 1. **Subjects:** Instrumental and vocal music. **Special Collections:** Collection of 33 1/3 and 78rpm recordings; 19th-century music (350 pieces). **Holdings:** 2000 books; 50,000 bound periodical volumes. **Subscriptions:** 51 journals and other serials. **Services:** Interlibrary loan; copying; library open to the public on a fee basis.

★17332★
VICTORIA GENERAL HOSPITAL - HEALTH SCIENCES LIBRARY (Med)
Halifax, NS, Canada B3H 2Y9 Phone: (902)428-2641
Samuel B. King, Libn.
Founded: 1972. **Staff:** Prof 1; Other 5. **Subjects:** Medicine, medical research, nursing, nursing education, allied health sciences, hospital administration and management. **Holdings:** 10,000 books; 5500 bound periodical volumes; 4000 pamphlets. **Subscriptions:** 550 journals and other serials; 10 newspapers. **Services:** Interlibrary loan; library open to the public with restrictions. **Automated Operations:** Computerized cataloging, acquisitions, and ILL. **Computerized Information Services:** DIALOG Information Services, MEDLARS; internal database. **Networks/Consortia:** Member of Nova Scotia On-Line Consortium. **Publications:** Acquisitions list; serials list. **Special Catalogs:** Catalog of Patient Education Resources of the Victoria General Hospital.

★17333★
VICTORIA TIMES-COLONIST - LIBRARY (Publ)
P.O. Box 300 Phone: (604)380-5211
Victoria, BC, Canada V8W 2N4 Corinne Wong, Libn.
Founded: 1955. **Staff:** Prof 1; Other 4. **Subjects:** Newspaper reference topics. **Holdings:** 5000 volumes; newspaper clipping and photograph collection; newspapers on microfilm; newspaper indexes. **Services:** Library for staff use only. **Remarks:** Published by Canadian Newspapers Ltd.

★17334★
VICTORIA UNION HOSPITAL - MEDICAL LIBRARY (Med)
1200 24th St., W. Phone: (306)764-1551
Prince Albert, SK, Canada S6V 5T4 Joan I. Ryan, Med.Rec.Libn.
Staff: 1. **Subjects:** Medicine, surgery, and gynecology. **Holdings:** 243 books; 350 bound periodical volumes. **Subscriptions:** 14 journals and other serials. **Services:** Library not open to the public.

VICTORIA UNIVERSITY
See: University of Toronto - Victoria University - Library (17001)

VICTORIA UNIVERSITY ARCHIVES
See: United Church of Canada/Victoria University Archives (14520)

VICTORIAN PERIODICAL LIBRARY
See: American Life Foundation and Study Institute - Americana Research Library (588)

★17335★
VICTORY MEMORIAL HOSPITAL - MEDICAL LIBRARY (Med)
1324 N. Sheridan Rd. Phone: (312)360-3000
Waukegan, IL 60085 Barbara Schaumberg, Med.Lib.Techn.
Founded: 1969. **Staff:** Prof 1. **Subjects:** Medicine, nursing, hospitals. **Holdings:** 514 volumes. **Subscriptions:** 45 journals and other serials. **Services:** Interlibrary loan; library not open to the public. **Networks/Consortia:** Member of Northeastern Illinois Library Consortium.

★17336★
VIDEO-DOCUMENTARY CLEARINGHOUSE - ARCHIVES (Aud-Vis)
Harbor Square, Suite 2201
700 Richards St. Phone: (808)523-2882
Honolulu, HI 96813-4631 Dr. Morton Cotlar, Exec.Dir.
Founded: 1977. **Staff:** Prof 2; Other 1. **Subjects:** Business administration, organizational administration, management, marketing, accounting, finance. **Holdings:** 15 AV programs. **Services:** Interlibrary loan; copying; archives open to the public on fee basis.

★17337★
VIDEO FREE AMERICA - LIBRARY (Aud-Vis)
442 Shotwell St. Phone: (415)648-9040
San Francisco, CA 94110 Joanne Kelly, Co-Dir.
Founded: 1970. **Staff:** 1. **Subjects:** Video, dance, individual artists. **Holdings:** 500 volumes. **Subscriptions:** 100 journals and other serials. **Services:** Library open to the public by appointment.

VIDEO IN LIBRARY
See: Satellite Video Exchange Society (12932)

★17338★
VIGO COUNTY HISTORICAL SOCIETY - HISTORICAL MUSEUM OF THE WABASH VALLEY - LIBRARY (Hist)
1411 S. 6th St. Phone: (812)235-9717
Terre Haute, IN 47802 David Buchanan, Exec.Dir.
Founded: 1958. **Staff:** Prof 1; Other 1. **Subjects:** Local history. **Holdings:** Figures not available. **Services:** Library open to the public by permission. **Publications:** Leaves of Thyme, quarterly.

★17339★
VIGO COUNTY PUBLIC LIBRARY - SPECIAL COLLECTIONS (Hist)
One Library Square Phone: (812)232-1113
Terre Haute, IN 47807 Clarence Brink, Coord., Ref.Serv.
Staff: Prof 3; Other 3. **Subjects:** State and local history, genealogy. **Special Collections:** Baertich Collection (2 VF drawers); Shriner Collection (4 VF drawers); family files (22 VF drawers); community affairs (108 VF drawers); local club and association records (26 boxes); Dr. Charles N. Combs Memorabilia (1 box); Eugene V. Debs Collection (2 boxes); Jane Dabney Shackelford Collection (1 box); Joseph Jenckes Collection (1 box); Theodore Dreiser/Paul Dresser Collection (1 box); J.A. Wickersham Scrapbook (1 box); League of Women Voters of Terre Haute Collection; Rotary Club of Terre Haute Collection. **Holdings:** 7800 books; 1285 bound periodical volumes; 381 maps and charts; 202 archival collections; 4340 reels of microfilm. **Subscriptions:** 57 journals and other serials. **Services:** Copying; collections open to the public for reference use only. **Automated Operations:** Computerized cataloging. **Computerized Information Services:** OCLC. **Networks/Consortia:** Member of INCOLSA, Stone Hills Area Library Services Authority (SHALSA). **Special Catalogs:** Main Special Collections (card); Community Archives (card). **Special Indexes:** Surname Index, irregular. **Staff:** Nancy Sherrill, Geneal.Libn.; Susan Dehler, Spec.Coll.Archv..

★17340★
VIGO COUNTY SCHOOL CORPORATION - INSTRUCTIONAL MATERIALS CENTER (Educ)
3000 College Ave. Phone: (812)238-4354
Terre Haute, IN 47803 Alice M. Reck, Coord.
Founded: 1966. **Staff:** Prof 2; Other 5. **Subjects:** Curriculum, professional education. **Holdings:** 10,448 books; 7671 transparency masters; 426 framed art prints; 987 slides; 2445 16mm films; 25 8mm films; 8 filmstrips; 85 sound filmstrips; 225 tapes; 371 videotapes; 10 realia; 1 map; 70 pieces of sculpture; 3 program instructions; 49 videodiscs; 44 motion picture loops; 16 kits; 23 computer disks. **Subscriptions:** 14 journals and other serials. **Services:** Copying; center open to the public with restrictions. **Automated Operations:** Computerized cataloging. **Computerized Information Services:** OCLC. **Networks/Consortia:** Member of INCOLSA. **Publications:** Bibliographies, irregular. **Staff:** Lorraine E. Brett, Cat..

VILLA ANNESLIE ARCHIVES
See: Polish Nobility Association (11422)

CARLOS VILLALONGIN DRAMATIC COMPANY ARCHIVES
See: University of Texas, Austin - Benson Latin American Collection (16917)

★17341★
VILLANOVA UNIVERSITY - LIBRARY SCIENCE LIBRARY (Info Sci)
Graduate Dept. of Library Science Phone: (215)645-4672
Villanova, PA 19085 Carolyn C. Walsh, Libn.
Staff: Prof 2; Other 1. **Subjects:** Library and information sciences, children's and young adult's literature, archives, computer science. **Special Collections:** Philadelphia Authors and Illustrators (200 items). **Holdings:** 22,000 books. **Subscriptions:** 265 journals and other serials. **Services:** Interlibrary loan; copying; library open to the public for reference use only. **Publications:** Pennsylvania Authors at a Glance; Philadelphia Children's Authors and Illustrators at a Glance; Annotated Bibliography of Periodical Holdings (book). **Staff:** Carol A. Kare, Cat..

★17342★
VILLANOVA UNIVERSITY - SCHOOL OF LAW - PULLING LAW LIBRARY (Law)
Garey Hall Phone: (215)645-7022
Villanova, PA 19085 Elizabeth Devlin, Act.Dir.
Founded: 1953. **Staff:** Prof 7; Other 13. **Subjects:** Law. **Special Collections:** Church and State. **Holdings:** 326,943 volumes and microforms. **Subscriptions:** 3225 journals and other serials; 14 newspapers. **Services:** Interlibrary loan; copying; library open to the public for reference use only. **Automated Operations:** Computerized cataloging. **Computerized Information Services:** LEXIS, WESTLAW, DIALOG Information Services, NEXIS, BRS Information Technologies, VU/TEXT Information Services, OCLC; MCI Mail (electronic mail service). **Networks/Consortia:** Member of Mid-Atlantic Law Library Cooperative (MALLCO). **Publications:** New Acquisitions, monthly. **Staff:** Maura Buri, Per.Libn.; Janet H. Dreher, Hd., Tech.Serv.; Zarin Bengali, Evening/Weekend Ref.Libn.; Nancy Armstrong, Ref.Libn.; Margaret Coyne, Circ.Libn..

★17343★
VILLE MARIE SOCIAL SERVICE CENTRE - LIBRARY (Soc Sci)
2155 Guy St., Suite 1010 Phone: (514)989-1885
Montreal, PQ, Canada H3H 2R9 Janet Sand Steinhouse, Libn.
Founded: 1976. **Staff:** Prof 1. **Subjects:** Social services, family, youth, aged. **Holdings:** Government publications. **Subscriptions:** 50 journals and other serials. **Services:** Interlibrary loan; copying; library open to the public by appointment. **Networks/Consortia:** Member of McGill Medical and Health Libraries Association (MMHLA). **Also Known As:** Centre de Services Sociaux Ville Marie.

VILLE DE MONTREAL - SERVICE DE L'URBANISME
See: Montreal City Planning Department (9273)

★17344★
VINCENNES UNIVERSITY - BYRON R. LEWIS HISTORICAL LIBRARY (Hist)
Vincennes, IN 47591 Phone: (812)885-4330
Robert R. Stevens, Dir.
Founded: 1967. **Staff:** Prof 1; Other 2. **Subjects:** Political, social, economic and general history of Lower Wabash Valley; university archives; oral history of Depression Era; genealogy. **Holdings:** 7500 volumes; manuscripts; photographs; maps; broadsides; newspapers; pamphlets. **Subscriptions:** 12 journals and other serials. **Services:** Limited area and genealogical research; library open to the public.

D.J. VINCENT MEDICAL LIBRARY
See: Riverside Methodist Hospital (12079)

G. ROBERT VINCENT VOICE LIBRARY
See: Michigan State University (8913)

JOHN VINCENT ARCHIVE
See: University of California, Los Angeles - Music Library (15981)

★17345★
VINELAND HISTORICAL AND ANTIQUARIAN SOCIETY - LIBRARY (Hist)
108 S. 7th St.
Box 35 Phone: (609)691-1111
Vineland, NJ 08360 Joseph E. Sherry, Libn.
Founded: 1864. **Staff:** Prof 1. **Subjects:** Genealogy and local history, Americana, antiques. **Special Collections:** Sheppard Genealogical Papers; Autograph Collection; Civil War Official Records; Bureau of American Ethnology Library. **Holdings:** 5000 books; bound local newspapers, 1861-1935; pamphlets and documents; census material on microfilm. **Services:** Copying; library open to the public on a limited schedule.

★17346★
THE VINEYARD - REAL ESTATE, SHOPPING CENTER & URBAN DEVELOPMENT INFORMATION CENTER (Bus-Fin, Plan)
50 W. Shaw Ave. Phone: (209)222-0182
Fresno, CA 93704 Richard Erganian, Info.Dir.
Staff: Prof 2; Other 1. **Subjects:** Real estate, shopping centers, urban and regional planning, architecture, mortgage financing, market research, landscaping. **Special Collections:** Shopping center, hotel, and mixed use development. **Holdings:** 4500 books; 210 bound periodical volumes; 2000 other cataloged items; 30 real estate transcripts; 20 shopping center development transcripts; 10 appraisal tapes and cassettes; 5 income property reports and transcripts; 25 video cassettes. **Subscriptions:** 250 journals and other serials; 25 newspapers. **Services:** Library open to real estate developers. **Special Catalogs:** Real Estate Information Sources. **Staff:** Aram Long, Staff Libn..

★17347★
VINNELL CORPORATION - CORPORATE/PROGRAM DEVELOPMENT LIBRARY
10530 Rosehaven St., Suite 600
Fairfax, VA 22030
Founded: 1932. **Subjects:** Military art and science, military education, vocational/technical education, job corps, specialized marketing information on Saudi Arabia and Southeast Asia. **Special Collections:** Photographs of corporate projects and personnel, 1932 to present (3000). **Holdings:** 250 books; 3000 proposals, reports, contracts; 20,000 military documents; 5000 other government documents; 1500 curriculum resources; 200 slides, cassettes, microfiche. **Remarks:** Presently inactive.

★17348★
VINSON & ELKINS - LAW LIBRARY (Law)
3055 First City Tower
1001 Fannin Phone: (713)651-2678
Houston, TX 77002 Karl T. Gruben, Libn.
Founded: 1917. **Staff:** Prof 3; Other 7. **Subjects:** Law - Texas, environmental, foreign and international, oil and gas. **Holdings:** 100,000 books; 1500 bound periodical volumes; microforms; audio cassettes; U.S. and Texas documents. **Subscriptions:** 300 journals and other serials. **Services:** Interlibrary loan; copying; library open to researchers with approval of librarian. **Computerized Information Services:** DIALOG Information Services, Pergamon ORBIT InfoLine, Inc., LEXIS, WESTLAW. **Staff:** David Blythe, Asst.Libn..

★17349★
VIRGIN ISLANDS DEPARTMENT OF PLANNING AND NATURAL RESOURCES - DIVISION OF LIBRARIES, ARCHIVES, AND MUSEUMS (Info Sci)
23 Dronningens Gade
Charlotte Amalie Phone: (809)774-3407
St. Thomas, VI 00802 Jeannette B. Allis, Dir.
Founded: 1920. **Staff:** Prof 17; Other 61. **Subjects:** General and reference topics. **Special Collections:** Von Scholton Collection (Caribbean, West Indian, and Virgin Island materials; 14,000 volumes; periodicals; newspapers; dissertations; manuscripts; maps; documents); Virgin Islands archives, 1655-1933 (on microfilm); newspapers, 1770 to present (on microfilm). **Holdings:** 119,000 books; U.N., U.S., and Virgin Islands government documents depository; manuscripts; clippings; archival materials; ephemera. **Subscriptions:** 354 journals and other serials. **Services:** Interlibrary loan; copying; microfilming; bureau open to the public. **Networks/Consortia:** Member of VILINET. **Publications:** Annual Reports, Virgin Islands Government Documents, quarterly; Caribbeana (union acquisitions list), irregular; occasional papers. **Special Catalogs:** Union List of Periodicals and Newspapers (book); Union Title File (card). **Special Indexes:** Local Newspaper index (card). **Remarks:** An alternate telephone number is 774-0630. **Formerly:** Virgin Islands Department of Conservation & Cultural Affairs - Bureau of Libraries and Museums. **Staff:** June A.V. Lindqvist, Cur., Von Scholton Coll.; Martin Gerbens, Hd., Caribbean Coll..

★17350★
VIRGIN ISLANDS ENERGY OFFICE - LIBRARY (Energy)
Lagoon Complex
Bldg. 3, Rm. 233
Frederiksted, VI 00840 Phone: (809)772-2616
Subjects: Energy policy. **Holdings:** 5000 books.

★17351★
VIRGINIA BAPTIST HISTORICAL SOCIETY - LIBRARY (Hist, Rel-Phil)
University of Richmond
Box 34 Phone: (804)289-8434
Richmond, VA 23173 Fred Anderson, Exec.Dir.
Founded: 1876. **Staff:** Prof 2; Other 2. **Subjects:** History - Virginia Baptist, Baptist, religious, church, Virginia State, Confederate, Colonial Virginia. **Special Collections:** Church manuscripts (2600). **Holdings:** 12,000 books; 650 bound periodical volumes; 95 VF drawers of manuscripts, documents, papers, diaries, journals. **Subscriptions:** 12 journals and other serials. **Services:** Copying; library open to the public by appointment. **Publications:** Virginia Baptist Register, annual - to members and by subscription; The Chronicle, quarterly - to members. **Special Indexes:** Index to Virginia Baptist Register; index to The Religious Herald, 1828-1874 (card).

★17352★
VIRGINIA BAPTIST HOSPITAL - BARKSDALE MEDICAL LIBRARY (Med)
3300 Rivermont Ave. Phone: (804)522-4505
Lynchburg, VA 24503 Anne M. Nurmi, Libn.
Staff: Prof 1. **Subjects:** Obstetrics and gynecology, pediatrics, internal medicine. **Holdings:** 600 books; 2000 bound periodical volumes; video cassettes. **Subscriptions:** 66 journals and other serials. **Services:** Interlibrary loan; copying; library open to the public for reference use only. **Computerized Information Services:** MEDLINE. **Networks/Consortia:** Member of Southeastern/Atlantic Regional Medical Library Services, Lynchburg Area Library Cooperative.

★17353★
VIRGINIA BEACH PUBLIC LIBRARY SYSTEM - MUNICIPAL REFERENCE LIBRARY (Soc Sci)
Municipal Center Phone: (804)427-4644
Virginia Beach, VA 23456 Kathleen G. Hevey, Municipal Ref.Coord.
Founded: 1972. **Staff:** Prof 2; Other 1. **Subjects:** Virginia Beach, public administration. **Special Collections:** Governmental and community affairs news clippings. **Holdings:** 2380 books and documents; 100 bound periodical volumes; 550 information files; 4000 microfiche. **Subscriptions:** 120 journals and other serials; 10 newspapers. **Services:** Interlibrary loan; copying; SDI; library open to the public for reference use only. **Automated Operations:** Computerized cataloging, acquisitions, and circulation. **Computerized Information Services:** DIALOG Information Services, LOGIN; LINUS, Pacific Telecommunication International, Inc. (PTI; electronic mail services). **Publications:** Information Briefs, bimonthly - for internal distribution only. **Special Indexes:** Newspaper clippings index (online). **Staff:** Helen M. Buonviri, Info.Spec..

★17354★
VIRGINIA BEACH PUBLIC LIBRARY SYSTEM - ROBERT S. WAHAB, JR. PUBLIC LAW LIBRARY (Law)
Municipal Center Phone: (804)427-4419
Virginia Beach, VA 23456-9002 Robert P. Miller, Jr., Law Libn.
Staff: Prof 2. **Subjects:** Law. **Holdings:** 8300 books; 200 bound periodical volumes. **Subscriptions:** 25 journals and other serials. **Services:** Interlibrary loan; copying; library open to the public for reference use only. **Staff:** Terry R. Mathieson, Info.Spec..

★17355★
VIRGINIA CHEMICALS, INC. - LIBRARY (Sci-Engr)
3340 W. Norfolk Rd. Phone: (703)483-7213
Portsmouth, VA 23703 Barbara Smith, Libn.
Staff: Prof 1. **Subjects:** Chemistry, chemical engineering, textiles, pulp and paper. **Holdings:** 2000 books; 3000 bound periodical volumes. **Subscriptions:** 82 journals and other serials. **Services:** Library not open to the public. **Computerized Information Services:** DIALOG Information Services, Pergamon ORBIT InfoLine, Inc., Occupational Health Services, Inc., MEDLINE.

★17356★
VIRGINIA COMMONWEALTH UNIVERSITY - JAMES BRANCH CABELL LIBRARY - SPECIAL COLLECTIONS AND ARCHIVES (Hum)
901 Park Ave.
VCU Box 2033 Phone: (804)367-1108
Richmond, VA 23284-2033 Dr. John H. Whaley, Interim Hd.
Founded: 1966. **Staff:** Prof 3; Other 2. **Subjects:** Contemporary Virginia authors, Southeastern American poetry, 20th century American cartoons and caricatures, book art. **Special Collections:** James Branch Cabell Collection (3000 books, notes, and manuscripts); Poetry Society of Virginia Memorial Collection (325 volumes); Richmond authors (250 volumes);

Giacomini Collection (Samuel Johnson and James Boswell; 500 volumes); Richmond Area Development Archives (310 feet); Virginia Health Sciences Archives (175 feet); Adele Clark Suffrage Collection (100 feet); New Virginia Review Library (600 books and current periodicals); Richmond YWCA Records (30 feet). **Holdings:** 8000 books; 1535 feet of manuscripts; 1250 theses; university archives. **Services:** Copying; collections open to the public. **Automated Operations:** Computerized cataloging, acquisitions, and serials. **Computerized Information Services:** BRS Information Technologies, OCLC. **Networks/Consortia:** Member of SOLINET. **Remarks:** Collection housed in 2 buildings, James Branch Cabell Library and Tompkins-McCaw Library. **Staff:** Jodi Koste, Archv.; Betsy Pittman, Archv..

★17357★
VIRGINIA COMMONWEALTH UNIVERSITY - MEDICAL COLLEGE OF VIRGINIA - TOMPKINS-MC CAW LIBRARY (Med)
509 N. 12th St.
Box 582 Phone: (804)786-0633
Richmond, VA 23298-0001 William J. Judd, Dir., Univ.Lib.Serv.
Founded: 1913. **Staff:** Prof 8; Other 26. **Subjects:** Medicine, dentistry, pharmacy, nursing, basic sciences, allied health sciences. **Holdings:** 210,543 bound volumes; institutional archives. **Subscriptions:** 3750 journals and other serials. **Services:** Interlibrary loan; SDI; library open to the public. **Automated Operations:** Computerized cataloging, serials, and circulation. **Computerized Information Services:** DIALOG Information Services, MEDLINE, BRS Information Technologies, NLM, OCLC. Performs searches on fee basis. **Networks/Consortia:** Member of SOLINET. **Publications:** Monthly Statistical Report; Library Handbook. **Staff:** Prudence Clark, Coll.Dev.Libn.; Christine Kush, ILL; Judith Robinson, Online Serv.; Jodi Koste, Archv.; Kevin Wah, Lrng.Rsrcs.Ctrs.; Dr. Virginia Crowe, Pub.Serv.Div.; Melanie Hillner, Info.Serv.Dept..

VIRGINIA ELECTRIC AND POWER COMPANY
See: Virginia Power (17371)

VIRGINIA HEALTH SCIENCES ARCHIVES
See: Virginia Commonwealth University - James Branch Cabell Library - Special Collections and Archives (17356)

★17358★
VIRGINIA HISTORICAL SOCIETY - LIBRARY (Hist)
428 North Blvd.
Box 7311 Phone: (804)358-4901
Richmond, VA 23221 Donald Haynes, Dir.
Founded: 1831. **Staff:** Prof 11; Other 6. **Subjects:** Virginiana, 16th-19th century Americana. **Special Collections:** Confederate imprints; 17th and 18th century English architecture. **Holdings:** 265,000 volumes; 7 million manuscripts; prints and engravings; maps and printed ephemera; sheet music; newspapers; paintings. **Subscriptions:** 330 journals and other serials. **Services:** Copying; library open to the public. **Staff:** Virginius C. Hall, Jr., Assoc.Dir.; Robert F. Strohm, Asst.Dir., Adm.; Frances Pollard, Ref.; Sarah M. Sartain, Bks. & Ser.; Howson W. Cole, Mss. & Archv.; Waverly Winfree, Mss. & Archv.; E. Lee Shepard, Mss. & Archv.; William Obrochta, Mss. & Archv..

VIRGINIA INSTITUTE
See: University of Richmond/Virginia Institute (16816)

★17359★
VIRGINIA INSTITUTE OF MARINE SCIENCE - LIBRARY (Biol Sci)
College of William and Mary
School of Marine Science Phone: (804)642-7114
Gloucester Point, VA 23062 Susan O. Barrick, Lib.Dir.
Founded: 1953. **Staff:** Prof 3; Other 1. **Subjects:** Marine biology and ecology, oceanography, aquaculture, Chesapeake Bay. **Special Collections:** Sport fishing collection; rare books. **Holdings:** 14,000 books; 24,000 bound periodical volumes; 500 volumes of VIMS Archives. **Subscriptions:** 800 journals and other serials. **Services:** Interlibrary loan; copying; library open to the public. **Automated Operations:** Computerized cataloging and serials. **Computerized Information Services:** DIALOG Information Services, OCLC. **Networks/Consortia:** Member of SOLINET. **Publications:** VIMS Publications List, annual; VIMS Contributions, annual; Chesapeake Bay Bibliography (book and online); Library Acquisitions List, bimonthly. **Remarks:** Alternate telephone numbers are 642-7115 and 642-7116. **Staff:** Janice Meadows, Cat./ILL; Diane Walker, Circ. & Rd.Serv..

★17360★
VIRGINIA MARINE SCIENCE MUSEUM - LIBRARY (Biol Sci)
717 General Booth Blvd. Phone: (804)425-3476
Virginia Beach, VA 23451 Lynn Clements, Educ.Prog.Coord.
Founded: 1985. **Staff:** Prof 14. **Subjects:** Marine science, Chesapeake Bay, museums and aquariums, local maritime history. **Holdings:** Figures not available. **Subscriptions:** 14 journals and other serials. **Services:** Library open to researchers.

VIRGINIA-MARYLAND REGIONAL COLLEGE OF VETERINARY MEDICINE
See: Virginia Polytechnic Institute and State University (17370)

★17361★
VIRGINIA MILITARY INSTITUTE - PRESTON LIBRARY (Hum, Sci-Engr)
Lexington, VA 24450 Phone: (703)463-6228
James E. Gaines, Hd.Libn.
Founded: 1839. **Staff:** Prof 7; Other 11. **Subjects:** Engineering, liberal arts. **Special Collections:** Civil War period; Virginia Military Institute archives. **Holdings:** 285,933 volumes; 137,151 government documents. **Subscriptions:** 861 journals and other serials; 31 newspapers. **Services:** Interlibrary loan; copying; library open to the public. **Computerized Information Services:** DIALOG Information Services, OCLC. **Networks/Consortia:** Member of SOLINET. **Publications:** Friends of Preston Library Newsletter; annual report. **Special Indexes:** Library Guide. **Staff:** Wylma P. Davis, Ref.Libn.; Janet S. Holly, Asst.Ref.Libn.; Winnie F. Fun, Tech.Serv.; Edward DeLong, AV Libn.; Diane B. Jacob, Archv..

★17362★
VIRGINIA MUSEUM OF FINE ARTS - LIBRARY (Art)
Boulevard & Grove Ave.
Box 7260 Phone: (804)257-0827
Richmond, VA 23221 Betty A. Stacy, Libn.
Founded: 1936. **Staff:** Prof 4. **Subjects:** Art history, decorative arts, painting, sculpture, theater. **Special Collections:** John Barton Payne Collection; John Koenig Collection (theater); Ellen Bayard Weedon Collection (Oriental studies); Gordon Strause Collection; Ike Bana Society Collection; John G. Hayes Decorative Arts Collection. **Holdings:** 52,000 books; 1200 bound periodical volumes; VF drawers of clippings; 728 boxes of museum publications; 660 boxes of auction catalogs. **Subscriptions:** 200 journals and other serials. **Services:** Copying; library open to the public for reference use only. **Staff:** Margaret Burcham, Lib.Asst..

★17363★
VIRGINIA POLYTECHNIC INSTITUTE AND STATE UNIVERSITY - ARCHIVES OF AMERICAN AEROSPACE EXPLORATION (Sci-Engr)
Special Collections Department
Carol M. Newman Library Phone: (703)961-6308
Blacksburg, VA 24061 Glenn L. McMullen, Hd., Spec.Coll.Dept.
Founded: 1986. **Staff:** Prof 3; Other 1. **Subjects:** Aeronautical engineering, space transportation and exploration. **Holdings:** Papers of Christopher Kraft (30 cubic feet), Samuel Herrick (60 cubic feet), John T. Parsons (200 cubic feet), Melvin Gough (20 cubic feet), Hartley Soule (2 cubic feet), Marjorie R. Townsend (2 cubic feet), Thornton L. Page (2 cubic feet), and James Randolph (4 cubic feet). **Services:** Copying; archives open to the public. **Staff:** Laura H. Katz, Mss.Cur..

★17364★
VIRGINIA POLYTECHNIC INSTITUTE AND STATE UNIVERSITY - ART & ARCHITECTURE LIBRARY (Art, Plan)
Cowgill Hall Phone: (703)961-6182
Blacksburg, VA 24061 Robert E. Stephenson, Art & Arch.Libn.
Staff: Prof 1; Other 4. **Subjects:** Architecture, art, urban affairs and planning, building construction, landscape architecture. **Holdings:** 55,700 volumes; 7125 microforms; 1823 files of planning materials; 30,500 architecture slides. **Subscriptions:** 525 journals and other serials. **Services:** Interlibrary loan; copying; library open to the public. **Automated Operations:** Computerized cataloging, acquisitions, and circulation. **Computerized Information Services:** DIALOG Information Services, OCLC, Knowledge Index, MEDLARS, WILSONLINE, CAS ONLINE, NASA/RECON; Virginia Tech Library System (VTLS; internal database). Performs searches on fee basis. Contact Person: Harry Kriz, Hd., Sys.Off., 961-6617. **Networks/Consortia:** Member of SOLINET. **Special Catalogs:** Planning vertical file catalog (card).

★17365★
VIRGINIA POLYTECHNIC INSTITUTE AND STATE UNIVERSITY - CAROL M. NEWMAN LIBRARY (Sci-Engr, Hum)
Blacksburg, VA 24061 Phone: (703)961-5593
Paul M. Gherman, Dir.
Founded: 1872. **Staff:** Prof 56; Other 108. **Subjects:** Agricultural sciences, architecture, biological and physical sciences, engineering, humanities, social sciences. **Special Collections:** Archive of Norfolk & Western Railway; Archive of Southern Railway Predecessors; Sherwood Anderson book collection; History of Technology; Southwest Virginiana; Western Americana. **Holdings:** 1.6 million books and bound periodical volumes; 115,000 maps; 3.6 million microforms; 6000 phonograph records; 125 audiotapes; 350 videotapes. **Subscriptions:** 23,000 journals and other serials; 78 newspapers. **Services:** Interlibrary loan; copying; library open to the public. **Automated Operations:** Computerized cataloging, acquisitions, serials, and circulation. **Computerized Information Services:** DIALOG Information Services, OCLC, MEDLARS, CAS ONLINE; Virginia Tech Library System (VTLS; internal database). Performs searches on fee basis. Contact Person: Harry Kriz, Hd., Sys.Off., 961-6617. **Networks/Consortia:** Member of SOLINET. **Publications:** Detailed Documentation of Virginia Tech Library System (VTLS). **Staff:** Ann Edwards, Act.Hd., Hum.Dept.; Gail McMullen, Act.Hd., Bibliog.Serv.; Paul D. Metz, Hd., User Serv.Dept.; Michael Cramer, Act.Hd., Acq.Dept.; Donald J. Kenney, Hd., Gen.Ref.Dept.; Mary R. Hinkle, Hd., Soc.Sci.Dept..

★17366★
VIRGINIA POLYTECHNIC INSTITUTE AND STATE UNIVERSITY - CENTER FOR HOSPITALITY RESEARCH & SERVICE (Bus-Fin)
Division of Hotel, Restaurant & Institutional Management
Hillcrest Hall, Rm. 15 Phone: (703)961-4567
Blacksburg, VA 24061 Michael D. Olsen, Ph.D., Exec.Dir.
Staff: Prof 2. **Subjects:** Hospitality service industries. **Holdings:** Figures not available. **Services:** Center not open to the public.

★17367★
VIRGINIA POLYTECHNIC INSTITUTE AND STATE UNIVERSITY - CENTER FOR THE STUDY OF SCIENCE IN SOCIETY - LIBRARY (Sci-Engr)
Price House Phone: (703)961-7687
Blacksburg, VA 24061 Robert A. Paterson, Dir.
Staff: 2. **Subjects:** Science and technology studies; history of science and technology. **Special Collections:** Richard Schallenberg Collection (history of science and technology). **Holdings:** 1100 books; unbound periodicals, reports, and manuscripts. **Subscriptions:** 17 journals and other serials. **Services:** Library open to the public.

★17368★
VIRGINIA POLYTECHNIC INSTITUTE AND STATE UNIVERSITY - GEOLOGY LIBRARY (Sci-Engr)
3040 Derring Hall Phone: (703)961-6101
Blacksburg, VA 24061 Patricia J. Morris, Geol.Libn.
Staff: Prof 1; Other 1. **Subjects:** Geology of Virginia, seismic geophysics, geochemistry, paleontology, mineralogy. **Holdings:** 33,000 volumes; 350 reels of microfilm; 10,000 microfiche; 10,000 maps; 38,000 aerial photographs. **Subscriptions:** 500 journals and other serials. **Services:** Interlibrary loan; copying; library open to the public. **Automated Operations:** Computerized circulation. **Computerized Information Services:** DIALOG Information Services, OCLC. Performs searches on fee basis. **Networks/Consortia:** Member of SOLINET. **Publications:** New Acquisitions List, bimonthly - free upon request.

★17369★
VIRGINIA POLYTECHNIC INSTITUTE AND STATE UNIVERSITY - INTERNATIONAL ARCHIVE OF WOMEN IN ARCHITECTURE (Art)
Special Collections Dept.
University Libraries Phone: (703)961-6308
Blacksburg, VA 24061 Laura H. Katz, Archv.
Founded: 1985. **Staff:** Prof 1. **Subjects:** Architecture, women. **Holdings:** 50 collections of photographs, architectural drawings, artwork, catalogs, and brochures. **Services:** Copying; archive open to the public.

★17370★
VIRGINIA POLYTECHNIC INSTITUTE AND STATE UNIVERSITY - VIRGINIA-MARYLAND REGIONAL COLLEGE OF VETERINARY MEDICINE - LIBRARY (Med)
CVM, Phase II Phone: (703)961-7666
Blacksburg, VA 24061 Victoria T. Kok, Vet.Med.Libn.
Founded: 1980. **Staff:** Prof 1; Other 2. **Subjects:** Clinical and preclinical veterinary medicine. **Holdings:** 1370 books; 500 bound periodical volumes; 300 slide sets and video cassettes. **Subscriptions:** 194 journals and other serials. **Services:** Interlibrary loan; SDI; library open to the public. **Automated Operations:** Computerized cataloging, acquisitions, serials, and circulation. **Computerized Information Services:** DIALOG Information Services, MEDLARS. Performs searches on fee basis. **Remarks:** An alternate telephone number is 961-6610.

★17371★
VIRGINIA POWER - LIBRARY & INFORMATION SERVICES (Energy, Sci-Engr)
One James River Plaza
Box 26666 Phone: (804)771-3657
Richmond, VA 23261 Barbara A. Wichser, Supv.
Founded: 1937. **Staff:** Prof 5; Other 4. **Subjects:** Electric power, nuclear power, environment, fuel resources, engineering, management. **Holdings:** 23,000 books; 960 bound periodical volumes; 79 shelves of government and industry reports; 40 shelves of pamphlets and clippings; 4 shelves of standards; 7000 microforms, including industry standards. **Subscriptions:** 700 journals and other serials; 185 newspapers. **Services:** Interlibrary loan; library open to the public by appointment. **Automated Operations:** Computerized cataloging, acquisitions, serials, and circulation. **Computerized Information Services:** DIALOG Information Services, Pergamon ORBIT InfoLine, Inc., LEXIS, NEXIS, Dun & Bradstreet Corporation, Utility Data Institute. **Formerly:** Virginia Electric and Power Company. **Staff:** Barbara A. Wichser, Supv.; Linda G. Royal, Info.Spec.; Mary Ann Dvorak, Assoc.Info.Spec.; Sheila D. Hedgecock, Assoc.Info.Spec..

★17372★
VIRGINIA STATE DEPARTMENT OF CONSERVATION AND HISTORIC RESOURCES - DIVISION OF HISTORIC LANDMARKS - ARCHIVES AND LIBRARY (Hist, Art)
221 Governor St. Phone: (804)786-3143
Richmond, VA 23230 Elizabeth P. Hoge, Archv.
Staff: Prof 1. **Subjects:** Architecture and history of buildings, structures, and sites in Virginia, 1600s to present. **Special Collections:** Mutual Assurance Company insurance policies for the State of Virginia; measured drawings of historic buildings. **Holdings:** 35,000 files; 150,000 photographs; slides; historic maps. **Services:** Copying; library open to the public for reference use only.

★17373★
VIRGINIA (State) DEPARTMENT OF CORRECTIONS - ACADEMY FOR STAFF DEVELOPMENT - LIBRARY (Soc Sci, Law)
500 N. Winchester Ave.
Box 2215 Phone: (703)943-3141
Waynesboro, VA 22980 Carmela Sperlazza Southers, Libn.
Staff: Prof 1; Other 1. **Subjects:** Criminal justice, management, psychology, juvenile delinquency, family therapy, training and development. **Holdings:** 5800 books; 69 bound periodical volumes; 250 16mm films; 117 filmstrips; 270 videotapes; 5 VF drawers; 34 slide/cassette sets. **Subscriptions:** 90 journals and other serials. **Services:** Interlibrary loan; copying; library open to the public by appointment. **Publications:** Acquisitions list, quarterly; AV resources list; subject bibliographies.

★17374★
VIRGINIA STATE DEPARTMENT OF CRIMINAL JUSTICE SERVICES - LIBRARY (Law, Soc Sci)
805 E. Broad St. Phone: (804)786-8478
Richmond, VA 23219 Stephen E. Squire, Libn.
Founded: 1982. **Staff:** Prof 1. **Subjects:** Criminal and juvenile justice planning and evaluation; crime prevention programs; domestic violence. **Holdings:** 6000 volumes; 10 VF drawers; 45 microfiche. **Subscriptions:** 250 journals and other serials. **Services:** Interlibrary loan; copying; library open to the public by appointment. **Networks/Consortia:** Member of Criminal Justice Information Exchange Group. **Publications:** Current Newsletters and Periodicals List, irregular - available upon request; List of Acquisitions, weekly - for internal distribution only.

★17375★
VIRGINIA STATE DEPARTMENT OF EDUCATION - DIVISION OF MANAGEMENT INFORMATION SERVICES - DATA UTILIZATION & REPORTING (Educ)
Box 6Q Phone: (804)225-2101
Richmond, VA 23216 M. Diane Wresinski, Supv.
Founded: 1960. **Staff:** Prof 2; Other 1. **Subjects:** Educational research and statistics. **Holdings:** Statistical reports and documents. **Services:** Copying; open to the public. **Publications:** Facing Up, annual; Membership Report, annual; School Census, triennial.

★17376★
VIRGINIA STATE DEPARTMENT OF GENERAL SERVICES - DIVISION OF CONSOLIDATED LABORATORY SERVICES LIBRARY (Sci-Engr)
1 N. 14th St. Phone: (804)786-7905
Richmond, VA 23219 Susan E. Wells, Adm. Staff Spec.
Founded: 1963. **Staff:** Prof 1. **Subjects:** Chemistry, forensic science, microbiology. **Holdings:** 2800 books; 500 bound periodical volumes. **Subscriptions:** 75 journals and other serials. **Services:** Library not open to the public.

★17377★
VIRGINIA STATE DEPARTMENT OF HIGHWAYS AND TRANSPORTATION - FILM LIBRARY (Aud-Vis)
1221 E. Broad St. Phone: (804)276-9600
Richmond, VA 23225 Nancy T. Arrowood, Film Libn.
Founded: 1968. **Staff:** Prof 2. **Subjects:** Transportation and highway safety. **Special Collections:** Films on all phases of highway safety. **Holdings:** 900 books; 1000 films. **Subscriptions:** 20 journals and other serials. **Services:** Interlibrary loan; library open to state residents. **Special Catalogs:** Film Catalog. **Staff:** Betty Stargardt, Film Libn..

★17378★
VIRGINIA STATE DEPARTMENT OF HIGHWAYS AND TRANSPORTATION - LOCATION & DESIGN PLAN LIBRARY (Plan)
1401 E. Broad St. Phone: (804)786-2521
Richmond, VA 23219 Robert W. Eacho, Off.Serv.Supv.
Staff: Prof 3. **Subjects:** Highway construction and right of way plans. **Holdings:** 60,000 survey books; 17,000 bound periodical volumes; 2 million cards. **Services:** Library not open to the public. **Automated Operations:** Computerized cataloging.

VIRGINIA STATE DEPARTMENT OF HIGHWAYS AND TRANSPORTATION - VIRGINIA TRANSPORTATION RESEARCH COUNCIL
See: Virginia Transportation Research Council - Library (17389)

★17379★
VIRGINIA STATE DEPARTMENT OF INFORMATION TECHNOLOGY - TELECOMMUNICATIONS DIVISION - TECHNICAL LIBRARY (Info Sci)
Eighth Street Office Bldg., Suite 700 Phone: (804)786-8497
Richmond, VA 23219 Jane A. Terrell, Libn./Mgr.
Founded: 1985. **Staff:** 1. **Subjects:** Telecommunications, data communications, telephony. **Holdings:** 500 books. **Subscriptions:** 35 journals and other serials; 12 newspapers. **Services:** Interlibrary loan; copying; SDI; library open to the public by appointment. **Automated Operations:** Computerized cataloging, acquisitions, serials, and circulation. **Computerized Information Services:** MAPPER (internal database). Performs searches free of charge.

★17380★
VIRGINIA STATE DEPARTMENT OF MINES, MINERALS, AND ENERGY - NATIONAL CARTOGRAPHIC INFORMATION CENTER (Sci-Engr)
Virginia State Division of Mineral Resources Library
Box 3667
Charlottesville, VA 22903 Avon L. Hudson, Libn.
Staff: 1. **Subjects:** Geology, mineral resources, remote sensing. **Holdings:** 1171 books; 3501 bound periodical volumes; 478 theses; 7292 maps; 23,890 pamphlets; 672 microforms. **Subscriptions:** 54 journals and other serials. **Services:** Center open to the public for reference use only.

★17381★
VIRGINIA STATE DIVISION OF ENERGY - ENERGY INFORMATION AND SERVICES CENTER (Energy)
2201 W. Broad St. Phone: (804)745-3245
Richmond, VA 23220 Kathy Erickson, Br.Chf.
Founded: 1975. **Staff:** Prof 2; Other 1. **Subjects:** Energy. **Holdings:** 9000 books; 2000 subject files. **Subscriptions:** 122 journals and other serials. **Services:** Center open to the public with restrictions. **Staff:** Jennifer Snead, Res.Spec..

★17382★
VIRGINIA STATE DIVISION OF LEGISLATIVE SERVICES - REFERENCE LIBRARY (Soc Sci)
Box 3-AG Phone: (804)786-3591
Richmond, VA 23208 Jay Baxa, Libn.
Founded: 1972. **Staff:** Prof 1. **Subjects:** Energy, taxation, juvenile delinquency, crime, children, economics, environment. **Special Collections:** Historical state reports; Virginia Statutes. **Holdings:** Figures not available. **Services:** Copying; library open to the public. **Computerized Information Services:** LEGISNET, DIALOG Information Services, VU/TEXT Information Services; internal databases. Performs searches free of charge. **Publications:** Topical Studies of the General Assembly of Virginia, irregular - free upon request.

★17383★
VIRGINIA STATE LAW LIBRARY (Law)
Supreme Court Bldg., 2nd Fl.
100 N. Ninth St. Phone: (804)786-2075
Richmond, VA 23219 Gail Warren, State Law Libn.
Staff: 3. **Subjects:** Law. **Holdings:** 85,000 books; 8500 bound periodical volumes. **Subscriptions:** 329 journals and other serials. **Services:** Copying; library open to the public with restrictions. **Remarks:** Maintained by Virginia Supreme Court.

★17384★
VIRGINIA STATE LIBRARY AND ARCHIVES (Hist, Info Sci)
11th St. at Capitol Square Phone: (804)786-8929
Richmond, VA 23219 Dr. Ella Gaines Yates, State Libn.
Founded: 1823. **Staff:** Prof 54; Other 83. **Subjects:** Virginiana, Southern and Confederate history, genealogy, social sciences, U.S. colonial history. **Special Collections:** Virginia newspapers; Virginia public records; Virginia maps; Confederate imprints. **Holdings:** 628,600 volumes; 86,115 maps; 30.3 million manuscripts; 222,900 reels of microfilm. **Subscriptions:** 1481 journals and other serials; 110 newspapers. **Services:** Interlibrary loan; copying; library open to the public. **Automated Operations:** Computerized cataloging and circulation. **Computerized Information Services:** OCLC; Virginia Tech Library System (VTLS; internal database); ALANET (electronic mail service). **Networks/Consortia:** Member of SOLINET. **Publications:** Virginia Cavalcade, quarterly - by subscription; Virginia State Library Publications - by subscription and exchange. **Special Catalogs:** CAVALIR, statewide union list (microfiche). **Staff:** Nolan T. Yelich, Dp. State Libn.; Dr. Louis H. Manarin, State Archv.; William J. Hubbard, Dir., Automated Sys.; William R. Chamberlain, Dir., Gen.Lib.; Richardia Johnson, Dir., Lib.Dev.; Dr. Jon K. Kukla, Asst.Dir., Pubn..

★17385★
VIRGINIA STATE LIBRARY FOR THE VISUALLY AND PHYSICALLY HANDICAPPED (Aud-Vis)
1901 Roane St. Phone: (804)786-8016
Richmond, VA 23222 Mary Ruth Halapatz, Lib.Dir.
Founded: 1958. **Staff:** Prof 2; Other 15. **Subjects:** General collection. **Holdings:** 3000 large print books; 65,000 talking books; 81,000 cassettes. **Subscriptions:** 46 journals and other serials. **Services:** Interlibrary loan; copying; volunteer tape recording program; library open to blind and physically handicapped; open to the rest of the public for reference use only. **Automated Operations:** Computerized circulation. **Networks/Consortia:** Member of National Library Service for the Blind & Physically Handicapped (NLS). **Publications:** Visual News (newsletter), quarterly. **Special Catalogs:** Catalog of large print holdings (book). **Staff:** Gwendolyn Goff, Asst.Libn.; Clayton Bowen, AV Techn..

VIRGINIA STATE OFFICE OF EMERGENCY & ENERGY SERVICES
See: Virginia State Division of Energy (17381)

★17386★
VIRGINIA STATE UNIVERSITY - JOHNSTON MEMORIAL LIBRARY - SPECIAL COLLECTIONS (Educ)
Box JJ Phone: (804)520-6171
Petersburg, VA 23803 Catherine V. Bland, Dean, Lib.Serv.
Founded: 1882. **Special Collections:** U.S. Government document depository; black studies; instructional materials; manuscripts. **Holdings:** Figures not available. **Services:** Interlibrary loan; copying; collections open to the public with restrictions. **Automated Operations:** Computerized cataloging. **Computerized Information Services:** DIALOG Information Services, OCLC. **Networks/Consortia:** Member of SOLINET.

★17387★
VIRGINIA STATE WATER CONTROL BOARD - LIBRARY (Env-Cons)
2111 N. Hamilton St.
Box 11143 Phone: (804)257-6340
Richmond, VA 23230 Patricia G. Vanderland, Libn.
Founded: 1974. **Staff:** Prof 1. **Subjects:** Water, water pollution, waste water, groundwater, toxins in water, environment. **Special Collections:** Virginia State Water Control Board publications (185); Environmental Protection Agency publications (2500). **Holdings:** 5000 books; 150 bound periodical volumes; 6000 pamphlets and reprints; 1800 unbound reports; 6300 microforms; government publications on water and environment. **Subscriptions:** 101 journals and other serials. **Services:** Interlibrary loan; copying; library open to the public for reference use only. **Publications:** Acquisitions List, quarterly.

★17388★
VIRGINIA THEOLOGICAL SEMINARY - BISHOP PAYNE LIBRARY (Rel-Phil)
Seminary Rd. & Quaker Lane Phone: (703)370-6602
Alexandria, VA 22304 J.H. Goodwin, Libn.
Founded: 1823. **Staff:** Prof 6; Other 2. **Subjects:** Theology. **Holdings:** 110,000 volumes. **Subscriptions:** 706 journals and other serials. **Services:** Interlibrary loan; copying; library open to the public for reference use only. **Automated Operations:** Computerized cataloging and circulation. **Computerized Information Services:** OCLC. **Networks/Consortia:** Member of Washington Theological Consortium, CAPCON. **Staff:** Josephine Dearborn, Asst.Libn..

★17389★
VIRGINIA TRANSPORTATION RESEARCH COUNCIL - LIBRARY (Trans)
Box 3817, University Sta. Phone: (804)293-1959
Charlottesville, VA 22903 Angela Andrews, Libn.
Founded: 1949. **Staff:** 1. **Subjects:** Road and transportation technology, construction and maintenance, traffic safety, environment. **Special Collections:** American Road and Transportation Archives (1340 pamphlets, maps, documents). **Holdings:** 1800 books; 88 bound periodical volumes; 12,300 reports and documents; 156 videotapes and microfiche; 4 drawers of papers by council authors. **Subscriptions:** 109 journals and other serials. **Services:** Interlibrary loan; copying; library open to the public. **Computerized Information Services:** DIALOG Information Services. **Remarks:** Council jointly sponsored by Virginia State Department of Highways and Transportation and University of Virginia.

★17390★
VIRGINIA UNION UNIVERSITY - WILLIAM J. CLARK LIBRARY - SPECIAL COLLECTIONS (Soc Sci)
1500 N. Lombardy St. Phone: (804)257-5820
Richmond, VA 23220 Wanda L. Crenshaw, Libn.
Founded: 1865. **Subjects:** Afro-American materials, with emphasis on Richmond Black history. **Holdings:** 10,543 volumes. **Services:** Interlibrary loan; copying; collections open to the public with special permit for reference use only. **Computerized Information Services:** Cooperative College Library Center (CCLC).

★17391★
VIRGINIAN-PILOT & LEDGER-STAR - LIBRARY (Publ)
150 W. Brambleton Ave. Phone: (804)446-2242
Norfolk, VA 23510 Ann Kinken Johnson, Hd.Libn.
Founded: 1947. **Staff:** Prof 2; Other 5. **Subjects:** Newspaper reference topics. **Services:** Library not open to the public except for brief reference questions by phone. **Special Indexes:** Index to Virginian-Pilot and Ledger-Star, 1947 to present. **Remarks:** Kirn Memorial Library (Norfolk Public Library) has copies of the newspapers on microfilm and is equipped to make copies.

★17392★
VISITING NURSE ASSOCIATION OF CHICAGO - LIBRARY (Med)
322 S. Green
Chicago, IL 60607-3599 Sarah Redinger, Libn.
Staff: Prof 1; Other 1. **Subscriptions:** Nursing, medicine. **Special Collections:** Patient Education literature (500 titles). **Holdings:** 2000 books; unbound periodicals. **Subscriptions:** 100 journals and other serials. **Services:** Interlibrary loan; copying; library open to the public by appointment only. **Automated Operations:** Computerized cataloging, acquisitions, and ILL. **Computerized Information Services:** OCLC. **Networks/Consortia:** Member of Greater Midwest Regional Medical Library Network, Chicago Library System.

★17393★
VISITING NURSE SERVICE, INC. - LIBRARY
328 E. Lakeside St.
Madison, WI 53715
Subjects: Nursing, public health, physical and speech therapy, occupational therapy, home health aids, mobile meals, social work. **Holdings:** Figures not available. **Remarks:** Presently inactive.

★17394★
VISKASE CORPORATION - TECHNICAL LIBRARY (Sci-Engr)
6855 W. 65th St. Phone: (312)496-4286
Chicago, IL 60638 Therese J. Manweiler, Tech.Info.Serv.
Founded: 1945. **Staff:** Prof 1. **Subjects:** Natural and synthetic high polymers; chemistry - food, organic, physical, polymer; packaging; chemical engineering. **Holdings:** 4500 books; 4000 bound periodical volumes; 500 unbound periodical volumes; dissertations; translations; trade literature. **Subscriptions:** 250 journals and other serials. **Services:** Interlibrary loan; library not open to the public.

★17395★
VISUAL COMMUNICATIONS - ASIAN PACIFIC AMERICAN PHOTOGRAPHIC ARCHIVES (Aud-Vis)
263 S. Los Angeles St., Rm. 307 Phone: (213)680-4462
Los Angeles, CA 90012 Linda Mabalot, Exec.Dir.
Staff: 8. **Subjects:** Asian American studies. **Holdings:** 300,000 historical and contemporary photographs and slides. **Services:** Copying; archives open to the public by appointment for reference use only. **Automated Operations:** Computerized photo indexing (in process).

★17396★
VITERBO COLLEGE - ZOELLER FINE ARTS LIBRARY (Art, Mus)
815 S. Ninth
La Crosse, WI 54601 Phone: (608)784-0040
Founded: 1970. **Staff:** 8. **Subjects:** Music, art, theater. **Holdings:** 4750 books; 1110 bound periodical volumes; 9623 scores; 3051 recordings; 268 tapes; 18 compact discs; 1100 plays. **Subscriptions:** 50 journals and other serials. **Services:** Library open to the public with restrictions. **Networks/Consortia:** Member of Wisconsin Interlibrary Services (WILS). **Staff:** Bruce Roby, Cat.; Sr. M. Annarose Glum, Circ.Libn..

★17397★
VITRO CORPORATION - LIBRARY (Sci-Engr)
14000 Georgia Ave. Phone: (301)231-2553
Silver Spring, MD 20910 Louis M. Morris, Proj.Hd./Libn.
Founded: 1948. **Staff:** Prof 1; Other 2. **Subjects:** Missiles and spacecraft, systems engineering, management, data processing, electronic engineering, ships, underwater acoustics, antisubmarine warfare. **Holdings:** 9246 books; 1135 bound periodical volumes; 19,790 technical correspondence; 650,000 standards and specifications, hardcopy and microfilm; 270 nautical charts. **Subscriptions:** 750 journals and other serials. **Services:** Interlibrary loan; copying; SDI; library open to the public with restrictions. **Automated Operations:** Computerized cataloging and circulation. **Computerized Information Services:** DIALOG Information Services, Pergamon ORBIT InfoLine, Inc., DTIC, Government-Industry Data Exchange Program (GIDEP). **Networks/Consortia:** Member of Interlibrary Users Association (IUA). **Publications:** List of new drawings and technical correspondence, daily; list of new technical reports, weekly; list of new books, monthly - all for internal distribution only. **Special Indexes:** Indexes to drawings of ballistic missiles, guided missiles, missile engineering; technical correspondence index; books, technical reports, and manuals index on COM - for internal distribution only.

R.G. VIVIAN ARCHIVE
See: U.S. Natl. Park Service - Branch of Cultural Research - Library (15257)

★17398★
VIVITAR CORPORATION - TECHNICAL LIBRARY (Sci-Engr)
9350 De Soto Ave. Phone: (818)700-2890
Chatsworth, CA 91311 S. Klang
Founded: 1975. **Subjects:** Photography, optics, engineering, mathematics, manufacturing, design. **Holdings:** 700 books; 200 bound periodical volumes. **Computerized Information Services:** Online systems. **Formerly:** Product Development & Manufacturing Division, located in Santa Monica, CA.

★17399★
VIZCAYA GUIDES LIBRARY (Art)
3251 S. Miami Ave. Phone: (305)579-2808
Miami, FL 33129 Dan Gayer, Lib.Chm.
Staff: 5. **Subjects:** Decorative arts, architecture, furniture, 15th-19th century history. **Special Collections:** James Deering house, furnishings, and gardens (folios; manuscripts; photographs; records; ledgers). **Holdings:** 2500 books; 85 bound periodical volumes; 15,000 slides. **Services:** Library open to the public with written application to the librarian.

★17400★
THE VOCATIONAL AND REHABILITATION RESEARCH INSTITUTE - RESOURCE CENTRE/LIBRARY (Med)
3304 33rd St., N.W. Phone: (403)284-1121
Calgary, AB, Canada T2L 2A6 Bob McGowan, Libn.
Staff: Prof 1. **Subjects:** Developmental disabilities, rehabilitation, vocational training, residential services. **Holdings:** 2500 books; 1200 manuscripts, reports, dissertations. **Subscriptions:** 80 serials. **Services:** Copying; library open to the public. **Automated Operations:** Computerized public access catalog, cataloging, and serials. **Computerized Information Services:** BRS Information Technologies; VRRI Research Database, Library Catalog Database, Reprint Database (internal databases); Disability Information Service of Canada (DISC) Network (electronic mail service).

TORAH VODAATH LIBRARY
See: Yeshiva Torah Vodaath and Mesifta (18164)

A.W. VODGES LIBRARY OF GEOLOGY AND PALEONTOLOGY
See: San Diego Society of Natural History - Natural History Museum Library (12782)

DR. PHILIP J. VOGEL LIBRARY
See: White Memorial Medical Center - Courville-Abbott Memorial Library (17834)

WILLIAM H. VOLCK MUSEUM
See: Pajaro Valley Historical Association (11030)

★17401★
VOLTARC TUBES INC. - LIBRARY (Sci-Engr)
74 Linwood Ave. Phone: (202)255-2633
Fairfield, CT 06430 Evlyn Perkins, Libn.
Staff: Prof 1; Other 1. **Subjects:** Lamp manufacturing. **Holdings:** 500 books; 5 VF drawers of patents; 5 VF drawers of clippings. **Subscriptions:** 60 journals and other serials. **Services:** Interlibrary loan; library not open to the public.

★17402★
VOLUNTARY ACTION CENTER OF THE ST. PAUL AREA - LIBRARY (Soc Sci)
251 Starkey St., Rm. 127 Phone: (612)227-3938
St. Paul, MN 55107 Therese Crisman, Exec.Dir.
Founded: 1975. **Subjects:** Management of volunteer programs. **Holdings:** 500 volumes. **Subscriptions:** 18 journals and other serials. **Services:** Copying; library open to the public.

★17403★
VOLUNTEER - THE NATIONAL CENTER (Soc Sci)
1111 N. 19th St., Suite 500 Phone: (703)276-0542
Arlington, VA 22209 Kay Drake-Smith, Dir., Info.Serv.
Founded: 1979. **Staff:** 1. **Subjects:** Volunteerism, citizen participation, nonprofit organization, leadership, administration, fundraising. **Holdings:** 10,000 published and unpublished documents. **Subscriptions:** 10 journals and other serials. **Services:** Free library research service for associates; fee for nonassociates. **Publications:** Voluntary Action Leadership; Volunteering; Volunteer Readership.

★17404★
VOLUSIA COUNTY LAW LIBRARY (Law)
Courthouse Annex, Rm. 208
125 E. Orange Ave. Phone: (904)257-6041
Daytona Beach, FL 32014 Rae Mastropierro, Law Libn.
Staff: Prof 1. **Subjects:** Law. **Holdings:** 23,500 books and periodicals. **Services:** Copying; library open to the public. **Remarks:** This library maintains branch libraries in DeLand and New Smyrna Beach.

★17405★
VOLUSIA COUNTY SCHOOL BOARD - RESOURCE LIBRARY (Educ)
729 Loomis Ave.
Box 1910 Phone: (904)255-6475
Daytona Beach, FL 32015 Nancy B. Martin, Supv., Media Rsrcs.
Founded: 1967. **Staff:** Prof 1; Other 1. **Subjects:** Education - all subjects K-12. **Special Collections:** Suitcase Museums (60). **Holdings:** 10,000 books; 96 bound periodical volumes; 12,000 AV programs and microfiche; 52 VF drawers; 4000 pamphlets. **Subscriptions:** 133 journals and other serials. **Services:** Interlibrary loan; library not open to the public. **Special Catalogs:** Printed materials and nonprint media catalogs, supplement 2/year.

VON BRAUN LIBRARY/ARCHIVES
See: Alabama Space and Rocket Center (140)

★17406★
SUNNY VON BULOW NATIONAL VICTIM ADVOCACY CENTER - LIBRARY (Soc Sci)
307 W. 7th St., Suite 1001 Phone: (817)877-3355
Fort Worth, TX 76107 Cindy Lea Arbelbide, Libn.
Staff: Prof 1. **Subjects:** Victims of violent crimes, legislation, national and local victim organizations. **Holdings:** Figures not available. **Services:** Library open to the public. **Special Catalogs:** Victims of Violent Crime.

VON KLEINSMID LIBRARY
See: University of Southern California (16887)

LEOPOLD VON RANKE LIBRARY
See: Syracuse University - George Arents Research Library for Special Collections (13858)

★17407★
VSE CORPORATION - TECHNICAL LIBRARY (Sci-Engr)
2550 Huntington Ave. Phone: (703)329-3222
Alexandria, VA 22303-1499 Merriel T. Whitehead, Tech.Libn.
Founded: 1965. **Staff:** Prof 1. **Subjects:** Engineering, physics, mathematics, environment. **Holdings:** 3500 books; 2000 vendor catalogs; Visual Search Microfilm file on military and federal specifications, standards, handbooks, and design engineering. **Subscriptions:** 75 journals and other serials. **Services:** Interlibrary loan; library not open to the public. **Publications:** New Acquisitions, monthly - for internal distribution only. **Special Catalogs:** Consolidated Master Cross Reference List; Cataloging Handbook H4-1 and H4-2 (all on microfiche).

★17408★
VSE CORPORATION - TECHNICAL LIBRARY (Sci-Engr)
1417 N. Battlefield Blvd. Phone: (804)547-4544
Chesapeake, VA 23320 Jo Collins, Tech.Libn.
Founded: 1980. **Staff:** Prof 1. **Subjects:** U.S. Navy ships, marine engineering. **Special Collections:** AFS (auxiliary fast stores) ships (800 technical manuals; 7600 drawings). **Holdings:** 1400 books; 400 vendor catalogs; 5000 aperture cards of drawings; 1600 drawings; 1000 microfiche. **Services:** Library not open to the public. **Special Catalogs:** Technical manuals, specifications, and test procedures catalog; catalog of drawings (both on cards). **Special Indexes:** Technical manuals bibliography lists.

★17409★
WABASH COUNTY HISTORICAL MUSEUM - HISTORICAL LIBRARY (Hist)
Memorial Hall — Phone: (219)563-0661
Wabash, IN 46992 — Jack M. Miller, Cur.
Founded: 1923. **Staff:** 2. **Subjects:** Indiana and Wabash County history, Civil War. **Holdings:** 1940 books; newspapers; manuscripts; documents. **Services:** Library open to the public for research on premises.

★17410★
WACKER SILICONES CORPORATION - SWS SILICONES - TECHNICAL LIBRARY (Sci-Engr)
3301 Sutton Rd. — Phone: (517)263-5711
Adrian, MI 49221 — Dr. George Wolf, Libn.
Subjects: Siloxanes, electronics, sealants, furniture, automotive products, petroleum, tire construction. **Holdings:** 400 books; 400 bound periodical volumes; 7 VF drawers of government publications and specifications; 3 VF drawers of reprints; 10 VF drawers of patents. **Subscriptions:** 90 journals and other serials; 10 newspapers. **Services:** Copying; library open to the public with prior approval. **Formerly:** Stauffer Chemical Company.

★17411★
WACO-MC LENNAN COUNTY LIBRARY - SPECIAL COLLECTIONS DEPARTMENT (Hist)
1717 Austin Ave. — Phone: (817)754-4694
Waco, TX 76701 — Sue Kethley, Spec.Coll.Libn.
Staff: Prof 2; Other 2. **Subjects:** Texas and local history, genealogy. **Holdings:** 13,075 books; 15,354 bound periodical volumes; 5640 reels of microfilm; 2583 microfiche. **Subscriptions:** 413 journals and other serials; 11 newspapers. **Services:** Copying; department open to the public. **Automated Operations:** Computerized cataloging. **Networks/Consortia:** Member of AMIGOS Bibliographic Council, Inc.. **Publications:** Heart of Texas Records, quarterly - by subscription.

★17412★
WADDELL AND REED, INC. - RESEARCH LIBRARY (Bus-Fin)
Box 1343 — Phone: (816)283-4072
Kansas City, MO 64141 — Betty J. Howerton, Hd.Libn.
Founded: 1962. **Staff:** Prof 1; Other 3. **Subjects:** Stock market, industries, corporation statistics, investments, mutual funds, economics. **Holdings:** 700 books; 75 bound periodical volumes; 3000 corporate files; 300 government documents; 42,000 10K and 10Q reports on microfiche. **Subscriptions:** 200 journals and other serials; 40 newspapers. **Services:** Library open to the public for reference use only, with limited access to corporation files.

MARION E. WADE CENTER
See: Wheaton College (17824)

E.H. WADEWITZ MEMORIAL LIBRARY
See: Graphic Arts Technical Foundation (5826)

★17413★
WADHAMS HALL SEMINARY - COLLEGE LIBRARY (Rel-Phil)
Riverside Dr. — Phone: (315)393-4231
Ogdensburg, NY 13669 — Sr. Helen Martin, Hd.Libn.
Founded: 1924. **Staff:** Prof 2; Other 1. **Subjects:** Scholastic philosophy, ascetical theology, classical languages, ecclesiastical history, undergraduate arts. **Holdings:** 75,995 books; 15,379 bound periodical volumes; 883 reels of microfilm; 2308 records; 1580 tapes; 131 videotapes. **Subscriptions:** 590 journals and other serials. **Services:** Interlibrary loan; copying; library open to the public. **Networks/Consortia:** Member of North Country Reference and Research Resources Council (NCRRRC). **Publications:** Monthly Acquisitions List; Patron's Brochure. **Staff:** Susan Campbell, ILL.

★17414★
WADLEY INSTITUTES OF MOLECULAR MEDICINE - RESEARCH INSTITUTE LIBRARY (Med)
9000 Harry Hines Blvd. — Phone: (214)351-8648
Dallas, TX 75235 — Kathryn Manning, Libn.
Founded: 1956. **Staff:** Prof 1. **Subjects:** Cancer, microbiology, hematology, biochemistry, immunology, genetics, interferon. **Holdings:** 11,629 volumes; 73 dissertations; 225 reprints; 6 VF drawers of unbound material. **Subscriptions:** 235 journals and other serials. **Services:** Interlibrary loan; copying; SDI; library open to all medical personnel. **Computerized Information Services:** MEDLINE. **Networks/Consortia:** Member of Dallas-Tarrant County Consortium of Health Science Libraries. **Publications:** Journal Clinical Hematology and Oncology, quarterly - to interested medical personnel and libraries. **Remarks:** An alternate telephone number is 351-8649.

★17415★
WADSWORTH ATHENEUM - AUERBACH ART LIBRARY (Art)
600 Main St. — Phone: (203)278-2670
Hartford, CT 06103 — John W. Teahan, Libn.
Staff: Prof 2. **Subjects:** Fine arts, museology, art education. **Special Collections:** Watkinson Collection (3000 volumes); Lewitt Collection of Artists' Books. **Holdings:** 22,000 volumes; 32 VF drawers; 200 feet of boxes of museum files; 120 feet of sales catalogs; 15 feet of bookplates. **Subscriptions:** 125 journals and other serials. **Services:** Interlibrary loan; copying; library open to the public for reference use only. **Special Indexes:** Index to Wadsworth Atheneum Bulletin; Index to Wadsworth Atheneum Exhibitions, 1910 to present. **Staff:** Karen McNulty, Asst.Libn..

WADSWORTH CENTER FOR LABORATORIES AND RESEARCH LIBRARY
See: New York State Department of Health (10100)

WADSWORTH MEDICAL LIBRARY
See: U.S. Veterans Administration (CA-Los Angeles) (15526)

★17416★
WAGNALLS MEMORIAL LIBRARY (Hist)
150 E. Columbus St. — Phone: (614)837-4765
Lithopolis, OH 43136 — Mrs. Jo Riegel, Lib.Dir.
Founded: 1924. **Staff:** 9. **Special Collections:** Books written by and belonging to Mabel Wagnalls-Jones; local history; letters written by O. Henry to Mabel Wagnalls-Jones; paintings by John Ward Dunsmore. **Subscriptions:** 160 journals and other serials. **Services:** Library open to the public. **Networks/Consortia:** Member of CALICO. **Staff:** Jerry W. Neff, Exec.Dir.; Sue Stebelton, Prog.Coord..

★17417★
WAGNER COLLEGE - HORRMANN LIBRARY - SPECIAL COLLECTIONS (Hum)
631 Howard Ave. — Phone: (718)390-3401
Staten Island, NY 10301 — Y. John Auh, Dir.
Founded: 1883. **Holdings:** U.S. Government documents depository; Edwin Markham Collection (10,000 volumes including poems, prose, clippings, Markham's works in translation, musical settings, recordings, and a line by line index to his poems); Early American and German-American Newspapers (118 reels of microfilm); Old English Literature (105,000 microforms). **Services:** Interlibrary loan; copying; collections open to the public with library card subscription. **Automated Operations:** Computerized cataloging. **Computerized Information Services:** DIALOG Information Services, BRS Information Technologies. **Networks/Consortia:** Member of New York Metropolitan Reference and Research Library Agency (METRO). **Publications:** Markham Review, semiannual.

★17418★
WAGNER FREE INSTITUTE OF SCIENCE - LIBRARY (Sci-Engr)
17th St. & Montgomery Ave. — Phone: (215)763-6529
Philadelphia, PA 19121 — John Graham, Dir.
Staff: 2. **Subjects:** Natural and physical sciences. **Holdings:** 25,000 volumes; 150,000 bound periodical volumes and pamphlets. **Subscriptions:** 10 journals and other serials. **Services:** Interlibrary loan; library open to the public.

WAGNER-KEVETTER LIBRARY
See: William Carter College & Evangelical Theological Seminary (2717)

ROBERT F. WAGNER LABOR ARCHIVES
See: New York University - Tamiment Library (10182)

ROBERT S. WAHAB, JR. PUBLIC LAW LIBRARY
See: Virginia Beach Public Library System (17354)

WAHLERT MEMORIAL LIBRARY
See: Loras College (7969)

WAHLQUIST LIBRARY
See: San Jose State University (12827)

MAGNUS WAHLSTROM LIBRARY
See: University of Bridgeport (15847)

WAIKIKI AQUARIUM
See: University of Hawaii (16200)

★17419★
WAINWRIGHT GENERAL HOSPITAL - MEDICAL LIBRARY (Med)
Box 820 Phone: (403)842-3324
Wainwright, AB, Canada T0B 4P0 Loretta Haire, Hea.Rec.Adm.
Staff: 1. **Subjects:** Medicine, nursing, hospital administration, allied health sciences. **Holdings:** 260 books. **Subscriptions:** 20 journals and other serials. **Services:** Library not open to the public.

★17420★
WAKE COUNTY MEDICAL CENTER - MEDICAL LIBRARY (Med)
3000 New Bern Ave. Phone: (919)755-8528
Raleigh, NC 27610 Karen K. Grandage, Dir., Lib./Info.Serv.
Staff: Prof 2; Other 3. **Subjects:** Medicine, pediatrics, orthopedics, nursing, hospital administration, allied health sciences. **Special Collections:** Staff development/training collection; Clinical Pastoral Education. **Holdings:** 8000 books; 2988 bound periodical volumes; 1000 AV programs. **Subscriptions:** 250 journals and other serials. **Services:** Interlibrary loan (fee); copying; library open to the public with permission of librarian. **Computerized Information Services:** MEDLARS, BRS Information Technologies. Performs searches on fee basis. **Networks/Consortia:** Member of North Carolina Area Health Education Centers Program Library and Information Services Network, Resources for Health Information (REHI). **Staff:** Beverly Richardson, Assoc.Dir., Lib./Info.Serv..

★17421★
WAKE FOREST UNIVERSITY - BABCOCK GRADUATE SCHOOL OF MANAGEMENT - LIBRARY (Bus-Fin)
Reynolda Sta.,
Box 7689 Phone: (919)761-5414
Winston-Salem, NC 27109 Jean B. Hopson, Lib.Dir.
Founded: 1970. **Staff:** Prof 1; Other 4. **Subjects:** General management. **Holdings:** 18,583 books; microforms. **Subscriptions:** 291 journals and other serials. **Services:** Interlibrary loan; copying; library open to the public. **Automated Operations:** Computerized cataloging and ILL. **Computerized Information Services:** OCLC, DIALOG Information Services; internal database. **Networks/Consortia:** Member of SOLINET. **Publications:** Management periodicals in university collections.

★17422★
WAKE FOREST UNIVERSITY - BAPTIST COLLECTION (Rel-Phil)
University Library Phone: (919)761-5472
Winston-Salem, NC 27109 John R. Woodard, Jr., Dir.
Founded: 1885. **Staff:** Prof 1; Other 1. **Subjects:** North Carolina Baptist history, Wake Forest University history. **Special Collections:** Manuscript records of 105 North Carolina Baptist churches; microfilm records of 923 North Carolina Baptist churches. **Holdings:** 11,567 books; 1641 bound periodical volumes; 381 private collections of personal papers; 1572 reels of microfilm; vertical file of North Carolina churches; biography file of North Carolina ministers. **Services:** Copying; will answer correspondence relating to Baptist history; collection open to the public. **Publications:** Newsletter, bimonthly; Special Bulletins, irregular. **Special Indexes:** Index to Biblical Recorder, the North Carolina Baptist newspaper (computerized).

★17423★
WAKE FOREST UNIVERSITY - BOWMAN GRAY SCHOOL OF MEDICINE - COY C. CARPENTER LIBRARY (Med)
300 S. Hawthorne Rd. Phone: (919)748-4691
Winston-Salem, NC 27103 Michael D. Sprinkle, Dir.
Founded: 1941. **Staff:** Prof 11; Other 23. **Subjects:** Medicine, nursing. **Holdings:** 37,326 books; 84,118 bound periodical volumes; 2731 AV programs; 1979 microforms. **Subscriptions:** 2213 journals and other serials. **Services:** Interlibrary loan; copying; SDI; library open to the public for reference use only. **Automated Operations:** Computerized public access catalog, cataloging, acquisitions, serials, and circulation. **Computerized Information Services:** MEDLINE, DIALOG Information Services, BRS Information Technologies, LS/2000, OCLC, WILSONLINE; internal database; OnTyme Electronic Message Network Service, DOCLINE, EasyLink, ALANET (electronic mail services). Performs searches on fee basis. **Networks/Consortia:** Member of SOLINET, Northwest AHEC Library Information Network. **Publications:** FOLIO (newsletter), monthly - to the public. **Staff:** Sherry Anderson, Assoc.Dir.; Carolyn Parker, Coord., Doc. Delivery Serv.; Madeleine Perez, Med.Ctr.Archv.; Bob Winslow, Pharm.D., Drug Info.Serv.Ctr.Dir.; Faye Foltz, Hd., Ser.Sect.; Becky Johnston, Hd., Cat.Sect.; Elizabeth Ladner, Ref.Libn./Comparative Med.; Janine Tillett, Ref.Libn./Educ.Progs.; Sara Ruona, Ref.Libn./Drug Info.Serv.Ctr.; Rochelle Kramer, Ref.Libn..

★17424★
WAKE FOREST UNIVERSITY - LAW LIBRARY (Law)
Reynolda Sta., Box 7206 Phone: (919)761-5438
Winston-Salem, NC 27109 Thomas M. Steele, Dir./Assoc.Prof. of Law
Founded: 1894. **Staff:** Prof 4; Other 5. **Subjects:** Law. **Holdings:** 107,020 books; 11,553 bound periodical volumes; 334,166 microfiche; 4447 reels of microfilm. **Subscriptions:** 2816 journals and other serials; 12 newspapers. **Services:** Interlibrary loan; copying; library open to the public. **Automated Operations:** Computerized cataloging, acquisitions, serials, and ILL. **Computerized Information Services:** WESTLAW, OCLC, LEXIS, NEXIS. **Networks/Consortia:** Member of SOLINET. **Staff:** Mary Louise Cobb, Asst.Libn., Adm. & Tech.Serv.; Glen Peter Ahlers, Hd., Pub.Serv.; Miriam A. Murphy, Ref./Tech.Serv.Libn..

WAKSMAN INSTITUTE OF MICROBIOLOGY LIBRARY
See: Rutgers University, the State University of New Jersey (12269)

JOHN & BERTHA E. WALDMANN MEMORIAL LIBRARY
See: New York University - Dental Center (10172)

★17425★
WALDO COUNTY LAW LIBRARY (Law)
Waldo County Courthouse
73 Church St.
Belfast, ME 04915 Phone: (207)338-2512
Staff: 3. **Subjects:** Law. **Holdings:** 5000 volumes. **Services:** Library open to the public.

WALDO GENERAL HOSPITAL
See: Fifth Avenue Medical Center (5006)

★17426★
WALDORF CORPORATION - TECHNICAL CENTER LIBRARY (Sci-Engr)
2250 Wabash Ave. Phone: (612)641-4125
St. Paul, MN 55114 Yolanda Dorso, Sec.
Subjects: Paper technology, chemistry, packaging, plastics and polymers. **Special Collections:** Institute of Paper Chemistry (abstracts, 1930 to present; 705 project reports and bibliographies). **Holdings:** 550 books; 129 bound periodical volumes; 100 miscellaneous published reports. **Formerly:** Champion International.

LIONEL A. WALFORD LIBRARY
See: U.S. Natl. Marine Fisheries Service - Sandy Hook Laboratory (15220)

★17427★
WALKER ART CENTER - STAFF REFERENCE LIBRARY (Art)
Vineland Place Phone: (612)375-7680
Minneapolis, MN 55403 Rosemary Furtak, Libn.
Founded: 1950. **Staff:** 2. **Subjects:** Contemporary art, art history, architecture, design, film, artists' books, graphics, photography, painting, sculpture. **Special Collections:** Artists' catalogs, 1940 to present; Audio/Video Archive; Edmund R. Ruben Film Study Collection. **Holdings:** 8000 books; 550 bound periodical volumes; 30,000 catalogs; vertical files. **Subscriptions:** 140 journals and other serials. **Services:** Copying; library open to the public by appointment. **Automated Operations:** Computerized cataloging. **Computerized Information Services:** OCLC. **Networks/Consortia:** Member of MINITEX. **Publications:** Design Quarterly. **Special Catalogs:** Walker Art Center exhibition catalogs. **Staff:** Mark Stanger, Asst.Libn.; Karen Dykstra, Slide Libn..

E.F. WALKER MEMORIAL LIBRARY
See: First Baptist Church (5026)

ELISHA WALKER STAFF LIBRARY
See: New York Infirmary Beekman Downtown Hospital (10032)

HASTINGS H. WALKER MEDICAL LIBRARY
See: Hawaii State Department of Health (6157)

HENRY B. WALKER, JR. MEMORIAL ART LIBRARY
See: Evansville Museum of Arts and Science - Library (4841)

★17428★
HIRAM WALKER HISTORICAL MUSEUM - REFERENCE LIBRARY (Hist)
254 Pitt St., W. Phone: (519)253-1812
Windsor, ON, Canada N9A 5L5 Alan Douglas, Cur.
Founded: 1958. **Staff:** 4. **Subjects:** Local history. **Holdings:** 969 books; 29 bound periodical volumes; 327 archival materials; 488 maps; 3089 photographs; 184 reels of microfilm; 1800 microfiche. **Subscriptions:** 26 journals and other serials. **Services:** Copying; library open to the public. **Remarks:** Maintained by the Windsor Public Library Board.

WALKER LIBRARY
See: American Council on Alcoholism, Inc. (467)

WALKER MANAGEMENT LIBRARY
See: Vanderbilt University - Jean and Alexander Heard Library (17285)

★17429★
WALKER MANUFACTURING CO. - LIBRARY
1201 Michigan Blvd.
Racine, WI 53402
Subjects: Automotive industry, business management. **Holdings:** 300 books; 50 bound periodical volumes; 3000 other cataloged items. **Remarks:** Presently inactive.

WALKER MEMORIAL HOSPITAL
See: Adventist Health Systems Sunbelt - Walker Memorial Hospital (68)

★17430★
WALKER MUSEUM - LIBRARY
Fairlee, VT 05045
Subjects: Art, architecture, classical archeology, music, theater. **Special Collections:** Japanese 18th century illustrated books (25 volumes); 15th-16th century calligraphy (10 volumes); Persian lithographed Shah Nameh. **Holdings:** 1000 books; 100 paintings, Civil War letters, woolen industry records. **Remarks:** Presently inactive.

★17431★
WALL STREET JOURNAL - LIBRARY (Bus-Fin, Publ)
World Financial Center
200 Liberty St.
New York, NY 10281 Lottie Lindberg, Libn.
Founded: 1903. **Staff:** Prof 2; Other 12. **Subjects:** Finance, business, investments. **Holdings:** Books; clippings file of The Wall Street Journal. **Services:** Library not open to the public. **Automated Operations:** Computerized cataloging and circulation. **Computerized Information Services:** Dow Jones News/Retrieval. **Special Indexes:** The Wall Street Journal Index, monthly with annual cumulation; Barron's Index, annual.

★17432★
WALLA WALLA COLLEGE - CURRICULUM LIBRARY (Educ)
Smith Hall Phone: (509)527-2221
College Place, WA 99324 Carolyn Wolters, Dir.
Founded: 1963. **Staff:** Prof 4; Other 3. **Subjects:** Vocational guidance, curriculum, social sciences, mathematics, science, health and physical education, language arts, administration. **Special Collections:** Teaching kits; career information files; Standardized Test File (83 titles); children's literature (9950 volumes). **Holdings:** 28,525 volumes; 13,000 pamphlets; 475 phonograph records; 3580 pictures; 150 maps and globes; 200 theses; 351 cassettes; 909 filmstrips; 208 transparencies; 1435 slides; 551 realia. **Subscriptions:** 11 journals and other serials. **Services:** Copying; library open to the public with valid library cards.

★17433★
WALLA WALLA COLLEGE - SCHOOL OF NURSING PROFESSIONAL LIBRARY (Med)
10345 S.E. Market Phone: (503)251-6115
Portland, OR 97216 Shirley A. Cody, Libn.
Founded: 1960. **Staff:** Prof 1; Other 1. **Subjects:** Nursing - administration, medical-surgical, parent-child, public health, psychiatric, mental health. **Holdings:** 8000 books; 1100 bound periodical volumes; 60 tape cassettes; 6 VF drawers of clippings; 2000 pamphlets; 20 slide/tape sets; 60 video cassettes; 60 filmstrips. **Subscriptions:** 125 journals and other serials. **Services:** Interlibrary loan; copying; library open to employees of Portland Adventist Medical Center and to the public with librarian's permission.

★17434★
WALLA WALLA COUNTY LAW LIBRARY (Law)
315 W. Main Phone: (509)529-9250
Walla Walla, WA 99362 Ben R. Forcier, Jr., Libn.
Staff: 1. **Subjects:** Law. **Holdings:** 30,000 volumes. **Services:** Library not open to the public.

JAMES A. WALLACE LIBRARY
See: Memphis Mental Health Institute (8671)

WALLACE LIBRARY
See: The Criswell College (3891)

LILA ACHESON WALLACE LIBRARY
See: Juilliard School (7298)

LOU WALLACE LIBRARY
See: Tennessee State Department of Agriculture (14012)

MADELEINE CLARK WALLACE LIBRARY
See: Wheaton College (17823)

WALLACE MEMORIAL LIBRARY
See: Rochester Institute of Technology (12113)

MIRIAM AND IRA D. WALLACH DIVISION OF ART, PRINTS & PHOTOGRAPHS
See: New York Public Library (10076)

FRANCES L.N. WALLER RESEARCH MUSEUM AND LIBRARY
See: Spotsylvania Historical Association, Inc. (13561)

★17435★
WALLINGFORD HISTORICAL SOCIETY, INC. - LIBRARY (Hist)
180 S. Main St.
Box 73 Phone: (203)269-3172
Wallingford, CT 06492 Mary I. Annis, Pres.
Staff: 1. **Subjects:** Local history, genealogy. **Holdings:** 450 books. **Services:** Library open to the public by appointment.

WALLOPS FLIGHT FACILITY
See: NASA (9511)

W.J. WALLS HERITAGE HALL ARCHIVES
See: Hood Theological Seminary - Livingstone College - Library (6449)

WALNUT CANYON NATIONAL MONUMENT
See: U.S. Natl. Park Service (15359)

★17436★
WALNUT CREEK HISTORICAL SOCIETY - SHADELANDS RANCH HISTORICAL MUSEUM - HISTORY ROOM (Hist)
2660 Ygnacio Valley Rd. Phone: (415)935-7871
Walnut Creek, CA 94598 Sherwood Burgess, Libn.
Founded: 1972. **Subjects:** Walnut Creek history. **Special Collections:** Joseph Reddeford Walker; Albert and Bessie Johnson; Seely-Hodges letters, 1852-1881 (94); Hiram Penniman family; bound collection of Walnut Kernel newspapers (37 years). **Holdings:** 500 books; 62 bound periodical volumes; 6 VF drawers of maps, manuscripts, files, records; 1300 photographs; 25 tapes; 120 unbound newspapers. **Services:** History room open to the public by appointment. **Publications:** Shadelands News, quarterly - to members. **Staff:** Elizabeth Isles, Musm.Dir..

LEWIS WALPOLE LIBRARY
See: Yale University (18139)

★17437★
WALSH COLLEGE OF ACCOUNTANCY AND BUSINESS ADMINISTRATION - LIBRARY (Bus-Fin)
3838 Livernois
Box 7006 Phone: (313)689-8282
Troy, MI 48007 Gloria B. Ellis, Dir.
Founded: 1965. **Staff:** Prof 3; Other 3. **Subjects:** Accounting, auditing, investments, business law, economics, money and banking, taxation, data processing and statistics. **Special Collections:** Annual reports of 1300 companies. **Holdings:** 18,000 volumes; 500 pamphlets; 500 ultrafiche; 60 C.P.A. audiotapes. **Subscriptions:** 350 journals and other serials; 11

newspapers. **Services:** Interlibrary loan; copying; library open to alumni and area businesses and professionals.

★17438★
WALSH YOUNG - LIBRARY (Law)
801 6th Ave., S.W., Suite 2800 Phone: (403)267-8400
Calgary, AB, Canada T2P 4A3 Gail Grout, Libn.
Staff: Prof 1. **Subjects:** Law. **Holdings:** 600 books; 2900 bound periodical volumes. **Subscriptions:** 82 journals and other serials. **Services:** Interlibrary loan; copying; library open to the public with restrictions.

WALSON ARMY HOSPITAL
See: U.S. Army Hospitals (14838)

★17439★
WALTER, CONSTON, ALEXANDER & GREEN, P.C. - LAW LIBRARY (Law)
90 Park Ave.
New York, NY 10016 Phone: (212)210-9526
Staff: Prof 1; Other 1. **Subjects:** Law - corporate, international, German. **Special Collections:** West German law (German and English materials). **Holdings:** 15,000 books. **Services:** Interlibrary loan; copying; SDI; library open to the public with lawyer's permission. **Computerized Information Services:** WESTLAW, DIALOG Information Services, VU/TEXT Information Services, NEXIS, LEXIS. Performs searches on fee basis. **Formerly:** Walter, Conston & Schurtman, P.C.

★17440★
WALTER, HAVERFIELD, BUESCHER AND CHOCKLEY - LAW LIBRARY (Law)
1215 Terminal Tower Phone: (216)781-1212
Cleveland, OH 44113 Leon Stevens, Libn.
Founded: 1932. **Staff:** Prof 1. **Subjects:** Law - tax, labor, business, general. **Holdings:** 13,000 books; 250 bound periodical volumes; briefs; memoranda. **Subscriptions:** 200 journals and other serials; 55 newspapers. **Services:** Library not open to the public. **Computerized Information Services:** LEXIS, NEXIS.

★17441★
JIM WALTER RESEARCH CORPORATION - TECHNICAL INFORMATION CENTER (Sci-Engr)
10301 9th St., N. Phone: (813)576-4171
St. Petersburg, FL 33702 Patricia Owen, Info.Spec.
Founded: 1966. **Staff:** Prof 1; Other 1. **Subjects:** Polymer chemistry, specialty chemicals, building materials, industrial safety, environmental health, paper chemistry. **Holdings:** 3500 books; 600 bound periodical volumes; 20 VF drawers of patents. **Subscriptions:** 200 journals and other serials. **Services:** Interlibrary loan; center not open to the public. **Computerized Information Services:** NLM, DIALOG Information Services, CAS ONLINE. **Networks/Consortia:** Member of Tampa Bay Library Consortium, Inc..

JOSEPH C. WALTER, JR. AND ELIZABETH C. WALTER GEOLOGY LIBRARY
See: University of Texas, Austin - Geology Library (16930)

★17442★
WALTERS ART GALLERY - LIBRARY (Art)
600 N. Charles St. Phone: (301)547-9000
Baltimore, MD 21201 Muriel L. Toppan, Ref.Libn.
Staff: Prof 2; Other 1. **Subjects:** Art - European, Greek, Roman, Egyptian, medieval; manuscripts; sculpture. **Holdings:** 80,000 volumes; 700 rare books; 782 illuminated manuscripts; 1400 incunabula. **Subscriptions:** 700 journals and other serials. **Services:** Copying; library open to the public by appointment. **Staff:** Elizabeth Fishman, Asst./Slide Libn.; Lilian M.C. Randall, Cur., Mss. & Rare Bks..

RAYMOND WALTERS COLLEGE
See: University of Cincinnati (16060)

★17443★
WALTHAM WESTON HOSPITAL & MEDICAL CENTER - MEDICAL LIBRARY (Med)
Hope Ave. Phone: (617)647-6261
Waltham, MA 02254-9116 Alison Coolidge, Libn.
Staff: Prof 1; Other 1. **Subjects:** Medicine, surgery, psychiatry, nursing, hospital administration. **Holdings:** 1000 books; 1600 bound periodical volumes; 2 VF drawers of pamphlets; 1200 volumes of unbound periodicals. **Subscriptions:** 153 journals and other serials. **Services:** Interlibrary loan; copying; SDI; library open to the public. **Automated Operations:** Computerized ILL. **Computerized Information Services:** MEDLINE; MEDLINK, ALANET, DOCLINE (electronic mail services). Performs searches on fee basis. **Networks/Consortia:** Member of Consortium for Information Resources (CIR).

★17444★
WALTON LANTAFF SCHROEDER & CARSON - LAW LIBRARY (Law)
900 Alfred I. DuPont Bldg.
169 E. Flagler St. Phone: (305)379-6411
Miami, FL 33131 Daniel Linehan, Libn.
Founded: 1934. **Subjects:** Law. **Holdings:** 34,000 volumes. **Services:** Library open to attorneys with prior permission.

★17445★
WANDERER PRESS - LIBRARY (Rel-Phil, Publ)
201 Ohio St. Phone: (612)224-5733
St. Paul, MN 55107-2096 Paul W. LeVoir, Ed.
Subjects: Catholic religion, theology, and philosophy. **Special Collections:** Papal Encyclicals, 1740 to present; The Wanderer newspaper, 1867 to present. **Holdings:** 2000 books; 25 reels of microfilm. **Subscriptions:** 50 journals and other serials; 50 newspapers. **Services:** Interlibrary loan; library open to the public by appointment.

★17446★
WANG INSTITUTE OF BOSTON UNIVERSITY - LIBRARY (Sci-Engr, Comp Sci)
72 Tyng Rd. Phone: (508)649-9731
Tyngsboro, MA 01879-2099 Francesca L. Denton, Libn.
Founded: 1980. **Staff:** Prof 2; Other 1. **Subjects:** Software engineering, computer programming languages, program methodology, project management, artificial intelligence, computer science. **Holdings:** 4000 books; 53 bound periodical volumes; 3000 technical reports. **Subscriptions:** 264 journals and other serials; 10 newspapers. **Services:** Interlibrary loan; copying; SDI; library open to the public by appointment. **Automated Operations:** Computerized public access catalog, cataloging, acquisitions, and circulation. **Computerized Information Services:** DIALOG Information Services, VU/TEXT Information Services; internal databases. Performs searches on fee basis. Contact Person: Martha E. Dionne, Asst.Libn., 649-9731, ext. 18. **Networks/Consortia:** Member of NELINET. **Formerly:** Wang Institute of Graduate Studies.

WANGENHEIM ROOM
See: San Diego Public Library (12781)

OWEN H. WANGENSTEEN HISTORICAL LIBRARY OF BIOLOGY AND MEDICINE
See: University of Minnesota - Biomedical Library - Owen H. Wangensteen Historical Library of Biology and Medicine (16455)

★17447★
WAR MEMORIAL MUSEUM OF VIRGINIA - RESEARCH LIBRARY (Mil)
9285 Warwick Blvd. Phone: (804)247-8523
Newport News, VA 23607 Eliza E. Embrey, Libn.
Staff: 1. **Subjects:** Military history. **Special Collections:** Rare books and documents on Spanish-American War, Civil War, World Wars I and II; uniform regulations; military manuals. **Holdings:** 14,000 books; 200 bound periodical volumes; 700 newspapers; 5000 items in historical files; 300 microfiche; 350 films; 25 oral history tapes. **Subscriptions:** 60 journals and other serials. **Services:** Copying; library open to the public by appointment for research use. **Special Catalogs:** Film catalog.

★17448★
WAR/WATCH FOUNDATION - LIBRARY (Soc Sci)
35 Benton St.
Box 487 Phone: (501)253-8900
Eureka Springs, AR 72632 Richard J. Parker, Exec.Dir.
Subjects: Conflict resolution, children and war, human cost of war, international law. **Holdings:** 1200 volumes.

CLARENCE WARD ART LIBRARY
See: Oberlin College (10612)

WARD MEMORIAL LIBRARY
See: Sacred Heart Seminary (12292)

ROBERT WARD ARCHIVES
See: Duke University - Music Library (4442)

WARDEN'S HOME MUSEUM
See: Washington County Historical Society (17476)

E.G. WARE LIBRARY
See: Garden Grove Historical Society (5467)

WARNE CLINIC
See: Pottsville Hospital and Warne Clinic (11492)

THOMAS WARNE HISTORICAL MUSEUM AND LIBRARY
See: Madison Township Historical Society (8299)

WARNER HOUSE LIBRARY
See: Constitution Island Association, Inc. (3696)

★17449★
WARNER-LAMBERT CANADA INC. - LIBRARY (Med)
2200 Eglinton Ave., E. Phone: (416)750-2360
Scarborough, ON, Canada MIL 2N3 Edna Allen, Libn.
Staff: 1. **Subjects:** Medicine, pharmacy, advertising and marketing. **Special Collections:** Clinical papers; current and historical promotional and product information. **Holdings:** 1500 books; 600 bound periodical volumes; 6000 nonbook items; vertical files; 600 tapes; 3500 microfiche; 200 archive files. **Subscriptions:** 200 journals and other serials. **Services:** Interlibrary loan; copying (both by special request); library open to the public by special request. **Computerized Information Services:** MEDLINE, TOXLINE, CAN/OLE, Pergamon ORBIT InfoLine, Inc.

★17450★
WARNER-LAMBERT COMPANY - CORPORATE LIBRARY (Med)
170 Tabor Rd. Phone: (201)540-2875
Morris Plains, NJ 07950 Nedra Behringer, Mgr., Corp.Lib.
Founded: 1945. **Staff:** Prof 7; Other 6. **Subjects:** Pharmaceuticals, medicine, pharmacology, chemistry, microbiology, dentistry, business. **Holdings:** 21,000 books; 21,000 bound periodical volumes; microfilm. **Subscriptions:** 600 journals and other serials. **Services:** Interlibrary loan. **Computerized Information Services:** Online systems. **Staff:** Verdelle B. Jones, Asst.Libn., Tech.Proc.; Mary Ammann, Sr.Lit.Sci.; Linda Warren, Supv., Lib.Oper.; Arlene F. Drucker, Sr.Lit.Sci.; Eric N. Goldschmidt, Sr.Lit.Assoc.; Charlotte Finneran, Lit.Sci..

★17451★
WARNER-LAMBERT/PARKE-DAVIS - RESEARCH LIBRARY (Biol Sci, Med)
2800 Plymouth Rd. Phone: (313)996-7000
Ann Arbor, MI 48105 Sharon Lehman, Mgr.
Founded: 1885. **Staff:** Prof 12; Other 4. **Subjects:** Chemistry, pharmacology, medicine, toxicology, microbiology, pathology. **Holdings:** 17,478 books; 15,118 bound periodical volumes; 3500 microfilm cassettes; 76,457 computerized and indexed product documents; 3767 reprints. **Subscriptions:** 900 journals and other serials. **Services:** Interlibrary loan (limited); library not open to the public. **Automated Operations:** Computerized cataloging, acquisitions, serials, and ILL. **Computerized Information Services:** DIALOG Information Services, Pergamon ORBIT InfoLine, Inc., BRS Information Technologies, NLM; PARDLARS (literature citations on company products; internal database). **Networks/Consortia:** Member of Greater Midwest Regional Medical Library Network, Metropolitan Detroit Medical Library Group (MDMLG), Michigan Library Consortium (MLC). **Staff:** Catherine E. McLoughlin, Supv., Lib.Serv.; Rose Cygan, Supv., Lit.Serv..

★17452★
WARNER, NORCROSS & JUDD - LIBRARY (Law)
900 Old Kent Bldg. Phone: (616)459-6121
Grand Rapids, MI 49503 Mary Lou Calvin, Libn.
Staff: Prof 1; Other 1. **Subjects:** Law. **Holdings:** 10,000 books; 750 bound periodical volumes. **Subscriptions:** 175 journals and other serials. **Services:** Library not open to the public. **Computerized Information Services:** LEXIS, DIALOG Information Services, WESTLAW. **Networks/Consortia:** Member of Michigan Library Consortium (MLC).

★17453★
WARNER-PACIFIC COLLEGE - OTTO F. LINN LIBRARY (Rel-Phil)
2219 S.E. 68th Ave. Phone: (503)775-4366
Portland, OR 97215 Alice Kienberger, Hd.Libn.
Founded: 1937. **Staff:** Prof 1. **Subjects:** Religion, natural and applied science, education, business, economics, social and behavioral science, music, health, physical education. **Special Collections:** Church of God Collection (Anderson, Indiana). **Holdings:** 52,500 books; 3000 bound periodical volumes; 40 theses and dissertations; 1500 AV programs relating to core program. **Subscriptions:** 250 journals and other serials; 5 newspapers. **Services:** Interlibrary loan; copying; library open to the public. **Computerized Information Services:** Online systems. **Staff:** Marilyn Neu, Circ.Libn..

WARNER RESEARCH COLLECTION
See: Burbank Public Library (2034)

★17454★
WARNER & STACKPOLE - LAW LIBRARY (Law)
28 State St. Phone: (617)725-1400
Boston, MA 02109 Brian J. Harkins, Libn.
Staff: Prof 1; Other 1. **Subjects:** Law. **Holdings:** 10,000 books. **Services:** Library not open to the public.

★17455★
WARREN COUNTY HISTORICAL SOCIETY - LIBRARY AND ARCHIVES (Hist)
Box 427 Phone: (814)723-1795
Warren, PA 16365 Mrs. Conrad Brunke, Libn.
Staff: 2. **Subjects:** History - local, state, Indian; genealogy; Quaker records; local authors. **Special Collections:** Harold C. Putnam Collection (local history and the inland rivers of the eastern United States; 95 linear feet); Joseph Wick Collection (background and history of construction of the Kinzua Dam; 9 linear feet); Byron Barnes Horton Collection (history of the Barnes, Hortons, and related families in New England and Pennsylvania; 37 linear feet). **Holdings:** 2000 books; 400 archival boxes of material from local and area families and businesses; 250 boxes of magnetic tapes. **Subscriptions:** 14 journals and other serials. **Services:** Copying; library open to the public with restrictions.

★17456★
WARREN COUNTY HISTORICAL SOCIETY - MUSEUM AND LIBRARY (Hist)
105 S. Broadway
Box 223 Phone: (513)932-1817
Lebanon, OH 45036 Thomas G. Kuhn, Dir.
Founded: 1940. **Staff:** Prof 1; Other 35. **Subjects:** Local history, genealogy, archeology, Warren County, Shaker records, agriculture. **Special Collections:** Shaker Library. **Holdings:** 1500 volumes; 1526 family files; 600 general county information files; 75,000 index cards of county residents; 350 reels of microfilm of court records, church census, newspapers, school records; 24 volumes of cemetery, marriage, and birth records; 87 bound copies of Ohio Historical Society quarterlies; Warren County court, census, school, and church records. **Subscriptions:** 20 journals and other serials. **Services:** Copying; library open to the public. **Publications:** Historicalog, monthly.

★17457★
WARREN COUNTY LAW LIBRARY (Law)
500 Justice Dr. Phone: (513)933-1381
Lebanon, OH 45036 Robert Watson, Libn.
Staff: 2. **Subjects:** Law. **Holdings:** 15,000 volumes. **Services:** Library open to the public.

★17458★
WARREN GENERAL HOSPITAL - MEDICAL STAFF LIBRARY (Med)
667 Eastland Ave., S.E. Phone: (216)399-7541
Warren, OH 44484 Nancy L. Bindas, Med.Libn.
Founded: 1965. **Staff:** 1. **Subjects:** Medicine, surgery, and allied health sciences. **Holdings:** 550 books; 500 bound periodical volumes; 480 Audio-Digest tapes and cassettes; 400 videotapes. **Subscriptions:** 48 journals and other serials. **Services:** Interlibrary loan; library not open to the public.

★17459★
WARREN HOSPITAL - MEDICAL LIBRARY (Med)
185 Roseberry St. Phone: (201)859-6728
Phillipsburg, NJ 08865 Esther Tews, Dir., Volunteer Serv.
Staff: Prof 1; Other 9. **Subjects:** Medicine. **Holdings:** 700 books. **Subscriptions:** 47 journals and other serials. **Services:** Interlibrary loan; library not open to the public. **Computerized Information Services:** Grateful Med.

★17460★
WARREN LIBRARY ASSOCIATION - LIBRARY - SPECIAL COLLECTIONS (Mus, Hist)
205 Market St. Phone: (814)723-4650
Warren, PA 16365 Deana Noack, Hd., Ref.
Founded: 1873. **Special Collections:** Petroleum history (450 items); popular American sheet music of show tunes, 1834-1955 (3590 items); Warren County newspapers, 1824 to present, on microfilm; historic Warren County photographs (460). **Services:** Interlibrary loan (none on sheet music); copying; collections open to the public. **Automated Operations:** Computerized cataloging and ILL. **Computerized Information Services:** OCLC, DIALOG Information Services. **Networks/Consortia:** Member of Pittsburgh Regional Library Center (PRLC).

LOUIS A. WARREN LINCOLN LIBRARY AND MUSEUM
See: Lincoln National Life Foundation (7872)

S.D. WARREN COMPANY
See: Scott Paper Company (13004)

★17461★
WARREN STATE HOSPITAL - MEDICAL LIBRARY (Med)
Box 249 Phone: (814)723-5500
Warren, PA 16365 Daryl G. Ellsworth, Libn./Supv.
Founded: 1930. **Staff:** Prof 2. **Subjects:** Psychiatry, neurology, psychology, medicine, nursing, occupational therapy, therapeutic activities, sociology. **Holdings:** 20,000 books; 1600 bound periodical volumes; 1400 audio cassettes. **Subscriptions:** 190 journals and other serials. **Services:** Interlibrary loan; copying; library open to professional and paraprofessional users. **Automated Operations:** Computerized cataloging and serials. **Computerized Information Services:** OCLC, DIALOG Information Services. **Networks/Consortia:** Member of Pennsylvania State Institutional Libraries, Northwest Interlibrary Cooperative of Pennsylvania (NICOP), Erie Area Health Information Library Cooperative (EAHILC). **Staff:** Helen Sweitzer, Libn..

BETTY WARRINGTON MEMORIAL
See: Krotona Institute of Theosophy - Krotona Library (7565)

★17462★
WARSAW HISTORICAL SOCIETY - LIBRARY (Hist)
15 Perry Ave. Phone: (716)786-3515
Warsaw, NY 14569 Kenneth M. Cole, Cur.
Founded: 1939. **Subjects:** Civil War and Wyoming County history. **Holdings:** 500 books; 100 years of local newspapers bound by years; local publications. **Services:** Library open to the public by appointment.

★17463★
WARWICK PUBLIC LIBRARY - CENTRAL CHILDREN'S LIBRARY (Hum)
600 Sandy Lane Phone: (401)739-5440
Warwick, RI 02886 Susan Humerickhouse, Hd., Ch.Serv.
Staff: Prof 2; Other 2. **Subjects:** Children's literature. **Special Collections:** Educational toys (165). **Holdings:** 30,000 books. **Subscriptions:** 10 journals and other serials. **Services:** Interlibrary loan; copying; library open to the public. **Automated Operations:** Computerized circulation. **Networks/Consortia:** Member of Western Interrelated Library System.

★17464★
WASCANA INSTITUTE OF APPLIED ARTS AND SCIENCES - RESOURCE & INFORMATION CENTRE (Educ)
4635 Wascana Pkwy.
Box 556 Phone: (306)787-4321
Regina, SK, Canada S4P 3A3 Pran Vohra, Supv./Chf.Libn.
Founded: 1972. **Staff:** Prof 2; Other 13. **Subjects:** Nursing, health sciences, dental nursing, agriculture, industrial arts, business. **Holdings:** 38,704 books and AV programs. **Subscriptions:** 450 journals and other serials; 8 newspapers. **Services:** Interlibrary loan; copying; SDI; center open to the public for reference use only. **Remarks:** Includes holdings of libraries at St. John Street Campus, Albert South Campus, Winnipeg North Campus, Maxwell Crescent Campus, and branch libraries in North Battleford, Yorkton and Moose Jaw.

★17465★
WASCANA REHABILITATION CENTRE - HEALTH SCIENCES LIBRARY (Med)
Ave. G & 23rd Ave. Phone: (306)359-9230
Regina, SK, Canada S4S 0A5 Darlene Jones, Dir.
Staff: 2. **Subjects:** Rehabilitation, gerontology, pediatrics, physically handicapped. **Holdings:** 2400 books; 1300 bound periodical volumes. **Subscriptions:** 100 journals and other serials. **Services:** Interlibrary loan; copying; library open to the public with restrictions. **Staff:** Lily Walter-Smith, Libn..

★17466★
WASECA COUNTY HISTORICAL SOCIETY - RESEARCH LIBRARY (Hist)
315 2nd Ave., N.E.
Box 314 Phone: (507)835-7700
Waseca, MN 56093 Mary Ellen Lucas, Res.Ck.
Founded: 1938. **Staff:** Prof 1. **Subjects:** Local and state history, genealogy. **Holdings:** 1000 books; 750 unbound documents; 70 reels of microfilm. **Services:** Copying; library open to the public. **Networks/Consortia:** Member of Southcentral Minnesota Inter-Library Exchange (SMILE), Waseca Interlibrary Resource Exchange (WIRE).

WASH INFORMATION CENTER
See: U.S. Agency for International Development - Water & Sanitation for Health Project - Information Center (14577)

WASHBURN OBSERVATORY
See: University of Wisconsin, Madison - Washburn Observatory (17158)

★17467★
WASHBURN UNIVERSITY OF TOPEKA - SCHOOL OF LAW LIBRARY (Law)
1700 College Ave. Phone: (913)295-6688
Topeka, KS 66621 John E. Christensen, Dir.
Founded: 1903. **Staff:** Prof 6; Other 7. **Subjects:** Law. **Special Collections:** U.S. Government documents depository, 1972 to present; Kansas documents depository; Nuclear Regulatory Commission documents depository. **Holdings:** 122,870 bound volumes; 77,545 volumes on microfiche; CIS microfiche, 1974-1982; U.S. Supreme Court records and briefs, 1974 to present, on microfiche. **Subscriptions:** 2906 journals and other serials. **Services:** Interlibrary loan; library open to the public with restrictions. **Computerized Information Services:** NewsNet, Inc., Dow Jones News/Retrieval, NEXIS, WESTLAW, Kansas Legislative Information System, DIALOG Information Services, LEXIS, OCLC. **Networks/Consortia:** Member of Mid-America Law School Library Consortium, Bibliographical Center for Research, Rocky Mountain Region, Inc. (BCR). **Staff:** Jan Brown, Doc.Libn.; Virgie Smith, Ref.Libn.; David Ensign, Assoc.Dir.; Martin Wisneski, Cat..

★17468★
WASHINGTON ADVENTIST HOSPITAL - HEALTH SCIENCES LIBRARY (Med)
7600 Carroll Ave. Phone: (301)891-5261
Takoma Park, MD 20912 Jeannine M. Hinkel, Libn./Supv.
Founded: 1928. **Staff:** Prof 1; Other 1. **Subjects:** Medicine, nursing, hospital administration. **Holdings:** 4000 volumes. **Subscriptions:** 300 journals and other serials; 10 newspapers. **Services:** Interlibrary loan; copying; SDI; library open to the public for reference use only. **Automated Operations:** Computerized serials, circulation, and ILL. **Computerized Information Services:** MEDLARS, DIALOG Information Services, BRS Information Technologies; DOCLINE (electronic mail service). Performs searches on fee basis. **Networks/Consortia:** Member of Maryland and D.C. Consortium of Resource Sharing (MADCORS), Maryland Association of Health Science Librarians, District of Columbia Health Sciences Information Network (DOCHSIN).

★17469★
WASHINGTON ARCHAEOLOGICAL RESEARCH CENTER - LIBRARY (Soc Sci)
Commons Hall 322
Washington State Univ. Phone: (509)335-8566
Pullman, WA 99164 Richard Bailey, Rec.Libn.
Founded: 1973. **Staff:** 1. **Subjects:** Archeology in Washington and the Pacific Northwest, anthropology, cultural resources management. **Holdings:** 4000 volumes; maps; photographs; slides. **Services:** Copying; graphic display services; library open to the public for reference use only.

★17470★
WASHINGTON AREA WOMEN'S CENTER - WAWC FEMINIST LIBRARY & ARCHIVES
1638 R St., N.W., No. 2
Washington, DC 20009
Subjects: Feminism, lesbianism, sexism. **Special Collections:** Lesbian Heritage archives, 1960 to present. **Holdings:** 1123 books; oral histories; Feminist Radio Network tapes. **Remarks:** Presently inactive.

★17471★
WASHINGTON BIBLE COLLEGE/CAPITAL BIBLE SEMINARY - OYER MEMORIAL LIBRARY (Rel-Phil)
6511 Princess Garden Pkwy. Phone: (301)552-1400
Lanham, MD 20706 Lyn S. Brown, Dir., Lib.Serv.
Founded: 1937. **Staff:** Prof 1; Other 2. **Subjects:** Evangelical theology, Bible, Christian education, missions and evangelism, Greek and Hebrew language studies, church history. **Holdings:** 44,500 books; 1235 bound periodical volumes; 672 filmstrips; microforms; 1581 cassette tapes; 1219 phonograph records; 140 transparency files; 672 religious teaching aid files; 580 VF folders of pamphlets. **Subscriptions:** 267 journals and other serials; 12 newspapers. **Services:** Interlibrary loan; copying; library open to the public with restrictions. **Automated Operations:** Computerized cataloging. **Networks/Consortia:** Member of CAPCON.

BOOKER T. WASHINGTON NATIONAL MONUMENT
See: U.S. Natl. Park Service (15256)

★17472★
WASHINGTON CATHEDRAL FOUNDATION - CATHEDRAL RARE BOOK LIBRARY (Rel-Phil, Rare Book)
Mount St. Alban, N.W.
Washington, DC 20016 Irwin H. Wensink, Chm., Lib.Comm.
Founded: 1965. **Subjects:** Biblical texts, liturgies, church history, theology, church music, ecclesiastical art and architecture. **Special Collections:** Carson Collection of American Bishops (manuscript material in the hand of most of the Bishops of the Protestant-Episcopal Church). **Holdings:** 4000 books and manuscripts. **Services:** Library open to the public by appointment. **Special Catalogs:** Catalogs of special exhibitions.

WASHINGTON COLLEGE OF LAW
See: American University (707)

WASHINGTON COUNTY FREE LIBRARY - WESTERN MARYLAND PUBLIC LIBRARIES
See: Western Maryland Public Libraries (17721)

★17473★
WASHINGTON COUNTY HISTORICAL ASSOCIATION - MUSEUM LIBRARY (Hist)
14th & Monroe Sts. Phone: (402)468-5740
Fort Calhoun, NE 68023 Genevieve Slader, Libn./Cur.
Founded: 1938. **Staff:** 2. **Subjects:** Local and state history, family histories. **Special Collections:** Artifacts and copies of military records of Fort Atkinson, 1819-1827; pioneer documents and letters; Lorenzo Crounse Personal Papers (Governor of Nebraska, 1893). **Holdings:** 600 books; 30 bound periodical volumes; 140 maps and atlases; 54 school reports; 80 manuscripts of letters, genealogies, pioneer reminiscences; 2400 photographs; 23 photograph albums; 2700 clippings. **Services:** Copying; library open to the public for reference use only. **Publications:** The Story of Fort Atkinson (pamphlet) - for sale; Fort on the Prairie (book); History of Washington County, 1876 (reprinted 1985 with index; booklet).

★17474★
WASHINGTON COUNTY HISTORICAL AND MUSEUM SOCIETY - LE MOYNE HOUSE LIBRARY (Hist)
LeMoyne House
49 E. Maiden St. Phone: (412)225-6740
Washington, PA 15301 Laura M. Liggett, Dir.
Founded: 1900. **Staff:** Prof 1. **Subjects:** County histories and biographies, Pennsylvania archives, family genealogies. **Special Collections:** Marriage records; abolitionist correspondence; cemetery records; county atlas and maps. **Holdings:** 1000 titles; old newspapers. **Services:** Library open to the public for reference use only.

★17475★
WASHINGTON COUNTY HISTORICAL SOCIETY - LIBRARY (Hist)
Stevens Memorial Musm.
307 E. Market St. Phone: (812)883-6495
Salem, IN 47167 Rae Etta Bordon
Founded: 1915. **Staff:** 2. **Subjects:** Genealogy, history, religion, biography, antiques. **Special Collections:** Newspapers, 1819 to present; The Christian Record, 1843-1884; Quaker Genealogies for Hinshaw and Blue River; family information (VF drawers). **Holdings:** 2000 books; 75 records; 255 genealogies; 36 cemetery record books; 80 church histories; 1340 family files; 206 reels of microfilm; 45 state histories; 60 Daughters of the American Revolution and Colonial Dames records; 400 files of general historical data; 2 Justice of Peace books; 13 records of 1923 survey of Washington County; 25 files of marriage affidavits, applications, and certificates; 1 file of deeds; booklets of clubs and lodges; 61 diaries; 34 account books; 34 township books; war and school records. **Services:** Copying; library open to the public on fee basis. **Special Indexes:** Index to Washington County newspapers; 1850 and 1860 census indexes. **Staff:** Dorothy Cottongim.

★17476★
WASHINGTON COUNTY HISTORICAL SOCIETY - WARDEN'S HOME MUSEUM - LIBRARY (Hist)
602 N. Main St.
Box 167 Phone: (612)439-5956
Stillwater, MN 55082 Yvette Bergeron Handy, Cur.
Staff: 2. **Subjects:** History - Washington County, Minnesota, St. Croix River Valley. **Holdings:** 100 volumes. **Services:** Library open to the public for reference use only.

★17477★
WASHINGTON COUNTY HOSPITAL - WROTH MEMORIAL LIBRARY (Med)
251 E. Antietam St. Phone: (301)824-8801
Hagerstown, MD 21740 Myra Binau, Coord., Lib.Serv.
Founded: 1953. **Staff:** Prof 1. **Subjects:** Medicine, nursing, and allied health sciences. **Holdings:** 5000 volumes; 8 VF drawers of pamphlets and clippings. **Subscriptions:** 178 journals and other serials. **Services:** Interlibrary loan; copying; library open to the public for reference use only. **Computerized Information Services:** BRS Information Technologies, DIALOG Information Services. Performs searches on fee basis. **Networks/Consortia:** Member of National Library of Medicine (NLM), Maryland Association of Health Science Librarians.

★17478★
WASHINGTON COUNTY LAW LIBRARY (Law)
Circuit Court House Phone: (301)791-3115
Hagerstown, MD 21740 Janna P. Johnson, Law Ck./Libn.
Staff: Prof 1. **Subjects:** Law. **Holdings:** Figures not available. **Subscriptions:** 18 journals and other serials. **Services:** Copying; library open to the public for reference use only. **Remarks:** Maintained by Washington County Bar Association.

★17479★
WASHINGTON COUNTY LAW LIBRARY (Law)
County Court House
205 Putnam St. Phone: (614)373-6623
Marietta, OH 45750 Patricia W. Wheeler, Libn.
Staff: Prof 1; Other 2. **Subjects:** Law. **Holdings:** 15,000 volumes. **Services:** Library open to the public for reference use only. **Computerized Information Services:** WESTLAW. Performs limited searches on fee basis.

★17480★
WASHINGTON COUNTY LAW LIBRARY (Law)
230 N.E. 2nd Ave. Phone: (503)648-8880
Hillsboro, OR 97124 Ann Karlen, Libn.
Founded: 1926. **Staff:** 2. **Subjects:** Law. **Holdings:** 15,000 volumes. **Services:** Copying; library open to the public.

★17481★
WASHINGTON COUNTY LAW LIBRARY (Law)
Courthouse Phone: (412)228-6747
Washington, PA 15301-6813 Charles G. Stock, Jr., Law Libn.
Founded: 1867. **Staff:** 1. **Subjects:** Law. **Holdings:** 18,400 volumes. **Services:** Library open to the public.

★17482★
WASHINGTON COUNTY MUSEUM - LIBRARY (Hist)
17677 N.W. Springville Rd. Phone: (503)645-5353
Portland, OR 97229 Joan H. Smith, Exec.Dir.
Staff: 2. **Subjects:** History, anthropology, cultural resources management. **Special Collections:** Washington County Collection (manuscripts; pamphlets; ephemera). **Holdings:** 100 books; 10,000 photographs; 72 reels of microfilm of Washington County newspapers; 100 cubic feet of manuscript materials; 40 oral history tapes; 3 cubic feet of clippings; 24 reels of microfilm of Washington County archival materials. **Services:** Copying; library open to the public for reference use only. **Networks/Consortia:** Member of Washington County Cooperative Library Services (WCCLS).

★17483★
WASHINGTON COUNTY MUSEUM OF FINE ARTS - LIBRARY (Art)
City Park, Box 423 Phone: (301)739-5727
Hagerstown, MD 21740 Jean Woods, Dir.
Founded: 1931. **Subjects:** Art, art history. **Holdings:** 3100 volumes. **Services:** Interlibrary loan; library open to the public for reference use only.

★17484★
WASHINGTON GAS LIGHT COMPANY - LIBRARY AND RECORDS CENTER (Bus-Fin, Energy)
6801 Industrial Rd. Phone: (703)750-7927
Springfield, VA 22151 Dr. Mahvash K. Momeni, Lib. & Rec.Adm.
Founded: 1944. **Staff:** Prof 3; Other 2. **Subjects:** Gas technology, energy, personnel administration, management. **Special Collections:** Company history. **Holdings:** 30,000 volumes. **Subscriptions:** 820 journals and other serials. **Services:** Interlibrary loan; library open to the public on a limited basis. **Automated Operations:** Computerized cataloging. **Computerized Information Services:** DIALOG Information Services, BRS Information Technologies, Dow Jones News/Retrieval, OCLC. Performs searches on fee basis. **Networks/Consortia:** Member of CAPCON. **Publications:** New in the Library; Corporate Library Bulletin, both monthly. **Staff:** Fred Simms, Info.Res..

★17485★
GEORGE WASHINGTON UNIVERSITY - MEDICAL CENTER - PAUL HIMMELFARB HEALTH SCIENCES LIBRARY (Med)
2300 Eye St., N.W. Phone: (202)994-3528
Washington, DC 20037 Shelley A. Bader, Dir.
Staff: Prof 14; Other 16. **Subjects:** Medicine and allied health sciences. **Holdings:** 20,000 books; 90,000 bound periodical volumes; 1200 titles of AV programs. **Subscriptions:** 1400 journals and other serials. **Services:** Interlibrary loan; copying; SDI; library open to the public with restrictions. **Automated Operations:** Computerized cataloging, serials, circulation, and acquisitions. **Computerized Information Services:** DIALOG Information Services, BRS Information Technologies, NLM, MEDLINE, PHILSOM; internal databases. **Networks/Consortia:** Member of Southeastern/Atlantic Regional Medical Library Services, District of Columbia Health Sciences Information Network (DOCHSIN), Consortium of Academic Health Science Libraries of the District of Columbia. **Publications:** Information Interface, 10/year - to Medical Center faculty, staff; to students upon request. **Staff:** Laurie Thompson, Asst.Dir., Lib.Oper.; Elaine Martin, Asst.Dir., Info. & Instr.Serv.; Anne Linton, Online Serv.Coord..

★17486★
GEORGE WASHINGTON UNIVERSITY - MELVIN GELMAN LIBRARY - SINO-SOVIET INFORMATION CENTER (Area-Ethnic)
2130 H St., N.W. Phone: (202)994-7105
Washington, DC 20052 Craig H. Seibert, Dir.
Staff: 4. **Subjects:** Soviet Union, China, Eastern Europe - political science, history, economics, geography, military; international communism. **Special Collections:** Joint Publications Research Service (J.P.R.S.); translations from foreign press: USSR, China, Korea; Foreign Broadcast Information Service (F.B.I.S.); China, USSR, Eastern Europe, Western Europe, Middle East, Africa, Southeast Asia, Latin America, Asia and Pacific; map collection. **Holdings:** 5000 books; 500 bound periodical volumes; 2000 other cataloged items; microforms. **Subscriptions:** 200 journals and other serials; 6 newspapers. **Services:** Interlibrary loan; copying; center open to the public. **Automated Operations:** Computerized cataloging, acquisitions, serials, and circulation. **Computerized Information Services:** DIALOG Information Services; INQUIRE (internal database). Performs searches on fee basis. Contact Person: Tracy Casorso, Dir., INQUIRE, 994-6973. **Networks/Consortia:** Member of Consortium of Universities of the Washington Metropolitan Area.

★17487★
GEORGE WASHINGTON UNIVERSITY - NATIONAL LAW CENTER - JACOB BURNS LAW LIBRARY (Law)
716 20th St., N.W.. Phone: (202)994-6648
Washington, DC 20052 Anita K. Head, Prof. of Law/Law Libn.
Founded: 1865. **Staff:** Prof 10; Other 17. **Subjects:** Law - Anglo-American, international, comparative. **Special Collections:** U.N. publications; records and briefs of U.S. Court of Customs and Patent Appeals; U.S. Supreme Court records and briefs, 1959 to present; selected U.S. Government documents depository. **Holdings:** 261,000 books; 500,000 microforms. **Subscriptions:** 3800 journals and other serials; 18 newspapers. **Services:** Interlibrary loan; government documents open to the public. **Automated Operations:** Computerized cataloging, acquisitions, and serials. **Computerized Information Services:** LEXIS, WESTLAW, VU/TEXT Information Services, BRS Information Technologies, DIALOG Information Services, NEXIS, ELSS (Electronic Legislative Search System), OCLC. **Networks/Consortia:** Member of CAPCON. **Publications:** Monthly Information Bulletin; Update; Library Guide. **Staff:** Randall J. Snyder, Assoc.Libn. for Adm..

★17488★
WASHINGTON HEALTH CARE ASSOCIATION - WHCA LIBRARY (Med)
2120 State Ave., N.E., Suite 102 Phone: (206)352-3304
Olympia, WA 98506 Diana North, Staff Libn.
Founded: 1985. **Staff:** Prof 1. **Subjects:** Long-term care, nursing, aging, medicine. **Holdings:** 220 books; 20 audiotapes; 2 slide sets. **Services:** Copying; library open to nursing homes and associate members in the state. **Automated Operations:** Computerized cataloging.

★17489★
WASHINGTON HOSPITAL - HEALTH SCIENCES LIBRARY (Med)
155 Wilson Ave. Phone: (412)225-7000
Washington, PA 15301 Mary D. Leif, Libn.
Staff: Prof 1; Other 2. **Subjects:** Medicine, nursing, paramedical sciences. **Holdings:** 7500 books; 1660 bound periodical volumes; 1500 AV programs; 20 VF drawers of pamphlets and clippings. **Subscriptions:** 275 journals and other serials. **Services:** Interlibrary loan; copying; library open to the public for reference use only. **Computerized Information Services:** MEDLINE. Performs searches on fee basis.

★17490★
WASHINGTON HOSPITAL CENTER - MEDICAL LIBRARY (Med)
110 Irving St., N.W., Rm. 2A-21 Phone: (202)877-6221
Washington, DC 20010 Mickey Cook, Dir.
Founded: 1958. **Staff:** Prof 4; Other 4. **Subjects:** Medicine, nursing, health administration, allied health sciences. **Holdings:** 12,000 books; 18,000 bound periodical volumes; 1100 volumes on microfilm; 700 AV programs; 1 file drawer of pamphlets. **Subscriptions:** 960 journals and other serials. **Services:** Interlibrary loan; library not open to the public. **Automated Operations:** Computerized cataloging. **Computerized Information Services:** MEDLINE, DIALOG Information Services, OCLC, BRS Information Technologies; OnTyme Electronic Message Network Service (electronic mail service). Performs searches on fee basis. **Networks/Consortia:** Member of District of Columbia Health Sciences Information Network (DOCHSIN), National Capital Area Hospital Council. **Publications:** News Log, monthly - for internal distribution only; annual report. **Staff:** Anne Swedenberg, Asst.Libn.; Mary Ryan, Asst.Libn.; Velora Jernigan, ILL Techn.; Nancy Terry, Asst.Libn..

★17491★
WASHINGTON & LEE UNIVERSITY - LAW LIBRARY (Law)
Lewis Hall Phone: (703)463-8540
Lexington, VA 24450 Sarah K. Wiant, Dir.
Staff: Prof 5; Other 10. **Subjects:** Law. **Special Collections:** Extensive early Virginia legal materials; annotated codes and statutes for all states, territories, and possessions, federal government; records and briefs of U.S. Supreme Court, 4th U.S. Circuit Court of Appeals, and Virginia Supreme Court; U.S. Government document depository; John W. Davis papers; Caldwell Butler papers on bankruptcy. **Holdings:** 259,862 volumes; microforms; 17,770 documents; 648 AV programs. **Subscriptions:** 3704 journals and other serials; 18 newspapers. **Services:** Interlibrary loan; copying; classroom videotaping; library open to the public. **Automated Operations:** Computerized cataloging. **Computerized Information Services:** VU/TEXT Information Services, DIALOG Information Services, WILSONLINE, NEXIS, LEXIS, WESTLAW, OCLC. **Publications:** Acquisitions List, monthly; Law Library Newsletter; Law Library Users Guide, annual; bibliographies on current legal issues. **Staff:** Jean Eisenhauer, Acq.Libn.; John P. Bissett, Cat.Libn.; Judy Stinson, Doc./Ref.Libn.; John Doyle, Assoc. Law Libn..

★17492★
WASHINGTON & LEE UNIVERSITY - SPECIAL COLLECTIONS DEPARTMENT (Hist)
University Library Phone: (703)463-8663
Lexington, VA 24450 Erin Foley, Spec.Coll.Libn.
Founded: 1939. **Staff:** Prof 2; Other 2. **Subjects:** Local history, genealogy, university history, Civil War, Robert E. Lee. **Special Collections:** Rockbridge Historical Society Collection (local history, genealogy; 130 cubic feet of papers); George West Diehl papers (genealogy, local history, religion; 37 cubic feet of papers); Michael Miley Collection (8000 glass plate negatives); G. William Whitehurst congressional papers (270 cubic

feet); Robert E. Lee papers (6 cubic feet of correspondence). **Holdings:** 334,000 books; 100,000 bound periodical volumes; 50,000 rare books; 84,000 government documents; 112,000 reels of microfilm; 1800 reels of film and videotape. **Subscriptions:** 1500 journals and other serials; 26 newspapers. **Services:** Interlibrary loan; copying; department open to the public. **Automated Operations:** Computerized cataloging. **Computerized Information Services:** DIALOG Information Services. Performs searches on fee basis. Contact Person: Richard Grefe, Ref. & Pub.Serv.Libn., 463-8648. **Staff:** Barbara Brown, Univ.Libn..

★17493★
WASHINGTON LIBRARY FOR THE BLIND AND PHYSICALLY HANDICAPPED (Aud-Vis)
821 Lenora St. Phone: (206)464-6930
Seattle, WA 98129 Jan Ames, Dir.
Founded: 1931. **Staff:** 21. **Subjects:** Blindness and disabilities. **Holdings:** 5000 braille books; 95,000 recorded books; 6000 ink print books. **Subscriptions:** 100 journals and other serials. **Services:** Readers' Services; Radio Reading Service; Braille Service; Taping Service; Aids for Print Handicapped. **Publications:** Newsletter. **Special Catalogs:** Talking book catalogs, braille catalogs, and cassette catalogs - most prepared by the National Library Service for the Blind and Physically Handicapped at the Library of Congress; Northwest Collection and Large Print catalogs for distribution to eligible borrowers and libraries. **Remarks:** Administered by Seattle Public Library. **Staff:** Karen Wallin, Mgr.; Robyn Foreman, Mgr..

★17494★
MARY BALL WASHINGTON MUSEUM AND LIBRARY, INC. (Hist)
Box 97 Phone: (804)462-7280
Lancaster, VA 22503-0097 Ann Lewis Burrows, Exec.Dir.
Founded: 1958. **Staff:** Prof 3; Other 15. **Subjects:** U.S. and Virginia history; county histories; genealogy. **Holdings:** 6000 books; 200 bound periodical volumes; historical research and family papers. **Subscriptions:** 10 journals and other serials. **Services:** Interlibrary loan; copying; library open to the public. **Publications:** Newsletter, quarterly.

★17495★
MARY WASHINGTON HOSPITAL - GORDON W. JONES MEDICAL LIBRARY (Med)
2300 Fall Hill Ave. Phone: (703)899-1597
Fredericksburg, VA 22401 Joan S. Bulley, Med.Libn.
Staff: Prof 1; Other 1. **Subjects:** Medicine, nursing, biomedical sciences, administration, management. **Holdings:** 900 books; 3000 bound periodical volumes. **Subscriptions:** 200 journals and other serials. **Services:** Interlibrary loan; copying; current awareness (limited); library open to the public with restrictions. **Computerized Information Services:** MEDLARS, BRS Information Technologies. Performs searches on fee basis.

WASHINGTON MEMORIAL LIBRARY
See: Valley Forge Historical Society - Washington Memorial Library (17248)

★17496★
WASHINGTON MEMORIAL LIBRARY - GENEALOGY DEPARTMENT - MIDDLE GEORGIA ARCHIVES (Hist)
1180 Washington Ave. Phone: (912)744-0821
Macon, GA 31201 Willard L. Rocker, Geneal.Libn.
Founded: 1923. **Staff:** Prof 2; Other 5. **Subjects:** Genealogy, history, county histories, heraldry, British genealogies. **Special Collections:** Stevens-Davis Memorial Collection (British and pre-Colonial history); J.W. Burke imprints; Georgia authors; Porter Horticultural Collection. **Holdings:** 15,317 books; 60 bound periodical volumes; 303 bound volumes of newspapers; 108 city directories; 4766 reels of microfilm; 1132 microfiche; 259 maps; 26 drawers of architectural drawings; 52 boxes of county and family histories. **Subscriptions:** 65 journals and other serials. **Services:** Copying; archives open to the public for reference use only. **Special Indexes:** Index to History of Jones County, Georgia; index to Macon Telegraph (newspaper), 1934-1987. **Remarks:** An alternate telephone number is 744-0820. **Staff:** Peer Ravnan, Archv..

★17497★
WASHINGTON METROPOLITAN AREA TRANSIT AUTHORITY - OFFICE OF PUBLIC AFFAIRS - LIBRARY
600 Fifth St., N.W., Rm. 2G-02
Washington, DC 20001
Defunct

★17498★
WASHINGTON MUTUAL SAVINGS BANK - INFORMATION CENTER & DIETRICH SCHMITZ MEMORIAL LIBRARY (Bus-Fin)
Box 834 Phone: (206)464-4494
Seattle, WA 98111 Marcella C. Gaar, Info.Off./Mgr.
Founded: 1970. **Staff:** Prof 1; Other 1. **Subjects:** Banking and finance, economics, investments, management, real estate. **Special Collections:** Seattle History (15 volumes); History of Washington State (6 volumes). **Holdings:** 2000 books; 250 reports; 12 VF drawers of annual reports; 8 VF drawers of ephemera and reports; 25 tapes and films; videotapes. **Subscriptions:** 175 journals and other serials; 12 newspapers. **Services:** Interlibrary loan; library open to the public for reference use by request. **Remarks:** Library located at 1101 2nd Ave., Seattle, WA 98101.

★17499★
WASHINGTON NATIONAL INSURANCE COMPANY - INFORMATION RESOURCES CENTER (Bus-Fin)
1630 Chicago Ave. Phone: (312)570-4865
Evanston, IL 60201 Eugenia D. Bryant, Hd.Libn.
Founded: 1956. **Staff:** Prof 3; Other 1. **Subjects:** Insurance - life, health, group; law; management; pensions. **Holdings:** 5800 books; 300 serials; 20 VF drawers; 750 reels of microfilm; 135 AV programs; 32 motion picture titles; company annual reports; Best's Insurance Reports, 1912 to present; proceedings of insurance associations; law reporters. **Subscriptions:** 180 journals and other serials. **Services:** Interlibrary loan; SDI; center open to qualified users for reference use only. **Computerized Information Services:** DIALOG Information Services, BRS Information Technologies, Dow Jones News/Retrieval, OCLC. **Networks/Consortia:** Member of ILLINET. **Publications:** Handbook; Periodicals Holdings List; AV Cassette and Film Lists. **Staff:** John Kadus, Tech.Serv.Libn.; Joyce Cox, Law Libn..

WASHINGTON NATIONAL RECORDS CENTER (Archives)
See: National Archives & Records Administration (9560)

WASHINGTON NEWS BUREAU SOUND ARCHIVE
See: Broadcast Pioneers Library (1897)

★17500★
WASHINGTON PARK ZOO - LIBRARY (Biol Sci)
4001 S.W. Canyon Rd.
Portland, OR 97221 Phone: (503)226-1561
Staff: Prof 1. **Subjects:** Zoology, animal husbandry, veterinary medicine, biology. **Special Collections:** Zoo periodicals. **Holdings:** 500 books. **Subscriptions:** 100 journals and other serials. **Services:** Library open to the public for reference use only.

★17501★
WASHINGTON POST - NEWS LIBRARY (Publ)
1150 15th St., N.W. Phone: (202)334-7341
Washington, DC 20071 Jennifer Belton, Dir., Info.Serv.
Founded: 1933. **Staff:** Prof 9; Other 16. **Subjects:** Newspaper reference topics. **Holdings:** 20,000 books; 6 million newspaper clippings; 30,000 pamphlets and documents; maps; pictures; microfilm. **Subscriptions:** 100 journals and other serials; 10 newspapers. **Services:** Interlibrary loan (fee); copying; SDI; library open to members of the press only. **Automated Operations:** Computerized cataloging, acquisitions, serials, and circulation. **Computerized Information Services:** NEXIS, DIALOG Information Services, VU/TEXT Information Services; PostHaste (internal database). Performs searches on fee basis. **Staff:** Richard Ploch, Ref.Dir.; Kathy Foley, Dp.Dir., Info.Serv.; Sandy Davis, Online Serv.Mgr.; Herb Pierson, Tech.Serv.Coord..

★17502★
WASHINGTON PROGRAM IN COMMUNICATIONS POLICY STUDIES - ANNENBERG SCHOOLS OF COMMUNICATION - LIBRARY (Info Sci)
1455 Pennsylvania Ave., N.W., Suite 200 Phone: (202)393-7100
Washington, DC 20004 Odell Dehart, Libn.
Founded: 1983. **Staff:** Prof 1. **Subjects:** Telecommunications, telephony. **Holdings:** 1500 books; 200 bound periodical volumes; 250 audio cassettes. **Subscriptions:** 75 journals and other serials. **Services:** Interlibrary loan; copying; library open to the public by appointment. **Computerized Information Services:** DIALOG Information Services. **Also Known As:** Washington Program/Annenberg Schools.

★17503★
WASHINGTON PSYCHOANALYTIC SOCIETY - HADLEY MEMORIAL LIBRARY (Med)
4925 MacArthur Blvd., N.W. Phone: (202)338-5453
Washington, DC 20007 Mary W. Allen, Libn.
Staff: Prof 1; Other 2. **Subjects:** Psychoanalysis, psychiatry, psychology, clinical and behavioral research. **Holdings:** 3200 books; 950 bound periodical volumes; 1200 unbound journals; 950 reprints. **Subscriptions:** 50 journals and other serials. **Services:** Interlibrary loan; copying; library open to professionals in psychoanalysis, psychiatry, and psychology and students in allied disciplines.

★17504★
WASHINGTON PUBLIC POWER SUPPLY SYSTEM - LIBRARY (Energy)
3000 George Washington Way
Box 968 Phone: (509)372-5120
Richland, WA 99352 Betty J. Hodges, Lib.Spec.
Staff: 2. **Subjects:** Engineering standards, nuclear power, power transmission. **Holdings:** 8800 books; 3800 standards; 3300 reports. **Subscriptions:** 167 journals and other serials. **Services:** Interlibrary loan; copying; library open to the public with restrictions.

WASHINGTON STAR LIBRARY
See: District of Columbia Public Library - Washingtoniana Division (4312)

★17505★
WASHINGTON STATE ATTORNEY GENERAL'S LIBRARY (Law)
Highways-Licenses Bldg., 7th Fl. Phone: (206)753-2681
Olympia, WA 98504 Phillip G. Bunker, Law Libn.
Staff: Prof 1. **Subjects:** Law, consumer protection, crime prevention. **Special Collections:** Attorney General's formal and informal opinions written on the state constitution with card index. **Holdings:** 12,328 books; 1620 bound periodical volumes; 150 boxes of Washington State Supreme Court briefs. **Subscriptions:** 25 journals and other serials; 12 newspapers. **Services:** Interlibrary loan; library not open to the public. **Publications:** A.G. Reports; Annual Law Enforcement Salary Survey; miscellaneous brochures, irregular. **Remarks:** Offices also maintained in Seattle, Spokane, and Tacoma. Figures include holdings for all locations.

★17506★
WASHINGTON STATE DEPARTMENT OF ECOLOGY - TECHNICAL LIBRARY (Env-Cons)
PV-11 Phone: (206)459-6150
Olympia, WA 98504 Barbara Colquhoun, Tech.Libn.
Staff: Prof 1; Other 1. **Subjects:** Water resources and quality, air quality, solid waste, environmental legislation, waste treatment, shorelines management, hazardous waste cleanup. **Special Collections:** Radioactive waste (100 items); publications of department and predecessor agencies. **Holdings:** 4000 books; 12,000 other cataloged items. **Services:** Interlibrary loan; copying; library open to the public. **Automated Operations:** Computerized public access catalog, cataloging, and serials. **Computerized Information Services:** DIALOG Information Services, Chemical Information Systems, Inc. (CIS). **Networks/Consortia:** Member of Western Library Network (WLN). **Publications:** Selected New Additions to Ecology Library, bimonthly - for internal distribution only. **Remarks:** This library is a branch of the Washington State Library.

★17507★
WASHINGTON STATE DEPARTMENT OF NATURAL RESOURCES - DIVISION OF GEOLOGY AND EARTH RESOURCES - LIBRARY (Sci-Engr)
Bldg. One, Rowe 6
4224 6th Ave., S.E. Phone: (206)459-6373
Lacey, WA 98503 Connie J. Manson, Sr.Libn.
Founded: 1901. **Staff:** Prof 1. **Subjects:** Geology, mining, mineral resources. **Holdings:** 16,000 volumes; 20,000 state and federal documents; 1000 technical reports; 1400 theses; 1400 U.S. Geological Survey topographic quadrangles of Washington; 1500 maps; vertical files. **Subscriptions:** 100 journals and other serials. **Services:** Copying; library open to the public for reference use only. **Computerized Information Services:** Bibliographic Information System (BIS; full bibliography of Washington geology and mineral resources, 1963-1987; internal database). Performs searches on fee basis. **Publications:** List of publications - available on request.

★17508★
WASHINGTON STATE DEPARTMENT OF NATURAL RESOURCES - PUBLIC LAND SURVEY OFFICE (Geog-Map)
1102 S. Quince St.
Mail Stop EV-11 Phone: (206)753-5337
Olympia, WA 98504 Donnell R. Fitch, Unit Supv./Surveyor
Founded: 1951. **Staff:** Prof 4; Other 1. **Subjects:** Cadastral and geodetic survey information. **Special Collections:** Survey information files. **Holdings:** 100,000 aperture cards of survey maps; 300 reels of microfilm of original government survey notes; 2000 field books from private surveyors. **Services:** Copying; office open to the public for a fee. **Staff:** Gary Herrick, Off.Mgr./Surveyor; Craig Granquist, Survey Techn..

★17509★
WASHINGTON STATE DEPARTMENT OF REVENUE - RESEARCH SECTION (Bus-Fin, Info Sci)
General Administration Bldg. AX-02 Phone: (206)753-5542
Olympia, WA 98504 Donn Smallwood, Asst.Dir., Res. & Plan.
Staff: 12. **Subjects:** Washington state and local government taxation and public finance, analysis of tax legislation, dissemination of statistical tax information. **Holdings:** Data series are maintained including collections and other statistics for state and local tax sources; publications and federal reports containing data on collections, activity levels, and public finance. **Services:** Documents available to public for reference use.

★17510★
WASHINGTON STATE DEPARTMENT OF TRADE AND ECONOMIC DEVELOPMENT - TOURISM DEVELOPMENT DIVISION (Rec)
101 General Administration Bldg., AX-13 Phone: (206)753-5600
Olympia, WA 98504-0613 W.D. Taylor, Dir.
Founded: 1957. **Subjects:** Promotional material on Washington State. **Holdings:** Maps and brochures. **Services:** Materials are available for promotional use.

★17511★
WASHINGTON STATE DEPARTMENT OF TRANSPORTATION - LIBRARY (Trans, Plan)
Transportation Bldg., KF-01 Phone: (206)753-2107
Olympia, WA 98504-5201 Barbara Russo, Libn.
Founded: 1968. **Staff:** Prof 1; Other 2. **Subjects:** Transportation administration; highway transportation; public transit including the world's largest ferry system; rail and air transportation in the areas of planning, design, construction, maintenance, operations, and safety. **Special Collections:** Comprehensive plans for cities and counties of Washington. **Holdings:** 1075 books; 7555 reports; 1000 microfiche; 880 comprehensive plans. **Subscriptions:** 300 journals and other serials. **Services:** Interlibrary loan; copying; library open to the public for reference use only. **Automated Operations:** Computerized serials and circulation. **Computerized Information Services:** DIALOG Information Services, LEGI-SLATE, OCLC; OnTyme Electronic Message Network Service (electronic mail service). **Networks/Consortia:** Member of Western Library Network (WLN). **Publications:** Monthly accessions list - for internal distribution only. **Remarks:** Library is a branch of the Washington State Library.

★17512★
WASHINGTON STATE DEPARTMENT OF VETERANS AFFAIRS - STAFF & MEMBER LIBRARY (Med)
Washington Veterans' Home Phone: (206)895-4727
Retsil, WA 98378 Belva Carter, Lib.Techn.
Founded: 1975. **Staff:** 4. **Subjects:** Geriatric medicine and nursing, long term care, autism, mental retardation, child welfare and abuse, gerontology. **Special Collections:** Aging (45 volumes); autism (38 volumes); mental retardation (35 volumes). **Holdings:** 5200 books; 2000 large print books. **Subscriptions:** 100 journals and other serials. **Services:** Interlibrary loan; library open to the public with restrictions on circulation. **Remarks:** The library is a part of the Washington State Library's Institution Library Services section.

★17513★
WASHINGTON STATE ENERGY OFFICE - LIBRARY (Energy)
809 Legion Way, S.E. Phone: (206)586-5078
Olympia, WA 98504 Gretchen K. Leslie, Sr.Libn.
Founded: 1978. **Staff:** Prof 1; Other 2. **Subjects:** Energy conservation, resources, and planning; alternative sources of energy. **Holdings:** 600 monographs; 2000 reports and documents. **Subscriptions:** 150 journals and other serials. **Services:** Interlibrary loan; SDI (for state agencies); library open to the public. **Computerized Information Services:** DIALOG Information Services, WILSONLINE. **Networks/Consortia:** Member of

Western Library Network (WLN). **Publications:** Washington State Energy Use Profile, 1960-1983; WSEO Dispatch (newsletter); fact sheets and technical notes on residential energy conservation; film list.

★17514★
WASHINGTON STATE HISTORICAL SOCIETY - LIBRARY (Hist)
315 N. Stadium Way Phone: (206)593-2830
Tacoma, WA 98403 Frank L. Green, Libn.
Founded: 1940. **Staff:** Prof 3. **Subjects:** Washington State history, Pacific Northwest history. **Special Collections:** Asahel Curtis Negative Collection. **Holdings:** 15,000 books; 200,000 pictures; 4000 manuscripts; 3000 pamphlets; 1017 reels of microfilm. **Subscriptions:** 35 journals and other serials. **Services:** Copying; research by mail; library open to the public. **Staff:** Elaine Miller, Photo.Libn.; Joy Werlink, Mss.Libn..

★17515★
WASHINGTON STATE LAW LIBRARY (Law)
Temple of Justice Phone: (206)753-6524
Olympia, WA 98504 C.E. Bolden, Dir.
Founded: 1920. **Staff:** Prof 4; Other 11. **Subjects:** Anglo-American law, government, jurisprudence. **Holdings:** 260,000 books; 10 VF drawers of pamphlets; 40 volumes of maps; 1600 volumes of appellate briefs. **Subscriptions:** 850 journals; 10 newspapers. **Services:** Interlibrary loan; copying; library open to the public. **Automated Operations:** Computerized cataloging, acquisitions, and serials. **Computerized Information Services:** DIALOG Information Services, WESTLAW, Washington Legislative Information System, WILSONLINE. Performs searches on fee basis and free of charge. Contact Person: Arthur J. Ruffier, Ref.. **Networks/Consortia:** Member of Western Library Network (WLN). **Publications:** Washington State legal documents - by exchange; Selected Recent Acquisitions List, bimonthly - free upon request. **Special Indexes:** Index to Washington State Attorney General Opinions. **Staff:** James Tsao, Chf. of Tech.Serv.; Cora Morley Ecklund, Cat..

★17516★
WASHINGTON STATE LIBRARY (Info Sci)
State Library Bldg., AJ-11 Phone: (206)753-5592
Olympia, WA 98504-0111 Nancy Zussy, State Libn.
Founded: 1853. **Staff:** Prof 87; Other 72. **Subjects:** Public administration, applied sciences, medicine and health, behavioral sciences, transportation, ecology, energy. **Special Collections:** Pacific Northwest History (15,455 items); Washington authors (6050 items). **Holdings:** 402,159 books; 63,000 bound periodical volumes; 1 million U.S. documents; 215,387 Washington state documents; 146,507 other state documents; 30,572 reels of microfilm; 375,000 microfiche; 58 VF drawers; 8120 AV titles, including 16mm films. **Subscriptions:** 5000 journals and other serials; 109 newspapers. **Services:** Interlibrary loan; copying; library open to the public. **Automated Operations:** Computerized cataloging, acquisitions, circulation, and interlibrary loan search. **Computerized Information Services:** DIALOG Information Services, MEDLARS, WILSONLINE, LEGISNET, Chemical Information Systems, Inc. (CIS), LEGI-SLATE, OCLC. **Networks/Consortia:** Member of Western Library Network (WLN), RLG. **Publications:** List of publications - available on request. **Special Catalogs:** Periodicals Holdings (microfiche); Washington State Publications (microfiche); AV Catalog (microfiche); Washington Authors (pamphlet); Recent Books and Pamphlets About Washington (pamphlet). **Staff:** Vicki R. Kreimeyer, Dp. State Libn.; Gene Bismuti, Chf., Off. of Plan. & Dev.; Bruce Ziegman, Act.Dir., WLN; Mary Moore, Chf., Lib.Plan. & Dev.Div.; Kristy Coomes, Chf., Pub.Serv.Div.; Rosemary Shold, Chf., Tech.Serv.Div..

★17517★
WASHINGTON STATE LIBRARY - EASTERN STATE HOSPITAL LIBRARY (Med)
Box A Phone: (509)299-4276
Medical Lake, WA 99022 Kathy Butler, Libn.
Founded: 1968. **Staff:** Prof 1; Other 1. **Subjects:** Psychiatry, nursing, medicine, mental health, social work. **Holdings:** 2230 books; 3 VF drawers. **Subscriptions:** 66 journals and other serials. **Services:** Interlibrary loan; copying; library open to the public. **Networks/Consortia:** Member of Western Library Network (WLN).

★17518★
WASHINGTON STATE LIBRARY - LAKELAND VILLAGE BRANCH LIBRARY (Med)
Box 200 Phone: (509)299-5089
Medical Lake, WA 99022 Kathy Butler, Inst.Libn.
Founded: 1968. **Staff:** Prof 1; Other 1. **Subjects:** Mental retardation, medicine. **Holdings:** 1471 books; 5 years back issues of unbound journals. **Subscriptions:** 66 journals and other serials. **Services:** Interlibrary loan; copying; library open to the public. **Networks/Consortia:** Member of Western Library Network (WLN).

★17519★
WASHINGTON STATE LIBRARY - RAINIER SCHOOL BRANCH LIBRARY (Med)
Box 600 Phone: (206)829-1111
Buckley, WA 98321 Lynn Red, Module Supv.
Staff: Prof 2; Other 2. **Subjects:** Mental retardation, developmental psychology, institutionalization, deaf/blind/retarded handicapped. **Holdings:** 3000 books; 1596 bound and unbound periodical volumes; 100 boxes of pamphlets; 15 boxes of periodical, book, and film catalogs in the field of retardation. **Subscriptions:** 163 journals and other serials; 30 newspapers. **Services:** Interlibrary loan; copying (limited); SDI; library open to the public. **Computerized Information Services:** MEDLINE. **Networks/Consortia:** Member of Western Library Network (WLN). **Publications:** Bibliographies, irregular. **Staff:** Herrick Heitman, Libn. I.

★17520★
WASHINGTON STATE LIBRARY - WASHINGTON UTILITIES & TRANSPORTATION COMMISSION - LIBRARY (Trans)
1300 Evergreen Park Dr., S.W., FY-11 Phone: (206)586-0900
Olympia, WA 98504 Mary Lu Hefley, Libn.
Staff: Prof 1; Other 1. **Subjects:** Utilities regulation - electric, gas, water, telecommunications; transportation regulation; regulatory policies and procedures. **Holdings:** 500 books; 1500 technical reports. **Subscriptions:** 302 journals and other serials. **Services:** Interlibrary loan; copying; library open to the public with restrictions. **Automated Operations:** Computerized cataloging, acquisitions, and serials. **Computerized Information Services:** DIALOG Information Services; internal database; OnTyme Electronic Message Network Service, Phonelink (electronic mail services). **Networks/Consortia:** Member of Western Library Network (WLN).

★17521★
WASHINGTON STATE LIBRARY - WESTERN STATE HOSPITAL BRANCH LIBRARY (Med)
Fort Steilacoom, WA 98494 Phone: (206)756-2635
Neal Van Der Voorn, Libn.
Founded: 1956. **Staff:** Prof 1; Other 2. **Subjects:** Psychiatry, clinical psychology, mental health, psychiatric nursing, psychiatric social work, medicine. **Holdings:** 5200 books; 375 tapes; 2 VF drawers of clippings, bibliographies, pamphlets. **Subscriptions:** 154 journals and other serials. **Services:** Interlibrary loan; copying; library open to the public if material is not available elsewhere. **Networks/Consortia:** Member of Western Library Network (WLN). **Publications:** In Touch, monthly - to hospital staff and residents. **Remarks:** Residents' library contains an additional 11,000 volumes.

★17522★
WASHINGTON STATE OFFICE OF SECRETARY OF STATE - DIVISION OF ARCHIVES AND RECORD MANAGEMENT (Hist)
Archives & Records Center
12th & Washington Phone: (206)753-5485
Olympia, WA 98504 Sidney McAlpin, State Archv.
Staff: Prof 8; Other 14. **Subjects:** State and local government records. **Special Collections:** Governors' Papers, 1854-1980; land records, 1858 to present; election returns; incorporation records, 1854 to present; Supreme Court records, 1854 to present; water rights, 1917 to present; legislative records, 1854 to present; state agency records, 1900 to present. **Holdings:** 7000 bound public records; 40,000 cubic feet of state and local archives; 120,000 cubic feet of records; 60,000 reels of microfilm. **Services:** Copying; research; division open to the public. **Automated Operations:** Computerized cataloging. **Computerized Information Services:** Spindex Archival Control System (internal database). **Publications:** General Guide to the Washington State Archives; list of other publications - available on request. **Remarks:** Territorial District Court records and other county records are held at five regional depositories operated by the division. **Staff:** David Owens, Dp. State Archv.; Dwight Ellenwood, Rec.Anl.; Everett Evans, Microfilm Supv.; Wayne Lawson, Rec.Ctr.Mgr.; David Hastings, Asst. State Archv.; Pat Hopkins, Res.Archv.; James Moore, Reg.Archv.; Tim Eckert, Reg.Archv.; Tim Fredrick, Reg.Archv.; Jay Rae, Reg.Archv.; Michael Betz, Docs.Cons..

★17523★
WASHINGTON STATE SCHOOL FOR THE DEAF - MC GILL LIBRARY (Educ)
611 Grand Blvd. Phone: (206)696-6223
Vancouver, WA 98661-4918 James D. Randall, Dir.
Staff: Prof 2; Other 6. **Subjects:** Elementary and secondary education. **Special Collections:** Education for the deaf (professional books; 500 titles). **Holdings:** 10,672 books; 60 bound periodical volumes; VF drawers; 226 videotapes; 2943 filmstrips; 545 film loops; 369 study prints; 250 microfiche; 44 charts. **Subscriptions:** 89 journals and other serials. **Services:** Interlibrary loan; copying; library open to the public with restrictions. **Automated Operations:** Computerized cataloging and acquisitions. **Networks/Consortia:** Member of Western Library Network (WLN). **Remarks:** Library is a part of the Learning Resource Center. **Staff:** Wanda Forcht, Hd.Libn..

★17524★
WASHINGTON STATE SUPERINTENDENT OF PUBLIC INSTRUCTION - RESOURCE INFORMATION CENTER (Educ)
Old Capitol Bldg., Fg-11 Phone: (206)753-6731
Olympia, WA 98504 Mrs. Bobbie J. Patterson, Coord.
Staff: Prof 1. **Subjects:** Education, curriculum materials. **Special Collections:** Excellence in education materials; Phi Delta Kappan Collection. **Holdings:** 200 books; complete ERIC microfiche collections. **Subscriptions:** 400 journals and other serials; 5 newspapers. **Services:** Interlibrary loan (limited); copying; center open to the public. **Networks/Consortia:** Member of Western Library Network (WLN).

★17525★
WASHINGTON STATE UNIVERSITY - GEORGE B. BRAIN EDUCATION LIBRARY (Educ)
130 Cleveland Hall Phone: (509)335-1591
Pullman, WA 99164-2110 Barbara Kemp, Hd., Hum./Soc.Sci./Pub.Serv.
Staff: Prof 2; Other 2. **Subjects:** Education. **Holdings:** 39,500 books, juvenile books, and textbooks; 11,225 bound periodical volumes; 20 cabinets of ERIC microfiche; 4 cabinets of journals on microfilm; 8 VF cabinets; 2 cabinets of monographs on microfilm; 4 VF cabinets of tests; 870 masters' projects; 675 kits and records. **Subscriptions:** 800 journals and other serials. **Services:** Interlibrary loan (fee); copying; SDI; library open to the public by registration and library card. **Automated Operations:** Computerized cataloging, acquisitions, and circulation. **Computerized Information Services:** DIALOG Information Services; internal database. Performs searches on fee basis. Contact Person: Carolyn Hook, Ref./Coll.Dev.Libn., 335-2691. **Networks/Consortia:** Member of Western Library Network (WLN). **Publications:** List of recent acquisitions, monthly. **Staff:** Linda Snook, Supv..

WASHINGTON STATE UNIVERSITY - INTERCOLLEGIATE CENTER FOR NURSING EDUCATION
See: Intercollegiate Center for Nursing Education (6960)

★17526★
WASHINGTON STATE UNIVERSITY - MANUSCRIPTS, ARCHIVES, & SPECIAL COLLECTIONS (Hist, Hum)
Pullman, WA 99164-5610 Phone: (509)335-6272
John F. Guido, Hd.
Staff: Prof 4; Other 5. **Subjects:** History - Pacific Northwest, agriculture, veterinary medicine; 20th century British literature; wildlife and outdoor recreation; ethnic history. **Special Collections:** Leonard and Virginia Woolf Library; Bloomsbury authors; Pacific Northwest Agricultural History Archives; Veterinary History; Pacific Northwest Publishers' Archives; 20th Century Music Archives; Angling; Germans from Russia; Small Presses; regional presses. **Holdings:** 20,000 volumes; manuscripts; photographs; audiotapes; maps; broadsides; theses and dissertations. **Services:** Copying.

★17527★
WASHINGTON STATE UNIVERSITY - OWEN SCIENCE AND ENGINEERING LIBRARY (Sci-Engr, Biol Sci)
Pullman, WA 99164-3200 Phone: (509)335-4181
Elizabeth P. Roberts, Hd.
Founded: 1892. **Staff:** Prof 7; Other 16. **Subjects:** Pure and applied sciences with special emphasis on engineering, biological sciences, chemistry, biochemistry, mathematics, and physical science. **Special Collections:** Mathematics. **Holdings:** 395,000 volumes; 33 cabinets of microfilm; 59 cabinets of microfiche. **Subscriptions:** 6395 journals and other serials. **Services:** Interlibrary loan; copying; library open to the public. **Automated Operations:** Computerized cataloging, acquisitions and circulation. **Computerized Information Services:** DIALOG Information Services, Pergamon ORBIT InfoLine, Inc., BRS Information Technologies, MEDLARS, CAS ONLINE, Pergamon ORBIT InfoLine, Inc., Chemical Information Systems, Inc. (CIS), WILSONLINE. Performs searches on fee basis. **Networks/Consortia:** Member of Western Library Network (WLN), Center for Research Libraries (CRL) Consortia, CLASS. **Publications:** Palouse Bibliography. **Special Indexes:** Index of Selected Publications of the WSU College of Agriculture, 1970-1982; Abstracts and Indexes Section Index; Atlas Index; Biographical Index; Environmental Impact Statement Index; Section; National Library of Medicine and National Agriculture Library KWIC Bibliography Index.

★17528★
WASHINGTON STATE UNIVERSITY - OWEN SCIENCE AND ENGINEERING LIBRARY - GEORGE W. FISCHER AGRICULTURAL SCIENCES BRANCH LIBRARY (Biol Sci, Agri)
C-2 Johnson Annex Phone: (509)335-2266
Pullman, WA 99164-7150 Betty Bienz, Supv.
Staff: 2. **Subjects:** Plant pathology, agronomy and soils, horticulture, landscape architecture and regional planning, forestry and range management, entomology, mycology. **Special Collections:** Plant pathology reprints (2300 volumes); professional and senior student projects (300 volumes). **Holdings:** 21,565 volumes; 87 reels of microfilm; 932 microfiche; 400 VF items. **Subscriptions:** 782 journals and other serials. **Services:** Interlibrary loan; copying; library open to the public. **Automated Operations:** Computerized public access catalog and circulation. **Computerized Information Services:** Online systems. **Networks/Consortia:** Member of Center for Research Libraries (CRL) Consortia, CLASS, Western Library Network (WLN). **Publications:** The Record (newsletter), annual - to the public.

★17529★
WASHINGTON STATE UNIVERSITY - PRIMATE RESEARCH CENTER LIBRARY
Pullman, WA 99164
Founded: 1957. **Subjects:** Psychology, ophthalmology, optometry, neurophysiology, biophysics. **Holdings:** 1758 books; 2400 bound periodical volumes; 38 VF drawers of reprints and preprints. **Remarks:** Presently inactive.

★17530★
WASHINGTON STATE UNIVERSITY - VETERINARY MEDICAL/PHARMACY LIBRARY (Med)
170 Wegner Hall Phone: (509)335-9556
Pullman, WA 99164-6512 Vicki F. Croft, Hd.
Staff: Prof 2; Other 2. **Subjects:** Veterinary and human medicine, pharmacy and pharmacology. **Holdings:** 20,600 books; 28,500 bound periodical volumes. **Subscriptions:** 1000 journals and other serials. **Services:** Interlibrary loan; copying; library open to the public. **Automated Operations:** Computerized cataloging, acquisitions, and circulation. **Computerized Information Services:** DIALOG Information Services, CAS ONLINE, BRS Information Technologies, VETNET, NLM; WSU Online Catalog (internal database). Performs searches on fee basis. Contact Person: Margaret Buchanan, Libn.. **Networks/Consortia:** Member of Western Library Network (WLN), CLASS. **Staff:** Lani Walton, Lib.Supv..

★17531★
WASHINGTON THEOLOGICAL UNION - LIBRARY (Rel-Phil)
9001 New Hampshire Ave. Phone: (301)439-0551
Silver Spring, MD 20903-3699 Carol R. Lange, Libn.
Staff: Prof 2; Other 4. **Subjects:** Theology. **Special Collections:** Franciscana; Carmelitana; Augustiniana. **Holdings:** 131,000 volumes. **Subscriptions:** 330 journals and other serials. **Services:** Interlibrary loan; copying; library open to the public. **Networks/Consortia:** Member of Washington Theological Consortium. **Publications:** Consortium Guide to Library Resources, updated as needed.

★17532★
WASHINGTON UNIVERSITY - ART & ARCHITECTURE LIBRARY (Plan, Art)
Steinberg Hall
Box 1061 Phone: (314)889-5268
St. Louis, MO 63130 Linda Lott, Art/Arch.Libn.
Founded: 1879. **Staff:** Prof 1; Other 2. **Subjects:** Art history, classical archeology, architecture, costume design, fine art techniques, East Asian art, building technology, urban planning and design, landscape architecture. **Special Collections:** East Asian Collection (Oriental art; 1361 volumes); Bryce Collection (architectural history; 576 volumes); Sorger Collection (historical costume; 243 volumes; 2 VF drawers of plates); Eames and Young Collection (architectural history; 273 volumes); rare

books (2471 volumes). **Holdings:** 67,657 volumes; 52 VF drawers of pamphlets and clippings. **Subscriptions:** 462 journals and other serials. **Services:** Interlibrary loan; copying; library open to the public for reference use only. **Automated Operations:** Computerized cataloging. **Computerized Information Services:** BRS Information Technologies, DIALOG Information Services, Pergamon ORBIT InfoLine, Inc. **Networks/ Consortia:** Member of Missouri Library Network (MLNC), St. Louis Regional Library Network, Center for Research Libraries (CRL) Consortia. **Special Catalogs:** Washington University Art and Architecture Library List of Serials.

★17533★
WASHINGTON UNIVERSITY - BIOLOGY LIBRARY (Biol Sci)
Life Sciences Bldg. Phone: (314)889-5405
St. Louis, MO 63130 Ruth Lewis, Libn.
Staff: Prof 1; Other 2. **Subjects:** Genetics, mycology, embryology, neurosciences, molecular biology, botany. **Holdings:** 46,286 volumes. **Subscriptions:** 473 journals and other serials. **Services:** Interlibrary loan; copying; library open to the public. **Automated Operations:** Computerized cataloging. **Computerized Information Services:** MEDLINE, Pergamon ORBIT InfoLine, Inc., DIALOG Information Services, BRS Information Technologies, STN International. **Networks/Consortia:** Member of Missouri Library Network (MLNC), St. Louis Regional Library Network, Center for Research Libraries (CRL) Consortia. **Publications:** Monthly acquisitions list - to other science libraries.

★17534★
WASHINGTON UNIVERSITY - CENTER FOR THE STUDY OF DATA PROCESSING - CSDP LIBRARY (Comp Sci)
Prince Hall
1 Brookings Dr.
Campus Box 1103 Phone: (314)889-5366
St. Louis, MO 63130 Darrel Youngman, Libn.
Staff: Prof 1; Other 6. **Subjects:** Data processing, programming languages, systems analysis and design, software engineering, communications. **Holdings:** 4100 books; 520 bound periodical volumes; 51 staff seminar notebooks; 1 VF drawer of miscellaneous materials; 78 slides of computer-generated graphics. **Subscriptions:** 225 journals and other serials; 15 newspapers. **Services:** Interlibrary loan; copying; library open to the public for reference use only. **Automated Operations:** Computerized cataloging. **Computerized Information Services:** DIALOG Information Services. **Publications:** Library Update, bimonthly.

★17535★
WASHINGTON UNIVERSITY - CHEMISTRY LIBRARY (Sci-Engr)
Louderman Hall Phone: (314)889-6591
St. Louis, MO 63130 Robert McFarland, Chem.Libn.
Founded: 1905. **Staff:** Prof 1; Other 1. **Subjects:** Chemistry - organic, inorganic, physical, biophysical; spectroscopy. **Holdings:** 28,213 volumes; 327 theses; 627 microfiche. **Subscriptions:** 401 journals and other serials. **Services:** Interlibrary loan; copying; library open to the public with restrictions. **Computerized Information Services:** DIALOG Information Services, Pergamon ORBIT InfoLine, Inc., MEDLINE, BRS Information Technologies, CAS ONLINE. Performs searches on fee basis. **Networks/ Consortia:** Member of Missouri Library Network (MLNC), St. Louis Regional Library Network, Center for Research Libraries (CRL) Consortia.

★17536★
WASHINGTON UNIVERSITY - DENTISTRY LIBRARY (Med)
School of Dental Medicine
4559 Scott Ave. Phone: (314)454-0385
St. Louis, MO 63110 Carol Murray, Libn.
Founded: 1928. **Staff:** Prof 1; Other 3. **Subjects:** Dentistry and related subjects, basic sciences. **Special Collections:** McKellop's Collection (historical dental literature). **Holdings:** 20,000 volumes. **Subscriptions:** 250 journals and other serials. **Services:** Interlibrary loan; library open to the public for reference use only.

★17537★
WASHINGTON UNIVERSITY - DEPARTMENT OF SPECIAL COLLECTIONS (Rare Book, Hum)
Olin Library Phone: (314)889-5495
St. Louis, MO 63130 Holly Hall, Hd.
Founded: 1962. **Staff:** Prof 2; Other 2. **Subjects:** 19th and 20th century English and American literature; history of printing and book arts; semeiology; Americana; St. Louis political and social welfare history; 16th century French literature, especially Pierre de Ronsard. **Special Collections:** Contemporary American and British writers; distinguished faculty and alumni papers; university records. **Holdings:** 39,106 volumes; 5000 ephemera; 250,000 manuscript items; 3000 cubic feet of archival records. **Subscriptions:** 50 journals and other serials. **Services:** Copying; collections open to the public with restrictions. **Automated Operations:** Computerized cataloging. **Special Catalogs:** Occasional exhibit catalogs; special subject area catalogs (card); A Guide to the Modern Literary Manuscripts Collections, 1985; The Samuel Beckett Collection, 1986. **Special Indexes:** Manuscript index (card); registers and special finding aids to manuscript collections and archives. **Staff:** Kevin Ray, Cur., Mss..

★17538★
WASHINGTON UNIVERSITY - EARTH AND PLANETARY SCIENCES LIBRARY (Sci-Engr)
Wilson Hall Phone: (314)889-5406
St. Louis, MO 63130 Clara McLeod, Libn.
Staff: Prof 1; Other 1. SJ Geology, geophysics, geochemistry, mineralogy, geomorphology, petrology, sedimentation, structural geology, paleontology, planetary science. **Special Collections:** State Geological Survey Publications; U.S. Geological Survey and Defense Mapping Agency map depository. **Holdings:** 27,620 volumes; 8078 documents; 947 reprints; 392 pamphlets; 83,278 maps. **Subscriptions:** 266 journals and other serials. **Services:** Interlibrary loan; copying; library open to qualified users for reference. **Automated Operations:** Computerized cataloging and acquisitions. **Computerized Information Services:** BRS Information Technologies, Pergamon ORBIT InfoLine, Inc., DIALOG Information Services, CAS ONLINE, STN International. **Networks/Consortia:** Member of Missouri Library Network (MLNC), St. Louis Regional Library Network, Center for Research Libraries (CRL) Consortia. **Publications:** Monthly acquisitions list.

★17539★
WASHINGTON UNIVERSITY - EAST ASIAN LIBRARY (Area-Ethnic, Hum)
Box 1061 Phone: (314)889-5155
St. Louis, MO 63130 Sachiko Morrell, Libn.
Founded: 1964. **Staff:** Prof 1; Other 1. **Subjects:** East Asia - language and literature, history, philosophy and religion, art history, social science, performing arts. **Special Collections:** Rare book collection; Robert S. Elegant Collection (4 cabinets of clippings, magazines, news releases from the Chinese cultural revolution). **Holdings:** 100,393 volumes; 1308 reels of microfilm; 1 cabinet of pamphlets; Taiwan Government documents. **Subscriptions:** 200 journals and other serials; 11 newspapers. **Services:** Interlibrary loan; copying; library open to the public. **Computerized Information Services:** BRS Information Technologies, Pergamon ORBIT InfoLine, Inc., DIALOG Information Services. **Networks/Consortia:** Member of Missouri Library Network (MLNC), St. Louis Regional Library Network, Center for Research Libraries (CRL) Consortia. **Publications:** Guide to Library Resources for Chinese Studies, 1978; Resource Sources for Chinese and Japanese Studies, 1976; List of Serials related to Chinese and Japanese Studies, 1973; A Guide to Library Resources for Japanese Studies, 1987.

★17540★
WASHINGTON UNIVERSITY - GAYLORD MUSIC LIBRARY (Mus)
6500 Forsyth Phone: (314)889-5560
St. Louis, MO 63130 Susanne Bell, Mus.Libn.
Founded: 1947. **Staff:** Prof 2; Other 2. **Subjects:** Music. **Special Collections:** Sheet Music (51,000 pieces). **Holdings:** 71,151 books, bound periodical volumes, and scores; 13,198 phonograph records; 4624 tapes. **Subscriptions:** 236 journals and other serials. **Services:** Interlibrary loan; copying; library open to visiting scholars for research. **Computerized Information Services:** BRS Information Technologies, Pergamon ORBIT InfoLine, Inc., DIALOG Information Services. **Networks/Consortia:** Member of Missouri Library Network (MLNC), St. Louis Regional Library Network, Center for Research Libraries (CRL) Consortia. **Special Indexes:** Title index to popular sheet music collection (cards); Composer Index to vocal and piano sheet music collection (cards).

★17541★
WASHINGTON UNIVERSITY - GEORGE WARREN BROWN SCHOOL OF SOCIAL WORK - LIBRARY & LEARNING RESOURCES CENTER (Soc Sci)
Box 1196 Phone: (314)889-6633
St. Louis, MO 63130 Michael E. Powell, Dir.
Staff: Prof 1; Other 1. **Subjects:** Social work, gerontology, mental health, health, children and youth services, social and economic development, family therapy, management. **Holdings:** 36,179 volumes; 2000 government documents; 1525 theses/dissertations; 4122 pamphlets; 113 reels of microfilm; 11 films, filmstrips, slides; 911 recording discs and tapes.

Subscriptions: 600 journals and other serials; 10 newspapers. **Services:** Interlibrary loan; copying; library open to those with library cards. **Publications:** Acquisitions list, monthly; bibliographies.

★17542★
WASHINGTON UNIVERSITY - KOPOLOW BUSINESS LIBRARY (Bus-Fin)
School of Business
Box 1133 Phone: (314)889-6334
St. Louis, MO 63130 Ronald Allen, Dir.
Founded: 1925. **Staff:** Prof 3; Other 3. **Subjects:** Finance, management, marketing, accounting, production, operations research. **Holdings:** 24,694 books; 200 working papers; 250,000 annual reports on microfiche; 4719 other microforms; 190 dissertations. **Subscriptions:** 394 journals and other serials; 11 newspapers. **Services:** Interlibrary loan; copying; library open to the public for reference use only. **Computerized Information Services:** BRS Information Technologies, DIALOG Information Services, Dow Jones News/Retrieval. Performs searches on fee basis. Contact Person: Kay Shehan, Asst.Bus.Libn., 889-6465. **Networks/Consortia:** Member of Missouri Library Network (MLNC). **Publications:** Recent Acquisitions, quarterly - available on request. **Formerly:** Business Administration Library. **Staff:** Magda Buday, Assoc.Libn..

★17543★
WASHINGTON UNIVERSITY - MATHEMATICS LIBRARY (Sci-Engr)
Cupples I, Rm. 15
Skinker & Lindell Blvds. Phone: (314)889-5048
St. Louis, MO 63130 Barbara Luszczynska, Math/CSDP Libn.
Staff: Prof 1. **Subjects:** Advanced mathematics. **Special Collections:** Australian National University Center for Mathematical Analysis research reports; Mathematical Sciences Research Institute preprints; Institute for Mathematics and its Applications abstracts. **Holdings:** 483 books; 3120 bound periodical volumes. **Subscriptions:** 103 journals and other serials. **Services:** Interlibrary loan; library open to the public for reference use only. **Computerized Information Services:** BRS Information Technologies, Pergamon ORBIT InfoLine, Inc., DIALOG Information Services, STN International. **Networks/Consortia:** Member of Missouri Library Network (MLNC), St. Louis Regional Library Network, Center for Research Libraries (CRL) Consortia.

★17544★
WASHINGTON UNIVERSITY - PFEIFFER PHYSICS LIBRARY (Sci-Engr)
Lindell & Skinker Blvds. Phone: (314)889-6215
St. Louis, MO 63130 B.M. Eickhoff, Physics Libn.
Staff: 2. **Subjects:** Astrophysics, atomic and nuclear physics, solid state physics, high energy particles, low temperature physics, cosmic rays, quantum mechanics, physical electronics, plasma physics, chemical physics, mathematics, mathematical physics, electronics, electrical and communications engineering, science history, astronomy, space physics. **Holdings:** 31,079 volumes. **Subscriptions:** 205 journals. **Services:** Interlibrary loan; copying; library open to the public for reference use only.

★17545★
WASHINGTON UNIVERSITY - REGIONAL PLANETARY IMAGE FACILITY - LIBRARY (Sci-Engr)
Dept. of Earth & Planetary Sciences
Campus Box 1169 Phone: (314)889-5679
St. Louis, MO 63130 Betty L. Weiss, Libn./Data Mgr.
Staff: Prof 1. **Subjects:** Planetary geology, space exploration missions, remote sensing, image processing. **Special Collections:** Space mission photographs and videodiscs. **Holdings:** 1250 books; 2000 digital tapes; microfiche sets; complete set of U.S. Geological Survey planetary maps. **Subscriptions:** 15 journals and other serials. **Services:** Copying; library open to the public by appointment. **Computerized Information Services:** Image Retrieval and Processing System (IRPS; internal database); NASA/MAIL, Telemail, SPAN (electronic mail services).

★17546★
WASHINGTON UNIVERSITY - SCHOOL OF LAW - FREUND LAW LIBRARY (Law)
Mudd Bldg.
One Brookings Dr.
Box 1120 Phone: (314)889-6459
St. Louis, MO 63130 Bernard D. Reams, Jr., Law Libn.
Staff: Prof 6; Other 10. **Subjects:** Law, taxation, urban affairs, international law. **Special Collections:** U.S. Supreme Court and Missouri Supreme Court Briefs; Ashman British Collection; Neuhoff Rare Book Collection; U.S. and Missouri documents depository. **Holdings:** 325,415 volumes; 774,943 microfiche; 54 microcards; 5376 reels of microfilm; 410 cassette tapes. **Subscriptions:** 3094 journals and other serials; 20 newspapers. **Services:** Interlibrary loan; copying; library open to the public on a limited schedule. **Automated Operations:** Computerized cataloging. **Computerized Information Services:** LEXIS, WESTLAW, DIALOG Information Services, ELSS (Electronic Legislative Search System), LEGI-SLATE. **Networks/Consortia:** Member of St. Louis Regional Library Network, Mid-America Law School Library Consortium. **Publications:** Select acquisitions list, quarterly - by request; bi-annual bibliography series - for sale. **Special Indexes:** Index to legislative histories (card). **Staff:** Mary Ann Nelson, Assoc.Dir.; Stuart D. Yoak, Assoc. Law Libn.-Adm.; Virginia Bryant, Cat.Libn.; Carol J. Gray, Doc.Libn.; Margaret McDermott, Ref.Libn..

★17547★
WASHINGTON UNIVERSITY - SCHOOL OF MEDICINE - DEPARTMENT OF PSYCHIATRY LIBRARY (Med)
4940 Audubon Ave.
St. Louis, MO 63110 Phone: (314)362-2454
Founded: 1963. **Staff:** Prof 1; Other 1. **Subjects:** Psychiatry, biochemistry, neurochemical pharmacology. **Holdings:** 1000 books; 20,000 bound periodical volumes; 3 VF drawers of department reprints. **Subscriptions:** 99 journals and other serials. **Services:** Library not open to the public.

★17548★
WASHINGTON UNIVERSITY - SCHOOL OF MEDICINE - MALLINCKRODT INSTITUTE OF RADIOLOGY LIBRARY (Med)
510 S. Kingshighway Blvd. Phone: (314)362-2978
St. Louis, MO 63110 William Totty, M.D., Lib.Dir.
Staff: 2. **Subjects:** Radiology. **Special Collections:** CIBA, Armed Forces Institute of Pathology, and American College of Radiology syllabi; Saunders monographs; Yearbook of Tumor Radiology. **Holdings:** 1105 books; 1510 bound periodical volumes; 377 videotapes; 96 slide lectures; 381 other cataloged items. **Subscriptions:** 64 journals and other serials. **Services:** Interlibrary loan; library not open to the public. **Automated Operations:** Computerized cataloging, serials, and circulation. **Computerized Information Services:** Institute for Scientific Information (ISI); BACS (internal database). **Staff:** Harriet Fieweger, Libn..

★17549★
WASHINGTON UNIVERSITY - SCHOOL OF MEDICINE LIBRARY (Med)
660 S. Euclid Ave. Phone: (314)362-7080
St. Louis, MO 63110 Prof. Susan Y. Crawford, Dir.
Founded: 1910. **Staff:** Prof 17; Other 34. **Subjects:** Medicine. **Special Collections:** Becker Ophthalmological Collection, C.I.D. - Max A. Goldstein Collection in Speech and Hearing (both printed); papers of William Beaumont, Joseph Erlanger, Leo Loeb, Evarts Graham, Helen Treadway Graham, E.V. Cowdry, Wendell Scott; school's early records. **Holdings:** 78,007 books; 131,305 bound periodical volumes; 2500 feet of archives; 2474 nonprint items. **Subscriptions:** 3101 journals and other serials. **Services:** Interlibrary loan; copying; clinical librarianship; library open to the public. **Automated Operations:** Computerized cataloging, acquisitions, serials, and circulation. **Computerized Information Services:** DIALOG Information Services, OCLC, BRS Information Technologies, NLM, Philnet; BACS (internal database); computer-assisted instruction. Performs searches on fee basis. Contact Person: Linda Salisbury, Assoc.Dir., Info.Serv., 362-7084. **Networks/Consortia:** Member of Midcontinental Regional Medical Library Program, St. Louis Regional Library Network. **Publications:** Library Guide; Selection and Acquisitions Manual; Archives Manual; Library Newsletter; Annual Report. **Staff:** Loretta Stucki, Assoc.Dir., Tech.Serv.; Barbara Halbrook, Dp.Dir.; Elizabeth Kelly, AssocDir., Access Serv.; Paul Anderson, Assoc.Dir., Spec.Coll.; Marion McGuinn, Asst.Dir., Rare Bks..

WASHINGTON UTILITIES & TRANSPORTATION COMMISSION
See: Washington State Library (17520)

WASHINGTON'S HEADQUARTERS STATE HISTORIC SITE
See: New York State Office of Parks, Recreation and Historic Preservation - Palisades Region (10133)

★17550★
WASHOE COUNTY LAW LIBRARY (Law)
Court House
Box 11130 Phone: (702)328-3250
Reno, NV 89520 Sandra Marz, Law Lib.Dir.
Founded: 1915. **Staff:** Prof 2; Other 4. **Subjects:** Law. **Special Collections:** Nevada gambling, water rights, and Indian law. **Holdings:** 33,622 books; 3125 bound periodical volumes; 2317 volumes in microform; 85 cassettes. **Subscriptions:** 233 periodicals. **Services:** Interlibrary loan; copying; library open to the public for reference use only. **Automated Operations:** Computerized cataloging. **Computerized Information Services:** WESTLAW, RLIN. **Publications:** Acquisitions list, monthly. **Staff:** Wilma Smith, Asst.Libn..

★17551★
WASHOE MEDICAL CENTER - MEDICAL LIBRARY (Med)
77 Pringle Way Phone: (702)785-5693
Reno, NV 89520 Sherry A. McGee, Dir., Med.Lib.
Founded: 1941. **Staff:** Prof 1; Other 1. **Subjects:** Medicine, nursing, allied health sciences. **Holdings:** 2093 books; 4949 bound periodical volumes. **Subscriptions:** 265 journals and other serials. **Services:** Interlibrary loan; copying; library open to the public for reference use only. **Computerized Information Services:** MEDLARS, DIALOG Information Services. Performs searches on fee basis. **Networks/Consortia:** Member of Northern California and Nevada Medical Library Group (NCNMLG), Nevada Medical Libraries Group (NMLG). **Publications:** Medical Library News, quarterly - to hospital staff, local libraries, and other interested persons.

★17552★
WASHTENAW COMMUNITY COLLEGE - LEARNING RESOURCE CENTER - SPECIAL COLLECTIONS (Educ)
4800 E. Huron River Dr. Phone: (313)973-3300
Ann Arbor, MI 48106 Adella B. Scott, Dir. of LRC
Founded: 1965. **Special Collections:** Professional Collection (higher education); Washtenaw Community College Archives. **Services:** Interlibrary loan; copying; collections open to the public. **Automated Operations:** Computerized cataloging. **Computerized Information Services:** DIALOG Information Services. **Networks/Consortia:** Member of Michigan Library Consortium (MLC), Washtenaw-Livingston Library Network (WLLN). **Publications:** Acquisitions List.

★17553★
WASHTENAW COUNTY METROPOLITAN PLANNING COMMISSION - LIBRARY (Plan)
Court House, Rm. 305
Box 8645 Phone: (313)994-2435
Ann Arbor, MI 48107 Eve Wuttke, Asst. to the Dir.
Founded: 1949. **Staff:** 1. **Subjects:** Planning, census of population and housing, recreation, statistics, transportation, water sewage and drainage, conservation, urban growth and renewal, zoning ordinances, land use plans, development plans, subdivision ordinances. **Holdings:** 5000 books, reports, and bound periodical volumes. **Subscriptions:** 15 journals and other serials. **Services:** Copying; library open to the public with permission.

WASON COLLECTION
See: Cornell University (3796)

★17554★
WASSAIC DEVELOPMENTAL CENTER - LIBRARY (Med)
Route 22 Phone: (914)877-6821
Wassaic, NY 12592 Cynthia Lyon, Sr.Libn.
Staff: Prof 1. **Subjects:** Mental retardation. **Holdings:** 2000 books; 3000 unbound periodicals. **Subscriptions:** 60 journals and other serials. **Services:** Interlibrary loan; library not open to the public. **Networks/Consortia:** Member of Southeastern New York Library Resources Council (SENYLRC).

WASSERMAN PUBLIC AFFAIRS LIBRARY
See: University of Texas, Austin (16945)

WATCH & CLOCK MUSEUM OF THE NAWCC
See: National Association of Watch and Clock Collectors, Inc. (9591)

★17555★
WATER INFORMATION CENTER, INC. (Env-Cons)
125 E. Bethpage Rd. Phone: (516)249-7634
Plainview, NY 11803 Fred Troise, Vice-Pres.
Founded: 1959. **Subjects:** Ground water, water supply, conservation, pollution, chemistry of water, water laws. **Holdings:** 500 books; 2000 bound periodical volumes; 3000 technical reports. **Subscriptions:** 40 journals and other serials. **Services:** Answers general and semi-technical questions, especially on ground water, by phone or mail as a free public service; center not open to general public. **Publications:** Water Newsletter, semimonthly; Ground Water Newsletter, semimonthly; International Water Report, quarterly - by subscription; Bibliographies: Water Publications of State Agencies; Geraghty & Miller's Groundwater Bibliography; The Water Atlas of the United States; Climates of the States; Water Resources of the World; Sources of Information in Water Resources. **Remarks:** Associated with Geraghty & Miller, Inc., groundwater consultants.

★17556★
WATER POLLUTION CONTROL FEDERATION - LIBRARY (Env-Cons)
601 Wythe St. Phone: (703)684-2400
Alexandria, VA 22314-1994 Berinda J. Ross, Asst.Mgr., Tech.Serv.
Founded: 1928. **Staff:** Prof 1; Other 1. **Subjects:** Water pollution control, water supply and resources, wastewater treatment and disposal, sludge treatment and disposal, collection systems, environmental engineering. **Special Collections:** National Commission on Water Quality publications. **Holdings:** 2000 books; 300 bound periodical volumes. **Subscriptions:** 35 journals and other serials. **Services:** Interlibrary loan; copying; library open to the public for reference use only. **Computerized Information Services:** DIALOG Information Services. Performs searches on fee basis. **Publications:** Journal WPCF; Operations Forum; Highlights; The Bench Sheet; newsletters; Manuals of Practice; Special Publications; Surveys. **Special Indexes:** Five-year index of Journal WPCF (book).

★17557★
WATER QUALITY ASSOCIATION - RESEARCH COUNCIL LIBRARY (Env-Cons)
4151 Naperville Rd. Phone: (312)369-1600
Lisle, IL 60532 Douglas R. Oberhamer, Exec.Dir.
Staff: 15. **Subjects:** Water quality, water conditioning, home water supply, water usage, industrial water conditioning, water softening, water pollution, geographic water data. **Special Collections:** U.S. Government publications on water quality and usage; water conditioning industry publications; International Water Quality Symposia Proceedings, 1965-1968, 1970, 1972. **Holdings:** 1000 books; industry papers; manuscripts; clippings; committee reports and pamphlets. **Subscriptions:** 40 journals and other serials. **Services:** Copying; library open to the public for reference use only.

★17558★
WATER RESOURCES ASSOCIATION OF THE DELAWARE RIVER BASIN - LIBRARY (Env-Cons)
Davis Rd.
Box 867 Phone: (215)783-0634
Valley Forge, PA 19481 Bruce E. Stewart, Exec.Dir.
Founded: 1959. **Subjects:** Water and related land resources. **Holdings:** 500 volumes.

WATER & SANITATION FOR HEALTH PROJECT
See: U.S. Agency for International Development - Water & Sanitation for Health Project - Information Center (14577)

★17559★
WATERBURY AMERICAN-REPUBLICAN - LIBRARY (Publ)
389 Meadow St. Phone: (203)574-3636
Waterbury, CT 06722 Mary B. Fuller, Libn.
Founded: 1926. **Staff:** Prof 1; Other 1. **Subjects:** Newspaper reference topics. **Holdings:** 1000 books; clippings; photographs and negatives; newspapers, 1884 to present, on microfilm. **Subscriptions:** 25 newspapers. **Services:** Copying; library open to the public with restrictions.

WATERBURY BAR LIBRARY
See: Connecticut State Library - Law Library at Waterbury (3666)

★17560★
WATERBURY HOSPITAL - HEALTH CENTER LIBRARY (Med)
64 Robbins St. Phone: (203)573-6136
Waterbury, CT 06721 Joan Ruszkowski, Dir.
Staff: Prof 1; Other 2. **Subjects:** Medicine, nursing, and allied health sciences. **Holdings:** 2719 books; 7227 bound periodical volumes; 4 VF drawers of pamphlets; 110 videotapes; 5 drawers of audiotapes. **Subscriptions:** 266 journals and other serials. **Services:** Interlibrary loan; copying; SDI; library open to the public with permission of librarian. **Computerized Information Services:** MEDLARS, BRS Information Technologies; DOCLINE (electronic mail service). **Networks/Consortia:** Member of Northwestern Connecticut Health Science Library Consortium, Connecticut Association of Health Science Libraries (CAHSL).

★17561★
WATERBURY STATE TECHNICAL COLLEGE - HELEN HAHLO LIBRARY (Sci-Engr)
750 Chase Pkwy. Phone: (203)575-8106
Waterbury, CT 06708 John Kiernan, Jr., Hd.Libn.
Founded: 1964. **Staff:** Prof 2; Other 1. **Subjects:** Electrical technology, data processing, chemical technology, mechanics, metallurgy, tools and manufacturing, industrial management. **Holdings:** 8836 books; 80 folders of pamphlets; 251 reels of microfilm. **Subscriptions:** 94 journals and other serials; 5 newspapers. **Services:** Interlibrary loan; copying; library open to the public with restrictions. **Networks/Consortia:** Member of Region One Cooperating Library Service Unit, Inc..

★17562★
WATERFORD HOSPITAL - HEALTH SERVICES LIBRARY (Med)
Waterford Bridge Rd. Phone: (709)364-0269
St. John's, NF, Canada A1E 4J8 Maisie Young, Libn.
Founded: 1969. **Staff:** 1. **Subjects:** Psychiatry, nursing, medicine, social work, psychology, pharmacology. **Holdings:** 2300 books; unbound periodicals; annual reports; manuscripts; pamphlets; AV programs. **Subscriptions:** 104 journals and other serials. **Services:** Interlibrary loan; copying; library open to the public by request.

★17563★
WATERLOO HISTORICAL SOCIETY - GRACE SCHMIDT ROOM OF LOCAL HISTORY (Hist)
85 Queen St., N. Phone: (519)743-0271
Kitchener, ON, Canada N2H 2H1
Susan Hoffman, Local Hist.Libn. & Archv.
Founded: 1984. **Subjects:** History - Kitchener, Waterloo County, Wellington County, general. **Special Collections:** Early issues of Waterloo County newspapers. **Holdings:** 500 books. **Services:** Interlibrary loan; copying; library open to the public. **Publications:** Waterloo Historical Society Annual Volume - to members. **Special Indexes:** Index to annual volumes. **Remarks:** Maintained in cooperation with Kitchener Public Library.

★17564★
WATERLOO LIBRARY AND HISTORICAL SOCIETY (Hist)
31 E. Williams St. Phone: (315)539-3313
Waterloo, NY 13165 Betty Kemak, Lib.Dir.
Founded: 1875. **Staff:** Prof 2. **Subjects:** Local history, antiques. **Holdings:** 18,000 books; pictures; maps; diaries; letters; organization minute books; 1000 town and county records. **Subscriptions:** 65 journals and other serials. **Services:** Interlibrary loan; copying; library open to the public with restrictions. **Automated Operations:** Computerized cataloging. **Networks/Consortia:** Member of Finger Lakes Library System. **Staff:** Michael Becker, Hd.Libn..

WATERS ASSOCIATES INC.
See: Millipore Corporation - Waters Chromatography Division (8995)

★17565★
WATERTOWN DAILY TIMES - LIBRARY (Publ)
260 Washington St. Phone: (315)782-1000
Watertown, NY 13601 Wendy Aschmann, Chf.Libn.
Founded: 1934. **Staff:** Prof 1; Other 3. **Subjects:** Newspaper reference topics, northern New York history. **Holdings:** 109 file cabinets of clippings; 669 reels of microfilm; 11 microfiche. **Services:** Copying; library open to the public by appointment only. **Networks/Consortia:** Member of North Country Reference and Research Resources Council (NCRRRC). **Special Indexes:** Index of obituary files (online). **Remarks:** Published by Johnson Newspaper Corporation.

★17566★
WATERTOWN HISTORICAL SOCIETY - ARCHIVES (Hist)
919 Charles St. Phone: (414)261-2796
Watertown, WI 53094 Judy Quam, Octagon House Mgr.
Subjects: First kindergarten, Margarethe Meyer Schurz, Carl Schurz, Octagon houses, local history. **Holdings:** 100 volumes; photographs; clippings.

★17567★
WATERTOWN HISTORICAL SOCIETY INC. - LIBRARY (Hist)
22 DeForest St. Phone: (203)274-4344
Watertown, CT 06795 Florence Crowell, Cur.
Founded: 1968. **Staff:** Prof 1. **Subjects:** Genealogy, local and state history, local authors. **Special Collections:** Collection of diaries of town's residents; town reports; oral histories; Watertown Town Times, 1947-1975, on microfilm. **Holdings:** 1200 books. **Services:** Library open to the public with permission required for circulation. **Automated Operations:** Computerized acquisitions. **Remarks:** An alternate telephone number is 274-1634. **Staff:** John Pillis, Pres..

★17568★
WATERVILLE HISTORICAL SOCIETY - LIBRARY AND ARCHIVES (Hist)
64 Silver St.
Waterville, ME 04901 Phone: (207)872-9439
Founded: 1903. **Subjects:** History - local, regional, state; Civil War. **Special Collections:** Diaries, 1753-1955; early textbooks (200); 19th century apothecary. **Holdings:** 1520 books; local newspaper, 1853-1906; early account books; old documents and letters; maps; old photographs. **Services:** Archives open to the public with restrictions. **Also Known As:** Redington Museum.

★17569★
WATERVILLE OSTEOPATHIC HOSPITAL - M.J. GERRIE, SR., MEDICAL LIBRARY (Med)
Kennedy Memorial Dr. Phone: (207)873-0731
Waterville, ME 04901 Mary Anne Libby, Lib.Serv.Coord.
Staff: Prof 1. **Subjects:** Medicine, surgery, osteopathy. **Holdings:** 150 books. **Subscriptions:** 40 journals and other serials. **Services:** Interlibrary loan; copying; library open to the public with restrictions. **Networks/Consortia:** Member of Health Science Library and Information Cooperative of Maine (HSLIC).

JESSIE BEACH WATKINS MEMORIAL LIBRARY
See: Seneca Falls Historical Society (13070)

★17570★
WATKINS WOOLEN MILL STATE HISTORIC SITE - RESEARCH LIBRARY (Hist)
Rte. 2, Box 270M Phone: (816)296-3357
Lawson, MO 64062 Ann M. Matthews, Historic Site Adm.
Staff: Prof 2; Other 3. **Subjects:** 19th century textile industry and farming. **Holdings:** 500 books; 2000 bound periodical volumes; 5000 pamphlets and letters. **Services:** Library open to the public for reference use only on request. **Remarks:** Maintained by Missouri State Division of Parks, Recreation, & Historic Preservation.

WATKINSON LIBRARY
See: Trinity College (14331)

ARTHUR R. WATSON LIBRARY
See: Baltimore Zoo (1277)

★17571★
WATSON CLINIC - MEDICAL LIBRARY (Med)
Box 95000 Phone: (813)687-4000
Lakeland, FL 33804-5000 Cheryl Dee, Lib.Dir.
Founded: 1945. **Staff:** Prof 1; Other 3. **Subjects:** Medicine. **Holdings:** 1800 books; 3000 bound periodical volumes; 550 cassettes. **Subscriptions:** 400 journals and other serials. **Services:** Interlibrary loan; copying; library open to the public by permission only. **Computerized Information Services:** MEDLINE, DIALOG Information Services.

EUGENE P. WATSON LIBRARY
See: Northwestern State University of Louisiana (10493)

JOHN BROWN WATSON MEMORIAL LIBRARY
See: University of Arkansas, Pine Bluff (15840)

THOMAS J. WATSON LIBRARY
See: Metropolitan Museum of Art (8828)

THOMAS J. WATSON LIBRARY OF BUSINESS AND ECONOMICS
See: Columbia University (3495)

THOMAS J. WATSON RESEARCH CENTER LIBRARY
See: IBM Corporation (6658)

WATSTORE
See: U.S. Geological Survey - Water Resources Division - National Water Data Storage & Retrieval System (15129)

DONALD B. WATT LIBRARY
See: Experiment in International Living - School for International Training (4849)

WATTS SCHOOL OF NURSING
See: Durham County Hospital Corporation (4463)

★17572★
WATTS STREET BAPTIST CHURCH - LIBRARY (Rel-Phil)
800 Watts St. Phone: (919)688-1366
Durham, NC 27705 Barbara Newnam, Libn.
Founded: 1960. **Staff:** Prof 1; Other 3. **Subjects:** Religion, children's literature. **Holdings:** 1000 books; 200 pamphlets. **Services:** Library open to the public with restrictions.

★17573★
WAUKEGAN HISTORICAL SOCIETY - JOHN RAYMOND MEMORIAL LIBRARY (Hist)
1917 N. Sheridan Rd.
Waukegan, IL 60087 Phone: (312)336-1859
Staff: 5. **Subjects:** Local history. **Special Collections:** Waukegan authors. **Holdings:** 1338 books; 3 bound newspapers; 12 VF drawers of pamphlets; 4 drawer case of slides; 1 cabinet of maps and posters; 4 portfolios of old newspapers; 4 VF drawers of photographs; 1 VF drawer of material on landmark buildings; 3 VF drawers of ephemera. **Services:** Copying; library open to the public. **Publications:** Historically Speaking, monthly - to members. **Special Indexes:** Index to books, photographs, and slides (card). **Staff:** Eloise Daydif, Co-Libn.; Marjorie Howe, Co-Libn..

★17574★
WAUKEGAN NEWS-SUN - LIBRARY (Publ)
100 Madison St. Phone: (312)689-6969
Waukegan, IL 60085 Barbara Apple, Hd.Libn.
Staff: Prof 2. **Subjects:** Newspaper reference topics. **Holdings:** 1200 books; 2900 reels of microfilm; photographs; newspaper clippings. **Subscriptions:** 15 journals and other serials; 25 newspapers. **Services:** Library not open to the public. **Computerized Information Services:** Battelle Automated Search Information System (BASIS). **Special Indexes:** News-Sun Microfilm Index (book); Editorial Index (card; book).

★17575★
WAUKESHA COUNTY FREEMAN DAILY NEWSPAPER - LIBRARY (Publ)
200 Park Pl.
Box 7 Phone: (414)542-2501
Waukesha, WI 53187 Deborah J. Kranitz, Libn.
Founded: 1965. **Staff:** Prof 1. **Subjects:** Newspaper reference topics. **Holdings:** Clipping files, 1965 to present; pictures, headshots, and negatives; bound volumes, 1859 to present, in storage; newspapers, 1859 to present, on microfilm; city directories; college and high school yearbooks; pamphlets. **Subscriptions:** 15 journals and other serials. **Services:** Library open to the public with restrictions. **Special Indexes:** Index of headshot photograph file.

★17576★
WAUKESHA COUNTY HISTORICAL MUSEUM - RESEARCH CENTER (Hist)
101 W. Main St. Phone: (414)548-7186
Waukesha, WI 53186 Jean Penn Loerke, Dir.
Staff: Prof 2; Other 2. **Subjects:** Local history and genealogy. **Special Collections:** Pioneer Notebooks (unpublished information on early pioneers of city and county; 82 volumes); county naturalization records. **Holdings:** 2700 books; 87 bound periodical volumes; 1 VF drawer of cemetery records; 1 VF drawer of census records; 40 VF drawers of newspaper clippings; 11,000 photographs; 10,000 negatives; 1800 slides. **Subscriptions:** 36 journals and other serials; 7 newspapers. **Services:** Copying; center open to adults for reference use only. **Publications:** Primary Bibliography for Research in Waukesha History; Family History Research in Waukesha County; list of other publications - available on request. **Staff:** Terry Becker, Res.Techn..

★17577★
WAUKESHA COUNTY TECHNICAL COLLEGE - WCTC LIBRARY (Educ)
800 Main St. Phone: (414)691-5316
Pewaukee, WI 53072 Ruth Ahl, Lib.Dir.
Staff: Prof 1; Other 6. **Subjects:** Nursing, allied health sciences, industrial arts, business, police and fire sciences, electronics, food service. **Special Collections:** NEWSBANK, Inc.; international trade; career collection. **Holdings:** 30,000 books; 27,000 unbound periodicals; 859 reels of microfilm; 125 films; 180 videotapes; 1285 audio cassettes; SAMS Photofact Service; ERIC microfiche. **Subscriptions:** 482 journals and other serials; 30 newspapers. **Services:** Interlibrary loan; copying; library open to the public with restrictions. **Automated Operations:** Computerized cataloging and circulation. **Computerized Information Services:** DIALOG Information Services. Performs searches on fee basis. Contact Person: Joyce Laabs, Circ./ILL.. **Networks/Consortia:** Member of Library Council of Metropolitan Milwaukee, Inc. (LCOMM), Wisconsin Interlibrary Services (WILS). **Publications:** WCTC film and videotape list, annual; WCTC periodical holdings list, annual. **Formerly:** Waukesha County Technical Institute.

★17578★
WAUKESHA MEMORIAL HOSPITAL - MEDICAL LIBRARY (Med)
725 American Ave. Phone: (414)544-2150
Waukesha, WI 53186 Linda Oddan, Med.Libn.
Founded: 1958. **Staff:** Prof 1. **Subjects:** Medicine, nursing, hospital administration. **Holdings:** 2100 books; 2500 bound periodical volumes; 9 VF drawers of pamphlets. **Subscriptions:** 200 journals and other serials. **Services:** Interlibrary loan; copying; library open to the public with restrictions. **Computerized Information Services:** DIALOG Information Services, MEDLINE, BRS Information Technologies; DOCLINE (electronic mail service). Performs searches on fee basis. **Networks/Consortia:** Member of Greater Midwest Regional Medical Library Network, Southeastern Wisconsin Health Science Library Consortium (SWHSL).

★17579★
WAUSAU INSURANCE COMPANIES - MEDIA AND REFERENCE SERVICES (Bus-Fin)
2000 Westwood Dr. Phone: (715)847-8504
Wausau, WI 54401 Douglas H. Lay, Mgr.
Founded: 1935. **Staff:** Prof 2; Other 3. **Subjects:** Insurance, industrial safety and health. **Holdings:** 11,000 books; 130 bound periodical volumes; 185 VF drawers of clippings; 850 AV programs. **Subscriptions:** 320 journals and other serials; 17 newspapers. **Services:** Interlibrary loan; library open to serious students and researchers. **Automated Operations:** Computerized cataloging, serials, and media booking. **Computerized Information Services:** DIALOG Information Services, Dun & Bradstreet Corporation, Insurance Information Institute (III). **Networks/Consortia:** Member of Wisconsin Valley Library Service (WVLS). **Publications:** Management Media Scan, quarterly - for internal distribution only. **Staff:** Donna S. Nuernberg, Ref.Serv.Spec..

★17580★
WAUWATOSA PRESBYTERIAN CHURCH - LIBRARY (Rel-Phil)
2366 N. 80th St.
Wauwatosa, WI 53213
Staff: Prof 1; Other 6. **Subjects:** Religion. **Holdings:** 1102 books. **Services:** Library not open to the public.

WAY & WILLIAMS COLLECTION
See: University of North Carolina, Greensboro (16644)

JOHN W. WAYLAND LIBRARY
See: Harrisonburg-Rockingham Historical Society and Museum (6049)

★17581★
WAYNE COMMUNITY COLLEGE - LEARNING RESOURCE CENTER (Educ)
Caller Box 8002 Phone: (919)735-5151
Goldsboro, NC 27533-8002 Dr. Shirley T. Jones, LRC Dean
Founded: 1957. **Staff:** Prof 7; Other 9. **Subjects:** Agriculture and natural resources, health occupations, dental occupations, business, liberal arts, engineering, mechanical vocations, aerospace maintenance technology, mathematics. **Special Collections:** Local genealogy collection. **Holdings:** 32,913 books; 29,732 microforms; 9634 AV programs. **Subscriptions:** 248 journals and other serials; 9 newspapers. **Services:** Interlibrary loan; copying; media production; center open to the public. **Staff:** Dot Elledge, Dir., Lib.Serv.; Malcalm Shearin, Dir., Media Prod.; Sue Potter, Dir., Directed Stud..

★17582★
WAYNE COUNTY HISTORICAL MUSEUM - LIBRARY (Hist)
1150 North A St. Phone: (317)962-5756
Richmond, IN 47374 Michele Bottorff, Dir.
Founded: 1930. **Staff:** Prof 3. **Subjects:** Local and Quaker history. **Special Collections:** Gaar Williams Collection (Chicago Tribune cartoonist); Victorian valentines (500); World War I posters. **Holdings:** 1000 books; 50

scrapbooks; records of the museum. **Subscriptions:** 15 journals and other serials. **Services:** Copying; library open to the public for reference use only. **Also Known As:** Julia Meek Gaar Wayne County Historical Museum. **Staff:** Charlotte Carpentier, Asst.Dir..

★17583★
WAYNE COUNTY HISTORICAL SOCIETY MUSEUM - LIBRARY (Hist)
21 Butternut St. Phone: (315)946-4943
Lyons, NY 14489 Marjory Allen Perez, County Hist.
Founded: 1949. **Staff:** 3. **Subjects:** Wayne County history and genealogy, western New York history. **Holdings:** 1800 volumes; 20 VF drawers of clippings, archives, pictures, pamphlets, scrapbooks. **Services:** Copying (limited); library open to the public for reference use only. **Publications:** The Aesthetic Heritage of a Rural Area, 1978; History of Pioneers Settlement of Phelps and Gorham Purchase.

★17584★
WAYNE COUNTY LAW LIBRARY ASSOCIATION (Law)
Wayne County Courthouse
107 W. Liberty St. Phone: (216)262-5561
Wooster, OH 44691 Betty K. Schuler, Libn.
Founded: 1903. **Subjects:** Law. **Holdings:** 20,000 volumes; microfiche. **Services:** Copying; library open to the public with restrictions. **Computerized Information Services:** LEXIS, DIALOG Information Services.

★17585★
WAYNE COUNTY REGIONAL LIBRARY FOR THE BLIND AND PHYSICALLY HANDICAPPED (Aud-Vis)
33030 Van Born Rd. Phone: (313)274-2600
Wayne, MI 48184 Pat Klemans, Reg.Libn.
Founded: 1931. **Staff:** Prof 4; Other 2. **Holdings:** 95,000 phonograph records and cassettes. **Services:** Interlibrary loan; copying; library serves the legally blind and physically handicapped. **Networks/Consortia:** Member of National Library Service for the Blind & Physically Handicapped (NLS).

★17586★
WAYNE HISTORICAL MUSEUM - HISTORICAL COMMISSION ARCHIVES (Hist)
One Town Square Phone: (313)722-0113
Wayne, MI 48184 Henry Goudy, Fac.Mgr.
Staff: 2. **Subjects:** Local history. **Holdings:** Clippings; manuscripts; documents; maps; genealogical material; cemetery inscriptions; church, school, and local government records; local biographies; photographs. **Services:** Archives open to the public.

★17587★
WAYNE PRESBYTERIAN CHURCH - LIBRARY (Rel-Phil)
125 E. Lancaster Ave.
Box 502 Phone: (215)688-8700
Wayne, PA 19087 Mary Augusterfer, Libn.
Staff: Prof 1; Other 2. **Subjects:** Bible study, Christian education, biography, fine arts, sociology. **Special Collections:** Hymnals. **Holdings:** 4500 books; records; cassettes; filmstrips; 13 rapid reading program portfolios; 70 college catalogs. **Subscriptions:** 10 journals and other serials. **Services:** Library open to the public with restrictions.

★17588★
WAYNE STATE COLLEGE - U.S. CONN LIBRARY (Educ)
200 E. 10 Phone: (402)375-2200
Wayne, NE 68787 Dr. Jack L. Middendorf, Dir.
Founded: 1910. **Staff:** Prof 7; Other 7. **Subjects:** Business, education, literature, social science. **Holdings:** 100,000 book titles; 3500 AV programs; 30,000 government documents (selective depository); 350,000 microform titles, including ERIC and U.S. Government microfiche collections. **Subscriptions:** 1000 journals and other serials. **Services:** Interlibrary loan; copying; AV production; library open to the public. **Computerized Information Services:** DIALOG Information Services. **Networks/Consortia:** Member of Northeast Library System. **Publications:** Connformation, monthly - to faculty. **Staff:** Janet Brumm, Tech.Serv.; Carole Schmidt, Instr.Rsrcs.; Jo Anne Bock, Govt.Doc.; Gail Egbers, Ref. & Bibliog.Instr.; Lois Spencer, AV Media Serv.; Diana Boone, Pub.Serv..

★17589★
WAYNE STATE UNIVERSITY - ARCHIVES OF LABOR AND URBAN AFFAIRS/UNIVERSITY ARCHIVES (Soc Sci, Bus-Fin)
Walter P. Reuther Library Phone: (313)577-4024
Detroit, MI 48202 Philip P. Mason, Dir.
Staff: Prof 13; Other 12. **Subjects:** American labor, urban affairs, civil rights, civil liberties, social reform, history of Wayne State University. **Special Collections:** Inactive files of United Auto Workers, American Federation of Teachers, The Newspaper Guild, United Farm Workers, Industrial Workers of the World, Air Line Pilots Association, Congress of Industrial Organizations, American Federation of State, County and Municipal Employees, and Association of Flight Attendants; personal papers of labor, political, and community leaders. **Holdings:** 11,000 books; 2600 bound periodical volumes; 49,000 linear feet of archives; 700,000 still photographs; 6000 audiotapes; 200 oral histories. **Subscriptions:** 200 journals and other serials. **Services:** Copying; archives open to qualified researchers. **Publications:** Newsletter, 3/year; A Guide to the Archives of Labor History and Urban Affairs, Wayne State University Press, 1974. **Staff:** Malvina Abonyi, Archv.; Patricia Bartkowski, Archv.; Margery Long, Archv.; Warner Pflug, Asst.Dir.; Thomas Featherstone, Archv.; Carolyn Davis, Archv./Libn.; Kathleen Schmeling, Archv.; Michael Smith, Archv.; Margaret Raucher, Archv.; Karen Krepps, Archv..

★17590★
WAYNE STATE UNIVERSITY - ARTHUR NEEF LAW LIBRARY (Law)
468 W. Ferry Mall Phone: (313)577-3925
Detroit, MI 48202 Georgia A. Clark, Hd., Law Lib.
Founded: 1927. **Staff:** Prof 5; Other 6. **Subjects:** Law and allied fields. **Special Collections:** Depository for U.S. Government documents (96,500); Michigan Legal Collection; Alwyn V. Freeman International Law Collection; U.S. and Michigan Supreme Courts Records and Briefs. **Holdings:** 235,432 volumes; 700,000 microform units. **Subscriptions:** 4048 journals and other serials; 35 newspapers. **Services:** Interlibrary loan; copying (limited); library open to the public. **Automated Operations:** Computerized cataloging, acquisitions, and circulation. **Computerized Information Services:** LEXIS, NOTIS, WESTLAW, NEXIS, OCLC. Performs searches on fee basis. Contact Person: Heather Braithwaite, Ref./Database Libn.. **Publications:** Law Library News, semimonthly; Recent Acquisitions List, semimonthly - both primarily for faculty distribution. **Staff:** Kanhya Kaul, Doc./Media Libn.; Janice Selberg, ILL/Ref.Libn..

★17591★
WAYNE STATE UNIVERSITY - FOLKLORE ARCHIVE (Hum, Area-Ethnic)
448 Purdy Library Phone: (313)577-4053
Detroit, MI 48202 Janet L. Langlois, Dir.
Founded: 1939. **Staff:** 2. **Subjects:** Oral, customary, and material culture of urban occupational and ethnic groups. **Special Collections:** International Library of African Music (authentic tribal music); Ivan Walton Collection of Michigan Folklore (Great Lakes folk music); Michigan State University Collection of Folk Narrative; Southern Upland Folklife Oral Histories (Southern whites in Detroit); Greek American Families in Detroit (oral histories; 75 tapes); Great Lakes Lighthouse Keepers (oral histories; 26 tapes); Bruce L. Harkness Poletown Photographic Exhibit (urban ethnic neighborhood; 487 black/white photographs). **Holdings:** 7000 separate collections of 3000 manuscripts, 1000 audiotape recordings, 500 phonograph records, popular publications, videotapes, slides, photographs, file cards. **Services:** Copying; archive open to the public. **Publications:** Annual Report; annotated holdings lists; Archive Study Series.

★17592★
WAYNE STATE UNIVERSITY - PURDY/KRESGE LIBRARY (Hum, Soc Sci)
5244 Gullen Mall Phone: (313)577-4043
Detroit, MI 48202 Lothar Spang, Hd.
Founded: 1973. **Staff:** Prof 12; Other 22. **Subjects:** Business and business administration, education, humanities, juvenile literature, library science, social work, social sciences. **Special Collections:** Leonard N. Simons Collection (Detroit and Michigan History); Eloise Ramsey Collection of Literature for Young People (12,000 items). **Holdings:** 1.1 million books; 201,600 bound periodical volumes; 308,269 documents (leaflets and bulletins only); 1.8 million microforms; 7607 curriculum guides; 65 VF drawers of pamphlets and clippings; 4591 films; 60,455 maps; 75 video cassettes; 1577 audio recordings. **Subscriptions:** 6665 journals and other serials; 92 newspapers. **Services:** Interlibrary loan; copying; SDI; library open to the public. **Automated Operations:** Computerized cataloging, acquisitions, serials, and circulation. **Computerized Information Services:** DIALOG Information Services, BRS Information Technologies, Pergamon ORBIT InfoLine, Inc., InfoTrac, WILSONLINE, SEARCH HELPER;

ALANET (electronic mail service). Performs searches on fee basis. Contact Person: Karen Bacsanyi, Database Coord., 577-4040. **Networks/Consortia:** Member of Michigan Library Consortium (MLC), Southeastern Michigan League of Libraries (SEMLOL). **Publications:** (WSU) Library leaflets; undergraduate guides to library use. **Staff:** Willie Edwards, Pub.Serv.Coord.; Donald Breneau, Asst.Dir.; Irene Bakewell, Found.Ctr.Coord.; Wesley Schram, Lib.Instr.; Gloria Sniderman, Educ.Libn.; Patricia Lynn, Ref.Libn.; David Rosenbaum, Ref.Libn.; William Kane, Ctr. for Bibliog.Instr..

★17593★
WAYNE STATE UNIVERSITY - SCHOOL OF MEDICINE - VERA PARSHALL SHIFFMAN MEDICAL LIBRARY (Med)
4325 Brush St. Phone: (313)577-1088
Detroit, MI 48201 Faith Van Toll, Dir.
Founded: 1949. **Staff:** Prof 6; Other 13. **Subjects:** Clinical medicine, pharmacy, and allied health sciences. **Holdings:** 66,782 books; 111,125 bound periodical volumes. **Subscriptions:** 2963 journals and other serials. **Services:** Interlibrary loan; copying; library open to the public with restrictions. **Automated Operations:** Computerized acquisitions. **Computerized Information Services:** NLM, BRS Information Technologies, DIALOG Information Services. **Staff:** Ruth Taylor, Pub.Serv.Libn.; Anaclare F. Evans, Cat./Hd., Tech.Serv.; Lora Robbins, Pub.Serv.Libn.; Jean Monroe, Pub.Serv.Libn..

★17594★
WAYNE STATE UNIVERSITY - SCIENCE AND ENGINEERING LIBRARY (Sci-Engr)
5048 Gullen Mall Phone: (313)577-4066
Detroit, MI 48234 Lothar Spang, Act.Hd.
Staff: Prof 5; Other 9. **Subjects:** Chemistry, biology, mathematics, engineering, computer science, physics, geology, nursing. **Special Collections:** Samuel Cox Hooker Chemistry Collection. **Holdings:** 198,044 books; 136,779 bound periodical volumes; 105,172 government documents; 78,534 microfiche; 1509 reels of microfilm; 455 microcards; 8213 maps. **Subscriptions:** 3137 journals and other serials. **Services:** Interlibrary loan; copying; library open to the public with restrictions. **Computerized Information Services:** DIALOG Information Services, BRS Information Technologies, Pergamon ORBIT InfoLine, Inc., CAS ONLINE. Performs searches on fee basis. **Networks/Consortia:** Member of Michigan Library Consortium (MLC), Southeastern Michigan League of Libraries (SEMLOL). **Publications:** Recent Additions List. **Staff:** Jill Rood, Ref.Libn.; William Hulsker, Ref.Libn.; Dr. James R. Ruffner, Ref.Libn.; Loren Mendelsohn, Ref.Libn..

WCRB LIBRARY
See: Charles River Broadcasting Company (2985)

WE CARE ABOUT SPECIAL CHILDREN MOBIL RESOURCE LIBRARY
See: North Shore University Hospital - Department of Health Education (10372)

WEAN MEDICAL LIBRARY
See: Trumbull Memorial Hospital (14359)

★17595★
WEATHER RESEARCH CENTER - LIBRARY (Sci-Engr)
3710 Mt. Vernon Phone: (713)529-3076
Houston, TX 77006 Dr. John C. Freeman, Dir., Res..
Founded: 1988. **Staff:** Prof 1. **Subjects:** Meteorology, oceanography, physics, hydrology, climatology. **Holdings:** 1000 books; government scientific publications; research papers; maps; microfilm. **Subscriptions:** 11 journals and other serials. **Services:** Interlibrary loan; copying; library open to the public for reference use only. **Formerly:** Institute for Storm Research.

★17596★
WEATHERDATA, INC. - LIBRARY (Aud-Vis, Sci-Engr)
833 N. Main St. Phone: (316)265-9127
Wichita, KS 67203 Patricia Cooper, Mgr., Graphics Serv.
Founded: 1981. **Subjects:** Weather. **Holdings:** Photographs and slides (most in color); videotapes; films; MacIntosh computer weather graphics library.

ANNIE BELLE WEAVER SPECIAL COLLECTIONS
See: West Georgia College - Irvine Sullivan Ingram Library (17652)

JENNIE E. WEAVER MEMORIAL LIBRARY
See: First United Methodist Church (5100)

DEL E. WEBB MEMORIAL LIBRARY
See: Loma Linda University (7927)

DEL E. WEBB MEMORIAL MEDICAL INFORMATION CENTER
See: Eisenhower Medical Center (4636)

★17597★
WEBB INSTITUTE OF NAVAL ARCHITECTURE - LIVINGSTON LIBRARY (Sci-Engr)
Crescent Beach Rd. Phone: (516)671-0439
Glen Cove, NY 11542-1398 David J. Zaehringer, Libn.
Founded: 1931. **Staff:** Prof 1; Other 1. **Subjects:** Naval architecture, marine engineering, engineering, science, literature, history, fine arts, philosophy, religion, social science. **Holdings:** 42,514 volumes; 5224 engineering reports; 1153 phonograph records; 1061 microforms; clippings and archives of W.H. Webb. **Subscriptions:** 269 journals and other serials; 6 newspapers. **Services:** Interlibrary loan; copying; library open to the public by appointment. **Publications:** Accession list, quarterly.

WEBB MEMORIAL LIBRARY
See: Penrose Hospital (11224)

★17598★
WEBER COUNTY LAW LIBRARY (Law)
Municipal Bldg., 4th Fl. Phone: (801)399-8466
Ogden, UT 84401 Grace A. Rost, Libn.
Founded: 1896. **Staff:** Prof 1. **Subjects:** Law. **Holdings:** 11,950 volumes. **Services:** Copying; library open to the public with restrictions.

WEBER MEMORIAL LIBRARY
See: San Antonio Community Hospital (12740)

★17599★
DANIEL WEBSTER COLLEGE - LIBRARY (Sci-Engr, Bus-Fin)
University Dr. Phone: (603)883-3556
Nashua, NH 03063 Patience K. Jackson, Lib.Dir.
Founded: 1966. **Staff:** Prof 4; Other 4. **Subjects:** Aeronautics, business administration, computers. **Special Collections:** Aeronautics; aviation history; air traffic control; computer systems; computer science. **Holdings:** 27,000 books. **Subscriptions:** 600 journals and other serials; 10 newspapers. **Services:** Interlibrary loan; copying; library open to the public. **Networks/Consortia:** Member of New Hampshire College & University Council Library Policy Committee (NHCUC). **Staff:** France Kelleher, Ref.Libn.; Mary Marks, Ref. & Ser.Libn.; Beth Rohning Barrett, Cat.Libn..

JEROME P. WEBSTER LIBRARY OF PLASTIC SURGERY
See: Columbia University - Augustus C. Long Health Sciences Library (3470)

JOHN P. WEBSTER LIBRARY
See: First Church of Christ Congregational (5061)

WEBSTER MEDICAL LIBRARY
See: Evanston Hospital (4840)

★17600★
NOAH WEBSTER FOUNDATION & HISTORICAL SOCIETY OF WEST HARTFORD - LIBRARY (Hist)
227 S. Main St. Phone: (203)521-5362
West Hartford, CT 06107 Sally Williams, Dir.
Founded: 1970. **Staff:** Prof 3. **Subjects:** Noah Webster, local history, the Congregational Church in Connecticut, local architecture and preservation, Connecticut colonial life and culture. **Special Collections:** Noah Webster Collection (rare books; manuscripts; letters); rare book collection (200). **Holdings:** 800 books; 10 VF drawers of West Hartford social history archives; tax records; 6 VF drawers of pictures, clippings, scrapbooks, letters. **Subscriptions:** 22 journals and other serials. **Services:** Interlibrary loan; copying; library open to the public with restrictions. **Publications:** Noah Webster, David C. Sargent, 1976; From Colonial Parish to Modern Suburb: A Brief Appreciation of West Hartford, Nelson R. Burr, 1976 - for sale; The Spectator, quarterly - to members. **Staff:** Criss Watson, Libn..

★17601★
WEBSTER & SHEFFIELD - LIBRARY (Law)
237 Park Ave. Phone: (212)808-6515
New York, NY 10017 Teresa E. Wrenn, Libn.
Staff: Prof 2; Other 2. **Subjects:** Law - corporate, public finance, securities, taxation. **Holdings:** 14,500 books; 350 bound periodical volumes; microfilm; microfiche. **Subscriptions:** 48 journals and other serials; 6

newspapers. **Services:** Interlibrary loan (limited); library not open to the public. **Automated Operations:** Computerized cataloging, acquisitions, serials, and circulation. **Computerized Information Services:** LEXIS, DIALOG Information Services, WESTLAW, Dow Jones News/Retrieval, VU/TEXT Information Services. **Staff:** Jo Cooper, Asst.Libn..

I.D. WEEKS LIBRARY
See: University of South Dakota - I.D. Weeks Library (16859)

A.T. WEHRLE MEMORIAL LIBRARY
See: Pontifical College Josephinum (11443)

G. WEIGEL ARCHIVES
See: Woodstock Theological Center - Library (18017)

WEIGEL LIBRARY OF ARCHITECTURE AND DESIGN
See: Kansas State University (7370)

★17602★
WEINBERG & GREEN, ATTORNEYS-AT-LAW - LIBRARY (Law)
100 S. Charles St. Phone: (301)332-8651
Baltimore, MD 21201 Sally J. Miles, Libn.
Staff: Prof 2; Other 3. **Subjects:** Law. **Holdings:** 20,000 books; 200 bound periodical volumes. **Subscriptions:** 150 journals and other serials. **Services:** Interlibrary loan; copying; SDI; library open to serious researchers by appointment. **Computerized Information Services:** LEXIS, NEXIS, DIALOG Information Services, WESTLAW. **Publications:** Acquisitions List, monthly - for internal distribution only. **Staff:** Allyn Simon, Asst.Libn..

JACK WEINBERG LIBRARY
See: Illinois State Psychiatric Institute (6718)

MAX AND EDITH WEINBERG LIBRARY
See: Temple Israel (13966)

★17603★
WEINBERG NATURE CENTER - LIBRARY (Biol Sci)
455 Mamaroneck Rd.
Scarsdale, NY 10583 Phone: (914)723-4784
Founded: 1958. **Subjects:** Botany, ornithology, forestry, geology, environmental education. **Holdings:** 550 books. **Subscriptions:** 25 journals and other serials. **Services:** Library open to the public for reference use only. **Remarks:** Maintained by Village of Scarsdale.

RABBI DUDLEY WEINBERG LIBRARY
See: Congregation Emanu-El B'ne Jeshurun (3624)

WEINER LIBRARY
See: Fairleigh Dickinson University (4892)

NORMAN D. WEINER PROFESSIONAL LIBRARY
See: Friends Hospital (5414)

WEINLOS MEDICAL LIBRARY
See: Misericordia Hospital (9093)

WEINREICH LIBRARY AND ARCHIVES OF YIDDISH LINGUISTICS
See: Yivo Institute for Jewish Research - Library and Archives (18173)

★17604★
ROBERT WEINSTEIN MARITIME HISTORICAL COLLECTION (Aud-Vis)
1253 S. Stanley Ave. Phone: (213)936-0558
Los Angeles, CA 90019 R. Weinstein, Owner
Subjects: Sailing ships of all countries and trades. **Holdings:** 250,000 original and copy photographs, glass negatives, clippings, post cards.

JOHN A. WEIR MEMORIAL LAW LIBRARY
See: University of Alberta (15802)

★17605★
PAUL WEIR COMPANY - LIBRARY
820 Davis St.
Evanston, IL 60201
Subjects: Coal, coal geology, mining engineering and laws, coal and mineral benefication. **Holdings:** 1000 books; 18 shelves of technical reports; 24 shelves of foreign publications; 36 shelves of state publications. **Remarks:** Presently inactive.

THEOFIELD G. WEIS LIBRARY
See: Columbia Union College (3468)

ALEX F. WEISBERG LIBRARY
See: Temple Emanu-El (13950)

EDWARD WEISS READING CENTER FOR THE VISUALLY IMPAIRED
See: Temple Beth El of Greater Buffalo - Library (13942)

★17606★
LOUIS A. WEISS MEMORIAL HOSPITAL - L. LEWIS COHEN MEMORIAL MEDICAL LIBRARY (Med)
4646 N. Marine Dr. Phone: (312)878-8700
Chicago, IL 60640 Iris Sachs, Med.Libn.
Staff: Prof 1. **Subjects:** Medicine, pre-clinical sciences. **Holdings:** 1100 books; 800 bound periodical volumes. **Subscriptions:** 131 journals and other serials. **Services:** Interlibrary loan; copying; SDI; library open to the public with restrictions. **Computerized Information Services:** NLM; DOCLINE (electronic mail service). **Networks/Consortia:** Member of Metropolitan Consortium of Chicago, ILLINET, Greater Midwest Regional Medical Library Network.

★17607★
WELBORN, DUFFORD, BROWN & TOOLEY, P.C. - LAW LIBRARY (Law)
1700 Broadway, Suite 1100 Phone: (303)861-8013
Denver, CO 80290-1199 Cori Arsenault, Firm Libn.
Founded: 1981. **Staff:** Prof 1. **Subjects:** Bankruptcy; real estate; taxation; law - oil and gas, environmental resources, mining, water. **Holdings:** Figures not available. **Subscriptions:** 94 journals and other serials. **Services:** Interlibrary loan; copying; library open to other law librarians. **Computerized Information Services:** LEXIS, NEXIS. **Publications:** Library Newsletter, bimonthly - for internal distribution only. **Special Indexes:** Index to local court rule changes (card).

WILLIAM H. WELCH MEDICAL LIBRARY
See: Johns Hopkins University - William H. Welch Medical Library (7249)

★17608★
WELD COUNTY DISTRICT COURT - LAW LIBRARY (Law)
Weld County Court House Phone: (303)356-4000
Greeley, CO 80632 Oleta B. Weber, Libn.
Founded: 1924. **Staff:** Prof 1. **Subjects:** Law. **Holdings:** 18,000 books; 265 bound periodical volumes; 12,100 reports; 650 laws; 1050 texts. **Services:** Copying; library open to the public.

★17609★
ROB & BESSIE WELDER WILDLIFE FOUNDATION - LIBRARY (Biol Sci)
Drawer 1400 Phone: (512)364-2643
Sinton, TX 78387 Vaunda Boscamp, Libn.
Founded: 1954. **Staff:** Prof 1; Other 2. **Subjects:** Natural history, ornithology, wildlife management, ecology and range management, environment and conservation, science and technology. **Special Collections:** Alexander Wetmore Library (former secretary of the Smithsonian Institution; 5274 volumes); Quillin Egg Collection. **Holdings:** 11,579 books; 1852 bound periodical volumes; 172 bound theses; 276 unbound reports and manuscripts; 500 archival items; 336 vertical files of Welder student contributions; 3254 vertical files of non-Welder reprints. **Subscriptions:** 99 journals and other serials. **Services:** Interlibrary loan; copying; library open to the public by appointment for reference use only. **Publications:** Reports and newsletters, biennial; Student Symposiums.

★17610★
WELDING INSTITUTE OF CANADA - TECHNICAL INFORMATION SERVICES (Sci-Engr)
391 Burnhamthorpe Rd., E. Phone: (416)845-9881
Oakville, ON, Canada L6J 6C9 Lorna Beresford, Tech.Info.Serv.
Founded: 1973. **Staff:** Prof 2; Other 1. **Subjects:** Welding, nondestructive testing, metallurgy. **Special Collections:** International Institute of Welding (IIW) documents (3500). **Holdings:** 500 books; 550 bound periodical volumes; 3 VF drawers. **Subscriptions:** 45 journals and other serials. **Services:** Interlibrary loan; copying; library open to institute members for reference use. **Computerized Information Services:** DIALOG Information Services, Pergamon ORBIT InfoLine, Inc., CAN/OLE; internal database.

Performs searches on fee basis. **Publications:** Welding Technology for Canada, quarterly - to corporate members; The Welding Source. **Staff:** Bruce F. Bryan, Libn..

WELDING RESEARCH COUNCIL - AMERICAN COUNCIL OF THE INTERNATIONAL INSTITUTE OF WELDING
See: American Council of the International Institute of Welding (470)

D.B. WELDON LIBRARY
See: University of Western Ontario (17090)

★17611★
WELEX HALLIBURTON COMPANY - ENGINEERING LIBRARY (Sci-Engr)
2135 Highway 6, S. Phone: (713)596-5495
Houston, TX 77077 Pat Farnell, Libn.
Founded: 1981. **Staff:** Prof 1. **Subjects:** Applied mathematics, nuclear science, computer software, electronics, geophysics, geology. **Holdings:** 1500 books. **Subscriptions:** 82 journals and other serials. **Services:** Interlibrary loan; library not open to the public. **Automated Operations:** Computerized acquisitions. **Computerized Information Services:** DIALOG Information Services. **Special Indexes:** Technical papers and reports index (card).

★17612★
WELLESLEY COLLEGE - ARCHIVES (Educ)
Wellesley, MA 02181 Phone: (617)235-0320
Wilma R. Slaight, Archv.
Staff: Prof 1; Other 1. **Subjects:** Wellesley College, women's education. **Holdings:** 3800 linear feet of archival material. **Services:** Copying; archives open to the public. **Computerized Information Services:** OCLC. **Networks/Consortia:** Member of NELINET, Boston Library Consortium.

★17613★
WELLESLEY COLLEGE - ART LIBRARY (Art)
Jewett Arts Center Phone: (617)235-0320
Wellesley, MA 02181 Richard McElroy, Art Libn.
Founded: 1883. **Staff:** Prof 1; Other 1. **Subjects:** Art history with emphasis on Western European, American, Far Eastern, and classical art and architecture; photography. **Holdings:** 37,329 volumes. **Subscriptions:** 144 journals and other serials. **Services:** Interlibrary loan; library not open to the public. **Automated Operations:** Computerized cataloging. **Computerized Information Services:** OCLC. **Networks/Consortia:** Member of NELINET, Boston Library Consortium.

★17614★
WELLESLEY COLLEGE - MARGARET CLAPP LIBRARY - SPECIAL COLLECTIONS (Hum, Hist)
Wellesley, MA 02181 Phone: (617)235-0320
Anne Anninger, Spec.Coll.Libn.
Staff: Prof 1; Other 2. **Special Collections:** English Poetry Collection (including Robert and Elizabeth Barrett Browning; 12,000 volumes); Durant Collection (19th century America; 10,000 volumes); Plimpton Collection (15th and 16th century Italian literature; 1200 volumes); Book Arts Collection (4600 volumes); Alcove of North American Languages (Indian languages; 280 volumes); Elbert Collection (slavery and Reconstruction; 800 volumes); Juvenile Collection (1000 volumes); John Ruskin Collection (900 volumes); Guy Walker Collection (illustrated books; 350 volumes). **Holdings:** 41,000 books; 20 linear feet of manuscripts and autographs. **Services:** Copying (limited); microfilming; collections open to the public.

★17615★
WELLESLEY COLLEGE - MUSIC LIBRARY (Mus)
Jewett Arts Center Phone: (617)235-0320
Wellesley, MA 02181 Ross Wood, Music Libn.
Founded: 1904. **Staff:** Prof 1; Other 1. **Subjects:** Music. **Holdings:** 23,927 volumes; 12,594 sound recordings. **Subscriptions:** 204 journals and other serials. **Services:** Interlibrary loan; library open to the public. **Automated Operations:** Computerized cataloging. **Computerized Information Services:** OCLC. **Networks/Consortia:** Member of NELINET, Boston Library Consortium, Boston Area Music Libraries (BAML).

★17616★
WELLESLEY COLLEGE - SCIENCE LIBRARY (Biol Sci, Sci-Engr, Comp Sci)
Science Center Phone: (617)235-0320
Wellesley, MA 02181 Irene S. Laursen, Sci.Libn.
Founded: 1976. **Staff:** Prof 1; Other 2. **Subjects:** Biological sciences, chemistry, computer science, geology, mathematics, physics, psychology. **Holdings:** 87,340 volumes. **Subscriptions:** 680 journals and other serials. **Services:** Interlibrary loan; copying; library open to the public with restrictions. **Automated Operations:** Computerized cataloging. **Computerized Information Services:** OCLC, DIALOG Information Services, WILSONLINE. **Networks/Consortia:** Member of NELINET, Boston Library Consortium.

★17617★
WELLESLEY HOSPITAL - LIBRARY (Med)
160 Wellesley St., E. Phone: (416)926-7071
Toronto, ON, Canada M4Y 1J3 Verla E. Empey, Dir.
Founded: 1967. **Staff:** Prof 1; Other 4. **Subjects:** Medicine, nursing, and hospital administration. **Holdings:** 12,000 books; 7300 bound periodical volumes; 2 VF drawers of bibliographies; 2 VF drawers of staff publications; 1500 AV programs; 4 VF drawers. **Subscriptions:** 365 journals and other serials. **Services:** Interlibrary loan; copying; SDI; library open to the public by appointment. **Computerized Information Services:** MEDLARS. Performs searches on fee basis.

★17618★
WELLINGTON COUNTY BOARD OF EDUCATION - EDUCATION LIBRARY (Educ)
500 Victoria Rd., N. Phone: (519)822-4420
Guelph, ON, Canada N1E 6K2 R.E. Monkhouse, Educ. Media Cons.
Founded: 1973. **Staff:** Prof 1; Other 2. **Subjects:** School librarianship, educational psychology, teaching, children's literature, curriculum support materials, special education. **Holdings:** 11,000 books; 900 bound periodical volumes; 8 drawers of current clippings. **Subscriptions:** 800 journals and other serials. **Services:** Interlibrary loan; SDI; periodical reprint and routing services; current awareness services; library open to the public by prior arrangement. **Automated Operations:** Computerized public access catalog, cataloging, and circulation. **Computerized Information Services:** DIALOG Information Services, UTLAS, QL Systems, Info Globe, BRS Information Technologies, CAN/OLE. **Publications:** T-L Talk; Educational Aids - both for internal distribution only. **Staff:** Paola Rowe, Educ.Libn..

★17619★
WELLINGTON COUNTY BOARD OF EDUCATION - TEACHER RESOURCE LIBRARY (Educ)
500 Victoria Rd. Phone: (519)822-4420
Guelph, ON, Canada N1E 6K2 R.E. Monkhouse, Educ. Media Cons.
Founded: 1982. **Staff:** 1. **Subjects:** Special education, reading, life skills, French language, primary education, speech and language. **Special Collections:** Approved textbook collection; AV programs in health education. **Holdings:** 18,500 books. **Services:** Library not open to the public. **Automated Operations:** Computerized cataloging. **Computerized Information Services:** Internal database. **Remarks:** Library located on Brighton St., Guelph, ON. **Publications:** TRL Bibliographies, irregular.

★17620★
WELLINGTON COUNTY MUSEUM - ARCHIVES (Hist)
R.R. 1 Phone: (519)846-5169
Fergus, ON, Canada N1M 2W3 Bonnie Callen, Archv.
Founded: 1977. **Staff:** 1. **Subjects:** Municipal records, genealogy, maps and plans. **Special Collections:** District of Wellington municipal records; genealogies (400). **Holdings:** 1000 books; 50 linear feet of municipal records and manuscripts; 8000 photographs; 600 maps; 400 reels of microfilm of newspapers, land abstracts, municipal records, and other items.

★17621★
WELLINGTON MANAGEMENT COMPANY - RESEARCH LIBRARY (Bus-Fin)
Box 823 Phone: (215)647-6000
Valley Forge, PA 19482 Jeanne Wilmer, Libn.
Staff: Prof 1; Other 1. **Subjects:** Corporate finance, industry. **Holdings:** 72 shelves of annual reports and financial information. **Subscriptions:** 60 journals and other serials; 15 newspapers. **Services:** Interlibrary loan; library open to the public by appointment. **Remarks:** Library located at 1300 Morris Dr., Wayne, PA 19087.

EARL H. WELLMAN, SR., MEMORIAL LIBRARY OF THE AFA
See: Aerophilatelic Federation of the Americas (78)

ANNA E. WELLS MEMORIAL LIBRARY
See: Manitoba Health (8364)

★17622★
WELLS FARGO BANK - HISTORY DEPARTMENT 921 (Hist)
420 Montgomery St. Phone: (415)396-4157
San Francisco, CA 94163 Grace A. Evans, Cur./Hist.Off.
Subjects: Wells Fargo and Company history, California gold rush and mining, staging and western transportation, history of banking and finance, San Francisco history, Californiana. **Special Collections:** Photographic Collection; Wiltsee Memorial Collection of Western Stamps, Franks and Postmarks. **Holdings:** 3600 books. **Subscriptions:** 15 journals and other serials. **Services:** Department open to qualified researchers by appointment.

★17623★
WELLS FARGO BANK - LIBRARY 0188-056 (Bus-Fin)
111 Sutter St., 5th Fl. Phone: (415)399-7357
San Francisco, CA 94163 Alice E. Hunsucker, V.P./Mgr.
Founded: 1890. **Staff:** Prof 3; Other 4. **Subjects:** Banking, finance. **Holdings:** 50,000 volumes; 24 drawers of microfiche. **Subscriptions:** 2200 journals and other serials; 32 newspapers. **Services:** Interlibrary loan; copying; library open to the public for reference use only. **Automated Operations:** public access catalog, cataloging, acquisitions, serials, and circulation. **Computerized Information Services:** DIALOG Information Services, Pergamon ORBIT InfoLine, Inc., Dow Jones News/Retrieval, NEXIS, VU/TEXT Information Services, DataTimes. **Publications:** New Acquisitions, monthly - for internal distribution only. **Remarks:** An alternate telephone number is 399-7356. **Staff:** Peggy Merbach, Ref.Libn.; Paul North, Tech.Serv./Ref..

WELLS FREEDOM ARCHIVES
See: Brigham Young University - Archives and Manuscripts Division (18209)

W. KEITH WELSH LIBRARY
See: North York General Hospital (10380)

EUDORA WELTY LIBRARY
See: Jackson/Hinds Library System (7141)

★17624★
WENHAM HISTORICAL ASSOCIATION AND MUSEUM - COLONEL TIMOTHY PICKERING LIBRARY (Hist)
132 Main St. Phone: (617)468-2377
Wenham, MA 01984 Eleanor E. Thompson, Dir.
Founded: 1952. **Staff:** 3. **Subjects:** Local history, decorative arts, fashions and costumes, herbals and horticulture, agriculture, domestic and farm animals, genealogy and town histories. **Special Collections:** Book collection of Massachusetts Society for Promoting Agriculture, founded 1792. **Holdings:** 2000 volumes; photographs; maps. **Services:** Library open to the public with restrictions.

★17625★
WENNER-GREN FOUNDATION FOR ANTHROPOLOGICAL RESEARCH - LIBRARY (Soc Sci)
1865 Broadway Phone: (212)957-8750
New York, NY 10023-7596 Annetherese Hirth, Off./Prog.Mgr.
Founded: 1941. **Subjects:** Cultural and physical anthropology, archeology. **Holdings:** 3000 volumes. **Subscriptions:** 96 journals and other serials. **Services:** Interlibrary loan; library open by appointment. **Publications:** Viking Fund Publications in Anthropology; Current Anthropology; annual report of the foundation.

WENRICH MEMORIAL LIBRARY
See: Landmark Society of Western New York (7649)

★17626★
WENTWORTH INSTITUTE OF TECHNOLOGY - ALUMNI LIBRARY (Sci-Engr)
550 Huntington Ave. Phone: (617)442-9010
Boston, MA 02115 Ann Montgomery Smith, Dir. of Libs.
Founded: 1954. **Staff:** Prof 7; Other 5. **Subjects:** Aeronautics; electronics; metals and materials; engineering technology - computer, civil, electrical, mechanical; architecture. **Holdings:** 64,000 volumes; 90 magazines and newspapers on microfilm; 1000 microfiche. **Subscriptions:** 475 journals and other serials. **Services:** Interlibrary loan; copying; library open to the public. **Automated Operations:** Computerized serials. **Computerized Information Services:** DIALOG Information Services. **Networks/Consortia:** Member of Fenway Library Consortium (FLC). **Staff:** Royce Byrd, Act.Dir., Lrng.Ctr.; Rocco Piccinino, Assoc.Dir. of Libs.; Barbara Coffey, Assoc.Libn.; Michael Logan, Tech.Serv.Libn.; Debra Mandel, Media Serv.Libn.; Priscilla Biondi, Circ.; Mary Ellen Flaherty, Archv..

★17627★
T.T. WENTWORTH, JR. MUSEUM - LIBRARY (Hist)
Box 7605 Phone: (904)438-3638
Pensacola, FL 32514-8605 T.T. Wentworth, Jr., Pres.
Founded: 1958. **Staff:** 2. **Subjects:** History of Florida, Escambia County, Pensacola. **Special Collections:** Rare books on Florida, Pensacola, and U.S. history. **Holdings:** 3000 books; 30 bound periodical volumes; 100 scrapbooks; 6000 newspapers, manuscripts, pictures, miscellaneous materials, and Fort Pickens material on microfilm. **Subscriptions:** 15 journals and other serials; 8 newspapers. **Services:** Library open to the public with restrictions.

A.R. WENTZ LIBRARY
See: Lutheran Theological Seminary (8135)

WENTZEL MEDICAL LIBRARY
See: Manatee Memorial Hospital (8341)

LILLIE B. WERNER HEALTH SCIENCES LIBRARY
See: Rochester General Hospital (12107)

★17628★
WERTHEIM SCHRODER AND COMPANY, INC. - RESEARCH LIBRARY (Bus-Fin)
200 Park Ave. Phone: (212)578-0427
New York, NY 10166 Beth Simon, Hd.Libn.
Founded: 1927. **Staff:** Prof 1; Other 4. **Subjects:** Finance, business, economics, industrial statistics. **Special Collections:** Robert Fisher Manuals of Obsolete Companies; historical stock price records. **Holdings:** 400 books; 375 reels of microfilm; 60,000 microfiche. **Subscriptions:** 50 journals and other serials; 12 newspapers. **Services:** Interlibrary loan; library open to clients and students by appointment. **Computerized Information Services:** DIALOG Information Services, Dow Jones News/Retrieval, NEXIS.

★17629★
CARL L. WESCHCKE LIBRARY (Rel-Phil)
16363 Norell Ave., N. Phone: (612)443-2321
Marine-on-St. Croix, MN 55047 Carl L. Weschcke, Pres.
Subjects: Astrology, Tantra, occultism, alchemy, witchcraft, Tarot. **Special Collections:** Bondage fetishism. **Holdings:** 20,000 books; 200 bound periodical volumes. **Subscriptions:** 25 journals and other serials. **Services:** Library open to the public with written application. **Remarks:** The library is associated with Llewellyn Publications.

★17630★
WESLEY BIBLICAL SEMINARY - LIBRARY (Rel-Phil)
Box 9938 Phone: (601)957-1315
Jackson, MS 39206 Wayne W. Woodward, Dir. of Lib.Serv.
Staff: Prof 1; Other 2. **Subjects:** Theology. **Holdings:** 33,453 books; 24 bound periodical volumes. **Subscriptions:** 165 journals and other serials. **Services:** Interlibrary loan; copying; library open to the public.

★17631★
WESLEY MEDICAL CENTER - H.B. MC KIBBIN HEALTH SCIENCE LIBRARY (Med)
550 N. Hillside Phone: (316)688-2715
Wichita, KS 67214 Jan Braden, Coord.
Founded: 1956. **Staff:** Prof 3; Other 3. **Subjects:** Medicine and nursing. **Holdings:** 31,000 books; 10,000 bound periodical volumes; 12,000 pamphlets; 3034 AV programs. **Subscriptions:** 501 journals and other serials. **Services:** Interlibrary loan; copying; library open to the public with physician's approval. **Computerized Information Services:** MEDLINE, DIALOG Information Services, BRS Information Technologies; internal database. **Networks/Consortia:** Member of Wichita Area Health Science Libraries. **Staff:** Leslie James, Libn.; Jane Tanner, Libn..

★17632★
WESLEY THEOLOGICAL SEMINARY - LIBRARY (Rel-Phil)
4500 Massachusetts Ave., N.W. Phone: (202)885-8691
Washington, DC 20016 Allen W. Mueller, Dir.
Founded: 1882. **Staff:** Prof 3; Other 3. **Subjects:** Theology, Bible, religion, philosophy, allied fields. **Special Collections:** Materials related to the former Methodist Protestant Church; Wesleyana. **Holdings:** 100,000 books; 19,000 bound periodical volumes; 1772 AV programs; 1173 tapes. **Subscriptions:** 650 journals; 10 newspapers. **Services:** Interlibrary loan; copying; library open to the public. **Automated Operations:** Computerized cataloging, acquisitions, and ILL. **Computerized Information Services:** OCLC; Bib-Base (internal database). **Networks/Consortia:** Member of Washington Theological Consortium, CAPCON.

★17633★
WESLEY UNITED METHODIST CHURCH - LIBRARY (Rel-Phil)
721 King St.
La Crosse, WI 54601 Phone: (608)782-3018
Founded: 1966. **Staff:** Prof 1; Other 5. **Subjects:** Religion, philosophy, literature, children's collection, social sciences, fine arts. **Holdings:** 2400 books; 84 filmstrips; 33 phonograph records; 2 VF drawers of pamphlets, study guides. **Services:** Library open to the public.

★17634★
WESLEY UNITED METHODIST CHURCH - RESOURCE LIBRARY (Rel-Phil)
400 Iowa Ave. Phone: (319)263-1596
Muscatine, IA 52761 Mary Ann Pedde, Christian Educ.Dir.
Founded: 1977. **Staff:** Prof 1; Other 1. **Subjects:** Christian education, Bible study, personal development, parenting, family relations, children's literature, Christian biographies and fiction. **Holdings:** 2500 books; phonograph records; media kits; games. **Subscriptions:** 16 journals and other serials. **Services:** Copying; library open to the public. **Networks/Consortia:** Member of Cokesbury Church Library Services (CLS). **Staff:** Connie Minnick, Libn..

★17635★
WESLEYAN CHURCH - ARCHIVES & HISTORICAL LIBRARY (Rel-Phil)
8050 Castleway Dr.
Box 50434 Phone: (317)576-1315
Indianapolis, IN 46250 Daniel L. Burnett, Dir.
Staff: 2. **Subjects:** History of The Wesleyan Church. **Holdings:** 5000 books; conference minute books; journals; photographs; correspondence. **Services:** Interlibrary loan; copying; library open to the public.

★17636★
WESLEYAN UNIVERSITY - LIBRARY - SPECIAL COLLECTIONS (Art, Hum)
Middletown, CT 06457 Phone: (203)347-9411
Elizabeth A. Swaim, Spec.Coll.Libn./Archv.
Founded: 1831. **Staff:** Prof 1; Other 1. **Subjects:** English and American literature and civilization, history of printing, Methodistica, Wesleyan University and Middletown history. **Special Collections:** Henry Bacon papers (architecture; 30 feet); Wilbur O. Atwater papers (agricultural chemistry; 13.5 feet); Gorham Munson and social credit (33 feet). **Holdings:** 20,000 books; 350 feet of manuscripts and archives. **Services:** Copying; collections open to the public by appointment.

★17637★
WESLEYAN UNIVERSITY - LIBRARY - WORLD MUSIC ARCHIVES (Mus)
Middletown, CT 06457 Phone: (203)347-9411
James Farrington, Mus.Libn.
Founded: 1965. **Staff:** Prof 2. **Subjects:** Ethnomusicology, non-Western music, Western nonclassical music. **Special Collections:** Music of North American Indians (especially Navajo ceremonial music), Java (music and language), Bali, Philippines, Japan, Korea, China, South India, British Isles, Greece, Afghanistan, Iran, Turkey, and West Africa. **Holdings:** 2600 audiotapes; 1000 sound discs; 120 videotapes; 4 VF drawers of indices, translations, and transcriptions. **Services:** Archives open to the public by appointment. **Networks/Consortia:** Member of NELINET.

★17638★
WESLEYAN UNIVERSITY - PSYCHOLOGY LIBRARY (Med)
Judd Hall Phone: (203)347-9411
Middletown, CT 06457 Shirley Schmottlach, Lib.Asst.
Founded: 1910. **Staff:** Prof 1. **Subjects:** Psychology, psychoanalysis, behavioral sciences, neurosciences, cognitive sciences. **Holdings:** 10,600 books; 7575 bound periodical volumes; 204 bound theses. **Subscriptions:** 200 journals and other serials. **Services:** Interlibrary loan; copying; library open to the public with restrictions.

★17639★
WESLEYAN UNIVERSITY - SCIENCE LIBRARY (Biol Sci, Sci-Engr)
Middletown, CT 06457 Phone: (203)347-9411
Cynthia Ostroff, Sci.Libn.
Founded: 1972. **Staff:** Prof 1; Other 4. **Subjects:** Astronomy, biology, chemistry, geology, mathematics, physics. **Special Collections:** History of Science (early editions; 888 volumes). **Holdings:** 125,725 volumes; 112,792 maps. **Subscriptions:** 940 journals and other serials. **Services:** Interlibrary loan; copying; library open to the public with permission. **Computerized Information Services:** DIALOG Information Services, BRS Information Technologies, WILSONLINE, CAS ONLINE. Performs searches on fee basis. **Publications:** Database Search Services; Science Journals.

★17640★
WESLEYAN UNIVERSITY - WOMEN'S CENTER - LIBRARY (Soc Sci)
Wesleyan Sta., Box 6195
Middletown, CT 06457 Phone: (203)347-9411
Founded: 1979. **Staff:** 5. **Subjects:** Women - health, history, sports, fiction, poetry, sexuality, spirituality, work, Third World, minority, arts; feminist theory. **Holdings:** 450 books; 3 drawers of subject files; directories. **Subscriptions:** 15 journals and other serials; 30 newsletters. **Services:** Library open to the public.

★17641★
WEST ALLIS MEMORIAL HOSPITAL - MEDICAL LIBRARY (Med)
8901 W. Lincoln Ave. Phone: (414)546-6162
West Allis, WI 53227 Joan A. Clausz, Med.Libn.
Staff: Prof 1. **Subjects:** Medicine. **Holdings:** 500 books; 900 bound periodical volumes. **Subscriptions:** 100 journals and other serials. **Services:** Interlibrary loan; library not open to the public. **Computerized Information Services:** BRS Information Technologies, MEDLARS. **Networks/Consortia:** Member of Southeastern Wisconsin Health Science Library Consortium (SWHSL).

★17642★
WEST BEND GALLERY OF FINE ARTS - LIBRARY (Art)
300 S. 6th Ave. Phone: (414)334-9638
West Bend, WI 53095 Thomas Lidtke, Exec.Dir.
Staff: Prof 1. **Subjects:** Art history and techniques. **Special Collections:** Letters, sketches, and documents of German American artist Carl von Marr, 1850-1936. **Holdings:** 1000 books. **Services:** Copying; library open to the public. **Special Catalogs:** Carl von Marr catalog.

★17643★
WEST CENTRAL GEORGIA REGIONAL HOSPITAL - LIBRARY (Med)
3000 Schatulga Rd.
Box 12435 Phone: (404)568-5236
Columbus, GA 31995-7499 Linda A. Sears, Libn.
Staff: Prof 1; Other 1. **Subjects:** Alcohol and drug abuse, bibliotherapy, brief and short-term therapy/counseling, consumer/patient education, forensic psychiatry, psychiatric nursing, psychiatric social work, psychology. **Holdings:** 3704 books; 246 bound periodical volumes; 624 AV programs. **Subscriptions:** 85 journals and other serials. **Services:** Interlibrary loan; copying; SDI; library open to the public with restrictions. **Computerized Information Services:** MEDLINE, BRS Information Technologies. **Networks/Consortia:** Member of Georgia Health Sciences Library Association (GHSLA), Georgia Interactive Network for Medical Information (GAIN), Georgia Library Information Network (GLIN), Health Science Libraries of Central Georgia (HSLCG), Southeastern/Atlantic Regional Medical Library Services. **Publications:** Library Manual; brochures; policy statements.

★17644★
WEST CENTRAL MINNESOTA HISTORICAL CENTER - LIBRARY (Hist)
University of Minnesota, Morris Phone: (612)589-2211
Morris, MN 56267 Dr. Wilbert H. Ahern, Dir.
Founded: 1973. **Staff:** 2. **Subjects:** Ethnicity in west central Minnesota, agribusiness, Minnesota politics and government, oral history, church history. **Special Collections:** Stevens County Census Computerization Project; The Great Depression in West Central Minnesota; Powerline Construction Oral History Project; World War II: The Home Front in Central Minnesota (oral history). **Holdings:** 650 linear feet of local history materials; oral history cassettes; microfilm. **Services:** Copying; library open to the public. **Remarks:** Maintained by the University of Minnesota, Morris.

★17645★
WEST CHESTER UNIVERSITY - FRANCIS HARVEY GREEN LIBRARY - SPECIAL COLLECTIONS (Educ)
West Chester, PA 19383 Phone: (215)436-3456
R. Gerald Schoelkopf, Spec.Coll.Libn.
Founded: 1871. **Staff:** Prof 1; Other 1. **Subjects:** Botanical history, history of Chester County and Pennsylvania, Chester County and Pennsylvania authors, physical education. **Special Collections:** William Darlington

Library (rare scientific and botanical materials); Chester County Cabinet Library; Philips Autograph Library; Shakespeare folios; Ehinger Library (historical material on physical education; 581 items); Chester County Collection; university archives (350 boxes). **Holdings:** 9100 books; 200 bound periodical volumes; 5 folio drawers; 40 VF drawers; 100 magnetic tapes; 6 boxes of microfilm; 70 oral history tapes. **Services:** Interlibrary loan; copying; collections open to the public for reference use, with borrowing privileges by special arrangement. **Automated Operations:** Computerized cataloging. **Computerized Information Services:** DIALOG Information Services, BRS Information Technologies, Pergamon ORBIT InfoLine, Inc., OCLC. **Networks/Consortia:** Member of PALINET, Tri-State College Library Cooperative (TCLC), Interlibrary Delivery Service of Pennsylvania (IDS), State System of Higher Education Libraries Council (SSHELCO). **Special Catalogs:** Computerized periodical list.

★17646★
WEST CHESTER UNIVERSITY - SCHOOL OF MUSIC LIBRARY (Mus)
Francis Harvey Green Library
High St. & Rosedale Ave. Phone: (215)436-2430
West Chester, PA 19383 Paul Emmons, Mus.Libn./Asst.Prof.
Founded: 1960. **Staff:** Prof 1; Other 1. **Subjects:** Music history, opera, instrumental music, jazz, contemporary music, American music. **Special Collections:** Gilbert and Sullivan (100 items). **Holdings:** 24,000 scores; 20,000 phonograph records. **Services:** Interlibrary loan; copying; library open to the public with restrictions. **Automated Operations:** Computerized, public access catalog, cataloging, serials, and circulation. **Computerized Information Services:** OCLC, DIALOG Information Services, BRS Information Technologies, Pergamon ORBIT InfoLine, Inc. **Networks/Consortia:** Member of PALINET, Tri-State College Library Cooperative (TCLC), Interlibrary Delivery Service of Pennsylvania (IDS), State System of Higher Education Libraries Council (SSHELCO). **Special Indexes:** Song title file; record analytic file; piano music file; women composers; early music file.

★17647★
WEST COAST CHRISTIAN COLLEGE - MC BRAYER LIBRARY (Rel-Phil)
6901 N. Maple Ave. Phone: (209)297-0598
Fresno, CA 93710 Edward E. Call, Hd.Libn.
Staff: Prof 1; Other 1. **Subjects:** Religion, philosophy, literature, psychology, social science, science. **Special Collections:** Pentecostal Studies Research; Studies in 7th Day Adventism; Studies in Christian Scientism. **Holdings:** 66,500 books; 141 bound periodical volumes; 2300 microforms; 5 films; 349 filmstrips; 91 video cassettes; 1102 audio cassettes; 105 reels of microfilm; 61 transparencies; 1344 phonograph records. **Subscriptions:** 710 journals and other serials; 7 newspapers. **Services:** Interlibrary loan; copying; center open to the public for reference use only. **Networks/Consortia:** Member of Areawide Library Network (AWLNET). **Formerly:** Hughes Memorial Research Pentecostal Center. **Staff:** Cindy Edwards, Circ.Libn..

WEST COAST LESBIAN COLLECTIONS, INC.
See: Mazer Collection (8587)

★17648★
WEST COAST UNIVERSITY - ELCONIN CENTER LIBRARY (Sci-Engr, Bus-Fin)
440 Shatto Place Phone: (213)487-4433
Los Angeles, CA 90020 Emma C. Gibson, Dir. of Libs.
Staff: Prof 2. **Subjects:** Management, engineering, computer science. **Holdings:** 15,000 books; unbound periodicals. **Subscriptions:** 300 journals and other serials; 7 newspapers. **Services:** Interlibrary loan; copying; library open to the public with restrictions. **Computerized Information Services:** DIALOG Information Services. Performs searches on fee basis.

★17649★
WEST END COLLEGIATE CHURCH - LIBRARY
West End Ave. at 77th St.
New York, NY 10024
Subjects: Religion. **Holdings:** 150 volumes. **Remarks:** Presently inactive.

★17650★
WEST END SYNAGOGUE - LIBRARY (Rel-Phil)
3810 West End Ave. Phone: (615)269-4592
Nashville, TN 37205 Annette Levy Ratkin, Dir.
Staff: Prof 1. **Subjects:** Judaica, children's literature, Yiddish. **Holdings:** 4400 books. **Services:** Interlibrary loan; copying; library open to the public.

★17651★
WEST FLORIDA REGIONAL MEDICAL CENTER - MEDICAL LIBRARY (Med)
8383 N. Davis Hwy.
Box 18900 Phone: (904)478-4460
Pensacola, FL 32523-8900 Kay Franklin, Dir./Med.Libn.
Founded: 1954. **Staff:** Prof 1; Other 2. **Subjects:** Clinical medicine, oncology. **Special Collections:** Chadbourne Collection (oncology; 90 books). **Holdings:** 1400 books. **Subscriptions:** 383 journals and other serials. **Services:** Interlibrary loan; library not open to the public. **Automated Operations:** Computerized serials. **Computerized Information Services:** NLM, BRS Information Technologies, DIALOG Information Services, AMA/NET.

★17652★
WEST GEORGIA COLLEGE - IRVINE SULLIVAN INGRAM LIBRARY - ANNIE BELLE WEAVER SPECIAL COLLECTIONS (Hist)
Carrollton, GA 30118 Phone: (404)836-3695
Myron W. House, Spec.Coll.Libn.
Founded: 1933. **Staff:** Prof 1. **Subjects:** West Georgia College archives, history of western Georgia, sacred harp music. **Special Collections:** Robert H. Claxton papers (5 linear feet); William H. Row papers (5 linear feet); Melvin T. Steely papers (1 linear foot); Alice Nix papers (1 linear foot); W. Benjamin Kennedy papers (1 linear foot); Thomas A. Bryson papers (13 linear feet); Robert D. Tisinger papers (2 linear feet); James E. Boyd papers (13 linear feet); Ward Pafford papers (4 linear feet); Tracy Stallings papers (10 linear feet); Sidney M. Jourard papers (76 linear feet); Association for Humanistic Education (1 linear foot); William G. Roll papers (18 linear feet); Fourth District A & M School Collection (144 items; 19 volumes); Irvine S. Ingram papers (50 linear feet); J. Ebb Duncan papers (4 linear feet); oral history collection (129 audio cassettes; 15 video cassettes). **Holdings:** 2312 volumes; 16,499 clippings, letters, photographs, maps; 223 feet of manuscript collections. **Services:** Copying; collections open to the public.

★17653★
WEST JERSEY HEALTH SYSTEM, EASTERN DIVISION - STAFF MEDICAL LIBRARY (Med)
Evesham Rd. Phone: (609)772-5494
Voorhees, NJ 08043 Jean I. Belsterling, Med.Libn.
Founded: 1976. **Staff:** Prof 1. **Subjects:** Medicine, nursing, patient education, administration. **Holdings:** 1000 books; 2000 bound periodical volumes; 35 AV programs. **Subscriptions:** 157 journals and other serials. **Services:** Interlibrary loan; copying; SDI; library open to the public for reference use only. **Computerized Information Services:** MEDLARS. **Networks/Consortia:** Member of Southwest New Jersey Consortium for Health Information Services, New Jersey Library Network.

★17654★
WEST LIBERTY STATE COLLEGE - ELBIN LIBRARY (Educ, Bus-Fin)
West Liberty, WV 26074 Phone: (304)336-8035
Donald R. Strong, Libn.
Founded: 1932. **Staff:** Prof 5; Other 8. **Subjects:** Education, economics, business. **Special Collections:** Krise Rare Book Collection (400 volumes); college archives (10 filing drawers; 130 file boxes; 43 volumes). **Holdings:** 194,000 books; 28,042 bound periodical volumes; 45,000 pamphlets, clippings, and pictures; 12,000 recordings and tapes; 30,000 microforms; 5800 reels of microfilm; 2109 filmstrips and slides. **Subscriptions:** 1170 journals and other serials; 14 newspapers. **Services:** Interlibrary loan; copying; library open to the public. **Computerized Information Services:** DIALOG Information Services. Performs searches on fee basis. **Networks/Consortia:** Member of Pittsburgh Regional Library Center (PRLC). **Publications:** Accessions List, monthly; Handbook. **Staff:** Heather Lyle, Acq.Libn.; Jeanne Schramm, Ref.Libn.; Nancy Sandercox, Cat.; Mrs. Francis Stewart, AV Libn.; Laurence Williams, Media Spec..

ROSCOE L. WEST LIBRARY
See: Trenton State College (14313)

★17655★
WEST SUBURBAN HOSPITAL MEDICAL CENTER - HEALTH INFORMATION CENTER (Med)
Erie at Austin Phone: (312)383-6200
Oak Park, IL 60302 Constance M. Gibbon, Libn.
Staff: Prof 1; Other 1. **Subjects:** Consumer health. **Holdings:** 900 books; 350 videotapes; pamphlets. **Subscriptions:** 25 journals and other serials. **Services:** Interlibrary loan; copying; center open to the public. **Automated Operations:** Computerized cataloging and acquisitions. **Computerized**

Information Services: MEDLINE, BRS Information Technologies. Performs searches on fee basis. **Networks/Consortia:** Member of Suburban Library System (SLS), Metropolitan Consortium of Chicago. **Publications:** Healthinfo - for internal distribution only.

★17656★
WEST SUBURBAN HOSPITAL MEDICAL CENTER - WALTER LAWRENCE MEMORIAL LIBRARY (Med)
Erie at Austin Phone: (312)383-6200
Oak Park, IL 60302 Eva Fels Eisenstein, Dir. of Lib. & Info.Serv.
Founded: 1978. **Staff:** Prof 1; Other 2. **Subjects:** Clinical medicine, nursing. **Holdings:** 4000 books; 10 VF drawers; 400 videotapes. **Subscriptions:** 350 journals and other serials; 5 newspapers. **Services:** Interlibrary loan; copying; SDI; library open to the public by appointment. **Computerized Information Services:** MEDLINE, BRS Information Technologies. **Networks/Consortia:** Member of Greater Midwest Regional Medical Library Network, Metropolitan Consortium of Chicago, Suburban Library System (SLS), Rush Affiliates Information Network (RAIN). **Publications:** Library News, quarterly - internal distribution and to colleagues upon request.

★17657★
WEST TENNESSEE HISTORICAL SOCIETY - LIBRARY (Hist)
Memphis State University
Box 111046
Memphis, TN 38111 Phone: (901)458-4696
Founded: 1935. **Staff:** Prof 1; Other 2. **Subjects:** Western Tennessee, Memphis and regional history. **Holdings:** 1000 books; 80 cubic feet of 19th and early 20th century manuscripts, scrapbooks, and articles including archives of the society and its predecessor organizations, 1857 to present. **Subscriptions:** 10 journals and other serials. **Services:** Copying; library open to the public. **Publications:** West Tennessee Historical Society Papers, annual. **Special Indexes:** Composite indexes to WTHS Papers and Guide to West Tennessee Historical Society Publications. **Remarks:** Library is part of Memphis State University Libraries - Special Collections.

★17658★
WEST VALLEY MEDICAL CENTER - HEALTH INFORMATION CENTER (Med)
1717 Arlington Phone: (208)459-4641
Caldwell, ID 83605 Jan Walters, Med.Libn.
Staff: Prof 1; Other 2. **Subjects:** Medicine, consumer health. **Holdings:** 276 books; 60 bound periodical volumes; 200 pamphlets; 300 other cataloged items. **Subscriptions:** 55 journals and other serials; 5 newspapers. **Services:** Interlibrary loan; copying; SDI; library open to the public with restrictions. **Automated Operations:** Computerized cataloging, acquisitions, and circulation. **Computerized Information Services:** MEDLINE, BRS Information Technologies, DIALOG Information Services; EMS (electronic mail service). **Networks/Consortia:** Member of Boise Valley Health Sciences Library Consortium, Pacific Northwest Regional Health Sciences Library Service. **Publications:** Health Information Newsletter.

★17659★
WEST VALLEY NUCLEAR SERVICES COMPANY, INC. - TECHNICAL LIBRARY (Sci-Engr)
10300 Rock Springs Rd. Phone: (716)942-4362
West Valley, NY 14171-0191 L. Yvonne Curry, Tech.Libn.
Founded: 1982. **Staff:** Prof 1. **Subjects:** Nuclear waste management; engineering - mechanical, civil, chemical. **Holdings:** 500 books; 3500 government contractor reports. **Subscriptions:** 85 journals and other serials; 5 newspapers. **Services:** Interlibrary loan; copying; SDI; library open to the public with restrictions. **Computerized Information Services:** DIALOG Information Services. **Networks/Consortia:** Member of Western New York Library Resources Council (WNYLRC). **Publications:** Technical Library Bulletin, monthly - available upon request.

WEST VIRGINIA PULP AND PAPER COMPANY
See: Westvaco Corporation (17803)

★17660★
WEST VIRGINIA SCHOOL OF OSTEOPATHIC MEDICINE - WVSOM LIBRARY (Med)
400 N. Lee St. Phone: (304)645-6270
Lewisburg, WV 24901-0827 Donna M. Hudson, Dir.
Staff: Prof 1; Other 5. **Subjects:** Medicine. **Holdings:** 11,000 books; 3000 bound periodical volumes; 4000 AV programs. **Subscriptions:** 400 journals and other serials; 5 newspapers. **Services:** Interlibrary loan; copying; library open to the public with restrictions. **Computerized Information Services:** MEDLINE. Performs searches on fee basis. **Publications:** WVSOM Newsletter, monthly.

★17661★
WEST VIRGINIA SCHOOLS FOR THE DEAF AND BLIND - SCHOOL FOR THE BLIND LIBRARY (Aud-Vis)
301 E. Main St. Phone: (304)822-3521
Romney, WV 26757 Leslie C. Durst, Coord., Lib.Serv.
Founded: 1963. **Staff:** Prof 2; Other 1. **Subjects:** General collection. **Special Collections:** Education of the visually impaired. **Holdings:** 10,000 talking books; 220 magnetic tapes; 2881 braille books; 3650 print books; 610 commercial sound recordings. **Subscriptions:** 60 journals and other serials; 9 newspapers. **Services:** Interlibrary loan; library not open to the public. **Networks/Consortia:** Member of National Library Service for the Blind & Physically Handicapped (NLS). **Staff:** Donna See, Libn..

★17662★
WEST VIRGINIA STATE ATTORNEY GENERAL - LAW LIBRARY (Law)
State Capitol, RM E-26 Phone: (304)348-2021
Charleston, WV 25305 Sue Harris, Libn.
Staff: Prof 1. **Subjects:** Law. **Holdings:** 8678 volumes. **Services:** Library not open to the public. **Computerized Information Services:** WESTLAW. **Publications:** Biennial Report & Opinions of Attorney General - for sale.

★17663★
WEST VIRGINIA STATE BOARD OF REHABILITATION - DIVISION OF REHABILITATION SERVICES - STAFF LIBRARY (Med)
Rehabilitation Center Phone: (304)766-4644
Institute, WV 25112-1004 Mrs. Jo Skiles, Staff Libn.
Staff: Prof 1. **Subjects:** Physical and vocational rehabilitation, behavioral sciences, management, medicine. **Special Collections:** Division of Vocational Rehabilitation research and development projects (52). **Holdings:** 11,241 books; 4800 monographs, reports, projects; 114 16mm films; 32 slides and cassettes; 174 videotapes. **Subscriptions:** 54 journals and other serials. **Services:** Interlibrary loan; copying; library open to the public with restrictions. **Special Catalogs:** Film catalog. **Formerly:** West Virginia State Board of Vocational Education - Division of Vocational Rehabilitation - Staff Development Library.

★17664★
WEST VIRGINIA STATE COMMISSION ON AGING - LIBRARY (Soc Sci)
State Capitol Phone: (304)348-2917
Charleston, WV 25305 Eleanor M. Keenan, Libn.
Staff: Prof 1. **Subjects:** Gerontology. **Holdings:** 9063 books; 7 shelves of newsletters, reports, bulletins; 5 VF drawers of pamphlets; 5 VF drawers of clippings. **Subscriptions:** 25 journals and other serials. **Services:** Interlibrary loan; copying; library open to the public. **Publications:** Annual progress report; occasional brochures.

★17665★
WEST VIRGINIA STATE DEPARTMENT OF AGRICULTURE - LIBRARY (Biol Sci, Agri)
Capitol Bldg. Phone: (304)348-2212
Charleston, WV 25305 Dr. Maria Gyulahazi, Libn.
Founded: 1973. **Staff:** Prof 1. **Subjects:** Entomology, plant pathology, regulation and inspection, forestry, animal health and breeding, pesticide regulations. **Special Collections:** Entomology (30,000 items). **Holdings:** 5000 books; 750 bound periodical volumes; 225 boxes of pamphlets; 8000 other cataloged items. **Subscriptions:** 70 journals and other serials. **Services:** Interlibrary loan; copying; library open to state agencies and college students with permission. **Computerized Information Services:** Internal database. **Publications:** Acquisition List for Books, quarterly; alphabetical and subject lists of journals.

★17666★
WEST VIRGINIA STATE DEPARTMENT OF CULTURE AND HISTORY - ARCHIVES AND HISTORY LIBRARY (Hist)
Cultural Center, Capitol Complex Phone: (304)348-0230
Charleston, WV 25305 Mary M. Jenkins, Libn.
Founded: 1905. **Staff:** Prof 6; Other 8. **Subjects:** West Virginia archives, history, genealogy; history - U.S., Civil War, colonial, military. **Special Collections:** Governors' papers (1500 linear feet); manuscripts (957 linear feet); Boyd Stutler-John Brown Collection (200 cubic feet); agency records; state documents (22,000); county court records (5800 reels of microfilm); newspapers (15,000 reels of microfilm and clippings); military and land records (2500 reels of microfilm). **Holdings:** 70,000 books; 10,000 bound periodical volumes; 6400 linear feet of state archives; 25,000 reels of microfilm; 10,000 photographs; 50,000 stories on newsfilm and videotape from four West Virginia television stations, 1955-1982; 6000 maps; 24 VF drawers of clippings. **Subscriptions:** 250 journals and other serials; 80

newspapers. **Services:** Copying; library open to the public for reference use only. **Publications:** West Virginia History, annual; Checklist of State Publications, quarterly. **Staff:** Fred Armstrong, Assoc.Dir.; Debra Basham, Archv.; Carol Vandevender, Per./Doc.Libn.; Richard Fauss, AV Archv.; Robert A.C. Mount, Photo.Archv.; Mary M. Jenkins, Libn..

★17667★
WEST VIRGINIA STATE DEPARTMENT OF EDUCATION - EDUCATIONAL MEDIA CENTER
1900 Washington St., E., Rm. B346
Charleston, WV 25305
Defunct

★17668★
WEST VIRGINIA STATE DEPARTMENT OF HEALTH - STATE HYGIENIC LABORATORY - LIBRARY (Med)
167 11th Ave. Phone: (304)348-3530
South Charleston, WV 25303 Jennifer J. Graley, Stenographer
Staff: 1. **Subjects:** Public health. **Holdings:** 500 books. **Subscriptions:** 12 journals and other serials. **Services:** Library open to the public with director's permission.

★17669★
WEST VIRGINIA STATE DEPARTMENT OF HIGHWAYS - PLANNING, RESEARCH, AND ENVIRONMENTAL STUDIES DIVISION - LIBRARY (Trans)
1900 Washington St., E.
Charleston, WV 25305 Phone: (304)348-3161
Subjects: Highway research. **Holdings:** 5000 volumes. **Services:** Copying; library open to universities and government agencies.

★17670★
WEST VIRGINIA STATE DEPARTMENT OF HIGHWAYS - RIGHT OF WAY DIVISION LIBRARY (Trans, Law)
1900 Washington St., E. Phone: (304)348-3195
Charleston, WV 25305 Richard D. Ricketts, Chf., Adm.Serv.
Founded: 1963. **Staff:** 1. **Subjects:** Real estate appraisal, eminent domain, highway severance and research studies, building costs, right of way operating manuals. **Holdings:** 1400 volumes; 2 VF drawers of pamphlets; 200 slides; appraisal cassette tapes. **Subscriptions:** 20 journals and other serials. **Services:** Library open to the public with permission. **Special Catalogs:** Appraisal subjects on cards.

★17671★
WEST VIRGINIA STATE DEPARTMENT OF NATURAL RESOURCES - DIVISION OF WATER RESOURCES - LIBRARY
1201 Greenbrier St.
Charleston, WV 25311
Subjects: Water, pollution, legislation. **Special Collections:** Environment Reporter (12 volumes). **Holdings:** State water basin studies and water quality reports; Environmental Protection Agency water pollution control reports and water resources planning; water resources data; journals of Water Pollution Control Federation; developing documents for proposed effluent limitations guidelines; economic analyses of proposed effective limitations; chemical and environmental engineering magazines. **Remarks:** Presently inactive.

★17672★
WEST VIRGINIA STATE GEOLOGICAL AND ECONOMIC SURVEY - LIBRARY (Sci-Engr)
Box 879 Phone: (304)292-6331
Morgantown, WV 26505 Ruth I. Hayhurst, Libn.
Founded: 1897. **Staff:** Prof 1. **Subjects:** Geology, petroleum, coal, oil, gas, allied sciences. **Holdings:** 6187 volumes; 9461 pamphlets. **Subscriptions:** 16 journals and other serials. **Services:** Library not open to the public.

★17673★
WEST VIRGINIA STATE LEGISLATIVE REFERENCE LIBRARY (Law)
Capitol Bldg., Rm. 206 W. Phone: (304)348-2153
Charleston, WV 25305 Mary Del Cont, Libn.
Founded: 1957. **Staff:** Prof 1. **Subjects:** Legislation, law, education, government and finance, taxation. **Holdings:** 3150 volumes; 7 VF drawers of legislative reports from other states; 3 VF files of reports of Council of State Governments; 4 VF drawers of newspaper clippings. **Subscriptions:** 37 journals and other serials. **Services:** Interlibrary loan; library open to the public. **Publications:** Reports of the Legislative Auditor's Office.

★17674★
WEST VIRGINIA STATE LIBRARY COMMISSION - FILM SERVICES DEPARTMENT (Aud-Vis)
Science and Cultural Center Phone: (304)348-3976
Charleston, WV 25305 Steve Fesenmaier, Hd. Film Serv.
Founded: 1976. **Staff:** Prof 2; Other 4. **Special Collections:** Appalachia (150 films); astronomy (10 films); women (100 films); feature films (1000); Les Blank Collection (20 films); foreign feature films (200); black history and culture (100 films). **Holdings:** 4500 16mm sound films. **Subscriptions:** 12 journals and other serials. **Services:** Interlibrary loan (within state); department open to the public. **Networks/Consortia:** Member of Educational Film Library Association. **Publications:** WVLC Film Services Newsletter, quarterly - to WV public libraries. **Special Indexes:** Pickfick Papers II and supplements; filmographies on energy, women, Appalachia, features. **Remarks:** Conducts state and local film workshops and annual film festival. **Staff:** Frani Fesenmaier, Asst.Hd..

★17675★
WEST VIRGINIA STATE LIBRARY COMMISSION - REFERENCE LIBRARY (Info Sci)
Cultural Center Phone: (304)348-2045
Charleston, WV 25305 Karen E. Goff, Ref.Libn.
Founded: 1929. **Staff:** Prof 2; Other 5. **Subjects:** Political science, public administration, social welfare, economics. **Holdings:** 81,146 volumes; 500 West Virginia reports and publications; 16,182 reels of microfilm of periodicals; 127,303 microfiche; U.S. Government documents depository. **Subscriptions:** 786 journals and other serials. **Services:** Interlibrary loan; copying; library open to the public. **Automated Operations:** Computerized cataloging, acquisitions, and circulation. **Computerized Information Services:** DIALOG Information Services. Performs searches on fee basis. **Publications:** West Virginia Library Commission Newsletter, quarterly. **Special Indexes:** Charleston Newspaper Index, annual. **Staff:** Candace Cooper, Doc.Libn..

★17676★
WEST VIRGINIA STATE SUPREME COURT OF APPEALS - STATE LAW LIBRARY (Law)
Capitol Bldg., Rm. E-320 Phone: (304)348-2607
Charleston, WV 25305 Richard Rosswurm, Supreme Court Law Libn.
Founded: 1863. **Staff:** Prof 2; Other 3. **Subjects:** Law. **Special Collections:** State Constitutional Convention Debates; G.P.O. Collection; English and Canadian law; West Virginia documents. **Holdings:** 100,000 books; 25,000 bound periodical volumes; 2500 pamphlets; microfiche; records and briefs of U.S. Supreme Court, 1963 to present. **Subscriptions:** 544 journals and other serials. **Services:** Interlibrary loan; copying; library open to the public. **Computerized Information Services:** WESTLAW. **Publications:** Annual Report to the State Supreme Court; Acquisitions List, irregular. **Special Catalogs:** Periodical Holdings. **Staff:** Marjorie Price, Asst. Law Libn.; Kimberly Crawford, Tech.Serv.Libn..

★17677★
WEST VIRGINIA STATE TAX DEPARTMENT - RESEARCH DIVISION - LIBRARY (Bus-Fin)
Capitol Bldg.
Charleston, WV 25305 Phone: (304)348-3478
Subjects: Taxation, energy, economic research. **Holdings:** 2000 books; reports.

★17678★
WEST VIRGINIA UNIVERSITY - COLLEGE OF BUSINESS AND ECONOMICS - BUREAU OF BUSINESS RESEARCH (Bus-Fin)
Box 6025 Phone: (304)293-5837
Morgantown, WV 26506 Tom S. Witt, Exec.Dir.
Staff: Prof 6; Other 14. **Subjects:** Business, economics, West Virginia economy, small business. **Holdings:** 2000 volumes; Association for Business and Economic Research, Bureau of Economic Analysis, Census Data Centers, and Conference Board publications. **Subscriptions:** 242 journals and other serials. **Services:** Bureau open to the public. **Computerized Information Services:** Bureau of Economic Analysis (BEA), Wharton Econometric; internal database; BITNET (electronic mail service). Performs searches on fee basis. **Publications:** University Research in Business and Economics, annual - for sale.

★17679★
WEST VIRGINIA UNIVERSITY - COLLEGE OF CREATIVE ARTS - MUSIC LIBRARY (Mus)
Morgantown, WV 26506-6111 Phone: (304)293-4505
John Core, Supv.
Staff: Prof 1; Other 12. **Subjects:** Music. **Special Collections:** Fry Jazz Archives (4000 pre-1945 phonograph records). **Holdings:** 13,000 books and bound periodical volumes; 13,350 scores; 850 reels of microfilm; 95 titles on microcards; 7000 phonograph records. **Subscriptions:** 160 journals and other serials. **Services:** Interlibrary loan; library open to the public with restrictions. **Networks/Consortia:** Member of Pittsburgh Regional Library Center (PRLC). **Special Catalogs:** Fry Archives catalog (card). **Formerly:** Creative Arts Center - Music Library.

★17680★
WEST VIRGINIA UNIVERSITY - LAW LIBRARY (Law)
Law School
Box 6135 Phone: (304)293-5309
Morgantown, WV 26506-6130 Camille M. Riley, Law Libn.
Staff: Prof 2; Other 6. **Subjects:** Law. **Holdings:** 146,680 volumes; 33,745 microfiche. **Subscriptions:** 2357 journals and other serials. **Services:** Interlibrary loan; copying; library open to the public. **Computerized Information Services:** LEXIS, WESTLAW. **Staff:** Carol S. Davis, Sr.Cat.Libn..

★17681★
WEST VIRGINIA UNIVERSITY - MEDICAL CENTER - CHARLESTON DIVISION - LEARNING RESOURCES CENTER (Med)
3110 MacCorkle Ave., S.E. Phone: (304)347-1285
Charleston, WV 25304 Patricia Powell, Hd.Libn.
Staff: Prof 2; Other 4. **Subjects:** Medicine, nursing. **Holdings:** 15,000 books; 14,000 bound periodical volumes; 1800 AV programs. **Subscriptions:** 525 journals and other serials. **Services:** Interlibrary loan; copying; center open to the public. **Automated Operations:** Computerized cataloging. **Computerized Information Services:** DIALOG Information Services, OCLC, MEDLINE. Performs searches on fee basis. **Networks/Consortia:** Member of Pittsburgh Regional Library Center (PRLC). **Publications:** Acquisitions list, monthly - by request; AV holdings list. **Remarks:** Includes the holdings of Charleston Area Medical Center - General Division - Medical Library. An alternate telephone number is 347-1282. **Staff:** Carol Bohlman, Staff Libn..

★17682★
WEST VIRGINIA UNIVERSITY - MEDICAL CENTER LIBRARY (Med)
Basic Sciences Bldg. Phone: (304)293-2113
Morgantown, WV 26506-6306 Robert Murphy, Dir.
Founded: 1954. **Staff:** Prof 5; Other 11. **Subjects:** Medicine, dentistry, pharmacy, nursing, hospital administration. **Special Collections:** Medicine in West Virginia; occupational respiratory diseases. **Holdings:** 48,200 books; 128,300 bound periodical volumes; 600 dissertations and theses; 6302 reels of microfilm containing 469 titles; 6152 microfiche containing 400 titles; 2500 slides and films. **Subscriptions:** 2300 journals and other serials. **Services:** Interlibrary loan; copying; SDI; library open to the public for reference use only. **Automated Operations:** Computerized cataloging and serials union list. **Computerized Information Services:** DIALOG Information Services, BRS Information Technologies, Pergamon ORBIT InfoLine, Inc., OCLC, CAS ONLINE; West Virginia Union List of Serials (internal database). Performs searches on fee basis for CAS ONLINE only. Contact Person: Jean Allyson McKee, Tech.Serv.. **Networks/Consortia:** Member of Pittsburgh Regional Library Center (PRLC), Southeastern/Atlantic Regional Medical Library Services. **Publications:** What's New, irregular. **Staff:** Marge Abel, Assoc.Dir.; Diane Morton, Pub.Serv.; Beth Hough, AV Serv..

★17683★
WEST VIRGINIA UNIVERSITY - OFFICE OF HEALTH SERVICE RESEARCH - LIBRARY (Med)
900 Chestnut Ridge Rd.
Morgantown, WV 26505 Phone: (304)293-2601
Subjects: Health demographics, health finances and management, diabetes. **Holdings:** Figures not available. **Computerized Information Services:** Internal databases.

★17684★
WEST VIRGINIA UNIVERSITY - WEST VIRGINIA AND REGIONAL COLLECTION (Hist)
University Library Phone: (304)293-3536
Morgantown, WV 26506 George Parkinson, Cur.
Founded: 1925. **Staff:** Prof 3; Other 9. **Subjects:** Appalachian, regional, state, and local history and genealogy. **Holdings:** 27,000 volumes; 22,310 reels of microfilm; 12,000 linear feet of manuscripts including 3000 collections, photographs, oral histories, folk music, and archival materials. **Computerized Information Services:** OCLC.

★17685★
WEST VIRGINIA WESLEYAN COLLEGE - ANNIE MERNER PFEIFFER LIBRARY (Hist)
College Ave. Phone: (304)473-8013
Buckhannon, WV 26201 Benjamin F. Crutchfield, Jr., Dir., Lib.Serv.
Founded: 1890. **Staff:** Prof 3; Other 5. **Subjects:** History of Methodist Church in West Virginia; history of Upshur County, West Virginia; Lincolniana. **Special Collections:** Charles Aubrey Jones Lincolniana (3000 items); Pearl S. Buck Manuscripts (68 Hollinger boxes; 200 file envelopes). **Holdings:** 150,000 volumes; 12,000 unbound periodicals; 5665 volumes in microform; 6217 AV programs. **Subscriptions:** 640 journals and other serials; 19 newspapers. **Services:** Interlibrary loan; copying (limited); library open to the public for reference use only. **Automated Operations:** Computerized cataloging. **Networks/Consortia:** Member of Pittsburgh Regional Library Center (PRLC). **Special Catalogs:** Media Catalog. **Staff:** Judith R. Martin, Cat.; Stephen E. Cresswell, Ref.Libn..

★17686★
WEST VOLUSIA MEMORIAL HOSPITAL - MEDICAL LIBRARY (Med)
Box 509 Phone: (904)734-3320
De Land, FL 32721-0509 Marjorie E. Cook, Lib.Mgr.
Staff: 1. **Subjects:** Medicine and allied health sciences. **Holdings:** 800 books; 150 bound periodical volumes; 2 Audio-Digest subscriptions. **Subscriptions:** 50 journals and other serials; 5 newspapers. **Services:** Interlibrary loan; copying; library open to the public with permission.

★17687★
WESTCHESTER COUNTY DEPARTMENT OF PARKS, RECREATION AND CONSERVATION - DELAWARE INDIAN RESOURCE CENTER (Area-Ethnic)
Ward Pound Ridge Reservation Phone: (914)763-3993
Cross River, NY 10518 Ed Kanze, Cur.
Founded: 1977. **Staff:** Prof 3. **Subjects:** Delaware culture, Native American herbalism, Algonkian tribes of the Eastern United States, Algonkian linguistics, Northeastern United States archeology, tribes of the greater New York area. **Special Collections:** Rare books on native cultures of Southern New York; taped oral history interviews with Delaware elders (50). **Holdings:** 1000 books; 500 bound periodical volumes; 10 file boxes of unbound material. **Services:** Copying; center open to the public by appointment for reference use only. **Staff:** Tim Barton, Asst.Cur..

★17688★
WESTCHESTER COUNTY HISTORICAL SOCIETY - LIBRARY (Hist)
75 Grasslands Rd. Phone: (914)592-4338
Valhalla, NY 10595 Elizabeth G. Fuller, Libn.
Founded: 1874. **Staff:** Prof 1. **Subjects:** Genealogy and history of Westchester County and New York State, history of New York City. **Special Collections:** French scrapbooks (43); Barron picture collection (New York City and the Revolutionary War; 225 volumes); Sanchi's Architecture of Westchester Picture Collection (8 VF drawers). **Holdings:** 5000 books; 350 bound periodical volumes; 8 VF drawers of manuscripts; 6 VF drawers of photographs; 12 VF drawers of clippings; 10 drawers of maps. **Subscriptions:** 27 journals and other serials. **Services:** Copying; library open to the public on fee basis.

★17689★
WESTCHESTER COUNTY MEDICAL CENTER - HEALTH SCIENCES LIBRARY (Med)
Eastview Hall Phone: (914)285-7033
Valhalla, NY 10595 Charlene Sikorski, Med.Libn.
Founded: 1925. **Staff:** Prof 1; Other 2. **Subjects:** Medicine, nursing, psychiatry, psychology, dentistry. **Holdings:** 12,000 volumes. **Subscriptions:** 180 journals and other serials. **Services:** Interlibrary loan; copying; library open to the public with permission of librarian. **Networks/Consortia:** Member of Health Information Libraries of Westchester (HILOW), BHSL, New York Metropolitan Reference and Research

Library Agency (METRO). **Publications:** Acquisitions List, quarterly; Orientation and Information Manual.

★17690★
WESTCHESTER ROCKLAND NEWSPAPERS - EDITORIAL LIBRARY (Publ)
One Gannett Dr. Phone: (914)694-5000
White Plains, NY 10604 Joan M. Reicherter, Libn.
Founded: 1987. **Subjects:** Newspaper reference topics. **Holdings:** Figures not available. **Services:** Interlibrary loan; library not open to the public. **Computerized Information Services:** DIALOG Information Services, NEXIS, VU/TEXT Information Services, DataTimes.

★17691★
WESTCOAST TRANSMISSION COMPANY LIMITED - LIBRARY (Energy)
1333 W. Georgia St., 14th Fl. Phone: (604)664-5517
Vancouver, BC, Canada V6E 3K9 Beatrice P. Yakimchuk, Libn.
Staff: Prof 2; Other 1. **Subjects:** Energy regulation and law. **Special Collections:** History of Westcoast Transmission Company (20 books; 2 drawers of clippings). **Holdings:** 8000 books; 1400 annual reports; 12 VF drawers; 4 VF drawers of clippings; 200 other cataloged items. **Subscriptions:** 200 journals and other serials; 20 newspapers. **Services:** Interlibrary loan; copying; library open to the public with restrictions. **Computerized Information Services:** DIALOG Information Services. **Staff:** Louise Barre, Asst.Libn..

★17692★
WESTERLY HOSPITAL - Z.T. TANG MEDICAL LIBRARY (Med)
Wells St. Phone: (401)596-6000
Westerly, RI 02891 Natalie V. Lawton, Libn.
Founded: 1956. **Staff:** Prof 1. **Subjects:** Medicine, surgery. **Holdings:** 838 books; 525 bound periodical volumes. **Subscriptions:** 52 journals and other serials. **Services:** Interlibrary loan; copying; library open to the public for reference use only by request. **Computerized Information Services:** MEDLINE, DOCLINE. **Networks/Consortia:** Member of Association of Rhode Island Health Sciences Librarians (ARIHSL).

★17693★
WESTERN CANADA AVIATION MUSEUM - LIBRARY (Sci-Engr)
Hangar T-2
958 Ferry Rd. Phone: (204)786-5503
Winnipeg, MB, Canada R3H 0Y8 K. Schmidt, Archv.
Founded: 1974. **Staff:** 2. **Subjects:** Aircraft, aviation. **Holdings:** 2554 books; 5 drawers of magnetic tapes, microfilm, records; aircraft technical manuals and catalogs; aviation magazines; R.C.A.F. histories; NASA reports; aviation textbooks. **Services:** Copying; library not open to the public.

★17694★
WESTERN CANADIAN UNIVERSITIES - MARINE BIOLOGICAL SOCIETY - DEVONIAN LIBRARY (Biol Sci)
Bamfield Marine Sta. Phone: (604)728-3301
Bamfield, BC, Canada V0R 1B0 Shirley Pakula, Libn.
Staff: 1. **Subjects:** Marine biology, ecology, plants, and mammals; biological oceanography; fisheries; aquaculture. **Special Collections:** K.D. Hobson Collection (reprints on polychaetes; 4 VF drawers); W.S. Hoar Collection (reprints on fish physiology). **Holdings:** 3000 books; 1061 bound periodical volumes; 1400 unbound journals; 2000 reports and bulletins; 40 VF drawers of reprints; 84 dissertations. **Subscriptions:** 38 journals and other serials. **Services:** Interlibrary loan; copying; library open to the public for reference use only.

★17695★
WESTERN CAROLINA UNIVERSITY - HUNTER LIBRARY - MAP ROOM (Geog-Map)
Cullowhee, NC 28723 Phone: (704)227-7316
Anita K. Oser, Hd.
Founded: 1980. **Staff:** Prof 1; Other 2. **Holdings:** 105 books; 85,020 maps; 393 atlases; 72 gazetteers; government documents. **Subscriptions:** 133 journals and other serials. **Services:** Interlibrary loan; copying; room open to the public. **Automated Operations:** Computerized cataloging.

★17696★
WESTERN CAROLINA UNIVERSITY - HUNTER LIBRARY - SPECIAL COLLECTIONS (Area-Ethnic, Biol Sci)
Cullowhee, NC 28723 Phone: (704)227-7474
Lewis Miller, Interim Hd., Spec.Coll. & Maps
Founded: 1953. **Subjects:** Western North Carolina, Cherokeee Indians. **Special Collections:** Appalachia (2000 volumes); spider behavior (200 volumes); Cherokee Documents in Foreign Archives Collection, 1632-1909 (manuscript sources from foreign archives relating specifically to the Cherokee and to southern Indians in general; 821 reels of microfilm). **Services:** Interlibrary loan; copying; collections open to the public. **Automated Operations:** Computerized cataloging and serials. **Computerized Information Services:** Online Manuscript Search Service (internal database). Performs searches free of charge. **Networks/Consortia:** Member of SOLINET.

★17697★
WESTERN CENTER ON LAW AND POVERTY, INC. - LIBRARY (Soc Sci)
3535 W. 6th St. Phone: (213)487-7211
Los Angeles, CA 90020 Richard A. Rothschild, Act.Libn.
Staff: Prof 1; Other 1. **Subjects:** Poverty, education, consumer protection, discrimination, employment, housing, health, welfare. **Holdings:** 5000 books; pamphlets; pleadings; reprints. **Subscriptions:** 60 journals and other serials. **Services:** Interlibrary loan; center open to the public with restrictions. **Computerized Information Services:** DIALOG Information Services, LEXIS; internal database.

★17698★
WESTERN CONNECTICUT STATE UNIVERSITY - RUTH A. HAAS LIBRARY - SPECIAL COLLECTIONS (Hist)
181 White St. Phone: (203)797-4052
Danbury, CT 06810-6885 Katherine J. Sholtz, Dir. of Lib.Serv.
Founded: 1903. **Staff:** Prof 11. **Special Collections:** Connecticut and Fairfield County history; Instructional Media Center; government documents (1700 linear feet); Young Business Collection. **Services:** Interlibrary loan; copying; collections open to the public for reference use only. **Automated Operations:** Computerized cataloging, acquisitions, and circulation. **Computerized Information Services:** OCLC, DIALOG Information Services, BRS Information Technologies. Performs searches on fee basis. **Networks/Consortia:** Member of NELINET. **Publications:** Library Handbook.

★17699★
WESTERN CONSERVATIVE BAPTIST SEMINARY - CLINE-TUNNELL LIBRARY (Rel-Phil)
5511 S.E. Hawthorne Blvd. Phone: (503)233-8561
Portland, OR 97215 Robert A. Krupp, Lib.Dir.
Founded: 1927. **Staff:** Prof 3; Other 4. **Subjects:** Religion, theology, psychology. **Special Collections:** Oregon Baptist history. **Holdings:** 70,400 books; 2330 bound periodical volumes; 4 VF drawers of pamphlets; 6450 AV programs. **Subscriptions:** 1250 journals and other serials; 10 newspapers. **Services:** Interlibrary loan; copying; library open to the public by registration and with limited loan privileges. **Automated Operations:** Computerized cataloging. **Computerized Information Services:** DIALOG Information Services, OCLC. **Publications:** Bibliography of Recent Acquisitions - to faculty and limited number of libraries. **Staff:** Karen Peterson, Cat.Libn.; Betty Lu Johnstone, Rd.Serv.Libn..

★17700★
WESTERN COSTUME COMPANY - RESEARCH LIBRARY (Hist)
5335 Melrose Ave. Phone: (213)469-1451
Los Angeles, CA 90038 Sally Nelson-Harb, Dir. of Res.
Staff: Prof 1; Other 1. **Subjects:** Clothing, military and civilian uniforms, insignia, medals and decorations, police uniforms, occupational clothing, sports clothing, ecclesiastical clothing, folk dress. **Special Collections:** Sears, Roebuck and Montgomery Ward clothing catalogs, 1895 to present (70). **Holdings:** 12,000 volumes; 107 VF drawers; 800 volumes of wardrobe photographs from 20th Century-Fox films, 1930-1975. **Subscriptions:** 60 journals and other serials. **Services:** Copying; library open to the public on a fee basis. **Special Indexes:** Index of clothing, especially uniforms, as worn by world police and military, occupational groups, the clergy, ethnic groups, and characters from literature, plays, movies, and television.

★17701★
WESTERN CURRICULUM COORDINATION CENTER (WCCC) - RESOURCE CENTER (Educ)
1776 University Ave., Wist 216 Phone: (808)948-6496
Honolulu, HI 96822 Gail M. Urago, Libn.
Staff: Prof 1; Other 4. **Subjects:** Vocational education and guidance. **Holdings:** 21,932 books; 4 VF drawers of pamphlets and clippings; 350 microfiche; 30 films; 125 filmstrips; 76 kits. **Services:** Interlibrary loan; center open to the public with restrictions. **Computerized Information Services:** Internal database. **Special Catalogs:** Special Groups (minorities and women); productivity; small engines; energy; computers and computer-assisted instruction; entrepreneurship. **Remarks:** Maintained by U.S. Department of Education. Center serves American Samoa, Arizona, California, Guam, Hawaii, Nevada, Northern Marianas, Trust Territory of the Pacific Isles.

★17702★
WESTERN EVANGELICAL SEMINARY - GEORGE HALLAUER MEMORIAL LIBRARY (Rel-Phil)
4200 S.E. Jennings Ave. Phone: (503)654-5182
Milwaukie, OR 97267 Gary Metzenbacher, Dir. of Lib.
Founded: 1947. **Staff:** Prof 2; Other 3. **Subjects:** Religion, theology, philosophy, ethics, marriage, family. **Holdings:** 52,000 books; 4000 bound periodical volumes; 19 filmstrips; 498 cassette tapes; 203 magnetic tapes; 73 reels of microfilm; 19 phonograph records; 150 maps; 308 multimedia kits; 11 videotapes; 82 volumes on microfiche. **Subscriptions:** 446 journals and other serials; 8 newspapers. **Services:** Interlibrary loan; copying; library open to the public. **Automated Operations:** computerized cataloging. **Computerized Information Services:** DIALOG Information Services, OCLC. Performs searches on fee basis. **Networks/Consortia:** Member of Cooperative Library Network of Clackamas County. **Publications:** Selected List of Books Processed, quarterly; Bulletin of the George Hallauer Memorial Library, quarterly - both for internal distribution only; Reference Tools for Theological Students, irregular. **Staff:** Patricia Kuehne, Asst.Dir.; Dennis Pinheiro, Cat.; Theresa Williams, Per..

★17703★
WESTERN FAIRS ASSOCIATION - LIBRARY (Bus-Fin)
1329 Howe Ave., Suite 202 Phone: (916)927-3100
Sacramento, CA 95825 Stephen J. Chambers, Exec.Dir.
Founded: 1945. **Staff:** 1. **Subjects:** Fair management, fair financing, horse racing, breeding, allied fair and agricultural subjects. **Special Collections:** Lou Merrill Oral History (growth of fairs in California; oral history interviews). **Holdings:** Figures not available. **Services:** Archives open to the public with restrictions.

WESTERN FEDERATION OF MINERS ARCHIVES
See: University of Colorado, Boulder - Western Historical Collection & University Archives (16084)

★17704★
WESTERN GAS MARKETING LTD. - LIBRARY (Sci-Engr, Energy)
530 8th Ave., S.W.
P.O. Box 500, Sta. M Phone: (403)269-5792
Calgary, AB, Canada T2P 3V6 Elizabeth A. Varsek, Supv., Lib.Serv.
Staff: Prof 1; Other 1. **Subjects:** Geology, petroleum and natural gas technology. **Holdings:** 1000 books; 60 bound periodical volumes; 200 other cataloged items. **Subscriptions:** 118 journals and other serials. **Services:** Interlibrary loan; library open to the public with librarian's permission. **Automated Operations:** Computerized cataloging. **Computerized Information Services:** DIALOG Information Services, Info Globe, Pergamon ORBIT InfoLine, Inc.; Envoy 100 (electronic mail service).

★17705★
WESTERN GEOPHYSICAL COMPANY OF AMERICA - R & D LIBRARY (Sci-Engr)
Box 2469
Houston, TX 77252 Phone: (713)974-3194
Founded: 1968. **Staff:** 1. **Subjects:** Geophysics, mathematics, geology, computer science, physics, engineering. **Holdings:** 4700 books; 800 bound periodical volumes; technical reports; maps; government documents. **Subscriptions:** 103 journals and other serials. **Services:** Interlibrary loan; library not open to the public. **Computerized Information Services:** NERAC, Inc., DIALOG Information Services. Performs searches on fee basis. **Publications:** New books list, quarterly. **Remarks:** Library located at 3600 Briarpark Dr., Houston, TX 77042.

★17706★
WESTERN HENNEPIN COUNTY PIONEERS ASSOCIATION, INC. - LIBRARY (Hist)
1953 W. Wayzata Blvd.
Box 332 Phone: (612)473-6557
Long Lake, MN 55356 Roger Avery Stubbs, Dir.
Founded: 1907. **Staff:** Prof 1; Other 10. **Subjects:** Local and family history. **Holdings:** 200 books; 25 bound periodical volumes; 1000 family histories; 15 municipal histories; vital records; church and business histories; maps. **Subscriptions:** 15 journals and other serials. **Services:** Library open to the public on a fee basis. **Publications:** Newsletter, quarterly - to the public.

WESTERN HERITAGE CENTER
See: National Cowboy Hall of Fame & Western Heritage Center (9649)

★17707★
WESTERN HIGHWAY INSTITUTE - RESEARCH LIBRARY (Trans)
1200 Bayhill Dr., Suite 112 Phone: (415)952-4900
San Bruno, CA 94066 Mae Frances Moore, Libn.
Founded: 1970. **Staff:** Prof 1. **Subjects:** Transportation, highways and bridges, engineering, motor vehicles, trucking. **Holdings:** 4000 volumes. **Subscriptions:** 20 journals and other serials. **Services:** Interlibrary loan; copying; library open to the public with restrictions.

★17708★
WESTERN HISTORICAL MANUSCRIPT COLLECTION/STATE HISTORICAL SOCIETY OF MISSOURI MANUSCRIPTS JOINT COLLECTION (Hist)
University of Missouri
23 Ellis Library Phone: (314)882-6028
Columbia, MO 65201 Nancy Lankford, Assoc.Dir.
Founded: 1943. **Staff:** Prof 12; Other 4. **Subjects:** History - Missouri, political, economic, agricultural, urban, labor, black, women's, frontier, religious, literary, social, science, steamboating, social reform and welfare, business. **Holdings:** 11,000 linear feet of manuscripts; 7300 reels of microfilm; 1975 audiotapes; 675 phonograph records; 150 video materials. **Services:** Interlibrary loan; copying; collection open to the public. **Publications:** Guide to the Western Historical Manuscripts Collection, 1952; supplement, 1956; finding aids (index, shelf list, and chronological file). **Remarks:** Collection contains the manuscript holdings of both the University of Missouri and the State Historical Society of Missouri. Offices are located at the four branches of the University of Missouri. Materials may be loaned among the four branches. **Staff:** Lynn Wolf Gentzler, Asst.Dir.; Laura Bullion, Sr.Mss.Spec.; Cynthia Stewart, Sr.Mss.Spec.; Kathleen Conway, Mss.Spec.; Elizabeth M. Uhlig, Mss.Spec.; Paula McNeill, Mss.Spec.; Sharon L. Fleming, Mss.Spec.; Randy Roberts, Sr.Mss.Spec.; Claudia Lane Powell, Doc.Cons.Spec.; Nancy Sandleback, Mss.Spec..

★17709★
WESTERN HISTORICAL MANUSCRIPT COLLECTION/STATE HISTORICAL SOCIETY OF MISSOURI MANUSCRIPTS JOINT COLLECTION (Hist)
302 Newcomb Hall
University of Missouri
5100 Rockhill Rd. Phone: (816)276-1543
Kansas City, MO 64110 David L. Boutros, Act.Assoc.Dir.
Staff: Prof 2; Other 2. **Subjects:** Kansas City history and architectural records, civic and political leadership, history of citizen action groups. **Holdings:** 3000 cubic feet of manuscripts. **Services:** Copying; collection open to the public with restrictions. **Remarks:** Collection contains the manuscript holdings of both the University of Missouri and the State Historical Society of Missouri. Offices are located at the four branches of the University of Missouri. Materials may be loaned among the four branches.

★17710★
WESTERN HISTORICAL MANUSCRIPT COLLECTION/STATE HISTORICAL SOCIETY OF MISSOURI MANUSCRIPTS JOINT COLLECTION (Hist)
Library, Rm. G-3
University of Missouri Phone: (314)341-4874
Rolla, MO 65401-0249 Mark C. Stauter, Assoc.Dir.
Staff: Prof 2. **Subjects:** History - Missouri, the Ozarks, mining and technology. **Special Collections:** Historical records of St. Joe Minerals Corporation (46 volumes); historical records of American Zinc Company (151 boxes). **Holdings:** 300 historical manuscript collections. **Services:** Interlibrary loan; copying; collection open to the public. **Remarks:** Collection contains the manuscript holdings of both the University of

Missouri and the State Historical Society of Missouri. Offices are located at the four branches of the University of Missouri. Materials may be loaned among the four branches. **Staff:** John F. Bradbury, Jr., Mss.Spec..

★17711★
WESTERN HISTORICAL MANUSCRIPT COLLECTION/STATE HISTORICAL SOCIETY OF MISSOURI MANUSCRIPTS JOINT COLLECTION (Hist, Soc Sci)
Thomas Jefferson Library
University of Missouri
8001 Natural Bridge Rd. Phone: (314)553-5143
St. Louis, MO 63121 Patricia L. Adams, Assoc.Dir.
Founded: 1968. **Staff:** Prof 2; Other 2. **Subjects:** History - state and local, women's, Afro-American, ethnic, education, immigration; socialism; 19th century science; environment; peace; religion; Missouri politics; social reform and welfare; photography; journalism; business; labor. **Special Collections:** Socialist Party of Missouri records; Oral History Program (800 tapes); Photograph Collection (55,000 images); League of Women Voters of Missouri (59 boxes); Papers of Irving Dilliard, Dr. Thomas A. Dooley, Margaret Hickey, Ernest and Deverne Calloway, Theodore Lentz, Alberta Slavin, Rep. William Hungate, Rep. Robert Young, Rep. James Symington, Lt. Governor Harriet Woods, Paul Preisler, Joseph Pulitzer (copy), Virginia Irwin, and Kay Drey; Coalition for the Environment; Committee for Environmental Information; KETC-TV; Metropolitan Church Federation; Sierra Club - Ozark Chapter; Nuclear Weapons Freeze Campaign; Health and Welfare Council; Bureau for Men; Dismas House; St. Louis Labor Council; Family and Children's Service of Greater St. Louis; Regional Commerce and Growth Association; Missouri Public Interest Research Group; Ethical Society of St. Louis; YMCA and YWCA of St. Louis. **Holdings:** 4500 linear feet of manuscripts, photographs, oral history tapes, and university archives. **Services:** Interlibrary loan (limited); copying of manuscripts, tape recordings, and photographs; library open to the public with restricted circulation. **Special Indexes:** Unpublished inventories to collections in repository. **Remarks:** Collection contains the manuscript holdings of both the University of Missouri and the State Historical Society of Missouri. Offices are located at the four branches of the University of Missouri. Materials may be loaned among the four branches. **Staff:** Kenn Thomas, Sr.Mss.Spec..

★17712★
WESTERN ILLINOIS UNIVERSITY - GEOGRAPHY & MAP LIBRARY (Geog-Map)
Macomb, IL 61455 Phone: (309)298-1171
John V. Bergen, Map Libn.
Founded: 1968. **Staff:** Prof 1; Other 1. **Subjects:** Maps of Illinois, U.S. topographic maps, thematic maps, geography, area and regional studies. **Special Collections:** Federal and state depositories; U.S. Geological Survey (67,000 maps); Defense Mapping Agency (36,000 maps); Illinois (12,000 maps; 12,000 air photographs, atlases, plat books). **Holdings:** 3300 books; 1000 periodical volumes; 3000 atlases; 170,000 maps; 13,000 air photos; 1000 pamphlets; 120 theses; 120 map information catalogs. **Subscriptions:** 80 journals and other serials. **Services:** Interlibrary loan (limited); copying; library open to the public.

★17713★
WESTERN ILLINOIS UNIVERSITY - MUSIC LIBRARY (Mus)
204 Browne Hall Phone: (309)298-1105
Macomb, IL 61455 Allie Wise Goudy, Mus.Libn.
Staff: Prof 1; Other 1. **Subjects:** Classical music. **Holdings:** 7000 books; 5000 bound periodical volumes; 5500 volumes of scores; 4700 phonograph records. **Subscriptions:** 100 journals and other serials. **Services:** Copying; library open to the public. **Publications:** Guides to the collection; bibliographies.

★17714★
WESTERN ILLINOIS UNIVERSITY - PHYSICAL SCIENCES LIBRARY (Sci-Engr)
Currens Hall Phone: (309)298-1407
Macomb, IL 61455 Kenneth Smejkal, Libn.
Founded: 1976. **Staff:** Prof 1; Other 1. **Subjects:** Physics, chemistry. **Holdings:** 20,600 books; 15,500 bound periodical volumes. **Subscriptions:** 465 journals and other serials. **Services:** Interlibrary loan; copying; library open to the public. **Computerized Information Services:** DIALOG Information Services, OCLC.

★17715★
WESTERN ILLINOIS UNIVERSITY - WESTERN ILLINOIS REGIONAL STUDIES COLLECTIONS (Hist)
Macomb, IL 61455 Phone: (309)298-2718
Dr. John E. Hallwas, Dir.
Founded: 1970. **Staff:** Prof 2; Other 2. **Subjects:** Western Illinois history and literature. **Special Collections:** Papers of Tom Railsback, Elton Fawks, Burl Ives, Phillip D. Jordan; Illinois Regional Archives Depository Collection (public records for the region); Icarian Collection; Regional Authors Collection. **Holdings:** 12,000 books; 6000 photographs; 10,000 VF items; 750 linear feet of records. **Services:** Copying; SDI; center open to the public. **Computerized Information Services:** OCLC. **Publications:** Western Illinois Regional Studies; Western Illinois Monograph Series.

★17716★
WESTERN INTERSTATE COMMISSION FOR HIGHER EDUCATION - LIBRARY (Educ)
Drawer P Phone: (303)497-0285
Boulder, CO 80301 Eileen Conway, Cons.Dir.
Founded: 1955. **Staff:** Prof 1; Other 1. **Subjects:** Higher education, mental health and human services, nursing, minority education. **Holdings:** 7000 books and documents; 1000 volumes of unbound periodicals; 2000 documents on microfiche. **Subscriptions:** 280 journals and other serials; 10 newspapers. **Services:** Interlibrary loan; copying; SDI; library open to the public. **Automated Operations:** Computerized serials and circulation. **Computerized Information Services:** DIALOG Information Services; Telemail (electronic mail service). Performs searches on fee basis. **Publications:** Acquisitions List, monthly - for internal distribution only.

WESTERN JEWISH HISTORY CENTER
See: Judah L. Magnes Memorial Museum (8308)

★17717★
WESTERN KENTUCKY UNIVERSITY - DEPARTMENT OF SPECIAL COLLECTIONS - FOLKLIFE ARCHIVES (Soc Sci)
Kentucky Bldg. Phone: (502)745-6086
Bowling Green, KY 42101 Patricia M. Hodges, Mss. & Archv.Supv.
Staff: Prof 1. **Subjects:** Folklore, folk songs and music, social folk customs, traditional arts, regional oral history. **Holdings:** 3650 cassettes and tapes; 2100 manuscripts; collections of folk songs, beliefs, speech, correspondence. **Services:** Copying (limited); archives open to the public. **Staff:** Sue Lynn Stone, Mss.Libn..

★17718★
WESTERN KENTUCKY UNIVERSITY - DEPARTMENT OF SPECIAL COLLECTIONS - KENTUCKY LIBRARY AND MUSEUM/UNIVERSITY ARCHIVES (Hist)
Bowling Green, KY 42101 Riley Handy, Hd., Spec.Coll.Dept.
Founded: 1931. **Staff:** Prof 6; Other 10. **Subjects:** Rare Kentuckiana, Mammoth Cave, Kentucky writers, Civil War, Shakers, Ohio Valley. **Special Collections:** Journals and writers of South Union Shaker Colony; Alice Hegan and Cale Young Rice Collection; McGregor Collection; Janice Holt Giles Collection; Tim Lee Carter Collection. **Holdings:** 35,000 books; 2000 bound periodical volumes; 60 VF drawers; 10,000 photographs; 375 land grants; 2000 postcards; 435 prints; Kentucky census, 1810-1910, on microfilm; 350 titles of Kentucky sheet music; scrapbooks; broadsides; maps. **Services:** Copying (limited); library open to the public for research and reference. **Publications:** Occasional house organs. **Special Indexes:** Current Kentucky periodicals index. **Staff:** Constance A. Mills, Ref.Libn.; Virginia Pearson, Ref.Libn.; Elaine Harrison, Mss.Libn.; Helen Knight, Univ.Archv.; Nancy Baird, Ref.Libn.; Nancy Solley, Ref.Libn..

★17719★
WESTERN LIFE INSURANCE COMPANY - LIBRARY (Bus-Fin)
Box 64271 Phone: (612)738-4589
St. Paul, MN 55164 Gayle Jansen, Libn.
Founded: 1978. **Staff:** 1. **Subjects:** Insurance, management. **Holdings:** 300 books; annual statements. **Subscriptions:** 120 journals and other serials; 8 newspapers. **Services:** Library not open to the public.

★17720★
WESTERN MARYLAND COLLEGE - ARCHIVES (Hist)
Hoover Library Phone: (301)848-7000
Westminster, MD 21157-4390 Alice G. Chambers, Archv.
Subjects: History of Western Maryland College, 1867 to present. **Holdings:** Photographs; noncurrent working papers; student records on microfilm; college journals and publications. **Services:** Archives open to the public by appointment.

★17721★
WESTERN MARYLAND PUBLIC LIBRARIES - REGIONAL LIBRARY (Bus-Fin, Educ)
100 S. Potomac St. Phone: (301)739-3250
Hagerstown, MD 21740 Mary S. Mallery, Reg.Libn.
Staff: Prof 3; Other 5. **Subjects:** Small business; auto, truck, and motorcycle repair; antiques and collectibles; Civil Service and vocational tests; small scale farming. **Holdings:** 46,000 books; 300 reels of microfilm; 1452 16mm films; 1000 automobile, truck, and motorcycle repair manuals; 887 video cassettes. **Services:** Interlibrary loan; copying; library open to the public with restrictions. **Automated Operations:** Online 16mm film booking system. **Computerized Information Services:** DIALOG Information Services, WILSONLINE. Performs searches free of charge. Contact Person: Darlene Koenig, Ref.Libn.. **Networks/Consortia:** Member of Maryland Interlibrary Organization (MILO), Maryland Interlibrary Loan Network (MILNET). **Special Catalogs:** Catalogs of 16mm films, video cassettes, and literacy books. **Remarks:** Library is maintained by the Washington County Free Library. **Staff:** Darlene Koenig, Ref.Libn.; Ralph E. DeVore, Pub.Rel.Dir.; Lawrence Springer, AV Libn..

★17722★
WESTERN MEDICAL CENTER - MEDICAL LIBRARY (Med)
1001 N. Tustin Ave. Phone: (714)835-3555
Santa Ana, CA 92705 Evelyn Simpson, Dir.
Staff: Prof 1; Other 2. **Subjects:** Medicine, nursing, surgery. **Holdings:** 4800 books; 5000 bound periodical volumes; 2300 Audio-Digest tapes (9 specialties); video cassettes. **Subscriptions:** 260 journals and other serials. **Services:** Interlibrary loan; copying; SDI; library open to the public with restrictions. **Computerized Information Services:** Online systems.

★17723★
WESTERN MEMORIAL REGIONAL HOSPITAL - HEALTH SCIENCE LIBRARY (Med)
West Valley Rd.
Box 2005 Phone: (709)637-5395
Corner Brook, NF, Canada A2H 6J7 Patricia Tilley, Libn.
Founded: 1968. **Staff:** Prof 1; Other 1. **Subjects:** Medicine, nursing, paramedical fields. **Holdings:** 2500 books; 1150 bound periodical volumes. **Subscriptions:** 167 journals and other serials. **Services:** Interlibrary loan; copying; library open to the public.

★17724★
WESTERN MICHIGAN UNIVERSITY - ARCHIVES AND REGIONAL HISTORY COLLECTIONS (Hist)
Kalamazoo, MI 49008 Phone: (616)383-1826
Wayne C. Mann, Dir.
Founded: 1957. **Staff:** Prof 2; Other 5. **Subjects:** History of Western Michigan University, local and regional history, genealogy. **Holdings:** 7000 books; 15,000 linear feet of manuscripts, photographs, and other archival materials. **Subscriptions:** 20 journals and other serials. **Services:** Copying; collection open to the public. **Special Indexes:** Comprehensive index to historic photographs. **Staff:** William K. Smith, Assoc.Dir.; Phyllis Burnham, Mss.Cat.; Barbara Taflinger, Archv.Cur..

★17725★
WESTERN MICHIGAN UNIVERSITY - BUSINESS LIBRARY (Bus-Fin)
Kalamazoo, MI 49008 Phone: (616)383-1926
David H. McKee, Hd.Libn.
Founded: 1958. **Staff:** Prof 4; Other 3. **Subjects:** Management, marketing, finance, accounting, business information systems, commercial law. **Holdings:** 38,645 books; 17,373 bound periodical volumes; 400 theses on microfilm; 25,000 corporate annual reports; 24 linear feet of business material; 300 linear feet of government documents. **Services:** Interlibrary loan; copying; library open to the public. **Automated Operations:** Computerized public access catalog and circulation. **Computerized Information Services:** DIALOG Information Services, BRS Information Technologies, Pergamon ORBIT InfoLine, Inc.; OLLI, CLSI (internal databases). Performs searches on fee basis. **Networks/Consortia:** Member of Michigan Library Consortium (MLC), Southwest Michigan Library Cooperative (SMLC), Center for Research Libraries (CRL) Consortia. **Publications:** Guide to Business Library Materials series; New Acquisitions List; Business Library Matters (newsletter). **Staff:** Donna Ring, Bus.Libn.; Mary Ellen Hegedus, Bus.Libn.; Hardy Carroll, Bus.Libn..

★17726★
WESTERN MICHIGAN UNIVERSITY - CENTER FOR WOMEN'S SERVICES - LIBRARY (Soc Sci)
331 Ellsworth Hall Phone: (616)383-6097
Kalamazoo, MI 49008 Darlene Mosher, Exec.Dir.
Staff: 1. **Subjects:** Women - health, financial status, careers, discrimination; displaced homemakers; nontraditional students and jobs; reentry women; equal pay for equal work. **Special Collections:** Local history of women's groups and causes; sex bias in textbooks in local public schools. **Holdings:** 1000 books; 9 VF drawers of clippings. **Subscriptions:** 20 journals and other serials. **Services:** Copying; library open to community members.

★17727★
WESTERN MICHIGAN UNIVERSITY - DOCUMENTS LIBRARY (Info Sci)
Waldo Library Phone: (616)383-1435
Kalamazoo, MI 49008 Michael McDonnell, Ref.Libn., Maps & Docs.
Founded: 1963. **Staff:** Prof 1; Other 2. **Subjects:** U.S. Government publications, 1963 to present; United Nations documents, 1946-1981; Michigan documents; U.S. Dept. of Energy documents (microfiche). **Special Collections:** 19th Century Serial Set (microcard). **Holdings:** 451,010 documents. **Services:** Interlibrary loan; copying; library open to the public. **Computerized Information Services:** DIALOG Information Services, OCLC, BRS Information Technologies; OLLI (internal database). Performs searches on fee basis. **Networks/Consortia:** Member of Southwest Michigan Library Cooperative (SMLC), Michigan Library Consortium (MLC), Center for Research Libraries (CRL) Consortia.

★17728★
WESTERN MICHIGAN UNIVERSITY - EDUCATION LIBRARY (Educ)
3300 Sangren Hall Phone: (616)383-1666
Kalamazoo, MI 49008 David J. Netz, Hd.Libn.
Founded: 1964. **Staff:** Prof 3; Other 4. **Subjects:** Educational research; education - higher, secondary, elementary; educational psychology; educational tests and measurement; educational law; comparative education. **Special Collections:** ERIC documents (215,000 titles; 270,000 microfiche); Curriculum Development Library (12,000 microfiche); children's and young people's books (2745); textbooks (13,270 elementary and secondary). **Holdings:** 51,458 books; 8065 bound periodical volumes; 6000 pamphlets; 2500 books on microfilm; 500 producers' catalogs. **Subscriptions:** 600 journals and other serials. **Services:** Interlibrary loan; copying; library open to the public with restrictions on circulation. **Automated Operations:** Computerized public access catalog and circulation. **Computerized Information Services:** DIALOG Information Services, BRS Information Technologies, Pergamon ORBIT InfoLine, Inc.; OLLI (internal database). **Networks/Consortia:** Member of Southwest Michigan Library Cooperative (SMLC), Michigan Library Consortium (MLC), Center for Research Libraries (CRL) Consortia. **Publications:** News, Views and Reviews; bibliographies and study guides; Education Library Link - all to College of Education Faculty. **Staff:** Maria Perez-Stable, Libn.; Patricia VanderMeer, Libn..

★17729★
WESTERN MICHIGAN UNIVERSITY - HARPER C. MAYBEE MUSIC & DANCE LIBRARY (Mus, Theater)
3008 Dalton Center Phone: (616)383-1817
Kalamazoo, MI 49008 Gregory Fitzgerald, Hd.Libn.
Founded: 1949. **Staff:** Prof 1; Other 1. **Subjects:** Music, dance. **Special Collections:** American vocal sheet music collection (1500 titles); WMU School of Music performance archives (1050 tapes); International Trumpet Guild Archives (300 items). **Holdings:** 12,255 books; 3600 bound periodical volumes; 12,800 scores; 10,500 phonograph records and tapes; 158 reels of microfilm; 79 microfiche; 1250 other cataloged items. **Subscriptions:** 110 journals and other serials. **Services:** Interlibrary loan; copying; library open to the public with restrictions on borrowing. **Automated Operations:** Computerized public access catalog and circulation. **Networks/Consortia:** Member of Southwest Michigan Library Cooperative (SMLC), Michigan Library Consortium (MLC), Center for Research Libraries (CRL) Consortia. **Publications:** Guides to collection and catalogs; Recent Acquisitions, 3/year; newsletter, semiannual - to faculty and staff. **Special Indexes:** Index to song collections; index to jazz recordings; index to International Trumpet Guild Archives recordings (online).

★17730★
WESTERN MICHIGAN UNIVERSITY - INSTITUTE OF CISTERCIAN STUDIES LIBRARY (Rel-Phil)
Hillside West Phone: (616)383-1969
Kalamazoo, MI 49008 Beatrice H. Beech, Hd.
Founded: 1973. **Staff:** Prof 1; Other 1. **Subjects:** Cisterciansia, history, monasticism. **Special Collections:** Editions of Bernard of Clairvaux (400 volumes); the rule of St. Benedict; medieval manuscripts; incunabula; early 16th-18th century books. **Holdings:** 7816 books; 471 bound periodical volumes; 96 manuscripts. **Services:** Interlibrary loan; copying; library open to the public. **Networks/Consortia:** Member of Southwest Michigan Library Cooperative (SMLC), Michigan Library Consortium (MLC), Center for Research Libraries (CRL) Consortia.

★17731★
WESTERN MICHIGAN UNIVERSITY - INSTITUTE OF PUBLIC AFFAIRS - ENVIRONMENTAL RESOURCE CENTER FOR COMMUNITY INFORMATION (Env-Cons, Plan)
Kalamazoo, MI 49008 Phone: (616)383-3983
Rudy Ziehl, Dir.
Staff: 1. **Subjects:** Environment, public policy, community planning. **Holdings:** 3000 titles; 8 VF drawers of cataloged items. **Services:** Copying; center open to the public for reference use only.

★17732★
WESTERN MICHIGAN UNIVERSITY - MAP LIBRARY (Geog-Map)
Waldo Library Phone: (616)383-1435
Kalamazoo, MI 49008 Michael McDonnell, Ref.Libn., Maps & Docs.
Founded: 1968. **Staff:** Prof 1; Other 2. **Subjects:** Domestic and foreign maps, antique maps of special historical interest, U.S. Geological Survey, U.S. Defense Mapping Agency, National Ocean Survey, U.S. Forest Service, Soil Conservation Service, national parks, city maps, topographic maps, aeronautical and nautical charts. **Special Collections:** Climatological data; historical maps and atlases; soil surveys; gazetteers. **Holdings:** 325 books; 65 bound periodical volumes; 1600 atlases; 177,839 maps. **Services:** Copying; library open to the public. **Computerized Information Services:** OCLC, DIALOG Information Services, BRS Information Technologies; OLLI (internal database). Performs searches on fee basis. **Networks/Consortia:** Member of Southwest Michigan Library Cooperative (SMLC), Michigan Library Consortium (MLC), Center for Research Libraries (CRL) Consortia.

★17733★
WESTERN MICHIGAN UNIVERSITY - PHYSICAL SCIENCES LIBRARY (Sci-Engr)
3376 Rood Hall Phone: (616)383-4943
Kalamazoo, MI 49008 Beatrice Sichel, Hd.Libn.
Founded: 1971. **Staff:** Prof 1; Other 1. **Subjects:** Mathematics, physics, geology, computer science, astronomy. **Holdings:** 42,458 books; 22,136 bound periodical volumes; 2485 geological maps; 143 reels of microfilm; 2181 microfiche. **Subscriptions:** 551 journals and other serials. **Services:** Interlibrary loan; copying; library open to the public. **Automated Operations:** Computerized public access catalog and circulation. **Computerized Information Services:** DIALOG Information Services, MATHFILE; OLLI (internal database). Performs searches on fee basis. **Networks/Consortia:** Member of Southwest Michigan Library Cooperative (SMLC), Michigan Library Consortium (MLC), Center for Research Libraries (CRL) Consortia.

★17734★
WESTERN MISSOURI MENTAL HEALTH CENTER - LIBRARY (Med)
600 E. 22nd St. Phone: (816)471-3000
Kansas City, MO 64108 Tyron Emerick, Med.Libn.
Founded: 1954. **Staff:** Prof 1. **Subjects:** Psychiatry, psychology, social science, psychological testing, psychoanalysis, drugs and alcohol. **Special Collections:** Works of Sigmund Freud. **Holdings:** 3400 books; 110 unbound periodical titles; 410 cassette tapes. **Subscriptions:** 90 journals and other serials. **Services:** Interlibrary loan; copying; library open to the public with permission. **Networks/Consortia:** Member of Kansas City Library Network, Inc. (KCLN), Kansas City Metropolitan Library Network (KCMLN).

★17735★
WESTERN MONTANA CLINIC - LIBRARY (Med)
515 W. Front St.
Box 7609 Phone: (406)721-5600
Missoula, MT 59807 Patricia A. Manlove, Libn.
Staff: Prof 1. **Subjects:** Medicine. **Holdings:** 500 books; 165 bound periodical volumes. **Subscriptions:** 165 journals and other serials. **Services:** Interlibrary loan; copying; library open to the public with restrictions. **Computerized Information Services:** MEDLARS; OnTyme Electronic Message Network Service (electronic mail service). **Networks/Consortia:** Member of Pacific Northwest Regional Health Sciences Library Service.

★17736★
WESTERN MUSEUM OF MINING & INDUSTRY - LIBRARY (Sci-Engr)
1025 North Gate Rd. Phone: (719)598-8850
Colorado Springs, CO 80921 Linda Le Mieux, Dir.
Subjects: Mining, metallurgy, electrical and mechanical engineering. **Holdings:** 7000 books; 400 bound periodical volumes; 45 other items; early engineering periodicals on microfilm. **Services:** Copying; library open to members and scholars. **Publications:** Newsletter; Annual Report; brochure.

★17737★
WESTERN NEW ENGLAND COLLEGE - SCHOOL OF LAW LIBRARY (Law)
1215 Wilbraham Rd. Phone: (413)782-1457
Springfield, MA 01119-2693 Donald J. Dunn, Law Libn.
Founded: 1973. **Staff:** Prof 6; Other 7. **Subjects:** Law. **Holdings:** 150,000 volumes; 80,000 volumes in microform. **Subscriptions:** 2777 journals and other serials; 10 newspapers. **Services:** Interlibrary loan; copying; library open to the public. **Automated Operations:** Computerized cataloging. **Computerized Information Services:** LEXIS, NEXIS, WESTLAW. **Networks/Consortia:** Member of Cooperating Libraries of Greater Springfield, A CCGS Agency (CLGS), New England Law Library Consortium (NELLCO). **Publications:** Selected List of New Acquisitions; Contents Pages of Legal Periodicals; Slipped Opinions, quarterly - all for internal distribution only; Reader's Guide; Self-Guided Tour, both annual. **Staff:** Bonnie Koneski-White, Assoc. Law Libn.; Susan C. Wells, Hd., Tech.Serv.; Howard E. Polonsky, Hd., Rd.Serv.; Michele Dill LaRose, Ref.Libn.; Christine Archambault, Cat.Libn..

WESTERN NEW YORK FORUM FOR AMERICAN ART
See: SUNY - College at Buffalo - Burchfield Art Center - Research Library (13763)

★17738★
WESTERN NEW YORK GENEALOGICAL SOCIETY, INC. - LIBRARY (Hist)
Box 338
Hamburg, NY 14075
Subjects: Genealogy and local history. **Special Collections:** McCabe Collection. **Holdings:** 350 books; 1500 unbound periodicals; 650 pamphlets, paperbacks, manuscripts, articles; genealogical society publications; 200 reels of microfilm. **Services:** Copying; library open to the public. **Remarks:** Library located in the Hamburg Historical Museum, 5859 S. Park Ave., Hamburg, NY 14075.

★17739★
WESTERN ONTARIO BREEDERS, INC. - LIBRARY (Agri)
Hwy. 59 N.
P.O. Box 457 Phone: (519)539-9831
Woodstock, ON, Canada N4S 7Y7 Howard D. Start, Dir.
Founded: 1946. **Subjects:** Livestock breeding, veterinary science. **Holdings:** 425 books and bound periodical volumes; breed journals; sire directories; sales catalogs. **Subscriptions:** 35 journals and other serials; 6 newspapers. **Services:** Library not open to the public.

★17740★
WESTERN OREGON STATE COLLEGE - LIBRARY - SPECIAL COLLECTIONS (Hist)
234 Monmouth Ave. Phone: (503)838-1220
Monmouth, OR 97361 Dr. Gary D. Jensen, Dir.
Founded: 1856. **Holdings:** John C. Higgins Memorial Collection of Pacific Northwest History and Culture. **Services:** Interlibrary loan; copying; collections open to the public for reference use only.

★17741★
WESTERN ORGANIZATION OF RESOURCE COUNCILS - LIBRARY (Env-Cons)
412 Stapleton Bldg. Phone: (406)252-9672
Billings, MT 59101 John Smillie
Founded: 1979. **Staff:** 1. **Subjects:** Natural resources, environment, energy. **Holdings:** Figures not available.

WESTERN PENNSYLVANIA BOTANICAL SOCIETY LIBRARY
See: Carnegie Museum of Natural History - Library (2688)

★17742★
WESTERN PENNSYLVANIA GENEALOGICAL SOCIETY - LIBRARY (Hist)
4338 Bigelow Blvd. Phone: (412)681-5533
Pittsburgh, PA 15213-2695 Helen M. Wilson, Libn.
Staff: Prof 2. **Subjects:** Genealogy, local history. **Holdings:** 1124 volumes; 170 archival items; 8 VF drawers of local obituaries; 35 feet of newsletters; 2000 pages of obituaries for persons born in Pennsylvania but living elsewhere. **Services:** Interlibrary loan; copying; library open to the public on fee basis. **Publications:** Quarterly; Jots From The Point; list of additional publications - available upon request. **Special Indexes:** Index to Members' Lineage Charts. **Remarks:** Collection is housed at the Historical Society of Western Pennsylvania. **Staff:** Donald L. Haggerty, Dir., Archv.-Lib..

★17743★
WESTERN PENTECOSTAL BIBLE COLLEGE - LIBRARY (Rel-Phil)
Box 1000 Phone: (604)222-2574
Clayburn, BC, Canada V0X 1E0 Rev. Laurence M. Van Kleek, Libn.
Founded: 1941. **Staff:** Prof 1; Other 3. **Subjects:** Humanities, social sciences, Bible, doctrinal and practical theology, world religions and cults, missions. **Special Collections:** Archive for Pentecostal Studies, includes Action, 1970 to present; Pentecostal Testimony, 1920 to present. **Holdings:** 26,412 books; 340 bound periodical volumes; 23 filmstrips; 445 audio recordings; 900 microforms; 700 pamphlets; 50 clippings; 175 yearbooks. **Subscriptions:** 250 journals and other serials. **Services:** Copying; library open to the public. **Computerized Information Services:** Internal database. **Publications:** WPBC Library Bulletin, irregular - to faculty, staff, and administration. **Special Indexes:** Indexes to denominational periodicals (mimeographed). **Remarks:** Library is located at 35235 Straiton Rd., Clayburn, BC V0X 1E0.

WESTERN POWER CORPORATION LIBRARY
See: Bechtel Power Corporation - Library (1449)

WESTERN PSYCHIATRIC INSTITUTE AND CLINIC
See: University of Pittsburgh (16784)

★17744★
WESTERN RAILROAD ASSOCIATION - LIBRARY (Trans)
222 S. Riverside Plaza, Suite 1200 Phone: (312)648-7800
Chicago, IL 60606 James N. Baker, Pres.
Founded: 1909. **Subjects:** Railroad tariffs, tariff supplements, division sheets. **Holdings:** 600 volumes. **Computerized Information Services:** Internal databases.

★17745★
WESTERN RAILWAY MUSEUM - LIBRARY (Trans)
5848 State Hwy. 12 Phone: (415)534-0071
Suisun City, CA 94585 Vernon J. Sappers, Chf.Libn.
Founded: 1969. **Staff:** Prof 1; Other 3. **Subjects:** Railroad - technology, history, fiction, maps. **Special Collections:** Vernon J. Sappers Collection (complete sets of Electric Railway Journal, Electric Traction; negative collection of 60,000 railroad subjects; bound sets of railroad employees timetables from major railroads of California); F.M. Smith Memorial Collection (corporate records of street railways serving Oakland, California, 1863-1946). **Holdings:** 5000 books; 100 bound periodical volumes; pamphlets; technical railroad newspaper clippings; maps; annual reports; timetables. **Services:** Library open to the public with recommendation from outside sources. **Remarks:** Maintained by Bay Area Electric Railroad Association.

★17746★
WESTERN RESEARCH INSTITUTE - LIBRARY (Energy, Sci-Engr)
University Sta., Box 3395 Phone: (307)721-2201
Laramie, WY 82071 Valerie Chilson, Libn.
Founded: 1947. **Staff:** Prof 1. **Subjects:** In-situ recovery research - oil shale, tar sands, coal gasification; geology; chemistry; hazardous waste management; engineering. **Special Collections:** Internal publications. **Holdings:** 3000 monographs; U.S. Bureau of Mines collection on microfiche; reports. **Subscriptions:** 70 journals and other serials. **Services:** Interlibrary loan; library open to the public by appointment. **Computerized Information Services:** DIALOG Information Services; internal database; DIALMAIL (electronic mail service).

★17747★
WESTERN RESERVE CARE SYSTEM - MEDICAL CENTER LIBRARIES (Med)
345 Oak Hill Ave. Phone: (216)747-0777
Youngstown, OH 44501 Patricia L. Augustine, Dir., Hea.Sci.Lib.
Staff: Prof 2; Other 2. **Subjects:** Clinical medicine, science and nursing. **Holdings:** 3014 books; 6196 bound periodical volumes; Audio-Digest tapes. **Subscriptions:** 318 journals and other serials. **Services:** Interlibrary loan; copying; libraries open to college students with librarian's permission. **Automated Operations:** Computerized cataloging. **Computerized Information Services:** DIALOG Information Services, MEDLINE. **Networks/Consortia:** Member of NEOUCOM Council Associated Hospital Librarians. **Remarks:** Western Reserve Care System maintains libraries at two units: Southside Medical Center and Northside Medical Center.

★17748★
WESTERN RESERVE HISTORICAL SOCIETY - LIBRARY (Hist)
10825 E. Blvd. Phone: (216)721-5722
Cleveland, OH 44106 Kermit J. Pike, Dir.
Founded: 1867. **Staff:** Prof 12; Other 5. **Subjects:** Ohio history, American genealogy, Civil War, slavery and abolitionism, ethnic history, American Revolution. **Special Collections:** Wallace H. Cathcart Shaker Collection; William P. Palmer Civil War Collection; David Z. Norton Napoleon Collection. **Holdings:** 218,800 books; 25,000 volumes of newspapers; 50,000 pamphlets; 5 million manuscripts; 26,000 reels of microfilm. **Subscriptions:** 322 journals and other serials; 50 newspapers. **Services:** Interlibrary loan; copying; library open to the public. **Special Catalogs:** Catalogs to manuscript, genealogy, and Shaker collections (all on cards). **Staff:** Ann Sindelar, Ref.Supv.; John Grabowski, Cur. of Mss.; Marian Sweton, Hd.Cat..

★17749★
WESTERN RESERVE PSYCHIATRIC HABILITATION CENTER - STAFF LIBRARY (Med)
1756 Sagamore Rd.
Box 305 Phone: (216)467-7131
Northfield, OH 44067 Pearlie McAlpine, Libn.
Staff: 1. **Subjects:** Psychiatry, psychiatric nursing, psychology, social service. **Holdings:** 500 books. **Subscriptions:** 55 journals and other serials. **Services:** Interlibrary loan; library not open to the public.

★17750★
WESTERN AND SOUTHERN LIFE INSURANCE CO. - LIBRARY (Bus-Fin)
400 Broadway Phone: (513)629-1393
Cincinnati, OH 45202 Patricia Billow, Libn.
Founded: 1952. **Staff:** Prof 1. **Subjects:** Business, insurance, recreation. **Holdings:** 3784 volumes; 4 VF drawers. **Subscriptions:** 41 journals and other serials. **Services:** Library not open to the public.

★17751★
WESTERN STATE HOSPITAL - LIBRARY (Med)
Box 1 Phone: (405)766-2311
Fort Supply, OK 73841 Kaye Statton, Lib.Techn.
Founded: 1950. **Staff:** Prof 1. **Subjects:** Substance abuse, psychiatry, psychology. **Holdings:** 2943 books; 23 bound periodical volumes; 50 boxes of booklets, pamphlets, and reports; 43 slide sets; 74 cassettes; 169 filmstrips; 27 films. **Subscriptions:** 73 journals and other serials; 25 newspapers. **Services:** Interlibrary loan; copying; library open to the public for reference use only. **Remarks:** Maintains a patients' library of 6500 volumes. **Formerly:** Western State Bradshaw Memorial Hospital.

★17752★
WESTERN STATE HOSPITAL - MEDICAL LIBRARY (Med)
Box 2500 Phone: (703)332-8307
Staunton, VA 24401-1405 Richard D. Wills, Med.Libn.
Staff: Prof 1; Other 1. **Subjects:** Psychology, psychiatry, general medicine, nursing. **Holdings:** 3600 books; 600 bound periodical volumes. **Subscriptions:** 117 journals and other serials. **Services:** Interlibrary loan; library open to the public. **Computerized Information Services:** BRS Information Technologies; DOCLINE (electronic mail service).

★17753★
WESTERN STATE HOSPITAL - PROFESSIONAL LIBRARY (Med)
Russellville Rd.
Box 2200 Phone: (502)886-4431
Hopkinsville, KY 42240 Margaret Crim Riley, Staff Libn.
Staff: Prof 1; Other 1. **Subjects:** Psychiatry, psychology, nursing, medicine, social work, management. **Holdings:** 2500 books; 240 bound periodical volumes; 50 cassettes relating to mental health care. **Subscriptions:** 58 journals and other serials. **Services:** Interlibrary loan; copying; library open to the public with restrictions.

WESTERN STATE HOSPITAL BRANCH LIBRARY
See: Washington State Library (17521)

★17754★
WESTERN STATE UNIVERSITY - COLLEGE OF LAW - LIBRARY (Law)
2121 San Diego Ave. Phone: (619)297-9700
San Diego, CA 92110 Karla M. Castetter, Assoc.Univ.Libn.
Staff: Prof 2; Other 10. **Subjects:** Law. **Holdings:** 35,000 books; 5000 bound periodical volumes; 26,700 volumes in microform; 150 videotapes; 100 audiotapes. **Subscriptions:** 1057 journals and other serials; 10 newspapers. **Services:** Interlibrary loan; library open to the public. **Computerized Information Services:** LEXIS, WESTLAW, OCLC. **Staff:** Christine M. Cheff, Ref. & Pub.Serv.Libn.

★17755★
WESTERN STATE UNIVERSITY - COLLEGE OF LAW - REIS LAW LIBRARY (Law)
1111 N. State College Blvd. Phone: (714)738-1000
Fullerton, CA 92631 Steven C. Perkins, Univ.Libn.
Founded: 1966. **Staff:** Prof 7; Other 19. **Subjects:** California and Anglo-American law. **Holdings:** 46,480 books; 3900 bound periodical volumes; 47,817 volumes in microform. **Subscriptions:** 400 journals; 2083 serials; 12 newspapers. **Services:** Interlibrary loan; copying; SDI; library open to the public with restrictions. **Automated Operations:** Computerized cataloging. **Computerized Information Services:** LEXIS, WESTLAW, NEXIS, DIALOG Information Services, ELSS (Electronic Legislative Search System). **Staff:** Sara Dobbins, Govt.Doc.Libn.; Carol J. Becker, Cat.; Monique Merrill, Acq. & Ser.Libn.; James Thompson, Ref.Libn..

★17756★
WESTERN STATES CHIROPRACTIC COLLEGE - W.A. BUDDEN MEMORIAL LIBRARY (Med)
2900 N.E. 132nd Ave. Phone: (503)256-3180
Portland, OR 97230 Kay Irvine, Hd.Libn.
Staff: Prof 2; Other 10. **Subjects:** Chiropractic, obstetrics, neurology, orthopedics, roentgenology. **Holdings:** 5000 books; 1000 bound periodical volumes. **Subscriptions:** 450 journals and other serials. **Services:** Interlibrary loan; copying; library open to the public. **Computerized Information Services:** DIALOG Information Services, MEDLINE. Performs searches on fee basis. **Networks/Consortia:** Member of Chiropractic Library Consortium (CLIBCON), Oregon Health Sciences Libraries Association (OHSLA), Portland Area Health Sciences Librarians. **Special Indexes:** Index to Chiropractic Literature. **Staff:** Sandra Loveland, Dir., Instr. Media Ctr..

★17757★
WESTERN THEOLOGICAL SEMINARY - BEARDSLEE LIBRARY (Rel-Phil)
Holland, MI 49423 Phone: (616)392-8555
Paul M. Smith, Libn.
Staff: Prof 3; Other 1. **Subjects:** Theology. **Holdings:** 85,000 books; 4200 bound periodical volumes; 350 linear feet of archives; 3200 slides; 2060 microforms. **Subscriptions:** 500 journals and other serials. **Services:** Interlibrary loan; copying; library open to the public with restrictions. **Automated Operations:** Computerized cataloging and acquisitions. **Computerized Information Services:** OCLC. **Networks/Consortia:** Member of Michigan Library Consortium (MLC). **Publications:** Reformed Review, 3/year.

★17758★
WESTERN UNION CORPORATION - LIBRARY
One Lake St.
Upper Saddle River, NJ 07458
Founded: 1921. **Subjects:** Telecommunications, telegraphy, electronics, satellites. **Special Collections:** History of telegraphy. **Holdings:** 11,000 books; 3000 bound periodical volumes; 300 monographs. **Remarks:** Presently inactive.

★17759★
WESTERN WASHINGTON UNIVERSITY - CENTER FOR PACIFIC NORTHWEST STUDIES (Hist)
Bellingham, WA 98225 Phone: (206)676-3125
Dr. James W. Scott, Dir.
Staff: 4. **Subjects:** History - Washington, Pacific Northwest, business. **Holdings:** 500 books; 100 bound periodical volumes; 600 volumes of bound newspapers; 300 cubic feet and 200 linear feet of business records; 90 cubic feet of manuscripts and personal collections; 26,000 photographs and negatives. **Services:** Copying; center open to the public for reference use only. **Publications:** Occasional Papers series; Guide to the Collections. **Remarks:** An alternate telephone number is 647-4776.

★17760★
WESTERN WASHINGTON UNIVERSITY - DEPARTMENT OF GEOGRAPHY AND REGIONAL PLANNING - MAP LIBRARY (Geog-Map)
Arntzen Hall 101 Phone: (206)676-3272
Bellingham, WA 98225 Karl Thompson, Act.Cur.
Founded: 1957. **Staff:** Prof 1; Other 6. **Subjects:** Maps, atlases. **Special Collections:** Maps emphasizing the Pacific Northwest, Canada, Mexico, and Circum-Pacific. **Holdings:** 865 atlases; 190,000 maps; 22,000 aerial photographs; 55 globes. **Services:** Copying; library open to the public for reference use only.

WESTERN WASHINGTON UNIVERSITY - ENVIRONMENTAL RESOURCE LIBRARY
See: Huxley College of Environmental Studies - Environmental Resource Library (6626)

★17761★
WESTERN WISCONSIN TECHNICAL COLLEGE - LIBRARY (Sci-Engr)
304 N. 6th St. Phone: (608)785-9142
La Crosse, WI 54602-0908 Thuan T. Pham, Hd.Libn.
Founded: 1966. **Staff:** Prof 2; Other 3. **Subjects:** Technology, health occupations, business administration, distributive education, adult education, home economics, agriculture. **Holdings:** 28,000 books and bound periodical volumes; 2500 reels of microfilm; 1200 microfiche; 8 VF drawers of pamphlets. **Subscriptions:** 450 journals and other serials; 30 newspapers. **Services:** Interlibrary loan; copying; library open to the public. **Formerly:** Western Wisconsin Technical College. **Staff:** Annette Neiderkorn, Ref.Libn..

★17762★
WESTERN WYOMING COMMUNITY COLLEGE - LIBRARY - SPECIAL COLLECTIONS (Hist)
3500 College Dr. Phone: (307)382-1700
Rock Springs, WY 82902-0428 Donna S. Snyder, Dir. of Lib.Serv.
Founded: 1959. **Staff:** Prof 2; Other 3. **Special Collections:** Wyoming documents (389); Smithsonian Institution annual reports, 1849-1969; Bureau of American Ethnology, 1880-1967; U.S. Government documents. **Holdings:** 32,000 books; 1801 bound periodical volumes; 14,756 microforms; 360 cassettes and AV programs; 24 computer software programs. **Subscriptions:** 316 journals and other serials; 31 newspapers. **Services:** Interlibrary loan; copying; collections open to the public. **Automated Operations:** Computerized cataloging and ILL. **Computerized Information Services:** BRS Information Technologies. Performs searches on fee basis. Contact Person: Pam Hiltner, Tech.Serv.. **Networks/Consortia:** Member of Western Wyoming Health Science Library Consortium. **Staff:** Robert Kalabus, Assoc.Libn./Hd., Tech.Serv..

★17763★
WESTERNERS INTERNATIONAL, A FOUNDATION - LIBRARY (Hist)
College Sta., Box 3485
Tucson, AZ 85722 W.K. Brown, Sec.-Treas.
Founded: 1944. **Subjects:** Western history. **Holdings:** 500 volumes; publications, documents, and correspondence of more than 100 local units called "Corrals" devoted to research and popularization of Western history. **Subscriptions:** 18 journals and other serials. **Services:** Library not open to the public.

WESTGATE FRIENDS LIBRARY
See: Society of Friends - Ohio Yearly Meeting (13324)

★17764★
WESTINGHOUSE CANADA LTD. - ELECTRONICS DIVISION LIBRARY (Sci-Engr)
777 Walker's Line
P.O. Box 5009
Burlington, ON, Canada L7R 4B3 Phone: (416)528-8811
Staff: Prof 1. **Subjects:** Electronics and electrical engineering, data processing. **Holdings:** 2000 books; trade literature from 1000 manufacturers; 1000 reports; 8000 military, government, and commercial specifications and standards; 25 VF drawers of pamphlets; 200 reels of microfilm. **Subscriptions:** 150 journals and other serials; 15 newspapers. **Services:** Interlibrary loan; copying; library open to the public for reference use only on request. **Publications:** Library Bulletin, irregular - for internal distribution only.

★17765★
WESTINGHOUSE ELECTRIC CORPORATION - BETTIS ATOMIC POWER LABORATORY - LIBRARY (Energy)
Box 79 Phone: (412)462-5000
West Mifflin, PA 15122-0079 Mary Louise Frazee, Libn.
Founded: 1949. **Staff:** Prof 4; Other 3. **Subjects:** Nuclear power. **Holdings:** 44,000 books and bound periodical volumes; internal technical reports and correspondence; Atomic Energy Commission reports. **Subscriptions:** 300 journals and other serials. **Services:** Interlibrary loan; library not open to the public. **Remarks:** Westinghouse Electric Corporation operates under contract to the U.S. Department of Energy.

★17766★
WESTINGHOUSE ELECTRIC CORPORATION - DEFENSE & ELECTRONIC CENTER - TECHNICAL INFORMATION CENTER (Sci-Engr)
MS 1138, Box 746 Phone: (301)765-2858
Baltimore, MD 21203 Joan L. Doerr, Supv.
Founded: 1961. **Staff:** Prof 3; Other 7. **Subjects:** Electronic communication engineering, systems engineering. **Holdings:** 20,000 books; 4000 bound periodical volumes; 100,000 technical reports on microfilm. **Subscriptions:** 450 journals and other serials. **Services:** Interlibrary loan; center not open to the public. **Automated Operations:** Computerized circulation. **Computerized Information Services:** DIALOG Information Services, BRS Information Technologies, Integrated Technical Information System (ITIS), DTIC.

★17767★
WESTINGHOUSE ELECTRIC CORPORATION - ELECTRICAL SYSTEMS DIVISION - TECHNICAL LIBRARY (Sci-Engr)
1501 S. Dixie Phone: (419)226-3210
Lima, OH 45804 Jack Witte, Mgr.
Staff: 1. **Subjects:** Electrical and electronic engineering. **Holdings:** 2200 books; 1100 bound periodical volumes; 8000 technical reports; 600 patents. **Subscriptions:** 100 journals and other serials. **Services:** Library not open to the public. **Computerized Information Services:** Online systems.

★17768★
WESTINGHOUSE ELECTRIC CORPORATION - ENGINEERING DIVISION - ENGINEERING LIBRARY
1447 Chestnut Ave.
Hillside, NJ 07205
Defunct

★17769★
WESTINGHOUSE ELECTRIC CORPORATION - HITTMAN NUCLEAR COMPANY - ENGINEERING LIBRARY (Energy)
9151 Rumsey Rd. Phone: (301)964-5000
Columbia, MD 21045 Karen Johnson, Sr.Sec.
Subjects: Environment, synthetic fuels, energy conservation, solar energy. **Holdings:** 2000 books; 10,000 technical reports.

★17770★
WESTINGHOUSE ELECTRIC CORPORATION - NAVAL REACTOR FACILITY LIBRARY (Energy)
Box 2068
Idaho Falls, ID 83401 Marcia J. Francis, Libn.
Founded: 1956. **Staff:** Prof 1; Other 6. **Subjects:** Atomic power. **Holdings:** 4000 books; 58,000 documents and technical reports. **Subscriptions:** 52 journals and other serials. **Services:** Library not open to the public.

★17771★
WESTINGHOUSE ELECTRIC CORPORATION - NUCLEAR ENERGY SYSTEMS - ADVANCED ENERGY SYSTEMS DIVISION - LIBRARY
Waltz Mill Site
Box 158
Madison, PA 15663
Defunct

★17772★
WESTINGHOUSE ELECTRIC CORPORATION - POWER GENERATION DIVISION - LIBRARY (Sci-Engr, Comp Sci)
The Quadrangle, MC 235
4400 Alafaya Trail Phone: (407)281-2170
Orlando, FL 32826-2399 Mary P. Maynard, Assoc.Libn.
Founded: 1931. **Staff:** Prof 1; Other 1. **Subjects:** Engineering, mathematics, computers, management, metallurgy. **Special Collections:** Westinghouse Historical Collection. **Holdings:** 2500 books; 1100 bound periodical volumes; 14,000 reports; 8000 microfiche. **Subscriptions:** 104 journals and other serials. **Services:** Interlibrary loan; library not open to the public. **Automated Operations:** Computerized circulation. **Computerized Information Services:** DIALOG Information Services, BRS Information Technologies, NEXIS; WCAP (internal database). **Publications:** New Books Listing, monthly; Newly Issued WORL Reports, monthly.

★17773★
WESTINGHOUSE ELECTRIC CORPORATION - POWER SYSTEMS - INFORMATION RESOURCE CENTER (Sci-Engr)
209 Energy Center East
Box 355 Phone: (412)373-4200
Pittsburgh, PA 15230 Cynthia A. Hodgson, Mgr., Info.Rsrcs.
Founded: 1955. **Staff:** Prof 6; Other 7. **Subjects:** Nuclear technology, engineering and industry, physics, business management and marketing computer applications. **Special Collections:** Three Mile Island and Chernobyl accidents. **Holdings:** 60,000 volumes; 300,000 technical reports in microform; 50,000 technical reports and documents; 1500 AV programs; 3000 pamphlets; 20,000 internal reports. **Subscriptions:** 650 journals and other serials. **Services:** Interlibrary loan; copying; center open to the public by appointment only. **Automated Operations:** Computerized cataloging, serials, and circulation. **Computerized Information Services:** DIALOG Information Services, BRS Information Technologies, Integrated Technical Information System (ITIS), NEXIS, Dow Jones News/Retrieval, Dun & Bradstreet Corporation, INVESTEXT, Dialcom, Inc., NewsNet, Inc., NRC Database. **Networks/Consortia:** Member of Pittsburgh Regional Library Center (PRLC). **Special Indexes:** KWOC Indexes to Nucleonics Week 1968-80, Selected Public Information on Nuclear Energy (SPINDEX) 1969-81, TMI related information. **Formerly:** Westinghouse Electric Corporation - Water Reactor Divisions. **Staff:** Carla Newsome, Info.Sys.Anl.; Barbara Spiegelman, Sr.Info.Spec.; Ann Chernega, Info.Anl.; Bob Sullivan, Sr.Info.Spec.; Wun-Yun Tsai, Sr.Info.Spec.; Jane Singer, Info.Spec..

★17774★
WESTINGHOUSE ELECTRIC CORPORATION - RESEARCH AND DEVELOPMENT CENTER - RESEARCH LIBRARY (Sci-Engr)
1310 Beulah Rd. Phone: (412)256-1610
Pittsburgh, PA 15235 Anita Newell, Mgr.
Founded: 1923. **Staff:** Prof 3; Other 4. **Subjects:** Chemistry, ceramics, electrical engineering, electronics, mathematics, magnetics, mechanical engineering, mechanical sciences, metallurgy, nuclear sciences, space sciences, physics. **Holdings:** 50,000 volumes. **Subscriptions:** 650 journals and other serials. **Services:** Library open to the public by special arrangement.

WESTINGHOUSE ELECTRIC CORPORATION - WATER REACTOR DIVISIONS
See: Westinghouse Electric Corporation - Power Systems (17773)

★17775★
WESTINGHOUSE ELECTRIC CORPORATION - WESTINGHOUSE NUCLEAR TRAINING CENTER - INFORMATION RESOURCE CENTER (Energy)
505 Shiloh Blvd.
Zion, IL 60099 Phone: (312)872-4585
Founded: 1970. **Staff:** 1. **Subjects:** Nuclear power, physics. **Holdings:** 500 books; 600 technical manuals; 150 videotapes; 5000 slides; 300 microfiche. **Subscriptions:** 25 journals and other serials; 6 newspapers. **Services:** Interlibrary loan; center not open to the public.

★17776★
WESTINGHOUSE ELECTRIC CORPORATION - WIPP TECHNICAL LIBRARY (Sci-Engr)
Box 2078 Phone: (505)885-8883
Carlsbad, NM 88220 Jamie A. Clarkston, Act.Tech.Libn.
Staff: 1. **Subjects:** Nuclear waste disposal, geology. **Special Collections:** U.S. Department of Energy Waste Isolation Pilot Plant (WIPP) materials. **Holdings:** 400 books; 4000 technical reports. **Subscriptions:** 105 journals and other serials. **Services:** Interlibrary loan; library not open to the public. **Computerized Information Services:** Integrated Technical Information System (ITIS), DIALOG Information Services.

★17777★
WESTINGHOUSE HANFORD COMPANY - DEPARTMENT OF ENERGY'S PUBLIC READING ROOM (Sci-Engr)
Federal Bldg., Rm. 157
Box 1970 Phone: (509)376-8583
Richland, WA 99352 Terri Traub, Pub.Info.Spec.
Founded: 1976. **Staff:** Prof 1. **Subjects:** Hanford Project, nuclear waste management. **Holdings:** 50 books; 6000 technical reports; 3500 microfiche. **Services:** Copying; room open to the public for reference use only. **Automated Operations:** Computerized cataloging. **Formerly:** Rockwell International - Rockwell Hanford Operations.

★17778★
WESTINGHOUSE HANFORD COMPANY - HANFORD SCIENCE CENTER - ENERGY & ENVIRONMENT LIBRARY (Energy, Env-Cons)
825 Jadwin
Box 800 Phone: (509)376-6374
Richland, WA 99352 Terri Traub, Pub.Info.Spec.
Staff: Prof 1. **Subjects:** Energy sources, environment. **Holdings:** 3000 books; teacher curriculum on energy and environment. **Subscriptions:** 30 journals and other serials. **Services:** Copying; library open to the public. **Publications:** Highlights, semiannual - to teachers. **Formerly:** Rockwell International - Rockwell Hanford Operations.

★17779★
WESTINGHOUSE MATERIALS CO. OF OHIO - FMPC LIBRARY (Sci-Engr, Energy)
Box 398704 Phone: (513)738-6534
Cincinnati, OH 45239 Rosemary H. Gardewing, Libn.
Founded: 1951. **Staff:** 2. **Subjects:** Atomic energy, chemistry, metallurgy. **Holdings:** 6000 books; 2000 bound periodical volumes; 30,000 technical reports; 200,000 technical reports in microform. **Subscriptions:** 225 journals and other serials. **Services:** Interlibrary loan; library not open to the public. **Computerized Information Services:** DIALOG Information Services. **Publications:** Library Accessions, bimonthly - for internal distribution only. **Remarks:** Operates under contract to the U.S. Department of Energy.

★17780★
WESTLAKE COMMUNITY HOSPITAL - LIBRARY (Med)
1225 Lake St. Phone: (312)681-3000
Melrose Park, IL 60160 Carol D. Strauss, Libn.
Staff: Prof 1. **Subjects:** Medicine, nursing, hospitals, health administration. **Holdings:** 750 books; 50 bound periodical volumes; 6 VF drawers of pamphlets. **Subscriptions:** 90 journals and other serials. **Services:** Interlibrary loan; library open to the public for reference use only. **Computerized Information Services:** BRS Information Technologies. **Networks/Consortia:** Member of Metropolitan Consortium of Chicago, Suburban Library System (SLS). **Publications:** Annual Report.

★17781★
WESTLAND MEDICAL CENTER - LIBRARY (Med, Biol Sci)
2345 Merriman Rd. Phone: (313)467-2459
Westland, MI 48185 L.A. Dorman, Lib.Dir.
Founded: 1949. **Staff:** Prof 2; Other 2. **Subjects:** Biological sciences. **Holdings:** 3464 books; 6000 bound periodical volumes; 343 Audio-Digest tapes. **Subscriptions:** 222 journals and other serials. **Services:** Interlibrary loan; SDI; library open to the public. **Computerized Information Services:** MEDLINE. **Networks/Consortia:** Member of Greater Midwest Regional Medical Library Network.

★17782★
WESTMINSTER ABBEY - LIBRARY (Rel-Phil)
Mission, BC, Canada V2V 4J2 Boniface Aicher, O.S.B., Libn.
Subjects: Theology, church history, scripture. **Holdings:** 32,000 books; 2000 bound periodical volumes; 3000 microfiche. **Subscriptions:** 70 journals and other serials; 15 newspapers. **Services:** Copying; library open to the public with restrictions.

★17783★
WESTMINSTER CHOIR COLLEGE - TALBOTT LIBRARY (Mus)
Hamilton Ave. at Walnut Ln. Phone: (609)921-3658
Princeton, NJ 08540 Sherry L. Vellucci, Dir.
Staff: Prof 6; Other 4. **Subjects:** Music - choral, organ, church. **Special Collections:** Choral music performance collection (over 4100 titles in multiple copy); Routley Collection of Books and Hymnals; Archives of the Organ Historical Society; Music Education Resource Center. **Holdings:** 26,000 volumes; 18,600 scores; 1000 microforms; 7000 sound recordings. **Subscriptions:** 135 journals and other serials. **Services:** Interlibrary loan (fee); copying; library open to the public with fee for circulation for area residents. **Automated Operations:** Computerized cataloging and acquisitions. **Computerized Information Services:** OCLC. **Networks/Consortia:** Member of PALINET. **Staff:** Jeanette Jacobson, Hd., Cat.; Nancy A. Wicklund, Hd., Rd.Serv.; Mary Benton, Acq.Libn.; Susan Flick, Choral Libn.; Marilyn Quinn, Cat..

★17784★
WESTMINSTER COLLEGE - WINSTON CHURCHILL MEMORIAL AND LIBRARY (Hist)
7th & Westminster Ave. Phone: (314)642-3361
Fulton, MO 65251-1299 Warren M. Hollrah, Musm.Mgr./Coll.Archv.
Staff: 3. **Subjects:** Sir Winston Churchill. **Special Collections:** Sir Christopher Wren; World War II; 20th century Anglo/American documents. **Holdings:** 1100 books; 530 reels of microfilm. **Services:** Library open to the public with restrictions. **Automated Operations:** Computerized cataloging. **Publications:** Memorial Memo, 3/year. **Remarks:** An alternate telephone number is 642-6648.

★17785★
WESTMINSTER INSTITUTE FOR ETHICS AND HUMAN VALUES - LIBRARY (Soc Sci)
361 Windermere Rd. Phone: (519)673-0046
London, ON, Canada N6G 2K3 Janet Baldock, Lib.Adm.Asst.
Subjects: Ethics - bioethics, legal, business and professional, philosophical; morality and population. **Holdings:** 1800 volumes; journal article and newspaper clipping files. **Subscriptions:** 51 journals and other serials. **Services:** Copying; library open to the public for reference use only. **Publications:** Westminster Affairs (newsletter), quarterly - free upon request. **Remarks:** The Westminster Institute for Ethics and Human Values is sponsored by Westminster College and the University of Western Ontario.

WESTMINSTER LAW LIBRARY
See: University of Denver - College of Law (16121)

★17786★
WESTMINSTER PRESBYTERIAN CHURCH - JOHN H. HOLMES LIBRARY (Rel-Phil)
Cleves-Warsaw & Nancy Lee Ln. Phone: (513)921-1623
Cincinnati, OH 45238 Esther Reher, Libn.
Founded: 1948. **Staff:** 1. **Subjects:** Bible, devotional materials, church work, religious education, family life, children's books. **Special Collections:** Bibles (including braille). **Holdings:** 5000 books. **Services:** Library open to church visitors.

★17787★
WESTMINSTER PRESBYTERIAN CHURCH - LIBRARY (Rel-Phil)
4400 N. Shartel Phone: (405)524-2204
Oklahoma City, OK 73118 J. Richard Hershberger, Assoc. Minister
Founded: 1950. **Staff:** Prof 1; Other 1. **Subjects:** Religion, church history, biography. **Holdings:** 1200 volumes. **Services:** Library open to the public with restrictions.

★17788★
WESTMINSTER PRESBYTERIAN CHURCH - LIBRARY (Rel-Phil)
2040 Washington Rd. Phone: (412)835-6630
Pittsburgh, PA 15241 Betty B. Brown, Lib.Dir.
Staff: Prof 2. **Subjects:** Religion, West Pennsylvania history. **Holdings:** 5000 books.

★17789★
WESTMINSTER PRESBYTERIAN CHURCH - LIBRARY (Rel-Phil)
2701 Cameron Mills Rd. Phone: (703)549-4766
Alexandria, VA 22302 Jane Campbell, Coord. of Christian Educ.
Founded: 1956. **Staff:** Prof 1; Other 2. **Subjects:** Religion. **Holdings:** 2100 books; phonograph records; audiotapes. **Subscriptions:** 11 journals and other serials. **Services:** Library open to the public.

★17790★
WESTMINSTER THEOLOGICAL SEMINARY - MONTGOMERY LIBRARY (Rel-Phil)
Chestnut Hill Phone: (215)887-5511
Philadelphia, PA 19118 John R. Muether, Libn.
Founded: 1929. **Staff:** Prof 3; Other 3. **Subjects:** Biblical studies, theology, church history, patristics. **Special Collections:** Bible texts and versions (1000); Reformed theology of 16th-20th centuries (2500 items). **Holdings:** 100,000 books; 10,000 bound periodical volumes; 600 reels of microfilm. **Subscriptions:** 800 journals and other serials. **Services:** Interlibrary loan; copying; library open to the public. **Automated Operations:** Computerized cataloging and acquisitions. **Computerized Information Services:** OCLC, BRS Information Technologies. **Networks/Consortia:** Member of PALINET, State System of Higher Education Libraries Council (SSHELCO). **Remarks:** Library located at Willow Grove Ave. & Church Rd., Glenside, PA 19038. **Staff:** Jane Patete, Cir.; Grace Mullen, Archv./Pub.Serv..

★17791★
WESTMORELAND COUNTY HISTORICAL SOCIETY - CALVIN E. POLLINS MEMORIAL LIBRARY (Hist)
Union Trust Bldg.
102 N. Main St. Phone: (412)836-1800
Greensburg, PA 15601 Linda E. Forish, Adm.Sec.
Staff: 3. **Subjects:** Local history, genealogy, fine and decorative arts, archeology. **Special Collections:** Early West Pennsylvania manuscript collections dealing with local area and individuals. **Holdings:** 1500 books; 12 VF drawers; 55 bound volumes of local newspapers; 12,000 documents; 24 reels of microfilm; 500 slides; 400 architectural drawings of Westmoreland County. **Services:** Copying; library open to the public on a fee basis. **Special Indexes:** Archival holdings indexes; Westmoreland County History, A Union List and Bibliography (paperback book) - for sale; indexes to fine and decorative arts collections.

★17792★
WESTMORELAND COUNTY LAW LIBRARY (Law)
202 Courthouse Square Phone: (412)834-2191
Greensburg, PA 15601 Betsey Laffey, Libn.
Staff: Prof 3. **Subjects:** Law. **Holdings:** 19,000 volumes. **Subscriptions:** 20 journals and other serials. **Services:** Interlibrary loan; copying; library open to the public. **Computerized Information Services:** WESTLAW. Performs searches on fee basis.

★17793★
WESTMORELAND HOSPITAL - LIBRARY AND HEALTH RESOURCE CENTER (Med)
532 W. Pittsburgh St. Phone: (412)832-4088
Greensburg, PA 15601-2282 Janet C. Petrak, Med.Libn.
Founded: 1959. **Staff:** Prof 1. **Subjects:** Medicine, nursing, surgery. **Special Collections:** History of nursing; Clinical Pastoral Education Program Support Collection. **Holdings:** 4000 books; 1499 bound periodical volumes. **Subscriptions:** 348 journals and other serials. **Services:** Interlibrary loan; copying; library open to the public for reference use only. **Computerized Information Services:** BRS Information Technologies. **Publications:** Library & Health Resource Center Newsletter.

★17794★
WESTMORELAND MUSEUM OF ART - ART REFERENCE LIBRARY (Art)
221 N. Main St.
Greensburg, PA 15601-1898 Phone: (412)837-1500
Founded: 1958. **Staff:** 1. **Subjects:** American and European artists and styles, American architecture, techniques of materials, history. **Holdings:** 10,200 books; 75 bound periodical volumes; 28,000 exhibition catalogs; 15,000 museum exchange bulletins and reports; 50,000 exhibition brochures. **Subscriptions:** 45 journals and other serials. **Services:** Copying; library open to the public for reference use only. **Publications:** Monthly brochures on exhibitions.

WESTON CLINICAL SCIENCE CENTER LIBRARY
See: University of Wisconsin, Madison - Center for Health Sciences Libraries (17122)

★17795★
WESTON COUNTY HISTORICAL SOCIETY - ANNA MILLER MUSEUM (Hist)
Box 516 Phone: (307)746-4188
Newcastle, WY 82701 Helen M. Larsen, Dir.
Founded: 1966. **Staff:** 2. **Subjects:** Wyoming and Western history; U.S. Congress. **Special Collections:** Frank W. Mondell, Wyoming Congressman, 1898-1922. **Holdings:** 50 bound periodical volumes; periodicals, 1860 to present; 100 items of ephemera, local history, clippings, pamphlets, booklets, manuscripts; 1400 local history photographs; 30 oral history tapes. **Subscriptions:** 12 journals and other serials. **Services:** Copying; library open to the public for reference use only. **Automated Operations:** Computerized acquisitions.

★17796★
WESTON RESEARCH CENTRE - INFORMATION RESOURCE CENTRE (Food-Bev)
1047 Yonge St. Phone: (416)922-5100
Toronto, ON, Canada M4W 2L2 Lusi Wong, Info.Mgr.
Founded: 1976. **Staff:** Prof 4; Other 2. **Subjects:** Food science, chemical analysis, microbiology, packaging, the senses. **Holdings:** 3000 volumes; 25 VF drawers of patents, manuscripts, pamphlets, clippings. **Subscriptions:** 250 journals and other serials. **Services:** Interlibrary loan; copying; SDI; center open to the public by appointment only. **Automated Operations:** Computerized cataloging, acquisitions, serials, and circulation. **Computerized Information Services:** DIALOG Information Services, BRS Information Technologies, QL Systems, CAN/OLE, Pergamon ORBIT InfoLine, Inc., Telesystemes Questel, Info Globe. Performs searches on fee basis. **Networks/Consortia:** Member of Sheridan Park Association - Library and Information Science Committee (LISC). **Publications:** Frontiers, monthly - to clients. **Special Indexes:** Index to internal project reports. **Staff:** Lu Chan, Asst.Mgr..

★17797★
ROY F. WESTON, INC. - CORPORATE INFORMATION CENTER (Env-Cons, Energy)
Weston Way Phone: (215)692-3030
West Chester, PA 19380 Margo Dinniman, Dir.
Founded: 1963. **Staff:** Prof 2; Other 2. **Subjects:** Pollution; waste - solid, nuclear, hazardous; environmental science; planning; energy. **Holdings:** 5000 books; 700 bound periodical volumes; 10,000 documents; 2500 microfiche. **Subscriptions:** 120 journals and other serials. **Services:** Interlibrary loan; center not open to the public. **Computerized Information Services:** DIALOG Information Services, Pergamon ORBIT InfoLine, Inc., DTIC, BRS Information Technologies, MEDLARS, OCLC, National Ground Water Information Center Data Base, Chemical Information Systems, Inc. (CIS), VU/TEXT Information Services, NewsNet, Inc., Dow Jones News/Retrieval.

★17798★
WESTON SCHOOL OF THEOLOGY - LIBRARY (Rel-Phil)
99 Brattle St. Phone: (617)868-3450
Cambridge, MA 02138 James Dunkly, Dir.
Founded: 1922. **Staff:** Prof 5; Other 8. **Subjects:** Theology, papal and conciliar documents, New Testament, Jesuitica. **Special Collections:** Arabic Collection (4000 volumes). **Holdings:** 260,000 volumes. **Subscriptions:** 1100 journals and other serials. **Services:** Interlibrary loan; copying; library open to the public with restrictions on circulation. **Automated Operations:** Computerized cataloging and ILL. **Computerized Information Services:** OCLC. **Networks/Consortia:** Member of NELINET, Boston Theological Institute Libraries. **Remarks:** Maintained jointly by Weston School of Theology and Episcopal Divinity School. **Staff:** Gayle Pershouse, Pub.Serv.Coord.; Paul LaCharite, Acq. & Res.Coord.; Jeanne Zudeck, Ser.Supv.; Anne Reece, Hd., Cat.; Colleen McHale O'Connor, Cat.; Judith Russell, Cat.Asst.; Barbara Holdorph, ILL Supv./Cat.Asst..

★17799★
WESTPOINT PEPPERELL - RESEARCH CENTER - INFORMATION SERVICES LIBRARY (Sci-Engr)
3300 23rd Dr. Phone: (404)645-4659
Valley, AL 36854 Mary Lou Dabbs, Supv.
Founded: 1944. **Staff:** Prof 1; Other 1. **Subjects:** Textiles, chemistry, textile testing, dyeing, fire retardancy, environmental pollution, engineering, industrial hygiene. **Holdings:** 9000 books; 3000 bound periodical volumes; 15 VF drawers of research reports; 4 VF drawers of patents; 4 VF drawers of reprints; 4000 microfiche; 4 VF drawers of catalogs, brochures, and manufacturing technical data. **Subscriptions:** 200 journals and other serials; 10 newspapers. **Services:** Interlibrary loan; copying; SDI; library open to students. **Computerized Information Services:** DIALOG Information Services, NLM. Performs searches on fee basis. **Publications:** Recent Accessions, quarterly - to technical supervisors.

★17800★
WESTRECO, INC. - FOOD RESEARCH AND DEVELOPMENT - LIBRARY (Food-Bev)
555 S. Fourth St.
Box 274 Phone: (315)598-1234
Fulton, NY 13069 Catherine A. Reed, Res.Libn.
Founded: 1955. **Staff:** Prof 1. **Subjects:** Confectionery industry; food processing; chemistry - industrial, physical, analytical; chemical engineering. **Special Collections:** Chocolate; cocoa. **Holdings:** 1577 books; 24 VF drawers of pamphlets, articles, clippings, newsletters. **Subscriptions:** 130 journals and other serials. **Services:** Interlibrary loan; library not open to the public. **Computerized Information Services:** DIALOG Information Services, BRS Information Technologies.

★17801★
WESTRECO, INC. - TECHNICAL LIBRARY (Food-Bev)
140 Boardman Rd. Phone: (203)355-0911
New Milford, CT 06776 Linda F. Carhuff, Hd.Libn.
Staff: Prof 2; Other 1. **Subjects:** Food science, analytical chemistry, nutrition. **Special Collections:** Company reports and files on food technology and agricultural research; chemical abstracts, 1907 to present (microfilm). **Holdings:** 3700 books; 1500 bound periodical volumes; 3300 patents; 20 VF drawers of pamphlets; 70 reels of microfilm of company records; metal corrosion articles; Pineapple Research Institute reports. **Subscriptions:** 220 journals and other serials. **Services:** Interlibrary loan; library open to the public for reference use only by arrangement. **Computerized Information Services:** DIALOG Information Services, NEXIS, Occupational Health Services, Inc; DIALMAIL (electronic mail service). **Networks/Consortia:** Member of Southwestern Connecticut Library Council (SWLC). **Staff:** Kathy Null, Libn..

WESTSIDE HOSPITAL LIBRARY
See: U.S. Veterans Administration (IL-Chicago) (15552)

★17802★
WESTVACO CORPORATION - FOREST SCIENCE LABORATORY LIBRARY (Agri)
Box 1950 Phone: (803)871-5000
Summerville, SC 29484 Roxy Rust, Libn.
Founded: 1982. **Staff:** Prof 1. **Subjects:** Forestry, forestry management, biometrics, forest genetics and soils. **Holdings:** 3500 books; 400 bound periodical volumes; 7000 U.S. Forest Service Experiment Station documents; 3000 clippings; 1100 company reports; 2000 institutional and miscellaneous publications. **Subscriptions:** 200 journals and other serials. **Services:** Interlibrary loan; copying; SDI; library open to the public for reference use only. **Automated Operations:** Computerized cataloging and ILL. **Computerized Information Services:** DIALOG Information Services, OCLC. **Networks/Consortia:** Member of SOLINET. **Publications:** FSL Library Book Acquistions List, monthly - for internal distribution only. **Special Indexes:** Information file index (book).

★17803★
WESTVACO CORPORATION - INFORMATION SERVICES CENTER (Sci-Engr)
Box 5207 Phone: (803)745-3401
North Charleston, SC 29406 Elizabeth D. De Liesseline, Info.Spec.
Staff: Prof 2; Other 2. **Subjects:** Papermaking, pulping, forestry, utilization of by-products. **Holdings:** 9000 volumes; 50,000 company reports; 15,000 patents; 2000 clippings. **Subscriptions:** 150 journals and other serials. **Services:** Interlibrary loan; center not open to the public. **Computerized Information Services:** Pergamon ORBIT InfoLine, Inc., DIALOG Information Services. **Publications:** Reports Bulletin, monthly. **Also Known As:** West Virginia Pulp and Paper Company. **Staff:** Barbara McDonald, Info.Spec..

★17804★
WESTVACO CORPORATION - LAUREL RESEARCH LIBRARY (Sci-Engr)
Johns Hopkins Rd. Phone: (301)792-9100
Laurel, MD 20707 Elizabeth Omar, Res.Libn.
Founded: 1967. **Staff:** Prof 1. **Subjects:** Chemistry - paper, polymer, organic, colloidal; paper physics; biotechnology; corrosion. **Special Collections:** Specialized collection of books, periodicals, and bibliographies on paper chemistry and physics. **Holdings:** 2200 books; 2500 bound periodical volumes. **Subscriptions:** 110 journals and other serials; 5 newspapers. **Services:** Interlibrary loan; library not open to the public. **Computerized Information Services:** Pergamon ORBIT InfoLine, Inc., DIALOG Information Services, STN International, Pergamon ORBIT InfoLine, Inc. **Networks/Consortia:** Member of National Capitol Area Interlibrary Loan Association.

★17805★
WESTVIEW CHRISTIAN REFORMED CHURCH - LIBRARY (Rel-Phil)
2929 Leonard St., N.W. Phone: (616)453-3105
Grand Rapids, MI 49504 Beatrice Dahnke, Libn.
Founded: 1900. **Staff:** Prof 1; Other 1. **Subjects:** Religion. **Holdings:** 2350 books. **Services:** Library not open to the public.

★17806★
WESTWOOD FIRST PRESBYTERIAN CHURCH - WALTER LORENZ MEMORIAL LIBRARY (Rel-Phil)
3011 Harrison Ave. Phone: (513)661-6846
Cincinnati, OH 45211 Marian B. McNair, Libn.
Founded: 1957. **Staff:** Prof 2; Other 9. **Subjects:** Religion, curriculum materials, children's books, fiction, biography. **Special Collections:** Henderson Collection (107 19th century books). **Holdings:** 3900 books; 3 VF drawers; 250 filmstrips, cassettes, records, slides; Presbyterian College bulletins. **Subscriptions:** 10 journals and other serials. **Services:** Interlibrary loan; library open to the public. **Publications:** Library Bulletin, monthly; Christian holidays; bibliographies for church school and adult study groups; Sponsored Workshops for Church Libraries in Cincinnati Presbytery.

★17807★
WETHERSFIELD HISTORICAL SOCIETY - OLD ACADEMY MUSEUM LIBRARY (Hist)
150 Main St. Phone: (203)529-7656
Wethersfield, CT 06109 Donald H. Axman, Libn./Archv.
Founded: 1932. **Staff:** Prof 4; Other 1. **Subjects:** Wethersfield history, genealogy, maritime history. **Special Collections:** Rushlight Club (history of lighting; 300 books and pamphlets); First Church of Christ archives; The Connecticut Horticultural Society library (1000 volumes). **Holdings:** 1000 books; 2000 photographs; 75 linear feet of account books, ship logs, letters, broadsides, maps, sermons, wallpaper, diaries, manuscripts. **Services:** Copying; library open to the public. **Publications:** Wethersfield Newsletter, quarterly; Local History, annual. **Staff:** Nora O. Howard, Dir..

ALEXANDER WETMORE LIBRARY
See: Rob & Bessie Welder Wildlife Foundation - Library (17609)

WEY MEMORIAL LIBRARY
See: Arnot-Ogden Memorial Hospital (950)

★17808★
WEYBURN MENTAL HEALTH CENTRE - LIBRARY (Med)
Box 1056 Phone: (306)842-5461
Weyburn, SK, Canada S4H 2L4 Merle St. Onge, Ck. Stenographer II
Staff: 1. **Subjects:** Psychiatry, psychology, social work, nursing, child and youth services, occupational therapy, vocational guidance. **Holdings:** 1545 volumes. **Subscriptions:** 37 journals and other serials; 6 newspapers. **Services:** Interlibrary loan; library open to students.

★17809★
CHARLES A. WEYERHAEUSER MEMORIAL MUSEUM - LIBRARY (Hist)
Box 239 Phone: (612)632-4007
Little Falls, MN 56345 Jan Warner, Exec.Dir.
Founded: 1975. **Staff:** Prof 1; Other 2. **Subjects:** Local history of Morrison County. **Special Collections:** Swanville News (defunct local newspaper; microfilm); Little Falls Daily Transcript, 1892-1982 (bound volumes); Minnesota State Census, 1865-1904 (microfilm); Works Progress Administration (WPA) Biographies of Morrison County; Pierz Journal; Motley Mercury and Motley Register. **Holdings:** 800 books. **Services:** Interlibrary loan; copying; library open to the public for reference use only.

Publications: News & Notes, quarterly. **Remarks:** Maintained by Morrison County Historical Society.

★17810★
WEYERHAEUSER COMPANY - ARCHIVES (Sci-Engr)
Tacoma, WA 98477 Phone: (205)924-5051
Donnie Crespo, Archv.
Staff: Prof 3; Other 2. **Subjects:** Weyerhaeuser Company, forest products, logging, lumber manufacturing, pulp/paperboard, Pacific Northwest. **Holdings:** 2000 cubic feet and 128 linear feet of archival material including correspondence and office files, 1900-1983, ledgers, journals, annual and financial reports, biographical files, speeches of company executives and personnel, company publications, minute books of the company, photographs of company facilities and operations, photographs of logging in the Northwest, films, oral history interviews, artifacts and memorabilia, maps. **Services:** Copying (limited); archives open to the public with restrictions. **Publications:** Weyerhaeuser Company Archives, 1981; The White River Lumber Company, 1979; Clemons Tree Farm, 1981; Weyerhaeuser Timber Company History 1900-1950. **Special Catalogs:** Shelf lists; content notes; descriptive catalogs. **Staff:** Pauline Larson, Asst.Archv..

★17811★
WEYERHAEUSER COMPANY - CORPORATE LIBRARY (Bus-Fin)
CH 1-W Phone: (206)924-3030
Tacoma, WA 98477 Karin H. Williams, Mgr.
Founded: 1952. **Staff:** Prof 11. **Subjects:** Business, economics, forestry, finance, law/tax, management, marketing. **Special Collections:** Annual reports of major national and foreign companies (5000 cataloged items); Conference Board collection; SRI Business Intelligence Program Audiovisual Collection (700 items). **Holdings:** 10,000 books; 8 drawers of maps; 4 VF drawers. **Subscriptions:** 450 journals and other serials; 40 newspapers. **Automated Operations:** Computerized cataloging, acquisitions, and serials. **Services:** Interlibrary loan; copying; SDI; library open to the public with restrictions. **Computerized Information Services:** DIALOG Information Services, Pergamon ORBIT InfoLine, Inc., BRS Information Technologies, Info Globe, NEXIS, LEXIS, Dow Jones News/Retrieval, Western Library Network (WLN); OnTyme Electronic Message Network Service (electronic mail service). **Networks/Consortia:** Member of Western Library Network (WLN). **Publications:** Bulletin of new services and holdings, monthly. **Remarks:** Maintains Law/Tax Library and Marketing & Economic Research Library. **Staff:** Carolyn Burns, Supv., Tech.Serv.; Linda McBroom, Ref.Libn.; Sandra Hanseling, Ref.Libn.; Jerry A. Eckrom, Acq.; Trisha Camozzi-Ekberg, Ref.Libn..

★17812★
WEYERHAEUSER COMPANY - SFRD TECHNICAL INFORMATION CENTER (Biol Sci)
Box 1060 Phone: (501)624-8545
Hot Springs, AR 71902 Evelyn Smith, Libn.
Staff: 1. **Subjects:** Forestry and related subjects. **Holdings:** 5000 pamphlets. **Subscriptions:** 75 journals and other serials. **Services:** Center open to the public with restrictions.

★17813★
WEYERHAEUSER COMPANY - TECHNICAL INFORMATION CENTER (Sci-Engr, Biol Sci)
WTC-TIC Phone: (206)924-6265
Tacoma, WA 98477 L.W. Martinez, Mgr., Tech.Info.Serv.
Founded: 1957. **Staff:** Prof 6; Other 5. **Subjects:** Wood and wood products, forestry, coatings, adhesives, paper chemistry, chemical engineering. **Holdings:** 20,000 books; 30,000 reports. **Subscriptions:** 803 journals and other serials. **Services:** Interlibrary loan; copying (both limited); SDI; center open to the public by permission. **Automated Operations:** Computerized public access catalog, cataloging, acquisitions, serials, and circulation. **Computerized Information Services:** DIALOG Information Services, Pergamon ORBIT InfoLine, Inc., STN International, OCLC, WILSONLINE, ESA/IRS. Performs searches on fee basis. **Publications:** Accession list, monthly - limited circulation; Journal Holdings list, annual; Patent Digest; Technology Awareness Updates. **Special Catalogs:** Journal subject list (computer printout). **Remarks:** An alternate telephone number is 924-6263.

★17814★
WEYERHAEUSER COMPANY - WESTERN FORESTRY RESEARCH CENTER - LIBRARY (Biol Sci)
Box 420 Phone: (206)736-8241
Centralia, WA 98531 Donna Loucks, Libn.
Founded: 1954. **Staff:** Prof 1; Other 1. **Subjects:** Forestry, biology, zoology, ecology, herbicides, pesticides, agronomy, genetics, physiology, dendrology. **Holdings:** 3000 books; 1000 bound periodical volumes; 40,000 reports; 200 dissertations. **Subscriptions:** 150 journals and other serials. **Services:** Copying; library open to the public for reference use only. **Automated Operations:** Computerized cataloging and serials. **Computerized Information Services:** DIALOG Information Services, Pergamon ORBIT InfoLine, Inc.; internal database. **Publications:** Weyerhaeuser Forestry Paper, irregular.

WEYERHAEUSER LIBRARY
See: Macalester College (8269)

★17815★
WHALE CENTER - LIBRARY (Biol Sci)
3929 Piedmont Ave. Phone: (415)654-6621
Oakland, CA 94611 Katherine Bertolucci, Hd.Libn.
Staff: Prof 2. **Subjects:** Whales and whaling - commercial and aboriginal; International Whaling Commission; marine sanctuaries; whale habitat; outer-continental shelf (OCS) lease sales. **Special Collections:** International Whaling Commission documents and reports. **Holdings:** 550 books; 100 bound periodical volumes; 16 VF drawers. **Services:** Copying; library open to the public for reference use only. **Publications:** Newsletters; action alerts; special publications on whaling; ethics; research. **Staff:** Anthony J. Pettinato, Asst.Libn..

★17816★
WHALING MUSEUM SOCIETY, INC. - LIBRARY (Biol Sci)
Main St.
Box 25 Phone: (516)367-3418
Cold Spring Harbor, NY 11724 Ann M. Gill, Exec.Dir.
Founded: 1936. **Staff:** Prof 7. **Subjects:** Whaling, whales, Cold Spring Harbor, marine mammal conservation, coastwise trade under sail, scrimshaw. **Special Collections:** Manuscript collections on whales, whaling, and Cold Spring Harbor (thousands of documents). **Holdings:** 2800 books; 10 drawers of archives; 6 drawers of photographs and prints; 12 reels of microfilm of logbooks. **Subscriptions:** 12 journals and other serials. **Services:** Copying; library open to the public with written application to director. **Publications:** A Whaling Account (newsletter); annual reports; pamphlets; miscellaneous publications; bibliographies.

★17817★
JAMES E. WHALLEY MUSEUM AND LIBRARY (Rec, Hist)
351 Middle St. Phone: (603)436-3712
Portsmouth, NH 03801 Lynn J. Sanderson, Pres.
Founded: 1962. **Staff:** Prof 1; Other 1. **Subjects:** Freemasonry; genealogy; history - New Hampshire, New Hampshire seacoast, Portsmouth. **Special Collections:** Masonic proceedings (500 items); published sermons and orations, 1758 to present; New Hampshire state papers (40 volumes); New Hampshire county histories (10); New Hampshire town histories (50); photograph collections (600); town and city directories (60). **Holdings:** 3600 books; 600 bound periodical volumes; 96 file drawers; 100 boxes; 1000 other cataloged items. **Services:** Copying; library open to the public by appointment.

★17818★
WHATCOM/ISLAND HEALTH SERVICES - LIBRARY (Med)
2901 Squalicum Pkwy. Phone: (206)734-5400
Bellingham, WA 98225 Betty Jo Jensen, Med.Libn.
Founded: 1975. **Staff:** Prof 1. **Subjects:** Medicine. **Holdings:** 600 books. **Subscriptions:** 80 journals and other serials. **Services:** Library not open to the public. **Computerized Information Services:** MEDLINE; OnTyme Electronic Message Network Service (electronic mail service). **Remarks:** Maintained jointly by St. Joseph and St. Luke's Hospitals. Street address and telephone listed above are for St. Joseph Hospital. St. Luke's Hospital's street address and telephone are 809 E. Chestnut St., 647-3815.

★17819★
WHEAT RIDGE REGIONAL CENTER - EMPLOYEE'S LIBRARY (Med)
10285 Ridge Rd. Phone: (303)424-7791
Wheat Ridge, CO 80033 Greg Rowe, Dir.
Staff: Prof 2; Other 2. **Subjects:** Mental retardation, behavior modification, developmental disabilities, child development, psychology, sociology, medicine. **Holdings:** 1145 books; 200 pamphlets. **Subscriptions:** 28 journals

and other serials. **Services:** Library not open to the public. **Networks/Consortia:** Member of Central Colorado Library System (CCLS).

★17820★
WHEATON COLLEGE - BILLY GRAHAM CENTER - ARCHIVES (Rel-Phil)
Wheaton, IL 60187 Robert Shuster, Dir. of Archv.
Founded: 1975. **Staff:** Prof 3; Other 3. **Subjects:** North American Protestant missions and evangelistic work. **Special Collections:** Billy Graham Evangelistic Association; records of Africa Inland Mission, Evangelical Foreign Mission Association, China Inland Mission, South America Mission, and National Religious Broadcasters; papers of Herbert J. Taylor, Paul Rader, R.A. Torrey, Kathryn Kuhlman, Aimee Semple McPherson, and Billy Sunday; Youth for Christ/USA archival materials. **Holdings:** 400 archival and manuscript collections; 20,000 photographs; 6000 audiotapes; 1200 reels of microfilm. **Services:** Interlibrary loan; copying; archives open to the public. **Automated Operations:** Computerized cataloging and acquisitions. **Publications:** From the Graham Center Archives, semiannual - by subscription; guides to special collections. **Staff:** Paul Ericksen, Archv.; Lannae Graham, Ref.Archv..

★17821★
WHEATON COLLEGE - BILLY GRAHAM CENTER - LIBRARY (Rel-Phil)
Wheaton, IL 60187 Phone: (312)260-5194
Ferne L. Weimer, Dir.
Staff: Prof 3; Other 4. **Subjects:** Christian evangelism and missions; history of revivalism; American church history; Celtic church history; patristics. **Special Collections:** Billy Graham Collection; Joint IMC/CBMS Missionary Archives (microfiche); Council for World Mission Archives (microfiche); Moravian Missions to the Indians (microfilm); Early American Imprints; Pamphlets in American History; Human Relations Area Files (microfiche). **Holdings:** 53,000 books; 3500 bound periodical volumes; 1000 theses and dissertations; microforms; imprints and pamphlets. **Subscriptions:** 500 journals and other serials. **Services:** Interlibrary loan; copying; SDI; library open to the public with restrictions. **Automated Operations:** Computerized cataloging. **Computerized Information Services:** OCLC. **Publications:** Resource Notes (newsletter); occasional papers of conferences; occasional short bibliographies. **Staff:** Janet Kennard, Tech.Serv.; Kenneth Gill, Coll.Dev..

★17822★
WHEATON COLLEGE - BUSWELL MEMORIAL LIBRARY (Rel-Phil, Hum)
501 E. Seminary Phone: (312)260-5101
Wheaton, IL 60187 P. Paul Snezek, Dir.
Founded: 1860. **Staff:** Prof 8; Other 11. **Subjects:** American history, religion and theology, American and English literature, science, education. **Special Collections:** Wheaton College archives; Mormonism; Hymnals; American Scientific Affiliation; Keswick Movement; Madeleine L'Engle; Malcolm Muggeridge; Frederich Buechner; John Bunyan; Samuel Johnson; James Boswell; Everett Mitchell; Robert Siegel; Norman Stone; Kenneth Taylor; Hans Rookmaaker. **Holdings:** 189,000 books; 29,300 bound periodical volumes; 166,400 microforms; 19,400 documents; 1800 audiotapes; 150 videotapes; 7400 scores; 6050 phonograph records. **Subscriptions:** 1155 journals and other serials; 19 newspapers. **Services:** Interlibrary loan; copying; library open to visiting scholars. **Automated Operations:** Computerized cataloging. **Computerized Information Services:** DIALOG Information Services, OCLC. **Networks/Consortia:** Member of ILLINET, LIBRAS Inc.. **Publications:** Collegii Bibliotheca; Library Handbook. **Staff:** Jolene Carlson, Hd., Pub.Serv.; Sharon Vance, Hd., Tech.Serv.; Mary Doresett, Hd., Spec.Serv.; Susan Fenton, Asst.Pub.Serv.; John Fawcett, Asst.Pub.Serv. & Mus.Libn.; Joanna Parks, Cat./Curric.Libn..

★17823★
WHEATON COLLEGE - MADELEINE CLARK WALLACE LIBRARY - FINE ARTS COLLECTION (Mus, Art)
Norton, MA 02766 Phone: (617)285-7722
Faith Dickhaut Kindness, Fine Arts Libn.
Founded: 1960. **Staff:** 1. **Subjects:** Art, music. **Holdings:** 25,000 volumes, including scores; 4900 sound recordings; 75,000 slides; 10,000 photographs. **Subscriptions:** 117 journals and other serials. **Services:** Interlibrary loan; copying; collection open to the public for reference use only. **Automated Operations:** Computerized cataloging. **Computerized Information Services:** OCLC, BRS Information Technologies, WILSONLINE, DIALOG Information Services. **Networks/Consortia:** Member of NELINET, Southeastern Massachusetts Cooperating Libraries (SMCL). **Remarks:** The Music Library is located in Watson Hall; the Art Collection is located in the Main Library. The Art Department slide and photograph collections are housed in Watson Hall.

★17824★
WHEATON COLLEGE - MARION E. WADE CENTER (Hum)
Wheaton, IL 60187-5593 Phone: (312)260-5908
Lyle W. Dorsett, Dir.
Founded: 1965. **Staff:** Prof 6. **Subjects:** English and American literature. **Special Collections:** Owen Barfield; G.K. Chesterton; C.S. Lewis (personal library); George MacDonald; J.R.R. Tolkien; Dorothy L. Sayers; Charles Williams. **Holdings:** 12,059 books; 169 bound periodical volumes; 266 bound dissertations; 49 reels of microfilm; 627 audiotapes; 81 videotapes; 25,000 manuscript letters; 426 file folders of manuscripts; 8 VF drawers of articles; artwork and photographs. **Subscriptions:** 34 journals and other serials. **Services:** Copying; center open to the public. **Publications:** SEVEN: An Anglo-American Literary Review, annual - by subscription. **Staff:** Marjorie Lamp Mead, Assoc.Dir.; Virginia Vail Kolb, Asst.Archv.; Betty Carter, Res.Asst..

★17825★
WHEATON COMMUNITY HOSPITAL - MEDICAL LIBRARY (Med)
401 12th St., N. Phone: (612)563-8226
Wheaton, MN 56296 Diana Johnson, Dir.
Staff: 1. **Subjects:** Medicine. **Holdings:** Figures not available. **Subscriptions:** 90 journals and other serials. **Services:** Interlibrary loan; copying; library open to the public with restrictions. **Networks/Consortia:** Member of Valley Medical Network (VMN).

★17826★
WHEATON HISTORICAL ASSOCIATION - LIBRARY & RESEARCH OFFICE (Hist)
Wheaton Village Phone: (609)825-6800
Millville, NJ 08332 Gay Le Cleire Taylor, Cur.
Staff: Prof 2. **Subjects:** Glass history and manufacture, American and European glass, Victorian life, antiques, American architecture. **Special Collections:** Charles B. Gardner Library (200 glass photographs and documents; 53 framed glass documents; 75 glass books). **Holdings:** 1200 books; 25 bound periodical volumes; 100 personal papers of T.C. Wheaton; 35 newspapers and pamphlets; 20 glass ledgers and indentures; 200 photographs of glass factories; 2000 glass slides. **Subscriptions:** 12 journals and other serials. **Services:** Copying; library open to the public by appointment.

★17827★
WHEDON CANCER FOUNDATION - LIBRARY (Med)
30 S. Scott St.
Box 683 Phone: (307)672-2941
Sheridan, WY 82801-0683 Nancy E. Peterson, Lib.Mgr.
Founded: 1981. **Staff:** 1. **Subjects:** Cancer, hospice care, medicine, current events. **Special Collections:** Hospice (250 articles); local medical group histories (3). **Holdings:** 75 books. **Services:** Interlibrary loan; copying; library open to the public for reference use only. **Computerized Information Services:** OCLC, MEDLARS; DOCLINE (electronic mail service). Performs searches free of charge for local physicians and libraries. **Networks/Consortia:** Member of Northeastern Wyoming Medical Library Consortium. **Special Catalogs:** Hospice (printout).

WHEELABRATOR TECHNOLOGIES, INC. - RUST INTERNATIONAL CORPORATION
See: Rust International Corporation (12248)

JOHN M. WHEELER LIBRARY
See: Edward S. Harkness Eye Institute (6024)

★17828★
WHEELING HOSPITAL, INC. - HENRY G. JEPSON MEMORIAL LIBRARY (Med)
Medical Park Phone: (304)243-3308
Wheeling, WV 26003 Rosella M. Saseen, Med.Libn.
Founded: 1936. **Staff:** Prof 1; Other 1. **Subjects:** Medicine, nursing, allied health sciences. **Holdings:** 2200 books; 118 bound periodical volumes; 612 cassettes; 5 VF drawers; pamphlet file. **Subscriptions:** 113 journals and other serials. **Services:** Copying; library open to physicians. **Computerized Information Services:** MEDLINE. **Networks/Consortia:** Member of Southeastern/Atlantic Regional Medical Library Services.

★17829★
WHEELWRIGHT MUSEUM OF THE AMERICAN INDIAN - MARY CABOT WHEELWRIGHT RESEARCH LIBRARY
(Area-Ethnic)
704 Camino Lejo
Box 5153 Phone: (505)982-4636
Santa Fe, NM 87502 Steve Rogers, Cur.
Founded: 1937. **Staff:** 1. **Subjects:** Navajo and American Indian - religion, culture, arts; comparative religions; the Southwest. **Special Collections:** Archival material on Navaho religion, sand paintings, chants, and Southwest Indian art. **Holdings:** 2000 books; 2300 bound periodical volumes; 100 Navaho religion manuscripts; 3000 sound recordings; 1000 slides of sandpaintings and reproductions; 100 Navajo music and prayer tapes. **Services:** Copying; library open to the public by appointment. **Publications:** Navaho Figurines Called Dolls; Introduction to Navaho Sandpaintings. **Special Catalogs:** Exhibition Catalogs - Native American Arts and Culture.

★17830★
WHIDDEN MEMORIAL HOSPITAL - LIBRARY (Med)
103 Garland St. Phone: (617)389-6270
Everett, MA 02149 Selma W. Eigner, Libn.
Staff: Prof 1. **Subjects:** Medicine, nursing, allied health sciences. **Holdings:** 1500 books; 115 bound periodical volumes; 4 shelves of clippings and pamphlets. **Subscriptions:** 69 journals and other serials. **Services:** Interlibrary loan; copying; library open to the public for reference use only. **Networks/Consortia:** Member of Massachusetts Health Sciences Library Network (MAHSLIN).

★17831★
WHIRLPOOL CORPORATION - TECHNICAL INFORMATION CENTER (Sci-Engr)
Monte Rd. Phone: (616)926-5323
Benton Harbor, MI 49022 Gene Heileman, Sr.Info.Spec.
Founded: 1964. **Staff:** Prof 2; Other 1. **Subjects:** Mechanical and electrical engineering, polymer science, food technology. **Holdings:** 7000 books. **Subscriptions:** 350 journals and other serials. **Services:** Interlibrary loan; center open to the public on request. **Automated Operations:** Computerized cataloging and circulation. **Computerized Information Services:** DIALOG Information Services, OCLC, NLM; WIN (Whirlpool Information Network; internal database). **Networks/Consortia:** Member of Michigan Library Consortium (MLC), Berrien Library Consortium. **Publications:** WIN Alert, monthly - for internal distribution only. **Staff:** Karen Heyn, Info.Spec..

JOHN C. WHITAKER LIBRARY
See: Forsyth Memorial Hospital (5266)

MAE M. WHITAKER LIBRARY
See: St. Louis Conservatory and Schools for the Arts (CASA) (12521)

★17832★
WHITE & CASE - LIBRARY (Law)
1155 Ave. of the Americas Phone: (212)819-7569
New York, NY 10036 John J. Banta, Chf. Law Libn.
Founded: 1901. **Staff:** Prof 5; Other 7. **Subjects:** Law. **Holdings:** 50,000 volumes. **Services:** Interlibrary loan; library not open to the public. **Computerized Information Services:** LEXIS, WESTLAW, Dow Jones News/Retrieval, DIALOG Information Services. **Remarks:** White & Case maintains branch libraries at their offices in London, Paris, Hong Kong, Singapore, Stockholm, Turkey, Tokyo, Los Angeles, CA, Miami, FL, and Washington, DC. **Staff:** Sara Wagschal, Asst.Libn.; Pauline Reid, Tax Libn.; Jane Towell, Br.Libn..

CHARLES E. WHITE MEMORIAL LIBRARY
See: University of Maryland, College Park Libraries (16376)

E.G. WHITE RESEARCH CENTER
See: Andrews University - James White Library - Special Collections (775)

ERNEST MILLER WHITE LIBRARY
See: Louisville Presbyterian Theological Seminary (8071)

G.W. BLUNT WHITE LIBRARY
See: Mystic Seaport Museum, Inc. (9481)

★17833★
WHITE HAVEN CENTER - STAFF LIBRARY
Oley Valley Rd.
White Haven, PA 18661
Founded: 1972. **Subjects:** Mental retardation, developmental disabilities. **Holdings:** 1600 books; 1 vertical file. **Remarks:** Presently inactive.

JAMES HERBERT WHITE LIBRARY
See: Mississippi Valley State University (9117)

JAMES WHITE LIBRARY
See: Andrews University - James White Library - Special Collections (775)

JOHN G. WHITE COLLECTION AND RARE BOOKS
See: Cleveland Public Library - Fine Arts and Special Collections Department - Special Collections Section - John G. White Collection and Rare Books (3318)

★17834★
WHITE MEMORIAL MEDICAL CENTER - COURVILLE-ABBOTT MEMORIAL LIBRARY (Med)
1720 Brooklyn Ave. Phone: (213)268-5000
Los Angeles, CA 90033 Joyce Marson, Libn.
Founded: 1920. **Staff:** Prof 2; Other 2. **Subjects:** Medicine, nursing, dietetics, paramedical sciences. **Special Collections:** Library of Dr. Philip J. Vogel. **Holdings:** 45,000 volumes; 8 VF drawers of pamphlets; tapes; phonograph records; filmstrips. **Subscriptions:** 460 journals and other serials. **Services:** Interlibrary loan; copying; library open to the public for reference use only. **Computerized Information Services:** MEDLINE. **Networks/Consortia:** Member of Pacific Southwest Regional Medical Library Service. **Staff:** Mary E. Flake, Ref.Libn..

★17835★
WHITE PLAINS HOSPITAL - MEDICAL LIBRARY (Med)
E. Post Rd. at Davis Ave. Phone: (914)681-1231
White Plains, NY 10601 Joan Giordano, Mgr., Med.Lib.
Staff: Prof 1; Other 1. **Subjects:** Medicine, nursing, allied health fields. **Special Collections:** Patient education (books; pamphlets; journals). **Holdings:** 1000 books; 2900 bound periodical volumes; VF of allied health subjects. **Subscriptions:** 160 journals and other serials. **Services:** Interlibrary loan; copying; SDI; library open to the public for reference use only. **Automated Operations:** Computerized ILL. **Computerized Information Services:** BRS Information Technologies, MEDLINE; DOCLINE (electronic mail service). Performs searches on fee basis. **Networks/Consortia:** Member of Health Information Libraries of Westchester (HILOW), New York Metropolitan Reference and Research Library Agency (METRO). **Publications:** Medical Library News, quarterly - for internal distribution only.

★17836★
WHITE RIVER VALLEY HISTORICAL SOCIETY MUSEUM - LIBRARY (Hist)
918 H St., S.E. Phone: (206)939-2783
Auburn, WA 98002 LaVerna J. Conrad, Libn.
Founded: 1970. **Staff:** Prof 1; Other 3. **Subjects:** Local Northwest history and genealogy, history of local industries. **Special Collections:** Histories of pioneer families. **Holdings:** 400 volumes; 25 boxes of pamphlets; 10 maps; 25 cassette tapes. **Services:** Library open to the public for reference use only.

ROBERT J. WHITE LAW LIBRARY
See: Catholic University of America - School of Law (2761)

ROBERT M. WHITE MEMORIAL LIBRARY
See: Paoli Memorial Hospital (11056)

WILLIAM ALANSON WHITE LIBRARY
See: St. Elizabeths Hospital - Health Sciences Library (12372)

WILLIAM ALLEN WHITE LIBRARY
See: Emporia State University (4695)

WILLIAM M. WHITE BUSINESS LIBRARY
See: University of Colorado, Boulder (16085)

★17837★
WHITE & WILLIAMS - LIBRARY (Law)
1234 Market St.
Philadelphia, PA 19107 Phone: (215)854-7126
Staff: Prof 1; Other 2. **Subjects:** Law. **Holdings:** 13,500 volumes. **Subscriptions:** 80 journals and other serials. **Services:** Interlibrary loan; library not open to the public. **Computerized Information Services:** LEXIS.

WHITEFORD MEMORIAL LIBRARY
See: Foreign Services Research Institute (5254)

WHITEHALL LIBRARY
See: Stonington Historical Society (13698)

ALFRED WHITEHEAD MEMORIAL MUSIC LIBRARY
See: Mount Allison University (9361)

★17838★
WHITMAN COLLEGE - MYRON EELLS LIBRARY OF NORTHWEST HISTORY (Hist)
Penrose Memorial Library
345 Boyer St.
Walla Walla, WA 99362 Phone: (509)527-5191
Subjects: Pacific Northwest - geography, education, politics, government, anthropology, Indians and native peoples, archeology, religion, missions, art, architecture; regional Indian art; historical fiction about the Northwest and Northwesterners; Lewis and Clark; the Oregon Trail. **Holdings:** 5200 books; 140 bound periodical volumes. **Services:** Interlibrary loan; copying. **Automated Operations:** Computerized cataloging and acquisitions.

★17839★
WHITMAN COLLEGE - NORTHWEST AND WHITMAN COLLEGE ARCHIVES (Hist)
Penrose Memorial Library
345 Boyer St. Phone: (509)527-5191
Walla Walla, WA 99362 Lawrence L. Dodd, Archv. & Cur.
Subjects: History of the city of Walla Walla, Walla Walla County, Whitman College, 1804 to present, and the Pacific Northwest. **Special Collections:** Papers of American Board of Commissioners for Foreign Missions-affiliated missionaries in the Pacific Northwest; missionary activities on the Skokomish Indian Reservation, 1874-1907; photographs and manuscripts of Indians of the Pacific Northwest coast; Walla Walla area business records; Whitman College archives; photographs of Walla Walla area. **Holdings:** 900 books; 125 periodicals. **Services:** Copying (limited); archives open to the public for reference use only. **Computerized Information Services:** Spindex III (Historical Records of Washington State).

★17840★
WHITMAN & RANSOM - LIBRARY (Law)
200 Park Ave. Phone: (212)351-3000
New York, NY 10166 Lynn Orfe, Libn.
Founded: 1920. **Staff:** Prof 2; Other 2. **Subjects:** Law, corporate law. **Special Collections:** Japanese Law (1600 volumes). **Holdings:** 9000 volumes. **Services:** Interlibrary loan; copying; library open to the public with restrictions. **Computerized Information Services:** DIALOG Information Services, LEXIS, WESTLAW, Dow Jones News/Retrieval, VU/TEXT Information Services. **Staff:** Allen Miller, Asst.Libn..

★17841★
WALT WHITMAN ASSOCIATION - LIBRARY (Hum)
328 Mickle St. Phone: (609)541-8280
Camden, NJ 08102 Denise Buzz, Dir.
Founded: 1920. **Staff:** Prof 1; Other 1. **Subjects:** Walt Whitman. **Special Collections:** 19th and 20th century American poetry. **Holdings:** 600 books. **Services:** Library open to the public by appointment. **Automated Operations:** Computerized cataloging. **Computerized Information Services:** RLIN. **Publications:** Mickle Street Review, annual. **Special Catalogs:** Mickle Street Review No. 9 (catalog of books and manuscripts in the Walt Whitman Library).

★17842★
WALT WHITMAN BIRTHPLACE ASSOCIATION - LIBRARY AND MUSEUM (Hum)
246 Old Walt Whitman Rd. Phone: (516)427-5240
Huntington Station, NY 11746 Barbara Bart, Dir.
Founded: 1949. **Staff:** 5. **Subjects:** Books by and about Walt Whitman. **Special Collections:** Translations and studies in foreign languages including Japanese and Catalan. **Holdings:** 350 books; artifacts; plaques; portraits; scrapbooks; rare monographs; catalogs; pamphlets; bibliographies; letters; broadsides; photostats of manuscripts; file of Walt Whitman Review; Walt Whitman Fellowship Papers. **Services:** Library open to the public for reference use only. **Publications:** Broadsides of Whitman prose and poetry - for sale; West Hills Review - A Walt Whitman Journal, annual - for sale.

★17843★
WHITNEY COMMUNICATIONS COMPANY - RESEARCH LIBRARY (Publ)
Time & Life Bldg., Rm. 4600
110 W. 51st St. Phone: (212)582-2300
New York, NY 10020 Andrea Zalaznick, Res.Mgr.
Founded: 1970. **Staff:** Prof 2. **Subjects:** Publishing, finance, business, broadcasting. **Special Collections:** New York Herald Tribune historical material. **Holdings:** 100 VF drawers of corporate records and archives of Whitney Communications Company. **Subscriptions:** 75 journals and other serials. **Services:** Library open to SLA members by appointment. **Computerized Information Services:** Dow Jones News/Retrieval; internal database. **Special Indexes:** Corporate files.

★17844★
ELI WHITNEY MUSEUM - LIBRARY
Box 6099
Hamden, CT 06517
Subjects: Antique arms. **Special Collections:** Photo archive (8000 transparencies of American and European arms and private collections); arms auction and sales catalogs, 1900 to present. **Holdings:** 1200 books. **Remarks:** Presently inactive.

WHITNEY INFORMATION SERVICES
See: General Electric Company - Corporate Research & Development (5527)

WHITNEY LIBRARY
See: New Haven Colony Historical Society (9956)

★17845★
WHITNEY MUSEUM OF AMERICAN ART - LIBRARY (Art)
945 Madison Ave. Phone: (212)570-3649
New York, NY 10021 May Castleberry, Libn.
Founded: 1931. **Staff:** Prof 1; Other 2. **Subjects:** American art, particularly of the 20th century. **Holdings:** 20,000 volumes; 200 periodical titles; 79 VF drawers of clippings on American artists. **Subscriptions:** 47 journals and other serials. **Services:** Library open by appointment to qualified researchers only.

JERE WHITSON MEMORIAL LIBRARY
See: Tennessee Technological University (14029)

★17846★
WHITTAKER COMMAND & CONTROL SYSTEMS, INC. - LIBRARY (Mil)
23670 Hawthorne Blvd.
Torrance, CA 90505
Subjects: Military and commercial systems and equipment. **Holdings:** 100 books; 2500 reports. **Subscriptions:** 10 journals and other serials. **Services:** Library not open to the public. **Formed by the merger of:** Whittaker Command Control Systems and Lee Telecommunications.

WHITTAKER CORPORATION - TASKER SYSTEMS DIVISION
See: Whittaker Electronic Systems (17847)

★17847★
WHITTAKER ELECTRONIC SYSTEMS - TECHNICAL LIBRARY (Sci-Engr)
1785 Voyager Ave.
Box 8000 Phone: (818)341-3010
Simi Valley, CA 93063-8000 Orlean A. Hinds, Libn.
Staff: Prof 1. **Subjects:** Engineering, electronics, management, mathematics. **Holdings:** 3200 books; military specifications and standards; patents; 12,000 unbound reports; 6000 reports on microfiche and microfilm. **Subscriptions:** 165 journals and other serials. **Services:** Library not open to the public. **Computerized Information Services:** DIALOG Information Services. **Remarks:** An alternate telephone number is (805)584-8200. **Formerly:** Whittaker Corporation - Tasker Systems Division.

★17848★
WHITTAKER TECHNICAL PRODUCTS, INC. - WHITTAKER-YARDNEY POWER SYSTEMS - TECHNICAL INFORMATION CENTER (Sci-Engr)
82 Mechanic St. Phone: (203)599-1100
Pawcatuck, CT 02891 Marion Durfee, Libn.
Founded: 1960. **Staff:** Prof 1. **Subjects:** Batteries, electrochemistry, chemistry, electrical engineering, metallurgy, plastics. **Holdings:** 1000 books. **Subscriptions:** 10 journals and other serials. **Services:** Center not open to the public. **Formerly:** Yardney Electric Corporation.

WHITTEN CENTER LIBRARY & MEDIA RESOURCE SERVICES
See: South Carolina State Department of Mental Retardation (13387)

★17849★
WHITTIER COLLEGE - DEPARTMENT OF GEOLOGY - FAIRCHILD AERIAL PHOTOGRAPHY COLLECTION (Geog-Map)
Whittier, CA 90608 Phone: (213)693-0771
Dallas D. Rhodes, Dir.
Founded: 1965. **Staff:** Prof 1; Other 3. **Subjects:** Aerial photographs, primarily of California, 1924-1965; partial coverage of 49 states and 29 countries. **Special Collections:** Fairchild Collection including 2350 flights (300,000 prints; 100,000 negatives; 500 photo-mosaic flight indexes; 500 orthophoto maps). **Services:** Interlibrary loan (fee); copying; collection open to the public on a fee basis. **Special Indexes:** Inventory of flights (looseleaf); Flight Index Maps.

★17850★
WHITTIER COLLEGE - SCHOOL OF LAW - LIBRARY (Law)
5353 W. 3rd St. Phone: (213)938-3621
Los Angeles, CA 90020 J. Denny Haythorn, Dir., Law Lib./Prof.
Staff: Prof 7; Other 5. **Subjects:** American law. **Holdings:** 158,330 volumes; 365 cassettes. **Subscriptions:** 2610 journals and other serials; 21 newspapers. **Services:** Interlibrary loan; copying; library open to attorneys, law students, and others wishing to use legal research materials. **Automated Operations:** Computerized cataloging. **Computerized Information Services:** WESTLAW, LEXIS, DIALOG Information Services, RLIN. **Networks/Consortia:** Member of CLASS. **Publications:** Whittier Law Review, quarterly - by subscription. **Staff:** Christopher Noe, Ref./Circ.; Rosanne Krikorian, Asst.Dir.; Christa Gowan, Ser.; Frank Gallegos, Cat.; Virbala Thaker, Govt.Docs..

★17851★
WHITTIER HOME ASSOCIATION - LIBRARY (Hist)
86 Friend St. Phone: (508)388-1337
Amesbury, MA 01913 Gloria Leslie, Cur.
Subjects: John Greenleaf Whittier. **Holdings:** Figures not available. **Services:** Library open to the public for reference use only on a limited schedule and for a fee. **Remarks:** The library at the Whittier home consists of books, pamphlets, newspapers, letters, and other documents which belonged to poet and abolitionist John Greenleaf Whittier. It is now being cataloged for the first time and will be available to visitors.

N. PAUL WHITTIER HISTORICAL AVIATION LIBRARY
See: San Diego Aero-Space Museum - N. Paul Whittier Historical Aviation Library (12758)

★17852★
WHITWORTH COLLEGE - SCIENCE LIBRARY (Sci-Engr)
Spokane, WA 99251 Phone: (509)489-3550
Hans E. Bynagle, Lib.Dir.
Founded: 1955. **Staff:** 1. **Subjects:** Chemistry, physics, geology, biology. **Holdings:** 3000 books; 1700 bound periodical volumes; 60 filmstrips; 750 microcards; 3 VF drawers of supply and book catalogs; 100 pamphlets. **Subscriptions:** 66 journals and other serials. **Services:** Interlibrary loan; copying; library open to the public for reference use only.

WHOOPING CRANE ARCHIVAL LIBRARY
See: Saskatchewan Museum of Natural History - Library (12913)

JOHN L. WHORTON MEDIA CENTER
See: First Baptist Church (5028)

JOHN A. WHYTE MEDICAL LIBRARY
See: Delaware Valley Medical Center - John A. Whyte Medical Library (4167)

WHYTE MUSEUM OF THE CANADIAN ROCKIES - ALPINE CLUB OF CANADA
See: Alpine Club of Canada (334)

★17853★
WHYTE MUSEUM OF THE CANADIAN ROCKIES - ARCHIVES-LIBRARY (Hist, Area-Ethnic)
Box 160 Phone: (403)762-2291
Banff, AB, Canada T0L 0C0 Edward J. Hart, Dir.
Founded: 1965. **Staff:** Prof 2; Other 2. **Subjects:** History, peoples, and natural history of the Canadian Rockies. **Holdings:** 4702 books and pamphlets; 141 bound periodical volumes; 520 manuscript collections; 280,000 photographs; 76 reels of microfilm; 400 audiotapes. **Subscriptions:** 39 journals and other serials; 7 newspapers. **Services:** Copying; archives open to the public for reference use only. **Publications:** The CAIRN Quarterly. **Special Indexes:** Inventory of the Catharine Robb Whyte Collection, 1987. **Remarks:** The museum also administers the Alpine Club of Canada Library. **Staff:** Mary Andrews, Libn.; Donald Bourdon, Hd.Archv..

HAROLD E. WIBBERLEY, JR. LIBRARY
See: Brazilian-American Cultural Institute, Inc. (1825)

★17854★
WICHITA ART ASSOCIATION, INC. - REFERENCE LIBRARY (Art)
9112 E. Central Phone: (316)686-6687
Wichita, KS 67206 Janet Murfin, Chm., Lib.Comm.
Founded: 1920. **Staff:** Prof 1; Other 4. **Subjects:** Art. **Holdings:** 3000 volumes. **Subscriptions:** 10 journals and other serials. **Services:** Library open to the public.

★17855★
WICHITA ART MUSEUM - LIBRARY (Art)
619 Stackman Dr. Phone: (316)268-4921
Wichita, KS 67203 Lois F. Crane, Libn.
Founded: 1935. **Staff:** Prof 1; Other 2. **Subjects:** American art, general art history. **Holdings:** 3230 books; 14 VF drawers; 5300 slides. **Subscriptions:** 41 journals and other serials. **Services:** Library open to the public for reference use only.

★17856★
WICHITA EAGLE-BEACON - LIBRARY (Publ)
825 E. Douglas
Box 820 Phone: (316)268-6554
Wichita, KS 67202 Sally Stratton, Libn.
Founded: 1912. **Staff:** Prof 2; Other 3. **Subjects:** Newspaper reference topics. **Holdings:** 1000 books; 400,000 clippings; 200,000 photographs; pamphlets; maps; microfilm. **Subscriptions:** 20 journals and other serials. **Services:** Library not open to the public. **Computerized Information Services:** Dow Jones News/Retrieval, VU/TEXT Information Services. **Staff:** Allan Tanner, Asst.Libn..

★17857★
WICHITA FALLS STATE HOSPITAL - THOMAS J. GALVIN MEMORIAL MEDICAL LIBRARY (Med)
Box 300 Phone: (817)692-1220
Wichita Falls, TX 76307 E. Joe Roberts, Libn.
Staff: 1. **Subjects:** Psychiatry, psychology, surgery and nursing, philosophy, anatomy, education, forensic medicine, history of medicine. **Special Collections:** Bassett Collection (anatomy); Baker and Baker Collection (neurology). **Holdings:** 3500 books; 50 bound periodical volumes; 1050 AV programs; 200 pamphlets; 100 medical reports. **Subscriptions:** 67 journals and other serials. **Services:** Interlibrary loan; copying; library open to the public with restrictions. **Computerized Information Services:** The Source Information Network, DIALOG Information Services, PaperChase. Performs searches on fee basis. **Networks/Consortia:** Member of TALON. **Publications:** Library Notes International, quarterly - free upon request.

★17858★
WICHITA GENERAL HOSPITAL - MEDICAL LIBRARY (Med)
1600 8th St. Phone: (817)723-1461
Wichita Falls, TX 76301 Marge Alexander, Dir. of Educ.
Founded: 1915. **Subjects:** Medicine, nursing. **Holdings:** 1000 books; 25 bound periodical volumes; 10 medical journals; 20 nursing journals. **Subscriptions:** 18 journals and other serials. **Services:** Interlibrary loan; library not open to the public.

★17859★
WICHITA PUBLIC LIBRARY - BUSINESS AND TECHNOLOGY DIVISION (Bus-Fin, Sci-Engr)
223 S. Main Phone: (316)262-0611
Wichita, KS 67202 Brian Beattie, Hd., Bus. & Tech.
Founded: 1950. **Staff:** Prof 3; Other 5. **Subjects:** Aeronautics, petroleum, geology, economics, mathematics, taxes, finances, firearms, automobiles, business management. **Holdings:** 90,128 volumes; Patent Gazette, 1872 to present, on microfilm; 22,839 pamphlets; 2737 auto repair manuals; 1385 telephone directories. **Subscriptions:** 304 journals and other serials; 6 newspapers. **Services:** Interlibrary loan; copying. **Automated Operations:** Computerized cataloging and circulation. **Computerized Information Services:** DIALOG Information Services. **Publications:** Occasional book lists and bibliographies. **Staff:** Jimmie Hooper, Asst.Dept.Hd.; Jayne Young, Asst. II.

★17860★
WICHITA-SEDGWICK COUNTY HISTORICAL MUSEUM - LIBRARY & ARCHIVES (Hist)
204 S. Main Phone: (316)265-9314
Wichita, KS 67202 Robert A. Puckett, Dir.
Staff: 2. **Subjects:** Local and state history. **Special Collections:** Complete collection of Wichita city directories, 1874 to present; M.C. Naftzger Collection (books on Wichita and Kansas history). **Holdings:** 600 books; 50 bound periodical volumes; 75 other cataloged items; 6 VF drawers of clippings. **Services:** Copying; library open to the public with restrictions. **Publications:** Heritage, quarterly.

★17861★
WICHITA STATE UNIVERSITY - DEPARTMENT OF CHEMISTRY - LLOYD MC KINLEY MEMORIAL CHEMISTRY LIBRARY (Sci-Engr)
1845 Fairmount Phone: (316)689-3120
Wichita, KS 67208 B. Jack McCormick
Founded: 1926. **Staff:** 1. **Subjects:** Chemistry. **Holdings:** 6000 books; 8000 bound periodical volumes; 1000 periodical volumes on microcard. **Subscriptions:** 130 journals and other serials. **Services:** Interlibrary loan; library open to the public for reference use only.

★17862★
WICHITA STATE UNIVERSITY - SPECIAL COLLECTIONS (Hist)
Abalh Library
Box 68 Phone: (316)689-3590
Wichita, KS 67208 Michael T. Kelly, Cur.
Staff: Prof 1; Other 1. **Subjects:** State and local history, congressional papers, radical pamphlets, history of printing, slavery and abolitionism, university archives, history of hypnotism/mesmerism, World War I aviation. **Special Collections:** Robert T. Aitchison Collection (history of printing; 1582 books); Tinterow Collection (history of hypnotism; 188 books); Merrill Collection of W.L. Garrison papers (abolitionists; 6 linear feet). **Holdings:** 4500 volumes; 330 Kansas maps; 719 linear feet of manuscript collections and pamphlets; 2400 theses; 109 linear feet of archival materials. **Services:** Interlibrary loan; copying; collections open to the public. **Automated Operations:** Computerized cataloging. **Publications:** Guide to the Collections, irregular; Illuminator, annual - to Library Associates. **Special Catalogs:** Manuscript registers.

★17863★
WICHITA STATE UNIVERSITY - THURLOW LIEURANCE MEMORIAL MUSIC LIBRARY (Mus)
Walter Duerksen Fine Arts Center Phone: (316)689-3029
Wichita, KS 67208 David L. Austin, Mus.Libn.
Founded: 1926. **Staff:** Prof 1; Other 2. **Subjects:** Music. **Special Collections:** Kansas Music Teachers' Association Archives; Thurlow Lieurance Archives. **Holdings:** 16,500 books; 1800 bound periodical volumes; 13,500 phonograph records; 21,500 scores. **Services:** Interlibrary loan; library open to the public. **Automated Operations:** Computerized cataloging, acquisitions, serials, and circulation. **Networks/Consortia:** Member of AMIGOS Bibliographic Council, Inc..

★17864★
WICKES COMPANIES - MARKETING LIBRARY (Bus-Fin)
26261 Evergreen Rd.
Box 999
Southfield, MI 48037 Phone: (313)355-8517
Founded: 1980. **Subjects:** Business, marketing. **Holdings:** 50 books; corporate annual and 10K reports. **Subscriptions:** 50 journals and other serials. **Services:** Interlibrary loan; library not open to the public.

★17865★
WIDE WORLD PHOTOS, INC. (Aud-Vis)
50 Rockefeller Plaza Phone: (212)621-1930
New York, NY 10020 Jim Donna, Dir.
Staff: Prof 35. **Subjects:** News, sports, and feature pictures on all subjects. **Holdings:** 50 million news and feature type pictures. **Services:** Pictures for newspaper and commercial use; photography assignments, distribution, and transmission of pictures; print and reproduction fees charged.

WIDENER UNIVERSITY - DELAWARE COUNTY HISTORICAL SOCIETY
See: Delaware County Historical Society (4148)

★17866★
WIDENER UNIVERSITY - DELAWARE LAW SCHOOL - LAW LIBRARY (Law)
Concord Pike
Box 7475 Phone: (302)478-5280
Wilmington, DE 19803 Eileen B. Cooper, Dir.
Founded: 1971. **Staff:** Prof 9; Other 11. **Subjects:** Law. **Holdings:** 126,000 books; 78,000 volumes in microform. **Subscriptions:** 600 journals and other serials; 11 newspapers. **Services:** Interlibrary loan; copying; library open to the public. **Automated Operations:** Computerized cataloging, acquisitions, serials, and ILL. **Computerized Information Services:** LEXIS, WESTLAW, DIALOG Information Services. **Networks/Consortia:** Member of Mid-Atlantic Law Library Cooperative (MALLCO), Delaware Library Consortium. **Staff:** Karin Thurman, Hd., Pub.Serv.; Jacqui Paul, Cat.; Mary Alice Peeling, Ser.Libn.; Janet Hirt, Ref.; Mary Jane Mallonee, Ref.; Lisa Clark, AV; Sandra Sadow, Acq.; Betsy Smith, Ref..

★17867★
WIDENER UNIVERSITY - WOLFGRAM MEMORIAL LIBRARY (Hum)
17th & Walnut Sts. Phone: (215)499-4066
Chester, PA 19013 Theresa Taborsky, Dir.
Founded: 1821. **Staff:** Prof 10; Other 15. **Subjects:** Arts and sciences, behavioral sciences, education, economics and management, engineering, nursing. **Special Collections:** Wolfgram Collection (English literature). **Holdings:** 134,928 volumes; 39,668 bound periodical volumes; 19,880 microforms; 8245 AV programs; vertical files. **Subscriptions:** 1840 journals and other serials. **Services:** Interlibrary loan; copying; library open to the public with restrictions. **Automated Operations:** Computerized cataloging, acquisitions, and serials. **Computerized Information Services:** BRS Information Technologies, DIALOG Information Services, VU/TEXT Information Services, OCLC. Performs searches on fee basis. Contact Person: Maria Varki, Ref., 499-4080. **Networks/Consortia:** Member of PALINET, Tri-State College Library Cooperative (TCLC), Interlibrary Delivery Service of Pennsylvania (IDS), Consortium for Health Information & Library Services (CHI). **Publications:** WolfGRAMS, 4/year - to academic community. **Remarks:** The Wolfgram Memorial Library houses the collections of the Delaware County Historical Society and the Lindsay Law Library. **Staff:** T. Cartularo, Ref.; D. Fidishun, AV; R. Goldstein, Cat. & Ser.; K.J. Kim, Pub.Serv.; P. Lenkowski, Ref.; D. Medzie, Acq.; P. O'Neill, Ref..

★17868★
WIDETT, SLATER & GOLDMAN P.C. - LIBRARY (Law)
60 State St. Phone: (617)227-7200
Boston, MA 02109 Sarah G. Connell, Hd. Law Libn.
Staff: Prof 1; Other 2. **Subjects:** Law - corporation, real estate, securities, antitrust, government contracts, banking, estate planning, family, hospital, probate, tax, bankruptcy, education, labor. **Special Collections:** Memoranda of Law Archives (200 legal memoranda). **Holdings:** 12,000 books; 500 bound periodical volumes. **Subscriptions:** 400 journals and other serials; 10 newspapers. **Services:** Interlibrary loan; copying; SDI; library open to the public with restrictions. **Computerized Information Services:** LEXIS, DISCLOSURE Online Database. **Publications:** WS&G Library News - to attorneys. **Special Catalogs:** Catalog to Memoranda of Law Archives (card).

WILLIAM E. WIENER ORAL HISTORY LIBRARY
See: American Jewish Committee (571)

WIGGANS HEALTH SCIENCES LIBRARY
See: Norwalk Hospital (10516)

★17869★
WIGGIN AND DANA - LIBRARY (Law)
195 Church St.
Box 1832
New Haven, CT 06508 Phone: (203)789-1511
Staff: 2. **Subjects:** Law. **Holdings:** 13,000 books. **Services:** Library not open to the public. **Computerized Information Services:** LEXIS, WESTLAW, DIALOG Information Services, Dow Jones News/Retrieval. **Staff:** Ellen R. Jarrett, Libn.; Rosemarie Kjerulf, Libn..

★17870★
WIGHT CONSULTING ENGINEERS, INC. - TECHNICAL LIBRARY (Sci-Engr)
127 S. Northwest Hwy. Phone: (312)381-1800
Barrington, IL 60010 Sally M. Trainer, Sec.
Staff: Prof 1; Other 2. **Subjects:** Water, sanitary engineering, city planning, transportation, environment, industrial waste. **Holdings:** 1800 books; 400 bound periodical volumes; 50 directories. **Subscriptions:** 30 journals and other serials; 5 newspapers. **Services:** Interlibrary loan; copying; library open to the public upon request.

★17871★
WILBERFORCE UNIVERSITY - REMBERT-STOKES LEARNING CENTER - ARCHIVES AND SPECIAL COLLECTIONS (Hist, Area-Ethnic)
Wilberforce, OH 45384 Phone: (513)376-2911
Jean Mulhern, Chf.Libn.
Staff: Prof 2; Other 3. **Subjects:** African Methodist Episcopal (A.M.E.) Church history; books by and about blacks, 19th century; history of Wilberforce University. **Special Collections:** A.M.E. Church conference minutes; papers of Bishop Reverdy Cassius Ransom, university president W.S. Scarborough, and Wilberforce professor Milton S.J. Wright. **Holdings:** 2000 books; 20 reels of microfilm; 10,000 uncataloged items. **Services:** Copying; collections open to the public by appointment. **Networks/Consortia:** Member of Southwest Ohio Council for Higher Education (SOCHE). **Publications:** Printed guides to some parts of collection. **Staff:** Jacqueline Y. Brown, Asst.Libn./Dir., Archv..

WILBOUR LIBRARY OF EGYPTOLOGY
See: Brooklyn Museum (1943)

PETER WILCOCK LIBRARY
See: Charles Camsell General Hospital (2284)

★17872★
G.N. WILCOX MEMORIAL HOSPITAL & HEALTH CENTER - MEDICAL LIBRARY (Med)
3420 Kuhio Hwy.
Lihue, HI 96766 Phone: (808)245-1100
Founded: 1971. **Staff:** 1. **Subjects:** Medicine. **Special Collections:** Doctors of Hawaii - in memoriam (5 volumes). **Holdings:** 400 books; 35 bound periodical volumes; 150 cassette tapes. **Subscriptions:** 70 journals and other serials. **Services:** Interlibrary loan; copying; library open to the public. **Networks/Consortia:** Member of Pacific Southwest Regional Medical Library Service.

WILCOX LIBRARY
See: William Penn College (11151)

★17873★
WILDERNESS LEADERSHIP INTERNATIONAL - OUTDOOR LIVING LIBRARY (Rec)
Wilderness Leadership Center
Box 770
North Fork, CA 93643 Miriam Darnall, Act.Libn.
Founded: 1970. **Subjects:** Wilderness survival, edible wild plants, camping, mountaineering, homestead skills, health. **Holdings:** 4000 books; 300 magazine articles, pamphlets, reprints; films; slide/tape sets.

★17874★
WILDLIFE MANAGEMENT INSTITUTE - LIBRARY (Env-Cons)
1101 Fourteenth St., N.W., Suite 725 Phone: (202)347-1774
Washington, DC 20005 Richard E. McCabe, Dir., Pubns.
Staff: Prof 9. **Subjects:** Wildlife and conservation. **Special Collections:** Complete Transactions of North American Wildlife and Natural Resources Conference; Proceedings of American Game Conference (complete set); American Game Bulletin (complete run). **Holdings:** 1000 volumes. **Subscriptions:** 50 journals and other serials. **Services:** Library open to the public with restrictions. **Special Indexes:** 40-year cumulative index to Transactions of North American Wildlife and Natural Resources Conference.

ERNEST A. WILDMAN SCIENCE LIBRARY
See: Earlham College (4484)

★17875★
WILDWOOD HISTORICAL COMMISSION - WILDWOOD LIBRARY OF NEW JERSEY HISTORY (Hist)
4400 New Jersey Ave., Rm. 214
Wildwood, NJ 08260 Phone: (609)522-2444
Founded: 1962. **Subjects:** State and local history, American history. **Holdings:** 1200 books; 2300 bound periodical volumes; 1400 school records; newspapers, 1899 to present; city records; clippings; photographs. **Services:** Library open to the public on limited schedule.

★17876★
JOHN WILEY AND SONS, INC. - INFORMATION CENTER (Publ)
605 Third Ave. Phone: (212)850-6050
New York, NY 10158 Helen Witsenhausen, Corp.Libn.
Staff: Prof 1. **Subjects:** Publishing, business and management, computers, higher education. **Holdings:** 500 books; 9 VF drawers of clippings. **Subscriptions:** 35 journals and other serials. **Services:** Center not open to the public. **Automated Operations:** Computerized cataloging and acquisitions. **Computerized Information Services:** DIALOG Information Services, NEXIS, Dow Jones News/Retrieval, CompuServe, Inc.; internal databases. Performs searches on fee basis. **Publications:** New acquisitions memo, monthly - for internal distribution only.

★17877★
WILKES, ARTIS, HEDRICK & LANE, CHARTERED - LAW LIBRARY (Law)
1666 K St., N.W., 11th Fl. Phone: (202)457-7871
Washington, DC 20006 David W. Lang, Law Libn.
Founded: 1926. **Staff:** Prof 2; Other 2. **Subjects:** Law - real estate, tax, communications, eminent domain, zoning; municipal affairs. **Holdings:** 20,000 books; 1260 bound periodical volumes; 2300 microfiche; 2100 ultrafiche; 61 audiotapes; 7 videotapes. **Subscriptions:** 114 journals and other serials. **Services:** Interlibrary loan; SDI; library open to the public by appointment. **Computerized Information Services:** NEXIS, LEXIS, DIALOG Information Services, Dow Jones News/Retrieval. **Publications:** D.C. Code Updater, monthly - by subscription; Library Report, weekly - for internal distribution only. **Special Indexes:** Index to FCC Daily Releases (book); D.C. Legislative Service (book); Subject Index to Bills of D.C. Council, quarterly - by subscription. **Staff:** Barbara S. Wilson, Asst.Libn..

★17878★
WILKES-BARRE GENERAL HOSPITAL - HOSPITAL LIBRARY (Med)
Auburn & River Sts. Phone: (717)829-8111
Wilkes-Barre, PA 18764 Rosemarie Kazda Taylor, Dir., Lib./Commun.
Founded: 1935. **Staff:** Prof 1; Other 1. **Subjects:** Medicine, nursing, allied health sciences, hospital administration. **Holdings:** 3312 books; 234 titles on microfilm; AV programs; 5 VF drawers of pamphlets; periodicals. **Subscriptions:** 395 journals and other serials. **Services:** Interlibrary loan; copying; SDI; library open to health personnel. **Automated Operations:** Computerized serials and circulation. **Computerized Information Services:** MEDLARS, DIALOG Information Services. Performs searches on fee basis. **Networks/Consortia:** Member of Northeastern Pennsylvania Bibliographic Center (NEPBC), Health Information Library Network of Northeastern Pennsylvania (HILNNEP), Greater Northeastern Regional Medical Library Program. **Special Indexes:** Medical Index, monthly - for internal distribution, area libraries, and by request.

★17879★
WILKES-BARRE LAW AND LIBRARY ASSOCIATION (Law)
Courthouse, Rm. 23 Phone: (717)822-6712
Wilkes-Barre, PA 18711 Lawrence H. Sindaco, Libn.
Staff: Prof 3. **Subjects:** Law. **Holdings:** 30,000 books; 200 bound periodical volumes. **Subscriptions:** 20 journals and other serials. **Services:** Copying; library open to those directly involved in the legal profession. **Publications:** Luzerne Legal Register, weekly.

★17880★
WILKES COLLEGE - EARTH AND ENVIRONMENTAL SCIENCES READING ROOM
Farley Library
Box 111
Wilkes-Barre, PA 18766
Subjects: Earth sciences, environmental sciences, urban planning, astronomy. **Special Collections:** Local acid mine drainage; local coal mining. **Holdings:** 1000 books; 100 bound periodical volumes; 3000 maps. **Remarks:** Presently inactive.

★17881★
WILKES COLLEGE - INSTITUTE OF REGIONAL AFFAIRS - LIBRARY
Box 111
Wilkes-Barre, PA 18766
Subjects: Government - local, state, in-service training; economic development; legislative reference (state). **Special Collections:** Flood Recovery Collection, 1972 (records of Flood Recovery Task Force, Inc.). **Holdings:** 5000 books; 2000 bound periodical volumes; 3000 pamphlets, studies, reports; 20 file cabinets of news clippings; 500 maps. **Remarks:** Presently inactive.

WILKES LIBRARY
See: Strayer College (13713)

WALTER L. WILKINS BIO-MEDICAL LIBRARY
See: U.S. Navy - Naval Health Research Center (15405)

★17882★
WILL COUNTY HISTORICAL SOCIETY - ARCHIVES (Hist)
803 S. State St. Phone: (815)838-5080
Lockport, IL 60441 Rose Bucciferro, Cur.
Subjects: History of Will County, Illinois, and the Illinois and Michigan Canal, 1830-1935; genealogy. **Holdings:** 350,000 archival materials, including property records, surname files, biographies, cemetery records. **Services:** Archives not open to the public. **Remarks:** Manual search services available by written request on a fee basis.

★17883★
WILLAMETTE UNIVERSITY - LAW LIBRARY (Law)
250 Winter St., S.E. Phone: (503)370-6386
Salem, OR 97301 Richard F. Breen, Jr., Law Libn.
Founded: 1883. **Staff:** Prof 3; Other 4. **Subjects:** Law. **Holdings:** 110,000 volumes. **Subscriptions:** 2200 journals and other serials; 7 newspapers. **Services:** Interlibrary loan; copying; library open to the public. **Automated Operations:** Computerized cataloging. **Computerized Information Services:** WESTLAW, OCLC. **Staff:** Mary Edith Gilbertson, Per.Libn.; Lysa Hall, Law Cat..

FRANCES E. WILLARD MEMORIAL LIBRARY
See: National Woman's Christian Temperance Union (9819)

★17884★
WILLARD LIBRARY OF EVANSVILLE - SPECIAL COLLECTIONS DEPARTMENT (Hist)
21 First Ave. Phone: (812)425-4309
Evansville, IN 47710 Joan M. Elliott, Spec.Coll.Libn.
Staff: Prof 2; Other 2. **Subjects:** History and genealogy of Evansville, Vanderburgh County, and the surrounding areas in Indiana, Illinois, and Kentucky, 1800 to present. **Special Collections:** Records of Willard Library and its predecessors; Southwest Indiana Historical Society collection; Vanderburgh Historical and Biographical Society collection; papers of Annie Fellows Johnston (author), Albion Fellows Bacon (social reformer), Norman A. Shane, Sr. (businessman and civic leader); radio newscast scripts; U.S. Weather Service, Evansville Station, records; photographic collections of local persons and subjects; Old Vanderburgh County Archives (county court records). **Holdings:** 7500 books; 4500 microforms; 500 linear feet of personal papers, city, township, and county records. **Services:** Interlibrary loan; copying (both limited); department open to public. **Networks/Consortia:** Member of Four Rivers Area Library Services Authority, INCOLSA. **Staff:** Antoinette Brinkman, Archv..

★17885★
WILLARD PSYCHIATRIC CENTER - HATCH LIBRARY (Med)
Hatch Bldg. Phone: (607)869-3111
Willard, NY 14588 Helen Bunting, Sr.Libn.
Founded: 1869. **Staff:** Prof 1. **Subjects:** Psychiatry, medicine, psychology, health sciences, nursing. **Holdings:** 3300 books; 1200 bound periodical volumes; 12 cubic feet of medical files. **Subscriptions:** 80 journals and other serials; 8 newspapers. **Services:** Interlibrary loan; copying; library open to the public with director's written permission. **Computerized Information Services:** New York State Library Data Base (internal database). **Networks/Consortia:** Member of South Central Research Library Council (SCRLC), Finger Lakes Library System. **Publications:** Library Quarterly (acquisitions list). **Special Indexes:** Monthly Journal Index (table of contents of journals received).

★17886★
WILLET STAINED GLASS STUDIOS - LIBRARY (Art)
10 E. Moreland Ave. Phone: (215)247-5721
Philadelphia, PA 19118 Helene Weis, Libn.
Founded: 1890. **Staff:** Prof 1. **Subjects:** Stained glass - historic and contemporary process; art. **Holdings:** 1000 volumes; 15,350 photographs; 20,000 slides; 4500 microforms; pictures; clippings. **Subscriptions:** 30 journals and other serials. **Services:** Interlibrary loan; copying; library open to qualified persons.

★17887★
WILLIAMS BROTHERS ENGINEERING COMPANY - TECHNICAL INFORMATION CENTER (Energy)
6600 S. Yale Ave. Phone: (918)496-5655
Tulsa, OK 74136 Kay Kittrell, Mgr.
Staff: Prof 1. **Subjects:** Pipeline engineering, petroleum industry, energy technology, environmental engineering, energy statistics. **Special Collections:** Liquid natural gas historical/technical data; pipeline maps. **Holdings:** 5000 books; 10,000 company reports; 487 reels of microfilm of association standards; 200 maps; 200 VF drawers of clippings and reprints. **Subscriptions:** 140 journals and other serials. **Services:** Copying; center open to the public with restrictions. **Computerized Information Services:** DIALOG Information Services. **Publications:** Newsletter, quarterly - for internal distribution only. **Special Catalogs:** Technical Reports Catalog (card); catalog of published papers of company personnel (card).

★17888★
C.S. WILLIAMS CLINIC - LIBRARY (Med)
901 Helena St. Phone: (604)368-5211
Trail, BC, Canada V1R 3X4 Dr. L. Simonetta, Lib.Chm.
Subjects: Medicine and allied health sciences. **Holdings:** 500 books; 1000 bound periodical volumes. **Subscriptions:** 10 journals and other serials. **Services:** Library open to area doctors only.

★17889★
WILLIAMS COLLEGE - CENTER FOR ENVIRONMENTAL STUDIES - MATT COLE MEMORIAL LIBRARY (Env-Cons)
Box 632 Phone: (413)597-2500
Williamstown, MA 01267 Marcella Rauscher, Res.Coord.
Founded: 1972. **Staff:** Prof 1. **Subjects:** Air pollution, coasts, energy, environmental health, environmental law, land use, natural resources, toxic substances, water resources, local and regional data and planning. **Holdings:** 3000 books; 1200 bound periodical volumes; 3100 EPA documents; 8000 other documents. **Subscriptions:** 250 journals and other serials. **Services:** Library open to the public.

★17890★
WILLIAMS COLLEGE - CHAPIN LIBRARY (Rare Book, Hum)
Stetson Hall, 2nd Fl.
Box 426 Phone: (413)597-2462
Williamstown, MA 01267 Robert L. Volz, Custodian
Founded: 1923. **Staff:** Prof 2; Other 1. **Special Collections:** Incunabula (550 volumes); English literature before 1700 (1500 volumes); English 18th and 19th century first editions (1800 volumes); Americana (1600 volumes); History of Science (500 volumes); Ornithology (250 volumes); Classical and European literature (1500 volumes); Bibles and liturgical books (300 volumes); Aldine Press (135 volumes); Graphic Arts and private press books (3000 volumes); Walt Whitman (600 items); William Saroyan (250 items); Edwin Arlington Robinson (400 items); Samuel Butler (1000 items); Rudyard Kipling (700 items); Joseph Conrad (140 items); Theodore Roosevelt (200 items); William Faulkner (450 items); pre-1600 codices (40 volumes); historical and literary manuscripts (1400 items); prints of historical subjects (500 items); English 17th and 18th century broadside ballads (130 items); C.B. Falls (1000 items); performing arts (3000 items). **Holdings:** 35,000 volumes. **Subscriptions:** 25 journals and other serials. **Services:** Copying; answers correspondence requests for bibliographical information; library open to the public with restrictions. **Automated Operations:** Computerized cataloging. **Networks/Consortia:** Member of SUNY/OCLC Library Network. **Publications:** Exhibition handlists; Book Decoration in America: 1890-1910 (1979); The Graphic Art of C.B. Falls (1982). **Special Catalogs:** Short-Title List of Books in the Chapin Library (1939); special card file for printers (place of printing, date of imprint,

binders); watermarks in incunabula; provenance; maps and illustrations; Catalog of the Collection of Samuel Butler (of Erewhon) in the Chapin Library (1945). **Staff:** Wayne G. Hammond, Asst.Libn..

E.K. WILLIAMS LAW LIBRARY
See: University of Manitoba (16351)

★17891★
WILLIAMS INTERNATIONAL - LIBRARY (Sci-Engr)
2280 W. Maple Rd.
Box 200 Phone: (313)624-5200
Walled Lake, MI 48088 Lydia O. Johnstone, Libn.
Staff: Prof 1; Other 1. **Subjects:** Aerodynamics, gas turbine engines, metallurgy. **Holdings:** 1200 books; 8500 documents; 3000 monographs. **Subscriptions:** 40 journals and other serials. **Services:** Interlibrary loan; library not open to the public. **Computerized Information Services:** Online systems.

JACK K. WILLIAMS LIBRARY
See: Texas A & M University at Galveston (14059)

JOHN A. WILLIAMS ARCHIVE
See: University of Rochester - Department of Rare Books and Special Collections (16820)

JOHN DAVIS WILLIAMS LIBRARY
See: University of Mississippi (16516)

JOHN R. WILLIAMS, SR., HEALTH SCIENCES LIBRARY
See: Highland Hospital (6286)

KEMPER AND LEILA WILLIAMS FOUNDATION - HISTORIC NEW ORLEANS COLLECTION
See: Historic New Orleans Collection (6327)

★17892★
WILLIAMS-KUEBELBECK & ASSOCIATES, INC. - LIBRARY (Bus-Fin)
1301 Shoreway Rd., Suite 317 Phone: (415)593-7600
Belmont, CA 94002 Karen S. Maskel, Libn.
Founded: 1972. **Staff:** Prof 1. **Subjects:** Real estate market, fiscal impact analysis. **Special Collections:** Real estate development; Marina Development (150 volumes). **Holdings:** 1100 books; 1600 unbound reports. **Subscriptions:** 150 journals and other serials. **Services:** Interlibrary loan; library not open to the public. **Computerized Information Services:** DIALOG Information Services. **Publications:** Newsletter, monthly; bibliographies - both for internal distribution only. **Special Catalogs:** Internal reports catalog (card).

PAUL WILLIAMS MEMORIAL RESOURCE CENTER
See: Investigative Reporters and Editors, Inc. (7085)

★17893★
ROGER WILLIAMS GENERAL HOSPITAL - HEALTH SCIENCES LIBRARY (Med)
825 Chalkstone Ave. Phone: (401)456-2036
Providence, RI 02908 Hadassah Stein, Libn.
Staff: Prof 1. **Subjects:** Medicine, nursing, allied health sciences. **Holdings:** 2200 books; 2800 bound periodical volumes; 600 indexes, clinics. **Subscriptions:** 182 journals and other serials. **Services:** Interlibrary loan; library not open to the public. **Computerized Information Services:** NLM. **Networks/Consortia:** Member of Association of Rhode Island Health Sciences Librarians (ARIHSL).

★17894★
ROGER WILLIAMS PARK - PARK MUSEUM OF NATURAL HISTORY & PLANETARIUM - MUSEUM LIBRARY/ RESOURCE CENTER (Hist)
Providence, RI 02905 Phone: (401)785-9450
Founded: 1896. **Subjects:** Natural history, local history, astronomy, Native American artifacts. **Special Collections:** Natural History Library; glassplate negative collection; natural history specimen collection. **Holdings:** Figures not available. **Services:** Center open to the public by appointment.

RONALD WILLIAMS LIBRARY
See: Northeastern Illinois University (10402)

SAMUEL C. WILLIAMS LIBRARY
See: Stevens Institute of Technology - Samuel C. Williams Library (13678)

T.F. WILLIAMS HEALTH SCIENCES LIBRARY
See: Monroe Community Hospital (9196)

DR. GEORGE S. WILLIAMSON HEALTH SCIENCES LIBRARY
See: Ottawa Civic Hospital (10947)

★17895★
WILLIAMSPORT HOSPITAL & MEDICAL CENTER - LEARNING RESOURCES CENTER (Med)
777 Rural Ave. Phone: (717)321-2266
Williamsport, PA 17701-3198 Michael Heyd, Dir.
Staff: Prof 1; Other 1. **Subjects:** Medicine, nursing, allied health sciences. **Special Collections:** Medical textbooks, 1850 to present. **Holdings:** 4482 books; 4319 bound periodical volumes; 329 filmstrip/cassette programs; 256 slide/cassette programs; 240 video cassette programs; 317 audio cassette programs; 5 16mm films. **Subscriptions:** 220 journals and other serials. **Services:** Interlibrary loan; copying; reference and bibliographic information; center open to the public for reference use only. **Computerized Information Services:** MEDLARS. Performs searches on fee basis. **Networks/Consortia:** Member of Susquehanna Library Cooperative, Central Pennsylvania Health Sciences Library Association (CPHSLA).

JEANNIE WILLIS MEMORIAL LIBRARY
See: Mc Gill University - Religious Studies Library (8212)

★17896★
WILLKIE FARR & GALLAGHER - LIBRARY (Law)
153 E. 53rd St. Phone: (212)935-8000
New York, NY 10022 Jane Huston, Dir., Lib.Serv.
Staff: Prof 8; Other 8. **Subjects:** Law - corporate, tax, real estate, trusts and estates, general. **Holdings:** 40,000 books; 400 bound periodical volumes; 5 cabinets of microforms. **Subscriptions:** 350 journals and other serials. **Services:** Interlibrary loan; library not open to the public. **Automated Operations:** Computerized cataloging. **Computerized Information Services:** DIALOG Information Services, BRS Information Technologies, Dow Jones News/Retrieval, NEXIS, LEXIS, NewsNet, Inc., WILSONLINE, WESTLAW, Advanceline, OCLC, Spectrum Ownership Profiles Online, TEXTLINE, DataTimes, VU/TEXT Information Services; MCI Mail (electronic mail service). **Staff:** Maryann O'Donnell, Cat.; Elise Lilly, Asst.Libn.; Robin Ahern, Corp.Libn.; Nancy Ciliberti, Br.Libn., DC Off.; Anthony Cocuzzi, Ref.Libn.; Lori Krevoruck, Ref.Libn.; Valerie Railey, Ref.Libn..

★17897★
WILLMAR PUBLIC SCHOOLS - EARLY CHILDHOOD FAMILY EDUCATION/COMMUNITY EDUCATION TOY LIBRARY (Educ)
c/o Willmar Public Library
Pioneerland Library System
410 S.W. 5th St. Phone: (612)235-3162
Willmar, MN 56201 Linda Cogelow, Coord.
Staff: 4. **Holdings:** 1250 toys; baby furniture. **Services:** Library open to members. **Publications:** Brochures, irregular. **Remarks:** Maintained by Early Childhood Family Education Department.

★17898★
WILLMAR REGIONAL TREATMENT CENTER - LIBRARY (Med)
Box 1128 Phone: (612)231-5934
Willmar, MN 56201 Henry L. Wagener, Libn.
Founded: 1917. **Staff:** Prof 1. **Subjects:** Alcoholism, psychiatric nursing, mental retardation. **Special Collections:** Brandes Memorial Library (special collection of books on alcoholism). **Holdings:** 2200 books. **Subscriptions:** 75 journals and other serials. **Services:** Interlibrary loan; copying; library open to the public with restrictions. **Networks/Consortia:** Member of Minnesota Department of Human Services Library Consortium.

BOB WILLS MEMORIAL ARCHIVE OF POPULAR MUSIC
See: Panhandle-Plains Historical Museum - Research Center (11051)

★17899★
WILLS EYE HOSPITAL AND RESEARCH INSTITUTE - ARTHUR J. BEDELL MEMORIAL LIBRARY (Med)
Ninth & Walnut Sts. Phone: (215)928-3288
Philadelphia, PA 19107 Fleur Weinberg, Libn.
Founded: 1832. **Staff:** Prof 1; Other 2. **Subjects:** Clinical and historical ophthalmology. **Special Collections:** Ophthalmic history. **Holdings:** 2500 books; 7600 bound periodical volumes; 200 Wills Quarterly Conference Papers; 2 VF drawers of Wills staff reprints; 5 VF drawers; 250,000 audiotapes, cassettes, slides; 78 video cassettes. **Subscriptions:** 125 journals

and other serials. **Services:** Interlibrary loan; library open to the public by appointment. **Computerized Information Services:** NLM.

★17900★
WILMER, CUTLER & PICKERING - LAW LIBRARY (Law)
2445 M St., N.W. Phone: (202)663-6771
Washington, DC 20037 Elaine Mitchell, Dir. of Info.Serv.
Staff: Prof 4; Other 9. **Subjects:** Law - antitrust, corporate, securities, tax, administrative. **Special Collections:** Legislative histories (500); bound Senate and House reports. **Holdings:** 45,000 books; 1500 bound periodical volumes. **Subscriptions:** 1200 journals and other serials; 20 newspapers. **Services:** Interlibrary loan; copying; library open to the public with restrictions. **Automated Operations:** Computerized cataloging and serials. **Computerized Information Services:** LEXIS, The Reference Service (REFSRV), DIALOG Information Services, Pergamon ORBIT InfoLine, Inc., WESTLAW, Dow Jones News/Retrieval, OCLC. **Staff:** Teresa Llewellyn, Dp.Dir.; Barclay Inge, Leg.Spec.; Dale Wright, Leg.Spec.; Bob Asztalos, Leg.Spec.; Douglas King, Leg.Spec..

WILMER MEMORIAL MEDICAL LIBRARY
See: Abington Memorial Hospital (14)

WILMER OPHTHALMOLOGICAL INSTITUTE
See: Johns Hopkins Hospital - Wilmer Ophthalmological Institute (7231)

★17901★
WILMETTE HISTORICAL MUSEUM - LIBRARY (Hist)
565 Hunter Rd. Phone: (312)256-5838
Wilmette, IL 60091 E. Ramm, Musm.Dir.
Founded: 1950. **Staff:** 1. **Subjects:** History and institutions of the village of Wilmette. **Holdings:** 500 books; 120 bound periodical volumes; 4000 photographs; 50 VF drawers of archival material. **Services:** Library open to the public with restrictions. **Special Indexes:** Subject index to photographs.

★17902★
WILMINGTON AREA HEALTH EDUCATION CENTER - LEARNING RESOURCE CENTER - LIBRARY (Med)
2131 S. 17th St. Phone: (919)343-0161
Wilmington, NC 28402-9990 Mrs. Spencer Kearns Sexton, Dir.
Staff: Prof 1; Other 6. **Subjects:** Internal medicine, nursing, oncology, cardiology, surgery, obstetrics and gynecology, allied health sciences. **Holdings:** 3000 books; 3000 bound periodical volumes; AV programs. **Subscriptions:** 250 journals and other serials. **Services:** Interlibrary loan; copying; SDI; library open to the public for reference use only. **Automated Operations:** Computerized cataloging, serials, and circulation. **Computerized Information Services:** BRS Information Technologies, NLM; internal database; OnTyme Electronic Message Network Service (electronic mail service). **Networks/Consortia:** Member of North Carolina Area Health Education Centers Program Library and Information Services Network. **Publications:** Newsletter - state distribution.

★17903★
WILMINGTON COLLEGE OF OHIO - PEACE RESOURCE CENTER - HIROSHIMA/NAGASAKI MEMORIAL COLLECTION (Soc Sci)
Pyle Center, Box 1183 Phone: (513)382-5338
Wilmington, OH 45177 Helen Redding, Dir.
Founded: 1975. **Staff:** 1. **Subjects:** Atomic bomb development, Hiroshima, Nagasaki, peace education, nonviolence. **Special Collections:** Hiroshima/Nagasaki Memorial Collection (in Japanese; 600 volumes). **Holdings:** 1100 books; 26 VF drawers; 103 AV programs. **Subscriptions:** 60 journals and other serials. **Services:** Interlibrary loan; collection open to the public. **Publications:** Newsletter, quarterly - to mailing list. **Special Catalogs:** Peace education resources catalog, irregular.

WILMINGTON HOSPITAL
See: Medical Center of Delaware (8608)

★17904★
WILMINGTON NEWS-JOURNAL COMPANY - LIBRARY (Publ)
831 Orange St. Phone: (302)573-2038
Wilmington, DE 19899 Charlotte Walker, Chf.Libn.
Founded: 1955. **Staff:** Prof 4; Other 3. **Subjects:** Newspaper reference topics. **Special Collections:** Company archives. **Holdings:** 1500 books; 92 VF drawers of photographs and art; city directories; 10 million clippings. **Subscriptions:** 150 journals and other serials; 10 newspapers. **Services:** Copying; library open to the public with restrictions. **Staff:** Katherine Fiedler, Libn.; George Stoica, Libn.; Cecilia James, Libn..

★17905★
WILMINGTON STAR-NEWS NEWSPAPERS, INC. - LIBRARY (Publ)
1103 S. 17th St.
Box 840 Phone: (919)343-2309
Wilmington, NC 28402 Shirley A. Moore, Libn.
Staff: Prof 1; Other 1. **Subjects:** Newspaper reference topics. **Holdings:** Wilmington Star and News, 1925 to present, on microfilm; local clipping files on microfilm. **Services:** Library open to the public on a limited schedule.

LORETTE WILMOT LIBRARY
See: Nazareth College of Rochester (9839)

★17906★
WILSHIRE BOULEVARD TEMPLE - SIGMUND HECHT LIBRARY (Rel-Phil)
3663 Wilshire Blvd. Phone: (213)388-2401
Los Angeles, CA 90010 Joan Kropf, Libn.
Staff: Prof 1; Other 1. **Subjects:** Judaica, Bible, philosophy, religion, Jewish history, education, language and literature, arts, sociology. **Special Collections:** World War II, 1939-1945: trials of the major war criminals (complete set). **Holdings:** 17,000 volumes; 100 pamphlets; 12 VF drawers of uncataloged pamphlets; 100 filmstrips. **Subscriptions:** 15 journals and other serials. **Services:** Interlibrary loan; library open to the public for reference use only.

★17907★
WILSON & COMPANY, ENGINEERS & ARCHITECTS - LIBRARY (Plan)
631 E. Crawford
Box 1640
Salina, KS 67402 Phone: (913)827-0433
Founded: 1932. **Subjects:** Planning - city, regional, industrial; industrial waste. **Holdings:** Figures not available. **Services:** Library not open to the public.

★17908★
WILSON COUNTY HISTORICAL SOCIETY - MUSEUM LIBRARY (Hist)
420 N. 7th Phone: (316)378-3965
Fredonia, KS 66736 Bonnie Forbes, Musm.Cur.
Founded: 1962. **Staff:** 2. **Subjects:** The West; Kansas; pioneer life; plains agriculture - tools, equipment, facilities. **Special Collections:** Original set of the Offical Records of the Civil War. **Holdings:** 400 books; 300 bound periodical volumes; 1050 indexed pictures; 68 indexed notebooks of clippings; 15 notebooks of clipped obituaries from last 40 years in Wilson County; 110 reels of microfilm of Wilson County newspapers; books of grade school local history essays, 1983-1984. **Services:** Copying; library open to the public for reference use only. **Publications:** Newsletter, 4/year.

CUNNINGHAM WILSON LIBRARY
See: St. Vincent's Hospital (12696)

CURTIS LAWS WILSON LIBRARY
See: University of Missouri, Rolla (16542)

EDMUND WILSON LIBRARY
See: University of Tulsa - Mc Farlin Library - Special Collections (17004)

EVAN WILSON TURKISH LIBRARY
See: Middle East Institute - George Camp Keiser Library (8944)

★17909★
WILSON FOODS CORPORATION - RESEARCH LIBRARY (Food-Bev)
4545 Lincoln Blvd. Phone: (405)525-4781
Oklahoma City, OK 73105 Joy Jones
Staff: 2. **Subjects:** Chemistry, food science. **Holdings:** 600 books. **Subscriptions:** 70 journals and other serials; 12 newspapers. **Services:** Library not open to the public.

WILSON HOSPITAL
See: United Health Services/Wilson Hospital (14539)

★17910★
WILSON, IHRIG & ASSOCIATES - LIBRARY (Sci-Engr)
5776 Broadway Phone: (415)658-6719
Oakland, CA 94618 Kash Gill, Mktg.Mgr.
Subjects: Acoustics theory; acoustics - architectural, industrial, general; rapid transit noise and vibration. **Holdings:** 500 books; 2000 reports; 2400 articles and reprints. **Subscriptions:** 50 journals and other serials. **Services:** Interlibrary loan (limited); copying; library open to the public by appointment. **Automated Operations:** Computerized cataloging. **Computerized Information Services:** DIALOG Information Services. Performs searches on fee basis.

★17911★
WILSON MEMORIAL HOSPITAL - LEARNING CENTER/ LIBRARY (Med)
1705 S. Tarboro St. Phone: (919)399-8253
Wilson, NC 27893 Rosa Edwards, Supv.
Founded: 1964. **Staff:** Prof 1; Other 1. **Subjects:** Medicine, nursing, and allied health sciences. **Holdings:** 2827 volumes; 1018 video cassettes; 252 slide sets; 396 filmstrips. **Subscriptions:** 90 journals and other serials. **Services:** Interlibrary loan; copying; library open to the public with restrictions. **Networks/Consortia:** Member of North Carolina Area Health Education Centers Program Library and Information Services Network. **Special Catalogs:** Audiovisual Catalog.

WILSON MEMORIAL LIBRARY
See: Aldersgate College (263)

★17912★
WILSON ORNITHOLOGICAL SOCIETY - JOSSELYN VAN TYNE MEMORIAL LIBRARY (Biol Sci)
Museum of Zoology
University of Michigan Phone: (313)764-0457
Ann Arbor, MI 48109 Janet G. Hinshaw, Libn.
Founded: 1930. **Staff:** 1. **Subjects:** Ornithology. **Holdings:** 1700 books; 2400 bound periodical volumes; 1000 boxes of pamphlets and reprints; 500 translations; 70 dissertations; 50 sound recordings. **Subscriptions:** 193 journals and other serials. **Services:** Interlibrary loan; direct mail loan service to members of Wilson Ornithological Society; library open to University of Michigan staff and students.

WILSON RECORDINGS COLLECTION
See: University of British Columbia (15878)

★17913★
WOODROW WILSON BIRTHPLACE FOUNDATION, INC. - RESEARCH LIBRARY & ARCHIVES (Hist)
20 N. Coalter St.
Box 24 Phone: (703)885-0897
Staunton, VA 24401 Dr. Katharine L. Brown, Exec.Dir.
Founded: 1973. **Staff:** Prof 2. **Subjects:** Life and times of President Woodrow Wilson; international affairs during World War I period; Wilson family members; American government, 1902-1921. **Special Collections:** Katherine C. Brand Collection (Life and Times of Woodrow Wilson; 500 volumes); Wallace M. McClure Collection (Woodrow Wilson and International Affairs; 1000 volumes). **Holdings:** 4000 books; 150 bound periodical volumes; 1000 pamphlets; 1000 pieces of Woodrow Wilson and family manuscripts; 10 boxes of period newspaper clippings; 20 boxes of period photographs; 12 drawers and 20 boxes of institutional archives. **Subscriptions:** 20 journals and other serials. **Services:** Library open to the public on request. **Staff:** Gertrude Middendorf, Libn..

★17914★
WOODROW WILSON INTERNATIONAL CENTER FOR SCHOLARS - LIBRARY (Soc Sci)
Smithsonian Institution Bldg. Phone: (202)357-2567
Washington, DC 20560 Zdenek V. David, Libn.
Founded: 1970. **Staff:** Prof 2; Other 2. **Subjects:** U.S. history and politics; American, East and West European, Latin American, Russian, and Asian studies; international security. **Special Collections:** Russian/Soviet Collection of the Kennan Institute (8600 volumes). **Holdings:** 26,000 books, documents, and bound periodical volumes; 8 VF drawers. **Subscriptions:** 500 journals and other serials; 25 newspapers. **Services:** Interlibrary loan; copying; library open to the public for reference use only. **Remarks:** Center is an autonomous branch of the Smithsonian Institution.

WOODROW WILSON LIBRARY
See: Library of Congress - Rare Book & Special Collections Division (7836)

WOODROW WILSON MEMORIAL LIBRARY
See: United Nations Headquarters - Dag Hammarskjold Library (14569)

WOODROW WILSON SCHOOL OF PUBLIC AND INTERNATIONAL AFFAIRS
See: Princeton University (11596)

★17915★
WILTON HISTORICAL SOCIETY, INC. - LIBRARY (Hist)
249 Danbury Rd. Phone: (203)762-7257
Wilton, CT 06897 Marilyn Gould, Dir.
Subjects: Connecticut and Wilton history and genealogy. **Special Collections:** Connecticut and New England maps. **Holdings:** 500 volumes; manuscript collection. **Services:** Copying; library open to the public for reference use only. **Remarks:** Library housed at the Wilton Public Library.

E.W. WIMBLE MEMORIAL LIBRARY
See: Harlem Valley Psychiatric Center (6026)

★17916★
WINCHESTER HISTORICAL SOCIETY - SOLOMON ROCKWELL HOUSE - ARCHIVE (Hist)
225 Prospect St. Phone: (203)379-8433
Winsted, CT 06098 Pauline Fancher, Cur.
Staff: Prof 1; Other 2. **Subjects:** Local history. **Holdings:** Books; photographs; maps; documents; 5000 glassplate negatives. **Services:** Archive open to the public by appointment. **Publications:** Brochure. **Remarks:** Curator can be reached at 379-6269. **Staff:** Lester Schaeffer, Libn.; Louella Francis, Asst.Libn..

★17917★
WINCHESTER MEDICAL CENTER - HEALTH SCIENCES LIBRARY (Med)
Box 3340 Phone: (703)665-5124
Winchester, VA 22601-2540 Beth A. Layton, Libn.
Staff: Prof 1. **Subjects:** Medicine, nursing, allied health sciences. **Holdings:** 450 books; 2000 bound periodical volumes. **Subscriptions:** 175 journals and other serials. **Services:** Interlibrary loan; copying; library open to the public by appointment. **Computerized Information Services:** BRS Information Technologies, MEDLARS. Performs searches on fee basis. **Networks/Consortia:** Member of Northern Virginia Hospital Libraries. **Publications:** Newsletter, bimonthly - for internal distribution only.

WINCHESTER REPEATING ARMS COMPANY ARCHIVES
See: Buffalo Bill Historical Center - Harold Mc Cracken Research Library (2013)

★17918★
WINDELS, MARX, DAVIES & IVES - LIBRARY (Law)
156 W. 56th St. Phone: (212)977-9600
New York, NY 10019 Joel Solomon, Libn.
Staff: Prof 1; Other 1. **Subjects:** Law - corporate, international, securities, tax, trusts and estates, banking. **Holdings:** 20,000 books; 550 bound periodical volumes. **Subscriptions:** 185 journals and other serials; 10 newspapers. **Services:** Interlibrary loan; library open to the public with restrictions. **Computerized Information Services:** LEXIS, DIALOG Information Services, NEXIS, National Automated Accounting Research System (NAARS). **Publications:** Library Newsletter, bimonthly.

★17919★
WINDSOR HISTORICAL SOCIETY, INC. - LIBRARY (Hist)
96 Palisado Ave. Phone: (203)688-3813
Windsor, CT 06095 Robert T. Silliman, Dir.
Founded: 1923. **Staff:** Prof 1; Other 12. **Subjects:** Local history, genealogy, biography. **Special Collections:** Account books; Bibles; Northeast history; history and genealogy of 1633 founding families; history of 20 daughter towns which were once part of Windsor. **Holdings:** 3000 books; 50 bound periodical volumes; 3000 other cataloged items; documents and historic pictures concerning Windsor and its people; 100 ephemeral files. **Services:** Copying; library open to the public for reference use only.

WINDSOR PUBLIC LIBRARY - HIRAM WALKER HISTORICAL MUSEUM
See: Hiram Walker Historical Museum (17428)

★17920★
WINDSOR PUBLIC LIBRARY - SPECIAL COLLECTIONS (Hist)
850 Ouellette Ave. Phone: (519)255-6770
Windsor, ON, Canada N9A 4M9 Gail P. Juris, Hd., Main Lib.
Subjects: Windsor local history, automotive history. **Special Collections:** Windsor Municipal Archives (1470 linear feet). **Holdings:** 2000 books, scrapbooks, pamphlets, oral history cassettes, microforms; government documents depository. **Services:** Interlibrary loan; copying; collection open to the public. **Automated Operations:** Computerized circulation. **Computerized Information Services:** DIALOG Information Services, Info Globe, WILSONLINE, CAN/OLE, Infomart. Performs searches free of charge. Contact Person: Marilyn Scase, Hd., Soc.Sci., 255-6764. **Special Indexes:** Windsor Star Index; index to local French newspapers.

★17921★
WINDSOR STAR - LIBRARY (Publ)
167 Ferry St. Phone: (519)256-5511
Windsor, ON, Canada N9A 4M5 Mary Jane Handy, Libn.
Founded: 1935. **Staff:** Prof 1; Other 5. **Subjects:** Newspaper reference topics. **Holdings:** 500 books; one million clippings; 1.5 million pictures; 5000 maps; 3 VF drawers of pamphlets; 24 drawers of microfilm of Windsor Star, 1893 to present; 200 other cataloged items. **Services:** Copying; library open to the public with restrictions. **Computerized Information Services:** Infomart. Performs searches on fee basis.

★17922★
WINE INSTITUTE - LIBRARY (Food-Bev)
165 Post St. Phone: (415)986-0878
San Francisco, CA 94108 Karen Thomas, Libn.
Founded: 1934. **Staff:** Prof 1. **Subjects:** Wine and winemaking, viticulture. **Special Collections:** California wine industry clippings and brochures spanning 50 years; wine labels; ephemera. **Holdings:** 3000 volumes. **Subscriptions:** 100 journals and other serials. **Services:** Library open to the public by appointment.

★17923★
WINEBRENNER THEOLOGICAL SEMINARY - LIBRARY (Rel-Phil)
701 E. Melrose Ave.
Box 478 Phone: (419)422-4824
Findlay, OH 45839-0478 Bur Shilling, Dir., Lib.Serv.
Founded: 1942. **Staff:** Prof 1; Other 2. **Subjects:** Church history, Old and New Testament, contemporary theology, homiletics, Christian education and practical theology, Christian ministries. **Special Collections:** Churches of God old and rare books; Churches of God history; John Winebrenner materials. **Holdings:** 32,426 books; 1803 bound periodical volumes; 398 other cataloged items; 8 VF of pamphlets. **Subscriptions:** 143 journals and other serials. **Services:** Interlibrary loan; copying; library open to the public. **Automated Operations:** Computerized cataloging. **Computerized Information Services:** OCLC. **Staff:** Florence Cook, Cat..

★17924★
WINEDALE HISTORICAL CENTER - LIBRARY (Hist)
Box 11 Phone: (409)278-3530
Round Top, TX 78954 Gloria Jaster, Adm.
Staff: 5. **Subjects:** Historic sites, furniture, decorative arts, agriculture. **Holdings:** 835 books; 75 bound periodical volumes; 200 other cataloged items; historic preservation documentation. **Subscriptions:** 38 journals and other serials. **Services:** Interlibrary loan; copying; library open to the public for reference use only. **Publications:** Quid Nunc (newsletter), quarterly - to friends of Winedale, members, and museums. **Remarks:** Maintained by University of Texas, Austin.

★17925★
WINFIELD STATE HOSPITAL AND TRAINING CENTER - PROFESSIONAL AND MEDICAL LIBRARY (Med)
Winfield, KS 67156 Phone: (316)221-1200
Janis McGlasson, Lib.Ck.
Staff: Prof 1. **Subjects:** Mental retardation, psychology, medicine, social work and welfare, education and special education, nursing. **Holdings:** 2400 books; 189 bound periodical volumes; 246 AV programs; 476 unbound periodical volumes; 398 indexes and abstracts in volumes; 15 theses; 3000 pamphlets and clippings. **Subscriptions:** 100 journals and other serials. **Services:** Interlibrary loan; copying; library open to the public. **Networks/Consortia:** Member of Midcontinental Regional Medical Library Program.

★17926★
WINNEBAGO COUNTY LAW LIBRARY (Law)
Courthouse Bldg., Suite 306
400 W. State St. Phone: (815)987-2514
Rockford, IL 61101-1221 Robert J. Lindvall, Law Libn.
Founded: 1975. **Staff:** Prof 1; Other 1. **Subjects:** General legal material; law - federal, Illinois, Wisconsin. **Holdings:** 17,000 volumes and microfiche. **Subscriptions:** 26 journals and other serials. **Services:** Interlibrary loan; copying; library open to the public. **Networks/Consortia:** Member of Northern Illinois Library System (NILS).

★17927★
WINNEBAGO MENTAL HEALTH INSTITUTE - MEDICAL LIBRARY (Med)
Box 9 Phone: (414)235-4910
Winnebago, WI 54985-0009 Mary Kotschi, Dir. of Lib.Serv.
Founded: 1873. **Staff:** Prof 2; Other 1. **Subjects:** Psychiatry, psychology, social service, counseling, hospital administration, nursing, sociology. **Holdings:** 6500 volumes; 8 VF drawers of pamphlets; 585 cassette tapes; 15 videotapes. **Subscriptions:** 183 journals and other serials. **Services:** Interlibrary loan; copying; library open to the public. **Computerized Information Services:** MEDLARS. **Networks/Consortia:** Member of Fox River Valley Area Library Consortium, Fox Valley Library Council.

★17928★
WINNIPEG ART GALLERY - CLARA LANDER LIBRARY (Art)
300 Memorial Blvd. Phone: (204)786-6641
Winnipeg, MB, Canada R3C 1V1 David W. Rozniatowski, Libn.
Founded: 1912. **Staff:** Prof 1. **Subjects:** History of art and painting, drawing, sculpture, ceramics, prints, architecture, antiques and photography. **Special Collections:** Canadiana (Eskimo and Indian art). **Holdings:** 19,000 books; 720 bound periodical volumes; 8500 exhibition catalogs; 844 reports; 666 folders of bulletins; 7000 folders of biographies of artists; 136 binders of archives. **Subscriptions:** 40 journals and other serials. **Services:** Interlibrary loan; copying; library open to the public; gallery membership is necessary for loan privileges. **Special Catalogs:** Exhibition catalogs.

★17929★
WINNIPEG BIBLE COLLEGE - REIMER LIBRARY (Rel-Phil)
Otterburne, MB, Canada R0A 1G0 Phone: (204)433-7488
Karin Friesen, Hd.Libn.
Staff: Prof 4; Other 25. **Subjects:** Theology, Old and New Testament. **Holdings:** 33,633 books; 1593 bound periodical volumes; 1004 book titles in microform; 114 periodical titles in microform; 1593 volumes in microform; 16 VF drawers; 259 scores; 592 sound recordings; 1539 cassette tapes; 580 choral music items; 102 media kits. **Subscriptions:** 368 journals and other serials. **Services:** Interlibrary loan; copying; library open to the public. **Staff:** Audrey Adrian-Neufeld, Asst.Libn.; Martha Loeppky, Asst.Libn.; Jennifer Kroeker, Asst.Libn..

★17930★
WINNIPEG CLINIC - LIBRARY (Med)
425 St. Mary Ave. Phone: (204)957-1900
Winnipeg, MB, Canada R3C 0N2 S. Loeppky, Libn.
Staff: Prof 1. **Subjects:** Medicine. **Holdings:** Figures not available. **Subscriptions:** 78 journals and other serials. **Services:** Interlibrary loan; copying; library open to the public with restrictions.

★17931★
WINNIPEG DEPARTMENT OF ENVIRONMENTAL PLANNING - LIBRARY (Plan)
395 Main St.
Winnipeg, MB, Canada R3B 3E1 Mrs. A. Thiesson, Libn.
Founded: 1960. **Staff:** Prof 1; Other 2. **Subjects:** City planning, local government, real estate trends, urban economics, geography. **Holdings:** 6600 books; pamphlets; 400 slides; 3050 reports; maps; microfiche. **Subscriptions:** 40 journals and other serials. **Services:** Interlibrary loan; library open to the public with restrictions on some material.

★17932★
WINNIPEG FREE PRESS - LIBRARY (Publ)
300 Carlton St. Phone: (204)943-9331
Winnipeg, MB, Canada R3C 3C1 Mrs. E. Langer, Libn.
Founded: 1923. **Staff:** 6. **Subjects:** Newspaper reference topics. **Special Collections:** Selected Canadian and Manitoba government documents. **Holdings:** 6800 volumes. **Subscriptions:** 125 journals and other serials. **Services:** Interlibrary loan; library not open to the public.

★17933★
WINNIPEG HEALTH SCIENCES CENTRE - LIBRARY SERVICES (Med)
700 McDermot Ave. Phone: (204)787-3416
Winnipeg, MB, Canada R3E 0T2
Ada M. Ducas, Dir., Educ.Rsrcs. & Lib.Serv.
Founded: 1981. **Staff:** Prof 1; Other 4. **Subjects:** Medicine, surgery, pediatrics, nursing, allied health sciences, hospital administration. **Holdings:** 8000 books; 300 bound periodical volumes; 1000 slides. **Subscriptions:** 400 journals and other serials. **Services:** Interlibrary loan; copying; SDI; services open to the public with restrictions. **Computerized Information Services:** MEDLARS. **Networks/Consortia:** Member of Manitoba Health Libraries Association (MHLA). **Publications:** Library Limelight (newsletter), quarterly - for internal distribution only.

★17934★
WINNIPEG SCHOOL DIVISION NO. 1 - TEACHERS LIBRARY AND RESOURCE CENTRE (Educ)
1180 Notre Dame Ave. Phone: (204)943-3541
Winnipeg, MB, Canada R3E 0P2 Gerald R. Brown, Chf.Libn.
Staff: Prof 3; Other 27. **Subjects:** Education and audiovisual education, library science, Canadiana, Manitobiana. **Special Collections:** Historical curriculum texts. **Holdings:** 18,308 books; 926 bound periodical volumes; 4401 AV programs; 27 VF drawers; 261 reels of microfilm; 2086 16mm film titles; 112 videotape titles. **Subscriptions:** 326 journals and other serials. **Services:** Interlibrary loan; copying; center open to the public with restrictions. **Publications:** Newsletter, monthly. **Special Catalogs:** 16mm Film Catalog; Microcomputer Software Catalog. **Staff:** Jean Baptist, Cons., Lib. Media Serv.; M. Green, Hd., Tech.Serv.; Corinne Tellier, Ref.Libn..

★17935★
WINNIPEG SOCIAL PLANNING COUNCIL - LIBRARY (Soc Sci)
412 McDermot Ave. Phone: (204)943-2561
Winnipeg, MB, Canada R3A 0A9 Ken Murdoch, Exec.Dir.
Subjects: Social welfare policy in Manitoba, Canada, and other selected areas. **Holdings:** Books; studies; reports. **Services:** Library open to the public for reference use only.

★17936★
WINONA MEMORIAL HOSPITAL - HEALTH SCIENCES LIBRARY (Med)
3232 N. Meridian Phone: (317)927-2248
Indianapolis, IN 46208 Donald H. Monroe, Jr., Med.Libn.
Founded: 1971. **Staff:** Prof 1. **Subjects:** Medicine, nursing, hospital administration, allied health sciences. **Holdings:** 1340 books; 1989 bound periodical volumes; 3 VF drawers of pamphlets. **Subscriptions:** 140 journals and other serials. **Services:** Interlibrary loan; library not open to the public. **Automated Operations:** Computerized cataloging. **Computerized Information Services:** NLM, BRS Information Technologies. **Networks/Consortia:** Member of Central Indiana Health Science Library Consortium, Central Indiana Area Library Services Authority (CIALSA), Greater Midwest Regional Medical Library Network, INCOLSA.

★17937★
WINROCK INTERNATIONAL - LIBRARY (Agri)
Petit Jean Mountain, Rte. 3 Phone: (501)727-5435
Morrilton, AR 72110 Joan Newton, Libn.
Staff: 2. **Subjects:** Agriculture, ruminant livestock, range management, public policy, appropriate technology systems, cropping and farming systems, research management. **Holdings:** 5000 books; 50 bound periodical volumes; 200 reports on microfiche; 2000 government documents; 10,000 slides; 12 VF drawers of miscellaneous material. **Subscriptions:** 416 journals and other serials; 10 newspapers. **Services:** Interlibrary loan; library open to the public for reference use only. **Computerized Information Services:** Online systems.

WINSLOW LIBRARY
See: Meadville Medical Center (8593)

WINSPEAR READING ROOM
See: University of Alberta - Humanities and Social Sciences Library (15801)

★17938★
WINSTON-SALEM FOUNDATION - FOUNDATION CENTER REGIONAL LIBRARY (Soc Sci)
229 First Union Bldg. Phone: (919)725-2382
Winston-Salem, NC 27101 Sara N. Willard, Libn.
Subjects: Foundations. **Special Collections:** North Carolina Foundation IRS Returns. **Holdings:** 35 volumes; 250 annual reports; source book profiles. **Services:** Copying; library open to the public. **Also Known As:** Donors Forum of Forsyth County.

★17939★
WINSTON-SALEM JOURNAL - REFERENCE DEPARTMENT (Publ)
418 N. Marshall Phone: (919)727-7275
Winston-Salem, NC 27102 Marilyn H. Rollins, Ref.Dept.Mgr.
Founded: 1947. **Staff:** Prof 4; Other 3. **Subjects:** Newspaper reference topics. **Holdings:** 1250 books; 50 bound periodical volumes; 3000 pamphlets; 2.5 million newspaper clippings; 370,000 photographs; 18,000 negatives; 1861 reels of microfilm of newspapers; 6 VF drawers of reports. **Subscriptions:** 200 journals and other serials; 53 newspapers. **Services:** Copying; department open to students for academic research by appointment. **Remarks:** Published by Piedmont Publishing Company.

★17940★
WINSTON-SALEM STATE UNIVERSITY - C.G. O'KELLY LIBRARY - SPECIAL COLLECTIONS (Educ)
Winston-Salem, NC 27110 Phone: (919)750-2440
Vicki S. Miller, Ref.Libn.
Founded: 1922. **Special Collections:** Curriculum Materials Center Collection (30,000 items); Black Studies Collection; School of Nursing Library (5000 items). **Services:** Interlibrary loan; copying; collections open to the public. **Automated Operations:** Computerized public access catalog, cataloging, acquisitions, serials, circulation, and reference. **Computerized Information Services:** OCLC, DIALOG Information Services; internal database. Performs searches on fee basis. Contact Person: Gwen Harris, Ref.Libn.. **Networks/Consortia:** Member of SOLINET.

★17941★
WINSTON & STRAWN - LIBRARY (Law)
2550 M St., N.W., Suite 500 Phone: (202)828-8400
Washington, DC 20037 Janet G. Baxter, Libn.
Founded: 1970. **Staff:** Prof 1; Other 1. **Subjects:** Law. **Holdings:** 6000 books; loose-leaf services. **Subscriptions:** 125 journals and other serials; 5 newspapers. **Services:** Interlibrary loan; library open to the public by appointment. **Automated Operations:** Computerized cataloging. **Computerized Information Services:** DIALOG Information Services, OCLC, LEXIS, NEXIS, WESTLAW; ABA/net, MCI Mail (electronic mail services). **Networks/Consortia:** Member of ILLINET. **Publications:** Library Bulletin (newsletter), monthly - for internal distribution only.

★17942★
WINSTON & STRAWN - LIBRARY (Law)
One 1st National Plaza Phone: (312)558-5740
Chicago, IL 60603 Donna M. Tuke, Chf.Libn.
Founded: 1857. **Staff:** Prof 3; Other 4. **Subjects:** Law - securities, antitrust, corporate, tax, labor, real estate. **Holdings:** 30,000 volumes; 10 boxes of ultrafiche; 1 drawer of microfiche; 60 reels of microfilm. **Subscriptions:** 250 journals and other serials. **Services:** Interlibrary loan; copying; library open to lawyers and other professionals for reference use only. **Automated Operations:** Computerized cataloging. **Computerized Information Services:** WESTLAW, Dow Jones News/Retrieval, PHINet FedTax Database, LEXIS, DIALOG Information Services, VU/TEXT Information Services, OCLC; internal database. **Networks/Consortia:** Member of Chicago Library System, ILLINET. **Publications:** Library Bulletin, monthly - to all attorneys.

★17943★
WINTER HAVEN HOSPITAL - J.G. CONVERSE MEMORIAL MEDICAL LIBRARY (Med)
200 Ave. F., N.E. Phone: (813)293-1121
Winter Haven, FL 33881 Henry Hasse, Media Mgr.
Founded: 1957. **Staff:** Prof 2. **Subjects:** Medicine, nursing, allied health sciences, community mental health. **Holdings:** 400 books; 1200 bound periodical volumes; 160 audio cassettes; 310 video cassettes. **Subscriptions:** 95 journals and other serials. **Services:** Interlibrary loan; copying; library open to the public for reference use only. **Computerized Information Services:** MEDLARS. Performs searches on fee basis. Contact Person: Agnes Kormendy, Asst.Libn..

★17944★
WINTER PARK MEMORIAL HOSPITAL - MEDICAL STAFF LIBRARY (Med)
200 N. Lakemont Ave. Phone: (407)646-7049
Winter Park, FL 32792 Patricia N. Cole, Med.Libn.
Staff: Prof 1; Other 2. **Subjects:** Medicine, surgery, nursing. **Holdings:** 2778 books; 7539 bound periodical volumes; 150 feet of unbound periodicals; 1450 tapes; 1 VF drawer of pamphlets. **Subscriptions:** 231 journals and other serials. **Services:** Interlibrary loan; copying; library open to the public for reference use only with permission of administration. **Publications:** Report to Chairman of Library Committee, bimonthly; New Acquisitions List, monthly - both for internal distribution only; bibliographies - to staff doctors, nurses, and students at local colleges and universities.

WILLIAM WINTER MARINE LIBRARY
See: College of Insurance - Insurance Society of New York - Library (3382)

★17945★
WINTERS GROUP - INFORMATION CENTER (Bus-Fin)
14 Franklin St. Phone: (716)546-7480
Rochester, NY 14607 Robert Berkman, Dir., Info.Serv.Dev.
Founded: 1984. **Staff:** Prof 1; Other 1. **Subjects:** Corporations, industries, new products, health care, banking, high technology, social services. **Holdings:** 50 books. **Subscriptions:** 50 journals and other serials; 20 newspapers. **Services:** Center not open to the public. **Computerized Information Services:** DIALOG Information Services; internal database. **Publications:** AI (Artificial Intelligence), monthly. **Remarks:** Company performs primary and secondary market research.

WINTERTHUR MUSEUM
See: Henry Francis Du Pont Winterthur Museum - Library (4424)

WINTERTHUR SWISS INSURANCE CO. - CITADEL ASSURANCE
See: Citadel Assurance (3222)

WINTHROP LABORATORIES
See: Sterling Drug, Inc. (13669)

★17946★
WINTHROP, STIMSON, PUTNAM AND ROBERTS - LIBRARY (Law)
40 Wall St. Phone: (212)530-7567
New York, NY 10005 Nancy J. Haab, Libn.
Founded: 1948. **Staff:** Prof 4; Other 5. **Subjects:** Law, public utilities. **Holdings:** 35,000 volumes. **Subscriptions:** 125 journals and other serials. **Services:** Interlibrary loan; library not open to the public. **Staff:** Faya Cohen, Asst.Libn.; Hilary Gold, Asst.Libn.; Sonja McDaniel, Cat..

★17947★
WINTHROP-UNIVERSITY HOSPITAL - MEDICAL LIBRARY (Med)
259 First St. Phone: (516)663-2280
Mineola, NY 11501 Virginia I. Cook, Med.Libn.
Staff: Prof 1; Other 5. **Subjects:** Medicine, surgery, nursing, and allied health sciences. **Holdings:** 2600 books; 7100 bound periodical volumes; 127 AV programs; 113 computer-assisted instruction programs; audiotapes; pamphlets. **Subscriptions:** 326 journals and other serials. **Services:** Interlibrary loan; library not open to the public. **Computerized Information Services:** NLM, BRS Information Technologies; DOCLINE (electronic mail service). **Networks/Consortia:** Member of Medical Library Center of New York (MLCNY), Long Island Library Resources Council, Inc. (LILRC), Medical & Scientific Libraries of Long Island (MEDLI). **Publications:** Acquisition list, quarterly.

WINTON HILL TECHNICAL CENTER
See: Procter & Gamble Company (11606)

★17948★
WIRE ASSOCIATION INTERNATIONAL - TECHNICAL INFORMATION CENTER (Sci-Engr)
1570 Boston Post Rd.
Box H Phone: (203)453-2777
Guilford, CT 06437 Ralph P. Edwards, Tech.Dir.
Staff: Prof 1; Other 1. **Subjects:** Wire technology; metallurgy; engineering - electrical, nonferrous, ferrous; fiber optics; fasteners. **Special Collections:** Complete run of Wire Journal (indexed, abstracted); complete run of Wire and Wire Products (48 volumes; indexed, abstracted). **Holdings:** 600 books; 80 bound periodical volumes. **Services:** Interlibrary loan; copying; center open to the public at director's discretion. **Computerized Information Services:** DIALOG Information Services. Performs searches on fee basis. **Publications:** Wire Association Conference Proceedings, annual; meeting proceedings; Technical Reports, irregular; technical handbooks and correspondence courses. **Special Indexes:** Wire Index (hardcopy of internal database holdings), updated annually.

WIRTANEN LIBRARY
See: Quincy Historical Society (11840)

WISCONSIN ARCHITECTURAL ARCHIVE
See: Milwaukee Public Library (9016)

WISCONSIN AREA RESEARCH CENTER ARCHIVES
See: University of Wisconsin, Oshkosh - University Libraries and Learning Resources - Special Collections (17175)

WISCONSIN CENTER FOR FILM AND THEATER RESEARCH
See: University of Wisconsin, Madison - Wisconsin Center for Film and Theater Research (17161)

★17949★
WISCONSIN CONSERVATORY OF MUSIC - LIBRARY (Mus)
1584 N. Prospect Ave. Phone: (414)276-5760
Milwaukee, WI 53202-2394 Raymond Lynn Mueller, Dir.
Founded: 1968. **Staff:** Prof 1; Other 2. **Subjects:** Music. **Holdings:** 26,000 books and scores; 6300 sound recordings. **Subscriptions:** 10 journals and other serials. **Services:** Interlibrary loan; copying; library open to the public for reference use only. **Publications:** Facsimile reprint of 12 Landler for Two Guitars, Opus 55, by Mauro Giuliani.

★17950★
WISCONSIN GAS COMPANY - CORPORATE AND LAW LIBRARY (Energy)
626 E. Wisconsin Ave. Phone: (414)291-6666
Milwaukee, WI 53202 Carolyn A. Simpson, Supv., Info.Rsrcs.
Founded: 1930. **Staff:** Prof 2; Other 1. **Subjects:** Natural gas, public utility regulation law, engineering, gas industries, corporation law. **Holdings:** 2000 books; 520 bound periodical volumes; 8 VF drawers of pamphlets. **Subscriptions:** 204 journals and other serials. **Services:** Interlibrary loan; copying; SDI; library open to the public by appointment. **Automated Operations:** Computerized cataloging, acquisitions, serials, and circulation. **Computerized Information Services:** DIALOG Information Services, Pergamon ORBIT InfoLine, Inc., VU/TEXT Information Services, A.G.A. GasNet, YankeeNet, WESTLAW; Wisconsin Economic Indicators/Milwaukee Economic Indicators (internal databases); A.G.A. GasNet (electronic mail service). **Networks/Consortia:** Member of Library Council of Metropolitan Milwaukee, Inc. (LCOMM), American Gas Association - Library Services (AGA-LSC). **Publications:** Information Resource Update, irregular. **Staff:** Linda Nordstrom, Coord., Info.Rsrcs..

★17951★
WISCONSIN HOSPITAL ASSOCIATION - MEMORIAL LIBRARY (Med)
5721 Odana Rd. Phone: (608)274-1820
Madison, WI 53719 Dexter N. Katzman, Libn.
Staff: Prof 1. **Subjects:** Health care and statistics, hospital administration, health careers, health insurance, labor relations, long-term care programs, hospital law and regulations. **Holdings:** 2200 books. **Subscriptions:** 80 journals and other serials. **Services:** Interlibrary loan; copying; library open to the public for reference use only. **Networks/Consortia:** Member of South Central Wisconsin Health Planning Area Cooperative, South Central Library System.

★17952★
WISCONSIN INDIANHEAD TECHNICAL COLLEGE, NEW RICHMOND CAMPUS - LEARNING RESOURCE CENTER (Sci-Engr)
1019 S. Knowles Ave. Phone: (715)246-6561
New Richmond, WI 54017 David D. Hartung, Libn.
Founded: 1969. **Staff:** Prof 1; Other 2. **Subjects:** Agriculture, business, general education, health occupations, home economics, trade and industry. **Special Collections:** Curriculum Library (1300 volumes; 350 AV programs). **Holdings:** 4640 books; 2300 AV programs. **Subscriptions:** 160 journals and other serials; 16 newspapers. **Services:** Interlibrary loan; center open to the public. **Networks/Consortia:** Member of Technical Information Exchange. **Also Known As:** Indianhead Technical College; WITC - New Richmond.

★17953★
WISCONSIN INDIANHEAD TECHNICAL INSTITUTE, SUPERIOR CAMPUS - LIBRARY (Educ)
600 N. 21st St. Phone: (715)394-6677
Superior, WI 54880 Donald Rantala, LRC Spec.
Founded: 1965. **Staff:** Prof 1; Other 2. **Subjects:** Nursing, mechanical design, electronics, business, data processing, marketing and advertising. **Holdings:** 10,000 books; 1500 pamphlets; 50 maps; theses; microfilm; slides; cassettes. **Subscriptions:** 170 journals and other serials; 25 newspapers. **Services:** Copying; library open to the public with restrictions.

★17954★
WISCONSIN INFORMATION SERVICE (Soc Sci)
161 W. Wisconsin Ave. Phone: (414)276-0760
Milwaukee, WI 53203 Judith H. Cohen, Dir.
Staff: Prof 2; Other 3. **Subjects:** Human services, especially in health and social work. **Holdings:** Files on 1100 Milwaukee area human service agencies. **Services:** Service open to the public by appointment. **Publications:** WIS data reports, monthly. **Special Indexes:** Alphabetical and numerical lists of agencies. **Staff:** Alice C. Henry, Assoc.Dir..

★17955★
WISCONSIN LUTHERAN SEMINARY - LIBRARY (Rel-Phil)
6633 W. Wartburg Circle Phone: (414)242-7209
Mequon, WI 53092 Rev. Martin O. Westerhaus, Libn.
Founded: 1863. **Staff:** Prof 2; Other 3. **Subjects:** Theology, church history. **Holdings:** 37,000 books; 2200 bound periodical volumes. **Subscriptions:** 281 journals and other serials. **Services:** Interlibrary loan; copying; library open to the public with restrictions. **Staff:** Rev. Robert M. Oswald, Tech.Serv..

WISCONSIN MUSIC ARCHIVES
See: University of Wisconsin, Madison - Mills Music Library (17143)

WISCONSIN REGIONAL PRIMATE RESEARCH CENTER
See: University of Wisconsin, Madison (17162)

★17956★
WISCONSIN SCHOOL FOR THE DEAF - JOHN R. GANT LIBRARY (Educ)
309 W. Walworth Ave. Phone: (414)728-6477
Delavan, WI 53115 Betty E. Watkins, Libn.
Founded: 1852. **Staff:** Prof 1. **Subjects:** Books of high interest-low vocabulary, professional library, K-12 general collection. **Special Collections:** Education of the deaf; captioned films for the deaf (1100). **Holdings:** 6000 books; 1700 filmstrips; 150 film loops; 500 microfiche; 16 drawers of transparencies. **Subscriptions:** 89 journals and other serials. **Services:** Interlibrary loan; copying; library open to the public with librarian's permission. **Publications:** Wisconsin Times, monthly - to patrons.

★17957★
WISCONSIN (State) DEPARTMENT OF DEVELOPMENT - LIBRARY (Bus-Fin)
123 W. Washington Ave.
Box 7970
Madison, WI 53707
Subjects: Economic and community development, small business, local government, tourism. **Special Collections:** Local, county, and regional planning commission reports; departmental archives. **Holdings:** 10,000 books. **Subscriptions:** 100 journals and other serials.

★17958★
WISCONSIN STATE DEPARTMENT OF EMPLOYEE TRUST FUNDS - LIBRARY (Bus-Fin)
201 E. Washington Ave., Rm. 171
Box 7931 Phone: (608)266-7387
Madison, WI 53707 John R. Wendorf, Prog.Asst./Libn.
Staff: Prof 1. **Subjects:** Pensions, insurance, social security. **Special Collections:** Collections of historical materials on various state pension and retirement programs; pamphlets of other states' retirement systems; congressional and state legislative history on retirement bills (10 VF drawers). **Holdings:** 300 books; 5 VF drawers of clippings; 2000 manuscripts and documents. **Subscriptions:** 50 journals and other serials. **Services:** Interlibrary loan; copying; library open to the public. **Automated Operations:** Computerized cataloging and acquisitions. **Publications:** Library summary of new acquisitions, monthly; List of Departmental Publications; Title List of Periodical/Newsletter Holdings.

★17959★
WISCONSIN STATE DEPARTMENT OF HEALTH & SOCIAL SERVICES - LIBRARY (Med, Soc Sci)
1 W. Wilson St., Rm. 630
Box 7850 Phone: (608)266-7473
Madison, WI 53707 Nancy J. Ahlquist, Libn.
Staff: Prof 1; Other 1. **Subjects:** Public health and welfare, corrections, community services, mental health, vocational rehabilitation. **Holdings:** 10,000 books; 401 bound periodical titles; 75 pamphlet boxes. **Subscriptions:** 400 journals and other serials. **Services:** Interlibrary loan; library not open to the public. **Automated Operations:** Computerized cataloging and ILL. **Computerized Information Services:** MEDLARS, BRS Information Technologies; DOCLINE (electronic mail service). **Publications:** Acquisition list, monthly - free upon request.

★17960★
WISCONSIN STATE DEPARTMENT OF INDUSTRY, LABOR & HUMAN RELATIONS - EMPLOYMENT & TRAINING LIBRARY (Bus-Fin)
201 E. Washington Ave.
Box 7944 Phone: (608)266-2832
Madison, WI 53707 Janet D. Pugh, Libn.
Staff: Prof 1; Other 1. **Subjects:** Labor, employment, demographics, Job Training Partnership Administration (JTPA), employment and training programs. **Holdings:** 10,000 books; government documents. **Subscriptions:** 80 journals and other serials. **Services:** Interlibrary loan; library open to the public for reference use only. **Publications:** Inform (acquisition list), bimonthly - to interested persons; Annotated Directory of Labor Market Information.

★17961★
WISCONSIN STATE DEPARTMENT OF JUSTICE - LAW LIBRARY (Law)
123 W. Washington, Rm. 349
Box 7857 Phone: (608)266-0325
Madison, WI 53707 Michael F. Bemis, Law Libn.
Founded: 1969. **Staff:** Prof 2; Other 1. **Subjects:** Wisconsin law, general law. **Special Collections:** Antitrust law; consumer protection; law enforcement and criminology; environmental protection. **Holdings:** 30,000 volumes; departmental and divisional publications. **Subscriptions:** 30 journals and other serials; 10 newspapers. **Services:** Library not open to the public, but arrangements may be made with librarian for use of materials. **Computerized Information Services:** LEXIS, NEXIS. **Publications:** Information bulletins, irregular - for internal distribution only. **Special Indexes:** Index digest to opinions of the Attorney General of Wisconsin, 1845-1972 (book with update on computer microfiche card). **Staff:** Sara Paul, Asst. Law Libn..

★17962★
WISCONSIN STATE DEPARTMENT OF NATURAL RESOURCES - BUREAU OF RESEARCH - TECHNICAL LIBRARY (Env-Cons)
3911 Fish Hatchery Rd. Phone: (608)275-3200
Fitchburg, WI 53711-5397 Amy L. Kindschi, Libn.
Founded: 1964. **Staff:** Prof 2; Other 1. **Subjects:** Fish, wildlife, water resources. **Special Collections:** Fish (Dr. Schneberger, Lyle Christensen, Warren Churchill); Wildlife (Richard Hunt, Carroll D. Besadny). **Holdings:** 4050 books; 562 bound periodical volumes; unbound reports; archival materials; dissertations; documents; microfiche; reprints; bureau publications. **Subscriptions:** 83 journals and other serials. **Services:** Interlibrary loan; copying; SDI; library open to the public for reference use only. **Automated Operations:** Computerized cataloging. **Computerized Information Services:** DIALOG Information Services. **Networks/Consortia:** Member of Wisconsin Interlibrary Services (WILS). **Publications:** Acquisitions List, quarterly; Periodical Holdings, irregular - both for internal distribution only. **Staff:** William N. Roark, Reprints & Archv.Libn..

★17963★
WISCONSIN STATE DEPARTMENT OF NATURAL RESOURCES - LIBRARY (Env-Cons)
Box 7921 Phone: (608)266-8933
Madison, WI 53707 Patricia S. Parsons, Dept.Libn.
Staff: Prof 1; Other 1. **Subjects:** Environmental protection, air pollution, solid waste and water quality management, natural resources, fish and wildlife. **Holdings:** 5500 books; 100 bound periodical volumes; 4500 other cataloged items. **Subscriptions:** 200 journals and other serials. **Services:** Interlibrary loan; library open to the public by appointment. **Automated Operations:** Computerized cataloging. **Computerized Information Services:** Chemical Information Systems, Inc. (CIS), DIALOG Information

Services. **Networks/Consortia:** Member of Multitype Advisory Library Committee (MALC). **Publications:** Shelflife (acquisitions list), irregular.

★17964★
WISCONSIN STATE DEPARTMENT OF NATURAL RESOURCES - MAC KENZIE ENVIRONMENTAL EDUCATION CENTER (Env-Cons)
W7303 Cty. 4 Phone: (608)635-4498
Poynette, WI 53955 Robert Wallen, Prog.Spec.
Staff: 1. **Subjects:** Natural resources, natural sciences, environment. **Holdings:** 700 books; 12 VF drawers of pamphlets and clippings; 2500 color slides. **Services:** Center open to the public with restrictions.

★17965★
WISCONSIN STATE DEPARTMENT OF NATURAL RESOURCES - SOUTHEAST DISTRICT LIBRARY (Env-Cons)
2300 N. Martin Luther King Jr. Dr. Phone: (414)562-9536
Milwaukee, WI 53212 Kathleen Schultz, Libn.
Staff: Prof 1. **Subjects:** Pollution and quality of air and water, fish and wildlife, solid waste management, parks and recreation, forestry. **Special Collections:** Departmental publications (500 technical bulletins, research reports, surface water reports); Environmental Protection Agency documents (1100). **Holdings:** 2600 books; 35 bound periodical volumes. **Subscriptions:** 78 journals and other serials. **Services:** Interlibrary loan; copying; SDI; library open to the public for reference use only.

WISCONSIN STATE DEPARTMENT OF PUBLIC INSTRUCTION - DIVISION OF LIBRARY SERVICES - COOPERATIVE CHILDREN'S BOOK CENTER
See: University of Wisconsin, Madison - Cooperative Children's Book Center (CCBC) (17126)

★17966★
WISCONSIN STATE DEPARTMENT OF PUBLIC INSTRUCTION - MICROCOMPUTER CENTER/LIBRARY
(Educ, Comp Sci)
125 S. Webster St., 3rd Fl.
Box 7841 Phone: (608)266-2529
Madison, WI 53707 Phillip Sager, Libn.
Founded: 1968. **Staff:** Prof 2; Other 1. **Subjects:** Educational administration, handicapped children, curriculum development, public administration, education and related social sciences, research, professional improvement, instructional materials, educational technology, library and information science. **Holdings:** 300 pamphlets; 300 journals; 3500 monographs; 1982-1983 curriculum development library on microfiche; complete ERIC microfiche collection; 300 microcomputer software packages; software reviews. **Subscriptions:** 350 journals and other serials. **Services:** Interlibrary loan; copying; computer demonstration center; library open to the public for reference use only. **Automated Operations:** Computerized cataloging. **Computerized Information Services:** DIALOG Information Services, BRS Information Technologies, LEXIS, NEXIS, SpecialNet; ALANET (electronic mail service). Performs searches on fee basis. **Networks/Consortia:** Member of Multitype Advisory Library Committee (MALC). **Publications:** New Acquisitions, monthly; WDP Brochure and request form - on request; subject bibliographies. **Staff:** Mary Fix, Instr. Software Spec..

★17967★
WISCONSIN STATE DEPARTMENT OF PUBLIC INSTRUCTION - SCHOOL FOR THE VISUALLY HANDICAPPED - LIBRARY (Aud-Vis)
1700 W. State St. Phone: (608)755-2967
Janesville, WI 53545 Jean Wolski, Libn.
Founded: 1850. **Staff:** Prof 1. **Subjects:** General collection. **Holdings:** 3000 print books; 280 tactile items; 3000 braille books; 5000 talking books; 3000 cassette books. **Subscriptions:** 60 journals and other serials. **Services:** Library services restricted to the visually handicapped and educators serving the visually impaired.

★17968★
WISCONSIN STATE DEPARTMENT OF TRANSPORTATION - LIBRARY (Trans)
4802 Sheboygan Ave., Rm. 901
Box 7913
Madison, WI 53707 Phone: (608)266-0724
Founded: 1961. **Staff:** Prof 1; Other 1. **Subjects:** Transportation planning, highways, urban transit, Wisconsin urban planning, transportation economics. **Special Collections:** Transportation (Highway) Research Board. **Holdings:** 4300 books; 200 unbound periodical volumes; 9500 reports; 300 pamphlets. **Subscriptions:** 200 journals and other serials. **Services:** Interlibrary loan; copying; library open to the public. **Networks/Consortia:** Member of Multitype Advisory Library Committee (MALC). **Publications:** Recent Acquisitions, monthly - to Department of Transportation staff and others upon request. **Staff:** Cordell Klyve, Libn.; Susan Fox, Libn..

★17969★
WISCONSIN STATE DIVISION FOR LIBRARY SERVICES - REFERENCE AND LOAN LIBRARY (Info Sci)
2109 S. Stoughton Rd. Phone: (608)266-1081
Madison, WI 53716 Sally J. Drew, Dir.
Founded: 1895. **Staff:** Prof 8; Other 21. **Subjects:** Biography, geography, religion, education, political science, music, recreation, library science, science and technology, crafts, collectibles, computing. **Holdings:** 157,000 volumes; 14,800 phonograph records; 250 compact discs; 5200 reels of microfilm of periodicals; 18,200 Wisconsin documents; 1020 mixed media kits; 6400 audiotapes; 90 films; 1300 videotapes; 3000 pamphlets; 165 video discs; video cassettes; filmstrips; slides; 16mm films; foreign and English language instruction sound recordings; Media Resources for Continuing Library Education and Staff Development. **Subscriptions:** 700 journals and other serials. **Services:** Interlibrary loan; copying; library is the state resource center for public and school libraries; other resource center libraries are searched for needed material to which requests are then referred. **Automated Operations:** Computerized cataloging. **Computerized Information Services:** BRS Information Technologies, WILSONLINE, DIALOG Information Services, OCLC. **Networks/Consortia:** Member of Wisconsin Interlibrary Services (WILS). **Publications:** Manual for Interlibrary Loan Service; selected lists of holdings. **Staff:** Virginia Potter, Ref.Supv.; Janice Lang, Tech.Serv.Supv.; Reid Harrsch, Acq. & Bibliog.Serv.Libn.; Mary Struckmeyer, ILL; Willeen Tretheway, AV Libn..

★17970★
WISCONSIN STATE JOURNAL/CAPITAL TIMES - LIBRARY
(Publ)
Box 8058 Phone: (608)252-6112
Madison, WI 53708 Ronald J. Larson, Hd.Libn.
Staff: Prof 1; Other 3. **Subjects:** Newspaper reference topics, local news and history, state news, state government, University of Wisconsin news. **Special Collections:** Joseph McCarthy; Frank Lloyd Wright. **Holdings:** 500 books; newspaper clippings; photographs; Wisconsin State Journal, 1852 to present, on microfilm; Capital Times, 1917 to present, on microfilm. **Services:** Copying; library open to the public on a limited schedule. **Automated Operations:** Computerized reference directory. **Computerized Information Services:** NEXIS.

WISCONSIN STATE LAW LIBRARY
See: Wisconsin State Supreme Court (17974)

★17971★
WISCONSIN (State) LEGISLATIVE REFERENCE BUREAU - REFERENCE AND LIBRARY SECTION (Soc Sci, Law)
State Capitol, Rm. 201 North Phone: (608)266-0341
Madison, WI 53702 H. Rupert Theobald, Bureau Chf.
Founded: 1901. **Staff:** Prof 12; Other 7. **Subjects:** State government - public administration, taxation, finance, education, public welfare, labor, conservation, energy, pollution, public health, agriculture, economic development, motor vehicle regulation, highway finance and development, legislative procedure, courts, civil rights, civil service, federal and local governments. **Special Collections:** Wisconsin session laws, statutes, legislative journals, and Supreme Court reports, 1848 to present; Opinions of the Attorney General, 1904 to present; Blue Books, 1858 to present; bound volumes of legislative bills, 1897 to present; archival depository of departmental reports in separate collection of state documents; legislative bill drafting records, 1927 to present. **Holdings:** 100,000 volumes, including an extensive number of unbound and microfiche volumes of clippings. **Subscriptions:** 300 journals and other serials. **Services:** Interlibrary loan; copying; bureau open to the public. **Computerized Information Services:** LEXIS, NEXIS, LEGISNET; ATMS (bill histories), STAIRS (Wisconsin statutes; internal databases). **Publications:** Research Bulletins; Informational Bulletins; Wisconsin Briefs; Wisconsin Facts; Comparative Facts, all irregular; Wisconsin Blue Book, biennial. **Special Catalogs:** State Document Catalog. **Special Indexes:** Index to legislation introduced in the Wisconsin Legislature since 1897. **Staff:** Mina Waldie, Supv.Libn.; Rose Arnold, Libn.; Janet Monk, Libn.; Marian Rogers, Libn.; Lawrence S. Barish, Res.Dir.; Peter Cannon, Res.Anl.; Amy Hague, Res.Anl.; Dick Pazen, Res.Anl.; Clark Radatz, Res.Anl.; Richard Roe, Res.Anl.; Gary Watchke, Res.Anl..

★17972★
WISCONSIN STATE MEDICAL SOCIETY - LIBRARY (Med)
330 E. Lakeside St.
Box 1109 Phone: (608)257-6781
Madison, WI 53701 Mary Angell, Mng.Ed.
Staff: 1. **Subjects:** Medicine. **Holdings:** 125 volumes. **Subscriptions:** 158 journals and other serials. **Services:** Library not open to the public. **Publications:** Wisconsin Medical Journal, monthly - to members of the Wisconsin State Medical Society.

★17973★
WISCONSIN STATE OFFICE OF THE COMMISSIONER OF INSURANCE - LIBRARY (Bus-Fin)
Box 7873 Phone: (608)266-3585
Madison, WI 53707 Shari Blasdel
Staff: Prof 1. **Subjects:** Insurance and its law. **Special Collections:** Wisconsin Insurance Report, 1895-1987. **Holdings:** 1000 books; 1400 bound periodical volumes; 35 cubic feet of unbound periodicals. **Subscriptions:** 30 journals and other serials. **Services:** Library open to the public with restrictions. **Remarks:** Library located at 123 W. Washington Ave., 7th Fl., Madison, WI 53703.

★17974★
WISCONSIN STATE SUPREME COURT - WISCONSIN STATE LAW LIBRARY (Law)
Box 7881 Phone: (608)266-1600
Madison, WI 53707-7881 Marcia J. Koslov, State Law Libn.
Founded: 1836. **Staff:** Prof 5; Other 6. **Subjects:** Law. **Special Collections:** Wisconsin Appendices & Briefs, 1836 to present; Wisconsin Court of Appeals Unpublished Opinions. **Holdings:** 135,000 volumes; 10,000 documents; 3600 reels of microfilm; 86,000 microfiche. **Subscriptions:** 640 journals and other serials. **Services:** Copying; library open to the public with restrictions on circulation. **Computerized Information Services:** LEXIS, NEXIS, WESTLAW, DIALOG Information Services, OCLC. Performs searches for attorneys and judges on fee basis. **Staff:** Dennis Austin, Dp. Law Libn.; M. Elaine Sharp, Asst.Libn., Tech.Serv.; Cheryl A. O'Connor, Asst.Libn., Rd.Serv.; Janice Pena, Asst.Libn., Rd.Serv.; Jane Colwin, Lib.Serv.Libn..

WISCONSIN VETERANS MUSEUMS - GRAND ARMY OF THE REPUBLIC MEMORIAL HALL MUSEUM
See: Grand Army of the Republic Memorial Hall Museum (5791)

★17975★
WISE COUNTY HISTORICAL SOCIETY, INC. - WISE COUNTY HISTORICAL COMMISSION ARCHIVE (Hist)
1602 S. Trinity
Box 427 Phone: (817)627-3732
Decatur, TX 76234 Rosalie Gregg, Chm.
Staff: 2. **Subjects:** Wise County history, family histories, cemetery records, census. **Special Collections:** Wise County Messenger and Decatur News (microfilm); Wise County, Tennessee, and Virginia census records; Civil War; Presidents; Texas Heritage Project; county histories. **Holdings:** Books; microfiche. **Services:** Copying; archive open to the public for reference use only; will answer mail inquiries. **Publications:** Newsletter, monthly. **Remarks:** An alternate telephone number is 627-5586.

★17976★
ISAAC M. WISE TEMPLE - RALPH COHEN MEMORIAL LIBRARY (Rel-Phil)
8329 Ridge Rd. Phone: (513)793-2556
Cincinnati, OH 45236 Judith S. Carsch, Libn.
Staff: Prof 1. **Subjects:** Judaica, Holocaust. **Holdings:** 15,000 books. **Subscriptions:** 23 journals and other serials. **Services:** Library open to the public with restrictions.

★17977★
WILLIAM N. WISHARD MEMORIAL HOSPITAL - PROFESSIONAL LIBRARY/MEDIA SERVICES (Med)
1001 W. 10th St. Phone: (317)630-7657
Indianapolis, IN 46202 Kirsten Quam, Mgr., Lib./Media Serv.Dept.
Staff: Prof 2; Other 5. **Subjects:** Medicine, nursing, health care administration. **Special Collections:** Emergency medical services (100 volumes). **Holdings:** 6000 books; 8000 bound periodical volumes; 1000 AV programs. **Subscriptions:** 250 journals and other serials. **Services:** Interlibrary loan; copying; current awareness service; library open to the public for reference use only. **Automated Operations:** Computerized cataloging and ILL. **Computerized Information Services:** OCLC, DIALOG Information Services, BRS Information Technologies, Pergamon ORBIT InfoLine, Inc., NLM; DOCLINE (electronic mail service). **Networks/Consortia:** Member of Central Indiana Health Science Library Consortium, Greater Midwest Regional Medical Library Network, INCOLSA. **Staff:** Susan H. Kent, Libn./Search Anl..

★17978★
WISTAR INSTITUTE OF ANATOMY & BIOLOGY - LIBRARY (Med)
36th & Spruce Sts. Phone: (215)898-3805
Philadelphia, PA 19104 J.A. Hunter, Libn.
Founded: 1894. **Staff:** Prof 1; Other 1. **Subjects:** Cancer, virus diseases, cytology, immunology, genetics, biochemistry. **Special Collections:** Personal library of General Isaac J. Wistar (including English and scientific classics, Americana, and history; 1000 volumes). **Holdings:** 3000 books; 9000 bound periodical volumes. **Subscriptions:** 182 journals and other serials. **Services:** Interlibrary loan; library open to the public for reference use only. **Computerized Information Services:** NLM, BRS Information Technologies, DIALOG Information Services, Pergamon ORBIT InfoLine, Inc., WILSONLINE.

R.D. WISWALL MEMORIAL LIBRARY
See: Vancouver Memorial Hospital (17264)

★17979★
WITCO CHEMICAL CORPORATION - GOLDEN BEAR DIVISION - QC/R & D LIBRARY (Sci-Engr)
Ferguson & Manor Rds.
Box 5446 Phone: (805)393-7110
Oildale, CA 93388 Euthene Snell, Libn.
Founded: 1948. **Staff:** 2. **Subjects:** Petroleum refining, lubricants, asphalt pavements, rubber, emulsions, instrumental analyses. **Holdings:** 2200 books; 670 bound periodical volumes; 5 catalogs; 5 VF drawers of internal technical reports; preprints; reprints; instrumental scans; 5 VF drawers of patents, technical documents, product development information; 5 VF drawers of government and industry specifications, qualifications, and contracts. **Subscriptions:** 47 journals and other serials. **Services:** Copying; library open to the public by appointment.

★17980★
WITCO CORPORATION - RESEARCH & DEVELOPMENT LIBRARY (Sci-Engr)
3200 Brookfield Phone: (713)433-7281
Houston, TX 77045 Helen K. Kim, Libn.
Staff: Prof 1. **Subjects:** Chemistry and applied technology. **Holdings:** Books; bound periodical volumes; reprints; reports; technical abstracts. **Subscriptions:** 96 journals and other serials. **Services:** Interlibrary loan; library not open to the public. **Computerized Information Services:** Pergamon ORBIT InfoLine, Inc., DIALOG Information Services, STN International. Performs searches on fee basis. **Publications:** Current Notes, monthly - for internal distribution only; New Acquisitions, semiannual; Selected Subject Bibliographies, irregular.

★17981★
WITCO CORPORATION - TECHNICAL INFORMATION CENTER (Sci-Engr)
100 Bauer Dr. Phone: (201)337-5812
Oakland, NJ 07436 Jo Therese Smith, Mgr., Tech.Info.Serv.
Founded: 1967. **Staff:** Prof 2. **Subjects:** Chemistry - organic, analytic, petroleum; chemical engineering. **Special Collections:** Petroleum technology; surfactant technology. **Holdings:** 14,000 books; 13,500 bound periodical volumes; 15 VF drawers of patents, pamphlets, reprints; 10 drawers of patents and journals on microfiche; Chemical Abstracts, 1980 to present. **Subscriptions:** 154 journals and other serials. **Services:** Interlibrary loan; SDI; center open to the public by appointment. **Computerized Information Services:** DIALOG Information Services, STN International, CAS ONLINE. **Networks/Consortia:** Member of New Jersey Library Network. **Publications:** Current Holdings List; Articles of Current Interest.

JOHN WITHERSPOON LIBRARY
See: Princeton University - Rare Books and Special Collections (11593)

★17982★
WITHLACOOCHEE REGIONAL PLANNING COUNCIL - LIBRARY (Plan)
1241 S.W. 10th St. Phone: (904)732-3307
Ocala, FL 32674-2798 Vivian A. Whittier, Mktg.Coord.
Staff: Prof 1. **Subjects:** Statistics, planning, land use, water, energy, criminal justice, census data. **Holdings:** 5000 bound periodical volumes; maps; technical reports. **Subscriptions:** 19 journals and other serials. **Services:** Copying; library open to the public with restrictions on lending.

Publications: Data Subscription Service (reports), quarterly; Bulletin; Final Inspection Report, biannual. **Remarks:** Most library materials are concerned with Citrus, Hernando, Levy, Marion, and Sumter counties.

RABBI LOUIS WITT MEMORIAL LIBRARY
See: Temple Israel (13968)

WITTE MEMORIAL MUSEUM
See: San Antonio Museum Association (12742)

★17983★
WITTENBERG UNIVERSITY - THOMAS LIBRARY (Rel-Phil)
Box 720 Phone: (513)327-7016
Springfield, OH 45501 John Montag, Dir.
Founded: 1845. **Staff:** Prof 7; Other 11. **Subjects:** Lutheran Church, Martin Luther, Reformation. **Special Collections:** Baltasar Gracian y Morales Collection; Wilhelm C. Berkenmeyer Colonial Parish Library (226 volumes); Susan V. Russell Tape Library (religious sermons); Archives, Ohio Synod Lutheran Church in America; University Archives; 19th century Ohio newspapers; Lutheran Reformation; Goldman Travel Collection (11,080 slides); Cyril F. DosPassos Collection of Lepidoptera (2500 volumes); diaries, papers, and etchings of Walter Tittle, American artist, 1883-1965; correspondence, manuscripts, and books of Dr. Martin C. Fischer, University of Cincinnati professor; Geiger Family papers, 1870-1910; hymnals (3700 volumes). **Holdings:** 333,870 books; 41,481 bound periodical volumes; 16,631 phonograph records; 44,130 AV programs; 35,000 volumes of Library of American Civilization and English Literature on microfiche; 5836 volumes on East Asia. **Subscriptions:** 1176 journals and other serials; 16 newspapers. **Services:** Interlibrary loan; copying; library open to the public. **Automated Operations:** Computerized cataloging. **Computerized Information Services:** DIALOG Information Services, CAS ONLINE, BRS Information Technologies, OCLC. **Networks/Consortia:** Member of OHIONET, Southwest Ohio Council for Higher Education (SOCHE). **Publications:** Library publications, irregular; selective accessions, semimonthly. **Special Indexes:** Indexes to Martin C. Fischer, Walter Tittle, and Geiger Family Papers collection; University Archives index (card). **Staff:** Velma Layman, Hd., Circ.; Don Gordon, Soc.Sci.Libn.; Regina Entorf, Spec.Coll.Libn.; Kathy Schulz, Hum.Libn.; Robert Klapthor, Sci.Libn.; Norman Pearson, Hd., Tech.Serv..

WNYC ARCHIVES
See: New York Public Library - Performing Arts Research Center - Rodgers & Hammerstein Archives of Recorded Sound (10082)

★17984★
WOFFORD COLLEGE - SANDOR TESZLER LIBRARY - ARCHIVES (Hist)
N. Church St. Phone: (803)585-4821
Spartanburg, SC 29301 Herbert Hucks, Jr., Archv.
Staff: Prof 1. **Subjects:** History of Wofford College, its alumni and faculty. **Holdings:** 1415 books; 565 bound periodical volumes; 850 cataloged items; manuscripts of books by faculty members; tape recordings of "From Dr. Snyder's Study" (1948-1949 broadcasts over local radio station WSPA; manuscripts, tapes, and broadcasts contained in 28 legal size filing cabinet drawers); college catalogs; yearbooks; college journals; alumni and faculty publications; Old Gold and Black (student newspaper); memorabilia; photographs. **Services:** Copying; archives open to the public for reference use only.

★17985★
WOFFORD COLLEGE - SANDOR TESZLER LIBRARY - LITTLEJOHN RARE BOOK ROOM (Rare Book)
N. Church St. Phone: (803)585-4821
Spartanburg, SC 29301 Oakley H. Coburn, Lib.Dir.
Founded: 1854. **Subjects:** South Caroliniana; private presses, including Wofford Library Press; 16th and 17th century books; Folio Society publications; 19th and 20th century children's books. **Special Collections:** Matthew Carey Collection (100 volumes); Haynes Brown Hymnal Collection (1200 volumes); Leonard Baskin/Gehenna Press Collection (100 volumes). **Holdings:** 10,000 books; 1000 bound periodical volumes. **Services:** Room open to the public by appointment with supervision. **Automated Operations:** Computerized cataloging. **Computerized Information Services:** DIALOG Information Services. **Publications:** Special Collections Checklists, Numbers 1-7; Wofford Bibliopolist.

★17986★
ALAN WOFSY FINE ARTS - REFERENCE LIBRARY (Art)
401 China Basin St. Phone: (415)986-3030
San Francisco, CA 94107 Adios Butler, Libn.
Subjects: Art of the book, graphics, architecture. **Special Collections:** Descriptive catalogs of artists. **Holdings:** 3000 books; 100 bound periodical volumes. **Publications:** San Francisco Review of Books, quarterly - by subscription.

JOHN G. WOLBACH LIBRARY
See: Harvard University - Observatory Library (6112)

★17987★
WOLF, BLOCK, SCHORR & SOLIS-COHEN - LIBRARY (Law)
Packard Bldg., 12th Fl. Phone: (215)977-2000
Philadelphia, PA 19102 John Duckett, Libn.
Founded: 1913. **Staff:** Prof 2; Other 3. **Subjects:** Law - corporate, real estate, labor, health, environmental; litigation. **Special Collections:** Tax law. **Holdings:** 14,000 volumes. **Subscriptions:** 75 journals and other serials. **Services:** Interlibrary loan; library open to the public by appointment. **Computerized Information Services:** LEXIS. **Staff:** Lisa McLean, Asst.Libn..

WOLF TRAP FOUNDATION FOR THE PERFORMING ARTS ARCHIVES
See: George Mason University - Fenwick Library - Special Collections and Archives (8509)

★17988★
THE HORACE L. WOLFE MEMORIAL LIBRARY (Mil)
Grand Central Station
Box 3514 Phone: (818)241-7284
Glendale, CA 91201 Douglas L. Evans, Libn.
Founded: 1954. **Staff:** Prof 2. **Subjects:** Espionage, sabotage, military intelligence, secret services, secret societies, cryptography. **Holdings:** 10,785 books; 3700 clippings. **Subscriptions:** 20 journals and other serials; 12 newspapers. **Services:** Library not open to the public. **Remarks:** Library serves as a reference source for television and motion picture industries and certain government agencies.

MAX & BEATRICE WOLFE LIBRARY
See: Beth Tzedec Congregation (1552)

★17989★
WOLFEBORO HISTORICAL SOCIETY - LIBRARY (Hist)
S. Main St.
Box 1066 Phone: (603)569-4997
Wolfeboro, NH 03894 Harrison D. Moore, Pres.
Staff: 1. **Subjects:** Local history and genealogy, 19th century fire engines. **Holdings:** Books; maps; scrapbooks of local events; town reports; old school records. **Services:** Library open to the public on a limited schedule.

WOLFGRAM MEMORIAL LIBRARY
See: Widener University (17867)

WOLFNER MEMORIAL LIBRARY FOR THE BLIND & PHYSICALLY HANDICAPPED
See: Missouri State Library - Wolfner Memorial Library for the Blind & Physically Handicapped (9134)

ISAAC N. WOLFSON LIBRARY
See: Letchworth Village Developmental Center (7764)

LOUIS WOLFSON MEDIA HISTORY CENTER
See: Miami-Dade Public Library (8861)

WOMACK ARMY COMMUNITY HOSPITAL
See: U.S. Army Hospitals (14841)

★17990★
WOMEN ARTISTS NEWS/MIDMARCH ARTS - ARCHIVES (Art)
Grand Central Sta., Box 3304 Phone: (212)666-6990
New York, NY 10163 K. Staroba
Founded: 1973. **Staff:** 2. **Subjects:** Art, women artists, women in art, women's organizations, art exhibitions. **Holdings:** 24 VF drawers of archival material on women in the arts; ephemera. **Subscriptions:** 25 journals and other serials. **Services:** Copying; archives open to the public by appointment. **Publications:** Women Artists News, quarterly; Guide to Women's Art Organizations, biennial; Whole Arts Directory, biennial with

quarterly update; Voices of Women (criticism, poetry, graphics); Women Artists of the World (essays, photographs, and reproductions of art works of women artists worldwide); Pilgrims & Pioneers: New England Women in the Arts (historical and contemporary; essays and photographs); American Women in Art: Works on Paper. **Remarks:** Published by Midmarch Associates. **Staff:** Cynthia Navaretta, Exec.Dir..

★17991★
WOMEN & INFANTS HOSPITAL OF RHODE ISLAND - HEALTH SCIENCES INFORMATION CENTER (Med)
101 Dudley St. Phone: (401)274-1100
Providence, RI 02905 Barbara Riter, Libn.
Founded: 1884. **Staff:** Prof 1; Other 2. **Subjects:** Obstetrics, gynecology, pediatrics. **Holdings:** 2000 books; 1650 bound periodical volumes. **Subscriptions:** 185 journals and other serials. **Services:** Interlibrary loan; copying; SDI; center open to the public with permission. **Computerized Information Services:** NLM. Performs searches on fee basis. **Networks/Consortia:** Member of Greater Northeastern Regional Medical Library Program, Consortium of Rhode Island Academic and Research Libraries, Inc. (CRIARL).

★17992★
WOMEN'S ACTION ALLIANCE, INC. - LIBRARY (Soc Sci)
370 Lexington Ave., Suite 603 Phone: (212)532-8330
New York, NY 10017 Paulette Brill, Info.Serv.
Founded: 1971. **Staff:** Prof 1. **Subjects:** Women's issues - child care, sex discrimination, marriage, divorce, family, health, employment, affirmative action, reproductive rights, legislation, organizations and centers, chemical dependency, AIDS, teenage pregancy. **Special Collections:** Files of national women's organizations and women's centers organized by state. **Holdings:** 2000 books; 2000 bound periodical volumes; 40 VF drawers. **Subscriptions:** 200 journals and other serials. **Services:** Interlibrary loan; library open to the public by appointment. **Automated Operations:** Computerized cataloging. **Publications:** List of publications - available upon request. **Special Indexes:** Employment resource list for New York City.

WOMEN'S AMERICAN ORT FEDERATION - BRAMSON ORT INSTITUTE
See: Bramson ORT Institute (1807)

★17993★
THE WOMEN'S BOOK EXCHANGE (Soc Sci)
408 W. Rosemary St.
Chapel Hill, NC 27514-3934 Phone: (919)942-1740
Founded: 1983. **Subjects:** Women's literature, women's studies, feminism, nonsexist children's literature. **Holdings:** 4000 books; 100 other cataloged items. **Services:** Exchange open to the public for referrals and reference; full service available to members. **Publications:** Women's Book Exchange Newsletter, irregular - to members. **Staff:** Spring E. Brooks, Co-Dir.; Melody Ivins, Co.-Dir..

★17994★
WOMEN'S CAREER CENTER - CAREER RESOURCE LIBRARY (Educ)
14 Franklin St., Suite 1200 Phone: (716)325-2274
Rochester, NY 14604 Sarah I. Hartwell, Dir., Info. & Rsrcs.
Staff: Prof 1. **Subjects:** Vocational guidance, career change, career management and development, outplacement and spouse relocation. **Holdings:** 800 books; 7000 articles in vertical files; Employer Information File on 700 local companies and organizations. **Subscriptions:** 35 journals and other serials. **Services:** Interlibrary loan; copying; consulting; library open to the public. **Publications:** Annotated subject bibliographies. **Special Indexes:** Index to local Employer Information File (card).

★17995★
WOMEN'S CENTER OF SOUTHEASTERN CONNECTICUT - LIBRARY (Soc Sci)
120 Broad St.
Box 572
New London, CT 06320 Phone: (203)447-0366
Staff: Prof 1. **Subjects:** Feminism, violence against women, health, women's issues. **Holdings:** 500 books; 25 bound periodical volumes; vertical files. **Subscriptions:** 15 journals and other serials; 5 newspapers. **Services:** Copying; library open to the public for reference use only.

★17996★
WOMEN'S COLLEGE HOSPITAL - MEDICAL LIBRARY (Med)
76 Grenville St. Phone: (416)323-6078
Toronto, ON, Canada M5S 1B2 Margaret Robins, Dir.
Founded: 1955. **Staff:** Prof 3; Other 3. **Subjects:** Dermatology, diabetes, perinatal medicine, obstetrics, gynecology, high risk pregnancy. **Holdings:** 3800 books; 3700 periodical volumes; 410 tapes; 410 video cassettes. **Subscriptions:** 256 journals and other serials. **Services:** Interlibrary loan (fee); library not open to the public.

★17997★
WOMEN'S EQUITY ACTION LEAGUE - NATIONAL INFORMATION CENTER ON WOMEN AND THE MILITARY (Mil)
1250 I St., N.W., Suite 305 Phone: (202)898-1588
Washington, DC 20005 Carolyn Becraft, Proj.Dir.
Staff: 1982. **Staff:** Prof 2; Other 2. **Subjects:** Women and the military, military families, veterans, retired military personnel, registration and the draft, employment and utilization. **Holdings:** 100 books; 2000 reports, manuscripts, dissertations; 9 VF drawers of clippings and articles. **Services:** Copying; center open to the public. **Automated Operations:** Computerized cataloging. **Computerized Information Services:** Internal database. **Publications:** WEAL Washington Report, 6/year - to subscribers and members. **Staff:** June Inuzuka, Legal Policy Anl..

★17998★
WOMEN'S HISTORY RESEARCH CENTER, INC. - WOMEN'S HISTORY LIBRARY (Hist, Soc Sci)
2325 Oak St. Phone: (415)548-1770
Berkeley, CA 94708 Laura X, Dir.
Founded: 1968. **Staff:** Prof 2; Other 20. **Subjects:** Women's health and mental health, women and law, black and Third World women, female artists, children, films by and/or about women, Soviet women. **Special Collections:** International Women's History Archive (850 periodical titles on microfilm). **Holdings:** 2000 books; 300 tapes; 54 reels of microfilm on health and law; 90 reels of microfilm of women's periodicals in Herstory Collection. **Services:** Library not open to the public. **Publications:** Directory of Films by and/or about Women; Female Artists Directory; Women & Health/Mental Health, Women & Law, and Herstory serials (microfilm) - all for sale.

★17999★
WOMEN'S INTERNATIONAL NETWORK (Soc Sci)
187 Grant St. Phone: (617)862-9431
Lexington, MA 02173 Fran P. Hosken, Ed.
Subjects: Women's development and health, women's economic development, property rights of women worldwide. **Special Collections:** Feminine genital mutilation. **Holdings:** Figures not available. **Subscriptions:** 40 journals and other serials; 10 newspapers. **Publications:** Childbirth Picture Book/Program; WIN News, quarterly; list of additional publications - available on request.

★18000★
WOMEN'S RESOURCE AND ACTION CENTER - SOJOURNER TRUTH WOMEN'S RESOURCE LIBRARY (Soc Sci)
130 N. Madison Phone: (319)335-1486
Iowa City, IA 52242 Cherry Muhanji, Libn.
Founded: 1976. **Staff:** Prof 1; Other 5. **Subjects:** Feminism. **Special Collections:** Complete holdings of Ain't I A Woman, 1970-1973 (feminist periodical). **Holdings:** 1700 books. **Subscriptions:** 100 journals and other serials. **Services:** Library open to the public. **Publications:** Women's Resource & Action Center News, monthly - by subscription and free local distribution.

★18001★
WOMEN'S RESOURCE CENTER LIBRARY (Soc Sci)
Bldg. T-9
University of California Phone: (415)642-4786
Berkeley, CA 94720 Nancy Humphreys, Lib.Coord.
Staff: Prof 1; Other 2. **Subjects:** Women's studies, women and work, financial aid, career resources for women; minority women; international issues. **Special Collections:** Catherine Scholten Collection on Women in American History (100 books); Bea Bain Collection on the Women's Movement (100 books); Margaret Monroe Drews Collection of Working Papers (the status of women in the U.S., 1950-1970; 12 VF drawers); Constance Barker Collection on Lesbian History (700 books); women's movement magazines of the 1970s. **Holdings:** 3000 books; 20,000 other cataloged items. **Subscriptions:** 60 journals and other serials. **Services:** Library open to the public for reference use only. **Publications:** Acquisitions list, quarterly; bibliographies, irregular; WLW (Women

Library Workers) Journal, quarterly. **Special Catalogs:** Tape catalog; journal and newsletter catalog (both on cards). **Special Indexes:** Vertical file index.

★18002★
WOOD COUNTY HISTORICAL SOCIETY - HISTORICAL MUSEUM LIBRARY (Hist)
13660 County Home Rd. Phone: (419)352-0967
Bowling Green, OH 43402 Lyle Fletcher, Archv.
Founded: 1955. **Staff:** Prof 1. **Subjects:** History of Wood County, Maumee Valley, and Ohio. **Holdings:** 150 books; maps; papers; periodicals. **Services:** Copying; library open to the public for reference use only. **Publications:** The Black Swamp Chanticleer, monthly. **Special Indexes:** Index of surnames in Leeson-Evers History of Wood County; Surname Index of the Pioneer Scrap Book of Wood County and the Maumee Valley by Charles Evers; index for 4 wood county atlases: Historical Atlas of the World (Wood County edition) 1875, Lucas and Part of Wood Counties, Ohio 1871, Atlas of Wood County 1886, and Atlas of Wood County 1912.

★18003★
WOOD COUNTY LAW LIBRARY (Law)
County Office Bldg., 1st Fl. Phone: (419)353-3921
Bowling Green, OH 43402 Judith L. Gill, Libn.
Staff: 2. **Subjects:** Law. **Holdings:** 19,000 books; 1100 bound periodical volumes; 250 volumes of legal opinions; tapes. **Subscriptions:** 50 journals and other serials. **Services:** Interlibrary loan; copying; library open to the public. **Computerized Information Services:** WESTLAW, VU/TEXT Information Services, DIALOG Information Services, Dow Jones News/Retrieval.

GENERAL LEONARD WOOD ARMY COMMUNITY HOSPITAL
See: U.S. Army Hospitals (14827)

GRANT WOOD ARCHIVES
See: Cedar Rapids Museum of Art - Herbert S. Stamats Art Library (2782)

★18004★
WOOD GUNDY INC. - LIBRARY (Bus-Fin)
100 Wall St.
New York, NY 10005 Phone: (212)344-0633
Staff: Prof 1. **Subjects:** Investment securities. **Holdings:** Figures not available.

★18005★
WOOD GUNDY INC. - LIBRARY (Bus-Fin)
P.O. Box 274
Royal Trust Tower Phone: (416)869-8100
Toronto, ON, Canada M5K 1M7 Anne Baumann, Libn.
Founded: 1964. **Staff:** Prof 3; Other 4. **Subjects:** Corporations and industry, investments, accounting, economics. **Special Collections:** Wood Gundy publications (145 binders); financial statements of private Canadian companies (8000 microfiche). **Holdings:** 5000 volumes. **Subscriptions:** 434 journals and other serials; 310 Statistics Canada titles. **Services:** Interlibrary loan; copying. **Computerized Information Services:** Info Globe, Infomart, Canada Systems Group (CSG), INVESTEXT, The Financial Post Information Service, Datasolve Ltd., DIALOG Information Services, Dow Jones News/Retrieval. **Publications:** Acquisitions list, monthly; list of Wood Gundy Research Reports, quarterly; periodicals list, annual - all for internal distribution only. **Special Indexes:** Index of Wood Gundy research reports, 1976 to present. **Staff:** Julie Brittain, Libn..

JOHN PENMAN WOOD LIBRARY OF NATIONAL DEFENSE
See: University of Pennsylvania (16737)

WOOD LIBRARY-MUSEUM OF ANESTHESIOLOGY
See: American Society of Anesthesiologists (664)

WOOD NEPAL LIBRARY
See: American Nepal Education Foundation - Wood Nepal Library (618)

SAMUEL J. WOOD LIBRARY
See: Cornell University - Medical College (3785)

WOOD TECHNICAL LIBRARY
See: U.S. Army - Health Services Command - Medical Research Institute of Chemical Defense (14757)

WOODBERRY POETRY ROOM
See: Harvard University (6126)

★18006★
WOODBURY COUNTY BAR ASSOCIATION - LAW LIBRARY (Law)
Woodbury County Courthouse, 6th Fl.
7th & Douglas Sts. Phone: (712)279-6609
Sioux City, IA 51101 Susan M. Dunn, Libn.
Staff: Prof 1; Other 1. **Subjects:** State and general law. **Holdings:** 12,100 volumes. **Services:** Copying; library open to the public.

★18007★
WOODBURY UNIVERSITY - LIBRARY (Bus-Fin, Art)
7500 Glenoaks Blvd.
Box 7846 Phone: (818)767-0888
Burbank, CA 91510-7846 Dr. William Stanley, Lib.Dir.
Founded: 1884. **Staff:** Prof 3; Other 4. **Subjects:** Economics, international business, art, architecture, interior decoration, management, fashion marketing and design, computers. **Holdings:** 54,327 books; 1888 bound periodical volumes; 47,819 microforms; 5045 slides, filmstrips, cassettes, and films. **Subscriptions:** 488 journals and other serials; 12 newspapers. **Services:** Interlibrary loan; copying; library open to the public for reference use only. **Staff:** Lydia Gonzales, Ref.; Martha Pike, Tech.Serv..

JOHN WOODENLEGS MEMORIAL LIBRARY
See: Dull Knife Memorial College (4447)

★18008★
WOODHULL MEDICAL AND MENTAL HEALTH CENTER - HEALTH SCIENCES LIBRARY (Med)
760 Broadway, Rm. 3A160 Phone: (718)963-8397
Brooklyn, NY 11206 Jo-Anne Richardson, Sr.Dept.Libn.
Founded: 1982. **Staff:** Prof 1; Other 2. **Subjects:** Medicine, allied health sciences. **Holdings:** 1000 books; 250 bound periodical volumes; 300 unbound journals. **Subscriptions:** 150 journals and other serials. **Services:** Interlibrary loan; library not open to the public. **Computerized Information Services:** BRS Information Technologies. **Networks/Consortia:** Member of Brooklyn-Queens-Staten Island Health Sciences Librarians (BQSI). **Remarks:** Alternate telephone numbers are 963-8216 and 963-8275. **Staff:** Shirley Buddin, Coord.Mgr..

★18009★
WOODLAKE LUTHERAN CHURCH - LIBRARY (Rel-Phil)
7525 Oliver Ave., S. Phone: (612)866-8449
Richfield, MN 55423 Jean Ellefson, Libn.
Founded: 1959. **Staff:** 13. **Subjects:** Religion and religious teaching, books of interest to adults and youth. **Holdings:** 5192 volumes; recordings; art. **Services:** Library not open to the public.

★18010★
WOODLAND HILLS PRESBYTERIAN CHURCH - NORMAN E. NYGAARD LIBRARY (Rel-Phil)
5751 Platt Ave.
Woodland Hills, CA 91367
Founded: 1973. **Staff:** 1. **Subjects:** Bible, philosophy, Christian beliefs and living, children's literature. **Holdings:** 1000 books; 75 audio cassette tapes. **Services:** Library open to the public.

★18011★
WOODLAND PARK ZOOLOGICAL GARDENS - LIBRARY (Biol Sci)
5500 Phinney Ave., N. Phone: (206)625-4550
Seattle, WA 98103 Mary C. Hopkins, Libn.
Founded: 1971. **Staff:** Prof 2; Other 2. **Subjects:** Wild and captive mammals, birds, and reptiles; amphibians; veterinary medicine; ecology; zoos and zookeeping. **Holdings:** 1017 books; pamphlets; microforms. **Subscriptions:** 63 journals and other serials. **Services:** Interlibrary loan; copying; library open to the public for reference use only. **Computerized Information Services:** DIALOG Information Services, NEXIS, LOGIN. **Staff:** Shirley Cotter, Lib.Supv..

WOODMAN ASTRONOMICAL LIBRARY
See: University of Wisconsin, Madison - Washburn Observatory (17158)

★18012★
WOODMEN ACCIDENT & LIFE COMPANY - LIBRARY (Bus-Fin)
1526 K St.
Box 82288 Phone: (402)476-6500
Lincoln, NE 68501 Virgene K. Sloan, Libn.
Founded: 1969. **Staff:** Prof 1. **Subjects:** Health and life insurance, law, office management, data processing, accounting, finance, economics.

Holdings: 3500 books; 60 films and filmstrips; 20 VF drawers of clippings, reports, policy forms, pamphlets; 40 videotapes; 300 audio cassettes. **Subscriptions:** 125 journals and other serials. **Services:** Library not open to the public. **Special Indexes:** Index of company magazine and bulletins (card).

ROBERT W. WOODRUFF LIBRARY
See: Atlanta University Center (1111)

D.S. WOODS EDUCATION LIBRARY
See: University of Manitoba (16350)

WOODS GORDON
See: Clarkson Gordon/Woods Gordon (3272)

★18013★
WOODS HOLE OCEANOGRAPHIC INSTITUTION - RESEARCH LIBRARY (Biol Sci, Sci-Engr)
Woods Hole, MA 02543 Phone: (508)548-1400
Carolyn P. Winn, Res.Libn.
Founded: 1932. **Staff:** Prof 2; Other 7. **Subjects:** Oceanography; marine geology, chemistry, and biology; ocean engineering; marine policy. **Special Collections:** Institution Archives and Data Collection (12,000 AV programs; 160,000 underwater photographs; 11,000 charts and atlases; 3000 films; 10,000 slides). **Holdings:** 12,000 books; 20,000 bound periodical volumes; 20,000 technical reports; 250,000 reprints. **Subscriptions:** 1500 journals and other serials. **Services:** Interlibrary loan; copying; library open to the public by permission of librarian. **Computerized Information Services:** DIALOG Information Services, BRS Information Technologies, CAS ONLINE, Pergamon ORBIT InfoLine, Inc., WILSONLINE. Performs searches on fee basis. Contact Person: Colleen Hurter, Lib.Asst.. **Publications:** Monthly accession announcement; WHOI report bibliography, annual; Collected Reprints, annual - on exchange. **Special Indexes:** Oceanographic Index. **Remarks:** Jointly maintained with the Marine Biological Laboratory, where the library's holdings are housed. **Staff:** William Dunkle, Data Libn..

★18014★
WOODSIDE RECEIVING HOSPITAL - STAFF RESOURCE LIBRARY/PATIENTS' LIBRARY (Med)
800 E. Indianola Ave. Phone: (216)788-8712
Youngstown, OH 44502 Louise M. Mulderig, Libn.
Founded: 1955. **Staff:** Prof 1. **Subjects:** Psychiatry, psychiatric nursing, mental illness, mental health, social services, psychotherapy. **Special Collections:** Large print collection (90 volumes); patients' library (includes the Yale Shakespeare). **Holdings:** 6200 books; 31 bound periodical volumes; 300 boxes of archives; 200 reports; 2000 pamphlets; 22 documents; 200 phonograph records; 10 drawers of filmstrips and cassette tapes; 450 items in picture files; 260 dissertations. **Subscriptions:** 110 journals and other serials; 11 newspapers. **Services:** Interlibrary loan; copying; library open to visiting state staff and relatives of institution staff. **Networks/Consortia:** Member of NEOUCOM Council Associated Hospital Librarians. **Publications:** Public relations posters and flyers, monthly; acquisitions update, monthly. **Special Catalogs:** Research bibliography catalogs.

CARTER G. WOODSON LIBRARY
See: Association for the Study of Afro-American Life and History, Inc. (1035)

CARTER G. WOODSON REGIONAL LIBRARY
See: Chicago Public Library - Carter G. Woodson Regional Library - Vivian G. Harsh Research Collection of Afro-American History & Literature (3067)

★18015★
LEIGH YAWKEY WOODSON ART MUSEUM - LIBRARY (Art)
12th & Franklin Sts. Phone: (715)845-7010
Wausau, WI 54401-5007 Marcia M. Theel, Off.Mgr.
Founded: 1976. **Staff:** Prof 1; Other 2. **Subjects:** Wildlife art, decorative arts, glass, art history, art techniques. **Holdings:** 1000 books. **Subscriptions:** 17 journals and other serials. **Services:** Copying; library open to the public by appointment only.

WOODSON RESEARCH CENTER
See: Rice University - Woodson Research Center (12040)

WOODSTOCK COLLEGE ARCHIVES
See: Georgetown University - Special Collections Division - Lauinger Memorial Library (5597)

★18016★
WOODSTOCK HISTORICAL SOCIETY, INC. - JOHN COTTON DANA LIBRARY (Hist)
26 Elm St. Phone: (802)457-1822
Woodstock, VT 05091 Linda Williamson, Assoc.Libn.
Staff: 3. **Subjects:** Woodstock history, antiques, Vermont history, Woodstock genealogy. **Special Collections:** Charles Dana's Account Books (102 volumes); old Woodstock newspapers. **Holdings:** 1500 books; 51 bound periodical volumes; 500 pamphlets; 42 maps; 250 VF folders of papers and manuscripts; account books and records of Woodstock merchants. **Services:** Library open on a limited schedule to qualified researchers. **Publications:** Woodstock's U.S. Senator Jacob Collamer (1944); Something About Old Woodstock (1952); The Vermont Heritage of George Perkins Marsh (1960); My Grandmother's and Other Tales (1968) - all for sale; The Dana House Collection (1974); Hiram Powers, Vermont Sculptor (1974). **Staff:** Vivian Bates, Libn..

★18017★
WOODSTOCK THEOLOGICAL CENTER - LIBRARY (Rel-Phil)
Georgetown University
Box 37445 Phone: (202)687-7513
Washington, DC 20013 Rev. Eugene M. Rooney, S.J., Hd.Libn.
Founded: 1869. **Staff:** Prof 2; Other 2. **Subjects:** Roman Catholic theology, patristics, Jesuitica, church history, moral theology, scripture, Catholic Americana. **Special Collections:** Rare Jesuitica; Teilhard de Chardin Collection; Halpern Collection of Engravings (religious art); Woodstock Archives; J.C. Murray Archives; G. Weigel Archives; early printed works. **Holdings:** 175,604 books; 30,800 bound periodical volumes; 17,188 rare books; 984 reels of microfilm; 1683 microfiche. **Subscriptions:** 650 journals and other serials. **Services:** Interlibrary loan; copying; library open to scholars for reference use. **Networks/Consortia:** Member of Consortium of Universities of the Washington Metropolitan Area. **Remarks:** Maintained by Maryland Province of the Society of Jesus. **Staff:** Paul S. Osmanski, Asst.Libn..

★18018★
WOODVIEW-CALABASAS PSYCHIATRIC HOSPITAL - LIBRARY (Med)
25100 Calabasas Rd. Phone: (818)888-7500
Calabasas, CA 91302 Ching-Fen Wu Tsiang, Libn.
Founded: 1968. **Staff:** Prof 1. **Subjects:** Psychiatry, nursing, general medicine. **Holdings:** 2000 books; 500 bound periodical volumes. **Subscriptions:** 25 journals and other serials. **Services:** Interlibrary loan; library open to medical and hospital staff. **Remarks:** Maintained by Hospital Corporation of America.

★18019★
WOODVILLE STATE HOSPITAL - PROFESSIONAL LIBRARY (Med)
Carnegie, PA 15106-3793 Phone: (412)645-6470
Elaine M. Gruber, Libn.
Founded: 1967. **Staff:** Prof 1; Other 1. **Subjects:** Psychiatry, psychology, behavioral sciences, psychiatric nursing, medicine. **Holdings:** 3000 books and bound periodical volumes. **Subscriptions:** 110 journals and other serials. **Services:** Interlibrary loan; copying (limited); library open to local mental health professionals. **Networks/Consortia:** Member of Greater Northeastern Regional Medical Library Program. **Publications:** Bulletin of recent acquisitions - for internal distribution only; newsletter, quarterly.

WOODWARD BIOMEDICAL LIBRARY
See: University of British Columbia (15879)

★18020★
WOODWARD-CLYDE CONSULTANTS - LIBRARY/ INFORMATION CENTER (Sci-Engr)
203 N. Golden Circle Dr. Phone: (714)835-6886
Santa Ana, CA 92705 Ute Hertel, Libn.
Staff: Prof 1. **Subjects:** Geology, engineering, geophysics, waste management, environmental sciences. **Holdings:** 8000 books; 630 unbound periodical volumes; 600 WCC reports; 15 file cabinets of maps; 2 file cabinets of reprints; microfiche. **Subscriptions:** 60 journals and other serials. **Services:** Interlibrary loan; copying; library open to the public by appointment. **Publications:** New Book List, quarterly. **Special Catalogs:** Project files catalog (card).

★18021★
WOODWARD-CLYDE CONSULTANTS, EASTERN REGION - WCC LIBRARY (Sci-Engr)
201 Willowbrook Blvd.
Box 290 Phone: (201)785-0700
Wayne, NJ 07470 Wendy L. Wallace, Libn.
Staff: Prof 1. **Subjects:** Civil and geotechnical engineering, geology, hydrology, environmental science, hazardous waste, seismology. **Special Collections:** Geologic Atlas of the United States. **Holdings:** Figures not available. **Subscriptions:** 20 journals and other serials. **Services:** Library not open to the public. **Computerized Information Services:** DIALOG Information Services.

★18022★
WOODWARD-CLYDE CONSULTANTS, WESTERN REGION - INFORMATION CENTER (Sci-Engr)
500 12th St., Suite Phone: (415)945-3447
Oakland, CA 94607 Margaret Crawford, Libn.
Founded: 1965. **Staff:** Prof 1. **Subjects:** Water, hazardous waste, environmental science, soil mechanics, earthquake engineering, geology, seismology. **Holdings:** 2500 books; 6000 reports; 5000 unbound periodicals; 8 VF drawers of pamphlets. **Subscriptions:** 250 journals and other serials. **Services:** Interlibrary loan; center not open to the public. **Computerized Information Services:** DIALOG Information Services.

★18023★
WOODWARD GOVERNOR CO. - WOODWARD LIBRARY (Sci-Engr)
5001 N. Second St. Phone: (815)877-7441
Rockford, IL 61101 Mabel Beaumont, Libn.
Founded: 1957. **Staff:** 2. **Subjects:** Prime movers, aircraft, governors, locomotives, electricity and machine shop practices. **Holdings:** 1200 volumes; 10 VF drawers of technical papers; 1 VF drawer of bulletins. **Subscriptions:** 150 journals and other serials. **Services:** Interlibrary loan; copying; library open to the public for reference use only by request. **Publications:** Prime Mover Control - monthly.

ROY J. WOODWARD MEMORIAL LIBRARY OF CALIFORNIANA
See: California State University, Fresno - Henry Madden Library - Department of Special Collections (2217)

★18024★
WOODWARD STATE HOSPITAL SCHOOL - STAFF LIBRARY (Med)
Woodward, IA 50276 Phone: (515)438-2600
Joy Averill, Libn.
Founded: 1962. **Staff:** Prof 1; Other 1. **Subjects:** Mental retardation, special education, psychology, leisure services, social services, medicine, nursing. **Holdings:** 4000 books; 8 VF drawers of pamphlets and reprints; 20 16mm films, 15 video cassettes. **Subscriptions:** 67 journals and other serials; 5 newspapers. **Services:** Interlibrary loan; library open to the public with restrictions. **Networks/Consortia:** Member of Polk County Biomedical Consortium (PCBC).

WOOLAROC MUSEUM
See: Frank Phillips Foundation, Inc. (11293)

LEONARD & VIRGINIA WOOLF LIBRARY
See: Washington State University - Manuscripts, Archives, & Special Collections (17526)

★18025★
WORCESTER ART MUSEUM - LIBRARY (Art)
55 Salisbury St. Phone: (508)799-4406
Worcester, MA 01609-3916 Kathy L. Berg, Libn.
Founded: 1909. **Staff:** Prof 2; Other 1. **Subjects:** American and European painting and prints, photography, Japanese prints. **Holdings:** 38,000 volumes; 132 linear feet of exhibition catalogs; 264 linear feet of sale and dealer catalogs. **Subscriptions:** 200 journals and other serials. **Services:** Interlibrary loan; copying; library open to the public for reference use only. **Networks/Consortia:** Member of Worcester Area Cooperating Libraries (WACL). **Special Indexes:** Card index to Worcester Art Museum objects published in Worcester Art Museum publication (by accession number). **Staff:** Cynthia L. Bolshaw, Slide Libn..

★18026★
WORCESTER CITY HOSPITAL - MEDICAL LIBRARY (Med)
26 Queen St. Phone: (508)799-8186
Worcester, MA 01610 Timothy D. Rivard, Med.Libn.
Founded: 1937. **Staff:** Prof 1; Other 1. **Subjects:** Medicine and allied health sciences. **Special Collections:** Burn care and rehabilitation. **Holdings:** 1500 books; 4500 bound periodical volumes. **Subscriptions:** 200 journals and other serials. **Services:** Interlibrary loan; copying; use of library for reference may be requested. **Automated Operations:** Computerized cataloging. **Computerized Information Services:** NLM, ESA/IRS; DOCLINE (electronic mail service). **Networks/Consortia:** Member of Worcester Area Cooperating Libraries (WACL), Central Massachusetts Consortium of Health Related Libraries (CMCHRL). **Remarks:** Maintained by Hospital Corporation of America.

★18027★
WORCESTER COUNTY HORTICULTURAL SOCIETY - LIBRARY (Agri, Biol Sci)
30 Tower Hill Rd. Phone: (508)869-6111
Boylston, MA 01505-1001 Julie A. O'Shea, Libn.
Staff: Prof 1. **Subjects:** Agriculture, botany, conservation, fruit culture, general horticulture, landscape design. **Special Collections:** 6 centuries of horticultural literature; 18th and 19th century fruitbooks (250). **Holdings:** 6000 books; 1000 bound periodical volumes; 300 seed, tool, plant, and equipment catalogs. **Subscriptions:** 25 journals and other serials. **Services:** Library open to the public for reference use only. **Publications:** Grow With Us (newsletter), bimonthly.

WORCESTER DISTRICT MEDICAL SOCIETY
See: University of Massachusetts Medical School & Worcester District Medical Society (16395)

★18028★
WORCESTER FOUNDATION FOR EXPERIMENTAL BIOLOGY - GEORGE F. FULLER LIBRARY (Biol Sci)
222 Maple St. Phone: (508)842-8921
Shrewsbury, MA 01545 Barbara Lee, Lib.Dir.
Founded: 1945. **Staff:** Prof 2; Other 2. **Subjects:** Molecular biology, chemistry, biochemistry, physiology, pharmacology, neurobehavioral sciences. **Holdings:** 8000 books; 25,000 bound periodical volumes; 4 VF drawers of chemical patents; 4 VF drawers of subject bibliographies; 4 VF drawers of clippings. **Subscriptions:** 200 journals and other serials. **Services:** Interlibrary loan; copying; SDI; library open to staffs and students of institutions of higher education in the community. **Computerized Information Services:** DIALOG Information Services, BRS Information Technologies, MEDLARS. **Networks/Consortia:** Member of Central Massachusetts Consortium of Health Related Libraries (CMCHRL). **Publications:** Monthly Acquisitions list; Periodicals list, annual; bibliographies. **Special Catalogs:** Collected reprints of Worcester Foundation authors (book); catalog of bound company annual reports, 1945 to present (book).

★18029★
WORCESTER HAHNEMANN HOSPITAL - MEDICAL LIBRARY (Med)
281 Lincoln St. Phone: (508)792-8567
Worcester, MA 01605 Annanaomi Sams, Libn.
Staff: Prof 1. **Subjects:** Medicine. **Special Collections:** Collection of Historic Medical Texts (40). **Holdings:** 230 books; 440 bound periodical volumes. **Subscriptions:** 75 journals and other serials. **Services:** Interlibrary loan; copying; SDI; library open to the public for reference use only. **Automated Operations:** Computerized ILL. **Computerized Information Services:** MEDLINE, BRS Information Technologies, MEDLARS. Performs searches on fee basis. **Networks/Consortia:** Member of Central Massachusetts Consortium of Health Related Libraries (CMCHRL), Massachusetts Health Sciences Library Network (MAHSLIN), North Atlantic Health Science Libraries (NAHSL). **Remarks:** An alternate telephone number is 792-8140.

★18030★
WORCESTER HAHNEMANN HOSPITAL - SCHOOL OF NURSING LIBRARY (Med)
281 Lincoln St. Phone: (508)792-8567
Worcester, MA 01605 Annanaomi Sams, Libn.
Founded: 1900. **Staff:** Prof 1. **Subjects:** Nursing and allied health sciences. **Special Collections:** Historical nursing books. **Holdings:** 1500 books; 800 bound periodical volumes; 100 videotapes; 25 models; 75 sound filmstrips. **Subscriptions:** 56 journals and other serials. **Services:** Interlibrary loan; copying; SDI; library open to the public for reference use only. **Automated Operations:** Computerized ILL. **Computerized Information Services:**

MEDLINE. Performs searches on fee basis. **Networks/Consortia:** Member of Central Massachusetts Consortium of Health Related Libraries (CMCHRL), Massachusetts Health Sciences Library Network (MAHSLIN).

★18031★
WORCESTER HISTORICAL MUSEUM - LIBRARY (Hist)
39 Salisbury St. Phone: (508)753-8278
Worcester, MA 01609 Mildred Sanders, Off.Mgr.
Founded: 1875. **Staff:** Prof 3. **Subjects:** Local history. **Holdings:** 20,000 volumes; photographs; maps; manuscripts; ephemera. **Services:** Copying (limited); library open to the public on a limited schedule. **Networks/ Consortia:** Member of Worcester Area Cooperating Libraries (WACL).

★18032★
WORCESTER LAW LIBRARY (Law)
County Court House Phone: (508)756-2441
Worcester, MA 01608 Mary A. Terpo, Law Libn.
Founded: 1842. **Staff:** Prof 1; Other 3. **Subjects:** Law. **Holdings:** 100,869 volumes; periodicals; 10 VF drawers of pamphlets; Reporter series on ultrafiche; Federal Register and State Session Laws on microfiche; Massachusetts Supreme Judicial Court Records and Briefs on microfiche. **Services:** Interlibrary loan; copying; library open to the public. **Publications:** Annual Report, 1844 to present. **Remarks:** Part of the Massachusetts State Trial Court; Marnie Warner, Law Lib.Coord.

★18033★
WORCESTER POLYTECHNIC INSTITUTE - GEORGE C. GORDON LIBRARY (Sci-Engr)
West St. Phone: (508)793-5411
Worcester, MA 01609 Albert G. Anderson, Jr., Hd.Libn.
Founded: 1865. **Staff:** Prof 9; Other 12. **Subjects:** Engineering, chemistry, environmental science, computer science, physics, life sciences, biomedicine, mathematics, city planning, history of science and technology. **Special Collections:** WPI Archives; History of Engineering. **Holdings:** 269,549 books; 44,710 bound periodical volumes; 14,771 technical reports; 2082 maps; 125 boxes and 25 files of archives; 8 VF drawers; 765,000 NASA, American Engineering Council (AEC), and NASA Test Support microfiche; 1915 recordings; 4544 videotapes, audio cassettes, film loops. **Subscriptions:** 1350 journals and other serials; 25 newspapers. **Services:** Interlibrary loan; copying; microfiche copying; transparencies made; library open to qualified users. **Automated Operations:** Computerized cataloging, serials, and circulation. **Computerized Information Services:** DIALOG Information Services, OCLC. Performs searches on fee basis. Contact Person: Joanne Williams, Ref.. **Networks/Consortia:** Member of NELINET, Worcester Area Cooperating Libraries (WACL), C/W MARS, Inc.. **Publications:** New Acquisitions list, monthly; Library Handbook. **Special Catalogs:** Fire Safety Material. **Staff:** Carmen Brown, Hd., Pub.Serv./Ref.; Helen Shuster, Hd., Tech.Serv.; Cornelia Pomeroy, Circ.; Diana Johnson, Ref./ILL; Donald Richardson, Tech.Rpt.; Lora Brueck, Spec.Coll.; Martha Gunnarson, Cat..

★18034★
WORCESTER PUBLIC LIBRARY - REFERENCE AND READER SERVICES (Soc Sci, Sci-Engr, Hum)
Salem Square Phone: (508)799-1655
Worcester, MA 01608 Joseph S. Hopkins, Hd.Libn.
Staff: Prof 26; Other 2. **Subjects:** History, art, music, social and political science, literature, travel, science and technology, business, religion, architecture. **Special Collections:** Worcester Collection; Grants Resource Center; U.S. Government documents depository. **Holdings:** 376,369 books; 58,612 bound periodical volumes; 317,329 government documents; 7000 recordings; Massachusetts State documents. **Subscriptions:** 959 journals and other serials; 63 newspapers. **Services:** Interlibrary loan; copying; services open to the public. **Automated Operations:** Computerized cataloging and circulation. **Computerized Information Services:** OCLC, DIALOG Information Services, WILSONLINE, VU/TEXT Information Services, BRS Information Technologies. **Networks/Consortia:** Member of C/W MARS, Inc.. **Staff:** Penelope B. Johnson, Assoc.Libn.; Paul Pelletier, Hd., Bus., Sci. & Tech.; Jane Peck, Hd., Hum. & Fine Arts; Leonard Lucas, Hd., Soc.Sci. & Hist.; Mary Frances Cooper, Hd., Ref. & Rd.Serv.; Nancy Gaudette, Worcester Coll.Libn.; Dorothy Johnson, Govt.Docs.; Charlene Sokal, Grants Ctr.; James Izatt, Per..

★18035★
WORCESTER STATE COLLEGE - LEARNING RESOURCES CENTER (Educ)
486 Chandler St. Phone: (508)793-8027
Worcester, MA 01602 Bruce Plummer, Dir.
Founded: 1874. **Staff:** Prof 7; Other 14. **Subjects:** Education, humanities. **Special Collections:** Education Resources Collection (11,000 elementary and secondary textbooks; 3000 curriculum guides; 1000 tests); Children's Collection (9000 juvenile volumes). **Holdings:** 160,000 books; 2000 bound periodical volumes; 47,000 microforms; 15,000 16mm films; 8mm film loops; slides; phonograph records; tapes; video cassettes. **Subscriptions:** 1000 journals and other serials; 10 newspapers. **Services:** Interlibrary loan; copying; television and photography studios; center open to the public. **Computerized Information Services:** DIALOG Information Services, OCLC. Performs searches on fee basis. **Networks/Consortia:** Member of Worcester Area Cooperating Libraries (WACL), C/W MARS, Inc., NELINET. **Publications:** Learning Resources Center Location Guide - to users. **Staff:** Betsey Brenneman, Acq.; Krishna Das Gupta, Tech.Serv.; Pamela McKay, Ref.; Ruth Greenslit, Circ.; Ruth Webber, Cat.; Bill Piekarski, Educ.Rsrcs.; Linda Snodgrass, Per..

★18036★
WORCESTER TELEGRAM AND GAZETTE, INC. - LIBRARY (Publ)
20 Franklin St. Phone: (508)793-9240
Worcester, MA 01613 Sharon C. Carter, Libn.
Founded: 1913. **Staff:** 7. **Subjects:** Newspaper reference topics; biography. **Special Collections:** Local and state history and biography. **Holdings:** 374 books; 2.3 million clippings; 481,000 graphics; Worcester Telegram, 1884 to present, on microfilm; Evening Gazette, 1866 to present, on microfilm. **Services:** Copying; library open to the public on written request only.

★18037★
WORCESTER VOCATIONAL SCHOOLS - GEORGE I. ALDEN LIBRARY (Educ)
26 Salisbury St. Phone: (508)799-1952
Worcester, MA 01608 Francesca M. Van Liew, Libn.
Founded: 1963. **Staff:** Prof 1. **Subjects:** Ophthalmics; welding; drafting; electronics; data processing; electric power and instrumentation; heating, ventilating, and air conditioning; architecture and construction; machine tool design. **Holdings:** 10,230 books. **Subscriptions:** 132 journals and other serials. **Services:** Library open to the public with restrictions. **Automated Operations:** Computerized cataloging and circulation.

WORDEN SCHOOL OF SOCIAL SERVICE
See: Our Lady of the Lake University (10957)

★18038★
WORK IN AMERICA INSTITUTE, INC. - LIBRARY (Bus-Fin)
700 White Plains Rd. Phone: (914)472-9600
Scarsdale, NY 10583 Cynthia C. Rubino, Mgr., Info.Serv.
Staff: Prof 2; Other 1. **Subjects:** Productivity, quality of working life, work innovations and design, industrial relations, personnel management. **Special Collections:** Publications of the former National Center for Productivity and Quality of Working Life (50 volumes). **Holdings:** 3000 books; 2200 file documents; 20,000 subject files of clippings, unpublished reports, technical documents. **Subscriptions:** 200 journals and other serials. **Services:** Library open to the public by appointment. **Special Indexes:** Subject Headings Index. **Staff:** Diane Rowan, Libn..

★18039★
WORKER'S COMPENSATION BOARD OF ONTARIO - DOWNSVIEW REHABILITATION CENTRE - MEDICAL LIBRARY (Med)
115 Torbarrie Rd. Phone: (416)244-1761
Downsview, ON, Canada M3L 1G8 Catherine W. Wilson, Libn.
Staff: 1. **Subjects:** Physical medicine, rehabilitation, orthopedics, neurology, psychiatry, psychology, physical and occupational therapy. **Holdings:** 1900 books; 248 bound periodical volumes. **Subscriptions:** 147 journals and other serials. **Services:** Interlibrary loan; library not open to the public.

★18040★
WORKING OPPORTUNITIES FOR WOMEN - RESOURCE CENTER (Soc Sci)
2700 University Ave., Suite 120 Phone: (612)647-9961
St. Paul, MN 55114-1016 Yvette Oldendorf, Dir.
Subjects: Women - employment, job seeking skills, assertiveness, careers, motherhood, minorities. **Holdings:** 600 books; 2 shelves of educational

bulletins. **Subscriptions:** 12 journals and other serials. **Services:** Copying; center open to the public for reference use only.

WORKSHOP IN POLITICAL THEORY & POLICY ANALYSIS
See: Indiana University (6804)

★18041★
WORLD AFFAIRS COUNCIL OF NORTHERN CALIFORNIA - LIBRARY (Soc Sci)
312 Sutter St., Suite 200 Phone: (415)982-2541
San Francisco, CA 94108 Lone C. Beeson, Hd.Libn.
Founded: 1947. **Staff:** Prof 2. **Subjects:** International relations, foreign policy, political science, economics, modern history. **Special Collections:** Newsletters and press releases from various embassies and information centers; U.S. Department of State documents. **Holdings:** 6000 books; 200 documents; 3000 pamphlets; 300 cassette tapes; maps. **Subscriptions:** 40 journals and other serials; 5 newspapers. **Services:** Copying; library open to the public with restrictions on borrowing. **Publications:** Booknotes, monthly - to members. **Staff:** Edith Malamud, Circ.Libn..

★18042★
WORLD ARCHEOLOGICAL SOCIETY - INFORMATION CENTER (Hist, Soc Sci)
Lake Rd. 65-48
HCR-1-Box 445 Phone: (417)334-2377
Hollister, MO 65672 Ron Miller, Dir.
Founded: 1971. **Staff:** Prof 2. **Subjects:** Archeology, anthropology, and art history of the world; Biblical archeology; museum science. **Special Collections:** Steve Miller Library of American Archaeology (1100 publications); democracy club; publications commendations; Bible repair project. **Holdings:** 6500 volumes; 7500 item clipping file; 2000 photographs, tapes, and slides. **Subscriptions:** 30 journals and other serials; 6 newspapers. **Services:** Full art service for researchers, authors, and others; center not open to the public. **Publications:** W.A.S. Fact Sheet; W.A.S. Newsletter and Special Publications, irregular - to the public. **Staff:** Mrs. Steve Miller, Asst.Dir..

★18043★
WORLD ASSOCIATION OF DOCUMENT EXAMINERS - WADE LIBRARY (Law)
111 N. Canal St. Phone: (312)930-9446
Chicago, IL 60606 Lee Arnold, Libn.
Founded: 1973. **Staff:** Prof 2; Other 3. **Subjects:** Handwriting, documents, paper and ink, law, trial procedure, psychology. **Holdings:** 7000 books. **Subscriptions:** 75 journals and other serials; 25 newspapers. **Services:** Library not open to the public. **Publications:** WADE Exchange, monthly; WADE Journal, quarterly. **Staff:** Martha Lindberg, Libn..

WORLD BANK
See: International Monetary Fund/World Bank (7046)

★18044★
WORLD BANK - LAW LIBRARY (Law)
1818 H St., N.W. (E-7014) Phone: (202)477-2128
Washington, DC 20433 Linda L. Thompson, Law Libn.
Founded: 1975. **Staff:** Prof 1; Other 1. **Subjects:** Law - international, foreign, comparative; arbitration; administrative tribunals. **Holdings:** 15,000 books. **Subscriptions:** 150 journals and other serials. **Services:** Interlibrary loan; library open to the public for reference use only on request. **Automated Operations:** Computerized cataloging and acquisitions. **Computerized Information Services:** LEXIS, NEXIS, DIALOG Information Services; internal database.

★18045★
WORLD BANK - SECTORAL LIBRARY (Soc Sci)
1818 H St., N.W., Rm. N 145 Phone: (202)676-0153
Washington, DC 20433 Sue Dyer, Libn.
Founded: 1984. **Staff:** Prof 7; Other 5. **Subjects:** Agriculture, population, health, transportation, energy, environment, mining, nutrition, telecommunications, women in development, education, water supply in the developing world. **Special Collections:** Cartography library (4000 titles). **Holdings:** 30,000 books; 100,000 microfiche. **Subscriptions:** 800 journals and other serials; 10 newspapers. **Services:** Interlibrary loan; copying; library open to the public with permission. **Automated Operations:** Computerized cataloging and acquisitions. **Computerized Information Services:** DIALOG Information Services, Pergamon ORBIT InfoLine, Inc., BRS Information Technologies, NewsNet, Inc., ESA/IRS, Telesystemes Questel, National Ground Water Information Center (NGWIC), WILSONLINE, MEDLARS, International Development Research Centre (IDRC); JOLIS (internal database). **Staff:** Karen Eggert, Hd., Cat.; Chris Windheuser, Map & Ref.Libn.; Jane Keneshea, Ref.Libn.; Alcione Amos, Acq.Libn.; So Young Choi, Cat.Libn.; Jean Malinasky, Cat.Libn..

WORLD BAPTIST FELLOWSHIP - ARLINGTON BAPTIST COLLEGE
See: Arlington Baptist College (929)

★18046★
WORLD BOOK INC. - RESEARCH LIBRARY (Publ)
Merchandise Mart Plaza Phone: (312)341-8777
Chicago, IL 60654 Mary S. Kayaian, Hd., Lib.Serv.
Founded: 1920. **Staff:** Prof 2; Other 3. **Subjects:** General reference, biography, statistics. **Holdings:** 22,000 volumes; 375 VF drawers of pamphlets and clippings; 3000 maps; 400 government publications; college catalogs. **Subscriptions:** 600 journals and other serials; 7 newspapers. **Services:** Interlibrary loan; library not open to the public. **Automated Operations:** Computerized cataloging, acquisitions, and serials. **Computerized Information Services:** DIALOG Information Services. **Networks/Consortia:** Member of ILLINET.

★18047★
WORLD CONFESSIONAL LUTHERAN ASSOCIATION - FAITH EVANGELICAL LUTHERAN SEMINARY - LIBRARY (Rel-Phil)
3504 N. Pearl St.
Box 7186 Phone: (206)752-2020
Tacoma, WA 98407 Rev. Osborne Y. Bruland, Libn.
Founded: 1969. **Staff:** Prof 1; Other 1. **Subjects:** Theology, church history, missions, homiletics. **Holdings:** 10,800 books; 120 bound periodical volumes. **Subscriptions:** 21 journals and other serials. **Services:** Interlibrary loan; library open to the public.

★18048★
WORLD CONGRESS OF GAY & LESBIAN JEWISH ORGANIZATIONS - RESOURCE LIBRARY (Soc Sci)
Box 18961
Washington, DC 20036
Founded: 1980. **Subjects:** Gay Jewish ideas, feminism and gay consciousness. **Holdings:** Journal articles; newsletters; religious and liturgical materials. **Services:** Library not open to the public. **Formerly:** Located in San Francisco, CA.

★18049★
WORLD DATA CENTER A - GLACIOLOGY INFORMATION CENTER (Sci-Engr)
CIRES, Campus Box 449
University of Colorado Phone: (303)492-5171
Boulder, CO 80309 Ann M. Brennan, Info.Spec.
Founded: 1957. **Staff:** Prof 1; Other 1. **Subjects:** All aspects of snow and ice, including snow cover, avalanches, glaciers, sea, river, lake ice, polar ice sheets, permafrost, paleoglaciology, ice physics. **Special Collections:** Historical glacier photograph collections (1880s-1960s). **Holdings:** 4750 books and technical reports; 10,000 reprints. **Subscriptions:** 90 journals and other serials. **Services:** Interlibrary loan; copying; SDI; will answer requests for information by correspondence; center open to the public. **Automated Operations:** Automated bibliographic file of holdings. **Computerized Information Services:** DIALOG Information Services, Pergamon ORBIT InfoLine, Inc.; Citation Data Base, Glacier Photo Index (internal databases). Performs searches on fee basis. **Publications:** Quarterly accessions list - free upon request.

★18050★
WORLD DATA CENTER A - OCEANOGRAPHY (Sci-Engr)
Natl. Oceanic and Atmospheric Adm. Phone: (202)673-5571
Washington, DC 20235 James Churgin, Dir.
Founded: 1957. **Staff:** Prof 3; Other 1. **Subjects:** Physical, chemical, and biological oceanographic data; current data; sea surface data. **Special Collections:** Oceanographic data from the International Geophysical Year, the International Indian Ocean Expedition, and other international cooperative oceanographic expeditions and projects; international data inventory forms. **Holdings:** Oceanographic data on log sheets, machine listings, and in publications for more than 850,000 stations. **Services:** Copying; utilizes Automatic Data Processing (ADP) facilities of the National Oceanographic Data Center; facility open to qualified scientists and persons interested in oceanography. **Publications:** Reports of Oceanographic Data Exchange, annual. **Special Catalogs:** Catalogue of Data, annual; Catalogue of Accessioned Publications, annual.

★18051★
WORLD DATA CENTER A - ROCKETS & SATELLITES - NATIONAL SPACE SCIENCE DATA CENTER (NSSDC) (Sci-Engr)
Code 630.2, Goddard Space Flight Ctr. Phone: (301)286-6695
Greenbelt, MD 20771 Dr. James I. Vette, Dir.
Subjects: Space science. **Special Collections:** Satellite and space probe experimental data. **Holdings:** 472,949 volumes; 30,000 microfiche; 68,292 tapes; 35,000 reels of microfilm; 1.67 million linear feet of photographs. **Services:** Copying; SDI; center open to the public by appointment. **Automated Operations:** Computerized cataloging, acquisitions, and files. **Computerized Information Services:** Internal databases. **Remarks:** Maintained by NASA.

★18052★
WORLD DATA CENTER A - SOLAR-TERRESTRIAL PHYSICS (Sci-Engr)
Natl. Oceanic and Atmospheric Adm.
E/GC2
325 Broadway Phone: (303)497-6323
Boulder, CO 80303 Joe H. Allen, Chf., STP Div.
Founded: 1957. **Staff:** Prof 9; Other 16. **Subjects:** Geomagnetism, ionospheric phenomena, solar and interplanetary phenomena, aurora, airglow, cosmic rays. **Special Collections:** Largest collection of solar-terrestrial data in the world. **Holdings:** 19 million feet of 35mm film; station booklets; 12,000 magnetic tapes; microfiche. **Services:** Copying; open to the public. **Automated Operations:** Computerized cataloging and circulation. **Computerized Information Services:** Online systems; Telemail (electronic mail service). **Publications:** Solar-Geophysical Data, monthly; UAG-Report Series, intermittent. **Special Catalogs:** Catalogs of data (by discipline, periodically). **Also Known As:** National Geophysical Data Center - Solar-Terrestrial Physics Division.

★18053★
WORLD FUTURES STUDIES FEDERATION - RESOURCE ROOM (Soc Sci)
2424 Maile Way, Rm. 721 A Phone: (808)948-6601
Honolulu, HI 96822 James Dator, Adm.Dir.
Founded: 1983. **Staff:** Prof 2; Other 1. **Subjects:** Education, communication and the media, science and technology, law and politics. **Holdings:** 500 books; 15 bound periodical volumes; 100 monographs; 5 file cabinets of reports and manuscripts; 1 file cabinet of research from the Commission on the Year 2000. **Subscriptions:** 12 journals and other serials. **Services:** Room open to the public by appointment.

WORLD HEALTH ORGANIZATION - PAN AMERICAN HEALTH ORGANIZATION
See: Pan American Health Organization (11044)

★18054★
WORLD HUNGER EDUCATION SERVICE - LIBRARY (Soc Sci, Agri)
1317 G St., N.W. Phone: (202)347-4441
Washington, DC 20005 Dr. Patricia L. Kutzner, Dir.
Founded: 1976. **Staff:** Prof 3; Other 1. **Subjects:** World food problems, development policy, appropriate technology, poverty. **Holdings:** 1000 books; U.S. Government and U.N. publications; unbound reports; pamphlets; documents. **Subscriptions:** 110 journals and other serials. **Services:** Library open to the public for reference use only. **Publications:** Hunger Notes, bimonthly - by subscription; Who's Involved with Hunger: An Organization Guide for Education and Advocacy. **Staff:** Robert Auerbach, Cat.Libn..

★18055★
THE WORLD INSTITUTE FOR ADVANCED PHENOMENOLOGICAL RESEARCH & LEARNING - LIBRARY AND ARCHIVES (Rel-Phil)
348 Payson Rd. Phone: (617)489-3696
Belmont, MA 02178 Anna-Teresa Tymieniecka, Pres.
Subjects: Phenomenology. **Holdings:** 500 books. **Subscriptions:** 15 journals and other serials. **Services:** Library open to the public with restrictions. **Publications:** Phenomenological Inquiry Beacon: A Review of Philosophical Ideas and Trends.

★18056★
WORLD JEWISH GENEALOGY ORGANIZATION - LIBRARY (Hist, Rel-Phil)
1533 60th St.
Box 420 Phone: (718)435-7878
Brooklyn, NY 11219 Rabbi N. Halberstam, Libn.
Staff: 1. **Subjects:** Judaica. **Holdings:** 10,000 books. **Services:** Library not open to the public. **Publications:** Bibliography and biography journal devoted to genealogy.

★18057★
WORLD LIFE RESEARCH INSTITUTE - LIBRARY (Biol Sci)
23000 Grand Terrace Rd. Phone: (714)825-4773
Colton, CA 92324 Bruce W. Halstead, Lib.Dir.
Founded: 1959. **Staff:** Prof 2; Other 2. **Subjects:** Marine biotoxins, venomous snakes, plant and insect biotoxins, dangerous marine animals, herbal and medicinal plants, biomedical history, biologically-active natural products. **Holdings:** 7000 volumes; 50 manuscripts; 18,000 reprints and pamphlets; bibliographic references on biotoxins; 4000 maps and pictures of poisonous plants and animals. **Subscriptions:** 20 journals and other serials. **Services:** Copying; library open to the public by appointment. **Publications:** Monographs on poisonous plants and animals; handbooks on immunology and nontoxic medical therapies. **Special Indexes:** Plant and animal poisons; traditional herbal medicine.

★18058★
WORLD LITHUANIAN ARCHIVES, INC. (Area-Ethnic)
5620 S. Claremont Phone: (312)434-4545
Chicago, IL 60636 Ceslovas V. Grincevicius, Dir.
Founded: 1946. **Staff:** Prof 2; Other 4. **Subjects:** Lithuania. **Special Collections:** Krupavicius Collection; Pakstas Collection; Danzvardis Consular Archive; Kreivenas Collection; official document repository of the World Lithuanian Community, Inc. **Holdings:** 30,000 books; 1100 bound periodical volumes; manuscripts; documents. **Subscriptions:** 50 journals and other serials; 12 newspapers. **Services:** Copying; archives open to the public. **Automated Operations:** Computerized cataloging. **Computerized Information Services:** Internal database. **Remarks:** Affiliated with Lithuanian Research and Studies Center, Inc. **Staff:** Leonardas Kerulis, Asst.Dir..

★18059★
WORLD MODELING ASSOCIATION - WMA LIBRARY (Bus-Fin)
Box 100 Phone: (914)737-8512
Croton-on-Hudson, NY 10520 Kathy Miller, Libn.
Staff: 3. **Subjects:** Fashion - careers, modeling, and merchandising; personal development. **Special Collections:** Photographic and Professional Modeling Collection. **Holdings:** 275 volumes; 28 manuscripts; clippings. **Subscriptions:** 18 journals and other serials. **Services:** Copying; library open to the public by mail inquiry only. **Publications:** Who's Who in Modeling - to school career guidance centers and individuals.

WORLD MUSIC ARCHIVES
See: Wesleyan University - Library (17637)

★18060★
WORLD PEACE THROUGH LAW CENTER - ARCHIVES (Law, Soc Sci)
1000 Connecticut Ave., N.W., Suite 800
Washington, DC 20036 Phone: (202)466-5428
Subjects: International law, human rights, international trade, law and technology, aviation and outer space, nuclear arms control. **Holdings:** Figures not available. **Services:** Archives not open to the public. **Publications:** The World Jurist (newsletter), bimonthly; Law/Technology (journal), quarterly; publications directory.

★18061★
WORLD PEACE THROUGH LAW CENTER - INFORMATION CENTER (Law)
1000 Connecticut Ave., N.W., Suite 800
Washington, DC 20036
Subjects: International law, law and technology, human rights, international trade, nuclear arms control. **Holdings:** 50 books and bound periodical volumes; U.N. documents. **Automated Operations:** Computerized circulation. **Publications:** List of publications - available on request.

★18062★
WORLD RESOURCES INSTITUTE - LIBRARY (Env-Cons, Agri)
1735 New York Ave., N.W. Phone: (202)638-6300
Washington, DC 20006 Susan N. Terry, Res.Libn.
Founded: 1982. **Staff:** Prof 1; Other 1. **Subjects:** Environment, pollution, agriculture, forestry, climate, energy. **Holdings:** 3000 books and reports; 16 VF drawers of pamphlets and clippings; studies. **Subscriptions:** 200 journals and other serials; 5 newspapers. **Services:** Interlibrary loan; library open to the public by appointment. **Automated Operations:** Computerized cataloging, acquisitions, and serials. **Computerized Information Services:** DIALOG Information Services, BRS Information Technologies, WILSONLINE; internal databases; Telecommunications Cooperative Network (TCN; electronic mail service). **Networks/Consortia:** Member of Interlibrary Users Association (IUA).

WORLD STUDENT CHRISTIAN FEDERATION - ARCHIVES
See: Yale University - Divinity School Library (18126)

★18063★
WORLD TRADE CENTER OF NEW ORLEANS - LIBRARY (Bus-Fin)
Two Canal St., Suite 2900 Phone: (504)529-1601
New Orleans, LA 70130 Mina L. Crais, Dir., Info.Serv.
Founded: 1946. **Staff:** Prof 1; Other 2. **Subjects:** Import and export trade, travel, international relations, economics, transportation. **Holdings:** 20,000 volumes; 350 foreign telephone directories; 700 U.S. telephone directories; 700 trade directories; 31 VF drawers of pamphlet material. **Subscriptions:** 450 journals and other serials. **Services:** Copying; library open to graduate students, government agencies, and other World Trade Centers. **Publications:** List of periodicals currently received, annuals, and World Trade Center Libraries; list of additional publications - available on request.

★18064★
WORLD TRADE CENTRE TORONTO - LIBRARY (Bus-Fin)
60 Harbour St. Phone: (416)863-2153
Toronto, ON, Canada M5J 1B7 Maria A. Escriu Fenn, Libn.
Founded: 1978. **Staff:** Prof 1. **Subjects:** International trade, marketing, importing and exporting, Canadian industries, economics. **Holdings:** 1200 publications; 12 VF drawers of clippings and annual reports. **Subscriptions:** 300 journals and other serials. **Services:** Copying; library open to WTC members only. **Computerized Information Services:** DIALOG Information Services, BRS Information Technologies, The Reference Service (REFSRV), Info Globe. **Remarks:** Maintained by Toronto Harbour Commissioners.

WORLD TRADE CENTRE VANCOUVER
See: Vancouver Board of Trade/World Trade Centre Vancouver (17262)

★18065★
WORLD UNIVERSITY ROUNDTABLE - WORLD UNIVERSITY LIBRARY (Rel-Phil)
Desert Sanctuary Regional Campus
Mescal-Salcido Rd.
Box 2470 Phone: (602)586-2985
Benson, AZ 85602 Howard John Zitko, Pres./Libn.
Founded: 1947. **Staff:** Prof 1; Other 1. **Subjects:** Metaphysics and philosophy, esoteric science, health, astrology, UFO phenomena, poetry. **Special Collections:** Rare books in religious philosophy. **Holdings:** 25,000 books; 250 bound periodical volumes; 100 boxes of unbound magazines, dissertations, essays, paperbacks; 1000 other cataloged items. **Subscriptions:** 25 journals and other serials. **Services:** Library open to the public for reference use only. **Publications:** World University Library, occasional - to members and the public; Liftoff (newsletter), bimonthly.

★18066★
WORLD VISION INTERNATIONAL - INFORMATION RESOURCE CENTER (Rel-Phil)
919 W. Huntington Dr. Phone: (818)303-8811
Monrovia, CA 91016 John E. Cooper, Dir., Res. & Info.Div.
Founded: 1970. **Staff:** 1. **Subjects:** World Christianity, missions, hunger, refugees, development. **Holdings:** 6634 books; 36 periodical titles; 36 VF drawers of geographic material; 2 lateral file drawers on North American mission organizations. **Subscriptions:** 67 journals and other serials. **Services:** Copying (limited); center not open to the public. **Automated Operations:** Computerized circulation. **Computerized Information Services:** The Source Information Network, EasyNet; AUTOLIB (internal database). **Special Indexes:** Index to book collection; index to people and organizations significant to world evangelization (computerized).

★18067★
WORLD WILDLIFE FUND-U.S. - CONSERVATION FOUNDATION - LIBRARY (Env-Cons)
1250 24th St., N.W. Phone: (202)797-4300
Washington, DC 20037 Barbara K. Rodes, Res.Libn.
Founded: 1949. **Staff:** 2. **Subjects:** Natural resource conservation, water resources, pollution, land use planning, wildlife and economic development, habitat preservation. **Holdings:** 10,000 volumes; clippings file. **Subscriptions:** 385 journals and other serials. **Services:** Interlibrary loan; library open to the public by appointment. **Computerized Information Services:** DIALOG Information Services. Performs searches on fee basis. **Publications:** Acquisitions List, monthly. **Staff:** Carla Langeveld, Asst.Libn..

★18068★
WORLD WITHOUT WAR COUNCIL - MIDWEST LIBRARY (Soc Sci)
421 S. Wabash Phone: (312)236-7459
Chicago, IL 60605 Robert Woito, Dir.
Staff: Prof 1; Other 2. **Subjects:** International relations and organizations, arms race and disarmament, human rights, nonviolence, world economic development, crisis issues, area studies, ethics and war. **Holdings:** 2000 books; reference files on organizations in war/peace field. **Subscriptions:** 10 journals and other serials. **Services:** Library open to the public. **Publications:** Newsletter, quarterly - free upon request.

★18069★
WORLD ZIONIST ORGANIZATION - AMERICAN SECTION - ZIONIST ARCHIVES AND LIBRARY (Area-Ethnic, Rel-Phil)
515 Park Ave. Phone: (212)753-2167
New York, NY 10022 Esther Togman, Dir. & Libn.
Founded: 1939. **Staff:** Prof 3; Other 1. **Subjects:** Israel, Zionism, Middle East, history of the Jews and Jewish life. **Holdings:** 50,000 books and pamphlets; 50,000 photographs; 977 reels of microfilm; slides; filmstrips; nonmusical and musical recordings; symphonic scores; folk music; maps and posters; 137 VF drawers of archival material. **Subscriptions:** 400 journals and other serials. **Services:** Interlibrary loan; copying; library open to the public. **Staff:** Ruth Fergenson, Libn.; Judy Wallach, Libn..

WORLDWIDE CHURCH OF GOD - AMBASSADOR COLLEGE
See: Ambassador College (371)

SOL WORTH ETHNOGRAPHIC FILM ARCHIVE
See: University of Pennsylvania - Annenberg School of Communications - Library (16725)

★18070★
WORTHINGTON HISTORICAL SOCIETY - LIBRARY (Hist)
50 W. New England Ave. Phone: (614)885-1247
Worthington, OH 43085 Lillian Skeele, Libn.
Staff: Prof 2. **Subjects:** Local history and genealogy, historic preservation, decorative arts, pioneer crafts, dolls, lace-making. **Holdings:** 800 books. **Services:** Interlibrary loan; copying; library open to the public by appointment.

WQED LIBRARY
See: Metropolitan Pittsburgh Public Broadcasting, Inc. (8831)

★18071★
WRATHER PORT PROPERTIES, LTD. - HISTORICAL ARCHIVES AND RESOURCE CENTER (Trans, Hist)
RMS Queen Mary & Spruce Goose
Box 8 Phone: (213)435-3511
Long Beach, CA 90801 Greg Mangum, Exhibits Mgr.
Founded: 1967. **Staff:** Prof 5. **Subjects:** RMS Queen Mary, Howard Hughes' Spruce Goose Flying Boat. **Special Collections:** Ship's Logs (145); Radio, Engine, Boiler, and Steam Logs; memoranda, letters, reports, papers for stores, crew, cargo, and drydocking (17 VF drawers and 200 linear feet). **Holdings:** 200 books; 100 bound periodical volumes; 10,000 photographs; 20 VF drawers of plans for mechanical and utilities installations; 250 menus; 45 passenger lists; 400 pieces of memorabilia, pamphlets, booklets, souvenirs; 200 bound reports, test results, plans; 4 VF drawers of plans and documents. **Services:** Center not open to the public; requests for materials and publications should be addressed to the Exhibits Department. **Publications:** Howard Hughes: His Achievements and Legacy; The Queen Mary: The Stateliest Ship - for sale. **Remarks:** Ninety percent of the material in the center was found on the ship. **Staff:** Bill M. Winberg, Archv.Adm..

JOHN HENRY WRENN LIBRARY
See: University of Texas, Austin - Harry Ransom Humanities Research Center (16931)

★18072★
WRIGHT INSTITUTE - GRADUATE DIVISION LIBRARY (Soc Sci)
2728 Durant Ave. Phone: (415)841-9230
Berkeley, CA 94704 Mary L. Parks, Libn.
Staff: Prof 1; Other 1. **Subjects:** Psychology, sociology, education, research methodology, Third World psychology. **Special Collections:** Dr. Abraham Maslow Collection (his complete private collection donated by his widow). **Holdings:** 10,000 books; 152 Wright Institute dissertations. **Subscriptions:** 36 journals and other serials. **Services:** Interlibrary loan; library open to the public only through faculty members' approval. **Computerized Information Services:** DIALOG Information Services. Performs searches on fee basis.

J.M. WRIGHT TECHNICAL SCHOOL
See: Connecticut State Board of Education (3651)

JOHN SHEPARD WRIGHT MEMORIAL LIBRARY
See: Indiana Academy of Science (6750)

★18073★
WRIGHT STATE UNIVERSITY - ARCHIVES & SPECIAL COLLECTIONS (Hist)
Dayton, OH 45435 Phone: (513)873-2092
Dr. Patrick B. Nolan, Hd. of Archv.
Staff: Prof 4; Other 4. **Subjects:** Aeronautics history, Wright Brothers, Ohio and local history, genealogy, Arthur Rackham. **Special Collections:** Early Aviation (1000 volumes); Miami Valley history (3000 volumes); Abraham Lincoln (500 volumes); university archives (100 cubic feet); manuscripts (1000 cubic feet). **Holdings:** 4100 books and bound periodical volumes; 30 cubic feet of Wright Brothers Papers; 24 cubic feet of James M. Cox Papers; 100 cubic feet of labor union records; 200 cubic feet of local business records; 40 cubic feet of local church records. **Services:** Copying; collections open to the public for reference use only. **Automated Operations:** Computerized cataloging. **Networks/Consortia:** Member of Southwest Ohio Council for Higher Education (SOCHE), Ohio Network of American History Research Centers. **Publications:** Guide to Manuscripts. **Special Catalogs:** Inventories or registers for manuscript collections; computer guide and COM catalog to local government records. **Staff:** Robert H. Smith, Jr., Supv. of Archv.; Dorothy Smith, Archv.; Vicky Cooper, Local Rec.Spec..

★18074★
WRIGHT STATE UNIVERSITY - SCHOOL OF MEDICINE - FORDHAM HEALTH SCIENCES LIBRARY (Med)
3640 Colonel Glenn Hwy. Phone: (513)873-2266
Dayton, OH 45401-0927 Audrey J. Kidder, Hea.Sci.Libn.
Founded: 1974. **Staff:** Prof 11; Other 19. **Subjects:** Medicine, human anatomy, microbiology, physiology, psychology, biochemistry. **Special Collections:** Ross A. McFarland Collection in Aerospace Medicine and Human Factors Engineering; Aerospace Medical Association Archives; H.T.E. Hertzburg Collection in Anthropometry. **Holdings:** 38,210 books; 45,374 bound periodical volumes; 2139 AV programs; 91 computer software programs. **Subscriptions:** 1360 journals and other serials. **Services:** Interlibrary loan; copying; SDI; library open to the public with restrictions. **Automated Operations:** Computerized cataloging, acquisitions, serials, and circulation. **Computerized Information Services:** MEDLINE, DIALOG Information Services, OCLC, PHILSOM, BRS Information Technologies, NASA/RECON, PaperChase; DOCLINE, OnTyme Electronic Message Network Service (electronic mail services). **Networks/Consortia:** Member of Southwest Ohio Council for Higher Education (SOCHE), Greater Midwest Regional Medical Library Network, OHIONET. **Special Catalogs:** Periodical holdings in the Health Sciences Library; Ross A. McFarland Catalogs and Inventory. **Staff:** Mary Ann Hoffman, Spec.Coll. & Serv.; Sarah S. Timmons, Assoc.Libn.; Mary Faulkner, Ref./ILL LIbn.; Narcissa Baker, Cat.Libn.; Douglas Kaylor, LRC; Christine Watson, Automation Coord.; Tamera Peach Lee, Circ.Libn..

W. HOWARD WRIGHT RESEARCH CENTER
See: Schenectady Chemicals, Inc. (12950)

★18075★
WM. WRIGLEY, JR. COMPANY - CORPORATE LIBRARY (Bus-Fin)
Wrigley Bldg.
410 N. Michigan Ave. Phone: (312)644-2121
Chicago, IL 60611-4287 Linda Hanrath, Corp.Libn.
Founded: 1978. **Staff:** Prof 1; Other 1. **Subjects:** Business, chewing gum industry. **Special Collections:** Company history (5 VF drawers). **Holdings:** 2000 volumes; 12 VF drawers. **Subscriptions:** 100 journals and other serials. **Services:** Interlibrary loan; SDI; library open to the public with restrictions. **Computerized Information Services:** DIALOG Information Services. **Networks/Consortia:** Member of Chicago Library System. **Publications:** Serials Holdings List, annual; New Library Acquisitions, quarterly.

★18076★
WM. WRIGLEY, JR. COMPANY - QUALITY ASSURANCE BRANCH LIBRARY (Sci-Engr)
3535 S. Ashland Ave. Phone: (312)523-4040
Chicago, IL 60609 Sandra L. McLeod, Tech.Libn.
Staff: Prof 1. **Subjects:** Quality assurance. **Holdings:** 250 titles. **Services:** Interlibrary loan; copying; SDI; library open to the public with restrictions. **Remarks:** The Research & Development Library, located at the same address, staffs and services the Quality Assurance Branch Library.

★18077★
WM. WRIGLEY, JR. COMPANY - RESEARCH & DEVELOPMENT LIBRARY (Food-Bev)
3535 S. Ashland Ave. Phone: (312)523-4040
Chicago, IL 60609 Sandra L. McLeod, Info.Spec.
Founded: 1972. **Staff:** Prof 2. **Subjects:** Chewing gum, food science and technology, flavors, chemistry, packaging, chemical engineering. **Special Collections:** Chewing gum patent file, 19th century to present (1300 patents). **Holdings:** 1400 books; 310 volumes of unbound periodicals. **Subscriptions:** 204 journals and other serials. **Services:** Interlibrary loan. **Computerized Information Services:** DIALOG Information Services. **Special Indexes:** Subject index to chewing gum patents (online).

WROTH MEMORIAL LIBRARY
See: Washington County Hospital (17477)

WSAZ-TV NEWS FILM ARCHIVE
See: Marshall University - James E. Morrow Library - Special Collections (8466)

★18078★
WUESTHOFF MEMORIAL HOSPITAL - HOSPITAL LIBRARY (Med)
110 Longwood Ave.
Box 6
Rockledge, FL 32955 Phone: (407)636-2211
Staff: Prof 1. **Subjects:** Medicine, surgery, nursing, allied health sciences. **Holdings:** 1936 books; 620 bound periodical volumes; 480 audio cassettes; 49 slide carrousels; 4 VF drawers of pamphlets. **Subscriptions:** 126 journals and other serials. **Services:** Interlibrary loan; copying; library open to the public with administrative approval.

WUPATKI NATIONAL MONUMENT
See: U.S. Natl. Park Service (15363)

★18079★
WYANDOT COUNTY HISTORICAL SOCIETY - WYANDOT MUSEUM - LIBRARY (Hist)
130 S. 7th St. Phone: (419)294-3857
Upper Sandusky, OH 43351 Bryan E. Long, Hd.Cur.
Subjects: Wyandot Mission, Indian artifacts. **Special Collections:** Normandy Home, 1852 (pioneer and Victorian furniture; toys; musical instruments; clothing; dishes; early history of Wyandot County). **Holdings:** 500 books. **Services:** Library open to the public for reference use only. **Staff:** Paula Cash, Asst.Cur..

★18080★
WYANDOTTE COUNTY HISTORICAL SOCIETY AND MUSEUM - HARRY M. TROWBRIDGE RESEARCH LIBRARY (Hist)
631 N. 126th St. Phone: (913)721-1078
Bonner Springs, KS 66012 Phylis A. Hancock, Archv.
Founded: 1956. **Staff:** Prof 1; Other 5. **Subjects:** Wyandotte County and Kansas City history; Wyandot, Shawnee, and Delaware Indians. **Special Collections:** J.R. Kelley Cooperage Company business papers and ledgers,

1903-1916 (36 cubic feet); proceedings of Congresses of mid-19th century; bound magazines and school texts of the late 19th century; Early, Conley, and Farrow Family Collections, 1763-1960 (30 cubic feet of papers, books, photographs). **Holdings:** 4000 books; 1000 bound periodical volumes; clippings; 150 reels of microfilm; 5000 photographs; maps. **Subscriptions:** 10 journals and other serials. **Services:** Copying; library open to the public with restrictions.

★18081★
WYANDOTTE COUNTY LAW LIBRARY (Law)
Wyandotte County Courthouse
710 N. 7th St. Phone: (913)573-2899
Kansas City, KS 66101 Jeanne Stanley, Law Libn.
Founded: 1925. **Staff:** 2. **Subjects:** Law. **Special Collections:** Blackstones Commentaries, 1761 (4 volumes). **Holdings:** 17,000 books. **Subscriptions:** 12 journals and other serials. **Services:** Copying; library open to students with recommendation from an attorney.

WYCLIFFE COLLEGE
See: University of Toronto - Wycliffe College - Leonard Library (17002)

WYETH-AYERST LABORATORIES
See: American Home Products Corporation - Wyeth-Ayerst Laboratories Division (535)

★18082★
WYETH-AYERST RESEARCH, INC. - INFORMATION CENTER (Sci-Engr, Med)
64 Maple St. Phone: (518)297-8294
Rouses Point, NY 12979-9985
George L. Curran, III, Sr.Libn. & Info.Spec.
Staff: Prof 2; Other 3. **Subjects:** Analytical and pharmaceutical chemistry, pharmacy, pharmacology, business management, quality control. **Holdings:** 5500 books; 4000 bound periodical volumes; chemical patents, 1974-1987, on microfilm; 600 volumes on microfilm; 100 cassette programs. **Subscriptions:** 500 serials. **Services:** Interlibrary loan; center not open to the public. **Automated Operations:** Computerized cataloging, acquisitions, serials, and circulation. **Computerized Information Services:** DIALOG Information Services, BRS Information Technologies, Occupational Health Services, Inc. (OHS), STN International, Chemical Information Systems, Inc. (CIS), Pergamon ORBIT InfoLine, Inc., Data-Star, NLM. **Networks/Consortia:** Member of New York State Interlibrary Loan Network (NYSILL), North Country Reference and Research Resources Council (NCRRRC), Northern New York Health Information Cooperative. **Publications:** Bulletin, quarterly - for internal distribution only. **Formerly:** Ayerst Laboratories, Inc. **Staff:** Tari L. Mc Tague, Info.Sci..

★18083★
WYETH, LTD. - WYETH RESOURCE LIBRARY (Med)
4455 Chesswood Dr. Phone: (416)630-0280
Downsview, ON, Canada M3J 2C2 Lesley Bailey, Prod.Info.Off.
Staff: 2. **Subjects:** Pharmacology - general, clinical, hormonal; psychiatry; gynecology; cardiovascular system. **Holdings:** 610 books; 723 bound periodical volumes; 10,000 reprints; 10 reports and current awareness publications. **Subscriptions:** 47 journals and other serials. **Services:** Library not open to the public. **Automated Operations:** Computerized cataloging. **Computerized Information Services:** DIALOG Information Services; internal database.

★18084★
WYLE LABORATORIES - WYLE RESEARCH LIBRARY (Sci-Engr)
128 Maryland St. Phone: (213)322-1763
El Segundo, CA 90245 Deborah Aber, Info.Dir.
Staff: Prof 1. **Subjects:** Noise control, acoustics. **Holdings:** 12,000 books; 50 bound periodical volumes. **Subscriptions:** 25 journals and other serials. **Services:** Interlibrary loan; library not open to the public. **Automated Operations:** Computerized cataloging. **Computerized Information Services:** DIALOG Information Services. **Formerly:** Technical Information Library.

★18085★
WYOMING HISTORICAL AND GEOLOGICAL SOCIETY - BISHOP MEMORIAL LIBRARY (Hist)
49 S. Franklin St. Phone: (717)823-6244
Wilkes-Barre, PA 18701 Margaret E. Craft, Libn.
Founded: 1858. **Staff:** Prof 3; Other 1. **Subjects:** Wyoming Valley and Pennsylvania history. **Special Collections:** Manuscripts relating chiefly to the Wilkes-Barre region of the Susquehanna Valley and the Wyoming Valley, 1750-1950 (1500 cubic feet). **Holdings:** 5000 books; 500 bound periodical volumes; 900 reels of microfilm of Wilkes-Barre newspapers, 1797-1950; 2500 photographs. **Subscriptions:** 15 journals and other serials. **Services:** Copying; library open to the public. **Publications:** Susquehanna Company Papers; Proceedings and Collections, irregular; Newsletter; guides to manuscript collections.

★18086★
WYOMING MEDICAL CENTER - MEDICAL LIBRARY (Med)
1233 E. 2nd St. Phone: (307)577-2450
Casper, WY 82601 J. Wilbert, Dir.
Staff: Prof 1; Other 1. **Subjects:** Medicine. **Holdings:** 810 books; 800 bound periodical volumes. **Subscriptions:** 111 journals and other serials. **Services:** Interlibrary loan; copying; library open to the public for reference use only. **Computerized Information Services:** MEDLARS, MEDLINE; DOCLINE (electronic mail service). Performs searches on fee basis. **Networks/Consortia:** Member of Muddy Mountain Health Sciences Library Consortium. **Publications:** New book list, monthly - for internal distribution only.

★18087★
WYOMING STATE ARCHIVES, MUSEUMS & HISTORICAL DEPARTMENT (Hist)
Barrett Bldg. Phone: (307)777-7519
Cheyenne, WY 82002-0130 David Kathka, Dir.
Staff: 70. **Subjects:** Wyoming and Western history; collection, preservation, and interpretation of historical, ethnological, and archeological materials. **Holdings:** 6500 volumes; 38,500 reels of microfilm of Wyoming newspapers, 1867 to present, National Archives materials, scrapbooks, manuscripts; maps and plats; documents; letters; ledgers; diaries; research collections; census records; oral histories; folklore; AV programs; territorial and state government records. **Subscriptions:** 75 journals and other serials. **Services:** Copying; department open to the public for reference use only with staff member present. **Publications:** Annals of Wyoming, semiannual; Wyoming History News, 6/year; calendar of Wyoming history; Buffalo Bones, Stories from Wyoming's Past. **Special Indexes:** Indexes to Annals of Wyoming, 1897-1974; Inventory of WPA Manuscripts Collection; Oral History index. **Remarks:** An alternate telephone number is 777-7014. **Staff:** Julia Yelvington, Hd., Archv.Div.; Roger Doherty, Hd., Historic Sites Div.; Tom Marceau, Hd., State Historic Presrv.Off..

★18088★
WYOMING (State) DEPARTMENT OF EDUCATION - COMPUTER CENTER (Educ)
Hathaway Bldg.
Cheyenne, WY 82002 Phone: (307)777-6254
Staff: Prof 1; Other 1. **Subjects:** K-12 science, mathematics, social studies, language arts, arts; education. **Holdings:** 100 education newsletters; 20 professional journals; 600 computer software diskettes. **Subscriptions:** 50 journals and other serials. **Services:** Interlibrary loan; center open to residents of Wyoming. **Computerized Information Services:** The Source Information Network (electronic mail service). **Networks/Consortia:** Member of Wyoming Library Network. **Publications:** Wyoming Educator (newsletter), monthly - for internal distribution only.

★18089★
WYOMING STATE DEPARTMENT OF HEALTH & SOCIAL SERVICE - PUBLIC HEALTH FILM LIBRARY (Med, Aud-Vis)
Hathaway Bldg., Rm. 518 Phone: (307)777-7363
Cheyenne, WY 82002-0710 Janet L. Manners, Film Libn.
Staff: 2. **Subjects:** Nursing, mental health, childbirth education, venereal diseases, dental health, school health. **Special Collections:** Rape Prevention; Family Violence. **Holdings:** 400 16mm films; 100 videotape and filmstrip programs. **Services:** Library open to the public with restrictions. **Special Catalogs:** Film Library Catalog. **Remarks:** Part of Division of Health and Medical Services.

★18090★
WYOMING (State) ECONOMIC DEVELOPMENT AND STABILIZATION BOARD - ECONOMIC DEVELOPMENT LIBRARY (Plan)
Herschler Bldg. Phone: (307)777-6430
Cheyenne, WY 82002 Anne W. McGowan, Lib.Mgr.
Staff: Prof 1. **Subjects:** Economic development, land use planning, water development, Wyoming statistics, mineral development. **Holdings:** 500 books; 5000 documents and reports. **Subscriptions:** 105 journals and other serials. **Services:** Interlibrary loan; copying; SDI; library open to the public.

★18091★
WYOMING STATE GAME AND FISH DEPARTMENT - LIBRARY (Env-Cons)
5400 Bishop Blvd. Phone: (307)777-5812
Cheyenne, WY 82002 Mary E. Link, Sec.
Staff: 1. **Subjects:** Wildlife and fisheries management, conservation. **Special Collections:** Departmental annual reports, 1898 to present; departmental publications; Wyoming Wildlife, 1936 to present (magazine). **Holdings:** 100 books; 700 bound periodical volumes; 2300 technical reports; 300 U.S. Geological Survey maps; 30 film titles; 15 videotape titles; 50,000 color slide and black/white negatives. **Subscriptions:** 45 journals and other serials; 8 newspapers. **Services:** Interlibrary loan; copying; library open to the public with restrictions.

WYOMING (State) GEOLOGICAL SURVEY
See: Geological Survey of Wyoming (5587)

★18092★
WYOMING STATE HIGHWAY DEPARTMENT - PLANNING AND ADMINISTRATION DIVISION - LIBRARY (Trans)
Box 1708 Phone: (307)777-7555
Cheyenne, WY 82002-9019 Timothy Carroll, Res.Engr.
Subjects: Transportation. **Holdings:** 1750 books. **Services:** Library not open to the public. **Computerized Information Services:** DIALOG Information Services.

★18093★
WYOMING STATE HOSPITAL - MEDICAL LIBRARY (Med)
Box 177 Phone: (307)789-3464
Evanston, WY 82930 William L. Matchinski, Prin.Libn.
Staff: Prof 2; Other 2. **Subjects:** Psychiatry, medicine, nursing, social work, psychology. **Holdings:** 2500 volumes. **Subscriptions:** 155 journals and other serials; 32 newspapers. **Services:** Interlibrary loan; copying; library open to the public with restrictions. **Networks/Consortia:** Member of Western Wyoming Health Science Library Consortium.

★18094★
WYOMING STATE LAW LIBRARY (Law)
Supreme Court Bldg. Phone: (307)777-7509
Cheyenne, WY 82002 Lisa Hoffmeister, Law Libn.
Founded: 1897. **Staff:** Prof 2; Other 1. **Subjects:** Law. **Holdings:** 78,000 volumes. **Subscriptions:** 425 journals and other serials. **Services:** Interlibrary loan (limited); copying; library open to the public. **Automated Operations:** Computerized cataloging. **Networks/Consortia:** Member of Bibliographical Center for Research, Rocky Mountain Region, Inc. (BCR). **Staff:** Kathy Carlson, Asst. Law Libn..

★18095★
WYOMING STATE LIBRARY (Info Sci)
Supreme Court & State Library Bldg. Phone: (307)777-7281
Cheyenne, WY 82002 Wayne H. Johnson, State Libn.
Founded: 1871. **Staff:** Prof 9; Other 22. **Subjects:** Wyoming, Western Americana, North American Indians, library science, cookbooks, art and architecture. **Special Collections:** Large print books (2983). **Holdings:** 151,556 books; 1208 bound periodical volumes; 18 VF drawers of U.S., Wyoming, and foreign materials; regional depository for U.S. Government publications (1.5 million); depository for Wyoming publications (5000). **Subscriptions:** 400 journals and other serials; 54 newspapers. **Services:** Interlibrary loan; copying; library open to the public. **Automated Operations:** Computerized cataloging, acquisitions, and circulation. **Computerized Information Services:** BRS Information Technologies, WILSONLINE, DIALOG Information Services. **Networks/Consortia:** Member of Bibliographical Center for Research, Rocky Mountain Region, Inc. (BCR), Health Sciences Information Network (HSIN), Wyoming Library Network. **Publications:** Annual Report; Annual Report of Wyoming Public Library Service; Outrider (newsletter); Wyoming Library Roundup; Wyoming Public Library Trustees Manual. **Special Catalogs:** Wyoming Union List of Serials; Large Print catalog; Directory of Wyoming Libraries; Wyoming Library Laws; Wyoming Public Library Standards. **Staff:** Beth Agar, Chf., Tech.Serv.; Gwen Rice, Chf., Ref. & ILL; Corky Walters, Chf., Coll.Dev. & Educ.; Jerome Krois, Lib.Dev.Off.; Karen Hedrick, Mgr., Acq.; Donna Jo Best, Chf., Bus.Off.; Linn Rounds, Pub.Info.Off..

★18096★
WYOMING STATE PLANNING COORDINATOR'S OFFICE - LIBRARY (Plan)
Herschler Bldg., 2nd Fl., E.
122 W. 25th Phone: (307)777-7574
Cheyenne, WY 82002 Sheryl Jeffries, Libn.
Founded: 1975. **Staff:** Prof 1. **Subjects:** Federal and state agencies, environment, higher education. **Holdings:** 4000 books; 6 VF drawers of documents; environmental impact statements. **Subscriptions:** 20 journals and other serials.

★18097★
WYOMING STATE TRAINING SCHOOL - MEDICAL LIBRARY (Med)
Lander, WY 82520 Phone: (307)332-5302
Bonnie V. Freimuth, Med. Inservice
Founded: 1981. **Staff:** Prof 1. **Subjects:** Mental retardation, epilepsy, neurological disorders, pediatric medicine, occupational and physical therapy. **Holdings:** 300 books. **Subscriptions:** 16 journals and other serials. **Services:** Interlibrary loan; copying; library open to state employees. **Computerized Information Services:** MEDLINE. **Networks/Consortia:** Member of Wind River Health Science Library Consortium.

★18098★
WYTHEVILLE COMMUNITY COLLEGE - KEGLEY LIBRARY - SPECIAL COLLECTIONS (Hist)
1000 E. Main St. Phone: (703)228-5541
Wytheville, VA 24382 Anna Ray Roberts, Coord., Lib.Serv.
Staff: Prof 2; Other 1. **Subjects:** Southwest Virginia history and genealogy. **Holdings:** 500 books; 86 bound periodical volumes; 300 historical maps; 500 oral history interviews; data on 103 local cemeteries; 4 VF drawers; 90 volumes of family history; 100 volumes of local history; 120 reels of microfilm. **Services:** Copying; collections open to the public.

X

★18099★
XAVIER SOCIETY FOR THE BLIND - NATIONAL CATHOLIC PRESS AND LIBRARY FOR THE VISUALLY HANDICAPPED (Aud-Vis)
154 E. 23rd St.
New York, NY 10010 Rev. Anthony F. LaBau, S.J., Dir.
Subjects: General collection. **Holdings:** 900 books in braille; 800 books in large type; 650 books on cassette. **Services:** Multiple copies of books and periodicals in all three forms available on free loan. **Publications:** Newsletter, weekly; Catholic Review, monthly (braille, large print, and cassette).

★18100★
XAVIER UNIVERSITY OF LOUISIANA - COLLEGE OF PHARMACY - LIBRARY (Med)
Palmetto & Pine Sts. Phone: (504)486-7411
New Orleans, LA 70125 Yvonne C. Hull, Libn.
Staff: Prof 1; Other 1. **Subjects:** Pharmacy, pharmacology, medicinal chemistry, pharmacognosy, clinical pathology, toxicology, drug interaction, public health, history of pharmacy. **Special Collections:** Collection of volumes dealing with medical and pharmaceutical information from the 19th century (150 volumes including antique chemical handbooks and pharmacopeias). **Holdings:** 4000 books; 2800 bound periodical volumes; 250 audio cassettes; 10 records; 3 films. **Subscriptions:** 100 journals and other serials. **Services:** Interlibrary loan; copying; SDI (limited); library open to the public for reference use only. **Remarks:** Library has initiated a Drug Information Center in cooperation with V.A. Hospital of New Orleans.

★18101★
XEROX CORPORATION - EL SEGUNDO TECHNICAL LIBRARY (Comp Sci)
701 S. Aviation Blvd., A3-25 Phone: (213)333-5222
El Segundo, CA 90245 Amy Feller, Tech.Info.Spec.
Founded: 1968. **Staff:** Prof 3; Other 2. **Subjects:** Computer science, electronics, microelectronics, management, marketing, telecommunications. **Holdings:** 4800 books; 1200 bound periodical volumes; 3000 reports and conference proceedings. **Subscriptions:** 280 journals and other serials; 15 newspapers. **Services:** Interlibrary loan; copying (limited); SDI. **Automated Operations:** Computerized cataloging and serials. **Computerized Information Services:** DIALOG Information Services, OCLC, BRS Information Technologies, Pergamon ORBIT InfoLine, Inc.; internal databases. **Networks/Consortia:** Member of CLASS, OCLC Pacific Network. **Publications:** Newsletter, monthly; Journal Holdings, annual. **Staff:** Kay Traylor, Sr.Tech.Info.Asst.; Sherrill Cohn, Cat.Libn..

★18102★
XEROX CORPORATION - LAW LIBRARY (Law)
Box 1600 Phone: (203)329-8700
Stamford, CT 06904 Ruth E. Gebhard, Act.Libn.
Founded: 1969. **Staff:** Prof 1; Other 1. **Subjects:** Law, business. **Holdings:** 15,000 volumes; 2 VF drawers of pamphlets; 6 drawers of cassette tapes; 6 drawers of annual reports; 2 drawers of foreign materials; 10 drawers of microfiche. **Subscriptions:** 104 journals and other serials. **Services:** Interlibrary loan; copying; library open to the public at discretion of librarian. **Computerized Information Services:** Pergamon ORBIT InfoLine, Inc., Dow Jones News/Retrieval, LEXIS, Pergamon ORBIT InfoLine, Inc., Official Airline Guides, Inc. (OAG), DIALOG Information Services, WESTLAW; internal databases. **Networks/Consortia:** Member of Southwestern Connecticut Library Council (SWLC).

★18103★
XEROX CORPORATION - LIBRARY SERVICES
1301 Ridgeview Dr.
Lewisville, TX 75067
Subjects: Business machines, electronic typing systems, communication equipment. **Special Collections:** Word processing; document creation centers; facsimile transmission. **Holdings:** 2000 books; 600 reports. **Remarks:** Presently inactive.

★18104★
XEROX CORPORATION - PALO ALTO RESEARCH CENTER - TECHNICAL INFORMATION CENTER (Comp Sci, Info Sci)
3333 Coyote Hill Rd. Phone: (415)494-4042
Palo Alto, CA 94304 Giuliana A. Lavendel, Mgr.
Founded: 1971. **Staff:** Prof 7; Other 9. **Subjects:** Computer and information science, physics, material science, electronics, psychology, education. **Special Collections:** Information systems and materials. **Holdings:** 13,000 books; 5000 bound periodical volumes; 10,000 external reports; 50,000 Xerox reports; microfilm; microfiche. **Subscriptions:** 750 journals and other serials. **Services:** Interlibrary loan; SDI; center open to the public by appointment. **Automated Operations:** Computerized cataloging, serials, and circulation. **Computerized Information Services:** DIALOG Information Services, Pergamon ORBIT InfoLine, Inc., BRS Information Technologies, NEXIS, LEXIS, Dow Jones News/Retrieval, RLIN; internal database. **Networks/Consortia:** Member of SOUTHNET, CLASS. **Publications:** Competitive Flyer, weekly; holdings list, annual; Update, weekly. **Special Catalogs:** Report list catalog. **Staff:** Alice Wilder, Supv., User Network; Katherine S. Jarvis, Supv., Tech.Info.; Maia Pindar, Sys.Spec..

★18105★
XEROX CORPORATION - TECHNICAL INFORMATION CENTER (Sci-Engr)
Box 305 Phone: (716)422-3505
Webster, NY 14580 Michael D. Majcher, Mgr.
Founded: 1960. **Staff:** Prof 18; Other 10. **Subjects:** Xerography, electrophotography, reprography, electronics, chemistry, physics, photography, materials and processes, computer science. **Special Collections:** Corporation Technical Archives. **Holdings:** 35,000 books; 8500 bound periodical volumes; 100,000 internal reports; 20,000 external reports; 45 VF drawers; 5500 reels of microfilm; 305,000 microfiche; 1.5 million patents. **Subscriptions:** 2000 journals and other serials. **Services:** Interlibrary loan; SDI; Xerox Telecopier Facsimile Service; center open to the public by appointment. **Automated Operations:** Computerized cataloging, acquisitions, serials, and circulation. **Computerized Information Services:** OCLC, LEXIS, NEXIS, TEXTLINE, MEDLARS, Dun & Bradstreet Corporation, Pergamon ORBIT InfoLine, Inc., NewsNet, Inc., Electronet/1, DIALOG Information Services, BRS Information Technologies, CAS ONLINE, Dow Jones News/Retrieval, Chemical Information Systems, Inc. (CIS); LINX Courier (electronic mail service). **Networks/Consortia:** Member of Rochester Regional Library Council (RRLC). **Publications:** TIC Users Guide; Internal Reports Accession List; Current Awareness Bulletin. **Staff:** David A. Mindel, Mgr., Tech.Serv.; Cecelia E. Rice, Mgr., Pub.Serv.; F. Belli, Mgr., Database/Indexing Serv..

XEROX CORPORATION - VERSATEC
See: Versatec (17319)

★18106★
XEROX RESEARCH CENTRE OF CANADA - TECHNICAL INFORMATION CENTRE (Sci-Engr)
2660 Speakman Dr. Phone: (416)823-7091
Mississauga, ON, Canada L5K 2L1
Betty A. Bassett, Mgr., Tech.Info.Serv.
Founded: 1974. **Staff:** Prof 1; Other 2. **Subjects:** Electrochemistry, polymer chemistry, colloid chemistry, surface science, electrophotography, xerography, control engineering, paper science, materials science. **Special Collections:** Internal technical reports (65,000). **Holdings:** 12,000 books; 9000 bound periodical volumes; 3000 reels of microfilm; 70,000 microfiche. **Subscriptions:** 400 journals and other serials; 8 newspapers. **Services:** Interlibrary loan; copying; SDI; center open to the public by appointment. **Automated Operations:** Computerized cataloging, acquisitions, circulation, and current awareness service. **Computerized Information Services:** DIALOG Information Services, Pergamon ORBIT InfoLine, Inc., BRS Information Technologies, STN International, Info Globe, CAN/OLE, Occupational Health Services, Inc., Pergamon ORBIT InfoLine, Inc., UTLAS, WILSONLINE; Ethernet (electronic mail service). **Networks/Consortia:** Member of Sheridan Park Association - Library and Information Science Committee (LISC). **Publications:** TIC Update, monthly; Serials Holdings List, annual.

★18107★
XEROX SPECIAL INFORMATION SYSTEMS - TECHNICAL LIBRARY (Sci-Engr)
250 N. Halstead St., M/S 1369 Phone: (818)351-2351
Pasadena, CA 91109 Frances A. Piatt, Res.Libn.
Founded: 1983. **Staff:** Prof 1. **Subjects:** Optics, artificial intelligence, computer science, languages. **Holdings:** 1322 books; 500 bound periodical volumes. **Subscriptions:** 83 journals and other serials. **Services:** Interlibrary

loan; library not open to the public. **Automated Operations:** Computerized serials and circulation. **Computerized Information Services:** DIALOG Information Services, BRS Information Technologies.

Y

Y-12 NUCLEAR PLANT
See: Martin Marietta Energy Systems Inc. - Libraries (8475)

★18108★
YADKIN COUNTY PUBLIC LIBRARY - PAUL PRICE DAVIS HISTORY ROOM (Hist)
243 E. Main St.
Box 607 Phone: (919)679-8792
Yadkinville, NC 27055 Malinda Sells, Br.Libn.
Founded: 1971. **Subjects:** Local and North Carolina history. **Holdings:** 660 volumes; 44 reels of microfilm of census data, marriage records, wills, deeds, estates, court minutes of county, 1851-1950; 12 drawers of family genealogies, local history; The Yadkin Ripple, The Enterprise, and The Tribune, all 1981 to present. **Services:** Interlibrary loan; Copying; room open to the public for reference use only. **Special Indexes:** Index of all surnames (card).

★18109★
YAKIMA COUNTY LAW LIBRARY (Law)
Yakima County Court House Phone: (509)457-5452
Yakima, WA 98901 Linda Von Essen, Law Libn.
Founded: 1932. **Staff:** Prof 1. **Subjects:** Law. **Holdings:** 16,500 volumes. **Services:** Interlibrary loan; copying; library open to the public with restrictions. **Automated Operations:** Computerized acquisitions.

★18110★
YAKIMA VALLEY GENEALOGICAL SOCIETY - LIBRARY (Hist)
Box 445 Phone: (509)248-1328
Yakima, WA 98907 Ellen Brzoska, Libn.
Founded: 1967. **Staff:** Prof 2; Other 18. **Subjects:** Genealogy; family, Yakima County, and central Washington history. **Special Collections:** Abstracts from old bound newspapers, 1884-1925; Daughters of the American Revolution, Daughters of Washington Pioneers collections. **Holdings:** 2000 volumes; 3000 bound periodical volumes; 100,000 card Yakima County cemetery file; 50,000 card Klickitat and Kittitas Counties cemetery file; 8 VF drawers of reports, clippings, pamphlets, and documents; 200 reels of microfilm and cassette tapes; 100 family history interview sheets. **Subscriptions:** 200 journals and other serials. **Services:** Interlibrary loan; copying; library open to the public for reference use only. **Publications:** Yakima Valley Genealogical Society Bulletin, quarterly. **Remarks:** The library is located at N. 3rd and East B St., Yakima, WA. **Staff:** Marge Karkau, Asst.Libn.; Wilbur Helm, ILL.

★18111★
YAKIMA VALLEY MUSEUM AND HISTORICAL ASSOCIATION - ARCHIVES (Hist)
2105 Tieton Dr. Phone: (509)248-0747
Yakima, WA 98902 Frances A. Hare, Archv.
Subjects: Area history and development, Yakima Indians, pioneers, irrigation history. **Special Collections:** Apple and pear box labels; William O. Douglas Collection (1500 books; slides; films; photographs); local newspaper, 1889-1952 (bound volumes). **Holdings:** 4425 books; 6231 photographs; clipping file; documents; manuscripts. **Subscriptions:** 25 journals and other serials. **Services:** Copying; archives open to the public by appointment for reference use only. **Remarks:** Includes the holdings of the Gannon Museum of Wagons.

★18112★
YAKIMA VALLEY REGIONAL LIBRARY - REFERENCE DEPARTMENT - CLICK RELANDER COLLECTION (Hist)
102 N. 3rd St. Phone: (509)452-8541
Yakima, WA 98901 Cynthia Garrick, Ref.Coord.
Subjects: Click Relander, Yakima newspaper publisher; Pacific Northwest history; Yakima and Wanapum Indians and their relationship with the U.S. government; Yakima Valley history and agriculture. **Holdings:** 169 boxes of letters, manuscripts, federal documents, photographs. **Services:** Copying; collection open to the public.

YALE CENTER FOR BRITISH ART
See: Yale University (18152)

★18113★
YALE CLUB OF NEW YORK CITY - LIBRARY (Hum)
50 Vanderbilt Ave. Phone: (212)661-2070
New York, NY 10017 Seth J. Ramson, Libn.
Founded: 1897. **Staff:** Prof 1; Other 1. **Subjects:** Literature, history, travel, biography, social sciences, art, music. **Special Collections:** Yale memorabilia and publications. **Holdings:** 45,000 volumes. **Subscriptions:** 100 journals and other serials. **Services:** Library not open to the public.

YALE COLLECTION OF HISTORICAL SOUND RECORDINGS
See: Yale University (18155)

YALE EDITIONS OF THE PRIVATE PAPERS OF JAMES BOSWELL
See: Yale University (18156)

★18114★
YALE UNIVERSITY - AFRICAN COLLECTION (Area-Ethnic)
Sterling Memorial Library, Rm. 317 Phone: (203)432-1883
New Haven, CT 06520 J. Moore D. Crossey, Cur.
Founded: 1963. **Staff:** Prof 1; Other 3. **Subjects:** Africa - languages, literature, history, art, politics, government, religion, education, economics, law, social conditions, civilizations, philosophy, natural history, big game hunting, travel, topography, mining. **Special Collections:** Howell Wright Collection of Rhodesiana and South Africana (5000 volumes). **Holdings:** 80,000 books; 75,000 bound periodical volumes; over 100 manuscript collections (original and in microform); 1000 reels of microfilm of newspapers, pamphlet collections, government documents; photographs; posters; postcards; pamphlets; broadsides; maps. **Subscriptions:** 1000 journals and other serials; 35 newspapers. **Services:** Interlibrary loan; copying; collection open to the public with restrictions. **Automated Operations:** Computerized cataloging, acquisitions, serials, and circulation. **Networks/Consortia:** Member of RLG, Center for Research Libraries (CRL) Consortia, Hartford Consortium for Higher Education. **Special Catalogs:** Catalog of Africa-related materials (1965 to present) arranged by African countries and/or subjects (card).

★18115★
YALE UNIVERSITY - AMERICAN ORIENTAL SOCIETY LIBRARY (Area-Ethnic)
Sterling Memorial Library, Rm. 329 Phone: (203)432-1842
New Haven, CT 06520 Mary Ann T. Itoga, Libn.
Founded: 1842. **Staff:** Prof 1. **Subjects:** Oriental civilizations - language, literature, history, culture. **Holdings:** 22,670 volumes. **Subscriptions:** 115 journals and other serials. **Services:** Collection open only to members of the society, Yale University personnel, and visiting scholars on application. **Networks/Consortia:** Member of RLG.

★18116★
YALE UNIVERSITY - ANTHROPOLOGY LIBRARY (Soc Sci)
Kline Science Library
Box 6666 Phone: (203)432-3439
New Haven, CT 06511 Howard D. Keith, Act.Libn. for the Sci.
Staff: 1. **Subjects:** Anthropology. **Holdings:** 18,461 volumes. **Subscriptions:** 205 journals and other serials. **Services:** Interlibrary loan; copying; library open to the public with permission. **Networks/Consortia:** Member of RLG, Center for Research Libraries (CRL) Consortia, Hartford Consortium for Higher Education.

★18117★
YALE UNIVERSITY - ART AND ARCHITECTURE LIBRARY (Art)
Art & Architecture Bldg.
Yale Sta., Box 1605A Phone: (203)432-2641
New Haven, CT 06520 Nancy S. Lambert, Libn.
Staff: Prof 3; Other 8. **Subjects:** History of art, architecture, city planning, painting, sculpture, graphic arts. **Special Collections:** Faber Birren Collection on color (books; photographs). **Holdings:** 89,247 volumes; 14,400 exhibition catalogs; 55 VF drawers of pamphlets; 17 VF drawers of city planning material; 283,951 slides; 170,266 photographs. **Subscriptions:** 504 journals and other serials. **Services:** Interlibrary loan; copying (both limited); library open to the public for reference use only; Special Borrower's Card available on a fee basis. **Networks/Consortia:** Member of RLG, Center for Research Libraries (CRL) Consortia, Hartford Consortium for Higher Education. **Staff:** Helen Chillman, Slide & Photo.Libn.; Christine De Vallet, Ref.Libn..

★18118★
YALE UNIVERSITY - ARTS OF THE BOOK COLLECTION (Publ, Art)
Sterling Memorial Library — Phone: (203)432-1712
New Haven, CT 06520 — R. Gay Walker, Cur.
Founded: 1967. **Staff:** Prof 1; Other 2. **Subjects:** Typography, book illustration and design, calligraphy, bookbinding, book-plates, private presses and fine printing. **Special Collections:** Caricature; trade cards; Western Americana prints; engraved views of Vienna; historic printing material including the Bibliographical Press (four presses and an extensive collection of printing types); engraved woodblocks; special archives of Fritz Kredel, Fritz Eichenberg, and Carl P. Rollins. **Holdings:** 14,000 books; 10,000 prints; type specimens; archive of student printing, including masters' theses from School of Graphic Design at Yale; 1 million bookplates. **Services:** Interlibrary loan; copying; collection open to the public. **Automated Operations:** Computerized cataloging and acquisitions. **Networks/Consortia:** Member of RLG, Hartford Consortium for Higher Education.

★18119★
YALE UNIVERSITY - ASTRONOMY LIBRARY (Sci-Engr)
J.W. Gibbs Laboratory
260 Whitney Ave.
Box 6666 — Phone: (203)432-3000
New Haven, CT 06511 — Pauline DiGioia, Lib.Serv.Asst.
Founded: 1871. **Staff:** 3. **Subjects:** Astronomy, astrophysics, celestial mechanics, physics, mathematics. **Special Collections:** Extensive collection of domestic and foreign observatory publications. **Holdings:** 16,232 books; 6000 bound periodical volumes; 800 shelf feet of observatory reprints. **Subscriptions:** 120 journals and other serials. **Services:** Interlibrary loan; copying; library open to the public for reference use only. **Networks/Consortia:** Member of RLG, Center for Research Libraries (CRL) Consortia, Hartford Consortium for Higher Education. **Publications:** Transactions of Yale University Observatory; Tables of the Motion of the Moon; The Evolution of Galaxies and Stellar Populations, 1977. **Special Catalogs:** Bright Star Catalog, 4th edition; Supplement to the Bright Star Catalog, 1983; General Catalog of Trigonometric Stellar Parallaxes and supplement 1963.

★18120★
YALE UNIVERSITY - BABYLONIAN COLLECTION (Hist)
Sterling Memorial Library
120 High St. — Phone: (203)432-1837
New Haven, CT 06520 — William W. Hallo, Cur.
Founded: 1912. **Staff:** Prof 5. **Subjects:** Assyriology; cuneiform; Sumerian, Akkadian, Hittite, Mesopotamian literature, archeology, and history; Semitics. **Special Collections:** Cuneiform texts from the collections of E.I. David, E.J. Banks, J.P. Morgan, Edwin T. Newell, General Theological Seminary. **Holdings:** 7000 books; 1200 bound periodical volumes; 1000 reprints; 35,577 cuneiform tablets and inscriptions; 3000 cylinder seals and stamp seals; 1000 other Ancient Near Eastern artifacts. **Subscriptions:** 25 journals and other serials. **Services:** Collection open to the public upon application to the curator. **Networks/Consortia:** Member of RLG, Center for Research Libraries (CRL) Consortia, Hartford Consortium for Higher Education. **Publications:** Yale Oriental Series - Babylonian Texts; Yale Oriental Series - Researches; Babylonian Inscriptions in the Collection of James B. Nies, Yale University; Goucher College Cuneiform Inscriptions; Babylonian Records in the Library of J. Pierpont Morgan; Yale Near Eastern Researches. **Remarks:** This library includes "the largest collection of cuneiform tablets and cylinder seals in the U.S.A." **Staff:** Gary Beckman, Asst.Cur.; Harvey Weiss, Archeo.Adv.; Ulla Kasten, Musm.Ed.; B.R. Foster, Assyriologist.

★18121★
YALE UNIVERSITY - BEINECKE RARE BOOK AND MANUSCRIPT LIBRARY (Rare Book, Hum)
Wall & High Sts. — Phone: (203)432-2959
New Haven, CT 06520 — Ralph W. Franklin, Dir.
Founded: 1963. **Staff:** Prof 13; Other 20. **Subjects:** Alchemy and the occult; Afro-American arts and letters; American, British, and European history and literature; British economic tracts; Congregationalism; exploration and travel; French illustrated books; German literature; Greek and Latin literature; history of education; history of printing; incunabula; Judaica; Latin America; Native American History and Languages; Near Eastern manuscripts; early British and American newspapers; ornithology; Oxford; papyri; playing cards; pre-1600 manuscripts; Russian books and manuscripts; sporting books; Theatre Guild; theology; Tibet; Western Americana. **Special Collections:** Leonie Adams, Aldus Manutius, Matthew Arnold, Asch, Joel Barlow, Barrie, Baskerville, Baskin, William Beckford, S.V. Benet, W.R. Benet, Boccaccio, Boswell, Hermann Broch, Browning, Buchan, Burney, Byron, Cabell, Carlyle, Rachel Carson, Sir Winston Churchill, Barrett Clark, Coleridge, Conrad, Cooper, Walter Crane, Defoe, Dickens, Hilda Doolittle, Norman Douglas, Muriel Draper, Katherine Dreier, Dryden, Jonathan Edwards, George Eliot, Maria Edgeworth, Arthur Davison Ficke, Fielding, Vardis Fisher, John Gould Fletcher, Paul Leicester Ford, Garrick, Jean Giono, Gissing, Goethe, Herman Hagedorn, Hutchins and Neith Boyce Hapgood, Hardy, Marsden Hartley, John Hersey, Hogg, Paul Horgan, Langston Hughes, Joseph Ireland, Washington Irving, Robinson Jeffers, James Weldon Johnson, Samuel Johnson, Joyce, Kafka, Kipling, Landor, D.H. Lawrence, Sinclair Lewis, Mabel Luhan, George Macdonald, William McFee, MacLeish, Norman MacLeod, Thomas Mann, F.T. Marinetti, Marquand, Masefield, Mencken, Meredith, Milton, George Moore, Sir Thomas More, Robert Nathan, O'Neill, James Gates Percival, Pope, Ezra Pound, James Purdy, Dorothy Richardson, Samuel Richardson, Rilke, Bruce Rogers, Ruskin, Shakespeare, Sheridan, Spenser, Gertrude Stein, Leo Stein, Stevenson, Stieglitz, Ezra Stiles, Swinburne, Tennyson, Thackeray, Tocqueville, Toklas, Trollope, Van Vechten, Walton, Robert Penn Warren, Rebecca West, Edith Wharton, Whitman, Wilder, William Carlos Williams, Edmund Wilson, Kurt Wolff, Wordsworth, Richard Wright, Eleanor Wylie. **Holdings:** 595,466 volumes; 2.25 million manuscripts. **Services:** Copying; library open to the public. **Networks/Consortia:** Member of RLG, Center for Research Libraries (CRL) Consortia, Hartford Consortium for Higher Education. **Staff:** Patricia Willis, Cur., Amer.Lit.Coll.; Vincent Giroud, Cur., Modern Bks. & Mss.; Robert Babcock, Cur., Early Bks. & Mss.; George Miles, Cur./W.Americana; Stephen Parks, Cur./Osborn Coll./Mss.; Christa Sammons, Cur./German Coll.; Patricia Middleton, Pub.Serv.Libn.; Suzanne Rutter, Tech.Serv.Libn.; Bruce Stark, Tech.Serv.Libn..

★18122★
YALE UNIVERSITY - BENJAMIN FRANKLIN COLLECTION (Hist)
Sterling Memorial Library, Rm. 230
Yale Sta., Box 1603A — Phone: (203)432-1815
New Haven, CT 06520 — Barbara Oberg, Ed.
Founded: 1935. **Subjects:** Books, portraits, medals, and other memorabilia relating to Benjamin Franklin and the American Revolution. **Holdings:** Figures not available. **Subscriptions:** 10 journals and other serials. **Services:** Copying; collection open to the public for reference use only. **Networks/Consortia:** Member of RLG, Center for Research Libraries (CRL) Consortia, Hartford Consortium for Higher Education. **Remarks:** The manuscripts, broadsides, and a portion of the printed material have been transferred to Beinecke Library.

★18123★
YALE UNIVERSITY - CLASSICS LIBRARY (Hum)
Phelps Hall
344 College St. — Phone: (203)432-0854
New Haven, CT 06520 — Carla M. Lukas, Lib.Serv.Asst.
Founded: 1892. **Staff:** Prof 1. **Subjects:** Greek and Latin classical literature, ancient history, art, archeology, papyrology. **Holdings:** 21,013 volumes. **Subscriptions:** 221 journals and other serials. **Services:** Interlibrary loan; copying; library open to the public by permission. **Networks/Consortia:** Member of RLG, Center for Research Libraries (CRL) Consortia, Hartford Consortium for Higher Education.

★18124★
YALE UNIVERSITY - COLLECTION OF THE LITERATURE OF THE AMERICAN MUSICAL THEATRE (Theater, Mus)
Sterling Memorial Library, Rm. 226 — Phone: (203)432-1795
New Haven, CT 06520 — Richard Warren, Jr., Cur.
Founded: 1954. **Subjects:** Musical shows produced on Broadway for profit. **Special Collections:** Manuscripts of Cole Porter and E.Y. Harburg. **Holdings:** Books; theater programs; pamphlets and clippings; phonograph records; sheet music; 349 scores. **Services:** Collection open to the public for reference use only by appointment. **Networks/Consortia:** Member of RLG, Center for Research Libraries (CRL) Consortia, Hartford Consortium for Higher Education.

★18125★
YALE UNIVERSITY - COWLES FOUNDATION FOR RESEARCH IN ECONOMICS - LIBRARY (Bus-Fin)
30 Hillhouse Ave. — Phone: (203)432-3697
New Haven, CT 06520 — Karlee Gifford, Libn.
Founded: 1932. **Staff:** Prof 1. **Subjects:** Economic theory; mathematical econometrics; macroeconomic, microeconomic, monetary, and game theory. **Holdings:** 11,956 volumes; 3000 reprints and unpublished articles; 600 Cowles Foundation papers. **Subscriptions:** 170 journals and other serials. **Services:** Interlibrary loan; copying; permission to use library may

be requested from director. **Networks/Consortia:** Member of RLG, Center for Research Libraries (CRL) Consortia, Hartford Consortium for Higher Education.

★18126★
YALE UNIVERSITY - DIVINITY SCHOOL LIBRARY (Rel-Phil)
409 Prospect St. Phone: (203)432-5290
New Haven, CT 06510 Stephen L. Peterson, Divinity Libn.
Founded: 1932. **Staff:** Prof 6; Other 13. **Subjects:** History of doctrine, biblical studies, missions, theology. **Special Collections:** Historical Library of Missions (90,000 items); archives of the Student Volunteer Movement (285 linear feet); archives of the World Student Christian Federation (110 linear feet); papers of American missionaries in China (400 linear feet); papers of John R. Mott (100 linear feet); missions pamphlet collection (250 linear feet); Historical Sermons Collection (75 linear feet); United Board for Christian Higher Education in Asia (475 linear feet); Council for World Mission (23,000 microfiche); Methodist Missionary Society (8700 microfiche); American Home Missionary Society (385 reels of microfilm); International Missionary Council/Conference of British Missionary Societies (2500 microfiche); American Board of Commissioners for Foreign Missions (858 reels of microfilm). **Holdings:** 351,000 volumes; 300 linear feet of other personal papers and archival collections. **Subscriptions:** 1700 journals and other serials; 8 newspapers. **Services:** Interlibrary loan; copying; library open to the public. **Automated Operations:** Computerized cataloging and acquisitions. **Networks/Consortia:** Member of RLG, Center for Research Libraries (CRL) Consortia. **Staff:** John Bollier, Asst.Libn.; Paul Stuehrenberg, Monographs Libn.; Rolfe Gjellstad, Ser.Libn.; Martha Smalley, Archv.; Suzanne Estelle-Holmer, Circ.Supv./ILL; Duane Harbin, Sys. & Plan.Mgr..

★18127★
YALE UNIVERSITY - EAST ASIAN COLLECTION (Hum, Area-Ethnic)
Sterling Memorial Library Phone: (203)432-1791
New Haven, CT 06520 Hideo Kaneko, Cur.
Staff: Prof 7; Other 9. **Subjects:** East Asian languages and literature, history, art, politics, government, economics, law, social conditions, religion, education, humanities, and social sciences. **Holdings:** 281,699 volumes in Chinese; 157,149 volumes in Japanese; 5377 volumes in Korean; 5124 reels of microfilm. **Services:** Interlibrary loan; copying; collection open to qualified outside users. **Networks/Consortia:** Member of RLG, Center for Research Libraries (CRL) Consortia, Hartford Consortium for Higher Education. **Remarks:** Includes holdings of the Sinological Seminar Library. **Staff:** Antony Marr, Assoc.Cur.; Boksoon Hahn, Hd.Cat.Libn.; Mitsuko Ichinose, Prin.Cat./Ref.Libn..

★18128★
YALE UNIVERSITY - ECONOMIC GROWTH CENTER COLLECTION (Soc Sci)
140 Prospect St. Phone: (203)432-3304
New Haven, CT 06520 Billie I. Salter, Libn. for Soc.Sci.
Founded: 1961. **Staff:** Prof 3; Other 5. **Subjects:** Economic data sources and surveys focusing primarily on the developing countries. **Holdings:** 48,994 volumes. **Subscriptions:** 4087 journals and other serials. **Services:** Interlibrary loan; copying; collection open to the public for reference use only, circulation limited to card holders. **Computerized Information Services:** RLIN. **Networks/Consortia:** Member of RLG, Center for Research Libraries (CRL) Consortia, Hartford Consortium for Higher Education. **Special Catalogs:** Shelf list arranged by country and subdivided by subject; subject classified catalog. **Remarks:** Library is a special collection within the Social Science Library. **Staff:** Edita R. Baradi, Acq.Libn.; Nenita A. Fernandez, Cat.Libn..

★18129★
YALE UNIVERSITY - ELIZABETHAN CLUB COLLECTION (Hum)
459 College St. Phone: (203)436-8535
New Haven, CT 06511 Stephen R. Parks, Libn.
Founded: 1911. **Subjects:** Elizabethan drama, 16th and 17th century. **Holdings:** 300 volumes, before 1700. **Services:** Copying; collection open to the public by arrangement. **Networks/Consortia:** Member of RLG, Center for Research Libraries (CRL) Consortia, Hartford Consortium for Higher Education. **Publications:** Newsletter, annual - to members; The Elizabethan Club of Yale University and its Library, 1986. **Remarks:** Readers may consult Elizabethan Club volumes, by arrangement, in the Beinecke Library.

★18130★
YALE UNIVERSITY - ENGINEERING AND APPLIED SCIENCE LIBRARY (Sci-Engr, Comp Sci)
Becton Center
15 Prospect St. Phone: (203)432-2928
New Haven, CT 06520 Elizabeth Hayes, Lib.Serv.Asst.
Founded: 1969. **Staff:** 2. **Subjects:** Applied sciences, engineering, computer sciences. **Holdings:** 35,247 volumes. **Subscriptions:** 494 journals and other serials. **Services:** Interlibrary loan; copying; library open to qualified users. **Networks/Consortia:** Member of RLG, Center for Research Libraries (CRL) Consortia.

★18131★
YALE UNIVERSITY - FORTUNOFF VIDEO ARCHIVE FOR HOLOCAUST TESTIMONIES (Hist)
Sterling Memorial Library, Rm. 331C Phone: (203)432-1879
New Haven, CT 06520 Joanne Rudof, Mgr.
Staff: Prof 2. **Subjects:** Holocaust. **Holdings:** 916 videotaped oral histories. **Services:** Archive open to the public. **Automated Operations:** Computerized cataloging. **Computerized Information Services:** RLIN. Performs searches free of charge. Contact Person: Sandra Rosen, Archv., 432-1881. **Networks/Consortia:** Member of RLG, Center for Research Libraries (CRL) Consortia, Hartford Consortium for Higher Education. **Publications:** Newsletter, irregular - available on request. **Special Catalogs:** Testimony inventories (typed).

★18132★
YALE UNIVERSITY - GEOLOGY LIBRARY (Sci-Engr)
Box 6666 Phone: (203)432-3157
New Haven, CT 06511 Hanford A. LeMay, Act.Hd.
Staff: Prof 1; Other 2. **Subjects:** Geology, paleontology, oceanography, meteorology. **Holdings:** 101,608 volumes; 182,462 maps, including U.S. Geological Survey geologic and topographic series; 14,000 reprints. **Subscriptions:** 2714 journals and other serials. **Services:** Interlibrary loan; copying; library open to the public with permission. **Networks/Consortia:** Member of RLG, Center for Research Libraries (CRL) Consortia, Hartford Consortium for Higher Education.

★18133★
YALE UNIVERSITY - INDOLOGICAL AND LINGUISTIC SEMINAR - LIBRARY (Hum)
302 Hall of Graduate Studies
320 York St. Phone: (203)432-2450
New Haven, CT 06520 Prof. Stanley Insler, Chm.
Subjects: Indology, descriptive and historical linguistics. **Special Collections:** Bequest of Franklin Edgerton; Edward E. Salisbury, Professor of Sanskrit. **Holdings:** 5579 volumes; 500 offprints. **Services:** Library open to the public by appointment. **Networks/Consortia:** Member of RLG, Center for Research Libraries (CRL) Consortia, Hartford Consortium for Higher Education.

★18134★
YALE UNIVERSITY - IRA V. HISCOCK EPIDEMIOLOGY AND PUBLIC HEALTH LIBRARY (Med)
60 College St. Phone: (203)785-2835
New Haven, CT 06520 Dena B. Vosper, Libn.
Founded: 1940. **Subjects:** Biostatistics, environmental health, epidemiology, health services administration. **Holdings:** 16,292 books. **Subscriptions:** 475 journals and other serials.

★18135★
YALE UNIVERSITY - JOHN HERRICK JACKSON MUSIC LIBRARY (Mus)
98 Wall St. Phone: (203)432-0495
New Haven, CT 06520 Harold E. Samuel, Libn.
Founded: 1917. **Staff:** Prof 4; Other 10. **Subjects:** Music. **Special Collections:** Complete manuscripts and papers of Richard Donovan, Lehman Engel, Henry Gilbert, Benny Goodman, Thomas de Hartmann, Charles E. Ives, J. Rosamond Johnson, Armin Loos, Leo Ornstein, Horatio Parker, Quincy Porter, Carl Ruggles, David Stanley Smith; Alec Templeton; Virgil Thomson; Kurt Weill; Lowell Mason Collection of Church Music (10,000 pieces); Marc Pincherle Collection (musical iconography; 1200 items). **Holdings:** 124,076 volumes; 80,570 pieces of sheet music; 16,791 phonograph records; microfilm. **Subscriptions:** 444 journals and other serials. **Services:** Interlibrary loan; copying; library open to the public for reference use only. **Networks/Consortia:** Member of RLG, Center for Research Libraries (CRL) Consortia, Hartford Consortium for Higher Education. **Staff:** Helen Bartlett, Hd.Cat.; Monica Slomski, Cat..

★18136★
YALE UNIVERSITY - KLINE SCIENCE LIBRARY (Biol Sci, Sci-Engr)
Kline Biology Tower, Rm. C-8 Phone: (203)432-3439
New Haven, CT 06520 Howard D. Keith, Act.Libn. for the Sci.
Staff: Prof 4; Other 10. **Subjects:** Biological sciences, physics, chemistry, conservation, oceanography. **Special Collections:** Evans Collection (bryology and lichenology). **Holdings:** 323,597 volumes; Atomic Energy Commission (AEC) documents on microfiche and microcard. **Subscriptions:** 2066 journals and other serials. **Services:** Interlibrary loan; copying; SDI; library open to qualified users with permission of librarian. **Computerized Information Services:** Online systems. **Networks/Consortia:** Member of RLG, Center for Research Libraries (CRL) Consortia, Hartford Consortium for Higher Education. **Staff:** Elizabeth E. Ferguson, Ref.Libn..

★18137★
YALE UNIVERSITY - LATIN AMERICAN COLLECTION (Area-Ethnic)
Sterling Memorial Library, Rm. 316 Phone: (203)432-1835
New Haven, CT 06520 Cesar Rodriguez, Cur.
Founded: 1907. **Staff:** Prof 1; Other 5. **Subjects:** Latin America - languages, literature, history, politics, government, economics, social conditions, religions, education, civilizations, art, law. **Special Collections:** Latin American Pamphlet Collection, 1600-1900 (social, political, and economic conditions in Latin America; 10,000 pamphlets). **Holdings:** 350,000 books. **Subscriptions:** 1289 journals and other serials; 22 newspapers. **Networks/Consortia:** Member of RLG, Center for Research Libraries (CRL) Consortia, Hartford Consortium for Higher Education. **Special Indexes:** Guide to Latin American Pamphlet Collection (book).

★18138★
YALE UNIVERSITY - LAW LIBRARY (Law)
127 Wall St. Phone: (203)432-1600
New Haven, CT 06520 Morris L. Cohen, Libn.
Staff: Prof 14; Other 28. **Subjects:** Law - Anglo-American, foreign, comparative, international. **Special Collections:** Blackstone Collection. **Holdings:** 755,766 volumes. **Subscriptions:** 7227 journals and other serials. **Services:** Interlibrary loan; copying; library open to qualified users. **Automated Operations:** Computerized cataloging, acquisitions, and serials. **Computerized Information Services:** LEXIS, WESTLAW. **Networks/Consortia:** Member of RLG, New England Law Library Consortium (NELLCO), Hartford Consortium for Higher Education. **Staff:** Gene P. Coakley, Fac.Serv.Libn.; Daniel L. Wade, Foreign Law Libn.; Robert E. Brooks, Hd.Ref.Libn.; Jo-Anne Giammattei, Acq.Libn.; Frances B. Woods, Hd., Cat.Dept.; J. Michael Hughes, Ref.Libn.; Mary Jane Kelsey, Asst.Libn., Tech.Serv.; Margaret Chisholm, Pub.Serv.Libn.; Martha Clark, Circ.Libn.; Ann J. Laeuchli, Assoc.Libn.; Fred Shapiro, Asst.Libn., Pub.Serv..

★18139★
YALE UNIVERSITY - LEWIS WALPOLE LIBRARY (Hist)
154 Main St. Phone: (203)677-2140
Farmington, CT 06032 Marle Devine, Libn.
Staff: Prof 4; Other 3. **Subjects:** Horace Walpole, Earl of Orford; 18th century caricatures and cartoons; 18th century English history; Wilmarth Sheldon Lewis; Strawberry Hill and Twickenham; William Mason; Thomas Gray; Thomas Chatterton. **Special Collections:** Horace Walpole's Library, 1717-1797 (1307 volumes; 1500 manuscripts); Strawberry Hill Press (500 volumes); 18th century satiric prints (8355); Sir Charles Hanbury Williams papers, 1708-1759 (93 volumes); Edward Weston papers, 1703-1770 (25 volumes); Keppel Family papers (9 volumes); Henry Seymour Conway papers, 1721-1795 (14 volumes). **Holdings:** 28,591 volumes; 330 bound manuscripts; 35 linear feet of manuscripts; 37,000 prints, drawings, paintings. **Subscriptions:** 26 journals and other serials. **Services:** Copying; library open to scholars by appointment. **Automated Operations:** Computerized cataloging. **Networks/Consortia:** Member of RLG.

★18140★
YALE UNIVERSITY - MANUSCRIPTS AND ARCHIVES (Hist)
Sterling Memorial Library Phone: (203)432-1740
New Haven, CT 06520 Katharine D. Morton, Hd., Mss. & Archv.
Founded: 1701. **Staff:** Prof 12; Other 6. **Subjects:** Yale history; Connecticut history; religion; World War I and II diplomacy; 19th century science and technology; Progressive Period; 20th century journalism, law, and political writing. **Special Collections:** Papers of Chester Bowles, Henry L. Stimson, Edward M. House, Jerome Frank, Walter Lippmann, Benjamin Silliman, John Lindsay, Dwight MacDonald; Crawford Theater Collection; Contemporary Medical Care and Health Policy Collection; University Archives. **Holdings:** 31,600 books; 51,500 bound periodical volumes; 300,000 photographs; 35,000 reels of microfilm; 28,219 linear feet of manuscripts. **Services:** Copying; archives open to the public. **Computerized Information Services:** RLIN. **Special Catalogs:** Card catalog for manuscripts. **Special Indexes:** Registers or indexes to manuscript collections. **Staff:** Judith A. Schiff, Chf.Res.Archv..

★18141★
YALE UNIVERSITY - MAP COLLECTION (Geog-Map)
Sterling Memorial Library, Map Rm. Phone: (203)432-1867
New Haven, CT 06520 Barbara B. McCorkle, Map Cur.
Founded: 1932. **Staff:** Prof 1; Other 1. **Subjects:** Historical map collection covering the entire world. **Special Collections:** E.L. Stevenson Collection (glass plates of early maps); Horace Brown Collection of early New England maps; Karpinski-Thorne Collection of rare and early atlases. **Holdings:** 2500 atlases; 208,261 maps. **Services:** Copying; collection open to the public for reference use only. **Networks/Consortia:** Member of RLG, Center for Research Libraries (CRL) Consortia, Hartford Consortium for Higher Education.

★18142★
YALE UNIVERSITY - MATHEMATICS LIBRARY (Sci-Engr)
12 Hillhouse Ave.
Yale Sta., Box 2155 Phone: (203)432-4179
New Haven, CT 06520 Paul J. Lukasiewicz, Lib.Serv.Asst.
Staff: 1. **Subjects:** Pure mathematics. **Holdings:** 21,028 volumes. **Subscriptions:** 330 journals and other serials. **Services:** Interlibrary loan; library open to the public for reference use only. **Networks/Consortia:** Member of RLG, Center for Research Libraries (CRL) Consortia, Hartford Consortium for Higher Education.

★18143★
YALE UNIVERSITY - MEDICAL LIBRARY (Med)
333 Cedar St.
Box 3333 Phone: (203)785-5354
New Haven, CT 06510 Bella Z. Berson, Assoc.Univ.Libn./Dir., Med.Lib
Founded: 1814. **Staff:** Prof 11; Other 27. **Subjects:** Medicine, nursing, public health, allied health sciences. **Special Collections:** History of medicine (90,000 volumes); George Milton Smith Collection (early ichthyology; 700 volumes); Edward Clark Streeter Collection (early weights and measures; 350 volumes; 3000 artifacts); Clement C. Fry Collection (2000 medical prints and drawings); medical and scientific incunabula. **Holdings:** 353,472 volumes; 50 manuscript codices before 1600. **Subscriptions:** 2507 journals and other serials. **Services:** Interlibrary loan; copying; SDI; library open to the public with restrictions. **Computerized Information Services:** NLM, DIALOG Information Services, RLIN, BRS Information Technologies. **Networks/Consortia:** Member of RLG, Center for Research Libraries (CRL) Consortia, Greater Northeastern Regional Medical Library Program. **Publications:** Users' Guide; Subject Bibliography; Medical Library Bulletin, all irregular. **Staff:** Ferenc A. Gyorgyey, Hist.Libn.; R. Kenny Fryer, Hd.Ref.Libn.; Carol Lawrence, Hd., Tech.Serv. & Coll.Dev.; Paula Ball, Asst.Hd., Tech.Serv.; Ann Paietta, Hd., Access Serv..

★18144★
YALE UNIVERSITY - ORNITHOLOGY LIBRARY (Biol Sci)
310 Bingham Lab., Peabody Museum
170 Whitney Ave.
Box 6666 Phone: (203)432-3793
New Haven, CT 06511 Eleanor H. Stickney, Sr.Musm.Asst.
Founded: 1959. **Staff:** Prof 1. **Subjects:** Ornithology. **Special Collections:** William R. Coe Collection. **Holdings:** 7776 volumes; 15,000 reprints. **Subscriptions:** 150 journals and other serials. **Services:** Interlibrary loan; copying; library open to the public by permission. **Networks/Consortia:** Member of RLG, Center for Research Libraries (CRL) Consortia, Hartford Consortium for Higher Education.

★18145★
YALE UNIVERSITY - SCHOOL OF DRAMA LIBRARY (Theater)
222 York St.
Yale Sta., Box 1903A Phone: (203)432-1554
New Haven, CT 06520 Pamela C. Jordan, Libn.
Staff: 1. **Subjects:** Plays by American, British, and foreign playwrights; history of the theater; theater architecture; drama criticism; costume and set design; stage lighting; acting; direction; production; theater administration. **Special Collections:** Abel Thomas (1200 books); Rockefeller Prints Collection (80,000 photographs); George Pierce Baker Collection; slide collections; History of Costume (1188 slides); Architecture, Interiors and Furnishings (1893 slides). **Holdings:** 24,952 volumes; 550 production books; 450 masters' theses; 132 dissertations; 80

scrapbooks of clippings. **Subscriptions:** 88 journals and other serials; 12 newspapers. **Services:** Interlibrary loan; copying; listening station; library open to the public for reference use only, circulation limited to Yale University card holders. **Networks/Consortia:** Member of RLG, Center for Research Libraries (CRL) Consortia, Hartford Consortium for Higher Education.

★18146★
YALE UNIVERSITY - SEELEY G. MUDD LIBRARY - GOVERNMENT DOCUMENTS CENTER (Info Sci)
38 Mansfield St.
Yale Sta., Box 2491 Phone: (203)432-3209
New Haven, CT 06520 Sandra K. Peterson, Docs.Libn.
Staff: Prof 2; Other 5. **Subjects:** American history, U.S. foreign relations, economics, U.S. Congress. **Special Collections:** U.S. federal document depository, 1859 to present; document depository for Canadian federal government, United Nations, European Communities, and Food Agriculture Organization; CIS U.S. Congressional Committee Prints, through 1969; CIS U.S. Congressional Committee Prints Microfiche Collection; CIS U.S. Senate Unpublished Hearings, 1824-1964 (on microfiche); nondepository document collection from the American Statistics Index and CIS Index to Publications of the U.S. Congress; Foreign Broadcast Information Service Daily Reports, 1946 to present (all areas); Declassified Documents Reference System (on microfiche); FAO Comprehensive Collection, 1978 to present (on microfiche). **Holdings:** 595,466 items; 78 drawers of microfiche. **Services:** Copying; center open to the public. **Computerized Information Services:** DIALOG Information Services, BRS Information Technologies. Performs searches on fee basis. **Networks/Consortia:** Member of RLG, Center for Research Libraries (CRL) Consortia, Hartford Consortium for Higher Education. **Publications:** Selected New Acquisitions: Government Documents Center, 8/year - for internal distribution only. **Special Indexes:** Index to Declassified Documents Reference System. **Remarks:** An alternate telephone number is 432-3212. **Staff:** Kathy Spurgeon, Asst.Docs.Libn..

★18147★
YALE UNIVERSITY - SEMITIC REFERENCE LIBRARY (Area-Ethnic)
314 Sterling Memorial Library
Yale University Library Phone: (203)432-1707
New Haven, CT 06520
Leonard Mathless, Act.Hd., Near East Cat.Div.
Founded: 1930. **Subjects:** Comparative Semitics; Hebrew, Arabic, and other Semitic languages (except Akkadian). **Holdings:** 1500 volumes. **Networks/Consortia:** Member of RLG, Center for Research Libraries (CRL) Consortia, Hartford Consortium for Higher Education.

YALE UNIVERSITY - SINOLOGICAL SEMINAR LIBRARY
See: Yale University - East Asian Collection (18127)

★18148★
YALE UNIVERSITY - SLAVIC & EAST EUROPEAN COLLECTIONS (Hum, Area-Ethnic)
Sterling Memorial Library Phone: (203)432-1861
New Haven, CT 06520 Tatiana Rannit, Cur.
Founded: 1961. **Staff:** Prof 1; Other 4. **Subjects:** East Europe - social sciences, humanities, linguistics, history. **Special Collections:** Joel Sumner Smith; Harrison Thomson; Mikhail Rostovtseff; George Vernadsky; Vasilii Tutcheff; Pilsudski archives (microfilm). **Holdings:** 245,000 books in Slavic and East European languages; 70,000 bound periodical volumes; 2 VF drawers of clippings; 38 archival collections; 21,000 titles on microfilm and microfiche; 142 shelves of pamphlet volumes; 1.75 aisles of Free Europe material. **Subscriptions:** 331 journals and other serials; 66 newspapers. **Networks/Consortia:** Member of RLG, Center for Research Libraries (CRL) Consortia, Hartford Consortium for Higher Education.

★18149★
YALE UNIVERSITY - SOCIAL SCIENCE LIBRARY (Soc Sci, Bus-Fin)
140 Prospect St.
Yale Sta., Box 1958 Phone: (203)432-3304
New Haven, CT 06520 Billie I. Salter, Libn.
Founded: 1972. **Staff:** Prof 8; Other 13. **Subjects:** Administrative sciences, business, economics and economic development, finance, health services administration, management, political science, sociology. **Special Collections:** Economic Growth Center Collection (government reports, surveys, statistical yearbooks, bulletins focusing on developing countries and their economies; 48,994 volumes); Social Science Data Archive (687 machine-readable data files of political and social surveys, voting records, and economic data sources); Roper Center Archives (public opinion polls; 64 drawers). **Holdings:** 69,248 volumes; corporate reports of New York Stock Exchange, selected other domestic companies, and foreign firms; 5 drawers of subject files; 14 drawers of political polls. **Subscriptions:** 2572 journals and other serials. **Services:** Interlibrary loan; copying; library open to the public for reference use only, circulation limited to card holders only. **Automated Operations:** Computerized cataloging. **Computerized Information Services:** DIALOG Information Services, RLIN, BRS Information Technologies. **Networks/Consortia:** Member of RLG, Center for Research Libraries (CRL) Consortia, Hartford Consortium for Higher Education. **Publications:** Social Science Data Archive's Directory of Data Holdings and Services. **Staff:** JoAnn L. Dionne, Ref.Libn. & Data Archv.; Judith O. Carnes, Ref.Libn. & Coll.Dev.; Edita R. Baradi, Acq.Libn.; Nenita A. Fernandez, Cat.Libn..

★18150★
YALE UNIVERSITY - SOUTHEAST ASIA COLLECTION (Area-Ethnic)
Sterling Memorial Library Phone: (203)432-1859
New Haven, CT 06520 Charles R. Bryant, Cur.
Staff: Prof 2; Other 2. **Subjects:** Social sciences and humanities of Southeast Asia: Burma, Thailand, Laos, Vietnam, Cambodia, Philippines, Malaysia, Brunei, Singapore, Indonesia. **Holdings:** 200,000 volumes. **Subscriptions:** 750 journals and other serials. **Services:** Interlibrary loan; copying. **Automated Operations:** Computerized cataloging, acquisitions, and serials. **Networks/Consortia:** Member of RLG, Center for Research Libraries (CRL) Consortia, Hartford Consortium for Higher Education. **Publications:** Checklist of Southeast Asian Serials, 1968. **Staff:** Ms. Lian Tie Kho, Libn..

★18151★
YALE UNIVERSITY - STERLING CHEMISTRY LIBRARY (Sci-Engr)
225 Prospect St. Phone: (203)432-3960
New Haven, CT 06520 Deborah A. Paolillo, Lib.Serv.Asst.
Founded: 1923. **Subjects:** Chemistry, biochemistry. **Holdings:** 14,961 volumes. **Subscriptions:** 163 journals and other serials. **Services:** Interlibrary loan; copying; library open to the public with restrictions. **Networks/Consortia:** Member of RLG, Center for Research Libraries (CRL) Consortia, Hartford Consortium for Higher Education.

★18152★
YALE UNIVERSITY - YALE CENTER FOR BRITISH ART - PHOTO ARCHIVE (Art)
2120 Yale Sta. Phone: (203)432-2846
New Haven, CT 06520 Dr. Anne-Marie Logan, Libn./Photo Archv.
Staff: 3. **Subjects:** British art - paintings, drawings, prints, and sculpture, 1500-1945 (emphasizing works dating before 1900). **Special Collections:** Photographs after works by British artists and foreigners working in Great Britain (100,000 black/white photographs); British School photographs in the Witt Collection, Courtauld Institute, London (4000 microfiche); Harold Jennings Collection (60 volumes containing 150,000 prints, photographs, and reproductions after paintings, drawings, and prints of British sitters). **Services:** Copying; archive open to the public. **Computerized Information Services:** Internal database. **Special Indexes:** Subject thesaurus of British Art (20,000 terms); Artist authority list for British Artists (4500 names); Computerized Census of British Art in North American Collections (12,000 records).

★18153★
YALE UNIVERSITY - YALE CENTER FOR BRITISH ART - RARE BOOK COLLECTION (Art, Rare Book)
2120 Yale Sta. Phone: (203)432-2814
New Haven, CT 06520 Joan M. Friedman, Cur. of Rare Bks.
Staff: Prof 2; Other 3. **Subjects:** British illustrated books, 15th-19th centuries; visual arts in Great Britain, 17th-19th centuries. **Special Collections:** Major J.R. Abbey Collection of Color-Plate Books. **Holdings:** 21,205 rare books and serials. **Services:** Copying; collection open to the public. **Automated Operations:** Computerized cataloging. **Computerized Information Services:** RLIN. **Special Catalogs:** Computerized catalog of illustrators, graphic techniques, provenance, imprints, bookbinding, and chronology. **Staff:** Elisabeth R. Fairman, Cat.Libn..

★18154★
YALE UNIVERSITY - YALE CENTER FOR BRITISH ART - REFERENCE LIBRARY (Art)
1080 Chapel St.
Yale Sta., Box 2120 Phone: (203)432-2846
New Haven, CT 06520 Dr. Anne-Marie Logan, Libn./Photo Archv.
Staff: Prof 1; Other 1. **Subjects:** British art - paintings, drawings, prints, sculpture, and architecture, 1500-1945. **Special Collections:** Sotheby and

Christies sales catalogues, 1734-1980; Victoria and Albert Museum oils, watercolors, miniatures, and RIBA architectural drawings; British Museum Satirical Prints; British Museum's Turner Bequest; Huntington Library drawings (all microfilm and photographs). **Holdings:** 9000 books; 1000 bound periodical volumes; 870 reels of microfilm; 7300 microfiche. **Subscriptions:** 60 journals and other serials. **Services:** Copying; library open to the public. **Automated Operations:** Computerized cataloging. **Computerized Information Services:** DIALOG Information Services; internal database. **Networks/Consortia:** Member of RLG.

★18155★
YALE UNIVERSITY - YALE COLLECTION OF HISTORICAL SOUND RECORDINGS (Aud-Vis)
Sterling Memorial Library Phone: (203)432-1795
New Haven, CT 06520 Richard Warren, Jr., Cur.
Founded: 1960. **Staff:** Prof 1; Other 2. **Subjects:** Phonograph recordings of historical interest in the fields of concert music, jazz, drama, politics, literature, documentary from the end of the 19th century to the present, with emphasis on history of performance practice in the arts. **Holdings:** 122,500 sound recordings; catalogs; lists; books; photographs; autograph letters, manuscripts, and other documents relating to the history of sound recording. **Subscriptions:** 20 journals and other serials. **Services:** Collection open to the public for reference use only by appointment. **Networks/Consortia:** Member of RLG, Center for Research Libraries (CRL) Consortia, Hartford Consortium for Higher Education. **Special Indexes:** The Rigler & Deutsch Record Index - a National Union Catalog of Sound Recordings - Part I; An Index to 78 rpm Sound Recordings in ARSC/AAA member libraries.

★18156★
YALE UNIVERSITY - YALE EDITIONS OF THE PRIVATE PAPERS OF JAMES BOSWELL (Hum)
Sterling Memorial Library, Rms. 330 and 331A Phone: (203)432-1864
New Haven, CT 06520 Rachel McClellan, Mgr.
Founded: 1949. **Staff:** Prof 3. **Subjects:** James Boswell. **Special Collections:** The Yale Boswell Collection, 1760-1795 (manuscript text and proofsheets of Tour to the Hebrides and Life of Johnson; 6000 letters to and from Mr. Boswell). **Networks/Consortia:** Member of RLG, Hartford Consortium for Higher Education.

★18157★
YALE UNIVERSITY - YALE FORESTRY LIBRARY (Biol Sci)
205 Prospect St. Phone: (203)432-5130
New Haven, CT 06511 Joseph A. Miller, Libn.
Founded: 1900. **Staff:** Prof 1; Other 3. **Subjects:** Forestry, environmental studies, ecology, biology, natural resources management, conservation, wildlife, land use, planning. **Holdings:** 130,000 books, bound periodical volumes, government documents, and reports; 175 newsletter titles; 900 dissertations; 500 maps; 2500 microforms. **Subscriptions:** 1150 journals and other serials. **Services:** Interlibrary loan; copying; library open to the public for reference use only. **Computerized Information Services:** FESR (Forestry and Environmental Studies Record; internal database). Performs searches on fee basis. **Networks/Consortia:** Member of RLG, Center for Research Libraries (CRL) Consortia. **Special Catalogs:** Dictionary Catalog, 12 volumes, published in 1962. **Also Known As:** Henry S. Graves Memorial Library.

★18158★
YAMAHA MOTOR CORPORATION USA - YAMAHA R&D MINNESOTA - RESEARCH LIBRARY (Sci-Engr)
1255 Main St. Phone: (612)755-2743
Coon Rapids, MN 55433 William B. Seath, Info.Mgr.
Founded: 1979. **Staff:** Prof 1; Other 2. **Subjects:** Engineering, business, management. **Special Collections:** Patent records; Society of Automotive Engineers papers; snowmobile laws; snowmobile accident records. **Holdings:** 500 books; 40 bound periodical volumes; 9 VF drawers. **Subscriptions:** 110 journals and other serials; 5 newspapers. **Services:** Interlibrary loan; library not open to the public. **Computerized Information Services:** Access to online systems.

★18159★
YANKEE ATOMIC ELECTRIC COMPANY - LIBRARY (Energy)
1671 Worcester Rd. Phone: (617)872-8100
Framingham, MA 01701-1101 Delores Markt, Lib.Techn.
Founded: 1980. **Staff:** 1. **Subjects:** Nuclear power. **Special Collections:** Nuclear Regulatory Commission reports; Electric Power Research Institute (EPRI) reports (microform); Federal Regulations, 1979 to present (microform); standards from American National Standards Institute (ANSI), American Nuclear Society (ANS), Institute of Electrical and Electronics Engineers (IEEE), American Society for Testing and Materials (ASTM). **Holdings:** 1106 books. **Subscriptions:** 327 journals and other serials. **Services:** Interlibrary loan; copying; SDI; library open to the public with restrictions. **Computerized Information Services:** DIALOG Information Services.

YARDNEY ELECTRIC CORPORATION
See: Whittaker Technical Products, Inc. - Whittaker-Yardney Power Systems (17848)

★18160★
YARMOUTH COUNTY HISTORICAL SOCIETY - RESEARCH LIBRARY AND ARCHIVES (Hist)
P.O. Box 39 Phone: (902)742-5539
Yarmouth, NS, Canada B5A 4B1 Helen J. Hall, Libn./Archv.
Staff: 1. **Subjects:** Local history and genealogy, shipping. **Holdings:** 1300 books; local newspapers, 1833-1960s; 16 VF drawers and 10 shelves of archival materials; manuscripts; maps; charts; clippings; pictures. **Subscriptions:** 20 journals and other serials. **Services:** Copying; library open to the public when staff is available. **Publications:** Newsletter, monthly; Early Vital Records of the Township of Yarmouth, N.S. **Special Indexes:** Index to Shipping of Yarmouth, N.S.

★18161★
YASODHARA ASHRAM SOCIETY - LIBRARY
Box 9
Kootenay Bay, BC, Canada V0B 1X0
Subjects: Yoga, religious and spiritual philosophy, Eastern religions. **Special Collections:** Extensive collection of works of Swami Sivananda Saraswati, many not available elsewhere in North America. **Holdings:** 3500 books; 400 Eastern magazines. **Remarks:** Presently inactive.

★18162★
YAVAPAI COUNTY LAW LIBRARY (Law)
County Courthouse, Fl. 4 Phone: (602)445-7450
Prescott, AZ 86301 Pam Mathwig, Law Libn.
Staff: 2. **Subjects:** Law. **Holdings:** 11,986 volumes. **Services:** Library not open to the public.

ALFRED A. YEE DIVISION
See: Leo A. Daly Company (4014)

YELLOWSTONE ASSOCIATION
See: U.S. Natl. Park Service (15364)

★18163★
YELLOWSTONE-BIGHORN RESEARCH ASSOCIATION - LIBRARY (Sci-Engr)
Box 2297
Billings, MT 59103 Vincent T. Larsen, Treas.
Founded: 1936. **Subjects:** Geology. **Special Collections:** N.H. Darton's personal collection. **Holdings:** 2300 volumes; geological manuscripts, reprints, and maps; herbarium contains plants from Montana and Wyoming: 81 families, 381 genera, 1028 species.

JEAN D. YEOMANS MEMORIAL LIBRARY
See: C.G. Jung Institute of Boston (7300)

YERKES OBSERVATORY LIBRARY
See: University of Chicago (16040)

YERKES REGIONAL PRIMATE CENTER
See: Emory University (4690)

★18164★
YESHIVA TORAH VODAATH AND MESIFTA - TORAH VODAATH LIBRARY (Rel-Phil)
425 E. Ninth St.
Brooklyn, NY 11218 Phone: (718)941-8000
Founded: 1918. **Staff:** Prof 1; Other 2. **Subjects:** Biblical exegesis, Talmud (and novellae on), Rabbinical responsa, Halachic literature, liturgy and homiletic literature, Jewish history, Hebrew and Yiddish literature, Hasidic literature. **Holdings:** 23,500 books; 575 bound periodical volumes; 600 unbound periodicals; 280 unbound pamphlets. **Subscriptions:** 65 journals and other serials. **Services:** Copying; library open to the public.

★18165★
YESHIVA UNIVERSITY - ALBERT EINSTEIN COLLEGE OF MEDICINE - D. SAMUEL GOTTESMAN LIBRARY (Med)
1300 Morris Park Ave. Phone: (212)430-3108
Bronx, NY 10461 Charlotte K. Lindner, Dir. of Lib.
Founded: 1955. **Staff:** Prof 6; Other 16. **Subjects:** Biochemistry, cell biology, medicine, molecular biology, pharmacology, physiology, genetics, anatomy, oncology, pathology, psychiatry, immunology. **Special Collections:** Gresser Collection (ophthalmology). **Holdings:** 68,946 books; 94,052 bound periodical volumes; 40 VF drawers of archival materials; 17,493 other cataloged items; 541 dissertations; 10,433 microforms. **Subscriptions:** 2472 journals and other serials. **Services:** Interlibrary loan; copying; SDI; library open to the public with restrictions. **Automated Operations:** Computerized cataloging. **Computerized Information Services:** MEDLARS, BRS Information Technologies. **Networks/Consortia:** Member of SUNY/OCLC Library Network, New York Metropolitan Reference and Research Library Agency (METRO), Medical Library Center of New York (MLCNY). **Publications:** Acquisitions List, bimonthly. **Staff:** Florence Schreibstein, Asst.Dir.; Clara Dunleavy, Chf.Ref.Libn.; Elsie Herzberg, Chf. of Circ.Dept.; Rachline Habousha, Asst.Ref.Libn.; James Swanton, Chf.Cat.; Norma Nelson, Asst.Ref.Libn.; Norman Flores, Circ.Lib..

★18166★
YESHIVA UNIVERSITY - ALBERT EINSTEIN COLLEGE OF MEDICINE - DEPARTMENT OF ANESTHESIOLOGY - LIBRARY (Med)
1300 Morris Park Ave.
Bldg. J, Rm. 1226 Phone: (212)430-5889
Bronx, NY 10461 Jill Foscaldi, Adm.
Subjects: Anesthesiology. **Holdings:** 200 books; 500 bound periodical volumes; 110 slide/tape sets. **Subscriptions:** 30 journals and other serials. **Services:** Library not open to the public.

★18167★
YESHIVA UNIVERSITY - ALBERT EINSTEIN COLLEGE OF MEDICINE - DEPARTMENT OF PSYCHIATRY - J. THOMPSON PSYCHIATRY LIBRARY (Med)
Bronx Municipal Hospital Center
NR 2E7A Phone: (212)430-5571
Bronx, NY 10461 Mary Nahon Galgan, Libn.
Staff: Prof 1; Other 1. **Subjects:** Psychiatry, psychoanalysis, social work, philosophy, history, literature, theology, arts. **Holdings:** 8000 books; 3300 bound periodical volumes; 6 VF drawers of reprints; 98 masters' dissertations. **Subscriptions:** 110 journals and other serials. **Services:** Library not open to the public.

★18168★
YESHIVA UNIVERSITY - ALBERT EINSTEIN COLLEGE OF MEDICINE - SURGERY LIBRARY (Med)
Jacobi Hospital, Rm. 613
Pelham Pkwy. & Eastchester Rd.
Bronx, NY 10461 Phone: (212)430-5800
Founded: 1965. **Subjects:** Surgery, medicine. **Holdings:** 571 books; 1448 bound periodical volumes; 2 drawers of reprints. **Subscriptions:** 21 journals and other serials. **Services:** Interlibrary loan; library not open to the public. **Publications:** Bibliographies - to department members.

★18169★
YESHIVA UNIVERSITY - HEDI STEINBERG LIBRARY (Rel-Phil)
Stern College for Women
245 Lexington Ave. Phone: (212)340-7720
New York, NY 10016 Prof. Edith Lubetski, Hd.Libn.
Founded: 1954. **Staff:** Prof 3; Other 3. **Special Collections:** Judaica and Hebraica (18,500 volumes). **Holdings:** 96,261 volumes. **Services:** Interlibrary loan; copying; library open to the public for reference use only. **Automated Operations:** Computerized cataloging and acquisitions. **Computerized Information Services:** DIALOG Information Services, BRS Information Technologies. **Networks/Consortia:** Member of New York Metropolitan Reference and Research Library Agency (METRO). **Publications:** Sifriya (newsletter), semiannual - for internal distribution only. **Staff:** Cherie Feiger, Pub.Serv.Libn./ILL; Libby Neiman, Ref.Libn.; Naomi Schwer Bricker, Ref.Libn..

★18170★
YESHIVA UNIVERSITY - MENDEL GOTTESMAN LIBRARY OF HEBRAICA AND JUDAICA (Rel-Phil)
500 W. 185th St. Phone: (212)960-5382
New York, NY 10033 Pearl Berger, Dean of Libs.
Founded: 1920. **Staff:** Prof 4; Other 3. **Subjects:** Rabbinics; Bible and Jewish commentaries; Hebrew and cognate languages; Jewish history, philosophy, literature. **Special Collections:** Vatican Collection; Lehman Collection (both on microfilm); rare books and manuscripts. **Holdings:** 163,000 books; 20,300 bound periodical volumes; 1120 reels of microfilm; 6400 microfiche; 1000 manuscripts. **Subscriptions:** 817 journals and other serials. **Services:** Interlibrary loan; copying; library open to the public for reference use only. **Automated Operations:** Computerized cataloging. **Computerized Information Services:** OCLC. **Networks/Consortia:** Member of New York Metropolitan Reference and Research Library Agency (METRO), Council of Archives and Research Libraries in Jewish Studies (CARLJS). **Publications:** Selected Recent Acquisitions, 3/year. **Special Catalogs:** Hebrew Incunabula - Mendel Gottesman Library of Hebraica and Judaica (1984). **Staff:** Leah Adler, Hd.Libn..

★18171★
YESHIVA UNIVERSITY - MUSEUM (Area-Ethnic, Hist)
2520 Amsterdam Ave. Phone: (212)960-5390
New York, NY 10033 Sylvia A. Herskowitz, Dir.
Staff: Prof 7; Other 3. **Subjects:** Jewish art, Judaica, Jewish history. **Special Collections:** Jewish history and communities around the world (photographs; documents; ceremonial objects; textiles; books). **Services:** Copying; museum open to the public with restrictions. **Special Catalogs:** Exhibition catalogs. **Staff:** Bonni-Dara Michaels, Cur..

★18172★
YESHIVA UNIVERSITY - POLLACK LIBRARY - LANDOWNE-BLOOM COLLECTION (Soc Sci)
500 W. 185th St. Phone: (212)960-5378
New York, NY 10033 John Moryl, Hd.Libn.
Founded: 1975. **Subjects:** Aging, Jewish social welfare. **Holdings:** 13,381 books; 10,000 pamphlets and documents; 2320 dissertations in microform. **Services:** Interlibrary loan; copying; collection open to the public for reference use only. **Automated Operations:** Computerized cataloging. **Computerized Information Services:** BRS Information Technologies, DIALOG Information Services, OCLC. **Networks/Consortia:** Member of New York Metropolitan Reference and Research Library Agency (METRO).

★18173★
YIVO INSTITUTE FOR JEWISH RESEARCH - LIBRARY AND ARCHIVES (Area-Ethnic, Hist)
1048 Fifth Ave. Phone: (212)535-6700
New York, NY 10028 Marek Web, Chf.Archv.
Founded: 1925. **Staff:** Prof 14; Other 15. **Subjects:** Yiddish language, literature, drama, folklore; East European Jewry; European Jewry in the 19th and 20th centuries; Jewish history; Jewish immigration to the U.S.; Jews under Nazi rule. **Special Collections:** Rare books; Rabbinics; Vilna Collection of periodicals; Nazi literature; Jewish music; archives of Jewish organizations; archives of ghettoes and concentration camps; captured Nazi documents; manuscripts of Yiddish writers; Weinreich Library and Archives of Yiddish Linguistics; Landsmanshaft Archive. **Holdings:** 315,000 volumes; 8500 linear feet of manuscript collections, records of institutions, individual collections, general records of the Yivo archives, photograph collections, art collections; 30 linear feet of tapes and recordings; 4800 reels of microfilm. **Subscriptions:** 486 journals and other serials. **Services:** Interlibrary loan; copying; library open to the public on a limited schedule. **Publications:** News of the Yivo, 3/year - to members; bibliographies on certain subjects (mimeographed). **Special Catalogs:** Library catalogs for special collections; guide to major collections in the Yivo Archives; archives' inventories and registers of individual collections. **Staff:** Zachary M. Baker, Hd.Libn.; Dina Abramowicz, Ref.Libn.; Stanley Bergman, Adm.Libn.; Bella Hass Weinberg, Cons.; Daniel Soyer, Archv.; Fruma Mohrer, Archv.; Eleanor Mlotek, Archv.; Rosaline Schwartz, Dir., Pub.Prog.; Samuel Norich, Exec.Dir.; Hannah Fryshdorf, Asst.Dir.; Adrienne Cooper, Asst.Dir..

YMCA
See: Young Men's Christian Associations of the United States of America - YMCA of the USA Archives (18228)

P.K. YONGE LABORATORY SCHOOL
See: University of Florida - P.K. Yonge Laboratory School (16157)

P.K. YONGE LIBRARY OF FLORIDA HISTORY
See: University of Florida (16158)

★18174★
YONKERS GENERAL HOSPITAL - MEDICAL LIBRARY (Med)
2 Park Ave. Phone: (914)964-7300
Yonkers, NY 10701 Phyllis Perez, Med.Libn.
Founded: 1965. **Staff:** Prof 1. **Subjects:** Internal medicine, surgery, gynecology, pathology, pediatrics, psychiatry. **Holdings:** 800 books; 300 bound periodical volumes; 3 VF drawers of pamphlets; cassettes. **Subscriptions:** 45 journals and other serials. **Services:** Interlibrary loan; copying; library open to the public. **Networks/Consortia:** Member of Health Information Libraries of Westchester (HILOW), Greater Northeastern Regional Medical Library Program.

★18175★
YONKERS HISTORICAL SOCIETY - LIBRARY (Hist)
7 Odell Plaza
Greystone P.O. Box 885 Phone: (914)969-5622
Yonkers, NY 10703 Olga C. Kourre, Libn.
Founded: 1952. **Subjects:** History - Yonkers, Westchester County, Hudson River; local authors. **Holdings:** 400 books; manuscripts; documents. **Services:** Library open to the public for reference use only.

★18176★
YONKERS PUBLIC LIBRARY - FINE ARTS DEPARTMENT (Art, Mus)
1500 Central Park Ave. Phone: (914)337-1500
Yonkers, NY 10710 Martha Powell, Hd., Fine Arts Dept.
Founded: 1962. **Staff:** Prof 3. **Subjects:** History of art, painting, sculpture, architecture, graphic arts, crafts, music, performing arts, photography and film arts, antique collecting. **Holdings:** 13,700 books; 27,000 recordings; 4500 cassettes; 625 compact discs; 7550 pieces of sheet music; 2000 slides; 3 file drawers of film catalogs; 17 file drawers of pictures; 5 file drawers of clippings. **Subscriptions:** 55 journals and other serials. **Services:** Interlibrary loan; copying; department open to the public with restrictions on borrowing. **Networks/Consortia:** Member of Westchester Library System. **Staff:** Ethel Petryczka; Martha Darcy; Mahin Hambly.

★18177★
YONKERS PUBLIC LIBRARY - INFORMATION SERVICES - TECHNICAL & BUSINESS DIVISION (Bus-Fin, Sci-Engr)
7 Main St. Phone: (914)337-1500
Yonkers, NY 10701 Frances C. Roberts, Act.Hd., Info.Serv.
Founded: 1938. **Staff:** Prof 6; Other 2. **Subjects:** Business and finance, transportation, engineering, automobiles, building trades, plumbing and heating, mathematics, physics, chemistry. **Special Collections:** Annual reports of most corporations; telephone directories of U.S. cities; state, business, and biographical directories; local history. **Holdings:** 19,500 books; 107 bound periodical volumes; Official Patent Gazette, 1925 to present; 7000 government depository publications; 17,000 pamphlets. **Subscriptions:** 240 journals and other serials. **Services:** Interlibrary loan; copying; division open to the public. **Computerized Information Services:** DIALOG Information Services; WESNEWS (internal database). Performs searches on fee basis.

★18178★
YORK BOROUGH BOARD OF EDUCATION - PROFESSIONAL LIBRARY (Educ)
2 Trethewey Dr.
Toronto, ON, Canada M6M 4A8 Phone: (416)653-2270
Founded: 1971. **Staff:** Prof 1; Other 2. **Subjects:** Education, sociology. **Special Collections:** Computer programs preview collection (200). **Holdings:** 15,000 books; 75 files of unbound reports; 1500 filmstrips and media kits; 50 drawers of pamphlets and clippings; 200 reels of microfilm; 4000 microfiche; ERIC on CD-ROM. **Subscriptions:** 300 journals and other serials; 6 newspapers. **Services:** Interlibrary loan; copying; SDI; library open to the public. **Automated Operations:** Computerized public access catalog, cataloging, acquisitions, serials, and circulation. **Computerized Information Services:** BRS Information Technologies, Info Globe, Pergamon ORBIT InfoLine, Inc., DIALOG Information Services; internal databases. **Publications:** New Books and Articles, 4/year. **Special Indexes:** Subject list of computer programs; subject and title guide to media kits. **Staff:** Pat Steenbergen, Libn.; Sheila Moll, Libn..

★18179★
YORK COLLEGE OF PENNSYLVANIA - SCHMIDT LIBRARY - SPECIAL COLLECTIONS (Hist)
Country Club Rd. Phone: (717)846-7788
York, PA 17405 Susan M. Campbell, Lib.Dir.
Staff: Prof 5; Other 12. **Subjects:** Abraham Lincoln. **Holdings:** Figures not available. **Services:** Interlibrary loan; copying; collections open to the public with restrictions. **Automated Operations:** Computerized cataloging and ILL. **Computerized Information Services:** DIALOG Information Services, RLIN. **Networks/Consortia:** Member of PALINET, Association of College Libraries of Central Pennsylvania (ACLCP).

★18180★
YORK COUNTY LAW LIBRARY (Law)
Court House Phone: (717)854-0754
York, PA 17401 Susan F. Hedge, Libn.
Founded: 1872. **Staff:** Prof 2. **Subjects:** Law. **Holdings:** 30,000 volumes. **Services:** Interlibrary loan; copying; library open to the public for reference use only. **Staff:** Mary Fitzgibbons, Asst.Libn..

★18181★
YORK COUNTY PLANNING COMMISSION - LIBRARY (Plan)
118 Pleasant Acres Rd.
York, PA 17402 Phone: (717)757-2647
Staff: 1. **Subjects:** Planning, land utilization, transportation, recreation, utilities, natural resources, statistics, housing, social and health planning, computerized information systems. **Holdings:** 6000 books and pamphlets; tapes. **Subscriptions:** 60 journals and other serials. **Services:** Interlibrary loan; copying; library open to the public. **Publications:** Planning Commission Newsletter, quarterly - to interested citizens and municipal officials; Housing Newsletter; Transportation Newsletter, both biennial. **Remarks:** Library is an affiliated data center of the Pennsylvania State Data Center.

★18182★
YORK-FINCH GENERAL HOSPITAL - THOMAS J. MALCHO MEMORIAL LIBRARY (Med)
2111 Finch Ave., W. Phone: (416)744-2500
Downsview, ON, Canada M3N 1N1 Mona Kakoschke, Med.Libn.
Staff: Prof 1. **Subjects:** Medicine, nursing, hospital administration. **Holdings:** 2000 books. **Subscriptions:** 210 journals. **Services:** Interlibrary loan; library not open to the public. **Computerized Information Services:** MEDLARS. **Networks/Consortia:** Member of Canadian Health Libraries Association, Ontario Hospital Libraries Association (OHLA).

★18183★
YORK HOSPITAL - HEALTH SCIENCES LIBRARY (Med)
15 Hospital Dr. Phone: (207)363-4321
York, ME 03909 Darryl Hamson, Libn.
Staff: 1. **Subjects:** Medicine, nursing, hospital administration. **Holdings:** 320 books; 480 bound periodical volumes. **Subscriptions:** 90 journals and other serials. **Services:** Interlibrary loan; copying; SDI; library open to the public. **Computerized Information Services:** BRS Information Technologies, WILSONLINE, NLM. Performs searches free of charge for professionals in community. **Networks/Consortia:** Member of Health Science Library and Information Cooperative of Maine (HSLIC). **Publications:** Library News (newsletter), quarterly - for internal distribution only.

★18184★
YORK HOSPITAL - LIBRARY (Med)
1001 S. George St. Phone: (717)771-2495
York, PA 17405 Barbara H. Bevan, Libn.
Founded: 1962. **Staff:** Prof 2; Other 4. **Subjects:** Medicine, nursing, health education. **Special Collections:** Health Education Resource Shelf (100 books; pamphlets; periodicals); Chaplaincy Collection (150 books). **Holdings:** 7753 books; 6285 bound periodical volumes. **Subscriptions:** 632 journals and other serials. **Services:** Interlibrary loan; copying; SDI; library open to the public with restrictions on borrowing. **Automated Operations:** Computerized cataloging. **Computerized Information Services:** BRS Information Technologies, MEDLARS; internal database. Performs searches on fee basis. Contact Person: Beth A. Evitts, Asst.Libn.. **Networks/Consortia:** Member of Central Pennsylvania Health Sciences Library Association (CPHSLA), University of Pennsylvania Affiliated Librarians, BHSL. **Publications:** Library Letter, irregular. **Special Indexes:** Periodical list (book, online); Health Education Books in Hospital & Public Libraries (book, online).

★18185★
YORK INSTITUTE MUSEUM - DYER LIBRARY (Hist)
371 Main St. Phone: (207)283-3861
Saco, ME 04072 Christine L. Bertsch, Act.Lib.Dir.
Subjects: History of York County and Maine, 1681-1900. **Holdings:** 100,000 deeds, indentures, letters, public documents, church records, municipal records, logbooks, business records, maps, plans, architectural drawings, photographs, glass negatives, 18th-19th century newspapers, diaries. **Services:** Interlibrary loan; copying; library open to the public. **Computerized Information Services:** Internal database. **Formerly:** Dyer-York Library and Museum.

★18186★
YORK INTERNATIONAL CORPORATION - ENGINEERING LIBRARY (Sci-Engr)
Box 1592-191A Phone: (717)771-7553
York, PA 17405-1592 Joyce Budesheim, Libn.
Founded: 1942. **Staff:** 1. **Subjects:** Refrigeration, air conditioning, engineering, metallurgy, heating, acoustics. **Holdings:** 2896 books; 1536 bound periodical volumes; 36 VF drawers of pamphlets; 2043 articles on microfilm; 6 VF drawers of standards and codes; 2 VF drawers of translations. **Subscriptions:** 85 journals and other serials. **Services:** Interlibrary loan; copying; library open to the public by special arrangement. **Publications:** Current Awareness Bulletin, quarterly - for internal distribution only.

★18187★
YORK RESEARCH CORPORATION - LIBRARY (Env-Cons)
One Research Dr.
Stamford, CT 06906 Phone: (203)325-1371
Founded: 1969. **Staff:** Prof 1. **Subjects:** Air and water pollution, chemistry, industrial hygiene, solid wastes, engineering. **Holdings:** 1800 books. **Subscriptions:** 90 journals and other serials. **Services:** Interlibrary loan; copying; SDI; library open to the public by appointment. **Networks/Consortia:** Member of Southwestern Connecticut Library Council (SWLC).

★18188★
YORK TECHNICAL COLLEGE - LIBRARY (Sci-Engr)
U.S. 21 Bypass Phone: (803)324-3130
Rock Hill, SC 29730 Amanda Yu, Libn.
Founded: 1964. **Staff:** Prof 1; Other 1. **Subjects:** Industrial arts, business, health sciences, engineering, liberal arts. **Holdings:** 20,324 books; 34,458 microforms; 30,210 slides; 3532 cassette tapes; 2763 transparencies; 458 videotapes; 1681 filmstrips. **Subscriptions:** 225 journals and other serials; 13 newspapers. **Services:** Interlibrary loan; copying; library open to residents of area.

★18189★
YORK UNIVERSITY - CENTRE FOR RESEARCH ON ENVIRONMENTAL QUALITY - CREQ RESEARCH CENTRE (Env-Cons)
Steacie Science Bldg., Rm. T114
4700 Keele St. Phone: (416)736-5028
North York, ON, Canada M3J 1P3 Mrs. C. Masaro
Staff: 1. **Subjects:** Environment, nuclear winter, acid rain. **Holdings:** Newspaper clippings. **Services:** Copying; center open to the public. **Publications:** Prospects for Mankind Series.

★18190★
YORK UNIVERSITY - CENTRE FOR RESEARCH ON LATIN AMERICA AND THE CARIBBEAN - CERLAC DOCUMENTATION CENTRE (Area-Ethnic)
204B Founders College
4700 Keele St. Phone: (416)736-5237
Downsview, ON, Canada M3J 1P3 Alan Simmons, Dir., CERLAC
Staff: Prof 2; Other 2. **Subjects:** Latin America and the Caribbean - sociology, economics, political science, history; Canadian-Latin American/Caribbean relations. **Special Collections:** Research reports and working papers from Latin American social science research centers in Argentina, Brazil, Chile, Ecuador, Mexico, Peru, Uruguay, Venezuela, and Costa Rica; reviews of the Organization for Economic Cooperation and Development (OECD) pertaining to Latin America; United Nations information and statistics; Brazilian government documents. **Holdings:** 1500 volumes; government research reports on microfilm and microfiche; Spanish, Portuguese, Italian journals. **Subscriptions:** 50 journals and other serials. **Services:** Copying; center open to the public by appointment. **Publications:** List of publications - available upon request. **Remarks:** Includes holdings of the Latin America Research Unit (LARU). **Staff:** Peter Landstreet, Dp.Dir..

★18191★
YORK UNIVERSITY - DEPARTMENT OF VISUAL ARTS - SLIDE LIBRARY (Art)
Fine Arts Phase II, Rm. 274 Phone: (416)667-3749
Toronto, ON, Canada M3J 1P3 Michele Metraux, Supv.
Staff: Prof 3; Other 4. **Subjects:** Painting, sculpture, architecture. **Special Collections:** Germain Bazin Collection of Photographs; Theodore A. Heinrich Slide Collection. **Holdings:** 180,000 35mm slides. **Subscriptions:** 35 journals and other serials. **Services:** Library open to faculty. **Staff:** Lillian Heinson, Asst. Slide Libn..

★18192★
YORK UNIVERSITY - EDUCATION DEVELOPMENT OFFICE - RESOURCE CENTRE (Educ)
4700 Keele St. Phone: (416)736-2100
North York, ON, Canada M3J 1P3 Janette M. Baker
Founded: 1976. **Staff:** Prof 1; Other 1. **Subjects:** Higher and adult education. **Holdings:** 1000 books; 5000 conference papers and reports; unbound periodicals. **Subscriptions:** 90 journals and other serials. **Services:** Copying; SDI; center open to the public with restrictions. **Automated Operations:** Computerized cataloging, acquisitions, and circulation. **Publications:** Orientations (newsletter), quarterly - for internal distribution only.

★18193★
YORK UNIVERSITY - FACULTY OF ARTS - WRITING WORKSHOP LIBRARY (Educ)
208 Strong College
4700 Keele St. Phone: (416)736-5134
Downsview, ON, Canada M3J 1P3 Sylvia Meade, Adm.Sec.
Subjects: Composition, how to write and teach special subjects. **Holdings:** 1100 books; 100 bound periodical volumes. **Services:** Interlibrary loan; library open to students and faculty.

★18194★
YORK UNIVERSITY - FACULTY OF EDUCATION - EDUCATION CENTRE (Educ)
North Tower, Rm. 828 Ross
4700 Keele St. Phone: (416)736-5259
Downsview, ON, Canada M3J 1P3 Elaine Leung, Supv.
Founded: 1974. **Staff:** Prof 1; Other 1. **Subjects:** Education. **Holdings:** 10,690 books; 716 kits; 846 filmstrips; 380 phonograph records. **Services:** Center not open to the public.

★18195★
YORK UNIVERSITY - FILM LIBRARY (Aud-Vis)
Scott Library
4700 Keele St. Phone: (416)667-2546
North York, ON, Canada M3J 1P3 Kathryn Elder, Film Libn.
Founded: 1970. **Staff:** Prof 1; Other 3. **Special Collections:** Dance in Canada: Jean A. Chalmers Choreographic Collection (53 video cassettes of work by contemporary Canadian choreographers); Labatt Breweries of Canada Sports Collection (350 films). **Holdings:** 1774 16mm film titles; 1421 video cassettes. **Services:** Films loaned to other Ontario universities. **Automated Operations:** Computerized cataloging. **Special Catalogs:** Annotated catalog with subject index (book). **Remarks:** Provides film reference service and obtains films from outside rental sources.

★18196★
YORK UNIVERSITY - FRENCH STUDIES DEPARTMENT - LIBRARY (Area-Ethnic)
Ross Bldg., Rm. 5556A
4700 Keele St. Phone: (416)736-5086
Downsview, ON, Canada M3J 1P3 Liliana Guadagnoli, Adm.Asst.
Staff: 3. **Subjects:** French studies. **Special Collections:** Bibliotheque de la Pleiade, 16th-19th centuries (French). **Holdings:** Figures not available. **Services:** Library not open to the public.

★18197★
YORK UNIVERSITY - GEOGRAPHY DEPARTMENT - TEACHING RESOURCES CENTRE (Geog-Map)
Ross Bldg., Rm. S405
4700 Keele St. Phone: (416)736-5108
Downsview, ON, Canada M3J 1P3 Michael Flosznik, Supv.
Staff: Prof 1; Other 4. **Subjects:** Geography - urban and historical Canada, biology, recreation, economic. **Special Collections:** Departmental papers, theses, dissertations; Census of Canada, 1961-1981 (incomplete). **Holdings:** 500 books; unbound periodicals. **Subscriptions:** 45 journals and other serials. **Services:** Center open to the public for reference use only.

Automated Operations: Computerized cataloging. **Computerized Information Services:** Internal database.

★18198★
YORK UNIVERSITY - GOVERNMENT DOCUMENTS/ ADMINISTRATIVE STUDIES LIBRARY (Bus-Fin, Info Sci)
113 Administrative Studies Bldg.
4700 Keele St. Phone: (416)736-5139
North York, ON, Canada M3J 1P3 Vivienne Monty, Hd.
Staff: Prof 3; Other 7. **Subjects:** Documents of the governments of Canada, Great Britain, United States; documents of United Nations, Organization for Economic Cooperation and Development, European Communities; management; public administration; capital markets; corporations; administrative behavior; arts management; executive development. **Holdings:** 150,000 documents (83,000 bound); 8622 reels of microfilm; 1.06 million microfiche and microcards; 2000 volume reference collection; 15,000 bound periodical volumes; microfiche data file on Canadian and American companies, mid-1950s-1972 for U.S. companies, mid-1950s to present for Canadian companies. **Subscriptions:** 6000 journals and other serials; 12 newspapers. **Services:** Interlibrary loan; copying; library open to the public. **Automated Operations:** Computerized cataloging and acquisitions. **Computerized Information Services:** DIALOG Information Services, CAN/OLE, BRS Information Technologies, QL Systems, The Reference Service (REFSRV), Info Globe, International Development Research Centre (IDRC). **Staff:** Elizabeth Watson, Ref.Libn.; D.K. Varma, Adm.Stud.Libn..

★18199★
YORK UNIVERSITY - INSTITUTE FOR SOCIAL RESEARCH - DATA ARCHIVE (Soc Sci)
4700 Keele St. Phone: (416)736-5061
North York, ON, Canada M3J 1P3 Prof. Gordon Darroch
Founded: 1968. **Staff:** Prof 11; Other 6. **Subjects:** Social sciences with Canadian focus; survey research - by mail, telephone, or interview, questionnaire design, measurement, programming, and data analysis. **Services:** Archive open to the public with restrictions. **Computerized Information Services:** Data archives (internal database). **Publications:** List of publications - available on request. **Special Catalogs:** Canadian Social Science Data Catalogue 1985.

★18200★
YORK UNIVERSITY - LAW LIBRARY (Law)
4700 Keele St. Phone: (416)736-2100
North York, ON, Canada M3J 1P3 Prof. B.J. Halevy, Libn.
Founded: 1892. **Staff:** Prof 5; Other 23. **Subjects:** Law. **Holdings:** 262,658 volumes; 86,055 volumes in microform. **Subscriptions:** 2404 journals and other serials. **Services:** Interlibrary loan; copying; library open to the public with fee for borrowing. **Automated Operations:** Computerized cataloging. **Computerized Information Services:** QL Systems. **Publications:** Acquisitions list, monthly; KF Canadian Adaptation Classification Schedule, quarterly. **Staff:** Judy Ginsberg, Asst. Law Libn.; Marianne Rogers, Ref.Libn.; Lucie Hamelin-Touloumis, Hd., Acq.; Monica Perot, Hd., Circ..

★18201★
YORK UNIVERSITY - LISTENING ROOM (Mus)
Scott Library, Rm. 409
4700 Keele St. Phone: (416)736-2100
North York, ON, Canada M3J 1P3
Julie M. Stockton, Listening Rm.Hd.
Founded: 1970. **Staff:** Prof 1; Other 2. **Subjects:** Music, theater, ethnomusicology, spoken word. **Special Collections:** CBC Ideas Collection (1750 reels of tape); International Library of African Music (213 phonograph records); Edith Fowke Collection (95 reels of field tapes); Robert and Anne Levine Collection of Archival Jazz and Blues (2500 phonograph records). **Holdings:** 51,500 books and scores; 26,500 phonograph records, compact discs, tapes, cassette tapes; 1000 scores on microfiche. **Subscriptions:** 12 journals and other serials. **Services:** Interlibrary loan; copying (limited); room open to library card holders. **Automated Operations:** Computerized circulation. **Publications:** Handbook; discographies on selected topics. **Special Indexes:** Ethnomusicology index.

★18202★
YORK UNIVERSITY - MAP LIBRARY (Geog-Map)
Scott Library, Rm. 115
4700 Keele St. Phone: (416)736-2100
North York, ON, Canada M3J 1P3 Kathleen M. Wyman, Map Libn.
Founded: 1970. **Staff:** Prof 1; Other 1. **Subjects:** Geography, cartography. **Holdings:** 4200 books and atlases; 83,860 maps; 122 wall maps; clipping file; pamphlet file; 3800 aerial photographs; file of articles on cartography; maps on slides. **Subscriptions:** 30 journals and other serials. **Services:** Interlibrary loan; copying; library open to the public. **Remarks:** Location of Canadian Ports Collection material.

★18203★
YORK UNIVERSITY - NELLIE LANGFORD ROWELL LIBRARY (Soc Sci)
202C Founders College
4700 Keele St. Phone: (416)736-2100
Downsview, ON, Canada M3J 1P3 C.M. Donald, Lib.Coord.
Founded: 1970. **Staff:** 5. **Subjects:** Women, women's studies, feminism. **Holdings:** 6000 books; 250 boxes of broadsides and ephemera. **Subscriptions:** 150 journals and other serials. **Services:** Library open to the public. **Publications:** Pamphlet series.

★18204★
YORK UNIVERSITY - SPECIAL COLLECTIONS (Hum)
Scott Library, Rm. 305
4700 Keele St.
North York, ON, Canada M3J 1P3 Phone: (416)736-2100
Founded: 1965. **Staff:** 1. **Subjects:** Canadian history, literature, and art; 20th century British literature. **Special Collections:** Auden; Day-Lewis; Isherwood; MacNeice; Spender; the Sitwells; Marsh; MacLeish. **Holdings:** 26,000 books; 6000 Canadian pamphlets. **Services:** Copying; collections open to the public. **Automated Operations:** Computerized cataloging and acquisitions.

★18205★
YORK UNIVERSITY - STEACIE SCIENCE LIBRARY (Sci-Engr, Comp Sci)
4700 Keele St. Phone: (416)736-5084
North York, ON, Canada M3J 1P3 Brian B. Wilks, Hd.
Founded: 1970. **Staff:** Prof 1; Other 6. **Subjects:** Mathematics, applied computational mathematics, chemistry, computer science, physics, biology, earth and atmospheric sciences. **Holdings:** 50,000 books; 60,000 bound periodical volumes; 28,500 microforms. **Subscriptions:** 1800 journals and other serials. **Services:** Interlibrary loan; copying; library open to the public for reference use only. **Automated Operations:** Computerized cataloging, acquisitions, and circulation. **Computerized Information Services:** DIALOG Information Services, BRS Information Technologies, Pergamon ORBIT InfoLine, Inc., CAN/SDI, CAN/OLE, QL Systems, MEDLARS, Info Globe, Telesystemes Questel, Infomart, WILSONLINE.

★18206★
YORK UNIVERSITY - UNIVERSITY ARCHIVES (Hist, Hum)
105 Scott Library
4700 Keele St. Phone: (416)736-2100
North York, ON, Canada M3J 1P3 Hartwell Bowsfield, Univ.Archv.
Founded: 1960. **Staff:** Prof 1; Other 1. **Special Collections:** Papers of Louis Applebaum (55 feet); Margaret Avison (1 foot); Bill Bissett (59 feet); Canadian Broadcasting Corporation TV Drama Scripts (476 feet); Canadian Speakers' and Writers' Service (84 feet); Canadian Theatre Review (40 feet); Harry Crowe (56 feet); William Esdaile (7 feet); Joseph O. Goodman (100 feet); Allan Grossman (61 feet); Robert Haynes (3 feet); William Jaffe (42 feet); Margaret Laurence (22 feet); Norman Levine (28 feet); Roy Mitchell (5 feet); Mavor Moore (115 feet); Northern Journey (6 feet); Province of Ontario Land Registry Books (916 feet); Operation Lifeline (24 feet); Joseph Bascom St. John (40 feet); Sitwell Family (9 feet); Richard Storr (36 feet); Toronto Real Estate Board Multiple Listings (450 feet); Toronto Telegram Photograph Collection (889 feet); United Electrical, Radio and Machine Workers of America, Local 507, Toronto (61 feet); Vaughan Township (45 feet); Ernest Vinci (86 feet); Herman Voaden (72 feet); Lady Victoria Welby (17 feet). **Holdings:** 4192 feet of manuscripts; 1067 feet of university records; 178 feet of university theses. **Services:** Copying; archives open to the public. **Publications:** Accession Bulletin, irregular.

YOSEMITE NATIONAL PARK
See: U.S. Natl. Park Service (15365)

★18207★
ARTHUR YOUNG & COMPANY - LIBRARY (Bus-Fin)
One IBM Plaza Phone: (312)645-3000
Chicago, IL 60611 Jack Holcomb, Libn.
Staff: 2. **Subjects:** Accounting, taxation. **Holdings:** 1200 books. **Subscriptions:** 400 journals and other serials; 20 newspapers. **Services:** Interlibrary loan; library not open to the public. **Automated Operations:** Computerized cataloging. **Computerized Information Services:** LEXIS, The Reference Service (REFSRV), DIALOG Information Services.

★18208★
ARTHUR YOUNG & COMPANY - LIBRARY (Bus-Fin)
277 Park Ave. Phone: (212)407-1975
New York, NY 10172 Nan C. Schubel, Libn.
Founded: 1953. **Staff:** Prof 4; Other 5. **Subjects:** Accounting and auditing, management consulting, taxation. **Holdings:** 5500 books; 115,000 microfiche. **Subscriptions:** 500 journals and other serials. **Services:** Interlibrary loan; copying; library open to clients and SLA members. **Automated Operations:** Computerized cataloging and serials. **Computerized Information Services:** NEXIS, Pergamon ORBIT InfoLine, Inc., Dow Jones News/Retrieval, DIALOG Information Services. **Publications:** Acquisitions List, bimonthly - to staff and other accounting firms. **Staff:** Robert Carlson, Asst.Libn.; Shabeer Khan, Asst.Libn..

ARTHUR YOUNG TAX LIBRARY
See: Arizona State University - Lloyd Bimson Memorial Library (908)

ARTHUR YOUNG TAX RESEARCH LIBRARY
See: San Diego State University - Bureau of Business & Economic Research Library (12783)

★18209★
BRIGHAM YOUNG UNIVERSITY - ARCHIVES AND MANUSCRIPTS DIVISION (Hist)
5030 Harold B. Lee Library Phone: (801)378-6372
Provo, UT 84602 E. Dennis Rowley, Cur./Univ.Archv.
Staff: Prof 7; Other 15. **Subjects:** Brigham Young University; Utah and the American West; the Mormon experience; arts and communication; motion pictures; literature; Mesoamerica; politics; history - European, ancient, medieval. **Special Collections:** Wells Freedom Archives. **Holdings:** 7500 linear feet of manuscripts; 5000 linear feet of archival material. **Services:** Copying; archives open to the public. **Computerized Information Services:** DIALOG Information Services, Pergamon ORBIT InfoLine, Inc., BRS Information Technologies, The Reference Service (REFSRV), OCLC; NOTIS, BITNET (electronic mail services). **Networks/Consortia:** Member of RLG, Utah College Library Council. **Staff:** Melva H. Richey, Asst.Univ.Archv.; Albert L. Winkler, Mss.Cat.; David J. Whittaker, Cur.; LeGrand L. Baker, Cur.; Harvard S. Heath, Cur.; James V. D'Arc, Cur..

★18210★
BRIGHAM YOUNG UNIVERSITY - ARCHIVES AND MANUSCRIPTS DIVISION - ARCHIVES OF RECORDED SOUND (Aud-Vis)
5030 Harold B. Lee Library Phone: (801)378-6372
Provo, UT 84602 E. Dennis Rowley, Cur.
Staff: Prof 1; Other 1. **Subjects:** Radio broadcasting, U.S. presidents, movie soundtracks, Utah and university history. **Special Collections:** Oral history interviews (700). **Holdings:** 45,000 tape recordings; 15,000 phonograph records. **Services:** Copying; archives open to the public. **Computerized Information Services:** RLIN.

★18211★
BRIGHAM YOUNG UNIVERSITY - ASIAN COLLECTION (Area-Ethnic)
1066 Harold B. Lee Library Phone: (801)378-4061
Provo, UT 84602 Gail King, Cur.
Founded: 1972. **Staff:** Prof 1. **Subjects:** Asia. **Holdings:** 38,000 books. **Subscriptions:** 115 journals and other serials; 5 newspapers. **Services:** Interlibrary loan; collection open to the public. **Automated Operations:** Computerized cataloging, serials, and circulation. **Computerized Information Services:** Internal database. Performs searches free of charge. **Networks/Consortia:** Member of RLG.

★18212★
BRIGHAM YOUNG UNIVERSITY - BEAN MUSEUM - RESEARCH LIBRARY (Biol Sci)
Provo, UT 84602 Phone: (801)378-4585
Jody Chandler, Bean Musm.Libn.
Founded: 1978. **Staff:** Prof 1; Other 1. **Subjects:** Taxonomy - botany, zoology. **Holdings:** 4700 books; 550 bound periodical volumes; 8000 taxonomic offprints. **Subscriptions:** 31 journals and other serials. **Services:** Interlibrary loan (through Harold B. Lee Library); copying; library open to the public. **Automated Operations:** Computerized public access catalog, cataloging, and acquisitions. **Computerized Information Services:** NOTIS; BITNET (electronic mail service). **Networks/Consortia:** Member of RLG, Utah College Library Council. **Special Catalogs:** Catalog of offprint collection (online).

★18213★
BRIGHAM YOUNG UNIVERSITY - COMPUTER AIDED MANUFACTURING LABORATORY - LIBRARY
105 D&TB
Provo, UT 84602
Founded: 1977. **Subjects:** Group technology, computer-aided design and manufacturing, robotics. **Holdings:** 3000 volumes. **Remarks:** Presently inactive.

★18214★
BRIGHAM YOUNG UNIVERSITY - DOCUMENTS AND MAP COLLECTION (Geog-Map, Info Sci)
1368 Harold B. Lee Library Phone: (801)378-6180
Provo, UT 84602 Therrin C. Dahlin, Docs.Libn.
Founded: 1955. **Staff:** Prof 3; Other 6. **Holdings:** Documents - U.S. Federal, state/municipal, Canadian, United States, Organization of American States; maps. **Services:** Interlibrary loan; copying; collection open to the public. **Automated Operations:** Computerized cataloging, acquisitions, serials, and circulation. **Computerized Information Services:** DIALOG Information Services, Pergamon ORBIT InfoLine, Inc., WILSONLINE, MEDLINE; BYLINE, NOTIS (internal databases); BITNET (electronic mail service). Performs searches on fee basis. Contact Person: Larry D. Benson, Pol.Sci./Econ.Libn., 378-3800. **Networks/Consortia:** Member of RLG, Utah College Library Council. **Staff:** Beverly J. Norton, Fed.Docs.Libn.; Richard E. Soares, Map Libn..

★18215★
BRIGHAM YOUNG UNIVERSITY - GLENN AND OLIVE NIELSON LIBRARY (Bus-Fin)
School of Management
410 N. Eldon Tanner Bldg. Phone: (801)378-3924
Provo, UT 84602 Gordon C. Casper, Dir.
Founded: 1982. **Staff:** Prof 2; Other 7. **Subjects:** Accounting, business and information management, managerial economics, organizational behavior, public administration. **Special Collections:** Ernst & Whinney Tax Library. **Holdings:** 5000 books; 450 bound periodical volumes; 40 drawers of microfiche. **Subscriptions:** 500 journals and other serials; 5 newspapers. **Services:** Interlibrary loan; copying; library open to the public. **Automated Operations:** Computerized cataloging, acquisitions, and serials. **Computerized Information Services:** DIALOG Information Services, Pergamon ORBIT InfoLine, Inc., NOTIS, WILSONLINE, NewsNet, Inc., LEXIS, NEXIS, Nikkei Telecom, InfoTrac; BITNET (electronic mail service). Performs searches on fee basis. **Networks/Consortia:** Member of Utah College Library Council. **Publications:** Subject Bibliographies. **Staff:** Linda C. Brown, Asst.Libn..

★18216★
BRIGHAM YOUNG UNIVERSITY - HUMANITIES AND ARTS DIVISION LIBRARY (Hum)
University Library Phone: (801)378-4005
Provo, UT 84602 Richard D. Hacken, Dept.Chm.
Staff: Prof 4; Other 8. **Subjects:** Literature, music, art, languages, speech, drama, theater arts, cinematic arts, library science. **Holdings:** Figures not available. **Services:** Interlibrary loan; copying; library open to the public. **Automated Operations:** Computerized cataloging, serials, and circulation. **Computerized Information Services:** DIALOG Information Services, Pergamon ORBIT InfoLine, Inc., RLIN, BRS Information Technologies, The Reference Service (REFSRV), OCLC. **Networks/Consortia:** Member of RLG, Utah College Library Council.

★18217★
BRIGHAM YOUNG UNIVERSITY - J. REUBEN CLARK LAW SCHOOL LIBRARY (Law)
Provo, UT 84602 Phone: (801)378-3593
David A. Thomas, Law Libn.
Founded: 1972. **Staff:** Prof 8; Other 40. **Subjects:** American and British Commonwealth law. **Holdings:** 238,000 books; 130,000 bound periodical volumes; 62,000 monographs; 50,000 government documents; 1500 other cataloged items; 69,000 volumes in microform. **Subscriptions:** 2825 journals and other serials; 38 newspapers. **Services:** Interlibrary loan; copying; library open to the public for legal research use only. **Computerized Information Services:** LEXIS, WESTLAW. **Networks/Consortia:** Member of RLG, Utah College Library Council, Northwest Consortium of Law Libraries. **Publications:** Foreign Law Classification Schedule, Class K (2nd edition); Abstracts of Book Reviews in Current Legal Periodicals, semimonthly; LC Subject Headings - KF: Cross-References; Legal Research Manual. **Staff:** Gary Hill, Ref.Libn.; Heinz Peter Mueller, Assoc. Law Libn.; Dennis Sears, Circ.Libn.; Ruth Jones, Doc.Libn.; Louisa Lyman, Acq.Libn.; Curt Conklin, Cat.Libn.; Robin Booth, Ser.Libn.; Gary Buckway, Sys.Libn..

★18218★
BRIGHAM YOUNG UNIVERSITY - MUSEUM OF PEOPLES AND CULTURES LIBRARY (Soc Sci)
Allen Hall Phone: (801)378-6112
Provo, UT 84602 Joel C. Janetski, Dir.
Staff: Prof 1; Other 12. **Subjects:** Archeology - Mesoamerican, Southwestern, historical. **Holdings:** 4000 books; 1500 bound periodical volumes. **Services:** SDI; library open to the public. **Publications:** Publications in Archaeology, annual.

★18219★
BRIGHAM YOUNG UNIVERSITY - RELIGION AND HISTORY DIVISION LIBRARY (Hist, Rel-Phil)
University Library Phone: (801)378-6198
Provo, UT 84602 Susan L. Fales, Dept.Chm.
Staff: Prof 4; Other 7. **Subjects:** History, religion, biography, genealogy, philosophy, geography, anthropology, archeology. **Holdings:** 500,000 books. **Services:** Interlibrary loan; copying; library open to the public. **Automated Operations:** Computerized cataloging, acquisitions, serials, and circulation. **Computerized Information Services:** DIALOG Information Services, Pergamon ORBIT InfoLine, Inc., BRS Information Technologies, NOTIS, RLIN, InfoTrac, OCLC; BITNET (electronic mail service). Performs searches on fee basis. **Networks/Consortia:** Member of RLG, Utah College Library Council, Center for Research Libraries (CRL) Consortia. **Staff:** Mark L. Grover, Lat.Amer.Stud.Libn.; Gary P. Gillum, Ancient & Near Eastern Stud.Libn.; Donald H. Howard, Hist./Religion Libn..

★18220★
BRIGHAM YOUNG UNIVERSITY - SCIENCE AND TECHNOLOGY LIBRARY (Sci-Engr)
University Library Phone: (801)378-2986
Provo, UT 84602 Richard Jensen, Dept.Chm.
Staff: Prof 5; Other 8. **Subjects:** Science and technology. **Holdings:** 470,000 volumes. **Subscriptions:** 5100 journals and other serials. **Services:** Interlibrary loan; copying; SDI; library open to the public. **Automated Operations:** Computerized public access catalog, cataloging, acquisitions, serials, and circulation. **Computerized Information Services:** DIALOG Information Services, STN International, WILSONLINE, BRS Information Technologies, RLIN, NLM; BITNET (electronic mail service). **Networks/Consortia:** Member of RLG, Utah College Library Council.

★18221★
BRIGHAM YOUNG UNIVERSITY - SOCIAL SCIENCE DEPARTMENT LIBRARY (Soc Sci)
Harold B. Lee Library Phone: (801)378-3809
Provo, UT 84602 Marvin Wiggins, Dept.Chm.
Staff: Prof 3; Other 7. **Subjects:** Psychology, sociology, family science, education, business/economics, social work, political science. **Holdings:** Figures not available. **Services:** Interlibrary loan; copying; SDI; library open to the public. **Automated Operations:** Computerized cataloging, acquisitions, serials, and circulation. **Computerized Information Services:** DIALOG Information Services, Pergamon ORBIT InfoLine, Inc., WILSONLINE, MEDLINE, NOTIS; BITNET (electronic mail service). Performs searches on fee basis. **Networks/Consortia:** Member of RLG, Utah College Library Council. **Remarks:** An alternate telephone number is 378-6346. **Staff:** Afton McG. Miner, Educ.Libn.; Larry Benson, Political Sci.Libn..

★18222★
BRIGHAM YOUNG UNIVERSITY - SPECIAL COLLECTIONS (Hist, Rel-Phil)
University Library Phone: (801)378-2932
Provo, UT 84602 Chad J. Flake, Cur.
Founded: 1956. **Staff:** Prof 3; Other 2. **Subjects:** Renaissance and Reformation; history of printing; Mormonism; Utah and Western history; 19th century American and English literature; typography; 17th century astronomy; 16th century European diplomatics. **Special Collections:** LeRoy Hafen Collection of Western American History; J. Reuben Clark Collection of Law and Religion; Mormon Americana; Victorian book collection; Tyrus Hillway Collection of Herman Melville; Marco Heidner Collection of 15th and 16th century printing. **Holdings:** 185,467 volumes; 25,000 pamphlets. **Subscriptions:** 15 newspapers. **Services:** Interlibrary loan; copying; collections open to the public. **Automated Operations:** Computerized cataloging, acquisitions, and serials. **Computerized Information Services:** DIALOG Information Services, Pergamon ORBIT InfoLine, Inc., BRS Information Technologies, The Reference Service (REFSRV), NOTIS, OCLC; BITNET (electronic mail service). **Networks/Consortia:** Member of RLG, Utah College Library Council. **Staff:** Scott H. Duvall, Asst.Cur., Spec.Coll..

★18223★
BRIGHAM YOUNG UNIVERSITY - UTAH VALLEY REGIONAL FAMILY HISTORY CENTER (Hist)
Harold B. Lee Library, Rm. 4386 Phone: (801)378-6200
Provo, UT 84602 F. Haws Durfey, Pres.
Founded: 1964. **Staff:** 1. **Subjects:** Genealogy. **Holdings:** Genealogical Society of Salt Lake City Library Catalog; primary and secondary source material in microform. **Services:** Copying; center open to the public. **Publications:** Newsletter and Information Sheet. **Special Indexes:** International Genealogical Index (89,000 births, christenings, and marriages arranged by state or country). **Remarks:** This library is a branch of the Church of Jesus Christ of Latter Day Saints - Family History Center in Salt Lake City and has access to their collection on a loan basis.

★18224★
BRIGHAM YOUNG UNIVERSITY, HAWAII CAMPUS - JOSEPH F. SMITH LIBRARY AND MEDIA CENTER (Rel-Phil, Hum)
55-220 Kulanui St.
BYU-HC Box 1966 Phone: (808)293-3850
Laie, HI 96762 Rex Frandsen, Dir.
Founded: 1955. **Staff:** Prof 8; Other 8. **Special Collections:** Pacific Islands (9000 books); Mormonism (4200 books); children's collection (2500 books); government documents; archives. **Holdings:** 135,000 books; 500,000 microforms; 1200 films; 1100 videotapes. **Services:** Interlibrary loan; copying; library open to the public on payment of annual fee. **Automated Operations:** Computerized public access catalog, cataloging, acquisitions, and circulation. **Computerized Information Services:** DIALOG Information Services, OCLC. **Publications:** Library Newsgram. **Staff:** Marynelle Chew, Cat./Govt.Doc.; Cheryle Makanui-Pyne, Ref.; Anita Henry, Acq.; Ed Jensen, Media; Dwight Miller, Pub.Serv.; Terry Webb, Ref.; Riley Moffat, Ref.; Allen Septon, Automation.

★18225★
YOUNG, CONAWAY, STARGATT & TAYLOR - LIBRARY (Law)
Rodney Sq. N., 11th Fl.
Box 391 Phone: (302)571-6680
Wilmington, DE 19899-0391 Robin Kershaw, Libn.
Staff: Prof 1. **Subjects:** Law. **Holdings:** 10,000 books. **Subscriptions:** 79 journals and other serials. **Services:** Library not open to the public.

★18226★
HOWARD YOUNG MEDICAL CENTER - HEALTH SCIENCE LIBRARY (Med)
Box 470 Phone: (715)356-8000
Woodruff, WI 54568 Rita Sieracki, Libn.
Founded: 1973. **Staff:** Prof 1. **Subjects:** Medicine, nursing. **Holdings:** 1000 volumes; 200 pamphlets; 100 video cassettes; 500 audio cassettes. **Subscriptions:** 110 journals and other serials. **Services:** Interlibrary loan; copying; library open to the public with restrictions. **Computerized Information Services:** MEDLINE. **Networks/Consortia:** Member of Northern Wisconsin Health Science Libraries Cooperative, Greater Midwest Regional Medical Library Network.

★18227★
YOUNG MEN'S CHRISTIAN ASSOCIATION OF METROPOLITAN HARTFORD, INC. - CAREER COUNSELING CENTER LIBRARY
160 Jewell St.
Hartford, CT 06103
Defunct

★18228★
YOUNG MEN'S CHRISTIAN ASSOCIATIONS OF THE UNITED STATES OF AMERICA - YMCA OF THE USA ARCHIVES (Soc Sci)
2642 University Ave.
St. Paul, MN 55114 Andrea Hinding, Archv.
Founded: 1877. **Staff:** Prof 1; Other 4. **Subjects:** History of the YMCA in the United States, Canada, and abroad, 1850 to present. **Special Collections:** Early Young Men's Societies publications, 1700-1850; biographical files on 200 YMCA leaders, 1850 to present; records of YMCA work in 80 countries, 1890 to present. **Holdings:** 6000 books; 2000 bound periodical volumes; 1200 linear feet of historical records; 125 reels of microfilm; 10,000 photographs; memorabilia. **Services:** Archives closed for on-site use until late 1988; limited phone and mail reference provided when

possible. **Remarks:** Archives are on deposit in the Social Welfare History Archives of the University of Minnesota Libraries.

★18229★
YOUNG MEN'S MERCANTILE LIBRARY ASSOCIATION - LIBRARY
414 Walnut St. Phone: (513)621-0717
Cincinnati, OH 45202 Jean M. Springer, Exec.Dir.
Subjects: General collection. **Holdings:** 200,000 volumes. **Services:** Library open to members only.

YOUNG MEN'S PHILANTHROPIC LEAGUE
See: Jewish Guild for the Blind (7210)

★18230★
MORRIS N. & CHESLEY V. YOUNG MNEMONICS LIBRARY (Soc Sci)
270 Riverside Dr. Phone: (212)233-2344
New York, NY 10025 Morris N. Young, M.D., Dir.
Founded: 1953. **Staff:** 2. **Subjects:** Memory, memory aids, mnemonics. **Holdings:** 5500 cataloged items; books; pamphlets; manuscripts; prints; articles; records; cassettes; games; 15,000 index cards. **Services:** Copying; library open to accredited researchers by appointment. **Publications:** Bibliography of Memory; How to Develop an Exceptional Memory; How to Read Faster and Remember More; The Magic of a Mighty Memory; William Stokes: Magician of Memory; The Magic of a Powerful Memory.

★18231★
YOUNG RADIATOR COMPANY - LIBRARY
2825 Four Mile Rd.
Racine, WI 53404
Founded: 1945. **Subjects:** Competitive heat transfer material, specifications, and data. **Holdings:** 600 volumes; 300 magazines; 1450 catalogs; 5700 folders; 10 volumes of patents; 1 VF drawer of clippings; 5 VF drawers; house organs; annual reports. **Remarks:** Presently inactive.

ROBERT A. AND VIVIAN YOUNG LAW LIBRARY
See: University of Arkansas, Fayetteville - School of Law (15834)

★18232★
YOUNG AND RUBICAM INC. - CORPORATE LIBRARY (Bus-Fin)
285 Madison Ave., 10th Fl. Phone: (212)953-3075
New York, NY 10017 Celestine G. Frankenberg, Dir. of Lib.Serv.
Founded: 1953. **Staff:** Prof 4; Other 3. **Subjects:** Advertising, marketing. **Special Collections:** Company histories; annual reports; cookbooks; art books; picture collection; competitive advertisers file. **Holdings:** 7500 volumes. **Subscriptions:** 250 journals and other serials. **Services:** Interlibrary loan; library not open to the public. **Computerized Information Services:** NEXIS, DIALOG Information Services, Market Analysis and Information Database (MAID).

WHITNEY M. YOUNG, JR. MEMORIAL LIBRARY OF SOCIAL WORK
See: Columbia University - Whitney M. Young, Jr. Memorial Library of Social Work (3496)

★18233★
YOUNG WOMEN'S CHRISTIAN ASSOCIATION - NATIONAL BOARD - LIBRARY (Soc Sci)
726 Broadway
New York, NY 10003 Elizabeth D. Norris, Libn./Hist.
Founded: 1959. **Staff:** Prof 1; Other 1. **Subjects:** Women, racism, sexism, civil rights, women's health, youth, voluntarism. **Special Collections:** Womans Press Publications, 1918-1952 (2500 volumes). **Holdings:** 10,000 books; 25 VF drawers of subject files, clippings, pamphlets, reports, catalogs. **Subscriptions:** 175 journals and other serials. **Services:** Interlibrary loan; copying; library open to students and scholars by referral. **Publications:** New Library Books, monthly - for internal distribution only. **Also Known As:** YWCA.

★18234★
YOUNG WOMEN'S CHRISTIAN ASSOCIATION OF MARIN - RESOURCE CENTER (Educ)
1000 Sir Francis Drake Blvd.
San Anselmo, CA 94960 Ann Kennedy, Ctr.Dir.
Staff: Prof 4; Other 3. **Subjects:** Career planning, self-help law, women's movement, county resources, political issues, health, counseling, children. **Holdings:** 300 books; 10 VF drawers; 4 scrapbooks; 130 tapes. **Subscriptions:** 14 journals and other serials. **Services:** Center open to the public for reference use only.

BARTON KYLE YOUNT MEMORIAL LIBRARY
See: American Graduate School of International Management (521)

YOUTH LIBERATION ARCHIVE
See: Temple University - Central Library System - Contemporary Culture Collection (13988)

★18235★
YOUTH NETWORK COUNCIL OF CHICAGO, INC. - ILLINOIS YOUTH SERVICE RESOURCE CENTER (Soc Sci)
321 S. Sixth St. Phone: (217)522-2663
Springfield, IL 62701 Carol Esarey, Prog.Adm
Founded: 1983. **Staff:** Prof 1; Other 1. **Subjects:** Youth and social services, community organization, juvenile justice, nonprofit organizations. **Holdings:** Figures not available. **Services:** Interlibrary loan; copying; center open to the public with restrictions. **Publications:** Newsline, quarterly - national distribution.

★18236★
YOUTH NETWORK COUNCIL, INC. - CLEARINGHOUSE (Soc Sci)
506 S. Wabash Ave. Phone: (312)427-2710
Chicago, IL 60605 Denis Murstein, Adm.Dir.
Founded: 1972. **Staff:** Prof 15; Other 2. **Subjects:** Alternative youth services, runaway youth, adolescent sexuality, youth employment, substance abuse, grantsmanship, juvenile justice, community development, public relations. **Holdings:** 500 books; 80 VF drawers of pamphlets; Federal Register, 1978 to present; videotapes. **Subscriptions:** 60 journals and other serials; 10 newspapers. **Services:** Interlibrary loan; copying; clearinghouse open to the public by appointment. **Publications:** Newsline, quarterly - by subscription; Reachout, Resource Guide to Substance Abuse in Metropolitan Chicago; Youth Employment & Training Guide; Resources for Youth; A Guide to Advocacy for Youth.

★18237★
YPSILANTI REGIONAL PSYCHIATRIC HOSPITAL - STAFF LIBRARY (Med)
Box A Phone: (313)434-3400
Ypsilanti, MI 48197 Bonnie A. Gasperini, Dir., Lib.Serv.
Staff: 1. **Subjects:** Activity therapy, psychiatry, nursing, psychology, social work, medicine, neurology. **Holdings:** Figures not available. **Services:** Interlibrary loan; library not open to the public. **Special Catalogs:** Audio Visual Media (card).

YUKON CHAMBER OF MINES
See: British Columbia and Yukon Chamber of Mines (1894)

★18238★
YUKON TERRITORY - DEPARTMENT OF EDUCATION - YUKON ARCHIVES (Hist)
Box 2703 Phone: (403)667-5321
Whitehorse, YT, Canada Y1A 2C6 Miriam McTiernan, Dir.
Founded: 1972. **Staff:** Prof 4; Other 3. **Subjects:** Yukon history and current development; Klondike gold rush; Yukon native people; northern pipelines; Alaska Highway; northern hydrocarbon development. **Special Collections:** Yukon Record Group I (central records of Yukon Government, 1894-1951; 475 meters); Dawson Mining Recorder (placer and quartz mining records, 1894-1971; 200 meters); White Pass and Yukon Route Records (transportation company records, 1898-1960; 25 meters); Anglican Church, Diocese of Yukon, 1888-1980 (7.5 meters). **Holdings:** 13,000 books; 215 bound periodical volumes; 1000 meters of territorial, municipal, federal government records; 310 meters of private manuscripts and corporate records; 1031 reels of microfilm; 7500 pamphlets; 8000 maps; 44,000 photographs; 173 films. **Subscriptions:** 100 journals and other serials; 40 newspapers. **Services:** Copying; duplication of photographs and maps; Public Reading Room open to the public. **Computerized Information Services:** DIALOG Information Services, QL Systems; Envoy 100 (electronic mail service). **Publications:** Checklist of Yukon Newspapers, 1898-1985; Yukon Native History and Culture: A Bibliography of Sources Available at the Yukon Archives; Hydrocarbon Development: A Yukon Perspective; From Sissons to Meyer: The Administrative Development of the Yukon Government, 1948-1979; Yukon Economic Planning Studies, 1965-1985, an annotated bibliography; Acquisitions List for Hydrocarbon Development, monthly; Information pamphlet; Access to Information (brochure); bibliographies; visual finding aids for photographs. **Special Indexes:** Inventories of government, private, and corporate records. **Staff:**

Diane Chisholm, Asst. Territorial Archv.; Charles Maier, Archv.; Eileen Edmunds, Libn.; Lynn McPherson, Archv..

★18239★
YUMA COUNTY LAW LIBRARY (Law)
219 W. 2nd St. Phone: (602)782-4534
Yuma, AZ 85364 Gerrie Regenscheid, Libn.
Staff: Prof 1. **Subjects:** Law. **Holdings:** 13,500 volumes. **Services:** Library not open to the public.

YWCA
See: Young Women's Christian Association (18233)

Z

★18240★
H.B. ZACHRY COMPANY - CENTRAL RECORDS AND LIBRARY (Plan)
Box 21130
San Antonio, TX 78285 Phone: (512)922-1213
Staff: 1. **Subjects:** Construction specifications, industrial relations, tax laws, electronic data processing, accounting procedures, building codes. **Holdings:** 1500 books; 60 bound periodical volumes; film; maps. **Subscriptions:** 135 journals and other serials. **Services:** Interlibrary loan; copying; library open to the public by permission.

H.B. ZACKRISON MEMORIAL LIBRARY
See: U.S. Army - Corps of Engineers - Construction Engineering Research Laboratory (14719)

ZAHN INSTRUCTIONAL MATERIALS CENTER
See: Temple University - Central Library System (13997)

ZALE LIBRARY
See: Bishop College - Zale Library (1624)

★18241★
ZANESVILLE ART CENTER - LIBRARY (Art)
620 Military Rd.
Zanesville, OH 43701 Phone: (614)452-0741
Staff: 5. **Subjects:** Art history, art techniques, aesthetics, world art, antiques. **Holdings:** 6288 books; 3000 filmstrips and slides. **Subscriptions:** 17 journals and other serials. **Services:** Library open to the public. **Publications:** Monthly Bulletin; Gallery Brochure.

ERICH ZEISL ARCHIVE
See: University of California, Los Angeles - Music Library (15981)

★18242★
ZEITLIN PERIODICALS COMPANY - LIBRARY (Publ)
817 S. La Brea Ave. Phone: (213)933-7175
Los Angeles, CA 90036 Stanley Zeitlin, Owner
Founded: 1925. **Staff:** Prof 1; Other 4. **Special Collections:** Back-issue periodicals. **Holdings:** 2 million periodicals. **Services:** Library open to the public by appointment.

★18243★
ZEITLIN & VER BRUGGE, BOOKSELLERS - LIBRARY
815 N. La Cienega Blvd.
Los Angeles, CA 90069
Defunct

★18244★
GEORGE A. ZELLER MENTAL HEALTH CENTER - PROFESSIONAL LIBRARY (Med)
5407 N. University Phone: (309)693-5272
Peoria, IL 61614 Barbara Haun, Libn.
Founded: 1967. **Staff:** Prof 1; Other 1. **Subjects:** Psychiatry, psychology, community mental health, geriatrics, sociology, general medicine. **Holdings:** 3000 books; 400 bound periodical volumes; 4 VF drawers. **Subscriptions:** 25 journals and other serials. **Services:** Interlibrary loan; copying; library open to students and professionals in the field. **Networks/Consortia:** Member of Heart of Illinois Library Consortium (HILC), ILLINET, Illinois Valley Library System, Illinois Department of Mental Health and Developmental Disabilities Library Services Network (LISN). **Publications:** New Book List, monthly - for internal distribution only. **Remarks:** Maintained by Illinois State Department of Mental Health and Developmental Disabilities.

MAX AND LORE ZELLER LIBRARY
See: C.G. Jung Institute of Los Angeles, Inc. - Max and Lore Zeller Library (7302)

★18245★
ZENITH ELECTRONICS CORPORATION - TECHNICAL LIBRARY (Sci-Engr)
1000 N. Milwaukee Ave. Phone: (312)391-8452
Glenview, IL 60025 Ruby K. Chu, Info.Mgr.
Staff: Prof 1; Other 2. **Subjects:** Physics, mathematics, electronics, engineering, chemistry. **Holdings:** 10,500 books; 5000 bound periodical volumes; pamphlet file. **Subscriptions:** 300 journals and other serials. **Services:** Interlibrary loan; library not open to the public. **Computerized Information Services:** Online systems.

ZILEVICIUS-KREIVENAS LITHUANIAN MUSIC ARCHIVE
See: Lithuanian Research and Studies Center, Inc. - Libraries (7889)

ZIMPRO INC.
See: Sterling Drug, Inc. (13670)

★18246★
ZINC INSTITUTE - INFORMATION SERVICE
292 Madison Ave.
New York, NY 10017
Defunct

★18247★
ZION MENNONITE CHURCH - LIBRARY (Rel-Phil)
149 Cherry Ln. Phone: (215)723-3592
Souderton, PA 18964 Gwen N. Hartzel, Libn.
Founded: 1945. **Staff:** 6. **Subjects:** Bible, Mennonite Church history, books for children and young people. **Holdings:** 5000 books. **Services:** Interlibrary loan; library open to the public.

ZION NATIONAL PARK
See: U.S. Natl. Park Service (15366)

★18248★
ZION UNITED CHURCH OF CHRIST - LIBRARY (Rel-Phil)
415 S. Main St.
North Canton, OH 44720 Phone: (216)499-6979
Staff: 2. **Subjects:** Religious literature. **Holdings:** 2000 books. **Services:** Library not open to the public. **Staff:** Margaril M. Deihel, Asst.Libn..

ZIONIST ARCHIVES AND LIBRARY
See: World Zionist Organization - American Section (18069)

ZIONIST YOUTH MOVEMENT
See: Hashomer Hatzair-Zionist Youth Movement (6128)

ZISKIND MEMORIAL LIBRARY
See: Temple Beth-El (13940)

★18249★
ZITTRER, SIBLIN, STEIN, LEVINE - LIBRARY (Bus-Fin)
4115 Sherbrooke St., W. Phone: (514)935-1117
Montreal, PQ, Canada H3Z 1K9 Norman Daitchman
Subjects: Accounting, auditing, tax. **Holdings:** 200 books. **Subscriptions:** 10 journals and other serials. **Services:** Library not open to the public.

ZIV LIBRARY OF TELEVISION PROGRAMS
See: University of Wisconsin, Madison - Wisconsin Center for Film and Theater Research (17161)

ZOECON RESEARCH INSTITUTE
See: Sandoz Crop Protection Corporation (12847)

ZOELLER FINE ARTS LIBRARY
See: Viterbo College (17396)

ZONDERVAN LIBRARY
See: Taylor University (13898)

★18250★
ZOOLOGICAL SOCIETY OF CINCINNATI - LIBRARY (Biol Sci)
3400 Vine St. Phone: (513)281-3700
Cincinnati, OH 45220 Bea Orendorff, Lib.Coord.
Founded: 1977. **Subjects:** Zoology, biology, natural history, environmental science, botany. **Special Collections:** Zoological Realia. **Holdings:** 3100 books; 100 bound periodical volumes; 3500 slides; 30 educational kits; 1200 vertical files. **Subscriptions:** 35 journals and other serials. **Services:** Library open to the public for reference use only on a limited schedule.

★18251★
ZOOLOGICAL SOCIETY OF PHILADELPHIA - LIBRARY (Biol Sci)
34th St. & Girard Ave. Phone: (215)243-1100
Philadelphia, PA 19104 Ellen Goldberg, Libn.
Staff: Prof 1. **Subjects:** Zoology, ornithology, mammalogy, herpetology, ichthyology, natural history, zoos and zoo management. **Holdings:** 3000 books; 75 bound periodical volumes; archival material; reports; theses. **Subscriptions:** 250 journals and other serials. **Services:** Interlibrary loan; copying; library open to the public by appointment. **Publications:** Monthly report - for internal distribution only.

★18252★
ZOOLOGICAL SOCIETY OF SAN DIEGO - ERNST SCHWARZ LIBRARY (Biol Sci)
San Diego Zoo
Box 551 Phone: (619)231-1515
San Diego, CA 92112-0551 Michaele M. Robinson, Mgr., Lib.Serv.
Founded: 1916. **Staff:** Prof 1; Other 1. **Subjects:** Vertebrate zoology, animal husbandry, animal behavior, wildlife conservation, veterinary medicine, horticulture. **Special Collections:** Charles E. Shaw Herpetological Library (300 books; 5000 reprints); Ernst Schwarz reprint collection (2000). **Holdings:** 11,000 books; 5000 bound periodical volumes; 15,000 reprints; 60 boxes of zoo annual reports and guidebooks; 54 linear feet of Zoological Society archives; 76 oral history audio- and videotapes. **Subscriptions:** 605 journals and other serials; 8 newspapers. **Services:** Interlibrary loan; copying; library open to the public with advance approval of library staff. **Automated Operations:** Computerized cataloging and serials. **Computerized Information Services:** OCLC, DIALOG Information Services. **Networks/Consortia:** Member of CLASS. **Publications:** Acquisitions list, monthly - for internal distribution only; Serials Holding List, updated annually; Guide to Library Services.

ANGELO ZOSA MEMORIAL LIBRARY
See: Horsham Clinic (6476)

ZUG MEMORIAL LIBRARY
See: Elizabethtown College (4656)

JACOB D. ZYLMAN MEMORIAL LIBRARY
See: Fairfax Hospital (4886)

International

A

ACADEMIA DE CIENCIAS DE LA REPUBLICA DE CUBA - CENTRO DE ESTUDIOS DE HISTORIA Y ORGANIZACION DE LA CIENCIA
See: Cuban Academy of Sciences - Center for the Study of the History and Organization of Science (18370)

ACADEMIA COLOMBIANA DE CIENCIAS EXACTAS, FISICAS Y NATURALES
See: Colombian Academy of Exact, Physical and Natural Sciences (18358)

★18253★
ACADEMIA SINICA - INSTITUTE OF ATOMIC ENERGY - LIBRARY (Energy, Sci-Engr)
No. 23
P.O. Box 275
Beijing, People's Republic of China Chen Xiongshu, Libn.
Founded: 1956. **Staff:** 31. **Subjects:** Nuclear science and engineering, mathematics, physical sciences, chemistry, electronics, electrical and mechanical engineering, metallurgy, environmental protection, biology, medicine. **Holdings:** 81,856 volumes; 1253 periodicals; 37,000 technical reports; 40,000 AV programs and microforms. **Services:** Interlibrary loan. **Publications:** New Book Reports, irregular; Library Newsletter, semiannual.

★18254★
ACADEMIA SINICA - INSTITUTE OF COAL CHEMISTRY - LIBRARY (Energy)
Yingze Jie
Taiyuan, Shanxi Province, People's Republic of China Fan Fubi, Libn.
Founded: 1961. **Staff:** 11. **Subjects:** Coal - chemistry, combustion, gasification, liquefaction; fuel chemistry; catalysis; carbon materials; fluidization; chemical reaction engineering; separation; analysis; testing; electronics. **Special Collections:** Coal chemistry; coal energy transformation; comprehensive utilization of coal and allied materials; academic reports on fuel chemistry, 1958 to present (in Chinese). **Holdings:** 40,761 volumes; 32,000 technical reports; 300,000 microforms and AV programs. **Subscriptions:** 1829 journals and other serials. **Services:** Copying. **Publications:** Journal of Fuel Chemistry and Technology.

★18255★
ACADEMIA SINICA - INSTITUTE OF GENETICS - LIBRARY (Biol Sci, Soc Sci)
Bldg. 17, Beishatan
Deshengmenwai
Beijing, People's Republic of China Phone: 1 446551
Subjects: Biological genetics, Marx, Engels, Lenin, Stalin, Chairman Mao, politics, economics, history, languages. **Holdings:** 19,100 volumes; 744 periodicals; 24 AV programs and microforms; threadbound ancient Chinese books. **Services:** Interlibrary loan.

★18256★
ACADEMIA SINICA - INSTITUTE OF SEMICONDUCTOR - LIBRARY (Sci-Engr)
P.O. Box 650
Beijing, People's Republic of China Xu Pengtai, Libn.
Founded: 1960. **Staff:** 20. **Subjects:** Semiconductor and integrated circuits, microelectronics. **Holdings:** 34,800 volumes; 770 periodicals; 2867 technical reports. **Services:** Interlibrary loan; copying. **Publications:** Brief News on Semiconductor Literature - for internal distribution only; bibliographies.

★18257★
ACADEMIA SINICA - LIBRARY (Sci-Engr, Area-Ethnic)
Wangfu Dajie
Beijing, People's Republic of China Phone: 1 553052
Staff: 360. **Subjects:** Natural sciences, new technology, scientific and technical problems affecting the national economy and defence construction. **Special Collections:** District histories; collected works of the Ming and Qing dynasties; stone tablet rubbings (30,000). **Holdings:** 1.1 million volumes; 25,000 periodicals; 750,000 scientific and technical reports; 450,000 volumes of threadbound Chinese ancient books; international abstract and index journals; proceedings and publications of worldwide scientific research organizations.

ACADEMY OF ATHENS - HELLENIC FOLKLORE RESEARCH CENTER
See: Hellenic Folklore Research Center (18464)

★18258★
ACADEMY OF SCIENCES OF THE U.S.S.R. - ASTRONOMICAL COUNCIL - CENTER FOR ASTRONOMICAL DATA - LIBRARY (Sci-Engr)
Pjatnitskaya, 48 Phone: 233-17-02
109017 Moscow, Union of Soviet Socialist Republics
M.S. Nikitina, Chf. of Lib.
Founded: 1947. **Staff:** Prof 2. **Subjects:** Astronomy, physics, mathematics, mechanics, electronics, philosophy. **Holdings:** 23,387 books; 28,130 bound periodical volumes; 44 microfiche. **Subscriptions:** 63 journals and other serials. **Services:** Interlibrary loan; library open to the public. **Computerized Information Services:** Internal database. **Remarks:** An alternate telephone number is 231-54-61.

★18259★
ACADEMY OF SOCIAL AND POLITICAL SCIENCES - ART HISTORY INSTITUTE - LIBRARY (Area-Ethnic, Art)
Calei Victoriei 196 Phone: 0 50 56 80
Bucharest 1, Romania Alexandra Revenco, Libn.
Subjects: Romania - art and artists, fine arts, music, theater, cinema. **Holdings:** 49,500 volumes. **Also Known As:** Institutul de Istoria Artei.

ACADEMY OF SOCIAL AND POLITICAL SCIENCES - INSTITUTE FOR SOUTHEAST EUROPEAN STUDIES
See: Institute for Southeast European Studies (18526)

★18260★
ACADEMY OF TRADITIONAL CHINESE MEDICINE - LIBRARY (Med)
Haiyuncang
Dongzhimennei Phone: 1 446661
Beijing, People's Republic of China Geng Jianting, Dp.Libn.
Founded: 1955. **Staff:** 23. **Subjects:** Traditional Chinese medicine, medicine, science, applied technology, medical and pharmaceutical research. **Special Collections:** Traditional Chinese medicine (70,000 volumes; manuscripts from different dynasties, 13th-19th century). **Holdings:** 200,000 volumes; 1890 periodicals. **Services:** Copying. **Publications:** Journal of Traditional Chinese Medicine; Traditional Chinese Medicine Abstracts; Traditional Chinese Medicine Bulletin; Foreign Medical Sciences, Traditional Chinese Medical Science and Medicine Series. **Special Catalogs:** Union Catalog of Books on Traditional Chinese Medicine.

ACTON LIBRARY
See: University of Cambridge - Library (18846)

ADELAIDE CIRCULATING LIBRARY
See: State Library of South Australia - Special Collections (18794)

★18261★
AFRICA INSTITUTE OF SOUTH AFRICA - LIBRARY (Area-Ethnic, Soc Sci)
P.O. Box 630 Phone: 12 28-6970
Pretoria 0001, Republic of South Africa Elizabeth Wessels, Libn.
Subjects: South Africa - political stability, international relations, intra-regional cooperation, socioeconomic change, education in multicultural societies. **Holdings:** 50,000 volumes. **Remarks:** Maintained by South Africa - Department of National Education.

★18262★
AFRICAN REGIONAL ORGANIZATION FOR STANDARDIZATION - LIBRARY (Sci-Engr)
P.O. Box 57363
Nairobi, Kenya Phone: 2 24561
Subjects: Industrial and socioeconomic development through scientific and technological applications. **Holdings:** 50,000 volumes of standards and documentation. **Computerized Information Services:** Internal database. **Remarks:** Telex: 22097 ARSO. **Also Known As:** Organisation Regionale Africaine de Normalisation.

★18263★
AFRICAN TRAINING AND RESEARCH CENTRE IN ADMINISTRATION FOR DEVELOPMENT - LIBRARY (Soc Sci)
P.O. Box 310
19, Abou-Al-Alae Al-Maari Phone: 36430
Tangier, Morocco E.S. Asiedu, Chf.
Subjects: Africa - local government, rural and urban development, organizational development, human resources, personnel management, training, and financial, project, and public enterprises management. **Holdings:** 18,000 volumes. **Subscriptions:** 350 journals and other serials. **Services:** Microform copying; library open to African libraries and government agencies. **Computerized Information Services:** Produces African Network of Administrative Information. **Publications:** Subject bibliographies. **Also Known As:** Centre Africain de Formation et de Recherche Administratives pour le Developpement.

AGRICULTURAL RESEARCH INSTITUTE OF SENEGAL - DAKAR-THIAROYE CENTER FOR OCEANOGRAPHIC RESEARCH
See: Dakar-Thiaroye Center for Oceanographic Research (18376)

AHMADU BELLO UNIVERSITY - INSTITUTE FOR AGRICULTURAL RESEARCH
See: Institute for Agricultural Research (18496)

★18264★
AHMEDABAD TEXTILE INDUSTRY'S RESEARCH ASSOCIATION - ATIRA LIBRARY (Sci-Engr, Bus-Fin)
Polytechnic Post Office Phone: 442671
Ahmedabad 380 015, India P.C. Shah, Mgr., Lib. & Info.Serv.
Subjects: Textile industry - technology, management, new products and processes; increasing industry productivity, quality, economy. **Holdings:** 29,000 volumes.

AKADEMIO INTERNACIA DE LA SCIENCOJ
See: International Academy of Sciences (18532)

ALGERIA - MINISTRY OF PUBLIC HEALTH - PASTEUR INSTITUTE OF ALGERIA
See: Pasteur Institute of Algeria (18682)

ALL INDIA INSTITUTE OF HYGIENE AND PUBLIC HEALTH
See: India - Ministry of Health and Family Welfare (18488)

ALLPORT LIBRARY AND MUSEUM OF FINE ARTS
See: State Library of Tasmania (18795)

★18265★
LISANDRO ALVARADO FOUNDATION - LIBRARY (Soc Sci, Area-Ethnic)
Apartado Postal 4518 Phone: 23482
Maracay 2101-A, Venezuela Maria Romero, Libn.
Subjects: Lake Valencia region of Venezuela - archeology, anthropology, ethnology, history. **Holdings:** 19,000 volumes.

C.W. ANDERSEN LIBRARY
See: Australian Society of Accountants (18284)

★18266★
ARAB CENTER FOR THE STUDY OF ARID ZONES AND DRY LANDS - ACSAD LIBRARY (Agri)
P.O. Box 2440 Phone: 755713
Damascus, Syrian Arab Republic Ouni Jalahej, Libn.
Subjects: Arid zones agriculture. **Holdings:** 22,000 volumes. **Remarks:** Affiliated with League of Arab Countries; represents 16 Arab nations. Telex: 412697.

★18267★
ARAB GULF STATES INFORMATION DOCUMENTATION CENTER (Info Sci)
P.O. Box 5063 Phone: 5564171
Baghdad, Iraq Dr. Jasim M. Jirjees, Dir.Gen.
Founded: 1981. **Staff:** Prof 23; Other 7. **Subjects:** Affairs of the Arab Gulf States, mass media, information science, journalism, documentation, computation, library science. **Holdings:** 10,000 books in Arabic; 7000 books in English; 3708 microfiche; 492 reels of microfilm; 118 clipping files on microfiche; dissertations; video cassettes; audio cassettes; slides; photographs; maps. **Subscriptions:** 718 journals and other serials; 50 newspapers. **Services:** Interlibrary loan; copying; SDI; microfilming; center

open to member institutions, students, scholars, researchers. **Computerized Information Services:** DIALOG Information Services; internal databases. Performs searches free of charge. Contact Person: Mr. Ra'ad Mahmud Al Zubaidi, Hd., Comp.Dept.. **Publications:** Information Documentation Journal, biennial; The Center Guide, biennial; additional publications available. **Remarks:** Center is composed of the following member states: United Arab Emirates, Bahrain, Saudi Arabia, Iraq, Oman, Qatar, Kuwait. An alternate telephone number is 5555962. Telex: 213627 GIDAC. **Formerly:** Gulf States Information Documentation Center. **Staff:** Mrs. Najeeba Nafi' AlRawi, Chf.Libn.; Mrs. Janan Ibrahim, Libn.; Nidal Abas, Libn..

★18268★
ARAB ORGANIZATION OF ADMINISTRATIVE SCIENCES - LIBRARY (Bus-Fin)
P.O. Box 17159 Phone: 6 811394
Amman, Jordan Ms. Azza Hammad, Hd., Lib. & Doc.
Subjects: Public administration and policy, business administration, finance, accounting. **Holdings:** 18,000 books; 1500 bound periodical volumes. **Services:** Copying; library open to the public. **Publications:** Bibliography, semiannual. **Remarks:** Telex: 21594 AOAS JO.

ARBEJDERBEVAEGELSENS BIBLIOTEK OG ARKIV
See: Danish Federation of Trade Unions - Library and Archive (18378)

★18269★
ARCHITECTURAL ASSOCIATION - LIBRARY (Plan)
34/36 Bedford Square
London WC1B 3ES, England Phone: 1 6360974
Subjects: Architecture. **Special Collections:** Slide library. **Holdings:** 22,000 volumes, including rare books; 41,000 classified periodical articles; technical reference materials. **Subscriptions:** 300 journals and other serials.

ARCHIVES DE LA BASTILLE
See: France - Bibliotheque Nationale - Bibliotheque de l'Arsenal (18419)

ARCHIVES OF THE ORDER OF ST. JOHN OF JERUSALEM
See: The National Library of Malta (18638)

ARGENTINA - MINISTRY OF DEFENSE - NATIONAL DIRECTORATE OF THE ANTARCTIC - ARGENTINE ANTARCTIC INSTITUTE
See: Argentine Antarctic Institute (18272)

ARGENTINA - MINISTRY OF THE ECONOMY - OBISPO COLOMBRES AGRO-INDUSTRIAL EXPERIMENT STATION
See: Obispo Colombres Agro-Industrial Experiment Station (18667)

ARGENTINA - MINISTRY OF EDUCATION AND JUSTICE - MIGUEL LILLO FOUNDATION
See: Miguel Lillo Foundation - Information Center (18592)

★18270★
ARGENTINA - NATIONAL ATOMIC ENERGY COMMISSION - DIVISION OF TECHNICAL INFORMATION - LIBRARY (Energy)
Avenida de Libertador, 8250 Phone: 1 707711
1429 Buenos Aires, Argentina Elsa Butierrez, Hd. of Lib.
Subjects: Atomic energy, nuclear sciences. **Holdings:** 32,900 volumes; 286,000 microfiche; 77,500 reports; International Nuclear Information System (INIS) magnetic tapes. **Subscriptions:** 1600 journals and other serials. **Computerized Information Services:** Internal database. **Publications:** CNEA Reports, irregular; Technical Notes, irregular - both available on exchange; bibliographies.

★18271★
ARGENTINA - OFFICE OF THE SECRETARY-GENERAL OF THE NAVY - DEPARTMENT OF NAVAL HISTORICAL STUDIES - LIBRARY (Mil)
Jefatura del Estado Mayor General de la Armada
Avenida Almirante Brown 401 Phone: 1 362-1130
1155 Buenos Aires, Argentina Dora Martinez, Libn.
Subjects: World and Argentine naval history. **Holdings:** 5500 volumes.

ARGENTINA - SECRETARIAT OF CULTURE - NATIONAL INSTITUTE FOR THE STUDY OF THE THEATER
See: National Institute for the Study of the Theater (18630)

★18272★
ARGENTINE ANTARCTIC INSTITUTE - LIBRARY (Sci-Engr)
Cerrito 1248 Phone: 1 44-0071
1010 Buenos Aires, Argentina Nidia Chiesa, Libn.
Subjects: Geology, geophysics, seismology, glaciology, physical and chemical oceanography, radiation, human and comparative physiology, animal biology, limnology, geomagnetism, ionospheric physics, auroras. **Holdings:** 8000 volumes. **Remarks:** Maintained by Argentina - Ministry of Defense - National Directorate of the Antarctic. **Also Known As:** Instituto Antartico Argentino.

★18273★
ASIAN INSTITUTE OF TECHNOLOGY - LIBRARY AND REGIONAL DOCUMENTATION CENTER (Sci-Engr)
P.O. Box 2754 Phone: 2 5290100
Bangkok 10501, Thailand Mr. H.A. Vespry, Dir.
Subjects: Engineering - geotechnical, foundation, earthquake; soil and rock mechanics; engineering geology. **Holdings:** 200,000 volumes. **Subscriptions:** 1400 journals and other serials. **Services:** Library open to Asian institutions and organizations. **Computerized Information Services:** Produces Asian Information Center for Geotechnical Engineering. Performs searches on fee basis. **Publications:** Bibliographies. **Remarks:** Center provides geotechnical information to developing countries. Telex: 84276.

★18274★
ASIAN VEGETABLE RESEARCH AND DEVELOPMENT CENTER - LIBRARY (Agri)
P.O. Box 42
Shanhua Phone: 583-7801
Tainan 74199, Taiwan Mr. Teng-hui Hwang, Sr.Libn.
Subjects: Vegetables - tomato, chinese cabbage, sweet potato, soybean, mungbean, radish, mustard green, common bean, pepper, cauliflower; tropical agriculture; nutrition; appropriate technology; horticultural research; plant breeding; marketing. **Holdings:** 19,740 volumes. **Computerized Information Services:** Produces Tropical Vegetable Information Services database. **Remarks:** Sponsored by U.S. Agency for International Development, the Republic of China, the Federal Republic of Germany, Korea, Japan, Thailand, and the Philippines. Telex: 73560 AVRDC.

★18275★
ASIATIC RESEARCH CENTER - LIBRARY (Area-Ethnic, Soc Sci)
Korea University
1-5Ka Anam-dong
Sungbuk-ku Phone: 2 922-4117
Seoul, Republic of Korea Il-Sun Lee, Libn.
Subjects: Contemporary problems in Asia, Korean studies, pre-1949 China, Southeast Asia studies, Japanese studies, communist societies, international relations and security problems. **Holdings:** 100,000 volumes. **Remarks:** Center is a component of Korea University.

★18276★
ASOCIACION ARGENTINA DE CULTURA INGLESA - BIBLIOTECA (Hum)
Suipacha 1333 Phone: 3934864
Buenos Aires, 1011 Argentina Beatriz E. De Lome, Libn.
Subjects: English culture - literature, history, philosophy, art, music, architecture, theater, law. **Holdings:** 36,345 books. **Services:** Interlibrary loan; library not open to the public.

ASSOCIATION POUR LE DEVELOPPEMENT DE LA RIZICULTURE EN AFRIQUE DE L'OUEST
See: West Africa Rice Development Association (18871)

★18277★
ASSOCIATION FRANCAISE DE NORMALISATION - CENTRE DE DOCUMENTATION (Sci-Engr)
Tour Europe
Cedex 07 Phone: 1 42 91 5616
F-92080 Paris La Defense, France Jocelyne Laurent, Resp.
Subjects: Technology, food and agriculture, safety, standardization. **Holdings:** 3000 books; 600 bound periodical volumes; 5000 microforms; 450,000 standards and specifications. **Services:** SDI; center open to the public. **Computerized Information Services:** Telesystemes Questel, DIALOG Information Services, Bank Group for Automation in Management (G.CAM), Pergamon ORBIT InfoLine, Inc. Performs searches on fee basis. **Remarks:** Telex: 611 974 F.

ASSOCIATION INTERNATIONALE FUTURIBLES
See: Futuribles International (18432)

ASSOCIATION INTERNATIONALE DE RECHERCHE APICOLE
See: International Bee Research Association - Library (18536)

ASSOCIATION OF UNIVERSITIES FOR RESEARCH IN ASTRONOMY, INC. - CERRO TOLOLO INTER-AMERICAN OBSERVATORY
See: Cerro Tololo Inter-American Observatory (18343)

ASTRONOMISCHES RECHEN-INSTITUT
See: Institute for Astronomical Computations (18499)

★18278★
ATHENS TECHNOLOGICAL ORGANIZATION - ATHENS CENTER OF EKISTICS - LIBRARY (Soc Sci)
24 Strat. Syndesmou St. Phone: 1 3623-216
GR-106 73 Athens, Greece Rodney J. Rooke, Hd.Libn.
Subjects: Development of human settlements. **Holdings:** 35,000 volumes. **Remarks:** Telex: 215227.

★18279★
AUSTRALIA - DEPARTMENT OF THE ATTORNEY-GENERAL & JUSTICE - LAW COURTS LIBRARY (Law)
Law Courts Bldg., 15th Level Phone: 02 230-8232
Sydney, NSW 2000, Australia Lynn Pollack, Libn.
Subjects: Law. **Special Collections:** Judges' papers. **Holdings:** 20,936 books; 110,609 bound periodical volumes; 24,622 microforms. **Services:** Interlibrary loan; copying; library open to the public with restrictions. **Computerized Information Services:** CLIRS Information Services, SCALE, LEXIS, DIALOG Information Services, Pergamon ORBIT InfoLine, Inc., QL Systems, CAN/LAW, ESTOPL, AUSINET, I.P. Sharp Associates Limited. **Publications:** List of publications - available on request. **Staff:** Juliet Dennison, Rd.Serv.Libn..

★18280★
AUSTRALIA - DEPARTMENT OF DEFENCE - DEFENCE REGIONAL LIBRARY VICTORIA/TASMANIA (Mil, Sci-Engr)
Defence Centre
350 St. Kilda Rd. Phone: 613 697 5383
Melbourne, VIC 3004, Australia Ms. E. Alexander, Reg.Libn.
Subjects: Engineering, military history, electronics, computers, military art and science, management. **Holdings:** 20,000 books; 3000 historical materials; 150 microforms. **Services:** Interlibrary loan; copying; SDI; library open to the public with restrictions. **Computerized Information Services:** DIALOG Information Services, Pergamon ORBIT InfoLine, Inc., ESA/IRS, AUSINET, Australian Bibliographic Network (ABN), AUSTRALIS. **Remarks:** Library is part of the Defence Information Services (DIS) Network whose headquarters is in Canberra, Australia. It has over 85 member libraries.

AUSTRALIA - DEPARTMENT OF HOUSING AND CONSTRUCTION - NATIONAL BUILDING TECHNOLOGY CENTRE
See: National Building Technology Centre (18619)

AUSTRALIA - NATIONAL LIBRARY OF AUSTRALIA
See: National Library of Australia (18632)

AUSTRALIAN ATOMIC ENERGY COMMISSION
See: Australian Nuclear Science and Technology Organisation (18283)

★18281★
AUSTRALIAN CAPITAL TERRITORY DEPARTMENT OF SCIENCE - BUREAU OF METEOROLOGY RESEARCH CENTRE - LIBRARY (Sci-Engr)
150 Lonsdale St. Phone: 3 669-4000
Melbourne, VIC 3001, Australia Pamela Tonkin, Libn.
Subjects: Meteorology. **Holdings:** 70,000 volumes.

AUSTRALIAN CLEARING HOUSE FOR PUBLICATIONS IN RECREATION SPORT AND TOURISM
See: Footscray Institute of Technology - Library (18418)

AUSTRALIAN DEVELOPMENT ASSISTANCE BUREAU - INTERNATIONAL TRAINING INSTITUTE
See: International Training Institute - Learning Resources Centre (18561)

AUSTRALIAN MEDICAL ASSOCIATION LIBRARY
See: Cumberland Area Health Services - Westmead Hospital - AMA Library (18371)

★18282★
AUSTRALIAN NATIONAL GALLERY - LIBRARY (Art)
G.P.O. Box 1150 Phone: 62 712532
Canberra, ACT 2614, Australia J. Margaret Shaw, Prin.Libn.
Staff: Prof 5; Other 8. **Subjects:** Art - Australian, Aboriginal, pre-Columbian, contemporary; photography; prints; Ballets Russes; Indonesian textiles. **Holdings:** 70,000 books; 30,000 bound periodical volumes; 20,000 microforms; manuscripts; extensive documentation collection. **Subscriptions:** 1500 journals and other serials. **Services:** Interlibrary loan; copying; library open to the public with restrictions. **Automated Operations:** Computerized public access catalog and cataloging. **Computerized Information Services:** DIALOG Information Services, AUSINET, RLIN. Performs searches on fee basis. Contact Person: Joan Bruce, Doc.Libn., 712531. **Special Indexes:** Australian National Gallery Library List of Periodicals (ANGALLOP). **Remarks:** Telex: AA 61500; Fax: 62 712529. **Staff:** John Thomson, Dp. & Ser.Libn.; Gillian Currie, Hd.Cat.; Jeni Allenby, ILL Off..

AUSTRALIAN NATIONAL UNIVERSITY - JOHN CURTIN SCHOOL OF MEDICAL RESEARCH
See: John Curtin School of Medical Research (18372)

★18283★
AUSTRALIAN NUCLEAR SCIENCE AND TECHNOLOGY ORGANISATION - LUCAS HEIGHTS RESEARCH LABORATORIES - LIBRARY (Energy)
Private Mail Bag No. 1 Phone: 2 543 3111
Menai, NSW 2234, Australia Yvonne M. Long, Act.Hd.Libn.
Subjects: Atomic energy research, radioisotopes, radioactive waste disposal, nuclear medicine, radiation protection, oil shales. **Holdings:** 45,000 books; 15,000 bound periodical volumes; 250,000 patents and documents; 400,000 microforms. **Services:** Interlibrary loan; copying; SDI; library open to the public with restrictions. **Computerized Information Services:** DIALOG Information Services, STN International, Pergamon ORBIT InfoLine, Inc., MEDLINE, Australian Bibliographic Network (ABN), INIS (International Nuclear Information System). Performs searches on fee basis. Contact Person: Wendy Bartlett, Rd.Serv.Libn., 543-3935. **Publications:** AAEC reprint titles. **Special Indexes:** AAEC periodicals list. **Remarks:** Library located at New Illawarra Rd., Lucas Heights, NSW 2234. Library is the Australian input center for International Nuclear Information System (INIS). **Formerly:** Australian Atomic Energy Commission.

★18284★
AUSTRALIAN SOCIETY OF ACCOUNTANTS - C.W. ANDERSEN LIBRARY (Bus-Fin)
170 Queen St. Phone: 3 606 9606
Melbourne, VIC 3000, Australia Joyce Korn, Ctrl.Libn.
Founded: 1887. **Staff:** Prof 4; Other 3. **Subjects:** Accounting, company law, taxation, auditing. **Special Collections:** ASA archival materials. **Holdings:** 30,000 books; 5000 bound periodical volumes; 1000 microforms; 5000 ASA seminar papers. **Subscriptions:** 700 journals and other serials; 6 newspapers. **Services:** Interlibrary loan; copying; SDI; library open to the public with restrictions. **Automated Operations:** Computerized cataloging. **Computerized Information Services:** Internal database. **Publications:** Library accessions list, monthly with annual cumulation; periodical and serials list. **Special Indexes:** Index to The Australian Accountant; index to overseas journal articles in The Australian Accountant. **Staff:** Jill Bright, Ref.Libn.; Pat McGregor, Sys.Libn..

★18285★
AUSTRALIAN WAR MEMORIAL - RESEARCH CENTRE (Mil)
G.P.O. Box 345
Canberra, ACT 2601, Australia Phone: 62 434211
Subjects: Australian military history, Australian Defence Force history. **Holdings:** 50,000 books; 4000 serial titles; 850,000 photographs; 4000 film titles; 5000 sound recordings; 4000 meters of official and personal papers and archival materials. **Services:** Interlibrary loan; copying; center open to the public. **Publications:** A General Guide to the Library Collections and Archives; Roll Call: A Guide to Genealogical Sources in the Australian War Memorial; Bibliographies of Military History; A Guide to the Personal, Family and Official Papers of C.E.W. Bean. **Remarks:** Telex: 61986.

★18286★
AUSTRIA - FEDERAL MINISTRY OF AGRICULTURE AND FORESTRY - LIBRARY (Agri, Biol Sci)
Stubenring 1 Phone: 222-7500
A-1011 Vienna, Austria Ingrid Gruner
Subjects: Agriculture, forestry, plant and animal production, environmental contaminants, agrarian policies, wildlife, hunting, vegetation and watershed management, farm mechanization, standardization. **Special Collections:** Torrent control (avalanches); Royal and Imperial Ministry of Agriculture collection (10,000 books). **Holdings:** 94,000 books; 526 bound periodical volumes. **Services:** Interlibrary loan; library open to the public with restrictions. **Also Known As:** Bundesministerium fur Land- und Forstwirtschaft.

AUSTRIA - MINISTRY OF FOREIGN AFFAIRS - DIPLOMATIC ACADEMY OF VIENNA
See: Diplomatic Academy of Vienna (18385)

AUSTRIA - MINISTRY OF SCIENCE & RESEARCH - GEOLOGICAL SURVEY OF AUSTRIA
See: Geological Survey of Austria (18436)

★18287★
AUSTRIAN INSTITUTE OF EAST AND SOUTHEAST EUROPEAN STUDIES - LIBRARY (Area-Ethnic)
Josefsplatz 6 Phone: 222 512 18 95
A-1010 Vienna, Austria Walter Lukan, Libn.
Subjects: East Europe - history, geography, economics, education and cultural relations, political science. **Holdings:** 23,500 books. **Subscriptions:** 800 journals and other serials. **Services:** Copying; library open to the public. **Remarks:** An alternate telephone number is 222 52 43 28. **Also Known As:** Oesterreichisches Ost- und Sudosteuropa-Institut.

B

BADEN-WURTEMBERG STÅTE MINISTRY OF SCIENCE AND ART - INSTITUTE FOR ASTRONOMICAL COMPUTATIONS
See: Institute for Astronomical Computations (18499)

BAHA'I WORLD CENTRE
See: The Universal House of Justice (18834)

BALAI BESAR PENELITIAN DAN PENGEMBANGAN INDUSTRI KERAJINAN DAN BATIK
See: Institute for Research and Development of Handicraft and Batik Industries (18520)

BANGLADESH - MINISTRY OF AGRICULTURE - AGRICULTURE AND FORESTRY DIVISION - BANGLADESH JUTE RESEARCH INSTITUTE
See: Bangladesh Jute Research Institute (18289)

★18288★
BANGLADESH AGRICULTURAL UNIVERSITY - COMMITTEE FOR ADVANCED STUDIES AND RESEARCH - LIBRARY (Agri)
Mymensingh, Bangladesh Abdun Nur, Libn.
Subjects: Agricultural economics and engineering, livestock, fisheries. **Holdings:** 71,000 volumes.

★18289★
BANGLADESH JUTE RESEARCH INSTITUTE - LIBRARY (Agri)
Manik Miah Ave.
Dacca 7, Bangladesh Abdur Rouf Mian, Libn.
Subjects: Jute, kenaf, and mesta fibers - production, development, technology. **Holdings:** 3800 volumes. **Subscriptions:** 1500 journals and other serials. **Remarks:** Maintained by Bangladesh - Ministry of Agriculture - Agriculture and Forestry Division.

★18290★
BATTELLE INSTITUTE E.V. - LIBRARY (Sci-Engr, Soc Sci)
Am Romerhof 35
Postfach 900160 Phone: 69 7908 2210
D-6000 Frankfurt am Main 90, Federal Republic of Germany
Dr. Wolfgang Kuhn, Libn.
Staff: Prof 4. **Subjects:** Physics, chemistry, biology, information processing, materials technology, economics, social sciences, energy and transportation systems. **Holdings:** 60,000 books; 50,000 bound periodical volumes. **Subscriptions:** 330 journals and other serials. **Services:** Copying; library open to the public by prior application.

BAVARIAN STATE MINISTRY FOR EDUCATION AND CULTURE - EAST EUROPEAN INSTITUTE, MUNICH
See: East European Institute, Munich (18389)

BAVARIAN STATE MINISTRY FOR SCIENCE AND CULTURE - INSTITUTE OF CONTEMPORARY HISTORY
See: Institute of Contemporary History (18502)

EVAN BEDFORD LIBRARY OF CARDIOLOGY
See: Royal College of Physicians of London - Library (18739)

★18291★
BEIJING AGRICULTURAL UNIVERSITY - LIBRARY (Agri, Biol Sci)
2 West Yuanmingyuan Lu Phone: 1 281103
Beijing, People's Republic of China Yang Zhimin, Dp.Libn.
Founded: 1949. **Staff:** 27. **Subjects:** Agriculture; genetic crop breeding; plant physiology, biochemistry, pathology; entomology; agricultural microbiology; animal husbandry; veterinary medicine; allied sciences and technology. **Special Collections:** Chinese and foreign publications on plant pathology, entomology, veterinary parasitology, pesticides, plant physiology and biochemistry, genetic breeding, fertilizers; ancient Chinese agricultural works (300 titles). **Holdings:** 404,982 volumes; 4211 periodicals. **Services:** Interlibrary loan; copying. **Publications:** Bulletin of Beijing Agricultural University; Journal of Plant Protection; Journal of Animal Breeding and Veterinary Medicine. **Remarks:** Includes the holdings of the former Tsin Hwa University, Peking University, North China University, and the Catholic University Agricultural Faculty.

★18292★
BEIJING COLLEGE OF LINGUISTICS - LIBRARY (Hum)
Dongsheng Lu
Haidian District Phone: 1 277531
Beijing, People's Republic of China Li Xinmin, Dp.Libn.
Founded: 1961. **Staff:** 26. **Subjects:** Chinese, English, French, Japanese, Spanish, German, and Arabian languages; philology; literature. **Holdings:** 303,675 volumes; 1097 periodicals; 1100 AV programs and microforms; threadbound ancient Chinese books. **Services:** Copying.

★18293★
BEIJING FILM ACADEMY - LIBRARY (Theater)
Zhuxinzhuang
Shahe
Beijing, People's Republic of China Phone: 1 275631
Founded: 1956. **Staff:** 16. **Subjects:** Literature, art, cinema. **Special Collections:** Playscripts (Chinese and translations of foreign movies; 4000 volumes). **Holdings:** 87,200 volumes; 291 periodicals; bound volumes of pre-Liberation movie magazines; slides; photographs. **Services:** Copying.

★18294★
BEIJING INSTITUTE OF FOREIGN TRADE - LIBRARY (Bus-Fin)
Xiaoguan
Andingmenwai Phone: 1 462161
Beijing, People's Republic of China Wang Zhihua, Libn.
Founded: 1954. **Staff:** 42. **Subjects:** World economics, international trade, languages. **Special Collections:** Remarkable editions of Chinese and foreign books (Chinese block-printed editions and hand copies of Ming and Qing dynasties; foreign editions of customhouse publications; 5000 volumes); Chinese customhouse publications, 1850s-1949. **Holdings:** 310,000 volumes; 604 periodicals. **Services:** Copying.

★18295★
BEIJING PETROLEUM DESIGN INSTITUTE - LIBRARY (Energy)
P.O. Box 10053 Phone: 1 445261
Beijing, People's Republic of China Qian Peiliang, Libn.
Staff: 8. **Subjects:** Petroleum processing; petrochemical technology, devices, equipment, machinery; oil product storage and transportation; water supply and drainage; heat; electricity; building structure; earthquake engineering; waste treatment; computers. **Holdings:** 160,000 volumes; 1000 periodicals; 5000 technical reports; 100 AV programs and microforms.

★18296★
BEIJING UNIVERSITY - LIBRARY (Soc Sci, Rel-Phil, Hum)
Haidian District Phone: 1 282471
Beijing, People's Republic of China Xie Daoyuan, Libn.
Founded: 1902. **Subjects:** Philosophy, politics, economics, language, literature, history, history of philosophy, history of literature. **Special Collections:** Chinese ancient books (1.6 million volumes); books in English, French, German, Spanish (500,000); Japanese books (200,000); Complete Works of Shakespeare, 1623; Dante; Schiller. **Holdings:** 3.3 million volumes; 15,000 back issues of periodicals. **Subscriptions:** 7000 journals and other serials. **Special Catalogs:** Catalog of Remarkable Edition Books Held by the Library; Catalog of Chinese History Books Held by the Library. **Special Indexes:** Subject index to Lu Xun's Articles.

★18297★
BELGIUM - MINISTRY OF ECONOMIC AFFAIRS - FONDS QUETELET LIBRARY (Soc Sci)
6, rue de l'Industrie Phone: 2 5127950
B-1040 Brussels, Belgium G. De Saedeleer, Hd.Libn.
Subjects: Economics, social sciences, statistics. **Holdings:** 600,000 volumes. **Subscriptions:** 3000 journals and other serials. **Services:** Library open to the public. **Computerized Information Services:** Internal database. Performs searches on fee basis.

★18298★
BELGIUM - MINISTRY OF NATIONAL EDUCATION - BIBLIOTHEQUE ROYALE DE BELGIQUE (Info Sci)
4, Boulevard de l'Empereur Phone: 2 519 53 11
B-1000 Brussels, Belgium Denise De Weerdt, Chef
Subjects: Library science, bibliography. **Special Collections:** Incunabula and early imprints; manuscripts (37,000); maps; Belgian music; engravings; coins and medals. **Holdings:** 2.9 million volumes. **Services:** Interlibrary loan; copying; SDI; library open to the public. **Computerized Information**

Services: BELINDIS, O.R.I., DIMDI, STN International, GENIOS, Data-Star, ESA/IRS, Telesystemes Questel, Juridial, GCAM, BNDO, Electronic Data Systems Ltd. (EDS), BLAISE Online Services, Finsbury Data Services Ltd., Datasolve Ltd., I/S Datacentralen (DC), ECHO, CELEX, DIALOG Information Services, Pergamon ORBIT InfoLine, Inc., CAS ONLINE, INFORDOC. Performs searches free of charge. Contact Person: Catherina Pletinckx-Oukhow. **Publications:** Bibliographie de Belgique, quarterly; bulletin, quarterly; additional publications available. **Special Catalogs:** Catalogue des manuscrits de la Bibliotheque royale de Belgique, 8/year; additional catalogs available. **Also Known As:** Bibliotheque Royale Albert 1er; Koninklijke Bibliotheek Albert I. **Staff:** Martin Wittek, Chf.Cons..

★18299★
BELGIUM - MINISTRY OF NATIONAL EDUCATION - GEMBLOUX STATE FACILITY OF AGRICULTURAL SCIENCES - LIBRARY (Agri)
B-5800 Gembloux, Belgium Phone: 61 29 58
Mrs. L. William, Libn.
Subjects: Agronomy, biology, soil and environmental sciences, animal and plant products, engineering, economics. **Holdings:** 100,000 volumes. **Also Known As:** Faculte des Sciences Agronomiques de l'Etat.

BELGIUM - MINISTRY OF NATIONAL EDUCATION - ROYAL BELGIAN OBSERVATORY
See: Royal Belgian Observatory (18733)

★18300★
BERMUDA BIOLOGICAL STATION FOR RESEARCH, INC. - EDWARD LAURENS MARK MEMORIAL LIBRARY (Biol Sci)
17 Biological Station Lane Phone: (809)29 71880
Ferry Reach GE 01, Bermuda A. Chiltern-Hunt, Libn.
Founded: 1947. **Staff:** Prof 1. **Subjects:** Marine biology and ecology, oceanography, geology. **Special Collections:** Bermuda Biological Station Special Publications (set of 28); Bermuda Biological Station Contributions (numbers 1 to 1000). **Holdings:** 16,000 volumes. **Subscriptions:** 154 journals and other serials. **Services:** Interlibrary loan; copying; library open to the public for reference use only. **Computerized Information Services:** DIALOG Information Services, Telemail. **Publications:** List of publications - available on request.

BERNHARD-NOCHT-INSTITUT FUER SCHIFFS- UND TROPENKRANKHEITEN
See: Bernhard Nocht Institute for Nautical and Tropical Medicine (18662)

★18301★
BHANDARKAR ORIENTAL RESEARCH INSTITUTE - LIBRARY (Area-Ethnic)
Pune 411004, India Phone: 56936
Prof. R.N. Dandekar, Dir.
Subjects: Sanskrit, Indology. **Holdings:** 50,000 books; 20,000 manuscripts. **Remarks:** Affiliated with University of Poona.

BIBLIOTECA CARLOS MONGE ALFARO
See: Universidad de Costa Rica - Direccion de Bibliotecas Documentacion e Informacion (18838)

BIBLIOTECA LUCCHESI PALLI
See: Italy - Ministero beni Cultrali - Biblioteca Nazionale Vittorio Emanuele III (18565)

BIBLIOTECA LUIS DEMETRIO TINOCO
See: Universidad de Costa Rica - Direccion de Bibliotecas Documentacion e Informacion (18838)

BIBLIOTECA NACIONAL JOSE MARTI
See: Cuba - Ministerio de Cultura (18369)

BIBLIOTECA NAZIONALE VITTORIO EMANUELE III
See: Italy - Ministero beni Cultrali - Biblioteca Nazionale Vittorio Emanuele III (18565)

BIBLIOTEKO HECTOR HODLER
See: Universala Esperanto-Asocio (18835)

BIBLIOTHEEK KONINKLIJKE NEDERLANDSE AKADEMIE VAN WETENSCHAPPEN
See: Royal Netherlands Academy of Arts and Sciences - Library (18747)

BIBLIOTHEEK VAN HET RUUSBROECGENOOTSCHAP
See: Universiteit Antwerpen - Universitaire Faculteiten Sint-Ignatius Antwerpen (18842)

★18302★
BIBLIOTHEQUE HISTORIQUE DE LA VILLE DE PARIS (Hist)
24, rue Pavee Phone: 1 42 74 44 44
F-75004 Paris, France M. Jean Derens, Chf.Cons.
Subjects: History of Paris, French Revolution, theater. **Special Collections:** Feminism; Dreyfus Affair; Jules Michelet; George Sand. **Holdings:** 700,000 books; 6000 bound periodical volumes; 200 microforms; 6000 volumes of manuscripts. **Services:** Copying; library open to the public. **Publications:** Publications de la Commission des Travaux historiques; Bulletin de la Bibliotheque et des Travaux Historiques. **Remarks:** Maintained by the city of Paris. **Staff:** Maria Deurbergue, Cons.; Maryse Goldemberg, Cons..

★18303★
BIBLIOTHEQUE NATIONALE ET UNIVERSITAIRE DE STRASBOURG (Hum, Sci-Engr, Law, Med)
5, rue du Marechal Joffre
Boite Postale 1029/F Phone: 88360068
F-67070 Strasbourg Cedex, France Lily Greiner, Cons. en chef/Adm.
Subjects: Humanities, science and technology, medicine, law, France. **Special Collections:** Regional collections; manuscripts; incunabula; papyrii; cuneiform tablets; ostraca; coins and medals. **Holdings:** 3 million books; maps; plans; seals; photographs. **Subscriptions:** 6076 journals and other serials. **Services:** Interlibrary loan; copying; library open to the public. **Computerized Information Services:** Online systems. Performs searches on fee basis. **Publications:** Bibliographie alsacienne; Papyrus grecs de la B.N.U.S. **Special Catalogs:** Catalogues collectifs de periodiques. **Remarks:** Library is part of France - Ministere de l'Education Nationale - Direction des Bibliotheques, des Musees et de l'Information Technique et Scientifique.

BIBLIOTHEQUE ROYALE ALBERT 1ER
See: Belgium - Ministry of National Education - Bibliotheque Royale de Belgique (18298)

BIBLIOTHEQUE DE LA SORBONNE
See: Universites de Paris I, III, IV, V, VII (18843)

BOLIVIA - MINISTRY OF AGRICULTURE AND CAMPESINO AFFAIRS - BOLIVIAN INSTITUTE OF AGRICULTURAL TECHNOLOGY
See: Bolivian Institute of Agricultural Technology (18305)

★18304★
BOLIVIAN INSTITUTE OF AGRICULTURAL TECHNOLOGY - INFORMATION CENTER (Agri)
Mendez Arcos No. 710 (Sopocahi) Phone: 2 370883
La Paz, Bolivia Danilsa Saravia Nieves, Lib.Hd.
Founded: 1975. **Staff:** Prof 8; Other 5. **Subjects:** Soils, seeds, husbandry health, agricultural economics, cereals. **Special Collections:** Agricultural Yearbook (magazines); annual research report. **Holdings:** 2548 books; 48 bound periodical volumes. **Subscriptions:** 12 journals and other serials; 7 newspapers. **Services:** Interlibrary loan; copying; center open to the public. **Automated Operations:** Computerized public access catalog and cataloging. **Publications:** Alerta, monthly. **Special Catalogs:** High Plateau Products. **Special Indexes:** Index of forages, soil, water, plant disease, etc. **Staff:** Hernan Rocabado.

★18305★
BOLIVIAN INSTITUTE OF AGRICULTURAL TECHNOLOGY - LIBRARY (Agri)
Casilla 5783
Avenida Camacho, 1471 Phone: 2 374289
La Paz, Bolivia Carmen Sotelo De Salazar, Libn.
Subjects: Oil-bearing plants, tropical and Andean crops, plant and animal breeding, horticulture, maize, sorghum and beans, tuber crops, wheat, rural sociology. **Holdings:** 40,000 volumes. **Remarks:** Maintained by Bolivia - Ministry of Agriculture and Campesino Affairs. **Also Known As:** Instituto Boliviano de Tecnologia Agropecuaria.

★18306★
JULES BORDET INSTITUTE - LIBRARY (Med)
1, rue Heger-Bordet Phone: 2 537 33 28
B-1000 Brussels, Belgium A. Bormans, Libn.
Subjects: Hematology, cancer, infectious diseases, endocrinology, pharmacology, experimental chemotherapy. **Holdings:** 75,000 volumes.

Remarks: Institute is the tumor center of Brussels University Medical School. **Also Known As:** Institut Jules Bordet.

★18307★
BOTANIC GARDENS OF ADELAIDE AND STATE HERBARIUM - LIBRARY (Biol Sci)
North Terrace Phone: 228 2320
Adelaide, SA, Australia Miss Gaye Denny, Libn.
Subjects: Taxonomic botany, applied horticulture, plant pathology. **Special Collections:** Floral Collection (440,775 specimens). **Holdings:** 19,370 volumes. **Remarks:** Maintained by Government of South Australia.

★18308★
BOTSWANA MINISTRY OF FINANCE AND DEVELOPMENTAL PLANNING - BOTSWANA TECHNOLOGY CENTER - LIBRARY (Sci-Engr)
Private Bag 0082 Phone: 314161
Gaborone, Botswana Tiro Maphage, Libn.
Subjects: Renewable energy sources, small-scale production, electronics, food processing, information collection and dissemination. **Holdings:** 3500 books. **Subscriptions:** 180 journals and other serials. **Remarks:** Telex: 2928.

★18309★
BRAZIL - MINISTERIO DA CULTURA - BIBLIOTECA NACIONAL (Info Sci)
Fundacao Nacional Pro-Memoria
Avenida Rio Branco, 219-39 Phone: 21 240 9229
Rio de Janeiro 20042, Brazil Elaine Perez, Hd., Info.Doc.Sect.
Subjects: General collection. **Special Collections:** Colecao Barbosa Machado; Colecao Conde da Barca; Colecao de Angelis; Colecao Salvador de Mendonca; Colecao Jose Antonio Marques; Colecao Teresa Cristina Maria; Colecao Wallenstein; Colecao Benedito Otoni. **Holdings:** 4 million books; 22,147 bound periodical volumes; 130,139 documents; 253,185 reels of microfilm, phonograph records, photographs, pieces of sheet music; 657,000 manuscripts. **Services:** Copying; SDI; library open to the public. **Publications:** List of publications available. **Staff:** Maria Alice Barroso, Gen.Dir..

★18310★
BRAZIL - MINISTRY OF AGRICULTURE - NATIONAL CENTER FOR AGRICULTURAL DOCUMENTARY INFORMATION - LIBRARY (Agri)
Caixa Postal 10.2432
Anexo I, Bloca B, Ala Oeste
70043 Brasilia DF, Brazil Phone: 61 2251101
Subjects: Agriculture, allied areas of natural science, technology, history, legislation. **Holdings:** 45,000 volumes; 190,000 documents on microfiche; 69,000 computer records. **Subscriptions:** 6700 serials. **Computerized Information Services:** AGROBASE (internal database). Performs searches on fee basis. **Publications:** Bibliografia Brasileira de Agricultura; Levantamentos Bibliograficos; additional publications available. **Also Known As:** Centro Nacional de Informacao Documental Agricola.

★18311★
BRAZIL - MINISTRY OF HEALTH - INSTITUTE OF HEALTH - LIBRARY (Med)
Avenida Dr. Eneas de Carvalho
Aguiar, 188-6
Caixa Postal 8027 Phone: 11 282-0962
Sao Paulo, Brazil Astrid B. Wiesel, Libn.
Subjects: Public health, health education, leprosy, tuberculosis, ophthalmology, mother and child care, nutrition, social medicine. **Holdings:** 40,000 volumes. **Also Known As:** Instituto de Saude.

BRAZIL - NATIONAL COUNCIL OF SCIENTIFIC AND TECHNOLOGICAL DEVELOPMENT
See: National Council of Scientific and Technological Development (18620)

BRAZIL - SECRETARY OF STATE FOR HEALTH - BUTANTAN INSTITUTE
See: Butantan Institute (18328)

★18312★
BRAZILIAN AGRICULTURAL RESEARCH CORPORATION - AGRICULTURAL RESEARCH CENTER FOR THE HUMID TROPICS - LIBRARY (Biol Sci)
Caixa Postal 48 Phone: 226-1941
66000 Belem, Brazil Celia Maria Lopes Pereira, Libn.
Subjects: Animal pathology, climatology, entomology, botany, phytopathology. **Holdings:** 150,000 volumes. **Also Known As:** Empresa Brasileira de Pesquisa Agropecuria - Centro de Pesquisa Agropecuaria do Tropica Umido.

★18313★
BRAZILIAN AGRICULTURAL RESEARCH CORPORATION - NATIONAL CENTER FOR AGRICULTURAL AND AGROINDUSTRIAL FOOD TECHNOLOGY - INFORMATION AND DOCUMENTATION SECTION (Food-Bev)
Avenida das Americas, 29501
Guaratiba Phone: 21 310 1353
23020 Rio de Janeiro, Brazil Maria Ruth Martins Leao, Libn.
Subjects: Food technology and science, chemistry, fats and oils, natural products, essential oils. **Holdings:** 5500 books; 22,000 bound periodical volumes; 800 patents; 250 dissertations; Chemical Abstracts, 1907 to present; Food Science & Technology Abstracts, 1969 to present; Food Science Abstracts, 1950 to present; Nutrition Abstracts, 1970 to present; Microbiology Abstracts, 1970 to present; Nucleic Acid Abstracts, 1971 to present. **Subscriptions:** 400 journals and other serials; 10 newspapers. **Services:** Interlibrary loan; copying; SDI. **Publications:** List of publications available. **Also Known As:** Empresa Brasileira de Pesquisa Agropecuaria - Centro Nacional de Pesquisa de Tecnologia Agroindustrial de Alimentos. **Staff:** Maria da Graca M. Silva, Abstractor.

BRAZILIAN INSTITUTE FOR INFORMATION IN SCIENCE AND TECHNOLOGY
See: National Council of Scientific and Technological Development (18620)

★18314★
BRION RESEARCH INSTITUTE OF TAIWAN - LIBRARY (Med)
116 Chung-ching South Rd., Section 3 Phone: 2 303 4828
Taipei 10743, Taiwan Yuchen Kao, Libn.
Subjects: Pharmaceuticals, Chinese medicine, herbs. **Holdings:** 30,000 volumes. **Remarks:** Affiliated with the Oriental Healing Arts Institute of Palo Alto, CA, USA.

BRITISH AND FOREIGN BIBLE SOCIETY LIBRARY
See: University of Cambridge - Library (18846)

★18315★
BRITISH INSTITUTE OF ARCHAEOLOGY AT ANKARA - LIBRARY (Soc Sci)
Tahran Caddesi 24, Kavaklidere Phone: 275487
Ankara, Turkey Dr. David H. French, Dir.
Subjects: Archeology in Turkey, epigraphy. **Holdings:** 20,000 volumes.

★18316★
BRITISH INSTITUTE OF MANAGEMENT - MANAGEMENT INFORMATION CENTRE (Bus-Fin)
Management House
Cottingham Rd. Phone: 536 204222
Corby, Northants NN17 1TT, England Bob Norton, Hd., Info.Serv.
Staff: Prof 11; Other 6. **Subjects:** Management, personnel management, education and training, industrial relations. **Special Collections:** Institute archives. **Holdings:** 70,000 books. **Subscriptions:** 400 journals and other serials. **Services:** Interlibrary loan; copying; SDI (all limited); center open to the public for reference use only. **Computerized Information Services:** DIALOG Information Services, Pergamon ORBIT InfoLine, Inc., Datasolve Ltd., BLAISE Online Services; ASSASSIN (internal database). Performs searches on fee basis. Contact Person: Jennie Butters, Prin.Info.Off.. **Publications:** Bibliographies; journals bulletin; acquisitions bulletin; management information notes and topics; general publications in information management. **Staff:** Sharon Barker, Prin.Libn.; Nick Parker, Libn.; Kate Rungman, Libn.; Sandra Yarwood, Libn.; Lorna Stewart, Libn.; Cathy Smith, Sr.Info.Off.; Simon Gotts, Sr.Info.Off.; Debbie Ellis, Sr.Info.Off.; Angela Haddon, Sr.Info.Off..

★18317★
BRITISH LIBRARY - HUMANITIES AND SOCIAL SCIENCES DIVISION - DEPARTMENT OF WESTERN MANUSCRIPTS (Hum)
Great Russell St. Phone: 1 636-1544
London WC1B 3DG, England Mrs. S.J. Tyacke, Dir. of Spec.Coll.
Subjects: Western manuscripts. **Special Collections:** Music; maps; topographical drawings; seals; ostraca. **Holdings:** 272,826 manuscripts; 4132 microforms. **Services:** Copying; department open to the public with restrictions. **Special Catalogs:** Catalogs of additional manuscripts published to 1955; catalogs of Arundel, Burney, Cotton, Harleian, Hargrave, Lansdowne, Royal, and Stowe Manuscripts. **Special Indexes:** Amalgamated index.

★18318★
BRITISH LIBRARY - HUMANITIES AND SOCIAL SCIENCES DIVISION - ORIENTAL COLLECTIONS (Area-Ethnic)
14 Store St. Phone: 1 636-1544
London WC1E 7DG, England Dr. Albertine Gaur, Dp.Dir.
Staff: Prof 24; Other 31. **Subjects:** Humanities and social sciences in the languages of Asia and North and Northeast Africa (350 languages or language groups represented). **Special Collections:** Early imprints; rare manuscripts. **Holdings:** 660,000 books; 7500 serial titles; 1100 newspapers; 5000 microforms; 42,000 manuscripts. **Services:** Interlibrary loan; copying; collections open to the public with readers' pass. **Computerized Information Services:** BLAISE Online Services. **Publications:** Newsletter, semiannual; annual report. **Remarks:** Department houses the national collections of books and manuscripts from Asia and North and Northeast Africa. **Formerly:** Department of Oriental Manuscripts and Printed Books.

BRITISH LIBRARY OF POLITICAL AND ECONOMIC SCIENCE
See: London School of Economics (18596)

★18319★
BRITISH MARITIME TECHNOLOGY LTD. - LIBRARY (Trans, Sci-Engr)
Wallsend Research Station
Wallsend Phone: 91 2625242
Tyne and Wear NE28 6UY, England J.G. Kerr, Tech.Info.Mgr.
Founded: 1945. **Staff:** Prof 3; Other 4. **Subjects:** Ship operation, offshore engineering, ship/offshore design, ocean engineering, fluid mechanics, maritime technology. **Holdings:** 5000 books; 500 bound periodical volumes; 30,000 other cataloged items. **Subscriptions:** 403 journals and other serials. **Services:** Interlibrary loan; copying; SDI; library open to the public with restrictions. **Automated Operations:** Computerized cataloging. **Computerized Information Services:** Internal database. Performs searches on fee basis. **Publications:** BMT Abstracts, monthly - by subscription. **Formerly:** British Ship Research Association. **Staff:** B.M. Miller, Libn..

★18320★
BRITISH MUSEUM (Natural History) - DEPARTMENT OF LIBRARY SERVICES (Biol Sci)
Cromwell Rd. Phone: 1 589-6323
London SW7 5BD, England Mr. R. Banks, Hd. of Lib.Serv.
Subjects: Natural history, zoology, botany, entomology, paleontology, mineralogy, ornithology. **Special Collections:** Linnaeus; Walsingham; Tweeddale; Owen; Sowerby; Gunther; Rothschild. **Holdings:** 800,000 books; 22,000 periodical titles; 20,000 microforms; 72,000 maps; 375,000 prints and drawings; 20,000 manuscripts. **Subscriptions:** 9000 journals and other serials. **Services:** Copying; department open to the public. **Computerized Information Services:** DIALOG Information Services, BLAISE Online Services. Performs searches on fee basis. Contact Person: Ms. Goodman, 589-6323, ext. 382. **Publications:** A Short History of the Libraries and List of Manuscripts and Original Drawings in the British Museum (Natural History). **Special Catalogs:** A Catalogue of the Richard Owen Collection of Palaeontological and Zoological Drawings in the British Museum (Natural History); Catalogue of the Drawings from Captain Cook's First Voyage; list of manuscripts and drawings; catalog of portraits.

BRITISH SHIP RESEARCH ASSOCIATION
See: British Maritime Technology Ltd. (18319)

BRITISH STANDARDS INSTITUTION
See: BSI (18321)

BRUSSELS UNIVERSITY - MEDICAL SCHOOL - JULES BORDET INSTITUTE
See: Jules Bordet Institute (18306)

★18321★
BSI - LIBRARY AND INFORMATION DEPARTMENT (Sci-Engr)
Linford Wood Phone: 908 220022
Milton Keynes, Bucks., MK14 6LE, England
Mrs. F.E. Abrams, Chf.Libn.
Staff: Prof 11; Other 9. **Subjects:** Standards, codes of practice, laws, regulations, and other technical requirements affecting the design, operation, or performance of a piece of equipment or a service; systems for certification, approval, or compliance. **Holdings:** 2000 volumes; 500,000 British, international, and foreign standards, technical regulations, specifications. **Subscriptions:** 400 journals and other serials. **Services:** Interlibrary loan; copying; SDI; translations; library open to members for reference use only. **Computerized Information Services:** DIALOG Information Services, Deutsches Informationszentrum fur Technische Regeln (DITR), Normes et Reglements Informations Automatisees Accessibles en Ligne (NORIANE), CAN-STAN; produces STANDARDLINE. Performs searches on fee basis (for members). Contact Person: Mrs. P. Heffernan, Serv.Libn., 220022, ext. 2032. **Publications:** Worldwide Standards Information (SDI service of new British and overseas standards added to the BSI Library, arranged by subject and country), monthly - by subscription; Overseas Standards Updating Service (members' lists of standards documents monitored for revisions, changes, etc.), monthly - by subscription. **Formerly:** British Standards Institution. **Staff:** Miss H. Ward, Sys.Libn..

BUCHAREST UNIVERSITY - INSTITUTE FOR SOUTHEAST EUROPEAN STUDIES
See: Institute for Southeast European Studies (18526)

★18322★
BULGARIA - COMMITTEE OF CULTURE - CYRIL AND METHODIUS NATIONAL LIBRARY (Area-Ethnic, Info Sci)
Blvd. Tolbuhin 11 Phone: 2 88-28-11
BG-1504 Sofia, Bulgaria Peter Karaangov, Info.Off.
Subjects: General collection. **Special Collections:** Music collection (41,684 items); graphic arts collection (115,291 items); archival collection (3.03 million archival materials); official publications (389,287). **Holdings:** 1.4 million books; 647,416 bound periodical volumes; 283,720 patents; 23,933 tapes and phonograph records; 214,024 microforms; 10,262 cartographic materials; 18,699 unpublished materials; 5206 manuscripts. **Services:** Interlibrary loan; copying; library open to the public with restrictions. **Publications:** National Bibliography of Bulgaria; Proceedings of the Cyril and Methodius National Library, annual; Bibliotekar, monthly. **Special Indexes:** Index of Bulgarian books; index of Bulgarian periodicals. **Remarks:** Serves as the National Library of Bulgaria. **Staff:** Dr. Alexandra Stojanova, Hd., Info.Ctr..

BULGARIA - MINISTRY OF NATIONAL EDUCATION - GEORGI DIMITROV HIGHER INSTITUTE OF PHYSICAL CULTURE
See: Georgi Dimitrov Higher Institute of Physical Culture (18384)

BULGARIA - MINISTRY OF NATIONAL EDUCATION - V.I. LENIN HIGHER INSTITUTE OF MECHANICAL AND ELECTRICAL ENGINEERING
See: V.I. Lenin Higher Institute of Mechanical and Electrical Engineering - Library (18590)

★18323★
BULGARIA MEDICAL ACADEMY - CENTER FOR SCIENTIFIC INFORMATION IN MEDICINE AND PUBLIC HEALTH - CENTRAL MEDICAL LIBRARY (Med)
1 Georgi Sofijski St.
BG-1431 Sofia, Bulgaria Phone: 2 522342
Subjects: Medicine, public health. **Holdings:** 600,000 volumes. **Subscriptions:** 7147 journals and other serials. **Services:** SDI; library open to the public. **Computerized Information Services:** MEDIK, Chorisont, Sirena, INIS (International Nuclear Information System), BIOSIS, INSPEC, COMPENDEX, CIS, EMBASE, VINITI. Performs searches on fee basis. **Publications:** Bibliographies. **Also Known As:** Tsentar za Nauchna Informacija po Meditsina i Zdraveopazvane.

★18324★
BULGARIA MEDICAL ACADEMY - INSTITUTE OF DERMATOLOGY AND VENEREOLOGY - LIBRARY (Med)
1 Georgi Sofiski St.
BG-1431 Sofia, Bulgaria Rene Todorova, Libn.
Subjects: Dermatology, allergies, occupational and oncological dermatoses, venereology, physiotherapy. **Holdings:** 50,000 volumes.

★18325★
BULGARIAN ACADEMY OF SCIENCES - CENTER FOR RESEARCH IN LINGUISTICS AND LITERATURE - LIBRARY (Area-Ethnic, Hum)
52 Capaev St.
BG-1113 Sofia, Bulgaria Phone: 2 72-20-58
Subjects: History of Bulgarian language and literature, Bulgarian dialects, Slavic literature, Balkan linguistics, comparative linguistics and literature. **Holdings:** 100,000 volumes. **Staff:** Marietta Cukova, Libn.; Ivanka Manova, Libn..

BUNDESINSTITUT FUER OSTWISSENSCHAFTLICHE UND INTERNATIONALE STUDIEN
See: Federal Institute for East European and International Studies (18406)

BUNDESINSTITUT FUR SPORTWISSENSCHAFT - FACHBEREICH DOKUMENTATION UND INFORMATION
See: Federal Institute for Sports Science - Documentation and Information Division (18407)

BUNDESMINISTERIUM FUR LAND- UND FORSTWIRTSCHAFT
See: Austria - Federal Ministry of Agriculture and Forestry (18286)

BUNDESMINISTERIUM FUR WISSENSCHAFT UND FORSCHUNG - BIBLIOTHEK DER GEOLOGISCHEN BUNDESANSTALT
See: Geological Survey of Austria (18436)

★18326★
BUREAU POUR L'ENSEIGNEMENT DE LA LANGUE ET DE LA CIVILISATION FRANCAISES A L'ETRANGER - CENTRE DE DOCUMENTATION ET D'INFORMATION (Hum, Educ)
9, rue Lhomond Phone: 1 47 07 42 73
F-75007 Paris, France C. De Quatrebarbes
Subjects: Teaching French as a foreign language, language teaching, French linguistics, teaching aids, linguistics, French culture. **Special Collections:** French textbooks for French as a foreign language, 1960 to present; foreign books (800). **Holdings:** 18,800 books; 4000 brochures. **Subscriptions:** 180 journals and other serials. **Services:** Center open to teachers of French and researchers on language teaching. **Publications:** Accession list, 9/year; bibliographies.

BUREAU INTERNATIONAL DE L'UNION POSTALE UNIVERSELLE
See: International Bureau of the Universal Postal Union (18538)

BURMA - MINISTRY OF EDUCATION - BURMA EDUCATIONAL RESEARCH BUREAU
See: Burma Educational Research Bureau (18327)

★18327★
BURMA EDUCATIONAL RESEARCH BUREAU - LIBRARY (Educ)
Institute of Education Compound
University P.O. 11041 Phone: 31468
Rangoon, Burma U. Maung Maung U, Chf.Libn.
Subjects: Educational research, teaching, learning, curriculum, measurement and evaluation, media in education. **Holdings:** 48,200 volumes. **Remarks:** Maintained by Burma - Ministry of Education.

★18328★
BUTANTAN INSTITUTE - LIBRARY (Biol Sci, Med)
Avenida Vital Brazil, 1500
Caixa Postal 65 Phone: 11 211-8211
01051 Sao Paulo, Brazil Denise Maria Mariotti, Chf.Libn.
Subjects: Biology, immunology, bacteriology, chemistry, pharmacology, herpetology, production of serums and vaccines. **Holdings:** 63,000 volumes. **Remarks:** Maintained by Brazil - Secretary of State for Health. **Also Known As:** Instituto Butantan.

★18329★
BYGGDOK/THE SWEDISH INSTITUTE OF BUILDING DOCUMENTATION - INFORMATION CENTER (Plan)
Haelsingegatan 49 Phone: 8 34 01 70
S-113 31 Stockholm, Sweden Bengt Eresund, Mng.Dir.
Founded: 1966. **Subjects:** Construction, building, architecture, planning, building services, environment. **Special Collections:** Swedish Council for Building Research reports (complete set). **Holdings:** 1000 linear meters of books. **Subscriptions:** 460 journals and other serials. **Services:** Interlibrary loan; copying; center open to the public with restrictions. **Computerized Information Services:** DIALOG Information Services, Pergamon ORBIT InfoLine, Inc., STN International, BODIL, BYGGFO, VA NYTT. Performs searches on fee basis. Contact Person: Monica Stroemberg. **Publications:** Byggreferat abstract journal; VA NYTT abstract journal. **Staff:** Bernhard Lindahl, Archv.; Barbro Widell, Libn.; Bodil Wennerlund, Libn.; John Squires, Libn..

C

★18330★
CAMEROON INSTITUTE OF INTERNATIONAL RELATIONS - LIBRARY (Soc Sci)
B.P. 1637 Phone: 22 03 05
Yaounde, United Republic of Cameroon
Eteminlem Minko Monique, Libn.
Subjects: International relations; political science; international law; diplomacy; economic, financial and technical problems affecting present and future relations of African states as well as other countries. **Holdings:** 10,000 volumes. **Remarks:** Maintained by University of Yaounde. **Also Known As:** Institut des Relations Internationales du Cameroun.

★18331★
CAMUNIAN CENTER FOR PREHISTORIC AND ETHNOLOGIC STUDIES - LIBRARY (Soc Sci, Hist)
25044 Capo di Ponte (Bs) Phone: 644 20 91
Valcomonica, Italy Bruna Facchini, Libn.
Subjects: Archeology, prehistoric art, ethnology, history of religions. **Special Collections:** Archives (documentation for studies in prehistoric art). **Holdings:** 20,000 volumes. **Also Known As:** Centro Camuno di Studi Preistorici e Etnologici.

CANTACUZINO INSTITUTE
See: Romania - Ministry of Health - Cantacuzino Institute (18730)

★18332★
CANTERBURY CATHEDRAL - LIBRARY-PRINTED BOOKS (Rel-Phil, Hist)
Cathedral House
11 The Precincts Phone: 227 658950
Canterbury, Kent CT1 2EH, England
Naomi Linnell, Kpr., Printed Bks.
Subjects: Slavery, church history, theology, early printing and science. **Special Collections:** Mendham Collection (15th-19th century anti-Papist materials; 6000 titles). **Holdings:** 40,000 books; 1000 bound periodical volumes; 19th century pamphlets. **Services:** Library open to the public by appointment with letter of introduction and identification. **Automated Operations:** Online catalog. **Computerized Information Services:** Online systems. Performs searches on fee basis. **Publications:** Information leaflets. **Remarks:** Canterbury Cathedral - Archives is maintained separately and is located at The Precincts, Canterbury, Kent CT1 2EG; Miss A.M. Oakley is the archivist.

★18333★
CAPITAL CONSTRUCTION COMMISSION OF CHINA - CONSTRUCTION AND BUILDING LIBRARY (Plan)
19 Chegongzhuang Dajie
West Suburb
Beijing, People's Republic of China Chang Qing, Libn.
Founded: 1956. **Staff:** 30. **Subjects:** Building construction and engineering, architecture, allied sciences. **Holdings:** 200,000 volumes; 1219 periodicals; 1500 technical reports. **Services:** Interlibrary loan; copying.

CARIBBEAN FOOD AND NUTRITION INSTITUTE
See: Pan American Health Organization (18675)

★18334★
CARIBBEAN INDUSTRIAL RESEARCH INSTITUTE - TECHNICAL INFORMATION SERVICE (Sci-Engr)
Tunapuna Post Office Phone: (809)663-4171
Trinidad, Trinidad and Tobago Nirupa Oudit, Prog.Ldr.
Founded: 1970. **Subjects:** Analytical and industrial chemistry; food technology; microbiology; biochemistry; materials technology; engineering - chemical, electronic, mechanical, industrial, civil; information science; patents and copyright. **Holdings:** 25,000 volumes. **Subscriptions:** 125 journals and other serials. **Services:** SDI; service open to business, manufacturers, processors, service organizations, and government agencies. **Computerized Information Services:** Online systems; internal database. Performs searches on fee basis. **Publications:** Accessions list, bimonthly.

CASA DE VELAZQUEZ
See: France - Ministere de l'Education - Velazquez House (18423)

★18335★
CENTER FOR ADVANCED STUDIES ON MODERN AFRICA AND ASIA - LIBRARY (Area-Ethnic)
13, rue du Four Phone: 1 43 26 96 90
F-75006 Paris, France Anne Malecot, Libn.
Subjects: Africa, Asia, the Pacific Basin, the Caribbean - social, political, administrative, and economic problems; sociopolitical and anthropological traditions. **Holdings:** 14,000 volumes. **Remarks:** Maintained by National Foundation of Political Sciences/Fondation Nationale des Sciences Politiques. **Also Known As:** Centre de Hautes Etudes sur l'Afrique et l'Asie Modernes.

CENTRE AFRICAIN DE FORMATION ET DE RECHERCHE ADMINISTRATIVES POUR LE DEVELOPPEMENT
See: African Training and Research Centre in Administration for Development - Library (18263)

★18336★
CENTRE DE CREATION INDUSTRIELLE - SERVICE DOCUMENTATION (Art, Plan)
Centre Georges Pompidou
F-75191 Paris Cedex 4, France Phone: 1 2771233
Founded: 1982. **Subjects:** Design - industrial, graphic, urban; architecture. **Holdings:** 10,000 volumes; photographs; AV programs. **Subscriptions:** 100 journals and other serials. **Services:** Service open to architects, urban designers, students, government agencies, and users of the Pompidou Centre. **Computerized Information Services:** Produces CECILE Data Base. Performs searches on fee basis. **Publications:** Bulletin Mensuel d'Information du Centre de Creation Industrielle CCI - by subscription.

CENTRE DE DOCUMENTATION POUR L'EDUCATION EN EUROPE
See: Documentation Centre for Education in Europe (18387)

CENTRE D'ETUDES ET RECHERCHES DE CHARBONNAGES DE FRANCE
See: Coal Mining Research Center of France (18355)

CENTRE DE HAUTES ETUDES SUR L'AFRIQUE ET L'ASIE MODERNES
See: Center for Advanced Studies on Modern Africa and Asia (18335)

CENTRE INTERNATIONAL DE DOCUMENTATION PARLEMENTAIRE
See: International Centre for Parliamentary Documentation (18540)

★18337★
CENTER FOR MATHEMATICS AND COMPUTER SCIENCE - LIBRARY (Sci-Engr, Comp Sci)
Kruislaan 413 Phone: 20 5929333
NL-1098 SJ Amsterdam, Netherlands Dr. Frank A. Roos, Libn.
Subjects: Pure and numerical mathematics, applied statistics, mathematical statistics, operations research, systems analysis, computer science. **Holdings:** 100,000 volumes. **Remarks:** Maintained by Netherlands Organization for the Advancement of Pure Science. **Also Known As:** Centrum voor Wiskunde en Informatica.

★18338★
CENTRE NATIONAL DE LA RECHERCHE SCIENTIFIQUE - BIBLIOTHEQUE DE SOCIOLOGIE DU CNRS (Soc Sci)
59, 61 rue Pauchet Phone: 1 40 25 11 80
F-75849 Paris Cedex 17, France Blandine Veith, Libn.
Staff: Prof 9. **Subjects:** Sociology. **Holdings:** 40,000 books. **Subscriptions:** 620 journals and other serials. **Services:** Interlibrary loan; copying; library open to social science researchers and students. **Special Catalogs:** Catalogue Collectif des Ouvrages Etrangers; Catalogue Collectif National (periodiques). **Formerly:** Centre d'Etudes Sociologiques - Library. **Staff:** Francoise Picard, Libn.; Marie Noelle Postic, Libn.; Jean Claude Darbois, Libn.; Beatrice De Peyret, Libn..

★18339★
CENTRE NATIONAL DE LA RECHERCHE SCIENTIFIQUE - CENTRE DE DOCUMENTATION SCIENTIFIQUE ET TECHNIQUE (Sci-Engr)
26, rue Boyer Phone: 1 43583559
F-75971 Paris Cedex 20, France
D. Pelissier, Hd., Diffusion & Transl.Serv.
Founded: 1939. **Subjects:** Physics, chemistry, biology, medicine, psychology, earth sciences, engineering, energy, food and agriculture, zoology, metallurgy, welding, building construction, mathematics. **Special**

Collections: Periodiques (serials). **Holdings:** 24,000 French scientific reports; 86,000 French scientific theses; 31,000 conference proceedings. **Subscriptions:** 13,000 journals and other serials. **Services:** Copying; SDI; translation; center open to the public. **Automated Operations:** Computerized cataloging. **Computerized Information Services:** DOBIS Canadian Online Library System, ESA/IRS, Telesystemes Questel, DIALOG Information Services; produces PASCAL M, PASCAL S. Performs searches on fee basis. **Publications:** PASCAL SIGMA, PASCAL THEMA, PASCAL FOLIO, PASCAL EXPLORE (4 part bibliographic bulletin series). **Special Catalogs:** Catalogue des periodiques recus (1982, supplements); Catalogue des rapports de fin de contrat DGRST (1968-1981, supplements); Catalogue des rapports scientifiques et techniques FRT (1982-1983); Catalogue des rapports de recherche sur l'environnement, annual. **Special Indexes:** Index permute des periodiques recus (1982, supplement); Liste des periodiques traduits (1980); Inventaire des theses soutenues devant les universites francaises, annual. **Remarks:** PASCAL is an acronym for Programme Applique a la Selection et a la Compilation Automatiques de la Litterature.

★18340★
CENTRE DE RECHERCHE ET D'ETUDES SUR LES SOCIETES MEDITERRANEENNES - BIBLIOTHEQUE (Area-Ethnic)
Maison de la Mediterranee
5, avenue Pasteur — Phone: 42 230386
F-13100 Aix en Provence, France — A. Raymond, Dir.
Subjects: Social, economic, political, geographic aspects of contemporary North Africa - Algeria, Libya, Morocco, Tunisia. **Holdings:** 20,000 volumes. **Subscriptions:** 200 journals and other serials. **Services:** Library open to researchers and educators. **Computerized Information Services:** Produces Maghreb Data Base. Performs searches on fee basis. Contact Person: Jean-Jacques Regnier or V. Michel.

CENTRE DE RECHERCHE OCEANOGRAPHIQUES DE DAKAR-THIAROYE
See: Dakar-Thiaroye Center for Oceanographic Research (18376)

CENTER FOR RESEARCH AND DOCUMENTATION OF EAST EUROPEAN JEWRY
See: Hebrew University of Jerusalem - Society for Research on Jewish Communities (18463)

★18341★
CENTRAL AMERICAN RESEARCH INSTITUTE FOR INDUSTRY - DOCUMENTATION AND INFORMATION DIVISION (Sci-Engr)
Avenida La Reforma, 4-47
Zona 10 — Phone: 2 310631
01010 Guatemala City, Guatemala
Rocio M. Marban, Hd., Doc. & Info.Div.
Founded: 1956. **Staff:** Prof 4; Other 4. **Subjects:** Technology, food industry, biotechnology, pulp and paper, industrial counseling. **Special Collections:** Central American standards (1140). **Holdings:** 35,000 books; 900 bound periodical volumes; reports; documents; reprints; microfiche; catalogs; directories; AV programs; diskettes. **Subscriptions:** 200 journals and other serials. **Services:** Interlibrary loan; copying; division open to the public for reference use only. **Automated Operations:** Computerized cataloging. **Computerized Information Services:** DIALOG Information Services, Pergamon ORBIT InfoLine, Inc., Telesystemes Questel, STN International; internal database; DIALMAIL, Dialcom Inc. (electronic mail services). Performs searches on fee basis. **Publications:** List of publications - available on request. **Remarks:** Institute was established by the governments of Costa Rica, El Salvador, Guatemala, Honduras, and Nicaragua, and maintains an office in each country. **Formerly:** Central American Institute of Research and Industrial Technology - Library. **Also Known As:** Instituto Centroamericano de Investigacion y Tecnologia Industriel (ICAITI). **Staff:** Rosa Regina de De La Vega, Libn..

★18342★
THE CENTRAL CONSERVATORY OF CHINA - BIBLIOTHECA (Mus)
43 Baojia Jie — Phone: 1 665336
Beijing, People's Republic of China — Song Kai, Dp.Libn.
Founded: 1950. **Staff:** 26. **Subjects:** Music, music theory, composition, conducting, national music and instruments, piano, orchestra and vocal music, opera in Chinese, Russian, Japanese, English, and other foreign languages. **Holdings:** 250,000 volumes; 275 periodicals; 150,000 AV programs and microforms; scores. **Services:** Copying. **Publications:** Selected Works on Chinese and Foreign Musicians; Selected Works on the Performing Art of Vocal Music.

CENTRO AGRONOMICO TROPICAL DE INVESTIGACION Y ENSENANSA (CATIE)
See: Tropical Agricultural Research and Training Center (18821)

CENTRO DE BIBLIOTECA E INFORMACION CIENTIFICA ENRIQUE MEJIA RUIZ
See: Universidad de Caldas (18837)

CENTRO CAMUNO DI STUDI PREISTORICI E ETNOLOGICI
See: Camunian Center for Prehistoric and Ethnologic Studies (18331)

CENTRO INTERAMERICANO DE INVESTIGACION Y DOCUMENTACION SOBRE FORMACION PROFESIONAL
See: Inter-American Center for Research and Documentation on Vocational Training (18530)

CENTRO INTERNACIONAL DE AGRICULTURA TROPICAL
See: International Center for Tropical Agriculture (18542)

CENTRO DE INVESTIGACION Y DESARROLLO "ING. JUAN C. VAN WYK"
See: Ing. Juan C. Van Wyck Center for Research and Development (18868)

CENTRO DE INVESTIGACIONES BIOLOGICAS
See: Scientific Research Council of Spain - Biological Research Center (18760)

CENTRO NACIONAL DE CONDICIONES DE TRABAJO
See: Spain - Ministry of Labour - National Institute of Occupational Safety and Health (18787)

CENTRO NACIONAL DE INFORMACAO DOCUMENTAL AGRICOLA
See: Brazil - Ministry of Agriculture - National Center for Agricultural Documentary Information - Library (18310)

CENTRO NACIONAL DE REFERENCIA DEL URUGUAY
See: Uruguay - Biblioteca Nacional - Centro Nacional de Documentacion Cientifica, Tecnica y Economica (18866)

CENTRO PANAMERICANO DE INGENIERIA SANITARIA Y CIENCIAS DEL AMBIENTE
See: Pan American Center for Sanitary Engineering and Environmental Sciences (18674)

CENTRO DE PESQUISAS E DESENVOLVIMENTO LEOPOLDO A. MIGUEZ DE MELLO
See: Leopolde A. Miguez de Mello Research and Development Center (18607)

CENTRO REGIONAL DE EDUCACION DE ADULTOS Y ALFABETIZACION FUNCIONAL PARA AMERICA LATINA
See: Mexico - Office of the Secretary of Public Education - Regional Center for Adult Education and Functional Development of Latin America (18605)

CENTRUM VOOR WISKUNDE EN INFORMATICA
See: Center for Mathematics and Computer Science (18337)

★18343★
CERRO TOLOLO INTER-AMERICAN OBSERVATORY - LIBRARY (Sci-Engr)
Casilla 603 — Phone: 213352
La Serena, Chile — Eugenia Barraza, Libn.
Subjects: Astronomy. **Holdings:** 12,300 volumes. **Remarks:** Operated by Association of Universities for Research in Astronomy, Inc. (AURA). **Also Known As:** Observatorio Interamericano de Cerro Tololo.

CHARBONNAGES DE FRANCE - COAL MINING RESEARCH CENTER OF FRANCE
See: Coal Mining Research Center of France (18355)

★18344★
CHARTERED INSTITUTE OF TRANSPORT - LIBRARY (Trans)
80 Portland Place
London W1N 4DP, England — Phone: 1 6369952
Subjects: Transportation, physical distribution. **Holdings:** 50,000 volumes. **Remarks:** Fax: 1 6369952.

J & W CHESTER SUBSCRIPTION LIBRARY
See: University of Sussex - University Library (18860)

★18345★
CHILDREN'S BOOK COUNCIL OF IRAN - LIBRARY (Hum)
Enghelab, Sevazar No. 69 Phone: 009821 6408074
Tehran, Iran Mrs. Nasrin-Dokht Em Khorasani, Libn.
Subjects: Children's and young adult literature. **Holdings:** 12,000 books and reference works; documents; dissertations; posters; disks.

★18346★
CHILE - MINISTRY OF PUBLIC HEALTH - PUBLIC HEALTH INSTITUTE OF CHILE - LIBRARY (Med)
Casilla 48
Avenida Marathon 1000 Phone: 2 490021
Santiago, Chile Maria Teresa Orostica, Libn.
Subjects: Clinical microbiology and immunology, medical bacteriology, virology, bromatology, bacteriology of tuberculosis, serology of syphilis. **Holdings:** 10,000 volumes. **Also Known As:** Instituto de Salud Publica de Chile.

★18347★
CHILE - NATIONAL COMMISSION FOR SCIENTIFIC AND TECHNOLOGICAL RESEARCH - DIRECTORATE FOR INFORMATION - TECHNICAL LIBRARY (Sci-Engr)
Casilla Postal 297-V
Canada 308 Phone: 2 744537
Santiago, Chile Ana Maria Prat, Dir. of Info.
Subjects: Science, technical information and documentation. **Holdings:** 5000 volumes. **Subscriptions:** 150 journals and other serials. **Services:** Copying; microfilming; translation. **Computerized Information Services:** Internal database. **Publications:** Serie Informacion y Documentacion, irregular; Serie Directorios; Serie Bibliografica.

★18348★
CHINA BUILDING TECHNOLOGY DEVELOPMENT CENTRE - LIBRARY (Plan)
19 Che Gong Zhuang St.
Beijing, People's Republic of China Phone: 1 8992613
Subjects: Building science and technology. **Holdings:** 200,000 volumes; documents. **Subscriptions:** 800 journals and other serials. **Services:** Copying; library open to engineers, architects, researchers, and workers in construction, production, education, and administration. **Computerized Information Services:** Internal database. **Publications:** Bibliography on Foreign Literature of Science and Technology, monthly.

★18349★
CHINA ENCYCLOPAEDIA PUBLISHING HOUSE - LIBRARY (Info Sci, Publ)
A1 East Waiguan Jie
Andingmenwai
Beijing, People's Republic of China Phone: 1 464389
Founded: 1979. **Staff:** 15. **Subjects:** Encyclopedias, reference books, yearbooks, directories, guides, chronological tables, and dictionaries published around the world. **Holdings:** 40,000 volumes; 600 periodicals. **Services:** Interlibrary loan; copying. **Publications:** Encyclopaedic Knowledge; Encyclopaedic Reference Materials; Encyclopaedic Yearbook.

★18350★
CHINESE ACADEMY OF MEDICAL SCIENCES - LIBRARY (Med)
9 Dongdan Santiao
Beijing, People's Republic of China Phone: 1 553731
Founded: 1957. **Staff:** 51. **Subjects:** Medicine, clinical medicine, environmental hygiene, nutrition. **Special Collections:** Philosophical Transactions of the Royal Society of London, 1665 to present; Chinese ancient books (1235 titles). **Holdings:** 134,000 volumes; 1715 technical reports; 3848 microforms and AV programs. **Subscriptions:** 9917 journals and other serials. **Services:** Interlibrary loan; copying. **Special Catalogs:** Foreign Sci-Tech Reference Material Catalog - Medical Sciences.

CHINESE ACADEMY OF SCIENCES - GUANGZHOU INSTITUTE OF ENERGY CONVERSION
See: Guangzhou Institute of Energy Conversion (18455)

★18351★
CHINESE ACADEMY OF SCIENCES - INSTITUTE OF OCEANOLOGY - LIBRARY (Sci-Engr, Biol Sci)
7 Nanhai Rd. Phone: 27 9062
Qingdao, People's Republic of China Peng Haiqing, Hd. of Lib.
Staff: Prof 15. **Subjects:** Physical oceanography; marine - geology, geophysics, biology, environment, chemistry; instrumentation. **Holdings:** 84,349 books; 42,361 bound periodical volumes; 24,960 unbound reports. **Subscriptions:** 1039 journals and other serials; 20 newspapers. **Services:** Interlibrary loan; copying; library open to the public. **Publications:** Bulletin of New Books. **Special Catalogs:** Catalog of periodical holdings; catalog of conference proceedings holdings. **Special Indexes:** Special technical reports index (card); conference proceedings index (card). **Staff:** Wang Zuxian, Sr.Libn.; Xu Minshu, Sr.Libn.; Shi Guiying, Sr.Libn..

★18352★
CHINESE ACADEMY OF SOCIAL SCIENCES - INSTITUTE OF NATIONALITY STUDIES - LIBRARY (Area-Ethnic)
Weigongcun
Western Suburb Phone: 1 890771
Beijing, People's Republic of China Chen Huaxiang, Libn.
Founded: 1958. **Staff:** 17. **Subjects:** Ethnology; nationality histories, languages, writings, literatures, customs; world nationalities; anthropology; race relations; religions; ethnic liberation movements. **Holdings:** 400,000 volumes.

CHINESE LANGUAGE AND RESEARCH CENTER
See: National University of Singapore (18649)

★18353★
CHINESE UNIVERSITY OF HONG KONG - UNIVERSITY LIBRARY (Hum)
Shatin, N.T., Hong Kong Phone: 0-6952301
Dr. David S. Yen
Subjects: General collection. **Special Collections:** Fine arts and archeology (6000 book and periodical titles); pre-1949 Chinese periodicals; 10th century blockprints and Chinese writings (2000 volumes and reprints); masters theses and Ph.D. dissertations. **Holdings:** 816,000 books; 121,000 bound periodical volumes; 128,000 microforms. **Services:** Interlibrary loan; copying; SDI; library open to the public with restrictions. **Computerized Information Services:** DIALOG Information Services, Datasolve Ltd. **Publications:** An Annotated Guide to Serial Publications of the Hong Kong Government; Serials of Hong Kong: 1845-1979; Newspapers of Hong Kong: 1841-1979; History of Medicine: An Annotated Bibliography of Titles at the Chinese University. **Special Catalogs:** Union Catalogue of Serials; Union Catalogue of Audio Visual Materials; Asian Fine Arts Collection: Union Catalogue: The Chinese University of Hong Kong; Catalogue of the Chinese Rare Books in the Libraries of the Chinese University of Hong Kong. **Remarks:** Telex: 50301 CUHK HX.

★18354★
CHONGQING DESIGN INSTITUTE - THE INFORMATION MATERIAL GROUP (Plan, Sci-Engr)
26 Gongren Jie
Daxigou, Central District Phone: 51942
Chongqing, Sichuan Province, People's Republic of China
Wei Qide, Libn.
Founded: 1951. **Staff:** 6. **Subjects:** Building design and structure, heating, ventilation, water supply and drainage, electricity, municipal administration. **Special Collections:** Ancient and modern architecture; photography; fine arts; building structure data. **Holdings:** 15,611 volumes; 60,551 technical reports; microforms; AV programs. **Subscriptions:** 186 journals and other serials. **Services:** Copying.

★18355★
COAL MINING RESEARCH CENTER OF FRANCE - LIBRARY (Sci-Engr, Env-Cons)
33, rue de la Baume Phone: 1 563 11 20
F-75008 Paris, France S. Perrenot, Libn.
Subjects: Coal, mining techniques, mine and industrial safety, air pollution, noise control. **Holdings:** 23,000 volumes. **Remarks:** Center is part of Charbonnages de France. **Also Known As:** Centre d'Etudes et Recherches de Charbonnages de France.

★18356★
COCOA RESEARCH INSTITUTE OF GHANA - LIBRARY
(Food-Bev, Agri)
P.O. Box 8 Phone: Tafo 51
Tafo-Akim, Ghana Mr. E.K. Tetteh, Chf.Lib.Off.
Subjects: Cocoa, coffee, cola, sheanut, and tallow - breeding, agronomy, soil nutrition, plant pathology, entomology, physiology, biochemistry. **Holdings:** 13,110 volumes.

★18357★
COLOMBIA - MINISTRY OF MINES & PETROLEUM - INSTITUTE FOR NUCLEAR AFFAIRS - LIBRARY (Energy)
Apartado Aereo 8595 Phone: 44 08 09
Bogota, Colombia Cecilia Briceno de Monroy, Hd.Libn.
Subjects: Peaceful uses of nuclear energy in health physics and nuclear medicine, industry, biochemistry, hydrology and sedimentology, geology, nuclear safety, metallurgy, reactors, chemistry, physics, electronics, uranium exploration, agriculture. **Holdings:** 60,000 volumes. **Remarks:** Telex: 42416 IAN BG. **Also Known As:** Instituto de Asuntos Nucleares.

★18358★
COLOMBIAN ACADEMY OF EXACT, PHYSICAL AND NATURAL SCIENCES - LIBRARY (Sci-Engr)
Carrera 3A No. 17-34
Apartado Aereo 44-763 Phone: 241 48 05
Bogota, Colombia Prof. Eduardo Caro, Libn.
Subjects: Natural sciences, mathematics, physics, geology, astronomy, history of sciences in Colombia. **Holdings:** 20,000 volumes. **Remarks:** Maintained by Colombia - Ministry of Education. **Also Known As:** Academia Colombiana de Ciencias Exactas, Fisicas y Naturales.

★18359★
COMMISSION OF THE EUROPEAN COMMUNITIES - SPECIALIZED DEPARTMENT FOR TERMINOLOGY AND COMPUTER APPLICATIONS - LIBRARY (Sci-Engr)
Batiment Jean Monnet A2/101 Phone: 43012389
Kirchberg, Luxembourg Mr. J. Goetschalckx, Hd.
Subjects: Terminology - agriculture, coal and steel technology, medicine, occupational health, nuclear science, transport, industry, official nomenclatures, economics, community regulations, data processing, civil engineering, information and documentation sciences. **Holdings:** 7500 volumes. **Subscriptions:** 200 journals and other serials. **Services:** Library open to terminologists and translators. **Computerized Information Services:** Produces Eurodicautom. Performs searches on fee basis. **Remarks:** Provides scientific and technical terms, definitions, contextual phrases, and abbreviations in the official languages of the European Communities.

COMMISSION SERICOLE INTERNATIONALE
See: International Sericultural Commission (18559)

★18360★
THE COMMONWEALTH INSTITUTE - LIBRARY AND RESOURCE CENTRE (Area-Ethnic)
Kensington High St.
London W8 6NQ, England Phone: 1 603 4535
Staff: Prof 3. **Subjects:** The Commonwealth - arts and literature, trade and development, education, community relations, commodities, languages, agriculture, sociology. **Holdings:** 60,000 AV programs. **Subscriptions:** 600 journals and other serials. **Services:** Interlibrary loan; copying; center open to the public. **Publications:** Commonwealth Bibliographies; reading lists; lists of materials; information leaflets. **Special Catalogs:** Exhibition catalogs. **Remarks:** Library and Resource Centre now divided into four sections: Commonwealth Information Centre, Educational Resource Centre, Staff & Research Library, and Compix Photographic Library. **Staff:** Roger Hughes, Libn., Staff & Res.Lib.; Christiane Keane, Libn., Info.Ctr.; Karen Peters, Libn., Educ.Rsrc.Ctr.; Maria Ockenden, Adm., Compix.

★18361★
COMMONWEALTH SCIENTIFIC AND INDUSTRIAL RESEARCH ORGANIZATION (CSIRO) - CSIRO WHEAT RESEARCH UNIT - LIBRARY (Agri)
Epping Rd.
Private Bag Phone: 888-9600
North Ryde, NSW 2113, Australia Jill Chambers, Libn.
Subjects: Quality, processing, and marketability of wheat and wheat products; cereals - triticale, barley, rice, oats. **Holdings:** 50,000 volumes.

★18362★
COMMONWEALTH SCIENTIFIC AND INDUSTRIAL RESEARCH ORGANIZATION (CSIRO) - DIVISION OF APPLIED PHYSICS - LIBRARY (Sci-Engr)
Bradfield Rd.
P.O. Box 218 Phone: 467-6097
Lindfield, NSW 2070, Australia Miss Robin Shelley-Jones, Act.Libn.
Subjects: Physics measurement and science, industrial physics, manufacturing technology, chemistry, engineering. **Special Collections:** Standards published by Standards Association of Australia. **Holdings:** 18,500 books; 900 serial titles. **Services:** Interlibrary loan; copying; SDI; library open to the public with lending through ILL. **Computerized Information Services:** DIALOG Information Services, Pergamon ORBIT InfoLine, Inc., CSIRO Australis. **Staff:** Anne Jack, Libn..

★18363★
COMMONWEALTH SCIENTIFIC AND INDUSTRIAL RESEARCH ORGANIZATION (CSIRO) - DIVISION OF TEXTILE PHYSICS - LIBRARY (Sci-Engr)
P.O. Box 7 Phone: 2 800211
Ryde, NSW 2112, Australia Pauline Quan, Libn.
Staff: Prof 1; Other 2. **Subjects:** Wool, textiles, robotics, computer systems. **Holdings:** 15,500 volumes. **Subscriptions:** 302 journals and other serials. **Services:** Interlibrary loan; copying; library open to the public by appointment. **Automated Operations:** Computerized public access catalog, cataloging, and circulation. **Computerized Information Services:** DIALOG Information Services.

★18364★
COMMONWEALTH SCIENTIFIC AND INDUSTRIAL RESEARCH ORGANIZATION (CSIRO) - INFORMATION RESOURCES UNIT (Sci-Engr, Info Sci)
314 Albert St. Phone: 3 4187 333
East Melbourne, VIC 3002, Australia Mr. P.H. Dawe, Act.Mgr.
Subjects: Science, science policy, librarianship, information science, communications, computers. **Holdings:** 10,000 books; 500,000 bound periodical volumes. **Services:** Interlibrary loan; copying; SDI; unit open to the public. **Computerized Information Services:** CSIRO Australis, DIALOG Information Services, ESA/IRS, AUSINET, Australian Bibliographic Network (ABN), Pergamon ORBIT InfoLine, Inc. Performs searches on fee basis. Contact Person: Penny Braybrook, Online Search Spec., 4187 335. **Publications:** Directory of CSIRO research in progress 1986; Research in progress databases; SALI: selected abstracts: library, information; scientific and technical research centres; renewable energy directory. **Special Indexes:** Renewable energy index.

CONGRESO DE LOS DIPUTADOS
See: Spain - Congress of Deputies (18786)

CONSEIL OECUMENIQUE DES EGLISES
See: World Council of Churches (18872)

CONSEIL OLEICOLE INTERNATIONAL
See: International Olive Oil Council (18555)

CONSEJO SUPERIOR DE INVESTIGACIONES CIENTIFICAS - INSTITUTO DE INFORMACION Y DOCUMENTACION EN CIENCIA Y TECNOLOGIA
See: Higher Council for Scientific Research - Institute for Information and Documentation in Science and Technology (18469)

CONSULTATIVE GROUP ON INTERNATIONAL AGRICULTURAL RESEARCH - INTERNATIONAL CENTER FOR TROPICAL AGRICULTURE
See: International Center for Tropical Agriculture (18542)

CONSULTATIVE GROUP ON INTERNATIONAL AGRICULTURAL RESEARCH - INTERNATIONAL INSTITUTE OF TROPICAL AGRICULTURE
See: International Institute of Tropical Agriculture (18551)

CONSULTATIVE GROUP ON INTERNATIONAL AGRICULTURAL RESEARCH - INTERNATIONAL LABORATORY FOR RESEARCH ON ANIMAL DISEASES
See: International Laboratory for Research on Animal Diseases (18552)

CONSULTATIVE GROUP ON INTERNATIONAL AGRICULTURAL RESEARCH - INTERNATIONAL RICE RESEARCH INSTITUTE
See: International Rice Research Institute (18558)

★18365★
JAMES COOK UNIVERSITY OF NORTH QUEENSLAND - LIBRARY (Area-Ethnic, Biol Sci, Med)
Townsville, QLD 4811, Australia Phone: 77 814472
John McKinlay, Univ.Libn.
Staff: Prof 15; Other 50. **Subjects:** General collection. **Special Collections:** North Queensland history and literature; tropical marine studies; tropical veterinary medicine. **Holdings:** 325,000 books; 130,000 bound periodical volumes; 65,000 AV programs; 25,000 microforms. **Subscriptions:** 4800 journals and other serials. **Services:** Interlibrary loan; copying; SDI; library open to the public. **Automated Operations:** Computerized cataloging, acquisitions, and circulation. **Computerized Information Services:** DIALOG Information Services, MEDLINE, AUSTRALIS, CAS ONLINE, Australian Bibliographic Network (ABN), Pergamon ORBIT InfoLine, Inc., ESA/IRS. Performs searches on fee basis. **Publications:** Library Guide. **Special Indexes:** Serials List.

★18366★
COOPERATIVE LEAGUE OF THE REPUBLIC OF CHINA - LIBRARY (Bus-Fin)
11-2 Fuchow St. Phone: 2 321-9343
Taipei, Taiwan Wen-pinn Tsai, Libn.
Subjects: Cooperatives, economics. **Holdings:** 10,000 volumes.

★18367★
COUNCIL FOR THE CARE OF CHURCHES - LIBRARY (Rel-Phil, Art)
83 London Wall Phone: 1 638-0971
London EC2M 5NA, England Janet Seeley, Libn.
Staff: Prof 1. **Subjects:** Ecclesiastical art and architecture, Anglican churches and cathedrals in England, conservation. **Special Collections:** National Survey of English Churches (guidebooks; photographs). **Holdings:** 12,000 books; 30 microforms; 20,000 files; 135,000 photographs; 11,000 slides. **Subscriptions:** 120 journals and other serials. **Services:** Interlibrary loan; copying; library open to the public by appointment. **Special Catalogs:** Slide library catalog. **Remarks:** Maintained by the General Synod of the Church of England.

★18368★
COUVENT DES DOMINICAINS - BIBLIOTHEQUE DE L'ECOLE BIBLIQUE ET ARCHEOLOGIQUE FRANCAISE DE JERUSALEM (Rel-Phil)
6 Nablus Rd.
P.O. Box 19053 Phone: 2 28 24 99
91 190 Jerusalem, Israel Marcel Sigrist, Ph.D.
Subjects: Bible, archeology and epigraphy of the ancient Near East. **Holdings:** 80,000 books; 300 bound periodical volumes. **Services:** Copying; library open to the public with restrictions. **Publications:** Revue biblique; Etudes Bibliques; Cahiers de la Revue biblique.

★18369★
CUBA - MINISTERIO DE CULTURA - BIBLIOTECA NACIONAL JOSE MARTI (Info Sci)
Avenida de Independencia
Plaza de la Revolucion
Havana, Cuba Miriam Martinez Crespo, Vice-Dir., Tech.Serv.
Subjects: General collection. **Special Collections:** 16th-19th century rare documents, books, periodicals, incunabula. **Holdings:** 1.8 million volumes; 17,000 scores; 8400 posters; 11,800 maps; 21,000 slides; 8500 phonograph records; 66,200 photographs; 45,000 manuscripts. **Services:** Interlibrary loan; copying; SDI; library open to the public. **Publications:** Revista de la Biblioteca Nacional Jose Marti; Bibliografia Cubana; bibliographic bulletins in the fields of fine arts, music, theater, dance, literature, and general cultural problems. **Special Indexes:** Indice General de Publicaciones Periodicas Cubanas de Ciencias Sociales y Humanidades; indice acumulativo de la Bibliografia Cubana. **Staff:** Dr. Julio Le Riverend Brusone, Dir..

★18370★
CUBAN ACADEMY OF SCIENCES - CENTER FOR THE STUDY OF THE HISTORY AND ORGANIZATION OF SCIENCE - C.J. FINLAY LIBRARY (Sci-Engr)
460 entre Amargura y Teniente Rey
Apartado 70 Phone: 60 2084
Havana, Cuba Lidia C. Patallo Bernardez, Libn.
Staff: Prof 4; Other 4. **Subjects:** Science of science; science policy; history, organization, and economy of science. **Special Collections:** History of science (6000 volumes); Cuba (6000 volumes); old and rare books (2500 volumes). **Holdings:** 94,800 books and pamphlets. **Services:** Interlibrary loan; SDI; library open to the public. **Publications:** Conferencias y estudios de Historia y Organizacion de la Ciencia. **Also Known As:** Academia de Ciencias de la Republica de Cuba - Centro de Estudios de Historia y Organizacion de la Ciencia.

★18371★
CUMBERLAND AREA HEALTH SERVICES - WESTMEAD HOSPITAL - AMA LIBRARY (Med)
Westmead, NSW 2145, Australia Phone: 02 633-6266
Linda Mulheron, Chf.Libn.
Founded: 1978. **Staff:** Prof 5; Other 4. **Subjects:** Epidemiology, bacteriology, virology, hematology, cytology, cytogenetics, tumors, pathology, medicine, surgery, pediatrics, psychiatry, radiation oncology, radiology. **Special Collections:** Australian Medical Association Library (5000 books and journals). **Holdings:** 18,000 books; 1970 tapes, slides, films, videotapes, audio cassettes. **Subscriptions:** 1600 journals and other serials. **Services:** Interlibrary loan; copying; SDI; library open to medical professionals and local medical students. **Computerized Information Services:** MEDLINE, DIALOG Information Services, Pergamon ORBIT InfoLine, Inc., Data-Star, ABN (Australian Bibliographic Network). Performs searches on fee basis. Contact Person: Bronwyn King, Ref.Libn., 633 6261. **Formerly:** New South Wales Department of Health - Institute of Clinical Pathology and Medical Research. **Staff:** Mrs. K. Kelly, Cat.Libn.; Ms. N. Stratton, AV Off.; Mrs. R. Zuther, Lib.Techn..

★18372★
JOHN CURTIN SCHOOL OF MEDICAL RESEARCH - LIBRARY (Med, Biol Sci)
P.O. Box 334 Phone: 492597
Canberra, ACT 2601, Australia Miss J. Nicholson, Libn.
Subjects: Immunology, microbiology, biochemistry, cancer research, vision, neurology. **Holdings:** 45,000 volumes. **Remarks:** School is part of the Australian National University.

★18373★
CYPRUS - DEPARTMENT OF STATISTICS AND RESEARCH - LIBRARY (Soc Sci, Bus-Fin)
13 Byron Ave. Phone: 2 30-2349
Nicosia 162, Cyprus Chr. Demosthenous, Clerical Off.
Subjects: Demography, agriculture, trade, industry, economics, statistics. **Special Collections:** Publications of United Nations, International Labour Office, Economic Commission for Europe; statistics of selected countries worldwide. **Holdings:** 10,261 books; statistical yearbooks. **Services:** Interlibrary loan; copying; library open to the public with restrictions. **Remarks:** Telex: 3399 MINFIN CY.

CYRIL AND METHODIUS NATIONAL LIBRARY
See: Bulgaria - Committee of Culture - Cyril and Methodius National Library (18322)

★18374★
CZECHOSLOVAKIA - GEOLOGICAL OFFICE - GEOLOGICAL SURVEY OF PRAGUE - LIBRARY (Sci-Engr)
Malostranske nam. 19 Phone: 533641
CS-118 21 Prague 1, Czechoslovakia Vera Krajickova, Ph.D., Libn.
Founded: 1919. **Subjects:** Prof 6; Other 1. **Subjects:** Geology, hydrogeology, geochemical prospecting, mineralogy, petrology, paleontology, chemical analysis. **Holdings:** 35,000 books; 13,650 monographs; 78,894 journals; 38,797 reprints; 3827 microfiche; 1353 other cataloged items. **Subscriptions:** 1100 journals and other serials. **Services:** Copying; library open to the public. **Computerized Information Services:** PASCAL-GEODE. **Publications:** News, monthly.

★18375★
CZECHOSLOVAKIA - MINISTRY OF FORESTRY AND WATER MANAGEMENT - WATER RESEARCH INSTITUTE - BRANCH INFORMATION CENTER (Biol Sci, Sci-Engr)
Podbabska 30 Phone: 2 329041
CS-160 62 Prague 6, Czechoslovakia Mr. J. Lauerman, Libn.
Founded: 1920. **Staff:** Prof 9; Other 8. **Subjects:** Hydraulics, hydrology, sanitary engineering, waste treatment, chemistry, physics, water supply, water pollution control, dam design. **Holdings:** 60,000 books; 462,390 bound periodical volumes. **Subscriptions:** 125 journals and other serials; 6 newspapers. **Services:** Interlibrary loan; copying; center open to the public. **Publications:** Prace a studie, annual; Vyzkum pro praxi, annual; VTEI, irregular. **Special Catalogs:** Hydrologicka bibliografie za rok, annual (book). **Also Known As:** Vyzkumny Ustav Vodohospodarsky. **Staff:** Ms. M. Bruhova, Ph.D., Intermediary; Ms. J. Plechacova, Res.Asst.; Ms. H. Havrankova, Transl.; Ms. M. Kuckova, Libn..

D

★18376★
DAKAR-THIAROYE CENTER FOR OCEANOGRAPHIC RESEARCH - LIBRARY (Biol Sci)
Route de Rufisque, Km. 10
B.P. 2241 Phone: 34-05-36
Dakar, Senegal Florent Diouf, Documentaliste
Subjects: Marine stocks, ecosystems, environment, marine economics, oceanography. **Holdings:** 21,500 volumes. **Remarks:** Maintained by Agricultural Research Institute of Senegal. **Also Known As:** Centre de Recherche Oceanographiques de Dakar-Thiaroye.

★18377★
DALIAN INSTITUTE OF TECHNOLOGY - LIBRARY (Sci-Engr)
40 Luanjincun Phone: 42102
Dalian, Liaoning Province, People's Republic of China
Guo Keren, Libn.
Founded: 1949. **Staff:** 71. **Subjects:** Mathematics, physics, engineering mechanics, harbor buildings, water conservancy and electricity supply, offshore construction, metals, mechanical engineering, equipment automation, derrick and transport machines, internal combustion ship engines, industrial use turbines, ship design and building, radio technology, industrial automation, computer manufacturing, chemical industry machinery, inorganic chemicals industry, automation and instrumentation of the chemical industry, intermediates and dyestuffs, organic chemistry, high polymer chemical industry, coal industry, engineering management. **Holdings:** 1.06 million volumes; 3690 periodicals; 30,000 technical reports; 500 AV programs and microforms. **Services:** Interlibrary loan; copying. **Publications:** Book and Information Work; Library and Readers; New Books; Scientific and Technical Reference Material; Translations of Scientific and Technical Literatures. **Special Catalogs:** Catalog of Chinese and Foreign Scientific and Technical Periodicals Held by the Library; Catalog of New Acquisitions of Scientific and Technical Publications.

★18378★
DANISH FEDERATION OF TRADE UNIONS - LIBRARY AND ARCHIVE (Bus-Fin, Soc Sci)
Rejsbygade 1 Phone: 1 24 15 22
DK-1759 Copenhagen V, Denmark Dr. Gerd Callesen
Subjects: Labor movement; trade unions; socialdemocratic, socialist, communist organizations; Socialism; Marxism; cultural and educational associations of the labor movement. **Special Collections:** Labor organization archives (50,000 photographs; 3000 posters; 600 banners; 7000 unprinted protocols and minutebooks; 3000 linear meters of manuscripts; oral history tapes; videotapes; personal papers of members of labor movement). **Holdings:** 75,000 books; 5500 periodical titles. **Services:** Interlibrary loan; copying; library open to the public. **Publications:** ABAs bibliografiske serie; International arbejderbevaegelse; Under de rode faner; Et arkiv bliver til. **Special Indexes:** Index to periodicals found in the library. **Also Known As:** Arbejderbevaegelsens Bibliotek og Arkiv. **Staff:** Borge Pedersen.

DANISH VETERINARY AND AGRICULTURAL LIBRARY
See: The Royal Veterinary and Agricultural University (18753)

DANMARKS BIBLIOTEKSSKOLES BIBLIOTEK
See: Royal School of Librarianship - Library (18750)

DANMARKS GEOLOGISKE UNDERSOGELSE
See: Geological Survey of Denmark (18437)

DARWIN LIBRARY
See: University of Cambridge - Library (18846)

★18379★
DARWINIAN INSTITUTE OF BOTANY - LIBRARY (Biol Sci)
Labarden, 200
Casilla de Correo 22 Phone: 743-4748
1642 San Isidro, Argentina Elena Silnicky De Vizer, Libn.
Subjects: Argentine flora, systematic botany, phytogeography, plant anatomy and cytogenetics, palynology. **Holdings:** 37,000 volumes. **Remarks:** Affiliated with the National Academy of Sciences of Buenos Aires and the National Council of Scientific and Technical Research. **Also Known As:** Instituto de Botanica "Darwinion."

★18380★
FRANCISCO JOSE DE CALDAS COLUMBIAN ORGANIZATION FOR SCIENTIFIC RESEARCH AND SPECIAL PROJECTS - NATIONAL INFORMATION SYSTEM (Sci-Engr)
Apartado Aereo 051580
Bogota, Colombia Phone: 274 06 60
Subjects: Agriculture, health, education, economics, industry, energy, environment, marine sciences. **Holdings:** Figures not available. **Publications:** Informativo SNI, bimonthly. **Remarks:** Maintained by Colombia - National Ministry of Education. **Also Known As:** Fondo Colombiano de Investigaciones Cientificas y Proyectos Especiales Francisco Jose de Caldas.

★18381★
DECHEMA - I & D INFORMATION SYSTEMS AND DATA BANKS DEPARTMENT (Sci-Engr)
Theodor-Heuss-Allee 25 Phone: 69 7564244
D-6000 Frankfurt am Main 97, Federal Republic of Germany
Dr. Reiner Eckermann, Dept.Hd.
Staff: Prof 3. **Subjects:** Chemical engineering and biotechnology - equipment manufacturing, plant design and construction, computer-aided design, mathematical models and methods, laboratory techniques, analytical chemistry, safety, dangerous materials, pollution control, energy and raw materials supply and conservation, chemical reaction engineering. **Holdings:** 15,000 volumes. **Subscriptions:** 300 journals and other serials. **Services:** SDI; inquiry service; department open to the public. **Automated Operations:** Computerized cataloging. **Computerized Information Services:** STN International, Informationssystem Karlsruhe (INKADATA), Data-Star; produces DECHEMA Chemical Engineering and Biotechnology Abstracts Data Bank, DECHEMA Biotechnology Equipment Suppliers Databank (BIOQUIP), European Coal Data Bank (COALDATA), DECHEMA Equipment Suppliers Data Base (DEQUIP), DECHEMA Research and Education Databank (DERES), DECHEMA Environmental Technology Equipment Databank (DETEQ), DECHEMA Thermophysical Property Data Bank (DETHERM), Chemical Industries Scheme for Assistance in Freight Emergencies (CHEMSAFE), DECHEMA Corrosion Data Base (DECOR). Performs searches on fee basis. Contact Person: Michael Groves, 7564-248. **Publications:** DECHEMA Chemistry Data Series; DECHEMA Corrosion Handbook; DECHEMA Monograph Series; publications in all areas of chemical engineering and biotechnology. **Special Catalogs:** Publications catalog. **Remarks:** DECHEMA is an acronym for Deutsche Gesellschaft fur Chemisches Apparatewesen, Chemische Technik und Biotechnologie e.V. **Staff:** Dagmar Lower, Supv..

★18382★
DEFENSE SCIENCE AND TECHNOLOGY ORGANISATION - MATERIALS RESEARCH LABORATORIES - LIBRARY (Mil, Sci-Engr)
P.O. Box 50 Phone: 319 4499
Ascot Vale, VIC 3032, Australia Malcolm McPherson, Sr.Libn.
Subjects: Research and development of defense materials, organic and physical chemistry, physics, metallurgy, explosives, ballistics, protection of personnel and equipment. **Holdings:** 50,000 volumes; 100,000 reports. **Subscriptions:** 500 journals and other serials.

★18383★
DEMEURE HISTORIQUE - LIBRARY (Hist)
57, quai de la Tournelle Phone: 1 43290286
F-75005 Paris, France Marquis De Breteuil, Exec.Off.
Founded: 1924. **Subjects:** French historic landmarks. **Holdings:** 500 volumes.

DENMARK - MINISTRY OF ENVIRONMENT AND NORDIC AFFAIRS - GEOLOGICAL SURVEY OF DENMARK
See: Geological Survey of Denmark (18437)

DEUTSCHE BIBLIOTHEK
See: Federal Republic of Germany - Deutsche Bibliothek (18408)

DEUTSCHE GESELLSCHAFT FUR CHEMISCHES APPARATEWESEN, CHEMISCHE TECHNIK UND BIOTECHNOLOGIE E.V.
See: DECHEMA (18381)

DEUTSCHE STIFTUNG FUR INTERNATIONALE ENTWICKLUNG
See: German Foundation for International Development (18444)

DEUTSCHES ARCHAEOLOGISCHES INSTITUT
See: German Archaeological Institute (18442)

DEUTSCHES ARCHAEOLOGISCHES INSTITUT - ABTEILUNG ATHEN
See: German Archaeological Institute - Athens Division (18440)

DEUTSCHES HYDROGRAPHISCHES INSTITUT
See: German Hydrographic Institute (18445)

DEUTSCHES INSTITUT FUR INTERNATIONALE PADAGOGISCHE FORSCHUNG
See: German Institute for International Educational Research (18446)

★18384★
GEORGI DIMITROV HIGHER INSTITUTE OF PHYSICAL CULTURE - LIBRARY (Rec, Educ)
1 Tina Kirkova St. Phone: 2 88-15-11
Sofia, Bulgaria M. Karparova, Libn.
Subjects: Physical culture and sports - medicine, physiology, psychology, history, organization and managment. **Holdings:** 101,000 volumes. **Remarks:** Maintained by Bulgaria - Ministry of National Education. **Also Known As:** Vish Institut za fizicheska kultura "Georgi Dimitrov."

★18385★
DIPLOMATIC ACADEMY OF VIENNA - LIBRARY (Soc Sci)
Favoritenstrasse 15 Phone: 222 65 72 72
A-1040 Vienna, Austria Dr. G. Loibl, Libn.
Subjects: International relations, law, and economics; foreign languages; history; diplomacy; politics. **Holdings:** 25,000 volumes. **Remarks:** Maintained by Austria - Ministry of Foreign Affairs. **Also Known As:** Diplomatische Akademie Wien.

DIPLOMATISCHE AKADEMIE WIEN
See: Diplomatic Academy of Vienna (18385)

DIXSON LIBRARY
See: State Library of New South Wales - Mitchell Library (18790)

★18386★
DOBRA IRON AND STEEL RESEARCH INSTITUTE - LIBRARY (Sci-Engr)
CS-739 51 Dobra, Czechoslovakia Phone: 23421
Boris Skandera, Hd.
Staff: Prof 36. **Subjects:** Metallurgy, steel production, extraction and treatment of metals, powder metallurgy, nonferrous metals, automation in the field of metallurgy, economics. **Holdings:** 900,000 volumes; 400,000 special materials. **Subscriptions:** 11,500 journals and other serials. **Services:** Interlibrary loan; copying; SDI; library open to the public. **Computerized Information Services:** DIALOG Information Services, Pergamon ORBIT InfoLine, Inc., Data-Star, STN International; produces INFORMETAL; internal database. Performs searches on fee basis. **Publications:** Hutnicke aktuality, 12/year - international exchange. **Also Known As:** Vyzkumny Ustav Hutnictvi Zeleza, Dobra.

★18387★
DOCUMENTATION CENTRE FOR EDUCATION IN EUROPE (Educ)
Council of Europe
Boite Postal 431 R6 Phone: 88 61 49 61
F-67006 Strasbourg Cedex, France Wilson Barrett
Founded: 1964. **Subjects:** Education. **Holdings:** 20,000 volumes. **Remarks:** Telex: 870943. **Also Known As:** Centre de Documentation pour l'Education en Europe.

E

★18388★
EAST CHINA INSTITUTE OF TEXTILE SCIENCE AND TECHNOLOGY - LIBRARY (Sci-Engr)
1882 West Yan'an Lu Phone: 522430
Shanghai, People's Republic of China Zhou Shiqiu, Libn.
Founded: 1951. **Staff:** 46. **Subjects:** Cotton and wool textile engineering, mechanical engineering, knitting, textiles, textile industry management, textile machinery, automation, instrumentation, synthetic fibers, dyeing and finishing, environmental control, chemical engineering. **Holdings:** 384,317 volumes; 2965 periodicals; 1047 technical reports; 360 AV programs and microforms. **Services:** Copying.

★18389★
EAST EUROPEAN INSTITUTE, MUNICH - LIBRARY (Hist, Area-Ethnic)
Scheinerstrasse 11 Phone: 89 98 38 21
D-8000 Munich 80, Federal Republic of Germany
Dr. Otto Boess, Libn.
Subjects: History and economy of Eastern Europe and the Soviet Union. **Holdings:** 120,000 volumes. **Remarks:** Affiliated with the Foundation for Research on Eastern Europe and the Bavarian State Ministry for Education and Culture. **Also Known As:** Osteuropa-Institut Munchen.

ECOLE POLYTECHNIQUE FEDERALE DE LAUSANNE
See: Swiss Federal Institute of Technology, Lausanne (18807)

★18390★
ECONOMIC AND SOCIAL COMMISSION FOR ASIA AND THE PACIFIC - NATURAL RESOURCES DIVISION - ENERGY RESOURCES SECTION - LIBRARY (Energy)
United Nations Bldg.
Rajadamnern Ave.
Bangkok 10200, Thailand Phone: 2 282-9161
Subjects: Energy assessment and planning, accelerated development and use of new and renewable sources of energy, conservation and efficient use of energy. **Holdings:** 20,000 volumes.

★18391★
ECUADORIAN INSTITUTE OF NATURAL SCIENCES - LIBRARY (Biol Sci, Env-Cons)
Casilla 408 Phone: 2 215-497
Quito, Ecuador Prof. Carlos A. Carrera, Libn.
Subjects: Natural resources, phytogeography, soil conservation and erosion, forestry, ecology of tropical forests. **Holdings:** 36,000 volumes. **Remarks:** Affiliated with Ecuador - Ministry of Public Education, Sports, and Culture. **Also Known As:** Instituto Ecuatoriano de Ciencias Naturales.

EDUCATIONAL INSTITUTE OF SCOTLAND LIBRARY
See: National Library of Scotland (18641)

EIDGENOESSISCHES INSTITUT FUER REAKTORFORSCHUNG
See: Swiss Federal Institutes of Technology - Swiss Federal Institute for Reactor Research (18809)

EIDGENOESSISCHES INSTITUT FUER SCHNEE- UND LAWINENFORSCHUNG
See: Switzerland - Federal Forest Office - Federal Institute for Snow and Avalanche Research (18810)

EIDGENOSSISCHE TECHNISCHE HOCHSCHULE
See: Swiss Federal Institute of Technology, Zurich (18808)

★18392★
ELECTRONICS AND TELECOMMUNICATIONS RESEARCH INSTITUTE - ETRI LIBRARY (Sci-Engr, Info Sci)
P.O. Box 8
Daedog Danji Phone: 822-4455
Chung Nam 300-31, Republic of Korea Dong Chin Woo, Hd. of Lib.
Subjects: Information technology, telecommunications, computer science, automation, semiconductors. **Holdings:** 50,000 volumes. **Remarks:** Maintained by Korea - Ministry of Science and Technology.

EMPRESA BRASILEIRA DE PESQUISA AGROPECUARIA - CENTRO DE PESQUISA AGROPECUARIA TROPICA UMIDO
See: Brazilian Agricultural Research Corporation - Agricultural Research Center for the Humid Tropics (18312)

★18393★
ENGLISH FOLK DANCE AND SONG SOCIETY - VAUGHAN WILLIAMS MEMORIAL LIBRARY (Mus)
Cecil Sharp House
2 Regent's Park Rd. Phone: 1 485 2206
London NW1 7AY, England Malcolm Taylor, Libn.
Subjects: Traditional music, song, dance, and customs; storytelling; social history; folk revivals. **Special Collections:** 20th century collections of traditional music, including Percy Grainger, Cecil Sharp, Ralph Vaughan Williams, James Carpenter, Mike Yates, and British Broadcasting Corporation (BBC; manuscripts; field recordings). **Holdings:** 15,000 books; 100 bound periodical volumes; 175 microforms; 25 manuscripts. **Services:** Interlibrary loan (limited); copying; library open to the public on fee basis. **Publications:** A List of Books for the Study of Folk Song; A List of Books for the Study of English Folk Dancing; Folk Music Collected in the British Isles: Some Manuscript and Recorded Collections Accessible to the Public; additional publications available - all for sale. **Special Catalogs:** Catalogs of: photographs, periodicals, leaflets, Cecil Sharp's informants, films, videos; Sound Library catalog. **Special Indexes:** Indexes to: song titles, dance titles, tune titles, folk plays.

EPITESUGYI ES VAROSFEJLESZTESI MINISZTERIUM - EPITESUGYI TAJEKOZTATASI KOZPONT
See: Hungary - Ministry of Building and Urban Development - Information Centre of Building (18480)

ERDELYI VILAGSZOVETSEG
See: Transylvanian World Federation (18819)

★18394★
ESPERANTO CULTURAL CENTRE - LIBRARY (Hum)
Postiers 27, Case Postale 771 Phone: 39 26 74 07
CH-2301 La Chaux-De-Fonds, Switzerland Claude Gacond, Dir.
Founded: 1968. **Subjects:** Esperanto. **Holdings:** 10,000 volumes. **Remarks:** Jointly maintained with the Centro De Dokumentado Kaj Exploro Pri La Lingua Internacia. **Also Known As:** Kultura Centro Esperantista.

ESTACION EXPERIMENTAL AGRO-INDUSTRIAL OBISPO COLOMBRES
See: Obispo Colombres Agro-Industrial Experiment Station (18667)

★18395★
ESZTERGOMI FOSZEKESEGYHAZI KONYVTAR (Rel-Phil)
Bajcsy Zsilinszky utca 28 Phone: 527
H-2500 Esztergom, Hungary Dr. Matyas Erdos, Dir.
Subjects: Religion. **Special Collections:** Lajos Batthiany; Mayer; Jakob Fugger. **Holdings:** 250,000 volumes; 1000 bound periodical volumes. **Services:** Interlibrary loan; copying; library open to the public with restrictions.

ETHIOPIA - MINISTRY OF CULTURE - THE NATIONAL LIBRARY AND ARCHIVES OF ETHIOPIA
See: The National Library and Archives of Ethiopia (18631)

★18396★
EUROPEAN ACADEMY OF FACIAL SURGERY - LIBRARY (Med)
107 Harley St. Phone: 1 935 3171
London W1, England P. Adlington
Founded: 1977. **Subjects:** Facial plastic surgery. **Holdings:** Videotapes.

★18397★
EUROPEAN BAPTIST FEDERATION - INTERNATIONAL BAPTIST THEOLOGICAL SEMINARY - LIBRARY (Rel-Phil)
Laerdalsgade 7
DK-2300 Copenhagen S, Denmark Phone: 1 590904
Subjects: Theology, missions, understanding between Baptists and other Christians. **Holdings:** 50,000 volumes. **Subscriptions:** 350 journals and other serials.

★18398★
EUROPEAN CENTER FOR APPLIED ECONOMIC RESEARCH - LIBRARY (Bus-Fin)
Steinengraben 42 Phone: 22 32 00
CH-4012 Basel, Switzerland Mr. Bodenstedt, Libn.
Subjects: Applied economics, innovation and new technology, market research, marketing, management consulting, economic analysis and policy consulting, regional policy and local authorities, technical infrastructure, energy, water, transportation, health policy. **Holdings:** 50,000 volumes. **Remarks:** Telex: 963 323 PROG.

★18399★
EUROPEAN CHIROPRACTORS' UNION - LIBRARY (Med)
Anglo-European Chiropractic College
13/15 Parkwood Rd. Phone: 202 431021
Bournemouth BH5 2DF, England A. Christensen, Pres.
Subjects: Chiropractic and life sciences. **Holdings:** 7000 books.

★18400★
EUROPEAN INSTITUTE OF ENVIRONMENTAL CYBERNETICS - LIBRARY (Sci-Engr, Biol Sci)
GR-162 32 Athens, Greece Phone: 1 363 5951
B.D. Georgeascu, Libn.
Founded: 1970. **Subjects:** Automation, biosciences, biotechnology, energy, information science, environmental and health control, management, nuclear studies, pollution control, space sciences. **Holdings:** 30,000 volumes.

★18401★
EUROPEAN ORGANIZATION FOR NUCLEAR RESEARCH - LIBRARY (Sci-Engr)
CH-1211 Geneva, Switzerland Phone: 22 836111
Dr. Alfred Gunther, Libn.
Subjects: Nuclear research. **Holdings:** 50,000 volumes; 25,000 periodicals; 80,000 reports and reprints. **Services:** Library open to scientists. **Remarks:** Organization is a center for research and not concerned with the development of nuclear power or weapons.

★18402★
EUROPEAN REGIONAL CLEARINGHOUSE FOR COMMUNITY WORK - LIBRARY (Soc Sci)
179, rue du Debarcadere
B-6001 Marcinelle, Belgium Mrs. Bertiaux
Founded: 1976. **Subjects:** Social work, gerontology. **Holdings:** 1500 volumes.

★18403★
EUROPEAN SPACE AGENCY (ESA) - LIBRARY (Sci-Engr)
8-10, rue Mario Nikis Phone: 42 73 76 54
F-75738 Paris, France R.J. Weiss, Chf.Libn.
Subjects: Astronomy, astrophysics, space plasma physics, advanced space technology, telecommunications, life sciences, material sciences, launcher technology, remote sensing by satellite. **Holdings:** 21,000 volumes; 600,000 microfiche; 6000 reports and standards. **Remarks:** The agency comprises three principal components: 1) European Space Research and Technology Center, located in Noordwijk, The Netherlands; 2) European Space Operations Center, located in Darmstadt, Federal Republic of Germany; and 3) European Space Research Institute, located in Rome, Italy.

★18404★
EXECUTIVE YUAN - COUNCIL OF AGRICULTURE - AGRICULTURAL SCIENCE INFORMATION CENTER (Agri)
14 Wen-Chou St. Phone: 2 3946222
Taipei 10616, Taiwan Wan-Jiun Wu, Dir.
Subjects: Agriculture, forestry, fisheries, animal husbandry, food science. **Holdings:** 5200 books; 1160 bound periodical volumes. **Services:** Copying; SDI; center open to the public. **Computerized Information Services:** Agricultural Science & Technology Information Management System (ASTIMS), DIALOG Information Services, BRS Information Technologies, Pergamon ORBIT InfoLine, Inc., ESA/IRS. Performs searches on fee basis. Contact Person: Ching-Whay Chung, Libn.. **Publications:** ASIC Universal Information Service System; List of Agricultural Journals/Periodicals; Bibliography of Agricultural Literature. **Also Known As:** ASIC.

F

★18405★
FACHINFORMATIONSZENTRUM KARLSRUHE GMBH. - LIBRARY (Sci-Engr, Energy)
D-7514 Eggenstein-Leopoldshafen 2, Federal Republic of Germany
Phone: 49 7247 824600
Dr. Werner Rittberger, Dir.
Subjects: Energy, nuclear research and technology, astronautics, aeronautics, space research, physics, mathematics and informatics, astronomy and astrophysics. **Holdings:** 83,000 monographs; 1.70 million reports. **Subscriptions:** 3092 journals and other serials. **Services:** Copying; SDI; library open to the public on a fee basis. **Computerized Information Services:** STN International, INKADATA. Performs searches on fee basis. **Formerly:** Information Center for Energy Physics Mathematics. **Also Known As:** Fachinformationszentrum Energie, Physik, Mathematik GmbH - FIZ Karlsruhe. **Staff:** Mrs. U. Keil, Hd., Lib.Div..

FACULTE DES SCIENCES AGRONOMIQUES DE L'ETAT
See: Belgium - Ministry of National Education - Gembloux State Facility of Agricultural Sciences - Library (18299)

★18406★
FEDERAL INSTITUTE FOR EAST EUROPEAN AND INTERNATIONAL STUDIES - LIBRARY (Area-Ethnic, Soc Sci)
Lindenbornstrasse 22
Phone: 57-47-0
D-5000 Cologne 30, Federal Republic of Germany
Stefan Mardak, Libn.
Subjects: International politics, international relations, Communism, Eastern Europe, Soviet Union. **Holdings:** 190,000 volumes. **Also Known As:** Bundesinstitut fuer Ostwissenschaftliche und Internationale Studien.

FEDERAL INSTITUTE FOR SNOW AND AVALANCHE RESEARCH
See: Switzerland - Federal Forest Office - Federal Institute for Snow and Avalanche Research (18810)

★18407★
FEDERAL INSTITUTE FOR SPORTS SCIENCE - DOCUMENTATION AND INFORMATION DIVISION - LIBRARY (Rec)
Carl-Diem-Weg 4
Phone: 221 4979
D-5000 Cologne 41, Federal Republic of Germany
Siegfried Lachenicht, Dir.
Subjects: Sports and sport science - sporting events, individual athletic performances, sports medicine, research; allied subjects. **Holdings:** 16,500 volumes; 25,000 reprints of journal articles. **Subscriptions:** 650 journals and other serials. **Services:** Library open to researchers, those involved with sports legislation, trainers, teachers, students, athletes, sports officials, sports reporters. **Computerized Information Services:** SPOLIT, SPOFOR. Performs searches on fee basis. **Also Known As:** Bundesinstitut fur Sportwissenschaft - Fachbereich Dokumentation und Information.

★18408★
FEDERAL REPUBLIC OF GERMANY - DEUTSCHE BIBLIOTHEK (Area-Ethnic, Hum, Info Sci)
Zeppelinallee 4-8
Phone: 69 75 661
D-6000 Frankfurt am Main, Federal Republic of Germany
Ute Valentin, Asst. to Gen.Dir.
Subjects: German publications and foreign German language publications, May 8, 1945 to present; foreign publications of translations of German works; foreign language publications about Germany. **Special Collections:** German Music Archives; German Exile Archives (works written by German-speaking emigrants, 1933-1945). **Holdings:** 2.6 million books; 544,032 bound periodical volumes; 236,839 AV programs; 282,284 microforms; 60,348 manuscripts. **Services:** Interlibrary loan; copying; SDI; library open to the public for reference use only. **Computerized Information Services:** BIBLIO-DATA. Performs searches on fee basis. Contact Person: Dr. Reinhold Buchbinder, 7566394. **Publications:** Deutsche Bibliographie. **Staff:** Dr. Gunther Pflug.

★18409★
FEDERAL REPUBLIC OF GERMANY - FEDERAL ENVIRONMENTAL AGENCY - ENVIRONMENTAL INFORMATION AND DOCUMENTATION SYSTEM - LIBRARY (Env-Cons)
Bismarckplatz 1
Phone: 30 8903305
D-1000 Berlin 33, Federal Republic of Germany
Dr. Klaus Luedcke
Staff: Prof 5; Other 12. **Subjects:** Environment, pollution, solid wastes, environmental chemicals and wastes, noise, environmental research, allied subjects. **Special Collections:** Sammlung Erhard (archives of solid waste, 1900 to present; 2000 books, journals, reports, photographs). **Holdings:** 65,000 volumes; 120,000 microforms. **Subscriptions:** 500 journals and other serials. **Services:** Interlibrary loan; copying; SDI; library open to the public with restrictions. **Automated Operations:** Computerized public access catalog. **Computerized Information Services:** Data-Star; produces ULIDAT, UFORDAT, AWIDAT, DABAWAS; internal database. **Special Catalogs:** Environmental Research Catalogue. **Also Known As:** Umweltbundesamt - Informations- und Dokumentationssystem Umwelt - Zentrale Fachbibliothek.

FEDERAL REPUBLIC OF GERMANY - FOREIGN MINISTRY - GERMAN ARCHAELOGICAL INSTITUTE
See: German Archaeological Institute (18442)

FEDERAL REPUBLIC OF GERMANY - MINISTRY OF RESEARCH AND TECHNOLOGY - INSTITUTE OF CONTEMPORARY HISTORY
See: Institute of Contemporary History (18502)

★18410★
FEDERAL REPUBLIC OF GERMANY - MINISTRY OF RESEARCH AND TECHNOLOGY - JUELICH NUCLEAR RESEARCH CENTER - LIBRARY (Energy, Sci-Engr)
Postfach 1913
Phone: 6 10
D-5170 Juelich 1, Federal Republic of Germany
Dr. Manz, Libn.
Subjects: Energy technology, materials research, nuclear research, reactor plants, nuclear fusion. **Holdings:** 340,000 books; 360,000 reports. **Also Known As:** Kernforschungsanlage Juelich.

FEDERAL REPUBLIC OF GERMANY - MINISTRY OF TRANSPORT - GERMAN HYDROGRAPHIC INSTITUTE
See: German Hydrographic Institute (18445)

★18411★
FEDERAL STATISTICAL OFFICE - LIBRARY (Sci-Engr)
Gustav-Stresemann-Ring 11
Phone: 061217 51
D-6200 Wiesbaden, Federal Republic of Germany
R.D. Steiger
Founded: 1948. **Staff:** Prof 9; Other 18. **Subjects:** Statistics, statistical methods, economics, demography, ecology, social sciences. **Special Collections:** International statistical publications. **Holdings:** 234,000 statistical publications; 1600 microfiche; 3000 clippings. **Subscriptions:** 6150 journals and other serials; 22 newspapers. **Services:** Interlibrary loan; copying; SDI; library open to the public. **Automated Operations:** Computerized public access catalog, cataloging, and serials. **Computerized Information Services:** STALIS (internal database). Performs searches free of charge. **Publications:** Current contents; SDI; accession list, all monthly; list of periodicals. **Also Known As:** Statistisches Bundesamt.

FINLAND - MINISTRY OF AGRICULTURE AND FORESTRY - FINNISH FOREST RESEARCH INSTITUTE
See: Finnish Forest Research Institute (18413)

FINLAND - MINISTRY OF AGRICULTURE AND FORESTRY - FINNISH GEODETIC INSTITUTE
See: Finnish Geodetic Institute (18414)

FINLAND - MINISTRY OF COMMERCE AND INDUSTRY - GEOLOGICAL SURVEY OF FINLAND
See: Geological Survey of Finland (18438)

FINLAND - MINISTRY OF EDUCATION - NATIONAL BOARD OF ANTIQUITIES
See: National Board of Antiquities (18618)

★18412★
FINLAND - MINISTRY OF SOCIAL AFFAIRS AND HEALTH - FINNISH CENTER FOR RADIATION AND NUCLEAR SAFETY - LIBRARY (Sci-Engr)
P.O. Box 268 Phone: 0 61671
SF-00101 Helsinki 15, Finland Armi Lankelin, Libn.
Subjects: Radiation protection. **Holdings:** 12,000 volumes. **Also Known As:** Sateilyturvakeskus.

FINLAND - TECHNICAL RESEARCH CENTRE OF FINLAND
See: Technical Research Centre of Finland (18816)

C.J. FINLAY LIBRARY
See: Cuban Academy of Sciences - Center for the Study of the History and Organization of Science (18370)

★18413★
FINNISH FOREST RESEARCH INSTITUTE - LIBRARY (Biol Sci)
Unioninkatu 40A Phone: 0 661401
SF-00170 Helsinki 17, Finland Liisa Ikavalko-Ahvonen, Libn.
Subjects: Forests and forest resources. **Holdings:** 45,000 books. **Remarks:** Maintained by Finland - Ministry of Agriculture and Forestry. **Also Known As:** Metsantutkimuslaitos.

★18414★
FINNISH GEODETIC INSTITUTE - LIBRARY (Sci-Engr)
Ilmalankatu 1A Phone: 0 410433
SF-00240 Helsinki, Finland Leena Kulju, Libn.
Subjects: Geodesy, gravimetry, photogrammetry, cartography. **Holdings:** 31,000 volumes. **Services:** Interlibrary loan; library open to the public. **Publications:** Publications and reports of the Finnish Geodetic Institute. **Remarks:** Maintained by Finland - Ministry of Agriculture and Forestry. **Also Known As:** Suomen Geodeettinen Laitos.

★18415★
FINNISH PULP AND PAPER RESEARCH INSTITUTE - TECHNICAL INFORMATION MANAGEMENT (Sci-Engr)
P.O. Box 136 Phone: 0 43711
SF-00101 Helsinki, Finland Jorma Paakko, Res.Mgr.
Staff: Prof 7; Other 12. **Subjects:** Pulp, paper, board, packaging. **Holdings:** 40,000 volumes. **Subscriptions:** 420 journals and other serials. **Services:** Interlibrary loan; copying; SDI; open to the public. **Automated Operations:** Computerized public access catalog and cataloging. **Computerized Information Services:** DIALOG Information Services, Pergamon ORBIT InfoLine, Inc., STN International; internal database. Performs searches on fee basis. Contact Person: Birgitta af Forselles, Info.Spec., 4371268. **Publications:** Weekly Survey of Periodicals; list of accessions; list of meetings. **Also Known As:** Oy Keskuslaboratorio - Centrallaboratorium Ab. **Staff:** Eija Ilveskorpi, Info.Spec.; Aimo Kaiku, Info.Spec..

★18416★
FINNISH STANDARDS ASSOCIATION SFS - INFORMATION SERVICE (Sci-Engr)
Bulevardi 5 A 7
P.O. Box 205 Phone: 0 645 601
SF-00121 Helsinki, Finland Marjatta Aarniala, Mgr.
Subjects: Finnish, international, and foreign standards. **Holdings:** 220,000 standards and documents. **Computerized Information Services:** Produces SFS Data Base. Performs searches on fee basis. **Publications:** SFS Tiedotus (list of new standards, drafts and draft technical regulations), bimonthly. **Special Catalogs:** SFS Catalogue (bilingual list of Finnish Standards Association Standards), annual with supplements. **Remarks:** Telex: 122303 stand sf; Fax: 358 0 643 147. **Also Known As:** Suomen Standardisoimisliitto SFS.

★18417★
HARRY FISCHEL INSTITUTE FOR RESEARCH IN TALMUD AND JEWISH LAW - LIBRARY (Law, Rel-Phil)
5 Hapisga St.
P.O. Box 16002
Jerusalem, Israel Phone: 2 416166
Subjects: Jewish law, ancient and medieval rabbinical works, codification of Jewish law, Jewish law as applied in Rabbinical Courts of Israel. **Holdings:** 40,000 volumes. **Remarks:** Maintained by Israel - Ministry of Religious Affairs.

FONDATION NATIONALE DES SCIENCES POLITIQUES - CENTRE DE HAUTES ETUDES SUR L'AFRIQUE ET L'ASIE MODERNES
See: Center for Advanced Studies on Modern Africa and Asia (18335)

FONDO COLOMBIANO DE INVESTIGACIONES CIENTIFICAS Y PROYECTOS ESPECIALES FRANCISCO JOSE DE CALDAS
See: Francisco Jose De Caldas Columbian Organization for Scientific Research and Special Projects (18380)

FONDS MONDIAL POUR LA CONSERVATION DE LA NATURE
See: World Wide Fund for Nature (18874)

FONDS QUETELET LIBRARY
See: Belgium - Ministry of Economic Affairs (18297)

★18418★
FOOTSCRAY INSTITUTE OF TECHNOLOGY - LIBRARY - AUSTRALIAN CLEARING HOUSE FOR PUBLICATIONS IN RECREATION SPORT AND TOURISM (Rec)
P.O. Box 64 Phone: 3 6884544
Footscray, VIC 3011, Australia Lea Giles-Peters, Coord.
Subjects: Sport, tourism, and recreation in Australia. **Holdings:** 80,000 volumes; 3000 AV programs. **Subscriptions:** 1000 journals and other serials. **Services:** Clearinghouse open to the public. **Computerized Information Services:** AUSINET; produces LeisureLine. Performs searches on fee basis. **Publications:** Australian Leisure Bibliography - for sale. **Special Indexes:** Australian Leisure Index, semiannual - by subscription.

FORSCHUNGSINSTITUT DER FRIEDRICH-EBERT STIFTUNG - BIBLIOTHEK DER SOZIALEN DEMOKRATIE
See: Research Institute of the Friedrich Ebert Foundation - Library of Social Democracy (18726)

FORSCHUNGSINSTITUT FUER INTERNATIONALE POLITIK UND SICHERHEIT
See: Research Institute for International Politics and Security (18727)

FORSCHUNGSINSTITUT UND NATURMUSEUM SENCKENBERG
See: Senckenberg Research Institute and Natural History Museum (18765)

FOUNDATION FOR RESEARCH ON EASTERN EUROPE - EAST EUROPEAN INSTITUTE, MUNICH
See: East European Institute, Munich (18389)

★18419★
FRANCE - BIBLIOTHEQUE NATIONALE - BIBLIOTHEQUE DE L'ARSENAL (Area-Ethnic, Hist, Hum)
1, rue de Sully Phone: 1 42 77 44 21
F-75004 Paris, France Jean-Claude Garreta, Cons. en chef
Subjects: 17th and 18th century France, French literature, history of books, heraldry. **Special Collections:** Archives de la Bastille (18th century; 2700 documents); Enfantin Collection (19th century socialism; 800 volumes); Lambert Collection (J.-K. Huysmans; 95 manuscripts). **Holdings:** 1 million books; 100 microforms; 15,000 manuscripts. **Services:** Interlibrary loan; copying; library open to the public with restrictions. **Special Catalogs:** Catalogue des manuscrits de la bibliotheque de l'Arsenal Paris 1885-1892 (9 volumes).

★18420★
FRANCE - BIBLIOTHEQUE NATIONALE - DEPARTEMENT DE LA PHONOTHEQUE NATIONALE ET DE L'AUDIOVISUEL (Aud-Vis)
2, rue de Louvois Phone: 1 47 03 88 20
F-75002 Paris, France Dominique Villemot, Chf., Pub.Serv.
Subjects: General collection. **Special Collections:** Romanian Collection, 1928; G. Massignon Ethnographic Collection, 1941-1966; Ch. Delaunay Collection, 1977; Nadia Boulanger Collection; Musee Charles Cros (350 old phonographs). **Holdings:** 4000 books; 500 serial titles; 1 million phonograph records, magnetic tapes, videotapes; 5000 AV programs. **Services:** Copying; department open to the public with restrictions. **Computerized Information Services:** Internal database. Performs searches free of charge. **Publications:** Phonographies: Faure, Poulenc, Milhaud. **Staff:** Marie France Calas, Dir..

★18421★
FRANCE - BIBLIOTHEQUE NATIONALE - MUSEE DE L'OPERA - BIBLIOTHEQUE (Mus, Theater)
Place Charles Garnier Phone: 1 47 42 07 02
F-75009 Paris, France Martine Kahane, Cons.
Subjects: Opera, ballet, music. **Special Collections:** Russian ballet; Taglioni; Rouche; Saint Leon; Garnier. **Holdings:** 85,000 books; 1500 serial titles; 130,000 drawings and prints. **Services:** Interlibrary loan; copying; library open to the public. **Special Catalogs:** Catalogs to circus collection, illustrated posters, and 19th century scenery drawings.

★18422★
FRANCE - BUREAU DE RECHERCHES GEOLOGIQUES ET MINIERES - SERVICE GEOLOGIQUE NATIONAL - DEPARTEMENT DOCUMENTATION ET INFORMATION GEOLOGIQUE (Sci-Engr)
Boite Postale 6009
F-45060 Orleans Cedex, France Phone: 38 643552
Subjects: Earth sciences - mineralogy, geochemistry, extraterrestrial geology, mineral deposits, economic geology, sedimentary and crystalline petrology, marine geology, stratigraphy, paleontology, hydrogeology, geomorphology, soil sciences, engineering geology. **Holdings:** 12,000 volumes; 25,000 maps. **Subscriptions:** 1500 journals and other serials. **Services:** SDI; department open to geologists. **Computerized Information Services:** Produces PASCAL-GEODE. Performs searches on fee basis. **Publications:** Bibliographic bulletin, 10/year.

★18423★
FRANCE - MINISTERE DE L'EDUCATION - VELAZQUEZ HOUSE - LIBRARY (Hum, Area-Ethnic)
Ciudad Universitaria Phone: 1 243 36 05
E-28040 Madrid, Spain Laurence Camous, Cons.
Subjects: Spain and Latin America - literature, arts, humanities, including history, geography, economy, art, hispanic anthropology, painting, sculpture, engraving, architecture, music, cinema. **Holdings:** 90,000 volumes; 1200 periodicals. **Also Known As:** Casa de Velazquez.

FRANCE - MINISTERE DE L'EDUCATION NATIONALE - BIBLIOTHEQUE NATIONALE ET UNIVERSITAIRE DE STRASBOURG
See: Bibliotheque Nationale et Universitaire de Strasbourg (18303)

FRANCE - MINISTRY OF EDUCATION - FRENCH INSTITUTE OF EASTERN ARCHEOLOGY
See: French Institute of Eastern Archeology (18428)

★18424★
FRANCISCAN BIBLICAL INSTITUTE - LIBRARY (Rel-Phil)
Via Dolorosa
P.O. Box 19424 Phone: 2 282936
Jerusalem 91140, Israel Fr. Tomislav Vuk, Libn.
Subjects: Biblical and Christian archeology, Judeo-Christianity, Bible. **Holdings:** 30,000 volumes. **Subscriptions:** 250 journals and other serials. **Publications:** Liber Annuus, annual; Collection Maior, Collection Minor, Analecta, Museum, irregular - distributed by Franciscan Printing Press. **Remarks:** Sponsored by Franciscan Custody of the Holy Land. **Also Known As:** Studium Biblicum Franciscanum.

FRANCISCAN CUSTODY OF THE HOLY LAND - FRANCISCAN BIBLICAL INSTITUTE
See: Franciscan Biblical Institute (18424)

★18425★
FRAUNHOFER SOCIETY - INFORMATION CENTRE FOR REGIONAL PLANNING AND BUILDING CONSTRUCTION (Plan)
Nobelstrasse 12 Phone: 711 6868500
D-7000 Stuttgart 80, Federal Republic of Germany
Mr. J. Acevedo-Alvarez, Engr.
Subjects: Regional and city planning, housing, civil engineering, building development, spatial structure, regulations, urban renewal, conservation, economics, regional policy, building politics and economics, standards, architecture, horticulture and landscaping, construction. **Holdings:** 40,000 volumes; 2 million references in card files. **Subscriptions:** 1500 journals and other serials. **Services:** SDI; center open to building and construction industry, government agencies, and other interested organizations and individuals. **Computerized Information Services:** Informationssystem Karlsruhe (INKA), CIBDOC. Performs searches on fee basis. **Publications:** New Literature Compilations (subject bibliographies), bimonthly; additional publications available. **Also Known As:** Fraunhofer-Gesellschaft - Informationszentrum Raum und Bau.

★18426★
FRENCH INSTITUTE OF ANDEAN STUDIES - LIBRARY (Area-Ethnic)
Apartado 278 Phone: 14 476070
Lima 18, Peru Zaida Janning de Sanchez, Libn.
Subjects: Andes - geology, anthropology, history, sociology, ethnology, geography. **Holdings:** 35,000 volumes. **Remarks:** Maintained by French Foreign Affairs Office. **Also Known As:** Institut Francais d'Etudes Andines.

★18427★
FRENCH INSTITUTE FOR ARCHAEOLOGY IN THE NEAR EAST - LIBRARY (Soc Sci, Area-Ethnic)
P.O. Box 11-1424 Phone: 917-511
Beirut, Lebanon Dr. Frank Braemer, Libn.
Subjects: Archeology and history of the Near East, fourth millenium B.C. to seventh century A.D. **Holdings:** 40,000 volumes. **Publications:** Bibliotheque Archeologique, 4-5/year (in French, German, English, Arabic). **Also Known As:** Institut Francais d'Archeologie du Proche-Orient.

★18428★
FRENCH INSTITUTE OF EASTERN ARCHEOLOGY - LIBRARY (Soc Sci, Area-Ethnic)
37 Sh. el Cheikh Aly Youssef (Mounira)
B.P. Qasr el Ainy 11562 Phone: 3 557142
Cairo, Egypt J.P. Corteggiani, Libn.
Subjects: Archeology, Egyptology, Coptology, Greek and Arabic languages, papyrology, Islam. **Holdings:** 60,000 volumes. **Remarks:** Maintained by France - Ministry of Education. **Also Known As:** Institut Francais d'Archeologie Orientale.

★18429★
FUNDACAO CASA DE RUI BARBOSA - BIBLIOTECA (Area-Ethnic, Law, Hum)
Rua Sao Clemente, 134 Phone: 21 2861297
22260 Rio de Janeiro, Brazil Maria Amelia Bianchini, Libn.
Subjects: History of Brazil, law, literature, philology. **Special Collections:** Cordel collection (popular literature originating in northeast Brazil; 6000 pamphlets). **Holdings:** 60,000 books; 2200 periodical titles. **Services:** Interlibrary loan; copying; library open to the public for reference use only. **Publications:** Bibliographies. **Remarks:** Telex: (21)37232 - RCBR. **Staff:** Beatriz Amaral de Salles Coelho, Hd.Libn..

FUNDACAO GETULIO VARGAS
See: Getulio Vargas Foundation (18869)

★18430★
FUNDACAO INSTITUTO BRASILEIRO DE GEOGRAFIA E ESTATISTICA (IBGE) - GERENCIA DE DOCUMENTACAO E BIBLIOTECA (Geog-Map, Soc Sci)
Avenida Franklin Roosevelt, 166 Phone: 21 220-7243
20021 Rio de Janeiro RJ, Brazil
Maria Beatriz Pontes de Carvalho, Dir.
Subjects: Statistics, geography, economics, demography, cartography, natural resources. **Special Collections:** Race books (early censuses); atlases; Brasiliana. **Holdings:** 40,000 books; 3000 bound periodical volumes; 9334 microfiche; 97 reels of microfilm. **Services:** Interlibrary loan; copying; library open to the public. **Computerized Information Services:** Internal database. Performs searches free of charge. **Publications:** Publicacoes editadas pelo IBGE (Volume 1: Periodicals; Volume 2: Monographs). **Special Catalogs:** Catalogo do IBGE 1986, 2nd edition. **Special Indexes:** Cumulated Index of Revista Brasileira de Estatistica, 1941-1981. **Remarks:** Telex: 2130939.

★18431★
FUNDACAO UNIVERSIDADE DE BRASILIA - BIBLIOTECA CENTRAL (Educ, Soc Sci, Med)
Campus Universitario
Asa Norte
Casilla Postal 15-2951 Phone: 61 2742412
Brasilia 70910, Brazil Murilo Bastos da Cunha, Dir.
Subjects: Mathematics, education, economics, social sciences, medicine, literature. **Special Collections:** Rare books (6000); classical studies (5000 volumes). **Holdings:** 500,000 books; 2056 microforms; 50 AV programs; 5 manuscripts. **Subscriptions:** 7080 journals and other serials. **Services:** Interlibrary loan; copying; library open to the public with restrictions.

Computerized Information Services: DIALOG Information Services, Telesystemes Questel. **Remarks:** Telex: 611083.

FUNDACION MIGUEL LILLO - CENTRO DE INFORMACION GEO-BIOLOGICA NOA
See: Miguel Lillo Foundation - Information Center (18592)

★18432★
FUTURIBLES INTERNATIONAL - LIBRARY (Bus-Fin)
55, rue de Varenne Phone: 1 42 22 63 10
F-75007 Paris, France Annie Palmantier, Exec.Sec.
Staff: Prof 2. **Subjects:** Futures studies, forecasting, planning. **Holdings:** 10,000 books. **Subscriptions:** 100 journals and other serials. **Services:** Interlibrary loan; library not open to the public. **Also Known As:** Association Internationale Futuribles. **Staff:** Laurence Faupin, Responsable.

G

★18433★
MAHATMA GANDHI INSTITUTE - LIBRARY (Area-Ethnic)
Mahatma Gandhi Institute Ave. Phone: 4-8021
Moka, Mauritius Chan Kam Lon, Libn.
Subjects: History and multiculturalism of Mauritius, oriental languages, oral traditions, demography, Indian immigration. **Holdings:** 30,000 volumes. **Remarks:** Maintained by Mauritius - Ministry of Education, Arts and Culture.

★18434★
GANSU PROVINCIAL ACADEMY OF SOCIAL SCIENCES - LIBRARY AND INFORMATION DEPARTMENT (Soc Sci)
Dajiazhuang
Shilidian
Lanzhou, Gansu Province, People's Republic of China
Wu Mingde, Libn.
Founded: 1978. **Staff:** 7. **Subjects:** Philosophy, economics, history, scientific socialism, literature, Marxism, Leninism, Maoism, population. **Special Collections:** Chinese ancient books; politics, economy, history, and culture of Lanzhou district. **Holdings:** 70,000 volumes; 350 periodicals; 100 AV programs and microforms. **Services:** Interlibrary loan (limited). **Publications:** Social Sciences.

★18435★
GENERAL AGREEMENT ON TARIFFS AND TRADE - GATT LIBRARY (Bus-Fin)
Centre William Rappard
154, rue de Lausanne Phone: 22 395295
CH-1121 Geneva 21, Switzerland Jany Grandjean, Libn.
Subjects: International trade, economics, monetary and customs policy, statistics. **Special Collections:** Complete collection of GATT documents and publications. **Holdings:** 18,000 books; 1800 statistical titles; 35 titles on microfiche. **Subscriptions:** 800 journals and other serials. **Services:** Interlibrary loan; copying; SDI; library open to the public with restrictions. **Publications:** List of publications received in the GATT Library, monthly; list of periodicals; list of statistical publications; current awareness bulletin, weekly.

GENERAL SYNOD OF THE CHURCH OF ENGLAND - COUNCIL FOR THE CARE OF CHURCHES
See: Council for the Care of Churches (18367)

GEOLOGIAN TUTKIMUSKESKUS
See: Geological Survey of Finland (18438)

★18436★
GEOLOGICAL SURVEY OF AUSTRIA - LIBRARY (Sci-Engr)
Rasumofskygasse 23 Phone: 222 72 56 74
A-1031 Vienna, Austria Dr. Tillfried Cernajsek, Hd.
Founded: 1849. **Staff:** Prof 3; Other 3. **Subjects:** Geological mapping, exploration for mineral resources, engineering geology, hydrogeology. **Special Collections:** Geoscientific maps (32,500); science archives. **Holdings:** 50,000 books; 170,000 bound periodical volumes; 8000 microforms; 6500 other cataloged items. **Subscriptions:** 961 journals and other serials. **Services:** Interlibrary loan; copying; library open to the public. **Computerized Information Services:** GEOKART, GEOLIT (internal databases). Performs searches free of charge. **Remarks:** Maintained by Austria - Ministry of Science and Research. Telex: 13 29 27. **Also Known As:** Bundesministerium fur Wissenschaft und Forschung - Bibliothek der Geologischen Bundesanstalt. **Staff:** Ingrid Riedl; Johanna Findl.

★18437★
GEOLOGICAL SURVEY OF DENMARK - LIBRARY (Sci-Engr)
Thoravej 31
DK-2400 Copenhagen NV, Denmark Phone: 1 10 66 00
Subjects: Geology, geochemistry, raw materials, groundwater, oil and gas, geothermal energy. **Remarks:** Survey is a research and advisory institution of Denmark - Ministry of Environment and Nordic Affairs. **Also Known As:** Danmarks Geologiske Undersogelse.

★18438★
GEOLOGICAL SURVEY OF FINLAND - LIBRARY (Sci-Engr)
Betonimiehenkuja 4 Phone: 46931
SF-02150 Espoo 15, Finland Helka Lauerma, Libn.
Founded: 1885. **Staff:** Prof 4; Other 3. **Subjects:** Geology, petrology, mineral resources, geophysics, geochemistry. **Holdings:** 101,000 volumes; 16,000 maps. **Subscriptions:** 800 journals and other serials. **Services:** Interlibrary loan; copying; SDI; library open to the public. **Computerized Information Services:** DIALOG Information Services, Pergamon ORBIT InfoLine, Inc.; FINNGEO (internal database). Performs searches on fee basis. Contact Person: Lahja Voutilainen, Hd.. **Remarks:** Maintained by Finland - Ministry of Commerce and Industry. **Also Known As:** Geologian Tutkimuskeskus. **Staff:** Jani Ilressaare, Finngeo; Liisa Vuorela, ILL.

★18439★
GEOLOGICAL SURVEY OF SOUTH AFRICA - LIBRARY (Sci-Engr)
208 Pretorius Ave.
Private Bag X112 Phone: 12 28-4230
Pretoria 0001, Republic of South Africa Mrs. L. Niebuhr, Libn.
Subjects: Geology - general, structural, petrographic, stratigraphic, paleontologic, sedimentologic; geophysics; mineral resources; fossil fuels; mineralogy; petrology; geochemistry; engineering geology. **Holdings:** 60,000 volumes. **Publications:** Bibliography and Subject Index of South African Geological Literature, annual. **Remarks:** Maintained by South Africa - Department of Mineral and Energy Affairs.

★18440★
GERMAN ARCHAEOLOGICAL INSTITUTE - ATHENS DIVISION - LIBRARY (Soc Sci)
Fidiou 1
GR-106 78 Athens, Greece Phone: 1 3620-270
Subjects: Archeological studies of Greece, prehistoric to Byzantine period. **Holdings:** 60,000 volumes; photographs. **Services:** Library open to the public with restrictions. **Also Known As:** Deutsches Archaeologisches Institut - Abteilung Athen. **Staff:** Dr. Axel Rugler, Libn.; Margit Heiber, Libn..

★18441★
GERMAN ARCHAEOLOGICAL INSTITUTE - COMMISSION FOR ANCIENT HISTORY AND EPIGRAPHY (Hist)
Amalienstrasse 736 Phone: 89 28 43 51
D-8000 Munich 40, Federal Republic of Germany Dr. K. Dietz, Libn.
Subjects: Ancient history, numismatics, epigraphy. **Holdings:** 19,000 volumes. **Also Known As:** Kommission fur Alte Geschichte und Epigraphik.

★18442★
GERMAN ARCHAEOLOGICAL INSTITUTE - LIBRARY (Soc Sci)
Podbielskiallee 69 Phone: 30 83 20 41
D-1000 Berlin 33, Federal Republic of Germany
Dr. Anneliese Peschlow
Staff: Prof 2; Other 1. **Subjects:** Classical archeology. **Holdings:** 60,000 volumes. **Services:** Library open to the public. **Automated Operations:** Computerized public access catalog. **Remarks:** Maintained by Federal Republic of Germany - Foreign Ministry. **Also Known As:** Deutsches Archaeologisches Institut. **Staff:** Helga Skottke, Libn..

★18443★
GERMAN ARCHAEOLOGICAL INSTITUTE - MADRID DIVISION - LIBRARY (Soc Sci)
Serrano, 159 Phone: 1 261 09 04
E-28002 Madrid, Spain Horst Zeschke, Libn.
Subjects: Archeology of the Iberian peninsula. **Holdings:** 37,000 volumes. **Also Known As:** Deutsches Archaeologisches Institut - Abteilung Madrid.

GERMAN EXILE ARCHIVES
See: Federal Republic of Germany - Deutsche Bibliothek (18408)

★18444★
GERMAN FOUNDATION FOR INTERNATIONAL DEVELOPMENT - DOCUMENTATION CENTER (Soc Sci)
Hans-Bockler-Strasse 5 Phone: 228 40010
D-5300 Bonn 3, Federal Republic of Germany Dr. Beate Brodmeier
Subjects: Developing countries - aid, development policy of national and international organizations, socioeconomic and cultural change. **Holdings:** 45,000 books; 380,000 clippings. **Subscriptions:** 750 journals and other serials. **Services:** Copying; SDI; center open to the public. **Computerized Information Services:** Internal database. Performs searches free of charge.

Publications: Bibliography of German Research on Developing Countries, annual - for sale; Recent Acquisitions, 2/year - free upon request. **Also Known As:** Deutsche Stiftung fur Internationale Entwicklung.

★18445★
GERMAN HYDROGRAPHIC INSTITUTE - LIBRARY (Sci-Engr, Agri)
Postfach 30 12 20 Phone: 40 3190478
D-2000 Hamburg 36, Federal Republic of Germany Gunter Heise
Founded: 1875. **Staff:** Prof 5; Other 4. **Subjects:** Hydrography, oceanography, navigation safety, geodesy, marine sciences, geophysics, nautical engineering, agricultural meteorology, worldwide climatological and meteorological observations. **Holdings:** 100,000 volumes. **Services:** Copying; library open to the public. **Remarks:** Maintained by Federal Republic of Germany - Ministry of Transport. Library located at Bernhard-Nocht-Strasse 78, D-2000 Hamburg 4, Federal Republic of Germany. Telex: 2 11 138 bmvhh d. **Also Known As:** Deutsches Hydrographisches Institut.

★18446★
GERMAN INSTITUTE FOR INTERNATIONAL EDUCATIONAL RESEARCH - LIBRARY AND DOCUMENTATION (Educ)
Schloss-Strasse 29-31
Postfach 900280 Phone: 69 77 02 45
D-6000 Frankfurt am Main 90, Federal Republic of Germany
Hartmut Muller, Libn.
Staff: Prof 10. **Subjects:** Education - general, comparative, vocational, technical; law; psychology; economics. **Special Collections:** Textbooks (19,000). **Holdings:** 155,000 books; 890 bound periodical volumes. **Subscriptions:** 660 journals and other serials. **Services:** Copying; SDI; library open to the public. **Automated Operations:** Computerized public access catalog. **Computerized Information Services:** DBI (Deutsches Bibliotheksinstitut), DIMDI, ECHO (European Commission Host Organization), INKADATA (Informationssystem Karlsruhe), Pergamon ORBIT InfoLine, Inc., Telesystemes Questel; PEDI, NEUTECH, INTERLIMES, TEST, ZEITDOK (internal databases). Performs searches on fee basis. Contact Person: Wieland Barth. **Publications:** Zeitungsdokumentation Bildungswesen, semimonthly - by subscription. **Special Catalogs:** Catalog of countries; catalog of corporate sources (both on cards). **Also Known As:** Deutsches Institut fur Internationale Padagogische Forschung.

★18447★
GERMAN IRON AND STEEL ENGINEERS ASSOCIATION - INSTITUTE FOR APPLIED RESEARCH - VDEH LIBRARY (Sci-Engr)
VDEh - Institut fur Angewandte Forschung
Sohnstrasse 65
D-4000 Dusseldorf 1, Federal Republic of Germany Phone: 211 67071
Subjects: Engineering and physical properties of iron and steel. **Holdings:** 100,000 volumes; standards. **Subscriptions:** 500 journals and other serials. **Services:** Library open to materials and design engineers. **Computerized Information Services:** Produces Materials Database Steel and Iron (STEELFACTS). **Also Known As:** Verein Deutscher Eisenhuttenleute - Betriebsforschungsinstitut.

GERMAN MUSIC ARCHIVES
See: Federal Republic of Germany - Deutsche Bibliothek (18408)

GESELLSCHAFT FUR INFORMATION UND DOKUMENTATION (GID) - GID-INFORMATIONSZENTRUM FUR INFORMATIONSWISSENSCHAFT UND -PRAXIS
See: Society for Information and Documentation - GID Information Center for Information Science and Information Work (18777)

★18448★
GHANA LIBRARY BOARD - RESEARCH LIBRARY ON AFRICAN AFFAIRS (Area-Ethnic, Soc Sci)
P.O. Box 2970 Phone: 228402
Accra, Ghana Christina D.T. Kwei, Libn.
Subjects: Anthropology, social studies, history, literature, economics, geography. **Special Collections:** Ghana National Collection. **Holdings:** 33,000 books; 550 bound periodical volumes; 3000 microforms. **Services:** Interlibrary loan; copying; library open to the public with restrictions. **Publications:** Special subject lists on African affairs; Ghana National Bibliography.

★18449★
EMILIO GOELDI MUSEUM - LIBRARY (Biol Sci, Soc Sci)
Avenida Magalhaes Barata, 376
Caixa Postal 399 Phone: 223-6414
6600 Belem, Brazil Jose Seixas Lourenco, Musm.Dir.
Subjects: Amazon region - anthropology, zoology, archeology, botany. **Special Collections:** Botanical collection (80,000 specimens). **Holdings:** 150,000 volumes. **Remarks:** Maintained by the National Council of Scientific and Technological Development. **Also Known As:** Museu Paraense Emilio Goeldi.

★18450★
GOETHE-INSTITUTE LONDON - LIBRARY (Area-Ethnic)
50 Princes Gate Exhibition Rd. Phone: 1 581 3344
London SW7 2PH, England Michael Stilkenboom, Hd.Libn.
Subjects: Germany - literature, art, social sciences, history. **Holdings:** 36,000 books; 8000 microforms; AV programs. **Services:** Interlibrary loan; copying; library open to the public. **Publications:** New acquisitions list; German Books from the British Market.

★18451★
GOKHALE INSTITUTE OF POLITICS AND ECONOMICS - LIBRARY (Soc Sci, Bus-Fin)
Deccan Gymkhana Phone: 54287
Pune 411 004, India Mrs. P. Wable, Asst.Libn.
Subjects: Economic and social problems of India - agricultural economics, regional development, urban studies, sociology, industrial research, demography, education, economic policy and planning, monetary economics and finance, foreign trade, economic history; economics of Eastern Europe. **Holdings:** 217,681 volumes. **Remarks:** Affiliated with University of Poona.

RAFAEL GARCIA GRANADOS LIBRARY
See: National Autonomous University of Mexico - Institute of Historical Research (18617)

★18452★
GREAT BRITAIN - DEPARTMENT OF HEALTH AND SOCIAL SECURITY - LIBRARY (Soc Sci, Med)
Alexander Fleming House
Elephant and Castle Phone: 1 407 5522
London SE1 6BY, England J.H. Wormald, Prin.Libn.
Founded: 1948. **Staff:** Prof 27; Other 26. **Subjects:** Health services, social security, social services, social policy, safety of medicines, health service buildings. **Holdings:** 200,000 volumes. **Subscriptions:** 2500 journals and other serials; 5 newspapers. **Services:** Interlibrary loan; copying; SDI; library open to research workers on application to librarian. **Automated Operations:** Computerized cataloging, acquisitions, serials, and routing. **Computerized Information Services:** Data-Star, DIALOG Information Services, Pergamon ORBIT InfoLine, Inc., Scicon Ltd.; produces DHSS-DATA. **Publications:** Health Service Abstracts, monthly; Social Service Abstracts, monthly; Nursing Research Abstracts, quarterly; Quality Assurance Abstracts, bimonthly; Social Security Library Bulletin, monthly; Current Literature on Occupational Pensions, monthly; Health Buildings Library Bulletin, monthly; Selected Abstracts on Occupational Diseases, quarterly.

GREATER LONDON COUNCIL - INFORMATION SERVICES GROUP
See: London Research Centre - Research Library (18595)

GREECE - MINISTRY OF JUSTICE - HELLENIC INSTITUTE OF INTERNATIONAL AND FOREIGN LAW
See: Hellenic Institute of International and Foreign Law (18465)

GROUP FOR THE ADVANCEMENT OF SPECTROSCOPIC METHODS AND PHYSICOCHEMICAL ANALYSIS - SPECTROSCOPIC INFORMATION CENTER
See: Groupement pour l'Avancement des Methodes Spectroscopiques et Physicochimique d'Analyse - Centre d'Information Spectroscopiques (18453)

★18453★
GROUPEMENT POUR L'AVANCEMENT DES METHODES SPECTROSCOPIQUES ET PHYSICOCHIMIQUE D'ANALYSE - CENTRE D'INFORMATION SPECTROSCOPIQUES (Sci-Engr)
88, boulevard Malesherbes Phone: 1 45639304
F-75008 Paris, France Mme. D. Sandino, Adjunct Dir.
Subjects: Spectroscopic data - infrared, ultraviolet, nuclear magnetic resonance, Raman, mass spectra. **Holdings:** 40,894 mass spectra; 264,255 infrared spectra; 44,099 ultraviolet spectra; 1135 Raman spectra; 57,867 nuclear magnetic resonance spectra. **Services:** Center open to members only. **Also Known As:** Group for the Advancement of Spectroscopic Methods and Physicochemical Analysis - Spectroscopic Information Center.

★18454★
GUANGZHOU ACADEMY OF FINE ARTS - LIBRARY (Art, Hum)
Xiaogang Xincun Phone: 51626
Guangzhou, Guangdong Province, People's Republic of China
Wang Yilun, Libn.
Founded: 1951. **Staff:** 10. **Subjects:** Fine arts, social sciences, literature. **Special Collections:** Original Chinese traditional paintings and stamps; albums of foreign paintings. **Holdings:** 141,096 volumes; 4213 periodicals. **Publications:** Fine Arts Bulletin.

★18455★
GUANGZHOU INSTITUTE OF ENERGY CONVERSION - LIBRARY (Energy)
81 Central Xianlie La
P.O. Box 1254 Phone: 75600
Guangzhou 510027, People's Republic of China
Zhang Huan-fen, Div.Chf.
Subjects: Energy conversion; biomass, solar, geothermal energy; waste heat recovery; waste incineration; fluidized bed combustion; electrical generators; heat storage; heat pumps; wave/ocean energy utilization. **Holdings:** 40,000 volumes. **Remarks:** Affiliated with the Chinese Academy of Sciences.

★18456★
GUATEMALA - MINISTRY OF EDUCATION - INSTITUTE OF ANTHROPOLOGY AND HISTORY - LIBRARY (Area-Ethnic, Soc Sci)
12 Avenida 11-65
Zona 1 Phone: 2 531570
Guatemala City, Guatemala Gloria Arroya Liquez, Libn.
Subjects: Central America - archeology, ethnology, linguistics, anthropology, arts, history. **Holdings:** 35,000 volumes. **Also Known As:** Instituto de Antropologia e Historia.

★18457★
GUJARAT VIDYA SABHA - SHETH BHOLABHAI JESHINGBHAI INSTITUTE OF LEARNING AND RESEARCH - LIBRARY (Area-Ethnic, Hum)
R.C. Marg Phone: 408862
Ahmedabad 380 009, Gujarat, India Vidula T. Mistry, Libn.
Subjects: Indian culture, history, archeology; iconography and painting; Sanskrit and Gujarati literature. **Holdings:** 64,000 volumes.

★18458★
GUJARAT VIDYAPITH - PEACE RESEARCH CENTER, AHMEDABAD - LIBRARY (Soc Sci)
Ashram Rd. Phone: 447292
Ahmedabad 380 014, Gujarat, India Mr. Kanubhai Shah, Libn.
Subjects: Peace, peace education, science and nonviolence, Gandhian thought, impact of war. **Holdings:** 10,000 volumes. **Remarks:** Gujarat Vidyapith was founded in 1920 by Mohandas Gandhi to work towards the establishment of a society based on truth and nonviolence. Telex: 121 254 GUVI.

★18459★
GULF ARAB STATES EDUCATIONAL RESEARCH CENTER - LIBRARY (Educ)
P.O. Box 25566 Phone: 835203
Safat, Kuwait Mohei A. Hak, Libn.
Founded: 1978. **Subjects:** Education in Arab countries - kindergarten through higher education, teacher training, teaching methods, educational objectives, special education, curriculum development, educational evaluation. **Holdings:** 12,000 volumes. **Remarks:** Affiliated with Regional Arab Bureau of Education. Telex: 44118.

GULF STATES INFORMATION DOCUMENTATION CENTER
See: Arab Gulf States Information Documentation Center (18267)

GYOGYSZERKUTATO INTEZET KV.
See: Institute for Drug Research (18505)

H

★18460★
HACETTEPE UNIVERSITY - LIBRARIES (Med, Sci-Engr, Soc Sci)
Ankara, Turkey Phone: 41-3117998
Mrs. Z. Sezen Tan
Subjects: Medicine, engineering, social sciences, physical therapy, dentistry, nursing. **Holdings:** 125,000 books; 200,000 bound periodical volumes; 22,000 AV programs; 200 manuscripts. **Services:** Interlibrary loan; copying; SDI; library open to the public with restrictions. **Special Catalogs:** Hacettepe University Periodicals Catalog. **Remarks:** Includes the holdings of the Medical Center Library and the Beytepe Campus Library. Telex: 42237 htk tr.

OTTO HAHN BIBLIOTHEK
See: Max Planck Institute for Biophysical Chemistry (18688)

HALLSTROM PACIFIC LIBRARY
See: International Training Institute - Learning Resources Centre (18561)

THOMAS HARDY WINE LIBRARY
See: State Library of South Australia - Special Collections (18794)

TOM HARRISSON MASS-OBSERVATION ARCHIVE
See: University of Sussex - University Library (18860)

HEBERDEN LIBRARY OF BRITISH ASSOCIATION OF RHEUMATOLOGY
See: Royal College of Physicians of London - Library (18739)

★18461★
HEBREW UNIVERSITY OF JERUSALEM - GIVAT RAM CAMPUS - JEWISH MUSIC RESEARCH CENTRE - LIBRARY (Mus, Area-Ethnic)
P.O. Box 503
Jerusalem 91004, Israel Phone: 2 584638
Subjects: Musical traditions and musical life of Jewish communities, ethnomusicology. **Special Collections:** Jacob Michael Collection of Jewish Music (2000 books; 6000 manuscripts and scores). **Holdings:** 15,000 volumes; 200,000 sound recordings and videotapes. **Remarks:** Center located next to the Music Department and National Sound Archive of the Jewish National and University Library.

★18462★
HEBREW UNIVERSITY OF JERUSALEM - HARRY S TRUMAN INSTITUTE FOR THE ADVANCEMENT OF PEACE - LIBRARY (Soc Sci, Area-Ethnic)
Mount Scopus Phone: 2 882300
Jerusalem 91905, Israel Cecile Panzer, Hd.Libn.
Subjects: Peace, Middle East, Asia, Africa, Latin America. **Holdings:** 50,000 volumes. **Subscriptions:** 200 journals and other serials; 100 newspapers.

★18463★
HEBREW UNIVERSITY OF JERUSALEM - SOCIETY FOR RESEARCH ON JEWISH COMMUNITIES - CENTER FOR RESEARCH AND DOCUMENTATION OF EAST EUROPEAN JEWRY - LIBRARY AND ARCHIVES (Area-Ethnic)
Mount Scopus
Jerusalem 91905, Israel Phone: 2 584271
Subjects: History, culture, social aspects of East European Jewry, especially Soviet Jewry. **Special Collections:** Archives. **Holdings:** 50,000 volumes. **Remarks:** "Contains the largest collection of books, periodicals, and archival materials on Soviet and East European Jewry in the West."

★18464★
HELLENIC FOLKLORE RESEARCH CENTER - LIBRARY (Area-Ethnic)
1 Dipla St. and 129 Syngrou Ave. Phone: 1 9344 811
Athens, Greece Dr. Anna Papamichael, Dir.
Subjects: Greek folklore. **Holdings:** 5800 volumes. **Remarks:** Maintained by Academy of Athens. **Also Known As:** Kentron Erevnis Ellinikis Laographias.

★18465★
HELLENIC INSTITUTE OF INTERNATIONAL AND FOREIGN LAW - LIBRARY (Law)
73 Solonos St.
Athens, Greece Phone: 1 3615-646
Subjects: Law - foreign, civil, commercial, international. **Holdings:** 20,000 volumes. **Services:** Library open to lawyers and public organizations. **Remarks:** Supervised by Greece - Ministry of Justice.

★18466★
HELSINKI UNIVERSITY OF TECHNOLOGY - UNIVERSITY LIBRARY (Sci-Engr)
Otaniementie 9 Phone: 0 4512824
SF-02150 Espoo, Finland Prof. Elin Tornudd, Dir.
Founded: 1849. **Staff:** Prof 25; Other 50. **Subjects:** Engineering - electrical, mechanical, civil, chemical; information technology; mining and metallurgy; chemistry; physics; mathematics; geology; industrial economy; architecture. **Special Collections:** Collection of reports on energy, environmental protection. **Holdings:** 300,000 books; 500,000 bound periodical volumes; 700,000 items on microfiche. **Subscriptions:** 5700 journals and other serials; 10 newspapers. **Services:** Interlibrary loan; copying; SDI; library open to the public. **Automated Operations:** Computerized public access catalog and cataloging. **Computerized Information Services:** DIALOG Information Services, Pergamon ORBIT InfoLine, Inc., ESA/IRS; produces TALI, TENTTU; EUSIDIC (European Association of Information Services; electronic mail service). Performs searches on fee basis. Contact Person: Dr. Sinikka Koskiala, Hd., Tech.Info.Dept., 4512825. **Publications:** Monographs Series OTA-kirjasto, irregular; accession lists, monthly. **Special Catalogs:** Dictionary catalog; list of current journals received. **Special Indexes:** Tekniikan Aikakauslenti Indeksi-TALI (KWIC index), annual.

★18467★
HENAN ACADEMY OF SCIENCES - GEOGRAPHY RESEARCH INSTITUTE - LIBRARY (Sci-Engr)
West Longhai Lu
Zhengzhou, Henan Province, People's Republic of China Phone: 9875
Founded: 1959. **Staff:** 4. **Subjects:** Earth sciences, meteorology, climatology, hydrography, hydrogeology, geomorphology, geology, soil science, economic geography, cartography, remote sensing, telemetering, environmental protection, paleogeography, historical geography. **Holdings:** 45,000 volumes; 5000 bound periodical volumes; 15,000 technical reports. **Publications:** Translations on Geography. **Special Catalogs:** Book Catalog; Reference Materials Catalog. **Remarks:** An alternate telephone number is 9487.

★18468★
JOHANN GOTTFRIED HERDER INSTITUTE - LIBRARY (Area-Ethnic)
Gisonenweg 7 Phone: 2 50 44
D-3550 Marburg, Federal Republic of Germany
Dr. Horst Von Chmielewski, Libn.
Subjects: Eastern Central Europe - geography, ethnography, and political, legal, economic, cultural history. **Holdings:** 250,000 volumes. **Also Known As:** Johann-Gottfried-Herder-Institut.

★18469★
HIGHER COUNCIL FOR SCIENTIFIC RESEARCH - INSTITUTE FOR INFORMATION AND DOCUMENTATION IN SCIENCE AND TECHNOLOGY - LIBRARY (Sci-Engr)
Joaquin Costa, 22
E-28006 Madrid, Spain Phone: 1 2614808
Subjects: Industrial chemistry, electrical engineering, electronics, metallurgy, farm engineering, agronomics, management, physics, life sciences, pharmacology, mathematics, astronomy, astrophysics. **Holdings:** 18,000 volumes; Spanish patents. **Subscriptions:** 2000 journals and other serials. **Services:** SDI; library open to the public. **Computerized Information Services:** Internal database. Performs searches on fee basis. **Also Known As:** Consejo Superior de Investigaciones Cientificas - Instituto de Informacion y Documentacion en Ciencia y Tecnologia.

L. HIRSZFELD INSTITUTE OF IMMUNOLOGY AND EXPERIMENTAL THERAPY
See: Polish Academy of Sciences - L. Hirszfeld Institute of Immunology and Experimental Therapy (18709)

HO SAMUT HAENG CHAT
See: National Library of Thailand (18642)

★18470★
HORTUS BOTANICUS NANJINGENSIS INSTITUTUM BOTANICUM - LIBRARY (Biol Sci)
Nanjing, Jiangsu Province, People's Republic of China Phone: 43375
Founded: 1954. **Staff:** 3. **Subjects:** Botany; plant taxonomy; horticulture; plants for medical use; plant protection, ecology, physiology, breeding; environmental protection; chemistry; agronomy. **Special Collections:** Flowers. **Holdings:** 23,601 volumes; 171 microforms and AV programs. **Subscriptions:** 1280 journals and other serials. **Services:** Interlibrary loan; copying. **Publications:** Jiangsu Flora; Research Papers of Nanjing Zhongshan Botanical Garden.

★18471★
HUBEI PROVINCIAL INSTITUTE FOR DRUG CONTROL - LIBRARY (Med)
235 Ziyang Lu
Wuhan, Hubei Province, People's Republic of China Phone: 71249
Founded: 1973. **Staff:** 2. **Subjects:** Pharmacy, medicament analysis for traditional Chinese medicine and western medicine, instrumental analysis, traditional Chinese medicine, biology, chemistry. **Holdings:** 12,973 volumes; 217 periodicals. **Services:** Interlibrary loan; copying. **Publications:** Hubei Chinese Herbal Medicine (2 volumes).

HUBRECHT LABORATORY LIBRARY
See: Royal Academy of Sciences - Netherlands Institute for Developmental Biology (18731)

★18472★
HUNAN TEACHERS COLLEGE - LIBRARY (Educ)
Yuelushan Phone: 82911
Changsha, Hunan Province, People's Republic of China
Wang Ziyun, Dp.Libn.
Founded: 1953. **Staff:** 61. **Subjects:** Teaching of politics, history, physical education, linguistics, foreign languages, mathematics, physics, chemistry, biology, earth sciences; education; philology. **Special Collections:** Chinese ancient books (487 titles; 5316 volumes); district histories of places of historical significance; Confucian classics and histories. **Holdings:** 1.09 million volumes. **Subscriptions:** 1216 journals and other serials. **Services:** Copying.

★18473★
HUNGARIAN ACADEMY OF SCIENCES - ARCHAEOLOGICAL INSTITUTE - LIBRARY (Soc Sci)
Uri utca 49
Postafiok 14
H-1250 Budapest, Hungary Dr. Magdolna Makkay-Tulok, Libn.
Subjects: Archeology - prehistory, classical, Roman, Middle Ages. **Holdings:** 32,000 volumes. **Also Known As:** Magyar Tudomanyos Akademia - Regeszeti Intezet.

★18474★
HUNGARIAN ACADEMY OF SCIENCES - ETHNOGRAPHICAL INSTITUTE - LIBRARY (Area-Ethnic)
I. Orszaghaz utca 30 Phone: 75 90 11
Budapest, Hungary Eva Falvy, Libn.
Subjects: Hungarian and general ethnography, folklore, and social and cultural anthropology. **Holdings:** 40,000 volumes. **Also Known As:** Magyar Tudomanyos Akademia - Neprajzi Kutato Csoportja.

★18475★
HUNGARIAN ACADEMY OF SCIENCES - INSTITUTE OF HISTORY - LIBRARY (Hist)
Uri utca 53 Phone: 1 759-011
H-1014 Budapest, Hungary Angela Borsos, Hd. of Lib.
Founded: 1949. **Staff:** Prof 7; Other 1. **Subjects:** Hungarian and world history - economics, politics, society, civilization, culture, ideologies. **Holdings:** 90,060 books; 10,002 bound periodical volumes; 3000 items on microfilm; 3010 other cataloged items. **Subscriptions:** 290 journals and other serials; 15 newspapers. **Services:** Interlibrary loan; copying; SDI; library open to researchers and students. **Computerized Information Services:** ABACUS, SCI (internal databases). **Publications:** Annual bibliography of Hungarian historical books. **Also Known As:** Magyar Tudomanyos Akademia - Tornettudomanyi Intezete.

★18476★
HUNGARIAN ACADEMY OF SCIENCES - INSTITUTE OF LINGUISTICS - LIBRARY (Hum)
I. Szentharomsag utca 2 Phone: 75 82 85
H-1014 Budapest, Hungary Mrs. G. Szathury, Libn.
Subjects: History and descriptive analysis of Hungarian language, general and applied linguistics. **Holdings:** 30,000 volumes. **Also Known As:** Magyar Tudomanyos Akademia - Nyelvtudomanyi Intezete.

★18477★
HUNGARIAN ACADEMY OF SCIENCES - INSTITUTE OF LITERARY STUDIES - LIBRARY (Hum)
Menesi utca 11-13 Phone: 665-861
H-1118 Budapest, Hungary Dr. Katalin S. Nemeth, Dir.
Subjects: Hungarian literature, literary history, literary criticism, especially the Marxist-Leninist approach. **Holdings:** 150,000 volumes. **Publications:** National Bibliography of Hungarian Literary History. **Also Known As:** Magyar Tudomanyos Akademia - Irodalomtudomanyi Intezet.

★18478★
HUNGARIAN ACADEMY OF SCIENCES - LIBRARY (Sci-Engr)
Roosevelt ter 9
H-1051 Budapest, Hungary Gyorgy Rozsa, Dir.
Subjects: Science. **Special Collections:** Department of Manuscripts; Collection of Old Books; Oriental Collections; Archives. **Holdings:** 1.4 million volumes. **Services:** Library open to the public. **Also Known As:** Magyar Tudomanyos Akademia.

★18479★
HUNGARY - CENTRAL STATISTICAL OFFICE - LIBRARY AND DOCUMENTATION SERVICE (Soc Sci)
Keleti Karoly utca 5
Postafiok 10 Phone: 358734
H-1024 Budapest, Hungary Dr. Istvan Csahok, Gen.Dir.
Subjects: Hungarian economic and social statistics, demography, data analysis and methods. **Holdings:** 600,000 volumes; 10,000 maps; 800 scientific manuscripts. **Subscriptions:** 2000 Hungarian and foreign journals and other serials. **Services:** Copying; library open to the public. **Computerized Information Services:** I.P. Sharp Associates Limited; internal databases. Performs searches on fee basis. **Publications:** Statistical Methods; Papers in Historical Statistics; Studies on Historical Statistics; Special Bibliographies. **Also Known As:** Kozponti Statisztikai Hivatal.

★18480★
HUNGARY - MINISTRY OF BUILDING AND URBAN DEVELOPMENT - INFORMATION CENTRE OF BUILDING - LIBRARY (Plan)
P.O. Box 83 Phone: 117317
H-1400 Budapest, Hungary Dr. Peter Hamvay, Dir.
Subjects: Building and construction in Hungary and worldwide. **Holdings:** 40,000 volumes; 22,500 product information documents; 21,000 translations; 24,000 study-tour reports; 7000 research reports; 49,000 documents, standards, patents, other cataloged items. **Services:** SDI; library open to government officials, planning and building firms, research organizations, private builders, and architects and engineers in building, civil engineering, and building materials industries. **Computerized Information Services:** Produces KGST-CMEA, STN-ICONDA, CIBORG (CIB Ongoing Research Group). Performs searches on fee basis. **Publications:** Accession lists. **Also Known As:** Epitesugyi es Varosfejlesztesi Miniszterium - Epitesugyi Tajekoztatasi Kozpont.

★18481★
HUNGARY - MINISTRY OF CONSTRUCTION AND CITY PLANNING - CENTRAL RESEARCH AND DESIGN INSTITUTE FOR THE SILICATE INDUSTRY - LIBRARY (Sci-Engr)
Becsi utca 126 Phone: 804 311
H-1034 Budapest, Hungary Istvan Somogyi, Libn.
Founded: 1953. **Staff:** Prof 6; Other 2. **Subjects:** Hungarian silicate industry, silicate chemistry, geology, mineralogy, chemistry, new technology, power engineering methods and systems, industrial sanitary engineering and environmental protection, new building materials. **Holdings:** 25,000 volumes. **Subscriptions:** 6500 journals and other serials. **Services:** Interlibrary loan; copying; library open to the public. **Also Known As:** Szilikatipari Kozponti Kutato es Tervezo Intezet.

★18482★
HUNGARY - MINISTRY OF EDUCATION AND CULTURE - NATIONAL EDUCATIONAL LIBRARY AND MUSEUM (Educ)
Honved utca 19 Phone: 1 126-862
H-1055 Budapest, Hungary Dr. Mayerne Zsadon Eva, Dept.Hd.
Subjects: Education - general, history, comparative; sociology; psychology. **Special Collections:** Textbooks; school annuals; foreign and Hungarian juvenile literature. **Holdings:** 287,600 books; 94,668 bound periodical volumes; 11,740 microforms; 6880 manuscripts. **Services:** Interlibrary loan; copying; SDI; library open to the public. **Publications:** Hungarian Educational Literature; International Educational Information; International Education; Educational News from Abroad; School Systems; Books and Education; Comparative Education Studies; Studies in History of Education; additional publications available. **Staff:** Balazs Mihaly, Dir.-Gen..

I

HUNGARY - NATIONAL TECHNICAL INFORMATION CENTRE AND LIBRARY
See: National Technical Information Centre and Library (18648)

IBERO-AMERIKANISCHES INSTITUT
See: Stiftung Preussischer Kulturbesitz (18797)

★18483★
IKEBANA INTERNATIONAL - LIBRARY (Art)
1-6 Kanda Surugadai, Chiyoda-ku Phone: 3 293-8188
Tokyo 101, Japan Keiko Ohta
Founded: 1956. **Subjects:** Ikebana (Japanese flower arranging). **Holdings:** Figures not available.

★18484★
IMEDE INTERNATIONAL MANAGEMENT DEVELOPMENT INSTITUTE - IMEDE LIBRARY (Bus-Fin)
Chemin de Bellerive 23 Phone: 21 26 71 12
CH-1007 Lausanne, Switzerland Silvia Farmanfarma, Dir., Lib.Serv.
Staff: Prof 3. **Subjects:** Management, business, economics. **Special Collections:** Company reports (800); IMEDE case studies (1425). **Holdings:** 10,000 books; 2250 bound periodical volumes; 850 microfiche; 36 reels of microfilm; 170 videotapes. **Subscriptions:** 370 journals and other serials; 30 newspapers. **Services:** Library open to the public by appointment. **Computerized Information Services:** Data-Star, Mead Data Central, MINITEL. **Publications:** IMEDE Library's Current Contents for Managers, biweekly; Additions to IMEDE Case Collection, bimonthly; Recent Additions to IMEDE Library, monthly. **Special Catalogs:** Author and subject catalogs (both on cards). **Staff:** Isabelle De Kaenel, Book Sect.; Monique Schultz, Per..

INDIA - BOARD OF EDUCATION - SILK AND ART SILK MILLS' RESEARCH ASSOCIATION
See: Silk and Art Silk Mills' Research Association - SASMIRA Library (18771)

★18485★
INDIA - COUNCIL OF SCIENTIFIC AND INDUSTRIAL RESEARCH - INDIAN NATIONAL SCIENTIFIC DOCUMENTATION CENTRE - INSDOC LIBRARY (Sci-Engr)
14, Satsang Vihar Marg
New Delhi 110067, India Phone: 665837
Subjects: All aspects of science and technology. **Holdings:** 124,068 volumes; 2500 reports; 1000 microforms. **Subscriptions:** 4610 journals and other serials. **Services:** SDI; library open to scientists and technologists in industry, government, universities, and research institutes. **Computerized Information Services:** Internal databases. Performs searches on fee basis. **Publications:** Bibliographies; Annals of Library Science and Documentation, quarterly; Russian Scientific & Technical Publications - An Accession List, bimonthly.

★18486★
INDIA - MINISTRY OF AGRICULTURE AND RURAL DEVELOPMENT - NATIONAL INSTITUTE OF RURAL DEVELOPMENT - CENTRE ON RURAL DOCUMENTATION (Agri, Soc Sci)
Rajendranagar Phone: 48001
Hyderabad 500 030, Andhra Pradesh, India K.A. Raju, Dir.
Subjects: Social sciences, rural development. **Holdings:** 48,000 volumes. **Remarks:** Institute is a center for research, training, consultancy, and documentation in rural development in India.

★18487★
INDIA - MINISTRY OF EDUCATION - CENTRAL INSTITUTE OF INDIAN LANGUAGES - LIBRARY (Hum)
Manasagnangotri Phone: 23820
Mysore 570 006, Karnataka, India C.R. Sulochana, Libn.
Subjects: Linguistics, Indian languages. **Holdings:** 50,000 volumes.

★18488★
INDIA - MINISTRY OF HEALTH AND FAMILY WELFARE - ALL INDIA INSTITUTE OF HYGIENE AND PUBLIC HEALTH - LIBRARY (Med)
110 Chittaranjan Ave. Phone: 345271
Calcutta 700 073, West Bengal, India Mr. A.K. Biswas, Libn.
Subjects: Public health, allied health sciences. **Holdings:** 51,610 volumes.

INDIA - MINISTRY OF TEXTILES - SILK AND ART SILK MILLS' RESEARCH ASSOCIATION
See: Silk and Art Silk Mills' Research Association - SASMIRA Library (18771)

INDIA - NATIONAL ARCHIVES OF INDIA
See: National Archives of India (18614)

★18489★
INDIAN AGRICULTURAL RESEARCH INSTITUTE - PUSA LIBRARY (Agri, Sci-Engr)
New Delhi 110 012, India Phone: 587438
A. Shoaib Ahsan, Hd., Lib.Serv.
Founded: 1905. **Staff:** Prof 52; Other 41. **Subjects:** Crop improvement - genetics, horticulture and fruit technology, vegetable crops, floriculture and landscaping, seed science and technology; crop production - agronomy, soil science and agricultural chemistry, agricultural physics and engineering; crop protection - mycology and plant pathology, entomology and insect pests, nematology and nematode pest, agricultural chemicals; basic sciences - biochemistry, plant physiology, microbiology; nuclear research in agrobiology; water technology; biotechnology; agro-energy; seed testing; bio-fertilizer. **Special Collections:** Plant sciences collection, 1597 to present; Research Bulletin Collection (45,000 field reports from agricultural experiment station); Blue-green Algae Collection. **Holdings:** 115,000 books; 235,000 bound periodical volumes; 10,000 dissertations. **Subscriptions:** 5100 journals and other serials; 12 newspapers. **Services:** Interlibrary loan; copying; SDI; library open to the public with letter of introduction from parent organization. **Publications:** Bibliography of Indian Agriculture; Developmental News in Agriculture; Futuristic Agriculture, all quarterly; monthly list of additions. **Special Catalogs:** Catalogue of IARI Library Serials (1967); Bibliography of IARI Contributions, 1905-1963; Bibliography of IARI Theses, 1936-1973; Information Sources in IARI Library; revised edition of IARI Library serials. **Special Indexes:** Index to classified part of IARI Library catalog; Index to classification numbers of species of insects, fungi, weeds, medicinal plants. **Formerly:** Indian Council of Agricultural Research.

INDIAN COUNCIL OF AGRICULTURAL RESEARCH
See: Indian Agricultural Research Institute (18489)

★18490★
INDIAN COUNCIL OF SOCIAL SCIENCE RESEARCH - SOCIAL SCIENCE DOCUMENTATION CENTRE - LIBRARY (Soc Sci)
35, Ferozshah Rd. Phone: 383186
New Delhi 110001, India Shri S.P. Agrawal, Dir.
Subjects: Anthropology, commerce, demography, economics, education, geography, history, law, management studies, political science, psychology, sociology, town and country planning. **Holdings:** 25,000 books; 1500 project reports and working papers. **Subscriptions:** 2000 journals and other serials. **Services:** Interlibrary loan; copying; translation; library open to social scientists. **Publications:** Bibliographies - by request.

INDIAN NATIONAL SCIENTIFIC DOCUMENTATION CENTRE
See: India - Council of Scientific and Industrial Research (18485)

INDONESIA - DEPARTMENT OF INDUSTRY - INSTITUTE FOR RESEARCH AND DEVELOPMENT OF HANDICRAFT AND BATIK INDUSTRIES
See: Institute for Research and Development of Handicraft and Batik Industries (18520)

★18491★
INDONESIAN INSTITUTE OF SCIENCES - CENTRE FOR SCIENTIFIC DOCUMENTATION AND INFORMATION (Sci-Engr)
Jalan Jenderal Gatot Subroto Kav. 10
P.O. Box 3065/Jkt. Phone: 21 583465
Jakarta 10002, Indonesia Miss Luwarsih Pringgoadisurjo, Hd.
Founded: 1965. **Staff:** Prof 83; Other 148. **Subjects:** Science, technology, social sciences, humanities. **Special Collections:** Women for Development (2435 titles); standards (11,383 titles). **Holdings:** 114,503 volumes; 15,713

report titles; 1517 patents; 1890 dissertations; 47,713 microforms. **Subscriptions:** 1435 journals and other serials. **Services:** Interlibrary loan; copying; SDI; center open to Indonesians without restrictions. **Automated Operations:** Computerized cataloging and acquisitions. **Computerized Information Services:** DIALOG Information Services; internal databases. Performs searches on fee basis. Contact Person: B. Sudarsono. **Publications:** Accessions list (books and microforms); Annual Report; Directory of Special Libraries and Information Sources in Indonesia; bibliographies on various technical topics; additional publications available. **Special Catalogs:** Union List of Serials; Union List of Indonesian Dissertations; catalog of microform holdings held by the centre. **Special Indexes:** Index of Indonesian Learned Periodicals; Index of Research and Survey Reports; Index of papers submitted to seminars, conferences, workshops, and meetings held in Indonesia. **Remarks:** Alternate telephone numbers are 510719 and 511065. Telex: 45875 IA. **Also Known As:** Lembaga Ilmu Pengetahuan Indonesia - Pusat Dokumentasi dan Informasi Ilmiah.

★18492★
INDUSTRIAL TECHNOLOGY RESEARCH INSTITUTE - UNION CHEMICAL LABORATORIES - LIBRARY (Sci-Engr)
321 Kuang-Fu Rd., Section 2 Phone: 72-1321
Hsinchu 30042, Taiwan Ms. A. Du, Libn.
Subjects: Chemistry, chemical engineering, polymers, biotechnology. **Holdings:** 40,000 volumes. **Remarks:** Telex: 31478 UCL ITRI.

INFORMATION CENTER FOR ENERGY PHYSICS MATHEMATICS
See: Fachinformationszentrum Karlsruhe GmbH. - Library (18405)

INSTITUCION MILA Y FONTANALS
See: Scientific Research Council of Spain - Mila and Fontanals Institution (18761)

★18493★
INSTITUT AFRICAIN POUR LE DEVELOPPEMENT ECONOMIQUE ET SOCIAL (INADES) - INADES-DOCUMENTATION (Bus-Fin, Soc Sci)
08 Boite Postal 8 Phone: 44-15-94
Abidjan 08, Ivory Coast Yves Morel, Dir.
Subjects: Africa - economy, development, agriculture, sociology, ethnology, politics, history, geography, religion. **Holdings:** 42,000 books; 300 bound periodical volumes; 400 titles in microform. **Services:** Interlibrary loan; copying; SDI; open to the public. **Publications:** Fichier Afrique (abstracts of papers about African countries); Commented Bibliographies (development in Africa). **Staff:** Marie-Paule Coing, Biblio.-Doc..

INSTITUT FUR DEUTSCHE SPRACHE
See: Institute for German Language (18511)

INSTITUT FUR DOKUMENTATION UND INFORMATION UBER SOZIALMEDIZIN UND OFFENTLICHES GESUNDHEITSWESEN
See: Institute for Documentation and Information in Social Medicine (18504)

INSTITUT FUR ENTWICKLUNGSFORSCHUNG UND ENTWICKLUNGSPOLITIK
See: Institute for Development Research and Development Policy (18503)

INSTITUT FRANCAIS D'ARCHEOLOGIE ORIENTALE
See: French Institute of Eastern Archeology (18428)

INSTITUT FRANCAIS D'ARCHEOLOGIE DU PROCHE-ORIENT
See: French Institute for Archaeology in the Near East (18427)

INSTITUT FRANCAIS D'ETUDES ANDINES
See: French Institute of Andean Studies (18426)

★18494★
INSTITUT FRANCAIS D'ETUDES ARABES DE DAMAS - BIBLIOTHEQUE (Area-Ethnic)
Boite Postal 344 Phone: 330 214-331 962
Damascus, Syrian Arab Republic Christian Velud
Subjects: Arabic and Islamic studies. **Special Collections:** Bulletin d'Etudes Orientales, 1928 to present. **Holdings:** Figures not available. **Publications:** Ahmad Sawqi, l'homme et l'oeuvre, 1977; Le personnage de la femme dans le roman et la nouvelle egyptiens de 1914 a 1960, 1979; Culture et education arabo-islamiques au Sam pendant les trois premiers siecles de l'Islam d'apres le Tarih Dimasq d'Ibn Asakir, 1981; additional publications available.

INSTITUT INTERNATIONAL DE PLANIFICATION DE L'EDUCATION
See: International Institute for Educational Planning (18548)

INSTITUT JULES BORDET
See: Jules Bordet Institute (18306)

INSTITUT FUR KIRCHLICHE ZEITGESCHICHTE
See: Institute for Contemporary Ecclesiastical History (18501)

INSTITUT NATIONAL D'ETUDES DEMOGRAPHIQUES
See: National Institute of Demographic Studies (18625)

★18495★
INSTITUT NATIONAL DE RECHERCHE EN INFORMATIQUE ET EN AUTOMATIQUE - CENTRE DE DOCUMENTATION (Comp Sci)
Boite Postale 105 Phone: 1 39 63 55 11
F-78153 Le Chesnay Cedex, France Mrs. Touzeau
Founded: 1967. **Staff:** Prof 9; Other 7. **Subjects:** Computer science, automation and control, applied mathematics. **Special Collections:** French theses in computer science; computer science proceedings; computer science research reports. **Holdings:** 15,000 books; 475 bound periodical volumes; 25,000 reports and theses. **Subscriptions:** 470 journals and other serials. **Services:** Interlibrary loan; copying; center open to the public. **Automated Operations:** Computerized public access catalog, cataloging, acquisitions, and circulation. **Computerized Information Services:** ESA/IRS, DIALOG Information Services, FIZ CHEMIE, Telesystemes Questel; BIB, TRAP, PERI-CF (internal databases). Performs searches free of charge. Contact Person: Nicole Szwarcbaum, 39 63 56 53. **Publications:** Bulletin de Liaison de la Recherche en Informatique et en Automatique, monthly; INRIATHEQUE (list of new acquisitions received), weekly; INRIA Information, monthly. **Special Catalogs:** Catalogue Collectif National des Publications en Serie. **Special Indexes:** Authors, titles, meetings (online).

INSTITUT PASTEUR
See: Pasteur Institute (18681)

INSTITUT PASTEUR D'ALGERIE
See: Pasteur Institute of Algeria (18682)

INSTITUT DES RELATIONS INTERNATIONALES DU CAMEROUN
See: Cameroon Institute of International Relations (18330)

INSTITUT FUR SEEVERKEHRWIRTSCHAFT UND LOGISTIK
See: Institute of Shipping Economics and Logistics - Library (18523)

INSTITUT FUR WELTWIRTSCHAFT IN KIEL - ZENTRALBIBLIOTHEK DER WIRTSCHAFTSWISSENSCHAFTEN
See: Kiel Institute of World Economics - National Library of Economics (18579)

INSTITUT FUR ZEITGESCHICHTE - BIBLIOTHEK
See: Institute of Contemporary History (18502)

★18496★
INSTITUTE FOR AGRICULTURAL RESEARCH - LIBRARY (Agri)
Ahmadu Bello University
Private Mail Bag 1044 Phone: 32571
Samaru, Zaria, Nigeria Rabiu Salami, Libn.
Subjects: Cereals, oilseeds, fibers, grain legumes and horticultural crops, soil and crop improvement, agricultural mechanization, farming systems. **Holdings:** 40,000 books and pamphlets. **Subscriptions:** 700 journals and other serials. **Remarks:** Affiliated with Ahmadu Bello University.

★18497★
INSTITUTE OF ANTHROPOLOGY - LIBRARY (Soc Sci, Biol Sci)
University of Coimbra Phone: 29051
P-3000 Coimbra, Portugal Maria Isilda Figueiras, Libn.
Subjects: Sociocultural and physical anthropology, social biology, human genetics, paleoanthropology. **Holdings:** 12,459 books; 11,982 bound periodical volumes. **Subscriptions:** 360 journals and other serials. **Services:**

Interlibrary loan; copying; library open to the public. **Publications:** Boletine Informativo, bimonthly - on exchange. **Remarks:** Affiliated with University of Coimbra and Portugal - Ministry of Education.

★18498★
INSTITUTE OF ARGENTINE STANDARDS - DOCUMENTATION CENTER (Sci-Engr)
Chile 1175 Phone: 1 37-3387
1098 Buenos Aires, Argentina Enzo Di Muro, Libn.
Founded: 1936. **Subjects:** Standards - electric, iron, construction, engineering. **Holdings:** 700,000 items. **Subscriptions:** 20 journals and other serials; 5 newspapers. **Services:** Interlibrary loan; copying; SDI; center open to the public. **Publications:** Dinamico, monthly - free by subscription. **Also Known As:** Instituto Argentino de Racionalizacion de Materiales - Centro de Documentacion.

★18499★
INSTITUTE FOR ASTRONOMICAL COMPUTATIONS - LIBRARY (Sci-Engr)
Moenchhofstrasse 12-14 Phone: 4 90 26
D-6900 Heidelberg 1, Federal Republic of Germany
Dr. Lutz Schmadel, Libn.
Subjects: Astronomy, astrophysics, celestial mechanics, dynamics of the galaxy. **Holdings:** 50,000 volumes. **Remarks:** Affiliated with Baden-Wurtemberg State Ministry of Science and Art. Telex: 461336. **Also Known As:** Astronomisches Rechen-Institut.

★18500★
INSTITUTE FOR BALKAN STUDIES - LIBRARY (Area-Ethnic)
Tsimiski 45
P.O. Box 10611 Phone: 225-365
Thessalonika 54110, Greece Thomy Verrou-Karakostas, Libn.
Subjects: Balkan region - history, culture, arts, language, folklore. **Holdings:** 17,000 books.

★18501★
INSTITUTE FOR CONTEMPORARY ECCLESIASTICAL HISTORY - LIBRARY (Rel-Phil, Hist)
Monchsberg 2a Phone: 84 25 21
A-5020 Salzburg, Austria Theodora Bogalin, Libn.
Subjects: Contemporary ecclesiastical history, Austrian history. **Holdings:** 7500 volumes. **Remarks:** Maintained by Internationales Forschungszentrum fur Grundfragen der Wissenschaften Salzburg. **Also Known As:** Institut fur Kirchliche Zeitgeschichte.

★18502★
INSTITUTE OF CONTEMPORARY HISTORY - LIBRARY (Area-Ethnic, Hist)
Leonrodstrasse 46b Phone: 89 18 00 26
D-8000 Munich 19, Federal Republic of Germany
Dr. Christoph Weisz, Libn.
Subjects: Contemporary history of the German Reich, Third Reich, and Federal Republic of Germany; emigration of Germans during the years 1933-1945; national socialism; Bavarian contemporary history. **Holdings:** 120,000 volumes. **Remarks:** Affiliated with Federal Republic of Germany - Ministry of Research and Technology and Bavarian State Ministry for Science and Culture. **Also Known As:** Institut fur Zeitgeschichte - Bibliothek.

★18503★
INSTITUTE FOR DEVELOPMENT RESEARCH AND DEVELOPMENT POLICY - LIBRARY (Bus-Fin, Soc Sci)
Ruhr-Universitat Bochum
Postfach 102148 Phone: 700 24 18
D-4630 Bochum, Federal Republic of GermanyDorothee Sensen, Libn.
Subjects: Development policy and strategy, economics of education, government and politics, economic and social geography, demography and sociology, agricultural policy, statistics and econometrics. **Holdings:** 40,000 volumes. **Remarks:** Maintained by Ruhr-University. Telex: 08 25 860. **Also Known As:** Institut fur Entwicklungsforschung und Entwicklungspolitik.

★18504★
INSTITUTE FOR DOCUMENTATION AND INFORMATION IN SOCIAL MEDICINE - LIBRARY (Med)
Postfach 201012
Westerfeldstrasse 35-37
D-4800 Bielefeld 1, Federal Republic of Germany Phone: 521 86033
Subjects: Addiction and alcoholism; environmental health and toxicology; epidemiology; medicine - industrial, legal, preventive, social, traffic; health education; occupational health; mental retardation; public health; medical sociology. **Special Collections:** German medical statistics. **Holdings:** 70,000 volumes; microfiche; AV programs. **Subscriptions:** 700 journals and other serials. **Services:** Library open to the public. **Computerized Information Services:** DIMDI; produces SOMED. **Remarks:** Maintained by the State Ministry of Labor, Health and Social Affairs of North Rhine-Westphalia. **Also Known As:** Institut fur Dokumentation und Information uber Sozialmedizin und Offentliches Gesundheitswesen.

★18505★
INSTITUTE FOR DRUG RESEARCH - LIBRARY (Med, Sci-Engr)
Szabadsagharcosok utja 47-49
Postafiok 82 Phone: 694-650
H-1325 Budapest, Hungary Dr. Judit Stverteczky, Hd., Res. Group
Founded: 1950. **Staff:** Prof 3; Other 3. **Subjects:** Organic chemistry, biochemistry, analytical chemistry, bioengineering, new drugs, medicine. **Holdings:** 15,248 books; 16,317 bound periodical volumes. **Subscriptions:** 109 journals and other serials; 9 newspapers. **Services:** Interlibrary loan; copying; SDI; library open to the public. **Computerized Information Services:** DIALOG Information Services, Data-Star, STN International. **Also Known As:** Gyogyszerkutato Intezet Kv.

★18506★
INSTITUTE OF DUNHUANG RELICS STUDY - LIBRARY (Hist)
Mogaoku
Dunhuang, Gansu Province, People's Republic of China
Founded: 1960. **Staff:** 11. **Subjects:** Fine arts archeology, Chinese western regions archeology, Buddhism. **Special Collections:** Dunhuang Study Collection (articles; sutras; Chinese ancient books and paintings). **Holdings:** 43,055 volumes; 200 periodicals; 50 technical reports; 5 AV programs and microforms. **Services:** Interlibrary loan. **Publications:** Dunhuang Study (magazine); Dunhuang Painted Sculpture; Dunhuang Frescoes; Dunhuang Artistic Treasures; Dunhuang (5 volumes).

★18507★
INSTITUTE OF ELECTRICAL RESEARCH - LIBRARY (Sci-Engr)
Apartado Postal 475 Phone: 14-38-99
62000 Cuernavaca, Mexico Dr. Jaime Pontigo, Libn.
Founded: 1975. **Subjects:** Power generation, transmission, distribution, and automation. **Holdings:** 35,000 volumes. **Also Known As:** Instituto de Investigaciones Electricas.

★18508★
INSTITUTE OF EUROPEAN STUDIES - VIENNA LIBRARY (Area-Ethnic, Bus-Fin)
Palais Corbelli
Johannesgasse 7 Phone: 222 512 22 601
A-1010 Vienna, Austria Cele Cerne, Libn.
Founded: 1955. **Staff:** Prof 3; Other 10. **Subjects:** Eastern European studies, arts, Austrian cultural studies, international business and economics, international relations, psychology. **Special Collections:** Scores; libretti. **Holdings:** 8500 books; students' term papers and essays; 170 audiotapes; 350 phonograph records. **Subscriptions:** 16 journals and other serials; 5 newspapers. **Services:** Interlibrary loan; library not open to the public. **Publications:** Annual Report. **Remarks:** Materials are in English. **Staff:** Fanny Schlogelhofer, Libn..

★18509★
INSTITUTE OF FISCAL STUDIES - LIBRARY (Bus-Fin)
Casado del Alisal 6 Phone: 1 227 15 07
E-28014 Madrid, Spain Antonio Pajuelo Macias, Libn.
Subjects: Public finance, taxation, economics. **Holdings:** 55,000 volumes. **Remarks:** Maintained by Spain - Ministry of Finance and Economy. **Also Known As:** Instituto de Estudios Fiscales.

★18510★
INSTITUTE OF FUNDAMENTAL TECHNOLOGICAL RESEARCH - LIBRARY (Sci-Engr)
ulica Swietokrzyska 21 Phone: 22 26-18-81
PL-00-049 Warsaw, Poland Aleksandra Krolikowska, Libn.
Subjects: Applied mechanics, acoustics, electrodynamics, nondestructive testing, energy research. **Holdings:** 80,000 volumes. **Remarks:** Affiliated with Polish Academy of Sciences. **Also Known As:** Instytut Podstawowych Problemow Techniki.

★18511★
INSTITUTE FOR GERMAN LANGUAGE - LIBRARY (Hum)
Friedrich-Karl-Strasse 12 Phone: 621 44011
D-6800 Mannheim 1, Federal Republic of Germany
Eva Teubert, Libn.
Subjects: Contemporary German language, linguistics, and literature. **Holdings:** 40,000 volumes; 10,000 tape recordings. **Subscriptions:** 200 journals and other serials. **Services:** Library open to institutions and scholars of German language and linguistics. **Computerized Information Services:** Internal databases. **Also Known As:** Institut fur Deutsche Sprache.

★18512★
INSTITUTE OF HISTORICAL, SOCIAL, AND POLITICAL STUDIES OF THE CENTRAL COMMITTEE OF THE ROMANIAN COMMUNIST PARTY - LIBRARY (Soc Sci)
Strada Ministerului 4 Phone: 17 01 06
Bucharest 70000, Romania Dr. Nicolae Popescu
Subjects: Communist party, revolutionary and democratic movements in Romania and other countries. **Holdings:** 100,000 volumes. **Also Known As:** Institutul de Studii Istorice si Social-Politice de pe Linga Comitetul Central al Partidului Comunist Roman.

★18513★
INSTITUTE OF LOGISTICS AND DISTRIBUTION MANAGEMENT - LIBRARY (Bus-Fin)
Douglas House
Queens Square Phone: 536 205500
Corby, Northamptonshire NN 17, England R.C. Horsley, Dir.Gen.
Founded: 1981. **Subjects:** Physical distribution of goods. **Holdings:** 250 volumes.

★18514★
INSTITUTE FOR MEDICAL INFORMATION - STATE MEDICAL LIBRARY (Med)
Vitezneho unora 31 Phone: 299956
CS-121 32 Prague 2, Czechoslovakia Daha Baborova
Subjects: Biomedicine, public health, health-related legislation. **Holdings:** 230,000 volumes; microfiche. **Subscriptions:** 1560 journals and other serials. **Services:** Interlibrary loan; copying; SDI; library open to the public. **Computerized Information Services:** Excerpta Medica, Czechoslovak Medical Literature Data Base. Performs searches free of charge. **Publications:** Bibliographies and abstracts of domestic and foreign literature; Bibliographia Medica Cechoslovaca, monthly. **Also Known As:** Ustav Vedeckych Lekarskych Informaci - Statni Lekarska Knihovna.

★18515★
INSTITUTE FOR PALESTINE STUDIES - LIBRARY (Area-Ethnic)
Anis Nsouli St., Off Verdun
P.O. Box 11-7164 Phone: 312-512
Beirut, Lebanon Mona Nsouli, Libn.
Founded: 1963. **Staff:** Prof 3; Other 2. **Subjects:** Palestine problem, Arab-Israeli conflict, Judaica, Zionism, Jewish-Arab relations. **Special Collections:** Rare books (pertaining to Mandate period); private papers; photograph collection; official correspondence, records, and private collections of the Public Record Office, London; League of Arab States and United Nations documents. **Holdings:** 29,000 books; 11,600 bound periodical volumes; pamphlet files; 3850 reels of microfilm; 400 maps; 200 theses. **Subscriptions:** 518 journals and other serials; 40 newspapers. **Services:** Interlibrary loan; copying; library open to the public with restrictions for security reasons. **Publications:** Accessions list, bimonthly. **Special Indexes:** Periodicals index. **Remarks:** An alternate telephone number is 814174. **Staff:** Leila Halavi, Asst.Libn., Cat.; Rima Awad, Asst.Libn., Doc..

INSTITUTE OF PAPUA NEW GUINEA STUDIES
See: Papua New Guinea - Department of Culture and Tourism (18679)

★18516★
INSTITUTE FOR PHILOLOGY AND FOLKLORISTICS - INSTITUTE FOR FOLKLORE RESEARCH - LIBRARY (Area-Ethnic)
Socijalisticke Revolucije 17/1V Phone: 440-880
YU-41000 Zagreb, Yugoslavia Anamarija Starcevic-Stambuk, Libn.
Subjects: Croatian folklore - oral and folk literature, popular literature, folk theater and dance, customs, urban folklore, ethnology and folkloristics, ethnomusicology. **Special Collections:** Folklore Archives (1250 unpublished manuscripts; 1980 tapes and cassettes; 210 phonograph records; films; 25,000 photographs and slides). **Holdings:** 19,000 volumes. **Remarks:** An alternate telephone number is 410-617. **Also Known As:** Zavod za Istrazivanje Folklora.

★18517★
INSTITUTE FOR PHYTOMEDICINE - SWISS BOTANICAL SOCIETY - LIBRARY (Biol Sci)
Universitatsstrasse 2
ETH-Zentrum
CH-8092 Zurich, Switzerland L. Konig, Libn.
Subjects: Botany. **Holdings:** 600,000 volumes. **Also Known As:** Schweizerische Botanische Gesellschaft.

★18518★
INSTITUTE FOR THE PROTECTION OF THE NATURAL AND CULTURAL HERITAGE OF SLOVENIA - LIBRARY (Hist, Env-Cons)
Plecnikov trg 2
Postanski Fah 176 Phone: 213-022
Ljubljana, Yugoslavia Mrs. Alenka Prunk, Libn.
Subjects: Slovenia - monument preservation and nature conservation. **Holdings:** 20,000 volumes. **Also Known As:** Zavod SR Slovenije za Varstvo Naravne in Kulturne Dediscine.

★18519★
INSTITUTE OF PUBLIC ADMINISTRATION - LIBRARY AND DOCUMENTS CENTER (Soc Sci, Bus-Fin)
P.O. Box 205 Phone: 4768888
Riyadh 11141, Saudi Arabia
Sorayye Al-Sorayye, Dir., Circ. & Ref.Serv.
Subjects: Public administration, management, law, financial administration, library and information sciences, computer science, economics, political science. **Special Collections:** Rare books on Saudi Arabia, Islam, and the Arabian Gulf States. **Holdings:** 162,182 books; 6400 bound periodical volumes; 37,925 documents; 150 AV programs; 13,248 microforms; maps; theses; films. **Services:** Interlibrary loan; copying; SDI; library open to the public. **Computerized Information Services:** DOBIS-LIBIS. Performs searches free of charge. **Publications:** Information Sources on Saudi Arabia, 2nd edition; Periodicals holdings list (in Arabic or in English); Bibliography of Saudi Government Publications in IPA Documents Center (in Arabic); Bibliography of IPA Publications; Maktabat Al-Idarah (periodical specializing in library science), quarterly. **Remarks:** Library holdings are in English and Arabic. An alternate telephone number is 4792127. Telex: 401160 IPADMN SJ or 404360 IPADMN SJ. **Staff:** Mostafa Sadhan, Dir.Gen. of Libs. & Docs.Ctr..

★18520★
INSTITUTE FOR RESEARCH AND DEVELOPMENT OF HANDICRAFT AND BATIK INDUSTRIES - IRDHBI LIBRARY (Art)
2 Jalan Kusumanegara Phone: 2557
Yogyakarta, Indonesia Slamet Rahayu, Libn.
Subjects: Handicraft and batik industries, rattan, wood carving. **Holdings:** 4300 volumes. **Remarks:** Maintained by Indonesia - Department of Industry. **Also Known As:** Balai Besar Penelitian dan Pengembangan Industri Kerajinan dan Batik.

★18521★
INSTITUTE FOR SCIENTIFIC, TECHNICAL AND ECONOMIC INFORMATION - TECHNICAL LIBRARY (Info Sci)
ul. Jasna 14/16
PL-00-041 Warsaw, Poland
Subjects: Scientific, technical, and economic information services and systems; information science; documentation. **Holdings:** 60,500 volumes. **Subscriptions:** 118 journals and other serials. **Computerized Information Services:** Online systems. **Publications:** Bibliographies. **Remarks:** Maintained by Poland - Ministry of Higher Education, Science and Technology. **Also Known As:** Instytut Informacji Naukowej, Technicznej i Ekonomicznej (IINTE).

★18522★
INSTITUTE OF SCIENTIFIC AND TECHNICAL INFORMATION OF CHINA - LIBRARY (Sci-Engr)
P.O. Box 640
Beijing, People's Republic of China Phone: 1 464746
Subjects: Science and technology. **Holdings:** 1 million research reports, proceedings, scientific and technical publications; 1.1 million microfiche; 4000 films. **Subscriptions:** 19,500 journals and other serials. **Services:** Library open to the public. **Computerized Information Services:** Chinese Pharmacy Abstracts data base (internal database). Performs searches on fee basis.

★18523★
INSTITUTE OF SHIPPING ECONOMICS AND LOGISTICS - LIBRARY (Trans)
Am Dom 5 A
D-2800 Bremen 1, Federal Republic of Germany Phone: 421 36805
Subjects: Shipping, shipbuilding industry. **Special Collections:** Biographical archives. **Holdings:** 45,000 volumes. **Computerized Information Services:** Internal database. **Also Known As:** Institut fur Seeverkehrwirtschaft und Logistik.

★18524★
INSTITUTE OF SOCIAL STUDIES - LIBRARY (Soc Sci)
P.O. Box 90733 Phone: 70 502321
NL-2509 LS The Hague, Netherlands Prof. D. Wolfson, Dir.
Subjects: Social policy, including development policy and the state, agricultural development, international economic issues, international relations, labor and development, women and development, urban-rural relations. **Holdings:** 60,000 volumes. **Subscriptions:** 550 journals and other serials. **Remarks:** Maintained by Netherlands - Ministry of Foreign Affairs.

★18525★
INSTITUTE OF SOUTHEAST ASIAN STUDIES - LIBRARY (Area-Ethnic, Soc Sci)
Heng Mui Keng Terrace
Pasir Panjang Phone: 7780955
Singapore 0511, Singapore Wan Lye Tim, Sr.Asst.Libn.
Subjects: Southeast Asia, international relations and strategic studies, economics, sociology and anthropology, history, demography. **Special Collections:** Photo archive (Southeast Asian ethnography). **Holdings:** 66,090 volumes; 6290 documents; 181,580 microforms; 600 files of press clippings; 300 rare book volumes. **Services:** Interlibrary loan; copying; library open to the public for reference use only. **Publications:** Tan Cheng Lock papers: a descriptive list, 1972; ASEAN: a bibliography; ASEAN: a bibliography II; additional publications available. **Remarks:** Telex: ISEAS RS37068. **Staff:** Ch'ng Kim-See, Libn..

★18526★
INSTITUTE FOR SOUTHEAST EUROPEAN STUDIES - LIBRARY (Area-Ethnic)
Blvd. Republicii 13
P.O. Box 22-159 Phone: 0 14 49 96
Bucharest, Romania Corina Mihailescu, Libn.
Subjects: Southeast Europe - history, philology, linguistics, literary history, art history, law. **Holdings:** 24,800 volumes. **Remarks:** Affiliated with Bucharest University and Academy of Social and Political Sciences. **Also Known As:** Institutul de Studii Sud-Est Europene.

★18527★
INSTITUTE OF SPACE AND ASTRONAUTICAL SCIENCE - ISAS LIBRARY (Sci-Engr)
6-1, Komaba, 4-Chome
Meguro-ku Phone: 3 467-1111
Tokyo 153, Japan Dr. Minoru Oda, Dir.-Gen.
Subjects: Space sciences, astronautics, satellites, new spacecraft technology, planetary sciences. **Holdings:** 89,390 volumes. **Also Known As:** Uchu Kagaku Kenkyusho.

INSTITUTIONEN FOR STRESSFORSKNING
See: Karolinska Institute - Department of Stress Research (18575)

INSTITUTO ANTARTICO ARGENTINO
See: Argentine Antarctic Institute (18272)

INSTITUTO DE ANTROPOLOGIA E HISTORIA
See: Guatemala - Ministry of Education - Institute of Anthropology and History - Library (18456)

INSTITUTO ARGENTINO DE RACIONALIZACION DE MATERIALES - CENTRO DE DOCUMENTACION
See: Institute of Argentine Standards - Documentation Center (18498)

INSTITUTO BOLIVIANO DE TECNOLOGIA AGROPECUARIA
See: Bolivian Institute of Agricultural Technology (18305)

INSTITUTO DE BOTANICA "DARWINION"
See: Darwinian Institute of Botany (18379)

INSTITUTO BUTANTAN
See: Butantan Institute (18328)

INSTITUTO CENTROAMERICANO DE INVESTIGACION Y TECNOLOGIA INDUSTRIEL (ICAITI)
See: Central American Research Institute for Industry (18341)

INSTITUTO ECUATORIANO DE CIENCIAS NATURALES
See: Ecuadorian Institute of Natural Sciences (18391)

★18528★
INSTITUTO DE ESTUDIOS ISLAMICOS - BIBLIOTECA GENERAL (Rel-Phil, Area-Ethnic)
Calle Rey de Bahamonde, 121
Vista Alegre, Surco Phone: 14 489720
Lima 33, Peru Dr. Antolin Bedoya Villacorta
Subjects: Cultural roots, Zionism, Islam in Latin America, colonialism of La Ummah. **Special Collections:** Libya; Iran; disinformation regarding pseudo-terrorism; luchas de liberacion; religion. **Holdings:** 15,000 volumes; 250 AV programs; 400 manuscripts. **Services:** Library not open to the public. **Computerized Information Services:** Online systems.

INSTITUTO INTERAMERICANO DO COOPERACION PARA LA AGRICULTURA (IICA)
See: Inter-American Institute for Cooperation on Agriculture (IICA) - Biblioteca Venezuela (18531)

INSTITUTO DE INVESTIGACIONES ESTETICAS
See: National Autonomous University of Mexico - Institute of Aesthetics Research (18616)

INSTITUTO DE INVESTIGACIONES HISTORICAS
See: National Autonomous University of Mexico - Institute of Historical Research (18617)

INSTITUTO LATINOAMERICANO DEL FIERRO Y EL ACERO
See: Latin American Iron and Steel Institute (18588)

INSTITUTO NACIONAL DE ESTUDIOS DEL TEATRO
See: National Institute for the Study of the Theater (18630)

INSTITUTO NACIONAL DE INVESTIGACIONES NUCLEARES
See: Mexico - National Institute of Nuclear Research - Nuclear Information and Documentation Center (18604)

INSTITUTO NACIONAL DE INVESTIGACIONES SOBRE RECURSOS BIOTICOS
See: National Institute for Research on Biological Sciences (18629)

INSTITUTO NACIONAL DE PESQUISAS DA AMAZONIA
See: National Institute of Amazon Research (18624)

INSTITUTO DE NUTRICION DE CENTROAMERICA Y PANAMA
See: Pan-American Health Organization - Nutrition Institute of Central America and Panama (18677)

INSTITUTO RIVA-AGUERO
See: Pontificia Universidad Catolica del Peru - Riva-Aguero Institute (18715)

INSTITUTO DE SALUD PUBLICA DE CHILE
See: Chile - Ministry of Public Health - Public Health Institute of Chile (18346)

★18529★
INSTITUTO TECNOLOGICO DE COSTA RICA - BIBLIOTECA (Sci-Engr)
Apartado 159 - 7050 Phone: 51-53-33
Cartago, Costa Rica Paulina Retana Acevedo
Subjects: Engineering, science. **Holdings:** 40,000 books; 2000 reprints. **Services:** Interlibrary loan; library open to the public with restrictions.

INSTITUTUL CANTACUZINO
See: Romania - Ministry of Health - Cantacuzino Institute (18730)

INSTITUTUL DE ISTORIA ARTEI
See: Academy of Social and Political Sciences - Art History Institute (18259)

INSTITUTUL NATIONAL DE METROLOGIE
See: National Institute of Metrology (18628)

INSTITUTUL DE STUDII ISTORICE SI SOCIAL-POLITICE DE PE LINGA COMITETUL CENTRAL AL PARTIDULUI COMUNIST ROMAN
See: Institute of Historical, Social, and Political Studies of the Central Committee of the Romanian Communist Party (18512)

INSTITUTUL DE STUDII SUD-EST EUROPENE
See: Institute for Southeast European Studies (18526)

INSTYTUT BADAN LITERACKICH
See: Polish Academy of Sciences - Literary Research Institute (18710)

INSTYTUT IMMUNOLOGII I TERAPII DOSWIADCZALNEJ IM. LUDWICKA HIRSZFELDA
See: Polish Academy of Sciences - L. Hirszfeld Institute of Immunology and Experimental Therapy (18709)

INSTYTUT INFORMACJI NAUKOWEJ, TECHNICZNEJ I EKONOMICZNEJ (IINTE)
See: Institute for Scientific, Technical and Economic Information (18521)

INSTYTUT MATKI I DZIECKA
See: Poland - Ministry of Health and Social Welfare - National Research Institute of Mother and Child (18704)

INSTYTUT PODSTAWOWYCH PROBLEMOW TECHNIKI
See: Institute of Fundamental Technological Research (18510)

INSTYTUT SZTUKI
See: Polish Academy of Sciences - Institute of Art (18707)

INTER-AMERICAN AGRICULTURAL DOCUMENTATION AND INFORMATION CENTER - BIBLIOTECA VENEZUELA
See: Inter-American Institute for Cooperation on Agriculture (IICA) - Biblioteca Venezuela (18531)

★18530★
INTER-AMERICAN CENTER FOR RESEARCH AND DOCUMENTATION ON VOCATIONAL TRAINING - LIBRARY (Educ)
Avenida Uruguay
Casilla de Correo 1761
Montevideo, Uruguay Phone: 98 17 44
Subjects: Vocational training in Latin American and Caribbean countries. **Holdings:** 21,000 volumes. **Remarks:** Maintained by Organizacion Interacional del Trabajo. **Also Known As:** Centro Interamericano de Investigacion y Documentacion sobre Formacion Profesional.

★18531★
INTER-AMERICAN INSTITUTE FOR COOPERATION ON AGRICULTURE (IICA) - BIBLIOTECA VENEZUELA (Agri)
Apartado Postal 55-2200 Coronado Phone: 29-02-22
San Jose, Costa Rica Ghislaine Poitevien, Hd.Libn.
Subjects: Agricultural policy planning, technology generation and transfer, rural development, agricultural marketing, animal health, plant protection. **Holdings:** 8000 books; 200 bound periodical volumes; 2000 microforms; IICA publications; statistical data collection. **Services:** Interlibrary loan; copying; SDI; library open to the public with restrictions. **Computerized Information Services:** DIALOG Information Services, AGRIS (International Information System for the Agricultural Sciences and Technology), AGRINTER, CAB (Commonwealth Agriculture Bureaux) ABSTRACTS. Performs searches on fee basis. Contact Person: Lina Roman, Bibliotecologa, 29-02-22, ext. 326. **Remarks:** Library is part of Inter-American Agricultural Documentation and Information Center. Telex: 2144-IICA. **Also Known As:** Instituto Interamericano do Cooperacion para la Agricultura (IICA) - Centro Interamericano de Documentacion e Informacion Agricola (CIDIA).

INTERNATIONAAL ARCHIEF VOOR DE VROUWENBEWEGING
See: International Archives for the Women's Movement (18534)

INTERNATIONAAL BELASTING DOCUMENTATIE BUREAU
See: International Bureau of Fiscal Documentation (18537)

★18532★
INTERNATIONAL ACADEMY OF SCIENCES - LIBRARY (Sci-Engr)
Kleinberger Weg 16 B Phone: 05251 64200
D-4790 Paderborn, Federal Republic of Germany Prof. Helmar Frank
Founded: 1985. **Subjects:** Scientific terminology and international academic standards in the fields of cybernetics, humanities, structural sciences, philosophy, natural sciences, and morphological sciences. **Holdings:** 300 volumes. **Also Known As:** Akademio Internacia de la Sciencoj.

★18533★
INTERNATIONAL AGENCY FOR RESEARCH ON CANCER - LIBRARY (Med)
150, cours Albert-Thomas Phone: 72 73 84 34
F-69372 Lyon Cedex 08 France Mrs. Agnes Nagy-Tiborcz, Libn.
Founded: 1967. **Staff:** Prof 2; Other 2. **Subjects:** Cancer, chemical carcinogenesis, cancer epidemiology, environmental carcinogenesis, virology/genetics, biostatistics. **Holdings:** 8000 books; 7000 bound periodical volumes; annual reports; World Health Organization documents. **Subscriptions:** 280 journals and other serials. **Services:** Interlibrary loan; copying; library open to the public on a limited schedule. **Computerized Information Services:** NLM, DIALOG Information Services. **Publications:** Library Bulletin. **Remarks:** Agency is the autonomous cancer research arm of the World Health Organization. **Staff:** Ms. H. Miido, Info.Sci..

★18534★
INTERNATIONAL ARCHIVES FOR THE WOMEN'S MOVEMENT (Soc Sci)
Postbus 19504 Phone: 20 244268
NL-1000 GM Amsterdam, Netherlands Sacha Vries, Lib.Asst.
Subjects: Women, women's movement. **Special Collections:** Archives (100 linear meters); photograph collection. **Holdings:** 30,000 books. **Services:** Interlibrary loan; copying; archives open to the public. **Remarks:** Jointly maintained by Netherlands - Ministry of Social Affairs and University of Amsterdam. Located at Keizersgracht 10, NL-1015 CN Amsterdam. **Also Known As:** Internationaal Archief voor de Vrouwenbeweging. **Staff:** Claire C. Posthumus, Libn..

INTERNATIONAL ATOMIC ENERGY AGENCY - INTERNATIONAL CENTER FOR THEORETICAL PHYSICS
See: International Center for Theoretical Physics (18541)

★18535★
INTERNATIONAL ATOMIC ENERGY AGENCY - LIBRARY (Energy)
Vienna International Center Postfach 100
Wagramer Strasse 5 A-1400 Vienna, Austria
Subjects: Research and development of practical applications of atomic energy for peaceful uses. **Holdings:** 51,000 books; 4000 periodicals, films, and documents; 35,000 technical reports. **Remarks:** The agency was founded under the auspices of UNESCO.

INTERNATIONAL BAPTIST THEOLOGICAL SEMINARY
See: European Baptist Federation (18397)

★18536★
INTERNATIONAL BEE RESEARCH ASSOCIATION - LIBRARY (Agri)
18 North Rd.
Cardiff CF1 3DY, Wales Phone: 222 372409
Subjects: Bee research; pollination, especially by bees. **Holdings:** 4000 books; 26,000 reprints and reports; 8000 photographs. **Subscriptions:** 750 journals and other serials. **Remarks:** Telex: 23152 monref G 8390. **Also Known As:** Association Internationale de Recherche Apicole.

★18537★
INTERNATIONAL BUREAU OF FISCAL DOCUMENTATION - LIBRARY (Bus-Fin)
Muiderpoort-Sarphatistraat 124
Postbus 20237
NL-1000 HE Amsterdam, Netherlands Phone: 20 267726
Subjects: International taxation. **Holdings:** 20,000 volumes. **Computerized Information Services:** Internal database. **Remarks:** Founded by International Fiscal Association. Telex: 13217 intax nl; Fax: 20 228658. **Also Known As:** Internationaal Belasting Documentatie Bureau.

★18538★
INTERNATIONAL BUREAU OF THE UNIVERSAL POSTAL UNION - LIBRARY (Bus-Fin)
CH-3000 Berne 15, Switzerland Phone: 31 43 22 11
William Reid, First Sec.
Subjects: Postal service. **Holdings:** 10,000 volumes. **Also Known As:** Bureau International de l'Union Postale Universelle.

★18539★
INTERNATIONAL CENTER FOR LIVING AQUATIC RESOURCES MANAGEMENT - ICLARM LIBRARY (Biol Sci)
MC, P.O. Box 1501
Makati Phone: 2 818-0466
Manila, Philippines Rosalinda M. Temprosa, Chf.Libn.
Founded: 1978. **Staff:** Prof 4; Other 1. **Subjects:** Fisheries, aquaculture, coastal resources management, biological research, economics. **Special Collections:** Newspaper clipping and reprint collection (fisheries and aquaculture; coastal resources management in tropical and developing countries). **Holdings:** 8000 books, monographs, theses, dissertations, conference proceedings, papers; CD-ROM. **Subscriptions:** 600 serial titles. **Services:** Interlibrary loan; copying; library open to the public for reference use only to fisheries and aquaculture researchers. **Automated Operations:** Computerized cataloging and serials. **Computerized Information Services:** DIALOG Information Services; internal database; SCIENCEnet (electronic mail service). Performs searches free of charge. **Publications:** Acquisitions list, quarterly - selective distribution; other publications available. **Remarks:** An alternate telephone number is 817-5255. **Staff:** Mrs. Norma Jhocson, Assoc.Libn.; Mrs. Erlinda B. Gonzalez, Asst.Libn.; Mrs. Nelia Balagapo, Asst.Libn..

★18540★
INTERNATIONAL CENTRE FOR PARLIAMENTARY DOCUMENTATION - LIBRARY (Law)
Place Petit-Saconnex
Case Postale 438 Phone: 22 34 41 50
CH-1211 Geneva 19, Switzerland D. Kordon
Founded: 1965. **Subjects:** Structure and working methods of all national parliaments. **Holdings:** 7000 volumes. **Remarks:** Telex: 28 97 84. **Also Known As:** Centre International de Documentation Parlementaire.

★18541★
INTERNATIONAL CENTER FOR THEORETICAL PHYSICS - LIBRARY (Sci-Engr)
Strada Costiera 11
Casella Postale 586 Phone: 40 2240215
I-34100 Trieste, Italy Maria Zingarelli, Libn.
Founded: 1964. **Subjects:** Physics - high energy, condensed matter, plasma, atomic, nuclear; applied mathematics; physics of the earth; atmosphere and oceans. **Holdings:** 40,000 volumes. **Services:** Interlibrary loan; library not open to the public. **Remarks:** Jointly maintained by the International Atomic Energy Agency and UNESCO. Telex: 460392 ICTPI.

★18542★
INTERNATIONAL CENTER FOR TROPICAL AGRICULTURE - LIBRARY (Agri)
Apartado Aereo 6713 Phone: 3 680111
Cali, Colombia Susan C. Harris, Hd., Commun. & Info.Sys.
Subjects: Agricultural technology, cassava, field beans, rice, pasture technology. **Holdings:** 30,000 volumes. **Remarks:** Maintained by the Consultative Group on International Agricultural Research. **Also Known As:** Centro Internacional de Agricultura Tropical.

★18543★
INTERNATIONAL CIVIL DEFENSE ORGANIZATION - DOCUMENTATION CENTER (Soc Sci)
10-12, Chemin de Surville
CH-1213 Geneva, Switzerland Phone: 22 934433
Subjects: Civil defense - organization, training, equipment. **Holdings:** 14,500 volumes. **Also Known As:** Organisation Internationale de Protection Civile.

★18544★
INTERNATIONAL COFFEE ORGANIZATION - LIBRARY (Food-Bev, Bus-Fin)
22 Berners St.
London W1P 4DD, England Phone: 1 5808591
Subjects: Coffee - production, price fluctuation, consumption; economic development of coffee-producing countries. **Holdings:** 10,000 volumes. **Computerized Information Services:** Produces COFFEELINE (10,000 bibliographic records). **Publications:** Library, monthly. **Remarks:** Telex: 267659 INTCAF G. **Also Known As:** Organisation Internationale du Cafe.

INTERNATIONAL CONRAD SOCIETY
See: British Institute of Management - Management Information Centre (18316)

INTERNATIONAL CONRAD SOCIETY
See: Polish Social and Cultural Association - Library (18712)

★18545★
INTERNATIONAL COUNCIL OF ENVIRONMENTAL LAW - LIBRARY (Law, Env-Cons)
Adenauerallee 214
D-5300 Bonn 1, Federal Republic of Germany Phone: 228 2692240
Subjects: Environmental law, environmental policy and administration. **Holdings:** 30,000 volumes. **Also Known As:** Conseil International du Droit de l'Environnement.

INTERNATIONAL COUNCIL OF MUSEUMS
See: UNESCO - International Council of Museums (18825)

★18546★
INTERNATIONAL COUNCIL OF SCIENTIFIC UNIONS - LIBRARY
51, boulevard de Montmorency
F-75016 Paris, France
Defunct

INTERNATIONAL EMBRYOLOGICAL INSTITUTE
See: Royal Academy of Sciences - Netherlands Institute for Developmental Biology (18731)

INTERNATIONAL INSTITUTE OF AGRICULTURE LIBRARY
See: United Nations - Food and Agriculture Organization - David Lubin Memorial Library (18829)

★18547★
INTERNATIONAL INSTITUTE FOR APPLIED SYSTEMS ANALYSIS - LIBRARY (Soc Sci)
Schloss Laxenburg
Schlossplatz 1 Phone: 715210
A-2361 Laxenburg, Austria Peter Popper, Hd.Libn.
Subjects: Social, economic, technological, and environmental development. **Holdings:** 12,000 volumes. **Remarks:** Telex: 079137.

★18548★
INTERNATIONAL INSTITUTE FOR EDUCATIONAL PLANNING - LIBRARY (Educ)
7-9, rue Eugene-Delacroix Phone: 1 45 04 28 12
F-75516 Paris, France Francoise Du Pouget, Libn.
Subjects: Educational planning; social, economic and political dynamics of educational development. **Holdings:** 30,000 volumes. **Remarks:** Institute is part of UNESCO. **Also Known As:** Institut International de Planification de l'Education.

INTERNATIONAL INSTITUTE FOR LAND RECLAMATION AND IMPROVEMENT
See: Netherlands - Ministry of Agriculture and Fisheries (18654)

★18549★
INTERNATIONAL INSTITUTE FOR LAND RECLAMATION AND IMPROVEMENT - LIBRARY (Agri)
Postbus 45
NL-6700 AA Wageningen, Netherlands Phone: 8370 19100
Subjects: Agricultural development, land and water management, soil sciences, remote sensing. **Holdings:** 40,000 volumes. **Publications:** Bibliographies. **Special Catalogs:** Catalog of publications. **Remarks:** Affiliated with International Agricultural Centre. Telex: 75230 VISI NL.

★18550★
INTERNATIONAL INSTITUTE FOR LIGURIAN STUDIES - LIBRARY (Area-Ethnic)
via Romana 39 bis
I-18012 Bordighera, Italy Phone: 263601
Subjects: History and archeology of ancient Liguria. **Holdings:** 46,000 volumes. **Also Known As:** Istituto Internazionale di Studi Liguri.

★18551★
INTERNATIONAL INSTITUTE OF TROPICAL AGRICULTURE - LIBRARY AND DOCUMENTATION CENTRE (Agri)
Oyo Rd.
Private Mail Bag 5320 Phone: 22 400300
Ibadan, Oyo State, Nigeria Dr. S.M. Lawani, Dir.
Founded: 1969. **Staff:** Prof 5; Other 10. **Subjects:** Tropical regions - food crops, agricultural research, soil and crop management, farming methods. **Special Collections:** World Report; CGIAR Center's Publications. **Holdings:** 30,760 books; 33,450 bound periodical volumes. **Subscriptions:** 1250 journals and other serials. **Services:** Interlibrary loan; copying; SDI; library open to the public. **Automated Operations:** Computerized public access catalog, cataloging, acquisitions, serials, and circulation. **Computerized Information Services:** Automated Library Service for Tropical Agriculture (internal database). **Publications:** A Guide to Library Database: What it does and how to use it; IITA Publications in Print (1986); A bibliography of yams and genus Dioscorea (2 volumes); Farming Systems in Africa: a working bibliography (book). **Special Catalogs:** Cowpeas (Vigna unguiculata L. Walp.; 4 volumes); IITA: Record of Publications (2 volumes). **Remarks:** Maintained by the Consultative Group on International Agricultural Research. **Staff:** G.O. Ibekwe, Libn.; J.I. Adeyomoye, Cat./Indexer; A.A. Azubuike, Bibliog./Indexer; O.O. Osaniyi, Acq.Libn..

★18552★
INTERNATIONAL LABORATORY FOR RESEARCH ON ANIMAL DISEASES - ILRAD LIBRARY (Med)
P.O. Box 30709 Phone: 2 592311
Nairobi, Kenya William Umbima, Libn.
Subjects: Immunology, parasitology, veterinary medicine. **Holdings:** 3000 volumes. **Subscriptions:** 200 journals and other serials. **Remarks:** Maintained by Consultative Group on International Agricultural Research. Telex: 22040 ILRAD.

★18553★
INTERNATIONAL LABOUR OFFICE - CENTRAL LIBRARY AND DOCUMENTATION BRANCH (Bus-Fin)
4, route des Morillons Phone: 22 99 86 76
CH-1211 Geneva 22, Switzerland Kate Wild, Chf.
Founded: 1919. **Staff:** Prof 30. **Subjects:** Industrial relations, labor law, employment, working conditions, vocational training, management, and labor-related aspects of economics, social and rural development, technological change. **Special Collections:** ILO publications, 1919 to present. **Holdings:** 1 million volumes; 47,000 microfiche; 1200 reels of microfilm. **Subscriptions:** 7500 journals and other serials. **Services:** Interlibrary loan; copying; SDI; library open to persons engaged in policymaking, planning, or research in social and labor fields. **Computerized Information Services:** ARAMIS, ESA/IRS, HRIN (Human Resource Information Network), Pergamon ORBIT InfoLine, Inc.; produces LABORDOC, LABORINFO. Performs searches free of charge. Contact Person: Andy Jesse, Lib.Sys.Coord., 99 86 28. **Publications:** International Labour Documentation (abstracting journal), monthly; occasional bibliographies; ILO Thesaurus. **Special Catalogs:** Subject Guide to Publications of the International Labour Office, 1980-1985 (1987). **Special Indexes:** Register of Periodicals in the ILO Library, semiannual update (microfiche). **Staff:** Linda Stoddart, Dp.Libn.; Liliana Canadas, Info.Serv.Coord.; Sue Luzy, Terminology Coord..

★18554★
INTERNATIONAL LIVESTOCK CENTRE FOR AFRICA (ILCA) - DOCUMENTATION CENTRE (Agri)
P.O. Box 5689 Phone: 183215
Addis Ababa, Ethiopia Azab Abraham, Libn.
Founded: 1977. **Staff:** Prof 9; Other 11. **Subjects:** Livestock production - forage plant production, ecology, economics, sociology. **Holdings:** 15,000 volumes; 25,000 microfiche. **Subscriptions:** 1200 journals and other serials. **Services:** SDI; center open to non-African users on fee basis. **Computerized Information Services:** Internal database. Performs searches on fee basis. **Publications:** Accessions bulletin, quarterly; bibliographies, irregular; photomap acquisitions, irregular. **Remarks:** Telex: 21207.

INTERNATIONAL NUCLEAR INFORMATION SYSTEM - AUSTRALIAN NUCLEAR SCIENCE AND TECHNOLOGY ORGANISATION
See: Australian Nuclear Science and Technology Organisation (18283)

★18555★
INTERNATIONAL OLIVE OIL COUNCIL - LIBRARY (Food-Bev)
Juan Bravo, 10, Piso 2
E-28006 Madrid, Spain Phone: 1 2759606
Subjects: Olives, olive oil. **Special Collections:** Bibliographical archives. **Holdings:** 2500 volumes. **Remarks:** Telex: 48197 IOOC.E. **Also Known As:** Conseil Oleicole International.

★18556★
INTERNATIONAL ORIENTEERING FEDERATION, SCIENTIFIC GROUP - LIBRARY (Rec)
Philippstrasse 68 Phone: 221 56 24 80
D-5000 Cologne 30, Federal Republic of Germany Dr. Helga Kolb
Founded: 1984. **Subjects:** Orienteering. **Holdings:** 400 volumes. **Also Known As:** Internationale Orientierungslauf Foderation, Wissenschaftliche Arbeitsgruppe.

★18557★
INTERNATIONAL POLAR MOTION SERVICE - IPMS LIBRARY (Sci-Engr)
International Latitude Observatory
Hoshi-ga-oka 2-12
Mizusawa City Phone: 24-7111
Iwate, Japan Mr. E. Onodera, Libn.
Subjects: Geodynamics, Earth's rotation, astronomy, geophysics. **Holdings:** 53,000 volumes. **Remarks:** Maintained by Japan - Ministry of Education, Science, and Culture - International Latitude Observatory.

★18558★
INTERNATIONAL RICE RESEARCH INSTITUTE - LIBRARY (Agri)
P.O. Box 933
Manila, Philippines Lina M. Vergara, Libn.
Subjects: Rice. **Holdings:** 78,034 books. **Subscriptions:** 3283 serials. **Services:** Copying; library open to the public. **Publications:** International Bibliography of Rice Research, annual. **Remarks:** Maintained by the Consultative Group on International Agricultural Research.

★18559★
INTERNATIONAL SERICULTURAL COMMISSION - LIBRARY (Biol Sci)
25, quai Jean-Jacques Rousseau
F-69350 La Mulatiere, France Phone: 7 8504198
Subjects: Silk. **Special Collections:** Biographical archives. **Holdings:** 10,000 historical and scientific books. **Remarks:** Sericulture is the production of raw silk by raising silk worms. Maintains documentation service. **Also Known As:** Commission Sericole Internationale.

★18560★
INTERNATIONAL TIN RESEARCH COUNCIL - ITRC LIBRARY (Sci-Engr)
Kingston Lane
Uxbridge
Middlesex UB8 3PJ, England Phone: 895 72406
Subjects: Tin, tin alloys and compounds, industrial processes involving tin. **Holdings:** 35,000 pamphlets; 43,000 abstracts; 2000 monographs.

★18561★
INTERNATIONAL TRAINING INSTITUTE - LEARNING RESOURCES CENTRE (Soc Sci)
Middle Head Rd. Phone: 2 9691888
Mosman, NSW 2091, Australia Peter Hopcraft, Libn.
Subjects: Developing countries, economic development, education, management, rural development, public administration. **Special Collections:** Rare book collection (500); Hallstrom Pacific Library. **Holdings:** 50,000 books; 15,000 bound periodical volumes; 800 AV programs and microforms. **Services:** Interlibrary loan; copying; SDI; library open to the public. **Computerized Information Services:** Internal database. **Special Indexes:** Periodical articles index, 1984 to present. **Remarks:** A part of the Australian Development Assistance Bureau.

INTERNATIONAL UNION FOR CONSERVATION OF NATURE AND NATURAL RESOURCES - WORLD WIDE FUND FOR NATURE
See: World Wide Fund for Nature (18874)

★18562★
INTERNATIONAL WORKING GROUP FOR THE CONSTRUCTION OF SPORTS AND LEISURE FACILITIES - IAKS LIBRARY (Plan)
Carl-Diem-Weg 3
D-5000 Cologne 41, Federal Republic of Germany Phone: 221 492991
Subjects: Planning, constructing, equipping, and maintaining recreation and sports facilities. **Holdings:** 8000 technical books, planning guidelines, research data. **Publications:** Literature Documentation, quarterly. **Remarks:** Maintains Documentation and Information Center of literature, films, photographs, slides, and a data bank. Telex: 8 881 792 IAKS. **Also Known As:** Internationaler Arbeitskreis Sport- und Freizeiteninrichtungen.

INTERNATIONALE ORIENTIERUNGSLAUF FODERATION, WISSENSCHAFTLICHE ARBEITSGRUPPE
See: International Orienteering Federation, Scientific Group (18556)

INTERNATIONALER ARBEITSKREIS SPORT- UND FREIZEITENINRICHTUNGEN
See: International Working Group for the Construction of Sports and Leisure Facilities (18562)

INTERNATIONALES FORSCHUNGSZENTRUM FUR GRUNDFRAGEN DER WISSENSCHAFTEN SALZBURG - INSTITUTE FOR CONTEMPORARY ECCLESIASTICAL HISTORY
See: Institute for Contemporary Ecclesiastical History (18501)

★18563★
IRAN - MINISTRY OF CULTURE AND HIGHER EDUCATION - IRANIAN DOCUMENTATION CENTRE - IRANDOC LIBRARY (Sci-Engr, Info Sci)
1188 Enqelab Ave.
P.O. Box 13185/1371 Phone: 21 662223
Tehran, Iran Mrs. M. Toufio, Libn.
Subjects: Science, technology, social sciences, library and information science. **Holdings:** 38,000 books and technical reports; 4500 periodicals; 8000 theses and dissertations. **Subscriptions:** 125 journals and other serials. **Services:** Library open to researchers and professionals.

IRAN - MINISTRY OF CULTURE AND HIGHER EDUCATION - NATIONAL LIBRARY OF IRAN
See: National Library of Iran (18635)

ISRAEL - MINISTRY OF RELIGIOUS AFFAIRS - HARRY FISCHEL INSTITUTE FOR RESEARCH IN TALMUD AND JEWISH LAW
See: Harry Fischel Institute for Research in Talmud and Jewish Law (18417)

★18564★
ISRAEL ATOMIC ENERGY COMMISSION - SOREQ NUCLEAR RESEARCH CENTER - LIBRARY AND TECHNICAL INFORMATION DEPARTMENT (Energy, Sci-Engr)
Yavne 70600, Israel Phone: 54 84380
Mrs. S. Weil, Hd.
Founded: 1952. **Staff:** Prof 9; Other 7. **Subjects:** Nuclear physics, chemistry, and engineering; lasers; electro-optics. **Holdings:** 60,000 volumes; 220,000 technical reports. **Subscriptions:** 280 journals and other serials. **Services:** Interlibrary loan; copying; SDI; library open to center staff and cooperating scientists. **Computerized Information Services:** DIALOG Information Services; internal database. **Publications:** Accession list of new books, bimonthly; accession list of new reports, biweekly; current journal subscriptions, annual.

ISTITUTO INTERNAZIONALE DI STUDI LIGURI
See: International Institute for Ligurian Studies (18550)

ISTITUTO NAZIONALE DI STUDI ROMANI
See: Italy - Ministry of Cultural Affairs - National Institute of Roman Studies (18566)

★18565★
ITALY - MINISTERO BENI CULTRALI - BIBLIOTECA NAZIONALE VITTORIO EMANUELE III (Info Sci, Hum, Theater)
Piazza Plebiscito
Palazzo Reale Phone: 81 40 28 42
Naples, Italy Maria Grazia Malates Pasqualitti, Dir.
Subjects: General collection with emphasis on humanities. **Special Collections:** Papyrus manuscripts; Biblioteca Lucchesi Palli (theater and cinema); Zagazzi Collection; Americana Collection; Neapolitan Collection. **Holdings:** 2 million books; 7442 bound periodical volumes; 18,522 documents; 2030 reels of microfilm; 12,379 manuscripts. **Services:** Interlibrary loan; copying; library open to the public with restrictions. **Publications:** Quarterly newsletter.

★18566★
ITALY - MINISTRY OF CULTURAL AFFAIRS - NATIONAL INSTITUTE OF ROMAN STUDIES - LIBRARY (Area-Ethnic)
Piazza dei Cavalieri di Malta 2 Phone: 57 43 442
I-00153 Rome, Italy Dr. Fernanda Roscetti, Dir.
Subjects: Ancient and modern Rome - archeology, sociology, language, literature. **Holdings:** 17,900 books. **Subscriptions:** 810 journals and other serials. **Also Known As:** Istituto Nazionale di Studi Romani.

J

★18567★
JANACEK ACADEMY OF MUSIC AND DRAMATIC ART - LIBRARY (Mus, Theater)
Gorkeho 11 Phone: 042-05-759841
CS-602 00 Brno, Czechoslovakia Jana Wagnerova, Promovany historik
Subjects: Music, theater, plays. **Holdings:** 30,000 books; 3500 bound periodical volumes; 35,000 pieces of music; 8000 phonograph records. **Services:** Interlibrary loan; library open to the public with restrictions. **Publications:** Monthly list of additions in the library. **Also Known As:** Janackova Akademie Muzickych Umeni - Ustredni Knihovna JAMU.

JANACKOVA AKADEMIE MUZICKYCH UMENI - USTREDNI KNIHOVNA JAMU
See: Janacek Academy of Music and Dramatic Art - Library (18567)

★18568★
JAPAN - MINISTRY OF AGRICULTURE, FORESTRY AND FISHERIES - FRUIT TREE RESEARCH STATION - LIBRARY (Agri)
2-1 Fujimoto
Yatabe Phone: 56-6416
Ibaraki 305, Japan Dr. Akira Yamaguchi, Dir.
Subjects: Agronomy; fruit trees - breeding techniques, pomology, plant protection. **Holdings:** 40,000 volumes.

★18569★
JAPAN - MINISTRY OF CONSTRUCTION - BUILDING RESEARCH INSTITUTE - LIBRARY (Plan)
1 Tatehara
Oho-machi
Tsukuba-gun Phone: 64-2151
Ibaraki, Japan Ms. K. Kimura, Libn.
Subjects: Housing and building economy, building materials, structural engineering, building production, environmental design and fire protection, urban planning, disaster prevention, new building techniques, energy, natural resources. **Holdings:** 30,000 volumes.

★18570★
JAPAN - MINISTRY OF EDUCATION - AGENCY FOR CULTURAL AFFAIRS - NATIONAL LANGUAGE RESEARCH INSTITUTE - LIBRARY (Hum)
3-9-14 Nisigaoka
Kita-ku Phone: 3 900-3111
Tokyo 115, Japan Kikuo Nomoto, Dir.
Founded: 1948. **Staff:** Prof 2. **Subjects:** Modern Japanese language studies, linguistics. **Special Collections:** Books printed in the Meiji era; books on Japanese dialects; Japanese language dictionaries printed before the Meiji era. **Holdings:** 74,680 volumes; 871 reels of microfilm; 355 records; 565 open-reel and cassette tapes. **Subscriptions:** 801 journals and other serials; 5 newspapers. **Services:** SDI; library open to the public with restrictions. **Publications:** Library News, irregular; Acquisition list, quarterly - both for internal distribution only; Bibliography of bibliographies of Japanese Language Researchers. **Also Known As:** Kokuritsu Kokugo Kenkyujo. **Staff:** Michiko Otsuko, Chf.Libn..

JAPAN - MINISTRY OF EDUCATION, SCIENCE, AND CULTURE - INTERNATIONAL LATITUDE OBSERVATORY - INTERNATIONAL POLAR MOTION SERVICE
See: International Polar Motion Service (18557)

★18571★
JAPAN - MINISTRY OF HEALTH AND WELFARE - INSTITUTE FOR POPULATION PROBLEMS - POPULATION REFERENCE CENTER (Soc Sci)
2-2 1-Chome
Kasumigaseki, Chiyoda-ku Phone: 3 591-4816
Tokyo, Japan Kiichi Yamaguchi, Act.Chf.
Subjects: Population; demography; population problems and policies in Japan, Asia, the world. **Holdings:** 100,000 volumes.

★18572★
JAPAN - MINISTRY OF TRANSPORT - SHIP RESEARCH INSTITUTE - LIBRARY (Trans, Sci-Engr)
38-1 6-Chome
Shinkawa, Mitaka Phone: 45-5171
Tokyo, Japan Kaitsu Saegusa, Libn.
Subjects: Shipbuilding, engineering. **Holdings:** 50,000 volumes.

JAPAN - THE NATIONAL DIET OF JAPAN
See: The National Diet of Japan (18621)

★18573★
JAPAN ATOMIC ENERGY RESEARCH INSTITUTE (JAERI) - DEPARTMENT OF TECHNICAL INFORMATION (Energy)
2-2-2 Uchisaiwai-cho
Chiyoda-ku Phone: 3 503-6111
Tokyo 100, Japan Dr. Yukio Ebinuma, Dir.
Founded: 1956. **Staff:** Prof 30; Other 5. **Subjects:** Nuclear science and technology. **Holdings:** 33,000 volumes; 1200 serial titles; 660,000 technical reports. **Services:** Library open to Japanese nuclear community. **Computerized Information Services:** INIS (International Nuclear Information System). Performs searches on fee basis.

JEWISH THEOLOGICAL SEMINARY OF AMERICA - SCHOCKEN INSTITUTE FOR JEWISH RESEARCH
See: Schocken Institute for Jewish Research (18758)

JUGOSLOVENSKI CENTAR ZA TEHNICKU I NAUCNU DOKUMENTACIJU
See: Yugoslav Center for Technical and Scientific Documentation (18877)

★18574★
C.G. JUNG INSTITUTE OF ZURICH - LIBRARY (Soc Sci)
Hornweg 28
CH-8700 Kusnacht, Switzerland Phone: 910 53 23
Staff: Prof 2; Other 5. **Subjects:** Analytical psychology, religion, folklore and fairy tales, ethnology, mythology, psychiatry, psychology. **Special Collections:** Privately published and unpublished manuscripts, records, and works by C.G. Jung; development of analytical psychology; picture archive (photographs; reproductions; paintings and drawings by patients undergoing psychological treatment); diploma theses. **Holdings:** 10,000 books. **Subscriptions:** 20 journals and other serials. **Services:** Copying; library open to the public by application to librarian. **Publications:** New acquisitions list, semiannual; theses title lists. **Also Known As:** C.G. Jung-Institut Zurich. **Staff:** Barbara Jarrett, Libn.; Verena Maag, Libn..

K

★18575★
KAROLINSKA INSTITUTE - DEPARTMENT OF STRESS RESEARCH - LIBRARY (Med)
P.O. Box 60205 Phone: 8 34 05 60
S-104 01 Stockholm, Sweden Isabella Levi, Info.Sci.
Subjects: Stress, psychosocial medicine. **Holdings:** 2000 volumes; 24,000 reprints, monographs, reports (online). **Computerized Information Services:** Internal database. **Remarks:** Sponsored by Swedish Medical Research Council and Swedish Work Environment Fund. Telex: 12442 FOTEX. **Also Known As:** Institutionen for Stressforskning.

★18576★
KAROLINSKA INSTITUTE - LIBRARY AND INFORMATION CENTER (Med)
Box 60201 Phone: 46 8 340560
S-104 01 Stockholm, Sweden Ake Lilliestam, Ph.D.
Founded: 1810. **Staff:** Prof 33; Other 42. **Subjects:** Medicine, dentistry, toxicology. **Holdings:** 531,000 volumes; 875 manuscripts. **Services:** Interlibrary loan; copying; SDI; library open to the public. **Automated Operations:** Computerized public access catalog and cataloging. **Computerized Information Services:** MEDLARS, NLM, DIALOG Information Services, ESA/IRS, MEDLINE, CANCERLIT (Cancer Literature), RTECS (Registry of Toxic Effects of Chemical Substances), Drugline, SWEMED, Nordser; produces MIC-KIBIC. Performs searches on fee basis. Contact Person: Elisabeth Kjellander, M.D., 232270. **Publications:** KIBIC-rapport, irregular; MIC News, bimonthly. **Special Catalogs:** List BioMed (Nordic Union Catalogue of Serials in Biomedicine). **Also Known As:** Karolinska Institutets Bibliotek och Informationscentral. **Staff:** Anita Klebom, Dp.Libn.; Goran Falkenberg, M.D., Hd. of MIC-KIBIC; Tor Ahlenius, Ph.D., Hd. of Sys.Dept.; Arnold Johansson, Info.Sci..

KEGYESRENDI KOZPONTI KONYVTAR
See: Piarist Central Library (18687)

KENTRON EREVNIS ELLINIKIS LAOGRAPHIAS
See: Hellenic Folklore Research Center (18464)

★18577★
KENYA INDUSTRIAL RESEARCH AND DEVELOPMENT INSTITUTE - LIBRARY (Sci-Engr)
P.O. Box 30650 Phone: 2 557762
Nairobi, Kenya Paul B. Imende, Libn.
Subjects: Agro-industrial research. **Holdings:** 15,000 volumes. **Remarks:** Maintained by Kenya - Ministry of Commerce and Industry.

★18578★
KENYA TRYPANSOMIASIS RESEARCH ORGANIZATION - LIBRARY (Med)
P.O. Box 362 Phone: 0154 32960-4
Kikuyu, Kenya Dr. A.R. Njogu, Dir.
Founded: 1977. **Subjects:** Tsetse flies, trypansomiasis. **Holdings:** Figures not available. **Remarks:** Telex: 25556.

KERNFORSCHUNGSANLAGE JUELICH
See: Federal Republic of Germany - Ministry of Research and Technology - Juelich Nuclear Research Center (18410)

★18579★
KIEL INSTITUTE OF WORLD ECONOMICS - NATIONAL LIBRARY OF ECONOMICS (Soc Sci)
Dusternbrooker Weg 120 Phone: 431 8841
D-2300 Kiel 1, Federal Republic of Germany
Dr. Erwin Heidemann, Dir.
Founded: 1914. **Subjects:** Economics, political economics, allied social sciences. **Holdings:** 1.6 million volumes; yearbooks; newspapers. **Subscriptions:** 19,000 journals and other serials. **Services:** SDI; library open to the public. **Publications:** Bibliographie der Wirtschaftswissenschaften, semiannual. **Also Known As:** Institut fur Weltwirtschaft in Kiel - Zentralbibliothek der Wirtschaftswissenschaften.

★18580★
KING ABDUL AZIZ RESEARCH CENTER - LIBRARY (Area-Ethnic)
P.O. Box 2945
King Faisal Hospital Rd. Phone: 1 4412316
Riyadh 11461, Saudi Arabia Naser Al-Khudhairi, Libn.
Subjects: Saudi Arabia - history, geography, literature, cultural and intellectual heritage; history of Arabian peninsula; Arab Islamic countries. **Holdings:** 24,000 volumes.

★18581★
KING FAISAL SPECIALIST HOSPITAL AND RESEARCH CENTRE - MEDICAL LIBRARY (Med)
P.O. Box 3354 Phone: 464-7272
Riyadh 11211, Saudi Arabia Biraj L. Brown, Act.Libn.
Subjects: Clinical medicine, nursing, health administration, computers. **Special Collections:** Falconry. **Holdings:** 15,000 books; 45,000 bound periodical volumes; 1500 AV programs; 1000 microforms. **Services:** Interlibrary loan; library open to the public with restrictions.

KOKURITSU KOKUGO KENKYUJO
See: Japan - Ministry of Education - Agency for Cultural Affairs - National Language Research Institute (18570)

KOMMISSION FUR ALTE GESCHICHTE UND EPIGRAPHIK
See: German Archaeological Institute - Commission for Ancient History and Epigraphy (18441)

KONINKLIJKE BIBLIOTHEEK
See: Netherlands - Royal Library (18655)

KONINKLIJKE BIBLIOTHEEK ALBERT I
See: Belgium - Ministry of National Education - Bibliotheque Royale de Belgique (18298)

★18582★
KONINKLIJKE NEDERLANDSE AKADEMIE VAN WETENSCHAPPEN - P.J. MEERTENS-INSTITUUT - BIBLIOTHEEK (Hum)
Keizersgracht 569-571 Phone: 020 234698
NL-1017 DR Amsterdam, Netherlands Mrs. L. Van Immerzeel, Hd.
Subjects: Dialectology, onomastics, folklore. **Holdings:** 50,000 books. **Services:** Interlibrary loan; copying; library open to the public with restrictions. **Staff:** Gemma Van der Spek.

KOREA - MINISTRY OF AGRICULTURE AND FISHERIES - RURAL DEVELOPMENT ADMINISTRATION
See: Rural Development Administration (18754)

KOREA - MINISTRY OF SCIENCE AND TECHNOLOGY - ELECTRONICS AND TELECOMMUNICATIONS RESEARCH INSTITUTE
See: Electronics and Telecommunications Research Institute (18392)

★18583★
KOREA ADVANCED ENERGY RESEARCH INSTITUTE - KAERI LIBRARY (Energy)
P.O. Box 7, Cheongryang Phone: 2 972 2081
Seoul 131, Republic of Korea Chong Hwae Kim, Libn.
Subjects: Nuclear science. **Holdings:** 325,800 volumes. **Remarks:** Maintained by Korea - Ministry of Science and Technology.

★18584★
KOREA INSTITUTE FOR INDUSTRIAL ECONOMICS AND TECHNOLOGY - LIBRARY (Sci-Engr, Bus-Fin)
P.O. Box 205
Cheong Ryang Phone: 2 965-6211
Seoul 131, Republic of Korea
Youn Kyun Mok, Dir., Dept. of Info.Rsrcs.
Subjects: Science and technology, industrial economics. **Holdings:** 40,000 volumes; 10,000 reports; 9000 noncurrent periodical titles. **Subscriptions:** 7500 journals and other serials. **Services:** SDI; library open to industry research and development institutes, academic institutions, government agencies. **Computerized Information Services:** AGRIS Data Base, Chemical Abstracts Service, COMPENDEX, INSPEC, Information Service in Mechanical Engineering (ISMEC), NTIS Bibliographic Data Base, World Patents Index (WPI); internal databases. Performs searches on fee basis. **Publications:** Bibliographies. **Remarks:** Maintains six regional information services branches.

KOREA UNIVERSITY - ASIATIC RESEARCH CENTER
See: Asiatic Research Center (18275)

KOZPONTI STATISZTIKAI HIVATAL
See: Hungary - Central Statistical Office (18479)

KULTURA CENTRO ESPERANTISTA
See: British Library - Humanities and Social Sciences Division - Oriental Collections (18318)

KULTURA CENTRO ESPERANTISTA
See: Esperanto Cultural Centre (18394)

KUNGL. BIBLIOTEKET
See: Sweden - Royal Library (18801)

KUNGLIGA TEKNISKA HOGSKOLANS BIBLIOTEK
See: Royal Institute of Technology - Library (18746)

★18585★
KYOTO UNIVERSITY - RESEARCH INSTITUTE FOR HUMANISTIC STUDIES - LIBRARY (Hum, Area-Ethnic)
Ushinomiya-cho
Yoshida, Sakyo-ku — Phone: 75 761-9583
Kyoto 606, Japan — Oguni Ken-ichi, Libn.
Staff: Prof 13; Other 7. **Subjects:** Humanities; Japan; China; Asia; Western civilization; history of fine arts, religions, science; social anthropology. **Holdings:** 412,000 books; 3623 bound periodical volumes. **Subscriptions:** 1537 journals and other serials; 12 newspapers. **Also Known As:** Zinbun Kagaku Kenkyusho. **Staff:** Ozaki Yujiro.

★18586★
KYUNGNAM UNIVERSITY - INSTITUTE FOR FAR EASTERN STUDIES - IFES LIBRARY (Area-Ethnic)
28-42 Samchung-dong
Chongro-ku
Seoul, Republic of Korea — Phone: 2 735-3202
Subjects: North Korea, China and the Soviet Union, United States and Japan, third world, economics of Communist countries. **Holdings:** 30,000 volumes. **Services:** Library open to scholars and students of Asian affairs.

L

★18587★
LANZHOU RAILWAY INSTITUTE - LIBRARY (Trans)
West Anning Lu Phone: 6223
Lanzhou, Gansu Province, People's Republic of China
Chen Heping, Libn.
Founded: 1958. **Staff:** 41. **Subjects:** Railway construction and transport, locomotives, communication signals, water supply and drainage. **Holdings:** 227,944 volumes; 908 periodicals. **Publications:** Chinese and Foreign New Books Quarterly.

★18588★
LATIN AMERICAN IRON AND STEEL INSTITUTE - ILAFA LIBRARY (Sci-Engr)
Dario Urzua, Numero 1994
Casilla 16065
Santiago 9, Chile Phone: 2 2237581
Subjects: Iron, steelmaking, allied subjects. **Holdings:** 10,000 documents. **Remarks:** Telex: 340 348 ILAFA CK. **Also Known As:** Instituto Latinoamericano del Fierro y el Acero.

LEAGUE OF ARAB COUNTRIES - ARAB CENTER FOR THE STUDY OF ARID ZONES AND DRY LANDS
See: Arab Center for the Study of Arid Zones and Dry Lands (18266)

★18589★
LEAGUE OF ARAB STATES - DOCUMENTATION AND INFORMATION CENTER (ALDOC) (Area-Ethnic)
37 Khereddine Pacha St. Phone: 1 890100
Tunis, Tunisia Mrs. Faria Zahawi, Dir.
Founded: 1981. **Staff:** 68. **Subjects:** Arab region - politics, economics, law, military and social concerns; international affairs; communication. **Special Collections:** Arab League documents; documents from other international organizations. **Holdings:** 26,000 volumes; 150 magnetic tapes; 11,000 microforms; 4000 clipping files. **Subscriptions:** 1600 journals and other serials. **Services:** Interlibrary loan; copying; SDI; center open to the public. **Automated Operations:** Computerized cataloging, acquisitions, serials, circulation, and indexing. **Computerized Information Services:** Online systems; internal databases. **Publications:** Accessions List, monthly; Current Contents Bulletin, monthly; Documentation Bulletin, quarterly; bibliographies; Aris-Net Newsletter, monthly; Info-Packs.

LEIDEN STATE UNIVERSITY - NATIONAL HERBARIUM OF THE NETHERLANDS
See: National Herbarium of the Netherlands (18623)

LEMBAGA ILMU PENGETAHUAN INDONESIA - PUSAT DOKUMENTASI DAN INFORMASI ILMIAH
See: Indonesian Institute of Sciences - Centre for Scientific Documentation and Information (18491)

★18590★
V.I. LENIN HIGHER INSTITUTE OF MECHANICAL AND ELECTRICAL ENGINEERING - LIBRARY (Sci-Engr)
Hristo Botev Students' Complex
Sofia, Bulgaria Phone: 2 63-61
Subjects: Education and training in mechanical and electrical engineering; electronics; automation and robotics; machine building. **Holdings:** 65,700 books; 10,500 bound periodical volumes. **Remarks:** Maintained by Bulgaria - Ministry of National Education.

★18591★
LIBRARY OF INNER MONGOLIA AUTONOMOUS REGION (Area-Ethnic)
People's Park Phone: Huhhot 4948
Huhhot, Inner Mongolia, People's Republic of China
Liang Jixiao, Libn.
Founded: 1950. **Staff:** 83. **Subjects:** General collection. **Special Collections:** Mongolian nationality and regional history. **Holdings:** 1.15 million volumes. **Subscriptions:** 2050 journals and other serials. **Services:** Copying. **Publications:** Library Work Newsletter, irregular.

★18592★
MIGUEL LILLO FOUNDATION - INFORMATION CENTER (Biol Sci)
Miguel Lillo, 251 Phone: 230159
4000 San Miguel de Tucuman, Argentina Prof. Natalia Schechaj
Founded: 1931. **Staff:** Prof 3; Other 8. **Subjects:** Botany, geology, zoology. **Special Collections:** Herbarium (70,000 specimens); A. Humboldt and A. Bonpland "Voyage aux Regions Equinoxiales". **Holdings:** 130,000 volumes. **Services:** Interlibrary loan; copying; center open to the public for reference use only. **Publications:** Informativo Lilloano, monthly. **Special Catalogs:** Publicaciones Periodicas Biblioteca Fundacion Miguel Lillo. **Remarks:** Maintained by Argentina - Ministry of Education and Justice. **Also Known As:** Fundacion Miguel Lillo - Centro de Informacion Geo-Biologica NOA.

★18593★
LINEN HALL LIBRARY (Area-Ethnic, Hist)
17 Donegall Square, N. Phone: 232 321707
Belfast BT1 5GD, Northern Ireland John Killen, Dp.Libn.
Staff: Prof 3; Other 10. **Subjects:** Irish and British history, biography, travel, topography. **Special Collections:** Northern Ireland Political Literature Collection; Belfast Printed Books Collection. **Holdings:** 200,000 books; 1000 microforms; 500 manuscripts. **Services:** Interlibrary loan; copying; library open to the public. **Staff:** John Gray, Libn..

★18594★
LINNEAN SOCIETY OF LONDON - LIBRARY (Biol Sci)
Burlington House
Piccadilly Phone: 1 434-4479
London W1V 0LQ, England Gina Douglas, Libn./Archv.
Subjects: Natural history, taxonomy, flora, fauna, evolutionary theory, history of biology. **Special Collections:** Linnean Collections (books, manuscripts, and specimens belonging to C. von Linne); manuscript collections. **Holdings:** 25,000 books; 75,000 bound periodical volumes; 1000 manuscripts. **Services:** Interlibrary loan; library open to the public by appointment. **Special Catalogs:** Catalogue of Manuscripts in the Library of the Linnean Society of London (4 volumes).

★18595★
LONDON RESEARCH CENTRE - RESEARCH LIBRARY (Plan, Soc Sci)
County Hall, Rm. 514 Phone: 1 633 7149
London SE1 7PB, England Richard Golland, Hd., Res.Lib.
Staff: Prof 15; Other 9. **Subjects:** Local government, town and county planning, traffic and transportation research, social services and planning, environment, noise, pollution, energy, public health, government finance and management, inner-city studies, architecture and building, civil engineering, housing, industry and employment. **Holdings:** 50,000 volumes; 60,000 pamphlets and reports; 20,000 microfiche; 15,000 slides. **Subscriptions:** 1000 journals and other serials. **Services:** Interlibrary loan; copying; SDI; library open to the public by appointment. **Computerized Information Services:** Produces ACOMPLINE, URBALINE. Performs searches on fee basis. **Publications:** Urban Abstracts, monthly. **Remarks:** Fax: 1 261 1710. **Formerly:** Greater London Council - Information Services Group. **Staff:** Annabel Davies, Dp.Hd..

★18596★
LONDON SCHOOL OF ECONOMICS - BRITISH LIBRARY OF POLITICAL AND ECONOMIC SCIENCE (Soc Sci, Bus-Fin)
10 Portugal St. Phone: 1 405-7686
London WC2A 2HD, England C.J. Hunt, Libn.
Founded: 1896. **Subjects:** Social sciences; economics; politics; sociology; modern political history; economic, social, and business history; history of economic thought. **Holdings:** 881,000 volumes. **Services:** Interlibrary loan; copying; library open to the public with restrictions. **Computerized Information Services:** DIALOG Information Services, ESA/IRS, BRS Information Technologies, Pergamon ORBIT InfoLine, Inc., Telesystemes Questel, Datasolve Ltd., BLAISE Online Services, Scicon Ltd. **Publications:** A London Bibliography of the Social Sciences, annual. **Special Catalogs:** Classified Catalogue of a Collection of Works on Publishing and Bookselling in the British Library of Political and Economic Science. **Remarks:** The British Library of Political and Economic Science serves both as the working library of the London School of Economics and as a national collection of material for research. Telex: 24655 BLPESG. **Staff:** D.A. Bovey, Hd., Rd.Serv..

DAVID LUBIN MEMORIAL LIBRARY
See: United Nations - Food and Agriculture Organization - David Lubin Memorial Library (18829)

M

★18597★
PETER MAC CALLUM CANCER INSTITUTE - CENTRAL CANCER LIBRARY (Med)
481 Little Lonsdale St. Phone: 3 6021333
Melbourne, VIC 3000, Australia Aina Zalitis, Chf.Libn.
Staff: Prof 2; Other 2. **Subjects:** Cancer, radiotherapy. **Holdings:** 8500 books; 7600 bound periodical volumes. **Subscriptions:** 220 journals and other serials. **Services:** Interlibrary loan; copying; SDI; library open to the public with restrictions. **Computerized Information Services:** MEDLINE, DIALOG Information Services, Pergamon ORBIT InfoLine, Inc. **Formerly:** Peter Mac Callum Hospital.

PAUL MC GUIRE MARITIME LIBRARY
See: State Library of South Australia - Special Collections (18794)

MAGYAR TUDOMANYOS AKADEMIA
See: Hungarian Academy of Sciences (18478)

MAGYARORSZAGI KEGYESTANITOREND/PIARISTAK - KEGYESRENDI KOZPONTI KONYVTAR
See: Piarist Central Library (18687)

MALAYSIA - MINISTRY OF CULTURE, YOUTH AND SPORTS - NATIONAL LIBRARY OF MALAYSIA
See: National Library of Malaysia (18637)

★18598★
MALAYSIAN RUBBER RESEARCH AND DEVELOPMENT BOARD - RUBBER RESEARCH INSTITUTE OF MALAYSIA - LIBRARY (Sci-Engr)
260 Jalan Ampang Phone: 4567033
50450 Kuala Lumpur, Malaysia J.S. Soosai, Libn.
Subjects: Natural rubber industry in Malaysia - plant science, crop protection, agronomy, agricultural economics, rubber chemistry and technology, polymer chemistry, analytical and applied chemistry, biological chemistry. **Holdings:** 70,000 volumes.

MALTA - THE NATIONAL LIBRARY OF MALTA
See: The National Library of Malta (18638)

★18599★
MANAGEMENT PROFESSIONALS ASSOCIATION - LIBRARY (Bus-Fin)
15 Ramanathan St.
T Nagar
Madras 600017, India Phone: 44 443216
Subjects: Management. **Special Collections:** Biographical archives. **Holdings:** 50,000 volumes. **Remarks:** Telex: 041 6489 MPA IN.

★18600★
MARGA INSTITUTE - LIBRARY (Area-Ethnic, Soc Sci)
61 Isipathana Mawatha Phone: 1 585186
Colombo 5, Sri Lanka Mrs. M. Nanayakkara, Chf.Libn.
Subjects: Development issues in Sri Lanka and Asia, socioeconomics. **Holdings:** 30,000 volumes. **Remarks:** Telex: 21642 MARGA.

★18601★
MARINE BIOLOGICAL ASSOCIATION OF THE UNITED KINGDOM - LIBRARY AND INFORMATION SERVICES (Biol Sci)
Citadel Hill Phone: 752 221761
Plymouth PL1 2PB, England Allen Varley, Hd.
Subjects: Marine biology, pollution, and chemistry; oceanography; fisheries; marine and estuarine ecology. **Special Collections:** Marine pollution (33,000 documents). **Holdings:** 15,000 books; 45,000 bound periodical volumes; 60,000 pamphlets and reprints. **Subscriptions:** 1400 journals and other serials. **Services:** Interlibrary loan; copying; SDI; library open to the public by appointment. **Computerized Information Services:** ECDIN (Environmental Chemicals Data and Information Network), IRPTC (International Register of Potentially Toxic Chemicals); produces ASFA (Aquatic Sciences and Fisheries Abstracts); SCIENCEnet (electronic mail service). Performs searches on fee basis. Contact Person: Mr. D.S. Moulder. **Publications:** Marine Pollution Research Titles (bulletin), monthly; Estuaries and Coastal Waters of the British Isles (bibliography), annual.

EDWARD LAURENS MARK MEMORIAL LIBRARY
See: Bermuda Biological Station for Research, Inc. (18300)

MAURITIUS - MINISTRY OF EDUCATION, ARTS AND CULTURE - MAHATMA GANDHI INSTITUTE
See: Mahatma Gandhi Institute (18433)

★18602★
MAURITIUS - MINISTRY OF EDUCATION, ARTS AND CULTURE - MAURITIUS INSTITUTE - LIBRARY (Biol Sci)
Chaussee Phone: 2-0639
Port Louis, Mauritius S. Ankiah, Hd.Libn.
Subjects: Fisheries biology. **Holdings:** 60,000 volumes.

★18603★
MAURITIUS SUGAR INDUSTRY RESEARCH INSTITUTE - MSIRI LIBRARY (Agri, Biol Sci)
Reduit, Mauritius Phone: 54-1061
Subjects: Sugar industry, agronomy, agricultural chemistry, botany and physiology, plant breeding, phytopathology, entomology, weed control, sugar technology, biometry, economics. **Holdings:** 20,600 books. **Subscriptions:** 670 journals and other serials. **Remarks:** Operates in cooperation with Mauritius - Ministry of Agriculture - Agricultural Services, Mauritius Chamber of Agriculture, and University of Mauritius. Telex: 44770.

P.J. MEERTENS-INSTITUT
See: Koninklijke Nederlandse Akademie van Wetenschappen (18582)

METSANTUTKIMUSLAITOS
See: Finnish Forest Research Institute (18413)

★18604★
MEXICO - NATIONAL INSTITUTE OF NUCLEAR RESEARCH - NUCLEAR INFORMATION AND DOCUMENTATION CENTER (Sci-Engr, Energy)
Apartado 18-1027
11800 Mexico, DF, Mexico
Subjects: Science and technology, energy, nuclear energy. **Holdings:** 30,000 volumes; 365,000 technical reports; magnetic tapes. **Subscriptions:** 665 journals and other serials. **Services:** Center open to institute staff and chief researchers of other institutions. **Also Known As:** Instituto Nacional de Investigaciones Nucleares.

★18605★
MEXICO - OFFICE OF THE SECRETARY OF PUBLIC EDUCATION - REGIONAL CENTER FOR ADULT EDUCATION AND FUNCTIONAL DEVELOPMENT OF LATIN AMERICA - LIBRARY (Educ)
Quinta Erendira s/n
Patzcuaro Phone: 2-00-05
Michoacan, Mexico Alicia Marquez Melgoza, Libn.
Subjects: Mexico, Latin America, Caribbean Area - adult education and rural development, literacy, educational communication and technology. **Holdings:** 50,000 volumes. **Also Known As:** Centro Regional de Educacion de Adultos y Alfabetizacion Funcional para America Latina.

★18606★
CHR. MICHELSEN INSTITUTE - DEPARTMENT OF SOCIAL SCIENCE AND DEVELOPMENT - LIBRARY (Soc Sci)
Fantoftvagen 38 Phone: 5 28 44 10
N-5036 Fantoft, Norway Kirsti Hagen Andersen, Hd.Libn.
Staff: Prof 2; Other 1. **Subjects:** Developing countries, economics, Southern and Eastern Africa, social anthropology, Southeast Asia. **Special Collections:** Documentation on developing problems and countries. **Holdings:** 25,000 books; 450 bound periodical volumes. **Services:** Interlibrary loan; copying; library open to the public. **Automated Operations:** Computerized cataloging. **Computerized Information Services:** DIALOG Information Services; internal database. **Special Catalogs:** Norwegian Development Research Catalogue, every 3 years; Nordic Union Catalogue of Periodicals Issued in Developing Countries.

★18607★
LEOPOLDE A. MIGUEZ DE MELLO RESEARCH AND DEVELOPMENT CENTER - LIBRARY (Energy)
Ilha do Fundao, Quadra 7 Phone: 270-2122
21910 Rio de Janeiro, Brazil Miriam Y. Couto, Libn.
Subjects: Petroleum, petrochemistry, oil refining, oil shale, biomass energy. **Holdings:** 30,000 volumes. **Remarks:** Maintained by Petroleo Brasileiro, S.A. Telex: 213 1219. **Also Known As:** Centro de Pesquisas e Desenvolvimento Leopoldo A. Miguez de Mello.

MILA AND FONTANALS INSTITUTION
See: Scientific Research Council of Spain - Mila and Fontanals Institution (18761)

MITCHELL LIBRARY
See: State Library of New South Wales - Mitchell Library (18790)

★18608★
MOORE THEOLOGICAL COLLEGE - LIBRARY (Rel-Phil)
1 King St.
Newtown, NW 2042, Australia Mr. Kim S. Robinson, Libn.
Subjects: Theology, religion. **Special Collections:** Rare book collection; Australiana collection. **Holdings:** 109,000 books. **Services:** Copying; library open to the public. **Special Catalogs:** Catalogue of the Bishop Broughton Memorial Library, Volume 1 (rare books).

MORTLOCK LIBRARY OF SOUTH AUSTRALIANA
See: State Library of South Australia (18793)

MUSEOVIRASTO
See: National Board of Antiquities (18618)

MUSEU PARAENSE EMILIO GOELDI
See: Emilio Goeldi Museum (18449)

★18609★
MUSEUM OF LONDON - LIBRARY (Hist)
150 London Wall Phone: 1 600 3699
London EC2Y 5HN, England Joanna Clark, Hd., Lib. & Doc.
Subjects: History and topography of London, social history, archeology. **Special Collections:** Tangye Collection (English Civil War and Interregnum; rare books and manuscripts); Bell Collection (Great Plague and Fire of London). **Holdings:** 25,000 books; 5000 bound periodical volumes; 50 oral history tapes; 100 manuscripts; maps of London, 16th century to present; records of archeological excavations in London, 1930s to present. **Services:** Interlibrary loan; copying; library open to the public by appointment.

N

★18610★
NANJING UNIVERSITY - LIBRARY (Area-Ethnic)
Hankou Lu Phone: 34651
Nanjing, Jiangsu Province, People's Republic of China
Fan Cunzhong, Univ. V.P./Libn.
Founded: 1902. **Staff:** 98. **Subjects:** Orientalism, bibliography, archeology. **Special Collections:** Chinese ancient books (1400 titles; 20,000 volumes); district histories, especially Jiangsu and Sichuan provinces (3500 titles; 37,000 volumes); books of rubbings from stone inscriptions (10,000 titles). **Holdings:** 1.85 million volumes. **Subscriptions:** 3862 journals and other serials. **Services:** Copying; library open to the public for research. **Special Catalogs:** Catalogue of Remarkable Editions of Chinese Ancient Books Held by the Library; Catalogue of District Histories Held by the Library.

NATIONAL ACADEMY OF SCIENCES OF BUENOS AIRES - DARWINIAN INSTITUTE OF BOTANY
See: Darwinian Institute of Botany (18379)

★18611★
NATIONAL AGRO-INDUSTRIAL UNION - AGRICULTURAL ACADEMY - CENTER FOR SCIENTIFIC, TECHNICAL AND ECONOMIC INFORMATION - CENTRAL AGRICULTURAL LIBRARY (Agri)
125 Lenin Blvd., Block No. 1
1113 Sofia, Bulgaria
Subjects: Agriculture, animal husbandry, veterinary medicine, agronomy, food industry. **Holdings:** 600,000 volumes; translations; microfilm; miscellanea. **Subscriptions:** 5000 journals and other serials. **Services:** Interlibrary loan; SDI; library open to government agencies. **Computerized Information Services:** BIOSIS, INIS (International Nuclear Information System), COMPENDEX, AGRIS. Performs searches on fee basis. **Publications:** Bibliographies. **Also Known As:** Natsionalen Agrarno-Promishlen Suyuz - Selskostopanska Akademiya - Tsentur za Naouchno-Technicheska i Ikonomicheska Infomatsiya.

★18612★
NATIONAL AGRO-INDUSTRIAL UNION - INSTITUTE OF MECHANIZATION & ELECTRIFICATION OF AGRICULTURE - LIBRARY (Agri)
3 Chaussee Bankja St. Phone: 2 2-52-43
1331 Sofia, Bulgaria Antoaneta Andonova, Libn.
Subjects: Agricultural machinery. **Holdings:** 17,500 volumes.

★18613★
NATIONAL AGRO-INDUSTRIAL UNION - RESEARCH INSTITUTE ON FRUIT GROWING - LIBRARY (Agri)
4004 Plovdiv, Bulgaria Phone: 7-80-81
Subjects: Mechanization of fruit-growing processes; agro-technology; field management; plant protection; breeding, propagation, physiology, economics of fruit-growing. **Holdings:** 22,160 volumes. **Staff:** Maria Kozhukharova, Libn.; Sophia Manolova, Libn..

★18614★
NATIONAL ARCHIVES OF INDIA - LIBRARY (Hist, Area-Ethnic)
Janpath Phone: 383436
New Delhi 110001, India Dr. R.K. Perti, Dir.
Subjects: India - history, political science, social sciences, education. **Special Collections:** Fort William College Collection; proscribed publications relating to freedom struggle; rare books. **Holdings:** 200,000 volumes; official gazettes and gazetteers; blue books; statutes; census reports; survey and settlement reports; travel accounts, civil lists; parliamentary papers relating to Indian affairs. **Services:** Interlibrary loan; library not open to the public. **Publications:** Patriotic poetry banned by the Raj; Patriotic writings banned by the Raj. **Staff:** Sh.R.C. Puri, Libn..

★18615★
NATIONAL ARCHIVES OF NORWAY - LIBRARY (Area-Ethnic, Hist)
Folke Bernadottes vei 21 Phone: 2 23 74 80
N-0862 Oslo 8, Norway Kirsten Julien, Libn.
Subjects: Scandinavian and Norwegian history, Norwegian biography and family history. **Holdings:** 60,000 volumes; 500 serials. **Services:** Interlibrary loan; library open to the public for reference use only. **Publications:** Riksarkivets Bibliotek Tilvekst (accession list). **Also Known As:** Norway - Riksarkivet - Biblioteket.

★18616★
NATIONAL AUTONOMOUS UNIVERSITY OF MEXICO - INSTITUTE OF AESTHETICS RESEARCH - LIBRARY (Art)
Ciudad Universitaria
Alvaro Obragon Phone: 5 48-41-17
04510 Mexico City, DF, Mexico Prof. Luis Rodriguez Serafin, Dir.
Subjects: Mexican arts - pre-Columbian, colonial, 19th century, modern, contemporary; literature; music; dance; theater; cinema. **Holdings:** 14,000 volumes. **Also Known As:** Instituto de Investigaciones Esteticas.

★18617★
NATIONAL AUTONOMOUS UNIVERSITY OF MEXICO - INSTITUTE OF HISTORICAL RESEARCH - RAFAEL GARCIA GRANADOS LIBRARY (Hist)
Ciudad de la Investigacion en Humanidades
Tercer Circuito Exterior
Zona Cultural/C.U. Phone: 655-13-44
Mexico City 04510 D.F., Mexico Marianela Heredia Abarca, Libn./Adm.
Founded: 1954. **Staff:** Prof 2; Other 5. **Subjects:** History of Mexico, Latin America, Spain; world history; writing of history; history of science and technology. **Special Collections:** Rafael Garcia Granados; Pedro Bosch-Gimpera; Juan Comas; Manuel Maldonado; Koerdell y Fernado Anaya Monroy. **Holdings:** 30,000 books; 5000 bound periodical volumes; 850 theses; 2000 pamphlets; 300 reels of microfilm; 1000 microfiche. **Subscriptions:** 380 journals and other serials. **Services:** Interlibrary loan; copying; SDI; library open to the public for reference use only. **Automated Operations:** Computerized cataloging. **Special Catalogs:** De articulos de publicaciones periodicas (incomplete). **Special Indexes:** De tesis sobre Historia de Mexico presentadas en Estados Unidos y Canada, reproducidas por University Microfilms International (book). **Also Known As:** Instituto de Investigaciones Historicas. **Staff:** Carmen Manzano, Chf., Lib.Serv..

★18618★
NATIONAL BOARD OF ANTIQUITIES - LIBRARY (Soc Sci, Art)
Postilokero 913
SF-00101 Helsinki 10, Finland Phone: 0 40251
Holdings: Archeology, ethnology, art history, museology. **Holdings:** 105,000 volumes. **Remarks:** Maintained by Finland - Ministry of Education. **Also Known As:** Museovirasto.

★18619★
NATIONAL BUILDING TECHNOLOGY CENTRE - NBTC LIBRARY (Plan)
87-101 Delhi Rd. Phone: 888-8888
North Ryde, NSW 2113, Australia Kaye Nolan, Libn.
Subjects: Building research, fire technology. **Holdings:** 26,000 volumes. **Remarks:** Maintained by Australia - Department of Housing and Construction. Telex: 123400.

NATIONAL COUNCIL OF SCIENTIFIC AND TECHNICAL RESEARCH - DARWINIAN INSTITUTE OF BOTANY
See: Darwinian Institute of Botany (18379)

★18620★
NATIONAL COUNCIL OF SCIENTIFIC AND TECHNOLOGICAL DEVELOPMENT - BRAZILIAN INSTITUTE FOR INFORMATION IN SCIENCE AND TECHNOLOGY - LIBRARY (Info Sci)
SCN, Quadra 2, Blocok
70710 Brasilia, DF, Brazil
Subjects: Library and information science, documentation, scientific and technological information policy. **Holdings:** 21,000 volumes; dissertations; pamphlets; microfiche. **Subscriptions:** 3815 journals and other serials. **Computerized Information Services:** Brazilian Union Catalog for Scientific and Technological Serials, Brazilian Bibliography in Science and Technology (internal databases). **Publications:** Bibliografias Especializadas Brasileiras/Specialized Brazilian Bibliographies; Ciencia da Informacao/Information Science (review); additional publications available. **Special Catalogs:** Catalogo Coletivo de Publicacoes Periodicas/National Union Catalog of Periodical Publications.

NATIONAL COUNCIL OF SCIENTIFIC AND TECHNOLOGICAL DEVELOPMENT - EMILIO GOELDI MUSEUM
See: Emilio Goeldi Museum (18449)

NATIONAL COUNCIL OF SCIENTIFIC AND TECHNOLOGICAL DEVELOPMENT - NATIONAL INSTITUTE OF AMAZON RESEARCH
See: National Institute of Amazon Research (18624)

★18621★
THE NATIONAL DIET OF JAPAN - LIBRARY (Info Sci)
10-1, Nagatacho 1 chome
Chiyoda-ku — Phone: 3 581-2331
Tokyo 100, Japan — Kiyohide Ibusuki, Libn.
Founded: 1948. **Subjects:** General collection. **Holdings:** 4.5 million volumes. **Services:** Interlibrary loan; copying; library open to the public with restrictions. **Automated Operations:** Computerized cataloging and serials. **Computerized Information Services:** DIALOG Information Services; Japanese Books System (internal database). Performs searches free of charge. **Publications:** Japanese National Bibliography, weekly; Directory of Japanese Scientific Periodicals, irregular. **Special Indexes:** Japanese Periodicals Index, quarterly; general index to the debates. **Remarks:** Provides library services for the Diet, government ministries and agencies, and the general public. **Staff:** Konosuke Hayashi, Dir., Lib.Coop.Dept..

NATIONAL FOUNDATION OF POLITICAL SCIENCES - CENTER FOR ADVANCED STUDIES ON MODERN AFRICA AND ASIA
See: Center for Advanced Studies on Modern Africa and Asia (18335)

★18622★
NATIONAL GEOLOGICAL LIBRARY (Sci-Engr)
275 Ganjiakou
Fuchengmenwai — Phone: 1 891982
Beijing, People's Republic of China — Deng Geming, Libn.
Founded: 1922. **Staff:** 55. **Subjects:** Geology, structure, stratigraphy, paleontology, rocks, minerals, mineral deposits, geophysics, geochemistry, hydrographic geology, engineering geology, analysis and identification of rocks and minerals, geological reconnaissance survey methods. **Special Collections:** Worldwide geological survey publications (emphasis on paleontology). **Holdings:** 170,000 volumes; 6000 periodicals; 800 AV programs and microforms. **Services:** Interlibrary loan; copying. **Computerized Information Services:** Internal database. **Special Catalogs:** Catalog of Chinese Scientific and Technical Literatures--Geology, bimonthly; Catalog of Foreign Scientific and Technical Literatures--Geology, bimonthly.

★18623★
NATIONAL HERBARIUM OF THE NETHERLANDS - LIBRARY (Biol Sci)
Rapenburg 70-74
P.O. Box 9514 — Phone: 273500
NL-2300 RA Leiden, Netherlands — Mr. L. Vogelenzang, Libn.
Subjects: Plant systematics, plant geography. **Holdings:** 28,000 books; 65,000 reprints and pamphlets; 100,000 microfiche. **Subscriptions:** 2100 journals and other serials. **Remarks:** Maintained by Leiden State University. **Also Known As:** Rijksherbarium.

★18624★
NATIONAL INSTITUTE OF AMAZON RESEARCH - LIBRARY (Biol Sci)
Estrada do Aleixo
Caixa Postal 478 — Phone: 236-9899
69000 Manaus, Amazonas, Brazil
Algenir Ferraz Suano Da Silva, Libn.
Subjects: Amazon region - botany, ecology, agronomy, natural resources, tropical silviculture, tropical diseases, limnology. **Holdings:** 226,400 volumes. **Remarks:** Maintained by National Council of Scientific and Technological Development. **Also Known As:** Instituto Nacional de Pesquisas da Amazonia.

★18625★
NATIONAL INSTITUTE OF DEMOGRAPHIC STUDIES - LIBRARY (Soc Sci)
27, rue du Commandeur — Phone: 43 20 13 45
F-75675 Paris 14, France — M. Todd, Hd., Lib.Serv.
Subjects: Demography. **Holdings:** 30,000 volumes. **Also Known As:** Institut National d'Etudes Demographiques.

★18626★
NATIONAL INSTITUTE OF DEVELOPMENT ADMINISTRATION - LIBRARY (Bus-Fin)
Klong Chan
Bangkapi — Phone: 2 377-7400
Bangkok 10240, Thailand — Assoc.Prof. Kamala Roong-uthai, Libn.
Subjects: Economic, social, and political development; marketing; finance; public administration. **Holdings:** 131,950 volumes. **Remarks:** Maintained by Thailand - Ministry of University Affairs.

★18627★
NATIONAL INSTITUTE FOR MEDICAL RESEARCH - LIBRARY (Med, Biol Sci)
P.O. Box 9653 — Phone: 30770
Dar es Salaam, United Republic of Tanzania — M.K. Franc, Libn.
Subjects: Parasitology, entomology, tropical medicine, public health. **Holdings:** 19,000 volumes. **Remarks:** Maintained by Tanzania - Ministry of Health and Social Welfare.

★18628★
NATIONAL INSTITUTE OF METROLOGY - LIBRARY (Sci-Engr)
Sos. Vitan-Birzesti 11 — Phone: 0 83 35 20
Bucharest 75669, Romania — Anca Dragan, Libn.
Subjects: Metrology; standards for physical quantities; calibration and measurement techniques; development of high precision instruments. **Holdings:** 50,000 volumes. **Also Known As:** Institutul National de Metrologie.

★18629★
NATIONAL INSTITUTE FOR RESEARCH ON BIOLOGICAL SCIENCES - INFORMATION DOCUMENTATION (Biol Sci)
Km. 2.5 Carretera Antigua a Coatepec
Apartado Postal 63 — Phone: 281 72974
Xalapa 91000, Veracruz, Mexico — Alma Aguilar Caceres, Hd.
Founded: 1976. **Staff:** Prof 3; Other 2. **Subjects:** Ecology, botany, biology, zoology, silviculture. **Holdings:** 17,000 books; 1500 technical reports; 500 maps; 12,026 microfiche; 33 records. **Subscriptions:** 617 journals and other serials. **Services:** Copying; open to local researchers and universities and others upon application. **Automated Operations:** Computerized cataloging. **Computerized Information Services:** DIALOG Information Services, BRS Information Technologies. Performs searches on fee basis. Contact Person: Dulce Ma. Salmones. **Publications:** Nuevas Adquisiciones, semiannual. **Also Known As:** Instituto Nacional de Investigaciones sobre Recursos Bioticos. **Staff:** Felisa Harrador, Pub.Serv.; Delfino Hernandez, Tech.Libn.; Patricia Flores, Tech.Libn..

★18630★
NATIONAL INSTITUTE FOR THE STUDY OF THE THEATER - LIBRARY (Theater)
Avenida Cordoba 1199 — Phone: 1 45-8634
1055 Buenos Aires, Argentina — Dr. Nestor Suarez Aboy, Dir.
Subjects: National theater of Argentina - heritage and history. **Holdings:** 8000 volumes; historic manuscript file; documents; pictures; costumes. **Remarks:** Maintained by Argentina - Secretariat of Culture. **Also Known As:** Instituto Nacional de Estudios del Teatro.

★18631★
THE NATIONAL LIBRARY AND ARCHIVES OF ETHIOPIA (Area-Ethnic, Info Sci)
P.O. Box 717 — Phone: 44 22 41
Addis Ababa, Ethiopia — Yonas Tilahun, Div.Hd.
Subjects: Ethiopiana, education, science and technology. **Special Collections:** Ethiopian manuscripts (1650); rare books; Ethiopiana (clippings; cuttings; bound newspapers). **Holdings:** 60,000 books; 10,000 bound periodical volumes; 40,000 patents and documents; 200 microforms; UN publications. **Services:** Interlibrary loan; copying; library open to the public. **Publications:** Ethiopian Publications, semiannual. **Special Indexes:** Index of Periodicals, semiannual. **Remarks:** Maintained by Ethiopia - Ministry of Culture. **Staff:** Arefaine Belay, Dept.Hd..

★18632★
NATIONAL LIBRARY OF AUSTRALIA (Area-Ethnic, Hum, Info Sci)
Parkes Place — Phone: 62 621111
Canberra, ACT 2600, Australia — Mr. W.M. Horton, Dir.-Gen.
Subjects: Australiana, Pacificana, representative literature in English and European languages. **Special Collections:** Ferguson, Petherick, and Rex Nan Kivell collections of Australiana. **Holdings:** 2.4 million books; 111,700 bound periodical volumes; 20,481 AV programs; 3.2 million microforms,

aerial photographs, maps, photographs, paintings, drawings, prints, scores, oral histories, tapes; 6400 meters of manuscripts. **Services:** Interlibrary loan; copying; SDI; library open to the public. **Computerized Information Services:** AUSINET, DIALOG Information Services, Pergamon ORBIT InfoLine, Inc., ESA/IRS, Australian Bibliographic Network (ABN), BLAISE Online Services, QL Systems, International Nuclear Information System (INIS). Performs searches on fee basis. Contact: Chief Librarian, Computer Search Services. **Publications:** Australian National Bibliography. **Special Catalogs:** National Union Catalogue of Serials (NUCOS). **Special Indexes:** Australian Public Affairs Information Index (APAIS).

★18633★
NATIONAL LIBRARY FOR THE BLIND (Aud-Vis)
Cromwell Rd.
Bredbury Phone: 61 494-0217
Stockport, Cheshire SK6 2SG, England Allan Leach, Dir.-Gen.
Subjects: General collection. **Special Collections:** Early tactile books (100); braille music (6000 pieces). **Holdings:** 350,000 volumes in braille, moon type, and large print; 1500 bound periodical volumes. **Services:** Interlibrary loan; copying; library open to the public. **Publications:** Guide to braille music - for sale.

NATIONAL LIBRARY OF BULGARIA
See: Bulgaria - Committee of Culture - Cyril and Methodius National Library (18322)

★18634★
NATIONAL LIBRARY OF CHINA (Info Sci, Area-Ethnic)
7 Wenjin St. Phone: 1 666331
Beijing, People's Republic of China Ding Zhigang, Dp.Libn.
Founded: 1910. **Subjects:** General collection. **Special Collections:** Wenyuange Collection (imperial library of Ming Dynasty); Wenjinge Collection (depository library of Four Vaults of Emperor Qianlong); Iron Lute and Copper Sword Mansion of Qu's Family Collection (total of 2.5 million rare books). **Holdings:** 5.4 million volumes; 60,000 periodicals; 260,000 technical reports; 90,000 AV programs and microforms; Chinese publications in 24 minority languages; hand copies, blockprint, and monograph editions of famous writers; inscribed tortoise shells and bones; books of rubbings; atlases. **Services:** Interlibrary loan; copying; library open to the public.

NATIONAL LIBRARY OF FINLAND
See: University of Helsinki - Library (18851)

★18635★
NATIONAL LIBRARY OF IRAN (Area-Ethnic, Info Sci)
30 Tir St. Phone: 21 673315
Tehran 11364, Iran Mrs. Poori Soltani, Hd., Lib.Res.Gp.
Staff: Prof 18; Other 60. **Subjects:** Iranology, Islamic studies, library and information science. **Special Collections:** Persian and Arabic manuscripts (12,000 volumes). **Holdings:** 265,000 books; 13,100 bound periodical volumes; 20,000 microforms. **Subscriptions:** 196 journals and other serials; 56 newspapers. **Services:** Copying; library open to the public with restrictions. **Publications:** National Bibliography of Iran; Directory of Iranian Periodicals; additional publications available. **Special Catalogs:** Catalog of manuscripts. **Remarks:** Maintained by Iran - Ministry of Culture and Higher Education. **Staff:** Mohammad Rajabi, Dir.; Mr. Kamran Fani; Mrs. Zohreh Alavi; Mr. Farhad Vaziri; Ms. Mandana Sadiq-Behzadi; Ms. Zahra Shadman-Valavi; Ms. Guiti Arian; Mr. Mehrdad Niknam-Vazifeh; Mr. Hoseyn Shahedi-Razavi; Mrs. Shirin Ta'avoni; Ms. Mahvash Behnam; Ms. Ma'sumeh Baqeri.

NATIONAL LIBRARY OF IRELAND
See: Republic of Ireland - Department of the Taoiseach (18724)

★18636★
NATIONAL LIBRARY OF JAMAICA (Area-Ethnic, Info Sci)
12 East St.
P.O. Box 823 Phone: (809)922-0620
Kingston, Jamaica Stephney Ferguson, Dir.
Subjects: Jamaica, West Indies. **Holdings:** 35,700 books; 31,212 AV programs; 23,575 microforms; 2027 manuscripts; newspapers; photographs; prints; maps. **Services:** Interlibrary loan; copying. **Publications:** Jamaican National Bibliography. **Special Indexes:** Index to the Daily Gleaner, 1975 to present.

★18637★
NATIONAL LIBRARY OF MALAYSIA (Area-Ethnic, Info Sci)
Wisma Thakurdas/Sachdev, 1st Fl.
Jalan Raja Laut Phone: 3 2923144
Kuala Lumpur 50572, Malaysia Dr. D.E.K. Wijasuriya, Act.Dir.-Gen.
Subjects: General collection. **Special Collections:** Malaysiana; Malay manuscripts; rare books. **Holdings:** 512,054 books; 11,970 serial titles; 1197 AV programs; 21,707 microforms; 321 manuscripts. **Services:** Interlibrary loan; copying; library open to the public. **Computerized Information Services:** DIALOG Information Services, FORMIS. Performs searches on fee basis. **Publications:** Malaysian National Bibliography. **Special Indexes:** Malaysian Periodical Index; Malaysian Newspaper Index; Malaysian Conference Index. **Remarks:** Maintained by Malaysia - Ministry of Culture, Youth and Sports.

★18638★
THE NATIONAL LIBRARY OF MALTA (Area-Ethnic, Hist, Info Sci)
36 Old Treasury St. Phone: 226585
Valletta, Malta John B. Sultana, Libn.
Subjects: Malta, Order of St. John. **Special Collections:** Archives of the Order of St. John of Jerusalem (also known as the Knights of Malta); early and old printed books. **Holdings:** 350,000 books; 10,000 manuscripts. **Services:** Interlibrary loan; copying; library open to the public. **Publications:** Malta National Bibliography, annual. **Special Catalogs:** Catalogue of the Records of the Order of St. John in the National Library of Malta (in progress).

★18639★
NATIONAL LIBRARY OF NEW ZEALAND - ALEXANDER TURNBULL LIBRARY (Area-Ethnic, Hum)
P.O. Box 12349 Phone: 4 743-000
Wellington, New Zealand Mr. J.E. Traue, Chf.Libn.
Subjects: New Zealand, Pacific, John Milton, English literature, voyages and travels, printing and the book. **Special Collections:** John Milton and the Seventeenth Century. **Holdings:** 205,000 books; 2000 linear meters of bound periodical volumes; 500,000 microforms; 2800 linear meters of manuscripts. **Services:** Copying; library open to the public. **Computerized Information Services:** New Zealand Bibliographic Network. Performs searches free of charge. Contact Person: Miss J. Horncy, Rd.Serv.Libn.. **Publications:** National Register of Archives and Manuscripts; Turnbull Library Record. **Special Catalogs:** Descriptive Catalogue of the Milton Collection.

★18640★
THE NATIONAL LIBRARY FOR PSYCHOLOGY AND EDUCATION (Soc Sci, Educ)
P.O. Box 50063 Phone: 8 15 18 20
S-104 05 Stockholm, Sweden Tomas Lidman, Lib.Dir.
Subjects: Psychology, education, special education, adult education, educational psychology. **Special Collections:** Swedish School Book Collection; ERIC microfiche collection. **Holdings:** 250,000 books; 850 bound periodical volumes; 300,000 patents and documents; Psyclitt and ERIC on CD-ROM. **Services:** Interlibrary loan; copying; SDI; library open to the public. **Computerized Information Services:** DIALOG Information Services, ESA/IRS, Telesystemes-Questel, DIMDI, MEDICINDATA, Norsk Senter for Informatikk A/S-NSI; SVEPP (Swedish Behavioral Sciences; internal database). Performs searches on fee basis. Contact Person: Gunilla Appelgren, Info.Spec.. **Publications:** Annual Bibliographies in Psychology and Education. **Remarks:** Maintained by Sweden - Ministry of Education.

★18641★
NATIONAL LIBRARY OF SCOTLAND (Area-Ethnic, Info Sci)
George IV Bridge Phone: 31 226 4531
Edinburgh EH1 1EW, Scotland Prof. E.F.D. Roberts, Libn.
Staff: 220. **Subjects:** Scotland, Scottish literature and history, Scots overseas. **Special Collections:** Astorga Collection (Spanish); Balfour Collection (Handel); Blaikie Collection (Jacobitism); Blairs (libraries of Scottish Roman Catholic communities at home and abroad - on deposit); Bute Collection (17th-18th century English plays); Dieterichs Collection (German Reformation); Educational Institute of Scotland Library; Glen Collection (Scottish music); Graham Brown Collection (alpine and mountaineering); Gray Collection (theology and classics, 15th-17th centuries); Hopkinson Collection (Berlioz and Verdi); Inglis Collection (Scottish music); Institute of Chartered Accountants (Antiquarian Collection - on deposit); Jolly Collection (theology, pre-1801); Lauriston Castle Collection (Scottish books, pamphlets, chap-books); Lloyd Collection (alpine and mountaineering); Macadam Collection (baking and confectionery); Mason Collection (children's books); Nichol Smith

Collection (French and English literature, 16th-18th centuries); Rosebery Collection (early and rare Scottish books and pamphlets); Scandinavian Collection (founded on Grimur Thorkelin's library); Hugh Sharp Collection (English and American first editions); Warden Collection (shorthand); Wordie Collection (polar exploration). **Holdings:** 5 million books; 70,000 bound manuscripts. **Subscriptions:** 18,000 journals and other serials. **Services:** Interlibrary loan; copying. **Automated Operations:** Computerized public access catalog and cataloging. **Publications:** Annual Report; Bibliography of Scotland, annual; catalog of publications - available upon request. **Special Catalogs:** Catalog of manuscripts; Gaelic Union Catalogue. **Special Indexes:** Current Periodicals in the National Library of Scotland; Directory of Scottish Newspapers.

★18642★
NATIONAL LIBRARY OF THAILAND (Area-Ethnic, Info Sci)
Samsen Rd. Phone: 2 281-5212
Bangkok 10300, Thailand
Mr. Prachark Wattananusit, Gift & Exch.Libn.
Subjects: History, literature, Buddhism, art, social and basic sciences. **Special Collections:** Praya Anumanrajadhon; Vichitravadakarn; music; Thai manuscripts and collections. **Holdings:** 1.2 million books; 1933 periodical titles; 24,771 AV programs; 5014 microforms; 132,490 manuscripts. **Services:** Interlibrary loan; copying; library open to the public. **Publications:** National bibliography; ISDS-SEA bulletin; bibliography of children's books. **Special Indexes:** Subject indexes. **Also Known As:** Ho Samut Haeng Chat. **Staff:** Mrs. Pranom Panya-ngam, Dir..

★18643★
NATIONAL METEOROLOGICAL LIBRARY (Sci-Engr)
London Rd. Phone: 344 420242
Bracknell, Berkshire RG12 2SZ, England Maurice E. Crewe, Libn.
Staff: Prof 10; Other 6. **Subjects:** Meteorology, climatology, hydrometeorology, oceanology, fluid dynamics, allied atmospheric sciences. **Special Collections:** Rare and historic meteorological literature. **Holdings:** 150,000 books; 50,000 pamphlets; 30,000 photographs; 30,000 microfiche. **Services:** Interlibrary loan; copying (both limited); library open to the public. **Automated Operations:** Computerized public access catalog, cataloging, and acquisitions. **Computerized Information Services:** ESA/IRS, DIALOG Information Services, KOMPASS ON LINE; MOLARS (Meteorological Office Library Accessions Retrieval System; internal database). Performs searches on fee basis. Contact Person: R.W. Mason, Info.Off., ext. 2712. **Publications:** Accessions List, monthly. **Special Catalogs:** Library Union Catalogue of Rare Books (published with the Royal Meteorological Society). **Staff:** R. Anderson-Jones, Classifier; N.S. Harrison, Classifier; K. Herrington, Vis. Aids Off..

NATIONAL MUSEUM OF ANTIQUITIES OF SCOTLAND - LIBRARY
See: National Museums of Scotland - Library (18644)

★18644★
NATIONAL MUSEUMS OF SCOTLAND - LIBRARY (Sci-Engr, Art, Biol Sci)
Chambers St. Phone: 31 225 7534
Edinburgh EH1 1JF, Scotland M.V. Mathew, Hd. of Lib.
Founded: 1985. **Staff:** Prof 7; Other 4. **Subjects:** Decorative arts, archeology, zoology, geology, history of science and technology. **Special Collections:** Society of Antiquaries of Scotland Library. **Holdings:** 95,000 books; 65,000 bound periodical volumes; 200 documents; 30 AV programs; 250 microforms; manuscripts. **Services:** Interlibrary loan; copying; library open to the public by appointment. **Remarks:** The National Museums of Scotland Library was formed by the amalgamation of the libraries of the Royal Scottish Museum, National Museum of Antiquities of Scotland, and Scottish United Services Museum.

★18645★
NATIONAL SCIENCE COUNCIL - SCIENCE AND TECHNOLOGY INFORMATION CENTER (Sci-Engr)
P.O. Box 4, Nankang Phone: 2 7822183
Taipei, Taiwan Dr. Tao-Hsing Ma, Dir.
Subjects: Science and technology. **Holdings:** 16,030 volumes; documents in microform. **Subscriptions:** 1318 journals and other serials. **Services:** SDI; center open to academic research and industrial communities. **Computerized Information Services:** DIALOG Information Services, Pergamon ORBIT InfoLine, Inc., BRS Information Technologies; internal databases. Performs searches on fee basis. **Publications:** STIC Newsletter, monthly.

★18646★
NATIONAL SWEDISH INSTITUTE FOR BUILDING RESEARCH - LIBRARY (Plan)
P.O. Box 785 Phone: 10 02 20
S-801 29 Gavle, Sweden Lena Berntler, Libn.
Subjects: Building, planning, architecture. **Holdings:** 25,000 books. **Services:** Interlibrary loan; copying; library open to the public. **Computerized Information Services:** DIALOG Information Services, ESA/IRS, ARAMIS, BYGGDOK. **Remarks:** Telex: 47396 BYGGFO. **Also Known As:** Statens Institut for Byggnadsforskning.

★18647★
NATIONAL SZECHENYI LIBRARY - CENTRE FOR LIBRARY SCIENCE AND METHODOLOGY (Info Sci)
Budavari Palota, F epulet Phone: 757533
H-1827 Budapest, Hungary Emoke Kovacs, Hd., Lib.Sci.Lib.
Subjects: Library and information science. **Holdings:** 57,000 volumes; 9500 study-tour reports, dissertations, translations, prospectuses; International Federation of Library Associations (IFLA) papers and publications; photographs; prints. **Services:** Interlibrary loan; copying; center open to Hungarian and foreign experts in librarianship and information science and students. **Publications:** Library and Documentation Literature (in Hungarian), quarterly; Hungarian Library and Information Science Abstracts (in English), semiannual; additional publications available. **Also Known As:** Orszabos Szechenyi Konyvtar - Konyvtartudomanyi es Modszertani Kozpont.

★18648★
NATIONAL TECHNICAL INFORMATION CENTRE AND LIBRARY (Sci-Engr)
P.O. Box 12
Muzeum u.17 Phone: 336300
H-1428 Budapest, Hungary Mihaly Agoston, Dir.Gen.
Subjects: Science, technology, applied economics. **Holdings:** 500,000 monographs and research reports; 320,000 bound periodical volumes; 630,000 translations. **Subscriptions:** 5300 journals and other serials. **Services:** Copying; SDI; library open to the public. **Computerized Information Services:** DIALOG Information Services, Pergamon ORBIT InfoLine, Inc., CAS ONLINE, Data-Star, IAEA/INIS, Tenders Electronic Daily (TED); internal database. Performs searches on fee basis. **Publications:** Hungarian R and D Abstracts: Science and Technology (in English), quarterly; Abstract Journals (21 subject sections); Technical Digest Journals (18 subject sections); Technical-Economic Digest Journals (5 subject sections); Technical Information Journals for Managers; Primary Journals in Science and Technology; other publications available - all in Hungarian. **Also Known As:** Orszagos Muszaki Informacios Kozpont es Konyvtar.

★18649★
NATIONAL UNIVERSITY OF SINGAPORE - CHINESE LANGUAGE AND RESEARCH CENTER - LIBRARY (Hum, Soc Sci)
10 Kent Ridge Crescent Phone: 7723328
Singapore 0511, Singapore Koh Thong Ngee, Libn.
Subjects: Chinese linguistics, humanities, social sciences. **Holdings:** 300,000 volumes. **Subscriptions:** 400 journals and other serials. **Remarks:** Library holdings are in Chinese. Telex: 33943 UNISPO.

★18650★
NATIONAL VACCINE & SERUM INSTITUTE - LIBRARY (Biol Sci, Med)
Sanjianfang, Chaoyang District Phone: 1 571161-1665
Beijing, People's Republic of China Yang Xichang, Libn.
Founded: 1919. **Staff:** 7. **Subjects:** Natural sciences, cytology, genetics, biochemistry, molecular biology, microbiology, preventive medicine, public health, medicine, clinical diagnosis, infectious diseases, oncology, experimental zoology. **Special Collections:** Medical biological products. **Holdings:** 21,109 volumes; 172 technical reports; 20 microforms and AV programs.. **Subscriptions:** 1342 journals and other serials. **Services:** Copying. **Publications:** Annual Review, irregular.

★18651★
NATIONALITIES CULTURE PALACE - LIBRARY (Area-Ethnic)
Xidan Phone: 1 668761-720
Beijing, People's Republic of China Li Zongju, Dp.Libn.
Founded: 1959. **Staff:** 32. **Subjects:** Chinese publications. **Special Collections:** 24 Chinese provincial languages, emphasis on Tibetan language (130,000 volumes); manuscripts in gold and silver; sutras written on palm leaves; rubbings from stone and bronze tablets; district histories. **Holdings:** 400,000 volumes. **Services:** Copying. **Special Catalogs:** Catalog

of Publications Held by the Library; Chronicle of National Affairs; Catalog of Collections in Ancient Tibetan. **Remarks:** An alternate telephone number is 668761-280.

NATSIONALEN AGRARNO-PROMISHLEN SUYUZ - SELSKOSTOPANSKA AKADEMIYA - TSENTUR ZA NAOUCHNO-TECHNICHESKA I IKONOMICHESKA INFOMATSIYA
See: National Agro-Industrial Union - Agricultural Academy - Center for Scientific, Technical and Economic Information (18611)

NEDERLANDS ORGANISATIE VOOR TOEGEPAST NATUURWETENSCHAPPELIJK ONDERZOEK
See: Netherlands Organization for Applied Scientific Research (18657)

★18652★
NETHERLANDS - CENTRAL BUREAU OF STATISTICS - LIBRARY (Soc Sci)
P.O. Box 959 Phone: 70 694341
NL-2270 AZ Voorburg, Netherlands T. Vreugdenhil, Libn.
Staff: Prof 21; Other 12. **Subjects:** Worldwide statistical data. **Holdings:** 290,000 volumes; 70,000 bound periodical volumes; 75,000 annual reports; 70,000 microfiche. **Subscriptions:** 9400 journals and other serials. **Services:** Interlibrary loan; copying; SDI; library open to the public. **Automated Operations:** Computerized cataloging and journal routing.

★18653★
NETHERLANDS - EDUCATION DEPARTMENT - ECONOMISCH-HISTORISCHE BIBLIOTHEEK (Bus-Fin)
Herengracht 220 Phone: 20 247270
NL-1016 BT Amsterdam, Netherlands Dr. J.J. Seegers
Subjects: History - economic, accounting, insurance. **Special Collections:** Accountancy prior to 1850 (3000 titles); history of economic thought. **Holdings:** 75,000 books; 25,000 bound periodical volumes; 10,000 documents. **Special Catalogs:** Economisch-Historische Katalogi; Katalogi bronvenoverzichlen.

★18654★
NETHERLANDS - MINISTRY OF AGRICULTURE AND FISHERIES - INTERNATIONAL INSTITUTE FOR LAND RECLAMATION AND IMPROVEMENT - LIBRARY (Agri)
Postbus 45 Phone: 8370 19100
NL-6700 AA Wageningen, Netherlands J.A.M. Kuijlen, Hd.Libn./Info.Spec.
Subjects: Soil science, water management, hydrology, irrigation and drainage, remote sensing, land-use planning. **Holdings:** 42,000 books; 16,000 bound periodical volumes. **Subscriptions:** 1500 journals and other serials. **Services:** Interlibrary loan; copying; SDI; library open to the public. **Automated Operations:** Computerized public access catalog, cataloging, and circulation. **Computerized Information Services:** ESA/IRS, DIMDI, DIALOG Information Services, Pergamon ORBIT InfoLine, Inc.; produces AGRALIN (Agricultural Literature Information System in the Netherlands). Performs searches on fee basis. **Publications:** Attenderingsbulletin Bibliotheek Staringgebouw: land, soil, water, 6/year. **Staff:** Mrs. L.A. Trouw, Doc.; P. Heikamp, Desk Off..

NETHERLANDS - MINISTRY OF FOREIGN AFFAIRS - INSTITUTE OF SOCIAL STUDIES
See: Institute of Social Studies - Library (18524)

NETHERLANDS - MINISTRY OF SOCIAL AFFAIRS - INTERNATIONAL ARCHIVES FOR THE WOMEN'S MOVEMENT
See: International Archives for the Women's Movement (18534)

★18655★
NETHERLANDS - ROYAL LIBRARY (Hum, Soc Sci, Law, Info Sci)
P.O. Box 90407 Phone: 70 140911
NL-2509 LK The Hague, Netherlands
Mr. W.G. Van Pijpen, Dp.Libn.
Subjects: Humanities, philosophy, psychology, religion, law, sociology, economics, language and literature, history and fine art, geography, education, political science. **Special Collections:** Medieval manuscripts; incunabula and post-incunabula; historical bindings; paper collection; chess literature. **Holdings:** 2.25 million bound volumes; 160,000 microforms; 7000 manuscripts. **Subscriptions:** 14,500 periodicals. **Services:** Interlibrary loan; copying; library open to the public. **Publications:** Treasures of the Royal Library; Bibliography of Translations of North and South Netherlandic Publications; Bibliography of Cartographic Materials in the Netherlands; special bibliographies. **Special Catalogs:** Cumulatieve Catalogus; Centrale catalogus van Periodieken (Union Catalog of Periodicals; book); exhibition catalogs. **Remarks:** Library located at Prins Willem Alexanderhof 5, NL-2595 BE The Hague, Netherlands. **Remarks:** Telex: 34402. **Also Known As:** Koninklijke Bibliotheek. **Staff:** Mr. J. Van Heijst, Libn.; Mr. A.W. Willemsen, Libn..

★18656★
NETHERLANDS FOREIGN TRADE AGENCY - LIBRARY (Bus-Fin)
Bezuidenhoutseweg 151 Phone: 70 797221
NL-2594 AG The Hague, Netherlands J.H. Ypma, Hd.
Subjects: Economics, international trade, foreign investment. **Holdings:** 100,000 volumes. **Subscriptions:** 1800 journals and other serials. **Services:** Library open to businesses, government agencies, and students. **Computerized Information Services:** DIALOG Information Services, Belgian Information and Dissemination Service (BELINDIS); internal database. Performs searches on fee basis.

NETHERLANDS INSTITUTE FOR DEVELOPMENTAL BIOLOGY
See: Royal Academy of Sciences - Netherlands Institute for Developmental Biology (18731)

NETHERLANDS ORGANIZATION FOR THE ADVANCEMENT OF PURE SCIENCE - CENTER FOR MATHEMATICS AND COMPUTER SCIENCE
See: Center for Mathematics and Computer Science (18337)

★18657★
NETHERLANDS ORGANIZATION FOR APPLIED SCIENTIFIC RESEARCH - CENTRAL LIBRARY (Sci-Engr)
Juliana van Stolberglaan 148 Phone: 70 496500
NL-2595 The Hague, Netherlands Mrs. T. Wagemakers, Dir.
Subjects: Applied research and development in the areas of industrial technology, energy, environment, food and nutrition, health, defense. **Holdings:** 250,000 volumes. **Also Known As:** Nederlands Organisatie voor Toegepast Natuurwetenschappelijk Onderzoek.

NEW SOUTH WALES DEPARTMENT OF HEALTH - INSTITUTE OF CLINICAL PATHOLOGY AND MEDICAL RESEARCH
See: Cumberland Area Health Services - Westmead Hospital - AMA Library (18371)

★18658★
NEW SOUTH WALES DEPARTMENT OF MAIN ROADS - LIBRARY (Sci-Engr)
309 Castlereagh St. Phone: 2 2186520
Sydney, NSW 2000, Australia Rosemary Bell, Sr.Libn.
Subjects: Civil and traffic engineering. **Holdings:** 66,000 books; 100 microforms. **Services:** Interlibrary loan; copying; library open to the public for reference use only. **Computerized Information Services:** ESA/IRS, AUSTRALIS, AUSINET. **Remarks:** Telex: AA 21825.

★18659★
NEW ZEALAND - DEPARTMENT OF SCIENTIFIC AND INDUSTRIAL RESEARCH - GRASSLANDS DIVISION - LIBRARY (Biol Sci, Agri)
Fitzherbert West
Private Bag Phone: 68-019
Palmerston North, New Zealand Cynthia M. Owen, Hd.Libn.
Subjects: Plant and pasture improvement in New Zealand and worldwide; agronomy; ecology; plant physiology; molecular genetics; seed technology; plant breeding; plant nutrition. **Holdings:** 35,070 volumes. **Remarks:** Telex: 31285.

★18660★
NEW ZEALAND - MINISTRY OF FORESTRY - FOREST RESEARCH INSTITUTE - LIBRARY (Agri, Biol Sci)
Private Bag Phone: 73 475-899
Rotorua, New Zealand Beryl Anderson, Libn.
Staff: Prof 3; Other 1. **Subjects:** Forest health, improvement, management, resources; wood technology; protection forestry - geohydrology, revegetation, plant and animal ecology. **Holdings:** 110,000 books and monographs; 8000 microfiche. **Subscriptions:** 1600 journals and other serials. **Services:** Interlibrary loan; copying; SDI; library open to the public. **Automated Operations:** Computerized cataloging, serials, and journal circulation. **Computerized Information Services:** DIALOG Information Services, Pergamon ORBIT InfoLine, Inc., CSIRONET, INFOS

(Information Network for Official Statistics). Performs searches on fee basis. Contact Person: Marilla Mullon, Dp.Libn.. **Publications:** Accessions list, monthly - to staff and selected libraries. **Formerly:** New Zealand Forest Service. **Staff:** Judy Prictor, Asst.Libn..

NEW ZEALAND - NATIONAL LIBRARY OF NEW ZEALAND
See: National Library of New Zealand (18639)

★18661★
NIGERIAN INSTITUTE OF INTERNATIONAL AFFAIRS - LIBRARY (Soc Sci)
13-15 Kofo Abayomi Rd.
Victoria Island — Phone: 1 615608
Lagos, Lagos State, Nigeria — Mr. A.O. Banjo, Dir., Lib. & Doc.Serv.
Subjects: Development of foreign policy, international politics, strategic studies, international economic relations, international law and organization. **Holdings:** 46,550 volumes. **Publications:** Library Information Bulletin. **Special Indexes:** Periodic: An Index to Current Journal Articles.

★18662★
BERNHARD NOCHT INSTITUTE FOR NAUTICAL AND TROPICAL MEDICINE - LIBRARY (Med)
Bernhard-Nocht-Strasse 74 — Phone: 31 10 24 05
D-2000 Hamburg 4, Federal Republic of Germany
Martina-Christine Koschwitz, Libn.
Subjects: Tropical diseases, medicine, infectious diseases, veterinary medicine, maritime virology, helminthology, protozoology, biochemistry, entomology, pathology, immune diagnosis. **Holdings:** 85,000 volumes. **Subscriptions:** 192 journals and other serials. **Services:** Interlibrary loan; copying; library open to the public. **Also Known As:** Bernhard-Nocht-Institut fuer Schiffs- und Tropenkrankheiten.

NORDISK FORSKNINGSINSTITUT FOR MALING OG TRYKFARVER
See: Scandinavian Paint and Printing Ink Research Institute - Library (18757)

NORDISKA AFRIKAINSTITUTET
See: Scandinavian Institute of African Studies (18756)

★18663★
NORDLEK COUNCIL - LIBRARY (Area-Ethnic)
Postfack 9104 — Phone: 08 937038
S-102 72 Stockholm, Sweden — Fredrik Bergh, Sec.Gen.
Subjects: Folk dancing. **Holdings:** 312 volumes. **Services:** Library not open to the public.

NORGES TEKNISK-NATURVITENSKAPELIGE FORSKNINGSRAD - NORGES BYGGFORSKNINGSINSTITUTT
See: Royal Norwegian Council for Scientific and Industrial Research - Norwegian Building Research Institute (18748)

NORSK POLARINSTITUTT
See: Norwegian Polar Research Institute (18666)

★18664★
NORTH EAST LONDON POLYTECHNIC - SCIENCE FICTION FOUNDATION RESEARCH LIBRARY (Hum)
Longbridge Rd. — Phone: 1 590 7722
Dagenham, Essex RM8 2AS, England — E.W. Chapman, Hon.Libn.
Subjects: Science fiction, fantasy. **Special Collections:** Pulp magazines, 1920s to present; critical works; Russian science fiction; Flat Earth Society papers; fanzines. **Holdings:** 12,750 books; 100 microforms; 100 manuscripts. **Services:** Copying; library open to the public. **Staff:** Joyce Day, Sec..

★18665★
NORTHERN TERRITORY DEPARTMENT OF EDUCATION - STATE REFERENCE LIBRARY OF THE NORTHERN TERRITORY - NORTHERN AUSTRALIA COLLECTION (Area-Ethnic)
25 Cavenagh St.
P.O. Box 42 — Phone: 89 897364
Darwin, NT 5790, Australia — Michael Loos, Sr.Libn.
Staff: Prof 2; Other 2. **Subjects:** Northern Australia. **Holdings:** 5915 books; 940 bound periodical volumes; 5740 pamphlets; 670 maps; 693 reels of microfilm; 916 films and videotapes; .5 meters of microfiche; 30,336 photographs. **Subscriptions:** 996 journals and other serials; 39 newspapers. **Services:** Copying; collection open to the public for reference use only. **Automated Operations:** Computerized public access catalog, cataloging, and acquisitions. **Computerized Information Services:** AUSINET, ABN (Australian Bibliographic Network). Performs searches free of charge. **Publications:** Occasional papers. **Special Indexes:** State Library Photograph Index (online). **Staff:** Ron Davis, Dir., Lib.Serv..

NORWAY - RIKSARKIVET
See: National Archives of Norway (18615)

NORWEGIAN BUILDING RESEARCH INSTITUTE
See: Royal Norwegian Council for Scientific and Industrial Research - Norwegian Building Research Institute (18748)

NORWEGIAN INSTITUTE OF TECHNOLOGY
See: University of Trondheim - Norwegian Institute of Technology (18863)

★18666★
NORWEGIAN POLAR RESEARCH INSTITUTE - LIBRARY (Sci-Engr)
P.O. Box 158
Rolfstangveien 12 — Phone: 2 12 36 50
N-1330 Oslo Lufthavn, Norway — Reidunn Lund, Libn.
Subjects: Norwegian Arctic and Antarctic - geology, geophysics, biology, expeditions. **Holdings:** 19,000 volumes. **Also Known As:** Norsk Polarinstitutt.

NUTRITION INSTITUTE OF CENTRAL AMERICA AND PANAMA
See: Pan-American Health Organization - Nutrition Institute of Central America and Panama (18677)

O

★18667★
OBISPO COLOMBRES AGRO-INDUSTRIAL EXPERIMENT STATION - LIBRARY (Agri)
Casilla de Correo 71
Obispo Colombres Phone: 16561
4000 San Miguel de Tucuman, Argentina Rolando Juarez, Libn.
Subjects: Sugarcane, citrus fruits, soybeans, cereals, dry beans, potatoes, beef and dairy production, bioenergy, gasohol. **Holdings:** 58,000 volumes. **Remarks:** Maintained by Argentina - Ministry of the Economy. **Also Known As:** Estacion Experimental Agro-Industrial Obispo Colombres.

OBSERVATOIRE ROYAL DE BELGIQUE
See: Royal Belgian Observatory (18733)

OBSERVATORIO INTERAMERICANO DE CERRO TOLOLO
See: Cerro Tololo Inter-American Observatory (18343)

OESTERREICHISCHES OST- UND SUDOSTEUROPA-INSTITUT
See: Austrian Institute of East and Southeast European Studies (18287)

★18668★
ORGANISATION OF EASTERN CARIBBEAN STATES, ECONOMIC AFFAIRS SECRETARIAT - LIBRARY (Bus-Fin)
P.O. Box 822 Phone: 462-1530
St. John's, Antigua-Barbuda Sue Evan-Wong, Doc.
Founded: 1981. **Subjects:** Economic integration within the Eastern Caribbean in the areas of trade and commercial policies, agriculture, industry, energy, tourism, and manpower development. **Holdings:** 8000 volumes. **Remarks:** Telex: 2157.

ORGANISATION DE LOS ESTADOS AMERICANOS - INSTITUTO INDIGENISTA INTERAMERICANO
See: Organization of American States - Inter-American Indian Institute (18669)

ORGANISATION INTERNATIONALE DU CAFE
See: International Coffee Organization (18544)

ORGANISATION INTERNATIONALE DE PROTECTION CIVILE
See: International Civil Defense Organization (18543)

ORGANISATION REGIONALE AFRICAINE DE NORMALISATION
See: African Regional Organization for Standardization (18262)

★18669★
ORGANIZATION OF AMERICAN STATES - INTER-AMERICAN INDIAN INSTITUTE - LIBRARY (Area-Ethnic)
Insurgentes Sur, 1690 Phone: 5 24-10-03
01030 Mexico, DF, Mexico Hilda Obregon, Libn.
Subjects: Indians of the Americas, anthropology. **Holdings:** 50,000 books. **Also Known As:** Organisation de los Estados Americanos - Instituto Indigenista Interamericano.

ORGANIZATION INTERNACIONAL DEL TRABAJO - INTER-AMERICAN CENTER FOR RESEARCH AND DOCUMENTATION ON VOCATIONAL TRAINING
See: Inter-American Center for Research and Documentation on Vocational Training (18530)

ORGANIZATION OF THE ISLAMIC CONFERENCE - RESEARCH CENTER OF ISLAMIC HISTORY, ART AND CULTURE
See: Research Center for Islamic History, Art and Culture (18725)

ORIENTAL HEALING ARTS INSTITUTE - BRION RESEARCH INSTITUTE OF TAIWAN
See: Brion Research Institute of Taiwan (18314)

ORSZAGOS MUSZAKI INFORMACIOS KOZPONT ES KONYVTAR
See: National Technical Information Centre and Library (18648)

ORSZAGOS SZECHENYI KONYVTAR - KONYVTARTUDOMANYI ES MODSZERTANI KOZPONT
See: National Szechenyi Library - Centre for Library Science and Methodology (18647)

OSTEUROPA-INSTITUT MUNCHEN
See: East European Institute, Munich (18389)

JOHN OXLEY LIBRARY
See: State Library of Queensland (18791)

OY KESKUSLABORATORIO - CENTRALLABORATORIUM AB
See: Finnish Pulp and Paper Research Institute (18415)

P

★18670★
PACIFIC REGIONAL SEMINARY - LIBRARY (Rel-Phil)
P.O. Box 1200 Phone: 22648
Suva, Fiji Rev. J.M. Pusateri, S.M., Libn.
Subjects: Catholic theology, religion, philosophy. **Special Collections:** Pacific Collection. **Holdings:** 10,000 books. **Services:** Interlibrary loan; copying; library open to the public.

★18671★
PAKISTAN - MINISTRY OF FOOD, AGRICULTURE AND COOPERATIVES - DEPARTMENT OF PLANT PROTECTION - LIBRARY (Biol Sci)
Jinnah Ave., Malir Halt Phone: 21 480111
Karachi 27, Pakistan Miss Nuzhat Mustafa, Libn.
Subjects: Entomology, mycology, plant pathology. **Holdings:** 14,000 volumes.

★18672★
PAKISTAN - PLANNING AND DEVELOPMENT DIVISION - PAKISTAN INSTITUTE OF DEVELOPMENT ECONOMICS - LIBRARY (Bus-Fin, Soc Sci)
Quaid-I-Azam University Campus
P.O. Box 1091 Phone: 826911
Islamabad, Pakistan Mr. Zafar Javed Naqvi, Libn.
Subjects: Economics, Islamic economics, demography, agricultural and rural development, industrial growth, international trade, fiscal and monetary policy, health, education, housing. **Holdings:** 23,380 volumes. **Remarks:** Telex: 5602 PIDE.

★18673★
PAKISTAN INSTITUTE OF COTTON RESEARCH AND TECHNOLOGY - LIBRARY (Sci-Engr)
Moulvi Tamizuddin Khan Rd. Phone: 21 512238
Karachi, Pakistan Miss Rafia Sultana, Libn.
Subjects: Textile technology. **Holdings:** 15,000 volumes. **Remarks:** Affiliated with Pakistan Central Cotton Committee.

★18674★
PAN AMERICAN CENTER FOR SANITARY ENGINEERING AND ENVIRONMENTAL SCIENCES - LIBRARY (Sci-Engr, Env-Cons)
Los Pinos
Urbanizacion Camacho Phone: 14 354135
Lima 12, Peru Carmen Nieto, Libn.
Subjects: Environmental health, sanitary engineering. **Holdings:** 18,000 volumes. **Remarks:** A regional center of the Pan American Sanitary Bureau - Environmental Health Program. Telex: 21052. **Also Known As:** Centro Panamericano de Ingenieria Sanitaria y Ciencias del Ambiente.

★18675★
PAN AMERICAN HEALTH ORGANIZATION - CARIBBEAN FOOD AND NUTRITION INSTITUTE - LIBRARY (Med, Food-Bev)
University of the West Indies, Mona Campus
P.O. Box 140 Phone: (809)927-1540-1
Kingston 7, Jamaica Yvonne Campbell, Libn.
Staff: Prof 1; Other 1. **Subjects:** Caribbean area - nutrition, food issues, public health. **Holdings:** 6000 books; 1071 bound periodical volumes; 1803 documents; 164 AV programs; theses. **Services:** Interlibrary loan; copying; SDI; library open to the public for reference use only. **Remarks:** Maintains a branch library at the University of West Indies campus in Trinidad.

★18676★
PAN AMERICAN HEALTH ORGANIZATION - CENTER FOR SANITARY ENGINEERING & ENVIRONMENTAL SCIENCES - INFORMATION & DOCUMENTATION NETWORK (Env-Cons, Sci-Engr)
Los Pinos 259
Urbanizacion Camacho Phone: 14 354135
Lima 12, Peru Orlando Arboleda, Mgr.
Subjects: Sanitation, water supply, sanitary and environmental engineering. **Holdings:** 24,000 volumes; documents. **Subscriptions:** 200 journals and other serials. **Services:** SDI. **Computerized Information Services:** REPINDEX, Directory of Water and Sanitation Institutions in Latin America and the Caribbean, MISCA Microthesaurus (internal databases). Performs searches on fee basis. **Publications:** TABCONT/CEPIS, bimonthly; REPIDISCA Newsletter, quarterly. **Special Indexes:** REPINDEX (author index, in Spanish), quarterly.

★18677★
PAN-AMERICAN HEALTH ORGANIZATION - NUTRITION INSTITUTE OF CENTRAL AMERICA AND PANAMA - LIBRARY (Med)
Carretera Roosevelt
Zona 11
Apartado Postal 1188 Phone: 723765
Guatemala City, Guatemala Lidia Lopez, Libn.
Subjects: Human and animal nutrition, public health, food technology. **Holdings:** 32,000 volumes. **Also Known As:** Instituto de Nutricion de Centroamerica y Panama.

★18678★
PAN AMERICAN INSTITUTE OF GEOGRAPHY AND HISTORY - LIBRARY (Geog-Map)
Ex-Arzobispado 29
Col. Observatorio
Mexico City 18, D.F., Mexico Phone: 905 2775888
Subjects: Cartography, geography, history, geophysics. **Holdings:** 150,000 volumes. **Computerized Information Services:** Internal database.

★18679★
PAPUA NEW GUINEA - DEPARTMENT OF CULTURE AND TOURISM - INSTITUTE OF PAPUA NEW GUINEA STUDIES - LIBRARY (Area-Ethnic)
P.O. Box 1432 Phone: 25-4644
Boroko, National Capital District, Papua New Guinea
Dr. John Kolia, Libn.
Subjects: Papua New Guinea - music, oral history, ethnology, literature, film. **Holdings:** 5000 volumes.

★18680★
PARLIAMENT OF ZIMBABWE - LIBRARY OF PARLIAMENT (Area-Ethnic, Soc Sci)
P.O. Box 8055 Causeway Phone: 700181
Harare, Zimbabwe W.H.C. Gurure, Chf.Libn.
Staff: Prof 6; Other 2. **Subjects:** Politics and government, social sciences, history and political biography, education, science and technology, English literature. **Special Collections:** Zimbabweana (500 items). **Holdings:** 100,030 volumes; 20,000 legal, official, and parliamentary documents; 60 microforms. **Subscriptions:** 300 journals and other serials; 25 newspapers. **Services:** Interlibrary loan; library not open to the public. **Publications:** Library Guide. **Special Indexes:** Newspaper index.

★18681★
PASTEUR INSTITUTE - LIBRARY (Biol Sci, Med)
25 et 28, rue du Docteur Roux Phone: 45 68 80 00
75015 Paris, France Mrs. Dubois, Chf.Libn.
Subjects: Microbiology, virology, immunology, biochemistry, cell and molecular biology, pharmacology, developmental biology, mycology, protozoology, medicine. **Holdings:** 120,000 volumes. **Also Known As:** Institut Pasteur.

★18682★
PASTEUR INSTITUTE OF ALGERIA - LIBRARY (Biol Sci)
Rue du Dr. Laveran Phone: 653496
Algiers, Algeria Jamila Arib, Libn.
Subjects: Microbiology, immunology, life sciences. **Holdings:** 55,000 volumes. **Remarks:** Sponsored by the Pasteur Institute in Paris. Also affiliated with Algeria - Ministry of Public Health. **Also Known As:** Institut Pasteur d'Algerie.

★18683★
PEOPLE'S REPUBLIC OF CHINA - MINISTRY OF COMMUNICATIONS - SHANGHAI SHIP AND SHIPPING RESEARCH INSTITUTE - LIBRARY (Trans)
60 Minsheng Lu
Shanghai, People's Republic of China Phone: 840438
Subjects: Shipping economics; ship evaluation, performance, structure, automation; marine engineering; marine navigation; navigation instruments and equipment; anti-corrosion and anti-fouling techniques for ships; computers. **Holdings:** 47,000 volumes; 1700 periodicals; 3800 technical reports. **Services:** Interlibrary loan; copying. **Publications:** Journal of Shanghai Ship and Shipping Research Institute; Navigation Science and

Technology Information, monthly; The Journal of Navigation of China, semiannual (all have contents and summaries in English) - all on exchange.

★18684★
PEOPLE'S REPUBLIC OF CHINA - MINISTRY OF LIGHT INDUSTRY - SALT INDUSTRY RESEARCH INSTITUTE - SCIENTIFIC AND TECHNICAL LIBRARY (Sci-Engr)
15 Yingkoudao
Tanggu District
Tianjin, People's Republic of China Ge Wenming, Libn.
Founded: 1955. **Staff:** 2. **Subjects:** Salt manufacturing technology, machinery, equipment; salt analysis; comprehensive utilization of sea water. **Holdings:** 5660 volumes; 634 periodicals; 7721 technical reports; 1900 AV programs and microforms. **Services:** Interlibrary loan (limited); copying. **Computerized Information Services:** Internal database.

PEOPLE'S REPUBLIC OF CHINA - NATIONAL GEOLOGICAL LIBRARY
See: National Geological Library (18622)

★18685★
PEOPLE'S REPUBLIC OF CHINA - STATE ADMINISTRATION OF PUBLICATIONS - ARCHIVES LIBRARY OF CHINESE PUBLICATIONS (Info Sci)
32 Bei Zhongbu Hutong
Dongcheng District Phone: 1 553694
Beijing, People's Republic of China Song Zhicheng, Libn.
Founded: 1950. **Staff:** 60. **Subjects:** Chinese Government documents. **Holdings:** 1 million volumes; 5000 periodicals; reproductions of paintings; picture-story books; textbooks; braille books; facsimiles of Chinese ancient and rare books. **Services:** Archives open to publishers only. **Special Catalogs:** National Catalogue of New Books, monthly; National General Catalogue, annual; Catalogue of Chinese Ancient Books, irregular; Catalogue of Translations of Foreign Classics, irregular; National General Catalogue of Juvenile Books, irregular.

PETERBOROUGH CATHEDRAL LIBRARY
See: University of Cambridge - Library (18846)

PETROLEO BRASILEIRO, S.A. - LEOPOLDO A. MIGUEZ DE MELLO RESEARCH AND DEVELOPMENT CENTER
See: Leopolde A. Miguez de Mello Research and Development Center (18607)

★18686★
PHILIPPINE INVENTION DEVELOPMENT INSTITUTE - PIDI LIBRARY (Sci-Engr)
General Santos Ave.
Bicutan, Taguig Phone: 2 822-09-61
Manila, Philippines Mrs. Levita Portugal, Libn.
Subjects: Local and foreign patents, science, technology, inventions. **Holdings:** 10,000 volumes. **Remarks:** Maintained by Philippines - Ministry of Science and Technology. Telex: 23312 RHPA.

PHILIPPINES - MINISTRY OF SCIENCE AND TECHNOLOGY - PHILIPPINE INVENTION DEVELOPMENT INSTITUTE
See: Philippine Invention Development Institute (18686)

★18687★
PIARIST CENTRAL LIBRARY (Rel-Phil)
Mikszath Kalman ter 1 Phone: 1 330-701
H-1444 Budapest 8, Hungary Dr. Laszlo Mihaly, Libn.
Subjects: Piarist authors. **Holdings:** 100,000 books; 8000 bound periodical volumes. **Remarks:** Maintained by Magyarorszagi Kegyestanitorend/Piaristak. **Also Known As:** Kegyesrendi Kozponti Konyvtar.

★18688★
MAX PLANCK INSTITUTE FOR BIOPHYSICAL CHEMISTRY - OTTO HAHN LIBRARY (Biol Sci, Sci-Engr)
Am Fassberg 2
Postfach 2841 Phone: 551 201 349
D-3400 Goettingen, Federal Republic of Germany
Bernhard Reuse, Hd.Libn.
Founded: 1947. **Staff:** Prof 3; Other 4. **Subjects:** Biochemistry, physics, neurobiology, spectroscopy, laser physics, molocular biology, biochemical kinetics, membrane physics, cell physiology, molecular genetics. **Holdings:** 32,000 books; 55,000 bound periodical volumes. **Subscriptions:** 760 journals and other serials; 14 newspapers. **Services:** Copying; library open to the public for reference use only. **Also Known As:** Max-Planck-Institut fuer Biophysikalische Chemie - Otto-Hahn-Bibliothek.

★18689★
MAX PLANCK INSTITUTE FOR BRAIN RESEARCH - LIBRARY (Med)
Deutschordenstrasse 46
Postfach 710409
D-6000 Frankfurt 71, Federal Republic of Germany
Phone: 89 6 70 41
Subjects: Brain research. **Holdings:** 18,000 volumes. **Also Known As:** Max-Planck-Institut fuer Hirnforschung.

★18690★
MAX PLANCK INSTITUTE FOR BREEDING RESEARCH - LIBRARY (Biol Sci)
Egelspfad Phone: 5 06 21
D-5000 Cologne 30, Federal Republic of Germany
Christa Weinke, Libn.
Subjects: Plant genetics. **Holdings:** 15,500 volumes. **Also Known As:** Max-Planck-Institut fuer Zuechtungforschung.

★18691★
MAX PLANCK INSTITUTE FOR COMPARATIVE PUBLIC LAW AND INTERNATIONAL LAW - LIBRARY (Law)
Berliner Strasse 48 Phone: 6221 48 21
D-6900 Heidelberg, Federal Republic of Germany
Joachim Schwietzke, Libn.
Holdings: Public law - foreign, international, comparative; international organizations. **Holdings:** 315,000 volumes. **Also Known As:** Max-Planck-Institut fuer Auslaendisches Oeffentliches Recht und Voelkerrecht.

★18692★
MAX PLANCK INSTITUTE FOR DEVELOPMENTAL BIOLOGY - LIBRARY (Med, Biol Sci)
Spemannstrasse 35 Phone: 60 13 17
D-7400 Tuebingen, Federal Republic of Germany Ursel Zeug, Libn.
Subjects: Virology, immunology, biology. **Holdings:** 27,700 books. **Subscriptions:** 350 journals and other serials. **Formerly:** Max-Planck-Institut fuer Virusforschung. **Also Known As:** Max-Planck-Institut fuer Entwicklungsbiologie.

★18693★
MAX PLANCK INSTITUTE FOR FOREIGN AND INTERNATIONAL PATENT, COPYRIGHT, AND COMPETITION LAW - LIBRARY (Law)
Siebertstrasse 3 Phone: 89 92461
D-8000 Munich 80, Federal Republic of Germany Dr. J. Straus, Libn.
Founded: 1966. **Staff:** Prof 5; Other 5. **Subjects:** Law - industrial property, copyright, competition, antitrust. **Holdings:** 70,000 books; 21,000 bound periodical volumes; 6000 microfiche. **Subscriptions:** 750 journals and other serials; 7 newspapers. **Services:** Copying; library open to the public by appointment. **Also Known As:** Max-Planck-Institut fuer Auslaendisches und Internationales Patent-, Urheber-, und Wettbewerbsrecht. **Staff:** Monika Valenta, Supv.Libn.; Sabine Von Brescius, Libn.; Mrs. Anke Rohrbacher, Libn.; Elke List, Libn..

★18694★
MAX PLANCK INSTITUTE FOR FOREIGN AND INTERNATIONAL PRIVATE LAW - LIBRARY (Law)
Mittelweg 187 Phone: 40 41271
D-2000 Hamburg 13, Federal Republic of Germany
Dr. Ralph Lansky, Lib.Dir.
Founded: 1926. **Staff:** Prof 12; Other 6. **Subjects:** Law - private international, private, economic, comparative; unification of law. **Holdings:** 270,000 volumes; 2500 other cataloged items. **Subscriptions:** 2000 journals and other serials; 12 newspapers. **Services:** Copying; library open to the public with restrictions. **Automated Operations:** Computerized serials. **Publications:** The Library of the Max Planck Institute for Foreign and International Private Law, Hamburg; Information and Regulations for Visitors on the Use of this Library (with bibliography, 1987). **Also Known As:** Max-Planck-Institut fuer Auslaendisches und Internationales Privatrecht. **Staff:** Dr. Juergen Goedan; Jutta Voss; Ruediger Baatz; Vera Klemp.

★18695★
MAX PLANCK INSTITUTE FOR FOREIGN AND INTERNATIONAL SOCIAL LAW - LIBRARY (Law)
Leopold Strasse 24
Postfach 440109 Phone: 89 38 60 21
D-8000 Munich 40, Federal Republic of Germany
Mrs. I. Deltaglia, Libn.
Subjects: Law - social, welfare, social security. **Holdings:** 25,000 volumes. **Also Known As:** Max-Planck-Institut fuer Auslaendisches und Internationales Sozialrecht.

★18696★
MAX PLANCK INSTITUTE OF HISTORY - LIBRARY (Hist)
Hermann-Foege-Weg 11 Phone: 49560
D-3400 Goettingen, Federal Republic of Germany Ursala Beiss, Libn.
Subjects: History - social, institutional, intellectual, economic, legal, educational. **Holdings:** 62,000 volumes. **Also Known As:** Max-Planck-Institut fuer Geschichte.

★18697★
MAX PLANCK INSTITUTE OF LIMNOLOGY - LIBRARY (Biol Sci)
August-Thienemann-Strasse 2
Postfach 165 Phone: 50 21
D-2320 Plon, Federal Republic of Germany Brigitte Lechner, Libn.
Subjects: Limnology, tropical ecology, plankton. **Holdings:** 11,000 volumes. **Also Known As:** Max-Planck-Institut fuer Limnologie.

★18698★
MAX PLANCK INSTITUTE FOR METALS RESEARCH - LIBRARY (Sci-Engr)
Heisenbergstrasse 1 Phone: 6860-229
D-7000 Stuttgart 80, Federal Republic of Germany
Ingeborg Jaiser, Libn.
Staff: Prof 3. **Subjects:** Solid state physics, semiconductors, electron microscopy, magnetism, superconductivity. **Holdings:** 10,000 books; 13,000 bound periodical volumes. **Subscriptions:** 299 journals and other serials. **Services:** Library not open to the public. **Remarks:** Telex: Nr. 7-255 555. **Also Known As:** Max-Planck-Institut fuer Metallforschung. **Staff:** Ute Muller, Libn.; Daniela Kabinova, Libn..

★18699★
MAX PLANCK INSTITUTE FOR NUTRITION PHYSIOLOGY - LIBRARY (Biol Sci, Med)
Rheinlanddamm 201 Phone: 1 20 61
D-4600 Dortmund 1, Federal Republic of Germany
Ute Graesiek, Libn.
Subjects: Biochemistry, physiology, metabolic processes. **Holdings:** 16,600 volumes. **Also Known As:** Max-Planck-Institut fuer Ernahrungsphysiologie.

★18700★
MAX PLANCK INSTITUTE OF PLASMA PHYSICS - LIBRARY (Sci-Engr)
Boltzmannstrasse 2 Phone: 3 29 91
D-8046 Garching, Federal Republic of Germany
Angelika Hohaus, Libn.
Subjects: Controlled nuclear fusion, plasma physics in the development of a fusion reactor. **Holdings:** 42,000 books; 21,000 bound periodical volumes; 50,000 reports. **Subscriptions:** 580 journals and other serials. **Services:** Library not open to the public. **Automated Operations:** Computerized cataloging. **Also Known As:** Max-Planck-Institut fuer Plasmaphysik.

★18701★
MAX PLANCK INSTITUTE FOR PSYCHIATRY - LIBRARY (Med)
Kraepelinstrasse 2 and 10 Phone: 30 622333
D-8000 Munich 40, Federal Republic of Germany
Angelika Kaufmann, Libn.
Subjects: Normal/abnormal function of the nerve system: neuromorphology, neurochemistry, primate behavior, neuropharmacology, neurophysiology; clinical research: adult psychiatry, neurology and neuroradiology, neuropsychology, child psychiatry, clinical chemistry, clinical neurophysiology, and experimental, social, and clinical psychology. **Holdings:** 38,000 volumes. **Remarks:** A branch library is maintained at Am Klopferspitz 18 A, D-8033 Martinsried, Federal Republic of Germany; telephone: 85 783529. **Also Known As:** Max-Planck-Institut fuer Psychiatrie. **Staff:** Judith Sidorenko-Wurm, Br.Libn..

★18702★
MAX PLANCK INSTITUTE FOR RADIO ASTRONOMY - LIBRARY (Sci-Engr)
Auf dem Huegel 69
D-5300 Bonn 1, Federal Republic of Germany Phone: 52 51
Subjects: Radio astronomy, radio spectroscopy. **Holdings:** 11,000 volumes. **Also Known As:** Max-Planck-Institut fuer Radioastronomie. **Staff:** Karina Kaulins, Libn.; Silke Niehaus-Weingartner, Libn..

★18703★
MAX PLANCK INSTITUTE FOR SYSTEM PHYSIOLOGY - LIBRARY (Med)
Rheinlanddamm 201 Phone: 120 640 80
D-4600 Dortmund 1, Federal Republic of Germany
Mrs. Ute Grzesiek, Libn.
Subjects: System physiology, solute transport in epithelia, differentiation of epithelial cells. **Holdings:** 16,000 volumes. **Also Known As:** Max-Planck-Institut fuer Systemphysiologie.

★18704★
POLAND - MINISTRY OF HEALTH AND SOCIAL WELFARE - NATIONAL RESEARCH INSTITUTE OF MOTHER AND CHILD - LIBRARY (Med)
Kasprzaka 17 Phone: 32-68-58
PL-01-211 Warsaw, Poland Wanda Foltyn, Libn.
Subjects: Reproduction, child growth and development. **Holdings:** 17,000 volumes. **Also Known As:** Instytut Matki i Dziecka.

POLAND - MINISTRY OF HIGHER EDUCATION, SCIENCE AND TECHNOLOGY - INSTITUTE FOR SCIENTIFIC, TECHNICAL AND ECONOMIC INFORMATION
See: Institute for Scientific, Technical and Economic Information (18521)

★18705★
POLISH ACADEMY OF SCIENCES - CENTER FOR STUDIES ON NON-EUROPEAN COUNTRIES - LIBRARY (Area-Ethnic)
ulica Nowy Swiat 72 Phone: 22 26-52-31
PL-00-330 Warsaw, Poland Irena Wojsz, Libn.
Subjects: Social and cultural problems of Asia, Africa, Latin America. **Holdings:** 50,000 volumes.

★18706★
POLISH ACADEMY OF SCIENCES - GDANSK LIBRARY (Hum, Soc Sci, Area-Ethnic)
Walowa 15 Phone: 31-22-51
PL-80-858 Gdansk, Poland Dr. Jadwiga Wroblewska
Subjects: Humanities, social sciences, maritime studies, Pomeranian and Gdansk affairs. **Holdings:** 467,826 books; 60,012 bound periodical volumes; 14,254 documents; 3056 AV programs; 4601 manuscripts; 15th-20th century: 54,881 prints; 6404 graphics; 6421 maps; 11,827 exlibrises/bookplates; 2627 numismatic materials. **Services:** Interlibrary loan; copying; library open to the public for reference use only. **Publications:** Libri Gedanenses, 1967-1975; Rocznik Gdanski, semiannual. **Special Catalogs:** Catalogs of manuscripts, old books, incunabula, graphics, maps, numismatics, exlibrises, photographs to 1945, books, 1800 to present. **Also Known As:** Polska Akademia Nauk - Biblioteka Gdanska. **Staff:** Zbigniew Nowak, Docent.

★18707★
POLISH ACADEMY OF SCIENCES - INSTITUTE OF ART - LIBRARY (Art, Mus, Theater)
ulica Dluga 26/28
P.O. Box 994 Phone: 31 31 49
00-950 Warsaw, Poland Dr. Wojciech Miszczuk, Hd.Libn.
Subjects: History and theory of fine arts, music, theater, film, and folklore. **Holdings:** 106,000 volumes. **Also Known As:** Instytut Sztuki.

POLISH ACADEMY OF SCIENCES - INSTITUTE OF FUNDAMENTAL TECHNOLOGICAL RESEARCH
See: Institute of Fundamental Technological Research (18510)

★18708★
POLISH ACADEMY OF SCIENCES - INSTITUTE OF THE HISTORY OF MATERIAL CULTURE - LIBRARY (Area-Ethnic, Soc Sci)
Swierczewskiego 105 Phone: 22 20-28-81
PL-00-140 Warsaw, Poland Piotr Podgorski, Libn.
Subjects: Prehistoric and medieval archeology of Poland; classical archeology; ethnology of Poland, Slavonic peoples, Central Asia,

Mesoamerica; history of material culture of medieval and modern Poland. **Holdings:** 60,000 volumes.

★18709★
POLISH ACADEMY OF SCIENCES - L. HIRSZFELD INSTITUTE OF IMMUNOLOGY AND EXPERIMENTAL THERAPY - LIBRARY (Med, Biol Sci)
ulica Czerska 12 Phone: 67-94-24
PL-53-114 Wroclaw, Poland Helena Kopec, Libn.
Subjects: Immunology, microbiology, biochemistry, experimental therapy. **Holdings:** 7500 books. **Subscriptions:** 9000 journals and other serials. **Remarks:** Telex: 7151210. **Also Known As:** Instytut Immunologii i Terapii Doswiadczalnej im. Ludwika Hirszfelda.

★18710★
POLISH ACADEMY OF SCIENCES - LITERARY RESEARCH INSTITUTE - LIBRARY (Hum)
ulica Nowy Swiat 72 Phone: 26-68-63
PL-00-330 Warsaw, Poland Edward Ruziewicz, Libn.
Staff: Prof 17; Other 5. **Subjects:** Literary theory, Polish literature and culture. **Holdings:** 166,000 books; 34,000 bound periodical volumes; 83,000 other cataloged items. **Subscriptions:** 500 journals and other serials. **Services:** Interlibrary loan; copying; library open to the public. **Also Known As:** Instytut Badan Literackich.

★18711★
POLISH INSTITUTE OF INTERNATIONAL AFFAIRS - DEPARTMENT FOR SCIENTIFIC INFORMATION - LIBRARY (Soc Sci)
1a ulica Warecka
Skrytka Pocztowa 1000 Phone: 22 27-28-26
PL-00-950 Warsaw, Poland Leszek Cyrzyk
Subjects: Contemporary international relations, international law, politics, military affairs, economics, social affairs. **Special Collections:** United Nations depository library; European Documentation Center of the European Economic Community; League of Nations publications. **Holdings:** 85,000 books; 35,000 bound periodical volumes; 5000 microforms. **Services:** Interlibrary loan; library open to academic users only. **Publications:** List of Acquisitions, bimonthly; selected bibliographies, irregular.

★18712★
POLISH SOCIAL AND CULTURAL ASSOCIATION - LIBRARY (Area-Ethnic)
238/246 King St. Phone: 1 741 1940
London W6 0RF, England Dr. Z. Zagodzinski
Founded: 1964. **Subjects:** Polish culture, history, literature; World War II. **Holdings:** 100,000 volumes. **Remarks:** Library is the seat of the International Conrad Society.

POLITECHNIKA WROCLAWSKA - BIBLIOTEKA GLOWNA I OSRODEK INFORMACJI NAUKOWO-TECHNICZNEJ
See: Technical University of Wroclaw - Main Library and Scientific Information Center (18817)

POLSKA AKADEMIA NAUK - BIBLIOTEKA GDANSKA
See: Polish Academy of Sciences - Gdansk Library (18706)

★18713★
PONTIFICAL INSTITUTE OF SPIRITUALITY OF THE TERESIANUM - LIBRARY (Rel-Phil)
Piazza San Pancrazio 5/a Phone: 6 58 23 62
I-00152 Rome, Italy Fr. Faustino Macchiella, Libn.
Subjects: Spiritual theology. **Holdings:** 150,000 volumes. **Publications:** Bibliographia Internationalis Spiritualitatis. **Also Known As:** Pontificio Instituto di Spiritualita del Teresianum.

★18714★
PONTIFICIA UNIVERSIDAD CATOLICA DEL PERU - BIBLIOTECA CENTRAL (Hum, Law, Hist)
Av. Universitaria Cuadra 18 s/n Phone: 14 622540
Lima 32, Peru Carmen Villanueva, Hd.
Staff: Prof 18; Other 62. **Subjects:** Literature, linguistics, history, law, pure sciences and engineering, social sciences, theology, arts. **Special Collections:** Coleccion Sabroso (political party documents); Coleccion Majluf; Coleccion Martin Adan (manuscripts of poems); Coleccion Universidades (original documents and publications from universities). **Holdings:** 250,000 books; 92,000 unbound periodical volumes; 30,000 documents; 35,000 slides. **Subscriptions:** 770 journals and other serials; 30 newspapers. **Services:** Interlibrary loan; copying; SDI; library open to the public with letter of presentation. **Automated Operations:** Computerized serials. **Computerized Information Services:** BIB-SOC, C-DOC (internal databases). **Publications:** Current awareness bulletins (social sciences, pure sciences, theology), bimonthly. **Remarks:** Maintains 8 campus libraries. **Staff:** Ana Maria Talavera, Hd., Tech.Serv..

★18715★
PONTIFICIA UNIVERSIDAD CATOLICA DEL PERU - RIVA-AGUERO INSTITUTE - LIBRARY (Area-Ethnic)
Jiron Camana 459 Phone: (14)277-678
Lima 1, Peru Alejandro Lostaunau, Libn.
Subjects: Peruvian history, hispanic literature. **Holdings:** 60,000 volumes. **Also Known As:** Instituto Riva-Aguero.

★18716★
PORTUGAL - MINISTERIO DA HABITADAO E OBRAS PUBLICAS - LABORATORIO NACIONAL DE ENGENHARIA CIVIL - LIBRARY (Sci-Engr)
Avenida do Brasil, 101 Phone: 1 882131
P-1799 Lisbon Codex, Portugal Eduardo Sampaio Franco, Res.Off.
Subjects: Building, construction and materials, structures, geotechnics, hydraulics, roads, airfields, dams. **Holdings:** 105,000 books; 1500 bound periodical volumes. **Services:** Copying; SDI; library open to the public. **Computerized Information Services:** Telesystemes Questel, DIALOG Information Services, ESA/IRS. Performs searches on fee basis. **Publications:** Technical papers, standards, specifications, handbooks.

PORTUGAL - MINISTRY OF EDUCATION - INSTITUTE OF ANTHROPOLOGY
See: Institute of Anthropology (18497)

PROGRAMA DE LAS NACIONES UNIDAS PARA EL MEDIO AMBIENTE
See: United Nations Environment Programme (18832)

★18717★
PRUSSIAN CULTURAL FOUNDATION - LIBRARY (Area-Ethnic, Law)
Potsdamer Strasse 33
Postfach 1407 Phone: 30 266-1
D-1000 Berlin 30, Federal Republic of Germany
Dr. Richard Landwehrmeyer, Dir.Gen.
Subjects: Jurisprudence; Oriental studies; Chinese, Japanese, Korean, and Southeast Asian studies; Eastern European studies; cartography; topography. **Special Collections:** Manuscripts (10,160 occidental manuscripts; 3130 incunabula; 4300 autographs; 425 collections of personal papers; rare printing and bindings, post-1500); music collection (20,680 musical manuscripts; 230,000 music printings; 13,000 libretti; musicology literature; Mendelssohn-Archive); maps and atlases, 16th-20th centuries (430,000 maps; 30,000 volumes of cartographic literature and atlases); Eastern European literature (390,000 volumes); Oriental manuscripts (32,370 manuscripts; 104,000 films of Nepalese, Indian, and Ethiopian manuscripts); East Asian literature (240,000 volumes); official publications (federal and state documents; parliamentary and government publications of 30 foreign states; publications of 70 international organizations; 30,000 volumes of old parliamentary papers); picture archive (5 million photographs, graphics, engravings, woodcuts, lithographs; 12,000 slides). **Holdings:** 3.7 million volumes; 605,000 microforms; 63,210 manuscripts. **Subscriptions:** 30,635 periodicals and newspapers. **Services:** Interlibrary loan; copying; library open to the public. **Computerized Information Services:** STN International, JURIS (Justice Retrieval and Inquiry System), DIMDI, DIALOG Information Services, Data-Star, Deutsches Bibliotheksinstitut (DBI), INKADATA (Informationssystem Karlsruhe), FIZ Technik, GID-IZ, ECHO (European Commission Host Organization). Performs searches on fee basis for Berlin residents. Contact Person: Johannes Ziegler, 266-2235. **Publications:** Jahresbericht; Mitteilungen, 3/year; additional publications available. **Special Catalogs:** Katalog der Bestande zum anglo-amerikanischen Recht (catalog of library holdings in Anglo-American Law); additional catalogs available. **Staff:** Dr. Gunter Baron, Dp.Dir..

PUSA LIBRARY
See: Indian Agricultural Research Institute (18489)

R

★18718★
RADIO FREE EUROPE/RADIO LIBERTY - RADIO LIBERTY RESEARCH - RFE/RL LIBRARY (Info Sci, Soc Sci)
D-8000 Munich 22, Federal Republic of Germany Keith Bush, Dir.
Subjects: East European, Soviet, and world affairs. **Special Collections:** Radio Liberty Samizdat Archive ("self-published writing" from the USSR). **Holdings:** 102,000 volumes - 35,000 in 6 East European languages, 29,000 in Russian and Soviet languages, 38,000 in western languages. **Subscriptions:** 600 Soviet, Western, and emigre newspapers and periodicals.

★18719★
RAILWAYS LIBRARY (Trans, Sci-Engr)
Daliushu North Stop
Xizhimenwai
Beijing, People's Republic of China Gao Wen, Dp.Libn.
Founded: 1950. **Staff:** 25. **Subjects:** Railroads, electric engineering, electronics, machinery, metallurgy, construction, chemical engineering. **Holdings:** 168,223 volumes; 116,594 other cataloged items. **Subscriptions:** 2200 journals and other serials. **Services:** Interlibrary loan; copying. **Special Catalogs:** Catalog of Foreign Periodicals for Subscription; Catalog of Foreign Books.

★18720★
RAPRA TECHNOLOGY - LIBRARY (Sci-Engr)
Shawbury
Shrewsbury, Shropshire SY4 4NR, England Phone: 939 250383
Subjects: Rubber, plastics, polymer synthesis. **Holdings:** 45,000 volumes, pieces of trade literature, standards, specifications, government reports. **Remarks:** Telex: 35134.

★18721★
RED NOTES ITALY BULLETIN - LIBRARY (Area-Ethnic)
BP 15
2A St. Paul's Rd.
London N1, England Phil Saunders
Founded: 1976. **Subjects:** Italian social, communist, revolutionary movements; Italian culture. **Holdings:** 200 volumes; newspapers; pamphlets.

REGIONAL ARAB BUREAU OF EDUCATION - GULF ARAB STATES EDUCATIONAL RESEARCH CENTER
See: Gulf Arab States Educational Research Center (18459)

★18722★
REGIONAL CONFERENCE ON INTERNATIONAL VOLUNTARY SERVICE - LIBRARY (Soc Sci)
Thomas-Mann-Strasse 52 Phone: 228 65 41 60
D-5300 Bonn 1, Federal Republic of Germany Bernard Gilson
Founded: 1964. **Subjects:** Cooperation between national volunteer organizations in developing countries. **Holdings:** 1000 volumes.

★18723★
REPUBLIC OF CHINA - MINISTRY OF EDUCATION - NATIONAL CENTRAL LIBRARY (Hum, Info Sci)
20 Chung Shan South Rd. Phone: 2 361-9132
Taipei 10040, Taiwan Chen-ku Wang, Dir.
Subjects: Chinese literature, library history and science. **Special Collections:** Chinese rare books. **Holdings:** 900,000 books; 75,000 bound periodical volumes; 19,300 patents and documents; 43,332 microforms; 170,000 volumes of manuscripts. **Services:** Interlibrary loan; copying; library open to the public with restrictions. **Computerized Information Services:** DIALOG Information Services, Mead Data Central. Performs searches on fee basis. Contact Person: Shu-fen Chen. **Publications:** National Bibliography of the Republic of China; A Selection of Newly-Received Western Book Titles; A Monthly Selection of Newly-Received Western Government Publications; Bulletin of the National Central Library; additional publications available. **Special Indexes:** Index to Chinese Periodical Literature of the Republic of China; additional indexes available.

★18724★
REPUBLIC OF IRELAND - DEPARTMENT OF THE TAOISEACH - NATIONAL LIBRARY OF IRELAND (Area-Ethnic, Info Sci)
Kildare St. Phone: 1 765521
Dublin 2, Ireland Michael Hewson, Dir.
Staff: Prof 14; Other 38. **Subjects:** Irish studies; official publications of Ireland, Great Britain, and Europe. **Special Collections:** Dix Collection (early Irish printings; circa 5000 items); Thom Collection (Irish and general literature, history, topography; circa 2000 items); Joly Collection (Irish history and topography, French history; 23,000 volumes). **Holdings:** 500,000 books; 10,000 reels of microfilm; 25,000 manuscripts. **Subscriptions:** 2070 journals and other serials; 90 newspapers. **Services:** Copying; library open to the public with restrictions. **Publications:** Annual report; Sources for the history of Irish Civilisation. **Special Indexes:** Clar Litridheacht na Nua-Ghaeilge 1850-1936 (Index to literature in Irish).

★18725★
RESEARCH CENTER FOR ISLAMIC HISTORY, ART AND CULTURE - IRCICA LIBRARY (Rel-Phil)
Barbaros Bulvari
Yildiz Sarayi
Seyir Kosku, Besiktas Phone: 1 160 59 89
Istanbul, Turkey Mr. Halit Eren, Libn.
Subjects: Islamic history, art, culture, history of science. **Holdings:** 17,000 volumes. **Remarks:** An affiliate of the Organization of the Islamic Conference. Telex: 26484 ISAM.

★18726★
RESEARCH INSTITUTE OF THE FRIEDRICH EBERT FOUNDATION - LIBRARY OF SOCIAL DEMOCRACY (Bus-Fin, Hist)
Godesberger Allee 149 Phone: 0228 8830
D-5300 Bonn 3, Federal Republic of Germany Horst Ziska, Chf.Libn.
Founded: 1969. **Staff:** Prof 34. **Subjects:** German and international labor history, social history, political party and trade union publications. **Holdings:** 300,000 books; 70,000 bound periodical volumes. **Services:** Interlibrary loan; copying; library open to the public. **Publications:** Bibliographie zur Geschichte der deutschen Arbeiterbewegung, quarterly. **Also Known As:** Forschungsinstitut der Friedrich-Ebert Stiftung - Bibliothek der Sozialen Demokratie.

★18727★
RESEARCH INSTITUTE FOR INTERNATIONAL POLITICS AND SECURITY - LIBRARY (Soc Sci)
Stiftung Wissenschaft und Politik Phone: 8178 700
D-8026 Ebenhausen, Federal Republic of Germany
Dietrich Seydel, Hd. of Doc.
Staff: Prof 30; Other 3. **Subjects:** International relations, security, economics; worldwide area studies. **Holdings:** 85,000 volumes; 6000 clippings files. **Subscriptions:** 1000 journals and other serials; 100 newspapers. **Services:** Library open to the public with restrictions. **Automated Operations:** Computerized cataloging, acquisitions, serials, and circulation. **Computerized Information Services:** IRIS (International Relations Information System; internal database). Performs searches on fee basis. Contact Person: Volker Steidle, 70271. **Also Known As:** Forschungsinstitut fuer Internationale Politik und Sicherheit. **Staff:** Gerhard Weiher; Peter Bottger; Matthias Bauermeister; Joachim Held.

RIJKSHERBARIUM
See: National Herbarium of the Netherlands (18623)

★18728★
RISO NATIONAL LABORATORY - RISO LIBRARY (Energy)
P.O. Box 49 Phone: 2 371212
DK-4000 Roskilde, Denmark Birgit Pedersen, Chf.Libn.
Founded: 1957. **Staff:** Prof 8; Other 12. **Subjects:** Energy - biomass, coal, wind, geothermal, nuclear, solar; oil, uranium, and other energy sources; air pollution and environmental issues; heating and power generation; reactors and thermal plants; waste heat utilization. **Holdings:** 60,000 volumes; 500,000 reports. **Subscriptions:** 1700 journals and other serials. **Services:** Interlibrary loan; copying; SDI; library open to the public. **Automated Operations:** Computerized cataloging, acquisitions, and circulation. **Computerized Information Services:** INIS (International Nuclear Information System), U.S. Department of Energy Energy Data Base (EDB), ESA/IRS, DIALOG Information Services, Pergamon ORBIT InfoLine, Inc.; produces Nordic Energy Index (NEI). Performs searches on fee basis. **Publications:** Acquisitions List, 2/week; Periodical Holdings, annual.

RIVA-AGUERO INSTITUTE
See: Pontificia Universidad Catolica del Peru - Riva-Aguero Institute (18715)

ROEMISCSH-GERMANISCHE KOMMISSION DES DEUTSCHEN ARCHAEOLOGISCHEN INSTITUTS
See: Roman-Germanic Commission of German Archaeological Institutes (18729)

★18729★
ROMAN-GERMANIC COMMISSION OF GERMAN ARCHAEOLOGICAL INSTITUTES - LIBRARY (Soc Sci)
Palmengartenstrasse 10-12 Phone: 69 752025
D-6000 Frankfurt am Main, Federal Republic of Germany
Dr. E. Schubert, Libn.
Subjects: European archeology, Stone Age through Middle Ages. **Holdings:** 60,000 volumes. **Also Known As:** Roemiscsh-Germanische Kommission des Deutschen Archaeologischen Instituts.

★18730★
ROMANIA - MINISTRY OF HEALTH - CANTACUZINO INSTITUTE - LIBRARY (Biol Sci)
Splaiul Independentei 103
C.P. 1-525 Phone: 13 97 20
Bucharest 70100, Romania Maria Lucia Sandu, Libn.
Subjects: Bacteriology, virology, parasitology. **Holdings:** 89,000 volumes. **Also Known As:** Institutul Cantacuzino.

ROSARIO NATIONAL UNIVERSITY - FACULTY OF EXACT SCIENCES AND ENGINEERING - ING. JUAN C. VAN WYCK CENTER FOR RESEARCH AND DEVELOPMENT
See: Ing. Juan C. Van Wyck Center for Research and Development (18868)

★18731★
ROYAL ACADEMY OF SCIENCES - NETHERLANDS INSTITUTE FOR DEVELOPMENTAL BIOLOGY - HUBRECHT LABORATORY LIBRARY (Biol Sci)
Uppsalalaan 8 Phone: 30 510211
NL-3584 CT Utrecht, Netherlands Dr. J.G. Bluemink, Hd. of Lib.
Staff: Prof 2; Other 1. **Subjects:** Developmental biology of animals and man; embryology - descriptive, experimental, molecular; recombinant DNA research; developmental genetics; regeneration; asexual reproduction and development; pattern formation. **Holdings:** 3050 books; 4000 bound periodical volumes; 141,000 reprints. **Subscriptions:** 75 journals and other serials. **Services:** Interlibrary loan; copying; library open to biologists and embryologists. **Automated Operations:** Computerized cataloging. **Computerized Information Services:** BIOSIS (BioSciences Information Service); internal database. **Remarks:** Fax: 0031-30-516464. **Formerly:** International Embryological Institute. **Staff:** Miss. O. Kruythof, Libn..

★18732★
ROYAL AERONAUTICAL SOCIETY - LIBRARY (Sci-Engr)
4 Hamilton Place Phone: 1 499-3515
London W1V 0BQ, England A.W.L. Nayler, Libn.
Founded: 1866. **Subjects:** Aerospace engineering and technology. **Special Collections:** Hodgson Collection (700 titles; 600 lithographs); Poynton Collection (100 titles). **Holdings:** 25,000 books; 1000 periodical titles; 75,000 documents; technical reports; photographs. **Subscriptions:** 300 journals and other serials. **Services:** Interlibrary loan; copying; library open to the public on fee basis. **Special Indexes:** Publications index, 1897-1977. **Remarks:** Telex: 262826 RAESOC; Fax: 1 499-6230.

★18733★
ROYAL BELGIAN OBSERVATORY - LIBRARY (Sci-Engr)
3, avenue Circulaire Phone: 2 375 24 84
B-1180 Brussels, Belgium P.H. Dale, Asst.Libn.
Subjects: Astronomy, astrophysics, geophysics, meteorology. **Holdings:** 120,000 volumes. **Remarks:** Maintained by Belgium - Ministry of National Education. Also serves the Royal Meteorological Institute of Belgium. **Also Known As:** Observatoire Royal de Belgique.

★18734★
ROYAL BOTANIC GARDEN, EDINBURGH - LIBRARY (Biol Sci)
Edinburgh EH3 5LR, Scotland Phone: 31 552 7171
Dr. B.J. Coppins, Chm., Lib.Comm.
Founded: 1670. **Subjects:** Botany, horticulture, early medicine and agriculture. **Special Collections:** Pre-Linnean literature; herbals; prints, paintings, and clippings collection; archival collection. **Holdings:** 45,000 books; 70,000 bound periodical volumes; 90 linear feet of microforms; 150,000 manuscripts. **Subscriptions:** 1774 journals and other serials. **Services:** Interlibrary loan; copying; library open to the public with restrictions. **Publications:** History of the Royal Botanic Garden Library, Edinburgh; Ericales bibliography. **Special Indexes:** Periodicals holding list.

★18735★
ROYAL BOTANIC GARDENS, KEW - LIBRARY & ARCHIVES (Biol Sci)
Richmond, Surrey TW9 3AE, England Phone: 1 940 1171
Miss S.M.D. FitzGerald, Chf.Libn. & Archv.
Staff: Prof 7; Other 7. **Subjects:** Plants - taxonomy, distribution, conservation, anatomy, genetics, biochemistry; economic botany; horticulture. **Special Collections:** Pre-Linnean and Linnean collections; botanical illustrations; archives. **Holdings:** 120,000 books; 37,000 bound periodical volumes; 20,000 microforms; 250,000 manuscripts. **Subscriptions:** 2000 journals and other serials. **Services:** Copying; library open to the public by appointment with written application. **Computerized Information Services:** DIALOG Information Services, DIALTECH. **Publications:** Selective bibliographies. **Special Catalogs:** Author and Classified Catalogue (9 volumes; 1974). **Remarks:** Telex: 296 694. **Staff:** John P. Flanagan, Dp.Libn.; Vicki Humphrey, Paper Cons..

★18736★
ROYAL BOTANIC GARDENS & NATIONAL HERBARIUM - LIBRARY (Biol Sci)
Birdwood Ave. Phone: 639424
South Yarra, VIC 3141, Australia H.M. Cohn, Libn.
Subjects: Botany - taxonomic, economic, history; horticulture; landscape architecture. **Holdings:** 36,000 books; 15,000 bound periodical volumes; 8500 microforms; 100 manuscripts. **Services:** Interlibrary loan; copying; library open to the public by appointment. **Special Indexes:** Indexes to Australian taxonomic literature, registered cultivars, botanical collectors and artists, and botanists. **Remarks:** Maintained by Victoria Department of Conservation, Forests and Lands.

★18737★
ROYAL COLLEGE OF NURSING - LIBRARY (Med)
20 Cavendish Square Phone: 1 409 3333
London W1M 0AB, England Miss A. Tucker
Subjects: Nursing, health service, education, psychology, management. **Special Collections:** Steinberg Collection of Nursing Research (400 thesis titles); historical collection (320 linear feet). **Holdings:** 40,000 books; 400 manuscripts. **Services:** Interlibrary loan; copying; SDI; library open to the public with restrictions. **Computerized Information Services:** Data-Star, DIALOG Information Services, ESA/IRS, Scicon Ltd. **Publications:** Nursing bibliography. **Special Catalogs:** Catalog to Steinberg Collection. **Staff:** Mrs. A. Bramley.

★18738★
ROYAL COLLEGE OF PHYSICIANS OF EDINBURGH - LIBRARY (Med)
9 Queen St. Phone: 31 225 7324
Edinburgh EH2 1JQ, Scotland Joan P.S. Ferguson, Libn.
Staff: Prof 2; Other 2. **Subjects:** History of medicine and Scottish medicine. **Special Collections:** Simpson Collection (obstetrics and gynecology); J.W. Ballantyne Collection (fetal pathology). **Holdings:** 300,000 volumes; 1000 volumes of manuscripts. **Subscriptions:** 128 journals and other serials. **Services:** Interlibrary loan; copying; library open to the public. **Publications:** Annual Report. **Special Catalogs:** A Catalogue of Sixteenth-Century Medical Books in Edinburgh Libraries - for sale. **Staff:** Iain Milne, Asst.Libn..

★18739★
ROYAL COLLEGE OF PHYSICIANS OF LONDON - LIBRARY (Med)
11 St. Andrew's Place Phone: 1 935-1174
London NW1 4LE, England Geoffrey Davenport, Libn.
Subjects: Medical history and biography. **Special Collections:** Library of Marquis of Dorchester, 1606-1680 (3000 volumes); Evan Bedford Library of Cardiology (history of cardiology; 1112 books and pamphlets; 215 bound periodical volumes); Heberden Library of British Association of Rheumatology (history of rheumatology; 1200 items); Willan Library of British Association of Dermatologists (history of dermatology; 500 books and pamphlets; 113 bound periodical volumes). **Holdings:** 50,000 volumes; 14 AV programs; 184 microforms; 18,000 manuscripts. **Services:** Interlibrary loan; copying; library open to bona fide researchers. **Special Catalogs:** Catalog of Evan Bedford Library of Cardiology; catalog of engraved portraits in the Royal College of Physicians of London.

★18740★
ROYAL COLLEGE OF SURGEONS OF ENGLAND - LIBRARY (Med)
35-43 Lincoln's Inn Fields Phone: 1 405-3474
London WC2A 3PN, England Ian F. Lyle, Libn.
Subjects: Surgery, pathology, anatomy, anesthesia, physiology, history of medicine. **Special Collections:** Hunter-Baillie Collection (1500 autograph letters and manuscripts); John Hunter and his pupils and contemporaries (1100 books, manuscripts, and autograph letters); engraved portraits (3000); medical bookplates (2000). **Holdings:** 60,000 books; 115,000 bound periodical volumes; 50 AV programs; 5000 manuscripts and autograph letters. **Services:** Interlibrary loan; copying; library open to the public with restrictions. **Computerized Information Services:** MEDLINE. Performs searches on fee basis. **Special Catalogs:** English books before 1701 in the Library of the Royal College of Surgeons.

★18741★
ROYAL COLLEGE OF VETERINARY SURGEONS - WELLCOME LIBRARY (Med)
32 Belgrave Square Phone: 1 235 6568
London SW1X 8QP, England Benita Horder, Libn.
Subjects: Veterinary science, animal husbandry, comparative medicine. **Special Collections:** Historical collection (2500 volumes); Henry Gray Collection (ornithology; 250 volumes). **Holdings:** 25,000 books. **Services:** Interlibrary loan; copying; SDI; library open to the public with restrictions. **Computerized Information Services:** DIALOG Information Services, BLAISE Online Services, IRS-DIALTECH, Data-Star, Pergamon ORBIT InfoLine, Inc. **Remarks:** Maintained by Royal College of Veterinary Surgeons' Trust Fund.

★18742★
ROYAL DUBLIN SOCIETY - LIBRARY (Area-Ethnic)
Ballsbridge Phone: 1 680645
Dublin 4, Ireland Alan R. Eager, Libn.
Subjects: Ireland, agriculture, fine arts, biography, literature. **Special Collections:** Ireland (80 volumes of pamphlets); Dante Collection (120 volumes). **Holdings:** 120,000 books; 80,000 bound periodical volumes; 20 microforms; 50 manuscripts. **Services:** Interlibrary loan; copying; SDI; library open to bona fide researchers. **Publications:** Annual List of Accessions.

★18743★
ROYAL GEOGRAPHICAL SOCIETY OF AUSTRALASIA, INC. - SOUTH AUSTRALIAN BRANCH - LIBRARY (Geog-Map, Area-Ethnic)
c/o State Library of South Australia
North Terrace
G.P.O. Box 419 Phone: 8 2238750
Adelaide, SA 5001, Australia Roslyn Blandy, Libn.
Staff: Prof 1. **Subjects:** Australia - discovery, exploration, description, travel; voyages and travels; geography; Australian aborigines; biography. **Special Collections:** The York Gate Geographical and Colonial Library (9300 volumes). **Holdings:** 15,000 books; 5500 bound periodical volumes; 15 reels of microfilm; 2200 pictorial records; 800 maps; 200 manuscripts. **Subscriptions:** 148 journals and other serials. **Services:** Interlibrary loan; copying; library open to the public for reference use only. **Special Catalogs:** Catalogue of the York Gate Library; Catalogue of the Manuscripts in the Library of the RGSASA.

★18744★
ROYAL GREENWICH OBSERVATORY - LIBRARY (Sci-Engr)
Herstmonceux Castle Phone: 323 833171
Hailsham, East Sussex BN27 1RP, England Jon Hutchins, Libn.
Subjects: Astronomy, geodesy, physics, history of science, science policy, chronometry and time. **Special Collections:** Airy Collection (astronomy, mathematics, voyages of discovery, science, chronometry; 1000 rare and pre-1830 books); archives of Astronomers Royal (150,000 manuscripts). **Holdings:** 30,000 books; 60,000 bound periodical volumes; 100 microforms; 3500 slides. **Services:** Interlibrary loan; copying; library open to the public with written application. **Computerized Information Services:** DIALOG Information Services, INSPEC, ESA/IRS, SIMBAD; internal database.

★18745★
ROYAL INSTITUTE OF INTERNATIONAL AFFAIRS - LIBRARY (Soc Sci)
Chatham House
10 St. James's Square Phone: 1 930 2233
London SW1Y 4LE, England Nicole Gallimore, Libn.
Subjects: International affairs, end of World War II to present. **Special Collections:** International press clippings library. **Holdings:** 160,000 books and pamphlets. **Subscriptions:** 650 journals and other serials.

★18746★
ROYAL INSTITUTE OF TECHNOLOGY - LIBRARY (Sci-Engr)
Valhallavagen 81 Phone: 8 790 70 80
S-100 44 Stockholm, Sweden Stephan Schwarz, Hd.Libn.
Subjects: Physical sciences, technology, engineering, architecture. **Special Collections:** History of Sciences and Technology. **Holdings:** 15,000 linear meters. **Services:** Interlibrary loan; copying; SDI; library open to the public. **Computerized Information Services:** Online systems. Performs searches on fee basis. Contact Person: Marie Wallin, 790 89 74. **Publications:** Stockholm papers in library and information science; Stockholm papers in history and philosophy of technology. **Also Known As:** Kungliga Tekniska Hogskolans Bibliotek.

ROYAL METEOROLOGICAL INSTITUTE OF BELGIUM
See: Royal Belgian Observatory (18733)

★18747★
ROYAL NETHERLANDS ACADEMY OF ARTS AND SCIENCES - LIBRARY (Med, Sci-Engr)
Kloveniersburgwal 29
P.O. Box 19121 Phone: 20 222902
NL-1000 GC Amsterdam, Netherlands Dr. J.A.W. Brak, Dir.
Staff: 53. **Subjects:** Medicine, biology, chemistry, physics, pharmacy, astronomy. **Holdings:** 330,000 volumes; 2 million microfiche. **Subscriptions:** 10,000 journals and other serials. **Services:** Interlibrary loan; copying; SDI; library open to the public. **Automated Operations:** Computerized cataloging, acquisitions, and serials. **Computerized Information Services:** INIS (International Nuclear Information System); internal databases. Performs searches on fee basis. **Remarks:** Fax: 20 220211. **Also Known As:** Bibliotheek Koninklijke Nederlandse Akademie van Wetenschappen. **Staff:** Dr. Th.W.J. Pieters; Dr. A.T. Hogenaar; Dr. R. Brandune; Dr. J.A. Dijkman.

★18748★
ROYAL NORWEGIAN COUNCIL FOR SCIENTIFIC AND INDUSTRIAL RESEARCH - NORWEGIAN BUILDING RESEARCH INSTITUTE - LIBRARY (Plan)
P.O. Box 322
Blindern Phone: 2 46 98 80
N-0314 Oslo 3, Norway Margareth Grini, Libn.
Subjects: Building, construction, building management. **Holdings:** 32,000 volumes. **Also Known As:** Norges Teknisk-Naturvitenskapelige Forskningsrad - Norges Byggforskningsinstitutt.

★18749★
ROYAL OBSERVATORY, HONG KONG - LIBRARY (Sci-Engr)
134A Nathan Rd. Phone: 3-7329200
Kowloon, Hong Kong Patrick P. Sham, Dir.
Founded: 1883. **Subjects:** Weather forecasting, tropical cyclones, climatology, tropical meteorology, hydrology, seismology, astronomy, time standards, air pollution, oceanography, disaster prevention, gravimetric surveys, metrication, metrology. **Holdings:** 31,800 volumes. **Publications:** Royal Observatory Almanac; Royal Observatory Calandar; Hong Kong Tide Tables, annual; Marine Climatological Summary Charts for the South China Sea, annual - on exchange; Daily Weather Charts; Monthly Weather Summaries; Meteorological Results Part I - Surface Observations, annual - on exchange; A Summary of Radiosonde-Radiowind Ascents made at King's Park, Hong Kong, annual - on exchange; Meteorological Results Part III - Tropical Cyclone Summaries, annual - on exchange; Occasional Papers, irregular; Technical Memoirs, irregular - on exchange; Technical Notes, irregular - on exchange; Technical Notes (Local), irregular - on exchange. **Remarks:** Observatory is Hong Kong's National Meteorological Service. Telex: 54777GEOPH HX; Fax: 3-7215034.

★18750★
ROYAL SCHOOL OF LIBRARIANSHIP - LIBRARY (Info Sci)
Birketinget 6 Phone: 1 58 60 66
DK-2300 Copenhagen S, Denmark Susanne Ornager, Chf.Libn.
Subjects: Library science, documentation, information. **Holdings:** 110,713 books; 1556 bound periodical volumes; 42 AV programs; 8942 microforms.

Services: Interlibrary loan; copying; SDI; library open to the public. **Computerized Information Services:** Library and Information Science Abstracts (LISA), NORDICOM. Performs searches free of charge. **Special Indexes:** Nordisk BDI-Index (online index of Nordic library and information literature). **Also Known As:** Danmarks Biblioteksskoles Bibliotek.

★18751★
ROYAL SCIENTIFIC SOCIETY - LIBRARY (Sci-Engr)
P.O. Box 925819 Phone: 844700
Amman, Jordan Sana Takrouri, Dp.Libn.
Founded: 1970. **Subjects:** Applied engineering. **Holdings:** 40,000 volumes. **Publications:** Monthly Accession List; Bibliography of Jordan; Current List of Periodical Holdings. **Remarks:** Society objective is to promote research and provide scientific and technological consultation relating to economic and social development in Jordan.

ROYAL SCOTTISH MUSEUM - LIBRARY
See: National Museums of Scotland - Library (18644)

ROYAL SHAKESPEARE THEATRE LIBRARY
See: Shakespeare Birthplace Trust - Shakespeare Centre Library (18766)

★18752★
ROYAL SOCIETY OF MEDICINE - LIBRARY (Med)
1 Wimpole St. Phone: 1 408 2119
London W1M 8AE, England David W.C. Stewart, Libn.
Subjects: Medicine, history of medicine. **Holdings:** 100,000 books; 400,000 bound periodical volumes; 500 microforms; 500 manuscripts. **Services:** Interlibrary loan; copying; SDI; library open to the public with restrictions. **Computerized Information Services:** DIALOG Information Services, Data-Star, BLAISE Online Services. Performs searches on fee basis. Contact Person: Linda Griffiths. **Publications:** Current periodicals list.

★18753★
THE ROYAL VETERINARY AND AGRICULTURAL UNIVERSITY - DANISH VETERINARY AND AGRICULTURAL LIBRARY (Med, Agri)
Bulowsvej 13
1870 Copenhagen V, Denmark Phone: 1 351788
Subjects: Veterinary science, agriculture, food science. **Holdings:** 391,643 books; 4030 bound periodical volumes; 200 microforms. **Services:** Interlibrary loan; copying; SDI; library open to the public. **Computerized Information Services:** DIALOG Information Services, DIMDI. Performs searches on fee basis.

RUBBER RESEARCH INSTITUTE OF MALAYSIA
See: Malaysian Rubber Research and Development Board (18598)

RUHR-UNIVERSITY - INSTITUTE FOR DEVELOPMENT RESEARCH AND DEVELOPMENT POLICY
See: Institute for Development Research and Development Policy (18503)

★18754★
RURAL DEVELOPMENT ADMINISTRATION - RDA LIBRARY (Agri)
250 Seodoon-dong Phone: 2101
Suweon 170, Republic of Korea Heu Noon, Lib.Dir.
Subjects: Agriculture, rural sociology. **Holdings:** 56,000 volumes. **Remarks:** Maintained by Korea - Ministry of Agriculture and Fisheries.

S

RUUSBROECGENOOTSCHAP CENTRUM VOOR SPIRITUALITEIT
See: Universiteit Antwerpen - Universitaire Faculteiten Sint-Ignatius Antwerpen (18842)

SALT INDUSTRY RESEARCH INSTITUTE
See: People's Republic of China - Ministry of Light Industry (18684)

★18755★
SALZBURG SEMINAR IN AMERICAN STUDIES - LIBRARY (Soc Sci, Law)
Schloss Leopoldskron
Postfach 129 Phone: 662 841 2330
A-5010 Salzburg, Austria Josephine V. Said, Libn.
Subjects: American law, history, and literature; social sciences; political science. **Special Collections:** Tapes of faculty lectures (600). **Holdings:** 10,000 books; 120 bound periodical volumes; 22 AV programs; 500 phonograph records. **Services:** Copying; library open to the public by appointment. **Publications:** Serial Holdings, annual. **Special Catalogs:** Catalog of music and spoken recordings (card). **Special Indexes:** Index to seminar session lectures (online). **Remarks:** Telex: 847 633701 SASEM A.

SATEILYTURVAKESKUS
See: Finland - Ministry of Social Affairs and Health - Finnish Center for Radiation and Nuclear Safety (18412)

★18756★
SCANDINAVIAN INSTITUTE OF AFRICAN STUDIES - LIBRARY (Area-Ethnic)
Postfack 1703 Phone: 155480
S-751 47 Uppsala, Sweden Ms. B. Fahlander, Libn.
Subjects: Developmental problems of modern Africa. **Holdings:** 30,000 volumes. **Remarks:** Institute is supported by the governments of Sweden, Denmark, Finland, Iceland, and Norway. **Also Known As:** Nordiska Afrikainstitutet.

★18757★
SCANDINAVIAN PAINT AND PRINTING INK RESEARCH INSTITUTE - LIBRARY (Sci-Engr)
Agern Alle 3 Phone: 57 03 55
DK-2970 Horsholm, Denmark Birthe Kaare Poulsen, Libn.
Subjects: Research, development, testing, and analysis of dry and wet coatings and printing inks. **Holdings:** 6000 volumes. **Remarks:** Institute serves Denmark, Sweden, Norway, and Finland. **Also Known As:** Nordisk Forskningsinstitut for Maling og Trykfarver.

★18758★
SCHOCKEN INSTITUTE FOR JEWISH RESEARCH - LIBRARY (Rel-Phil)
6 Balfour St. Phone: 2 631288
Jerusalem 92102, Israel Esther Ben-David, Libn.
Subjects: Jewish mysticism, medieval Jewish poetry, Halacha, Hasidism, prayer, Jewish history. **Special Collections:** Special editions and early printings; prayer books. **Holdings:** Figures not available. **Services:** Copying; library open to persons with a letter of introduction from a known scholar or institution. **Remarks:** Maintained by Jewish Theological Seminary of America. **Staff:** S. Friedman, Prof..

SCHWEIZERISCHE BOTANISCHE GESELLSCHAFT
See: Institute for Phytomedicine - Swiss Botanical Society (18517)

SCIENCE FICTION FOUNDATION RESEARCH LIBRARY
See: North East London Polytechnic (18664)

★18759★
SCIENCE MUSEUM - LIBRARY (Sci-Engr)
South Kensington Phone: 1 938 8220
London SW7 5NH, England Prof. R. Fox
Subjects: Science, technology, history of science and technology. **Special Collections:** Pictorial and archival collection. **Holdings:** 600,000 volumes; British patents; trade literature; microforms. **Services:** Copying; library open to the public. **Computerized Information Services:** Online systems. Performs searches on fee basis. Contact Person: Mr. I.E.D. Carter. **Publications:** Bibliographies; additional publications available - all for sale.

★18760★
SCIENTIFIC RESEARCH COUNCIL OF SPAIN - BIOLOGICAL RESEARCH CENTER - LIBRARY (Biol Sci)
Velazquez 144 Phone: 1 261 18 00
E-28006 Madrid, Spain Antonia Hermida, Libn.
Subjects: Biology, biomedicine. **Holdings:** 69,000 volumes. **Also Known As:** Centro de Investigaciones Biologicas.

★18761★
SCIENTIFIC RESEARCH COUNCIL OF SPAIN - MILA AND FONTANALS INSTITUTION - LIBRARY (Hum)
Calle Egipciacas 15 Phone: 3 242 34 89
E-08001 Barcelona, Spain Maria Antonia Callis, Chf.Libn.
Subjects: Medieval and modern history, musicology, cultural anthropology and ethnology, geography, classic and romance philology, archeology, pedagogics, philosophy and religion, art, literature. **Holdings:** 53,470 volumes. **Remarks:** Telex: 99560 DCCSI. **Also Known As:** Institucion Mila y Fontanals.

★18762★
SCIENTIFIC RESEARCH INSTITUTE OF WATER CONSERVANCY AND HYDROELECTRIC POWER - LIBRARY (Energy, Sci-Engr)
10 West Chegongzhuang Lu
West Suburb Phone: 1 890781
Beijing, People's Republic of China Shen Conggang, Libn.
Founded: 1956. **Staff:** 7. **Subjects:** Science; applied mathematics; mechanics - fluid, hydraulic, soil, rock, structural, aerodynamic; geological geography; meteorology; geomorphology; hydrogeology; irrigation works; soil improvement; engineering - hydropower, electrical, civil, hydraulic; electrotechnics; automation. **Holdings:** 108,824 volumes; 2150 periodicals; 618 AV programs and microforms. **Services:** Interlibrary loan; copying. **Publications:** Journal of Water Conservancy; Silt Research; reports of research results - all on exchange.

★18763★
SCIENTIFIC & TECHNICAL LIBRARY OF HIGHWAY & WATERWAY TRANSPORT (Trans)
12 West Beihuan Lu
Beijing, People's Republic of China
Founded: 1964. **Staff:** 40. **Subjects:** Bridge engineering, road construction and maintenance machinery, motor transport and maintenance, communication engineering, port and channel engineering, shipbuilding, canals and navigation, navigation, navigation marks, shipyards and docks, rescue and salvage. **Holdings:** 78,500 volumes; 3280 periodicals; 46,000 technical reports; 50 AV programs and microforms. **Services:** Interlibrary loan; copying. **Computerized Information Services:** Internal database. **Publications:** Road Transport Abstracts; Water Transport Abstracts; New Books on Communication and Transportation. **Special Catalogs:** Union Catalogue of Foreign Periodicals Held by Departments of Communication; catalogs of Chinese scientific and technical materials on land and water transport; communication science and technology product catalogs.

★18764★
SCIENTIFIC AND TECHNICAL RESEARCH COUNCIL OF TURKEY - TURKISH SCIENTIFIC AND TECHNICAL DOCUMENTATION CENTER (Sci-Engr)
Ataturk Bulvari 221
Kavaklidere Phone: 26 27 70
Ankara, Turkey Rezzan Kockar, Libn.
Founded: 1966. **Subjects:** Basic and applied sciences, agriculture, economics, industry, industrial management, medicine, information and library science. **Holdings:** 10,000 volumes. **Subscriptions:** 600 journals and other serials. **Services:** SDI; center open to the public. **Computerized Information Services:** Internal database. Performs searches on fee basis. **Also Known As:** Turkiye Bilimsel ve Teknik Arastirma Kurumu.

SCOTTISH UNITED SERVICES MUSEUM - LIBRARY
See: National Museums of Scotland - Library (18644)

★18765★
SENCKENBERG RESEARCH INSTITUTE AND NATURAL HISTORY MUSEUM - LIBRARY (Biol Sci)
Senckenberglage 25 Phone: 069-75 42 1
D-6000 Frankfurt am Main 1, Federal Republic of Germany
Friedrich Schepky, Libn.
Subjects: Botany, ecology, geological paleontology, hydrobiology, marine biology and geology, paleo-anthropology, zoology. **Holdings:** 250,000 volumes. **Also Known As:** Forschungsinstitut und Naturmuseum Senckenberg.

SERVICIO DE INVESTIGACION PREHISTORICA
See: Valencia Province - Service for Prehistoric Research (18867)

★18766★
SHAKESPEARE BIRTHPLACE TRUST - SHAKESPEARE CENTRE LIBRARY (Theater)
Henley St. Phone: 789 204016
Stratford-upon-Avon, Warwickshire CV37 6QW, England
Marian J. Pringle, Sr.Libn.
Subjects: Shakespeare, Warwickshire, theater, Elizabethan England. **Special Collections:** Royal Shakespeare Theatre Library, 1879 to present; Bram Stoker Collection of Henry Irving; Wheler and Saunders Collections of Warwickshire Documents. **Holdings:** 40,000 books; 1000 bound periodical volumes; 50,000 documents and manuscripts; 200 video titles; 200 phonograph records, tapes, films; 200 reels of microfilm; 100 microfiche titles; 6000 photographs; 10,000 prints and drawings. **Services:** Copying; library open to the public with restrictions. **Staff:** Dr. Levi Fox, Dir.; Robert Bearman, Sr.Archv..

★18767★
SHANGHAI INSTITUTE OF PHARMACEUTICAL INDUSTRY - LIBRARY (Med, Biol Sci)
1320 West Beijing Lu Phone: 539828
Shanghai, People's Republic of China Wang Xianglin, Libn.
Founded: 1956. **Staff:** 14. **Subjects:** Pharmacy, medicine, microbiology, organic and analytical chemistry, biochemistry, chemical engineering. **Holdings:** 35,376 volumes; 28,536 bound periodical volumes; 36 AV programs; 7 journals on microcard. **Subscriptions:** 609 journals and other serials. **Services:** Copying. **Publications:** Collected Abstracts of Annual Meeting Papers - on exchange. **Special Indexes:** Medicines (card, microfiche).

★18768★
SHANGHAI LIBRARY (Hum, Sci-Engr, Area-Ethnic)
325 W. Nanjing Lu Phone: 563176
Shanghai, People's Republic of China Gu Tinglong, Libn.
Founded: 1952. **Staff:** 545. **Subjects:** Philosophy, social sciences, natural sciences, applied sciences. **Special Collections:** Song, Yuan, Ming dynasties; The Six Dynasties, 222-589 A.D. (manuscripts); Sui and Tang dynasties; Ming and Qing writers (handwritten copies; manuscripts); early revolutionary documents. **Holdings:** 7 million volumes; technical reports; 11,250 reels of microfilm; 140,000 phonograph records; 1020 audiotapes; pre-liberation newspapers and magazines. **Subscriptions:** 14,449 journals and other serials. **Holdings:** Interlibrary loan; copying. **Special Catalogs:** Catalog of Shanghai Library Collection of Local Histories; Catalog of Works and Translations by Guo Moruo; Shanghai Union Catalog of New Foreign Books; additional catalogs available. **Special Indexes:** National Index of Newspapers and Periodicals: Philosophy and Social Sciences series; National Index of Newspapers and Periodicals: Science and Technology series - domestic distribution only.

SHANGHAI SHIP AND SHIPPING RESEARCH INSTITUTE
See: People's Republic of China - Ministry of Communications (18683)

★18769★
SHENKAR COLLEGE OF TEXTILE TECHNOLOGY AND FASHION - LIBRARY (Sci-Engr, Art)
12 Anna Frank St. Phone: 3 7521133
Ramat-Gan 52526, Israel Paula Ostfeld
Subjects: Textile technology and machinery, fashion, fashion history, apparel industry, production management. **Special Collections:** History of Costumes (250 items); Pollak Collection (108 items). **Holdings:** 17,000 books; 250 periodical titles. **Services:** Interlibrary loan; copying; library open to the public. **Computerized Information Services:** DIALOG Information Services. Performs searches on fee basis. **Special Catalogs:** Catalog of New Books in the Library, annual. **Remarks:** Telex: 341118 BXTV-IL, ext. 5790.

SHETH BHOLABHAI JESHINGBHAI INSTITUTE OF LEARNING AND RESEARCH
See: Gujarat Vidya Sabha (18457)

★18770★
SHOE AND LEATHER RESEARCH INSTITUTE - LIBRARY (Sci-Engr)
CH-762 65 Gottwaldov, Czechoslovakia Phone: 23151
Jarmila Dvorakova, Libn.
Subjects: Leather and shoemaking technology, equipment and machinery, shoemaking materials, tannery effluent treatment. **Holdings:** 50,000 volumes. **Remarks:** Telex: 067 337. **Also Known As:** Vyzkumny Ustav Kozedelny.

★18771★
SILK AND ART SILK MILLS' RESEARCH ASSOCIATION - SASMIRA LIBRARY (Sci-Engr, Bus-Fin)
Sasmira Marg
Worli Phone: 493 5351
Bombay 400 025, India Mrs. S.R. Taggarsi, Libn.
Staff: Prof 4; Other 3. **Subjects:** Textiles and allied subjects, management and marketing, pure and applied sciences, engineering, economics, social sciences. **Special Collections:** Indian Standards on Textiles; BISFA Rules; Novelty Fabric Design Samples; press clippings. **Holdings:** 9117 books; 5980 bound periodical volumes; 7528 other cataloged items. **Subscriptions:** 202 journals and other serials; 8 newspapers. **Services:** Interlibrary loan; copying; library open to the public for reference use only. **Publications:** Man-Made Textiles in India; SASMIRA Bulletin; SASMIRA Digest. **Special Catalogs:** Selected list of books; list of dissertations; list of current periodicals and ad-hoc publications. **Special Indexes:** Index of the articles published in Man-Made Textiles in India; Index of Papers presented in Technology Conferences from 1970-1985. **Remarks:** Affiliated with India - Board of Education and India - Ministry of Textiles. **Staff:** Mr. G.D. Saraf, Asst.Libn.; Mr. S.R. Deshpande, Asst.Libn..

★18772★
SINGAPORE - MINISTRY OF COMMUNITY DEVELOPMENT - NATIONAL LIBRARY - REFERENCE SERVICES DIVISION (Area-Ethnic, Info Sci)
Stamford Rd. Phone: 65 330 9660
Singapore 0617, Singapore Alice Loh, Hd.
Founded: 1958. **Staff:** Prof 10; Other 18. **Subjects:** Southeast Asia, Asian children's literature, business, science and technology, humanities, social science, fine arts. **Special Collections:** Southeast Asia Collection (microforms and rare books; 85,373 volumes); Asian Collection of Children's Books (13,883 volumes). **Holdings:** 233,375 books; 25,183 bound periodical volumes; 16,073 reels of microfilm; 62,794 microfiche; 25,311 AV programs. **Subscriptions:** 7672 journals and other serials; 42 newspapers. **Services:** Interlibrary loan; copying; SDI; division open to the public. **Automated Operations:** Computerized public access catalog, cataloging, acquisitions, serials, and circulation. **Computerized Information Services:** DIALOG Information Services, Pergamon ORBIT InfoLine, Inc., QL/SEARCH, AUSTRALIS; NALINET (internal database). Performs searches on fee basis. Contact Person: Chan Fook Weng, Hd., Bus./Sci./Tech.Sect., 330 9661. **Publications:** Books about Singapore, biennial - free upon request; Government Services Directory, biennial - for sale; guides to the special reference collections; subject bibliographies - both for sale. **Special Catalogs:** Masterlist of Southeast Asian Microforms Supplement, 1978-1983 (microfiche). **Special Indexes:** Singapore Periodicals Index (SPI), annual (book). **Remarks:** Telex: RS 26620 NATLIB. Fax: 3309611. **Staff:** Miss Lim Kek Hwa, Hd., Southeast Asia Sect.; Miss Chan Luck, Hd., Hum. & Soc.Sci.Sect.; Mrs. V. Perumbulavil, Hd., Asian Coll. of Ch.Bks.; Mrs. Rokiah Mentol, NLDC-SEA Consortium Off..

★18773★
SINGAPORE - MINISTRY OF NATIONAL DEVELOPMENT - PARKS AND RECREATION DEPARTMENT - BOTANIC GARDENS - LIBRARY (Biol Sci)
Cluny Rd. Phone: 65 4741165
Singapore 1025, Singapore Christina Soh, Lib.Techn.
Subjects: Taxonomic and floristic botany, especially in Southeast Asia. **Holdings:** 15,600 volumes.

★18774★
SINT-ANDRIESABDIJ VAN DE BENEDICTYNEN TE BRUGGE - BIBLIOTHEEK VAN DE SINT-ANDRIESABDIJ (Rel-Phil)
Zevenkerken 4 Phone: 50 38 01 36
B-8200 Brugge 2, Belgium J.D. Broekaert, Biblio.
Subjects: Theology, missiology, monasticism. **Special Collections:** Regel van Sint-Benedictus (850 volumes); Newmaniana (1100 books); Central Africa (6000 books). **Holdings:** 140,000 volumes. **Services:** Interlibrary loan; library open to the public with restrictions.

SOCIETE DE LEGISLATION COMPAREE
See: Society of Comparative Legislation (18775)

SOCIETY OF ANTIQUARIES OF SCOTLAND - LIBRARY
See: National Museums of Scotland - Library (18644)

★18775★
SOCIETY OF COMPARATIVE LEGISLATION - LIBRARY (Law)
28, rue Saint-Guillaume
F-75007 Paris, France Phone: 1 4544467
Subjects: Comparative law, foreign law. **Holdings:** 100,000 volumes. **Also Known As:** Societe de Legislation Comparee.

★18776★
SOCIETY FOR COPTIC ARCHAEOLOGY - LIBRARY (Area-Ethnic)
222 Ramses Ave.
Abbassiya Phone: 2 824252
Cairo, Egypt Dr. Margit Thot, Libn.
Subjects: Coptic language, literature, history, art, thought, theology; papyrology. **Holdings:** 12,000 volumes.

★18777★
SOCIETY FOR INFORMATION AND DOCUMENTATION - GID INFORMATION CENTER FOR INFORMATION SCIENCE AND INFORMATION WORK (Info Sci, Comp Sci)
P.O. Box 710363
Lyonner Strasse 44-48 Phone: 69 66871
D-6000 Frankfurt am Main 71, Federal Republic of Germany
Dr. Peter Budinger, Hd.
Founded: 1977. **Subjects:** Methodology of information and documentation; information processing, systems, networks; computational linguistics. **Holdings:** 50,000 monographs, reports, standards. **Subscriptions:** 360 journals and other serials. **Services:** SDI; center open to the public on fee basis. **Computerized Information Services:** INFODATA (internal database). Performs searches on fee basis. **Publications:** Directory of Journals Held by the GID Information Center, biennial; additional publications available. **Also Known As:** Gesellschaft fur Information und Dokumentation (GID) - GID-Informationszentrum fur Informationswissenschaft und -Praxis.

SOCIETY FOR RESEARCH ON JEWISH COMMUNITIES
See: Hebrew University of Jerusalem - Society for Research on Jewish Communities (18463)

★18778★
SOUTH AFRICA - DEPARTMENT OF AGRICULTURE AND WATER SUPPLY - SOIL AND IRRIGATION RESEARCH INSTITUTE - LIBRARY (Agri)
Private Bag X79 Phone: 28-4048
Pretoria 0001, Republic of South Africa Miss E. Prinsloo, Libn.
Subjects: Soil and water research, irrigation. **Holdings:** 20,000 volumes.

SOUTH AFRICA - DEPARTMENT OF MINERAL AND ENERGY AFFAIRS - GEOLOGICAL SURVEY OF SOUTH AFRICA
See: Geological Survey of South Africa (18439)

SOUTH AFRICA - DEPARTMENT OF NATIONAL EDUCATION - AFRICA INSTITUTE OF SOUTH AFRICA
See: Africa Institute of South Africa (18261)

★18779★
SOUTH AFRICA - DEPARTMENT OF NATIONAL EDUCATION - SOUTH AFRICAN LIBRARY (Area-Ethnic, Info Sci)
P.O. Box 496 Phone: 21 24-6320
Cape Town 8000, Republic of South Africa Mr. P.E. Westra, Dir.
Staff: Prof 26; Other 60. **Subjects:** Africana-Southern Africa, humanities. **Special Collections:** Grey Collection (115 medieval illuminated manuscripts); Dessinian Collection (17th-18th century); Fairbridge Collection (19th century); Pama Collection (heraldry and genealogy); Cape and South Africa newspaper collection (35,000 newspapers; photographs). **Holdings:** 600,000 books; 160,000 bound periodical volumes; 74,000 microforms; 35,000 manuscripts. **Services:** Interlibrary loan; copying; library open to the public. **Automated Operations:** Computerized cataloging, acquisitions, serials, and circulation. **Computerized Information Services:** Internal databases. Performs searches free of charge. Contact Person: Mr. Prinsloo, 24-6321. **Publications:** Quarterly Bulletin; Grey Bibliographies; Reprint Series; Newspapers on Microfilm. **Special Indexes:** Cape Town English Press Index. **Staff:** Mr. A.S. Kericham, Dp.Dir..

★18780★
SOUTH AFRICA - STATE LIBRARY (Area-Ethnic, Soc Sci, Info Sci)
P.O. Box 397 Phone: 12 218931
Pretoria 0001, Republic of South Africa
Prof. Reginald Brand Zaaiman, Dir.
Founded: 1887. **Staff:** Prof 65; Other 96. **Subjects:** Africana, politics, economics. **Special Collections:** Legal Deposit Collection for South Africa, 1916 to present (newspapers; periodicals; official publications depository for U.S. Government, U.N., World Bank); bibliographies; maps (21,000); documents on printing; official publications of Southern African states; banned (restricted circulation) documents; library science documents. **Holdings:** 1 million books; 60,000 bound periodical volumes; 150,000 microforms. **Subscriptions:** 5500 journals and other serials; 300 newspapers. **Services:** Interlibrary loan; copying; library open to the public. **Automated Operations:** Computerized cataloging and acquisitions. **Computerized Information Services:** DOBIS-LIBIS, S.A. Bibliographic and Information Network (SABINET). Performs searches free of charge. Contact Person: Mrs. Jo Bishoff, Chf.Libn.. **Publications:** Informat - Information Bulletin of the State Library, bimonthly - worldwide distribution; bibliographies, reprints, newspapers, periodicals (microfilm); contributions to library science. **Special Catalogs:** Joint Catalogue of Monographs; Periodicals in Southern African Libraries (PISAL). **Special Indexes:** Index to South Africa Government Gazette; Index to Gazettes of Ciskei, Transkei, Venda, and Bophuthatswana. **Remarks:** Library located at Cor. Andries and Vermeulen St., Pretoria. **Formerly:** South Africa - Department of National Education - State Library. **Staff:** Mr. A.G.C. Olivier, Asst.Dir.; Mrs. M.A. Botha, Asst.Dir..

★18781★
SOUTH AFRICAN INSTITUTE OF RACE RELATIONS - LIBRARY (Soc Sci)
Auden House
68 de Korte St.
Braamfontein Phone: 724-4441
Johannesburg, Republic of South Africa J. Morrison, Libn.
Subjects: Race relations, human rights. **Holdings:** 5000 volumes.

★18782★
SOUTH CHINA ACADEMY/COLLEGE OF TROPICAL CROPS - LIBRARY (Agri)
Baodaoxincun
Danxian
Hainan Island, Guangdong Province, People's Republic of China
Yu Hongfei, Libn.
Founded: 1958. **Staff:** 22. **Subjects:** Tropical crops, tropical economic crops, rubber plants. **Special Collections:** Planting and processing of Malaysian rubber. **Holdings:** 175,700 volumes. **Subscriptions:** 710 journals and other serials. **Publications:** Chinese Journal of Tropical Crops (1980).

★18783★
SOUTH-WEST AFRICA SCIENTIFIC SOCIETY - LIBRARY (Area-Ethnic)
P.O. Box 67 Phone: 225372
Windhoek 9000, Namibia Mrs. J. Bieker, Libn.
Subjects: Namibia - history, archeology, ethnology, zoology, botany, geology. **Holdings:** 7000 volumes.

★18784★
SOUTHEAST ASIAN FISHERIES DEVELOPMENT CENTER - SEAFDEC LIBRARY (Biol Sci)
Secretariat 956 Rama IV Rd.
Olympia Bldg. Bangkok 10 500, Thailand
Subjects: Aquaculture, marine technology, postharvest technology. **Holdings:** 50,000 volumes. **Remarks:** SEAFDEC coordinates activities in Japan, Malaysia, the Philippines, Singapore, and Thailand.

★18785★
SOUTHEAST ASIAN MINISTERS OF EDUCATION ORGANIZATION - SEAMED REGIONAL CENTER FOR EDUCATION IN SCIENCE AND MATHEMATICS - LIBRARY (Educ)
11700 Glugor Phone: 883266
Penang, Malaysia Mr. Thoh Khye Juat, Libn.
Subjects: Science and mathematics education. **Holdings:** 21,250 volumes; 720 pamphlets. **Subscriptions:** 200 journals and other serials.

★18786★
SPAIN - CONGRESS OF DEPUTIES - LIBRARY (Law, Soc Sci)
Floridablanca s/n Phone: 1 4 29 51 93
E-28014 Madrid, Spain Alicia Martin Gonzalez, Chf.
Subjects: Law, political science, history, economics, sociology. **Special Collections:** Spanish parliamentary history before and during the constitutional period (bibliography; original documents); elections; 15th century incunabula (81); 16th-17th century rare books (257); 19th century pamphlets; parliamentary activity films and photographs. **Holdings:** 100,000 book titles; 1500 periodical titles; 5000 AV programs; 25 titles in microform. **Services:** Interlibrary loan; copying; library open to historians and researchers. **Computerized Information Services:** IBERLEX, Communitatis Europae Lex (CELEX), CRONOS Data Bank, ECHO, COMEXT Data Bank; ARGO (internal database). **Publications:** Recent acquisitions information; Congress of Deputies Library history; Library and Archives holdings publications. **Special Catalogs:** Periodical catalog. **Remarks:** Telex: 46.685 HEMIE. **Also Known As:** Congreso de los Diputados - Biblioteca. **Staff:** Manuel Gonzalo, Dir. of Res. & Doc..

SPAIN - MINISTRY OF FINANCE AND ECONOMY - INSTITUTE OF FISCAL STUDIES
See: Institute of Fiscal Studies (18509)

★18787★
SPAIN - MINISTRY OF LABOUR - NATIONAL INSTITUTE OF OCCUPATIONAL SAFETY AND HEALTH - CENTRO NACIONAL DE CONDICIONES DE TRABAJO (Med)
Calle Dulcet, s/n Phone: 3 932044500
E-08034 Barcelona, Spain Jaume Llacuna Morera
Staff: Prof 6; Other 5. **Founded:** 1972. **Subjects:** Occupational health and safety, occupational medicine, industrial hygiene, industrial toxicology, ergonomics, safety education. **Holdings:** 15,000 volumes; reports; reprints. **Subscriptions:** 200 journals and other serials. **Services:** Copying; SDI; center open to the public. **Computerized Information Services:** Seguridad e Higiene en el Trabajo Bibliograf (internal database). Performs searches on fee basis. **Publications:** Boletin Bibliografico (current awareness bulletin), monthly; Erga Bibliografico (1988).

SQUIRE LAW LIBRARY
See: University of Cambridge - Library (18846)

★18788★
SRI LANKA - DEPARTMENT OF CENSUS AND STATISTICS - LIBRARY (Soc Sci)
11/1 Independence Ave. Phone: 1 598445
Colombo 7, Sri Lanka M.D.H. Goonatillake, Libn.
Subjects: Statistics, mathematics, demography, computer science, economics, agriculture. **Special Collections:** Sri Lanka census reports, 1871 to present; blue books; publications of United Nations and foreign statistical organizations. **Holdings:** 1479 books; 7210 bound periodical volumes; 4124 documents. **Services:** Interlibrary loan; SDI; library open to the public. **Publications:** List of Current Acquisitions and Guide to Periodical Literature; Annotated List of Departmental Publications; List of the Latest Publications of the Department.

★18789★
SRI LANKA TEA BOARD - TEA RESEARCH INSTITUTE OF SRI LANKA - LIBRARY (Food-Bev, Agri)
St. Coombs
Talawakele, Sri Lanka Phone: Hatton 601
Subjects: Tea cultivation and processing, agriculture, agro-industrial sciences. **Holdings:** 20,000 volumes. **Subscriptions:** 250 journals and other serials.

STAATSBIBLIOTHEK PREUSSISCHER KULTURBESITZ
See: Prussian Cultural Foundation - Library (18717)

★18790★
STATE LIBRARY OF NEW SOUTH WALES - MITCHELL LIBRARY (Area-Ethnic)
Macquarie St. Phone: 2 230 1466
Sydney, NSW 2000, Australia Margy Burn, Mgr.
Subjects: New South Wales, Australia, Southwest Pacific region. **Special Collections:** Dixson Library. **Holdings:** 501,880 volumes; 57,049 microforms; 7109.5 linear meters of manuscripts. **Services:** Copying; library open to the public with restrictions on use of original materials. **Computerized Information Services:** AUSINET, Australian Bibliographic Network (ABN), DIALOG Information Services. **Publications:** Printed guides to selected collections.

★18791★
STATE LIBRARY OF QUEENSLAND (Hist, Info Sci)
William St. Phone: 7 221 8400
Brisbane, QLD 4000, Australia Michael Hallam, Adm.Off.
Subjects: General collection. **Special Collections:** John Oxley Library (25,000 photographs; early Queensland newspapers; private manuscripts; early Australian printed material); rare books collection. **Holdings:** 758,823 books; 57,171 bound periodical volumes; 109,392 AV programs; 66,984 microforms. **Services:** Interlibrary loan; library open to the public. **Computerized Information Services:** DIALOG Information Services, Pergamon ORBIT InfoLine, Inc., AUSINET. Performs searches on fee basis. Contact Person: June Anthony. **Publications:** Annual Report; Directory of State and Public Library Services in Queensland; Public Libraries in Queensland: Statistical Bulletin. **Remarks:** Maintained by the Library Board of Queensland. **Staff:** Mr. S.L. Ryan, State Libn..

★18792★
STATE LIBRARY OF SOUTH AUSTRALIA - CHILDREN'S LITERATURE RESEARCH COLLECTION (Hum)
North Terrace
G.P.O. Box 419 Phone: 8 223 8742
Adelaide, SA 5001, Australia Juliana Bayfield, Libn. in Charge
Subjects: Children's literature - Australian, English, American, European. **Holdings:** 45,000 books; 1000 microfiche; 150 toys and games; ephemera. **Services:** Interlibrary loan (limited); copying; SDI; collection open to the public.

★18793★
STATE LIBRARY OF SOUTH AUSTRALIA - MORTLOCK LIBRARY OF SOUTH AUSTRALIANA (Area-Ethnic)
North Terrace
G.P.O. Box 419 Phone: 8 223 8760
Adelaide, SA 5001, Australia Margy Burn, Mgr.
Staff: Prof 21; Other 14. **Subjects:** South Australia, Northern Territory of Australia to 1911. **Special Collections:** Sir Donald Bradman Collection of Cricketing Memorabilia; oral history collection. **Holdings:** 75,000 volumes; 10,000 serial titles; 74,000 photographs; 7500 manuscripts. **Services:** Copying; library open to the public. **Automated Operations:** Computerized cataloging. **Computerized Information Services:** Australian Bibliographic Network (ABN). **Special Indexes:** Bibliographic, geographic, and subject indexes to archival collections and print media (on cards). **Remarks:** Library is the central repository for the preservation of South Australia nongovernment records. **Staff:** Euan M. Miller, State Libn.; Liz Moulton, Rd.Serv.Libn..

★18794★
STATE LIBRARY OF SOUTH AUSTRALIA - SPECIAL COLLECTIONS (Hist)
North Terrace
G.P.O. Box 419 Phone: 8 223 8718
Adelaide, SA 5001, Australia Valmai Hankel, Fine Bks.Libn.
Subjects: Shipping, wine, book production and history, Australian ethnology, jazz music. **Holdings:** Paul McGuire Maritime Library (2000 volumes); A.D. Edwardes Collection (8000 photographs, mainly of sailing ships); Arbon-Le Maistre Collection (photographs, mainly of powered ships); Thomas Hardy Wine Library (1000 volumes); Mountford-Sheard Collection (life of Australian ethnologist C.P. Mountford; 13,000 manuscripts, photographs, slides); John Purches Collection (jazz; 20,000 78rpm phonograph records; 4000 wax cylinders); Adelaide Circulating Library (popular literature, 1900-1975; 40,000 volumes); private press collections; modern fine book production collections. **Services:** Copying; collections open to the public.

★18795★
STATE LIBRARY OF TASMANIA (Area-Ethnic, Info Sci)
91 Murray St. Phone: 307011
Hobart, TAS 7000, Australia T.E. Meredith, Sr.Libn., Plan. & Dev.
Subjects: Tasmaniana, maritime history, Antarctica. **Special Collections:** Tasmaniana Library (111,000 items); Allport Library and Museum of Fine Arts. **Holdings:** 1.2 million books; 115,000 bound periodical volumes; 11,000 AV programs; 50,000 microforms; 60,000 musical recordings; 8000 maps. **Services:** Interlibrary loan; copying; SDI; library open to the public. **Computerized Information Services:** Australian Bibliographic Network (ABN), AUSINET, BRS Information Technologies, CSIRONET, DIALOG Information Services, ESA/IRS, MEDLINE, Pergamon ORBIT InfoLine, Inc., WILSONLINE. Performs searches free of charge (fee for printout only). **Special Indexes:** Tasmanian Index (newspaper and periodical items; card); Tasmanian Index of Community Organisations (TICO; online). **Staff:** D. Warwick Dunstan, State Libn..

★18796★
STATE LIBRARY OF VICTORIA (Hum, Info Sci)
304-328 Swanston St. Phone: 3 6699888
Melbourne, VIC 3000, Australia Moira MacKinnon, Dir., Info.Serv.
Subjects: General collection. **Special Collections:** Latrobe Collection of Australiana and Victoriana; Art, Music, and the Performing Arts Library; M.V. Anderson Chess Collection. **Holdings:** 1.27 million volumes; 8894 sound recordings; 326,500 pictures; 1700 linear meters of manuscripts. **Services:** Interlibrary loan; copying; library open to the public. **Computerized Information Services:** Australian Bibliographic Network (ABN), AUSTRALIS, BRS Information Technologies, COOL-CAT, Data-Star, DIALOG Information Services, I.P. Sharp Associates Limited, MEDLINE, Pergamon ORBIT InfoLine, Inc., WILSONLINE, Performs searches free of charge. **Publications:** Victorian Government Publications, 1976 to present; Directory of Government Libraries in Victoria; Directory of Public Libraries in Victoria; monographs, irregular. **Staff:** Jane La Scala, State Libn..

STATE REFERENCE LIBRARY OF THE NORTHERN TERRITORY
See: Northern Territory Department of Education (18665)

STATENS GEOTEKNISKA INSTITUT
See: Swedish Geotechnical Institute (18803)

STATENS INSTITUT FOR BYGGNADSFORSKNING
See: National Swedish Institute for Building Research - Library (18646)

STATENS VAG- OCH TRAFIKINSTITUT (VTI)
See: Swedish Road and Traffic Research Institute (18805)

STATISTICS SWEDEN
See: Sweden - Statistics Sweden - Library (18802)

STATISTISCHES BUNDESAMT
See: Federal Statistical Office (18411)

STATISTISKA CENTRALBYRANS BIBLIOTEK
See: Sweden - Statistics Sweden - Library (18802)

★18797★
STIFTUNG PREUSSISCHER KULTURBESITZ - IBERO-AMERIKANISCHES INSTITUT - BIBLIOTHEK (Area-Ethnic)
Potsdamer Strasse 37
Postfach 1247 Phone: 030 266-5
D-1000 Berlin 30, Federal Republic of Germany
Dr. Dietrich Briesemeister, Prof.
Subjects: Latin American studies. **Holdings:** 610,000 volumes; 51,800 maps; 15,500 phonograph records; 22,600 slides; 4500 photographs; 19,620 microforms; 100 manuscripts; scores. **Services:** Interlibrary loan; copying; library open to the public. **Computerized Information Services:** Online systems. Performs searches free of charge. Contact Person: Dr. Ulrich Menge, 2662520. **Publications:** List of publications - available on request. **Remarks:** Telex: 183160 staab d.

★18798★
STOCKHOLM INTERNATIONAL PEACE RESEARCH INSTITUTE - LIBRARY (Soc Sci, Mil)
Pipers vag 28 Phone: 559700
S-171 73 Solna, Sweden Janet Meurling, Libn.
Subjects: Disarmament and arms control; military technology and expenditure; arms trade; strategy. **Holdings:** 14,000 volumes. **Subscriptions:** 320 journals and other serials; 12 newspapers. **Services:** Interlibrary loan; library open to the public by appointment. **Computerized Information Services:** Internal database. **Staff:** Gunnel Von Dobeln, Hd., Doc. & Lib.

STUDIUM BIBLICUM FRANCISCANUM
See: Franciscan Biblical Institute (18424)

SUOMEN GEODEETTINEN LAITOS
See: Finnish Geodetic Institute (18414)

SUOMEN STANDARDISOIMISLIITTO SFS
See: Finnish Standards Association SFS (18416)

★18799★
SVENSKA LITTERATURSALLSKAPET ARKIV I FINLAND (Area-Ethnic)
Fabiansgatan 7 B Phone: 0-90-176165
SF-00180 Helsinki, Finland Eeva Kairisalo
Subjects: Swedish ethnology and folklore. **Holdings:** Manuscripts. **Services:** Copying; archive open to the public with restrictions.

★18800★
SWAZILAND NATIONAL LIBRARY SERVICE (Area-Ethnic, Info Sci)
P.O. Box 1461 Phone: 42633
Mbabane, Swaziland Mr. B.J.K. Kingsley, Dir.
Subjects: General collection. **Special Collections:** Swaziana; United Nations documents and government publications (20,000). **Holdings:** 140,000 books. **Subscriptions:** 200 journals and other serials. **Services:** Interlibrary loan; copying; SDI; library open to the public. **Publications:** Accessions lists; National Bibliography; SDI lists. **Special Catalogs:** Subject catalogs. **Remarks:** Maintains 13 urban and branch libraries.

SWEDEN - MINISTRY OF EDUCATION - THE NATIONAL LIBRARY FOR PSYCHOLOGY AND EDUCATION
See: The National Library for Psychology and Education (18640)

SWEDEN - MINISTRY OF TRANSPORT AND COMMUNICATIONS - SWEDISH GEOTECHNICAL INSTITUTE
See: Swedish Geotechnical Institute (18803)

SWEDEN - NATIONAL BOARD OF EDUCATION LIBRARY
See: Sweden - Statistics Sweden - Library (18802)

SWEDEN - NATIONAL BOARD OF HEALTH AND WELFARE LIBRARY
See: Sweden - Statistics Sweden - Library (18802)

★18801★
SWEDEN - ROYAL LIBRARY (Area-Ethnic, Info Sci)
Box 5039 Phone: 8 24 10 40
S-102 41 Stockholm, Sweden Lars Tynell, Natl.Libn.
Staff: 265. **Subjects:** General collection. **Special Collections:** Swedish Collection; old Swedish and Icelandic manuscripts; incunabula; elzeviers. **Holdings:** 3 million volumes. **Services:** Interlibrary loan; copying; library open to the public. **Automated Operations:** Computerized cataloging. **Computerized Information Services:** LIBRIS. **Publications:** AKB-mikro; Svensk Bokforteckning (National Bibliography); Acta. **Special Catalogs:** Accessionskatalog (foreign books acquired by Swedish research libraries), annual. **Also Known As:** Kungl. Biblioteket.

★18802★
SWEDEN - STATISTICS SWEDEN - LIBRARY (Sci-Engr, Soc Sci)
S-115 81 Stockholm, Sweden Phone: 8 783 40 00
Malkon Lindmark, Chf.Libn.
Founded: 1858. **Staff:** Prof 11; Other 10. **Subjects:** Statistics, statistical methodology, demography, health and welfare, education. **Holdings:** 260,000 volumes. **Subscriptions:** 4404 journals and other serials. **Services:** Interlibrary loan; copying; library open to the public. **Automated Operations:** Computerized cataloging. **Computerized Information Services:** LIBRIS. **Publications:** Statistik Fran Enskilda Lander; Statistik Fran Internationella Organ (annual lists of serials in the library) - both for sale. **Remarks:** Incorporates the National Board of Health and Welfare Library and National Board of Education Library. **Formerly:** Sweden - Ministry of Finance. **Also Known As:** Statistiska Centralbyrans Bibliotek.

★18803★
SWEDISH GEOTECHNICAL INSTITUTE - LIBRARY (Sci-Engr)
Olaus Magnus vag 35
S-581 01 Linkoping, Sweden Phone: 11 51 00
Subjects: Soil mechanics, foundation engineering. **Holdings:** 70,000 titles. **Remarks:** Maintained by Sweden - Ministry of Transport and Communications. Telex: 501 25 VTISGI. **Also Known As:** Statens Geotekniska Institut.

THE SWEDISH INSTITUTE OF BUILDING DOCUMENTATION
See: BYGGDOK/The Swedish Institute of Building Documentation (18329)

★18804★
SWEDISH INTERNATIONAL DEVELOPMENT AUTHORITY - SIDA LIBRARY (Soc Sci)
Birger Jarlsgata 61, 9th Fl.
S-105 25 Stockholm, Sweden Phone: 8 728 51 00
Staff: Prof 2; Other 1. **Subjects:** Third World, especially South Asia, Southeast Asia, East and South Africa, Nicaragua; developing countries; development theories and economics; multilateral and bilateral assistance; education; health; rural development; agriculture; industry; women in development. **Holdings:** 30,000 books; maps; statistics; newspapers. **Subscriptions:** 450 journals and other serials. **Services:** Interlibrary loan; copying; library open to the public. **Computerized Information Services:** LIBRIS. **Publications:** Acquisitions list, monthly - to libraries and interested parties; SIDA-library periodicals; U-bit, monthly.

SWEDISH MEDICAL RESEARCH COUNCIL - DEPARTMENT OF STRESS RESEARCH
See: Karolinska Institute - Department of Stress Research (18575)

★18805★
SWEDISH ROAD AND TRAFFIC RESEARCH INSTITUTE - INFORMATION AND DOCUMENTATION SECTION - LIBRARY (Trans)
S-581 01 Linkoping, Sweden Phone: 13 11 52 00
Sigvard Tim, Hd.
Subjects: Roads, traffic, vehicles, road users, traffic safety, allied topics. **Holdings:** 35,000 volumes. **Subscriptions:** 650 journals and other serials. **Services:** SDI; library open to the public. **Computerized Information Services:** ESA/IRS, DIALOG Information Services, Pergamon ORBIT InfoLine, Inc., International Road Research Documentation (IRRD) data base; ROADLINE (internal database). Performs searches on fee basis. **Remarks:** Telex: 50125 VTISGI S. **Also Known As:** Statens Vag- och Trafikinstitut (VTI).

★18806★
SWEDISH SOCIETY OF MEDICINE - LIBRARY (Med)
P.O. Box 558 Phone: 8 24 33 50
S-101 27 Stockholm, Sweden Goran Falkenberg, M.D., Hd.Libn.
Founded: 1808. **Staff:** Prof 2; Other 1. **Subjects:** Medical ethics, history of medicine. **Holdings:** 20,000 books; 30,000 bound periodical volumes; rare medical books. **Services:** Interlibrary loan; library not open to the public. **Publications:** List of periodicals. **Special Catalogs:** Descriptive catalog of older books (in progress). **Remarks:** Library located at Klara Ostra Kyrkogata 10, Stockholm, Sweden. **Staff:** Gunilla Sonden, Asst..

SWEDISH WORK ENVIRONMENT FUND - DEPARTMENT OF STRESS RESEARCH
See: Karolinska Institute - Department of Stress Research (18575)

SWISS BOTANICAL SOCIETY
See: Institute for Phytomedicine - Swiss Botanical Society (18517)

★18807★
SWISS FEDERAL INSTITUTE OF TECHNOLOGY, LAUSANNE - LIBRARY (Sci-Engr)
EPFL-Ecublens
CH-1015 Lausanne, Switzerland Phone: 47 11 11
Subjects: Civil engineering, rural engineering and surveying, mechanical engineering, renewable energy resources, electrical engineering, physics, chemical engineering, mathematics, materials science, architecture. **Holdings:** 200,000 books. **Subscriptions:** 1800 journals and other serials. **Services:** Library open to engineers and architects. **Also Known As:** Ecole Polytechnique Federale de Lausanne.

★18808★
SWISS FEDERAL INSTITUTE OF TECHNOLOGY, ZURICH - LIBRARY (Sci-Engr)
Ramistrasse 101
ETH-Zentrum Phone: 1 256 22 11
CH-8092 Zurich, Switzerland Dr. J.P. Sydler, Dir.
Subjects: Mathematics; physics; chemistry; biology; earth sciences; astronomy; computer science; materials; pharmacy; agriculture; forestry; engineering - mechanical, electrical, civil, environmental; water management, surveying; architecture; humanities; social sciences. **Holdings:** 3.1 million volumes. **Subscriptions:** 9000 journals and other serials. **Remarks:** Telex: 817 379 EHHG. **Also Known As:** Eidgenossische Technische Hochschule.

★18809★
SWISS FEDERAL INSTITUTES OF TECHNOLOGY - SWISS FEDERAL INSTITUTE FOR REACTOR RESEARCH - LIBRARY (Energy)
CH-5303 Wuerenlingen, Switzerland Phone: 99 21 11
Dr. S. Huwyler, Libn.
Subjects: Nuclear energy, nuclear reactors, allied sciences. **Holdings:** 20,000 books; 100,000 reports. **Subscriptions:** 450 journals and other serials. **Remarks:** Telex: 827417. **Also Known As:** Eidgenoessisches Institut fuer Reaktorforschung.

★18810★
SWITZERLAND - FEDERAL FOREST OFFICE - FEDERAL INSTITUTE FOR SNOW AND AVALANCHE RESEARCH - LIBRARY (Sci-Engr)
Weissfluhjoch Phone: 83 532 64
CH-7620 Davos, Switzerland Mrs. E. Huelsmann, Libn.
Subjects: Snow, avalanches. **Holdings:** 20,000 titles. **Formerly:** Switzerland - Federal Administration for Forestry. **Also Known As:** Eidgenoessisches Institut fuer Schnee- und Lawinenforschung.

★18811★
SYRIA - MINISTRY OF CULTURE AND NATIONAL GUIDANCE - DIRECTORATE GENERAL OF ANTIQUITIES AND MUSEUMS - LIBRARY (Area-Ethnic, Hist)
Damascus, Syrian Arab Republic Phone: 228566
Rihab Dahood, Libn.
Subjects: Syria - material culture, archeology, art history, history. **Holdings:** 30,000 volumes. **Remarks:** Telex: 412491 MUSEUM. **Also Known As:** Direction Generale des Antiquites et des Musees.

SZILIKATIPARI KOZPONTI KUTATO ES TERVEZO INTEZET
See: Hungary - Ministry of Construction and City Planning - Central Research and Design Institute for the Silicate Industry (18481)

T

★18812★
TAIWAN AGRICULTURAL RESEARCH INSTITUTE - LIBRARY (Agri, Biol Sci)
189 Chung-Cheng Rd.
Wu-Feng Phone: 4 330-2301
Taichung 41301, Taiwan Miss Shu-Hui Pan, Libn.
Staff: Prof 1; Other 2. **Subjects:** Agronomy, applied zoology, horticulture, agricultural chemistry, plant pathology, agricultural engineering. **Holdings:** 53,000 books; 6885 bound periodical volumes. **Subscriptions:** 1200 journals and other serials; 12 newspapers. **Services:** Interlibrary loan; copying; SDI; library open to the public for reference use only.

★18813★
TAIWAN SUGAR CORPORATION - TAIWAN SUGAR RESEARCH INSTITUTE - LIBRARY (Food-Bev, Agri)
54 Sheng Chan Rd. Phone: 267-1911
Tainan 700, Taiwan Miss Y.H. Ting, Libn.
Subjects: Sugar industry in Taiwan; sugarcane breeding, processing, engineering; soil science; biological control of pests. **Holdings:** 40,000 volumes. **Remarks:** Telex: 4554 TAINAN.

TANZANIA - MINISTRY OF HEALTH AND SOCIAL WELFARE - NATIONAL INSTITUTE FOR MEDICAL RESEARCH
See: National Institute for Medical Research (18627)

★18814★
TANZANIA - NATIONAL CENTRAL LIBRARY - TANZANIA NATIONAL DOCUMENTATION CENTRE (TANDOC) (Sci-Engr, Bus-Fin)
P.O. Box 9283 Phone: 26121
Dar es Salaam, United Republic of Tanzania
Mr. E.A. Mwinyimvua, Prin.Libn.
Subjects: Appropriate technology, agriculture, education, public health, economic development, industry and commerce. **Holdings:** 750,000 volumes; documents; reports. **Subscriptions:** 2500 journals and other serials. **Services:** Copying; center open to the public. **Publications:** Bibliographies; Directory of Libraries in Tanzania; Periodicals in the National Central Library; additional publications available.

★18815★
TATE GALLERY - LIBRARY (Art)
Millbank Phone: 1 821 1313
London SW1P 4RG, England Beth Houghton, Libn.
Staff: Prof 5; Other 3. **Subjects:** Modern art, 1870 to present; British art, 16th century to present; museology; conservation. **Holdings:** 30,000 books; 2000 periodical titles; 100,000 current exhibition catalogs; 2000 artists' books. **Subscriptions:** 750 journals and other serials. **Services:** Interlibrary loan; copying; library open to the public with restrictions. **Publications:** Bibliographies. **Staff:** Meg Duff, Acq.Libn.; Elisabeth Bell, Exch.Libn.; Krzysztof Cieszkowski, Cat.; Jane Savidge, Cat..

TEA RESEARCH INSTITUTE OF SRI LANKA
See: Sri Lanka Tea Board (18789)

★18816★
TECHNICAL RESEARCH CENTRE OF FINLAND - INFORMATION SERVICE (Sci-Engr)
Vuorimiehentie 5 Phone: 0 4561
SF-02150 Espoo, Finland Sauli Laitinen, Dir.
Founded: 1947. **Staff:** Prof 26; Other 42. **Subjects:** Technology - general, energy, information, process, building and community development, manufacturing. **Holdings:** 118,000 books; 25,000 bound periodical volumes; 11,700 travel reports; 87,200 reports on microfiche. **Subscriptions:** 2400 journals and other serials. **Services:** Interlibrary loan; copying; SDI; service open to the public. **Automated Operations:** Computerized cataloging, acquisitions, serials, circulation, and ILL. **Computerized Information Services:** BRS Information Technologies, Chemical Information Systems, Inc. (CIS), Cornell Computer Services (CCS), DIALOG Information Services, Dow Jones News/Retrieval, EBSCO Subscription Services, I.P. Sharp Associates Limited, Info Globe, LEXIS, NEXIS, NewsNet, Inc., OCLC, Pergamon ORBIT InfoLine, Inc., QL Systems, RLIN, STN International, The Source Information Network, Timeplace, Inc., VU/TEXT Information Services, WILSONLINE, Western Library Network (WLN), BELINDIS (Belgian Information and Dissemination Service), BLAISE Online Services, British Maritime Technology Ltd., CMO/Maritime Information Centre, Data-Star, Datasolve Ltd., DBI (Deutsches Bibliotheksinstitut), DIMDI, ECHO (European Commission Host Organization), ESA/IRS, Finsbury Data Services, Ltd., FIZ Technik, G.CAM (Groupement de la Caisse des Depots Automatisation pour le Management), GID (Gesellschaft fur Information und Dokumentation), INKADATA (Informationssystem Karlsruhe), KOMPASS ON LINE, Leatherhead Food Research Association, Telesystemes Questel, Thermodata-Thermdoc Data Bank, VINITI (Vsesoyuznyi Institut Nauchnoy i Teknicheskoy Informatsii), AffarsData, ALIS (Automated Library Information System), ARAMIS, BIBSYS, BYGGDOK (Institutet for Byggdokumentation), DataArkiv AB, Datacentralen (I/S), IDC-KTHB (Information and Documentation Center of the Royal Institute of Technology Library), LIBRIS, ROADLINE, NSI (Norsk Senter for Informatikk A/S), QZ (Stockholm University Computing Center), RECODEX, TESS Sokservice, Helecon, TENTTU. Performs searches on fee basis. Contact Person: Pirkko Eskola, Hd., Res. & Info.Serv.Sect., 4564410. **Publications:** List of new publications acquired, 12/year - by subscription; Periodica, annual - free upon request; list of new travel reports on scientific and technological conferences abroad, 5/year - by subscription; list of new research reports published by Technical Research Centre of Finland, 12/year - by subscription; bulletin of new and ongoing research projects at Technical Research Centre of Finland, 12/year - by subscription; Informaatiopalvelu Tiedottaa (newsletter), semiannual - free upon request. **Special Catalogs:** Travel reports register (card); Research Register (online). **Staff:** Ritva Sundquist, Hd., Doc. Delivery Serv.; Herttu Tirronen, Hd., Publ.Sect..

TECHNICAL UNIVERSITY LIBRARY OF NORWAY
See: University of Trondheim - Norwegian Institute of Technology (18863)

★18817★
TECHNICAL UNIVERSITY OF WROCLAW - MAIN LIBRARY AND SCIENTIFIC INFORMATION CENTER (Sci-Engr)
Wybrzeze Wyspianskiego 27 Phone: 202305
PL-50-370 Wroclaw, Poland Dr. Henryk Szarski, Dir.
Staff: Prof 108; Other 62. **Subjects:** Mathematics; physics; chemistry; architecture; engineering - civil, chemical, electric, mechanical; biochemistry; cybernetics; materials science; earth science; systems theory; environmental sciences. **Holdings:** 700,000 volumes. **Subscriptions:** 2578 journals and other serials. **Services:** SDI; library open to the public. **Automated Operations:** Computerized cataloging. **Computerized Information Services:** INIS (International Nuclear Information System), COMPENDEX, INSPEC, ISMEC, PASCAL; SEBAN (internal database). Performs searches on fee basis. **Remarks:** An alternate telephone number is 212707. Telex: 071-53-71 bg pw pl. **Also Known As:** Politechnika Wroclawska - Biblioteka Glowna i Osrodek Informacji Naukowo-Technicznej.

THAILAND - MINISTRY OF UNIVERSITY AFFAIRS - NATIONAL INSTITUTE OF DEVELOPMENT ADMINISTRATION
See: National Institute of Development Administration (18626)

THAILAND - NATIONAL LIBRARY OF THAILAND
See: National Library of Thailand (18642)

★18818★
TIAN YI GE LIBRARY (Area-Ethnic)
Ningbo, Zhejiang Province, People's Republic of China
Founded: 1561. **Subjects:** Chinese writings - Confucian classics, history, philosophy, belles-lettres. **Special Collections:** Rare editions of Song, Yuan, Ming, and Qing dynasties block-printed editions, handcopies of Ming and Qing manuscripts, rectified editions, copper and wooden type editions (total of 80,000 volumes); Ming dynasty district histories (271 titles); registers of candidates and papers of Imperial Examinations of Ming dynasty (389 titles). **Holdings:** 300,000 volumes.

★18819★
TRANSYLVANIAN WORLD FEDERATION - LIBRARY (Area-Ethnic)
Rua Pedro Zolcsak, 221
Sao Bernardo do Campo Phone: 11 448-8855
Sao Paulo, Brazil Ilona Abaligeti, Sec.
Founded: 1968. **Subjects:** Hungarians in Transylvania and Moldavia in Rumania. **Holdings:** 190 volumes; archival materials. **Remarks:** Telex: 44536 CSAK BR. **Also Known As:** Erdelyi Vilagszovetseg.

★18820★
TRINIDAD AND TOBAGO - MINISTRY OF EDUCATION - CENTRAL LIBRARY SERVICES - WEST INDIAN REFERENCE LIBRARY (Area-Ethnic)
81 Belmont Circular Rd. Phone: 62-41130
Belmont, Trinidad and Tobago Pearl Springer, Libn.
Subjects: West Indies - history, culture, literature, social studies. **Holdings:** 10,445 books; 1739 bound periodical volumes; 50 cassette tapes. **Services:** Interlibrary loan; library open to the public. **Staff:** Angela Bernard, Dir., Lib.Serv..

★18821★
TROPICAL AGRICULTURAL RESEARCH AND TRAINING CENTER - LIBRARY (Agri)
7170 CATIE Phone: 56-64-31
Turrialba, Costa Rica Ana Maria Arias, Dir. of Lib.
Subjects: Agriculture, farming systems, animal husbandry, agroforestry, genetic resources, pastures, watershed management, conservation, cocoa and coffee production. **Holdings:** 70,000 volumes. **Remarks:** Maintains field units in Honduras, Guatemala, Nicaragua, Panama, and El Salvador. Telex: 8005 CATIE. **Also Known As:** Centro Agronomico Tropical de Investigacion y Ensenansa (CATIE).

HARRY S TRUMAN INSTITUTE FOR THE ADVANCEMENT OF PEACE
See: Hebrew University of Jerusalem (18462)

TSENTAR ZA NAUCHNA INFORMACIJA PO MEDITSINA I ZDRAVEOPAZVANE
See: Bulgaria Medical Academy - Center for Scientific Information in Medicine and Public Health (18323)

TURKIYE BILIMSEL VE TEKNIK ARASTIRMA KURUMU
See: Scientific and Technical Research Council of Turkey - Turkish Scientific and Technical Documentation Center (18764)

U

ALEXANDER TURNBULL LIBRARY
See: National Library of New Zealand (18639)

UCHU KAGAKU KENKYUSHO
See: Institute of Space and Astronautical Science - ISAS Library (18527)

UMWELTBUNDESAMT - INFORMATIONS- UND DOKUMENTATIONSSYSTEM UMWELT - ZENTRALE FACHBIBLIOTHEK
See: Federal Republic of Germany - Federal Environmental Agency - Environmental Information and Documentation System - Library (18409)

★18822★
UNESCO - COMPUTERIZED DOCUMENTATION AND LIBRARY SECTION (Educ, Sci-Engr)
7, place de Fontenoy — Phone: 1 568-1000
F-75700 Paris, France — Mr. M. Pobukovsky, Libn.
Subjects: Education, science, culture. **Holdings:** 150,000 volumes. **Also Known As:** United Nations Educational, Scientific, and Cultural Organization.

★18823★
UNESCO - INSTITUTE FOR EDUCATION - LIBRARY (Educ)
Feldbrunnenstrasse 58 — Phone: 44 78 43
D-2000 Hamburg 13, Federal Republic of Germany
Ursula Giere, Libn.
Subjects: Comparative education, educational research, lifelong education, curriculum development, learning strategies, evaluation, teacher training, literacy, continuing education in developing countries. **Holdings:** 45,000 volumes.

UNESCO - INTERNATIONAL ATOMIC ENERGY AGENCY
See: International Atomic Energy Agency (18535)

★18824★
UNESCO - INTERNATIONAL BUREAU OF EDUCATION - DOCUMENTATION CENTRE (Educ)
P.O. Box 199 — Phone: 22 98 14 55
CH-1211 Geneva 20, Switzerland
Liliane Berney, Chf., Doc. & Info. Unit
Staff: Prof 3; Other 6. **Subjects:** UNESCO member states - educational organization, school systems, educational policies and reform. **Special Collections:** ERIC microfiche collection. **Holdings:** 100,000 books and documents; 1000 periodicals; 200 AV programs; 280,000 microfiche. **Services:** Interlibrary loan; copying; center open to the public. **Automated Operations:** Computerized public access catalog, cataloging, acquisitions, serials, and circulation. **Computerized Information Services:** DIALOG Information Services, Pergamon ORBIT InfoLine, Inc., Telesystemes Questel; IBEDOC, IBECENT (internal databases); UNESCO, ICC (electronic mail services). Performs searches on fee basis. **Publications:** Thematic bibliographies; directories. **Remarks:** Center located at 15, route des Morillons, 1218 Grand-Saconnex, Geneva, Switzerland.

UNESCO - INTERNATIONAL CENTER FOR THEORETICAL PHYSICS
See: International Center for Theoretical Physics (18541)

★18825★
UNESCO - INTERNATIONAL COUNCIL OF MUSEUMS - ICOM DOCUMENTATION CENTRE (Hum)
1, rue Miollis — Phone: 1 47340500
F-75732 Paris Cedex 15, France — Susanne Peters, Hd.
Subjects: Museology. **Special Collections:** Museum catalogs (26,000). **Holdings:** 3500 books; 1000 unbound periodicals; 7000 microfiche. **Services:** Copying; center open to the public with restrictions. **Computerized Information Services:** ICOMMOS (internal database). Performs searches free of charge. **Publications:** International Museological Bibliography, annual; Basic Museum Bibliography, irregular; Directory of African Museums; Directory of Asian Museums.

UNESCO - INTERNATIONAL INSTITUTE FOR EDUCATIONAL PLANNING
See: International Institute for Educational Planning (18548)

★18826★
UNESCO - REGIONAL OFFICE FOR EDUCATION IN ASIA AND THE PACIFIC - LIBRARY AND DOCUMENTATION SERVICE (Educ)
P.O. Box 1425, G.P.O. — Phone: 2 391-0879
Bangkok 10501, Thailand — Mr. Ekok Djaka, Chf.
Subjects: Education, culture, communication, social and human sciences, natural science. **Holdings:** 50,000 monographs; 3200 bound periodical volumes; 30,000 documents; 1500 microforms. **Services:** Interlibrary loan; service open to the public. **Computerized Information Services:** Computerized Documentation Service/Integrated Set of Information Systems (CDS/ISIS). **Publications:** Accessions list; book reviews; bibliographies. **Special Indexes:** Periodicals of Asia and the Pacific.

★18827★
UNESCO - REGIONAL OFFICE FOR SCIENCE AND TECHNOLOGY FOR SOUTH AND CENTRAL ASIA - ROSTSCA LIBRARY (Sci-Engr)
UNESCO House
15 Jor Bagh — Phone: 618092
New Delhi 110 003, India — Mrs. Tripta Sondhi, Doc.
Subjects: Science and technology, education, culture, communications. **Special Collections:** ROSTSCA reports; UNESCO publications; appropriate technology (120 volumes). **Holdings:** 24,000 books; 750 periodicals; 60 films, video cassettes, audiotapes; posters; photographs. **Services:** Interlibrary loan; copying (limited); library open to the public.

★18828★
UNION OF BANANA-EXPORTING COUNTRIES - LIBRARY (Food-Bev)
Calle 50 — Panama 5, Panama
Edificio del Bank of America, Piso 7
Apartado 4273
Phone: 636062
Subjects: Banana - production, exportation, transport, commercialization, pricing. **Holdings:** 10,000 volumes. **Remarks:** Serves Colombia, Costa Rica, Dominican Republic, Guatemala, Honduras, Nicaragua, Panama, and Venezuela. Telex: 2568. **Also Known As:** Union de Paises Exportadores de Banano.

★18829★
UNITED NATIONS - FOOD AND AGRICULTURE ORGANIZATION - DAVID LUBIN MEMORIAL LIBRARY (Biol Sci, Agri)
Via delle Terme di Caracalla — Phone: 6 5797 3703
I-00100 Rome, Italy — Carole Joling, Chf.Libn.
Subjects: Agriculture, food and nutrition, fisheries, forestry, rural development, animal production. **Special Collections:** FAO publications, 1945 to present; International Institute of Agriculture Library, 1905-1945; incunabula (32). **Holdings:** 1 million volumes; 120,000 documents; 90,000 microfiche; 4 manuscripts. **Subscriptions:** 3500 journals and other serials. **Services:** Interlibrary loan; copying; SDI; library open to experts. **Automated Operations:** Computerized public access catalog, cataloging, and acquisitions. **Computerized Information Services:** DIALOG Information Services, ESA/IRS. Performs searches on fee basis. **Publications:** FAO Documentation on Microfiche - by subscription; New Books in the DLML, monthly. **Special Catalogs:** Aglinet Union List; COM Catalogs of FAO Documentation, 1976 to present.

★18830★
UNITED NATIONS - INTERNATIONAL COURT OF JUSTICE - LIBRARY (Law)
Peace Palace
Carnegieplein 2 — Phone: 70 924441
NL- 2517 KJ The Hague, Netherlands — Arthur C. Eyffinger, Libn.
Subjects: International public law, International Court of Justice. **Special Collections:** Permanent Court of International Justice publications; International Court of Justice publications. **Holdings:** 13,000 books; 17,000 bound periodical volumes; 50,000 United Nations documents; 500 microforms. **Services:** Library not open to the public. **Publications:** Annual Bibliography of the International Court of Justice. **Staff:** Mrs. R.S.B. Van Megen, Dp.Libn..

UNITED NATIONS - WORLD METEOROLOGICAL ORGANIZATION
See: World Meteorological Organization (18873)

★18831★
UNITED NATIONS CENTER FOR REGIONAL DEVELOPMENT - UNCRD LIBRARY (Soc Sci)
Nagono 1-47-1
Nakamura-ku Phone: 561-9377
Nagoya 450, Japan Josefa S. Edralin, Info.Sys.Plan.
Subjects: Regional development and planning in developing countries. **Holdings:** 12,000 books. **Subscriptions:** 500 journals and other serials. **Remarks:** Maintained by United Nations Department of Technical Cooperation for Development. Telex: J59620 UNCENTRE.

UNITED NATIONS EDUCATIONAL, SCIENTIFIC, AND CULTURAL ORGANIZATION
See: UNESCO (18822)

★18832★
UNITED NATIONS ENVIRONMENT PROGRAMME - REGIONAL OFFICE FOR LATIN AMERICA - LIBRARY (Env-Cons)
Presidente Masaryk, 29, Piso 5
11570 Mexico, D.F., Mexico Alicia Gomez Navarro
Founded: 1972. **Subjects:** Environmental protection in Latin America and the Caribbean. **Holdings:** 6000 volumes. **Remarks:** Telex: 017-71-055 ECLAME. **Also Known As:** Programa de las Naciones Unidas para el Medio Ambiente.

★18833★
UNITED NATIONS INSTITUTE FOR NAMIBIA - LIBRARY (Area-Ethnic)
P.O. Box 33811 Phone: 216468
Lusaka, Namibia Mr. P.C. Kullen, Libn.
Subjects: Namibia - liberation struggle to post-independence reconstruction. **Holdings:** 10,000 monographs; 40,000 documents. **Subscriptions:** 150 journals and other serials. **Remarks:** Telex: 41960.

★18834★
THE UNIVERSAL HOUSE OF JUSTICE - BAHA'I WORLD CENTRE - LIBRARY (Rel-Phil)
16 Golomb Ave.
P.O. Box 155 Phone: 972 4 372433
31 001 Haifa, Israel William P. Collins, Hd.Libn.
Subjects: Bahai faith, Babi faith (Babism), comparative religion, Iran, Islam. **Special Collections:** A.L.M. Nicolas Collection (Shaykhi, Babi, and Baha'i manuscripts and books; 250); Baha'i faith, 1977 to present (25,000 clippings). **Holdings:** 22,000 books; 850 bound periodical volumes; 48,000 pamphlets; 500 AV programs; 2000 microforms; 200 manuscripts. **Services:** Copying; library open to accepted researchers only. **Automated Operations:** Computerized cataloging. **Computerized Information Services:** DIALOG Information Services. **Remarks:** An alternate telephone number is 372440. **Staff:** Elizabeth Jenkerson, Ref.Libn.; Louise Mould, Hd.Cat.; Carol Clyde, Acq.Libn.; Bryn Deamer, Per.Asst.; Janet Beavers, Per.Libn..

★18835★
UNIVERSALA ESPERANTO-ASOCIO - BIBLIOTEKO HECTOR HODLER (Hum)
Nieuwe Binnenweg 176 Phone: 10 436 10 44
NL-3015 BJ Rotterdam, Netherlands Rob Moerbeek
Subjects: Esperanto literature, history of Esperanto movement and organizations, interlinguistics. **Holdings:** 13,013 books; 150 bound periodical volumes. **Services:** Library open to the public for reference use only. **Remarks:** Telex: 23721 uea nl.

★18836★
UNIVERSIDAD DE LOS ANDES - BIBLIOTECA GENERAL (Sci-Engr, Hum)
Apartado Aereo 4976
Carrera 1-Este, 18-A-10 Phone: 2-81-58-24
Bogota, Colombia Angela Maria Mejia de Restrepo, Dir.
Subjects: Science; engineering - electrical, mechanical, civil, industrial; computer sciences; humanities. **Special Collections:** Antique and rare books. **Holdings:** 75,000 titles; 6000 documents; 4500 nonbook materials; United Nations university publications depository. **Services:** Interlibrary loan; copying; library open to the public with restrictions. **Computerized Information Services:** DIALOG Information Services. Performs searches on fee basis. Contact Person: Luz Marina Guerrero, Hd., Info./Doc.Serv.. **Publications:** Incunables de la Universidad de los Andes; Libros publicados entre 1501 y 1600; La Expedicion Botamica. **Staff:** Balbina Chavarro Olaya, Hd., Coll.Dev..

★18837★
UNIVERSIDAD DE CALDAS - CENTRO DE BIBLIOTECA E INFORMACION CIENTIFICA ENRIQUE MEJIA RUIZ (Med, Agri)
Apartado Aereo 275 Phone: 968-855-240
Manizales, Colombia Elsie Duque de Ramirez, Dir.
Subjects: Medicine, agriculture, veterinary medicine, law, education, social sciences, humanities. **Holdings:** 30,000 books; 25,000 bound periodical volumes; 300 AV programs; 100 microforms; 50 manuscripts. **Services:** Interlibrary loan; copying; SDI; library open to the public. **Computerized Information Services:** MEDLARS, MEDLINE. Performs searches on fee basis.

★18838★
UNIVERSIDAD DE COSTA RICA - DIRECCION DE BIBLIOTECAS DOCUMENTACION E INFORMACION (Sci-Engr, Hum, Med, Law)
Ciudad Universitaria "Rodrigo Facio" Phone: 25-7372
San Jose, Costa Rica Licda Aurora Zamora Gonzalez, Dir.
Subjects: Religion, humanities, literature, history, geography, medicine, philosophy, education, philology, chemistry, computer science, geology, mathematics, architecture, economics, physics, engineering, law, pharmacy and pharmacology. **Special Collections:** Rare books; atomic energy collection. **Holdings:** 271,576 books; 21,542 AV programs; theses. **Subscriptions:** 9704 journals and other serials. **Services:** Interlibrary loan; copying; SDI; library open to the public with restrictions. **Computerized Information Services:** DIALOG Information Services. Performs searches on fee basis. Contact Person: Licda Flora Li Chen, Bibliotecarias. **Publications:** Boletin Bibliografico; Boletines Diseminacion de la Informacion; Publicacion Trabajos Finales de Graduacion; Publicacion "Serie Bibliografica." **Remarks:** Includes the holdings of the following libraries: Biblioteca Carlos Monge Alfaro, Biblioteca Luis Demetrio Tinoco, Biblioteca Facultad de Derecho, and Biblioteca Facultad de Farmacia. Telex: UNICORI.

★18839★
UNIVERSIDAD NACIONAL AUTONOMA DE MEXICO - DIRECCION GENERAL DE BIBLIOTECAS - BIBLIOTECA CENTRAL (Hum, Soc Sci)
Ciudad Universitaria
Circuito Interior Phone: 915 550-52-15
Mexico City, DF 04510, Mexico Adolfo Rodriguez Gallardo, Dir.Gen.
Subjects: Humanities, social sciences, physical sciences, medicine, health sciences, arts. **Special Collections:** Rare books (16th-19th centuries). **Holdings:** 350,000 books; 40,000 bound periodical volumes; 5000 microforms. **Services:** Interlibrary loan; copying; library open to the public. **Computerized Information Services:** LIBRUNAM. Contact Person: Angela Pacheco. **Publications:** List of publications - available on request. **Special Catalogs:** Catalogo Colectivo de Publicaciones Periodicas de la UNAM; Informe de Labores de la Direccion General de Bibliotecas. **Staff:** Eugenio Romero Hernandez, Subdir., Serv..

UNIVERSIDAD DEL NORTE - UNIDAD DE BIBLIOTECA Y DOCUMENTACION
See: University of North - Library and Documentation Unit (18854)

★18840★
UNIVERSIDAD SANTA MARIA LA ANTIGUA - BIBLIOTECA (Bus-Fin, Law)
Apartado 6-16
96 El Dorado Phone: 60 63 11
Panama City, Panama Emeterio Quintero Ramos, Libn.
Subjects: Mathematics, finance, economics, management, Catholicism, accounting, law. **Special Collections:** Panamanian collection (4000 volumes). **Holdings:** 35,623 books; 8000 bound periodical volumes; 1000 theses. **Services:** Library open to the public with restrictions. **Publications:** New Books List, monthly. **Remarks:** An alternate telephone number is 60 62 84.

★18841★
UNIVERSIDADE FEDERAL DO RIO GRANDE DO SUL - BIBLIOTECA CENTRAL (Soc Sci, Hist)
Avenida Paulo Gama
Caixa Postal 2303 Phone: 24-2431
90001 Porto Alegre RS, Brazil Zita Catarina Prates de Oliveira, Dir.
Subjects: Social sciences, philosophy, history. **Special Collections:** Rare books (7000 volumes). **Holdings:** 408,184 books; 13,131 bound periodical volumes; 217,445 nonbook materials. **Services:** Interlibrary loan; copying; SDI; library open to the public. **Computerized Information Services:** DIALOG Information Services, Pergamon ORBIT InfoLine, Inc.,

Telesystemes Questel, STN International, ARUANDA, SINORTEC/INMETRO, PRODASEN, BSP/IBICT. Performs searches on fee basis. Contact Person: Heloisa Schreiner, Libn., 31-2355, ext. 41. **Publications:** Periodicos Correntes da UFRGS; Bibliotec; annual report. **Remarks:** Maintains 27 branch libraries. Telex: 051 1055.

UNIVERSITATSBIBLIOTHEK HANNOVER UND TECHNISCHE INFORMATIONSBIBLIOTHEK
See: University Library of Hannover and Technical Information Library (18852)

★18842★
UNIVERSITEIT ANTWERPEN - UNIVERSITAIRE FACULTEITEN SINT-IGNATIUS ANTWERPEN - BIBLIOTHEEK VAN HET RUUSBROECGENOOTSCHAP (Rel-Phil)
Prinsstraat 13 Phone: 3 220 41 11
B-2000 Antwerp, Belgium Frans Hendrickx, Libn.
Subjects: History of ascetic and mystic devotion, history of spirituality, church history, cloisters, religious art and folklore. **Special Collections:** Rare books, 1470-1800 (35,000); saints and devotional prints (35,000); manuscripts, 12th-20th centuries (500). **Holdings:** 103,000 volumes; 600 reels of microfilm. **Services:** Interlibrary loan; copying; library open to the public. **Computerized Information Services:** VUBIS. Performs searches on fee basis. **Remarks:** Telex: 33.599 UFSIA B. **Also Known As:** Ruusbroecgenootschap Centrum voor Spiritualiteit.

★18843★
UNIVERSITES DE PARIS I, III, IV, V, VII - BIBLIOTHEQUE DE LA SORBONNE (Hist, Sci-Engr, Hum)
47, rue des Ecoles Phone: 1 40.46.30.27
F-75230 Paris Cedex 05, France Claude Jolly, Dir.
Subjects: Classical history; linguistics; literature - French, Slavic, foreign; history of science and technology; psychology; sociology; philosophy; history; religious studies; university history. **Special Collections:** Archives de l'ancienne universite; early theology and history. **Holdings:** 3.2 million books; 13,000 bound periodical volumes; 2141 manuscripts. **Services:** Interlibrary loan; copying; library open to the public with restrictions. **Computerized Information Services:** FRANCIS (French Retrieval Automated Network for Current Information in Social and Human Sciences), CAPOU, Hispabib, teletheses, Frantext. Performs searches on fee basis. Contact Person: Nicole Pierre, Cons., 40.46.31.06. **Publications:** Melanges de la Bibliotheque de la Sorbonne (8 volumes); Les Bibliotheques des Universites de Paris - both for sale; Listes Annuelles des Theses de Lettres. **Special Catalogs:** Catalogue des Theses de Doctorat; Catalogue Collectif National des Publications en Serie; Repertoire des Bibliotheques - all for sale.

UNIVERSITY OF ADELAIDE - WAITE AGRICULTURAL RESEARCH INSTITUTE
See: Waite Agricultural Research Institute (18870)

UNIVERSITY OF AMSTERDAM - INTERNATIONAL ARCHIVES FOR THE WOMEN'S MOVEMENT
See: International Archives for the Women's Movement (18534)

★18844★
UNIVERSITY OF BARCELONA - CENTRE FOR INTERNATIONAL HISTORICAL STUDIES - CEHI LIBRARY (Area-Ethnic, Hist)
Carrer de Brusi, 61 Phone: 3 200 45 67
E-08006 Barcelona, Spain Jordi Planes, Hd., Res.
Subjects: Spain - contemporary history, Spanish Civil War, Francoist period, modern social movements, national liberation movements. **Holdings:** 20,000 books; 5000 bound periodical volumes; documents; microforms. **Services:** Copying; library open to the public for reference use only. **Publications:** Estudis d'Historia Agraria. **Special Indexes:** Indice Historico Espanol.

★18845★
UNIVERSITY OF BRISTOL - UNIVERSITY LIBRARY (Hum)
Tyndall Ave. Phone: 272 303030
Bristol BS8 1TJ, England Norman Higham, Libn.
Subjects: Arts, engineering, law, medicine, social sciences. **Special Collections:** English Novel to 1850; Penguin Books Collection; business histories; early science and philosophy; British General Election addresses; I.K. Brunel workbooks and papers (railroad builder/engineer); Pinney papers (17th-19th century); landscape gardening; Wiglesworth Ornithological Library. **Holdings:** 1 million books, periodicals, and pamphlets; 130,000 microforms; manuscripts. **Services:** Interlibrary loan. **Computerized Information Services:** DIALOG Information Services, Data-Star, Pergamon ORBIT InfoLine, Inc., DIMDI, Scicon Ltd. **Remarks:** Telex: 265871.

★18846★
UNIVERSITY OF CAMBRIDGE - LIBRARY (Rare Book, Hum, Sci-Engr)
West Rd. Phone: 223 333000
Cambridge CB3 9DR, England Dr. F.W. Ratcliffe, Univ.Libn.
Staff: Prof 44; Other 188. **Subjects:** Theology, religion, philosophy, psychology, social sciences, law, sciences, fine arts, entertainment and sports, technology, engineering, agriculture, anthropology, archeology, genealogy, history, geography, Western literature, linguistics, Oriental languages and literature, bibliography. **Special Collections:** Acton Library; adversaria (printed books with annotations); almanacs; armorial bindings; Madden Collection of Ballads, 1750-1850 (16,354 broadsides); bookplates and book stamps; book sales catalogs; Cambridge Collection; chapbooks, 1750-1850 (3500); Darwin Library; early English printed books, 1501-1701; Ely diocesan and chapter records; incunabula (4300); Bradshaw Collection of Irish Books; Peterborough Cathedral Library; portraits; Taylor-Schechter Genizah Collection (100,000 fragments of vellum and paper from the depository of an ancient synagogue in Cairo); university archives, 13th century to the present (charters of privilege; letters and mandates; records of the University Press, 16th-early 20th century; plans for university buildings; university papers); War Collection (World War I; pamphlets and ephemeral publications); British and Foreign Bible Society Library. **Holdings:** 4.15 million volumes; 680,000 reels of microfilm; 910,000 maps; 85,300 manuscripts. **Services:** Interlibrary loan; copying; library open to the public with restrictions. **Automated Operations:** Computerized public access catalog, cataloging, and circulation. **Computerized Information Services:** Online systems. Performs searches on fee basis. **Publications:** Bibliographies; guides to the library; Libraries Information Bulletin, monthly - available on request. **Special Catalogs:** Catalogs to: AV material, ballads, Cambridge Collection, chapbooks, dissertations, Far Eastern books, incunabula, manuscripts, maps and atlases, microforms, music, official publications, pamphlets, university archives; additional published catalogs of special collections - for sale. **Remarks:** Includes the holdings of the Squire Law Library, the Scientific Periodicals Library, and the Medical Library.

★18847★
UNIVERSITY OF CAPE TOWN - CENTRE FOR AFRICAN STUDIES - LIBRARY (Area-Ethnic)
Leslie Social Science Bldg.
Rondebosch 7700, Republic of South Africa Phone: 650-2308
Subjects: South Africa, Africa. **Holdings:** 7500 volumes.

UNIVERSITY OF COIMBRA - INSTITUTE OF ANTHROPOLOGY
See: Institute of Anthropology (18497)

★18848★
UNIVERSITY OF COLOGNE - CENTRAL ARCHIVES FOR EMPIRICAL SOCIAL RESEARCH (Soc Sci)
Bachemer Strasse 40 Phone: 221 444086
D-5000 Cologne 41, Federal Republic of Germany
Dr. Erwin K. Scheuch, Dir.
Founded: 1960. **Subjects:** Surveys - social, population, panel studies, cross-national studies; survey methodology. **Holdings:** 10,000 monographs, reports, unpublished papers; complete primary materials for 1400 surveys. **Services:** Archives open to the public with restrictions. **Computerized Information Services:** Internal database. Performs searches on fee basis. **Publications:** List of Archive Holdings; additional publications available. **Staff:** Ekkehard Mochmann, Mgr..

★18849★
UNIVERSITY OF DUSSELDORF - RESEARCH DIVISION FOR PHILOSOPHY INFORMATION AND DOCUMENTATION - PHILOSOPHY INFORMATION SERVICE (Rel-Phil)
Universitatstrasse 1 Phone: 211 3112913
D-4000 Dusseldorf 1, Federal Republic of Germany
Dr. Norbert Henrichs, Hd.
Founded: 1967. **Staff:** Prof 3; Other 7. **Subjects:** Philosophy, philosophy of science, logic, anthropology, metaphysics, ethics. **Special Collections:** Letters of Philosophers, 1750-1850 (300,000 pages). **Holdings:** 70,000 volumes. **Subscriptions:** 150 journals and other serials. **Services:** Interlibrary loan; SDI; service open to the public. **Automated Operations:** Computerized public access catalog, cataloging, and serials. **Computerized Information Services:** Produces Epistolographie Data Base; PHILIS (internal database). Performs searches free of charge.

★18850★
UNIVERSITY OF GRONINGEN - POLEMOLOGICAL INSTITUTE - LIBRARY (Soc Sci)
Heresingel 13 Phone: 635655
NL-9711 ER Groningen, Netherlands Ms. Digna Van Boven, Libn.
Subjects: Conflicts in the international system; theories of international relations; relations between U.S and their allies, 1945 to present; conflict, political violence, and war; armament; arms race; defense expenditures; effects of war; conflict resolution and peace. **Holdings:** 13,000 books. **Subscriptions:** 200 journals and other serials. **Also Known As:** Polemologisch Instituut.

★18851★
UNIVERSITY OF HELSINKI - LIBRARY (Hum, Info Sci)
Unioninkatu 36
P.O. Box 312 Phone: 0 191 2740
SF-00171 Helsinki, Finland Inger Osterman, Libn./Hd., Pub.Serv.
Subjects: Humanities. **Special Collections:** National Library of Finland; Slavonic Collection, 1828-1917 (300,000 volumes); 200 other special collections. **Holdings:** 2.5 million volumes; 150,000 microforms. **Services:** Interlibrary loan; copying; SDI; library open to the public. **Computerized Information Services:** KDOK/Minttu, DIALOG Information Services. Performs searches on fee basis. **Publications:** Finnish national bibliography; bibliographies - both for sale. **Remarks:** National Library of Finland is an archival collection; no interlibrary loans or circulation are allowed.

★18852★
UNIVERSITY LIBRARY OF HANNOVER AND TECHNICAL INFORMATION LIBRARY (Sci-Engr)
Universitatsbibliothek und T13
Welfengarten 1B Phone: 511 7622268
D-3000 Hannover 1, Federal Republic of Germany
Dr. Gerhard Schlitt, Dir.
Founded: 1959. **Staff:** Prof 75; Other 134. **Subjects:** Engineering, physics, mathematics, chemistry. **Holdings:** 3 million volumes; 1 million reels of microfilm. **Subscriptions:** 22,000 journals and other serials. **Services:** Interlibrary loan; copying; library open to the public. **Automated Operations:** Computerized cataloging. **Computerized Information Services:** DIALOG Information Services, ESA/IRS, STN International, DIMDI, Zeitschriftendatenbank (ZDB). Performs searches on fee basis. **Special Catalogs:** Periodicals list: ZV 89. **Remarks:** Serves as central national library for science and engineering. **Also Known As:** Universitatsbibliothek Hannover und Technische Informationsbibliothek. **Staff:** Jobst Tehnzen, Dp.Libn.; Christoph-Hubert Schutte, Dp.Libn..

UNIVERSITY OF MAURITIUS - MAURITIUS SUGAR INDUSTRY RESEARCH INSTITUTE
See: Mauritius Sugar Industry Research Institute (18603)

★18853★
UNIVERSITY OF NIAMEY - RESEARCH INSTITUTE FOR THE HUMANITIES - LIBRARY (Hum)
B.P. 318 Phone: 72-31-41
Niamey, Niger M. Saidou Harouna, Libn.
Subjects: Sociology, linguistics, archeology, history, geography. **Holdings:** 17,000 volumes.

★18854★
UNIVERSITY OF NORTH - LIBRARY AND DOCUMENTATION UNIT (Sci-Engr)
Avenida Angamos, 0610
Casilla Postal 1280 Phone: 251611
Antofagasta, Chile Drahomira Srytrova Tomasova
Subjects: Exact sciences, engineering, architecture, economy, humanities. **Special Collections:** Chilean history (1300 items); thesis collection (2000); historical archives (13 items). **Holdings:** 74,000 books; 52,000 bound periodical volumes; 6500 documents; 16,800 AV programs. **Services:** Interlibrary loan; copying; SDI; unit open to the public with restrictions. **Special Catalogs:** Repertorios: Serie I, Repertorio Bibliografico; Repertorios: Serie II, Repertorio Documental (bibliographic catalogs of information about the reality of northern Chile). **Remarks:** Telex: 225097 UNORT CL. **Also Known As:** Universidad del Norte - Unidad de Biblioteca y Documentacion.

★18855★
UNIVERSITY OF OSLO - INSTITUTE FOR SOCIAL ANTHROPOLOGY - LIBRARY (Soc Sci)
P.O. Box 1091 Blindern Phone: 2 45 65 26
N-0317 Oslo 3, Norway Ms. Per Pharo, Libn.
Subjects: Social anthropology, ethnic relations, migration, peasant economy and development, symbolic anthropology, culture of complex societies, migrants in Norway. **Holdings:** 30,000 volumes.

★18856★
UNIVERSITY OF OSLO LIBRARY (Biol Sci, Med, Law, Info Sci)
Drammensveien 42 Phone: 2 553630
N-0255 Oslo 2, Norway Jan Erik Roed, Libn.
Subjects: Natural sciences, medicine, dentistry, law, humanities, theology, social sciences. **Holdings:** 4 million books; 550,000 microforms; 40,000 manuscripts. **Services:** Interlibrary loan; copying; SDI; library open to the public. **Computerized Information Services:** UBO:BOK. Performs searches on fee basis. **Publications:** National Bibliography. **Remarks:** Library is the legal depository for Norway and serves as the national library.

★18857★
UNIVERSITY OF PETROLEUM AND MINERALS - RESEARCH INSTITUTE - LIBRARY (Energy)
Dhahran 31261, Saudi Arabia Phone: 8603319
Subjects: Petroleum and gas, energy resources, geology, minerals, water resources, environment, metrology, standards, materials, economic and industrial research. **Holdings:** 200,000 volumes.

★18858★
UNIVERSITY OF THE PHILIPPINES - ASIAN CENTER - LIBRARY (Area-Ethnic)
Diliman Phone: 96-18-21
Quezon City, Philippines Violeta V. Encarnacion, Libn.
Subjects: Philippines - history, culture, politics. **Holdings:** 26,240 volumes.

UNIVERSITY OF POONA - BHANDARKAR ORIENTAL RESEARCH INSTITUTE
See: Bhandarkar Oriental Research Institute (18301)

UNIVERSITY OF POONA - GOKHALE INSTITUTE OF POLITICS AND ECONOMICS
See: Gokhale Institute of Politics and Economics (18451)

★18859★
UNIVERSITY OF SIND - INSTITUTE OF SINDHOLOGY - RESEARCH LIBRARY (Area-Ethnic)
Jamshoro, Sind, Pakistan Phone: 221 71125
Gul Mohammad N. Mughol, Libn.
Founded: 1962. **Staff:** Prof 2; Other 24. **Subjects:** Sind - history, literature, religion, fine arts, linguistics, social science. **Special Collections:** Sind archives (4851 archival materials). **Holdings:** 80,000 books; 10,000 bound periodical volumes; 1210 manuscripts; 6930 dissertations; 370 reels of microfilm. **Subscriptions:** 45 journals and other serials; 18 newspapers. **Services:** Copying; library open to the public for reference use only. **Automated Operations:** Computerized public access catalog. **Special Catalogs:** Catalogue of Manuscripts, Sindhi periodicals, and list of archival material. **Staff:** Sayed Ghullam Mohammed Shah, Classifier.

★18860★
UNIVERSITY OF SUSSEX - UNIVERSITY LIBRARY (Soc Sci, Hum)
Falmer Phone: 273 678163
Brighton BN1 9QL, England A.N. Peasgood, Libn.
Subjects: General collection. **Special Collections:** European Communities documents; Paris Commune of 1871 (2500 items); Rudyard Kipling papers; papers of Leonard and Virginia Woolf; Tom Harrisson Mass-observation Archive; sheet music (the former J & W Chester Subscription Library; 50,000 pieces). **Holdings:** 430,000 books; 145,000 bound periodical volumes; 5000 AV programs; 720,000 microforms; 1500 boxes of manuscripts. **Services:** Interlibrary loan; copying; SDI; library open to the public with restrictions. **Computerized Information Services:** DIALOG Information Services, ESA/IRS, STN International, Data-Star, Pergamon InfoLine, BLAISE Online Services. Performs searches on fee basis. **Publications:** Handlists of Special Collections. **Remarks:** Telex: 265871.

★18861★
UNIVERSITY OF TOKYO - EARTHQUAKE RESEARCH INSTITUTE - LIBRARY (Sci-Engr)
1-1 Yayoi, 1-Chome
Bunkyo-ku
Tokyo, 113 Japan Phone: 3 812-2111
Subjects: Seismology. **Holdings:** 39,000 volumes.

★18862★
UNIVERSITY OF TOKYO - INSTITUTE OF INDUSTRIAL SCIENCE - LIBRARY (Sci-Engr)
22-1 Roppongi, 7-Chome
Minato-ku
Tokyo 106, Japan Phone: 402-6231
Subjects: Applied physics and mechanics, mechanical engineering, naval architecture, industrial chemistry, metallurgy, building, civil engineering, instrumentation, composite materials, functional electronics. **Holdings:** 132,000 volumes. **Remarks:** Telex: 0242 3216 IISTYO.

★18863★
UNIVERSITY OF TRONDHEIM - NORWEGIAN INSTITUTE OF TECHNOLOGY - TECHNICAL UNIVERSITY LIBRARY OF NORWAY (Sci-Engr, Art)
N-7034 Trondheim, Norway Phone: 7 595110
Mrs. Randi Gjersvik, Dir.
Founded: 1912. **Staff:** Prof 11; Other 52. **Subjects:** Science and technology, architecture, art, trade. **Holdings:** 910,000 volumes; 160,000 standards; 2.9 million patents; 243,000 reports on microfiche. **Subscriptions:** 8000 journals and other serials; 40 newspapers. **Services:** Interlibrary loan; copying; SDI; library open to the public. **Automated Operations:** Computerized public access catalog, cataloging, acquisitions, and ILL. **Computerized Information Services:** ESA/IRS, DIALOG Information Services, Pergamon ORBIT InfoLine, Inc., Telesystemes Questel, STN International; internal databases. Performs searches on fee basis. **Publications:** Research reports, irregular. **Remarks:** Serves as the central technical library of Norway. DIANE, a Norwegian national service center for online users, is located within the library.

★18864★
UNIVERSITY OF VIENNA - INSTITUTE OF BOTANY AND BOTANICAL GARDEN - LIBRARY (Biol Sci)
Rennweg 14 Phone: 222 78 71 01
A-1030 Vienna, Austria Dr. Liselotte Niklas, Libn.
Staff: Prof 2; Other 1. **Subjects:** Electron microscopy, comparative phytochemistry, algae and lichens, morphology, palynology, cytogenetics, systematics, evolution of spermatophytes, tropical botany and geobotany. **Holdings:** 14,000 books; 40,000 bound periodical volumes; monographs; reprints. **Subscriptions:** 250 journals and other serials. **Services:** Interlibrary loan; copying; library open to the public. **Staff:** Dr. Robert Stangl, Asst.Libn.; Dr. Karin Vetschera, Asst.Libn..

★18865★
UNIVERSITY OF THE WEST INDIES - MAIN LIBRARY (Agri, Soc Sci, Sci-Engr)
St. Augustine, Trinidad and Tobago Phone: 663-1439
Dr. Alma T. Jordan, Univ.Libn.
Subjects: Agriculture, engineering, social sciences, natural sciences, humanities. **Special Collections:** West Indian Collection. **Holdings:** 244,310 books; 42,720 bound periodical volumes; 18,749 microforms; 6947 AV programs; 3166 manuscripts. **Services:** Interlibrary loan; copying; SDI; library open to the public with restrictions. **Computerized Information Services:** DIALOG Information Services, Pergamon ORBIT InfoLine, Inc., WILSONLINE, AGRIS (International Information System for the Agricultural Sciences and Technology), CARBIB. Performs searches on fee basis. Contact Person: Shirley Evelyn, Hd., Rd.Serv.. **Special Indexes:** CARINDEX: Science and Technology; CARINDEX: Social Sciences and Humanities; CAGRINDEX: Abstracts of the agricultural literature of the English-Speaking Caribbean. **Remarks:** Telex: 24-520 UWI-WG.

UNIVERSITY OF YAOUNDE - CAMEROON INSTITUTE OF INTERNATIONAL RELATIONS
See: Cameroon Institute of International Relations (18330)

★18866★
URUGUAY - BIBLIOTECA NACIONAL - CENTRO NACIONAL DE DOCUMENTACION CIENTIFICA, TECNICA Y ECONOMICA (Sci-Engr)
18 de Julio 1790 Phone: 2 4 41 72
Montevideo, Uruguay Elena Castro De Blengini, Dir.
Subjects: Information science, science and technology. **Holdings:** 1000 books; 200 serial titles. **Services:** Interlibrary loan; copying; SDI; center open to the public with restrictions. **Publications:** Directorio de Servicios de Informacion y Documentacion en el Uruguay. **Special Indexes:** Uruguay: Indice de publicaciones periodicas en ciencia y tecnologia, 1981-1983. **Also Known As:** Centro Nacional de Referencia del Uruguay.

USTAV VEDECKYCH LEKARSKYCH INFORMACI - STATNI LEKARSKA KNIHOVNA
See: Institute for Medical Information (18514)

V

★18867★
VALENCIA PROVINCE - SERVICE FOR PREHISTORIC RESEARCH - LIBRARY (Hist, Soc Sci)
Calle de la Corona, 36 Phone: 331 71 64
E-46003 Valencia, Spain Consuelo Martin Piera, Libn.
Founded: 1927. **Staff:** Prof 2; Other 3. **Subjects:** Prehistory, archeology. **Holdings:** 17,450 books; 10,550 bound periodical volumes. **Subscriptions:** 756 journals and other serials. **Services:** Interlibrary loan; copying; library open to the public. **Publications:** Serie de Trabajos Varios, irregular; Archivo de Prehistoria Levantina, irregular; La Labor del Servicio de Investigacion Prehistorica y su Museo en el pasado ano, annual. **Also Known As:** Servicio de Investigacion Prehistorica. **Staff:** Carmen Baguena Barrachina, Asst.Libn..

★18868★
ING. JUAN C. VAN WYCK CENTER FOR RESEARCH AND DEVELOPMENT - LIBRARY (Sci-Engr)
Berutti y Rio Bamba Phone: 81-3194
2000 Rosario, Argentina E. Sisti, Libn.
Subjects: Engineering, material technology, structural analysis, metallurgy, nuclear technology. **Holdings:** 41,175 volumes. **Remarks:** Maintained by Rosario National University - Faculty of Exact Sciences and Engineering. **Also Known As:** Centro de Investigacion y Desarrollo "Ing. Juan C. Van Wyk."

★18869★
GETULIO VARGAS FOUNDATION - LIBRARY (Soc Sci, Bus-Fin)
Caixa Postal 9052 Phone: 21 551-1542
20000 Rio de Janeiro RJ, Brazil Marietta Latorre, Libn.
Subjects: Economics, public law, political science, public administration, foreign trade, psychology, contemporary Brazilian history, education, sociology. **Holdings:** 121,870 volumes. **Also Known As:** Fundacao Getulio Vargas.

VAUGHAN WILLIAMS MEMORIAL LIBRARY
See: English Folk Dance and Song Society (18393)

VELAZQUEZ HOUSE
See: France - Ministere de l'Education - Velazquez House (18423)

VEREIN DEUTSCHER EISENHUTTENLEUTE - BETRIEBSFORSCHUNGSINSTITUT
See: German Iron and Steel Engineers Association - Institute for Applied Research (18447)

VICTORIA DEPARTMENT OF CONSERVATION, FORESTS AND LANDS - ROYAL BOTANIC GARDENS & NATIONAL HERBARIUM
See: Royal Botanic Gardens & National Herbarium (18736)

VISH INSTITUT ZA FIZICHESKA KULTURA "GEORGI DIMITROV"
See: Georgi Dimitrov Higher Institute of Physical Culture (18384)

VYZKUMNY USTAV HUTNICTVI ZELEZA, DOBRA
See: Dobra Iron and Steel Research Institute (18386)

VYZKUMNY USTAV KOZEDELNY
See: Shoe and Leather Research Institute (18770)

VYZKUMNY USTAV VODOHOSPODARSKY
See: Czechoslovakia - Ministry of Forestry and Water Management - Water Research Institute (18375)

W

★18870★
WAITE AGRICULTURAL RESEARCH INSTITUTE - LIBRARY (Agri, Biol Sci)
Glen Osmond, SA 5064, Australia Phone: 372 2310
Ms. K.L. Baudinette, Libn.
Founded: 1925. **Staff:** Prof 2; Other 5. **Subjects:** Crop, pasture, and animal production; agricultural biochemistry; agronomy; crop ecology; genetics; plant breeding; animal husbandry; systematic botany; entomology; plant physiology and pathology; soil science; horticulture. **Holdings:** 46,000 volumes. **Services:** Interlibrary loan; copying; SDI. **Automated Operations:** Computerized public access catalog and cataloging. **Computerized Information Services:** DIALOG Information Services, CSIRONET, STN International, Australian Bibliographic Network (ABN). Performs searches on fee basis. **Remarks:** Maintained by University of Adelaide.

WELLCOME LIBRARY
See: Royal College of Veterinary Surgeons (18741)

★18871★
WEST AFRICA RICE DEVELOPMENT ASSOCIATION - WARDA LIBRARY (Food-Bev, Agri)
E.J. Roye Memorial Bldg.
Ashmun St.
P.O. Box 1019 Phone: 221466
Monrovia, Liberia Alassane Diallo, Libn.
Subjects: Rice production, food crops in the tropics. **Holdings:** 15,000 volumes. **Also Known As:** Association pour le Developpement de la Riziculture en Afrique de l'Ouest.

WEST INDIAN REFERENCE LIBRARY
See: Trinidad and Tobago - Ministry of Education - Central Library Services (18820)

WIGLESWORTH ORNITHOLOGICAL LIBRARY
See: University of Bristol - University Library (18845)

WILLAN LIBRARY OF BRITISH ASSOCIATION OF DERMATOLOGISTS
See: Royal College of Physicians of London - Library (18739)

★18872★
WORLD COUNCIL OF CHURCHES - ECUMENICAL LIBRARY (Rel-Phil)
150, route de Ferney
Boite Postale 66
CH-1211 Geneva 20, Switzerland Phone: 22 916111
Subjects: Ecumenical fellowship of Eastern and Oriental Orthodox, Lutheran, Reformed, Methodist, Anglican, Old Catholic, Pentecostal, Baptist, United, and Independent denominations around the world. **Holdings:** 87,000 volumes; 10,000 boxes of archival materials. **Also Known As:** Conseil Oecumenique des Eglises.

WORLD HEALTH ORGANIZATION - INTERNATIONAL AGENCY FOR RESEARCH ON CANCER
See: International Agency for Research on Cancer (18533)

★18873★
WORLD METEOROLOGICAL ORGANIZATION - WMO LIBRARY (Sci-Engr)
P.O. Box 5
41, ave. Giuseppe-Motta Phone: 22 34 64 00
CH-1211 Geneva, Switzerland Miss Favre, Libn.
Subjects: Weather prediction, world climate, tropical meteorology, monitoring environmental pollution, weather modification. **Holdings:** 35,000 volumes. **Remarks:** Organization is a specialized agency of the United Nations. Telex: 23 260.

★18874★
WORLD WIDE FUND FOR NATURE - LIBRARY (Env-Cons)
c/o World Conservation Centre
Avenue du Mont-Blanc
CH-1196 Gland, Switzerland Phone: 22 647181
Subjects: Conservation of the natural environment, ecological processes necessary to life on earth. **Holdings:** 10,000 books; 10,000 color slides; 10,000 black/white photographs of nature and wildlife. **Subscriptions:** 400 journals and other serials. **Remarks:** Affiliated with International Union for Conservation of Nature and Natural Resources. Telex: 419618 wwf ch. Fax: 22 044238. **Also Known As:** Fonds Mondial pour la Conservation de la Nature.

★18875★
WUHAN COLLEGE OF GEODESY, PHOTOGRAMMETRY AND CARTOGRAPHY - LIBRARY (Geog-Map, Sci-Engr)
23 Loyu Lu Phone: 72202
Wuchang, Hubei Province, People's Republic of China
Yuan Jianxing, Dp.Libn.
Founded: 1956. **Staff:** 38. **Subjects:** Surveying, geodesy, photogrammetry, cartography, satellite geodesy, astronomy, gravity, optical instruments, computer hardware and software, lasers, remote sensing, automatic control. **Holdings:** 331,146 volumes; 2315 periodicals; 2117 technical reports. **Services:** Copying.

Y

THE YORK GATE GEOGRAPHICAL AND COLONIAL LIBRARY
See: Royal Geographical Society of Australasia, Inc. - South Australian Branch - Library (18743)

★18876★
YORK MINSTER - LIBRARY (Rel-Phil, Hist)
Dean's Park — Phone: 0904 25308
York YO1 2JD, England — C.B.L. Barr, Sub-Libn.
Subjects: Theology; religion; church history; York Minster - history, work, architecture, art; York and Yorkshire - history, churches, local booktrade; religious literature, art, architecture. **Special Collections:** York and Yorkshire history (30,000 print and manuscript materials); English Civil War (1500 items); music (1250 print and manuscript materials); Minster archives (manuscripts). **Holdings:** 100,000 volumes; 50 microforms; 700 manuscripts. **Services:** Copying; library open to the public. **Special Catalogs:** Catalog of manuscript music; catalog of printed music. **Staff:** Canon J. Toy, Canon Libn..

★18877★
YUGOSLAV CENTER FOR TECHNICAL AND SCIENTIFIC DOCUMENTATION (Sci-Engr)
Slobodana Penezica-Krcuna 29-31
P.O. Box 724 — Phone: 11 644-250
11000 Belgrade, Yugoslavia — Alexsic Miodrag, Dir.
Founded: 1952. **Subjects:** Scientific, technical, and economic information. **Holdings:** 1 million volumes. **Subscriptions:** 5000 journals and other serials. **Services:** Library open to the public. **Publications:** Bibliographies. **Remarks:** Telex: 12497. **Also Known As:** Jugoslovenski Centar za Tehnicku i Naucnu Dokumentaciju.

Z

ZAVOD ZA ISTRAZIVANJE FOLKLORA
See: Institute for Philology and Folkloristics - Institute for Folklore Research (18516)

ZAVOD SR SLOVENIJE ZA VARSTVO NARAVNE IN KULTURNE DEDISCINE
See: Institute for the Protection of the Natural and Cultural Heritage of Slovenia (18518)

ZIMBABWE - PARLIAMENT OF ZIMBABWE
See: Parliament of Zimbabwe (18680)

ZINBUN KAGAKU KENKYUSHO
See: Kyoto University - Research Institute for Humanistic Studies (18585)

Appendix A

NETWORKS AND CONSORTIA

All libraries in this directory were asked for information concerning the networks and consortia in which they participate. This appendix is a geographic list by state of approximately 400 cooperative organizations and their addresses based on the responses given by librarians. These groups range in scope and sophistication from local informal arrangements to larger regional and national organizations.

Networks well known by their acronym, such as NELINET or MINITEX, are listed under it; others appear under their complete name. When a network is known by more than one name, that information is noted in the entry and the variant name or acronym can be found in the cumulative index arranged in alphabetical order at the end of the Appendix.

UNITED STATES

ALABAMA

★N1★
ALABAMA HEALTH LIBRARIES ASSOCIATION (ALHELA)
c/o Library
Carraway Methodist Medical Center
1600 N. 26th St. Phone: (205)226-6265
Birmingham, AL 35234 Ms. Bobby Powell, Archv.

★N2★
JEFFERSON COUNTY HOSPITAL LIBRARIANS' ASSOCIATION
Department of Surgery
University of Alabama at Birmingham
University Sta. Phone: (205)934-7044
Birmingham, AL 35294 Marian Brennan, Pres.
Address rotates annually.

★N3★
ALABAMA LIBRARY EXCHANGE, INC. (ALEX)
Box 443 Phone: (205)532-5965
Huntsville, AL 35804 Lee E. Pike, Dir.

★N4★
NETWORK OF ALABAMA ACADEMIC LIBRARIES (NAAL)
Alabama Commission on Higher Education
One Court Square, Suite 221 Phone: (205)269-2700
Montgomery, AL 36197-0001 Dr. Sue O. Medina, Dir.

ALASKA

★N5★
ALASKA LIBRARY NETWORK (ALN)
c/o Alaska State Library
P.O. Box G Phone: (907)465-2910
Juneau, AK 99811 Judy Monroe, Coord.

ARIZONA

★N6★
MARICOPA BIOMEDICAL LIBRARIANS (MABL)
c/o Health Science Library
Good Samaritan Medical Center
Box 2989
Phoenix, AZ 85062 Phone: (602)239-4353
Address and phone number given are those of member library.

CALIFORNIA

★N7★
METROPOLITAN COOPERATIVE LIBRARY SYSTEM (MCLS)
2235 N. Lake Ave., Suite 106 Phone: (818)798-1146
Altadena, CA 91001 Holly Millard, Sys.Dir.

★N8★
KERN HEALTH SCIENCE LIBRARIES CONSORTIUM
c/o Kern Health Science Library
1830 Flower St.
Bakersfield, CA 93305 Phone: (805)326-2227

★N9★
PENINSULA LIBRARY SYSTEM (PLS)
25 Tower Rd. Phone: (415)349-5538
Belmont, CA 94002 Linda Crowe, Sys.Dir.

★N10★
TRANSPORTATION RESEARCH SERVICES INFORMATION NETWORK (TRISNET)
c/o Institute of Transportation Studies Library
University of California
412 McLaughlin Hall
Berkeley, CA 94720
Address is that of member library.

★N11★
NORTHERN CALIFORNIA AND NEVADA MEDICAL LIBRARY GROUP (NCNMLG)
2140 Shattuck Ave.
Box 2105
Berkeley, CA 94704

★N12★
OCLC PACIFIC NETWORK
250 W. First St., Suite 330 Phone: (714)621-9998
Claremont, CA 91711 Terry Zinser, Dir.

★N13★
LOS ANGELES COUNTY HEALTH SCIENCES LIBRARY CONSORTIUM
c/o Health Sciences Library
Rancho Los Amigos Medical Center
7601 E. Imperial Hwy.
Downey, CA 90242

★N14★
AREAWIDE LIBRARY NETWORK (AWLNET)
2420 Mariposa St. Phone: (209)488-3229
Fresno, CA 93721 Sharon Vandercook, Ref.Coord.
Affiliated with the San Joaquin Valley Library System.

★N15★
SAN JOAQUIN VALLEY LIBRARY SYSTEM (SJVLS)
2420 Mariposa St. Phone: (209)488-3185
Fresno, CA 93721 John Kallenberg, Sys.Adm.

★N16★
INLAND EMPIRE MEDICAL LIBRARY COOPERATIVE
c/o Library Service
V.A. Hospital
11201 Benton St.
Loma Linda, CA 92357
Address rotates annually.

★N17★
SOUTHERN CALIFORNIA ANSWERING NETWORK (SCAN)
Los Angeles Public Library
630 W. 5th St. Phone: (213)612-3216
Los Angeles, CA 90071 Evelyn Greenwald, Dir.

★N18★
PACIFIC SOUTHWEST REGIONAL MEDICAL LIBRARY SERVICE
Biomedical Library
Center for the Health Sciences
University of California
Los Angeles, CA 90024 Phone: (213)825-1200
Region 7 of the Regional Medical Library Program serving AZ, CA, HI, and NV.

★N19★
NORTH SAN JOAQUIN HEALTH SCIENCES LIBRARY CONSORTIUM
Stanlislaus County Medical Library
Scenic General Hospital
Modesto, CA 95352

★N20★
MONTEREY BAY AREA COOPERATIVE LIBRARY SYSTEM (MOBAC)
MPC Library Bldg.
980 Fremont Blvd. Phone: (408)646-4256
Monterey, CA 93940 Mary Layman, Coord.

★N21★
BAY AREA LIBRARY AND INFORMATION NETWORK (BALIN)
125 14th St.
Oakland, CA 94612
A multi-type library organization affiliated with the Bay Area Library and Information System (BALIS).

★N22★
BAY AREA LIBRARY AND INFORMATION SYSTEM (BALIS)
125 14th St. Phone: (415)839-6001
Oakland, CA 94612 Ruth Foley Metz, Sys.Coord.

★N23★
HEWLETT-PACKARD LIBRARY/INFORMATION NETWORK
Corporate Library
Hewlett-Packard Company
1501 Page Mill Rd.
Palo Alto, CA 94304 Phone: (415)857-3092

★N24★
INLAND EMPIRE ACADEMIC LIBRARIES COOPERATIVE (IEALC)
c/o California Baptist College
8432 Magnolia Ave.
Riverside, CA 92504
Address rotates annually.

★N25★
SACRAMENTO AREA HEALTH SCIENCES LIBRARIES GROUP (SAHSL)
5380 Elvas Ave. Phone: (916)452-2671
Sacramento, CA 95819 K.D. Proffit, Libn.
Address rotates annually.

★N26★
SAN BERNARDINO, INYO, RIVERSIDE COUNTIES UNITED LIBRARY SERVICES (SIRCULS)
312 W. 20th St., Suite D Phone: (714)882-7577
San Bernardino, CA 92405 Vaughn Simon, Dir.

★N27★
LEARNING RESOURCES COOPERATIVE
County Office of Education
6401 Linda Vista Rd. Phone: (619)693-6800
San Diego, CA 92111 Dr. Marvin Barbula, Coord.
Address rotates annually.

★N28★
KAISER PERMANENTE LIBRARY SYSTEM (KPLS)
c/o Health Sciences Library
Kaiser Permanente Medical Center
4647 Zion Ave.
San Diego, CA 92120 Phone: (619)584-5285
Address and phone number given are those of member library.

★N29★
BAY AREA REFERENCE CENTER (BARC)
San Francisco Public Library
Civic Center Phone: (415)558-2941
San Francisco, CA 94102 Fauneil McInnis, Dir.

★N30★
SAN FRANCISCO BIOMEDICAL LIBRARY GROUP
c/o Medical Library
Mt. Zion Hospital and Medical Center
1600 Divisadero St. Phone: (415)885-7378
San Francisco, CA 94115 Angela Wesling, Coord.
Address rotates annually.

★N31★
SOUTHNET
180 W. San Carlos St. Phone: (408)294-2345
San Jose, CA 95113 Mary Clare Sprott, Ref.Coord.

★N32★
CLASS
1415 Koll Circle, Suite 101 Phone: (408)289-1756
San Jose, CA 95112-4698 Ron Miller, Exec.Dir.
Also known as Cooperative Library Agency for Systems and Services.

★N33★
MEDICAL LIBRARY CONSORTIUM OF SANTA CLARA VALLEY
c/o Santa Clara Valley Medical Center
Milton J. Chatton Medical Library
751 S. Bascom Ave. Phone: (408)299-5660
San Jose, CA 95128 Joan Gerteis, Chm.
Chairmanship and address rotate biennially. Also known as Santa Clara County Medical Library Consortium.

★N34★
SOUTH BAY COOPERATIVE LIBRARY SYSTEM (SBCLS)
180 W. San Carlos St. Phone: (408)294-7332
San Jose, CA 95113 Craig R. Conover, Sys.Dir.

★N35★
NURSING INFORMATION CONSORTIUM OF ORANGE COUNTY (NICOC)
Medical Library
Western Medical Center
1001 N. Tustin Ave. Phone: (714)533-6220
Santa Ana, CA 92705 Evelyn Simpson, Co.Dir.

★N36★
RLG
Jordan Quadrangle Phone: (415)328-0920
Stanford, CA 94305 La Vonne Gallo, Mgr.
Operates the Research Libraries Information Network (RLIN). Also known as Research Libraries Group, Inc.

★N37★
49-99 COOPERATIVE LIBRARY SYSTEM
Stockton-San Joaquin County Public Library
605 N. El Dorado St. Phone: (209)944-8649
Stockton, CA 95202 Janet Kase, Dir.

★N38★
TOTAL INTERLIBRARY EXCHANGE (TIE)
Box 771 Phone: (805)652-7516
Ventura, CA 93002-0771 Susan K. Soy, Sys.Dir.

COLORADO

★N39★
COLORADO COUNCIL OF MEDICAL LIBRARIANS
c/o Medical Library
Denver General Hospital
775 Bannock St.
Denver, CO 80204 Phone: (303)893-7421
Address rotates annually.

★N40★
BIBLIOGRAPHICAL CENTER FOR RESEARCH, ROCKY MOUNTAIN REGION, INC. (BCR)
1777 S. Bellaire, Suite 425 Phone: (303)691-0550
Denver, CO 80222 David H. Brunell, Exec.Dir.
See also the library listing for this network in the main section.

★N41★
COLORADO ALLIANCE OF RESEARCH LIBRARIES (CARL)
777 Grant St., Suite 304 Phone: (303)861-5319
Denver, CO 80203 Ward Shaw, Exec.Dir.

★N42★
DENVER AREA HEALTH SCIENCES LIBRARY CONSORTIUM
c/o Medical Library
Rocky Mountain Hospital
4701 E. 9th Ave. Phone: (303)393-5784
Denver, CO 80220 Patricia O. Perry, Libn.
Address rotates annually.

★N43★
SOUTHWEST REGIONAL LIBRARY SERVICE SYSTEM (SWRLSS)
201 12th St.
Drawer B Phone: (303)247-4782
Durango, CO 81302 S. Jane Ulrich, Dir.

★N44★
HIGH PLAINS REGIONAL LIBRARY SERVICE SYSTEM
800 8th Ave., Suite 341 Phone: (303)356-4357
Greeley, CO 80631 Nancy Knepel, Dir.

★N45★
HONEYWELL INFORMATION NETWORK (HIN)
c/o Honeywell TID
4800 E. Dry Creek Rd.
Littleton, CO 80122 Phone: (303)773-4829
Address rotates annually.

★N46★
ARKANSAS VALLEY REGIONAL LIBRARY SERVICE SYSTEM
205 W. Abriendo Ave. Phone: (303)542-2156
Pueblo, CO 81004 Donna R. Jones, Dir.

CONNECTICUT

★N47★
SOUTHWESTERN CONNECTICUT LIBRARY COUNCIL (SWLC)
Bridgeport Public Library
925 Broad St. Phone: (203)367-6439
Bridgeport, CT 06604 Ann M. Neary, Adm.

★N48★
HEALTH INFORMATION LIBRARIES OF WESTCHESTER (HILOW)
c/o Gray Carter Library
Greenwich Hospital
Perryridge Rd. Phone: (203)863-3000
Greenwich, CT 06830 Carmel Fedors, Pres.
Address rotates annually.

★N49★
SOUTHERN CONNECTICUT LIBRARY COUNCIL (SCLC)
2901 Dixwell Ave. Phone: (203)248-5898
Hamden, CT 06518 Sharon W. Hupp, Dir.
Address changes periodically.

★N50★
HARTFORD CONSORTIUM FOR HIGHER EDUCATION
30 Elizabeth St. Phone: (203)236-1203
Hartford, CT 06105 Ruth W. Billyou, Coord.

★N51★
CONNECTICUT ASSOCIATION OF HEALTH SCIENCE LIBRARIES (CAHSL)
c/o Middlesex Memorial Hospital
28 Crescent St. Phone: (203)347-9471
Middletown, CT 06457 Evelyn Breck, Pres.
Address rotates annually.

★N52★
REGION ONE COOPERATING LIBRARY SERVICE UNIT, INC.
c/o Silas Bronson Library
267 Grand St. Phone: (203)756-6149
Waterbury, CT 06702 Leo N. Flanagan, Reg.Coord.

★N53★
CAPITOL REGION LIBRARY COUNCIL (CRLC)
599 Matianuck Ave. Phone: (203)549-0404
Windsor, CT 06095 Ms. Dency Sargent, Coord.

DELAWARE

★N54★
KENT LIBRARY NETWORK (KLN)
c/o Delaware Tech and Community College
Terry Campus Phone: (302)736-5404
Dover, DE 19901 Joe Gates, Asst.Libn.
Address rotates biennially.

★N55★
LIBRARIES IN THE NEW CASTLE COUNTY SYSTEM (LINCS)
c/o Concord Pike Library
3406 Concord Pike Phone: (302)478-7961
Wilmington, DE 19803 Mark Titus, Pres.
Address rotates annually.

★N56★
WILMINGTON AREA BIOMEDICAL LIBRARY CONSORTIUM (WABLC)
Delaware Academy of Medicine
1925 Lovering Ave. Phone: (302)656-1629
Wilmington, DE 19806 Gail P. Gill

DISTRICT OF COLUMBIA

★N57★
NASA AEROSPACE RESEARCH INFORMATION NETWORK (ARIN)
NASA Headquarters, Code NTT-1 Phone: (202)453-2927
Washington, DC 20546 Adelaide Del Frate, Adm.Libn.

★N58★
CAPCON
1717 Massachusetts Ave., N.W., Suite 100
Washington, DC 20036 Phone: (202)745-7722

★N59★
CONSORTIUM OF UNIVERSITIES OF THE WASHINGTON METROPOLITAN AREA
1717 Massachussetts Ave., N.W., Suite 101 Phone: (202)332-1894
Washington, DC 20036 Dr. Darrell Lemke, Coord., Lib

★N60★
ERIC
National Institute of Education
U.S. Dept. of Education
555 New Jersey Ave., N.W. Phone: (202)628-9180
Washington, DC 20208-1101 Charles W. Hoover, Chf.
Also known as Education Resources Information Center.

★N61★
FEDLINK
Federal Library & Information Center Committee
Library of Congress
Adams Bldg., Rm. 1026C Phone: (202)287-6454
Washington, DC 20540 Milton McGee, Coord.
Also known as Federal Library and Information Network.

★N62★
FOREST SERVICE INFORMATION NETWORK/FORESTRY ONLINE (FS INFO)
U.S. Forest Service
RPE, Rm. 809
Box 96090 Phone: (703)235-3442
Washington, DC 20013-6090 Chris A. Johnson, Proj.Ldr.

★N63★
HEALTH SCIENCES CONSORTIUM
c/o Dahlgren Memorial Library
Medical Center, Georgetown University
3900 Reservoir Rd., N.W. Phone: (202)625-2195
Washington, DC 20007 Naomi C. Broering, Libn.

★N64★
INTERLIBRARY USERS ASSOCIATION (IUA)
c/o Urban Institute Library
2100 M St., N.W. Phone: (202)857-8686
Washington, DC 20037 Camille A. Motta, Pres.
Address rotates annually.

★N65★
METROPOLITAN WASHINGTON LIBRARY COUNCIL
Council of Governments
1875 I St., N.W., Suite 200 Phone: (202)223-6800
Washington, DC 20006 Mollyne Honor-Forte, Dir.

★N66★
NATIONAL LIBRARY SERVICE FOR THE BLIND & PHYSICALLY HANDICAPPED (NLS)
Library of Congress
1291 Taylor St., N.W. Phone: (202)287-5100
Washington, DC 20542 Frank Kurt Cylke, Dir.
Regional and subregional libraries in this network are listed in Appendix B. See also the library listing for this network in the main section.

★N67★
NATIONAL NATURAL RESOURCES LIBRARY AND INFORMATION SYSTEM (NNRLIS)
Natural Resources Library
U.S. Dept. of the Interior
18th and C Sts., N.W. Phone: (202)343-5815
Washington, DC 20240 Philip M. Haymond, Coord.
See also the library listing for this network under U.S. Dept. of the Interior - Natural Resources Library in the main section.

★N68★
VALNET
Library Division 142D
Veterans Administration
810 Vermont Ave., N.W. Phone: (202)233-2711
Washington, DC 20420 Karen Renninger, Chf., Lib.Div
Also known as Veterans Administration Library Network.

★N69★
WASHINGTON THEOLOGICAL CONSORTIUM
487 Michigan Ave., N.E.
Washington, DC 20017 Dr. Daniel F. Martensen, Dir.

FLORIDA

★N70★
TAMPA BAY MEDICAL LIBRARY NETWORK
VA Medical Center
Box 527
Bay Pines, FL 33504

★N71★
MIAMI HEALTH SCIENCES LIBRARY CONSORTIUM (MHSLC)
Box 561542
Miami, FL 33156-1542 Celia Steinberg, Coord.

★N72★
FLORIDA LIBRARY INFORMATION NETWORK (FLIN)
State Library
R. A. Gray Bldg.
Tallahassee, FL 32301-0821 Phone: (904)487-2651

★N73★
TAMPA BAY LIBRARY CONSORTIUM, INC.
c/o Merl Kelce Library
401 W. Kennedy Blvd.
Tampa, FL 33606 Phone: (813)253-3333
Address and phone number given are those of member library.

★N74★
PALM BEACH COUNTY HEALTH SCIENCES LIBRARY CONSORTIUM
Richard S. Beinecke Medical Library
Good Samaritan Health Systems, Inc.
Box 3166 Phone: (305)650-6315
West Palm Beach, FL 33402 Linda O'Callaghan, Liaison
Address rotates annually.

GEORGIA

★N75★
GEORGIA LIBRARY INFORMATION NETWORK (GLIN)
Division of Public Library Services
Georgia Department of Education
156 Trinity Ave., S.W.
Atlanta, GA 30303 — Faye Elmore, Cons.

★N76★
CCLC
159 Ralph McGill Blvd., Suite 602 — Phone: (404)659-6886
Atlanta, GA 30365 — Hillis D. Davis, Dir.
Also known as Cooperative College Library Center, Inc.

★N77★
GEORGIA HEALTH SCIENCES LIBRARY ASSOCIATION (GHSLA)
School of Nursing Library
Georgia Baptist Hospital
300 Boulevard, N.E., Box 411 — Phone: (404)653-4000
Atlanta, GA 30312 — Susan Wright, Coord.
Address rotates annually.

★N78★
SOLINET
400 Colony Sq. Plaza Level
1201 Peachtree St., N.E. — Phone: (404)892-0943
Atlanta, GA 30361 — Frank P. Grisham, Exec.Dir.
Also known as Southeastern Library Network.

★N79★
UNIVERSITY CENTER IN GEORGIA, INC.
c/o Georgia State University
University Plaza
Box 1033 — Phone: (404)658-2668
Atlanta, GA 30303 — Charles B. Bedford, Dir.

★N80★
SOUTH GEORGIA ASSOCIATED LIBRARIES
c/o Brunswick Junior College — Phone: (912)264-7270
Brunswick, GA 31523-5101 — J. Allen Spivey, Sec./Treas.
Address rotates periodically.

★N81★
GEORGIA INTERACTIVE NETWORK FOR MEDICAL INFORMATION (GAIN)
c/o Medical Library, School of Medicine
Mercer University
1550 College St. — Phone: (912)744-2515
Macon, GA 31207 — Joceyln Rankin, Dir.

IDAHO

★N82★
BOISE VALLEY HEALTH SCIENCES LIBRARY CONSORTIUM
c/o Health Sciences Library
St. Alphonsus Regional Medical Center
Boise, ID 83706
Address is that of member library.

★N83★
SOUTHEAST IDAHO HEALTH INFORMATION CONSORTIUM
c/o Eastern Idaho Regional Medical Center
Health Sciences Library
Box 2077
Idaho Falls, ID 83403-2077 — Phone: (208)529-6077
Address rotates annually.

ILLINOIS

★N84★
AREAWIDE HOSPITAL LIBRARY CONSORTIUM OF SOUTHWESTERN ILLINOIS (AHLC)
c/o St. Joseph Hospital
915 E. Fifth St. — Phone: (618)463-5284
Alton, IL 62002-6434 — Betty Byrd, Coord.

★N85★
LIBRAS INC.
c/o Aurora University
347 S. Gladstone Ave.
Aurora, IL 60507

★N86★
HEART OF ILLINOIS LIBRARY CONSORTIUM (HILC)
Bromenn Health Care
807 N. Main St. — Phone: (309)827-4321
Bloomington, IL 61701 — Sue Stroyan, Coord.
Address rotates biennially.

★N87★
ILLINOIS VALLEY LIBRARY SYSTEM
c/o Medical Staff Library
Graham Hospital Association
210 W. Walnut St.
Canton, IL 61520 — Phone: (309)647-5240
Address and phone number given are those of member library.

★N88★
ASSOCIATION OF CHICAGO THEOLOGICAL SCHOOLS
c/o Library
Meadville/Lombard Theological School
5701 S. Woodlawn Ave. — Phone: (312)753-3196
Chicago, IL 60637 — Rev. Neil W. Gerdes, Libn.
Address rotates biennially.

★N89★
ILLINOIS HEALTH LIBRARIES CONSORTIUM
Meat Industry Information Center
National Livestock & Meat Board
444 N. Michigan Ave.
Chicago, IL 60611 — William D. Siarny, Jr., Coord.

★N90★
GREATER MIDWEST REGIONAL MEDICAL LIBRARY NETWORK
Library of the Health Sciences
Health Sciences Center, Univ. of Illinois
1750 W. Polk St. — Phone: (312)996-2464
Chicago, IL 60612 — Irwin Pizer, Coord.
Region 3 of the Regional Medical Library Program serving IA, IL, IN, KY, MI, MN, ND, OH, SD, WI.

★N91★
CENTER FOR RESEARCH LIBRARIES (CRL) CONSORTIA
6050 S. Kenwood Ave. — Phone: (312)955-4545
Chicago, IL 60637 — Donald B. Simpson, Pres.

★N92★
CHICAGO ACADEMIC LIBRARY COUNCIL (CALC)
c/o Library
Roosevelt University
430 S. Michigan Ave. — Phone: (312)341-3640
Chicago, IL 60605 — Adrian Jones, Chm.
Address rotates annually.

★N93★
JUDAICA LIBRARY NETWORK OF CHICAGO
c/o Norman and Helen Asher Library
Spertus College of Judaica
618 S. Michigan Ave. — Phone: (312)922-9012
Chicago, IL 60605 — Richard W. Marcus, Coord.

★N94★
METROPOLITAN CONSORTIUM OF CHICAGO
Stromberg Library
Swedish Covenant Hospital
5145 N. California Ave.
Chicago, IL 60625 Phone: (312)878-8200
Also known as Chicago Metropolitan Consortium.

★N95★
RIVER BEND LIBRARY SYSTEM (RBLS)
Box 125 Phone: (309)799-3155
Coal Valley, IL 61240 Mary Root, Coord.

★N96★
ILLINOIS DEPARTMENT OF MENTAL HEALTH AND DEVELOPMENTAL DISABILITIES LIBRARY SERVICES NETWORK (LISN)
Elgin Mental Health Center
750 S. State St. Phone: (312)742-1040
Elgin, IL 601201020 Jennifer Ford, Coord.

★N97★
PRIVATE ACADEMIC LIBRARIES OF ILLINOIS (PALI)
c/o Learning Resource Center
National College of Education
2840 Sheridan Rd.
Evanston, IL 60201 Phone: (312)256-5150

★N98★
U.S.A. TOY LIBRARY ASSOCIATION
1800 Pickwick Ave.
Glenview, IL 60025 Judith Q. Iacuzzi, Exec.Dir.

★N99★
SANGAMON VALLEY ACADEMIC LIBRARY CONSORTIUM (SVALC)
c/o Schewe Library
Illinois College
Jacksonville, IL 62650

★N100★
NORTHEASTERN ILLINOIS LIBRARY CONSORTIUM
c/o Corporate Library
Hollister Incorporated
2000 Hollister Dr. Phone: (312)680-1000
Libertyville, IL 60048 Elizabeth A. Cunningham, Libn.
Coordinator rotates annually.

★N101★
RUSH AFFILIATES INFORMATION NETWORK (RAIN)
c/o West Suburban Hospital Library
Erie at Austin Phone: (312)383-6200
Oak Park, IL 60302 Julia Faust, Coord.
Address rotates annually.

★N102★
CHICAGO AND SOUTH CONSORTIUM
Medical Library
Palos Community Hospital
80th Ave. & McCarthy Rd.
Palos Heights, IL 60463 Phone: (312)361-4500
Address rotates biennially.

★N103★
UPSTATE CONSORTIUM OF MEDICAL AND ALLIED LIBRARIES IN NORTHERN ILLINOIS
c/o Health Care Library
Swedish American Hospital
1400 Charles St. Phone: (815)968-4400
Rockford, IL 61108-1257 Sharon Montana, Med.Libn.
Address rotates annually.

★N104★
CAPITAL AREA CONSORTIUM
c/o St. John's Hospital
Health Science Library
800 E. Carpenter
Springfield, IL 62769 Kitty Wrigley, Coord.
Address rotates biennially.

★N105★
ILLINET
Illinois State Library
275 Centennial Bldg.
Springfield, IL 62756
Also known as Illinois Library and Information Network.

★N106★
ILLINOIS STATE DATA CENTER COOPERATIVE (ISDCC)
Illinois State Bureau of the Budget
605 Stratton Office Bldg.
401 S. Spring St.
Springfield, IL 62706 Phone: (217)782-3500

★N107★
CHAMPAIGN-URBANA CONSORTIUM
c/o Library
Mercy Hospital
1400 W. Park Phone: (217)337-2283
Urbana, IL 61801 Harriet Williamson, Coord.
Address rotates periodically. An alternate telephone number is 337-2299.

INDIANA

★N108★
STONE HILLS AREA LIBRARY SERVICES AUTHORITY (SHALSA)
112 N. Walnut, Suite 500 Phone: (812)334-8347
Bloomington, IN 47401 Sara Laughlin, Coord.

★N109★
NORTHEASTERN INDIANA HEALTH SCIENCE LIBRARY CONSORTIUM
Caylor-Nickel Clinic
311 S. Scott St. Phone: (219)824-3500
Bluffton, IN 46714 Pat Niblick, Coord.
Address and phone number given are those of member library.

★N110★
SOUTHEASTERN INDIANA AREA LIBRARY SERVICES AUTHORITY (SIALSA)
718 Third St. Phone: (812)372-0691
Columbus, IN 47201 Louise D. Schlesinger, Act.Dir.

★N111★
EASTERN INDIANA AREA LIBRARY SERVICES AUTHORITY (EIALSA)
R.R. 1, Box 76-A Phone: (317)378-0216
Daleville, IN 47334 Mary Frautschi, Adm.

★N112★
EVANSVILLE AREA HEALTH SCIENCES LIBRARIES CONSORTIUM
c/o Library
St. Mary Medical Center
3700 Washington Ave. Phone: (812)479-4151
Evansville, IN 47750 E. Jane Saltzman, Coord.

★N113★
FOUR RIVERS AREA LIBRARY SERVICES AUTHORITY
Old Vanderburgh County Courthouse, Rm. 11 Phone: (812)425-1946
Evansville, IN 44708 Ida L. McDowell, Coord.

★N114★
TRI-ALSA
900 Webster St.
Box 2270
Fort Wayne, IN 46801-2270 Jane Raifsnider, Coord.
Also known as Area 3 Library Services Authority.

★N115★
INCOLSA
1100 W. 42nd St. Phone: (317)926-3361
Indianapolis, IN 46208 B. Evans Markuson, Exec.Dir.
Also known as Indiana Cooperative Library Services Authority.

★N116★
CENTRAL INDIANA AREA LIBRARY SERVICES AUTHORITY (CIALSA)
1100 W. 42nd St.
Indianapolis, IN 46208
Phone: (317)926-6561
Judith Wegener, Exec.Dir.

★N117★
CENTRAL INDIANA HEALTH SCIENCE LIBRARY CONSORTIUM
c/o V.A. Medical Center Library
1481 Tenth St.
Indianapolis, IN 46202
Address rotates annually.
Phone: (317)635-7401
Judith Alfred, Coord.

★N118★
AREA 2 LIBRARY SERVICES AUTHORITY (ALSA 2)
209 Lincolnway, E.
Mishawaka, IN 46544
Phone: (219)255-5262
Martha Stratton, Coord.

IOWA

★N119★
POLK COUNTY BIOMEDICAL CONSORTIUM (PCBC)
c/o Library, Bldg. 6
Des Moines Area Community College
2006 S. Ankeny Blvd.
Ankeny, IA 50021
Address rotates biennially.
Phone: (515)964-6573
Diana Messersmith, Ref.Libn.

★N120★
LINN COUNTY LIBRARY CONSORTIUM (LCLC)
Health Services Library
701 - 10th St., S.E.
Cedar Rapids, IA 52403
Address rotates annually.
Phone: (319)398-6166
Joy Stoker-Hadow, Libn.

★N121★
QUAD CITY AREA BIOMEDICAL CONSORTIUM
c/o St. Joseph Mercy Hospital
1410 N. Fourth St.
Clinton, IA 52732
Phone: (319)243-5900
Kris Paulsen, Lrng.Rsrc.Techn.

★N122★
MID-AMERICA LAW SCHOOL LIBRARY CONSORTIUM
c/o Law Library
Drake University
Des Moines, IA 50311
Address rotates biennially.
Phone: (515)271-2141
John D. Edwards, Chm.

★N123★
IOWA COMPUTER ASSISTED NETWORK (ICAN)
State Library
Capitol Complex
E. 12th & Grand
Des Moines, IA 50319
Phone: (515)281-6920
Rinda Kramme, Networking Assoc

KANSAS

★N124★
KANSAS LIBRARY NETWORK
Kansas State Library
State Capitol, 3rd Fl.
Topeka, KS 66612
Phone: (913)296-3296
Michael Piper, Exec.Asst.

KENTUCKY

★N125★
STATE ASSISTED ACADEMIC LIBRARY COUNCIL OF KENTUCKY (SAALCK)
c/o Western Kentucky University Library
Bowling Green, KY 42101-3576
Address rotates annually.
Phone: (502)745-2904
Earl Wassam, Dir., Lib.Serv.

★N126★
KENTUCKY LIBRARY NETWORK, INC. (KLN)
300 Coffee Tree Rd.
Box 458
Frankfort, KY 40602
Phone: (502)875-7000
Linda B. Reel, Exec.Dir.

★N127★
KENTUCKY HEALTH SCIENCES LIBRARY CONSORTIUM
c/o V.A. Hospital Library
800 Zorn Ave.
Louisville, KY 40202
Address rotates biennially.
Phone: (502)895-3401
James F. Kastner, Pres.

★N128★
TEAM-A LIBRARIANS
c/o Southern Baptist Theological Seminary
2825 Lexington Rd.
Louisville, KY 40280
Phone: (502)897-4807
Dr. Ronald F. Deering
Also known as Theological Education Association of Mid-America Librarians.

★N129★
EASTERN KENTUCKY HEALTH SCIENCE INFORMATION NETWORK (EKHSIN)
c/o Camden-Carroll Library
Morehead State University
Morehead, KY 40351
Phone: (606)784-4301
Betty S. Ison, Coord.

LOUISIANA

★N130★
HEALTH SCIENCES LIBRARY ASSOCIATION OF LOUISIANA
c/o Medical Library
V.A. Medical Center
Alexandria, LA 71301
Phone: (318)473-0010
Address and phone number given are those of member library.

MAINE

★N131★
HEALTH SCIENCE LIBRARY AND INFORMATION COOPERATIVE OF MAINE (HSLIC)
V.A. Medical Center
Box 395
Togus, ME 04330
Phone: (207)623-8411

MARYLAND

★N132★
MARYLAND INTERLIBRARY ORGANIZATION (MILO)
Enoch Pratt Free Library
State Library Resource Center
400 Cathedral St.
Baltimore, MD 21201
Phone: (301)396-5328
Eleanor Jo Rodger, Chf.

★N133★
SOUTHEASTERN/ATLANTIC REGIONAL MEDICAL LIBRARY SERVICES
Health Science Library
University of Maryland
111 S. Greene St.
Baltimore, MD 21201
Phone: (301)528-2855
Carol G. Jenkins, Exec.Dir.
Region 2 of the Regional Medical Program serving AL, DC, FL, GA, MD, MS, NC, SC, TN, VA, and WV. A toll-free telephone number is (800)638-6093.

★N134★
NATIONAL LIBRARY OF MEDICINE (NLM)
8600 Rockville Pike
Bethesda, MD 20894
Phone: (301)496-4777
Becky Lyon-Hartmann, Coord.
See also the library listing for this network in the main section.

★N135★
CRIMINAL JUSTICE INFORMATION EXCHANGE GROUP
c/o National Institute of Justic/NCJRS
Box 6000 Phone: (301)251-5500
Rockville, MD 20850 J. H. Anderson, NCJRS Commun.
A toll-free telephone number is (800)751-3420.

★N136★
DISTRICT OF COLUMBIA HEALTH SCIENCES INFORMATION NETWORK (DOCHSIN)
c/o American Occupational Therapy Foundation
Box 1725 Phone: (301)948-9626
Rockville, MD 20850 Mary S. Binderman, Pres.
Address and phone number given are those of member library.

MASSACHUSETTS

★N137★
WELEXACOL
c/o Horn Library
Babson College Phone: (617)239-4473
Babson Park, MA 02157 Alma Maller, Pres.
Address rotates biennially. Also known as Wellesley-Lexington Area Cooperating Libraries.

★N138★
NORTHEASTERN CONSORTIUM FOR HEALTH INFORMATION (NECHI)
c/o Beverly Public Library Phone: (617)922-0310
Beverly, MA 01915 Suzanne Nicolson, Libn.
Address rotates annually.

★N139★
ESSEX COUNTY COOPERATING LIBRARIES (ECCL)
Library
Beverly Hospital
Herrick St. Phone: (617)922-3000
Beverly, MA 01915 Ann Kowalski
Address rotates annually.

★N140★
BOSTON AREA MUSIC LIBRARIES (BAML)
c/o Music Library
Boston University
771 Commonwealth Ave. Phone: (617)353-3705
Boston, MA 02215 Frank Gramenz, Coord.
Address rotates periodically.

★N141★
BOSTON BIOMEDICAL LIBRARY CONSORTIUM
c/o Agoos Medical Library
Beth Israel Hospital
330 Brookline Ave. Phone: (617)735-4225
Boston, MA 02215 Margo Coletti, Ch.
Address rotates annually.

★N142★
BOSTON LIBRARY CONSORTIUM
Boston Public Library, Rm. 339
666 Boylston St. Phone: (617)262-0380
Boston, MA 02117 Ann C. Schaffner, Coord.

★N143★
SOUTHEASTERN MASSACHUSETTS COOPERATING LIBRARIES (SMCL)
c/o Clement C. Maxwell Library
Bridgewater State College Phone: (617)697-1256
Bridgewater, MA 02324 William Boyle, Coord.

★N144★
LIBRARIES AND INFORMATION FOR NURSING CONSORTIUM (LINC)
c/o School of Nursing Library
St. Elizabeth's Hospital
159 Washington St. Phone: (617)789-2304
Brighton, MA 02135 Robert L. Loud, Libn.

★N145★
NEW ENGLAND LAW LIBRARY CONSORTIUM (NELLCO)
Law School Library
c/o Harvard University
Langdell Hall
Cambridge, MA 02138 Phone: (617)495-3176

★N146★
BOSTON THEOLOGICAL INSTITUTE LIBRARIES
45 Frances Ave. Phone: (617)495-5780
Cambridge, MA 02138 Barbara McNamara, Coord.

★N147★
DIGITAL LIBRARY NETWORK
555 Virginia Rd., VR03-3/W5 Phone: (617)264-3433
Concord, MA 01742 Joyce Ward, Coord.

★N148★
CONSORTIUM FOR INFORMATION RESOURCES (CIR)
C.G. Tedeschi Library
Framingham Union Hospital
115 Lincoln St. Phone: (617)879-7111
Framingham, MA 01701 Sandra Clevesy, Adm.

★N149★
COOPERATING LIBRARIES OF GREATER SPRINGFIELD, A CCGS AGENCY (CLGS)
c/o Learning Resources Center
Holyoke Community College
303 Homestead Ave. Phone: (413)538-7000
Holyoke, MA 01040 Elizabeth Sheehan, Dir.

★N150★
NORTHEAST CONSORTIUM OF COLLEGES AND UNIVERSITIES IN MASSACHUSETTS (NECCUM)
51 Lawrence St. Phone: (617)686-3183
Lawrence, MA 01841 Dr. Tara Elyssa, Exec.Dir.

★N151★
NELINET
385 Elliot St. Phone: (617)969-0400
Newton, MA 02164 Ms. Laima Mockus, Exec. Dir.
Also known as New England Library Information Network.

★N152★
WESTERN MASSACHUSETTS HEALTH INFORMATION CONSORTIUM
c/o Cooley Dickinson Hospital
30 Locust St. Phone: (413)584-4090
North Hampton, MA 01060 Richard H. Dolloff, Med.Libn.

★N153★
C/W MARS, INC.
1 Sunset Lane Phone: (617)755-3323
Paxton, MA 01612 David T. Sheehan, Mgr.

★N154★
MASSACHUSETTS HEALTH SCIENCES LIBRARY NETWORK (MAHSLIN)
c/o Mack Memorial Library
Salem Hospital
81 Highland Ave. Phone: (617)741-1200
Salem, MA 01970 Jennie McGee, Pres.
Address rotates annually.

★N155★
GTE LIBNET
GTE Laboratories Library
40 Sylvan Rd.
Waltham, MA 02254 Phone: (617)890-8460

★N156★
WORCESTER AREA COOPERATING LIBRARIES (WACL)
Learning Resource Center, Rm. 301
Worcester State College Phone: (617)754-3964
Worcester, MA 01602 Gladys E. Wood, Res.Asst.

★N157★
CENTRAL MASSACHUSETTS CONSORTIUM OF HEALTH RELATED LIBRARIES (CMCHRL)
c/o Medical School Library
University of Massachusetts
Worcester, MA 01605
Phone: (617)856-2511
Faith Anttila, Adm.

MICHIGAN

★N158★
WASHTENAW-LIVINGSTON LIBRARY NETWORK (WLLN)
Washtenaw County Library
4133 Washtenaw Ave.
Ann Arbor, MI 48107
Phone: (313)971-6056
Mary Croteau, Lib.Dir.

★N159★
DETROIT AREA LIBRARY SERVICE (DALS)
Detroit Public Library
5201 Woodward Ave.
Detroit, MI 48202
Phone: (313)833-3997

★N160★
DETROIT ASSOCIATED LIBRARIES REGION OF COOPERATION
c/o Detroit Public Library
5201 Woodward Ave.
Detroit, MI 48202
Phone: (313)833-3997
Lesley C. Loke, Coord.

★N161★
FLINT AREA HEALTH SCIENCE LIBRARY NETWORK (FAHSLN)
Hurley Medical Center
1 Hurley Plaza
Flint, MI 48502
Phone: (313)766-0454
Marilyn Schleg, Pres.
Address rotates periodically.

★N162★
LAKELAND AREA LIBRARY NETWORK (LAKENET)
c/o Lakeland Library Cooperative
60 Library Plaza, N.E.
Grand Rapids, MI 49503
Phone: (616)456-4426
Harriet Field, Coord.

★N163★
MICHIGAN LIBRARY CONSORTIUM (MLC)
6810 S. Cedar St., Suite 8
Lansing, MI 48911
Phone: (517)694-4242
Kevin C. Flaherty, Exec.Dir.

★N164★
CAPITOL AREA LIBRARY NETWORK (CALNET)
Library Service Center
407 N. Cedar St.
Mason, MI 48854
Phone: (517)676-2147
Kathleen M. Vera

★N165★
MICHIGAN HEALTH SCIENCES LIBRARIES ASSOCIATION (MHSLA)
1000 Houghton Ave.
Saginaw, MI 48602-5398
Phone: (517)771-6846
Stephanie John, Pres.
Address rotates annually.

MINNESOTA

★N166★
NORTHERN LIGHTS LIBRARY NETWORK (NLLN)
17th & Jefferson
Box 845
Alexandria, MN 56308-0845
Phone: (612)762-1032
Joan B. Larson, Coord.

★N167★
PRAIRIE LIBRARY NETWORK
c/o Community Health Science Library
St. Francis Medical Center
415 Oak St.
Breckenridge, MN 56520
Karen Engstrom, Dir.

★N168★
ARROWHEAD PROFESSIONAL LIBRARIES ASSOCIATION (APLA)
Health Sciences Library
St. Mary's Medical Center
407 E. Third St.
Duluth, MN 55805
Phone: (218)726-4396
Elizabeth Sobczak, Libn.
Address rotates annually.

★N169★
VALLEY MEDICAL NETWORK (VMN)
c/o Education Resource Center
Lake Region Hospital
Fergus Falls, MN 56537
Phone: (218)736-5475
Connie Schulz, Pres.
Address rotates annually.

★N170★
SOUTHCENTRAL MINNESOTA INTER-LIBRARY EXCHANGE (SMILE)
Box 3031
Mankato, MN 56001
Phone: (507)389-5108
Lucy Lowry, Coord.

★N171★
MINITEX
33 Wilson Library
University of Minnesota
309 19th Ave., S.
Minneapolis, MN 55455
Phone: (612)624-6353
William DeJohn, Dir.
See also the library listing for this network in the main section. Also known as Minnesota Interlibrary Telecommunications Exchange.

★N172★
TWIN CITIES BIOMEDICAL CONSORTIUM (TCBC)
Hennepin County Medical Center Library
701 Park Ave.
Minneapolis, MN 55415
Phone: (612)347-2710
Patty Williams, Coord.
Address rotates annually.

★N173★
MINNESOTA DEPARTMENT OF HUMAN SERVICES LIBRARY CONSORTIUM
Oak Terrace Nursing Home
14500 County Rd. 67
Minnetonka, MN 55345
Phone: (612)934-4100
Susan Ager, Coord.

★N174★
CENTRAL MINNESOTA LIBRARIES EXCHANGE (CMLE)
c/o Learning Resources, Rm. 122
St. Cloud State University
St. Cloud, MN 56301
Phone: (612)255-2950
Patricia E. Peterson, Coord.

★N175★
MINNESOTA THEOLOGICAL LIBRARIES ASSOCIATION (MTLA)
c/o Luther-Northwestern Seminary Library
2375 Como Ave.
St. Paul, MN 55108
Phone: (612)641-3225
Address is that of member library.

★N176★
COOPERATING LIBRARIES IN CONSORTIUM (CLIC)
c/o James J. Hill Reference Library
80 W. Fourth St.
St. Paul, MN 55102
Phone: (612)699-0724
Terry Metz, Coord.

★N177★
CAPITOL AREA LIBRARY CONSORTIUM (CALCO)
Information Services Center
Minnesota Department of Transportation
B26A Transportation Bldg.
St. Paul, MN 55155
Phone: (612)296-1741
Pam Cornell, Pres.
Address rotates annually.

★N178★
METRONET
226 Metro Square Bldg.
7th & Robert Sts.
St. Paul, MN 55101
Phone: (612)224-4801
Metronet was created to foster cooperation among all types of libraries and media centers in a seven county area.

★N179★
METROPOLITAN LIBRARY SERVICE AGENCY (MELSA)
Griggs-Midway Bldg., Rm. 322 S.
1821 University Ave. Phone: (612)645-5731
St. Paul, MN 55104-3083 William M. Duncan, Exec.Dir.

MISSISSIPPI

★N180★
CENTRAL MISSISSIPPI COUNCIL OF MEDICAL LIBRARIES
c/o Luther Manship Medical Library
St. Dominic-Jackson Memorial Hospital
969 Lakeland Dr.
Jackson, MS 39216 Phone: (601)982-0121
Address and phone number given are those of member library.

★N181★
CENTRAL MISSISSIPPI LIBRARY COUNCIL
Hood Library
Jackson, MS 39202 Phone: (601)968-5947
Address rotates annually.

★N182★
MISSISSIPPI BIOMEDICAL LIBRARY CONSORTIUM
c/o Medical Library
U.S. Air Force Medical Center
Keesler Air Force Base, MS 39534 Phone: (601)377-6042
Address rotates annually. An alternate telephone number is 377-6249.

MISSOURI

★N183★
MID-MISSOURI LIBRARY NETWORK (MMLN)
100 W. Broadway
Box 1267 Phone: (314)442-7115
Columbia, MO 65205 Frederick J. Raithel, Dir.

★N184★
KANSAS CITY METROPOLITAN LIBRARY NETWORK (KCMLN)
3675 S. Noland Rd., Suite 215 Phone: (816)461-7001
Independence, MO 64055 Edyth Dalton, Coord.

★N185★
CHIROPRACTIC LIBRARY CONSORTIUM (CLIBCON)
Cleveland Chiropractic College
6401 Rockhill Rd. Phone: (816)333-8230
Kansas City, MO 64131 Marcia M. Thomas, Pres.
Address rotates annually.

★N186★
KANSAS CITY LIBRARY NETWORK, INC. (KCLN)
c/o Medical Library
St. Luke's Hospital
44th & Wornall Rd. Phone: (816)932-2333
Kansas City, MO 64111 Karen Horst, Pres.

★N187★
NORTHWEST MISSOURI LIBRARY NETWORK
1904B North Belt Hwy.
St. Joseph, MO 64506 Phone: (816)364-3386

★N188★
ST. LOUIS REGIONAL LIBRARY NETWORK
9929 Manchester Rd., Suite 258 Phone: (314)968-2489
St. Louis, MO 63122-1915 Dr. Arthur R. Taylor, Adm.
Multi-type network with 111 members.

★N189★
MISSOURI LIBRARY NETWORK (MLNC)
12166 Old Big Bend Blvd., Suite 215 Phone: (314)965-7030
St. Louis, MO 63122-6834 Mary Ann Mercante, Dir.

★N190★
SOUTHWEST MISSOURI LIBRARY NETWORK
c/o Springfield-Greene County Library
397 E. Central
Box 737 Phone: (417)869-4621
Springfield, MO 65801 Shannon Roy, Coord.

MONTANA

★N191★
HELENA AREA HEALTH SCIENCES LIBRARY CONSORTIUM (HAHSLC)
c/o Medical Reference Library
Shodair Children's Hospital
Box 5539 Phone: (406)442-1980
Helena, MT 59604 Suzy Holt, Info.Spec.

NEBRASKA

★N192★
LINCOLN HEALTH SCIENCE LIBRARY GROUP
Library Service (142D)
Medical Center
U.S. Veterans Administration Phone: (402)489-3802
Lincoln, NE 68510 Ruth Boettcher, Pres.
Address rotates annually.

★N193★
NEBASE
Nebraska Library Commission
1420 P St. Phone: (402)471-2045
Lincoln, NE 68508 Pat Gildersleeve, Coord.

★N194★
MIDCONTINENTAL REGIONAL MEDICAL LIBRARY PROGRAM
McGoogan Library of Medicine
University of Nebraska Medical Center
42nd & Dewey Ave.
Omaha, NE 68105-1065 Phone: (402)559-4326
Region 4 of the Regional Medical Library Program serving CO, KS, MO, NE, UT, and WY. A toll free telephone number for Nebraska residents is (800)633-7654.

NEVADA

★N195★
INFORMATION NEVADA
Nevada State Library
Capitol Complex Phone: (702)885-5165
Carson City, NV 89710 Danna G. Sturm, ILL Libn.

★N196★
NEVADA MEDICAL LIBRARIES GROUP (NMLG)
Medical Library
Nevada Mental Health Institute
480 Galletti Way
Sparks, NV 89431-5574 Phone: (702)322-6961

NEW HAMPSHIRE

★N197★
SUBSTANCE ABUSE LIBRARIANS AND INFORMATION SPECIALISTS (SALIS)
Project CORK Resource Centre
Dartmouth Medical School Phone: (603)646-7540
Hanover, NH 03755 Virginia Rolett, Coord.
Address rotates annually.

★N198★
NORTH ATLANTIC HEALTH SCIENCE LIBRARIES (NAHSL)
c/o Dana Biomedical Library
Hanover, NH 03756
Phone: (603)646-7660
John Bundy, Ch.
Address rotates annually.

★N199★
NORTH COUNTRY CONSORTIUM (NCC)
c/o Littleton Hospital
107 Cottage St.
Littleton, NH 03561
Phone: (603)444-7731
Linda L. Ford, Med.Libn.
Address rotates periodically.

★N200★
NEW HAMPSHIRE COLLEGE & UNIVERSITY COUNCIL LIBRARY POLICY COMMITTEE (NHCUC)
Notre Dame College Library
2321 Elm St.
Manchester, NH 03104
Phone: (603)669-3432
Douglas W. Lyon, Coord.

NEW JERSEY

★N201★
PINELANDS CONSORTIUM
Library, UMDNJ
401 Haddon Ave.
Camden, NJ 08103
Phone: (609)346-6800
Janice Skicka, Coord.

★N202★
NORTHWEST REGIONAL LIBRARY COOPERATIVE
31 Fairmount Ave.
Chester, NJ 07930
Keith Michael Fiels, Reg.Coord

★N203★
SOCIETY FOR COOPERATIVE HEALTHCARE AND RELATED EDUCATION (SCHARE)
MacKay Library
Union County College
Cranford, NJ 07016
Phone: (201)276-5710
Carol Dreyer, Coord.

★N204★
NEW JERSEY ACADEMIC LIBRARY NETWORK
c/o Music Branch Library
Wilson Bldg. 615
Glassboro State College
Glassboro, NJ 08028
Phone: (609)445-7306
Marjorie Travaline, Libn.

★N205★
SOUTH JERSEY REGIONAL LIBRARY COOPERATIVE
Midway Professional Center, Suite 102
8 N. White House Pike
Hammond, NJ 08037
Karen D. Hyman, Dir.

★N206★
AT & T BELL LABORATORIES LIBRARY NETWORK
Crawfords Corner Rd.
Holmdel, NJ 07733
Phone: (201)949-3456
F.H. Spaulding, Dir.

★N207★
COSMOPOLITAN BIOMEDICAL LIBRARY CONSORTIUM (CBLC)
Library
Hospital Center at Orange
188 S. Essex Ave.
Orange, NJ 07051
Phone: (201)266-2000
Jeanette Merkl, V.P.
Address rotates annually.

★N208★
BERGEN-PASSAIC HEALTH SCIENCES LIBRARY CONSORTIUM
c/o St. Joseph's Medical Center
Patterson, NJ 07503
Phone: (201)977-2104
Address and phone number given are those of member library.

★N209★
EDUCOM
Rosedale Rd.
Box 364
Princeton, NJ 08540
Phone: (609)291-7575

★N210★
HEALTH SCIENCES LIBRARY ASSOCIATION OF NEW JERSEY
c/o Library
Health Research and Educational Trust of New Jersey 746-760
Alexander Rd., CN-1
Princeton, NJ 08543-0001
Phone: (609)275-4230
Michelle Volesko, Coord.

★N211★
MONMOUTH-OCEAN BIOMEDICAL INFORMATION CONSORTIUM (MOBIC)
c/o Medical Library
Community Memorial Hospital
99 Hwy. 37, W.
Toms River, NJ 08753
Phone: (201)240-8117
Address rotates annually.

★N212★
CENTRAL JERSEY HEALTH SCIENCE LIBRARIES ASSOCIATION
c/o Health Science Library
St. Francis Medical Center
601 Hamilton Ave.
Trenton, NJ 08629
Phone: (609)559-5068
Donna Barlow, Libn.

NEW MEXICO

★N213★
NEW MEXICO CONSORTIUM OF BIOMEDICAL AND HOSPITAL LIBRARIES
Lovelace Medical Library
5400 Gibson Blvd., S.E.
Albuquerque, NM 87108
Phone: (505)262-7158
Jeane E. Strub, Coord.

NEW YORK

★N214★
NEW YORK STATE INTERLIBRARY LOAN NETWORK (NYSILL)
Division of Library Development
New York State Library
Cultural Education Center
Albany, NY 12230
Phone: (518)474-7732
Jane G. Rollins, Assoc.

★N215★
SUNY/OCLC LIBRARY NETWORK
Central Administration
State University of New York
State University Plaza
Albany, NY 12246
Phone: (518)434-8141
Glyn T. Evans, Dir.

★N216★
NEW YORK METROPOLITAN REFERENCE AND RESEARCH LIBRARY AGENCY (METRO)
57 Willoughby St.
Brooklyn, NY 11201
Phone: (718)852-8700
Joan Neumann, Dir.
Also known as METRO.

★N217★
BROOKLYN-QUEENS-STATEN ISLAND HEALTH SCIENCES LIBRARIANS (BQSI)
c/o Coney Island Hospital
2601 Ocean Pkwy.
Brooklyn, NY 11235
Phone: (718)615-4299
Ronnie Joan Mark, Pres.
Address rotates biennially.

★N218★
WESTERN NEW YORK LIBRARY RESOURCES COUNCIL (WNYLRC)
180 Oak St. Phone: (716)852-3844
Buffalo, NY 14203 Joyce D. Everingham, Exec.Dir.

★N219★
LIBRARY CONSORTIUM OF HEALTH INSTITUTIONS IN BUFFALO (LCHIB)
Abbott Hall
SUNY at Buffalo Phone: (716)831-3351
Buffalo, NY 14214 C. Bertuca, Hd., Dissem.Serv.
Consortum consists of eight teaching hospital libraries and the university's Health Sciences Library.

★N220★
NORTH COUNTRY REFERENCE AND RESEARCH RESOURCES COUNCIL (NCRRRC)
Box 568 Phone: (315)386-4569
Canton, NY 13617 Richard H. Kimball, Exec.Dir.

★N221★
MEDICAL & SCIENTIFIC LIBRARIES OF LONG ISLAND (MEDLI)
c/o Shell Library
Nassau Academy of Medicine
1200 Stewart Ave. Phone: (516)832-2320
Garden City, NY 11530 Pamela Kerns, Pres.

★N222★
SOUTHEASTERN NEW YORK LIBRARY RESOURCES COUNCIL (SENYLRC)
Rt. 299
Box 879
Highland, NY 12528-0879 Phone: (914)691-2734
Maintains the Southeastern Bibliographic Center (SEBC).

★N223★
EDUCATIONAL FILM LIBRARY ASSOCIATION
c/o Audiovisual Resource Center
Cornell University
8 Research Park Phone: (607)255-2090
Ithaca, NY 14850 Carol Doolittle, AV Coord.

★N224★
SOUTH CENTRAL RESEARCH LIBRARY COUNCIL (SCRLC)
215 N. Cayuga St. Phone: (607)273-9106
Ithaca, NY 14850 Janet E. Steiner, Exec.Dir.

★N225★
MEDICAL LIBRARY CENTER OF NEW YORK (MLCNY)
5 E. 102nd St., 7th Fl. Phone: (212)427-1630
New York, NY 10029 William D. Walker, Dir.
See also the library listing for this network in the main section.

★N226★
GREATER NORTHEASTERN REGIONAL MEDICAL LIBRARY PROGRAM
New York Academy of Medicine Library
2 E. 103rd St. Phone: (212)876-8763
New York, NY 10029-5293 Kay Mills Due, Assoc.Dir.
Region 1 of the Regional Medical Library Program serving CT, DE, ME, MA, NH, NJ, NY, PA, RI, VT, and PR.

★N227★
CONSORTIUM OF FOUNDATION LIBRARIES
c/o Carnegie Corporation of New York
437 Madison Ave. Phone: (212)371-3200
New York, NY 10022 Patricia Haynes, Chm.

★N228★
COUNCIL OF ARCHIVES AND RESEARCH LIBRARIES IN JEWISH STUDIES (CARLJS)
330 7th Ave., 21st Fl. Phone: (212)490-2280
New York, NY 10001 Abraham Atik, Coord.
Affiliated with the World Council on Jewish Archives, Jerusalem.

★N229★
MANHATTAN-BRONX HEALTH SCIENCES LIBRARY GROUP
c/o International Center for the Disabled
340 E. 24th St.
New York, NY 10010

★N230★
NORTHERN NEW YORK HEALTH INFORMATION COOPERATIVE
c/o Medical Library
Champlain Valley Physicians Hospital
100 Beekman St. Phone: (518)561-2000
Plattsburgh, NY 112901 Christina Ransom, Med.Libn.

★N231★
ASSOCIATED COLLEGES OF THE ST. LAWRENCE VALLEY, INC. (ACSLV)
Raymond Hall
SUNY - College at Potsdam Phone: (315)265-2790
Potsdam, NY 13676 Judy C. Chittenden

★N232★
ROCHESTER REGIONAL LIBRARY COUNCIL (RRLC)
339 East Ave., Rm. 300 Phone: (716)232-7930
Rochester, NY 14604 Janet M. Welch, Dir.

★N233★
CAPITAL DISTRICT LIBRARY COUNCIL FOR REFERENCE & RESEARCH RESOURCES (CDLC)
2255 Story Ave. Phone: (518)382-2001
Schenectady, NY 12309-5315 Charles D. Custer, Exec.Dir.
See also the library listing for this network in the main section.

★N234★
LONG ISLAND LIBRARY RESOURCES COUNCIL, INC. (LILRC)
Melville Library Bldg., Suite E5310 Phone: (516)632-6650
Stonybrook, NY 11794-3399 Herbert Biblo, Exec.Dir.
See also the library listing for this network in the main section.

★N235★
CENTRAL NEW YORK LIBRARY RESOURCES COUNCIL (CENTRO)
763 Butternut St. Phone: (315)478-6080
Syracuse, NY 13208 James M. Turner, Jr.,Exec.Dir.

★N236★
HEALTH RESOURCES COUNCIL OF CENTRAL NEW YORK (HRCCNY)
SUNY
Health Science Center at Syracuse - Library
766 Irving Ave.
Syracuse, NY 13210 Phone: (315)473-4580
Address rotates annually.

★N237★
LIBRARY EXCHANGE AND RESOURCES NETWORK (LEARN)
Mohawk Valley Psychiatric Center
1400 Noyes St.
Utica, NY 13502 Phone: (315)797-6600
Address rotates periodically.

NORTH CAROLINA

★N238★
NORTH CAROLINA AREA HEALTH EDUCATION CENTERS PROGRAM LIBRARY AND INFORMATION SERVICES NETWORK
Health Sciences Library, 223H
University of North Carolina Phone: (919)962-0700
Chapel Hill, NC 27514 Lynne K. Siemers, Hd.

★N239★
TRIANGLE RESEARCH LIBRARIES NETWORK (TRLN)
c/o Wilson Library 024-A
University of North Carolina at Chapel Hill
Chapel Hill, NC 27514 Phone: (919)962-8022

★N240★
CAPE FEAR HEALTH SCIENCES INFORMATION CONSORTIUM
c/o Medical Library
Womack Army Community Hospital
U.S. Army Hospitals — Phone: (919)396-0205
Fort Bragg, NC 28307-5000 — Cecilia C. Edwards, Med.Libn.
Address rotates annually.

★N241★
RESOURCES FOR HEALTH INFORMATION (REHI)
Medical Library
Wake County Medical Center
3000 New Bern Ave. — Phone: (919)755-8529
Raleigh, NC 28610 — B.S. Richardson, Assoc.Dir.

★N242★
NORTH CAROLINA INFORMATION NETWORK (IN-WATS)
Interlibrary Services Branch
Division of State Library
109 E. Jones St. — Phone: (919)733-3683
Raleigh, NC 27611 — Sue Farr, Hd., ILL Serv.Br.

★N243★
NEW JERSEY HEALTH SCIENCES LIBRARY NETWORK (NJHSN)
c/o Learning Resource Center
Central Carolina Technical College
1105 Kelly Dr. — Phone: (919)775-5401
Sanford, NC 27330 — Patricia Regenberg, Chm.

★N244★
NORTHWEST AHEC LIBRARY INFORMATION NETWORK
Northwest Area Health Education Center
Bowman Gray School of Medicine
Winston-Salem, NC 27103 — Phyllis Gillikin, Coord.

NORTH DAKOTA

★N245★
NORTH DAKOTA NETWORK FOR KNOWLEDGE
North Dakota State Library
Liberty Memorial Bldg.
Capitol Grounds
Bismarck, ND 58505 — Phone: (701)224-2490

OHIO

★N246★
GREATER CINCINNATI LIBRARY CONSORTIUM (GCLC)
3333 Vine St., Suite 605 — Phone: (513)751-4422
Cincinnati, OH 45220 — JoAnn Johnson, Exec.Dir.

★N247★
OHIONET
1500 West Lane Ave. — Phone: (614)486-2966
Columbus, OH 43221 — Ronald E. Diener, Exec.Dir.
Also known as Ohio Library Network.

★N248★
CENTRAL OHIO HOSPITAL LIBRARY CONSORTIUM
Medical Library
Riverside Methodist Hospital
3535 Olentangy River Rd. — Phone: (614)261-5230
Columbus, OH 43214 — Ms. Jo Yeoh, Coord.

★N249★
OHIO NETWORK OF AMERICAN HISTORY RESEARCH CENTERS
Archives
Ohio Historical Society
1985 Velma Ave. — Phone: (614)297-2510
Columbus, OH 43211 — Dennis East, Archv.

★N250★
SOUTHWEST OHIO COUNCIL FOR HIGHER EDUCATION (SOCHE)
2900 Acosta St., Suite 141 — Phone: (513)278-9105
Dayton, OH 45420 — Dr. Pressley C. McCoy, Pres.

★N251★
CONSORTIUM OF UNIVERSITY FILM CENTERS (CUFC)
c/o Audio Visual Services
330 KSU Library
Kent State University — Phone: (216)672-3456
Kent, OH 44242 — John Kerstetter, Act.Exec.Dir.

★N252★
NEOUCOM COUNCIL ASSOCIATED HOSPITAL LIBRARIANS
Ocasek Regional Medical Information Center — Phone: (216)325-2511
Rootstown, OH 44272 — Karen Brewer, Lib.Dir.
Also known as Council of Hospital Librarians.

★N253★
HEALTH SCIENCE LIBRARIANS OF NORTHWEST OHIO (HSLNO)
c/o Burns Health Sciences Library
Mercy Hospital
2238 Jefferson Ave.
Toledo, OH 43624 — Phone: (419)259-1327
Address is that of member library.

★N254★
NEOMARL
c/o William F. Maag Library
Youngstown State University — Phone: (216)742-3676
Youngstown, OH 44555 — David C. Genaway, Ch.
Also known as Northeast Ohio Major Academic and Research Libraries. Address rotates annually.

OKLAHOMA

★N255★
GREATER OKLAHOMA CITY AREA HEALTH SCIENCES LIBRARY CONSORTIUM (GOAL)
Box 60918
Oklahoma City, OK 73106 — Sherry Greenwood, Coord.

★N256★
BHSL
Library
Oklahoma Children's Memorial Hospital
Box 26307 — Phone: (405)271-5699
Oklahoma City, OK 73126 — Jean Cavett, Lib.Dir.

★N257★
OKLAHOMA TELECOMMUNICATIONS INTERLIBRARY SYSTEM (OTIS)
Oklahoma Department of Libraries
200 N.E. 18th St. — Phone: (405)521-2502
Oklahoma City, OK 73105 — Mary Hardin, ILL Libn.

★N258★
TULSA AREA LIBRARY COOPERATIVE (TALC)
400 Civic Center — Phone: (918)592-7893
Tulsa, OK 74103 — Jo Ann King, Coord.

★N259★
OKLAHOMA HEALTH SCIENCES LIBRARY ASSOCIATION (OHSLA)
c/o L.C. Baxter Library
Oklahoma Osteopathic Hospital
744 W. Ninth
Tulsa, OK 74127 — Jane Cooper, Pres.
Address rotates annually.

OREGON

★N260★
MARINE-VALLEY HEALTH INFORMATION NETWORK (MARVHIN)
c/o Learning Resources Center
Linn-Benton Community College
6500 S.W. Pacific Blvd. Phone: (503)928-2361
Albany, OR 97321 S. Charlene Fella, Coord.
A multi-type network comprised of 36 member libraries.

★N261★
WASHINGTON COUNTY COOPERATIVE LIBRARY SERVICES (WCCLS)
17880 S.W. Blanton St.
Box 5129 Phone: (503)642-1544
Aloha, OR 97006 Donna M. Selle, Coord.

★N262★
ASSOCIATION OF VISUAL SCIENCE LIBRARIANS (AVSL)
c/o Library
Pacific University Phone: (503)357-6151
Forest Grove, OR 97116 Laurel Gregory, Optometry Libn
Address rotates biennially.

★N263★
SOUTHERN OREGON LIBRARY FEDERATION (SOLF)
Jackson County Library
413 W. Main St.
Medford, OR 97501

★N264★
OREGON HEALTH INFORMATION NETWORK (OHIN)
Oregon Health Sciences University Library
3181 S.W. Sam Jackson Rd.
Box 573 Phone: (503)225-8026
Portland, OR 97207 Steve Teich, Coord.

★N265★
PORTLAND AREA HEALTH SCIENCES LIBRARIANS
c/o Health Sciences Library
Eastmoreland General Hospital
2900 S.E. Steele St.
Portland, OR 97202 Phone: (503)234-0411
Address and phone number given are those of member library.

★N266★
OREGON HEALTH SCIENCES LIBRARIES ASSOCIATION (OHSLA)
c/o Health Sciences Library & Information Center
Salem Hospital, 665 Winter St., S.E.
Box 14001 Phone: (503)370-5559
Salem, OR 97309 Susan Dyer, Hea.Sci.Libn.
Address and phone number given are those of member library.

PENNSYLVANIA

★N267★
LEHIGH VALLEY ASSOCIATION OF INDEPENDENT COLLEGES, INC. (LVAIC)
Moravian College Phone: (215)691-6131
Bethlehem, PA 18018 Galen Godbey

★N268★
CONSORTIUM FOR HEALTH INFORMATION & LIBRARY SERVICES (CHI)
15th St. & Upland Ave. Phone: (215)447-6163
Chester, PA 19013 Kathleen Vick, Exec. Dir.

★N269★
NORTHWEST INTERLIBRARY COOPERATIVE OF PENNSYLVANIA (NICOP)
Erie County Library System
3 S. Perry Sq. Phone: (814)452-2333
Erie, PA 16501 James R. Przepasniak, Coord.
Address rotates annually.

★N270★
CENTRAL PENNSYLVANIA HEALTH SCIENCES LIBRARY ASSOCIATION (CPHSLA)
c/o Medical Library
Lancaster General Hospital Phone: (717)299-5511
Lancaster, PA 17604 Claudette Strohm, Pres.
Address rotates annually.

★N271★
STATE SYSTEM OF HIGHER EDUCATION LIBRARIES COUNCIL (SSHELCO)
c/o Library
University of Mansfield Phone: (717)662-4672
Mansfield, PA 16933 Dr. Larry L. Nesbit, Coord.
Address rotates biennially.

★N272★
TRI-COUNTY LIBRARY CONSORTIUM
New Castle Public Library
207 E. North St.
New Castle, PA 16101-3691 Phone: (412)658-6659

★N273★
CONFEDERATION OF STATE & STATE RELATED INSTITUTIONS
c/o Professional Staff Library, Bldg. 11
Norristown State Hospital
Stanbridge and Sterigere Sts. Phone: (215)270-1369
Norristown, PA 19401 Frieda Liem, Libn.

★N274★
ERIE AREA HEALTH INFORMATION LIBRARY COOPERATIVE (EAHILC)
Library, Oil City Area Health Center, Inc.
174 E. Bissell Ave.
Box 1068 Phone: (814)677-1744
Oil City, PA 16301 Ann L. Lucas, Libn.
Address rotates annually.

★N275★
SOUTHEASTERN PENNSYLVANIA THEOLOGICAL LIBRARY ASSOCIATION (SEPTLA)
Austen K. DeBlois Library
Eastern Baptist Seminary
Lancaster at City Line Phone: (215)896-5000
Philadelphia, PA 19151-1495 Tom Gilbert, Pres.

★N276★
HEALTH SCIENCES LIBRARY CONSORTIUM
3700 Market St., Suite 307 Phone: (215)222-1532
Philadelphia, PA 19104 Joseph Scorza, Dir.

★N277★
DELAWARE VALLEY AUDIOVISUAL EXCHANGE (DAVE)
c/o Methodist Hospital
2301 S. Broad St. Phone: (215)952-9404
Philadelphia, PA 19148 Sara Richardson, Libn.
Address rotates annually.

★N278★
DELAWARE VALLEY INFORMATION CONSORTIUM (DEVIC)
c/o Health Sciences Library
University of Pennsylvania Medical Center
51 N. 39th St. Phone: (215)662-9181
Philadelphia, PA 19104 Kathy Ahrens, Coord.

★N279★
PALINET
3401 Market St., Suite 262 Phone: (215)382-7031
Philadelphia, PA 19104 Dr. J.G. Schoenung, Exec.Dir.
See also the library listing for this network in the main section.
Formerly: Library Catalogue of Pennsylvania; PALINET/ULC.

★N280★
MID-ATLANTIC LAW LIBRARY COOPERATIVE (MALLCO)
c/o Law Library
University of Pittsburgh
3900 Forbes Ave. Phone: (412)434-6293
Pittsburgh, PA 15260 Jenni Parrish, Dir.
Address and phone number given are those of member library.

★N281★
ASSOCIATION FOR LIBRARY INFORMATION (AFLI)
Duquesne University Library
Pittsburgh, PA 15282
Phone: (412)434-6138
Paul J. Pugliese, Exec.Dir.

★N282★
INTERLIBRARY DELIVERY SERVICE OF PENNSYLVANIA (IDS)
c/o Pittsburgh Regional Library Ctr.
Chatham College
Pittsburgh, PA 15232
Phone: (412)441-6409
Chuck Broadbent, Exec.Dir.

★N283★
PITTSBURGH-EAST HOSPITAL LIBRARY COOPERATIVE
c/o Forbes Center for Gerontology
Frankstown Ave. at Washington Blvd.
Pittsburgh, PA 15206
Address and presidency rotate irregularly.

★N284★
PITTSBURGH REGIONAL LIBRARY CENTER (PRLC)
Beatty Hall
Chatham College
Pittsburgh, PA 15232
Phone: (412)441-6409
Betty Anderson, Lib.Serv.Mgr.

★N285★
BERKS COUNTY LIBRARY ASSOCIATION (BCLA)
Box 7545
Reading, PA 19603
Kathryn A. Joffred, Pres.

★N286★
TRI-STATE COLLEGE LIBRARY COOPERATIVE (TCLC)
Rosemont College Library
Rosemont, PA 19010
Jude D. O'Shea

★N287★
HEALTH INFORMATION LIBRARY NETWORK OF NORTHEASTERN PENNSYLVANIA (HILNNEP)
c/o Medical Library
V.A. Medical Center
Wilkes-Barre, PA 18711
Phone: (717)824-3521
Bruce Reid, Chm.
Address rotates periodically.

★N288★
NORTHEASTERN PENNSYLVANIA BIBLIOGRAPHIC CENTER (NEPBC)
D. Leonard Corgan Library
King's College
14 W. Jackson St.
Wilkes-Barre, PA 18711
Phone: (717)826-5841
Terrence Mech, Dir.

★N289★
SUSQUEHANNA LIBRARY COOPERATIVE
c/o Library
Lycoming College
Williamsport, PA 17701
Phone: (717)321-4082
Bruce M. Hurlbert, Ch.
Address and chair rotate periodically.

RHODE ISLAND

★N290★
ASSOCIATION OF RHODE ISLAND HEALTH SCIENCES LIBRARIANS (ARIHSL)
c/o Health Science Library
Our Lady of Providence Unit, St. Joseph Hospital
21 Peace St.
Providence, RI 02907

★N291★
RHODE ISLAND INTERRELATED LIBRARY NETWORK
95 Davis St.
Providence RI 02908
Phone: (401)277-2726
Bruce Daniels, Dir.

★N292★
CONSORTIUM OF RHODE ISLAND ACADEMIC AND RESEARCH LIBRARIES, INC. (CRIARL)
Rockefeller Library
Brown University
Providence, RI 02912
Phone: (401)863-2162
Arthur P. Young, Chm.

SOUTH CAROLINA

★N293★
CHARLESTON HIGHER EDUCATION CONSORTIUM (CHEC)
Library
The Citadel Military College of South Carolina
Charleston, SC 29409
Phone: (803)792-5116
Dr. Richard Wood, Chm.
Address rotates annually.

★N294★
SOUTH CAROLINA HEALTH INFORMATION NETWORK (SCHIN)
Medical Library, School of Medicine
Medical University of S. Carolina
171 Ashley Ave.
Charleston, SC 29403
Phone: (803)792-2352

★N295★
COLUMBIA AREA MEDICAL LIBRARIANS' ASSOCIATION (CAMLA)
Professional Library
William S. Hall Psychiatric Institute
Box 202
Columbia, SC 29202
Phone: (803)758-5370
Neeta N. Shaw, Coord.

TENNESSEE

★N296★
TENNESSEE HEALTH SCIENCE LIBRARY ASSOCIATION (THSLA)
Learning Center
Jackson-Madison County General Hospital
708 W. Forest Ave.
Jackson, TN 38301
Phone: (901)425-6024
Linda G. Farmer, Pres.
Address and phone number given are those of member library.

★N297★
TRI-CITIES AREA HEALTH SCIENCES LIBRARIES CONSORTIUM
Quillen-Dishner College of Medicine Library
East Tennessee State University
Box 23290A
Johnson City, TN 37614
Phone: (615)928-6426
Janet Fisher, Asst. Dean

★N298★
KNOXVILLE AREA HEALTH SCIENCES LIBRARY CONSORTIUM (KAHSLC)
c/o Preston Medical Library
1924 Alcoa Hwy.
Knoxville, TN 37920
Phone: (615)544-9525
Lynn Yeomans Gard, Libn.
Address rotates annually.

★N299★
ASSOCIATION OF MEMPHIS AREA HEALTH SCIENCES LIBRARIES (AMAHSL)
Center for the Health Sciences Library
University of Tennessee
800 Madison Ave.
Memphis, TN 38163
Phone: (901)528-5634

TEXAS

★N300★
TEXAS STATE LIBRARY COMMUNICATIONS NETWORK (TSLCN)
Texas State Library
Box 12927 Phone: (512)463-5465
Austin, TX 78711 Edward Seidenberg, Mgr.

★N301★
APLIC INTERNATIONAL CENSUS NETWORK
c/o Population Research Center
1800 Main Bldg.
University of Texas Phone: (512)471-5514
Austin, TX 78712 Doreen S. Goyer, Libn.
Also known as Association of Population/Family Planning Libraries and Information Centers Census Network.

★N302★
TAMU CONSORTIUM OF MEDICAL LIBRARIES
Medical Sciences Library
Texas A & M University Phone: (409)845-7427
College Station, TX 77843 Virginia Algermissen, Dir.

★N303★
COASTAL BEND HEALTH SCIENCES LIBRARY CONSORTIUM
Memorial Medical Center
2606 Hospital Blvd.
Box 5280 Phone: (512)881-4198
Corpus Christi, TX 78405 Angelica Hinojosa, Coord.

★N304★
AMIGOS BIBLIOGRAPHIC COUNCIL, INC.
11300 N. Central Expy., Suite 321 Phone: (214)750-6130
Dallas, TX 75243 Louella V. Wetherbee, Exec.Dir

★N305★
ASSOCIATION FOR HIGHER EDUCATION OF NORTH TEXAS (AHE)
17811 Waterview Pkwy., Suite 125 Phone: (214)231-7211
Dallas, TX 75252-8016 Katherine P. Jagoe, Dir.

★N306★
DALLAS-TARRANT COUNTY CONSORTIUM OF HEALTH SCIENCE LIBRARIES
c/o C.B. Sacher Library
St. Paul Hospital
5909 Harry Hines Blvd. Phone: (214)879-2390
Dallas, TX 75235 Barbara Miller, Coord.
Address rotates annually.

★N307★
TALON
Health Science Center Library
University of Texas
5323 Harry Hines Blvd. Phone: (214)688-2085
Dallas, TX 75235-9049 Regina Harris Lee, Coord.
Region 5 of the Regional Medical Library Program. TALON is an acronym for the five states served by the program - TX, AR, LA, OK, and NM. Also known as South Central Regional Medical Library Program.

★N308★
SOUTH CENTRAL ACADEMIC MEDICAL LIBRARIES CONSORTIUM (SCAMEL)
c/o Health Sciences Library
Texas College of Osteopathic Medicine
Camp Bowie at Montgomery Phone: (817)735-2464
Fort Worth, TX 76107 Bobby R. Carter, Treas.

★N309★
NORTHEAST TEXAS LIBRARY SYSTEM (NETLS)
625 Austin Phone: (214)494-7192
Garland, TX 75040 Elizabeth Crabb, Coord.

★N310★
HOUSTON AREA RESEARCH LIBRARY CONSORTIUM (HARLIC)
Houston Academy of Medicine
Texas Medical Center Library, Jones Library Bldg.
1133 M.D. Anderson Blvd. Phone: (713)797-1230
Houston, TX 77030 Richard Lyders, Pres.
Address and presidency rotate biennially.

★N311★
COUNCIL OF RESEARCH & ACADEMIC LIBRARIES (CORAL)
Box 290236 Phone: (512)695-8008
San Antonio, TX 78280-1636 Irene Scharf, Exec.Dir.

★N312★
HEALTH ORIENTED LIBRARIES OF SAN ANTONIO (HOLSA)
c/o Baptist Memorial Hospital
111 Dallas St. Phone: (512)222-8431
San Antonio, TX 78286 Ruth Libby, Libn.
Address rotates annually.

★N313★
PAISANO CONSORTIUM OF LIBRARIES
2602 N. Ben Jordan Phone: (512)576-3157
Victoria, TX 77901 Dr. S. Joe McCord, Coord.
Address rotates with coordinator.

UTAH

★N314★
UTAH HEALTH SCIENCES LIBRARY CONSORTIUM
Medical Library
Primary Children's Medical Center
320 12th Ave. Phone: (801)521-1301
Salt Lake City, UT 84103 Amy Owen, Exec.Sec.

VIRGINIA

★N315★
AMERICAN GAS ASSOCIATION - LIBRARY SERVICES (AGA-LSC)
1515 Wilson Blvd.
Arlington, VA 22219 Phone: (801)841-8400

★N316★
TRALINET
HQ TRADOC, TRALINET Center
ATLS, Bldg. 117 Phone: (804)727-4491
Fort Monroe, VA 23651-5117 James H. Byrn, Dir.
Also known as U.S. Army Training & Doctrine Command (TRADOC) Library & Information Network.

★N317★
SOUTHWESTERN VIRGINIA HEALTH INFORMATION LIBRARIANS
Health Sciences Library
Rockingham Memorial Hospital
235 Cantrell Ave. Phone: (703)982-2463
Harrisonburg, VA 22801-3293 Ilene Smith, Ch.
Address rotates annually.

★N318★
TIDEWATER HEALTH SCIENCES LIBRARIES (THSL)
c/o Library
Eastern Virginia Medical School
Box 1980
Norfolk, VA 23501 Phone: (804)446-5849
Address rotates annually.

★N319★
RICHMOND AREA LIBRARIES COOPERATIVE
c/o E. Claiborne Robins School of
Business Library
University of Richmond
Richmond, VA 23173 Phone: (804)289-8666
Address and phone number given are those of member library.

WASHINGTON

★N320★
COUNCIL ON BOTANICAL HORTICULTURAL LIBRARIES
Lawrence Pierce Library
Rhododendron Species Foundation
2525 S. 336th St., Box 3798
Federal Way, WA 98063-3798
Phone: (206)927-6960
Mrs. George Harrison, Chm.

★N321★
NORTHWEST CONSORTIUM OF LAW LIBRARIES
Washington State Law Library
Temple of Justice
Olympia, WA 98504-0502
Phone: (206)753-6526
C.E. Bolden, Ch.
Address rotates annually.

★N322★
WESTERN LIBRARY NETWORK (WLN)
Washington State Library
AJ-11W
Olympia, WA 98504-0111
Phone: (206)459-6518
N.A. Stussy, Exec.Dir.

★N323★
SEATTLE AREA HOSPITAL LIBRARY CONSORTIUM (SAHLC)
Medical Library
Group Health Eastside
2700 152nd, N.E.
Redmond, WA 98052
Phone: (206)883-5431
Mary Lumsden, Pres.
Address and phone number given are those of member library.

★N324★
PACIFIC NORTHWEST REGIONAL HEALTH SCIENCES LIBRARY SERVICE
Health Sciences Library and Information Center
University of Washington
Seattle, WA 98195
Phone: (206)543-8262
Gerald J. Oppenheimer, Dir.
Region 6 of the Regional Medical Library Program serving AK, ID, MI, OR, and WA.

WEST VIRGINIA

★N325★
HUNTINGTON HEALTH SCIENCE LIBRARY CONSORTIUM
Health Science Libraries
Marshall University School of Medicine
Huntington, WV 25701
Phone: (304)696-6426
Edward Dzierzak, Chm.

WISCONSIN

★N326★
FOX VALLEY LIBRARY COUNCIL
225 N. Oneida St.
Appleton, WI 54911
Rick Krumwiede, Chm.

★N327★
NORTHEAST WISCONSIN INTERTYPE LIBRARIES (NEWIL)
c/o Nicolet Federated Library System
515 Pine St.
Green Bay, WI 54301
Phone: (414)497-3468
Mary Schmidt, Coord.

★N328★
FOX RIVER VALLEY AREA LIBRARY CONSORTIUM
St. Vincent Hospital - Health Science Library
835 S. Van Buren St.
Box 13508
Green Bay, WI 54305
Address rotates biennially.

★N329★
WISCONSIN INTERLIBRARY SERVICES (WILS)
728 State St., Rm. 464
Madison, WI 53706

★N330★
MULTITYPE ADVISORY LIBRARY COMMITTEE (MALC)
1922 University Ave.
Madison, WI 53705
Phone: (608)231-1052
Patricia Lund, Dir.

★N331★
SOUTH CENTRAL WISCONSIN HEALTH PLANNING AREA COOPERATIVE
c/o Library
St. Marys Hospital Medical Center
707 S. Mills St.
Madison, WI 53715

★N332★
WISCONSIN AREA RESEARCH CENTER NETWORK
State Historical Society of Wisconsin
816 State St.
Madison, WI 53706
Phone: (608)262-3338

★N333★
SOUTHEASTERN WISCONSIN HEALTH SCIENCE LIBRARY CONSORTIUM (SWHSL)
c/o Health Science Learning Center
St. Francis Hospital
3237 S. 16th St.
Milwaukee, WI 53215
Phone: (414)647-5156
Patricia Malmberg, Coord.

★N334★
LIBRARY COUNCIL OF METROPOLITAN MILWAUKEE, INC. (LCOMM)
814 W. Wisconsin Ave.
Milwaukee, WI 53233
Phone: (414)271-8470
Janis Trebby, Exec.Dir.

★N335★
NORTHERN WISCONSIN HEALTH SCIENCE LIBRARIES COOPERATIVE
c/o Library
St. Michael's Hospital
900 Illinois Ave.
Stevens Point, WI 54481
Phone: (715)346-5091
Barb DeWeerd, Coord.
Address rotates biennially.

★N336★
WISCONSIN VALLEY LIBRARY SERVICE (WVLS)
400 First St.
Wausau, WI 54401
Phone: (715)847-5535
Heather Eldred, Dir.

WYOMING

★N337★
WYOMING LIBRARY NETWORK
c/o Wyoming State Library
Supreme Court & State Library Bldg.
Cheyenne, WY 82002
Phone: (307)777-7281
Wayne H. Johnson, State Libn.
Address and phone number given are those of member library.

★N338★
SOUTHEAST WYOMING HEALTH SCIENCE LIBRARY CONSORTIUM
Family Practice Library
821 E. 18th St.
Cheyenne, WY 82001-4393
Phone: (307)777-7911

★N339★
NORTHEASTERN WYOMING MEDICAL LIBRARY CONSORTIUM
c/o Library
Campbell County Memorial Hospital
Box 3011
Gillette, WY 82716
Phone: (307)682-8811
Address rotates annually.

★N340★
WIND RIVER HEALTH SCIENCE LIBRARY CONSORTIUM
c/o Medical Library
Wyoming State Training School
8204 State Hwy. 789
Lander, WY 82520
Phone: (307)332-5302
Bonnie V. Freimuth, Coord.

★N341★
HEALTH SCIENCES INFORMATION NETWORK (HSIN)
c/o Science & Technology Library
University of Wyoming
University Sta., Box 3262
Laramie, WY 82071 Bonnie R. Mack, Coord.

Canada

ALBERTA

★N342★
ALBERTA GOVERNMENT LIBRARIES' COUNCIL (AGLC)
c/o Alberta Legislature Library
Cooperative Government Library Services Section
9th Fl., Legislature Annex, 9718 107th St.
Edmonton, AB, Canada T5K 2C8 Phone: (403)427-3837

★N343★
NORTHERN ALBERTA HEALTH LIBRARIES GROUP
AHP Library
Alberta Hospital Ponoka
P.O. Box 1000 Phone: (403)783-3351
Ponoka, AB, Canada T0C 2H0 Peter Managhan, Staff Libn.
Address and phone number given are those of member library.

NOVA SCOTIA

★N344★
NOVA SCOTIA ON-LINE CONSORTIUM
Dalhousie University
W.K. Kellog Health Sciences Library
Tupper Bldg. Phone: (902)424-2458
Halifax, NS, Canada B3H 4H7 Carol Webb

ONTARIO

★N345★
HAMILTON/WENTWORTH DISTRICT HEALTH LIBRARY NETWORK
Health Sciences Library
McMaster University
1200 Main St., W. Phone: (416)525-9140
Hamilton, ON, Canada L8N 3Z5 Linda Panton, Coord.

★N346★
CANADIAN HEALTH LIBRARIES ASSOCIATION
Health Sciences Library
McMaster University
1200 Main St., W
Hamilton, ON, Canada L8N 3Z5 Phone: (416)525-9140

★N347★
ONTARIO LIBRARY SERVICE - ESCARPMENT
1133 Central Ave. Phone: (416)544-2780
Hamilton, ON, Canada L8K 1N7 June E. Wilson, Dir.

★N348★
SHERIDAN PARK ASSOCIATION - LIBRARY AND INFORMATION SCIENCE COMMITTEE (LISC)
Sheridan Park Research Community
2275 Speakman Dr. Phone: (416)823-6160
Mississauga, ON, Canada L5K 1B1 Eileen Gordon, Coord.
Network of librarians in research centers, members of Sheridan Park Association.

★N349★
CANADIAN ASSOCIATION OF RESEARCH LIBRARIES (CARL)
Office of University Chief Librarian
University of Ottawa
65 Hastey St.
Ottawa, ON, Canada K1N 9A5 Phone: (613)564-5864

★N350★
ONTARIO HOSPITAL LIBRARIES ASSOCIATION (OHLA)
Children₉s Hospital of Eastern Ontario
401 Smythe Rd. Phone: (613)737-7600
Ottawa, ON, Canada KYH 8L1 Margaret Taylor, Pres.

★N351★
ONTARIO COUNCIL OF UNIVERSITY LIBRARIES (OCUL)
Library
Brock University Phone: (416)688-5550
St. Catharines, ON, Canada L2S 3A1 James Hogan, Chm.
Address rotates biennially.

★N352★
BIBLIOCENTRE
80 Cowdray Court Phone: (416)299-1515
Scarbourough, ON, Canada M1S 4N1 Doug Wentzel, Dir.

★N353★
DISABILITY RESEARCH LIBRARY NETWORK
c/o CRCD Resource Center
Canadian Rehabilitation Council for the Disabled
One Yonge St., Suite 2110
Toronto, ON, Canada M5E 1E5

★N354★
EDUCATION LIBRARIES SHARING OF RESOURCES NETWORK (ELSOR)
Metropolitan Toronto School Board
45 York Mills Rd. Phone: (416)489-3332
Willowdale, ON, Canada M2P lB6 Carol Williams, Coord.

QUEBEC

★N355★
MONTREAL HEALTH LIBRARIES ASSOCIATION (MHLA)
Medical Library
Royal Victoria Hospital
687 Pine Ave., W. Phone: (514)842-1251
Montreal, PQ, Canada H3A 1A1 Janet Joyce, Pres.
Address rotates annually.

★N356★
ASSOCIATION DES BIBLIOTHEQUES DE LA SANTE AFFILIEES A L'UNIVERSITE DE MONTREAL (ABSAUM)
c/o Bibliotheque de la Sante
Universite de Montreal
CP 6128, Succursale A Phone: (514)343-6826
Montreal, PQ, Canáda H3C 3J7 Lise Lambert, Sec.

★N357★
AGRICULTURE CANADA NETWORK OF LIBRARY SERVICES
c/o Agriculture Canada Res. Station
2560 Hochelaga Blvd.
Ste. Foy, PQ, Canada G1V 2J3
Address is that of member library.

All numbers refer to networks and consortia listed in geographic order in Appendix A. An asterick before an entry number indicates that a cross reference has been made from this title.

D

E

F

G

H

I

J

K

L

M

N

O

P

Q

R

S

T

U

V

W

Appendix B

Regional and Subregional Libraries for the Blind and Physically Handicapped

In cooperation with a network of regional and subregional libraries, the Library of Congress provides free library services to persons who are unable to read or use standard printed materials because of visual or physical impairment. Books and magazines in recorded form (talking books) or in braille are delivered to eligible readers by postage-free mail and are returned in the same manner. Specially designed phonographs and cassette players are also loaned free to persons borrowing talking books.

This list contains three elements: the addresses, telephone numbers, and names of librarians in charge of each of the regional and subregional libraries in the network. The regional library or libraries listed under each state provide a full range of library services to handicapped readers. In many states, readers receive talking books through subregional libraries, which are local public libraries having collections of current materials and direct access to the resources of their regional libraries. In addition, they offer handicapped readers reference and reader's advisory services.

Regional libraries are listed after the state heading. Subregional libraries within the state are listed next, arranged alphabetically by the city in which they are located. Some states contain more than one regional library. In this case, a remark is added to the entry to signify which portion of the state is served by a particular regional library.

American citizens certified eligible for such services who reside in foreign countries receive library service from:

Consumer Relations Section
National Library Service for the Blind and Physically Handicapped
Library of Congress
1291 Taylor Street, N.W.
Washington, DC 20542
Phone: (202)287-6397

Alabama

Alabama Public Library Service - Alabama Regional Library for the Blind & Physically Handicapped
6030 Monticello Dr. — Phone: (205)277-7330
Montgomery, AL 36130 — Mr. Hulen E. Bivins
TDD number is 272-0830. The toll-free telephone number for state residents is (800)392-5671.

Public Library of Anniston & Calhoun County - Library for the Blind & Handicapped
108 E. 10th St. — Phone: (205)237-8501
Box 308 — Mrs. Deenie M. Culver
Anniston, AL 36202

Houston-Love Memorial Library - Department for the Blind & Physically Handicapped
Box 1369 — Phone: (205)793-9767
Dothan, AL 36301 — Mary Sue Carte

Huntsville Subregional Library for the Blind & Physically Handicapped
Box 443 — Phone: (205)536-0022
Huntsville, AL 35804 — Joyce L. Smith

Alabama Institute for the Deaf & Blind - Library and Resource Center for the Blind & Physically Handicapped
705 South St. — Phone: (205)362-1500
Box 698 — Gloria S. Lemaster
Talladega, AL 35160

Tuscaloosa Public Library - Subregional Library for the Blind & Physically Handicapped
1801 River Rd. — Phone: (205)345-5820
Tuscaloosa, AL 35401 — Barbara B. Jordan

Alaska

Alaska State Library - Services for the Blind & Physically Handicapped
650 W. International Airport Rd. — Phone: (907)561-1003
Anchorage, AK 99518-1393 — Mary Jennings

Arizona

Arizona State Library for the Blind & Physically Handicapped
1030 N. 32nd St. — Phone: (602)255-5578
Phoenix, AZ 85008 — Richard C. Peel
The toll-free telephone number for state residents is (800)255-5578.

Flagstaff City-Coconino County Library - Library Special Services
300 W. Aspen — Phone: (602)779-7670
Flagstaff, AZ 86001 — Mary Mohr
TDD number is 779-7670.

Prescott Talking Book Library
215 E. Goodwin — Phone: (602)445-8110
Prescott, AZ 86301 — Ms. Jan Marr

Arkansas

Arkansas State Library for the Blind & Physically Handicapped
One Capitol Mall Phone: (501)371-1155
Little Rock, AR 72201 Cleotta Mullen

Ozarks Regional Library - Library for the Blind & Handicapped, Northwest
217 E. Dickson St. Phone: (501)442-6253
Fayetteville, AR 72701 Rachel Anne Ames

Fort Smith Public Library - Library for the Blind & Handicapped
61 S. 8th Phone: (501)783-0229
Fort Smith, AR 72901-2480 Mary Nigh

Crowley Ridge Regional Library - Library for the Blind & Physically Handicapped, Northeast
315 W. Oak Phone: (501)935-5133
Jonesboro, AR 72401 Ruth Ball

Columbia-Lafayette-Ouachita-Calhoun Regional Library - Library for the Blind & Handicapped, Southwest
220 E. Main St. Phone: (501)234-1991
Box 668 Christine McDonald
Magnolia, AR 71753

California

Braille Institute of America, Inc. - Library
741 N. Vermont Ave. Phone: (213)663-1111
Los Angeles, CA 90029 Phyllis Cairns
This regional library serves southern California. The toll-free telephone number for residents within the service area is (800)252-9486.

California State Library - Braille & Talking Book Library
600 Broadway Phone: (916)322-4090
Sacramento, CA 95818 Donine Hedrick
This regional library serves northern California. The toll-free telephone number for residents within the service area is (800)952-5666.

Fresno County Free Library - Blind & Handicapped Services
770 N. San Pablo Ave. Phone: (209)488-3217
Fresno, CA 93728
TDD number is 488-3209. The toll-free telephone number for state residents is (800)742-1011.

San Francisco Public Library for the Blind & Print Handicapped
3150 Sacramento St. Phone: (415)558-5035
San Francisco, CA 94115 Martha Heverly
TDD number is 864-1112.

Colorado

Colorado State Library - Services for the Blind & Physically Handicapped
1313 Sherman St. Phone: (303)866-2081
Denver, CO 80203 Barbara Goral
The toll-free telephone number for state residents is (800)332-5852.

Connecticut

Connecticut State Library - Library for the Blind & Physically Handicapped
198 West St. Phone: (203)566-2151
Rocky Hill, CT 06067 Ms. Dale Wierzbicki
The toll-free telephone number for state residents is (800)842-4516.

Delaware

Delaware Division of Libraries - Library for the Blind & Physically Handicapped
43 S. Dupont Hwy. Phone: (302)736-4748
Box 639 Mr. Lee Steele
Dover, DE 19903
The toll-free telephone number for state residents is (800)282-8676.

District of Columbia

District of Columbia Reigonal Library for the Blind & Physically Handicapped
901 G St., N.W., Rm. 215 Phone: (202)727-2142
Washington, DC 20001 Grace J. Lyons
TDD number is 727-2255.

Florida

Florida Divisioı of Blind Services - Library for the Blind & Physically Handicapped
420 Platt St. Phone: (904)254-3824
Box 2299 Donald John Weber
Daytona, FL 32015
TDD number is 254-3824. The toll-free telephone number for state residents is (800)342-5627.

Manatee County Central Library - Talking Book Service
1301 Barcarrota Blvd., W. Phone: (813)749-7113
Bradenton, FL 33505 Mary Peach
TDD number is 749-7113.

Broward County Talking Book Library
100 S. Andrews Ave. Phone: (305)765-5999
Fort Lauderdale, FL 33301 Joann Block
TDD number is 357-7413.

Jacksonville Public Libraries - Talking Book Library
2809 Commonwealth Ave. Phone: (904)388-6135
Jacksonville, FL 32205 Gloria E. Zittrauer

Miami-Dade Public Library System - Dade County Talking Book Library
150 N.E. 79th St. Phone: (305)751-8687
Miami, FL 33138 Barbara L. Moyer
TDD number is 758-6599.

Orange County Library System - Talking Book Section
101 E. Central Blvd. Phone: (305)425-4694
Orlando, FL 32801 Dan Kennedy
TDD number is 425-5668.

Tampa-Hillsborough County Public Library System - Tampa Subregional Library
900 N. Ashley St. Phone: (813)223-8349
Tampa, FL 33602 Jeannette Martin
TDD number is 223-8858.

Palm Beach County Public Library System - Talking Book Library
3650 Summit Blvd. Phone: (305)686-0895
West Palm Beach, FL 33406 Mrs. Pat W. Soule

Georgia

Georgia Library for the Blind & Physically Handicapped
1050 Murphy Ave., S.W. Phone: (404)656-2465
Atlanta, GA 30310 Jim DeJarnatt

Dougherty County Public Library - Albany Talking Book Center
300 Pine Ave. Phone: (912)431-2920
Albany, GA 31701 Kathryn R. Sinquefield

Athens Regional Library - Talking Book Center
435 N. Lumpkin St. Phone: (404)354-2625
Athens, GA 30601 Janet Wright
TDD number is 354-2620.

Augusta-Richmond County Public Library - Talking Book Center
425 9th St. Phone: (404)821-2625
Augusta, GA 30901 Gary Swint

Southwest Georgia Regional Library - Talking Book Center
Shotwell & Monroe Sts. Phone: (912)246-3895
Bainbridge, GA 31717 Laura S. Harrison

Brunswick-Glynn County Regional Library - Talking Book Center
208 Gloucester St. Phone: (912)267-1212
Brunswick, GA 31523 Cheryl Stiles

Chattahoochee Valley Regional Library - Talking Book Center
1120 Bradley Dr. Phone: (404)327-0211
Columbus, GA 31995 Crawford B. Pike

Oconee Regional Library - Talking Book Center
806 Highland Ave. Phone: (912)275-3322
Box 100 Katharine Clark
Dublin, GA 31021

Chestatee Regional Library - Talking Book Center
322 Oak St., Suite 5 Phone: (404)535-5738
Gainesville, GA 30501 Dorothy Dickinson

Cherokee Regional Library - Talking Book Center
305 S. Duke St. Phone: (404)638-2992
Lafayette, GA 30728 Robert L. Manning

Washington Memorial Library - Talking Book Center
1180 Washington Ave. Phone: (912)744-0877
Macon, GA 31201 Rebecca M. Sherrill

Sara Hightower Regional Library - Talking Book Center
606 Broad St. Phone: (404)295-6167
Rome, GA 30161 Sue Frazier
TDD number is 295-6167.

Chatham-Effingham-Liberty Regional Library - Talking Book Center
2002 Bull St. Phone: (912)234-5127
Savannah, GA 31499 Linda Field
The toll-free telephone number for residents within the service area is (800)342-4455.

South Georgia Regional Library - Talking Book Center
110 W. Central Ave. Phone: (912)333-5210
Valdosta, GA 31601 Frank Bonney

Guam

Guam Public Library for the Blind & Physically Handicapped
Nieves M. Flores Memorial Library Phone: (671)472-6417
254 Martyr St. Pauline V. Concepcion
Agana, GU 96910
This is a Hawaiian subregional library.

HAWAII

Hawaii State Library for the Blind & Physically Handicapped
402 Kapahulu Ave. Phone: (808)732-7767
Honolulu, HI 96815 Lydia S. Ranger
TDD number is 732-7767.

Idaho

Idaho State Library - Blind & Physically Handicapped Library Services
325 W. State St. Phone: (208)334-2117
Boise, ID 83702 Evva L. Larson
The toll-free telephone number for state residents is (800)233-4931.

Illinois

Illinois Regional Library for the Blind & Physically Handicapped
1055 W. Roosevelt Rd. Phone: (312)738-9210
Chicago, IL 60608 James Pletz
The toll-free telephone number for state residents is (800)331-2351.

Shawnee Library System
Greenbriar Rd. Phone: (618)985-3713
Carterville, IL 62918 Joan Laskaris
TDD number is 985-3711.

Chicago Library Service for the Blind & Physically Handicapped
1055 W. Roosevelt Rd. Phone: (312)738-9200
Chicago, IL 60608 Carol Reeder

River Bend Library System - Talking Books Program
220 W. 23rd Ave.
Box 125 Phone: (309)799-3155
Coal Valley, IL 61240 Dee Canfield

Lewis & Clark Library System
R.R. 4, Box 368 Phone: (618)656-3216
Edwardsville, IL 62025 Mary Lou Kampwerth
The toll-free telephone number for residents within the service area is (800)642-9545.

Cumberland Trail Library System
12th & McCawley Phone: (618)662-9335
Flora, IL 62839 Eileen Sheppard
The toll-free telephone number for state residents is (800)325-0440.

Western Illinois Library System - Talking Books Library
1518 S. Henderson Phone: (309)343-2380
Galesburg, IL 61401 Ronald Winner
The toll-free telephone number for state residents is (800)223-1853.

Dupage Library System - Subregional Library for the Blind & Physically Handicapped
127 S. 1st St. Phone: (312)232-8457
Geneva, IL 60134 Sharon Hoffman

North Suburban and Suburban Library Systems - Surburban Audio Visual Service for the Blind & Physically Handicapped
920 Barnsdale Rd. Phone: (312)352-7671
La Grange Park, IL 60525 Leon L. Drolet, Jr.

Corn Belt, Lincoln Trail, and Rolling Prairie Library Systems - Service to the Blind & Physically Handicapped
1809 W. Hovey Ave. Phone: (309)454-2711
Normal, IL 61761 Clara E. Castelo
The toll-free telephone number for residents within the service area is (800)322-9164.

Starved Rock Library System - Subregional Library for the Blind & Physically Handicapped
900 Hitt St. Phone: (815)434-7537
Ottawa, IL 61350 Sandra Donahue
The toll-free telephone number for residents within the service area is (800)892-7882.

Illinois Valley Library System
845 Brenkman Dr. Phone: (309)353-4110
Pekin, IL 61554 Valerie Brenkman

Great River Library System - Talking Book Library
515 York St. Phone: (217)223-2560
Quincy, IL 62301 Karen Gray
The toll-free telephone number for residents within the service area is (800)252-0889.

Northern Illinois Library System - Services for the Blind & Physically Handicapped
4034 E. State St. Phone: (815)229-0330
Rockford, IL 61108 Mr. Chris Anthon

Bur Oak Library System - Services for the Blind & Physically Handicapped
405 Earl Rd. Phone: (815)729-2039
Shorewood, IL 60436 Mary Moss

Kaskaskia Library System
306 N. Main St. Phone: (618)235-4220
Box 325 Linda Gapsewicz
Smithton, IL 62285

Indiana

Indiana State Library - Division for the Blind & Physically Handicapped
140 N. Senate Ave. Phone: (317)232-3684
Indianapolis, IN 46204 Lissa Shanahan
The toll-free telephone number for state residents is (800)622-4970.

Bartholomew County Public Library
Fifth & Lafayette Phone: (812)379-1277
Columbus, IN 47201 Wilma J. Perry

Elkhart Public Library - Blind & Physically Handicapped Services
300 S. Second St. Phone: (219)522-2665
Elkhart, IN 46516 Kay McCarroll

Evansville-Vanderburgh County Public Library - Talking Books Service
22 South East Fifth Phone: (812)428-8235
Evansville, IN 47708 Barbara Shanks

Allen County Public Library - Readers Services Department
900 Webster St. Phone: (219)424-7241
Box 2270 Paul Deane
Fort Wayne, IN 46801

Lake County Public Library - Talking Book Service
1919 W. 81st Ave. Phone: (219)769-3541
Merrillville, IN 46410 Joanne Panasuk
TDD number is 769-3541, ext. 240. The toll-free telephone number for residents within the service area is (800)552-8950.

Iowa

Iowa Commission for the Blind - Library
524 Fourth St. Phone: (515)281-7999
Des Moines, IA 50309 Catherine Ford
The toll-free number for state residents is (800)362-2587.

Kansas

Kansas State Library - Division for the Blind & Physically Handicapped
ESU Memorial Union Phone: (316)343-7124
1200 Commercial Caroline G. Longmoor
Emporia, KS 66801
The toll-free telephone number for state residents is (800)362-0699.

Central Kansas Library System Headquarters - Talking Book Service
1409 Williams St. Phone: (316)792-2393
Great Bend, KS 67530 Ms. Jerri Robinson
The toll-free telephone number for residents within the service area is (800)362-2642.

South Central Kansas Library System - Subregional Talking Book Library
901 N. Main Phone: (316)663-5441
Hutchinson, KS 67501 Karen Socha
The toll-free telephone number for residents within the service area is (800)362-2615.

Kansas City, Kansas Public Library - Kansas Braille Library
625 Minnesota Ave. Phone: (913)621-3073
Kansas City, KS 66101 Troy Gordon
This library is a braille lending library only.

Manhattan Public Library
Juliette & Poyntz Phone: (913)776-4741
Manhattan, KS 66502 Lois Hartley
The toll-free telephone number for residents within the service area is (800)432-2796.

Northwest Kansas Library System - Talking Books
408 N. Norton Phone: (913)877-5148
Norton, KS 67654 Clarice Howard
The toll-free telephone number for residents within the service area is (800)432-2858.

Topeka Public Library - Talking Books
1515 W. 10th St. Phone: (913)233-2040
Topeka, KS 66604 Marlene F. Hendrick
TDD number is 233-3277. The toll-free telephone number for residents within the service area is (800)432-2925.

Wichita Public Library - Talking Books Department
223 South Main Phone: (316)262-0611
Wichita, KS 67202 Betty C. Spriggs
TDD number is 262-3972. The toll-free telephone number for residents within the service area is (800)362-2869.

Kentucky

Kentucky Library for the Blind & Physically Handicapped
300 Coffee Tree Rd. Phone: (502)875-7000
Box 818 Richard Feindel
Frankfort, KY 40602
The toll-free telephone number for state residents is (800)372-2968.

Northern Kentucky Talking Book Library
502 Scott St. Phone: (606)491-7610
Covington, KY 41011 Alice Manchikes

Louisville Free Public Library - Talking Book Library
301 W. York St. Phone: (502)561-8625
Louisville, KY 40203 Maxine Harris Surratt
TDD number is 561-8621.

Louisiana

Louisiana State Library - Section for the Blind & Physically Handicapped
760 Riverside, N. Phone: (504)342-4944
Baton Rouge, LA 70802 Richard Smith
The toll-free telephone number for state residents is (800)543-4702.

Maine

Maine State Library - Library Services for the Blind & Physically Handicapped
State House, Sta. 64 Phone: (207)289-3328
Augusta, ME 04333 Benita Davis
The toll-free telephone number for state residents is (800)452-8793.

Bangor Public Library
145 Harlow St. Phone: (207)947-8336
Bangor, ME 04401 Judith Leighton
The toll-free telephone number for residents within the service area is (800)432-7860.

Cary Library
107 Main St. Phone: (207)532-3967
Houlton, ME 04730 Norma Watson

Lewiston Public Library
105 Park St. Phone: (207)783-2331
Lewiston, ME 04240 Muriel Landry

Portland Public Library - Talking Books Department
5 Monument Square Phone: (207)773-4761
Portland, ME 04101 Janice Littlefield
The toll-free telephone number for residents within the service area is (800)442-6384.

Waterville Public Library
73 Elm St. Phone: (207)873-4779
Waterville, ME 04901 Meta Vigue

Maryland

Maryland State Library for the Blind & Physically Handicapped
1715 N. Charles St. Phone: (301)333-2668
Baltimore, MD 21201 Lance C. Finney
The toll-free telephone number for state residents is (800)492-5627.

Montgomery County Department of Public Libraries - Special Needs Library
6400 Democracy Blvd. Phone: (301)493-2555
Bethesda, MD 20817 Martha Spencer
TDD number is 424-0066.

Prince George's County Memorial Library - Talking Book Center
6530 Adelphi Rd. Phone: (301)779-9330
Hyattsville, MD 20782 Shirley J. Tuthill

Massachusetts

Massachusetts Regional Library for the Blind & Physically Handicapped
Perkins School for the Blind Phone: (617)924-3434
175 N. Beacon St. Patricia Kirk
Watertown, MA 02172
The toll-free telephone number for state residents is (800)852-3133.

Worcester Public Library - Talking Book Library
Salem Square Phone: (617)799-1730
Worcester, MA 01608 Marlene Temsky
TDD number is 799-1724. The toll-free telephone number for residents within the service area is (800)922-8326.

Michigan

Library of Michigan - Library for the Blind & Physically Handicapped
735 E. Michigan Ave. Phone: (517)373-1593
Box 30007 Margaret Wolfe
Lansing, MI 48909
This regional library serves the entire state of Michigan except Wayne County. TDD number is 373-1592. The toll-free telephone number for residents within the service area is (800)992-9012.

Wayne County Regional Library for the Blind & Physically Handicapped
33030 Van Born Rd. Phone: (313)274-2600
Wayne, MI 48184 Steve Gulvezan
This regional library serves only Wayne County. TDD number is 326-1080.

Northland Library Cooperative - Library For the Blind & Physically Handicapped
316 E. Chisholm Phone: (517)356-1622
Alpena, MI 49707 Susan S. Williams

Washtenaw County Library - Library For the Blind & Physically Handicapped
4133 Washtenaw Ave. Phone: (313)971-6059
Box 8645 Mary E. Udoji
Ann Arbor, MI 48107

Willard Subregional Library
7 W. Van Buren Phone: (616)968-8166
Battle Creek, MI 49016 Beverly Brown

Downtown Detroit Subregional Library for the Blind & Physically Handicapped
121 Gratiot Ave. Phone: (313)224-0580
Detroit, MI 48226 Alva Fuquay
TDD number is 224-0584.

Farmington Community Library - Oakland County Subregional Library
32737 W. Twelve Mile Rd. Phone: (313)553-0300
Farmington Hills, MI 48018 Carole Hund
TDD number is 553-0320.

Mideastern Michigan Library Cooperative - Library for the Blind & Physically Handicapped
G-4195 W. Pasadena Ave. Phone: (313)732-1120
Flint, MI 48504 Joyce Wheat

Kent County Library System - Library for the Blind & Physically Handicapped
775 Ball Ave., N.E. Phone: (616)774-3262
Grand Rapids, MI 49503 Linda Waltman
TDD number is 531-6800.

Capital Area Library for the Blind & Physically Handicapped
Box 30007 Phone: (517)373-1593
Lansing, MI 48909 Edith Darling Heezen
The toll-free telephone number for state residents is (800)992-9012.

Upper Peninsula Library for the Blind & Physically Handicapped
217 N. Front St. Phone: (906)228-7697
Marquette, MI 49855 Suzanne Dees
The toll-free telephone number for residents within the service area is (800)562-8985.

Macomb Library for the Blind & Physically Handicapped
16480 Hall Rd. Phone: (313)286-1580
Mt. Clemens, MI 48044 Margaret Hachey

Muskegon County Library for the Blind & Physically Handicapped
635 Ottawa St. Phone: (616)724-6257
Muskegon, MI 49442 Faith Jernigan

Blue Water Library Federation - Blind & Physically Handicapped Library
210 McMorran Blvd. Phone: (313)982-3600
Port Huron, MI 48060 Debra Oyler

Southwest Michigan Library for the Blind & Physically Handicapped
300 Library Lane Phone:(616)323-3714
Portage, MI 49002 Ann Niedzielski
TDD number is 327-6727. The toll-free telephone number for residents within the service area is (800)554-0054.

Grand Traverse Area Library for the Blind & Physically Handicapped
322 Sixth St. Phone: (616)922-4824
Traverse City, MI 49684 Carol Hubbell

Minnesota

Minnesota Library for the Blind & Physically Handicapped
Braille and Sight Saving School Phone: (507)332-3279
Box 68 Myrna Wright
Faribault, MN 55021
The toll-free telephone number for state residents is (800)722-0550.

Mississippi

Mississippi Library Commission - Service for the Handicapped
5455 Executive Place Phone: (601)354-7208
Jackson, MS 39206 JoEllen Ostendorf

Missouri

Wolfner Memorial Library for the Blind & Physically Handicapped
Truman State Office Bldg., 2nd Fl. Phone: (314)751-8720
Box 387 Elizabeth Echles
Jefferson City, MO 65102
The toll-free telephone number for state residents is (800)392-2614.

Montana

Montana State Library - Division for the Blind & Physically Handicapped
1515 E. Sixth Ave. Phone: (406)444-2064
Helena, MT 59620 Darleen Tiensvold
The toll-free telephone number for state residents is (800)332-3400.

Nebraska

Nebraska Library Commission - Library for the Blind & Physically Handicapped
1420 P St. Phone: (402)471-2045
Lincoln, NE 68508 David Oertli
The toll-free telephone number for state residents is (800)742-7691.

North Platte Public Library - Blind & Physically Handicapped Program
120 W. 4th St. Phone: (308)532-6424
North Platte, NE 69101 Brenda Behsman
This subregional library may be called collect.

Nevada

Nevada State Library and Archives - Talking Book Program
Capitol Complex Phone: (702)885-5154
Carson City, NV 89710 Mrs. Leslie M. Hester
TDD number is 885-5160. The toll-free telephone number for state residents is (800)922-2880.

Las Vegas-Clark County Library District - Special Services
1401 E. Flamingo Rd. Phone: (702)733-3610
Las Vegas, NV 89119 Ann Langevin
TDD number is 369-9517.

New Hampshire

New Hampshire State Library - Division of Library Services to the Handicapped
17 S. Fruit St. Phone: (603)271-3429
Concord, NH 03301 Eileen Keim
The toll-free telephone number for state residents is (800)592-0300.

New Jersey

New Jersey Library for the Blind & Handicapped
2300 Stuyvesant Ave. Phone: (609)292-6450
Trenton, NJ 08618 Marya Hunsicker
TDD number is 633-7250. The toll-free telephone number for state residents is (800)792-8322.

New Mexico

New Mexico State Library for the Blind & Physically Handicapped
325 Don Gaspar Phone: (505)827-3829
Santa Fe, NM 87503 Ms. Glee Wenzel
The toll-free telephone number for state residents is (800) 432-5515.

New York

New York State Library for the Blind & Visually Handicapped
Cultural Education Center Phone: (518)474-5935
Empire State Plaza Jane Somers
Albany, NY 12230
This regional library serves the entire state of New York except New York City and Long Island. The toll-free telephone number for state residents is (800)342-3688.

New York Public Library - Library for the Blind & Physically Handicapped
166 Ave. of the Americas Phone: (212)925-1011
New York, NY 10013 Barbara Nugent
This regional library serves only New York City and Long Island.

Suffolk Cooperative Library System - Talking Books Plus
627 N. Sunrise Service Rd. Phone: (516)286-1600
Bellport, NY 11713 Julie Klauber
TDD number is 286-4546.

Nassau Library System - Talking Books
900 Jerusalem Ave. Phone: (516)292-8920
Uniondale, NY 11553 Myra Grimes
TDD number is 579-8585.

North Carolina

North Carolina Library for the Blind & Physically Handicapped - Department of Cultural Resources
1811 North Blvd. Phone: (919)733-4376
Raleigh, NC 27635-0001 Charles H. Fox
The toll-free telephone number for state residents is (800)662-7726.

North Dakota

South Dakota State Library for the Handicapped
State Library Bldg. Phone: (701)781-2604
800 Governors Dr. Daniel W. Boyd
Pierre, SD 57501
North Dakota is served by the South Dakota Regional Library. TDD number is (605)773-4914. The toll-free telephone numbers for North Dakota residents are (800)843-9948 and (800)843-7927.

Ohio

Cincinnati Regional Library for the Blind & Physically Handicapped
Library Square
800 Vine St. Phone: (513)369-6074
Cincinnati, OH 45202 Carol Heideman
This regional library serves southern Ohio. TDD number is 369-6072. The toll-free telephone number for residents within the service area is (800)582-0335.

Cleveland Public Library - Library for the Blind & Physically Handicapped
325 Superior Ave. Phone:(216)623-2911
Cleveland, OH 44114 Barbara T. Mates
This regional library serves northern Ohio. TDD number is 566-8294. The toll-free telephone number for residents within the service area is (800)362-1262.

Oklahoma

Oklahoma Library for the Blind & Physically Handicapped
1108 N.E. 36th St. Phone: (405)521-3514
Oklahoma City, OK 73111

Tulsa City-County Library System - Special Services
400 Civic Center Phone: (918)592-7922
Tulsa, OK 74103 Ellen Ontko
TDD number is 592-7965.

Oregon

Oregon State Library Talking Book and Braille Services
State Library Bldg. Phone: (503)378-3849
555 13th St., N.E. Kathleen McHarg
Salem, OR 97310
The toll-free telephone number for state residents is (800)452-0292. The toll-free telephone number for Portland residents is 224-0610.

Pennsylvania

Free Library of Philadelphia - Library for the Blind & Physically Handicapped
919 Walnut St. Phone: (215)925-3213
Philadelphia, PA 19107 Michael P. Coyle
This regional library serves eastern Pennsylvania. The toll-free telephone number for residents within the service area is (800)222-1754.

Carnegie Library of Pittsburgh - Library for the Blind & Physically Handicapped
4724 Baum Blvd. Phone: (412)687-2440
Pittsburgh, PA 15213 Sue O. Murdock
This regional library serves western Pennsylvania. The toll-free telephone number for residents within the service area is (800)242-0586.

Puerto Rico

Puerto Rico Regional Library for the Blind & Physically Handicapped
520 Ponce de Leon Ave. Phone: (809)723-2519
Stop 8½, Puerto de Tierra Evelyn Rodriguez
SanJuan, PR 00901

Rhode Island

Rhode Island Department of State Library Services - Regional Library for the Blind & Physically Handicapped
95 Davis St. Phone: (401)277-2726
Providence, RI 02908 Barbara L. Wilson
TDD number is 277-2726. The toll-free telephone number for state residents is (800)662-5141.

South Carolina

South Carolina State Library - Department for the Blind & Physically Handicapped
301 Gervais St.
Box 821 Phone: (803)737-9970
Columbia, SC 29202 Frances K. Case
The toll-free telephone number for state residents is (800)922-7818.

South Dakota

South Dakota State Library for the Handicapped
State Library Bldg. Phone: (605)773-3514
800 Governors Dr. Daniel W. Boyd
Pierre, SD 57501
TDD number is 773-4914. The toll-free telephone number for state residents is (800)592-1841. This regional library also serves North Dakota.

Tennessee

Tennessee Regional Library for the Blind & Physically Handicapped
Tennessee State Library & Archives Phone: (615)741-3915
403 Seventh Ave., N. Miss Francis H. Ezell
Nashville, TN 37219
TDD number is 255-6956. The toll-free telephone number for state residents is (800)342-3308.

Texas

Texas State Library - Division for the Blind & Physically Handicapped
1201 Brazos
Box 12927, Capitol Sta. Phone: (512)463-5458
Austin, TX 78711 Mr. Dale Propp
TDD number is 463-5449. The toll-free telephone number for state residents is (800)252-9605.

Utah

Utah State Library Commission - Division for the Blind & Physically Handicapped
2150 S. 300 W., Suite 16 Phone: (801)466-6363
Salt Lake City, UT 84115 Gerald A. Buttars
The toll-free telephone number for state residents is (800)662-5540. This regional library also serves Wyoming. The toll-free telephone number for residents in Wyoming and other western states is (800)453-4293.

Vermont

Vermont Department of Libraries - Special Services Unit
Box 1870, RD No. 4 Phone: (802)828-3273
Montpelier, VT 05602 Josephine Hess

Virgin Islands

Virgin Islands Regional Library for the Blind & Physically Handicapped
Lagoon Complex No. 3 Phone: (809)772-2250
Fredericksted Michael John Herz
St. Croix, VI 00840

Virginia

Virginia State Library for the Visually & Physically Handicapped
1901 Roane St. Phone: (804)786-8016
Richmond, VA 23222 Mary Ruth Halapatz
TDD number is 786-8863. The toll-free telephone number for state residents is (800)552-7015.

Alexandria Library - Talking Book Service
826 Slaters Lane Phone: (703)838-4298
Alexandria, VA 22314 Patricia Bates
TDD number is 838-4568.

Fairfax County Public Library - Special Services
6209 Rose Hill Dr. Phone: (703)971-0030
Alexandria, VA 22310 Jeanette A. Studley
TDD number is 971-6612.

Arlington County Department of Libraries - Talking Book Service
1015 N. Quincy St. Phone: (703)284-8149
Arlington, VA 22201 Roxanne Barnes
TDD number is 525-3086.

Hampton Subregional Library for the Blind & Physically Handicapped
4207 Victoria Blvd. Phone: (804)727-6630
Hampton, VA 23669 Mary Sue Newman
TDD number is 727-6630.

Newport News Public Library System - Library Service for the Blind & Physically Handicapped
112 Main St. Phone: (804)877-9488
Newport News, VA 23601 Julie M. Hewin
TTY number is 599-6475.

Roanoke City Public Library System - Department of Extention Services
706 S. Jefferson St. Phone: (703)981-2921
Roanoke, VA 24011 Rebecca Cooper

Staunton Public Library - Talking Book Center
19 S. Market St. Phone: (703)885-6215
Staunton, VA 24401 Velma Harner

Virginia Beach Public Library - Special Services Division
930 Independence Blvd. Phone: (804)464-9175
Virginia Beach, VA 23455 Marilyn W. Mortensen
TDD number is 464-9136.

Washington

Washington Library for the Blind & Physically Handicapped
821 Lenora St. Phone: (206)464-6930
Seattle, WA 98129 Ms. Jan Ames
TDD number is 464-6930
The toll-free telephone number for state residents is (800)542-0866.

West Virginia

West Virginia Library Commission - Services for the Blind & Physically Handicapped
Science & Culture Center Phone: (304)348-4061
Greenbrier & Washington Sts. Judith Duncan
Charleston, WV 25305
The toll-free telephone number for state residents is (800)642-8674.

Kanawha County Public Library - Services for the Blind & Physically Handicapped
123 Capitol St. Phone: (304)343-4646
Charleston, WV 25301 Jay Pauley

Cabell County Public Library - Services for the Blind & Physically Handicapped
455 9th St. Plaza Phone: (304)523-9451
Huntington, WV 25701 Suzanne L. Marshall

Parkersburg & Wood County Public Library - Services for the Blind & Physically Handicapped
3100 Emerson Ave. Phone: (304)485-6564
Parkersburg, WV 26101 Kim Flanigan
The toll-free telephone number for state residents is (800)642-8674.

West Virginia School for the Blind
301 E. Main St. Phone: (304)822-3521
Romney, WV 26003 Donna See

Ohio County Public Library
52 16th St. Phone: (304)232-0244
Wheeling, WV 26003 Rosalie Galloway

Wisconsin

Wisconsin Regional Library for the Blind & Physically Handicapped
813 W. Wells St. Phone: (414)278-3045
Milwaukee, WI 53233 Ms. Corliss Rice
The toll-free telephone number for state residents is (800)242-8822.

Brown County Library - Special Services Division
515 Pine St. Phone: (414)497-3473
Green Bay, WI 54301 Angela Basten
TDD number is 432-1758.

Wyoming

Utah State Library Commission - Division for the Blind & Physically Handicapped
2150 S. 300 W., Suite 16 Phone: (801)466-6363
Salt Lake City, UT 84115 Gerald A. Buttar
Wyoming is served by the Utah Regional Library. The toll-free telephone number for residents of Wyoming and other western states is (800)453-4293.

Appendix C

Patent Depository Libraries

The libraries listed below have been designated as patent depositories by the U.S. Patent and Trademark Office and are open for public use. Each of the patent depository libraries offers the publications of the patent classification system (i.e., The Manual of Classification, Index to the U.S. Patent Classification, Classification Definitions, etc.) and provides technical staff assistance to aid individuals in gaining effective access to patent information.

Depending upon the library, the patents may be available in bound volumes, in microform, on computer, or in some combination thereof. The collections are organized in patent number sequence. Facilities for making copies are generally provided for a fee. Not all depository libraries have equally complete collections, however. Some libraries have available the entire patent collection dating back to 1790, while other libraries have collections of much more limited scope. Therefore it is advisable to contact the particular library in advance about its collection size and hours of service to the public in order to ensure that a meaningful search in the chosen area of technology can be conducted.

Alabama

Auburn University Libraries
Ralph Brown Draughon Library
Science and Technology Department
Auburn University, AL 36849
(205) 826-4500 Ext: 21

Birmingham Public Library Government Documents Department
2100 Park Place
Birmingham, AL 35203
(205) 226-3680

Alaska

Anchorage Municipal Libraries
Z.J. Loussac Public Library
3600 Denali St.
Anchorage, AK 99503-6903
(907) 261-2907

Arizona

Arizona State University
Daniel E. Noble Science and Engineering Library
Tempe, AZ 85287
(602) 965-7609

Arkansas

Arkansas State Library
State Library Services
1 Capitol Mall
Little Rock, AR 77201-1081
(501) 371-2090

California

Los Angeles Public Library
Science & Technology Department
307 W. Seventh St.
Los Angeles, CA 90014
(213) 612-3274

California State Library
Government Publications Section
Library-Courts Building
Box 942837
Sacramento, CA 94237-0001
(916) 322-4572

San Diego Public Library
Science & Industry Section
820 E St.
San Diego, CA 92101
(619) 236-5813

Patent Information Clearinghouse
Sunnyvale Public Library
1500 Partridge Ave., Bldg. No. 7
Sunnyvale, CA 94087
(408) 730-7290

Colorado

Denver Public Library
Business, Science & Technology
1357 Broadway
Denver, CO 80203
(303) 571-2122

Connecticut

Science Park Patent Depository
25 Science Park, Suite 654
New Haven, CT 06511
(203) 786-5447

Delaware

University of Delaware, Newark Library
Reference Department
Newark, DE 19717-5267
(302) 451-2965

District of Columbia

Howard University
Undergraduate Library
500 Howard Place
Washington, DC 20059
(202) 636-5060

Florida

Broward County Main Library
Government Documents Department
100 S. Andrews Ave.
Fort Lauderdale, FL 33301
(305) 357-7444

Miami-Dade Public Library
Business and Science Department
101 W. Flagler St.
Miami, FL 33130-2585
(305) 375-2665

Georgia

Georgia Institute of Technology
Price Gilbert Memorial Library
Department of Microforms
Atlanta, GA 30332-0999
(404) 894-4508

Idaho

University of Idaho Library
Moscow, ID 83843
(208) 885-6235

Illinois

Chicago Public Library
Business/Science/Technology Department
425 N. Michigan Ave.
Chicago, IL 60611
(312) 269-2865

Illinois State Library
Reference Department
Centennial Building
Springfield, IL 62756
(217) 782-5430

Indiana

Indianapolis-Marion County Public Library
Business, Science and Technology Division
Box 211
Indianapolis, IN 46206
(317) 269-1741

Kentucky

Louisville Free Public Library
Government Documents Division
Fourth & York Sts.
Louisville, KY 40203

Louisiana

Louisiana State University
Troy H. Middleton Library
Business Administration/Government Documents Department
Baton Rouge, LA 70803
(504) 388-2570

Maryland

University of Maryland, College Park Libraries
Engineering & Physical Sciences Library
Reference Services
College Park, MD 20742
(301) 454-3037

Massachusetts

University of Massachusetts, Amherst
Physical Sciences Library
Graduate Research Center
Amherst, MA 01003
(413) 545-1370

Boston Public Library
Science Reference Department
Copley Square
Box 286
Boston, MA 02117
(617) 536-5400 Ext: 265

Michigan

University of Michigan
Engineering-Transportation Library
312 UGL
Ann Arbor, MI 48109-1185
(313) 764-7494

Detroit Public Library
Technology and Science Department
5201 Woodward Ave.
Detroit, MI 48202
(313) 833-1450

Minnesota

Minneapolis Public Library and Information Center
Technology and Science Department
300 Nicollet Mall
Minneapolis, MN 55401
(621) 372-6570

Missouri

Linda Hall Library
Documents Department
5109 Cherry St.
Kansas City, MO 64110
(816) 363-4600

St. Louis Public Library
Applied Science Department
1301 Olive St.
St. Louis, MO 63103
(314) 241-2288 Ext: 390

Montana

Montana College of Mineral Science and Technology Library
Butte, MT 59701
(406) 496-4284

Nebraska

University of Nebraska, Lincoln
Engineering Library
Nebraska Hall, 2nd Fl., W.
Lincoln, NE 68588-0410
(402) 472-3411

Nevada

University of Nevada, Reno
Getchell Library
Government
Publications Department
Reno, NV 89557-0044
(702) 784-6579

New Hampshire

University of New Hampshire
University Library
Patent Collection
Durham, NH 03824
(603) 862-1777

New Jersey

Newark Public Library
Science and Technology Division
5 Washington St.
Box 630
Newark, NJ 07101-0630
(201) 733-7815 or (201)733-7786

New Mexico

University of New Mexico
General Library
Government Publications and Maps Department
Albuquerque, NM 87131
(505) 277-5441

New York

New York State Library
Sciences/Health Sciences/Technology Reference Services
Cultural Education Center
Empire State Plaza
Albany, NY 12230
(518) 474-7040

Buffalo and Erie County Public Library
Science and Technology Department
Lafayette Square
Buffalo, NY 14203
(716) 846-7101

New York Public Library Annex
Patents Collection
521 W. 43rd St.
New York, NY 10036-4396
(212) 714-8529

North Carolina

North Carolina State University
D.H. Hill Library
Documents Department
Box 7111
Raleigh, NC 27695-7111
(919) 737-3280

Ohio

Public Library of Cincinnati and Hamilton County
Science and Technology Department
800 Vine St.
Cincinnati, OH 45202-2071
(513) 369-6936

Cleveland Public Library
Documents Collection
325 Superior Ave.
Cleveland, OH 44114-1271
(216) 623-2870

Ohio State University Libraries
Special Materials
1858 Neil Ave. Mall
Columbus, OH 43210
(614) 292-6286

Toledo-Lucas County Public Library
Science and Technology Department
325 Michigan St.
Toledo, OH 43624
(419) 255-7055 Ext: 212

Oklahoma

Oklahoma State University
Edmon Law Library
Documents Department
Stillwater, OK 74078-0375
(405) 624-6546

Oregon

Oregon State Library
Documents Section
State Library Building
Salem, OR 97310
(503) 378-4239

Pennsylvania

Free Library of Philadelphia
Documents Department
Logan Square
Philadelphia, PA 19103
(215) 686-5330

Carnegie Library of Pittsburgh
Science & Technology Department
4400 Forbes Ave.
Pittsburgh, PA 15213
(412) 622-3138

Pennsylvania State University Libraries
Documents Section
C207 Pattee Library
University Park, PA 16802
(814) 865-4861

Rhode Island

Providence Public Library
Business-Industry-Science-Patent Department
150 Empire St.
Providence, RI 02903
(401) 521-8726

South Carolina

Medical University of South Carolina
Library
177 Ashley Ave.
Charleston, SC 29425
(803) 792-2372

Tennessee

Memphis and Shelby County Public Library and Information Center
Business/Science Department
1850 Peabody Ave.
Memphis, TN 38104
(901) 725-8876

Vanderbilt University
Stevenson Science Library
419 21st Ave., S.
Nashville, TN 37240-0007
(615) 322-2775

Texas

University of Texas, Austin
McKinney Engineering Library
Rm. 1.3 ECJ
Austin, TX 78713
(512) 471-1610

Texas A&M University
Sterling C. Evans Library
Documents Division
College Station, TX 77843-5000
(409)845-2551

Dallas Public Library
Government Publications Division
1515 Young St.
Dallas, TX 75201
(214) 670-1468

Rice University
Fondren Library
Division of Government Publications and Special Resources
6100 S. Main
Houston, TX 77251-1892
(713) 527-8101 Ext: 2587

Utah

University of Utah
Marriott Library
Documents Division
Salt Lake City, UT 84112
(801) 581-8394

Virginia

Virginia Commonwealth University
University Library Services
Government Documents
901 Park Ave.
Box 2033
Richmond, VA 23284-0001
(804) 257-1104

Washington

University of Washington
Engineering Library, FH-15
Seattle, WA 98195
(206) 543-0740

Wisconsin

University of Wisconsin, Madison
Kurt F. Wendt Library
Technical Reports Center
215 N. Randall Ave.
Madison, WI 53706
(608) 262-6845

Milwaukee Public Library
Science, Business and Technology Department
814 W. Wisconsin Ave.
Milwaukee, WI 53233-2385
(414) 278-3247 or (414)278-3000

Appendix D

Regional Government Depository Libraries

Free information from the federal government on a broad range of subjects is available to all Americans through the U.S. Government Printing Office Depository Library Program. Fifty-four regional depositories receive every unclassified government publication of interest to the public, and have undertaken the responsibility of retaining this material permanently, in paper or microfiche format. Interlibrary loan and reference services are also provided. A listing of regional depositories with their addresses and telephone numbers follows.

Alabama

Auburn University, Montgomery Library
Documents Department
Montgomery, AL 36193
(205)279-9110 Ext: 253

University of Alabama Library
Reference Department/Documents
Box S
University, AL 35486
(205)348-6046

Arizona

Arizona State Department of Library, Archives & Public Records
State Capitol
1700 W. Washington
Phoenix, AZ 85007
(602)255-5240

University of Arizona Library
Government Documents Department
Tucson, AZ 85721
(602)621-4871

Arkansas

Arkansas State Library
Documents Service Section
One Capitol Mall
Little Rock, AR 72201
(501)371-2090

California

California State Library
Government Publications Service
Library & Courts Bldg.
914 Capitol Mall
Box 942837
Sacramento, CA 94237-0001
(916)445-2825

Colorado

University of Colorado, Boulder
Norlin Library
Government Publications Division
Campus Box 184
Boulder, CO 80309
(303)492-8834

Denver Public Library
Business, Science & Government Publications Department
1357 Broadway
Denver, CO 80203
(303)571-2122

Connecticut

Connecticut State Library
231 Capitol Ave.
Hartford, CT 06106
(203)566-4777

Florida

University of Florida Libraries
Documents Library
254 Library West
Gainesville, FL 32611
(904)392-0367

Georgia

University of Georgia Libraries
Government Documents Department
Athens, GA 30602
(404)542-8949

Hawaii

University of Hawaii
Hamilton Library
Government Documents Collection
2550 The Mall
Honolulu, HI 96822
(808)948-8230

Idaho

University of Idaho Library
Documents Section
Moscow, ID 83843
(208)885-6344

Illinois

Illinois State Library
Government Documents
Centennial Bldg.
Springfield, IL 62706
(217)782-5012

Indiana

Indiana State Library
Serials Section
140 N. Senate Ave.
Indianapolis, IN 46204
(317)232-3686

Iowa

University of Iowa Libraries
Government Publications Department
Iowa City, IA 52242
(319)353-3318

Kansas

University of Kansas
Spencer Research Library
Documents Collection
Lawrence, KS 66045
(913)864-4662

Kentucky

University of Kentucky
Margaret I. King Library
Government Publications/Map Department
Lexington, KY 40506-0039
(606)257-3139

Louisiana

Louisiana State University
Troy H. Middleton Library
Government Documents Department
Baton Rouge, LA 70803
(504)388-2570

Louisiana Tech University
Prescott Memorial Library
Documents Department
Tech Sta., Box 10318
Ruston, LA 71272
(318)257-4962

Maine

University of Maine, Orono
Raymond H. Fogler Library
Tri-State Regional Documents Depository
Orono, ME 04469
(207)581-1680

Maryland

University of Maryland, College Park Libraries
McKeldin Library
Government Documents/Map Room
College Park, MD 20742
(301)454-3034

Massachusetts

Boston Public Library
Government Documents, Microtext, Newspapers
Copley Square
Box 286
Boston, MA 02117
(617)536-5400 Ext: 226

Michigan

Detroit Public Library
5201 Woodward Ave.
Detroit, MI 48202
(313)833-1409

Library of Michigan
Government Documents
Box 30007
Lansing, MI 48909
(517)373-1593

Minnesota

University of Minnesota
Government Publications Library
409 Wilson Library
309 19th Ave., S.
Minneapolis, MN 55455
(612)624-5073

Mississippi

University of Mississippi
J.D. Williams Library
Documents Department
University, MS 38677
(601)232-5857

Missouri

University of Missouri, Columbia
Ellis Library
Government Documents
Columbia, MO 65201
(314)882-6733

Montana

University of Montana
Maureen & Mike Mansfield Library
Documents Department
Missoula, MT 59812
(406)243-6700

Nebraska

Nebraska State Library Commission
Federal Documents Department
1420 P St.
Lincoln, NE 68508-1683
(402)471-2045

Nevada

University of Nevada, Reno Library
Government Publications Department
Reno, NV 89557
(702)784-6579

New Jersey

Newark Public Library
U.S. Documents Division
5 Washington St.
Box 630
Newark, NJ 07101-0630
(201)733-7812

New Mexico

University of New Mexico
General Library
Government Publications & Maps Dept.
Albuquerque, NM 87131
(505)277-7180

New Mexico State Library
325 Don Gaspar
Santa Fe, NM 87503
(505)827-3800

New York

New York State Library
Documents Control
Cultural Education Center
Empire State Plaza
Albany, NY 12230
(518)474-5563

North Carolina

University of North Carolina, Chapel Hill
Wilson Library
BA/SS Division Documents
Chapel Hill, NC 27514
(919)962-1151

North Dakota

North Dakota State University Library
Government Documents Department
Fargo, ND 58105-5599
(701)237-7008

University of North Dakota
Chester Fritz Library
Documents Department
Grand Forks, ND 58202
(701)777-4630

Ohio

State Library of Ohio
Documents Section
65 S. Front St.
Columbus, OH 43266-0334
(614)462-7061

Oklahoma

Oklahoma State Department of Libraries
Government Documents
200 N.E. 18th St.
Oklahoma City, OK 73105
(405)521-2502

Oklahoma State University Library
Documents Department
Stillwater, OK 74078
(405)624-6546

Oregon

Portland State University Library
Box 1151
Portland, OR 97207
(503)229-3673

Pennsylvania

Pennsylvania State Department of Education
State Library of Pennsylvania
Government Publications Section
Box 1601
Harrisburg, PA 17105
(717)787-3752

South Carolina

Clemson University
Robert Muldrow Cooper Library
Documents Department
Clemson, SC 29631
(803)656-5174

University of South Carolina
Thomas Cooper Library
Documents/Microform Department
Columbia, SC 29208
(803)777-4841

Texas

Texas State Library
Public Services Department
1201 Brazos
Box 12927
Austin, TX 78711
(512)463-5455

Texas Tech University Library
Documents Department
Lubbock, TX 79409
(806)742-2268

Utah

Utah State University
Merrill Library and Learning Resources Center, UMC-30
Documents Department
Logan, UT 84322
(801)750-2682

Virginia

University of Virginia
Alderman Library
Government Documents
Charlottesville, VA 22901
(804)924-3133

Washington

Washington State Library
Documents Section
State Library Bldg., AJ-11
Olympia, WA 98504-0111
(206)753-5592

West Virginia

West Virginia University Library
Government Documents Section
Box 6069
Morgantown, WV 26506
(304)293-3640

Wisconsin

State Historical Society of Wisconsin Library
Government Publications Section
816 State St.
Madison, WI 53706-1482
(608)262-3421

Milwaukee Public Library
Documents Division
814 W. Wisconsin Ave.
Milwaukee, WI 53233
(414)278-3000

Wyoming

Wyoming State Library
Supreme Court & State Library Bldg.
Cheyenne, WY 82002
(307)777-7281

Appendix E

United Nations Depository Libraries

The following list contains the names of libraries throughout the world that house United Nations documents and publications, with international entries appearing after United States entries. The entries are arranged geographically by state or country and city. Within each city, the entries are arranged alphabetically according to the name of the parent institution or library. Users are advised to contact a particular library directly to ascertain the extent of its holdings.

UNITED STATES

California

University of California, Berkeley
General Library
Government Documents Library
Berkeley, CA 94720
(415) 642-2568

Los Angeles Public Library
Social Sciences, Philosophy and Religion Department
630 W. Fifth St.
Los Angeles, CA 90071
(213) 612-0503

University of California, Los Angeles
University Research Library
405 Hilgard Ave.
Los Angeles, CA 90024
(213) 825-1201

Stanford University Libraries
Jonsson Library of Government Documents
Stanford, CA 94305
(415) 723-2727

Colorado

University of Colorado, Boulder
Norlin Library
Government Publications Division
Campus Box 184
Boulder, CO 80309
(303) 492-8834

Connecticut

Yale University Library
Seeley G. Mudd Library
Government Documents Center
38 Mansfield St.
Yale Sta., Box 2491
New Haven, CT 06520
(203) 432-3209

District of Columbia

Library of Congress
Serial & Government Publications Division
James Madison Memorial Bldg., Rm. LM-133
Washington, DC 20540
(202) 287-5690

United Nations Information Centre
1889 F St., N.W.
Washington, DC 20006
(202) 289-8670

Florida

Nova University Law Library
3100 S.W. 9th Ave.
Fort Lauderdale, FL 33315
(305) 760-5766

Florida State University
Robert Manning Strozier Library
Documents-Maps Department
Tallahassee, FL 32306
(904) 644-5211

Hawaii

University of Hawaii
Public Services - Government Documents, Maps & Microforms
Hamilton Library
2550 The Mall
Honolulu, HI 96822
(808) 948-8230

Illinois

Illinois Institute of Technology
Chicago Kent Law School Library
Library of International Relations
77 S. Wacker Dr.
Chicago, IL 60606
(312) 567-5014

University of Chicago
Joseph Regenstein Library
1100 E. 57th St.
Chicago, IL 60637
(312) 962-7874

Northwestern University Library
Government Publications Department
1935 Sheridan Rd.
Evanston, IL 60201
(312) 491-7658

University of Illinois
Education and Social Science Library
100 Main Library
1408 W. Gregory Dr.
Urbana, IL 61801
(217) 333-2305

Indiana

Indiana University Libraries
Government Publications Department
Bloomington, IN 47405
(812) 335-6924

Indiana University
School of Law Library
735 W. New York St.
Indianapolis, IN 46202
(317) 274-4027

Iowa

University of Iowa Libraries
Government Publications Department
Iowa City, IA 52242
(319) 353-4450

Kansas

University of Kansas Libraries
Documents Collection
117 Spencer Research Library
Lawrence, KS 66045-2800
(913) 864-4662

Kentucky

University of Kentucky
Margaret I. King Library
Government Publications/Map Department
Lexington, KY 40506-0039
(606) 257-3139

Louisiana

Louisiana State University
Troy H. Middleton Library
Business Administration/Government Documents Department
Baton Rouge, LA 70803
(504) 388-2570

Maryland

Johns Hopkins University
Milton S. Eisenhower Library
Government Publications/Maps/Law Department
Charles & 34th Sts.
Baltimore, MD 21218
(301) 338-8360

Massachusetts

Boston Public Library
Government Documents, Microtext, Newspapers
Copley Square
Box 286
Boston, MA 02117
(617) 536-5400

Harvard University
Harvard College Library
Government Documents Division
Cambridge, MA 02138
(617) 495-2401

Michigan

University of Michigan
Harlan Hatcher Graduate Library
Documents Center
Ann Arbor, MI 48109-1205
(313)764-0410

Minnesota

University of Minnesota
Government Publications Library
409 Wilson Library
309 19th Ave., S.
Minneapolis, MN 55455
(612) 624-5073

Nevada

University of Nevada, Reno
University Library
Government Publications Department
Reno, NV 89557
(702) 784-6579

New Jersey

Princeton University Library
Documents Division
United Nations Collection
Princeton, NJ 08544
(609) 452-3211

New York

Cornell University Libraries
Serials Department
Ithaca, NY 14853
(607) 256-4144

Columbia University
Law School Library
435 W. 116th St.
New York, NY 10027
(212) 280-3737

Council on Foreign Relations Library
58 E. 68th St.
New York, NY 10021
(212) 734-0400

New York Public Library
Economic and Public Affairs Division
5th Ave. & 42nd St., Rm. 228
New York, NY 10018
(212) 930-0750

New York University
Elmer Holmes Bobst Library
United Nations Collection
70 Washington Sq., S.
New York, NY 10012
(212) 998-2610

North Carolina

University of North Carolina, Chapel Hill
Davis Library 080A
BA/SDS International Documents
Bldg. 024A
Chapel Hill, NC 27514
(919) 962-1301

Ohio

Cleveland Public Library
Social Sciences Department
325 Superior Ave.
Cleveland, OH 44114-1271
(216) 623-2860

Pennsylvania

University of Pennsylvania
Population Studies Center
Demography Library
3718 Locust Walk
Philadelphia, PA 19104-6298
(215) 898-5375

Puerto Rico

Catholic University of Puerto Rico
Monsignor Juan Fremiot Torres Oliver Law Library
Ave. Las Americas
Ponce, PR 00732
(809) 844-4150

University of Puerto Rico
Biblioteca General
Zenobia y Juan Ramon Jiminez Collection
Box 22933, UPR Sta.
Rio Piedras, PR 00931
(809) 764-0000

Rhode Island

Brown University
John D. Rockefeller, Jr. Library
Documents Department
Providence, RI 02912
(401) 863-2167

Tennessee

Vanderbilt University Library
Serials
419 21st Ave., S.
Nashville, TN 37203
(615) 322-2838

Texas

University of Texas, Austin
Documents Collection
General Libraries, PCL 2.400
Austin, TX 78713-7330
(512) 471-3813

Utah

University of Utah
Marriott Library
Documents Division
Salt Lake City, UT 84112
(801) 581-8394

Virginia

University of Virginia
Alderman Library
Government Documents
Charlottesville, VA 22901
(804) 924-3026

Washington

University of Washington Libraries
Government Publications Division
Suzzallo Library, FM-25
Seattle, WA 98195
(206) 543-1937

INTERNATIONAL

Afghanistan

Kabul University
Library
Kabul, Afghanistan

United Nations Information Centre
Shah Mahmoud Ghazi Watt
P.O. Box 5
Kabul, Afghanistan

Algeria

Bibliotheque Nationale d'Algerie
Ave. Dr. Frantz Fanon
Algiers, Algeria

Centre d'Information des Nations Unies
19, ave. Chahid El Quali Mustapha Sayed
B.P. 823
Algiers, Algeria

Argentina

Centro de Informacion de las Naciones Unidas
Junin 1930 (bis), 1er piso
Buenos Aires, 1113 Argentina

Congreso de la Nacion
Biblioteca
Rivadavia 1850
C.P. 1033
Buenos Aires, Argentina

Departamento de Documentacion e Informacion Internacional
Paseo Colon 533-7o piso
Buenos Aires, 1063 Argentina

Universidad Nacional de Cordoba
Biblioteca Mayor
Centro de Documentacion
Casilla de Correos 63
Cordoba, 5000 Argentina

Biblioteca Depositaria de las Naciones Unidas
Editorial Rio Negro
9 de julio 733, Casilla de Correo 450
General Roca, 8332 Argentina

Municipalidad de Gral Pueyrredon
Biblioteca Depositaria de las Naciones Unidas
Olavarria 2508
Mar del Plata, 7600 Argentina

Universidad Nacional de Cuyo
Biblioteca Central
Casilla de Correo 420
Mendoza, 5500 Argentina

Biblioteca Argentina "Dr. Juan Alvarez"
Pasage Dr. Juan Alvarez 1550
Rosario, 2000 Argentina

Australia

Australian Capital Territory

Australian Parliamentary Library
Parliament House
Canberra, ACT 2600, Australia

National Library of Australia
Gift and Exchange Section (D139/1)
Canberra, ACT 2600, Australia

New South Wales

State Library of New South Wales
Government Publications
Macquarie St.
Sydney, NSW 2000, Australia

United Nations Information Centre
National Mutual Centre
44 Market St., 16th Fl.
P.O. Box 4045
Sydney, NSW 2001, Australia

Queensland

State Library of Queensland
William St.
Brisbane, QLD 4000, Australia

South Australia

The State Library of South Australia
Acquisitions Section
P.O. Box 415, GPO
Adelaide, SA 5001, Australia

Victoria

State Library of Victoria
Government Publications
328 Swanston St.
Melbourne, VIC 3000, Australia

Western Australia

The Library Board of Western Australia
Alexander Library Bldg.
Perth Cultural Center
Perth, WA 6000, Australia

Austria

Osterreichische Nationalbibliothek
Josefsplatz 1
A-1015 **Vienna,** Austria

United Nations Information Service
Vienna Information Centre
P.O. Box 500
A-1400 **Vienna,** Austria

Bahrain

Ministry of Education
Directorate of Public Libraries
Manama Public Library
P.O. Box 43
Manama, Bahrain

United Nations Information Centre
King Faisal Rd., Gufool
P.O. Box 26004
Manama, Bahrain

Bangladesh

Dhaka University
Library
Dhaka 2, Bangladesh

United Nations Information Centre
GPO Box 3658
Dhaka 100, Bangladesh

Barbados

University of the West Indies
Cave Hill Campus
Bridgetown, Barbados

Belgium

Bibliotheque du Parlement
Palais de la Nation
Rue de la Loi
B-1040 **Brussels,** Belgium

Bibliotheque Royale Albert 1er
Section des Documents Officiels
Blvd. de l'Empereur 4
B-1000 **Brussels,** Belgium

United Nations Information Centre and Liaison Office
Rue d'Arlon 108
B-1040 **Brussels,** Belgium

Katholieke Universiteit Leuven
Bibliotheekcentrale
Mgr. Ladeuzeplein 21
B-3000 **Leuven,** Belgium

Centre General de Documentation de l'Universite Catholique de Louvain
Place Cardinal Mercier 31
B-1348 **Louvain-la-neuve,** Belgium

Benin

Universite Nationale du Be
Bibliotheque Universitaire
B.P. 526
Cotonou, Benin

Bhutan

Thimpu Public Library
Thimpu P.O.
Thimpu, Bhutan

Bolivia

Centro de Informacion de las Naciones Unidas
Edificio Naciones Unidas
Plaza Isabel la Catolica
Apdo. 686
La Paz, Bolivia

Biblioteca Nacional de Bolivia
Espana 25
Sucre, Bolivia

Botswana

National Library of Botswana
Gaborone, Botswana

Brazil

Biblioteca da Camara dos Deputados
Secao de Colecones Especiais
Centro de Documentacao e Informacao
Palacio do Congreso Nacional
Brasilia, DF 70160 Brazil

Universidad Federal do Rio Grande do Sul
Faculdade de Dereito
Biblioteca-Depositaria das Nacoes Unidas
Ave. Joao Passoa 6/No
Porto Alegre, RS 90000 Brazil

Biblioteca Nacional do Rio de Janeiro
Ave. Rio Branco 219
Rio de Janeiro, RJ 20042 Brazil

Centro de Informacaos das Nacoes Unidas
Palacio Itamaraty
Ave. Marechal Floriano 196
Rio de Janeiro, RJ 20060 Brazil

Biblioteca Mario de Andrade
Rueda Consolacao 94
C.P. 8170
Sao Paulo, SP 01302, Brazil

Burkina Faso

United Nations Information Centre
218, rue de la Gare
B.P. 135
Ouagadougou, Burkina Faso

Bulgaria

Sofiiski Universitet "Kliment Ohridsky"
Biblioteca
15 Blvd. Ruski
Sofia, Bulgaria

Burma

National Library
Municipal Bldg., 2nd Fl.
Rangoon, Burma

United Nations Information Centre
281 Manawhari Rd.
P.O. Box 230
Rangoon, Burma

Burundi

Centre d'Information des Nations Unies
Ave. de la Poste 7
Place de l'Independence
B.P. 2160
Bujumbura, Burundi

Cameroon

Centre d'Information des Nations Unies
Immeuble Kamden rue Joseph Clere
B.P. 836
Yaounde, Cameroon

Canada

Alberta

University of Alberta
Humanities and Social Sciences Library
Government Publications
Edmonton, AB T6G 2J8
(403) 432-3776

British Columbia

University of British Columbia
University Library
Government Publications & Microforms Divisions
Vancouver, BC V6T 1W3
(604) 228-2584

Manitoba

Manitoba Legislative Library
Manitoba Archives Building
200 Vaughan St., Main Fl., E.
Winnipeg, MB R3C 1T8
(204) 945-4330

New Brunswick

University of New Brunswick
Harriet Irving Library
Government Documents Department
P.O. Box 7500
Fredericton, NB E3B 5H5
(506) 453-4752

Nova Scotia

Dalhousie University Library
Documents Section
Halifax, NS B3H 4H8
(902) 424-3634

Ontario

Queen's University at Kingston
Documents Library
Mackintosh-Corry Hall
Kingston, ON K7L 3N6
(613) 545-6313

University of Ottawa
Bibliotheque Morisset
Documents Officiels
65 Hastey St.
Ottawa, ON K1N 9A5
(613) 231-6880

Canadian Institute of International Affairs
15 King's College Circle
Toronto, ON M5S 2V9
(416) 979-1851

University of Toronto Library
Government Publications Division
Toronto, ON M5S 1A5
(416) 978-3931

Quebec

McGill University
McLennan Library
Government Documents Department
3459 McTavish St.
Montreal, PQ H3A 1Y1
(514) 392-5063

Universite de Montreal
Bibliotheque des Sciences Humaines et Sociales
Publications Officielles
C.P. 6128, Succursale A
Montreal, PQ H3C 3J7
(514) 343-7430

Universite Laval Bibliotheque
Services des Documents Officiels
Cite Universitaire
Ste. Foy, PQ G1K 7P4
(418) 656-3344

Saskatchewan

University of Saskatchewan
Murray Memorial Library
Government Publications Department
Saskatoon, SK S7N 0W0
(306) 966-5986

Chile

Biblioteca Nacional
Oficina de Canje y Donaciones
Ave. Bernardo O'Higgins 651
Santiago, Chile

Comision Economica para America Latina y el Caribe
Servicio de Informacion
Edificio Naciones Unidas
Ave. Dag Hammarskjold
Santiago, Chile

Unidad de Organismos Internacionales
Hemeroteca-Biblioteca del Congreso Nacional
Huerfanos 1117 2o piso
Santiago, Chile

People's Republic of China

National Library of Beijing
United Nations Material Section
Beijing 7, People's Republic of China

Chong-Qing Library
Chong-Qing, People's Republic of China

Shanghai Library
325 Nanjing Rd., W.
Shanghai, 200003, People's Republic of China

Colombia

Biblioteca Nacional
Calle 24, No. 5-60
Apdo. aereo 27600
Bogota, Colombia

Centro de Informacion de las Naciones Unidas
Calle 27, No. 12-65, piso 2
Apdo. aereo 058964
Bogota, Colombia

Universidad del Valle
Departamento de Bibliotecas
Apdo. aereo 25360
Cali, Colombia

Congo

Centre d'Information des Nations Unies
Ave. Pointe-Hollandaise
Quartier M'Pila
B.P. 465
Brazzaville, Congo

Costa Rica

Universidad Nacional
Escuela de Relaciones Internacionales
Centro de Documentacion "Luis y Felipe Molina"
Apdo. 437
Heredia, Costa Rica

Biblioteca Nacional
Apdo. 10.008
San Jose, Costa Rica

Cuba

Biblioteca Nacional "Jose Marti"
Havana, Cuba

Cyprus

Ministry of Education
Library
Nicosia, Cyprus

Czechoslovakia

Univerzitna Kniznica
Michalska 1
CS-814 17 **Bratislava,** Czechoslovakia

Universitni Knihovna
Keninovna 5/7
CS-601 87 **Brno,** Czechoslovakia

Knihovna Federalniho Shromazdeni CSSR
Vinahradska 1
CS-110 02 **Prague,** Czechoslovakia

Statni Knihovna CSR
Klementinum 190
CS-110 01 **Prague** 1, Czechoslovakia

United Nations Information Centre
Panska 5
CS-110 00 **Prague** 1, Czechoslovakia

Denmark

Statsbiblioteket
Section for International Organisations' Publications
Universitetsparken
DK-8000 **Arhus** C, Denmark

Det Kongelige Bibliotek
Kontoret fur Internationale Publikationer
Christians Brygge 8
DK-1219 **Copenhagen** K, Denmark

United Nations Information Centre
H.C. Andersens Blvd. 37
DK-1533 **Copenhagen** V, Denmark

Dominican Republic

Universidad Autonoma de Santo Domingo
Biblioteca Central
Santo Domingo, Dominican Republic

Ecuador

Biblioteca Nacional
Casa de la Cultura Ecuadoriana
12 de Octubre y ave. Patria
Quito, Ecuador

Egypt

Universite d'Alexandrie
Faculte de Droit d'Alexandrie
Alexandria, Egypt

Dar-el kutub al-wataniyah
Bab-el-Khala
Cairo, Egypt

United Nations Information Centre
Tagher Bldg.
1 Osoris St.
P.O. Box 262
Cairo, Egypt

El Salvador

Biblioteca Nacional de El Salvador
8a Ave. Norte 228
San Salvador, El Salvador

Centro de Informacion de las Naciones Unidas
Paseo General Escalon y
87 Ave. Norte
Apdo Postal 2157
San Salvador, El Salvador

England

Birmingham Central Library
Chamberlin Square
Birmingham B3 3HQ, England

The University of Sussex
The Institute of Development Studies
The Library
Falmer
Brighton BN1 9RE, England

Cambridge University
Library
Official Publications Department
West Road
Cambridge CB3 9DR, England

Liverpool City Libraries
Liverpool L3 8EW, England

The British Library
Reference Division
Department of Printed Books
London WC1B 3DG, England

London School of Economic and Political Science
British Library of Political and Economic Science
London WC2A 2AE, England

The Royal Institute of International Affairs
The Library
10 St. James Square
London SW1Y 4LE, England

United Nations Information Centre
Ship House
20 Buckingham Gate
London SW1E 6LB, England

Manchester Public Libraries
Central Library
Book Services Department
St. Peter's Square
Manchester M2 5PD, England

Oxford University
Bodleian Library
Official Papers
Broad St.
Oxford 0X1 3BG, England

Ethiopia

Addis Ababa University
Library
Addis Ababa, Ethiopia

United Nations Information Service
Economic Commission for Africa
Africa Hall
P.O. Box 3001
Addis Ababa, Ethiopia

Fiji

The University of the South Pacific
Library
P.O. Box 1168
Suva, Fiji

Finland

Abo Akademi
Forenta Nationernas Deposatory
Gezeluingatan 2
SF-20500 **Abo** 50, Finland

Eduskunnan Kirjasto
SF-00102 **Helsinki,** Finland

Tampereen Yliopiston Kirjasto
P.O. Box 617
SF-33101 **Tampere** 10, Finland

France

Fonds des Nations Unies
Bibliotheque Interuniversitaire
d'Aix-Marseilles
3, ave. Robert-Schuman
F-13626 **Aix-en-Provence,** France

Bibliotheque Interuniversitaire de Lyon
18, quai Claude Bernard
F-69363 **Lyon Cedex** 2, France

Universite de Nancy
Bibliotheque
Section Centrale
11, Place Carnot
F-54042 **Nancy Cedex,** France

Bibliotheque Cujas de Droit et Sciences Economiques
Service des Publications Internationales
2, rue Cujas
F-75005 **Paris,** France

Bibliotheque de l'Assemblee Nationale
Service de la Documentation Etrangere
126, rue de l'Universite
F-75355 **Paris,** France

Bibliotheque Nationale
Service des Publications Officielles
58, rue de Richelieu
F-75084 **Paris Cedex** 02, France

Centre d'Information des Nations Unies
1, rue Miollis
F-75732 **Paris Cedex** 15, France

Fondation Nationale des Sciences Politiques
27, rue Saint Guillaume
F-75006 **Paris,** France

Bibliotheque Nationale et Universitaire
Section Droit
5, rue du Marechal Joffre
B.P. 1029/F
F-57070 **Strasbourg Cedex,** France

Bibliotheque Interuniversitaire de Bordeaux
Droit et Sciences Economiques
Allee Maine de Biran, Domaine Universitaire
F-33405 **Talence,** France

Gabon

Bibliotheque Nationale Gabonaise
B.P. 1188
Libreville, Gabon

German Democratic Republic

Deutsche Staatsbibliothek
Unter der Linden 8
DDR-1086 **Berlin,** German Democratic Republic

Friedrich-Schiller-Universitat
Institut fur Volkerrecht
DDR-69 **Jena,** German Democratic Republic

Deutsche Bucherei
Deutscher Platz
DDR-7010 **Leipzig,** German Democratic Republic

Federal Republic of Germany

Freie Universitat Berlin
Universitatsbibliothek
D-1000 **Berlin** 33, Federal Republic of Germany

Staatsbibliothek Preussischer Kulturbesitz
Abt. Amtsdruckschriften Umtausch-Internationale
Organisationen
Potsdamer Strasse 30
Postfach 1407
D-1000 **Berlin** 30, Federal Republic of Germany

Universitatsbibliothek Bochum
Universitatstrasse 150
Postfach 10 21 48
D-4630 **Bochum** 1, Federal Republic of Germany

Deutscher Bundestag
Bibliothek
Internationale Organisationen
Bundeshaus
Gorresstrasse 15
D-5300 **Bonn** 12, Federal Republic of Germany

HWWA - Institut fur Wirtschaftsforschung-Hamburg
Bibliothek
Neuer Jungfernstieg 21
D-2000 **Hamburg** 36, Federal Republic of Germany

Max Planck-Institut fur Auslandisches Offentliches Recht und Volkerrecht
Berliner Strasse 48
D-6900 **Heidelberg** 1, Federal Republic of Germany

Institut fur Internationales Recht an der Universitat Kiel
D-2300 **Kiel** 1, Federal Republic of Germany

Bayerische Staatsbibliothek
Munchen
Postfach 34-0150
D-8000 **Munich** 34, Federal Republic of Germany

Ghana

Ghana Library Board
Accra, Ghana

United Nations Information Centre
Gamel Abdul Nassar/Liberia Rds.
P.O. Box 2339
Accra, Ghana

University of Ghana
Balme Library
P.O. Box 24
Legon, Ghana

Greece

Bibliotheque de la Chambre des Deputes Helleniques
Ancien Palais Royal
Athens, Greece

Bibliotheque Nationale
Athens, Greece

United Nations Information Centre
36 Amalia Ave.
GR-10558 **Athens,** Greece

Institute of International Public Law and International Relations
Megalou Alexandrou 15 and Hadji Sts.
Thessaloniki, Greece

Guatemala

Biblioteca National
5a Avenida, 7-26 Zona 1
Guatemala City, Guatemala

Guinea

Bibliotheque Nationale
Centre National et de Documentation
B.P. 516
Conakry, Guinea

Guinea-Bissau

Bissau Bibliotheca
Instituto Nacional de Estudios e Pesquisa
Complexo Escolar
14 de Novembro Bairro
Cobornel
C.P. 112
Bissau, Guinea-Bissau

Guyana

University of Guyana
Library
Georgetown, Guyana

Honduras

Universidad Nacional Autonoma
Sistema Bibliotecario de Honduras
Ciudad Universitaria
Tegucigalpa, D.C., Honduras

Hong Kong

Urban Council Public Libraries
Kwong Sang Hong Bldg.
296A Hennessy Rd., 1st Fl.
Hong Kong, Hong Kong

Hungary

Orszaggyulesi Konyvtar
Kossuth Lajos ter 1-3
H-1357 **Budapest,** Hungary

Iceland

Landsbokasafn Islands
Reykjavik, Iceland

India

University of Bombay
University Library
K.P. Patil Marg Fort
Bombay 400032, India

National Library
Foreign Official Documents Division
Belvedere
Calcutta 700027, India

Punjab University
Department of Laws
Library
Chandigarh, India

University of Delhi
Delhi School of Economics
Ratan Tata Library
Delhi 110007, India

Karnatak University
Library
Pavate Nagar
Dharwad 580003, India

Osmania University
Library
Hyderabad 500007 A.P., India

Connemara Public Library
Madras 600008, India

Indian Council of World Affairs
Library
Sapru House
Barakhamba Rd.
New Delhi 110001, India

Parliament Library
Acquisition Section
Parliament House
New Delhi 110001, India

United Nations Information Centre
55 Lodi Estate
New Delhi 110003, India

Servants of India Society
Library
Pune 411004, India

Kerala University
Library
Trivandrum 695034, India

Banares Hindu University
Library
Varanasi 221005, **Uttar Pradesh,** India

Indonesia

Dewan Perwakilan Rakjat Rupublik Indonesia
Jakarta, Indonesia

National Library of Indonesia
Jalan Salemba Raya 28
P.O. Box 3624
Jakarta 10002, Indonesia

United Nations Information Centre
Gedung Dewan Pers, 5th Fl.
32-34 Jalan Kebon Sirih
Jakarta, Indonesia

Iran

Shiraz University
College of Arts and Science
Mulla Sadra Library
Shiraz, Iran

Center for Graduate International Studies
Faculty of Law and Political Science
Library
Ave. Shareza
P.O. Box 41-3729
Teheran 14, Iran

Library of the Majlis
Teheran, Iran

United Nations Information Centre
Ave. Gandhi
43 Street No. 3
P.O. Box 1555
Teheran, Iran

Iraq

United Nations Information Service
Economic and Social Commission for Western Asia
Amiriya, Airport St.
P.O. Box 27
Baghdad, Iraq

University of Baghdad
Central Library
Waziriya
Baghdad, Iraq

University of Basrah
Central Library
Basrah, Iraq

University of Mosul
Central Library
Mosul, Iraq

Ireland

National Library of Ireland
Kildare St.
Dublin, Ireland

Northern Ireland

Belfast Public Libraries
Central Library
Belfast BT1 EA, Northern Ireland

Israel

The Jewish National and University Library
General Reading Room
United Nations Collection
P.O. Box 503
Jerusalem 91-004, Israel

The Knesset
Library
Jerusalem, Israel

Italy

Biblioteca Nazionale Centrale
Piazza Cavalleggeri, 1a
I-50122 **Florence,** Italy

Universita Cattolica del Sacro Cuore
Biblioteca-Ufficio Scambi Periodici
Largo Gemelli 1
I-20123 **Milan,** Italy

Universita di Padova
Istituto di Diritto Pubblico
Seminario de Diritto Internazionale
Via VIII Febbraio 2
I-35122 **Padua,** Italy

Bibliotheque de l'Institut International pour l'Unification du Droit Prive (UNIDROIT)
DL-178
Via Panisperna 28
I-00184 **Rome,** Italy

Centro d'Informazione delle Nazioni Unite
Palazzetto Venezia
Piazza San Marco 50
Rome, Italy

Societa Italiana per la Organizzazione Internazionale
Via San Marco 3
I-00186 **Rome,** Italy

Istituto di Diritto Internazionale e Legislazione Comparata
Facolta de Giurisprudenza
Piazzale Europa 1
I-34127 **Triest,** Italy

Ivory Coast

Bibliotheque Nationale
Abidjan, Ivory Coast

Jamaica

National Library of Jamaica
12 East St.
P.O. Box 823
Kingston, Jamaica

University of the West Indies
Library
Mona, Jamaica

Japan

Kyushu United Nations Depository Library
5th Fl., Denki Bldg., Daiichi Bekkan
1-82-2 Watanabe-Dori Chuo-Ku
Fukuoka 810, Japan

Seinan Gakuin University
Library
Fukuoka 814, Japan

Hiroshima Municipal Central Library
United Nations Depository Library
3-1 Motomachi, Nakaku
Hiroshima 730, Japan

Kobe University
Research Institute for Economics and Business Administration
Rokkodai-cho, Nada-Ku
Kobe, Japan

Kyoto United Nations Depository Library
2nd Fl., Kyoto Shimbun Bldg., Karasumya-Ebisugawa dori
Nakakyo-ku
Kyoto 604, Japan

Nihon University
College of International Relations
Library
2-31-145, Bunkyo-Cho
Mishima, Shizuoka 411, Japan

Aichi-Ken Kinro-Kaikan
Aichi Prefectural Labour Centre
United Nations Depository Library
2-32-1 Tsurumai
Showa-ku
Nagoya 466, Japan

University of Ryukyus
University Library
Nishihara-Chome
Okinawa 903-01, Japan

Hokkaido University
University Library
Kita-Ru, N.9, W.7
Sapporo, Japan

Tohoku University
Library
United Nations Depository Library
75 Katahira-Cho
Kawauchi
Sendai-Shi 980, Japan

National Diet Library
1-10-1 Nagata-Cho, Chiyoda-ku
Tokyo 100, Japan

United Nations Information Centre
Shin Aoyama Bldg. Nishikan, 22nd Fl.
1-1-1 Minami Aoyama
Minato-ku
Tokyo 107, Japan

University of Tokyo
Library
United Nations Depository Library
Hongo 7-Chome, Bunkyo-Ku
Tokyo 113, Japan

Jordan

University of Jordan
Library
Amman, Jordan

Democratic Kampuchea

Bibliotheque Nationale
c/o MP du Kampuchea Democratique
486 Ihetsabarn-Nimit Nua Rd.
Lard Yao, Bangkhen
Bangkok 9, Thailand

Kenya

United Nations Information Centre
United Nations Office
P.O. Box 34135
Gigiri
Nairobi, Kenya

University of Nairobi
Library
P.O. Box 30197
Nairobi, Kenya

Republic of Korea

Korea University
Library
1 Anam-dong
Seoul 132-00, Republic of Korea

National Assembly Library
Acquisition and Exchange Division
Yoi-dong 1, Yeongdeungpo-gu
Seoul, Republic of Korea

Kuwait

Kuwait University
United Nations Publications Library
P.O. Box 5486
Kuwait, Kuwait

Ministry of Foreign Affairs
The Library
Kuwait, Kuwait

Lebanon

United Nations Information Centre
Fakhoury Bldg.
Montee Bain Militaire
P.O. Box 4656
Beirut, Lebanon

Lesotho

United Nations Information Centre
Corner Kiligmom and Hilton Rds.
Opposite Sanlam Centre
P.O. Box 301
Maseru 100, Lesotho

National University of Lesotho
Library
Roma 180, Lesotho

Liberia

United Nations Information Centre
LBDI Bldg.
Tubman Blvd.
P.O. Box 274
Monrovia, Liberia

University of Liberia
Libraries
Monrovia, Liberia

Libyan Arab Jamahiriya

Garyounis University
Central Library Administration
P.O. Box 1308
Benghazi, Libyan Arab Jamahiriya

Central Bank of Libya
Economic Research Library
King Saud St.
Tripoli, Libyan Arab Jamahiriya

United Nations Information Centre
Muzaffar Al Aftas St.
Hay El-Andalous, P.O. Box 286
Tripoli, Libyan Arab Jamahiriya

Luxembourg

Bibliotheque Nationale
37, blvd. F.D. Roosevelt
Luxembourg, Luxembourg

Madagascar

Bibliotheque Universitaire
Antananarivo, Madagascar

Centre d'Information des Nations Unies
22, rue Rainitovo
Antsahavola
B.P. 1348
Antananarivo, Madagascar

Malawi

University of Malawi
Libraries
P.O. Box 280
Zomba, Malawi

Malaysia

National Library of Malaysia
Gifts, Exchange & Depository Unit
1st Fl., Wisma S.Y.S.
338, Jalan Raja Laut
Kuala Lumpur, Malaysia

Malta

Royal Malta Library
Old Treasury St.
Valletta, Malta

Mauritius

The University of Mauritius
Library
Reduit, Mauritius

Mexico

Centro de Informacion de las Naciones
Unidas
Presidente Mazaryk No. 29, 7 piso
11570 **Mexico City**, DF, Mexico

Hemeroteca Nacional
Centro Cultural Universitario
Delegacion Coyoacan
Apdo. Postal 22-1999
Mexico 1400-D.F.
04510 **Mexico City**, DF, Mexico

Universidad Autonoma de Nuevo Leon
Facultad de Economia
Biblioteca "Consuelo Meyer L."
Apdo. Postal 288
Monterrey, NL, Mexico

Universidad Veracruzana
Instituto de Investigaciones y Estudios
Superiores Economicos y Sociales
20 de Noviembre Oriente
375 Apdo. Postal 67
C.P. 91030 Xalapa
Xalapa, Mexico

Mongolia

Gosudarstvennaia Publichnaia Biblioteka
MNR
Ulan-Bator, Mongolia

Morocco

United Nations Information Centre
Angle Charia Ibnouzaid et Zankat
Roundanat
No. 6
B.P. 601
Rabat, Morocco

Universite Mohamed V
Faculte des Sciences Juridiques,
Economiques et Sociales
Blvd. des Nations Unies
Rabat-Agdal, Morocco

Nepal

Tribhuvan University
Library
Kirtipur
Kathmandu, Nepal

United Nations Information Centre
P.O. Box 107
Pulchowk
Kathmandu, Nepal

Netherlands

Universiteit van Amsterdam
Seminarium voor Volkenrecht en
Internationale Betrekkingen
Bibliotheek Verenigde Naties Doc.
BG Gebouw I, Grimburgwal 10
NL-1012 GA **Amsterdam**, Netherlands

Bibliotheek der Rijksuniversiteit Te
Groning
Oude Kihk in 't Jatstraat 5
Postbus 559
NL-9700 AN **Groningen**, Netherlands

Koninklijke
Koninklijke Bibliotheek
Prins Willem Alexanderhof 5
NL-2595 BE **The Hague**, Netherlands

Bibliotheek Rijksuniversiteit Leiden
Tijdschriftenafdeling
P.O. Box 9501
NL-2300 RA **Leiden**, Netherlands

Katholieke Universiteit
Universiteitsbibliotheek
Erasmuslaan 36
NL-6525 GG **Nijmegen**, Netherlands

New Zealand

Auckland Public Libraries
P.O. Box 4138
Auckland 1, New Zealand

General Assembly Library
Parliament House
Wellington 1, New Zealand

Victoria University of Wellington
The Library (Periodicals)
United Nations Collection
Private Bag
Wellington, New Zealand

Nicaragua

Biblioteca Nacional
Managua, Nicaragua

Centro de Informacion de Naciones Unidas
Bolonia, de Plaza Espana
2 Cuadras Abajo
P.O. Box 3260
Managua, Nicaragua

Niger

Ecole Nationale d'Administration de Niamey
Niamey, Niger

Nigeria

University of Ife
Library
Ife-Ife, Nigeria

National Library of Nigeria
P.M.B. 12626
Lagos, Nigeria

United Nations Information Centre
17 Kingsway Rd., Ikoyi
P.O. Box 1068
Lagos, Nigeria

University of Nigeria
Nnamdi Azikiwe Library
Nsukka, Nigeria

University College Library
P.M.B. 5323
Port Harcourt, Nigeria

Ahmadu Bello University
Kashim Ibrahim Library
Zaria, Nigeria

Norway

Universitetsbiblioteket i Bergen
N-5000 **Bergen**, Norway

Nobelinstituttet
Biblioteket
Drammensveien 19
N-0255 **Oslo** 2, Norway

Universitet Biblioteket
Erling Skakkes GT 47c
N-7000 **Trondheim**, Norway

Pakistan

National Assembly
Library
Ramna-5
Islamabad, Pakistan

Quaid-I-Azam University
Central Library
P.O. Box 1090
Islamabad, Pakistan

United Nations Information Centre
House No. 26
88th St., Ramna 6/3
P.O. Box 1107
Islamabad, Pakistan

University of Sind
Central Library
Jamshoro, Pakistan

Karachi University
Library
Karachi 32, Pakistan

Punjab University
Library
1, Shari Al-Biruni
Lahore 2/12, Pakistan

University of Peshawar
Library
Peshawar, Pakistan

Panama

Biblioteca Nacional
Panama, Panama

Centre de Informacion de las Naciones Unidas
Urbanizacion Obarrio
Calle 54 y Ave. Tercesa Sur Case No. 17
P.O. Box 6-5083 El Dorado
Panama, Panama

Papua New Guinea

University of Papua New Guinea
Library
P.O. Box 319 University P.O.
Boroko, Papua New Guinea

Paraguay

Biblioteca Nacional
Asuncion, Paraguay

Centro de Informacion de las Naciones Unidas
Calle Estrella y Chile
Edificio City, 3er Piso
Casilla de Correo 1107
Asuncion, Paraguay

Peru

Biblioteca del Congreso
Camada de Diputados
Plaza Bolivar
Lima, Peru

Biblioteca Nacional
Lima, Peru

Centro de Informacion de las Naciones Unidas
Mariscal Blas Cerdena 450, San Isidro
Apdo. Postal 14-0199
Lima, Peru

Philippines

University of Mindanao
Bolton St.
Davao City, Philippines

Central Philippine University
Libraries
Iloilo City 5901, Philippines

The National Library
Public Documents Division
T.M. Kalaw St.
Ermita, **Manila**, Philippines

United Nations Information Centre
NEDA Bldg., Ground Fl.
106 Amorsollo St.
Legaspi Village, Makaki
Metro **Manila**, Philippines

Parliamentary Library Service
Batasang Pambansa
National Government Center
Quezon City, Metro **Manila**, Philippines

University of the Philippines
College of Law
The Library
Bocobo Hall
Diliman
Quezon City 3004, Philippines

Poland

Biblioteka Sejmowa
PL-00-902 **Warsaw**, Poland

Polski Instityt Spraw Miedzynarodowych
Polish Institute of International Affairs
Department of Scientific Information and the Library
Ul. Warecka 1A
P.O. Box 1000
PL-00-950 **Warsaw**, Poland

Zaklad Uzepelniania Zbiorow
Biblioteka Narodowa
ul. Hankiewicza 1
PL-00-973 **Warsaw**, Poland

Portugal

Biblioteca Geral de Universidade
Coimbra, Portugal

Biblioteca Nacional de Lisboa
Lisbon 5, Portugal

United Nations Information Centre
Rua Latino Coelho No. 1
Edificio Aviz Bloco A1-10o
P-1000 **Lisbon**, Portugal

Romania

Academiei Republicii Socialiste Romania
Biblioteca
Bucharest, Romania

Centrul de Informare al Onu
rue Aurel Vlaicu 16
P.O. Box 1-701
Bucharest, Romania

Rwanda

Universite Nationale du Rwanda
Bibliotheque
Butare, Rwanda

Samoa

The Melson Memorial Public Library
Apia, Samoa

Saudi Arabia

King Abdulaziz University
Library
Deanship of Library Affairs
Special Collections
P.O. Box 3711
Jeddah 21481, Saudi Arabia

State Public Library
Riyadh, Saudi Arabia

Scotland

National Library of Scotland
Official Papers Unit
George IV Bridge
Edinburgh EH1 1EW, Scotland

The Mitchell Library
Glasgow, G3 7DN, Scotland

Senegal

Assemblee Nationale
Secretariat General
Section de la Bibliotheque
Dakar, Senegal

Centre d'Information des Nations Unies
9, Allees Robert Delmas
B.P. 154
Dakar, Senegal

Universite de Dakar
Bibliotheque
Dakar, Senegal

Sierra Leone

University of Sierra Leone
Fourah Bay College Library
Documents Collection
P.O. Box 87
Freetown, Sierra Leone

Singapore

National Library
Gifts and Exchange Section
Stamford Rd.
Singapore 0617, Singapore

Somalia

University Institute of Somalia
Mogadishu, Somalia

Republic of South Africa

Library of Parliament
Cape Town, Republic of South Africa

South African Library
P.O. Box 496
Cape Town 18000, Republic of South Africa

State Library
United Nations Collection
P.O. Box 397
Pretoria 0001, Republic of South Africa

Spain

Universidad de Barcelona
Facultad de Derecho
Biblioteca Depositaria de Naciones Unidas
Zona Universitaria-Pedralbes
Diagonal 684
E-08034 **Barcelona,** Spain

Biblioteca de la Escuela Diplomatica
Paseo Juan XXIII, No. 5
E-28040 **Madrid,** Spain

Biblioteca Nacional
Seccion de Publicaciones Oficiales
Paseo de Recoletos, 20
Madrid 1, Spain

Centro de Informacion de Naciones Unidas
Ave. General Peron, 32-1o
P.O. Box 3.400
E-28080 **Madrid,** Spain

Universidad de Valencia
Facultad de Derecho
Biblioteca
Valencia, Spain

Sri Lanka

The Bar Association
Hultsdorp
Colombo 12, Sri Lanka

United Nations Information Centre
202-204 Bauddhaloka Mawatha
P.O. Box 1505
Colombo 7, Sri Lanka

Sudan

University of Juba
Library
P.O. Box 82
Juba, Sudan

United Nations Information Centre
Gasser Ave.
Khartoum East
St. 15 Block No. 3
P.O. Box 1992
Khartoum, Sudan

University of Khartoum
Library
Khartoum, Sudan

Surinam

Anton de Kom Universiteit
United Nations Depository Library
Onaflhandelijkheidshotel
Kleine Waterstraat 10-12
Paramaribo, Surinam

Swaziland

Swaziland National Library Service
Headquarters
P.O. Box 1461
Mbabane, Swaziland

Sweden

Goteborgs Universitetsbibliotek
P.O. Box 5096
S-402 22 **Gothenborg,** Sweden

Lunds Universitetsbibliotek
P.O. Box 3
S-221 00 **Lund,** Sweden

Riksdagsbiblioteket
S-100 12 **Stockholm,** Sweden

Dag Hammarskjold Library
P.O. Box 644
S-75127 **Uppsala** 1, Sweden

Switzerland

Eidgenossische Parlaments- und Zentralbibliothek
Bundeshaus West
CH-3003 **Bern,** Switzerland

Bibliotheque Publique et Universitaire de Geneve
CH-1211 **Geneva** 4, Switzerland

Institut Universitaire des Hautes Etudes Internationales
Bibliotheque
132, rue de Lausanne
CH-1211 **Geneva** 21, Switzerland

United Nations Information Service
United Nations Office at Geneva
Palais des Nations
CH-1211 **Geneva** 10, Switzerland

Syrian Arab Republic

Damascus University
United Arab Library
Damascus, Syrian Arab Republic

United Republic of Tanzania

United Nations Information Centre
Matasalamat Bldg., 1st Fl.
Samora Machel Ave.
P.O. Box 9224
Dar es Salaam, United Republic of Tanzania

University of Dar es Salaam
Library
P.O. Box 35092
Dar es Salaam, United Republic of Tanzania

Thailand

National Library
Bangkok 3, Thailand

United Nations Information Service
Economic and Social Commission for Asia and the Pacific
United Nations Bldg.
Rajadamnern Ave.
Bangkok 10200, Thailand

Togo

Bibliotheque Nationale du Togo
Lome, Togo

Centre d'Information des Nations Unies
107 Blvd. du 13 Janvier
B.P. 911
Lome, Togo

Trinidad and Tobago

United Nations Information Centre
15 Keate St.
P.O. Box 130
Port-of-Spain, Trinidad and Tobago

University of the West Indies
Library
St. Augustine, Trinidad and Tobago

Tunisia

Centre d'Information des Nations Unies
61 blvd. Bab Benat
B.P. 863
Tunis, Tunisia

Universite de Tunis
Faculte de Droit et des Sciences Politiques et Economiques
Campus universitaire
Tunis, Tunisia

Turkey

Milli Kutuphan Baskanligi
Bahcelievler
Ankara, Turkey

United Nations Information Office
197 Ataturk Bulvari
P.K. 407
Ankara, Turkey

Istanbul Universitesi Kutuphanesi
University Library
Beyazit, Besim Omer Pasa Cad. No. 15
Istanbul, Turkey

Uganda

Makere University
Library
Kampala, Uganda

Union of Soviet Socialist Republics

Akademia Nauk Ukrainskoi SSR
Centralnaya Nauchnaya
Biblioteka
Ul. Vladimirskaya 62
Kiev 17, Union of Soviet Socialist Republics

Leningradskogo Gosudarstvennogo Universiteta Imeni A.A. Zhdanova
Nauchnaya Biblioteka Im. M. Gorky
7/9 Universitetskaia nab.
Leningrad 199164, Union of Soviet Socialist Republics

Gosudarstvennaya Biblioteka BSSR Imeni V.I. Lenin
Lrasnoarmeiakaia 9
Minsk 30, Union of Soviet Socialist Republics

Gosudarstvennaya Biblioteka SSR Imeni V.I. Lenin
Moscow, Union of Soviet Socialist Republics

Informatcionnyi Centr Oon
4/16 Ulitsa Lunacharskogo 1
Moscow 121002, Union of Soviet Socialist Republics

Institut Nauchnoi Informatii po Obschestvennym Naukami
Academii Nauk SSSR
Moscow 13-418, Union of Soviet Socialist Republics

Vilnaius Valstybinis V. Kapsuko Vardo Universitetas
Moksline Biblioteka
Vilnius 232633, Union of Soviet Socialist Republics

United Arab Emirates

United Arab Emirates University
Library
P.O. Box 1441
Al-Ain, United Arab Emirates

Uruguay

Biblioteca Nacional
Ave. 18 de Julio 1790
Casilla de Correo 452
Montevideo, Uruguay

Venezuela

Biblioteca Nacional
Caracas, Venezuela

Viet Nam

Viet Nam National Library
International Exchange Service
31 Trang thi
10 000 **Hanoi,** Viet Nam

Virgin Islands

Enid M. Baa Library and Archives
P.O. Box 390
Charlotte Amalie, St. Thomas 00801

Wales

The National Library of Wales
Abersystwyth SY23 3BU, Wales

University College
The Arts and Social Studies Library
United Nations Depository Library
P.O. Box 78
Cardiff CF1 1XL, Wales

Yemen Arab Republic

Sana'a University
Library
Sana'a, Yemen Arab Republic

Yugoslavia

Informacioni Centar Ujedinjenih Nacija
Svetozara Markovica 58
P.O. Box 157
YU-11001 **Belgrade,** Yugoslavia

Institut za Medjunarodnu Politiku i Privredu
Biblioteka
Belgrade, Yugoslavia

Skupstina Sfrj
Odelenje Inostrane Dokumentacije
TRG Marksa 1 Engelsa 13
Belgrade, Yugoslavia

Universizitet u Beogradu
Pravni Facultet
Biblioteka
YU-11000 **Belgrade,** Yugoslavia

Univerza v Ljubljani
Pravna Fakulteta
YU-61000 **Ljubljana,** Yugoslavia

Univerzitet "Dzemal Bijedic"
Univerzitetska Biblioteka
Trg "14 Februar"
Postanski Pretinac 168
YU-88000 **Mostar,** Yugoslavia

Univerzitet Kiril i Metodi Skofoje
Praven Fakultet
Biblioteka
Skopje, Yugoslavia

Sveuciliste u Zagrebu
Pravni Fakultet
Biblioteka
YU-41001 **Zagreb,** Yugoslavia

Zaire

Centre d'Information des Nations Unies
Batiment Deuxieme Republique
Blvd. du 30 Juin
B.P. 7248
Kinshasa, Zaire

Zambia

President's Citizenship College
Library
Mulungushi
P.O. Box 80415
Kabwe, Zambia

United Nations Information Centre
P.O. Box 32905
Lusaka, Zambia

University of Zambia
Library
P.O. Box 32379
Lusaka, Zambia

Zimbabwe

United Nations Information Centre
Dolphin House
123 Moffat St./Union Ave.
P.O. Box 4408
Harare, Zimbabwe

Appendix F

World Bank Depository Libraries

The institutions listed below have been designated as official World Bank depository libraries. They provide free public access to books published for the World Bank by university presses, country and economic studies, technical papers, annual reports, statistical publications, and selected public information material. Collections are open to the public during normal business hours and, in most instances, accessible without charge. Listings appear in alphabetical order by name of country and, in countries with more than one library, by name of city. Users should address requests for additional information to:

The World Bank
Publications Department
Mr. Taverekere Srikantaiah,
Chf., Publications Sales Unit
1818 H St., N.W., Rm. H-2167
Washington, DC 20433

Algeria

Institut Superior de Gestion et de Planification
Bibliotheque
Rue Hadj Messaoud Nourredine
Baha (Ex. Lido) Borg El Kiffane
Algiers, Algeria

Argentina

Secretaria de Planificacion
Biblioteca
Hipolito Yrigoyen 250-8 piso Of 801-C
Buenos Aires, 1310 Argentina

Universidad Nacional del Litoral
Facultad de Ciencias Economicas
Biblioteca
25 de Mayo 1783
Santa Fe, 3000 Argentina

Australia

National Library of Australia
Selection Acquisition & Serials
Canberra, ACT 2600, Australia

Bahrain

Gulf Polytechnic
Library
P.O. Box 32038
Isa Town, Bahrain

Bangladesh

Bangladesh Academy for Rural Development
Library
Kotbari
Comilla, Bangladesh

Bangladesh Public Administration Training Centre
Library
Savar Dhaka, Bangladesh

CIRDAP
Library
Chameli House 17 Topkhana Rd.
GPO Box 2883
Dhaka 2, Bangladesh

Botswana

University of Botswana
Library
Private Bag 0022
Gaborone, Botswana

Brazil

CENDEC
Library
SGAN quadra 908 Modulo E
Brasilia, DF 70740, Brazil

Burkina Faso

Institut National de la Statistique et de la Demographie
Bibliotheque
Direction Generale
B.P. 374
Ouagadougou, Burkina Faso

Burundi

Centre de Perfectionnement et de Formation en Cours d'Emploi (CPF)
B.P. 732
10 route rumonge
Bujumbura, Burundi

Cameroon

Institut Panafricain pour le Developpement du CPF
Centre de Documentation
B.P. 4078
Littoral
Douala, Cameroon

University Center Dschang
Library
P.O. Box 255
Dschang, Cameroon

Chile

Oficina de Planificacion Nacional
Biblioteca
Ahumada 48 piso 4
Santiago, Chile

Escuele de Negocios de Valparaiso
Biblioteca
Casilla 846
Balmaceda 1625
Vina del Mar, Chile

People's Republic of China

Bank of China
Institute of International Finance
Division of Statistics and Library
Xijiao Minxiang 17
Beijing, People's Republic of China

Central Institute of Finance and Banking
Library
Beijing, People's Republic of China

Institute of World Economy and Politics
Library
Chinese Academy of Social Sciences
5 Jianguomen Dajie
Beijing, People's Republic of China

Ministry of Finance
External Finance Department
World Bank Division Library
San Li He
Beijing, People's Republic of China

National Library of China
The United Nations Materials Section
7 Wen Jin St.
Beijing, People's Republic of China

The People's University of China
Library
39 Hai Dian Rd.
Beijing, People's Republic of China

Quinghua University
School of Economics and Management
Library
Beijing, People's Republic of China

State Planning Commission of People's Republic of China Library
38 Yuetan Nan Jie
San Li He
Beijing, People's Republic of China

Jilin University
International Exchange Section
Library
Changchun, People's Republic of China

Guangdong Provincial Academy of Social Sciences Library
222 Yue Xiu Bei Rd.
Guangzhou, People's Republic of China

Wuhan University
Department of Economics Library
Wuhan
Hubei, People's Republic of China

University of Nanjing
Economics Department
Library
Nanjing, People's Republic of China

Institute for World Economy
Library
Fudan University
220 Handan Rd.
Shanghai, People's Republic of China

Shanghai Academy of Social Sciences
Library
1575 Van Hong Du Rd.
Shanghai, People's Republic of China

Shanghai University of Finance and Economics
Research School
369 North Nhung-shan Rd. I
Shanghai, 200 081 People's Republic of China

Nankai University
Economic School Center of Information
94 Weijin Rd.
Tianjin, People's Republic of China

Colombia

Universidad Externado de Colombia
Biblioteca
Calle 12 No. 1-17 Este
Bogota, Colombia

Universidad del Valle
Seccion Documentos Organismos Internacionales
Apartado Aereo 25360
Cali, Colombia

Universidad de Antioquia
Centro de Documentacion
Apartado Aereo 1226
Medellin, Colombia

Costa Rica

INCAE
Biblioteca
Apartado 960
4050 **Alajuela,** Costa Rica

Instituto de Investigaciones en Ciencias Economicas
Biblioteca
Universidad de Costa Rica
San Jose, Costa Rica

Cyprus

Middle East Marketing Research Bureau (MEMRB)
Library
P.O. Box 2098
Nicosia, Cyprus

Denmark

Copenhagen School of Economics and Business
Library
Rosenorns Alle 31
DK-1970 **Copenhagen V,** Denmark

Ecuador

Pontificia Universidad Catolica del Ecuador
Biblioteca
Quito, Ecuador

Egypt

Institute of National Planning
Documentation and Publishing Centre
Salah Salem St.
Nasr City
Cairo, Egypt

El Salvador

Consejo Nacional de Planificacion y Coordinacion Economica
Biblioteca
Casa Presidential
San Salvador, El Salvador

England

British Library
Great Russell St.
London WC1B 3DG, England

Ethiopia

Addis Ababa University Library
Documents Department
P.O. Box 1176
Addis Ababa, Ethiopia

Fiji

University of the South Pacific
Library (Gifts and Exchanges)
P.O. Box 1168
Suva, Fiji

The Gambia

National Investment Board
Library
78 Wellington St.
Banjul, The Gambia

Ghana

University of Ghana
Library
P.O. Box 25
Legon
Accra, Ghana

University of Cape Coast
Library
University Post Office
Cape Coast, Ghana

Greece

Centre of Planning and Economic Research (KEPE)
Library
22 Hippokratous St.
GR-10680 **Athens,** Greece

Institute of International Public Law and International Relations of Thessaloniki
Library
Leof. Meg. Alexandrou 15 & Hadji
GR-54640 **Thessaloniki,** Greece

Guyana

Bank of Guyana
Library
P.O. Box 1003
Georgetown, Guyana

Honduras

Consejo Superior de Planificacion Economica
Biblioteca
P.O. Box 1327
Tegucigalpa, DC, Honduras

Hungary

National Bank of Hungary
Library
T 8 Szabadsaq
H-1850 **Budapest,** Hungary

India

Indian Institute of Management
Vikram Sarabhai Library
Vastrapur
Ahmedabad 380015, India

Guru Nanak Dev University
Punjab School of Economics
Library
Amritsar Punjab 143005, India

Institute for Social and Economic Change
Library
Nagarbhavi
Bangalore 560072, India

University of Bombay
Jawaharlal Nehru Library
Vidyanagari Campus
Kalina Santacruz (E)
Bombay 400098, India

Indian Statistical Institute
Library
203 Barrackpore Trunk Rd.
Calcutta 700035, India

Karnatak University
Library
Pavate Nagar
Dharwad Karnataka 580003, India

Centre for Economic and Social Studies
Library
Nizamia Observatory Campus
Begumpet
Hyderabad 500016, India

Giri Institute of Development Studies
Library
Sector "O" Aliganj Housing Scheme
Lucknow U.P. 226020, India

Institute for Financial Management and Research
Library
30 Kothari Rd.
Nungambakkam
Madras 600034, India

Administrative Training Institute
Library
Nainital U.P., India

Indian Institute of Public Administration
Library
Ring Rd. Indraprastha Estate
New Delhi 110002, India

Institute of Economic Growth
Library
University Enclave
New Delhi 110007, India

Punjabi University
Department of Economics
Patiala Punjab 147002, India

Gokhale Institute of Politics and Economics
Library
Pune Maharashtra 411004, India

Ravishankar University
Library
Raipur M.P. 492010, India

Annamalai University
Library
Annamalainagar
South Arcot District 608002, India

Kerala University
Library
Trivandrum Kerala 695034, India

Indonesia

Bandung Institute of Technology
Central Library
Jalan Ganesya 10
Bandung, Indonesia

Bogor Agricultural University
Library
Kampus IPB Darwaga
Bogor, Indonesia

Universitas Udayana
Jalan P B Sudiram
Denpasar Bali, Indonesia

Atma Jaya Research Centre
Library
Jalan Jenderal Sudirman 49A
P.O. Box 2639
Jakarta 10001, Indonesia

Institut Keguruan Dan Ilmu
Library
Pendidikan Negeri
Kampus IKIP
Manado Sulawesi Utara, Indonesia

Institut Teknologi Sepuluh Nopember
Kampus ITS Keputih Sukolilo
Surabaya Jawa Timur, Indonesia

Universitas Hasanuddin
Kampus Unhas
Jl Mesjid Raya 55
Ujung Pandang, Indonesia

Ivory Coast

Institut Africain pour le Developpement Economique et Social
Bibliotheque
08 B.P. 8
Abidjan 08, Ivory Coast

Jamaica

Planning Institute of Jamaica
Library
39-41 Barbados Ave.
Kingston 5, Jamaica

Republic of Korea

Korea Development Institute
Library
207-41 Chungryangri-Dong
Dongdaemun-Ku
Seoul 131, Republic of Korea

Kuwait

The Arab Planning Institute
Library
P.O. Box 5834
13059 **Safat,** Kuwait

Lesotho

The National University of Lesotho
Library
P.O. Box 180
Roma, Lesotho

Malawi

Ministry of Agriculture
Chitedze Agricultural Research Station
Library
P.O. Box 158
Lilongwe, Malawi

Malaysia

Asian and Pacific Development Centre
Library
Persiaran Duta
P.O. Box 12224
01-02 **Kuala Lumpur,** Malaysia

SEACEN Centre
Library
46350 **Petaling Jaya,** Malaysia

Malta

Central Bank of Malta
Library
Valletta, Malta

Mauritius

University of Mauritius
Library
Reduit, Mauritius

Mexico

Banco de Mexico
Biblioteca
Apartado Postal 98 Bis
06059 **Mexico City,** DF, Mexico

Morocco

Centre National de Documentation
Bibliotheque
B.P. 826
Charii Maa Al Ainain
Haut-Aqdal, Morocco

Nepal

Tribhuvan University
Central Library
Kirtipur, Nepal

Netherlands

Royal Tropical Institute
Central Library
United Nations Collection
Mauritskade 63
1092 AD **Amsterdam,** Netherlands

Nicaragua

Instituto Centroamericano de Administracion de Empresas
Biblioteca
Apartado Postal 2485
Managua, Nicaragua

Nigeria

Nigerian Institute of Social and Economic Research
Library
PMB 5
U I Post Office
Ibadan Oyo, Nigeria

Bayero University Library
PMB 3011
Kano, Nigeria

Nigerian Industrial Development Bank
Library
P.O. Box 2357
Lagos, Nigeria

University of Nigeria
Nnamdi Azikiwe Library
Nsukka, Nigeria

The Polytechnic of Sokoto State
College of Administration
Library
PMB 2126
Sokoto, Nigeria

Pakistan

University of Agriculture
Library
Faisalabad, Pakistan

Pakistan Institute of Development Economics
Library
P.O. Box 1091
Islamabad, Pakistan

Applied Economic Research Centre
Library
University of Karachi
P.O. Box 8403
Karachi 32, Pakistan

Punjab Economic Research Institute
Library
74-B-II Gulberg III
Lahore, Pakistan

Pakistan Academy for Rural Development
Library
Academy Town
Peshawar, Pakistan

University of Baluchistan
Library
Sariab Rd.
Quetta, Pakistan

Papua New Guinea

University of Papua New Guinea
Library
University P.O. Box 319
National Capital District, Papua New Guinea

Philippines

University of San Carlos
Library
P del Rosario St.
Cebu City 6401, Philippines

University of the Philippines at Los Banos College
Library
Laguna 3720, Philippines

Panay State Polytechnic College
Library
Mambusao Capiz, Philippines

NEDA
Library
NEDA Sa Pasig
Amber Ave.
Metro Manila, Philippines

University of the Philippines
School of Economics
Library
Diliman
Quezon City 3004, Philippines

Poland

Uniwersytet Jagiellonski W. Krakowie
Centrum Badan nad Zadluzeniem Rojwojem
ul Golebia 24
31-007 **Kracow,** Poland

Norodowy Bank Polski
President's Office
Swietokrzyska 11/21
00-950 **Warsaw,** Poland

Portugal

Universidade do Minho
Servicos de Documentacao
Largo do Paco
P-4719 **Braga Codex,** Portugal

Instituto Universitario de Beira Interior
Library
Rua Marques d'Avila e Bolama
P-6200 **Covilha,** Portugal

Romania

Institutul de Economie Mondiala
Library
Blvd. Republic II 12 Sector 3
70348 **Bucharest,** Romania

Saudi Arabia

Ministry of Planning
Library and Documentation Department
Riyadh 11182, Saudi Arabia

Senegal

Centre Africain d'Etudes Superieures en Gestion
Bibliotheque
Blvd. General Degaulle X Malick SY
B.P. 1497/3802
Dakar, Senegal

South Africa

State Library
Special Collections
P.O. Box 397
Pretoria 0001, South Africa

University of South Africa
Sanlam Library
P.O. Box 392
Pretoria 0001, South Africa

Spain

Escuela Superior de Administracion y Direccion de Empresas (ESADE)
Avenida de Pedralbes 60-62
E-08034 **Barcelona,** SP

Sri Lanka

Ceylon Institute of Scientific and Industrial Research
Technical Library and Information Service
Colombo 7, Sri Lanka

University of Sri Jayewardenepura
Library
Nugegoda, Sri Lanka

Sudan

University of Juba
Library
P.O. Box 82
Juba, Sudan

Arab Organization for Agricultural Development
Library
4 El Gama'a Ave.
P.O. Box 474
Khartoum, Sudan

Swaziland

University of Swaziland
Library
Private Bag
Kaluwesi, Swaziland

Switzerland

United Nations Library
Specialized Agencies Collections
Palais des Nations, Rm. B-121
CH-1211 **Geneva** 10, Switzerland

Tanzania

Eastern and Southern African Management Institute
Library
P.O. Box 3030
Arusha, Tanzania

Thailand

National Institute of Development Administration
Ministry of University Affairs
Library
Klongchan Bangkapi
Bangkok 10240, Thailand

Trinidad and Tobago

The University of West Indies
Library
St. Augustine, Trinidad and Tobago

Tunisia

Faculte de Droit et des Sciences Politiques et Economiques
Bibliotheque
Campus Universitaire
Tunis Belvedere, Tunisia

Turkey

Cukurova Universitesi
Library
Kutuphanesi
Adana, Turkey

SESRTCIC
Library
Hemsehri Sokak No. 1
Gazi Osman Pasa
Ankara, Turkey

Ege Universitesi
Tarim Fakultesi
Department of Agricultural Economics
Library
Bornova
Izmir, Turkey

United Arab Emirates

Sharjah Chamber of Commerce and Industry
Library
P.O. Box 580
Sharjah, United Arab Emirates

Uruguay

Oficina de Planeamiento y Presupuesto
Edificio Libertad
Biblioteca
Montevideo, Uruguay

United States of America

United Nations
Dag Hammarskjold Library
Acquisition Section
Grand Central P.O. Box 2000
New York, NY 10163

United Nations
UNECA
Library
P.O. Box 5834
New York, NY 10163-5834

Library of Congress
Copyright Office
Rm. 438 C
Washington, DC 20559

Vanuatu

Central Bank of Vanuatu
Library
P.O. Box 271
Port Vila, Vanuatu

Venezuela

IESA
Biblioteca
Apartado 1640
Caracas 1010A, Venezuela

Yugoslavia

Institute of Economic Sciences
Library
Zmaj Jovina 12
P.O. Box 611
YU-11001 **Belgrade,** Yugoslavia

Nacionalna Sveucilsna Biblioteka
Information Resources Center
Marulicev trg 21
YU-41001 **Zagreb,** Yugoslavia

Zaire

Centre d'Etudes pour l'Action Sociale (CEPAS)
Bibliotheque
BP 5717
Kinshasa-Gombe, Zaire

Zambia

The University of Zambia
Rural Development Studies Bureau
Library
P.O. Box 30900
Lusaka, Zambia

Zimbabwe

National Free Library of Zimbabwe
P.O. Box 1773
Bulawayo, Zimbabwe

Abbreviations

(State, Province and Territory)

UNITED STATES

AL	Alabama	MT	Montana
AK	Alaska	NE	Nebraska
AZ	Arizona	NV	Nevada
AR	Arkansas	NH	New Hampshire
CA	California	NJ	New Jersey
CO	Colorado	NM	New Mexico
CT	Connecticut	NY	New York
DE	Delaware	NC	North Carolina
DC	District of Columbia	ND	North Dakota
FL	Florida	OH	Ohio
GA	Georgia	OK	Oklahoma
HI	Hawaii	OR	Oregon
ID	Idaho	PA	Pennsylvania
IL	Illinois	RI	Rhode Island
IN	Indiana	SC	South Carolina
IA	Iowa	SD	South Dakota
KS	Kansas	TN	Tennessee
KY	Kentucky	TX	Texas
LA	Louisiana	UT	Utah
ME	Maine	VT	Vermont
MD	Maryland	VA	Virginia
MA	Massachusetts	WA	Washington
MI	Michigan	WV	West Virginia
MN	Minnesota	WI	Wisconsin
MS	Mississippi	WY	Wyoming
MO	Missouri		

U.S. TERRITORIES

AS	American Samoa	PR	Puerto Rico
GU	Guam	VI	Virgin Islands

CANADA

AB	Alberta	NS	Nova Scotia
BC	British Columbia	ON	Ontario
MB	Manitoba	PE	Prince Edward Island
NB	New Brunswick	PQ	Quebec
NF	Newfoundland	SK	Saskatchewan
NT	Northwest Territories	YT	Yukon Territory

Abbreviations

Foreign Country Codes

AA	Algeria
AR	Argentina
AU	Australia
AT	Austria
BD	Bangladesh
BE	Belgium
BM	Bermuda
BO	Bolivia
BW	Botswana
BR	Brazil
BG	Bulgaria
BU	Burma
CM	United Republic of Cameroon
CL	Chile
CH	People's Republic of China
CO	Colombia
CR	Costa Rica
CU	Cuba
CS	Czechoslovakia
DK	Denmark
EC	Ecuador
EG	Egypt
EN	England
ET	Ethiopia
FJ	Fiji
FI	Finland
FR	France
FG	Federal Republic of Germany
GH	Ghana
GR	Greece
GT	Guatemala
HK	Hong Kong
HU	Hungary
IN	India
ID	Indonesia
IR	Iran
IQ	Iraq
IE	Ireland
IL	Israel
IT	Italy
JM	Jamaica
JP	Japan
KR	Republic of Korea
KW	Kuwait
LB	Lebanon
LR	Liberia
LU	Luxembourg
MY	Malaysia
MT	Malta
MU	Mauritius
MX	Mexico
MO	Morocco
NM	Namibia
NL	Netherlands
NZ	New Zealand
NE	Niger
NG	Nigeria
NT	Northern Ireland
NO	Norway
PK	Pakistan
PA	Panama
PG	Papua New Guinea
PE	Peru
PH	Philippines
PL	Poland
PT	Portugal
RO	Romania
SA	Saudi Arabia
SW	Scotland
SN	Senegal
SG	Singapore
SX	Republic of South Africa
SP	Spain
SQ	Sri Lanka
SZ	Swaziland
SE	Sweden
SI	Switzerland
SY	Syrian Arab Republic
TW	Taiwan (Republic of China)
TZ	United Republic of Tanzania
TH	Thailand
TT	Trinidad and Tobago
TN	Tunisia
TR	Turkey
SU	Union of Soviet Socialist Republics
UY	Uruguay
VE	Venezuela
WL	Wales
YU	Yugoslavia
ZB	Zimbabwe

SUBJECT INDEX

Entries 1-10570, Part 1 • Entries 10571-18877, Part 2
Entries are arranged geographically under each subject. The order in which they appear is as follows: U.S. states and territories, Canadian provinces, and foreign countries. Geographical abbreviations with their definitions may be found on pages 1922 and 1923. The abbreviation INTL separates foreign from U.S. and Canadian entries.

Subject Index

Subject Index

Subject Index

Subject Index

Subject Index